The
American Heritage®
College Dictionary

FOURTH EDITION

Houghton Mifflin Company
Boston • New York

Visit our website: www.houghtonmifflinbooks.com

The American Heritage college dictionary.-- 4th ed.
    p.cm.
  Based on the fourth ed. of the American Heritage
  dictionary.
  ISBN 0-618-09848-8 (thumb edge) --
  ISBN 0-618-19604-8 (deluxe binding)
   1. English language--Dictionaries. 2. Americanisms. I
  Houghton Mifflin Company. II. American Heritage
  dictionary.

PE1628 .A6227 2002
423--dc21
                                                    2001039826

Manufactured in the United States of America

Table of Contents

Preface

Each new edition of a dictionary documents a language at a particular point in time. Because language changes—new words are created, existing words develop new uses, the way we pronounce words varies, and attitudes about language shift over time—even the best dictionaries need to be revised and updated periodically. This new Fourth Edition of *The American Heritage College Dictionary* appears only nine years after its predecessor, but in those nine years enough has happened to require the addition of 7,500 new words and senses to its vocabulary and to prompt many other changes in its pages. The Fourth Edition has many new computer and Internet terms along with newly coined words in science, politics, and the arts. Other timely changes include the addition of biographical entries for newly prominent people and the updating of our entries for US towns, cities, and states with statistics from the 2000 census.

But this Dictionary is more than just a record of the English language at the start of the 21st century, and it does much more than provide accurate answers to specific questions about words. It is a multifaceted book, designed to present many different opportunities to learn about our language—how it has changed throughout its long history, how it should be used to best effect, how its widely accepted usage stands in relation to its many local flavors and social variations.

In short, this book is meant to be a companion to anyone wishing to explore the English language in all its dimensions. This is why we have carefully redesigned its pages to invite exploring and sustained reading. We sought out new typefaces and researched 2,500 new photographs, drawings, and maps to enhance the body of the text and to make discovery easier, so that one page will actually lead to another.

A hallmark of American Heritage Dictionaries has always been their clear defining style, and this Dictionary stands among the most readable in that great tradition. The editors revised scores of thousands of definitions, both for accuracy and for general readability. We also increased the number of example sentences by a third over the previous edition to provide more concrete ways of grasping a meaning.

To be sure, technology has helped us in all these efforts. We use computers to search and analyze large files of data, looking for evidence of new words and new uses of existing words. We use the Internet to gather additional information about words and to check their usage. We communicate with consultants in specialty areas by e-mail and present them with the information we extract from our databases. But the improvements we make in our dictionaries only come as a result of the professionalism and hard work of the people who use these sophisticated tools. Making substantive improvements to such an expansive reference work requires the close examination of evidence and the insistence on making every line of every entry as accessible and useful as possible.

One of the most important strengths of this Dictionary is the abundance of guidance it provides on how to use words. Language change is not limited to new contributions to the vocabulary and the emergence of technical meanings. The way we use words, along with the way we think about and react to words, also changes over time. A usage once considered trendy or unappealing can often become widely accept-

ed as speakers grow accustomed to it. To track these developments, we have continued our research in consultation with the chair of our Usage Panel, linguist Geoffrey Nunberg. As part of this effort, we send surveys on usage issues to our Usage Panel, a group of 200 writers, scholars, and others whose livelihood depends on their using language to great effect. We use these surveys as the basis for writing and revising many of the Usage Notes in the Dictionary. Thus, the Fourth Edition has Notes discussing usages that were once considered incorrect but have since become predominant (*cohort, nauseous*) and usages that continue to provoke strong negative reactions despite being widely used for decades (*critique, impact*). The Dictionary also has Notes that offer guidance on controversial terms for members of specific social groups (*Anglo, Hispanic*) and on words with controversial or varying pronunciations (*banal, harass*).

But knowing what to expect when choosing one word or another in standard contexts affords but one view of the language landscape. This Dictionary contains a variety of other note programs that allow you to build a more sophisticated picture of the world of words. Hundreds of Notes discuss groups of synonyms, often distinguishing nuances of meaning among them (*defend, method, superfluous*). Other Notes call out regionalisms—words whose use is limited to a certain region of our country. These words (*dragonfly, pone, you-all*) give our language much of its distinctive character. And because language varies not just by region but also by social factors like age and group identity, the Fourth Edition contains an entirely new series of Notes, called Our Living Language Notes, that show how language varies among groups and changes in time (*as far as, rap*[4], *za*).

Like its predecessors, the Fourth Edition is distinguished by highly informative etymologies that have been researched and revised according to the latest scholarship. Many of these etymologies are fleshed out in Word History Notes that tell the stories behind words (*bug, Hoosier, typhoon*). In addition, the highly acclaimed Appendix of Indo-European Roots was revised for this edition by its author, Calvert Watkins. This Appendix, unique to American Heritage Dictionaries, allows you to trace words that have very different spellings but share a core meaning back to their ancestors in the prehistoric language that gave rise to the Indo-European language family. Thus you can learn that the words *dairy, dough, fiction, lady,* and *paradise* all derive from a common root, *dheigh-*, meaning "to form, shape." No other dictionary on the market today provides such an in-depth appreciation of the words we use.

Our aim in making this book has been to provide a dictionary of the highest quality at an affordable price for college students—indeed, for anyone who has a need or desire to learn more about words. In this regard, I believe we have succeeded. Few investments could be more prudent than the purchase of this Dictionary. My confidence in saying this is really a measure of the pride I have in the intelligence and dedication of our editors and production staff, in the expert assistance of our consultants, and in the professionalism of everyone else who contributed to this book's completion.

Joseph P. Pickett
Vice President and Executive Editor

Editorial and Production Staff

Special Contributors and Consultants

Usage

Geoffrey Nunberg, PhD, Xerox Palo Alto Research Center
and Stanford University

Dialects

Allan A. Metcalf, PhD, Professor of English, MacMurray
College

Indo-European Roots

Calvert Watkins, PhD, Victor S. Thomas Professor of
Linguistics and the Classics, Harvard University

Language Variation and Change

Natalie Schilling Estes, PhD, Assistant Professor,
Department of Linguistics, Georgetown University
John R. Rickford, PhD, Martin Luther King, Jr.,
Centennial Professor of Linguistics, Stanford University

Etymology Consultants

Carib Languages

Spike Gildea, PhD, Associate Professor of Linguistics, Rice
University

Chinese

Jun Qian, PhD, Associate Professor of English, Beijing
University

Hawaiian

William H. Wilson, PhD, Professor of Hawaiian and
Hawaiian Studies, University of Hawaii

Inuit/Eskimo Languages

Jerrold M. Sadock, PhD, Glen A. Lloyd Distinguished
Service Professor, Department of Linguistics, University
of Chicago

Iranian Languages

P. Oktor Skjærvø, PhD, Aga Khan Professor of Iranian,
Department of Near Eastern Languages and
Civilizations, Harvard University

Semitic Roots

John Huehnergard, PhD, Professor of Semitic Philology,
Department of Near Eastern Languages and
Civilizations, Harvard University

Turkic Languages

Alexander Lehrman, PhD, Department of Foreign
Languages and Literatures, University of Delaware

Special Consultants

Anthropology

Rosemary A. Joyce, PhD, Associate Professor of
Anthropology, University of California, Berkeley

Architecture

James S. Ackerman, PhD, Arthur Kingsley Porter
Professor of Fine Arts, Harvard University

Cinema

Mark Garrett Cooper, PhD, Assistant Professor,
Department of English, Florida State University

Dance

Thomas Guzman-Sanchez, Urban Dance Scholar and
Historian, Los Angeles

Law

Sanford N. Katz, JD, Professor of Law, Boston College

Mathematics

Keith Conrad, PhD, Zassenhaus Assistant Professor,
Department of Mathematics, Ohio State University

Military Science and Weapons

Dennis E. Showalter, PhD, Professor of History, Colorado
College

Music

Edmund J. Goehring, PhD, Assistant Professor, Program
of Liberal Studies, University of Notre Dame
Ivan Kreilkamp, PhD

Nautical

Richard Sherwood

Philosophy

Tamar Szabó Gendler, PhD, Assistant Professor, Department of Philosophy, Syracuse University

Religion

William A. Graham, PhD, Professor of the History of Religion and Islamic Studies, Department of Near Eastern Languages and Civilizations, Harvard University (Islamic)

Miriam L. Levering, PhD, Associate Professor, Department of Religious Studies, University of Tennessee, Knoxville (Asian)

Science and Technology

Christopher D. Bedford, CCM, Chief Meteorologist, Sailing Weather Services

Rufus W. Burlingame, PhD, Senior Scientist, INOVA Diagnostics, San Diego (Genetics, Immunology, Biochemistry)

Chryssostomos Chryssostomidis, PhD, Department Head, Department of Ocean Engineering, Massachusetts Institute of Technology, Director, MIT Sea Grant College Program

Bryan E. Dutton, PhD, Assistant Professor, Department of Biology, Western Oregon University, Monmouth OR (Botany)

William S. Haubrich, MD, Division of Gastroenterology, Scripps Clinical Research Foundation (Retired) (Medicine)

William McCloskey, PharmD, Associate Professor of Clinical Pharmacy, Director of the Drug Information Center, Massachusetts College of Pharmacy and Allied Health Sciences (Pharmacology)

R. Dwayne Ramey, PhD, Assistant Professor of Physics, Tennessee State University (Physics and Astronomy)

Nada Stotland, MD, Chair, Department of Psychiatry, Illinois Masonic Medical Center, Chicago IL; Professor, Department of Psychiatry, Rush University Medical College (Psychology/Psychiatry)

Lawrence G. Weathers, Science Coordinator and Project Director, Systems Dynamics in K–12 Education, Harvard Public Schools, Harvard MA (Physics)

Timothy Webster (Computer Science)

Sports

Mike Meserole, Author, essayist, editor

Previous Contributors and Consultants

G.W. Abernathy	John A. Garraty	Robert N. Mory
Michael Adams	Ives Goddard	Ted J. Murphy
Donald C.S. Allison	The Very Rev. Dmitri Griegorieff	Joseph M. Patwell
Richard Allsopp	Maura Hadro	Mara Peets
Deborah W. Anderson	Van A. Harvey	Lee Pederson
William Ira Bennett	H. Kristina Haugland	Martha Fairman Phelps
Stephen A. Bladey	Marvin L. Herzog	J.W. Pierce
Daniel P. Bolger	Nicholas Hotton III	Sr. Mary Dominic Pitts, OP
William S. Bonds	Martin E. Huld	Rosemary Previte
Jim Boyle	Ann-Marie Imbornoni	Daniel G. Prior
Heywood Hale Broun	David B. Johnson	C.E. Ray, Jr.
Sheila Ewing Browne	Brian D. Joseph	Frank E. Reynolds
Neal D. Buffaloe	Lionel S. Joseph	Carol Rigsby
Craig M. Carver	David A. Jost	David W. Ruddy
Hipólito Rafael Chacón	Sara E. Kimball	David L. Scott
Susan S. Chicoski	Hilary Kornblith	Richard Evans Schultes
George N. Clements	Henry Kučera	Marion Severynse
F.J. Collier	Robert M. Landis	Ihsan A. Al-Shehbaz
Jim A. Craig	Jonathan P. Latimer	P. Adams Sitney
Robert W. Creamer	Alexander Lehrman	Anne H. Soukhanov
Thomas Creamer	James P. Marciano	Anne D. Steinhardt
Donna Cremans	Lynn Margulis	Richard F. Townsend
Mary Davenport	Sharon L. Marshall	James Trefil
Pamela Burton DeVinne	Martin E. Marty	Jack D. Van Horn
Patrick S. Diehl	Richard P. McBrien	Rex E. Wallace
Kaethe Ellis	Vincent P. McCarren	Mary Waters
Brooks B. Ellwood	Rima Elkin McKinzey	David M. Weeks
R.J. Emry	Paul Mendes-Flohr	Roger D. Woodard
Frank Espey	Ann Marie Menting	David M. Yerkes
Paul G. Evenson	Reuven Merkin	R. David Zorc
Edward F. Ford	Marilyn S. Miller	

The Usage Panel

J. Edward Gates Lexicographer; editor; Professor Emeritus of English, Indiana State University

James Gleick Author; columnist

Philip Gourevitch Writer

Francine du Plessix Gray Writer

Georgia M. Green Professor of Linguistics; writer

Stephen Greenblatt The Harry Levin Professor of Literature, Harvard University

Linda Gregerson Poet; Professor of English, University of Michigan

Alma Guillermoprieto Writer; staff writer, *The New Yorker*

Patricia Hampl Writer; Regents' Professor of English, University of Minnesota

Liane Hansen Radio correspondent

Robert Hass Former US Poet Laureate

The Hon. Mark O. Hatfield Formerly US Senator from Oregon

William Least Heat-Moon Author

Mark Helprin Writer; editor; Senior Fellow, Hudson Institute

Oscar Hijuelos Author; recipient, Pulitzer Prize and Rome Prize

Douglas R. Hofstadter Professor of Cognitive Science and Computer Science; Director, Center for Research on Concepts and Cognition, Indiana University; recipient, Pulitzer Prize

Jenny Holzer Artist; writer

Gloria Hom Educator and consultant; Professor of Economics, Mission College; member, California State University Board of Trustees; member, Board of Trustees, Dominican College of San Rafael

Garrett Hongo Writer

Laurence Horn Professor; author

Fanny Howe Poet; novelist

Sue Hubbell Science and nature essayist

The Hon. Shirley M. Hufstedler Attorney; formerly US Secretary of Education; formerly Judge, US Court of Appeals for the Ninth Circuit

Molly Ivins Journalist; columnist; author

Jennifer James, PhD Cultural anthropologist; writer

Joyce Johnson Writer; recipient, National Book Critics Circle Award

Erica Jong Poet; novelist; essayist

June M. Jordan Poet; Professor of African American Studies and Women's Studies, University of California, Berkeley

Alfred E. Kahn Robert Julius Thorne Professor Emeritus of Economics, Cornell University; formerly Economic Adviser to the President of the United States

Roger Kahn Author; journalist

Wendy Kaminer Writer

Alice Kaplan Professor of Romance Studies and Literature; Director, Center for French and Francophone Studies, Duke University

Justin Kaplan Writer; recipient, Pulitzer Prize and National Book Award

Stanley Kauffmann Film critic for *The New Republic*

Trudy Kehret-Ward Educator, University of California, Berkeley; writer

Garrison Keillor Author; radio host

Elizabeth T. Kennan, PhD Formerly President, Mount Holyoke College

Tracy Kidder Writer

Jamaica Kincaid Author

Florence King Writer; critic and columnist

Maxine Hong Kingston Writer; recipient, National Book Award, National Book Critics Circle Award, Anisfield-Wolf Race Relations Award, and PEN USA West Award in Fiction

Galway Kinnell Poet; Erich Maria Remarque Professor of Creative Writing, New York University; recipient, Pulitzer Prize

The Hon. Jeremy K.B. Kinsman Canadian Ambassador to Russia

The Hon. Jeane J. Kirkpatrick Diplomat; writer; educator; formerly US Ambassador to the United Nations

Ed Koren Cartoonist/captionist, *The New Yorker*

Jane Kramer Writer, *The New Yorker*; author

Maxine Kumin Writer; formerly Consultant in Poetry, Library of Congress; recipient, Pulitzer Prize

Robert Kuttner Founder, co-editor, *The American Prospect*; columnist, *Business Week, The Boston Globe*

David Leavitt Novelist; Professor of English, University of Florida

Wendy Lesser Writer; Editor, *The Threepenny Review*

Anthony Lewis Columnist, *The New York Times*

Flora Lewis Columnist

Robert E. Lewis Lexicographer; Professor of English, University of Michigan; Editor in Chief, *Middle English Dictionary*

Sara Lawrence Lightfoot Emily Hargroves Fisher Professor of Education, Harvard University

Phillip Lopate Writer; Professor of English, Hofstra University

Lois Lowry Author

Claudine B. Malone Management consultant; formerly Associate Professor, Harvard Business School

William Manchester Writer; Professor of History Emeritus, Wesleyan University; Fellow, Pierson College, Yale University

Robert Manning Writer; editor; formerly Editor in Chief, *The Atlantic Monthly*

Greil Marcus Historian; essayist; critic

Suzanne R. Massie Writer; lecturer on Russian history and culture; Fellow, Harvard Russian Research Center

Armistead Maupin Author

Alice E. Mayhew Editorial Director, Simon & Schuster

The Hon. Eugene McCarthy Writer; poet; lecturer; formerly US Senator from Minnesota

Mary McGrory Journalist; columnist; recipient, Pulitzer Prize

Terrence McNally Playwright

Leonard Michaels Professor of English, University of California, Berkeley

Hassan Minor, Jr. Vice President for Government Affairs, Howard University

Lorrie Moore Writer; Professor of English, University of Wisconsin

Lance Morrow Essayist, Time; University Professor, Boston University

The Hon. Daniel Patrick Moynihan US Senator from New York; formerly Professor of Political Science

Bharati Mukherjee Professor; writer; winner, National Book Critics Circle Award

Alice Munro Author

Cullen Murphy Managing Editor, *The Atlantic Monthly*

Thomas M.T. Niles President, United States Council for International Business

Marsha Norman Playwright

Mary Oliver Poet; Professor, Bennington College

Cynthia Ozick Novelist; essayist; member, American Academy of Arts and Letters

Margaret Sayers Peden Translator

Ivars Peterson Mathematics/Physics Editor, *Science News*

Steven Pinker Peter de Florez Professor of Psychology, Massachusetts Institute of Technology; writer

Robert Pinsky Poet; translator; US Poet Laureate; Professor of English, Boston University

Robert S. Pirie President and Chief Executive Officer, Rothschild Inc.

Katha Pollitt Writer; Contributing Editor, *The Nation*

Alvin F. Poussaint, MD Professor of Psychiatry, Harvard Medical School

Usage in *The American Heritage Dictionary*

GEOFFREY NUNBERG

Viewed in retrospect, controversies over usage usually seem incomprehensibly trivial. It is hard for us to fathom why Jonathan Swift should have railed against the shortening of *mobile vulgus* to *mob* or why Benjamin Franklin should have written to Noah Webster complaining about the use of *improve* to mean "ameliorate." Even comparatively recent controversies have a quaint air about them: most people under 50 would be hard-put to understand what in the world critics of the 1960s had in mind when they described the verb *contact* as an "abomination" and a "lubricious barbarism."

This does not necessarily mean that there was never any substance to these controversies—or that there is nothing of importance at stake in the issues that modern critics worry over, even if it is certain that most of them will strike our successors as no less trivial than Swift's and Franklin's complaints seem to us. In his time, Swift may have been within his rights to complain about *mob,* which began as an affectation of aristocratic swells. The fact that the word later settled into middle-aged respectability doesn't retroactively excuse its youthful flippancy. And *contact* started as business jargon before it was generally adopted as a useful verb. Perhaps current jargon like *incentivize* will develop along the same lines, but it doesn't follow that critics have no justification for objecting to it now.

Past controversies should put us on our guard against viewing these disputes too narrowly. Disputes about usage are always proxy wars. What is important is not the particular words and expressions that critics seize on at a given moment but the underlying mental vices that they (often temporarily) exemplify—for example, foppery, pretension, or foggy thinking. Language criticism is instructive only when it takes words as its occasion rather than as its object.

After all, even if you set out to violate every stricture in the most comprehensive usage guide you could find, your derelictions would affect only a small proportion of your vocabulary and would make only the tiniest dent in the overall quality of your prose. This Dictionary contains over 300 Usage Notes and comments that deal with thousands of words and usages. That is a good deal more than are found in most dictionaries and usage handbooks, but at a conservative estimate, an educated speaker of English knows around 100,000 words and constructions. These can be combined in an infinite number of ways, almost all of them infelicitous—for there are many more ways of getting a word wrong than of getting it right.

So usage criticism has had to provide critical methods rather than lists. A book that contents itself with giving the "right" answer on a few hundred traditional questions of usage can have little claim on the attention of serious readers. Usage is not like orthography, and usage debates are not adjudicated like spelling bees. Quite the contrary: the most "authoritative" writers on usage have usually been indifferent to the dictates of received wisdom. H.W. Fowler had no patience with the rules stating that *none* must be singular or that *whose* should not be used with an inanimate antecedent. Most of his contemporaries would have disagreed, and so too would many modern critics. But it is not Fowler's judgments that readers venerate; it is his skill as a litigant.

Still, modern controversies about usage are different from these earlier discussions in important ways. The 18th- and 19th-century grammarians may have argued heatedly about particular points of usage, but they were usually in tacit agreement about the central premise of language criticism: that some forms of expression are preferable to others. Today that assumption is itself controversial. Modern debates about usage often take the form of engagements in a battle between ostensibly irreconcilable philosophical camps. On one side of the field is ranged the party of science, the "descriptivists," who hold that all standards are ultimately based on the facts of use, and that the business of dictionaries and usage books is simply to record those facts in a neutral way. On the other side stand the "prescriptivists," who insist that language is subject to a higher morality and that people who care about the state of the language have an obligation to defend traditional values in the face of growing laxity and permissiveness.

For all the passionate intensity of the partisans, most concerned onlookers have watched the battle with a certain bemusement, for each party does seem to be partly right—and partly wrong. Clearly there was much to criticize in traditional usage writing. A lot of it *was* mere pedantry and ritual schoolroom lore, and it was unquestionably sullied by a strain of snobbery. A large part of usage writing has been dedicated to demonstrating that the speech forms of Standard English—the variety that happens to have been adopted by the educated middle classes—are inherently superior to the forms found in other varieties. There is a strong case to be made for using Standard English as the common medium of public communication of all types, but the point can be made without visiting unwarranted ridicule on the speakers of nonstandard varieties—an approach that ultimately damages the credit of serious language criticism itself.

Usage doctrines must change with the times. It is not just that the language itself changes, so that words that were once controversial become unexceptionable, but that the critical principles themselves must be reevaluated in every age. English today is used for new purposes and in new media, and its discourses have been opened to groups that were linguistically disenfranchised in the past. A responsible program of language criticism must take all of this into account, without at the same time abandoning a commitment to the fundamental linguistic virtues of simplicity, clarity, and intelligibility. The language is too important to be left to nostalgic reveries. But it is also too important to be exempt from critical review.

Usage in This Dictionary

In the treatment of usage, the editors of this Dictionary have been mindful of the dictum of the linguist Antoine Meillet: "Every word has its story." We do not believe that all usage questions can be evaluated by recourse to any single criterion or principle, whether of "use" or "tradition." Rather, we have tried to set up the Usage Notes as miniature critical exercises and to provide, as space allows, the kinds of information that readers will require to resolve questions to their own satisfaction. This information falls into three broad categories: information about use, summaries and analyses of critical arguments, and observations about the opinions of writers and critics.

Use The doctrine that correctness rests on use is as close to a timeless truth as anything ever said about language. But like all timeless truths, it is largely an empty frame that every age shapes to fit its own worldview. *Of course* the rules of the language are determined by use, but whose? Where use is uniform, the question does not arise. It is a curious fact of English that the phrase *more than one* takes a singular verb, despite its sense: *More than one student* has *left.* Doubtless it would be more logical to say *More than one student* have *left;* but it would not be English.

Unfortunately, usage is often divided, sometimes unaccountably, but more often according to social or geographical differences. Sometimes local custom is the only determinant, and we find as many standards as there are speech communities. But in other cases people do insist that there must be one general standard, usually the one determined by the practice of educated middle-class speakers. This Dictionary records facts about the use of items like these either with usage labels such as *Nonstandard* (see the Guide to the Dictionary on page xiv) or, in particularly complicated cases, in the Usage Notes. Take the past tense forms of *sneak.* Many people still object to the form *snuck,* including a majority of the Usage Panel. But in recent years *snuck* has become increasingly frequent in reputable writing, and while *sneaked* is still more prevalent in edited prose by a factor of about 3 to 1, the use of *snuck* is 20 percent more common now than it was in 1985. Clearly it is no longer possible to apply the label *Nonstandard* to *snuck.* When we are dealing with something so straightforward as a past tense form, where no logical or semantic subtleties arise, acceptability depends on nothing more than widespread educated use.

But while the practice of the educated middle class generally determines what counts as Standard English, it does not have the last word in all matters of divided usage. For example, a great many educated speakers use *ironic* to mean simply "coincidental," as in *It's ironic that he was also using a borrowed bat when he hit a grand slam last week against the Dodgers.* This use, then, is unquestionably Standard English, and it is certainly the responsibility of a dictionary to record it. But people still consider *ironic* a literary sort of word, and so long as literary folk continue to use *ironic* in a narrower sense, a dictionary also has a responsibility to note that in this case the general use is sometimes at odds with the use of the writers and critics who have particular authority about the notion in question.

Criticism Custom fixes the rules of language, but it does not justify them. Even complete uniformity of use doesn't make a practice exempt from critical review. There was a time when everybody used *fish* to refer to whales, but the practice was abandoned in light of new zoological evidence. And until quite recently, everybody used the words *man* and *men* to refer to all humans, but many people have abandoned that practice in the light of new conceptions of gender equality.

The prescriptive tradition had its origins in the Age of Criticism as a method no different in kind from the criticism of artistic works or of civil society in general. Eighteenth-century writers established the battery of principles to which usage might be held accountable—the

familiar arguments from analogy, logic, etymology, and meaning, among others. Granted, they often applied these principles with the overzealous love of rules and systems that they brought to all their critical enterprises, and the "logic" that they invoked was sometimes of dubious relevance to the facts of English. It is fair to criticize the double negative in a sentence like *I didn't see nothing* on the grounds that it is associated with nonstandard varieties of English. But one cannot fault the construction on logical grounds without also being prepared to assert as well the illogicality of standard French and Italian, in which standard negation involves the use of more than one negative word.

Still, the fact that particular prescriptive arguments are sometimes unsound does not vitiate the case for criticism in general, but only requires that we go about it in a more sophisticated way. Modern linguistics teaches us that the logic of language structure is a good deal more subtle and elusive than traditional grammarians supposed, and it has provided us with analytical tools that can capture distinctions and subtleties that elude the sometimes coarse apparatus of traditional, Latin-based school grammar. We have made use of techniques like these in the Notes, in the course of analyzing a number of vexed grammatical questions (see, for example, the entries at *different, myself, plus,* and *than,* and at *he*[1] and *man*).

Opinion: The Role of the Usage Panel Custom can provide precedents and criticism can provide principles, but each has to be evaluated at the bar of opinion. Dictionaries register received opinion at every turn—on what other grounds would one label a usage *Vulgar* or *Offensive?* But it is often useful to have a more explicit way of gauging the opinions of people with a critical interest in the language. This is the role of the Dictionary's Usage Panel, a group of some 200 well-known writers, critics, and scholars (a list of Panel members can be found on pages viii–x). Panel members are regularly surveyed on a broad range of usage questions, from the distinction between *nauseous* and *nauseating* to the status of innovations like *lifestyle* or the use of *grow* as a transitive verb in business contexts. The results of these surveys are included in many of the Usage Notes.

The Usage Panel should not be thought of as an academy empowered to rule on all questions of disputed usage. That is an expedient that the English-speaking world has rejected since the 18th century, and in a world where English is established as the language of a heterogeneous international community, the idea that any group or individual might arrogate the authority to fix standards seems not only illiberal but absurd.

Indeed, the Panel is rarely in a position to "rule" on disputes, since its opinions are often divided. Sometimes, it is true, the Panelists seem to speak with a single voice. In surveys from the 1960s, for example, 99 percent rejected *between you and I* and *ain't I* in formal writing. But the Panel's judgment on questions like these merely reflects the predominant practices of Standard English. The survey results are far more interesting when they involve questions that are matters of dispute among educated speakers. When 52 percent of the Panel rejects the use of *anxious* to mean "eager," and 59 percent of the Panel rejects *enormity* to mean "largeness," such divided responses can give a rough indication of just how broadly various critical concerns are shared by educated speakers. Ultimately, readers will want to make up their own minds about each of such usage issues, but the opinions of the Panel may provide a useful point of reference.

The Scope of Coverage

The Traditional Canon The first things that come to mind when we speak of "usage questions" are points of grammar and diction that have occupied critics for a century or more: the differences between *who* and *whom*, *between* and *among*; the qualification of absolute terms like *unique* and *infinite*; and so forth. To be sure, over the years the traditional canon has accumulated a good deal of unexamined grammatical lore that does not hold up well under scrutiny; see for example the Notes at *and* and *preposition*[1]. But we believe that canonical issues like these give language criticism its historical continuity, and that it is the task of a dictionary to evaluate them anew for each generation. In fact, these points still constitute the largest single category among the Dictionary's Usage Notes.

New Words, New Issues The Dictionary's treatment of usage has been extended to cover a variety of words and expressions that bear on the issues facing the language at the beginning of the 21st century. One class of these new entries deserves special mention. Digital technologies have had a sweeping effect on the language in recent years, as evidenced by the hundreds of new words and new senses that appear for the first time in the Dictionary. These include not just technical terms like *active-matrix*, *applet*, *metatag*, and *object-oriented*, but words that suggest the broad cultural influence of the technologies, such as *chatroom*, *dotcommer*, *cyperpunk*, *netiquette*, and *netizen*. And with these words have come new usage problems particular to this domain. When does one capitalize the word *web*? When does one use the word *virtual* as opposed to *digital*, or the prefix *cyber–* as opposed to the prefix *e–*? Is it *compact disc* or *compact disk*? Are there 1,000,000 or 1,048,576 bytes in a megabyte? Of course, some technologies are changing too rapidly for norms to become fixed, but it is important at least to signal that these new forms are part of the domain of criticism.

Other items have a more general provenance, such as the use of *holocaust* to mean simply "disaster" or the use of *ad hominem* as applied to a personal attack. And then there are the words we use to talk about the language itself. In recent years, for example, items like *Standard English* and *Black English* have figured prominently in public debates about the language, and these issues are dealt with in Usage Notes.

Usage and Social Diversity Over the last 30 years, one of the most radical changes in the scope of language criticism has been its extension to a wide range of usages involving questions of social diversity. There have been widespread public discussions, for example, about the names of groups defined along lines of ethnicity, religion, race, physical capacity, and sexual orientation. Some of these discussions are summarized in Usage Notes at words like *Anglo, Asian, black, Chicano, color, deaf, gay, gender, handicapped, Hispanic, homosexual, Jew, Latina,* and *Native American.*

In matters like these, of course, a dictionary has no authority to dictate "correct" usage (at least not in the linguistic sense of the term). Most of these words are subject to a great deal of variation, even among members of the groups they apply to, and their connotations and use can change very rapidly. But dictionaries can help by providing information on the social and linguistic backgrounds of these questions, which can be quite complex—information that may spare some readers from resorting to unnecessary circumlocution and others from giving inadvertent offense.

Usage and Gender With a few exceptions (as with *black* and *gay*), the usage questions raised by the names of ethnic and other groups are socially complicated but linguistically simple. The replacement of one such word by another rarely raises grammatical difficulties or creates ancillary linguistic problems. But gender differences are so extensively and intricately woven into the fabric of the language that efforts to change usage often require a great deal of attentiveness and linguistic ingenuity. So it is not surprising that the debate over these issues has been particularly energetic. These questions are discussed in Usage Notes at *–ess*, *gender, he*[1], *hero, lady, man, Ms., person,* and *they*.

With these items, as with the names of ethnic and social categories, we have tried to present the linguistic and social background that readers will require to make informed decisions about the issues. Because the linguistic program of feminism has called for such extensive and varied changes in usage, we have also made an effort to gauge its overall effects on the attitudes and practice of writers with regard to particular words and constructions. The results of Usage Panel surveys have been particularly instructive here, since they show how selective educated speakers have been in adopting or rejecting patterns of usage. The Panel's divisions with respect to some of these items are not likely to be resolved in the near future. But these are precisely the kinds of controversies that ensured the vitality of language criticism in the 18th and 19th centuries. Here, as elsewhere, achieving uniformity is not what matters. Indeed, that goal seems antithetical to the genius of English, whose strength has always resided in its capacity to accommodate heterogeneity, whether in regional or social variation. What draws us together as speakers of English is not our sameness but our ability to find in our differences the occasion for lively critical discussion.

Guide to the Dictionary

This Guide explains the conventions used in presenting the great array of information contained in the Dictionary, enabling you to find and understand that information quickly and easily.

Guidewords

A pair of boldface guidewords, together with the page number, appears on each page. The word on the top represents the first boldface entry on that page of the Dictionary. The word on the bottom represents the last boldface entry on that page. Thus, **braided** and **branch** and all the entries that fall alphabetically between them are entered and defined on page 174.

The Entry Words: Alphabetical Order

Each entry word, printed in boldface type, is set slightly to the left of the text column. All entries—including biographical and geographic names, abbreviations, symbols, and compounds of two or more words—are listed in strict alphabetical order:

> **abs**
> **ABS**
> **Absalom**
> **Absaroka Range**
> **Absaroke**
> **abscess**

For the sake of convenience, proper names are listed according to their most important element, such as a surname shared by a number of important people. In these cases, the alphabetical sequence applies only to those letters preceding the first comma. Thus in the list below, the personal name **James, Henry** appears before the geographical entry **James Bay**.

> **James**
> **James¹, Saint**
> **James², Saint**
> ......
> **James, Henry**
> **James, Jesse**
> **James, William**
> **James Bay**
> **Jamesian**
> **James River**

Superscript numbers. Words with identical spellings but different etymologies are entered separately and have superscript, or raised, numbers:

> **tick¹** (tĭk) *n.* **1.** A light sharp clicking sound made repeatedly by a machine, such as a clock. . . . [ME *tek,* light tap.]
> **tick²** (tĭk) *n.* **1.** Any of numerous small bloodsucking parasitic arachnids of the family Ixodidae, many of which transmit febrile diseases, such as Lyme disease. . . . [ME *tik,* perh. < OE *ticca.*]

Syllabification

An entry word and its inflected and derived forms are divided into syllables by means of centered dots:

> **ac·e·tate** (ăs′ĭ-tāt′) *n.*

In entries such as *ethyl acetate* that consist of two or more words separated by spaces, the words without centered dots are divided into syllables at their own places in the Dictionary.

Pronunciations are syllabified for the sake of clarity. The syllabication of the pronunciation may not match the syllabification of the entry word because the division of the pronunciation follows phonological rules, while the division of the entry word reflects the long-established practices of printers and editors in breaking words at the end of a line.

Variants

Though standardization of English in the United States is more extensive than at any earlier time, many variant spellings and stylings remain in common use. All variants shown in this Dictionary are acceptable in any context unless indicated otherwise by a restrictive label, such as a dialect label. Variants, set in boldface type, are of two kinds: equal and unequal.

Equal variants. The word *or* joining an entry word and its variant form or forms indicates that these forms occur with virtually equal frequency in edited sources, based on our electronic and printed citational evidence:

> **on·line** or **on-line** (ŏn′līn′, ôn′-) *adj.*

Unequal variants. The word *also* joining an entry word and its variant form or forms indicates that the variant form occurs less frequently:

> **am·bi·ance** also **am·bi·ence** (ăm′bē-əns, äɴ-byäɴs′) *n.*

Variants that occur more than ten entries away from the main entry word in alphabetical order are entered as separate cross-references at the appropriate places in the alphabetical word list:

> **me·di·e·val** also **me·di·ae·val** (mē′dē-ē′vəl, mĕd′ē-, mĭ-dē′-vəl) *adj.*
> **me·di·ae·val** (mē′dē-ē′vəl, mĕd′ē-, mĭ-dē′vəl) *adj.* Variant of **medieval.**

British variants. A number of variants consist of spellings preferred in British English. These variants, such as *defence* and *colour,* are labeled *Chiefly British.* They are entered at their own alphabetical places but are not given at the entries to which they relate:

> **de·fence** (dĭ-fĕns′) *n. & v. Chiefly British* Variant of **defense.**

Part-of-speech Labels

The following italicized labels indicate parts of speech:

adj.	adjective
adv.	adverb
conj.	conjunction

def.art.	definite article
indef.art.	indefinite article
interj.	interjection
_n._	noun
prep.	preposition
pron.	pronoun
_v._	verb

These italicized labels indicate inflected forms:

| _pl._ | plural |
| _sing._ | singular |

These italicized labels are used for the traditional classification of verbs:

_tr._	transitive
intr.	intransitive
aux.	auxiliary

The labels for word elements are:

| _pref._ | prefix |
| _suff._ | suffix |

Entries that are abbreviations, such as _A.M._ and _blvd._, are labeled _abbr._

Certain entries do not carry labels. They include contractions (_I'll_), symbols (_Fe_, the symbol for iron), trademarks (_Walkman_), and the word elements _–i–_ and _–o–_, which never occur in initial or final position in a word.

Sometimes an entry word fulfills more than one grammatical function. For example, _current_ can be an adjective (_current pricing; current negotiations_) and a noun (_a current of air; the swift current of a river; electric current_). In such cases the different parts of speech are defined within a single entry called a _combined entry_. The shift in grammatical function is indicated by a special symbol (❖) followed by the appropriate part-of-speech label. If the syllabication or pronunciation differs, it is also included. Inflected forms are given if necessary and are followed by definitions:

> **re·bel** (rĭ-bĕl′) _intr.v._ **-belled, -bel·ling, -bels 1.** To refuse allegiance to and oppose by force an established government or ruling authority. **2.** To resist or defy an authority or a generally accepted convention. **3.** To feel or express strong unwillingness or repugnance: _rebelled at the suggestion._ ❖ _n._ **reb·el** (rĕb′əl) One who rebels or is in rebellion.

Inflected Forms

An inflected form of a word differs from the main entry form by the addition of a suffix or by a change in its base form to indicate grammatical features such as number, person, mood, or tense.

Inflected forms follow the part-of-speech label. They are set in boldface type, divided into syllables, and given pronunciations as necessary. Inflected forms are usually shortened to the last syllable of the entry word plus the inflectional ending. Irregular inflected forms are spelled out to the extent required for clarity. When inflected forms are shortened, each shortened inflected form is preceded by a boldface hyphen:

> **cap·i·tal·ize** (kăp′ĭ-tl-īz′) _v._ **-ized, -iz·ing, -iz·es**

Principal parts of verbs. The principal parts of verbs are entered in this order: _past tense, past participle, present participle,_ and _third person singular present tense._ When

the past tense and the past participle are identical, one form represents both:

> **fly¹** (flī) _v._ **flew** (flо̄о̄), **flown** (flōn), **fly·ing, flies** (flīz)
> **walk** (wôk) _v._ **walked, walk·ing, walks**

Comparison of adjectives and adverbs. Adjectives and adverbs whose comparative and superlative degrees can be formed by adding _–er_ and _–est_ to the unchanged word show these comparative and superlative suffixes immediately after the part-of-speech label:

> **high** (hī) _adj._ **high·er, high·est**

Irregular comparative and superlative forms are given in full.

> **bad** (băd) _adj._ **worse,** (wûrs), **worst** (wûrst)

Plurals of nouns. Plurals of nouns other than those formed regularly by adding the suffixes _–s_ or _–es_ are shown and labeled _pl._:

> **mouse** (mous) _n., pl._ **mice** (mīs)

When a noun has a regular and an irregular plural form, both forms appear, with the most common shown first:

> **a·quar·i·um** (ə-kwâr′ē-əm) _n., pl._ **-i·ums** or **-i·a** (-ē-ə)

Regular plurals are also shown when spelling might be a problem:

> **ra·di·o** (rā′dē-ō) _n., pl._ **-os**
> **hon·ey** (hŭn′ē) _n., pl._ **-eys**

A noun that is chiefly or exclusively plural in both form and meaning is labeled _pl.n._:

> **cat·tle** (kăt′l) _pl.n._ **1.** Any of various chiefly domesticated mammals of the genus _Bos,_ including cows, steers, bulls, and oxen, often raised for meat and dairy products.

A noun that is always plural in form but is not necessarily used with a plural verb is labeled like this:

> **aer·o·bics** (â-rō′bĭks) _n._ (_used with a sing. or pl. verb_) **1.** A system of physical conditioning designed to enhance circulatory and respiratory efficiency that involves vigorous, sustained exercise, such as jogging, swimming, or cycling. **2.** A program of physical fitness that involves such exercise. [< AEROBIC.]

> **pol·i·tics** (pŏl′ĭ-tĭks) _n._ **1.** (_used with a sing. verb_) **a.** The art or science of government or governing, esp. the governing of a political entity, such as a nation, and the administration and control of its internal and external affairs. **b.** Political science.

Separate entries for inflected forms. Irregular inflected forms are entered separately in the Dictionary when they occur more than ten entries away from the main entry word:

> **men** (mĕn) _n._ Plural of **man.**

Such entries carry a part-of-speech label and are given pronunciations as necessary.

Some verbs, such as _do, be,_ and _have,_ have archaic inflected forms, such as _dost, art,_ and _hadst,_ that occur frequently enough to justify their inclusion in this Dictionary. These forms are also entered separately:

> **dost** (dŭst) _v. Archaic_ A second person singular present tense of **do¹.**

Labels

This Dictionary uses various labels to indicate entries related to particular subject areas, to provide guidance regarding various levels of usage, and to indicate words indigenous to specific geographic areas.

Subject labels. A subject label identifies the special area of knowledge to which an entry word or a definition applies:

> **tri·mor·phic** (trī-môr′fĭk) also **tri·mor·phous** (-fəs) *adj.* **1.** *Biology* Having or occurring in three differing forms. **2.** *Chemistry* Crystallizing in three distinct forms.

Status labels. Status labels indicate that an entry word or a definition is limited to a particular level or style of usage. All words and definitions not restricted by such a label should be regarded as appropriate for use in all contexts.

Nonstandard. This, the most restrictive label in the Dictionary, is applied to forms and usages that educated speakers and writers consider unacceptable:

> **an·y·ways** (ĕn′ē-wāz′) *adv. Nonstandard* In any case.

Usage Problem. The label *Usage Problem* warns of possible difficulties involving grammar, diction, and writing style. A word or definition so labeled is discussed in a Usage Note:

> **snuck** (snŭk) *v. Usage Problem* A past tense and a past participle of **sneak.** See Usage Note at **sneak.**

Offensive. This label is reserved for words and expressions such as racial, ethnic, or gender slurs that are not only derogatory and insulting to the person to whom they are directed but also a discredit to the one using them. This label may occur alone or in combination as *Offensive Slang.*

Vulgar. This label warns of social taboos attached to a word; it may appear alone or in combination as *Vulgar Slang.*

Slang. This label indicates a style of language that is distinguished by a striving for rhetorical effect through the use of extravagant, often facetious figures of speech. Some forms of slang occur in most cultivated speech but not in formal discourse. An example of a word labeled *Slang* is:

> **white-knuck·le** (hwīt′nŭk′əl, wīt′-) also **white-knuck·led** (-əld) *adj. Slang* Characterized by tense nervousness or apprehension.

Informal. Those whose speech is standard use not only the language of formal discourse but also the language of conversation. The great majority of words are acceptable at both levels, though many words that are acceptable in conversation with friends and colleagues would be unsuitable in the formal prose of an article written for publication in the journal of a learned society, for example. An example of an entry labeled *Informal* is:

> **whirl·y·bird** (hwûr′lē-bûrd′, wûr′-) *n. Informal* A helicopter.

Temporal labels. Temporal labels signal words or senses whose use in modern English is uncommon.

Archaic. This label is applied to words and senses that once

were common but are now rare. Specifically, this label is attached to entry words and senses for which there is only sporadic evidence in print after 1755:

> **en·ter·tain·ment** (ĕn′tər-tān′mənt) *n.* . . . **5.** *Archaic* Maintenance; support.

Obsolete. The label *Obsolete* is used with entry words and senses no longer in active use, except, for example, in literary quotations. Specifically, this label is attached to entry words and senses for which there is little or no printed evidence since 1755. Sense 6 of *entertainment* is an example:

> **6.** *Obsolete* Employment.

English-language labels. This Dictionary contains a number of labels noting the restriction of particular entry words and senses to specific areas of the English-speaking world. Here is a typical example of a word labeled *Chiefly British:*

> **win·kle²** (wĭng′kəl) *tr.v.* **-kled, -kling, -kles** *Chiefly British* To pry, extract, or force from a place or position. Often used with *out.*

Other English-language labels are:

Australian	*Caribbean*	*Scots*
Canadian	*Irish*	*South African*

Dialect labels. When a word or sense is commonly used in a specific area of the United States and little used—even if known—in other areas, it has been given a dialect label.

> **bo·da·cious** also **bow·da·cious** (bō-dā′shəs) or **bar·da·cious** (bär-) *Southern & South Midland US*

This Dictionary uses dialect labels singly and in various combinations ranging from the very general (*Regional*) to the very specific (*New Orleans*). The very specific labels, which are self-explanatory, serve as descriptors of geographic regions such as cities, states, and interstate areas. For a list of these labels see page xxvii.

Cross-references

A cross-reference signals that additional information about one entry can be found at another entry. Cross-references have two main functions: to avoid needless duplication of information and to indicate where further discussion of a word occurs.

The entry referred to is printed in boldface type preceded by a brief descriptive or instructional phrase:

> **bade** (băd, bād) *v.* A past tense of **bid.**

The cross-reference indicates that *bade* is a past tense at the entry *bid,* where further information about the entry can be found.

The word *See* is also used to introduce certain cross-references:

> **feath·er·edge** (fĕth′ər-ĕj′) *n.* . . . **2.** See **deckle edge.**

A full definition is given at the entry referred to, in this case *deckle edge.*

A cross-reference referring to only one definition in an entry having two or more definitions contains that definition number:

tsar (zär, tsär) *n.* Variant of **czar**[1].

Some cross-references refer to tables. The boldface term in the cross-reference is the entry at which the table can be found:

kro·na[2] (krō′nə) *n., pl.* **-nor** (-nôr′, -nər) See table at **currency.**

Order of Senses

Entries containing more than one sense are arranged for the convenience of contemporary dictionary users with the central and often the most commonly sought meanings first. Senses and subsenses are grouped to show their relationships with each other. For example, in the entry for *fatal* shown below, the commonly sought meaning "Causing or capable of causing death" appears first and the now obsolete sense "Having been destined; fated" comes last in the series of five:

fa·tal (fāt′l) *adj.* **1.** Causing or capable of causing death. **2.** Causing ruin or destruction; disastrous. **3.** Of decisive importance; fateful. **4.** Concerning or determining one's fate: *the fatal thread of life.* **5.** *Obsolete* Having been destined; fated.

Division of senses. Boldface letters before senses indicate that two or more subsenses are closely related:

phe·nom·e·non (fĭ-nŏm′ə-nŏn′, -nən) *n., pl.* **-na** (-nə) **1.** . . . **2.** *pl.* **-nons a.** An unusual, significant, or unaccountable fact or occurrence; a marvel. **b.** A remarkable or outstanding person; a paragon. See Syns at **wonder.**

In a combined entry the senses are numbered in separate sequences after each part of speech:

back·fire (băk′fīr′) *n.* **1.** An explosion of prematurely ignited fuel or of unburned exhaust gases in an internal-combustion engine. **2.** The backward escape of gases or cartridge fragments when a gun is fired. **3.** Fire started to control an oncoming forest or prairie fire by burning an area in its path. ❖ *intr.v.* **-fired, -fir·ing, -fires 1.** To explode in the manner of or make the sound of a backfire. **2.** To start or use a backfire. **3.** To produce an unexpected, undesired result.

Information applicable only to a particular sense or subsense is shown after the number or letter of that sense or subsense:

ra·dix (rā′dĭks) *n.* . . . **1.** *Biology* A root or point of origin. **2.** *Mathematics* The base of a system of numbers, such as 10 in the decimal system.

In this entry the subject label *Biology* applies only to the first sense; the subject label *Mathematics*, only to the second sense.

Labels and other information applicable to all senses in an entry with more than one part of speech appear before the first part of speech in that entry:

kedge (kĕj) *Nautical n.* A light anchor used to warp a vessel. ❖ *v.* **kedged, kedg·ing, kedg·es** —*tr.* To warp (a vessel) by using a light anchor. —*intr.* To move by using a light anchor.

The positioning of the label *Nautical* before the noun part-of-speech label, the first such label in the entry, indicates that *Nautical* applies to the entire combined entry—in this case, the noun and the verb.

Explanatory notes. Words whose meanings do not permit standard definitions have explanatory notes, beginning with *Used* or *Often used.* Words requiring notes of this

kind include function words, interjections, intensives, some auxiliary verbs, and words labeled *Offensive* and *Offensive Slang.* An example is the explanatory note at the interjection *ugh:*

Used to express horror, disgust, or repugnance.

Illustrative Examples

Illustrative examples, which follow the definitions and are set in italic type, show the entry words in typical contexts. Here is an instance of the use of a quoted illustration:

bloom[1] (blo͞om) *n.* . . . . **3.** A fresh, rosy complexion: *"She was short, plump, and fair, with a fine bloom"* (Jane Austen).

Illustrative examples that are not direct quotations appear in entries such as the verb *speak:*

speak (spēk) *v.* **spoke** (spōk), **spo·ken** (spō′kən), **speak·ing, speaks** —*intr.* . . . **4a.** To make a statement in writing: *The biography speaks of loneliness.*

Phrasal Verbs

A phrasal verb is an expression consisting of a verb and either an adverb or a preposition that together have a unitary meaning that cannot be deduced from the sum total of the meanings of its constituent parts. Phrasal verbs, set in boldface type and introduced by the heading **—phrasal verbs,** follow the main definitions and precede the idioms, if any are present. Phrasal verbs are listed in alphabetical order:

set[1] (sĕt) *v.* **set, set·ting, sets** —*tr.* **1.** To put in a specified position; place. . . . . **—phrasal verbs: set about** To begin or start. **set apart 1.** To reserve for a specific use. **2.** To make noticeable. **set aside 1.** To separate and reserve for a special purpose. **2.** To discard or reject. **3.** To declare invalid; annul or overrule. **set at** To attack or assail. **set back 1.** To slow down the progress of; hinder. **2.** *Informal* To cost.

Idioms

An idiom is an expression consisting of two or more words having a meaning that cannot be deduced from the sum total of the meanings of its constituent parts. Idioms, set in boldface type and introduced by the heading **—idioms,** are fully defined in the last part of an entry. Idioms are listed in alphabetical order:

take (tāk) *v.* **took** (to͝ok), **tak·en** (tā′kən), **tak·ing, takes** —*tr.* **1.** To get into one's possession by force, skill, or artifice. . . . . **—idioms: on the take** *Informal* Taking or seeking to take bribes or illegal income. **take a bath** *Informal* To experience serious financial loss. **take account of** To take into consideration. . . . **take it on the chin** *Slang* To endure punishment, suffering, or defeat. **take it or leave it** To accept or reject unconditionally.

Etymologies

Etymologies appear in square brackets following the definitions. An etymology traces the history of a word from one language to another as far back in time as can be determined with reasonable certainty. The most recent stage before Modern English is given first, with each earlier stage following in sequence:

cab·in (kăb′ĭn) *n.* **1.** A small, roughly built house. . . . [ME *caban* < OFr. *cabane* < O Provençal *cabana* < LLat. *capanna.*]

A language name, linguistic form, and brief definition, or gloss, of that form are given for each stage of the derivation. In order to avoid redundancy, however, a language, form, or gloss is not repeated if it is identical to the corresponding item in the immediately preceding stage. In the example shown for *cabin*, the different Middle English, Old French, and Late Latin forms have the same gloss, which is the same as the first definition of the Modern English word *cabin*: "small, roughly built house."

Content of etymologies.

The etymologies in this Dictionary are designed to be as readable as possible. The traditional language of descriptive grammar is used to identify parts of speech and various grammatical and morphological forms and processes, such as *diminutive, frequentative, variant, stem, past participle,* and *metathesis.* All of these terms are fully defined entries in the Dictionary. Likewise, every language that is cited in an etymology either is a Dictionary entry or is glossed in the etymology itself.

Sometimes a stage in the history of a word is not attested, yet there is reasonable certainty from comparative evidence about what the missing linguistic form looked like and what language it belonged to. These unattested forms are preceded by an asterisk indicating their hypothetical nature:

cer·tain (sûr′tn) *adj.* **1.** Definite; fixed. **2.** Sure to come or happen; inevitable. **3.** Established beyond doubt or question; indisputable. . . . [ME < OFr. < VLat. *certānus < Lat. certus, p. part. of cernere, to determine. See krei- in App.]

If a word is taken from the name of a person or place, such names are identified with pertinent information as to time or place. The etymology usually stops there, although a further etymology of the name itself is occasionally given.

Some words are not given etymologies. These include interjections, trademarks, and ethnic names that are Anglicizations of the group's name for itself. A large and important group of words not given explicit etymologies consists of compounds and derivatives, such as *sodium chloride, emergence,* and *euploid,* formed in English from words or word elements that are themselves entries in the Dictionary. If only a portion of an entry is used in an etymology, the unused portion of the entry is enclosed within parentheses:

bal·lis·to·car·di·o·gram (bə-lĭs′tō-kär′dē-ə-grăm′) *n.* A recording made by a ballistocardiograph. [BALLIST(IC) + CARDIOGRAM.]

Derivatives such as *emergence,* from *emerge,* in which only the final vowel of one constituent has been deleted, are assumed to be sufficiently understandable not to need etymologies.

Indo-European roots.

It is remarkable that the great bulk of the now vast vocabulary of English can be traced back to the reconstructed ancestral language called Proto-Indo-European. The etymologies in this Dictionary take many such words back to their earliest ascertainable origins either in Proto-Indo-European or in the prehistoric stage of one of its chief branches, such as Germanic or Celtic. Each word is traced back to its earliest documentary attestation in its own etymology, then cross-referred to the Appendix of Indo-European Roots found at the end of the Dictionary by a cross-reference like "See **krei-** in App.", as shown in the etymology of *certain*. An introductory essay by Professor Calvert Watkins discusses some of the cultural inferences that may be drawn from this material (see pages 1598–1603). Also included are an explanatory Guide to the Appendix (pages 1604–1605), a table of the principal sound correspondences (pages 1606–1607), and a diagram of the Indo-European languages on the endpapers.

Style of etymologies.

The etymologies present a great deal of complex information in a small space, and for this reason certain typographic and stylistic conventions are used. The symbol < indicates origin of any kind—by inheritance, borrowing, derivation, or composition. When a compound word is split into its component elements, a colon introduces these parts. Each element is traced in turn to its further origins. Parentheses enclose the further history of a part of a compound:

pseud·e·pig·ra·pha (sōō′dĭ-pĭg′rə-fə) *pl.n.* **1.** Spurious writings, esp. writings that are falsely attributed to biblical characters or times. . . . [Gk. < neut. pl. of *pseudepigraphos,* falsely ascribed : *pseudēs,* false; see PSEUDO– + *epigraphein,* to inscribe (*epi-,* epi- + *graphein,* to write; see **gerbh-** in App.).]

At times it is necessary to cross-refer from one etymology to another, either to avoid repeating part of a lengthy and complex derivation or to indicate the close relationship between two different Modern English words:

bat³ (băt) *tr.v.* **bat·ted, bat·ting, bats** To wink or flutter: *bat one's eyelashes.* [Prob. var. of BATE².]

A word or word element in an etymology printed in small capitals is an entry in the Dictionary and should be referred to for more etymological information. Linguistic forms that are not Modern English words appear in italics, and glosses and language names appear in roman type.

The transliterations of Greek, Russian, Arabic, and Hebrew are shown at the Table of Alphabets on page 40. Old English thorn (ᚦ) and edh (ð) are both given as *th,* whereas Old Norse thorn is spelled as *th* and the phonemically distinct edh as *dh.* In Latin all long vowels are marked with macrons. Mandarin Chinese forms are given in the Pinyin system. The transcription of African and Native American languages occasionally requires the use of symbols—usually drawn from the International Phonetic Alphabet—whose values will be apparent to specialists but are not discussed here.

Undefined Forms

At the end of many entries additional boldface words appear without definitions—words either formed from the entry word by the addition of suffixes or otherwise closely and clearly related to the entry word or the entry word itself with a different part of speech. These *run-on entries* are related in basic meaning to the entry word but may have different grammatical functions, as indicated by their part-of-speech labels. Multisyllabic run-ons are divided into syllables and show primary and secondary stresses as needed. Pronunciations are included as required:

ex·cuse (ĭk-skyōōz′) *tr.v.* . . . [ME *excusen < OFr. excuser < Lat. excūsāre : ex-, ex- + causa,* accusation; see CAUSE.] —**ex·cus′a·ble** *adj.* —**ex·cus′a·ble·ness** *n.* —**ex·cus′a·bly** *adv.* —**ex·cus′er** *n.*

Notes

This Dictionary contains five types of Notes: Synonym

Paragraphs, Usage Notes, Word Histories, Regional Notes, and Our Living Language Notes. An explanation of each type follows.

Synonym Paragraphs. Synonyms of special interest are listed after the entry for the central word in the group. Synonym paragraphs are introduced by the heading SYNONYMS. There are two kinds of synonym paragraphs. The first consists of a group of undiscriminated, alphabetically ordered words sharing a single, irreducible meaning. These synonyms are presented in illustrative examples following a core definition. An example of an undiscriminated synonym paragraph appears at the entry for *close*. Antonyms, if applicable, appear at the end of the paragraph.

The second kind of paragraph consists of fully discriminated synonyms ordered in a way that reflects their interrelationships. A brief sentence explaining the initial point of comparison of the words is given, followed by explanations of their connotations and varying shades of meaning, along with illustrative examples. An example of a discriminated synonym paragraph appears at the entry for *curious*.

Every synonym in a synonym paragraph is cross-referenced to that synonym paragraph. Sometimes a word is discussed in more than one synonym paragraph. Cross-references are given to all the synonym paragraphs that include that word.

Usage Notes. The Usage Notes following many entries present important information and guidance on matters of grammar, diction, pronunciation, and registers and nuances of usage. For a discussion of usage and our Usage Panel, see Geoffrey Nunberg's essay on pages xi–xiii.

Many Notes, such as those at *disinterested* and *prioritize*, contain opinions of the Usage Panel about the acceptability or conventionality of words, especially as used in formal Standard English contexts. Others, such as those at *criterion* and *principal*, are more explanatory in nature and do not refer to Panel opinions. Entries of words discussed in the Notes have cross-references to the entry at which the Note appears. If an entry that has a Note is discussed in a Note at another entry, the cross-reference to that entry is given immediately following the Usage Note.

Word Histories. This Dictionary provides Word History paragraphs at some entries whose etymologies are of particular interest. In these paragraphs the bare facts of the etymology are expanded to give a fuller understanding of how important linguistic processes operate, how words move from one language to another, and how the history of an individual word can be related to historical and cultural developments. For example, the history of the word *mosquito* involves borrowing from Spanish and Portuguese into English, as its etymology reveals, but the Word History also describes its relationship to words such as *musket*.

Regional Notes. This Dictionary contains hundreds of words and meanings whose occurrence is restricted to certain areas of the United States. Some entries contain Regional Notes explaining in detail a point of dialect. For example, the word *dragonfly* is widespread in American English, but dialect terms for the insect abound. These dialect terms are discussed in the Regional Note at the end of the entry. The entries discussed in Regional Notes are fully cross-referenced.

Our Living Language Notes. Since language varies not just by region but also by social group, this Dictionary contains Notes that discuss the social aspect of words. Like regionalisms, some of these words and constructions fall outside Standard usage. Others are limited to a particular social group, such as teenagers. But most are widely recognized, and some have been incorporated into the Standard language. Some Notes, such as those at *be* or *zero copula*, explain the patterns of usage of particular constructions and describe the linguistic situations under which they are and are not used, in order to show how they fit into the broader phenomenon of language. Other Notes, such as the one at *comparative*, explain the linguistic processes governing certain constructions that might at first appear to be errors or anomalies, relating such constructions to similar examples in earlier times and showing them to have traveled a different path from their standard counterparts for centuries. Still other Notes, such as those at *cool, schlock*, and *za*, describe groups of words that have arisen from the lingo of particular subcultures, such as jazz musicians, speakers of Yiddish, and teenagers.

Style Manual

This section of the Dictionary discusses and illustrates the basic, generally accepted stylistic conventions of American English. Over 300 verbal illustrations, many of which are quotations from the citation files of *The American Heritage Dictionary,* exemplify and augment the more than 100 rules delineating the proper use of capital letters, italics, and punctuation marks.

Unfortunately, the space constraints inherent in a college-level dictionary such as this one preclude discussion of all aspects of English grammar, stylistics, and diction. Hence, we recommend that readers seeking in-depth guidance to the use of graceful English prose consult one of the many books on the subject, such as *Keys for Writers,* 3rd ed., by Ann Raimes (Boston: Houghton Mifflin, 2002, ISBN 0-618-11523-4).

Capitalization

The following should be capitalized:

Beginnings

1. The first word of a sentence:

Some diseases are acute; others are chronic.
Aren't you my new neighbor?
Great! Let's go!

2. The first word of a direct quotation, except when it is a split quotation closely woven into the sentence:

Helen asked, "Do you think Satie was a serious composer?"
"For me," I answered, "he was simply amusing."
G.B. Shaw said, "Assassination is the extreme form of censorship."

3. The first word of each line in a poem in traditional verse:

Poets that lasting marble seek
Must carve in Latin or in Greek.
    —Edmund Waller

Proper names

4. The names of people, of organizations and their members, of councils and congresses, and of historical periods and events:

Albert Einstein	a Democrat
Marie Curie	the Nuclear Regulatory
the Free and Accepted	Commission
Masons	the Potsdam Conference
a Mason	the House of Representatives
Roman Catholic Church	the Middle Ages
a Catholic	World War II
the Republican Party	the Battle of the Bulge

5. The names of places and geographic divisions, districts, regions, and locales:

Boston	Arctic Circle
Virginia	Western Hemisphere
France	South Pole
Fifth Avenue	Torrid Zone
Golden Gate Bridge	Continental Divide

Middle East	the South
Far West	the East
Mountain States	the West
Gulf Coast	the Midwest
the North	the Southwest

But do not capitalize words designating points of the compass unless a specific region is referred to:

Turn south onto I-95.

6. The names of rivers, lakes, mountains, and oceans:

Connecticut River	Blue Ridge Mountains
Lake Geneva	Pacific Ocean

7. The names of ships, airplanes, and space vehicles:

USS *Kitty Hawk*
Lindbergh's *Spirit of St. Louis*
Voyager II

8. The names of nationalities, races, peoples, and languages:

Canadians	Bantu
Maori	German
Caucasian	Old High German

9. Words derived from proper names, when used in their primary senses:

Chinese emperors
Moroccan cities

But do not capitalize these derivations if they are used as integral elements of compound words having their own distinct meanings:

chinese red (i.e., a specific shade of red)
moroccan leather (i.e., a specific kind of leather)

Titles of people

10. Words indicating familial relationships when preceding a person's name and forming a title:

Aunt Mary
Grandmother Walker

but

my aunt, Mary Smith
her grandmother, Mrs. Walker

11. Titles—civil, military, royal and noble, religious, and honorary—when preceding a name:

Justice Ginsburg	Lord Nelson
General Marshall	Pope John Paul II
Mayor White	Professor Malone
Queen Elizabeth II	

12. All references to the President and Vice President of the United States:

President Eisenhower
Vice President Humphrey
the President
the Vice President

Titles of publications and artistic works

13. All words except definite and indefinite articles, prepositions, and conjunctions within titles of literary, dramatic, artistic, and musical works:

the novel *All Quiet on the Western Front*
the short story "The Nose"
an article entitled "The Finiteness of Natural Language"
Byron's poem "The Prisoner of Chillon"
the play *Cat on a Hot Tin Roof*
Van Gogh's *Wheat Field and Cypress Trees*
Bartok's *Concerto for Orchestra*

14. *The* in the title of a newspaper if it is considered an integral part of the publication's entire title:

The Wall Street Journal
the New York *Daily News*

Salutations and complimentary closes

15. The first word of the salutation and of the complimentary close of a letter:

My dear Joyce
Dear Mr. Atkins
Sincerely yours
Yours sincerely

Epithets

16. Epithets used as substitutes for the names of people or places:

the Iron Chancellor
the Big Apple

Personifications

17. Words used in personification:

I met Murder in the way—/He had a mask like Castlereagh.
—Percy Bysshe Shelley

The pronoun I

18. The pronoun *I*:

Peter and I went to the store.
"May I be excused?"

Names for God in various religions, and sacred works

19. Names for God, and for sacred books:

God and His blessings   Allah
the Almighty   the Bible
the Holy Spirit   the Koran
Jehovah   the Talmud
Krishna   the Upanishads

Days, months, and holidays

20. Days of the week, months of the year, holidays, and holy days:

Monday   Ramadan
January   Easter
Labor Day   Día de los Muertos
Passover   Elul

Courts

21. The names of specific judicial courts:

The Supreme Court of the United States
the United States Court of Appeals for the Fourth Circuit
Court of Justice of the European Communities

Treaties and laws

22. The names of treaties, pacts, accords, acts, laws, and specific amendments:

Panama Canal Treaty
Treaty of Versailles
Warsaw Pact
Geneva Accords
the Labor Management Relations Act
the Sherman Antitrust Law
the First Amendment to the Constitution

Trademarks and service marks

23. Registered trademarks and service marks:

Kleenex
Xerox
Comsat
Soap Box Derby

Scientific terms

24. The names of geological eras, periods, epochs, and strata and the names of prehistoric divisions:

The Paleozoic Era
the Precambrian Period
the Pleistocene Epoch
Age of Reptiles
the Bronze Age

25. The names of constellations, planets, and stars:

the Milky Way
the Southern Cross
Jupiter
Mars
Venus
Polaris

26. Genus—but not species—names in binomial nomenclature:

Chrysanthemum leucanthemum
Corvus corax
Rana pipiens

27. New Latin names of classes, families, and all groups higher than genera in botanical and zoological nomenclature:

Gastropoda
Nematoda

But do not capitalize English adjectives and nouns derived from these New Latin names:

gastropod
a nematode

Abbreviations and acronyms

28. Many abbreviations and acronyms (consult this Dictionary when in doubt about styling):

Nov.   MBA
Tues.   UNESCO
Lt Col   MIRV
NW   OPEC

Italics

1. Indicate titles of books, plays, and very long poems:

For Whom the Bell Tolls
The Little Foxes
Paradise Lost

2. Indicate the titles of magazines and newspapers:

American Heritage magazine
The Wall Street Journal
the New York *Daily News*

Note that *The* is capitalized and italicized in publication titles only if it is considered an integral part of the entire title.

3. Set off the titles of motion pictures and radio and television series:

Four Weddings and a Funeral
All Things Considered
Masterpiece Theater

4. Indicate the titles of long musical compositions:

Messiah
Die Götterdämmerung
Bartok's *Concerto for Orchestra*
Elgar's *Enigma Variations*

5. Set off the names of paintings and sculpture:

Mona Lisa   *Pietà*
Guernica   *The Burghers of Calais*

6. Indicate words, letters, or numbers used as such:

The word *buzz* is onomatopoeic.
Can't means *won't* in his lexicon.
She formed her *n*'s like *u*'s.
A *6* looks like an inverted *9*.

7. Indicate foreign words and phrases not yet assimilated into English:

editors, machinists, *pâtissiers*, barbers, and hoboes
his *Sturm und Drang* period

8. Indicate the names of plaintiff and defendant in legal citations:

Madison v. *Kingsley*

9. Emphasize a word or phrase:

When you are quoted on the six o'clock news, you have *arrived*.

This device should be used sparingly.

10. Distinguish the New Latin names of genera, species, subspecies, and varieties in botanical and zoological nomenclature:

Homo sapiens
Sciurus carolinensis
Brassica oleracea var. *botrytis*

Do not italicize phyla, classes, orders, and families in botanical and zoological nomenclature:

Gastropoda   Nematoda

11. Set off the names of ships, planes, and spacecraft:

USS *Kitty Hawk*
Spirit of St. Louis
Voyager II

Punctuation

Apostrophe   '

1. Indicates the possessive case of singular and plural nouns, indefinite pronouns, and surnames combined with designations such as *Jr., Sr.,* and *II*:

her aunt's house   someone's bright idea
their aunts' houses   John Stone, Jr.'s car
the children's toys   the John Stone, Jrs.' car
Keats's "Ode to Psyche"

2. Indicates joint possession when used with the last of two or more nouns in a series:

Smith and Roe's report

3. Indicates individual possession when used with each of two or more nouns in a series:

Smith's, Roe's, and Doe's reports

4. Indicates the plurals of figures, letters, or words when this is not clear without the apostrophe:

6's and 7's
x's, *y*'s, and *z*'s
an article with too many *also*'s

However:

the 1930s   88s and 99s   MBAs

5. Indicates the omission of letters in contractions:

isn't   couldn't   that's   o'clock

6. Indicates the omission of figures in dates:

the class of '67

Brackets   [ ]

1. Enclose words or passages in quotations to indicate the insertion of material written by someone other than the original writer:

. . . On these two commandments hang [are based] all the Law and the Prophets.
And summer's lease [allotted time] hath all too short a date [duration]. . . .

Morgan then asserted that [Riley] has been mistaken.

2. Enclose material inserted within matter already in parentheses:

(Washington [DC], January, 1983)

Colon   :

1. Introduces words, phrases, or clauses that explain, amplify, or summarize what has preceded:

Suddenly I knew where we were: Paris.
The army was cut to pieces: more than fifty thousand men had been captured or killed.
The lasting influence of Greece's dramatic tradition is indicated by words still in our vocabulary: *chorus, comedy,* and *drama*.
She has three sources of income: salary, stock dividends, and interest from savings accounts.

2. Introduces a long quotation:

In his Gettysburg Address, Lincoln said: "Four score and seven years ago our fathers brought forth on this continent, a new nation, conceived in Liberty, and dedicated to the proposition that all men are created equal. . . ."

3. Introduces a list:

Among the conjunctive adverbs are the following: *so, therefore, hence, however, nevertheless, moreover, accordingly,* and *besides.*

4. Separates chapter and verse numbers in reference to biblical quotations:

Esther 2:17

5. Separates city from publisher in footnotes and bibliographies:

Boston: Houghton Mifflin, 2001.

6. Separates hour and minute in time designations:

1:30 P.M.   a 9:15 class

7. Follows the salutation in a business letter:

Dear Sir or Madam:
Dear Mr. Johnson:
Members of the Board:

Comma ,

1. Separates the clauses of a compound sentence connected by a coordinating conjunction:

There is a difference between the musical works of Mozart and Haydn, and it is a difference worth discovering.
He didn't know where they got such an idea, but he didn't disagree.

The comma may be omitted in short compound sentences in which the connection between the clauses is close:

She understood the situation and she was furious.
He got in the car and he drove and drove.

The comma is not used before a conjunction that joins two compound verbs in an independent clause:

We worked hard on the project but could not finish in time.
I can see the post office but not the bank.

2. Separates *and* or *or* from the preceding item in a series of three or more:

Lights of red, green, and blue wavelengths may be mixed to produce all colors.
The radio, television set, and stereo were arranged on one shelf.
Would you rather have ice cream, cake, or pie for dessert?

3. Often separates two or more adjectives and usually separates three or more adjectives modifying the same noun if *and* could be used between them without changing the meaning:

a solid, heavy gate
a large, high-ceilinged room
a grainy, old, black-and-white film

but

a polished mahogany desk
a silver metallic element

4. Sets off a nonrestrictive clause or phrase (one that if eliminated would not change the meaning of the sentence):

The thief, who had entered through the window, went straight to the safe.

The comma should not be used when the clause is restrictive (essential to the meaning of the sentence):

The thief who had entered through the window went straight to the safe; the other burglar searched for the silverware.

5. Sets off words or phrases in apposition to a noun or noun phrase:

Plato, the famous Greek philosopher, was a pupil of Socrates.
The composer of *Tristan and Isolde,* Richard Wagner, was a leading exponent of German romanticism.

The comma should not be used if such words or phrases further specify the noun that precedes:

The Greek philosopher Plato was a pupil of Socrates.
The composer Richard Wagner was a leading exponent of German romanticism.
The Dostoevsky novel *Crime and Punishment* was required reading.

6. Sets off transitional words and short expressions that require a pause in reading or speaking:

Unfortunately, Mrs. Lee hadn't read many Russian novels.
Peter lives with his family, of course.
Indeed, the sight of him gave me quite a jolt.

7. Sets off words used to introduce a sentence:

No, I haven't seen her.
Well, why don't you do as I ask?

8. Sets off a subordinate clause or a long phrase that precedes a principal clause:

By the time they finally found the restaurant, they were no longer hungry.
After the army surrendered, the general was taken prisoner.
Of all the illustrations in the book, the most striking are those that show the beauty of the mosaics.

9. Sets off short quotations and sayings:

Jo told him, "Come tomorrow for dinner."
The candidate said, "Actions speak louder than words."
"I don't know if I can," he said, "but maybe I will."

10. Indicates the omission of a word or words:

To err is human; to forgive, divine.

11. Sets off the year from the month in full dates:

Louis XVI of France was guillotined on January 21, 1793.

but also possible

Louis XVI of France was guillotined in January 1793.

12. Sets off city and state in geographical names:

Boston, Massachusetts, is the most populous city in New England.

512 Peaks Street
Bedford, VA 24523

13. Separates series of four or more figures into thousands, millions, and so on:

57,395   100,000

The comma is not used in this way in dates or pagination:

the year 1776   page 1100

14. Sets off words used in direct address:

Ms. Stone, please submit your report as soon as possible.
Thank you, Sandy, for your help.
The forum is open to questions, ladies and gentlemen.

15. Separates a tag question from the rest of the sentence:

You did say that you had the book, didn't you?
Beethoven's *Eroica* is on the program, isn't it?

16. Sets off any sentence elements that might be misunderstood if the comma were not used:

Some time after, the actual date was set.
To Pat, Chris was just a nuisance.
Whenever possible, friends provide moral support.

17. Follows the salutation in a personal letter and the complimentary close in a business or personal letter:

Dear Patsy,   Sincerely yours,

18. Sets off titles and degrees from surnames and from the rest of a sentence:

John T. Brown, Jr.
Michael A. Callahan, SJ
Maria I. Martin, MD, presented the case.

Dash —

1. Indicates a sudden break or abrupt change in continuity:

Well, you see, I—I've—I'm just not sure.
He seemed very upset about—I never knew what.
And then the problem—if it is a problem—can be solved.

2. Sets apart an explanatory or defining phrase:

Foods high in protein—meats, fish, eggs, and cheese—should be a part of one's daily diet.
We suddenly realized what the glittering gems were—emeralds.

3. Sets apart parenthetical material:

He stares soulfully heavenward—to the great delight of the audience—when he plays Chopin.
Allen—who had a lean face, a long nose, and cold blue eyes—was a stern man.

4. Marks an unfinished sentence:

Well, then, I'll simply tell her that I—
"But if the plane is late—" he began.

5. Sets off a summarizing phrase or clause:

Noam Chomsky, Morris Halle, Roman Jakobson—these are among America's most prominent linguists.

6. Sets off the name of an author or source, as at the end of a quotation:

There never was a good war, or a bad peace.
—Benjamin Franklin

Ellipses ...

1. Indicate, by three spaced points, the omission of words or sentences within quoted matter:

This ended, the power of the council . . . and the former regents were put on trial.

2. Indicate, by four spaced points, the omission of words at the end of a sentence:

Nor have we been wanting in Attentions to our British Brethren. . . . They too have been deaf to the Voice of Justice. . . .

3. Indicate, when extended the length of a line, the omission of one or more lines of poetry:

Come away, O human child!
....
For the world's more full of weeping
than you can understand.
—William Butler Yeats

4. Are sometimes used as a device to catch and hold the reader's interest, especially in advertising copy:

To help you Move and Grow
with the Rigors of
Business in the 21st century . . .
and Beyond.
—*The Journal of Business Strategy*

Exclamation Point !

1. Terminates an emphatic or exclamatory sentence:

Go home immediately!
You can't be serious!
What a ball game that was!

2. Terminates an emphatic interjection:

Bravo!

Hyphen -

1. Indicates that part of a word of more than one syllable has been carried over from one line to the next:

Anatole France's actual name was Jacques Anatole Thibault.

2. Joins the elements of some compounds:

great-grandfather
cure-all
ne'er-do-well

3. Joins the elements of compound modifiers preceding nouns:

a well-dressed woman   a four-hour seminar
high-school athletics   a two-thirds share
a fire-and-brimstone sermon

4. Indicates that two or more compounds share a single base:

three- and four-volume sets   six- and seven-year-olds

5. Separates the prefix and root in some combinations:

prefix + proper noun or adjective   anti-American
                                        pro-American

some prefixes ending in a vowel   de-escalate
+ root beginning with a vowel   co-anchor

stressed prefix + root word if   re-form/reform
absence of hyphen could cause   re-cover/recover
misunderstanding of meanings   re-create/recreate

6. Substitutes for the word *to* between figures or words:

pages 12-24
the years 1790-1980
the Boston-New York shuttle

7. Punctuates compound numbers from 21 through 99 that are written out:

thirty-five years of age
a man who is thirty-five
two hundred thirty-one dollars

Parentheses ( )

1. Enclose material that is not an essential part of the sentence and that if not included would not alter its meaning:

In an hour's time (some say less) the firefighters had extinguished the blaze.
It was a dream (although a hazy one) of an ideal, poverty-free state.
Susan doesn't feel (and why should she?) that she should pay higher rent.

2. Often enclose letters or figures to indicate subdivisions of a series:

A movement in sonata form consists of the following sections: (a) the exposition; (b) the development; and (c) the recapitulation, which is often followed by a coda.

3. Enclose figures following and confirming written-out numbers, especially in legal and business documents:

Delivery will be made in sixty (60) days.

4. Enclose abbreviations of written-out words when the abbreviations are used for the first time in a text and may be unfamiliar to the reader:

The study regarding anti-ballistic missiles (ABMs) is classified.

Period   .

1. Terminates a complete declarative or mild imperative sentence:

The carved ornamentation of the façade dates back to the fourteenth century.
Come home when you can.
Would you please sign here.

2. Follows some abbreviations:

Jan.	St.	Inc.
etc.	Ave.	Ltd.
Rev.	pp.	Op. cit.

Question Mark   ?

1. Terminates a direct question:

What are your editorial skills?
Who is there?

but

I wonder who said, "Speak softly and carry a big stick."
He asked when Harry planned to leave.

2. Indicates uncertainty:

Ferdinand Magellan (1480?–1521)

Quotation Marks   " " ' '

Double quotation marks

1. Enclose direct quotations:

"What was Berlin like during the war?" she asked.
"Ladies and gentlemen," the store manager said, "shoes are on sale today."
Arnold Toynbee wrote that "though not lovable" Caesar was "fascinating."
Will Rogers said: "Things in our country run in spite of government. Not by aid of it."

2. Enclose words or phrases to clarify their meaning or to indicate that they are being used in a special way:

"Dey" is a title formerly given to governors of Algiers.
By "brace" we mean the bracket and line joining two or more staves of music.
"The Big Apple" is a name for New York City.

3. Set off the translation of a foreign word or phrase:

déjà vu, "already seen"

4. Set off the titles of series of books, of articles or chapters in publications, of essays, of short stories and poems, of individual television and radio programs, and of songs and short musical pieces:

"The Horizon Concise History" series
"Some Notes on Case Grammar in English"

Chapter 9, "Four in Freedom"
Gogol's "The Nose"
Shelley's "Ode to the West Wind"
"The Tonight Show"
Schubert's "Death and the Maiden"

Single quotation marks

Enclose quotations within quotations:

"To me," he said, "the key word for modern business people is 'entrepreneurship.'"
Mary said, "I heard the thief yell, 'Quick! Let's get out of here!'"

Put commas and periods inside closing colons closing quotation marks; put semicolons and colons outside. Other punctuation, such as exclamation points and question marks, should be put inside the closing quotation marks only if it is part of the matter quoted.

Semicolon   ;

1. Separates the clauses of a compound sentence having no coordinating conjunction:

The questions are provided by the analyst; the answers come from the data.
Many industries were paralyzed by the strike; factory owners left the district, taking their money with them.

2. Separates the clauses of a compound sentence in which the clauses contain internal punctuation, even when the clauses are joined by a conjunction:

Picnic baskets in hand, we walked to the beach, chose a sunny spot, and spread out the blankets; and the rest of the group followed us in a dune buggy.

3. Separates elements of a series in which items already contain commas:

Among the guests were Mary Adams; her daughter, Elaine; Henry Abrams, formerly of the Redding Institute; and two couples whom I had never met.

4. Separates clauses of a compound sentence joined by a conjunctive adverb, such as *nonetheless*, *however*, or *hence*:

We demanded a refund; however, the manufacturer refused to give us one.

5. May be used instead of a comma to signal longer pauses; for dramatic effect:

But I want you to know that when I cross the river my last conscious thoughts will be of the Corps; and the Corps; and the Corps.

—General Douglas MacArthur

Virgule   /

1. Separates successive divisions in an extended date:

the fiscal year 1982/83

2. Represents the word *per*:

800 ft./sec.   4,000 gal./min.

3. Means *or* between the words *and* and *or*:

matters of linguistic and/or sociological importance
Take skis and/or ice skates when you visit New England in the winter.

4. Separates two or more lines of poetry that are quoted and run in on successive lines of a text:

The actor had a memory lapse when he came to the lines "Why? all delights are vain, but that most vain/ Which, with pain purchas'd, doth inherit pain" and had to improvise.

Abbreviations and Labels
Used in This Dictionary

Abbreviated Language Names Used in Etymologies

Afr.	Afrikaans
Am.Sp.	American Spanish
AN	Anglo-Norman
Ar.	Arabic
Aram.	Aramaic
Balt.	Baltic
Brit.	British
Canadian Fr.	Canadian French
Celt.	Celtic
Chin.	Chinese
Dan.	Danish
Du.	Dutch
E.	English
Egypt.	Egyptian
Finn.	Finnish
Flem.	Flemish
Fr.	French
Gael.	Gaelic
Ger.	German
Gk.	Greek
Gmc.	Germanic
Goth.	Gothic
Heb.	Hebrew
HGer.	High German
Hung.	Hungarian
Icel.	Icelandic
IE	Indo-European
Ir.	Irish
Iran.	Iranian
Ir.Gael.	Irish Gaelic
Ital.	Italian
J.	Japanese
Lat.	Latin
LGer.	Low German
L.Gk.	Late Greek
Lith.	Lithuanian
LLat.	Late Latin
Louisiana Fr.	Louisiana French
MDu.	Middle Dutch
ME	Middle English
Med.Gk.	Medieval Greek
Med.Lat.	Medieval Latin
MFlem.	Middle Flemish
MHGer.	Middle High German
MIr.	Middle Irish
MLGer.	Middle Low German
Mod.Gk.	Modern Greek
Mod.Heb.	Modern Hebrew
MPers.	Middle Persian
N.Amer.Fr.	North American French
NLat.	New Latin
Norman Fr.	Norman French
Norw.	Norwegian
ODan.	Old Danish
OE	Old English
OFr.	Old French
OHGer.	Old High German
OIr.	Old Irish
OIran.	Old Iranian
OItal.	Old Italian
OLat.	Old Latin
ON	Old Norse
ONFr.	Old North French
OPers.	Old Persian
OPort.	Old Portuguese
ORuss.	Old Russian
OSpan.	Old Spanish
OSwed.	Old Swedish
Penn. Dutch	Pennsylvania Dutch
Pers.	Persian
Pidgin E.	Pidgin English
Pol.	Polish
Port.	Portuguese
Prov.	Provençal
Rom.	Romanian
Russ.	Russian
Sc.	Scots
Scand.	Scandinavian
Sc. Gael.	Scottish Gaelic
Skt.	Sanskrit
Slav.	Slavic
Sp.	Spanish
Swed.	Swedish
Turk.	Turkish
VLat.	Vulgar Latin

Other Abbreviations and Symbols Used in This Dictionary

abbr.	abbreviation
adj.	adjective
adv.	adverb
approx.	approximately
aug.	augmentative
cent.	century, centuries
comp.	comparative
conj.	conjunction
dial.	dialectal
dim.	dimunitive
esp.	especially
fem.	feminine
freq.	frequentative
fut.	future
imit.	imitative
imper.	imperative
indic.	indicative
interj.	interjection
intr.	intransitive
L	Late
M	Middle
masc.	masculine
Med.	Medieval
Mod.	Modern
n.	noun

neut.	neuter
O	Old
orig.	origin, originally
p.	past
part.	participle, participial
p.part.	past participle
p.t.	past tense
perh.	perhaps
pers.	person
pl.	plural
pl.n.	plural noun
poss.	possibly
pr.	present
pr.part.	present participle
pr.t.	present tense
pref.	prefix
prep.	preposition
prob.	probably
pron.	pronoun
redup.	reduplication
sing.	singular
St.	Saint
suff.	suffix
superl.	superlative
t.	tense
tr.	transitive
transl.	translation
ult.	ultimately
usu.	usually
v.	verb
var.	variant, variants
*	unattested
<	derived from
+	combined with
?	Origin unknown

Dialect labels

This Dictionary uses dialect labels singly and in various combinations ranging from the very general (*Regional*) to the very specific (*New Orleans*). The very specific labels, which are self-explanatory, serve as descriptors of geographic regions such as cities, states, and interstate areas.

Major areas of distribution. Major, generalized areas of dialect distribution are labeled as follows and can occur in any number of combinations:

Northern US—from New Jersey and Pennsylvania north to New England and west to Washington and Oregon

Southern US—from southern Maryland along the coastal plains of Virginia, North and South Carolina, Georgia, Florida, Alabama, Mississippi, and Louisiana to eastern Texas and also including the "Upper South" as defined in the section "Midwestern and Midland"

Eastern US—the Atlantic states from Maine to Florida, also including Vermont, New Hampshire, and upstate New York

Western US—west of the 98th meridian, which extends southward from the Dakotas to central Oklahoma and Texas

Subcategories of distribution. Within the major areas are these subcategories, the labels for which also can occur in various combinations:

For the north:

New England—Maine, New Hampshire, Vermont, Massachusetts, Connecticut, and Rhode Island

Northeastern US—New England, New York State, Pennsylvania, and New Jersey

Upper Northern or *Inland Northern US*—western upstate New York; northwest Pennsylvania; northern Ohio, Indiana, and Illinois; Michigan; Wisconsin; and Minnesota

Lower Northern or *North Midland US*—southern New Jersey and Pennsylvania; northern Delaware, Maryland, and West Virginia; Ohio; Indiana; Illinois; Iowa; and Nebraska

Upper Midwest—Minnesota, Iowa, North and South Dakota, and Nebraska

Northwestern US or *Pacific Northwest*—Washington, Oregon, Idaho, Montana, and Wyoming

For the south:

Southeastern US—North and South Carolina, Georgia, Florida, Tennessee, Alabama, and Mississippi

Upper Southern or *South Midland US*—southern Delaware, Maryland, West Virginia, Ohio, Indiana, and Illinois; western Virginia and North Carolina; northern Georgia, Alabama, Mississippi, and Louisiana; Tennessee; Kentucky; Arkansas; and eastern Oklahoma

Lower Southern US—Florida, Georgia, Alabama, Mississippi, Louisiana, and eastern Texas

Eastern Lower Southern or *South Atlantic US*—North and South Carolina, Georgia, and Florida

For the east:

Central Atlantic US—Delaware; Washington, DC; eastern Virginia, Maryland, and Pennsylvania; and southern New Jersey

North Atlantic Coast—Maine, Massachusetts, Rhode Island, Connecticut, southeast New York State, and northern New Jersey

For the west:

Southwestern US—Oklahoma, Texas, New Mexico, Arizona, and southern California

Midwestern and Midland. In addition to these labels, two labels that overlap with but lie outside the overall scheme are used. Midwestern US designates regional terms that occur throughout the area from Michigan westward to the Dakotas and from Ohio westward to Kansas, an area that includes parts of several dialect areas. Midland US, a term previously used in American dialect geography, includes the Lower North and the Upper South. The collective label Midland is distinguished from the label Midwestern, which does not include the South. Two Midland words are *umbrella plant* for *May apple* and *snake feeder* for *dragonfly*.

Gullah. The label Gullah refers not to a region but to the distinctive dialect of English that is spoken by African Americans who live on the coast and coastal islands of Georgia, South Carolina, and northern Florida.

Pronunciation

The pronunciation enclosed in parentheses follows the boldface entry word. If an entry word and a variant to that entry have the same pronunciation, the pronunciation follows the variant. If the variant or variants do not have the same pronunciation as the entry word, pronunciations follow the forms to which they apply. Differing or variant pronunciations are given whenever necessary. If an entry or a variant requires more than one pronunciation, subsequent pronunciations show only those syllables that are different in sound quality or stress from the first pronunciation or that are necessary for clarity.

Pronunciation symbols. The symbols in this dictionary enable you to produce a satisfactory pronunciation with no more than a quick reference to the key. All pronunciations given here are acceptable in all circumstances. When more than one pronunciation is given, the first is assumed to be the most common, but the difference in frequency may be insignificant.

A list of pronunciation symbols used in this Dictionary is given below in the column headed Symbols. The column headed Examples contains words chosen to illustrate how the AHD symbols are pronounced. The letters that correspond in sound to the AHD symbols are shown in boldface. The nonalphabetical symbol (ə) is called a *schwa*. It is used in this Dictionary to represent a reduced vowel, a vowel that receives the weakest level of stress within a word. The schwa sound varies, sometimes according to the vowel it is representing and often according to the sounds surrounding it:

> **sis·ter** (sĭs′tər)
> **a·bun·dant** (ə-bŭn′dənt)

For most words, a single set of symbols can represent the pronunciation found in each regional variety of American English. You will supply those features of your own regional speech that are called forth by the pronunciation key in this Dictionary. The pronunciations are exclusively those of educated speech.

Stress. The relative emphasis with which the syllables of a word or phrase are spoken, called *stress*, is indicated in three different ways. The strongest, or primary, stress is marked with a bold mark (′). An intermediate, or secondary, level of stress is marked with a similar but lighter mark (′). The weakest stress is unmarked. Words of one syllable show no stress mark.

PRONUNCIATION KEY

Symbols	Examples	Symbols	Examples	Symbols	Examples	Symbols	Examples
ă	pat	îr	p**ier**	p	**p**o**p**	zh	vi**s**ion, plea**s**ure,
ā	pay	j	**j**u**dg**e	r	**r**oa**r**		**g**ara**g**e
âr	c**are**	k	**k**i**ck**, **c**at, pi**q**ue	s	**s**au**c**e	ə	**a**bout, it**e**m,
ä	f**a**ther	l	**l**id, need**le*** (nēd′l)	sh	**sh**ip, di**sh**		edi**b**le, gall**o**p,
b	**b**i**b**	m	**m**u**m**	t	**t**igh**t**, stopp**ed**		circ**u**s
ch	**ch**ur**ch**	n	**n**o, sudd**en*** (sŭd′n)	th	**th**in	ər	butt**er**
d	**d**ee**d**, mille**d**	ng	thi**ng**	th	**th**is		
ě	p**e**t	ŏ	p**o**t	ŭ	c**u**t	**Foreign**	
ē	b**ee**	ō	t**oe**	ûr	**ur**ge, t**er**m,	œ	*French* f**eu**
f	**f**i**f**e, **ph**ase, rou**gh**	ô	c**augh**t, p**aw**, f**or**,		f**ir**m, w**or**d,		*German* sch**ö**n
g	**g**a**g**		h**o**rrid, h**oar**se **		h**ear**d	ü	*French* t**u**
h	**h**at	oi	n**oi**se	v	**v**al**v**e		*German* **ü**ber
hw	**wh**ich	ōō	t**oo**k	w	**w**ith	ᴋʜ	*German* i**ch**
ĭ	p**i**t	ōō	b**oo**t	y	**y**es		*Scottish* lo**ch**
ī	p**ie**, b**y**	ou	**ou**t	z	**z**ebra, **x**ylem	ɴ	*French* bo**n**

* In English the consonants *l* and *n* often constitute complete syllables by themselves.

** Regional pronunciations of *-or-* vary. In pairs such as **for, four**; **horse, hoarse**; and **morning, mourning**, the vowel varies between (ô) and (ō). In this Dictionary these vowels are represented as (ô) and (ō). A similar

follows: **for** (fôr), **four** (fôr, fōr); **horse** (hôrs), **hoarse** (hôrs, hōrs); and **morning** (môr′nĭng), **mourning** (môr′nĭng, mōr′-). A similar variant occurs in words such as **coral, forest,** and **horrid,** where the pronunciation of *or* varies between (ôr) and (ŏr): **forest** (fôr′ĭst, fŏr′-).

Aa

a¹ or **A** (ā) *n., pl.* **a's** or **A's** also **as** or **As 1.** The first letter of the modern English alphabet. **2.** Any of the speech sounds represented by the letter *a.* **3.** The first in a series. **4.** Something shaped like the letter A. **5. A** The best or highest in quality or rank: *grade A milk.* **6.** *Music* **a.** The sixth tone in the scale of C major or the first tone in the relative minor scale. **b.** A key or scale in which A is the tonic. **7. A** One of the four major blood groups in the ABO system. —*idiom:* **from A to Z** Completely; thoroughly.

a² (ə; ā *when stressed*) *indef.art.* **1.** Used before nouns and noun phrases that denote a single but unspecified person or thing: *a region.* **2.** Used before terms that denote number, amount, quantity, or degree: *only a few voters; a bit more rest.* **3a.** Used before a proper name to denote a type or a member of a class: *the wisdom of a Socrates.* **b.** Used before a mass noun to indicate a single type or example: *a dry wine.* **4.** The same: *birds of a feather.* **5.** Any: *not a drop to drink.* [ME, var. of *an,* an. See AN¹.]

> **USAGE NOTE** In writing, the form *a* is used before a word beginning with a consonant sound, regardless of its spelling (*a frog, a university*). The form *an* is used before a word beginning with a vowel sound (*an orange, an hour*). • *An* was also once a common variant before words beginning with *h* in which the first syllable was unstressed; thus 18th-century authors wrote either *a historical* or *an historical* but *a history,* not *an history.* This usage made sense in that people often did not pronounce the initial *h* in words such as *historical* and *heroic,* but by the late 19th century educated speakers usually pronounced it, and the practice of writing *an* before such words began to die out. Nowadays it survives primarily before the words *historical* and *historic.*

a³ (ə) *prep.* In every; to each; per: *once a month; one dollar a pound.* [ME < OE *an,* in.]

a⁴ (ə) *aux.v. Informal* Have: *He'd a come if he could.* [ME, alteration of *haven,* to have. See HAVE.]

a⁵ *abbr.* **1.** acceleration **2.** are (measurement)

A *abbr.* **1.** accusative **2.** *Games* ace **3.** across **4.** adenine **5.** alto **6.** ampere **7.** or **Å** angstrom **8.** area

a. *abbr.* **1.** acre **2.** adjective **3.** *Latin* anno (in the year) **4.** *Latin* annus (year) **5.** anode **6.** answer **7.** *Latin* ante (before) **8.** anterior

a–¹ or **an–** *pref.* Without; not: *amoral.* [Gk. See **ne** in App.]

a–² *pref.* **1.** On; in: *abed.* **2.** In the act of: *aborning.* **3.** In the direction of: *astern.* **4.** In a specified state or condition: *abuzz.* [ME < OE < *an,* on.]

> **OUR LIVING LANGUAGE** Prefixing *a–* to verb forms that end in *–ing,* as in *a-hunting* and *a-fishing,* was once fairly common in vernacular US speech, particularly in the highland areas of the South and in the Southwest. Such verb forms derive from an Old English construction in which a preposition, usually *on,* was placed in front of a verbal noun—a verb to which *–ing* had been added to indicate that the action was extended or ongoing. Gradually such prepositions were shortened to *a–.* The *–ing* forms came to be regarded as present participles rather than verbal nouns. Eventually *a–* disappeared from many dialects, including Standard English in the United States and Great Britain, although it is still retained today in some isolated dialect areas, particularly among older speakers. Today, speakers who use the *a–* prefix do not use it randomly; it is only used with *–ing* words that function as part of a verb phrase, as in *She was a-running.*

A1C *abbr.* airman first class

a·a or **aa** (ä′ä) *n.* Lava having a rough surface. [Hawaiian *'a'ā,* to burn, aa.]

AA *abbr.* **1.** *Bible* Acts of the Apostles **2.** Alcoholics Anonymous **3.** antiaircraft **4.** Associate in Arts

AAA *abbr.* **1.** Agricultural Adjustment Administration **2.** Amateur Athletic Association **3.** antiaircraft artillery

AAAL *abbr.* American Academy of Arts and Letters

AAAS *abbr.* American Association for the Advancement of Science

Aa·chen (ä′kən, ä′кнən) also **Aix-la-Cha·pelle** (āks′lä-shə-pĕl′, ĕks′-) A city of W Germany near the Belgian and Dutch borders. Pop. 246,671.

aah (ä) *interj.* Used to express pleasure, satisfaction, surprise, or great joy. —**aah** *v. & n.*

Aal·borg (ôl′bôrg′) See **Ålborg.**

Aal·to (äl′tō), **Alvar** 1898–1976. Finnish architect and furniture designer noted for his use of contrasting materials.

A and R *abbr.* artists and repertory

AAPSS *abbr.* American Academy of Political and Social Sciences

AAR *abbr.* against all risks

aard·vark (ärd′värk′) *n.* A burrowing mammal (*Orycteropus afer*) of southern Africa, having a stocky, hairy body, large ears, and a long tubular snout. [Obsolete Afr. : *aarde,* earth (< MDu. *aerde*) + *vark,* pig (< MDu. *varken;* see **porko–** in App.).]

aard·wolf (ärd′wŏolf′) *n.* A mammal (*Proteles cristatus*) native to southern and eastern Africa that resembles the hyena and feeds mainly on termites and insect larvae. [Afr. : *aarde,* earth; see AARDVARK + *wolf,* wolf (< MDu.; see w**ļ**k**″o–** in App.).]

Aa·re (är′ə) or **Aar** (är) A river of central and N Switzerland flowing c. 295 km (183 mi) to the Rhine R.

Aar·hus (ôr′hōōs′) See **Århus.**

Aar·on (âr′ən, ăr′–) In the Bible, the elder brother of Moses who helped lead the Hebrews out of Egypt.

Aaron, Henry Louis Known as "Hank." b. 1934. Amer. baseball player who retired (1976) with a total of 755 home runs.

Aa·ron·ic (â-rŏn′ĭk, ă-rŏn′–) also **Aa·ron·i·cal** (-ĭ-kəl) *adj.* **1.** Of, having to do with, or characteristic of Aaron. **2.** *Mormon Church* Of or having to do with the lower order of priests.

Aa·ron's rod (âr′ənz, ăr′–) *n. Architecture* A rod-shaped molding decorated with a design of leaves, scrolls, or a twined serpent. [After the blossoming rod of Aaron in Numbers 17:8.]

AARP *abbr.* American Association of Retired Persons

AAS *abbr.* Associate in Applied Sciences

AAU *abbr.* Amateur Athletic Union

AAUP *abbr.* American Association of University Professors

AAUW *abbr.* American Association of University Women

AAVE *abbr.* African American Vernacular English

ab (ăb) *n. Slang* An abdominal muscle. Often used in the plural.

Ab (ăb, äv, ôv) *n.* Variant of **Av.**

AB¹ (ā′bē′) *n.* One of the four major blood groups in the ABO system.

AB² *abbr.* **1.** airman basic **2.** Alberta **3.** *Latin* Artium Baccalaureus (Bachelor of Arts)

ab–¹ *pref.* Away from: *aboral.* [Lat. See **apo–** in App.]

ab–² *pref.* Used to indicate an electromagnetic unit in the centimeter-gram-second system: *abcoulomb.* [< ABSOLUTE.]

a·ba (ə-bä′, ä′bə) *n.* **1.** A fabric woven of the hair of camels or goats. **2.** A loose-fitting sleeveless garment made of this fabric, traditionally worn by Arabs. [Ar. *'abā'.*]

A·ba (ä′bə) A city of SE Nigeria WNW of Lagos. Pop. 210,700.

ABA *abbr.* **1.** abscisic acid **2.** American Bankers Association **3.** American Bar Association **4.** American Booksellers Association

ab·a·ca also **ab·a·cá** (ăb′ə-kä′, ä′bə-) *n.* **1.** A bananalike plant (*Musa textilis*) native to the Philippines. **2.** The fibers obtained from the stalks of this plant. [Sp. *abacá* < Tagalog *abaka.*]

a·back (ə-băk′) *adv.* **1.** By surprise. **2.** *Nautical* In such a way that the wind pushes against the forward side of a sail or sails. **3.** *Archaic* Back; backward.

A·ba·co and Cays (ăb′ə-kō′; kēz, kāz) An island group in the Atlantic Ocean E of S FL.

ab·a·cus (ăb′ə-kəs, ə-băk′əs) *n., pl.* **ab·a·cus·es** or **ab·a·ci** (ăb′ə-sī′, ə-băk′ī′) **1.** A computing device consisting of a frame holding parallel rods strung with movable counters. **2.** *Architecture* A slab on the top of the capital of a column. [ME < Lat. < Gk. *abax, abak-,* counting board, perh. < Heb. *'ābāq,* dust.]

Hank Aaron

Ab·a·dan (ăb′ə-dän′, äb′ə-dän′) A city of SW Iran on **Abadan Island** at the head of the Persian Gulf. Pop. 296,081.

a·baft (ə-băft′) *prep. Nautical* Toward the stern from. [ME *on baft* : *on,* at; see ON + *baft,* to the rear (< OE *beæftan,* behind : *be,* by, at; see **ambhi** in App. + *æftan,* behind; see **apo–** in App.).]

ab·a·lo·ne (ăb′ə-lō′nē, ăb′ə-lō′–) *n.* Any of various large edible marine gastropods of the genus *Haliotis,* having an ear-shaped shell with a row of holes along the outer edge and a pearly interior. [Am.Sp. *abulón.*]

ab·am·pere (ăb-ăm′pîr′) *n.* The centimeter-gram-second electromagnetic unit of current equal to ten amperes.

a·ban·don (ə-băn′dən) *tr.v.* **-doned, -don·ing, -dons 1.** To withdraw one's support or help from, esp. in spite of duty; desert: *abandon a friend in trouble.* **2.** To give up by leaving or ceasing to operate or inhabit, esp. as a result of danger: *abandoned the ship.* **3.** To surrender one's claim to, right to, or interest in; give up entirely. See Syns at **relinquish. 4.** To cease trying to continue; desist from: *abandoned the search.* **5.** To yield (oneself) completely, as to emotion. ❖ *n.* **1.** Unbounded enthusiasm; exuberance. **2.** A complete surrender of inhibitions. [ME *abandounen* < OFr. *abandoner* < *a bandon* : *a,* at (< Lat. *ad*) + *bandon,* control; see **bhā–** in App.] —**a·ban′don·ment** *n.*

a·ban·doned (ə-băn′dənd) *adj.* **1.** Deserted; forsaken. **2.** Exuberantly enthusiastic. **3.** Recklessly unrestrained.

abacus

a·base (ə-bās′) *tr.v.* **a·based, a·bas·ing, a·bas·es** To lower in rank, prestige, or esteem. See Syns at **degrade.** [ME *abassen* < OFr. *abaissier* : Lat. *ad-*, ad- + VLat. **bassiāre* (< Med.Lat. *bassus*, low).] —**a·base′ment** *n.*

a·bash (ə-băsh′) *tr.v.* **a·bashed, a·bash·ing, a·bash·es** To make ashamed or uneasy; disconcert. [ME *abaishen*, to lose one's composure < OFr. *esbahir, esbahiss-* : *es-*, intensive pref. (< Lat. *ex-*; see EX–) + *baer*, to gape; see BAY².] —**a·bash′ment** *n.*

a·ba·sia (ə-bā′zhə) *n.* Impaired muscular coordination in walking. [A–¹ + Gk. *basis*, step; see g**ᵂā**- in App. + –IA¹.]

a·bate (ə-bāt′) *v.* **a·bat·ed, a·bat·ing, a·bates** —*tr.* **1.** To reduce in amount, degree, or intensity; lessen. See Syns at **decrease. 2.** To deduct from an amount; subtract. **3.** *Law* **a.** To put an end to. **b.** To make void. —*intr.* **1.** To fall off in degree or intensity; subside. **2.** *Law* To become void. [ME *abaten* < OFr. *abatre*, to beat down : *a-*, to (< Lat. *ad-*; see AD–) + *batre*, to beat; see BATTER¹.]

a·bate·ment (ə-bāt′mənt) *n.* **1.** Diminution in amount, degree, or intensity; moderation. **2.** The amount lowered; a reduction.

ab·a·tis (ăb′ə-tē′, -tĭs) *n., pl.* **-tis** (-tēz′) or **-tis·es** (-tĭ-sĭz) A defensive obstacle made by laying felled trees on top of each other with branches, sometimes sharpened, facing the enemy. [Fr., pile of things thrown down < OFr. *abateis*; akin to *abattre*, to throw down. See ABATE.]

ab·at·toir (ăb′ə-twär′) *n.* **1.** A slaughterhouse. **2.** Something likened to a slaughterhouse. [Fr. < *abattre*, to strike down < OFr. See ABATE.]

ab·ax·i·al (ăb-ăk′sē-əl) *adj.* Located away from or on the opposite side of the axis, as of an organ or organism.

a·bay·a (ə-bī′ə) *n.* A loose, usu. black robe worn by Muslim women, esp. in Arabic-speaking regions, covering the body from head to toe and often worn with a headscarf and veil. [Colloquial Ar. *'abāya* < Ar. *'abā'a*, var. of *'abā'*, aba.]

Abb. *abbr.* **1.** abbess **2.** abbot

Ab·ba (ăb′ə, ä′bə) *n.* **1.** *Bible* In the New Testament, God. **2. abba** Used as a title of honor for bishops and patriarchs in some Christian churches of Egypt, Syria, and Ethiopia. [ME *abba* < Gk. See ABBOT.]

ab·ba·cy (ăb′ə-sē) *n., pl.* **-cies** The office, term, or jurisdiction of an abbot. [ME *abbatie* < LLat. *abbatia* < *abbās, abbat-*, abbot. See ABBOT.]

Ab·bas·sid (ă-băs′ĭd′, ăb′ə-sĭd′) also **Ab·bas·side** (ă-băs′ĭd′, ăb′ə-sĭd′) An Arabic dynasty (750–1258) named for al-Abbas (566?–652), paternal uncle of Muhammad.

ab·ba·tial (ə-bā′shəl) *adj.* Of or having to do with an abbey, abbot, or abbess. [ME *abbacyal* < LLat. *abbātiālis* < *abbās, abbāt-*, abbot. See ABBOT.]

ab·bé (ăb′ā′, ă-bā′) *n. Roman Catholic Church* **1.** Used as a title for the superior of a monastery in a French-speaking area. **2.** Used as a title for a cleric in major or minor orders in a French-speaking area. [Fr. < OFr. *abbé* < LLat. *abbās*, abbot. See ABBOT.]

ab·bess (ăb′ĭs) *n.* **1.** The superior of a convent. **2.** Used as a title for such a person. [ME *abesse* < OFr. < LLat. *abbātissa* < *abbās, abbāt-*, abbot. See ABBOT.]

Ab·be·vil·li·an (ăb′ə-vĭl′ē-ən) *adj.* Of or relating to the earliest Paleolithic archaeological sites in Europe, characterized by bifacial stone hand axes. [After *Abbeville*, a city of northern France.]

ab·bey (ăb′ē) *n., pl.* **-beys 1.** A monastery supervised by an abbot. **2.** A convent supervised by an abbess. **3.** A church that is or once was part of a monastery or convent. [ME < OFr. *abaie* < LLat. *abbātia*. See ABBACY.]

ab·bot (ăb′ət) *n.* **1.** The superior of a monastery. **2.** Used as a title for such a person. [ME *abbod* < OE < LLat. *abbās, abbāt-* < Gk. *abba, abbās* < Aram. *'abbā, 'abbā*, the father, my father < *'ab*, father.]

Abbott (ăb′ət), **Berenice** 1898–1991. Amer. photographer known esp. for her black-and-white portraits of New York City.

Abbott, Sir **John Joseph Caldwell** 1821–93. Canadian politician who served as prime minister (1891–92).

Abbott, Robert Sengstacke 1868–1940. Amer. newspaper publisher who founded and edited (1905–40) the *Chicago Defender*, an early advocate of African-American civil rights.

Abbott, William Known as "**Bud.**" 1898–1974. Amer. comedian noted for his partnership with Lou Costello.

abbr. or **abbrev.** *abbr.* abbreviation

ab·bre·vi·ate (ə-brē′vē-āt′) *tr.v.* **-at·ed, -at·ing, -ates 1.** To make shorter. **2.** To reduce (a word or phrase) to a shorter form intended to represent the full form. [ME *abbreviaten* < LLat. *abbreviāre, abbreviāt-* : ad-, ad- + *breviāre*, to shorten (< *brevis*, short).] —**ab·bre′vi·a′tor** *n.*

ab·bre·vi·a·tion (ə-brē′vē-ā′shən) *n.* **1.** The act or product of shortening. **2.** A shortened form of a word or phrase used chiefly in writing, such as *USMC* for *United States Marine Corps.*

ABC (ā′bē-sē′) *n.* **1.** The alphabet. Often used in the plural: *learned her ABCs.* **2.** The rudiments of a subject, esp. reading and writing. Often used in the plural.

ab·cou·lomb (ăb-kōō′lŏm′, -lōm′) *n.* The centimeter-gram-second electromagnetic unit of charge, equal to ten coulombs.

ABC soil *n.* Soil in which three distinct layers can be seen in vertical section.

ABD (ā′bē-dē′) *n.* A person who is a candidate for a doctorate and has completed all requirements for the degree except the dissertation. [*a*(ll) *b*(ut) *d*(issertation).]

Ab·di·as (ăb-dī′əs) See **Obadiah¹.**

ab·di·cate (ăb′dĭ-kāt′) *v.* **-cat·ed, -cat·ing, -cates** —*tr.* To relinquish (power or responsibility) formally. —*intr.* To relinquish formally a high office or responsibility. [Lat. *abdicāre, abdicāt-*, to disclaim : *ab-*, away; see AB–¹ + *dīcāre*, to proclaim; see **deik-** in App.] —**ab′di·ca·ble** (-kə-bəl) *adj.* —**ab′di·ca′tion** *n.* —**ab′di·ca′tor** *n.*

ab·do·men (ăb′də-mən, ăb-dō′mən) *n.* **1.** The part of the body that lies between the thorax and the pelvis and encloses the stomach, intestines, liver, spleen, and pancreas. **2.** The corresponding region in vertebrates other than mammals. **3.** The posterior segment of the body in arthropods. [Lat. *abdōmen*, belly. See dhē- in App.] —**ab·dom′i·nal** (ăb-dŏm′ə-nəl) *adj.* —**ab·dom′i·nal·ly** *adv.*

ab·dom·i·no·plas·ty (ăb-dŏm′ə-nō-plăs′tē, -nə-) *n., pl.* **-ties** Plastic surgery of the abdomen in which excess fatty tissue and skin are removed, usu. for cosmetic purposes. [Lat. *abdōmen, abdōmin-*, belly + -PLASTY.]

ab·du·cens (ăb-dōō′sənz, -dyōō′-) *n., pl.* **ab·du·cen·tes** (ăb′dōō-sĕn′tēz′, -dyōō-) Either of the sixth pair of cranial nerves that convey motor impulses to the rectus muscle on the lateral side of each eye. [< Lat. *abdūcēns*, pr. part. of *abdūcere*, to take away. See ABDUCT.]

ab·duct (ăb-dŭkt′) *tr.v.* **-duct·ed, -duct·ing, -ducts 1.** To carry off by force; kidnap. **2.** *Physiology* To draw away from the midline of the body or from an adjacent part or limb. [Lat. *abdūcere, abduct-* : *ab-*, away; see AB–¹ + *dūcere*, to lead; see **deuk-** in App.] —**ab·duct·ee′** *n.* —**ab·duc′tion** *n.*

ab·duc·tor (ăb-dŭk′tər) *n.* **1.** One, such as a kidnapper, who abducts. **2.** *Anatomy* A muscle that draws a body part, such as a finger, away from the midline of the body or of an extremity.

Ab·dul-Jab·bar (ăb-dŏōl′jə-bär′), **Kareem** Orig. Lew Alcindor. b. 1947. Amer. basketball player and all-time leading scorer in the National Basketball Association.

Ab·dul·lah ibn-Hu·sein (ăb′dŏō-lä′ ĭb′n-hōō-sān′) 1882–1951. Transjordanian emir (1921–46) and first king of independent Jordan (1946–51).

a·beam (ə-bēm′) *adv.* At right angles to the fore-and-aft line of a ship.

a·be·ce·dar·i·an (ā′bē-sē-dâr′ē-ən) *n.* **1.** One who teaches or studies the alphabet. **2.** One who is just learning; a beginner or novice. ❖ *adj.* **1.** Having to do with the alphabet. **2.** Being arranged alphabetically. **3.** Elementary or rudimentary. [ME < Med.Lat. *abecedārium*, alphabet < LLat. *abecedārius*, alphabetical : the names of the letters A B C D + *-ārius*, -ary.]

a·bed (ə-bĕd′) *adv.* In bed.

A·bed·ne·go (ə-bĕd′nĭ-gō′) In the Bible, a young man who emerged unharmed from the fiery furnace of Babylon.

A·bel (ā′bəl) In the Bible, the son of Adam and Eve who was slain by his elder brother, Cain.

Abel, Sir **Frederick Augustus** 1827–1902. British chemist who invented cordite (1889) with Sir James Dewar.

Ab·e·lard (ăb′ə-lärd′) also **A·bé·lard** (ä-bā-lär′), **Peter** or **Pierre** 1079–1142. French theologian and philosopher whose nominalist application of the principles of ancient Greek logic to medieval Catholic Church doctrines led to heresy charges.

a·bele (ə-bēl′) *n.* See **white poplar.** [Du. *abeel* < OFr. *aubel* < Med.Lat. *albellus*, dim. of Lat. *albus*, white. See **albho-** in App.]

a·bel·mosk (ā′bəl-mŏsk′) *n.* A hairy annual or biennial plant (*Abelmoschus moschatus*) native to tropical Asia and having yellow flowers with crimson centers. [NLat. *abelmoschus* < Ar. *'abū l-musk*, musk source : *'abū*, father, source of + *al-*, the + *musk*, musk (< Pers. *mušk*; see MUSK).]

Ab·e·na·ki (ă′bə-nä′kē, ăb′ə-năk′ē) or **Ab·na·ki** (ăb-nä′kē, äb-) *n., pl.* **Abenaki** or **-kis** or **Abnaki** or **-kis 1.** A member of any of various Native American peoples formerly inhabiting northern New England and southeast Canada, with present-day populations in Maine and southern Quebec. **2.** A member of a confederacy of Abenaki and other peoples formed in the mid-18th century in opposition to the Iroquois confederacy and the English colonists. **3.** Either or both of the two Eastern Algonquian languages of the Abenaki peoples. [Prob. Montagnais *wabanākiwek*, dawn land people, Abenaki.]

ABEND *abbr. Computer Science* abnormal end of task

A·be·o·ku·ta (ä′bē-ō-kōō′tə) A city of SW Nigeria N of Lagos. Pop. 301,000.

Ab·er·deen (ăb′ər-dēn′) **1.** (*also* ăb′ər-dēn′) A city of NE Scotland on the North Sea. Pop. 218,220. **2.** A city of NE SD NE of Pierre. Pop. 24,658.

Aberdeen An·gus (ăng′gəs) *n.* A breed of black hornless beef cattle that originated in Scotland. [After *Aberdeen* and *Angus*, former counties of Scotland.]

Ab·er·nath·y (ăb′ər-năth′ē), **Ralph David** 1926–90. Amer. civil rights leader who was president (1968–77) of the Southern Christian Leadership Conference.

ab·er·rant (ă-bĕr′ənt, ăb′ər-) *adj.* **1.** Deviating from the proper or expected course. **2.** Deviating from what is normal; untrue to type. ❖ *n.* One that is aberrant. [Lat. *aberrāns, aberrant-*, pr. part. of *aberrāre*, to go astray. See ABERRATION.] —**ab·er′rance, ab·er′ran·cy** *n.* —**ab·er′rant·ly** *adv.*

abbey
Mosteiro de Santa Maria, Alcobaça, Portugal

Ralph Abernathy
speaking at a 1968 press conference

USAGE NOTE Traditionally *aberrant* has been pronounced with stress on the second syllable. A pronunciation with stress on the first syllable, however, has become equally common and may eventually supplant the older pronunciation. This change is owing perhaps to the influence of the words *aberration* and *aberrated*, which are stressed on the first syllable. The Usage Panel was divided almost evenly on the subject: 45 percent preferred the older pronunciation and 50 percent preferred the newer one. The remaining 5 percent of the Panelists said they use both pronunciations.

ab·er·ra·tion (ăb′ə-rā′shən) *n.* **1.** A deviation from the proper or expected course. **2.** A departure from the normal or typical. **3.** *Psychology* A disorder or abnormal alteration in one's mental state. **4a.** A defect of focus, such as blurring in an image. **b.** A physical defect in an optical element, as in a lens, that causes such an imperfection. **5.** The apparent displacement of the position of a celestial body in the direction of motion of an observer on Earth, caused by the motion of Earth and the finite velocity of light. **6.** *Genetics* A deviation in the normal structure or number of chromosomes in an organism. [Lat. *aberrātiō, aberrātiōn-*, diversion < *aberrātus*, p. part. of *aberrāre*, to go astray : *ab-*, away from; see AB–[1] + *errāre*, to stray.]

a·bet (ə-bĕt′) *tr.v.* **a·bet·ted, a·bet·ting, a·bets** **1.** To approve, encourage, and support (an action or a plan of action); urge and help on. **2.** To urge, encourage, or help (a person). [ME *abetten* < OFr. *abeter*, to entice : *a-*, to (< Lat. *ad–*; see AD–) + *beter*, to bait; see bheid- in App.] —**a·bet′ment** *n.* —**a·bet′tor, a·bet′ter** *n.*

ab ex·tra (ăb ĕk′strə) *adv.* From without. [Lat. *ab extrā* : *ab*, from + *extrā*, outside.]

a·bey·ance (ə-bā′əns) *n.* The condition of being temporarily set aside; suspension: *held the plan in abeyance.* [AN, var. of OFr. *abeance*, desire < *abaer*, to gape at : *a-*, at (< Lat. *ad–*; see AD–) + *baer*, to gape; see BAY[2].] —**a·bey′ant** *adj.*

ab·far·ad (ăb-făr′ăd′, -əd) *n.* The centimeter-gram-second electromagnetic unit of capacitance, equal to one billion farads.

ab·hen·ry (ăb-hĕn′rē) *n., pl.* **-ries** The centimeter-gram-second electromagnetic unit of inductance, equal to one billionth of a henry.

ab·hor (ăb-hôr′) *tr.v.* **-horred, -hor·ring, -hors** To regard with horror or loathing; detest. [ME *abhorren* < Lat. *abhorrēre*, to shrink from : *ab-*, from; see AB–[1] + *horrēre*, to shudder.] —**ab·hor′rer** *n.*

ab·hor·rence (ăb-hôr′əns, -hŏr′-) *n.* **1.** One that is disgusting or loathsome. **2.** A feeling of repugnance or loathing.

ab·hor·rent (ăb-hôr′ənt, -hŏr′-) *adj.* **1.** Disgusting, loathsome, or repellent. **2.** Feeling repugnance or loathing. **3.** *Archaic* Being strongly opposed. —**ab·hor′rent·ly** *adv.*

A·bib (ä-vēv′) *n.* The seventh month of the year in the Hebrew calendar, corresponding to Nisan. [Heb. *'ābîb*, young barley, spring, Abib.]

a·bid·ance (ə-bīd′ns) *n.* **1.** The act or condition of abiding; continuance. **2.** Adherence; compliance.

a·bide (ə-bīd′) *v.* **a·bode** (ə-bōd′) *or* **a·bid·ed** (ə-bīd′ĭd), **a·bid·ing, a·bides** —*tr.* **1.** To put up with; tolerate: *can't abide delays.* See Syns at **bear**[1]. **2.** To wait patiently for. **3.** To withstand: *a plastic that abides great heat.* —*intr.* **1.** To remain in a place. **2.** To continue to be sure or firm; endure. See Syns at **stay**[1]. **3.** To dwell or sojourn. —*idiom:* **abide by** To conform to; comply with: *abided by the rules.* [ME *abiden* < OE *ābīdan* : *ā-*, intensive pref. + *bīdan*, to remain; see bheidh- in App.] —**a·bid′er** *n.*

a·bid·ing (ə-bī′dĭng) *adj.* Lasting for a long time; enduring: *an abiding love of music.* —**a·bid′ing·ly** *adv.*

Ab·i·djan (ăb′ĭ-jän′) The largest city and former cap. of Côte d'Ivoire, in the S part on the Gulf of Guinea. Pop. 1,929,079.

ab·i·et·ic acid (ăb′ē-ĕt′ĭk) *n.* A yellowish resinous powder, C₁₉H₂₉COOH, isolated from rosin and used in lacquers, varnishes, and soaps. [< Lat. *abiēs, abiet-*, silver fir.]

Ab·i·gail (ăb′ĭ-gāl′) In the Bible, the wife of David.

Ab·i·lene (ăb′ə-lēn′) A city of W-central TX WSW of Fort Worth; founded 1881. Pop. 115,930.

a·bil·i·ty (ə-bĭl′ĭ-tē) *n., pl.* **-ties** **1.** The quality of being able to do something, esp. the physical, mental, financial, or legal power to accomplish something. **2.** A natural or acquired skill or talent. **3.** The quality of being suitable for or receptive to a specified treatment; capacity: *the ability of a computer to be configured for use as a file server.* [ME *abilite* < OFr. *habilite* < Lat. *habilitās* < *habilis*, handy. See ABLE.]

–ability *or* **–ibility** *suff.* Ability, inclination, or suitability for a specified action or condition: *teachability.* [ME *-abilitie* < OFr. *-abilite* < Lat. *-ābilitās* < *-ābilis, -able.*]

ability grouping *n.* See **tracking** 1.

ab in·i·ti·o (ăb ĭ-nĭsh′ē-ō′) *adv.* From the beginning. [Lat. *ab initiō* : *ab*, from + *initiō*, ablative of *initium*, beginning.]

ab in·tra (ĭn′trə) *adv.* From within. [Lat. *ab intrā* : *ab*, from + *intrā*, within.]

a·bi·o·gen·e·sis (ā′bī-ō-jĕn′ĭ-sĭs) *n.* The supposed development of living organisms from nonliving matter. —**a′bi·o·ge·net′ic** (-jə-nĕt′ĭk), **a′bi·o·ge·net′i·cal·ly** —**a′bi·og′e·nist** (-ŏj′ə-nĭst) *n.*

a·bi·o·gen·ic (ā′bī-ō-jĕn′ĭk) *adj.* Not produced by living organisms. —**a′bi·o·gen′i·cal·ly** *adv.*

a·bi·o·log·i·cal (ā′bī-ə-lŏj′ĭ-kəl) *adj.* Not associated with or derived from living organisms. —**a′bi·o·log′i·cal·ly** *adv.*

a·bi·ot·ic (ā′bī-ŏt′ĭk) *adj.* Nonliving. —**a·bi·o′sis** (-ō′sĭs) *n.* —**a·bi·ot′ic·al·ly** *adv.*

Ab·i·tib·i Lake (ăb′ĭ-tĭb′ē) A lake of E Ontario and SW Quebec, Canada; source of the **Abitibi River,** which flows c. 370 km (230 mi) to an arm of James Bay.

ab·ject (ăb′jĕkt′, ăb-jĕkt′) *adj.* **1.** Brought low in condition or status. **2.** Being of the most contemptible kind: *abject cowardice.* **3.** Being of the most miserable kind; wretched: *abject poverty.* [ME, outcast < Lat. *abiectus*, p. part. of *abicere*, to cast away : *ab-*, from; see AB–[1] + *iacere*, to throw.] —**ab′ject′ly** *adv.* —**ab·ject′ness, ab·jec′tion** *n.*

ab·jure (ăb-jŏor′) *tr.v.* **-jured, -jur·ing, -jures** **1.** To renounce under oath; forswear. **2.** To recant solemnly; repudiate: *abjure one's beliefs.* **3.** To give up (an action or practice, for example); abstain from. [ME *abjuren* < OFr. *abjurer* < Lat. *abiūrāre* : *ab-*, away; see AB–[1] + *iūrāre*, to swear.] —**ab′ju·ra′tion** *n.* —**ab·jur′er** *n.*

Ab·khaz (ăb-kăz′, ăb-käz′) *also* **Ab·kha·zian** (ăb-kā′zhən, -zē-ən, -kä′-) *n., pl.* **Abkhaz** *or* **-khaz·es 1.** A native or inhabitant of Abkhazia. **2.** The Northwest Caucasian language of Abkhazia, also spoken in Georgia and Turkey. [Russ.]

Ab·kha·zia (ăb-kā′zhə, -zē-ə, -kä′-, äb-) An autonomous republic of NW Georgia bordering on Russia and the Black Sea.

Ab·kha·zian (ăb-kā′zhən, -zē-ən, -kä′-, äb-) *n.* Variant of **Abkhaz.** ❖ *adj.* Of or relating to Abkhazia or the Abkhaz.

abl. *abbr. Grammar* ablative

ab·late (ă-blāt′) *v.* **-lat·ed, -lat·ing, -lates** —*tr.* **1.** *Medicine* To excise (a body tissue, for example). **2.** To remove by erosion, melting, evaporation, or vaporization. —*intr.* To become ablated. [Back-formation < ABLATION.] —**ab·la′tor** *n.*

ab·la·tion (ă-blā′shən) *n.* **1.** Surgical excision of a body part or tissue. **2.** The reduction of a glacier by erosion, melting, evaporation, or vaporization. **3.** *Aerospace* The reduction or removal of a usu. heat-protective surface material by aerodynamic friction. [LLat. *ablātiō, ablātiōn-* < Lat. *ablātus*, p. part. of *auferre*, to carry away : *ab-*, away; see AB–[1] + *lātus*, carried; see telə- in App.]

ab·la·tive[1] (ăb′lə-tĭv) *adj.* Of, relating to, or being a grammatical case indicating separation, direction away from, sometimes manner or agency, and the object of certain verbs. ❖ *n.* **1.** The ablative case. **2.** A word in this case. [ME < Lat. *ablātīvus* < *ablātus*, carried away. See ABLATION.]

ab·la·tive[2] (ă-blā′tĭv) *adj.* **1.** Of, relating to, or capable of ablation. **2.** Tending to ablate. [< ABLATION.]

ab·la·tive absolute (ăb′lə-tĭv) *n.* In Latin grammar, an adverbial phrase syntactically independent from the rest of the sentence and containing a noun or pronoun plus an adjunct, usu. a participle or adjective, with both elements in the ablative case.

ab·laut (ăb′lout′, äp′-) *n.* A vowel change, characteristic of Indo-European languages, that accompanies a change in grammatical function. [Ger. : *ab*, off (< MHGer. < OHGer. *aba*; see **apo-** in App.) + *Laut*, sound (< MHGer. *lūt* < OHGer. *hlūt*; see **kleu-** in App.).]

a·blaze (ə-blāz′) *adj.* **1.** Being on fire: *The house is ablaze.* **2.** Radiant with bright color: *a maple tree ablaze in autumn.* **3.** Fervent or excited. —**a·blaze′** *adv.*

a·ble (ā′bəl) *adj.* **a·bler, a·blest** **1.** Having sufficient power or resources: *able to pay.* **2.** *Usage Problem* Susceptible to action or treatment: *The brakes were able to be fixed.* **3.** Especially capable or talented. [ME < OFr. < Lat. *habilis* < *habēre*, to handle. See **ghabh-** in App.] —**a′bly** (ā′blē) *adv.*

USAGE NOTE The construction *able to* takes an infinitive to show the subject's ability to accomplish an action: *We were able to get a grant for the project from a large corporation.* Some people think this construction should be avoided when the subject does not have an ability, as in sentences with passive constructions with the verb *be*, as in *The problem was able to be solved,* since the *problem* has no ability to solve the problem. In such cases *can* or *could* can usually be substituted: *The problem could be solved.* By contrast, passives with *get* ascribe a more active role to their subjects, and here the *able to* construction can be used: *He was able to get himself accepted by a top law school.*

–able *or* **–ible** *suff.* **1.** Susceptible to, capable of, or worthy of a specified action: *debatable.* **2.** Inclined or given to a specified state or action: *changeable.* [ME < OFr. < Lat. *-ābilis, -ibilis* : *-ā-* and *-i-*, thematic vowels + *-bilis,* adj. suff.]

a·ble-bod·ied (ā′bəl-bŏd′ēd) *adj.* Physically strong and healthy.

able-bodied seaman *n.* See **able seaman.**

a·ble·ism (ā′bə-lĭz′əm) *n.* Discrimination against people with disabilities, esp. physical disabilities. —**a′ble·ist** *adj. & n.*

able seaman *n.* An experienced seaman certified to perform all routine duties at sea.

a·bloom (ə-bloōm′) *adj.* Being in bloom; flowering.

ab·lu·tion (ə-bloō′shən, ă-bloō′-) *n.* **1.** A washing or cleansing of the body. **2.** The liquid so used. [ME *ablucioun* < Lat. *ablūtiō, ablūtiōn-* < *ablūtus*, p. part. of *abluere*, to wash away : *ab-*, away;

ă	pat	oi	boy
ā	pay	ou	out
âr	care	ŏŏ	took
ä	father	ōō	boot
ĕ	pet	ŭ	cut
ē	be	ûr	urge
ĭ	pit	th	thin
ī	pie	th	this
îr	pier	hw	which
ŏ	pot	zh	vision
ō	toe	ə	about,
ô	paw		item

Stress marks:
′ (primary);
′ (secondary), as in
lexicon (lĕk′sĭ-kŏn′)

see AB-[1] + *-luere*, to wash; see **leu(ə)-** in App.] —**ab•lu′tion•ar•y** (-shə-nĕr′ē) *adj.*

ABM *abbr.* antiballistic missile

abn *abbr.* airborne

Ab•na•ki (ăb-nä′kē, ä-bä-) *n.* Variant of **Abenaki.**

ab•ne•gate (ăb′nĭ-gāt′) *tr.v.* **-gat•ed, -gat•ing, -gates 1.** To give up (rights or a claim, for example); renounce. **2.** To deny (something) to oneself. [Lat. *abnegāre, abnegāt-,* to refuse : *ab-,* away; see AB-[1] + *negāre,* to deny; see **ne** in App.] —**ab′ne•ga′tor** *n.*

ab•ne•ga•tion (ăb′nĭ-gā′shən) *n.* Self-denial.

ab•nor•mal (ăb-nôr′məl) *adj.* Not typical, usual, or regular; not normal; deviant. [Alteration (influenced by AB-[1]) of obsolete *anormal* < Med.Lat. *anormālis,* blend of LLat. *abnormis* (Lat. *ab-,* away from; see AB-[1] + Lat. *norma,* rule; see **gnō-** in App.) and *anōmalus;* see ANOMALOUS.] —**ab•nor′mal•ly** *adv.*

ab•nor•mal•i•ty (ăb′nôr-măl′ĭ-tē) *n., pl.* **-ties 1.** The condition of not being normal. **2.** A phenomenon or occurrence that is not normal.

abnormal psychology *n.* The study of mental disorders, maladaptive behaviors, and certain mental phenomena such as dreams and hypnosis.

Ab•o or **ab•o** (ăb′ō) *n., pl.* **-os** *Offensive Slang* Used as a disparaging term for an Australian Aborigine.

a•board (ə-bôrd′, ə-bōrd′) *adv.* **1.** On board a passenger vehicle. **2.** At the side; alongside. **3.** In or into a group, organization, or business. **4.** *Baseball* On base. ❖ *prep.* On board of; on; in. [ME *abord : a-,* on; see A-[2] + *bord,* ship (< OE *bord*).]

a•bode (ə-bōd′) *v.* A past tense and past participle of **abide.** ❖ *n.* **1.** A dwelling place; a home. **2.** The act of abiding; a sojourn. [ME *abod,* home < *abiden,* to wait. See ABIDE.]

ab•ohm (ăb-ōm′) *n.* The centimeter-gram-second electromagnetic unit of resistance, equal to one billionth of an ohm.

a•boil (ə-boil′) *adv. & adj.* **1.** At a boil; boiling. **2.** In an excited or tumultuous state.

a•bol•ish (ə-bŏl′ĭsh) *tr.v.* **-ished, -ish•ing, -ish•es 1.** To do away with; annul. **2.** To destroy completely. [ME *abolisshen* < OFr. *abolir, aboliss-* < Lat. *abolēre.*] —**a•bol′ish•a•ble** *adj.* —**a•bol′ish•er** *n.* —**a•bol′ish•ment** *n.*

ab•o•li•tion (ăb′ə-lĭsh′ən) *n.* **1.** The act of doing away with or the state of being done away with; annulment. **2.** Abolishment of slavery. [Lat. *abolitiō, abolitiōn-* < *abolitus,* p. part. of *abolēre,* to abolish.] —**ab′o•li′tion•ar′y** (-lĭsh′ə-nĕr′ē) *adj.*

ab•o•li•tion•ism (ăb′ə-lĭsh′ə-nĭz′əm) *n.* Advocacy of the abolition of slavery. —**ab′o•li′tion•ist** *n.*

ab•o•ma•sum (ăb′ō-mā′səm) *n., pl.* **-sa** (-sə) The fourth division of the stomach in ruminant animals, in which digestion takes place. —**ab′o•ma′sal** (-səl) *adj.*

A-bomb (ā′bŏm′) *n.* See **atom bomb** 1.

a•bom•i•na•ble (ə-bŏm′ə-nə-bəl) *adj.* **1.** Unequivocally detestable; loathsome. **2.** Thoroughly unpleasant or disagreeable. [ME *abhominable* < OFr. < Lat. *abōminābilis* < *abōminārī,* to abhor. See ABOMINATE.] —**a•bom′i•na•bly** *adv.*

abominable snowman *n.* A hairy humanlike animal reportedly inhabiting the high Himalaya Mountains.

a•bom•i•nate (ə-bŏm′ə-nāt′) *tr.v.* **-nat•ed, -nat•ing, -nates** To detest thoroughly; abhor. [Lat. *abōminārī, abōmināt-,* to deprecate as a bad omen : *ab-,* away; see AB-[1] + *ōmen,* omen.] —**a•bom′i•na′tor** *n.*

a•bom•i•na•tion (ə-bŏm′ə-nā′shən) *n.* **1.** Abhorrence; disgust. **2.** A cause of abhorrence or disgust.

ab•o•ral (ă-bôr′əl, ă-bōr′-) *adj.* Located opposite to or away from the mouth. —**ab•o′ral•ly** *adv.*

ab•o•rig•i•nal (ăb′ə-rĭj′ə-nəl) *adj.* **1.** Having existed in a region from the beginning. **2a.** Of or relating to aborigines. **b.** often **Aboriginal** Of or relating to the indigenous peoples of Australia. ❖ *n.* also **Aboriginal** An aborigine. —**ab′o•rig′i•nal•ly** *adv.*

ab•o•rig•i•ne (ăb′ə-rĭj′ə-nē) *n.* **1a.** A member of the indigenous or earliest known population of a region. **b.** often **Aborigine** A member of any of the indigenous peoples of Australia. **2. aborigines** The flora and fauna native to a geographic area. [< Lat. *aborīginēs,* original inhabitants : *ab,* from; see AB-[1] + *orīgine,* ablative of *orīgō,* beginning; see ORIGIN.]

a•born•ing (ə-bôr′nĭng) *adv.* While coming into being or being created. ❖ *adj.* Coming into being or being created.

a•bort (ə-bôrt′) *v.* **a•bort•ed, a•bort•ing, a•borts** —*intr.* **1.** To give birth prematurely or before term; miscarry. **2.** To cease growth before full development or maturation. **3.** To terminate an operation or procedure before completion. —*tr.* **1a.** To cause to terminate (a pregnancy) prematurely, esp. before the fetus is viable. **b.** To cause the expulsion of (an embryo or fetus) before it is viable. **c.** To give premature birth to (an embryo or fetus). **2.** To interfere with the development of; conclude prematurely: *abort plans for a corporate takeover.* **3.** To terminate before completion: *abort a takeoff.* **4.** To stop the progress of (a disease, for example). ❖ *n.* **1.** The act of terminating an operation or procedure before completion. **2.** *Computer Science* A procedure to terminate execution of a program when an unrecoverable error or malfunction occurs. [Lat. *abortāre,* freq. of *aborīrī, abort-,* to disappear, miscarry : *ab-,* away; see AB-[1] + *orīrī,* to appear; see **er-** in App.]

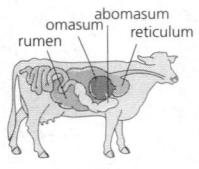

omasum · abomasum
rumen · reticulum

abomasum

a•bor•ti•fa•cient (ə-bôr′tə-fā′shənt) *adj.* Causing abortion. ❖ *n.* A substance or device used to induce abortion.

a•bor•tion (ə-bôr′shən) *n.* **1a.** Induced termination of pregnancy, involving expulsion and destruction of the embryo or fetus, esp. before it is capable of survival. **b.** A procedure that results in such termination. **2.** A miscarriage. **3.** Cessation of normal growth, esp. of a body part, prior to full development or maturation. **4.** An aborted organism. **5.** Something malformed or incompletely developed; a monstrosity.

a•bor•tion•ist (ə-bôr′shə-nĭst) *n.* One who performs abortions.

a•bor•tive (ə-bôr′tĭv) *adj.* **1.** Failing to accomplish an intended objective; fruitless. **2.** *Biology* Partially or imperfectly developed. **3.** Causing or meant to cause abortion; abortifacient. —**a•bor′tive•ly** *adv.* —**a•bor′tive•ness** *n.*

ABO system (ā′bē-ō′) *n.* A classification system for human blood that identifies four major blood types, A, B, AB, and O, based on the presence or absence of two antigens, A and B, on red blood cells.

a•bound (ə-bound′) *intr.v.* **a•bound•ed, a•bound•ing, a•bounds 1.** To be great in number or amount. **2.** To be fully supplied or filled. See Syns at **teem**[1]. [ME *abounden* < OFr. *abonder* < Lat. *abundāre,* to overflow : *ab-,* away; see AB-[1] + *undāre,* to flow (< *unda,* wave; see **wed-** in App.).]

a•bout (ə-bout′) *adv.* **1.** Approximately; nearly: *about an hour.* **2.** Almost: *The job is about done.* **3.** To a reversed position or direction. **4.** In no particular direction: *wandering about.* **5.** All around; on every side: *look about for help.* **6.** In the area or vicinity; near: *spoke to spectators standing about.* **7.** In succession; one after another: *Turn about is fair play.* **8a.** On the verge of doing something. Used with the infinitive: *The chorus is about to sing.* **b.** Used to show determination or intention in negative constructions with an infinitive: *I am not about to concede the point.* ❖ *prep.* **1.** On all sides of; surrounding. **2.** In the vicinity of; around: *explored the streams about the estate.* **3.** Almost the same as; close to; near. **4a.** In reference to; relating to; concerned with: *a book about snakes.* **b.** In the act or process of: *While you're about it, please clean your room.* **5.** In the possession or innate character of: *Keep your wits about you.* ❖ *adj.* **1.** Moving here and there; astir: *The patient is up and about.* **2.** Being in evidence or existence: *Rumors are about concerning his resignation.* [ME < OE *onbūtan : on-,* in (< *on*) + *būtan,* outside; see **ud-** in App.]

a•bout-face (ə-bout′fās′) *n.* **1a.** The act of pivoting to face in the opposite direction from the original. **b.** A military command to turn clockwise 180°. **2.** A total change of attitude or viewpoint. —**a•bout′-face′** *v.*

a•bove (ə-bŭv′) *adv.* **1.** On high; overhead: *the clouds above.* **2.** In heaven; heavenward. **3a.** Upstairs: *in the dining room above.* **b.** To a degree that is over zero: *15° above.* **4.** In or to a higher place. **5.** In an earlier part of a given text. **6.** In or to a higher rank or position: *the ranks of major and above.* ❖ *prep.* **1.** Over or higher than. **2.** Superior to in rank, position, or number; greater than: *put principles above expediency.* **3.** Beyond the level or reach of: *heard above the music.* **4.** In preference to. **5.** Too honorable to bend to: *above petty intrigue.* **6.** More than: *above normal temperature.* **7.** Upstream of: *a dam positioned above the town.* **8.** North of: *Utah is above Arizona.* ❖ *n.* **1.** An earlier part of a given text. **2.** The person or persons already referred to in a text. ❖ *adj.* Appearing earlier in the same text: *the above interpretation.* —*idiom:* **above all** Over and above all other considerations. [ME *aboven* < OE *abūfan : a-,* on; see A-[2] + *būfan,* above; see **upo** in App.]

a•bove•board (ə-bŭv′bôrd′, -bōrd′) *adv. & adj.* Without deceit or trickery; straightforward in manner. [Orig. a gambling term referring to the fact that a gambler could not engage in trickery when the hands were above the gaming table.]

a•bove•ground (ə-bŭv′ground′) *adj.* **1.** Situated on or above the surface of the ground. **2.** Operating or existing within the establishment; conventional: *published in the aboveground press.* —**a•bove′ground′** *adv.*

a•bove•men•tioned (ə-bŭv′mĕn′shənd) *adj.* Mentioned previously. ❖ *n.* The one or ones mentioned previously.

ab o•vo (ăb ō′vō) *adv.* From the beginning. [Lat. *ab ōvō : ab,* from + *ōvō,* ablative of *ōvum,* egg.]

Abp. *abbr.* archbishop

ab•ra•ca•dab•ra (ăb′rə-kə-dăb′rə) *n.* **1.** A magical charm or incantation having the power to ward off disease or disaster. **2.** Foolish or unintelligible talk. [LLat., magical formula.]

a•brad•ant (ə-brād′nt) *n.* An abrasive. ❖ *adj.* Abrasive.

a•brade (ə-brād′) *tr.v.* **a•brad•ed, a•brad•ing, a•brades 1.** To wear down or rub away by friction; erode. **2.** To make weary through constant irritation; wear down spiritually. [Lat. *abrādere,* to scrape off : *ab-,* away; see AB-[1] + *rādere,* to scrape.] —**a•brad′a•ble** *adj.*

A•bra•ham (ā′brə-hăm′) In the Bible, the first patriarch and progenitor of the Hebrew people.

a•bra•sion (ə-brā′zhən) *n.* **1.** The process of wearing down or rubbing away by means of friction. **2a.** A scraped or worn area. **b.** A scraped area, as on the skin, resulting from injury or irritation. [Med.Lat. *abrāsiō, abrāsiōn-* < Lat. *abrāsus,* p. part. of *abrādere,* to scrape off. See ABRADE.]

a•bra•sive (ə-brā′sĭv, -zĭv) *adj.* **1.** Causing abrasion. **2.** Harsh and rough in manner: *an abrasive personality.* ❖ *n.* A substance that abrades. —**a•bra′sive•ly** *adv.* —**a•bra′sive•ness** *n.*

ab•re•act (ăb′rē-ăkt′) *tr.v.* **-act•ed, -act•ing, -acts** To release (repressed emotions) by acting out, as in behavior or the imagination, the situation causing the conflict. [Transl. of Ger. *abreagieren* : *ab-*, away + *reagieren*, to react.] —**ab′re•ac′tion** *n.*

a•breast (ə-brĕst′) *adv.* **1.** Side by side: *ships docked two abreast.* **2.** Up to date: *keeping abreast of the news.*

a•bridge (ə-brĭj′) *tr.v.* **a•bridged, a•bridg•ing, a•bridg•es 1.** To reduce the length of (a written text); condense. **2.** To cut short; curtail. [ME *abregen* < OFr. *abregier* < LLat. *abbreviāre*, to shorten. See ABBREVIATE.] —**a•bridg′er** *n.*

a•bridg•ment also **a•bridge•ment** (ə-brĭj′mənt) *n.* **1.** The act of abridging or the state of being abridged. **2.** A written text that has been abridged.

a•broach (ə-brōch′) *adj.* **1.** Opened or positioned so that a liquid, such as wine, can be let out. **2.** In a state of action; astir. [ME *abroche* : *a-*, on, in; see A–[2] + *broche*, a pointed object, spigot; see BROACH[1].]

a•broad (ə-brôd′) *adv. & adj.* **1.** Out of one's own country. **2.** In a foreign country or countries. **3.** Away from one's home. **4.** In circulation; at large. **5.** Covering a large area; widely. **6.** Not on target; in error. ❖ *n.* A foreign country or countries in which to live or travel: *"Do you like abroad or hate it?"* (John le Carré). [ME *abrod* : *a-*, in, on; see A–[2] + *brod*, broad; see BROAD.]

ab•ro•gate (ăb′rə-gāt′) *tr.v.* **-gat•ed, -gat•ing, -gates** To abolish, do away with, or annul. [Lat. *abrogāre, abrogāt-* : *ab-*, away; see AB–[1] + *rogāre*, to ask; see **reg-** in App.] —**ab′ro•ga′tion** *n.*

a•brupt (ə-brŭpt′) *adj.* **1.** Unexpectedly sudden: *an abrupt change in the weather.* **2.** Surprisingly and unceremoniously curt; brusque: *an abrupt answer made in anger.* **3.** Touching on one subject after another with sudden transitions: *abrupt prose.* **4.** Steeply inclined. See Syns at **steep**[1]. **5.** *Botany* Terminating suddenly rather than gradually; truncate: *an abrupt leaf.* [Lat. *abruptus*, p. part. of *abrumpere*, to break off : *ab-*, away; see AB–[1] + *rumpere*, to break; see **reup-** in App.] —**a•brupt′ly** *adv.* —**a•brupt′ness** *n.*

a•brup•tion (ə-brŭp′shən) *n.* An instance of suddenly breaking away or off.

A•bruz•zi also **A•bruz•zi e Mo•li•se** (ä-bro͞ot′sē ā mô-lē′zĕ, ə-bro͞ot′-) A region of central Italy bordering on the Adriatic Sea.

abs *abbr.* absolute temperature

ABS *abbr.* antilock braking system

Ab•sa•lom (ăb′sə-ləm) In the Bible, a son of David who staged a revolt against his father's kingship and was killed in the ensuing battle.

Ab•sa•ro•ka Range (ăb-sär′ə-kə) A section of the Rocky Mts. in NW WY and S MT, rising to 4,007.7 m (13,140 ft).

Ab•sa•ro•ke (ăb-sär′ə-kə) *n., pl.* **Absaroke** or **-kes** See **Crow.** [Crow, children of the long-beaked bird.]

ab•scess (ăb′sĕs′) *n.* A localized collection of pus in part of the body, surrounded by an inflamed area. ❖ *intr.v.* **-scessed, -scess•ing, -scess•es** To form an abscess. [Lat. *abscessus*, separation, abscess < p. part. of *abscēdere*, to go away, slough, form an abscess (poss. transl. of Gk. *apostēma*, distance, abscess < *aphistasthai*, to withdraw, slough, form an abscess) : *ab-*, away; see AB–[1] + *cēdere*, to go.]

ab•scise (ăb-sīz′) *v.* **-scised, -scis•ing, -scis•es** —*tr.* To cut off; remove. —*intr.* To shed by abscission. [Lat. *abscīdere, abscīs-* : *ab-*, away; see AB–[1] + *caedere*, to cut.]

ab•scis•sa (ăb-sĭs′ə) *n., pl.* **-scis•sas** or **-scis•sae** (-sĭs′ē) *Symbol* **x** The coordinate representing the position of a point along a line perpendicular to the *y*-axis in a plane Cartesian coordinate system. [NLat. *(līnea) abscissa*, (line) cut off < Lat. *abscissa*, fem. p. part. of *abscindere*, to abscise. See ABSCISSION.]

ab•scis•sion (ăb-sĭzh′ən) *n.* **1.** The act of cutting off. **2.** *Botany* The shedding of leaves, flowers, or fruits following the formation of the abscission zone. [Lat. *abscissiō, abscissiōn-* < *abscissus*, p. part. of *abscindere*, to cut off : *ab-*, ab- + *scindere*, to cut.]

abscission zone *n.* The region at the base of a plant part, such as a leaf, where the formation of a cork layer results in the separation of that part from the plant body.

ab•scond (ăb-skŏnd′) *intr.v.* **-scond•ed, -scond•ing, -sconds** To leave quickly and secretly and hide, often to avoid arrest or prosecution. [Lat. *abscondere*, to hide : *abs-*, *ab-*, away; see AB–[1] + *condere*, to put; see **dhē-** in App.] —**ab•scond′er** *n.*

ab•seil (äp′zīl′, -sīl′, ăb′-) *intr.v.* **-seiled, -seil•ing, -seiled** To rappel. [Ger. *abseilen*, to descend at the end of a rope : *ab*, down, off; see ABLAUT + *Seil*, rope (< MHGer. < OHGer.).]

ab•sence (ăb′səns) *n.* **1.** The state of being away. **2.** The time during which one is away. **3.** Lack; want: *an absence of leadership.* **4.** The state of being absent-minded; inattentiveness.

ab•sent (ăb′sənt) *adj.* **1.** Not present; missing: *absent friends.* **2.** Not existent; lacking: *Morality is absent.* **3.** Exhibiting or feeling inattentiveness: *an absent nod.* ❖ *tr.v.* (ăb-sĕnt′) **-sent•ed, -sent•ing, -sents** To keep (oneself) away: *They absented themselves from the debate.* ❖ *prep.* Without. [ME < OFr. < Lat. *absēns, absent-*, pr. part. of *abesse*, to be away : *ab-*, away; see AB–[1] + *esse*, to be; see **es-** in App.] —**ab′sent•ly** *adv.*

ab•sen•tee (ăb′sən-tē′) *n.* One that is absent. ❖ *adj.* **1.** Of or relating to one that is absent. **2.** Not in residence: *a building owned by an absentee landlord.* See Usage Note at **–ee**[1].

absentee ballot *n.* A ballot marked and mailed in advance by a voter away from the place where he or she is registered.

ab•sen•tee•ism (ăb′sən-tē′ĭz′əm) *n.* **1.** Habitual failure to appear, esp. for work or other regular duty. **2.** The rate of occurrence of habitual absence from work or duty.

ab•sent-mind•ed (ăb′sənt-mīn′dĭd) *adj.* Deep in thought and heedless of present circumstances or activities; preoccupied. —**ab′sent-mind′ed•ly** *adv.* —**ab′sent-mind′ed•ness** *n.*

absent without leave *adj.* Absent from one's assigned military post or duties without official permission; AWOL.

ab•sinthe also **ab•sinth** (ăb′sĭnth) *n.* **1.** A perennial aromatic European herb *(Artemisia absinthium).* **2.** A green liqueur having a bitter anise or licorice flavor and a high alcohol content, prepared from absinthe and other herbs. [ME, wormwood < OFr. < Lat. *absinthium* < Gk. *apsinthion.*]

ab•so•lute (ăb′sə-lo͞ot′, ăb′sə-lo͞ot′) *adj.* **1.** Perfect in quality or nature; complete. **2.** Not mixed; pure. See Syns at **pure. 3a.** Not limited by restrictions or exceptions; unconditional: *absolute trust.* **b.** Unqualified in extent or degree; total: *absolute silence.* See Usage Note at **infinite. 4.** Unconstrained by constitutional or other provisions: *an absolute ruler.* **5.** Not to be doubted or questioned; positive: *absolute proof.* **6.** *Grammar* **a.** Of, relating to, or being a word, phrase, or construction that is isolated syntactically from the rest of a sentence. **b.** Of, relating to, or being a transitive verb when its object is implied but not stated. **c.** Of, relating to, or being an adjective or pronoun that stands alone when the noun it modifies is implied but not stated. **7.** *Physics* **a.** Relating to measurements or units of measurement derived from fundamental units of length, mass, and time. **b.** Relating to absolute temperature. ❖ *n.* **1.** Something that is absolute. **2. Absolute** *Philosophy* **a.** Something regarded as the ultimate basis of all thought and being. Used with *the.* **b.** Something regarded as independent of and unrelated to anything else. [ME *absolut* < Lat. *absolūtus*, unrestricted, p. part. of *absolvere*, to absolve : *ab-*, away; see AB–[1] + *solvere*, to loosen; see **leu-** in App.] —**ab′so•lute′ness** *n.*

absolute alcohol *n.* Ethyl alcohol containing no more than one percent water.

absolute ceiling *n.* The maximum altitude above sea level at which an aircraft or missile can maintain horizontal flight under standard atmospheric conditions.

absolute convergence *n.* The mathematical property by which the sum of the absolute values of the terms in a series converge. —**absolutely convergent** *adj.*

absolute humidity *n.* The amount of water vapor present in a unit volume of air, usu. expressed in kilograms per cubic meter.

ab•so•lute•ly (ăb′sə-lo͞ot′lē, ăb′sə-lo͞ot′lē) *adv.* **1.** Definitely and completely; unquestionably. **2.** *Grammar* **a.** In a manner that does not take an object. **b.** In an absolute relationship.

absolute magnitude *n.* The intrinsic magnitude of a celestial body computed as if viewed from a distance of 10 parsecs, or 32.6 light-years.

absolute music *n.* Instrumental music that is free of any explicit verbal reference or program.

absolute pitch *n.* **1.** The precise pitch of an isolated tone, as established by its rate of vibration measured on a standard scale. **2.** *Music* The ability to identify any pitch heard or produce any pitch referred to by name.

absolute scale *n.* **1.** A scale of temperature with absolute zero as the minimum. **2.** The Kelvin scale.

absolute temperature *n.* Temperature measured or calculated on an absolute scale.

absolute value *n.* **1.** The numerical value of a real number without regard to its sign. For example, the absolute value of –4 (written |–4|) is 4. **2.** The modulus of a complex number, equal to the square root of the sum of the squares of the real and imaginary parts of the number.

absolute zero *n.* The theoretical temperature at which substances possess no thermal energy, equal to –273.15°C, or –459.67°F.

ab•so•lu•tion (ăb′sə-lo͞o′shən) *n.* **1.** The act of absolving or the state of being absolved. **2.** The formal remission of sin imparted by a priest. [ME < OFr. < Lat. *absolūtiō*, acquittal < *absolūtus*, p. part. of *absolvere*, to absolve. See ABSOLUTE.]

ab•so•lut•ism (ăb′sə-lo͞o′tĭz′əm) *n.* **1a.** A political theory holding that all power should be vested in one authority. **b.** A form of government in which all power is vested in a single authority. **2.** An absolute doctrine, principle, or standard. —**ab′so•lut′ist** *n.* —**ab′so•lu•tis′tic** (-lo͞o-tĭs′tĭk) *adj.*

ab•so•lu•tive (ăb′sə-lo͞o′tĭv) *adj.* In ergative languages, of or relating to the grammatical case of the subject of an intransitive verb and the object of a transitive verb. —**ab′so•lu′tive** *n.*

ab•solve (əb-zŏlv′, -sŏlv′) *tr.v.* **-solved, -solv•ing, -solves 1.** To pronounce clear of guilt or blame. **2.** To relieve of a requirement or obligation. **3a.** To grant a remission of sin to. **b.** To pardon or remit (a sin). [ME *absolven* < Lat. *absolvere.* See ABSOLUTE.] —**ab•solv′a•ble** *adj.* —**ab•solv′er** *n.*

ab•sorb (əb-sôrb′, -zôrb′) *tr.v.* **-sorbed, -sorb•ing, -sorbs 1.** To take (something) in through or as through pores or interstices. **2.** To occupy the full attention, interest, or time of; engross. **3.** *Physics* To retain (radiation, for example) wholly, without reflection

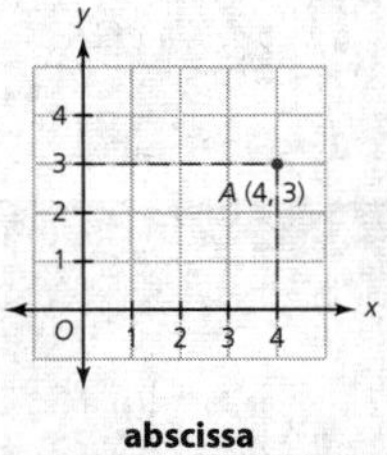

abscissa
The coordinates for *A* are (4,3); the abscissa is 4.

ă	pat	oi	boy
ā	pay	ou	out
âr	care	o͝o	took
ä	father	o͞o	boot
ĕ	pet	ŭ	cut
ē	be	ûr	urge
ĭ	pit	th	thin
ī	pie	*th*	this
îr	pier	hw	which
ŏ	pot	zh	vision
ō	toe	ə	about, item
ô	paw		

Stress marks:
′ (primary);
′ (secondary), as in
lexicon (lĕk′sĭ-kŏn′)

or transmission. **4.** To take in; assimilate. **5.** To learn; acquire: *absorb a lesson.* **6.** To receive (an impulse) without echo or recoil: *a bumper that absorbs impact.* **7.** To take over (a cost or costs). **8.** To endure; accommodate. [ME, to swallow up < OFr. *absorber* < Lat. *absorbēre : ab-,* away; see AB–[1] + *sorbēre,* to suck.] —**ab·sorb′a·bil′i·ty** *n.* —**ab·sorb′a·ble** *adj.* —**ab·sorb′er** *n.* —**ab·sorb′ing·ly** *adv.*

ab·sor·be·fa·cient (ăb-sôr′bə-fā′shənt, -zôr′-) *adj.* Inducing or causing absorption. ❖ *n.* A medicine or agent that induces absorption. [ABSORBE(NT) + –FACIENT.]

ab·sor·bent (ăb-sôr′bənt, -zôr′-) *adj.* Capable of absorbing. ❖ *n.* A substance that is capable of absorbing. —**ab·sor′ben·cy** *n.*

ab·sorp·tance (ăb-sôrp′təns, -zôrp′-) *n.* The ratio of absorbed to incident radiation. [ABSORPT(ION) + –ANCE.]

ab·sorp·tion (ăb-sôrp′shən, -zôrp′-) *n.* **1.** The act or process of absorbing or the condition of being absorbed. **2.** A state of mental concentration. [Lat. *absorptiō, absorptiōn-* < *absorptus,* p. part. of *absorbēre,* to absorb. See ABSORB.] —**ab·sorp′tive** (-tĭv) *adj.* —**ab′sorp·tiv′i·ty** *n.*

absorption spectrum *n.* The spectrum formed when electromagnetic radiation traverses an absorbing medium, resulting in a pattern of dark bands or lines specific to the medium.

ab·squat·u·late (ăb-skwŏch′ə-lāt′) *intr.v.* **-lat·ed, -lat·ing, -lates** *Midwestern & Western US* **1a.** To depart in a hurry; abscond: *"Your horse has absquatulated!"* (Robert M. Bird). **b.** To die. **2.** To argue. [Mock-Latinate formation, purporting to mean "to go off and squat elsewhere."]

REGIONAL NOTE The vibrant energy of American English sometimes appears in the use of Latin affixes to create jocular pseudo-Latin "learned" words. Midwestern and Western US *absquatulate* has a prefix *ab–,* "away from," and a suffix *–ate,* "to act upon in a specified manner," affixed to a nonexistent base form *–squatul–,* probably suggested by *squat.* Another such coinage is Northern *busticate,* which joins *bust* with *–icate* by analogy with verbs like *medicate.* Southern *argufy* joins *argue* to a redundant *–fy,* "to make, cause to become." Today, these creations are most used in regions of the United States where change is slow.

ab·stain (ăb-stān′, əb-) *intr.v.* **-stained, -stain·ing, -stains 1.** To refrain from something by one's own choice. **2.** To refrain from voting. [ME *absteinen,* to avoid < OFr. *abstenir* < Lat. *abstinēre,* to hold back : *abs-, ab-,* away; see AB–[1] + *tenēre,* to hold; see **ten-** in App.] —**ab·stain′er** *n.*

ab·ste·mi·ous (ăb-stē′mē-əs, əb-) *adj.* **1.** Eating and drinking in moderation. **2a.** Sparingly used or consumed. **b.** Restricted to bare necessities. [< Lat. *abstēmius : abs-, ab-,* away; see AB–[1] + **tēmum,* liquor, var. of *tēmētum.*] —**ab·ste′mi·ous·ly** *adv.* —**ab·ste′mi·ous·ness** *n.*

ab·sten·tion (ăb-stěn′shən, əb-) *n.* **1.** The act or habit of deliberate self-denial. **2.** An abstaining vote or voter. [LLat. *abstentiō, abstentiōn-* < *abstentus,* p. part. of Lat. *abstinēre,* to hold back. See ABSTAIN.]

ab·sti·nence (ăb′stə-nəns) *n.* **1.** The act or practice of refraining from indulging an appetite. **2.** Abstention from alcoholic beverages. [ME < OFr. *abstenance* < Lat. *abstinentia* < *abstinēns, abstinent-,* pr. part. of *abstinēre,* to hold back. See ABSTAIN.] —**ab′sti·nent** *adj.* —**ab′sti·nent·ly** *adv.*

ab·stract (ăb-străkt′, ăb′străkt′) *adj.* **1.** Considered apart from concrete existence. **2.** Not applied or practical; theoretical. **3.** Difficult to understand; abstruse: *abstract philosophical problems.* **4.** Impersonal, as in attitude or views. **5.** Having an intellectual and affective artistic content that depends solely on intrinsic form rather than on narrative content or pictorial representation. ❖ *n.* (ăb′străkt′) **1.** A statement summarizing the important points of a text. **2.** Something abstract. ❖ *tr.v.* (ăb-străkt′) **-stract·ed, -stract·ing, -stracts 1.** To take away; remove. **2.** To remove without permission; filch. **3.** To consider (a quality, for example) without reference to a particular example or object. **4.** (ăb′străkt′) To summarize; epitomize. **5.** To create artistic abstractions of. [ME < Lat. *abstractus,* p. part. of *abstrahere,* to draw away : *abs-, ab-,* away; see AB–[1] + *trahere,* to draw.] —**ab·stract′er** *n.* —**ab·stract′ly** *adv.* —**ab·stract′ness** *n.*

ab·stract·ed (ăb-străk′tĭd, ăb′străk′-) *adj.* **1.** Removed or separated from something else; apart. **2.** Lost or deep in thought; preoccupied. —**ab·stract′ed·ly** *adv.* —**ab·stract′ed·ness** *n.*

abstract expressionism *n.* A movement in abstract painting that flourished in the US after World War II until the early 1960s, characterized by a spontaneous process.

ab·strac·tion (ăb-străk′shən, əb-) *n.* **1a.** The act or process of abstracting or the state of having been abstracted. **b.** An abstract concept, idea, or term. **c.** An abstract quality. **2.** Preoccupation; absent-mindedness. **3.** An abstract work of art. —**ab·strac′tion·al, ab·strac′tive** *adj.*

ab·strac·tion·ism (ăb-străk′shə-nĭz′əm) *n.* The theory and practice of abstract art. —**ab·strac′tion·ist** *n.*

abstract noun *n.* A noun that denotes an abstract or intangible concept, such as *envy* or *joy.*

abstract of title *n.* A brief history of the transfers of a piece of land, including all claims that could be made against it.

ab·struse (ăb-strōōs′, əb-) *adj.* Difficult to understand; recondite. [Lat. *abstrūsus,* p. part. of *abstrūdere,* to hide : *abs-, ab-,*

away; see AB–[1] + *trūdere,* to push.] —**ab·struse′ly** *adv.* —**ab·struse′ness** *n.*

ab·surd (əb-sûrd′, -zûrd′) *adj.* **1.** Ridiculously incongruous or unreasonable. **2.** Of, relating to, or manifesting the view that there is no order or value in the universe. **3.** Of or relating to absurdism or the absurd. ❖ *n.* The condition in which humans exist in a meaningless, irrational universe. Used chiefly with *the.* [Lat. *absurdus,* out of tune, absurd.] —**ab·sur′di·ty** (-sûr′dĭ-tē, -zûr′-), **ab·surd′ness** *n.* —**ab·surd′ly** *adv.*

ab·surd·ism (əb-sûr′dĭz-əm, -zûr′-) *n.* **1.** A philosophy holding that humans exist in a meaningless, irrational universe. **2.** An act or instance of the ridiculous. —**ab·surd′ist** *adj. & n.*

A·bu-Bakr (ä′bōō-bä′kər) also **A·bu Bekr** (ä′bōō běk′ər) 573–634. First caliph of the Muslim empire (632–634).

A·bu Dha·bi (ä′bōō dä′bē) A sheikdom and city of E Arabia on the Persian Gulf. The city is the cap. of the United Arab Emirates. Pop. 242,975.

a·build·ing (ə-bĭl′dĭng) *adj.* In the process of being built or of building.

A·bu·ja (ä-bōō′jä) The cap. of Nigeria, in the central part, NE of Lagos.

A·bu·kir or **A·bu Qir** (ä′bōō-kîr′, äb′ōō-) A village of N Egypt in the Nile R. delta on the **Bay of Abukir;** site of Adm. Horatio Nelson's victory over a French fleet (1798).

a·bu·li·a (ə-bōō′lē-ə, -byōō′-) *n.* Loss or impairment of the ability to make decisions or act independently. [NLat. < Gk. *abouliā,* indecision : *a-,* without; see A–[1] + *boulē,* will; see **gʷelə-** in App.] —**a·bu′lic** (-lĭk) *adj.*

a·bun·dance (ə-bŭn′dəns) *n.* **1.** A great or plentiful amount. **2.** Fullness to overflowing. **3.** Affluence; wealth. **4.** The actual or relative amount of an element or isotope that exists in a given sample of material, such as a meteorite.

a·bun·dant (ə-bŭn′dənt) *adj.* **1.** Occurring in or marked by abundance; plentiful. **2.** Abounding with; rich: *land abundant in wildlife.* [ME *aboundant* < OFr. *abundant* < Lat. *abundāns, abundant-,* pr. part. of *abundāre,* to overflow. See ABOUND.] —**a·bun′dant·ly** *adv.*

a·buse (ə-byōōz′) *tr.v.* **a·bused, a·bus·ing, a·bus·es 1.** To use wrongly or improperly; misuse. **2.** To hurt or injure by maltreatment; ill-use. **3.** To force sexual activity on; rape or molest. **4.** To assail with contemptuous, coarse, or insulting words; revile. ❖ *n.* (ə-byōōs′) **1.** Improper use or handling; misuse: *drug abuse.* **2.** Physical maltreatment. **3.** Sexual abuse. **4.** An unjust or wrongful practice. **5.** Insulting or coarse language: *verbal abuse.* [ME *abusen* < OFr. *abuser* < *abus,* improper use < Lat. *abūsus,* p. part. of *abūtī,* to misuse : *ab-,* away; see AB–[1] + *ūtī,* to use.] —**a·bus′er** *n.*

A·bu Sim·bel (ä′bōō sĭm′bəl, -běl) A village of S Egypt on the Nile R.; site of massive rock temples that were raised (1964–66) to avoid flooding from the Aswan High Dam.

a·bu·sive (ə-byōō′sĭv, -zĭv) *adj.* **1.** Characterized by improper or wrongful use: *abusive utilization of public funds.* **2.** Using or containing insulting or coarse language. **3.** Causing physical injury to another. **4.** Relating to or practicing sexual abuse. —**a·bu′sive·ly** *adv.* —**a·bu′sive·ness** *n.*

a·but (ə-bŭt′) *v.* **a·but·ted, a·but·ting, a·buts** —*intr.* To touch or end at one end or side; lie adjacent. —*tr.* **1.** To border upon or end at; be next to. **2.** To support as an abutment. [ME *abutten* < OFr. *abouter,* to border on (*a-,* to < Lat. *ad-;* see AD– + *bouter,* to strike; see **bhau-** in App.) and < OFr. *abuter,* to end at (< *but,* end; see BUTT[4].] —**a·but′ter** *n.*

a·but·ment (ə-bŭt′mənt) *n.* **1.** The act or process of abutting. **2a.** Something that abuts. **b.** The point of contact of two abutting objects or parts. **3a.** The part of a structure that bears the weight or pressure of an arch. **b.** A structure that supports the end of a bridge. **c.** A structure that anchors the cables of a suspension bridge.

a·buzz (ə-bŭz′) *adj.* Filled with or as if with a buzzing sound.

ab·volt (ăb′vōlt′) *n.* The centimeter-gram-second electromagnetic unit of potential difference, equal to one hundred-millionth of a volt.

A·by·dos (ə-bī′dŏs) **1.** An ancient town of Asia Minor on the Asiatic coast of the Hellespont in modern-day Turkey; scene of the legendary tale of Hero and Leander. **2.** An ancient city of S Egypt on the Nile R. NW of Thebes; burial site for kings of the earliest dynasties.

a·bysm (ə-bĭz′əm) *n.* An abyss. [ME *abime* < OFr. *abisme* < VLat. **abissimus,* alteration of LLat. *abyssus.* See ABYSS.]

a·bys·mal (ə-bĭz′məl) *adj.* **1.** Resembling an abyss in depth; unfathomable. **2.** Very profound; limitless: *abysmal misery.* **3.** Very bad. —**a·bys′mal·ly** *adv.*

a·byss (ə-bĭs′) *n.* **1.** An immeasurably deep chasm, depth, or void. **2a.** The primeval chaos out of which it was believed that the earth and sky were formed. **b.** The abode of evil spirits; hell. [ME *abissus* < LLat. *abyssus* < Gk. *abussos,* bottomless : *a-,* without; see A–[1] + *bussos,* bottom.]

a·bys·sal (ə-bĭs′əl) *adj.* **1.** Abysmal; unfathomable. **2.** Of or relating to the great depths of the oceans. **3.** Of or relating to the region of the ocean bottom between the bathyal and hadal zones, from depths of approx. 3,000 to 6,000 meters (10,000 to 20,000 feet).

Abu Simbel
top: Great Temple of
Rameses II
bottom: Temple of Queen
Nefertari

Ab·ys·sin·i·a (ăb′ĭ-sĭn′ē-ə) See **Ethiopia.** —**Ab′ys·sin′i·an** *adj. & n.*

Abyssinian cat *n.* A slender shorthaired cat of a breed developed from Near Eastern stocks, having a reddish-brown coat tipped with small black markings.

Ab·zug (ăb′zŏŏg′, -zŭg′), **Bella** 1920–98. Amer. politician noted for her support of feminism and the peace movement.

Ac[1] The symbol for the element **actinium.**

Ac[2] *abbr. Bible* Acts of the Apostles

AC *abbr.* **1.** alternating current **2.** area code

ac. *abbr.* **1.** acre **2.** air-cool

a.c. *abbr. Latin* ante cibum (before meals)

a/c *abbr.* **1.** account **2.** account current **3.** or **AC** air conditioning

ac– *pref.* Variant of **AD–** 1.

-ac *suff.* Used to form adjectives from nouns: *ammoniac.* [NLat. *-acus* < Gk. *-akos.*]

a·ca·cia (ə-kā′shə) *n.* **1.** Any of various often spiny trees or shrubs of the genus *Acacia* in the pea family, having heads or spikes of small flowers. **2.** Any of several other leguminous plants. **3.** See **gum arabic.** [ME < Lat. < Gk. *akakiā.*]

ac·a·deme (ăk′ə-dēm′) *n.* **1a.** The academic environment, community, or world. **b.** Academic life. **2.** A place in which instruction is given to students. **3.** A scholar, esp. a pedant. [< Lat. *Acadēmīa,* the Academy. See ACADEMY.]

ac·a·de·mi·a (ăk′ə-dē′mē-ə) *n.* The academic community; academe. [NLat. *acadēmīa* < Lat., the Academy. See ACADEMY.]

ac·a·dem·ic (ăk′ə-dĕm′ĭk) *adj.* **1.** Of, relating to, or characteristic of a school, esp. one of higher learning. **2a.** Relating to studies that are liberal or classical. **b.** Relating to scholarly performance: *a student's academic average.* **3.** Of or belonging to a scholarly organization. **4.** Scholarly to the point of being unaware of the outside world. **5.** Based on formal education. **6.** Formalistic or conventional. **7.** Theoretical or speculative. **8.** Having no practical purpose or use. ❖ *n.* **1.** A member of an institution of higher learning. **2.** One who has an academic viewpoint or a scholarly background. —**ac′a·dem′i·cal·ly** *adv.*

academic freedom *n.* Liberty to teach, pursue, and discuss knowledge without restriction or interference.

ac·a·de·mi·cian (ăk′ə-də-mĭsh′ən, ə-kăd′ə-) *n.* **1.** An academic. **2.** A member of an art, literary, or scientific academy or society.

ac·a·dem·i·cism (ăk′ə-dĕm′ĭ-sĭz′əm) also **a·cad·e·mism** (ə-kăd′ə-mĭz′əm) *n.* Traditional formalism, esp. in art.

ac·a·dem·ics (ăk′ə-dĕm′ĭks) *n. (used with a pl. verb)* College or university courses and studies.

a·cad·e·my (ə-kăd′ə-mē) *n., pl.* **-mies** **1.** A school for special instruction. **2.** A secondary or college-preparatory school, esp. a private one. **3a.** The academic community; academe. **b.** Higher education in general. Used with *the.* **c.** A society of scholars, scientists, or artists. **4. Academy a.** Plato's school for advanced education. **b.** Platonism. **c.** The disciples of Plato. [Lat. *Acadēmīa,* the school where Plato taught < Gk. *Akadēmeia.*]

A·ca·di·a (ə-kā′dē-ə) A region and former French colony of E Canada, chiefly in Nova Scotia but also including New Brunswick, Prince Edward I., Cape Breton I., and the coastal area from the St. Lawrence R. S into ME.

A·ca·di·an (ə-kā′dē-ən) *adj.* Of or relating to Acadia or its people, language, or culture. ❖ *n.* **1a.** One of the early French settlers of Acadia. **b.** A descendant of these settlers, esp. a Cajun. **2.** A dialect of French spoken by the Acadians.

a·can·tha (ə-kăn′thə) *n., pl.* **-thae** (-thē) A sharp spiny part or structure, such as the spinous process of a vertebra. [NLat. < Gk. *akantha,* thorn.]

acantho– or **acanth–** *pref.* Thorn: *acanthocephalan.* [< Gk. *akanthos,* thorn plant. See ACANTHUS.]

a·can·tho·ceph·a·lan (ə-kăn′thə-sĕf′ə-lən) also **a·can·tho·ceph·a·lid** (-lĭd) *n.* See **spiny-headed worm.** [< NLat. *Acanthocephala,* phylum name : ACANTHO– + Gk. *kephalē,* head; see –CEPHALOUS.] —**a·can′tho·ceph′a·lan** *adj.*

a·can·thoid (ə-kăn′thoid′) *adj.* Shaped like a thorn or spine.

ac·an·thop·ter·yg·i·an (ăk′ən-thŏp′tə-rĭj′ē-ən) *n.* Any of a large group of fishes of the superorder Acanthopterygii, having bony skeletons and spiny rays in the dorsal and anal fins. [< NLat. *Acanthopterygiī,* superorder name : ACANTHO– + Gk. *pterux, pterug-,* wing, fin; see **pet-** in App.] —**ac′an·thop′ter·yg′i·an** *adj.*

a·can·thus (ə-kăn′thəs) *n., pl.* **-thus·es** or **-thi** (-thī′) **1.** Any of various perennial herbs or small shrubs of the genus *Acanthus,* native to the Mediterranean and having pinnately lobed basal leaves with spiny margins. **2.** *Architecture* A design patterned after the leaves of one of these plants, used esp. on the capitals of Corinthian columns. [NLat. *Acanthus,* genus name < Gk. *akanthos,* thorn plant < *akantha,* thorn.]

a·cap·ni·a (ā-kăp′nē-ə) *n.* A condition marked by the presence of less than the normal amount of carbon dioxide in the blood and tissues. [NLat. < Lat. *acapnus,* without smoke < Gk. *akapnos : a-,* not; see A–[1] + *kapnos,* smoke.]

a cap·pel·la (ä′ kə-pĕl′ə) *adv. Music* Without instrumental accompaniment. [Ital. : *a,* in the manner of + *cappella,* chapel, choir.]

Ac·a·pul·co (ăk′ə-pŏŏl′kō, ä′kä-pŏŏl′kô) A city of S Mexico on the Pacific Ocean. Pop. 301,902.

ac·ar·bose (ăk′är-bōs′) *n.* A drug used in the management of mild diabetes mellitus that acts to reduce blood glucose levels. [A–[1] + CARB(O)– + –OSE[2].]

ac·a·ri·a·sis (ăk′ə-rī′ə-sĭs) *n.* Infestation with or disease caused by mites. [ACAR(ID) + –IASIS.]

ac·a·rid (ăk′ə-rĭd) *n.* An arachnid of the order Acarina, which includes the mites and ticks. [< NLat. *Acaridae,* family name < *Acarus,* type genus < Gk. *akari,* a mite.] —**ac′a·rid** *adj.*

a·car·pous (ā-kär′pəs) *adj. Botany* **1.** Producing no fruit; sterile. **2.** Having no fruit.

ac·a·rus (ăk′ər-əs) *n., pl.* **-ri** (-rī′) A mite, esp. one of the genus *Acarus.* [NLat. *Acarus.* See ACARID.]

a·cat·a·lec·tic (ā-kăt′l-ĕk′tĭk) *adj.* Having a metrically complete pattern, esp. having the full number of syllables in the final foot. Used of verse. [LLat. *acatalēcticus* < Gk. *akatalēktikos : a-,* not; see A–[1] + *katalēktikos,* incomplete; see CATALECTIC.]

a·cau·date (ā-kô′dāt′) also **a·cau·dal** (ā-kôd′l) *adj.* Having no tail.

a·cau·les·cent (ā′kô-lĕs′ənt) *adj. Botany* Stemless or apparently so.

acc. *abbr.* accusative

Ac·cad (ăk′ăd′, ä′kăd′) See **Akkad.**

ac·cede (ăk-sēd′) *intr.v.* **-ced·ed, -ced·ing, -cedes** **1.** To give one's consent, often at the insistence of another; concede. See Syns at **assent. 2.** To arrive at or come into an office or dignity: *accede to the throne.* **3.** To become a party to an agreement. [ME *acceden,* to come near < Lat. *accēdere,* to go near : *ad-, ad-* + *cēdere,* to go.] —**ac·ced′ence** (-sēd′ns) *n.* —**ac·ced′er** *n.*

ac·cel·er·an·do (ä-chĕl′ə-rän′dō) *adv. & adj. Music* Gradually accelerating in time. [Ital., pr. part. of *accelerare,* to hasten < Lat. *accelerāre.* See ACCELERATE.]

ac·cel·er·ant (ăk-sĕl′ər-ənt) *n.* A substance, such as a petroleum distillate, that is used as a catalyst.

ac·cel·er·ate (ăk-sĕl′ə-rāt′) *v.* **-at·ed, -at·ing, -ates** —*tr.* **1.** To increase the speed of. **2.** To cause to occur sooner than expected. **3.** To cause to develop or progress more quickly. **4.** To reduce the time required for (an academic course, for example). **5.** *Physics* To change the velocity of. —*intr.* **1.** To move or act faster. **2.** To develop or progress faster than usual. [Lat. *accelerāre, accelerāt-* : *ad-,* intensive pref.; see AD– + *celerāre,* to quicken (< *celer,* swift).] —**ac·cel′er·a′tive** *adj.*

ac·cel·er·a·tion (ăk-sĕl′ə-rā′shən) *n.* **1a.** The act of accelerating. **b.** The process of being accelerated. **2.** *Physics* The rate of change of velocity with respect to time.

acceleration of gravity *n.* The acceleration of freely falling bodies under the influence of terrestrial gravity, equal to approx. 9.81 meters (32 feet) per second per second.

ac·cel·er·a·tor (ăk-sĕl′ə-rā′tər) *n.* **1.** A device, esp. the gas pedal of a motor vehicle, for increasing speed. **2.** *Chemistry* A substance that increases the speed of a reaction. **3.** *Physics* A particle accelerator.

accelerator board *n.* A printed circuit board that enhances a computer's performance by substituting a faster microprocessor without replacing the entire motherboard.

accelerator mass spectrometry *n.* Mass spectroscopy in which a particle accelerator is used to disassociate molecules, ionize atoms, and accelerate the ions.

ac·cel·er·o·graph (ăk-sĕl′ər-ə-grăf′) *n.* An accelerometer equipped to measure and record ground motion during an earthquake.

ac·cel·er·om·e·ter (ăk-sĕl′ə-rŏm′ĭ-tər) *n.* An instrument used to measure acceleration. [ACCELER(ATION) + –METER.]

ac·cent (ăk′sĕnt′) *n.* **1.** The relative prominence of a particular syllable of a word by greater intensity or by variation or modulation of pitch or tone. **2.** Vocal prominence or emphasis given to a particular syllable, word, or phrase. **3.** A characteristic pronunciation, esp.: **a.** One determined by the regional or social background of the speaker. **b.** One determined by the phonetic habits of the speaker's native language carried over to his or her use of another language. **4.** A mark or symbol used in the printing and writing of certain languages to indicate the vocal quality to be given to a particular letter: *an acute accent.* **5.** A mark or symbol used in printing and writing to indicate the stressed syllables of a spoken word. **6.** Rhythmically significant stress in a line of verse. **7.** *Music* **a.** Emphasis given to a note, as by an increase in volume or extended duration. **b.** A mark representing this. **8.** *Mathematics* **a.** A mark used as a superscript to distinguish among variables represented by the same symbol. **b.** A mark used as a superscript to indicate the first derivative of a variable. **9.** A mark or one of several marks used as a superscript to indicate a unit, such as feet (′) and inches (″) in linear measurement. **10.** A distinctive feature or quality, as in a decorative style. **11.** Particular importance or interest; emphasis. See Syns at **emphasis.** ❖ *tr.v.* (ăk′sĕnt′, ăk-sĕnt′) **-cent·ed, -cent·ing, -cents** **1.** To stress or emphasize the pronunciation of. **2.** To mark with a printed accent. **3.** To focus attention on; accentuate. [ME < OFr. < Lat. *accentus,* accentuation : *ad-, ad-* + *cantus,* song (< *canere,* to sing; see **kan-** in App.)]

ac·cen·tu·al (ăk-sĕn′chŏŏ-əl) *adj.* **1.** Of or relating to accent. **2.** Based on stress accents: *accentual rhythm.* [< Lat. *accentus,* accent. See ACCENT.] —**ac·cen′tu·al·ly** *adv.*

acanthus
atop a Corinthian column

Acapulco

acciaccatura
A. grace note
B. principal note

ac·cen·tu·ate (ăk-sĕn′chōō-āt′) *tr.v.* **-at·ed, -at·ing, -ates** **1.** To stress or emphasize; intensify. **2.** To pronounce with a stress or accent. **3.** To mark with an accent. [Med.Lat. *accentuāre, accentuāt-* < Lat. *accentus,* accent. See ACCENT.] —**ac·cen′tu·a′tion** *n.*

ac·cept (ăk-sĕpt′) *v.* **-cept·ed, -cept·ing, -cepts** —*tr.* **1.** To receive (something offered), esp. with gladness or approval: *accepted a glass of water; accepted their contract.* **2.** To admit to a group, organization, or place: *accepted me as a new member.* **3a.** To regard as proper, usual, or right: *Such customs are widely accepted.* **b.** To regard as true; believe in: *accepted the new theory.* **c.** To understand as having a specific meaning. **4.** To endure resignedly or patiently: *accept one's fate.* **5a.** To answer affirmatively: *accept an invitation.* **b.** To agree to take (a duty or responsibility). **6.** To be able to hold (something applied or inserted): *This wood will not accept oil paints.* **7.** To receive officially: *accept the report.* **8.** To consent to pay, as by a signed agreement. **9.** *Medicine* To receive (a transplanted organ or tissue) without rejection by the immune system. —*intr.* To receive something, esp. with favor. Often used with *of.* [ME *accepten* < Lat. *acceptāre,* freq. of *accipere,* to receive : *ad-, ad-* + *capere,* to take; see **kap-** in App.]

ac·cept·a·ble (ăk-sĕp′tə-bəl) *adj.* **1.** Worthy of being accepted: *an acceptable compromise.* **2.** Adequate to satisfy a need, requirement, or standard; satisfactory. —**ac·cept′a·bil′i·ty, ac·cept′a·ble·ness** *n.* —**ac·cept′a·bly** *adv.*

ac·cep·tance (ăk-sĕp′təns) *n.* **1.** The act or process of accepting. **2.** The state of being accepted or acceptable. **3.** Favorable reception; approval. **4.** Belief in something; agreement. **5a.** A formal indication by a debtor of willingness to pay a time draft or bill of exchange. **b.** A written instrument so accepted. **6.** *Law* Compliance by one party with the terms and conditions of another's offer so that a contract becomes legally binding between them.

ac·cep·tant (ăk-sĕp′tənt) *adj.* Accepting willingly.

ac·cep·ta·tion (ăk′sĕp-tā′shən) *n.* **1.** The usual or accepted meaning, as of a word or expression. See Syns at **meaning.** **2.** Favorable reception; approval.

ac·cept·ed (ăk-sĕp′tĭd) *adj.* Widely encountered, used, or recognized: *an accepted treatment for pneumonia.*

ac·cept·er (ăk-sĕp′tər) *n.* **1.** One that accepts. **2.** Variant of **acceptor** 1.

ac·cep·tor (ăk-sĕp′tər) *n.* **1.** also **ac·cept·er** One who signs a time draft or bill of exchange. **2.** *Chemistry* **a.** The reactant in an induced reaction that has an increased rate of reaction in the presence of the inductor. **b.** An atom, molecule, or ion that receives a component from a donor, esp. an atom that receives two electrons for the formation of a molecular bond.

ac·cess (ăk′sĕs) *n.* **1.** A means of approaching, entering, exiting, or making use of; a passage. **2.** The act of approaching. **3.** The right to approach, enter, exit, communicate with, or make use of. **4.** Increase by addition. **5.** An outburst or onset: *an access of rage.* ❖ *tr.v.* **-cessed, -cess·ing, -cess·es** To obtain access to, esp. by computer: *accessed her bank account online.* [ME *acces,* a coming to < OFr. < Lat. *accessus,* p. part. of *accēdere,* to arrive : *ad-, ad-* + *cēdere,* to come.]

ac·ces·si·ble (ăk-sĕs′ə-bəl) *adj.* **1.** Easily approached or entered. **2.** Easily obtained: *accessible money.* **3.** Easy to talk to or get along with. **4.** Easily swayed or influenced. —**ac·ces′si·bil′i·ty, ac·ces′si·ble·ness** *n.* —**ac·ces′si·bly** *adv.*

ac·ces·sion (ăk-sĕsh′ən) *n.* **1.** The attainment of a dignity or rank: *the queen's accession to the throne.* **2a.** Something that has been acquired or added; an acquisition. **b.** An increase by means of something added. *Law* **a.** The addition to or increase in value of property by means of improvements or natural growth. **b.** The right of a proprietor to ownership of such addition or increase. **4.** Agreement or assent. **5.** Access; admittance. **6.** A sudden outburst. ❖ *tr.v.* **-sioned, -sion·ing, -sions** To record (paintings, for example) in the order of acquisition. —**ac·ces′sion·al** *adj.*

ac·ces·sor·ize (ăk-sĕs′ə-rīz′) *v.* **ized, -iz·ing, -iz·es** —*tr.* To furnish with accessories. —*intr.* To wear or select accessories.

ac·ces·so·ry (ăk-sĕs′ə-rē) *n., pl.* **-ries** **1a.** A subordinate or supplementary item; an adjunct. **b.** Something nonessential but desirable that contributes to an effect or result. **2.** *Law* **a.** One who incites, aids, or abets a lawbreaker in the commission of a crime but is not present at the time of the crime. **b.** One who aids a criminal after the commission of a crime but was not present at the time of the crime. ❖ *adj.* **1.** Having a secondary, supplementary, or subordinate function. **2.** *Law* Serving to aid or abet a lawbreaker, either before or after the commission of the crime, without being present at the time the crime was committed. [ME *accessorie* < Med.Lat. *accessōrius* < *accessor,* helper < Lat. *accessus,* approach. See ACCESS.] —**ac′ces·so′ri·al** (ăk′sĕs-sôr′ē-əl, -sōr-) *adj.* —**ac·ces′so·ri·ly** *adv.* —**ac·ces′so·ri·ness** *n.*

accessory after the fact *n., pl.* **accessories after the fact** *Law* See **accessory** 2b.

accessory before the fact *n., pl.* **accessories before the fact** *Law* See **accessory** 2a.

accessory fruit *n.* A fruit, such as the pear or strawberry, that develops from a ripened ovary or ovaries but includes a significant portion derived from nonovarian tissue.

accessory nerve *n.* Either of the 11th pair of cranial nerves,

which convey motor impulses to the pharynx and muscles of the upper thorax, back, and shoulders.

access time *n.* *Computer Science* The average time lag between a request for information stored on a component, such as the hard drive, and its delivery.

ac·ciac·ca·tu·ra (ä-chä′kə-tŏōr′ə) *n.* *Music* An ornament note one half step or one whole step below a principal note, sounded at the same time as the principal note, adding dissonance to a harmony. [Ital. < *acciaccare,* to crush.]

ac·ci·dence (ăk′sĭ-dəns, -dĕns′) *n.* The section of morphology that deals with the inflections of words. [ME < LLat. *accidentia* < Lat. *accidēns, accident-,* accident. See ACCIDENT.]

ac·ci·dent (ăk′sĭ-dənt, -dĕnt′) *n.* **1a.** An unexpected, undesirable event, esp. one resulting in damage or harm. **b.** An unforeseen incident. **2.** Lack of intention; chance: *met by accident.* **3.** *Logic* A circumstance or attribute that is not essential to the nature of something. [ME, chance event < OFr. < Lat. *accidēns, accident-,* pr. part. of *accidere,* to happen : *ad-, ad-* + *cadere,* to fall.]

ac·ci·den·tal (ăk′sĭ-dĕn′tl) *adj.* **1.** Occurring unexpectedly, unintentionally, or by chance. **2.** *Music* Of or relating to an accidental. ❖ *n.* **1.** A property, factor, or attribute that is not essential. **2.** *Music* **a.** A sign indicating the alteration of a note by one or two semitones or the cancellation of a previous sign. **b.** A note that has been marked with such a sign. —**ac′ci·den′tal·ly, ac′ci·dent′ly** *adv.*

accident insurance *n.* Insurance against bodily injury or death because of accident.

ac·ci·dent-prone (ăk′sĭ-dənt-prōn′) *adj.* Having or susceptible to having a greater than average number of accidents or mishaps.

ac·cip·i·ter (ăk-sĭp′ĭ-tər) *n.* A hawk of the genus *Accipiter,* characterized by short wings and a long tail. [Lat., hawk. See **pet-** in App.] —**ac·cip′i·trine** (-trīn′, -trĭn) *adj.*

ac·claim (ə-klām′) *v.* **-claimed, -claim·ing, -claims** —*tr.* **1.** To praise enthusiastically and often publicly; applaud. See Syns at **praise.** **2.** To acknowledge or declare with enthusiastic approval: *He was acclaimed teacher of the year.* —*intr.* To shout approval. ❖ *n.* Enthusiastic applause; acclamation. [< Lat. *acclāmāre : ad-, ad-* + *clāmāre,* to shout; see **kelə-** in App.] —**ac·claim′er** *n.*

ac·cla·ma·tion (ăk′lə-mā′shən) *n.* **1.** A shout or salute of enthusiastic approval. **2.** An oral vote, esp. an enthusiastic vote of approval without formal ballot. [Lat. *acclāmātiō, acclāmātiōn-* < *acclāmātus,* p. part. of *acclāmāre,* to shout at. See ACCLAIM.] —**ac·clam′a·to′ry** (ə-klăm′ə-tôr′ē, -tōr′ē) *adj.*

ac·cli·mate (ə-klī′mĭt, ăk′lə-māt′) *tr. & intr.v.* **-mat·ed, -mat·ing, -mates** To accustom or become accustomed to a new environment or situation; adapt. [Fr. *acclimater : a-,* to (< Lat. *ad-;* see AD-) + *climat,* climate (< OFr.; see CLIMATE).]

ac·cli·ma·tion (ăk′lə-mā′shən) *n.* **1.** The process of acclimating or of becoming acclimated. **2.** Acclimatization.

ac·cli·ma·ti·za·tion (ə-klī′mə-tĭ-zā′shən) *n.* The physiological adaptation of an animal or plant to changes in climate or environment, such as light, temperature, or altitude.

ac·cli·ma·tize (ə-klī′mə-tīz′) *v.* **-tized, -tiz·ing, -tiz·es** —*tr.* **1.** To acclimate. **2.** To adapt (oneself), esp. to environmental or climatic changes. —*intr.* To become acclimated or adapted. —**ac·cli′ma·tiz′er** *n.*

ac·cliv·i·ty (ə-klĭv′ĭ-tē) *n., pl.* **-ties** An upward slope. [Lat. *acclīvitās < acclīvis,* uphill : *ad-, ad-* + *clīvus,* slope; see **klei-** in App.]

ac·co·lade (ăk′ə-lād′, -läd′) *n.* **1a.** An expression of approval; praise. **b.** A special acknowledgment; an award. **2.** A ceremonial embrace, as of greeting. **3.** Ceremonial bestowal of knighthood. ❖ *tr.v.* **-lad·ed, -lad·ing, -lades** To praise or honor. [Fr., an embrace, accolade < *accoler,* to embrace < OFr. *acoler* < VLat. **accolāre* : Lat. *ad-, ad-* + Lat. *collum,* neck; see **kʷel-** in App.]

ac·com·mo·date (ə-kŏm′ə-dāt′) *v.* **-dat·ed, -dat·ing, -dates** —*tr.* **1.** To do a favor or service for; oblige. **2.** To provide for; supply with. **3.** To hold comfortably without crowding: *This diner accommodates 50 patrons.* **4.** To make suitable; adapt. See Syns at **adapt.** **5.** To allow for; consider: *a proposal that accommodates taxpayers' interests.* **6.** To settle; reconcile. —*intr.* **1.** To adapt oneself; become adjusted. **2.** *Physiology* To become adjusted, as the eye to focusing on distant objects. [Lat. *accommodāre, accommodāt-,* to fit : *ad-, ad-* + *commodus,* suitable; see COMMODIOUS.] —**ac·com′mo·da′tive** *adj.* —**ac·com′mo·da′tor** *n.*

ac·com·mo·dat·ing (ə-kŏm′ə-dā′tĭng) *adj.* Helpful and obliging. —**ac·com′mo·dat′ing·ly** *adv.*

ac·com·mo·da·tion (ə-kŏm′ə-dā′shən) *n.* **1.** The act of accommodating or the state of being accommodated. **2.** Something that meets a need; a convenience. **3. accommodations a.** Room and board; lodgings. **b.** A seat, compartment, or room on a public vehicle. **4.** Reconciliation or settlement of opposing views. **5.** *Physiology* The automatic adjustment in the focal length of the lens of the eye to permit retinal focus of images of objects at varying distances. **6.** A financial favor.

ac·com·mo·da·tion·ist (ə-kŏm′ə-dā′shə-nĭst) *n.* One that compromises with or adapts to the viewpoint of the opposition. —**ac·com′mo·da′tion·ist** *adj.*

accommodation ladder *n.* A portable ladder hung from the side of a ship.

ac•com•pa•ni•ment (ə-kŭm′pə-nē-mənt, ə-kŭmp′nē-) *n.* **1.** *Music* A vocal or instrumental part that supports another, often solo, part. **2.** Something that accompanies something else; a concomitant. **3.** Something added for embellishment, completeness, or symmetry; a complement.

ac•com•pa•nist (ə-kŭm′pə-nĭst, ə-kŭmp′nĭst) *n.* A performer who plays or sings a musical accompaniment.

ac•com•pa•ny (ə-kŭm′pə-nē, ə-kŭmp′nē) *v.* **-nied, -ny•ing, -nies** —*tr.* **1.** To be or go with as a companion. **2.** To add to; supplement. **3.** To coexist or occur with. **4.** *Music* To perform an accompaniment to. —*intr. Music* To play an accompaniment. [ME *accompanien* < OFr. *acompagnier* : *a-*, to (< Lat. *ad-*; see AD–) + *compaignon*, companion; see COMPANION[1].]

SYNONYMS *accompany, conduct, escort, chaperon* These verbs mean to be with or to go with another or others. *Accompany* suggests going on an equal basis: *She went accompanied by her colleague. Conduct* implies guidance of others: *The usher conducted us to our seats. Escort* stresses protective guidance: *escorting the candidate through the crowd. Chaperon* specifies adult supervision of young persons: *teachers chaperoning students.*

ac•com•plice (ə-kŏm′plĭs) *n.* An associate in wrongdoing, esp. one who aids another in a criminal act. [Alteration of COMPLICE.]

ac•com•plish (ə-kŏm′plĭsh) *tr.v.* **-plished, -plish•ing, -plish•es 1.** To succeed in doing; bring to pass. **2.** To reach the end of; complete. [ME *accomplisshen* < OFr. *acomplir, acompliss-*, to complete : *a-*, *to* (< Lat. *ad-*; see AD–) + *complir*, to complete (< Lat. *complēre*, to fill out; see COMPLETE).] —**ac•com′plish•a•ble** *adj.* —**ac•com′plish•er** *n.*

ac•com•plished (ə-kŏm′plĭsht) *adj.* **1.** Skilled; expert: *an accomplished pianist.* **2.** Having many social graces; polished or refined. **3.** Unquestionable; indubitable.

ac•com•plish•ment (ə-kŏm′plĭsh-mənt) *n.* **1.** The act of accomplishing or the state of being accomplished; completion. **2.** Something completed successfully; an achievement. **3.** An acquired skill or expertise. **4.** Social poise and grace.

ac•cord (ə-kôrd′) *v.* **-cord•ed, -cord•ing, -cords** —*tr.* **1.** To cause to conform or agree; bring into harmony. **2.** To grant, esp. as being due or appropriate. **3.** To bestow upon: *I accord you my blessing.* —*intr.* To be in agreement, unity, or harmony. ❖ *n.* **1.** Agreement; harmony. **2.** A settlement or compromise of conflicting opinions. **3.** A settlement of points at issue between nations. **4.** Spontaneous or voluntary desire to take a certain action: *on their own accord.* [ME *accorden* < OFr. *acorder* < Med.Lat. *accordāre*, to bring into agreement : Lat. *ad-*, ad- + Lat. *cor, cord-*, heart; see **kerd-** in App.]

ac•cor•dance (ə-kôr′dns) *n.* **1.** Agreement; conformity: *in accordance with your instructions.* **2.** The act of granting.

ac•cor•dant (ə-kôr′dnt) *adj.* Being in agreement or harmony; consonant. —**ac•cor′dant•ly** *adv.*

ac•cord•ing as (ə-kôr′dĭng) *conj.* **1.** Corresponding to the way in which; precisely as. **2.** Depending on whether; if.

ac•cord•ing•ly (ə-kôr′dĭng-lē) *adv.* **1.** In accordance; correspondingly. **2.** So; consequently.

according to *prep.* **1.** As stated or indicated by; on the authority of: *according to historians.* **2.** In keeping with: *according to instructions.* **3.** As determined by: *a list arranged according to the alphabet.*

ac•cor•di•on (ə-kôr′dē-ən) *n.* A portable instrument with a small keyboard and free metal reeds that sound when air is forced past them by pleated bellows operated by the player. ❖ *adj.* Having folds or bends like the bellows of an accordion: *accordion pleats.* [Ger. *Akkordion* < *Akkord*, chord < Fr. *accord*, harmony < OFr. *acorder*, to accord < Med.Lat. *accordāre*, to bring into agreement. See ACCORD.] —**ac•cor′di•on•ist** *n.*

ac•cost (ə-kôst′, ə-kŏst′) *tr.v.* **-cost•ed, -cost•ing, -costs 1.** To approach and speak to boldly or aggressively, as with a demand. **2.** To solicit for sex. [Fr. *accoster* < OFr. < Med.Lat. *accostāre*, to adjoin : Lat. *ad-*, ad- + Lat. *costa*, side.]

ac•couche•ment (ä′ko͞osh-mäɴ′) *n.* A confinement during childbirth; a lying-in. [Fr. < *accoucher*, to assist in childbirth < OFr. : *a-*, to (< Lat. *ad-*; see AD–) + *coucher*, to lay down; see COUCH.]

ac•count (ə-kount′) *n.* **1.** A narrative or record of events. **2a.** A reason given for a particular action or event. **b.** A report relating to one's conduct. **c.** A basis or ground: *no reason to worry on that account.* **3a.** A formal banking, brokerage, or business relationship established to provide for financial transactions. **b.** A precise list or enumeration of financial transactions. **c.** Money deposited for checking, savings, or brokerage use. **d.** A customer having a business or credit relationship with a firm. **4.** Worth, standing, or importance. **5.** Profit or advantage: *turned her writing skills to good account.* ❖ *tr.v.* **-count•ed, -count•ing, -counts** To consider as being; deem. See Usage Note at **as**[1]. —***phrasal verb:* account for 1.** To constitute the governing or primary factor for: *Bad weather accounted for the delay.* **2.** To provide an explanation or justification for: *couldn't account for my time.* —***idioms:* call to account 1.** To challenge or contest. **2.** To hold answerable for. **on account** On credit. **on account of** Because of; for the sake of: *"We got married on account of the baby"* (Anne Tyler). **on no account** Under no circumstances. **on (one's) own account 1.** For oneself. **2.** On one's own; by oneself. **take into account** To take into consideration; allow for. [ME < OFr. *acont* < *aconter*, to reckon : *a-*, to (< Lat. *ad-*; see AD–) + *cunter*, to count (< Lat. *computāre*, to sum up; see COMPUTE).]

ac•count•a•ble (ə-koun′tə-bəl) *adj.* **1.** Liable to being called to account; answerable. See Syns at **responsible. 2.** That can be explained: *an accountable phenomenon.* —**ac•count′a•bil′i•ty, ac•count′a•ble•ness** *n.* —**ac•count′a•bly** *adv.*

ac•coun•tant (ə-koun′tənt) *n.* One that keeps, audits, and inspects financial records and prepares financial and tax reports. —**ac•coun′tan•cy** (-tən-sē) *n.*

account executive *n.* A person, as in an advertising or a public relations firm, who manages clients' accounts.

ac•count•ing (ə-koun′tĭng) *n.* The bookkeeping methods involved in making a financial record of business transactions and in the preparation of statements concerning the assets, liabilities, and operating results of a business.

ac•cou•ter or **ac•cou•tre** (ə-ko͞o′tər) *tr.v.* **-tered, -ter•ing, -ters** or **-tred, -tre•ing, -tres** To outfit and equip, as for military duty. [Fr. *accoutrer* < OFr. *acoustrer*, arrange, equip : *a-*, to (< Lat. *ad-*; see AD–) + *coustrer*, sew; see COUTURE.]

ac•cou•ter•ment or **ac•cou•tre•ment** (ə-ko͞o′tər-mənt, -trə-) *n.* **1a.** An ancillary item of equipment or dress. Often used in the plural. **b.** Military equipment other than uniforms and weapons. Often used in the plural. **2. accouterments** Outward forms of recognition; trappings. **3.** *Archaic* The act of accoutering.

Ac•cra (ăk′rə, ə-krä′) The cap. of Ghana, in the SE part on the Gulf of Guinea. Pop. 859,640.

ac•cred•it (ə-krĕd′ĭt) *tr.v.* **-it•ed, -it•ing, -its 1.** To ascribe or attribute to; credit with. **2a.** To supply with credentials or authority; authorize. **b.** To appoint as an ambassador to a foreign government. **3a.** To attest to and approve as meeting a prescribed standard. See Syns at **approve. b.** To recognize (an institution of learning) as maintaining those standards requisite for its graduates to gain admission to other reputable institutions of higher learning or achieve credentials for professional practice. **4.** To believe. [Fr. *accréditer* : *a-*, to (< Lat. *ad-*; see AD–) + *crédit*, credit (< OFr.; see CREDIT).] —**ac•cred′i•ta′tion** *n.*

ac•crete (ə-krēt′) *v.* **-cret•ed, -cret•ing, -cretes** —*tr.* To make larger or greater, as by increased growth. —*intr.* **1.** To grow together; fuse. **2.** To grow or increase gradually, as by addition. [Back-formation < ACCRETION.]

ac•cre•tion (ə-krē′shən) *n.* **1a.** Growth or increase in size by gradual external addition, fusion, or inclusion. **b.** Something added externally to promote such growth or increase. **2.** *Biology* The growing together or adherence of parts that are normally separate. **3.** *Geology* **a.** The addition of land mass to a continent through plate tectonic processes. **b.** Slow addition to land by deposition of water-borne sediment. **4.** *Astronomy* An increase in the mass of a celestial object by the collection of surrounding interstellar gases and objects by gravity. [Lat. *accrētiō, accrētiōn-* < *accrētus*, p. part. of *accrēscere*, to grow. See ACCRUE.] —**ac•cre′tion•ar′y** (-shə-nĕr′ē), **ac•cre′tive** *adj.*

ac•cru•al (ə-kro͞o′əl) *n.* **1.** The act or process of accumulating; an increase. **2.** Something that accumulates or increases.

ac•crue (ə-kro͞o′) *v.* **-crued, -cru•ing, -crues** —*intr.* **1.** To come to one as a gain, addition, or increment: *interest accruing in my savings account.* **2.** To increase, accumulate, or come about as a result of growth. **3.** To come into existence as a claim that is legally enforceable. —*tr.* To accumulate over time: *I have accrued 15 days of sick leave.* [ME *acreuen*, ult. < Lat. *accrēscere*, to grow : *ad-*, ad- + *crēscere*, to arise; see **ker-**[2] in App.] —**ac•cru′a•ble** *adj.*

acct. *abbr.* **1.** account **2.** accountant

ac•cul•tur•ate (ə-kŭl′chə-rāt′) *v.* **-at•ed, -at•ing, -ates** —*tr.* To cause (a society, for example) to change by the process of acculturation. —*intr.* To change by acculturation.

ac•cul•tur•a•tion (ə-kŭl′chə-rā′shən) *n.* **1.** The modification of the culture of a group or individual as a result of contact with a different culture. **2.** The process by which the culture of a particular society is instilled in a human from infancy onward. —**ac•cul′tur•a′tion•al** *adj.* —**ac•cul′tur•a′tive** *adj.*

ac•cum•bent (ə-kŭm′bənt) *adj.* Lying down; reclining. [Lat. *accumbēns, accumbent-*, pr. part. of *accumbere*, to recline at table : *ad-*, ad- + *cumbere*, to recline.]

ac•cu•mu•late (ə-kyo͞om′yə-lāt′) *v.* **-lat•ed, -lat•ing, -lates** —*tr.* To gather or pile up; amass. See Syns at **gather.** —*intr.* To mount up; increase. [Lat. *accumulāre, accumulāt-* : *ad-*, ad- + *cumulāre*, to pile up (< *cumulus*, heap).] —**ac•cu′mu•la•ble** (-lə-bəl) *adj.*

ac•cu•mu•la•tion (ə-kyo͞om′yə-lā′shən) *n.* **1.** The act of gathering or amassing, as into a heap. **2.** The process of growing into a large amount or heap. **3.** An amount that has accumulated or been accumulated.

ac•cu•mu•la•tive (ə-kyo͞om′yə-lā′tĭv, -lə-tĭv) *adj.* **1.** Characterized by or showing the effects of accumulation; cumulative. **2.** Tending to accumulate. —**ac•cu′mu•la•tive•ly** *adv.*

ac•cu•mu•la•tor (ə-kyo͞om′yə-lā′tər) *n.* **1.** One that accumulates. **2.** A register or electric circuit in a calculator or computer, in which the results of arithmetical and logical operations are formed. **3.** *Chiefly British* An automobile storage battery.

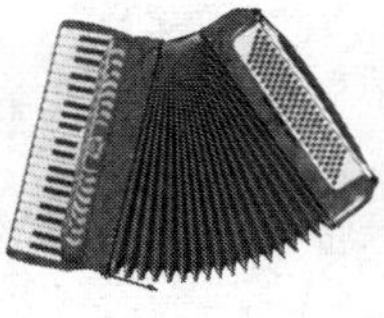

accordion

ă	pat	oi	boy
ā	pay	ou	out
âr	care	o͝o	took
ä	father	o͞o	boot
ĕ	pet	ŭ	cut
ē	be	ûr	urge
ĭ	pit	th	thin
ī	pie	*th*	this
îr	pier	hw	which
ŏ	pot	zh	vision
ō	toe	ə	about, item
ô	paw		

Stress marks:
′ (primary);
′ (secondary), as in
lexicon (lĕk′sĭ-kŏn′)

ac·cu·ra·cy (ăk′yər-ə-sē) *n.* **1.** Conformity to fact. **2.** Precision; exactness.

ac·cu·rate (ăk′yər-ĭt) *adj.* **1.** Conforming exactly to fact; errorless. **2.** Deviating only slightly or within acceptable limits from a standard. **3.** Capable of providing a correct reading or measurement. **4.** Acting or performing with care and precision; meticulous. [Lat. *accūrātus*, done with care, p. part. of *accūrāre*, to do with care : *ad-*, ad- + *cūrāre*, to care for (< *cūra*, care; see CURE).] —**ac′cu·rate·ly** *adv.* —**ac′cu·rate·ness** *n.*

ac·curs·ed (ə-kûr′sĭd, ə-kûrst′) also **ac·curst** (ə-kûrst′) *adj.* **1.** Abominable; hateful. **2.** Being under a curse; doomed. [ME *acursed*, p. part. of *acursen*, to put a curse on : *a-*, intensive pref. (< OE *ā-*) + OE *cursian*, to curse (< *curs*, curse).] —**ac·curs′ed·ly** *adv.* —**ac·curs′ed·ness** *n.*

accus. *abbr.* accusative

ac·cu·sa·tion (ăk′yōō-zā′shən) *n.* **1.** An act of accusing or the state of being accused. **2.** A charge of wrongdoing that is made against a person or other party.

ac·cu·sa·tive (ə-kyōō′zə-tĭv) *adj.* **1.** Of, relating to, or being the grammatical case that is the direct object of a verb or the object of certain prepositions. **2.** Accusatory. ❖ *n.* **1.** The accusative case. **2.** A word in this case. [ME *acusatif* < OFr. < Lat. *(cāsus) accūsātīvus*, (case) of accusation (mistranslation of Gk. *aitiātikē (ptōsis)*, causal (case), (case) indicating the thing caused by the verb < *aitiā*, cause, also accusation, charge) < *accūsātus*, p. part. of *accūsāre*; see ACCUSE.] —**ac·cu′sa·tive·ly** *adv.*

ac·cu·sa·to·ry (ə-kyōō′zə-tôr′ē, -tōr′ē) also **ac·cu·sa·to·ri·al** (-tôr′ē-əl, -tōr′-) *adj.* Containing or implying accusation: *an accusatorial glare.* —**ac·cu′sa·to′ri·ly** *adv.*

ac·cuse (ə-kyōōz′) *v.* **-cused, -cus·ing, -cus·es** —*tr.* **1.** To charge with a shortcoming or error. **2.** To charge formally with a wrongdoing. —*intr.* To make a charge of wrongdoing against another. [ME *acusen* < Lat. *accūsāre* : *ad-*, ad- + *causa*, lawsuit.] —**ac·cus′er** *n.* —**ac·cus′ing·ly** *adv.*

ac·cused (ə-kyōōzd′) *n.* The defendant or defendants in a criminal case.

ac·cus·tom (ə-kŭs′təm) *tr.v.* **-tomed, -tom·ing, -toms** To familiarize, as by constant practice, use, or habit: *I have accustomed myself to working long hours.* [ME *accustomen* < OFr. *acostumer* : *a-*, to (< Lat. *ad-*; see AD-) + *costume*, custom; see CUSTOM.]

ac·cus·tomed (ə-kŭs′təmd) *adj.* **1.** Frequently practiced, used, or experienced; customary. See Syns at **usual.** **2.** Being in the habit of: *I am accustomed to sleeping late.* **3.** Having been adapted to the existing environment and conditions.

AC/DC (ā′sē-dē′sē) *adj.* *Slang* Having a bisexual orientation. [< the likening of a bisexual person to an appliance that works on either alternating or direct current.]

ace (ās) *n.* **1a.** A single spot or pip on a playing card, die, or domino. **b.** A playing card, die, or domino having one spot or pip. **2.** In racket games: **a.** A serve that one's opponent fails to return. **b.** A point scored by such a serve. **3.** The act of hitting a golf ball in the hole with one's first shot. **4.** A military aircraft pilot who has destroyed five or more enemy aircraft. **5.** An expert in a given field. ❖ *adj.* Top-notch; first-rate. ❖ *tr.v.* **aced, ac·ing, ac·es 1.** To serve an ace against in racket games. **2.** To hit an ace on (a hole) in golf. **3.** *Slang* To get the better of (someone). **4.** *Slang* **a.** To receive a grade of A on: *aced the exam.* **b.** To perform with distinction on: *aced the interview.* —**idioms: ace in the hole** A hidden advantage or resource kept in reserve until needed. **within an ace of** On the verge of; very near to. [ME *as* < OFr. < Lat. *as*.]

–acean *suff.* **1.** Variant of –aceous. **2.** An organism belonging to a taxonomic group: *cetacean.* [< NLat. *-ācea*, neut. pl. of *-āceus*, -aceous.]

a·ce·di·a (ə-sē′dē-ə) *n.* Spiritual torpor and apathy; ennui. [LLat. < Gk. *akēdeia*, indifference : *a-*, a-; see A–[1] + *kēdos*, care.]

ACE inhibitor (ās) *n.* Any of a class of drugs used to treat hypertension and heart failure. [*a(ngiotensin) c(onverting) e(nzyme) inhibitor.*]

a·cel·lu·lar (ā-sĕl′yə-lər) *adj.* Containing no cells; not made of cells.

–aceous or **–acean** *suff.* **1a.** Of or relating to: *amylaceous.* **b.** Resembling or having the nature of: *amentaceous.* **2.** Belonging to a taxonomic group: *orchidaceous.* [Lat. *-āceus.*]

a·ceph·a·lous (ā-sĕf′ə-ləs) *adj.* **1.** *Biology* Headless or lacking a clearly defined head. **2.** Having no leader. [< Med.Lat. *acephalus* < Gk. *akephalos* : *a-*, without; see A–[1] + *kephalē*, head; see CEPHALOUS.]

a·ce·qui·a (ə-sā′kē-ə) *n.* *Southwestern US* An irrigation canal. [Sp. < Ar. *as-sāqiya* : *al-*, the + *sāqiya*, irrigation ditch, fem. active part. of *saqā*, to give to drink.]

ac·er·ate (ăs′ə-rāt′) also **ac·er·at·ed** (-rā′tĭd) *adj.* Acerose. [< Lat. *ācer*, sharp. See ak- in App.]

ac·er·bate (ăs′ər-bāt′) *tr.v.* **-bat·ed, -bat·ing, -bates** To vex or annoy. [Lat. *acerbāre*, *acerbāt-*, to make harsh < *acerbus*, harsh. See ACERBIC.]

a·cer·bic (ə-sûr′bĭk) also **a·cerb** (ə-sûrb′) *adj.* Sour or bitter, as in taste, character, or tone. [< Lat. *acerbus*. See ak- in App.] —**a·cer′bi·cal·ly** *adv.*

a·cer·bi·ty (ə-sûr′bĭ-tē) *n., pl.* **-ties** Sourness or acidness of taste, character, or tone.

acerose
needles of the white pine

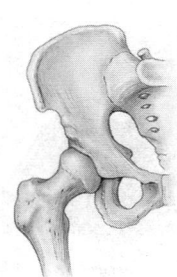

acetabulum
hip ball-and-socket joint

ac·e·ro·la (ăs′ə-rō′lə) *n.* See **Barbados cherry.** [Sp., prob. < Ar. dialectal *az-zeror, az-za′rūr* < Ar. *az-zu′rūr*, : *al-*, the + *zu′rūr*, medlar.]

ac·er·ose (ăs′ə-rōs′) *adj.* Needlelike, as the leaves of pine; acerate. [NLat. *acerōsus*, incorrect use (as if < Lat. *acus*, needle, or *ācer*, sharp) of Lat. *acerōsus*, full of chaff < Lat. *acus*, *acer-*, chaff. See ak- in App.]

acet– *pref.* Variant of aceto-.

ac·e·tab·u·lum (ăs′ĭ-tăb′yə-ləm) *n., pl.* **-la** (-lə) **1.** *Anatomy* The cup-shaped cavity at the base of the hipbone into which the head of the femur fits. **2.** *Zoology* The cavity in the body of an insect into which the leg fits. **3.** *Zoology* A cup-shaped structure, such as the sucker of a tapeworm. [Lat. *acētābulum*, vinegar cup < *acētum*, vinegar. See ACETUM.] —**ac′e·tab′u·lar** (-lər) *adj.*

ac·e·tal (ăs′ĭ-tăl′) *n.* **1.** A colorless, flammable, volatile liquid, $CH_3CH(OC_2H_5)_2$, used in cosmetics and as a solvent. **2.** Any of the class of compounds formed from aldehydes combined with alcohol. [ACET(O)– + AL(COHOL).]

ac·et·al·de·hyde (ăs′ĭ-tăl′də-hīd′) *n.* A colorless flammable liquid, C_2H_4O, used to manufacture acetic acid, perfumes, and drugs.

a·cet·a·mide (ə-sĕt′ə-mīd′, ăs′ĭt-ăm′ĭd′) *n.* The crystalline amide of acetic acid, CH_3CONH_2, used as a solvent and wetting agent and in lacquers and explosives.

a·cet·a·min·o·phen (ə-sĕt′ə-mĭn′ə-fən, ăs′ə-) *n.* A crystalline compound, $C_8H_9NO_2$, used in medicine to relieve pain and reduce fever. [ACET(O)– + AMINO– + PHEN(OL).]

ac·et·an·i·lide (ăs′ĭt-ăn′l-īd′) *n.* A white crystalline compound, $C_6H_5NH(COCH_3)$, formerly used to relieve pain and reduce fever. [ACET(O)– + ANIL(INE) + –IDE.]

ac·e·tate (ăs′ĭ-tāt′) *n.* **1.** A salt or ester of acetic acid. **2.** Cellulose acetate or any of various products, esp. fibers, derived from it.

a·ce·tic (ə-sē′tĭk) *adj.* Of, relating to, or containing acetic acid or vinegar. [< Lat. *acētum*, vinegar. See ACETUM.]

acetic acid *n.* A clear colorless organic acid, CH_3COOH, with a distinctive pungent odor, used as a solvent and in the manufacture of rubber, plastics, and acetate fibers, for example.

a·ce·ti·fy (ə-sē′tə-fī′, ə-sĕt′ə-) *tr. & intr.v.* **-fied, -fy·ing, -fies** To convert to or become converted to acetic acid or vinegar. —**a·ce′ti·fi·ca′tion** (-fĭ-kā′shən) *n.* —**a·ce′ti·fi·er** *n.*

aceto– or **acet–** *pref.* **1.** Acetic acid: *acetify.* **2.** Acetyl: *acetanilide.* [< Lat. *acētum*, vinegar. See ACETUM.]

ac·e·to·a·ce·tic acid (ăs′ĭ-tō-ə-sē′tĭk, ə-sē′tō-) *n.* A ketone body, CH_3COCH_2COOH, excreted in the urine in certain diabetic conditions.

ac·e·tone (ăs′ĭ-tōn′) *n.* A colorless, volatile, extremely flammable liquid ketone, CH_3COCH_3, widely used as an organic solvent. —**ac′e·ton′ic** (-tŏn′ĭk) *adj.*

acetone body *n.* See **ketone body.**

a·ce·tous (ə-sē′təs, ăs′ĭ-təs) *adj.* **1.** Of, relating to, or producing acetic acid or vinegar. **2.** Having an acetic taste; sour-tasting. [ME, sour < Med.Lat. *acētōsus*, vinegary < Lat. *acētum*, vinegar. See ACETUM.]

a·ce·tum (ə-sē′təm) *n.* **1.** Vinegar. **2.** An acetic acid solution of a drug. [Lat. *acētum*. See ak- in App.]

a·ce·tyl (ə-sĕt′l, ăs′ĭ-tl) *n.* The acetic acid radical CH_3CO. —**ac′e·tyl′ic** (ăs′ĭ-tĭl′ĭk) *adj.*

a·cet·y·late (ə-sĕt′l-āt′) *tr.v.* **-lat·ed, -lat·ing, -lates** To bring an acetyl group into (an organic molecule). —**a·cet′y·la′tion** *n.*

a·cet·yl·cho·line (ə-sĕt′l-kō′lēn′) *n.* A white crystalline derivative of choline, $C_7H_{17}NO_3$, that is involved in the transmission of nerve impulses in the body.

a·cet·yl·cho·li·nes·ter·ase (ə-sĕt′l-kō′lə-nĕs′tə-rās′, -rāz′) *n.* Any of various enzymes that catalyze the hydrolysis of acetylcholine.

a·ce·tyl-co·A (ə-sĕt′l-kō′ā′, ăs′ĭ-tl-) *n.* See **acetyl coenzyme A.**

acetyl coenzyme A *n.* A compound, $C_{25}H_{38}N_7O_{17}P_3S$, that functions as a coenzyme in many biological acetylation reactions and is formed as an intermediate in the oxidation of carbohydrates, fats, and proteins.

a·cet·y·lene (ə-sĕt′l-ēn′, -ən) *n.* A colorless, highly flammable or explosive gas, C_2H_2, used for metal welding and cutting and as an illuminant. —**a·cet′y·len′ic** (ə-sĕt′l-ĕn′ĭk) *adj.*

acetylene series *n.* A series of unsaturated aliphatic hydrocarbons having chemical properties resembling acetylene and the general formula C_nH_{2n-2}.

a·ce·tyl·sal·i·cyl·ic acid (ə-sĕt′l-săl′ĭ-sĭl′ĭk) *n.* See **aspirin** 1.

ace·y-deuc·y (ā′sē-dōō′sē, -dyōō′) *n.* A variation of backgammon. [Alteration of ACE + DEUCE[1].]

A·chae·a (ə-kē′ə) also **A·cha·ia** (ə-kī′ə, -kā′-) An ancient region of S Greece in the Peloponnesus on the Gulf of Corinth. The **Achaean League**, formed in the early 3rd cent. B.C., defeated Sparta but was eventually beaten by the Romans, who annexed Achaia in 146 B.C.

A·chae·an (ə-kē′ən) also **A·cha·ian** (ə-kā′ən, -kī′-) *n.* **1.** A native or inhabitant of Achaea. **2.** One of a Hellenic people believed to have inhabited the Peloponnesus and to have created the Mycenaean civilization. **3.** A Greek, esp. of the Mycenaean era. —**A·chae′an** *adj.*

A·chae·me·nid (ə-kē′mə-nĭd, -kĕm′ə-) also **A·chae·me·ni·**

an (ăk'ə-mēn'ē-ən) *adj.* Of or relating to the dynasty that ruled the Persian Empire. ❖ *n.* A member or subject of this dynasty. [After *Achaemenes*, legendary ancestor of Cyrus II, founder of the dynasty.]

ach·a·la·sia (ăk'ə-lā'zhə) *n.* The failure of a ring of muscle fibers, such as a sphincter of the esophagus, to relax. [NLat. : A⁻¹ + Gk. *khalasis*, relaxation (< *khalân*, to loosen).]

A·cha·tes (ə-kā'tēz) *n.* **1.** *Greek & Roman Mythology* The faithful companion of Aeneas in Virgil's *Aeneid*. **2.** A loyal friend.

ache (āk) *intr.v.* **ached, ach·ing, aches 1.** To suffer a dull, sustained pain. **2.** To feel sympathy or compassion. **3.** To yearn painfully. ❖ *n.* **1.** A dull, steady pain. **2.** A longing or desire; a yen. **3.** A painful sorrow. [ME *aken* < OE *acan*.]

A·che·be (ä-chā'bā), **Chinua** b. 1930. Nigerian writer whose works include the novel *Things Fall Apart* (1958).

a·chene (ā-kēn') *n.* A small, dry, indehiscent one-seeded fruit with a thin wall. [NLat. *achēnium* : Gk. *a*-, without; see A⁻¹ + Gk. *khainein*, to yawn.] —**a·che'ni·al** (-nē-əl) *adj.*

A·cher·nar (ā'kər-när') *n.* A star in the constellation Eridanus that is one of the brightest stars in the sky. [< Ar. *'aḥīr an-nahr*, the end of the river (referring to the star's position in the constellation Eridanus) : *'aḥīr*, last, end + *al*-, the + *nahr*, river.]

Ach·er·on (ăk'ə-rŏn', -rən) *n. Greek Mythology* The river of woe, one of the five rivers of Hades.

Ach·e·son (ăch'ĭ-sən), **Dean Gooderham** 1893–1971. Amer. public official who helped establish NATO.

A·cheu·li·an also **A·cheu·le·an** (ə-shōō'lē-ən) *adj.* Of or relating to a stage of tool culture of the Lower Paleolithic Period between the second and third interglacial periods, characterized by flaked bifacial hand axes. [Fr. *acheuléen*, after St. *Acheul*, a hamlet in northern France.]

a·chieve (ə-chēv') *v.* **a·chieved, a·chiev·ing, a·chieves** —*tr.* **1.** To perform or carry out with success; accomplish. **2.** To attain with effort or despite difficulty. See Syns at **reach.** —*intr.* To accomplish something successfully; perform at a standard or above standard level: *skills needed to achieve in school.* [ME *acheven* < OFr. *achever* < *a chief (venir)*, (to come) to a head. See CHIEF.] —**a·chiev'a·ble** *adj.* —**a·chiev'er** *n.*

a·chieve·ment (ə-chēv'mənt) *n.* **1.** The act of accomplishing or finishing. **2.** Something accomplished successfully, esp. by means of exertion, skill, or perseverance.

Ach·ill (ăk'ĭl) A mountainous and barren island off the NW coast of Ireland. At its W end is **Achill Head.**

ach·il·le·a (ăk'ə-lē'ə, ə-kĭl'ē-ə) *n.* See **yarrow.** [NLat. *Achillēa*, genus name < Lat., a plant that healed wounds < Gk. *akhilleios*, of Achilles, plant that healed wounds < *Akhilleus*, Achilles.]

A·chil·les (ə-kĭl'ēz) *n. Greek Mythology* The hero of Homer's *Iliad*, the son of Peleus and Thetis and slayer of Hector.

A·chil·les' heel (ə-kĭl'ēz) *n.* A seemingly small but actually crucial weakness. [< Achilles being vulnerable only in the heel.]

Achilles tendon *n.* The large tendon connecting the heel bone to the calf muscle of the leg.

a·chi·o·te (ä'chē-ō'tē, -tĕ) *n.* See **annatto.** [Am.Sp. < Nahuatl *achiotl*.]

ach·la·myd·e·ous (ăk'lə-mĭd'ē-əs, ā'klə-) *adj.* Having no perianth, as the flowers of a willow.

a·chlor·hy·dri·a (ā'klôr-hī'drē-ə, ā'klôr-) *n.* Absence of hydrochloric acid in the gastric secretions of the stomach. [A⁻¹ + CHLOR(O)- + HYDR(O)- + -IA¹.] —**a·chlor·hy'dric** (-drĭk) *adj.*

a·cho·li·a (ā-kō'lē-ə) *n.* A decrease in or an absence of bile secretion. [NLat. : A⁻¹ + Gk. *kholē*, bile; see **ghel-** in App.]

A·cho·ma·wi (ä-chō'mə-wē') *n., pl.* **Achomawi** or **-wis 1.** A member of a Native American people inhabiting northeast California. **2.** The language of the Achomawi. [Achomawi *ažumaawi*, river people < *ažuma*, it flows, river.]

a·chon·drite (ā-kŏn'drīt') *n.* A stony meteorite that contains no chondrules. —**a'chon·drit'ic** (-drĭt'ĭk) *adj.*

a·chon·dro·pla·sia (ā-kŏn'drō-plā'zhə, -zhē-ə) *n.* Improper development of cartilage at the ends of the long bones, resulting in a form of congenital dwarfism. —**a·chon'dro·plas'tic** (-plăs'tĭk) *adj.*

ach·ro·mat·ic (ăk'rə-măt'ĭk) *adj.* **1.** Of or relating to color having zero saturation or hue, such as white or black. **2.** Refracting light without spectral color separation. **3.** *Biology* Difficult to stain with standard dyes. Used of cells or tissues. **4.** *Music* Having only the diatonic tones of the scale. [< Gk. *akhrōmatos* : *a*-, without; see A⁻¹ + *khrōma, khrōmat*-, color.] —**ach'ro·mat'i·cal·ly** *adv.* —**a·chro'ma·tism** (ā-krō'mə-tĭz'əm), **a·chro'ma·tic'i·ty** (-tĭs'ĭ-tē) *n.*

achromatic lens *n.* A combination of lenses made of different glass, used to produce images free of chromatic aberrations.

a·chro·ma·tin (ā-krō'mə-tĭn) *n.* The part of a cell nucleus that remains less colored than the rest when stained or dyed. [ACHROMAT(IC) + -IN.] —**a·chro'ma·tin'ic** *adj.*

a·chro·ma·tize (ā-krō'mə-tīz') *tr.v.* **-tized, -tiz·ing, -tiz·es** To rid of color; render achromatic.

a·chro·mic (ā-krō'mĭk) *adj.* Having no color; colorless. [A⁻¹ + CHROM(O)- + -IC.]

ach·y (ā'kē) *adj.* **-i·er, -i·est** Experiencing aches. —**ach'i·ness** *n.*

a·cic·u·la (ə-sĭk'yə-lə) *n., pl.* **-lae** (-lē') A slender needlelike part

or structure, such as the crystals of certain minerals. [Lat., hairpin, dim. of *acus*, needle. See **ak-** in App.] —**a·cic'u·late** (-lĭt, -lāt'), **a·cic'u·lat'ed** (-lā'tĭd) *adj.*

a·cic·u·lar (ə-sĭk'yə-lər) *adj.* Having the shape of a needle.

ac·id (ăs'ĭd) *n.* **1.** *Chemistry* **a.** Any of a class of substances whose aqueous solutions are characterized by a sour taste, the ability to turn blue litmus red, and the ability to react with bases and certain metals to form salts. **b.** A substance that yields hydrogen ions when dissolved in water. **c.** A substance that can act as a proton donor. **d.** A substance that can accept a pair of electrons to form a covalent bond. **2.** A substance having a sour taste. **3.** The quality of being sarcastic, bitter, or scornful. **4.** *Slang* See LSD¹. ❖ *adj.* **1.** *Chemistry* **a.** Of, relating to, or containing an acid. **b.** Having a high concentration of acid. **c.** Having the characteristics of an acid. **2a.** Having a pH of less than 7. **b.** Having a relatively high concentration of hydrogen ions. **3.** *Geology* Containing a large proportion of silica. **4.** Having a sour taste. **5.** Biting, sarcastic, or scornful. [< Lat. *acidus*, sour < *acēre*, to be sour. See **ak-** in App.] —**ac'id·ly** *adv.* —**ac'id·ness** *n.*

ac·i·dan·the·ra (ăs'ĭ-dăn'thər-ə) *n.* Any of several ornamental African plants of the genus *Acidanthera*, having fibrous corms, swordlike leaves, and large fragrant flowers. [NLat. : Gk. *akis, akid*-, needle; see **ak-** in App. + NLat. *anthera*; see ANTHER.]

ac·i·de·mi·a (ăs'ĭ-dē'mē-ə) *n.* Abnormal acidity of the blood.

ac·id-fast (ăs'ĭd-făst') *adj.* Not decolorized by acid after staining, as bacteria that retain dye after an acid rinse. —**ac'id-fast'ness** *n.*

a·cid·ic (ə-sĭd'ĭk) *adj.* **1.** Acid. **2.** Tending to form an acid.

a·cid·i·fy (ə-sĭd'ə-fī') *tr. & intr.v.* **-fied, -fy·ing, -fies** To make or become acid. —**a·cid'i·fi'a·ble** *adj.* —**a·cid'i·fi·ca'tion** (-fĭ-kā'shən) *n.* —**a·cid'i·fi'er** *n.*

ac·i·dim·e·ter (ăs'ĭ-dĭm'ĭ-tər) *n.* A hydrometer used to determine the specific gravity of acid solutions. —**a·cid'i·met'ric** (ə-sĭd'ə-mĕt'rĭk) *adj.* —**ac'i·dim'e·try** *n.*

a·cid·i·ty (ə-sĭd'ĭ-tē) *n.* **1.** The state, quality, or degree of being acid. **2.** Hyperacidity.

ac·i·do·phil·ic (ăs'ĭ-dō-fĭl'ĭk) also **ac·i·doph·i·lus** (-dŏf'ə-ləs) *adj.* **1.** Growing well in an acid medium. **2.** Easily stained with acid dyes. —**a·cid'o·phil'** (ə-sĭd'ə-fĭl'), **a·cid'o·phile'** (-fĭl') *n.*

acidophilus milk *n.* Milk fermented by bacterial cultures that thrive in dilute acid. [NLat. *acidophilus*, specific epithet of several species of bacteria : ACID + *-philus*, -philous.]

ac·i·do·sis (ăs'ĭ-dō'sĭs) *n.* An abnormal increase in the acidity of the body's fluids, caused either by accumulation of acids or by depletion of bicarbonates. —**ac'i·dot'ic** (-dŏt'ĭk) *adj.*

acid precipitation *n.* Precipitation having an abnormally high acidity as a result of interactions with atmospheric pollutants.

acid rain *n.* Acid precipitation falling as rain.

acid reflux *n.* See **gastroesophageal reflux.**

acid rock *n.* Rock music having a prominent repetitive beat and lyrics that suggest psychedelic experiences.

acid test *n.* A decisive or critical test, as of worth or quality. [< the testing of gold in nitric acid.]

a·cid·u·late (ə-sĭj'ə-lāt') *tr. & intr.v.* **-lat·ed, -lat·ing, -lates** To make or become slightly acid. [ACIDUL(OUS) + -ATE¹.] —**a·cid'u·la'tion** *n.*

a·cid·u·lous (ə-sĭj'ə-ləs) *adj.* Slightly sour in taste or in manner. [< Lat. *acidulus*, dim. of *acidus*, sour. See ACID.]

ac·i·du·ri·a (ăs'ĭ-dŏor'ē-ə, -dyŏor'-) *n.* A condition marked by the presence of acid in the urine.

ac·i·nar (ăs'ĭ-nər, -när') *adj.* Of or relating to an acinus.

ac·i·nus (ăs'ə-nəs) *n., pl.* **-ni** (-nī') One of the small saclike dilations composing a compound gland. [Lat., berry.] —**a·cin'ic** (ə-sĭn'ĭk), **ac'i·nous** *adj.*

ack-ack (ăk'ăk') *n. Slang* **1.** An antiaircraft gun. **2.** Antiaircraft fire. [British telephone code for AA, abbr. for ANTIAIRCRAFT.]

ac·knowl·edge (ăk-nŏl'ĭj) *tr.v.* **-edged, -edg·ing, -edg·es 1a.** To admit the existence, reality, or truth of. **b.** To recognize as being valid or having force or power. **2a.** To express recognition of. **b.** To express thanks or gratitude for. **3.** To report the receipt of: *acknowledge a letter.* **4.** *Law* To certify or notarize as legally binding. [Prob. blend of ME *knowlechen*, to acknowledge (< *knouen*, to know; see KNOW) and ME *aknouen*, to recognize (< OE *oncnāwan*, to know : *on*-, on < *on* + *cnāwan*, to know; see KNOW).] —**ac·knowl'edge·a·ble** *adj.*

ac·knowl·edged (ăk-nŏl'ĭjd) *adj.* Commonly accepted or recognized.

ac·knowl·edg·ment or **ac·knowl·edge·ment** (ăk-nŏl'ĭj-mənt) *n.* **1.** The act of admitting or owning to something. **2.** Recognition of another's existence, validity, authority, or right. **3.** A response in return for something done. **4.** An expression of thanks or a token of appreciation. **5.** A formal declaration made to authoritative witnesses to ensure legal validity.

a·clin·ic line (ā-klĭn'ĭk) *n.* See **magnetic equator.** [< Gk. *aklinēs*, not inclining to either side : *a*-, not; see A⁻¹ + *klīnein*, to lean; see **klei-** in App.]

ACLU *abbr.* American Civil Liberties Union

ACM *abbr.* asbestos-containing material

ac·me (ăk'mē) *n.* The highest point, as of achievement or development: *at the acme of her career.* [Gk. *akmē*. See **ak-** in App.]

achene
left to right: sunflower, dandelion, and swamp beggar ticks

ă pat	oi boy
ā pay	ou out
âr care	ŏŏ took
ä father	ōō boot
ĕ pet	ŭ cut
ē be	ûr urge
ĭ pit	th thin
ī pie	th this
îr pier	hw which
ŏ pot	zh vision
ō toe	ə about,
ô paw	item

Stress marks:
' (primary);
' (secondary), as in
lexicon (lĕk'sĭ-kŏn')

ac·ne (ăk′nē) *n.* An inflammatory disease of the sebaceous glands and hair follicles of the skin that is marked by pimples or pustules, esp. on the face. [NLat., prob. < misreading of Gk. *akmē*, point, facial eruption. See ACME.] —**ac′ned** *adj.*

acne rosacea *n.* See rosacea.

a·coe·lo·mate (ə-sē′lə-māt′) *n.* An animal that lacks a coelom, exhibits bilateral symmetry, and possesses a digestive cavity. [NLat. *Acoelomata*, group name : A-¹ + Gk. *koilōma, koilōmat-*, cavity; see COELOM.] —**a·coe′lo·mate** (-lə-mĭt) *adj.*

a·coe·lous (ā-sē′ləs) *adj.* Lacking a true body cavity or digestive tract. [A-¹ + COEL(OM) +-OUS.]

ac·o·lyte (ăk′ə-līt′) *n.* **1.** One who assists the celebrant in the performance of liturgical rites. **2.** A devoted follower or attendant. [ME *acolit* < OFr. < Med.Lat. *acolytus* < Gk. *akolouthos*, attendant. See ANACOLUTHON.]

A·co·ma¹ (ăk′ə-mə, -mô′, ä′kə-) *n.*, *pl.* **Acoma** or **-mas 1.** A member of a Pueblo people, the founders of Acoma. **2.** Their Keresan language. [Acoma, people of the white rock.]

A·co·ma² (ăk′ə-mə, -mô′, ä′kə-) A pueblo of W-central NM W of Albuquerque; founded c. 1100–1250 and regarded as the oldest continuously inhabited US community. Pop. 2,802.

A·con·ca·gua (ăk′ən-kä′gwə, ä′kən-) A mountain, 7,025.4 m (23,034 ft), in the Andes of W Argentina.

ac·o·nite (ăk′ə-nīt′) *n.* **1.** Any of various, usu. poisonous perennial herbs of the genus *Aconitum.* **2.** The dried leaves and roots of these plants, which yield a poisonous alkaloid that is used in herbal preparations. [Fr. *aconit* < Lat. *aconītum* < Gk. *akonīton*, perh. < neut. of *akonītos*, without dust or struggle : *a-*, without; see A-¹ + *konis*, dust.]

a·corn (ā′kôrn′, ā′kərn) *n.* The fruit of an oak, consisting of a single-seeded, thick-walled nut set in a woody, cuplike base. [ME *akorn* < OE *æcern*.]

acorn squash *n.* A type of winter squash shaped somewhat like an acorn and having yellow to orange flesh.

acorn worm *n.* Any of a class (Enteropneusta) of hemichordate, wormlike animals that are equipped with an acornlike proboscis used for digging and collecting food.

a·cous·tic (ə-kōō′stĭk) *adj.* also **a·cous·ti·cal** (-stĭ-kəl) **1.** Of or relating to sound, the sense of hearing, or the science of sound. **2a.** Designed to carry sound or to aid in hearing. **b.** Designed to absorb or control sound: *acoustic tile.* **3.** *Music* Of or being an instrument that does not produce or enhance sound electronically: *an acoustic guitar.* ❖ *n. Music* An acoustic instrument. [Gk. *akoustikos*, pertaining to hearing < *akouein*, to hear. See kous- in App.] —**a·cous′ti·cal·ly** *adv.*

ac·ous·ti·cian (ăk′ōō-stĭsh′ən) *n.* A specialist in acoustics.

acoustic nerve *n.* See auditory nerve.

a·cous·tics (ə-kōō′stĭks) *n.* **1.** (*used with a sing. verb*) The scientific study of sound. **2.** (*used with a pl. verb*) The total effect of sound, esp. as produced in an enclosed space.

acoustic spectrography *n.* A technique for studying sound by separating it into its component frequencies.

ACP *abbr.* American College of Physicians

acpt. *abbr.* acceptance

ac·quaint (ə-kwānt′) *tr.v.* **-quaint·ed, -quaint·ing, -quaints 1a.** To cause to come to know: *Let me acquaint you with my family.* **b.** To make familiar: *acquainted myself with the controls.* **2.** To inform: *Acquaint us with your plans.* [ME *aqueinten* < OFr. *acointier* < Med.Lat. *accognitāre* < Lat. *accognitus*, p. part. of *accognōscere*, to know perfectly : *ad-*, intensive pref.; see AD- + *cognōscere*, to know; see COGNITION.]

ac·quain·tance (ə-kwān′təns) *n.* **1a.** Knowledge of a person that is less intimate than friendship. **b.** A relationship based on such knowledge: *struck up an acquaintance.* **2.** A person whom one knows. **3.** Knowledge or information. —**ac·quain′tance·ship′** *n.*

acquaintance rape *n.* Rape perpetrated by someone known to the victim.

ac·quaint·ed (ə-kwān′tĭd) *adj.* **1.** Known by or familiar with another. **2.** Informed or familiar: *acquainted with the facts.*

ac·qui·esce (ăk′wē-ĕs′) *intr.v.* **-esced, -esc·ing, -esc·es** To consent or comply passively or without protest. See Syns at **assent.** [Lat. *acquiēscere* : *ad-*, ad- + *quiēscere*, to rest.]

USAGE NOTE When *acquiesce* takes a preposition, it is usually used with *in* (*acquiesced in the ruling*) but sometimes with *to* (*acquiesced to her parents' wishes*). *Acquiesced with* is obsolete.

ac·qui·es·cence (ăk′wē-ĕs′əns) *n.* **1.** Passive assent or agreement without protest. **2.** The state of being acquiescent.

ac·qui·es·cent (ăk′wē-ĕs′ənt) *adj.* Disposed or willing to acquiesce. —**ac′qui·es′cent·ly** *adv.*

ac·quire (ə-kwīr′) *tr.v.* **-quired, -quir·ing, -quires 1.** To gain possession of: *acquire 100 shares of stock.* **2.** To get by one's own efforts: *acquire knowledge.* **3.** To gain through experience; come by: *acquired a dislike of television.* **4.** To locate (a moving object) with a tracking system, esp. radar. [ME *acquere* < OFr. *aquerre* < Lat. *acquīrere*, to add to : *ad-*, ad- + *quaerere*, to seek, get.] —**ac·quir′a·ble** *adj.* —**ac·quir′er** *n.*

ac·quired (ə-kwīrd′) *adj.* **1.** Of or relating to a disease, condition, or characteristic that is not congenital but develops after birth. **2.** Resulting from exposure to something, such as an anti-

gen or antibiotic: *an acquired antibody.*

acquired character *n.* A nonhereditary change in a plant or animal in response to the environment.

acquired immune deficiency syndrome *n.* AIDS.

acquired immunity *n.* Immunity obtained either from the development of antibodies in response to exposure to an antigen, as from vaccination, or from the transmission of antibodies, as from mother to fetus.

acquired taste *n.* One that is unpleasant on immediate experience or is likeable only after being experienced repeatedly.

ac·quire·ment (ə-kwīr′mənt) *n.* **1.** The act of acquiring. **2.** An attainment, such as a skill.

ac·qui·si·tion (ăk′wĭ-zĭsh′ən) *n.* **1.** The act of acquiring. **2.** Something acquired. [ME *adquisicioun*, attainment < Lat. *acquisitiō, acquisitiōn-* < *acquisitus*, p. part. of *acquīrere*, to acquire. See ACQUIRE.]

ac·quis·i·tive (ə-kwĭz′ĭ-tĭv) *adj.* **1.** Characterized by a strong desire to gain and possess. **2.** Tending to acquire and retain information: *an acquisitive mind.* —**ac·quis′i·tive·ly** *adv.* —**ac·quis′i·tive·ness** *n.* —**ac·quis′i·tor** (-tər) *n.*

ac·quit (ə-kwĭt′) *tr.v.* **-quit·ted, -quit·ting, -quits 1.** *Law* To clear from a charge or accusation. **2.** To release or discharge from a duty. **3.** To conduct (oneself) in a specified manner: *acquitted herself well at the interview.* **4.** *Obsolete* To repay. [ME *aquiten* < OFr. *aquiter* : *a-*, to (< Lat. *ad-*; see AD–) + *quite*, free, clear (< Med.Lat. *quittus*, var. of Lat. *quiētus*, p. part. of *quiēscere*, to rest).] —**ac·quit′ter** *n.*

ac·quit·tal (ə-kwĭt′l) *n.* **1.** Judgment by a court that a defendant is not guilty of a crime. **2.** The state of being found not guilty.

ac·quit·tance (ə-kwĭt′ns) *n.* A written release from an obligation, specifically a receipt indicating payment in full.

a·cre (ā′kər) *n.* **1.** A unit of area in the US Customary System, equal to 160 square rods, 4,840 square yards, or 43,560 square feet. **2. acres** Property in the form of land; estate. **3.** A large quantity. Often used in the plural. **4.** *Archaic* A field or plot of arable land. [ME *aker*, field, acre < OE *æcer*. See **agro-** in App.]

a·cre·age (ā′kər-ĭj, ā′krĭj) *n.* Area of land measured in acres.

a·cre-foot (ā′kər-fŏŏt′) *n.* The volume of water, 43,560 cubic feet, that will cover an area of one acre to a depth of one foot.

a·cre-inch (ā′kər-ĭnch′) *n.* One twelfth of an acre-foot, equal to 3,630 cubic feet.

ac·rid (ăk′rĭd) *adj.* **1.** Unpleasantly sharp or bitter to the taste or smell. **2.** Caustic in language or tone. [< Lat. *ācer*, sharp (prob. modeled on ACID).] —**a·crid′i·ty** (ə-krĭd′ĭ-tē), **ac′rid·ness** *n.* —**ac′rid·ly** *adv.*

ac·ri·dine (ăk′rĭ-dēn′) *n.* A coal tar derivative, $C_{13}H_9N$, that is used in the manufacture of dyes and synthetics.

ac·ri·fla·vine (ăk′rə-flā′vēn′, -vĭn) *n.* A brown or orange powder, $C_{14}H_{14}N_3Cl$, used as a topical antiseptic. [Blend of ACRIDINE and FLAVIN.]

ac·ri·mo·ni·ous (ăk′rə-mō′nē-əs) *adj.* Bitter and sharp in language or tone; rancorous: *an acrimonious debate.* —**ac′ri·mo′ni·ous·ly** *adv.* —**ac′ri·mo′ni·ous·ness** *n.*

ac·ri·mo·ny (ăk′rə-mō′nē) *n.* Bitter, sharp animosity, esp. in speech or behavior. [Lat. *ācrimōnia*, sharpness < *ācer*, sharp. See **ak-** in App.]

A·cris·i·us (ə-krĭz′ē-əs) *n. Greek Mythology* A king of Argos and father of Danaë who was killed by his grandson Perseus.

acro- or **acr-** *pref.* **1a.** Top; summit: *acropetal.* **b.** Height: *acrophobia.* **2a.** Tip; beginning: *acronym.* **b.** Extremity of the body: *acromegaly.* [< Gk. *akros*, extreme. See **ak-** in App.]

ac·ro·bat (ăk′rə-băt′) *n.* One who is skilled in feats of balance and agility in gymnastics. [Fr. *acrobate* < Gk. *akrobatēs* : *akros*, high; see ACRO- + *bainein, bat-*, to walk; see gʷā- in App.] —**ac′ro·bat′ic** *adj.* —**ac′ro·bat′i·cal·ly** *adv.*

ac·ro·bat·ics (ăk′rə-băt′ĭks) *n.* **1a.** (*used with a pl. verb*) The gymnastic moves of an acrobat. **b.** (*used with a sing. or pl. verb*) The art, skill, or performance of an acrobat. **2.** (*used with a pl. verb*) A display of great skill and agility: *vocal acrobatics.*

ac·ro·cen·tric (ăk′rō-sĕn′trĭk) *adj.* Having the centromere near one end of the chromosome so that one chromosomal arm is long and the other is short. —**ac′ro·cen′tric** *n.*

ac·ro·ceph·a·ly (ăk′rə-sĕf′ə-lē) *n.* See oxycephaly. —**ac′ro·ce·phal′ic** (-sə-făl′ĭk) *adj.*

a·cro·le·in (ə-krō′lē-ĭn) *n.* A colorless, flammable, poisonous liquid aldehyde, CH_2CHCHO, having an acrid odor and vapors irritating to the eyes. [ACR(ID) + OLEIN.]

ac·ro·meg·a·ly (ăk′rō-mĕg′ə-lē) *n.* A disease marked by enlargement of the bones of the extremities and face, caused by overactivity of the pituitary gland. [Fr. *acromégalie* < Gk. *akron*, top, extremity (< neut. of *akros*, extreme; see ACRO-) + Gk. *megas, megal-*, big; see **meg-** in App.] —**ac′ro·me·gal′ic** (-mĭ-găl′ĭk) *adj.*

a·cro·mi·on (ə-krō′mē-ən) *n.* The outer end of the scapula. [NLat. *acrōmion* < Gk. *akrōmion* : *akros*, extreme; see **ak-** in App. + *ōmos*, shoulder.] —**a·cro′mi·al** *adj.*

ac·ro·nym (ăk′rə-nĭm′) *n.* A word formed from the initial letters or parts of a series of words, such as *PAC* for political *a*ction *c*ommittee. [ACR(O)– + –ONYM.] —**ac′ro·nym′ic, a·cron′y·mous** (ə-krŏn′ə-məs) *adj.*

a·crop·e·tal (ə-krŏp′ĭ-tl) *adj.* Developing from the base toward

acorn squash
white acorn squash

the apex of a plant. —**a•crop′e•tal•ly** *adv.*

ac•ro•pho•bi•a (ăk′rə-fō′bē-ə) *n.* An abnormal fear of high places. —**ac′ro•phobe′** *n.* —**ac′ro•pho′bic** (-fō′bĭk) *adj. & n.*

a•crop•o•lis (ə-krŏp′ə-lĭs) *n.* **1.** The fortified height or citadel of an ancient Greek city. **2.** A raised area holding a building or buildings, esp. in a pre-Columbian city. [Gk. *akropolis* : *akron*, top; see ACROMEGALY + *polis*, city.]

ac•ro•some (ăk′rə-sōm′) *n.* A caplike structure at the end of a spermatozoon that produces enzymes aiding in egg penetration. [ACRO– + –SOME³.] —**ac′ro•so′mal** (-sō′məl) *adj.*

a•cross (ə-krôs′, ə-krŏs′) *prep.* **1.** On, at, or from the other side of: *across the street.* **2.** So as to cross; through: *drew lines across the paper.* **3.** From one side of to the other: *a bridge across a river.* **4.** Into contact with: *came across my old friend.* ❖ *adv.* **1.** From one side to the other. **2.** On or to the opposite side. **3.** Crosswise; crossed. **4.** So as to be comprehensible or successful: *put our idea across.* [ME *acrois* < AN *an croiz* : *an*, in (< Lat. *in*; see IN–²) + *croiz*, cross (< Lat. *crux*; see CROSS).]

a•cross-the-board (ə-krôs′thə-bôrd′, -bōrd′, ə-krŏs′-) *adj.* **1.** Including or applying to all categories or members. **2.** Of or being a racing wager whereby equal amounts are bet on the same contestant to win, place, and show.

a•cros•tic (ə-krô′stĭk, ə-krŏs′tĭk) *n.* **1.** A poem or series of lines in which certain letters, usu. the first, form a name or motto. **2.** See **word square.** [Fr. *acrostiche* < OFr. < Gk. *akrostikhis* : *akron*, head, end; see ACROMEGALY + *stikhos*, line; see **steigh-** in App.] —**a•cros′tic** *adj.* —**a•cros′ti•cal•ly** *adv.*

a•cryl•a•mide (ə-krĭl′ə-mīd′) *n.* A readily polymerized amide, C_3H_5NO, derived from acrylic acid and used in synthetic fibers and sewage treatment. [ACRYL(IC ACID) + AMIDE.]

ac•ry•late resin (ăk′rə-lāt′) *n.* Any of a class of acrylic resins used esp. in emulsion paints, adhesives, and plastics.

a•cryl•ic (ə-krĭl′ĭk) *n.* **1.** An acrylic resin. **2.** A paint containing acrylic resin. **3.** A painting done in acrylic resin. **4.** An acrylic fiber. [ACR(OLEIN) + –YL + –IC.] —**a•cryl′ic** *adj.*

acrylic acid *n.* An easily polymerized, colorless corrosive liquid, $H_2C{:}CHCOOH$, used as a monomer for acrylate resins.

acrylic fiber *n.* Any of numerous synthetic fibers polymerized from acrylonitrile.

acrylic resin *n.* Any of numerous thermoplastic polymers of acrylic acid, methacrylic acid, esters of these acids, or acrylonitrile, used esp. to produce paints and plastics.

ac•ry•lo•ni•trile (ăk′rə-lō-nī′trəl, -trēl, -trīl) *n.* A colorless liquid organic compound, $H_2C{:}CHCN$, used in the manufacture of acrylic rubber and fibers. [ACRYL(IC RESIN) + NITRILE.]

ACS *abbr.* American College of Surgeons

act (ăkt) *n.* **1.** The process of doing or performing something: *the act of thinking.* **2.** Something done or performed; a deed: *a charitable act.* **3.** A product, such as a statute or decree, resulting from a decision by a legislative or judicial body. **4.** A written record of proceedings or transactions. **5a.** One of the major divisions of a play or opera. **b.** A performance or entertainment that usu. forms part of a longer presentation. **6.** A manifestation of insincerity; a pose. ❖ *v.* **act•ed, act•ing, acts** —*tr.* **1.** To play the part of; assume the dramatic role of: *act Lady Macbeth.* **2.** To perform (a role) on the stage. **3a.** To behave like or pose as. **b.** To behave in a manner suitable for: *Act your age.* —*intr.* **1.** To behave or comport oneself: *act like a born leader.* **2.** To perform in a dramatic role or roles. **3.** To be suitable for performance: *This scene acts well.* **4.** To behave affectedly or unnaturally; pretend. **5.** To appear or seem to be: *The dog acted ferocious.* **6.** To carry out an action: *The governor acted on the bill.* **7.** To operate or function in a specific way: *His mind acts quickly.* **8.** To serve or function as a substitute: *A coin can act as a screwdriver.* **9.** To produce an effect: *The drug acts slowly.* ***—phrasal verbs:*** **act out 1a.** To perform in or as if in a play; represent dramatically: *act out a story.* **b.** To realize in action: *act out a theory.* **2.** To express (unconscious impulses, for example) in an overt manner without conscious understanding or regard for social appropriateness. **act up 1.** To misbehave. **2.** To malfunction. **3.** *Informal* To become painful or troublesome again. ***—idioms:*** **clean up (one's) act** *Slang* To improve one's behavior or performance. **get (one's) act together** *Slang* To get organized. [ME < OFr. *acte* < Lat. *āctus*, a doing, and *āctum*, a thing done, both < p. part. of *agere*, to drive, do. See **ag-** in App.] —**ac′ta•bil′i•ty** *n.* —**act′a•ble** *adj.*

USAGE NOTE While the words *act* and *action* can both mean "a deed" as well as "the process of doing," there is a tendency for *act* to refer to a deed and for *action* to refer to the process of doing. The demands of meaning or idiom will often require one word or the other. For instance, *class act* and *class action* are not interchangeable; similarly, a person may want *a piece of the action,* but not *a piece of the act.*

ACT¹ (ā′sē-tē′) *n.* A trademark for a standardized college entrance examination.

ACT² *abbr.* Australian Capital Territory

Ac•tae•on (ăk-tē′ən) *n. Greek Mythology* A hunter who, having seen Artemis bathing, was turned into a stag and killed by his own dogs.

ACTH (ā′sē′tē-āch′) *n.* A hormone produced by the anterior lobe of the pituitary gland that stimulates the secretion of hormones by the adrenal cortex. [A(DRENO)C(ORTICO)T(ROPIC) H(ORMONE).]

ac•tin (ăk′tĭn) *n.* A protein found in muscle that together with myosin functions in muscle contraction. [Lat. *āctus*, motion; see ACT + –IN.]

ac•ti•nal (ăk′tĭ-nəl, ăk-tī′-) *adj.* Of or relating to the part of a radially symmetric animal from which the tentacles radiate or the side on which the oral area is found. —**ac′ti•nal•ly** *adv.*

act•ing (ăk′tĭng) *adj.* **1.** Temporarily assuming the duties of another. **2.** Appropriate for dramatic performance: *an acting comedy.* ❖ *n.* **1.** The occupation of an actor or actress. **2.** Performance as an actor or actress.

ac•tin•i•a (ăk-tĭn′ē-ə) also **ac•tin•i•an** (-ən) *n., pl.* **-i•ae** (-ē-ē′) also **-i•ans** A sea anemone or a related animal. [NLat. *Actīnia*, genus name < Gk. *aktīs*, *aktīn-*, ray. See ACTINO–.]

ac•tin•ic (ăk-tĭn′ĭk) *adj.* Of, relating to, resulting from, or showing actinism. —**ac•tin′i•cal•ly** *adv.*

actinic ray *n.* Photochemically active radiation, as of the sun.

ac•ti•nide (ăk′tə-nīd′) *n.* Any of a series of chemically similar, radioactive elements with atomic numbers ranging from 89 (actinium) through 103 (lawrencium). [ACTIN(IUM) + –IDE.]

ac•ti•nism (ăk′tə-nĭz′əm) *n.* The intrinsic property in radiation that produces photochemical activity.

ac•tin•i•um (ăk-tĭn′ē-əm) *n. Symbol* **Ac** A radioactive element that is found in uranium ores. Its longest-lived isotope is Ac 227, with a half-life of 21.7 years. Atomic number 89; melting point 1,050°C; boiling point (estimated) 3,200°C; specific gravity (calculated) 10.07; valence 3. See table at **element.** [< Gk. *aktīs*, *aktīn-*, ray (< its radioactivity).]

actino– or **actin–** *pref.* **1.** Radial in form: *actinoid.* **2.** Actinic radiation: *actinometer.* [< Gk. *aktīs*, *aktīn-*, ray.]

ac•ti•noid (ăk′tə-noid′) *adj.* Having a radial form, as a starfish.

ac•tin•o•lite (ăk-tĭn′ə-līt′) *n.* A greenish variety of amphibole.

ac•ti•no•mere (ăk-tĭn′ə-mîr′) *n.* One of the segments forming the body of a radially symmetric animal.

ac•ti•nom•e•ter (ăk′tə-nŏm′ĭ-tər) *n.* Any of several radiometric instruments used chiefly for meteorological measurements of terrestrial and solar radiation. —**ac′ti•no•met′ric** (-nō-mĕt′rĭk), **ac′ti•no•met′ri•cal** *adj.* —**ac′ti•nom′e•try** *n.*

ac•ti•no•mor•phic (ăk′tə-nō-môr′fĭk) also **ac•ti•no•mor•phous** (-fəs) *adj. Botany* Capable of being divided into equal halves along any diameter, as the flowers of the rose; radially symmetrical. —**ac′ti•no•mor′phy** *n.*

ac•ti•no•my•ces (ăk′tə-nō-mī′sēz′) *n., pl.* **actinomyces** Any of various filamentous, mostly anaerobic microorganisms of the genus *Actinomyces,* which includes the causative agents of actinomycosis. [NLat. *Actinomycēs*, genus name : ACTINO– + Gk. *mukēs*, fungus.]

ac•ti•no•my•cete (ăk′tə-nō-mī′sēt′, -mī-sēt′) *n.* Any of various filamentous or rod-shaped, often pathogenic microorganisms of the order Actinomycetales that are found in soil. —**ac′ti•no•my•ce′tal** (-mī-sēt′l) *adj.*

ac•ti•no•my•cin (ăk′tə-nō-mī′sĭn) *n.* Any of various red, often toxic polypeptide antibiotics obtained from soil bacteria.

ac•ti•no•my•co•sis (ăk′tə-nō-mī-kō′sĭs) *n.* An inflammatory disease of cattle, hogs, and sometimes humans, caused by microorganisms of the genus *Actinomyces* and characterized by lumpy tumors. —**ac′ti•no•my•cot′ic** (-kŏt′ĭk) *adj.*

ac•ti•non (ăk′tə-nŏn′) *n.* A radioactive, inert gaseous isotope of radon, with a half-life of 3.92 seconds. [ACTIN(IUM) + –ON².]

ac•ti•no•u•ra•ni•um (ăk′tə-nō-yo͝o-rā′nē-əm) *n.* The isotope of uranium with mass number 235, fissionable with relatively low-energy neutrons. [ACTIN(IUM) + URANIUM.]

ac•tion (ăk′shən) *n.* **1.** The state or process of acting or doing. **2.** A deed. See Usage Note at **act. 3.** Organized activity to accomplish an objective: *required drastic action.* **4.** The causation of change by the exertion of power or a natural process: *the action of a drug on the pulse.* **5.** A movement or a series of movements. **6.** Manner of movement: *a gearshift with smooth action.* **7.** Habitual, vigorous activity. **8.** Behavior or conduct. Often used in the plural. **9a.** The operating parts of a mechanism. **b.** The manner in which such parts operate. **c.** The manner in which a musical instrument can be played; playability. **10.** The series of events that form the plot of a story or play. **11.** The appearance of animation of a figure in painting or sculpture. **12.** *Law* A judicial proceeding undertaken against another. **13a.** Armed encounter; combat. **b.** A military engagement. **14.** Activity or excitement.

ac•tion•a•ble (ăk′shə-nə-bəl) *adj.* Giving cause for legal action: *an actionable statement.* —**ac′tion•a•bly** *adv.*

action painting *n.* A style of abstract painting that uses techniques such as the dribbling or splashing of paint to achieve a spontaneous effect. —**action painter** *n.*

action potential *n.* A momentary change in electrical potential on the surface of a nerve or muscle cell that takes place when it is stimulated, esp. by the transmission of a nerve impulse.

Ac•ti•um (ăk′shē-əm, -tē-) A promontory and ancient town of W Greece; site of Octavian's victory over Mark Antony and Cleopatra (31 B.C.).

ac•ti•vate (ăk′tə-vāt′) *tr.v.* **-vat•ed, -vat•ing, -vates 1.** To set in motion; make active or more active. **2.** To organize or create (a military unit, for example). **3.** To treat (sewage) with aeration and bacteria to aid decomposition. **4.** *Chemistry* To accelerate a

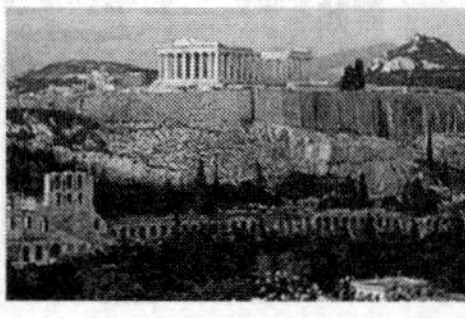

acropolis
view of the south slope and the Stoa of Eumenes at the Acropolis, Athens

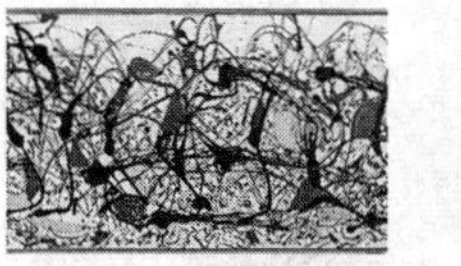

action painting
detail from *Summertime: Number 9A,* 1948, by Jackson Pollock

ă pat	oi boy
ā pay	ou out
âr care	o͝o took
ä father	o͞o boot
ĕ pet	ŭ cut
ē be	ûr urge
ĭ pit	th thin
ī pie	*th* this
îr pier	hw which
ŏ pot	zh vision
ō toe	ə about, item
ô paw	

Stress marks:
′ (primary);
′ (secondary), as in
lexicon (lĕk′sĭ-kŏn′)

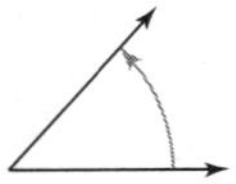

acute angle

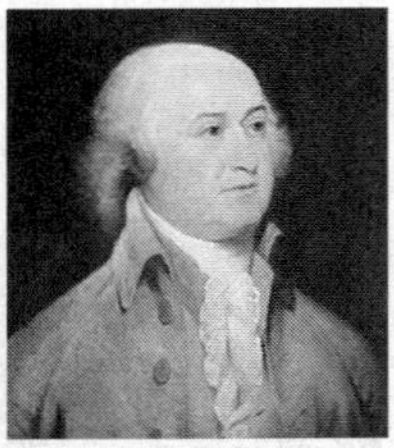

John Adams
1793 portrait by John Trumbull

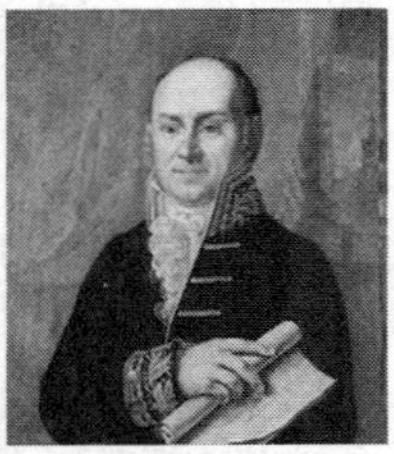

John Quincy Adams
1815 portrait by Pieter van Huffel (1769–1844)

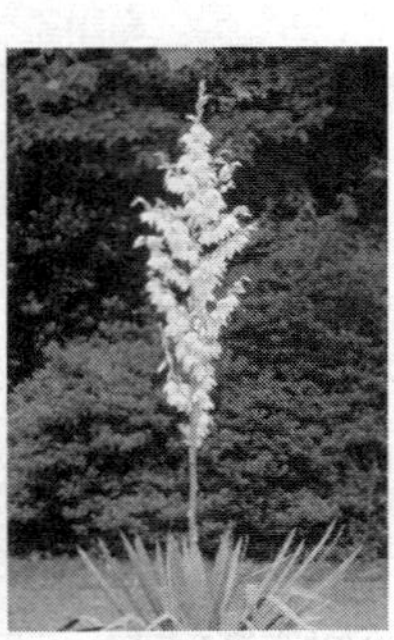

Adam's-needle
Yucca filamentosa

reaction in, as by heat. **5.** *Physics* To make (a substance) radioactive. **6.** *Biology* To convert (compounds) into biologically active derivatives. **—ac′ti•va′tion** *n.* **—ac′ti•va′tor** *n.*

ac•ti•vat•ed charcoal (ăk′tə-vā′tĭd) *n.* A highly absorbent form of carbon made by heating granulated charcoal and used primarily for purifying gases and deodorization.

activation analysis *n.* A method for analyzing a material for its component chemical elements by bombarding it with nuclear particles or gamma rays and identifying the resultant radiations.

ac•tive (ăk′tĭv) *adj.* **1.** Being in physical motion. **2.** Functioning or capable of functioning. **3a.** Marked by energetic activity; busy. **b.** Involving or requiring physical exertion and energy: *an active workout.* **4a.** Marked by or involving direct participation: *played an active role.* **b.** Currently in use or effect: *an active membership.* **c.** Openly acknowledged or expressed: *an active dislike.* **5.** Being in a state of action: *an active volcano.* **6.** Producing an intended action or effect: *active ingredients.* **7.** Producing profit, interest, or dividends. **8.** *Grammar* **a.** Indicating that the subject of the sentence is performing or causing the action of the verb. For example, in *His manner impressed them, impressed* is in the active voice. **b.** Expressing action rather than a state of being. Used of verbs such as *run* or *speak.* **9.** Being on full military duty and receiving full pay. ❖ *n.* **1.** *Grammar* **a.** The active voice. **b.** A construction or form in the active voice. **2.** A participating member of an organization: *union actives.* [ME *actif* < OFr. < Lat. *āctīvus* < *āctus*, p. part. of *agere*, to drive, do. See **ag-** in App.] **—ac′tive•ly** *adv.* **—ac′tive•ness** *n.*

active immunity *n.* Immunity resulting from the development of antibodies in response to the presence of an antigen.

ac•tive-ma•trix (ăk′tĭv-mā′trĭks) *adj.* Of or relating to a liquid-crystal display that uses individual transistors to control the charges on each cell in the liquid-crystal layer.

active site *n.* The part of an enzyme at which catalysis of the substrate occurs.

active transport *n.* The movement of a substance across a cell membrane by means of chemical energy in the direction opposite to normal diffusion.

ac•tive•wear (ăk′tĭv-wâr′) *n.* Sportswear.

ac•tiv•ism (ăk′tə-vĭz′əm) *n.* The use of direct, often confrontational action, such as a demonstration or strike, in opposition to or support of a cause. **—ac′tiv•ist** *n.* & *adj.* **—ac•tiv•ist′ic** *adj.*

ac•tiv•i•ty (ăk-tĭv′ĭ-tē) *n., pl.* **-ties 1.** The state of being active. **2.** Energetic action or movement; liveliness. **3a.** A specified pursuit or action. **b.** An educational procedure intended to stimulate learning through experience. **4.** The intensity of a radioactive source. **5.** The ability to take part in a chemical reaction. **6.** A physiological process: *respiratory activity.*

act of God *n., pl.* **acts of God** A manifestation of a usu. violent or destructive natural force, such as an earthquake, that is beyond human power to prevent or control.

ac•to•my•o•sin (ăk′tə-mī′ə-sĭn) *n.* The system of actin and myosin that, with other substances, constitutes muscle fiber and is responsible for muscular contraction. [ACT(IN) + MYOSIN.]

ac•tor (ăk′tər) *n.* **1.** A theatrical performer. **2.** One who takes part; a participant. [ME *actour*, doer, prob. < Lat. *āctor* < *āctus*, p. part. of *agere*, to drive, do. See **ag-** in App.]

ac•tress (ăk′trĭs) *n.* A woman who is an actor. See Usage Note at **–ess.**

Acts of the Apostles (ăkts) *pl.n.* (*used with a sing. verb*) See table at **Bible.**

ac•tu•al (ăk′cho͞o-əl) *adj.* **1.** Existing and not merely potential or possible. **2.** Being, existing, or acting at the present moment; current. **3.** Based on fact: *an actual account of the accident.* [ME < OFr., active < LLat. *āctuālis* < Lat. *āctus*, p. part. of *agere*, to drive, do. See **ag-** in App.]

ac•tu•al•i•ty (ăk′cho͞o-ăl′ĭ-tē) *n., pl.* **-ties 1.** The state or fact of being actual; reality. **2.** An actual condition or fact. Often used in the plural.

ac•tu•al•ize (ăk′cho͞o-ə-līz′) *v.* **-ized, -iz•ing, -iz•es** *—tr.* **1.** To realize in action or make real: *"More flexible life patterns could . . . nurture and renew our spirits through opportunities to actualize personal dreams"* (Fred Best). **2.** To describe or portray realistically. *—intr.* To become actual. **—ac′tu•al•i•za′tion** (-ə-lĭ-zā′shən) *n.*

ac•tu•al•ly (ăk′cho͞o-ə-lē) *adv.* **1.** In fact; in reality: *That tree is actually a fir, not a pine.* **2.** Used to express wonder, surprise, or incredulity: *I actually won!*

ac•tu•ar•y (ăk′cho͞o-ĕr′ē) *n., pl.* **-ies** A statistician who computes insurance risks and premiums. [Lat. *āctuārius*, secretary of accounts < *ācta*, records < neut. pl. p. part. of *agere*, to drive, do. See **ag-** in App.] **—ac′tu•ar′i•al** (-âr′ē-əl) *adj.* **—ac′tu•ar′i•al•ly** *adv.*

ac•tu•ate (ăk′cho͞o-āt′) *tr.v.* **-at•ed, -at•ing, -ates 1.** To put into motion or action; activate. **2.** To move to action: *a speech that actuated dissent.* [Med.Lat. *āctuāre, āctuāt-* < Lat. *āctus*, act. See ACT.] **—ac′tu•a′tion** *n.* **—ac′tu•a′tor** *n.*

a•cu•i•ty (ə-kyo͞o′ĭ-tē) *n.* Acuteness of vision or perception. [ME *acuite* < OFr., ult. < Lat. *acūtus*, sharp. See ACUTE.]

a•cu•le•ate (ə-kyo͞o′lē-ĭt, -āt′) *adj.* **1.** *Biology* Having a stinger, as a bee or wasp. **2.** *Botany* Having sharp prickles. [Lat. *acūleātus* < *acūleus*, sting, dim. of *acus*, needle. See ACUMEN.]

ac•u•men (ăk′yə-mən, ə-kyo͞o′-) *n.* Quickness and keenness of judgment or insight. [Lat. *acūmen* < *acuere*, to sharpen < *acus*, needle. See **ak-** in App.]

USAGE NOTE The pronunciation (ə-kyo͞o′mən), with stress on the second syllable, is an older, traditional pronunciation reflecting the word's Latin origin. In recent years it has been supplanted as the most common pronunciation of the word by a variant with stress on the first syllable, (ăk′yə-mən). In a recent survey, 68 percent of the Usage Panelists chose this as their pronunciation, while 29 percent preferred the pronunciation with stress on the second syllable. The remaining 3 percent of the Panelists said they use both pronunciations.

a•cu•mi•nate (ə-kyo͞o′mə-nĭt, -nāt′) *adj.* Tapering to a point: *acuminate leaves.* ❖ *tr.v.* (-nāt′) **-nat•ed, -nat•ing, -nates** To make sharp; taper. [Lat. *acūminātus*, p. part. of *acūmināre*, to sharpen < *acūmen*, acuteness. See ACUMEN.] **—a•cu′mi•na′tion** *n.*

ac•u•pres•sure (ăk′yə-prĕsh′ər) *n.* See **shiatsu.** [ACU(PUNCTURE) + PRESSURE.]

ac•u•punc•ture (ăk′yo͞o-pŭngk′chər) *n.* A therapeutic technique based on traditional Chinese medicine, in which needles are inserted into the body at specific points, as to relieve pain. [Lat. *acus*, needle; see **ak-** in App. + PUNCTURE.] **—ac′u•punc′tur•ist** *n.*

a•cute (ə-kyo͞ot′) *adj.* **1.** Having a sharp point or tip. **2.** Keenly perceptive or discerning. See Syns at **sharp. 3.** Reacting readily to stimuli or impressions; sensitive. **4.** Of great importance or consequence; crucial: *an acute lack of funds.* **5.** Extremely sharp or severe; intense: *acute pain.* **6.** *Medicine* **a.** Having a rapid onset and a short, severe course: *acute disease.* **b.** Afflicted with an acute disease. **7.** *Music* High in pitch; shrill. **8.** *Geometry* Having an acute angle: *an acute triangle.* [Lat. *acūtus*, p. part. of *acuere*, to sharpen < *acus*, needle. See **ak-** in App.] **—a•cute′ly** *adv.* **—a•cute′ness** *n.*

acute accent *n.* A mark (´) indicating: **a.** that a vowel is close or tense, as *é* in French *été.* **b.** that a vowel or syllable has a high or rising pitch, as in Chinese or Ancient Greek. **c.** that a vowel is long, as in Czech *dobrá.* **d.** that the syllable in which the vowel appears is stressed, as in Spanish *fácil.*

acute angle *n.* An angle of less than 90°.

acute care *n.* Short-term medical treatment, usu. in a hospital, for patients having an acute illness or injury or recovering from surgery.

ACV *abbr.* **1.** actual cash value **2.** air-cushion vehicle

a•cy•clic (ā-sī′klĭk, ā-sĭk′lĭk) *adj.* **1.** *Botany* Not cyclic: *an acyclic flower.* **2.** *Chemistry* Having an open-chain molecular structure.

a•cy•clo•vir (ā-sī′klō-vîr, -klə-) *n.* A synthetic purine nucleoside analog, $C_8H_{10}N_5O_3$, used in the treatment of certain herpesvirus infections. [A–[1] + CYCLO– + VIR(AL) or VIR(US).]

ac•yl (ăs′əl) *n.* *Chemistry* A radical having the general formula RCO-, derived from an organic acid. [AC(ID) + –YL.]

ad[1] (ăd) *n.* An advertisement.

ad[2] (ăd) *n.* An advantage in tennis.

AD *abbr.* **1.** active duty **2.** air-dried

A.D. or **a.d.** *abbr.* anno Domini

ad– *pref.* **1. ac–** or **af–** or **ag–** or **al–** or **ap–** or **as–** or **at–** Toward; to. Before *c, f, g, k, l, p, q, s,* and *t, ad-* is usu. assimilated to *ac-, af-, ag-, ac-, al-, ap-, ac-, as-,* and *at-*, respectively. **2.** Near; at: *adrenal.* [Lat. < *ad*, to.]

–ad *suff.* In the direction of; toward: *cephalad.* [< Lat. *ad*, to.]

A•da (ā′də) *n.* A programming language, based on Pascal and developed for the US Department of Defense. [After Augusta *Ada* Byron, Countess of Lovelace (1815–52).]

ADA *abbr.* **1.** American Dental Association **2.** American Diabetes Association **3.** Americans for Democratic Action **4.** Americans with Disabilities Act **5.** assistant district attorney

ad•age (ăd′ĭj) *n.* A traditional saying; a proverb. [Fr. < OFr. < Lat. *adagium.*]

USAGE NOTE It is sometimes claimed that the expression *old adage* is redundant, inasmuch as a saying must have a certain tradition behind it to count as an *adage* in the first place. But the word *adage* is first recorded by the *Oxford English Dictionary* in the phrase *old adage,* showing that this redundancy itself is very old. Such idiomatic redundancy is paralleled by similar phrases such as *young whelp.*

a•da•gio (ə-dä′jō, -jē-ō′, -zhō, -zhē-ō) *adv.* & *adj.* *Music* In a slow tempo. ❖ *n., pl.* **-gios 1.** *Music* A slow passage, movement, or work. **2.** A section of a pas de deux requiring great skill in lifting, balancing, and turning. [Ital. : *ad-*, at (< Lat.; see AD–) + *agio*, ease (< O Provençal *aize* < OFr. *aise*; see EASE).]

Ad•am[1] (ăd′əm) In the Bible, the first man and the husband of Eve.

Ad•am[2] (ăd′əm) *adj.* Of or relating to the neoclassic style of furniture and architecture originated by Robert and James Adam.

Adam, Robert 1728–92. British neoclassic architect and designer who collaborated with his brother **James** (1730–94).

Ad•am-and-Eve (ăd′əm-ənd-ēv′) *n.* See **puttyroot.**

ad•a•mant (ăd′ə-mənt, -mănt′) *adj.* Impervious to pleas or reason; stubbornly unyielding. ❖ *n.* **1.** A stone once believed to be impenetrable in its hardness. **2.** An extremely hard substance. [< ME, a hard precious stone < OFr. *adamaunt* < Lat. *adamās, adamant-* < Gk., unconquerable, hard steel, diamond.]

ad·a·man·tine (ăd′ə-măn′tēn′, -tīn′, -tĭn) *adj.* **1.** Made of or resembling adamant. **2.** Having the hardness or luster of a diamond. **3.** Unyielding; inflexible.

Ad·ams (ăd′əmz), **Abigail Smith** 1744–1818. First Lady of the US (1797–1801).

Adams, Ansel 1902–84. Amer. photographer noted for his black-and-white photographs of the wilderness.

Adams, Brooks 1848–1927. Amer. historian who theorized that civilizations rise and fall according to a pattern of economic growth and decline.

Adams, Charles Francis 1807–86. Amer. public official who served as ambassador to Great Britain during the Civil War.

Adams, Henry Brooks 1838–1918. Amer. historian noted for his autobiography, *The Education of Henry Adams* (1918).

Adams, John 1735–1826. The first Vice President (1789–97) and second President (1797–1801) of the US. He was a major figure during the drafting of the Declaration of Independence and the Constitution.

Adams, John Quincy 1767–1848. The sixth President of the US (1825–29). He later served in the House of Representatives (1831–48), where he advocated antislavery measures.

Adams, Mount A peak, 3,753.6 m (12,307 ft), in the Cascade Range of SW WA.

Adams, Samuel 1722–1803. Amer. Revolutionary leader whose agitations spurred Bostonians toward rebellion against British occupation and rule.

Ad·am's apple (ăd′əmz) *n.* The slight projection at the front of the throat formed by the largest cartilage of the larynx. [Ult. transl. of Fr. *pomme d'Adam,* pomegranate, Adam's apple (sense influenced by Ar. *rummāna,* pomegranate, Adam's apple).]

Adam's Bridge also **Ra·ma's Bridge** (rä′məz) A chain of shoals between India and Sri Lanka.

Ad·am's-nee·dle (ăd′əmz-nēd′l) *n.* Any of several related, stemless or nearly stemless plants of the genus *Yucca.* [< the spines on its leaves.]

Adam's Peak A mountain, 2,244.8 m (7,360 ft), in S-central Sri Lanka; a pilgrimage site for Buddhists, Hindus, and Muslims.

A·da·na (ä′də-nə, ə-dä′nə) A city of S Turkey near the Mediterranean; probably founded by the Hittites. Pop. 1,047,300.

a·dapt (ə-dăpt′) *v.* **a·dapt·ed, a·dapt·ing, a·dapts** —*tr.* To make suitable to a specific use or situation. —*intr.* To become adapted. [ME *adapten* < Lat. *adaptāre* : *ad-,* ad- + *aptāre,* to fit (< *aptus,* fitting; see APT.]] —**a·dapt′ed·ness** *n.*

SYNONYMS *adapt, accommodate, adjust, conform, fit, reconcile* These verbs mean to make suitable to or consistent with a particular situation or use: *adapted themselves to city life; can't accommodate myself to the new requirements; adjusting their behavior to the rules; conforming her life to accord with her moral principles; fit the punishment to the crime; couldn't reconcile his gentle words with his hostile actions.* **ANTONYM** *unfit*

a·dapt·a·ble (ə-dăp′tə-bəl) *adj.* Capable of adapting or of being adapted. —**a·dapt′a·bil′i·ty, a·dapt′a·ble·ness** *n.*

ad·ap·ta·tion (ăd′ăp-tā′shən) *n.* **1a.** The act or process of adapting. **b.** The state of being adapted. **2a.** Something that is changed or changes to become suitable to a new situation. **b.** A composition recast into a new form: *an adaptation of a novel for the stage.* **3.** *Biology* A usu. hereditary alteration in an organism that facilitates its survival and reproduction. **4.** *Physiology* The responsive adjustment of a sense organ, such as the eye, to varying conditions, such as light intensity. **5.** Change in behavior in response to new surroundings. —**ad′ap·ta′tion·al** *adj.* —**ad′ap·ta′tion·al·ly** *adv.*

a·dapt·er also **a·dap·tor** (ə-dăp′tər) *n.* One that adapts, such as a device used to connect different pieces of apparatus.

a·dap·tion (ə-dăp′shən) *n.* Adaptation.

a·dap·tive (ə-dăp′tĭv) *adj.* **1.** Relating to or exhibiting adaptation. **2.** Readily capable of adapting or of being adapted. —**a·dap′tive·ly** *adv.* —**a·dap·tiv′i·ty** (-tĭv′ĭ-tē) *n.*

adaptive radiation *n.* Diversification of a species or single ancestral type into several forms that are each adaptively specialized to a specific environmental niche.

A·dar (ä-där′, ä′där) *n.* The sixth month of the year in the Jewish calendar. See table at **calendar.** [Heb. *'ădār* < Akkadian *adaru, addaru,* month corresponding to parts of February and March.]

Adar She·ni (shā-nē′) *n.* An extra month of the Hebrew year, having 29 days, added in leap years after the regular month of Adar. See table at **calendar.** [Heb. *'ădār šēnî,* second Adar : *'ădār,* Adar; see ADAR + *šēnî,* second.]

ad·ax·i·al (ăd-ăk′sē-əl) *adj.* Located on the side nearest to the axis of an organ or organism.

ADC *abbr.* **1.** aide-de-camp **2.** Aid to Dependent Children **3.** Air Defense Command

add (ăd) *v.* **add·ed, add·ing, adds** —*tr.* **1.** To combine into a sum. **2.** To join or unite so as to increase in size, quantity, quality, or scope: *added 12 inches to the deck.* **3.** To say or write further. —*intr.* **1.** To find a sum in arithmetic. **2.** To constitute an addition: *an exploit that will add to her reputation.* **3.** To make or create

ate an addition. —*phrasal verb:* **add up 1.** To be reasonable, plausible, or consistent; make sense. **2.** To amount to an expected total. —*idiom:* **add up to** To constitute; amount to: *The revisions added up to a lot of work.* [ME *adden* < Lat. *addere* : *ad-,* ad- + *dare,* to give; see dō- in App.] —**add′a·ble, add′i·ble** *adj.*

ADD *abbr.* attention deficit disorder

Ad·dams (ăd′əmz), **Jane** 1860–1935. Amer. social reformer and pacifist who founded Chicago's Hull House (1889) and shared the 1931 Nobel Peace Prize.

ad·dax (ăd′ăks′) *n.* An antelope (*Addax nasomaculatus*) of northern Africa having long twisted horns. [Lat., of African orig.]

ad·dend (ăd′ĕnd′, ə-dĕnd′) *n.* Any of a set of numbers to be added. [Short for ADDENDUM.]

ad·den·dum (ə-dĕn′dəm) *n., pl.* **-da** (-də) Something added or to be added, esp. a supplement to a book. [Lat., neut. gerundive of *addere,* to add. See ADD.]

add·er[1] (ăd′ər) *n.* One that adds, esp. a computational device that performs arithmetic addition.

ad·der[2] (ăd′ər) *n.* **1.** See viper 1. **2.** Any of several nonvenomous snakes popularly believed to be harmful. [ME < *an addre,* alteration of *a naddre,* a snake < OE *nǣdre,* snake.]

WORD HISTORY The biblical injunction to be wise as serpents and innocent as doves looks somewhat alien in Middle English "Loke ye be prudent as neddris and symple as dowves." *Neddris* would be *adders* in Modern English, with a different meaning and form. *Adder,* an example of specialization in meaning, no longer refers to just any serpent or snake, as it once did, but now denotes only specific kinds of snakes. *Adder* also illustrates a process known as false splitting, or juncture loss: the word came from Old English *nǣdre* and kept its *n* into the Middle English period, but later during that stage of the language people started analyzing the phrase *a naddre* as *an addre*—the false splitting that has given us *adder.* Such false splitting also resulted in an initial *n* getting lost in the original forms of *apron, umpire,* and a variety of other English words.

Ad·der·ley (ăd′ər-lē), **Julian** Known as "Cannonball." 1928–75. Amer. jazz saxophonist who promoted the musical styles known as soul jazz and bop.

ad·der's-mouth (ăd′ərz-mouth′) *n.* Any of various chiefly terrestrial orchids of the genus *Malaxis,* having small, often greenish flowers. [< the resemblance of its flowers to the open mouths of snakes.]

ad·der's-tongue (ăd′ərz-tŭng′) *n.* **1.** See adder's-tongue fern. **2.** See dogtooth violet.

adder's-tongue fern *n.* Any of various ferns in the genus *Ophioglossum,* having leaves divided into a simple sterile blade and a slender, spikelike spore-bearing segment. [< the resemblance of the spike at the base of the frond to a snake's tongue.]

ad·dict (ə-dĭkt′) *tr.v.* **-dict·ed, -dict·ing, -dicts 1.** To cause to become physiologically or psychologically dependent on a habit-forming substance. **2.** To occupy or involve (oneself) habitually or compulsively. Used in the passive: *was addicted to video games.* ❖ *n.* (ăd′ĭkt) **1.** One who is addicted, as to narcotics. **2.** A devoted adherent or fan. [Lat. *addīcere,* addict-, to sentence : *ad-,* ad- + *dīcere,* to adjudge; see deik- in App.] —**ad·dic′tive** *adj.*

ad·dic·tion (ə-dĭk′shən) *n.* The quality or condition of being addicted, esp. to a habit-forming substance.

ad·dic·tive (ə-dĭk′tĭv) *adj.* **1.** Causing or tending to cause addiction: *an addictive substance.* **2.** Characterized by or susceptible to addiction: *an addictive personality.*

add-in (ăd′ĭn′) *n.* **1.** Something designed or intended for use in conjunction with another. **2.** An accessory software program that extends an existing application's capabilities. —**add′-in′** *adj.*

Ad·dis Ab·a·ba (ăd′ĭs ăb′ə-bə, ä′dĭs ä′bə-bä′) The cap. of Ethiopia, in the center on a high plateau; held by the Italians from 1936 to 1941. Pop. 2,316,400.

Ad·di·son (ăd′ĭ-sən), **Joseph** 1672–1719. English essayist, poet, and statesman known for his elegant prose style. —**Ad′di·so′ni·an** (-sō′nē-ən) *adj.*

Ad·di·son's disease (ăd′ĭ-sənz) *n.* A disease caused by failure of adrenocortical function and characterized by darkening of the skin, anemia, weakness, and low blood pressure. [After Thomas Addison (1793–1860), British physician.]

ad·di·tion (ə-dĭsh′ən) *n.* **1.** The act or process of adding, esp. of combining numbers into a sum. **2.** Something added, such as a room to a building. —*idioms:* **in addition** Also; as well. **in addition to** Over and above; besides. [ME < OFr. < Lat. *additiō, additiōn-* < *additus,* p. part. of *addere,* to add. See ADD.] —**ad·di′tion·al** *adj.* —**ad·di′tion·al·ly** *adv.*

ad·di·tive (ăd′ĭ-tĭv) *n.* A substance that is added in small amounts to something else to improve, strengthen, or otherwise alter it. ❖ *adj.* **1.** Marked by or involving addition. **2.** Of or being any of the primary colors red, green, or blue, whose wavelengths may be mixed with one another to produce all other spectral colors. —**ad′di·tive·ly** *adv.* —**ad′di·tiv′i·ty** *n.*

additive identity *n.* An element that in a given mathematical system leaves unchanged any element to which it is added.

additive inverse *n.* See inverse 2b.

ad·dle (ăd′l) *v.* **-dled, -dling, -dles** —*tr.* To muddle; confuse:

Jane Addams

addax
Addax nasomaculatus

ă	pat	oi	boy
ā	pay	ou	out
âr	care	ŏŏ	took
ä	father	ōō	boot
ĕ	pet	ŭ	cut
ē	be	ûr	urge
ĭ	pit	th	thin
ī	pie	*th*	this
îr	pier	hw	which
ŏ	pot	zh	vision
ō	toe	ə	about,
ô	paw		item

Stress marks:
′ (primary);
′ (secondary), as in
lexicon (lĕk′sĭ-kŏn′)

The heat addled his brain. See Syns at **confuse.** —*intr.* **1.** To become confused. **2.** To become rotten, as an egg. [< ME *adel,* rotten < OE *adel,* pool of excrement.]

ad·dle·pat·ed (ăd′l-pā′tĭd) *adj.* **1.** Muddled; confused. **2.** Eccentric; peculiar. **3.** Senseless; mad.

add-on (ăd′ŏn′, -ôn′) *n.* **1.** One thing added as a supplement to another. **2.** *Computer Science* **a.** See **add-in** 2. **b.** A hardware device added to a computer to increase its capabilities. **3.** An additional amount or charge.

ad·dress (ə-drĕs′) *tr.v.* **-dressed, -dress·ing, -dress·es** **1.** To speak to: *addressed me in low tones.* **2.** To make a formal speech to. **3.** To direct (a spoken or written comment) to someone's attention: *Address your remarks to the manager.* **4.** To mark with a destination: *address a letter.* **5a.** To direct the efforts of (oneself): *address oneself to a task.* **b.** To deal with; manage. **6.** *Sports* To adjust the club behind (a golf ball) before a stroke. ❖ *n.* **1.** (*also* ăd′rĕs′) **a.** A description of the location of a person or organization, as placed on mail as directions for delivery: *wrote the address on the envelope.* **b.** The location at which a particular organization or person may be found or reached: *went to her address but no one was home.* **2.** (*also* ăd′rĕs′) *Computer Science* **a.** A name or number used in information storage or retrieval assigned to a specific memory location. **b.** The memory location identified by this name or number. **c.** A name or a sequence of characters that designates an e-mail account or a specific network site. **3.** A formal spoken or written communication. **4.** A formal speech. **5.** Courteous attentions. Often used in the plural. **6.** The manner or bearing of a person, esp. in conversation. **7.** Skill and grace in dealing with people or situations. [ME *adressen,* to direct < OFr. *adresser* < VLat. **addīrēctiāre* : Latin *ad-,* ad- + VLat. **dīrēctiāre,* to straighten < Lat. *dīrēctus,* p. part. of *dīrigere,* to direct; see DIRECT).] —**ad·dress′a·ble** *adj.* —**ad·dress′er, ad·dress′or** *n.*

ad·dress·ee (ăd′rĕ-sē′, ə-drĕs′ē′) *n.* The one to whom something is addressed.

ad·duce (ə-dōōs′, ə-dyōōs′) *tr.v.* **-duced, -duc·ing, -duc·es** To cite as an example or means of proof in an argument. [Lat. *addūcere,* to bring to : *ad-,* ad- + *dūcere,* to lead; see **deuk-** in App.] —**ad·duce′a·ble, ad·duc′i·ble** *adj.*

ad·duct (ə-dŭkt′, ă-dŭkt′) *tr.v.* **-duct·ed, -duct·ing, -ducts** *Physiology* To draw inward toward the median axis of the body or toward an adjacent part or limb. ❖ *n.* A chemical compound formed by the addition of two or more substances. [Back-formation < ADDUCTOR.] —**ad·duc′tion** *n.* —**ad·duc′tive** *adj.*

ad·duc·tor (ə-dŭk′tər) *n.* A muscle that adducts a body part. [NLat. < Lat. *addūcere, adduct-,* to bring to, contract. See ADDUCE.]

–ade *suff.* A sweetened beverage of: *limeade.* [ME < OFr., ult. < Lat. *-āta,* fem. of *-ātus,* -ate. See –ATE[1].]

Ad·e·laide (ăd′l-ād′) A city of S Australia NW of Melbourne; founded 1836. Met. area pop. 1,071,100.

A·dé·lie Coast also **A·dé·lie Land** (ə-dā′lē) A region of Antarctica near George V Coast, under French sovereignty.

Adélie penguin *n.* A common Antarctic penguin (*Pygoscelis adeliae*) that has white underparts and a black back and head.

a·demp·tion (ə-dĕmp′shən) *n.* The disposal by a testator of property bequeathed in a will so as to invalidate the bequest. [Lat. *adēmptiō, adēmptiōn-,* a taking away < *adēmptus,* p. part. of *adimere,* to take away : *ad-,* ad- + *emere,* to buy, take.]

A·den (äd′n, ād′n) **1.** A former British colony and protectorate of S Arabia, part of Southern Yemen (now Yemen) since 1967. **2.** A city of S Yemen on the Gulf of Aden; cap. of Southern Yemen (1967–90). Pop. 400,783.

Aden, Gulf of An arm of the Arabian Sea between Yemen on the Arabian Peninsula and Somalia in E Africa.

A·de·na (ə-dē′nə) *n.* A Native American culture centered in the Ohio River valley from about the tenth century B.C. to about the second century A.D., noted esp. for its circular earthworks and elaborate burial mounds. [After the *Adena* Mound in Adena, Ohio.]

Ad·en·au·er (ăd′n-ou′ər, ăd′-), **Konrad** 1876–1967. First chancellor of West Germany (1949–63).

ad·e·nec·to·my (ăd′n-ĕk′tə-mē) *n., pl.* **-mies** Surgical excision of a gland.

ad·e·nine (ăd′n-ēn′, -ĭn) *n.* A purine base, $C_5H_5N_5$, that is the constituent involved in base-pairing with thymine in DNA and with uracil in RNA.

ad·e·ni·tis (ăd′n-ī′tĭs) *n.* Inflammation of a lymph node or gland.

adeno– or **aden–** *pref.* Gland: *adenectomy.* [< Gk. *adēn, aden-.*]

ad·e·no·car·ci·no·ma (ăd′n-ō-kär′sə-nō′mə) *n.* A malignant tumor originating in glandular tissue. —**ad′e·no·car′ci·nom′a·tous** (-nŏm′ə-təs, -nō′mə-təs) *adj.*

ad·e·no·hy·poph·y·sis (ăd′n-ō-hī-pŏf′ĭ-sĭs) *n.* The anterior lobe of the pituitary gland. —**ad′e·no·hy·poph′y·se′al, ad′e·no·hy·poph′y·si′al** (-pŏf′ĭ-sē′əl) *adj.*

ad·e·noid (ăd′n-oid′) *n.* One of two masses of lymphoid tissue at the back of the nose in the upper part of the throat that when swollen may obstruct breathing. Often used in the plural. ❖ *adj.* Of or relating to lymphatic glands or lymphoid tissue.

ad·e·noi·dal (ăd′n-oid′l) *adj.* **1.** Of or relating to the adenoids. **2.** Suggestive of the vocal sound caused by enlarged adenoids.

Adélie penguin
Pygoscelis adeliae

ad·e·no·ma (ăd′n-ō′mə) *n., pl.* **-mas** or **-ma·ta** (-mə-tə) A benign epithelial tumor having a glandular origin and structure. —**ad′e·nom′a·toid′** (ăd′n-ōm′ə-toid′) *adj.* —**ad′e·nom′a·tous** (-ōm′ə-təs) *adj.*

a·den·o·sine (ə-dĕn′ə-sēn′) *n.* A nucleoside, $C_{10}H_{13}N_5O_4$, that is a structural component of nucleic acids and the major molecular component of ADP, AMP, and ATP. [Blend of ADENINE and RIBOSE.]

adenosine diphosphate *n.* ADP.

adenosine mon·o·phos·phate (mŏn′ō-fŏs′fāt′) *n.* **1.** AMP. **2.** Cyclic AMP.

adenosine triphosphate *n.* ATP.

ad·e·no·sis (ăd′n-ō′sĭs) *n., pl.* **-ses** (-sēz′) A disease of a gland, esp. one marked by abnormal formation or enlargement.

ad·e·no·vi·rus (ăd′n-ō-vī′rəs) *n.* Any of a group of DNA-containing viruses that cause conjunctivitis and respiratory infections in humans. [ADENO(ID) + VIRUS.] —**ad′e·no·vi′ral** *adj.*

a·den·yl·ate cy·clase (ə-dĕn′l-ĭt sĭ′klăs, -klāz, ăd′n-ĭl′ĭt) also **a·den·yl cyclase** (ə-dĕn′l, ăd′n-ĭl) *n.* An enzyme that catalyzes the formation of cyclic AMP from ATP. [ADEN(INE) + –YL + –ATE[2] + CYCL(O)– + –ASE.]

ad·e·nyl·ic acid (ăd′n-ĭl′ĭk) *n.* See AMP. [ADEN(INE) + –YL + –IC + ACID.]

a·dept (ə-dĕpt′) *adj.* Very skilled. See Syns at **proficient.** ❖ *n.* (ăd′ĕpt′) A highly skilled person; an expert. [Lat. *adeptus,* p. part. of *adipīscī,* to attain : *ad-,* ad- + *apīscī,* to grasp.] —**a·dept′ly** *adv.* —**a·dept′ness** *n.*

ad·e·quate (ăd′ĭ-kwĭt) *adj.* **1.** Sufficient to meet a need. **2.** Barely satisfactory or sufficient. [Lat. *adaequātus,* p. part. of *adaequāre,* to equalize : *ad-,* ad- + *aequāre,* to make equal < *aequus,* equal.] —**ad′e·qua·cy** (-kwə-sē), **ad′e·quate·ness** *n.* —**ad′e·quate·ly** *adv.*

à deux (ä′ dœ′) *adj.* Involving two persons. ❖ *adv.* With only two persons involved. [Fr. : *à,* by, at + *deux,* two.]

ad fem·i·nam (ăd fĕm′ī-năm′, -nəm) *adj.* Appealing to irrelevant personal considerations concerning women. See Usage Note at **ad hominem.** [Lat. *ad,* to + *fēminam,* accusative of *fēmina,* woman.] —**ad fem′i·nam′** *adv.*

ADH *abbr.* antidiuretic hormone

ADHD *abbr.* attention deficit hyperactivity disorder

ad·here (ăd-hîr′) *v.* **-hered, -her·ing, -heres** —*intr.* **1.** To stick fast; remain attached. **2.** To be a devoted follower or supporter. **3.** To carry out a plan, scheme, or operation without deviation. —*tr.* To cause to adhere; make stick. [Fr. *adhérer* < Lat. *adhaerēre,* to stick to : *ad-,* ad- + *haerēre,* to hold.]

ad·her·ence (ăd-hîr′əns, -hĕr′-) *n.* **1.** The process or condition of adhering. **2.** Faithful attachment; devotion.

ad·her·ent (ăd-hîr′ənt, -hĕr′-) *n.* A supporter, as of a cause or individual. ❖ *adj.* **1.** Sticking or holding fast. **2.** *Botany* Joined but not united. —**ad·her′ent·ly** *adv.*

ad·he·sion (ăd-hē′zhən) *n.* **1.** The act or state of adhering. **2.** Attachment or devotion; loyalty. **3.** Assent or agreement to join. **4.** *Physics* The molecular force that attracts or binds dissimilar substances. **5.** *Medicine* A fibrous band of scar tissue that binds together normally separate anatomical structures. [Fr. *adhésion* < Lat. *adhaesiō, adhaesiōn-* < *adhaesus,* p. part. of *adhaerēre,* to adhere. See ADHERE.]

ad·he·si·ot·o·my (ăd-hē′zē-ŏt′ə-mē) *n., pl.* **-mies** Surgical division or separation of adhesions.

ad·he·sive (ăd-hē′sĭv, -zĭv) *adj.* **1.** Tending to adhere; sticky. **2.** Gummed so as to adhere. ❖ *n.* A substance, such as paste or cement, that provides adhesion. —**ad·he′sive·ly** *adv.* —**ad·he′sive·ness** *n.*

adhesive tape *n.* A tape lined on one side with an adhesive.

ad hoc (ăd hŏk′, hōk′) *adv.* For the specific purpose or situation at hand. ❖ *adj.* **1.** Formed for or concerned with one specific purpose: *an ad hoc committee.* **2.** Improvised; impromptu. [Lat. : *ad,* to + *hoc,* neut. accusative of *hic,* this.]

ad hom·i·nem (hŏm′ə-nĕm′, -nəm) *adj.* Appealing to personal considerations rather than to logic or reason. [Lat. : *ad,* to + *hominem,* accusative of *homō,* man.] —**ad hom′i·nem′** *adv.*

USAGE NOTE The phrase *ad hominem* is used to denote an argument designed to appeal to the listener's emotions rather than to reason, as in the sentence *The Republicans' evocation of pity for the small farmer struggling to maintain his property is a purely ad hominem argument for reducing inheritance taxes.* This usage appears to be waning; only 37 percent of the Usage Panel finds this sentence acceptable. The phrase now chiefly describes an argument based on the failings of an adversary rather than on the merits of the case: *Ad hominem attacks on one's opponent are a tried-and-true strategy for people who have a case that is weak.* Ninety percent of the Panel finds this sentence acceptable. • A modern coinage patterned on *ad hominem* is *ad feminam.* Though some would argue that this neologism is unnecessary because the Latin word *homo* refers to humans generically, rather than to the male sex, in some contexts *ad feminam* has a more specific meaning than *ad hominem,* being used to describe attacks on women as women or because they are women, as in "Their recourse . . . to ad feminam attacks evidences the chilly climate for women's leadership on campus" (Donna M. Riley).

ad•i•a•bat•ic (ăd′ē-ə-băt′ĭk, ā′dī-ə-) *adj.* Of, relating to, or being a reversible thermodynamic process occurring without gain or loss of heat or change in entropy. [< Gk. *adiabatos*, impassable : *a-*, not; see A–[1] + *diabatos*, passable (*dia*, dia- + *batos*, passable < *bainein*, to go; see g^{w}ā- in App.).] **—ad′i•a•bat′i•cal•ly** *adv.*

a•dieu (ə-dyo͞o′, ə-do͞o′) *interj.* Used to express farewell. ❖ *n., pl.* **a•dieus** or **a•dieux** (ə-dyo͞oz′, ə-do͞oz′) A farewell. [ME < OFr. *a dieu*, (I commend you) to God : *a*, to (< Lat. *ad*) + *Dieu*, God (< Lat. *deus*; see **dyeu-** in App.).]

A•di•ge (ä′dĭ-jā′, ä′dē-jĕ′) A river of NE Italy rising in the Alps and flowing c. 410 km (255 mi) to the Adriatic Sea.

ad in•fi•ni•tum (ăd ĭn′fə-nī′təm) *adv. & adj.* To infinity; having no end. [Lat. *ad*, to + *īnfīnītum*, accusative of *īnfīnītus*, infinite.]

ad in•ter•im (ĭn′tər-əm) *adv.* In or for the meantime; temporarily. ❖ *adj.* Acting or done ad interim; temporary. [Lat. *ad*, to, for + *interim*, the meantime.]

ad•i•os (ä′dē-ōs′) *interj.* Used to express farewell. [Sp. *adiós*, prob. transl. of French *à dieu*. See ADIEU.]

a•dip•ic acid (ə-dĭp′ĭk) *n.* A white crystalline dicarboxylic acid, $C_6H_{11}O_4$, that is derived from oxidation of various fats, is slightly soluble in water, and is used esp. in the manufacture of nylon. [< Lat. *adeps*, *adip-*, fat.]

ad•i•po•cere (ăd′ə-pō-sîr′) *n.* A brown, fatty waxlike substance that forms on dead animal tissues in response to moisture. [ADIPO(SE) + Lat. *cēra*, wax.]

ad•i•po•cyte (ăd′ə-pō-sīt′) *n.* See **fat cell.**

ad•i•pose (ăd′ə-pōs′) *adj.* Of, relating to, or composed of animal fat; fatty. ❖ *n.* The fat found in adipose tissue. [NLat. *adipōsus* < Lat. *adeps*, *adip-*, fat.]

adipose tissue *n.* A type of connective tissue that contains stored cellular fat.

Ad•i•ron•dack chair (ăd′ə-rŏn′dăk′) *n.* An outdoor armchair having an angled back and seat made of wide, usu. wooden slats.

Adirondack Mountains A group of mountains in NE NY between the St. Lawrence R. and the Mohawk R. Part of the Appalachian system, the range rises to 1,629.9 m (5,344 ft).

ad•it (ăd′ĭt) *n.* An almost horizontal entrance to a mine. [Lat. *aditus*, access < p. part. of *adīre*, to approach : *ad-*, ad + *īre*, to go; see **ei-** in App.]

adj. *abbr.* **1.** adjective **2.** adjunct **3. Adj.** adjutant

ad•ja•cen•cy (ə-jā′sən-sē) *n., pl.* **-cies 1.** The state of being adjacent; contiguity. **2.** A thing that is adjacent.

ad•ja•cent (ə-jā′sənt) *adj.* **1.** Close to; lying near: *adjacent cities.* **2.** Next to; adjoining: *adjacent garden plots.* [ME < Lat. *adiacēns*, *adiacent-*, pr. part. of *adiacēre*, to lie near : *ad-*, ad- + *iacēre*, to lie.] **—ad•ja′cent•ly** *adv.*

adjacent angle *n.* Either of two angles having a common side and a common vertex.

ad•jec•tive (ăj′ĭk-tĭv) *n.* **1.** *Grammar* The part of speech that modifies a noun or other substantive by limiting, qualifying, or specifying and often distinguished in English by one of several suffixes, such as *-ous*, *-er*, and *-est*, or by preceding a noun or nominal phrase. **2.** A word belonging to this part of speech. ❖ *adj.* **1.** *Grammar* Of, relating to, or functioning as an adjective. **2.** Not standing alone; derivative or dependent. [ME < OFr. *adjectif* < LLat. *adiectīvus* < *adiectus*, p. part. of *adicere*, to add to : *ad-*, ad- + *iacere*, to throw.] **—ad′jec•ti′val** (-tī′vəl) *adj.* **—ad′jec•ti′val•ly** *adv.* **—ad′jec•tive•ly** *adv.*

ad•join (ə-join′) *v.* **-joined, -join•ing, -joins** *—tr.* **1.** To be next to; be contiguous to: *property that adjoins ours.* **2.** To attach; append. *—intr.* To be contiguous. [ME *ajoinen* < OFr. *ajoindre*, *ajoin-* < Lat. *adiungere*, to join to : *ad-*, ad- + *iungere*, to join; see **yeug-** in App.]

ad•join•ing (ə-joi′nĭng) *adj.* Neighboring; contiguous.

ad•journ (ə-jûrn′) *v.* **-journed, -journ•ing, -journs** *—tr.* To suspend until a later stated time. *—intr.* **1.** To suspend proceedings to another time or place. **2.** To move from one place to another: *We adjourned to the living room.* [ME *ajournen* < OFr. *ajourner* : *a-*, to (< Lat. *ad-*; see AD–) + *jour*, day (< LLat. *diurnum* < Lat. *diurnus*, daily < *diēs*, day; see **dyeu-** in App.).] **—ad•journ′ment** *n.*

Adjt. *abbr.* adjutant

ad•judge (ə-jŭj′) *tr.v.* **-judged, -judg•ing, -judg•es 1a.** To determine or decide by judicial procedure; adjudicate. **b.** To order judicially; rule. **c.** To award by law. **d.** To sentence; condemn. **2.** To regard or deem. [ME *ajugen* < OFr. *ajuger* < Lat. *adiūdicāre*. See ADJUDICATE.]

ad•ju•di•cate (ə-jo͞o′dĭ-kāt′) *v.* **-cat•ed, -cat•ing, -cates** *—tr.* **1.** To hear and settle (a case). **2.** To study and settle (a dispute). *—intr.* To act as a judge. [Lat. *adiūdicāre*, *adiūdicāt-*, to award to (judicially) : *ad-*, ad- + *iūdicāre*, to judge (< *iūdex*, judge; see JUDGE).] **—ad•ju′di•ca′tion** *n.* **—ad•ju′di•ca′tive** *adj.* **—ad•ju′di•ca′tor** *n.*

ad•junct (ăj′ŭngkt′) *n.* **1.** Something attached to another in a dependent or subordinate position. **2.** A person associated with another in a subordinate or auxiliary capacity. **3.** *Grammar* A clause or phrase added to a sentence that amplifies its meaning. ❖ *adj.* **1.** Added or connected in a subordinate or auxiliary capacity. **2.** Attached to a faculty or staff in a temporary or auxiliary capacity: *an adjunct professor of history.* [< Lat. *adiūnctus*, p. part. of *adiungere*, to join to. See ADJOIN.] **—ad•junc′tion** (ə-jŭngk′shən) *n.* **—ad•junc′tive** *adj.*

ad•ju•ra•tion (ăj′ə-rā′shən) *n.* An earnest, solemn appeal. **—ad•jur′a•to′ry** (ə-jo͝or′ə-tôr′ē, -tōr′ē) *adj.*

ad•jure (ə-jo͝or′) *tr.v.* **-jured, -jur•ing, -jures 1.** To command or enjoin solemnly, as under oath. **2.** To appeal to or entreat earnestly. [ME *adjuren* < Lat. *adiūrāre*, to swear to : *ad-*, ad- + *iūrāre*, to swear.] **—ad•jur′er, ad•ju′ror** *n.*

ad•just (ə-jŭst′) *v.* **-just•ed, -just•ing, -justs** *—tr.* **1.** To change so as to match or fit. **2.** To bring into proper relationship. **3.** To adapt or conform, as to new conditions. See Syns at **adapt. 4.** To make more effective or efficient: *adjust the timing of a car.* **5.** To settle; resolve. **6.** To decide how much is to be paid on (an insurance claim). *—intr.* To adapt oneself; conform. [Obsolete Fr. *adjuster* < OFr. *ajoster* < VLat. **adiūxtāre*, to put close to : Lat. *ad-*, ad- + Lat. *iūxtā*, near; see **yeug-** in App.] **—ad•just′a•ble** *adj.* **—ad•just′a•bly** *adv.* **—ad•just′er, ad•jus′tor** *n.*

ad•just•a•ble-rate mortgage (ə-jŭst′ə-bəl-rāt′) *n.* A mortgage whose interest rate is raised or lowered at periodic intervals according to the prevailing interest rates in the market.

ad•just•ed (ə-jŭs′tĭd) *adj.* **1.** Arranged or changed so as to match, conform, or function, esp. in a specified way: *an improperly adjusted scale.* **2.** Having achieved psychological balance, esp. regarding others or the demands of everyday life: *a poorly adjusted teenager.*

ad•just•ment (ə-jŭst′mənt) *n.* **1.** The act of adjusting or the state of being adjusted. **2.** A means of adjusting. **3.** Settlement of a debt or claim. **4.** A modification, fluctuation, or correction: *an adjustment on a bill.*

ad•ju•tant (ăj′ə-tənt) *n.* **1.** A staff officer who helps a commanding officer with administrative affairs. **2.** An assistant. **3.** See **marabou** 1. [< Lat. *adiūtāns*, *adiūtant-*, pr. part. of *adiūtāre*, to help. See AID.] **—ad′ju•tan•cy** *n.*

adjutant general *n., pl.* **adjutants general 1.** An adjutant of a unit having a general staff. **2.** An officer in charge of the National Guard in one of the US states. **3. Adjutant General** The chief administrative officer, a major general, of the US Army.

adjutant stork *n.* See **marabou** 1.

ad•ju•vant (ăj′ə-vənt) *n.* **1.** An agent added to a drug to increase or aid its effect. **2.** An immunological agent that increases antigenic response. [< Lat. *adiuvāns*, *adiuvant-*, pr. part. of *adiuvāre*, to help. See AID.]

ADL *abbr.* **1.** activities of daily living **2.** Anti-Defamation League

Ad•ler (ăd′lər, äd′-), **Alfred** 1870–1937. Austrian psychiatrist who theorized that neurotic behavior is an overcompensation for feelings of inferiority. **—Ad•le′ri•an** (ăd-lîr′ē-ən) *adj.*

Ad•ler (ăd′lər), **Cyrus** 1863–1940. Amer. religious leader who was president of the Jewish Theological Seminary of America (1924–40).

Ad•ler (ăd′lər), **Mortimer Jerome** b. 1902. Amer. educator and philosopher whose works include *How to Read a Book* (1940).

ad lib (ăd lĭb′) *adv.* In an unrestrained manner; spontaneously. [Short for AD LIBITUM.]

ad-lib (ăd-lĭb′) *v.* **-libbed, -lib•bing, -libs** *—tr.* To improvise and deliver extemporaneously. *—intr.* To engage in improvisation, as in a speech. ❖ *n.* (ăd′lĭb′) Something, such as a joke, that is improvised. ❖ *adj.* Improvised; extemporaneous. **—ad-lib′ber** *n.*

ad lib•i•tum (ăd lĭb′ĭ-təm) *adj.* *Music* At the discretion of the performer. Used chiefly as a direction giving license to alter or omit a part. [Lat. *ad*, according to + *libitum*, p. part. of *libēre*, to please.]

ad loc. *abbr.* *Latin* ad locum (to, or at, the place)

ADM or **Adm.** *abbr.* admiral

ad•man (ăd′măn′) *n.* A man who designs, writes, acquires, or sells advertising.

ad•meas•ure (ăd-mĕzh′ər) *tr.v.* **-ured, -ur•ing, -ures** To divide and distribute proportionally; apportion. [ME *amesuren* < OFr. *amesurer* : *a-*, to (< Lat. *ad-*; see AD–) + *mesurer*, to measure (< LLat. *mēnsūrāre*, to measure < Lat. *mēnsūra*, measure; see MEASURE).] **—ad•meas′ure•ment** *n.* **—ad•meas′ur•er** *n.*

Ad•me•tus (ăd-mē′təs) *n.* *Greek Mythology* A king of Thessaly and husband of Alcestis.

ad•min•is•ter (ăd-mĭn′ĭ-stər) *v.* **-tered, -ter•ing, -ters** *—tr.* **1.** To have charge of; manage. **2a.** To give or apply in a formal way: *administer the last rites.* **b.** To apply as a remedy: *administer a sedative.* **c.** To direct the taking of (an oath). **3.** To mete out; dispense: *administer justice.* **4.** To manage or dispose of (a trust or estate) under a will or official appointment. **5.** To impose, offer, or tender (an oath, for example). *—intr.* **1.** To manage as an administrator. **2.** To minister: *administering to every whim.* [ME *administren* < OFr. *administrer* < Lat. *administrāre* : *ad*, ad- + *ministrāre*, to manage (< *minister*, *ministr-*, servant; see MINISTER).] **—ad•min′is•tra•ble** (-ĭ-strə-bəl) *adj.* **—ad•min′is•trant** *adj. & n.*

ad•min•is•trate (ăd-mĭn′ĭ-strāt′) *tr.v.* **-trat•ed, -trat•ing, -trates** To administer.

ad•min•is•tra•tion (ăd-mĭn′ĭ-strā′shən) *n.* **1.** The act or process of administering, esp. the management of a government or large institution. **2.** The activity of a government or state in the exercise of its powers and duties. **3a.** often **Administration** The

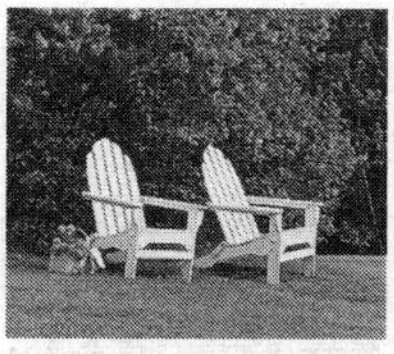

Adirondack chair

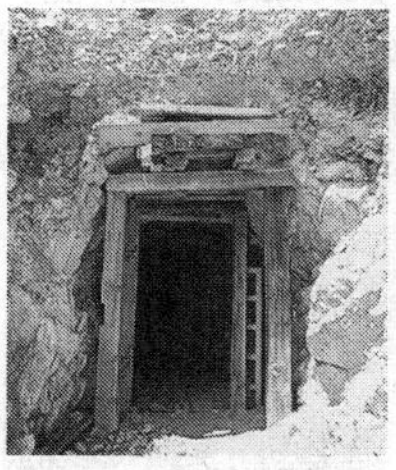

adit
Eureka Mine, Death Valley, California

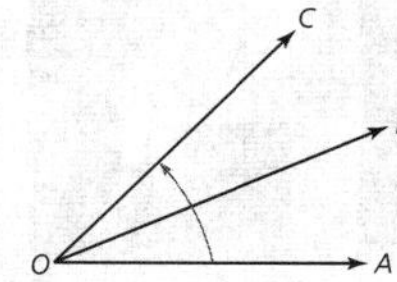

adjacent angle
The common vertex is *O*; angle *AOB* is adjacent to angle *BOC.*

ă pat	oi boy
ā pay	ou out
âr care	o͝o took
ä father	o͞o boot
ĕ pet	ŭ cut
ē be	ûr urge
ĭ pit	th thin
ī pie	*th* this
îr pier	hw which
ŏ pot	zh vision
ō toe	ə about, item
ô paw	

Stress marks:
′ (primary);
′ (secondary), as in
lexicon (lĕk′sĭ-kŏn′)

group of people who constitute the executive branch of a government **b.** The group of people who manage an institution. **c.** The term of office of an executive officer or a body. **4.** *Law* Management and disposal of a trust or estate. **5.** The administering of something, such as medicine or an oath. —**ad·min′is·tra′tive** (-strā′tĭv, -strə-) *adj.* —**ad·min′is·tra′tive·ly** *adv.*

ad·min·is·tra·tor (ăd-mĭn′ĭ-strā′tər) *n.* **1.** One who administers, such as a manager in a business, school, or government. **2.** *Law* One appointed to administer an estate.

ad·mi·ra·ble (ăd′mər-ə-bəl) *adj.* Deserving admiration. —**ad′mi·ra·ble·ness** *n.* —**ad′mi·ra·bly** *adv.*

ad·mi·ral (ăd′mər-əl) *n.* **1.** The commander in chief of a fleet. **2.** A flag officer. **3a.** A commissioned rank in the US Navy or Coast Guard that is above vice admiral and below Admiral of the Fleet. **b.** One who holds the rank of admiral, Admiral of the Fleet, rear admiral, or vice admiral. **4.** Any of various brightly colored butterflies of the genera *Limenitis* and *Vanessa*. **5.** *Archaic* The ship carrying an admiral; flagship. [ME *amiral, admiral* < OFr. and < Med.Lat. *amīrālis, admīrālis,* both < Ar. *'amīr al-* . . ., commander of the . . . (as in *'amīr al-baḥr,* commander of the sea) : *'amīr,* commander; see EMIR + *al-,* the.]

Admiral of the Fleet *n.* **1.** The highest rank in the US Navy, equivalent to General of the Army. **2.** One who holds this rank.

ad·mi·ral·ty (ăd′mər-əl-tē) *n., pl.* **-ties 1a.** A court exercising jurisdiction over all maritime cases. **b.** Maritime law. **2. Admiralty** The department of the British government that once had control over all naval affairs.

Admiralty Islands A group of volcanic islands of Papua New Guinea in the SW Pacific.

Admiralty Range A mountain group of Antarctica on the N coast of Victoria Land NW of Ross Sea.

ad·mi·ra·tion (ăd′mə-rā′shən) *n.* **1.** A feeling of pleasure, wonder, and approval. **2.** An object of wonder and esteem; a marvel. **3.** *Archaic* Wonder.

ad·mire (ăd-mīr′) *v.* **-mired, -mir·ing, -mires** —*tr.* **1.** To regard with pleasure, wonder, and approval. **2.** To have a high opinion of; esteem or respect. **3.** *Chiefly New England & Upper Southern US* To enjoy (something). **4.** *Archaic* To marvel or wonder at. —*intr. New England & Upper Southern US* To marvel at something. Often used with *at.* [Fr. *admirer* < OFr. *amirer* < Lat. *admīrārī,* to wonder at : *ad-, ad-* + *mīrārī,* to wonder (< *mīrus,* wonderful).] —**ad·mir′er** *n.* —**ad·mir′ing·ly** *adv.*

ad·mis·si·ble (ăd-mĭs′ə-bəl) *adj.* **1.** Acceptable; allowable: *admissible evidence.* **2.** Worthy of admission. —**ad·mis′si·bil′i·ty, ad·mis′si·ble·ness** *n.* —**ad·mis′si·bly** *adv.*

ad·mis·sion (ăd-mĭsh′ən) *n.* **1a.** The act of admitting or allowing to enter. **b.** The state of being allowed to enter. **2.** Right to enter; access. **3.** The price required or paid for entering. **4.** A confession, as of having committed a crime. **5.** A voluntary acknowledgment of truth. **6.** A fact or statement granted or admitted; a concession. [ME < Lat. *admissiō, admissiōn-* < *admissus,* p. part. of *admittere,* to admit. See ADMIT.] —**ad·mis′sive** (-mĭs′ĭv) *adj.*

ad·mit (ăd-mĭt′) *v.* **-mit·ted, -mit·ting, -mits** —*tr.* **1.** To permit to enter: *A crack in the wall admitted some light.* **2.** To provide the right or a means of entrance to: *a ticket that admits four.* **3.** To permit to exercise the rights, functions, or privileges of: *admitted to the bar.* **4.** To have room for; accommodate. **5.** To afford opportunity for; permit: *We must admit no delay.* **6.** To grant to be real, valid, or true; acknowledge: *admit the truth.* **7.** To grant as true or valid; concede. —*intr.* **1.** To afford possibility: *The problem admits of no solution.* **2.** To allow entrance: *a door admitting to the hall.* **3.** To make acknowledgment. [ME *amitten, admitten* < OFr. *amettre, admettre* < Lat. *admittere* : *ad-, ad-* + *mittere,* to send.]

ad·mit·tance (ăd-mĭt′ns) *n.* **1.** The act of admitting or entering. **2.** Permission or right to enter. **3.** *Symbol* Y *Electricity* The reciprocal of impedance.

ad·mit·ted·ly (ăd-mĭt′ĭd-lē) *adv.* By general admission; confessedly.

ad·mix (ăd-mĭks′) *tr. & intr.v.* **-mixed, -mix·ing, -mix·es** To mix; blend. [Back-formation < obsolete *admixt,* mixed into < ME < Lat. *admixtus,* p. part. of *admiscēre,* to mix into : *ad-, ad-* + *miscēre,* to mix; see **meik-** in App.]

ad·mix·ture (ăd-mĭks′chər) *n.* **1.** The act of mixing or the state of being mixed. **2.** Something produced by mixing; a mixture. **3.** Something added in mixing. See Syns at **mixture.**

ad·mon·ish (ăd-mŏn′ĭsh) *tr.v.* **-ished, -ish·ing, -ish·es 1.** To reprove gently; warn. **2.** To caution; warn. **3.** To remind of an obligation or duty. [ME *amonishen, admonishen,* alteration of *amonesten* < OFr. *amonester, admonester* < VLat. **admonestāre* < Lat. *admonēre* : *ad-, ad-* + *monēre,* to warn; see **men-¹** in App.] —**ad·mon′ish·er** *n.* —**ad·mon′ish·ing·ly** *adv.* —**ad·mon′ish·ment** *n.*

SYNONYMS *admonish, reprove, rebuke, reprimand, reproach* These verbs mean to correct or caution critically. *Admonish* implies the giving of advice or a warning: *"A gallows erected on an eminence admonished the offenders of the fate that awaited them"* (William Hickling Prescott). *Reprove* usually suggests gentle criticism: *With a quick look the teacher reproved the child for interrupting. Rebuke* and *reprimand* both refer to sharp, often angry

admiral
red admiral
Vanessa atalanta

adobe
San Miguel Mission Church,
Santa Fe, New Mexico

criticism: *"Some of the most heated criticism . . . has come from the Justice Department, which rarely rebukes other agencies in public"* (Howard Kurtz). *"A committee* [at the university] *asked its president to reprimand a scientist who tested gene-altered bacteria on trees"* (New York Times). *Reproach* usually refers to regretful or unhappy criticism: *"Every other author may aspire to praise; the lexicographer can only hope to escape reproach"* (Samuel Johnson).

ad·mo·ni·tion (ăd′mə-nĭsh′ən) *n.* **1.** Mild reproof. **2.** Cautionary advice or warning. [ME *amonicioun* < OFr. *amonition* < Lat. *admonitiō, admonitiōn-* < *admonitus,* p. part. of *admonēre,* to admonish. See ADMONISH.]

ad·mon·i·to·ry (ăd-mŏn′ĭ-tôr′ē, -tōr′ē) *adj.* Expressing admonition.

ad·nate (ăd′nāt′) *adj. Biology* United to a different part or organ. [Lat. *adnātus,* var. of *agnātus,* p. part. of *agnāscī,* to grow upon. See AGNATE.] —**ad·na′tion** *n.*

ad nau·se·am (ăd nô′zē-əm) *adv.* To a disgusting or ridiculous degree. [Lat. *ad,* to + *nauseam,* accusative of *nausea,* sickness.]

ad·nex·a (ăd-nĕk′sə) *pl.n.* Accessory or adjoining anatomical parts. [Lat., neut. pl. of *adnexus,* p. part. of *adnectere,* to bind to. See ANNEX.] —**ad·nex′al** *adj.*

a·do (ə-do͞o′) *n.* Bustle; fuss; bother. [ME < the phrase *at do* : *at,* to (used with infinitive) (< ON *at;* see **ad-** in App.) + *do,* do; see DO¹.]

a·do·be (ə-dō′bē) *n.* **1a.** A sun-dried brick of clay and straw. **b.** The clay or soil from which this brick is made. **2.** A structure built with this brick. [Sp. < Ar. *aṭ-ṭūba,* the brick : *aṭ-* + *ṭūba,* brick (< *ṭūb,* bricks < Coptic *tōbe, tōōbe* < Egypt. *ḏbt,* brick).]

a·do·bo (ä-dō′bō) *n., pl.* **-bos** A Philippine dish of marinated meat or fish seasoned with garlic and spices. [Sp. < OSpan. *adobar,* to stew < OFr. *adouber,* to dub, arm, prepare, of Gmc. orig.]

ad·o·les·cence (ăd′l-ĕs′əns) *n.* **1.** The period of development from the onset of puberty to maturity. **2.** A period of development between youth and maturity.

ad·o·les·cent (ăd′l-ĕs′ənt) *adj.* **1.** Of or relating to adolescence. **2.** Characteristic of adolescence; immature. ❖ *n.* A person who has undergone puberty but not reached maturity. [ME < OFr. < Lat. *adolēscēns, adolēscent-,* pr. part. of *adolēscere,* to grow up : *ad-, ad-* + *alēscere,* to grow, inchoative of *alere,* to nourish.]

Ad·o·nai (ä′dô-nī′, -noi′) *n.* Lord. Used in Judaism as a spoken substitute for the ineffable name of God. [Heb. *'ăḏōnāy,* my lord : *'āḏôn,* lord + *-ay,* my.]

A·don·is (ə-dŏn′ĭs, ə-dō′nĭs) *n.* **1.** *Greek Mythology* A beautiful young man loved by Aphrodite. **2.** often **adonis** A very handsome young man. [Gk. *Adōnis,* of Phoenician orig.; akin to Heb. *'ăḏônāy,* my lord, Adonai.]

a·dopt (ə-dŏpt′) *tr.v.* **a·dopt·ed, a·dopt·ing, a·dopts 1.** To take into one's family through legal means and raise as one's own child. **2a.** To take and follow (a course of action, for example). **b.** To take up and make one's own: *adopt a new idea.* **3.** To vote to accept: *adopt a resolution.* **4.** To choose as standard or required in a course: *adopt a new line of English textbooks.* [ME *adopten* < OFr. *adopter* < Lat. *adoptāre* : *ad-, ad-* + *optāre,* to choose.] —**a·dopt′a·bil′i·ty** *n.* —**a·dopt′a·ble** *adj.* —**a·dop′tee** *n.* —**a·dop′tion** *n.*

USAGE NOTE One refers to an *adopted* child but to *adoptive* parents. Either adjective, however, can refer to places: *her adopted* (or *adoptive*) *country.*

a·dop·tive (ə-dŏp′tĭv) *adj.* **1.** Of or having to do with adoption. **2.** Related by adoption: *adoptive parents.* See Usage Note at **adopt.** —**a·dop′tive·ly** *adv.*

a·dor·a·ble (ə-dôr′ə-bəl, ə-dōr′-) *adj.* **1.** Delightful, lovable, and charming. **2.** Worthy of adoration. —**a·dor′a·bil′i·ty, a·dor′a·ble·ness** *n.* —**a·dor′a·bly** *adv.*

ad·o·ra·tion (ăd′ə-rā′shən) *n.* **1.** The act of worship. **2.** Profound love or regard.

a·dore (ə-dôr′, ə-dōr′) *v.* **a·dored, a·dor·ing, a·dores** —*tr.* **1.** To worship as God or a god. **2.** To regard with deep, often rapturous love. See Syns like **revere¹.** **3.** To like very much: *adores mink coats.* —*intr.* To worship. [ME *adouren* < OFr. *adourer* < Lat. *adōrāre,* to pray to : *ad-, ad-* + *ōrāre,* to pray.] —**a·dor′er** *n.* —**a·dor′ing·ly** *adv.*

a·dorn (ə-dôrn′) *tr.v.* **a·dorned, a·dorn·ing, a·dorns 1.** To make beautiful or attractive. **2.** To put ornaments on; decorate. [ME *adornen* < OFr. *adourner* < Lat. *adōrnāre* : *ad-, ad-* + *ōrnāre,* to decorate.] —**a·dorn′er** *n.*

a·dorn·ment (ə-dôrn′mənt) *n.* **1.** The act of adorning. **2.** Something that adorns; an ornament.

A·dour (ə-do͞or′) A river of SW France rising in the Pyrenees and flowing c. 338 km (210 mi) to the Bay of Biscay.

ADP¹ (ā′dē′pē′) *n.* A nucleotide, $C_{10}H_{15}N_5O_{10}P_2$, composed of adenosine and two phosphate groups, that is converted to ATP for the storage of energy. [A(DENOSINE) D(I)P(HOSPHATE).]

ADP² *abbr.* automatic data processing

A·dras·te·a (ə-drăs′tē-ə) *n.* A satellite of Jupiter. [Lat. *Adrāstēa,* a daughter of Jupiter < Gk. *Adrásteia.*]

ad rem (ăd rĕm) *adj.* Relevant; pertinent. ❖ *adv.* To the point; relevantly. [Lat. : *ad,* to + *rem,* accusative of *rēs,* matter, thing.]

ad·re·nal (ə-drē′nəl) *adj.* **1.** At, near, or on the kidneys. **2.** Of or relating to the adrenal glands or their secretions. ❖ *n.* An adrenal gland. [AD- + RENAL.] —**ad're•nal•ly** *adv.*

adrenal gland *n.* Either of two small endocrine glands, one located above each kidney, consisting of the cortex, which secretes several steroid hormones, and the medulla, which secretes epinephrine.

A•dren•a•lin (ə-drĕn′ə-lĭn) A trademark used for a medicinal preparation of epinephrine.

a•dren•a•line (ə-drĕn′ə-lĭn) *n.* See **epinephrine** 1.

ad•re•nal•ize (ə-drē′nə-līz′, ə-drĕn′ə-) *tr.v.* **-ized, -iz•ing, -izes** To stir up and spur to action.

ad•re•ner•gic (ăd′rə-nûr′jĭk) *adj.* **1.** Activated by or releasing epinephrine or an epinephrinelike substance, esp. in the sympathetic nervous system. **2.** Having physiological effects like those of epinephrine. [ADREN(ALINE) + -ERGIC.] —**ad're•ner'gi•cal•ly** *adv.*

a•dre•no•chrome (ə-drē′nō-krōm′, -nə-) *n.* A naturally occurring chemical formed during the oxidation of epinephrine. [ADREN(ALINE) + CHROME.]

ad•re•no•cor•ti•cal (ə-drē′nō-kôr′tĭ-kəl) *adj.* Of, relating to, or derived from the cortex of an adrenal gland. [ADREN(AL) + CORTICAL.]

ad•re•no•cor•ti•co•ster•oid (ə-drē′nō-kôr′tĭ-kō-stîr′oid, -stĕr′-) *n.* Any of various steroids derived from the cortex of an adrenal gland. [ADREN(AL) + CORTICOSTEROID.]

ad•re•no•cor•ti•co•trop•ic (ə-drē′nō-kôr′tĭ-kō-trŏp′ĭk, -trō′pĭk) also **ad•re•no•cor•ti•co•troph•ic** (-trŏf′ĭk, -trō′fĭk) *adj.* Stimulating or otherwise acting on the cortex of an adrenal gland. [ADREN(AL) + CORTICO- + -TROPIC.]

adrenocorticotropic hormone also **adrenocorticotrophic hormone** *n.* ACTH.

ad•re•no•cor•ti•co•trop•in (ə-drē′nō-kôr′tĭ-kō-trŏp′ĭn, -trō′pĭn) also **ad•re•no•cor•ti•co•troph•in** (-trŏf′ĭn, trō′fĭn) *n.* See **ACTH.** [ADREN(AL) + CORTICOTROPIN.]

A•dri•an IV (ā′drē-ən) Orig. Nicholas Breakspear. 1100?–59. English-born pope (1154–59).

Adrian, Edgar Douglas. 1st Baron Adrian. 1889–1977. British physiologist who shared a 1932 Nobel Prize.

A•dri•a•no•ple (ā′drē-ə-nō′pəl) See **Edirne.**

A•dri•at•ic Sea (ā′drē-ăt′ĭk) An arm of the Mediterranean Sea between Italy and the Balkan Peninsula.

a•drift (ə-drĭft′) *adv. & adj.* **1.** Drifting or floating freely; not anchored. **2.** Without direction or purpose.

a•droit (ə-droit′) *adj.* **1.** Dexterous; deft. **2.** Skillful and adept under pressing conditions. See Syns at **dexterous.** [Fr. < *à droit*: *à,* to (< Lat. *ad*) + *droit,* right (< Lat. *dīrēctus;* see DIRECT.] —**a•droit′ly** *adv.* —**a•droit′ness** *n.*

ad•sci•ti•tious (ăd′sĭ-tĭsh′əs) *adj.* Not inherent or essential; derived from something outside. [< Lat. *adscītus,* p. part. of *adscīscere,* to adopt: *ad-,* ad- + *scīscere,* to accept, inchoative of *scīre,* to know.]

ADSL *abbr.* Asymmetric Digital Subscriber Line

ad•sorb (ăd-sôrb′, -zôrb′) *tr.v.* **-sorbed, -sorb•ing, -sorbs** To take up by adsorption. [AD- + Lat. *sorbēre,* to suck.] —**ad•sorb′a•bil•i•ty** *n.* —**ad•sorb′a•ble** *adj.*

ad•sor•bate (ăd-sôr′bĭt, -bāt′, -zôr′-) *n.* An adsorbed substance.

ad•sor•bent (ăd-sôr′bənt, -zôr′-) *adj.* Capable of adsorption. ❖ *n.* An adsorptive material, such as activated charcoal.

ad•sorp•tion (ăd-sôrp′shən, -zôrp′-) *n.* The accumulation of gases, liquids, or solutes on the surface of a solid or liquid. [< ADSORB.] —**ad•sorp′tive** (-tĭv) *adj.*

ad•su•ki bean (ăd-sōō′kē, -zōō′-) *n.* Variant of **adzuki bean.**

ad•u•lar•i•a (ăj′ə-lâr′ē-ə, -lăr′-) *n.* A variety of transparent or translucent orthoclase. [Ital. < Fr. *adulaire,* after *Adula,* a mountain group of southeast Switzerland.]

ad•u•late (ăj′ə-lāt′) *tr.v.* **-lat•ed, -lat•ing, -lates** To praise or admire excessively. [Back-formation < ADULATION.] —**ad′u•la′tor** *n.* —**ad′u•la•to′ry** (-lə-tôr′ē, -tōr′ē) *adj.*

ad•u•la•tion (ăj′ə-lā′shən) *n.* Excessive flattery or admiration. [ME *adulacioun* < OFr. < Lat. *adūlātiō, adūlātiōn-* < *adūlātus,* p. part. of *adūlārī,* to flatter.]

a•dult (ə-dŭlt′, ăd′ŭlt) *n.* **1.** One who has attained maturity or legal age. **2.** *Biology* A fully grown, mature organism. ❖ *adj.* **1.** Fully developed and mature. **2.** Intended for or befitting adults: *adult education.* **3.** Containing or dealing in explicitly sexual material; pornographic: *adult movies.* [< Lat. *adultus,* p. part. of *adolēscere,* to grow up. See ADOLESCENT.] —**a•dult′hood′** *n.* —**a•dult′ness** *n.*

a•dul•ter•ant (ə-dŭl′tər-ənt) *n.* A substance that adulterates. ❖ *adj.* Serving to adulterate.

a•dul•ter•ate (ə-dŭl′tə-rāt′) *tr.v.* **-at•ed, -at•ing, -ates** To make impure by adding extraneous, improper, or inferior ingredients. [Lat. *adulterāre, adulterāt-,* to pollute. See al- in App.] —**a•dul′ter•a′tion** *n.* —**a•dul′ter•a′tor** *n.*

a•dul•ter•er (ə-dŭl′tər-ər) *n.* One who commits adultery.

a•dul•ter•ess (ə-dŭl′trĭs, -tər-ĭs) *n.* A woman who commits adultery. See Usage Note at **-ess.**

a•dul•ter•ine (ə-dŭl′tə-rīn′, -rĕn′) *adj.* **1.** Characterized by adulteration; spurious. **2.** Unauthorized by law; illegal. **3.** Born of

adultery. [Lat. *adulterīnus* < *adulter,* adulterer, perh. back-formation < *adulterāre,* to pollute. See ADULTERATE.]

a•dul•ter•ous (ə-dŭl′tər-əs, -trəs) *adj.* Relating to, inclined to, or marked by adultery. —**a•dul′ter•ous•ly** *adv.*

a•dul•ter•y (ə-dŭl′tə-rē, -trē) *n., pl.* **-ies** Voluntary sexual intercourse between a married person and a partner other than the lawful spouse. [ME < OFr. *adultere* < Lat. *adulterium* < *adulter,* adulterer. See ADULTERATE.]

a•dult-on•set diabetes (ə-dŭlt′ŏn′sĕt, -ôn′-) *n.* See **diabetes mellitus.**

ad•um•brate (ăd′əm-brāt′, ə-dŭm′-) *tr.v.* **-brat•ed, -brat•ing, -brates 1.** To give a sketchy outline of. **2.** To prefigure indistinctly; foreshadow. **3.** To disclose partially or guardedly. **4.** To overshadow; shadow or obscure. [Lat. *adumbrāre, adumbrāt-,* to represent in outline: *ad-,* ad- + *umbra,* shadow.] —**ad′um•bra′tion** *n.* —**ad•um′bra•tive** (ə-dŭm′brə-tĭv) *adj.* —**ad•um′bra•tive•ly** *adv.*

a•dust (ə-dŭst′) *adj.* **1.** Burned; scorched. **2.** *Archaic* Browned by the sun; sunburned. **3.** *Archaic* Melancholy in appearance or temperament; gloomy. [ME < Lat. *adustus,* p. part. of *adūrere,* to set fire to: *ad-,* ad- + *ūrere,* to burn.]

adv. *abbr.* **1.** adverb **2.** *Latin* adversus (against)

ad va•lo•rem (ăd′ və-lôr′əm, -lōr′-) *adj.* In proportion to the value: *ad valorem duties on imported goods.* [NLat. *ad valōrem* : Lat. *ad,* to + LLat. *valōrem,* accusative of *valor,* value.]

ad•vance (ăd-văns′) *v.* **-vanced, -vanc•ing, -vanc•es** —*tr.* **1.** To move or cause to move forward: *advance a chess piece.* **2.** To put forward; propose or suggest: *advanced a novel theory during the seminar.* **3.** To aid the growth or progress of: *advanced the cause of freedom.* **4.** To raise in rank; promote. **5.** To cause to occur sooner: *advance a deadline.* **6.** To raise in amount or rate; increase. **7.** To pay (money or interest) before due. **8.** To supply or lend, esp. on credit. —*intr.* **1.** To go or move forward or onward. **2.** To make progress; improve. **3.** To rise in rank, position, or value. ❖ *n.* **1.** The act or process of moving or going forward. **2.** A forward move; an improvement: *an advance in research.* **3.** An increase of price or value. **4. advances** Opening approaches to secure acquaintance or favor. **5a.** The furnishing of funds or goods on credit. **b.** The funds or goods so furnished. **6.** Payment of money before due. **7.** Preparation, esp. publicity, done prior to an event. ❖ *adj.* **1.** Made or given ahead of time: *an advance payment.* **2.** Going before, in front, or forward. —*idioms:* **in advance** Ahead of time; beforehand. **in advance of** In front of; ahead of. [ME *avauncen* < OFr. *avauncer* < VLat. **abantiāre* < Lat. *abante,* from before : *ab-,* ab- + *ante,* before; see **ant-** in App.] —**ad•vanc′er** *n.*

SYNONYMS *advance, forward, foster, further, promote* These verbs mean to cause to move ahead, as toward a goal: *advance a worthy cause; forwarding their own interests; fostered friendly relations; furthering your career; efforts to promote sales.*

USAGE NOTE *Advance* as a noun is used for forward movement (*the advance of the army*) or for progress or improvement in a figurative sense. *Advancement* is used mainly in the figurative sense: *career advancement.* In this use, moreover, there is a distinction between the two terms deriving from the transitive and intransitive forms of the verb *advance.* Thus, *the advance of science* means simply the progress of science, whereas *the advancement of science* implies progress resulting from the action of an agent or force: *The purpose of the legislation was the advancement of science.*

---

ad•vanced (ăd-vănst′) *adj.* **1.** Highly developed or complex. **2.** Being at a higher level than others: *an advanced textbook.* **3.** Ahead of the times; progressive: *advanced teaching methods.* **4.** Far along in course or time: *an advanced stage of illness.*

advanced standing *n.* The status of a college student granted credit for courses taken elsewhere.

advance guard *n.* A detachment of troops sent ahead of a main force to reconnoiter and provide protection.

advance man or **ad•vance•man** (ăd-văns′măn′) *n.* A man who travels ahead to arrange scheduling, publicity, and security for someone making a public appearance.

ad•vance•ment (ăd-văns′mənt) *n.* **1.** A forward step; an improvement. **2.** Development; progress: *the advancement of knowledge.* **3.** A promotion, as in rank. **4.** The act of moving forward. See Usage Note at **advance.**

ad•van•tage (ăd-văn′tĭj) *n.* **1.** A beneficial factor or combination of factors. **2.** Benefit or profit; gain: *It is to your advantage to invest wisely.* **3.** A relatively favorable position: *Good education gave us the advantage.* **4.** *Sports* **a.** The first point scored in tennis after deuce. **b.** The resulting score. ❖ *tr.v.* **-taged, -tag•ing, -tag•es** To afford profit or gain to; benefit. —*idioms:* **take advantage of 1.** To put to good use; avail oneself of: *take advantage of all opportunities.* **2.** To profit selfishly by; exploit: *took advantage of the customer.* **to advantage** To good effect; favorably. [ME *avantage* < OFr. < *avant,* before < Lat. *abante,* from before. See ADVANCE.]

ad•van•ta•geous (ăd′văn-tā′jəs, -vən-) *adj.* Affording advantage; beneficial. See Syns at **beneficial.** —**ad′van•ta′geous•ly** *adv.* —**ad′van•ta′geous•ness** *n.*

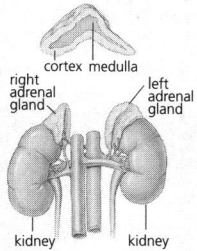

adrenal gland
top: cross section of a right adrenal gland
bottom: placement of adrenal glands relative to kidneys

cortex medulla
right adrenal gland
left adrenal gland
kidney   kidney

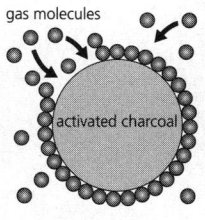

gas molecules
activated charcoal

adsorption
Activated charcoal in a gas mask attracts toxic gas molecules, allowing the person wearing the mask to breathe fresh air.

ă pat oi boy
ā pay ou out
âr care ŏŏ took
ä father ōō boot
ĕ pet ŭ cut
ē be ûr urge
ĭ pit th thin
ī pie th this
îr pier hw which
ŏ pot zh vision
ō toe ə about,
ô paw   item

Stress marks:
′ (primary);
′ (secondary), as in
lexicon (lĕk′sĭ-kŏn′)

ad·vect (ăd-vĕkt′) *tr.v.* **-vect·ed, -vect·ing, -vects 1.** To convey horizontally by advection. **2.** To transport (a substance) by advection. [Back-formation < ADVECTION.]

ad·vec·tion (ăd-vĕk′shən) *n.* **1.** The transfer of an atmospheric property, such as temperature, by the movement of air, esp. horizontally. **2.** The rate of change of an atmospheric property caused by the horizontal movement of air. **3.** The horizontal movement of water, as in an ocean current. [Lat. *advectiō, advection-*, act of conveying < *advectus,* p. part. of *advehere,* to carry to : *ad-,* ad- + *vehere,* to carry; see **wegh-** in App.]

ad·vent (ăd′vĕnt′) *n.* **1.** A coming or arrival: *the advent of the computer.* **2.** also **Advent** *Christianity* **a.** The liturgical period preceding Christmas, observed by many Christians as a season of prayer, fasting, and penitence. **b.** The coming of Jesus at the Incarnation. **c.** See **Second Coming.** [ME, the Advent season < OFr. < Lat. *adventus,* arrival < p. part. of *advenīre,* to come to : *ad-,* ad- + *venīre,* to come; see **gʷā-** in App.]

Ad·vent·ist (ăd′vĕn′tĭst, ăd-vĕn′-) *n.* A member of any of several Christian denominations that believe the Second Coming and the end of the world are near. —**Ad′vent·ism** *n.*

ad·ven·ti·tia (ăd′vĕn-tĭsh′ə, -vən-) *n.* The membranous outer covering of an organ or a blood vessel. [NLat. < *adventīcius,* foreign. See ADVENTITIOUS.] —**ad′ven·ti′tial** *adj.*

ad·ven·ti·tious (ăd′vĕn-tĭsh′əs, -vən-) *adj.* **1.** Not inherent but added extrinsically. **2.** *Biology* Of or belonging to a structure that develops in an unusual place. [< Lat. *adventīcius,* foreign < *adventus,* arrival. See ADVENT.] —**ad′ven·ti′tious·ly** *adv.* —**ad′ven·ti′tious·ness** *n.*

ad·ven·tive (ăd-vĕn′tĭv) *adj.* Not native to and not fully established in a new habitat or environment: *an adventive weed.* ❖ *n.* An adventive organism. [< Lat. *adventus,* arrival. See ADVENT.] —**ad·ven′tive·ly** *adv.*

Advent Sunday *n.* The first Sunday of Advent in Western Christianity.

ad·ven·ture (ăd-vĕn′chər) *n.* **1.** A hazardous or uncertain undertaking. **2.** An unusual or exciting experience. **3.** Participation in hazardous or exciting experiences: *the love of adventure.* **4.** A financial speculation or business venture. ❖ *v.* **-tured, -tur·ing, -tures** *—tr.* **1.** To venture upon; undertake or try. **2.** To expose to danger or risk; hazard. *—intr.* **1.** To take a risk; dare. **2.** To proceed despite risks. [ME *aventure* < OFr. < Lat. *adventūrus,* fut. part. of *advenīre,* to arrive. See ADVENT.]

ad·ven·tur·er (ăd-vĕn′chər-ər) *n.* **1.** One that seeks adventure. **2.** A soldier of fortune. **3.** A heavy speculator in stocks, business, or trade. **4.** One that attempts to gain wealth and social position by unscrupulous means.

ad·ven·ture·some (ăd-vĕn′chər-səm) *adj.* Disposed to engage in risky activities or enterprises. —**ad·ven′ture·some·ly** *adv.* —**ad·ven′ture·some·ness** *n.*

ad·ven·tur·ess (ăd-vĕn′chər-ĭs) *n.* A woman who seeks social and financial advancement by unscrupulous means. See Usage Note at **-ess.**

ad·ven·tur·ism (ăd-vĕn′chə-rĭz′əm) *n.* Involvement in risky enterprises, esp. in international affairs. —**ad·ven′tur·ist** *adj. & n.* —**ad·ven′tur·is′tic** *adj.*

ad·ven·tur·ous (ăd-vĕn′chər-əs) *adj.* **1.** Inclined to undertake new and daring enterprises. **2.** Hazardous; risky. —**ad·ven′tur·ous·ly** *adv.* —**ad·ven′tur·ous·ness** *n.*

ad·verb (ăd′vûrb) *n.* **1.** The part of speech that modifies a verb, adjective, or other adverb. **2.** Any of the words belonging to this part of speech, such as *rapidly.* [ME *adverbe* < OFr. < Lat. *adverbium* (transl. of Gk. *epirrhēma*) : *ad-,* in relation to; see AD- + *verbum,* word; see **wer-**¹ in App.]

ad·ver·bi·al (ăd-vûr′bē-əl) *adj.* Of, relating to, or being an adverb. ❖ *n.* An adverbial element or phrase. —**ad·ver′bi·al·ly** *adv.*

ad ver·bum (ăd-vûr′bəm) *adv.* Word for word; verbatim. [Lat. : *ad,* in accordance with + *verbum,* word.]

ad·ver·sar·i·al (ăd′vər-sâr′ē-əl) *adj.* Relating to or characteristic of an adversary.

ad·ver·sar·y (ăd′vər-sĕr′ē) *n., pl.* **-ies 1.** An opponent; an enemy. **2. Adversary** The Devil; Satan. Often used with *the.* [ME *adversarie* < Lat. *adversārius,* enemy < *adversus,* against. See ADVERSE.]

ad·ver·sa·tive (ăd-vûr′sə-tĭv) *adj.* Expressing antithesis or opposition: *the adversative conjunction but.* ❖ *n.* A word that expresses antithesis or opposition. [Lat. *adversātīvus < adversātus,* p. part. of *adversārī,* to oppose < *adversus,* against. See ADVERSE.] —**ad·ver′sa·tive·ly** *adv.*

ad·verse (ăd-vûrs′, ăd′vûrs′) *adj.* **1.** Acting or serving to oppose; antagonistic: *adverse criticism.* **2.** Contrary to one's interests or welfare; harmful or unfavorable: *adverse circumstances.* **3.** Moving in an opposite or opposing direction: *adverse currents.* **4.** *Archaic* Placed opposite. [ME < OFr. *advers* < Lat. *adversus,* p. part. of *advertere,* to turn toward : *ad-,* ad- + *vertere,* to turn; see **wer-**² in App.] —**ad·verse′ly** *adv.* —**ad·verse′ness** *n.*

ad·ver·si·ty (ăd-vûr′sĭ-tē) *n., pl.* **-ties 1.** A state of hardship or affliction; misfortune. **2.** A calamitous event.

ad·vert¹ (ăd-vûrt′) *intr.v.* **-vert·ed, -vert·ing, -verts 1.** To turn attention. Used with *to.* **2.** To call attention; refer. Used with *to: advert to a problem.* [ME *adverten* < OFr. *advertir,* to notice < Lat.

advertere, to turn toward. See ADVERSE.]

ad·vert² (ăd′vûrt) *n. Chiefly British* An advertisement.

ad·ver·tise (ăd′vər-tīz′) *v.* **-tised, -tis·ing, -tis·es** *—tr.* **1.** To make public announcement of, esp. to proclaim the qualities or advantages of (a product or business) so as to increase sales. **2.** To make known; call attention to: *advertised my intention to resign.* **3.** To warn or notify: *"This event advertises me that there is such a fact as death"* (Henry David Thoreau). *—intr.* **1.** To call the attention of the public to a product or business. **2.** To inquire or seek in a public notice, as in a newspaper. [ME *advertisen,* to notify < OFr. *advertir, advertiss-,* to notice. See ADVERT¹.] —**ad′ver·tis′er** *n.*

ad·ver·tise·ment (ăd′vər-tīz′mənt, ăd-vûr′tĭs-, -tĭz-) *n.* **1.** The act of advertising. **2.** A notice, such as a poster or a paid announcement in the print, broadcast, or electronic media, designed to attract public attention or patronage.

ad·ver·tis·ing (ăd′vər-tī′zĭng) *n.* **1.** The activity of attracting public attention to a product or business, as by paid announcements in the print, broadcast, or electronic media. **2.** The business of designing and writing advertisements. **3.** Advertisements considered as a group.

ad·ver·to·ri·al (ăd′vər-tôr′ē-əl, -tōr′-) *n.* An advertisement promoting the interests or opinions of a corporate sponsor, often presented in such a way as to resemble an editorial. [ADVER(TISEMENT) + (EDI)TORIAL.]

ad·vice (ăd-vīs′) *n.* **1.** Opinion about what could or should be done about a situation or problem; counsel. **2.** Information communicated; news. Often used in the plural: *advices from an ambassador.* [ME *avis, advice* < OFr. *avis < (ester) a vis,* to seem : *a,* to (< Lat. *ad*) + *vis,* seen (< Lat. *vīsum,* what seems (good) < neut. p. part. of *vidēre,* to see; see **weid-** in App.).]

SYNONYMS *advice, counsel, recommendation* These nouns denote an opinion as to a decision or course of action: *sound advice for the unemployed; accepted my attorney's counsel; will follow your recommendation.*

ad·vis·a·ble (ăd-vī′zə-bəl) *adj.* Worthy of being recommended or suggested; prudent. —**ad·vis′a·bil′i·ty, ad·vis′a·ble·ness** *n.* —**ad·vis′a·bly** *adv.*

ad·vise (ăd-vīz′) *v.* **-vised, -vis·ing, -vis·es** *—tr.* **1.** To offer advice to; counsel. **2.** To recommend; suggest: *advised patience.* **3.** *Usage Problem* To inform; notify. *—intr.* **1.** To take counsel; consult: *advised with her boss.* **2.** To offer advice. [ME *avisen, advisen* < OFr. *aviser < avis,* advice. See ADVICE.] —**ad·vis′er, ad·vis′or** *n.*

ad·vised (ăd-vīzd′) *adj.* **1.** Thought out; considered. Often used in combination: *well-advised; ill-advised.* **2.** Informed: *Keep me advised of further developments.*

ad·vis·ed·ly (ăd-vī′zĭd-lē) *adv.* With careful consideration.

ad·vi·see (ăd-vī-zē′) *n.* One that is advised.

ad·vise·ment (ăd-vīz′mənt) *n.* Careful consideration: *Your request will be taken under advisement.*

ad·vi·so·ry (ăd-vī′zə-rē) *adj.* **1.** Empowered to advise: *an advisory committee.* **2.** Relating to or containing advice: *an advisory memorandum.* ❖ *n., pl.* **-ries** A report giving information, esp. a warning: *a weather advisory.*

ad·vo·ca·cy (ăd′və-kə-sē) *n.* The act of pleading or arguing in favor of something, such as a cause; active support.

ad·vo·cate (ăd′və-kāt′) *tr.v.* **-cat·ed, -cat·ing, -cates** To speak, plead, or argue in favor of. See Syns at **support.** ❖ *n.* (-kĭt, -kāt′) **1.** One that argues for a cause; a supporter or defender: *an advocate of civil rights.* **2.** One that pleads in another's behalf; an intercessor. **3.** A lawyer. [< ME *advocat,* lawyer < OFr. *advocat* < Lat. *advocātus,* p. part. of *advocāre,* to summon for counsel : *ad-,* ad- + *vocāre,* to call; see **wekʷ-** in App.] —**ad′vo·ca′tion** *n.* —**ad′vo·ca′tor** *n.* —**ad·voc′a·to′ry** (ăd-vŏk′ə-tôr′ē, -tōr′ē, ăd′və-kə-) *adj.*

ad·vow·son (ăd-vou′zən) *n.* The right in English ecclesiastical law of presentation to a vacant benefice. [ME *avouson* < OFr. *avoeson* < Med.Lat. *advocātia* < Lat. *advocātiō,* a summoning < *advocāre,* to summon. See ADVOCATE.]

ad·wom·an (ăd′wŏom′ən) *n.* A woman who designs, writes, acquires, or sells advertising.

ad·y·tum (ăd′ĭ-təm) *n., pl.* **-ta** (-tə) The sanctum in an ancient temple. [Lat. < Gk. *aduton < adutos,* not to be entered : *a-,* not; see A-¹ + *duein,* to enter.]

adz or **adze** (ădz) *n.* An axlike tool with a curved blade at right angles to the handle, used for shaping wood. [ME *adese* < OE *adesa.*]

adz

Ad·zhar·i·a or **A·jar·i·a** (ə-jär′ē-ə) An autonomous republic of SW Georgia bordering on the Black Sea and Turkey. —**Ad·zhar′** (ə-jär′) *n.* —**Ad·zhar′i·an** *adj. & n.*

ad·zu·ki bean (ăd-zōō′kē) also **ad·su·ki bean** (-sōō′-, -zōō′-)

n. 1. An erect or twining East Asian herb (*Vigna angularis*) of the pea family, having edible sprouts and reddish seeds used to make flour. **2.** A seed of this plant. [J. *azuki*.]

ae·des (ā-ēʹdēz) *n., pl.* **aedes** A mosquito of the genus *Aëdes,* including *A. aegypti,* which transmits diseases such as yellow fever and dengue. [NLat. *Aëdēs,* genus name < Gk. *aēdēs,* unpleasant : *a-,* not; see A–¹ + *ēdos,* pleasure; see **swād-** in App.] —a·eʹdine (-dīn, -dēn) *adj.*

ae·dile (ēʹdīl) *n.* An elected official of ancient Rome who was responsible for public works and games, markets, the grain supply, and the water supply. [Lat. *aedīlis* < *aedēs,* house.]

Ae·ga·de·an Isles (ē-gāʹdē'ən) also **Ae·ga·tes** (-tēz) See Egadi Islands.

Ae·ge·an (ĭ-jēʹən) *adj.* **1.** Of or relating to the Aegean Sea. **2.** Of or relating to the Bronze Age civilization that flourished in the Aegean area, as at Crete.

Aegean Sea An arm of the Mediterranean off SE Europe between Greece and Turkey. The **Aegean Islands** include the Cyclades, the Dodecanese, and the Sporades.

Ae·geus (ēʹjōos, ēʹjē-əs) *n. Greek Mythology* A king of Athens and the father of Theseus.

Ae·gi·na (ĭ-jīʹnə) An island off SE Greece in the Saronic Gulf of the Aegean Sea near Athens.

Aeg·ir (ăgʹər, ĕjʹīr) *n. Mythology* The Norse god of the sea.

ae·gis also **e·gis** (ēʹjĭs) *n.* **1.** Protection: *a child under the aegis of the courts.* **2.** Sponsorship; patronage: *a concert held under the aegis of the parents' association.* **3.** Guidance, direction, or control. **4.** *Greek Mythology* The goatskin shield or breastplate of Zeus, later of Athena, carrying at its center the head of Medusa. [Lat. < Gk. *aigis,* goatskin, skin shield, aegis < *aix, aig-,* goat.]

Ae·gis·thus (ĭ-jĭsʹthəs) *n. Greek Mythology* The son of Thyestes and lover of Clytemnestra who helped Clytemnestra kill Agamemnon upon Agamemnon's return from the Trojan War.

Ae·gos·pot·a·mi (ēʹgəs-pŏtʹə-mī') or **Ae·gos·pot·a·mos** (-mŏs') A river and ancient town of S Thrace in present-day W Turkey; site of the final battle of the Peloponnesian War, in which the Spartans destroyed the Athenian fleet (405 B.C.).

Ael·fric (ălʹfrĭk) Also called "Grammaticus." 955?–1020? Anglo-Saxon abbot whose works include *Lives of the Saints* and a Latin grammar.

–aemia *suff.* Variant of **–emia.**

Ae·ne·as (ĭ-nēʹəs) *n. Greek & Roman Mythology* The Trojan hero of the *Aeneid* who escaped the sack of Troy and wandered for seven years before settling in Italy.

a·e·ne·ous or **a·e·ne·us** (ā-ēʹnē-əs) *adj.* Brassy or golden green in color. [< Lat. *aēneus,* of bronze < *aes,* bronze.]

Ae·o·li·an (ē-ōʹlē-ən) *adj.* **1.** Of or relating to Aeolis or its people or culture. **2.** *Greek Mythology* Of or relating to Aeolus. **3.** **aeolian** Variant of **eolian.** ❖ *n.* **1.** One of a Hellenic people of central Greece that occupied Aeolis and Lesbos around 1100 B.C. **2.** See Aeolic 1.

Aeolian harp *n.* An instrument consisting of an open box over which are stretched strings that sound when the wind passes over them. [< AEOLIAN, relating to Aeolus, god of the winds.]

Ae·o·lic (ē-ōʹlĭk) *n.* **1.** A group of dialects of ancient Greek spoken by the Aeolians. **2.** Any of several verse forms built around a central choriamb, used esp. by Sappho and Alcaeus.

Ae·o·lis (ēʹō-lĭs) or **Ae·o·li·a** (ē-ōʹlē-ə) An ancient region of W Asia Minor in present-day Turkey.

Ae·o·lus (ēʹə-ləs) *n.* **1.** *Greek Mythology* The god of the winds. **2.** A king of Thessaly and ancestor of the Aeolians. [Lat. < Gk. *Aiolos* < *aiolos,* quick, changeable.]

ae·on (ēʹŏn', ēʹən) *n.* Variant of **eon.**

ae·o·ni·an (ē-ōʹnē-ən) *adj.* Variant of **eonian.**

ae·py·or·nis (ēʹpē-ôrʹnĭs) *n.* A genus of extinct, large, flightless birds native to Madagascar. [NLat. *Aepyornis,* genus name : Gk. *aipus,* high + Gk. *ornis,* bird.]

aer·ate (ârʹāt) *tr.v.* **-at·ed, -at·ing, -ates** **1.** To supply with air or expose to the circulation of air. **2.** To expose to oxygen, as in the oxygenation of the blood by respiration. **3.** To supply or charge (liquid) with a gas, esp. to charge with carbon dioxide. —aerʹa·tion *n.*

aer·a·tor (ârʹāʹtər) *n.* One that aerates, as a machine for aerating turf or a device for aerating liquids.

aer·i·al (ârʹē-əl, ā-îrʹē-əl) *adj.* **1.** Of, in, or caused by the air. **2.** Living in the air. **3.** Reaching high into the air; lofty. **4.** Suggestive of air, as in lightness; airy. **5.** Unsubstantial; imaginary. **6.** Of, for, or by means of aircraft: *aerial photography.* **7.** *Botany* Growing or borne above the ground or water: *aerial roots.* ❖ *n.* (ârʹē-əl) A radio antenna, esp. one suspended in or extending into the air. [< Lat. *āerius* < Gk. *āerios* < *āēr,* air.]

aer·i·al·ist (ârʹē-ə-lĭst) *n.* An acrobat who performs in the air, as on a trapeze or tightrope.

aerial ladder *n.* A ladder that can be extended to reach high places, esp. one mounted on a fire engine.

aerial yam *n.* See air potato.

aer·ie or **aer·y** also **ey·rie** or **ey·ry** (ârʹē, îrʹē) *n., pl.* **-ies 1.** The nest of a bird, such as an eagle, built on a cliff or other high place. **2.** A house or stronghold perched on a height. [Med.Lat. *aeria* < OFr. *aire* < Lat. *ārea,* open space, threshing-floor.]

aero- or **aer-** *pref.* **1a.** Air; atmosphere: *aeroballistics.* **b.** Gas:

osol. **2.** Aviation: *aeronautics.* [Gk. *āero-* < *āēr,* air.]

aer·o·al·ler·gen (ârʹō-ălʹər-jən) *n.* Any of various airborne substances, such as pollen or spores, that can cause an allergic response.

aer·o·bal·lis·tics (ârʹō-bə-lĭsʹtĭks) *n.* (*used with a sing. verb*) Ballistics, esp. of missiles, in the atmosphere. —aerʹo·bal·lisʹtic *adj.*

aer·o·bat·ics (ârʹō-bătʹĭks) *n.* (*used with a sing. or pl. verb*) Stunts, such as rolls and loops, performed in an aircraft. [AERO- + (ACRO)BATICS.] —aerʹo·batʹ *n.* —aerʹo·batʹic *adj.*

aer·obe (ârʹōb) *n.* An organism, such as a bacterium, requiring oxygen to live. [Fr. *aérobie* : Gk. *āēr,* air; see AERO- + Gk. *bios,* life; see gʷeiə- in App.]

aer·o·bic (â-rōʹbĭk) *adj.* **1.** *Biology* **a.** Living or occurring only in the presence of oxygen: *aerobic bacteria.* **b.** Of or relating to aerobes. **2.** Involving or improving oxygen consumption by the body: *aerobic exercise.* **3.** Relating to or used in aerobics: *aerobic shoes.* —aerʹo·bi·cal·ly *adv.*

aer·o·bics (â-rōʹbĭks) *n.* (*used with a sing. or pl. verb*) **1.** A system of physical conditioning designed to enhance circulatory and respiratory efficiency that involves vigorous, sustained exercise, such as jogging, swimming, or cycling. **2.** A program of physical fitness that involves such exercise. [< AEROBIC.]

aer·o·bi·ol·o·gy (ârʹō-bī-ŏlʹə-jē) *n.* The study of the sources, dispersion, and effects of airborne biological materials, such as pollen, spores, and microorganisms. —aerʹo·bi·o·logʹi·cal (-ə-lŏjʹĭ-kəl) *adj.* —aerʹo·bi·o·logʹi·cal·ly *adv.*

aer·o·bi·um (â-rōʹbē-əm) *n.* See aerobe. [NLat. *āerobium* < AEROBE.]

aer·o·brak·ing (ârʹō-brāʹkĭng) *n.* The use of atmospheric drag rather than onboard thrusters to reduce the velocity of a satellite or spacecraft.

aer·o·cul·ture (ârʹō-kŭlʹchər) *n.* See aeroponics. [AERO- + (AGRI)CULTURE.]

aer·o·drome (ârʹə-drōm') *n. Chiefly British* An airdrome.

aer·o·dy·nam·ic (ârʹō-dī-nămʹĭk) also **aer·o·dy·nam·i·cal** (-ĭ-kəl) *adj.* **1.** Of or relating to aerodynamics. **2.** Designed to reduce wind drag. —aerʹo·dy·namʹi·cal·ly *adv.*

aer·o·dy·nam·ics (ârʹō-dī-nămʹĭks) *n.* (*used with a sing. verb*) The dynamics of bodies moving relative to gases, esp. the interaction of moving objects with the atmosphere. —aerʹo·dy·namʹi·cist (-ĭ-sĭst) *n.*

aer·o·dyne (ârʹə-dīn') *n.* A heavier-than-air aircraft deriving lift from motion. [AERO- + Gk. *dunamis,* power (< *dunasthai,* to be able; see deu-² in App.).]

aer·o·em·bo·lism (ârʹō-ĕmʹbə-lĭzʹəm) *n.* Embolism that occurs as a result of the entrance of air bubbles into a blood vessel after surgical procedures or trauma.

aer·o·foil (ârʹō-foil') *n. Chiefly British* Variant of **airfoil.**

aer·o·gel (ârʹə-jĕl') *n.* A highly porous solid formed from a gel, such as silica gel, in which the liquid is replaced with a gas.

aer·o·gram also **aer·o·gramme** (ârʹə-grăm') *n.* An airmail letter in the form of a lightweight sheet of stationery that folds into its own envelope. [AERO- + (TELE)GRAM.]

aer·o·lite (ârʹə-līt') also **aer·o·lith** (-lĭth') *n.* A chiefly siliceous meteorite. —aerʹo·litʹic (-lĭtʹĭk) *adj.*

aer·ol·o·gy (â-rŏlʹə-jē) *n.* Meteorology of the total vertical extent of the atmosphere as opposed to the study of the atmosphere near Earth's surface. —aerʹo·logʹic (ârʹō-lŏjʹĭk), aerʹo·logʹi·cal *adj.* —aer·olʹo·gist *n.*

aer·o·mag·net·ics (ârʹō-măg-nĕtʹĭks) *n.* (*used with a sing. verb*) The science of magnetic characteristics associated with atmospheric conditions. —aerʹo·mag·netʹic *adj.* —aerʹo·mag·netʹi·cal·ly *adv.*

aer·o·me·chan·ics (ârʹō-mĭ-kănʹĭks) *n.* (*used with a sing. verb*) The science of the motion and equilibrium of air and other gases, comprising aerodynamics and aerostatics. —aerʹo·me·chanʹi·cal *adj.* —aerʹo·me·chanʹi·cal·ly *adv.*

aer·o·med·i·cine (ârʹō-mĕdʹĭ-sĭn) *n.* The medical study and treatment of physiological and psychological disorders associated with atmospheric or space flight. —aerʹo·medʹi·cal (-kəl) *adj.*

aer·o·me·te·or·o·graph (ârʹō-mēʹtē-ôrʹə-grăf', -ōrʹ-) *n.* An aircraft instrument for simultaneously recording temperature, atmospheric pressure, and humidity.

aer·om·e·ter (â-rŏmʹĭ-tər) *n.* An instrument for determining the weight and density of air or another gas.

aer·o·naut (ârʹə-nôt') *n.* A pilot of a lighter-than-air craft, such as a balloon. [AERO- + Gk. *nautēs,* sailor.]

aer·o·nau·tic (ârʹə-nôʹtĭk) also **aer·o·nau·ti·cal** (-tĭ-kəl) *adj.* Of or relating to aeronautics. —aerʹo·nauʹti·cal·ly *adv.*

aer·o·nau·tics (ârʹə-nôʹtĭks) *n.* (*used with a sing. verb*) **1.** The design and construction of aircraft. **2.** The theory and practice of aircraft navigation.

aer·o·neu·ro·sis (ârʹō-nōō-rōʹsĭs, -nyōō-) *n.* Nervous exhaustion attributed to prolonged piloting of aircraft.

aer·on·o·my (â-rŏnʹə-mē) *n.* The study of planetary atmospheres, esp. of regions of ionized gas in Earth's upper atmosphere. —aerʹo·nomʹic, aerʹo·nomʹi·cal *adj.* —aerʹo·nomʹist *n.*

aer·o·pause (ârʹō-pôz') *n.* The region of the atmosphere above which aircraft cannot fly.

aerobics

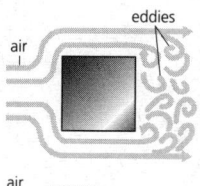

aerodynamics
top: high drag on a less
aerodynamic shape
bottom: low drag on a
more aerodynamic shape

ă	pat	oi	boy
ā	pay	ou	out
âr	care	ŏŏ	took
ä	father	ōō	boot
ĕ	pet	ŭ	cut
ē	be	ûr	urge
ĭ	pit	th	thin
ī	pie	th	this
îr	pier	hw	which
ŏ	pot	zh	vision
ō	toe	ə	about,
ô	paw		item

Stress marks:
ʹ (primary);
ʹ (secondary); as in
lexicon (lĕkʹsĭ-kŏn')

aer·o·pha·gia (âr′ə-fā′jə) *n.* The abnormal, spasmodic swallowing of air.

aer·o·pho·bi·a (âr′ə-fō′bē-ə) *n.* An abnormal fear of air, esp. drafts.

aer·o·phore (âr′ə-fôr′, -fōr′) *n.* An early portable breathing apparatus, formerly used in diving and mining.

aer·o·phyte (âr′ə-fīt′) *n.* See **epiphyte**.

aer·o·plane (âr′ə-plān′) *n. Chiefly British* Variant of **airplane**.

aer·o·pon·ics (âr′ə-pŏn′ĭks) *n.* (*used with a sing. verb*) A technique for growing plants without soil by suspending them and constantly misting the roots with nutrient-laden water. [AERO- + (HYDRO)PONICS.]

aer·o·sol (âr′ə-sôl′, -sŏl′) *n.* **1.** A gaseous suspension of fine solid or liquid particles. **2.** A substance, such as paint, packaged under pressure with a gaseous propellant for release as a spray of fine particles. [AERO- + SOL(UTION).]

aer·o·space (âr′ō-spās′) *adj.* **1.** Of or relating to Earth's atmosphere and the space beyond. **2.** Of or relating to the science or technology of flight. —**aer′o·space′** *n.*

aerospace medicine *n.* See **aeromedicine**.

aer·o·stat (âr′ō-stăt′) *n.* An aircraft, esp. a balloon or dirigible, that derives its lift from the buoyancy of surrounding air. [Fr. *aérostat* : Gk. *āero-*, aero-; see AERO- + Gk. *statos*, standing; see STATO-.] —**aer′o·stat′ic, aer′o·stat′i·cal** *adj.*

aer·o·stat·ics (âr′ō-stăt′ĭks) *n.* (*used with a sing. verb*) The science of gases in equilibrium and of the equilibrium of balloons or aircraft under changing atmospheric flight conditions.

aer·o·ther·mo·dy·nam·ics (âr′ō-thûr′mō-dī-năm′ĭks) *n.* **1.** (*used with a sing. verb*) The study of the thermodynamics of gases, esp. at high relative velocities. **2.** (*used with a pl. verb*) The thermodynamics of such gases. —**aer′o·ther′mo·dy·nam′ic** *adj.*

aer·y¹ (âr′ē, ā′ə-rē) *adj.* **-i·er, -i·est** Ethereal. [Lat. *āerius*, of the air. See AERIAL.]

aer·y² (âr′ē, îr′ē) *n.* Variant of **aerie**.

Aes·chy·lus (ĕs′kə-ləs, ē′skə-) 525–456 B.C. Greek tragic dramatist whose surviving plays include the *Oresteia* trilogy (458). —**Aes′chy·le′an** (-lē′ən) *adj.*

Aes·cu·la·pi·us (ĕs′kyə-lā′pē-əs) *n. Roman Mythology* The god of medicine and healing. [Lat. *Aesculapius*, Gk. *Asklēpios, Asklā-pios*, Asclepius.] —**Aes′cu·la′pi·an** *adj.*

Ae·sir (ā′sîr′, ā′zîr′) *pl.n. Mythology* The Norse gods. [ON, pl. of *āss*, god.]

Ae·sop (ē′sŏp, -sŏp′) 6th cent. B.C. Greek fabulist traditionally considered the author of *Aesop's Fables*. —**Ae·so′pi·an** (ē-sō′pē-ən), **Ae·sop′ic** (ē-sŏp′ĭk) *adj.*

aes·the·sia or **es·the·sia** (ĕs-thē′zhə) *n.* The ability to feel or perceive sensations. [Back-formation < ANESTHESIA.]

aes·thete or **es·thete** (ĕs′thēt) *n.* **1.** One who cultivates an unusual sensitivity to beauty, as in art or nature. **2.** One whose admiration of beauty is regarded as excessive or affected. [Back-formation < AESTHETIC.]

aes·thet·ic or **es·thet·ic** (ĕs-thĕt′ĭk) *adj.* **1.** Relating to aesthetics. **2.** Of or concerning the appreciation of beauty or good taste: *the aesthetic faculties.* **3.** Characterized by a heightened sensitivity to beauty. ❖ *n.* A conception of what is artistically valid or beautiful. [Ger. *ästhetisch* < NLat. *aesthēticus* < Gk. *aisthētikos*, of sense perception < *aisthēta*, perceptible things < *aisthanesthai*, to perceive.] —**aes·thet′i·cal·ly** *adv.*

aes·the·ti·cian or **es·the·ti·cian** (ĕs′thĭ-tĭsh′ən) *n.* **1.** One versed in the theory of beauty and artistic expression. **2.** One skilled in giving facials and other beauty treatments.

aes·thet·i·cism or **es·thet·i·cism** (ĕs-thĕt′ĭ-sĭz′əm) *n.* Devotion to and pursuit of the beautiful; sensitivity to artistic beauty and refined taste. **2.** The doctrine that beauty is the basic principle from which all other principles are derived.

aes·thet·ics or **es·thet·ics** (ĕs-thĕt′ĭks) *n.* (*used with a sing. verb*) **a.** The branch of philosophy that deals with the nature and expression of beauty, as in the fine arts. **b.** In Kantian philosophy, the branch of metaphysics concerned with the laws of perception. **2.** (*used with a sing. verb*) The study of the psychological responses to beauty and artistic experiences. **3.** (*used with a sing. or pl. verb*) A conception of what is artistically valid or beautiful: *minimalist aesthetics.* **4.** (*used with a sing. or pl. verb*) An artistically beautiful or pleasing appearance: *"They're looking for quality construction, not aesthetics"* (Ron Schram).

aes·ti·val (ĕs′tə-vəl) *adj.* Variant of **estival**.

aes·ti·vate (ĕs′tə-vāt′) *v.* Variant of **estivate**.

aes·ti·va·tion (ĕs′tə-vā′shən) *n.* Variant of **estivation**.

Aeth·el·red II (ĕth′əl-rĕd′) See **Ethelred II**.

Ae·ther (ē′thər) *n. Greek Mythology* The personification of the clear upper air breathed by the Olympians. [Lat. *Aethēr* < Gk. *aithēr*, upper air.]

ae·ti·ol·o·gy (ē′tē-ŏl′ə-jē) *n.* Variant of **etiology**.

Aet·na (ĕt′nə), **Mount** See Mount **Etna**.

Ae·to·li·a (ē-tō′lē-ə, -tōl′yə) An ancient region of central Greece. The **Aetolian League**, formed in 290 B.C., was defeated by the Achaeans later in the 3rd cent. —**Ae·to′li·an** *adj. & n.*

AF *abbr.* **1.** air force **2.** audio frequency

af- *pref.* Variant of **ad-** 1.

a·far (ə-fär′) *adv.* From, at, or to a great distance: *saw it afar off;*

traveled afar. ❖ *n.* A long distance: *Tales from afar.* [ME *afer* < *on fer*, far, and < *of fer*, from afar < OE *feor*, far, from afar. See FAR.]

A·fars and Is·sas (ə-färs′; ĭ′səs) See **Djibouti** 1.

AFB *abbr.* air force base

AFDC *abbr.* Aid to Families with Dependent Children

a·feard also **a·feared** (ə-fîrd′) *adj. Southern & Midland US* Afraid. [ME *afered* < OE *āfǣred*, p. part. of *āfǣran*, to frighten : *ā-*, intensive pref. + *fǣran*, to frighten (< *fǣr*, danger; see FEAR).]

a·feb·rile (ā-fĕb′rəl, ā-fē′brəl) *adj.* Having no fever.

af·fa·ble (ăf′ə-bəl) *adj.* **1.** Easy and pleasant to speak to; approachable. **2.** Gentle and gracious: *an affable smile.* [ME *affabil* < OFr. *affable* < Lat. *affabilis* < *affārī*, to speak to : *ad-*, ad- + *fārī*, to speak; see **bhā-** in App.] —**af′fa·bil′i·ty** *n.* —**af′fa·bly** *adv.*

af·fair (ə-fâr′) *n.* **1.** Something done or to be done; business. **2. affairs** Transactions and other matters of professional or public business: *affairs of state.* **3a.** An occurrence, object, or matter: *The senator's death was a tragic affair.* **b.** A social function. **4.** A matter of personal concern. **5. affairs** Personal business: *get one's affairs in order.* **6.** A matter causing public scandal and controversy: *the Dreyfus affair.* **7.** A sexual relationship between two people who are not married to each other. [ME *affaire* < OFr. *afaire* < *a faire*, to do : *a*, to (< Lat. *ad*) + *faire*, to do (< *facere*; see **dhē-** in App.).]

af·faire d'a·mour (ä-fâr′ dä-mōōr′) *n., pl.* **af·faires d'amour** (ä-fâr′) A love affair. [Fr. : *affaire*, affair + *de*, of + *amour*, love.]

af·faire de coeur (ä-fâr′ də kœr′) *n., pl.* **af·faires de coeur** (ä-fâr′) A love affair. [Fr. : *affaire*, affair + *de*, of + *cœur*, heart.]

af·faire d'hon·neur (ä-fâr′ dô-nœr′) *n., pl.* **af·faires d'hon·neur** (ä-fâr′) An affair of honor; a duel. [Fr. : *affaire*, affair + *de*, of + *honneur*, honor.]

af·fect¹ (ə-fĕkt′) *tr.v.* **-fect·ed, -fect·ing, -fects 1.** To have an influence on or effect a change in: *Inflation affects buying power.* **2.** To act on the emotions of; touch or move. **3.** To attack or infect, as a disease. ❖ *n.* (ăf′ĕkt′) **1.** Feeling or emotion, esp. as manifested by facial expression or body language. **2.** *Obsolete* A disposition, feeling, or tendency. [Lat. *afficere*, affect-, to do to, act on : *ad-*, ad- + *facere*, to do; see **dhē-** in App.]

> **USAGE NOTE** *Affect¹* and *effect* have no senses in common. As a verb *affect¹* is most commonly used in the sense of "to influence" (*how smoking affects health*). *Effect* means "to bring about or execute": *measures designed to effect savings.*

af·fect² (ə-fĕkt′) *tr.v.* **-fect·ed, -fect·ing, -fects 1.** To put on a false show of; simulate: *affected a British accent.* **2a.** To have or show a liking for: *affects dramatic clothes.* **b.** *Archaic* To fancy; love. **3.** To tend to by nature; tend to assume: *a substance that affects crystalline form.* **4.** To imitate; copy: *"Spenser, in affecting the ancients, writ no language"* (Ben Jonson). [ME *affecten* < Lat. *affectāre*, to strive after, freq. of *afficere*, affect-, to affect, influence. See AFFECT¹.] —**af·fect′er** *n.*

af·fec·ta·tion (ăf′ĕk-tā′shən) *n.* **1.** A show, pretense, or display. **2a.** Behavior that is assumed rather than natural; artificiality. **b.** A particular habit adopted to give a false impression. [Lat. *affec-tātiō, affectātiōn-* < *affectātus*, p. part. of *affectāre*, to strive after. See AFFECT².]

af·fect·ed¹ (ə-fĕk′tĭd) *adj.* **1.** Acted upon, influenced, or changed. **2.** Emotionally stirred or moved. **3.** Infected or attacked, as by disease. [< AFFECT¹.]

af·fect·ed² (ə-fĕk′tĭd) *adj.* **1.** Assumed or simulated to impress others: *an affected accent.* **2.** Speaking or behaving in an artificial way to make an impression. **3.** Disposed or inclined. [< AFFECT².] —**af·fect′ed·ly** *adv.* —**af·fect′ed·ness** *n.*

af·fect·ing (ə-fĕk′tĭng) *adj.* Inspiring or capable of inspiring strong emotion; moving. [< AFFECT¹.] —**af·fect′ing·ly** *adv.*

af·fec·tion (ə-fĕk′shən) *n.* **1.** A tender feeling toward another; fondness. See Syns at **love**. **2.** Feeling or emotion. Often used in the plural. **3.** A disposition to feel, do, or say; a propensity. [ME *affeccioun* < OFr. *affection* < Lat. *affectiō, affectiōn-* < *affectus*, p. part. of *afficere*, to affect, influence. See AFFECT¹.] —**af·fec′tion·al** *adj.* —**af·fec′tion·al·ly** *adv.*

af·fec·tion·ate (ə-fĕk′shə-nĭt) *adj.* **1.** Having or showing fond feelings or affection; loving and tender. **2.** *Obsolete* Inclined or disposed. —**af·fec′tion·ate·ly** *adv.* —**af·fec′tion·ate·ness** *n.*

af·fec·tive (ə-fĕk′tĭv) *adj. Psychology* **1.** Influenced by or resulting from the emotions. **2.** Concerned with or arousing feelings or emotions; emotional. —**af·fec′tive·ly** *adv.* —**af·fec·tiv′i·ty** (ăf′ĕk-tĭv′ĭ-tē) *n.*

affective disorder *n.* A mental disorder characterized by a persistent, pervasive alteration in mood.

af·fect·less (ăf′fĕkt′lĭs) *adj.* Having or showing no emotion; unfeeling. —**af′fect′less·ness** *n.*

af·fen·pin·scher (ăf′ən-pĭn′shər) *n.* Any of a breed of small dogs of European origin, having wiry shaggy hair and a tufted muzzle. [Ger. : *Affe*, ape (< MHGer. < OHGer. *affo*) + *Pinscher*, a type of dog with ears operated on or "pinched" to make them stand up (< E. PINCH).]

af·fer·ent (ăf′ər-ənt) *adj.* Carrying inward to a central organ or section, as nerves that conduct impulses from the periphery of the body to the spinal cord. [Lat. *afferēns, afferent-*, pr. part. of *afferre*, to bring toward : *ad-*, ad- + *ferre*, to bring; see **bher-¹** in App.] —**af′fer·ent·ly** *adv.*

af·fi·ance (ə-fī′əns) *tr.v.* **-anced, -anc·ing, -anc·es** To bind in a pledge of marriage; betroth. [< ME *affiaunce*, assurance < OFr. < *affier*, to trust to < Med.Lat. *affīdāre* : Lat. *ad-*, ad- + Lat. *fīdus*, faithful; see **bheidh-** in App.]

af·fi·ant (ə-fī′ənt) *n.* One who makes an affidavit. [< *affy*, to make affidavit < ME *affien*, to trust < OFr. *affier*, to promise. See AFFIANCE.]

af·fi·da·vit (ăf′ĭ-dā′vĭt) *n.* A written declaration made under oath before an authorized official. [Med.Lat. *affīdāvit* < third pers. sing. perfect t. of Lat. *affīdāre*, to pledge. See AFFIANCE.]

af·fil·i·ate (ə-fīl′ē-āt′) *v.* **-at·ed, -at·ing, -ates** —*tr.* **1.** To adopt or accept as a member, subordinate, or branch. **2.** To associate (oneself) as a member, subordinate, or employee: *affiliated herself with a new law firm.* **3.** To assign the origin of. —*intr.* To become closely connected or associated. ❖ *n.* (-ē-ĭt, -āt′) A person or organization associated with another as a subordinate, subsidiary, or member: *network affiliates.* [Med.Lat. *affiliāre*, to adopt : Lat. *ad-*, ad- + Lat. *fīlius*, son.] —**af·fil′i·a′tion** *n.*

af·fine (ə-fīn′) *adj. Mathematics* **1.** Of or relating to a transformation of coordinates that is equivalent to a linear transformation followed by a translation. **2.** Of or relating to the geometry of affine transformations. [Fr. *affin*, closely related < OFr. See AFFINED.]

af·fined (ə-fīnd′) *adj.* **1.** Linked by a close relationship. **2.** Beholden to another; bound. [Fr. *affiné* < OFr. *affin*, closely related < Lat. *affinis*, related by marriage : Lat. *ad-*, ad- + *fīnis*, boundary.]

af·fin·i·ty (ə-fīn′ĭ-tē) *n., pl.* **-ties** **1.** A natural attraction or feeling of kinship. **2.** Relationship by marriage. **3.** An inherent similarity between persons or things. **4.** *Biology* A relationship or resemblance in structure between species that suggests a common origin. **5.** *Immunology* The attraction between an antigen and an antibody. **6.** *Chemistry* An attraction or force between particles that causes them to combine. [ME *affinite* < OFr. *afinite* < Lat. *affīnitās* < *affīnis*, related by marriage. See AFFINED.]

af·firm (ə-fûrm′) *v.* **-firmed, -firm·ing, -firms** —*tr.* **1.** To declare positively or firmly; maintain to be true. **2.** To support or uphold the validity of; confirm. —*intr. Law* To declare solemnly and formally but not under oath. [ME *affermen* < OFr. *afermer* < Lat. *affirmāre* : *ad-*, ad- + *firmāre*, to strengthen (< *firmus*, strong).] —**af·firm′a·ble** *adj.* —**af·firm′a·bly** *adv.* —**af·fir′mant** *adj. & n.* —**af·firm′er** *n.*

af·fir·ma·tion (ăf′ər-mā′shən) *n.* **1.** The act of affirming or the state of being affirmed; assertion. **2.** Something declared to be true; a positive statement or judgment. **3.** *Law* A solemn declaration given in place of a statement made under oath.

af·fir·ma·tive (ə-fûr′mə-tĭv) *adj.* **1.** Asserting that something is true or correct. **2.** Giving assent or approval; confirming: *an affirmative vote.* **3.** Positive; optimistic: *an affirmative outlook.* **4.** *Logic* Of, relating to, or being a proposition that affirms something about the subject, such as the statement *Apples have seeds.* ❖ *n.* **1.** A word or statement of agreement or assent, such as the word *yes.* **2.** The side in a debate that upholds the proposition. ❖ *adv. Informal* Used in place of the response "yes" to express confirmation or consent. —**af·fir′ma·tive·ly** *adv.*

affirmative action *n.* A policy or a program that seeks to redress past discrimination by increasing opportunities for underrepresented groups, as in employment.

af·fix (ə-fīks′) *tr.v.* **-fixed, -fix·ing, -fix·es** **1.** To secure to something; attach: *affix a label to a package.* **2.** To impute; attribute: *affix blame.* **3.** To place at the end; append: *affix a postscript to a letter.* **4.** *Grammar* To add as an affix. ❖ *n.* (ăf′ĭks′) **1.** Something that is attached, joined, or added. **2.** *Linguistics* A word element, such as a prefix or suffix, that can only occur attached to a base, stem, or root. [Med.Lat. *affīxāre*, freq. of Lat. *affīgere*, affix- : *ad-*, ad- + *fīgere*, to fasten.] —**af·fix′a·ble** *adj.* —**af′fix′al** *adj.* —**af·fix′er** *n.*

af·fla·tus (ə-flā′təs) *n.* A strong creative impulse; divine inspiration. [Lat. *afflātus* < p. part. of *afflāre*, to breathe on : *ad-*, ad- + *flāre*, to blow.]

af·flict (ə-flĭkt′) *tr.v.* **-flict·ed, -flict·ing, -flicts** To inflict grievous physical or mental suffering on. [ME *afflighten* < *afflight*, disturbed, frightened < Lat. *afflīctum*, p. part. of *afflīgere*, to cast down : *ad-*, ad- + *flīgere*, to strike.] —**af·flict′er** *n.* —**af·flic′tive** *adj.* —**af·flic′tive·ly** *adv.*

af·flic·tion (ə-flĭk′shən) *n.* **1.** A condition of pain, suffering, or distress. **2.** A cause of pain, suffering, or distress. See Syns at **burden**[1].

af·flu·ence (ăf′lōō-əns, ə-flōō′-) *n.* **1.** A plentiful supply of material goods; wealth. **2.** A great quantity; an abundance. **3.** A flowing to or toward a point; afflux.

af·flu·en·cy (ăf′lōō′ən-sē, ə-flōō′-) *n.* Affluence.

af·flu·ent (ăf′lōō-ənt, ə-flōō′-) *adj.* **1.** Generously supplied with money, property, or possessions; prosperous or rich. **2.** Plentiful; abundant. **3.** Flowing freely; copious. ❖ *n.* **1.** A stream or river that flows into a larger one; a tributary. **2.** A person who is well-off financially. [ME, abundant, flowing < OFr. < Lat. *affluēns, affluent-*, pr. part. of *affluere*, to abound in : *ad-*, ad- + *fluere*, to flow.] —**af′flu·ent·ly** *adv.*

af·flux (ăf′lŭks′) *n.* A flow to or toward an area, esp. of blood or other fluid to a body part. [Med.Lat. *affluxus* < Lat., p. part. of *affluere*, to flow to. See AFFLUENT.]

af·ford (ə-fôrd′, ə-fōrd′) *tr.v.* **-ford·ed, -ford·ing, -fords** **1.** To have the financial means for; bear the cost of: *I can afford a new car.* **2.** To be able to spare or give up: *can't afford an hour for lunch.* **3.** To manage or bear without serious risk: *can afford to be tolerant.* **4.** To make available; provide: *a sport affording good exercise.* [ME *aforthen* < OE *geforthian*, to carry out : *ge-*, perfective pref.; see YCLEPT + *forthian*, to further (< *forth*, forth, forward; see *per*[1] in App.).] —**af·ford′a·bil·i·ty** *n.* —**af·ford′a·ble** *adj.* —**af·ford′a·bly** *adv.*

af·for·est (ə-fôr′ĭst, -fŏr′-) *tr.v.* **-est·ed, -est·ing, -ests** To convert (open land) into a forest by planting trees or their seeds. [Med.Lat. *afforestāre* : Lat. *ad-*, ad- + Med.Lat. *forestāre* (< *forēsta*, forest; see FOREST).] —**af·for′es·ta′tion** *n.*

af·fray (ə-frā′) *n.* A noisy quarrel or brawl. ❖ *tr.v.* **-frayed, -fray·ing, -frays** *Archaic* To frighten. [ME < OFr. *effrei, esfrei* < *esfraier, esfreer*, to disturb. See **prī-** in App.]

af·fri·cate (ăf′rĭ-kĭt) *n.* A speech sound consisting of a stop consonant followed by a fricative; for example, the initial sounds of *child* and *joy*. [Lat. *affricātus*, p. part. of *affricāre*, to rub against : *ad-*, ad- + *fricāre*, to rub.]

af·fric·a·tive (ə-frĭk′ə-tĭv) *adj.* Of, relating to, or forming an affricate. ❖ *n.* See **affricate.**

af·fright (ə-frīt′) *tr.v.* **-fright·ed, -fright·ing, -frights** To arouse fear in; terrify. ❖ *n.* **1.** Great fear; terror. **2.** A cause of terror. [ME *afrighten* < OE *āfyrhtan* < *ā-*, intensive pref. + *fyrhtan*, to frighten (< *fyrhto*, fright).] —**af·fright′ment** *n.*

af·front (ə-frŭnt′) *tr.v.* **-front·ed, -front·ing, -fronts** **1.** To insult intentionally, esp. openly. **2a.** To meet defiantly; confront. **b.** *Obsolete* To meet or encounter face to face. ❖ *n.* An open or intentional offense or insult. [ME *afrounten* < OFr. *afronter* : Lat. *ad-*, ad- + Lat. *frōns, front-*, face; see FRONT.]

af·fu·sion (ə-fyōō′zhən) *n.* A pouring on of liquid, as in baptism. [LLat. *affūsiō, affūsiōn-* < Lat. *affūsus*, p. part. of *affundere*, to pour on : *ad-*, ad- + *fundere*, to pour; see **gheu-** in App.]

Afg. *abbr.* Afghanistan

Af·ghan (ăf′găn′, -gən) *adj.* Of or relating to Afghanistan or its people, language, or culture. ❖ *n.* **1.** A native or inhabitant of Afghanistan; an Afghani. **2.** See **Pashto.** **3. afghan** A coverlet or shawl of wool, knitted or crocheted in colorful geometric designs. **4.** An Afghan hound. [Pers. *afghān*, an Afghan.]

Afghan hound *n.* A large, slender hunting dog having long thick hair, a pointed muzzle, and drooping ears.

af·ghan·i (ăf-găn′ē, -gä′nē) *n., pl.* **-ghan·is** See table at **currency.** [Pashto *afghānī*, Afghani. See AFGHANI.]

Afghani *adj.* Of or relating to Afghanistan; Afghan. ❖ *n., pl.* **-ghan·is** A native or inhabitant of Afghanistan; an Afghan. [Pashto *afghānī* < *afghān*, Afghan.]

Af·ghan·i·stan (ăf-găn′ĭ-stăn′) A country of SW-central Asia; crisscrossed by invasion routes since ancient times. Cap. Kabul. Pop. 18,879,000.

a·fi·cio·na·do (ə-fĭsh′ē-ə-nä′dō, -fĭs′ē-, -fē′sē-) *n., pl.* **-dos** An enthusiastic admirer or follower; a fan. [Sp., p. part. of *aficionar*, to induce a liking for < *afición*, liking < Lat. *affectiō, affectiōn-*. See AFFECTION.]

a·field (ə-fēld′) *adv.* **1.** Off the usual or desired track. See Syns at **amiss.** **2.** Away from one's home or usual environment. **3.** To or on a field.

a·fire (ə-fīr′) *adv. & adj.* **1.** On fire. **2.** Intensely interested.

AFL *abbr.* **1.** American Federation of Labor **2.** American Football League

a·flame (ə-flām′) *adv. & adj.* **1.** On or as if on fire. **2.** Keenly excited and interested.

af·la·tox·in (ăf′lə-tŏk′sĭn) *n.* Any of a group of toxic compounds produced by certain molds, esp. *Aspergillus flavus*, that contaminate stored food supplies such as animal feed and peanuts. [NLat. *A(spergillus) flā(vus)*, species name (ASPERGILLUS + Lat. *flāvus*, yellow) + TOXIN.]

AFL-CIO *abbr.* American Federation of Labor and Congress of Industrial Organizations

a·float (ə-flōt′) *adv. & adj.* **1.** In a floating position or condition. **2.** On a boat or ship away from the shore; at sea. **3.** In circulation; prevailing: *Rumors are afloat.* **4.** Awash; flooded. **5.** Drifting about; moving without guidance. **6.** Free or out of difficulty, esp. financial difficulty.

a·flut·ter (ə-flŭt′ər) *adj.* **1.** Being in a flutter; fluttering: *with flags aflutter.* **2.** Nervous and excited.

a·foot (ə-fōōt′) *adv. & adj.* **1.** On foot; walking. **2.** In the process of being carried out; astir: *plans afoot to resign.*

a·fore (ə-fôr′, ə-fōr′) *adv., prep., & conj. Southern & Midland US* Before. [ME < OE *onforan* : *on-*, at (< *on*) + *foran*, before (< *fore*; see FORE).]

a·fore·men·tioned (ə-fôr′měn′shənd, -fōr′-) *adj.* Mentioned previously. ❖ *n.* The one or ones mentioned previously.

a·fore·said (ə-fôr′sĕd′, -fōr′-) *adj.* Spoken of earlier.

a·fore·thought (ə-fôr′thôt′, -fōr′-) *adj.* Planned or intended beforehand; premeditated: *malice aforethought.*

a·fore·time (ə-fôr′tīm′, -fōr′-) *Archaic adv.* At a former or past time; previously. ❖ *adj.* Earlier; former.

a for·ti·o·ri (ä fôr′tē-ôr′ē, ä fôr′tē-ō′rī′) *adv.* For a still stronger reason; all the more. [Lat. *ā fortiōrī* : *ā, ab*, from + *fortiōrī*, ablative of *fortior*, stronger.]

Afghanistan [map]

a·foul of (ə-foul′) *prep.* **1.** In or into collision, entanglement, or conflict with. **2.** In trouble with: *ran afoul of the law.*

AFP *abbr.* alpha-fetoprotein

Afr. *abbr.* **1.** Africa **2.** African

a·fraid (ə-frād′) *adj.* **1.** Filled with fear: *afraid of ghosts; afraid to die.* **2.** Having feelings of aversion or unwillingness: *afraid to show emotion.* **3.** Filled with regret or concern: *I'm afraid you're wrong.* [ME *affraied*, p. part. of *affraien*, to frighten < OFr. *esfraier, esfreer*, to disturb, of Gmc. orig. See **prī–** in App.]

SYNONYMS *afraid, apprehensive, fearful* These adjectives mean filled with fear: *afraid of snakes; feeling apprehensive before surgery; fearful of criticism.*

A-frame (ā′frām′) *n.* A structure, such as a house, with steeply angled sides that meet at the top in the shape of the letter A.

af·reet also **af·rit** (ăf′rēt′, ə-frēt′) *n.* A powerful evil spirit or monstrous demon in Arabic mythology. [Ar. *'ifrīt.*]

a·fresh (ə-frĕsh′) *adv.* Once more; anew; again: *start afresh.*

Af·ri·ca (ăf′rĭ-kə) The second-largest continent, S of Europe between the Atlantic and Indian oceans.

Af·ri·can (ăf′rĭ-kən) *adj.* Of or relating to Africa or its peoples, languages, or cultures. ❖ *n.* **1.** A native or inhabitant of Africa. **2.** A person of African descent.

Af·ri·ca·na (ăf′rĭ-kä′nə, -kăn′ə, -kā′nə) *n. (used with a pl. verb)* Materials, such as books, documents, or art objects, relating to the history or culture of African peoples.

African American also **Af·ri·can-A·mer·i·can** (ăf′rĭ-kən-ə-mĕr′ĭkən) *n.* A Black American of African ancestry. See Usage Note at **black.** —**Af′ri·can-A·mer′i·can** *adj.*

African American Vernacular English *n.* Any of the nonstandard varieties of English spoken by African Americans. See Usage Note at **Black English.**

African buffalo *n.* A large, often fierce buffalo (*Syncerus caffer*) of central Africa, having massive, downward curving horns.

African daisy *n.* Any of several African plants in the composite family, esp. those in the genera *Arctotis, Gerbera,* and *Lonas,* that have showy flower heads.

Af·ri·can·der or **Af·ri·kan·der** (ăf′rĭ-kăn′dər) *n.* Any of a breed of tall red cattle originally developed in South Africa and having a humped back and large spreading horns. [Obsolete Afr., an African < *Afrikaan* (on the model of *Hollander,* Hollander). See AFRIKANER.]

Af·ri·can·ism (ăf′rĭ-kə-nĭz′əm) *n.* **1.** A characteristic African cultural feature. **2.** A linguistic feature of an African language occurring in a non-African language.

Af·ri·can·ist (ăf′rĭ-kə-nĭst) *n.* A specialist in African affairs, cultures, or languages.

Af·ri·can·ized bee (ăf′rĭ-kə-nīzd′) *n.* A hybrid strain of honeybee introduced into Brazil in the mid-1950s and distinguished by aggressive traits such as the tendency to mass swarm and sting with great frequency.

African lily *n.* A South African rhizomatous plant (*Agapanthus africanus*) having funnel-shaped flowers grouped in umbels.

African marigold *n.* An aromatic annual Mexican plant (*Tagetes erecta*) in the composite family, having pinnately lobed leaves and showy, solitary yellow to orange flower heads.

African oil palm *n.* See **oil palm** 1.

African sleeping sickness *n.* See **sleeping sickness** 1.

African swine fever *n.* See **hog cholera.**

African violet *n.* Any of various East African herbs of the genus *Saintpaulia,* having a basal leaf rosette and a showy cluster of violet or sometimes pink or white flowers.

Af·ri·kaans (ăf′rĭ-käns′, -känz′) *n.* A language that developed from 17th-century Dutch and is an official language of South Africa. ❖ *adj.* Of or relating to Afrikaans or Afrikaners. [Afr. < Du. *Afrikaansch,* African < Lat. *Āfricānus.* See AFRIKANER.]

Af·ri·ka·ner (ăf′rĭ-kä′nər) *n.* An Afrikaans-speaking South African of European ancestry, esp. one descended from 17th-century Dutch settlers. [Afr., an African < Du. < *Afrikaan* < Lat. *Āfricānus* < *Āfrica,* Africa < *Āfer, Āfr–,* an African.]

af·rit (ăf′rēt′, ə-frēt′) *n.* Variant of **afreet.**

Af·ro (ăf′rō) *n., pl.* **-ros** A rounded, thick, tightly curled hair style. ❖ *adj.* African in style or origin. [Prob. short for AFRO-AMERICAN.]

Afro– *pref.* African: *Afro-Asiatic.* [< Lat. *Āfer, Āfr–,* an African.]

Af·ro-A·mer·i·can (ăf′rō-ə-mĕr′ĭ-kən) *n.* A Black American of African ancestry; an African American. See Usage Note at **black.** —**Af′ro-A·mer′i·can** *adj.*

Af·ro-A·si·at·ic (ăf′rō-ā′zhē-ăt′ĭk, -shē-, -zē-) *n.* A large family of languages spoken in northern Africa and southwest Asia, comprising the Semitic, Chadic, Cushitic, Berber, Omotic, and ancient Egyptian languages; formerly known as Hamito-Semitic. —**Af′ro-A′si·at′ic** *adj.*

Af·ro-Car·ib·be·an (ăf′rō-kăr′ĭ-bē′ən, -kə-rĭb′ē-ən) *adj.* **1.** Combining African and other, usu. European cultural elements as found in the Caribbean region. **2.** Of or relating to Afro-Caribbeans or their history or culture. ❖ *n.* A native or inhabitant of the Caribbean region who is of African ancestry.

Af·ro·cen·tric (ăf′rō-sĕn′trĭk) *adj.* Centered or focused on Africa or African peoples, esp. in relation to historical or cultural influence. —**Af′ro·cen′trism** *n.* —**Af′ro·cen′trist** *adj. & n.*

Af·ro-Cu·ban (ăf′rō-kyōō′bən) *adj.* **1.** Combining African and other cultural elements as found in Cuban society. **2.** Of or relating to Afro-Cubans or their history or culture. ❖ *n.* A Cuban of African ancestry.

aft (ăft) *adv. & adj.* At, in, toward, or close to the stern of a vessel or the rear of an aircraft or spacecraft. [ME *afte,* back < OE *æftan,* behind. See **apo–** in App.]

AFT *abbr.* American Federation of Teachers

af·ter (ăf′tər) *prep.* **1a.** Behind in place or order: *Z comes after Y.* **b.** Next to or lower than in order or importance. **2.** In quest or pursuit of: *He is after your job.* **3.** Concerning: *asked after you.* **4.** Subsequent in time to; at a later time than: *come after dinner.* **5.** Subsequent to and because of or regardless of: *They are still friends after all their differences.* **6.** Following continually: *year after year.* **7.** In the style of or in imitation of: *satires after Horace.* **8.** In honor or commemoration of: *was named after her mother.* **9.** In accordance with; in conformity to: *a person after my own heart.* **10.** Past the hour of: *five minutes after three.* **11.** *Irish* Used with a present participle to indicate action that has just been completed: *"Sure I'm after seeing him not five minutes ago"* (James Joyce). ❖ *adv.* **1.** Behind; in the rear. **2.** At a later or subsequent time; afterward: *departed shortly after.* ❖ *adj.* **1.** Subsequent in time or place; later; following: *in after years.* **2.** Located near the stern of a vessel or the rear or an aircraft or spacecraft. ❖ *conj.* Following or subsequent to the time that: *I saw them after I arrived.* —**idiom: after all** In spite of everything to the contrary; nevertheless: *We took a plane after all.* [ME < OE *æfter.* See **apo–** in App.]

af·ter·birth (ăf′tər-bûrth′) *n.* The placenta and fetal membranes expelled from the uterus following birth.

af·ter·burn·er (ăf′tər-bûr′nər) *n.* **1.** A device for augmenting the thrust of a jet engine by burning additional fuel with the uncombined oxygen in the hot exhaust gases. **2.** A device for burning or chemically altering unburned or partially burned carbon compounds in exhaust gases.

af·ter·care (ăf′tər-kâr′) *n.* **1.** Follow-up care provided after a medical procedure or treatment program. **2.** Care provided to children after school, esp. in an organized setting. —**af′ter·care′** *adj.*

af·ter·clap (ăf′tər-klăp′) *n.* An unexpected aftereffect.

af·ter·damp (ăf′tər-dămp′) *n.* An asphyxiating mixture of gases, primarily nitrogen and carbon dioxide, left in a mine after a fire or an explosion. [AFTER + DAMP, gas.]

af·ter·deck (ăf′tər-dĕk′) *n.* The part of a ship's deck past amidships toward the stern.

af·ter·ef·fect (ăf′tər-ĭ-fĕkt′) *n.* An effect following its cause after some delay.

af·ter·glow (ăf′tər-glō′) *n.* **1.** The atmospheric glow that remains for a short time after sunset. **2.** The light emitted after removal of a source of energy, esp. the emission of light from a phosphor after removal of excitation. **3.** A lingering impression of past glory or success.

af·ter·hours (ăf′tər-ourz′) *adj.* **1.** Occurring after closing time: *after-hours socializing.* **2.** Open after a legal or established closing time: *an after-hours club.*

af·ter·im·age (ăf′tər-ĭm′ĭj) *n.* A visual image that persists after the visual stimulus causing it has ceased to act.

af·ter·life (ăf′tər-līf′) *n.* **1.** A life or existence believed to follow death. **2.** The part of one's life that follows a particular event.

af·ter·mar·ket (ăf′tər-mär′kĭt) *n.* The market for parts and accessories used in the upkeep or enhancement of a previous purchase, as of a car or computer. —**af′ter·mar′ket** *adj.*

af·ter·math (ăf′tər-măth′) *n.* **1.** A consequence, esp. of a disaster: *famine as an aftermath of drought.* **2.** A period of time following a disaster: *in the aftermath of war.* **3.** A second growth or crop in the same season, as of grass after mowing. [AFTER + obsolete *math,* mowing (< OE *mǣth*; see **mē–²** in App.).]

af·ter·most (ăf′tər-mōst′) *adj.* **1.** Nearest the stern; farthest aft. **2.** Nearest the end or rear; hindmost or last.

af·ter·noon (ăf′tər-nōōn′) *n.* **1.** The part of day from noon until sunset. **2.** The latter part: *in the afternoon of life.*

af·ter·pains (ăf′tər-pānz′) *pl.n.* Cramps or pains following childbirth, caused by contractions of the uterus.

af·ter·piece (ăf′tər-pēs′) *n.* A short comic piece performed after a play.

af·ter·school (ăf′tər-skōōl′) *adj.* **1.** Taking place following school classes: *afterschool activities.* **2.** Providing care for and educational enhancement to children in the hours following school classes. ❖ *n.* An afterschool program.

af·ter-shave (ăf′tər-shāv′) *n.* A usu. fragrant lotion for use on the face after shaving.

af·ter·shock (ăf′tər-shŏk′) *n.* **1.** A quake of lesser magnitude following a large earthquake in the same area. **2.** A further reaction following the shock of a disturbing occurrence.

af·ter·taste (ăf′tər-tāst′) *n.* **1.** A taste persisting in the mouth after the substance that caused it is no longer present. **2.** A feeling that remains after an event or experience.

af·ter-tax also **af·ter·tax** (ăf′tər-tăks′) *adj.* Remaining after payment, esp. of income taxes: *after-tax profits.*

af·ter·thought (ăf′tər-thôt′) *n.* An idea, response, or explanation that occurs to one after an event or decision.

A-frame

African buffalo
Syncerus caffer

af·ter·time (ăf′tər-tīm′) *n.* The time to come; the future.

af·ter·ward (ăf′tər-wərd) also **af·ter·wards** (-wərdz) *adv.* At a later time; subsequently.

af·ter·word (ăf′tər-wûrd′) *n.* See **epilogue** 2.

af·ter·world (ăf′tər-wûrld′) *n.* A world believed to exist for those in the afterlife.

aft·most (ăft′mōst′) *adj.* Farthest aft; aftermost.

Ag The symbol for the element **silver** 1. [< Lat. *argentum*, silver. See ARGENT.]

AG *abbr.* **1.** adjutant general **2.** attorney general

ag– *pref.* Variant of **ad–** 1.

a·ga also **a·gha** (ä′gə, ăg′ə) *n.* Used as a title for a male civil or military leader, esp. in Turkey. [Turk. *ağa* < O Turkic *aqa*, older brother.]

A·ga·de (ə-gä′də) See **Akkad** 2.

a·gain (ə-gĕn′) *adv.* **1.** Once more; anew: *try again.* **2.** To a previous place, position, or state: *left home but went back again.* **3.** Furthermore; moreover. **4.** On the other hand: *She might go, and again she might not.* **5.** In return; in response. [ME (influenced by ON *ĩ gegn*, again) < OE *ongeagn*, against.]

a·gainst (ə-gĕnst′) *prep.* **1.** In a direction or course opposite to: *row against the current.* **2.** So as to come into forcible contact with: *waves dashing against the shore.* **3.** In contact with so as to rest or press on: *leaned against the tree.* **4.** In hostile opposition or resistance to: *struggle against fate.* **5.** Contrary to; opposed to: *against my better judgment.* **6.** In competition with: *raced against the record holder.* **7.** In contrast with the background of: *white clouds against the blue sky.* **8.** In preparation for; in anticipation of: *food stored against winter.* **9.** As a defense or safeguard from: *protection against the cold.* **10.** To the account or debt of: *drew a check against my bank balance.* **11.** Directly opposite to; facing. [ME, alteration of *againes* < OE *ongeagn*.]

A·ga Khan III (ä′gə kän′) 1877–1957. Indian leader of the Ismaili Muslim sect. His grandson Prince Karim (b. 1936) succeeded him as **Aga Khan IV.**

a·ga·lac·ti·a (ā-gə-lăk′tē-ə, -shē-ə, ăg′ə-) *n.* Absence of or faulty secretion of milk following childbirth. [NLat. < Gk. *agalaktia*, lack of milk : *a-*, without; see A–[1] + *gala, galakt-*, milk; see **melg-** in App.]

a·ga·ma (ä-gä′mə, ăg′ə-) *n.* Any of various small, long-tailed, insect-eating lizards of the family Agamidae, found in the Old World tropics. [Am.Sp., of Cariban orig.]

Ag·a·mem·non (ăg′ə-mĕm′nŏn′, -nən) *n. Greek Mythology* The king of Mycenae and leader of the Greeks in the Trojan War and the father of Orestes, Electra, and Iphigenia; killed by his wife Clytemnestra upon returning from Troy.

a·gam·ete (ā-găm′ēt′, ā′gə-mēt′) *n.* An asexual reproductive cell, such as a spore. [< Gk. *agametos*, unmarried, var. of *agamos*. See AGAMIC.]

a·gam·ic (ā-găm′ĭk) also **ag·a·mous** (ăg′ə-məs) *adj.* Occurring or reproducing without the union of male and female cells; asexual or parthenogenetic. [< LLat. *agamus*, unmarried < Gk. *agamos* : *a-*, without; see A–[1] + *gamos*, marriage; see –GAMY.] **—a·gam′i·cal·ly** *adv.*

a·gam·ma·glob·u·lin·e·mi·a (ā-găm′ə-glŏb′yə-lə-nē′mē-ə) *n.* A deficiency of gamma globulins in the blood.

a·gam·o·gen·e·sis (ā-găm′ə-jĕn′ĭ-sĭs, ăg′ə-mō-) *n.* Asexual reproduction, as by budding, cell division, or parthenogenesis. [Gk. *agamos*, unmarried; see AGAMIC + –GENESIS.]

A·ga·na (ə-gä′nyə, ä-gä′nyä) The cap. of Guam, on the W coast of the island. Pop. 1,139.

ag·a·pan·thus (ăg′ə-păn′thəs) *n.* See **African lily.** [NLat. *Agapanthus*, genus name : Gk. *agapē*, love + Gk. *anthos*, flower.]

a·gape[1] (ə-gāp′, ə-găp′) *adv. & adj.* **1.** In a state of wonder or amazement, as with the mouth wide open. **2.** Wide open.

a·ga·pe[2] (ä-gä′pā, ä′gə-pā′) *n.* **1.** *Christianity* Love as revealed in Jesus, spiritual and selfless. **2.** Love that is spiritual, not sexual, in its nature. **3.** *Christianity* In the early Christian Church, the love feast accompanied by Eucharistic celebration. [Gk. *agapē*, love.]

a·gar (ä′gär′, ā′gär′) also **a·gar-a·gar** (ä′gär-ä′gär′, ä′gär-ä′-) *n.* **1.** A gelatinous material derived from certain marine algae and used as a base for bacterial culture media and a stabilizer and thickener in many food products. **2.** A culture medium containing this material. [Short for Malay *agar-agar*.]

ag·a·ric (ăg′ər-ĭk, ə-găr′ĭk) *n.* **1.** Any of various mushrooms of the genera *Agaricus* or *Fomes* or related genera, having large umbrellalike caps with numerous gills beneath. **2.** The dried fruiting body of certain fungal species in the genus *Fomes*, formerly used in medicine. [ME *agarik*, a kind of fungus < Lat. *agaricum* < Gk. *agarikon* < *Agaria*, a town in Sarmatia.]

a·ga·rose (ā′gə-rōs′, -rōz′, ăg′ə-) *n.* A polysaccharide obtained from agar and used as a medium for gel electrophoresis procedures. [AGAR + –OSE[2].]

Ag·as·siz (ăg′ə-sē), **(Jean) Louis (Rodolphe)** 1807–73. Swissborn Amer. naturalist and geologist noted for his study of fossil fish.

Agassiz, Lake A glacial lake of the Pleistocene Epoch extending across NW MN, NE ND, S Manitoba, and SW Ontario.

ag·ate (ăg′ĭt) *n.* **1.** A fine-grained variety of quartz with colored bands or irregular clouding. **2.** *Games* A playing marble made of agate or a glass imitation of it; an aggie. **3.** A tool with agate parts, such as a burnisher tipped with agate. **4.** *Printing* A type size, approximately 5½ points. [ME *achate, agaten* < OFr. *acate, agate*, alteration (influenced by Gk. *agathē*, good) of Lat. *achātēs* < Gk. *akhātēs*.]

agate line *n.* A measure of space, usu. one column wide and ¼₁₄ inch deep, used esp. for classified advertisements.

a·ga·ve (ə-gä′vē, ə-gā′-) *n.* Any of numerous plants of the genus *Agave*, native to hot, dry regions of the New World and having basal rosettes of tough sword-shaped leaves. [NLat. *Agave*, genus name : Gk. *agauē*, fem. of *agauos*, noble.]

age (āj) *n.* **1.** The length of time that one has existed; duration of life. **2.** The time of life when a person becomes qualified to assume certain civil and personal rights and responsibilities; legal age: *under age; of age.* **3.** One of the stages of life: *at an awkward age.* **4.** The state of being old; old age: *hair white with age.* **5.** often **Age** **a.** A period in the history of humankind marked by a distinctive characteristic or person: *the computer age.* **b.** A period in the history of the earth, usu. shorter than an epoch: *the Ice Age.* **6a.** The period of history during which a person lives: *a product of his age.* **b.** A generation: *ages yet unborn.* **7. ages** *Informal* An extended period of time: *left ages ago.* ❖ *v.* **aged, ag·ing, ag·es** *—tr.* **1.** To cause to become old. **2.** To cause to mature or ripen under controlled conditions: *aging wine.* *—intr.* **1.** To become old. **2.** To manifest traits associated with old age. **3.** To develop a certain quality of ripeness; become mature: *cheese aging at room temperature.* See Syns at **mature.** *—idiom:* **come of age** To reach maturity. [ME < OFr. *aage* < VLat. **aetāticum* < Lat. *aetās, aetāt-*, age. See **aiw-** in App.] **—ag′er** *n.*

–age *suff.* **1a.** Collection; mass: *sewerage.* **b.** Amount: *footage.* **2.** Relationship; connection: *parentage.* **3.** Condition; state: *vagabondage.* **4a.** Action: *blockage.* **b.** Result of an action: *breakage.* **5.** Residence or place of: *vicarage.* **6.** Charge or fee: *cartage.* [ME < OFr. < VLat. **-āticum*, abstract n. suff. < Lat. *-āticum*, n. and adj. suff.]

ag·ed (ā′jĭd) *adj.* **1.** Being of advanced age; old. **2.** Characteristic of old age. **3.** (ājd) Having reached the age of: *aged three.* **4.** (ājd) Brought to a desired ripeness or maturity: *aged cheese.* **5.** *Geology* Approaching the base level of erosion. ❖ *n.* Elderly people considered as a group. **—ag′ed·ly** *adv.* **—ag′ed·ness** *n.*

A·gee (ā′jē), **James** 1909–55. Amer. writer noted esp. for his novel *A Death in the Family* (1957).

age group *n.* All the people of a particular age or range of ages.

age·ing (ā′jĭng) *n. Chiefly British* Variant of **aging.**

age·ism also **ag·ism** (ā′jĭz′əm) *n.* Discrimination based on age. **—age′ist** *adj. & n.*

age·less (āj′lĭs) *adj.* **1.** Seeming never to grow old. **2.** Existing forever; eternal. **—age′less·ly** *adv.* **—age′less·ness** *n.*

Ag·e·nais (ä′zhə-nā′) or **Ag·e·nois** (-nwä′) A historical region of SW France.

a·gen·cy (ā′jən-sē) *n., pl.* **-cies 1.** The condition of being in action; operation. **2.** The means or mode of acting; instrumentality. **3.** A business or service authorized to act for others: *an employment agency.* **4.** An administrative division of a government or an international body. [Med.Lat. *agentia* < Lat. *agēns, agent-*, pr. part. of *agere*, to do. See AGENT.]

agency shop *n.* An establishment in which a union represents all employees regardless of union membership but requires that nonmembers pay union dues or fees.

a·gen·da (ə-jĕn′də) *n., pl.* **-das** A list or program of things to be done or considered. [Lat., pl. of *agendum*, agendum. See AGENDUM.]

> **USAGE NOTE** In Modern English a phrase such as *item on the agenda* expresses the sense of the Latin singular form *agendum*, and the plural form *agenda* is used as a singular noun to denote the set or list of such items, as in *The agenda for the meeting has not yet been set.* If a plural of *agenda* is required, the form should be *agendas.*

a·gen·dum (ə-jĕn′dəm) *n., pl.* **-da** (-də) also **-dums** Something to be done, esp. an item on a program or list. [Lat., neut. gerundive of *agere*, to do. See **ag–** in App.]

a·gen·e·sis (ā-jĕn′ĭ-sĭs) *n.* Absence or incomplete development of an organ or body part.

a·gent (ā′jənt) *n.* **1.** One that acts or has the power or authority to act. **2.** One empowered to act for or represent another: *an insurance agent.* **3.** A means by which something is done or caused; an instrument. **4.** A force or substance that causes a change: *a chemical agent.* **5.** A representative or official of a government: *an FBI agent.* **6.** A spy. **7.** *Linguistics* The noun or noun phrase that specifies the person through whom or the means by which an action is effected. ❖ *v.* **a·gent·ed, a·gent·ing, a·gents** *—tr.* To act as an agent for; represent. *—intr.* To act as an agent or representative for: *agent a book.* [ME < Lat. *agēns, agent-*, pr. part. of *agere*, to do. See **ag–** in App.]

Agent Orange *n.* A herbicide containing trace amounts of the toxic contaminant dioxin that was used in the Vietnam War to defoliate areas of forest. [< the orange identifying strip on drums in which it was stored.]

a·gent pro·vo·ca·teur (ä-zhän′ prô-vô′kä-tœr′) *n., pl.* **a·gents pro·vo·ca·teurs** (ä-zhän′ prô-vô′kä-tœr′) A person em-

ă	pat	oi	boy
ā	pay	ou	out
âr	care	ŏŏ	took
ä	father	ōō	boot
ĕ	be	ŭ	cut
ē	be	ûr	urge
ĭ	pit	th	thin
ī	pie	th	this
îr	pier	hw	which
ŏ	pot	zh	vision
ō	toe	ə	about,
ô	paw		item

Stress marks:
′ (primary);
′ (secondary), as in
lexicon (lĕk′sĭ-kŏn′)

ployed to incite suspected persons to commit acts that will make them liable to punishment. [Fr. : *agent*, agent + *provocateur*, instigator.]

age of consent *n.* The age at which a person is legally considered competent to give consent, as to sexual intercourse.

age of reason *n.* **1.** An era in which rationalism prevails, esp. the period of the Enlightenment in England, France, and the United States. **2.** An age at which a person is considered capable of making reasoned judgments.

age-old (āj′ōld′) *adj.* Very old or of long standing.

ag•er•a•tum (ăj′ə-rā′təm) *n.* **1.** Any of various New World plants of the genus *Ageratum* in the composite family, esp. *A. houstonianum*, having showy, colorful flower heads. **2.** Any of several other plants having flower clusters similar to the ageratum. [NLat. *Agēratum*, genus name < Gk. *agēratos*, a plant (perh. rosemary) < neut. of *agēratos*, ageless : *a-*, without; see A–¹ + *gēras*, old age.]

A•ges•i•la•us II (ə-jĕs′ə-lā′əs) 444?–360? B.C. Spartan king (399?–360?) who defended Sparta during the Corinthian War (394–387).

age spot *n.* See **liver spot.**

ag•gie¹ (ăg′ē) *n.* A playing marble. [AG(ATE) + –IE.]

ag•gie² (ăg′ē) *n. Informal* **1.** An agricultural school or college. **2.** A student enrolled at such a school or college. [AG(RICULTURAL) + –IE.]

ag•gior•na•men•to (ə-jôr′nə-mĕn′tō) *n., pl.* **-tos** The process of bringing an institution or organization up to date; modernization. [Ital. < *aggiornare*, to update : *a-*, to (< Lat. *ad-*; see AD–) + *giorno*, day (< Lat. *diurnus*, daily; see DIURNAL.)]

ag•glom•er•ate (ə-glŏm′ə-rāt′) *tr. & intr.v.* **-at•ed, -at•ing, -ates** To form or collect into a rounded mass. ❖ *adj.* (-ər-ĭt) Gathered into a rounded mass. ❖ *n.* (-ər-ĭt) **1.** A confused or jumbled mass; a heap. **2.** A volcanic rock consisting of rounded and angular fragments fused together. [Lat. *agglomerāre, agglomerāt-*, to mass together : *ad-*, ad- + *glomerāre*, to form into a ball (< *glomus, glomer-*, ball).] **—ag•glom′er•a•tive** (-ə-rā′tĭv, -ər-ə-tĭv) *adj.* **—ag•glom′er•a•tor** *n.*

ag•glom•er•a•tion (ə-glŏm′ə-rā′shən) *n.* **1.** The act or process of gathering into a mass. **2.** A confused or jumbled mass.

ag•glu•ti•nate (ə-glōōt′n-āt′) *v.* **-nat•ed, -nat•ing, -nates** *—tr.* **1.** To cause to adhere, as with glue. **2.** *Linguistics* To form (words) by combining words or words and word elements. **3.** *Physiology* To cause (red blood cells or bacteria) to clump together. *—intr.* **1.** To join together into a group or mass. **2.** *Linguistics* To form words by agglutination. **3.** *Physiology* To clump together; undergo agglutination. ❖ *n.* See **agglutination** 2. [Lat. *agglūtināre, agglūtināt-* : *ad-*, ad- + *glūtināre*, to glue (< *glūten*, glue).] **—ag•glu′ti•nant** *adj. & n.*

ag•glu•ti•na•tion (ə-glōōt′n-ā′shən) *n.* **1.** The act or process of agglutinating; adhesion of distinct parts. **2.** A clumped mass of material formed by agglutination. **3.** *Physiology* The clumping together of red blood cells or bacteria, usu. in response to a particular antibody. **4.** *Linguistics* The formation of words from morphemes that retain their original forms and meanings with little change during the combination process.

ag•glu•ti•na•tive (ə-glōōt′n-ā′tĭv, -ə-tĭv) *adj.* **1.** Tending toward, concerning, or characteristic of agglutination. **2.** *Linguistics* Of or being a language characterized by agglutination.

ag•glu•ti•nin (ə-glōōt′n-ĭn) *n.* A substance, such as an antibody, that causes agglutination. [AGGLUTIN(ATION) + –IN.]

ag•glu•tin•o•gen (ăg′lōō-tĭn′ə-jən, ə-glōōt′n-) *n.* An antigen that stimulates the production of a particular agglutinin, such as an antibody. [AGGLUTIN(IN) + –GEN.] **—ag′glu•tin′o•gen′ic** (ăg′lōō-tĭn′ə-jĕn′ĭk, ə-glōōt′n-) *adj.*

ag•grade (ə-grād′) *tr.v.* **-grad•ed, -grad•ing, -grades** To fill and raise the level of (the bed of a stream) by deposition of sediment. **—ag′gra•da′tion** (ăg′rə-dā′shən) *n.* **—ag′gra•da′tion•al** *adj.*

ag•gran•dize (ə-grăn′dīz′, ăg′rən-) *tr.v.* **-dized, -diz•ing, -diz•es** **1.** To increase the scope of; extend. **2.** To make greater in power, influence, stature, or reputation. **3.** To make appear greater; exaggerate: *aggrandize an argument.* [Fr. *agrandir, agrandiss-* < OFr. : *a-*, to (< Lat. *ad-*; see AD–) + *grandir*, to grow larger (< Lat. *grandīre < grandis*, large).] **—ag•gran′dize•ment** (ə-grăn′dĭz-mənt, -dīz′-) *n.* **—ag•gran′diz′er** *n.*

ag•gra•vate (ăg′rə-vāt′) *tr.v.* **-vat•ed, -vat•ing, -vates** **1.** To make worse or more troublesome. **2.** To rouse to exasperation or anger; provoke. [Lat. *aggravāre, aggravāt-* : *ad-*, ad- + *gravāre*, to burden (< *gravis*, heavy; see gʷerə- in App.).] **—ag′gra•vat′ing•ly** *adv.* **—ag′gra•va′tive** *adj.*

USAGE NOTE *Aggravate* comes from the Latin verb *aggravāre,* which meant "to make heavier," that is, "to add to the weight of." It also had the extended senses "to annoy" and "to oppress." Some people claim that *aggravate* can only mean "to make worse," and not "to irritate," on the basis of the word's etymology. But, in fact, this sense existed in Latin, and in English it dates back to the 17th century. It is accepted by 68 percent of the Usage Panel.

ag•gra•vat•ed assault (ăg′rə-vā′tĭd) *n.* Any of various assaults that are more serious than a common assault, esp. one performed

with an intent to commit a crime.

ag•gra•va•tion (ăg′rə-vā′shən) *n.* **1.** The act of aggravating or the state of being aggravated. **2.** A source of continuing, increasing irritation or trouble. **3.** Exasperation.

ag•gre•gate (ăg′rī-gĭt) *adj.* **1.** Constituting or amounting to a whole; total: *aggregate sales.* **2.** *Botany* Crowded or massed into a dense cluster. **3.** Composed of a mixture of minerals separable by mechanical means. ❖ *n.* **1.** A total considered with reference to its constituent parts. **2.** The mineral materials used in making concrete. ❖ *tr.v.* (-gāt′) **-gat•ed, -gat•ing, -gates** **1.** To gather into a mass, sum, or whole. **2.** To amount to; total. **—idiom: in the aggregate** Taken into account as a whole. [ME *aggregat* < Lat. *aggregātus*, p. part. of *aggregāre*, to add to : *ad-*, ad- + *gregāre*, to collect (< *grex, greg-*, flock).] **—ag′gre•gate•ly** *adv.* **—ag′gre•ga′tion** *n.* **—ag′gre•ga′tive** *adj.* **—ag′gre•ga′tor** *n.*

aggregate fruit *n.* A fruit, such as the raspberry, consisting of many individual small fruits derived from separate ovaries within a single flower, borne on a common receptacle.

ag•gress (ə-grĕs′) *intr.v.* **-gressed, -gress•ing, -gress•es** To initiate an attack, war, quarrel, or fight. [Fr. *agresser* < Lat. *aggredī, aggress-*, to attack : *ad-*, ad- + *gradī*, to go; see ghredh- in App.]

ag•gres•sion (ə-grĕsh′ən) *n.* **1.** The act of initiating hostilities or invasion. **2.** The practice or habit of launching attacks. **3.** Hostile or destructive behavior or actions.

ag•gres•sive (ə-grĕs′ĭv) *adj.* **1.** Characterized by aggression. **2.** Inclined toward hostile behavior. **3.** Assertive, bold, and enterprising. **4.** Intense or harsh, as in color. **5.** Fast growing; tending to spread quickly: *an aggressive tumor.* **6.** Of or relating to medical treatment that is more vigorous or intensive than usual. **—ag•gres′sive•ly** *adv.* **—ag•gres′sive•ness** *n.*

ag•gres•sor (ə-grĕs′ər) *n.* One that engages in aggression.

ag•grieve (ə-grēv′) *tr.v.* **-grieved, -griev•ing, -grieves** **1.** To distress; afflict. **2.** To inflict an injury or injuries on. [ME *agreven* < OFr. *agrever* < Lat. *aggravāre*, to make worse. See AGGRAVATE.]

ag•grieved (ə-grēvd′) *adj.* **1.** Feeling distress or affliction. **2.** Treated wrongly; offended. **3.** *Law* Treated unjustly, as by denial of one's legal rights. **—ag•griev′ed•ly** (ə-grē′vĭd-lē) *adv.* **—ag•griev′ed•ness** *n.*

ag•gro (ăg′rō) *n., pl.* **-gros** *Chiefly British Slang* **1.** Irritation and exasperation. **2.** Aggressive behavior. ❖ *adj. Slang* **1.** Aggressive or violent. **2.** Daring and skillful, esp. in sports. [Short for AGGRAVATION and AGGRESSION.] **—ag′gro** *adj.*

a•gha (ä′gə, ăg′ə) *n.* Variant of **aga.**

a•ghast (ə-găst′) *adj.* Struck by shock, terror, or amazement. [ME *agast*, p. part. of *agasten*, to frighten : *a-*, intensive pref. (< OE ā-) + *gasten*, to frighten (< OE *gǣstan < gāst*, ghost).]

ag•ile (ăj′əl, -īl′) *adj.* **1.** Characterized by quickness, lightness, and ease of movement; nimble. **2.** Mentally quick or alert: *an agile mind.* [Fr. < Lat. *agilis < agere*, to drive, do. See ag- in App.] **—ag′ile•ly** *adv.* **—ag′ile•ness** *n.*

a•gil•i•ty (ə-jĭl′ĭ-tē) *n.* The state or quality of being agile; nimbleness. [ME *agilite* < OFr. < Med.Lat. *agilitās* < Lat. *agilis.* See AGILE.]

a•gin (ə-gĭn′) *Chiefly Upper Southern US prep.* **1.** Against. **2.** Opposed to: *I'm agin him.* **3.** Next to; beside; near. **4.** By or before (a specified time). ❖ *conj.* By the time that. [Regional var. of AGAINST.]

REGIONAL NOTE *Agin* has a wide spectrum of senses in the regional speech of those who pronounce it this way. Indeed, these regional senses are tied to the pronunciation, for standard English *against* does not quite capture the full implication of the assertion "*I'm agin him*"—that is, "opposed to him and all that he stands for." Another regional sense recalls the original literal Old English sense of "facing; next to" (see the first four senses of *against* in the *Oxford English Dictionary*), where standard English would have *by: Their house is agin the mountain. Agin* may be used figuratively with regard to time, meaning "by or before (a specified time)," in Upper Southern dialects:"*I'll be there agin daylight*" (North Carolina informant in DARE).

A•gin•court (ăj′ĭn-kôrt′, -kōrt′) A village of N France; site of Henry V of England's decisive defeat of the French (1415).

ag•ing (ā′jĭng) *n.* **1.** The process of growing old or maturing. **2.** A process for imparting the properties of age.

ag•ism (ā′jĭz′əm) *n.* Variant of **ageism.**

ag•i•ta (ăj′ĭ-tə, ä′jĭ-) *n.* Acid indigestion. [Ital. < *agitare*, to agitate < Lat. *agitāre.* See AGITATE.]

ag•i•tate (ăj′ĭ-tāt′) *v.* **-tat•ed, -tat•ing, -tates** *—tr.* **1.** To cause to move with violence or sudden force. **2.** To upset; disturb: *agitated by the news.* **3.** To arouse interest in (a cause, for example). *—intr.* To stir up interest: *agitate for a tax reduction.* [Lat. *agitāre, agitāt-*, freq. of *agere*, to drive, do. See ag- in App.] **—ag′i•tat′ed•ly** (-tā′tĭd-lē) *adv.* **—ag′i•ta′tive** *adj.*

ag•i•ta•tion (ăj′ĭ-tā′shən) *n.* **1.** The act of agitating or the state of being agitated. **2.** Extreme emotional disturbance; perturbation. **3.** The stirring up of public interest in a matter of controversy. **—ag′i•ta′tion•al** *adj.*

ag•i•ta•to (ăj′ĭ-tä′tō) *adv. & adj. Music* In a restless, agitated style. [Ital., p. part. of *agitare* < Lat. *agitāre*, to agitate. See AGITATE.]

ag·i·ta·tor (ăj′ĭ-tā′tər) *n.* **1.** One who agitates, esp. one who engages in political agitation. **2.** An apparatus that shakes or stirs.

ag·it·prop (ăj′ĭt-prŏp′) *n.* Political propaganda, esp. favoring communism. [Russ., short for *otdel agitatsii i propagandy*, incitement and propaganda section of the central and local committees of the Russ. Communist Party); name changed in 1934.]

A·gla·ia (ə-glā′ə, -glī′-) *n. Greek Mythology* One of the three Graces.

a·gleam (ə-glēm′) *adv. & adj.* Brightly shining.

ag·let (ăg′lĭt) *n.* **1.** A tag or sheath, as of plastic, on the end of a lace, cord, or ribbon to help it pass through eyelet holes. **2.** A similar ornamental device. [ME < OFr. *aguillette*, dim. of *aguille*, needle < VLat. *acūcula* < LLat. *acucula*, dim. of Lat. *acus*, needle. See **ak-** in App.]

a·gley (ə-glī′, -glā′, -glē′) *adv.* Scots Off to one side; awry. [A–² + Sc. *gley*, to squint (< ME *glien*, poss. of Scand. orig.).]

a·glit·ter (ə-glĭt′ər) *adv. & adj.* Glittering; sparkling.

a·glow (ə-glō′) *adv. & adj.* In a glow; glowing.

a·gly·cone (ə-glī′kōn′) or **a·gly·con** (-kŏn) *n.* The nonsugar component of a glycoside molecule. [*a-*, together (< Gk. *ha-*; see HAPLOID) + GLYC(O)- + -ONE.]

ag·nate (ăg′nāt′) *adj.* **1.** Related on the male side. **2.** Coming from a common source; akin. ❖ *n.* A relative on the male side only. [Lat. *agnātus*, p. part. of *agnāscī*, to become an agnate : *ad-*, ad- + *nāscī*, to be born; see **genə-** in App.] —**ag·nat′ic** (ăg-năt′ĭk) *adj.* —**ag·nat′i·cal·ly** *adv.* —**ag·na′tion** *n.*

Ag·nes (ăg′nĭs), Saint. d. c. A.D. 304. Roman Christian traditionally venerated as a martyr and the patron saint of young girls.

Ag·new (ăg′nōō′, -nyōō′), **Spiro Theodore** 1918–96. Vice President of the US (1969–73); resigned.

Ag·ni (ŭg′nē) *n.* The Hindu god of fire. [Skt. *Agniḥ* < *agniḥ*, fire.]

ag·no·men (ăg-nō′mən) *n., pl.* **-nom·i·na** (-nŏm′ə-nə) An additional cognomen given to a Roman citizen, often in honor of military victories. [Lat. : *ad-*, ad- (influenced by *agnōscere*, to recognize) + *nōmen*, name; see **nō-men-** in App.]

Ag·non (ăg′nôn′), **Shmuel Yosef** 1888–1970. Polish-born Israeli writer who shared the 1966 Nobel Prize for literature.

ag·no·sia (ăg-nō′zhə) *n.* Loss of the ability to interpret sensory stimuli. [Gk. *agnōsiā*, ignorance : *a-*, without; see A–¹ + *gnōsis*, knowledge (< *gignōskein*, to know; see **gnō-** in App.)]

ag·nos·tic (ăg-nŏs′tĭk) *n.* **1.** One who believes that there is no proof of the existence of God but does not deny the possibility that God exists. **2.** One who is doubtful or noncommittal about something. ❖ *adj.* **1.** Relating to or being an agnostic. **2.** Noncommittal: *"I favored European unity, but I was agnostic about the form it should take"* (Henry A. Kissinger). [A–¹ + GNOSTIC.] —**ag·nos′ti·cal·ly** *adv.* —**ag·nos′ti·cism** (-tĭ-sĭz′əm) *n.*

Ag·nus De·i (ăg′nəs dē′ĭ′, än′yōōs dā′ē, ăg′nōōs′) *n. Christianity* **1.** Lamb of God; Jesus. **2.** A liturgical prayer to Jesus in its musical setting. [LLat. *Agnus Deī* : Lat. *agnus*, lamb + Lat. *deī*, genitive of *deus*, god.]

a·go (ə-gō′) *adv. & adj.* Gone by; past: *two years ago.* **2.** In the past: *ages ago.* [ME, p. part. of *agon*, to go away < OE *āgān* : *ā-*, intensive pref. + *gān*, to go; see **ghē-** in App.]

a·gog (ə-gŏg′) *adj.* Full of anticipation or excitement; eager. [ME *agogge* < OFr. *en gogue*, in merriment : *en*, in (< Lat. *in*; see IN–²) + *gogue*, merriment.] —**a·gog′** *adv.*

à go·go or **a go·go** (ä gō′gō′) *adv.* In a fast and lively manner: *dancing à gogo.* ❖ *n., pl.* **-gos** A nightclub. [Fr. *à gogo*, galore < OFr. *a gogo* : *a*, to (< Lat. *ad*) + *gogo* (prob. reduplicated form of *gogue*, merriment).]

–agogue or **–agog** *suff.* A substance that stimulates the flow of: *emmenagogue*. [Fr. < LLat. *-agōgus* < Gk. *-agōgos* < *agōgos*, drawing off < *agein*, to lead, drive. See **ag-** in App.]

ag·on (ăg′ŏn, -ōn, ä-gōn′) *n., pl.* **a·gon·es** (ə-gō′nēz) **1.** A conflict, esp. between the protagonist and antagonist in literature or drama. **2.** The part of an ancient Greek drama, esp. a comedy, in which two characters engage in verbal dispute. **3.** A contest in ancient Greece, as in athletics or music. [Gk. *agōn*. See AGONY.]

ag·o·nal (ăg′ə-nəl) *adj.* Associated with or relating to great pain, esp. the agony of death.

a·gone (ə-gôn′, ə-gŏn′) *adv. & adj. Archaic* Gone by; past. [ME *agon*, p. part. of *agon*, to go away. See AGO.]

a·gon·ic (ā-gŏn′ĭk, ə-gŏn′-) *adj.* Having no angle. [< Gk. *agōnos* : *a-*, without; see A–¹ + *gōniā*, angle; see DIAGONAL.]

agonic line *n.* An imaginary line on the earth's surface connecting points where the magnetic variation is zero.

ag·o·nist (ăg′ə-nĭst) *n.* **1.** One involved in a struggle. **2.** *Physiology* A contracting muscle that is resisted by another muscle. **3.** *Biochemistry* A drug or other chemical that can combine with a receptor on a cell to produce a reaction typical of a naturally occurring substance. [LLat. *agōnista*, contender < Gk. *agōnistēs* < *agōn*, contest. See AGONY.]

ag·o·nis·tic (ăg′ə-nĭs′tĭk) also **ag·o·nis·ti·cal** (-tĭ-kəl) *adj.* **1.** Striving to overcome in argument; combative. **2.** Struggling to achieve effect. **3.** Of or relating to contests, originally those of the ancient Greeks. —**ag′o·nis′ti·cal·ly** *adv.*

ag·o·nize (ăg′ə-nīz′) *v.* **-nized, -niz·ing, -niz·es** —*intr.* **1.** To suffer extreme pain or great anguish: *agonize over a decision.* **2.** To make a great effort; struggle. —*tr.* To cause great pain or anguish to. [Med.Lat. *agōnizāre* < Gk. *agōnizesthai*, to struggle

< *agōn*, contest. See AGONY.] —**ag′o·niz′ing·ly** *adv.*

ag·o·ny (ăg′ə-nē) *n., pl.* **-nies** **1.** The suffering of intense physical or mental pain. **2.** The struggle that precedes death. **3.** A sudden or intense emotion: *an agony of doubt.* **4.** A violent, intense struggle. [ME *agonie* < OFr. < LLat. *agōnia* < Gk. *agōniā* < *agōn*, struggle < *agein*, to drive. See **ag-** in App.]

ag·o·ra (ăg′ər-ə) *n., pl.* **-o·rae** (ə-rē′) or **-o·ras** A gathering place, esp. an ancient Greek marketplace. [Gk. *agorā*.]

ag·o·ra·pho·bi·a (ăg′ər-ə-fō′bē-ə, -gôr′ə-) *n.* Fear of open or public places. [Gk. *agorā*, marketplace + –PHOBIA.] —**ag′o·ra·pho′bic** *adj. & n.*

a·gou·ti (ə-gōō′tē) *n., pl.* **-tis** or **-ties** **1.** A burrowing rodent of the genus *Dasyprocta*, native to tropical America and usu. having brown fur streaked with gray. **2.** The alternation of light and dark bands of color in some furs. [Fr. < Am.Sp. *agutí* < Guarani *acutí*.]

AGP *abbr.* accelerated graphics port

agr– *pref.* Variant of **agro–**.

A·gra (ä′grə) A city of N-central India on the Jumna R. SE of New Delhi; site of the Taj Mahal. Pop. 891,790.

a·graffe also **a·grafe** (ə-grăf′) *n.* **1.** A clasp on armor and clothing. **2.** A cramp iron for holding stones together in building. [Fr. *agrafe* < *agrafer*, to hook onto : *a-*, to (< Lat. *ad-*; see AD–) + *grafer*, to hook (< *grafe*, hook < OHGer. *krāpfo*).]

a·gran·u·lo·cy·to·sis (ā-grăn′yə-lō-sī-tō′sĭs) *n.* An acute disease marked by high fever and loss of circulating granular white blood cells.

ag·ra·pha also **Ag·ra·pha** (ăg′rə-fə) *pl.n.* The sayings of Jesus not written in the canonical Gospels. [Gk. < neut. pl. of *agraphos*, unwritten : *a-*, not; see A–¹ + *graphein*, to write; see **gerbh-** in App.]

a·graph·i·a (ā-grăf′ē-ə) *n.* Loss of the ability to write. [A–¹ + Gk. *graphein*, to write; see **gerbh-** in App. + –IA¹.] —**a·graph′ic** *adj.*

a·grar·i·an (ə-grâr′ē-ən) *adj.* **1.** Relating to the land and its ownership, cultivation, and tenure. **2.** Relating to agricultural or rural matters. ❖ *n.* A person who favors equitable distribution of land. [< Lat. *agrārius* < *ager, agr-*, field. See **agro-** in App.] —**a·grar′i·an·ly** *adv.*

a·grar·i·an·ism (ə-grâr′ē-ə-nĭz′əm) *n.* A movement for equitable distribution of land and for agrarian reform.

a·gree (ə-grē′) *v.* **a·greed, a·gree·ing, a·grees** —*intr.* **1.** To grant consent; accede: *We agreed to her suggestion.* **2.** To come into or be in accord, as of opinion: *I agree with you on that.* See Syns at **assent. 3.** To come to an understanding or to terms: *We agreed on the price.* **4.** To be compatible or in correspondence: *The copy agrees with the original.* **5.** To be suitable, pleasing, or healthful: *Spicy food does not agree with me.* **6.** *Grammar* To correspond in gender, number, case, or person. —*tr.* To grant or concede: *They agreed that we should go.* [ME *agreen* < OFr. *agreer* < VLat. *aggrātāre* : Lat. *ad-*, ad- + Lat. *grātus*, pleasing.]

a·gree·a·ble (ə-grē′ə-bəl) *adj.* **1.** To one's liking; pleasing: *agreeable weather.* **2.** Suitable; conformable. **3.** Ready to consent or submit. —**a·gree′a·bil′i·ty, a·gree′a·ble·ness** *n.* —**a·gree′a·bly** *adv.*

a·gree·ment (ə-grē′mənt) *n.* **1.** The act of agreeing. **2.** Harmony of opinion; accord. **3.** An arrangement regarding a method of action; a covenant. **4.** *Law* **a.** A properly executed and legally binding contract. **b.** The writing or document embodying this contract. **5.** *Grammar* Correspondence in gender, number, case, or person between words.

agri– *pref.* Variant of **agro–**.

ag·ri·busi·ness (ăg′rə-bĭz′nĭs) *n.* Farming engaged in as a large-scale business operation.

A·gric·o·la (ə-grĭk′ə-lə), **Gnaeus Julius** A.D. 37–93. Roman soldier and governor of Britain (77–84).

ag·ri·cul·ture (ăg′rĭ-kŭl′chər) *n.* The science, art, and business of cultivating soil, producing crops, and raising livestock; farming. [ME < Lat. *agricultūra* : *agrī*, genitive of *ager*, field; see **agro-** in App. + *cultūra*, cultivation; see CULTURE.] —**ag′ri·cul′tur·al** *adj.* —**ag′ri·cul′tur·al·ly** *adv.* —**ag′ri·cul′tur·ist, ag′ri·cul′tur·al·ist** *n.*

A·gri·gen·to (ä′grĭ-jĕn′tō, ăg′rĭ-) A city of SW Sicily, Italy, overlooking the Mediterranean; founded c. 580 B.C. Pop. 51,931.

ag·ri·mo·ny (ăg′rə-mō′nē) *n., pl.* **-nies** **1.** Any of various perennial herbaceous plants of the genus *Agrimonia*, having pinnately compound leaves and spikelike clusters of small yellow flowers. **2.** Any of several similar or related plants, such as the hemp agrimony. [ME < OFr. *aigremoine* < Lat. *agrimōnia* (influenced by OFr. *aigre*, sour), alteration of *argemōnia* < Gk. *argemōnē*, poppy, poss. < *argos*, white. See **arg-** in App.]

A·grip·pa (ə-grĭp′ə), **Marcus Vipsanius** 63–12 B.C. Roman soldier who commanded the victorious fleet at Actium (31).

Ag·rip·pi·na (ăg′rə-pī′nə, -pē′-) Known as "the Elder." 13 B.C.?–A.D. 33. Roman matron and mother of Caligula.

Ag·rip·pi·na² (ăg′rə-pī′nə, -pē′-) Known as "the Younger." A.D. 15?–59. Roman empress who murdered her husband, Claudius, and plotted so that her son by a previous marriage, Nero, would become emperor.

ag·ri·tour·ism (ăg′rĭ-tōōr′ĭz′əm) also **ag·ro·tour·ism** (-rō-) *n.* Tourism in which tourists experience rural farming at close hand. —**ag′ri·tour′ist** *n.*

agouti

agro– or **agri–** or **agr–** *pref.* **1.** Field; soil: *agrology.* **2.** Agriculture: *agroindustrial.* [< Gk. *agros* and Lat. *ager, agr-,* field.]

ag·ro·bi·o·log·i·cal (ăg′rō-bī-ŏl′ə-jē) *n.* The study of plant nutrition and growth as related to soil condition. —**ag′ro·bi′o·log′i·cal** (-ə-lŏj′ĭ-kəl) *adj.* —**ag′ro·bi·ol′o·gist** *n.*

ag·ro·chem·i·cal (ăg′rə-kĕm′ĭ-kəl) also **ag·ri·chem·i·cal** (ăg′rī-) *n.* **1.** A chemical, such as an insecticide, that improves the production of crops. **2.** A chemical or product derived from plants.

ag·ro·for·est·ry (ăg′rō-fôr′ĭ-strē, -fŏr′-) *n.* A system of land use in which harvestable plants, such as trees, are grown near crops or on pastureland to preserve or enhance the productivity of the land.

ag·ro·in·dus·tri·al (ăg′rō-ĭn-dŭs′trē-əl) *adj.* Of or relating to the production or supply of various needs, such as water or power, for agriculture and industry.

a·grol·o·gy (ə-grŏl′ə-jē) *n.* The applied science of soils in relation to crops. —**ag′ro·log′ic** (ăg′rə-lŏj′ĭk), **ag′ro·log′i·cal** *adj.* —**ag′ro·log′i·cal·ly** *adv.* —**a·grol′o·gist** *n.*

a·gron·o·my (ə-grŏn′ə-mē) *n.* The application of soil and plant science to soil management and crop production; scientific agriculture. —**ag′ro·nom′ic** (ăg′rə-nŏm′ĭk), **ag′ro·nom′i·cal** *adj.* —**a·gron′o·mist** *n.*

ag·ros·tol·o·gy (ăg′rə-stŏl′ə-jē) *n.* The study of grasses. [Gk. *agrōstis,* a kind of wild grass (< *agros,* field; see AGRO–) + –LOGY.] —**ag′ros·tol′o·gist** *n.*

a·ground (ə-ground′) *adv. & adj.* **1.** Onto or on a shore, reef, or the bottom of a body of water: *a ship that ran aground.* **2.** On the ground: *combat aircraft aloft and aground.*

a·gua·ca·te (ä′gwə-kä′tē) *n.* The avocado. [Am.Sp. < Nahuatl *ahuacatl.*]

A·guas·ca·lien·tes (ä′gwäs-kä-lyĕn′tĕs) A city of central Mexico NE of Guadalajara; built over an intricate system of ancient tunnels. Pop. 293,152.

a·gue (ā′gyōo) *n.* **1.** A condition marked by alternating periods of chills, fever, and sweating. **2.** A chill or fit of shivering. [ME < OFr. *(fievre) ague,* sharp (fever) < Med.Lat. *(febris) acūta* < Lat., fem. of *acūtus.* See ACUTE.] —**a′gu·ish** (ā′gyōo-ĭsh) *adj.* —**a′gu·ish·ly** *adv.* —**a′gu·ish·ness** *n.*

A·gui·nal·do (ä′gē-näl′dō), **Emilio** 1869–1964. Philippine revolutionary leader.

A·gul·has (ə-gŭl′əs), **Cape** A rugged headland of South Africa, the southernmost point of Africa.

ah (ä) *interj.* Used to express various emotions, such as satisfaction, surprise, or pain.

A.h. *abbr.* ampere-hour

A.H. or **a.h.** *abbr. Latin* **1.** anno Hebraico **2.** anno Hegirae

a·ha (ä-hä′) *interj.* Used to express surprise or pleasure.

AHA *abbr.* **1.** American Heart Association **2.** American Hospital Association

A·hab (ā′hăb′) 9th cent. B.C. King of Israel and husband of Jezebel.

a·head (ə-hĕd′) *adv.* **1.** At or to the front or head. **2a.** In advance; before: *pay ahead.* **b.** In or into the future; for the future: *planned ahead.* **3a.** In an advanced position registering the future: *Set the clock ahead.* **b.** At or to a different time; earlier or later: *moved the appointment ahead.* **4a.** In a forward direction; onward: *The train moved ahead.* **b.** In the prescribed direction for normal use: *Roll the tape ahead.* **5.** In or into a more advantageous position: *get ahead in life.* —*idiom:* **be ahead** To be winning or in a superior position.

ahead *prep.* **1.** In front of. **2.** In advance of; at an earlier time than: *arrived ahead of the others.* **3.** In a superior or advanced position to; more successful than.

a·hem (ə-hĕm′) *interj.* Used to attract attention or express doubt or warning.

a·him·sa (ə-hĭm′sä′) *n.* A Jain, Buddhist, and Hindu doctrine expressing belief in the sacredness of all living creatures and urging the avoidance of harm and violence. [Skt. *ahimsā : a–,* not; see **ne** in App. + *himsā,* injury (< *himsati,* he injures).]

a·his·tor·i·cal (ā′hĭ-stôr′ĭ-kəl, -stŏr′-) *adj.* Unconcerned with or unrelated to history.

Ah·ma·da·bad or **Ah·me·da·bad** (ä′mə-də-bäd′) A city of NW India N of Mumbai (Bombay); founded 1412. Pop. 2,876,710.

a·hold (ə-hōld′) *n.* Hold; grip: *took ahold of my arm.*

–aholic or **–oholic** *suff.* One that is addicted to or compulsively in need of: *workaholic.* [< alteration of (ALC)OHOLIC.]

A horizon *n.* In ABC soil, the topsoil.

a·hoy (ə-hoi′) *interj.* Used to hail a ship or a person or to attract attention.

Ah·ri·man (ä′rĭ-mən) *n.* The chief spirit of evil in Zoroastrianism. [Pers. *ahriman* < MPers. *ahraman* < Avestan *angrō mainiiuš,* the evil spirit : *angra,* evil + *mainiiuš,* spirit; see **men-¹** in App.]

A·hu·ra Maz·da (ä-hoor′ə măz′də) *n.* The chief deity of Zoroastrianism, the creator of the world, the source of light, and the embodiment of good. [Avestan *ahurō mazdā,* the Wise Lord : *ahurō,* lord + *mazdā-,* wise; see **men-¹** in App.]

Ah·vaz or **Ah·waz** (ä-wäz′) A city of SW Iran NNE of Basra, Iraq; built on ruins of an ancient Persian city. Pop. 828,380.

Ah·ven·an·maa (ä′və-nän-mä′) also **Åland Islands** (ĭland,

aiguille
the Matterhorn, near Zermatt, Switzerland

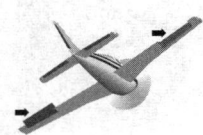

aileron
To bank to the left, a pilot must raise the left aileron and lower the right aileron.

ō′länd′) A Finnish archipelago in the Baltic Sea at the entrance to the Gulf of Bothnia.

ai (ī) *n.* See **sloth** 2. [Port., of Tupian orig.]

AI *abbr.* **1.** artificial insemination **2.** artificial intelligence

a.i. *abbr. Latin* ad interim (in the meantime)

aid (ād) *intr. & tr.v.* **aid·ed, aid·ing, aids** To help or furnish with help, support, or relief. ❖ *n.* **1.** The act or result of helping; assistance. **2a.** An assistant or helper. **b.** A device that assists: *visual aids.* **c.** A hearing aid. **3.** An aide or aide-de-camp. **4.** A payment to a lord by a vassal in medieval England. [ME *aiden* < OFr. *aider* < Lat. *adiūtāre,* freq. of *adiuvāre,* to help : *ad-,* to + *iuvāre,* to help.] —**aid′er** *n.*

aide (ād) *n.* **1.** An assistant; a helper: *a nurse's aide.* **2.** An aide-de-camp. [Fr. < *aider,* to aid. See AID.]

aide-de-camp (ād′dĭ-kămp′) *n., pl.* **aides-de-camp** A military officer acting as secretary and confidential assistant to a superior officer of general or flag rank. [Fr. : *aide,* assistant + *de,* of + *camp,* camp.]

aide-mé·moire (ād′măm-wär′, ĕd-) *n., pl.* **aide-mémoire** or **aide-mémoires** **1.** A memorandum setting forth the major points of a proposed discussion or agreement. **2.** Something that serves as an aid to memory. [Fr. : *aide,* aid + *mémoire,* memory.]

aid·man (ād′măn′) *n.* A member of an army medical corps attached to a field unit. [Short for *medical aid man.*]

AIDS (ādz) *n.* A severe immunological disorder caused by HIV, resulting in a defect in cellular immunity causing increased susceptibility to opportunistic infections and certain rare cancers. [A(CQUIRED) I(MMUNE) D(EFICIENCY) S(YNDROME).]

AIDS-re·lat·ed complex (ādz′rĭ-lā′tĭd) *n.* ARC.

ai·grette or **ai·gret** (ā-grĕt′, ā′grĕt′) *n.* **1.** An ornamental tuft of upright plumes, esp. the tail feathers of an egret. **2.** An ornament resembling a tuft of plumes. [Fr., egret < OFr. See EGRET.]

ai·guille (ā-gwēl′) *n.* **1.** A sharp, pointed mountain peak. **2.** A needle-shaped drill for boring holes in rock or masonry. [Fr., needle < OFr. See AGLET.]

ai·guil·lette (ā′gwə-lĕt′) *n.* An ornamental cord worn on the shoulder of a military uniform. [Fr. See AGLET.]

Ai·ken (ā′kən), **Conrad Potter** 1889–1973. Amer. writer who won a 1930 Pulitzer Prize for *Selected Poems.*

ai·ki·do (ī′kē-dō′, ī-kē′dō) *n.* A Japanese art of self-defense that uses holds and locks to exploit an opponent's strength to one's own advantage. [J. *aikidō : ai,* mutual + *ki,* spirit (< M Chin. *khi*) + *dō,* art (< M Chin. *daw′, thaw*).]

ail (āl) *v.* **ailed, ail·ing, ails** —*intr.* To feel ill or have pain. —*tr.* To cause physical or mental pain or uneasiness to; trouble. See Syns at **trouble.** [ME *eilen* < OE *eglian < egle,* troublesome.]

ai·lan·thus (ā-lăn′thəs) *n.* Any of several deciduous Asian trees of the genus *Ailanthus,* esp. the tree of heaven. [NLat. *Ailanthus,* genus name, alteration (influenced by Gk. *anthos,* flower) of Ambonese *ai lanto,* tree of heaven : *ai,* tree + *lanto,* heaven.]

ai·le·ron (ā′lə-rŏn′) *n.* Either of two movable flaps on the wings of an airplane, used to control rolling and banking. [Fr., dim. of *aile,* wing < OFr. < Lat. *āla.*]

Ai·ley (ā′lē, ī′lē), **Alvin, Jr.** 1931–89. Amer. choreographer whose works draw upon African-American styles and themes.

ail·ment (āl′mənt) *n.* A physical or mental disorder, esp. a mild illness.

ai·lu·ro·phile (ī-loor′ə-fīl′, ā-loor′-) *n.* One who loves cats. [Gk. *ailouros,* cat + –PHILE.]

ai·lu·ro·phobe (ī-loor′ə-fōb′, ā-loor′-) *n.* One who hates or fears cats. [Gk. *ailouros,* cat + –PHOBE.] —**ai·lu′ro·pho′bi·a** *n.*

aim (ām) *v.* **aimed, aim·ing, aims** —*tr.* **1.** To direct (a weapon) toward an intended target. **2.** To direct toward or intend for a particular goal or group: *aimed the marketing at teenagers.* —*intr.* **1.** To direct a weapon. **2.** To determine a course: *aim for a better education.* **3.** To propose to do something; intend. ❖ *n.* **1a.** The act of aiming. **b.** Skill at hitting a target: *perfect aim.* **2a.** The line of fire of an aimed weapon. **b.** The degree of accuracy of a weapon. **3.** A purpose or intention toward which one's efforts are directed. See Syns at **intention.** **4.** *Obsolete* A target; a mark. **5.** *Obsolete* A conjecture; a guess. [ME *aimen* < OFr. *esmer,* to estimate (< Lat. *aestimāre*) and < OFr. *aesmer* (< VLat. **ad estimāre* : Lat. *ad-,* ad- + Lat. *aestimāre,* to estimate).]

aim·less (ām′lĭs) *adj.* Devoid of direction or purpose. —**aim′less·ly** *adv.* —**aim′less·ness** *n.*

ain (ān) *adj. Scots* Own.

ain't (ānt) *Nonstandard* **1.** Am not. **2.** Used also as a contraction for *are not, is not, has not,* and *have not.*

USAGE NOTE The use of *ain't* goes back to the 18th century, and the contraction has been strongly condemned as a mark of ignorance since the 1800s. Nevertheless, it has remained in use by educated speakers wishing to strike a jocular or popular note, especially in fixed expressions such as *Say it ain't so.* • The stigmatization of *ain't* leaves us with no happy alternative for use in first-person questions. The widely used *Aren't I?,* though illogical, was found acceptable for use in speech by a majority of the Usage Panel in an earlier survey, but in writing there is no acceptable substitute for the admittedly stilted *Am I not?*

Ain·tab (īn-täb′) See **Gaziantep.**

Ai·nu (ī′nōo) *n., pl.* **Ainu** or **-nus 1.** A member of an indigenous people of Japan. **2.** The language of the Ainu. [Ainy *aynu*, person.]

ai•o•li (ī-ō′lē, ā-ō′-) *n.* A sauce of garlic, egg yolks, lemon juice, and olive oil. [Provençal : *ai*, garlic (< Lat. *allium*) + *oli*, oil (< Lat. *oleum*; see OIL).]

air (âr) *n.* **1a.** A colorless, odorless, gaseous mixture, mainly nitrogen (approx. 78 percent) and oxygen (approx. 21 percent) with lesser amounts of other gases. **b.** This mixture with varying amounts of moisture and particulate matter, enveloping the earth; the atmosphere. **2a.** The sky; the firmament. **b.** A giant void; nothingness: *vanished into thin air.* **3.** A breeze or wind. **4.** Aircraft: *traveled to Asia by air.* **5a.** Public utterance; vent: *gave air to their grievances.* **b.** The electronic broadcast media. **6.** A characteristic impression; an aura. **7.** Personal bearing, appearance, or manner; mien. **8. airs** An affected pose; affectation. **9.** *Music* **a.** A melody or tune, esp. in the soprano or tenor range. **b.** A solo with or without accompaniment. **10.** Air conditioning. **11.** *Archaic* Breath. ❖ *v.* **aired, air•ing, airs** —*tr.* **1.** To expose so that air can dry or freshen; ventilate. **2.** To give vent to publicly: *airing my pet peeves.* See Syns at **vent**¹. **3.** To broadcast on television or radio. —*intr.* To be broadcast on television or radio. ***—idioms:* in the air** Abroad; prevalent: *Excitement was in the air.* **up in the air** Not yet decided; uncertain. [Partly < ME *air*, gas, atmosphere (< OFr. < Lat. *āēr* < Gk.) and partly < Fr. *air*, nature, quality, place of orig. (< Lat. *ager*, place, field; see AGRICULTURE, and Lat. *ārea*, open space, threshing floor; see AREA). N., sense 9 < Fr. *air*, tune < Ital. *aria.* See ARIA.]

air bag *n.* **1.** An automotive restraint consisting of a bag that is designed to inflate upon collision. **2.** A large, strong, rubber inflatable bag used to lift a vehicle or heavy machinery or debris that has trapped a person.

air ball *n.* *Basketball* A shot that misses the backboard, rim, and net.

air base *n.* A base for military aircraft.

air bladder *n.* **1.** An air-filled structure in many fishes that functions to maintain buoyancy or aid in respiration. **2.** See **float** 2.

air•boat (âr′bōt′) *n.* See **swamp boat.**

air•borne (âr′bôrn′, -bōrn′) *adj.* **1.** Carried by or through the air: *airborne pollen.* **2.** Transported in aircraft. **3.** In flight; flying.

air brake *n.* **1.** A brake operated by compressed air. **2.** A surface that can be projected into the airflow to increase drag; a spoiler.

air•brush (âr′brŭsh′) *n.* An atomizer using compressed air to spray a liquid on a surface. ❖ *tr.v.* **-brushed, -brush•ing, -brush•es** To spray with an airbrush.

air•burst (âr′bûrst′) *n.* Explosion of a bomb or shell in the atmosphere.

air•bus or **air bus** (âr′bŭs′) *n., pl.* **-bus•es** or **-bus•ses** A commercial passenger jet with a short to medium range.

air chamber *n.* **1.** An enclosure filled with air for a special purpose. **2.** A chamber in which air elastically compresses and expands to regulate the flow of a fluid.

air-con•di•tion (âr′kən-dĭsh′ən) *tr.v.* **-tioned, -tion•ing, -tions** To subject to, provide with, or ventilate by air conditioning.

air conditioner *n.* An apparatus for controlling, esp. lowering, the temperature and humidity of an enclosed space.

air conditioning *n.* **1.** The state of temperature and humidity produced by an air conditioner. **2.** An air conditioner or system of air conditioners.

air-cool (âr′ko͞ol′) *tr.v.* **-cooled, -cool•ing, -cools 1.** To cool by a flow of air. **2.** To air-condition.

air cover *n.* **1.** Protective use of military aircraft during ground operations. **2.** The aircraft used to support ground troops.

air•craft (âr′krăft′) *n., pl.* **aircraft** A machine or device that is capable of atmospheric flight.

aircraft carrier *n.* A large naval vessel designed as a mobile air base.

air•crew (âr′kro͞o′) *n.* The crew operating an aircraft.

air cushion *n.* **1.** Trapped air that supports a vehicle a short distance above land or water. **2.** A device that uses trapped air to absorb the shock of motion. **—air′-cush′ion** (âr′ko͝osh′ən), **air′-cush′ioned** (-ənd) *adj.*

air-cushion vehicle *n.* A usu. propeller-driven vehicle for traveling over land or water on a supportive cushion of air.

air dam *n.* A strip of metal or plastic fitted beneath the front bumper of a car, intended to enhance aerodynamics and stability by blocking the flow of turbulent air under the vehicle.

air•date (âr′dāt′) *n.* The date on which a program is scheduled for broadcast.

air door *n.* A strong current of air that is used instead of a door.

air•drome (âr′drōm′) *n.* **1.** An airport. **2.** A military air base.

air•drop (âr′drŏp′) *n.* A delivery by parachute. ❖ *tr. & intr.v.* **-dropped, -drop•ping, -drops** To drop or be dropped from an aircraft.

air-dry (âr′drī′) *tr.v.* **-dried, -dry•ing, -dries** To dry by exposure to the air. ❖ *adj.* Sufficiently dry so that further exposure to air does not yield more moisture to be evaporated.

Aire•dale (âr′dāl′) *n.* A large terrier of a breed having long legs and a wiry tan coat marked with black. [After *Airedale*, a valley of north-central England.]

air•fare (âr′fâr′) *n.* Fare for travel by aircraft.

air•field (âr′fēld′) *n.* **1.** The area of fields and runways where aircraft can take off and land. **2.** An airport.

air•flow (âr′flō′) *n.* **1.** A flow of air. **2.** The motion of air around a moving object.

air•foil (âr′foil′) *n.* A part or surface, such as a wing or rudder, that controls stability or lift.

air force *n.* **1.** The aviation branch of a country's armed forces. **2.** A unit of the US Air Force larger than a division and smaller than a command.

air•frame (âr′frām′) *n.* The structure of an aircraft, such as an airplane, helicopter, or rocket, exclusive of its power plant.

air•freight (âr′frāt′) *n.* **1.** A system of transporting freight by air. **2.** The amount charged for transporting freight by air. **—air′freight′** *v.*

air gas *n.* See **producer gas.**

air•glow (âr′glō′) *n.* A faint photochemical luminescence in the upper atmosphere.

air gun *n.* A gun discharged by compressed air.

air•head¹ (âr′hĕd′) *n.* *Slang* A silly, unintelligent person.

air•head² (âr′hĕd′) *n.* An area of hostile or enemy-controlled territory secured by paratroops or air-assault forces. [AIR + (BEACH)HEAD.]

air hole *n.* **1.** A hole through which gas or air may pass. **2.** An opening in the frozen surface of water. **3.** See **air pocket.**

air hunger *n.* See **dyspnea.**

air•ing (âr′ĭng) *n.* **1.** Exposure to air for freshening or drying. **2.** Exposure to open air for exercise or the promotion of health. **3.** Exposure to public attention. **4.** A broadcast.

air lane *n.* A regular route of travel for aircraft.

air•less (âr′lĭs) *adj.* **1.** Having no air. **2.** Lacking fresh air; stuffy. **3.** Lacking movement of air; still. **—air′less•ness** *n.*

air letter *n.* See **aerogram.**

air•lift (âr′lĭft′) *n.* **1.** A system of transporting troops, passengers, or supplies by air, as when surface routes are blocked. **2.** A flight in such a system. ❖ *tr.v.* **-lift•ed, -lift•ing, -lifts** To transport in an airlift.

air•line (âr′līn′) *n.* **1.** A system for scheduled air transport of passengers and freight. **2.** A business providing such a system.

air•lin•er (âr′lī′nər) *n.* A passenger airplane operated by an airline.

air lock *n.* **1.** An airtight chamber in which air pressure can be regulated. **2.** A bubble or pocket of air or vapor that stops the normal flow of fluid, as in a pipe.

air•mail (âr′māl′) *tr.v.* **-mailed, -mail•ing, -mails** To send (a letter, for example) by air. ❖ *n.* **air mail** also **airmail 1.** The system of conveying mail by aircraft. **2.** Mail conveyed by aircraft. ❖ *adj.* Of, relating to, or for use with air mail.

air•man (âr′mən) *n.* **1.** An enlisted person in the US Air Force ranking above airman basic and below airman first class. **2.** An enlisted person in the US Navy working with aircraft. **3.** An aviator.

airman basic *n.* An enlisted person in the US Air Force ranking below airman.

airman first class *n.* An enlisted person in the US Air Force ranking above airman and below senior airman.

air mass *n.* A large body of air with only small horizontal variations of temperature, pressure, and moisture.

air mattress *n.* An inflatable airtight sack on which to sleep or float in water.

Air Medal *n.* A decoration awarded by the US Army, Air Force, or Navy for meritorious conduct in flight operations.

air mile *n.* A unit of distance in air travel, equal to one international nautical mile (6,076.115 feet).

air•mo•bile also **air-mo•bile** (âr′mō′bəl, -bēl, -bīl) *adj.* Capable of being transported and deployed to a combat zone or between sites.

air piracy *n.* **1.** The hijacking or wrongful seizure of an aircraft. **2.** The illegal reception and descrambling of television signals relayed by satellite. **—air pirate** *n.*

air•plane (âr′plān′) *n.* A winged vehicle capable of flight, generally heavier than air and driven by jet engines or propellers.

air plant *n.* See **epiphyte.**

air•play (âr′plā′) *n.* The broadcasting of a recording on the air over radio or television.

air pocket *n.* A downward air current that causes an aircraft to lose altitude abruptly.

air police *n.* The military police of an air force.

air•port (âr′pôrt′, -pōrt′) *n.* A place where aircraft can take off and land, usu. having hangars, refueling facilities, and accommodations for passengers and cargo.

air potato or **air-po•ta•to** (âr′pə-tā′tō) *n.* A tropical Old World yam *(Dioscorea bulbifera)* having potatolike tubers.

air•pow•er or **air power** (âr′pou′ər) *n.* **1.** The organized use of aircraft and missiles for military purposes and foreign policy. **2.** The tactical and strategic strength of a country's air force.

air pump *n.* A pump for compressing, removing, or forcing a flow of air.

air raid *n.* An attack by military aircraft.

air rifle *n.* A low-powered rifle that uses compressed air or gas to fire small pellets.

air right *n.* A right to develop the space above a building or other structure. Often used in the plural.

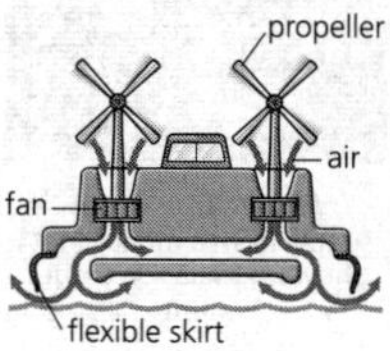

air-cushion vehicle
front cutaway view of a flexible skirt model hovercraft

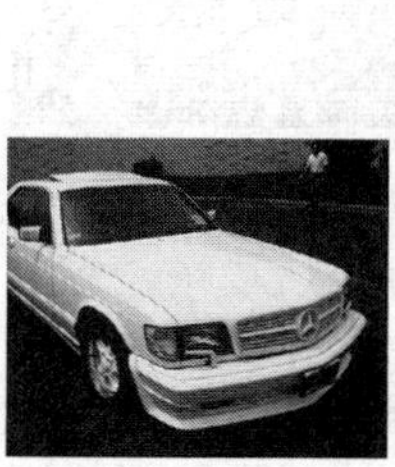

air dam

ă	pat	oi	boy
ā	pay	ou	out
âr	care	o͝o	took
ä	father	o͞o	boot
ĕ	pet	ŭ	cut
ē	be	ûr	urge
ĭ	pit	th	thin
ī	pie	*th*	this
îr	pier	hw	which
ŏ	pot	zh	vision
ō	toe	ə	about, item
ô	paw		

Stress marks:
′ (primary);
′ (secondary), as in
lexicon (lĕk′sĭ-kŏn′)

air sac *n.* **1.** An air-filled space in the body of a bird that forms a connection between the lungs and bone cavities. **2.** See **alveolus** 3. **3.** A saclike thin-walled enlargement in the trachea of an insect.

air•screw (âr′skrōō′) *n. Chiefly British* An airplane propeller.

air shed *n.* **1.** The air supply of a given region. **2.** The geographic region that shares an air supply. [AIR + (WATER)SHED.]

air•ship (âr′shĭp′) *n.* A self-propelled lighter-than-air craft with directional control surfaces.

air•sick (âr′sĭk′) *adj.* Suffering from airsickness.

air•sick•ness (âr′sĭk′nĭs) *n.* Nausea, vomiting, or dizziness induced by the motion that occurs during air flight.

air•space or **air space** (âr′spās′) *n.* **1.** The portion of the atmosphere above a particular land area. **2a.** The space occupied by an aircraft. **b.** A designated sector of space. **3.** See **airtime** 1.

air speed *n.* The speed, esp. of an aircraft, relative to the air.

air splint *n.* An inflatable cylinder used to immobilize injured limbs.

air spring *n.* See **air cushion** 2.

air strike *n.* An air attack on a ground or naval target.

air•strip (âr′strĭp′) *n.* See **landing strip.**

airt (ârt) *n. Scots* A cardinal point on the compass. [ME *art* < Sc. Gael. *aird* < OIr. *aird*, point of the compass.]

air taxi *n.* A small aircraft that makes short local flights.

air•tight (âr′tīt′) *adj.* **1.** Impermeable by air. **2.** Having no weak points; sound: *an airtight excuse.*

air•time (âr′tīm′) *n.* **1.** The time during which a radio or television station is broadcasting. **2.** The time of a broadcast.

air-to-air (âr′tə-âr′) *adj.* Operating between or designed to be fired from rockets or aircraft in flight.

air-to-sur•face (âr′tə-sûr′fĭs) *adj.* Operating from or designed to be fired from aircraft at targets on the ground.

air vesicle *n.* See **float** 2.

air walk *n.* An aboveground passageway connecting two buildings.

air•wave (âr′wāv′) *n.* The medium used for the transmission of radio and television signals. Often used in the plural.

air•way (âr′wā′) *n.* **1.** A passageway or shaft in which air circulates. **2a.** See **air lane. b.** See **airline** 2.

air•wor•thy (âr′wûr′thē) *adj.* Being in fit condition to fly: *airworthy avionics.* —**air′wor′thi•ness** *n.*

air•y (âr′ē) *adj.* **-i•er, -i•est** **1.** Of, relating to, or having the constitution of air. **2.** High in the air; lofty. **3.** Open to the air: *airy chambers.* **4.** Performed in the air; aerial. **5.** Immaterial; illusory: *an airy apparition.* **6.** Speculative, impractical, or vacuous: *airy theories.* **7.** Light; delicate. **8.** Haughty; affected: *an airy wave of the hand.* **9.** Light-hearted; merry: *an airy mood.* —**air′i•ly** *adv.* —**air′i•ness** *n.*

SYNONYMS *airy, diaphanous, ethereal, filmy, gauzy, gossamer, sheer, transparent, vaporous* These adjectives mean so light and insubstantial as to resemble air or a thin film: *airy curtains blowing at the window; a diaphanous veil; ethereal mist; the filmy wings of a moth; gauzy clouds; gossamer cobwebs; sheer silk stockings; transparent chiffon; vaporous shadows at dusk.*

air•y-fair•y (âr′ē-fâr′ē) *Chiefly British Slang n., pl.* **-ies** One that is insubstantial or impractical. ❖ *adj.* Insubstantial or impractical.

A•i•sha also **A•ye•sha** (ä′ē-shä′) 611–678. The wife of Muhammad who led a revolt against his successor, Ali.

aisle (īl) *n.* **1.** A part of a church separated from the nave by pillars or columns. **2.** A passageway between rows of seats. **3.** A passageway for indoor traffic. [Alteration (influenced by ISLE and Fr. *aile*, wing) of ME *ele* < OFr., wing of a building < Lat. *āla*.]

Aisne (ān) A river of N France rising in the Argonne Forest and flowing c. 266 km (165 mi) to the Oise R.

ait (āt) *n. Chiefly British* A small island. [ME *eit* < OE *īgeth*, dim. of *īg, īeg*, island. See ISLAND.]

aitch (āch) *n.* The letter *h.* [Fr. *hache*.]

aitch•bone (āch′bōn′) *n.* **1.** The rump bone, esp. of cattle. **2.** The cut of beef containing the rump bone. [Alteration (influenced by AITCH) of ME *hach-boon* < *an hach-boon*, an aitchbone, alteration of *a nachebon* : *nache*, buttock (< OFr. < LLat. *naticās*, accusative pl. of *natica*, buttock < Lat. *natis*) + *bon*, bone; see BONE.]

Aix-en-Pro•vence (āk′săn-prō-väns′, ĕk′-) A city of SE France N of Marseille; founded 123 B.C. Pop. 123,778.

Aix-la-Cha•pelle (āks′lä-shä-pĕl′, ĕks′-) See **Aachen.**

A•jac•cio (ä-yä′chō) A city of W Corsica, France, on the **Gulf of Ajaccio,** an inlet of the Mediterranean Sea; birthplace of Napoleon Bonaparte. Pop. 54,089.

A•jan•ta (ə-jŭn′tə) A village of W-central India SW of Amravati. Nearby caves dating from c. 200 B.C. to A.D. 650 contain remarkable examples of Buddhist art.

a•jar (ə-jär′) *adv. & adj.* Partially opened: *left the door ajar.* [ME *on char* : *on*, in; see ON + *char*, turn (< OE *cierr*).]

A•jar•i•a (ə-jär′ē-ə) See **Adzharia.**

A•jax (ā′jăks′) *n. Greek Mythology* **1.** The son of Telamon of Salamis and a warrior of great stature and prowess who fought against Troy. **2.** The son of Ileus of Locris and a warrior of small stature and arrogant character who fought against Troy.

Aj•man (ăj-män′) A sheikdom of E Arabia, part of the United Arab Emirates on the Persian Gulf. Pop. 3,725.

Aj•mer (ŭj-mîr′) A city of NW India SW of Delhi; founded c. A.D. 145. Pop. 402,700.

A•jodh•ya (ə-yōd′yə) See **Ayodhya.**

AK *abbr.* Alaska

AK-47 (ā′kā′fôr′tē-sĕv′ən) *n.* A clip-fed, gas-operated assault rifle of Soviet design having a caliber of 7.62 millimeters and used throughout the world by armed forces and paramilitary organizations. [Russ. *A(vtomat) K(alashnikova)*, automatic gun of Kalashnikov, after Viktor Timeevich *Kalashnikov* (born 1919), Soviet arms engineer.]

AKA *abbr.* also known as

A•kan (ä′kän′) *n., pl.* **Akan** or **A•kans** **1.** A Niger-Congo language spoken in parts of Ghana and the Côte d'Ivoire. **2.** A member of a people of Ghana and the Côte d'Ivoire. —**A′kan′** *adj.*

a•kar•y•o•cyte (ā-kăr′ē-ō-sīt′) *n.* A cell having no nucleus.

A•ka•shi (ä-kä′shē) A city of SW Honshu, Japan, on **Akashi Strait,** the E end of the Inland Sea. Pop. 280,795.

Ak•bar (ăk′bär) Known as "the Great." 1542–1605. Emperor of India (1556–1605) who conquered most of N India.

AKC *abbr.* American Kennel Club

ak•ee also **ac•kee** (ăk′ē, ə-kē′) *n.* **1.** A tropical western African evergreen tree (*Blighia sapida*) having leathery red and yellow fruits. **2.** The edible ripe aril of this tree. [Poss. Kru *akee* or Akan (Twi) *aŋkye*, wild cashew.]

A•khe•na•ton or **A•khe•na•ten** (ä′kə-nät′n, äk-nät′n) also **Ikh•na•ton** (ĭk-nät′n) Orig. Amenhotep IV. d. c. 1358 B.C. King of Egypt (1375?–1358?) who initiated worship of the sun god Aton.

Akh•ma•to•va (ək-mä′tə-və), **Anna** Pseudonym of Anna Andreevna Gorenko. 1889–1966. Russian poet whose work is noted for its lyrical beauty and intensity.

A•ki•ba ben Jo•seph (ä-kē′bə′ bĕn jō′zəf, -səf, ə-kē′və) A.D. 50?–132. Jewish religious leader whose works include a reinterpretation of the Halakah.

A•ki•hi•to (ä′kē-hē′tō) b. 1933. Emperor of Japan (since 1989).

a•kim•bo (ə-kĭm′bō) *adv.* In or into a position in which the hands are on the hips and the elbows are bowed outward: *standing akimbo.* ❖ *adj.* **1.** Placed in such a way as to have the hands on the hips and the elbows bowed outward: *with arms akimbo.* **2.** Being in a bent, bowed, or arched position. [ME *in kenebowe* : *in*, in; see IN[1] + *kenebowe* (*kene-*, of unknown meaning + *bowe*, bow, bend; see BOW[3].]

a•kin (ə-kĭn′) *adj.* **1.** Of the same kin; related by blood. **2.** Having a similar quality or character; analogous. **3.** *Linguistics* Sharing a common origin or an ancestral form.

a•ki•ne•sia (ā′kə-nē′zhə, -kī-) *n.* Loss of normal motor function, resulting in impaired muscle movement. [Gk. *akinēsiā* : *a-*, without; see A–[1] + *kinēsis*, motion; see –KINESIS.] —**a′ki•net′ic** (-nĕt′ĭk) *adj.*

A•ki•ta (ä-kē′tə, ä′kī-tä′) A city of NW Honshu, Japan, on the Sea of Japan. Pop. 307,862.

Ak•kad also **Ac•cad** (ăk′ăd′, ä′käd′) **1.** An ancient region of Mesopotamia in N Babylonia; reached the height of its power in the 3rd millennium B.C. **2.** also **A•ga•de** (ə-gä′də) An ancient city of Mesopotamia; cap. of the Akkadian empire.

Ak•ka•di•an (ə-kä′dē-ən) *n.* **1.** A native or inhabitant of ancient Akkad. **2.** The Semitic language of Mesopotamia. —**Ak•ka′di•an** *adj.*

Ak•ron (ăk′rən) A city of NE OH SSE of Cleveland. Its first rubber factory was est. in 1869 by B.F. Goodrich (1841–88). Pop. 217,074.

Ak•sum or **Ax•um** (äk′sōōm′) A town of N Ethiopia; cap. of an empire that controlled much of N Ethiopia (1st–8th cent. A.D.).

Ak•tyu•binsk (äk-tyōō′bĭnsk) See **Aqtöbe.**

Al The symbol for the element **aluminum.**

AL *abbr.* **1.** Alabama **2.** *Baseball* American League **3.** Arab League **4.** artificial light

al– *pref.* Variant of **ad–** 1.

–al¹ *suff.* Of, relating to, or characterized by: *parental.* [ME < OFr. < Lat. *-ālis, -adj. suff.*]

–al² *suff.* Action; process: *retrieval.* [ME *-aille* < OFr. < Lat. *-ālia* < neut. pl. of *-ālis.*]

–al³ *suff.* Aldehyde: *citronellal.* [< AL(DEHYDE).]

a•la (ā′lə) *n., pl.* **a•lae** (ā′lē) **1.** *Zoology* A wing or winglike structure or part. **2.** *Anatomy* A flat, winglike anatomic process or part, esp. of bone. **3.** *Botany* The flattened border of some stems, fruits, and seeds, or either one of the two side petals of certain flowers in the pea family. [Lat. *āla*, wing.]

Ala. *abbr.* Alabama

à la also **a la** (ä′ lä, ä′ lə, ăl′ə) *prep.* In the style or manner of. [Fr., short for *à la mode de*, in the manner of.]

Al•a•bam•a¹ (ăl′ə-băm′ə) *n., pl.* **Alabama** or **-as** **1.** A member of a tribe of the Creek confederacy formerly inhabiting southern Alabama and now located in eastern Texas. **2.** The Muskogean language of the Alabama.

Al•a•bam•a² (ăl′ə-băm′ə) A state of the SE US; admitted as the 22nd state in 1819. Cap. Montgomery. Pop. 4,447,100. —**Al′a•ba′mi•an** (-bā′mē-ən), **Al′a•bam′an** adj. & n.

Alabama River A river formed in central AL N of Montgomery and flowing c. 507 km (315 mi) to the Tombigbee R. N of Mobile.

Akbar the Great
detail from a manuscript showing Akbar on a tiger hunt

akee
Blighia sapida

Akhenaton
statue of Akhenaton and Nefertiti

al·a·bas·ter (ăl′ə-băs′tər) *n.* **1.** A dense translucent, white or tinted fine-grained gypsum. **2.** A variety of hard calcite, translucent and sometimes banded. **3.** A pale yellowish pink to yellowish gray. [ME *alabastre* < OFr. < Lat. *alabaster* < Gk. *alabastros, alabastos,* poss. of Egypt. orig.]

à la carte also **a la carte** (ä′ lə kärt′, ăl′ə) *adv. & adj.* With a separate price for each item on the menu. [Fr. : *à,* by + *la,* the + *carte,* menu.]

a·lack (ə-lăk′) *interj.* Used to express sorrow, regret, or alarm. [On the model of ALAS. See LACK.]

a·lac·ri·ty (ə-lăk′rĭ-tē) *n.* **1.** Cheerful willingness; eagerness. **2.** Speed or quickness; celerity. [Lat. *alacritās < alacer,* lively.] —**a·lac′ri·tous** (-təs) *adj.*

A·lad·din (ə-lăd′n) *n.* In the *Arabian Nights,* a boy who acquires a magic lamp and a magic ring with which he can summon two jinn to fulfill any desire.

a·lae (ā′lē) *n.* Plural of **ala.**

A·lai (ä′lī′) A mountain range of SW Kyrgyzstan extending c. 322 km (200 mi) W from the Chinese border and rising to 5,880.4 m (19,280 ft).

à la king (ä′ lə kĭng′, ăl′ə) *adj.* Cooked in a cream sauce with green pepper or pimiento and mushrooms.

al·a·me·da (ăl′ə-mē′də, -mä′-) *n. Southwestern US* A tree-shaded promenade or public park. [Sp. < *álamo,* poplar, alamo.]

Al·a·mein (ăl′ə-mān′), **El** See **El Alamein.**

al·a·mo (ăl′ə-mō′) *n., pl.* **-mos** *Southwestern US* A poplar tree, esp. a cottonwood. [Sp. *álamo.*]

Alamo A church built after 1744 as part of a mission in San Antonio TX; besieged and taken by Mexico (1836) during the Texas Revolution.

a·la·mode (ä′lə-mōd′, ăl′ə-) *n.* A lustrous plain-weave silk fabric for head coverings and scarfs. [< À LA MODE.]

à la mode (ä′ lə mōd′, ăl′ə) *adj.* **1.** According to the prevailing style. **2.** Served with ice cream. [Fr. : *à,* in + *la,* the + *mode,* fashion.]

Al·a·mo·gor·do (ăl′ə-mə-gôr′dō) A city of S-central NM NE of Las Cruces; first atomic bomb detonated nearby on Jul. 16, 1945. Pop. 35,582.

Å·land Islands (ā′lənd, ō′länd′) See **Ahvenanmaa.**

al·a·nine (ăl′ə-nēn′) *n.* A crystalline amino acid, $C_3H_7NO_2$, that is a constituent of many proteins. [Ger. *Alanin,* ult. < *Aldehyd,* aldehyde. See ALDEHYDE.]

a·lar (ā′lər) or **a·la·ry** (ā′lə-rē) *adj.* **1.** Resembling, containing, or composed of wings or alae. **2.** *Anatomy* Concerned with the armpit; axillary. [Lat. *ālāris < āla,* wing.]

Al·ar (ăl′är) A trademark used for daminozide.

A·lar·cón (ä′lär-kōn′), **Pedro Antonio de** 1833–91. Spanish writer whose novels include *The Three-Cornered Hat* (1874).

Al·ar·ic (ăl′ər-ĭk) A.D. 370?–410. King of the Visigoths (395–410) who plundered Greece in 395 and conquered Rome in 410.

a·larm (ə-lärm′) *n.* **1.** A sudden fear caused by the realization of danger. **2.** A warning of danger. **3.** A device that serves to warn of danger by a sound or signal. **4.** The sounding mechanism of an alarm clock. **5.** A call to arms. ❖ *tr.v.* **a·larmed, a·larm·ing, a·larms** **1.** To fill with alarm; frighten. See Syns at **fear. 2.** To give warning to. [ME < OFr. *alarme* < OItal. *allarme < all'arme,* to arms : *alla,* to the (< Lat. *ad illa : ad,* to + *illa,* neut. pl. of *ille,* that); see al- in App.) + *arme,* arms (< Lat. *arma;* see ar- in App.).] —**a·larm′ing·ly** *adv.*

alarm clock *n.* A clock that can be set to sound a bell or buzzer at a desired hour.

a·larm·ist (ə-lär′mĭst) *n.* A person who needlessly alarms others, as by inventing or spreading false or exaggerated rumors of impending danger. —**a·larm′ism** *n.*

a·la·rum (ə-lär′əm, -lăr′-) *n.* A warning or alarm, esp. a call to arms. [ME *alarom,* var. of *alarme,* alarm. See ALARM.]

a·las (ə-lăs′) *interj.* Used to express sorrow, regret, grief, compassion, or apprehension or danger or evil. [ME < OFr. *a las, helas,* ah (I am) miserable < Lat. *lassus,* weary.]

A·las·ka (ə-lăs′kə) A state of the US in extreme NW North America, separated from the other mainland states by British Columbia, Canada; admitted as the 49th state in 1959. Cap. Juneau. Pop. 626,932. —**A·las′kan** *adj. & n.*

Alaska, Gulf of An inlet of the Pacific Ocean between the Alaska Peninsula and Alexander Archipelago.

Alaska Highway Formerly **Al·can Highway** (ăl′kăn′) A road extending 2,450.5 km (1,523 mi) from Dawson Creek, British Columbia, to Fairbanks AK; built in 1942.

Alaska Native also **Alaskan Native** *n.* A member of any of the aboriginal peoples of Alaska, including American Indian, Eskimo, and Aleut peoples. See Usage Note at **Native American.**

Alaskan king crab *n.* See **king crab** 1.

Alaskan malamute *n.* A malamute.

Alaska Peninsula A peninsula of S-central to SW AK between the Bering Sea and the Pacific Ocean.

Alaska Range A mountain range of S-central AK rising to 6,197.6 m (20,320 ft) at Mt. McKinley.

Alaska Standard Time *n.* Standard time in the ninth time zone west of Greenwich, England, reckoned at 135° west and used throughout Alaska except for the western Aleutian Islands.

A·la-Tau (ăl′ə-tou′, ä′lə-) Several mountain ranges of the Tien

Shan in central Asia, E Kyrgyzstan, and SE Kazakhstan.

a·late (ā′lāt′) also **a·lat·ed** (ā′lā′tĭd) *adj.* Having winglike extensions or parts; winged. [Lat. *ālātus < āla,* wing.]

Al·a·va (ăl′ə-və), **Cape** A cape of NW WA; the westernmost point of the coterminous US.

alb (ălb) *n.* A long white linen robe with tapered sleeves worn by a priest at Mass. [ME *albe* < OE < Med.Lat. *alba < (vestis) alba,* white (garment), fem. of Lat. *albus,* white. See **albho-** in App.]

Alb. *abbr.* **1.** Albania **2.** Albanian

Al·ba (ăl′bə), **Duke of.** See Duke of **Alva.**

Alba. *abbr.* Alberta

Al·ba·ce·te (ăl′bə-sā′tē, äl′vä-thě′tě) A city of SE Spain WSW of Valencia. Pop. 132,448.

al·ba·core (ăl′bə-kôr′, -kōr′) *n., pl.* **albacore** or **-cores** A large marine fish (*Thunnus alalunga*) having edible flesh. [Port. *albacor* < Ar. *al-bakūra : al-,* the + *bakūra,* albacore.]

Alba Lon·ga (lông′gə, lŏng′-) A city of ancient Latium in central Italy SE of Rome; founded before 1100 B.C. and the legendary birthplace of Romulus and Remus.

Al·ba·ni·a (ăl-bā′nē-ə, -bān′yə, ôl-) A country of SE Europe on the Adriatic Sea; became a republic in 1925. Cap. Tiranë. Pop. 3,414,000.

Al·ba·ni·an (ăl-bā′nē-ən, -bān′yən, ôl-) *adj.* Of or relating to Albania or its people, language, or culture. ❖ *n.* **1.** A native or inhabitant of Albania. **2.** The Indo-European language of the Albanians.

Al·ba·no (äl-bä′nō) A lake of central Italy SE of Rome in an extinct volcanic crater.

Al·ba·ny (ôl′bə-nē) **1.** A city of SW GA SE of Columbus. Pop. 76,939. **2.** The cap. (since 1797) of NY, in the E part on the Hudson R.; founded in the early 17th cent. as Fort Orange and renamed Albany in 1664. Pop. 95,658.

Albany River A river rising in W Ontario, Canada, and flowing c. 982 km (610 mi) to James Bay.

al·ba·tross (ăl′bə-trôs′, -trŏs′) *n., pl.* **albatross** or **-tross·es 1.** Any of several large web-footed birds constituting the family Diomedeidae, chiefly of the oceans of the Southern Hemisphere. **2a.** A constant, worrisome burden. **b.** An obstacle to success. [Prob. alteration (influenced by Lat. *albus,* white) of *alcatras,* pelican < Port. or Sp. *alcatraz* < Ar. *al-ġaṭṭās : al-,* the + *ġaṭṭās,* diver, sea eagle (< *ġaṭasa,* to plunge, dive). Sense 2, after the *albatross* in *The Rime of the Ancient Mariner* by Samuel Taylor Coleridge, which the mariner killed and had to wear around his neck as a penance.]

al·be·do (ăl-bē′dō) *n., pl.* **-dos 1.** The fraction of incident electromagnetic radiation reflected by a surface. **2.** The spongy white tissue on the inside of the rind of citrus fruit. [LLat. *albēdō,* whiteness < Lat. *albus,* white. See **albho-** in App.]

Al·bee (ôl′bē, ŏl′-), **Edward Franklin** b. 1928. Amer. playwright whose works include *Who's Afraid of Virginia Woolf?* (1962).

al·be·it (ôl-bē′ĭt, ăl-) *conj.* Even though; although; notwithstanding: *a clear albeit cold day.* [ME *al be it : al,* even if; see ALL + *be,* subjunctive of *ben,* to be; see BE + *it,* it; see IT.]

Al·be·marle Sound (ăl′bə-märl′) A large body of generally fresh water in NE NC separated from the Atlantic Ocean by a narrow barrier island.

Al·bé·niz (äl-bě′nēs), **Isaac** 1860–1909. Spanish composer of piano works based on Spanish folk music.

Al·bers (ăl′bərz, ŏl′-), **Josef** 1888–1976. German-born Amer. painter whose works include *Homage to the Square* (1950–59).

Al·bert (ăl′bərt), **Prince.** 1819–61. German-born consort (1840–61) of Victoria.

Albert I 1875–1934. King of the Belgians (1909–34) who led the forces that reconquered Belgium (1918) during World War I.

Albert II b. 1934. King of the Belgians (crowned in 1993).

Albert, Lake also **Mo·bu·to Lake** (mə-bōō′tō, mō-) or **Albert Ny·an·za** (nī-ăn′zə, nyän′-) A shallow lake of E-central Africa in the Great Rift Valley between Uganda and Congo (formerly Zaire).

Al·ber·ta (ăl-bûr′tə) A province of W Canada between British Columbia and Saskatchewan; joined the confederation in 1905. Cap. Edmonton. Pop. 2,696,826. —**Al·ber′tan** *adj. & n.*

Al·ber·ti (ăl-bâr′tē), **Leon Battista** 1404–72. Italian mathematician and artist whose treatises introduced classical ideas into Renaissance art.

Albert Nile Part of the upper Nile R. in NW Uganda.

Al·ber·tus Mag·nus (ăl-bûr′təs măg′nəs), **Saint.** 1206?–80. German religious philosopher.

al·bes·cent (ăl-bĕs′ənt) *adj.* Becoming white; whitish. [Lat. *albēscēns, albēscent-,* pr. part. of *albēscere,* to become white < *albus,* white. See **albho-** in App.]

Al·bi·gen·ses (ăl′bĭ-jĕn′sēz′) *pl.n.* The members of a Catharist religious sect of southern France in the 12th and 13th centuries, condemned for heresy and persecuted during the Inquisition. [Med.Lat. *Albigēnsēs,* pl. of *Albigēnsis,* inhabitant of *Albiga,* Albi, a town of southern France where the sect was dominant.] —**Al′bi·gen′sian** (-shən, -sē-ən) *adj. & n.* —**Al′bi·gen′sian·ism** *n.*

al·bi·nism (ăl′bə-nĭz′əm) *n.* **1.** Congenital absence of pigmentation or coloration. **2.** The condition of being an albino. [Fr. *albi-*

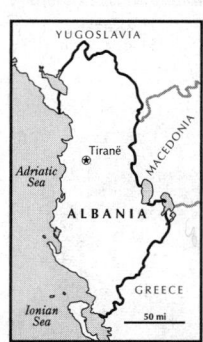

alabaster
Egyptian vessel in the form
of a lotus flower

Albania

ă	pat	oi	boy
ā	pay	ou	out
âr	care	oo	took
ä	father	oo	boot
ĕ	pet	ŭ	cut
ē	be	ûr	urge
ĭ	pit	th	thin
ī	pie	th	this
îr	pier	hw	which
ŏ	pot	zh	vision
ō	toe	ə	about,
ô	paw		item

Stress marks:
′ (primary);
′ (secondary); as in
lexicon (lĕk′sĭ-kŏn′)

nisme < Ger. *Albinismus* < *Albino,* albino < Port. See ALBINO.] —**al′bi•nis′tic** *adj.*

al•bi•no (ăl-bī′nō) *n., pl.* **-nos 1.** A person or animal with albinism, resulting in extremely pale skin and light hair and having usu. pinkish eyes with varying degrees of visual impairment. **2.** A plant that lacks chlorophyll. [Port. < *albo,* white < Lat. *albus.* See **albho-** in App.]

Al•bi•on (ăl′bē-ən) England or Great Britain.

al•bite (ăl′bīt) *n.* A white feldspar, NaAlSi₃O₈, that is one of the common rock-forming plagioclase group. [Lat. *albus,* white; see **albho-** in App. + -ITE¹.] —**al•bit′ic** (-bĭt′ĭk), **al•bit′i•cal** (-ĭ-kəl) *adj.*

Al•boin (ăl′boin, -bō-ĭn) d. 572. King of the Lombards (565?–572) who led the Germanic invasion of Italy.

Ål•borg also **Aal•borg** (ôl′bôrg′) A city of N Denmark NNE of Århus; chartered 1342. Pop. 157,270.

Al•bright (ôl′brīt, ōl′-), **Horace Marden** 1890–1987. Amer. conservationist and cofounder of the National Park Service.

Albright, Madeleine Korbel b. 1937. Czechoslovakian-born Amer. diplomat; first woman appointed as US secretary of state.

al•bum (ăl′bəm) *n.* **1.** A book with blank pages for the insertion and preservation of collections, as of stamps. **2a.** A phonograph record, esp. a long-playing record stored in a slipcase. **b.** A set of musical recordings stored together in jackets under one binding. **c.** The bound set of jackets for such a set. **d.** A recording of different musical pieces. **3.** A printed collection of musical compositions, pictures, or literary selections. **4.** A tall printed book, often having profuse illustrations and short, sentimental texts. [Lat., blank tablet < neut. of *albus,* white. See **albho-** in App.]

al•bu•men (ăl-byōō′mən) *n.* **1.** The white of an egg. **2.** See **albumin.** [Lat. *albūmen* < *albus,* white. See **albho-** in App.]

al•bu•min (ăl-byōō′mĭn) *n.* A class of simple water-soluble proteins that coagulate on being heated and are found esp. in egg white, blood, and milk. [ALBUM(EN) + -IN.] —**al•bu′mi•nous** *adj.*

al•bu•mi•noid (ăl-byōō′mə-noid′) *n.* See **scleroprotein.** ❖ *adj.* also **al•bu•mi•noi•dal** (-byōō′mə-noid′l) Composed of or resembling albumin.

al•bu•mi•nu•ri•a (ăl-byōō′mə-nŏŏr′ē-ə, -nyŏŏr-) *n.* The presence of albumin in the urine. —**al•bu′mi•nu′ric** (-nŏŏr′ĭk, -nyŏŏr′-) *adj.*

al•bu•mose (ăl′byə-mōs′, -mōz′) *n.* A class of substances derived from albumins and formed by the enzymatic breakdown of proteins during digestion. [Fr. : *albumine,* albumin; see ALBUMIN + *-ose,* -ose; see -OSE².]

Al•bu•quer•que (ăl′bə-kûr′kē) A city of central NM on the Rio Grande SW of Santa Fe; founded 1706. Pop. 448,607.

Albuquerque, Affonso de Known as "Affonso the Great." 1453–1515. Portuguese colonial administrator considered the founder of the E Portuguese empire.

al•bu•ter•ol (ăl-byōō′tə-rôl′, -rōl′) *n.* A bronchodilator used in the treatment of asthma and other obstructive lung diseases. [Prob. alteration of earlier *salbutamol* (influenced by AL(COHOL) and perh. TER(TIARY)) : *sal(icyl),* the radical of salicylic acid (< Fr. *salicyle;* see SALICYLIC ACID) + BUT(YL) + AM(INE) + -OL¹.]

Al•cae•us (ăl-sē′əs) fl. 611?–580 B.C. Greek poet who reputedly invented Alcaic verse.

Al•ca•ic (ăl-kā′ĭk) *adj.* Of or relating to a verse form consisting of strophes having four tetrametric lines. [LLat. *Alcaicus,* of Alcaeus < Gk. *Alkaïkos* < *Alkaios,* Alcaeus.] —**Al•ca′ic** *n.*

al•cai•de also **al•cay•de** (ăl-kī′dē) *n.* The commander or governor of a fortress in Spain or Portugal. [Sp. < Ar. *al-qā'id,* the commander : *al-,* the + *qā'id,* leader, active part. of *qāda,* to lead.]

Al•ca•lá de He•na•res (ăl′kə-lä′ dä hĕ-när′əs, äl′kä-lä′ thĕ ĕ-nä′rĕs) A town of central Spain ENE of Madrid; birthplace of Cervantes. Pop. 159,355.

al•cal•de (ăl-käl′dē, äl-käl′dĕ) *n.* The mayor or chief judicial official of a Spanish town. [Sp. < Ar. *al-qāḍī* : *al-,* the + *qāḍī,* judge, active part. of *qaḍā,* to judge.]

Al•can Highway (ăl′kăn′) See **Alaska Highway.**

Al•ca•traz (ăl′kə-trăz′) A rocky island of W CA in San Francisco Bay; a military prison from 1859 to 1933 and a federal prison until 1963.

al•caz•ar (ăl-kăz′ər, -kä′zər, ăl′kə-zär′) *n.* A Spanish palace or fortress, originally one built by the Moors. [Sp. *alcázar* < Ar. *alqaṣr* : *al,* the + *qaṣr,* castle (< Lat. *castra,* fort, pl. of *castrum,* camp).]

Al•ces•tis (ăl-sĕs′tĭs) *n.* Greek Mythology The wife of Admetus, who agreed to die in his place and was later rescued from Hades by Hercules.

al•che•mist (ăl′kə-mĭst) *n.* A practitioner of alchemy. —**al′che•mis′tic, al′che•mis′ti•cal** *adj.*

al•che•my (ăl′kə-mē) *n.* **1.** A medieval chemical philosophy having as its asserted aims the transmutation of base metals into gold, the discovery of the panacea, and the preparation of the elixir of longevity. **2.** A seemingly magical power or process of transmuting: *"He wondered by what alchemy it was changed, so that what sickened him one hour, maddened him with hunger the next"* (Marjorie K. Rawlings). [ME *alkamie* < OFr. *alquemie* < Med.Lat. *alchymia* < Ar. *al-kīmiyā'* : *al-,* the + *kīmiyā',* chemistry (< L.Gk. *khēmeia, khumeia,* perh. < Gk. *Khēmiā,* Egypt).]

—**al•chem′i•cal** (ăl-kĕm′ĭ-kəl), **al•chem′ic** *adj.* —**al′che•mize′** (ăl′kə-mīz′) *v.* —**al•chem′ist** *n.* —**al′che•mize′** (ăl′kə-mīz′) *v.* —**al•chem′ist** *n.*

Al•ci•bi•a•des (ăl′sə-bī′ə-dēz′) 450?–404 B.C. Athenian politician and general who changed allegiance three times during the Peloponnesian War (431–404).

Alc•me•ne (ălk-mē′nē) *n.* Greek Mythology Amphitryon's wife and mother of Hercules by Zeus.

al•co•hol (ăl′kə-hôl′, -hŏl′) *n.* **1.** A colorless volatile flammable liquid, C₂H₅OH, synthesized or obtained by fermentation of sugars and starches and used as a solvent and in drugs and intoxicating beverages: *he drinks too much alcohol.* **2.** Alcoholic beverages. **3.** Any of a series of hydroxyl compounds having the general formula CₙH₂ₙ₊₁OH, including ethanol and methanol. [Med.Lat., fine metallic powder, esp. of antimony < Ar. *al-kuḥl* : *al-,* the + *kuḥl,* powder of antimony.]

WORD HISTORY The *al-* in *alcohol* may alert some readers to the fact that this is a word of Arabic descent, as is the case with *algebra* and *alkali. Al-* is the Arabic definite article corresponding to *the* in English. The origin of *–cohol* is less obvious, however. Its Arabic ancestor was *kuḥl,* a fine powder most often made from antimony and used by women to darken their eyelids. Arabic chemists came to use *al-kuḥl* to mean "any fine powder produced in a number of ways, including the process of heating a substance to a gaseous state and then recooling it." The English word *alcohol,* derived through Medieval Latin from Arabic, is first recorded in 1543 in this sense. Arabic chemists also used *al-kuḥl* to refer to other substances, such as essences that were obtained by distillation. This sense of *alcohol* is first found in English in 1672. One of these distilled essences, known as "alcohol of wine," is the constituent of fermented liquors that causes intoxication. This essence took over the term *alcohol* for itself, and it has since come to refer to the liquor that contains this essence as well as to a class of chemical compounds such as methanol.

al•co•hol•ic (ăl′kə-hô′lĭk, -hŏl′ĭk) *adj.* **1.** Related to or resulting from alcohol. **2.** Containing or preserved in alcohol. **3.** Suffering from alcoholism. ❖ *n.* A person who suffers from alcoholism. —**al•co•hol′i•cal•ly** *adv.*

al•co•hol•ism (ăl′kə-hô-lĭz′əm, -hŏ-) *n.* A disorder characterized by the excessive consumption of and dependence on alcoholic beverages, leading to physical and psychological impairment.

al•co•hol•om•e•ter (ăl′kə-hô-lŏm′ĭ-tər) also **al•co•hol•me•ter** (ăl′kə-hôl-mē′tər, -hŏl-) *n.* An instrument used to determine the amount of alcohol in a liquid. —**al′co•hol•om′e•try** *n.*

Al•cott (ôl′kət, -kŏt, ōl′-), **Amos Bronson** 1799–1888. Amer. educator and transcendentalist reformer.

Alcott, Louisa May 1832–88. Amer. writer and reformer best known for her novel *Little Women* (1868–69).

al•cove (ăl′kōv′) *n.* **1.** A recess or partly enclosed extension connected to or forming part of a room. **2.** A secluded structure, such as a bower, in a garden. [Fr. *alcôve* < Sp. *alcoba* < Ar. *al-qubba,* the vault : *al-,* the + *qubba,* vault.]

Al•cuin (ăl′kwĭn) 735?–804. Anglo-Saxon prelate and scholar who was a leader in the revival of learning.

Al•cy•o•ne (ăl-sī′ə-nē) *n.* **1.** Greek Mythology The daughter of Aeolus who in grief over the death of her husband threw herself into the sea and was changed into a kingfisher. **2.** Greek Mythology A nymph, one of the Pleiades. **3.** Astronomy The brightest star in the Pleiades. [Lat. < Gk. *Alkuonē < alkuōn,* kingfisher.]

Ald. *abbr.* **1.** alderman **2.** alderwoman

Al•dan (äl-dän′) A river of SE Russia rising in the Stanovoy Range and flowing c. 2,253 km (1,400 mi) around the **Aldan Plateau** to the Lena R. N of Yakutsk.

Al•deb•a•ran (ăl-dĕb′ər-ən) *n.* A bright double star in the constellation Taurus. [ME *Aldeboran* < Med.Lat. *Aldebaran* < Ar. *addabarān* : *al-,* the + *dabarān,* following (the Pleiades) (< *dabara,* to follow).]

al•de•hyde (ăl′də-hīd′) *n.* **1.** Any of a class of highly reactive organic chemical compounds obtained by oxidation of primary alcohols, characterized by the common group CHO, and used in resins, dyes, and organic acids. **2.** See **acetaldehyde.** [Ger. *Aldehyd* < NLat. *al. dehyd.,* short for *alcohol dehydrogenātum,* dehydrogenized alcohol.]

Al•den (ôl′dən), **John** 1599?–1687. Pilgrim colonist known for his courtship of Priscilla Mullins (b. c. 1602).

al den•te (ăl dĕn′tĕ, äl dĕn′tä) *adj.* Cooked just enough to be firm. [Ital. : *al,* to the + *dente,* tooth.] —**al den′te** *adv.*

al•der (ôl′dər) *n.* **1.** Any of various deciduous shrubs or trees of the genus *Alnus,* native chiefly to northern temperate regions and having toothed leaves and fruits in woody conelike catkins. **2.** The wood of these plants, used in carvings and furniture. [ME < OE *alor.*]

Al•der (ăl′dər), **Kurt** 1902–58. German chemist who shared a 1950 Nobel Prize.

al•der•man (ôl′dər-mən) *n.* **1.** A member of a municipal legislative body. **2.** A member of the higher branch of the municipal or borough council in England and Ireland before 1974. **3a.** A noble of high rank or authority in Anglo-Saxon England. **b.** The chief officer of a shire in Anglo-Saxon England. [ME, a person of high rank < OE *ealdorman* : *ealdor,* elder, chief (< *eald,* old) + *man,*

Madeleine Albright

alcazar
Segovia, Spain

Louisa May Alcott

alder
white alder
Alnus rhombifolia

man; see MAN.] —**al′der·man·cy** (-sē) *n.* —**al′der·man′ic** (-măn′ĭk) *adj.*

Al·der·ney[1] (ôl′dər-nē) A British island in the Channel Is. separated from the French coast by the **Race of Alderney.**

Al·der·ney[2] (ôl′dər-nē) *n., pl.* **-neys** One of a breed of dairy cattle originally raised in the Channel Islands.

al·der·wom·an (ôl′dər-wŏŏm′ən) *n.* A woman who is a member of a municipal legislative body. [ALDER(MAN) + WOMAN.]

al·di·carb (ăl′dĭ-kärb′) *n.* A crystalline compound, $C_7H_{14}N_2O_2S$, used in agriculture as a pesticide. [(*propion)ald(ehyde)* + *(methyl)carb(amoyloxime)*, two of its constituents.]

al·dol (ăl′dôl′, -dōl′, -dŏl′) *n.* **1.** A thick colorless to yellow liquid, $C_4H_8O_2$, obtained from acetaldehyde and used in perfumery and as a solvent. **2.** A similar aldehyde. [ALD(EHYDE) + -OL[1].]

al·dol·ase (ăl′də-lās′) *n.* An enzyme in certain living tissues that catalyzes the breakdown of a fructose ester into triose sugars.

al·dose (ăl′dōs′, -dōz′) *n.* Any of a class of monosaccharide sugars containing an aldehyde group. [ALD(EHYDE) + -OSE[1].]

al·dos·ter·one (ăl-dŏs′tə-rōn′) *n.* A steroid hormone secreted by the cortex of an adrenal gland that regulates the salt and water balance in the body. [ALD(EHYDE) + STER(OL) + -ONE.]

al·dos·ter·on·ism (ăl-dŏs′tə-rō-nĭz′əm, ăl′dō-stĕr′ə-) *n.* A disorder marked by excessive secretion of aldosterone, resulting in muscle weakness and cardiovascular abnormalities.

al·drin (ôl′drĭn) *n.* An insecticide containing a naphthalene-derived compound, $C_{12}H_8Cl_6$. [After Kurt ALDER.]

Al·drin (ôl′drĭn, ŏl′-), **Edwin Eugene, Jr.** Known as "Buzz." b. 1930. Amer. astronaut who was the second person to walk on the moon (Jul. 20, 1969).

Al·dus Ma·nu·tius (ôl′dəs mə-nōō′shəs, -shē-əs, -nyōō′-, ŏl′-) See Aldus **Manutius.**

ale (āl) *n.* **1.** A fermented alcoholic beverage similar to but heavier than beer. **2.** A serving of this beverage. [ME < OE *ealu, alu.* See **alu-** in App.]

a·le·a·to·ry (ā′lē-ə-tôr′ē, -tōr′ē) *adj.* **1.** Dependent on chance, luck, or an uncertain outcome. **2.** Of or characterized by gambling. **3.** also **a·le·a·to·ric** (ā′lē-ə-tôr′ĭk, -tōr′-) *Music* Using or consisting of sounds chosen by the performer or left to chance. [Lat. *aleātōrius < āleātor,* gambler < *alea,* game of chance, die.]

a·lec·i·thal (ā-lĕs′ə-thəl) *adj.* Having little or no yolk: *an alecithal egg.* [A-[1] + LECITH(IN) + -AL[1].]

A·lec·to (ə-lĕk′tō) *n. Greek & Roman Mythology* One of the Furies.

a·lee (ə-lē′) *adv.* At, on, or to the leeward side.

al·e·gar (ăl′ĭ-gər, ā′lĭ-) *n.* Vinegar made from ale. [ME, blend of *ale,* ale. See ALE and *vinegar,* vinegar; see VINEGAR.]

ale·house (āl′hous′) *n.* A place where ale is sold and served.

A·lei·chem (ä-lā′kĕm, -ᴋʜĕm), **Sholem** or **Shalom** Orig. Solomon Rabinowitz. 1859–1916. Russian-born Jewish humorist noted for his stories and plays.

A·leix·an·dre (ä′lĕk-sän′drə), **Vicente** 1898–1984. Spanish poet who won the 1977 Nobel Prize for literature.

A·lek·san·drovsk (ăl′ĭk-sän′drəfsk, ə-lĭk-sän′-) See Zaporizhzhya.

Al·e·man·ni (ăl′ə-măn′ī) *pl.n.* A group of Germanic tribes that settled in and near Alsace during the fourth century A.D. and were defeated by the Franks in 496. [Lat. *Alemannī* < Gmc. orig. See **man-**[1] in App.]

Al·e·man·nic (ăl′ə-măn′ĭk) *n.* **1.** A group of High German dialects spoken in Alsace, Switzerland, and parts of southern Germany. **2.** The Germanic dialect of the Alemanni. ❖ *adj.* **1.** Of or relating to the Alemannic dialects. **2.** Of or relating to the Alemanni or their language.

A·lem·bert (ăl′əm-bâr′, ă-län-bĕr′), **Jean Le Rond d'** 1717–83. French mathematician and philosopher who wrote the influential *Treatise of Dynamics* (1743).

a·lem·bic (ə-lĕm′bĭk) *n.* **1.** An apparatus consisting of two vessels connected by a tube, formerly used for distilling. **2.** A device that purifies or alters by a process comparable to distillation. [ME *alambic* < OFr. < Med.Lat. *alembicus* < Ar. *al-'anbīq : al-,* the + *'anbīq,* still (< Gk. *ambix,* cup).]

a·leph (ä′lĕf, -ləf) *n.* The first letter of the Hebrew alphabet. [Heb. *'āleph* < Phoenician **'alp,* ox, first letter of the Phoenician alphabet.]

a·leph-null (ä′lĕf-nŭl′, -ləf-) *n.* The first of the transfinite cardinal numbers.

A·lep·po (ə-lĕp′ō) also **A·lep** (ə-lĕp′) A city of NW Syria near the Turkish border; inhabited perhaps as early as the 6th millennium B.C. Pop. 1,542,000.

a·lert (ə-lûrt′) *adj.* **1.** Vigilantly attentive: *alert to danger.* See Syns at **aware. 2.** Mentally responsive and perceptive. **3.** Brisk or lively in action: *the bird's alert hopping.* ❖ *n.* **1.** A signal that warns of danger: *Sirens sounded the alert.* **2.** A condition or period of heightened watchfulness or preparation for action. ❖ *tr.v.* **a·lert·ed, a·lert·ing, a·lerts** To notify of approaching danger or action. —**idiom: on the alert** Watchful and prepared for danger, emergency, or opportunity. [Fr. *alerte* < Ital. *all' erta,* on the lookout : *alla,* to the, on the (< Lat. *ad illam,* to that : *ad,* to, to AD- + *illam,* fem. accusative of *ille,* that) + *erta,* lookout < p. part. of *ergere,* to raise (< Lat. *ērigere,* to raise; see ERECT).] —**a·lert′ly** *adv.* —**a·lert′ness** *n.*

A·leut (ə-lōōt′, ăl′ē-ōōt′) *n., pl.* **Aleut** or **A·leuts 1.** A member of a Native American people inhabiting the Aleutian Islands and coastal areas of southwest Alaska. **2.** Either or both of the two languages of the Aleut. See Usage Note at **Native American.** [Russ.]

A·leu·tian (ə-lōō′shən) *adj.* Of or relating to the Aleut, their language, or their culture. ❖ *n.* A native or inhabitant of the Aleutian Islands, esp. an Aleut.

Aleutian Islands A chain of rugged volcanic islands of SW AK curving c. 1,931 km (1,200 mi) W from the Alaska Peninsula; under Russian control from 1741 until 1867.

Aleutian Range A mountain chain of SW AK extending W along the Alaska Peninsula and the Aleutian Is. to Attu I.

A level *n. Chiefly British* The later of two standardized tests in a secondary school subject, used for university admissions. [*A(dvanced) level.*]

ale·wife[1] (āl′wīf′) *n., pl.* **-wives** (-wīvz′) A fish (*Alosa pseudoharengus*) closely related to the herrings and native to North American Atlantic waters and some inland lakes. [Prob. alteration (influenced by ALEWIFE[2]) of obsolete *allowes,* a type of shad < Fr. *alose,* shad < OFr. < LLat. *alausa.*]

ale·wife[2] (āl′wīf′) *n., pl.* **-wives** (-wīvz′) A woman who keeps an alehouse.

al·ex·an·der also **Al·ex·an·der** (ăl′ĭg-zăn′dər) *n.* A cocktail made with crème de cacao, sweet cream, and brandy or gin. [< the name *Alexander.*]

Alexander I[1] 1777–1825. Czar of Russia (1801–25) whose plans to liberalize his country's government were forestalled by wars with Napoleon I.

Alexander I[2] Orig. Alexander Obrenović. 1876–1903. King of Serbia (1889–1903) whose efforts to increase his power at the expense of the national assembly led to his assassination.

Alexander I[3] 1888–1934. King of Yugoslavia (1921–34) who unified the peoples of Serbia, Croatia, and Slovenia (1929).

Alexander I Island An island in Bellingshausen Sea off the coast of the Antarctic Peninsula.

Alexander II 1818–81. Czar of Russia (1855–81) who emancipated the serfs in 1861.

Alexander III[1] Known as "Alexander the Great." 356–323 B.C. King of Macedonia (336–323) and conqueror of Asia Minor, Syria, Egypt, Babylonia, and Persia.

Alexander III[2] d. 1181. Pope (1159–81) who established papal supremacy.

Alexander VI 1431–1503. Pope (1492–1503) noted as a patron of the arts.

Alexander Archipelago A group of more than 1,000 islands off SE AK.

Alexander Nev·ski (nĕv′skē, nĕf′-) 1220?–63. Russian national hero who defeated the Swedes (1240).

Alexander of Tunis, 1st Earl. Title of Harold Rupert Leofric George Alexander. 1891–1969. British field marshal in World War II.

Alexander Se·ve·rus (sə-vîr′əs) A.D. 208?–235. Emperor of Rome (222–235) who succeeded his cousin Heliogabalus.

Al·ex·an·der·son (ăl′ĭg-zăn′dər-sən), **Ernst Frederick Werner** 1878–1975. Swedish-born Amer. electrical engineer who demonstrated the first practical television system (1930).

Alexander the Great See Alexander III[1].

Al·ex·an·dra (ăl′ĭg-zăn′drə, -zän′-) 1872–1918. Last czarina of Russia (1894–1917).

Al·ex·an·dret·ta (ăl′ĭg-zăn-drĕt′ə) See Iskenderun.

Al·ex·an·dri·a (ăl′ĭg-zăn′drē-ə) **1.** A city of N Egypt on the Mediterranean Sea at the W tip of the Nile Delta. Founded in 332 B.C., it was famous for its libraries and pharos (lighthouse), one of the Seven Wonders of the World. Pop. 3,380,000. **2.** An independent city of N VA on the Potomac R. opposite Washington DC; laid out in 1749. Pop. 128,283.

Al·ex·an·dri·an (ăl′ĭg-zăn′drē-ən) *adj.* **1.** Of or relating to Alexander the Great. **2.** Of or relating to Alexandria, Egypt. **3.** Of, characteristic of, or belonging to a school of Hellenistic literature, science, and philosophy located at Alexandria in the last three centuries B.C.

al·ex·an·drine also **Al·ex·an·drine** (ăl′ĭg-zăn′drĭn) *n.* **1.** A line of English verse in iambic hexameter, usu. with a caesura after the third foot. **2.** A line of French verse consisting of 12 syllables, usu. with a caesura after the sixth syllable. ❖ *adj.* Characterized by or composed of alexandrines. [Fr. *alexandrin* < OFr. < *Alexandre,* title of a romance about Alexander the Great written in this meter.]

al·ex·an·drite (ăl′ĭg-zăn′drīt′) *n.* A greenish chrysoberyl that appears red in artificial light, used as a gemstone. [Ger. *Alexandrit,* after ALEXANDER I[1].]

a·lex·i·a (ə-lĕk′sē-ə) *n.* Loss of the ability to read. [A-[1] + Gk. *lexis,* speech (< *legein,* to speak; see **leg-** in App.) + -IA[1].]

a·lex·in (ə-lĕk′sĭn) *n. Biochemistry* Complement. [Gk. *alexein,* to ward off + -IN.]

A·lex·is I Mi·khai·lo·vich (ä-lĕk′sĭs; mĭ-kī′lə-vĭch, mə-ᴋʜī′-) 1629–76. Czar of Russia (1645–76) who implemented a code of law that established serfdom (1649).

A·lex·i·us I Com·ne·nus (ə-lĕk′sē-əs; kŏm-nē′nəs) 1048–1118. Emperor of Byzantium (1081–1118) whose reign was

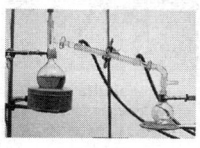

alembic

Alexander the Great
detail from a first-century
A.D. Roman mosaic
depicting the Battle of Issus

ă	pat	oi	boy
ā	pay	ou	out
âr	care	ŏŏ	took
ä	father	ōō	boot
ĕ	pet	ŭ	cut
ē	be	ûr	urge
ĭ	pit	th	thin
ī	pie	th	this
îr	pier	hw	which
ŏ	pot	zh	vision
ō	toe	ə	about,
ô	paw		item

Stress marks:
′ (primary);
′ (secondary), as in
lexicon (lĕk′sĭ-kŏn′)

marked by the First Crusade (1096–99).

al·fal·fa (ăl-făl′fə) *n.* A southwest Asian perennial herb (*Medicago sativa*) with compound leaves and clusters of usu. blue-violet flowers, cultivated as a pasture and hay crop. [Sp. < Ar. *alfasfasa* : *al-*, the + *fasfasa*, alfalfa (var. of *fisfisa* < Pers. *aspist*, clover).]

alfalfa weevil *n.* A weevil (*Hypera postica*) native to Europe that has widely infested North American alfalfa crops.

Al Fay·yam (ăl′ fä-ōōm′, fĭ-, äl′) A city of N Egypt on the Nile R. SSW of Cairo. Pop. 250,000.

Al·fie·ri (äl-fē-âr′ē, äl-fyâr′ē), Conte **Vittorio** 1749–1803. Italian playwright whose works influenced Italian nationalism.

al·fil·a·ri·a or **al·fil·e·ri·a** (ăl-fĭl′ə-rē′ə) *n.* An annual Mediterranean plant (*Erodium cicutarium*) having pinnately dissected leaves and small pink or purple flowers and used for spring forage in the western United States. [Am.Sp. *alfilerillo*, a cactus with sharp pointed leaves < Sp., dim. of *alfiler*, pin < Ar. *al-hilāl*, the thorn : *al-*, the + *hilāl*, thorn (< *halla*, to pierce).]

Al·föld also **Great Al·föld** (ôl′föld) An extensive plain of central Hungary extending into N Serbia and W Romania. The **Little Alföld** lies in NW Hungary and SW Slovakia.

Al·fon·so I (äl-fŏn′zō, äl-fōn′sō) 1110?–85. King of Portugal (1139–85) who won Portuguese independence from Castile (1139).

Alfonso XIII 1886–1941. King of Spain (1886–1931) who abdicated on the establishment of a republican government.

al·for·ja (äl-fôr′hä, äl-) *n. Western US* A saddlebag. [Sp. < OSpan. < Ar. *al-hurj* : *al-*, the + *hurj*, saddlebag; akin to Pers. *khurjīn*.]

Al·fred (ăl′frĭd) Known as "the Great." 849–899. King of the West Saxons (871–899) noted as a scholar and lawmaker.

al·fres·co (ăl-frĕs′kō) *adv.* In the fresh air: *dined alfresco.* ❖ *adj.* Taking place outdoors: *an alfresco conference.* [Ital. *al fresco*, in the fresh (air) : *al*, in the (*a*, to, in < Lat. *ad* + *il*, the, < Lat. *ille*; see **al-** in App.) + *fresco*, fresh.]

Alg. *abbr.* Algeria

al·ga (ăl′gə) *n., pl.* **-gae** (-jē) Any of various chiefly aquatic, eukaryotic, photosynthetic organisms, ranging from single-celled forms to the giant kelp. [Lat., seaweed.] —**al′gal** (ăl′gəl) *adj.*

al·gar·ro·ba or **al·ga·ro·ba** (ăl′gə-rō′bə) *n.* **1a.** See **mesquite** b. **b.** The edible pod of this plant. **2.** See **carob** 1. [Am.Sp. *mesquite* < Sp. *carob* < Ar. *al-harrūba* : *al-*, the + *harrūba*, carob pod (< *harrūb*, carob).]

Al·gar·ve (äl-gär′və) A medieval Moorish kingdom in present-day S Portugal.

al·ge·bra (ăl′jə-brə) *n.* **1.** A branch of mathematics in which symbols, usu. letters, represent numbers or members of a specified set and are used to represent quantities and to express general relationships that hold for all members of the set. **2.** A set together with a pair of binary operations defined on the set. Usually, the set and the operations include an identity element, and the operations are commutative or associative. [ME, bone-setting, and Ital., algebra, both < Med.Lat. < Ar. *al-jabr* (*wa-l-muqābala*), the restoration (and the compensation), addition (and subtraction) : *al-*, the + *jabr*, bone-setting, restoration (< *jabara*, to set (bones), restore).] —**al′ge·bra′ist** (-brā′ĭst) *n.*

al·ge·bra·ic (ăl′jə-brā′ĭk) *adj.* **1.** Of or relating to algebra. **2.** Of or relating to an expression, equation, or function in which only numbers, variables, and a finite number of arithmetic operations are contained or used. —**al′ge·bra′i·cal·ly** *adv.*

algebraic number *n.* A number that is a root of a polynomial equation with rational coefficients.

Al·ge·ci·ras (ăl′jĭ-sîr′əs, äl′hĕ-thē′räs) A city of S Spain on the **Bay of Algeciras** opposite Gibraltar. Pop. 101,256.

Al·ger (ăl′jər), **Horatio** 1832–99. Amer. writer of inspirational adventure books, such as *Ragged Dick* (1867).

Al·ge·ri·a (ăl-jîr′ē-ə) A country of NW Africa on the Mediterranean; gained independence from France in 1962. Cap. Algiers. Pop. 27,325,000. —**Al·ge′ri·an** *adj. & n.*

–algia *suff.* Pain: *neuralgia.* [Gk. < *algos*, pain.]

al·gi·cide (ăl′jĭ-sīd′) *n.* A substance used to kill or inhibit the growth of algae. [ALG(A) + -CIDE.] —**al′gi·cid′al** (-sīd′l) *adj.*

al·gid (ăl′jĭd) *adj.* Cold; chilly. [Lat. *algidus* < *algēre*, to be cold.] —**al·gid′i·ty** (-jĭd′ĭ-tē) *n.*

Al·giers (ăl-jîrz′) The cap. of Algeria, in the N part on the **Bay of Algiers**, an arm of the Mediterranean. Pop. 1,523,000.

al·gin (ăl′jĭn) *n.* Any of several derivatives of a gelatinous substance extracted from brown algae and widely used to thicken, stabilize, emulsify, or suspend. [ALG(A) + -IN.]

algo– *pref.* Pain: *algophobia.* [< Gk. *algos*, pain.]

al·goid (ăl′goid′) *adj.* Of or resembling algae.

Al·gol (ăl′gŏl′, -gôl′) *n.* A double, eclipsing variable star in the constellation Perseus. [Ar. *al-gūl* : *al-*, the + *gūl*, ghoul; see GHOUL.]

ALGOL also **Algol** *n.* An algebraic computer language for solving problems using algorithms. [*alg(orithmic-)o(riented) l(anguage).*]

al·go·lag·ni·a (ăl′gō-lăg′nē-ə) *n.* Sexual gratification that is derived from inflicting or experiencing pain. [NLat. : ALGO- + Gk. *lagneia*, lust (< *lagnos*, lustful).] —**al′go·lag′nic** *adj.* —**al′go·lag′nist** *n.*

al·gol·o·gy (ăl-gŏl′ə-jē) *n.* See **phycology**. [ALG(A) + -LOGY.]

—**al′go·log′i·cal** (ăl′gə-lŏj′ĭ-kəl) *adj.* —**al′go·log′i·cal·ly** *adv.* —**al′gol′o·gist** *n.*

Al·gon·ki·an (ăl-gŏng′kē-ən) *n.* See **Proterozoic**. [After the *Algonkin* Indians. See ALGONQUIN.]

Al·gon·qui·an (ăl-gŏng′kwē-ən, -kē-ən) also **Al·gon·ki·an** (-kē-ən) *n., pl.* Algonquian or **-ans** also Algonkian or **-ans 1.** A family of North American Indian languages spoken from Labrador to the Carolinas between the Atlantic coast and the Rocky Mountains. **2.** A member of a people traditionally speaking an Algonquian language. [< ALGONQUIN.] —**Al·gon′qui·an** *adj.*

Al·gon·quin (ăl-gŏng′kwĭn, -kĭn) also **Al·gon·kin** (-kĭn) *n., pl.* Algonquin or **-quins** also Algonkin or **-kins 1.** A member of any of various Native American peoples inhabiting the Ottawa River valley of Quebec and Ontario. **2.** Any of the varieties of Ojibwa spoken by the Algonquin. [Canadian Fr. < Malecite *elakómkwik*, they are our relatives.]

al·go·pho·bi·a (ăl′gə-fō′bē-ə) *n.* An abnormal fear of pain.

al·go·rism (ăl′gə-rĭz′əm) *n.* **1.** The Arabic system of numeration; the decimal system. **2.** Computation with Arabic figures. [ME *algorisme* < OFr. < Med.Lat. *algorismus*, after Muhammad ibn-Musa al-KHWARIZMI.]

al·go·rithm (ăl′gə-rĭth′əm) *n.* A step-by-step problem-solving procedure, esp. an established, recursive computational procedure with a finite number of steps. [Variant (prob. influenced by ARITHMETIC) of ALGORISM.] —**al′go·rith′mic** (-rĭth′mĭk) *adj.*

algorithmic language *n.* A programming language in which an algorithm can be expressed accurately.

al·gor mor·tis (ăl′gər môr′tĭs) *n.* The cooling of the body after death. [Lat. *algor*, coolness + *mortis*, genitive of *mors*, death.]

Al·gren (ôl′grĭn), **Nelson** 1909–81. Amer. writer whose works include *The Man with the Golden Arm* (1949).

Al·ham·bra (ăl-hăm′brə, äl-äm′brə) A citadel overlooking Granada, Spain; built by Moorish kings in the 12th and 13th cent.

Al Hil·lah (ăl hĭl′ə, äl) A city of central Iraq S of Baghdad; built c. 1100. Pop. 268,834.

Al Hu·day·dah (ăl hōō-dā′də, -dī′-) or **Ho·dei·da** (hō-dā′də) A city of W Yemen on the Red Sea. Pop. 246,068.

A·li (ä-lē′) 600?–661. Muslim caliph (656–661). After his assassination Islam was divided into Sunnite and Shiite sects.

Ali, Muhammad Orig. Cassius Marcellus Clay. b. 1942. Amer. prizefighter who won the world heavyweight title (1964, 1974, and 1978).

A·li·ák·mon (äl-yäk′môn, ä′lē-äk′-) A river, c. 322 km (200 mi), of N Greece.

a·li·as (ā′lē-əs, āl′yəs) *n.* **1.** An assumed name: *worked under an alias.* **2.** *Electronics* A false signal in telecommunication links from beats between signal frequency and sampling frequency. ❖ *adv.* Also known as: *Johnson, alias Johns.* [Lat. *aliās*, otherwise, at another time < fem. accusative pl. of *alius*, other. See **al-** in App.]

a·li·as·ing (ā′lē-ə-sĭng, āl′yə-) *n.* **1.** The appearance of jagged distortions in curves and diagonal lines in computer graphics because the resolution is limited or diminished. **2.** The static distortion in digital sound caused by a low sampling rate.

A·li Ba·ba (ä′lē bä′bə, äl′ē) A poor woodcutter in the *Arabian Nights* who enters a thieves' treasure cave by saying, "Open, Sesame!"

al·i·bi (ăl′ə-bī′) *n., pl.* **-bis 1.** *Law* a. A form of defense whereby a defendant attempts to prove absence from the scene of the crime. **b.** The fact or state of absence when a crime was committed. **2.** *Usage Problem* An explanation offered to avoid blame or justify action; an excuse. ❖ *intr.v.* **-bied, -bi·ing, -bis** *Usage Problem* To make an excuse for oneself. [Lat., elsewhere < *alius*, other (on the model of *ibi*, there). See **al-** in App.]

USAGE NOTE When used as a noun, *alibi* in its nonlegal sense of "an excuse" is acceptable in written usage to almost half of the Usage Panel. As a verb (*They never alibi*), it is unacceptable in written usage to a large majority of the Panel.

al·i·ble (ăl′ə-bəl) *adj.* Having nutrients; nourishing. [Lat. *alibilis* < *alere*, to nourish.]

Al·i·can·te (ăl′ĭ-kän′tē, ä′lē-kän′tē) A city of SE Spain on the Mediterranean Sea S of Valencia. Pop. 267,421.

al·i·cy·clic (ăl′ĭ-sī′klĭk, -sĭk′lĭk) *adj.* Of or relating to organic compounds having both aliphatic and cyclic characteristics or structures. [ALI(PHATIC) + CYCLIC.]

al·i·dade (ăl′ĭ-dād′) also **al·i·dad** (-dăd′) *n.* **1.** An indicator or a sighting apparatus on a plane table for angular measurement. **2.** A topographic surveying and mapping instrument for determining directions, consisting of a telescope and attached parts. [Fr. < Med.Lat. *alidada*, sighting rod < Ar. *al-ʿiḍāda*, the revolving radius of a circle : *al-*, the + *ʿiḍāda*, revolving radius, alternate form of *ʿaḍud*, humerus (< *ʿaḍada*, to lop, cut (trees)).]

a·li·en (ā′lē-ən, āl′yən) *adj.* **1.** Owing political allegiance to another country or government; foreign: *alien residents.* **2.** Belonging to, characteristic of, or constituting another and very different place, society, or person; strange. **3.** Dissimilar, inconsistent, or opposed: *emotions alien to her temperament.* ❖ *n.* **1.** An unnaturalized foreign resident of a country. **2.** A person from another and very different family, people, or place. **3.** A person not included in a group; an outsider. **4.** A creature from outer space: *an invasion of aliens.* **5.** *Ecology* An organism living or occurring in a

alfalfa
Medicago sativa

Algeria

Alhambra
the Court of the Lions

region to which it is not native. ❖ *tr.v.* **-ened, -en•ing, -ens** *Law* To transfer (property) to another; alienate. [ME < OFr. < Lat. *aliēnus* < *alius*, other. See **al-** in App.] **—al′ien•a•bil′i•ty** *n.* **—al′ien•a•ble** *adj.* **—al′ien•ee′** *n.*

al•ien•age (āl′yə-nĭj, ā′lē-ə-) *n.* The official status of an alien.

al•ien•ate (āl′yə-nāt′, ā′lē-ə-) *tr.v.* **-at•ed, -at•ing, -ates 1.** To make unfriendly or hostile; estrange. **2.** To make withdrawn or unresponsive; isolate or dissociate emotionally: *The numbing labor alienated the workers.* **3.** To cause to be transferred; turn away: *"He succeeded . . . in alienating the affections of my only ward"* (Oscar Wilde). **4.** *Law* To transfer (property or a right) to another, esp. by an act of the owner rather than by inheritance. [Lat. *aliēnāre, aliēnāt-* < Lat. *aliēnus*, alien. See ALIEN.] **—al′ien•a′tor** *n.*

al•ien•a•tion (āl′yə-nā′shən, ā′lē-ə-) *n.* **1.** The act of alienating or the condition of being alienated. **2.** Emotional isolation or dissociation. **3.** *Law* The act of propery transfer.

a•li•form (ā′lə-fôrm′, ăl′ə-) *adj. Biology* Shaped like a wing; alar. [Lat. *āla*, wing + –FORM.]

A•li•garh (ăl′ĭ-gär′, ä′lē-gŭr′) A city of N-central India SE of Delhi. Pop. 480,520.

a•light¹ (ə-līt′) *intr.v.* **a•light•ed** or **a•lit** (ə-lĭt′), **a•light•ing, a•lights 1.** To land, as after flight: *a sparrow alighting on a branch.* **2.** To set down, as from a vehicle; dismount: *alight from a carriage.* **3.** To come by chance: *alight on a solution.* [ME *alighten* < OE *ālīhtan* : *ā-*, intensive pref. + *līhtan*, to relieve of a burden (< *līht*, light; see LIGHT²).]

a•light² (ə-līt′) *adj.* **1.** Burning; lighted. **2.** Illuminated: *The sky was alight with stars.* [ME, p. part. of *alighten*, to set on fire < OE *ālīhtan*, to illuminate : *ā-*, intensive pref. + *līhtan*, to shine (< *lēoht*, a light; see LIGHT¹).] **—a•light′** *adv.*

a•lign (ə-līn′) *v.* **a•ligned, a•lign•ing, a•ligns** *—tr.* **1.** To arrange in a line or make parallel: *align the car with the curb.* **2.** To adjust to produce a proper relationship or orientation: *align the truck wheels.* **3.** To ally (oneself, for example) with one party or cause: *aligned themselves with the traders.* *—intr.* **1.** To adhere to a prescribed course of action. **2.** To move or be adjusted into proper relationship or orientation. [Fr. *aligner* < OFr. : *a-*, to (< Lat. *ad-*; see AD–) + *ligne*, line (< Lat. *līnea*; see LINE¹).] **—a•lign′er** *n.*

a•lign•ment (ə-līn′mənt) *n.* **1.** Linear or parallel positioning. **2a.** The process of adjusting parts so that they are in proper relative position: *Gears need alignment.* **b.** The condition of having parts so adjusted. **3.** A ground plan: *Building blueprints include an alignment.* **4.** The act of aligning or the condition of being aligned. **5.** *Sports* An arrangement or positioning of players.

a•like (ə-līk′) *adj.* Resembling closely; similar: *The twins are alike.* ❖ *adv.* In the same manner or to the same degree: *They dress alike.* [ME *alich* (influenced by ON *ālīkr*), blend of *ilich* (< OE *gelīc*) and *anlich* (< OE *onlīc*).] **—a•like′ness** *n.*

al•i•ment (ăl′ə-mənt) *n.* **1.** Something that nourishes; food. **2.** Something that supports or sustains. ❖ *tr.v.* (-mĕnt′) **-ment•ed, -ment•ing, -ments** To provide sustenance, such as food. [ME < Lat. *alimentum* < *alere*, to nourish.] **—al′i•men′tal** (-mĕn′tl) *adj.* **—al′i•men′tal•ly** *adv.*

al•i•men•ta•ry (ăl′ə-mĕn′tə-rē, -trē) *adj.* **1.** Concerned with food, nutrition, or digestion. **2.** Providing nourishment.

alimentary canal *n.* The mucous membrane-lined tube of the digestive system extending from the mouth to the anus and including the pharynx, esophagus, stomach, and intestines.

al•i•men•ta•tion (ăl′ə-mĕn-tā′shən) *n.* **1.** The act or process of giving or receiving nourishment. **2.** Support; sustenance.

al•i•mo•ny (ăl′ə-mō′nē) *n., pl.* **-nies 1.** *Law* An allowance for support made under court order to a divorced or separated person by the former partner, usu. the chief provider prior to separation. **2.** A means of livelihood; maintenance. [Lat. *alimōnia*, sustenance < *alere*, to nourish.]

A-line (ā′līn′) *adj.* Having a fitted top and a flared bottom: *an A-line dress.* [< garments being shaped like a capital *A*.]

al•i•phat•ic (ăl′ə-făt′ĭk) *adj.* Of or relating to a group of organic chemical compounds with carbon atoms linked in open chains. [< Gk. *aleiphar, aleiphat-*, oil < *aleiphein*, to anoint with oil.]

al•i•quot (ăl′ĭ-kwŏt′, -kwət) *adj.* Of or relating to an exact divisor of a quantity, esp. of an integer. ❖ *n.* An aliquot part. [Lat. *aliquot*, several : *alius*, some; see **al-** in App. + *quot*, how many; see **kʷo-** in App.]

a•lit (ə-lĭt′) *v.* A past tense and a past participle of **alight¹**.

a•lit•er•ate (ā-lĭt′ər-ĭt) *adj.* Able to read but not interested in reading. **—a•lit′er•a•cy** *n.* **—a•lit′er•ate** *n.*

a•live (ə-līv′) *adj.* **1.** Having life; living. **2.** In existence or operation; active: *keep hopes alive.* **3.** Full of living or moving things: *a pool alive with trout.* **4.** Active; animated; lively: *a face alive with mischief.* **—*idiom:* alive to** Aware of; sensitive to. [ME : *a-*, in a specified state; see A–² + *live*, life (< OE *līf*; see LIFE).] **—a•live′ness** *n.*

a•li•yah (ä′lē-ä′, ə-lē′ə) *n., pl.* **-yahs** or **-yot** (ä′lē-ōt′) The immigration of Jews to Israel. [Heb. *ʿălīyâ*, ascent < *ʿālâ*, to ascend.]

a•liz•a•rin (ə-lĭz′ər-ĭn) also **a•liz•a•rine** (-ĭn, -ə-rēn′) *n.* An orange-red crystalline compound, $C_{14}H_6O_2(OH)_2$, used in making dyes. [Fr. *alizarine* < *alizari*, madder root < Sp., prob. < Ar. *al-ʿuṣāra*, the juice : *al-*, the + *ʿuṣārah*, juice (< *ʿaṣara*, to squeeze).]

al•ka•hest (ăl′kə-hĕst′) *n.* The hypothetical universal solvent sought by alchemists. [Med.Lat. *alchahest*.]

al•ka•les•cent (ăl′kə-lĕs′ənt) *adj.* Becoming alkaline; slightly alkaline. [ALKAL(I) + –ESCENT.] **—al′ka•les′cence, al′ka•les′cen•cy** *n.*

al•ka•li (ăl′kə-lī′) *n., pl.* **-lis** or **-lies 1.** A carbonate or hydroxide of an alkali metal, the aqueous solution of which is bitter, slippery, caustic, and usu. basic in reactions. **2.** Any of various soluble mineral salts found in natural water and arid soils. **3.** Alkali metal. **4.** A substance having highly basic properties. [ME, alkaline substance from calcined plant ashes < Med.Lat. < Ar. *al-qily*, the ashes, lye, potash : *al-*, the + *qily*, ashes (< *qalā*, to fry).]

alkali metal *n.* Any of a group of soft, white, low-density, low-melting, highly reactive metallic elements, including lithium, sodium, potassium, rubidium, cesium, and francium.

al•ka•lim•e•ter (ăl′kə-lĭm′ĭ-tər) *n.* An apparatus for measuring alkalinity. **—al′ka•lim′e•try** *n.*

al•ka•line (ăl′kə-lĭn, -līn′) *adj.* **1.** Of, relating to, or containing an alkali. **2a.** Having a pH greater than 7. **b.** Having a relatively low concentration of hydrogen ions.

alkaline earth *n.* An oxide of an alkaline-earth metal.

al•ka•line-earth metal (ăl′kə-lĭn-ûrth′, -līn′-) *n.* Any of the metallic elements, esp. calcium, strontium, magnesium, barium, and usu. beryllium and radium.

al•ka•lin•i•ty (ăl′kə-lĭn′ĭ-tē) *n.* The alkali concentration or alkaline quality of an alkali-containing substance.

al•ka•lize (ăl′kə-līz′) also **al•ka•lin•ize** (-lə-nīz′) *v.* **-lized, -liz•ing, -liz•es** also **-lin•ized, -lin•iz•ing, -lin•iz•es** *—tr.* To make alkaline. *—intr.* To become an alkali. **—al′ka•li•za′tion** (-lĭ-zā′shən) *n.*

al•ka•loid (ăl′kə-loid′) *n.* Any of various nitrogenous organic compounds occurring chiefly in vascular plants and often having toxic, stimulant, or analgesic properties. [ALKAL(I) + –OID.] **—al′ka•loi′dal** (-loid′l) *adj.*

al•ka•lo•sis (ăl′kə-lō′sĭs) *n.* Abnormally high alkalinity of the body fluids. [ALKAL(I) + –OSIS.] **—al′ka•lot′ic** (-lŏt′ĭk) *adj.*

al•kane (ăl′kān′) *n.* Any member of the alkane series. [ALK(YL) + –ANE.]

alkane series *n.* A group of saturated open-chain hydrocarbons having the general formula C_nH_{2n+2}, the most abundant of which is methane.

al•kene (ăl′kēn′) *n.* Any of a series of unsaturated, open-chain hydrocarbons with one or more carbon-carbon double bonds, having the general formula C_nH_{2n}. [ALK(YL) + –ENE.]

Al Kha•lil (äl kä-lēl′, KHä-) See **Hebron.**

Alk•maar (älk′mär′) A town of N Netherlands NNW of Amsterdam; chartered 1254. Pop. 83,892.

al•ky (ăl′kē) *n., pl.* **-kies** *Slang* An alcoholic. [Shortening and alteration of ALCOHOLIC + –Y³.]

al•kyd (ăl′kĭd) *n.* A widely used durable synthetic resin derived from glycerol and phthalic anhydride. [ALKY(L) + (ACI)D.]

al•kyl (ăl′kəl) *n.* A monovalent radical, such as ethyl, having the general formula C_nH_{2n+1}. [Ger. *Alkohol*, alcohol (< Med.Lat. *alcohol*, antimony; see ALCOHOL) + –YL.]

al•kyl•ate (ăl′kə-lāt′) *tr.v.* **-at•ed, -at•ing, -ates** To add one or more alkyl groups to (a compound).

al•kyl•a•tion (ăl′kə-lā′shən) *n.* A process in which an alkyl group is added to or substituted in a compound, as in the reaction of alkenes with alkanes to make high-octane fuels.

al•kyne also **al•kine** (ăl′kīn′) *n.* Any of a series of open-chain hydrocarbons with a carbon-carbon triple bond and the general formula C_nH_{2n-2}. [ALKY(L) + –(I)NE².]

all (ôl) *adj.* **1.** Being or representing the entire number, amount, or quantity: *All the windows are open.* See Syns at **whole. 2.** Constituting, being, or representing the total extent or the whole: *all Christendom.* **3.** Being the utmost possible of: *in all seriousness.* **4.** Every: *got into all manner of trouble.* **5.** Any whatsoever: *beyond all doubt.* **6.** *Pennsylvania* Finished; used up: *The apples are all.* See Regional Note at **gum band. 7.** *Informal* Being more than one: *Who all came?* See Regional Note at **you-all.** ❖ *n.* The whole of one's resources or energy; everything one has: *They gave their all.* ❖ *pron.* **1.** The entire number, amount, or quantity; totality: *All that I have is yours.* **2.** Everyone; everything: *justice for all.* ❖ *adv.* **1.** Wholly; completely: *all wrong.* **2.** Each; apiece: *a score of five all.* **3.** So much: *all the better.* **—*idioms:* all along** From the beginning; throughout. **all but** Nearly; almost: *all but crying with relief.* **all in** Tired; exhausted. **all in all** Everything being taken into account: *All in all, it seemed fair.* **all of** *Informal* Not more than: *all of five minutes.* **all that** *Informal* To the degree expected. **all the same** Nevertheless: *I was ill but went all the same.* **all told** With everything considered; in all: *All told, we won ten games.* **at all 1.** In any way. **2.** To any extent. **in all** Considering everything; all together: *I bought four hats, in all.* [ME *al* < OE *eall*.]

OUR LIVING LANGUAGE Among the newest ways of introducing direct speech in the United States is the construction consisting of a form of *be* with *all*, as in *I'm all, "I'm not gonna do that!" And she's all, "Yes you are!"* This construction is particularly common in the animated speech of young people in California and elsewhere on the West Coast, who use it more frequently than the informal East Coast alternatives, *be like* and *go*, as in *He's like* (or *goes*), *"I'm not gonna do that!"* These indicators of direct

Muhammad Ali
photographed in 1974

ă	pat	oi	boy
ā	pay	ou	out
âr	care	ŏŏ	took
ä	father	ōō	boot
ĕ	pet	ŭ	cut
ē	be	ûr	urge
ĭ	pit	th	thin
ī	pie	*th*	this
îr	pier	hw	which
ŏ	pot	zh	vision
ō	toe	ə	about, item
ô	paw		

Stress marks:
′ (primary);
′ (secondary), as in
lexicon (lĕk′sĭ-kŏn′)

speech tend to be used more often with pronoun subjects (*He's all*, "*I'm not....*") than with nouns (*The man's all*, "*I'm not....*"), and with the historical present (*He's all....*) than with the past (*He was all....*). All of these locutions can introduce a gesture or facial expression rather than a quotation, as in *He's all....* followed by a shrug of the shoulders. *Be all* and *be like* can also preface a statement that sums up an attitude, as in "*I'm all 'No way!'*" See Note at **like²**.

all– *pref.* Variant of **allo–**.
al·la breve (äl′ə brĕv′, ä′lə brĕv′ā) *adv.* & *adj. Music* In cut time. [Ital. : *alla*, according to the + *breve*, breve.]
Al·lah (äl′ə, ä′lə) *n.* God, esp. in Islam. [Ar. *Allāh* : *al–*, the + *'ilāh*, god.]
Al·la·ha·bad (äl′ə-hə-băd′, ä′lə-hə-bäd′) A city of N-central India E of Varanasi; a pilgrimage site for Hindus. Pop. 792,858.
all-A·mer·i·can (ôl′ə-mĕr′ĭ-kən) *adj.* **1.** Typical or representative of the people of the United States or their ideals. **2.** *Sports* Chosen as the best United States amateur at a particular position or event. **3.** Composed entirely of people or materials from the United States. **4.** Of all the American nations: *an all-American conference.* ❖ *n.* often **All-American** An all-American athlete.
al·lan·toid (ə-lăn′toid′) also **al·lan·toi·dal** (äl′ən-toid′l) *adj.* **1.** Of or having an allantois. **2.** Shaped like a sausage. ❖ *n.* See **allantois.** [NLat. *allantoīdes.* See ALLANTOIS.]
al·lan·to·in (ə-lăn′tō-ĭn) *n.* A crystalline oxidation product, $C_4H_6N_4O_3$, of uric acid that is the metabolic end product of vertebrate purine oxidation and promotes tissue growth. [ALLANTO(IS) + –IN.]
al·lan·to·is (ə-lăn′tō-ĭs) *n.*, *pl.* **al·lan·to·i·des** (äl′ən-tō′ĭ-dēz′) A membranous sac in the embryos of mammals, birds, and reptiles that helps form the umbilical cord and placenta in mammals. [NLat. < *allantoīdes* < Gk. *allantoeidēs*, sausage-shaped : *allas, allant-*, sausage + *-oeidēs*, -oid.] —**al′lan·to′ic** (äl′ən-tō′ĭk) *adj.*
al·lar·gan·do (ä′lär-gän′dō) *adv.* & *adj. Music* In a gradually broadening style and slowing tempo. [Ital., pr. part. of *allargare*, to broaden : *al–*, to (< Lat. *ad–*; see AD–) + *largare*, to broaden (< *largo*, broad < Lat. *largus*).]
all-a·round (ôl′ə-round′) also **all-round** (ôl′round′) *adj.* **1.** Comprehensive in extent or depth. **2.** Able to do many things well; versatile.
al·lay (ə-lā′) *tr.v.* **-layed, -lay·ing, -lays 1.** To reduce the intensity of; relieve: *allay back pains.* See Syns at **relieve. 2.** To calm or pacify; set to rest: *allay fears.* [ME *aleien* < OE *ālecgan*, to lay down : *ā-*, intensive pref. + *lecgan*, to lay; see LAY¹.] —**al·lay′er** *n.*
all clear *n.* A signal, usu. by siren, that a danger has passed.
al·le·ga·tion (äl′ĭ-gā′shən) *n.* **1.** Something affirmed; an assertion. **2.** The act of alleging. **3.** An unproven assertion: *The charges were mere allegations.* **4.** *Law* An assertion that must be proved or supported with evidence. [Fr. *allégation* < Lat. *allēgātiō, allēgātiōn–* < *allēgātus*, p. part. of *allēgāre*, to dispatch, adduce : *ad-*, ad- + *lēgāre*, to depute; see LEGATE.]
al·lege (ə-lĕj′) *tr.v.* **-leged, -leg·ing, -leg·es 1.** To assert; affirm: *alleged innocence.* **2.** To assert without or before proof: *The indictment alleges bribery.* **3.** To state in support or denial of a claim or accusation: *allege insanity.* **4.** *Archaic* To present as an authority. [ME *alleggen* < OFr. *alegier*, to vindicate, justify (influenced by *aleguer*, to give a reason) < *esligier*, to pay a fine, justify oneself < LLat. **exlītigāre*, to clear at law : Lat. *ex-*, out; see EX– + Lat. *lītigāre*, to sue; see LITIGATE.] —**al·lege′a·ble** *adj.* —**al·leg′er** *n.*
al·leged (ə-lĕjd′, ə-lĕj′ĭd) *adj.* Represented in a certain way without proof; supposed. —**al·leg′ed·ly** (ə-lĕj′ĭd-lē) *adv.*

USAGE NOTE In their zeal to protect the rights of the accused, newspapers and law enforcement officials sometimes misuse *alleged.* Someone arrested for murder may be only an *alleged* murderer, for example, because no charge has been proved, but is a real, not an *alleged,* suspect in that his or her status as a suspect is not in doubt. Similarly, if the money from a safe is known to have been stolen and not merely mislaid, then we may safely speak of a theft without having to qualify our description with *alleged.*

Al·le·ghe·ny Mountains (äl′ĭ-gā′nē) also **Al·le·ghe·nies** (-nēz) A range forming the W part of the Appalachian Mts., extending from N PA to SW VA and rising to c. 1,483 m (4,862 ft).
Allegheny River A river rising in N-central PA and flowing c. 523 km (325 mi) to join the Monongahela R. at Pittsburgh and form the Ohio R.
al·le·giance (ə-lē′jəns) *n.* **1.** Loyalty or the obligation of loyalty, as to a nation, sovereign, or cause. **2.** The obligations of a vassal to a lord. [ME *alligeaunce*, alteration of *ligeaunce* < OFr. *ligeance* < *lige*, liege. See LIEGE.] —**al·le′giant** *adj.*
al·le·gor·i·cal (äl′ĭ-gôr′ĭ-kəl, -gôr′-) also **al·le·gor·ic** (-ĭk) *adj.* Of, characteristic of, or containing allegory. —**al′le·gor′i·cal·ly** *adv.*
al·le·go·rize (äl′ĭ-gô-rīz′, -gô-, -gə-) *v.* **-rized, -riz·ing, -riz·es** —*tr.* **1.** To express as an allegory. **2.** To interpret allegorically. —*intr.* To use allegory. —**al′le·go′ri·za′tion** (-gôr′ĭ-zā′shən, -gôr′-, -gôr′-) *n.* —**al′le·go′riz′er** *n.*

al·le·go·ry (äl′ĭ-gôr′ē, -gôr′ē) *n.*, *pl.* **-ries 1a.** The representation of abstract ideas or principles by characters, figures, or events in narrative, dramatic, or pictorial form. **b.** A story, picture, or play employing such representation. **2.** A symbolic representation. [ME *allegorie* < Lat. *allēgoria* < Gk. < *allēgorein*, to interpret allegorically : *allos*, other; see **al-** in App. + *agoreuein*, to speak publicly (< *agorā*, marketplace).] —**al′le·go′rist** *n.*
al·le·gret·to (äl′ĭ-grĕt′ō, ä′lĭ-) *Music adv.* & *adj.* In a moderately quick tempo. ❖ *n.*, *pl.* **-tos** An allegretto passage or movement. [Ital., dim. of *allegro*, allegro. See ALLEGRO.]
al·le·gro (ə-lĕg′rō, ə-lā′grō) *Music adv.* & *adj.* In a quick, lively tempo. ❖ *n.*, *pl.* **-gros** An allegro passage or movement. [Ital. < Lat. *alacer*, lively.]
al·lele (ə-lēl′) *n.* One member of a pair or series of genes that occupy a specific position on a specific chromosome. [Ger. *Allel*, short for *Allelomorph*, allelomorph < E. ALLELOMORPH.] —**al·lel′ic** (ə-lē′lĭk, ə-lĕl′ĭk) *adj.* —**al·lel′ism** *n.*
al·le·lo·morph (ə-lē′lə-môrf′, ə-lĕl′ə-) *n.* An allele. [Gk. *allēlōn*, mutually (< *allos*, other; see **al-** in App.) + –MORPH.] —**al·le′lo·mor′phic** *adj.* —**al·le′lo·mor′phism** *n.*
al·le·lop·a·thy (ə-lē-lŏp′ə-thē, ä′lə-) *n.* The inhibition of growth in one species of plants by chemicals from another species. [Gk. *allēlōn*, reciprocally (< *allos*, another; see al- in App.) + –PATHY.] —**al·le′lo·path′ic** (ə-lē′lə-păth′ĭk, ə-lĕl′ə-) *adj.*
al·le·lu·ia (äl′ə-loo′yə) *interj.* Hallelujah. [ME < Med.Lat. < L.Gk. *allelouia* < Heb. *halləlû-yāh*, praise God. See HALLELUJAH.]
al·le·mande (äl′ə-mänd′, -mänd′, äl′ə-mänd′, -mänd′) *n.* **1a.** A stately 16th-century dance in duple meter. **b.** A composition written to or as if to accompany this dance, often beginning a suite. **2.** A lively 18th-century dance in triple meter. [Fr., fem. of *allemand*, Ger. < Lat. *Alemannī*, an ancient Gmc. tribe. See ALEMANNI.]
Al·len (äl′ən), **Ethan** 1738–89. Amer. Revolutionary soldier whose Green Mountain Boys helped capture Fort Ticonderoga (1775).
Allen, Grace Ethel Cecile Rosalie Known as "Gracie." 1906–64. Amer. comedian best remembered as the confused but unflappable foil to her husband and stage partner, George Burns.
Allen, Richard 1760–1831. Amer. cleric who was the first bishop of the African Methodist Episcopal Church (1816–31).
Allen, William 1532–94. English Roman Catholic cardinal who directed the work on the Douay Bible.
Allen, Woody b. 1935. Amer. actor, writer, and filmmaker whose films include *Annie Hall* (1977).
Al·len·by (äl′ən-bē), **1st Viscount.** Title of Edmund Henry Hynman. 1861–1936. British field marshal during World War I.
Al·len·de Gos·sens (ä-yĕn′dē gô′sēns), **Salvador** 1908–73. Chilean president (1970–73) who was killed in a coup d'état.
Al·len·ti·ac (ə-lĕn′tē-äk′) *n.*, *pl.* **Allentiac** or **-acs 1.** A member of a South American Indian people of west-central Argentina. **2.** The extinct language of the Allentiac. [Sp. *alentiaco*.] —**Al·len′ti·ac′** *adj.*
Al·len·town (äl′ən-toun′) A city of E PA NNW of Philadelphia; founded 1762. Pop. 106,632.
Allen wrench *n.* A tool consisting of an L-shaped bar with a hexagonal head, used to turn screws with hexagonal sockets. [Orig. a trademark.]
al·ler·gen (äl′ər-jən) *n.* A substance, such as pollen, that causes an allergy. [Ger. *Allergen* : *Aller(gie)*, allergy; see ALLERGY + -gen (< Fr. *-gène*; see –GEN).] —**al′ler·gen′ic** (-jĕn′ĭk) *adj.*
al·ler·gic (ə-lûr′jĭk) *adj.* **1.** Of, characterized by, or caused by an allergy. **2.** Having an allergy. **3.** *Informal* Having a dislike; averse: *allergic to work.*
al·ler·gist (äl′ər-jĭst) *n.* A physician specializing in the diagnosis and treatment of allergies.
al·ler·gy (äl′ər-jē) *n.*, *pl.* **-gies 1.** An abnormally high sensitivity to certain substances, such as pollens or foods, often causing sneezing, itching, and skin rashes. **2.** *Informal* An aversion; antipathy: *an allergy to cocktail parties.* [Ger. *Allergie* : Gk. *allos*, other; see ALLO– + Gk. *ergon*, action; see **werg-** in App.]
al·le·thrin (äl′ə-thrĭn′) *n.* A synthetic clear or amber-colored viscous insecticide, $C_{19}H_{26}O_3$, similar to pyrethrin. [ALL(YL) + (PYR)ETHRIN.]
al·le·vi·ate (ə-lē′vē-āt′) *tr.v.* **-at·ed, -at·ing, -ates** To make more bearable: *a drug that alleviates cold symptoms.* See Syns at **relieve.** [ME *alleviaten* < LLat. *alleviāre, alleviāt-*, to lighten : Lat. *ad-*, ad- + *levis*, light; see **legwh-** in App.] —**al·le′vi·a′tor** *n.*
al·le·vi·a·tive (ə-lē′vē-ā′tĭv) also **al·le·vi·a·to·ry** (-ə-tôr′ē, -tôr′ē) *adj.* Reducing pain or severity; palliative.
al·ley¹ (äl′ē) *n.*, *pl.* **-leys 1.** A narrow street or passageway between or behind city buildings. **2.** A path between rows or trees in a garden or park. **3.** A straight narrow course or track; a lane. **4.** Either of the parallel lanes on a tennis court, which widen the inbounds area for doubles play. **—idiom: up (one's) alley** *Informal* Compatible with one's interests or qualifications. [ME *alei* < OFr. *alee* < *aller*, to walk < Lat. *ambulare*. See AMBULATE.]
al·ley² (äl′ē) *n.*, *pl.* **-leys** *Games* A large playing marble, often used as the shooter. [Short for ALABASTER.]
alley cat *n.* A homeless or stray cat.
al·ley-oop (äl′ē-oop′) *n. Basketball* **1.** A play in which a pass is lobbed above the basket and a player jumps up and attempts to

catch the ball and score before returning to the floor. **2.** The pass made in such a play. ❖ *interj.* Used to signal the start of a strenuous activity, such as lifting. [Fr. *allez-oop*, cry of circus acrobat about to leap < *allez*, pl. imper. of *aller*, to go < OFr. *aler*, to walk. See ALLEY¹.]

al·ley·way (ăl′ē-wā′) *n.* A narrow passage between buildings.

all-fired (ôl′fīrd′) *adv. Informal* Used as an intensive: *Don't be so all-fired aggressive.* [Alteration of *hell-fired.*]

All Fools' Day *n.* See **April Fools' Day.**

all fours *pl.n.* (*used with a sing. verb*) Any of several card games in which points are scored in four ways: for the high trump, the low trump, the jack of trumps, and the game.

all get-out also **all get out** (gĕt′out′) *n. Informal* The utmost degree imaginable: *raced like all get-out.*

all hail *interj.* Used to express acclamation, a welcome, or a greeting.

All·hal·low·mas (ôl′hăl′ō-məs) *n. Archaic* All Saints' Day. [ME *Alhalwemesse* < OE *ealra hālgena mæsse* : *ealra*, genitive pl. of *eall*, all + *hālgena*, genitive pl. of *hālga*, saint (< *hālig*, holy; see HOLY) + *mæsse*, Mass; see MASS.]

All·hal·lows (ôl′hăl′ōz) *n.* See **All Saints' Day.** [ME *al halwes* : *al*, all; see ALL + *halwes*, pl. of *halwe*, saint (< OE *hālga*; see ALLHALLOWMAS).]

all-heal or **all·heal** (ôl′hēl′) *n.* Any of several plants, such as the valerian, used in herbal medicine and reputed to have healing powers.

al·li·a·ceous (ăl′ē-ā′shəs) *adj.* Of or resembling onion, garlic, or similar plants of the genus *Allium,* esp. in taste and smell. [Lat. *allium,* garlic + –ACEOUS.]

al·li·ance (ə-lī′əns) *n.* **1a.** A close association of nations or other groups, formed to advance common interests: *an alliance of labor unions.* **b.** A formal agreement establishing such an association, esp. an international treaty. **2.** A connection based on kinship or marriage. **3.** Close similarity in nature or type; affinity: *the alliance between mathematics and music.* **4.** The act of becoming allied or the condition of being allied. [ME < OFr. *aliance* < *alier,* to ally. See ALLY.]

al·lied (ə-līd′, ăl′īd′) *adj.* **1.** Joined or united: *allied tribes.* **2.** Similar; related: *art and allied studies.* **3. Allied** Of or relating to the Allies.

Al·lier (ä-lyā′) A river rising in S-central France and flowing c. 410 km (255 mi) to the Loire R.

al·li·ga·tor (ăl′ĭ-gā′tər) *n.* **1.** Either of two large reptiles, *Alligator mississipiensis* of the southeast United States or *A. sinensis* of China, having sharp teeth, powerful jaws, and a broader, shorter snout than the crocodile. **2.** Leather from the hide of one of these reptiles. **3.** A tool or fastener with strong, adjustable, often toothed jaws. [Alteration of Sp. *el lagarto,* the lizard : *el,* the (< Lat. *ille,* that; see **al–** in App.) + *lagarto,* lizard (< Lat. *lacertus*).]

alligator clip *n.* A spring-loaded clip with serrated jaws, often used to make temporary electrical connections.

alligator pear *n.* See **avocado** 1. [By folk ety. < Am.Sp. *aguacate,* avocado (the trees are said to grow in areas infested by alligators). See AGUACATE.]

alligator snapper *n.* See **alligator snapping turtle.**

alligator snapping turtle *n.* A large freshwater snapping turtle (*Macroclemys temminckii*) of the south-central United States, having a rough carapace and powerful hooked jaws.

all-im·por·tant (ôl′ĭm-pôr′tnt) *adj.* Of the greatest importance; crucial. —**all′-im·por′tance** *n.*

all-in·clu·sive (ôl′ĭn-klōō′sĭv) *adj.* Including everything; comprehensive. —**all′-in·clu′sive·ness** *n.*

al·lit·er·ate (ə-lĭt′ə-rāt′) *v.* **-at·ed, -at·ing, -ates** —*intr.* **1.** To use alliteration in speech or writing. **2.** To have or contain alliteration. —*tr.* To form or arrange with alliteration. [Back-formation < ALLITERATION.]

al·lit·er·a·tion (ə-lĭt′ə-rā′shən) *n.* The repetition of the same sounds, usu. consonants, esp. at the beginning of words, as in "*on scrolls of silver snowy sentences*" (Hart Crane). [< AD– + Lat. *littera,* letter.]

al·lit·er·a·tive (ə-lĭt′ə-rā′tĭv, -ər-ə-) *adj.* Of, showing, or characterized by alliteration. —**al·lit′er·a′tive·ly** *adv.*

al·li·um (ăl′ē-əm) *n.* Any of numerous, usu. bulbous plants of the genus *Allium* in the lily family, with long stalks bearing variously colored flowers and including onions and garlic. [Lat., garlic.]

all-night (ôl′nīt′) *adj.* **1.** Continuing all through the night: *an all-night party.* **2.** Open all during the night.

all night·er or **all-night·er** (ôl′nī′tər) *n. Informal* A project or event lasting all through the night, esp. an intense bout of study or work.

allo *abbr.* allegro

allo– or **all–** *pref.* **1.** Other; different: *allopatric.* **2.** Isomeric: *allocholesterol.* [Gk. *allos,* other. See **al–** in App.]

al·lo·an·ti·bod·y (ăl′ō-ăn′tĭ-bŏd′ē) *n.,* pl. **-ies** An antibody produced by or derived from the same species as that of the alloantigen with which it reacts.

al·lo·an·ti·gen (ăl′ō-ăn′tĭ-jən) *n.* A protein or other antigenic substance present in only some members of a species and therefore able to stimulate alloantibody production in those members that lack it.

al·lo·ca·ble (ăl′ə-kə-bəl) *adj.* Capable of being allocated.

al·lo·cate (ăl′ə-kāt′) *tr.v.* **-cat·ed, -cat·ing, -cates 1.** To reserve for a purpose; designate: *allocate room for books.* **2.** To distribute by a plan; allot: *allocate rations.* [Med.Lat. *allocāre, allocāt–* : Lat. *ad-,* ad- + Lat. *locāre,* to place (< *locus,* place).] —**al′lo·cat′a·ble** *adj.* —**al′lo·ca′tion** *n.* —**al′lo·ca·tor** *n.*

SYNONYMS *allocate, appropriate, designate, earmark* These verbs mean to set aside for a specified purpose: *allocated time for recreation; appropriated funds for public education; designated a location for the new hospital; money earmarked for a vacation.*

al·lo·cu·tion (ăl′ə-kyōō′shən) *n.* A formal authoritative speech; an address. [Lat. *allocūtiō, allocūtiōn–* < *allocūtus,* p. part. of *alloquī,* to speak to : *ad-,* ad- + *loquī,* to speak.]

al·log·a·my (ə-lŏg′ə-mē) *n.* See **cross-fertilization** 1.

al·lo·ge·ne·ic (ăl′ə-jə-nē′ĭk) also **al·lo·gen·ic** (-jĕn′ĭk) *adj.* Being genetically different but from the same species. [ALLO– + Gk. *geneā,* race; see **genə–** in App. + –IC.] —**al′lo·ge·ne′i·cal·ly** *adv.*

al·lo·graft (ăl′ə-grăft′) *n.* A graft of tissue from an allogeneic donor.

al·lo·graph (ăl′ə-grăf′) *n.* **1.** A variant shape of a letter. **2.** A letter or letters that can represent one phoneme, as *f* and *gh* can represent the phoneme /f/. **3.** Writing, esp. a signature, made by one person for another. —**al′lo·graph′ic** *adj.*

al·lom·er·ism (ə-lŏm′ə-rĭz′əm) *n.* Consistency in crystalline form with variation in chemical composition. —**al·lom′er·ous** *adj.*

al·lom·e·try (ə-lŏm′ĭ-trē) *n.* The study of the change in proportion of various parts of an organism as a consequence of growth. —**al′lo·met′ric** (ăl′ə-mĕt′rĭk) *adj.*

al·lo·morph¹ (ăl′ə-môrf′) *n.* See **paramorph.** —**al′lo·mor′phic** *adj.* —**al′lo·mor′phism** *n.*

al·lo·morph² (ăl′ə-môrf′) *n.* Any of the variant forms of a morpheme. [ALLO– + MORPH(EME).] —**al′lo·mor′phic** *adj.* —**al′lo·mor′phism** *n.*

al·longe (ə-lŭnj′, ä-lônzh′) *n., pl.* **-longes** (ə-lŭn′jĭz, ä-lônzh′) See **rider** 3. [Fr. < *allonger,* to lengthen < OFr. *alongier.* See LUNGE.]

al·lo·nym (ăl′ə-nĭm′) *n.* The name of a person, usu. historical, assumed by a writer. [Fr. *allonyme* : Gk. *allos,* other; see ALLO– + Gk. *onoma,* name; see **nō-men–** in App.] —**al·lon′y·mous** (ə-lŏn′ə-məs) *adj.* —**al·lon′y·mous·ly** *adv.*

al·lo·path (ăl′ə-păth′) also **al·lop·a·thist** (ə-lŏp′ə-thĭst) *n.* One who practices or advocates allopathy.

al·lop·a·thy (ə-lŏp′ə-thē) *n.* A method of treating disease with remedies causing effects different from those of the disease itself. —**al′lo·path′ic** (ăl′ə-păth′ĭk) *adj.* —**al′lo·path′i·cal·ly** *adv.*

al·lo·pat·ric (ăl′ə-păt′rĭk) *adj. Ecology* Occurring in separate, nonoverlapping geographic areas, esp. when unable to crossbreed because of the separation. [ALLO– + Gk. *patrā,* fatherland (< *patēr, patr–,* father; see **pətər–** in App.) + –IC.] —**al′lo·pat′ri·cal·ly** *adv.* —**al·lop·a·try** (ə-lŏp′ə-trē) *n.*

al·lo·phane (ăl′ə-fān′) *n.* An amorphous translucent mineral, essentially hydrous aluminum silicate. [< Gk. *allophanēs,* appearing otherwise : *allos,* other; see ALLO– + *phainesthai, phan–,* to appear, passive of *phainein,* to show.]

al·lo·phone (ăl′ə-fōn′) *n.* **1.** A predictable phonetic variant of a phoneme. For example, the aspirated *t* of *top* and the unaspirated *t* of *stop* are allophones of the English phoneme /t/. **2.** or **Allophone** *Canadian* A person whose native language is other than French or English. [ALLO– + PHONE(ME).] —**al′lo·phon′ic** (-fŏn′ĭk) *adj.*

al·lo·pol·y·ploid (ăl′ə-pŏl′ē-ploid′) *adj.* Having two or more complete sets of chromosomes derived from different species. —**al′lo·pol′y·ploid** *n.* —**al′lo·pol′y·ploi′dy** *n.*

al·lo·pu·ri·nol (ăl′ō-pyŏŏr′ə-nôl′, -nŏl′, -nōl′) *n.* A drug, $C_5H_4N_4O$, used to treat gout because it inhibits the synthesis of uric acid. [ALLO– + PURIN(E) + –OL².]

all-or-none (ôl′ər-nŭn′) *adj.* Characterized by either a complete response or a total lack of response or effect.

all-or-noth·ing (ôl′ər-nŭth′ĭng) *adj.* **1.** Involving either complete success or failure, with no intermediate result. **2.** Refusing to accept less than all demands; uncompromising.

al·lo·saur (ăl′ə-sôr′) or **al·lo·sau·rus** (ăl′ə-sôr′əs) *n.* A carnivorous dinosaur of the late Jurassic and early Cretaceous Periods, similar to but smaller than the tyrannosaur. [NLat. *Allosaurus,* genus name : Gk. *allos,* other; see ALLO– + Gk. *sauros,* lizard.]

al·lo·ster·ic (ăl′ə-stĕr′ĭk) *adj.* Of or involving binding of a regulatory substance to an enzyme at a site other than the enzymatically active one. —**al′lo·ster′i·cal·ly** *adv.* —**al·los′ter·y** (ə-lŏs′tə-rē) *n.*

al·lot (ə-lŏt′) *tr.v.* **-lot·ted, -lot·ting, -lots 1.** To parcel out; distribute or apportion: *allot land.* **2.** To assign as a portion; allocate: *allot time to each speaker.* [ME *alotten* < OFr. *aloter* : *a-,* to (< Lat. *ad-;* see AD–) + *lot,* portion (of Gmc. orig.).] —**al·lot′tee′** *n.*

al·lot·ment (ə-lŏt′mənt) *n.* **1.** The act of allotting. **2.** Something allotted. **3.** A portion of military pay regularly deducted and set aside, as for insurance.

al·lo·trans·plant (ăl′ō-trăns′plănt′) *tr.v.* **-plant·ed, -plant·**

ă	pat	oi	boy
ā	pay	ou	out
âr	care	ŏŏ	took
ä	father	ōō	boot
ĕ	pet	ŭ	cut
ē	be	ûr	urge
ĭ	pit	th	thin
ī	pie	*th*	this
îr	pier	hw	which
ŏ	pot	zh	vision
ō	toe	ə	about,
ô	paw		item

Stress marks:
′ (primary);
′ (secondary), as in
lexicon (lĕk′sĭ-kŏn′)

ing, -plants To transfer (an organ or body tissue) between two genetically different individuals of the same species. ❖ *n.* An organ or tissue so transferred. —**al′lo·trans′plan·ta′tion** *n.*

al·lo·trope (ăl′ə-trōp′) *n.* A structurally differentiated form of an element that exhibits allotropy. [Back-formation < ALLOTROPY.]

al·lot·ro·py (ə-lŏt′rə-pē) *n.* The existence, esp. in the solid state, of two or more crystalline or molecular structural forms of an element. —**al′lo·trop′ic** (ăl′ə-trŏp′ĭk, -trō′pĭk), **al′lo·trop′i·cal** *adj.* —**al′lo·trop′i·cal·ly** *adv.*

all′ ot·ta·va (ăl′ə-tä′və, äl′ō-) *adv. & adj.* Ottava. [Ital. : *all′,* at the + *ottava,* octave.]

al·lo·type (ăl′ə-tīp′) *n.* **1.** A biological specimen that is the opposite sex of a holotype. **2.** *Immunology* An antibody with a variant molecular region that is detectable as an antigen by members of the same species having a different structure in the same region. —**al′lo·typ′ic** (-tĭp′ĭk) *adj.* —**al′lo·ty′py** (-tī′pē) *n.*

all out *adv.* With every possible effort: *worked all out.*

all-out (ôl′out′) *adj.* Using all available means or resources.

all over *adv.* **1.** Over the whole area or extent: *embroidered all over.* **2.** Everywhere: *searched all over.* **3.** In all respects. —**idiom: be all over** To attack verbally; reprimand severely.

all-o·ver also **all·o·ver** (ôl′ō′vər) *adj.* Covering an entire surface: *wallpaper with an all-over pattern.*

all-o·vers (ôl′ō′vərz) *pl.n. Informal* A feeling of great unease or extreme nervousness.

al·low (ə-lou′) *v.* **-lowed, -low·ing, -lows** —*tr.* **1.** To let do or happen; permit: *We allow smoking only in restricted areas.* **2.** To permit the presence of: *No pets allowed.* **3.** To permit to have: *allow oneself a treat.* **4.** To make provision for; assign: *Allow time for a break.* **5.** To plan for in case of need: *allowed room for shrinkage.* **6.** To grant as a discount or in exchange: *allowed me 20 dollars on my old typewriter.* **7.** *Chiefly Upper Southern US* **a.** To admit; concede: *I allowed he was right.* **b.** To think; suppose. **c.** To assert; declare. —*intr.* **1.** To offer a possibility; admit: *The poem allows of several interpretations.* **2.** To take a possibility into account; make allowance. [ME *allouen,* to approve, permit < OFr. *alouer* < Lat. *allaudāre,* to praise (*ad-,* intensive pref.; see AD- + *laudāre,* to praise; see LAUD) and < Med.Lat. *allocāre,* to assign; see ALLOCATE.] —**al·low′a·ble** *adj.* —**al·low′a·bly** *adv.*

al·low·ance (ə-lou′əns) *n.* **1.** The act of allowing. **2.** An amount allowed or granted: *a weekly allowance of two eggs.* **3.** Something, such as money, given regularly or for a specific purpose: *a travel allowance.* **4.** A price reduction, esp. in exchange for used merchandise: *an allowance on an old car.* **5.** A consideration for possibilities or modifying circumstances: *made allowances for rush-hour traffic.* **6.** An allowed deviation in dimension of closely mating machine parts. ❖ *tr.v.* **-anced, -anc·ing, -anc·es 1.** To put on a fixed allowance. **2.** To dispense in fixed quantities; ration.

al·low·ed·ly (ə-lou′ĭd-lē) *adv.* By general admission.

al·loy (ăl′oi′, ə-loi′) *n.* **1.** A homogeneous mixture or solid solution of two or more metals, the atoms of one replacing or occupying interstitial positions between the atoms of the other: *Brass is an alloy of zinc and copper.* **2.** A mixture; an amalgam. **3.** The relative degree of mixture with a base metal; fineness. **4.** Something added that lowers value or purity. ❖ *tr.v.* (ə-loi′, ăl′oi′) **-loyed, -loy·ing, -loys 1.** To combine (metals) to form an alloy. **2.** To combine; mix: *idealism that was alloyed with political skill.* **3.** To debase by adding an inferior element. [Alteration (influenced by Fr. *aloi*) of obsolete *allay* < ME *alay* < ONFr. *allai* < *allayer,* to alloy < Lat. *alligāre,* to bind : *ad-,* ad- + *ligāre,* to bind.]

all-pur·pose (ôl′pûr′pəs) *adj.* Serving many purposes.

all right *adj.* **1a.** In proper or satisfactory operational or working order: *Were the tires all right?* **b.** Acceptable; agreeable: *Delaying the repair is all right by me.* **c. all-right** (ôl′rīt′) *Informal* Satisfactory; good: *an all-right movie.* **2.** Correct. **3.** Average; mediocre: *The show was just all right, not great.* **4.** Uninjured; safe. **5.** Fairly healthy; well: *I feel all right.* ❖ *adv.* **1.** Satisfactorily; adequately: *did all right.* **2.** Very well; yes. Used as a reply to a question or to introduce a declaration: *All right, I'll go.* **3.** Without a doubt: *It's cold, all right.*

USAGE NOTE *All right,* usually pronounced as if it were a single word, probably should have followed the same orthographic development as *already* and *altogether.* But despite its use by a number of reputable authors, the spelling *alright* has never been accepted as a standard variant.

all-round (ôl′round′) *adj.* Variant of **all-around.**

All Saints′ Day *n.* November 1, the day on which a Christian feast honoring all the saints is observed.

All Souls′ Day *n. Roman Catholic Church* November 2, when special prayers are offered for souls in purgatory.

all·spice (ôl′spīs′) *n.* **1.** A tropical American evergreen tree (*Pimenta dioica*) having opposite simple leaves and small white flowers clustered in cymes. **2.** The dried, nearly ripe berries of this plant used as a spice, esp. in baking.

all-star (ôl′stär′) *adj.* Made up wholly of star performers. ❖ *n. Sports* One chosen for a team of star players.

all-time (ôl′tīm′) *adj.* Exceeding all others up to the present.

al·lude (ə-lōōd′) *intr.v.* **-lud·ed, -lud·ing, -ludes** To make an indirect reference. [Lat. *allūdere,* to play with : *ad-,* ad- + *lūdere,* to play (< *lūdus,* play).]

USAGE NOTE *Allude* and *allusion* are often used where the more general terms *refer* and *reference* would be preferable. *Allude* and *allusion* apply to indirect references in which the source is not specifically identified: "*Well, we'll always have Paris,*" *he told the travel agent, in an allusion to Casablanca. Refer* and *reference,* unless qualified, usually imply specific mention of a source: *I will refer to Hamlet for my conclusion: As Polonius says, "Though this be madness, yet there is method in't."* See Usage Note at **refer.**

al·lure (ə-lōōr′) *v.* **-lured, -lur·ing, -lures** —*tr.* To attract with something desirable; entice: *Promises allure the unwary.* —*intr.* To be highly, often subtly attractive: *charms that still allure.* ❖ *n.* The power to attract; enticement. [ME *aluren* < OFr. *alurer* : *a-,* to (< Lat. *ad-;* see AD–) + *loirre,* bait (of Gmc. orig.).] —**al·lure′ment** *n.* —**al·lur′er** *n.* —**al·lur′ing·ly** *adv.*

al·lu·sion (ə-lōō′zhən) *n.* **1.** The act of alluding; indirect reference: *The candidate criticized them by allusion.* **2.** An instance of indirect reference. See Usage Note at **allude.** [LLat. *allūsiō, allūsiōn-,* a playing with < Lat. *allūsus,* p. part. of *allūdere,* to play with. See ALLUDE.]

al·lu·sive (ə-lōō′sĭv) *adj.* Characterized by indirect references. —**al·lu′sive·ly** *adv.* —**al·lu′sive·ness** *n.*

al·lu·vi·al (ə-lōō′vē-əl) *adj.* Of, relating to, or found in alluvium: *alluvial soil; alluvial gold.*

alluvial fan *n.* A fan-shaped accumulation of alluvium deposited at the mouth of a ravine or at the juncture of a tributary stream with the main stream.

al·lu·vi·on (ə-lōō′vē-ən) *n.* **1.** See **alluvium. 2.** The flow of water against a shore or bank. **3.** Inundation by water; flood. **4.** *Law* The increasing of land area along a shore by deposited alluvium or water recession. [Lat. *alluviō, alluviōn-* < *alluere,* to wash against : *ad-,* ad- + *-luere,* to wash; see **leu(ə)-** in App.]

al·lu·vi·um (ə-lōō′vē-əm) *n., pl.* **-vi·ums** or **-vi·a** (-vē-ə) Sediment that is deposited by flowing water, as in a riverbed or delta. [Med.Lat., flood < neut. of Lat. *alluvius,* alluvial < *alluere,* to wash against. See ALLUVION.]

al·ly (ə-lī′, ăl′ī) *v.* **-lied, -ly·ing, -lies** —*tr.* **1.** To place in a friendly association, as by treaty. **2.** To unite or connect in a personal relationship, as in friendship or marriage. —*intr.* To enter into an alliance. ❖ *n., pl.* **-lies 1.** One allied with another, esp. by treaty: *an ally of France.* **2.** One in helpful association with another. See Syns at **partner. 3. Allies a.** The nations allied against the Central Powers of Europe during World War I, including Russia, France, Great Britain, and later the United States. **b.** The nations, primarily Great Britain, France, the Soviet Union, and the United States, allied against the Axis during World War II. [ME *allien* < OFr. *alier* < Lat. *alligāre,* to bind to. See ALLOY.]

al·lyl (ăl′əl) *n.* The univalent unsaturated organic radical C₃H₅. [Lat. *allium,* garlic + –YL (so called because it was first obtained from garlic).] —**al·lyl′ic** (ə-lĭl′ĭk) *adj.*

Al·ma·gest (ăl′mə-jĕst′) *n.* **1.** A comprehensive treatise on astronomy, geography, and mathematics compiled by Ptolemy about A.D. 150. **2. almagest** Any of several medieval treatises on astronomy or alchemy. [ME *almageste* < OFr. < Ar. *al-majisti* : *al-,* the + Gk. *megistē,* greatest, fem. of *megistos,* greatest, superl. of *megas,* great; see **meg-** in App.]

al·ma ma·ter or **Al·ma Ma·ter** (ăl′mə mä′tər, äl′mə) *n.* **1.** The school, college, or university that one has attended. **2.** The anthem of an institution of higher learning. [< Lat. *Alma Māter,* nourishing mother (epithet of certain goddesses) : *alma,* fem. of *almus,* nourishing + *māter,* mother.]

al·ma·nac (ôl′mə-năk′, ăl′-) *n.* **1.** An annual publication including weather forecasts, astronomical information, tide tables, and other tabular information. **2.** A usu. annual publication composed of various lists, charts, and other information in one or many fields. [ME *almenak* < Med.Lat. *almanach,* perh. < L.Gk. *almenikhiaka,* ephemeris.]

Al Ma·na·mah (ăl mə-năm′ə, äl mə-nä′mə) See **Manama.**

al·man·dine (ăl′mən-dēn′) also **al·man·dite** (-dīt′) *n.* A deep violet-red garnet, FeAl₂Si₃O₁₂, found in metamorphic rocks and used as a gemstone. [Alteration of obsolete *alabandyne* < ME *alabandine* < LLat. (*gemma*) *alabandina,* (gem) of Alabanda < *Alabanda,* a town of ancient Asia Minor.]

Al·ma-Tad·e·ma (ăl′mə-tăd′ə-mə), Sir **Lawrence** 1836–1912. Dutch-born British painter noted for his romantic works.

Al·ma·ty (ăl′mə-tē′) Formerly **Al·ma-A·ta** (ăl′mə-ä′tə, äl-mä′ə-tä′) The former cap. of Kazakhstan, in the SE part. Pop. 1,176,000.

al·me·mar (äl-mē′mär) *n. Judaism* See **bema** 1. [Med. Heb. ′al-mēmār < Ar. *al-minbar,* the pulpit : *al-,* the + *minbar,* pulpit (prob. < Ethiopic *manbar,* seat, pulpit, or *manbār,* seat, throne, both < *nabara,* to sit).]

Al·me·ri·a (ăl′mə-rē′ə, äl′mĕ-) A city of SE Spain on the **Gulf of Almería,** an arm of the Mediterranean. Pop. 157,540.

al·might·y (ôl-mī′tē) *adj.* **1.** Having absolute power: *almighty God.* **2.** *Informal* Great; extreme: *an almighty din.* ❖ *adv. Informal* Used as an intensive: *almighty scared.* ❖ *n.* **Almighty** God. Used with *the.* [ME *almighti* < OE *ealmihtig* : *eall,* all + *mihtig,*

mighty (< *miht*, might; see MIGHT[1]).] —**al•might′i•ly** *adv.*

al•mond (ä′mənd, äl′-, ôl′-, ăm′ənd) *n.* **1a.** A deciduous tree (*Prunus dulcis*) native to Asia and northern Africa and having alternate simple leaves, pink flowers, and leathery fruits. **b.** The ellipsoidal kernel of this tree, either eaten as a nut or used for extraction of an oil. **2.** Any of several other plants, esp. those with almondlike fruits or seeds. **3.** Something having the oval form of an almond. **4.** A pale tan. [ME < OFr. *almande* < OFr. < LLat. *amandula*, alteration of Lat. *amygdala* < Gk. *amugdalē*.]

al•mo•ner (äl′mə-nər, ä′mə-) *n.* **1.** One who distributes alms. **2.** *Chiefly British* A hospital social worker. [ME *aumoner* < OFr. *aumonier* < *amosne*, alms < LLat. *eleēmosyna*. See ALMS.]

al•most (ôl′mōst′, ôl-mōst′) *adv.* Slightly short of; not quite; nearly: *almost time to go.* See Usage Note at **none**. [ME < OE *ealmǣst* : *eall*, all + *mǣst*, most; see MOST.]

alms (ämz) *pl.n.* Money or goods given to the poor. [ME *almes* < OE *ælmesse* < LLat. *eleēmosyna* < Gk. *eleēmosunē*, pity, charity < *eleēmōn*, pitiful < *eleos*, pity.]

alms•house (ämz′hous′) *n.* **1.** A poorhouse. **2.** *Chiefly British* A home for the poor that is maintained by private charity.

alms•man (ämz′mən) *n.* One, usu. a man, dependent on alms.

al•ni•co (äl′nĭ-kō′) *n.* Any of several hard, strong alloys of iron, aluminum, nickel, cobalt, and sometimes copper, niobium, or tantalum, used to make strong permanent magnets. [AL(UMINUM) + NI(CKEL) + CO(BALT).]

al•oe (äl′ō) *n.* **1.** Any of various chiefly African plants of the genus *Aloe*, having rosettes of succulent leaves and long stalks bearing tubular flowers. **2.** See **aloe vera**. **3. aloes** (*used with a sing. verb*) A laxative drug obtained from the juice of a certain species of aloe. [ME < OE *aluwe* < Lat. *aloē* < Gk.] —**al′o•et′ic** (äl′ō-ĕt′ĭk) *adj.*

aloe ver•a (vĕr′ə, vîr′ə) *n.* **1.** A species of aloe (*Aloe vera*) native to the Mediterranean region. **2.** The mucilaginous juice or gel from the leaves of this plant, used for its soothing and healing properties. [*Aloe*, aloe plant + *vēra*, fem. of *vērus*, true.]

A•lo•fi (ä-lō′fē) The cap. of Niue, on the W coast of the island. Pop. 960.

a•loft (ə-lôft′, ə-lŏft′) *adv.* **1.** In or into a high place; high or higher up. **2.** *Nautical* At or toward the upper rigging. ❖ *prep.* On or above. [ME < ON *ā lopt* : *ā*, in + *lopt*, air.]

a•log•i•cal (ā-lŏj′ĭ-kəl) *adj.* Beyond the bounds of logic. —**a•log′i•cal•ly** *adv.* —**a•log′i•cal•ness** *n.*

a•lo•ha (ə-lō′ə, -hə, ä-lō′hä′) *interj. Chiefly Hawaii* Used as a traditional greeting or farewell. [Hawaiian.]

al•o•in (äl′ō-ĭn) *n.* A bitter, yellow crystalline compound obtained from the aloe and used as a laxative. [ALO(E) + –IN.]

a•lone (ə-lōn′) *adj.* **1.** Being apart from others; solitary. **2.** Being without anyone or anything else; only. **3.** Considered separately from all others of the same class. **4.** Being unequaled. ❖ *adv.* **1.** Without others. **2.** Without help: *cooked alone.* **3.** Exclusively; only: *The credit is hers alone.* [ME : *al*, all; see ALL + *one*, one; see ONE.] —**a•lone′ness** *n.*

> **SYNONYMS** *alone, lonely, lonesome, solitary* These adjectives describe lack of companionship. *Alone* emphasizes being apart from others but does not necessarily imply unhappiness: *"I am never less alone, than when I am alone"* (James Howell). *Lonely* connotes painful awareness of being alone: *" 'No doubt they are dead,' she thought, and felt . . . sadder and . . . lonelier for the thought"* (Ouida). *Lonesome* emphasizes a plaintive desire for companionship: *"You must . . . not be lonesome because I'm not at home"* (Charles Dickens). *Solitary* often stresses physical isolation that is self-imposed: *I thoroughly enjoyed my solitary meal.*

a•long (ə-lông′, ə-lŏng′) *prep.* **1.** Over the length of: *walked along the path.* **2.** On a line or course parallel and close to; continuously beside: *trees along the avenue.* **3.** In accordance with: *split along party lines.* ❖ *adv.* **1.** Forward; onward: *Farther along, we passed a hitchhiker.* **2.** As a companion: *brought a friend along.* **3.** In accompaniment or association; together: *packed an atlas along with other books.* See Usage Note at **together**. **4.** With one; at hand. **5.** *Informal* Advanced to some degree: *along in years.* [ME < OE *andlang*, extending opposite : *and-*, facing; see *ant-* in App. + *lang*, long; see LONG[1].]

a•long•shore (ə-lông′shôr′, -shōr′, ə-lŏng′-) *adv.* Along, near, or by the shore.

a•long•side (ə-lông′sīd′, ə-lŏng′-) *adv.* Along, near, at, or to the side. ❖ *prep.* By the side of; side by side with.

> **USAGE NOTE** In its prepositional use *alongside* may be accompanied by *of*: *The barge lay alongside* (or *alongside of*) *the pier.*

a•loof (ə-lōōf′) *adj.* Distant physically or emotionally; reserved and remote: *stood apart with aloof dignity.* ❖ *adv.* At a distance but within view; apart. [A–[2] + LUFF, windward part of a ship (obsolete).] —**a•loof′ly** *adv.* —**a•loof′ness** *n.*

al•o•pe•cia (äl′ə-pē′shə, -shē-ə) *n.* Loss of hair; baldness. [Lat. *alōpecia*, fox mange < Gk. *alōpekiā* < *alōpex*, fox. See w|p-ē- in App.] —**al′o•pe′cic** (-pē′sĭk) *adj.*

a•loud (ə-loud′) *adv.* **1.** By voice; orally: *Read aloud.* **2.** Loudly: *crying aloud for help.*

alp (älp) *n.* **1.** A high mountain. **2.** A very large mound or mass. [Back-formation < the ALPS.]

---

al•pac•a (äl-păk′ə) *n., pl.* **alpaca** or **-as 1.** A domesticated South American mammal (*Lama pacos*), related to the llama and having fine long wool. **2a.** The wool of this mammal. **b.** Cloth made from alpaca. **c.** A coat made of this cloth. **3.** A glossy cotton or rayon and wool fabric. [Am.Sp. < Aymara *allpaca*.]

al•pen•glow (äl′pən-glō′) *n.* A rosy glow that suffuses snow-covered mountain peaks at dawn or dusk on a clear day. [Partial transl. of Ger. *Alpenglühen* : *Alpen*, Alps + *glühen*, to glow.]

al•pen•horn (äl′pən-hôrn′) *n.* A curved wooden horn, sometimes as long as 6 meters (approx. 20 feet), used by Alpine herders to call cows. [Ger. : *Alpen*, Alps + *Horn*, horn (< MHGer. < OHGer.; see ker-[1] in App.).]

al•pen•stock (äl′pən-stŏk′) *n.* A mountaineer's long, iron-pointed staff. [Ger. : *Alpen*, Alps + *Stock*, staff (< MHGer. *stoc* < OHGer.).]

al•pes•trine (äl-pĕs′trĭn) *adj.* Growing at high altitudes; alpine or subalpine. [< Med.Lat. *alpestris* < Lat. *Alpēs*, the Alps.]

al•pha (äl′fə) *n.* **1.** The first letter of the Greek alphabet. **2.** The first one; the beginning. **3.** *Chemistry* The first position from a designated carbon atom in an organic molecule at which an atom or radical may be substituted. **4.** *Astronomy* The brightest or main star in a constellation. **5.** The mathematical estimate of the return on a security when the return on the market as a whole is zero. ❖ *adj.* **1.** Being the highest ranked or most dominant individual of one's sex. Used of social animals. **2.** *Chemistry* Closest to the functional group of atoms in an organic molecule. **3.** Alphabetical. [Gk. < Phoenician *'alp*, ox, first letter of the Phoenician alphabet.]

al•pha-ad•re•ner•gic (äl′fə-ăd′rə-nûr′jĭk) *adj.* Of, relating to, or being an alpha-receptor.

alpha-adrenergic receptor *n.* See **alpha-receptor**.

alpha and omega *n.* **1.** The first and the last. **2.** The most important part.

al•pha•bet (äl′fə-bĕt′, -bĭt) *n.* **1.** The letters of a language, arranged in the order fixed by custom. **2.** A system of characters or symbols representing sounds or things. **3.** A set of basic parts or elements. See tables on pages 40 and 41. [ME *alphabete* < Lat. *alphabētum* < Gk. *alphabētos* : *alpha*, alpha; see ALPHA + *bēta*, beta; see BETA.]

al•pha•bet•i•cal (äl′fə-bĕt′ĭ-kəl) also **al•pha•bet•ic** (-bĕt′ĭk) *adj.* **1.** Arranged in the customary order of the letters of a language. **2.** Of, relating to, or expressed by an alphabet. —**al′pha•bet′i•cal•ly** *adv.*

al•pha•bet•ize (äl′fə-bĭ-tīz′) *tr.v.* **-ized, -iz•ing, -iz•es 1.** To arrange alphabetically. **2.** To supply with an alphabet. —**al′pha•bet′i•za′tion** (-bĕt′ĭ-zā′shən) *n.* —**al′pha•bet′iz′er** *n.*

al•pha-block•er (äl′fə-blŏk′ər) *n.* A drug that opposes the excitatory effects of norepinephrine released from sympathetic nerve endings at alpha-receptors.

Alpha Cen•tau•ri (sĕn-tôr′ē) *n.* A multiple star in the constellation Centaurus, 4.4 light-years from Earth.

Alpha Cru•cis (krōō′sĭs) *n.* A double star in the constellation Southern Cross.

al•pha-fe•to•pro•tein (äl′fə-fē′tō-prō′tēn, -tē-ĭn) *n.* An antigen produced in the liver of a fetus that is present in amniotic fluid and is used in the detection of certain fetal abnormalities.

alpha helix *n.* A structure of proteins, characterized by a spiral chain of amino acids. —**al′pha-hel′i•cal** (äl′fə-hĕl′ĭ-kəl, -hē′lĭ-) *adj.*

al•pha-hy•drox•y acid (äl′fə-hī-drŏk′sē) *n.* Any of various fruit acids that are capable of trapping moisture in the skin and initiating the formation of collagen.

al•pha•nu•mer•ic (äl′fə-nōō-mĕr′ĭk, -nyōō-) also **al•pha•mer•ic** (-fə-mĕr′ĭk) *adj.* Consisting of or using letters, numbers, punctuation marks, and mathematical and other conventional symbols: *an alphanumeric code.* [ALPHA(BETIC) + NUMERIC(AL).] —**al′pha•nu•mer′i•cal** *n.* —**al′pha•nu•mer′i•cal•ly** *adv.*

alpha particle *n.* A positively charged particle, consisting of two protons and two neutrons.

alpha privative *n.* The prefix *a-* or *an-* before vowels, used in Greek and in English words borrowed from Greek to express absence or negation.

alpha ray *n.* A stream of alpha particles.

al•pha-re•cep•tor (äl′fə-rĭ-sĕp′tər) *n.* A site in the autonomic nervous system in which excitatory responses occur when adrenergic agents, such as epinephrine, are released.

alpha rhythm *n.* See **alpha wave**.

al•pha-to•coph•e•rol (äl′fə-tō-kŏf′ə-rôl′, -rōl′) *n.* An alcohol, $C_{29}H_{50}O_2$, obtained from wheat germ oil or produced synthetically and exhibiting the most potent vitamin E activity of the tocopherols.

alpha wave *n.* A pattern of smooth, regular electrical oscillations in the human brain, having a frequency of 8 to 13 hertz, that occur when a person is awake and relaxed.

Al•phe•us (äl-fē′əs) A river of the Peloponnesus in S Greece flowing c. 113 km (70 mi) to the Ionian Sea.

al•pine (äl′pīn′) *adj.* **1. Alpine** Of or relating to the Alps or their inhabitants. **2.** Of or relating to high mountains. **3.** *Biology* Living or growing above the timberline. **4.** *Sports* **a.** Intended for or concerned with mountaineering. **b. Alpine** Of or relating to down-

---

alpaca
Lama pacos

alpenhorn

ă	pat	oi	boy
ā	pay	ou	out
âr	care	ŏŏ	took
ä	father	ōō	boot
ĕ	pet	ŭ	cut
ē	be	ûr	urge
ĭ	pit	th	thin
ī	pie	*th*	this
îr	pier	hw	which
ŏ	pot	zh	vision
ō	toe	ə	about,
ô	paw		item

Stress marks:
′ (primary);
′ (secondary), as in
lexicon (lĕk′sĭ-kŏn′)

hill racing and slalom skiing events. [ME < Lat. *Alpīnus* < *Alpēs*, the Alps.]

al·pin·ist also **Al·pin·ist** (ăl′pə-nĭst) *n.* A mountain climber. —**al′pin·ism** *n.*

Alps (ălps) A mountain system of S-central Europe, c. 805 km (500 mi) long and 161 km (100 mi) wide, curving in an arc from the Riviera to the Balkan Peninsula and rising to 4,810.2 m (15,771 ft).

al·read·y (ôl-rĕd′ē) *adv.* **1.** By this or a specified time; before. **2.** So soon: *Are you quitting already?* **3.** *Informal* Used as an intensive: *Enough already.* [ME *alredi* : *al*, all; see ALL + *redi*, ready; see READY.]

al·right (ôl-rīt′) *adv. Nonstandard* All right. See Usage Note at **all right.**

ALS *abbr.* **1.** amyotrophic lateral sclerosis **2.** autograph letters, signed

Al·sace (ăl-săs′, -sās′) A region and former province of E France. Along with neighboring Lorraine, it was annexed by Germany in 1871 and returned to France by the Treaty of Versailles (1919).

Al·sa·tian (ăl-sā′shən) *adj.* Of or relating to Alsace or its inhabitants or culture. ❖ *n.* **1.** A native or inhabitant of Alsace. **2.** *Chiefly British* A German shepherd.

Al·sek (ăl′sĕk′) A river of NW Canada and SE AK flowing c. 418 km (260 mi) to the Pacific Ocean.

al·sike clover (ăl′sīk′) *n.* A perennial European clover (*Trifolium hybridum*) grown as a pasture and hay plant. [After *Alsike*, near Uppsala in eastern Sweden.]

al·so (ôl′sō) *adv.* **1.** In addition; besides. **2.** Likewise; too. ❖ *conj.*

TABLE OF ALPHABETS

Because it is more convenient to use a single system of spelling to represent the speech sounds of many different languages, words from languages that use other writing systems are usually transliterated into Roman characters. The transliterations shown here are those used in the etymologies in this Dictionary for four of the most important non-Roman alphabets. The names of the Hebrew and Greek letters are also entered and defined in the Dictionary as English nouns. (In some cases the English spelling differs from the transliterated letter name shown here, chiefly in the absence of diacritical marks—for example English **omega** versus Greek **ōmega**.) The Cyrillic letters shown are those used in modern Russian. For the history of the English alphabet, see "Development of the Alphabet."

HEBREW			ARABIC						GREEK				CYRILLIC		
				Forms											
Forms	Name	Sound	1	2	3	4	Name	Sound	Forms	Name	Sound		Forms		Sound
א	'aleph	'	ا	ا			'alif	'	A α	alpha	a		А а		a
	bēth	b	ب	ب	ب	ب	bā	b	B β	bēta	b		Б б		b
	gimel	g	ت	ت	ت	ت	tā	t	Γ γ	gamma	g (n)		В в		v
	dāleth	d	ث	ث	ث	ث	thā	t	Δ δ	delta	d		Г г		g
	hē	h	ج	ج	ج	ج	jīm	j	E ε	epsīlon	e		Д д		d
	vāv, wāw	w	ح	ح	ح	ح	hā	ḥ	Z ζ	zēta	z		Е е Ё ё		e, ë[1]
	zayin	z	خ	خ	خ	خ	khā	ḫ	H η	ēta	ē		Ж ж		zh
	ḥeth	ḥ	د	د			dāl	d	Θ θ	thēta	th		З з		z
	ṭeth	ṭ	ذ	ذ			dhāl	d	I ι	iōta	i		И и Й й		i, ī
	yodh	y	ر	ر			rā	r	K κ	kappa	k		К к		k
	kāph	k	ز	ز			zāy	z	Λ λ	lambda	l		Л л		l
	lāmedh	l	س	س	س	س	sīn	s	M μ	mū	m		М м		m
	mēm	m	ش	ش	ش	ش	shīn	š	N ν	nū	n		Н н		n
	nūn	n	ص	ص	ص	ص	ṣād	ṣ	Ξ ξ	xī	x		О о		o
	samekh	s	ض	ض	ض	ض	ḍād	ḍ	O ο	omīkron	o		П п		p
	'ayin	'	ط	ط	ط	ط	ṭā	ṭ	Π π	pī	p		Р р		r
	pē	p	ظ	ظ	ظ	ظ	ẓā	ẓ	P ρ	rhō	r (rh)		С с		s
	ṣadhe	ṣ	ع	ع	ع	ع	'ayn	'	Σ σ, ς	sīgma	s		Т т		t
	qōph	q	غ	غ	غ	غ	ghayn	ġ	T τ	tau	t		У у		u
	rēsh	r	ف	ف	ف	ف	fā	f	Υ υ	upsīlon	u		Ф ф		f
	sin	ś	ق	ق	ق	ق	qāf	q	Φ φ	phī	ph		Х х		kh
	shin	š	ك	ك	ك	ك	kāf	k	X χ	chī, khī	kh		Ц ц		ts
	tāv, tāw	t	ل	ل	ل	ل	lām	l	Ψ ψ	psī	ps		Ч ч		ch
			م	م	م	م	mīm	m	Ω ω	ōmega	ō		Ш ш		sh
			ن	ن	ن	ن	nūn	n					Щ щ		shch
			ه	ه	ه	ه	hā	h					Ъ ъ		[2]
			و	و			wāw	w					Ы ы		y
			ي	ي	ي	ي	yā	y					Ь ь		[3]
													Э э		e
													Ю ю		yu
													Я я		ya

Vowels are not represented in normal Hebrew writing, but for certain purposes they are indicated by a system of subscript and superscript dots. The transliterations with subscript dots are pharyngeal consonants as in Arabic. The second forms shown are used when the letter falls at the end of a word.

The different forms in the four numbered columns are used when the letters are in: 1. isolation; 2. juncture with a previous letter; 3. juncture with letters on both sides; 4. juncture with a following letter.

Long vowels are represented by the consonants 'alif (for ā), wāw (for ū), and yā (for ī). Short vowels are not usually written; they can, however, be indicated by the following signs: 'fatha (for a), kesra (for i), and ' damma (for u).

Transliterations with subscript dots represent "emphatic" or pharyngeal consonants, which are pronounced in the usual way except that the pharynx is tightly narrowed during articulation. When two dots are placed over the hā, the new letter thus formed is called tā marbūta, and is pronounced (t).

The superscript on an initial vowel or rhō represents aspiration or "rough breathing," and is transliterated by h. Lack of aspiration on an initial vowel is indicated by the superscript ', called the smooth breathing. When gamma precedes kappa, xī, khī, or another gamma, it has the value ng (as in Engl. sing) and is transliterated n. The second lowercase form of sigma is used only in the final position.

[1]The variant ё occurs only in stressed position, and is pronounced as (ô) or (yô).

[2]This letter, called the "hard sign," is very rare in modern Russian. It indicates that the previous consonant remains hard (not palatalized) even when followed by a front vowel.

[3]This letter, called the "soft sign," indicates that the previous consonant is soft (palatalized) even when a front vowel does not follow.

ă pat
ā pay
âr care
ä father
ĕ pet
ē be
ĭ pit
ī pie
îr pier
ŏ pot
ō toe
ô paw

oi boy
ou out
ŏŏ took
ōō boot
ŭ cut
ûr urge
th thin
th this
hw which
zh vision
ə about, item

Stress marks:
′ (primary);
′ (secondary), as in
lexicon (lĕk′sĭ-kŏn′)

And in addition: *It's a pretty cat, also friendly.* [ME < OE *ealswā* : *eall,* all + *swā,* so; see SO¹.]

al·so-ran (ôl′sō-răn′) *n.* **1.** A horse that does not win, place, or show in a race. **2.** A loser in a competition. **3.** One that has little talent or success.

al·stroe·me·ri·a (ăl′strə-mîr′ē-ə) *n.* Any of several South American perennial herbs of the genus *Alstroemeria,* with vari-

ously colored, showy blooms. [NLat. *Alstroemeria,* genus name, after Baron Clas *Alstroemer* (1736–94), Swedish naturalist.]

alt (ălt) *adj.* Pitched in the first octave above the treble staff. ❖ *n.* **1.** The first octave above the treble staff. **2.** A note or tone in the alt octave. [Lat. *altus,* high.]

alt. *abbr.* **1.** alteration **2.** alternate **3.** altitude

Alta. *abbr.* Alberta

DEVELOPMENT OF THE ALPHABET

In early forms of writing such as hieroglyphics, pictorial signs represented whole words or syllables. By around 1500 B.C. the Canaanites, a Semitic-speaking people living in ancient Palestine and Syria, began to use such signs to stand for individual speech sounds, writing them from right to left. A version of this alphabet was adopted by their successors the Phoenicians, who simplified the forms and added several new ones. Trade with the Phoenicians brought the alphabet to the early Greeks, who reassigned some of the Semitic consonant symbols to vowel sounds such as (a), (e), (ē), and (o). The Greeks also split the Semitic *wāw* into two letters, *wau* (later called *digamma,* "double gamma," whose sound (w) was lost in classical Greek but whose form survives in modern F) and *u* (later *u psīlon,* "simple u"), the ancestor of modern U, V, W, and Y.

In Italy, a western variant of the Greek alphabet was adopted by the Etruscans. Our modern letters derive from the Romans, who adapted the Etruscan script for monumental inscriptions and wrote from left to right. Because Etruscan writing did not distinguish between the sounds of *c* and *g,* the Romans created the new letter G by adding a stroke to C. The classical Greek Y and Z were added to represent the sounds (ü) and (z) in words borrowed from Greek. The English alphabet reached its total of 26 letters only after medieval scribes added *w* (originally written *uu*) and Renaissance printers separated the variant pairs *i/j* and *u/v.*

During the Middle Ages, the Roman capitals evolved into uncials and then to Carolingian minuscules and Italic cursive script, which are the prototypes of many modern printed and handwritten letters.

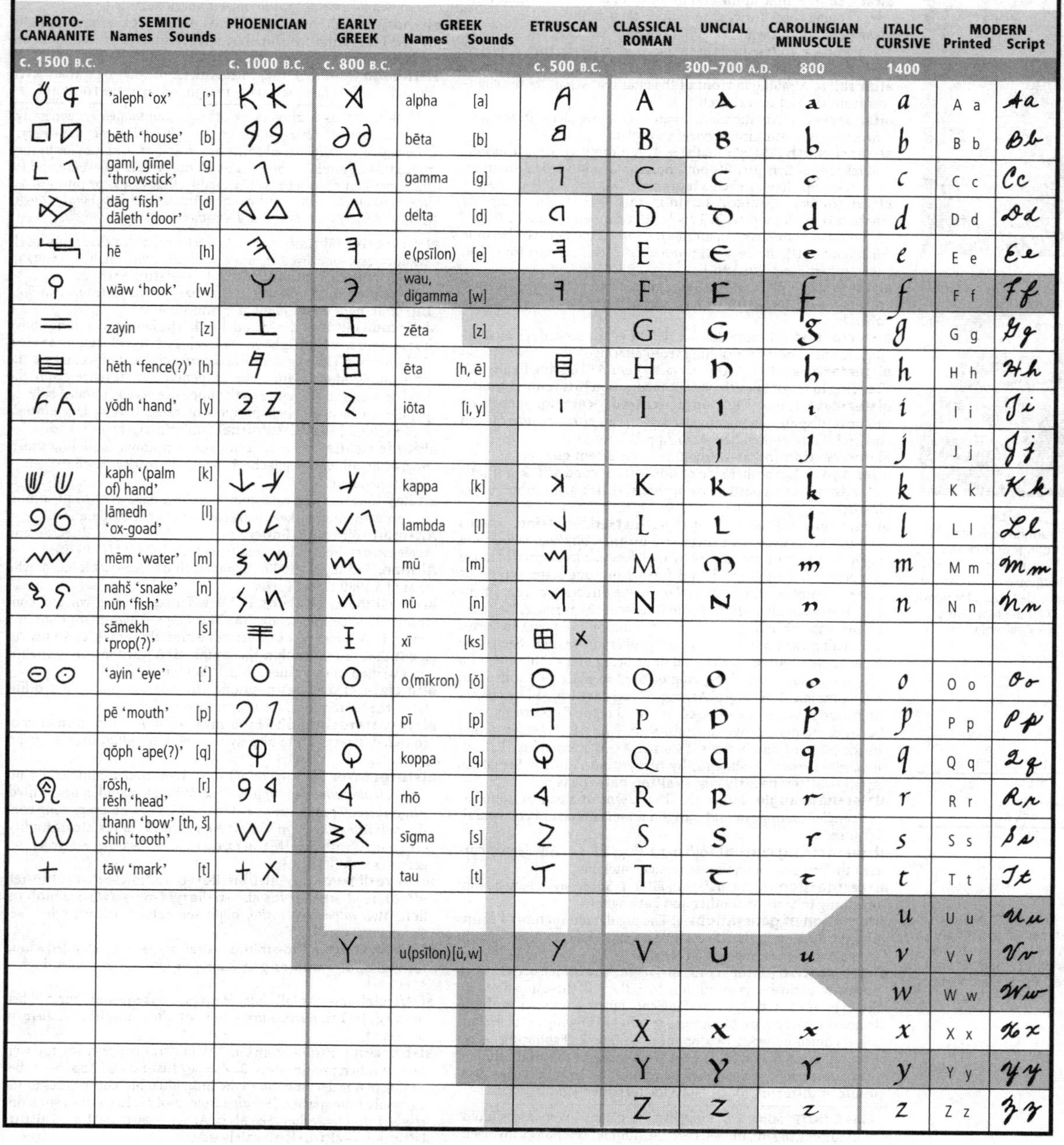

PROTO-CANAANITE	SEMITIC Names	Sounds	PHOENICIAN	EARLY GREEK	GREEK Names	Sounds	ETRUSCAN	CLASSICAL ROMAN	UNCIAL	CAROLINGIAN MINUSCULE	ITALIC CURSIVE	MODERN Printed	Script
c. 1500 B.C.			c. 1000 B.C.	c. 800 B.C.			c. 500 B.C.		300–700 A.D.	800	1400		
𐤀	'aleph 'ox'	[']	K K	X	alpha	[a]	A	A	A	a	a	A a	Aa
	bēth 'house'	[b]	9 9	∂∂	bēta	[b]	B	B	B	b	b	B b	Bb
L	gaml, gīmel 'throwstick'	[g]	1	1	gamma	[g]	7	C	C	c	C	C c	Cc
	dāg 'fish' dāleth 'door'	[d]	△ △	△	delta	[d]	◁	D	ठ	d	d	D d	Dd
	hē	[h]	∃	∃	e(psilon)	[e]	∃	E	E	e	e	E e	Ee
	wāw 'hook'	[w]	Y	ʔ	wau, digamma	[w]	∃	F	F	f	f	F f	Ff
=	zayin	[z]	I	I	zēta	[z]		G	G	g	g	G g	Gg
	hēth 'fence(?)'	[h]	月	目	ēta	[h, ē]	目	H	h	h	h	H h	Hh
	yōdh 'hand'	[y]	2 Z	Ƨ	iōta	[i, y]	I	I	I	ı	i	I i	Ii
									J	j	j	J j	Jj
Ш Ш	kaph '(palm of) hand'	[k]	↓ ↓	↯	kappa	[k]	X	K	K	k	k	K k	Kk
9 6	lāmedh 'ox-goad'	[l]	L L	√1	lambda	[l]	↳	L	L	l	l	L l	Ll
∿∿	mēm 'water'	[m]	ξ ๓	M	mū	[m]	๓	M	๓	m	m	M m	Mm
	nahš 'snake' nūn 'fish'	[n]	≶ ५	N	nū	[n]	५	N	N	n	n	N n	Nn
	sāmekh 'prop(?)'	[s]	₮	Ⱦ	xī	[ks]	⊞ X						
⊖ ⊙	'ayin 'eye'	[']	O	O	o(mīkron)	[ō]	O	O	O	o	o	O o	Oo
	pē 'mouth'	[p]	ʔ 1	1	pī	[p]	⌐	P	P	p	p	P p	Pp
	qōph 'ape(?)'	[q]	φ	Φ	koppa	[q]	Q	Q	q	q	q	Q q	Qq
	rōsh, rēsh 'head'	[r]	9 ٩	4	rhō	[r]	◁	R	R	r	r	R r	Rr
ⴓ	thann 'bow' [th, š] shin 'tooth'		W	≷ ≷	sīgma	[s]	Z	S	S	ſ	s	S s	Ss
+	tāw 'mark'	[t]	+ X	T	tau	[t]	T	T	τ	τ	t	T t	Tt
											u	U u	Uu
				Y	u(psīlon) [ü, w]		Y	V	U	u	v	V v	Vv
											w	W w	Ww
								X	x	x	x	X x	Xx
								Y	Y	Υ	y	Y y	Yy
								Z	Z	z	z	Z z	Zz

Al·ta California (ăl´tə) also **Upper California** The Spanish possessions along the Pacific coast N of the peninsula of Baja California.

Al·ta·ic (ăl-tā´ĭk) *n.* A proposed language family of Europe and Asia that includes the Turkic, Tungusic, and Mongolian subfamilies. ❖ *adj.* **1.** Of or relating to the Altai Mountains. **2.** Of or relating to Altaic.

Al·tai Mountains or **Al·tay Mountains** (ăl-tī´) A mountain system of central Asia, mostly in E Kazakhstan, S-central Russia, and W Mongolia, rising to 4,508.8 m (14,783 ft).

Al·tair (ăl-tîr´, -tär´, ăl´tîr´, -tär´) *n.* A variable double star in the constellation Aquila. [Ar. *(an-nasr) aṭ-ṭā'ir*, the flying (eagle) : *al-*, the + *ṭā'ir*, flying, active part. of *ṭāra*, to fly.]

Al·ta·mi·ra (ăl´tə-mîr´ə, äl´tä-mē´rä) A group of caverns of N Spain WSW of Santander; noted for specimens of Paleolithic art (discovered 1879).

al·tar (ôl´tər) *n.* **1.** An elevated place or structure before which religious ceremonies may be enacted or upon which sacrifices may be offered. **2.** A structure, typically a table, before which the divine offices are recited and upon which the Eucharist is celebrated in Christian churches. [ME *auter* < OE *altar* and OFr. *auter*, both < Lat. *altāre*.]

altar boy *n.* A boy who is an altar server.

altar call *n.* A time at the end of a Protestant service when worshipers may come forward to profess their faith.

altar girl *n.* A girl who is an altar server.

al·tar·piece (ôl´tər-pēs´) *n.* A piece of artwork that is placed above and behind an altar.

altar rail *n.* A railing in front of the altar that separates the chancel from the rest of a church.

altar server *n.* An attendant to an officiating cleric in the performance of a liturgical service; an acolyte.

alt·az·i·muth (ălt-ăz´ə-məth) *n.* **1.** A mounting for astronomical telescopes that permits both horizontal and vertical rotation. **2.** A telescope having such a mounting. [ALT(ITUDE) + AZIMUTH.]

al·ter (ôl´tər) *v.* **-tered, -ter·ing, -ters** —*tr.* **1.** To change or make different; modify. **2.** To adjust (a garment) for a better fit. **3.** To castrate or spay (an animal). —*intr.* To change or become different. [ME *alteren* < OFr. *alterer* < Med.Lat. *alterāre* < Lat. *alter*, other. See **al-** in App.]

al·ter·a·ble (ôl´tər-ə-bəl) *adj.* That can be altered: *alterable clothing.* —**al´ter·a·bil´i·ty, al´ter·a·ble·ness** *n.* —**al´ter·a·bly** *adv.*

al·ter·a·tion (ôl´tə-rā´shən) *n.* **1.** The act or procedure of altering. **2.** The condition resulting from altering.

al·ter·a·tive (ôl´tər-ā´tĭv, -tər-ə-tĭv) *adj.* **1.** Tending to alter. **2.** Tending to restore health. ❖ *n.* A medication that restores health.

al·ter·cate (ôl´tər-kāt´) *intr.v.* **-cat·ed, -cat·ing, -cates** To argue or dispute vehemently; wrangle. [Lat. *altercārī, altercāt-*, to quarrel < *alter*, other. See **al-** in App.]

al·ter·ca·tion (ôl´tər-kā´shən) *n.* A vehement quarrel.

alter ego *n.* **1.** Another side of oneself; a second self. **2.** An intimate friend or a constant companion. [Lat. : *alter*, other + *ego*, I, self.]

al·ter·nate (ôl´tər-nāt´, ăl´-) *v.* **-nat·ed, -nat·ing, -nates** —*intr.* **1a.** To occur in a successive manner: *day alternating with night.* **b.** To act or proceed by turns: *The students alternated at the computer.* **2.** To pass back and forth from one state, action, or place to another. **3.** *Electricity* To reverse direction at regular intervals in a circuit. —*tr.* **1.** To do or execute by turns. **2.** To cause to alternate. ❖ *adj.* (-nĭt) **1.** Happening or following in turns; succeeding each other continuously: *alternate seasons.* See Usage Note at **alternative. 2.** Relating to or being every other one of a series: *alternate lines.* **3.** Serving or used in place of another: *an alternate plan.* **4.** *Botany* **a.** Arranged singly at each node, as leaves on different sides of a stem. **b.** Arranged regularly between other parts, as stamens between petals. ❖ *n.* (-nĭt) **1.** A person acting in the place of another; a substitute. **2.** An alternative. [Lat. *alternāre, alternāt-* < *alternus*, by turns < *alter*, other. See **al-** in App.] —**al´ter·nate·ly** *adv.* —**al´ter·nate·ness** *n.*

alternate angle (ôl´tər-nĭt, ăl´-) *n.* One of a pair of nonadjacent angles on opposite sides of a transversal that cuts two parallel lines.

al·ter·nat·ing current (ôl´tər-nā´tĭng, ăl´-) *n.* An electric current that reverses direction at regular intervals.

al·ter·na·tion (ôl´tər-nā´shən, ăl´-) *n.* Successive change from one thing or state to another and back again.

alternation of generations *n.* The regular alternation of forms of reproduction in the life cycle of an organism, such as between sexual and asexual reproductive cycles.

al·ter·na·tive (ôl-tûr´nə-tĭv, ăl-) *n.* **1a.** The choice between two mutually exclusive possibilities. **b.** Either of these possibilities. See Syns at **choice. 2.** *Usage Problem* One of a number of things from which one must be chosen. ❖ *adj.* **1.** Allowing or necessitating a choice between two or more things. **2.** Espousing or reflecting values that are different from those of the establishment or mainstream: *an alternative newspaper.* **3.** *Usage Problem* Substitute or different; other. —**al·ter´na·tive·ly** *adv.*

is exactly two, because of the word's historical relation to Latin *alter*, "the other of two." Resistance to this view seems to be waning: In our 1999 ballot, 66 percent of the Panel accepted the sentence *Of the three alternatives, the first is the least distasteful,* compared with 49 percent in an earlier survey. • It is also increasingly acceptable to use *alternative* to refer to a variant or substitute in cases where there is no element of choice involved, as in *We will do our best to secure alternative employment for employees displaced by the closing of the factory.* This sentence is now acceptable to 75 percent of the Usage Panel, versus only 40 percent in an earlier survey. • *Alternative* should not be confused with *alternate.* Correct usage requires *The class will meet on alternate* (not *alternative*) *Tuesdays.*

alternative medicine *n.* A variety of therapeutic or preventive health care practices, such as homeopathy and herbal medicine, that do not follow generally accepted medical methods and may not have a scientific explanation for their effectiveness.

al·ter·na·tor (ôl´tər-nā´tər, ăl´-) *n.* An electric generator that produces alternating current.

al·the·a also **al·thae·a** (ăl-thē´ə) *n.* **1.** See **rose of Sharon** 1. **2.** See **hollyhock.** [Lat., mallows < Gk. *althaia < althainein*, to heal.]

Al·thing (äl´thĭng, ôl´-) *n.* The parliament of Iceland, the oldest assembly in Europe, first convened in 930. [ON *althing*, parliament, whole assembly : *allr*, all + *thing*, assembly.]

alt·horn or **Alt·horn** (ält´hôrn´) *n.* Any of several upright, valved brass wind instruments. [Ger. : *alt*, alto (< Ital. *alto*; see ALTO) + *Horn*, horn; see ALPENHORN.]

al·though (ôl-thō´) *conj.* Regardless of the fact that; even though. [ME : *al*, all; see ALL + *though*, though; see THOUGH.]

al·tim·e·ter (ăl-tĭm´ĭ-tər) *n.* An instrument for determining elevation, esp. one used in aircraft. [Lat. *altus*, high + -METER.] —**al´ti·met´ric** (ăl´tə-mĕt´rĭk) *adj.* —**al·tim´e·try** *n.*

al·ti·pla·no (äl´tĭ-plä´nō) *n., pl.* **-nos** A high plateau. [Am.Sp. : Lat. *altus*, high + Lat. *plānum*, plain; see PLANE[1].]

al·ti·tude (ăl´tĭ-tōōd´, -tyōōd´) *n.* **1.** The height of a thing above a reference level, esp. above sea level. **2.** A high location or area. **3.** *Astronomy* The angular distance of a celestial object above the horizon. **4.** *Mathematics* The perpendicular distance from the base of a geometric figure to the opposite vertex, parallel side, or parallel surface. **5.** High position or rank. [ME < Lat. *altitūdō < altus*, high.] —**al´ti·tu´di·nal** (-tōōd´n-əl, -tyōōd´-) *adj.*

altitude sickness *n.* A collection of symptoms, including shortness of breath and headache, brought on by decreased oxygen in the atmosphere.

alt key (ôlt) *n.* A key on a computer keyboard pressed in combination with another key to execute an alternate operation.

Alt·man (ôlt´mən), **Robert** b. 1925. Amer. film director and screenwriter whose film credits include *M*A*S*H* (1970).

Altman, Sidney b. 1939. Canadian-born Amer. biologist who shared a 1989 Nobel Prize.

al·to (ăl´tō) *n., pl.* **al·tos 1.** A low female singing voice; a contralto. **2.** A countertenor. **3a.** The range between soprano and tenor. **b.** A singer whose voice lies within this range. **c.** An instrument that sounds within this range. **d.** A vocal or instrumental part written within this range. [Ital. < Lat. *altus*, high.]

alto clef *n.* The C clef positioned to indicate that the third line from the bottom of a staff represents middle C.

al·to·cu·mu·lus (ăl´tō-kyōō´myə-ləs) *n.* A cloud formation of rounded, fleecy, white or gray masses. [Lat. *altus*, high + CUMULUS.]

al·to·geth·er (ôl´tə-gĕth´ər) *adv.* **1.** Entirely; completely; utterly: *an altogether new approach.* **2.** With all included or counted: *Altogether, 20 people came.* **3.** On the whole; with everything considered: *Altogether, I'm sorry it happened.* ❖ *n.* A state of nudity. Often used with *the.* [ME *al togeder* : *al*, all; see ALL + *togeder*, together; see TOGETHER.]

al·to-re·lie·vo also **al·to-ri·lie·vo** (ăl´tō-rĭ-lē´vō, ăl´tō-rĕl-yā´vō) *n., pl.* **-vos** also **-ri·lie·vi** (-rĕl-yā´vē) See **high relief.** [Ital. *altorilievo : alto*, high; see ALTO + *rilievo*, relief; see BAS-RELIEF.]

al·to·strat·us (ăl´tō-strāt´əs, -strā´təs) *n.* An extended cloud formation of bluish or gray sheets or layers. [Lat. *altus*, high + STRATUS.]

al·tri·cial (ăl-trĭsh´əl) *adj.* Helpless, naked, and blind when hatched. [< Lat. *altrīx, altrīc-*, fem. of *altor*, nourisher < *alere*, to nourish.]

al·tru·ism (ăl´trōō-ĭz´əm) *n.* **1.** Unselfish concern for the welfare of others; selflessness. **2.** *Zoology* Instinctive cooperative behavior that is detrimental to the individual but contributes to the survival of the species. [Fr. *altruisme*, prob. < Ital. *altrui*, someone else < Lat. *alter*, other. See **al-** in App.] —**al´tru·ist** *n.* —**al´tru·is´tic** *adj.* —**al´tru·is´ti·cal·ly** *adv.*

altar
top: Buddhist temple with offerings of fruit and flowers
bottom: Mission San Antonio de Padua, founded 1771, near Monterey, California

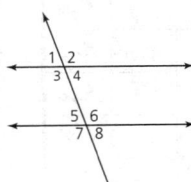

alternate angle
Angles 3,6 and 4,5 are alternate interior angles; angles 1,8 and 2,7 are alternate exterior angles.

Al U·bay·yid (ăl′ ŏo-bā′ĭd, äl′) See **El Obeid.**

al·u·la (ăl′yə-lə) *n., pl.* **-lae** (-lē′) A small joint in the middle of a bird's wing that is homologous with the thumb. [NLat., dim. of Latin *āla*, wing.] **—al′u·lar** (-lər) *adj.*

al·um[1] (ăl′əm) *n.* Any of various double sulfates of a trivalent metal, such as aluminum, chromium, or iron, and a univalent metal, such as potassium or sodium, esp. aluminum potassium sulfate, AlK(SO₄)₂·12H₂O. [ME < OFr. < Lat. *alūmen*.]

a·lum[2] (ə-lŭm′) *n. Informal* An alumna or alumnus.

a·lu·mi·na (ə-lōo′mə-nə) *n.* Any of several forms of aluminum oxide, Al₂O₃, occurring naturally as corundum, in bauxite, and with various impurities as ruby, sapphire, and emery. [NLat. *alūmina* < Lat. *alūmen, alūmin-*, alum.]

a·lu·mi·nate (ə-lōo′mə-nāt′, -nĭt) *n.* A chemical compound containing aluminum as part of a negative ion.

a·lu·mi·nif·er·ous (ə-lōo′mə-nĭf′ər-əs) *adj.* Containing or yielding aluminum, alumina, or alum. [Lat. *alūmen, alūmin-*, alum + −FEROUS.]

a·lu·min·i·um (ăl′yə-mĭn′ē-əm) *n. Chiefly British* Variant of **aluminum.**

a·lu·mi·nize (ə-lōo′mə-nīz′) *tr.v.* **-nized, -niz·ing, -niz·es** To coat or cover with aluminum or aluminum paint.

a·lu·mi·nous (ə-lōo′mə-nəs) *adj.* Of, relating to, or containing aluminum or alum.

a·lu·mi·num (ə-lōo′mə-nəm) *n. Symbol* **Al** A silvery-white, ductile metallic element, found chiefly in bauxite. A good conductor, it is used in light, corrosion-resistant alloys. Atomic number 13; atomic weight 26.98; melting point 660.2°C; boiling point 2,467°C; specific gravity 2.69; valence 3. See table at **element.** [ALUMIN(A) + −(I)UM.]

aluminum oxide *n.* See **alumina.**

aluminum plant *n.* A succulent herb (*Pilea cadierei*) often grown as a houseplant for its silver-colored leaves.

aluminum sulfate *n.* A crystalline compound, Al₂(SO₄)₃, used in papermaking and water purification.

a·lum·na (ə-lŭm′nə) *n., pl.* **-nae** (-nē′) A woman graduate or former student of a school, college, or university. See Usage Note at **alumnus.** [Lat., fem. of *alumnus*, pupil. See ALUMNUS.]

a·lum·nus (ə-lŭm′nəs) *n., pl.* **-ni** (-nī′) A male graduate or former student of a school, college, or university. [Lat., pupil < *alere*, to nourish.]

> **USAGE NOTE** *Alumnus* and *alumna* both come from Latin and preserve Latin plurals. *Alumnus* is a masculine noun whose plural is *alumni*, and *alumna* is a feminine noun whose plural is *alumnae*. Coeducational institutions usually use *alumni* for graduates of both sexes. But those who object to masculine forms in such cases may prefer the phrase *alumni and alumnae* or the form *alumnae/i*, which is the choice of many women's colleges that have begun to admit men.

al·um·root (ăl′əm-rōot′, -rŏot′) *n.* Any of various North American perennials of the genus *Heuchera* having palmately lobed basal leaves and leafless stalks. [< the use of its root as an astringent.]

al·u·nite (ăl′yə-nīt′) *n.* A gray to white mineral, chiefly K₂Al₆(OH)₆(SO₄)₃. [Fr. < *alun*, alum < Lat. *alūmen*.]

Al·va (ăl′və, äl′vä) also **Al·ba** (ăl′bə), Duke of. Title of Fernando Álvarez de Toledo. 1508–82. Spanish colonial administrator of the Netherlands (1567–73).

Al·va·ra·do (ăl′və-rä′dŏ, äl′vä-rä′thŏ), **Pedro de** 1485–1541. Spanish governor of Guatemala.

Al·va·rez (ăl′və-rĕz′), **Luis Walter** 1911–88. Amer. physicist who won a 1968 Nobel Prize.

al·ve·o·lar (ăl-vē′ə-lər) *adj.* **1.** Of or relating to an alveolus. **2.** *Anatomy* **a.** Relating to the jaw section containing the tooth sockets. **b.** Relating to the alveoli of the lungs. **3.** *Linguistics* Formed with the tip of the tongue touching or near the inner ridge of the gums of the upper front teeth, as the English (t). ❖ *n. Linguistics* An alveolar sound. **—al·ve′o·lar·ly** *adv.*

al·ve·o·late (ăl-vē′ə-lĭt) *adj.* Having a honeycombed surface. **—al·ve′o·la′tion** (-lā′shən) *n.*

al·ve·o·lus (ăl-vē′ə-ləs) *n., pl.* **-li** (-lī′) **1.** A small angular cavity or pit. **2.** A tooth socket in the jawbone. **3.** A tiny, thin-walled, capillary-rich sac in the lungs where the exchange of oxygen and carbon dioxide takes place. [Lat., small hollow, dim. of *alveus*, a hollow < *alvus*, belly.]

al·ways (ôl′wāz, -wĭz, -wēz) *adv.* **1.** At all times; invariably: *always late.* **2.** For all time; forever: *They will always be friends.* **3.** At any time; in any event: *You can always resign if you're unhappy.* [ME *alweis* : *alwei*, always (< OE *ealne weg* : *ealne*, accusative of *eall*, all + *weg*, way; see **wegh-** in App.) + *-es*, adv. suff.; see *-S*³.]

Al·yce clover or **al·yce clover** (ăl′ĭs) *n.* A tropical Asiatic herb (*Alysicarpus vaginalis*) with alternate simple leaves and reddish flowers. [Prob. by folk ety. < NLat. *Alysicarpus*, genus name : Gk. *halusis*, chain; see **wel-** in App. + Gk. *karpos*, fruit; see −CARP.]

a·lys·sum (ə-lĭs′əm) *n.* **1.** See **sweet alyssum. 2.** Any of various chiefly Mediterranean weeds or ornamentals of the genus *Alyssum* in the mustard family. **3.** See **hoary alyssum.** [NLat. *Alyssum*, genus name < Lat. *alysson*, kind of madder < Gk. *alusson*, a plant believed to cure rabies : *a-*, not; see A−¹ + *lussa*, rabies; see **w[l]k**ʷ**o-** in App.]

Alz·hei·mer's disease (älts′hī-mərz, ălts′-, ôlts′-, ôlz′-) *n.* A disease marked by the loss of cognitive ability, usu. over 10 to 15 years, that is associated with the accumulation of abnormal protein deposits in the brain and cortical atrophy. [After Alois *Alzheimer* (1864–1915), German neurologist.]

am (ăm) *v.* First person singular present indicative of **be.** [ME < OE *eom.* See **es-** in App.]

Am[1] The symbol for the element **americium.**

Am[2] *abbr. Bible* Amos

AM *abbr.* **1.** airmail **2.** amplitude modulation **3.** *Latin* artium magister (Master of Arts)

Am. *abbr.* **1.** America **2.** American

A.M. *abbr.* **1.** or **a.m** *Latin* anno mundi (in the year of the world) **2.** also **a.m.** or **a.m** ante meridiem

> **USAGE NOTE** By definition, *12 A.M.* denotes midnight, and *12 P.M.* denotes noon. There is sufficient confusion over the meanings of A.M. and P.M. when the hour is 12 to make it advisable to use *12 noon* and *12 midnight* where clarity is required.

AMA *abbr.* American Medical Association

A·ma·do (ə-mä′dŏo), **Jorge** 1912–2001. Brazilian writer whose works include *Dona Fior and Her Two Husbands* (1966).

A·ma·ga·sa·ki (ä′mə-gä-sä′kē) A city of S Honshu, Japan, on Osaka Bay. Pop. 496,313.

a·mah also **a·ma** (ä′mə, ä′mä) *n.* A housemaid, esp. a wet nurse, in Asia. [Port. *ama*, nurse < Med.Lat. *amma*, mother.]

Am·a·lek·ite (ăm′ə-lĕk′-īt′, ə-măl′ĭ-kīt′) *n.* A member of an ancient nomadic people of Canaan. [Heb. *'ămālēqī < 'ămālēq*, Amalek (name of a city).]

a·mal·gam (ə-măl′gəm) *n.* **1.** Any of various alloys of mercury with other metals, esp. **a.** An alloy of mercury and silver used in dental fillings. **b.** An alloy of mercury and tin used in silvering mirrors. **2.** A combination of diverse elements; a mixture. See Syns at **mixture.** [ME < OFr. *amalgame* < Med.Lat. *amalgama*, prob. alt. < Gk. *malagma*, soft mass.]

a·mal·ga·mate (ə-măl′gə-māt′) *v.* **-mat·ed, -mat·ing, -mates** *—tr.* **1.** To combine into a unified or integrated whole; unite. **2.** To alloy (a metal) with mercury. *—intr.* **1.** To become combined; unite. **2.** To blend with another metal. **—a·mal′ga·ma′tive** *adj.* **—a·mal′ga·ma′tor** *n.*

a·mal·ga·ma·tion (ə-măl′gə-mā′shən) *n.* **1.** The act of amalgamating or the condition resulting from this act. **2.** A consolidation or merger. **3.** The production of an alloy of mercury.

Am·al·the·a (ăm′əl-thē′ə) *n.* A satellite of Jupiter. [Lat. *Amalthēa*, nymph who nursed the infant Jupiter with goat's milk < Gk. *Amaltheia*.]

a·man·dine (ä′mən-dēn′, ăm′ən-) *adj.* Prepared or garnished with almonds: *sole amandine.* [Fr. < *amande*, almond < OFr. *almande.* See ALMOND.]

am·a·ni·ta (ăm′ə-nī′tə, -nē′-) *n.* Any of various mushrooms in the genus *Amanita.* [NLat. *Amānīta*, genus name < Gk. *amānītai*, a fungus.]

a·man·ta·dine (ə-măn′tə-dēn′) *n.* An antiviral drug, C₁₀H₁₇N· HCl, also used in the treatment of Parkinson's disease. [Alteration of *adamantane*, a hydrocarbon + −INE².]

a·man·u·en·sis (ə-măn′yŏo-ĕn′sĭs) *n., pl.* **-ses** (-sēz) One who is employed to take dictation or copy manuscripts. [Lat. *āmanuēnsis < (servus) ā manū*, (slave) at handwriting : *ā, ab*, by; see AB−¹ + *manū*, ablative of *manus*, hand; see **man-**² in App.]

am·a·ranth (ăm′ə-rănth′) *n.* **1.** Any of various annuals of the genus *Amaranthus*, including several weeds, ornamentals, and food plants. **2.** An imaginary flower that never fades. **3.** A deep reddish purple to dark or grayish purplish red. **4.** A dark red to purple azo dye. [NLat. *Amaranthus*, genus name, alteration of Lat. *amarantus* < Gk. *amarantos*, unfading : *a-*, not; see A−¹ + *marainein*, to wither; see **mer-** in App.]

am·a·ran·thine (ăm′ə-rănth′thĭn, -thĭn′) *adj.* **1.** Of, relating to, or resembling the amaranth. **2.** Eternally beautiful and unfading; everlasting. **3.** Deep purple-red.

am·a·relle (ăm′ə-rĕl′) *n.* A type of sour cherry. [Ger. < Med.Lat. *amārellum* < Lat. *amārus*, bitter.]

am·a·ret·to (ăm′ə-rĕt′ŏ) *n., pl.* **-tos** An Italian liqueur flavored with almond. [Ital., dim. of *amaro*, bitter < Lat. *amārus.*]

Am·a·ril·lo (ăm′ə-rĭl′ŏ, -rĭl′ŏ) A city of N TX in the Panhandle N of Lubbock. Pop. 173,627.

am·a·ryl·lis (ăm′ə-rĭl′ĭs) *n.* **1.** Any of several chiefly tropical American bulbous plants of the genus *Hippeastrum*, grown as ornamentals. **2.** See **belladonna lily. 3.** Any of several similar or related plants. [NLat. *Amaryllis*, genus name < Lat., name of a shepherdess < Gk. *Amaryllis.*]

a·mass (ə-măs′) *v.* **a·massed, a·mass·ing, a·mass·es** *—tr.* **1.** To gather together for oneself, as for one's pleasure or profit; accumulate. See Syns at **gather. 2.** To accumulate or assemble a large quantity of; collect. *—intr.* To come together; collect. [ME, to amass < OFr. *amasser*, to assemble : *a-*, to (< Lat. *ad-*; see AD−) + *masser*, to gather together (< Lat. *massa*, lump, mass; see MASS).] **—a·mass′a·ble** *adj.* **—a·mass′er** *n.* **—a·mass′ment** *n.*

A·ma·te·ra·su (ä′mä-tĕ-rä′sŏo) *n.* The central Shinto deity, a sun goddess believed to be the ancestor of the Japanese royal family.

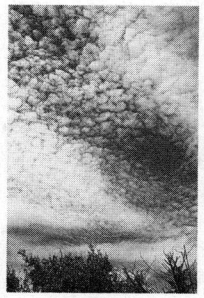

altocumulus

amaryllis

ă	pat	oi boy
ā	pay	ou out
âr	care	ŏo took
ä	father	ōo boot
ĕ	pet	ŭ cut
ē	be	ûr urge
ĭ	pit	th thin
ī	pie	th this
îr	pier	hw which
ŏ	pot	zh vision
ō	toe	ə about,
ô	paw	item

Stress marks:
′ (primary);
′ (secondary), as in
lexicon (lĕk′sĭ-kŏn′)

am·a·teur (ăm′ə-tûr′, -tər, -chŏŏr′, -chər, -tyŏŏr′) *n.* **1.** A person who engages in an art, science, study, or athletic activity as a pastime rather than a profession. **2.** An athlete who has never accepted money, or who accepts money under restrictions specified by a regulatory body, for participating in a competition. **3.** One lacking the skill of a professional. ❖ *adj.* **1.** Of, relating to, or performed by an amateur. **2.** Made up of amateurs. **3.** Not professional; unskillful. [Fr. < Lat. *amātor*, lover < *amāre*, to love.] —**am′a·teur·ism** *n.*

am·a·teur·ish (ăm′ə-tûr′ĭsh, -chŏŏr′-, -tyŏŏr′-) *adj.* Characteristic of an amateur; not professional. —**am′a·teur·ish·ly** *adv.* —**am′a·teur·ish·ness** *n.*

A·ma·ti (ä-mä′tē), **Nicolò** or **Nicola** 1596–1684. Italian violin maker who succeeded his father and grandfather in the family business.

am·a·tive (ăm′ə-tĭv) *adj.* Inclined toward love, esp. sexual love; amorous. [Med.Lat. *amātīvus*, capable of love < *amātus*, p. part. of Lat. *amāre*, to love.] —**am′a·tive·ly** *adv.* —**am′a·tive·ness** *n.*

am·a·tol (ăm′ə-tôl′, -tŏl) *n.* An explosive mixture of ammonium nitrate and trinitrotoluene. [< AM(MONIUM) + (TRINITRO)TOL(UENE).]

am·a·to·ry (ăm′ə-tôr′ē, -tōr′ē) *adj.* Relating to or inclined toward love, esp. sexual love; amorous. [Lat. *amātōrius* < *amātor*, lover. See AMATEUR.]

am·au·ro·sis (ăm′ô-rō′sĭs) *n.* Total loss of vision, esp. when occurring without pathological changes to the eye. [Gk. *amaurōsis* < *amauros*, dark.] —**am′au·rot′ic** (-rŏt′ĭk) *adj.*

a·maze (ə-māz′) *v.* **a·mazed, a·maz·ing, a·maz·es** —*tr.* **1.** To affect with great wonder; astonish. See Syns at **surprise**. **2.** *Obsolete* To bewilder; perplex. —*intr.* To cause great wonder or astonishment. ❖ *n.* Amazement; wonder. [< ME *masen*, to bewilder, and < *amased*, bewildered (< OE *āmasod*), both < OE *āmasian*, to bewilder : *ā-*, intensive pref. + **masian*, to confuse.] —**a·maz′ed·ly** (ə-mā′zĭd-lē) *adv.* —**a·maz′ed·ness** *n.*

a·maze·ment (ə-māz′mənt) *n.* **1.** A state of extreme surprise or wonder; astonishment. **2.** *Obsolete* Bewilderment; perplexity.

Am·a·zon (ăm′ə-zŏn′, -zən) *n.* **1.** *Greek Mythology* A member of a nation of women warriors reputed to have lived in Scythia. **2.** often **amazon** A tall, aggressive, strong-willed woman. [ME < Lat. *Amāzōn* < Gk. *Amazōn*, prob. < Scythian (Iran.) **hamazan*, fighting together.]

Am·a·zo·ni·a (ăm′ə-zō′nē-ə) The vast basin of the Amazon R. in N South America.

Am·a·zo·ni·an (ăm′ə-zō′nē-ən) *adj.* **1.** Of or relating to the Amazon River or Amazonia. **2.** Characteristic of or resembling an Amazon. **3.** often **amazonian** Strong and aggressive. Used of women.

am·a·zon·ite (ăm′ə-zə-nīt′) *n.* A green variety of microcline. [After the AMAZON (RIVER).]

Amazon River A river flowing c. 6,275 km (3,900 mi) from N Peru across N Brazil to a wide delta on the Atlantic Ocean.

amazon stone *n.* See amazonite.

am·bage (ăm′bĭj) *n.* *Archaic* **1.** Ambiguity. Often used in the plural. **2.** **ambages** Winding ways or indirect proceedings. [Back-formation < ME *ambages*, equivocation < Lat. *ambāges* : *amb-, ambi-*, around; see AMBI- + *agere*, to drive; see **ag-** in App.] —**am·ba′gious** (ăm-bā′jəs) *adj.*

am·bas·sa·dor (ăm-băs′ə-dər, -dôr′) *n.* **1.** A diplomatic official of the highest rank appointed and accredited as representative in residence by one government or sovereign to another. **2.** A diplomatic official heading his or her country's permanent mission to certain international organizations. **3.** An authorized messenger or representative. **4.** An unofficial representative: *ambassadors of goodwill.* [ME *ambassadour* < OFr. *ambassadeur* < Med.Lat. *ambactia*, mission < Lat. *ambactus*, servant, ult. of Celt. orig. See **ag-** in App.] —**am·bas·sa·do′ri·al** (-dôr′ē-əl, -dōr′-) *adj.* —**am·bas′sa·dor·ship′** *n.*

am·bas·sa·dress (ăm-băs′ə-drĭs) *n.* A woman ambassador. See Usage Note at **-ess.**

am·beer (ăm′bîr′) *n. Chiefly Southern US* Tobacco juice. [Alteration (influenced by BEER with reference to color and foam of the spittle) of AMBER (< its color).]

am·ber (ăm′bər) *n.* **1.** A hard translucent yellow, orange, or brownish-yellow fossil resin, used for making jewelry. **2.** A brownish yellow. ❖ *adj.* **1.** Having the color of amber; brownish-yellow. **2.** Made of or resembling amber. [ME *ambre* < OFr. < Med.Lat. *ambra, ambar* < Ar. *'anbar*, ambergris, amber.]

am·ber·gris (ăm′bər-grĭs′, -grēs′) *n.* A waxy substance formed in the intestines of sperm whales and used in perfume. [ME < OFr. *ambre gris* : *ambre*, amber; see AMBER + *gris*, gray; see GRISAILLE.]

am·ber·jack (ăm′bər-jăk′) *n., pl.* **amberjack** or **-jacks** A food and game marine fish of the genus *Seriola.* [AMBER + JACK, a fish.]

ambi- *pref.* Both: *ambiversion.* [Lat., around. See **ambhi** in App.]

am·bi·ance also **am·bi·ence** (ăm′bē-əns, äN-byäNs′) *n.* The special atmosphere or mood created by a particular environment. [Fr. < *ambiant*, surrounding < Lat. *ambiēns, ambient-.* See AMBIENT.]

am·bi·dex·ter·i·ty (ăm′bĭ-dĕk-stĕr′ĭ-tē) *n.* **1.** The state or quality of being ambidextrous. **2.** Deceit or hypocrisy.

am·bi·dex·trous (ăm′bĭ-dĕk′strəs) *adj.* **1.** Able to use both hands with equal facility. **2.** Unusually skillful; adroit. **3.** Deceptive or hypocritical. [Alteration of archaic *ambidexter* < ME, double dealer < Med.Lat. : Lat. *ambi-*, on both sides; see AMBI- + Lat. *dexter*, right-handed; see **deks-** in App.] —**am′bi·dex′trous·ly** *adv.*

am·bi·ent (ăm′bē-ənt) *adj.* Surrounding; encircling: *ambient sound.* [Lat. *ambiēns, ambient-*, pr. part. of *ambīre*, to surround : *amb-, ambi-*, around; see AMBI- + *īre*, to go; see **ei-** in App.]

am·bi·gu·i·ty (ăm′bĭ-gyōō′ĭ-tē) *n., pl.* **-ties 1.** Doubtfulness or uncertainty as regards interpretation: *moral ambiguity.* **2.** Something of doubtful meaning: *a poem full of ambiguities.*

am·big·u·ous (ăm-bĭg′yōō-əs) *adj.* **1.** Open to more than one interpretation: *an ambiguous reply.* **2.** Doubtful or uncertain. [< Lat. *ambiguus*, uncertain < *ambigere*, to go about : *amb-, ambi-*, around; see AMBI- + *agere*, to drive; see **ag-** in App.]

am·bi·po·lar (ăm′bĭ-pō′lər) *adj.* Operating in two directions simultaneously.

am·bi·sex·u·al (ăm′bĭ-sĕk′shōō-əl) *adj.* **1.** Having a sexual orientation to persons of either sex; bisexual. **2.** Suited to either sex; unisex: *ambisexual fashion.* —**am′bi·sex′u·al** *n.* —**am′bi·sex′u·al′i·ty** (-ăl′ĭ-tē) *n.*

am·bit (ăm′bĭt) *n.* **1.** An external boundary; a circuit. **2.** Sphere or scope. [Lat. *ambitus* < p. part. of *ambīre*, to go around. See AMBIENT.]

am·bi·tion (ăm-bĭsh′ən) *n.* **1a.** An eager or strong desire to achieve something. **b.** The object or goal desired. **2.** Desire for exertion or activity; energy: *no ambition for dancing.* [ME *ambicioun*, excessive desire for honor, power, or wealth < OFr. *ambicion* < Lat. *ambitiō, ambitiōn-* < *ambitus*, p. part. of *ambīre*, to go around (for votes). See AMBIENT.]

am·bi·tious (ăm-bĭsh′əs) *adj.* **1.** Full of, characterized by, or motivated by ambition. **2.** Greatly desirous; eager: "*I am not ambitious of ridicule*" (Edmund Burke). **3.** Requiring or showing much effort; challenging. —**am·bi′tious·ly** *adv.* —**am·bi′tious·ness** *n.*

am·biv·a·lence (ăm-bĭv′ə-ləns) *n.* **1.** The coexistence of opposing attitudes or feelings. **2.** Uncertainty or indecisiveness as to which course to follow. [Ger. *Ambivalenz* : Lat. *ambi-, ambi-* + Lat. *valentia*, vigor (< *valēns, valent-*, pr. part. of *valēre*, to be strong).]

am·biv·a·lent (ăm-bĭv′ə-lənt) *adj.* Exhibiting or feeling ambivalence.

am·bi·ver·sion (ăm′bĭ-vûr′zhən, -shən) *n.* A personality trait including the qualities of both introversion and extroversion. [AMBI- + (INTRO)VERSION or (EXTRO)VERSION.] —**am′bi·vert′** (-vûrt′) *n.*

am·ble (ăm′bəl) *intr.v.* **-bled, -bling, -bles 1.** To walk slowly or leisurely; stroll. **2.** To move along at an easy gait by using both legs on one side alternately with both on the other. Used of a horse. ❖ *n.* **1.** An unhurried or leisurely walk. **2.** An easy gait, esp. that of a horse. [ME *amblen* < OFr. *ambler* < Lat. *ambulāre*, to walk.] —**am′bler** *n.*

Am·bler (ăm′blər), **Eric** 1909–98. British writer noted for his suspense novels, including *A Passage of Arms* (1959).

am·blyg·o·nite (ăm-blĭg′ə-nīt′) *n.* A white or greenish mineral, (Li,Na)Al(PO₄)(F,OH), that is an important source of lithium. [Ger. *Amblygonit* < Gk. *amblugōnios*, obtuse-angled : *amblus*, blunt + *gōniā*, angle; see **genu-** in App.]

am·bly·o·pi·a (ăm′blē-ō′pē-ə) *n.* Dimness of vision, esp. when occurring in one eye without apparent physical defect. [NLat. *amblyōpia* < Gk. *ambluōpiā* < *ambluōpos*, dim-sighted : *amblus*, dim + *ōps, ōp-*, eye; see MYOPIA.] —**am′bly·o′pic** (-ō′pĭk, -ŏp′ĭk) *adj.*

am·bo (ăm′bō) *n., pl.* **am·bos** or **am·bo·nes** (ăm-bō′nēz) One of the two raised stands in early Christian churches from which parts of the service were chanted or read. [Med.Lat. < Gk. *ambōn*, raised edge.]

Am·bon (ăm′bôn) also **Am·boi·na** (ăm-boi′nə) An island of E Indonesia in the Moluccas near Ceram.

Am·bo·nese (ăm′bə-nēz′, -nēs′, ăm′-) or **Am·boi·nese** (-boi-) *n., pl.* **Ambonese** or **Amboinese 1.** A native or inhabitant of Ambon. **2.** The Austronesian language of Ambon.

Am·brose (ăm′brōz′), **Saint.** A.D. 340?–397. Bishop of Milan (374–397) who imposed orthodoxy on the early Christian Church. —**Am·bro′sian** (ăm-brō′zhən) *adj.*

am·bro·sia (ăm-brō′zhə, -zhē-ə) *n.* **1.** *Greek & Roman Mythology* The food of the gods, thought to confer immortality. **2.** Something with an esp. delicious flavor or fragrance. [Lat. < Gk. *ambrosiā* < *ambrotos*, immortal, immortalizing : *a-*, not; see A-¹ + *-mbrotos*, mortal; see **mer-** in App.]

am·bro·sial (ăm-brō′zhəl, -zhē-əl) also **am·bro·sian** (-zhən, -zhē-ən) *adj.* **1.** Suggestive of ambrosia; fragrant or delicious. **2.** Of or worthy of the gods. —**am·bro′sial·ly** *adv.*

am·bro·type (ăm′brō-tīp′) *n.* An early type of photograph made by imaging a negative on glass backed by a dark surface. [Gk. *ambrotos*, immortal; see AMBROSIA + TYPE.]

am·bry (ăm′brē) *n., pl.* **-bries 1.** *Chiefly British* A pantry. **2.** A niche that is located near the altar of a church for the safekeeping of sacred vessels and vestments. [ME *almerie*, place for safekeeping < OFr. *almarie* < Med.Lat. *almārium* < Lat. *armārium*, closet < *arma*, tools. See ARM².]

ambs·ace (ăm′zās′) *n.* **1.** *Games* Double aces. **2.** Bad luck; misfortune. **3.** The smallest amount possible or the most worthless thing. [ME *ambes as* < OFr. : Lat. *ambās*, fem. accusative of *ambō*, both + *as*, unit.]

am·bu·lac·rum (ăm′byə-lăk′rəm, -lā′krəm) *n., pl.* **-lac·ra** (-lăk′rə, -lā′krə) One of the areas on the undersurface of echinoderms, from which the tube feet project. [Lat. *ambulācrum*, walk planted with trees < *ambulāre*, to walk.] —**am′bu·lac′ral** *adj.*

am·bu·lance (ăm′byə-ləns) *n.* A specially equipped vehicle used to transport the sick or injured. [Fr. < *(hôpital) ambulant*, mobile (hospital) < Lat. *ambulāns, ambulant-*, pr. part. of *ambulāre*, to walk. See **ambhi** in App.]

ambulance chaser *n. Slang* **1.** A lawyer who obtains clients by persuading accident victims to sue for damages. **2.** A lawyer avid for clients.

am·bu·lant (ăm′byə-lənt) *adj.* Moving or walking about. [Fr. < Lat. *ambulāns, ambulant-*, pr. part. of *ambulāre*, to walk. See AMBULANCE.]

am·bu·late (ăm′byə-lāt′) *intr.v.* **-lat·ed, -lat·ing, -lates** To walk from place to place; move about. [Lat. *ambulāre, ambulāt-*, to walk. See **ambhi** in App.] —**am′bu·la′tion** *n.*

am·bu·la·to·ry (ăm′byə-lə-tôr′ē, -tōr′ē) *adj.* **1.** Of, relating to, or adapted for walking. **2a.** Capable of walking: *an ambulatory patient.* **b.** Of or relating to medical care or services provided on an outpatient basis. **3.** *Law* That can be changed or revoked. ❖ *n., pl.* **-ries** A covered place for walking. —**am′bu·la·to′ri·ly** *adv.*

ambulatory surgery *n.* Surgery performed on a person who is admitted to and discharged from a hospital on the same day.

am·bus·cade (ăm′bə-skād′, ăm′bə-skād′) *n.* An ambush. ❖ *tr.v.* **-cad·ed, -cad·ing, -cades** To attack suddenly and without warning from a concealed place; ambush. [Fr. *embuscade* (< OFr. *embuschier*, to ambush), and < OItal. *imboscata* < fem. p. part. of *imboscare*, to ambush, both < O Frankish **boscu*, bush, woods.] —**am′bus·cad′er** *n.*

am·bush (ăm′bŏŏsh) *n.* **1.** The act of lying in wait to attack by surprise. **2.** A sudden attack made from a concealed position. **3a.** Those hiding in order to attack by surprise. **b.** The hiding place used for this. **4.** A hidden peril or trap. ❖ *tr.v.* **-bushed, -bushing, -bush·es** To attack from a concealed position. [ME *embush* < OFr. *embusche* < *embuschier*, to ambush < Frankish **boscu*, bush, woods.] —**am′bush′er** *n.*

Am·chit·ka (ăm-chĭt′kə) An island off W AK in the W Aleutians.

a·me·ba (ə-mē′bə) *n.* Variant of **amoeba.**

am·e·bi·a·sis also **am·oe·bi·a·sis** (ăm′ə-bī′ə-sĭs) *n.* An infection caused by amoebas, esp. *Entamoeba histolytica.*

a·me·bo·cyte (ə-mē′bə-sīt′) *n.* Variant of **amoebocyte.**

a·me·lio·rate (ə-mēl′yə-rāt′) *tr. & intr.v.* **-rat·ed, -rat·ing, -rates** To make or become better; improve. [Alteration of MELIORATE.] —**a·mel′io·ra′tive** *adj.*

a·me·lio·ra·tion (ə-mēl′yə-rā′shən) *n.* **1.** The act or an instance of ameliorating. **2.** The state of being ameliorated.

a·men (ā-mĕn′, ä-mĕn′) *interj.* Used at the end of a prayer or a statement to express assent or approval. [ME < OE < LLat. *āmēn* < Gk. < Heb. *'āmēn*, certainly, verily < *'āman*, to be firm.]

A·men also **A·mon** or **Am·mon** (ä′mən) *n. Mythology* The Egyptian god of life and reproduction, represented as a man with a ram's head.

a·me·na·ble (ə-mē′nə-bəl, ə-mĕn′ə-) *adj.* **1.** Responsive to advice, authority, or suggestion; willing. **2.** Responsible to higher authority; accountable. See Syns at **responsible.** **3.** Susceptible or open, as to testing or criticism. [Prob. alteration of ME *menable* < OFr. < *mener*, to lead < Lat. *mināre*, to drive < *minārī*, to threaten < *minae*, threats.] —**a·me′na·bil′i·ty, a·me′na·ble·ness** *n.* —**a·me′na·bly** *adv.*

a·mend (ə-mĕnd′) *v.* **a·mend·ed, a·mend·ing, a·mends** —*tr.* **1.** To change for the better; improve: *amended the earlier proposal.* **2.** To remove the faults or errors in; correct. See Syns at **correct.** **3.** To alter (a legislative measure, for example) formally by adding, deleting, or rephrasing. **4.** To enrich (soil), esp. by mixing in organic matter or sand. —*intr.* To better one's conduct; reform. [ME *amenden* < OFr. *amender* < Lat. *ēmendāre* : *ē-, ex-*, ex- + *mendum*, fault.]

a·men·da·to·ry (ə-mĕn′də-tôr′ē, -tōr′ē) *adj.* Serving or tending to amend; corrective.

a·mend·ment (ə-mĕnd′mənt) *n.* **1.** The act of changing for the better; improvement. **2.** A correction or alteration. **3a.** The process of formally altering a document or record. **b.** A statement of such an alteration: *the 19th Amendment to the Constitution.* **4.** A material, such as organic matter, mixed into soil to improve growing conditions.

a·mends (ə-mĕndz′) *pl.n. (used with a sing. or pl. verb)* Recompense for grievance or injury. [ME *amendes* < OFr., pl. of *amende*, reparation, to amend. See AMEND.]

A·men·ho·tep III (ä′mən-hō′tĕp, ăm′ən-) also **Am·e·no·phis III** (ăm′ə-nō′fĭs) King of Egypt (1411?–1375 B.C.) who sponsored the building of many monuments.

Amenhotep IV See **Akhenaton.**

a·men·i·ty (ə-mĕn′ĭ-tē, ə-mē′nĭ-) *n., pl.* **-ties 1.** The quality of being pleasant or attractive; agreeableness. **2.** Something that

contributes to physical or material comfort. **3.** A feature that increases attractiveness or value. **4. amenities** Social courtesies. [ME *amenite* < OFr. < Lat. *amoenitās* < *amoenus*, pleasant.]

a·men·or·rhe·a or **a·men·or·rhoe·a** (ā-mĕn′ə-rē′ə) *n.* Abnormal suppression or absence of menstruation. [A–¹ + Gk. *mēn*, month; see ME-¹ in App. + −RRHEA.] —**a·men′or·rhe′ic** *adj.*

a·men·sa·lism (ā-mĕn′sə-lĭz′əm) *n.* A relationship between organisms in which one species is harmed and the other species is unaffected. [Prob. A–¹ + (COM)MENSALISM.]

am·ent¹ (ăm′ənt, ā′mənt) *n.* See **catkin.** [Lat. *āmentum*, strap.]

a·ment² (ā′mĕnt′, ā′mənt) *n.* A person with severely deficient intellectual capacity. [< Lat. *āmēns, āment-*, insane : *ā-, ab-*, out of; see AB–¹ + *mēns*, mind; see **men-**¹ in App.]

am·en·ta·ceous (ăm′ən-tā′shəs, ā′mən-) *adj.* **1.** Resembling or consisting of a catkin. **2.** Bearing catkins.

a·men·tia (ā-mĕn′shə, -shē-ə) *n.* Insufficient mental development. [Lat. *āmentia*, madness, senselessness < *āmēns, āment-*, insane. See AMENT².]

Amer. *abbr.* **1.** America **2.** American

A·mer·a·sian (ăm′ə-rā′zhən, -shən) *n.* A person of American and Asian descent. [AMER(ICAN) + ASIAN.] —**Am′er·a′sian** *adj.*

USAGE NOTE *Amerasian* is not a synonym for either *Asian American* or *Eurasian*, being used primarily with reference to children fathered in Asia by American servicemen of varying ethnic and racial backgrounds. In contrast, *Asian American* is typically used of a person whose parents are both ethnic Asians but who by birth or naturalization is an American citizen, while *Eurasian* designates a person of mixed Asian and European, or white, parentage. Though many Amerasians are, ethnically speaking, also Eurasians, in practice the two terms do not overlap very much, with *Amerasian* continuing to be restricted in usage to the historical context of the Korean and Vietnam wars.

A·mer·i·ca (ə-mĕr′ĭ-kə) **1.** The United States. **2.** Also **the A·mer·i·cas** (-kəz) The landmasses and islands of North America, Central America, and South America.

A·mer·i·can (ə-mĕr′ĭ-kən) *adj.* **1.** Of or relating to the United States of America or its people, language, or culture. **2.** Of or relating to North or South America, the West Indies, or the Western Hemisphere. **3.** Of or relating to any of the Native American peoples. **4.** Indigenous to North or South America. Used of plants and animals. ❖ *n.* **1.** A native or inhabitant of America. **2.** A citizen of the United States. **3.** American English. —**A·mer′i·can·ness** *n.*

A·mer·i·ca·na (ə-mĕr′ə-kä′nə, -kăn′ə, -kā′nə) *n.* **1.** *(used with a sing. or pl. verb)* Materials relating to American history, folklore, or geography or considered to be typical of American culture. **2.** *(used with a sing. verb)* The culture of America.

American Beauty *n.* A type of rose bearing large, long-stemmed purplish-red flowers.

American cheese *n.* A mild, white to yellow cheddar.

American chestnut *n.* An eastern North American deciduous tree (*Castanea dentata*).

American eagle *n.* See **bald eagle.**

American elk *n.* See **wapiti.**

American elm *n.* A North American deciduous tree (*Ulmus americana*) having double serrate leaves and winged fruits.

American English *n.* The English language as used in the United States.

American Falls A section, 50.9 m (167 ft) high, of Niagara Falls in W NY N of Buffalo.

American foxhound *n.* Any of a breed of foxhounds having drooping ears and usu. a black, tan, and white coat.

American Indian *n.* A member of any of the peoples indigenous to the Americas except the Eskimos, Aleuts, and Inuits. —**American Indian** *adj.*

USAGE NOTE In principle, *American Indian* can apply to all native peoples throughout the Americas except the Eskimos, Aleuts, and Inuits, but in practice it is generally restricted to the peoples of the United States and Canada. For native peoples in the rest of the hemisphere, usage generally favors *Indian* by itself or, less frequently, the contractions *Amerindian* or *Amerind*. See Usage Notes at **First Nation, Indian, Native American.**

A·mer·i·can·ism (ə-mĕr′ĭ-kə-nĭz′əm) *n.* **1.** A custom, trait, or tradition originating in the United States. **2.** A word, phrase, or idiom characteristic of American English. **3.** Allegiance to the United States and its customs and institutions.

A·mer·i·can·ist (ə-mĕr′ĭ-kə-nĭst) *n.* **1.** One who studies a facet of America. **2.** A specialist in American aboriginal cultures or languages. **3.** One that is sympathetic to the United States and its policies.

A·mer·i·can·ize (ə-mĕr′ĭ-kə-nīz′) *v.* **-ized, -iz·ing, -iz·es** —*tr.* **1.** To make American in form, style, or character. **2.** To assimilate into American culture. **3.** To bring under American influence or control. —*intr.* To become American, as in spirit. —**A·mer′i·can·i·za′tion** (-kə-nĭ-zā′shən) *n.*

American kestrel *n.* See **sparrow hawk** 2.

American plan *n.* A system of hotel management in which a guest pays a fixed daily rate for room and meals.

American Revolution *n.* The war between the American colo-

American elm
Ulmus americana

ă	pat	oi	**boy**
ā	pay	ou	**out**
âr	care	ŏŏ	**took**
ä	father	ōō	**boot**
ĕ	pet	ŭ	**cut**
ē	be	ûr	**urge**
ĭ	pit	th	**thin**
ī	pie	th	**this**
îr	pier	hw	**which**
ŏ	pot	zh	**vision**
ō	toe	ə	**about,**
ô	paw		**item**

Stress marks:
′ (primary);
′ (secondary), as in
lexicon (lĕk′sĭ-kŏn′)

nies and Great Britain (1775–83), leading to the formation of the independent United States.

American saddle horse *n.* A three- or five-gaited high-stepping saddle horse of a breed originating in Kentucky.

American Samoa An unincorporated territory of the US in the S Pacific NE of Fiji comprising the E islands of the Samoan archipelago; administered by the US since 1899. Cap. Pago Pago. Pop. 32,279.

American Sign Language *n.* The primary sign language used by deaf and hearing-impaired people in the United States and Canada.

American Spanish *n.* The Spanish language as used in the Western Hemisphere.

American Staf•ford•shire terrier (stăf′ərd-shîr′, -shər) *n.* A strong muscular terrier of an American breed, originally developed for dogfighting.

American Standard Version *n.* A revised version of the King James Bible published in the United States in 1901.

A•mer•i•cas (ə-mĕr′ĭ-kəz), **the** See **America** 2.

am•er•i•ci•um (ăm′ə-rĭsh′ē-əm) *n. Symbol* **Am** A white metallic synthetic element of the actinide series; its longest-lived isotopes, Am 241 and Am 243, are used as radiation sources in research. Atomic number 95; specific gravity 11.7; valence 3, 4, 5, 6. See table at **element.** [After AMERICA.]

Am•er•in•di•an (ăm′ə-rĭn′dē-ən) also **Am•er•ind** (ăm′ə-rĭnd′) *n.* An American Indian. See Usage Note at **Native American.** [AMER(ICAN) + INDIAN.] —**Am′er•in′di•an, Am′er•ind′, Am′er•in′dic** *adj.*

Ames (āmz) A city of central IA N of Des Moines. Pop. 50,731.

Am•es•lan (ăm′ĭ-slăn′) *n.* See **American Sign Language.**

Ames test *n.* A test used to determine the mutagenic potential of a substance. [After Bruce *Ames* (born 1928), American biochemist.]

am•e•thyst (ăm′ə-thĭst) *n.* **1.** A purple transparent quartz used as a gemstone. **2.** A moderate purple to grayish reddish purple. [ME *amatist* < OFr. < Lat. *amethystus* < Gk. *amethustos,* not drunk, remedy for intoxication, amethyst : *a-,* not; see A–¹ + *methuskein,* to intoxicate (< *methuein,* to be drunk < *methu,* wine).] —**am′e•thys′tine** (-thĭs′tĭn, -tīn′) *adj.*

am•e•tro•pi•a (ăm′ĭ-trō′pē-ə) *n.* Any of various eye abnormalities resulting from faulty refraction. [Gk. *ametros,* without measure (*a-,* without; see A–¹ + *metron,* measure; see METER¹) + –OPIA.] —**am′e•trop′ic** (-trŏp′ĭk, -trō′pĭk) *adj.*

Amex *abbr.* American Stock Exchange.

Am•ga (äm-gä′) A river rising in E Russia and flowing c. 1,287 km (800 mi) to the Aldan R. E of Yakutsk.

Am•gun (äm-go͞on′) A river of SE Russia flowing c. 788 km (490 mi) to the Amur R.

Am•har•ic (ăm-hăr′ĭk, äm-hä′rĭk) *n.* A Semitic language that is the official language of Ethiopia. [After *Amhara,* a former kingdom of northwest Ethiopia.] —**Am•har′ic** *adj.*

Am•herst (ăm′ərst, -hərst) A town of W MA NE of Northampton; birthplace of Emily Dickinson. Pop. 34,874.

Am•herst (ăm′ərst), **Jeffrey.** Baron Amherst. 1717–97. British general in North America during the French and Indian War.

a•mi•a•ble (ā′mē-ə-bəl) *adj.* **1.** Friendly and agreeable in disposition; good-natured and likable. **2.** Cordial; sociable; congenial. [ME < OFr. < LLat. *amīcābilis.* See AMICABLE.] —**a′mi•a•bil′i•ty, a′mi•a•ble•ness** *n.* —**a′mi•a•bly** *adv.*

am•i•an•thus (ăm′ē-ăn′thəs) also **am•i•an•tus** (-təs) *n.* A fine silky asbestos. [Lat. *amiantus* < Gk. *amiantos,* undefiled : *a-,* not; see A–¹ + *miantos,* defiled (< *miainein,* to defile).]

am•i•ca•ble (ăm′ĭ-kə-bəl) *adj.* Characterized by or exhibiting friendliness or goodwill. [ME < LLat. *amīcābilis* < Lat. *amīcus,* friend.] —**am′i•ca•bil′i•ty, am′i•ca•bly** *adv.*

am•ice (ăm′ĭs) *n.* A liturgical vestment consisting of an oblong piece of white linen worn around the neck and shoulders and partly under the alb. [ME, prob. < OFr. *amis,* pl. of *amit* < Lat. *amictus,* mantle < p. part. of *amicīre,* to wrap around : *am-, ambi-,* around; see AMBI– + *iacere,* to throw.]

a•mi•cus cu•ri•ae (ə-mē′kəs kyo͞or′ē-ē′) *n., pl.* **a•mi•ci curiae** (ə-mē′kē) A party uninvolved in a particular litigation but allowed to advise the court on a matter of law concerning the litigation. [Lat. *amīcus cūriae* : *amīcus,* friend + *cūriae,* genitive of *cūria,* court.]

a•mid (ə-mĭd′) also **a•midst** (ə-mĭdst′) *prep.* Surrounded by; in the middle of. [ME : *a-,* in; see A–² + *mid,* middle (< OE *midde,* middle; see **medhyo–** in App.).]

am•ide (ăm′īd′, -ĭd) *n.* **1.** An organic compound containing the CONH₂ radical. **2.** A compound with a metal replacing hydrogen in ammonia. [AM(MONIA) + –IDE.] —**a•mid′ic** (ə-mĭd′ĭk, ă-mĭd′-) *adj.*

am•i•dol (ăm′ĭ-dôl′, -dōl′, -dŏl′) *n.* A colorless crystalline compound, C₆H₃(NH₂)₂OH·2HCl, used as a photographic developer. [Orig. a Ger. trademark.]

a•mid•ships (ə-mĭd′shĭps′) also **a•mid•ship** (-shĭp′) *adv.* Midway between the bow and the stern or between the port and starboard sides.

a•midst (ə-mĭdst′) *prep.* Variant of **amid.** [ME *amiddes* : *amidde;* see AMID + *-es,* adverbial suff.; see –S³.]

Am•i•ens (ăm′ē-ənz, ä-myăN′) A city of N France on the

Somme R. N of Paris; settled in pre-Roman times. Pop. 131,880.

a•mi•go (ə-mē′gō) *n., pl.* **-gos** A friend. [Sp. < Lat. *amīcus.*]

A•min Da•da (ä-mēn′ dä-dä′, dä′dä), **Idi** b. c. 1925. Ugandan dictator (1971–79) who fled the country after a coup d'état.

A•min•di•vi Islands (ä′mĭn-dē′vē) A group of islands in the Arabian Sea off SW India.

a•mine (ə-mēn′, ăm′ēn) *n.* Any of a group of organic compounds derived from ammonia by replacing one or more hydrogen atoms by a hydrocarbon radical. [AM(MONIUM) + –INE².]

–amine *suff.* Amine: *diamine.* [< AMINE.]

a•mi•no (ə-mē′nō, ăm′ə-nō′) *adj.* Relating to an amine or other chemical compound containing an NH₂ group combined with a nonacid organic radical. [< AMINO–.]

amino– *pref.* Containing NH₂ combined with a nonacid organic radical: *aminopyrine.* [< AMINE.]

amino acid *n.* Any of various organic compounds containing an amino group (NH₂), a carboxylic acid group (COOH), and any of various other side groups, esp. any of the 20 compounds that link together to form proteins.

a•mi•no•ben•zo•ic acid (ə-mē′nō-bĕn-zō′ĭk, ăm′ə-) *n.* Any of three benzoic acid derivatives, C₇H₇NO₂, esp. the para-form, which is part of the vitamin B complex.

a•mi•no•phe•nol (ə-mē′nō-fē′nôl, -nŏl, ăm′ə-) *n.* One of three organic compounds with composition C₆H₄NH₂OH.

am•i•noph•yl•line (ăm′ə-nŏf′ə-lĭn) *n.* A theophylline derivative, C₁₆H₂₄N₁₀O₄, used as a bronchodilator. [AMINO + (THEO)PHYLLINE.]

a•mi•no•py•rine (ə-mē′nō-pī′rēn, ăm′ə-nō-) *n.* A crystalline compound, C₁₃H₁₇N₃O, formerly used to reduce fever and relieve pain. [AMINO– + (ANTI)PYRINE.]

a•mir (ə-mîr′, ä-mîr′) *n.* Variant of **emir.**

A•mis (ā′mĭs), **Sir Kingsley** 1922–95. British writer whose novels include *Lucky Jim* (1954).

A•mish (ä′mĭsh, ăm′ĭsh) *n.* An orthodox Anabaptist sect that exists today primarily in Ohio and southeast Pennsylvania. [Ger. *amisch,* after Jacob *Amman,* 17th-cent. Swiss Mennonite bishop.] —**A′mish** *adj.*

a•miss (ə-mĭs′) *adj.* **1.** Out of proper order. **2.** Not in perfect shape; faulty. ❖ *adv.* In an improper, defective, unfortunate, or mistaken way. [ME *amis,* prob. < ON *ā mis,* so as to miss : *ā,* on + *mis,* act of missing.]

SYNONYMS *amiss, afield, astray, awry, wrong* These adverbs mean not in the right or expected way: *spoke amiss; straying far afield; afraid the letter would go astray; thinking awry; plans that went wrong.* **ANTONYM** *aright*

---

am•i•trip•tyl•ine (ăm′ĭ-trĭp′tə-lēn′) *n.* A tricyclic antidepressant drug, C₂₀H₂₃N. [Perh. AMI(NO)– + alteration of TRYPT(OPHAN) + –YL + –INE².]

am•i•ty (ăm′ĭ-tē) *n., pl.* **-ties** Peaceful relations; friendship. [ME *amite* < OFr. < VLat. **amīcitās* < Lat. *amīcus,* friend.]

Am•man (ä-män′, ä′män) The cap. of Jordan, in the N-central part; known as Philadelphia during Roman and Byzantine times. Pop. 965,000.

am•me•ter (ăm′mē′tər) *n.* An instrument that measures electric current in amperes. [A(MPERE) + –METER.]

am•mine (ăm′ēn′, ă-mēn′) *n.* Any of a class of inorganic coordination compounds of ammonia and a metallic salt. [AMM(ONIA) + –INE².] —**am′mi•no′** (ăm′ə-nō′, ə-mē′nō) *adj.*

am•mo (ăm′ō) *n. Informal* Ammunition.

Am•mon¹ (ăm′ən) *n.* Variant of **Amen.**

Am•mon² (ăm′ən) An ancient kingdom E of the Jordan R. in present-day NW Jordan.

am•mo•ni•a (ə-mōn′yə) *n.* **1.** A colorless pungent gas, NH₃, used to manufacture fertilizers and nitrogen-containing chemicals. **2.** See **ammonium hydroxide.** [NLat. < Lat. *(sāl) ammōniacus,* (salt) of Amen < Gk. *Ammōniakos,* from *Ammon,* Amen (from its having been obtained from a region near the temple of Amen in Libya).]

am•mo•ni•ac¹ (ə-mō′nē-ăk′) also **am•mo•ni•a•cal** (ăm′ə-nī′kəl) *adj.* Of, containing, or similar to ammonia.

am•mo•ni•ac² (ə-mō′nē-ăk′) *n.* A strong-smelling gum resin from a plant (*Dorema ammoniacum*), valued as an essential oil and for its medicinal properties. [ME *ammoniak* < Lat. *ammōniacum* < *Ammōniacus,* of Amen < Gk. *Ammōniakos.* See AMMONIA.]

am•mo•ni•ate (ə-mō′nē-āt′) *tr.v.* **-at•ed, -at•ing, -ates** To treat or combine with ammonia. ❖ *n.* A compound that contains ammonia. —**am•mo′ni•a′tion** *n.*

ammonia water *n.* See **ammonium hydroxide.**

am•mon•i•fi•ca•tion (ə-mŏn′ə-fĭ-kā′shən, ə-mō′nə-) *n.* **1.** Impregnation with ammonia or an ammonium compound. **2.** Production of ammonia or ammonium compounds in the decomposition of organic matter.

am•mon•i•fy (ə-mŏn′ə-fī′, ə-mō′nə-) *tr. & intr.v.* **-fied, -fy•ing, -fies** To subject or be subjected to ammonification. —**am•mon′i•fi′er** *n.*

am•mo•nite (ăm′ə-nīt′) also **am•mo•noid** (-noid′) *n.* The coiled fossil shell of an extinct mollusk abundant in the Cretaceous Period. [NLat. *Ammōnītēs* < Lat. *(cornū) Ammōnis,* (horn) of Amen, ammonite, genitive of *Ammōn,* Amen < Gk.]

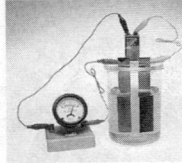

ammeter

ammonite

—am•mo•nit•ic (-nĭt′ĭk) adj.

Ammonite n. 1. A member of a Semitic people living in ancient Ammon. 2. The Semitic language of the Ammonites. [< LLat. *Ammōnītēs*, the Ammonites < Heb. *'ammônî*, Ammonite < *'ammôn*, Ammon, perh. < Canaanite *'amm*, paternal kinsman, kin.]

am•mo•ni•um (ə-mō′nē-əm) n. The univalent chemical ion NH_4^+, derived from ammonia. [AMMON(IA) + –IUM.]

ammonium bicarbonate n. A crystalline salt, NH_4HCO_3, used in fire-extinguishing compounds and in baking powder.

ammonium carbamate n. A salt, a carbonate of ammonium, $NH_4NH_2CO_2$, that is a component of smelling salts.

ammonium carbonate n. 1. A carbonate of ammonium, $(NH_4)_2CO_3$. 2. The white, crystalline double salt of ammonium bicarbonate and ammonium carbamate, NH_4HCO_3·NH_2COONH_4 produced commercially and used in smelling salts.

ammonium chloride n. A slightly hygroscopic white crystalline compound, NH_4Cl, used in dry cells.

ammonium hydroxide n. A colorless, basic, aqueous solution of ammonia, NH_4OH, used as a cleanser and in the manufacture of textiles, rayon, rubber, fertilizer, and plastic.

ammonium nitrate n. A colorless crystalline salt, NH_4NO_3, used in fertilizers, explosives, and solid rocket propellants.

ammonium phosphate n. A phosphate of ammonium, esp. $(NH_4)_2HPO_4$, used as a fire retardant and in fertilizers.

ammonium sulfate n. A brownish-gray to white crystalline salt, $(NH_4)_2SO_4$, used in fertilizers and water purification.

ammonium thiocyanate n. A colorless crystalline compound, NH_4SCN, used in dyeing fabrics and electroplating.

am•mo•noid (ăm′ə-noid′) n. Variant of **ammonite**.

am•mu•ni•tion (ăm′yə-nĭsh′ən) n. 1. Projectiles, such as bullets and shot, that can be fired from guns or otherwise propelled. 2. Nuclear, biological, chemical, or explosive materials that are used as weapons. 3. Objects used as missiles in offense or defense. 4. A means of attacking or defending an argument, thesis, or point of view. [Obsolete Fr. *amunition* < *l'amunition*, the provisioning, alteration of *la munition* < OFr. < Lat. *mūnītiō, mūnītiōn-,* fortification. See MUNITION.]

ammunition clip n. See **cartridge clip**.

Amn abbr. airman

Am•ne Ma•chin Shan (ăm′nē mə-jĭn′ shän) A range of mountains of W-central China, rising to 7,164.5 m (23,490 ft) at **Amne Machin**.

am•ne•sia (ăm-nē′zhə) n. Partial or total loss of memory. [Gk. *amnēsiā,* forgetfulness, prob. alteration of *amnēstiā* < *amnēstos,* not remembered : a-, not; see A–¹ + *mimnēskein, mnē-,* to remember; see men-¹ in App.] —**am•ne′si•ac′** (-nē′zē-ăk′, -zhē-ăk′), **am•ne′sic** (-zĭk, -sĭk) n. & adj. —**am•nes′tic** (-nĕs′tĭk) adj.

am•nes•ty (ăm′nĭ-stē) n., pl. **-ties** A general pardon granted by a government, esp. for political offenses. ❖ tr.v. **-tied, -ty•ing, -ties** To grant a general pardon to. [Lat. *amnēstia* < Gk. *amnēstiā.* See AMNESIA.]

am•ni•o•cen•te•sis (ăm′nē-ō-sĕn-tē′sĭs) n., pl. **-ses** (-sēz) A procedure in which amniotic fluid is drawn out of the uterus and analyzed to determine genetic abnormalities in or the sex of the fetus. [NLat. *amniocentēsis* : AMNION + Gk. *kentēsis,* act of pricking (< *kentein,* to prick).]

am•ni•on (ăm′nē-ən) n., pl. **-ni•ons** or **-ni•a** (-nē-ə) A thin, fluid-filled membranous sac that encloses the embryo or fetus of a mammal, bird, or reptile. [Gk. *amnīon.*] —**am′ni•ot′ic** (-ŏt′ĭk), **am′ni•on′ic** (-ŏn′ĭk) adj.

am•ni•os•co•py (ăm′nē-ŏs′kə-pē) n., pl. **-pies** Examination of the fetus using an optical instrument that is inserted directly into the amniotic cavity. [AMNIO(N) + –SCOPY.] —**am′ni•o•scope′** (-ə-skōp′) n.

am•ni•ote (ăm′nē-ōt′) n. Any of a group of vertebrates that have an amnion during embryonic development, including reptiles, birds, and mammals. [< NLat. *amniōta,* amniotes < Gk. *amnīon,* amnion (influenced by AMNIOTIC).]

am•o•bar•bi•tal (ăm′ō-bär′bĭ-tăl′) n. A barbiturate, $C_{11}H_{18}N_2O_3$, used as a sedative and a hypnotic. [AM(YL) + BARBITAL.]

a•moe•ba also **a•me•ba** (ə-mē′bə) n., pl. **-bas** also **-bae** (-bē) A one-celled protozoan of the genus *Amoeba* or related genera having no definite form and moving by means of pseudopods. [NLat., genus name < Gk. *amoibē,* change < *ameibein,* to change.] —**a•moe′bic, a•me′bic** (-bĭk) adj.

am•oe•bi•a•sis (ăm′ə-bī′ə-sĭs) n. Variant of **amebiasis**.

amoebic dysentery n. Dysentery caused by the amoeba *Entamoeba histolytica.*

a•moe•bo•cyte also **a•me•bo•cyte** (ə-mē′bə-sīt′) n. A cell having amoeboid form or motion. [AMOEB(A) + –CYTE.]

a•moe•boid (ə-mē′boid′) adj. Of or resembling an amoeba, esp. in changeability of form and means of locomotion.

a•mok (ə-mŭk′, ə-mŏk′) adv. & adj. Variant of **amuck**.

a•mo•le (ə-mō′lē) n. 1. The root, bulb, or other plant part of several North American plants, such as species of *Agave, Chlorogalum,* and *Yucca,* used as a soap. 2. A plant so used. [Am.Sp. < Nahuatl *amolli.*]

A•mon (ä′mən) n. Variant of **Amen**.

a•mong (ə-mŭng′) also **a•mongst** (ə-mŭngst′) prep. 1. In the midst of; surrounded by: *a pine tree among cedars.* 2. In the group, number, or class of: *She is among the wealthy.* 3. In the company of; in association with: *traveling among a group of tourists.* 4. By many or the entire number of; with many: *a custom among the Greeks.* 5. By the joint action of: *Among us, we will finish.* 6. With portions to each of: *Distribute this among you.* 7. Each with the other: *Don't fight among yourselves.* See Usage Note at **between**. [ME < OE *āmang* : ā, in; see A–² + *gemang,* throng.]

a•mon•til•la•do (ə-mŏn′tl-ä′dō, ä-mōn′tē-ä′-) n., pl. **-dos** A pale dry sherry. [Sp. : a-, to (< Lat. *ad–*; see AD–) + *Montilla,* a town of S Spain.]

a•mor•al (ā-môr′əl, ā-mŏr′-) adj. 1. Not admitting of moral distinctions or judgments; neither moral nor immoral. 2. Lacking moral sensibility; not caring about right and wrong. —**a•mor′al•ism, a′mo•ral′i•ty** (ā′mô-rălĭ-tē, -mə-) n. —**a•mor′al•ly** adv.

am•o•ret•to (ăm′ə-rĕt′ō, ä′mə-) n., pl. **-ti** (-tē) or **-tos** A cupid. [Ital., dim. of *Amore,* Cupid < Lat. *Amor < amor,* love. See AMOROUS.]

am•o•rist (ăm′ər-ĭst) n. 1. One dedicated to love, esp. sexual love. 2. One who writes about love. [Lat. *amor,* love; see AMOROUS + –IST.]

Am•o•rite (ăm′ə-rīt′) n. A member of one of several ancient Semitic peoples primarily inhabiting Canaan and Babylonia. [< Heb. *'ĕmōrî,* Amorite < Akkadian *amurrû,* westerner, Amorite < *amurru,* western geographical and tribal designation, perh. < Sumerian *martu,* westerner, country to the west of Sumer.] —**Am′o•rite′** adj.

am•o•rous (ăm′ər-əs) adj. 1. Strongly attracted or disposed to love, esp. sexual love. 2. Indicative of love or sexual desire: *an amorous glance.* 3. Of or associated with love. 4. Being in love; enamored. [ME < OFr. *amoureus* < Med.Lat. *amōrōsus* < Lat. *amor,* love < *amāre,* to love.] —**am′or•ous•ly** adv. —**am′or•ous•ness** n.

a•mor•phism (ə-môr′fĭz′əm) n. The state or quality of being amorphous.

a•mor•phous (ə-môr′fəs) adj. 1. Lacking definite form; shapeless. 2. Of no particular type; anomalous. 3. Lacking organization; formless. 4. Lacking distinct crystalline structure. [< Gk. *amorphos* : a-, without; see A–¹ + *morphē,* shape.] —**a•mor′phous•ly** adv. —**a•mor′phous•ness** n.

am•or•ti•za•tion (ăm′ər-tĭ-zā′shən, ə-môr′-) n. **1a.** The act or process of amortizing. **b.** The money set aside for this purpose. **2.** For a bond bought at a premium, the periodic subtraction from its current yield of a proportionate share of the premium between the purchase date and the maturity date.

am•or•tize (ăm′ər-tīz′, ə-môr′-) tr.v. **-tized, -tiz•ing, -tiz•es 1.** To liquidate (a debt) by installment payments or payment into a sinking fund. 2. To write off an expenditure for (office equipment, for example) by prorating over a certain period. [ME *amortisen,* to alienate in mortmain < OFr. *amortir, amortiss-* < VLat. **admortīre,* to deaden : Lat. *ad-,* ad- + Lat. *mors, mort-,* death; see mer–¹ in App.] —**am′or•tiz′a•ble** adj.

A•mos¹ (ā′məs) A Hebrew prophet of the 8th cent. B.C. [Heb. *'āmôs,* carried (by the divinity; sense uncertain) < *'āmas,* to carry.]

A•mos² (ā′məs) n. See table at **Bible**. [After AMOS¹.]

a•mount (ə-mount′) n. 1. The total of two or more quantities; the aggregate. 2. A number; a sum. 3. A principal plus its interest. 4. The full effect or meaning; import. 5. Quantity: *a great amount.* ❖ intr.v. **a•mount•ed, a•mount•ing, a•mounts 1.** To add up in number or quantity. 2. To add up in import or effect: *That plan will never amount to much.* 3. To be equivalent or tantamount: *accusations that amount to an indictment.* [< ME *amounten,* to ascend < OFr. *amonter < amont,* upward < Lat. *ad montem,* to the hill : *ad,* to + *mōns, mont-,* hill.]

a•mour (ə-mŏŏr′) n. A love affair, esp. an illicit one. [ME < OFr. < O Provençal < Lat. *amor,* love. See AMOROUS.]

a•mour-pro•pre (ä-mŏŏr-prŏp′rə) n. Respect for oneself; self-esteem. [Fr. : *amour,* love + *propre,* own.]

a•mox•i•cil•lin (ə-mŏk′sĭ-sĭl′ĭn) n. A semisynthetic penicillin, $C_{16}H_{19}N_3O_5S$, having an antibacterial spectrum of action similar to that of ampicillin. [AM(INO) + (HYDR)OX(Y) + (PEN)ICILLIN.]

A•moy¹ (ä-moi′) See **Xiamen**.

A•moy² (ä-moi′, ă-moi′) n. The variety of Chinese spoken in and around Xiamen in southeast China. [After *Amoy* (Xiamen).]

amp (ămp) n. *Informal* 1. An ampere. 2. An amplifier.

AMP (ā′ĕm-pē′) n. A mononucleotide, $C_{10}H_{14}N_5O_7P$, found in animal cells and reversibly convertible to ADP and ATP; adenosine monophosphate. [A(DENOSINE) M(ONO)P(HOSPHATE).]

am•per•age (ăm′pər-ĭj, ăm′pîr′-) n. The strength of an electric current expressed in amperes.

am•pere (ăm′pîr′) n. 1. A unit of electric current in the meter-kilogram-second system, equal to the current that, flowing in two parallel wires one meter apart, produces a force of 2×10^{-7} newtons per meter. 2. A unit specified as one International coulomb per second and equal to 0.999835 ampere. See table at **measurement**. [After André Marie AMPÈRE.]

Am•père (ăm′pîr′, äN-pĕr′), **André Marie** 1775–1836. French physicist and mathematician.

am•pere-hour (ăm′pîr-our′) n. The electric charge transferred by a current of one ampere in one hour.

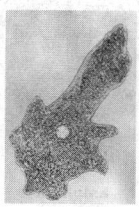
amoeba
Amoeba proteus

ă	pat	oi	boy
ā	pay	ou	out
âr	care	ŏŏ	took
ä	father	ōō	boot
ĕ	pet	ŭ	cut
ē	be	ûr	urge
ĭ	pit	th	thin
ī	pie	th	this
îr	pier	hw	which
ŏ	pot	zh	vision
ō	toe	ə	about,
ô	paw		item

Stress marks:
′ (primary);
′ (secondary); as in
lexicon (lĕk′sĭ-kŏn′)

am·pere-turn (ăm′pîr-tûrn′) *n.* A unit of magnetomotive force in the meter-kilogram-second system equal to the force of one turn of a conducting loop carrying a current of one ampere.

am·per·sand (ăm′pər-sănd′) *n.* The character or sign (&) representing the word *and.* [Alteration of *and per se and,* & (the sign) by itself (means) *and.*]

am·phet·a·mine (ăm-fĕt′ə-mēn′, -mĭn) *n.* **1.** A colorless volatile liquid, $C_9H_{13}N$, used in medicine as a central nervous system stimulant and known for its use as an illegal drug. **2.** A derivative of amphetamine, such as dextroamphetamine. [A(LPHA) + M(ETHYL) + PH(ENYL) + ET(HYL) + AMINE.]

amphi– *pref.* **1.** Both: *amphibiotic.* **2.** On both sides: *amphistylar.* **3.** Around: *amphithecium.* [Lat. < Gk. < *amphi,* on both sides, around. See **ambhi** in App.]

am·phi·ar·thro·sis (ăm′fē-är-thrō′sĭs) *n., pl.* **-ses** (-sēz) A type of articulation between bony surfaces that permits limited motion and is connected by ligaments or elastic cartilage.

am·phib·i·an (ăm-fĭb′ē-ən) *n.* **1.** A cold-blooded smooth-skinned vertebrate of the class Amphibia that hatches as an aquatic larva with gills and transforms into an adult having air-breathing lungs. **2.** An animal capable of living both on land and in water. **3.** An aircraft that can take off and land on either land or water. **4.** A vehicle that can operate both on land and in water. [< NLat. *Amphibia,* class name < Gk., neut. pl. of *amphibios,* amphibious : *amphi-,* amphi- + *bios,* life; see **gʷei∂-** in App.]

am·phi·bi·ot·ic (ăm′fə-bī-ŏt′ĭk) *adj.* Living in water during an early stage of development and on land during the adult stage.

am·phib·i·ous (ăm-fĭb′ē-əs) *adj.* **1.** *Biology* Living or able to live on land and in water. **2.** Able to operate both on land and in water: *amphibious tanks.* **3.** Relating to or organized for a military landing by naval and land forces. **4.** Of a mixed or twofold nature. [< Lat. *amphibius* < Gk. *amphibios.* See AMPHIBIAN.] —**am·phib′i·ous·ly** *adv.* —**am·phib′i·ous·ness** *n.*

am·phi·bole (ăm′fə-bōl′) *n.* Any of a large group of structurally similar hydrated double silicate minerals, such as hornblende. [Fr. < LLat. *amphibolus,* ambiguous < Gk. *amphibolos,* doubtful < *amphiballein,* to throw on either side : *amphi-,* amphi- + *ballein,* to throw; see **gʷelə-** in App.] —**am′phi·bol′ic** (-bŏl′ĭk) *adj.*

am·phib·o·lite (ăm-fĭb′ə-līt′) *n.* A metamorphic rock composed chiefly of amphibole with minor plagioclase and little quartz. —**am·phib′o·lit′ic** (-lĭt′ĭk) *adj.*

am·phib·o·lous (ăm-fĭb′ə-ləs) *adj.* Having a grammatical structure that allows of two interpretations; equivocal. [< LLat. *amphibolus.* See AMPHIBOLE.]

am·phi·brach (ăm′fə-brăk′) *n.* A trisyllabic metrical foot having one accented or long syllable between two unaccented or short syllables, as in *remember.* [Lat. *amphibrachys* < Gk. *amphibrakhus : amphi-,* amphi- + *brakhus,* short.]

am·phic·ty·o·ny (ăm-fĭk′tē-ə-nē) *n., pl.* **-nies** A league of neighboring ancient Greek states sharing a common religious center or shrine, esp. the one at Delphi. [Gk. *Amphiktuonia* < *amphiktuones,* var. of *amphiktiones,* neighbors : *amphi-,* on the periphery; see AMPHI– + *ktizein,* to settle; see **tkei-** in App.] —**am·phic′ty·on′ic** (-ŏn′ĭk) *adj.*

am·phi·dip·loid (ăm′fī-dĭp′loid′) *adj.* Having a diploid set of chromosomes derived from each parent. —**am′phi·dip′loid** *n.* —**am′phi·dip′loi·dy** *n.*

am·phim·a·cer (ăm-fĭm′ə-sər) *n.* A trisyllabic metrical foot having an unaccented or short syllable between two accented or long syllables, as in *Peter Pan.* [Lat. *amphimacrus* < Gk. *amphimakros : amphi-,* amphi- + *makros,* long.]

am·phi·mix·is (ăm′fə-mĭk′sĭs) *n., pl.* **-mix·es** (-mĭk′sēz′) The union of the sperm and egg in sexual reproduction. [AMPHI– + Gk. *mixis,* a mingling (< *meignunai, mik-,* to mingle; see **meik-** in App.).] —**am′phi·mic′tic** (-mĭk′tĭk) *adj.*

Am·phi·on (ăm-fī′ən) *n. Greek Mythology* The son of Zeus and twin brother of Zethus, with whom he built a wall around Thebes by charming the stones into place with his lyre.

am·phi·ox·us (ăm′fē-ŏk′səs) *n.* See **lancelet.** [AMPHI– + Gk. *oxus,* sharp; see **ak-** in App.]

am·phi·pod (ăm′fə-pŏd′) *n.* A crustacean of the order Amphipoda with a laterally compressed body and no carapace. [< NLat. *Amphipoda,* order name : AMPHI– + NLat. *-poda,* -pod.]

am·phi·pro·style (ăm-fĭp′rō-stīl′, ăm′fī-prō′stīl′) *adj. Architecture* Having a set of columns at each end but none along the sides. [Lat. *amphiprostylos* < Gk. *amphiprostulos : amphi-,* amphi- + *prostulos,* with pillars in front; see PROSTYLE.] —**am·phip′ro·style′** *n.*

am·phis·bae·na (ăm′fĭs-bē′nə) *n. Mythology* A serpent having a head at each end of its body. [ME *amphibena* < Lat. *amphisbaena* < Gk. *amphisbaina : amphis,* both ways (< *amphi-,* amphi-) + *bainein,* to go; see **gʷā-** in App.]

am·phi·sty·lar (ăm′fī-stī′lər) *adj.* Having columns at both front and back or on each side, as in some Greek temples. [< AMPHI– + Gk. *stulos,* pillar; see **stā-** in App.]

am·phi·the·a·ter (ăm′fə-thē′ə-tər) *n.* **1.** An oval or round structure having tiers of seats rising gradually outward from a central open space or arena. **2.** An arena for contests and spectacles. **3.** A level area surrounded by upward sloping ground. **4.** An upper, sloping gallery with seats for spectators, as in a thea-

amphibian
amphibious aircraft

amphora

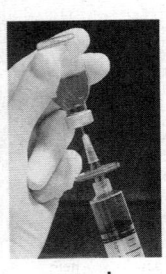

ampoule

ter. [ME *amphitheatre* < Lat. *amphitheatrum* < Gk. *amphitheātron : amphi-,* amphi- + *theātron,* theater; see THEATER.] —**am′phi·the·at′ric** (-ăt′rĭk), **am′phi·the·at′ri·cal** *adj.* —**am′phi·the·at′ri·cal·ly** *adv.*

am·phi·the·ci·um (ăm′fə-thē′shē-əm, -sē-əm) *n., pl.* **-ci·a** (-shē-ə, -sē-ə) The outer layer of cells of the spore-containing capsule of a moss. [NLat. : AMPHI– + Gk. *thēkion,* dim. of *thēkē,* receptacle; see **dhē-** in App.]

Am·phi·tri·te (ăm′fī-trī′tē) *n. Greek Mythology* A Nereid, goddess of the sea and the wife of Poseidon.

am·phit·ro·pous (ăm-fĭt′rə-pəs) *adj.* Partly inverted and attached near the center to the funiculus.

Am·phit·ry·on (ăm-fĭt′rē-ən) *n. Greek Mythology* A king of Thebes and the husband of Alcmene.

am·pho·ra (ăm′fər-ə) *n., pl.* **-pho·rae** (-fə-rē′) or **-pho·ras** A two-handled, narrow-necked Greek or Roman jar for wine or oil. [ME < Lat. < Gk. *amphoreus,* short for *amphiphoreus : amphi-,* amphi- + *phoreus,* bearer (< *pherein,* to bear; see **bher-**[1] in App.).] —**am′pho·ral** *adj.*

am·pho·ter·ic (ăm′fə-tĕr′ĭk) *adj.* Having the characteristics of an acid and a base and capable of reacting chemically as either. [< Gk. *amphoteros,* each of two < *amphō,* both.]

am·pho·ter·i·cin B (ăm′fə-tĕr′ĭ-sĭn) *n.* An antibiotic derived from strains of the actinomycete *Streptomyces nodosus* and used in treating systemic fungal infections. [AMPHOTERIC + –IN.]

amp hr *abbr.* ampere-hour

am·pi·cil·lin (ăm′pĭ-sĭl′ĭn) *n.* A semisynthetic penicillin, $C_{16}H_{19}N_3O_4S$, effective against a wide range of gram-negative and gram-positive bacteria and used to treat a variety of infections. [Blend of AMINO– and PENICILLIN.]

am·ple (ăm′pəl) *adj.* **-pler, -plest 1.** Of large size, amount, extent, or capacity. **2a.** Large in degree, kind, or quantity: *an ample reward.* **b.** More than enough: *ample evidence.* **3.** Fully sufficient for a purpose: *ample food for all.* [ME < OFr. < Lat. *amplus.*] —**am′ple·ness** *n.* —**am′ply** (-plē) *adv.*

am·plex·i·caul (ăm-plĕk′sĭ-kôl′) *adj.* Clasping the stem, as the base of a leaf. [Lat. *amplexus,* an embracing < p. part. of *amplectī,* to embrace (*am-, ambi-,* around; see AMBI– + *plectere,* to twine; see **plek-** in App.) + Lat. *caulis,* stem.]

am·pli·fi·ca·tion (ăm′plə-fĭ-kā′shən) *n.* **1.** The act or result of amplifying, enlarging, or extending. **2a.** An addition to or expansion of a statement or an idea. **b.** A statement with such an addition. **3.** *Electronics* See **gain**[1] **4. 4.** *Genetics* The process by which extra copies of a gene or a DNA sequence are formed.

am·pli·fi·er (ăm′plə-fī′ər) *n.* **1.** One that amplifies, enlarges, or extends. **2.** *Electronics* A device, esp. one using transistors or electron tubes, that amplifies an electrical signal.

am·pli·fy (ăm′plə-fī′) *v.* **-fied, -fy·ing, -fies** —*tr.* **1.** To make larger or more powerful; increase. **2.** To add to, as by illustrations; make complete. **3.** To exaggerate. **4.** To produce amplification of: *amplify an electrical signal.* —*intr.* To write or discourse at length; expatiate. [ME *amplifien* < OFr. *amplifier* < Lat. *amplificāre : amplus,* large + *-ficāre,* -fy.]

am·pli·tude (ăm′plĭ-tood′, -tyood′) *n.* **1.** Greatness of size; magnitude. **2.** Fullness; copiousness. **3.** Breadth or range, as of intelligence. **4.** *Astronomy* The angular distance along the horizon from true east or west to the intersection of the vertical circle of a celestial body with the horizon. **5.** *Physics* The maximum absolute value of a periodically varying quantity. **6.** *Mathematics* **a.** The maximum absolute value of a periodic curve measured along its vertical axis. **b.** The angle made with the positive horizontal axis by the vector representation of a complex number. **7.** *Electronics* The maximum absolute value reached by a voltage or current waveform. [Lat. *amplitūdō* < *amplus,* large.]

amplitude modulation *n. Electronics* **1.** The encoding of a carrier wave by variation of its amplitude in accordance with an input signal. **2.** A broadcast system that uses amplitude modulation.

am·poule also **am·pule** or **am·pul** (ăm′pool, -pyool) *n.* A small glass or plastic container sealed to preserve the sterility of its contents and used esp. to hold hypodermic injection solution. [Fr. < OFr. < Lat. *ampulla.* See AMPULLA.]

am·pul·la (ăm-pool′ə, -pŭl′ə) *n., pl.* **-pul·lae** (-pool′ē, -pŭl′ē) **1.** A nearly round bottle with two handles used by the ancient Romans for wine, oil, or perfume. **2.** *Ecclesiastical* A vessel for consecrated wine or holy oil. **3.** *Anatomy* A small dilatation in a canal or duct, esp. in the semicircular canal. [ME < OE < Lat., dim. of *amphora.* See AMPHORA.] —**am·pul′lar** *adj.*

am·pu·tate (ăm′pyoo-tāt′) *tr.v.* **-tat·ed, -tat·ing, -tates** To cut off (a part of the body), esp. by surgery. [Lat. *amputāre, amputāt-,* to cut around : *am-, ambi-,* around; see AMBI– + *putāre,* to cut.] —**am′pu·ta′tion** *n.* —**am′pu·ta′tor** *n.*

am·pu·tee (ăm′pyoo-tē′) *n.* A person with one or more amputated limbs.

Am·ra·va·ti (əm-rä′və-tē, ăm-) A town of central India W of Nagpur. Pop. 261,404.

am·ri·ta also **am·ree·ta** (ŭm-rē′tə) *n.* **1.** The ambrosia, prepared by the Hindu gods, that bestows immortality. **2.** The immortality thus bestowed. [Skt. *amṛtam : a-,* without; see **ne** in App. + *mṛtam,* death; see **mer-** in App.]

Am·rit·sar (əm-rĭt′sər) A city of NW India near the Pakistan border; founded 1577. Pop. 708,835.

AMS *abbr.* **1.** Agricultural Marketing Service **2.** auditory memory span

am·sinck·i·a (ăm-sĭngk′ē-ə) *n.* An annual herb of the genus *Amsinckia,* of southern California, with pubescent herbage and coiled, yellow to orange flowers. [NLat. *Amsinckia,* genus name, after Wilhelm *Amsinck* (died 1831), German botanist.]

Am·ster·dam (ăm′stər-dăm′) The constitutional cap. of the Netherlands, in the W part on an inlet of the Ijsselmeer. Pop. 721,976.

am·trac also **am·track** (ăm′trăk′) *n.* A small, flatbottom amphibious vehicle that moves along finned tracks and carries troops from ship to shore. [AM(PHIBIOUS) + TRAC(TOR).]

amu *abbr.* atomic mass unit

a·muck (ə-mŭk′) also **a·mok** (ə-mŭk′, ə-mŏk′) *adv.* **1.** In a frenzy to do violence or kill: *Rioters ran amuck.* **2.** In or into a confused manner: *The plans went amuck.* **3.** In or into an uncontrolled state or a state of extreme activity: *gentrification run amuck.* ❖ *adj.* Crazed with murderous frenzy. [Malay *amok.*]

A·mu Dar·ya (ä′mōō där′yə, ə-mōō′ dür-yä′) Formerly **Ox·us** (ŏk′səs) A river of central Asia flowing c. 2,574 km (1,600 mi) from the Pamir Mts. to the S Aral Sea.

am·u·let (ăm′yə-lĭt) *n.* An object worn esp. around the neck as a charm against evil or injury. [Lat. *amulētum.*]

A·mund·sen (ä′mənd-sən, ä′mōōn-), **Roald** 1872–1928. Norwegian explorer who in 1911 became the first person to reach the South Pole.

Amundsen Gulf An inlet of the Arctic Ocean in Northwest Terrs., Canada; navigated by Roald Amundsen during his 1903–05 expedition.

Amundsen Sea An arm of the S Pacific off the coast of Marie Byrd Land, Antarctica.

A·mur River (ä-mōōr′) also **Hei·long Jiang** (hä′lông′ jyäng′) A river of NE Asia flowing c. 2,896 km (1,800 mi) mainly along the border between China and Russia.

a·muse (ə-myōōz′) *tr.v.* **a·mused, a·mus·ing, a·mus·es 1.** To occupy in an agreeable, pleasing, or entertaining fashion. **2.** To cause to laugh or smile from pleasure. **3.** *Archaic* To delude or deceive. [ME < OFr. *amuser,* to stupefy : *a-,* to (< Lat. *ad-;* see AD–) + *muser,* to stare stupidly; see MUSE.] —**a·mus′a·ble** *adj.* —**a·mus′er** *n.* —**a·mu′sive** *adj.*

a·muse·ment (ə-myōōz′mənt) *n.* **1.** The state of being amused, entertained, or pleased. **2.** Something that amuses, entertains, or pleases.

amusement park *n.* A commercial enterprise that offers rides, games, and other entertainment.

a·mus·ing (ə-myōō′zĭng) *adj.* **1.** Entertaining or pleasing. **2.** Arousing laughter. —**a·mus′ing·ly** *adv.* —**a·mus′ing·ness** *n.*

AMVETS *abbr.* American Veterans

a·myg·da·la (ə-mĭg′də-lə) *n., pl.* **-lae** (-lē) An almond-shaped mass of gray matter in the anterior portion of the temporal lobe. [Lat., almond < Gk. *amugdalē.*]

a·myg·dale (ə-mĭg′dāl) *n.* An amygdule. [< Lat. *amygdala,* almond. See AMYGDALA.]

a·myg·da·lin (ə-mĭg′də-lĭn) *n.* A glycoside, C₂₀H₂₇NO₁₁, found in plant parts of many members of the rose family. [< LLat. *amygdalus,* almond tree < Gk. *amygdalos.*]

a·myg·da·line (ə-mĭg′də-līn, -lĭn′) *adj.* Of, relating to, or like an almond. [Lat. *amygdalīnus* < Gk. *amugdalinos* < *amugdalē,* almond.]

a·myg·da·loid (ə-mĭg′də-loid′) *n.* A volcanic rock containing many amygdules. ❖ *adj.* also **a·myg·da·loi·dal** (ə-mĭg′də-loi′dl) **1.** Shaped like an almond. **2.** *Anatomy* Of or relating to the amygdala. **3.** Resembling a volcanic rock that contains amygdules. [Lat. *amygdala,* almond; see AMYGDALA + –OID.]

amygdaloid nucleus *n.* See **amygdala.**

a·myg·dule (ə-mĭg′dyōōl) *n.* A small gas bubble in igneous rock filled with secondary minerals such as quartz. [Lat. *amygdala,* almond (< its shape); see AMYGDALA + (NOD)ULE.]

am·yl (ăm′əl) *n.* The univalent organic radical, C₅H₁₁, occurring in many organic compounds in eight isomeric forms. [Lat. *am(ylum),* starch + –YL.]

am·y·la·ceous (ăm′ə-lā′shəs) *adj.* Of, relating to, or resembling starch; starchy.

amyl acetate *n.* An organic compound, CH₃COOC₅H₁₁, used as a flavoring agent.

amyl alcohol *n.* Any of eight isomers of the alcohol composition C₅H₁₁OH, one of which is the principal constituent of fusel oil.

am·y·lase (ăm′ə-lās′, -lāz′) *n.* Any of a group of enzymes that convert starch to carbohydrate derivatives and are present in saliva, pancreatic juice, and parts of plants.

amyl nitrite *n.* A volatile yellow liquid, C₅H₁₁NO₂, used formerly in medicine as a vasodilator and used illicitly as a mood enhancer.

amylo– or **amyl–** *pref.* Starch: *amylose.* [< Lat. *amylum,* starch. See AMYLUM.]

am·y·loid (ăm′ə-loid) *n.* **1.** A starchlike substance. **2.** *Pathology* A hard waxy deposit of protein and polysaccharides resulting from tissue degeneration. ❖ *adj.* Starchlike.

am·y·loid·o·sis (ăm′ə-loi-dō′sĭs) *n.* A disorder marked by the deposition of amyloid in various organs and tissues of the body.

am·y·lol·y·sis (ăm′ə-lŏl′ĭ-sĭs) *n.* Conversion of starch to sug-

ars by the action of enzymes or acids. —**am′y·lo·lyt′ic** (-lō-lĭt′ĭk) *adj.*

am·y·lop·sin (ăm′ə-lŏp′sĭn) *n.* The starch-digesting amylase produced by the pancreas. [AMYLO– + (TRY)PSIN.]

am·y·lose (ăm′ə-lōs′, -lōz′) *n.* **1.** The inner portion of a starch granule, consisting of relatively soluble polysaccharides. **2.** A polysaccharide.

am·y·lum (ăm′ə-ləm) *n.* Starch. [Lat. < Gk. *amulon,* starch < neut. of *amulos,* not ground at a mill : *a-,* not; see A–¹ + *mulē,* mill; see **melə-** in App.]

a·my·o·to·ni·a (ā′mī-ə-tō′nē-ə) *n.* Lack of muscle tone.

a·my·o·tro·phic lateral sclerosis (ā′mī-ə-trō′fĭk, -trŏf′ĭk, ā-mī′-) *n.* A chronic, progressive, and usu. terminal disease marked by gradual degeneration of the nerve cells in the central nervous system that control voluntary muscle movement.

an¹ (ən; ăn *when stressed*) *indef.art.* The form of *a* that is used before words beginning with a vowel sound: *an advertisement; an hour; an umbrella.* See Usage Notes at *a²,* **every.** [ME < OE *ān,* one. See **oi-no-** in App.]

an² also **an′** (ən, ăn *when stressed*) *conj. Archaic* And if; if. [ME, short for *and,* and < OE. See AND.]

AN *abbr.* airman, Navy

an. *abbr. Latin* **1.** anno (in the year) **2.** ante (before)

an– *pref.* Variant of **a–¹.**

–an¹ *suff.* **1.** Of, relating to, or resembling: *brachyuran.* **2.** One relating to, belonging to, or resembling: *librarian.* [ME < OFr. < Lat. *-ānus,* adj. and n. suff.]

–an² *suff.* **1.** Unsaturated carbon compound: *urethan.* **2.** Anhydride of a carbohydrate: *dextran.* [Alteration of –ANE.]

an·a¹ (ăn′ə, ä′nə) *n., pl.* **ana** or **-as 1.** A collection of various materials that reflect the character of a person or place: *ana of Oman.* **2.** An item in such a collection. See –ANA. [< NLat. *-āna,* as in titles of such collections. See –ANA.]

an·a² (ăn′ə) *adv.* Both in the same quantity. Used in prescriptions. [ME < Med.Lat. < Gk. *ana,* at the rate of.]

ANA *abbr.* **1.** American Newspaper Association **2.** American Nurses Association **3.** Association of National Advertisers

ana– *pref.* **1.** Upward; up: *anabolism.* **2.** Backward; back: *anaplasia.* **3.** Again; anew: *anaphylaxis.* [Gk. < *ana,* up.]

–ana or **–iana** *suff.* A collection of items relating to a specified person or place: *Americana.* [NLat. *-āna* < Lat., neut. pl. of *-ānus,* adj. and n. suff. See –AN¹.]

an·a·bae·na (ăn′ə-bē′nə) *n.* Any of various freshwater algae of the genus *Anabaena* that can give drinking water a bad taste and odor. [NLat. *Anabaena,* genus name < Gk. *anabainein,* to go up : *ana-, ana-* + *bainein,* to go; see **gʷā-** in App.]

An·a·bap·tist (ăn′ə-băp′tĭst) *n.* A member of a 16th-century Reformation movement believing in baptism as a witness of a believer's profession of faith and in separation of church from state. [< L.Gk. *anabaptizein,* to baptize again : Gk. *ana-, ana-* + Gk. *baptizein,* to baptize (< *baptein,* to dip).] —**An′a·bap′tism** *n.*

an·a·bas (ăn′ə-băs′) *n.* A freshwater fish of the family Anabantidae, native to Africa and southeast Asia. [Gk. *anabās,* aorist part. of *anabainein,* to go up, climb. See ANABAENA.]

a·nab·a·sis (ə-năb′ə-sĭs) *n., pl.* **-ses** (-sēz′) **1.** An advance; an expedition. **2.** A large-scale military advance, specifically the unsuccessful Greek mercenary expedition across Asia Minor in 401 B.C. led by Cyrus the Younger, as described by Xenophon. [Gk. < *anabainein,* to go up. See ANABAENA.]

an·a·bat·ic (ăn′ə-băt′ĭk) *adj.* Of or relating to rising wind currents. [Gk. *anabatikos,* skilled in mounting < *anabainein,* to rise. See ANABAENA.]

an·a·bi·o·sis (ăn′ə-bī-ō′sĭs) *n.* **1.** A restoration to life from a deathlike condition; resuscitation. **2.** A state of suspended animation, esp. one in which certain aquatic invertebrates can survive long droughts. [Gk. *anabiōsis* < *anabioun,* to return to life : *ana-, ana-* + *bioun,* to live (< *bios,* life; see **gʷeiə-** in App.).] —**an′a·bi·ot′ic** (-ŏt′ĭk) *adj.*

anabolic steroid *n.* A group of synthetic hormones that promote the storage of protein and the growth of tissue.

a·nab·o·lism (ə-năb′ə-lĭz′əm) *n.* The phase of metabolism in which simple substances are synthesized into the complex materials of living tissue. [ANA– + (META)BOLISM.] —**an′a·bol′ic** (ăn′ə-bŏl′ĭk) *adj.*

a·nach·ro·nism (ə-năk′rə-nĭz′əm) *n.* **1.** Representation of someone as existing or something as happening in other than the chronological, proper, or historical order. **2.** One that is out of its proper or chronological order. [Fr. *anachronisme* < NLat. *anachronismus* < L.Gk. *anakhronismos* < *anakhronizesthai,* to be an anachronism : Gk. *ana-, ana-* + Gk. *khronizein,* to take time (< *khronos,* time).] —**a·nach′ro·nis′tic, a·nach′ro·nous** (-nəs) *adj.* —**a·nach′ro·nis′ti·cal·ly, a·nach′ro·nous·ly** *adv.*

an·a·cli·sis (ăn′ə-klī′sĭs, ə-năk′lĭ-) *n.* Psychological dependence on others. [Gk. *anaklisis,* a leaning back < *anaklīnein,* to lean on : *ana-,* see ANA– + *klīnein,* to lean; see **klei-** in App.] —**an′a·clit′ic** (-klĭt′ĭk) *adj.*

an·a·co·lu·thon (ăn′ə-kə-lōō′thŏn′) *n., pl.* **-thons** or **-tha** (-thə) An abrupt change within a sentence to a second construction inconsistent with the first; for example, *I warned that if he drinks, what will become of him?* [LLat. < L.Gk. *anakolouthon,* in-

ă	pat	oi	boy
ā	pay	ou	out
âr	care	ŏŏ	took
ä	father	ōō	boot
ĕ	pet	ŭ	cut
ē	be	ûr	urge
ĭ	pit	th	thin
ī	pie	th	this
îr	pier	hw	which
ŏ	pot	zh	vision
ō	toe	ə	about,
ô	paw		item

Stress marks:
′ (primary);
′ (secondary), as in
lexicon (lĕk′sĭ-kŏn′)

consistency in logic < Gk., neut. of *anakolouthos*, inconsistent : *an*-, not; see A–¹ + *akolouthos*, following (*a*-, together; see sem-¹ in App. + *keleuthos*, path).] **—an′a·co·lu′thic** *adj.*

an·a·con·da (ăn′ə-kŏn′də) *n.* **1.** A large nonvenomous arboreal snake (*Eunectes murinus*) of tropical South America that suffocates its prey. **2.** A similar or related snake. [Perh. alteration of Sinhalese *henakandayā*, whip snake.]

A·nac·re·on (ə-năk′rē-ən) 563?–478? B.C. Greek poet noted for his songs praising love and wine.

A·nac·re·on·tic (ə-năk′rē-ŏn′tĭk) *adj.* Of or resembling the poems of Anacreon. ❖ *n.* A poem in the style of Anacreon.

an·a·cru·sis (ăn′ə-krōō′sĭs) *n.* **1.** One or more unstressed syllables at the beginning of a line of verse, before the reckoning of the normal meter begins. **2.** *Music* See upbeat 1. [NLat. *anacrūsis* < Gk. *anakrousis*, beginning of a tune < *anakrouein*, to strike up a song : *ana*-, ana- + *krouein*, to push.]

an·a·dam·a bread (ăn′ə-dăm′ə) *n.* *New England* A loaf of bread made of white flour, cornmeal, and molasses. [?]

an·a·dem (ăn′ə-dĕm′) *n.* *Archaic* A wreath or garland for the head. [Lat. *anadēma* < Gk. < *anadein*, to bind up : *ana*-, ana- + *dein*, to bind.]

an·a·di·plo·sis (ăn′ə-də-plō′sĭs) *n.*, *pl.* **-ses** (-sēz) Rhetorical repetition at the beginning of a phrase of the word or words with which the previous phrase ended. [LLat. *anadiplōsis* < Gk. < *anadiploun*, to redouble : *ana*-, ana- + *diploun*, to double (< *diplous*, double; see **dwo-** in App.).]

a·nad·ro·mous (ə-năd′rə-məs) *adj.* Migrating up rivers from the sea to breed in fresh water. Used of fish. [< Gk. *anadromos*, running up : *ana*-, ana- + *dromos*, a running.]

A·na·dyr (ä′nə-dîr′) A river of NE Russia rising in the **Anadyr Plateau** and flowing c. 1,118 km (695 mi) to **Anadyr Bay,** an inlet of the Bering Sea.

a·nae·mi·a (ə-nē′mē-ə) *n.* Variant of **anemia.**

a·nae·mic (ə-nē′mĭk) *adj.* Variant of **anemic.**

an·aer·obe (ăn′â-rōb′, ăn-âr′ōb′) *n.* An organism, such as a bacterium, that can live without oxygen. **—an′aer·o′bic** (ăn′ə-rō′bĭk, -âr-ō′bĭk) *adj.* **—an′aer·o′bi·cal·ly** *adv.*

an·aer·o·bi·o·sis (ăn′ə-rō′bī-ō′sĭs, ăn′â-rō′-) *n.* Life sustained without oxygen. **—an′aer·o′bi·ot′ic** (-ŏt′ĭk) *adj.*

an·aes·the·sia (ăn′ĭs-thē′zhə) *n.* Variant of **anesthesia.**

an·aes·the·si·ol·o·gist (ăn′ĭs-thē′zē-ŏl′ə-jĭst) *n.* Variant of **anesthesiologist.**

an·aes·the·si·ol·o·gy (ăn′ĭs-thē′zē-ŏl′ə-jē) *n.* Variant of **anesthesiology.**

an·aes·thet·ic (ăn′ĭs-thĕt′ĭk) *adj.* & *n.* Variant of **anesthetic.**

an·naes·the·tist (ə-nĕs′thĭ-tĭst) *n.* Variant of **anesthetist.**

an·aes·the·tize (ə-nĕs′thĭ-tīz′) *v.* Variant of **anesthetize.**

an·a·gen·e·sis (ăn′ə-jĕn′ĭ-sĭs) *n.* A pattern of evolution resulting in linear descent with no splitting of the population.

an·a·glyph (ăn′ə-glĭf′) *n.* An ornament carved in low relief. [< LLat. *anaglyphus*, carved in low relief < Gk. *anagluphos* : *ana*-, ana- + *gluphein*, to carve.] **—an′a·glyph′ic, an′a·glyp′tic** (-glĭp′tĭk) *adj.*

an·a·go·ge also **an·a·go·gy** (ăn′ə-gō′jē) *n.*, *pl.* **-ges** also **-gies** A mystical interpretation of a word, passage, or text, esp. scriptural exegesis that detects allusions to heaven or to the afterlife. [LLat. *anagōgē* < L.Gk., spiritual uplift < *anagein*, to lift up : *ana*-, ana- + *agein*, to lead; see **ag-** in App.] **—an′a·gog′ic** (-gŏj′ĭk), **an′a·gog′i·cal** *adj.* **—an′a·gog′i·cal·ly** *adv.*

an·a·gram (ăn′ə-grăm′) *n.* **1.** A word or phrase formed by reordering the letters of another word or phrase, such as *satin* to *stain.* **2. anagrams** (*used with a sing. verb*) A game in which players form words from a group of randomly picked letters. [NLat. *anagramma* < Gk. *anagrammatismos* < *anagrammatizein*, to rearrange letters in a word : *ana*-, from bottom to top; see ANA- + *gramma*, *grammat*-, letter; see **gerbh-** in App.] **—an′a·gram·mat′ic** (-grə-măt′ĭk), **-mat′i·cal·ly** *adj.* **—an′a·gram·mat′i·cal·ly** *adv.*

an·a·gram·ma·tize (ăn′ə-grăm′ə-tīz′) *tr.v.* **-tized, -tiz·ing, -tiz·es** To make an anagram of. [L.Gk. *anagrammatizein*, to rearrange letters in a word. See ANAGRAM.]

An·a·heim (ăn′ə-hīm′) A city of S CA SE of Los Angeles. Pop. 328,014.

A·ná·huac (ə-nä′wäk′) An extensive plateau of central Mexico; center of a pre-Columbian Aztec civilization.

a·nal (ā′nəl) *adj.* **1.** Of, relating to, or near the anus. **2a.** In psychoanalytic theory, of or relating to the second stage of psychosexual development during which gratification derives from sensations associated with the anus. **b.** Anal-expulsive or analretentive. [< Lat. *ānus*, anus.] **—a′nal·ly** *adv.*

an·al·cime (ə-năl′sēm′) also **an·al·cite** (-sīt′) *n.* A zeolite, NaAlSi₂O₆·H₂O, found in certain basalts. [Fr. < Gk. *analkimos*, weak (< its weak electric power) : *an*-, not; see A–¹ + *alkimos*, brave (< *alkē*, strength).] **—an′al·cim′ic** *adj.*

an·a·lects (ăn′ə-lĕkts′) also **an·a·lec·ta** (ăn′ə-lĕk′tə) *pl.n.* Selections from or parts of a literary work or group of works. [Gk. *analekta*, selected things < neut. pl. of *analektos*, gathered together < *analegein*, to gather : *ana*-, ana- + *legein*, to gather; see **leg-** in App.] **—an′a·lec′tic** *adj.*

an·a·lem·ma (ăn′ə-lĕm′ə) *n.* A graduated scale in the shape of a figure eight, indicating the sun's declination and the equation of time for every day of the year. [Lat., sundial < Gk. *analēmma*

< *analambanein*, to take up. See ANALEPTIC.]

an·a·lep·tic (ăn′ə-lĕp′tĭk) *adj.* Restorative or stimulating, as a drug or medication. ❖ *n.* A medication used as a central nervous system stimulant. [Gk. *analēptikos* < *analambanein*, to take up : *ana*-, ana- + *lambanein*, to take.]

a·nal-ex·pul·sive (ā′nəl-ĭk-spŭl′sĭv) *adj.* In psychoanalytic theory, of or relating to personality traits, such as conceit, ambition, and generosity, associated with infantile pleasure in expelling feces.

an·al·ge·si·a (ăn′əl-jē′zē-ə, -zhə) *n.* A deadening or absence of pain without loss of consciousness. [Gk. *analgēsiā* < *an*-, without; see A–¹ + *algēsiā*, pain (< *algein*, to feel pain < *algos*, pain).] **—an′al·get′ic** (-jĕt′ĭk) *adj.*

an·al·ge·sic (ăn′əl-jē′zĭk, -sĭk) *n.* A medication that reduces or eliminates pain. ❖ *adj.* Of or causing analgesia.

an·a·log (ăn′ə-lôg′, -lŏg′) *n.* & *adj.* Variant of **analogue.**

analog computer also **analogue computer** *n.* A computer in which numerical data are represented by measurable physical variables, such as electrical voltage.

an·a·log·i·cal (ăn′ə-lŏj′ĭ-kəl) *adj.* Of, expressing, composed of, or based on an analogy. **—an′a·log′i·cal·ly** *adv.*

a·nal·o·gist (ə-năl′ə-jĭst) *n.* One who seeks or reasons by analogy.

a·nal·o·gize (ə-năl′ə-jīz′) *v.* **-gized, -giz·ing, -giz·es** *—tr.* To make an analogy of or concerning. *—intr.* To reason by or use analogy.

a·nal·o·gous (ə-năl′ə-gəs) *adj.* **1.** Similar in such a way as to permit analogy. **2.** *Biology* Similar in function but not in structure and evolutionary origin. [< Lat. *analogus* < Gk. *analogos*, proportionate : *ana*-, according to; see ANA- + *logos*, proportion; see **leg-** in App.] **—a·nal′o·gous·ly** *adv.* **—a·nal′o·gous·ness** *n.*

an·a·logue also **an·a·log** (ăn′ə-lôg′, -lŏg′) *n.* **1.** Something that bears an analogy to something else. **2.** *Biology* An organ or structure similar in function to one in another kind of organism but of dissimilar evolutionary origin. **3.** *Chemistry* A structural derivative of a parent compound that often differs from it by a single element. ❖ *adj.* often **analog 1.** Of or relating to a device that expresses changes in data by continuously varying a physical quantity, such as voltage, rather than as discreet digital values. **2.** *Computer Science* Of or relating to an analog computer. [Fr., analogous, analogue < Med.Lat. *analogus* < Gk. *analogos*, proportionate. See ANALOGOUS.]

a·nal·o·gy (ə-năl′ə-jē) *n.*, *pl.* **-gies 1a.** Similarity in some respects between things that are otherwise dissimilar. **b.** A comparison based on such similarity. **2.** *Biology* Correspondence in function or position between organs of dissimilar evolutionary origin or structure. **3.** A form or instance of logical inference, based on the assumption that if two things are alike in some respects, they must be alike in other respects. **4.** *Linguistics* The process by which words or morphemes are re-formed or created on the model of existing grammatical patterns in a language, as exemplified by *helped* replacing *holp* and *holpen* as the past tense and past participle of *help* on the model of verbs such as *yelp, yelped, yelped.* [ME *analogie* < OFr. < Lat. *analogia* < Gk. *analogiā* < *analogos*, proportionate. See ANALOGOUS.]

an·al·pha·bet·ic (ăn-ăl′fə-bĕt′ĭk) *adj.* **1.** Not alphabetical. **2.** Unable to read; illiterate. ❖ *n.* One who is unable to read; an illiterate. [< Gk. *analphabētos*, not knowing the alphabet : *an*-, not; see A–¹ + *alphabētos*, alphabet; see ALPHABET.]

a·nal-re·ten·tive (ā′nəl-rĭ-tĕn′tĭv) *adj.* In psychoanalytic theory, of or relating to personality traits, such as meticulousness, avarice, and obstinacy, originating in infantile pleasure in retention of feces.

a·nal·y·sand (ə-năl′ĭ-sănd′) *n.* A person who is being psychoanalyzed. [< ANALYZE, on the model of MULTIPLICAND.]

a·nal·y·sis (ə-năl′ĭ-sĭs) *n.*, *pl.* **-ses** (-sēz′) **1a.** The separation of a whole into its constituent parts for individual study. **b.** A study of such constituent parts and their interrelationships in making up a whole. **2.** *Chemistry* **a.** The separation of a substance into its constituent elements to determine either their nature (qualitative analysis) or their proportions (quantitative analysis). **b.** The stated findings of such a procedure. **3.** *Mathematics* **a.** A branch of mathematics principally involving calculus, sequences, and series and concerned with limits and convergence. **b.** The method of proof in which a known truth is sought as a consequence of deductions from that which is to be proved. **4.** *Linguistics* The use of function words such as prepositions instead of inflectional endings to express a grammatical relationship; for example, *the paw of the dog* instead of *the dog's paw.* **5.** Psychoanalysis. **6.** Systems analysis. [Med.Lat. < Gk. *analusis*, a dissolving < *analūein*, to undo : *ana*-, throughout; see ANA- + *lūein*, to loosen; see **leu-** in App.]

an·a·lyst (ăn′ə-lĭst) *n.* **1.** One that analyzes. **2.** A practitioner of psychoanalysis. **3.** A systems analyst.

an·a·lyt·ic (ăn′ə-lĭt′ĭk) or **an·a·lyt·i·cal** (-ĭ-kəl) *adj.* **1.** Of or relating to analysis or analytics. **2.** Dividing into elemental parts or basic principles. **3.** Reasoning from a perception of the parts and interrelations of a subject. **4.** Expert in or using analysis, esp. in thinking: *an analytic mind.* **5.** *Logic* Following necessarily; tautologous. **6.** *Mathematics* **a.** Using or capable of being subjected to a methodology involving algebra or other methods of mathematical analysis. **b.** Proving a known truth by reasoning from that which is to be proved. **7.** *Linguistics* Expressing a grammatical category with two or more words instead of an inflected form. **8.** Psychoanalytic. [Med.Lat. *analyticus* < Gk. *analutikos* < *analûein,* to resolve. See ANALYSIS.] —**an·a·lyt′i·cal·ly** *adv.*

analytical balance *n.* A balance for chemical analysis.

analytic geometry *n.* The analysis of geometric structures and properties principally by algebraic operations on variables defined in terms of position coordinates.

analytic philosophy *n.* **1.** A philosophical school of the 20th century whose central methodology is the analysis of concepts or language. **2.** Philosophy as professionally practiced in the United States and Great Britain in the 20th century.

an·a·lyt·ics (ăn′ə-lĭt′ĭks) *n.* (*used with a sing. or pl. verb*) The branch of logic dealing with analysis.

an·a·lyze (ăn′ə-līz′) *tr.v.* **-lyzed, -lyz·ing, -lyz·es 1.** To examine methodically by separating into parts and studying their interrelations. **2.** *Chemistry* To make a chemical analysis of. **3.** *Mathematics* To make a mathematical analysis of. **4.** To psychoanalyze. [Perh. < Fr. *analyser* < *analyse,* analysis < Gk. *analusis.* See ANALYSIS.] —**an·a·lyz′a·ble** *adj.* —**an·a·ly·za′tion** (-lĭ-zā′shən) *n.* —**an·a·lyz′er** *n.*

SYNONYMS *analyze, anatomize, dissect* These verbs mean to separate into constituent parts for study: *analyze a chemical substance; anatomizing the doctrine of free enterprise; medical students dissecting cadavers.*

an·am·ne·sis (ăn′ăm-nē′sĭs) *n., pl.* **-ses** (-sēz) **1.** A recalling to memory; recollection. **2.** A complete medical history as recalled by a patient. [Gk. *anamnēsis* < *anamimnēskein,* to remind : *ana-,* ana- + *mnēskein,* to recall; see men-[1] in App.] —**an′am·nes′tic** (-nĕs′tĭk) *adj.* —**an′am·nes′ti·cal·ly** *adv.*

an·a·mor·phic (ăn′ə-môr′fĭk) *adj.* Relating to, having, or producing different optical imaging effects along mutually perpendicular radii. [ANA- + —MORPH + -IC.]

an·a·mor·pho·sis (ăn′ə-môr′fə-sĭs) *n., pl.* **-ses** (-sēz′) **1a.** An image that appears distorted unless viewed from a special angle or with a special instrument. **b.** The production of such an image. **2.** Evolutionary increase in complexity of form and function. [NLat. *anamorphōsis* < Gk. *anamorphoun,* to transform : Gk. *ana-,* ana- + Gk. *morphē,* shape.]

An·an·ke (ə-năng′kē, ə-nän′-) *n.* A satellite of Jupiter. [Gk. *Anankē,* mother (by Jupiter) of Adrasteia, distributor of rewards and punishments < *anankē,* necessity.]

an·a·pest also **an·a·paest** (ăn′ə-pĕst′) *n.* **1.** A metrical foot of two short syllables followed by one long one, as in *at the park.* **2.** A line of verse using this meter. [Lat. *anapaestus* < Gk. *anapaistos* : *ana-,* ana- + *paiein, pais-,* to strike (so called because an anapest is a reversed dactyl).] —**an·a·pes′tic** *adj.*

an·a·phase (ăn′ə-fāz′) *n.* The stage of mitosis and meiosis in which the chromosomes move to opposite ends of the nuclear spindle.

a·naph·o·ra (ə-năf′ər-ə) *n.* **1.** The repetition of a word or phrase at the beginning of several successive verses, clauses, or paragraphs. **2.** *Linguistics* The use of a linguistic unit, such as a pronoun, to refer back to another unit, such as a noun or noun phrase. [LLat. < Gk. < *anapherein,* to bring back : *ana-,* ana- + *pherein,* to carry; see bher-[1] in App.] —**an′a·phor′ic** (ăn′ə-fôr′ĭk, -fôr′-) *adj.*

an·aph·ro·dis·i·a (ăn-ăf′rə-dĭz′ē-ə, -dĭzh′ə) *n.* Decline or absence of sexual desire. [Gk. *anaphrodīsia,* want of power to inspire love : *an-,* without; see A-[1] + *aphrodīsia,* sexual pleasures; see APHRODISIAC.] —**an·aph′ro·dis′i·ac′** (ăn-ăf′rə-dĭz′ē-ăk′) *adj. & n.*

anaphylactic shock *n.* A sudden, severe, and sometimes fatal allergic reaction marked by a sharp drop in blood pressure, urticaria, and breathing difficulties caused by exposure to a foreign substance after a preliminary exposure.

an·a·phy·lax·is (ăn′ə-fə-lăk′sĭs) *n.* **1.** Hypersensitivity esp. in animals to a substance, induced by a small preliminary exposure to the substance. **2.** See **anaphylactic shock.** [ANA- + (PRO)PHYLAXIS.] —**an′a·phy·lac′tic** (-lăk′tĭk), **an′a·phy·lac′toid** (-lăk′toid′) *adj.* —**an′a·phy·lac′ti·cal·ly** *adv.*

an·a·pla·sia (ăn′ə-plā′zhə) *n.* Reversion of cells to an immature or a less differentiated form, as in most malignant tumors.

an·a·plas·tic (ăn′ə-plăs′tĭk) *adj.* Of or characterized by cells that have become less differentiated.

A·ná·po·lis (ə-nä′pōō-lĭs) A city of central Brazil SE of Brasília. Pop. 239,047.

an·arch (ăn′ärk) *n.* An adherent of anarchy or a leader practicing it. [Back-formation < ANARCHY.]

an·ar·chic (ăn-är′kĭk) or **an·ar·chi·cal** (-kĭ-kəl) *adj.* **1a.** Of, like, or supporting anarchy. **b.** Likely to produce or result in anarchy. **2.** Lacking order or control. —**an·ar′chi·cal·ly** *adv.*

an·ar·chism (ăn′ər-kĭz′əm) *n.* **1.** The theory or doctrine that all forms of government are unnecessary, oppressive, and undesirable and should be abolished. **2.** Advocacy of or an active attempt to realize anarchism. —**an′ar·chis′tic** (-kĭs′tĭk) *adj.*

an·ar·chist (ăn′ər-kĭst) *n.* An advocate of or a participant in anarchism.

an·ar·cho-syn·di·cal·ism (ăn-är′kō-sĭn′dĭ-kə-lĭz′əm) *n.* Syn-

dicalism. [ANARCH(Y) + SYNDICALISM.]

an·ar·chy (ăn′ər-kē) *n., pl.* **-chies 1.** Absence of political authority. **2.** Political disorder and confusion. **3.** Absence of any cohesive principle, such as a common purpose. [NLat. *anarchia* < Gk. *anarkhiā* < *anarkhos,* without a ruler : *an-,* without; see A-[1] + *arkhos,* ruler; see -ARCH.]

an·ar·thri·a (ăn-är′thrē-ə) *n.* Loss of the motor ability that enables speech. [NLat. < Gk. *anarthros,* not articulated. See ANARTHROUS.] —**an·ar′thric** (-thrĭk) *adj.*

an·ar·throus (ăn-är′thrəs) *adj.* **1.** *Linguistics* Lacking an article. Used esp. of Greek nouns. **2.** *Zoology* Lacking joints. [< Gk. *anarthros,* not articulated : *an-,* without; see A-[1] + *arthron,* joint.]

an·a·sar·ca (ăn′ə-sär′kə) *n.* A general accumulation of serous fluid in various tissues and body cavities. [ME < Med.Lat. : Gk. *ana-,* throughout; see ANA- + Gk. *sarx, sark-,* flesh.] —**an′a·sar′cous** (-sär′kəs) *adj.*

A·na·sa·zi (ä′nə-sä′zē) *n., pl.* **Anasazi** or **-zis 1.** A Native American culture flourishing in southern Colorado and Utah and northern New Mexico and Arizona from about A.D. 100, whose descendants include the present-day Pueblo peoples. **2.** A member of a people sharing this culture. [Navajo *anaasází* < *anaa'bisází,* enemy's ancestors : *anaa',* enemy + *bisází,* ancestors.]

an·as·tig·mat (ăn-ăs′tĭg-măt′) *n.* An anastigmatic lens.

an·as·tig·mat·ic (ăn-ăs′tĭg-măt′ĭk) *adj.* Free from astigmatism. Used of a compound lens.

a·nas·to·mose (ə-năs′tə-mōz′, -mōs′) *v.* **-mosed, -mos·ing, -mos·es** —*tr.* To join by anastomosis. —*intr.* To be connected by anastomosis, as blood vessels. [Back-formation < ANASTOMOSIS.]

a·nas·to·mo·sis (ə-năs′tə-mō′sĭs) *n., pl.* **-ses** (-sēz) **1.** The connection of separate parts of a branching system in a network. **2.** *Medicine* The surgical connection of separate or severed tubular hollow organs in a continuous channel. [LLat. *anastomōsis* < Gk., outlet < *anastomoun,* to furnish with a mouth : *ana-,* ana- + *stoma,* mouth.] —**a·nas′to·mot′ic** (-mŏt′ĭk) *adj.*

a·nas·tro·phe (ə-năs′trə-fē) *n.* Inversion of the normal syntactic order of words. [LLat. *anastrophē* < Gk. < *anastrephein,* to turn upside-down : *ana-,* ana- + *strephein,* to turn.]

an·a·tase (ăn′ə-tās′, -tāz′) *n.* A blue or light yellow to brown crystalline mineral, the rarest form of titanium dioxide, TiO_2, used as a pigment, esp. in paint. [Fr. < Gk. *anatasis,* extension (< its long crystals) < *anateinein,* to extend : *ana-,* ana- + *teinein, ta-,* to stretch; see ten- in App.]

a·nath·e·ma (ə-năth′ə-mə) *n., pl.* **-mas 1.** An ecclesiastical ban, curse, or excommunication. **2.** A vehement denunciation; a curse. **3.** One that is cursed or damned. **4.** One that is reviled, loathed, or shunned: *took a position that was anathema to the party's platform.* [LLat., an accursed thing < Gk. < *anatithenai,* to dedicate : *ana-,* ana- + *tithenai, the-,* to put; see dhē- in App.]

a·nath·e·ma·tize (ə-năth′ə-mə-tīz′) *tr.v.* **-tized, -tiz·ing, -tiz·es** To proclaim an anathema on; curse. [LLat. *anathematīzāre* < Gk. *anathematizein* < *anathema, anathemat-,* anathema. See ANATHEMA.] —**a·nath′e·ma·ti·za′tion** (-tĭ-zā′shən) *n.*

An·a·to·li·a (ăn′ə-tō′lē-ə, -tōl′yə) The Asian part of Turkey, usu. considered synonymous with Asia Minor.

An·a·to·li·an (ăn′ə-tō′lē-ən) *adj.* **1.** Of or relating to Anatolia or its people, language, or culture. **2.** Of or relating to a branch of Indo-European that includes Hittite and other languages of ancient Anatolia. ❖ *n.* **1.** A native or inhabitant of Anatolia. **2.** The Anatolian languages.

an·a·tom·i·cal (ăn′ə-tŏm′ĭ-kəl) also **an·a·tom·ic** (-tŏm′ĭk) *adj.* **1.** Concerned with anatomy. **2.** Concerned with dissection. **3.** Related to the structure of an organism. —**an′a·tom′i·cal·ly** *adv.*

anatomically correct *adj.* Representing the body or a body part, esp. a sex organ, in a physiologically accurate manner.

a·nat·o·mist (ə-năt′ə-mĭst) *n.* An expert in or a student of anatomy.

a·nat·o·mize (ə-năt′ə-mīz′) *tr.v.* **-mized, -miz·ing, -miz·es 1.** To dissect (an organism) to study the structure and relation of its parts. **2.** To analyze minutely. See Syns at **analyze.** —**a·nat′o·mi·za′tion** (-mī-zā′shən) *n.*

a·nat·o·my (ə-năt′ə-mē) *n., pl.* **-mies 1.** The bodily structure of a plant or an animal or of any of its parts. **2.** The science of the shape and structure of organisms and their parts. **3.** A treatise on anatomic science. **4.** Dissection of a plant or animal to study the structure and interrelation of its parts. **5.** A skeleton. **6.** The human body. **7.** A detailed examination or analysis. [ME *anatomie* < LLat. *anatomia* < Gk. *anatomē,* dissection : *ana-,* ana- + *tomē,* a cutting (< *temnein,* to cut).]

a·nat·ro·pous (ə-năt′rə-pəs) *adj. Botany* Completely inverted so that the micropyle faces downward and is near the base of the funiculus. —*an anatropous ovule.*

An·ax·ag·o·ras (ăn′ăk-săg′ər-əs) 500?–428 B.C. Greek philosopher who held that each particle composing an object contains mixtures of all the object's qualities.

A·nax·i·man·der (ə-năk′sə-măn′dər) 611–547 B.C. Greek philosopher and astronomer who speculated that the universe arose out of the separation of opposite qualities from one primordial substance.

A·na·ya (ə-nī′yə), **Rudolfo** b. 1937. Amer. writer whose works

ă	pat	oi	boy
ā	pay	ou	out
âr	care	ŏŏ	took
ä	father	ōō	boot
ĕ	pet	ŭ	cut
ē	be	ûr	urge
ĭ	pit	th	thin
ī	pie	th	this
îr	pier	hw	which
ŏ	pot	zh	vision
ō	toe	ə	about,
ô	paw		item

Stress marks:
′ (primary);
′ (secondary), as in
lexicon (lĕk′sĭ-kŏn′)

include the novel *Bless Me, Ultima* (1972).

ANC *abbr.* African National Congress

–ance *suff.* **1.** State or condition: *absorptance.* **2.** Action: *continuance.* [ME < OFr. < Lat. *-antia*, n. suff. (*-āns, -ant-*, -ant + *-ia*, n. suff.) and < Lat. *-entia* (*-ēns, -ent-*, -ent + *-ia*, n. suff.).]

an•ces•tor (ăn′sĕs′tər) *n.* **1.** A person from whom one is descended, esp. more remote than a grandparent; a forebear. **2.** A forerunner or predecessor. **3.** *Law* The person from whom one inherits an estate. **4.** *Biology* The organism or stock from which later kinds evolved. [ME *auncestre* < OFr. < Lat. *antecessor*, predecessor < *antecessus*, p. part. of *antecēdere*, to precede : *ante-*, ante- + *cēdere*, to go.]

> **SYNONYMS** ancestor, forebear, forefather, progenitor These nouns denote a person from whom one is descended: *ancestors who were farmers; land once owned by his forebears; laws handed down from our forefathers; our progenitors' wisdom.* **ANTONYM** descendant

an•ces•tral (ăn-sĕs′trəl) *adj.* Of, relating to, or evolved from an ancestor or ancestors. —**an•ces′tral•ly** *adv.*

an•ces•try (ăn′sĕs′trē) *n., pl.* **-tries 1.** Ancestral descent or lineage. **2.** Ancestors as a group. [ME *auncestrie*, alteration (influenced by *auncestre*, ancestor) of OFr. *ancesserie* < *ancessour*, ancestor < Lat. *antecessor*. See ANCESTOR.]

an•cho (ăn′chō′, än′-) *n., pl.* **-chos** A dried poblano pepper. [Am.Sp. (*chile*) *ancho*, wide (chili) < Sp. < OSpan. < Lat. *amplus.* See AMPLE.]

an•chor (ăng′kər) *n.* **1.** *Nautical* A heavy object attached to a vessel and lowered overboard to keep the ship in place either by its weight or by its flukes, which grip the bottom. **2.** A rigid point of support, as for securing a rope. **3.** A source of security or stability. **4.** *Sports* **a.** An athlete who performs the last stage of a competition. **b.** The end of a tug-of-war team. **5.** An anchorperson. ❖ *v.* **-chored, -chor•ing, -chors** —*tr.* **1.** To hold fast by or as if by an anchor. **2.** *Sports* To serve as anchor for (a team or competition). **3.** To narrate or coordinate (a newscast). —*intr. Nautical* To drop anchor or lie at anchor. [ME *anker, ancher* < OE *ancor* < Lat. *ancora, anchora* < Gk. *ankura.*]

an•chor•age (ăng′kər-ĭj) *n.* **1.** A place for anchoring. **2.** A fee charged for anchoring. **3.** The act of anchoring or the condition of being at anchor. **4.** A means of securing or stabilizing.

Anchorage A city of S AK SSW of Fairbanks; founded 1915. Pop. 260,283.

an•cho•ress (ăng′kər-ĭs) *n.* A woman who has retired into religious seclusion. [ME *anchoryse, ankres* < *ancre*, anchorite < OE *ancra* < OIr. *anchara* < LLat. *anachōrēta.* See ANCHORITE.]

an•cho•rite (ăng′kə-rīt′) also **an•cho•ret** (-rĕt′) *n.* One who has retired into religious seclusion. [ME < Med.Lat. *anchōrīta* < LLat. *anachōrēta* < L.Gk. *anakhōrētēs* < *anakhōrein*, to retire : *ana-, ana-* + *khōrein*, to withdraw (< *khōros*, place).] —**an′cho•rit′ic** (-rĭt′ĭk) *adj.*

an•chor•man (ăng′kər-măn′) *n.* **1.** A man who narrates or coordinates a newscast. **2.** A man who is an anchor in a competition, such as a relay race.

an•chor•per•son (ăng′kər-pûr′sən) *n.* An anchorman or an anchorwoman.

an•chor•wom•an (ăng′kər-wŏom′ən) *n.* **1.** A woman who narrates or coordinates a newscast. **2.** A woman who is an anchor in a competition, such as a relay race.

an•cho•vy (ăn′chō′vē, ăn-chō′vē) *n., pl.* **anchovy** or **-vies** A herringlike marine fish of the family Engraulidae, esp. the European fish *Engraulis encrasicholus*, widely used in cooking. [Sp. *anchova*, poss. < VLat. **apiuva*, ult. < Gk. *aphuē.*]

an•chy•lose (ăng′kə-lōs′, -lōz′) *v.* Variant of **ankylose**.

an•chy•lo•sis (ăng′kə-lō′sĭs) *n.* Variant of **ankylosis**.

an•cien ré•gime (äN-syăN′ rā-zhēm′) *n.* **1.** The French political and social system prior to the Revolution of 1789. **2.** *pl.* **an•ciens ré•gimes** (äN-syăN′ rā-zhēm′) A sociopolitical or other system that no longer exists. [Fr. : *ancien*, old + *régime*, regime.]

an•cient[1] (ān′shənt) *adj.* **1.** Of great age; very old. **2.** Of or relating to the far past, esp. before the fall of the Western Roman Empire (A.D. 476). See Syns at **old**. **3.** Old-fashioned; antiquated. **4.** Having the qualities associated with age, wisdom, or long use; venerable. ❖ *n.* **1.** A very old person. **2.** A person who lived long ago. **3. ancients a.** The ancient Greeks and Romans. **b.** The ancient Greek and Roman authors. [ME *auncien* < OFr. < VLat. **anteānus* : Lat. *ante*, before; see ant- in App. + *-ānus*, adj. and n. suff.] —**an′cient•ly** *adv.* —**an′cient•ness** *n.*

an•cient[2] (ān′shənt) *n.* **1.** *Archaic* An ensign; a flag. **2.** *Obsolete* A flag-bearer or lieutenant. [Alteration of ENSIGN.]

ancient history *n.* **1.** The history of times long past. **2.** *Informal* Common knowledge, esp. of a recent event that has lost its original impact or importance.

an•cil•lar•y (ăn′sə-lĕr′ē) *adj.* **1.** Subordinate; secondary. **2.** Auxiliary; helping: *an ancillary pump.* ❖ *n., pl.* **-ies 1.** Something subordinate to something else, as a workbook to a textbook. **2.** *Archaic* A servant. [< Lat. *ancilla*, maidservant, fem. dim. of *anculus*, servant. See kʷel- in App.]

An•co•hu•ma (äng′kə-hōō′mə, äng′kō-ōō′mä) A mountain, c. 6,554 m (21,490 ft), of W Bolivia.

an•con (ăng′kŏn′) *n., pl.* **-co•nes** (-kō′nēz) A projecting bracket

that carries the upper elements of a cornice in classical architecture; a console. [Lat. *ancōn* < Gk. *ankōn*, elbow.]

–ancy *suff.* Condition or quality: *buoyancy.* [Lat. *-antia* and *-entia*; see –ANCE.]

an•cy•lo•sto•mi•a•sis (ăn′sə-lō-stō-mī′ə-sĭs, ăng′kə-lō-) *n.* A disease caused by hookworm infestation and marked by progressive anemia. [NLat. *Ancylostoma*, hookworm genus (Gk. *ankulos*, curved + Gk. *stoma*, mouth) + –IASIS.]

An•cy•ra (ăn-sī′rə) See **Ankara**.

and (ənd, ən; ănd *when stressed*) *conj.* **1.** Together with; in addition to; as well as. Used to connect words, phrases, or clauses with the same grammatical function. **2.** Added to; plus: *Two and two makes four.* **3.** Used to indicate result: *Give her a chance, and she'll do fine.* **4.** *Informal To.* Used between finite verbs, such as *go, come, try, write*, or *see*: *try and find it; come and see.* See Usage Note at **try**. **5.** *Archaic* If: *and it pleases you.* —**idioms: and so forth** (or **on**) **1.** And other unspecified things of the same class: *books, magazines, and so forth.* **2.** Further in the same manner. **and then some** With considerably more in addition. [ME < OE. See an in App.]

> **USAGE NOTE** It is frequently asserted that sentences beginning with *and* or *but* express "incomplete thoughts" and are therefore incorrect. But this rule has been ignored by writers from Shakespeare to Joyce Carol Oates. When asked whether they paid attention to the rule in their own writing, 24 percent of the Usage Panel answered "always or usually," 36 percent answered "sometimes," and 40 percent answered "rarely or never." See Usage Notes at **both, but, with**.

AND *n.* A logical operator that returns a true value only if both operands are true. [< AND.]

and. *abbr.* andante

ANDA *abbr.* abbreviated new drug application

An•da•lu•sia (ăn′də-lōō′zhə, -shē-ə, -shē-ə) A region of S Spain on the Mediterranean Sea, the Strait of Gibraltar, and the Atlantic Ocean. —**An′da•lu′sian** (-zhən, -shən) *adj. & n.*

an•da•lu•site (ăn′də-lōō′sīt′) *n.* A hard, grayish-white to pinkish brown mineral, Al_2SiO_5, occurring as nearly square prisms, often with cruciform cross sections, in metamorphic rock. [After ANDALUSIA.]

An•da•man•ese (ăn′də-mə-nēz′, -nēs′) *n., pl.* **Andamanese 1.** also **An•da•man** (ăn′də-mən) A member of an indigenous people of the Andaman Islands. **2.** The language of the Andamanese, of no known linguistic affiliation. —**An′da•man•ese′** *adj.*

Andaman Islands A group of Indian islands in the E Bay of Bengal S of Myanmar (Burma); separated from the Malay Peninsula by the **Andaman Sea**, an arm of the Bay of Bengal.

an•dan•te (än-dän′tā, ăn-dän′tē) *Music adv. & adj.* In a moderately slow tempo. ❖ *n.* An andante passage or movement. [Ital. < pr. part. of *andare*, to walk, ult. perh. < Lat. *ambulāre.* See ambhi in App.]

an•dan•ti•no (än′dän-tē′nō, ăn′dän-) *Music adv. & adj.* In a tempo either slightly faster or slower than andante. ❖ *n., pl.* **-nos** An andantino passage or movement. [Ital., dim. of *andante*, andante. See ANDANTE.]

An•der•sen (ăn′dər-sən), **Hans Christian** 1805–75. Danish writer whose fairy tales include "The Ugly Duckling."

An•der•son (ăn′dər-sən), **Carl David** 1905–91. Amer. physicist who won a 1936 Nobel Prize.

Anderson, Dame **Judith** 1898–1992. Australian-born actress noted for her roles in the plays of Shakespeare and Eugene O'Neill.

Anderson, Marian 1897–1993. Amer. contralto who was the first African-American singer to perform at the Metropolitan Opera (1955).

Anderson, Maxwell 1888–1959. Amer. playwright whose works include *Winterset* (1935).

Anderson, Sherwood 1876–1941. Amer. writer noted esp. for *Winesburg, Ohio* (1919).

Anderson River A river of NW Northwest Terrs., Canada, meandering c. 748 km (465 mi) to an arm of the Arctic Ocean.

An•der•son•ville (ăn′dər-sən-vĭl′) A village of SW-central GA NNE of Americus; site of a notorious Confederate prison during the Civil War.

An•des (ăn′dēz) A mountain system of W South America extending c. 8,045 km (5,000 mi) along the Pacific coast from Venezuela to Tierra del Fuego and rising to more than 6,710 m (22,000 ft). —**An′de•an** (ăn′dē-ən, ăn-dē′ən) *adj. & n.*

an•de•site (ăn′dĭ-zīt′) *n.* A gray, fine-grained volcanic rock, chiefly plagioclase and feldspar. [After the ANDES.]

and•i•ron (ănd′ī′ərn) *n.* One of a pair of metal supports for logs in a fireplace. [ME *aundiren*, alteration (influenced by ME *iren*, iron) of OFr. *andier*, of Celt. orig.]

> **REGIONAL NOTE** A number of words formerly limited to one region of the US are now used throughout the country. *Andiron* was once Northern, contrasting with Southern *dog iron* and *fire dog.* The Southern terms remain limited to that region, but *andiron* is now everywhere. Other formerly Northern words that have become national include *faucet*, contrasting with Southern *spigot*, and *frying pan*, contrasting with Midland and Upper

anchor
top to bottom: Danforth, admiralty, and stockless anchors

Marian Anderson

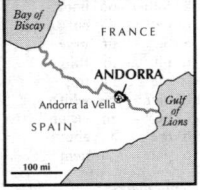

Andorra

Southern *skillet*. Southern words that are now used nationwide include *feisty* and *gutters*. See Regional Note at **frying pan**.

and/or (ăn'dôr') *conj.* Used to indicate that either or both of the items connected by it are involved.

USAGE NOTE *And/or* is widely used in legal and business writing. Its use in general writing to mean "one or the other or both" is acceptable but can appear stilted. See Usage Note at **or**[1].

An·dor·ra (ăn-dôr'ə, -dŏr'ə) A country of SW Europe between France and Spain in the E Pyrenees. Cap. Andorra la Vella (pop. 14,928). Pop. 65,000. —**An·dor'ran** *adj. & n.*

an·dou·ille (ăn-do͞o'ē) *n.* A spicy smoked sausage made with pork and garlic, used esp. in Cajun cooking. [Fr. < OFr. *andoille* < Med.Lat. *inductilia*, things to be introduced < *inductilis*, introduceable < Lat. *inductus*, p. part. of *indūcere*, to introduce into a casing. See INDUCE.]

An·dra·da e Sil·va (ăn-drä'də ĕ sēl'və), **José Bonifácio de** 1763?–1838. Brazilian politician, scientist, and poet who led the movement for independence from Portugal.

an·dra·dite (ăn'drə-dīt) *n.* A green to brown or black calcium-iron garnet, $Ca_3Fe_2(SiO_4)_3$. [After José Bonifácio de ANDRADA E SILVA.]

An·dré (ăn'drā, ăn'drē), **John** 1751–80. British army officer hanged as a spy in the American Revolution for conspiring with Benedict Arnold.

An·dre·a del Sar·to (ăn-drā'ə dĕl sär'tō) 1486–1531. Italian painter whose works epitomize Florentine classicism.

An·dre·a·nof Islands (ăn'drē-ăn'əf, -ôf, ăn'drē-ä'nəf) A group of islands of SW AK in the central Aleutian Is.

An·dre·ev or **An·dre·yev** (ăn-drā'əf, -yəf), **Leonid Nikolaevich** 1871–1919. Russian writer noted esp. for his short stories.

An·drew (ăn'dro͞o), Saint. One of the 12 Apostles. According to legend, he was martyred at Patrai (c. A.D. 60).

An·drić (ăn'drĭch), **Ivo** 1892–1975. Yugoslavian writer who won the 1961 Nobel Prize for literature.

andro– or **andr–** *pref.* **1.** Male; masculine: *androgen*. **2.** Stamen or anther: *androecium*. [Gk. < *anēr, andr-*, man. See **ner-** in App.]

an·dro·cen·tric (ăn'drō-sĕn'trĭk) *adj.* Centered or focused on men, often to the neglect or exclusion of women: *an androcentric view of history.* —**an'dro·cen'trism** *n.* —**an'dro·cen'trist** *n.*

An·dro·cles (ăn'drə-klēz') also **An·dro·clus** (-kləs) *n.* A legendary Roman spared in the arena by a lion that remembered him for having removed a thorn from its paw.

an·droe·ci·um (ăn-drē'shē-əm, -shəm) *n., pl.* **-ci·a** (-shē-ə, -shə) The stamens of a flower considered as a group. [NLat. : ANDR(O)- + Gk. *oikion*, dim. of *oikos*, house; see **weik-** in App.] —**an·droe'cial** (-shəl) *adj.*

an·dro·gen (ăn'drə-jən) *n.* A steroid hormone, such as testosterone or androsterone, that develops and maintains masculine characteristics. —**an·dro·gen'ic** (-jĕn'ĭk) *adj.*

an·drog·e·nize (ăn-drŏj'ə-nīz') *tr.v.* **-nized, -niz·ing, -niz·es** To treat with male hormones, usu. in large doses. —**an·drog'e·ni·za'tion** (-nī-zā'shən) *n.*

an·dro·gyne (ăn'drə-jīn') *n.* An androgynous individual. [Fr. < OFr. < Lat. *androgynus*. See ANDROGYNOUS.]

an·drog·y·nous (ăn-drŏj'ə-nəs) *adj.* **1.** *Biology* Having both female and male characteristics; hermaphroditic. **2.** Being neither distinguishably masculine nor feminine. [< Lat. *androgynus*, hermaphrodite < Gk. *androgunos* : *andro-*, andro- + *gunē*, woman; see –GYNOUS.] —**an·drog'y·nous·ly** *adv.* —**an·drog'y·ny** (-ə-nē) *n.*

an·droid (ăn'droid') *adj.* Having human features. ❖ *n.* An automaton made from biological materials to resemble a human.

An·drom·a·che (ăn-drŏm'ə-kē) *n. Greek Mythology* The wife of Hector, captured by the Greeks at the fall of Troy.

an·drom·e·da (ăn-drŏm'ĭ-də) *n.* Any of several shrubs of the genera *Pieris* or *Andromeda* or their relatives. [< ANDROMEDA.]

Andromeda *n. Greek Mythology* **1.** The daughter of Cepheus and Cassiopeia and wife of Perseus, who rescued her from a sea monster. **2.** A constellation in the Northern Hemisphere, containing a spiral galaxy visible to the naked eye. [Lat. < Gk. *Andromedē*.]

An·dro·pov (ăn-drŏp'ôf), **Yuri** 1914–84. Soviet politician who was general secretary of the Communist Party (1982–84).

An·dros (ăn'drəs) **1.** The largest island of the Bahamas, in the W part of the archipelago. **2.** (*also* ăn'drôs') An island of SE Greece in the Aegean; colonized by Athens in the 5th cent. B.C.

An·dros (ăn'drŏs, -drəs), **Sir Edmund** 1637–1714. English colonial administrator in America.

An·dros·cog·gin (ăn'drə-skŏg'ĭn) A river of NE NH and SW ME flowing c. 253 km (157 mi) to the Kennebec R. near the ME coast.

an·dros·ter·one (ăn-drŏs'tə-rōn') *n.* An androgen excreted in urine. [ANDRO- + STER(OL) + -ONE.]

-androus *suff.* Having a specified number or kind of stamens: *monandrous*. [< NLat. *-andrus* < Gk. *-andros*, having men < *anēr, andr-*, man. See **ner-** in App.]

-andry *suff.* **1.** The condition of having a specified kind or number of husbands: *monandry*. **2.** The condition of having a specified kind or number of stamens: *polyandry*. [Gk. *-andria* < *anēr, andr-*, man. See **ner-** in App.]

-ane *suff.* A saturated hydrocarbon: *hexane*. [Variant of –ENE, –INE[2] and –ONE.]

an·ec·dot·al (ăn'ĭk-dōt'l) *adj.* **1.** also **an·ec·dot·ic** (-dŏt'ĭk) Of, characterized by, or full of anecdotes. **2.** Based on casual observations or indications rather than rigorous or scientific analysis. —**an'ec·dot'al·ist** *n.* —**an'ec·dot'al·ly** *adv.*

an·ec·dote (ăn'ĭk-dōt') *n.* **1.** A short account of an interesting or humorous event. **2.** *pl.* **-dotes** or **-do·ta** (-dō'tə) Secret or hitherto undivulged particulars of history or biography. [Fr. < Gk. *anekdota*, unpublished items : *an-*, not; see A–[1] + *ekdota*, neut. pl. of *ekdotos*, published (< *ekdidonai*, to publish : *ek-*, out; see ECTO– + *didonai*, *do-*, to give; see **dō-** in App.).] —**an'ec·do'tist** *n.*

an·ec·dot·ic (ăn'ĭk-dŏt'ĭk) also **an·ec·dot·i·cal** (-ĭ-kəl) *adj.* **1.** Given to telling anecdotes. **2.** Variant of **anecdotal** 1. —**an'ec·dot'i·cal·ly** *adv.*

an·e·cho·ic (ăn'ĕ-kō'ĭk) *adj.* Neither having nor producing echoes: *an anechoic chamber.*

a·ne·mi·a also **a·nae·mi·a** (ə-nē'mē-ə) *n.* A pathological deficiency in the oxygen-carrying component of the blood, measured in unit volume concentrations of hemoglobin, red blood cell volume, or red blood cell number. [NLat. < Gk. *anaimiā* : *an-*, without; see A–[1] + *haima*, blood.]

a·ne·mic also **a·nae·mic** (ə-nē'mĭk) *adj.* **1.** Of, relating to, or suffering from anemia. **2.** Lacking vitality; listless and weak. —**a·ne'mi·cal·ly** *adv.*

anemo– *pref.* Wind: *anemometer*. [< Gk. *anemos*, wind. See **anə-** in App.]

a·nem·o·cho·ry (ə-nĕm'ə-kôr'ē, -kôr'ē) *n.* Dispersal of seeds, fruits, or other plant parts by wind.

an·e·mom·e·ter (ăn'ə-mŏm'ĭ-tər) *n.* An instrument for measuring wind force and velocity.

an·e·mom·e·try (ăn'ə-mŏm'ĭ-trē) *n.* Measurement of wind force and velocity. —**an'e·mo·met'ri·cal** *adj.*

a·nem·o·ne (ə-nĕm'ə-nē) *n.* **1.** Any of various perennial herbs of the genus *Anemone*, having palmately lobed leaves and large flowers. **2.** A sea anemone. [Lat. *anemōnē* < Gk., prob. < *anemos*, wind (perh. because the petals are lost easily in wind).]

anemone fish *n.* A small, brightly colored marine fish of the genus *Amphiprion*, found near sea anemones.

an·e·moph·i·lous (ăn'ə-mŏf'ə-ləs) *adj.* Pollinated by wind-dispersed pollen.

an·en·ceph·a·ly (ăn'ən-sĕf'ə-lē) *n., pl.* **-lies** Congenital absence of most of the brain and spinal cord. —**an'en·ce·phal'ic** (-sə-făl'ĭk) *adj.*

a·nent (ə-nĕnt') *prep.* Regarding; concerning. [ME < OE *onefn*, near : *on*, on + *efn*, even.]

an·er·oid (ăn'ə-roid') *adj.* Not using liquid. [Fr. *anéroïde* : Gk. *a-*, without; see A–[1] + L.Gk. *nēron*, water; see **newo–** in App.]

aneroid barometer *n.* A barometer in which variations of atmospheric pressure are indicated by the relative bulges of a thin elastic metal disk covering a partially evacuated chamber.

an·es·the·sia also **an·aes·the·sia** (ăn'ĭs-thē'zhə) *n.* **1.** Loss of sensation, esp. tactile sensibility, induced by disease, injury, acupuncture, or an anesthetic. **2.** Insensibility to pain, induced by an anesthetic. **3.** A drug that induces partial or total loss of sensation in the body and may be topical, local, regional, or general. [NLat. *anaesthēsia* < Gk. *anaisthēsiā*, insensibility : *an-*, without; see A–[1] + *aisthēsis*, feeling (< *aisthanesthai*, *aisthē-*, to feel; see **au-** in App.).]

WORD HISTORY The following passage, written on November 21, 1846, by Oliver Wendell Holmes, a physician-poet and the father of the Supreme Court justice of the same name, allows us to pinpoint the entry of *anesthesia* and *anesthetic* into English: "Every body wants to have a hand in a great discovery. All I will do is to give you a hint or two as to names—or the name—to be applied to the state produced and the agent. The state should, I think, be called 'Anaesthesia' [from the Greek word *anaisthēsia*, "lack of sensation"]. This signifies insensibility.... The adjective will be 'Anaesthetic.' Thus we might say the state of Anaesthesia, or the anaesthetic state." This citation is taken from a letter to William Thomas Green Morton, who in October of that year had successfully demonstrated the use of ether at Massachusetts General Hospital in Boston. Although *anaesthesia* is recorded in Nathan Bailey's *Universal Etymological English Dictionary* in 1721, it is clear that Holmes really was responsible for its entry into the language. The *Oxford English Dictionary* has several citations for *anesthesia* and *anesthetic* in 1847 and 1848, indicating that the words gained rapid acceptance.

an·es·the·si·ol·o·gist also **an·aes·the·si·ol·o·gist** (ăn'ĭs-thē'zē-ŏl'ə-jĭst) *n.* A physician specializing in anesthesiology.

an·es·the·si·ol·o·gy also **an·aes·the·si·ol·o·gy** (ăn'ĭs-thē'zē-ŏl'ə-jē) *n.* The medical study and application of anesthetics.

an·es·thet·ic also **an·aes·thet·ic** (ăn'ĭs-thĕt'ĭk) *adj.* **1.** Relating to or resembling anesthesia. **2.** Causing anesthesia. **3.** Insensitive. ❖ *n.* An agent that causes loss of sensation with or without the loss of consciousness. [< Gk. *anaisthētos*, without feeling : *an-*, without; see A–[1] + *aisthētos*, perceptible (< *aisthanesthai*, *aisthē-*, to feel; see ANESTHESIA).] —**an'es·thet'i·cal·ly** *adv.*

anemone
*top: Anemone blanda
bottom:* fish-eating
anemone
Urticina piscivora

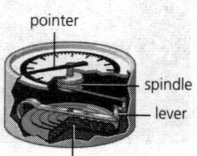

pointer

spindle
lever

vacuum chamber

aneroid barometer
Expansion or contraction of the vacuum chamber, caused by a change in air pressure, forces the pointer to move.

ă	pat	oi	boy
ā	pay	ou	out
âr	care	o͞o	took
ä	father	o͞o	boot
ĕ	pet	ŭ	cut
ē	be	ûr	urge
ĭ	pit	th	thin
ī	pie	*th*	this
îr	pier	hw	which
ŏ	pot	zh	vision
ō	toe	ə	item
ô	paw		item

Stress marks:
' (primary);
' (secondary), as in
lexicon (lĕk'sĭ-kŏn')

a·nes·the·tist also **a·naes·the·tist** (ə-něs′thĭ-tĭst) *n.* A person trained to administer anesthetics.

a·nes·the·tize also **a·naes·the·tize** (ə-něs′thĭ-tīz′) *tr.v.* **-tized, -tiz·ing, -tiz·es** To induce anesthesia in. —**a·nes′the·ti·za′tion** (-tĭ-zā′shən) *n.*

an·es·trous (ăn-ěs′trəs) *adj.* **1.** Not exhibiting estrus. **2.** Of or relating to anestrus.

an·es·trus (ăn-ěs′trəs) *n.* An interval of sexual inactivity between two periods of estrus in female mammals that breed cyclically.

A·ne·to (ə-nā′tō, ä-ně′-), **Pico de** A peak, 3,406.2 m (11,168 ft), in the Pyrenees of NE Spain near the French border.

an·eu·ploid (ăn′yə-ploid′) *adj.* Having a chromosome number that is not a multiple of the haploid number for the species. ❖ *n.* An aneuploid cell or organism. —**an′eu·ploi′dy** (-yə-ploi′dē) *n.*

an·eu·rysm (ăn′yə-rĭz′əm) *n.* A localized, pathological, blood-filled dilatation of a blood vessel caused by a disease or weakening of the vessel's wall. [ME *aneurisme*, ult. < Gk. *aneurusma* < *aneurein*, to dilate : *ana-*, throughout; see ANA– + *eurus*, wide.] —**an′eu·rys′mal** (-məl) *adj.*

a·new (ə-nōō′, ə-nyōō′) *adv.* **1.** Once more; again. **2.** In a new and different way or form. [ME : *a*, of (< OE *of*; see OF) + *new*, new thing (< OE *nīwe*; see NEW) or *a-*, on; see A–² + *new*.]

an·frac·tu·os·i·ty (ăn-frăk′chōō-ŏs′ĭ-tē) *n., pl.* **-ties 1.** The condition or quality of having many twists and turns. **2.** A winding channel, passage, or crevice. **3.** A complicated or involved process.

an·frac·tu·ous (ăn-frăk′chōō-əs) *adj.* Full of twists and turns; tortuous. [LLat. *anfractuōsus* < Lat. *anfrāctus*, winding : *am-, ambi-*, around; see AMBI– + *frāctus*, p. part. of *frangere*, to break; see **bhreg-** in App.]

Ang. *abbr.* Angola

An·ga·ra (ăn′gə-rä′) A river of E-central Russia flowing c. 1,850 km (1,150 mi) from Lake Baikal to the Yenisey R.

An·garsk (ăn-gärsk′) A city of SE-central Russia on the Angara R. near Irkutsk. Pop. 267,910.

an·ga·ry (ăn′gə-rē) also **an·gar·i·a** (ăng-gâr′ē-ə) *n.* The legal right of a belligerent to seize, use, or destroy a neutral's property if full compensation is made. [LLat. *angaria*, service to a lord < Gk. *angareia*, impressment for public service < *angaros*, conscript courier.]

Angel Fall

an·gel (ān′jəl) *n.* **1a.** A typically benevolent celestial being that acts as an intermediary between heaven and earth, esp. in Christianity, Judaism, Islam, and Zoroastrianism. **b.** A representation of such a being, esp. in Christianity, conventionally in the image of a human figure with a halo and wings. **2.** *Christianity* The last of the nine orders of angels in medieval angelology. **3.** A guardian spirit or guiding influence. **4a.** A kind and lovable person. **b.** One who manifests goodness, purity, and selflessness. **5.** *Informal* A financial backer of an enterprise. [ME < OE *engel* or OFr. *angele*, both < LLat. *angelus* < L.Gk. *angelos* < Gk., messenger.] —**an·gel′ic** (ăn-jěl′ĭk), **an·gel′i·cal** *adj.* —**an·gel′i·cal·ly** *adv.*

angel cake *n.* Angel food cake.

angel dust *n. Slang* Phencyclidine.

An·ge·le·no (ăn′jə-lē′nō) *n., pl.* **-nos** A native or inhabitant of Los Angeles. [Am.Sp. *Angeleño*, after LOS ANGELES.]

Angel Fall or **Falls** A waterfall, c. 980 m (3,212 ft), in SE Venezuela; highest uninterrupted waterfall in the world.

an·gel·fish (ăn′jəl-fĭsh′) *n., pl.* **angelfish** or **-fish·es 1.** A brightly colored fish of the family Pomacanthidae, having a laterally compressed body. **2.** A South American freshwater fish (*Pterophyllum scalare*) having a laterally compressed, usu. striped body.

angel food cake *n.* A light sponge cake.

angel hair *n.* Pasta in long, extremely thin strands.

an·gel·i·ca (ăn-jěl′ĭ-kə) *n.* **1a.** Any of various herbs of the genus *Angelica* in the parsley family, having pinnately compound leaves and flowers in compound umbels, esp. *A. archangelica.* **b.** The edible stem, leaf, or root of *Angelica archangelica.* **2.** often **Angelica** A sweet white wine or liqueur. [Med.Lat. *(herba) angelica*, angelic (herb), angelica < LLat., fem. of *angelicus*, angelic < L.Gk. *angelikos* < Gk., of a messenger < *angelos*, messenger.]

angelica tree *n.* See **Hercules′ club.**

An·gel·i·co (ăn-jěl′ĭ-kō′), **Fra.** Also known as Giovanni da Fiesole. 1400?–55. Italian Dominican friar and painter of the Florentine school.

An·gell (ăn′jəl), **Sir Norman** 1872–1967. British economist who won the 1933 Nobel Peace Prize.

an·gel·ol·o·gy (ān′jəl-ŏl′ə-jē) *n.* The branch of theology having to do with angels.

Maya Angelou

An·ge·lou (ăn′jə-lōō′), **Maya** Orig. Marguerite Johnson. b. 1928. Amer. writer known for her autobiographical novels, including *I Know Why the Caged Bird Sings* (1970).

angel shark *n.* Any of several raylike sharks of the genus *Squatina*, having a broad flat head and body.

an·gel's trumpet (ăn′jəlz) *n.* Any of several New World plants of the genera *Brugmansia* or *Datura*, having large, variously colored trumpet-shaped flowers and containing belladonna.

An·ge·lus also **an·ge·lus** (ăn′jə-ləs) *n. Roman Catholic Church* **1.** A devotional prayer at morning, noon, and night to commemorate the Annunciation. **2.** A bell rung as a call to recite this

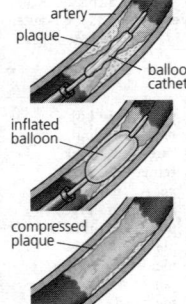

artery
plaque
balloon catheter
inflated balloon
compressed plaque

angioplasty
balloon angioplasty

prayer. [Med.Lat. < LLat., angel (first word of the devotion). See ANGEL.]

an·ger (ăng′gər) *n.* A strong feeling of displeasure or hostility. ❖ *v.* **-gered, -ger·ing, -gers** —*tr.* To make angry; enrage or provoke. —*intr.* To become angry. [ME < ON *angr*, sorrow.]

> **SYNONYMS** *anger, rage, fury, ire, wrath, resentment, indignation* These nouns denote varying degrees of marked displeasure. *Anger,* the most general, is unspecific as to intensity: *vented my anger by shouting.* *Rage* and *fury* imply intense, explosive, often destructive emotion: *smashed the glass in a fit of rage; directed his fury at the murderer.* *Ire* is frequently encountered in literature: "The best way to escape His ire/Is, not to seem too happy" (Robert Browning). *Wrath* applies especially to fervid anger that seeks vengeance or punishment: *the wrath of God.* *Resentment* refers to indignant smoldering anger generated by a sense of grievance: *deep resentment that led to a strike.* *Indignation* is righteous anger at something wrongful, unjust, or evil: "*public indignation about takeovers causing people to lose their jobs*" (Allan Sloan).

an·ger·ly (ăng′gər-lē) *adv. Archaic* Angrily.

An·ge·vin (ăn′jə-vĭn) *adj.* **1.** Relating to the historical region and former province of Anjou, France. **2.** Relating to the House of Anjou, esp. the Plantagenets, who descended from Geoffrey, Count of Anjou (died 1151). [Fr. < OFr. < Med.Lat. *Andegavīnus* < *Andegavia*, Anjou, France.]

an·gi·na (ăn-jī′nə, ăn′jə-) *n.* **1.** Angina pectoris. **2.** A condition, such as severe sore throat, marked by spasmodic attacks of suffocating pain. [Lat., quinsy < Gk. *ankhonē*, a strangling.] —**an·gi′nal** *adj.* —**an′gi·nose′** (-nōs′) *adj.*

angina pec·to·ris (pěk′tər-ĭs) *n.* Severe paroxysmal pain in the chest associated with an insufficient blood supply to the heart. [NLat. : Lat. *angina*, quinsy + *pectoris*, genitive of *pectus*, chest.]

angio– *pref.* **1.** Blood and lymph vessel: *angiogram.* **2.** Pericarp: *angiosperm.* [NLat. < Gk. *angeio-* < *angeion*, vessel, blood vessel, dim. of *angos*, vessel.]

an·gi·o·car·di·og·ra·phy (ăn′jē-ō-kär′dē-ŏg′rə-fē) *n.* Examination of the heart and associated blood vessels by x-rays following the injection of a radiopaque substance. —**an′gi·o·car′di·o·graph′ic** (-ə-grăf′ĭk) *adj.*

an·gi·o·gen·e·sis (ăn′jē-ō-jĕn′ĭ-sĭs) *n., pl.* **-ses** (-sēz′) The formation of new blood vessels. —**an′gi·o·gen′ic** (-jĕn′ĭk) *adj.*

an·gi·o·gram (ăn′jē-ə-grăm′) *n.* An x-ray of one or more blood vessels produced by angiography and used in diagnosing pathological conditions.

an·gi·og·ra·phy (ăn′jē-ŏg′rə-fē) *n.* Examination of the blood vessels using x-rays following the injection of a radiopaque substance. —**an′gi·o·graph′ic** (-ə-grăf′ĭk) *adj.*

an·gi·ol·o·gy (ăn′jē-ŏl′ə-jē) *n.* The study of blood and lymph vessels.

an·gi·o·ma (ăn′jē-ō′mə) *n., pl.* **-mas** or **-ma·ta** (-mə-tə) A tumor that is composed chiefly of lymph and blood vessels. —**an′gi·o′ma·tous** (-ō′mə-təs, -ŏm′ə-) *adj.*

an·gi·op·a·thy (ăn′jē-ŏp′ə-thē) *n., pl.* **-thies** Any of several diseases of the blood or lymph vessels.

an·gi·o·plas·ty (ăn′jē-ō-plăs′tē) *n., pl.* **-ties** The surgical repair of a blood vessel, either by inserting a balloon-tipped catheter to unblock it or by reconstructing part of the vessel.

an·gi·o·sar·co·ma (ăn′jē-ō-sär-kō′mə) *n.* A malignant tumor arising from vascular tissue.

an·gi·o·sperm (ăn′jē-ə-spûrm′) *n.* A plant whose ovules are enclosed in an ovary; a flowering plant.

an·gi·o·ten·sin (ăn′jē-ō-tĕn′sĭn) *n.* Any of three polypeptide hormones, one of which is a powerful vasoconstrictor, that function in the body in controlling arterial pressure. [ANGIO– + TENS(ION) + –IN.]

Ang·kor (ăng′kôr, -kōr) A region in NW Cambodia including two Hindu temple complexes, Angkor Wat (12th cent.) and Angkor Thom (13th cent.).

Angl. *abbr.* Anglican

an·gle[1] (ăng′gəl) *intr.v.* **-gled, -gling, -gles 1.** To fish with a hook and line. **2.** To try to get something by artful means: *angle for a promotion.* ❖ *n. Obsolete* A fishhook or fishing tackle. [ME *anglen* < *angel*, fishhook < OE.]

an·gle[2] (ăng′gəl) *n.* **1.** *Mathematics* **a.** The figure formed by two lines diverging from a common point. **b.** The figure formed by two planes diverging from a common line. **c.** The rotation required to superimpose either of two such lines or planes on the other. **d.** The space between such lines or surfaces. **e.** A solid angle. **2.** A sharp or projecting corner, as of a building. **3a.** The place, position, or direction from which an object is presented to view. **b.** An aspect, as of a problem, seen from a specific point of view. **4.** *Slang* A devious method; a scheme. ❖ *v.* **-gled, -gling, -gles** —*tr.* **1.** To turn or direct (something) at an angle: *angled the chair toward the window.* **2.** *Informal* To impart a biased point of view to: *angled the story so as to criticize.* —*intr.* To continue along or turn at an angle or by angles: *The path angled through the woods.* [ME < OFr. < Lat. *angulus.*]

Angle *n.* A member of a Germanic people that migrated to England from southern Jutland in the fifth and sixth centuries A.D. [< Lat. *Anglī*, the Angles, of Gmc. orig.]

angle bracket *n.* **1.** Either of a pair of symbols, < >, used to enclose written material. **2.** *Mathematics* Either of these symbols, used esp. together to indicate quantities to be treated as a unit.

angle iron *n.* A length of steel or iron bent at a right angle along its long side, used as a support or structural framework.

angle of attack *n.* The acute angle between the chord of an airfoil and a line representing the undisturbed relative airflow.

angle of incidence *n.* The angle formed by a ray incident on a surface and a perpendicular to the surface at the point of incidence.

angle of reflection *n.* The angle formed by a reflected ray and a perpendicular to the surface at the point of reflection.

angle of refraction *n.* The angle formed by a refracted ray and a perpendicular to the refracting surface at the point of refraction.

angle of yaw *n.* The angle between an aircraft's longitudinal axis and its line of travel, as seen from above.

angle plate *n.* A right-angled metal bracket that is used on the faceplate of a lathe to hold the pieces that are being worked.

an·gler (ăng′glər) *n.* **1.** One who fishes with a hook. **2.** A schemer.

an·gler·fish (ăng′glər-fĭsh′) *n., pl.* **anglerfish** or **-fish·es** A marine fish of the order Lophiiformes or Pediculati, having a long dorsal fin ray suspended over the mouth that serves to attract prey.

An·gle·sey or **An·gle·sea** (ăng′gəl-sē) An island of NW Wales in the Irish Sea; site of druidic ruins, esp. dolmens.

an·gle·site (ăng′glĭ-sīt′) *n.* A lead sulfate mineral, PbSO₄, occurring in colorless or tinted crystals and formed by the weathering of lead ore. [After ANGLESEY.]

an·gle·worm (ăng′gəl-wûrm′) *n.* A worm used as bait in fishing.

An·gli·a (ăng′glē-ə) England.

An·gli·an (ăng′glē-ən) *adj.* Of or relating to East Anglia or to the Angles. ❖ *n.* **1.** An Angle. **2.** The Old English dialects of Mercia and Northumbria.

An·gli·can (ăng′glĭ-kən) *adj.* **1.** Of, relating to, or characteristic of the Church of England or any related church, such as the Protestant Episcopal Church. **2.** Of or relating to England or the English. ❖ *n.* A member of the Church of England or of any related church. [Med.Lat. *Anglicānus*, English < *Anglicus* < LLat. *Anglī*, the Angles. See ANGLE.]

Anglican Church *n.* The Church of England and other churches in complete agreement with it as to doctrine and discipline and in communion with the Archbishop of Canterbury.

An·gli·can·ism (ăng′glĭ-kə-nĭz′əm) *n.* The faith, doctrine, system, and practice of the Anglican Church.

An·gli·ce (ăng′glĭ-sē′) *adv.* In the English form: *Firenze,* Anglice *Florence.* [Med.Lat. *Anglicē* < *Anglicus,* English. See ANGLICAN.]

An·gli·cism also **an·gli·cism** (ăng′glĭ-sĭz′əm) *n.* **1.** A word, phrase, or idiom characteristic of or peculiar to the English language. **2.** A typically English quality. [< Med.Lat. *Anglicus,* English. See ANGLICAN.]

An·gli·cist (ăng′glĭ-sĭst) *n.* A specialist in English language and literature.

An·gli·cize also **an·gli·cize** (ăng′glĭ-sīz′) *v.* **-cized, -ciz·ing, -ciz·es** —*tr.* To make English or similar to English in form, idiom, style, or character. —*intr.* To become English in form or character. —**An′gli·ci·za′tion** (-sī-zā′shən) *n.*

an·gling (ăng′glĭng) *n.* Fishing with a hook and line and usu. a rod.

An·glo also **an·glo** (ăng′glō) *n., pl.* **-glos 1.** *Informal* An Anglo-American. **2.** An English-speaking person, esp. a white North American who is not of Hispanic or French descent. [Short for ANGLO-AMERICAN.] —**An′glo** *adj.*

Anglo– *pref.* England; English: *Anglo-Saxon.* [NLat. < Lat. *Anglī,* the English people. See ANGLE.]

An·glo-A·mer·i·can (ăng′glō-ə-mĕr′ĭ-kən) *n.* An American, esp. one from the United States, whose language and ancestry are English. ❖ *adj.* **1.** Of, relating to, or between England and America, esp. the United States. **2.** Of or relating to Anglo-Americans.

An·glo-Cath·o·lic (ăng′glō-kăth′lĭk, -kăth′ə-lĭk) *n.* An Anglican whose convictions stress sacramental worship. —**An′glo-Cath′o·lic** *n.*

An·glo·cen·tric (ăng′glō-sĕn′trĭk) *adj.* Centered or focused on England or the English, esp. in relation to historical or cultural influence. —**An′glo·cen′trism** *n.*

An·glo-French (ăng′glō-frĕnch′) *adj.* Of, relating to, or between England and France or their peoples; English and French. ❖ *n.* See **Anglo-Norman** 2.

An·glo-In·di·an (ăng′glō-ĭn′dē-ən) *adj.* Of, relating to, or between England and India. ❖ *n.* **1.** A person of English and Indian descent. **2.** A person of English birth or ancestry living in India. **3.** The variety of English used in India.

An·glo-I·rish (ăng′glō-ī′rĭsh) *n.* **1.** An English native living in Ireland. **2.** An Irish native living in England. **3.** One of mixed Irish and English ancestry. **4.** See **Irish English.** —**An′glo-I′rish** *adj.*

An·glo-Lat·in (ăng′glō-lăt′n) *n.* Medieval Latin as used in England.

An·glo·ma·ni·a (ăng′glō-mā′nē-ə, -mān′yə) *n.* A strong predilection for anything English.

An·glo-Nor·man (ăng′glō-nôr′mən) *n.* **1.** One of the Normans who lived in England after the Norman Conquest of England in 1066 or a descendant of these settlers. **2a.** The dialect of Old French, derived chiefly from Norman French, that was used by the Anglo-Normans. **b.** The form of this dialect used in English law until the 17th century. —**An′glo-Nor′man** *adj.*

An·glo·phile (ăng′glə-fīl′) also **An·glo·phil** (-fĭl) *n.* One who admires England, its people, and its culture. —**An′glo·phile,** **An′glo·phil′ic** (ăng′glə-fĭl′ĭk) *adj.* —**An′glo·phil′i·a** (-fĭl′ē-ə) *n.*

An·glo·phobe (ăng′glə-fōb′) *n.* One who dislikes or fears England, its people, or its culture. —**An′glo·pho′bi·a** *n.* —**An′glo·pho′bic** *adj.*

An·glo·phone also **an·glo·phone** (ăn′glə-fōn′) *n.* An English-speaking person, esp. one in a country where two or more languages are spoken. —**An′glo·phon′ic** (-fŏn′ĭk) *adj.*

An·glo-Sax·on (ăng′glō-săk′sən) *n.* **1.** A member of one of the Germanic peoples who settled in Britain in the fifth and sixth centuries. **2.** A descendant of the Anglo-Saxons, who were dominant in England until the Norman Conquest of 1066. **3.** See **Old English** 1. **4.** A person of English ancestry. ❖ *adj.* Of, relating to, or characteristic of Anglo-Saxons, their descendants, or their language or culture; English.

An·go·la (ăng-gō′lə, ăn-) A country of SW Africa on the Atlantic Ocean; achieved independence from Portugal in 1975. Cap. Luanda. Pop. 8,140,000. —**An·go′lan** *adj. & n.*

An·go·ra¹ (ăng-gôr′ə, -gôr′ə, ăng′gər-ə) See **Ankara.**

An·go·ra² (ăng-gôr′ə, -gôr′ə) *n.* **1.** often **angora a.** The hair of the Angora goat or Angora rabbit. **b.** A yarn or fabric made from either of these fibers. **2.** An Angora cat. **3.** An Angora goat. **4.** An Angora rabbit. [After *Angora* (Ankara), Turkey.]

Angora cat *n.* A domestic cat having long silky hair.

Angora goat *n.* A domestic goat having long silky hair.

Angora rabbit *n.* A domestic rabbit having long, soft, usu. white hair.

an·gos·tu·ra bark (ăng′gə-stoŏr′ə, -styoŏr′ə) *n.* The bitter aromatic bark of either of two South American trees (*Galipea officinalis* or *Cusparia trifoliata*), used as a flavoring in bitters and as a tonic. [After *Angostura* (Ciudad Bolívar), Venezuela.]

An·gou·mois (äN′goō-mwä′) A historical region and former province of W France; occupied by Gallic peoples in pre-Roman times and a French duchy after 1515.

an·gry (ăng′grē) *adj.* **-gri·er, -gri·est 1.** Feeling or showing anger; incensed or enraged: *angry at a rude neighbor; angry at a salesclerk.* **2.** Indicative of or resulting from anger: *an angry silence.* **3.** Having a menacing aspect; threatening: *angry clouds moving in.* **4.** *Chiefly New England & Midland US* Inflamed and painful: *an angry sore.* [ME *angri* < *anger,* anger. See ANGER.] —**an′gri·ly** *adv.*

angry young man *n.* **1.** One of a group of English writers of the 1950s whose works are characterized by social protest. **2.** A critic of economic or social injustice.

angst¹ (ängkst) *n.* A feeling of anxiety or apprehension often accompanied by depression. [Ger. < MHGer. *angest* < OHGer. *angust.*]

angst² *abbr.* angstrom

ang·strom or **ång·strom** (ăng′strəm) *n.* A unit of length equal to one hundred-millionth (10⁻⁸) of a centimeter, used esp. to specify radiation wavelengths. [After Anders Jonas ÅNGSTRÖM.]

Ång·ström (ăng′strəm, ŏng′strœm), **Anders Jonas** 1814–74. Swedish physicist and astronomer who founded the science of spectroscopy.

ang·strom unit (ăng′strəm) *n.* See **angstrom.**

An·guil·la (ăng-gwĭl′ə, ăn-) An island of the British West Indies in the N Leeward Is.; settled by the British in the 17th cent., it became a dependency of Britain in 1971.

an·guish (ăng′gwĭsh) *n.* Agonizing physical or mental pain; torment. ❖ *v.* **-guished, -guish·ing, -guish·es** —*tr.* To cause to feel or suffer anguish. —*intr.* To feel or suffer anguish. [ME *angwisse* < OFr. *anguisse* < Lat. *angustiae,* distress < *angustus,* narrow.]

an·guished (ăng′gwĭsht) *adj.* Feeling, expressing, or caused by anguish: *anguished screams for help.*

an·gu·lar (ăng′gyə-lər) *adj.* **1.** Having, forming, or consisting of an angle or angles. **2.** Measured by an angle or by degrees of an arc. **3.** Bony and lean; gaunt: *an angular face.* **4.** Lacking grace or smoothness; awkward: *an angular gait.* [Lat. *angulāris* < *angulus,* angle.] —**an′gu·lar·ly** *adv.* —**an′gu·lar·ness** *n.*

angular acceleration *n.* The rate of change of angular velocity with respect to time.

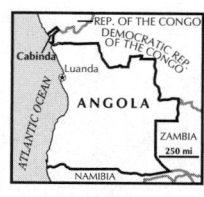

Angola

Angora cat

ă	pat	oi	boy
ā	pay	ou	out
âr	care	oŏ	took
ä	father	oō	boot
ĕ	pet	ŭ	cut
ē	be	ûr	urge
ĭ	pit	th	thin
ī	pie	th	this
îr	pier	hw	which
ŏ	pot	zh	vision
ō	toe	ə	about,
ô	paw		item

Stress marks:
′ (primary);
′ (secondary), as in
lexicon (lĕk′sĭ-kŏn′)

angular gyrus *n.* A region of the inferior parietal lobe of the brain that is involved in the processing of auditory and visual input and in the comprehension of language.

an·gu·lar·i·ty (ăng′gyə-lăr′ĭ-tē) *n., pl.* **-ties 1.** The quality or condition of being angular. **2. angularities** Angular forms, outlines, or corners.

angular momentum *n.* **1.** The vector product of the position vector and the linear momentum of a particle. **2.** The vector sum of the angular momentums of each component particle of an extended body.

angular velocity *n.* The rate of change of angular displacement with respect to time.

an·gu·late (ăng′gyə-lĭt, -lāt′) *adj.* Having angles or an angular shape. ❖ *tr. & intr.v.* (-lāt′) **-lat·ed, -lat·ing, -lates** To make or become angular. —**an′gu·late·ly** *adv.*

an·gu·la·tion (ăng′gyə-lā′shən) *n.* **1.** The formation of angles. **2.** An angular part, position, or formation.

an·he·do·ni·a (ăn′hē-dō′nē-ə) *n.* The absence of pleasure or the ability to experience it. [NLat. *anhēdonia* : Gk. *an-*, without; see A–[1] + Gk. *hēdonē*, pleasure; see **swād-** in App.] —**an′he·don′ic** (-dŏn′ĭk) *adj.*

an·hin·ga (ăn-hĭng′gə) *n.* Any of a genus (*Anhinga*) of long-necked birds having a pointed bill and inhabiting tropical and subtropical America. [Port. < Tupi *ayingá*.]

An·hui (än′hwē′) also **An·hwei** (-hwā′, -wā′) A province of E-central China; given provincial status in the 17th cent. Cap. Hefei. Pop. 56,180,813.

an·hy·dride (ăn-hī′drīd′) *n.* A chemical compound formed from another by the removal of water. [ANHYDR(OUS) + –IDE.]

an·hy·drite (ăn-hī′drīt) *n.* A colorless to white mineral of anhydrous calcium sulfate, $CaSO_4$. [ANHYDR(OUS) + –ITE[1].]

an·hy·drous (ăn-hī′drəs) *adj.* Without water, esp. water of crystallization. [< Gk. *anudros* : *an-*, without; see A–[1] + *hudōr*, water; see **wed-** in App.]

a·ni (ä-nē′) *n., pl.* **a·nis** Any of several chiefly tropical American birds of the genus *Crotophaga*, related to the cuckoo and having black plumage and a long tail. [Am.Sp. *aní* or Port. *ani*, both < Tupi *ani*.]

an·il (ăn′ĭl) *n.* The indigo plant or the blue dye obtained from it. [Fr. < Port. < Ar. *an-nīl*, the indigo plant : *al-*, the + Pers. *nīl*, indigo plant (< Skt. *nīlī* < *nīla-*, dark blue).]

an·ile (ăn′īl′, ā′nīl′) *adj.* **1.** Of or like an old woman. **2.** Senile. [Lat. *anīlis* < *anus*, old woman.] —**a·nil′i·ty** (ə-nĭl′ĭ-tē) *n.*

an·i·line also **an·i·lin** (ăn′ə-lĭn) *n.* A colorless, oily, poisonous benzene derivative, $C_6H_5NH_2$, used in the manufacture of rubber, dyes, resins, pharmaceuticals, and varnishes. ❖ *adj.* Derived from aniline. [ANIL + –INE[2].]

a·ni·lin·gus (ā′nə-lĭng′gəs) *n.* Oral stimulation of the anus. [NLat. : Lat. *ānus*, anus + Lat. *lingere*, to lick; see **leigh-** in App.]

anim. *abbr.* animato

an·i·ma (ăn′ə-mə) *n.* **1.** The inner self of an individual; the soul. **2.** In Jungian psychology: **a.** The unconscious or true inner self of an individual as opposed to the persona. **b.** The feminine inner personality, as present in men. [Lat. See **anə-** in App.]

an·i·mad·ver·sion (ăn′ə-măd-vûr′zhən, -shən) *n.* **1.** Strong criticism. **2.** A critical or censorious remark. [Lat. *animadversiō, animadversiōn-* < *animadversus*, p. part. of *animadvertere*, to turn the mind toward. See ANIMADVERT.]

an·i·mad·vert (ăn′ə-măd-vûrt′) *intr.v.* **-vert·ed, -vert·ing, -verts** To remark or comment critically, usu. with strong disapproval or censure. [ME *animadverten* < Lat. *animadvertere* : *animus*, mind; see **anə-** in App. + *advertere*, to turn toward; see ADVERSE.]

an·i·mal (ăn′ə-məl) *n.* **1.** A multicellular organism of the kingdom Animalia, characterized by a capacity for locomotion, non-photosynthetic metabolism, pronounced response to stimuli, restricted growth, and fixed bodily structure. **2.** An animal organism other than a human, esp. a mammal. **3.** A person who behaves in a bestial or brutish manner. **4.** A person considered with respect to the physical nature. **5.** A person having a specified aptitude or set of interests: "*that rarest of musical animals, an instrumentalist who is as comfortable on a podium with a stick as he is playing his instrument*" (Lon Tuck). ❖ *adj.* **1.** Relating to, characteristic of, or derived from an animal or animals: *animal fat.* **2.** Relating to the physical nature of people: *animal instincts.* [ME < Lat. < *animāle*, neut. of *animālis*, living < *anima*, soul. See **anə-** in App.]

animal cracker *n.* A small, animal-shaped cookie.

an·i·mal·cule (ăn′ə-măl′kyōōl) also **an·i·mal·cu·lum** (-kyə-ləm) *n., pl.* **-cules** also **-cu·la** (-kyə-lə) **1.** A microscopic or minute organism, such as an amoeba or paramecium. **2.** *Archaic* A tiny animal, such as a mosquito. [NLat. *animalculum*, dim. of Lat. *animal*, animal. See ANIMAL.]

animal heat *n.* The heat generated in the body of a warm-blooded vertebrate.

animal husbandry *n.* The branch of agriculture concerned with the care and breeding of domestic animals.

an·i·mal·ism (ăn′ə-mə-lĭz′əm) *n.* **1.** Enjoyment of vigorous, robust health and physical drives. **2.** Indifference to all but the physical appetites. **3.** *Philosophy* The doctrine that all humans are merely animals that have no spiritual nature. —**an′i·mal·ist** *n.*

an′i·mal·is′tic (-lĭs′tĭk) *adj.*

an·i·mal·i·ty (ăn′ə-măl′ĭ-tē) *n., pl.* **-ties 1.** The characteristics or nature of an animal. **2.** The animal kingdom. **3.** The animal instincts of humans.

an·i·mal·ize (ăn′ə-mə-līz′) *tr.v.* **-ized, -iz·ing, -iz·es 1.** To cause (another) to behave like an animal. **2.** To depict or represent as an animal. —**an′i·mal·i·za′tion** (-mə-lĭ-zā′shən) *n.*

animal kingdom *n.* A main classification of living organisms that includes all animals.

animal magnetism *n.* **1.** A special presence held to aid in hypnotism. **2.** Magnetic personal charm. **3.** Sex appeal.

animal pole *n. Embryology* The portion of an egg that is opposite the vegetal pole and that contains the nucleus and most of the cytoplasm.

animal rights *pl.n.* The rights to humane treatment claimed on behalf of animals.

animal spirits *pl.n.* The vitality of good health.

animal starch *n.* See **glycogen**.

an·i·mate (ăn′ə-māt′) *tr.v.* **-mat·ed, -mat·ing, -mates 1.** To give life to; fill with life. **2.** To impart interest or zest to; enliven. **3.** To fill with spirit, courage, or resolution; encourage. **4.** To inspire to action; prompt. **5.** To impart motion or activity to. **6.** To make, design, or produce so as to create the illusion of motion. ❖ *adj.* (ăn′ə-mĭt) **1.** Possessing life; living. **2.** Of or relating to animal life as distinct from plant life. **3.** Belonging to the class of nouns that stand for living things: *The word dog is animate; the word car is inanimate.* [Lat. *animāre, animāt-* < *anima*, soul. See **anə-** in App.] —**an′i·ma·cy** (-mə-sē) *n.*

an·i·mat·ed (ăn′ə-mā′tĭd) *adj.* **1.** Having life; alive. **2.** Filled with activity, vigor, or spirit; lively. **3.** Made in the form of an animated cartoon. —**an′i·mat·ed·ly** *adv.*

animated cartoon *n.* A motion picture or television film consisting of a photographed series of drawings, objects, or computer graphics that simulates motion by recording very slight, continuous changes in the images.

an·i·ma·tion (ăn′ə-mā′shən) *n.* **1.** The act, process, or result of imparting life, interest, spirit, motion, or activity. **2.** The quality or condition of being alive, active, spirited, or vigorous. **3a.** The preparation of animated cartoons. **b.** An animated cartoon.

an·i·ma·tism (ăn′ə-mĭ-tĭz′əm) *n.* A belief that all animate and inanimate objects are infused with a common life force. —**an′i·ma·tist** *adj. & n.* —**an′i·ma·tis′tic** *adj.*

a·ni·ma·to (ä′nē-mä′tō) *adv. & adj. Music* In an animated or lively manner. [Ital., p. part. of *animare*, to animate < Lat. *animāre*. See ANIMATE.]

an·i·ma·tor (ăn′ə-mā′tər) *n.* **1.** One that provides or imparts life, interest, spirit, or vitality. **2.** One who designs, develops, or produces an animated cartoon.

an·i·ma·tron·ics (ăn′ə-mə-trŏn′ĭks) *n.* (*used with a sing. verb*) The technology employing electronics to animate motorized puppets. [ANIMA(TION) + (ELEC)TRONICS.] —**an′i·ma·tron′ic** *adj.*

an·i·me (ăn′ə-mā′) *n.* A style of animation developed in Japan, characterized by stylized colorful art, futuristic settings, violence, and sex. [J., short for *animēshon*, animation < E. ANIMATION.]

an·i·mism (ăn′ə-mĭz′əm) *n.* **1.** The belief in the existence of individual spirits that inhabit natural objects and phenomena. **2.** The belief in the existence of spiritual beings that are separate from bodies. **3.** The theory that an immaterial force animates the universe. [< Lat. *anima*, soul. See **anə-** in App.] —**an′i·mist** *n.* —**an′i·mis′tic** *adj.*

an·i·mos·i·ty (ăn′ə-mŏs′ĭ-tē) *n., pl.* **-ties 1.** Bitter hostility or open enmity; active hatred. **2.** A hostile feeling or act. [ME *animosite* < OFr. < LLat. *animōsitās*, courage < Lat. *animōsus*, bold < *animus*, soul, spirit. See **anə-** in App.]

an·i·mus (ăn′ə-məs) *n.* **1.** An attitude that informs one's actions; disposition. **2.** A feeling of animosity; ill will. **3.** In Jungian psychology, the masculine inner personality, as present in women. [Lat. See **anə-** in App.]

an·i·on (ăn′ī′ən) *n.* A negatively charged ion, esp. the ion that migrates to an anode in electrolysis. [< Gk., neut. pr. part. of *anienai*, to go up : *ana-*, ana- + *ienai*, to go; see **ei-** in App.] —**an′i·on′ic** (-ŏn′ĭk) *adj.* —**an′i·on′i·cal·ly** *adv.*

an·ise (ăn′ĭs) *n.* **1.** An annual Mediterranean herb (*Pimpinella anisum*) in the parsley family, cultivated for its seedlike fruits and oil. **2.** Anise seed. [ME *anis* < OFr. < Lat. *anīsum* < Gk. *annēson, annison.*]

an·i·sei·ko·ni·a (ăn-ī′sī-kō′nē-ə) *n.* A condition in which the shape and size of the ocular image differ in each eye. [< ANIS(O)- + Gk. *eikōn*, image.] —**an′i·sei·kon′ic** (-kŏn′ĭk) *adj.*

anise seed or **an·i·seed** (ăn′ĭ-sēd′) *n.* The seedlike fruit of the anise.

an·i·sette (ăn′ĭ-sĕt′, -zĕt′) *n.* A liqueur flavored with anise. [Fr., dim. of *anis*, anise < OFr. See ANISE.]

aniso- or **anis-** *pref.* Unequal; dissimilar: *anisogamy.* [< Gk. *anīsos* : *an-*, not; see A–[1] + *īsos*, equal.]

an·i·so·gam·ete (ăn-ī′sō-găm′ēt, -gə-mēt′, ăn′ī-) *n.* See **heterogamete**.

an·i·sog·a·my (ăn′ī-sŏg′ə-mē) *n.* A union between two gametes that differ in size or form. —**an′i·so·gam′ic** (-sə-găm′ĭk) *adj.*

an·i·so·me·tro·pi·a (ăn-ī′sə-mĭ-trō′pē-ə) *n.* A condition in which the refractive power of one eye differs from that of the other. [ANISO– + Gk. *metron*, measure; see METER[1] + –OPIA.] —**an′i·so′me·tro′pic** (-trŏp′ĭk, -trō′pĭk) *adj.*

an·i·so·trop·ic (ăn-ī′sə-trŏp′ĭk, -trō′pĭk) *adj.* **1.** Not isotropic. **2.** *Physics* Having different properties in different directions. —**an′i·so·trop′i·cal·ly** *adv.* —**an′i·sot′ro·pism** (-sŏt′rə-pĭz′əm), **an′i·sot′ro·py** (-sŏt′rə-pē) *n.*

An·jou[1] (ăn′jōō′, än-zhōō′) A historical region and former province of NW France; annexed to the French crown lands in the 1480s.

An·jou[2] (ăn′zhōō, -jōō) *n.* A variety of pear with green skin and firm smooth flesh. [After ANJOU[1].]

An·ka·ra (ăng′kər-ə, äng′-) Formerly **An·cy·ra** (ăn-sī′rə) and **An·go·ra** (ăng-gôr′ə, -gōr′ə, äng′gər-ə) The cap. of Turkey, in the W-central part; replaced Istanbul as the cap. in 1923. Pop. 2,782,200.

an·ker·ite (ăng′kə-rīt′) *n.* A white, gray, or red iron-rich dolomitic or carbonate mineral, Ca(Fe,Mg,Mn)(CO₃)₂. [After Matthias Joseph Anker (1771–1843), Austrian mineralogist.]

ankh (ăngk) *n.* A cross shaped like a T with a loop at the top, esp. as used in ancient Egypt as a symbol of life. [Egypt. *'nḫ*, life.]

an·kle (ăng′kəl) *n.* **1.** The joint formed by the articulation of the lower leg bones with the talus. **2.** The slender section of the leg immediately above the foot. [ME *ancle, ankel*, partly < OE *anclēow* and partly of Scand. orig.]

an·kle·bone (ăng′kəl-bōn′) *n.* See talus[1] 1.

an·klet (ăng′klĭt) *n.* **1.** An ornament worn around the ankle. **2.** A sock that reaches just above the ankle.

an·ky·lo·saur (ăng′kə-lō-sôr′) or **an·ky·lo·sau·rus** (ăng′kə-lō-sôr′əs) *n.* A large herbivorous dinosaur of the Cretaceous Period, having a squat, heavily armored body and a clubbed tail. [NLat. *Ankylosaurus*, genus name : Gk. *ankulos*, crooked, bent + Gk. *sauros*, lizard.]

an·ky·lose also **an·chy·lose** (ăng′kə-lōs′, -lōz′) *v.* **-losed, -los·ing, -los·es** —*tr.* To join or consolidate by ankylosis. —*intr.* To become joined or consolidated by ankylosis. [Back-formation < ANKYLOSIS.]

an·ky·lo·sis also **an·chy·lo·sis** (ăng′kə-lō′sĭs) *n.* **1.** *Anatomy* The consolidation of bones to form a single unit. **2.** *Pathology* The stiffening and immobility of a joint as the result of disease, trauma, surgery, or abnormal bone fusion. [NLat. < Gk. *ankulōsis*, stiffening of the joints < *ankuloun*, to crook, bend < *ankulos*, crooked, bent.] —**an′ky·lot′ic** (-lŏt′ĭk) *adj.*

an·la·ge also **An·la·ge** (än′lä′gə) *n., pl.* **-ges** or **-gen** (-gən) The initial clustering of embryonic cells from which a part or organ develops; a primordium. [Ger., fundamental principle < MHGer. *anlāge*, request : *ane-*, on (< OHGer. *ana-*; see an- in App.) + *lāge*, act of laying (< OHGer. *lāga*; see legh- in App.).]

Ann (ăn), **Cape** A peninsula of NE MA NE of Gloucester.

An·na I·va·nov·na (ä′nə ē-vä′nəv-nə) 1693–1740. Empress of Russia (1730–40) who ordered an attack on Turkey (1736).

an·nal·ist (ăn′ə-lĭst) *n.* One who writes annals; a chronicler.

an·nals (ăn′əlz) *pl.n.* **1.** A chronological record of the events of successive years. **2.** A descriptive account or record; a history. **3.** A journal in which the records and reports of a learned field are compiled. [Lat. *(librī) annālēs*, yearly (books), annals, pl. of *annālis*, yearly < *annus*, year.]

An·nam (ə-năm′, ăn′ăm′) A region and former kingdom of central Vietnam on the South China Sea; ruled by China from 111 B.C. to A.D. 939. —**An′na·mese′, An′nam·ite′** *adj. & n.*

An·nan (ăn′ən), **Kofi** b. 1938. Ghanaian diplomat who was appointed secretary-general of the United Nations in 1996. He shared the 2001 Nobel Peace Prize.

An·nap·o·lis (ə-năp′ə-lĭs) The cap. of MD, in the central part on an inlet of Chesapeake Bay; site of the US Naval Academy (founded 1845). Pop. 35,838.

Annapolis Royal A town of W Nova Scotia, Canada, on an arm of the Bay of Fundy; founded as **Port Royal** by the French in 1605 and renamed by the British after 1710.

An·na·pur·na (ăn′ə-pŏŏr′nə, -pûr′-) A massif of the Himalaya Mts. in N-central Nepal rising to 8,083.7 m (26,504 ft) at **Annapurna I. Annapurna II** is 7,942.5 m (26,041 ft).

Ann Arbor A city of SE MI W of Detroit; seat of the University of Michigan (founded 1817). Pop. 114,024.

an·nat·to (ə-nä′tō) *n., pl.* **-tos 1.** A tropical American evergreen shrub or small tree (*Bixa orellana*), having heart-shaped leaves and showy flowers. **2.** The seed of this plant, used as a coloring and as a flavoring. **3.** A yellowish-red dyestuff obtained from the seed aril of this plant. [Of Cariban orig.]

Anne (ăn) 1665–1714. Queen of Great Britain and Ireland (1702–14); last monarch of the Stuart line.

an·neal (ə-nēl′) *v.* **-nealed, -neal·ing, -neals** —*tr.* **1.** To subject (glass or metal) to a process of heating and slow cooling to reduce brittleness. **2.** To strengthen or harden. —*intr.* To become strengthened or hardened. [ME *anelen* < OE *onǣlan*, to set fire to : *on-*, on (< *on*; see ON) + *ǣlan*, to kindle.]

An·ne·cy (ăn′ə-sē′, än-sē′) A city of S France in the Alps on **Lake Annecy** ENE of Lyons. Pop. 49,965.

an·ne·lid (ăn′ə-lĭd) also **an·nel·i·dan** (ə-nĕl′ĭ-dən) *n.* Any of various worms or wormlike animals of the phylum Annelida, characterized by an elongated, cylindrical, segmented body. ❖ *adj.* Of or belonging to the phylum Annelida. [< NLat. *Annelida*, phylum name < Fr. *annelés*, pl. p. part. of *anneler*, to ring < OFr. *anel*, ring < Lat. *ānellus*, dim. of *ānus*, ring.]

Anne of Austria 1601–66. Wife of Louis XIII of France and regent (1643–61) for her son Louis XIV.

Anne of Cleves (klēvz) 1515–57. Queen of England (Jan.–Jul. 1540) as the fourth wife of Henry VIII.

an·nex (ə-nĕks′, ăn′ĕks) *tr.v.* **-nexed, -nex·ing, -nex·es 1.** To append or attach, esp. to a larger or more significant thing. **2.** To incorporate (territory) into an existing political unit. **3.** To add or attach, as an attribute, condition, or consequence. ❖ *n.* (ăn′ĕks′, ăn′ĭks) **1.** A building added on to or situated near a main one. **2.** An addition that is made to a record or other document. [ME *annexen* < OFr. *annexer* < Lat. *annectere, annex-*, to connect : *ad-*, ad- + *nectere*, to bind.] —**an′nex·a′tion** (ăn′ĭk-sā′shən) *n.* —**an′nex·a′tion·al** *adj.* —**an′nex·a′tion·ism** *n.* —**an′nex·a′tion·ist** *n.*

an·nexe (ăn′ĭks) *n. Chiefly British* Variant of annex.

An·nie Oak·ley (ăn′ē ōk′lē) *n.* A free ticket or pass. [After *Annie* OAKLEY (< the association of the punched ticket with one of her bullet-riddled targets).]

an·ni·hi·late (ə-nī′ə-lāt′) *v.* **-lat·ed, -lat·ing, -lates** —*tr.* **1a.** To destroy completely. **b.** To reduce to nonexistence. **c.** To defeat decisively; vanquish. **2.** To nullify or render void; abolish. —*intr. Physics* To participate in annihilation. [LLat. *annihilāre, annihilāt-* : Lat. *ad-*, ad- + Lat. *nihil*, nothing; see ne in App.] —**an·ni′hi·la·bil′i·ty** (-lə-bĭl′ĭ-tē) *n.* —**an·ni′hi·la·ble** (-lə-bəl) *adj.* —**an·ni′hi·la′tive** (-lā′tĭv, -lə-) *adj.* —**an·ni′hi·la′tor** *n.*

an·ni·hi·la·tion (ə-nī′ə-lā′shən) *n.* **1a.** The act or process of annihilating. **b.** Utter destruction. **2.** *Physics* The phenomenon in which a particle and an antiparticle meet and are converted to energy approx. equivalent to the sum of their masses.

an·ni·ver·sa·ry (ăn′ə-vûr′sə-rē) *n., pl.* **-ries 1.** The annually recurring date of a past event. **2.** A celebration commemorating such a date. [ME *anniversarie* < Med.Lat. *(diēs) anniversāria*, anniversary (day) < Lat., fem. of *anniversārius*, returning yearly : *annus*, year + *versus*, p. part. of *vertere*, to turn; see wer-² in App.]

an·no Dom·i·ni (ăn′ō dŏm′ə-nī′, -nē′) *adv.* In a specified year of the Christian era. [Med.Lat. *annō Dominī*, in the year of (our) Lord : Lat. *annō*, ablative of *annus*, year + Lat. *Dominī*, genitive of *Dominus*, Lord.]

anno He·bra·i·co (hĭ-brā′ĭ-kō) *adv.* In a specified year of the Jewish calendar. [NLat. *annō Hebrāico* : Lat. *annō*, ablative of *annus*, year + Lat. *Hebrāicō*, ablative of *Hebrāicus*, Heb.]

anno He·gi·rae (hĭ-jī′rē, hĕj′ər-ē′) *adv.* In a specified year of the Islamic calendar. [NLat. *annō Hegirae*, in the year of the Hegira : Lat. *annō*, ablative of *annus*, year + NLat. *Hegirae*, genitive of *Hegira*, Hegira.]

an·no·tate (ăn′ō-tāt′) *v.* **-tat·ed, -tat·ing, -tates** —*tr.* To add commentary or notes to; gloss. —*intr.* To gloss a text. [Lat. *annotāre, annotāt-*, to note down : *ad-*, ad- + *notāre*, to write (< *nota*, note; see gnō- in App.).] —**an′no·ta′tive** *adj.* —**an′no·ta′tor** *n.*

an·no·ta·tion (ăn′ō-tā′shən) *n.* **1.** The act or process of adding commentary or notes. **2.** A critical or explanatory note.

an·nounce (ə-nouns′) *v.* **-nounced, -nounc·ing, -nounc·es** —*tr.* **1.** To make known publicly. **2.** To proclaim the presence of: *announce a caller*. **3.** To provide an indication of beforehand; foretell. **4.** To provide running comments on: *announce a football game*. —*intr.* **1.** To declare one's candidacy. **2.** To provide running comments. [ME *announcen* < OFr. *anoncier* < Lat. *annūntiāre* : *ad-*, ad- + *nūntiāre*, to report (< *nūntius*, messenger).] —**an·nounc′er** *n.*

an·nounce·ment (ə-nouns′mənt) *n.* **1a.** The act of making known publicly. **b.** Something announced. **c.** A broadcast message, such as a commercial. **2.** An engraved or printed statement or notice.

an·noy (ə-noi′) *v.* **-noyed, -noy·ing, -noys** —*tr.* **1.** To cause irritation to by troublesome acts. **2.** To harass or disturb by repeated attacks. —*intr.* To be annoying. [ME *anoien* < OFr. *anoier, ennuyer* < VLat. **inodiāre*, to make odious < Lat. *in odiō*, odious : *in*, in; see IN-² + *odiō*, ablative of *odium*, hatred.]

an·noy·ance (ə-noi′əns) *n.* **1.** The act of annoying or the state of being annoyed. **2.** A cause of irritation or vexation.

an·noy·ing (ə-noi′ĭng) *adj.* Causing vexation or irritation; troublesome: *an annoying cough.* —**an·noy′ing·ly** *adv.*

an·nu·al (ăn′yōō-əl) *adj.* **1.** Happening every year; yearly: *an annual medical examination.* **2.** Of, relating to, or determined by a year: *an annual income.* **3.** *Botany* Living or growing for one year or season. ❖ *n.* **1.** A periodical published yearly; a yearbook. **2.** *Botany* A plant that completes its life cycle in one growing season. [ME *annuel* < OFr. < LLat. *annuālis*, ult. < Lat. *annus*, year.]

an·nu·al·ize (ăn′yōō-ə-līz′) *tr.v.* **-ized, -iz·ing, -iz·es** To calculate to reflect a rate based on a full year.

annual ring *n.* The layer of wood formed in a plant during a single year.

an·nu·i·tant (ə-nōō′ĭ-tənt, ə-nyōō′-) *n.* One that receives or is qualified to receive an annuity.

ankh

annual ring
cross section from the trunk of a loblolly pine

ă	pat	oi	boy
ā	pay	ou	out
âr	care	ŏŏ	took
ä	father	ōō	boot
ĕ	pet	ŭ	cut
ē	be	ûr	urge
ĭ	pit	th	thin
ī	pie	th	this
îr	pier	hw	which
ŏ	pot	zh	vision
ō	toe	ə	about,
ô	paw		item

Stress marks:
′ (primary);
′ (secondary), as in
lexicon (lĕk′sĭ-kŏn′)

an·nu·i·ty (ə-nōō′ĭ-tē, ə-nyōō′-) *n., pl.* **-ties 1a.** The annual payment of an income. **b.** The right to receive this payment or the obligation to make this payment. **2.** A contract or agreement by which one receives fixed payments on an investment for a lifetime or for a specified number of years. [ME *annuite* < AN < Med.Lat. *annuitās* < Lat. *annuus*, yearly < *annus*, year.]

an·nul (ə-nŭl′) *tr.v.* **-nulled, -nul·ling, -nuls 1.** To make or declare void or invalid; nullify. **2.** To obliterate: *a memory annulled by time.* [ME *annullen* < OFr. *annuler* < LLat. *annullāre* : Lat. *ad-*, ad- + Lat. *nullus*, none; see **ne** in App.]

an·nu·lar (ăn′yə-lər) *adj.* Shaped like or forming a ring. [Lat. *ānulāris* < *ānulus*, ring. See ANNULUS.] —**an′nu·lar′i·ty** (-lăr′ĭ-tē) *n.*

annular eclipse *n.* A solar eclipse in which the moon covers all but a bright ring around the circumference of the sun.

annular ligament *n.* The fibrous band of tissue that surrounds the ankle joint or the wrist joint.

an·nu·late (ăn′yə-lĭt, -lāt′) also **an·nu·lat·ed** (-lā′tĭd) *adj.* Having or consisting of rings or ringlike segments. [Lat. *ānulātus* < *ānulus*, ring. See ANNULUS.]

an·nu·la·tion (ăn′yə-lā′shən) *n.* **1.** The act or process of forming rings. **2.** A ringlike structure, segment, or part.

an·nu·let (ăn′yə-lĭt) *n.* A ringlike molding around the capital of a pillar. [Lat. *ānulus*, ring; see ANNULUS + -ET.]

an·nul·ment (ə-nŭl′mənt) *n.* **1.** An act of making or declaring void. **2.** The invalidation of a marriage by means of a declaration stating that the marriage was never valid.

an·nu·lus (ăn′yə-ləs) *n., pl.* **-lus·es** or **-li** (-lī′) **1.** A ringlike figure, part, structure, or marking. **2a.** A ring of cells around the sporangia of many ferns that functions in spore release. **b.** A ring found around the stipes of certain mushrooms. **3.** *Mathematics* The region bounded by two concentric circles. [Lat. *ānulus*, ring, dim. of *ānus*.]

an·nun·ci·ate (ə-nŭn′sē-āt′) *tr.v.* **-at·ed, -at·ing, -ates** To announce; proclaim: *annunciate a policy.* [Lat. *annūntiāre*, *annūntiāt-*. See ANNOUNCE.]

an·nun·ci·a·tion (ə-nŭn′sē-ā′shən) *n.* **1.** The act of announcing. **2.** An announcement; a proclamation. **3. Annunciation** *Christianity* **a.** The angel Gabriel's announcement to the Virgin Mary of the Incarnation. **b.** The feast celebrating this event, traditionally observed on March 25.

an·nun·ci·a·tor (ə-nŭn′sē-ā′tər) *n.* One that announces, esp. an electrical signaling device used to indicate the sources of calls on a switchboard. —**an·nun′ci·a·to·ry** (-ə-tôr′ē, -tōr′ē) *adj.*

an·nus mi·rab·i·lis (ăn′əs mĭ-răb′ə-lĭs, ăn′ē) *n., pl.* **an·ni mi·ra·bi·les** (ăn′ī mĭ-răb′ə-lēz, ăn′ē) A year of wonders. [NLat. *annus mīrabilis* : Lat. *annus*, year + Lat. *mīrabilis*, wondrous.]

an·ode (ăn′ōd′) *n.* **1.** A positively charged electrode, as of a storage battery. **2.** The negatively charged terminal of a primary cell or of a storage battery that is supplying current. [Gk. *anodos*, a way up : *ana-*, ana- + *hodos*, way.] —**a·nod′ic** (ə-nŏd′ĭk), **a·nod′al** (ə-nōd′l) *adj.*

an·o·dize (ăn′ə-dīz′) *tr.v.* **-dized, -diz·ing, -diz·es** To coat (a metal) electrolytically with a protective or decorative oxide. [ANOD(E) + -IZE.] —**an′o·di·za′tion** (-dĭ-zā′shən) *n.*

an·o·dyne (ăn′ə-dīn′) *adj.* **1.** Capable of soothing or eliminating pain. **2.** Relaxing: *anodyne novels about country life.* ❖ *n.* A comforter or a reliever of pain. [Lat. *anōdynus* < Gk. *anōdunos*, free from pain : *an-*, without; see A-[1] + *odunē*, pain; see **ed-** in App.]

a·noint (ə-noint′) *tr.v.* **a·noint·ed, a·noint·ing, a·noints 1.** To apply oil, ointment, or a similar substance to. **2.** To put oil on during a religious ceremony. **3.** To choose by or as if by divine intervention. [ME *enointen* < OFr. *enoint*, p. part. of *enoindre* < Lat. *inunguere, inūnct-* : *in-*, on; see IN-[2] + *unguere*, to smear.] —**a·noint′ment** *n.*

A·noint·ing of the Sick (ə-noin′tĭng) *n. Roman Catholic Church* The sacrament of anointing a critically ill or weak person with prayers for recovery and an act of penance or confession.

a·no·le (ə-nōl′ē) *n.* Any of various chiefly tropical New World lizards of the genus *Anolis*, characterized by the ability to change color. [Fr. *anolis*, of Cariban orig.]

a·nom·a·lous (ə-nŏm′ə-ləs) *adj.* **1.** Deviating from the usual or common order, form, or rule. **2.** Equivocal, as in classification or nature. [< LLat. *anōmalos* < Gk., uneven : prob. < *an-*, not; see A-[1] + *homalos*, even (< *homos*, same; see **sem-[1]** in App.).] —**a·nom′a·lous·ly** *adv.*

a·nom·a·ly (ə-nŏm′ə-lē) *n., pl.* **-lies 1.** Deviation or departure from the usual or common order, form, or rule. **2.** One that is peculiar, irregular, abnormal, or difficult to classify. **3.** *Astronomy* The angular deviation, as observed from the sun, of a planet from its perihelion. —**a·nom′a·lis′tic** (-lĭs′tĭk) *adj.* —**a·nom′a·lis′ti·cal·ly** *adv.*

an·o·mie or **an·o·my** (ăn′ə-mē) *n.* **1.** Social instability caused by erosion of standards and values. **2.** Alienation and purposelessness experienced by a person or a class as a result of a lack of standards, values, or ideals. [Fr. < Gk. *anomiā*, lawlessness < *anomos*, lawless : *a-*, without; see A-[1] + *nomos*, law; see **nem-** in App.] —**a·nom′ic** (ə-nŏm′ĭk, ə-nō′mĭk) *adj.*

a·non (ə-nŏn′) *adv.* **1.** At another time; later. **2.** In a short time; soon. **3.** *Archaic* At once; forthwith. —**idiom: ever (or now) and anon** Time after time; now and then. [ME, at once < OE *on ān* :

on, in + *ān*, one; see oi-no- in App.]

anon. *abbr.* anonymous

an·o·nym (ăn′ə-nĭm′) *n.* **1.** An anonymous person. **2.** A pseudonym. [Fr. *anonyme* < LLat. *anōnymus*, anonymous. See ANONYMOUS.]

an·o·nym·i·ty (ăn′ə-nĭm′ĭ-tē) *n., pl.* **-ties 1.** The quality or state of being unknown or unacknowledged. **2.** One that is unknown or unacknowledged.

a·non·y·mous (ə-nŏn′ə-məs) *adj.* **1.** Having an unknown or unacknowledged name: *an anonymous author.* **2.** Having an unknown or withheld authorship or agency: *an anonymous letter.* **3.** Having no distinctive character or individuality. [< LLat. *anōnymus* < Gk. *anōnumos*, nameless : *an-*, without; see A-[1] + *onuma*, name (influenced by earlier *nōnumnos*, nameless).] —**a·non′y·mous·ly** *adv.*

a·noph·e·les (ə-nŏf′ə-lēz′) *n.* Any of various mosquitoes of the genus *Anopheles*, which can carry the malaria parasite. [NLat. *Anôphelês*, genus name < Gk. *anôphelês*, useless : *an-*, without; see A-[1] + *ophelos*, advantage, use (influenced by earlier *nōphelês*, useless).] —**a·noph′e·line′** (-līn′, -lĭn) *adj.*

an·o·rak (ăn′ə-răk′) *n.* A heavy jacket with a hood; a parka. [Inuit *annoraaq*.]

an·o·rec·tic (ăn′ə-rĕk′tĭk) also **an·o·ret·ic** (-rĕt′ĭk) *adj.* **1.** Marked by loss of appetite. **2.** Causing loss of appetite. **3.** Of or affected with anorexia nervosa. ❖ *n.* **1.** One who is affected with anorexia nervosa. **2.** An anorectic drug. [< Gk. *anorektos*, without appetite : *an-*, not; see A-[1] + *orektos*, verbal adj. of *oregein*, to reach out for.]

an·o·rex·i·a (ăn′ə-rĕk′sē-ə) *n.* **1.** Loss of appetite, esp. as a result of disease. **2.** Anorexia nervosa. [Gk. *anorexiā* : *an-*, without; see A-[1] + *orexis*, appetite (< *oregein*, to reach out for; see **reg-** in App.).]

anorexia ner·vo·sa (nûr-vō′sə) *n.* A psychophysiological disorder usu. occurring in young women, characterized by a fear of obesity, a distorted self-image, a persistent unwillingness to eat, and severe weight loss. [NLat. *anorexia nervōsa* : *anorexia*, anorexia + *nervōsa*, fem. of *nervōsus*, nervous.]

an·o·rex·ic (ăn′ə-rĕk′sĭk) *adj.* **1.** Affected with anorexia nervosa. **2.** Anorectic. —**an′o·rex′ic** *n.*

an·or·thite (ăn-ôr′thīt) *n.* A rare plagioclase feldspar with high calcium oxide content occurring in igneous rocks. [< Gk. *an-*, not; see A-[1] + *orthos*, straight (< its oblique crystals).]

an·or·tho·site (ăn-ôr′thə-sīt′) *n.* A variety of diorite consisting chiefly of feldspar. [Fr. *anorthose*, a kind of feldspar (Gk. *an-*, not; see A-[1] + Gk. *orthos*, straight) + -ITE[1].] —**an·or′tho·sit′ic** (-sĭt′ĭk) *adj.*

an·os·mi·a (ăn-ŏz′mē-ə) *n.* Loss of the sense of smell. [NLat. : Gk. *an-*, without; see A-[1] + Gk. *osmē*, odor.] —**an·os′mic** *adj.*

an·oth·er (ə-nŭth′ər) *adj.* **1.** One more; an additional: *another cup of coffee.* **2.** Distinctly different from the first. **3.** Some other: *another day.* ❖ *pron.* **1.** An additional one. **2.** A different one. **3.** One of an undetermined number or group: *one reason or another.* [ME *on other* : *on*, one; see ONE + *other*, other; see OTHER.]

A·nou·ilh (ä-nōō′ē), **Jean** 1910–87. French playwright whose works include *Antigone* (1944).

an·ov·u·lant (ăn′ŏv′yə-lənt) *n.* A drug that suppresses ovulation. [AN- + OVUL(ATION) + -ANT.] —**an·ov′u·lant** *adj.*

an·o·vu·la·tion (ăn-ō′vyə-lā′shən, -ŏv′yə-) *n.* The failure, cessation, or suppression of ovulation.

an·o·vu·la·to·ry (ăn-ō′vyə-lə-tôr′ē, -tōr′ē, -ŏv′yə-) *adj.* **1.** Relating to or causing the suppression of ovulation. **2.** Not associated with or influenced by ovulation.

an·ox·e·mi·a (ăn′ŏk-sē′mē-ə) *n.* An abnormal reduction in the oxygen content of the blood. [AN- + OX(O)- + -EMIA.] —**an′ox·e′mic** *adj.*

an·ox·i·a (ăn-ŏk′sē-ə) *n.* **1.** Absence of oxygen. **2.** A pathological deficiency of oxygen, esp. hypoxia. [AN- + OX(O)- + -IA[1].] —**an·ox′ic** (-ŏk′sĭk) *adj.*

An·que·til (än-kə-tēl′), **Jacques** 1934–87. French cyclist who won the Tour de France (1957 and 1961–64).

an·sate (ăn′sāt′) *adj.* Having a handle or a part resembling a handle. [Lat. *ānsātus* < *ānsa*, handle.]

ansate cross *n.* See ankh.

An·schluss (än′shlŏŏs′) *n.* A political union, esp. the one unifying Nazi Germany and Austria in 1938. [Ger., annexation < *anschliessen*, to enclose, annex : *an*, on (< MHGer. *ane* < OHGer. *ana*; see **an-** in App.) + *schliessen*, to close (< MHGer. *sliezen* < OHGer. *sliozan*).]

An·selm (ăn′sĕlm), **Saint** 1033–1109. Italian-born English theological philosopher best known for his ontological argument for the existence of God.

an·ser·ine (ăn′sə-rīn′, -rĭn) *adj.* **1.** Of or belonging to the subfamily Anserinae, which comprises the geese. **2.** Of or resembling a goose; gooselike. [Lat. *ānserīnus*, pertaining to geese < *ānser*, goose. See **ghans-** in App.]

An·shan (än′shän′) A city of NE China SSW of Shenyang. Pop. 2,478,650.

ANSI *abbr.* American National Standards Institute

an·swer (ăn′sər) *n.* **1a.** A spoken or written reply. **b.** A correct reply. **2a.** A solution. **b.** A correct solution. **3.** An act in retaliation or response: *Our only possible answer was to sue.* **4.** Something

anole
knight anole
Anolis equestris

anorak

markedly similar to another of the same class: *cable TV's answer to the commercial networks' sportscasts.* **5.** *Law* A defendant's defense against charges. ❖ *v.* **-swered, -swer·ing, -swers** *—intr.* **1.** To speak, write, or act as a return. **2.** To be liable or accountable: *answer for your actions.* **3.** To serve the purpose; suffice: *"Often I do use three words where one would answer"* (Mark Twain). **4.** To correspond; match: *I answer a dog answering to that description.* *—tr.* **1.** To speak, write, or act as a return to; respond to. **2.** To respond correctly to. **3.** To fulfill the demands or needs of; serve. **4.** To conform or correspond to: *The suspect answers the description.* [ME *answere* < OE *andswaru*.]

SYNONYMS answer, respond, reply, retort These verbs relate to action taken in return to a stimulus. *Answer, respond,* and *reply,* the most general, all mean to speak, write, or act in response: *Please answer my question. Did you expect the President to respond personally to your letter? The opposing team scored three runs; the home team replied with two of their own. Respond* also denotes a reaction, either voluntary (*A bystander responded to the victim's need for help*) or involuntary (*She responded in spite of herself to the puppy's antics*). To *retort* is to answer verbally in a quick, caustic, or witty manner: *She won the debate by retorting sharply to her opponent's questions.* See also Syns at **satisfy.**

an·swer·a·ble (ăn′sər-ə-bəl) *adj.* **1.** Subject to being called to answer; accountable. See Syns at **responsible. 2.** That can be answered or refuted: *an answerable charge.* **3.** *Archaic* **a.** Suitable. **b.** Corresponding. **—an′swer·a·bil′i·ty, an′swer·a·ble·ness** *n.* **—an′swer·a·bly** *adv.*

an·swer·back (ăn′sər-băk′) *n.* A response to a transmission made over a two-way radio.

an·swer·ing machine (ăn′sər-ĭng) *n.* A device for answering one's telephone and recording callers' messages.

answering service *n.* A business service that answers its clients' telephone calls and conveys messages to the clients.

ant (ănt) *n.* Any of various social insects of the family Formicidae, living in colonies that have a complex social organization. **—idiom: ants in (one's) pants** *Slang* A state of restless impatience. [ME *amte* < OE *ǣmete*.]

ant. *abbr.* antonym

Ant. *abbr.* Antarctica

ant– *pref.* Variant of **anti–.**

–ant *suff.* **1a.** Performing, promoting, or causing a specified action: *acceptant.* **b.** Being in a specified state or condition: *flippant.* **2a.** One that performs, promotes, or causes a specified action: *deodorant.* **b.** One that undergoes a specified action: *inhalant.* [ME < OFr. < Lat. *-āns, -ant-,* pr. part. suff. of verbs in *-āre.*]

an·ta (ăn′tə) *n., pl.* **-tae** (-tē) A pilaster or rectangular column forming the end of a projecting lateral wall, as in some Greek temples. [< Lat. *antae,* pilasters.]

ant·ac·id (ănt-ăs′ĭd) *adj.* Counteracting or neutralizing acidity, esp. of the stomach. ❖ *n.* A substance that neutralizes acid.

An·tae·us (ăn-tē′əs) *n. Greek Mythology* A giant wrestler who could not be defeated as long as he remained in contact with the earth.

an·tag·o·nism (ăn-tăg′ə-nĭz′əm) *n.* **1.** Hostility that results in active resistance, opposition, or contentiousness. **2.** The condition of being an opposing principle, force, or factor: *the antagonism of capitalism and socialism.* **3.** *Biochemistry* Interference in the physiological action of a chemical substance by another having a similar structure.

an·tag·o·nist (ăn-tăg′ə-nĭst) *n.* **1.** One who contends against another; an adversary. **2.** The principal character in opposition to the protagonist or hero of a narrative or drama. **3.** *Physiology* A muscle that counteracts the action of another muscle. **4.** *Biochemistry* A chemical substance that interferes with the physiological action of another. **—an·tag′o·nis′tic** *adj.* **—an·tag′o·nis′ti·cal·ly** *adv.*

an·tag·o·nize (ăn-tăg′ə-nīz′) *tr.v.* **-nized, -niz·ing, -niz·es 1.** To incur the dislike of; provoke hostility or enmity in. **2.** To counteract. [Gk. *antagōnizesthai,* to struggle against : *anti-, anti-* + *agōnizesthai,* to struggle (< *agōn,* contest; see AGONY).]

An·ta·kya (än-täk′yä) also **An·ti·och** (ăn′tē-ŏk′) A city of S Turkey near the Mediterranean; founded c. 300 B.C. Pop. 137,200.

An·tal·ya (än-täl′yä) A city of SW Turkey on the **Gulf of Antalya,** an inlet of the Mediterranean Sea. Pop. 497,200.

An·ta·na·na·ri·vo (ăn′tə-năn′ə-rē′vō, än′tə-nä′nə-) Formerly **Ta·na·na·rive** (tə-năn′ə-rēv′, tä-nä-nä-rēv′) The cap. of Madagascar, in the E-central part; founded in the 17th cent. Pop. 700,000.

Ant·arc·ti·ca (ănt-ärk′tĭ-kə, -är′tĭ-) A continent lying chiefly within the Antarctic Circle and asymmetrically centered on the South Pole; first explored in the early 1800s. **—Ant·arc′tic** *adj. & n.*

Antarctic Archipelago See **Palmer Archipelago.**

Antarctic Circle The parallel of latitude approx. 66°33′ S that forms the boundary between the South Temperate and South Frigid zones.

Antarctic Ocean The waters surrounding Antarctica, the S extensions of the Atlantic, Pacific, and Indian oceans.

Antarctic Peninsula also **Palm·er Peninsula** (pä′mər) A region

of Antarctica extending N toward South America.

An·tar·es (ăn-târ′ēz, -tär′-) *n.* A giant red binary star, the brightest in the constellation Scorpio. [Gk. *Antarēs : anti-,* rivaling; see ANTI– + *Arēs,* Ares, the planet Mars.]

ant bear *n.* A large anteater (*Myrmecophaga jubata*), native to South America and having white stripes that run along both sides of its body.

ant cow *n.* An aphid that yields a substance on which ants feed.

an·te (ăn′tē) *n.* **1.** *Games* The stake that each poker player puts into the pool. See Syns at **bet. 2.** A price to be paid, esp. as one's share; cost. ❖ *v.* **-ted** or **-teed, -te·ing, -tes** *—tr.* **1.** *Games* To put (one's stake) into the pool in poker. **2.** To pay. *—intr.* **1.** *Games* To put one's stake into the pool in poker. **2.** To pay up. [< Lat., before. See **ant-** in App.]

ante– *pref.* **1.** Prior to; earlier: *antenatal.* **2.** In front of; before: *anteroom.* [Lat. < *ante,* before. See **ant–** in App.]

ant·eat·er (ănt′ē′tər) *n.* **1.** Any of several tropical American mammals of the family Myrmecophagidae, which feed on ants and termites. **2.** Any of several other animals that feed on ants.

an·te·bel·lum (ăn′tē-bĕl′əm) *adj.* Belonging to the period before a war, esp. the American Civil War. [< Lat. *ante bellum,* before the war : *ante,* before; see ANTE + *bellum,* war.]

an·te·cede (ăn′tĭ-sēd′) *tr.v.* **-ced·ed, -ced·ing, -cedes** To precede. [Lat. *antecēdere : ante-, ante-* + *cēdere,* to go.] **—an′te·ce′dence** (-sēd′ns) *n.*

an·te·ce·dent (ăn′tĭ-sēd′nt) *adj.* Going before; preceding. ❖ *n.* **1.** One that precedes another. **2a.** A preceding occurrence, cause, or event. **b. antecedents** The important events and occurrences in one's early life. **3. antecedents** One's ancestors. **4.** *Grammar* The word, phrase, or clause that determines what a pronoun refers to, as *the children* in *The teacher asked the children where they were going.* **5.** *Mathematics* The first term of a ratio. **6.** *Logic* The conditional member of a hypothetical proposition. **—an′te·ce′dent·ly** *adv.*

an·te·ces·sor (ăn′tĭ-sĕs′ər) *n.* One who precedes; a predecessor. [ME *antecessour,* forebear < Lat. *antecessor,* forerunner, predecessor in office < *antecessus,* p. part. of *antecēdere,* to go before. See ANTECEDE.]

an·te·cham·ber (ăn′tē-chām′bər) *n.* An anteroom. [Fr. *antichambre : anti-,* before (< Lat. *ante-*; see ANTE–) + *chambre,* chamber (< OFr. *chaumbre;* see CHAMBER).]

an·te·choir (ăn′tĭ-kwīr′) *n.* A place in front of the choir reserved for the clergy and choir members.

an·te·date (ăn′tĭ-dāt′) *tr.v.* **-dat·ed, -dat·ing, -dates 1.** To precede in time. **2a.** To assign to a date earlier than that of the actual occurrence. **b.** To date as of a time before that of actual execution: *antedate a check.* ❖ *n.* A date given to an event or document that is earlier than the actual date.

an·te·di·lu·vi·an (ăn′tĭ-də-loo′vē-ən) *adj.* **1.** Extremely old and antiquated. See Syns at **old. 2.** *Bible* Occurring or belonging to the era before the Flood. [ANTE– + Lat. *dīluvium,* flood; see DILUVIAL.] **—an′te·di·lu′vi·an** *n.*

an·te·fix (ăn′tē-fĭks′) *n., pl.* **-fix·es** or **-fix·a** (-fĭk′sə) An ornament on the eaves of a tiled roof meant to conceal the joints between the rows of tiles. [< Lat. *antefixa,* pl. of *antefixum,* something fastened in front < *antefixus,* fastened in front : *ante-, ante-* + *fixus,* fastened, p. part. of *fīgere,* to fasten.] **—an′te·fix′al** *adj.*

an·te·lope (ăn′tl-ōp′) *n., pl.* **antelope** or **-lopes 1a.** Any of various swift-running ruminant mammals of the family Bovidae, having long horns. **b.** An animal that resembles a true antelope. **2.** Leather made from the hide of the antelope. [ME, heraldic beast, prob. < OFr. *antelop,* savage beast with sawlike horns < Med.Lat. *anthalopus* < L.Gk. *antholops.*]

an·te·me·rid·i·an (ăn′tē-mə-rĭd′ē-ən) *adj.* Of, relating to, or taking place in the morning. [Lat. *antemerīdiānus : ante-, ante-* + *merīdiānus,* of noon; see MERIDIAN.]

an·te me·rid·i·em (ăn′tē mə-rĭd′ē-əm) *adv. & adj.* Before noon. Used chiefly to specify the hour. See Usage Note at **A.M.** [Lat. *ante,* before + *merīdiem,* accusative of *merīdiēs,* noon.]

an·te·mor·tem (ăn′tē-môr′təm) *adj.* Preceding death. [< Lat. *ante mortem,* before death : *ante,* before; see ANTE– + *mortem,* accusative of *mors, mort-,* death. See MORTAL.]

an·te·na·tal (ăn′tē-nāt′l) *adj.* Occurring before birth; prenatal: *antenatal diagnostic procedures.* **—an′te·na′tal·ly** *adv.*

an·ten·na (ăn-tĕn′ə) *n., pl.* **-ten·nae** (-tĕn′ē) **1a.** *Zoology* One of the paired, flexible, segmented sensory appendages on the head of an insect, myriapod, or crustacean. **b.** Something likened to this sensory appendage: *sensitive public relations antennae.* **2.** *pl.* **-nas** An apparatus for sending or receiving electromagnetic waves. [Med.Lat. < Lat., sail yard, transl. of Gk. *keraia,* insect feeler, yardarm.] **—an·ten′nal** *adj.*

an·ten·nule (ăn-tĕn′yōōl) *n. Zoology* A small antenna or similar organ. [Fr., dim. of *antenne,* antenna < Med.Lat. *antenna,* sail yard. See ANTENNA.]

an·te·pen·di·um (ăn′tē-pĕn′dē-əm) *n., pl.* **-di·a** (-dē-ə) A hanging for an altar, lectern, or pulpit. [Med.Lat. : Lat. *ante-,* ante- + *pendēre,* to hang.]

an·te·pe·nult (ăn′tē-pē′nŭlt′, -pĭ-nŭlt′) *n.* The third syllable from the end in a word, such as *te* in *antepenult.* [< LLat. *antepaenultima* < fem. of *antepaenultimus,* antepenultimate. See ANTEPENULTIMATE.]

antefix

antenna
close-up of cecropia moth
antennae

ă	pat	oi	boy
ā	pay	ou	out
âr	care	ōō	took
ä	father	ōō	boot
ĕ	pet	ŭ	cut
ē	be	ûr	urge
ĭ	pit	th	thin
ī	pie	th	this
îr	pier	hw	which
ŏ	pot	zh	vision
ō	toe	ə	about,
ô	paw		item

Stress marks:
′ (primary);
′ (secondary), as in
lexicon (lĕk′sĭ-kŏn′)

an·te·pe·nul·ti·mate (ăn′tē-pĭ-nŭl′tə-mĭt) *adj.* Coming before the next to the last in a series. ❖ *n.* An antepenult. [< LLat. *antepaenultimus* : Lat. *ante-*, ante- + Lat. *paenultimus*, next to last; see PENULT.]

an·te·ri·or (ăn-tîr′ē-ər) *adj.* **1.** Placed before or in front. **2.** Occurring before in time; earlier. **3.** *Anatomy* **a.** Located near or toward the head in lower animals. **b.** Located on or near the front of the body in higher animals. **c.** Located on or near the front of an organ or on the ventral surface of the body in humans. **4.** *Botany* Facing away from the axis or stem. [Lat., comp. of *ante*, before. See ANT- in App.] —**an·te′ri·or′i·ty** (-ôr′ĭ-tē, -ŏr′-) *n.* —**an·te′ri·or·ly** *adv.*

An·te·ro (ăn-târ′ō), Mount A peak, 4,352 m (14,269 ft), in the Sawatch Mts. of central CO.

an·te·room (ăn′tē-rōōm′, -rŏŏm′) *n.* An outer room that opens into another room, often used as a waiting room.

ant·he·li·on (ănt-hē′lē-ən, ăn-thē′-) *n.*, *pl.* **-li·a** (-lē-ə) or **-ons** A luminous white area occasionally seen opposite the sun on the parhelic circle. [Gk. *anthēlion* < neut. of *anthēlios*, opposite the sun : *anti-*, anti- + *hēlios*, sun; see **sāwel-** in App.]

ant·hel·min·tic (ănt′hĕl-mĭn′tĭk, ăn′thĕl-) also **ant·hel·min·thic** (-thĭk) *adj.* Acting to expel or destroy parasitic intestinal worms. [ANT(I)– + Gk. *helmins*, helminth-, worm; see **wel-** in App.] —**ant′hel·min′tic** *n.*

an·them (ăn′thəm) *n.* **1.** A hymn of praise or loyalty. **2.** A choral composition having a sacred or moralizing text. **3.** A popular song, esp. a rock song felt to sum up the attitudes or feelings of a period or social group. [ME *anteme* < OE *antefn* < LLat. *antiphōna* < L.Gk. < neut. pl. of *antiphōnos*, sounding in answer : *anti-*, in return; see ANTI– + *phōnē*, voice; see **bhā-** in App.]

an·the·mi·on (ăn-thē′mē-ən) *n.*, *pl.* **-mi·a** (-mē-ə) A pattern of honeysuckle or palm leaves in a radiating cluster, used as a motif in Greek art. [Gk., dim. of *anthemon*, flower < *anthos*.]

an·ther (ăn′thər) *n.* The pollen-bearing part of the stamen. [Med.Lat. *anthēra*, pollen < Lat., a medicine extracted from flowers < Gk. < fem. of *anthēros*, flowery < *anthos*, flower.]

an·ther·id·i·um (ăn′thə-rĭd′ē-əm) *n.*, *pl.* **-i·a** (-ē-ə) A sperm-producing organ occurring in seedless plants, fungi, and algae. [NLat. : *anthēra*, anther; see ANTHER + *-idium*, diminutive suff. (< Gk. *-idion*).] —**an′ther·id′i·al** *adj.*

an·ther·o·zoid (ăn′thər-ə-zō′ĭd) *n.* A male gamete produced by an antheridium.

an·the·sis (ăn-thē′sĭs) *n.*, *pl.* **-ses** (-sēz) The period during which a flower is fully open and functional. [Gk. *anthēsis*, flowering < *anthein*, to bloom < *anthos*, flower.]

ant·hill (ănt′hĭl′) *n.* A mound of soil, sand, or dirt formed by ants or termites in digging or building a nest.

antho– *pref.* Flower: *anthozoan*. [Gk. < *anthos*, flower.]

an·thol·o·gize (ăn-thŏl′ə-jīz′) *v.* **-gized**, **-giz·ing**, **-giz·es** —*intr.* To compile or publish an anthology. —*tr.* To include (material) in an anthology. —**an·thol′o·gist** *n.*

an·thol·o·gy (ăn-thŏl′ə-jē) *n.*, *pl.* **-gies** A collection of literary pieces. [Med.Gk. *anthologiā*, collection of epigrams < Gk., flower gathering < *anthologein*, to gather flowers : *antho-*, antho- + *logos*, a gathering (< *legein*, to gather; see **leg-** in App.).] —**an′tho·log′i·cal** (ăn′thə-lŏj′ĭ-kəl) *adj.*

An·tho·ny (ăn′thə-nē), Saint. A.D. 250?–350? Egyptian ascetic monk considered to be the founder of Christian monasticism.

Anthony, Susan Brownell 1820–1906. Amer. feminist leader; cofounded the National Woman Suffrage Association (1869).

Anthony of Padua, Saint. 1195–1231. Portuguese-born Franciscan friar.

an·tho·zo·an (ăn′thə-zō′ən) *n.* Any of a class (Anthozoa) of marine organisms, such as the corals and sea anemones, that have radial segments and grow singly or in colonies. —**an′tho·zo′an, an′tho·zo′ic** (-zō′ĭk) *adj.*

an·thra·cene (ăn′thrə-sēn′) *n.* A crystalline hydrocarbon, $C_{14}H_{10}$, extracted from coal tar and used in making dyes and organic chemicals. [Gk. *anthrax*, anthrak-, charcoal + –ENE.]

an·thra·cite (ăn′thrə-sīt′) *n.* A type of coal that has a high carbon content and little volatile matter and burns with a clean flame. [Prob. ult. < Gk. *anthrakitis*, a kind of coal < *anthrax*, anthrak-, charcoal.] —**an′thra·cit′ic** (-sĭt′ĭk) *adj.*

an·thra·co·sis (ăn′thrə-kō′sĭs) *n.* See black lung. [NLat. : Gk. *anthrax*, anthrak-, charcoal + –OSIS.]

an·thra·qui·none (ăn′thrə-kwĭ-nōn′, -kwĭn′ōn′) *n.* A yellow crystalline powder, $C_{14}H_8O_2$, that is insoluble in water and used chiefly in the manufacture of dyes. [ANTHRA(CENE) + QUINONE.]

an·thrax (ăn′thrăks′) *n.* **1.** An infectious, usu. fatal disease of warm-blooded animals that can be transmitted to humans and is caused by the bacterium *Bacillus anthracis.* **2.** *pl.* **-thra·ces** (-thrə-sēz′) A lesion caused by anthrax. [ME *antrax*, malignant boil < Lat. *anthrax*, carbuncle < Gk.]

an·throp·ic (ăn-thrŏp′ĭk) also **an·throp·i·cal** (-ĭ-kəl) *adj.* Of or relating to humans or the era of human life. [Gk. *anthrōpikos* < *anthrōpos*, human being.]

anthropo– *pref.* Human: *anthropometry.* [Gk. *anthrōpo-* < *anthrōpos*, human being.]

an·thro·po·cen·tric (ăn′thrə-pə-sĕn′trĭk) *adj.* **1.** Regarding humans as the central element of the universe. **2.** Interpreting reality exclusively in terms of human values and experience. —**an′-**

thro·po·cen′tri·cal·ly *adv.* —**an′thro·po·cen·tric′i·ty** (-trĭs′ĭ-tē) *n.* —**an′thro·po·cen′trism** *n.*

an·thro·po·gen·e·sis (ăn′thrə-pə-jĕn′ĭ-sĭs) *n.* The scientific study of the origin and development of humans.

an·thro·po·gen·ic (ăn′thrə-pə-jĕn′ĭk) *adj.* **1.** Of or relating to anthropogenesis. **2.** Caused by humans: *anthropogenic degradation of the environment.* —**an′thro·po·gen′i·cal·ly** *adv.*

an·thro·pog·ra·phy (ăn′thrə-pŏg′rə-fē) *n.* The branch of anthropology that deals with the geographical distribution of specific human cultures. —**an′thro·po·graph′ic** (-pə-grăf′ĭk) *adj.* —**an′thro·po·graph′i·cal·ly** *adv.*

an·thro·poid (ăn′thrə-poid′) *adj.* **1.** Resembling a human, esp. in shape or outward appearance. **2.** Of or belonging to the group of great apes of the family Pongidae. **3.** Resembling or characteristic of an ape; apelike. ❖ *n.* An ape of the family Pongidae. —**an′thro·poi′dal** (-poid′l) *adj.*

an·thro·pol·o·gy (ăn′thrə-pŏl′ə-jē) *n.* The scientific study of the origin, the behavior, and the physical, social, and cultural development of humans. —**an′thro·po·log′ic** (-pə-lŏj′ĭ-kəl), **an′thro·po·log′i·cal** (-ĭk) *adj.* —**an′thro·po·log′i·cal·ly** *adv.* —**an′thro·pol′o·gist** *n.*

an·thro·pom·e·try (ăn′thrə-pŏm′ĭ-trē) *n.* The study of the measurement of the human body for use in anthropological classification and comparison. —**an′thro·po·met′ric** (-pə-mĕt′rĭk), **an′thro·po·met′ri·cal** (-rĭ-kəl) *adj.* —**an′thro·po·met′ri·cal·ly** *adv.* —**an′thro·pom′e·trist** *n.*

an·thro·po·mor·phism (ăn′thrə-pə-môr′fĭz′əm) *n.* Attribution of human characteristics to inanimate objects, animals, or natural phenomena. —**an′thro·po·mor′phic** *adj.* —**an′thro·po·mor′phi·cal·ly** *adv.*

an·thro·po·mor·phize (ăn′thrə-pə-môr′fīz) *v.* **-phized**, **-phiz·ing**, **-phiz·es** —*tr.* To ascribe human characteristics to. —*intr.* To ascribe human characteristics to things not human. —**an′thro·po·mor′phi·za′tion** (-fĭ-zā′shən) *n.*

an·thro·po·mor·phous (ăn′thrə-pə-môr′fəs) *adj.* **1.** Having or suggesting human form and appearance. **2.** Ascribing human characteristics to things not human.

an·thro·pop·a·thism (ăn′thrə-pŏp′ə-thĭz′əm) *n.* Attribution of human feelings to things not human. [L.Gk. *anthrōpopathēs*, involved in human suffering (< Gk., having human feelings < *anthrōpopathein*, to have human feelings : *anthrōpo-*, anthropo- + *pathos*, feeling; see PATHOS) + –ISM.]

an·thro·poph·a·gus (ăn′thrə-pŏf′ə-gəs′) *n.*, *pl.* **-gi** (-jī′) A person who eats human flesh; a cannibal. [Lat. *anthrōpophagus* < Gk. *anthrōpophagos*, man-eating : *anthrōpo-*, anthropo- + *-phagos*, *-phagous.*] —**an′thro·po·phag′ic** (-pə-făj′ĭk), **an′thro·poph′a·gous** (-pŏf′ə-gəs) *adj.* —**an′thro·poph′a·gy** (-jē) *n.*

an·thro·pos·o·phy (ăn′thrə-pŏs′ə-fē) *n.* A system of beliefs and practices based on the teachings of Rudolph Steiner and maintaining that by correct training and personal discipline one can experience the spiritual world. [ANTHROPO– + (THEO)SOPHY.] —**an′thro·po·soph′i·cal** (-pə-sŏf′ĭ-kəl) *adj.* —**an′thro·pos′o·phist** *n.*

an·thur·i·um (ăn-thŏŏr′ē-əm) *n.* Any of various evergreen tropical American plants of the genus *Anthurium*, grown as ornamentals. [NLat. *Anthūrium*, genus name : ANTH(O)– + Gk. *ourā*, tail; see **ors-** in App.]

an·ti (ăn′tī, -tē) *n.*, *pl.* **-tis** A person who is opposed to something, such as a group, policy, proposal, or practice. ❖ *prep.* Opposed to; against. [< ANTI–.] —**an′ti** *adj.*

anti– or **ant–** *pref.* **1a.** Opposite: *antimere.* **b.** Opposing; against: *antibusiness.* **c.** Counteracting; neutralizing: *antacid.* **d.** Destroying: *antiaircraft.* **2a.** Inverse: *antilogarithm.* **b.** Displaying opposite characteristics: *antihero.* [Gk. < *anti*, opposite. See **ant-** in App.]

an·ti·ag·ing (ăn′tē-ā′jĭng, ăn′tī-) *adj.* Intended to prevent, delay, or reduce the degenerative effects of aging.

an·ti·air·craft (ăn′tē-âr′krăft′, ăn′tī-) *adj.* Designed for defense against aircraft or missile attack. ❖ *n.* An antiaircraft weapon.

an·ti-A·mer·i·can (ăn′tē-ə-mĕr′ĭ-kən, ăn′tī-) *adj.* Opposed or hostile to the government, official policies, or people of the United States. —**an′ti-A·mer′i·can·ism** *n.*

an·ti·an·dro·gen (ăn′tē-ăn′drə-jən, ăn′tī-) *n.* A substance that inhibits the biological effects of androgenic hormones. —**an′ti·an′dro·gen′ic** (-jĕn′ĭk) *adj.*

an·ti·anx·i·e·ty (ăn′tē-ăng-zī′ĭ-tē, ăn′tī-) *adj.* Preventing or reducing anxiety: *an antianxiety drug.*

an·ti·ar·rhyth·mic (ăn′tē-ə-rĭth′mĭk, ăn′tī-) *adj.* Preventing or alleviating irregularities in the force or rhythm of the heart. ❖ *n.* An antiarrhythmic substance.

an·ti-art (ăn′tē-ärt′, ăn′tī-) *n.* Art, specifically Dada, that rejects traditional art forms and theories.

an·ti·at·om (ăn′tē-ăt′əm, ăn′tī-) *n.* An atom composed of antiparticles.

an·ti·bal·lis·tic missile (ăn′tĭ-bə-lĭs′tĭk, ăn′tī-) *n.* A defensive missile designed to intercept and destroy a ballistic missile in flight.

an·ti·bar·y·on (ăn′tē-băr′ē-ŏn′, ăn′tī-) *n.* The antiparticle of a baryon.

Susan B. Anthony
engraving by
G.E. Perine & Co.

anticipation
harmonic anticipation

An·tibes (äN-tēb′) A city of SE France on the Riviera between Nice and Cannes. Pop. 62,859.

an·ti·bi·o·sis (ăn′tē-bī-ō′sĭs, ăn′tī-) *n.* **1.** An association between two or more organisms that is detrimental to at least one of them. **2.** The antagonistic association between an organism and the metabolic substances produced by another.

an·ti·bi·ot·ic (ăn′tĭ-bī-ŏt′ĭk, ăn′tī-) *n.* A substance, such as penicillin, produced by or derived from certain microorganisms, including fungi and bacteria, that can destroy or inhibit the growth of other microorganisms. ❖ *adj.* **1.** Of or relating to antibiotics. **2.** Of or relating to antibiosis. **3.** Destroying life or preventing the inception or continuance of life. —**an′ti·bi·ot′i·cal·ly** *adv.*

an·ti-Black or **an·ti-black** (ăn′tē-blăk′, ăn′tī-) *adj.* Hostile or opposed to Black people.

an·ti·bod·y (ăn′tĭ-bŏd′ē) *n.* A protein produced by B cells that is secreted into the blood or lymph in response to a specific antigen; an immunoglobulin. [Transl. of Ger. *Antikörper* : *anti-*, antagonistic (< Lat. *anti-*, anti-) + *Körper*, body.]

an·ti·busi·ness (ăn′tē-bĭz′nĭs, ăn′tī-) *adj.* Hostile to business, esp. to big corporations.

an·tic (ăn′tĭk) *n.* **1.** A ludicrous or extravagant act; a caper. **2.** *Archaic* A buffoon, esp. a performing clown. ❖ *adj.* Ludicrously odd; fantastic. [< Ital. *antico*, ancient (used of grotesque designs on some ancient Roman artifacts) < Lat. *antīquus*, former, old. See **ant-** in App.] —**an′ti·cal·ly** *adv.*

an·ti·cat·a·lyst (ăn′tē-kăt′l-ĭst, ăn′tī-) *n.* **1.** A substance that retards or arrests a chemical reaction. **2.** A substance that reduces or destroys the effectiveness of a catalyst.

an·ti·cath·ode (ăn′tē-kăth′ōd′, ăn′tī-) *n.* An electrode that is the target in a cathode-ray tube, esp. in an x-ray tube.

an·ti·chlor (ăn′tĭ-klôr′, -klōr′, ăn′tī-) *n.* A substance used to neutralize the excess chlorine or hypochlorite left after bleaching textiles, fiber, or paper pulp. [ANTI- + CHLOR(INE).] —**an′ti·chlo·ris′tic** (-klə-rĭs′tĭk) *adj.*

an·ti·choice (ăn′tē-chois′, ăn′tī-) *adj.* Opposed to the right of women to have the choice to terminate a pregnancy by induced abortion.

an·ti·cho·li·ner·gic (ăn′tē-kō′lə-nûr′jĭk, ăn′tī-) *adj.* Inhibiting or blocking the physiological action of acetylcholine at a receptor site. —**an′ti·cho′li·ner′gic** *n.*

an·ti·christ (ăn′tĭ-krīst′, ăn′tī-) *n.* **1.** An enemy of Christ. **2. Antichrist** The great antagonist expected by the early Church to cause chaos and corruption in the last days before the Second Coming. **3.** A false Christ. [ME *Antecrist* < OFr. and < OE, both < LLat. *Antichrīstus* < L.Gk. *Antikhrīstos* : Gk. *anti-*, anti- + Gk. *Khrīstos*; see CHRIST.]

an·tic·i·pant (ăn-tĭs′ə-pənt) *adj.* **1.** Coming or acting in advance: *clouds anticipant of a storm.* **2.** Expectant; anticipating: *anticipant of victory.* ❖ *n.* One who anticipates.

an·tic·i·pate (ăn-tĭs′ə-pāt′) *tr.v.* **-pat·ed, -pat·ing, -pates 1.** To feel or realize beforehand; foresee: *hadn't anticipated the crowds at the zoo.* **2.** To look forward to, esp. with pleasure; expect: *anticipated a pleasant hike in the country.* **3.** To act so as to mitigate, nullify, or prevent: *anticipated the storm by boarding up the windows.* **4.** To cause to happen in advance; accelerate. **5.** To use in advance. **6.** To pay (a debt) before it is due. [Lat. *anticipāre, anticipāt-*, to take before : *ante-*, ante- + *capere*, to take; see **kap-** in App.] —**an·tic′i·pat′a·ble** *adj.* —**an·tic′i·pa′tor** *n.* —**an·tic′i·pa·to·ry** (-pə-tôr′ē, -tōr′ē) *adj.*

an·tic·i·pa·tion (ăn-tĭs′ə-pā′shən) *n.* **1.** The act of anticipating. **2.** An expectation. **3.** Foreknowledge, intuition, and presentiment. **4.** The use or assignment of funds before they are legitimately available for use. **5.** *Music* Introduction of one note of a new chord on a weak beat before the previous chord is resolved.

an·tic·i·pa·tive (ăn-tĭs′ə-pā′tĭv, -pə-tĭv) *adj.* Expectant. —**an·tic′i·pa′tive·ly** *adv.*

an·ti·cler·i·cal (ăn′tē-klĕr′ĭ-kəl, ăn′tī-) *adj.* Opposed to the influence of the church or the clergy in political affairs. —**an′ti·cler′i·cal·ism** *n.*

an·ti·cli·max (ăn′tē-klī′măks′, ăn′tī-) *n.* **1.** A decline viewed in disappointing contrast to previous events: *the anticlimax of a brilliant career.* **2.** Something trivial that concludes a series of significant events: *all that followed was anticlimax.* **3.** A sudden descent from the impressive or significant to the ludicrous or inconsequential. —**an′ti·cli·mac′tic** (-klī-măk′tĭk) *adj.* —**an′ti·cli·mac′ti·cal·ly** *adv.*

an·ti·cli·nal (ăn′tē-klī′nəl, ăn′tī-) *adj.* **1.** Sloping downward in opposite directions. **2.** *Botany* Of or relating to the plane of a cell division perpendicular to the surface of a plant organ.

an·ti·cline (ăn′tĭ-klīn′) *n. Geology* A fold with strata sloping downward on both sides from a common crest.

an·ti·clock·wise (ăn′tē-klŏk′wīz, ăn′tī-) *adv. & adj.* Counterclockwise.

an·ti·co·ag·u·lant (ăn′tē-kō-ăg′yə-lənt, ăn′tī-) *n.* A substance that prevents the clotting of blood. ❖ *adj.* Acting as an anticoagulant.

an·ti·co·don (ăn′tē-kō′dŏn, ăn′tī-) *n.* A triplet of adjacent nucleotides in transfer RNA that binds to a corresponding codon in messenger RNA and designates a specific amino acid during protein synthesis.

an·ti·col·li·sion (ăn′tē-kə-lĭzh′ən, ăn′tī-) *adj.* Serving to prevent midair collisions.

an·ti·com·pet·i·tive (ăn′tē-kəm-pĕt′ĭ-tĭv, ăn′tī-) *adj.* Discouraging competition among businesses.

an·ti·con·vul·sant (ăn′tē-kən-vŭl′sənt, ăn′tī-) *n.* A drug that prevents or relieves convulsions. —**an′ti·con·vul′sive** (-sĭv) *adj.*

An·ti·cos·ti (ăn′tĭ-kô′stē, -kŏs′tē) An island of E Quebec, Canada, at the head of the Gulf of St. Lawrence.

an·ti·cy·clone (ăn′tē-sī′klōn′, ăn′tī-) *n.* An extensive system of winds spiraling outward from a high-pressure center, circling clockwise in the Northern Hemisphere and counterclockwise in the Southern Hemisphere. —**an′ti·cy·clon′ic** (-klŏn′ĭk) *adj.*

an·ti·de·pres·sant (ăn′tē-dĭ-prĕs′ənt, ăn′tī-) *n.* A drug used to prevent or relieve depression. —**an′ti·de·pres′sant, an′ti·de·pres′sive** (-prĕs′ĭv) *adj.*

an·ti·de·riv·a·tive (ăn′tē-dĭ-rĭv′ə-tĭv, ăn′tī-) *n.* See **indefinite integral.**

an·ti·deu·ter·on (ăn′tē-dōō′tə-rŏn′, -dyōō′-, ăn′tī-) *n.* The antimatter equivalent of deuteron.

an·ti·di·u·ret·ic hormone (ăn′tē-dī′ə-rĕt′ĭk, ăn′tī-) *n.* See **vasopressin.**

an·ti·dote (ăn′tĭ-dōt′) *n.* **1.** A remedy or other agent used to neutralize or counteract the effects of a poison. **2.** An agent that relieves or counteracts: *jogging as an antidote to nervous tension.* ❖ *tr.v.* **-dot·ed, -dot·ing, -dotes** To relieve or counteract with an antidote. [ME < Lat. *antidotum* < Gk. *antidoton* < *antididonai*, to give as a remedy against : *anti-*, anti- + *didonai*, do-, to give; see **dō-** in App.] —**an′ti·dot′al** (-dōt′l) *adj.* —**an′ti·dot′al·ly** *adv.*

USAGE NOTE *Antidote* may be followed by *to, for,* or *against*: *an antidote to boredom; an antidote for snakebite; an antidote against inflation.*

---

an·ti·e·lec·tron (ăn′tē-ĭ-lĕk′trŏn′, ăn′tī-) *n.* See **positron.**

an·ti·en·zyme (ăn′tē-ĕn′zīm′, ăn′tī-) *n.* A substance that neutralizes or counteracts the actions of an enzyme. —**an′ti·en′zy·mat′ic** (-zĭ-măt′ĭk, -zī-), **an′ti·en·zy′mic** (-zī′mĭk) *adj.*

an·ti·es·tab·lish·ment (ăn′tē-ĭ-stăb′lĭsh-mənt, ăn′tī-) *adj.* Marked by opposition or hostility to conventional principles. —**an′ti·es·tab′lish·men·tar′i·an** *n.* —**an′ti·es·tab′lish·men·tar′i·an·ism** *n.*

An·ti·e·tam (ăn-tē′təm) A creek of N-central MD emptying into the Potomac R.; site of a major Civil War battle (1862).

an·ti·feb·rile (ăn′tē-fĕb′rəl, -fē′brəl, -brīl′, ăn′tī-) *n.* An agent that reduces fever. —**an′ti·feb′rile** *adj.*

an·ti·fed·er·al·ist also **An·ti·fed·er·al·ist** (ăn′tē-fĕd′ər-ə-lĭst, -fĕd′rə-lĭst, ăn′tī-) *n.* An opponent of the ratification of the US Constitution. —**an′ti·fed′er·al·ist** *adj.* —**an′ti·fed′er·al·ism** *n.*

an·ti·fer·til·i·ty (ăn′tē-fər-tĭl′ĭ-tē, ăn′tī-) *adj.* Capable of reducing or eliminating fertility; contraceptive.

an·ti·foul·ing paint (ăn′tē-fou′lĭng, ăn′tī-) *n.* Paint that counteracts or prevents the fouling of underwater surfaces.

an·ti·freeze (ăn′tĭ-frēz′) *n.* A substance, such as ethylene glycol, mixed with another liquid to lower its freezing point.

an·ti·gal·ax·y (ăn′tē-găl′ək-sē, ăn′tī-) *n.* A galaxy that is made up of antimatter.

an·ti·gen (ăn′tĭ-jən) also **an·ti·gene** (-jēn′) *n.* A substance that when introduced into the body stimulates the production of an antibody. —**an′ti·gen′ic** (-jĕn′ĭk) *adj.* —**an′ti·gen′i·cal·ly** *adv.* —**an′ti·ge·nic′i·ty** (-jə-nĭs′ĭ-tē) *n.*

An·tig·o·ne (ăn-tĭg′ə-nē) *n. Greek Mythology* The daughter of Oedipus and Jocasta who performed funeral rites over her brother's body in defiance of Creon.

An·tig·o·nus I (ăn-tĭg′ə-nəs) 382–301 B.C. King of Macedonia (306–301) who was one of Alexander III's generals.

an·ti·grav·i·ty (ăn′tē-grăv′ĭ-tē, ăn′tī-) *n.* The hypothetical effect of reducing or canceling a gravitational field. —**an′ti·grav′i·ty** *adj.*

An·ti·gua and Bar·bu·da (ăn-tē′gə, bär-bōō′də) A country in

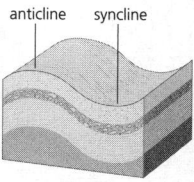

anticline   syncline

anticline

Antigua and Barbuda

an′ti·a·bor′tion *adj.*
an′ti·al·ler′gic *adj.*
an′ti·bac·te′ri·al *adj. & n.*
an′ti·can′cer *adj.*
an′ti·can′cer·ous *adj.*
an′ti·cho′li·nes′ter·ase *n.*
an′ti·crime′ *adj.*
an′ti·di·ar·rhe′al *n. & adj.*

an′ti·fem′i·nism *n.*
an′ti·fem′i·nist *adj. & n.*
an′ti·fun′gal *adj. & n.*
an′ti·fluor′i·da′tion·ist *n.*
an′ti·in·fec′tive *adj. & n.*
an′ti·in·flam′ma·to′ry *adj. & n.*
an′ti·in·tel′lec′tu·al *adj. & n.*

an′ti·in·tel′lec′tu·al·ism *n.*
an′ti·mi·tot′ic *adj. & n.*
an′ti·noise′ *adj.*
an′ti·par′a·sit′ic *adj. & n.*
an′ti·pol·lu′tion *adj.*
an′ti·pov′er·ty *adj.*
an′ti·slav′er·y *adj. & n.*
an′ti·smog′ *adj.*

an′ti·sub′ma·rine′ *adj.*
an′ti·take′o′ver *adj.*
an′ti·tank′ *adj.*
an′ti·ter′ror·ism *n.*
an′ti·ter′ror·ist *adj.*
an′ti·theft′ *adj.*
an′ti·tu′mor *adj.*
an′ti·war′ *adj.*

ă	pat	oi	boy
ā	pay	ou	out
âr	care	ŏŏ	took
ä	father	ōō	boot
ĕ	be	ŭ	cut
ē	be	ûr	urge
ĭ	pit	th	thin
ī	pie	*th*	this
îr	pier	hw	which
ŏ	pot	zh	vision
ō	toe	ə	about,
ô	paw		item

Stress marks:
′ (primary);
′ (secondary), as in
lexicon (lĕk′sĭ-kŏn′)

the N Leeward Is. of the Caribbean comprising Antigua, Barbuda, and Redonda; achieved independence in 1981. Cap. St. John's. Pop. 72,000. —**An·ti′guan** adj. & n.

an·ti·he·li·um (ăn′tē-hē′lē-əm, ăn′tī-) n. The antimatter equivalent of helium.

an·ti·he·mo·phil·ic factor (ăn′tē-hē′mə-fĭl′ĭk, ăn′tī-) n. A protein substance in blood plasma that participates in and is essential for the blood-clotting process.

an·ti·he·ro also **an·ti·he·ro** (ăn′tē-hîr′ō, ăn′tī-) n., pl. **-roes** A main character in a dramatic or narrative work who lacks traditional heroic qualities, such as idealism or courage. —**an′ti·he·ro′ic** (-hĭ-rō′ĭk) adj. —**an′ti·her′o·ism** (-hĕr′ō-ĭz′əm) n.

an·ti·he·ro·ine or **an·ti·her·o·ine** (ăn′tē-hĕr′ō-ĭn, ăn′tī-) n. A woman protagonist who lacks the qualities of a traditional hero or who acts counter to traditional expectations of women.

an·ti·his·ta·mine (ăn′tē-hĭs′tə-mēn′, -mĭn, ăn′tī-) n. A drug used to counteract the physiological effects of histamine production, as in allergic reactions. —**an′ti·his′ta·min′ic** (-mĭn′ĭk) adj.

an·ti·hy·dro·gen (ăn′tē-hī′drə-jən, ăn′tī-) n. The antimatter equivalent of hydrogen.

an·ti·hy·per·ten·sive (ăn′tē-hī′pər-tĕn′sĭv, ăn′tī-) adj. Reducing or controlling high blood pressure. —**an′ti·hy′per·ten′sive** n.

an·ti·knock (ăn′tī-nŏk′) n. A substance, such as tetraethyl lead, added to gasoline to reduce engine knock.

An·ti-Leb·a·non Range (ăn′tē-lĕb′ə-nən) A mountain range on the Syria-Lebanon border, rising to 2,815.8 m (9,232 ft).

an·ti·lep·ton (ăn′tē-lĕp′tŏn, ăn′tī-) n. The antiparticle of a lepton.

An·til·les (ăn-tĭl′ēz) The islands of the West Indies except for the Bahamas, separating the Caribbean Sea from the Atlantic Ocean and divided into the **Greater Antilles** to the N and the **Lesser Antilles** to the E.

an·ti·lock (ăn′tē-lŏk′, ăn′tī-) adj. Of or being a motor vehicle braking system that electronically monitors and adjusts individual wheel speeds during braking to prevent the wheels from locking.

an·ti·log (ăn′tē-lôg′, -lŏg′, ăn′tī-) n. An antilogarithm.

an·ti·log·a·rithm (ăn′tē-lô′gə-rĭth′əm, -lŏg′ə-, ăn′tī-) n. The number for which a given logarithm stands; for example, where log x equals y, then x is the antilogarithm of y. —**an′ti·log′a·rith′mic** adj.

an·ti·ma·cas·sar (ăn′tī-mə-kăs′ər) n. A protective covering for the backs of chairs and sofas. [ANTI- + Macassar, a brand of hair oil.]

an·ti·mag·net·ic (ăn′tē-măg-nĕt′ĭk, ăn′tī-) adj. Impervious to the effect of a magnetic field; resistant to magnetization.

an·ti·ma·lar·i·al (ăn′tē-mə-lâr′ē-əl, ăn′tī-) adj. Preventing or relieving the symptoms of malaria. ❖ n. A drug used to treat malaria.

an·ti·mat·ter (ăn′tī-măt′ər, ăn′tī-) n. A form of matter that is identical to ordinary matter except that it is composed of antielectrons, antiprotons, and antineutrons.

an·ti·mere (ăn′tī-mîr′) n. A part in the body of a bilaterally or radially symmetric animal that corresponds to an opposite or similar part. —**an′ti·mer′ic** (-mĕr′ĭk) adj.

an·ti·me·tab·o·lite (ăn′tē-mĭ-tăb′ə-līt′, ăn′tī-) n. A substance that closely resembles an essential metabolite and therefore interferes with physiological reactions involving it. —**an′ti·met′a·bol′ic** (-mĕt′ə-bŏl′ĭk) adj.

an·ti·mi·cro·bi·al (ăn′tē-mī-krō′bē-əl, ăn′tī-) also **an·ti·mi·cro·bic** (-bĭk) adj. Capable of destroying or inhibiting the growth of microorganisms. —**an′ti·mi′cro′bial** n.

an·ti·mis·sile (ăn′tē-mĭs′əl, ăn′tī-) adj. Designed to intercept and destroy another missile in flight: an antimissile missile.

an·ti·mo·ni·al (ăn′tē-mō′nē-əl) adj. Of or containing antimony. ❖ n. A medicine containing antimony.

an·ti·mo·ny (ăn′tə-mō′nē) n. Symbol **Sb** An element having several allotropes, the most common of which is a brittle, silver-white crystalline metal. It is used in alloys, esp. with lead in battery plates, and in flame-proofing compounds. Atomic number 51; atomic weight 121.76; melting point 630.5°C; boiling point 1,380°C; specific gravity 6.691; valence 3, 5. See table at **element**. [ME antimonie < Med.Lat. antimōnium, perh. < Ar. al-'iṯmid : al-, the + 'iṯmid, antimony (perh. < Gk. stimmi; see STIBINE).]

an·ti·ne·o·plas·tic (ăn′tē-nē′ə-plăs′tĭk, ăn′tī-) adj. Inhibiting or preventing the growth or development of malignant cells. —**an′ti·ne′o·plas′tic** n.

an·ti·neu·tri·no (ăn′tē-nōō-trē′nō, -nyōō-, ăn′tī-) n., pl. **-nos** The antiparticle of the neutrino.

an·ti·neu·tron (ăn′tē-nōō′trŏn, -nyōō′-, ăn′tī-) n. The antiparticle of the neutron.

an·ti·node (ăn′tī-nōd′) n. For a standing wave, the region or point of maximum amplitude between adjacent nodes.

an·ti·nome (ăn′tə-nōm′) n. One that is contradictory or opposite to another. [ANTI- + Gk. nomos, law; see ANTINOMY.]

an·ti·no·mi·an (ăn′tə-nō′mē-ən) n. An adherent of antinomianism. ❖ adj. **1.** Of or relating to antinomianism. **2.** Opposed to the fixed meaning or universality of moral law. [< Med.Lat. Antinomī, antinomians, pl. of antinomus, opposed to the moral law :

Gk. anti-, anti- + Gk. nomos, law; see **nem-** in App.]

an·ti·no·mi·an·ism (ăn′tī-nō′mē-ə-nĭz′əm) n. **1.** Theology The doctrine or belief that the Gospel frees Christians from obedience to any law, whether scriptural, civil, or moral, and that salvation is attained solely through faith and divine grace. **2.** The belief that moral laws are relative rather than fixed or universal.

an·tin·o·my (ăn-tĭn′ə-mē) n., pl. **-mies 1.** Contradiction or opposition, esp. between two laws or rules. **2.** A contradiction between equally reasonable principles or conclusions; a paradox. [Lat. antinomia < Gk. antinomiā : anti-, anti- + nomos, law; see **nem-** in App.] —**an′ti·nom′ic** (ăn′tī-nŏm′ĭk) adj.

an·ti·nov·el (ăn′tē-nŏv′əl, ăn′tī-) n. A fictional work that lacks traditional elements of the novel, such as a coherent plot. —**an′ti·nov′el·ist** n.

an·ti·nu·cle·ar (ăn′tē-nōō′klē-ər, -nyōō′-, ăn′tī-) adj. **1.** Opposing the production or use of nuclear power or nuclear weaponry. **2.** Reacting with the components of a cell nucleus.

an·ti·nu·cle·on (ăn′tē-nōō′klē-ŏn′, -nyōō′-, ăn′tī-) n. The antiparticle of a nucleon.

an·ti·nuke (ăn′tē-nōōk′, -nyōōk′, ăn′tī-) adj. Antinuclear. —**an′ti·nuk′er** n.

An·ti·och (ăn′tē-ŏk′) **1.** An ancient town of Phrygia N of present-day Antalya, Turkey. **2.** See **Antakya**. **3.** A city of W CA NE of Oakland on the San Joaquin R. Pop. 90,532.

An·ti·o·chus (ăn-tī′ə-kəs) A Seleucid dynasty ruling in Syria (280–264 B.C.), including **Antiochus III** (242–187, ruled 223–187), known as "the Great," who conquered much of Asia Minor before 190.

an·ti·ox·i·dant (ăn′tē-ŏk′sĭ-dənt, ăn′tī-) n. **1.** A chemical compound or substance that inhibits oxidation. **2.** A substance, such as vitamin E or beta carotene, thought to protect body cells from the damaging effects of oxidation.

an·ti·par·ti·cle (ăn′tē-pär′tĭ-kəl, ăn′tī-) n. A subatomic particle, such as an antiproton, having the same mass, lifetime, and spin as its corresponding particle but having the opposite electric charge, intrinsic parity, and direction of magnetic moment.

an·ti·pas·to (ăn′tē-päs′tō, ăn′tī-) n., pl. **-tos** or **-ti** (-tē) An appetizer usu. consisting of an assortment of foods, such as smoked meats, cheese, fish, and vegetables. [Ital. : anti-, before (< Lat. ante-; see ANTE-) + pasto, food (< Lat. pāstus, p. part. of pāscere, to feed; see **pā-** in App.]

An·tip·a·ter (ăn-tĭp′ə-tər) 398?–319 B.C. Macedonian general and regent (334–323 and 321–319).

an·tip·a·thet·ic (ăn-tĭp′ə-thĕt′ĭk) also **an·tip·a·thet·i·cal** (-ĭ-kəl) adj. **1a.** Having or showing a strong aversion or repugnance. **b.** Opposed in nature or character; antagonistic: antipathetic factions. **2.** Causing a feeling of antipathy; repugnant. —**an′tip′a·thet′i·cal·ly** adv.

an·tip·a·thy (ăn-tĭp′ə-thē) n., pl. **-thies 1.** A strong feeling of aversion or repugnance. **2.** An object of aversion. [Lat. antipathīa < Gk. antipatheia < antipathēs, of opposite feelings : anti-, anti- + pathos, feeling; see PATHOS.]

an·ti·pe·ri·od·ic (ăn′tē-pîr′ē-ŏd′ĭk, ăn′tī-) adj. Preventing regular recurrence of disease symptoms, as in malaria. —**an′ti·pe′ri·od′ic** n.

an·ti·per·son·nel (ăn′tē-pûr′sə-nĕl′, ăn′tī-) adj. Designed to inflict death or bodily injury rather than material destruction: antipersonnel grenades.

an·ti·per·spi·rant (ăn′tē-pûr′spər-ənt, ăn′tī-) n. An astringent preparation for decreasing perspiration. —**an′ti·per′spi·rant** adj.

an·ti·phlo·gis·tic (ăn′tē-flō-jĭs′tĭk, ăn′tī-) adj. Reducing inflammation or fever; anti-inflammatory. —**an′ti·phlo·gis′tic** n.

an·ti·phon (ăn′tə-fŏn′) n. **1.** A liturgical text sung responsively. **2.** A short liturgical text sung responsively preceding or following a psalm or canticle. **3.** A response; a reply. [LLat. antiphōna, sung responses. See ANTHEM.]

an·tiph·o·nal (ăn-tĭf′ə-nəl) adj. **1.** Of or like an antiphon. **2.** Responsive, as in antiphony. **3.** Occurring or responding in turns; alternating. ❖ n. An antiphonary. —**an·tiph′o·nal·ly** adv.

an·tiph·o·nar·y (ăn-tĭf′ə-nĕr′ē) n., pl. **-ies** A bound collection of antiphons, esp. of the Divine Office.

an·tiph·o·ny (ăn-tĭf′ə-nē) n., pl. **-nies 1.** Responsive or antiphonal singing or chanting. **2.** A composition that is sung responsively; an antiphon. **3.** A responsive or reciprocal interchange, as of ideas or opinions.

an·tiph·ra·sis (ăn-tĭf′rə-sĭs) n. The ironic or humorous use of a word or phrase in a sense contrary to its normal meaning, as in a babe of 40 years. [LLat. < Gk. < antiphrazein, to express by the opposite : anti-, anti- + phrazein, to speak; see PHRASE.]

an·tip·o·dal (ăn-tĭp′ə-dəl) adj. **1.** Of, on, or relating to the opposite side or sides of the earth. **2.** Diametrically opposed; exactly opposite.

an·tip·ode (ăn′tĭ-pōd′) n. A direct or diametrical opposite. [Back-formation < ANTIPODES.]

an·tip·o·des (ăn-tĭp′ə-dēz′) pl.n. **1.** Any two places or regions that are on diametrically opposite sides of the earth. **2.** (used with a sing. or pl. verb) The exact opposite or contrary of something; an antipode. [ME, people with feet opposite ours < Lat. < Gk. < pl. of antipous, with the feet opposite : anti-, anti- + pous, pod-, foot; see **ped-** in App.] **—an•tip′o•de′an** *adj.*

Antipodes 1. Australia and New Zealand. Usu. used informally. 2. A group of rocky islands of the S Pacific Ocean SE of New Zealand; so named by 19th-cent. British sailors because the islands are diametrically opposite Greenwich, England.

an•ti•pope (ăn′tĭ-pōp′) *n.* A person claiming to be or elected pope in opposition to the one chosen by church law, as during a schism. [ME < OFr. *antipape* < Med.Lat. *antipāpa* : Lat. *anti-*, anti- + *pāpa*, pope; see POPE.]

an•ti•pro•ton (ăn′tē-prō′tŏn′, ăn′tī-) *n.* The antiparticle of the proton.

an•ti•pru•rit•ic (ăn′tē-prŏo-rĭt′ĭk, ăn′tī-) *adj.* Preventing or relieving itching: *an antipruritic agent.* **—an′ti•pru•rit′ic** *n.*

an•ti•psy•chot•ic (ăn′tē-sī-kŏt′ĭk, ăn′tī-) *adj.* Counteracting or diminishing the symptoms of psychotic disorders. ❖ *n.* An antipsychotic medication.

an•ti•py•ret•ic (ăn′tē-pī-rĕt′ĭk, ăn′tī-) *adj.* Reducing fever. ❖ *n.* A medication that reduces fever. **—an′ti•py•re′sis** (-rē′sĭs) *n.*

an•ti•py•rine (ăn′tē-pī′rēn) *n.* A toxic white powder, $C_{11}H_{12}N_2O$, used in medicine as a topical analgesic. [Orig. a trademark.]

an•ti•quar•i•an (ăn′tĭ-kwâr′ē-ən) *adj.* 1. Of or relating to the study or collecting of antiquities. 2. Dealing in or having to do with old or rare books. ❖ *n.* One who studies, collects, or deals in antiquities. **—an′ti•quar′i•an•ism** *n.*

an•ti•quark (ăn′tē-kwôrk′, ăn′tī-) *n.* The antiparticle of a quark.

an•ti•quar•y (ăn′tĭ-kwĕr′ē) *n., pl.* **-ies** An antiquarian. [Lat. *antīquārius* < *antīquus*, old. See ANTIQUE.]

an•ti•quate (ăn′tĭ-kwāt′) *tr.v.* **-quat•ed, -quat•ing, -quates** 1. To make obsolete or old-fashioned. 2. To antique. [LLat. *antīquāre*, *antīquāt-*, to make old < Lat., to leave in an old state < *antīquus*, old. See ANTIQUE.] **—an′ti•qua′tion** *n.*

an•ti•quat•ed (ăn′tĭ-kwā′tĭd) *adj.* 1. Too old to be fashionable, suitable, or useful; outmoded. See Syns at **old.** 2. Very old; aged. **—an′ti•quat′ed•ness** *n.*

an•tique (ăn-tēk′) *adj.* 1. Belonging to, made in, or typical of an earlier period. See Syns at **old.** 2. Of, from, or characteristic of ancient times, esp. of ancient Greece or Rome. 3. Of or dealing in antiques. 4. Old-fashioned: *an antique appearance.* ❖ *n.* 1. An object, esp. a piece of furniture, esteemed for its age. 2. The style or manner of ancient times. ❖ *v.* **-tiqued, -tiqu•ing, -tiques** *—tr.* To give the appearance of an antique to: *antique an oak chest.* *—intr.* To hunt or shop for antiques. [Fr. < Lat. *antīquus.* See **ant-** in App.] **—an•tique′ly** *adv.* **—an•tique′ness** *n.*

an•tiqu•er (ăn-tē′kər) *n.* One who treats or finishes new furniture so as to make it appear antique.

an•tiq•ui•ty (ăn-tĭk′wĭ-tē) *n., pl.* **-ties** 1. Ancient times, esp. the times preceding the Middle Ages. 2. The people, esp. the writers and artisans, of ancient times. 3. The quality of being old or ancient; considerable age: *art of great antiquity.* 4. Something, such as an object or a relic, from ancient times. Often used in the plural.

an•ti•ra•chit•ic (ăn′tē-rə-kĭt′ĭk, ăn′tī-) *adj.* Curing or preventing rickets: *antirachitic drugs.* **—an′ti•ra•chit′ic** *n.*

an•ti•re•jec•tion (ăn′tē-rĭ-jĕk′shən, ăn′tī-) *adj.* Preventing rejection of a transplanted tissue or organ.

an•ti-roll bar *n.* See **anti-sway bar.**

An•ti•sa•na (ăn′tĭ-sä′nə) An active volcano, c. 5,760 m (18,885 ft), of N-central Ecuador in the Andes SE of Quito.

an•ti•sat•el•lite (ăn′tē-săt′l-īt′, ăn′tī-) *adj.* Directed against enemy satellites: *antisatellite weapons.*

an•ti•scor•bu•tic (ăn′tē-skôr-byŏo′tĭk, ăn′tī-) *adj.* Curing or preventing scurvy. **—an′ti•scor•bu′tic** *n.*

an•ti•se•cre•to•ry (ăn′tē-sĭ-krē′tə-rē, ăn′tī-) *adj.* Inhibiting or decreasing secretion, esp. gastric secretions. **—an′ti•se•cre′to•ry** *n.*

an•ti-Sem•ite (ăn′tē-sĕm′īt′, ăn′tī-) *n.* One who discriminates against or is hostile or prejudiced toward Jews. **—an′ti-Se•mit′ic** (-sə-mĭt′ĭk) *adj.*

an•ti-Sem•i•tism (ăn′tē-sĕm′ĭ-tĭz′əm, ăn′tī-) *n.* 1. Hostility or prejudice toward Jews or Judaism. 2. Discrimination against Jews.

an•ti•sense (ăn′tē-sĕns′, ăn′tī-) *adj.* Of or relating to a nucleotide sequence of DNA or RNA that is complementary to and capable of inactivating a specific messenger RNA molecule.

an•ti•sep•sis (ăn′tĭ-sĕp′sĭs) *n.* Destruction of disease-causing microorganisms to prevent infection.

an•ti•sep•tic (ăn′tĭ-sĕp′tĭk) *adj.* 1. Of, relating to, or producing antisepsis. 2. Capable of preventing infection by inhibiting the growth of microorganisms. 3. Thoroughly clean; aseptic. See Syns at **clean.** 4. Of or associated with the use of antiseptics. 5a. Devoid of enlivening or enriching qualities. b. Free of disturbing or unpleasant features; sanitized: *an antiseptic version of history.* ❖ *n.* A substance that inhibits the growth of disease-causing microorganisms. **—an′ti•sep′ti•cal•ly** *adv.*

an•ti•se•rum (ăn′tĭ-sîr′əm) *n., pl.* **-se•rums** or **-se•ra** (-sîr′ə) Human or animal serum containing antibodies that are specific for one or more antigens.

an•ti•smok•ing (ăn′tē-smō′kĭng, ăn′tī-) *adj.* Opposed to or prohibiting the smoking of tobacco, esp. in public.

an•ti•so•cial (ăn′tē-sō′shəl, ăn′tī-) *adj.* 1. Shunning the society of others; not sociable. 2. Hostile to or disruptive of the established social order; violating accepted mores. 3. Antagonistic toward or disrespectful of others; rude. **—an′ti•so′cial•ly** *adv.*

antisocial personality disorder *n.* A personality disorder characterized by chronic antisocial behavior and violation of the law and the rights of others.

an•ti•spas•mod•ic (ăn′tē-spăz-mŏd′ĭk, ăn′tī-) *adj.* Relieving or preventing spasms, esp. of smooth muscle. ❖ *n.* An antispasmodic agent.

an•ti•stat•ic (ăn′tē-stăt′ĭk, ăn′tī-) also **an•ti•stat** (-stăt′) *adj.* Preventing or inhibiting the buildup of static electricity. **—an′ti•stat′ic** *n.*

An•tis•the•nes (ăn-tĭs′thə-nēz′) 444?–371? B.C. Greek philosopher who founded the Cynic school.

an•tis•tro•phe (ăn-tĭs′trə-fē) *n.* 1. The second stanza, and those like it, in a poem with alternating stanzas in contrasting metrical form. 2. The second division of the triad of a Pindaric ode, having the same form as the strophe. 3a. The choral movement in classical Greek drama in the opposite direction from that of the strophe. b. The part of a choral ode sung while this movement is executed. [LLat. *antistrophē*, antistrophe of Gk. tragedy < Gk., strophic correspondence < *antistrephein*, to turn back : *anti-*, back; see ANTI- + *strephein*, to turn; see STROPHE.] **—an′ti•stroph′ic** (ăn′tĭ-strŏf′ĭk) *adj.* **—an′ti•stroph′i•cal•ly** *adv.*

an•ti-sway bar (ăn′tē-swā′, ăn′tī-) *n.* A metal bar connecting the left and right suspension systems at the front or rear of an automobile or a truck, used to stabilize the chassis against sway.

an•ti•ter•ror•ist (ăn′tē-tĕr′ər-ĭst, ăn′tī-) *adj.* Intended to prevent or counteract terrorism. **—an′ti•ter′ror•ism** *n.*

an•tith•e•sis (ăn-tĭth′ĭ-sĭs) *n., pl.* **-ses** (-sēz′) 1. Direct contrast; opposition. 2. The direct or exact opposite. 3a. A figure of speech in which contrasting ideas are juxtaposed in balanced or parallel grammatical structures. b. The second and contrasting part of such a juxtaposition. 4. The second stage of the Hegelian dialectic, representing the opposite of the thesis. [LLat. < Gk. < *antitithenai*, to oppose : *anti-*, anti- + *tithenai*, *the-*, to set; see **dhē-** in App.]

an•ti•thet•i•cal (ăn′tĭ-thĕt′ĭ-kəl) also **an•ti•thet•ic** (-ĭk) *adj.* 1. Of, relating to, or expressing antithesis. 2. Diametrically opposed. [< Med.Lat. *antitheticus* < Gk. *antithetikos* < *antithenai*, to oppose. See ANTITHESIS.] **—an′ti•thet′i•cal•ly** *adv.*

an•ti•tox•ic (ăn′tē-tŏk′sĭk, ăn′tī-) *adj.* 1. Counteracting a toxin or poison. 2. Of, relating to, or containing an antitoxin.

an•ti•tox•in (ăn′tē-tŏk′sĭn, ăn′tī-) *n.* 1. An antibody formed in response to and capable of neutralizing a specific biological toxin. 2. An animal or human antitoxic serum used to prevent or treat diseases caused by biological toxins, such as tetanus and diphtheria.

an•ti•trade (ăn′tĭ-trād′) *n.* The westerly winds above the surface trade winds of the tropics, which become the prevailing westerly winds of the middle latitudes. Often used in the plural.

an•ti•trust (ăn′tĭ-trŭst′, ăn′tī-) *adj.* Opposing or intended to regulate business monopolies, such as trusts or cartels, esp. in the interest of promoting competition.

an•ti•tus•sive (ăn′tē-tŭs′ĭv, ăn′tī-) *adj.* Capable of relieving or suppressing coughing. [ANTI- + Lat. *tussis*, cough; see TUSSIS + -IVE.] **—an′ti•tus′sive** *n.*

an•ti•type (ăn′tĭ-tīp′) *n.* 1. One that is foreshadowed by or identified with an earlier symbol or type. 2. An opposite or contrasting type. [Med.Lat. *antitypus* < L.Gk. *antitupos*, copy, antitype < Gk., corresponding, representing : *anti-*, equal to, like; see ANTI- + *tupos*, print, impression.] **—an′ti•typ′i•cal** (-tĭp′ĭ-kəl) *adj.*

an•ti-u•to•pi•a (ăn′tē-yōo-tō′pē-ə, ăn′tī-) *n.* 1. An imaginary place or society marked by misery and oppression; a dystopia. 2. A work describing an anti-utopia. **—an′ti-u•to′pi•an** *adj. & n.*

an•ti•ven•in (ăn′tē-vĕn′ĭn, ăn′tī-) *n.* 1. An antitoxin active against animal or insect venom. 2. An animal serum containing antivenins, used to treat poisoning caused by animal or insect venom. [ANTI- + VEN(OM) + -IN.]

an•ti•vi•rus (ăn′tē-vī′rəs, ăn′tī-) *n.* A software program designed to identify and remove a computer virus. **—an′ti•vi′ral** (-rəl) *adj.*

an•ti•vi•ta•min (ăn′tē-vī′tə-mĭn, ăn′tī-) *n.* A substance that destroys or inhibits the metabolic action of a vitamin.

an•ti•white also **an•ti•white** (ăn′tē-hwīt′, wīt′, ăn′tī-) *adj.* Hostile to or prejudiced against white people.

ant•ler (ănt′lər) *n.* One of a pair of bony deciduous growths, usu. elongated and branched, on the head of a member of the deer family. [ME *aunteler* < OFr. *antoillier* < VLat. **antoculāre*, *anteoculāre* : Lat. *ante-*, ante- + Lat. *oculāris*, of the eye; see OCULAR.] **—ant′lered** *adj.*

Ant•li•a (ănt′lē-ə) *n.* A constellation in the Southern Hemisphere near Hydra and Vela. [Lat. *antlia*, pump < Gk. *antliā*, ship's hold, bilge water < *antlos*.]

ant lion *n.* 1. Any of various insects of the family Myrmeleontidae, the adults of which resemble dragonflies. 2. The large-jawed larva of the ant lion, which digs a conical crater in the sand to trap insects for food.

An•to•ni•nus Pius (ăn′tə-nī′nəs) A.D. 86–161. Emperor of

antler
top to bottom: roe deer, elk, and moose antlers

ă	pat	oi	boy
ā	pay	ou	out
âr	care	ŏo	took
ä	father	ōo	boot
ĕ	pet	ŭ	cut
ē	be	ûr	urge
ĭ	pit	th	thin
ī	pie	th	this
îr	pier	hw	which
ŏ	pot	zh	vision
ō	toe	ə	about,
ô	paw		item

Stress marks:
′ (primary);
′ (secondary), as in
lexicon (lĕk′sĭ-kŏn′)

Rome (138–161) who was the successor of Hadrian.

An•to•ni•on•i (ăn-tō′nē-ō′nē), **Michelangelo** b. 1912. Italian filmmaker whose works include *L'Avventura* (1959).

An•to•ni•us (ăn-tō′nē-əs), **Marcus** See **Mark Antony.**

an•to•no•ma•sia (ăn′tə-nə-mā′zhə) *n.* **1.** The substitution of a title or epithet for a proper name. **2.** The substitution of a personal name for a common noun to designate a member of a group, as in calling a traitor a "Benedict Arnold." [Lat. < Gk. *antonomazein*, to name instead : *anti-*, instead of; see ANTI- + *onomazein*, to name (< *onoma*, name; see **nŏ-men-** in App.).]

an•to•nym (ăn′tə-nĭm′) *n.* A word having a meaning opposite to that of another word: *The word* wet *is an antonym of the word* dry. [ANT(I)- + –ONYM.] —**an′to•nym′ic** *adj.* —**an•ton′y•mous** (ăn-tŏn′ə-məs) *adj.* —**an•ton′y•my** *n.*

an•tre (ăn′tər) *n.* A cavern; a cave. [Fr. < Lat. *antrum.* See AN-TRUM.]

an•trorse (ăn′trôrs′) *adj. Biology* Directed forward and upward, as the hairs on certain plant stems. [NLat. *antrōrsum* < Lat. *anterior*, before (perh. after *intrōrsum*, inwards < *interior*, inside). See ANTERIOR.] —**an′trorse′ly** *adv.*

an•trum (ăn′trəm) *n., pl.* **-tra** (-trə) **1.** A cavity or chamber, esp. one in a bone. **2.** Either of the sinuses in the bones of the upper jaw, opening into the nasal cavity. [LLat., cavity in the body < Lat., cave < Gk. *antron.*] —**an′tral** *adj.*

ant•sy (ănt′sē) *adj.* **-si•er, -si•est** *Slang* **1.** Restless or impatient; fidgety: *The wait made the children antsy.* **2.** Nervous; apprehensive. [Perh. < the incessant motions of ants.]

An•tung (än′tŏŏng′) See **Dandong.**

Ant•werp (ănt′twərp) also **An•vers** (än-vâr′) A city of N Belgium on the Scheldt R. N of Brussels; a center of the diamond industry since the 15th cent. Pop. 490,524.

A•nu•bis (ə-nōō′bĭs, ə-nyōō′-) *n. Mythology* The jackal-headed Egyptian god who conducted the dead to judgment.

a•nu•ran (ə-nŏŏr′ən, ə-nyŏŏr′-) *n.* See **salientian.** [< NLat. *Anūra*, order of frogs and toads : A–[1] + Gk. *ourā*, tail; see ors- in App.]

an•u•re•sis (ăn′yə-rē′sĭs) *n.* **1.** Inability to urinate. **2.** See anuria. [A–[1] + Gk. *ourēsis*, urination (< *ourein*, to urinate < *ouron*, urine).] —**an′u•ret′ic** (-rĕt′ĭk) *adj.*

a•nu•ri•a (ə-nŏŏr′ē-ə, ə-nyŏŏr′-) *n.* The absence of urine formation. —**a•nu′ric** (ə-nŏŏr′ĭk, ə-nyŏŏr′-) *adj.*

a•nu•rous (ə-nŏŏr′əs, ə-nyŏŏr′-) *adj.* Having no tail; tailless.

a•nus (ā′nəs) *n., pl.* **a•nus•es** The opening at the lower end of the alimentary canal through which solid waste is eliminated. [ME < Lat. *ānus*, ring, anus.]

an•vil (ăn′vĭl) *n.* **1a.** A heavy block of iron or steel with a smooth, flat top on which metals are shaped by hammering. **b.** Something resembling an anvil. **2.** The fixed jaw in a set of calipers. **3.** *Anatomy* See **incus** 1. [ME *anfilt* < OE. See **pel-**[2] in App.]

anx•i•e•ty (ăng-zī′ĭ-tē) *n., pl.* **-ties 1a.** A state of uneasiness and apprehension. **b.** A cause of anxiety: *Air travel can be an anxiety.* **2.** *Psychology* A state of apprehension, uncertainty, and fear resulting from the anticipation of a threatening event or situation. **3.** Eager, often agitated desire: *anxiety to make a good impression.* [Lat. *ānxietās* < *ānxius*, anxious. See ANXIOUS.]

anvil
blacksmith forming
horseshoe on an anvil

SYNONYMS *anxiety, worry, care, concern, solicitude* These nouns refer to troubled states of mind. *Anxiety* suggests feelings of fear and apprehension: *"Resentment and rage over this devious form of manipulation cannot surface in the child. . . . At the most, he will experience feelings of anxiety, shame, insecurity, and helplessness"* (Alice Miller). *Worry* implies persistent doubt or fear: *"Having come to a decision the lad felt a sense of relief from the worry that had haunted him"* (Edgar Rice Burroughs). *Care* denotes a state of mind burdened by responsibilities: *The old man's face was worn with care.* *Concern* stresses serious thought combined with emotion: *"Concern for man himself and his fate must always form the chief interest of all technical endeavors"* (Albert Einstein). *Solicitude* is active and sometimes excessive concern for another's well-being: *"Animosity had given way . . . to worried solicitude for Lindbergh's safety"* (Warren Trabant).

anxiety attack *n.* See **panic attack.**

anx•i•o•lyt•ic (ăng′zē-ō-lĭt′ĭk, -sē-, ăngk′sē-) *adj.* Preventing or reducing anxiety; antianxiety. ❖ *n.* An antianxiety medication; a tranquilizer. [ANXI(ETY) + –LYTIC.]

anx•ious (ăngk′shəs, ăng′shəs) *adj.* **1.** Uneasy and apprehensive about something uncertain; worried. **2.** Attended with, showing, or causing anxiety: *an anxious night.* **3.** *Usage Problem* Eagerly or earnestly desirous. [< Lat. *ānxius* < *angere*, to torment.] —**anx′ious•ly** *adv.* —**anx′ious•ness** *n.*

USAGE NOTE *Anxious* has a long history of use roughly as a synonym for *eager*, but many prefer that *anxious* be used only when its subject is worried or uneasy about the anticipated event. Fifty-two percent of the Usage Panel rejects *anxious* in the sentence *We are anxious to see the new show of British sculpture at the museum.* But general adoption of *anxious* to mean "eager" is understandable, at least in colloquial discourse, since it provides a means of adding emotional urgency to an assertion. In this way, it resembles the informal adjective *dying* in sentences such as *I'm dying to see your new baby.*

ao dai

an•y (ĕn′ē) *adj.* **1.** One, some, every, or all without specification: *Are there any messages for me? Any child would love that.* **2.** Exceeding normal limits, as in size or duration: *I never stay for any length of time.* ❖ *pron.* (*used with a sing. or pl. verb*) Any one or more persons, things, or quantities: *Any of those books is suitable.* ❖ *adv.* To any degree or extent; at all: *didn't feel any better.* [ME *ani* < OE *ænig.* See **oi-no-** in App.]

USAGE NOTE When used as a pronoun, *any* can take either a singular or plural verb, depending on how it is construed: *Any of these books is suitable* (that is, *any one*). *But are any* (that is, *some*) *of them available?* • The construction *of any* is often used in informal contexts to mean "of all," as in *He is the best known of any living playwright.* In an earlier survey this example was unacceptable in writing to 67 percent of the Usage Panel. • *Any* is also used to mean "at all" before a comparative adjective or adverb in questions and negative sentences: *Is she any better?* This usage is entirely acceptable. The related use of *any* to modify a verb, as in *It didn't hurt any,* is considered informal and should be avoided in writing. See Usage Notes at **every, they.**

An•yang (än′yäng′) **1.** A city of E China NNE of Zhengzhou; one of the earliest centers of Chinese civilization. Pop. 616,803. **2.** A city of NW South Korea, a suburb of Seoul. Pop. 481,291.

an•y•bod•y (ĕn′ē-bŏd′ē, -bŭd′ē) *pron.* Any person; anyone. See Usage Notes at **anyone, every, he**[1]. ❖ *n.* A person of consequence: *Everybody who is anybody was at the party.*

an•y•how (ĕn′ē-hou′) *adv.* **1.** In whatever way or manner; however: *I'll cook it anyhow you like.* **2.** Carelessly; haphazardly. **3a.** In any case; at least: *I think they're asleep; anyhow, they're quiet.* **b.** Nevertheless: *It's crazy, but I believe it anyhow.*

an•y•more (ĕn′ē-môr′, -mōr′) *adv.* **1a.** Any longer; now: *Do they make this model anymore?* **b.** From now on: *We won't quarrel anymore.* **2.** *Chiefly Midland US* Nowadays.

REGIONAL NOTE In standard American English the word *anymore* is often found in negative sentences: *They don't live here anymore.* But *anymore* is widely found in regional American English in positive sentences with the meaning "nowadays": *"We use a gas stove anymore"* (Oklahoma informant in DARE). Its use, which appears to be spreading, is centered in the South Midland and Midwestern states, as well as in the Western states that received settlers from those areas.

an•y•one (ĕn′ē-wŭn′, -wən) *pron.* Any person.

USAGE NOTE The one-word form *anyone* is used to mean "any person." The two-word form *any one* is used to mean "whatever one (person or thing) of a group." *Anyone may join* means that admission is open to everybody. *Any one may join* means that admission is open to one person only. When followed by *of,* only *any one* can be used: *Any one* (not *anyone*) *of you may join.* • *Anyone* is often used in place of *everyone,* as in *She is the most thrifty person of anyone I know.* In an earlier survey 64 percent of the Usage Panel found this sentence unacceptable in writing. • *Anyone* and *anybody* are singular terms and always take a singular verb. See Usage Note at **they.**

an•y•place (ĕn′ē-plās′) *adv.* To, in, or at any place; anywhere.

an•y•thing (ĕn′ē-thĭng′) *pron.* Any object, occurrence, or matter whatever. ❖ *adv.* To any degree or extent; at all: *They aren't anything like last year's team.* ❖ *n.* Something or someone of importance: *"Jeremy never was anything"* (Anne Tyler). —**idioms: anything but** By no means; not at all: *anything but happy.* **anything goes** Anything is permissible or likely to be tolerated.

an•y•time (ĕn′ē-tīm′) *adv.* At any time.

an•y•way (ĕn′ē-wā′) *adv.* **1.** In any way or manner whatever: *Do the job anyway you can.* **2.** In any case; at least: *I don't know why; anyway, it's gone.* **3.** Nevertheless; regardless: *It rained but they played anyway.*

an•y•ways (ĕn′ē-wāz′) *adv. Nonstandard* In any case.

an•y•where (ĕn′ē-hwâr′, -wâr′) *adv.* **1.** To, in, or at any place. **2.** To any extent or degree; at all: *not anywhere near completion.* **3.** Used to indicate limits of variation: *anywhere from 300 to 400.* ❖ *n.* Any place whatsoever.

an•y•wise (ĕn′ē-wīz′) *adv. Nonstandard* In any case.

An•zac (ăn′zăk′) *n.* A soldier from New Zealand or Australia. [A(ustralian and) N(ew) Z(ealand) A(rmy) C(orps).] —**An′zac′** *adj.*

An•zi•o (ăn′zē-ō, än′tsyō) A town of central Italy on the Tyrrhenian Sea SSE of Rome; site of Allied landing (1944). Pop. 27,094.

a/o *abbr.* account of

ao dai (ou′ dī′, ô′) *n., pl.* **ao dais** The traditional dress of Vietnamese women, consisting of a long tunic slit on the sides and worn over loose trousers. [Vietnamese *áo dài* : *áo,* tunic (< M Chin. ʔ*aw,* padded coat) + *dài,* long (< M Chin. *daj, thaj*).]

AOH *abbr.* Ancient Order of Hibernians

A-OK also **A-O•kay** (ā′ō-kā′) *adj. Informal* Perfectly all right: *It's A-OK with me if you want to leave.* —**A-OK** *adv. & n.*

Ao•mo•ri (ou′mə-rē, ä′ō-môr′ē) A city of N Honshu, Japan, on **Aomori Bay.** Pop. 288,291.

A-one also **A-1** (ā′wŭn′) *adj. Informal* First-class; excellent. [< classification for ships in The Lloyd's Register of Shipping.]

AOR *abbr.* **1.** album-oriented radio **2.** album-oriented rock

A·o·rang·i (ä′ō-räng′gē) See Mount **Cook.**

a·o·rist (ā′ər-ĭst) *n.* **1.** A verb form in some languages, such as Classical Greek, that expresses action without indicating its completion or continuation. **2.** A verb form in some languages, such as Classical Greek, that in the indicative mood expresses past action. [< Gk. *aoristos,* indefinite, aorist t. : *a-,* not; see A–¹ + *horistos,* definable (< *horizein,* to define; see HORIZON).]

a·or·ta (ā-ôr′tə) *n., pl.* **-tas** or **-tae** (-tē) The main trunk of the systemic arteries, carrying blood from the left side of the heart to the arteries of all limbs and organs except the lungs. [NLat. < Gk. *āortē* < *āeirein,* to raise.] —**a·or′tal, a·or′tic** *adj.*

aortic arch *n.* One of a series of paired arteries in a vertebrate embryo that connects the ventral arterial system to the dorsal arterial system.

a·ou·dad (ä′ōō-dăd′, ou′dăd′) *n.* A wild sheep (*Ammotragus lervia*) of northern Africa having long curved horns and beardlike hair on the neck and chest. [Fr. < Berber *audad.*]

AP *abbr.* **1.** also **A/P** accounts payable **2.** advanced placement **3.** airplane **4.** air police **5.** american plan **6.** antipersonnel **7.** Associated Press

ap–¹ *pref.* Variant of **ad–** 1.

ap–² *pref.* Variant of **apo–.**

APA *abbr.* **1.** American Philological Association **2.** American Philosophical Association **3.** American Psychiatric Association **4.** American Psychological Association

a·pace (ə-pās′) *adv.* **1.** Rapidly; swiftly. **2.** So as to keep up the requisite momentum; abreast. [ME *a pas* < OFr. : *a,* to (< Lat. *ad*) + *pas,* step; see PACE¹.]

a·pache (ə-päsh′, ä-päsh′) *n., pl.* **a·paches** (ə-päsh′, ä-päsh′) **1.** A member of the Parisian underworld. **2.** A thug; a ruffian. [Fr. < *Apache,* Apache Indian. See APACHE.]

A·pach·e (ə-păch′ē) *n., pl.* **Apache** or **-es 1.** A member of a Native American people inhabiting the southwest United States and northern Mexico. **2.** Any of the Apachean languages of the Apache. [Am.Sp., prob. < Zuni *?aapaču,* pl. of *paču,* Navajo.]

A·pach·e·an (ə-päch′ē-ən) *n.* **1.** The subgroup of Athabaskan comprising the languages of the Apache and Navajo. **2.** A speaker of any of these languages.

Ap·a·lach·i·co·la (ăp′ə-lăch′ĭ-kō′lə) A river of NW FL flowing c. 180 km (112 mi) from the GA border to **Apalachicola Bay,** an inlet of the Gulf of Mexico.

ap·a·nage (ăp′ə-nĭj) *n.* Variant of **appanage.**

Ap·a·po·ris (ä′pə-pôr′ĕs, -pôr′) A river rising in S-central Colombia and flowing c. 805 km (500 mi) to the Japurá R.

ap·a·re·jo (ăp′ə-rā′hō, -rä′ō) *n., pl.* **-jos** *Southwestern US* A packsaddle made of a stuffed leather pad. [Am.Sp. < Sp., equipment < *aparejar,* to prepare < VLat. **appariculāre,* see APPAREL.]

a·part (ə-pärt′) *adv.* **1a.** At a distance in place, position, or time: *two feet apart.* **b.** Away from another or others: *live apart.* **2.** In or into parts or pieces: *split apart.* **3.** One from another: *I can't tell the twins apart.* **4.** Aside or in reserve, as for a separate use or purpose: *funds set apart for the project.* **5.** As a distinct item or entity: *Quality sets it apart.* **6.** So as to except or exclude from consideration; aside: *Joking apart, I think you're crazy.* ❖ *adj.* Set apart; isolated. Used after a noun or in the predicate: *a people existing as a world apart.* [ME < OFr. *a part : a,* to (< Lat. *ad*) + *part,* side (< Lat. *pars, part-*; see PART).] —**a·part′ness** *n.*

apart from *prep.* With the exception of; besides: *Apart from a few scratches, the car was undamaged.*

a·part·heid (ə-pärt′hīt′, -hāt′) *n.* **1.** An official policy of racial segregation formerly practiced in South Africa against non-whites. **2.** Any policy or practice of separating or segregating groups. **3.** The condition of being separated from others; segregation. [Afr. : Du. *apart,* separate (< Fr. *à part,* apart; see APART) + Du. *-heid,* -hood.]

a·part·ment (ə-pärt′mənt) *n.* **1.** A room or suite designed as a residence and usu. located in a building occupied by more than one household. **2.** An apartment building: *high-rise apartments.* **3.** A room. **4.** **apartments** *Chiefly British* A suite of rooms set aside for a particular purpose or person. [Fr. *appartement* < Ital. *appartamento < appartare,* to separate < *a parte,* apart : *a,* to (< Lat. *ad*) + *parte,* side (< Lat. *pars, part-*; see PART).]

apartment building *n.* A building divided into apartments.

apartment house *n.* See **apartment building.**

ap·a·tet·ic (ăp′ə-tĕt′ĭk) *adj. Zoology* Relating to or characterized by coloration serving as natural camouflage. [Gk. *apatētikos,* deceptive < *apatētēs,* deceiver < *apateuein,* to cheat < *apatē,* deceit.]

ap·a·thet·ic (ăp′ə-thĕt′ĭk) also **ap·a·thet·i·cal** (-ĭ-kəl) *adj.* **1.** Lacking interest or concern; indifferent. **2.** Lacking emotion; unresponsive. [< APATHY, on the model of PATHETIC.] —**ap′a·thet′i·cal·ly** *adv.*

ap·a·thy (ăp′ə-thē) *n.* **1.** Lack of interest or concern, esp. in matters of general importance or appeal; indifference. **2.** Lack of emotion or feeling; impassiveness. [Lat. *apathīa < Gk. apatheia < apathēs,* without feeling : *a-,* without; see A–¹ + *pathos,* feeling.]

ap·a·tite (ăp′ə-tīt′) *n.* A natural, variously colored calcium phosphate, Ca₅(PO₄)₃(F,Cl,OH), used in the manufacture of fertilizers. [Gk. *apatē,* deceit (< its often being mistaken for other minerals).]

a·pat·o·saur (ə-păt′ə-sôr′) or **a·pat·o·sau·rus** (ə-păt′ə-**sôr′əs)** *n.* A very large herbivorous dinosaur of the genus *Apatosaurus* (formerly *Brontosaurus*) of the late Jurassic Period, having a long neck and tail and a relatively small head. [NLat. *Apatosaurus,* unreal lizard, genus name : Gk. *apatē,* untruth, lie + Gk. *sauros,* lizard.]

APB *abbr.* all points bulletin

APC *abbr.* armored personnel carrier

ape (āp) *n.* **1a.** Any of various large, tailless Old World primates of the family Pongidae, including the chimpanzee, gorilla, and orangutan. **b.** A monkey. **2.** A mimic or imitator. **3.** *Informal* A clumsy or boorish person. ❖ *tr.v.* **aped, ap·ing, apes** To mimic slavishly but often with an absurd result. See Syns at **imitate.** —*idiom:* **go ape** *Informal* To become wildly excited or enthusiastic: *went ape at the party.* [ME < OE *apa.*] —**ap′er** *n.*

A·pel·doorn (ăp′əl-dôrn′, -dōrn′, ä′pəl-) A city of E-central Netherlands N of Arnhem. Pop. 149,147.

A·pel·les (ə-pĕl′ēz) fl. 4th cent. B.C. Greek painter whose works are known only from descriptions in ancient writings.

ape-man (āp′măn′) *n.* **1.** Any of various extinct primates sometimes considered intermediate in evolution between the anthropoid apes and modern humans. Not in scientific usage. **2.** A person or creature held to combine characteristics of apes and humans.

Ap·en·nines (ăp′ə-nīnz′) A mountain system extending from NW Italy to the Strait of Messina and rising to 2,915.8 m (9,560 ft).

a·per·çu (ä′pĕr-sü′) *n., pl.* **-çus** (-sü′) **1.** A discerning perception; an insight: *"Her schmoozy but magisterial aperçus inspired widespread emulation among the young"* (Roy Blount, Jr.). **2.** A short outline or summary; a synopsis. [Fr. < p. part. of *apercevoir,* to perceive : *a-,* to (< Lat. *ad–*; see AD–) + *percevoir,* to perceive (< OFr. *perceivre*; see PERCEIVE).]

a·pe·ri·ent (ə-pîr′ē-ənt) *adj.* Gently stimulating evacuation of the bowels; laxative. ❖ *n.* A mild laxative. [Lat. *aperiēns, aperient-,* pr. part. of *aperīre,* to open.]

a·pe·ri·od·ic (ā′pîr-ē-ŏd′ĭk) *adj.* **1.** Lacking periodicity; irregular. **2.** *Physics* Without periodic vibrations. —**a′pe·ri·od′i·cal·ly** *adv.* —**a′pe·ri·o·dic′i·ty** (-ō-dĭs′ĭ-tē) *n.*

a·pé·ri·tif (ä-pĕr′ĭ-tēf′) *n.* An alcoholic drink taken before a meal. [Fr. < OFr. *aperitif,* purgative < Med.Lat. *aperitīvus < LLat. apertīvus < Lat. apertus,* p. part. of *aperīre,* to open.]

ap·er·ture (ăp′ər-chər) *n.* **1.** An opening, such as a hole, gap, or slit. **2.** A usu. adjustable opening in an optical instrument, such as a camera, that limits the amount of light that can enter. [ME < Lat. *apertūra < apertus,* p. part. of *aperīre,* to open.] —**ap′er·tur′al** *adj.*

a·pet·al·ous (ā-pĕt′l-əs) *adj.* Having no petals. —**a·pet′al·y** (ā-pĕt′l-ē) *n.*

a·pex (ā′pĕks) *n., pl.* **a·pex·es** or **a·pi·ces** (ā′pĭ-sēz′, ăp′ĭ-) **1.** The highest point; the vertex: *the apex of a hill.* **2.** The point of culmination. **3.** The usu. pointed end of an object; the tip: *the apex of a leaf.* [Lat.]

Ap·gar score (ăp′gär) *n.* A system of assessing the health of a newborn by rating heart rate, respiration, muscle tone, skin color, and response to stimuli, with a perfect score being 10. [After Virginia Apgar (1909–74), American physician.]

a·phaer·e·sis or **a·pher·e·sis** (ə-fĕr′ĭ-sĭs) *n., pl.* **-ses** (-sēz′) The loss of one or more sounds from the beginning of a word, as in *till* for *until.* [LLat. < Gk. *aphairesis < aphairein,* to take away : *apo-,* apo- + *hairein,* to take.] —**aph′ae·ret′ic** (ăf′ə-rĕt′ĭk) *adj.*

a·pha·gi·a (ə-fā′jē-ə, -jə) *n.* Loss of the ability to swallow.

aph·a·nite (ăf′ə-nīt′) *n.* A dense homogeneous rock with constituents too fine to be seen by the naked eye. [< Gk. *aphanēs,* unseen : *a-,* not; see A–¹ + *phainesthai, phan-,* to appear, passive of *phainein,* to show.] —**aph′a·nit′ic** (-nĭt′ĭk) *adj.*

a·pha·sia (ə-fā′zhə) *n.* Partial or total loss of the ability to articulate ideas or comprehend language, resulting from brain damage caused by injury or disease. [Gk. < *aphatos,* speechless : *a-,* not; see A–¹ + *phatos,* spoken, speakable (< *phanai,* to speak; see –PHASIA).] —**a·pha′si·ac′** (-zē-ăk′) *n.* —**a·pha′sic** (-zĭk, -sĭk) *adj. & n.*

a·phe·li·on (ə-fē′lē-ən, ə-fēl′yən) *n., pl.* **-li·a** (-lē-ə) The point on the orbit of a celestial body that is farthest from the sun. [< NLat. *aphēlium* : Gk. *apo-,* apo- + Gk. *hēlios,* sun; see sāwel- in App.]

a·pher·e·sis (ā′fə-rē′sĭs) *n.* **1.** *Linguistics* Variant of **aphaeresis. 2. aph·er·e·sis** (ăf′ə-rē′sĭs) *Medicine* A procedure in which blood is drawn from a donor and separated into its components, some of which are retained, such as plasma or platelets, and the remainder of which are returned by transfusion to the donor.

aph·e·sis (ăf′ĭ-sĭs) *n., pl.* **-ses** (-sēz′) The loss of an initial, usu. unstressed vowel, as in *cute* from *acute.* [Gk., a release < *aphīenai,* to let go : *apo-,* apo- + *hīenai, he-,* to send.] —**a·phet′ic** (ə-fĕt′ĭk) *adj.* —**a·phet′i·cal·ly** *adv.*

a·phid (ā′fĭd, ăf′ĭd) *n.* Any of various small soft-bodied insects of the family Aphididae that feed by sucking sap from plants. [NLat. *Aphis, Aphid-,* type genus.] —**a·phid′i·an** (ə-fĭd′ē-ən) *adj. & n.*

aphid lion *n.* The larva of any of several insects of the family Chrysopidae, such as the lacewing, that feed on aphids.

a·phis (ā′fĭs, ăf′ĭs) *n., pl.* **a·phi·des** (ā′fĭ-dēz′, ăf′ĭ-) An aphid,

aoudad
Ammotragus lervia

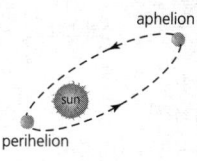

aphelion

perihelion

aphelion

esp. of the genus *Aphis*. [NLat. *Aphis*, genus name.]

a·pho·ni·a (ā-fō′nē-ə) *n.* Loss of the voice resulting from disease, injury to the vocal cords, or various psychological causes. [NLat. *aphōnia* < Gk. *aphōniā*, speechlessness < *aphōnos*, voiceless : *a-*, without; see A—¹ + *phōnē*, voice; see **bhā-** in App.] **—a·phon′ic** (ā-fŏn′ĭk, ā-fō′nĭk) *adj.*

aph·o·rism (ăf′ə-rĭz′əm) *n.* **1.** A terse statement of a truth or opinion; an adage. **2.** A brief statement of a principle. [Fr. *aphorisme* < OFr. < LLat. *aphorismus* < Gk. *aphorismos* < *aphorizein*, to delimit, define : *apo-*, apo- + *horizein*, to delimit, define; see HORIZON.] **—aph′o·rist** *n.* **—aph′o·ris′tic** (-rĭs′tĭk) *adj.* **—aph′o·ris′ti·cal·ly** *adv.*

aph·o·rize (ăf′ə-rīz′) *intr.v.* **-rized, -riz·ing, -riz·es** To express oneself in or as if in aphorisms.

a·pho·tic (ā-fō′tĭk) *adj.* **1.** Having no light. **2.** Of or relating to the region of a body of water that is not reached by sunlight and in which photosynthesis is unable to occur.

aph·ro·di·si·ac (ăf′rə-dē′zē-ăk′, -dĭz′ē-) *adj.* Arousing or intensifying sexual desire. ❖ *n.* Something, such as a drug or food, having such an effect. [Gk. *aphrodīsiakos* < *aphrodīsia*, sexual pleasures < neut. pl. of *aphrodīsios*, of Aphrodite < *Aphroditē*, Aphrodite. See APHRODITE.] **—aph′ro·di·si′a·cal** (-dī-zī′ĭ-kəl) *adj.*

aph·ro·di·te (ăf′rə-dī′tē) *n.* A brightly colored butterfly (*Argynnis aphrodite*) of North America. [< APHRODITE.]

Aphrodite *n. Greek Mythology* The goddess of love and beauty. [Gk. *Aphroditē*, prob. ult. < Phoenician *ʾaštart, Astarte (influenced by Gk. *aphros*, foam).]

API *abbr.* **1.** application programming interface **2.** Asian and Pacific Islander

A·pi·a (ə-pē′ə, ä′pē-ä′) The cap. of Samoa, on the N coast of Upolu I. Pop. 32,099.

a·pi·an (ā′pē-ən) *adj.* Of, relating to, or having the characteristics of bees. [< Lat. *apis*, bee.]

a·pi·ar·i·an (ā′pē-âr′ē-ən) *adj.* Relating to bees or the keeping and care of bees.

a·pi·a·rist (ā′pē-ə-rĭst, -ĕr′ĭst) *n.* See **beekeeper.**

a·pi·ar·y (ā′pē-ĕr′ē) *n., pl.* **-ies** A place where bees are kept, esp. a place where bees are raised for honey. [Lat. *apiārium*, beehive < *apis*, bee.]

a·pi·cal (ā′pĭ-kəl, ăp′ĭ-) *adj.* **1.** Of, relating to, located at, or constituting an apex. **2.** *Linguistics* Of, relating to, or articulated with the tip of the tongue, as (t), (d), and (s). [< Lat. *apex, apic-*, top.] **—ap′i·cal·ly** *adv.*

a·pi·ces (ā′pĭ-sēz′, ăp′ĭ-) *n.* A plural of **apex.**

a·pic·u·late (ə-pĭk′yə-lĭt) *adj.* Ending abruptly with a sharp flexible tip: *an apiculate leaf.* [< NLat. *apiculus*, sharp point, dim. of Lat. *apex, apic-*, point.]

a·pi·cul·ture (ā′pĭ-kŭl′chər) *n.* The raising and care of bees for commercial or agricultural purposes. [Lat. *apis*, bee + CULTURE.] **—a′pi·cul′tur·al** *adj.* **—a′pi·cul′tur·ist** *n.*

a·piece (ə-pēs′) *adv.* To or for each one; each: *an apple apiece.* [ME *a pece* : *a*, a; see A² + *pece*, piece; see PIECE.]

A·pis (ā′pĭs) *n.* A sacred bull of the ancient Egyptians.

ap·ish (ā′pĭsh) *adj.* **1.** Resembling an ape. **2.** Slavishly or foolishly imitative. **3.** Silly; outlandish. **—ap′ish·ly** *adv.*

a·piv·o·rous (ā-pĭv′ər-əs) *adj.* Feeding on bees. [Lat. *apis*, bee + -VOROUS.]

a·pla·cen·tal (ā′plə-sĕn′tl) *adj.* Having no placenta, as marsupials and monotremes.

ap·la·nat·ic (ăp′lə-năt′ĭk) *adj.* Of or relating to optical systems that correct for spherical aberration. [< A—¹ + Gk. *planāsthai*, to wander; see pela-² in App.]

a·plas·tic anemia (ā-plăs′tĭk) *n.* A form of anemia caused by bone marrow disease or exposure to toxic agents and impairing the capacity of the bone marrow to generate red blood cells.

a·plen·ty (ə-plĕn′tē) *adj.* In plentiful supply; abundant. **—a·plen′ty** *adv.*

ap·lite (ăp′līt′) *also* **hap·lite** (hăp′-) *n.* A fine-grained, light-colored granitic rock consisting primarily of orthoclase and quartz. [Ger. *Aplit* < Gk. *haplous*, single. See HAPLOID.] **—ap·lit′ic** (ă-plĭt′ĭk) *adj.*

a·plomb (ə-plŏm′, ə-plŭm′) *n.* Self-confident assurance. [Fr. < OFr. *a plomb*, perpendicularly : *a*, according to (< Lat. *ad-*; see AD–) + *plomb*, lead weight (< Lat. *plumbum*, lead).]

ap·ne·a *also* **ap·noe·a** (ăp′nē-ə, ăp-nē′ə) *n.* Temporary absence or cessation of breathing. [NLat. *apnoea* < Gk. *apnoia* : *a-*, without; see A—¹ + *pnoiā, -pnoia*, breathing (< *pnein*, to breathe).] **—ap·ne′ic** *adj. & n.*

A·po (ä′pō) The highest mountain, 2,956.1 m (9,692 ft), of the Philippines, an active volcano on SE Mindanao.

APO *abbr.* Army Post Office

apo- *or* **ap-** *pref.* **1a.** Away from; off: *aphelion.* **b.** Separate: *apocarpous.* **2.** Without; not: *apogamy.* **3.** Related to; derived from: *apomorphine.* **4.** Metasomatic: *apophyllite.* [Gk. < *apo*, away from. See **apo-** in App.]

Apoc. *abbr. Bible* **1.** Apocalypse **2.** Apocrypha

a·poc·a·lypse (ə-pŏk′ə-lĭps′) *n.* **1a.** **Apocalypse** *Bible* The Book of Revelation. **b.** Any of various anonymous Jewish or Christian texts from around the second century B.C. to the second century A.D. containing prophetic or symbolic visions, esp. of the imminent destruction of the world. **2.** Great or total devastation: *nuclear apocalypse.* **3.** A prophetic disclosure; a revelation. [ME *Apocalipse* < LLat. *Apocalypsis* < Gk. *apokalupsis*, revelation, Apocalypse < *apokaluptein*, to uncover : *apo-*, apo- + *kaluptein*, to cover; see **kel-¹** in App.]

a·poc·a·lyp·tic (ə-pŏk′ə-lĭp′tĭk) *also* **a·poc·a·lyp·ti·cal** (-tĭ-kəl) *adj.* **1.** Of or relating to an apocalypse. **2.** Involving or portending doom or vast devastation. **3.** Marked by usu. exaggerated predictions of or allusions to a disastrous outcome. **4.** Revelatory or prophetic. **—a·poc′a·lyp′ti·cal·ly** *adv.*

ap·o·car·pous (ăp′ə-kär′pəs) *adj.* Having carpels that are free from one another. Used of a single flower with two or more separate pistils. **—ap′o·car′py** (ăp′ə-kär′pē) *n.*

ap·o·chro·mat·ic (ăp′ə-krō-măt′ĭk) *adj.* Corrected for both chromatic and spherical aberration, as a lens.

a·poc·o·pe (ə-pŏk′ə-pē) *n.* The loss of one or more sounds from the end of a word, as in Modern English *sing* from Middle English *singen.* [LLat. < Gk. *apokopē* < *apokoptein*, to cut off : *apo-*, apo- + *koptein*, to cut.]

ap·o·crine (ăp′ə-krĭn, -krīn′, -krēn′) *adj.* Of or relating to a type of glandular secretion in which the apical portion of the secreting cell is released along with the secretory products. [Prob. < Gk. *apokrīnein*, to set apart : *apo-*, apo- + *krīnein*, to separate; see **krei-** in App.]

A·poc·ry·pha (ə-pŏk′rə-fə) *n. (used with a sing. or pl. verb)* **1.** *Bible* The biblical books included in the Vulgate and accepted in the Roman Catholic and Orthodox canon but considered noncanonical by Protestants. See table at **Bible.** **2.** Various early Christian writings proposed as additions to the New Testament but rejected by the major canons. **3. apocrypha** Writings or statements of questionable authorship or authenticity. [ME *apocripha*, not authentic < LLat. *apocrypha*, the Apocrypha < Gk. *Apokrupha*, neut. pl. of *apokruphos*, secret, hidden < *apokruptein*, to hide away : *apo-*, apo- + *kruptein, kruph-*, to hide.]

a·poc·ry·phal (ə-pŏk′rə-fəl) *adj.* **1.** Of questionable authorship or authenticity. **2.** Erroneous; fictitious. **3. Apocryphal** *Bible* Of or relating to the Apocrypha. **—a·poc′ry·phal·ly** *adv.*

ap·o·dal (ăp′ə-dl) *also* **ap·o·dous** (-dəs) *adj.* Having no limbs, feet, or footlike appendages. [< Gk. *apous* : *a-*, without; see A—¹ + *pous, pod-*, foot; see **ped-** in App.]

ap·o·dic·tic (ăp′ə-dĭk′tĭk) *adj.* Necessarily or demonstrably true; incontrovertible. [Lat. *apodīcticus* < Gk. *apodeiktikos* < *apodeiktos*, demonstrable < *apodeiknunai*, to demonstrate : *apo-*, apo- + *deiknunai*, to show; see **deik-** in App.] **—ap′o·dic′ti·cal·ly** *adv.*

a·pod·o·sis (ə-pŏd′ə-sĭs) *n., pl.* **-ses** (-sēz′) The main clause of a conditional sentence, as *We'll go* in *We'll go if we can.* [LLat. < Gk. < *apodidonai*, to give back : *apo-*, apo- + *didonai*, to give; see **dō-** in App.]

ap·o·en·zyme (ăp′ō-ĕn′zīm) *n.* The protein part of an enzyme, to which the coenzyme attaches to form an active enzyme.

a·pog·a·my (ə-pŏg′ə-mē) *n. Botany* The development of an embryo without the occurrence of fertilization. **—ap′o·gam′ic** (ăp′ə-găm′ĭk), **a·pog′a·mous** *adj.*

ap·o·gee (ăp′ə-jē) *n.* **1a.** The point in the orbit of the moon or of an artificial satellite most distant from the center of the earth. **b.** The point in an orbit most distant from the body being orbited. **2.** The farthest or highest point; the apex. [Fr. *apogée* < NLat. *apogaeum* < Gk. *apogaion* < neut. of *apogaios*, far from the earth : *apo-*, apo- + *gaia*, earth.] **—ap′o·ge′an** (-jē′ən) *adj.*

ap·o·lip·o·pro·tein (ăp′ə-lĭp′ə-prō′tēn′, -tē-ĭn, -lī′pō-) *n.* Any of various proteins that combine with a lipid to form a lipoprotein and are a constituent of chylomicrons, HDL, LDL, and VLDL.

a·po·lit·i·cal (ā′pə-lĭt′ĭ-kəl) *adj.* **1.** Having no interest in or association with politics. **2.** Having no political importance. **—a′po·lit′i·cal·ly** *adv.*

A·pol·li·naire (ə-pŏl′ə-nâr′), **Guillaume** 1880–1918. French poet and leading figure in avant-garde circles.

A·pol·lo (ə-pŏl′ō) *n. Greek & Roman Mythology* **1.** The god of prophecy, music, medicine, and poetry, sometimes identified with the sun. **2. apollo,** *pl.* **-los** A young man of great physical beauty. [Lat. *Apollō* < Gk. *Apollōn.*]

Ap·ol·lo·ni·an (ăp′ə-lō′nē-ən) *adj.* **1.** *Greek & Roman Mythology* Of or relating to Apollo or his cult. **2.** *often* **apollonian** Clear, harmonious, and restrained.

a·pol·o·get·ic (ə-pŏl′ə-jĕt′ĭk) *also* **a·pol·o·get·i·cal** (-ĭ-kəl) *adj.* **1.** Offering or expressing an apology or excuse: *an apologetic smile.* **2.** Self-deprecating; humble: *an apologetic manner.* **3.** Serving as a formal justification or defense: *an apologetic treatise.* ❖ *n.* A formal defense or apology. [ME, formal defense < Lat. *apologēticus* < Gk. *apologētikos*, suitable for defense < *apologeisthai*, to defend oneself verbally < *apologos*, apology, story. See APOLOGUE.] **—a·pol′o·get′i·cal·ly** *adv.*

a·pol·o·get·ics (ə-pŏl′ə-jĕt′ĭks) *n. (used with a sing. verb)* **1.** The branch of theology that is concerned with defending or proving Christian doctrines. **2.** Formal argumentation in defense of something, such as a position or system.

ap·o·lo·gi·a (ăp′ə-lō′jē-ə, -jə) *n.* A formal defense or justification. [Lat., apology. See APOLOGY.]

a·pol·o·gist (ə-pŏl′ə-jĭst) *n.* A person who defends or justifies something, such as a doctrine, policy, or institution.

a·pol·o·gize (ə-pŏl′ə-jīz′) *intr.v.* **-gized, -giz·ing, -giz·es 1.** To excuse or regretfully acknowledge a fault or offense. **2.** To defend or justify formally. —**a·pol′o·giz′er** *n.*

ap·o·logue (ăp′ə-lôg′, -lŏg′) *n.* A moral fable, esp. one having animals or inanimate objects as characters. [Fr. < Lat. *apologus* < Gk. *apologos* : *apo-*, apo- + *logos*, speech; see **leg-** in App.]

a·pol·o·gy (ə-pŏl′ə-jē) *n., pl.* **-gies 1.** An acknowledgment expressing regret or asking pardon for a fault or offense. **2a.** A formal justification or defense. **b.** An explanation or excuse. **3.** An inferior substitute: *The cot was a poor apology for a bed.* [Lat. *apologia* < Gk. *apologiā* : *apo-*, apo- + *logos*, speech; see **leg-** in App.]

a·po·lune (ăp′ə-lōōn′) *n.* The point of an orbit around the moon farthest from the moon's center. [APO– + Lat. *lūna*, moon.]

ap·o·mict (ăp′ə-mĭkt′) *n.* A plant that reproduces or is reproduced by apomixis. [Back-formation < *apomictic*, produced by apomixis : APO– + Gk. *miktos*, mixed (< *meignunai*, *mik-*, to mix).] —**ap′o·mic′tic** *adj.* —**ap′o·mic′tic·al·ly** *adv.*

ap·o·mix·is (ăp′ə-mĭk′sĭs) *n.* Reproduction without meiosis or formation of gametes. [APO– + Gk. *mixis*, a mingling (< *meignunai*, *mik-*, to mingle; see **meik-** in App.).]

ap·o·mor·phine (ăp′ə-môr′fēn′) *n.* A poisonous white crystalline alkaloid, $C_{17}H_{17}NO_2$, derived from morphine and used medicinally to induce vomiting.

ap·o·neu·ro·sis (ăp′ə-nōō-rō′sĭs, -nyōō-) *n., pl.* **-ses** (-sēz′) A fibrous membrane, resembling a flattened tendon, that serves to bind muscles together or connect muscle to bone. [Gk. *aponeurōsis* < *aponeurousthai*, to become tendinous : *apo-*, apo- + *neuron*, sinew.] —**ap′o·neu·rot′ic** (-rŏt′ĭk) *adj.*

a·poph·a·sis (ə-pŏf′ə-sĭs) *n.* Allusion to something by denying that it will be mentioned, as in *I will not mention their corruption.* [LLat. < Gk. *apophanai*, to say no : *apo-*, apo- + *phanai*, to say; see **bhā-** in App.]

ap·o·phthegm (ăp′ə-thĕm′) *n.* Variant of **apothegm.**

a·poph·y·ge (ə-pŏf′ə-jē) *n.* The outward curve at the top and bottom of a column where the shaft joins the capital or base. [Gk. *apophugē* < *apopheugein*, to flee : *apo-*, apo- + *pheugein*, *phug-*, to flee.]

a·poph·yl·lite (ə-pŏf′ə-līt′, ăp′ə-fĭl′īt′) *n.* A white crystalline mineral, essentially $KCa_4Si_8O_{20}(OH)\cdot8H_2O$.

a·poph·y·sis (ə-pŏf′ĭ-sĭs) *n., pl.* **-ses** (-sēz′) **1.** *Anatomy* A natural swelling, projection, or outgrowth of an organ or a part. **2.** *Geology* A branch from a dike or vein. [NLat. < Gk. *apophusis* < *apophuein*, to send out branches : *apo-*, apo- + *phuein*, to grow; see **bheuə-** in App.] —**a·poph′y·sate′** (-sāt′), **a·poph′y·se·al** (-sē′əl) *adj.*

ap·o·plec·tic (ăp′ə-plĕk′tĭk) *adj.* **1.** Of, resembling, or produced by apoplexy: *an apoplectic fit.* **2a.** Having or inclined to have apoplexy. **b.** Exhibiting symptoms associated with apoplexy. **3.** Extremely angry; furious. —**ap′o·plec′ti·cal·ly** *adv.*

ap·o·plex·y (ăp′ə-plĕk′sē) *n.* **1.** Sudden impairment of neurological function, esp. when resulting from a cerebral hemorrhage; a stroke. **2.** A sudden effusion of blood into an organ or tissue. **3.** A fit of extreme anger; rage. [ME *apoplexie* < OFr. < LLat. *apoplēxia* < Gk. *apoplēssein*, to cripple by a stroke : *apo-*, intensive pref.; see APO– + *plēssein*, *plēk-*, to strike; see **plāk-** in App.]

ap·op·to·sis (ăp′əp-tō′sĭs, ăp′ə-tō′-) *n.* A natural process of cell death in which cells disintegrate into membrane-bound particles that are then eliminated, as by shedding.

a·po·ri·a (ə-pôr′ē-ə, ə-pōr′-) *n.* **1.** A figure of speech in which the speaker expresses or purports to be in doubt about a question. **2.** An insoluble contradiction or paradox in a text's meanings. [Gk. *aporiā*, difficulty of passing < *aporos*, impassable : *a-*, without; see A–¹ + *poros*, passage; see **per-²** in App.]

ap·o·se·mat·ic coloration (ăp′ə-sə-măt′ĭk) *n.* See **warning coloration.**

ap·o·si·o·pe·sis (ăp′ə-sī′ə-pē′sĭs) *n., pl.* **-ses** (-sēz) A sudden breaking off of a thought in the middle of a sentence, as though the speaker were unwilling or unable to continue. [LLat. *aposiōpēsis* < Gk. *aposiōpān*, to become silent : *apo-*, intensive pref.; see APO– + *siōpān*, to be silent (< *siōpē*, silence).] —**ap′o·si′o·pet′ic** (-pĕt′ĭk) *adj.*

ap·o·spor·y (ăp′ə-spôr′ē, -spōr′ē, -ə-pŏs′pə-rē) *n.* The development of a gametophyte from a sporophyte without meiosis. —**a·pos′por·ous** (ə-pŏs′pər-əs) *adj.*

a·pos·ta·sy (ə-pŏs′tə-sē) *n., pl.* **-sies** Abandonment of one's beliefs, as in a religion or a cause. [ME *apostasie* < OFr. < LLat. *apostasia*, defection < L.Gk. *apostasiā* < Gk. *apostasis*, revolt < *aphistanai*, to revolt : *apo-*, away + *histanai*, *sta-*, to stand, place; see **stā-** in App.]

a·pos·tate (ə-pŏs′tāt′, -tĭt) *n.* One who has abandoned one's beliefs, such as one's religion or a cause. [ME < OFr. < LLat. *apostata* < Gk. *apostatēs* < *aphistanai*, to revolt. See APOSTASY.] —**a·pos′tate** *adj.*

a pos·te·ri·o·ri (ä′ pŏ-stîr′ē-ôr′ī, -ôr′ē, -ōr′ī, -ōr′ē, ä′, ā′) *adj.* **1.** Derived by or relating to the process of reasoning from facts or particulars to general principles or from effects to causes; inductive; empirical. **2.** Knowable from or justified by appeal to experience. [Med.Lat. *ā posteriōrī* : Lat. *ā*, from + Lat. *posteriōrī*, ablative of *posterior*, later.]

---

a·pos·tle (ə-pŏs′əl) *n.* **1a. Apostle** One of a group made up esp. of the 12 disciples chosen by Jesus to preach the gospel. **b.** A missionary of the early Christian Church. **c.** A leader of the first Christian mission to a country or region. **2.** One of the 12 members of the administrative council in the Mormon Church. **3.** One who pioneers a movement or belief: *an apostle of conservation.* [ME < OE *apostol* and < OFr. *apostle*, both < LLat. *apostolus* < Gk. *apostolos*, messenger < *apostellein*, to send off : *apo-*, away + *stellein*, to send; see **stel-** in App.] —**a·pos′tle·hood′** *n.* —**a·pos′tle·ship′** *n.*

A·pos·tles' Creed (ə-pŏs′əlz) *n.* A Christian creed ascribed to the 12 Apostles and used in public worship services in the West.

a·pos·to·late (ə-pŏs′tə-lāt′, -lĭt) *n.* **1.** The office or duties of an apostle. **2.** An association for the dissemination of a religion or doctrine. [LLat. *apostolātus* < *apostolus*, apostle. See APOSTLE.]

ap·os·tol·ic (ăp′ə-stŏl′ĭk) also **ap·os·tol·i·cal** (-ĭ-kəl) *adj.* **1.** Of or relating to an apostle. **2a.** Of or relating to the 12 Apostles, their teaching, or their practices. **b.** Of or relating to a succession of spiritual authority from the 12 Apostles. **c.** *Roman Catholic Church* Of or relating to the pope; papal.

apostolic delegate *n. Roman Catholic Church* A representative of the Vatican to a country having no formal relations with it.

Apostolic Father *n.* A church father of the first or second century A.D. said to have received instruction from the 12 Apostles or from their disciples.

a·pos·tro·phe¹ (ə-pŏs′trə-fē) *n.* The superscript sign (') used to indicate the omission of a letter or letters from a word, the possessive case, or the plurals of numbers, letters, and abbreviations. [Fr. < LLat. *apostrophus* < Gk. *apostrophos* < *apostrephein*, to turn away : *apo-*, apo- + *strephein*, to turn.] —**ap′os·troph′ic** (ăp′ə-strŏf′ĭk) *adj.*

a·pos·tro·phe² (ə-pŏs′trə-fē) *n.* A rhetorical device in which a speaker or writer addresses an absent person, an abstraction, or an inanimate object. [LLat. *apostrophē* < Gk. < *apostrephein*, to turn away. See APOSTROPHE¹.] —**ap′os·troph′ic** (ăp′ə-strŏf′ĭk) *adj.* —**a·pos′tro·phize′** (ə-pŏs′trə-fīz′) *v.*

a·poth·e·car·ies' measure (ə-pŏth′ĭ-kĕr′ēz) *n.* A system of liquid volume measure used in pharmacy, now largely replaced by the metric system.

apothecaries' weight *n.* A system of weights used in pharmacy and based on an ounce equal to 480 grains and a pound equal to 12 ounces, now largely replaced by the metric system.

a·poth·e·car·y (ə-pŏth′ĭ-kĕr′ē) *n., pl.* **-ies 1.** One that prepares and sells medicines; a pharmacist. **2.** See **pharmacy 2.** [ME *apotecarie* < OFr. *apotecaire* and < Med.Lat. *apothēcārius*, both < Lat. *apothēca*, storehouse < Gk. *apothēkē* : *apo-*, away; see APO– + *thēkē*, receptacle; see **dhē-** in App.]

ap·o·the·ci·um (ăp′ə-thē′sē-əm, -shē-) *n., pl.* **-ci·a** (-sē-ə, -shē-ə) A disk-shaped or cup-shaped ascocarp of some lichens and the fungi Ascomycetes. [< Lat. *apothēca*, storehouse. See APOTHECARY.] —**ap′o·the′cial** (-shəl) *adj.*

ap·o·thegm also **ap·o·phthegm** (ăp′ə-thĕm′) *n.* A terse, witty, instructive saying; a maxim. [Gk. *apophthegma* < *apophthengesthai*, to speak plainly : *apo-*, intensive pref.; see APO– + *phthengesthai*, to speak.] —**ap′o·theg·mat′ic** (-thĕg-măt′ĭk), **ap′o·theg·mat′i·cal** (-ĭ-kəl) —**ap′o·theg·mat′i·cal·ly** *adv.*

ap·o·them (ăp′ə-thĕm′) *n.* The perpendicular distance from the center of a regular polygon to any of its sides. [APO– + Gk. *thema*, something laid down; see THEME.]

a·poth·e·o·sis (ə-pŏth′ē-ō′sĭs, ăp′ə-thē′ə-sĭs) *n., pl.* **-ses** (-sēz) **1.** Exaltation to divine rank or stature; deification. **2.** Elevation to a preeminent or transcendent position; glorification. **3.** An exalted or glorified example: *the apotheosis of courage.* [LLat. *apotheōsis* < Gk. < *apotheoun*, to deify : *apo-*, change; see APO– + *theos*, god; see **dhēs-** in App.]

a·poth·e·o·size (ə-pŏth′ē-ə-sīz′, ăp′ə-thē′ə-sīz′) *tr.v.* **-sized, -siz·ing, -siz·es** To glorify; exalt.

ap·o·tro·pa·ic (ăp′ə-trō-pā′ĭk) *adj.* Intended to ward off evil. [< Gk. *apotropaios* < *apotrepein*, to ward off : *apo-*, apo- + *trepein*, to turn.] —**ap′o·tro·pa′i·cal·ly** *adv.*

app (ăp) *n. Informal* A computer application. [Short for APPLICATION.]

Ap·pa·la·chi·a (ăp′ə-lā′chē-ə, -chə, -lăch′ē-ə, -lăch′ə) A region of the E US including the Appalachian Mts. —**Ap′pa·la′chi·an** *adj.*

Appalachian Mountains also **Ap·pa·la·chi·ans** (ăp′ə-lā′chē-ənz, -chənz, -lăch′ē-ənz, -lăch′ənz) A mountain system of E North America extending c. 2,574 km (1,600 mi) from E Canada to central AL and rising to 2,038.6 m (6,684 ft).

Appalachian Trail A hiking path of the E US extending c. 3,298 km (2,050 mi) from central ME to N GA.

ap·pall (ə-pôl′) *tr.v.* **-palled, -pall·ing, -palls** To fill with consternation or dismay. [ME *apallen*, to grow faint < OFr. *apalir* : *a-*, to (< Lat. *ad-*; see AD–) + *palir*, to grow pale (< *pale*, pale < Lat. *pallidus* < *pallēre*, to grow pale).]

ap·pall·ing (ə-pôl′ĭng) *adj.* Causing consternation or dismay; frightful: *appalling conditions.* —**ap·pall′ing·ly** *adv.*

Ap·pa·loo·sa (ăp′ə-lōō′sə) *n.* A breed of saddle horse characteristically having a spotted rump. [?]

ap·pa·nage also **ap·a·nage** (ăp′ə-nĭj) *n.* **1.** A source of reve-

Appaloosa

ă	pat	oi	boy
ā	pay	ou	out
âr	care	ŏŏ	took
ä	father	ōō	boot
ĕ	pet	ŭ	cut
ē	be	ûr	urge
ĭ	pit	th	thin
ī	pie	th	this
îr	pier	hw	which
ŏ	pot	zh	vision
ō	toe	ə	item
ô	paw		

Stress marks:
′ (primary);
′ (secondary), as in
lexicon (lĕk′sĭ-kŏn′)

nue given by a sovereign for the maintenance of a member of the ruling family. **2.** Something extra offered to or claimed as due to a party; a perquisite. **3.** A rightful or customary accompaniment or adjunct. [Fr. *apanage* < OFr. < *apaner*, to make provisions for, poss. < Med.Lat. *appānāre* : Lat. *ad-*, ad- + Lat. *pānis*, bread; see pā- in App.]

ap·pa·rat (ăp′ə-rät′, ä′pə-rät′) *n.* See **apparatus** 2. [Russ., the government organization < Ger., a political organization < Lat. *apparātus*, preparation. See APPARATUS.]

ap·pa·ra·tchik (ä′pə-rä′chĭk) *n., pl.* **-tchiks** or **-tchi·ki** (-chē-kē) **1.** A member of a Communist apparat. **2.** An unquestioningly loyal subordinate, esp. of a political leader or organization. [Russ. < *apparat*, apparat. See APPARAT.]

ap·pa·rat·us (ăp′ə-rät′əs, -rä′təs) *n., pl.* **apparatus** or **-us·es 1a.** An appliance or device for a particular purpose. **b.** An integrated group of materials or devices used for a particular purpose. **2a.** The means by which a function is performed or executed. **b.** A political organization or an underground political movement. **3.** *Physiology* A group of organs that collectively perform a specific function or process: *the digestive apparatus.* **4.** The critical and source material that accompanies an edition of a text. [Lat. *apparātus*, preparation < p. part. of *apparāre*, to prepare : *ad-*, ad- + *parāre*, to prepare.]

ap·par·el (ə-păr′əl) *n.* **1.** Clothing, esp. outer garments; attire. **2.** A covering or adornment. ❖ *tr.v.* **-eled, -el·ing, -els** or **-elled, -el·ling, -els 1.** To clothe or dress. **2.** To adorn or embellish. [ME *appareil* < OFr. *apareil*, preparation < *apareillier*, to prepare, poss. < VLat. **appariculāre* < Lat. *apparāre*. See APPARATUS.]

ap·par·ent (ə-păr′ənt, ə-pâr′-) *adj.* **1.** Readily seen; visible. **2.** Readily understood; clear or obvious. **3.** Appearing as such; seeming: *an apparent advantage.* [ME < OFr. *aparant*, pr. part. of *aparoir*, to appear. See APPEAR.] —**ap·par′ent·ly** *adv.* —**ap·par′ent·ness** *n.*

SYNONYMS *apparent, clear, clear-cut, distinct, evident, manifest, obvious, patent, plain* These adjectives mean readily seen, perceived, or understood: *angry for no apparent reason; a clear danger; clear-cut evidence of tampering; distinct fingerprints; evident hostility; manifest pleasure; obvious errors; patent advantages; making my meaning plain.*

---

apparent horizon *n.* See **horizon** 1.

apparent magnitude *n.* See **magnitude** 2.

ap·pa·ri·tion (ăp′ə-rĭsh′ən) *n.* **1.** A ghostly figure; a specter. **2.** A sudden or unusual sight. **3.** The act of appearing; appearance. [ME *apparicioun* < OFr. < LLat. *appāritiō, appāritiōn-*, an appearance < Lat. *appāritus*, p. part. of *appārēre*, to appear. See APPEAR.] —**ap·pa·ri′tion·al** *adj.*

ap·par·i·tor (ə-păr′ĭ-tər) *n.* An official formerly sent to carry out the orders of a civil or ecclesiastical court. [ME < Lat. *appāritor* < *appāritus*, p. part. of *appārēre*, to appear. See APPEAR.]

ap·peal (ə-pēl′) *n.* **1.** An earnest or urgent request, entreaty, or supplication. **2.** A resort to a higher authority or greater power, as for sanction: *an appeal to reason.* **3.** *Law* **a.** The transfer of a case from a lower to a higher court for a review of the lower court's decision. **b.** A case so transferred. **c.** A request for such a review. **4.** The power of attracting interest: *a city with appeal for tourists.* ❖ *v.* **-pealed, -peal·ing, -peals** —*intr.* **1.** To make an earnest or urgent request. **2.** To have recourse, as for corroboration; resort. **3.** *Law* To make or apply for an appeal. **4.** To be attractive or interesting. —*tr. Law* To transfer or apply to transfer (a case) to a higher court for an appeal. [ME *apel* < OFr. < *apeler*, to appeal < Lat. *appellāre*, to entreat. See *pel-²* in App.] —**ap·peal′a·bil′i·ty** *n.* —**ap·peal′a·ble** *adj.* —**ap·peal′er** *n.*

ap·pear (ə-pîr′) *intr.v.* **-peared, -pear·ing, -pears 1.** To become visible. **2.** To come into existence: *New viruses appear periodically.* **3.** To seem or look to be: *appeared unhappy.* **4.** To seem likely. **5.** To come before the public: *has appeared in plays.* **6.** *Law* To present oneself formally before a court. [ME *aperen* < OFr. *aparoir, aper-* < Lat. *appārēre* : *ad-*, ad- + *pārēre*, to show.]

ap·pear·ance (ə-pîr′əns) *n.* **1.** The act or an instance of coming into sight. **2.** The act or an instance of coming into public view: *a rare personal appearance.* **3.** Outward aspect: *an untidy appearance.* **4.** Something that appears; a phenomenon. **5.** A superficial aspect; a semblance: *an appearance of wealth.* **6. appearances** Outward indications; circumstances.

ap·pease (ə-pēz′) *tr.v.* **-peased, -peas·ing, -peas·es 1.** To bring peace, quiet, or calm to; soothe. **2.** To satisfy or relieve: *appease one's thirst.* **3.** To pacify or attempt to pacify (an enemy) by granting concessions, often at the expense of principle. See Syns at **pacify.** [ME *appesen* < OFr. *apesier* : *a-*, to (< Lat. *ad-*; see AD-) + *pais*, peace (< Lat. *pāx).*] —**ap·peas′a·ble** *adj.* —**ap·peas′a·bly** *adv.* —**ap·peas′er** *n.*

ap·pease·ment (ə-pēz′mənt) *n.* **1a.** An act of appeasing. **b.** The condition of being appeased. **2.** The policy of granting concessions to potential enemies in order to maintain peace.

ap·pel·lant (ə-pĕl′ənt) *Law adj.* Of or relating to an appeal; appellate. ❖ *n.* One who appeals a court decision. [ME < OFr. *apelant* < pr. part. of *apeler*, to appeal. See APPEAL.]

ap·pel·late (ə-pĕl′ĭt) *adj.* Having the power to hear court appeals and to review court decisions. [Lat. *appellātus*, p. part. of *appellāre*, to entreat. See APPEAL.]

ap·pel·la·tion (ăp′ə-lā′shən) *n.* **1.** A name, title, or designation. **2.** The act of naming. **3.** A protected name under which a wine may be sold. [ME *appelacion* < OFr. *appelation* < Lat. *appellātiō, appellātiōn-* < *appellātus*, p. part. of *appellāre*, to entreat. See APPEAL. Sense 3 < Fr. *appellation (d'origine contrôlée)*, (registered vintage) trade name < OFr. *appelation*.]

ap·pel·la·tive (ə-pĕl′ə-tĭv) *adj.* **1.** Of or relating to the assignment of names. **2.** *Grammar* Of or relating to a common noun. ❖ *n.* A name or descriptive epithet. [ME, common (n.) < OFr. *appelatif* < LLat. *appellātīvus* < Lat. *appellātus*, p. part. of *appellāre*, to call upon, entreat. See APPEAL.] —**ap·pel′la·tive·ly** *adv.*

ap·pel·lee (ăp′ə-lē′) *n. Law* One against whom an appeal is taken. [Fr. *appelé* < OFr. *apele* < p. part. of *apeler*, to appeal. See APPEAL.]

ap·pend (ə-pĕnd′) *tr.v.* **-pend·ed, -pend·ing, -pends 1.** To add as a supplement or appendix: *appended a note to the report.* **2.** To fix to; attach: *append a charm to the bracelet.* [Lat. *appendere*, to hang upon : *ad-*, ad- + *pendere*, to hang.]

ap·pend·age (ə-pĕn′dĭj) *n.* **1.** Something added or attached to a larger or more important entity; an adjunct. **2.** *Biology* A part or organ that is joined to the axis or trunk of a body.

ap·pen·dant (ə-pĕn′dənt) *adj.* **1.** Affixed as an appendage. **2.** Accompanying; attendant. **3.** Belonging to a land grant as a subsidiary right in English law. —**ap·pen′dant** *n.*

ap·pen·dec·to·my (ăp′ən-dĕk′tə-mē) *n., pl.* **-mies** Surgical removal of the vermiform appendix. [APPEND(IX) + −ECTOMY.]

ap·pen·di·ci·tis (ə-pĕn′dĭ-sī′tĭs) *n.* Inflammation of the vermiform appendix. [NLat. < Lat. *appendix, appendic-*, appendage. See APPENDIX.]

ap·pen·dic·u·lar (ăp′ən-dĭk′yə-lər) *adj.* Of, relating to, or consisting of an appendage or appendages, esp. the limbs. [< Lat. *appendicula*, dim. of *appendix, appendic-*, appendix. See APPENDIX.]

ap·pen·dix (ə-pĕn′dĭks) *n., pl.* **-dix·es** or **-di·ces** (-dĭ-sēz′) **1a.** An appendage. **b.** A collection of supplementary material, usu. at the end of a book. **2.** *Anatomy* **a.** The vermiform appendix. **b.** A supplementary or accessory part of a body organ or structure. [Lat. < *appendere*, to hang upon. See APPEND.]

ap·per·ceive (ăp′ər-sēv′) *tr.v.* **-ceived, -ceiv·ing, -ceives** To perceive (something) by apperception. [Back-formation < APPERCEPTION.]

ap·per·cep·tion (ăp′ər-sĕp′shən) *n.* **1.** Conscious perception with full awareness. **2.** The process of understanding by which newly observed qualities of an object are related to past experience. [NLat. *apperceptiō, apperceptiōn-* : Lat. *ad-*, ad- + Lat. *perceptiō*, perception; see PERCEPTION.] —**ap′per·cep′tive** (-sĕp′tĭv) *adj.*

ap·per·tain (ăp′ər-tān′) *intr.v.* **-tained, -tain·ing, -tains** To belong as a proper function or part; pertain. [ME *appertenen* < OFr. *apartenir* < VLat. **appartenēre* < LLat. *appertinēre* : *ad-*, ad- + *pertinēre*, to belong; see PERTAIN.]

ap·pe·stat (ăp′ĭ-stăt′) *n.* The area in the brain that is believed to regulate appetite and food intake. [APPE(TITE) + −STAT.]

ap·pe·tence (ăp′ĭ-təns) *n.* **1.** A strong craving or desire. **2.** A tendency or propensity. **3.** A natural attraction or affinity. [Prob. Fr. *appétence* < Lat. *appetentia* < *appetēns, appetent-*, pr. part. of *appetere*, to strive after. See APPETITE.] —**ap′pe·ten·cy** *n.* —**ap′pe·tent** *adj.*

ap·pe·tite (ăp′ĭ-tīt′) *n.* **1.** An instinctive physical desire, esp. for food or drink. **2.** A strong wish or urge. [ME *apetit* < OFr. < Lat. *appetītus*, strong desire < p. part. of *appetere*, to strive after : *ad-*, ad- + *petere*, to seek; see *pet-* in App.] —**ap′pe·ti·tive** (ăp′ĭ-tī′tĭv, ə-pĕt′ĭ-tĭv) *adj.*

ap·pe·tiz·er (ăp′ĭ-tī′zər) *n.* A food or drink served usu. before a meal to stimulate the appetite.

ap·pe·tiz·ing (ăp′ĭ-tī′zĭng) *adj.* Appealing to or stimulating the appetite. —**ap′pe·tiz′ing·ly** *adv.*

Ap·pi·an Way (ăp′ē-ən) An ancient Roman road between Rome and Capua, later extended to Brindisi.

ap·plaud (ə-plôd′) *v.* **-plaud·ed, -plaud·ing, -plauds** —*intr.* To express approval, esp. by clapping. —*tr.* **1.** To express approval of, esp. by clapping. **2.** To commend highly; praise: *applauded her decision.* [ME *applauden* < Lat. *applaudere* : *ad-*, ad- + *plaudere*, to clap.] —**ap·plaud′a·ble** *adj.* —**ap·plaud′a·bly** *adv.* —**ap·plaud′er** *n.*

ap·plause (ə-plôz′) *n.* **1.** Approval expressed esp. by clapping. **2.** Praise; commendation. [Med.Lat. *applausus* < p. part. of Lat. *applaudere*, to applaud. See APPLAUD.]

ap·ple (ăp′əl) *n.* **1a.** A deciduous tree (*Malus pumila*) having alternate simple leaves and white or pink flowers. **b.** The firm, edible, usu. rounded fruit of this tree. **2a.** Any of several other plants, esp. those with fruits like the apple. **b.** The fruit of any of these plants. —*idiom:* **apple of (one's) eye** One that is treasured. [ME *appel* < OE *æppel.*]

apple green *n.* A moderate or vivid yellow green to light or strong yellowish green. —**ap′ple-green′** (ăp′əl-grēn′) *adj.*

ap·ple·jack (ăp′əl-jăk′) *n.* **1.** Brandy distilled from hard cider. **2.** An alcoholic drink made from frozen hard cider.

ap·ple-pie (ăp′əl-pī′) *adj. Informal* **1.** Perfect; exemplary: *apple-pie order.* **2.** often **apple pie** Of or relating to values regarded as typically American.

ap•ple-pol•ish (ăp′əl-pŏl′ĭsh) v. -ished, -ish•ing, -ish•es *Informal* —*intr.* To seek favor by toadying. —*tr.* To seek favor with. —**apple polisher, ap′ple-pol′ish•er** n.

ap•ple•sauce (ăp′əl-sôs′) n. **1.** Apples stewed to a pulp and sometimes sweetened or spiced. **2.** *Slang* Nonsense.

Ap•ple•seed (ăp′əl-sēd′), **Johnny** See John **Chapman.**

ap•plet (ăp′lĭt) n. *Computer Science* A minor application program that is usu. portable between operating system platforms. [APPL(ICATION) + −ET.]

Ap•ple•ton (ăp′əl-tən) A city of E WI on the Fox R. SW of Green Bay. Pop. 70,087.

Appleton, Sir **Edward Victor** 1892–1965. British physicist who won a 1947 Nobel Prize.

ap•pli•ance (ə-plī′əns) n. **1.** A device that performs a specific function, esp. an electrical device, such as a toaster, for household use. **2.** A dental or surgical device that performs a therapeutic or corrective function. [< APPLY.]

ap•pli•ca•ble (ăp′lĭ-kə-bəl, ə-plĭk′ə-) adj. That can be applied; appropriate. —**ap′pli•ca•bil′i•ty** n. —**ap′pli•ca•bly** adv.

ap•pli•cant (ăp′lĭ-kənt) n. One that applies, as for a job. [ME < Lat. *applicāns*, pr. part. of *applicāre*, to affix. See APPLY.]

ap•pli•ca•tion (ăp′lĭ-kā′shən) n. **1.** The act of applying. **2.** Something applied, such as a curative agent. **3a.** The act of putting something to a special use. **b.** A specific use to which something is put: *the application of science to industry.* **4.** The capacity of being usable; relevance. **5.** Close attention; diligence: *application to her work.* **6a.** A request, as for employment. **b.** The form or document on which such a request is made. **7.** *Computer Science* A computer program with a user interface. ❖ adj. also **applications** *Computer Science* Of or being a computer program designed for a specific task or use: *applications software.* [ME *applicacion* < OFr. < Lat. *applicātiō, applicātiōn-* < *applicātus*, p. part. of *applicāre*, to affix. See APPLY.]

ap•pli•ca•tive (ăp′lĭ-kā′tĭv, ə-plĭk′ə-) adj. **1.** Characterized by actual application; applied. **2.** Practical; applicatory. —**ap′pli•ca′tive•ly** adv.

ap•pli•ca•tor (ăp′lĭ-kā′tər) n. An instrument for applying something, such as medicine or glue.

ap•pli•ca•to•ry (ăp′lĭ-kə-tôr′ē, -tôr′ē, ə-plĭk′ə-) adj. Readily applicable; practical.

ap•plied (ə-plīd′) adj. Put into practice: *applied physics.*

ap•pli•qué (ăp′lĭ-kā′) n. A decoration or ornament made by cutting pieces of one material and applying them to the surface of another. [Fr., p. part. of *appliquer*, to apply < Lat. *applicāre*, to affix. See APPLY.] —**ap′pli•qué′** v.

ap•ply (ə-plī′) v. -plied, -ply•ing, -plies —*tr.* **1.** To bring into nearness or contact with something; put on, upon, or to. **2.** To put to or adapt for a special use: *applies all her money to her mortgage.* **3.** To put into action: *applied the brakes.* **4.** To devote (oneself or one's efforts) to something: *applied myself to my studies.* —*intr.* **1.** To be pertinent or relevant. **2.** To request or seek, as employment: *will apply for benefits.* [ME *applien* < OFr. *aplier* < Lat. *applicāre*, to affix : *ad-*, ad- + *plicāre*, to fold together; see **plek-** in App.] —**ap′pli•a•ble** adj.

ap•pog•gia•tu•ra (ə-pŏj′ə-tōōr′ə) n. *Music* An embellishing note, usu. one step above or below the note it precedes. [Ital. < *appoggiato*, p. part. of *appoggiare*, to lean on < VLat. **appodiāre* : Lat. *ad-*, ad- + Lat. *podium*, support; see PODIUM.]

ap•point (ə-point′) tr.v. -point•ed, -point•ing, -points **1.** To select or designate to fill a position. **2.** To set by authority or by mutual agreement: *will appoint a date for the examination.* **3.** To furnish; equip. **4.** *Law* To direct the disposition of (property) to a person in exercise of a power granted by a preceding deed. [ME *appointen* < OFr. *apointer, apointier*, to arrange < *a point*, to the point : *a*, to (Lat. *ad*) + *point*, point; see POINT.]

ap•point•ee (ə-poin′tē′, ăp′oin-) n. **1.** One who is appointed to a position. **2.** *Law* One granted a power of appointment of property.

ap•poin•tive (ə-poin′tĭv) adj. Relating to or filled by appointment: *an appointive office.*

ap•point•ment (ə-point′mənt) n. **1a.** The act of appointing someone to a position. **b.** The position to which one has been appointed. **2.** An arrangement to do something or meet someone at a particular time and place. See Syns at **engagement. 3. appointments** Furnishings, fittings, or equipment. **4.** *Law* The act of directing the disposition of property by virtue of a power granted for this purpose.

ap•poin•tor (ə-poin′tər, ə-poin′tôr′) n. One that executes a power of appointment of property.

Ap•po•mat•tox (ăp′ə-măt′əks) A town of S-central VA E of Lynchburg. Robert E. Lee surrendered to Ulysses S. Grant at **Appomattox Courthouse** on Apr. 9, 1865, ending the Civil War.

ap•por•tion (ə-pôr′shən, -pōr′-) tr.v. -tioned, -tion•ing, -tions To divide and assign according to a plan; allot: "The tendency persists to apportion blame as suits the circumstances" (Natalie Angier). [Fr. *apportionner* < OFr. : *a-*, to (< Lat. *ad-*, ad) + *portionner*, to divide into portions (< *portion*, portion; see PORTION).]

ap•por•tion•ment (ə-pôr′shən-mənt, -pōr′-) n. **1a.** The act of apportioning. **b.** The condition of having been apportioned. **2a.** The proportional distribution of the number of members of the US House of Representatives on the basis of the population of

each state. **b.** Allotment of direct taxes on the basis of state population.

ap•pose (ă-pōz′) tr.v. -posed, -pos•ing, -pos•es To place in proximity; juxtapose. [Prob. AD− + -*pose* (as in COMPOSE).]

ap•po•site (ăp′ə-zĭt) adj. Strikingly appropriate and relevant. [Lat. *appositus*, p. part. of *appōnere*, to put near : *ad-*, ad- + *pōnere*, to put; see **apo-** in App.] —**ap′po•site•ly** adv. —**ap′po•site•ness** n.

ap•po•si•tion (ăp′ə-zĭsh′ən) n. **1.** *Grammar* **a.** A construction in which a noun or noun phrase is placed with another as an explanatory equivalent, both having the same syntactic relation to the other elements in the sentence; for example, *Copley* and *the painter* in *The painter Copley was born in Boston.* **b.** The relationship between such nouns or noun phrases. **2.** A placing side by side or next to each other. **3.** *Biology* The growth of successive layers of a cell wall. [ME *apposicioun* < Lat. *appositiō, appositiōn-* < *appositus*, p. part. of *appōnere*, to put near. See APPOSITE.] —**ap′po•si′tion•al** adj. —**ap′po•si′tion•al•ly** adv.

ap•pos•i•tive (ə-pŏz′ĭ-tĭv) adj. Of, relating to, or being in apposition. ❖ n. *Grammar* A word or phrase that is in apposition. —**ap•pos′i•tive•ly** adv.

ap•prais•al (ə-prā′zəl) n. **1.** The act or an instance of appraising. **2.** An expert or official valuation, as for taxation.

ap•praise (ə-prāz′) tr.v. -praised, -prais•ing, -prais•es **1.** To evaluate, esp. in an official capacity. **2.** To estimate the quality, amount, size, and other factors of; judge. See Syns at **estimate.** [ME *appreisen*, poss. < OFr. *aprisier* < LLat. *appretiāre* < Lat. *appretiāre* : Lat. *ad-*, ad- + Lat. *pretium*, price.] —**ap•prais′a•ble** adj. —**ap•praise′ment** n. —**ap•prais′er** n.

ap•pre•cia•ble (ə-prē′shə-bəl) adj. Possible to estimate, measure, or perceive: *appreciable changes in temperature.* See Syns at **perceptible.** —**ap•pre′cia•bly** adv.

ap•pre•ci•ate (ə-prē′shē-āt′) v. -at•ed, -at•ing, -ates —*tr.* **1.** To recognize the quality, significance, or magnitude of: *appreciated their freedom.* **2.** To be fully aware of; realize. **3.** To be thankful or show gratitude for: *I appreciate your help.* **4.** To admire greatly; value. **5.** To raise in value, esp. over time. —*intr.* To increase in value, esp. over time. [LLat. *appretiāre, appretiāt-*, to appraise. See APPRAISE.] —**ap•pre′ci•a′tor** n. —**ap•pre′cia•to•ry** (-shə-tôr′ē, -tôr′ē) adj.

SYNONYMS appreciate, value, prize, esteem, treasure, cherish These verbs mean to have a highly favorable opinion of someone or something. *Appreciate* applies especially to high regard based on critical assessment, comparison, and judgment: *As immigrants, they appreciated their newfound freedom. Value* implies high regard for the importance or worth of the object: "*In principle, the modern university values . . . the free exchange of ideas*" (Eloise Salholz). *Prize* often suggests pride of possession: "*the nonchalance prized by teen-agers*" (Elaine Louie). *Esteem* implies respect: "*If he had never esteemed my opinion before, he would have thought highly of me then*" (Jane Austen). *Treasure* and *cherish* stress solicitous care and affectionate regard: *We treasure our freedom.* "*They seek out the Salish Indian woman . . . to learn the traditions she cherishes*" (Tamara Jones).

ap•pre•ci•a•tion (ə-prē′shē-ā′shən) n. **1.** Recognition of the quality, value, significance, or magnitude of people and things. **2.** A judgment or opinion, esp. a favorable one. **3.** An expression of gratitude. **4.** Awareness or delicate perception, esp. of aesthetic qualities or values. **5.** A rise in value, esp. over time.

ap•pre•cia•tive (ə-prē′shə-tĭv, -shē-ā′tĭv) adj. Showing gratitude or recognition of worth. —**ap•pre′cia•tive•ly** adv.

ap•pre•hend (ăp′rĭ-hĕnd′) v. -hend•ed, -hend•ing, -hends —*tr.* **1.** To take into custody; arrest. **2.** To grasp mentally; understand: *apprehends geopolitical issues.* **3.** To become conscious of, as through the senses; perceive. —*intr.* To understand something. [ME *apprehenden* < OFr. *apprehender* < Lat. *apprehendere*, to seize : *ad-*, ad- + *prehendere*, to grasp; see **ghend-** in App.]

SYNONYMS apprehend, comprehend, understand, grasp These verbs denote perception of the nature and significance of something. *Apprehend* denotes both mental and intuitive awareness: "*Intelligence is quickness to apprehend*" (Alfred North Whitehead). Both *comprehend* and *understand* stress complete realization and knowledge: "*To comprehend is to know a thing as well as that thing can be known*" (John Donne). "*No one who has not had the responsibility can really understand what it is like to be President*" (Harry S. Truman). To *grasp* is to seize an idea firmly: "*We have grasped the mystery of the atom and rejected the Sermon on the Mount*" (Omar N. Bradley).

ap•pre•hen•si•ble (ăp′rĭ-hĕn′sə-bəl) adj. Capable of being understood: *apprehensible truths.* —**ap′pre•hen′si•bly** adv.

ap•pre•hen•sion (ăp′rĭ-hĕn′shən) n. **1.** Fearful or uneasy anticipation of the future; dread. **2.** The act of seizing or capturing; arrest. **3.** The ability to apprehend; understanding. [ME *apprehencioun*, perception < OFr. < LLat. *apprehēnsiō, apprehēnsiōn-* < Lat. *apprehēnsus*, p. part. of *apprehendere*, to seize. See APPREHEND.]

ap•pre•hen•sive (ăp′rĭ-hĕn′sĭv) adj. **1.** Anxious or fearful about the future; uneasy: *apprehensive about the future.* See Syns at **afraid. 2.** Capable of understanding and quick to apprehend.

ă	pat	oi	boy
ā	pay	ou	out
âr	care	ōō	took
ä	father	ōō	boot
ĕ	pet	ŭ	cut
ē	be	ûr	urge
ĭ	pit	th	thin
ī	pie	th	this
îr	pier	hw	which
ŏ	pot	zh	vision
ō	toe	ə	about,
ô	paw		item

Stress marks:
′ (primary);
′ (secondary), as in
lexicon (lĕk′sĭ-kŏn′)

—**ap′pre•hen′sive•ly** *adv.* —**ap′pre•hen′sive•ness** *n.*

ap•pren•tice (ə-prĕn′tĭs) *n.* **1.** One bound by legal agreement to work in return for instruction, as in a trade. **2.** One who is learning a trade or occupation, esp. as a member of a labor union. **3.** A beginner; a learner. ❖ *tr.v.* **-ticed, -tic•ing, -tic•es** To place or take on as a beginner or learner. [ME *apprentis* < OFr. *aprentis* < VLat. **apprenditīcius* < **apprenditus*, alteration of Lat. *apprehēnsus*, p. part. of *apprehendere*, to seize. See APPREHEND.] —**ap•pren′tice•ship′** *n.*

ap•pressed (ə-prĕst′) *adj.* Lying flat or pressed closely against something, as hairs on certain plant stems. [< Lat. *appressus*, p. part. of *apprimere*, to press down : *ad-*, ad- + *premere*, to press.]

ap•prise (ə-prīz′) *tr.v.* **-prised, -pris•ing, -pris•es** To give notice to; inform: *apprised us of our rights.* [Fr. *apprendre, appris-* < OFr. *aprendre*, to learn < Lat. *apprehendere, apprēndere.* See APPRENTICE.]

ap•prize (ə-prīz′) *tr.v.* **-prized, -priz•ing, -priz•es** To appreciate; value.

ap•proach (ə-prōch′) *v.* **-proached, -proach•ing, -proach•es** —*intr.* **1.** To come near or nearer, as in space or time. **2.** *Sports* To make an approach, as in golf. —*tr.* **1.** To come or go near or nearer to. **2.** To come close to, as in appearance or quality; approximate: *The performance approaches perfection.* **3.** To make a proposal or overtures to with a specific end in view. **4.** To begin to deal with or work on: *approached the task.* ❖ *n.* **1.** The act of approaching. **2.** A fairly close resemblance; an approximation. **3.** A means of reaching something; an access. **4.** The method used in dealing with or accomplishing. **5.** An advance or overture made by one person to another. **6.** *Sports* **a.** The golf stroke following the drive from the tee. **b.** The steps taken prior to a competitive maneuver, as by a bowler before delivering the ball. **c.** The part of the area behind the foul line in a bowling alley. [ME *approchen* < OFr. *aprochier* < LLat. *appropiāre* : Lat. *ad-*, ad- + Lat. *propius*, nearer, comp. of *prope*, near; see **per**[1] in App.]

ap•proach•a•ble (ə-prō′chə-bəl) *adj.* **1.** Possible to approach; accessible: *a mountain retreat approachable by helicopter.* **2.** Easy to talk to or deal with; friendly. —**ap•proach′a•bil′i•ty** *n.*

ap•pro•bate (ăp′rə-bāt′) *tr.v.* **-bat•ed, -bat•ing, -bates** To sanction officially; authorize. [ME *approbaten* < Lat. *approbāre, approbāt-*, to approve. See APPROVE.] —**ap′pro•ba′tive, ap•pro′ba•to′ry** (ə-prō′bə-tôr′ē, -tōr′ē) *adj.*

ap•pro•ba•tion (ăp′rə-bā′shən) *n.* **1.** An expression of warm approval; praise. **2.** Official approval.

ap•pro•pri•a•ble (ə-prō′prē-ə-bəl) *adj.* That can be appropriated: *appropriable funds.*

ap•pro•pri•ate (ə-prō′prē-ĭt) *adj.* Suitable for a particular person, condition, occasion, or place; fitting. ❖ *tr.v.* (-āt′) **-at•ed, -at•ing, -ates 1.** To set apart for a specific use. See Syns at **allocate. 2.** To take possession of or make use of exclusively for oneself, often without permission. [ME *appropriat* < LLat. *appropriātus*, p. part. of *appropriāre*, to make one's own : Lat. *ad-*, ad- + Lat. *proprius*, own; see **per**[1] in App.] —**ap•pro′pri•ate•ly** *adv.* —**ap•pro′pri•ate•ness** *n.* —**ap•pro′pri•a′tive** (-ā′tĭv) *adj.* —**ap•pro′pri•a′tor** *n.*

ap•pro•pri•a•tion (ə-prō′prē-ā′shən) *n.* **1.** The act of appropriating. **2a.** Something appropriated, esp. public funds. **b.** A legislative act authorizing the expenditure of an amount of public funds.

ap•prov•al (ə-pro͞o′vəl) *n.* **1.** The act of approving. **2.** An official approbation; a sanction. **3.** Favorable regard; commendation. —***idiom:* on approval** For examination or trial by a customer without the obligation to buy: *took the dress on approval.*

ap•prove (ə-pro͞ov′) *v.* **-proved, -prov•ing, -proves** —*tr.* **1.** To consider right or good; think or speak favorably of. **2.** To consent to officially or formally; confirm or sanction. **3.** *Obsolete* To prove or attest. —*intr.* To show, feel, or express approval. [ME *approven* < OFr. *aprover* < Lat. *approbāre* : *ad-*, ad- + *probāre*, to test (< *probus*, good; see **per**[1] in App.).] —**ap•prov′a•ble** *adj.* —**ap•prov′ing•ly** *adv.*

SYNONYMS *approve, endorse, sanction, certify, accredit, ratify* These verbs mean to express a favorable opinion or signify satisfaction or acceptance. *Approve* means to consider right or good, but it can also denote official consent: *"The colonel or commanding officer approves the sentence of a regimental court-martial"* (Charles James). *Endorse* implies the public expression of support: *a speech endorsing the party's candidate. Sanction* usually implies official authorization: *The privilege of voting is a right sanctioned by law. Certify* and *accredit* imply official approval based on compliance with requirements or standards: *"The proper officers, comparing every article with its voucher, certified them to be right"* (Benjamin Franklin). *The board will not accredit substandard schools.* To *ratify* is to invest officially with legal authority: *"Amendments . . . shall be valid . . . when ratified by the Legislatures of three fourths of the several States"* (US Constitution, Article V).

ap•prox•i•mant (ə-prŏk′sə-mənt) *n.* A speech sound, such as a glide, produced by narrowing but not blocking the vocal tract, as by placing the tongue near the hard palate.

ap•prox•i•mate (ə-prŏk′sə-mĭt) *adj.* **1.** Almost exact or correct: *the approximate time.* **2.** Very similar; closely resembling: *sketched an approximate likeness.* **3.** *Botany* Close together but not united. ❖ *v.* (-māt′) **-mat•ed, -mat•ing, -mates** —*tr.* **1.** To come close to; be nearly the same as: *approximates the real thing.* **2.** To bring near or together. —*intr.* To come near or close, as in degree or quality. [ME < LLat. *approximātus*, p. part. of *approximāre*, to approach : Lat. *ad-*, ad- + *proximāre*, to come near (< *proximus*, nearest; see **per**[1] in App.).] —**ap•prox′i•mate•ly** *adv.*

ap•prox•i•ma•tion (ə-prŏk′sə-mā′shən) *n.* **1.** The act, process, or result of approximating. **2.** *Mathematics* An inexact result adequate for a given purpose. —**ap•prox′i•ma′tive** (-mā′tĭv) *adj.* —**ap•prox′i•ma′tive•ly** *adv.*

ap•pur•te•nance (ə-pûr′tn-əns) *n.* **1.** Something added to a more important thing; an appendage. **2. appurtenances** Equipment, such as clothing or tools, used for a specific purpose; gear. **3.** *Law* A right, privilege, or property that is considered incident to the principal property for purposes such as passage of title. [ME *appurtenaunce* < AN *apurtenance* < VLat. **appertinentia* < LLat. *appertinēns, appertinent-*, pr. part. of *appertinēre*, to appertain. See APPERTAIN.] —**ap•pur′te•nant** *adj.*

APR *abbr.* annual percentage rate

Apr. *abbr.* April

a•prax•i•a (ā-prăk′sē-ə) *n.* Loss of the ability to perform coordinated movements or manipulate objects in the absence of motor or sensory impairment. [Gk. *apraxiā*, inaction : *a-*, without; see A–[1] + *prāxis*, action; see PRAXIS.] —**a•prac′tic** (ā-prăk′tĭk), **a•prax′ic** (ā-prăk′sĭk) *adj.*

a•près (ä′prā, ăp′rā) *prep.* After. Often used in combination: *an après-dinner entertainment; a concert après dinner.* [Fr. < OFr. < LLat. *ad pressum* : *ad*, to + *pressum*, nearby (< neut. of Lat. *pressus*, p. part. of *premere*, to press closely).]

a•près-ski (ä′prā-skē′, ăp′rā-) *adj.* Concerned with or designed for use after skiing: *après-ski wear.* [Fr. : *après*, after + *ski*, skiing.] —**a′près-ski′** *n.*

a•pri•cot (ăp′rĭ-kŏt′, ā′prĭ-) *n.* **1a.** A deciduous tree *(Prunus armeniaca)* having alternate leaves and clusters of flowers. **b.** The edible yellow-orange fruit of this tree. **2.** A moderate, light, or strong orange to strong orange yellow. [Alteration of earlier *abrecock*, ult. < Ar. *al-barqūq*, the plum : *al-*, the + *barqūq*, plum (< Gk. *praikokion*, apricot < Lat. *praecoquus*, ripe early : *prae-*, pre- + *coquere*, to cook, ripen; see **pek**^{w}- in App.).]

A•pril (ā′prəl) *n.* The fourth month of the year in the Gregorian calendar. See table at **calendar.** [ME < Lat. *aprīlis.*]

April fool *n.* **1.** The victim of a joke or trick played on April Fools' Day. **2.** The joke or trick so played.

April Fools' Day *n.* April 1, celebrated in various countries and marked by the playing of practical jokes.

a pri•o•ri (ä′ prē-ôr′ē, -ōr′ē, ā′ prī-ôr′ī, -ōr′ī′) *adj.* **1.** Proceeding from a known or assumed cause or principle to a necessarily related effect or instance; deductive. **2a.** Relating to or derived by reasoning without reference to particular facts or experience. **b.** Knowable without appeal to particular experience. **3.** Made before or without examination; not supported by factual study. [Med.Lat. *ā priōrī* : Lat. *ā*, from + Lat. *priōrī*, ablative of *prior*, former.] —**a′pri•o′ri** *adv.* —**a′pri•or′i•ty** (-ôr′ĭ-tē, -ŏr′-) *n.*

a•pron (ā′prən) *n.* **1a.** A garment worn over the front of the body to protect clothing. **b.** Something that resembles this garment in appearance or function. **2.** The paved strip in front of and around airport hangars and terminal buildings. **3.** The part of a stage in a theater extending in front of the curtain. **4.** A covering or structure, as along a shoreline or below a dam, for protection against erosion. **5.** A continuous conveyor belt. **6.** An area covered by sand and gravel deposited at the front of a glacial moraine. **7.** A border of slightly longer grass that surrounds a green on a golf course. ❖ *tr.v.* **a•proned, a•pron•ing, a•prons** To cover, protect, or provide with an apron. [ME < *an apron*, alteration of *a napron* < OFr. *naperon*, dim. of *nape*, tablecloth < Lat. *mappa*, napkin. See MAP.]

apron string *n.* The string of an apron. Usu. used with *tied* to indicate control: *tied to her mother's apron strings.*

ap•ro•pos (ăp′rə-pō′) *adj.* Being opportune and to the point. ❖ *adv.* **1.** At an appropriate time; opportunely. **2.** By the way; incidentally. ❖ *prep.* With regard to; concerning: *Apropos our date, I can't go.* [Fr. *à propos* : *à*, to (< OFr. *a* < Lat. *ad*) + *propos*, purpose (< Lat. *prōpositum* < neut. p. part. of *prōpōnere*, to intend; see PROPOSE).]

apropos of *prep.* With reference to; speaking of.

apse (ăps) *n.* **1.** *Architecture* A semicircular or polygonal, usu. domed projection of a building, esp. of a church. **2.** *Astronomy* Apsis. [Variant of APSIS.] —**ap′si•dal** (ăp′sĭ-dəl) *adj.*

ap•sis (ăp′sĭs) *n., pl.* **-si•des** (-sĭ-dēz′) **1.** *Architecture* An apse. **2.** *Astronomy* The point of greatest or least distance of the orbit of a celestial body from a center of attraction. [LLat. < Lat., arch, vault < Gk. *hapsis* < *haptein*, to fasten.]

apt (ăpt) *adj.* **1.** Exactly suitable; appropriate: *an apt reply.* **2.** Having a natural tendency; inclined: *apt to take offense.* See Usage Note at **liable. 3.** Quick to learn or understand: *an apt student.* [ME < OFr. *apte* < Lat. *aptus*, p. part. of *apere*, to fasten.] —**apt′ly** *adv.* —**apt′ness** *n.*

apt. *abbr.* apartment

ap•ter•al (ăp′tər-əl) *adj.* Having no columns along the sides. Used esp. of a classical temple. [< Gk. *apteros*, wingless : *a-*, with-

aquacade

aqueduct
the Pont du Gard near Nîmes, France, built by the Romans in the first century B.C.

Saint Thomas Aquinas

out; see A–[1] + *pteron*, wing; see –PTER.]
ap•ter•ous (ăp′tər-əs) *adj.* Having no wings or winglike extensions: *an apterous insect.*
ap•ter•yx (ăp′tə-rĭks′) *n.* See **kiwi** 1. [NLat. *Apteryx*, genus name : A–[1] + Gk. *pterux*, wing; see **pet-** in App.]
ap•ti•tude (ăp′tĭ-to͞od′, -tyo͞od′) *n.* **1.** An inherent ability, as for learning; a talent. **2.** Quickness in understanding; intelligence. **3.** The condition of being suitable; appropriateness. [ME, tendency < LLat. *aptitūdō*, aptitude < Lat. *aptus*, apt. See APT.] **—ap′ti•tu′di•nal** (-to͞od′n-əl, -tyo͞od′-) *adj.* **—ap′ti•tu′di•nal•ly** *adv.*
aptitude test *n.* A standardized test designed to measure the ability of a person to develop skills or acquire knowledge.
Ap•u•lei•us (ăp′yə-lē′əs), **Lucius** fl. 2nd cent. A.D. Roman Neo-Platonist philosopher and satirist best known for *The Golden Ass.*
A•pu•lia (ə-po͞ol′yə) also **Pu•glia** (po͞o′lyä) A region of SE Italy on the Adriatic Sea. Its S portion is the heel of the Italian "boot."
A•pu•re (ä-po͞o′rĕ) A river of W-central Venezuela rising in the Andes of Colombia and flowing c. 805 km (500 mi) to the Orinoco R.
A•pu•rí•mac (ä′pə-rē′mäk) A river of S Peru rising in the Andes and flowing c. 885 km (550 mi) to the Ucayali R.
A•pus (ā′pəs) *n.* A constellation in the Southern Hemisphere near Musca and Pavo. [Lat. *apūs*, a kind of swallow < Gk. *apous*, without feet, sand martin : *a-*, without; see A–[1] + *pous*, foot; see **ped-** in App.]
ap•y•rase (ăp′ə-rās′, -rāz′) *n.* Any of various enzymes that catalyze the hydrolysis of ATP, causing the release of phosphate and energy. [A(DENOSINE) + PYR(O)– + (PHOSPHAT)ASE.]
A•qa•ba (ä′kə-bə, ăk′ə-), **Gulf of** An arm of the Red Sea between the Sinai Peninsula and NW Saudi Arabia.
Aq•tö•be (äk′tœ-bĕ′) also **Ak•tyu•binsk** (äk-tyo͞o′bĭnsk) A city of W Kazakhstan NW of Astrakhan; founded 1869. Pop. 264,000.
aq•ua (ăk′wə, ä′kwə) *n., pl.* **aq•uae** (ăk′wē, ä′kwī′) or **aq•uas 1.** Water. **2.** An aqueous solution. **3.** A light bluish green to light greenish blue. [ME < Lat. See **akʷ-ā-** in App.] **—aq′ua** *adj.*
aqua– *pref.* Water: *aquacade.* [< Lat. *aqua*, water. See AQUA.]
aq•ua•cade (ăk′wə-kād′, ä′kwə-) *n.* An entertainment spectacle of swimmers and divers. [AQUA– + (CAVAL)CADE.]
aq•ua•cul•ture (ăk′wə-kŭl′chər, ä′kwə-) *n.* **1.** The cultivation of food fish or shellfish under controlled conditions. **2.** *Botany* Hydroponics. **—aq′ua•cul′tur•al** *adj.* **—aq′ua•cul′tur•ist** *n.*
aq•ua•farm•ing (ăk′wə-fär′mĭng, ä′kwə-) *n.* See **aquaculture.** **—aq′ua•farm′** *n. & v.* **—aq′ua•farm′er** *n.*
aqua for•tis also **aq•ua•for•tis** (ăk′wə-fôr′tĭs, ä′kwə-) *n.* See **nitric acid.** [NLat. : Lat. *aqua*, water + Lat. *fortis*, strong.]
Aq•ua-Lung (ăk′wə-lŭng′, ä′kwə-) A trademark used for an underwater breathing apparatus.
aq•ua•ma•rine (ăk′wə-mə-rēn′, ä′kwə-) *n.* **1.** A transparent blue-green variety of beryl, used as a gemstone. **2.** A pale blue to light greenish blue. [Lat. *aqua marīna*, seawater : *aqua*, water; see AQUA + *marīna*, of the sea; see MARINE.]
aq•ua•naut (ăk′wə-nôt′, ä′kwə-) *n.* A scuba diver trained to work or take part in scientific research in underwater installations. [AQUA– + Gk. *nautēs*, sailor.]
aqua re•gi•a (rē′jē-ə, rē′jə) *n.* A corrosive, fuming, volatile mixture of hydrochloric and nitric acids, used for testing and dissolving metals. [NLat. *aqua rēgia* : Lat. *aqua*, water + Lat. *rēgia*, fem. of *rēgius*, royal (because it dissolves gold, the "royal metal").]
aq•ua•relle (ăk′wə-rĕl′, ä′kwə-) *n.* A painting that is done in transparent watercolors. [Fr. < obsolete Ital. *acquarella*, water color, dim. of *acqua*, water < Lat. *aqua.* See **akʷ-ā-** in App.] **—aq′ua•rel′list** *n.*
a•quar•ist (ə-kwâr′ĭst) *n.* One who maintains an aquarium.
a•quar•i•um (ə-kwâr′ē-əm) *n., pl.* **-i•ums** or **-i•a** (-ē-ə) **1.** A water-filled enclosure in which living fish or other aquatic animals and plants are kept. **2.** A place for the public exhibition of aquatic life. [Lat. *aquārium*, source of water < neut. of *aquārius*, of water < *aqua*, water. See **akʷ-ā-** in App.]
A•quar•i•us (ə-kwâr′ē-əs) *n.* **1.** A constellation in the equatorial region of the Southern Hemisphere near Pisces and Aquila. **2a.** The 11th sign of the zodiac in astrology. **b.** One who is born under this sign. [ME < Lat., water carrier, the constellation Aquarius < *aqua*, water. See AQUA.]
a•quat•ic (ə-kwăt′ĭk, ə-kwŏt′-) *adj.* **1.** Consisting of, relating to, or being in water. **2.** Living or growing in, on, or near the water: *aquatic animals.* **3.** Taking place in or on the water: *an aquatic sport.* ❖ *n.* **1.** An organism that lives in, on, or near the water. **2. aquatics** *Sports* Athletic activities performed in or on the water. [ME *aquatique* < OFr. < Lat. *aquāticus* < *aqua*, water. See **akʷ-ā-** in App.] **—a•quat′i•cal•ly** *adv.*
aq•ua•tint (ăk′wə-tĭnt′, ä′kwə-) *n.* **1.** A process of etching that produces several tones by varying the etching time of different areas of a copper plate. **2.** An etching made by this process. [Fr. *aquatinte* < Ital. *acquatinta* : *acqua*, water (< Lat. *aqua*; see AQUA) + *tinta*, dyed (< Lat. *tincta*, fem. p. part. of *tingere*, to dye).] **—aq′ua•tint′** *v.* **—aq′ua•tint′er, aq′ua•tint′ist** *n.*
a•qua•vit (ä′kwə-vēt′) *n.* A strong liquor distilled from potato or grain mash and flavored with caraway seed. [Swed., Dan., and Norw. *akvavit* < Med.Lat. *aqua vītae*, highly distilled spirits : Lat. *aqua*, water + Lat. *vītae*, genitive of *vīta*, life.]
aqua vi•tae (vī′tē) *n.* Strong distilled alcohol. [ME *aqua vite* < Med.Lat. *aqua vītae.* See AQUAVIT.]
aq•ue•duct (ăk′wĭ-dŭkt′) *n.* **1a.** A pipe or channel that transports water from a remote source, usu. by gravity. **b.** A bridgelike structure supporting a conduit or canal. **2.** *Anatomy* A channel or passage in an organ or a body part, esp. for conveying fluid. [Lat. *aquaeductus* : *aquae*, genitive of *aqua*, water; see AQUA + *ductus*, a leading; see DUCT.]
a•que•ous (ā′kwē-əs, ăk′wē-) *adj.* **1.** Relating to, similar to, containing, or dissolved in water; watery. **2.** *Geology* Formed from matter deposited by water. [< Med.Lat. *aqueus* < Lat. *aqua*, water. See AQUA.]
aqueous humor *n.* The clear, watery fluid circulating in the chamber of the eye between the cornea and the lens.
aqui– *pref.* Water: *aquifer.* [Lat. < *aqua*, water. See **akʷ-ā-** in App.]
aq•ui•fer (ăk′wə-fər, ä′kwə-) *n.* An underground layer, as of earth, that yields water. **—a•quif′er•ous** (ə-kwĭf′ər-əs) *adj.*
Aq•ui•la (ăk′wə-lə) *n.* A constellation in the Northern Hemisphere and the Milky Way near Aquarius and Serpens Cauda. [ME < Lat. *aquila*, eagle, the constellation Aquila.]
aq•ui•le•gi•a (ăk′wə-lē′jē-ə, -lē′jə) *n.* See **columbine.** [Med. Lat. *aquilēgia.*]
aq•ui•line (ăk′wə-līn′, -lĭn) *adj.* **1.** Of or relating to an eagle. **2.** Curved or hooked like an eagle's beak. [Lat. *aquilīnus* < *aquila*, eagle.] **—aq′ui•lin′i•ty** (-lĭn′ĭtē) *n.*
A•qui•nas (ə-kwī′nəs), Saint **Thomas** 1225–74. Italian theologian and philosopher best known for his *Summa theologica* (1266–73).
A•qui•no (ä-kē′nō), **Corazón Cojuangco** b. 1933. Philippine politician and president (1986–92).
Aq•ui•taine (ăk′wĭ-tān′) A historical region of SW France between the Pyrenees and the Garonne R.
Aq•ui•ta•ni•a (ăk′wĭ-tā′nē-ə) A Roman division of SW Gaul extending from the Pyrenees to the Garonne R.; conquered by Julius Caesar in 56 B.C.
a•quiv•er (ə-kwĭv′ər) *adj.* Marked by quivering.
ar[1] (är) *n.* Variant of **are[2].**
ar[2] (är) *n.* The letter *r.* [ME *arre* < LLat. *er.*]
Ar The symbol for the element **argon.**
AR *abbr.* **1.** also **A/R** accounts receivable **2.** Arkansas
Ar. *abbr.* **1.** Arabia **2.** Arabic **3.** army regulation
–ar *suff.* Of, relating to, or resembling: *polar.* [ME < OFr. *-er* < Lat. *-āris*, var. of *-ālis*, -al.]
A•ra (âr′ə) *n.* A constellation in the Southern Hemisphere near Norma and Telescopium. [Lat. *āra*, altar, Ara. See **as-** in App.]
Ar•ab (ăr′əb) *n.* **1.** A member of a Semitic people inhabiting Arabia, whose language and Islamic religion spread widely throughout the Middle East and northern Africa from the seventh century. **2.** A member of an Arabic-speaking people. **3.** An Arabian horse. **4.** *Offensive Slang* A waif. [Fr. *Arabe* < Lat. *Arabs* < Gk. *Araps, Arab-* < Ar. *ʿarab.*] **—Ar′ab** *adj.*
Arab. *abbr.* Arabic
ar•a•besque (ăr′ə-bĕsk′) *n.* **1.** A ballet position in which the dancer stands on one leg with the other extended to the back. **2.** A complex ornate design of intertwined floral, foliate, and geometric figures. **3.** *Music* An ornate whimsical composition, esp. for the piano. **4.** An intricate or elaborate pattern or design: "*the complex arabesque of a camera movement*" (Nigel Andrews). ❖ *adj.* In the fashion of or formed as an arabesque. [Fr. < Ital. *arabesco*, in Arabian fashion < *Arabo*, an Arab < Lat. *Arabus* < *Arabs.* See ARAB.]
A•ra•bi•a (ə-rā′bē-ə) also **A•ra•bi•an Peninsula** (-bē-ən) A peninsula of SW Asia between the Red Sea and the Persian Gulf. Politically, it includes Saudi Arabia, Yemen, Oman, the United Arab Emirates, Qatar, Bahrain, and Kuwait.
A•ra•bi•an (ə-rā′bē-ən) *adj.* Of or concerning Arabia or the Arabs; Arab. ❖ *n.* **1.** A native or inhabitant of Arabia. **2.** An Arabian horse.
Arabian camel *n.* See **dromedary.**
Arabian Desert A desert of E Egypt between the Nile Valley and the Red Sea.
Arabian Gulf See **Persian Gulf.**
Arabian horse *n.* Any of a breed of swift horses native to Arabia.
Arabian Sea The NW part of the Indian Ocean between Arabia and W India.
Ar•a•bic (ăr′ə-bĭk) *adj.* Of or relating to Arabia, the Arabs, their language, or their culture. ❖ *n.* A Semitic language consisting of numerous dialects that is the principal language of Arabia, Jordan, Syria, Iraq, Lebanon, Egypt, and parts of northern Africa.
a•rab•i•ca (ə-răb′ĭ-kə) *n.* **1a.** A species of coffee, *Coffea arabica*, originating in Ethiopia and widely cultivated for its seeds. **b.** The beanlike seed of this plant. **2.** The coffee brewed from the seed of this plant. [NLat. *(Coffea) arabica*, species name < Lat., fem. of *Arabicus*, from Arabia < Gk. *Arabikos* < *Araps, Arab-*, an Arab. See ARAB.]
Arabic numeral *n.* One of the numerical symbols 1, 2, 3, 4, 5, 6, 7, 8, 9, or 0.
a•rab•i•nose (ə-răb′ə-nōs′, ăr′ə-bə-) *n.* A crystalline pentose sugar, $C_5H_{10}O_5$, obtained from plant polysaccharides such as gums and hemicelluloses. [(GUM) ARAB(IC) + –IN + –OSE[2].]
Ar•ab•ist (ăr′ə-bĭst) *n.* **1.** A specialist in the Arabic language or

arabesque
top: ballet dancer
bottom: detail of a wall in Marrakesh, Morocco

Arabian horse

ă	pat	oi	boy
ā	pay	ou	out
âr	care	o͝o	took
ä	father	o͞o	boot
ĕ	pet	ŭ	cut
ē	be	ûr	urge
ĭ	pit	th	thin
ī	pie	*th*	this
îr	pier	hw	which
ŏ	pot	zh	vision
ō	toe	ə	about, item
ô	paw		

Stress marks:
′ (primary);
′ (secondary), as in
lexicon (lĕk′sĭ-kŏn′)

culture. **2.** One favorably disposed to Arab concerns.

ar·a·ble (ăr′ə-bəl) *adj.* Fit for cultivation, as by plowing. ❖ *n.* Land fit to be cultivated. [ME < OFr. < Lat. *arābilis* < *arāre*, to plow.] —**ar′a·bil′i·ty** *n.*

Arab League also **League of Arab States** An association of Arab states est. in 1945 to promote cooperation among member nations in economic and social development and in foreign policy matters.

A·ra·ca·ju (ä-rä′kä-zhoo′) A city of E-central Brazil near the Atlantic Ocean SSE of Recife. Pop. 401,676.

ar·a·chi·don·ic acid (ăr′ə-kĭ-dŏn′ĭk) *n.* An unsaturated fatty acid, $C_{20}H_{32}O_2$, found in animal fats that is essential in human nutrition. [< *arachidic*, of the groundnut < NLat. *Arachis*, groundnut genus < Gk. *arakis, arakid-*, dim. of *arakos*, a leguminous plant.]

A·rach·ne (ə-răk′nē) *n. Greek Mythology* A young woman who challenged Athena to a weaving contest and was turned into a spider.

a·rach·nid (ə-răk′nĭd) *n.* Any of various arthropods of the class Arachnida, characterized by four pairs of segmented legs and a body divided into two regions. [< NLat. *Arachnida*, class name < Gk. *arakhnē*, spider.] —**a·rach′ni·dan** (-nĭ-dən) *adj. & n.*

a·rach·noid (ə-răk′noid′) *adj.* **1.** *Anatomy* Of, relating to, or being a delicate membrane enclosing the spinal cord and brain. **2.** Of, relating to, or resembling arachnids. ❖ *n.* **1.** See **arachnid. 2.** *Anatomy* The arachnoid membrane. [NLat. *arachnoīdēs* < Gk. *arakhnoeidēs*, cobweblike : *arakhnē*, spider + *-oeidēs*, -oid.]

a·rach·no·pho·bi·a (ə-răk′nə-fō′bē-ə, -nō-) *n.* An abnormal fear of spiders. [ARACHN(ID) + −PHOBIA.]

Ar·a·fat (ăr′ə-făt′, är′ə-fät′), **Yasir** b. 1929. Leader of the Palestine Liberation Organization who shared the 1994 Nobel Peace Prize and was elected president of the Palestine Authority (1996).

A·ra·fu·ra Sea (ä′rə-foo′rə) A shallow part of the W Pacific Ocean separating New Guinea from Australia.

Ar·a·gon (ăr′ə-gŏn′) A region and former kingdom of NE Spain; united with Castile in 1479 to form the nucleus of modern Spain. —**Ar′a·go·nese′** (ăr′ə-gə-nēz′, -nēs′) *adj. & n.*

A·ra·gon (ä-rä-gôn′), **Louis** 1897–1982. French writer who was a founder of literary surrealism.

a·rag·o·nite (ə-răg′ə-nīt′, ăr′ə-gə-) *n.* An orthorhombic mineral form of crystalline calcium carbonate. [After ARAGON.]

A·ra·guai·a or **A·ra·gua·ya** (ä′rə-gwī′ə) A river rising in central Brazil and flowing c. 2,092 km (1,300 mi) to the Tocantins R.

A·raks (ə-räks′) or **A·ras** (ə-räs′) Formerly **A·rax·es** (ə-răk′sēz) A river rising in NE Turkey and flowing c. 965 km (600 mi) along the Turkey-Armenia and Azerbaijan-Iran borders.

Ar·al Sea (ăr′əl) An inland sea E of the Caspian Sea between S Kazakhstan and NW Uzbekistan. Once the fourth-largest inland body of water, it is fast disappearing because of diversion of its two sources, the Amu Darya and the Syr Darya.

Ar·am (âr′əm, är′-, ā′răm) In the Bible, an ancient country of SW Asia, roughly coextensive with present-day Syria.

Ar·a·ma·ic (ăr′ə-mā′ĭk) *n.* A Semitic language, originally of the ancient Arameans. —**Ar′a·ma′ic** *adj.*

a·ra·me (ä′rə-mä, ə-rä′-) *n.* An edible seaweed. [J.]

Ar·a·me·an or **Ar·a·mae·an** (ăr′ə-mē′ən) *adj.* Of or relating to Aram, its inhabitants, or their language. ❖ *n.* **1.** One of a group of Semitic peoples inhabiting Aram and parts of Mesopotamia from the 11th to the 8th century B.C. **2.** See **Aramaic.**

ar·a·mid fiber (ăr′ə-mĭd) *n.* A strong, heat-resistant fiber formed of polymers, used in bulletproof vests and radial tires. [AR(OMATIC) + (POLY)AMID(E).]

Ar·an Islands (ăr′ən) Three small islands of W Ireland at the entrance to Galway Bay.

A·ra·nya·ka (ăr′ə-nyä′kə, -nyə-) *n.* Any of several Sanskrit religious and philosophical treatises intended to be read by hermits in the quiet of the forest. [Skt. *Āraṇyakam* < neut. sg. of *āraṇyaka-*, of the forest < *āraṇya-* < *araṇyam*, foreign land, wilderness, forest < *arana-*, distant, foreign. See al- in App.]

A·rap·a·ho also **A·rap·a·hoe** (ə-răp′ə-hō′) *n., pl.* **Arapaho** or **-hos** also **Arapahoe** or **-hoes 1.** A member of a Native American people formerly inhabiting eastern Colorado and southeast Wyoming, with present-day populations in Oklahoma and central Wyoming. **2.** The Algonquian language of the Arapaho. [Crow *aaraxpéahu*, those with many tattoos.]

ar·a·pai·ma (ăr′ə-pī′mə) *n.* A large South American freshwater food fish (*Arapaima gigas*), up to 3 meters (10 feet) in length. [Am.Sp. or Port., both prob. of Tupian orig.]

Ar·a·rat (ăr′ə-rät′), **Mount** A massif, c. 5,168 m (16,945 ft), of extreme E Turkey; traditional resting place of Noah's ark.

A·ras (ə-räs′) See **Araks.**

A·rau·ca (ə-rou′kə) A river rising in N Colombia and flowing c. 805 km (500 mi) to the Orinoco R. in Venezuela.

Ar·au·ca·ni·an (är′ô-kā′nē-ən) also **A·rau·can** (ə-rô′kən) *n.* **1.** A member of a group of South American Indian peoples of south-central Chile and western Argentina, including the Mapuche. **2.** The family of languages spoken by the Araucanians. [Sp. *araucano* < *Arauco*, a former province of S-central Chile.] —**Ar′au·ca′ni·an** *adj.*

ar·au·car·i·a (ăr′ou-kâr′ē-ə) *n.* Any of several evergreen trees of the genus *Araucaria*, having awl-shaped leaves and whorled

Yasir Arafat

arborvitae
American arborvitae
Thuja occidentalis

branches. [< Sp. *araucaria*, (tree) of Arauco, a former province of S-central Chile.]

Ar·a·wak (ăr′ə-wäk′) *n., pl.* **Arawak** or **-waks 1.** A member of a South American Indian people formerly inhabiting much of the Greater Antilles and now living chiefly in certain regions of Guiana. **2.** The Arawakan language of the Arawak.

Ar·a·wa·kan (ăr′ə-wä′kən) *n., pl.* **Arawakan** or **-kans 1.** A member of a group of Indian peoples living in parts of Colombia, Venezuela, Guiana, the Amazon basin of Brazil, Paraguay, Bolivia, Peru, and formerly most of the Greater Antilles. **2.** The family of languages spoken by the Arawakan peoples. —**Ar′a·wa′kan** *adj.*

A·rax·es (ə-răk′sēz) See **Araks.**

ar·ba·lest also **ar·ba·list** (är′bə-lĭst) *n.* A medieval missile launcher designed on the principle of the crossbow. [ME *arblast* < OE < OFr. *arbaleste* < LLat. *arcuballista* : Lat. *arcus*, bow + Lat. *ballista*, ballista; see BALLISTA.] —**ar′ba·lest′er** (-lĕs′tər) *n.*

Ar·be·la (är-bē′lə) An ancient town of Assyria in present-day N Iraq. Its name is sometimes given to the battle fought at Gaugamela, c. 97 km (60 mi) away, in which Alexander the Great defeated Darius III in 331 B.C.

Ar·bil (îr′bĭl, är′-) or **Ir·bil** (îr′-) A city of N Iraq N of Baghdad; built on the site of ancient Arbela. Pop. 485,968.

ar·bi·ter (är′bĭ-tər) *n.* **1.** One chosen to judge or decide a disputed issue; an arbitrator. **2.** One who has the power to judge or ordain at will: *an arbiter of fashion.* [ME *arbitre* < OFr. < Lat. *arbiter* < Phoenician (Punic) **arb, surety, guarantee.]

ar·bi·tra·ble (är′bĭ-trə-bəl) *adj.* **1.** Subject to arbitration. **2.** Appropriate for referral to an arbitrator.

ar·bi·trage (är′bĭ-träzh′) *n.* The purchase of securities on one market for immediate resale on another market. ❖ *intr.v.* **-traged, -trag·ing, -trag·es** To be involved in arbitrage. [ME, arbitration < OFr. < *arbitrer*, to judge < Lat. *arbitrārī*, to give judgment. See ARBITRATE.]

ar·bi·tra·geur (är′bĭ-trä-zhûr′) also **ar·bi·tra·ger** (är′bĭ-trä′zhər) *n.* One that engages in arbitrage. [Fr. < *arbitrage*, arbitration. See ARBITRAGE.]

ar·bi·tral (är′bĭ-trəl) *adj.* Of or relating to arbiters or arbitration.

ar·bi·tra·ment (är-bĭt′rə-mənt) *n.* **1.** The act of arbitrating; arbitration. **2.** The judgment of an arbitrator. [ME *arbitrement* < OFr. < *arbitrer*, to judge. See ARBITRAGE.]

ar·bi·trar·y (är′bĭ-trĕr′ē) *adj.* **1.** Determined by chance, whim, or impulse: *arbitrary division of the group into halves.* **2.** Based on or subject to individual judgment or preference. **3.** Established by a court or judge rather than a specific law or statute. **4.** Not limited by law; despotic: *the arbitrary rule of a dictator.* [ME *arbitrarie* < Lat. *arbitrārius* < *arbiter, arbitr-*, arbiter. See ARBITER.] —**ar′bi·trar′i·ly** (-trâr′ə-lē) *adv.* —**ar′bi·trar′i·ness** *n.*

ar·bi·trate (är′bĭ-trāt′) *v.* **-trat·ed, -trat·ing, -trates** —*tr.* **1.** To judge or decide in or as in the manner of an arbitrator. **2.** To submit to settlement or judgment by arbitration. —*intr.* **1.** To serve as an arbitrator. **2.** To submit a dispute to arbitration. [Lat. *arbitrārī, arbitrāt-*, to give judgment < *arbiter, arbitr-*, arbiter. See ARBITER.] —**ar′bi·tra′tive** (-trā′tĭv) *adj.*

ar·bi·tra·tion (är′bĭ-trā′shən) *n.* The process by which the parties to a dispute submit their differences to the judgment of an impartial person or group appointed by mutual consent or statutory provision.

ar·bi·tra·tor (är′bĭ-trā′tər) *n.* **1.** A person chosen to settle the issue between parties engaged in a dispute. **2.** One having the ability or power to make authoritative decisions; an arbiter.

ar·bor¹ (är′bər) *n.* **1.** A shady place in a garden or park, often made of rustic work or latticework on which plants are grown. [ME *erber* < OFr. *erbier*, garden < *erbe*, herb. See HERB.]

ar·bor² (är′bər) *n.* **1.** An axis or shaft supporting a rotating part on a lathe. **2.** A bar for supporting cutting tools. **3.** A spindle of a wheel, as in clocks. **4.** *pl.* **ar·bo·res** (är′bə-rēz′) A tree, as opposed to a shrub. [Fr. *arbre* < Lat. *arbor*, tree.]

Arbor Day *n.* An unofficial holiday observed in the United States, usu. in April, for the public planting of trees.

ar·bo·re·al (är-bôr′ē-əl, -bŏr′-) *adj.* **1.** Relating to or resembling a tree. **2.** Living in trees; arboreous: *arboreal apes.* [< Lat. *arboreus* < *arbor*, tree.] —**ar′bo′re·al·ly** *adv.*

ar·bo·re·ous (är-bôr′ē-əs, -bŏr′-) *adj.* **1.** Relating to or resembling a tree. **2.** Living in trees; arboreal. **3.** Having many trees; wooded.

ar·bo·res·cent (är′bə-rĕs′ənt) *adj.* Having the size, form, or characteristics of a tree; treelike. [Lat. *arborēscēns, arborescent-*, pr. part. of *arborēscere*, to grow to be a tree < *arbor*, tree.] —**ar′bo·res′cence** *n.*

ar·bo·re·tum (är′bə-rē′təm) *n., pl.* **-tums** or **-ta** (-tə) A place where an extensive variety of woody plants are cultivated for scientific, educational, and ornamental purposes. [Lat. *arborētum*, place grown with trees < *arbor*, tree.]

ar·bo·ri·cul·ture (är′bər-ĭ-kŭl′chər, är-bôr′ĭ-, -bŏr′-) *n.* The planting and care of woody plants, esp. trees. —**ar′bo·ri·cul′tur·al** *adj.*

ar·bo·ri·o rice (âr-bôr′ē-ō, -bŏr′-) *n.* A rounded, medium-grain rice from Italy. [After *Arborio*, town in the Po valley in Italy where the rice is grown.]

ar·bor·ist (är′bər-ĭst) *n.* A specialist in the care of woody plants, esp. trees. [< Lat. *arbor*, tree.]

ar·bo·ri·za·tion (är′bər-ĭ-zā′shən) *n.* **1.** A branching treelike shape or arrangement, as that of the dendrite of a nerve cell. **2.** The formation of a treelike shape or arrangement.

ar·bo·rize (är′bə-rīz′) *intr.v.* **-rized, -riz·ing, -riz·es** To have or produce branching formations, as the capillaries. [< Lat. *arbor*, tree.]

ar·bor·vi·tae also **ar·bor vi·tae** (är′bər-vī′tē) *n.* **1a.** Any of several North American or eastern Asian evergreen trees or shrubs of the genus *Thuja*, having flattened branchlets with opposite scalelike leaves. **b.** Any similar plant of the genus *Platycladus* or *Thujopsis.* **2.** *Anatomy* The white nerve tissue of the cerebellum. [< NLat. *arbor vītae*, tree of life : Lat. *arbor*, tree + Lat. *vītae*, genitive of *vīta*, life.]

ar·bour (är′bər) *n.* Chiefly British Variant of **arbor**[1].

ar·bo·vi·rus (är′bə-vī′rəs) *n.* Any of a large group of viruses transmitted by arthropods that include the causative agents of encephalitis and dengue. [*ar(thropod-)bo(rne) virus.*] **—ar′bo·vi′ral** *adj.* **—ar′bo·vi·rol′o·gy** (är′bō-vī-rŏl′ə-jē) *n.*

Ar·bus (är′bəs), **Diane** 1923–71. Amer. photographer best known for her portraits of unconventional subjects.

ar·buth·not (är-bŭth′nət, är′bəth-nŏt′), **John** 1667–1735. Scottish physician noted for his anti-Whig pamphlets.

ar·bu·tus (är-byōō′təs) *n.* **1.** Any of various broad-leaved evergreen trees or shrubs of the genus *Arbutus* that are native chiefly to warm regions in the Americas and Europe. **2.** The trailing arbutus. [Lat. *arbutus*, arbutus.]

arc (ärk) *n.* **1.** Something shaped like a curve or arch: *the arc of a rainbow.* **2.** *Mathematics* A segment of a circle. **3.** An electric arc. **4.** *Astronomy* The apparent path of a celestial body as it rises above and falls below the horizon. ❖ *intr.v.* **arced** (ärkt), **arc·ing** (är′kĭng), **arcs** **1.** To form an arc. **2.** To move or seem to move in a curved path. [ME *ark* < OFr. *arc* < Lat. *arcus.*]

ARC[1] (ärk) *n.* A combination of symptoms, including fever, blood abnormalities, and susceptibility to opportunistic infections, that is a precursor to AIDS in some individuals infected with HIV. [A(IDS)-R(ELATED) C(OMPLEX).]

ARC[2] *abbr.* American Red Cross

ar·cade (är-kād′) *n.* **1.** A series of arches supported by columns, piers, or pillars. **2.** A roofed passageway or lane, esp. one with shops on either side. **3.** A commercial establishment featuring coin-operated games. ❖ *tr.v.* **-cad·ed, -cad·ing, -cades** To provide with or form into an arcade. [Fr. < Ital. *arcata* < *arco*, arch < Lat. *arcus.*]

Ar·ca·di·a[1] (är-kā′dē-ə) also **Ar·ca·dy** (är′kə-dē) A region of ancient Greece in the Peloponnesus. Its isolated inhabitants proverbially lived a simple, pastoral life.

Ar·ca·di·a[2] also **ar·ca·di·a** (är-kā′dē-ə) *n.* A region offering rural simplicity and contentment.

Ar·ca·di·an (är-kā′dē-ən) *adj.* **1.** Of or relating to the ancient Greek region of Arcadia or its people, language, or culture. **2.** often **arcadian** Rustic, peaceful, and simple; pastoral. ❖ *n.* **1.** A native or inhabitant of ancient Arcadia. **2.** often **arcadian** One who leads or prefers a simple, rural life. **3.** The dialect of ancient Greek used in Arcadia.

ar·cane (är-kān′) *adj.* Known or understood by only a few. See Syns at **mysterious.** [Lat. *arcānus*, secret < *arca*, chest.]

ar·ca·num (är-kā′nəm) *n., pl.* **-na** (-nə) *or* **-nums 1.** A deep secret; a mystery. **2.** often **arcana** Specialized knowledge that is mysterious to the average person: *"knows the arcana of police procedure"* (George F. Will). **3.** A secret essence or remedy; an elixir. [Lat. *arcānum* < neut. of *arcānus*, secret. See ARCANE.]

arc-bou·tant (är′bōō-tän′) *n., pl.* **arcs-bou·tants** (är′bōō-tän′) Flying buttress. [Fr. : *arc*, arch (< see ARC) + *boutant*, pr. part. of *bouter*, to thrust (< OFr.; see BUTT[1]).]

arc cosecant *n.* The inverse of the cosecant function.

arc cosine *n.* The inverse of the cosine function.

arc cotangent *n.* The inverse of the cotangent function.

arch[1] (ärch) *n.* **1.** A structure forming the curved, pointed, or flat upper edge of an open space and supporting the weight above it, as in a doorway. **2.** A structure shaped like an inverted U. **3.** A curve with the ends down and the middle up: *the arch of a raised eyebrow.* **4.** *Anatomy* A curved or bowlike structure, esp. either of two arched sections of the bony structure of the foot. ❖ *v.* **arched, arch·ing, arch·es** *—tr.* **1.** To provide with an arch: *arch a passageway.* **2.** To cause to form an arch or similar curve. **3.** To bend backward. **4.** To span: *"the rude bridge that arched the flood"* (Ralph Waldo Emerson). *—intr.* To form an arch or archlike curve. [ME < OFr. *arche* < VLat. **arca* < Lat. *arcus.*]

arch[2] (ärch) *adj.* **1.** Chief; principal. **2.** Mischievous; roguish. [< ARCH-[1].] **—arch′ly** *adv.* **—arch′ness** *n.*

arch. *abbr.* **1.** archaic **b.** archaism **2.** archipelago **3.** architecture

arch-[1] *pref.* **1.** Chief; highest; most important: *archenemy.* **2.** Extreme or most characteristic of its kind: *archconservative.* [ME *arche-* < OE *ærce-* and < OFr. *arche-*, both < Lat. *archi-* < Gk. *arkhi-*, *archi-*.]

arch-[2] *pref.* Variant of **archi-**.

-arch *suff.* Ruler; leader: *matriarch.* [ME *-arche* < OFr. < LLat. *-archa* < Lat. *-archēs* < Gk. *-arkhos* < *arkhos*, ruler < *arkhein*, to rule.]

Ar·chae·an (är-kē′ən) *adj.* Variant of **Archean.**

ar·chae·bac·te·ri·um (är′kē-băk-tîr′ē-əm) *n., pl.* **-ri·a** An archaeon. [ARCHAE(O)- + BACTERIUM.]

archaeo– or **archeo–** *pref.* Ancient; earlier; primitive: *archaeopteryx.* [NLat. < Gk. *arkhaio-* < *arkhaios*, ancient. See ARCHAIC.]

ar·chae·o·as·tron·o·my (är′kē-ō-ə-strŏn′ə-mē) *n.* The study of the knowledge, interpretations, and practices of ancient cultures regarding celestial objects or phenomena. **—ar′chae·o·as·tron′o·mer** *n.* **—ar′chae·o·as′tro·nom′i·cal** (-ăs′trə-nŏm′ĭ-kəl) *adj.*

ar·chae·ol·o·gy or **ar·che·ol·o·gy** (är′kē-ŏl′ə-jē) *n.* The study of past human life and culture by the examination of material remains, such as graves, tools, and pottery. [Fr. *archéologie* < NLat. *archaeologia* < Gk. *arkhaiologiā*, antiquarian lore : *arkhaio-*, archaeo- + *-logiā*, -logy.] **—ar′chae·o·log′i·cal** (-ə-lŏj′ĭ-kəl), **ar′chae·o·log′ic** *adj.* **—ar′chae·ol′o·gist** *n.*

ar·chae·on or **Ar·chae·on** (är′kē-ŏn′) *n., pl.* **-chae·a** (-kē-ə) Any of a group of bacterialike microorganisms comprising a division of the Prokaryotae and usu. thriving in extreme environments, often classified as a separate domain in taxonomic systems based on similarities of DNA sequences.

ar·chae·op·ter·yx (är′kē-ŏp′tər-ĭks) *n.* An extinct primitive bird of the genus *Archaeopteryx* of the Jurassic Period, having lizardlike characteristics, such as a long, bony tail. [NLat. *Archaeopteryx*, genus name : ARCHAEO- + Gk. *pterux*, bird, wing; see **pet-** in App.]

Ar·chae·o·zo·ic (är′kē-ə-zō′ĭk) *adj. & n.* Variant of **Archeozoic.**

ar·cha·ic (är-kā′ĭk) also **ar·cha·i·cal** (-ĭ-kəl) *adj.* **1.** also **Ar·chaic** Of, relating to, or characteristic of a much earlier, more primitive period. **2.** No longer current or applicable; antiquated. See Syns at **old. 3.** Of or characteristic of words and language that were once in regular use but are now rare and used chiefly to suggest an earlier style or period. [Gk. *arkhaïkos*, old-fashioned < *arkhaios*, ancient < *arkhē*, beginning < *arkhein*, to begin.] **—ar·cha′i·cal·ly** *adv.*

Archaic Latin *n.* Latin from the beginning of the 6th to the beginning of the 1st century B.C.

archaic smile *n.* A representation of the human mouth with slightly upturned corners, characteristic of early Greek sculpture. [After the Archaic Period of ancient Greek sculpture.]

ar·cha·ism (är′kē-ĭz′əm, -kā-) *n.* **1.** An archaic word, phrase, or other expression. **2.** An archaic style, quality, or usage. [NLat. *archaeismus*, < Gk. *arkhaismos* < *arkhaios*, ancient. See ARCHAIC.] **—ar′cha·ist** *n.* **—ar′cha·is′tic** (-ĭs′tĭk) *adj.*

ar·cha·ize (är′kē-īz′, -kā-) *v.* **-ized, -iz·ing, -iz·es** *—tr.* To give an archaic quality to; make archaic. *—intr.* To use archaisms in order to suggest the past. **—ar′cha·iz′er** *n.*

arch·an·gel (ärk′ān′jəl) *n.* **1.** A high-ranking angel. **2.** **archangels** The eighth of the nine orders of angels. [ME < LLat. *archangele* < LLat. *archangelus* < L.Gk. *arkhangelos* : Gk. *arkh-*, archi- + Gk. *angelos*, angel.] **—arch′an·gel′ic** (-ăn-jĕl′ĭk) *adj.*

Archangel See **Arkhangelsk.**

arch·bish·op (ärch-bĭsh′əp) *n.* A bishop of the highest rank, heading an archdiocese or province. [ME *archebishop* < OE *arcebisceop* < LLat. *archiepiscopus* < L.Gk. *arkhiepiskopos* : Gk. *arkhi-*, archi- + Gk. *episkopos*, bishop; see BISHOP.]

arch·bish·op·ric (ärch-bĭsh′əp-rĭk) *n.* **1.** The rank, office, or term of an archbishop. **2.** The area under an archbishop's jurisdiction; an archdiocese.

arch·con·ser·va·tive (ärch′kən-sûr′və-tĭv) *adj.* Highly conservative, esp. in political viewpoint. **—arch′con·ser′va·tive** *n.*

arch·dea·con (ärch-dē′kən) *n.* A church official with powers delegated from a bishop. [ME *archedeken* < OE *arcediacon* < LLat. *archidiāconus* < L.Gk. *arkhidiākonos* : Gk. *arkhi-*, archi- + L.Gk. *diākonos*, deacon.] **—arch′dea′con·ate** (-kə-nĭt) *n.* **—arch′dea′con·ship′** *n.*

arch·dea·con·ry (ärch-dē′kən-rē) *n., pl.* **-ries 1.** The rank or office of an archdeacon. **2.** The district or residence of an archdeacon.

arch·di·o·cese (ärch-dī′ə-sĭs, -sēs′, -sēz′) *n.* The district under an archbishop's jurisdiction. **—arch′di·oc′e·san** (-ŏs′ĭ-sən) *adj.*

arch·du·cal (ärch-dōō′kəl, -dyōō′-) *adj.* Of or relating to an archduke or archduchy. [Fr. *archiducal* < *archiduc*, archduke. See ARCHDUKE.]

arch·duch·ess (ärch-dŭch′ĭs) *n.* **1.** The wife or widow of an archduke. **2.** A woman holding an archduchy in her own right. **3.** Used as a title for such a noblewoman. [Fr. *archiduchesse*, fem. of *archiduc*, archduke. See ARCHDUKE.]

arch·duch·y (ärch-dŭch′ē) *n., pl.* **-ies** The territory over which an archduke or an archduchess has authority. [Fr. *archiduché* < obsolete Fr. *archeduché* < *arche-*, arch- + *duché*, duchy (< OFr. *duche*; see DUCHY.]

arch·duke (ärch-dōōk′, -dyōōk′) *n.* **1.** In certain royal families, a nobleman having a rank equivalent to that of a sovereign prince. **2.** Used as a title for such a nobleman. [Obsolete Fr. *archeduc* : *arche-*, arch- (< OFr.; see ARCH-[1]) + *duc*, duke (< OFr.; see DUKE.]

Ar·che·an also **Ar·chae·an** (är-kē′ən) *adj.* Of or belonging to

arch[1]
semicircular arch
A. keystone
B. voussoirs
C. springers
D. imposts

archaic smile
Greek marble kore

ă	pat	oi	boy
ā	pay	ou	out
âr	care	ŏŏ	took
ä	father	ōō	boot
ĕ	pet	ŭ	cut
ē	be	ûr	urge
ĭ	pit	th	thin
ī	pie	*th*	this
îr	pier	hw	which
ŏ	pot	zh	vision
ō	toe	ə	about,
ô	paw		item

Stress marks:
′ (primary);
′ (secondary), as in
lexicon (lĕk′sĭ-kŏn′)

the earlier of the two divisions of Precambrian time, from approx. 3.8 to 2.5 billion years ago, characterized by an atmosphere with little free oxygen and the development of unicellular life. See table at **geologic time**. ❖ *n.* The Archean Eon or its deposits. [< Gk. *arkhaios*, ancient. See ARCHAIC.]

arched (ärcht) *adj.* **1.** Forming an arch or a curve like that of an arch. **2.** Provided, made, or covered with an arch.

ar•che•go•ni•um (är′kĭ-gō′nē-əm) *n., pl.* **-ni•a** (-nē-ə) An egg-producing organ occurring in mosses, ferns, and most gymnosperms. [NLat. < Gk. *arkhegonos*, original : *arkhe-, arkhi-,* archi- + *gonos,* offspring; see **genə-** in App.] —**ar′che•go′ni•al** *adj.* —**ar′che•go′ni•ate** (-īt) *adj.*

arch•en•e•my (ärch-ĕn′ə-mē) *n.* **1.** A principal enemy. **2.** often **Archenemy** The Devil; Satan. Used with *the.*

ar•chen•ter•on (är-kĕn′tə-rŏn′, -tər-ən) *n.* The central cavity of the gastrula. —**ar′chen•ter′ic** (är′kĕn-tĕr′ĭk) *adj.*

archeo– *pref.* Variant of **archaeo–.**

ar•che•ol•o•gy (är′kē-ŏl′ə-jē) *n.* Variant of **archaeology.**

Ar•che•o•zo•ic also **Ar•chae•o•zo•ic** (är′kē-ə-zō′ĭk) *n.* See **Archean.**

arch•er (är′chər) *n.* **1.** One that shoots with a bow and arrow. **2. Archer** See **Sagittarius.** [ME < OFr. *archier* < LLat. *arcārius,* alteration of *arcuārius,* maker of bows < Lat. *arcus,* bow.]

arch•er•fish (är′chər-fĭsh′) *n., pl.* **archerfish** or **-fish•es** Any of various freshwater fishes of the family Toxotidae that spit at insects and prey on those knocked into the water.

arch•er•y (är′chə-rē) *n.* **1.** The art, sport, or skill of shooting with a bow and arrow. **2.** The equipment of an archer. **3.** A group of archers.

ar•che•type (är′kĭ-tīp′) *n.* **1.** An original model or type after which other similar things are patterned; a prototype. **2.** An ideal example of a type; quintessence: *an archetype of the successful entrepreneur.* **3.** In Jungian psychology, an inherited pattern of thought or symbolic imagery derived from past collective experience and present in the individual unconscious. [Lat. *archetypum* < Gk. *arkhetupon* < neut. of *arkhetupos,* original : *arkhe-, arkhi-,* archi- + *tupos,* model, stamp.] —**ar′che•typ′al** (-tī′pəl), **ar′che•typ′ic** (-tĭp′ĭk), **ar′che•typ′i•cal** *adj.* —**ar′che•typ′i•cal•ly** *adv.*

arch•fiend (ärch-fēnd′) *n.* **1.** A principal fiend. **2. Archfiend** The Devil; Satan. Used with *the.*

archi– or **arch–** *pref.* **1.** Chief; highest; most important: *archiepiscopal.* **2.** Earlier; primitive: *archenteron.* [Fr. *archi-* and Ital. *arci-,* both < Lat. *archi-* < Gk. *arkhi-, arkh-* < *arkhein,* to begin, rule.]

ar•chi•di•ac•o•nal (är′kĭ-dī-ăk′ə-nəl) *adj.* Of or having to do with an archdeacon or an archdeacon's office. [ME < LLat. *archidiāconus,* archdeacon. See ARCHDEACON.]

ar•chi•di•ac•o•nate (är′kĭ-dī-ăk′ə-nĭt) *n.* The office or position of an archdeacon. [Med.Lat. *archidiāconātus* < LLat. *archidiāconus,* archdeacon. See ARCHDEACON.]

ar•chi•e•pis•co•pal (är′kē-ĭ-pĭs′kə-pəl) *adj.* Of or having to do with an archbishop or an archbishopric. [Med.Lat. *archiepiscopālis* < LLat. *archiepiscopus,* archbishop. See ARCHBISHOP.] —**ar′chi•e•pis′co•pal′i•ty** (-păl′ĭ-tē) *n.* —**ar′chi•e•pis′co•pal•ly** *adv.* —**ar′chi•e•pis′co•pate** *n.*

ar•chil (är′kĭl, -chĭl) *n.* Variant of **orchil.**

ar•chi•man•drite (är′kə-măn′drīt′) *n. Eastern Orthodox Church* **1.** A cleric ranking below a bishop. **2.** The head of a monastery or a group of monasteries. **3.** Used as an honorific title for an unmarried priest. [LLat. *archimandrīta* < L.Gk. *arkhimandrītēs* : Gk. *arkhi-,* archi- + L.Gk. *mandra,* monastery (< Gk., cattle pen).]

Archimedean screw *n.* An ancient apparatus for raising water, consisting of either an inclined spiral tube or a broad-threaded screw. [After ARCHIMEDES.]

Ar•chi•me•des (är′kə-mē′dēz) 287?–212 B.C. Greek mathematician, engineer, and physicist; one of the most important intellectual figures of antiquity. —**Ar′chi•me′de•an** (-mē′dē-ən, -mĭ-dē′-) *adj.*

Ar•chi•me•des′ screw (är′kə-mē′dēz) *n.* See **Archimedean screw.**

ar•chine also **ar•shin** (är-shēn′) *n.* A unit of length formerly used in Russia and Turkey, equal to about 71 centimeters (28 inches). [Russ. *arshin* < Tatar *arshyn,* an ell; akin to Turk. *arşin* < MPers. *ārešn,* cubit < OPers. *arašn-,* ell.]

ar•chi•pel•a•go (är′kə-pĕl′ə-gō′) *n., pl.* **-goes** or **-gos 1.** A large group of islands. **2.** A sea containing many scattered islands. [Ital. *Arcipelago,* the Aegean Sea, alteration (influenced by *arci-,* chief, archi-) of Med.Lat. *Ēgēopelagus* : Lat. *Aegaeus, Ēgēus,* Aegean (< Gk. *Aigaios*) + Lat. *pelagus,* sea (< Gk. *pelagos,* sea).] —**ar′chi•pe•lag′ic** (-pə-lăj′ĭk) *adj.*

Ar•chi•pen•ko (är′kə-pĕng′kō), **Alexander Porfirievich** 1887–1964. Russian-born Amer. sculptor noted for his cubist work.

ar•chi•tect (är′kĭ-tĕkt′) *n.* **1.** One who designs and supervises the construction of buildings or other large structures. **2.** One that plans or devises: *the chief architect of war.* [Lat. *architectus* < Gk. *arkhitektōn* : *arkhi-,* archi- + *tektōn,* builder.]

ar•chi•tec•ton•ic (är′kĭ-tĕk-tŏn′ĭk) also **ar•chi•tec•ton•i•cal** (-ĭ-kəl) *adj.* **1.** Of or relating to architecture or design. **2.** Having qualities, such as design and structure, that are characteristic of architecture. **3.** *Philosophy* Of or relating to the scientific system-

archivolt

arctic fox
Alopex lagopus
in winter coat

atization of knowledge. [Lat. *architectonicus,* architectural < Gk. *arkhitektonikos* < *arkhitektōn,* architect. See ARCHITECT.]

ar•chi•tec•ton•ics (är′kĭ-tĕk-tŏn′ĭks) *n. (used with a sing. verb)* **1.** The science of architecture. **2.** Structural design: *the architectonics of a fugue.* **3.** *Philosophy* The systematization of knowledge.

ar•chi•tec•ture (är′kĭ-tĕk′chər) *n.* **1.** The art and science of designing and erecting buildings. **2.** Buildings and other large structures: *brick-and-adobe architecture of the Southwest.* **3.** A style and method of design and construction: *Byzantine architecture.* **4.** Orderly arrangement of parts; structure: *the architecture of a novel.* **5.** The overall design or structure of a computer system or microprocessor. [Lat. *architectūra* < *architectus,* architect. See ARCHITECT.] —**ar′chi•tec′tur•al** *adj.* —**ar′chi•tec′tur•al•ly** *adv.*

ar•chi•trave (är′kĭ-trāv′) *n.* **1.** The lowermost part of an entablature in classical architecture. **2.** The molding around a door or window. [Fr. < OFr. < OItal. : *archi-,* archi- + *trave,* beam (< Lat. *trabs, trab-*).]

ar•chi•val (är-kī′vəl) *adj.* Of, relating to, kept in, or suitable for archives.

ar•chive (är′kīv′) *n.* **1.** A place or collection containing records, documents, or other materials of historical interest. Often used in the plural. **2.** *Computer Science* **a.** A long-term storage area for backup copies of files or for inactive files. **b.** A file containing one or more compressed files for more efficient storage and transfer. **3.** A repository for memories or information: *the archive of the mind.* ❖ *tr.v.* **-chived, -chiv•ing, -chives 1.** To place or store in an archive. **2.** *Computer Science* To copy or compress (a file) into an archive. [< Fr. *archives* < Lat. *archīva* < Gk. *arkheia,* pl. of *arkheion,* town hall < *arkhē,* government < *arkhein,* to rule.]

ar•chi•vist (är′kə-vĭst, -kī′-) *n.* One who is in charge of archives.

ar•chi•volt (är′kə-vōlt′) *n.* A decorative molding carried around an arched wall opening. [Ital. *archivolto* or Fr. *archivolte* (Fr. < Ital.) : *arco,* arch (< Lat. *arcus*) + *volta,* vault (< Lat. *volūta*; see VAULT[1]).]

arch•lib•er•al (ärch′lĭb′ər-əl, -lĭb′rəl) *adj.* Highly liberal, esp. politically. —**arch′lib′er•al** *n.*

ar•chon (är′kŏn′, -kən) *n.* **1.** A high official; a ruler. **2.** One of the nine principal magistrates of ancient Athens. **3.** An authoritative figure; a leader. [Lat. *archōn* < Gk. *arkhōn* < pr. part. of *arkhein,* to rule.] —**ar′chon•ship′** *n.*

ar•cho•saur (är′kə-sôr′) *n.* A reptile of the subclass Archosauria, which includes the dinosaurs, pterosaurs, and modern crocodilians. [NLat. *Archosauria,* subclass name : Gk. *arkhos,* ruler + Gk. *sauros,* lizard.]

arch•priest (ärch′prēst′) *n. Roman Catholic Church* **1a.** Used formerly as a title for a priest holding first rank among the members of a cathedral chapter. **b.** An honorific title applied to a priest. **2.** *Eastern Orthodox Church* The highest rank a married priest can hold. [ME *archeprest* < OFr. *archeprestre* < LLat. *archipresbyter* < L.Gk. *arkhipresbuteros* : Gk. *arkhi-,* archi- + Gk. *presbuteros,* priest; see PRESBYTER.]

arch•ri•val (ärch′rī′vəl) *n.* A principal rival.

arch•way (ärch′wā′) *n.* **1.** A passageway under an arch. **2.** An arch over an entrance or passageway.

–archy *suff.* Rule; government: *oligarchy.* [< words such as (MON)ARCHY.]

ar•ci•form (är′sə-fôrm′) *adj.* Formed in the shape of an arc. [Lat. *arci-* (< *arcus,* bow) + –FORM.]

arc lamp *n.* An electric light in which a current traverses a gas between two electrodes and generates an arc that produces light.

ar•co (är′kō) *adv. & adj. Music* With a bow. Used chiefly as a direction to indicate the resumption of bowing after a pizzicato passage. [Ital. < Lat. *arcus.*]

arc secant *n.* The inverse of the secant function.

arc sine *n.* The inverse of the sine function.

arc tangent *n.* The inverse of the tangent function.

arc•tic (ärk′tĭk, är′tĭk) *adj.* Extremely cold; frigid. See Syns at **cold.** ❖ *n.* A warm waterproof overshoe. [Alteration (influenced by Lat. *arcticus*) of ME *artic,* northern < Med.Lat. *articus* < Lat. *arcticus* < Gk. *arktikos* < *arktos,* bear, the northern constellation Ursa Major. See **r̥tko-** in App.]

Arc•tic (ärk′tĭk, är′tĭk) A region between the North Pole and the N timberlines of North America and Eurasia. —**Arc′tic** *adj.*

Arctic Archipelago A group of more than 50 large islands of N Canada, in the Arctic Ocean.

arctic char *n.* A char (*Salvelinus alpinus*) native to the fresh waters of Alaska and northern Canada.

Arctic Circle The parallel of latitude approx. 66°33′ N that forms the boundary between the North Temperate and North Frigid zones.

arctic fox also **Arctic fox** *n.* A fox (*Alopex lagopus*) of Arctic regions, having fur that is white or light gray in winter and brown or blue-gray in summer.

Arctic Ocean The waters surrounding the North Pole between North America and Eurasia; covered year-round by pack ice.

Arctic Red River A river rising in W Northwest Terrs., Canada, and flowing c. 499 km (310 mi) to the Mackenzie R.

arctic tern also **Arctic tern** *n.* A tern (*Sterna paradisaea*) that typically migrates from the Arctic to the Antarctic and back each year.

Arc·tu·rus (ärk-tŏŏr′əs, -tyŏŏr′-) *n.* The fourth-brightest star in the sky and the brightest in the constellation Boötes. [ME < Lat. *Arctūrus* < Gk. *Arktouros* : *arktos*, bear; see **r̥tko-** in App. + *ouros*, guard (< its position behind Ursa Major).]

ar·cu·ate (är′kyŏŏ-ĭt, -āt′) also **ar·cu·at·ed** (-ā′tĭd) *adj.* Having the form of a bow; curved. [Lat. *arcuātus*, p. part. of *arcuāre*, to bend like a bow < *arcus*, bow.] —**ar′cu·ate·ly** *adv.*

ar·cu·a·tion (är′kyŏŏ-ā′shən) *n.* **1.** The process of curving or the condition of being curved. **2.** The use of arches or vaults in building.

arc welding *n.* Welding that uses an electric arc to provide heat.

–ard or **–art** *suff.* One that habitually or excessively is in a specified condition or performs a specified action: *drunkard.* [ME < OFr., of Gmc. orig.]

ar·deb (är′dĕb′) *n.* A unit of dry measure in the Middle East, standardized in Egypt to equal 198 liters (5.62 US bushels). [Ar. dialectal *′ardabb* < Aram. *′rdb* or Coptic *artab* or Gk. *artabē*, all prob. of OPers. orig.]

Ar·den (är′dn), **Forest of** A wooded area of central England W of Stratford-upon-Avon; setting for Shakespeare's *As You Like It.*

Ar·dennes (är-dĕn′) A plateau region of N France, SE Belgium, and N Luxembourg; site of heavy fighting in World War I and World War II.

ar·dent (är′dnt) *adj.* **1.** Expressing or characterized by warmth of feeling; passionate: *an ardent lover.* **2.** Displaying or characterized by strong enthusiasm or devotion; fervent. **3a.** Burning; fiery. **b.** Glowing; shining: *ardent eyes.* [ME *ardaunt* < OFr. *ardant* < Lat. *ārdēns, ārdent-*, pr. part. of *ārdēre*, to burn. See **as-** in App.] —**ar′den·cy** (-dn-sē) *n.* —**ar′dent·ly** *adv.*

ardent spirits *pl.n.* Strong alcoholic liquors.

ar·dor (är′dər) *n.* **1.** Fiery intensity of feeling. **2.** Strong enthusiasm or devotion; zeal. **3.** Intense heat or glow. [ME *ardour* < OFr. < Lat. *ārdor* < *ārdēre*, to burn. See **as-** in App.]

ar·dour (är′dər) *n. Chiefly British* Variant of **ardor.**

ar·du·ous (är′jŏŏ-əs) *adj.* **1.** Demanding great effort or labor; difficult: *"the arduous work of preparing a Dictionary of the English Language"* (Thomas Macaulay). **2.** Testing severely the powers of endurance; strenuous: *an arduous war.* **3.** Hard to traverse, climb, or surmount. [< Lat. *arduus*, high, steep.] —**ar′du·ous·ly** *adv.* —**ar′du·ous·ness** *n.*

are¹ (är) *v.* Second person singular and plural and first and third person plural present indicative of **be.** [ME *aren* < OE *aron.* See **er-** in App.]

are² (âr, är) also **ar** (är) *n.* A metric unit of area equal to 100 square meters (119.6 square yards). [Fr. < Lat. *ārea*, open space. See AREA.]

ar·e·a (âr′ē-ə) *n.* **1.** A roughly bounded part of a surface; a region: *the New York area.* **2.** A surface, esp. an open, unoccupied piece of ground: *a landing area.* **3.** A distinct part or section set aside for a specific function: *a storage area.* **4.** A division of experience, activity, or knowledge; a field: *the area of finance.* **5.** An open, sunken space next to a building; an areaway. **6.** The extent of a planar region or of the surface of a solid measured in square units. **7.** *Computer Science* A section of storage set aside for a particular purpose. [Lat. *ārea*, open space; poss. akin to *ārēre*, to be dry. See ARID.] —**ar′e·al** *adj.* —**ar′e·al·ly** *adv.*

area code *n.* A three-digit number assigned to a geographical area used before a seven-digit telephone number when placing a call to, and sometimes from within, that area.

ar·e·a·way (âr′ē-ə-wā′) *n.* **1.** A small sunken area allowing access or light and air to basement doors or windows. **2.** An often narrow passageway between buildings.

a·re·ca (ə-rē′kə, âr′ĭ-kə) *n.* Any of certain tropical Old World palms, such as those in the genus *Areca.* [Port. < Malayalam *aṭekka*, areca nut < Tamil *aṭaikkāy.*]

areca nut *n.* See **betel nut.**

a·re·na (ə-rē′nə) *n.* **1a.** An enclosed area for the presentation of sports events and spectacles. **b.** A building housing such an area. **2.** A place or scene where forces contend or events unfold: *the political arena.* **3.** The area in the center of an ancient Roman amphitheater where contests and other spectacles were held. [Lat. *harēna, arēna*, sand, a sand-strewn place of combat in an amphitheater, perh. of Etruscan orig.]

ar·e·na·ceous (âr′ə-nā′shəs) *adj.* **1.** Resembling, derived from, or containing sand. **2.** Growing in sandy areas. [< Lat. *harēnāceus, arēnāceus* : *harēna, arēna*, sand; see ARENA + -*āceus*, -aceous.]

arena theater *n.* A theater in which the stage is at the center of the auditorium and is surrounded by seats.

A·rendt (âr′ənt, är′-), **Hannah** 1906–75. German-born Amer. historian and political theorist whose works include *The Origins of Totalitarianism* (1951).

aren't (ärnt, är′ənt) Contraction of *are not.* See Usage Note at **ain't.**

a·re·o·la (ə-rē′ə-lə) also **a·re·ole** (âr′ē-ōl′) *n., pl.* **-lae** (-lē′) or **-las** also **-oles** (-ōlz′) **1. areole** *Biology* A small space or interstice in a tissue or part. **2.** *Anatomy* A small ring of color around a center portion, as about the nipple of the breast. [Lat. *āreola*, small open space, dim. of *ārea*, open place. See AREA.] —**a·re′o·lar, a·re′o·late** (-lĭt) *adj.* —**a·re′o·la′tion** *n.*

Ar·e·op·a·gite (âr′ē-ŏp′ə-jīt′, -gīt′) *n.* A member of the Areopagus. —**Ar′e·op·a·git′ic** (-jĭt′ĭk, -gīt′-) *adj.*

Ar·e·op·a·gus (âr′ē-ŏp′ə-gəs) *n.* The highest judicial and legislative council of ancient Athens. [Lat. < Gk. *Areios pagos, Areiopagos*, hill of Ares, Areopagus (where the tribunal met) : *Areios*, of Ares (< *Arēs*, Ares) + *pagos*, stiff mass, hill (< *pēgnunai*, pag-, to stick, stiffen).]

a·re·pa (ə-rā′pə) *n.* A baked or fried cornmeal cake of traditional Colombian cuisine. [Cariban *ərepa*, maize.]

A·re·qui·pa (ä′rə-kē′pə, ä′rĕ-kē′pä) A city of S Peru at the foot of El Misti; founded 1540. Pop. 624,500.

Ar·es (âr′ēz) *n. Greek Mythology* The god of war.

a·rête (ə-rāt′) *n.* A sharp, narrow mountain ridge or spur. [Fr. < OFr. *areste*, fishbone, spine < LLat. *arista*, awn, fishbone < Lat., awn.]

ar·e·thu·sa (âr′ə-thōō′zə, -sə) *n.* See **swamp pink.** [< Lat. *Arethūsa*, a wood nymph < Gk. *Arethousa.*]

A·re·ti·no (ä′rə-tē′nō, är′-), **Pietro** 1492–1556. Italian writer and satirist best known for his six volumes of letters.

A·rez·zo (ä-rĕt′sō) A city of central Italy on the Arno R. SE of Florence; orig. an Etruscan settlement. Pop. 91,535.

arg. *abbr.* argent

ar·gal (är′gəl) *n.* Variant of **argol.**

ar·ga·li (är′gə-lē) *n., pl.* **argali** or **-lis** A wild sheep (*Ovis ammon*) of central and northern Asia having large, spirally curved horns. [Mongolian *arghali*, mountain ewe.]

ar·gent (är′jənt) *n.* **1.** *Heraldry* The metal silver, represented by the color white. **2.** *Archaic* Silver or something resembling it. [ME < OFr. < Lat. *argentum*, silver. See **arg-** in App.]

ar·gen·tic (är-jĕn′tĭk) *adj.* Of or containing silver.

ar·gen·tif·er·ous (är′jən-tĭf′ər-əs) *adj.* Bearing or producing silver.

Ar·gen·ti·na (är′jən-tē′nə) A country of SE South America extending from Bolivia to Tierra del Fuego, an island it shares with Chile; proclaimed its independence from Spain in 1816. Cap. Buenos Aires. Pop. 34,180,000. —**Ar′gen·tine′** (-tēn′, -tīn′), **Ar′gen·tin′e·an** (-tĭn′ē-ən) *adj. & n.*

ar·gen·tine (är′jən-tīn′, -tēn′) *adj.* Relating to or resembling silver; silvery. ❖ *n.* **1.** Silver. **2.** Any of various silvery metals. [ME < OFr. *argentin* < Lat. *argentīnus* < *argentum*, silver. See **arg-** in App.]

ar·gen·tite (är′jən-tīt′) *n.* A valuable silver ore, Ag₂S, with a lead-gray color and metallic luster.

ar·gil (är′jĭl) *n.* Clay, esp. a white clay used by potters. [ME *argilla* < Lat. < Gk. *argillos.* See **arg-** in App.]

ar·gil·la·ceous (är′jə-lā′shəs) *adj.* Containing, made of, or resembling clay; clayey. [< Lat. *argillāceus* : *argilla*, argil; see ARGIL + -*āceus*, -aceous.]

ar·gil·lite (är′jə-līt′) *n.* A metamorphic rock, intermediate in structure between shale and slate. [Lat. *argilla*, argil; see ARGIL + -ITE¹.]

ar·gi·nase (är′jə-nās′, -nāz′) *n.* An enzyme found primarily in the liver that catalyzes the hydrolysis of arginine to form urea and ornithine. [< Ger. *Arginin*, arginine. See ARGININE.]

ar·gi·nine (är′jə-nēn′) *n.* An amino acid, $C_6H_{14}N_4O_2$, obtained from plant and animal protein. [Ger. *Arginin*, poss. < Gk. *arginoeis*, bright. See **arg-** in App.]

Ar·give (är′jīv′, -gīv′) *adj.* **1.** Of or relating to Argos or Argolis. **2.** Of or relating to Greece or the Greeks. ❖ *n.* A Greek, esp. an inhabitant of Argos or Argolis. [Lat. *Argīvus* < Gk. *Argeios* < ARGOS.]

Ar·go (är′gō′) *n.* **1.** *Greek Mythology* The ship in which Jason sailed in search of the Golden Fleece. **2.** Formerly, a constellation in the Southern Hemisphere, now divided into the constellations Carina, Puppis, Pyxis, and Vela. [Lat. *Argō* < Gk.]

ar·gol (är′gôl) also **ar·gal** (-gəl) *n.* Crude potassium bitartrate, a byproduct of winemaking. [ME *argoile* < AN *argoil*, ult. < Lat. *argilla*, clay. See ARGIL.]

Ar·go·lis (är′gə-lĭs) An ancient region of S Greece in the E Peloponnesus on the **Gulf of Argolis,** an inlet of the Aegean Sea.

ar·gon (är′gŏn′) *n. Symbol* **Ar** A colorless, inert gaseous element constituting approx. one percent of Earth's atmosphere, used in electric bulbs and fluorescent tubes and as an inert gas shield in arc welding. Atomic number 18; atomic weight 39.948; melting point −189.2°C; boiling point −185.7°C. See table at **element.** [< Gk. *ārgon*, neut. of *ārgos*, idle, inert : *a-*, without; see A-¹ + *ergon*, work; see **werg-** in App.]

ar·go·naut (är′gə-nôt′) *n.* See **paper nautilus.** [Lat. *Argonauta*, genus name, back-formation < Lat. *Argonautae*, Argonauts. See ARGONAUT.]

Argonaut *n.* **1.** *Greek Mythology* One who sailed with Jason on the *Argo* in search of the Golden Fleece. **2.** also **argonaut** A person who is engaged in a dangerous but rewarding quest; an adventurer. [< Lat. *Argonautae*, Argonauts < Gk. *Argonautēs*, Argonaut : *Argō*, the ship *Argo* + *nautēs*, sailor (< *naus*, ship).]

Ar·gonne (är-gŏn′, är′gŏn) A wooded region of NE France between the Meuse and Aisne rivers; site of major battles during World War I and World War II.

Ar·gos (är′gŏs, -gəs) A city of ancient Greece in the E Peloponnesus near the head of the Gulf of Argolis; inhabited since the early Bronze Age.

ar·go·sy (är′gə-sē) *n., pl.* **-sies 1a.** A large merchant ship. **b.** A fleet of ships. **2.** A rich source or supply: *an argosy of adventure*

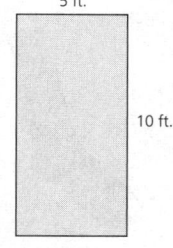

5 ft.

10 ft.

area
To calculate the area of a rectangle, multiply the length by the width. The area of this rectangle is 50 square feet.

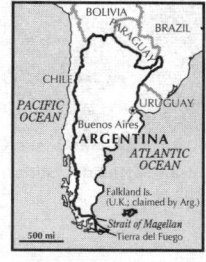

Argentina

ă	pat	oi	boy
ā	pay	ou	out
âr	care	ŏŏ	took
ä	father	ōō	boot
ĕ	pet	ŭ	cut
ē	be	ûr	urge
ĭ	pit	th	thin
ī	pie	th	this
îr	pier	hw	which
ŏ	pot	zh	vision
ō	toe	ə	about,
ô	paw		item

Stress marks:
′ (primary);
′ (secondary), as in
lexicon (lĕk′sĭ-kŏn′)

lore. [Alteration of obsolete *ragusye* < Ital. *ragusea*, vessel of Ragusa (Dubrovnik).]

ar·got (är′gō, -gət) *n.* A specialized vocabulary or set of idioms used by a particular group: *thieves′ argot.* [Fr.]

ar·gu·a·ble (är′gyōō-ə-bəl) *adj.* **1.** Open to argument: *an arguable question.* **2.** That can be argued plausibly; defensible in argument: *arguable points of law.* —**ar′gu·a·bly** *adv.*

ar·gue (är′gyōō) *v.* **-gued, -gu·ing, -gues** —*tr.* **1.** To put forth reasons for or against; debate. **2.** To attempt to prove by reasoning; maintain or contend. **3.** To give evidence of; indicate: *"Similarities cannot always be used to argue descent"* (Isaac Asimov). **4.** To persuade or influence (another), as by presenting reasons. —*intr.* **1.** To put forth reasons for or against something: *argued for dismissal of the case.* **2.** To engage in a quarrel; dispute. [ME *arguen* < OFr. *arguer* < Lat. *argūtāre,* to babble, chatter, freq. of *arguere,* to make clear. See **arg-** in App.] —**ar′gu·er** *n.*

ar·gu·fy (är′gyə-fī′) *Chiefly Southern US v.* **-fied, -fy·ing, -fies** —*tr.* To dispute (a point). —*intr.* To argue aimlessly; wrangle. See Regional Note at **absquatulate.** —**ar′gu·fi′er** *n.*

ar·gu·ment (är′gyə-mənt) *n.* **1a.** A discussion in which disagreement is expressed; a debate. **b.** A quarrel; a dispute. **c.** *Archaic* A reason or matter for dispute or contention: *"sheath'd their swords for lack of argument"* (Shakespeare). **2a.** A course of reasoning aimed at demonstrating truth or falsehood. **b.** A fact or statement put forth as proof or evidence; a reason: *an argument for buying a house.* **c.** A set of statements in which one follows logically as a conclusion from the others. **3a.** A summary or short statement of the plot or subject of a literary work. **b.** A topic; a subject. **4.** *Logic* The minor premise in a syllogism. **5.** *Mathematics* **a.** The independent variable of a function. **b.** The amplitude of a complex number. **6.** *Computer Science* A value used to evaluate a procedure or subroutine. **7.** *Linguistics* In generative grammar, any of various positions occupied by a noun phrase in a sentence. [ME < OFr. < Lat. *argūmentum* < *arguere,* to make clear. See ARGUE.]

ar·gu·men·ta·tion (är′gyə-mən-tā′shən) *n.* **1.** The presentation and elaboration of an argument or arguments. **2.** Deductive reasoning in debate. **3.** A debate.

ar·gu·men·ta·tive (är′gyə-mĕn′tə-tĭv) *adj.* **1.** Given to arguing; disputatious. **2.** Of or marked by argument. —**ar′gu·men′ta·tive·ly** *adv.* —**ar′gu·men′ta·tive·ness** *n.*

argyle
argyle sock

SYNONYMS *argumentative, combative, contentious, disputatious, quarrelsome, scrappy* These adjectives mean given to or fond of arguing: *an argumentative child; a combative teenager; a contentious mood; a disputatious lawyer; a quarrelsome drinker; a scrappy litigator.*

ar·gu·men·tum (är′gyə-mĕn′təm) *n., pl.* **-ta** (-tə) *Logic* An argument, demonstration, or appeal to reason. [Lat. *argūmentum.* See ARGUMENT.]

Ar·gun River (är-gōōn′) also **Er·gun He** (ĕr′gōōn′ hĕ′, ĕr′gwän′ hŭ′) A river of E-central Asia rising in NE China and flowing c. 1,529 km (950 mi) along the Russian-China border.

Ar·gus (är′gəs) *n.* **1.** *Greek Mythology* A giant with 100 eyes who was made guardian of Io and was later slain by Hermes. **2.** An alert or watchful person; a guardian. [Lat. < Gk. *Argos.*]

Ar·gus-eyed (är′gəs-īd′) *adj.* Extremely observant; vigilant.

ar·gus pheasant (är′gəs) *n.* A large bird (*Argusianus argus*) of southeast Asia having tail feathers with eyelike spots. [After ARGUS, whose hundred eyes were given to a peacock's tail.]

ar·gy-bar·gy (är′gē-bär′gē) *n., pl.* **-gies** *Chiefly British Slang* A lively or disputatious discussion. [Sc., redup. of *argie,* argument < ARGUE.]

ar·gyle also **ar·gyll** (är′gīl′) *n.* **1.** A knitting pattern of varicolored diamond shapes on a solid background. **2.** A sock knit in this pattern. [After Clan Campbell of *Argyle, Argyll,* a former county of western Scotland, originally from the pattern of their tartan.]

ar·hat (är′hət) *n. Buddhism* In Hinayana, one who has attained enlightenment. [Skt. < pr. part. of *arhati,* he deserves.]

Är·hus also **Aar·hus** (ôr′hōōs′) A city of central Denmark on Århus Bay, an arm of the Kattegat. Pop. 250,404.

a·ri·a (ä′rē-ə) *n.* **1.** A solo vocal piece with instrumental accompaniment, as in an opera. **2.** An air; a melody. [Ital., air, melody < Lat. *āera,* accusative of *āēr,* air < Gk.]

Ar·i·ad·ne (ăr′ē-ăd′nē) *n. Greek Mythology* The daughter of Minos and Pasiphaë who gave Theseus the thread with which he found his way out of the Minotaur's labyrinth.

Ar·i·an¹ (âr′ē-ən, ăr′-) *adj.* **1.** Of or relating to Arianism. **2.** Of or relating to Arius. ❖ *n.* A believer in Arianism.

Ar·i·an² (âr′ē-ən, ăr′-) *n.* One who is born under the sign of Aries. —**Ar′i·an** *adj.*

-arian *suff.* Believer in; advocate of: *utilitarian.* [Lat. *-ārius,* -ary + -AN¹.]

Jean-Bertrand Aristide

Ar·i·an·ism (âr′ē-ə-nĭz′əm, ăr′-) *n.* The doctrines of Arius, denying that Jesus was of the same substance as God and holding instead that he was only the highest of created beings, viewed as heretical by most Christian churches.

A·ri·as San·chez (ä′rē-äs sän′chĕs), Oscar b. 1941. Costa Rican politician who won the 1987 Nobel Peace Prize.

a·ri·bo·fla·vi·no·sis (ā-rī′bō-flā′və-nō′sĭs, -bə-) *n.* A condition caused by the dietary deficiency of riboflavin, characterized by mouth lesions and seborrhea.

ar·id (ăr′ĭd) *adj.* **1.** Lacking moisture, esp. having insufficient rainfall to support trees or woody plants. **2.** Lacking interest or feeling; lifeless and dull: *an arid performance.* [Lat. *āridus* < *ārēre,* to be dry. See **as-** in App.] —**a·rid′i·ty** (ə-rĭd′ĭ-tē), **ar′id·ness** *n.*

Ar·i·el (âr′ē-əl) *n.* A satellite of Uranus. [After ARIEL, a mischievous sprite in *The Tempest* by William Shakespeare.]

Ar·ies (âr′ēz, âr′ē-ēz′) *n.* **1.** A constellation in the Northern Hemisphere near Taurus and Pisces. **2a.** The first sign of the zodiac in astrology. **b.** *pl.* **Aries** One who is born under this sign. [ME, zodiacal sign Aries < Lat. *ariēs,* ram, zodiacal sign Aries.]

a·ri·et·ta (ä′rē-ĕt′ə) also **a·ri·ette** (-ĕt′) *n.* A short aria. [Ital., dim. of *aria,* aria. See ARIA.]

a·right (ə-rīt′) *adv.* In a proper manner; correctly. [ME < OE *ariht : a-²* + *riht,* right; see *riht.*]

A·rik·a·ra (ə-rĭk′ər-ə) *n., pl.* **Arikara** or **-ras 1.** A member of a Native American people formerly inhabiting the Missouri River valley from Kansas into the Dakotas and now located in western North Dakota. **2.** The Caddoan language of the Arikara.

ar·il (ăr′əl) *n.* A fleshy, usu. brightly colored cover of a seed. [Med.Lat. *arillus,* grape seed.] —**ar′iled, ar′il·late** (-lāt′, -lĭt) *adj.*

a·ri·o·so (ä′rē-ō′sō, -zō) *n., pl.* **-sos 1.** A style used in opera and oratorio, similar to but more melodic than recitative. **b.** A passage rendered in this style. **2.** A usu. short vocal solo having the melodic style but not the form of an aria. ❖ *adv. & adj.* In a melodic style like that of an aria. [Ital. < *aria,* aria. See ARIA.]

A·ri·os·to (är′ē-ŏs′tō, -ô′stō, är′-), **Ludovico** or **Lodovico** 1474–1533. Italian writer best known for *Orlando Furioso* (1532).

a·rise (ə-rīz′) *intr.v.* **a·rose** (ə-rōz′), **a·ris·en** (ə-rĭz′ən), **a·ris·ing, a·ris·es 1.** To get up, as from a sitting or reclining position; rise. **2.** To awaken and get up: *arose at dawn.* **3.** To move upward; ascend. **4.** To come into being; originate. **5.** To result, issue, or proceed. See Syns at **stem¹.** [ME *arisen* < OE *ārīsan : ā-,* intensive pref. + *rīsan,* to rise; see RISE.]

a·ris·ta (ə-rĭs′tə) *n., pl.* **-tae** (-tē) or **-tas** A bristlelike part or appendage, such as the awn of grains and grasses. [Lat., beard of grain, spike.] —**a·ris′tate** (-tāt) *adj.*

Ar·is·tar·chus (är′ĭ-stär′kəs) 217?–145? B.C. Greek grammarian and critic.

Aristarchus of Samos fl. 270 B.C. Greek astronomer who was among the first to propose that the earth moves around the sun.

Ar·is·tide (är′ĭs-tēd′, ä′rēs-), **Jean-Bertrand** b. 1953. Haitian priest and politician who was the first elected president of Haiti (1991–96).

Ar·is·ti·des also **Ar·is·tei·des** (är′ĭ-stī′dēz) Known as "the Just." 530?–468? B.C. Athenian statesman and general who fought at Marathon (490) and Salamis (480).

Ar·is·tip·pus of Cyrene (är′ĭ-stĭp′əs) 435?–366? B.C. Greek philosopher who founded the Cyrenaic school.

ar·is·toc·ra·cy (är′ĭ-stŏk′rə-sē) *n., pl.* **-cies 1.** A hereditary ruling class; nobility. **2a.** Government by a ruling class. **b.** A state or country having this form of government. **3a.** Government by the citizens deemed to be best qualified to lead. **b.** A state having such a government. **4.** A group or class considered superior to others. [LLat. *aristocratia,* government by the best < Gk. *aristokratiā : aristos,* best + *kratos,* power; see −CRACY.]

a·ris·to·crat (ə-rĭs′tə-krăt′, ăr′ĭs-) *n.* **1.** A member of a ruling class or of the nobility. **2.** A person having the tastes, manners, or other characteristics of the aristocracy. **3.** A person who advocates government by an aristocracy. **4.** One considered the best of its kind: *the aristocrat < aristocratie,* aristocracy < OFr. < LLat. *aristocratia.* See ARISTOCRACY.] —**a·ris′to·crat′ic, a·ris′to·crat′i·cal** *adj.* —**a·ris′to·crat′i·cal·ly** *adv.*

Ar·is·toph·a·nes (är′ĭ-stŏf′ə-nēz) 448?–388? B.C. Athenian playwright whose works include *Lysistrata* (411).

Ar·is·to·te·li·an also **Ar·is·to·te·le·an** (är′ĭ-stə-tē′lē-ən, -tĕl′yən, ə-rĭs′tə-) *adj.* Of or relating to Aristotle or to his philosophy. ❖ *n.* **1.** A follower of Aristotle or his teachings. **2.** A person whose thinking and methods tend to be empirical, scientific, or commonsensical. —**Ar·is′to·te′li·an·ism** *n.*

Aristotelian logic *n.* **1.** Aristotle's deductive method of logic, esp. the theory of the syllogism. **2.** The formal logic based on Aristotle's and dealing with the relations between propositions in terms of their form instead of their content.

Ar·is·tot·le (är′ĭ-stŏt′l) 384–322 B.C. Greek philosopher who studied under Plato and tutored Alexander the Great. His works on logic, metaphysics, and the natural sciences profoundly influenced Western thought.

Aristotle
bronze bust

a·rith·me·tic (ə-rĭth′mĭ-tĭk) *n.* **1.** The mathematics of integers, rational numbers, real numbers, or complex numbers under addition, subtraction, multiplication, and division. **2.** A book on arithmetic. [ME *arsmetike* < OFr. *arismetique* < Med.Lat. *arismetica,* alteration of Lat. *arithmētica* < Gk. *arithmētikē (tekhnē),* (art) of counting, fem. of *arithmētikos < arithmein,* to count < *arithmos,* number.] —**ar′ith·met′ic** (är′ĭth-mĕt′ĭk), **ar′ith·met′i·cal** (-ĭ-kəl) *adj.* —**ar′ith·met′i·cal·ly** *adv.* —**a·rith·me·ti·cian** (-tĭsh′ən) *n.*

ar·ith·met·ic mean (är′ĭth-mĕt′ĭk) *n.* The value obtained by dividing the sum of a set of quantities by the number of those quantities.

ar·ith·met·ic progression (ăr′ĭth-mĕt′ĭk) *n.* A sequence in which each term after the first is formed by adding a constant to the preceding term.

–arium *suff.* A place or device containing or associated with: *planetarium.* [Lat., neut. of *-ārius,* -ary.]

A·ri·us (ə-rī′əs, âr′ē-, âr′-) A.D. 256?–336. Greek Christian theologian and founder of Arianism who was condemned as a heretic.

Ariz. *abbr.* Arizona

A·ri·zo·na (ăr′ĭ-zō′nə) A state of the SW US on the Mexican border; admitted as the 48th state in 1912. Cap. Phoenix. Pop. 5,130,632. —**Ar′i·zo′nan, Ar′i·zo′ni·an** *adj. & n.*

Ar·ju·na (ûr′jə-nə, -jōō-) *n. Hinduism* The warrior prince in the *Bhagavad-Gita* to whom Krishna expounds the nature of being and the way humans can come to know God.

ark (ärk) *n.* **1.** often **Ark** *Bible* The chest containing the Ten Commandments written on stone tablets, carried by the Hebrews during their desert wanderings. **2.** often **Ark** *Judaism* The Holy Ark. **3.** *Bible* The boat built by Noah for survival during the Flood. **4.** A shelter or refuge. [ME < OE *arc* < Gmc. **arka* < Lat. *arca,* chest.]

Ark. *abbr.* Arkansas

Ar·kan·sas (är′kən-sô′) A state of the S-central US on the Mississippi R.; admitted as the 25th state in 1836. Cap. Little Rock. Pop. 2,673,400. —**Ar·kan′san** (är-kăn′zən) *adj. & n.*

Ar·kan·sas River (är′kən-sô′, är-kăn′zəs) A river of the S-central US rising in central CO and flowing c. 2,333 km (1,450 mi) to the Mississippi R. in SE AR.

Ar·kan·sas stone (är′kən-sô′) *n.* A stone used for sharpening and grinding metals, esp. the metal blades of knives.

Ark·han·gelsk (är-kän′gĕlsk, -кНän′-) or **Arch·an·gel** (ärk′ān′jəl) A city of NW Russia on the Northern Dvina R. near its mouth on the White Sea. Pop. 409,886.

Ark of the Covenant *n. Bible* See ark 1.

Ark·wright (ärk′rīt′), Sir **Richard** 1732–92. British inventor who patented a machine for spinning cotton thread (1769).

Ar·len (är′lən), **Harold** 1905–86. Amer. composer whose songs include "Over the Rainbow."

Arles (ärlz, ärl) **1.** A medieval kingdom (933–1246) of E and SE France. **2.** A city of S-central France on the Rhone R. delta; founded in Roman times. Pop. 52,593.

Ar·ling·ton (är′lĭng-tən) **1.** A city of N TX midway between Dallas and Fort Worth. Pop. 332,969. **2.** A county and unincorporated city in N VA across the Potomac R. from Washington DC; site of **Arlington National Cemetery,** where American war dead and other notables are buried. Pop. 189,453.

arm¹ (ärm) *n.* **1.** An upper limb of the human body, connecting the hand and wrist to the shoulder. **2.** A part similar to a human arm, such as the projection from a central support in a machine. **3.** Something, such as a sleeve on a garment, that is designed to cover or support the human arm. **4.** A relatively narrow extension jutting out from a large mass: *an arm of the sea.* **5.** An administrative or functional branch. **6.** Power or authority: *the long arm of the law.* **7.** *Sports* The skill of throwing or pitching a ball well. —**idioms: an arm and a leg** *Slang* An excessively high price. **at arm's length** At such a distance that physical or social contact is discouraged: *kept the newcomer at arm's length.* **with open arms** With great cordiality. [ME < OE *earm.*] —**armed** (ärmd) *adj.*

arm² (ärm) *n.* **1.** A weapon, esp. a firearm: *nuclear arms.* **2.** A branch of a military force. **3. arms a.** Warfare: *a call to arms.* **b.** Military service: *volunteers under arms.* **4. arms a.** *Heraldry* Bearings. **b.** Insignia, as of a state, official, family, or organization. ❖ *v.* **armed, arm·ing, arms** —*intr.* **1.** To supply or equip oneself with weaponry. **2.** To prepare oneself for warfare or conflict. —*tr.* **1.** To equip with weapons. **2.** To equip with what is needed for effective action. **3.** To provide with something that strengthens or protects. **4.** To prepare (a weapon) for use or operation. —**idiom: up in arms** Extremely upset; indignant. [< ME *armes,* weapons < OFr., pl. of *arme,* weapon < Lat. *arma,* weapons. V., ME *armen* < OFr. *armer* < Lat. *armāre* < *arma,* arms.] —**armed** (ärmd) *adj.* —**arm′er** *n.*

ARM *abbr.* adjustable-rate mortgage

Arm. *abbr.* **1.** Armenia **2.** Armenian

ar·ma·da (är-mä′də, -mā′-) *n.* **1.** A fleet of warships. **2.** A large group of moving things. [Sp. < Med.Lat. *armāta.* See ARMY.]

ar·ma·dil·lo (är′mə-dĭl′ō) *n., pl.* **-los** Any of several burrowing edentate mammals (family Dasypodidae) with armorlike bony plates, native to southern North America and South America. [Sp., dim. of *armado,* armored, p. part. of *armar,* to arm < Lat. *armāre* < *arma,* arms.]

Ar·ma·ged·don (är′mə-gĕd′n) *n.* **1.** *Bible* The scene of a final battle between the forces of good and evil, prophesied to occur at the end of the world. **2.** A decisive or catastrophic conflict. [LLat. *Armagedōn* < Gk. < Heb. *har mǝgiddô,* the mountain region of Megiddo : *har,* mountain + *mǝgiddô,* Megiddo.]

Ar·magh (är-mä′, är′mä) An urban district of S Northern Ireland; reputedly founded by Saint Patrick. Pop. 12,700.

Ar·ma·gnac¹ (är′mən-yăk′) A historical region of SW France; noted for its viniculture.

ar·ma·gnac² (är′mən-yăk′) *n.* A dry brandy. [After ARMAGNAC¹.]

ar·ma·ment (är′mə-mənt) *n.* **1.** The weapons and supplies of war with which a military unit is equipped. **2.** All the military forces and war equipment of a country. Often used in the plural. **3.** A military force equipped for war. **4.** The process of arming for war. [Lat. *armāmenta,* tools < *arma,* arms. See ARM².]

ar·ma·men·tar·i·um (är′mə-mĕn-târ′ē-əm) *n., pl.* **-i·ums** or **-i·a** (-ē-ə) **1.** The complete equipment of a physician or medical institution, including books, supplies, and instruments. **2.** The complete range of materials available or used for a task. [Lat. *armāmentārium,* arsenal < *armāmenta,* tools. See ARMAMENT.]

ar·ma·ture (är′mə-chŏŏr′, -chər) *n.* **1.** *Electricity* **a.** The rotating part of a dynamo. **b.** The moving part of an electromagnetic device such as a relay, buzzer, or loudspeaker. **c.** A piece of soft iron connecting the poles of a magnet. **2.** *Biology* A protective covering, structure, or organ of an animal or a plant, such as the shell of a turtle. **3.** A framework serving as a supporting core for the material used to make a sculpture. [ME, armor < OFr. < Lat. *armātūra,* equipment < *armātus,* p. part. of *armāre,* to arm. See ARM².]

arm·band (ärm′bănd′) *n.* A band worn around the upper arm, often as identification or as a symbol of mourning or protest.

arm candy *n. Slang* An attractive person who accompanies another to public gatherings but is not romantically involved with that person.

arm·chair (ärm′châr′) *n.* A chair with side structures to support the arms. ❖ *adj.* Remote from active involvement.

armed forces *pl.n.* The military forces of a country.

Ar·me·ni·a¹ (är-mē′nē-ə, -mēn′yə) A republic and former kingdom of Asia Minor S of Georgia; a constituent republic of the USSR from 1936 to 1991. Cap. Yerevan. Pop. 3,548,000.

Ar·me·ni·a² (är-mē′nē-ə, -nyə) A city of W-central Colombia W of Bogotá. Pop. 192,409.

Ar·me·ni·an (är-mē′nē-ən, -mēn′yən) *adj.* Of or relating to Armenia or its people, language, or culture. ❖ *n.* **1a.** A native or inhabitant of Armenia. **b.** A person of Armenian ancestry. **2.** The Indo-European language of the Armenians.

Armenian Church *n.* An autonomous Christian church established in Armenia in the fourth century A.D.

arm·ful (ärm′fŏŏl′) *n.* The amount that an arm or arms can hold.

arm·hole (ärm′hōl′) *n.* An opening in a garment for an arm.

ar·mi·ger (är′mə-jər) *n.* **1.** A bearer of armor for a knight; a squire. **2.** A person entitled to bear heraldic arms. [Med.Lat. < Lat., arms-bearing : *arma,* arms + *gerere,* to carry.]

ar·mil·lar·y sphere (är′mə-lĕr′ē, är-mĭl′ə-rē) *n.* An old astronomical model used to display the principal celestial circles. [Transl. of Fr. *sphère armillaire* < Lat. *armilla,* bracelet < *armus,* shoulder.]

Ar·min·i·an (är-mĭn′ē-ən) *adj.* Of or relating to the theology of Jacobus Arminius and his followers, who rejected the Calvinist doctrines of predestination and election and who believed that human free will is compatible with God's sovereignty. —**Ar·min′i·an** *n.* —**Ar·min′i·an·ism** *n.*

Ar·min·i·us (är-mĭn′ē-əs) also **Ar·min** (-mĕn′) 17? B.C.–A.D. 21. German hero who defeated the Romans in A.D. 9.

Arminius, Jacobus 1560–1609. Dutch theologian who opposed the predestinarianism of John Calvin.

ar·mi·stice (är′mĭ-stĭs) *n.* A temporary cessation of fighting by mutual consent; a truce. [Fr. < NLat. *armistitium* : Lat. *arma,* arms; see ARM² + Lat. *-stitium,* a stopping; see stā- in App.]

Armistice Day *n.* November 11, formerly observed in the United States in commemoration of the signing of the armistice ending World War I in 1918. Since 1954 it has been incorporated into the observances of Veterans Day.

arm·let (ärm′lĭt) *n.* **1.** A band worn on the arm for ornament or identification. **2.** A small arm, as of the sea.

arm·load (ärm′lōd′) *n.* The amount that can be carried in one arm or both arms: *an armload of laundry.*

arm·lock (ärm′lŏk′) *n.* A wrestling hold in which the opponent's arm is held so that it cannot be moved.

ar·moire (ärm-wär′, ärm′wär′) *n.* A large, often ornate cabinet or wardrobe. [Fr. *armoire* < OFr. *armaire* < Lat. *armārium,* chest < *arma,* tools.]

ar·mor (är′mər) *n.* **1.** A defensive covering worn to protect the body against weapons. **2.** A tough, protective covering, such as the metallic plates on tanks or warships. **3.** A safeguard or protection. **4a.** The combat arm that deploys armored vehicles, such as tanks. **b.** The armored vehicles of an army. ❖ *tr.v.* **-mored, -mor·ing, -mors** To cover with armor. [ME *armure* < OFr. *armeure* < Lat. *armātūra,* equipment. See ARMATURE.]

ar·mor-clad (är′mər-klăd′) *adj.* Covered with or wearing armor: *armor-clad warships.*

ar·mored personnel carrier (är′mərd) *n.* An armored vehicle, usu. equipped with treads, used to transport infantry.

ar·mor·er (är′mər-ər) *n.* **1.** A manufacturer of weapons, esp. firearms. **2.** An enlisted person in charge of maintenance and repair of the small arms of a military unit. **3.** One that makes or repairs armor.

ar·mo·ri·al (är-môr′ē-əl, -mōr′-) *adj.* Of or relating to heraldry or heraldic arms. ❖ *n.* A book or treatise on heraldry. [< ME *armorie,* arms < OFr. *armeurerie* < *armeure.* See ARMOR.]

Ar·mor·ic (är-môr′ĭk, -mōr′-) also **Ar·mor·i·can** (-ĭ-kən) *adj.*

armadillo
nine-banded armadillo
Dasypus novemcinctus

Armenia¹

ă pat	oi boy
ā pay	ou out
âr care	ŏŏ took
ä father	ōō boot
ĕ pet	ŭ cut
ē be	ûr urge
ĭ pit	th thin
ī pie	th this
îr pier	hw which
ŏ pot	zh vision
ō toe	ə about,
ô paw	item

Stress marks:
′ (primary);
′ (secondary); as in
lexicon (lĕk′sĭ-kŏn′)

Of or relating to Armorica or its people, language, or culture. ❖ *n.* **1.** A native or inhabitant of Armorica. **2.** See **Breton** 2.

Ar•mor•i•ca (är-môr′ĭ-kə, -mōr′-) The NW part of France, esp. Brittany.

armor plate *n.* Specially formulated hard steel plate used to cover warships, vehicles, and fortifications. —**ar′mor-plat′ed** (är′mər-plā′tĭd) *adj.*

ar•mor•y (är′mə-rē) *n., pl.* **-ies 1a.** A storehouse for arms; an arsenal. **b.** A building for storing arms and military equipment, esp. one serving as headquarters for military reserve personnel. **2.** An arms factory.

ar•mour (är′mər) *n. & v. Chiefly British* Variant of **armor.**

arm•pit (ärm′pĭt′) *n.* The hollow under the upper part of the arm at the shoulder.

arm•rest (ärm′rĕst′) *n.* A support for the arm, as on a piece of furniture or within a motor vehicle.

Arm•strong (ärm′strông′), **Edwin Howard** 1890–1954. Amer. engineer who developed frequency modulation (1933).

Armstrong, Louis Known as "Satchmo." 1900–71. Amer. trumpeter who greatly influenced the development of jazz.

Armstrong, Neil Alden b. 1930. Amer. astronaut who as commander of Apollo 11 became the first person to walk on the moon (Jul. 20, 1969).

arm wrestling or **arm-wres•tling** (ärm′rĕs′lĭng) *n.* A form of wrestling in which two opponents sit facing each other with usu. right hands interlocked and elbows firmly planted and attempt to force each other's arm down. —**arm′-wres′tle** *v.*

ar•my (är′mē) *n., pl.* **-mies 1a.** A large body of people organized and trained for land warfare. **b.** often **Army** The entire military land forces of a country. **c.** A tactical and administrative military unit consisting of a headquarters, two or more corps, and auxiliary forces. **2.** A large group of people organized for a specific cause: *the construction army that built the canal.* **3.** A multitude; a host: *an army of waiters.* [ME *armee* < OFr. < Med.Lat. *armāta* < Lat., fem. p. part. of *armāre,* to arm < *arma,* arms.]

army ant *n.* Any of various tropical ants of the family Formicidae that move in swarms and subsist on other insects.

army group *n.* An operational military formation consisting of two or more armies and their supporting elements.

ar•my•worm (är′mē-wûrm′) *n.* A caterpillar belonging to either of two genera of moth, *Pseudaletia* or *Spodoptera,* large groups of which destroy crops and other vegetation.

Arne (ärn), **Thomas Augustine** 1710–78. British composer whose works include the song "Rule, Britannia."

Arn•hem (är′nəm) A city of E Netherlands on the lower Rhine R. ESE of Utrecht. Pop. 133,471.

Arnhem Land A region of N Australia W of the Gulf of Carpentaria.

ar•ni•ca (är′nĭ-kə) *n.* **1.** Any of various perennial herbs of the genus *Arnica* in the composite family, having opposite simple leaves. **2.** A tincture of the dried flower heads of the European species *A. montana,* applied externally to reduce pain and inflammation. [NLat. *Arnica,* genus name.]

Ar•no (är′nō) A river of central Italy rising in the N Apennines and flowing c. 241 km (150 mi) to the Ligurian Sea.

Ar•nold (är′nəld), **Benedict** 1741–1801. Amer. Revolutionary general and traitor who fled to England in 1781.

Arnold, Matthew 1822–88. British poet and critic whose works include "Dover Beach" (1867).

Arnold, Thomas 1795–1842. British educator and historian; headmaster of Rugby School (1827–42).

A•roe Islands (ä′rōō) See **Aru Islands.**

ar•oid (är′oid′, âr′-) *n.* Any of various perennial herbs in the arum family, including houseplants such as the dieffenbachia and philodendron. [AR(UM) + -OID.] —**ar′oid′** *adj.*

a•roint (ə-roint′) *tr.v. Archaic* Used in the imperative to express an order of dismissal. [?]

a•ro•ma (ə-rō′mə) *n.* **1a.** A quality that can be perceived by the olfactory sense. See Syns at **smell. b.** A pleasant characteristic odor, as of a plant, spice, or food. **2.** A distinctive, intangible quality; an aura: *the aroma of success.* [Alteration (influenced by Lat. *arōma,* spice) of ME *aromat,* aromatic substance < OFr. < Lat. *arōmata,* pl. of *arōma* < Gk., aromatic herb.]

a•ro•ma•ther•a•py (ə-rō′mə-thĕr′ə-pē) *n., pl.* **-pies** The use of selected fragrant substances in lotions and inhalants in an effort to affect mood and promote health.

ar•o•mat•ic (är′ə-mät′ĭk) *adj.* **1.** Having an aroma; fragrant or sweet-smelling. **2.** *Chemistry* Of, relating to, or containing one or more six-carbon rings characteristic of the benzene series and related organic groups. ❖ *n.* An aromatic plant, substance, or compound. —**ar′o•mat′i•cal•ly** *adv.* —**ar′o•mat′ic•ness** *n.*

ar•o•ma•tic•i•ty (är′ə-mə-tĭs′ĭ-tē, ə-rō′mə-) *n., pl.* **-ties** Aromatic quality or character, esp. the distinctive structure or properties of the aromatic chemical compounds.

a•ro•ma•tize (ə-rō′mə-tīz′) *tr.v.* **-tized, -tiz•ing, -tiz•es 1.** To make aromatic or fragrant. **2.** *Chemistry* To convert a substance into an aromatic compound. —**a•ro′ma•ti•za′tion** (-tĭ-zā′shən) *n.*

A•roos•took (ə-rōōs′tək, -rōōs′-) A river rising in N ME and flowing c. 225 km (140 mi) to the St. John R. in New Brunswick, Canada.

Neil Armstrong
photographed in 1969

a•rose (ə-rōz′) *v.* Past tense of **arise.**

a•round (ə-round′) *adv.* **1a.** On all sides: *dirty clothes lying around.* **b.** In close to all sides from all directions: *a field bordered around with trees.* **2.** In a circle or with a circular motion: *spun around twice.* **3.** In circumference or perimeter: *two miles around.* **4.** In succession or rotation: *seasons that rolled around each year.* **5.** In or toward the opposite direction or position: *wheeled around.* **6a.** To or among various places; here and there: *wander around.* **b.** To a specific place: *Come around again.* **7.** In or near one's current location: *waited around for the next flight.* **8.** From the beginning to the end: *frigid weather the year around.* **9.** Approximately; about: *weighed around 30 pounds.* ❖ *prep.* **1.** On all sides of: *trees around the field.* **2.** In such a position as to encircle or surround: *a sash around the waist.* **3a.** Here and there within; throughout: *around the country.* **b.** In the immediate vicinity of; near: *She lives around Norfolk.* **4.** On or to the farther side of: *the house around the corner.* **5.** So as to pass, bypass, or avoid: *got around the difficulty.* **6.** Approximately at: *woke up around seven.* **7.** In such a way as to have a basis or center in: *an economy focused around farming.* ❖ *adj.* **1.** Being in existence: *Our old dog is no longer around.* **2.** Being in evidence; present: *Is the store manager around?* —*idiom:* **have been around** *Informal* To have had many and varied experiences. [ME : prob. *a-,* in; see A–[2] + *round,* circle; see ROUND[1].]

a•round-the-clock (ə-round′thə-klŏk′) *adj.* Variant of **round-the-clock.**

a•rouse (ə-rouz′) *v.* **a•roused, a•rous•ing, a•rous•es** —*tr.* **1.** To awaken from or as if from sleep. **2.** To stir up; excite: *The odd sight aroused our curiosity.* **3.** To stimulate sexual desire in. —*intr.* To be or become aroused. [< ROUSE, on the model of such pairs as *rise, arise.*] —**a•rous′al** *n.*

Arp (ärp), **Jean** or **Hans** 1887–1966. French artist noted for his abstract reliefs and three-dimensional sculptures.

ARP *abbr.* Address Resolution Protocol

Ar•pád (är′päd) d. 907. Hungarian national hero who founded the first Hungarian dynasty (c. 884).

ar•peg•gi•ate (är-pĕj′ē-āt′) *tr.v.* **-at•ed, -at•ing, -ates 1.** To play or sing (a chord) in arpeggio. **2.** To represent (the tones of a chord) as separate notes, as on a staff. —**ar•peg′gi•a′tor** *n.*

ar•peg•gi•o (är-pĕj′ē-ō′, -pĕj′ō) *n., pl.* **-os 1.** The sounding of the tones of a chord in rapid succession rather than simultaneously. **2.** A chord that is played or sung in this manner. [Ital. < *arpeggiare,* to play the harp < *arpa,* harp, of Gmc. orig. See HARP.]

ar•pent (är-pän′) *n.* Any of various French units of land measurement, esp. one used in parts of Canada and the southern United States and equal to about 0.4 hectare (0.85 acre). [Fr. < OFr. < Lat. *arepennis,* half acre. See **per**[1] in App.]

ar•que•bus (är′kə-bəs, -kwə-) *n.* Variant of **harquebus.**

arr. *abbr.* **1.** arranged **2a.** arrival **b.** arrived

ar•rack (är′ək, ə-räk′) *n.* A strong alcoholic drink of the Middle East and the Far East. [Ar. *'araq,* sweat, strong clear liquor made from raisins < *'ariqa,* to sweat.]

ar•raign (ə-rān′) *tr.v.* **-raigned, -raign•ing, -raigns 1.** *Law* To call (an accused person) before a court to answer the charge made against him or her by indictment, information, or complaint. **2.** To call to account; accuse. [ME *arreinen* < OFr. *araisnier* < VLat. **adratiōnāre,* to call to account : Lat. *ad-,* ad- + Lat. *ratiō-, ratiōn-,* account; see REASON.] —**ar•raign′er** *n.* —**ar•raign′ment** *n.*

Ar•ran (är′ən) An island of W Scotland in the Firth of Clyde.

ar•range (ə-rānj′) *v.* **-ranged, -rang•ing, -rang•es** —*tr.* **1.** To put into a specific order or relation; dispose: *arrange shoes in a neat row.* **2.** To plan or prepare for. **3.** To bring about an agreement concerning; settle: *"It has been arranged for him by his family to marry a girl of his own class"* (Edmund Wilson). **4.** *Music* To reset (a composition) for other instruments or voices or as another style of performance. —*intr.* **1.** To come to an agreement. **2.** To make preparations; plan. [ME *arengen* < OFr. *arengier* : *a-,* to (< Lat. *ad-;* see AD–) + *rengier,* to put in a line (< *reng,* line).] —**ar•rang′er** *n.*

SYNONYMS *arrange, marshal, order, organize, sort, systematize* These verbs mean to distribute or dispose persons or things properly or methodically: *arranging figures numerically; to marshal all relevant facts for presentation; ordered my chaotic life; organized the fundraiser; sorted the sweaters by color; systematizing the assorted files.*

ar•range•ment (ə-rānj′mənt) *n.* **1.** The act or process of arranging. **2.** The condition, manner, or result of being arranged; disposal. **3.** A collection of things that have been arranged. **4.** A provision or plan made in preparation for an undertaking. Often used in the plural. **5.** An agreement or settlement; a disposition. **6.** *Music* **a.** An adaptation of a composition for other instruments or voices or for another style of performance. **b.** A composition so arranged.

ar•rant (är′ənt) *adj.* Completely such; thoroughgoing: *an arrant fool.* [Variant of ERRANT.] —**ar′rant•ly** *adv.*

ar•ras (är′əs) *n., pl.* **arras 1.** A wall hanging; a tapestry. **2.** A curtain or wall hanging, esp. one of Flemish origin. [ME, after *Arras,* city of N France that was a medieval tapestry center.]

ar•ray (ə-rā′) *tr.v.* **-rayed, -ray•ing, -rays 1.** To set out for display or use; place in an orderly arrangement. **2.** To dress in finery; adorn. ❖ *n.* **1.** An orderly, often imposing arrangement: *an array of royal jewels.* **2.** An impressively large number, as of persons or objects. **3.** Splendid attire; finery. **4.** *Mathematics* **a.** An arrangement of quantities in rows and columns, as in a matrix. **b.** Numerical data linearly ordered by magnitude. **5.** *Computer Science* An arrangement of memory elements in one or more planes. [ME *arraien* < AN *arraier* < VLat. **arrēdāre*.]

ar·ray·al (ə-rāʹəl) *n.* **1.** The act or process of arranging in an orderly or imposing manner. **2.** Something so arranged.

ar·rear·age (ə-rîrʹĭj) *n.* **1.** The state of being behind in the fulfillment of obligations or of being overdue in payment. **2.** A payment owed.

ar·rears (ə-rîrzʹ) *pl.n.* **1.** An unpaid overdue debt or unfulfilled obligation. **2.** The state of being behind in fulfilling obligations: *in arrears.* [ME *arrers* < *arrere*, behind < OFr. *arere* < VLat. **ad retrō*, backward : Lat. *ad*, to + Lat. *retrō*, behind.]

ar·rest (ə-rĕstʹ) *v.* **-rest·ed, -rest·ing, -rests** —*tr.* **1.** To stop; check: *arrested the growth of the tumor.* **2.** To seize and hold under the authority of law. **3.** To capture and hold briefly (the attention, for example); engage. —*intr.* To undergo cardiac arrest. ❖ *n.* **1a.** The act of detaining in legal custody: *the arrest of a criminal suspect.* **b.** The state of being so detained: *a criminal under arrest.* **2.** A device for stopping motion, esp. of a moving part. **3.** The act of stopping or the condition of being stopped. [ME *aresten* < OFr. *arester* < VLat. **arrestāre* : Lat. *ad-*, ad- + Lat. *restāre*, to stand still (*re-*, re- + *stāre*, to stand; see **stā-** in App.).] —**ar·restʹer, ar·resʹtor** *n.* —**ar·restʹment** *n.*

ar·rest·ee (ə-rĕs-tēʹ) *n.* One who is under arrest.

ar·rest·ing (ə-rĕsʹtĭng) *adj.* Attracting and holding the attention; striking. —**ar·restʹing·ly** *adv.*

Ar·rhe·ni·us (ə-rēʹnē-əs, ä-rāʹ-), **Svante August** 1859–1927. Swedish chemist who won a 1903 Nobel Prize.

ar·rhyth·mi·a (ə-rĭthʹmē-ə) *n.* An irregularity in the force or rhythm of the heartbeat. [NLat. < Gk. *arruthmia*, lack of rhythm < *arruthmos*, unrhythmical : *a-*, without; see **A-¹** + *rhuthmos*, rhythm.]

ar·rhyth·mic (ə-rĭthʹmĭk) *adj.* Lacking rhythm or regularity of rhythm. —**ar·rhythʹmi·cal·ly** *adv.*

ar·ri·ba (ə-rēʹbə) *interj.* Used as an exclamation of pleasure, approval, or elation. [Sp. < Lat. *ad rīpam*, on the shore : *ad*, to + *rīpa*, shore.]

ar·ri·ère-ban (ârʹē-âr-bänʹ, -bănʹ) *n.* **1.** A medieval royal proclamation by which vassals were summoned to military service. **2.** The vassals summoned. [Fr. < OFr. *ariere-ban*, alteration (influenced by *arere*, behind) of *herban*; see **koro-** in App.]

ar·ri·ère-pen·sée (ârʹē-âr-päN-sāʹ) *n.* A mental reservation. [Fr. : *arrière*, in back (< OFr. *arere*; see ARREARS) + *pensée*, thought (< *penser*, to think; see PENSIVE).]

ar·ris (ârʹĭs) *n., pl.* **arris** or **-ris·es** The sharp edge or ridge formed by two surfaces meeting at an angle, as in a molding. [Alteration of OFr. *areste*, fishbone, spine. See ARÊTE.]

ar·ri·val (ə-rīʹvəl) *n.* **1.** The act of arriving. **2.** One that arrives or has arrived. **3.** The reaching of a goal or objective as a result of effort or a process.

ar·rive (ə-rīvʹ) *intr.v.* **-rived, -riv·ing, -rives** **1.** To reach a destination. **2.** To come at length; take place: *The day of reckoning has arrived.* **3.** To achieve success or recognition. —*phrasal verb:* **arrive at** To reach through effort or a process. [ME *ariven* < OFr. *ariver* < VLat. **arrīpāre*, to reach the shore : Lat. *ad-*, ad- + Lat. *rīpa*, shore.] —**ar·rivʹer** *n.*

ar·ri·viste (ă-rē-vēstʹ) *n.* **1.** A person who has recently attained high position or great power but not general acceptance or respect; an upstart. **2.** A social climber; a bounder. [Fr. < *arriver*, to arrive < OFr. *ariver.* See ARRIVE.]

ar·ro·ba (ə-rōʹbə) *n.* **1.** A unit of weight formerly used in Spanish-speaking countries, equal to about 11.3 kilograms (25 pounds). **2.** A unit of weight formerly used in Portuguese-speaking countries, equal to about 14.4 kilograms (32 pounds). [Sp. and Port., both < Ar. *ar-rubʻ*, the quarter (of a quintal) : *al-*, the + *rubʻ*, quarter.]

ar·ro·gance (ărʹə-gəns) *n.* The state or quality of being arrogant; overbearing pride.

ar·ro·gant (ărʹə-gənt) *adj.* **1.** Having or displaying a sense of overbearing self-worth or self-importance. **2.** Marked by or arising from a feeling or assumption of one's superiority toward others. See Syns at **proud.** [ME *arrogaunt* < OFr. < Lat. *arrogāns, arrogant-*, pr. part. of *arrogāre*, to arrogate. See ARROGATE.] —**arʹro·gant·ly** *adv.*

ar·ro·gate (ărʹə-gātʹ) *tr.v.* **-gat·ed, -gat·ing, -gates** **1.** To take or claim for oneself without right; appropriate. **2.** To ascribe on behalf of another in an unwarranted manner. [Lat. *arrogāre, arrogāt-* : *ad-*, ad- + *rogāre*, to ask; see **reg-** in App.] —**arʹro·gaʹtion** *n.* —**arʹro·gaʹtive** *adj.* —**arʹro·gaʹtor** *n.*

ar·ron·disse·ment (ă-rôNʹdēs-mäNʹ) *n.* **1.** The chief administrative subdivision of a department in France. **2.** A municipal subdivision in some large French cities. [Fr. < OFr., rounded projection on a wall < *arrondir, arrondiss-*, to round out : *a-*, to (< Lat. *ad-*; see AD–) + *rondir*, to make round (< *rond*, round; see ROUND¹).]

ar·row (ărʹō) *n.* **1.** A missile having a straight thin shaft with a

pointed head at one end and often flight-stabilizing vanes at the other, meant to be shot from a bow. **2.** Something that is similar to an arrow in form or function. [ME *arwe* < OE.]

ar·row·head (ărʹō-hĕdʹ) *n.* **1.** The pointed striking tip of an arrow, typically a wedge-shaped stone or fitted metal cap. **2.** Something having the shape of an arrowhead. **3a.** Any of various aquatic or wetland perennial plants of the genus *Sagittaria*, having arrowhead-shaped leaves. **b.** The edible tubers of the Eurasian species *S. sagittifolia* or of the North American species *S. latifolia.*

ar·row·root (ărʹō-rootʹ, -rootʹ) *n.* **1a.** A starch obtained from a tropical American perennial herb (*Maranta arundinacea*). **b.** The rhizome of this plant, eaten as a vegetable or used for starch extraction. **c.** The plant itself. **2a.** The edible starch obtained from plants in the genera *Canna* and *Tacca*. **b.** Any of these plants. [By folk ety. < Arawak *aru-aru*, meal of meals (< its use to draw poison from arrow wounds).]

ar·row·wood (ărʹō-woŏdʹ) *n.* Any of several North American species of viburnum having straight tough stems formerly used by certain Native American peoples to make arrows.

arrow worm *n.* Any of various small slender marine worms of the phylum Chaetognatha.

ar·roy·o (ə-roiʹō) *n., pl.* **-os** **1.** A deep gully cut by an intermittent stream; a dry gulch. **2.** A brook; a creek. [Sp. < VLat. **arrugius*, gold mine, underground passage, var. of Lat. *arrugia*, a galleried mine.]

ARS *abbr.* Agricultural Research Service

Ar·sa·cid (ärʹsə-sĭd, är-sāʹ-) *adj.* Of or relating to the Parthian dynasty that ruled Persia and parts of Asia Minor from c. 250 B.C. until its overthrow in A.D. 224. ❖ *n.* A member or subject of this dynasty. [After *Arsaces* (fl. 250 B.C.), founder of the dynasty.]

arse (ärs) *n. Chiefly British Slang* Variant of **ass²**.

ar·se·nal (ärʹsə-nəl) *n.* **1.** A governmental establishment for the storing, development, manufacturing, testing, or repairing of arms and other war materiel. **2.** A stock of weapons. **3.** A store or supply. [Ital. *arsenale* < obsolete *arzanale, darsena* < Ar. *aṣ ṣināʻa*, manufacture, industry, and *dār-aṣ-ṣināʻa*, place of manufacture : *dār*, house (< *dāra*, to turn, revolve) + *al-*, the + *ṣināʻa*, manufacture (< *ṣanaʻa*, to make).]

ar·se·nate (ärʹsə-nĭt, -nātʹ) *n.* A salt or ester of arsenic acid.

ar·se·nic (ärʹsə-nĭk) *n.* **1.** *Symbol* **As** A poisonous metallic element having three allotropes, of which the gray form is the most common. Arsenic compounds are used in insecticides and solid-state doping agents. Atomic number 33; atomic weight 74.922; valence 3, 5. Gray arsenic melts at 817°C (at 28 atm pressure), sublimes at 613°C, and has a specific gravity of 5.73. See table at **element**. **2.** Arsenic trioxide. ❖ *adj.* **ar·senʹic** (är-sĕnʹĭk) Of or containing arsenic, esp. with valence 5. [ME *arsenik* < OFr. < Lat. *arsenicum* < Gk. *arsenikon*, yellow orpiment, alteration of Syriac *zarnīkā*, of Iran. orig. See **ghel-** in App.]

arsenic acid (är-sĕnʹĭk) *n.* A poisonous translucent crystalline compound, H_3AsO_4, used to manufacture arsenates.

ar·sen·i·cal (är-sĕnʹĭ-kəl) *adj.* Of or containing arsenic. ❖ *n.* A drug or preparation containing arsenic.

ar·se·nic trioxide (ärʹsə-nĭk) *n.* A poisonous amorphous powder, As_2O_3, used in rat poisons.

ar·se·nide (ärʹsə-nĭdʹ) *n.* A compound of arsenic with a more electropositive element.

ar·se·ni·ous (är-sēʹnē-əs) *adj.* Of or containing arsenic, esp. with valence 3.

ar·se·no·py·rite (ärʹsə-nō-pīʹrīt) *n.* An arsenic ore, FeAsS.

ar·shin (är-shēnʹ) *n.* Variant of **archine**.

ar·sine (är-sēnʹ, ärʹsēnʹ) *n.* A poisonous gas, H_3As, used as a solid-state doping agent. [ARS(ENIC) + –INE².]

ar·sis (ärʹsĭs) *n., pl.* **-ses** (-sēzʹ) **1a.** The short or unaccented part of a metrical foot, esp. in quantitative verse. **b.** The accented or long part of a metrical foot, esp. in accentual verse. **2.** *Music* The upbeat or unaccented part of a measure. [ME, raising of the voice < LLat., raising of the voice, accented part of a metrical foot < Gk., raising of the foot (marking the upbeat), unaccented part of a metrical foot < *aeirein*, to lift.]

ar·son (ärʹsən) *n.* The crime of maliciously, voluntarily, and willfully setting fire to one's own or another's property for an improper purpose. [AN < LLat. *ārsiō, ārsiōn-* < Lat. *ārsus*, p. part. of *ārdēre*, to burn. See **as-** in App.] —**arʹson·ist** *n.*

ars·phen·a·mine (ärs-fĕnʹə-mēnʹ) *n.* A hygroscopic powder, $C_{12}H_{12}As_2N_2O_2 \cdot 2HCl \cdot 2H_2O$, formerly used to treat spirochetal infections such as syphilis. [ARS(ENIC) + PHEN(YL) + AMINE.]

art¹ (ärt) *n.* **1.** Human effort to imitate, supplement, alter, or counteract the work of nature. **2a.** The conscious production or arrangement of sounds, colors, forms, or other elements in a manner that affects the sense of beauty, specifically the production of the beautiful in a graphic or plastic medium. **b.** The study of these activities. **c.** The product of these activities; human works of beauty considered as a group. **3.** High quality of conception or execution; aesthetic value. **4.** A field or category of art, such as music. **5.** A nonscientific branch of learning; one of the liberal arts. **6a.** A system of principles and methods employed in the performance of a set of activities: *the art of building.* **b.** A trade or craft that applies such a system: *the art of the lexicographer.* **7a.** Skill that is attained by study, practice, or observation: *the art of the baker.* **b.** Skill arising from the exercise of intuitive

arrowhead
broad-leaved arrowhead
Sagittaria latifolia

faculties: *"Self-criticism is an art not many are qualified to practice"* (Joyce Carol Oates). **8a. arts** Artful devices, stratagems, and tricks. **b.** Artful contrivance; cunning. **9.** *Printing* Illustrative material. [ME < OFr. < Lat. *ars, art-*.]

art² (ərt; ärt *when stressed*) *v. Archaic* A second person singular present indicative of **be.** [ME < OE *eart.* See **er-** in App.]

art. *abbr.* article

-art *suff.* Variant of **-ard.**

Ar•ta•xer•xes I (är′tə-zûrk′sēz′) d. 424 B.C. King of Persia (465–425) who sanctioned Judaism in Jerusalem.

Artaxerxes II d. 359 B.C. King of Persia (404–359) whose reign was marked by a peace agreement with Sparta (386).

art dec•o also **Art Dec•o** (dĕk′ō) *n.* A decorative and architectural style of the period 1925–40, characterized by geometric designs, bold colors, and the use of plastic and glass. [Fr. *Art Déco* < *Exposition Internationale des Arts Décoratifs et Industriels Modernes*, a 1925 exposition in Paris, France.]

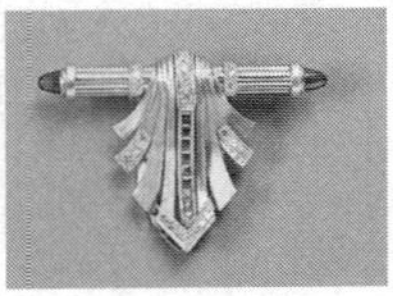

art deco
platinum, sapphire, and diamond clip

ar•te•fact (är′tə-făkt′) *n.* Variant of **artifact.**

Ar•te•mis (är′tə-mĭs) *n. Greek Mythology* The virgin goddess of the hunt and the moon and the twin sister of Apollo. [Gk.]

ar•te•mis•i•a (är′tə-mĭzh′ē-ə, -mĭzh′ə, -mĭz′ē-ə) *n.* Any of various aromatic plants of the genus *Artemisia* in the composite family, having green or grayish foliage and discoid flower heads. [ME *artemesie*, mugwort < OFr. < Lat. *artemisia* < Gk. *artemisiā*, wormwood, after *Artemis*, Artemis (to whom it was sacred).]

ar•te•ri•al (är-tîr′ē-əl) *adj.* **1.** Of, like, or in an artery or arteries. **2.** Of, relating to, or being the blood in the arteries that has absorbed oxygen in the lungs and is bright red. **3.** Being a main road or channel with many branches: *an arterial route.* ❖ *n.* A through road or street. **—ar•te′ri•al•ly** *adv.*

ar•te•ri•al•ize (är-tîr′ē-ə-līz′) *tr.v.* **-ized, -iz•ing, -iz•es** To convert (venous blood) into arterial blood. **—ar•te′ri•al•i•za′tion** (-lĭ-zā′shən) *n.*

arterio– *pref.* Artery: *arteriovenous.* [Gk. *artērio-* < *artēriā*, artery.]

ar•te•ri•og•ra•phy (är-tîr′ē-ŏg′rə-fē) *n., pl.* **-phies** Examination of the arteries using x-rays following injection of a radiopaque substance. **—ar•te′ri•o•gram′** (-ə-grăm′) *n.* **—ar•te′ri•o•graph′ic** (-ə-grăf′ĭk) *adj.*

ar•te•ri•ole (är-tîr′ē-ōl′) *n.* One of the small terminal branches of an artery, esp. one connected to a capillary. [NLat. *artēriola*, dim. of Lat. *artēria*, artery < Gk. *artēriā*.] **—ar•te′ri•o′lar** (-ō′lər, -ə-lər) *adj.*

ar•te•ri•o•scle•ro•sis (är-tîr′ē-ō-sklə-rō′sĭs) *n.* A chronic disease in which thickening, hardening, and loss of elasticity of the arterial walls result in impaired blood circulation. **—ar•te′ri•o•scle•rot′ic** (-rŏt′ĭk) *adj.*

ar•te•ri•o•ve•nous (är-tîr′ē-ō-vē′nəs) *adj.* Of, relating to, or connecting both arteries and veins.

ar•te•ri•tis (är′tə-rī′tĭs) *n.* Inflammation of an artery.

ar•ter•y (är′tə-rē) *n., pl.* **-ies 1.** *Anatomy* Any of a branching system of muscular elastic tubes that carry blood from the heart to cells, tissues, and organs. **2.** A major route of transportation into which local routes flow. See Syns at **way.** [ME *arterie* < Lat. *artēria* < Gk. *artēriā*, windpipe, artery.]

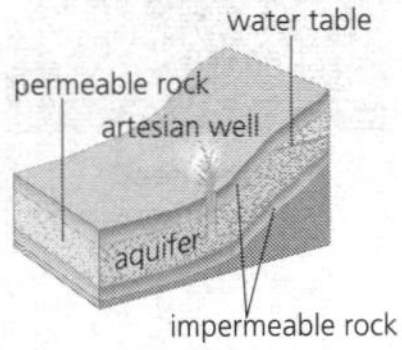

artesian well
A water table higher than the well ensures water pressure will consistently force water into an artesian well.

ar•te•sian well (är-tē′zhən) *n.* A well drilled through impermeable strata to reach water capable of rising to the surface by internal hydrostatic pressure. [Fr. *artésien* < OFr. *artesien*, of Artois < *Arteis*, Artois, France.]

Ar•te•vel•de (är′tə-vĕl′də), **Jacob van** 1290?–1345. Flemish political leader who maintained the neutrality of Flanders during Anglo-French hostilities.

art film *n.* A serious film intended to be artistic, often experimental and not for mass appeal.

art form *n.* An activity or a piece of artistic work that can be regarded as a medium of artistic expression.

art•ful (ärt′fəl) *adj.* **1.** Exhibiting art or skill. **2.** Skillful in accomplishing a purpose, esp. by the use of cunning or craft. **3.** Artificial. **—art′ful•ly** *adv.* **—art′ful•ness** *n.*

ar•thral•gia (är-thrăl′jə, -jē-ə) *n.* Neuralgic pain in a joint or joints. **—ar•thral′gic** (-jĭk) *adj.*

ar•thri•tis (är-thrī′tĭs) *n.* Joint inflammation, usu. accompanied by pain, swelling, and stiffness, resulting from infection, trauma, degenerative changes, metabolic disturbances, or other causes. **—ar•thrit′ic** (-thrĭt′ĭk) *adj. & n.* **—ar•thrit′i•cal•ly** *adv.*

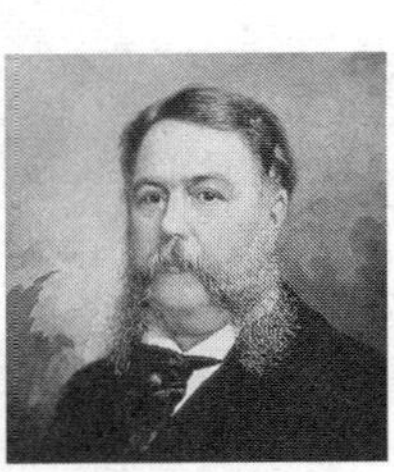

Chester A. Arthur

arthro– or **arthr–** *pref.* Joint: *arthropathy.* [Gk. < *arthron*, joint.]

ar•throd•e•sis (är-thrŏd′ĭ-sĭs, är′thrə-dē′sĭs) *n., pl.* **-ses** (-sēz) The surgical fixation of a joint by artificially induced ankylosis, resulting in bone fusion. [ARTHRO– + Gk. *desis*, binding together (< *dein*, to bind).]

ar•throg•ra•phy (är-thrŏg′rə-fē) *n.* Examination of the interior of a joint using x-rays following the injection of a radiopaque substance. **—ar′thro•gram′** (är′thrə-grăm′) *n.*

ar•thro•gry•po•sis (är′thrə-grə-pō′sĭs) *n.* **1.** The permanent fixation of a joint in a contracted position. **2.** A congenital disorder marked by generalized stiffness of the joints. [ARTHRO– + LLat. *grȳpōsis*, hooking (< L.Gk. *grūpōsis* < Gk. *grūpousthai*, to become hooked < *grūpos*, hook-nosed).]

ar•thro•mere (är′thrə-mîr′) *n.* One of the segments or divisions in the body of a jointed animal, such as an arthropod. **—ar′thro•mer′ic** (är′thrə-mĕr′ĭk, -mîr′ĭk) *adj.*

ar•throp•a•thy (är-thrŏp′ə-thē) *n., pl.* **-thies** A disease or abnormality of a joint.

ar•thro•pod (är′thrə-pŏd′) *n.* Any of numerous invertebrate animals of the phylum Arthropoda, including insects and arachnids, that are characterized by a chitinous exoskeleton and a segmented body with jointed appendages. [< NLat. *Arthropoda*, phylum name : ARTHRO– + NLat. *-poda*, -pod.] **—ar′thro•pod** *adj.* **—ar•throp′o•dan** (är-thrŏp′ə-dən), **ar•throp′o•dal** (-dəl) *adj.*

ar•thros•co•py (är-thrŏs′kə-pē) *n., pl.* **-pies** Examination of a joint using an endoscope that is inserted through a small incision. **—ar′thro•scope′** (är′thrə-skōp′) *n.* **—ar′thro•scop′ic** (-skŏp′ĭk) *adj.* **—ar′thro•scop′ic•al•ly** *adv.*

ar•thro•sis (är-thrō′sĭs) *n., pl.* **-ses** (-sēz) **1.** An articulation or joint between bones. **2.** A degenerative disease of a joint. [Gk. *arthrōsis*, jointing < *arthroun*, to fasten by a joint < *arthron*, joint.]

ar•throt•o•my (är-thrŏt′ə-mē) *n., pl.* **-mies** Surgical incision into a joint.

Ar•thur (är′thər) *n.* The legendary sixth-century king of the Britons who held court at Camelot.

Arthur, Chester Alan 1829–86. The 21st President of the US (1881–85) who became President after the assassination of James A. Garfield.

Ar•thu•ri•an (är-thoor′ē-ən) *adj.* Of or relating to King Arthur and his Knights of the Round Table.

ar•ti•choke (är′tĭ-chōk′) *n.* **1a.** A Mediterranean thistlelike plant *(Cynara scolymus)* in the composite family, having pinnately divided leaves. **b.** The edible immature flower head of this plant. **2.** The Jerusalem artichoke. [Ult. < OSpan. *alcarchofa* < Ar. *al-ḫaršuf* : *al-*, the + *ḫuršūf, ḫaršuf*, artichoke.]

ar•ti•cle (är′tĭ-kəl) *n.* **1.** An individual thing or element of a class; a particular item: *articles of food.* **2.** A given section or item of a series in a written document. **3.** A nonfiction literary composition that forms an independent part of a publication, as of a newspaper. **4.** *Grammar* **a.** The part of speech used to indicate nouns and to specify their application. **b.** Any of the words belonging to this part of speech. In English, the indefinite articles are *a* and *an* and the definite article is *the.* **5.** A particular part or subject; a specific matter or point. ❖ *tr.v.* **-cled, -cling, -cles** To bind by articles in a contract. [ME < OFr. < Lat. *articulus*, joint, article, dim. of *artus*, joint (transl. of Gk. *arthron*, joint, article).]

article of faith *n., pl.* **articles of faith** A very basic belief not to be doubted.

ar•tic•u•la•ble (är-tĭk′yə-lə-bəl) *adj.* That can be articulated: *articulable doubts.*

ar•tic•u•lar (är-tĭk′yə-lər) *adj.* Of or relating to a joint or joints. [ME *articuler* < Lat. *articulāris* < *articulus*, small joint. See ARTICLE.] **—ar•tic′u•lar•ly** *adv.*

ar•tic•u•late (är-tĭk′yə-lĭt) *adj.* **1.** Endowed with the power of speech. **2.** Composed of distinct meaningful syllables or words. **3.** Expressing oneself easily in clear and effective language: *an articulate speaker.* **4.** Marked by the use of clear, expressive language. **5.** *Anatomy* Consisting of sections united by joints; jointed. ❖ *v.* (är-tĭk′yə-lāt′) **-lat•ed, -lat•ing, -lates** —*tr.* **1.** To pronounce distinctly and carefully; enunciate. **2.** To utter (a sound) by making the necessary movements of the speech organs. **3.** To express in coherent verbal form; give words to. **4.** To fit together into a coherent whole; unify. **5.** *Anatomy* To unite by forming joints or a joint. **6.** *Architecture* To give visible or concrete expression to: *a design that strongly articulates windows and doors.* —*intr.* **1.** To speak clearly and distinctly. **2.** To utter a speech sound. **3.** *Anatomy* To form a joint; be jointed. [Lat. *articulātus*, p. part. of *articulāre*, to divide into joints, utter distinctly < *articulus*, small joint. See ARTICLE.] **—ar•tic′u•late•ly** *adv.* **—ar•tic′u•late•ness, ar•tic′u•la•cy** (-lə-sē) *n.*

ar•tic•u•la•tion (är-tĭk′yə-lā′shən) *n.* **1.** The act of vocal expression; utterance: *an articulation of the plan.* **2a.** The act or manner of producing a speech sound. **b.** A speech sound, esp. a consonant. **3a.** A jointing together or being jointed together. **b.** The method or manner of jointing. **4.** *Anatomy* **a.** A joint between bones. **b.** A movable joint between inflexible parts of the body of an animal. **5.** *Botany* **a.** A joint between two separable parts, as a leaf and a stem. **b.** A node or space on a stem between two nodes. **—ar•tic′u•la•to′ry** (-lə-tôr′ē, -tōr′ē), **ar•tic′u•la′tive** (-lā′tĭv, -lə-tĭv) *adj.*

ar•tic•u•la•tor (är-tĭk′yə-lā′tər) *n.* **1.** One that articulates. **2.** One of the organs of speech, such as the lips or tongue.

ar•ti•fact also **ar•te•fact** (är′tə-făkt′) *n.* **1.** An object produced or shaped by human craft, esp. one of archaeological or historical interest. **2.** A typical product or result: *"The act of looking at a naked model was an artifact of male supremacy"* (Philip Weiss). **3.** A structure or feature not normally present but produced by an external agent or action. **4.** An inaccurate observation or effect resulting from investigative or experimental error. [< Lat. *arte*, ablative of *ars*, art + *factum*, something made (< neut. p. part. of *facere*, to make; see **dhē-** in App.).] **—ar′ti•fac′tu•al** (-făk′chōō-əl) *adj.*

ar•ti•fice (är′tə-fĭs) *n.* **1.** An artful or crafty expedient; a stratagem. **2.** Subtle but base deception; trickery. **3.** Cleverness or skill; ingenuity. [Fr. < OFr., craftsmanship < Lat. *artificium* < *artifex*, *artific-*, craftsman : *ars*, *art-*, art + *-fex*, maker; see **dhē-** in App.]

ar•tif•i•cer (är-tĭf′ĭ-sər) *n.* **1.** A skilled worker; a craftsperson. **2.**

One that contrives, devises, or constructs something.

ar•ti•fi•cial (är′tə-fĭsh′əl) *adj.* **1.** Made or brought about by human action or influence. **2.** Imitating something natural; simulated: *artificial teeth.* **3.** Not genuine or natural: *an artificial smile.* [ME < OFr. < Lat. *artificiālis,* belonging to art < *artificium,* craftsmanship. See ARTIFICE.] **—ar′ti•fi′ci•al′i•ty** (-fĭsh′ē-ăl′ĭ-tē) *n.* **—ar′ti•fi′cial•ly** *adv.*

SYNONYMS *artificial, synthetic, ersatz, simulated* These adjectives refer to what is made by humans rather than natural in origin. *Artificial* is broadest in meaning and connotation: *an artificial sweetener; artificial flowers. Synthetic* often implies the use of a chemical process to produce a substance that will look or function like the original, often with certain advantages: *synthetic rubber.* An *ersatz* product is a transparently inferior imitation: *ersatz mink. Simulated* often refers to a substitute for or imitation of a costlier substance: *simulated diamonds.*

artificial horizon *n.* An instrument showing a line about which an aircraft's pitching and banking movements appear on a flight indicator.

artificial insemination *n.* Introduction of semen into the vagina or uterus without sexual contact.

artificial intelligence *n.* **1.** The ability of a computer or other machine to perform activities thought to require intelligence. **2.** The branch of computer science concerned with developing machines with this ability.

artificial language *n.* An invented language based on a set of prescribed rules and developed for a specific purpose, such as computer programming.

artificial life *n.* The simulation of biological phenomena through the use of computer models, robotics, or biochemistry.

artificial respiration *n.* A mechanical or manual procedure used to restore or maintain respiration in a person who has stopped breathing.

artificial selection *n.* Human intervention in animal or plant reproduction to ensure that desirable traits are represented in successive generations.

ar•til•ler•ist (är-tĭl′ər-ĭst) *n.* An artillery soldier; a gunner.

ar•til•ler•y (är-tĭl′ə-rē) *n., pl.* **-ies 1.** Large-caliber crew-operated weapons, such as cannon and missile launchers. **2.** The branch of an army that specializes in the use of such weapons. **3.** The science of the use of guns; gunnery. **4.** Early weapons, such as catapults, for discharging missiles. [ME *artillerie* < OFr. < *artillier,* to equip, perh. alteration of *atiller* < VLat. **apticulāre* < Lat. *aptāre,* to fit, adapt < *aptus,* apt. See APT.]

ar•til•ler•y•man (är-tĭl′ə-rē-mən) *n.* An artillery soldier.

ar•ti•o•dac•tyl (är′tē-ō-dăk′təl) *n.* Any of various hoofed mammals of the order Artiodactyla that have an even number of toes on each foot. [< NLat. *Artiodactyla,* order name : Gk. *artios,* even + Gk. *daktulos,* toe.] **—ar′ti•o•dac′tyl, ar′ti•o•dac′ty•lous** (-tə-ləs) *adj.*

ar•ti•san (är′tĭ-zən, -sən) *n.* A skilled manual worker; a craftsperson. [Prob. Fr. < Ital. *artigiano* < VLat. **artitiānus* < Lat. *artītus,* skilled in the arts, p. part. of *artīre,* to instruct in the arts < *ars, art-,* art.] **—ar′ti•san•ship′** *n.*

art•ist (är′tĭst) *n.* **1.** One who creates imaginative works of aesthetic value, esp. in the fine arts. **2.** One whose work shows great creativity or skill: *a culinary artist.* **3.** One who works in the performing arts. **4.** One who is adept at an activity, esp. trickery or deceit: *a con artist.* [Fr. *artiste* < OFr., lettered person < Med.Lat. *artista* < Lat. *ars, art-,* art.]

ar•tiste (är-tēst′) *n.* **1.** A skilled public performer, esp. a singer or dancer. **2.** A person with artistic pretensions. [Fr. See ARTIST.]

ar•tis•tic (är-tĭs′tĭk) *adj.* **1.** Of or relating to art or artists. **2.** Sensitive to or appreciative of art or beauty. **3.** Showing imagination and skill. **—ar•tis′ti•cal•ly** *adv.*

art•ist•ry (är′tĭ-strē) *n.* **1.** Artistic ability: *a sculptor of great artistry.* **2.** Artistic quality or craft: *the artistry of a poem.*

art•less (ärt′lĭs) *adj.* **1.** Having or displaying no guile, cunning, or deceit. See Syns at **naive. 2.** Free of artificiality; natural: *artless charm.* **3.** Lacking art, knowledge, or skill; uncultured and ignorant. **4.** Poorly made or done; crude. **—art′less•ly** *adv.* **—art′less•ness** *n.*

art nou•veau also **Art Nou•veau** (är′ nōō-vō′, ärt′) *n.* A style of decoration and architecture of the late 19th and early 20th centuries, marked by the depiction of leaves and flowers in flowing, sinuous lines. [Fr. : *art,* art + *nouveau,* new.]

Ar•tois (är-twä′) A historical region and former province of N France near the English Channel.

Arts and Crafts Movement *n.* A movement in architecture and the decorative arts in England and the United States from about 1870 to 1920, characterized by simplicity of design and the handcrafting of objects from local materials.

art song *n.* A lyric song intended to be sung in recital, usu. accompanied by a piano.

art•sy (ärt′sē) *adj.* **-si•er, -si•est** *Informal* Arty.

art•sy-craft•sy (ärt′sē-krăft′sē) *adj. Informal* **1.** Of or relating to handicrafts or the decorative arts. **2.** Self-consciously artistic.

art•work (ärt′wûrk′) *n.* **1.** Work in the graphic or plastic arts, esp. small decorative objects. **2.** An illustrative and decorative element used in a printed work.

art•y (är′tē) *adj.* **-i•er, -i•est** *Informal* **1.** Of or relating to artists or the fine arts. **2.** Showily or affectedly artistic. **—art′i•ly** *adv.* **—art′i•ness** *n.*

A•ru•ba (ə-rōō′bə) An island of the Netherlands Antilles N of the Venezuela coast.

a•ru•gu•la (ə-rōō′gə-lə) *n.* A Mediterranean plant *(Eruca vesicaria* subsp. *sativa)* having flowers with purple-veined yellowish-white petals and edible leaves. [Prob. Ital. dialectal < Lat. *ērūca,* cabbage.]

A•ru Islands also **A•roe Islands** (ä′rōō) An island group of E Indonesia, part of the Moluccas in the Arafura Sea SW of New Guinea.

ar•um (ăr′əm, âr′-) *n.* **1.** Any of several Old World plants, such as the cuckoopint, of the genus *Arum,* having basal arrowhead-shaped leaves. **2.** Any of several related plants, such as the water arum. [Lat., wake-robin < Gk. *aron.*]

a•rus•pex (ə-rŭs′pĕks′) *n.* Variant of **haruspex.**

A•ru•wi•mi (är′ə-wē′mē, ăr′-) A river of central Africa rising in NE Congo (formerly Zaire) near Lake Albert and flowing c. 1,287 km (800 mi) to the Congo R.

ARV *abbr. Bible* American Revised Version

Ar•vad•a (är-văd′ə) A city of N-central CO, a suburb of Denver. Pop. 102,153.

ARVIN *abbr.* Army of the Republic of Vietnam

-ary *suff.* **1.** Of or relating to: *bacillary.* **2.** One that relates to or is connected with: *boundary.* [ME *-arie* < OFr. < Lat. *-ārius,* adj. and n. suff.]

Ar•y•an (âr′ē-ən, ăr′-) *n.* **1.** Indo-Iranian. No longer in technical use. **2.** A member of the people who spoke Proto-Indo-European. No longer in technical use. **3.** A member of any people speaking an Indo-European language. No longer in technical use. **4.** In Nazism, a non-Jewish Caucasian, esp. of Nordic type, held to be part of a master race. [< Skt. *ārya-,* compatriot, Aryan.] **—Ar′y•an** *adj.*

WORD HISTORY It is one of the ironies of history that *Aryan,* a word that nowadays primarily refers to the blond-haired, blue-eyed physical ideal of Nazi Germany, originally referred to a people who looked vastly different. Its history starts with the tribal self-designation of the ancient Indo-Iranians, Indo-European peoples who inhabited parts of what are now Iran, Afghanistan, and India. Their name for themselves was **arya–* or **ārya–,* appearing in, among other things, the Sanskrit word for the upper crust of ancient Indian society. The Sanskrit word, rendered in English as *Aryan,* and its relatives became known to European scholars in the 18th century. In the 1830s, the German Friedrich Schlegel, an important early Indo-Europeanist, argued that **arya–* was not limited to Indo-Iranian but was in fact the ancient Indo-European name for themselves. Thus "Aryan" came to be thought of as synonymous with "Indo-European," and in this sense entered the general scholarly consciousness of the day. Not much later, it was proposed that the original homeland of the Indo-Europeans had been in northern Europe (a hypothesis now discredited). From this, it was but a small leap to think of the Indo-Europeans ("Aryans") as having had northern European looks. While these theories were playing themselves out, certain anti-Semitic scholars in Germany took to viewing German Jews as the main non-Aryan people because of their Semitic roots; a distinction thus arose in their minds between Jews and the "true Aryan" Germans, a distinction that later furnished unfortunate fodder for the racial theories of the Nazis.

ar•y•te•noid (ăr′ĭ-tē′noid′, ə-rĭt′n-oid′) *n.* **1.** Either of two small, pitcher-shaped cartilages at the back of the larynx to which the vocal cords are attached. **2.** A muscle connected to either of these cartilages. **3.** Any of several small mucous glands in front of these cartilages. [NLat. *arytaenoīdēs* < Gk. *arutainoeidēs,* shaped like a ladle : *arutaina,* fem. var. of *arutēr,* ladle (< *aruein,* to draw water) + *-oeidēs,* -oid.] **—ar′y•te′noid′, ar′y•te•noi′dal** *adj.*

as[1] (ăz; əz *when unstressed*) *adv.* **1.** To the same extent or degree; equally: *sings as sweetly as a nightingale.* **2.** For instance: *large carnivores, as the lion.* **3.** When taken into consideration in a specified relation or form: *this as distinguished from that.* ❖ *conj.* **1.** To the same degree or quantity that. Often used as a correlative after *so* or *as: as sweet as sugar.* **2.** In the same manner or way that: *Think as I think.* **3.** At the same time that; while: *slipped as I ran.* **4.** For the reason that; because: *went to bed early, as I was exhausted.* **5.** With the result that: *so foolish as to lie.* **6.** Though: *Ridiculous as it seems, it's true.* **7.** In accordance with which or with the way in which: *The cafe is fine as such places go.* **8.** *Informal* That: *I don't know as I can answer.* ❖ *pron.* **1.** That; which; who. Used after *same* or *such: I received the same grade as you did.* **2.** *Chiefly Upper Southern US* Who, whom, which, or that: *Those as want to can come.* ❖ *prep.* **1.** In the role, capacity, or function of: *acting as mediator.* **2.** In a manner similar to; the same as: *They thought as one.* ***—idioms:* as is** *Informal* Just the way it is, with no changes or modifications. **as it were** In a manner of speaking; as if such were so. [ME < OE *ealswā.* See ALSO.]

USAGE NOTE Traditionally, a distinction has been drawn between the constructions *as . . . as* and *so . . . as.* The *so . . . as* con-

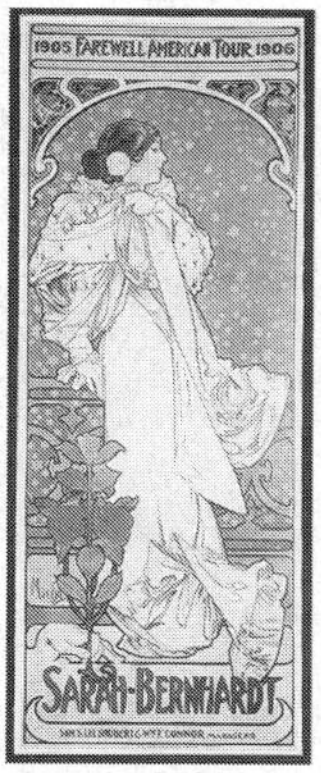

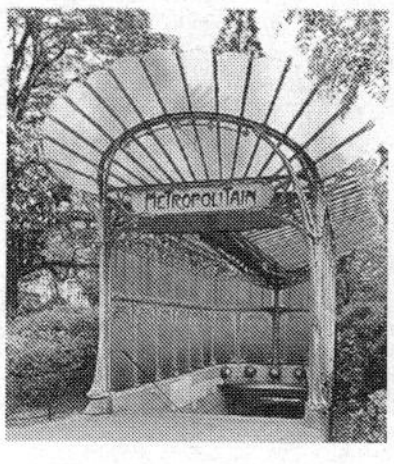

art nouveau
top: poster by Alphonse Mucha (1860–1939) featuring Sarah Bernhardt on her farewell American tour
bottom: metro entrance, Paris, designed by Hector Guimard (1867–1942)

ă	pat	oi	boy
ā	pay	ou	out
âr	care	ŏŏ	took
ä	father	ōō	boot
ĕ	pet	ŭ	cut
ē	be	ûr	urge
ĭ	pit	th	thin
ī	pie	*th*	this
îr	pier	hw	which
ŏ	pot	zh	vision
ō	toe	ə	about, item
ô	paw		

Stress marks:
′ (primary);
′ (secondary), as in
lexicon (lĕk′sĭ-kŏn′)

struction was required in negative sentences (as in Shakespeare's "*'tis not so deep as a well*"), in questions (as in *Is it so bad as that?*), and in certain *if* clauses (as in *If it is so bad as you say, leave*). But in American English the use of *as . . . as* is now acceptable in all contexts. • In a comparison involving both *as . . . as* and *than*, one should write *He is as smart as, or smarter than, his brother*, not *He is as smart or smarter than his brother*, which remains unacceptable in formal style. • *As* should be preceded by a comma when it expresses a causal relation, as in *She won't be coming, as we didn't invite her*. When used to express a time relation, *as* is not preceded by a comma: *She was finishing the painting as I walked into the room*. • *As* is sometimes used superfluously to introduce the complements of verbs like *consider, deem,* and *account,* as in *They considered it as a landmark decision*. This usage may have arisen by analogy *regard* and *esteem,* with which *as* is standardly used in this way. But the use of *as* with verbs like *consider* is not sufficiently well established to be acceptable in writing. See Usage Notes at **like²**, **so¹**, **than**.

as² (ăs) *n., pl.* **as•ses** (ăs′ēz′, ăs′ĭz) **1.** An ancient Roman coin of copper or copper alloy. **2.** An ancient Roman unit of weight equal to about one troy pound. [Lat.]

As The symbol for the element **arsenic** 1.

AS *abbr.* **1.** also **a/s** air speed **2.** American Samoa **3.** Anglo-Saxon **4.** antisubmarine **5.** Associate in Science

As. *abbr.* Asia

as– *pref.* Variant of **ad–** 1.

as•a•fet•i•da also **as•a•foet•i•da** (ăs′ə-fĕt′ĭ-də) *n.* A bitter, foul-smelling resinous material from the roots of several plants of the genus *Ferula* in the parsley family, formerly used in medicine. [ME < Med.Lat. : *asa,* gum (< Pers. *azā,* mastic) + Lat. *fetida,* fem. of *fetidus,* stinking; see FETID.]

A•sa•hi•ka•wa (ä′sə-hē-kä′wə, ä′sä-hē′kä-wä) also **A•sa•hi•ga•wa** (ä′sə-hē-gä′wə, ä′sä-hē′gä-wä) A city of W-central Hokkaido, Japan. Pop. 362,176.

A•sa•ma (ə-sä′mə), **Mount** An active volcano, 2,543.7 m (8,340 ft), of central Honshu, Japan, near Nagano.

a•sa•na (ä′sə-nə) *n.* Any of various bodily positions that are assumed in yogic excercise. [Skt. *āsanam,* a sitting posture < *āste,* he sits.]

A•san•te (ə-sän′tē) *n.* Variant of **Ashanti¹**.

ASAP *abbr.* as soon as possible

as•bes•tos (ăs-bĕs′təs, ăz-) *n.* Either of two incombustible, chemical-resistant, fibrous mineral forms of impure magnesium silicate. [ME *asbestus* < Lat. *asbestos,* mineral or gem < Gk., mineral or gem, unslaked lime < *asbestos,* unquenchable : *a–,* not; see A–¹ + *sbennunai, sbes–,* to quench.] —**as•bes′tine** (-tĭn), **as•bes′tic** (-tĭk) *adj.*

as•bes•to•sis (ăs′bĕs-tō′sĭs, ăz′-) *n.* A chronic, progressive lung disease caused by prolonged inhalation of asbestos particles. [ASBEST(OS) + –OSIS.] —**as′bes•tot′ic** (-tŏt′ĭk) *adj.*

As•bur•y (ăz′bə-rē), **Francis** 1745–1816. British-born Amer. cleric; first American Methodist Episcopal bishop.

ASCAP *abbr.* American Society of Composers, Authors, and Publishers

a•scared (ə-skârd′) *adj. Chiefly Southern & Midland US* Afraid. [Prob. blend of AFRAID and *scared,* p. part. of SCARE.]

as•ca•ri•a•sis (ăs′kə-rī′ə-sĭs) *n.* Infestation or disease caused by the parasitic roundworm *Ascaris lumbricoides.* [ASCAR(ID) + –IASIS.]

as•ca•rid (ăs′kə-rĭd) *n.* Any of various nematode worms of the family Ascaridae. [Sing. of ascarides, intestinal worms < ME < Med.Lat. *ascaridēs,* pl. of *ascaris* < Gk. *askaris.*]

ASCE *abbr.* American Society of Civil Engineers

as•cend (ə-sĕnd′) *v.* **-cend•ed, -cend•ing, -cends** —*intr.* **1.** To go or move upward; rise. **2.** To slope upward. **3.** To rise from a lower level or station; advance. —*tr.* **1.** To move upward upon or along; climb. **2.** To succeed to; occupy: *ascended the throne upon her father's death.* [ME *ascenden* < OFr. *ascendre* < Lat. *ascendere* : *ad–, ad–* + *scandere,* to climb.] —**as•cend′a•ble, as•cend′i•ble** *adj.*

as•cen•dance also **as•cen•dence** (ə-sĕn′dəns) *n.* Ascendancy.

as•cen•dan•cy also **as•cen•den•cy** (ə-sĕn′dən-sē) *n.* Superiority or decisive advantage; domination.

as•cen•dant also **as•cen•dent** (ə-sĕn′dənt) *adj.* **1.** Inclining or moving upward; rising. **2.** Dominant in position or influence; superior. ❖ *n.* **1.** The state of being dominant or in control. **2.** In astrology, the point of the ecliptic or the zodiac sign that rises in the east at a given time, esp. a birth. **3.** An ancestor.

as•cend•er (ə-sĕn′dər) *n.* **1.** One that ascends. **2.** The part of the tall lowercase letters, such as *b* and *h,* that extends above the other lowercase letters. **3.** A letter with such a part.

as•cend•ing (ə-sĕn′dĭng) *adj.* **1.** Moving, going, or growing upward. **2.** Moving or progressing toward a higher level or degree. **3.** *Botany* Growing or directing upward from a curved or slanted base. —**as•cend′ing•ly** *adv.*

ascending rhythm *n.* See **rising rhythm**.

as•cen•sion (ə-sĕn′shən) *n.* **1.** The act or process of ascending; ascent. **2.** *Astronomy* The rising of a star above the horizon. **3. Ascension a.** In Christianity, the bodily rising of Jesus into heaven 40 days after his Resurrection. **b.** A feast celebrating this event,

observed on Ascension Day. [ME *ascensioun* < OFr. *ascention* < Lat. *ascēnsiō, ascēnsiōn- < ascēnsus,* p. part. of *ascendere,* to ascend. See ASCEND.] —**as•cen′sion•al** *adj.*

Ascension Day *n.* The 40th day after Easter, on which the Christian feast of the Ascension is observed.

Ascension Island A British island in the S Atlantic NW of St. Helena; named by Portuguese explorers (1501).

as•cent (ə-sĕnt′) *n.* **1.** The act or process of rising or going upward. **2.** An advancement, esp. in social status. **3.** An upward slope or incline. **4.** A going back in time or genealogical succession. [< ASCEND, on the model of DESCENT.]

as•cer•tain (ăs′ər-tān′) —*tr.* **-tained, -tain•ing, -tains 1.** To discover with certainty, as through examination or experimentation. See Syns at **discover**. **2.** *Archaic* To make certain and precise. [ME *acertainen,* to inform < OFr. *acertener, ascertain–* : *a–,* to (< Lat. *ad–;* see AD–) + *certain,* certain; see CERTAIN.] —**as′cer•tain′a•ble** *adj.* —**as′cer•tain′a•bly** *adv.* —**as′cer•tain′ment** *n.*

as•cet•ic (ə-sĕt′ĭk) *n.* One who renounces material comforts for austere self-discipline, esp. as an act of religious devotion. ❖ *adj.* **1.** Leading a life of self-discipline and self-denial, esp. for spiritual improvement. See Syns at **severe**. **2.** Relating to or characteristic of an ascetic; self-denying and austere. [L.Gk. *askētikos* < Gk. *askētēs,* practitioner, hermit, monk < *askein,* to work.] —**as•cet′i•cal•ly** *adv.*

as•cet•i•cism (ə-sĕt′ĭ-sĭz′əm) *n.* **1.** The principles and practices of an ascetic; self-denial and austerity. **2.** The doctrine that the ascetic life releases the soul from bondage to the body and permits union with the divine.

Asch (ăsh), **Sholem** or **Shalom** 1880–1957. Polish-born Amer. Yiddish writer whose works include *The Nazarene* (1939).

As•cham (ăs′kəm), **Roger** 1515–68. English scholar who advocated the use of the vernacular in literature.

as•ci (ăs′ī′, -kī′) *n.* Plural of ascus.

as•cid•i•an (ə-sĭd′ē-ən) *n.* See **sea squirt**. [< NLat. *Ascidia,* genus name < Gk. *askidion,* dim. of *askos,* wineskin.]

as•cid•i•um (ə-sĭd′ē-əm) *n., pl.* **-i•a** (-ē-ə) *Botany* A pitcher-shaped or bottle-shaped part or organ. [NLat. < Gk. *askidion,* dim. of *askos,* wineskin.] —**as•cid′i•ate′** *adj.* —**as•cid′i•form′** (-ə-fôrm′) *adj.*

ASCII (ăs′kē) *n. Computer Science* A standard for assigning numerical values to the letters in the Roman alphabet and to typographical characters. [A(merican) S(tandard) C(ode for) I(nformation) I(nterchange).]

as•ci•tes (ə-sī′tēz) *n., pl.* ascites An abnormal accumulation of serous fluid in the abdominal cavity. [ME *aschites* < LLat. *ascītēs* < Gk. *askītēs < askos,* belly, wineskin.] —**as•cit′ic** (-sĭt′ĭk) *adj.*

As•cle•pi•us (ə-sklē′pē-əs) *n. Greek Mythology* Apollo's son, the god of medicine.

asco– *pref.* Ascus: *ascospore.* [NLat. < Gk. *askos,* bag, wineskin.]

as•co•carp (ăs′kə-kärp′) *n.* An ascus-bearing structure found in ascomycetous fungi.

as•co•go•ni•um (ăs′kə-gō′nē-əm) *n., pl.* **-ni•a** (-nē-ə) The female reproductive organ of ascomycetous fungi.

as•co•my•cete (ăs′kō-mī′sēt′, -mī-sēt′) *n.* Any of various fungi characterized by the presence of sexually produced spores formed within an ascus. —**as′co•my•ce′tous** (-sē′təs) *adj.*

as•cor•bate (ə-skôr′bāt, -bĭt) *n.* A salt of ascorbic acid. [ASCORB(IC ACID) + –ATE².]

a•scor•bic acid (ə-skôr′bĭk) *n.* A crystalline vitamin, $C_6H_8O_6$, found in citrus fruits, tomatoes, potatoes, and leafy green vegetables and used to prevent scurvy. [A–¹ + SCORB(UT)IC.]

as•co•spore (ăs′kə-spôr′, -spōr′) *n.* A sexually produced fungal spore in an ascus. —**as′co•spo′rous** (-spôr′əs, -spōr′-, ăs-kŏs′pər-əs), **as′co•spor′ic** (-spôr′ĭk, -spōr′-) *adj.*

as•cot (ăs′kət, -kŏt′) *n.* A broad neck scarf knotted so that one end lies flat on the other. [After the racetrack near ASCOT.]

As•cot (ăs′kət) A village of S-central England SW of London; site of the Royal Ascot horse races since 1711.

as•cribe (ə-skrīb′) *tr.v.* **-cribed, -crib•ing, -cribes 1.** To attribute to a specified cause, source, or origin. **2.** To assign as a quality or characteristic: *ascribed jealousy to the critics.* [ME *ascriben* < OFr. *ascrivre* < Lat. *ascrībere* : *ad–,* ad– + *scrībere,* to write; see skrībh– in App.] —**a•scrib′a•ble** *adj.*

as•crip•tion (ə-skrĭp′shən) *n.* **1.** The act of ascribing. **2.** A statement that ascribes. [Lat. *ascrīptiō, ascrīptiōn-,* addendum < *ascrīptus,* p. part. of *ascrībere,* to ascribe. See ASCRIBE.] —**as•crip′tive** *adj.*

ASCU *abbr.* Association of State Colleges and Universities

As•cu•lum (ăs′kyə-ləm) An ancient Roman town of SE Italy; site of Pyrrhus's victory (279 B.C.).

as•cus (ăs′kəs) *n., pl.* **as•ci** (ăs′ī′, -kī′) A membranous, often club-shaped structure in which typically eight ascospores form through sexual reproduction of ascomycetes. [NLat. < Gk. *askos,* bag.]

ASE *abbr.* American Stock Exchange

–ase *suff.* Enzyme: *amylase.* [< DIASTASE.]

a•sep•sis (ə-sĕp′sĭs, ā-) *n.* **1.** The state of being free of pathogenic microorganisms. **2.** The process of removing pathogenic microorganisms or protecting against infection by such organisms.

a·sep·tic (ə-sĕp′tĭk, ā-) *adj.* **1a.** Free of pathogenic microorganisms. **b.** Protecting against infection by pathogenic microorganisms: *aseptic surgery.* **2.** Lacking animation or emotion. —**a·sep′ti·cal·ly** *adv.* —**a·sep′ti·cism** *n.*

a·sex·u·al (ā-sĕk′shōō-əl) *adj.* **1.** Having no evident sex or sex organs; sexless. **2.** Relating to, produced by, or involving reproduction without the union of male and female gametes, as in binary fission. **3.** Lacking interest in or desire for sex. —**a·sex′u·al′i·ty** (-ăl′ĭ-tē) *n.* —**a·sex′u·al·ly** *adv.*

as far as *conj.* To the degree or extent that: *She returned at six, as far as I know.* ❖ *prep. Usage Problem* Concerning; regarding.

USAGE NOTE In standard usage, *as far as* is a conjunction that begins a subordinate clause. But it is sometimes used as a preposition meaning "as for" or "regarding," especially in speech. A large majority of the Usage Panel frowns upon this usage. Eighty percent find the *as far as* construction in this sentence unacceptable: *As far as something to do on the weekend, we didn't even have miniature golf.* Eighty-four percent reject the sentence *The Yankees are still very much alive, as far as the divisional race.* Further, 89 percent object to *as far as* when followed by a noun clause, as in *As far as how Koresh got shot, we don't know yet.*

OUR LIVING LANGUAGE Despite the admonitions detailed in the Usage Note, recent research indicates that speakers are increasingly dropping the verbal part of the *as far as* construction, as in *As far as a better house, I don't want one* (instead of *As far as a better house is concerned . . .*). This trend is more noticeable in speech than in writing. We can infer that this syntactic change is ongoing because teenagers and young adults omit *is/are concerned* and *go/went* in these constructions more often than older speakers do. • Like other examples of language variation and change, a number of constraints that we follow regularly, although unconsciously, govern the dropping of the verb in *as far as* constructions. For instance, if *as far as* precedes a personal pronoun or one whose point of view is being represented (*as far as he is concerned*), the verb cannot be deleted (notice that *as far as he* is strikingly ungrammatical). The longer and more complex the noun or sentence that follows *as far as,* the more likely the verb is to be omitted. Thus, *As far as getting a better house to live in, we . . .* is more likely to be uttered than *As far as a house, we. . . .* The very similar phrase *so far as* is found within verbless constructions in complex sentences that use gerunds as early as the 19th century, as in Jane Austen's novel *Emma:* "so far as our living with Mr. Churchill at Enscombe, it is settled."

as for *prep.* With regard to.

As·gard (ăs′gärd′, äz′-) *n. Mythology* The heavenly residence of the Norse gods and slain heroes of war. [ON *Āsgardhr* : *āss,* god + *gardhr,* enclosure; see **gher-** in App.]

ash¹ (ăsh) *n.* **1.** The grayish-white to black powdery residue from something that is burned. **2.** *Geology* Pulverized particulate matter ejected by volcanic eruption. **3.** The mineral residue of incinerated organic matter, used in pet foods. **4. ashes** Ruins. **5. ashes** Bodily remains, esp. after cremation or decay. ❖ *tr.v.* **ashed, ash·ing, ash·es** To reduce or convert to ash. [ME *asshe* < OE *æsce.* See **as-** in App.]

ash² (ăsh) *n.* **1.** Any of various chiefly deciduous trees of the genus *Fraxinus,* having opposite, pinnately compound leaves. **2.** The strong elastic wood of this tree. **3.** *Linguistics* The letter æ in Old English and some phonetic alphabets, representing the vowel sound of *ash.* [ME *asshe* < OE *æsc.*]

a·shamed (ə-shāmd′) *adj.* **1.** Feeling shame or guilt. **2.** Feeling inferior, inadequate, or embarrassed. **3.** Reluctant through fear of humiliation or shame: *ashamed to ask.* [ME < OE *āsceamod,* p. part. of *āsceamian,* to feel shame : *ā-,* intensive pref. + *sceamian,* to feel shame.] —**a·sham′ed·ly** (-shā′mĭd-lē) *adv.*

A·shan·ti (ə-shăn′tē, ə-shän′-) also **A·san·te** (-sän′tē) *n., pl.* **Ashanti** or **-tis** also **Asante** or **-tes 1.** A member of an Akan people of Ghana, formerly united in the Ashanti kingdom. **2.** The Twi language of the Ashanti.

A·shan·ti (ə-shăn′tē, -shän′-) A region and former kingdom of W Africa in present-day central Ghana; formed in the late 17th cent. and annexed to the British Gold Coast colony in 1901.

Ash·ber·y (ăsh′bĕr′ē, -bə-rē), **John** b. 1927. Amer. poet whose works include *Self-Portrait in a Convex Mirror* (1975).

ash·cake (ăsh′kāk′) *n. Chiefly Southern US* See **johnnycake.** See Regional Note at **johnnycake.** [< its being baked in hot ashes.]

ash·can or **ash can** (ăsh′kăn′) *n.* **1.** A large, usu. metal receptacle for trash. **2.** *Slang* A depth charge.

Ashcan school *n.* A group of US painters of the early 20th century who painted realistic scenes of everyday urban life.

Ash·dod (ăsh′dŏd′, äsh-dôd′) A city of SW Israel on the Mediterranean W of Jerusalem near the site of ancient **Ashdod,** an important Philistine city center. Pop. 68,900.

Ashe (ăsh), **Arthur Robert, Jr.** 1943–93. Amer. tennis player who won singles titles at the US Open (1968) and Wimbledon (1975).

ash·en¹ (ăsh′ən) *adj.* **1.** Consisting of ashes. **2.** Resembling ashes, esp. in color; very pale: *a face ashen with grief.*

ash·en² (ăsh′ən) *adj.* Of or relating to wood from the ash tree.

Ash·er (ăsh′ər) In the Bible, a son of Jacob and the forebear of one of the tribes of Israel.

Ashe·ville (ăsh′vĭl′) A city of W NC in the Blue Ridge WNW of Charlotte; site of Thomas Wolfe's home. Pop. 68,889.

Ash·ga·bat (ăsh′gä-bät′) also **Ash·kha·bad** (-kä-bäd′, -кнä-bät′) A city of S-central Turkmenistan near the Iranian border; founded as a fortress in 1881. Pop. 407,000.

Ash·ke·lon or **Ash·qe·lon** (ăsh′kə-lŏn′, ăsh′kĕ-lôn′) An ancient city of SW Palestine on the Mediterranean Sea; inhabited as early as the 3rd millennium B.C.

Ash·ke·naz·i (ăsh′kə-nä′zē) *n., pl.* **-naz·im** (-näz′ĭm, -nä′zĭm) A member of the branch of European Jews, historically Yiddish-speaking, who settled in central and northern Europe. [< Med. Heb. *'ăškănāzî* < *'ăškănaz,* Germany, adoption of Heb. *'ăškănaz,* one of Noah's grandsons and of a neighboring people, perh. alteration of earlier *'aškúz,* Scythians; akin to Akkadian *ašguzai, iškuzai* < OPers. *Saka-, Skúča-.*] —**Ash′ke·naz′ic** (-nä′zĭk) *adj.*

ash·lar (ăsh′lər) *n.* **1a.** A squared block of building stone. **b.** Masonry of such stones. **2.** A thin dressed rectangle of stone for facing walls. [ME *assheler* < OFr. *aisselier,* board < *aissele* < Med.Lat. *axicellus* < Lat. *assis.*]

a·shore (ə-shôr′, ə-shōr′) *adv.* **1.** To or onto the shore: *driven ashore by the wind.* **2.** On land: *spent the day ashore.*

as how *conj. Informal* That: *The child allowed as how he had already done his homework.*

ash·ram (ăsh′rəm) *n. Hinduism* **1.** A usu. secluded residence of a religious community and its guru. **2.** One of the four stages of an individual's life. [Skt. *āśramaḥ* : *ā-,* to + *śramaḥ,* toil, penance, austerity (< *śramati,* he toils, practices austerity).]

Ash·ton (ăsh′tən), Sir **Frederick** 1906–88. British choreographer whose ballets include *The Dream* (1964).

Ash·ton-un·der-Lyne (ăsh′tən-ŭn-dər-līn′) A borough of NW England, a suburb of Manchester. Pop. 218,800.

Ash·to·reth (ăsh′tə-rĕth′) *n., pl.* **Ash·ta·roth** (-rŏth′) See **Astarte.** [Heb. *'aštōret,* taboo-deformation (with the vowels of *bōšet,* shame) of earlier *'ašteret.*]

ash·tray (ăsh′trā′) *n.* A receptacle for tobacco ashes and cigarette and cigar butts.

A·shur (ä′shoōr′) also **As·sur** (ä′soōr′, ä′shoōr′) *n. Mythology* The principal Assyrian deity.

A·shur·ba·ni·pal (ä′shoōr-bä′nə-päl′) also **As·sur·ba·ni·pal** (ä′soōr-) fl. 7th cent. B.C. King of Assyria (669–626) who was a noted patron of literature and the arts.

Ash Wednesday *n.* The seventh Wednesday before Easter and the first day of Lent, when many Christians receive a mark of ashes on the forehead to indicate penitence and mortality.

ash·y (ăsh′ē) *adj.* **-i·er, -i·est 1.** Of, relating to, or covered with ashes. **2.** Of the color of ashes; pale. —**ash′i·ness** *n.*

ASI *abbr.* air speed indicator

A·sia (ā′zhə, ā′shə) The largest continent, occupying the E part of the Eurasian landmass and its adjacent islands; separated from Europe by the Ural Mts.

A·si·a·go (ä′sē-ä′gō, ä-syä′-) *n.* A yellow Italian cheese suitable for grating when aged. [After *Asiago,* Italy, commune where it originated.]

Asia Minor A peninsula of W Asia between the Black Sea and the Mediterranean; generally coterminous with Asian Turkey.

A·sian (ā′zhən, ā′shən) *adj.* Of or relating to Asia or its peoples, languages, or cultures. ❖ *n.* **1.** A native or inhabitant of Asia. **2.** A person of Asian descent.

USAGE NOTE The term *Asian* is now preferred for persons of South and East Asian ancestry, such as Indians, Southeast Asians, Chinese, Koreans, and Japanese, in place of *Oriental,* an older term for some of these groups. Indonesians and Filipinos are properly termed *Asian,* since their island groups are considered part of the Asian continent, but not the Melanesians, Micronesians, and Polynesians of the central and southern Pacific, who are now often referred to collectively as *Pacific Islanders.* Though strictly speaking all inhabitants of Asia are *Asians,* in practice the term is not used to refer to the peoples of Southwest Asia, who are more usually designated *Middle* or *Near Easterners.*

Asian American also **A·sian-A·mer·i·can** (ā′zhən-ə-mĕr′ĭ-kən, ā′shən-) *n.* A US citizen or resident of Asian descent. See Usage Note at **Amerasian.** —**A′sian-A·mer′i·can** *adj.*

Asian influenza *n.* Influenza caused by the most common influenza virus (type A), first isolated in China in 1957.

A·sian·i·za·tion (ā′zhə-nĭ-zā′shən) *n.* The act or process of making or becoming Asian in character, culture, or outlook.

Asian pear *n.* See **sand pear.**

Asian tiger mosquito *n.* A mosquito (*Aeder albopictus*), native to Asia and now present in parts of subtropical and tropical America, that transmits dengue and yellow fever.

A·si·at·ic (ā′zhē-ăt′ĭk, -shē-, -zē-) *adj.* Asian: *travels in Asiatic Russia; the Asiatic elephant.* ❖ *n. Often Offensive* An Asian.

Asiatic cholera *n.* See **cholera 1.**

a·side (ə-sīd′) *adv.* **1.** To or toward the side: *step aside.* **2.** Out of one's thoughts or mind: *put doubt aside.* **3.** Apart: *time set aside for fun.* **4.** In reserve; away. **5.** Set out of the way; dispensed with: *Joking aside, can you swim 15 miles?* ❖ *n.* **1.** A piece of dialogue supposedly not heard by the other actors on stage. **2.** A remark made in an undertone so as to be inaudible. **3.** A parenthetical departure; a digression.

ash²
white ash
Fraxinus americana

Arthur Ashe

ă	pat	oi	boy
ā	pay	ou	out
âr	care	oō	took
ä	father	oō	boot
ĕ	pet	ŭ	cut
ē	be	ûr	urge
ĭ	pit	th	thin
ī	pie	th	this
îr	pier	hw	which
ŏ	pot	zh	vision
ō	toe	ə	about,
ô	paw		item

Stress marks:
′ (primary);
′ (secondary), as in
lexicon (lĕk′sĭ-kŏn′)

aside from *prep.* Excluding; except for.

as if *conj.* **1.** In the same way that it would be if: *ran as if she were chased.* **2.** That: *It seemed as if the work would never end.*

As·i·mov (ăz′ĭ-môv′, -mŏv′), **Isaac** 1920–92. Russian-born Amer. scientist and writer whose works include *The Foundation Trilogy* (1963).

as·i·nine (ăs′ə-nīn′) *adj.* **1.** Utterly stupid or silly. **2.** Of or like an ass. [Lat. *asininus,* of an ass < *asinus,* ass.] —**as′i·nine′ly** *adv.* —**as′i·nin′i·ty** (-nĭn′ĭ-tē) *n.*

ask (ăsk) *v.* **asked, ask·ing, asks** —*tr.* **1.** To put a question to. **2.** To seek an answer to. **3.** To seek information about: *asked directions.* **4a.** To make a request of: *asked me for a loan.* **b.** To make a request for. Often used with an infinitive or clause: *asked to go along on the trip; asked that he be allowed to stay out late.* **5.** To require or call for as a price or condition: *asked ten dollars for the book.* **6.** To expect or demand: *ask too much.* **7.** To invite. **8.** *Archaic* To publish, as marriage banns. —*intr.* **1.** To inquire; seek information. **2.** To make a request: *asked for help.* —**idiom: ask for it (or trouble)** *Informal* To persist in an action although it may result in difficulty or punishment. [ME *asken* < OE *āscian, āscian.*] —**ask′er** *n.*

SYNONYMS ask, question, inquire, query, interrogate, examine, quiz These verbs mean to seek information. *Ask* is the most neutral term: *asked me what was wrong; ask too many questions. Question* implies careful and continuous asking: *The prosecutor questioned the witness. Inquire* refers to a simple request for information: *will inquire how we can help. Query* usually suggests settling a doubt: *The proofreader queried the spelling of the word. Interrogate* applies especially to official questioning: *The detectives interrogated the suspects. Examine* refers particularly to close and detailed questioning to ascertain a person's knowledge or qualifications: *Only lawyers who have been examined and certified by the bar association are admitted to practice. Quiz* denotes the informal examination of students: *The teacher quizzed the pupils on the state capitals.*

a·skance (ə-skăns′) also **a·skant** (ə-skănt′) *adv.* **1.** With disapproval, suspicion, or distrust. **2.** With a sideways glance; obliquely. [?]

a·skew (ə-skyōō′) *adv. & adj.* To one side; awry: *rugs lying askew.* [Prob. A–² + SKEW.]

ask·ing price (ăs′kĭng) *n.* The price asked for an item.

ASL *abbr.* American Sign Language

a·slant (ə-slănt′) *adv. & adj.* At a slant; obliquely. ❖ *prep.* Obliquely over or across.

a·sleep (ə-slēp′) *adj.* **1.** In a state of sleep; sleeping. **2a.** Inactive; dormant. **b.** Indifferent: *politicians asleep to minority needs.* **3.** Numb, esp. from reduced blood circulation: *My leg is asleep.* **4.** Dead. ❖ *adv.* **1.** In or into a state of sleep. **2.** In or into a state of apathy or indifference. **3.** Into a state of numbness. **4.** Into death.

as long as *conj.* **1.** During the time that: *I'll stay as long as you need me.* **2.** Since: *As long as you've offered, I accept.* **3.** On the condition that.

a·slope (ə-slōp′) *adv. & adj.* At a slope or slant.

a·slosh (ə-slŏsh′) *adv. & adj.* Awash.

As·ma·ra (ăz-mä′rə) The cap. and largest city of Eritrea, in the central part of the country. Pop. 358,100.

ASME *abbr.* American Society of Mechanical Engineers

As·mo·de·us (ăz′mə-dē′əs, ăs′-) *n.* A figure originally viewed as king of the demons in Jewish demonology and later as a mischievous sprite. [Med.Lat. *Asmodaeus* < Mishnaic Heb. *'ašmǝday* < Avestan *Aēšma-daēva-,* spirit of anger : *aēšma-,* anger; see **eis-** in App. + *daēva-,* spirit, demon; see **dyeu-** in App.]

A·so (ä′sō′), **Mount** also **A·so-san** (ä′sō-sän′) A volcanic mountain of central Kyushu, Japan, topped by one of the world's largest calderas and rising to 1,593 m (5,223 ft).

a·so·cial (ā-sō′shəl) *adj.* **1.** Not social. **2.** Avoiding or averse to the society of others; not sociable. **3.** Unable or unwilling to conform to normal standards of social behavior; antisocial. **4.** Inconsiderate of others; self-centered. ❖ *n.* One that exhibits behavior and characteristics deemed asocial.

as of *prep.* On; at: *The project was terminated as of January 1.*

A·so·ka (ə-sō′kə, -shō′-) Known as "the Great." d. 232 B.C. King of Magadha (273–232) who adopted Buddhism as the state religion.

asp (ăsp) *n.* Any of several venomous snakes of Africa, Asia, and Europe, such as the small cobra *Naja haje.* [ME *aspis* < Lat. < Gk.]

as·par·a·gin·ase (ə-spăr′ə-jə-nās′, -nāz′) *n.* An enzyme isolated from bacteria that catalyzes the hydrolysis of asparagine.

as·par·a·gine (ə-spăr′ə-jēn′) *n.* A crystalline amino acid, $C_4H_8N_2O_3$, found in many proteins, present in large amounts in some plants, and easily hydrolyzed to aspartic acid. [ASPARAG(US) + −INE².]

as·par·a·gus (ə-spăr′ə-gəs) *n.* **1.** The tender shoots of a Eurasian plant (*Asparagus officinalis*), eaten as a vegetable. **2.** Any of various perennial plants of the Old World genus *Asparagus* with leaflike stems, scalelike leaves, and small flowers. [Late ME *sperage, sparage* < Med.Lat. *sparagus* < Lat. *asparagus* < Gk. *aspharagos, asparagos.*]

asparagus beetle *n.* A small spotted beetle (*Crioceris asparagi*) that infests and damages asparagus plants.

asparagus pea *n.* An Asiatic twining herb (*Psophocarpus tetragonolobus*) having tuberous roots and long four-angled pods.

as·par·tame (ăs′pər-tām′, ə-spär′-) *n.* An artificial sweetener, $C_{14}H_{18}N_2O_5$, formed from aspartic acid. [ASPART(IC ACID) + (PHENYL)A(LANINE) + M(ETHYL) + E(STER).]

a·spar·tate (ə-spär′tāt) *n.* A salt or ester of aspartic acid. [ASPART(IC ACID) + −ATE².]

as·par·tic acid (ə-spär′tĭk) *n.* A nonessential amino acid, $C_4H_7NO_4$, found esp. in young sugar cane and sugar-beet molasses. [< ASPARAGUS (< its being obtained from an amino acid found in asparagus).]

as·par·to·kin·ase (ə-spär′tō-kī′nās) *n.* An enzyme that catalyzes aspartic acid phosphorylation by ATP. [ASPART(IC ACID) + KINASE.]

As·pa·sia (ă-spā′zhə) fl. c. 440 B.C. Greek courtesan and lover of Pericles who was noted for her wisdom, wit, and beauty.

ASPCA *abbr.* American Society for the Prevention of Cruelty to Animals

as·pect (ăs′pĕkt) *n.* **1.** A particular look or facial expression; mien. **2.** Appearance to the eye, esp. from a specific vantage point. **3.** A way in which something can be viewed by the mind: *all aspects of the situation.* **4.** A position facing or commanding a given direction; an exposure. **5.** A side or surface facing a particular direction. **6.** The configuration of the stars or planets in relation to one another, thought by astrologers to influence human affairs. **7.** *Grammar* A property of verbs that indicates inception, duration, completion, habituality, or other modes of action or being. **8.** *Archaic* An act of looking or gazing. [ME < Lat. *aspectus,* a view < p. part. of *aspicere,* to look at : *ad-, ad-* + *specere,* to look; see **spek-** in App.] —**as·pec′tu·al** (ă-spĕk′chōō-əl) *adj.*

aspect ratio *n.* **1.** The width-to-height ratio of a film or television image. **2.** The span-to-mean-chord ratio of an airfoil.

as·pen (ăs′pən) *n.* Any of several trees of the genus *Populus* having leaves attached by flat leafstalks so that they flutter in the wind. ❖ *adj.* **1.** Of or relating to one of these trees. **2.** Shaking like aspen leaves. [ME *aspe* < OE *æspe.*]

Aspen A city of W-central CO in the Sawatch Range of the Rocky Mts.; founded c. 1879. Pop. 5,049.

as·per·ate (ăs′pə-rāt′) *tr.v.* **-at·ed, -at·ing, -ates** To make uneven; roughen. [Lat. *asperāre, asperāt-* < *asper,* rough.]

As·per·ger's syndrome (ăs′pər-gərz) *n.* A psychiatric disorder, usu. of childhood, characterized by impairments in social interaction and repetitive behavior patterns. [After Hans *Asperger* (1906–80), Austrian pediatrician.]

as·per·ges (ə-spûr′jēz) *n. Roman Catholic Church* The ceremony of sprinkling the altar, clergy, and congregation with holy water. [< Lat. *aspergēs (mē),* you will sprinkle (me), the first words of the rite, second pers. sing. fut. t. of *aspergere,* to sprinkle. See ASPERSE.]

as·per·gil·lo·sis (ăs′pər-jə-lō′sĭs) *n.* An infection caused by fungi of the genus *Aspergillus.* [ASPERGILL(US) + −OSIS.]

as·per·gil·lum (ăs′pər-jĭl′əm) or **as·per·gill** (-jĭl) *n., pl.* **-gil·la** (-jĭl′ə) or **-gil·lums** *Roman Catholic Church* An instrument, such as a brush, used for sprinkling holy water. [NLat. < Lat. *aspergere,* to sprinkle. See ASPERSE.]

as·per·gil·lus (ăs′pər-jĭl′əs) *n., pl.* **-gil·li** (-jĭl′ī′) Any of various fungi of the genus *Aspergillus,* which includes many common molds. [NLat. *Aspergillus,* genus name < *aspergillum,* aspergill (< its resemblance to an aspergillum brush). See ASPERGILLUM.]

as·per·i·ty (ă-spĕr′ĭ-tē) *n., pl.* **-ties 1a.** Roughness or harshness, as of surface, sound, or climate. **b.** Severity; rigor. **2.** A slight projection from a surface; a point or bump. **3.** Harshness of manner; ill temper or irritability. [ME *asperite* < OFr. *asprete* < Lat. *asperitās* < *asper,* rough.]

as·perse (ə-spûrs′) *tr.v.* **-persed, -pers·ing, -pers·es 1.** To spread falsely or damaging charges or insinuations against. **2.** To sprinkle, esp. with holy water. [ME, to besprinkle < Lat. *aspergere, aspers-* : *ad-, ad-* + *spargere,* to strew.] —**as·per′sive** (-sĭv, -zĭv) *adj.*

as·per·sion (ə-spûr′zhən, -shən) *n.* **1a.** An unfavorable or damaging remark; slander: *Don't cast aspersions.* **b.** The act of defaming or slandering. **2.** A sprinkling, esp. with holy water.

as·phalt (ăs′fôlt′) *n.* **1.** A brownish-black solid or semisolid mixture of bitumens obtained from native deposits or as a petroleum byproduct, used in paving, roofing, and waterproofing. **2.** Mixed asphalt and crushed stone gravel or sand, used for paving or roofing. ❖ *tr.v.* **-phalted, -phalt·ing, -phalts** To pave or coat with asphalt. [ME *aspalt* < Med.Lat. *asphaltus* < Gk. *asphaltos.*] —**as·phal′tic** *adj.*

as·phal·tite (ăs′fôl-tīt′) *n.* A solid dark-colored complex of hydrocarbons found in natural veins and deposits.

asphalt jungle *n.* A large urban or inner-city area, esp. when characterized as congested and dangerous.

a·spher·ic (ā-sfîr′ĭk, ā-sfĕr′-) also **a·spher·i·cal** (-ĭ-kəl) *adj.* Varying slightly from sphericity with only slight aberration, as a lens.

as·pho·del (ăs′fə-dĕl′) *n.* **1a.** Any of several chiefly Mediterranean plants of the genera *Asphodeline* and *Asphodelus* in the lily family, having linear leaves and elongate flower clusters. **b.** Any of several other plants, such as the bog asphodel. **2.** In Greek poetry and mythology, the flowers of Hades and the dead, sacred to

Isaac Asimov

aspen
quaking aspen
Populus tremuloides

Persephone. **3.** In early English and French poetry, the daffodil. [Lat. *asphodelus* < Gk. *asphodelos.*]

as•phyx•i•a (ăs-fĭk′sē-ə) *n.* An extreme decrease in the amount of oxygen in the body, leading to unconsciousness or death. [NLat. < Gk. *asphuxiā,* stopping of the pulse : *a-,* not; see A–¹ + *sphuxis,* heartbeat (< *sphuzein, sphug-,* to throb).]

as•phyx•i•ant (ăs-fĭk′sē-ənt) *adj.* Inducing or tending to induce asphyxia. —**as•phyx′i•ant** *n.*

as•phyx•i•ate (ăs-fĭk′sē-āt′) *v.* **-at•ed, -at•ing, -ates** —*tr.* To cause asphyxia in; smother. —*intr.* To undergo asphyxia; suffocate. —**as•phyx′i•a′tion** *n.* —**as•phyx′i•a′tor** *n.*

as•pic¹ (ăs′pĭk) *n.* A clear jelly usu. made of stock and gelatin and used as a garnish or to make a mold. [Fr. < *aspic,* asp (< the resemblance of the jelly's coloration to an asp's). See ASPIC².]

as•pic² (ăs′pĭk) *n. Archaic* An asp. [Fr. < OFr., alteration of *aspe* < Lat. *aspis.* See ASP.]

as•pi•dis•tra (ăs′pĭ-dĭs′trə) *n.* Any of several eastern Asian plants of the genus *Aspidistra* in the lily family, esp. *A. elatior,* cultivated as a houseplant for its evergreen basal leaves and bell-shaped flowers. [NLat. *Aspidistra,* genus name < Gk. *aspis, aspid-,* shield.]

as•pi•rant (ăs′pər-ənt, ə-spīr′-) *n.* One who aspires, as to advancement, honors, or a high position. —**as′pi•rant** *adj.*

as•pi•rate (ăs′pə-rāt′) *tr.v.* **-rat•ed, -rat•ing, -rates 1.** *Linguistics* **a.** To pronounce (a vowel or word) with the initial release of breath associated with English *h,* as in *hurry.* **b.** To follow (a consonant, esp. a stop) with a clearly audible puff of breath, as in English *pit.* **2.** To draw (something) into the lungs; inhale. **3.** *Medicine* **a.** To remove an abnormal accumulation of (a liquid or gas) from the body by aspiration. **b.** To suction (a body part or growth, for example) for the removal of a liquid or gas. ❖ *n.* (-pər-ĭt) **1.** *Linguistics* **a.** The speech sound represented by English *h.* **b.** The puff of air accompanying the release of a stop. **c.** A speech sound followed by a puff of breath. **2.** *Medicine* Matter removed by aspiration. [Lat. *aspīrāre, aspīrāt-,* to breath on : *ad-,* ad- + *spīrāre,* to breathe.]

as•pi•ra•tion (ăs′pə-rā′shən) *n.* **1.** Expulsion of breath in speech. **2.** *Linguistics* **a.** Aspirated pronunciation of a consonant. **b.** A speech sound produced with an aspirate. **3.** The act of breathing in; inhalation. **4.** *Medicine* The process of removing fluids or gases from the body with a suction device. **5a.** A desire for high achievement. **b.** An object of such desire.

as•pi•ra•tor (ăs′pə-rā′tər) *n.* **1.** A device for removing liquids or gases by suction, esp. from a body cavity. **2.** A suction pump used to create a partial vacuum.

as•pir•a•to•ry (ə-spīr′ə-tôr′ē, -tōr′ē) *adj.* Of, relating to, or suited for breathing or suction.

as•pire (ə-spīr′) *intr.v.* **-pired, -pir•ing, -pires 1.** To have a great ambition or ultimate goal; desire strongly: *aspired to stardom.* **2.** To strive toward an end. **3.** To soar. [ME *aspiren* < *aspirer* < Lat. *aspīrāre,* to desire. See ASPIRATE.] —**as•pir′er** *n.* —**as•pir′ing•ly** *adv.*

as•pi•rin (ăs′pər-ĭn, -prĭn) *n.* **1.** A crystalline compound, $CH_3COOC_6H_4COOH$, derived from salicylic acid and used in medicine to relieve pain, reduce fever, and prevent blood clotting. **2.** A tablet of aspirin. [Orig. a trademark.]

a•squint (ə-skwĭnt′) *adv. & adj.* With a sidelong glance. [ME : *a-,* on; see A–² + *-squint;* akin to *skwyn,* in *of skwyn,* obliquely.]

As•quith (ăs′kwĭth), **Herbert Henry.** 1st Earl of Oxford and Asquith. 1852–1928. British prime minister (1908–16).

ASR *abbr.* air-sea rescue

as regards *prep.* In regard to.

ass¹ (ăs) *n., pl.* **ass•es** (ăs′ĭz) **1.** Any of several hoofed mammals of the genus *Equus,* closely related to the horses but with smaller build and longer ears and including the domesticated donkey. **2.** A vain, silly, or aggressively stupid person. [ME *asse* < OE *assa,* perh. of Celt. orig., ult. < Lat. *asinus.*]

ass² (ăs) *n., pl.* **ass•es** (ăs′ĭz) *Vulgar Slang* **1a.** The buttocks. **b.** The anus. **2.** Sexual intercourse. [ME *ars* < OE *ears.* See **ors-** in App.]

As•sad (ä-säd′), **Hafez al-** 1928?–2000. Syrian politician who seized control of the government in 1970 and served as president (1971–2000).

as•sa•gai (ăs′ə-gī′) *n.* Variant of **assegai.**

as•sai¹ (ä-sī′) *n., pl.* **-sais 1.** Any of several feather-leaved South American palms, esp. *Euterpe edulis* and *E. oleracea,* that are sources of heart of palm. **2.** A beverage made from the fleshy purple fruit of one of these palms. [Port. *assaí* < Tupi *assahi.*]

as•sai² (ä-sī′) *adv. Music* Very. [Ital. < VLat. **ad satis,* to sufficiency. See ASSET.]

as•sail (ə-sāl′) *tr.v.* **-sailed, -sail•ing, -sails 1.** To attack with or as if with violent blows; assault. **2.** To attack verbally. **3.** To trouble; beset: *assailed by doubts.* [ME *assailen* < OFr. *asalir, asaill-* < VLat. **assalīre,* var. of Lat. *assilīre,* to jump on : *ad-,* onto; see AD– + *salīre,* to jump.] —**as•sail′a•ble** *adj.* —**as•sail′ant, as•sail′er** *n.* —**as•sail′er** *n.* —**as•sail′ment** *n.*

As•sam (ă-săm′) A former kingdom of extreme NE India, now a state separated from the rest of the country by Bangladesh.

As•sam•ese (ăs′ə-mēz′, -mēs′) *adj.* Of or relating to Assam or its people, language, or culture. ❖ *n., pl.* **Assamese 1.** A native or inhabitant of Assam. **2.** The Indic language of the Assamese.

as•sas•sin (ə-săs′ĭn) *n.* **1.** One who murders by surprise attack, esp. one who carries out a plot to kill a prominent person. **2. Assassin** A member of a secret Muslim order that killed Crusaders and others. [Fr. < Med.Lat. *assassīnus* < Ar. *ḥaššāšīn,* pl. of *ḥaššāš,* hashish user < *ḥašīš,* hashish. See HASHISH.]

as•sas•si•nate (ə-săs′ə-nāt′) *tr.v.* **-nat•ed, -nat•ing, -nates 1.** To murder (a prominent person) by surprise attack, as for political reasons. **2.** To destroy or injure treacherously. —**as•sas′si•na′tion** *n.* —**as•sas′si•na′tive** *adj.* —**as•sas′si•na′tor** *n.*

assassin bug *n.* Any of various predatory bugs of the family Reduviidae, which have powerful beaks used to prey on other insects or modified to suck blood from mammals.

As•sa•teague Island (ăs′ə-tēg′) An island off MD and VA separating Chincoteague Bay from the Atlantic Ocean.

as•sault (ə-sôlt′) *n.* **1.** A violent physical or verbal attack. **2a.** A military attack, such as one launched against a fortified place. **b.** The concluding stage of an attack at which close combat occurs. **3.** *Law* **a.** An unlawful threat or attempt to do bodily injury to another. **b.** The act or an instance of unlawfully threatening or attempting to injure another. **4a.** *Law* Sexual assault. **b.** Rape. ❖ *v.* **-sault•ed, -sault•ing, -saults** —*tr.* **1.** To make an assault upon; attack. **2.** To rape. —*intr.* To make an assault. [ME *assaut* < OFr. < VLat. **assaltus,* var. of Lat. *assultus* < p. part. of *assilīre,* to jump on. See ASSAIL.] —**as•sault′er** *n.*

assault and battery *n.* An assault upon a victim that is carried out by striking the victim, knocking the victim down, or otherwise doing violence to the victim.

as•saul•tive (ə-sôl′tĭv) *adj.* Inclined to or suggestive of violent attack.

assault rifle *n.* An automatic or semiautomatic rifle designed for use in military attacks.

assault weapon *n.* An infantry weapon, such as an assault rifle, designed for individual use.

as•say (ăs′ā′, ă-sā′) *n.* **1a.** Qualitative or quantitative analysis of a metal or ore to determine its components. **b.** A substance to be so analyzed. **c.** The result of such an analysis. **2.** A bioassay. **3.** An analysis or examination. **4.** *Archaic* An attempt; an essay. ❖ *tr.v.* (ă-sā′, ăs′ā′) **-sayed, -say•ing, -says 1a.** To subject (a metal, for example) to chemical analysis so as to determine the strength or quality of its components. **b.** To bioassay. **2.** To examine by trial or experiment; put to a test: *assay one's ability to speak Chinese.* **3.** To evaluate; assess. See Syns at **estimate. 4.** To attempt; try. [ME < OFr. *essai, assai.* See ESSAY.] —**as•say′a•ble** *adj.* —**as•say′er** *n.*

as•se•gai or **as•sa•gai** (ăs′ə-gī′) *n.* **1.** A light spear or lance, esp. one with a short shaft and long blade for close combat, used by Bantu peoples of southern Africa. **2.** A southern African tree *(Curtisia dentata)* having wood used for spears or lances. [Obsolete Fr. *azagaie,* prob. < OSpan. *azagayah* < Ar. *az-zaġāya* : *al-,* the + Berber *zaġāya,* spear.]

as•sem•blage (ə-sĕm′blĭj) *n.* **1a.** The act of assembling. **b.** The state of being assembled. **2.** A collection of people or things; a gathering. **3.** A fitting together of parts, as in a machine. **4.** A sculptural composition of miscellaneous objects. —**as•sem′blag•ist** *n.*

as•sem•ble (ə-sĕm′bəl) *v.* **-bled, -bling, -bles** —*tr.* **1.** To bring or call together into a group or whole: *assembled the jury.* **2.** To fit together the parts or pieces of. —*intr.* To gather together; congregate. See Syns at **gather.** [ME *assemblen* < OFr. *assembler* < VLat. **assimulāre* : Lat. *ad-,* ad- + Lat. *simul,* together; see **sem-¹** in App.]

as•sem•bler (ə-sĕm′blər) *n.* **1.** One that assembles. **2.** *Computer Science* A program that produces executable machine code from symbolic assembly language.

as•sem•bly (ə-sĕm′blē) *n., pl.* **-blies 1a.** The act of assembling. **b.** The state of being assembled. **2.** A group gathered for a common reason, as for a religious or social purpose. **3. Assembly** The lower house of certain US state legislatures. **4a.** The putting together of manufactured parts to make a completed product. **b.** A set of parts so assembled. **5.** A signal for troops to come together in formation. **6.** *Computer Science* The automatic translation of symbolic code into machine code.

assembly language *n.* A programming language that is a close approximation of the binary machine code.

assembly line *n.* **1.** An arrangement of workers, machines, and equipment in which the product being assembled passes consecutively from operation to operation until completed. **2.** A process in which finished products are turned out in a mechanically efficient, though impersonal, manner.

as•sem•bly•man (ə-sĕm′blē-mən) *n.* A man who is a member of a legislative assembly.

Assembly of God *n.* A Pentecostal congregation founded in the United States in 1914.

as•sem•bly•wom•an (ə-sĕm′blē-wo͝om′ən) *n.* A woman who is a member of a legislative assembly.

as•sent (ə-sĕnt′) *intr.v.* **-sent•ed, -sent•ing, -sents** To agree, as to a proposal; concur. ❖ *n.* **1.** Agreement; concurrence: *reached assent on a course of action.* **2.** Acquiescence; consent: *gave my assent to the plan.* [ME *assenten* < OFr. *assentir* < Lat. *assentārī* : *ad-,* ad- + *sentīre,* to feel.] —**as•sent′er, as•sen′tor** *n.* —**as•sent′ing•ly** *adv.* —**as•sen′tive** *adj.*

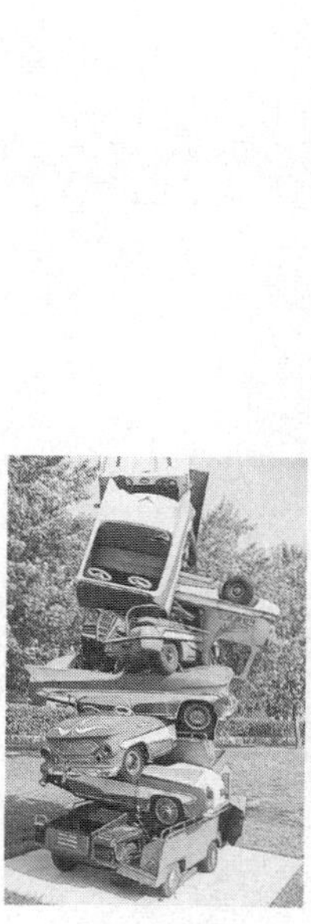

assemblage
Merry Go Straight, Montreal, Canada; 1990 fiberglass sculpture by Arman (b. 1928)

ă	pat	oi	boy
ā	pay	ou	out
âr	care	o͝o	took
ä	father	o͞o	boot
ĕ	pet	ŭ	cut
ē	be	ûr	urge
ĭ	pit	th	thin
ī	pie	*th*	this
îr	pier	hw	which
ŏ	pot	zh	vision
ō	toe	ə	about,
ô	paw		item

Stress marks:
′ (primary);
′ (secondary), as in
lexicon (lĕk′sĭ-kŏn′)

SYNONYMS *assent, agree, accede, acquiesce, consent, concur, subscribe* These verbs denote acceptance of and often belief in another's views, proposals, or actions. *Assent* implies agreement, especially as a result of deliberation: *assented to our suggestion. Agree* and *accede* are related in the sense that assent has been reached after discussion or persuasion, but *accede* implies that one person or group has yielded to the other: *"It was not possible to agree to a proposal so extraordinary and unexpected"* (William Robertson). *"In an evil hour this proposal was acceded to"* (Mary E. Herbert). *Acquiesce* suggests passive assent because of inability or unwillingness to oppose: *I acquiesced in their decision despite my misgivings. Consent* implies voluntary agreement: *My parents consented to my marriage. Concur* suggests that one has reached the same conclusion as another independently: *"I concurred with our incumbent in getting up a petition against the Reform Bill"* (George Eliot). *Subscribe* indicates hearty approval: *"I am contented to subscribe to the opinion of the best-qualified judge of our time"* (Sir Walter Scott).

as·sen·ta·tion (ăs′ĕn-tā′shən) *n.* Hasty, typically servile agreement with another's opinions.

as·sert (ə-sûrt′) *tr.v.* **-sert·ed, -sert·ing, -serts 1.** To state or express positively; affirm. **2.** To defend or maintain (one's rights, for example). **—idiom: assert oneself** To act boldly or forcefully, esp. in defending one's rights or stating an opinion. [Lat. *asserere, assert-* : *ad-,* ad- + *serere,* to join.] **—as·sert′a·ble, as·sert′i·ble** *adj.* **—as·sert′er, as·ser′tor** *n.*

as·sert·ed (ə-sûr′tĭd) *adj.* Confidently stated to be so but without proof; alleged. **—as·sert′ed·ly** *adv.*

as·ser·tion (ə-sûr′shən) *n.* **1.** The act of asserting. **2.** Something declared or stated positively, often with no support or attempt at proof. **—as·ser′tion·al** *adj.*

as·ser·tive (ə-sûr′tĭv) *adj.* Inclined to bold or confident assertion; aggressively self-assured. **—as·ser′tive·ly** *adv.* **—as·ser′tive·ness** *n.*

as·ses[1] (ăs′ēz′, ăs′īz) *n.* Plural of **as**[2].

ass·es[2] (ăs′ĭz) *n.* Plural of **ass**[1].

ass·es[3] (ăs′ĭz) *n. Vulgar Slang* Plural of **ass**[2].

as·sess (ə-sĕs′) *tr.v.* **-sessed, -sess·ing, -sess·es 1.** To estimate the value of (property) for taxation. **2.** To set or determine the amount of (a payment). **3.** To charge with a special payment. **4.** To determine the value, significance, or extent of; appraise. See Syns at **estimate**. **5.** *Sports* To charge (a foul or penalty) against a player, coach, or team. [ME *assessen* < OFr. *assesser* < Lat. *assidēre, assess-,* to sit by as an assistant judge : *ad-,* ad- + *sedēre,* to sit; see **sed-** in App.] **—as·sess′a·ble** *adj.*

as·sess·ment (ə-sĕs′mənt) *n.* **1.** The act of assessing; appraisal. **2.** An amount assessed, as for taxation.

as·ses·sor (ə-sĕs′ər) *n.* **1.** An official who evaluates property for taxation. **2.** An assistant to a judge or magistrate, usu. selected for special knowledge in a particular area. **—as′ses·so′ri·al** (ăs′ə-sôr′ē-əl, -sōr′-) *adj.*

as·set (ăs′ĕt′) *n.* **1.** A useful or valuable quality, person, or thing; an advantage or a resource. **2.** A valuable item that is owned. **3. assets a.** *Accounting* The entries on a balance sheet showing all properties and claims against others that may be applied to cover the liabilities of a person or business, such as cash, stock, and goodwill. **b.** The entire property owned by a person, esp. a bankrupt, that can be used to settle debts. [Back-formation < E. *assets,* sufficient goods to settle a testator's debts and legacies < AN *asetz* < *asez,* enough < VLat. **ad satis,* to sufficiency : Lat. *ad,* to + Lat. *satis,* enough.]

as·sev·er·ate (ə-sĕv′ə-rāt′) *tr.v.* **-at·ed, -at·ing, -ates** To declare seriously or positively; affirm. [Lat. *asseverāre, asseverāt-* : *ad-,* ad- + *sevērus,* serious.] **—as·sev′er·a′tion** *n.* **—as·sev′er·a′tive** (-ə-rā′tĭv, -ər-ə-tĭv) *adj.*

ass·hole (ăs′hōl′) *n. Vulgar Slang* **1.** The anus. **2.** A thoroughly contemptible, detestable person. [**ASS**[2] + **HOLE**.]

as·sib·i·late (ə-sĭb′ə-lāt′) *tr.v.* **-lat·ed, -lat·ing, -lates** To pronounce with a hissing sound; make sibilant. [**AD-** + **SIBILATE**.] **—as·sib′i·la′tion** *n.*

as·si·du·i·ty (ăs′ĭ-dōō′ĭ-tē, -dyōō′-) *n., pl.* **-ties 1.** Persistent diligence; unflagging effort. **2.** Constant personal attention and often obsequious solicitude. Often used in the plural.

as·sid·u·ous (ə-sĭj′ōō-əs) *adj.* **1.** Constant in application or attention; diligent. **2.** Unceasing; persistent. [< Lat. *assiduus* < *assidēre,* to attend to : *ad-,* ad- + *sedēre,* to sit; see **sed-** in App.] **—as·sid′u·ous·ly** *adv.* **—as·sid′u·ous·ness** *n.*

as·sign (ə-sīn′) *tr.v.* **-signed, -sign·ing, -signs 1.** To set apart for a purpose; designate. **2.** To select for a duty or office; appoint. **3.** To give out as a task; allot. **4.** To ascribe; attribute. **5.** *Law* To transfer (property, rights, or interests) from one to another. **6.** To place (a person or a military unit) under a specific command. **❖** *n. Law* An assignee. [ME *assignen* < OFr. *assigner* < Lat. *assignāre* : *ad-,* ad- + *signāre,* to mark (< *signum,* sign; see **sek**ʷ-¹ in App.).] **—as·sign′a·bil′i·ty** *n.* **—as·sign′a·ble** *adj.* **—as·sign′a·bly** *adv.* **—as·sign′er** *n.*

as·sig·na·tion (ăs′ĭg-nā′shən) *n.* **1.** The act of assigning. **2.** Something assigned, esp. an allotment. **3.** An appointment for a meeting between lovers; a tryst. See Syns at **engagement**. **—as′sig·na′tion·al** *adj.*

as·signed risk (ə-sīnd′) *n.* A poor risk that an insurance company is compelled to cover under state laws.

as·sign·ee (ə-sī′nē′, ăs′ī-nē′) *n.* **1.** A party to which a transfer of property, rights, or interest is made. **2.** One appointed to act for another; a deputy or agent.

as·sign·ment (ə-sīn′mənt) *n.* **1.** The act of assigning. **2.** Something, such as a task, that is assigned. See Syns at **task**. **3.** A position to which one is assigned. **4.** *Law* **a.** The transfer of a claim, right, interest, or property from one to another. **b.** The instrument by which this transfer is effected.

as·sign·or (ə-sī′nôr′, ə-sī′nər, ăs′ə-nôr′) *n. Law* One that makes an assignment.

as·sim·i·la·ble (ə-sĭm′ə-lə-bəl) *adj.* That can be assimilated. **—as·sim′i·la·bil′i·ty** *n.*

as·sim·i·late (ə-sĭm′ə-lāt′) *v.* **-lat·ed, -lat·ing, -lates** *—tr.* **1.** *Physiology* **a.** To consume and incorporate (nutrients) into the body after digestion. **b.** To transform (food) into living tissue by the process of anabolism; metabolize constructively. **2.** To incorporate and absorb into the mind. **3.** To make similar; cause to resemble. **4.** *Linguistics* To alter (a sound) by assimilation. **5.** To absorb (a minority) into the prevailing culture. *—intr.* To become assimilated. [ME *assimilaten* < Lat. *assimilāre, assimilāt-,* to make similar to : *ad-,* ad- + *similis,* like; see **sem-**¹ in App.] **—as·sim′i·la′tor** *n.*

as·sim·i·la·tion (ə-sĭm′ə-lā′shən) *n.* **1a.** The act or process of assimilating. **b.** The state of being assimilated. **2.** *Physiology* The conversion of nutriments into living tissue; constructive metabolism. **3.** *Linguistics* The process by which a sound becomes similar or identical to an adjacent or nearby sound. For example, the prefix *in-* becomes *im-* in *impossible* by assimilation to the labial *p* of *possible.* **4.** The process whereby a minority group gradually adopts the customs and attitudes of the majority.

as·sim·i·la·tion·ism (ə-sĭm′ə-lā′shə-nĭz′əm) *n.* A policy of furthering cultural or racial assimilation. **—as·sim′i·la′tion·ist** *adj. & n.*

as·sim·i·la·tive (ə-sĭm′ə-lā′tĭv) also **as·sim·i·la·to·ry** (-lə-tôr′ē, -tōr′ē) *adj.* Marked by or causing assimilation.

As·sin·i·boin also **As·sin·i·boine** (ə-sĭn′ə-boin′) *n., pl.* **Assiniboin** or **-boins** also **Assiniboine** or **-boines 1.** A member of a Native American people formerly inhabiting southern Manitoba and now located in Montana, Alberta, and Saskatchewan. **2.** The Siouan language of the Assiniboin. [Fr. *Assiniboine,* of Ojibwa orig.] **—As·sin′i·boin′** *adj.*

Assiniboine A river of S-central Canada rising in S Saskatchewan and flowing c. 949 km (590 mi) to the Red R. at Winnipeg, Manitoba.

As·si·si (ə-sē′zē, -sē, ə-sĭs′ē) A town of central Italy ESE of Perugia; home of Saint Francis of Assisi. Pop. 19,000.

as·sist (ə-sĭst′) *v.* **-sist·ed, -sist·ing, -sists** *—tr.* To help or support, esp. as a subordinate or supplement; aid. *—intr.* **1.** To give aid or support. **2.** To be present, as at a conference. **❖** *n.* **1.** An act of giving aid; help. **2.** *Sports* **a.** A fielding and throwing of a baseball that enables a teammate to put out a runner. **b.** A pass, as in basketball or ice hockey, that enables a teammate to score. **3.** A mechanical device providing aid. [ME *assisten* < OFr. *assister* < Lat. *assistere* : *ad-,* ad- + *sistere,* to stand; see **stā-** in App.] **—as·sist′er** *n.*

as·sis·tance (ə-sĭs′təns) *n.* **1.** The act of assisting. **2.** Aid; help: *financial assistance.*

as·sis·tant (ə-sĭs′tənt) *n.* One that assists; a helper. **❖** *adj.* **1.** Holding an auxiliary position; subordinate. **2.** Giving aid; auxiliary.

assistant professor *n.* A college or university teacher who ranks above an instructor and below an associate professor.

as·sis·tant·ship (ə-sĭs′tənt-shĭp′) *n.* An academic position that carries a stipend and usu. involves part-time teaching or research, given to a qualified graduate student.

as·sist·ed living (ə-sĭs′tĭd) *n.* A living arrangement in which people with special needs reside in a facility that provides help with everyday tasks.

assisted reproduction *n.* The use of medical techniques, such as drug therapy or in vitro fertilization, to enhance fertility.

assisted suicide *n.* Suicide accomplished with the aid of another person, esp. a physician.

as·size (ə-sīz′) *n.* **1a.** A session of a court. **b.** A decree or edict rendered at such a session. **2a.** An ordinance regulating weights and measures and the weights and prices of articles of consumption. **b.** The standards so established. **3.** *Law* A judicial inquest, the writ by which it is instituted, or the verdict of the jurors. **4. assizes a.** One of the periodic county court sessions formerly held in England and Wales. **b.** The time or place of such sessions. [ME *assise* < OFr. < p. part. of *asseoir,* to seat < Lat. *assidēre,* to sit beside : *ad-,* ad- + *sedēre,* to sit; see **ASSIDUOUS**.]

assn. *abbr.* association

assoc. *abbr.* **1.** associate **2.** association

as·so·ci·a·ble (ə-sō′shē-ə-bəl, -shə-bəl) *adj.* That can be associated: *words associable with politics.* **—as·so′ci·a·bil′i·ty** *n.*

as·so·ci·ate (ə-sō′shē-āt′, -sē-) *v.* **-at·ed, -at·ing, -ates** *—tr.* **1.** To join as a partner, ally, or friend. **2.** To connect or join together; combine. **3.** To connect in the mind or imagination. *—intr.* **1.** To join in or form a league, union, or association. **2.** To keep company. ❖ *n.* (-ĭt, -āt′) **1.** A person united with another or others in an act or business; a partner or colleague. **2.** A companion; a comrade. **3.** An attendant circumstance. **4.** A member of an institution or society with only partial status or privileges. **5.** often **Associate** An associate's degree. ❖ *adj.* (-ĭt, -āt′) **1.** Joined with another or others and having equal or nearly equal status: *an associate editor.* **2.** Having partial status or privileges: *an associate member of the club.* **3.** Following or accompanying; concomitant. [ME *associaten* < Lat. *associāre, associāt-* : *ad-,* ad- + *socius,* companion; see **sekʷ-¹** in App.]

associate professor *n.* A college or university professor who ranks above an assistant professor and below a professor.

as·so·ci·ate's degree (ə-sō′shē-ĭts′, -āts′, -sē-) *n.* An academic degree conferred by a two-year college upon completing the prescribed course of study.

as·so·ci·a·tion (ə-sō′sē-ā′shən, -shē-) *n.* **1.** The act of associating or the state of being associated. **2.** An organized body of people who have an interest in common; a society. **3a.** A mental connection or relation between thoughts, feelings, ideas, or sensations. **b.** A remembered or imagined feeling, emotion, idea, or sensation linked to a person, object, or idea. **4.** *Chemistry* Any of various processes of combination depending on relatively weak chemical bonding. **5.** *Ecology* A large number of organisms in a specific geographic area constituting a community with one or two dominant species. —**as·so′ci·a′tion·al** *adj.*

association area *n.* An area of the cerebral cortex where motor and sensory functions are integrated.

association football *n. Chiefly British* Soccer.

as·so·ci·a·tion·ism (ə-sō′sē-ā′shə-nĭz′əm, ə-sō′shē-) *n.* The psychological theory that association is the basis of all mental activity. —**as·so′ci·a′tion·ist** *adj. & n.* —**as·so′ci·a′tion·is′tic** *adj.*

as·so·ci·a·tive (ə-sō′shə-tĭv, -sē-ə-tĭv, -shē-ā′tĭv, -sē-) *adj.* **1.** Of, marked by, resulting from, or causing association. **2.** *Mathematics* Independent of grouping. For example, if *a* + (*b* + *c*) = (*a* + *b*) + *c,* the operation indicated by + is associative. —**as·so′ci·a·tive·ly** *adv.*

as·soil (ə-soil′) *tr.v.* **-soiled, -soil·ing, -soils** *Archaic* **1.** To absolve; pardon. **2.** To atone for. [ME *assoilen* < OFr. *assoldre, assoil-* < Lat. *absolvere,* to set free : *ab-,* away; see **AB-¹** + *solvere,* to loosen; see **leu-** in App.]

as·so·nance (ăs′ə-nəns) *n.* **1.** Resemblance of sound, esp. of vowels in stressed syllables, as in: *"that dolphin-torn, that gong-tormented sea"* (William Butler Yeats). **2.** Rough similarity; approximate agreement. [Fr. < Lat. *assonāre,* to respond to : *ad-,* ad- + *sonāre,* to sound.] —**as′so·nant** *adj. & n.* —**as′so·nan′tal** (-năn′tl) *adj.*

as·sort (ə-sôrt′) *v.* **-sort·ed, -sort·ing, -sorts** —*tr.* **1.** To separate into groups according to kind; classify. **2.** To supply with (a variety, as of goods). —*intr.* **1.** To agree in kind; fall into the same class. **2.** To associate with others. [ME *assorte* < OFr. *assorter* : *a-,* to (< Lat. *ad-*; see **AD-**) + *sorte,* kind (< Lat. *sors, sort-,* chance, lot).] —**as·sor′ta·tive** (ə-sôr′tə-tĭv) *adj.* —**as·sort′er** *n.*

as·sort·ed (ə-sôr′tĭd) *adj.* **1.** Consisting of a number of different kinds: *assorted sizes.* See Syns at **miscellaneous. 2.** Separated according to kind or class. **3.** Suited or matched. Often used in combination: *well-assorted accessories.*

as·sort·ment (ə-sôrt′mənt) *n.* **1.** The act of assorting; separation into classes. **2.** A collection of various kinds; a variety.

ASSR *abbr.* Autonomous Soviet Socialist Republic

asst. *abbr.* assistant

as·suage (ə-swāj′) *tr.v.* **-suaged, -suag·ing, -suag·es 1.** To make (something unpleasant) less intense or severe: *assuage grief.* See Syns at **relieve. 2.** To satisfy or appease (thirst, for example). **3.** To pacify or calm: *assuage insecurity.* [ME *asswagen* < OFr. *assuagier* < VLat. **assuāviāre* : Lat. *ad-,* ad- + Lat. *suāvis,* delightful, sweet; see **swād-** in App.] —**as·suage′ment** *n.*

as·sua·sive (ə-swā′sĭv, -zĭv) *adj.* Soothing; calming. [**AD-** + **SUASIVE** (sense influenced by **ASSUAGE**).]

as·sume (ə-sōōm′) *tr.v.* **-sumed, -sum·ing, -sumes 1.** To take upon oneself: *assume responsibility.* **2.** To undertake the duties of (an office). **3.** To take on; adopt. **4.** To put on; don. **5.** To affect the appearance or possession of; feign. **6.** To take for granted; suppose: *assumed that prices would rise.* See Syns at **presume. 7.** To take over or receive without justification; seize: *assume control.* **8.** To take up or receive into heaven. [ME *assumen* < Lat. *assūmere* : *ad-,* ad- + *sūmere,* to take.] —**as·sum′a·ble** *adj.* —**as·sum′a·bly** *adv.*

as·sumed (ə-sōōmd′) *adj.* **1.** Adopted or used so as to deceive; pretended. **2.** Taken for granted; supposed. —**as·sum′ed·ly** (ə-sōō′mĭd-lē) *adv.*

as·sum·ing (ə-sōō′mĭng) *adj.* Presumptuous; arrogant. ❖ *conj.* On the assumption that; supposing: *Assuming the house is for sale, would you buy it?* —**as·sum′ing·ly** *adv.*

as·sump·sit (ə-sŭmp′sĭt) *n.* **1.** An agreement or promise made orally or in writing not under seal; a contract. **2.** A legal action to enforce or recover damages for a breach of such an agreement. [NLat. *assūmpsit* < third pers. sing. perfect t. of Lat. *assūmere,* to undertake. See **ASSUME.**]

as·sump·tion (ə-sŭmp′shən) *n.* **1.** The act of taking to or upon oneself: *assumption of an obligation.* **2.** The act of taking posses-

sion or asserting a claim. **3.** The act of taking for granted. **4.** Something taken for granted or accepted as true without proof; a supposition. **5.** Presumption; arrogance. **6.** *Logic* A minor premise. **7. Assumption a.** In Christianity, the bodily taking up of the Virgin Mary into heaven after her death. **b.** A feast celebrating this event, observed on August 15. [ME *assumpcion* < Lat. *assūmptiō, assūmptiōn-,* adoption < *assūmptus,* p. part. of *assūmere,* to adopt. See **ASSUME.**]

as·sump·tive (ə-sŭmp′tĭv) *adj.* **1.** Characterized by assumption. **2.** Taken for granted; assumed. **3.** Presumptuous; assuming. —**as·sump′tive·ly** *adv.*

As·sur (ä′sŏŏr′, ä′shŏŏr′) *n.* Variant of **Ashur.**

as·sur·ance (ə-shŏŏr′əns) *n.* **1.** The act of assuring. **2.** A statement or indication that inspires confidence; a guarantee or pledge. **3.** Freedom from doubt; certainty. See Syns at **certainty. 4.** Self-confidence. **5.** Excessive self-confidence; presumption. **6.** *Chiefly British* Insurance, esp. life insurance.

As·sur·ba·ni·pal (ä′sŏŏr-bä′nə-päl′) See **Ashurbanipal.**

as·sure (ə-shŏŏr′) *tr.v.* **-sured, -sur·ing, -sures 1.** To state positively, as to remove doubt. **2.** To cause to feel sure. **3.** To give confidence to; reassure. **4.** To make certain; ensure. **5.** To make safe or secure. **6.** *Chiefly British* To insure, as against loss. [ME *assuren* < OFr. *assurer* < VLat. **assēcūrāre,* to make sure : Lat. *ad-,* ad- + Lat. *sēcūrus,* secure; see **SECURE.**] —**as·sur′a·ble** *adj.* —**as·sur′er** *n.*

as·sured (ə-shŏŏrd′) *adj.* **1.** Made certain; guaranteed. **2.** Exhibiting confidence or authority. **3.** *Chiefly British* Insured. ❖ *n., pl.* **assured** or **sureds** See **insured.** —**as·sur′ed·ly** (-ĭd-lē) *adv.* —**as·sur′ed·ness** *n.*

as·sur·gent (ə-sûr′jənt) *adj.* **1.** Rising or tending to rise. **2.** *Botany* Slanting or curving upward; ascending. [Lat. *assurgēns, assurgent-,* pr. part. of *assurgere,* to rise up to : *ad-,* ad- + *surgere,* to rise; see **SURGE.**] —**as·sur′gen·cy** *n.*

As·syr·i·a (ə-sîr′ē-ə) An ancient empire and civilization of W Asia in the upper valley of the Tigris R.; reached the height of its power between the 9th and 7th cent. B.C.

As·syr·i·an (ə-sîr′ē-ən) *adj.* Of or relating to Assyria or its people, language, or culture. ❖ *n.* **1.** A native or inhabitant of Assyria. **2.** See **Akkadian** 2. **3.** The Assyrian dialects of Akkadian.

As·syr·i·ol·o·gy (ə-sîr′ē-ŏl′ə-jē) *n.* The study of the civilization and language of Assyria. —**As·syr′i·ol′o·gist** *n.*

AST *abbr.* **1.** Alaska Standard Time **2.** Atlantic Standard Time

-ast *suff.* One associated with: *ecdysiast.* [< Lat. *-astēs* < Gk., n. suff.]

A·staire (ə-stâr′), **Fred** 1899–1987. Amer. dancer and actor whose films include *Top Hat* (1935).

A·sta·na (ə-stä′nə) The cap. of Kazakhstan, in the N-central part; shifted from Almaty in 1997. Pop. 287,000.

As·tar·te (ə-stär′tē) *n. Mythology* An ancient Semitic goddess of love and war, being the Phoenician, Syrian, and Canaanite counterpart to Ishtar. [Gk. *Astartē* < Phoenician **aštart.*]

a·sta·sia (ə-stā′zhə) *n.* Inability to stand because of motor incoordination. [Gk., unsteadiness < *astatos,* unsteady : *a-,* not; see **A-¹** + *statos,* standing; see **stā-** in App.]

a·stat·ic (ā-stăt′ĭk) *adj.* **1.** Unsteady; unstable. **2.** *Physics* Having no particular directional characteristics. —**a·stat′i·cal·ly** *adv.* —**a·stat′i·cism** *n.*

as·ta·tine (ăs′tə-tēn′, -tĭn) *n. Symbol* **At** A radioactive halogen element. Its longest-lived isotope has a mass number of 210 and a half-life of 8.3 hours. Atomic number 85; melting point 302ºC; boiling point 337ºC; valence probably 1, 3, 5, 7. See table at **element.** [Gk. *astatos,* unstable; see **ASTASIA** + **-INE².**]

as·ter (ăs′tər) *n.* **1.** Any of various plants of the genus *Aster* in the composite family, having radiate flower heads and a usu. yellow disk. **2.** The China aster. **3.** *Biology* A star-shaped structure formed in the cytoplasm of a cell and having raylike fibers that surround the centrosome during mitosis. [Lat. *astēr,* a plant < Gk., star, type of daisy. See **ster-** in App.]

as·te·ri·at·ed (ă-stîr′ē-ā′tĭd) *adj. Mineralogy* Exhibiting asterism. [< Gk. *asterios,* starry < *astēr,* star. See **ster-** in App.]

as·ter·isk (ăs′tə-rĭsk′) *n.* A star-shaped figure (*) used chiefly to indicate an omission, a reference to a footnote, or an unattested word, sound, or affix. ❖ *tr.v.* **-isked, -isk·ing, -isks** To mark with an asterisk. [ME < LLat. *asteriscus* < Gk. *asteriskos,* dim. of *astēr,* star. See **ster-** in App.]

as·ter·ism (ăs′tə-rĭz′əm) *n.* **1.** *Printing* Three asterisks in a triangular formation used to call attention to a following passage. **2.** *Astronomy* A cluster of stars smaller than a constellation. **3.** *Mineralogy* A six-rayed figure produced in some crystal structures by reflected or transmitted light. [Gk. *asterismos,* constellation < *astēr,* star. See **ster-** in App.] —**as′ter·is′mal** *adj.*

a·stern (ə-stûrn′) *adv. & adj. Nautical* **1.** Behind a vessel. **2.** At or to the stern of a vessel. **3.** With or having the stern foremost; backward.

aster
New England aster
Aster novae-angliae

ă pat	oi boy
ā pay	ou out
âr care	ŏŏ took
ä father	ōō boot
ĕ pet	ŭ cut
ē be	ûr urge
ĭ pit	th thin
ī pie	th this
îr pier	hw which
ŏ pot	zh vision
ō toe	ə about,
ô paw	item

Stress marks:
′ (primary);
′ (secondary), as in
lexicon (lĕk′sĭ-kŏn′)

a·ster·nal (ā-stûr′nəl) *adj.* **1.** Not connected to the sternum. **2.** Lacking a sternum.

as·ter·oid (ăs′tə-roid′) *n.* **1.** *Astronomy* Any of numerous small celestial bodies that revolve around the sun, with characteristic diameters between a few and several hundred kilometers. **2.** *Zoology* See **starfish.** ❖ *adj.* also **as·ter·oi·dal** (ăs′tə-roid′l) Star-shaped. [< Gk. *asteroeidēs,* starlike : *astēr,* star; see **ster-** in App. + *-oeidēs,* -oid.]

asteroid belt *n.* The region of the solar system between the orbits of Mars and Jupiter, where most of the asteroids are found.

as·the·ni·a (ăs-thē′nē-ə) *n.* Loss or lack of bodily strength; weakness; debility. [NLat. < Gk. *astheneia < asthenēs,* weak : *a-,* without; see A–¹ + *sthenos,* strength.]

as·then·ic (ăs-thĕn′ĭk) *adj.* **1.** Relating to or exhibiting asthenia; weak. **2.** Having a slender, lightly muscled physique. ❖ *n.* A person having such a physique.

as·the·no·pi·a (ăs′thə-nō′pē-ə) *n.* Weakness or fatigue of the eyes, usu. accompanied by headache and dimming of vision. [ASTHEN(IA) + –OPIA.] —**as′the·nop′ic** (-nŏp′ĭk) *adj.*

as·then·o·sphere (ăs-thĕn′ə-sfîr′) *n.* A zone of the earth's mantle that lies beneath the lithosphere and consists of several hundred kilometers of deformable rock. [Gk. *asthenēs,* weak; see ASTHENIA + SPHERE.]

asth·ma (ăz′mə, ăs′-) *n.* A chronic respiratory disease, often arising from allergies, marked by sudden recurring attacks of labored breathing, chest constriction, and coughing. [ME *asma* < Med.Lat. < Gk. *asthma.*] —**asth·mat′ic** (-măt′ĭk) *adj.* & *n.* —**asth·mat′i·cal·ly** *adv.*

as though *conj.* As if: *looked as though they were mad.*

As·ti (ä′stē) A city in NW Italy SE of Turin; noted for its sparkling wines. Pop. 76,950.

a·stig·ma·tism (ə-stĭg′mə-tĭz′əm) *n.* A visual defect in which the unequal curvature of one or more refractive surfaces of the eye, usu. the cornea, prevents light rays from focusing at one point on the retina, resulting in blurred vision. [A–¹ + Gk. *stigma, stigmat-,* point (< *stizein, stig-,* to tattoo).] —**as′tig·mat′ic** (ăs′tĭg-măt′ĭk) *adj.* & *n.* —**as′tig·mat′i·cal·ly** *adv.*

a·stir (ə-stûr′) *adj.* **1.** Moving about; being in motion. **2.** Having gotten out of bed.

ASTM *abbr.* American Society for Testing and Materials

as to *prep.* **1.** With regard to: *We are puzzled as to how it happened.* **2.** According to: *chosen as to ability.*

a·stom·a·tous (ā-stŏm′ə-təs, ā-stō′mə-) also **as·tom·ous** (ăs′tə-məs) or **a·stom·a·tal** (ā-stŏm′ə-tl, ā-stō′mə-) *adj.* Having no mouth or oral opening.

a·ston·ish (ə-stŏn′ĭsh) *tr.v.* **-ished, -ish·ing, -ish·es** To fill with sudden wonder or amazement: *results that astonished the researchers.* See Syns at **surprise.** [Prob. alteration of ME *astonen* < OFr. *estoner* < VLat. **extonāre* : Lat. *ex-,* ex- + Lat. *tonāre,* to thunder; see **(s)tenə-** in App.] —**a·ston′ish·ing·ly** *adv.*

a·ston·ish·ment (ə-stŏn′ĭsh-mənt) *n.* **1.** Great surprise or amazement. **2.** A cause of amazement; a marvel.

As·tor (ăs′tər), **Nancy Witcher Langhorne.** Viscountess Astor. 1879–1964. Amer.-born British politician who was the first woman elected to the House of Commons (1919–45).

As·to·ri·a (ă-stôr′ē-ə, -stōr′-) A city of NW OR; founded as a fur-trading post in 1811, the first permanent American settlement along the Pacific coast. Pop. 9,813.

a·stound (ə-stound′) *tr.v.* **a·stound·ed, a·stound·ing, a·stounds** To astonish and bewilder. See Syns at **surprise.** [< ME *astoned,* p. part. of *astonen, astonien,* to amaze. See ASTONISH.] —**a·stound′ing·ly** *adv.*

a·strad·dle (ə-străd′l) *adv.* **1.** In a straddling position; astride. **2.** Across or over both sides. ❖ *prep.* So as to straddle or bridge; astride.

astragal

as·tra·gal (ăs′trə-gəl) *n.* A narrow convex molding often having the form of beading. [Lat. *astragalus* < Gk. *astragalos.* See **ost-** in App.]

as·trag·a·lus (ə-străg′ə-ləs) *n., pl.* **-li** (-lī′) See **talus¹** 1. [NLat. < Gk. *astragalos,* vertebra. See **ost-** in App.] —**as·trag′a·lar** *adj.*

as·tra·khan also **as·tra·chan** (ăs′trə-kăn′, -kən) *n.* **1.** The curly, wavy wool of young lambs from Astrakhan. **2.** A fabric with a curly looped pile, made to resemble this wool.

As·tra·khan (ăs′trə-kăn′, ä-strä-кнän′) A city of SW Russia on the Volga R. delta. Pop. 507,710.

as·tral (ăs′trəl) *adj.* **1.** Of, relating to, or resembling the stars. **2.** *Biology* Of, relating to, or shaped like the mitotic aster; star-shaped. **3.** Of or relating to a supersensible body believed by theosophists to coexist with and survive the death of the human physical body: *astral projection.* [LLat. *astrālis* < Lat. *astrum,* star < Gk. *astron.* See **ster-** in App.] —**as′tral·ly** *adv.*

a·stray (ə-strā′) *adv.* **1.** Away from the correct path or direction. See Syns at **amiss.** **2.** Away from the right or good, as in thought or behavior. [ME < OFr. *estraie,* p. part. of *estraier,* to stray. See STRAY.] —**a·stray′** *adj.*

a·stride (ə-strīd′) *adv.* **1.** With a leg on each side: *riding astride.* **2.** With the legs wide apart. ❖ *prep.* **1.** On or over and with a leg on each side of. **2.** Situated on both sides of. **3.** Lying across or over; spanning.

as·trin·gent (ə-strĭn′jənt) *adj.* **1.** Tending to draw together or constrict body tissues; styptic. **2.** Sharp and penetrating; pungent

astrobleme
Meteor Crater, near
Winslow, Arizona

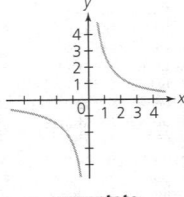

astrolabe

(chart)

or severe: *astringent remarks.* ❖ *n.* A substance that draws together body tissues and stops the flow of blood or other secretions. [Lat. *astringēns, astringent-,* pr. part. of *astringere,* to bind fast : *ad-,* ad- + *stringere,* to bind.] —**as·trin′gen·cy** —**as·trin′gent·ly** *adv.*

astro– or **astr–** *pref.* **1a.** Star: *astrophysics.* **b.** Celestial body: *astrometry.* **c.** Outer space: *astronaut.* **2.** The aster of a cell: *astrosphere.* [Gk. < *astron,* star. See **ster-** in App.]

as·tro·bi·ol·o·gy (ăs′trō-bī-ŏl′ə-jē) *n.* See **exobiology.** —**as′tro·bi′o·log′i·cal** (-ə-lŏj′ĭ-kəl) *adj.*

as·tro·bleme (ăs′trə-blēm′, -blēm′) *n.* A scar on the earth's surface left from the impact of a meteorite. [ASTRO– + Gk. *blēma,* missile, wound (< *ballein,* to throw; see **gʷelə-** in App.).]

as·tro·chem·is·try (ăs′trō-kĕm′ĭ-strē) *n.* The chemistry of stars and interstellar space. —**as′tro·chem′ist** *n.*

as·tro·cyte (ăs′trə-sīt′) *n.* A star-shaped cell, esp. a neuroglial cell of nervous tissue. —**as′tro·cyt′ic** (-sĭt′ĭk) *adj.*

as·tro·dome (ăs′trə-dōm′) *n.* A transparent dome on the top of an aircraft, through which celestial observations are made.

as·tro·ge·ol·o·gy (ăs′trō-jē-ŏl′ə-jē) *n.* The geology of celestial bodies. —**as′tro·ge·ol′o·gist** *n.*

as·tro·labe (ăs′trə-lāb′) *n.* A medieval instrument used to determine the altitude of the sun or other celestial bodies. [ME *astrelabie* < OFr. *astrelabe* < Med.Lat. *astrolabium* < Gk. *astrolabon,* planisphere : *astro-, astro-* + *lambanein, lab-,* to take.]

as·trol·o·gy (ə-strŏl′ə-jē) *n.* **1.** The study of the positions and aspects of celestial bodies in the belief that they have an influence on the course of natural earthly occurrences and human affairs. **2.** *Obsolete* Astronomy. [ME *astrologie* < OFr. < Lat. *astrologia* < Gk. *astrologiā* : *astro-, astro-* + *-logiā,* -logy.] —**as·trol′o·ger** *n.* —**as′tro·log′i·cal** (ăs′trə-lŏj′ĭ-kəl), **as′tro·log′ic** *adj.* —**as′tro·log′i·cal·ly** *adv.*

as·trom·e·try (ə-strŏm′ĭ-trē) *n.* The scientific measurement of the positions and motions of celestial bodies. —**as′tro·met′ric** (ăs′trō-mĕt′rĭk), **as′tro·met′ri·cal** *adj.*

as·tro·naut (ăs′trə-nôt′) *n.* A person trained to pilot, navigate, or otherwise participate as a crew member of a spacecraft. [ASTRO– + Gk. *nautēs,* sailor (< *naus,* ship).]

as·tro·nau·tics (ăs′trə-nô′tĭks) *n.* (*used with a sing. or pl. verb*) The science and technology of space flight. —**as′tro·nau′tic, as′tro·nau′ti·cal** *adj.* —**as′tro·nau′ti·cal·ly** *adv.*

as·tro·nav·i·ga·tion (ăs′trō-năv′ĭ-gā′shən) *n.* See **celestial navigation.** —**as′tro·nav′i·ga′tor** *n.*

as·tron·o·mer (ə-strŏn′ə-mər) *n.* One who specializes in astronomy.

as·tro·nom·i·cal (ăs′trə-nŏm′ĭ-kəl) also **as·tro·nom·ic** (-nŏm′ĭk) *adj.* **1.** Of or relating to astronomy. **2.** Of enormous magnitude; immense. —**as′tro·nom′i·cal·ly** *adv.*

astronomical unit *n.* A unit of length equal to the mean distance from Earth to the sun, approx. 150 million kilometers (93 million miles).

as·tron·o·my (ə-strŏn′ə-mē) *n.* The scientific study of matter in outer space, such as the positions, dimensions, energy, and evolution of stars and planets. [ME *astronomie* < OFr. < Lat. *astronomia* < Gk. *astronomiā* : *astro-, astron-* + *-nomia,* -nomy.]

as·tro·pho·tog·ra·phy (ăs′trō-fə-tŏg′rə-fē) *n.* Astronomical photography. —**as′tro·pho·tog′ra·pher** *n.* —**as′tro·pho′to·graph′ic** (-fō′tə-grăf′ĭk) *adj.*

as·tro·phys·ics (ăs′trō-fĭz′ĭks) *n.* (*used with a sing. verb*) The branch of astronomy that deals with the physics of stellar phenomena. —**as′tro·phys′i·cal** *adj.* —**as′tro·phys′i·cist** (-fĭz′ĭ-sĭst) *n.*

as·tro·sphere (ăs′trō-sfîr′) *n.* **1.** The central portion of a cell aster exclusive of the rays. **2.** The entire cell aster with the exception of the centrosome.

As·tro·Turf (ăs′trō-tûrf′) A trademark used for an artificial grasslike ground covering.

As·tu·ri·as (ă-stoŏr′ē-əs, -tyoŏr′-, äs-toō′ryäs) A region and former kingdom of NW Spain; conquered by Rome in the 2nd cent. B.C. —**As·tu′ri·an** *adj.* & *n.*

Asturias, Miguel Ángel 1899–1974. Guatemalan writer who won the 1966 Nobel Prize for literature.

as·tute (ə-stoōt′, ə-styoōt′) *adj.* Having or showing shrewdness and discernment, esp. with respect to one's own concerns. [Lat. *astūtus < astus,* craft. See **wes-¹** in App.] —**as·tute′ly** *adv.* —**as·tute′ness** *n.*

As·ty·a·nax (ă-stī′ə-năks′) *n.* *Greek Mythology* The son of Hector and Andromache, killed when the Greeks conquered Troy.

a·sty·lar (ā-stī′lər) *adj.* Not having columns or pilasters. [A–¹ + Gk. *stūlos,* pillar; see **stā-** in App. + –AR.]

A·sun·ción (ä-soōn′syōn′) The cap. of Paraguay, in the S part on the Paraguay R. Pop. 546,637.

a·sun·der (ə-sŭn′dər) *adv.* **1.** Into separate parts. **2.** Apart from each other. [ME < OE *on sundran* : *on,* on + *sundran,* separately (< *sunder*).] —**a·sun′der** *adj.*

ASV *abbr.* American Standard Version

As·wan (ăs′wän, äs-wän′, äs-) A city of S Egypt at the First Cataract of the Nile R. near the **Aswan High Dam** (dedicated 1971). Pop. 220,000.

a·swarm (ə-swôrm′) *adj.* Filled or overrun, as with moving objects or beings; teeming.

as well as *conj.* And in addition: *courageous as well as strong.* ❖ *prep.* In addition to: *Bob as well as Jim works here.*

a•swirl (ə-swûrl′) *adj.* Moving with a swirling motion.

a•swoon (ə-swo͞on′) *adv. & adj.* In a faint or swoon. [ME *aswowne*, ult. < OE *geswōgen*, fainted, p. part. of **swōgan*, to lose consciousness.]

a•sy•lum (ə-sī′ləm) *n.* **1.** An institution for the care of people who require organized supervision or assistance. **2.** A place offering protection and safety; a shelter. **3.** A place formerly constituting an inviolable refuge for criminals or debtors. **4.** The protection afforded by a sanctuary. **5.** Protection and immunity from extradition granted by a government to a political refugee from another country. [ME *asilum*, refuge < Lat. *asȳlum* < Gk. *asūlon*, sanctuary < neut. of *asūlos*, inviolable : *a-*, without; see A–¹ + *sūlon*, right of seizure.]

a•sym•met•ric (ā′sĭ-mĕt′rĭk) also **a•sym•met•ri•cal** (-rĭ-kəl) *adj.* **1.** Having no balance or symmetry. **2.** *Chemistry* Of or relating to a carbon atom bonded to four different atoms or groups, resulting in a molecule that cannot be superimposed on its mirror image; chiral. **—a′sym•met′ri•cal•ly** *adv.*

a•sym•me•try (ā-sĭm′ĭ-trē) *n.* Lack of balance or symmetry.

a•symp•to•mat•ic (ā′sĭmp-tə-măt′ĭk) *adj.* Causing or showing no disease symptoms. **—a′symp•to•mat′i•cal•ly** *adv.*

as•ymp•tote (ăs′ĭm-tōt′, -ĭmp-) *n.* A line whose distance to a given curve tends to zero. An asymptote may or may not intersect its associated curve. [Ult. < Gk. *asumptōtos*, not intersecting : *a-*, not; see A–¹ + *sumptōtos*, intersecting (< *sumpiptein*, to converge : *sun-*, syn- + *piptein*, *ptō-*, to fall; see **pet-** in App.).] **—as′ymp•tot′ic** (-tŏt′ĭk), **as′ymp•tot′i•cal** *adj.* **—as′ymp•tot′i•cal•ly** *adv.*

a•syn•ap•sis (ā′sĭ-năp′sĭs) *n., pl.* **-ses** (-sēz) The failure of homologous chromosomes to pair during meiosis.

a•syn•chro•nism (ā-sĭng′krə-nĭz′əm) or **a•syn•chron•y** (-krə-nē) *n.* Lack of concurrence; absence of synchronism. **—a•syn′chro•nous** (-nəs) *adj.* **—a•syn′chro•nous•ly** *adv.*

a•syn•de•ton (ə-sĭn′dĭ-tŏn′) *n.* The omission of conjunctions from constructions in which they would normally be used, as in *"Are all thy conquests, glories, triumphs, spoils,/Shrunk to this little measure?"* (Shakespeare). [LLat. < Gk. *asundeton* < neut. of *asundetos*, without conjunctions : *a-*, not; see A–¹ + *sundetos*, bound together (< *sundein*, to bind together : *sun-*, syn- + *dein*, to bind).] **—as′yn•det′ic** (ăs′ĭn-dĕt′ĭk) *adj.* **—as′yn•det′i•cal•ly** *adv.*

a•syn•tac•tic (ā′sĭn-tăk′tĭk) *adj.* Not conforming to accepted patterns of syntax.

As•yut (ä-syo͞ot′) A city of E-central Egypt on the Nile R. Pop. 321,000.

at (ăt; ət *when unstressed*) *prep.* **1a.** In or near the area occupied by; in or near the location of: *at the market.* **b.** In or near the position of: *at the center of the page.* **2.** To or toward the direction of, esp. for a specific purpose: *Questions came at us from all sides.* **3.** Present during; attending: *at the dance.* **4.** Within the interval or span of: *at a glance.* **5.** In the state of: *at peace.* **6.** In the activity or field of: *good at math.* **7.** To or using the rate, extent, or amount of; to the point of: *at 350°F.* **8.** On, near, or by the time or age of: *at three o'clock.* **9.** On account of; because of: *rejoice at a victory.* **10.** By way of; through: *exited at the rear gate.* **11.** In accord with; following: *at my request.* **12.** Dependent upon: *at the mercy of the court.* **13.** Occupied with: *at work.* **—*idiom:* at it** *Informal* Engaged in verbal or physical conflict: *The neighbors are at it again.* [ME < OE *æt.*]

At¹ The symbol for the element **astatine.**

At² *abbr.* ampere-turn

AT *abbr.* **1.** air temperature **2.** also a/t antitank **3.** automatic transmission

at– *pref.* Variant of **ad–** 1.

At•a•ca•ma Desert (ăt′ə-kăm′ə, ä′tä-kä′mä) An arid region of NW Chile, one of the driest areas in the world.

A•ta•hual•pa (ä′tə-wäl′pə) also **A•ta•ba•li•pa** (-bä′lĭ-pä′) 1502?–33. Last independent Incan emperor of Peru (1532–33).

At•a•lan•ta (ăt′ə-lăn′tə) *n. Greek Mythology* A hunter who, having agreed to marry any man who could defeat her in a footrace, was outrun by Hippomenes, who dropped three golden apples, which she paused to pick up.

at•a•man (ăt′ə-măn′) *n., pl.* **-mans** A Cossack chief. [Russ. < South Turkic, leader of an armed band : *ata*, father + *-man*, augmentative suff.]

at•a•mas•co lily (ăt′ə-măs′kō) *n.* A bulbous plant *(Zephyranthes atamasco)* of the southeast United States, having a solitary flower on a long stalk. [Virginia Algonquian *attamusco.*]

At•a•türk (ăt′ə-tûrk′, ä-tä-tûrk′), **Kemal** See **Kemal Atatürk.**

at•a•vism (ăt′ə-vĭz′əm) *n.* **1.** The reappearance of a characteristic after several generations of absence, usu. caused by the chance recombination of genes. **2.** An individual or a part that exhibits atavism. **3.** The return of a trait or previous behavior after a period of absence. [Fr. *atavisme* < Lat. *atavus*, ancestor : *atta*, father + *avus*, grandfather.] **—at′a•vist** *n.* **—at′a•vis′tic** *adj.* **—at′a•vis′ti•cal•ly** *adv.*

a•tax•i•a (ə-tăk′sē-ə) also **a•tax•y** (ə-tăk′sē) *n.* Loss of the ability to coordinate muscular movement. [Gk. *ataxiā*, disorder : *a-*, not; see A–¹ + *taxis*, order.] **—a•tax′ic** *adj. & n.*

At•ba•ra (ăt′bər-ə, ät′-) A river of NE Africa rising in NW Ethiopia and flowing c. 805 km (500 mi) to the Nile R. in E Sudan.

at bat *n. Baseball* A player's official turn to bat, counted in figuring a batting average unless the player is hit by the ball, makes a sacrifice hit, is walked, or is interfered with.

ate (āt) *v.* Past tense of **eat.**

A•te (ā′tē, ä′tē, ä′tā) *n. Greek Mythology* The personification of criminal rashness and consequent punishment.

–ate¹ *suff.* **1a.** Having: *nervate.* **b.** Characterized by: *Latinate.* **c.** Resembling: *lyrate.* **2a.** One characterized by: *laminate.* **b.** Rank; office: *rabbinate.* **3.** To act upon in a specified way: *acidulate.* [Ult. < Lat. *-ātus*, p. part. suff. of verbs in *-āre.*]

–ate² *suff.* **1.** A derivative of a specified chemical compound or element: *aluminate.* **2.** A salt or ester of a specified acid whose name ends in *-ic: acetate.* [NLat. *-ātum* < Lat., neut. of *-ātus*, p. part. suff. of verbs in *-āre.*]

at•e•lec•ta•sis (ăt′l-ĕk′tə-sĭs) *n., pl.* **-ses** (-sēz′) **1.** Total or partial collapse of the lung. **2.** Incomplete expansion of the lungs at birth. [NLat. : Gk. *atelēs*, incomplete (*a-*, not; see A–¹ + *telos*, end; see TELO–) + Gk. *ektasis*, stretching out (< *ekteinein*, to stretch out : *ek-*, out; see ECTO– + *teinein*, to stretch; see EPITASIS).]

at•el•ier (ăt′l-yā′) *n.* A workshop or studio. [Fr. < OFr. *astelier*, carpenter's shop < *astele*, splinter < LLat. *astella*, alteration of Lat. *astula*, dim. of *assis*, board.]

a tem•po (ä tĕm′pō) *adv. & adj. Music* In the tempo originally designated; resuming the initial tempo of a section or movement after a deviation from it. [Ital. : *a*, in + *tempo*, time.]

a•tem•po•ral (ā-tĕm′pər-əl) *adj.* Independent of time.

A•ten (ät′n) *n.* Variant of **Aton.**

At•get (ät-zhā′), **Jean Eugène** 1856–1927. French photographer noted for his documentary photographs of Paris.

Ath•a•bas•ca or **Ath•a•bas•ka** (ăth′ə-băs′kə) A river rising in the Rocky Mts. of SW Alberta, Canada, and flowing c. 1,231 km (765 mi) to **Lake Athabasca** on the border between N Alberta and Saskatchewan.

Ath•a•bas•kan or **Ath•a•bas•can** (ăth′ə-băs′kən) also **Ath•a•pas•can** (-păs′-) *n.* **1.** A group of related North American Indian languages including the Apachean languages and languages of Alaska, northwest Canada, and coastal Oregon and California. **2.** A member of an Athabaskan-speaking people. [After Lake ATHABASCA < Cree *athapaskaaw*, there is scattered grass.] **—Ath′a•bas′kan** *adj.*

Athanasian Creed *n.* A Christian creed of the early fifth century, originally attributed to Athanasius.

Ath•a•na•sius (ăth′ə-nā′shəs), Saint. A.D. 293?–373. Greek patriarch of Alexandria. **—Ath′a•na′sian** (-zhən) *adj. & n.*

A•thar•va-Ve•da (ə-tär′və-vā′də, -vē′-) *n.* One of the four Vedas, consisting mostly of spells of black and white magic. [Skt. *Atharvavedaḥ* : *atharvā*, priest + *vedaḥ*, sacred lore, knowledge, Veda; see **weid-** in App.]

a•the•ism (ā′thē-ĭz′əm) *n.* **1a.** Disbelief in or denial of the existence of God or gods. **b.** The doctrine that there is no God or gods. **2.** Godlessness; immorality. [Fr. *athéisme* < *athée*, atheist < Gk. *atheos*, godless : *a-*, without; see A–¹ + *theos*, god; see **dhēs-** in App.] **—a′the•ist** *n.* **—a′the•is′tic** (-ĭs′tĭk), **a′the•is′ti•cal** (-tĭ-kəl) *adj.* **—a′the•is′ti•cal•ly** *adv.*

ath•e•ling (ăth′ə-lĭng, ăth′-) *n.* An Anglo-Saxon nobleman or prince. [ME < OE *ætheling.*]

Ath•el•stan (ăth′əl-stăn′) 895?–939. King of Mercia and Wessex (924?–939) who established control over England.

A•the•na (ə-thē′nə) also **A•the•ne** (-nē) *n. Greek Mythology* The goddess of wisdom, the practical arts, and warfare.

ath•e•nae•um also **ath•e•ne•um** (ăth′ə-nē′əm) *n.* **1.** An institution, such as a literary club, for the promotion of learning. **2.** A place, such as a library, where printed materials are available. [LLat. *Athēnaeum*, a Roman school, after Gk. *Athēnaion*, the temple of Athena < *Athēna*, Athena.]

A•the•ni•an (ə-thē′nē-ən) *adj.* Of or relating to Athens, Greece, or its people. ❖ *n.* A citizen of Athens, Greece.

Ath•ens (ăth′ənz) **1.** The cap. of Greece, in the E part near the Saronic Gulf; reached the height of its power in the 5th cent. B.C. and became the cap. of modern Greece in 1834. Pop. 885,737. **2.** A city of NE GA ENE of Atlanta; founded 1785. Pop. 101,489.

ath•er•o•gen•e•sis (ăth′ər-ō-jĕn′ĭ-sĭs) *n.* Formation of atheromatous deposits. [ATHERO(MA) + –GENESIS.] **—ath′er•o•gen′ic** (-jĕn′ĭk) *adj.* **—ath′er•o•gen•i′ci•ty** (-jə-nĭs′ĭ-tē) *n.*

ath•er•o•ma (ăth′ə-rō′mə) *n., pl.* **-mas** or **-ma•ta** (-mə-tə) A deposit or degenerative accumulation of lipid-containing plaques on the innermost layer of the wall of an artery. [Lat. *athērōma*, tumor full of pus that is like gruel < Gk. < *athēra*, gruel.] **—ath′er•o•ma•to′sis** (-tō′sĭs) *n.* **—ath′er•om′a•tous** (-rŏm′ə-təs, -rō′mə-) *adj.*

ath•er•o•scle•ro•sis (ăth′ə-rō-sklə-rō′sĭs) *n.* A form of arteriosclerosis characterized by the deposit of atheromatous plaques on the innermost layer of the walls of large and medium-sized arteries. [ATHERO(MA) + SCLEROSIS.] **—ath′er•o•scle•rot′ic** (-rŏt′ĭk) *adj.* **—ath′er•o•scle•rot′i•cal•ly** *adv.*

a•thirst (ə-thûrst′) *adj.* **1.** Strongly desirous; eager: *athirst for freedom.* **2.** *Archaic* Thirsty.

ath•lete (ăth′lēt′) *n.* A person possessing the natural or acquired traits necessary for physical exercise or sports, esp. those per-

Atahualpa
contemporary drawing depicting Atahualpa's arrest by Pizarro

Athena
Greek bronze statuette of Athena with an owl, symbol of her wisdom

ă pat	oi boy		
ā pay	ou out		
âr care	o͝o took		
ä father	o͞o boot		
ĕ pet	ŭ cut		
ē be	ûr urge		
ĭ pit	th thin		
ī pie	*th* this		
îr pier	hw which		
ŏ pot	zh vision		
ō toe	ə about, item		
ô paw			

Stress marks:
′ (primary);
′ (secondary), as in
lexicon (lĕk′sĭ-kŏn′)

formed in competitive contexts. [ME < Lat. *āthlēta* < Gk. *āthlētēs*, contestant < *āthlein*, to contend, poss. < *āthlos*, contest.]

ath•lete's foot (ăth′lēts) *n.* A contagious fungal infection of the skin usu. affecting the feet, characterized by itching and scaling; ringworm of the foot.

ath•let•ic (ăth-lĕt′ĭk) *adj.* **1.** Of or relating to athletics or athletes. **2.** Characterized by or involving physical activity or exertion. **3.** Physically strong; muscular. See Syns at **muscular.** —**ath•let′i•cal•ly** *adv.* —**ath•let′i•cism** (-lĕt′ĭ-sĭz′əm) *n.*

ath•let•ics (ăth-lĕt′ĭks) *n.* (*used with a sing. or pl. verb*) **1.** Activities that require physical skill and stamina. **2.** The principles or system of training and practice for such activities.

athletic supporter *n.* An elastic support for the male genitals, worn esp. in athletic or other strenuous activity.

ath•o•dyd (ăth′ə-dĭd′) *n.* A simple, essentially tubular jet engine, such as a ramjet. [A(ERO)- + TH(ERM)ODY(NAMIC) + D(UCT).]

at-home (ət-hōm′, ăt-) *n.* also **at home** An informal reception in one's home. ❖ *adj.* **1.** Being or occurring in one's home: *at-home care.* **2.** Designed for or appropriate for one's home.

–athon *suff.* An activity continuing for an extended period of time: *phonathon.* [< (MAR)ATHON.]

Ath•os (ăth′ŏs, ā′thŏs, ā′thôs), Mount A peak, c. 2,034 m (6,670 ft), of NE Greece; site of the monastic community of **Mount Athos,** founded in the 10th cent.

a•thwart (ə-thwôrt′) *adv.* **1.** From side to side; crosswise or transversely. **2.** So as to thwart or oppose; perversely. ❖ *prep.* **1.** From one side to the other of; across: *"the Stars that shoot athwart the Night"* (Alexander Pope). **2.** Contrary to; against. [ME < *a-*, on; see A–² + *thwert,* across; see THWART.]

a•tilt (ə-tĭlt′) *adv. & adj.* **1.** In a tilted position; inclined upward. **2.** Tilting or as if tilting with a lance.

a•tin•gle (ə-tĭng′gəl) *adj.* Experiencing a prickling sensation, as from excitement.

–ation *suff.* **1a.** Action or process: *strangulation.* **b.** The result of an action or process: *acculturation.* **2.** State, condition, or quality of: *eburnation.* [ME *-acioun* < OFr. *-ation* < Lat. *-ātiō, -ātiōn-,* n. suff. : *-ā-,* stem vowel of verbs in *-āre* + *-tiō, -tiōn-,* abstract n. suff.]

A•ti•tlán (ä′tē-tlän′) A lake of SW Guatemala amid three inactive volcanoes, including **Atitlán,** 3,539.2 m (11,604 ft).

–ative *suff.* Of, relating to, or associated with: *talkative.* [ME < OFr. *-atif, -ative* < Lat. *-ātīvus* < *-ātus,* p.part. suff. See –ATE¹.]

At•ka Island (ăt′kə, ät′-) An island of SW AK in the central Aleutian Is.; site of a major World War II military base.

Atka mackerel *n.* A food fish (*Pleurogrammus monopterygius*) native to northern Pacific waters.

Atl. *abbr.* Atlantic

At•lan•ta (ăt-lăn′tə) The cap. of GA, in the NW part; founded as Terminus in 1837 and renamed Atlanta in 1845. Pop. 416,474. —**At•lan′tan** *n.*

At•lan•te•an¹ (ăt′lăn-tē′ən, ăt-lăn′tē-) *adj.* Of, relating to, or like Atlas. [< Gk. *Atlās, Atlant-,* Atlas. See ATLAS.]

At•lan•te•an² (ăt′lăn-tē′ən, ăt-lăn′tē-) *adj.* Of or relating to Atlantis.

at•lan•tes (ăt-lăn′tēz) *n. Architecture* Plural of **atlas²** 1.

At•lan•tic (ăt-lăn′tĭk) *n.* The Atlantic Ocean. ❖ *adj.* **1.** Of, in, or near the Atlantic Ocean. **2.** Of, on, or near the eastern coast of the United States. **3.** Of or concerning countries bordering the Atlantic Ocean, esp. those of Europe and North America. [ME *Atlantik* < Lat. (*mare*) *Atlanticum,* Atlantic (sea) < Gk. (*pelagos*) *Atlantikos* < *Atlās, Atlant-,* Atlas, Mount Atlas (in west Africa, on which the heavens were believed to rest). See **telə-** in App.]

Atlantic City A resort city of SE NJ on the Atlantic Ocean. Pop. 40,517.

Atlantic croaker *n.* A small silvery food fish (*Micropogonias undulatus*) common in Atlantic waters south of Massachusetts.

Atlantic Intracoastal Waterway A system of inland waterways along the Atlantic coast of the US extending from Cape Cod to S FL and forming part of the Intracoastal Waterway.

At•lan•ti•cism (ăt-lăn′tĭ-sĭz′əm) *n.* A policy of cooperation between western Europe and North America. —**At•lan′ti•cist** *n.*

Atlantic Ocean The second-largest ocean, divided into the **North Atlantic** and the **South Atlantic** and extending from the Arctic to the Antarctic between the E Americas and W Europe and Africa.

Atlantic Provinces The E Canadian provinces of New Brunswick, Prince Edward I., Nova Scotia, and Newfoundland.

Atlantic salmon *n.* A species of salmon (*Salmo salar*) native to northern Atlantic waters and valued as a food fish.

Atlantic Standard Time *n.* Standard time in the fourth time zone west of Greenwich, England, reckoned at 60° west and used, for example, in Puerto Rico.

At•lan•tis (ăt-lăn′tĭs) *n. Mythology* A legendary island in the Atlantic Ocean, said to have sunk during an earthquake.

at•las¹ (ăt′ləs) *n.,* pl. **-las•es 1.** A book or bound collection of maps, sometimes with supplementary illustrations and graphic analyses. **2.** A volume of tables, charts, or plates illustrating a particular subject: *an anatomical atlas.* [After ATLAS, probably from depictions of him holding the world on his shoulders that appeared on the frontispieces of early works of this kind.]

at•las² (ăt′ləs) *n.,* pl. **-es 1.** pl. **at•lan•tes** (ăt-lăn′tēz) *Architec-*

Atlantic salmon
female Atlantic salmon
Salmo salar

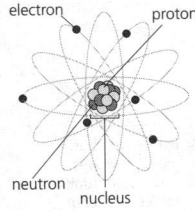

electron   proton

neutron
nucleus

atom
carbon atom

ture A figure of a man used as a supporting column, as for an entablature or balcony. **2.** *Anatomy* The top or first cervical vertebra of the neck, which supports the skull. [< ATLAS.]

Atlas *n.* **1.** *Greek Mythology* A Titan condemned by Zeus to support the heavens upon his shoulders. **2.** A satellite of Saturn. **3.** **atlas** A person who supports a great burden. [Gk. *Atlās.* See **telə-** in App.]

Atlas Mountains A system of ranges and plateaus of NW Africa extending from SW Morocco to N Tunisia and rising to 4,167.8 m (13,665 ft).

at•la•tl (ăt-lät′l) *n.* A throwing device usu. consisting of a stick fitted with a thong or socket to steady the butt of a spear or dart and extend the length it travels. [Nahuatl < *atla,* to throw.]

At•li (ăt′lē) *n.* In the *Volsunga Saga,* a husband of Gudrun.

atm or **atm.** *abbr. Physics* atmosphere

ATM *abbr.* **1.** asynchronous transfer mode **2.** automated teller machine

at•man (ät′mən) *n. Hinduism* **1.** The individual soul or essence. **2. Atman** The eternal, unchanging essence that is indistinguishable from the essence of the universe. [Skt. *ātmā, ātman-,* breath, spirit.]

at•mom•e•ter (ăt-mŏm′ĭ-tər) *n.* An instrument that measures the rate of water evaporation. [Gk. *atmos,* vapor + –METER.]

at•mos•phere (ăt′mə-sfîr′) *n.* **1.** The gaseous mass surrounding a celestial body, esp. the one surrounding the earth. **2.** The air or climate in a specific place. **3.** *Physics* A unit of pressure equal to the air pressure at sea level, 14.7 pounds per square inch, or approx. 1.01325×10^5 pascals. **4.** A dominant intellectual or emotional environment or attitude: *an atmosphere of distrust.* **5.** The dominant tone or mood of a work of art. **6.** An aesthetic quality or effect associated with a particular place. [NLat. *atmosphaera* : Gk. *atmos,* vapor; see **wet-¹** in App. + Lat. *sphaera,* sphere; see SPHERE.]

at•mos•pher•ic (ăt′mə-sfĕr′ĭk, -sfîr′-) also **at•mos•pher•i•cal** (-ĭ-kəl) *adj.* **1.** Of, relating to, or existing in the atmosphere. **2.** Produced by, dependent on, or coming from the atmosphere. **3.** Resembling or suggestive of the atmosphere: *a painting with an atmospheric glow.* **4.** Intended to evoke a particular emotional tone or aesthetic quality. —**at•mos•pher′i•cal•ly** *adv.*

atmospheric pressure *n.* Pressure caused by the weight of the atmosphere, a maximum at sea level and reducing with increasing altitude.

at•mos•pher•ics (ăt′mə-sfĕr′ĭks, -sfîr′-) *n.* **1.** (*used with a sing. verb*) **a.** Electromagnetic radiation produced by natural phenomena such as lightning. **b.** Radio interference produced by electromagnetic radiation. **2.** (*used with a pl. verb*) **a.** Features, events, or statements intended to create a particular mood. **b.** The mood so created.

at. no. *abbr.* atomic number

a•toll (ăt′ôl′, -ŏl′, ā′tôl′, ā′tŏl′) *n.* A ringlike coral island and reef that nearly or entirely encloses a lagoon. [Maldivian *atolu;* prob. akin to Sinhalese *ätul,* interior (< the interior lagoon), prob. < Skt. **antala-,* var. of *antara-.*]

at•om (ăt′əm) *n.* **1a.** A part or particle considered to be an irreducible constituent of a specified system. **b.** The irreducible indestructible material unit postulated by ancient atomism. **2.** An extremely small part, quantity, or amount. **3.** *Physics & Chemistry* **a.** The smallest unit of an element, characteristically remaining undivided in chemical reactions and consisting of a dense, central, positively charged nucleus surrounded by a system of electrons. **b.** This unit regarded as a source of nuclear energy. [ME *attome* < Lat. *atomus* < Gk. *atomos,* indivisible, atom : *a-,* not; see A–¹ + *tomos,* cutting (< *temnein,* to cut).]

atom bomb *n.* **1.** An explosive weapon of great destructive power derived from the release of energy in the fission of atomic nuclei. **2.** A bomb deriving its destructive power from the release of nuclear energy.

a•tom•ic (ə-tŏm′ĭk) *adj.* **1.** Of or relating to an atom or atoms. **2.** Of or employing nuclear energy: *atomic weapons.* **3.** Very small; infinitesimal. —**a•tom′i•cal•ly** *adv.*

atomic age also **Atomic Age** *n.* The era defined by the discovery, applications, and consequences of nuclear energy.

atomic bomb *n.* See **atom bomb** 1.

atomic clock *n.* An extremely precise timekeeping device regulated in correspondence with a characteristic invariant frequency of an atomic or molecular system.

atomic energy *n.* See **nuclear energy.**

a•tom•ic•i•ty (ăt′ə-mĭs′ĭ-tē) *n.* **1.** The state of being composed of atoms. **2.** *Chemistry* **a.** The number of atoms in a molecule. **b.** Valence.

atomic mass *n.* The mass of an atom, usu. expressed in atomic mass units.

atomic mass unit *n.* A unit of mass equal to 1/12 the mass of an atom of carbon 12, which is assigned a mass of 12.

atomic number *n. Symbol* **Z** The number of protons in an atomic nucleus.

atomic pile *n.* An early type of nuclear reactor consisting of alternating layers of uranium pellets and purified graphite bricks, designed to create a sustained fission reaction.

atomic reactor *n.* See **nuclear reactor.**

atomic weight *n.* The average mass of an atom of an element, usu. expressed relative to the atomic mass of carbon 12.

at•om•ism (ăt′ə-mĭz′əm) *n. Philosophy* **1.** The ancient theory that simple, minute, indivisible, and indestructible particles are the components of the entire universe. **2.** A theory that social institutions, values, and processes arise solely from the acts and interests of individuals, who are thus the only true subject of analysis. —**at′om•ist** *n.*

at•om•is•tic (ăt′ə-mĭs′tĭk) also **at•om•is•ti•cal** (-tĭ-kəl) *adj.* **1.** Of or relating to atoms or atomism. **2.** Consisting of many separate, often disparate elements. —**at′om•is′ti•cal•ly** *adv.*

at•om•ize (ăt′ə-mīz′) *tr.v.* **-ized, -iz•ing, -iz•es 1.** To reduce to or separate into atoms. **2.** To reduce to tiny particles or a fine spray. **3.** To break into small fragments. **4.** To subject to bombardment with atomic weapons. —**at′om•i•za′tion** (-ĭ-zā′shən) *n.*

at•om•iz•er (ăt′ə-mī′zər) *n.* A device for converting a substance, esp. a perfume or medicine, to a fine spray.

atom smasher *n.* A particle accelerator.

atom trap *n.* See **laser trap.**

at•o•my (ăt′ə-mē) *n., pl.* **-mies** *Archaic* **1.** A tiny particle. **2.** A tiny being. [< Lat. *atomī,* pl. of *atomus,* atom. See ATOM.]

A•ton also **A•ten** (ät′n) *n. Mythology* An Egyptian god of the sun, regarded during the reign of Akhenaton as the only god.

a•ton•al (ā-tō′nəl) *adj. Music* Lacking a tonal center or key; characterized by atonality. —**a•ton′al•ly** *adv.*

a•ton•a•list (ā-tō′nə-lĭst) *n.* One who composes atonal music.

a•to•nal•i•ty (ā′tō-năl′ĭ-tē) *n., pl.* **-ties** *Music* **1.** The absence of a tonal center and of harmonies derived from a diatonic scale corresponding to such a center; lack of tonality. **2.** A compositional style lacking a tonal center and its derived harmonies.

a•tone (ə-tōn′) *v.* **a•toned, a•ton•ing, a•tones** —*intr.* **1.** To make amends, as for a sin or fault. **2.** *Archaic* To agree. —*tr.* **1.** To expiate. **2.** *Archaic* To conciliate; appease. **3.** *Obsolete* To reconcile or harmonize. [ME *atonen,* to be reconciled < *at one,* in agreement : *at;* see AT + *one,* one; see ONE.] —**a•ton′a•ble, a•tone′a•ble** *adj.* —**a•ton′er** *n.*

a•tone•ment (ə-tōn′mənt) *n.* **1.** Amends or reparation made for an injury or wrong; expiation. **2a.** Reconciliation or an instance of reconciliation between God and humans. **b.** also **Atonement** *Christianity* The reconciliation between God and humans brought about by the life and death of Jesus. **3.** *Obsolete* Reconciliation; concord.

a•ton•ic (ā-tŏn′ĭk) *adj.* **1.** Not accented: *an atonic syllable.* **2.** *Pathology* Relating to, caused by, or exhibiting lack of muscle tone. ❖ *n.* A word, syllable, or sound that is unaccented. [< Gk. *atonos.* See ATONY.] —**a•ton′ic′i•ty** (ā′tŏ-nĭs′ĭ-tē, ăt′n-ĭs-) *n.*

at•o•ny (ăt′ə-nē, ăt′n-ē) *n.* **1.** Lack of normal muscle tone. **2.** Lack of accent or stress. [LLat. *atonia* < Gk. *atoniā* < *atonos,* slack : *a-,* without; see A⁻¹ + *tonos,* stretching, tone; see TONE.]

a•top (ə-tŏp′) *adv.* To, on, or at the top. ❖ *prep.* On top of.

a•top•ic (ā-tŏp′ĭk) *adj.* Of, relating to, or caused by a hereditary predisposition toward certain hypersensitivity reactions, such as hay fever or asthma, upon exposure to specific antigens. [< Gk. *atopiā,* unusualness < *atopos,* out of the way : *a-,* not; see A⁻¹ + *topos,* place.] —**at′o•py** (ăt′ə-pē) *n.*

-ator *suff.* One that acts in a specified manner: *radiator.* [Lat. *-ātor : -ā-,* stem vowel of verbs in *-āre* + *-tor,* agent n. suff. (later reanalyzed as *-ātus, -ate* + *-or,* -or).]

-atory *suff.* **1a.** Of or relating to: *perspiratory.* **b.** Tending to: *amendatory.* **2.** One that is connected with: *reformatory.* [< Lat. *-ātōrius* and *-ātōrium,* both < *-ātor,* -ator.]

ATP (ā′tē′pē′) *n.* An adenosine-derived nucleotide, $C_{10}H_{16}N_5O_{13}P_3$, that supplies energy to cells through its hydrolysis to ADP. [A(DENOSINE) T(RI)P(HOSPHATE).]

ATP•ase (ā′tē-pē′ās, -āz) *n.* An enzyme that catalyzes the hydrolysis of ATP to ADP; adenosine triphosphatase.

at•ra•bil•ious (ăt′rə-bĭl′yəs) also **at•ra•bil•i•ar** (-bĭl′ē-ər) *adj.* **1.** Inclined to melancholy. **2.** Having a peevish disposition; surly. [< Lat. *ātra bīlis,* black bile (transl. of Gk. *melankholiā*) : *ātra,* fem. of *āter,* black + *bīlis,* bile.] —**at′ra•bil′ious•ness** *n.*

a•trem•ble (ə-trĕm′bəl) *adj.* Being in a state of shaking or trembling, as from fear or excitement.

a•tre•sia (ə-trē′zhə, -zhē-ə) *n.* **1.** The absence or closure of a normal body orifice or passage such as the anus or intestine. **2.** The degeneration and resorption of an ovarian follicle before it reaches maturity. [NLat. *atrēsia* : Gk. *a-,* not, without; see A⁻¹ + Gk. *trēsis,* perforation, orifice; see **terə-¹** in App.] —**a•tre′sic** (-zĭk, -sĭk) *adj.*

A•treus (ā′trōos, ā′trē-əs) *n. Greek Mythology* A king of Mycenae, father of Agamemnon and Menelaus.

atrial natriuretic factor *n.* A hormone produced by the right atrium of the heart that stimulates the excretion of sodium by the kidneys and helps regulate blood pressure.

a•tri•o•ven•tric•u•lar (ā′trē-ō-vĕn-trĭk′yə-lər) *adj.* Of, relating to, or involving the atria and the ventricles of the heart.

atrioventricular node *n.* A small mass of specialized muscle fibers, located in the wall of the right atrium of the heart, that transmits impulses from the sinoatrial node to the ventricles.

a•tri•um (ā′trē-əm) *n., pl.* **a•tri•a** (ā′trē-ə) or **-ums 1.** *Architecture* A rectangular court, as: **a.** A usu. skylighted central area in some modern buildings. **b.** The open area in the center of an an-

cient Roman house. **c.** The forecourt of a building, enclosed on three or four sides with porticoes. **2.** *Anatomy* A body cavity or chamber, esp. either of the upper chambers of the heart that receives blood from the veins and forces it into a ventricle. [Lat. *ātrium.*] —**a′tri•al** *adj.*

a•tro•cious (ə-trō′shəs) *adj.* **1.** Extremely evil or cruel; monstrous. **2.** Exceptionally bad; abominable. [< Lat. *atrōx, atrōc-,* frightful, cruel.] —**a•tro′cious•ly** *adv.* —**a•tro′cious•ness** *n.*

a•troc•i•ty (ə-trŏs′ĭ-tē) *n., pl.* **-ties 1.** Appalling or atrocious condition, quality, or behavior; monstrousness. **2.** An appalling or atrocious act, situation, or object, esp. an act of cruelty inflicted by an armed force on civilians or prisoners.

at•ro•phy (ăt′rə-fē) *n., pl.* **-phies 1.** *Pathology* A wasting or decrease in size of a body organ, tissue, or part owing to disease, injury, or lack of use: *muscular atrophy.* **2.** A wasting away, deterioration, or diminution: *intellectual atrophy.* ❖ *v.* **-phied, -phy•ing, -phies** —*tr.* To affect with atrophy. —*intr.* To waste away or deteriorate. [LLat. *atrophia* < Gk. *atrophiā* < *atrophos,* ill-nourished : *a-,* without; see A⁻¹ + *trophē,* food.] —**a•troph′ic** (ā-trŏf′ĭk) *adj.*

at•ro•pine (ăt′rə-pēn′, -pĭn) also **at•ro•pin** (-pĭn) *n.* A poisonous crystalline alkaloid, $C_{17}H_{23}NO_3$, obtained from belladonna and other related plants and used to dilate the pupil of the eye and as an antispasmodic. [< NLat. *Atropa,* genus name of belladonna < Gk. *Atropos,* Atropos. See ATROPOS.]

At•ro•pos (ăt′rə-pŏs′, -pəs) *n. Greek Mythology* One of the three Fates, the cutter of the thread of destiny. [Gk. < *atropos,* inexorable : *a-,* not; see A⁻¹ + *tropos,* changeable; see –TROPOUS.]

at sign *n.* The symbol (@) for the word *at.*

At•si•na (ăt-sē′nə) *n., pl.* **Atsina** or **-nas 1.** A member of a Native American people formerly inhabiting the plains of northern Montana and southern Saskatchewan, with a present-day population in north-central Montana. **2.** The Algonquian language of the Atsina.

att. *abbr.* **1.** attached **2.** attention **3.** Att. attorney

at•ta•boy (ăt′ə-boi′) *interj. Informal* Used to show encouragement or approval to a boy or man. [Alteration of *That's the boy!*]

at•tach (ə-tăch′) *v.* **-tached, -tach•ing, -tach•es** —*tr.* **1.** To fasten, secure, or join: *attached the wires to the post.* **2.** To connect as an adjunct or associated condition or part: *issues attached to this legislation.* **3.** To affix or append; add: *attached riders to the document.* **4.** To ascribe or assign: *attached no significance to the threat.* **5.** To bind by emotional ties, as of affection: *I am attached to my family.* **6.** To assign to a military unit temporarily. **7.** *Law* To seize by legal writ. —*intr.* To adhere, belong, or relate: *Prestige attaches to this position.* [ME *attachen* < OFr. *attachier,* alteration of *estachier* < *estache,* stake, of Gmc. orig.] —**at•tach′a•ble** *adj.* —**at•tach′er** *n.*

at•ta•ché (ăt′ə-shā′, ă-tă-) *n.* **1.** One assigned to a diplomatic mission to serve in a particular capacity. **2.** An attaché case. [Fr. < p. part. of *attacher,* to attach < OFr. *attachier.* See ATTACH.]

attaché case *n.* A rigid briefcase, usu. having a lock.

at•tached (ə-tăcht′) *adj.* **1.** *Architecture* Joined to or by a wall, esp. by sharing a wall with another building. **2.** *Biology* Living in a permanently fixed state in the adult stage.

at•tach•ment (ə-tăch′mənt) *n.* **1.** The act of attaching or the condition of being attached. **2.** Something, such as a tie or band, that attaches one thing to another. **3.** A bond, as of affection; fond regard. **4a.** A supplementary part; an accessory. **b.** A supplementary document attached to a primary document. **5.** *Law* **a.** Legal seizure of property or a person. **b.** The writ ordering such a seizure.

at•tack (ə-tăk′) *v.* **-tacked, -tack•ing, -tacks** —*tr.* **1.** To set upon with violent force. **2.** To criticize strongly or hostilely. **3.** To start work on with purpose and vigor: *attack a problem.* **4.** To begin to affect harmfully: *The disease attacked the nervous system.* —*intr.* To make an attack; launch an assault. ❖ *n.* **1.** The act or an instance of attacking; an assault. **2.** An expression of strong criticism; hostile comment: *newspaper attacks.* **3.** *Sports* **a.** An offensive action in a sport or game. **b.** The players executing such an action. **4a.** The initial movement in a task. **b.** A method or procedure. **5.** An episode or onset of a disease, esp. an occurrence of a chronic disease. **6.** The experience or beginning of a feeling, need, or desire. **7a.** *Music* The beginning or manner of beginning a piece, passage, or tone. **b.** Decisiveness and clarity in artistic expression. [Fr. *attaquer* < OFr. < OItal. *estaccare,* of Gmc. orig.] —**at•tack′er** *n.*

at•ta•girl (ăt′ə-gûrl′) *interj. Informal* Used to show encouragement or approval to a girl or woman. [Alteration of *That's the girl!*]

at•tain (ə-tān′) *v.* **-tained, -tain•ing, -tains** —*tr.* **1.** To gain as an objective; achieve. **2.** To arrive at, as by persistence or the passage of time. See Syns at **reach.** —*intr.* To succeed in a directed effort or progression. [ME *atteignen* < OFr. *ataindre, ataign-,* to reach < VLat. **attangere* < Lat. *attingere* : *ad-,* ad- + *tangere,* to touch; see **tag-** in App.] —**at•tain′a•bil′i•ty, at•tain′a•ble•ness** *n.* —**at•tain′a•ble** *adj.*

at•tain•der (ə-tān′dər) *n.* **1.** In the ancient common law, the state of an offender who had been sentenced for a capital offense. **2.** *Obsolete* Dishonor. [ME *atteindre,* act of attainting < OFr. *ataindre,* to convict, affect, attainder. See ATTAIN.]

at·tain·ment (ə-tān′mənt) *n.* **1.** The act of attaining or the condition of being attained. **2.** Something that is attained.

at·taint (ə-tānt′) *tr.v.* **-taint·ed, -taint·ing, -taints 1.** To impart stigma to; disgrace. **2.** To pass a sentence of attainder against. **3.** *Archaic* To infect or corrupt, as with illness or vice. **4.** *Archaic* To accuse. ❖ *n.* **1.** *Obsolete* Attainder. **2.** *Archaic* A disgrace; a stigma. [ME *attainten* < OFr. *ataint,* p. part. of *ataindre,* to affect. See AT-TAIN.]

at·tar (ăt′ər) also **ot·tar** (ŏt′ər) or **ot·to** (ŏt′ō) *n.* A fragrant essential oil or perfume obtained from flowers: *attar of roses.* [Pers. *'aṭir,* perfumed < Ar., aromatic < *'aṭira,* to be fragrant.]

At·tar (ăt′ər, ə-tär′) d. c. 1229. Persian poet and mystic best known for his allegory *Conference of the Birds.*

At·ta·wa·pis·kat (ăt′ə-wə-pĭs′kət) A river, c. 748 km (465 mi), of N Ontario, Canada, flowing from **Attawapiskat Lake** into James Bay.

at·tempt (ə-tĕmpt′) *tr.v.* **-tempt·ed, -tempt·ing, -tempts 1a.** To try (to do something). **b.** To try to perform, make, or achieve: *attempt a difficult dive.* **2.** *Archaic* To tempt. **3.** *Archaic* To attack with the intention of subduing. ❖ *n.* **1.** An effort or a try. **2.** An attack; an assault. [ME *attempten* < OFr. *attempter* < Lat. *attemptāre : ad-,* ad- + *temptāre,* to test.] —**at·tempt′a·ble** *adj.* —**at·tempt′er** *n.*

at·tend (ə-tĕnd′) *v.* **-tend·ed, -tend·ing, -tends** —*tr.* **1.** To be present at: *attended class.* **2.** To accompany as a circumstance or follow as a result: *The speech was attended by wild applause.* **3a.** To accompany or wait upon as a companion or servant. **b.** To take care of. See Syns at *tend*[2]. **4.** To take charge of. **5.** To listen to; heed: *attended my every word.* **6.** *Archaic* To wait for; expect. —*intr.* **1.** To be present. **2.** To take care; give attention: *attended to that problem.* **3.** To apply or direct oneself: *attended to their business.* **4.** To pay attention. **5.** To remain ready to serve; wait. **6.** *Obsolete* To delay or wait. [ME *attenden* < OFr. *atendre* < Lat. *attendere,* to heed : *ad-,* ad- + *tendere,* to stretch; see **ten-** in App.] —**at·tend′er** *n.*

at·ten·dance (ə-tĕn′dəns) *n.* **1.** The act of attending. **2.** The persons or number of persons who are present. **3.** The frequency with which a person is present.

at·ten·dant (ə-tĕn′dənt) *n.* **1.** One who attends or waits on another. **2.** One who is present. **3.** An accompanying thing or circumstance; a concomitant. ❖ *adj.* **1.** Being present: *ships and attendant sailors.* **2.** Accompanying or following as a result: *attendant circumstances.* —**at·ten′dant·ly** *adv.*

at·tend·ee (ə-tĕn′dē′, ăt′ĕn-) *n.* One who is present at or attends a function. See Usage Note at **-ee**[1].

at·tend·ing (ə-tĕn′dĭng) *adj.* **1.** Being the principal supervising physician. **2.** Being a physician on the regular medical staff of a hospital. —**at·tend′ing** *n.*

at·ten·tion (ə-tĕn′shən) *n.* **1.** Concentration of the mental powers; a close observing or listening. **2.** The ability or power to concentrate mentally. **3.** Observant consideration; notice. **4.** Consideration or courtesy. **5.** **attentions** Acts of courtesy or consideration, esp. by a suitor. **6.** A military posture, with the body erect and heels together. ❖ *interj.* Used as a command to assume an erect military posture. [ME *attencioun* < Lat. *attentiō, attentiōn-* < *attentus,* p. part. of *attendere,* to heed. See ATTEND.] —**at·ten′tion·al** *adj.*

attention deficit disorder *n.* A syndrome, usu. diagnosed in childhood, marked by impulsiveness, a short attention span, and often hyperactivity.

attention deficit hyperactivity disorder *n.* Attention deficit disorder in which hyperactivity is present.

attention span *n.* The length of time during which a person can concentrate on a subject or idea.

at·ten·tive (ə-tĕn′tĭv) *adj.* **1.** Giving care or attention; watchful: *attentive to detail.* **2.** Marked by devoted attention to the pleasure or comfort of others. See Syns at **thoughtful.** —**at·ten′tive·ly** *adv.* —**at·ten′tive·ness** *n.*

at·ten·u·ate (ə-tĕn′yōō-āt′) *v.* **-at·ed, -at·ing, -ates** —*tr.* **1.** To make slender, fine, or small. **2.** To reduce, as in force or amount; weaken. **3.** To lessen the density of; rarefy. **4.** *Biology* To make (bacteria or viruses) less virulent. **5.** *Electronics* To reduce (the amplitude of an electrical signal) with little or no distortion. —*intr.* To become thin, weak, or fine. ❖ *adj.* (-yōō-ĭt) **1.** Reduced or weakened, as in strength, value, or virulence. **2.** *Botany* Gradually tapering to a point. [Lat. *attenuāre, attenuāt- : ad-,* ad- + *tenuāre,* to make thin (< *tenuis,* thin; see **ten-** in App.).] —**at·ten′u·a′tion** *n.*

at·ten·u·a·tor (ə-tĕn′yōō-ā′tər) *n.* A device that attenuates an electrical signal.

at·test (ə-tĕst′) *v.* **-test·ed, -test·ing, -tests** —*tr.* **1.** To affirm to be correct, true, or genuine. **2.** To certify by signature or oath. **3.** To supply or be evidence of: *Her fine work attests her ability.* **4.** To put under oath. —*intr.* To bear witness; give testimony: *attested to their good faith.* ❖ *n.* Attestation. [Lat. *attestārī : ad-,* ad- + *testārī,* to be witness (< *testis,* witness; see **trei-** in App.).] —**at·test′ant** *n.* —**at·tes·ta·tion** (ăt′ĕs-tā′shən, ăt′ə-stā′-) *n.* —**at·test′er, at·tes′tor** *n.*

at·tic (ăt′ĭk) *n.* **1.** A story directly below the roof of a building. **2.** A low wall or story above the cornice of a classical façade. [< *Attic story,* story of a building enclosed by one decorative structure

placed above another, much taller decorative structure, usu. involving the Attic order, an architectural order having square columns of any of the basic five orders < Fr. *attique* < *attique,* Attic < Lat. *Atticus.* See ATTIC.]

Attic *adj.* **1.** Of or relating to ancient Attica, Athens, or the Athenians. **2.** Characterized by purity, simplicity, and elegant wit: *Attic prose.* ❖ *n.* The ancient Greek dialect of Attica. [Lat. *Atticus* < Gk. *Attikos* < *Attikē,* Attica.]

At·ti·ca (ăt′ĭ-kə) An ancient region of E-central Greece surrounding Athens.

At·ti·cism (ăt′ĭ-sĭz′əm) *n.* **1.** A characteristic feature of Attic Greek. **2.** **atticism** A concise and elegant expression.

At·ti·la (ăt′l-ə, ə-tĭl′ə) A.D. 406?–453. King of the Huns (433?–453) who invaded the Roman Empire.

at·tire (ə-tīr′) *tr.v.* **-tired, -tir·ing, -tires** To dress or clothe, esp. in elaborate garments. ❖ *n.* **1.** Clothing or array; apparel. **2.** The antlers of a deer. [ME *atiren* < OFr. *atirier : a-,* to (< Lat. *ad-*; see AD-) + *tire,* order, rank; see TIER[1].]

at·ti·tude (ăt′ĭ-tōōd′, -tyōōd′) *n.* **1.** A position of the body or manner of carrying oneself: *stood in a graceful attitude.* **2a.** A state of mind or a feeling; a disposition: *a positive attitude.* **b.** An arrogant or hostile state of mind or disposition. **3.** The orientation of an aircraft's axes relative to a reference line or plane. **4.** The orientation of a spacecraft relative to its direction of motion. **5.** A position in which a ballet dancer stands on one leg with the other raised and bent at the knee. [Fr. < Ital. *attitudine* < LLat. *aptitūdō, aptitūdin-,* faculty. See APTITUDE.] —**at′ti·tu′di·nal** (-tōōd′n-əl, -tyōōd′-) *adj.*

attitude

at·ti·tu·di·nize (ăt′ĭ-tōōd′n-īz′, -tyōōd′-) *intr.v.* **-nized, -niz·ing, -niz·es** To assume an affected attitude; posture.

Att·lee (ăt′lē), Clement Richard 1883–1967. British politician who served as prime minister (1945–51).

attn. *abbr.* attention

atto- *pref.* One quintillionth (10⁻¹⁸): *attotesla.* [< Dan. or Norw. *atten,* eighteen < ON *āttjān.* See **oktō(u)** in App.]

at·torn (ə-tûrn′) *intr.v.* **-torned, -torn·ing, -torns** To agree to remain as a tenant of property after the transfer of its ownership. [ME *attournen* < OFr. *atorner,* to assign to : *a-,* to (< Lat. *ad-*; see AD-) + *torner,* to turn; see TURN.] —**at·torn′ment** *n.*

at·tor·ney (ə-tûr′nē) *n., pl.* **-neys** A person legally appointed by another to act as an agent in the transaction of business, esp. one licensed to act in legal proceedings. [ME *attourney* < OFr. *atorne* < p. part. of *atorner,* to appoint. See ATTORN.] —**at·tor′ney·ship′** *n.*

attorney-at-law (ə-tûr′nē-ət-lô′) *n., pl.* **at·tor·neys-at-law** (-nēz-) An attorney.

attorney general *n., pl.* **attorneys general** or **attorney generals 1.** The chief law officer and legal counsel of a government. **2. Attorney General** The head of the US Department of Justice and a member of the President's cabinet.

at·tract (ə-trăkt′) *v.* **-tract·ed, -tract·ing, -tracts** —*tr.* **1.** To cause to draw near or adhere by physical force: *Magnetic poles are attracted to their opposites.* **2.** To arouse or compel the admiration or attention of: *We were attracted by the display of lights.* —*intr.* To possess or use the power of attraction. [ME *attracten* < Lat. *attrahere, attract- : ad-,* ad- + *trahere,* pull.] —**at·tract′a·ble** *adj.*

at·trac·tant (ə-trăk′tənt) *n.* A substance, such as a pheromone, that attracts insects or other animals.

at·trac·tion (ə-trăk′shən) *n.* **1.** The act or capability of attracting. **2.** The quality of attracting; charm. **3.** Something that attracts or is intended to attract. **4a.** The electric or magnetic force exerted by oppositely charged particles, tending to draw them together. **b.** The gravitational force exerted by one body on another.

at·trac·tive (ə-trăk′tĭv) *adj.* **1.** Having the power to attract. **2.** Pleasing to the eye or mind; charming. —**at·trac′tive·ly** *adv.* —**at·trac′tive·ness** *n.*

at·trac·tor (ə-trăk′tər) *n.* also **at·tract·er** One that attracts. **2.** *Physics* A set of physical properties toward which a system tends to evolve, regardless of the starting conditions of the system.

at·trib·ute (ə-trĭb′yōōt) *tr.v.* **-ut·ed, -ut·ing, -utes 1.** To relate to a cause or source; ascribe. **2.** To regard as the work of a specified agent, place, or time: *attributed the painting to Titian.* ❖ *n.* **at·tri·bute** (ăt′rə-byōōt′) **1.** A quality or characteristic inherent in or ascribed to someone or something. **2.** An object associated with and serving to identify a character, personage, or office. **3.** *Grammar* A word or phrase syntactically subordinate to another word or phrase that it modifies; for example, *my sister's* and *brown* in *my sister's brown dog.* [Lat. *attribuere, attribūt- : ad-,* ad- + *tribuere,* to allot; see TRIBUTE.] —**at·trib′ut·a·ble** *adj.* —**at·trib′ut·er, at·trib′u·tor** *n.*

at·tri·bu·tion (ăt′rə-byōō′shən) *n.* **1.** The act of attributing, esp. the act of establishing a particular person as the creator of a work of art. **2.** Something related to a particular possessor; an attribute. —**at′tri·bu′tion·al** *adj.*

at·trib·u·tive (ə-trĭb′yə-tĭv) *n. Grammar* A word or word group that is placed adjacent to the noun it modifies without a linking verb; for example, *pale* in *the pale girl.* ❖ *adj.* **1.** *Grammar* Of, relating to, or being an attributive. **2.** Of or having the nature of an attribution or attribute. —**at·trib′u·tive·ly** *adv.*

at•trit (ə-trĭt′) also **at•trite** (ə-trīt′) *tr.v.* **-trit•ted, -trit•ting, -trits** also **-trit•ed, -trit•ing, -trites 1.** To lose (personnel, for example) by attrition. **2.** To destroy or kill (troops, for example) by firepower. [Back-formation < ATTRITION.]

at•tri•tion (ə-trĭsh′ən) *n.* **1.** A rubbing away or wearing down by friction. **2.** A gradual diminution in number or strength because of constant stress. **3.** A gradual reduction in membership or personnel, as through retirement or death. **4.** Repentance for sin motivated by fear of punishment rather than by love of God. [ME *atricioun*, regret, breaking < OFr. *attrition*, abrasion < LLat. *attrītiō*, *attrītiōn-*, act of rubbing against < Lat. *attrītus*, p. part. of *atterere*, to rub against : *ad-*, against; see AD– + *terere*, to rub; see **terə-**[1] in App.] **—at•tri′tion•al** *adj.*

At•tu (ăt′to͞o′) An island of SW AK in the Aleutian Is.

At•tucks (ăt′əks), **Crispus** 1723?–70. Amer. patriot killed in the Boston Massacre.

at•tune (ə-to͞on′, ə-tyo͞on′) *tr.v.* **-tuned, -tun•ing, -tunes 1.** To bring into a harmonious or responsive relationship: *is attuned to market demands.* **2.** *Music* To tune (an instrument).

Atty. *abbr.* attorney

Atty. Gen. *abbr.* Attorney General

a•twit•ter (ə-twĭt′ər) *adj.* Being in a state of nervous excitement; twittering: *a crowd atwitter with expectation.*

At•wood (ăt′wo͝od′), **Margaret Eleanor** b. 1939. Canadian writer known esp. for her novels, including *The Handmaid's Tale* (1985).

at. wt. *abbr.* atomic weight

a•typ•i•cal (ā-tĭp′ĭ-kəl) also **a•typ•ic** (-ĭk) *adj.* Not conforming to type; unusual or irregular. **—a′typ•i•cal′i•ty** (-kăl′ĭ-tē) *n.* **—a•typ′i•cal•ly** *adv.*

Au The symbol for the element **gold** 1a. [< Lat. *aurum*, gold.]

AU *abbr.* astronomical unit

A.U. or **a.u.** *abbr.* angstrom unit

au•bade (ō-bäd′) *n.* **1.** A song or instrumental composition concerning or evoking daybreak. **2.** A poem or song of or about lovers separating at dawn. [Fr. < OFr. *albade* < O Provençal *albada* < *alba*, dawn, aubade < Lat., fem. of *albus*, white. See **albho-** in App.]

Aube (ōb) A river of NE France flowing c. 225 km (140 mi) to the Seine R. NNW of Troyes.

au•ber•gine (ō′bĕr-zhēn′, ō′bər-jēn) *n.* See **eggplant** 1. [Fr. < Catalan *albergína* < Ar. *al-bāḏinjān*, the eggplant : *al-*, the + Pers. *bādenjān*, *bādengān*, eggplant.]

Au•brey (ô′brē), **John** 1626–97. English antiquarian best known for his *Brief Lives,* published posthumously.

au•burn (ô′bərn) *n.* A moderate reddish brown to brown. [ME < OFr. *auborne*, blond < Lat. *alburnus*, whitish < *albus*, white. See **albho-** in App.] **—au′burn** *adj.*

Au•bus•son (ō′bə-sən, -sôN′) *n.* A tapestry or carpet woven in Aubusson, a city of central France, or similar to the ones made there.

A.U.C. *abbr. Latin* **1.** ab urbe condita (from the founding of the city [of Rome, traditionally regarded as 753 B.C.]) **2.** anno urbis conditae (in the year from the founding of the city [of Rome, traditionally regarded as 753 B.C.])

Auck•land (ôk′lənd) A city of New Zealand on an isthmus of NW North I. Pop. 316,900.

au cou•rant (ō′ ko͞o-räN′) *adj.* Fully informed on current affairs; up-to-date. [Fr. : *au*, in the + *courant*, current.]

auc•tion (ôk′shən) *n.* **1.** A public sale in which property or goods are sold to the highest bidder. **2.** *Games* The bidding in bridge. ❖ *tr.v.* **-tioned, -tion•ing, -tions** To sell at or by an auction: *auctioned off the inventory.* [Lat. *auctiō*, *auctiōn-* < *auctus*, p. part. of *augēre*, to increase.]

auction bridge *n.* A variety of bridge in which tricks made in excess of the contract are scored toward game.

auc•tion•eer (ôk′shə-nîr′) *n.* One that conducts an auction. ❖ *tr.v.* **-eered, -eer•ing, -eers** To sell at auction.

auc•to•ri•al (ôk-tôr′ē-əl, -tōr′-) *adj.* Of or relating to an author. [< Lat. *auctor*, author. See AUTHOR.]

au•cu•ba (ô′kyə-bə) *n.* Any of several Asian evergreen shrubs of the genus *Aucuba*, esp. *A. japonica*, grown as an ornamental. [NLat. *Aucuba*, genus name : poss. < J. *auku*, green + J. *ba*, leaved.]

au•da•cious (ô-dā′shəs) *adj.* **1.** Fearlessly, often recklessly daring; bold. See Syns at **brave. 2.** Unrestrained by propriety; insolent. **3.** Spirited and original. [Fr. *audacieux* < OFr. *audace*, boldness < Lat. *audācia* < *audāx*, *audāc-*, bold < *audēre*, to dare < *avidus*, avid. See AVID.] **—au•da′cious•ly** *adv.* **—au•da′cious•ness** *n.*

au•dac•i•ty (ô-dăs′ĭ-tē) *n., pl.* **-ties 1.** Fearless daring; intrepidity. **2.** Bold or insolent heedlessness of restraints, as of those imposed by propriety. **3.** An act or instance of intrepidity or insolent heedlessness.

Au•den (ôd′n), **W(ystan) H(ugh)** 1907–73. British-born Amer. poet whose works include *The Dance of Death* (1933).

au•di•ble (ô′də-bəl) *adj.* That is heard or that can be heard. ❖ *n. Football* An offensive play or a defensive formation called at the line of scrimmage. [LLat. *audībilis* < Lat. *audīre*, to hear.] **—au′di•bil′i•ty, au′di•ble•ness** *n.* **—au′di•bly** *adv.*

au•di•ence (ô′dē-əns) *n.* **1a.** Those assembled at a performance, for example, or attracted by a radio or television program. **b.** The readership for printed matter. **2.** A body of adherents; a following. **3.** A formal hearing, as with a state dignitary. **4.** An opportunity to be heard or to express one's views. **5.** The act of hearing or attending. [ME < OFr. < Lat. *audientia* < *audiēns*, *audient-*, pr. part. of *audīre*, to hear.]

au•dile (ô′dīl′) *adj.* Of or relating to hearing; auditory. [< Lat. *audīre*, to hear. See **au-** in App.]

au•di•o (ô′dē-ō′) *adj.* **1.** Of or relating to humanly audible sound. **2.** Of or relating to the broadcasting, reception, or reproduction of sound. ❖ *n., pl.* **-di•os 1.** The part of television or movie equipment that has to do with sound. **2.** The broadcasting, reception, or reproduction of sound. **3.** Audible sound. **4.** A sound signal. [< AUDIO–.]

audio– *pref.* **1.** Hearing: *audio-lingual.* **2.** Sound: *audiophile.* [< Lat. *audīre*, to hear. See **au-** in App.]

audio frequency *n.* A range of frequencies, usu. from 15 hertz to 20,000 hertz, audible to the normal human ear.

au•di•o•gram (ô′dē-ə-grăm′) *n.* A graphic record of hearing ability for sound frequencies, used to measure hearing loss.

au•di•o-lin•gual (ô′dē-ō-lĭng′gwəl) *adj.* Relating to a system of language acquisition that stresses speaking and listening.

au•di•ol•o•gy (ô′dē-ŏl′ə-jē) *n.* The study of hearing, esp. hearing defects and their treatment. **—au′di•o•log′i•cal** (-ə-lŏj′ĭ-kəl) *adj.* **—au′di•ol′o•gist** *n.*

au•di•om•e•ter (ô′dē-ŏm′ĭ-tər) *n.* An instrument for measuring hearing activity for tones of normally audible frequencies. **—au′di•o•met′ric** (-ō-mĕt′rĭk) *adj.* **—au′di•om′e•try** *n.*

au•di•o•phile (ô′dē-ə-fīl′) *n.* A person having an ardent interest in stereo or high-fidelity sound reproduction.

au•di•o•spec•trog•ra•phy (ô′dē-ō-spĕk-trŏg′rə-fē) *n.* See **acoustic spectrography.**

au•di•o•tape (ô′dē-ō-tāp′) *n.* **1.** A relatively narrow magnetic tape used to record sound for subsequent playback. **2.** A tape recording of sound. ❖ *tr.v.* **-taped, -tap•ing, -tapes** To record (sound) on magnetic tape.

au•di•o-vis•u•al also **au•di•o•vis•u•al** (ô′dē-ō-vĭzh′o͞o-əl) *adj.* **1.** Both audible and visible. **2.** Of or relating to materials, such as films, that present information in audible and pictorial form. ❖ *n.* An aid, other than printed matter, that uses sight or sound to present information.

au•dit (ô′dĭt) *n.* **1.** An examination of records or financial accounts to check their accuracy. **2.** An adjustment or correction of accounts. **3.** An examined and verified account. ❖ *v.* **-dit•ed, -dit•ing, -dits** *—tr.* **1.** To examine, verify, or correct the financial accounts of. **2.** To attend (a course) without requesting or receiving academic credit. *—intr.* To examine financial accounts. [ME (influenced by *auditor*, auditor) < Lat. *audītus*, a hearing < p. part. of *audīre*, to hear.]

au•di•tion (ô-dĭsh′ən) *n.* **1.** A trial performance, as by an actor, to demonstrate suitability or skill. **2.** The sense or power of hearing. **3.** The act of hearing. ❖ *v.* **-tioned, -tion•ing, -tions** *—intr.* To take part in an audition: *auditioned for the lead role.* *—tr.* To evaluate (a person) in an audition. [Lat. *audītiō*, *audītiōn-* < *audītus*, p. part. of *audīre*, to hear.]

au•di•tive (ô′dĭ-tĭv) *adj.* Of or relating to hearing; auditory.

au•di•tor (ô′dĭ-tər) *n.* **1.** One that audits accounts. **2.** One who audits a course. **3.** One who hears; a listener. [ME < AN *auditour* < Lat. *audītor*, listener < *audīre*, to hear.]

au•di•to•ri•um (ô′dĭ-tôr′ē-əm, -tōr′-) *n., pl.* **-ri•ums** or **-ri•a** (-tôr′ē-ə, -tōr′-) **1.** A large room to accommodate an audience in a building. **2.** A large building for public meetings or performances. [Lat. < *audīre*, to hear.]

au•di•to•ry (ô′dĭ-tôr′ē, -tōr′ē) *adj.* Of or relating to hearing, the organs of hearing, or the sense of hearing. [LLat. *audītōrius* < Lat. *audīre*, to hear.]

auditory nerve *n.* Either of the eighth pair of cranial nerves that divides to form the cochlear nerve and the vestibular nerve.

Au•du•bon (ô′də-bŏn′, -bən), **John James** 1785–1851. Haitian-born Amer. ornithologist and artist best known for *The Birds of America* (1827–38).

Auf•klä•rung (ouf′klā′ro͝ong) *n.* The Enlightenment. [Ger. : *auf*, up (< MHGer. *ūf* < OHGer.; see **upo** in App.) + *Klärung*, a making clear (< *klären*, to make clear < MHGer. *klæren* < *klār*, clear < Lat. *clārus*; see CLEAR).]

auf Wie•der•seh•en (ouf vē′dər-zā′ən) *interj.* Used to express farewell. [Ger. : *auf*, until + *Wiedersehen*, seeing again.]

aug. *abbr.* augmentative

Aug. *abbr.* August

Au•ge•an (ô-jē′ən) *adj.* **1.** Exceedingly filthy from long neglect. **2.** Requiring heroic efforts of cleaning or correction. [After *Augeas*, legendary Greek king who did not clean his stable for 30 years.]

au•gend (ô′jĕnd′) *n.* A quantity to which the addend is added. [Lat. *augendum*, a thing to be increased < neut. gerundive of *augēre*, to increase.]

au•ger (ô′gər) *n.* **1a.** Any of various hand tools, typically having a threaded shank and cross handle, used for boring holes in wood or ice. **b.** A drill bit. **2a.** A machine having a rotating helical shaft for boring into the earth. **b.** A rotating helical shaft used to convey material, as in a snow blower. ❖ *tr.v.* **-gered, -ger•ing, -gers**

auger
industrial auger

ă pat	oi boy
ā pay	ou out
âr care	o͝o took
ä father	o͞o boot
ĕ pet	ŭ cut
ē be	ûr urge
ĭ pit	th thin
ī pie	*th* this
îr pier	hw which
ŏ pot	zh vision
ō toe	ə about, item
ô paw	

Stress marks:
′ (primary);
′ (secondary), as in
lexicon (lĕk′sĭ-kŏn′)

To drill or bore using an auger. [ME < *an auger*, alteration of *a nauger* < OE *nafogār*, auger. See **nobh-** in App.]

aught¹ also **ought** (ôt) *pron.* Anything whatever: *"Neither of his parents had aught but praise for him"* (Louis Auchincloss). ❖ *adv.* Archaic In any respect; at all. [ME < OE *āuht.* See **aiw-** in App.]

aught² also **ought** (ôt) *n.* **1.** A cipher; zero. **2.** Archaic Nothing. [< *an aught*, alteration of *a naught.* See NAUGHT.]

au·gite (ô′jīt′) *n.* A dark-green to black pyroxene mineral, (Ca,Na)(Mg,Fe,Al)(Si,Al)₂O₆, that contains large amounts of aluminum, iron, and magnesium. [Lat. *augītēs,* a precious stone < Gk. *augītēs* < *augē,* brightness.]

aug·ment (ôg-mĕnt′) *v.* **-ment·ed, -ment·ing, -ments** —*tr.* **1.** To make (something already developed or well under way) greater, as in size or extent: *Rain augmented the floodwaters.* **2.** *Linguistics* To add an augment to. —*intr.* To become augmented. See Syns at **increase.** ❖ *n.* (ôg′mĕnt′) *Linguistics* The prefixation of a vowel accompanying a past tense, esp. of Greek and Sanskrit verbs. [ME *augmenten* < OFr. *augmenter* < LLat. *augmentāre* < Lat. *augmentum,* an increase < *augēre,* to increase.] —**aug·ment′a·ble** *adj.* —**aug·ment′er** *n.*

aug·men·ta·tion (ôg′mĕn-tā′shən) *n.* **1.** The act or process of augmenting. **2.** The condition of being augmented. **3.** Something that augments. **4.** *Music* The presentation of a theme in notes of usu. double time value.

aug·men·ta·tive (ôg-mĕn′tə-tĭv) *adj.* **1.** Having the ability or tendency to augment. **2.** *Grammar* Increasing the size, force, or intensity of the meaning of an adjacent word, as *up* does in *eat up.* ❖ *n. Grammar* An augmentative word.

aug·ment·ed (ôg-mĕn′tĭd) *adj. Music* Larger by a semitone than the corresponding major or perfect interval.

au gra·tin (ō grät′n, grăt′n, grä-tăn′) *adj.* Covered with bread crumbs and sometimes butter and grated cheese and then browned in an oven. [Fr. : *au,* with the + *gratin,* scraping from the pan.]

Augs·burg (ôgz′bûrg′, ouks′bŏŏrk′) A city of S Germany WNW of Munich; founded c. 14 B.C. Pop. 264,764.

au·gur (ô′gər) *n.* **1.** One of a group of ancient Roman religious officials who foretold events by interpreting signs and omens. **2.** A seer or prophet; a soothsayer. ❖ *v.* **-gured, -gur·ing, -gurs** —*tr.* **1.** To predict, esp. from signs or omens; foretell. **2.** To serve as an omen of; betoken. —*intr.* **1.** To make predictions from signs or omens. **2.** To be a sign or omen. [ME < Lat.] —**au′gu·ral** (ô′gyə-rəl) *adj.*

au·gu·ry (ô′gyə-rē) *n., pl.* **-ries 1.** The art, ability, or practice of auguring; divination. **2.** A sign of something coming; an omen. [ME *augurie* < OFr. < Lat. *augurium* < *augur,* augur.]

au·gust (ô-gŭst′) *adj.* **1.** Inspiring awe or admiration; majestic. See Syns at **grand. 2.** Venerable because of age or rank. [Lat. *augustus.*] —**au·gust′ly** *adv.* —**au·gust′ness** *n.*

Au·gust (ô′gəst) *n.* The eighth month of the year in the Gregorian calendar. See table at **calendar.** [ME < OE < Lat. (*mēnsis*) *Augustus,* (month) of Augustus, after AUGUSTUS.]

Au·gus·ta (ô-gŭs′tə, ə-gŭs′-) **1.** A city of E GA on the SC border NNW of Savannah. Pop. 199,775. **2.** The cap. of ME, in the SW part on the Kennebec R. NNE of Portland; first settled in 1628. Pop. 18,560.

Au·gus·tan (ô-gŭs′tən) *adj.* **1.** Of or characteristic of Augustus or his reign or times. **2.** Of or characteristic of English literature during the early 18th century. —**Au·gus′tan** *n.*

Au·gus·tine¹ (ô′gə-stēn′, ô-gŭs′tĭn), Saint. A.D. 354–430. Early Christian church father and philosopher who profoundly influenced Christianity in his writings, esp. *Confessions* (397) and *City of God* (413–426), and served (396–430) as the bishop of Hippo.

Au·gus·tine² (ô′gə-stēn′, ô-gŭs′tĭn) also **Aus·tin** (ô′stən), Saint. Called "Apostle of the English." d. c. 604. Italian-born missionary and first archbishop of Canterbury (ordained 598).

Au·gus·tin·i·an (ô′gə-stĭn′ē-ən) *adj.* **1.** Of or relating to Saint Augustine of Hippo or his doctrines. **2.** Of or being any religious order following or influenced by the rule of Saint Augustine. ❖ *n.* **1.** A follower of the principles and doctrines of Saint Augustine. **2.** A monk or friar of an Augustinian order. —**Au′gus·tin′i·an·ism, Au·gus′tin·ism** (ô-gŭs′tĭ-nĭz′əm) *n.*

Au·gus·tus (ô-gŭs′təs) Orig. Octavian. 63 B.C.–A.D. 14. First emperor of Rome (27 B.C.–A.D. 14).

au jus (ō zhōōs′, zhŭ′) *adj.* Served with the natural juices or gravy: *roast beef au jus.* [Fr. : *au,* with the + *jus,* juice.]

auk (ôk) *n.* Any of several northern diving sea birds in the family Alcidae, such as the razor-billed auk, having a chunky body, short wings, and webbed feet. [Norw. *alk* < ON *ālka.*]

auk·let (ôk′lĭt) *n.* Any of various small auks of the genus *Aethia* and related genera of northern Pacific coasts and waters.

auld (ôld) *adj. Scots* Old.

auld lang syne (ôld′ lăng zīn′, sīn′) *n.* The times gone past; the good old days. [Sc. : *auld,* old + *lang,* long + *syne,* since.]

Aum (ōm) *n. Hinduism & Buddhism* Variant of **Om².**

au na·tu·rel (ō′ năch′ə-rĕl′, ō′ nä-tü-rĕl′) *adj.* **1a.** Nude. **b.** In a natural state: *an au naturel hairstyle.* **2.** Cooked simply. [Fr. : *au,* in the + *naturel,* natural (state).]

Aung San Suu Kyi (ông′ săn′ sōō′ chē′) b. 1945. Burmese political leader who won the 1991 Nobel Peace Prize.

Au·nis (ō-nēs′) A historical region and former province of W

Augustus
depicted in a cameo, a
detail from the Cross of
Lothar

Aung San Suu Kyi

aurora borealis

France on the Atlantic Ocean; became part of the crown lands in 1373.

aunt (ănt, änt) *n.* **1.** The sister of one's father or mother. **2.** The wife of one's uncle. **3.** Used as a form of address for an older woman, esp. by children. [ME *aunte* < AN < Lat. *amita,* paternal aunt.] —**aunt′hood** *n.*

aunt·ie also **aunt·y** (ăn′tē, än′-) *n., pl.* **-ies** *Informal* Aunt.

au pair (ō pâr′) *n.* A young foreigner who does domestic work for a family in exchange for room and board and a chance to learn the family's language. [Fr. : *au,* at the + *pair,* equal.]

au·ra (ôr′ə) *n., pl.* **au·ras** or **au·rae** (ôr′ē) **1.** An invisible breath, emanation, or radiation. **2.** A distinctive but intangible quality that seems to surround a person or thing; atmosphere. **3.** *Pathology* A sensation that precedes the onset of certain disorders, such as an attack of migraine. [ME, gentle breeze < Lat. < Gk. *aurā,* breath.]

au·ral¹ (ôr′əl) *adj.* Of, relating to, or perceived by the ear. [< Lat. *auris,* ear. See **ous-** in App.] —**au′ral·ly** *adv.*

au·ral² (ôr′əl) *adj.* Characterized by or relating to an aura.

Au·rang·a·bad (ou-rŭng′gə-bäd′, -ə-bäd′) A town of W India ENE of Mumbai (Bombay); founded 1610. Pop. 573,272.

Au·rang·zeb also **Au·rung·zeb** (ôr′əng-zĕb′) 1618–1707. Hindustani emperor (1658–1707) who expanded the empire.

au·re·ate (ôr′ē-ĭt) *adj.* **1.** Of a golden color; gilded. **2.** Inflated and pompous in style. [ME *aureat* < LLat. *aureātus* < *aureus,* golden < *aurum,* gold.]

Au·re·lian (ô-rēl′yən, ô-rē′lē-ən) Orig. Lucius Domitius Aurelianus. A.D. 212?–275. Emperor of Rome (270–275) who regained Britain, Gaul, Spain, Syria, and Egypt for the empire.

au·re·ole (ôr′ē-ōl′) also **au·re·o·la** (ô-rē′ə-lə) *n.* **1.** A circle of light or radiance surrounding the head or body of a representation of a deity or holy person; a halo. **2.** *Astronomy* See **corona** 1a. [ME < LLat. (*corōna*) *aureola,* golden (crown), fem. of Lat. *aureolus,* golden < *aureus* < *aurum,* gold.]

Au·re·o·my·cin (ôr′ē-ō-mī′sĭn) A trademark used for chlortetracycline.

au re·voir (ō′ rə-vwär′) *interj.* Used to express farewell. [Fr. : *au,* till the + *revoir,* seeing again.]

au·ric (ôr′ĭk) *adj.* Of, relating to, derived from, or containing gold, esp. with valence 3. [< Lat. *aurum,* gold.]

au·ri·cle (ôr′ĭ-kəl) *n.* **1.** *Anatomy* **a.** The outer projecting portion of the ear. **b.** See **atrium** 2. **2.** *Biology* An earlobe-shaped part, process, or appendage, esp. at the base of an organ. [ME, auricle of the heart < OFr., little ear < Lat. *auricula,* ear, earlier dim. of *auris,* ear. See **ous-** in App.] —**au′ri·cled** (-kəld) *adj.*

au·ric·u·la (ô-rĭk′yə-lə) *n., pl.* **-las** or **-lae** (-lē′) **1.** A central European primrose (*Primula auricula*) having large yellow flowers grouped in umbels. **2.** Any of numerous hybrids of this species with other primroses. [Lat., auricle. See AURICLE.]

au·ric·u·lar (ô-rĭk′yə-lər) *adj.* **1.** Of or relating to the sense of hearing or the organs of hearing. **2.** Perceived by or spoken into the ear. **3.** Shaped like an ear or an earlobe; having earlike parts or extensions. **4.** Of or relating to an auricle of the heart. [ME *auriculer,* spoken into the ear < LLat. *auriculāris* < Lat. *auricula,* ear. See AURICLE.] —**au·ric′u·lar·ly** *adv.*

au·ric·u·late (ô-rĭk′yə-lĭt, -lāt′) also **au·ric·u·lat·ed** (-lāt′ĭd) *adj.* **1.** Having ears, auricles, or earlobe-shaped parts or extensions. **2.** Shaped like an earlobe. [< Lat. *auricula,* auricle. See AURICLE.] —**au·ric′u·late·ly** *adv.*

au·rif·er·ous (ô-rĭf′ər-əs) *adj.* Containing gold; gold-bearing. [< Lat. *aurifer,* gold-bearing : *aurum,* gold + *-fer,* -fer.]

au·ri·form (ôr′ə-fôrm′) *adj.* Shaped like an ear. [Lat. *auris,* ear; see **ous-** in App. + -FORM.]

Au·ri·ga (ô-rī′gə) *n.* A constellation in the Northern Hemisphere near Lynx and Perseus that contains the bright star Capella. [Lat. *aurīga,* charioteer, Auriga. See **ōs-** in App.]

Au·ri·gnac (ôr′ēn-yäk′) A village of S France at the foot of the Pyrenees; site of caves containing prehistoric relics.

Au·rig·na·cian (ôr′ĭg-nā′shən, ôr′ēn-yā′-) *adj.* Of or relating to the Old World Upper Paleolithic culture between Mousterian and Solutrean, associated with early *Homo sapiens.* [After AURIGNAC.]

au·rochs (ou′rŏks′, ôr′ŏks′) *n., pl.* **aurochs 1.** See **urus.** 2. See **wisent.** [Obsolete Ger., var. of Ger. *Auerochs* < MHGer. *ūrohse* < OHGer. *ūrohso* : *ūro,* aurochs + *ohso,* ox; see **uks-en-** in App.]

au·ro·ra (ə-rôr′ə, ə-rōr′ə) *n., pl.* **-ras** or **-rae** (ə-rôr′ē, ə-rōr′ē) **1.** A luminous atmospheric phenomenon sometimes visible in the night sky in northern or southern regions of the earth and thought to be caused by charged particles from the sun entering the earth's magnetic field. **2.** The dawn. [ME, dawn < Lat. *aurōra.* See **aus-** in App.] —**au·ro′ral, au·ro′re·an** (-ē-ən) *adj.* —**au·ro′ral·ly** *adv.*

Aurora¹ *n. Roman Mythology* The goddess of the dawn. [Lat. *Aurōra.* See AURORA.]

Aurora² **1.** A city of N-central CO, a suburb of Denver. Pop. 276,393. **2.** A city of NE IL on the Fox R. W of Chicago. Pop. 142,990.

aurora aus·tra·lis (ô-strā′lĭs) *n., pl.* **aurora aus·tra·lis·es** (-lĭ-sĭz′) or **aurorae australis** An aurora that occurs in southern regions of the earth. [NLat. *aurōra austrālis* : Lat. *aurōra,* dawn + Lat. *austrālis,* southern.]

aurora bo·re·al·is (bôr′ē-ăl′ĭs, bŏr′-) *n.*, *pl.* **aurora bo·re·al·is·es** (-ĭ-sĭz) or **aurorae borealis** An aurora that occurs in northern regions of the earth. [NLat. *aurōra boreālis*: Lat. *aurōra*, dawn + Lat. *boreālis*, northern.]

au·rous (ôr′əs) *adj.* Of or relating to gold, esp. with valence 1. [Lat. *aurum*, gold + -OUS.]

Au·rung·zeb (ôr′əng-zĕb′) See Aurangzeb.

AUS *abbr.* Army of the United States

Aus. *abbr.* **1a.** Australia **b.** Australian **2a.** Austria **b.** Austrian

Ausch·witz (oush′vĭts′) See Oświęcim.

aus·cul·tate (ô′skəl-tāt′) *tr.v.* **-tat·ed, -tat·ing, -tates** *Medicine* To examine by auscultation. [Back-formation < AUSCULTATION.] —**aus′cul·ta·tive, aus·cul′ta·to·ry** (ô-skŭl′tə-tôr′ē, -tōr′ē) *adj.*

aus·cul·ta·tion (ô′skəl-tā′shən) *n.* **1.** The act of listening. **2.** *Medicine* The act of listening for sounds made by internal organs to help diagnose certain disorders. [Lat. *auscultātiō, auscultātiōn-* < *auscultātus*, p. part. of *auscultāre*, to listen to. See ous- in App.]

aus·form (ôs′fôrm′) *tr.v.* **-formed, -form·ing, -forms** To subject (esp. steel) to deformation, quenching, and tempering to improve its wear properties. [AUS(TENITIC) + (DE)FORM.]

aus·land·er (ou′slĕn′dər, -slän′-) *n.* A foreigner. [Ger. *Ausländer* < *Ausland*, foreign country : *aus-*, away (< MHGer. *ūz-* < OHGer. < *ūz*, out, away; see ud- in App.) + *Land*, land; see HINTERLAND.]

aus·pex (ô′spĕks′) *n.*, *pl.* **aus·pi·ces** (ô′spĭ-sēz′) An augur of ancient Rome, esp. one who interpreted omens derived from the observation of birds. [Lat. See AUSPICE.]

aus·pi·cate (ô′spĭ-kāt′) *tr.v.* **-cat·ed, -cat·ing, -cates** To begin or inaugurate with a ceremony for good luck. [Lat. *auspicārī, auspicāt-* < *auspex, auspic-*, bird augur. See AUSPICE.]

aus·pice (ô′spĭs) *n.*, *pl.* **aus·pi·ces** (ô′spĭ-sĭz, -sēz′) **1.** Protection or support; patronage. Often used in the plural. **2.** A sign indicative of future prospects; an omen. **3.** Observation of and divination from birds. [Lat. *auspicium*, bird divination, auspices < *auspex, auspic-*, bird augur. See awi- in App.]

aus·pi·cious (ô-spĭsh′əs) *adj.* **1.** Attended by favorable circumstances; propitious. See Syns at favorable. **2.** Successful; prosperous. —**aus·pi′cious·ly** *adv.* —**aus·pi′cious·ness** *n.*

Aus·sie (ô′sē, ô′zē) *n.* *Informal* A native or inhabitant of Australia. [< AUS(TRALIAN).] —**Aus′sie** *adj.*

Aust. *abbr.* **1a.** Australia **b.** Australian **2a.** Austria **b.** Austrian

Aus·ten (ô′stən), Jane 1775–1817. British writer whose novels include *Pride and Prejudice* (1813) and *Emma* (1816).

aus·ten·ite (ô′stə-nīt′) *n.* A nonmagnetic solid solution of ferric carbide or carbon in iron, used in making corrosion-resistant steel. [After Sir William Chandler Roberts-Austen (1843–1902), British metallurgist.] —**aus′ten·it′ic** (-ĭt′ĭk) *adj.*

aus·tere (ô-stîr′) *adj.* **-ter·er, -ter·est 1.** Severe or stern in disposition or appearance; somber and grave: *the austere figure of a Puritan minister.* **2.** Strict or severe in discipline; ascetic: *a desert nomad's austere life.* **3.** Having no adornment or ornamentation; bare. See Syns at severe. [ME < OFr. < Lat. *austērus* < Gk. *austēros*.] —**aus·tere′ly** *adv.* —**aus·tere′ness** *n.*

aus·ter·i·ty (ô-stĕr′ĭ-tē) *n.*, *pl.* **-ties 1.** The quality of being austere. **2.** Severe and rigid economy: *wartime austerity.* **3.** An austere habit or practice.

Aus·ter·litz (ô′stər-lĭts′, ous′tər-) A town of S Czech Republic; site of Napoleon's decisive defeat of the Russian and Austrian armies (Dec. 2, 1805).

Aus·tin¹ (ô′stən) See Saint Augustine².

Aus·tin² (ô′stən, ŏs′tən) The cap. of TX, in the S-central part; chosen as cap. in 1870. Pop. 656,562.

Aus·tin³ (ô′stən, ŏs′tən), **Stephen Fuller** 1793–1836. Amer. colonizer who helped Texas gain its independence from Mexico (1836).

Austl. *abbr.* Australia

aus·tral (ô′strəl) *adj.* Of, relating to, or coming from the south. [Lat. *austrālis* < *auster, austr-*, south.]

Aus·tral·a·sia (ô′strə-lā′zhə, -shə) **1.** The islands of the S Pacific, including Australia, New Zealand, and New Guinea. **2.** Broadly, all of Oceania. —**Aus′tral·a′sian** *adj. & n.*

Aus·tra·lia (ô-strāl′yə) **1.** The world's smallest continent, SE of Asia between the Pacific and Indian oceans. **2.** A commonwealth comprising the continent of Australia, Tasmania, two external territories, and several dependencies; first formed as a federation in 1901. Cap. Canberra. Pop. 17,843,000.

Aus·tra·lian (ô-strāl′yən) *adj.* **1.** Of or relating to Australia or its peoples, languages, or cultures. **2.** *Ecology* Of, relating to, or being the zoogeographic region that includes Australia and the islands adjacent to it. ❖ *n.* **1.** A native or inhabitant of Australia. **2.** A member of the Aboriginal peoples of Australia. **3.** Any of the languages of the Aboriginal peoples of Australia.

Australian Alps A chain of mountain ranges of SE Australia in the Great Dividing Range, rising to 2,231.4 m (7,316 ft).

Australian ballot *n.* A printed ballot that bears the names of all candidates and the texts of propositions and is distributed to the voter at the polls and marked in secret.

Australian crawl *n.* A crawl stroke in swimming that is executed with a flutter kick to each arm stroke.

Australian terrier *n.* A small dog of a breed originally bred in

Australia, having a coarse blackish coat with tan markings.

Aus·tra·loid (ô′strə-loid′) *adj. Anthropology* Of or being a human racial classification distinguished esp. by dark skin and curly hair and including peoples indigenous to Australia and southeast Asia. [AUSTRAL(IAN) + -OID.] —**Aus′tra·loid′** *n.*

aus·tra·lo·pith·e·cine (ô-strā′lō-pĭth′ĭ-sēn′, -sĭn′) *n.* Any of several extinct humanlike primates of the genus *Australopithecus*, known chiefly from Pleistocene fossil remains found in southern and eastern Africa. [< NLat. *Australopithēcus*, genus name : Lat. *austrālis*, southern; see AUSTRAL + *pithēcus*, ape (< Gk. *pithēkos*).] —**aus·tra′lo·pith′e·cine** *adj.*

Aus·tra·sia (ô-strā′zhə, -shə) The E portion of the kingdom of the Franks from the 6th to the 8th cent., including parts of E France, W Germany, and the Netherlands. —**Aus·tra′sian** *adj. & n.*

Aus·tri·a (ô′strē-ə) A landlocked country of central Europe; orig. a Roman and Carolingian territory and later a powerful empire ruled by the Hapsburgs. Cap. Vienna. Pop. 8,031,000. —**Aus′tri·an** *adj. & n.*

Aus·tri·a-Hun·ga·ry (ô′strē-ə-hŭng′gə-rē) A former dual monarchy (1867–1918) of central Europe consisting of Austria, Hungary, Bohemia, and parts of Poland, Romania, Slovenia, Croatia, and Italy. —**Aus′tro-Hun·gar′i·an** (ô′strō-hŭng-gâr′ē-ən) *adj. & n.*

Austro-¹ *pref.* Southern: *Austro-Asiatic.* [< Lat. *auster, austr-*, south. See aus- in App.]

Austro-² *pref.* Austria; Austrian: *Austro-Hungarian.*

Aus·tro-A·si·at·ic (ô′strō-ā′zhē-ăt′ĭk, -shē-, -zē-) *n.* A family of languages of southeast Asia once dominant in northeast India and Indochina, including Mon-Khmer and Munda. —**Aus′tro-A′si·at′ic** *adj.*

Aus·tro·ne·sia (ô′strō-nē′zhə, -shə) The islands of the Pacific Ocean, including Indonesia, Melanesia, Micronesia, and Polynesia.

Aus·tro·ne·sian (ô′strō-nē′zhən, -shən) *adj.* Of or relating to Austronesia or its peoples, languages, or cultures. ❖ *n.* A family of languages that includes the Formosan, Indonesian, Malay, Melanesian, Micronesian, and Polynesian subfamilies.

aut- *pref.* Variant of **auto-**.

au·ta·coid (ô′tə-koid′) *n.* An organic substance from one part of an organism transported by blood, lymph, or sap to another part where it exerts a physiologic effect. [AUT(O)- + Gk. *akos*, cure + -OID.] —**au′ta·coi′dal** (-koid′l) *adj.*

au·tarch (ô′tärk) *n.* An absolute ruler; a despot. [Gk. *autarkhos*, self-governing, autarch. See AUTARCHY¹.]

au·tar·chy¹ (ô′tär′kē) *n.*, *pl.* **-chies 1.** Absolute rule or power; autocracy. **2.** A country under such rule. [< Gk. *autarkhos*, self-governing, autarch : *auto-*, auto- + *arkhos*, ruler (< *arkhein*, to rule).] —**au·tar′chic** (-kĭk), **au·tar′chi·cal** *adj.*

au·tar·chy² (ô′tär′kē) *n.* Variant of **autarky**.

au·tar·ky or **au·tar·chy** (ô′tär′kē) *n.*, *pl.* **-kies** or **-chies 1.** A policy of national self-sufficiency and nonreliance on imports or economic aid. **2.** A self-sufficient region or country. [Gk. *autarkeia*, self-sufficiency < *autarkēs*, self-sufficient : *auto-*, auto- + *arkein*, to suffice.] —**au·tar′kic, au·tar′ki·cal** *adj.*

au·te·col·o·gy (ô′tĭ-kŏl′ə-jē) *n.* The branch of ecology that studies the biological relationship between an individual organism or species and its environment. —**au′te·co·log′i·cal** (-kə-lŏj′ĭ-kəl) *adj.*

au·teur (ō-tûr′) *n.* A filmmaker, usu. a director, who exercises creative control and has a strong personal style. [Fr. < OFr. *autor*, author. See AUTHOR.] —**au·teur′ist** *adj. & n.*

au·teur·ism (ō-tûr′ĭz′əm) *n.* See auteur theory.

auteur theory *n.* Belief in the primary creative importance of the director in filmmaking.

au·then·tic (ô-thĕn′tĭk) *adj.* **1.** Conforming to fact and therefore worthy of trust, reliance, or belief. **2.** Having a claimed and verifiable origin or authorship; not counterfeit or copied. **3.** *Music* **a.** Of or being a medieval mode having a range from its final tone to the octave above it. **b.** Of or being a cadence with the dominant chord immediately preceding the tonic chord. **4.** *Obsolete* Authoritative. [ME *autentik* < OFr. *autentique* < LLat. *authenticus* < Gk. *authentikos* < *authentēs*, author.] —**au·then′ti·cal·ly** *adv.*

au·then·ti·cate (ô-thĕn′tĭ-kāt′) *tr.v.* **-cat·ed, -cat·ing, -cates** To establish the authenticity of; prove genuine. —**au·then′ti·ca′tion** *n.* —**au·then′ti·ca′tor** *n.*

au·then·tic·i·ty (ô′thĕn-tĭs′ĭ-tē) *n.* The quality or condition of being authentic, trustworthy, or genuine.

au·thor (ô′thər) *n.* **1a.** The original writer of a literary work. **b.** One who writes professionally. **2.** An originator or creator. **3.** **Author** God. ❖ *tr.v.* **-thored, -thor·ing, -thors** To assume responsibility for the content of (a published or an unpublished text). [ME *auctour* < OFr. *autor* < Lat. *auctor*, creator < *auctus*, p. part. of *augēre*, to create.] —**au·thor′i·al** (ô-thôr′ē-əl, ô-thŏr′-) *adj.*

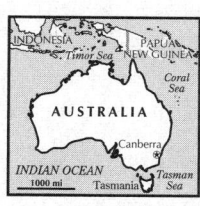

Australia

Austria

ă	pat	oi	boy
ā	pay	ou	out
âr	care	ŏŏ	took
ä	father	ōō	boot
ĕ	pet	ŭ	cut
ē	be	ûr	urge
ĭ	pit	th	thin
ī	pie	th	this
îr	pier	hw	which
ŏ	pot	zh	vision
ō	toe	ə	about,
ô	paw		item

Stress marks:
′ (primary);
′ (secondary), as in
lexicon (lĕk′sĭ-kŏn′)

au·thor·i·tar·i·an (ə-thôr′ĭ-târ′ē-ən, ə-thŏr′-, ô-thôr′-, ô-thŏr′-) *adj.* **1.** Characterized by or favoring absolute obedience to authority, as against individual freedom. **2.** Of, relating to, or expecting unquestioning obedience. —**au·thor′i·tar′i·an** *n.* —**au·thor′i·tar′i·an·ism** *n.*

au·thor·i·ta·tive (ə-thôr′ĭ-tā′tĭv, ə-thŏr′-, ô-thôr′-, ô-thŏr′-) *adj.* **1.** Having or arising from authority; official. **2.** Known to be accurate or excellent; highly reliable. **3.** Wielding authority; commanding. —**au·thor′i·ta′tive·ly** *adv.* —**au·thor′i·ta′tive·ness** *n.*

au·thor·i·ty (ə-thôr′ĭ-tē, ə-thŏr′-, ô-thôr′-, ô-thŏr′-) *n., pl.* **-ties 1a.** The power to enforce laws, exact obedience, command, determine, or judge. **b.** One that is invested with this power, esp. a government or body of government officials: *land titles issued by the civil authority.* **2.** Power assigned to another; authorization: *Deputies were given authority to make arrests.* **3.** A public agency or corporation with administrative powers in a specified field: *a city transit authority.* **4a.** An accepted source of expert information or advice: *a noted authority on birds.* **b.** A quotation or citation from such a source: *biblical authorities for a moral argument.* **5.** Justification; grounds: *On what authority do you make such a claim?* **6.** A conclusive statement or decision that may be taken as a guide or precedent. **7.** Power to influence or persuade resulting from knowledge or experience. **8.** Confidence derived from experience or practice; firm self-assurance. [ME *auctorite* < OFr. *autorite* < Lat. *auctōritās, auctōritāt-* < *auctor,* creator. See AUTHOR.]

au·thor·i·za·tion (ô′thər-ĭ-zā′shən) *n.* **1.** The act of authorizing. **2.** Something that authorizes; a sanction.

au·thor·ize (ô′thə-rīz′) *tr.v.* **-ized, -iz·ing, -iz·es 1.** To grant authority or power to. **2.** To give permission for; sanction. **3.** To be sufficient grounds for; justify. [ME *auctorisen* < OFr. *autoriser* < Med.Lat. *auctōrizāre* < Lat. *auctor,* author. See AUTHOR.] —**au′thor·iz′er** *n.*

Au·thor·ized Version (ô′thə-rīzd′) *n.* See **King James Bible.**

au·thor·ship (ô′thər-shĭp′) *n.* **1.** The act, fact, or occupation of writing. **2.** Source or origin, as of a book or idea.

au·tism (ô′tĭz′əm) *n.* A psychiatric disorder of childhood characterized by marked deficits in communication and social interaction, preoccupation with fantasy, and abnormal behavior patterns. —**au′tist** *n.* —**au·tis′tic** (-tĭk) *adj. & n.* —**au·tis′ti·cal·ly** *adv.*

au·to (ô′tō) *n., pl.* **-tos** An automobile. ❖ *intr.v.* **-toed, -to·ing, -tos** To go by or ride in a car. [Short for AUTOMOBILE.]

auto– or **aut–** *pref.* **1.** Self; same: *autogamy.* **2.** Automatic: *autopilot.* [Gk. < *autos,* self.]

au·to·an·ti·bod·y (ô′tō-ăn′tĭ-bŏd′ē) *n.* An antibody that reacts with the cells, tissues, or native proteins of the organism in which it is formed.

au·to·bahn (ô′tə-bän′, ou′tō-) *n.* An expressway in Germany and German-speaking countries. [Ger. : *Auto,* automobile; see AUTO + *Bahn,* road < MHGer. *ban.* See gʷhen- in App.]

au·to·bi·og·ra·phy (ô′tō-bī-ŏg′rə-fē) *n., pl.* **-phies** The biography of a person by that person. —**au′to·bi′o·graph′ic** (-bī′ə-grăf′ĭk), **au′to·bi′o·graph′i·cal** *adj.* —**au′to·bi′o·graph′i·cal·ly** *adv.*

au·to·bus (ô′tō-bŭs′) *n., pl.* **-bus·es** or **-bus·ses** A motor coach; a bus.

au·to·ca·tal·y·sis (ô′tō-kə-tăl′ĭ-sĭs) *n., pl.* **-ses** (-sēz′) Catalysis of a chemical reaction by one of the products of the reaction. —**au′to·cat′a·lyt′ic** (-kăt′l-ĭt′ĭk) *adj.* —**au′to·cat′a·lyt′i·cal·ly** *adv.*

au·toch·thon (ô-tŏk′thən) *n., pl.* **-thons** or **-tho·nes** (-thə-nēz′) **1.** One of the earliest known inhabitants of a place; an aborigine. **2.** *Ecology* An indigenous plant or animal. [Gk. *autokhthōn* : *auto-,* auto- + *khthōn,* earth; see **dhghem-** in App.]

au·toch·tho·nous (ô-tŏk′thə-nəs) also **au·toch·tho·nal** (-thə-nəl) or **au·toch·thon·ic** (ô′tŏk-thŏn′ĭk) *adj.* **1.** Originating where found; indigenous. **2.** *Biology* Originating or formed in the place where found. —**au·toch′thon·ism, au·toch′tho·ny** *n.* —**au·toch′tho·nous·ly** *adv.*

au·to·clave (ô′tō-klāv′) *n.* A strong, pressurized, steam-heated vessel, as for sterilization or cooking. [Fr. : Gk. *auto-,* auto- + Lat. *clāvis,* key (< its being self-locking from the pressurization).]

au·toc·ra·cy (ô-tŏk′rə-sē) *n., pl.* **-cies 1.** Government by a single person having unlimited power; despotism. **2.** A country or state governed by a person with unlimited power.

au·to·crat (ô′tə-krăt′) *n.* **1.** A ruler having unlimited power; a despot. **2.** A person with unlimited power or authority: *a corporate autocrat.* [Fr. *autocrate* < Gk. *autokratēs,* ruling by oneself : *auto-,* auto- + *-kratēs,* -crat.] —**au′to·crat′ic, au′to·crat′i·cal** *adj.* —**au′to·crat′i·cal·ly** *adv.*

au·to·da·fé (ô′tō-də-fā′, ou′tō-) *n. pl* **au·tos-da-fé** (ô′tōz-, ou′tōz-) **1.** Public announcement of the sentences imposed by the Inquisition. **2.** The public execution of those sentences by secular authorities, esp. by burning at the stake. [Port. *auto da fé* : *auto,* act + *da,* of the + *fé,* faith.]

au·to·de·struct (ô′tō-dĭ-strŭkt′) *intr.v.* **-struct·ed, -struct·ing, -structs** To destroy itself or oneself; self-destruct. [AUTO- + (SELF-)DESTRUCT.]

au·to·di·dact (ô′tō-dī′dăkt′) *n.* A self-taught person. [< Gk. *autodidaktos,* self-taught : *auto-,* auto- + *didaktos,* taught; see DIDACTIC.] —**au′to·di·dac′tic** *adj.*

au·to·dyne (ô′tə-dīn′) *n.* A heterodyne radio device in which one tube serves simultaneously as oscillator and detector. [AUTO– + (HETERO)DYNE.] —**au′to·dyne′** *adj.*

au·toe·cious (ô-tē′shəs) *adj.* Having all stages of a life cycle occurring on the same host. [< AUTO- + Gk. *oikos,* house; see **weik-** in App.] —**au·toe′cism** (-sĭz′əm) *n.*

autoerotic asphyxia *n.* A form of sexual masochism in which oxygen flow to the brain is reduced, as by controlled strangulation, in order to enhance the pleasure of masturbation.

au·to·er·o·tism (ô′tō-ĕr′ə-tĭz′əm) or **au·to·e·rot·i·cism** (-ĭ-rŏt′ĭ-sĭz′əm) *n.* **1.** Self-satisfaction of sexual desire, as by masturbation. **2.** The arousal of sexual feeling without an external stimulus. —**au′to·e·rot′ic** (-ĭ-rŏt′ĭk) *adj.*

au·tog·a·my (ô-tŏg′ə-mē) *n.* **1.** *Botany* Self-fertilization in plants. **2.** *Biology* The union of nuclei within and arising from a single cell, as in certain protozoans and fungi. —**au′to·gam′ic** (ô′tō-găm′ĭk), **au·tog′a·mous** *adj.*

au·to·gen·e·sis (ô′tō-jĕn′ĭ-sĭs) also **au·tog·e·ny** (ô-tŏj′ə-nē) *n.* See **abiogenesis.** —**au′to·ge·net′ic** (-jə-nĕt′ĭk) *adj.* —**au′to·ge·net′i·cal·ly** *adv.*

au·tog·e·nous (ô-tŏj′ə-nəs) also **au·to·gen·ic** (ô′tə-jĕn′ĭk) *adj.* **1.** Produced from within; self-generating. **2.** *Medicine* Originating with the individual to whom applied: *an autogenous graft.* —**au·tog′e·nous·ly** *adv.*

au·to·gi·ro also **au·to·gy·ro** (ô′tō-jī′rō) *n., pl.* **-ros** An aircraft powered by a conventional propeller and supported in flight by a freewheeling horizontal rotor that provides lift. [Orig. a trademark.]

au·to·graft (ô′tō-grăft′) *n.* A tissue or organ grafted into a new position on the same individual.

au·to·graph (ô′tə-grăf′) *n.* **1.** A person's own signature or handwriting. **2.** A manuscript in the author's handwriting. ❖ *tr.v.* **-graphed, -graph·ing, -graphs 1.** To write one's name or signature on or in; sign. **2.** To write in one's own handwriting. ❖ *adj.* Written in the writer's own handwriting. [LLat. *autographum* < neut. of Lat. *autographus,* written with one's own hand < Gk. *autographos* : *auto-,* auto- + *graphein,* to write; see –GRAPH.] —**au′to·graph′ic, au′to·graph′i·cal** *adj.* —**au′to·graph′i·cal·ly** *adv.*

au·tog·ra·phy (ô-tŏg′rə-fē) *n.* **1.** The writing of something in one's own handwriting. **2.** Autographs considered as a group.

Au·to·harp (ô′tō-härp′) A trademark used for a musical instrument similar to a zither.

au·to·hyp·no·sis (ô′tō-hĭp-nō′sĭs) *n.* **1.** The act or process of hypnotizing oneself. **2.** A self-induced hypnotic state. —**au′to·hyp·not′ic** (-nŏt′ĭk) *adj.*

au·to·im·mune (ô′tō-ĭ-myoon′) *adj.* Of or relating to an immune response by the body against one of its own cells, molecules, or tissues. —**au′to·im·mu′ni·ty** *n.* —**au′to·im·mu′ni·za′tion** (-ĭm′yə-nə-zā′shən) *n.*

au·to·in·fec·tion (ô′tō-ĭn-fĕk′shən) *n.* Infection, such as recurrent boils, caused by bacteria, viruses, or parasites that persist on or in the body.

au·to·in·oc·u·la·tion (ô′tō-ĭ-nŏk′yə-lā′shən) *n.* **1.** Inoculation with a vaccine made from microorganisms obtained from the recipient's body. **2.** An infection by a disease that has spread from a different part of the body. —**au′to·in·oc′u·la·ble** *adj.*

au·to·in·tox·i·ca·tion (ô′tō-ĭn-tŏk′sĭ-kā′shən) *n.* Self-poisoning caused by endogenous microorganisms, metabolic wastes, or other toxins produced within the body.

au·to·load·ing (ô′tō-lō′dĭng) *adj.* Semiautomatic.

au·tol·o·gous (ô-tŏl′ə-gəs) *adj.* Derived or transferred from the same individual's body. [AUTO- + *-logous,* as in HOMOLOGOUS.]

au·tol·y·sate (ô-tŏl′ĭ-sāt′, -zāt′) *n.* An end product of autolysis.

au·tol·y·sin (ô-tŏl′ĭ-sĭn, ô′tə-lī′sĭn) *n.* A substance, such as an enzyme, that is capable of destroying the cells or tissues of an organism within which it is produced.

au·tol·y·sis (ô-tŏl′ĭ-sĭs) *n.* The destruction of tissues or cells of an organism by the action of substances produced within the organism. —**au′to·lyt′ic** (ô′tə-lĭt′ĭk) *adj.*

au·to·mak·er (ô′tō-mā′kər) *n.* A manufacturer of automotive vehicles; a carmaker.

au·to·mate (ô′tə-māt′) *v.* **-mat·ed, -mat·ing, -mates** —*tr.* **1.** To convert to automatic operation: *automate a factory.* **2.** To control or operate by automation. —*intr.* To convert to or make use of automation: *a company that chose to automate for greater efficiency.* [Back-formation < AUTOMATION.] —**au′to·mat′a·ble** *adj.*

au·to·mat·ed teller machine (ô′tə-mā′tĭd) *n.* An unattended computer terminal that provides banking services.

au·to·mat·ic (ô′tə-măt′ĭk) *adj.* **1a.** Acting or operating in a manner essentially independent of external influence or control: *an automatic switch.* **b.** Self-regulating. **2a.** Acting or done without volition or conscious control; involuntary. **b.** Acting or done as if by machine; mechanical: *an automatic reply to a question.* **3a.** Capable of firing continuously until ammunition is exhausted or the trigger is released. **b.** Semiautomatic: *an automatic pistol.* ❖

n. 1. An automatic machine or device. **2a.** An automatic firearm. **b.** A semiautomatic firearm. **3.** A transmission or a motor vehicle with an automatic gear-shifting mechanism. **—idiom: on automatic** Functioning by or as if by automatic machine or device. [< Gk. *automatos* : *auto-*, auto- + *-matos*, willing; see **men-**¹ in App.] **—au′to•mat′i•cal•ly** *adv.* **—au•to•ma•tic′i•ty** (-mə-tĭs′ĭ-tē) *n.*

automatic pilot *n.* **1.** A navigation mechanism, as on an aircraft, that automatically maintains a preset course. **2.** A state of mind in which one acts without deliberate effort or self-awareness.

automatic writing *n.* Writing performed without conscious thought, typically by spontaneous free association or as a spiritual medium.

au•to•ma•tion (ô′tə-mā′shən) *n.* **1.** The automatic operation or control of equipment, a process, or a system. **2.** The techniques and equipment used to achieve automatic operation or control. **3.** The condition of being automatically controlled or operated. [< AUTOMATIC.]

au•tom•a•tism (ô-tŏm′ə-tĭz′əm) *n.* **1a.** The state or quality of being automatic. **b.** Automatic mechanical action. **2.** *Philosophy* The theory that the body is a machine whose functions are accompanied but not controlled by consciousness. **3.** *Physiology* **a.** The involuntary functioning of a body structure that is not under conscious control, such as the beating of the heart. **b.** The reflexive action of a body part. **4.** *Psychology* Mechanical, seemingly aimless behavior characteristic of various mental disorders. [< Lat. *automaton*, automaton. See AUTOMATON.] **—au•tom′a•tist** *n.*

au•tom•a•tize (ô-tŏm′ə-tīz′) *tr.v.* **-tized, -tiz•ing, -tiz•es 1.** To make automatic. **2.** To turn into an automaton. [< AUTOMATIC.] **—au•tom′a•ti•za′tion** (-tĭ-zā′shən) *n.*

au•tom•a•ton (ô-tŏm′ə-tən, -tŏn′) *n., pl.* **-tons** or **-ta** (-tə) **1.** A self-operating machine or mechanism, esp. a robot. **2.** One that behaves or responds in a mechanical way. [Lat., self-operating machine < Gk. < neut. of *automatos*, self-acting. See AUTOMATIC.] **—au•tom′a•tous** *adj.*

au•to•mo•bile (ô′tə-mō-bēl′, -mō′bēl′) *n.* A self-propelled passenger vehicle that usu. has four wheels and an internal-combustion engine, used for land transport. [Fr. : Gk. *auto-*, auto- + Fr. *mobile*, mobile (< OFr.; see MOBILE).] **—au′to•mo•bile′** *adj.* **—au′to•mo•bil′ist** *n.*

au•to•mo•tive (ô′tə-mō′tĭv) *adj.* **1.** Moving by itself; self-propelling or self-propelled. **2.** Relating to self-propelled vehicles.

au•to•nom•ic (ô′tə-nŏm′ĭk) *adj.* *Physiology* **a.** Of, relating to, or controlled by the autonomic nervous system. **b.** Occurring involuntarily; automatic. **c.** Resulting from internal stimuli; spontaneous. **—au′to•nom′i•cal•ly** *adv.*

autonomic nervous system *n.* The part of the vertebrate nervous system that regulates involuntary action, as of the intestines, heart, and glands.

au•ton•o•mous (ô-tŏn′ə-məs) *adj.* **1.** Not controlled by others or by outside forces; independent. **2.** Independent in mind or judgment; self-directed. **3a.** Independent of the laws of another state or government; self-governing. **b.** Of or relating to a self-governing entity. **c.** Self-governing with respect to local or internal affairs: *an autonomous region of a country.* **4.** Autonomic. [< Gk. *autonomos* : *auto-*, auto- + *nomos*, law; see **nem-** in App.] **—au•ton′o•mous•ly** *adv.*

au•ton•o•my (ô-tŏn′ə-mē) *n., pl.* **-mies 1.** The condition or quality of being autonomous. **2a.** Self-government or the right of self-government; self-determination. **b.** Self-government with respect to local or internal affairs. **3.** A self-governing state, community, or group. [Gk. *autonomiā* < *autonomos*, self-ruling. See AUTONOMOUS.] **—au•ton′o•mist** *n.*

au•to•nym (ô′tə-nĭm′) *n.* A name by which a people or social group refers to itself. [AUT(O)- + −ONYM.]

au•to•pen (ô′tō-pĕn′) *n.* A mechanical device used for writing imitations of a personal signature.

au•toph•a•gy (ô-tŏf′ə-jē) *n.* The process of self-digestion of a cell through the action of its own enzymes.

au•to•pi•lot (ô′tō-pī′lət) *n.* Automatic pilot. **—idiom: on autopilot** *Informal* Without conscious thought or effort.

au•to•plas•ty (ô′tō-plăs′tē) *n.* Surgical repair or reconstruction of a body part using tissue taken from another part of the body. **—au′to•plas′tic** *adj.* **—au′to•plas′ti•cal•ly** *adv.*

au•to•pol•y•ploid (ô′tō-pŏl′ē-ploid′) *adj.* Having more than two sets of chromosomes all derived from the same species. ❖ *n.* An autopolyploid organism. **—au′to•pol′y•ploi′dy** *n.*

au•top•sy (ô′tŏp′sē, ô′təp-) *n., pl.* **-sies 1.** Examination of a cadaver to determine or confirm the cause of death. **2.** A critical assessment or examination after the fact. ❖ *tr.v.* **-sied, -sying, -sies** To subject to an autopsy. [Gk. *autopsiā*, a seeing for oneself : *auto-*, auto- + *opsis*, sight; see **ok**ʷ- in App.] **—au′top′sic, au′top′si•cal** or **au′top′sist** *n.*

au•to•ra•di•o•gram (ô′tō-rā′dē-ō-grăm′) *n.* See **autoradiograph.**

au•to•ra•di•o•graph (ô′tō-rā′dē-ō-grăf′) *n.* An image recorded on a photographic film or plate produced by the radiation emitted from a specimen containing a radioactively labeled isotope. **—au′to•ra′di•o•graph′ic** *adj.* **—au′to•ra′di•og′ra•phy** (-ŏg′rə-fē) *n.*

au•to•route (ô′tō-rōōt′) *n.* An expressway in France and French-speaking countries. [Fr. : *auto*, automobile; see AUTO + *route*, road (< OFr.; see ROUTE).]

au•to•some (ô′tə-sōm′) *n.* A chromosome that is not a sex chromosome. **—au′to•so′mal** (-sō′məl) *adj.* **—au′to•so′mal•ly** *adv.*

au•to•stra•da (ô′tō-strä′də, ou′tō-) *n.* An expressway in Italy. [Ital. : *auto*, automobile; see AUTO + *strada*, street (< LLat. *strāta*, paved road; see STREET).]

au•to•sug•ges•tion (ô′tō-səg-jĕs′chən) *n.* *Psychology* The process by which a person induces self-acceptance of an opinion, belief, or plan of action. **—au′to•sug•gest′** *v.* **—au′to•sug•gest′i•bil′i•ty** (-ə-bĭl′ĭ-tē) *n.* **—au′to•sug•gest′i•ble** *adj.* **—au′to•sug•ges′tive** (-tĭv) *adj.*

au•tot•o•my (ô-tŏt′ə-mē) *n.* The spontaneous casting off of a body part, such as the tail of certain lizards, esp. when the organism is injured or under attack. **—au′to•tom′ic** (ô′tə-tŏm′ĭk), **au′tot′o•mous** *adj.* **—au•tot′o•mize′** *v.*

au•to•tox•e•mi•a also **au•to•tox•ae•mi•a** (ô′tō-tŏk-sē′mē-ə) *n.* See **autointoxication.**

au•to•tox•in (ô′tō-tŏk′sĭn) *n.* A poison that acts on the organism in which it is generated. **—au′to•tox′ic** *adj.*

au•to•trans•form•er (ô′tō-trăns-fôr′mər) *n.* An electrical transformer in which the primary and secondary coils have some or all windings in common.

au•to•troph (ô′tə-trŏf′, -trōf′) *n.* An organism capable of synthesizing its own food from inorganic substances, using light or chemical energy. **—au′to•troph′ic** (-trŏf′ĭk, -trō′fĭk) *adj.* **—au′to•troph′i•cal•ly** *adv.* **—au•tot′ro•phy** (ô-tŏt′rə-fē) *n.*

au•to•work•er (ô′tō-wûr′kər) *n.* A worker in the automobile industry.

au•tumn (ô′təm) *n.* **1.** The season of the year between summer and winter, lasting from the autumnal equinox to the winter solstice and from September to December in the Northern Hemisphere; fall. **2.** A period of maturity verging on decline. ❖ *adj.* **1.** Of, having to do with, occurring in, or appropriate to the season of autumn. **2.** Grown during the season of autumn. [ME *autumpne* < OFr. *autompne* < Lat. *autumnus.*] **—au•tum′nal** (ô-tŭm′nəl) *adj.* **—au•tum′nal•ly** *adv.*

autumnal equinox *n.* **1.** The point at which the ecliptic intersects the celestial equator, the sun having a southerly motion. **2.** The moment at which the sun passes through the autumnal equinox, about September 23, marking the beginning of autumn in the Northern Hemisphere.

autumn crocus *n.* A corm-producing European and North African plant (*Colchicum autumnale*) with flowers in the fall.

au•tun•ite (ô-tŭn′īt′, ô′tə-nīt) *n.* A yellowish fluorescent minor ore of uranium with the composition $Ca(UO_2)_2(PO_4)_2 \cdot 10–12H_2O$. [After *Autun*, a city of E-central France.]

Au•vergne (ō-vûrn′, ō-vĕrn′) A historical region and former province of central France traversed by the **Auvergne Mountains,** a chain of extinct volcanoes.

aux. *abbr.* **1.** auxiliary **2.** auxiliary verb

aux•e•sis (ôg-zē′sĭs, ôk-sē′-) *n.* Growth resulting from increase in cell size without cell division. [Gk. *auxēsis*, growth < *auxanein*, *auxē-*, to grow.] **—aux•et′ic** (ôg-zĕt′ĭk) *adj.* **—aux•et′i•cal•ly** *adv.*

aux•il•ia•ry (ôg-zĭl′yə-rē, -zĭl′ə-rē) *adj.* **1.** Giving assistance or support; helping. **2.** Acting as a subsidiary; supplementary: *the main library and its auxiliary branches.* **3.** Held in or used as a reserve: *an auxiliary power generator.* **4.** *Nautical* Equipped with a motor as well as sails. **5.** *Grammar* Of, relating to, or being an auxiliary verb. ❖ *n., pl.* **-ries 1.** An individual or group that assists or functions in a supporting capacity. **2.** A member of a foreign body of troops serving a country in war. **3.** *Grammar* An auxiliary verb. **4.** *Nautical* **a.** A sailing vessel equipped with a motor. **b.** A vessel that is designed for and used in instances and services other than combat. [ME < Lat. *auxiliārius* < *auxilium*, help.]

auxiliary verb *n.* A verb, such as *have*, *can*, or *will*, that accompanies the main verb in a clause and helps make distinctions in mood, voice, aspect, and tense.

aux•in (ôk′sĭn) *n.* Any of several plant hormones that regulate various functions, including cell elongation. [< Gk. *auxein*, to grow.] **—aux•in′ic** *adj.* **—aux•in′i•cal•ly** *adv.*

aux•o•troph (ôk′sə-trŏf′, -trōf′) *n.* An auxotrophic organism. [Back-formation < AUXOTROPHIC.]

aux•o•troph•ic (ôk′sə-trŏf′ĭk, -trō′fĭk) *adj.* Requiring one or more specific substances for growth and metabolism that can no longer be synthesized because of mutational changes. [Gk. *auxein*, to increase.]

aux. v. *abbr.* auxiliary verb

Av (äv, ôv) also **Ab** (äb, äv, ôv) *n.* The 11th month of the year in the Jewish calendar. See table at **calendar.** [Mishnaic Heb. *'āb* < Akkadian *abu*, a month name (July/August).]

AV *abbr.* **1.** audio-visual **2.** Authorized Version

av. *abbr.* **1.** Av. avenue **2.** average **3.** avoirdupois

a.v. or **a/v** *abbr.* ad valorem

a•vail (ə-vāl′) *v.* **a•vailed, a•vail•ing, a•vails** —*tr.* To be of use or advantage to; help: *Nothing could avail the dying patient.* —*intr.* To be of use, value, or advantage; serve. ❖ *n.* Use, benefit, or advantage: *labored to no avail.* **—idiom: avail (oneself) of** To

ă	pat	oi	boy
ā	pay	ou	out
âr	care	ŏŏ	took
ä	father	ōō	boot
ĕ	be	ŭ	cut
ē	be	ûr	urge
ĭ	pit	th	thin
ī	pie	th	this
îr	pier	hw	which
ŏ	pot	zh	vision
ō	toe	ə	about,
ô	paw		item

Stress marks:
′ (primary);
′ (secondary); as in
lexicon (lĕk′sĭ-kŏn′)

make use of. [ME *availen* : *a*-, intensive pref. (< Lat. *ad*-; see AD–) + OFr. *valoir, vail*-, to be worth (< Lat. *valēre*, to be strong).] —**a·vail′ing·ly** *adv.*

a·vail·a·ble (ə-vā′lə-bəl) *adj.* **1.** Present and ready for use; at hand; accessible. **2.** Capable of being gotten; obtainable. **3.** Qualified and willing to serve or assist. **4a.** *Chemistry* Capable of being used in a chemical reaction. **b.** *Botany* Capable of being used by plants as a nutrient. —**a·vail′a·bil′i·ty, a·vail′a·ble·ness** *n.* —**a·vail′a·bly** *adv.*

av·a·lanche (ăv′ə-lănch′) *n.* **1.** A fall or slide of a large mass, as of snow or rock, down a mountainside. **2.** A massive or overwhelming amount; a flood. ❖ *v.* **-lanched, -lanch·ing, -lanch·es** —*intr.* To fall or slide in a massive or overwhelming amount. —*tr.* To overwhelm; inundate. [Fr.; akin to Provençal *lavanca*, ravine, perh. ult. < Lat. *lābī*, to slip.]

avalanche lily *n.* A western North American corm-producing plant (*Erythronium grandiflorum*) in the lily family. [So called because it grows near the snow line and blooms when the snow begins to melt.]

Av·a·lon (ăv′ə-lŏn′) *n.* In Arthurian legend, an island paradise in the western seas to which King Arthur went at his death.

Avalon Peninsula A large, irregularly shaped peninsula of SE Newfoundland, Canada.

a·vant-garde (ä′vänt-gärd′, ăv′änt-) *n.* A group active in the invention and application of new techniques in a given field, esp. in the arts. ❖ *adj.* Of, relating to, or being part of the avant-garde. [Fr. < OFr., vanguard. See VANGUARD.] —**a′vant-gard′ism** *n.* —**a′vant-gard′ist** *n.*

A·var (ä′vär) *n., pl.* **Avar** or **A·vars 1.** A member of a people whose empire, centered in southern Hungary, reached its peak in the late sixth and early seventh centuries. **2a.** A member of a modern-day people of southern Dagestan and neighboring areas of Azerbaijan. **b.** Their Caucasian language.

av·a·rice (ăv′ə-rĭs) *n.* Immoderate desire for wealth; cupidity. [ME < OFr. < Lat. *avāritia* < *avārus*, greedy < *avēre*, to desire.]

av·a·ri·cious (ăv′ə-rĭsh′əs) *adj.* Immoderately desirous of wealth or gain; greedy. —**av′a·ri′cious·ly** *adv.* —**av′a·ri′cious·ness** *n.*

a·vas·cu·lar (ā-văs′kyə-lər) *adj.* Not associated with or supplied by blood vessels. —**a·vas′cu·lar′i·ty** (-lăr′ĭ-tē) *n.*

a·vast (ə-văst′) *interj. Nautical* Used as a command to stop or desist. [< MDu. *hou vast*, hold fast : *hou, houd*, imper. of *houden*, to hold + *vast*, fast.]

av·a·tar (ăv′ə-tär′) *n.* **1.** The descent to earth of a Hindu deity, esp. Vishnu, in human or animal form. **2.** An embodiment, as of a quality or concept; an archetype. **3.** A temporary manifestation or aspect of a continuing entity. [Skt. *avatārah,* descent (of a deity from heaven), avatar : *ava*, down + *tarati*, he crosses; see **terə-²** in App.]

a·vaunt (ə-vônt′, ə-vänt′) *adv.* Hence; away. [ME, forward < OFr. *avant* < Lat. *abante* : *ab*-, from; see AB-¹ + *ante*, before; see ANTE-.]

AVC *abbr.* American Veterans Committee

avdp. *abbr.* avoirdupois

a·ve (ä′vā) *n.* **1.** An expression of greeting or farewell. **2. Ave** *Roman Catholic Church* Hail Mary. [ME < Lat. *avē*.]

Ave. *abbr.* avenue

A·vel·la·ne·da (ä-vĕl′yä-nĕ′dä, ä-vĕ′yä-, ä-vĕ′zhä-) A city of E Argentina near Buenos Aires. Pop. 346,620.

A·ve Ma·ri·a (ä′vā mə-rē′ə) *n. Roman Catholic Church* See **Hail Mary** 1. [ME < Med.Lat. *Avē Marīa*.]

a·venge (ə-vĕnj′) *tr.v.* **a·venged, a·veng·ing, a·veng·es 1.** To inflict a punishment or penalty in return for; revenge: *avenge a murder.* **2.** To take vengeance on behalf of. [ME *avengen* < OFr. *avengier* : *a*-, to (< Lat. *ad*-; see AD–) + *vengier*, to vindicate (< Lat. *vindicāre*, to claim; see VINDICATE).] —**a·veng′er** *n.* —**a·veng′ing·ly** *adv.*

av·ens (ăv′ənz) *n., pl.* **avens 1.** Any of various perennial herbs of the genus *Geum* in the rose family. **2.** The mountain avens. [ME *avence* < OFr. < Med.Lat. *avencia.*]

Av·en·tine (ăv′ən-tīn′, -tēn′) One of the seven hills of ancient Rome; settled by plebes in 456 B.C. —**Av′en·tine′** *adj.*

a·ven·tu·rine (ə-vĕn′chə-rēn′, -rĭn′) also **a·ven·tu·rin** (-rĭn) *n.* **1.** An opaque or semitranslucent brown glass flecked with small metallic particles, often of copper or chromic oxide. **2.** Any of several varieties of quartz or feldspar flecked with particles of mica, hematite, or other materials. [Fr. < *aventure*, accident. See ADVENTURE.] —**a·ven′tu·rine′** *adj.*

av·e·nue (ăv′ə-nōō′, -nyōō′) *n.* **1.** A wide street or thoroughfare. **2a.** A broad roadway lined with trees. **b.** *Chiefly British* The drive leading from the main road up to a country house. **3.** A means of access or approach. [Fr. < OFr., arrival < fem. p. part. of *avenir*, to approach < Lat. *advenīre*, to come to. See ADVENT.]

A·ven·zo·ar (ăv′ən-zō′är) 1090?–1162. Spanish-Arab physician and writer.

a·ver (ə-vûr′) *tr.v.* **a·verred, a·ver·ring, a·vers 1.** To affirm positively; declare. **2.** *Law* **a.** To assert formally as a fact. **b.** To justify or prove. [ME *averren* < OFr. *averer* < VLat. **adverāre* : Lat. *ad*-, ad- + Lat. *vērus*, true; see **wērə-o-** in App.] —**a·ver′ment** *n.* —**a·ver′ra·ble** *adj.*

av·er·age (ăv′ər-ĭj, ăv′rĭj) *n.* **1.** *Mathematics* **a.** A number that

typifies a set of numbers of which it is a function. **b.** See **arithmetic mean.** **2a.** An intermediate level or degree. **b.** The usual or ordinary kind or quality. **3.** *Sports* The ratio of successful performances divided by total opportunities for successful performance: *a batting average of .274.* **4.** *Law* **a.** The loss of a ship or cargo, caused by damage at sea. **b.** The incurrence of such damage or loss. **c.** The equitable distribution of such a loss. **d.** A charge incurred through such a loss. **5.** *Nautical* Small expenses or charges that are usu. paid by the master of a ship. ❖ *adj.* **1.** *Mathematics* Of, relating to, or being an average. **2.** Intermediate between extremes, as on a scale. **3.** Usual or ordinary in kind or character. **4.** Assessed in accordance with the law of averages. ❖ *v.* **-aged, -ag·ing, -ag·es** —*tr.* **1.** *Mathematics* To calculate the average of. **2.** To do or have an average of: *averaged an hour a day.* **3.** To distribute proportionally. —*intr.* **1.** To be or amount to an average: *Costs averaged out to 5 dollars per day.* **2.** To buy more shares of the same security at a lower or higher price in order to decrease or increase the average price of one's position in relation to the current market. Used with *down* or *up.* [< ME *averay*, charge above the cost of freight < OFr. *avarie* < OItal. *avaria*, duty < Ar. *'awārīya*, damaged goods < *'awār*, blemish < *'awira*, to be damaged.] —**av′er·age·ly** *adv.* —**av′er·age·ness** *n.*

SYNONYMS *average, medium, mediocre, fair, middling, indifferent, tolerable* These adjectives indicate a middle position on a scale of evaluation. *Average* and *medium* apply to what is midway between extremes and imply both sufficiency and lack of distinction: *a novel of average merit; an orange of medium size. Mediocre* stresses the undistinguished aspect of what is average: *"The caliber of the students . . . has gone from mediocre to above average"* (Judy Pasternak). What is *fair* is passable but substantially below excellent: *in fair health. Middling* refers to a ranking between average and mediocre: *gave a middling performance. Indifferent* suggests neutrality: *"His home, alas, was but an indifferent attic"* (Edward Everett Hale). Something *tolerable* is merely acceptable: *prepared a tolerable meal.*

A·ver·no (ä-vĕr′nō) Ancient name **A·ver·nus** (ə-vûr′nəs) A small crater lake of S Italy near the Tyrrhenian Sea W of Naples; regarded by the ancient Romans as the entrance to the underworld.

A·ver·ro·ës or **A·ver·rho·ës** (ə-vĕr′ō-ēz′, ăv′ə-rō′ēz) also **Ibn Rushd** (ĭb′ən rōōsht′) 1126–98. Spanish-Arab physician and philosopher best known for his commentaries on Aristotle.

a·verse (ə-vûrs′) *adj.* Having a feeling of opposition, distaste, or aversion; strongly disinclined. [Lat. *āversus*, p. part. of *āvertere*, to turn away. See AVERT.] —**a·verse′ly** *adv.* —**a·verse′ness** *n.*

a·ver·sion (ə-vûr′zhən, -shən) *n.* **1.** A fixed, intense dislike; repugnance. **2.** The cause or object of such a feeling. **3.** *Psychology* Avoidance of something because of its association with an unpleasant or painful stimulus. **4.** *Obsolete* The act of turning away or averting.

aversion therapy *n.* A type of behavior therapy designed to modify antisocial habits or addictions by creating a strong association with a disagreeable or painful stimulus.

a·ver·sive (ə-vûr′sĭv, -zĭv) *adj. Psychology* Causing avoidance of something by the use of an unpleasant or punishing stimulus, as in behavior modification. —**a·ver′sive·ly** *adv.* —**a·ver′sive·ness** *n.*

a·vert (ə-vûrt′) *tr.v.* **a·vert·ed, a·vert·ing, a·verts 1.** To turn away: *avert one's eyes.* **2.** To ward off (something about to happen); prevent. [ME *averten* < OFr. *avertir* < Lat. *āvertere* : *ā-, ab-*, away from; see AB-¹ + *vertere*, to turn; see **wer-²** in App.] —**a·vert′i·ble, a·vert′a·ble** *adj.*

A·ves·ta (ə-vĕs′tə) *n.* The body of sacred writings of the Zoroastrian religion. [Short for ZEND-AVESTA.]

A·ves·tan (ə-vĕs′tən) *n.* The eastern dialect of Old Iranian, in which the Avesta is written. ❖ *adj.* Of or relating to Avestan or the Avesta.

avg. *abbr.* average

av·gas (ăv′găs′) *n.* Gasoline formulated for use in piston-driven airplanes. [*av(iation) gas(oline).*]

a·vi·an (ā′vē-ən) *adj.* Of, relating to, or characteristic of birds. [< Lat. *avis*, bird. See **awi-** in App.]

a·vi·ar·y (ā′vē-ĕr′ē) *n., pl.* **-ies** A large enclosure for confining birds. [Lat. *aviārium* < *avis*, bird. See **awi-** in App.] —**a′vi·a·rist** (-ə-rĭst, -ĕr′ĭst) *n.*

a·vi·ate (ā′vē-āt′, ăv′ē-) *intr.v.* **-at·ed, -at·ing, -ates** To operate an aircraft; fly. [Back-formation < AVIATION.]

a·vi·a·tion (ā′vē-ā′shən, ăv′ē-) *n.* **1.** The operation of aircraft. **2.** The design, development, and production of aircraft. **3.** Military aircraft. [Fr. < Lat. *avis*, bird. See **awi-** in App.]

aviation medicine *n.* See **aeromedicine.**

a·vi·a·tor (ā′vē-ā′tər, ăv′ē-) *n.* One who operates an aircraft; a pilot. [Fr. *aviateur* < *aviation*, aviation. See AVIATION.]

aviator glasses *pl.n.* Eyeglasses having a lightweight metal frame and oval lenses that narrow toward the bridge of the nose.

a·vi·a·trix (ā′vē-ā′trĭks, ăv′ē-) *n.* A woman who operates an aircraft; a woman pilot.

Av·i·cen·na (ăv′ĭ-sĕn′ə) 980–1037. Persian physician and philosopher noted for his *Canon of Medicine.*

a·vi·cul·ture (ā′vĭ-kŭl′chər, ăv′ĭ-) *n.* The raising, keeping, and

aviator glasses

care of birds. [Lat. *avis*, bird; see **awi-** in App. + CULTURE.] —a′vi•cul′tur•ist *n.*

av•id (ăv′ĭd) *adj.* **1.** Having an ardent desire or craving; greedy: *avid for adventure.* **2.** Marked by keen interest and enthusiasm: *an avid sports fan.* [Lat. *avidus < avēre*, to desire.] —av′id•ly *adv.*

av•i•din (ăv′ĭ-dĭn) *n.* A protein found in uncooked egg white that binds to and inactivates biotin, sometimes causing a deficiency. [AVID + (BIOT)IN < its affinity for biotin.]

a•vid•i•ty (ə-vĭd′ĭ-tē) *n., pl.* **-ties 1.** Ardent desire or craving; eagerness. **2.** Keen interest or enthusiasm: *followed the tournament with avidity.* **3.** *Chemistry* **a.** The dissociation-dependent strength of an acid or base. **b.** Degree of affinity.

a•vi•fau•na (ā′və-fô′nə, ăv′ə-) *n.* The birds of a specific region, habitat, or period. [Lat. *avis*, bird; see **awi-** in App. + FAUNA.] —a′vi•fau′nal *adj.*

A•vi•gnon (ä-vē-nyôN′) A city of SE France on the Rhone R.; seat of the papacy from 1309 to 1378. Pop. 89,132.

Á•vi•la (ä′və-lə, ä′vē-lä) A town of central Spain WNW of Madrid. Pop. 42,165.

Á•vi•la Ca•ma•cho (ä′vē-lä′ kə-mä′chō), **Manuel** 1897–1955. Mexican general and president (1940–46).

A•vi•lés (ä′və-läs′, ä′vē-lĕs′) A town of NW Spain on an inlet of the Bay of Biscay. Pop. 89,992.

a•vi•on•ics (ā′vē-ŏn′ĭks, ăv′ē-) *n.* **1.** (*used with a sing. verb*) The science and technology of the development and use of electronic devices in aeronautics and astronautics. **2.** (*used with a pl. verb*) The electronic systems, equipment, and other devices so developed. [AVI(ATION) + (ELECTR)ONICS.] —a′vi•on′ic *adj.*

a•vir•u•lent (ā-vîr′yə-lənt, ā-vîr′ə-) *adj.* Not virulent. —a•vir′u•lence *n.*

a•vi•ta•min•o•sis (ā-vī′tə-mĭ-nō′sĭs) *n., pl.* **-ses** (-sēz) A disease, such as scurvy, beriberi, or pellagra, caused by deficiency of one or more essential vitamins. —a•vi′ta•min•ot′ic (-nŏt′ĭk) *adj.*

AV node (ā′vē′) *n.* See **atrioventricular node.**

av•o•ca•do (ăv′ə-kä′dō, ä′və-) *n., pl.* **-dos 1a.** A tropical American tree (*Persea americana*) having oval or pear-shaped fruit with leathery skin, yellowish-green flesh, and a large seed. **b.** The edible fruit of this tree. **2.** A dull green. [Am.Sp., alteration (influenced by obsolete Sp. *avocado*, lawyer) of Nahuatl *ahuacatl.*]

av•o•ca•tion (ăv′ō-kā′shən) *n.* **1.** An activity taken up in addition to one's regular work or profession, usu. for enjoyment; a hobby. **2.** One's regular work or profession. **3.** *Archaic* A distraction or diversion. [Lat. *āvocātiō, āvocātiōn-*, diversion < *āvocātus*, p. part. of *āvocāre*, to call away : *ā-, ab-*, away; see AB–¹ + *vocāre*, to call; see **wek**ʷ- in App.] —av′o•ca′tion•al *adj.* —av′o•ca′tion•al•ly *adv.*

av•o•cet (ăv′ə-sĕt′) *n.* Any of several long-legged shore birds of the genus *Recurvirostra*, characterized by a long, slender, upturned beak. [Fr. *avocette* < Ital. *avocetta.*]

A•vo•ga•dro (ä′və-gä′drō, ä′vō-), **Amedeo** 1776–1856. Italian chemist and physicist.

A•vo•ga•dro's law (ä′və-gä′drōz, ä′vō-) *n.* The principle that equal volumes of all gases under identical conditions of pressure and temperature contain the same number of molecules.

Avogadro's number also **Avogadro number** *n. Symbol* **N** The number of molecules in a mole of a substance, approx. 6.0225 ×10²³.

a•void (ə-void′) *tr.v.* **a•void•ed, a•void•ing, a•voids 1.** To stay clear of; shun: *avoided heavy traffic by leaving early.* **2.** To keep from happening: *avoid illness.* **3.** *Law* To annul or make void; invalidate. **4.** *Obsolete* To void or expel. [ME *avoiden* < AN *avoider*, var. of OFr. *esvuidier* : *es-*, out (< Lat. *ex-*; see EX–) + *vuidier*, to empty (< *voide*, empty; see VOID).] —a•void′a•ble *adj.* —a•void′a•bly *adv.* —a•void′ance (ə-void′ns) *n.* —a•void′er *n.*

av•oir•du•pois (ăv′ər-də-poiz′) *n.* **1.** Avoirdupois weight. **2.** *Informal* Weight or heaviness, esp. of a person. [ME *avoir de pois*, commodities sold by weight, alteration of OFr. *aveir de peis*, goods of weight : *aveir, avoir*, to have (< Lat. *habēre*; see ABLE) + *de*, of (< Lat. *dē-*, from; see DE–) + *peis, pois*, weight (< VLat. **pēsum*, < Lat. *pēnsum*, p. part. of *pendere*, to hang).]

avoirdupois weight *n.* A system of weights and measures based on a pound containing 16 ounces or 7,000 grains and equal to 453.59 grams.

A•von (ā′vŏn, ā′vən, ăv′ən) also **Upper Avon** A river of S-central England flowing 154.5 km (96 mi) to the Severn R.; known for its associations with Shakespeare.

a•vouch (ə-vouch′) *tr.v.* **a•vouched, a•vouch•ing, a•vouch•es 1.** To declare the provable truth or validity of; affirm. **2.** To corroborate or confirm; vouch for. **3.** To accept responsibility for (an action, for example); acknowledge. **4.** To avow; confess. [ME *avouchen*, to cite as a warrant < OFr. *avochier* < Lat. *advocāre*, to summon. See ADVOCATE.]

a•vow (ə-vou′) *tr.v.* **a•vowed, a•vow•ing, a•vows 1.** To acknowledge openly, boldly, and unashamedly; confess: *avow guilt.* **2.** To state positively. See ADVOCATE. —a•vow′a•ble *adj.* —a•vow′a•bly *adv.* —a•vow′ed•ly (-ĭd-lē) *adv.* —a•vow′er *n.*

a•vow•al (ə-vou′əl) *n.* A frank admission or acknowledgment.

---

a•vulse (ə-vŭls′) *tr.v.* **a•vulsed, a•vuls•ing, a•vuls•es** To separate, cut, or tear off by avulsion. [Lat. *āvellere, āvuls-*, to tear off : *ā-, ab-*, away; see AB–¹ + *vellere*, to pull.]

a•vul•sion (ə-vŭl′shən) *n.* **1.** The forcible tearing away of a body part by trauma or surgery. **2.** The sudden movement of soil from one property to another as a result of a flood or a shift in the course of a boundary stream.

a•vun•cu•lar (ə-vŭng′kyə-lər) *adj.* **1.** Of or having to do with an uncle. **2.** Similar to an uncle, esp. in benevolence or tolerance. [< Lat. *avunculus*, maternal uncle.]

aw (ô) *interj.* Used to express sympathy, tenderness, disapproval, or disbelief.

AW *abbr.* **1.** aircraft warning **2.** Articles of War **3.** automatic weapon

a.w. *abbr.* **1.** also **A/W** actual weight **2.** all water

AWACS (ā′wăks) *n., pl.* **AWACS** An airborne surveillance system that is capable of tracking a large number of aircraft from a great distance. [A(irborne) W(arning) A(nd) C(ontrol) S(ystem).]

a•wait (ə-wāt′) *v.* **a•wait•ed, a•wait•ing, a•waits** —*tr.* **1a.** To wait for. **b.** To be in a state of abeyance until: *a contract awaiting signature.* **2.** To be in store for: *Death awaits us all.* **3.** *Obsolete* To lie in ambush for. —*intr.* **1.** To wait. **2.** To be in store. [ME *awaiten* < ONFr. *awaitier* : *a-*, on (< Lat. *ad-*; see AD–) + *waitier*, to watch; see WAIT.]

a•wake (ə-wāk′) *v.* **a•woke** (ə-wōk′) or **a•waked, a•waked** or **a•wok•en** (ə-wō′kən), **a•wak•ing, a•wakes** —*tr.* **1.** To rouse from sleep; waken. **2.** To stir the interest of; excite. **3.** To stir up (memories, for example). —*intr.* **1.** To wake up. **2.** To become alert. **3.** To become aware or cognizant: *awoke to reality.* See Usage Note at **wake¹.** ❖ *adj.* **1.** Conscious; not asleep. **2.** Vigilant; watchful. See Syns at **aware.** [ME *awaken* < OE *āwacan : ā-*, intensive pref. + *wacan*, wake; see WAKE¹.]

a•wak•en (ə-wā′kən) *tr. & intr.v.* **-ened, -en•ing, -ens** To awake; waken. See Usage Note at **wake¹.** [ME *awakenen* < OE *āwæcnian : ā-*, up; see A–² + *wæcnian*, to waken; see WAKEN.] —a•wak′en•er *n.*

a•ward (ə-wôrd′) *tr.v.* **a•ward•ed, a•ward•ing, a•wards 1.** To grant as merited or due: *awarded prizes.* **2.** To give as legally due: *awarded damages to the plaintiff.* ❖ *n.* **1.** Something awarded or granted, as for merit. **2.** A decision, such as one made by a judge or arbitrator. [ME *awarden* < AN *awarder*, to decide (a legal case), var. of ONFr. *eswarder : es-*, out (< Lat. *ex*; see EX–) + *warder*, to judge, guard.] —a•ward′a•ble *adj.* —a•ward′er *n.*

a•ward•ee (ə-wôr-dē′) *n.* The recipient of an award.

a•ware (ə-wâr′) *adj.* **1.** Having knowledge or cognizance: *aware of a sound.* **2.** *Archaic* Vigilant; watchful. [ME, var. of *iwar* < OE *gewær.*] —a•ware′ness *n.*

avocado
Persea americana

SYNONYMS *aware, cognizant, conscious, sensible, awake, alert, watchful, vigilant* These adjectives mean mindful or heedful. *Aware* implies knowledge gained through one's own perceptions or by means of information: *I am aware that the legislation passed. Cognizant* is a formal equivalent of *aware:* "Our research indicates that the nation's youth are cognizant of the law" (Jerry D. Jennings). *Conscious* emphasizes the recognition of something sensed or felt: "an importance . . . of which even Americans are barely conscious" (William Stanley Jevons). *Sensible* implies knowledge gained through intuition or intellectual perception: "I am sensible that the mention of such a circumstance may appear trifling" (Henry Hallam). To be *awake* is to have full consciousness of something: "as much awake to the novelty of attention in that quarter as Elizabeth herself" (Jane Austen). *Alert* stresses quickness to recognize and respond: *alert to career opportunities. Watchful* and *vigilant* imply looking out for what is dangerous or potentially so: *the toddler's watchful parent; kept a vigilant eye out for forest fires.*

avocet
American avocet
Recurvirostra americana

a•wash (ə-wŏsh′, ə-wôsh′) *adv.* **1.** Washed by the sea. **2.** At the surface level of a body of water, so as to be washed by waves. ❖ *adj.* **1.** Level with or washed by waves. **2.** Overflowing with or as if with water: *awash in cash.* **3.** Floating on or as if in water.

A•wash River (ä′wäsh′) also **Ha•wash River** (hä′-) A river of E Ethiopia flowing c. 805 km (500 mi) to the Danakil Desert.

a•way (ə-wā′) *adv.* **1.** From a particular thing or place: *Go away!* **2a.** At or to a distance in space or time: *We live a block away from the park.* **b.** At or by a considerable interval: *away back in time.* **3a.** In a different direction; aside: *glanced away.* **b.** On the way: *get away early.* **4.** In or into storage or safekeeping: *put the toys away.* **5.** Out of existence or notice: *The music faded away.* **6.** So as to remove, separate, or eliminate: *cleared away the debris.* **7.** From one's possession: *gave the tickets away.* **8.** Continuously; steadily: *toiling away.* **9.** Freely; at will: *Fire away!* ❖ *adj.* **1.** Absent: *The neighbors are away.* **2.** Distant, as in space or time: *The city is miles away.* **3.** Played on an opponent's field or grounds: *an away game.* **4.** In golf, having the ball lying farthest from the hole. **5.** *Baseball* Out. [ME < OE *aweg : a-*, on; see A–¹ + *weg*, way; see **wegh-** in App.]

awe (ô) *n.* **1.** A mixed emotion of reverence, respect, dread, and wonder inspired by authority, genius, great beauty, or might. **2.** *Archaic* **a.** The power to inspire dread. **b.** Dread. ❖ *tr.v.* **awed, aw•ing, awes** To inspire with awe. [ME < ON *agi.*]

a•wea•ry (ə-wîr′ē) *adj. Archaic* Tired; weary.

ă pat	oi boy
ā pay	ou out
âr care	ŏŏ took
ä father	ōō boot
ĕ pet	ŭ cut
ē be	ûr urge
ĭ pie	th thin
ī pie	th this
îr pier	hw which
ŏ pot	zh vision
ō toe	ə about,
ô paw	item

Stress marks:
′ (primary);
′ (secondary), as in
lexicon (lĕk′sĭ-kŏn′)

a·weath·er (ə-wĕth′ər) *adv.* To the windward side.

a·weigh (ə-wā′) *adj. Nautical* Hanging clear of the bottom. Used of an anchor.

awe·some (ô′səm) *adj.* **1.** Inspiring awe: *an awesome thunderstorm.* **2.** Expressing awe. **3.** *Slang* Remarkable; outstanding. —**awe′some·ly** *adv.* —**awe′some·ness** *n.*

awe·struck (ô′strŭk′) also **awe·strick·en** (-strĭk′ən) *adj.* Full of awe.

aw·ful (ô′fəl) *adj.* **1.** Extremely bad or unpleasant; terrible. **2.** Commanding awe: *"this sea, whose gently awful stirrings seem to speak of some hidden soul beneath"* (Herman Melville). **3.** Filled with awe, esp.: **a.** Filled with or displaying great reverence. **b.** *Obsolete* Afraid. **4.** Formidable in nature or extent. ❖ *adv. Informal* Extremely; very. [ME *aweful,* awe-inspiring, blend of *awe,* awe; see AWE, and **ayfull,* awful (< OE *egefull* : *ege,* dread + *-full,* -ful).] —**aw′ful·ly** *adv.* —**aw′ful·ness** *n.*

a·while (ə-hwīl′, ə-wīl′) *adv.* For a short time.

USAGE NOTE *Awhile,* an adverb, is never preceded by a preposition, such as *for,* but the two-word form *a while* may be preceded by a preposition. In writing each of the following is acceptable: *stay awhile; stay for a while; stay a while* (but not *stay for awhile*).

a·whirl (ə-hwûrl′, ə-wûrl′) *adj.* **1.** Having a whirling motion; spinning: *leaves awhirl in the wind.* **2.** Being in a state of excitement or confusion. —**a·whirl′** *adv.*

awk·ward (ôk′wərd) *adj.* **1.** Not graceful; ungainly. **2a.** Not dexterous; clumsy. **b.** Clumsily or unskillfully performed. **3a.** Difficult to handle or manage. **b.** Difficult to effect; uncomfortable: *an awkward pose.* **4a.** Marked by or causing embarrassment or discomfort. **b.** Requiring great tact and skill. [ME *awkeward,* in the wrong way : *awke,* wrong (< ON *öfugr,* backward; see **apo-** in App.) + *-ward,* -ward.] —**awk′ward·ly** *adv.* —**awk′ward·ness** *n.*

awl (ôl) *n.* A pointed tool for making holes, as in wood or leather. [ME *aul,* prob. blend of OE *æl* and OE *awel,* fleshhook.]

awn (ôn) *n.* A slender, bristlelike appendage found on the spikelets of many grasses. [ME *awne* < ON *ögn* or < OE *agen;* see **ak-** in App.] —**awned** *adj.* —**awn′less** *adj.*

awn·ing (ô′nĭng) *n.* A rooflike structure, often made of canvas or plastic, that serves as a shelter, as over a storefront, window, door, or deck. [?]

a·woke (ə-wōk′) *v.* A past tense of **awake.**

a·wok·en (ə-wō′kən) *v.* A past participle of **awake.**

AWOL or **awol** (ā′wôl′) *adj.* Absent without leave. ❖ *n.* One who is absent without leave.

a·wry (ə-rī′) *adv.* **1.** In a position that is turned or twisted toward one side; askew. **2.** Away from the correct course; amiss. See Syns at **amiss.** —**a·wry′** *adj.*

ax¹ or **axe** (ăks) *n., pl.* **ax·es** (ăk′sĭz) **1.** A tool with a bladed head mounted crosswise on a handle, used for felling trees or chopping wood. **2.** A similar implement used as a cutting tool or weapon. **3.** *Informal* A sudden termination of employment. **4.** *Slang* A musical instrument, esp. a guitar. ❖ *tr.v.* **axed, ax·ing, ax·es** **1.** To chop or fell with or as if with an ax. **2.** *Informal* To remove ruthlessly or suddenly. —*idiom:* **ax to grind** A selfish or ulterior aim. [ME < OE *æx.*]

ax² (ăks) *v.* **axed, ax·ing, ax·es** *Nonstandard* Variant of **ask.**

OUR LIVING LANGUAGE *Ax,* a common nonstandard variant of *ask,* is often identified as an especially salient feature of African American Vernacular English. While it is true that the form is frequent in the speech of African Americans, it used to be common in the speech of white Americans as well, especially in New England. This should not be surprising since *ax* is a very old word in English, having been used in England for over 1,000 years. In Old English we find both *āscian* and *ācsian,* and in Middle English both *asken* and *axen.* Moreover, the forms with *cs* or *x* had no stigma associated with them; Chaucer, for example, used *asken* and *axen* interchangeably. The forms in *x* arose from the forms in *sk* by a linguistic process called *metathesis,* in which two sounds are reversed. The *x* thus represents (ks), the flipped version of (sk). Metathesis is a common linguistic process around the world and does not arise from a defect in speaking. Nevertheless, *ax* has become stigmatized as substandard—a fate that has befallen other words, such as *ain't,* that were once perfectly acceptable in literate circles.

axolotl

ax. *abbr.* **1.** axiom **2.** axis

ax·el (ăk′səl) *n.* A jump in figure skating that is initiated from the outer forward edge of one skate, followed by one and one-half midair turns and a return to the outer backward edge of the other skate. [After *Axel* Paulsen (1856–1938), Norwegian figure skater.]

Axel Hei·berg (hī′bûrg′) An island of N Nunavut, Canada, in the Arctic Ocean W of Ellesmere I.

Ax·el·rod (ăk′səl-rŏd′), **Julius** b. 1912. Amer. biochemist who shared a 1970 Nobel Prize.

a·xen·ic (ā-zĕn′ĭk, ā-zē′nĭk) *adj.* Not contaminated by or associated with any other living organisms. Usu. used of cultures of microorganisms. [A—¹ + Gk. *xenikos,* foreign (< *xenos,* stranger; see **ghos-ti-** in App.).] —**a·xen′i·cal·ly** *adv.*

ax·es¹ (ăk′sēz′) *n.* Plural of **axis.**

ax·es² (ăk′sĭz) *n.* Plural of **ax¹.**

ax·i·al (ăk′sē-əl) *adj.* **1.** Relating to, characterized by, or forming an axis. **2.** Located on, around, or in the direction of an axis. —**ax′i·al′i·ty** (-ăl′ĭ-tē) *n.* —**ax′i·al·ly** *adv.*

axial skeleton *n.* The bones constituting the head and trunk of a vertebrate body.

ax·il (ăk′sĭl) *n.* The upper angle between a lateral organ, such as a leafstalk, and the stem that bears it. [Lat. *axilla,* armpit.]

ax·ile (ăk′sīl) *adj.* Situated along the central axis of an ovary having two or more locules: *axile placentation.* [AX(IS) + —ILE¹.]

ax·il·la (ăk-sĭl′ə) *n., pl.* **-lae** (-lē′) or **-las** **1.** The armpit. **2.** A body part analogous to the armpit, such as the hollow under a bird's wing. [Lat.]

ax·il·lar (ăk-sĭl′ər, ăk′sə-lər) or **ax·il·lar·y** (ăk′sə-lĕr′ē) *n., pl.* **axillars** or **-ies** One of the feathers in the axilla of a bird's wing.

ax·il·lar·y (ăk′sə-lĕr′ē) *adj.* **1.** *Anatomy* Of, relating to, or located near the axilla. **2.** *Botany* Of, relating to, or located in an axil.

axillary bud *n.* A lateral bud.

ax·i·ol·o·gy (ăk′sē-ŏl′ə-jē) *n.* The study of the nature of values and value judgments. [Gk. *axios,* worth; see **ag-** in App. + —LOGY.] —**ax′i·o·log′i·cal** (-ə-lŏj′ĭ-kəl) *adj.* —**ax′i·o·log′i·cal·ly** *adv.* —**ax′i·ol′o·gist** *n.*

ax·i·om (ăk′sē-əm) *n.* **1.** A self-evident or universally recognized truth. **2.** An established rule, principle, or law. **3.** A principle that is accepted as true without proof as the basis for argument; a postulate. [ME < OFr. *axiome* < Lat. *axiōma, axiōmat-* < Gk. < *axios,* worthy. See **ag-** in App.] —**ax′i·o·mat′ic** (-ĭ-măt′ĭk), **ax′i·o·mat′i·cal** (-ĭ-kəl) *adj.* —**ax′i·o·mat′i·cal·ly** *adv.*

ax·i·on (ăk′sē-ŏn′) *n.* A hypothetical boson having no charge or spin and small mass, proposed to explain the existence of certain symmetries of the strong nuclear force. [AXI(AL) + —ON¹.]

ax·is (ăk′sĭs) *n., pl.* **ax·es** (ăk′sēz′) **1.** A straight line about which a body or geometric object rotates or may be conceived to rotate. **2.** *Mathematics* **a.** A line serving to orient a geometric object, esp. a line about which the object is symmetric. **b.** A reference line along which coordinates are measured. **3.** A center line to which parts of a structure or body may be referred. **4.** An imaginary line to which elements of a work of art are referred for measurement or symmetry. **5.** *Anatomy* **a.** The second cervical vertebra. **b.** Any of various central structures, such as the spinal column or standard abstract lines used as a positional referent. **6.** *Botany* The main stem or central part about which plant parts are arranged. **7.** One of three mutually perpendicular lines that define the orientation of an aircraft. **8.** A line through the optical center of a lens that is perpendicular to both its surfaces. **9.** One of three or four imaginary lines used to define the faces of a crystal. **10a.** An alliance of powers, such as nations, to promote mutual interests and policies. **b. Axis** The alliance of Germany and Italy in 1936, later including Japan and other nations, that opposed the Allies in World War II. [ME < Lat.]

axis deer *n.* A deer (*Axis axis*) of central Asia having a brown coat with white spots. [Lat. *axis,* a spotted Indian quadruped.]

ax·i·sym·met·ric (ăk′sē-sĭ-mĕt′rĭk) also **ax·i·sym·met·ri·cal** (-rĭ-kəl) *adj.* Having symmetry around an axis. —**ax′i·sym·met′ri·cal·ly** *adv.* —**ax′i·sym′me·try** *n.*

ax·le (ăk′səl) *n.* **1.** A supporting shaft or member on or with which a wheel or a set of wheels revolves. **2a.** The spindle of an axletree. **b.** Either end of an axletree. [ME *axel* < ON *öxull.*]

ax·le·tree (ăk′səl-trē′) *n.* A crossbar or rod supporting a vehicle, such as a cart, that has terminal spindles on which the wheels revolve. [Blend of ME *axel,* axle; see AXLE, and ME *axtre,* axletree (*ax* < OE *eax* + *tre,* tree; see TREE).]

ax·man (ăks′mən) *n.* **1.** One who wields an ax. **2.** *Slang* One assigned to perform a task involving ruthless reduction, as of a work force.

Ax·min·ster (ăks′mĭn′stər) *n.* A carpet with stiff backing and a soft, colorful cut pile usu. arranged in a complex pattern. [After *Axminster,* a town of southwest England.]

ax·o·lotl (ăk′sə-lŏt′l) *n.* Any of several salamanders of the genus *Ambystoma,* native to Mexico and the western United States, that become sexually mature without undergoing metamorphosis. [Nahuatl.]

ax·on (ăk′sŏn′) also **ax·one** (-sōn′) *n.* The process of a nerve fiber that conducts impulses away from the body of the nerve cell. [Gk. *axōn,* axis.] —**ax′on·al** (ăk′sə-nəl, ăk-sōn′əl) *adj.*

ax·o·neme (ăk′sə-nēm′) *n.* **1.** The bundle of fibrils that constitutes the central core of a cilium or flagellum. **2.** The axial thread of a chromosome. [Gk. *axōn,* axis + *nēma,* thread; see **(s)nē-** in App.] —**ax′o·ne′mal** *adj.*

ax·o·no·met·ric (ăk′sə-nō-mĕt′rĭk) *adj.* Of or relating to a projection in which an object is drawn with its horizontal and vertical axes to scale but with its curved lines and diagonals distorted. [< *axonometry* : Gk. *axōn,* axis + —METRY.]

ax·o·plasm (ăk′sə-plăz′əm) *n.* The cytoplasm of an axon. [Gk. *axōn* + —PLASM.] —**ax′o·plas′mic** (-plăz′mĭk) *adj.*

Ax·um (ăk′sōom′) See **Aksum.**

ay¹ (ī) *interj.* Used before *me* to express distress or regret.

ay² (ī) *n. & adv.* Variant of **aye¹.**

ay³ (ā) *adv.* Variant of **aye².**

a·yah (ä′yə, ä′ə, ī′ə) *n.* A native maid or nursemaid in India.

[Hindi *āyā* < Port. *aia*, nursemaid < Lat. *avia*, grandmother.]

a·ya·hua·sca (ī′yə-wä′skə, ä′yə-) *n.* A hallucinogenic brew made from a tropical South American vine of the genus *Banisteriopsis*, mixed with other psychotropic plants, used esp. in rituals by certain Amazonian Indian peoples. [Am.Sp. < Quechua, rope of the dead, narcotic : *aya*, corpse + *huasca*, rope.]

a·ya·tol·lah (ī′yə-tō′lə, -tō-lä′) *n. Islam* **1.** A high-ranking Shiite religious authority regarded as worthy of imitation in matters of religious law and interpretation. **2.** Used as a title for such a leader. [Pers. *āyatollāh* < Ar. *āyatu llāh*, sign of God : *āyatu*, bound form of *āya*, sign, Koranic verse + *allāh*, Allah; see ALLAH.]

aye[1] also **ay** (ī) *n.* An affirmative vote or voter. ❖ *adv.* Yes; yea. [Perh. < ME **aye : ay*, always; see AYE[2] + *ye*, yes; see YEA.]

aye[2] also **ay** (ā) *adv.* Always; ever. [ME *ai* < ON *ei*. See aiw- in App.]

aye-aye (ī′ī′) *n.* A nocturnal lemur (*Daubentonia madagascariensis*) native to Madagascar, having a long bushy tail and rodentlike teeth. [Fr. < Malagasy *aiay*, prob. imit. of its cry.]

A·ye·sha (ä′ē-shä′) See **Aisha**.

AYH *abbr.* American Youth Hostels

a·yin (ī′ĭn) *n.* The 16th letter of the Hebrew alphabet. [Heb. *'ayin*, eye, ayin.]

Ay·ma·ra (ī′mä-rä′, ī′mə-) *n., pl.* **Aymara** or **-ras 1.** A member of a South American Indian people inhabiting parts of Bolivia and Peru. **2.** The Aymaran language of the Aymara.

Ay·ma·ran (ī′mä-rän′) *n.* A subgroup of the Quechumaran languages, the most important language being Aymara. ❖ *adj.* Of or relating to the Aymara or their language or culture.

A·yodh·ya also **A·jodh·ya** (ə-yōd′yə) A village of N India near Faizabad; a pilgrimage center sacred to Hindus.

Ayr (âr) A burgh of SW Scotland at the mouth of the **Ayr River** on the Firth of Clyde. Pop. 48,600.

Ayr·shire (âr′shĭr, -shər) *n.* Any of various brown and white dairy cattle of a breed that originated in Ayr, Scotland.

a-yuh (ā′yə, ĭ′yə, ā-yŭ′) *interj. New England* Used to express agreement.

A·yur·ve·da (ī′yər-vā′də, -vē′-) *n.* The ancient Hindu science of health and medicine, based on maintaining balance among the five elements earth, air, fire, water, and ether. [Skt. *āyurvedaḥ* : *āyuḥ*, life, health; see aiw- in App. + *vedah*, knowledge, lore; see weid- in App.] —**A′yur·ve′dic** *adj.*

Ayurvedic medicine *n.* A holistic approach to health care that is based on principles of Ayurveda and designed to maintain or improve health through the use of dietary modification, massage, yoga, herbal preparations, and other measures.

A·yut·thay·a (ä-yōō′tə-yä′) A city of S-central Thailand on an island in the Chao Phraya R. N of Bangkok; founded c. 1350. Pop. 55,130.

AZ *abbr.* Arizona

az. *abbr.* azimuth

az– *pref.* Variant of **azo-**.

a·zal·ea (ə-zāl′yə) *n.* Any of various shrubs of the genus *Rhododendron*, having showy, variously colored flowers. [Gk. *azaleā* < fem. of *azaleos*, dry (so called because it grows in dry soil, or from the texture of its wood). See **as-** in App.]

a·zan (ä-zän′) *n. Islam* The summons to a prayer service. [Ar. *'aḏān < 'aḏḏana*, to call to prayer, derived stem of *'aḏina*, to listen < *'uḏn*, ear.]

A·za·ni·a (ə-zā′nē-ə, ə-zān′yə) *South Africa.* The term is often used by Black African nationalists. —**A·za′ni·an** *adj. & n.*

az·a·thi·o·prine (ăz′ə-thī′ə-prēn′) *n.* An immunosuppressive agent used esp. to prevent organ rejection in kidney transplant recipients. [Prob. < AZ(O)– + THIO– + P(U)RINE.]

A·za·zel (ə-zā′zəl, ăz′ə-zĕl′) *n. Bible* The evil spirit in the wilderness to whom a scapegoat was sent on the Day of Atonement. [Heb. *'ăzā'zēl*, perh. corruption of *'ăzaz-'ēl*, God has been strong (personal name) : *'āzaz*, reduced form of *'āzaz*, he is strong + *'ēl*, God.]

a·ze·o·trope (ə-zē′ə-trōp′, ā′zē-) *n.* A mixture of two or more substances that retains the same composition in the vapor state as in the liquid state. [A–[1] + Gk. *zein*, to boil; see ZEOLITE + Gk. *-tropos*, turning; see –TROPOUS.] —**a′ze·o·trop′ic** (ā′zē-ə-trŏp′ĭk, -trō′pĭk) *adj.* —**a′ze·ot′ro·py** (-ŏt′rə-pē) *n.*

A·zer·bai·jan (ăz′ər-bī-jän′, ä′zər-) A republic and former kingdom of Transcaucasia N of Iran; a constituent republic of the USSR from 1936 to 1991. Cap. Baku. Pop. 7,472,000.

A·zer·bai·ja·ni (ăz′ər-bī-jä′nē, ä′zər-) *adj.* Of or relating to Azerbaijan or its people, language, or culture. ❖ *n., pl.* **-nis 1.** A native or inhabitant of Azerbaijan. **2.** The Turkic language of Azerbaijan.

A·zer·i (ə-zĕr′ē) *n., pl.* **-is 1.** A member of a Turkic people of

Azerbaijan and adjacent areas of Armenia and northern Iran; an Azerbaijani. **2.** The Azerbaijani language.

az·ide (ăz′īd, ā′zīd) *n.* A chemical compound that contains the group N₃. —**az′i·do** (az′ĭ-dō′) *adj.*

az·i·do·thy·mi·dine (ə-zī′dō-thī′mĭ-dēn′, ə-zē′-, ăz′ī-) *n.* AZT.

A·zil·ian (ə-zĭl′yən) *adj.* Of or relating to a Mesolithic western European culture. [After Le Mas d'*Azil*, a village of southern France.]

az·i·muth (ăz′ə-məth) *n.* **1.** The horizontal angular distance from a reference direction, usu. the northern point of the horizon, to the point where a vertical circle through a celestial body intersects the horizon, usu. measured clockwise. **2.** The horizontal angle of the observer's bearing in surveying, measured clockwise from a referent direction. **3.** The lateral deviation of a projectile or bomb. [ME *azimut* < OFr. < Ar. *as-sumūt*, pl. of *as-samt*, the way, compass bearing : *al-*, the + *samt*, way (< Lat. *sēmita*, path).] —**az′i·muth′al** (-mŭth′əl) *adj.* —**az′i·muth′al·ly** *adv.*

azimuthal equidistant projection *n.* A map projection of the earth designed so that a straight line from the central point on the map to any other point gives the shortest distance between the two points.

az·ine (ăz′ēn, ā′zēn′) *n.* A six-membered heterocyclic compound that contains nitrogen and carbon atoms.

azine dye *n.* Any of various dyes derived from phenazine.

az·o (ăz′ō, ā′zō) *adj.* Containing a nitrogen group, esp. N=N. [< AZO–.]

azo– or **az–** *pref.* Containing a nitrogen group, esp. one attached at both ends in a covalent bond to other groups: *azole*. [< Fr. *azote*, nitrogen < Gk. *a-*, not; see A–[1] + Gk. *zōē*, life (< the fact that nitrogen does not support respiration); see g*ʷ*eiə- in App.]

azo dye *n.* Any of various red, brown, or yellow acidic or basic dyes derived from amino compounds.

a·zo·ic (ā-zō′ĭk) *adj.* Of or relating to geologic periods that precede the appearance of life.

az·ole (ăz′ōl′, ā′zōl′) *n.* A class of organic compounds having a five-membered heterocyclic ring with two double bonds.

a·zon·al (ā-zō′nəl) *adj.* **1.** Not divided into zones. **2.** *Geology* Of or relating to soils characterized by poorly developed horizons and by a strong resemblance to the parent material.

a·zon·ic (ā-zŏn′ĭk, ā-zō′nĭk) *adj.* Not restricted to a particular zone or region; not local.

A·zores (ā′zôrz, ā′zōrz, ə-zôrz′, ə-zōrz′) A group of volcanic islands in the N Atlantic Ocean c. 1,448 km (900 mi) W of mainland Portugal, of which they are administrative districts. —**A·zor′e·an, A·zor′i·an** *adj. & n.*

az·o·te·mi·a (ăz′ə-tē′mē-ə, ā′zə-) *n.* See **uremia**. [Fr. *azote*, nitrogen; see AZO– + –EMIA.] —**az′o·te′mic** (-mĭk) *adj.*

az·oth (ăz′ŏth, -ōth) *n.* Mercury considered in alchemy to be the primary source of all metals. [ME *azoc* < OFr. < Ar. *az-zā'uq*, the mercury : *al-*, the + *zā'uq*, mercury (< Syriac *zīwag*, of Iran. orig.; see g*ʷ*eiə- in App.]

a·zo·to·bac·ter (ā-zō′tə-băk′tər) *n.* Any of various rod-shaped, nitrogen-fixing bacteria of the genus *Azotobacter*, found in soil and water. [Fr. *azote*, nitrogen; see AZO– + BACTER(IA).]

az·o·tu·ri·a (ăz′ə-tŏŏr′ē-ə, -tyŏŏr′-) *n.* Increase of nitrogenous substances, esp. urea, in the urine. [Fr. *azote*, nitrogen; see AZO– + –URIA.]

A·zov (ăz′ôf, ā′zôf, ə-zôf′), **Sea of** The N arm of the Black Sea between SW Russia and SE Ukraine.

AZT (ā′zē-tē′) *n.* A nucleoside analogue that inhibits the replication of retroviruses such as HIV. [AZ(IDO)T(HYMIDINE).]

Az·tec (ăz′tĕk′) *n.* **1.** A member of a people of central Mexico whose civilization was at its height at the time of the Spanish conquest in the early 16th century. **2.** The Nahuatl language of the Aztecs. ❖ *adj.* also **Az·tec·an** (-tĕk′ən) Of or relating to the Aztecs or their language, culture, or empire. [Sp. *Azteca* < Nahuatl *Aztecatl*, one who comes from the place of the cranes : *áztatl*, crane + *-tēcatl*, suff.]

Az·tlán (äz-tlän′) **1.** The original Aztec homeland, held to have been located in NW Mexico. **2.** The American Southwest, specifically the territory of N Mexico ceded to the US in 1848. Used esp. by Chicano-rights activists.

az·ure (ăzh′ər) *n.* **1a.** A light purplish blue. **b.** *Heraldry* The color blue. **2.** The blue sky. [ME < OFr. *azur* < Med.Lat. *azura* < Ar. *al-lāzaward*, the azure : *al-*, the + *lāzaward*, azure (< Pers. *lājward*, lapis lazuli).]

az·ur·ite (ăzh′ə-rīt′) *n.* An azure-blue vitreous mineral, Cu₃(CO₃)₂(OH)₂, used as a copper ore and as a gemstone.

a·zy·gous (ā-zī′gəs) *adj.* Occurring singly; not one of a pair, as a vein or muscle.

Az Zar·qā' (äz zär′kä) A city of Jordan NE of Amman. Pop. 359,000.

Azerbaijan

ă **pat**	oi **boy**	
ā **pay**	ou **out**	
âr **care**	ŏŏ **took**	
ä **father**	ōō **boot**	
ĕ **pet**	ŭ **cut**	
ē **be**	ûr **urge**	
ĭ **pit**	th **thin**	
ī **pie**	th **this**	
îr **pier**	hw **which**	
ŏ **pot**	zh **vision**	
ō **toe**	ə **about,**	
ô **paw**	**item**	

Stress marks:
′ (primary);
′ (secondary), as in
lexicon (lĕk′sĭ-kŏn′)

Bb

b¹ (bē) or **B** (bē) *n., pl.* **b's** or **B's** also **bs** or **Bs 1.** The second letter of the modern English alphabet. **2.** Any of the speech sounds represented by the letter *b*. **3.** The second in a series. **4.** Something shaped like the letter B. **5.** The second best or second highest in quality or rank: *a mark of B in English.* **6.** *Music* **a.** The seventh tone in the scale of C major or the second tone in the relative minor scale. **b.** A key or scale in which B is the tonic. **7. B** One of the four major blood groups in the ABO system.

b² *abbr.* **1.** *Physics* barn **2.** or **B** bel **3.** bottom quark **4.** breadth

B¹ 1. The symbol for the element **boron. 2.** The symbol for **magnetic flux density.**

B² or **b** *abbr.* **1.** baryon number **2.** *Baseball* base **3.** *Music* bass **4.** billion **5.** bishop (chess)

b. *abbr.* **1.** book **2.** born

B. *abbr.* **1.** Baumé scale **2.** bay

Ba The symbol for the element **barium.**

BA *abbr.* **1.** Bachelor of Arts **2.** bathroom **3.** batting average

baa (bă, bä) *intr.v.* **baaed, baa·ing, baas** To make a bleating sound, as a goat. ❖ *n.* The bleat of a sheep or goat. [Imit.]

Ba·al (bā′əl, bäl, bāl) *n., pl.* **Baals** or **Ba·al·im** (bā′ə-lĭm, bä′lĭm) **1.** Any of various local fertility and nature gods of the ancient Semitic peoples considered to be false gods by the Hebrews. **2.** often **baal** A false god or idol. [Heb. *ba'al,* lord, Baal.]

Baal·bek (bäl′bĕk′, bä′əl-) Formerly **He·li·op·o·lis** (hē′lē-ŏp′ə-lĭs) A town of E Lebanon NE of Beirut; noted for its extensive Roman ruins. Pop. 24,000.

Baal Shem Tov (bäl′ shĕm′ tŏv′) Orig. Israel ben Eliezer. 1700?–60. Polish-born Jewish leader who founded Hasidism.

Ba·ath·ist also **Ba′ath·ist** (bä′ä-thĭst) *n.* A member of a pan-Arab socialist political party active principally in Syria and Iraq. [After the *Ba'ath* Party < Ar. *ba'ṭ,* revival < *ba'ata,* to send, evoke, awaken.] —**Ba′ath·ism** *n.*

Bab (bäb), **the** Title of Ali Mohammad of Shiraz. 1819?–50. Persian founder of Babism.

ba·ba (bä′bə) *n.* A leavened rum cake, usu. made with raisins. [Fr. < Pol., old woman.]

Ba·bar (bä′bər) See **Baber.**

ba·bas·su (bä′bə-sōō′) *n.* A Brazilian feather-leaved palm (*Orbignya barbosiana*) bearing seeds that yield an edible vegetable oil. [Port. *babaçu* < Tupi *babassú, ibabassú* : *ibá,* fruit + *-bassú,* var. of *-assú, -guassú,* big.]

Bab·bage (băb′ĭj), **Charles** 1792–1871. British mathematician and inventor of a forerunner to the modern computer.

Bab·bitt (băb′ĭt) *n.* A self-satisfied person concerned chiefly with business and middle-class ideals such as material success. [After George F. *Babbitt,* the main character in the novel *Babbitt* by Sinclair Lewis.] —**Bab′bitt·ry** *n.*

Babbitt, Irving 1865–1933. Amer. humanist and scholar who founded the New Humanism movement.

Babbitt, Milton Byron b. 1916. Amer. composer whose works combine serial music and electronic effects.

babbitt metal *n.* Any of several soft, silvery antifriction alloys composed of tin usu. with small amounts of copper and antimony. [After Isaac *Babbitt* (1799–1862), American inventor who patented such an alloy.]

bab·ble (băb′əl) *v.* **-bled, -bling, -bles** —*intr.* **1.** To utter a meaningless confusion of words or sounds. **2.** To talk foolishly or idly; chatter. **3.** To make a low, murmuring sound, as flowing water. —*tr.* **1.** To utter rapidly and indistinctly. **2.** To utter carelessly; blurt out. ❖ *n.* **1.** Inarticulate or meaningless talk or sounds. **2.** Idle talk; prattle. **3.** A low, murmuring sound. [ME *babelen.*] —**bab′bler** *n.*

babe (bāb) *n.* **1.** A baby; an infant. **2.** An innocent or naive person. **3.** *Slang* A young woman. **4.** *Informal* Sweetheart; dear. Used as a term of endearment. [ME.]

ba·bel also **Ba·bel** (băb′əl, bā′bəl) *n.* **1.** A confusion of sounds or voices. **2.** A scene of noise and confusion. [After BABEL.]

Ba·bel (bā′bəl, băb′əl) In the Bible, a city (now thought to be Babylon) in Shinar where God confounded an attempt to build a tower into heaven by confusing the language of its builders into many mutually incomprehensible languages.

Bab el Man·deb (băb′ ĕl män′dĕb) A strait, 27.4 km (17 mi) wide, between the Arabian Peninsula and E Africa linking the Red Sea with the Gulf of Aden.

Ba·ber also **Ba·bar** or **Ba·bur** (bä′bər) Orig. Zahir ud-Din Mohammed. 1483–1530. Mongol conqueror of India who founded the Mogul dynasty.

ba·be·sia (bə-bē′zhə) *n.* A genus of parasitic sporozoans of the family Babesiidae that infect mammalian red blood cells. [NLat. *Babesia,* genus name, after Victor *Babeş* (1854–1926), Rom. bacteriologist.]

ba·be·si·o·sis (bə-bē′zē-ō′sĭs) also **bab·e·si·a·sis** (băb′ĭ-zī′ə-sĭs) *n.* **1.** A tick-borne infection of animals that is caused by species of *Babesia.* **2.** A disease of human red blood cells caused by *Babesia* species.

Ba·bian Jiang (bä′byän′ jyäng′) See **Black River** 1.

bab·i·ru·sa also **bab·i·rus·sa** or **bab·i·rous·sa** (băb′ə-rōō′sə, bä′bə-) *n.* A wild pig (*Babyrousa babyrussa*) of the East Indies, having upward-curving tusks in the male. [Malay *babirusa* : *babi,* hog + *rusa,* deer.]

Bab·ism (bä′bĭz′əm) *n.* A 19th-century outgrowth of Shiism that sought to reform Islam by advocating egalitarianism and by forbidding polygamy and trading in slaves.

Ba·bi Yar (bä′bē yär′, bä′byē) A ravine outside Kiev in N-central Ukraine where the Jews of the city were killed by German troops (1941).

bab·ka (băb′kə) *n.* A coffee cake flavored with orange rind, rum, almonds, and raisins. [Pol., dim. of *baba,* old woman.]

ba·boon (bă-bōōn′) *n.* **1.** Any of several large terrestrial African and Asian monkeys of the family Cercopithecidae, esp. of the genus *Papio* and related genera, characterized by a doglike muzzle and a short tail. **2.** *Slang* A brutish person; a boor. [ME *babewin* < OFr. *babuin,* gaping figure, gargoyle, baboon, perh. blend of OFr. *babine,* muzzle, and *babau,* grimace.] —**ba·boon′er·y** *n.* —**ba·boon′ish** *adj.*

Ba·bruysk or **Bo·bruysk** (bə-brōō′ĭsk) A city of S Belarus SE of Minsk; founded in the 16th cent. Pop. 226,000.

ba·bu also **ba·boo** (bä′bōō) *n., pl.* **-bus** also **-boos 1.** Used as a Hindi courtesy title for a man, equivalent to *Mr.* **2a.** A Hindu clerk who is literate in English. **b.** *Offensive* A native of India who has acquired some education in English. [Hindi *bābū,* father.]

ba·bul (bə-bōōl′) *n.* A tropical African tree (*Acacia nilotica*) that yields a gum similar to gum arabic and has a bark used in tanning. [Pers. *bābul.*]

ba·bush·ka (bə-bōōsh′kə) *n.* A woman's head scarf, folded triangularly and worn tied under the chin. [Russ., grandmother, dim. of *baba,* woman.]

Ba·bu·yan Islands (bä′bōō-yän′) An island group of the Philippines separated from the N coast of Luzon by the **Babuyan Channel.**

ba·by (bā′bē) *n., pl.* **-bies 1a.** A very young child; an infant. **b.** An unborn child; a fetus. **c.** The youngest member of a family or group. **d.** A very young animal. **2.** An adult or young person who behaves in an infantile way. **3.** *Slang* A girl or young woman. **4.** *Informal* Sweetheart; dear. Used as a term of endearment. **5.** *Slang* An object of personal concern: *That boat is your baby.* ❖ *adj.* **-i·er, -iest 1.** Of or having to do with a baby. **2.** Infantile or childish. **3.** Smaller than others of the same kind: *baby vegetables.* ❖ *tr.v.* **-bied, -by·ing, -bies** To pamper like a baby; coddle. [ME.] —**ba′by·hood′** *n.* —**ba′by·ish** *adj.*

Baby Bell *n.* Any of the seven regional telephone companies created in 1984 when AT&T was ordered to divest itself of its local telephone service operations. [< *(Ma) Bell,* nickname for Bell Telephone Company, after Alexander Graham BELL.]

baby blue *n.* A very light to very pale greenish or purplish blue.

ba·by-blue-eyes (bā′bē-blōō′īz′) *pl.n. (used with a sing. or pl. verb)* An annual plant (*Nemophila menziesii*) native to California and having blue flowers with white centers.

baby boom *n.* A large increase in the birthrate, esp. the one in the United States from the later 1940s through the early 1960s. —**ba′by-boom′** *adj.*

baby boomer also **ba·by-boom·er** (bā′bē-bōō′mər) *n.* A member of a baby-boom generation.

baby bust *n.* A sudden decline in the birthrate, esp. the one in the United States from about 1961 to 1981. —**baby buster** *n.*

baby carriage *n.* A four-wheeled carriage, often with a hood that folds back, used for wheeling an infant about.

baby grand *n.* A small grand piano about 1.5 meters (5 feet) long.

Bab·y·lon¹ (băb′ə-lən, -lŏn′) The cap. of ancient Babylonia, in Mesopotamia on the Euphrates R.; est. as cap. c. 1750 B.C. and site of the Hanging Gardens, one of the Seven Wonders of the World.

Bab·y·lon² (băb′ə-lən, -lŏn′) *n.* **1.** A city or place of great luxury, sensuality, and often vice and corruption. **2.** A place of captivity or exile.

Bab·y·lo·ni·a (băb′ə-lō′nē-ə, -lōn′yə) An ancient empire of Mesopotamia in the Euphrates R. valley. It declined after 562 B.C.

and fell to the Persians in 539 B.C.

Bab·y·lo·ni·an (băb′ə-lō′nē-ən) *adj.* **1.** Of or relating to Babylonia or Babylon or their people, culture, or language. **2.** Marked by a luxurious, pleasure-seeking, and often immoral way of life. ❖ *n.* **1.** A native or inhabitant of Babylon or Babylonia. **2.** The form of Akkadian used in Babylonia.

ba·by-proof (bā′bē-prōōf′) *adj.* Made safe for babies or young children; childproof. ❖ *tr.v.* **-proofed, -proof·ing, -proofs** To make safe for babies or young children; childproof.

ba·by's breath (bā′bēz) *n.* Any of several Eurasian plants of the genus *Gypsophila*, such as *G. paniculata*, having numerous small white flowers in profusely branched panicles.

ba·by-sit (bā′bē-sĭt′) *v.* **-sat** (-săt′), **-sit·ting, -sits** —*intr.* To act as a babysitter. —*tr.* To take care of.

WORD HISTORY One normally would expect the agent noun *babysitter* with its *–er* suffix to come from the verb *baby-sit*, as *diver* comes from *dive*, but in fact *babysitter* is first recorded in 1937, ten years earlier than the first appearance of *baby-sit.* Thus, the verb was derived from the agent noun rather than the other way around, and presents a good example of back-formation. Other examples of verbs that were back-formed from pre-existing nouns include *burgle* (first recorded in 1872) from *burglar* (first recorded in the late 1200s) and *diagnose* (first recorded in 1861) from *diagnosis* (first recorded in 1681).

ba·by·sit·ter also **ba·by-sit·ter** (bā′bē-sĭt′ər) *n.* **1.** A person engaged to care for one or more children when the parents or guardians are not at home. **2.** A person who watches over someone or something.

baby tooth *n.* See **milk tooth.**

Ba·cău (bə-kou′) A city of E Romania NNE of Bucharest. Pop. 206,995.

bac·ca·lau·re·ate (băk′ə-lôr′ē-ĭt) *n.* **1.** See **bachelor's degree. 2.** A farewell address delivered to a graduating class. [Med. Lat. *baccalaureātus < baccalārius,* bachelor (influenced by *laureātus,* crowned with laurel). See BACHELOR.]

bac·ca·rat (bä′kə-rä′, băk′ə-) *n.* A card game in which the winner is the player who holds two or three cards totaling closest to nine. [Fr. *baccara* < Provençal.]

bac·cate (băk′āt′) *adj.* **1.** Resembling a berry in texture or form; berrylike. **2.** Bearing berries. [< Lat. *bacca,* berry.]

Bac·chae (băk′ē) *pl.n.* *Greek & Roman Mythology* The priestesses and women followers of Bacchus. [Gk. *Bakkhai,* pl. of *Bakkhē,* female worshiper of Bacchus < *Bakkhos,* Bacchus.]

bac·cha·nal (băk′ə-năl′, -näl′, băk′ə-nəl) *n.* **1.** A participant in the Bacchanalia. **2.** The Bacchanalia. Often used in the plural. **3.** A drunken or riotous celebration. **4.** A reveler. ❖ *adj.* Of or relating to the worship of Bacchus. [< Lat. *Bacchānālia,* Bacchanalia. See BACCHANALIA.]

Bac·cha·na·lia (băk′ə-nāl′yə, -nā′lē-ə) *n., pl.* **Bacchanalia 1.** The ancient Roman festival in honor of Bacchus. **2.** **bacchanalia** A riotous drunken festival; a revel. [Lat. *Bacchānālia < Bacchus,* Bacchus < Gk. *Bakkhos.*] —**Bac′cha·na′lian** *adj. & n.*

bac·chant (bə-kănt′, -känt′, băk′ənt) *n., pl.* **bac·chants** or **bac·chan·tes** (bə-kăn′tēz, -kän′-, -kănts′, -känts′) **1.** *Greek & Roman Mythology* A priest or votary of Bacchus. **2.** A boisterous reveler. [Lat. *bacchāns, bacchant-,* pr. part. of *bacchārī,* to celebrate the festival of Bacchus < Bacchus < Gk. *Bakkhos.*] —**bac·chan·tic** (-kăn′tĭk) *adj.*

bac·chan·te (bə-kăn′tē, -kän′-, -kănt′, -känt′) *n.* *Greek & Roman Mythology* A priestess or female votary of Bacchus. [Fr. < Lat. *bacchāns, bacchant-.* See BACCHANT.]

Bac·chic (băk′ĭk) *adj.* **1.** *Greek & Roman Mythology* Of or relating to Bacchus. **2.** **bacchic** Drunken and carousing; bacchanalian.

Bac·chus (băk′əs) *n.* *Greek & Roman Mythology* See **Dionysus.** [Lat. < Gk. *Bakkhos.*]

bach also **batch** (băch) *Informal n.* A bachelor. ❖ *intr.v.* **bached, bach·ing, bach·es** also **batched, batch·ing, batch·es** To live alone and keep house as a bachelor. —*idiom:* **bach it** To bach. [Short for BACHELOR.] —**bach** *n.*

Bach (bäкн, bäk), **Johann Sebastian** 1685–1750. German composer and organist of the late baroque period. Four of his children also became musicians: **Wilhelm Friedemann** (1710–84); **Carl Philipp Emanuel** (1714–88); **Johann Christoph Friedrich** (1732–95); and **Johann Christian** (1735–82).

bach·e·lor (băch′ə-lər, băch′lər) *n.* **1.** An unmarried man. **2.** A person who has completed the undergraduate curriculum of a college or university and holds a bachelor's degree. **3.** A male animal, esp. a young fur seal, that does not mate during the breeding season. **4.** A young knight in the service of another knight in feudal times. [ME *bacheler,* squire, youth, bachelor < OFr. < Med.Lat. *baccalārius,* tenant farmer, perh. of Celt. orig.] —**bach′e·lor·dom, bach′e·lor·hood, bach′e·lor·ship′** *n.*

bach·e·lor's button (băch′ə-lərz, băch′lərz) *n.* **1.** See **cornflower. 2.** Any of several plants that have buttonlike flowers or flower heads.

bachelor's degree *n.* An academic degree conferred by a college or university upon those who complete the undergraduate curriculum.

bac·il·lar·y (băs′ə-lĕr′ē, bə-sĭl′ə-rē) also **ba·cil·lar** (bə-sĭl′ər, băs′ə-lər) *adj.* **1.** Shaped like a rod or rods. **2a.** Consisting of

small rods or rodlike structures. **b.** Caused by, relating to, or resembling bacilli: *bacillary dysentery.* [< BACILLUS.]

ba·cil·lus (bə-sĭl′əs) *n., pl.* **-cil·li** (-sĭl′ī′) **1.** Any of various rod-shaped, spore-forming aerobic bacteria of the genus *Bacillus* that often occur in chains. **2.** Any of various bacteria. [LLat., dim. of Lat. *baculum,* rod.]

bac·i·tra·cin (băs′ĭ-trā′sĭn) *n.* A polypeptide antibiotic obtained from a strain of a bacterium (*Bacillus subtilis*) and used as a topical ointment to treat certain bacterial infections, esp. those caused by cocci. [BACI(LLUS) + Margaret *Tracy,* an American child in whose blood it was first isolated + –IN.]

back¹ (băk) *n.* **1a.** The posterior portion of the human body between the neck and the pelvis. **b.** The analogous dorsal region in other animals. **2.** The backbone or spine. **3.** The part or area farthest from the front. **4.** The part that is less seen or used: *the back of a photograph.* **5.** The reverse side, as of a coin. **6.** A part that supports or strengthens from the rear: *the back of a couch.* **7a.** The part of a book where the pages are stitched or glued together into the binding. **b.** The binding itself. **8.** *Sports* **a.** A player who takes a position behind the front line in certain games, such as football. **b.** This playing position. ❖ *v.* **backed, back·ing, backs** —*tr.* **1.** To cause to move backward or in a reverse direction: *Back the car up.* **2.** To furnish or strengthen with a back or backing. **3.** To provide with financial or moral support; support or endorse. See Syns at **support. 4.** To provide with musical accompaniment. Often used with *up.* **5.** To bet or wager on. **6.** To adduce evidence in support of; substantiate: *backed the argument with facts.* **7.** To form the back or background of. —*intr.* **1.** To move backward: *backed out of the garage.* **2.** To shift in a counterclockwise direction. Used of the wind. ❖ *adj.* **1.** Located or placed in the rear: *a back entrance.* **2.** Distant from a center of activity; remote. **3.** Of a past date; not current: *a back issue.* **4.** Being owed or due from an earlier time: *back pay.* **5.** Being in a backward direction. **6.** *Linguistics* Pronounced with the back of the tongue, as *oo* in *cool.* ❖ *adv.* **1.** At, to, or toward the rear or back; backward. **2.** In, to, or toward a former location. **3.** In, to, or toward a former condition. **4.** In, to, or toward a past time. **5.** In reserve or concealment. **6.** In check or under restraint: *held the crowd back.* **7.** In reply or return. —*phrasal verbs:* **back away** To withdraw from a position; retreat. **back down** To withdraw from a position, opinion, or commitment. **back off** To retreat or draw away. **back out 1.** To withdraw from (an enterprise or a plan) before completion. **2.** To fail to keep a commitment or promise. **back up 1.** To cause to stop and accumulate. **2.** To accumulate or be stopped. **3.** *Computer Science* To make a backup of (a program or file). —*idioms:* **back and fill 1.** *Nautical* To maneuver a vessel in a narrow channel by adjusting the sails so as to let the wind in and out of them in alteration. **2.** To vacillate in one's actions or decisions. **back to back** Consecutively and without interruption. [ME *bak* < OE *bæc.*] —**back′less** *adj.*

back² (băk) *n.* A shallow vat or tub used chiefly by brewers. [Du. *bak* < Fr. *bac* < OFr., boat < VLat. **baccus,* vessel, prob. of Celt. orig.]

back·ache (băk′āk′) *n.* An ache or pain in the back, esp. the lower back.

back and forth *adv.* Backward and forward; to and fro. —**back′-and-forth′** (băk′ən-fôrth′, -fōrth′) *n. & adj.*

back·beat (băk′bēt′) *n.* A sharp rhythmic accent on the second and fourth beats of a measure in 4/4 time, characteristic of rock music. [BACK(GROUND) + BEAT.]

back·bench (băk′bĕnch′) *n.* **1.** *Chiefly British* The rear benches in the House of Commons where junior members of Parliament sit. **2.** New members of Congress considered as a group. —**back·bench′er** *n.*

back·bite (băk′bīt′) *v.* **-bit** (-bĭt′), **-bit·ten** (-bĭt′n), **-bit·ing, -bites** —*tr.* To speak spitefully or slanderously about (another). —*intr.* To speak spitefully or slanderously. —**back′bit′er** *n.*

back·board (băk′bôrd′, -bōrd′) *n.* **1.** A board placed under or behind something or someone to provide firmness or support. **2.** *Basketball* The elevated vertical board from which the basket projects.

back·bone (băk′bōn′) *n.* **1.** The vertebrate spine or spinal column. **2.** Something that resembles a backbone. **3.** A main support or sustaining factor. **4a.** A ridge forming the principal axis of a mountain. **b.** The principal mountain range of a region. **5.** *Chemistry* The main chain of atoms in a polymer. **6.** Strength of character; determination. —**back′boned′** *adj.*

back·break·ing (băk′brā′kĭng) *adj.* Demanding great exertion; arduous and exhausting. —**back′break′er** *n.*

back-check (băk′chĕk′) *intr.v.* **-checked, -check·ing, -checks** To check or defend against an ice hockey opponent while skating back toward one's own goal. —**back′-check′er** *n.*

back·cloth (băk′klôth′, -klŏth′) *n.* See **backdrop 1.**

back·coun·try (băk′kŭn′trē) *n.* A sparsely inhabited rural region.

back·court (băk′kôrt′, -kōrt′) *n.* **1.** *Sports* The part of a court between the service line and the base line in tennis and other net games. **2.** *Basketball* **a.** The half of the court that a team defends. **b.** The portion of the frontcourt farthest from the basket. **c.** The two guards on one team.

back·cross (băk′krôs′, -krŏs′) *tr.v.* **-crossed, -cross·ing,**

Johann Sebastian Bach

ă	pat	oi	boy
ā	pay	ou	out
âr	care	ōō	took
ä	father	ōō	boot
ĕ	pet	ŭ	cut
ē	be	ûr	urge
ĭ	pit	th	thin
ī	pie	th	this
îr	pier	hw	which
ŏ	pot	zh	vision
ō	toe	ə	about,
ô	paw		item

Stress marks:
′ (primary);
′ (secondary), as in
lexicon (lĕk′sĭ-kŏn′)

-cross·es To cross (a hybrid) with one of its parents or with an individual genetically identical to one of its parents. ❖ *n.* **1.** The act of making such a cross. **2.** An individual resulting from such a cross.

back·date (băk′dāt′) *tr.v.* **-dat·ed, -dat·ing, -dates** To mark or supply with a date that is earlier than the actual date: *backdate a check.*

back dive *n.* A dive in which the diver, standing on the end of the board or platform with the back to the water, leaps up and rotates backward.

back·door (băk′dôr′, -dōr′) *adj.* Secret or surreptitious; clandestine: *a backdoor romance.* **—back′door′** *adv.*

back·drop (băk′drŏp′) *n.* **1.** A painted cloth hung at the back of a stage set. **2.** The setting, as of a historical event; the background.

backed (băkt) *adj.* Having or furnished with a back or backing.

back·er (băk′ər) *n.* **1.** One that backs a person, group, or enterprise. **2.** A person who bets on a contestant.

back·field (băk′fēld′) *n.* **1.** *Football* **a.** The players stationed behind the line of scrimmage. **b.** The positions filled by these players. **c.** The area in which these players line up. **2.** *Sports* The primarily defensive players on a soccer, field hockey, or Rugby team.

back·fill (băk′fĭl′) *n.* Material used to refill an excavated area. ❖ *tr.v.* **-filled, -fill·ing, -fills** To refill (an excavated area) with such material.

back·fire (băk′fīr′) *n.* **1.** An explosion of prematurely ignited fuel or of unburned exhaust gases in an internal-combustion engine. **2.** The backward escape of gases or cartridge fragments when a gun is fired. **3.** Fire started to control an oncoming forest or prairie fire by burning an area in its path. ❖ *intr.v.* **-fired, -fir·ing, -fires 1.** To explode in the manner of or make the sound of a backfire. **2.** To start or use a backfire. **3.** To produce an unexpected, undesired result.

back·fit (băk′fĭt′) *tr.v.* **-fit·ted** or **-fit, -fit·ting, -fits** To retrofit.

back·flip (băk′flĭp′) *intr.v.* **-flipped, -flip·ping, -flips** To perform a backward somersault, esp. in the air. ❖ *n.* A backward somersault.

back·flow (băk′flō′) *n.* A flow of fluid in the opposite direction of its regular flow.

back-for·ma·tion or **back formation** (băk′fôr-mā′shən) *n.* **1.** A new word created by removing an affix from another word, as *vacuum clean* from *vacuum cleaner*, or by removing what is thought to be an affix, as *pea* from the earlier English plural *pease.* **2.** The process of forming words in this way.

back·gam·mon (băk′găm′ən) *n.* A board game for two persons, played with pieces whose moves are determined by throws of dice. [BACK¹ + GAMMON¹.]

back·ground (băk′ground′) *n.* **1.** The ground or scenery located behind something. **2a.** The part of a pictorial representation that provides relief for the objects in the foreground. **b.** The general scene or surface against which designs, patterns, or figures are represented or viewed. **3.** A position or area of relative inconspicuousness or unimportance. **4.** The circumstances and events surrounding or leading up to an event or occurrence. **5.** A person's experience, training, and education. **6.** Subdued music played esp. as an accompaniment to dialogue. **7a.** Sound that interferes with an audio recording. **b.** Low-level radiation, as from radioactive decay, in the natural environment. **—back′ground′** *v.*

back·hand (băk′hănd′) *n.* **1.** *Sports* **a.** A stroke or motion made with the back of the hand facing outward and the arm moving forward. **b.** A pass or shot in hockey made with the back of the blade of the stick. **c.** A catch made in baseball by reaching across the body with the palm turned toward the ball. **2.** Handwriting characterized by letters that slant to the left. ❖ *adj.* Backhanded. ❖ *adv.* With a backhanded stroke or motion. ❖ *tr.v.* **-hand·ed, -hand·ing, -hands** *Sports* To perform, catch, or hit with a backhand.

back·hand·ed (băk′hăn′dĭd) *adj.* **1.** *Sports* Made with or using a backhand. **2.** Oblique or roundabout. **—back′hand′ed·ly** *adv.* **—back′hand′ed·ness** *n.*

back·hoe (băk′hō′) *n.* An excavator whose bucket is attached to a hinged pole on a boom and drawn backward to the machine when in operation. **—back′hoe′** *v.*

back·ing (băk′ĭng) *n.* **1.** Something forming a back: *the backing of a carpet.* **2a.** Support or aid: *financial backing.* **b.** Approval or endorsement.

back·lash (băk′lăsh′) *n.* **1.** A sudden or violent backward whipping motion. **2.** An antagonistic reaction to a trend, development, or event. **3.** A snarl formed in the part of a fishing line that is wound around the reel. **4.** The play resulting from loose connections between gears or other mechanical elements. **—back′lash′** *v.*

back·light (băk′līt′) *n.* A type of spotlight, used in photography, that illuminates a subject from behind. ❖ *tr.v.* **-light·ed** or **-lit** (-lĭt′), **-light·ing, -lights** To illuminate from behind.

back·list (băk′lĭst′) *n.* A publisher's list of older titles kept in print.

back·log (băk′lŏg′, -lôg′) *n.* **1.** A reserve supply or source. **2.** An accumulation, esp. of unfinished work or unfilled orders. **3.** A large log at the back of a fire in a fireplace. ❖ *v.* **-logged, -log·ging, -logs** *—tr.* To acquire (something) as a backlog. *—intr.* To become a backlog; accumulate.

back dive

backhand
tennis player

backhoe

back matter *n.* Material, such as an index or appendix, that follows the main body of a book.

back mutation *n.* A reversal process whereby a gene that has undergone mutation returns to its previous state.

back nine *n.* The second half of an 18-hole golf course.

back office *n.* The internal operations of an organization that are not accessible or visible to the general public.

back·pack (băk′păk′) *n.* **1.** A knapsack, often mounted on a lightweight frame, that is worn on a person's back, as to carry camping supplies. **2.** A piece of equipment designed to be used while being carried on the back. ❖ *v.* **-packed, -pack·ing, -packs** *—intr.* To hike while carrying a backpack. *—tr.* To carry in a backpack. **—back′pack′er** *n.* **—back′pack′ing** *n.*

back·ped·al (băk′pĕd′l) *intr.v.* **-aled, -al·ing, -als** or **-alled, -al·ling, -als 1.** To move the pedals of a bicycle or similar vehicle backward, esp. to apply a brake. **2.** To move backward, esp. in boxing or football. **3.** To retreat or withdraw from a previous stand.

back·rest (băk′rĕst′) *n.* A rest or support for the back.

Back River A river of central Nunavut, Canada, flowing c. 965 km (600 mi) to an inlet S of Boothia Peninsula.

back·room (băk′room′, -room′) *n.* or **back room 1.** A room located at the rear. **2.** The meeting place used by an inconspicuous controlling group. ❖ *adj.* **1.** Of, relating to, or taking place in a backroom. **2.** Marked by inconspicuous control and maneuvering: *backroom politics.*

back·rush (băk′rŭsh′) *n.* The seaward return of water after the landward motion of a wave.

back·saw (băk′sô′) *n.* A saw that is reinforced by a metal band along its back edge.

back·scat·ter (băk′skăt′ər) *n.* **1.** The deflection of radiation or particles by electromagnetic or nuclear forces through angles greater than 90° to the initial direction of travel. **2.** The radiation or particles so deflected. **—back′scat′ter·v** *v.*

back seat *n.* **1.** A seat in the back, esp. of a vehicle. **2.** A subordinate position, as in a group or hierarchy.

back-seat driver (băk′sēt′) *n.* **1.** A passenger who gives unsolicited advice to the driver of a motor vehicle. **2.** A person who persists in giving unsolicited advice.

back·set (băk′sĕt′) *n.* **1.** A setback or reversal. **2.** An eddy or countercurrent in water.

back·shore (băk′shôr′, -shōr′) *n.* The area of shore between the average high-tide mark and the vegetation, affected by waves only during severe storms.

back·side (băk′sīd′) *n.* *Informal* The buttocks; the rump.

back·slap (băk′slăp′) *v.* **-slapped, -slap·ping, -slaps** *—intr.* To demonstrate effusive goodwill. *—tr.* To demonstrate effusive goodwill toward (another). **—back′slap′per** *n.*

back·slash (băk′slăsh′) *n.* A backward virgule (\ ).

back·slide (băk′slīd′) *intr.v.* **-slid** (-slĭd′), **-slid·ing, -slides** To revert to sin or wrongdoing. **—back′slid′er** *n.*

back·space (băk′spās′) *—intr.* **-spaced, -spac·ing, -spac·es** To move the cursor on a computer screen or the carriage of a typewriter back one or more spaces by striking the key used for this purpose. ❖ *n.* The backspacing key.

back·spin (băk′spĭn′) *n.* A spin that tends to retard, arrest, or reverse the linear motion of an object, esp. of a ball.

back·splash (băk′splăsh′) *n.* An upright surface or border, as of tile, that protects the wall behind a sink or stove.

back·stab (băk′stăb′) *tr.v.* **-stabbed, -stab·bing, -stabs** To attack (someone) unfairly, esp. in an underhand, deceitful manner. **—back′stab′ber** *n.*

back·stage (băk′stāj′) *adv.* **1.** In or toward the area behind the performing space in a theater, esp. the dressing rooms. **2.** In secret; privately. ❖ *adj.* (băk′stāj′) **1.** Of, relating to, occurring in, or situated behind the performing area of a theater. **2.** Concealed from the public; private.

back·stairs (băk′stârz′) also **back·stair** (-stâr′) *adj.* Furtively carried on; clandestine: *backstairs gossip.*

back·stay (băk′stā′) *n.* **1.** A stay extending from the top of a mast aft to a ship's side or stern to help support the mast. **2.** A supporting device at or for the back of something else.

back·stitch (băk′stĭch′) *n.* A stitch made by inserting the needle at the midpoint of a preceding stitch so that the stitches overlap by half lengths. **—back′stitch′** *v.*

back·stop (băk′stŏp′) *n.* A screen or fence used to prevent a ball from going far out of a playing area. ❖ *tr.v.* **-stopped, -stop·ping, -stops** To serve as a backstop for.

back·stretch (băk′strĕch′) *n.* The part of an oval racecourse opposite the homestretch.

back·stroke (băk′strōk′) *n.* **1.** *Sports* A swimming stroke executed with the swimmer lying on the back. **2.** A backhanded stroke or motion. **3.** A stroke or motion in the direction of an original starting point. **—back′stroke′** *v.* **—back′strok′er** *n.*

back·swept (băk′swĕpt′) *adj.* Swept, angled, or slanting backward: *a backswept hairstyle.*

back·swim·mer (băk′swĭm′ər) *n.* Any of various aquatic bugs of the family Notonectidae that swim on their backs by means of broadened, oarlike hind legs.

back·swing (băk′swĭng′) *n.* The initial part of a stroke, in which one moves a racket or club, for instance, to the position from which forward motion begins.

back•sword (băk′sôrd′, -sōrd′) *n.* **1.** A sword with only one cutting edge. **2.** A one-handed fencing stick; a singlestick.

back talk *n.* Insolent or impudent retorts.

back-to-back (băk′tə-băk′) *adj.* Consecutive; successive.

back•track (băk′trăk′) *intr.v.* **-tracked, -track•ing, -tracks 1.** To go back over the course by which one has come. **2.** To return to a previous point or subject, as in a lecture. **3.** To reverse one's position or policy.

back•up (băk′ŭp′) *n.* **1a.** A reserve or substitute. **b.** *Computer Science* A copy of a program or file stored separately from the original. **2a.** Support or backing. **b.** *Music* A background accompaniment. **3.** An overflow or accumulation caused by clogging or by a stoppage. ❖ *adj.* Extra; standby.

back•ward (băk′wərd) *adj.* **1.** Directed or facing toward the back or rear. **2.** Done or arranged so as to be opposite to previous occurrence or normal use. **3.** Unwilling to act; reluctant; shy. **4.** Behind in progress or development: *backward technology.* ❖ *adv.* or **back•wards** (-wərdz) **1.** To or toward the back or rear. **2.** With the back leading. **3.** In a reverse manner or order. **4.** To, toward, or into the past. **5.** Toward a worse or less advanced condition. —**back′ward•ly** *adv.* —**back′ward•ness** *n.*

> **USAGE NOTE** As adverbs, *backward* and *backwards* are interchangeable: *stepped backward; a mirror facing backwards.* In Standard English, however, the adjective has no -*s*: *a backward view.*

back•wash (băk′wŏsh′, -wôsh′) *n.* **1a.** A backward flow of water, as from oars. **b.** See **backrush. 2.** A backward flow of air, as from an aircraft propeller. **3.** A result of an event.

back•wa•ter (băk′wô′tər, -wŏt′ər) *n.* **1.** Water held or pushed back, as by a dam or current. **2.** A place or situation regarded as isolated, stagnant, or backward.

back•woods (băk′wŏŏdz′) *pl.n.* (used with a sing. or pl. verb) **1.** Heavily wooded, uncultivated, thinly settled areas. **2.** An area that is far from population centers or that is held to be culturally backward.

back•yard also **back yard** (băk′yärd′) *n.* A yard at the rear of a house.

Ba•co•lod (bä-kō′lôd′) A city of NW Negros I. in the S-central Philippines. Pop. 343,048.

ba•con (bā′kən) *n.* The salted and smoked meat from the back and sides of a pig. [ME < OFr., of Gmc. orig.]

Bacon¹, Francis. 1st Baron Verulam and Viscount Saint Albans. 1561–1626. English philosopher and essayist who proposed a theory of scientific knowledge based on observation and experiment that came to be known as the inductive method. —**Ba•co′ni•an** (bä-kō′nē-ən) *adj. & n.*

Bacon², Francis 1909–92. Irish-born British painter whose works often convey feelings of terror.

Bacon, Nathaniel 1647–76. English-born Amer. colonist in Virginia who led Bacon's Rebellion (1676).

Bacon, Roger Known as "Doctor Mirabilis." 1214?–92. English scientist and philosopher who wrote *Opus Majus* (1267).

bac•te•re•mi•a (băk′tə-rē′mē-ə) *n.* The presence of bacteria in the blood. —**bac′te•re′mic** (-mĭk) *adj.* —**bac′te•re′mi•cal•ly** *adv.*

bac•te•ri•a (băk-tîr′ē-ə) *n.* Plural of **bacterium.**

bac•te•ri•al (băk-tîr′ē-əl) *adj.* Relating to or caused by bacteria. —**bac′te′ri•al•ly** *adv.*

bac•te•ri•cide (băk-tîr′ĭ-sīd′) *n.* A substance that destroys bacteria. —**bac•te′ri•cid′al** (-sīd′l) *adj.*

bacterio– or **bacteri–** or **bacter–** *pref.* Bacteria; bacterial: *bacteriology.* [< NLat. *bactērium,* bacterium. See BACTERIUM.]

bac•te•ri•ol•o•gy (băk-tîr′ē-ŏl′ə-jē) *n.* The study of bacteria, esp. in relation to medicine and agriculture. —**bac•te′ri•o•log′ic** (-ə-lŏj′ĭk), **bac′te′ri•o•log′i•cal** *adj.* —**bac′te′ri•o•log′i•cal•ly** *adv.* —**bac′te′ri•ol′o•gist** *n.*

bac•te•ri•ol•y•sis (băk-tîr′ē-ŏl′ĭ-sĭs) *n., pl.* **-ses** (-sēz′) Dissolution or destruction of bacteria. —**bac′te′ri•o•lyt′ic** (-ə-lĭt′ĭk) *adj.*

bac•te•ri•o•phage (băk-tîr′ē-ə-fāj′) *n.* A virus that infects and lyses certain bacteria. —**bac′te′ri•o•phag′ic** (-făj′ĭk) *adj.* —**bac•te′ri•oph′a•gy** (-ŏf′ə-jē) *n.*

bac•te•ri•o•rho•dop•sin (băk-tîr′ē-ō-rō-dŏp′sĭn) *n.* A purple pigment similar to rhodopsin and produced by archaea of the genus *Halobacterium* that converts sunlight directly into chemical energy.

bac•te•ri•o•sta•sis (băk-tîr′ē-ō-stā′sĭs) *n., pl.* **-ses** (-sēz) The inhibition of growth, but not the killing, of bacteria.

bac•te•ri•o•stat (băk-tîr′ē-ō-stăt′) *n.* An agent, such as a chemical or biological material, that inhibits bacterial growth. —**bac•te′ri•o•stat′ic** *adj.*

bac•te•ri•um (băk-tîr′ē-əm) *n., pl.* **-te•ri•a** (-tîr′ē-ə) Any of the unicellular prokaryotic microorganisms of the class Schizomycetes, which vary in morphology and nutritional requirements and may be free-living, saprophytic, or pathogenic. [NLat. *bactērium* < Gk. *baktērion,* dim. of *baktron,* rod.]

bac•te•ri•u•ri•a (băk-tîr′ē-yŏŏr′ē-ə) *n.* The presence of bacteria in urine.

bac•te•rize (băk′tə-rīz′) *tr.v.* **-rized, -riz•ing, -riz•es** To change the composition of (something) by means of bacterial action.

—**bac′te•ri•za′tion** (-rĭ-zā′shən) *n.*

bac•te•roid (băk′tə-roid′) *adj.* Resembling bacteria in appearance or action. ❖ *n.* Any of various structurally modified bacteria, such as those occurring on the root nodules of leguminous plants.

Bac•tra (băk′trə) See **Balkh.**

Bac•tri•a (băk′trē-ə) An ancient country of SW Asia; destroyed c. 130 B.C. by nomadic tribes. —**Bac′tri•an** *adj. & n.*

Bactrian camel *n.* A two-humped camel (*Camelus bactrianus*) native to central and southwest Asia.

bac•u•li•form (băk′yə-lə-fôrm′, bə-kyŏŏ′lə-) *adj.* Rod-shaped. [Lat. *baculum,* stick + –FORM.]

bad¹ (băd) *adj.* **worse** (wûrs), **worst** (wûrst) **1.** Not achieving an adequate standard; poor. **2.** Evil; sinful. **3.** Vulgar or obscene: *bad language.* **4.** Disobedient or naughty. **5.** Disagreeable, unpleasant, or disturbing: *bad news.* **6.** Unfavorable: *bad reviews.* **7.** Not fresh; rotten or spoiled. **8.** Injurious in effect; detrimental: *bad habits.* **9.** Not working properly; defective. **10.** Full of or exhibiting faults or errors: *bad grammar.* **11.** Having no validity; void: *bad checks.* **12.** Being so far behind in repayment as to be considered a loss: *bad loans.* **13.** Severe; intense: *a bad cold.* **14a.** Being in poor health or in pain: *I feel bad today.* **b.** Being in poor condition; diseased: *bad lungs.* **15.** Sorry; regretful: *She feels bad about it.* **16. bad•der, bad•dest** *Slang* Very good; great. ❖ *n.* Something that is below standard or expectations. ❖ *adv. Usage Problem* Badly. —**idioms: in bad** *Informal* In trouble or disfavor. **my bad** *Slang* Used to acknowledge that one is at fault. **not half (or so) bad** *Informal* Reasonably good. [ME *badde.*] —**bad′ness** *n.*

> **USAGE NOTE** *Bad* is often used as an adverb in sentences such as *We need water bad.* This usage is common in informal speech but is widely regarded as unacceptable in formal writing. In an earlier survey the sentence *His tooth ached so bad he could not sleep* was unacceptable to 92 percent of the Usage Panel. • The adverb *badly* is often used as the complement of verbs such as *feel,* as in *I felt badly about the whole affair,* where the choice of *badly* as opposed to *bad* may convey an implication that the distress is emotional, rather than physical. This usage is now widespread and is supported by analogy to the use of other adverbs with *feel* (as in *We feel strongly about this issue*). In an earlier survey a majority of the Usage Panel accepted this use of *badly* in speech, though *bad* is less likely to occasion objections.

bad² (băd) *v. Archaic* A past tense of **bid.**

Ba•da•joz (bä′də-hōz′, -thä-hōth′) A city of SW Spain on the Guadiana R. near the Portugal border. Pop. 124,579.

Ba•da•lo•na (bä′də-lō′nə, -thä-lō′nä) A city of NE Spain, a suburb of Barcelona. Pop. 218,725.

bad•ass (băd′ăs′) *Vulgar Slang n.* A mean-tempered or belligerent person. ❖ *adj.* Mean; belligerent.

bad blood *n.* Enmity or bitterness.

bade (băd, bād) *v.* A past tense of **bid.**

Ba•den (bäd′n) A historical region of SW Germany.

Ba•den-Ba•den (bäd′n-bäd′n) A city of SW Germany in the Black Forest near the French border; founded as a Roman garrison in the 3rd cent. A.D. Pop. 48,622.

Ba•den-Pow•ell (bäd′n-pō′əl), Sir **Robert Stephenson Smyth** 1857–1941. British soldier who founded the Boy Scouts (1908) and with his sister **Agnes** (1858–1945) the Girl Guides (1910).

badge (băj) *n.* **1a.** A device or emblem worn as an insignia of rank, office, or membership in an organization. **b.** An emblem given as an award or honor. **2.** A characteristic mark. [ME *bagge* < Norman Fr. *bage.*] —**badge** *v.*

badg•er (băj′ər) *n.* **1.** Any of several carnivorous burrowing mammals of the family Mustelidae, such as *Taxidea taxus* of North America, having short legs and long claws on the front feet. **2.** The fur or hair of this mammal. **3.** Any of several similar mammals, such as the ratel. ❖ *tr.v.* **-ered, -er•ing, -ers** To harass or pester persistently. See Syns at **harass.** [Perh. < BADGE.]

bad•i•nage (băd′n-äzh′) *n.* Light, playful banter. [Fr. < *badin,* joker < Provençal *badar,* to gape < Lat. *bātāre.*]

bad•lands (băd′lăndz′) *pl.n.* Barren land characterized by roughly eroded ridges, peaks, and mesas.

Badlands also **Bad Lands** A heavily eroded arid region of SW SD and NW NE.

bad•ly (băd′lē) *adv.* **worse** (wûrs), **worst** (wûrst) **1.** In a bad manner. **2.** Very much; greatly. See Usage Note at **bad¹.**

bad•min•ton (băd′mĭn′tən, -mĭt′n) *n.* A sport played by volleying a shuttlecock over a high net by means of a light racket. [After *Badminton,* the Duke of Beaufort's country seat in western England.]

bad•mouth or **bad-mouth** (băd′mouth′, -mouth′) *tr.v.* **-mouthed, -mouth•ing, -mouths** *Informal* To criticize or disparage, often spitefully or unfairly.

BAE *abbr.* **1.** Bachelor of Aeronautical Engineering **2.** Bachelor of Agricultural Engineering **3.** Bachelor of Architectural Engineering **4.** Bachelor of Art Education **5.** Bachelor of Arts in Education

Bae•da (bē′də) See **Bede.**

Bae•de•ker (bā′dĭ-kər) *n.* A guidebook to countries or a country. [After the guidebooks published by Karl BAEDEKER.]

Baedeker, Karl 1801–59. German publisher who originated his series of guidebooks in 1829.

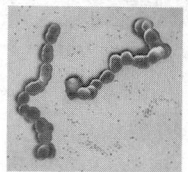
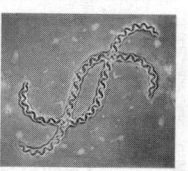

bacterium
top: rod-shaped bacteria
center: chains of ball-shaped *Streptococci*
bottom: spiral-shaped *Leptospira interrogans*

ă	pat	oi	boy
ā	pay	ou	out
âr	care	ŏŏ	took
ä	father	ōō	boot
ĕ	pet	ŭ	cut
ē	be	ûr	urge
ĭ	pit	th	thin
ī	pie	th	this
îr	pier	hw	which
ŏ	pot	zh	vision
ō	toe	ə	about,
ô	paw		item

Stress marks:
′ (primary);
′ (secondary); as in
lexicon (lĕk′sĭ-kŏn′)

BAEd *abbr.* Bachelor of Arts in Education

Ba·ez (bī-ĕz′, bī′ĕz′), **Joan** b. 1941. Amer. folk singer and political activist.

Baf·fin (băf′ĭn) A region of NE Nunavut, Canada.

Baffin, William 1584?–1622. English explorer who led expeditions (1612–16) in search of the Northwest Passage.

Baffin Bay An ice-clogged body of water between NE Canada and Greenland connecting the Arctic Ocean with the Atlantic.

Baffin Island An island of NE Nunavut, Canada, W of Greenland.

baf·fle (băf′əl) *tr.v.* **-fled, -fling, -fles** **1.** To frustrate or check (a person) by confusing or perplexing; stymie. **2.** To impede the force or movement of. ❖ *n.* **1.** A usu. static device that regulates the flow of a fluid or light. **2.** A partition that prevents interference between sound waves in a loudspeaker. [Perh. blend of Sc. Gael. *bauchle,* to denounce, revile publicly, and Fr. *bafouer,* to ridicule.] —**baf′fle·ment** *n.* —**baf′fler** *n.*

bag (băg) *n.* **1a.** A container of flexible material that is used for carrying or storing items. **b.** A handbag; a purse. **c.** A piece of hand luggage. **d.** An organic sac or pouch, such as an udder. **2.** An object that resembles a pouch. **3.** The amount that a bag can hold. **4.** An amount of game taken or legally permitted to be taken. **5.** *Baseball* A base. **6.** *Slang* An area of interest or skill. **7.** *Slang* A woman considered ugly or unkempt. ❖ *v.* **bagged, bag·ging, bags** —*tr.* **1.** To put into a bag. **2.** To cause to bulge like a pouch. **3.** To capture or kill (game). **4.** *Slang* To fail to attend purposely; skip. **b.** To stop doing or considering; abandon: *bagged their suggestion.* —*intr.* **1.** To put into or as if into a bag. **2.** To hang loosely. **3.** To swell out; bulge. —*idioms:* **bag and baggage 1.** With all one's belongings. **2.** To a complete degree; entirely. **in the bag** Assured of a successful outcome; virtually accomplished or won. [ME *bagge* < ON *baggi.*] —**bag′ful** *n.* —**bag′ger** *n.*

ba·gasse (bə-găs′) *n.* The dry fibrous residue remaining after the extraction of juice from sugar cane, used as a source of cellulose. [Fr. < Sp. *bagazo,* dregs < Lat. *bāca,* berry.]

bag·a·telle (băg′ə-tĕl′) *n.* **1.** An insignificant thing. **2.** A short, light piece of verse or music. **3.** A game played on an oblong table with a cue and balls. [Fr. < Ital. *bagatella,* dim. of dialectal *bagata,* little property, poss. < Lat. *bāca,* berry.]

Bage·hot (băj′ət), **Walter** 1826–77. British economist and social scientist who wrote *The English Constitution* (1867).

ba·gel (bā′gəl) *n.* A glazed, ring-shaped roll with a chewy texture, made from dough that is dropped into nearly boiling water and then baked. [Yiddish *beygl* < MHGer. **bougel,* dim. of *bouc,* ring < OHGer. *boug.*]

bag·gage (băg′ĭj) *n.* **1.** The trunks, bags, and parcels of a traveler; luggage. **2.** The movable equipment and supplies of an army. **3.** Superfluous or burdensome practices, regulations, ideas, or traits. **4a.** A woman prostitute. **b.** An impudent girl or woman. [ME *bagage* < OFr. *bague,* bundle, perh. of Gmc. orig. Sense 4, perh. < Fr. *bagasse* < Provençal *bagassa,* ult. < Ar. *baġī,* prostitute < *baġa,* to fornicate.]

bag·ging (băg′ĭng) *n.* Material used for making bags.

bag·gy (băg′ē) *adj.* **-gi·er, -gi·est** Bulging or hanging loosely: *baggy trousers.* —**bag′gi·ly** *adv.* —**bag′gi·ness** *n.*

Bagh·dad or **Bag·dad** (băg′dăd′) The cap. of Iraq, in the central part on the Tigris R.; founded in the 8th cent. Pop. 3,841,268.

bag lady *n. Slang* A homeless woman, esp. one in a big city, who carries her possessions with her, as in a shopping bag.

bag·man (băg′mən) *n.* **1.** *Slang* A person who collects money, as for racketeers. **2.** *Chiefly British* A traveling salesman.

ba·gnio (băn′yō, bän′-) *n., pl.* **-gnios 1.** A brothel. **2.** *Obsolete* A prison for slaves in Asian countries. **3.** *Obsolete* A public bathhouse in Italy or Turkey. [Ital. *bagno,* bath < Lat. *balneum* < Gk. *balaneion.*]

bag of waters *n.* See **water bag.**

bag·pipe (băg′pīp′) *n.* A musical instrument having a flexible bag inflated either by a tube with valves or by bellows, a double-reed melody pipe, and from one to four drone pipes. Often used in the plural. —**bag′pipe′** *v.* —**bag′pip′er** *n.*

ba·guette (bă-gĕt′) *n.* **1a.** A gem cut in the form of a narrow rectangle. **b.** The form of such a gem. **2.** *Architecture* A narrow convex molding. **3.** A small narrow loaf of French bread. [Fr., rod < Ital. *bacchetta,* dim. of *bacchio,* rod < Lat. *baculum,* stick.]

bag·wig (băg′wĭg′) *n.* A wig with the back hair encased in a small silk sack, worn in the 18th century.

bag·worm (băg′wûrm′) *n.* Any of several moths of the family Psychidae that construct fibrous cases of silk in which the plant-feeding larvae and wingless adult females live.

bah (bä, bă) *interj.* Used to express rejection or contempt.

Ba·ha'i (bä-hä′ē, bə-hī′) *adj.* Of or relating to a religion founded in 1863 in Persia and emphasizing the spiritual unity of all humankind. ❖ *n.* A teacher of or a believer in this faith. [Pers. *bahā'ī,* a follower of *Bahā'ullāh* < Ar. *bahā'u llāh,* the splendor of God < *bahā'u,* bound form of *bahā',* splendor < *bahā,* to be empty, be beautiful.] —**Ba·ha'ism** (bə-hä′ĭz′əm, -hī′-) *n.* —**Ba·ha'ist** *n.*

Ba·ha·mas (bə-hä′məz) also **Ba·ha·ma Islands** (-mə) An island country in the Atlantic Ocean E of FL and Cuba; gained independence from Great Britain in 1973. Cap. Nassau. Pop.

268,000. —**Ba·ha·mi·an** (-hā′mē-ən, -hä′-), **Ba·ha·man** (-hä′mən, -hä′-) *adj.* & *n.*

Ba·ha·sa Indonesia (bä-hä′sə) *n.* See **Indonesian 4.** [Indonesian, Indonesian language < Skt. *bhāṣā,* speech, language.]

Bahasa Ma·lay (mə-lā′) also **Bahasa Me·la·yo** (mə-lä′yoō) *n.* See **Malay 2.** [Malay *bahasa Melayu,* Malay language : *bahasa,* speech, language (< Skt. *bhāṣā*) + *Melayu,* Malay.]

Ba·ha·ul·lah (bä-hä′oō-lä′) 1817–92. Persian religious leader who founded the Baha'i religion (1863).

Ba·ha·wal·pur (bə-hä′wəl-poŏr′, -hä′wəl-poōr′) A region and former princely state of E-central Pakistan between the Sutlej R. and the Indian border.

Ba·hi·a (bə-hē′ə, bä-ē′ə) See **Salvador.** —**Ba·hi′an** *adj.* & *n.*

Ba·hí·a Blan·ca (bə-hē′ə bläng′kə, bä-ē′ə vläng′kä) A city of E Argentina on the **Bahía Blanca,** an inlet of the Atlantic Ocean SW of Buenos Aires. Pop. 255,145.

ba·hi·a grass (bə-hē′ə) *n.* A perennial tropical American grass (*Paspalum notatum*) grown in warm regions for forage, soil binding, and turf. [After *Bahia* (Salvador), Brazil.]

Bah·rain or **Bah·rein** (bä-rān′) A country comprising an archipelago of low sandy islands in the Persian Gulf between Qatar and Saudi Arabia; gained independence from Great Britain in 1971. Cap. Manama, on **Bahrain Island.** Pop. 549,000. —**Bah·rain′i** *adj.* & *n.*

Bahr el Gha·zal (bâr′ ĕl′ gə-zăl′, bär′ ĕl′ gä-zäl′) A river of SW Sudan flowing c. 805 km (500 mi) to Lake No, where it joins the Bahr el Jebel.

Bahr el Jeb·el (jĕb′əl) A river, c. 956 km (594 mi), of S Sudan, a section of the White Nile.

baht (bät) *n., pl.* **bahts** or **baht** See table at **currency.** [Thai *bāt.*]

ba·hu·vri·hi (bŭ′hoō-vrē′hē) *n., pl.* **-his** A compound word functioning as an adjective whose last element is in origin a noun, such as *high-fiber* in the phrase *high-fiber diet.* [Skt. *bahuvrīhiḥ,* having much rice (an example of the type) : *bahu-,* much + *vrīhiḥ,* rice.]

Bai·kal or **Bay·kal** (bī-kôl′, -kŏl′), **Lake** A lake of S-central Russia; the world's deepest lake, with a maximum depth of 1,742.2 m (5,712 ft).

bail[1] (bāl) *n.* **1.** Security, usu. a sum of money, exchanged for the release of an arrested person as a guarantee of that person's appearance for trial. **2.** Release from imprisonment provided by the payment of such money. **3.** A person who provides this security. ❖ *tr.v.* **bailed, bail·ing, bails 1.** To secure the release of by providing security. **2.** To release (a person) for whom security has been paid. **3.** *Informal* To extricate from a difficult situation: *bailed me out.* **4.** To transfer (property) to another for a special purpose but without permanent transference of ownership. [ME, custody < OFr. < *baillier,* to take charge of < Lat. *bāiulāre,* to carry a load < *bāiulus,* carrier of a burden.] —**bail′er** *n.*

bail[2] (bāl) *v.* **bailed, bail·ing, bails** —*tr.* **1.** To remove (water) from a boat with a container. **2.** To empty (a boat) of water by bailing. —*intr.* To empty a boat of water by bailing. ❖ *n.* A container used for bailing. —*phrasal verb:* **bail out 1.** To parachute from an aircraft; eject. **2.** To abandon a project. [< ME *baille,* bucket < OFr. < VLat. **bāiula,* water container < Lat. *bāiulāre,* to carry a load.] —**bail′er** *n.*

bail[3] (bāl) *n.* **1.** The arched, hooplike handle of a container, such as a pail. **2.** An arch or hoop, such as one of those used to support the top of a covered wagon. **3.** A hinged bar on a typewriter that holds the paper against the platen. **4.** The pivoting U-shaped part of a fishing reel that guides the line during rewinding. [ME *beil,* perh. < OE **bēgel* or of Scand. orig.]

bail[4] (bāl) *n.* **1.** *Chiefly British* A pole or bar used to confine or separate animals. **2.** *Sports* One of the two crossbars that form the top of a wicket used in the game of cricket. [OFr. dialectal, prob. < Lat. *baculum,* stick.]

bail·a·ble (bā′lə-bəl) *adj.* **1.** Eligible for bail: *a bailable defendant.* **2.** Allowing or admitting of bail: *a bailable offense.*

bail·ee (bā-lē′) *n.* A person to whom property is bailed.

bai·ley (bā′lē) *n., pl.* **-leys 1.** The outer wall of a castle. **2.** The space enclosed by this outer wall. [ME *bailli* < OFr. *baille,* prob. < Lat. *bacula,* pl. of *baculum,* log, stick.]

Bailey, Nathan or **Nathaniel** d. 1742. British lexicographer who compiled the *Universal Etymological English Dictionary* (1721).

Bailey bridge *n.* A steel bridge designed to be shipped in parts and assembled rapidly. [After Sir Donald *Bailey* (1901–85), British engineer.]

bail·ie (bā′lē) *n.* **1.** A Scottish municipal officer similar to an English alderman. **2.** *Obsolete* A bailiff. [ME *baillie,* town official < OFr., var. of *baillis.* See BAILIFF.]

bail·iff (bā′lĭf) *n.* **1.** A court attendant entrusted with duties such as the maintenance of order in court. **2.** An official who assists a British sheriff, able to execute writs, processes, and arrests. **3.** *Chiefly British* An overseer of an estate; a steward. [ME *baillif* < OFr. *baillis, baillif-,* overseer of an estate, steward < Med.Lat. **bāiulīvus* < Lat. *bāiulus,* carrier.]

bail·i·wick (bā′lə-wĭk′) *n.* **1.** A person's specific area of interest, skill, or authority. **2.** The office or district of a bailiff. [ME *bailliwik : baillif,* bailiff; see BAILIFF + *wik,* town (< OE *wīc* < Lat. *vīcus;* see VICINITY).]

bail·ment (bāl′mənt) *n.* **1.** The process of providing bail for an

Joan Baez

bagpipe

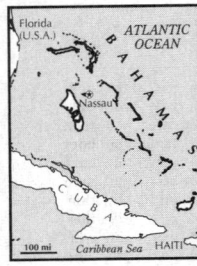

Bahamas

accused person. **2.** The act of delivering goods or personal property to another in trust.

bail·or (bāʹlər, bā-lôrʹ) *n.* One who bails property to another.

bail·out (bālʹoutʹ) *n.* A rescue from financial difficulties.

bails·man (bālzʹmən) *n.* One who provides bail or security.

bairn (bârn) *n. Scots* A child. [ME *barn* < OE *bearn.* See **bher-**¹ in App.]

bait¹ (bāt) *n.* **1a.** Food or other lure placed on a hook or in a trap and used in the taking of fish, birds, or other animals. **b.** Something, such as a worm, used for this purpose. **2.** An enticement; a temptation. **3.** *Archaic* A stop for food or rest during a trip. ❖ *v.* **bait·ed, bait·ing, baits** —*tr.* **1.** To place a lure in (a trap) or on (a fishing hook). **2.** To entice, esp. by trickery or strategy. **3.** To set dogs upon (a chained animal, for example) for sport. **4.** To attack or torment, esp. with insults or ridicule. **5.** To tease. **6.** To feed (an animal), esp. on a journey. —*intr. Archaic* To stop for food or rest during a trip. [ME < ON *beita,* food, fodder, fish bait. V. < ON *beita,* to put animals to pasture, hunt with dogs; see **bheid-** in App.] —**baitʹer** *n.*

> **USAGE NOTE** Note that the idiom *bated breath* contains the word *bated* ("abated, suspended"), not the more familiar *baited.*

bait² (bāt) *v.* Variant of **bate**².

bait and switch *n.* A sales tactic in which a bargain-priced item is used to attract customers who are then encouraged to purchase a more expensive similar item.

bait·fish (bātʹfĭshʹ) *n. Chiefly Chesapeake Bay & North Atlantic Coast* A small fish used for fishing bait.

baize (bāz) *n.* An often bright-green cotton or woolen material used chiefly as a cover for gaming tables. [Fr. *baies* < pl. of *bai,* bay-colored < Lat. *badius.*]

Ba·ja California (bäʹhä) also **Lower California** A mountainous peninsula of W Mexico extending SSE between the Pacific Ocean and the Gulf of California S of the US border.

Ba·jan (bāʹjən) *n.* A Barbadian. ❖ *adj.* Of or characteristic of Barbados. [Shortening and alteration of BARBADIAN.]

bake (bāk) *v.* **baked, bak·ing, bakes** —*tr.* **1.** To cook (food) with dry heat, esp. in an oven. **2.** To harden or dry (something) by subjecting to heat. —*intr.* **1.** To bake food. **2.** To become hardened or dry by baking. ❖ *n.* **1a.** The act or process of baking. **b.** An amount baked. **2.** A social gathering at which food is baked and served. [ME *baken* < OE *bacan.*]

bak·er (bāʹkər) *n.* **1.** One that bakes bread, cakes, or pastries. **2.** A portable oven.

Baker, Josephine 1906–75. Amer.-born French entertainer who became a popular jazz dancer and singer in Paris during the 1920s and 1930s.

Baker, Mount A peak, 3,287.3 m (10,778 ft), of NW WA in the Cascade Range E of Bellingham.

Baker, Sir Samuel White 1821–93. British explorer who founded a settlement at Ceylon (1848) and was the first European to sight Lake Albert (1864).

Baker Lake A lake of S Nunavut, Canada.

bak·er's dozen (bāʹkərz) *n.* A group of 13. [< the custom of adding an extra roll so that 12 would not weigh light.]

Ba·kers·field (bāʹkərz-fēldʹ) A city of S-central CA at the S end of the San Joaquin Valley NNW of Los Angeles. Pop. 247,057.

bak·er·sheet (-shētʹ) *n. Maine* See **dripping pan.**

bak·er·y (bāʹkə-rē) *n., pl.* **-ies** A place where products such as bread, cake, and pastries are baked or sold.

bake·shop (bākʹshŏpʹ) *n.* See **bakery.**

Bakh·ta·ran (bäkʹtə-ränʹ, вäкн'tä-) A city of W Iran WSW of Tehran; founded in the 4th cent. A.D. Pop. 665,636.

bak·ing powder (bāʹkĭng) *n.* A mixture of baking soda, starch, and an acidic compound such as cream of tartar that acts as a leavening agent when mixed with a liquid.

baking soda *n.* A white crystalline compound, $NaHCO_3$, with a slightly alkaline taste, used in effervescent salts and beverages, in fire extinguishers, and as an antacid.

ba·kla·va (bäʹklə-vä′, bäʹklə-vä′) *n.* A dessert made of layers of phyllo, chopped nuts, and honey. [Turk.]

bak·sheesh (bǎkʹshēsh′, bǎk-shēshʹ) *n., pl.* **baksheesh** A gratuity, tip, or bribe paid to expedite service, esp. in some Near Eastern countries. [Pers. *bakhshish,* present < MPers. *bakhshishn* < *bakhshīdan, bakhsh-,* to give presents < Avestan *bakhsh-.* See **bhag-** in App.]

Bakst (bäkst), **Léon Nikolaevich** 1866–1924. Russian painter and scenic designer who modernized theater design.

Ba·ku (bä-kōōʹ) The cap. of Azerbaijan, on the W shore of the Caspian Sea; acquired by Russia in 1806. Pop. 1,150,000.

Ba·ku·nin (bə-kōōʹnĭn, -nyĭn), **Mikhail Aleksandrovich** 1814–76. Russian anarchist and political theorist.

bal·a·cla·va (bǎlʹə-klä′və) *n.* A woolen hood covering the head and neck, worn in cold climates. [After BALAKLAVA.]

Ba·la·ki·rev (bə-läʹkĭ-rəf′), **Mili Alekseevich** 1837–1910. Russian composer whose works include the symphonic poems *Tamara* and *Russia.*

Bal·a·kla·va also **Bal·a·cla·va** (bǎlʹə-klä′və, -klä′və) A section of Sevastopol in the Crimea of S Ukraine; site of the charge of the Light Brigade (1854) during the Crimean War.

bal·a·lai·ka (bǎlʹə-līʹkə) *n.* A Russian musical instrument with a triangular body and three strings. [Russ. *balalaĭka,* of Turkic orig.]

bal·ance (bǎlʹəns) *n.* **1.** A weighing device, esp. one consisting of a rigid beam horizontally suspended at its center, with identical pans hung at either end. **2.** A state of equilibrium or parity. **3.** The power or means to decide. **4a.** A state of bodily equilibrium: *thrown off balance by a gust of wind.* **b.** The ability to maintain bodily equilibrium: *has good balance.* **5.** A stable mental or psychological state. **6.** A harmonious arrangement of parts or elements, as in a design. See Syns at **proportion. 7.** An influence or force tending to produce equilibrium; counterpoise. **8.** The difference in magnitude between opposing forces or influences. **9.** *Accounting* **a.** Equality of totals in the debit and credit sides of an account. **b.** The difference between such totals, either on the credit or the debit side. **10.** Something that is left over; a remainder. **11.** *Chemistry* Equality of mass and net electric charge of reacting species on each side of an equation. **12.** *Mathematics* Equality with respect to the net number of reduced symbolic quantities on each side of an equation. **13.** A balance wheel. **14.** **Balance** See **Libra** 1, 2a. ❖ *v.* **-anced, -anc·ing, -anc·es** —*tr.* **1.** To determine the weight of (something) in a weighing device. **2.** To compare by turning over in the mind: *balanced the pros and cons.* **3.** To bring into or maintain in a state of equilibrium. **4.** To act as an equalizing weight or force to; counterbalance. **5.** *Accounting* **a.** To compute the difference between the debits and credits of (an account). **b.** To reconcile or equalize the sums of the debits and credits of (an account). **c.** To settle by paying what is owed. **6.** To bring into or keep in equal or satisfying proportion or harmony. **7.** *Mathematics* To bring (an equation) into balance. **8.** *Chemistry* To bring (an equation) into balance. **9.** To move toward and then away from (a dance partner). —*intr.* **1.** To be in or come into equilibrium. **2.** To be equal or equivalent. **3.** To sway or waver as if losing or regaining equilibrium. **4.** To balance a dance partner. —*idioms:* **in the balance** In an undetermined and often critical position. **on balance** Taking everything into consideration; all in all. [ME *balaunce* < OFr. < VLat. **bilancia,* having two scale pans < Lat. *bilānx : bi-,* two; see **dwo-** in App. + *lānx,* scale.]

balance beam *n.* **1.** A horizontal raised beam used in gymnastic competition for balancing exercises. **2.** A competitive gymnastics event performed on this beam.

balance of payments *n.* A systematic record of a nation's total payments to and receipts from foreign countries.

balance of power *n.* Distribution of power in which no single nation is able to dominate or interfere with others.

balance of trade *n.* The difference in value between the total exports and total imports of a nation during a specific period.

bal·anc·er (bǎlʹən-sər) *n.* **1.** One that balances. **2.** See **halter**².

balance sheet *n.* A dated statement of a business or institution that lists the assets, debts, and owners' investment.

balance wheel *n.* **1.** A wheel that regulates rate of movement in machine parts, as in a watch. **2.** A stabilizing influence.

Bal·an·chine (bǎlʹən-chēn′, bǎlʹən-chēn′), **George** 1904–83. Russian-born Amer. ballet director who choreographed more than 100 ballets, including *Firebird* (1950).

bal·as (bǎlʹəs) *n.* A rose-red to orange spinel used as a semiprecious gem. [ME < OFr. *balais* and < OSpan. *balax;* both akin to Med.Lat. *balascus* < Ar. *balaḥṣ* < Pers. *Badakhshān,* a region of NE Afghanistan.]

ba·la·ta (bə-läʹtə) *n.* The nonelastic rubber obtained from the latex of the South American tree *Manilkara bidentata.* [Am.Sp. < Tupi and Galibi.]

Bal·a·ton (bǎlʹə-tŏn′, bŏlʹŏ-tôn′), **Lake** A lake of W-central Hungary SW of Budapest.

bal·bo·a (bǎl-bōʹə) *n.* See table at **currency.** [After Vasco Núñez de BALBOA.]

Balboa, Vasco Núñez de 1475–1517. Spanish explorer and colonial governor who claimed the Pacific Ocean for Spain (1513).

bal·brig·gan (bǎl-brĭgʹən) *n.* A knitted, unbleached cotton fabric for underwear. [After *Balbriggan,* a seaport of eastern Ireland.]

Balch (bôlch), **Emily Greene** 1867–1961. Amer. economist and sociologist who shared the 1946 Nobel Peace Prize.

bal·co·ny (bǎlʹkə-nē) *n., pl.* **-nies 1.** A platform that projects from the wall of a building and is surrounded by a railing, balustrade, or parapet. **2.** A gallery that projects over the main floor in a theater or auditorium. [Ital. *balcone* < OItal., scaffold, of Gmc. orig.] —**balʹco·nied** (-nēd) *adj.*

bald (bôld) *adj.* **bald·er, bald·est 1.** Lacking hair on the head. **2.** Lacking a natural or usual covering: *a bald spot on the lawn.* **3.** Lacking treads: *a bald tire.* **4.** *Zoology* Having white feathers or markings on the head. **5.** Lacking ornamentation; unadorned. **6.** Undisguised; blunt. [ME *balled,* prob. < *bal,* ball. See BALL¹.] —**baldʹly** *adv.* —**baldʹness** *n.*

bal·da·chin (bôlʹdə-kĭn, bǎlʹ-) also **bal·da·chi·no** (bǎlʹdə-kēʹnō) *n., pl.* **-chins** also **-chi·nos 1.** A rich fabric of silk and gold brocade. **2.** A canopy of fabric carried in church processions or placed over an altar, throne, or dais. **3.** *Architecture* A structure built in the form of a canopy, esp. over an altar. [Ital. *baldacchino* < OItal. < *Baldacco,* Baghdad.]

bald cypress *n.* A deciduous coniferous tree (*Taxodium*

Bahrain

Josephine Baker

distichum) native to the southeast United States and having alternate awl-shaped leaves and globose cones.

bald eagle *n.* A North American eagle (*Haliaeetus leucocephalus*) characterized by a brownish-black body and a white head and tail in the adult.

Bal·der or **Bal·dur** (bôl′dər) *n. Mythology* The Norse god of light. [ON *Baldr* < *ballr, baldr,* brave.]

bal·der·dash (bôl′dər-dăsh′) *n.* Nonsense. [Poss. alteration of Med.Lat. *balductum,* posset.]

bald-faced (bôld′fāst′) *adj.* **1.** Brash; undisguised: *a bald-faced lie.* **2.** *Zoology* Having a white face or face markings.

bald·head (bôld′hĕd′) *n.* **1.** A person whose head is bald. **2.** Any of several birds having white markings on the head. —**bald′-head′ed** (-ĭd) *adj.*

bald·ing (bôl′dĭng) *adj.* Becoming bald.

bald·pate (bôld′pāt′) *n.* **1.** See **baldhead 1. 2.** The widgeon of North America. —**bald′pat′ed** (-pā′tĭd) *adj.*

bal·dric (bôl′drĭk) *n.* A belt worn across the chest to support a sword or bugle. [ME *baudrik* < OFr. *baudre* and < MHGer. *balderich.*]

Bald·win (bôld′wĭn) *n.* An American variety of apple with red or yellow and red skin. [After Loammi *Baldwin* (1745–1897), American engineer.]

Baldwin I 1058–1118. King of Jerusalem (1100–18) who took part in the First Crusade (1096–99).

Baldwin, James Arthur 1924–87. Amer. writer whose works include *Notes of a Native Son* (1955).

Baldwin, Roger Nash 1884–1981. Amer. civil rights activist who helped found the American Civil Liberties Union (1918).

bale¹ (bāl) *n.* A large package of material tightly bound with twine or wire: *a bale of hay.* ❖ *tr.v.* **baled, bal·ing, bales** To wrap in a bale or in bales. [ME < OFr.] —**bal′er** *n.*

bale² (bāl) *n.* **1.** Evil. **2.** Mental suffering; anguish. [ME < OE *bealu.*]

Bal·e·ar·ic Islands (băl′ē-ăr′ĭk) An archipelago in the W Mediterranean off the E coast of Spain.

ba·leen (bə-lēn′) *n.* See **whalebone** 1. [ME *balene* < OFr. *baleine* < Lat. *balaena,* whale < Gk. *phalaina.*]

baleen whale *n.* Any of several usu. large whales of the suborder Mysticeti, such as the right whale, having a symmetrical skull, two blowholes, and whalebone plates instead of teeth.

bale·ful (bāl′fəl) *adj.* **1.** Portending evil; ominous. **2.** Harmful or malignant in intent or effect. —**bale′ful·ly** *adv.* —**bale′ful·ness** *n.*

> **USAGE NOTE** *Baleful* and *baneful* overlap in meaning, but *baleful* usually applies to that which is menacing or foreshadows evil: *a baleful look. Baneful* is said most often of that which is actually harmful or destructive: *baneful effects of war.*

bald eagle
Haliaeetus leucocephalus

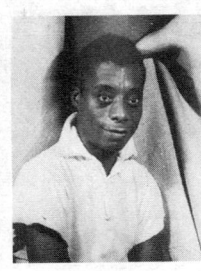

James Baldwin
1955 photograph by Carl
Van Vechten (1880–1964)

Bal·four (băl′fŏŏr′, -fôr′, -fōr′), **Arthur James** 1848–1930. British politician who served as prime minister (1902–05) and foreign secretary (1916–19).

Ba·li (bä′lē) An island of S Indonesia in the Lesser Sundas E of Java.

Ba·lik·pa·pan (bä′lĭk-pä′pän) A city of Indonesia in SE Borneo on an inlet of Makassar Strait. Pop. 280,675.

Ba·li·nese (bä′lə-nēz′, -nēs′) *adj.* Of or relating to Bali or its people, language, or culture. ❖ *n., pl.* **Balinese 1.** A native or inhabitant of Bali. **2.** The Indonesian language of Bali.

Balinese cat *n.* A domestic cat that is a hybrid between the Persian and Siamese and has long silky fur.

balk (bôk) *v.* **balked, balk·ing, balks** —*intr.* **1.** To stop short and refuse to go on. **2.** To refuse obstinately or abruptly: *She balked at the idea.* **3.** *Baseball* To make an illegal motion before pitching, allowing base runners to advance one base. —*tr.* **1.** To check or thwart by or as if by an obstacle. **2.** *Archaic* To let go by; miss. ❖ *n.* **1.** A hindrance, check, or defeat. **2.** *Baseball* An illegal move made by a baseball pitcher. **3.** *Games* One of the spaces between the cushion and the balk line on a billiard table. **4a.** An unplowed strip of land. **b.** A ridge between furrows. **5.** A wooden beam or rafter. [ME *balken,* to plow up in ridges < *balk,* ridge < OE *balca* and < ON *balkr,* beam.] —**balk′er** *n.*

Bal·kan (bôl′kən) *adj.* **1.** Of or relating to the Balkan Peninsula or the Balkan Mountains. **2.** Of or relating to the Balkan States or their inhabitants. ❖ *pl.n.* **Bal·kans** (bôl′kənz) The Balkan States.

Bal·kan·ize or **bal·kan·ize** (bôl′kə-nīz′) *tr.v.* **-ized, -iz·ing, -iz·es** To divide (a region or territory) into small, often hostile units. [< the political division of the Balkans in the early 20th cent.] —**Bal′kan·i·za′tion** *n.*

Balkan Mountains also **Bal·kans** (bôl′kənz) A mountain range of SE Europe extending from E Serbia to the Black Sea and rising to 2,377.2 m (7,794 ft).

Balkan Peninsula A peninsula of SE Europe bounded by the Black Sea, the Sea of Marmara, and the Aegean, Mediterranean, Ionian, and Adriatic seas. The **Balkan States** include Albania, Bulgaria, continental Greece, SE Romania, European Turkey, Yugoslavia, and the former Yugoslavian republics Slovenia, Croatia, Bosnia and Herzegovina, and Macedonia.

Balkh (bălk) Formerly **Bac·tra** (băk′trə) An ancient city in present-day N Afghanistan; legendary birthplace of the prophet Zoroaster.

Bal·khash (băl-käsh′, băl-kăsh′, -кнäsh′), **Lake** A shallow lake of SE Kazakhstan, having saline water in the E and fresh water in the W.

balk line also **balk·line** (bôk′lĭn′) *n.* A line parallel to one end of a billiard table, from behind which opening shots with the cue ball are made.

balk·y (bô′kē) *adj.* **-i·er, -i·est 1.** Given to stopping and refusing to go on: *a balky horse.* **2.** Difficult to operate or start: *a balky switch.* —**balk′i·ness** *n.*

ball¹ (bôl) *n.* **1.** A spherical or almost spherical object or entity: *a steel ball; a ball of flame.* **2.** *Sports* **a.** Any of various rounded movable objects used in various athletic activities and games. **b.** Such an object moving, thrown, hit, or kicked in a particular manner. **c.** A game, esp. baseball or basketball, played with such an object. **d.** A pitched baseball that does not pass through the strike zone and is not swung at by the batter. **3a.** A solid spherical or pointed projectile, such as one shot from a cannon. **b.** Projectiles of this kind considered as a group. **4.** A rounded part or protuberance, esp. of the body. **5. balls** *Vulgar Slang* **a.** The testicles. **b.** Courage, esp. when reckless. **c.** Great presumptuousness. ❖ *v.* **balled, ball·ing, balls** —*tr.* **1.** To form into a ball. **2.** *Vulgar Slang* To have sexual intercourse with. —*intr.* **1.** To become formed into a ball. **2.** *Vulgar Slang* To have sexual intercourse. —*phrasal verb:* **ball up** To confuse; bungle. —*idiom:* **on the ball** *Informal* **1.** Alert, competent, or efficient. **2.** Relating to qualities, such as competence or knowledge, that are necessary for success. [ME *bal,* prob. < OE **beall.*]

ball² (bôl) *n.* **1.** A formal gathering for social dancing. **2.** *Informal* An extremely enjoyable time or experience: *We had a ball during our vacation.* [Fr. *bal* < OFr. < *baller,* to dance < LLat. *ballāre* < Gk. *ballizein.* See **gᵂelə-** in App.]

Ball, John d. 1381. English agitator who was executed for his role in the Peasants' Revolt (1381).

Ball, Lucille 1911–89. Amer. actress best known as the star of the situation comedy *I Love Lucy* (1951–57).

bal·lad (băl′əd) *n.* **1a.** A narrative poem, often of folk origin and intended to be sung, consisting of simple stanzas and usu. having a refrain. **b.** The music for such a poem. **2.** A popular song esp. of a romantic or sentimental nature. [ME *balade,* poem or song in stanza form < OFr. *ballade* < O Provençal *balada,* song sung while dancing < *balar,* to dance < LLat. *ballāre.* See **BALL²**.] —**bal·lad′ic** (bə-lăd′ĭk, bă-) *adj.*

bal·lade (bə-läd′, bă-) *n.* **1.** A verse form usu. consisting of three stanzas of eight or ten lines each along with a brief envoy, with all stanzas and the envoy ending in the same one-line refrain. **2.** *Music* A composition, usu. for the piano, having the romantic or dramatic quality of a narrative poem. [ME *balade.* See **BALLAD**.]

bal·lad·eer (băl′ə-dîr′) *n.* A singer of ballads.

bal·lad·ist (băl′ə-dĭst′) *n.* A singer or composer of ballads.

bal·lad·ry (băl′ə-drē) *n.* Ballads considered as a group.

ballad stanza *n.* A four-line stanza often used in ballads, rhyming in the second and fourth lines and having four metrical feet in the first and third lines and three in the second and fourth.

ball-and-sock·et joint (bôl′ən-sŏk′ĭt) *n.* **1.** A synovial joint, such as the shoulder or hip joint, in which a spherical knob or knoblike part of one bone fits into a cavity or socket of another, permitting some degree of motion in every direction. **2.** A similar joint in a mechanical device.

bal·last (băl′əst) *n.* **1.** Heavy material that is placed in the hold of a ship or the gondola of a balloon to enhance stability. **2a.** Coarse gravel or crushed rock laid to form a bed for roads or railroads. **b.** The gravel ingredient of concrete. **3.** Something that gives stability, esp. in character. ❖ *tr.v.* **-last·ed, -last·ing, -lasts 1.** To stabilize or provide with ballast. **2.** To fill (a railroad bed) with ballast. [Perh. < OSwed. or ODan. *barlast* : *bar,* mere, bare + *last,* load.]

ball bearing *n.* **1.** A friction-reducing bearing consisting essentially of a ring-shaped track containing freely revolving hard metal balls against which a rotating shaft or other part turns. **2.** A hard ball used in such a bearing.

ball boy *n.* **1.** A male attendant on a tennis court who collects the ball when out of play. **2.** A boy in charge of the extra balls used in practice or those out of play.

ball cock *n.* A self-regulating device controlling the water supply in a tank, cistern, or toilet by a float connected to a valve that opens or closes with a change in water level.

bal·le·ri·na (băl′ə-rē′nə) *n.* **1.** A principal woman dancer in a ballet company. **2.** A woman ballet dancer. [Ital. < *ballare,* to dance < LLat. *ballāre* < Gk. *ballizein.* See **BALL²**.]

bal·let (bă-lā′, băl′ā′) *n.* **1.** A classical dance form characterized by grace and precision of movement and by elaborate formal gestures, steps, and poses. **2.** A theatrical presentation of this dance form, usu. with musical accompaniment, costumes, and scenery, conveying a story or theme. **3.** A musical composition written or used for this dance form. **4.** A company or group that performs ballet. [Fr. < Ital. *balletto,* dim. of *ballo,* dance < *ballare,* to dance. See **BALLERINA**.] —**bal·let′ic** (bă-lĕt′ĭk) *adj.*

bal·let·o·mane (bă-lĕt′ə-mān′) *n.* An ardent admirer of the ballet. [Fr. : *ballet,* ballet; see **BALLET** + *-mane,* ardent admirer (< Gk. *-manēs;* see **MANIA**).] —**bal·let′o·ma′ni·a** (-mā′nē-ə, -mān′yə) *n.*

ball·flow·er (bôl′flou′ər) *n. Architecture* An ornament in the form of a ball cupped in the petals of a circular flower.

ball game also **ball·game** (bôl′gām′) *n.* **1.** A game, esp. baseball, that is played with a ball. **2.** *Slang* **a.** A competition. **b.** A particular condition or set of circumstances.

ball girl *n.* **1.** A woman attendant on a tennis court who collects the ball when it is out of play. **2.** A girl in charge of the extra balls used in practice or those that are out of play.

bal·lis·ta (bə-lĭs′tə) *n., pl.* **-tae** (-tē′) An ancient and medieval engine of warfare used to hurl heavy projectiles. [Lat. < Gk. *ballistēs* < *ballein*, to throw. See gʷelə- in App.]

bal·lis·tic (bə-lĭs′tĭk) *adj.* Of or relating to ballistics. **—idiom:** **go ballistic** *Slang* To become very angry or irrational. [< BALLISTA.] **—bal·lis′ti·cal·ly** *adv.*

ballistic missile *n.* A projectile that assumes a free-falling trajectory after an internally guided, self-powered ascent.

bal·lis·tics (bə-lĭs′tĭks) *n.* (*used with a sing. verb*) **1a.** The study of the dynamics of projectiles. **b.** The study of the flight characteristics of projectiles. **2a.** The study of the functioning of firearms. **b.** The study of the firing, flight, and effects of ammunition. ❖ *adj.* Of, relating to, or engaging in the study of ballistics. **—bal·lis·ti′cian** (bǎl′ĭ-stĭsh′ən) *n.*

bal·lis·to·car·di·o·gram (bə-lĭs′tō-kär′dē-ə-grăm′) *n.* A recording made by a ballistocardiograph. [BALLIST(IC) + CARDIOGRAM.]

bal·lis·to·car·di·o·graph (bə-lĭs′tō-kär′dē-ə-grăf′) *n.* A device used to determine the volume of blood passing through the heart in a specific period of time and the force of cardiac contraction by measuring the body's recoil as blood is ejected from the ventricles with each heartbeat. [BALLIST(IC) + CARDIOGRAPH.] **—bal·lis′to·car′di·og′ra·phy** (-ŏg′rə-fē) *n.*

ball joint *n.* See **ball-and-socket joint** 2.

ball lightning *n.* A rare form of lightning in the shape of a glowing red ball, thought to consist of ionized gas.

bal·lo·net (bǎl′ə-nā′) *n.* A gasbag inside a balloon or a nonrigid airship that is inflated or deflated to control buoyancy. [Fr. *ballonnet*, dim. of *ballon*, balloon. See BALLOON.]

bal·loon (bə-lōon′) *n.* **1a.** A flexible bag designed to be inflated with hot air or with a gas that is lighter than the surrounding air, causing it to rise and float in the atmosphere. **b.** Such a bag with sufficient capacity to lift a payload. **c.** Such a bag shaped like a figure or object when inflated. **2.** A usu. round or oblong inflatable rubber bag used as a toy. **3.** *Medicine* A sac inserted into a body cavity or tube and distended with air or gas for therapeutic purposes. **4.** An outline containing the words that a cartoon character is saying. ❖ *v.* **-looned, -loon·ing, -loons** **—intr.** **1.** To ascend or ride in a balloon. **2.** To expand or swell out like a balloon. **3.** To increase or rise quickly. **—tr.** To cause to expand by or as if by inflating. ❖ *adj.* Suggestive of a balloon, as in shape. [Fr. *ballon* < Ital. dialectal *ballone*, augmentative of *balla*, ball, of Gmc. orig.] **—bal·loon′ist** *n.*

balloon mortgage *n.* A short-term mortgage in which small periodic payments are made until the completion of the term, at which time the balance is due as a single lump-sum payment.

balloon payment *n.* A final loan payment that is significantly larger than the payments preceding it.

balloon sail *n.* A comparatively large foresail used when going before the wind to supplement or replace a jib.

balloon tire *n.* A wide pneumatic tire, inflated to low pressure, used esp. in certain early bicycles and motor vehicles.

bal·lot (bǎl′ət) *n.* **1.** A sheet of paper or a card used to cast or register a vote. **2.** The act, process, or method of voting, esp. in secret. **3.** A list of candidates running for office; a ticket. **4.** The total of all votes cast in an election. **5.** The right to vote; franchise. **6.** A small ball once used to register a secret vote. ❖ *intr.v.* **-lot·ed, -lot·ing, -lots** **1.** To cast a ballot; vote. **2.** To draw lots. [Ital. *ballotta*, a small ball used to register a vote, dim. of dialectal *balla*, ball, of Gmc. orig.] **—bal′lot·er** *n.*

ballot box *n.* **1.** A box in which a voter deposits a marked ballot. **2.** The process of voting, esp. in secret.

bal·lotte·ment (bə-lŏt′mənt) *n. Medicine* A palpatory technique for detecting or examining a floating object in the body. [Fr. < *ballotter*, to toss < Ital. *ballotta*, dim. of dialectal *balla*, ball. See BALLOON.]

ball·park (bôl′pärk′) *n.* **1.** A park or stadium in which ball games are played. **2.** *Slang* The approximate range: *an estimate in the ballpark.* **—ball′park′** *adj.*

ball-peen hammer (bôl′pēn′) *n.* A hammer having one end of the head hemispherical and used in working metal.

ball·play·er (bôl′plā′ər) *n.* One who plays a ball game, esp. baseball.

ball·point (bôl′point′) *n.* A pen having as its writing point a small ball bearing that transfers ink stored in a cartridge onto a writing surface.

ball·room (bôl′rōōm′, -rŏom′) *n.* A large room for dancing.

ballroom dance *n.* Any of various social dances, such as the fox trot, tango, or waltz, in which couples follow a conventional pattern of steps. **—ballroom dancing** *n.*

balls·y (bôl′zē) *adj.* **-i·er, -i·est** *Vulgar Slang* Very tough and courageous, often recklessly or presumptuously so.

ball valve *n.* A valve regulated by a free-floating ball that moves

in response to fluid or mechanical pressure.

bal·ly·hoo (bǎl′ē-hōo′) *n., pl.* **-hoos** **1.** Sensational or clamorous advertising or publicity. **2.** Noisy shouting or uproar. ❖ *tr.v.* **-hooed, -hoo·ing, -hoos** To advertise or publicize by sensational methods. [?]

bal·ly·rag (bǎl′ē-răg′) *v.* Variant of **bullyrag.**

balm (bäm) *n.* **1a.** A chiefly Mediterranean perennial herb (*Melissa officinalis*) in the mint family, used as a seasoning or for tea. **b.** Any of several related plants in the mint family, such as the horse balm. **2.** Any of various aromatic resins from several trees and shrubs, esp. the balm of Gilead. **3.** An aromatic salve or oil. **4.** A pleasing aromatic fragrance. **5.** A soothing, healing, or comforting agent or quality. [ME *baume, balsam* < OFr. *basme* < Lat. *balsamum.* See BALSAM.]

bal·ma·caan (bǎl′mə-kǎn′, -kän′) *n.* A loose, full overcoat with raglan sleeves, originally made of rough woolen cloth. [After *Balmacaan*, an estate near Inverness, Scotland.]

balm of Gil·e·ad (gĭl′ē-əd, -ǎd′) *n.* **1a.** Any of several trees or shrubs of the genus *Commiphora*, esp. *C. opobalsamum*, of Arabia and Somalia. **b.** See **myrrh** 1. **2.** A poplar tree of hybrid origin, with heart-shaped leaves. [After GILEAD, known for its balm.]

Bal·mor·al (bǎl-môr′əl, -mŏr′-) *n.* **1.** A brimless Scottish cap with a flat round top. **2.** often **balmoral** A heavy laced walking shoe. [After *Balmoral* Castle in northeast Scotland.]

bal mu·sette (bǎl′ mōō-zět′) *n.* A dance hall in France, with music provided by an accordion band. [Fr. : *bal*, dance + *musette*, musette.]

balm·y (bä′mē) *adj.* **-i·er, -i·est** **1.** Having the quality or fragrance of balm; soothing. **2.** Mild and pleasant: *a balmy breeze.* **3.** *Slang* Eccentric in behavior. **—balm′i·ly** *adv.* **—balm′i·ness** *n.*

bal·ne·al (bǎl′nē-əl) *adj.* Of or relating to baths or bathing. [< Lat. *balneum*, bath. See BAGNIO.]

bal·ne·ol·o·gy (bǎl′nē-ŏl′ə-jē) *n.* The science of baths or bathing, esp. the study of the therapeutic use of mineral baths. [Lat. *balneum*, bath; see BAGNIO + -LOGY.]

ba·lo·ney[1] (bə-lō′nē) *n., pl.* **-neys** Variant of **bologna.**

ba·lo·ney[2] also **bo·lo·ney** (bə-lō′nē) *n. Slang* Nonsense. ❖ *interj.* Used to express disagreement or exasperation. [Alteration (influenced by BALONEY[1]) of BULLSHIT.]

bal·sa (bôl′sə) *n.* **1.** A tropical American tree (*Ochroma pyramidale*) having wood that is soft, light in weight, and used in insulation, floats, and crafts such as model airplanes. **2.** The wood of this tree. [Sp.]

bal·sam (bôl′səm) *n.* **1a.** Any of several aromatic resins that contain considerable amounts of benzoic acid, cinnamic acid, or both, or their esters. **b.** Any of several other fragrant plant resins, such as Canada balsam. **c.** A similar substance, esp. a fragrant ointment used as medication; a balm. **2.** Any of various trees yielding an aromatic resinous substance. **3.** See **jewelweed.** [Lat. *balsamum* < Gk. *balsamon*, of Semitic orig.; akin to Heb. *bōsem, bāśām*, balsam.]

balsam fir *n.* A North American tree (*Abies balsamea*) having a pyramidal shape and flat needles.

bal·sam·ic (bôl-sǎm′ĭk) *adj.* **1.** Of, relating to, or resembling balsam. **2.** Containing or yielding balsam.

balsamic vinegar *n.* **1.** An aromatic vinegar of Modena, Italy, made from white Trebbiano grape juice that is heated and aged in wooden barrels. **2.** Any of various similar vinegars. [< *balsamic*, restorative, curative (transl. of Ital. *aceto balsamico*).]

bal·sam·if·er·ous (bôl′sə-mĭf′ər-əs) *adj.* Yielding balsam.

balsam poplar *n.* A poplar (*Populus balsamifera*) of northern North America having ovate leaves.

Bal·sas (bôl′səs, bäl′-) A river flowing c. 724 km (450 mi) from S-central Mexico to the Pacific Ocean.

Balt (bôlt) *n.* **1.** A member of a Baltic-speaking people. **2.** A native or inhabitant of Lithuania, Latvia, or Estonia. [< Med.Lat. *Balthae*, Balts.]

Bal·tha·zar also **Bal·tha·sar** (bǎl-thā′zər, bǎl′thə-zär′) One of the three Magi.

Bal·tic (bôl′tĭk) *adj.* **1.** Of or relating to the Baltic Sea, the Baltic States, or a Baltic-speaking people. **2.** Of or relating to the branch of the Indo-European language family that contains Latvian, Lithuanian, and Old Prussian. ❖ *n.* The Baltic language branch.

Baltic Sea An arm of the Atlantic Ocean in N Europe bounded by Denmark, Sweden, Finland, Estonia, Latvia, Lithuania, Poland, and Germany.

Baltic States Estonia, Latvia, and Lithuania.

Bal·ti·more (bôl′tə-môr′, -mōr′) A city of N MD on an arm of Chesapeake Bay NE of Washington DC. Pop. 651,154. **—Bal′ti·mor′e·an** *n.*

Baltimore, Lord. See **Calvert.**

Baltimore oriole *n.* An eastern subspecies of the northern oriole, of which the male is bright orange and black and the female olive brown with white wing bars. [After Lord BALTIMORE.]

Bal·to-Sla·vic (bôl′tō-slä′vĭk, -slǎv′ĭk) *n.* A branch of the Indo-European language family that consists of the Baltic and Slavic languages. **—Bal′to-Sla′vic** *adj.*

Ba·lu·chi (bə-lōo′chē) also **Ba·loch** (-lōch′) *n., pl.* **Baluchi** or **-chis** also **Baluch** or **-lu·ches** (-lōo′chəz) **1.** A member of a traditionally nomadic Muslim people of Baluchistan. **2.** The Iranian language of the Baluchi.

ball-peen hammer

balsam fir
Abies balsamea

ă	pat	oi	boy
ā	pay	ou	out
âr	care	ŏŏ	took
ä	father	ōō	boot
ĕ	pet	ŭ	cut
ē	be	ûr	urge
ĭ	pit	th	thin
ī	pie	th	this
îr	pier	hw	which
ŏ	pot	zh	vision
ō	toe	ə	about,
ô	paw		item

Stress marks:
′ (primary);
′ (secondary), as in
lexicon (lĕk′sĭ-kŏn′)

Ba·lu·chi·stan (bə-lōō′chĭ-stän′) A desert region of W Pakistan bounded by Iran, Afghanistan, and the Arabian Sea.

bal·us·ter (băl′ə-stər) *n.* **1a.** One of the upright, usu. rounded supports of a balustrade. **b.** An upright support, such as a furniture leg, having a similar shape. **2.** One of the supporting posts of a handrail. [Fr. *balustre* < Ital. *balaustro* < *balaustra*, pomegranate flower (< a resemblance to the post) < Lat. *balaustium* < Gk. *balaustion*.]

bal·us·trade (băl′ə-strād′) *n.* A rail and the row of balusters or posts that support it, as along the front of a gallery. [Fr. < Ital. *balaustrata* < *balaustro*, baluster. See BALUSTER.]

Bal·zac (bôl′zăk′, băl′-, băl-zăk′), **Honoré de** 1799–1850. French writer who portrayed the panorama of French society in *La Comédie Humaine.* —**Bal·zac′i·an** (-zăk′ē-ən) *adj.*

BAM *abbr.* **1.** Bachelor of Applied Mathematics **2.** Bachelor of Arts in Music

Ba·ma·ko (bä′mə-kō′) The cap. of Mali, in the SW part on the Niger R.; a center of Muslim learning during the Mali empire (c. 11th–15th cent.). Pop. 658,275.

Bam·ba·ra (băm-bä′rä) *n., pl.* -**ra** or -**ras 1.** A member of a people of the upper Niger River valley. **2.** The Mandingo language of the Bambara, used as a lingua franca in Mali.

bam·bi·no (băm-bē′nō, bäm-) *n., pl.* -**nos** or -**ni** (-nē) **1.** A child; a baby. **2.** A representation of the infant Jesus. [Ital., dim. of *bambo*, child.]

bam·boo (băm-bōō′) *n., pl.* -**boos 1.** Any of various usu. woody, temperate or tropical grasses of the genera *Arundinaria, Bambusa, Dendrocalamus, Phyllostachys,* or *Sasa,* sometimes reaching heights of 20 to 30 meters (66 to 98 feet). **2.** The jointed, often hollow stems of these plants, used in construction and crafts. [Back-formation < earlier *bambos* (taken as pl.) < Du. *bamboes,* of Malay or Dravidian orig.]

Bamboo Curtain *n.* A political and ideological barrier between the West and the Communist countries of Asia after the Chinese revolution of 1949.

bamboo shoot *n.* The young shoot of certain species of the bamboo genera *Dendrocalamus* and *Phyllostachys,* sliced, cooked, and eaten as a vegetable, esp. in East Asian cuisine.

bam·boo·zle (băm-bōō′zəl) *tr.v.* -**zled**, -**zling**, -**zles** *Informal* To take in by elaborate methods of deceit; hoodwink. [?] —**bam·boo′zle·ment** *n.*

ban (băn) *tr.v.* **banned, ban·ning, bans 1.** To prohibit, esp. by official decree. See Syns at **forbid. 2.** *South African* Under the former system of apartheid, to deprive (one suspected of illegal activity) of the right of free movement and association with others. **3.** *Archaic* To curse. ❖ *n.* **1.** An excommunication or condemnation by church officials. **2.** A prohibition imposed by law or official decree. **3.** Censure, condemnation, or disapproval, esp. by the public. **4.** A curse; an imprecation. **5.** A summons to arms in feudal times. [ME *bannen,* to summon, banish, curse < OE *bannan,* to summon, and < ON *banna,* to prohibit, curse; see **bhā-** in App.]

ba·nal (bə-năl′, bā′nəl, bə-näl′) *adj.* Drearily commonplace and often predictable; trite. [Fr. < OFr., shared by tenants in a feudal jurisdiction < *ban,* summons to military service, of Gmc. orig. See **bhā-** in App.] —**ba·nal′ize′** *v.* —**ba·nal′ly** *adv.*

USAGE NOTE The pronunciation of *banal* varies among educated speakers of American English. In our 2001 survey, (bə-năl′) is preferred by 58 percent of the Usage Panel, (bā′nəl) by 28 percent, and (bə-näl′) by 13 percent (this pronunciation is more common in British English). None of these pronunciations should be considered incorrect.

ba·nal·i·ty (bə-năl′ĭ-tē, bā-) *n., pl.* -**ties 1.** The condition or quality of being banal; triviality. **2.** Something that is trite, obvious, or predictable; a commonplace.

ba·nan·a (bə-năn′ə) *n.* **1.** Any of several treelike Asian herbs of the genus *Musa,* esp. *M. acuminata,* having a crown of large leaves and a hanging fruit cluster. **2.** The elongated, edible fruit of these plants, having a thick yellow to red skin and white, aromatic, seedless pulp. [Port. and Sp. < Wolof, Mandingo, and Fulani.]

banana oil *n.* **1.** A liquid mixture of amyl acetate and usu. nitrocellulose, having a bananalike odor and used as a solvent or flavoring agent. **2.** See **amyl acetate. 3.** *Slang* Insincere flattery; nonsensical exaggeration.

banana republic *n.* A small country that is economically dependent on a single export commodity, such as bananas, and is typically governed by a dictator or the armed forces.

ba·nan·as (bə-năn′əz) *adj. Slang* Crazy. [< BANANA, crazy person.]

banana seat *n.* An elongated bicycle seat that usu. curves upward in the back. [< its shape.]

banana slug *n.* A large slug (*Ariolimax columbianus*) of northwestern North America, typically having a bright yellow body with black spots.

banana split *n.* A dessert consisting of ice cream and usu. flavored syrups, nuts, and whipped cream served on a banana that has been split lengthwise.

Ba·na·ras (bə-när′əs, -ēz) See **Varanasi.**

Ba·nat (bə-nät′, bä′nät′) A region of SE-central Europe extending across W Romania, NE Yugoslavia, and S Hungary.

ba·nau·sic (bə-nô′sĭk, -zĭk) *adj.* **1.** Merely mechanical; routine. **2.** Of or relating to a mechanic. [Gk. *banausikos* < *banausos,* mechanic.]

Ban·croft (băn′krôft′, -krŏft′, băng′-), **George** 1800–91. Amer. historian and diplomat who founded (1845) the naval academy at Annapolis.

band¹ (bănd) *n.* **1.** A thin strip of flexible material used to encircle and bind one object or hold a number of objects together. **2.** A strip or stripe that contrasts with something else in color, texture, or material. **3.** A narrow strip of fabric used to trim, finish, or reinforce clothing. **4.** Something that constrains or binds morally or legally. **5.** A simple ungrooved ring, esp. a wedding ring. **6a.** A neckband or collar. **b. bands** The two strips hanging from the front of a collar as part of the dress of certain clerics, scholars, and lawyers. **c.** A high collar popular in the 16th and 17th centuries. **7a.** *Biology* A chromatically, structurally, or functionally differentiated strip or stripe in or on an organism. **b.** *Anatomy* A cordlike tissue that connects or holds structures together. **8.** *Physics* **a.** A specific range of wavelengths or frequencies of electromagnetic radiation. **b.** A range of closely spaced electron energy levels in solids, the distribution and nature of which determine the electrical properties of a material. **9.** A cord or strip across the back of a book to which the sheets or quires are attached. ❖ *tr.v.* **band·ed, band·ing, bands 1.** To tie, bind, or encircle with or as if with a band. **2.** To mark or identify with or as if with a band. [ME *bende* (< OE *bend* and OFr. *bande, bende,* of Gmc. orig.) and ME *bond, band* (< ON *band*); see **bhendh-** in App.]

band² (bănd) *n.* **1a.** A group of people. **b.** A group of animals. **2.** A group of musicians who perform as an ensemble. **3a.** *Anthropology* A self-sufficient subdivision of a tribe, esp. among hunter-gatherers. **b.** *Canadian* An aboriginal group officially recognized by the Canadian government. ❖ *v.* **band·ed, band·ing, bands** —*tr.* To assemble or unite in a group. —*intr.* To form a group; unite. [Earlier *bande* < OFr., banner, troop identified by its standard, of Gmc. orig.]

band·age (băn′dĭj) *n.* A strip of material such as gauze used to protect, immobilize, compress, or support an injured body part. ❖ *tr.v.* -**aged, -ag·ing, -ag·es** To apply a bandage to. [Fr. < OFr. *bande,* band, strip. See BAND¹.] —**band′ag·er** *n.*

Band-Aid (bănd′ād′) A trademark used for a small adhesive bandage with gauze in the center.

ban·dan·na or **ban·dan·a** (băn-dăn′ə) *n.* A large handkerchief usu. figured and brightly colored. [Prob. Port. < Hindi *bāndhnū,* tie-dyeing < *bāndhnā,* to tie < Skt. *bandhati,* he ties. See **bhendh-** in App.]

Ban·dar Se·ri Be·ga·wan (bŭn′dər sĕr′ē bə-gä′wən) The cap. of Brunei, on the N coast of Borneo. Pop. 49,902.

Ban·da Sea (băn′də, bän′-) An arm of the Pacific Ocean in E Indonesia SE of Sulawesi and N of Timor. It includes the **Banda Islands,** a group of volcanic islands S of Ceram.

B & B *abbr.* bed-and-breakfast

band·box (bănd′bŏks′) *n.* A lightweight cylindrical box used to hold small articles of apparel.

B & E *abbr.* breaking and entering

ban·deau (băn-dō′) *n., pl.* -**deaux** (-dōz′) or -**deaus 1.** A narrow hair band. **2.** A brassiere. [Fr. < OFr. *bandel,* dim. of *bande,* band, strip. See BAND¹.]

band·ed (băn′dĭd) *adj.* Having bands or stripes.

ban·de·ril·la (băn′də-rē′ə, -rēl′yə) *n.* A barbed dart that is thrust into the bull's neck or shoulder muscles in a bullfight. [Sp., dim. of *bandera,* banner < VLat. *bandāria.* See BANNER.]

ban·de·ril·le·ro (băn′də-rē-âr′ō, -rēl-yâr′ō) *n., pl.* -**ros** One who implants banderillas during a bullfight. [Sp. < *banderilla,* banderilla. See BANDERILLA.]

ban·de·role or **ban·de·rol** (băn′də-rōl′) also **ban·ne·rol** (băn′ə-rōl′) *n.* **1.** A narrow forked flag or streamer. **2.** An inscribed representation of a ribbon or scroll. [Fr. < Ital. *banderuola,* dim. of *bandiera,* banner < VLat. *bandāria.* See BANNER.]

ban·di·coot (băn′dĭ-kōōt′) *n.* **1.** Any of several large rats of the genera *Bandicota* and *Nesokia* of southeast Asia. **2.** Any of several ratlike marsupials of the family Peramelidae of Australia and adjacent islands. [Telugu *bantikokku* : *banti,* ball + *kokku,* long beak.]

ban·dit (băn′dĭt) *n.* **1.** A robber, esp. with a gun. **2.** An outlaw; a gangster. **3.** One who cheats or exploits others. **4.** *Slang* A hostile aircraft, esp. a fighter. —*idiom:* **make out like a bandit** *Slang* To be highly successful in a given enterprise. [Ital. *bandito* < *bandire,* to band together, prob. of Gmc. orig. See **bhā-** in App.] —**ban′dit·ry** *n.*

Ban·djar·ma·sin (băn′jər-mä′sĭn, bän′-) See **Banjarmasin.**

band·lead·er (bănd′lē′dər) *n.* One who conducts a musical band, esp. a dance band.

band·mas·ter (bănd′măs′tər) *n.* A bandleader, esp. of a military, circus, or concert band.

ban·dog (băn′dôg′, -dŏg′) *n.* A dog kept chained as a watchdog or because of its ferocious aggressiveness. [ME *band-dogge* : *band,* leash, band + *dogge,* dog; see BAND¹ + DOG.]

ban·do·leer or **ban·do·lier** (băn′də-lîr′) *n.* A belt that is fitted with small pockets or loops for carrying cartridges and is worn across the chest by soldiers. [Fr. *bandoulière* < Sp. *bandolera*

balustrade

bamboo
golden bamboo
Phyllostachys aurea

band shell
Hollywood Bowl,
Los Angeles

dim. of *banda,* band, of Gmc. orig.]

ban•do•ne•on (băn-dō′nē-ŏn′) *n.* A small accordion esp. popular in Latin America. [Am.Sp. *bandoneón* < Ger. *Bandonion, Bandoneon* : Heinrich *Band* (1821–60), German inventor + *(Akkord)ion,* accordion; see ACCORDION.] —**ban•do′ne•on•ist** (-ə-nĭst) *n.*

ban•dore (băn′dôr′, -dōr′) also **ban•do•ra** (băn-dôr′ə, -dōr′ə) *n.* A Renaissance musical instrument resembling a guitar. [Port. *bandurra* < LLat. *pandūra* < Gk. *pandoura.*]

band•pass filter (bănd′păs′) *n.* A filter designed to transmit only a specified band of electromagnetic frequencies.

band saw *n.* A power saw for woodworking, consisting of a toothed metal band coupled to and driven around two wheels.

band shell also **band•shell** (bănd′shĕl′) *n.* A bandstand with a concave, almost hemispheric wall at the rear that serves as a sounding board.

bands•man (băndz′mən) *n.* A musician who plays in a band.

band•stand (bănd′stănd′) *n.* **1.** An outdoor stand or platform, often roofed, for a band or orchestra. **2.** An indoor stand or platform for musicians and other performers.

Ban•dung (bän′do͝ong′) A city of Indonesia in W Java SE of Jakarta; founded by the Dutch in 1810. Pop. 1,462,637.

band•wag•on (bănd′wăg′ən) *n.* **1.** *Music* An elaborately decorated wagon used to transport musicians in a parade. **2.** *Informal* A cause or party that attracts increasing numbers of adherents. **3.** *Informal* A current trend. —**band′wag′on•ing** *n.*

band•width (bănd′wĭdth′, -wĭth′) *n.* **1.** The numerical difference between the upper and lower frequencies of an electromagnetic radiation band, esp. an assigned range of radio frequencies. **2.** The amount of data that can be passed along a communications channel in a given period of time.

ban•dy (băn′dē) *tr.v.* **-died, -dy•ing, -dies 1a.** To toss or throw back and forth. **b.** To hit (a ball, for example) back and forth. **2a.** To give and receive (words, for example); exchange. **b.** To discuss in a casual or frivolous manner. ❖ *adj.* Bowed or bent in an outward curve: *bandy legs.* ❖ *n., pl.* **-dies** *Sports* **1.** A game resembling field hockey but played on ice by skaters. **2.** A stick, bent at one end, used in this game. [?]

ban•dy-leg•ged (băn′dē-lĕg′ĭd, -lĕgd′) *adj.* Bowlegged.

bane (bān) *n.* **1.** Fatal injury or ruin. **2a.** A cause of harm, ruin, or death. **b.** A source of persistent annoyance. **3.** A deadly poison. [ME, destroyer < OE *bana.* See **gʷhen-** in App.]

bane•ber•ry (bān′bĕr′ē) *n.* **1.** Any of several perennial herbs of the genus *Actaea,* native to northern temperate regions and having terminal berry clusters. **2.** The poisonous berry of such an herb.

bane•ful (bān′fəl) *adj.* Causing harm, ruin, or death; harmful. See Usage Note at **baleful.** —**bane′ful•ly** *adv.*

Banff (bămf) A town of SW Alberta, Canada, in the Rocky Mts. near Lake Louise. It is a popular winter resort. Pop. 6,098.

bang¹ (băng) *n.* **1.** A sudden loud noise, as of an explosion. **2.** A sudden loud blow or bump. **3.** *Informal* A sudden burst of action. **4.** *Slang* A sense of excitement; a thrill. ❖ *v.* **banged, bang•ing, bangs** —*tr.* **1.** To strike heavily and often repeatedly; bump. **2.** To close suddenly and loudly; slam. **3.** To handle noisily or violently. **4.** *Vulgar Slang* To have sexual intercourse with. —*intr.* **1.** To make a sudden loud, explosive noise. **2.** To crash noisily against or into something. ❖ *adv.* **1.** Exactly; precisely: *bang on the target.* **2.** Suddenly; abruptly: *cut the conversation bang off.* ***—phrasal verbs:*** **bang away 1.** To assail insistently, esp. with questions. **2.** To work diligently and often at length. **bang up** To damage extensively. [Prob. < ON, a hammering.]

bang² (băng) *n.* A fringe of short hair cut straight across the forehead. Often used in the plural. ❖ *tr.v.* **banged, bang•ing, bangs** To cut (hair) in bangs. [< BANG¹.]

bang³ (băng) *n.* Variant of **bhang.**

Ban•ga•lore (băng′gə-lôr′, -lōr′) A city of S-central India W of Chennai (Madras); founded 1537. Pop. 2,660,088.

bangalore torpedo *n.* A piece of metal pipe filled with an explosive, used to clear a path through barbed wire or to detonate land mines. [After BANGALORE.]

bang•er (băng′ər) *n. Chiefly British* **1.** A sausage. **2.** A noisy old car. **3.** A firework that explodes with a sudden loud noise.

Bang•ka or **Ban•ka** (băng′kə) An island of W Indonesia in the Java Sea separated from Sumatra by the **Strait of Bangka.**

bang•kok (băng′kŏk′, băng-kŏk′) *n.* A hat made of finely woven straw. [After BANGKOK.]

Bangkok also **Krung Thep** (gro͝ong tĕp′) The cap. of Thailand, in the SW near the Gulf of Siam. Pop. 5,876,000.

Bang•la•desh (bäng′glə-dĕsh′, băng′-) A country of S Asia on the Bay of Bengal; once a province of Pakistan (1947–71). Cap. Dhaka. Pop. 117,787,000. —**Bang′la•desh′i** *adj.* & *n.*

ban•gle (băng′gəl) *n.* **1.** A rigid bracelet or anklet, esp. one with no clasp. **2.** An ornament that hangs from a bracelet or necklace. [Hindi *baṅgrī,* glass bracelet.]

Ban•gor (băng′gôr, -gər) A city of S-central ME on the Penobscot R.; settled in 1769. Pop. 31,473.

Bang's disease (băngz) *n.* See **brucellosis** 2. [After Bernhard Laurits Frederik *Bang* (1848–1932), Danish veterinarian.]

Ban•gui (bäng-gē′, bäN-) The cap. of Central African Republic, in the S part on the Ubangi R. Pop. 473,817.

bang-up (băng′ŭp′) *adj. Informal* Very good; excellent. [< BANG¹.]

Bang•we•u•lu (băng′wē-o͞o′lo͞o), **Lake** A shallow lake on a plateau of NE Zambia.

ban•ian (băn′yən) *n.* Variant of **banyan.**

ban•ish (băn′ĭsh) *tr.v.* **-ished, -ish•ing, -ish•es 1.** To force to leave a place by official decree; exile. **2.** To drive away; expel: *banished fear.* [ME *banishen* < OFr. *banir, baniss-,* of Gmc. orig. See **bhā-** in App.] —**ban′ish•er** *n.* —**ban′ish•ment** *n.*

SYNONYMS *banish, exile, expatriate, deport, transport, extradite* These verbs mean to send away from a country or state. *Banish* applies to forced departure by official decree: *banished from the kingdom. Exile* specifies either voluntary or involuntary departure from one's own country because of adverse circumstances: *The royal family was exiled after the uprising. Expatriate* pertains to departure that is sometimes forced but often voluntary and may imply change of citizenship: *expatriated because of political beliefs. Deport* denotes the official act of expelling an alien: *deported for entering the country illegally. Transport* pertains to sending a convict abroad, usually to a penal colony: *transported offenders to Devil's Island. Extradite* applies to the delivery of an accused or convicted person to the state or country having jurisdiction over him or her: *will extradite the terrorists.*

ban•is•ter also **ban•nis•ter** (băn′ĭ-stər) *n.* **1.** A handrail, along with all of its supporting structures. **2.** One of the vertical supports of a handrail on a staircase. [Variant of BALUSTER.]

Ban•ja Lu•ka (bän′yə lo͞o′kə) A city of NW Bosnia and Herzegovina NW of Sarajevo; became part of Yugoslavia after World War I. Pop. 142,644.

Ban•jar•ma•sin also **Ban•djar•ma•sin** (bän′jər-mä′sĭn, bän′-) A city of Indonesia on a delta island of S Borneo; part of a Hindu kingdom in the 14th cent. Pop. 381,286.

ban•jo (băn′jō) *n., pl.* **-jos** or **-joes** A usu. fretted stringed instrument having a narrow neck and a hollow circular body with a covering of skin or plastic under the bridge. [Akin to Jamaican E. *banja,* fiddle; prob. akin to Kimbundu and Tshiluba *mbanza,* a plucked stringed instrument.] —**ban′jo•ist** *n.*

Ban•jul (bän′jo͞ol′) Formerly **Bath•urst** (băth′ərst) The cap. of Gambia, on an island at the mouth of the Gambia R. Pop. 49,181.

bank¹ (băngk) *n.* **1.** A piled-up mass, as of snow or clouds. **2.** A steep natural incline. **3.** An artificial embankment. **4.** The slope of land adjoining a body of water. Often used in the plural. **5.** A large elevated area of a sea floor. Often used in the plural. **6.** *Games* The cushion of a billiard or pool table. **7.** The lateral inward tilting, as of a vehicle, in turning or negotiating a curve. ❖ *v.* **banked, bank•ing, banks** —*tr.* **1.** To border or protect with a ridge or embankment. **2.** To pile up; amass: *banked earth along the wall.* **3.** To cover (a fire), as with ashes, to ensure continued low burning. **4.** To construct with a slope rising to the outside edge. **5a.** To tilt (an aircraft) laterally and inwardly in flight. **b.** To tilt (a motor vehicle) laterally and inwardly when negotiating a curve. **6.** *Games* To strike (a billiard ball) so that it rebounds from the table cushion. **7.** *Sports* To play (a ball or puck) in such a way as to make it glance off a surface. —*intr.* **1.** To rise in or take the form of a bank. **2.** To tilt an aircraft or a motor vehicle laterally when turning. [ME, of Scand. orig.]

bank² (băngk) *n.* **1a.** A business establishment where money is kept for saving or commercial purposes or is invested, supplied for loans, or exchanged. **b.** The offices or building housing such an establishment. **2.** *Games* **a.** The funds of a gambling establishment. **b.** The funds held by a dealer or banker in some gambling games. **c.** The reserve pieces, cards, chips, or play money in some games from which players may draw. **3a.** A stock for future or emergency use: *a grain bank.* **b.** *Medicine* A supply of human tissues or other materials, such as blood, held in reserve for future use. **4.** A place of safekeeping or storage. **5.** *Obsolete* A moneychanger's table or place of business. ❖ *v.* **banked, bank•ing, banks** —*tr.* To deposit in or as if in a bank. —*intr.* **1.** To transact business with or maintain an account in a bank. **2.** To operate a bank. ***—phrasal verb:*** **bank on** To have confidence in; rely on. [ME *banke* < Fr. *banque* < OItal. *banca,* bench, moneychanger's table < OHGer. *banc.*]

bank³ (băngk) *n.* **1.** A set of similar or matched things arranged in a row, esp.: **a.** A set of elevators. **b.** A row of keys on a keyboard. **2.** *Nautical* **a.** A bench for rowers in a galley. **b.** A row of oars in a galley. **3.** *Printing* The lines of type under a headline. ❖ *tr.v.* **banked, bank•ing, banks** To arrange in a row: *"Every street was banked with purple-blooming trees"* (Doris Lessing). [ME, bench < OFr. *banc* < LLat. *bancus,* of Gmc. orig.]

Ban•ka (băng′kə) See **Bangka.**

bank•a•ble (băng′kə-bəl) *adj.* **1.** Acceptable to or at a bank. **2.** Guaranteed to bring profit. —**bank′a•bil′i•ty** *n.*

bank acceptance *n.* A draft or bill of exchange drawn upon and accepted by a bank.

bank account *n.* Funds deposited in a bank that are credited to and subject to withdrawal by the depositor.

bank annuity *n. Chiefly British* See **consol.**

bank bill *n.* See **bank note.**

bank•book (băngk′bo͝ok′) *n.* A book in which a depositor's withdrawals and deposits are recorded by the bank.

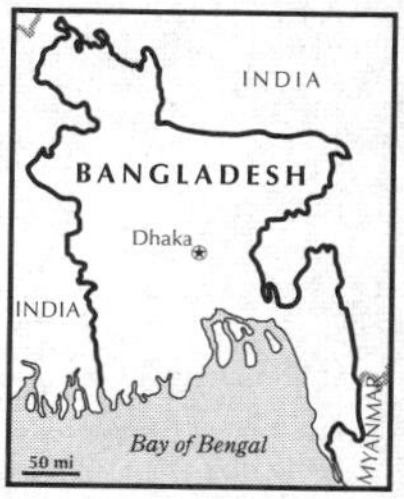

Bangladesh

banjo

ă	pat	oi	boy
ā	pay	ou	out
âr	care	o͝o	took
ä	father	o͞o	boot
ĕ	pet	ŭ	cut
ē	be	ûr	urge
ĭ	pit	th	thin
ī	pie	*th*	this
îr	pier	hw	which
ŏ	pot	zh	vision
ō	toe	ə	about, item
ô	paw		

Stress marks:
′ (primary);
′ (secondary), as in
lexicon (lĕk′sĭ-kŏn′)

bank·card (băngk′kärd′) *n.* A card issued by a bank authorizing the holder to receive bank services and often functioning as a debit card.

bank discount *n.* The interest on a loan computed in advance and deducted at the time the loan is made.

bank·er¹ (băng′kər) *n.* **1.** One serving as a bank officer or owner. **2.** *Games* The player in charge of the bank in some gambling games. —**bank′er·ly** *adj.*

bank·er² (băng′kər) *n.* One engaged in cod fishing off Newfoundland.

bank·er³ (băng′kər) *n.* A workbench used by a mason or sculptor. [< BANK³, bench (obsolete).]

bank·er's acceptance (băng′kərz) *n.* See **bank acceptance**.

bank·ers' hours (băng′kərz) *pl.n.* A short working day.

bank holiday *n.* **1.** A day on which banks are legally closed. **2.** *Chiefly British* A legal holiday when banks must stay closed.

bank·ing (băng′kĭng) *n.* **1.** The business of a bank. **2.** The occupation of a banker.

ban·kit (băng′kĭt) *n. Southern Louisiana & East Texas* Variant of **banquette** 2.

bank note *n.* A note issued by a bank promising to pay a sum to the bearer on demand and acceptable as money.

bank paper *n.* **1.** Bank notes considered as a group. **2.** Securities, drafts, and other commercial paper acceptable by a bank.

bank rate *n.* The rate of discount established by a country's central bank.

bank·roll (băngk′rōl′) *n.* **1.** A roll of paper money. **2.** *Informal* One's ready cash. ❖ *tr.v.* **-rolled, -roll·ing, -rolls** *Informal* To underwrite the expense of (a business venture, for example). —**bank′roll′er** *n.*

bank·rupt (băngk′rŭpt′, -rəpt) *n.* **1.** *Law* A debtor judged legally insolvent. **2.** A person who is totally lacking in a specified resource or quality. ❖ *adj.* **1a.** Having been legally declared financially insolvent. **b.** Financially ruined; impoverished. **2a.** Depleted of valuable qualities or characteristics. **b.** Totally depleted; destitute. **c.** Being in a ruined state. ❖ *tr.v.* **-rupt·ed, -rupt·ing, -rupts** **1.** To cause to become financially bankrupt. **2.** To ruin: *bankrupted their credibility.* [Fr. *banqueroute* < Ital. *banca rotta*, broken counter (< the practice of breaking the counters of bankrupt bankers) : *banca*, moneychanger's table; see BANK² + *rotta*, p. part. of *rompere*, to break (< Lat. *rumpere*; see reup- in App.).] —**bank′rupt·cy** (-rəpt-sē, -rap-sē) *n.* —**bank′rup′tive** *adj.*

Banks (băngks), Sir **Joseph** 1743–1820. British botanist who circumnavigated the globe (1768–71) with James Cook and cataloged many species of plant and animal life.

bank shot *n.* **1.** A shot in billiards in which the player causes a ball to rebound off a cushion. **2.** A shot in basketball in which the ball glances off the backboard before reaching the basket.

bank·si·a (băngk′sē-ə) *n.* Any of various Australian evergreen shrubs or trees of the genus *Banksia*, with narrow leaves, usu. yellow flowers, and small fruits in conelike clusters. [After Sir Joseph BANKS.]

Banks Island An island of N Northwest Terrs., Canada, in the Arctic Ocean W of Victoria I.

Ban·ne·ker (băn′ĭ-kər), **Benjamin** 1731–1806. Amer. mathematician and astronomer noted for his almanac (1792–1802).

ban·ner (băn′ər) *n.* **1a.** A piece of cloth on a staff used as a standard by a monarch, military commander, or knight. **b.** The flag of a nation, state, or army. **2.** A piece of cloth bearing a motto or legend, as of a club. **3.** A headline spanning the width of a newspaper page. **4.** *Botany* See **standard** 9. ❖ *adj.* Unusually good; outstanding. ❖ *tr.v.* **-nered, -ner·ing, -ners** *Informal* To give a banner headline to in a newspaper. [ME *banere* < OFr. *baniere* < VLat. **bandāria* < LLat. *bandum*, of Gmc. orig.]

ban·ner·et¹ (băn′ər-ĭt, -ə-rĕt′) also **ban·ner·ette** (băn′ə-rĕt′) *n.* A small banner. [ME *baneret* < OFr. *banerete*, dim. of *baniere*, banner. See BANNER.]

ban·ner·et² (băn′ər-ĭt, -ə-rĕt′) *n.* A feudal knight ranking between a knight bachelor and a baron. [ME *baneret* < OFr. < *baniere*, banner. See BANNER.]

ban·ne·rol (băn′ə-rōl′) *n.* Variant of **banderole**.

ban·nis·ter (băn′ĭ-stər) *n.* Variant of **banister**.

Bannister, Roger b. 1929. British runner who was the first person to run the mile in under four minutes (1954).

ban·nock (băn′ək) *n.* **1.** A flat, usu. unleavened bread made of oatmeal or barley flour. **2.** *Northern US, esp. New England* Thin cornbread baked on a griddle. [ME *bannok* < OE *bannuc*, of Celt. orig.]

Bannock *n., pl.* **Bannock** or **-nocks** **1.** A member of a Native American people inhabiting southeast Idaho and western Wyoming. **2.** The variety of Northern Paiute spoken by the Bannock.

Ban·nock·burn (băn′ək-bûrn′, băn′ăk-bûrn′) A town of central Scotland NNE of Glasgow on the **Bannock River**, a tributary of the Forth; site of Robert the Bruce's defeat of the English under Edward II (1314).

banns also **bans** (bănz) *pl.n.* An announcement, esp. in a church, of an intended marriage. [ME *banes*, pl. of *ban*, proclamation < OE *gebann* and < OFr. *ban* (of Gmc. orig.; see bhā- in App.).]

ban·quet (băng′kwĭt) *n.* **1.** An elaborate, sumptuous repast. **2.** A ceremonial dinner honoring a particular guest or occasion. ❖ *tr. & intr.v.* **-quet·ed, -quet·ing, -quets** To honor at or partake of a banquet. [OFr., dim. of *banc*, bench. See BANK³.] —**ban′quet·er** *n.*

banquet room *n.* A large room suitable for banquets.

ban·quette (băng-kĕt′) *n.* **1.** A platform lining a trench or parapet wall on which soldiers may stand when firing. **2.** also **ban·kit** (băng′kĭt) *Southern Louisiana & East Texas* A raised sidewalk. See Regional Note at *beignet*. **3.** A long upholstered bench placed against or built into a wall. **4.** A ledge or shelf, as on a buffet. [Fr. < Provençal *banqueta*, dim. of *banca*, bench, of Gmc. orig.]

bans (bănz) *pl.n.* Variant of **banns**.

ban·shee also **ban·shie** (băn′shē) *n.* A female spirit in Gaelic folklore believed to presage, by wailing, a death in a family. [Ir. Gael. *bean sídhe*, woman of the fairies, banshee : *bean*, woman (< OIr. *ben*; see g‴en- in App.) + *sídhe*, fairy (< OIr. *síde*, fairy mound; see sed- in App.).]

ban·tam (băn′təm) *n.* **1.** Any of various breeds of small domestic fowl that are often miniatures of larger breeds. **2.** A small but aggressive and spirited person. ❖ *adj.* **1.** Diminutive; miniature. **2.** Aggressive and spirited. [After *Bantam*, a region of western Java, Indonesia.]

ban·tam·weight (băn′təm-wāt′) *n.* **1.** A professional boxer weighing more than 112 and not more than 118 pounds (approx. 51–53.5 kilograms), heavier than a flyweight and lighter than a featherweight. **2.** A contestant of a similar weight in various sports.

ban·ter (băn′tər) *n.* Good-humored, playful conversation. ❖ *v.* **-tered, -ter·ing, -ters** —*tr.* To speak to in a playful or teasing way. —*intr.* To exchange mildly teasing remarks. [?] —**ban′ter·er** *n.* —**ban′ter·ing·ly** *adv.*

Ban·ting (băn′tĭng), Sir **Frederick Grant** 1891–1941. Canadian physiologist who shared a 1923 Nobel Prize.

bant·ling (bănt′lĭng) *n.* A young child. [?]

Ban·tu (băn′tōō) *n., pl.* **Bantu** or **-tus** **1.** A member of any of numerous linguistically related peoples of central and southern Africa. **2.** A group of more than 400 closely related languages spoken in central, east-central, and southern Africa, belonging to the South Central subgroup of the Niger-Congo language family. [< Proto-Bantu **bantu*, people : **ba-*, pl. human pref. + **-ntu*, entity.] —**Ban′tu** *adj.*

Ban·tu·stan (băn′tōō-stăn′) *n. Offensive* Any of the former Black homelands in South Africa. [< BANTU (on the model of HINDUSTAN).]

ban·yan also **ban·ian** (băn′yən) *n.* A tropical Indian fig tree (*Ficus benghalensis*) with aerial roots that descend from the branches and develop into additional trunks. [Short for *banyan tree*, merchants' tree < Port. *banian*, Hindu merchant < Gujarati *vāṇiyo* < Skt. *vāṇijaḥ*. See wen- in App.]

ban·zai (bän-zī′) *n.* A Japanese battle cry or patriotic cheer. [J., (may you live) ten thousand years : *ban*, ten thousand (< M Chin. *muanh, uan*) + *zai*, year (< M Chin. *swiajh, suaj*).]

ba·o·bab (bā′ō-băb′, bä′-) *n.* Any of several tropical trees of the genus *Adansonia*, esp. the African (*A. digitata*), with a water-filled trunk, palmately compound leaves, and edible gourdlike fruits. [Poss. < North African Ar. *būhibab*, fruit of many seeds < Ar. *'abū hibāb*, source of seeds : *'ab*, father, source + *hibāb*, of *habb*, seed.]

Bao·ding also **Pao·ting** (bou′dĭng′) A city of NE China SSW of Beijing. Pop. 594,966.

Bao·tou also **Pao·tow** (bou′tō′) A city of N China on the Huang He (Yellow R.) W of Hohhot. Pop. 1,075,920.

Bap. or **Bapt.** *abbr.* Baptist.

bap·tism (băp′tĭz′əm) *n.* **1.** A Christian sacrament marked by the symbolic use of water and resulting in the recipient's admission into the Christian community. **2.** An initiation, purification, or naming ceremony or experience. [ME *baptisme* < OFr. < LLat. *baptismus* < Gk. *baptismos* < *baptizein*, to baptize. See BAPTIZE.] —**bap·tis′mal** *adj.* —**bap·tis′mal·ly** *adv.*

baptism of fire *n.* **1.** A soldier's first experience of combat conditions. **2.** A severe ordeal experienced for the first time.

Bap·tist (băp′tĭst) *n.* **1.** A member of an evangelical Protestant church of congregational polity, believing in baptism of voluntary, conscious believers. **2. baptist** One that baptizes. [ME, baptizer < OFr. *baptiste* < LLat. *baptista* < Gk. *baptistēs* < *baptizein*, to baptize. See BAPTIZE.] —**Bap′tist** *adj.*

bap·tis·ter·y also **bap·tis·try** (băp′tĭ-strē) *n., pl.* **-ies** also **-tries** **1.** A part of a church or a separate building used for baptizing. **2.** A font used for baptism. [ME *baptisterie* < OFr. < LLat. *baptistērium* < Gk. *baptistērion* < *baptizein*, to baptize. See BAPTIZE.]

bap·tize (băp-tīz′, băp′tīz′) *v.* **-tized, -tiz·ing, -tiz·es** —*tr.* **1.** To admit into Christianity through baptism. **2a.** To cleanse or purify. **b.** To initiate. **3.** To give a Christian name to; christen. —*intr.* To administer baptism. [ME *baptizen* < OFr. *baptiser* < LLat. *baptīzāre* < Gk. *baptizein* < *baptein*, to dip.] —**bap·tiz′er** *n.*

bar¹ (bär) *n.* **1.** A relatively long, straight, rigid piece of solid material used as a fastener, support, barrier, or structural or mechanical member. **2a.** A solid oblong block of a substance, such as soap or candy. **b.** A rectangular block of a precious metal. **3.** *Sports* **a.** A horizontal bar. **b.** A horizontal rod that marks the height to be cleared in high jumping or pole vaulting. **4.** A stan-

baobab
Adansonia digitata

dard, expectation, or degree of requirement: *Her work set a high bar for others.* **5.** Something that impedes or prevents action or progress. **6.** A ridge, as of sand on a shore, that is formed by the action of tides or currents. **7.** A narrow marking, such as a stripe. **8.** A narrow strip worn on a military uniform indicating rank or service. **9.** *Heraldry* A pair of horizontal parallel lines across a shield. **10.** *Law* **a.** The nullification, defeat, or prevention of a claim or action. **b.** The process by which nullification, defeat, or prevention is achieved. **11.** The railing in a courtroom enclosing the area where the judges and lawyers sit, witnesses are heard, and prisoners are tried. **12.** A place of judgment; a tribunal. **13a.** Attorneys considered as a group. **b.** The profession of law. **14.** *Music* **a.** A vertical line drawn through a staff to mark off a measure. **b.** A measure. **15.** Variant of **barre. 16a.** A counter for serving drinks, esp. alcoholic drinks, and sometimes food. **b.** An establishment or room with such a counter. ❖ *tr.v.* **barred, barring, bars 1.** To fasten securely with a long, straight, rigid piece of material. **2.** To shut in or out with or as if with bars. **3.** To obstruct or impede; block. **4.** To keep out; exclude. **5.** To rule out; except. **6.** To mark with stripes or bands. **7.** *Law* To stop (a claim or action) by objection. ❖ *prep.* Except for; excluding. —*idiom:* **behind bars** In prison. [ME *barre* < OFr. < VLat. **barra.*]

bar² (bär) *n.* A unit of pressure equal to one million (10^6) dynes per square centimeter. [Gk. *baros,* weight. See **gʷerǝ-** in App.]

BAR *abbr.* Browning automatic rifle

bar. *abbr.* **1a.** barometer **b.** barometric **2.** barrel

Bar. *abbr. Bible* Baruch

bar– *pref.* Variant of **baro–.**

Ba·rab·bas (bǝ-rǎb'ǝs) In the New Testament, the condemned thief whose release, instead of that of Jesus, was demanded of Pilate by the multitude.

Ba·ra·cal·do (bär'ǝ-käl'dō, bä'rä-) A city of N Spain, a suburb of Bilbao. Pop. 105,088.

Ba·ra·co·a (bär'ǝ-kō'ǝ, bä'rä-) A city of SE Cuba on the Atlantic coast; the oldest settlement in Cuba. Pop. 35,754.

Ba·rak (bǝ-räk'), **Ehud** b. 1942. Israeli politician who served as prime minister from 1999–2001.

Ba·ra·ka (bǝ-rä'kǝ), **Imamu Amiri** Orig. LeRoi Jones. b. 1934. Amer. writer whose works focus on racial conflict.

Ba·ra·nof Island (bǎr'ǝ-nôf', -nŏf', bǝ-rä'nǝf) An island off SE AK in the Alexander Archipelago.

Ba·ra·nov (bǝ-rä'nǝf), **Aleksandr Andreevich** 1746–1819. Russian fur trader and first governor of the Russian colony of Alaska.

bar·a·the·a (bǎr'ǝ-thē'ǝ) *n.* A soft fabric of silk and cotton, silk and wool, or all wool. [?]

barb¹ (bärb) *n.* **1.** A sharp point projecting in reverse direction to the main point of a weapon or tool, as on an arrow. **2.** A cutting remark. **3.** *Zoology* One of the parallel filaments projecting from the main shaft of a feather. **4.** *Botany* A short, sharply hooked bristle or hairlike projection. **5.** See **barbel¹. 6.** Any of various Old World freshwater fishes of the genus *Barbus* or *Puntius* and related genera. **7.** A linen covering for a woman's head, throat, and chin worn in medieval times. ❖ *tr.v.* **barbed, barbing, barbs** To provide or furnish with a barb. [ME *barbe* < OFr., beard < Lat. *barba.* See **bhardh-ā-** in App.]

barb² (bärb) *n.* **1.** A horse of a breed introduced by the Moors into Spain from northern Africa that resembles the Arabians. **2.** One of a breed of domestic pigeons that is similar to the carrier and has dark plumage. [Fr. *barbe* < Ital. *barbero,* Berber < VLat. **Barbaria,* Barbary States < Lat. *barbarus,* barbarous. See BARBAROUS.]

Bar·ba·dos (bär-bä'dōs', -dōz', -dǝs) An island country of the E West Indies; achieved independence from Great Britain in 1966. Cap. Bridgetown. Pop. 261,000. —**Bar·ba'di·an** *adj. & n.*

Barbados cherry *n.* **1.** A tropical American evergreen shrub (*Malpighia glabra*) having red cherrylike edible fruits. **2.** The fruit of this plant.

bar·bar·i·an (bär-bâr'ē-ǝn) *n.* **1.** A member of a people considered by another nation or group to have a primitive civilization. **2.** A fierce, brutal, or cruel person. **3.** An insensitive, uncultured person; a boor. [Fr. *barbarien* < *barbare,* barbarous < Lat. *barbarus.* See BARBAROUS.] —**bar·bar'i·an** *adj.* —**bar·bar'i·an·ism** *n.*

bar·bar·ic (bär-bǎr'ĭk) *adj.* **1.** Of, relating to, or characteristic of barbarians. **2.** Marked by crudeness or lack of restraint in taste, style, or manner. [Lat. *barbaricus* < Gk. *barbarikos* < *barbaros,* foreign.] —**bar·bar'i·cal·ly** *adv.*

bar·ba·rism (bär'bǝ-rĭz'ǝm) *n.* **1.** An act, trait, or custom characterized by ignorance or crudity. **2a.** The use of words, forms, or expressions considered incorrect or unacceptable. **b.** A specific word, form, or expression so used. [Lat. *barbarismus,* incorrect use of a language, barbarism < Gk. *barbarismos* < *barbarizein,* to behave or speak like a barbarian < *barbaros,* non-Greek, foreign.]

bar·bar·i·ty (bär-bǎr'ĭ-tē) *n., pl.* **-ties 1.** Savage brutality or cruelty in actions or conduct. **2.** A cruel or savage act. **3.** *Usage Problem* Crudity; coarseness. See Usage Note at **barbarism.**

bar·ba·rize (bär'bǝ-rīz') *tr. & intr.v.* **-rized, -riz·ing, -riz·es** To make or become crude, savage, or barbarous. —**bar'ba·ri·za'tion** (-rĭ-zā'shǝn) *n.*

Bar·ba·ros·sa¹ (bär'bǝ-rŏs'ǝ, -rôs'ǝ) European name for Khair ed-Din. d. 1546. Greek-born Turkish corsair who with his brother **Arouj** (d. 1518) ravaged the coasts of Spain, Italy, and Greece.

Bar·ba·ros·sa² (bär'bǝ-rŏs'ǝ, -rôs'ǝ) See **Frederick I.**

bar·ba·rous (bär'bǝr-ǝs) *adj.* **1.** Primitive in culture and customs; uncivilized. **2.** Lacking refinement or culture; coarse. **3.** Characterized by savagery; very cruel. See Syns at **cruel. 4.** Marked by the use or occurrence of barbarisms in language. [< Lat. *barbarus* < Gk. *barbaros,* non-Greek, foreign.] —**bar'ba·rous·ly** *adv.* —**bar'ba·rous·ness** *n.*

Bar·ba·ry (bär'bǝ-rē, -brē) A region of N Africa on the Mediterranean coast between Egypt and the Atlantic Ocean; used as a base by pirates from the 16th to the 19th cent.

Barbary ape *n.* A tailless monkey (*Macaca sylvana*) of Gibraltar and northern Africa.

Barbary Coast 1. The Mediterranean coastal area of Barbary and the Barbary States. **2.** A waterfront area of San Francisco CA in the years after the 1849 gold rush.

Barbary sheep *n.* See **aoudad.**

Barbary States The North African states of Algeria, Tunisia, Tripoli, and Morocco, esp. from the 16th to the 19th cent.

bar·bas·co (bär-bäs'kō) *n., pl.* **-cos 1.** Any of several tropical American plants containing a substance that can stun or paralyze fish. **2.** Any of several Mexican plants of the genus *Dioscorea* having a root that yields an extract used for synthetic steroid hormones. [Am.Sp. < Sp., mullein, allection (poss. influenced by *barba,* beard) of *verbasco* < Lat. *verbascum.*]

bar·bate (bär'bāt') *adj.* Having a beard; bearded. [Lat. *barbātus* < *barba,* beard. See BARB¹.]

bar·be·cue (bär'bĭ-kyōō') *n.* **1.** A grill, pit, or outdoor fireplace for roasting meat. **2a.** A whole animal carcass or section thereof cooked over an open fire or on a spit. **b.** A social gathering, usu. outdoors, at which food is cooked over an open flame. ❖ *tr.v.* **-cued, -cu·ing, -cues** To cook over live coals or an open fire. [Am.Sp. *barbacoa,* of Taino orig.]

barbed (bärbd) *adj.* **1.** Having barbs. **2.** Cutting; stinging: *barbed criticism.* —**barb'ed·ness** (-bĭd-nĭs) *n.*

barbed wire *n.* Twisted strands of fence wire with barbs at regular intervals.

bar·bel¹ (bär'bǝl) *n.* One of the slender, whiskerlike tactile organs extending from the head of certain fishes. [Obsolete Fr. < OFr. < Med.Lat. *barbula,* dim. of LLat. *barbus,* beard < Lat. *barba.* See **bhardh-ā-** in App.]

bar·bel² (bär'bǝl) *n.* Any of several Old World freshwater fish of the genus *Barbus,* esp. *B. barbus,* having usu. four barbels on the upper jaw. [ME < OFr. < Med.Lat. **barbellus,* dim. of *barbus* < Lat. *barba,* beard. See BARBEL¹.]

bar·bell (bär'bĕl') *n.* A bar with adjustable weights at each end, lifted for sport or exercise. [BAR¹ + (DUMB)BELL.]

bar·bel·late (bär'bǝ-lāt', bär-bĕl'ĭt, -āt') *adj. Botany* Finely or minutely barbed. [< NLat. *barbella,* dim. of Latin *barba,* beard. See **bhardh-ā-** in App.]

bar·ber (bär'bǝr) *n.* One who cuts hair and shaves or trims beards professionally. ❖ *v.* **-bered, -ber·ing, -bers** —*tr.* **1.** To cut the hair of. **2.** To shave or trim the beard of. —*intr.* To work as a barber. [ME < OFr. *barbour* < Med.Lat. *barbātor* < Lat. *barba,* beard. See **bhardh-ā-** in App.]

Barber, Samuel 1910–81. Amer. composer whose works include the opera *Vanessa* (1958).

bar·ber·ry (bär'bĕr'ē) *n.* Any of various shrubs of the genus *Berberis* having often clustered leaves, small yellow flowers, and red, orange, or blackish berries. [ME *berberie* < Med.Lat. *berberis.*]

bar·ber·shop (bär'bǝr-shŏp') *n.* A barber's place of business. ❖ *adj.* Of or relating to the performance of sentimental songs for unaccompanied, usu. male voices in four-part harmony.

bar·ber's itch (bär'bǝrz) *n.* Inflammation of the hair follicles of skin that has been shaved, usu. caused by a staphyloccocal infection or fungus.

bar·bet (bär'bĭt) *n.* Any of various brightly colored tropical birds of the family Capitonidae that have a broad bristled bill and are related to the toucans. [Prob. < BARB¹.]

bar·bette (bär-bĕt') *n.* **1.** A platform or mound of earth within a fort from which guns are fired over the parapet. **2.** An armored protective cylinder around a revolving gun turret on a warship. [Fr., dim. of *barbe,* beard. See BARB¹.]

bar·bi·can (bär'bĭ-kǝn) *n.* A tower or other fortification on the approach to a castle or town, esp. one at a gate or drawbridge. [ME < OFr. *barbacane* < Med.Lat. *barbacana* < Pers. *barbārkhāna* : *barbār,* guard (< OIran. **parivāraka-,* protective) + *khān,* house (< MPers.).]

bar·bi·cel (bär'bĭ-sĕl') *n.* One of the minute hooked projections extending from and interlocking with the barbules of a feather. [NLat. *barbicella,* dim. of Latin *barba,* beard. See **bhardh-ā-** in App.]

bar·bi·tal (bär'bĭ-tôl', -tǎl') *n.* A barbiturate, $C_8H_{12}N_2O_3$, a crystalline powder used as a sedative and hypnotic esp. in the form of sodium barbital. [BARBIT(URIC ACID) + -AL³.]

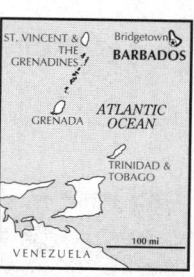
Barbados

barbel¹
bullhead catfish

ă	pat	oi	boy
ā	pay	ou	out
âr	care	ŏŏ	took
ä	father	ōō	boot
ĕ	pet	ŭ	cut
ē	be	ûr	urge
ĭ	pit	th	thin
ī	pie	th	this
îr	pier	hw	which
ŏ	pot	zh	vision
ō	toe	ǝ	about,
ô	paw		item

Stress marks:
' (primary);
' (secondary), as in
lexicon (lĕk'sĭ-kŏn')

bar·bi·tu·rate (bär-bĭch′ər-ĭt, -ə-rāt′, bär′bĭ-tōōr′ĭt, -āt′, -tyōōr′-, bär-bĭch′ə-wĭt) *n.* **1.** A salt or ester of barbituric acid. **2.** Any of a group of barbituric acid derivatives that act as central nervous system depressants and are used as sedatives or hypnotics. See Usage Note at **February**. [BARBITUR(IC ACID) + −ATE².]

bar·bi·tu·ric acid (bär′bĭ-tōōr′ĭk, -tyōōr′-) An organic acid, $C_4H_3O_3N_2$, used in the manufacture of barbiturates and some plastics. [Partial transl. of German *Barbitursäure* : barb- (perh. < the name *Barbara*) + -itur (ult. < *Ur(in)*, urine < Lat. *ūrīna*) + *Säure*, acid.]

Bar·bi·zon (bär′bĭ-zŏn′) *adj.* Of, relating to, or typical of a 19th-century group of landscape painters in France that included Millet. [After *Barbizon*, a village of north-central France.]

Bar·bu·da (bär-bōō′də) An island of Antigua and Barbuda in the West Indies N of Antigua; privately owned from 1691 to 1872. —**Bar·bu′dan** *adj. & n.*

bar·bule (bär′byōōl) *n. Zoology* A small barb or pointed projection, esp. fringing the edges of the barbs of feathers. [Lat. *barbula*, dim. of *barba*, beard. See **bhardh-ā-** in App.]

barb·wire (bärb′wīr′) *n.* Barbed wire.

bar·ca (bär′kə) *n.* A double-ended boat, skiff, or barge used in the Mediterranean. [Ital. *barca*. See BARK³.]

bar·ca·role also **bar·ca·rolle** (bär′kə-rōl′) *n.* **1.** A Venetian gondolier's song with a rhythm suggestive of rowing. **2.** A composition imitating such a song. [Fr. < Ital. *barcaruola* < *barcaruolo*, gondolier < *barca*, boat < Lat.]

Bar·ce·lo·na (bär′sə-lō′nə) A city of NE Spain on the Mediterranean; long a center of Catalan separatism. Pop. 1,770,296.

Barcelona chair A trademark used for a wide armless chair with leather cushions on a double X-shaped steel frame.

BArch *abbr.* Bachelor of Architecture

bar chart *n.* See **bar graph**.

bar code *n.* A series of vertical bars of varying widths, in which each of the digits zero through nine are represented by a different pattern of bars that can be read by a laser scanner, used esp. for computerized inventory control.

bard¹ (bärd) *n.* **1.** One of an ancient Celtic order of minstrel poets who composed and recited verses celebrating heroic exploits. **2.** A poet, esp. a lyric poet. [ME < Ir. and Sc. Gael. *bard* and < Welsh *bardd*.] —**bard′ic** *adj.*

bard² also **barde** (bärd) *n.* A piece of armor used to protect or ornament a horse. ❖ *tr.v.* **bard·ed**, **bard·ing**, **bards 1.** To equip (a horse) with bards. **2.** To cover (meat) in pieces of bacon or fat to preserve moisture during cooking. [ME *barde* < OFr. < OItal. *barda* < Ar. *barda'a*, packsaddle < Pers. *pardah*. See PURDAH.]

bar·da·cious (bär′dā′shəs) *adj. & adv. Southern & South Midland US* Variant of **bodacious**.

Bar·deen (bär-dēn′), **John** 1908–91. Amer. physicist who shared a Nobel Prize in 1956 and in 1972.

Bar·dot (bär-dō′), **Brigitte** b. 1935? French actress whose films include *And God Created Woman* (1956).

bare¹ (bâr) *adj.* **bar·er**, **bar·est 1.** Lacking the usual or appropriate covering or clothing; naked. **2.** Exposed to view; undisguised. **3.** Lacking the usual furnishings, equipment, or decoration. **4.** Having no addition, adornment, or qualification. **5.** Just sufficient; mere. **6.** *Obsolete* Bareheaded. ❖ *tr.v.* **bared**, **bar·ing**, **bares 1.** To make bare; uncover or reveal. **2.** To expose: *bared its teeth.* [ME *bar* < OE *bær*.] —**bare′ness** *n.*

bare² (bâr) *v. Archaic* A past tense of **bear¹**.

bare·back (bâr′băk′) also **bare·backed** (-băkt′) *adv. & adj.* On a horse or other animal with no saddle.

bare·boat (bâr′bōt′) *n.* A boat that is chartered without a crew and usu. without provisions. —**bare′boat′ing** *n.*

bare bones *pl.n. Informal* The basic elements or essentials: *bare bones of a plan.* —**bare′-bones′** *adj.* [*bâr′bōnz′*]

bare·faced (bâr′fāst′) *adj.* **1a.** Having no face covering. **b.** Having no beard. **2.** Without disguise; unconcealed. **3.** Undisguisedly bold; brazen. —**bare′fac·ed·ly** (-fā′sĭd-lē, -fāst′lē) *adv.* —**bare′fac′ed·ness** *n.*

bare·foot (bâr′fōōt′) also **bare·foot·ed** (-fōōt′ĭd) *adv. & adj.* With nothing on the feet; unshod: *walking barefoot in the grass.*

barefoot doctor *n.* A lay health care worker, esp. in rural China, trained in such activities as first aid.

ba·rege also **ba·rège** (bə-rĕzh′) *n.* A sheer fabric woven of silk or cotton and wool, used for women's apparel. [Fr. *barège*, after *Barèges*, a town in France.]

bare·hand·ed (bâr′hăn′dĭd) *adv. & adj.* With no covering on the hands: *fought barehanded.* —**bare′hand′ed·ness** *n.*

bare·head·ed (bâr′hĕd′ĭd) *adv. & adj.* With no covering on the head. —**bare′head′ed·ness** *n.*

Ba·reil·ly also **Ba·re·li** (bə-rā′lē) A city of N India ESE of Delhi; founded in the 16th cent. Pop. 587,211.

bare·knuck·le (bâr′nŭk′əl) *adj.* **1.** Wearing no gloves: *fought bare-knuckle.* ❖ *adj.* **1.** Wearing no gloves. **2.** *Slang* Of a fiercely implacable character.

bare·leg·ged (bâr′lĕg′ĭd, -lĕgd′) *adv. & adj.* With the legs uncovered: *ran barelegged.* —**bare′leg′ged·ness** *n.*

bare·ly (bâr′lē) *adv.* **1.** By a very little; hardly: *barely saw the road in the fog.* **2.** In a scanty manner; sparsely.

bare·na·ked (bâr′nā′kĭd, -nĕk′ĭd) *adj. & adv. Chiefly Northern US* With no clothes on.

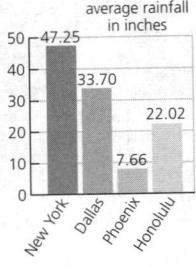

barge
on the Mississippi River

[bar graph]

average rainfall in inches

New York	Dallas	Phoenix	Honolulu
47.25	33.70	7.66	22.02

bar graph
the average annual rainfall
of several US cities

REGIONAL NOTE The chiefly Northern US expression *bare-naked* illustrates the linguistic process of redundancy, not always acceptable in Standard English but productive in regional dialect speech. A redundant expression combines two words that mean the same thing, thereby intensifying the effect. In *buck-naked*, used chiefly in the South Atlantic and Gulf States, *buck* is possibly an alteration of *butt*, "buttocks." If so, *bum-naked*, heard in various parts of the country, and *bare-ass(ed)*, attested in the Northeastern US, represent the same idea.

Bar·ents (bär′ənts, bâr′-), **Willem** 1550?–97. Dutch Arctic explorer who led several expeditions (1594–97) in search of the Northeast Passage.

Barents Sea A shallow section of the Arctic Ocean N of Norway and NW Russia.

barf (bärf) *tr. & intr.v.* **barfed**, **barf·ing**, **barfs** *Slang* To vomit. [Prob. imit.] —**barf** *n.*

bar·fly (bär′flī′) *n. Slang* One who frequents bars.

bar·gain (bär′gĭn) *n.* **1.** An agreement between parties fixing obligations that each promises to carry out. **2a.** An agreement establishing the terms of a sale or exchange of goods or services. **b.** Property acquired or services rendered as a result of such an agreement. **3.** Something offered or acquired at a price advantageous to the buyer. ❖ *v.* **-gained**, **-gain·ing**, **-gains** —*intr.* **1.** To negotiate the terms of an agreement, as to sell. **2.** To engage in collective bargaining. **3.** To arrive at an agreement. —*tr.* To exchange; trade. —*phrasal verb:* **bargain for** (or **on**) To count on; expect. —*idiom:* **into** (or **in**) **the bargain** Over and above what is expected; in addition. [ME < OFr. *bargaigne*, haggling < *bargaignier*, to haggle, of Gmc. orig.] —**bar′gain·er** *n.*

bargain basement *n.* A store basement where goods are sold at reduced prices. —**bar′gain-base′ment** *adj.*

bar·gain·ing chip (bär′gə-nĭng) *n.* Something, esp. an inducement or concession, used as leverage in negotiations.

barge (bärj) *n.* **1a.** A large, usu. flatbottom freight boat that is generally unpowered and towed or pushed by other craft. **b.** A large, open pleasure boat used for parties or formal ceremonies. **2.** An admiral's powerboat. ❖ *v.* **barged**, **barg·ing**, **barg·es** —*tr.* To carry by barge. —*intr.* **1.** To move clumsily. **2.** To intrude or interrupt, esp. rudely: *barged into the meeting.* [ME < OFr. < Lat. *barca*, boat.]

barge·board (bärj′bôrd′, -bōrd′) *n.* A board, often ornately carved, attached to a pitched roof in front of a gable. [?]

barg·ee (bär-jē′) *n. Chiefly British* A bargeman. [BARGE + −EE².]

bar·gel·lo (bär-zhĕl′ō) *n., pl.* **-los** A needlepoint stitch that produces zigzag lines. [After the *Bargello*, a museum in Florence, Italy.]

barge·man (bärj′mən) *n.* The captain or a crew member of a barge.

bar graph *n.* A graph consisting of parallel bars with lengths proportional to the frequency of specified quantities in a data set.

Bar Harbor A resort town of SE ME on Mount Desert I. Pop. 2,680.

bar·hop (bär′hŏp′) *intr.v.* **-hopped**, **-hop·ping**, **-hops** *Slang* To patronize a series of bars during an evening.

Ba·ri (bä′rē) A city of SE Italy on the Adriatic Sea; became part of the kingdom of Naples in 1557. Pop. 341,273.

bar·i·at·rics (băr′ē-ăt′rĭks) *n.* (*used with a sing. verb*) The branch of medicine that deals with obesity. [BAR(O)- + −IATRICS.] —**bar′i·at′ric** *adj.* —**bar′i·a·tri′cian** (-ə-trĭsh′ən) *n.*

ba·ril·la (bə-rĭl′yə, -rē′yə) *n.* **1.** Either of two Mediterranean saltworts (*Salsola kali* or *S. soda*) or a similar plant (*Halogeton sativus*). **2.** The crude sodium carbonate ash obtained from these plants. [Sp. *barrilla*.]

Bar·ing (bâr′ĭng), **Alexander.** 1st Baron Ashburton. 1774–1848. British public official who concluded the treaty between Great Britain and the US that defined the border between Canada and ME (1842).

bar·ite (bär′īt, băr′-) also **ba·ry·tes** (bə-rī′tēz) *n.* A crystalline mineral of barium sulfate, BaSO₄, used in paint and as the chief source of barium chemicals. [Gk. *barus*, heavy; see **gʷerə-** in App. + −ITE¹.]

bar·i·tone also **bar·y·tone** (băr′ĭ-tōn′) *n.* **1a.** A male singer or voice with a range higher than a bass and lower than a tenor. **b.** An instrument that sounds within this range. **c.** A vocal or instrumental part written in this range. **2.** A valved brass instrument similar to but larger than the euphonium. [Ital. *baritono* < Gk. *barutonos*, deep sounding : *barus*, heavy; see **gʷerə-** in App. + *tonos*, tone; see TONE.]

bar·i·um (bâr′ē-əm, băr′-) *n. Symbol* **Ba** A soft alkaline-earth metal used to deoxidize copper. Atomic number 56; atomic weight 137.33; melting point 725°C; boiling point 1,140°C; specific gravity 3.50; valence 2. See table at **element**. [BAR(YTA) + −IUM.] —**bar′ic** (-ĭk) *adj.*

barium sulfate *n.* A fine white powder, BaSO₄, used as a pigment, a contrast medium in x-ray photography of the digestive tract, and a filler for textiles, rubbers, and plastics.

bark¹ (bärk) *n.* **1.** The harsh sound uttered by a dog. **2.** A sound similar to a dog's bark. ❖ *v.* **barked**, **bark·ing**, **barks** —*intr.* **1.** To utter a bark. **2.** To make a sound similar to a bark. **3.** To speak sharply; snap. **4.** To work as a barker. —*tr.* To utter in a loud, harsh voice. —*idiom:* **bark up the wrong tree** To misdirect one's energies. [< ME *berken,* to bark < OE *beorcan.*]

bark² (bärk) *n.* **1.** The tough outer covering of the stems and roots of trees and other woody plants. **2.** A specific kind of bark used for a special purpose, as in medicine. ❖ *tr.v.* **barked, bark‧ing, barks 1.** To remove bark from (a tree or log). **2.** To rub the skin off of; abrade. **3.** To treat medically, tan, or dye using bark. [ME < ON *börkr.*] —**bark′y** *adj.*

bark³ also **barque** (bärk) *n.* **1.** A sailing ship with from three to five masts, all of them square-rigged except the aftermast, which is fore-and-aft rigged. **2.** A small vessel propelled by oars or sails. [ME *barke,* boat < OFr. *barque* < OItal. *barca* < Lat.]

bark beetle *n.* Any of various beetles of the family Scolytidae that burrow beneath the bark of trees, causing extensive damage.

bar‧keep‧er (bär′kē′pər) also **bar‧keep** (-kēp′) *n.* **1.** One who owns a bar that sells alcoholic drinks. **2.** See **bartender.**

bar‧ken‧tine also **bar‧quen‧tine** (bär′kən-tēn′) *n.* A sailing ship with from three to five masts of which only the foremast is square-rigged, the others being fore-and-aft rigged. [Prob. BARK³ + (BRIG)ANTINE.]

bark‧er¹ (bär′kər) *n.* **1.** One that makes a bark or a barking sound. **2.** An employee who stands before the entrance to a show and solicits customers with a loud sales spiel.

bark‧er² (bär′kər) *n.* One that removes bark from trees or logs or prepares it for tanning.

bark‧ing deer (bär′kĭng) *n.* See **muntjac.** [< the sound of its call.]

bar‧le‧duc also **Bar-le-Duc** (bär′lĭ-dook′) *n.* A savory preserve made of white currants or gooseberries. [After *Bar-le-Duc,* a town of northeast France.]

bar‧ley (bär′lē) *n.* **1.** A grass in the genus *Hordeum,* native to temperate regions and having flowers in terminal, often long-awned spikes. **2.** The grain of *H. vulgare* or its varieties, used for malt and cereal. [ME < OE *bærlic.*]

bar‧ley‧corn (bär′lē-kôrn′) *n.* **1.** The grain of barley. **2.** A unit of measure equal to the length of a grain of barley, or about ⅓ inch (0.85 centimeter).

barley sugar *n.* A clear hard candy made by boiling down sugar, formerly with an extract of barley added.

bar‧low (bär′lō′) *n.* An inexpensive, one- or two-bladed pocketknife. [After *Barlow,* the family of its makers, two brothers in Sheffield, England.]

Barlow, Joel 1754–1812. Amer. poet and diplomat whose works include "The Hasty Pudding" (1796).

barm (bärm) *n.* The yeasty foam that rises to the surface of fermenting malt liquors. [ME *berme* < OE *beorma,* yeast.]

bar‧maid (bär′mād′) *n.* A woman who serves drinks in a bar.

bar‧man (bär′mən) *n.* A man who serves drinks in a bar.

Bar‧me‧cid‧al (bär′mĭ-sīd′l) or **Bar‧me‧cide** (bär′mĭ-sīd′) *adj.* Plentiful or abundant in appearance only; illusory. [After *Barmecide,* a nobleman in *The Arabian Nights* who served an imaginary feast to a beggar.]

bar mitz‧vah or **bar miz‧vah** (bär mĭts′və) *n.* **1.** *Judaism* The ceremony that initiates and recognizes a 13-year-old Jewish boy as an adult responsible for his moral and religious duties. **2.** A boy so recognized. ❖ *tr.v.* **-vahed, -vah‧ing, -vahs** To confirm in the ceremony of bar mitzvah. [Heb. *bar miṣwâ* : Aram. *bar,* son + Heb. *miṣwâ,* command, commandment; see MITZVAH.]

barm‧y (bär′mē) *adj.* **-i‧er, -i‧est 1.** Full of barm; foamy. **2.** Eccentric; daft. [Sense 2, alteration of BALMY.]

barn (bärn) *n.* **1.** A farm building used to store farm products and shelter livestock. **2.** A large shed for the housing of vehicles. **3.** A particularly large, typically bare building. **4.** *Physics* A unit of area equal to 10⁻²⁴ square centimeters, used to measure cross sections in nuclear physics. [ME *bern* < OE *berærn* : *bere,* barley + *ærn,* house.]

Bar‧na‧bas (bär′nə-bəs), Saint. fl. 1st cent. A.D. Christian convert and missionary with Saint Paul to Cyprus and Asia Minor.

bar‧na‧cle (bär′nə-kəl) *n.* **1.** Any of various marine crustaceans of the subclass Cirripedia that in the adult stage form a hard shell and remain attached to submerged surfaces, such as rocks. **2.** The barnacle goose. [ME, barnacle goose < OFr. *bernacle* < Med.Lat. *bernacula,* dim. of *bernaca,* perh. < OIr. *báirneach,* limpet.] —**bar′na‧cled** *adj.*

barnacle goose *n.* A waterfowl *(Branta leucopsis)* of northern Europe and Greenland that breeds in the Arctic and has a white face with a black streak between the eyes and bill.

Bar‧nard (bär′nərd, bär-närd′), **Christiaan Neethling** 1923–2001. South African surgeon who performed the first human heart transplant (1967).

Bar‧na‧ul (bär′nə-ool′) A city of S-central Russia on the Ob R. S of Novosibirsk. Pop. 595,298.

barn‧burn‧er (bärn′bûr′nər) *n. Informal* An extremely impressive event or successful outcome.

barn dance *n.* A social gathering, often held in a barn, with music and square dancing.

Bar‧ne‧veldt or **Bar‧ne‧veld** (bär′nə-vĕlt′), **Jan van Olden** 1547–1619. Dutch public official who negotiated a treaty with Spain (1609) and opposed certain Calvinist doctrines; executed for treason.

barn owl *n.* A predatory nocturnal bird *(Tyto alba)* having a

white heart-shaped face, buff-brown upper plumage, and pale underparts, often nesting in buildings.

Barns‧ley (bärnz′lē) A municipal borough of N England N of Sheffield. Pop. 225,800.

barn‧storm (bärn′stôrm′) *v.* **-stormed, -storm‧ing, -storms** —*intr.* **1.** To travel around the countryside making political speeches, giving lectures, or presenting theatrical performances. **2.** To appear, as at fairs, in exhibitions of stunt flying and parachute jumping. **3.** To travel around an area appearing in exhibition sports events, esp. baseball games. —*tr.* To travel in this manner. —**barn′storm′er** *n.*

barn swallow *n.* A widely distributed bird *(Hirundo rustica)* that nests in barns and caves and has a deeply forked tail, a dark-blue back, and tan underparts.

Bar‧num (bär′nəm), **P(hineas) T(aylor)** 1810–91. Amer. showman who established The Greatest Show on Earth (1871).

barn‧yard (bärn′yärd′) *n.* The area surrounding a barn, often enclosed by a fence. ❖ *adj.* Smutty; earthy.

barnyard grass *n.* Any of certain grasses in the genus *Echinochloa,* esp. the Old World annual species *E. crusgalli,* used sometimes for forage and widespread as a weed.

baro- or **bar-** *pref.* Weight; pressure: *barometer.* [< Gk. *baros,* weight. See gʷerə- in App.]

Ba‧ro‧da (bə-rō′də) See **Vadodara.**

Ba‧ro‧graph (bär′ə-grăf′) *n.* A recording barometer. —**bar′o‧graph′ic** *adj.*

Ba‧ro‧ja y Nes‧si (bə-rō′hə ē nĕs′ē, bä-rō′hä), **Pío** 1872–1956. Spanish writer known esp. for his novels with a Basque setting.

Ba‧ro‧lo (bä-rō′lō′, bə-) *n.* A full-bodied red wine produced in Italy. [After *Barolo* in the Piedmont region of Italy.]

ba‧rom‧e‧ter (bə-rŏm′ĭ-tər) *n.* **1.** An instrument for measuring atmospheric pressure, used esp. in weather forecasting. **2.** Something that shows fluctuations; an indicator. —**bar′o‧met′ric** (bär′ə-mĕt′rĭk), **bar′o‧met′ri‧cal** *adj.* —**bar′o‧met′ri‧cal‧ly** *adv.* —**ba‧rom′e‧try** *n.*

bar‧on (bär′ən) *n.* **1a.** A British nobleman of the lowest rank. **b.** A nobleman, ranked differently in various countries. **c.** also **Baron** Used as the title for such a nobleman. **2a.** A male feudal tenant holding his rights and title directly from a superior. **b.** A lord or nobleman; a peer. **3.** A man with great wealth and influence in a specified sphere of activity. [ME < OFr., prob. of Gmc. orig.]

bar‧on‧age (bär′ə-nĭj) *n.* **1.** Peers considered as a group. **2.** Barons and baronesses considered as a group. **3.** The rank or dignity of a baron or baroness.

bar‧on‧ess (bär′ə-nĭs) *n.* **1.** The wife or widow of a baron. **2a.** A British noblewoman of the lowest rank. **b.** A noblewoman, ranked differently in various countries. **3.** also **Baroness** Used as the title for such a noblewoman.

bar‧on‧et (bär′ə-nĭt, bär′ə-nĕt′) *n.* **1.** A man holding a British hereditary title reserved for commoners, ranking immediately below the barons. **2.** also **Baronet** Used as the title for such a man. [ME, dim. of *baron,* baron. See BARON.]

bar‧on‧et‧age (bär′ə-nĭ-tĭj, -nĕt′ĭj) *n.* **1.** Baronets and baronetesses considered as a group. **2.** Baronetcy.

bar‧on‧et‧cy (bär′ə-nĭt-sē, -nĕt′sē) *n., pl.* **-cies** The rank or dignity of a baronet or baronetess.

bar‧on‧et‧ess (bär′ə-nĭ-tĭs, bär′ə-nĕt′ĭs) *n.* **1.** A woman holding a British hereditary title of honor reserved for commoners, ranking immediately below the barons. **2.** also **Baronetess** Used as the title for such a woman.

ba‧rong (bə-rông′, -rŏng′) *n.* A long, broad, leaf-shaped knife used by the Moros. [Malay *parang,* parang.]

ba‧ro‧ni‧al (bə-rō′nē-əl) *adj.* **1.** Of or relating to a baron or barony. **2.** Suited for or befitting a baron; stately and grand.

bar‧o‧ny (bär′ə-nē) *n., pl.* **-nies 1.** The domain of a baron or baroness. **2.** The rank or dignity of a baron or baroness.

ba‧roque (bə-rōk′) *adj.* **1.** also **Baroque** Of or being a style in art and architecture developed in Europe from the early 17th to mid-18th century, emphasizing dramatic, often strained effect and typified by elaborate ornamentation and overall balance of disparate parts. **2.** also **Baroque** *Music* Of or being a composition style that flourished in Europe from about 1600 to 1750, marked by expressive dissonance and elaborate ornamentation. **3.** Marked by rich and sometimes incongruous ornamentation. **4.** Irregular in shape. ❖ *n.* also **Baroque** The baroque style or period in art, architecture, or music. [Fr. < Ital. *barocco,* imperfect pearl, and < Port. *barroco.*] —**ba‧roque′ly** *adv.*

bar‧o‧re‧cep‧tor (bär′ə-rĭ-sĕp′tər) *n.* A sensory nerve ending that is stimulated by pressure changes, esp. one in the blood vessel walls.

bar‧o‧saur (bär′ə-sôr′) or **bar‧o‧sau‧rus** (bär′ə-sôr′əs) *n.* Any of various large sauropod dinosaurs of the genus *Barosaurus* of the late Jurassic Period, closely related to the diplodocus. [NLat. *Barosaurus,* genus name : Gk. *baros,* weight; see BARO- + Gk. *sauros,* lizard.]

Ba‧rot‧se‧land (bə-rŏt′sē-lănd′) A former kingdom of central Africa, now the W part of Zambia.

ba‧rouche (bə-roosh′) *n.* A four-wheeled carriage with a collapsible top, two double seats opposite each other, and a box seat outside for the driver. [Ger. *Barutsche* < Ital. *biroccio* < VLat.

barn swallow
Hirundo rustica

baroque
top: Bernini's *The Ecstasy of St. Theresa*
bottom: façade of St. Paul's Cathedral, London

ă	pat	oi	boy
ā	pay	ou	out
âr	care	oŏ	took
ä	father	oō	boot
ĕ	pet	ŭ	cut
ē	be	ûr	urge
ĭ	pit	th	thin
ī	pie	th	this
îr	pier	hw	which
ŏ	pot	zh	vision
ō	toe	ə	about,
ô	paw		item

Stress marks:
′ (primary);
′ (secondary), as in
lexicon (lĕk′sĭ-kŏn′)

birotium < LLat. *birotus*, two-wheeled : Lat. *bi-*, bi-; see **dwo-** in App. + Lat. *rota*, wheel.]

barque (bärk) *n.* Variant of **bark³**.

bar·quen·tine (bär′kən-tēn′) *n.* Variant of **barkentine**.

Bar·qui·si·me·to (bär′kə-sə-mā′tō, -kē-sē-mě′-) A city of NW Venezuela WSW of Caracas; founded 1552. Pop. 692,599.

bar·rack¹ (băr′ək) *tr.v.* **-racked, -rack·ing, -racks** To house (soldiers, for example) in quarters. ❖ *n.* **1.** Quarters for military personnel. Often used in the plural. **2.** A large building for temporary occupancy. Often used in the plural. [< Fr. *baraques*, barracks < Sp. *barracas*, soldiers' tents.]

bar·rack² (băr′ək) *v.* **-racked, -rack·ing, -racks** —*intr.* **1.** *Chiefly British* To jeer or shout at a player, speaker, or team. **2.** *Australian* To shout support for a team. —*tr.* *Chiefly British* To shout against; jeer at. [Perh. < Ir. dialectal *barrack*, to brag; akin to BRAG.] —**bar′rack·er** *n.*

bar·racks bag (băr′əks) *n.* A cloth bag, usu. with a drawstring, for the storage of clothing or laundry.

bar·ra·coon (băr′ə-kōōn′) *n.* A barracks in which slaves or convicts were formerly held in temporary confinement. [Sp. *barracón*, augmentative of *barraca*, hut. See BARRACK¹.]

bar·ra·cu·da (băr′ə-kōō′də) *n., pl.* **barracuda** or **-das** Any of various fierce, mostly tropical marine fishes of the genus *Sphyraena* that resemble pike and have a projecting lower jaw with fanglike teeth. [Am.Sp. < Sp. dialectal *barraco*, overlapping tooth.]

bar·rage¹ (bär′ij) *n.* An artificial obstruction built in a watercourse to increase its depth or to divert its flow. [Fr. < *barrer*, to bar < *barre*, bar < OFr. See BAR¹.]

bar·rage² (bə-räzh′) *n.* **1a.** A heavy curtain of artillery fire directed in front of allies to protect them. **b.** A rapid, concentrated missile discharge. **2.** An overwhelming outpouring, as of words: *a barrage of criticism.* [Fr. *(tir de) barrage*, barrier (fire). See BARRAGE¹.] —**bar·rage′** *v.*

barrage balloon *n.* A balloon anchored over a military objective to support nets that hinder enemy aircraft.

bar·ra·mun·da (băr′ə-mŭn′də) also **bar·ra·mun·di** (-dē) *n., pl.* **barramunda** or **-das** also **barramundi** or **-dis** Any of several Australian food fishes, such as the lungfish. [Prob. of Aboriginal orig.]

bar·ran·ca (bə-răng′kə) also **bar·ran·co** (-kō) *n., pl.* **-cas** also **-cos** *Southwestern US* **1.** A deep ravine or gorge. **2.** A bluff. [Sp., prob. of Iberian orig.]

Bar·ran·quil·la (băr′ən-kē′ə, -yä, bä′rän-) A city of N Colombia on the Magdalena R.; founded 1629. Pop. 917,486.

bar·ra·tor also **bar·ra·ter** (băr′ə-tər) *n.* One who engages in barratry. [ME *barateor* < OFr. *barateour*, swindler < *barater*, to cheat, perh. < VLat. *prattāre* < Gk. *prāttein*, to do.]

bar·ra·try (băr′ə-trē) *n., pl.* **-tries** **1.** The offense of persistently instigating lawsuits, typically groundless ones. **2.** Sale or purchase of positions in church or state. [ME *barratrie*, the sale of church offices < OFr. *baraterie*, deception, malversation < *barater*, to cheat. See BARRATOR.] —**bar′ra·trous** (-trəs) *adj.*

Barr body (bär) *n.* The condensed, inactive X-chromosome found in the nuclei of somatic cells of most female mammals. [After Murray Llewellyn *Barr* (1908–95), Canadian anatomist.]

barre also **bar** (bär) *n.* **1.** A handrail fixed to a wall, as in a dance studio, used by ballet dancers as a support in certain exercises. **2.** A fingering technique used with fretted stringed instruments in which a finger is laid across the fretboard to stop the strings. [Fr. < OFr. < VLat. *barra*, of Gaulish orig.]

barred (bärd) *adj.* Marked with bars or stripes.

barred owl *n.* A large North American owl (*Strix varia*) having barred brownish breast plumage, a streaked belly, and a strident hoot.

bar·rel (băr′əl) *n.* **1.** A large cylindrical container, usu. made of staves bound with hoops, with a flat top and bottom of equal diameter. **2.** The quantity that a barrel with a given or standard capacity will hold. **3.** Any of various units of volume or capacity. In the US Customary System it varies, as a liquid measure, from 31 to 42 gallons (120 to 159 liters) as established by law or usage. **4.** The cylindrical part or hollow shaft of any of various mechanisms, as: **a.** The cylindrical metal part of a firearm through which the bullet travels. **b.** A cylinder that contains a movable piston. **c.** The drum of a capstan. **d.** The cylinder within the mechanism of a timepiece that contains the mainspring. **5.** The trunk of a quadruped animal, such as a horse. **6.** *Informal* A large quantity. **7.** *Slang* An act or an instance of moving rapidly, often recklessly, in a motor vehicle. ❖ *adj.* Likened to a barrel, as in shape: *a barrel chest.* ❖ *v.* **-reled, -rel·ing, -rels** or **-relled, -rel·ling, -rels** —*tr.* To put or pack in a barrel. —*intr.* *Slang* To move at a high speed. —*idioms:* **on the barrel** (or **barrelhead**) Giving or requesting no credit: *paid cash on the barrel.* **over a barrel** In an awkward position from which extrication is difficult. [ME *barel* < OFr. *baril*.]

barrel cactus *n.* Any of several cacti, esp. in the genera *Ferocactus* and *Echinocactus,* having unbranched, globular to columnar, ribbed, spiny stems.

barrel chair *n.* A large upholstered chair having a high rounded back resembling a half barrel.

bar·rel·ful (băr′əl-fool′) *n., pl.* **-fuls** The amount that a barrel can hold.

barrel cactus
fishhook barrel cactus

bar·rel·head (băr′əl-hěd′) *n.* The flat top of a barrel.

bar·rel·house (băr′əl-hous′) *n.* **1.** A disreputable old-time saloon or house of prostitution. **2.** An early style of jazz characterized by boisterous piano playing, group improvisation, and a two-beat rhythm.

barrel organ *n.* A mechanical instrument on which a tune is played by the action of a revolving cylinder fitted with pegs or pins that open pipe valves supplied by a bellows.

barrel roll *n.* A flight maneuver in which an airplane makes a complete rotation on its longitudinal axis while approximately maintaining its original direction.

barrel vault *n.* A simple continuous vault, typically semicircular in cross section.

bar·ren (băr′ən) *adj.* **1a.** Not producing offspring. **b.** Incapable of producing offspring. **2.** Lacking vegetation. **3.** Unproductive of results or gains; unprofitable. See Syns at **futile**. **4.** Devoid of something specified. **5.** Lacking in liveliness or interest. ❖ *n.* A tract of unproductive land, often with a scrubby growth of trees. Often used in the plural. [ME *barreine* < OFr. *baraigne*, perh. of Gmc. orig.] —**bar′ren·ly** *adv.* —**bar′ren·ness** *n.*

Barren Grounds A treeless region of N Canada NW of Hudson Bay and E of the Mackenzie R. basin.

barren strawberry *n.* A low-growing, eastern North American perennial herb (*Waldsteinia fragarioides*) having strawberrylike leaves, yellow flowers, and small, dry, inedible fruit.

bar·rette (bə-rět′) *n.* A small clasp for holding hair in place. [Fr., dim. of *barre,* bar < OFr. See BAR¹.]

bar·ri·cade (băr′ĭ-kād′, băr′ĭ-kād′) *n.* **1.** A structure set up to obstruct the passage of an enemy. **2.** Something that serves as an obstacle; a barrier. ❖ *tr.v.* **-cad·ed, -cad·ing, -cades** **1.** To close off or block with a barricade. **2.** To keep in or out by such means. [Fr. < *barrique,* barrel < O Provençal *barrica* < VLat. **barrīca.* See EMBARGO.] —**bar′ri·cad′er** *n.*

Bar·rie (băr′ē), Sir J(ames) M(atthew) 1860–1937. British writer whose works include the play *Peter Pan* (1904).

bar·ri·er (băr′ē-ər) *n.* **1.** A structure built to bar passage. **2.** Something immaterial that obstructs or impedes. **3.** *Physiology* A membrane, tissue, or mechanism that blocks the passage of certain substances. **4.** *Ecology* A physical or biological factor that limits the migration, interbreeding, or free movement of individuals or populations. **5.** A boundary or limit. **6.** Something that separates or holds apart. **7.** A movable gate that keeps racehorses in line before a race. **8.** The palisades or fences enclosing the lists of a medieval tournament. Often used in the plural. **9.** *Geology* An ice barrier. [ME *barrer* < OFr. *barriere* < VLat. **barrāria* < **barra,* bar.]

barrier island *n.* A long narrow sand island that is parallel to the mainland and serves to protect the coast from erosion.

barrier reef *n.* A long narrow ridge of coral or rock parallel to and near a coastline from which it is separated by a lagoon too deep for coral growth.

bar·ring (bär′ing) *prep.* Assuming no occurrence of; excepting.

bar·ri·o (bä′rē-ō′, băr′-) *n., pl.* **-os** **1.** An urban district or quarter in a Spanish-speaking country. **2.** A chiefly Spanish-speaking community or neighborhood in a US city. [Sp. < Ar. *barrī,* of an open area < *barr,* open area.]

bar·ris·ter (băr′ĭ-stər) *n. Chiefly British* A lawyer admitted to the bar in the superior courts. [Prob. blend of BAR¹ and obsolete *legister,* legist; see LEGIST.]

bar·room (bär′rōōm′, -rŏŏm′) *n.* A room or building in which alcoholic beverages are sold at a bar.

bar·row¹ (băr′ō) *n.* **1.** A handbarrow. **2.** A wheelbarrow. [ME *barowe* < OE **bearwe.* See **bher-¹** in App.]

bar·row² (băr′ō) *n.* A large mound of earth or stones placed over a burial site. [ME *bergh* < OE *beorg,* hill. See **bhergh-** in App.]

bar·row³ (băr′ō) *n.* A male pig castrated prior to sexual maturity. [ME *barow* < OE *bearg.*]

Barrow, Point The northernmost point of AK, in the NW on the Arctic Ocean. The nearby city of **Barrow** has research and government facilities. Pop. 3,469.

Bar·ry (băr′ē), Sir **Charles** 1795–1860. British architect who designed the Houses of Parliament in London (1839).

Barry, Philip 1896–1949. Amer. playwright whose works include *The Philadelphia Story* (1939).

Bar·ry·more (băr′ĭ-môr′, -môr′) Family of Amer. actors, including **Lionel** (1878–1954), his sister **Ethel** (1879–1959), and their brother **John** (1882–1942), "the Great Profile."

bar sinister *n.* **1.** A heraldic bend or baton sinister, held to signify bastardy. Not in technical use. **2.** A hint or proof of such birth.

bar·stool (bär′stōōl′) *n.* A usu. high stool with a cushioned seat, used chiefly as seating for patrons at a bar.

Bart. *abbr.* baronet

bar·tend·er (bär′těn′dər) *n.* One who mixes and serves alcoholic drinks at a bar. —**bar′tend′** *v.*

bar·ter (bär′tər) *v.* **-tered, -ter·ing, -ters** —*intr.* To trade goods or services without money. —*tr.* To trade (goods or services) without money. ❖ *n.* **1.** The act or practice of bartering. **2.** Something bartered. ❖ *adj.* Of, relating to, or being based on bartering. [ME *barteren,* prob. < OFr. *barater.* See BARRATOR.] —**bar′ter·er** *n.*

Barth (bärth), **John Simmons** b. 1930. Amer. writer whose novels include *The Sot-Weed Factor* (1960).

Barth (bärt, bärth), **Karl** 1886–1968. Swiss Protestant theologian who advocated a return to the principles of the Reformation. —**Barth′i•an** *adj.*

Barthes (bärt), **Roland** 1915–80. French critic who applied semiology to literary and social criticism.

Bar•thol•di (bär-thŏl′dē, -tôl-dē′), **Frédéric Auguste** 1834–1904. French sculptor best known for the Statue of Liberty in New York Harbor (dedicated 1886).

Bar•tho•lin's gland (bär′tl-ĭnz, -thə-lĭnz) *n.* Either of two small glands located on either side of the vaginal orifice that secrete a lubricating mucus. [After Caspar *Bartholin* (1585–1629), Danish physician.]

Bar•thol•o•mew (bär-thŏl′ə-myo͞o′), Saint. Sometimes called Nathanael. One of the 12 Apostles, who according to tradition was martyred in Armenia.

bar•ti•zan (bär′tĭ-zən, bär′tĭ-zăn′) *n.* A small overhanging turret on a wall or tower. [Alteration of *bratticing*, timberwork < BRATTICE.] —**bar′ti•zaned** *adj.*

Bart•lett (bärt′lĭt) *n.* A comon variety of pear with yellowish skin and juicy flesh. [After Enoch *Bartlett* (1779–1860).]

Bartlett, John 1820–1905. Amer. publisher and editor who compiled *Familiar Quotations* (1855).

Bar•tók (bär′tŏk′, -tôk′), **Béla** 1881–1945. Hungarian pianist and composer whose works combine Eastern European folk music with dissonant harmonies. —**Bar•tók′i•an** *adj.*

Bar•to•lom•me•o (bär-tŏl′ə-mā′ō, -tō′lōm-mā′ō), **Fra** 1475?–1517. Italian painter of the Florentine school whose works include *Madonna della Misericordia* (1515).

Bar•ton (bär′tn), **Clara** 1821–1912. Amer. administrator who did battlefield relief work during the Civil War and organized the American Red Cross (1881).

Bar•tram (bär′trəm), **John** 1699–1777. Amer. botanist who established the first botanical garden in the colonies (1728). His son **William Bartram** (1739–1823) was also a botanist.

Bar•uch (bâr′ək, bə-ro͝ok′) *n.* See table at **Bible.**

Ba•ruch (bə-ro͞ok′), **Bernard Mannes** 1870–1965. Amer. financier, public official, and political adviser.

bar•ware (bär′wâr′) *n.* The glassware and other items used to prepare alcoholic drinks.

bar•y•cen•ter (băr′ĭ-sĕn′tər) *n.* See **center of mass.** [Gk. *barus*, heavy; see **gʷerə-** in App. + CENTER.]

bar•y•on (băr′ē-ŏn′) *n.* Any of a family of subatomic particles that participate in strong interactions, are composed of three quarks, and are generally more massive than mesons. [Gk. *barus*, heavy; see **gʷerə-**[1] in App. + –ON[1].] —**bar′y•on′ic** *adj.*

baryon number *n.* A quantum number equal to the difference between the number of baryons and the number of antibaryons in a system of subatomic particles.

Ba•rysh•ni•kov (bə-rĭsh′nĭ-kôf′), **Mikhail Nikolayavich** b. 1948. Soviet-born ballet dancer and choreographer who performed with the Kirov Ballet in Leningrad and later with the American Ballet Theater.

bar•y•sphere (băr′ĭ-sfîr) *n.* See **centrosphere** 2. [Gk. *barus*, heavy; see **gʷerə-** in App. + SPHERE.]

ba•ry•ta (bə-rī′tə) *n.* Any of several barium compounds. [NLat. < Gk. *barutēs*, weight < *barus*, heavy. See **gʷerə-** in App.]

ba•ry•tes (bə-rī′tēz) *n.* Variant of **barite.**

bar•y•tone (băr′ĭ-tōn′) *n.* **1.** *Music* Variant of **baritone. 2.** *Linguistics* A word with a heavy stress or pitch accent on its penultimate syllable.

BAS *abbr.* **1.** Bachelor of Agricultural Science **2.** Bachelor of Applied Science

bas•al (bā′səl, -zəl) *adj.* **1a.** Of, at, relating to, or forming a base. **b.** *Botany* Located at or near the base of any plant part. **2.** Of primary importance; basic. —**bas′al•ly** *adv.*

basal body *n.* A cellular organelle associated with the formation of cilia and flagella and similar to the centriole in structure.

basal cell *n. Biology* A type of cell found in the deepest layer of the epithelium.

basal ganglion *n.* Any of several masses of gray matter embedded in the cerebral hemispheres that are involved in the regulation of voluntary movement.

basal granule *n.* See **basal body.**

basal metabolic rate *n.* The rate at which energy is used by an organism at complete rest, measured in humans by the heat given off per unit time and expressed as the calories released per kilogram of body weight or per square meter of body surface per hour.

basal metabolism *n.* The minimum amount of energy required to maintain vital functions in an organism at complete rest, measured by the basal metabolic rate in a fasting individual who is awake, resting, and comfortably warm.

ba•salt (bə-sôlt′, bā′sôlt′) *n.* **1.** A hard, dense, dark igneous rock composed chiefly of plagioclase, pyroxene, and olivine and often having a glassy appearance. **2.** A kind of hard unglazed pottery. [Lat. *basaltēs*, alteration of *basanītēs*, touchstone < Gk. *basanītēs (lithos)* < *basanos*, of Egypt. orig.] —**ba•sal′tic** (-sôl′tĭk) *adj.*

BASc *abbr.* **1.** Bachelor of Agricultural Science **2.** Bachelor of Applied Science

bas•cule (băs′kyo͞ol) *n.* A device or structure, such as a drawbridge, counterbalanced so that when one end is lowered the other is raised. [Fr., seesaw : *bas*, low (< Med.Lat. *bassus*) + *cul*, bottom (< Lat. *cūlus*, rump; see **(s)keu-** in App.).]

base[1] (bās) *n.* **1a.** The lowest or bottom part. **b.** *Biology* The part of an animal or plant organ nearest its point of attachment. **2a.** A supporting part or layer; a foundation. **b.** A basic or underlying element; an infrastructure. **3.** The fundamental principle or underlying concept of a system or theory; a basis. **4.** A fundamental ingredient; a chief constituent: *a paint with an oil base.* **5.** The fact, observation, or premise from which a reasoning process is begun. **6a.** *Games* A starting point, safety area, or goal. **b.** *Baseball* Any one of the four corners of an infield, marked by a bag or plate. **7.** A center of organization, supply, or activity; a headquarters. **8a.** A fortified center of operations. **b.** A supply center for a large force of military personnel. **9.** A facial cosmetic used to even out the complexion or provide a surface for other makeup; a foundation. **10.** *Architecture* The lowest part of a structure, such as a wall, considered as a separate unit. **11.** *Heraldry* The lower part of a shield. **12.** *Linguistics* A morpheme or morphemes regarded as a form to which affixes or other bases may be added. **13.** *Mathematics* **a.** The side or face of a geometric figure to which an altitude is or is thought to be drawn. **b.** The number that is raised to various powers to generate the principal counting units of a number system. **c.** The number raised to the logarithm of a designated number in order to produce that designated number. **14.** A line used as a reference for measurement or computations. **15.** *Chemistry* **a.** Any of a large class of compounds, including the hydroxides and oxides of metals, having the ability to react with acids to form salts. **b.** A substance that yields hydroxyl ions when dissolved in water. **c.** A molecular or ionic substance capable of combining with a proton to form a new substance. **d.** A substance that can donate a pair of electrons for a covalent bond with an acid. **16.** *Electronics* **a.** The region in a transistor between the emitter and the collector. **b.** The electrode attached to this region. **17.** *Biochemistry* One of the purines (adenine and guanine) or pyrimidines (cytosine, thymine, and uracil) in DNA or RNA. ❖ *adj.* **1.** Forming or serving as a base: *a base layer of soil.* **2.** Situated at or near the base or bottom: *a base camp.* **3.** *Chemistry* Of, relating to, or containing a base. ❖ *tr.v.* **based, bas•ing, bas•es 1.** To form or provide a base for: *based the new company in Portland.* **2.** To find a basis for; establish: *based her conclusions on the report.* **3.** To assign to a base; station. —***idiom:* off base** Badly mistaken. [ME < OFr. < Lat. *basis* < Gk. See **gʷā-** in App.]

base[2] (bās) *adj.* **bas•er, bas•est 1a.** Having or showing a contemptible, mean-spirited, or selfish lack of human decency. **b.** Devoid of high values or ethics. **c.** Inferior in value or quality. **2.** Containing inferior substances: *a base metal.* **3.** *Archaic* Of low birth, rank, or position. ❖ *n. Obsolete* A bass singer or voice. [ME *bas*, low < OFr. < Med.Lat. *bassus.*] —**base′ly** *adv.* —**base′ness** *n.*

base•ball (bās′bôl′) *n.* **1.** A game played with a bat and ball by two teams of nine players, each team playing alternately in the field and at bat, the players at bat having to run a course of four bases laid out in a diamond pattern in order to score. **2.** The ball used in this game.

base•board (bās′bôrd′, -bōrd′) *n.* A molding that conceals the joint between an interior wall and the floor.

base•born (bās′bôrn′) *adj.* **1.** Ignoble; contemptible. **2a.** Born to unmarried parents. **b.** Of humble birth.

base•burn•er (bās′bûr′nər) *n.* A coal stove with a hopper that replenishes itself from above as fuel is burned.

base hit *n. Baseball* A hit by which the batter reaches base safely without an error, fielder's choice, or force play.

Ba•sel (bä′zəl) A city of N Switzerland on the Rhine R.; one of Europe's oldest intellectual centers. Pop. 175,781.

base•less (bās′lĭs) *adj.* Having no basis or foundation in fact.

base level *n.* The lowest level to which a land surface can be reduced by the action of running water.

base line *n.* **1a.** A line serving as a basis, as for measurement. **b.** A measurement, calculation, or location used as a basis for comparison. **2.** *Baseball* An area within which a base runner must stay when running between bases. **3.** *Sports* The boundary line at either end of a court, as in tennis.

base•man (bās′mən) *n. Baseball* A player assigned to field at first, second, or third base.

base•ment (bās′mənt) *n.* **1.** The substructure or foundation of a building. **2.** The lowest habitable story of a building, usu. below ground level. **3.** *Geology* The oldest rocks in a given area, usu. consisting of undifferentiated igneous and metamorphic rocks underlying sedimentary strata. **4.** *Slang* The last place or lowest level, as in competitive standings. **5.** *Chiefly New England* A public toilet, esp. one in a school. [Prob. BASE[1] + –MENT (perh. influenced by Fr. *soubassement*, subfoundation).]

basement membrane *n.* A thin delicate layer of connective tissue underlying the epithelium of many organs.

ba•sen•ji (bə-sĕn′jē) *n., pl.* **-jis** A dog of a breed from Africa, having a short reddish-brown coat and characterized by the absence of a bark. [Of Bantu orig.; akin to Tshiluba *ba-senji*, inhabitants of the hinterland : *ba-*, pl. n. pref. + *-senji*, hinterland.]

base on balls *n., pl.* **bases on balls** *Baseball* An advance to first

bartizan
El Morro fortress,
San Juan, Puerto Rico

Clara Barton

bascule
a bascule bridge

ă	pat	oi	boy
ā	pay	ou	out
âr	care	o͝o	took
ä	father	o͞o	boot
ĕ	pet	ŭ	cut
ē	be	ûr	urge
ĭ	pit	th	thin
ī	pie	*th*	this
îr	pier	hw	which
ŏ	pot	zh	vision
ō	toe	ə	about,
ô	paw		item

Stress marks:
′ (primary);
′ (secondary), as in
lexicon (lĕk′sĭ-kŏn′)

base that is awarded to a batter who takes four pitches that are balls.

base pair *n.* The pair of nitrogenous bases, consisting of a purine linked by hydrogen bonds to a pyrimidine, that connects the complementary strands of a DNA molecule or of hybrid molecules joining DNA and RNA.

base-pair·ing (bās'pâr'ĭng) *n.* The hydrogen bonding of complementary nitrogenous bases, one purine and one pyrimidine, in DNA and in hybrid molecules joining DNA and RNA.

base pay *n.* An amount or a rate of compensation for a specified position of employment or activity excluding any other payments or allowances.

base runner *n. Baseball* A member of the team at bat who has safely reached or is trying to reach a base. —**base'run'ning** (bās'rŭn'ĭng) *n.*

ba·ses (bā'sēz') *n.* Plural of **basis.**

bash (băsh) *v.* **bashed, bash·ing, bash·es** —*tr.* **1.** To strike with a heavy crushing blow. **2.** To beat or assault severely. **3.** *Informal* To criticize (another) harshly, accusatorially, and threateningly. —*intr. Informal* To engage in harsh, accusatory, threatening criticism. ❖ *n.* **1.** *Informal* A heavy crushing blow. **2.** *Slang* A celebration; a party. [?] —**bash'er** *n.*

Ba·shan (bā'shən) An ancient region of Palestine NE of the Sea of Galilee.

ba·shaw (bə-shô') *n.* a pasha. [Ar. *bāshā* < Turk. *paşa.* See PASHA.]

bash·ful (băsh'fəl) *adj.* **1.** Shy, self-conscious, and awkward in the presence of others. See Syns at **shy¹. 2.** Characterized by, showing, or resulting from shyness, self-consciousness, or awkwardness. [< ME *basshe* < *basshed,* p. part. of *basshen,* to be discomfited, prob. var. of *abaishen.* See ABASH.] —**bash'ful·ly** *adv.* —**bash'ful·ness** *n.*

basi– or **baso–** *pref.* **1.** Base; lower part: *basipetal.* **2.** Chemical base; chemically basic: *basophil.* [< Lat. *basis,* base. See BASIS.]

ba·sic (bā'sĭk) *adj.* **1.** Of, relating to, or forming a base; fundamental. **2.** Of, being, or serving as a starting point or basis: *a set of basic woodworking tools.* **3.** *Chemistry* **a.** Of or relating to a base. **b.** Containing a base, esp. in excess of acid. **c.** Alkaline. **4.** *Geology* Containing little silica, as certain igneous rocks. ❖ *n.* **1.** An essential, fundamental element or entity: *the basics of math.* **2.** Basic training. —**ba·sic'i·ty** (-sĭs'ĭ-tē) *n.*

BASIC or **Basic** *n.* A simple programming language. [*B(eginner's) A(ll-purpose) S(ymbolic) I(nstruction) C(ode).*]

ba·si·cal·ly (bā'sĭ-kə-lē, -klē) *adv.* **1.** In a basic way; fundamentally or essentially. **2.** For the most part; chiefly.

basic process *n.* A method of steel production that uses a furnace lined with a basic refractory material.

ba·sid·i·o·carp (bə-sĭd'ē-ō-kärp') *n.* A basidium-bearing structure found in basidiomycetous fungi. [BASIDI(UM) + –CARP.]

ba·sid·i·o·my·cete (bə-sĭd'ē-ō-mī'sēt', -mī-sēt') *n.* Any of a large group of fungi bearing sexually produced spores on a basidium. [BASIDI(UM) + –MYCETE.] —**ba·sid'i·o·my·ce'tous** (-mī-sē'təs) *adj.*

ba·sid·i·o·spore (bə-sĭd'ē-ə-spôr', -spōr') *n.* A sexually produced fungal spore borne on a basidium. —**ba·sid'i·o·spo'rous** *adj.*

ba·sid·i·um (bə-sĭd'ē-əm) *n., pl.* **-i·a** (-ē-ə) A small, specialized, club-shaped structure typically bearing four basidiospores at the tips of minute projections. [BAS(I) + Lat. *-idium,* dim. suff. (< Gk. *-idion*).] —**ba·sid'i·al** *adj.*

Ba·sie (bā'sē), **William** Known as "Count Basie." 1904–84. Amer. jazz pianist, band leader, and composer famous for his Big Band sound.

ba·si·fixed (bā'sə-fĭkst') *adj. Botany* Attached by the base.

ba·si·fy (bā'sə-fī') *tr.v.* **-fied, -fy·ing, -fies** *Chemistry* **1.** To convert into a base. **2.** To make alkaline. —**ba'si·fi·ca'tion** (-fĭ-kā'shən) *n.* —**ba'si·fi'er** *n.*

bas·il (băz'əl, băz'zəl) *n.* **1a.** An Old World aromatic annual herb (*Ocimum basilicum*) in the mint family, cultivated for its leaves. **b.** The leaves of this plant used as a seasoning. **2.** Any of various plants in the genus *Ocimum,* native to warm regions and having aromatic foliage. [ME < OFr. *basile* < Med.Lat. *basilicum* < Gk. *basilikon* < neut. of *basilikos,* royal. See BASILICA.]

Bas·il (băz'əl, băz'zəl, -səl), Saint. Known as "Basil the Great." A.D. 330?–379? Greek Christian leader who was bishop of Caesarea after A.D. 370.

Ba·si·lan Islands (bä-sē'län') A group of islands in the S Philippines separated from SW Mindanao by the narrow **Basilan Strait. Basilan Island** is the largest in the group.

bas·i·lar (băs'ə-lər) also **bas·i·lar·y** (-lĕr'ē) *adj.* Of, relating to, or located at or near the base, esp. the base of the skull. [NLat. *basilāris* < Lat. *basis,* base. See BASIS.]

bas·i·lect (băs'ə-lĕkt') *n.* The variety of speech most unlike the prestige variety, esp. in an area where a creole is spoken. [BASI– + (DIA)LECT.]

ba·sil·i·ca (bə-sĭl'ĭ-kə) *n.* **1a.** An ancient Roman public building having a central nave with an apse at one or both ends and two side aisles formed by rows of columns. **b.** A Christian church of a similar design. **2.** *Roman Catholic Church* A church that has been accorded certain privileges by the pope. [Lat. < Gk. *basilikē* < fem. of *basilikos,* royal < *basileus,* king.] —**ba·sil'i·can** (-kən) *adj.*

Ba·si·li·ca·ta (bə-zēl'ĭ-kä'tə, bä-zē'lē-kä'tä) A region of S Italy bordering on the Tyrrhenian Sea and the Gulf of Taranto and forming the instep of the Italian "boot."

bas·i·lisk (băs'ə-lĭsk', băz'-) *n.* **1.** A legendary serpent or dragon with lethal breath and glance. **2.** Any of various tropical American lizards of the genus *Basiliscus,* having a crest on the head, back, and tail. [ME < OFr. *basilisc* < Lat. *basiliscus* < Gk. *basiliskos,* dim. of *basileus,* king.]

ba·sin (bā'sĭn) *n.* **1a.** An open, shallow, usu. round container used esp. for holding liquids. **b.** The amount that such a vessel can hold. **2.** A washbowl; a sink. **3a.** An enclosed area of a river or harbor designed so that water level is unaffected by tidal changes. **b.** A small enclosed or partly enclosed body of water. **4.** A region drained by a single river system: *the Amazon basin.* **5.** *Geology* **a.** A large bowl-shaped depression in the surface of the land or ocean floor, esp. one in which sediments have accumulated. **b.** A tract of land in which the rock strata are tilted toward a common center. [ME < OFr. *bacin* < VLat. **baccīnum* < **baccus,* container, of Celt. orig.] —**ba·sin'al** *adj.*

bas·i·net (băs'ə-nĕt', băs'ə-nĭt) *n.* A small steel helmet having a point and often a visor. [ME < OFr. *bacinet,* dim. of *bacin,* basin. See BASIN.]

ba·sip·e·tal (bā-sĭp'ĭ-tl, -zĭp'-) *adj. Botany* Of or relating to growth, development, or movement from the apex down to the base. —**ba·sip'e·tal·ly** *adv.*

ba·sis (bā'sĭs) *n., pl.* **-ses** (-sēz') **1.** A foundation upon which something rests. **2.** The chief constituent; the fundamental ingredient. **3.** The fundamental principle. **4.** An underlying circumstance or condition: *is paid on a weekly basis.* [ME < Lat. < Gk. See gʷā– in App.]

basis point *n.* One hundredth of a percent, used in measuring yield differences among bonds.

bask (băsk) *intr.v.* **basked, bask·ing, basks 1.** To expose oneself to pleasant warmth. **2.** To take great pleasure or satisfaction. [ME *basken.*]

Bas·ker·ville (băs'kər-vĭl'), **John** 1706–75. British printer and typographer who produced a notable edition of Virgil (1757) and designed the typeface that bears his name.

bas·ket (băs'kĭt) *n.* **1a.** A container made of interwoven material, such as rushes. **b.** The amount that a basket can hold. **2.** An item resembling such a container in shape or function. **3.** A usu. open gondola suspended from a hot-air balloon. **4.** A group of related things, such as financial securities. **5.** *Basketball* **a.** Either of the two elevated goals, each having a metal hoop and a suspended, open-bottomed circular net. **b.** The score made by throwing the ball through this goal. **6.** *Sports* A circular structure at the base of a ski pole, used to prevent the pole from sinking into the snow. [ME < AN < VLat. **baskauta,* of Celt. orig.] —**bas'ket·ful'** *n.*

bas·ket·ball (băs'kĭt-bôl') *n.* **1.** A game played between two teams of five players each, the object being to throw the ball through an elevated basket on the opponent's side of the rectangular court. **2.** The ball used in this game.

basket case *n.* **1.** *Slang* One that is in a completely hopeless or useless condition. **2.** *Offensive Slang* A person, esp. a soldier, who has had all four limbs amputated.

basket fish *n.* See **basket star.**

basket hilt *n.* A sword hilt with a basket-shaped guard.

Basket Maker *n.* **1.** Any of several early periods of Anasazi culture characterized by the use of basketry, dry farming, and coiled pottery. **2.** A member of the people of this culture.

bas·ket-of-gold (băs'kĭt-əv-gōld') *n.* A shrubby perennial European herb (*Aurinia saxatilis*) with small golden-yellow flowers.

bas·ket·ry (băs'kĭ-trē) *n.* **1.** The craft or process of making baskets or objects woven like baskets. **2.** Baskets and similar woven objects considered as a group.

basket star *n.* Any of various marine organisms of the class Ophiuroidea, having slender, branching, interlaced arms.

basket weave *n.* A textile weave of double threads interlaced to produce a checkered pattern like that of a woven basket.

bask·ing shark (băs'kĭng) *n.* A shark (*Cetorhinus maximus*) that measures up to about 12 meters (40 feet) in length, feeds on plankton, and often floats near the surface of water.

bas·ma·ti rice (bäs-mä'tē) *n.* An aromatic long-grain rice from India. [Hindi *bāsmatī,* fragrant < *bās,* fragrance, perfume < Skt. *vāsaḥ.*]

bas mitz·vah or **bas miz·vah** (bäs mĭts'və) *n. & v.* Variants of **bat mitzvah.**

baso– *pref.* Variant of **basi–.**

ba·so·phil (bā'sə-fĭl, -zə-) also **ba·so·phile** (-fīl', -fĭl) *n.* A cell, esp. a white blood cell, having granules that stain readily with basic dyes. —**ba'so·phil'ic** or **ba·soph'i·lous** (bə-sŏf'ə-ləs) *adj.*

Ba·so·tho (bə-sō'tō, -sōō'tōō) *n., pl.* **Basotho** or **-thos 1.** A Sotho-speaking people of Lesotho and adjacent parts of South Africa. **2.** A member of this people.

basque (băsk) *n.* A woman's close-fitting bodice. [Fr., skirt of a garment, alteration (perh. influenced by *Basque,* Basque) of OFr. *baste* < Ital. *basta,* tuck, poss. of Gmc. orig.]

Basque *n.* **1.** A member of a people of unknown origin inhabiting the western Pyrenees and the Bay of Biscay. **2.** The Basque language, of no known linguistic affiliation. [Fr., prob. < Lat. *Vascō*

basil
sweet basil
Ocimum basilicum

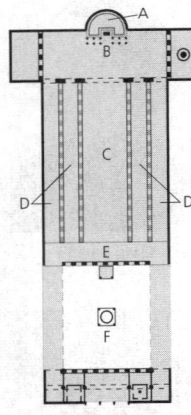

basilica
after a plan of fourth-century St. Peter's, Rome
A. apse
B. transept
C. nave
D. aisles
E. narthex
F. atrium

basketry

perh. < Basque *Euskadi.*] —**Basque** *adj.*

Basque Provinces A region comprising three provinces of N Spain on the Bay of Biscay.

Bas•ra (bäs′rə, bŭs′-) A port city of SE Iraq on the Shatt al Arab near the Persian Gulf. Pop. 406,296.

bas-re•lief (bä′rĭ-lēf′) *n.* See **low relief.** [Fr. < Ital. *bassorilievo* : *basso,* low (< Med.Lat. *bassus*) + *rilievo,* relief (< *rilevare,* to raise < Lat. *relevāre;* see RELIEVE).]

bass[1] (băs) *n., pl.* **bass** or **bass•es 1.** Any of several North American freshwater fishes of the family Centrarchidae. **2.** Any of various marine fishes of the family Serranidae, such as the sea bass. [ME **bars,* perch < OE *bærs.*]

bass[2] (bās) *n.* **1.** A low-pitched sound or tone. **2.** The tones in the lowest register of an instrument. **3a.** A male singing voice of the lowest range. **b.** A singer who has such a voice. **c.** An instrument that sounds within this range. **d.** A vocal or instrumental part written within this range. **4.** An instrument, esp. a double bass, that produces tones in a low register. [ME *bas,* lowest musical part < *bas,* low. See BASE[2].] —**bass** *adj.*

bass clef (bās) *n.* A symbol showing that the fourth line from the bottom of a staff represents the F below middle C.

bass drum (bās) *n.* A large drum having a cylindrical body and two heads and producing a low resonant sound.

Basse•terre (băs-târ′, bäs-) The cap. of St. Kitts–Nevis, on St. Kitts I. in the Leeward Is. of the West Indies. Pop. 14,161.

Basse-Terre (băs-târ′, bäs-) The cap. of the French overseas department of Guadeloupe, on the S end of **Basse-Terre Island** in the Leeward Is. of the West Indies. Pop. 29,522.

bas•set horn (băs′ĭt) *n.* A tenor clarinet, pitched in F, having a wider bell and greater range than a standard clarinet. [Partial transl. of Ger. *Bassetthorn* : *Bassett,* type of low-pitched string instrument (ult. < Ital. *basso,* low; see BASSO) + *Horn,* horn (< the resemblance of early models to hunting horns).]

basset hound *n.* A hunting dog of a breed originating in France, with a long body, short legs, and long ears. [Fr. *short, basset hound,* dim. of *basse,* fem. of *bas,* low. See BASE[2].]

bass fiddle (bās) *n.* See **double bass.**

bass horn (bās) *n.* **1.** A large, valved, brass wind instrument with a bass pitch; a tuba or a sousaphone. **2.** An instrument similar to the serpent but shaped like a bassoon, used primarily in military bands in the early 19th century.

bas•si•net (băs′ə-nĕt′, băs′ə-nĕt′) *n.* An oblong basketlike bed for an infant. [Fr., small basin, dim. of *bassin,* basin < OFr. *bacin.* See BASIN.]

bass•ist (bā′sĭst) *n.* One who plays a bass instrument.

bas•so (băs′ō, bä′sō) *n., pl.* **bas•sos** or **bas•si** (bä′sē) **1.** A bass singer, esp. operatic. **2.** An instrumental part written for a bass instrument. [Ital. < Med.Lat. *bassus,* low.]

bas•soon (bə-sōōn′, bă-) *n.* A low-pitched woodwind instrument having a double reed, a long wooden body, and a U-shaped tube leading to the mouthpiece. [Fr. *basson* < Ital. *bassone,* augmentative of *basso,* bass. See BASSO.] —**bas•soon′ist** *n.*

bas•so pro•fun•do (băs′ō prə-fŭn′dō, bä′sō prə-fōōn′dō) *n., pl.* **basso pro•fun•dos** or **bas•si pro•fun•di** (bä′sē prə-fōōn′dē) **1.** A deep bass singing voice. **2.** A singer who has such a voice. [Ital. : *basso,* bass + *profondo,* deep.]

bas•so-re•lie•vo (băs′ō-rĭ-lē′vō) *n., pl.* **-vos** See **low relief.** [Ital. *bassorilievo.* See BAS-RELIEF.]

Bass Strait (băs) A channel between Tasmania and SE Australia connecting the Indian Ocean with the Tasman Sea.

bass viol (bās) *n.* **1.** See **double bass. 2.** See **viola da gamba.**

bass•wood (băs′wo͝od′) *n.* **1.** See **linden. 2.** The soft, light-colored wood of any species of linden. [*bass,* linden bark (alteration of BAST) + WOOD[1].]

bast (băst) *n.* **1.** See **phloem. 2.** Bast fiber. [ME < OE *bæst.*]

bas•tard (băs′tərd) *n.* **1.** A child born out of wedlock. **2.** Something that is of irregular, inferior, or dubious origin. **3.** *Slang* A person, esp. one who is held to be mean or disagreeable. ❖ *adj.* **1.** Born of unwed parents; illegitimate. **2.** Not genuine; spurious. **3.** Resembling a known kind or species but not truly such. [ME < OFr., prob. of Gmc. orig.; akin to O Frisian *bōst,* marriage.] —**bas′tard•ly** *adj.*

bas•tard•ize (băs′tər-dīz′) *tr.v.* **-ized, -iz•ing, -iz•es 1.** To lower in quality or character; debase. **2.** To declare or prove (someone) to be a bastard. —**bas′tard•i•za′tion** (-tər-dĭ-zā′shən) *n.*

bastard toadflax *n.* Any of various hemiparasitic plants of the genus *Comandra,* having clusters of small flowers.

bastard wing *n.* See **alula.**

bas•tard•y (băs′tər-dē) *n.* **1.** The condition of being born of unwed parents; illegitimacy. **2.** The begetting of a bastard.

baste[1] (bāst) *tr.v.* **bast•ed, bast•ing, bastes** To sew with large running stitches to hold together temporarily. [ME *basten* < OFr. *bastir,* of Gmc. orig.] —**bast′er** *n.*

baste[2] (bāst) *tr.v.* **bast•ed, bast•ing, bastes** To moisten (meat, for example) periodically with a liquid, esp. while cooking. [ME *basten.*] —**bast′er** *n.*

baste[3] (bāst) *tr.v.* **bast•ed, bast•ing, bastes 1.** To beat vigorously; thrash. **2.** To lambaste. [Prob. of Scand. orig.; akin to ON *beysta.*]

Bas•tet (bä′stĕt) *n. Mythology* An ancient Egyptian goddess, daughter of Ra and agent of his vengeance, often depicted as a lioness or cat.

bast fiber *n.* Any of various durable fibers found in the phloem of certain plants, esp. flax, hemp, and jute.

bas•tille (bă-stēl′) *n.* A prison; a jail. [Fr. < OFr., fortress, alteration of *bastide* < O Provençal *bastida* < *bastir,* to build, of Gmc. orig.]

Bastille Day *n.* July 14, observed in France in commemoration of the storming of the Paris Bastille in 1789.

bas•ti•na•do (băs′tə-nā′dō, -nä′-) also **bas•ti•nade** (-nād′, -näd′) *n., pl.* **-does** also **-nades 1.** A beating with a stick or cudgel, esp. on the soles of the feet. **2.** A stick or cudgel. ❖ *tr.v.* **-doed, -do•ing, -does** also **-nad•ed, -nad•ing, -nades** To subject to a beating; thrash. [Alteration of Sp. *bastonada* < *baston,* stick < VLat. **bastō, *bastōn-.*]

bas•tion (băs′chən, -tē-ən) *n.* **1.** A projecting part of a fortification. **2.** A well-fortified position. **3.** One that is considered similar to a defensive stronghold. [Fr. < OFr. *bastillon* < *bastille,* fortress. See BASTILLE.] —**bas′tioned** *adj.*

bast•naes•ite (băst′nə-sīt′) *n.* A yellowish to reddish-brown mineral, $(Ce,La)CO_3(F,OH)$, that is a source of rare-earth elements. [After *Bastnäs,* a mine in south-central Sweden.]

Bas•togne (bă-stōn′, bă-stôn′yə) A town of SE Belgium near the Luxembourg border; a crucial point in the Battle of the Bulge (Dec. 1944–Jan. 1945). Pop. 11,386.

Ba•su•to•land (bə-sōō′tō-lănd′) See **Lesotho.**

bat[1] (băt) *n.* **1.** A stout wooden stick; a cudgel. **2.** A blow, such as one delivered with a stick. **3.** *Baseball* A rounded club, wider at the hitting end, used to strike the ball. **4.** *Sports* **a.** A club used in cricket, having a broad, flat-surfaced hitting end and a narrow handle. **b.** The racket used in various games, such as table tennis. ❖ *v.* **bat•ted, bat•ting, bats** —*tr.* **1.** To hit with or as if with a bat. **2.** *Baseball* **a.** To cause (a run) to be scored while at bat: *batted in a run.* **b.** To have (a certain percentage) as a batting average. **3.** *Informal* To produce in a hurried or an informal manner: *bat out a speech.* **4.** *Informal* To discuss or consider at length. —*intr.* **1.** *Baseball* **a.** To use a bat. **b.** To have a turn at bat. **2.** *Slang* To wander about aimlessly. ***—idioms:* at bat** *Sports* Taking one's turn to bat, as in baseball or cricket. **go to bat for** To give assistance to; defend. **off the bat** Without hesitation; immediately. [ME, perh. partly of Celt. orig., and partly < OFr. *batte,* pounding implement, flail (< *batre,* to beat; see BATTER[1]).]

bat[2] (băt) *n.* Any of various nocturnal flying mammals of the order Chiroptera, having membranous wings that extend from the forelimbs to the hind limbs or tail and anatomical adaptations for echolocation. ***—idiom:* have bats in (one's) belfry** To behave in an eccentric, bizarre manner. [Alteration of ME *bakke,* of Scand. orig.]

bat[3] (băt) *tr.v.* **bat•ted, bat•ting, bats** To wink or flutter: *bat one's eyelashes.* [Prob. var. of BATE[2].]

bat[4] (băt) *n. Slang* A binge; a spree. [Prob. < *batter,* spree.]

bat. *abbr.* battalion

BAT *abbr.* Bachelor of Arts in Teaching

Ba•taan (bə-tăn′, -tän′) A peninsula of W Luzon, Philippines, between Manila Bay and the South China Sea. US and Philippine World War II troops surrendered to the Japanese here in 1942.

Ba•ta•vi•a (bə-tā′vē-ə) See **Jakarta.**

bat•boy (băt′boi′) *n.* A boy who is employed by a baseball team to look after its equipment, esp. the bats.

batch[1] (băch) *n.* **1.** An amount produced at one baking. **2.** A quantity required for or produced as the result of one operation: *a batch of cement.* **3.** A group of persons or things. **4.** *Computer Science* A set of data or jobs to be processed in a single program run. ❖ *tr.v.* **batched, batch•ing, batch•es** To assemble or process as a batch. [ME *bache,* prob. < OE **bæcce* < *bacan,* to bake.]

batch[2] (băch) *n.* & *v. Informal* Variant of **bach.**

bate[1] (bāt) *tr.v.* **bat•ed, bat•ing, bates 1.** To lessen the force or intensity of; moderate: *"To his dying day he bated his breath a little when he told the story"* (George Eliot). **2.** To take away; subtract. [ME *baten,* short for *abaten.* See ABATE.]

bate[2] also **bait** (bāt) *intr.v.* **bat•ed, bat•ing, bates** also **bait•ed, bait•ing, baits** To flap the wings wildly. [ME *baten* < OFr. *batre,* to beat. See BATTER[1].]

ba•teau also **bat•teau** (bă-tō′) *n., pl.* **-teaux** (-tōz′) **1.** *Canada & New England* A long, light, flatbottom boat with a sharply pointed bow and stern. **2.** *South Atlantic & Gulf States* A small, light, flatbottom rowboat. [Canadian and Louisiana Fr. < Fr., boat < OFr. *batel* < OE *bāt.* See **bheid-** in App.]

Bates (bāts), **Katherine Lee** 1859–1929. Amer. educator and writer best known for her poem "America the Beautiful."

Bates•i•an mimicry (bāt′sē-ən) *n.* A form of protective mimicry in which a species closely resembles an unpalatable or harmful species and therefore is avoided by predators. [After Henry Walter *Bates* (1825–92), British naturalist.]

Bate•son (bāt′sən), **William** 1861–1926. British biologist who experimentally proved Mendel's theories on heredity.

BATF *abbr.* Bureau of Alcohol, Tobacco, and Firearms

bat•fish (băt′fĭsh′) *n., pl.* **batfish** or **-fish•es** Any of various marine anglerfishes of the family Ogcocephalidae, having a retractable appendage above the mouth.

bat•fowl (băt′foul′) *intr.v.* **-fowled, -fowl•ing, -fowls** To catch

bass clef

basset hound

ă	pat	oi	boy
ā	pay	ou	out
âr	care	o͝o	took
ä	father	ōō	boot
ĕ	pet	ŭ	cut
ē	be	ûr	urge
ĭ	pit	th	thin
ī	pie	*th*	this
îr	pier	hw	which
ŏ	pot	zh	vision
ō	toe	ə	about, item
ô	paw		

Stress marks:
′ (primary);
′ (secondary), as in
lexicon (lĕk′sĭ-kŏn′)

roosting birds at night by blinding them with a light and then hitting or netting them.

bat·girl (băt′gûrl′) *n.* A girl who is employed by a baseball team to look after its equipment, esp. the bats.

bath[1] (băth, bäth) *n., pl.* **baths** (băthz, băthz, băths, bäths) **1a.** The act of soaking or cleansing the body, as in water or steam. **b.** The water used for cleansing the body. **2a.** A bathtub. **b.** A bathroom. **3.** A building equipped for bathing. **4.** A resort providing therapeutic baths; a spa. Often used in the plural. **5a.** A liquid in which something is dipped or soaked for processing: *an acid bath.* **b.** A container holding such a liquid. **6.** A medium, such as oil or sand, that controls the temperature of objects placed in it. [ME < OE *bæth.*]

bath[2] (băth) *n.* An ancient Hebrew unit of liquid measure, equal to about 38 liters (10 US gallons). [Heb. *bat.*]

Bath (băth, bäth) A city of SW England SE of Bristol; famous for its Georgian architecture and its hot mineral springs. Pop. 84,100.

Bath chair (băth, bäth) *n.* A hooded wheelchair used esp. for invalids, typically at a spa. [After BATH.]

bathe (bāth) *v.* **bathed, bath·ing, bathes** —*intr.* **1.** To take a bath. **2.** To go into the water, as for swimming. **3.** To become immersed in or as if in liquid. —*tr.* **1.** To immerse in liquid; wet. **2.** To wash in a liquid. **3.** To apply a liquid to for healing or soothing purposes. **4.** To seem to wash or pour over; suffuse. [ME *bathen* < OE *bathian.*] —**bath′er** *n.*

ba·thet·ic (bə-thĕt′ĭk) *adj.* Characterized by bathos. [Prob. blend of BATHOS and PATHETIC.] —**ba·thet′i·cal·ly** *adv.*

bath·house (băth′hous′, bäth′-) *n.* A building with bathing facilities or with dressing rooms for swimmers.

bathing cap (bā′thĭng) *n.* An elastic cap worn by swimmers.

bathing suit *n.* A swimsuit.

bath·mat (băth′măt′, bäth′-) *n.* A mat used in front of a bathtub or shower to absorb water or prevent slipping.

bath·o·lith (băth′ə-lĭth′) *n.* A mass of igneous rock that has melted and intruded surrounding strata. —**bath′o·lith′ic** *adj.*

ba·thom·e·ter (bə-thŏm′ĭ-tər) *n.* An instrument used to measure the depth of water.

ba·thos (bā′thŏs′, -thôs′) *n.* **1a.** An abrupt, unintended transition in style from the exalted to the commonplace, producing a ludicrous effect. **b.** An anticlimax. **2a.** Insincere or grossly sentimental pathos. **b.** Banality; triteness. [Gk., depth < *bathus*, deep.]

bath·robe (băth′rōb′, bäth′-) *n.* A loose-fitting robe worn before and after bathing and for lounging.

bath·room (băth′rōōm′, -rōōm′, bäth′-) *n.* A room with facilities for bathing and usu. also containing a sink and toilet. —*idiom:* **go to the bathroom** *Informal* To defecate or urinate.

bath salts (băth, bäth) *pl.n.* A perfumed crystalline substance for softening bathwater.

Bath·she·ba (băth-shē′bə, băth′shə-) In the Bible, the wife of Uriah and later of David.

bath·tub (băth′tŭb′, bäth′-) *n.* A tub for bathing.

Bath·urst (băth′ərst′) See Banjul.

bathy- or **batho-** *pref.* **1.** Deep; depth: *batholith.* **2.** Deep-sea: *bathysphere.* [< Gk. *bathus*, deep, and < Gk. *bathos*, depth (< *bathus*).]

bath·y·al (băth′ē-əl) *adj.* Of or relating to the region of the ocean bottom between the sublittoral and abyssal zones, from depths of 200 to 4,000 meters (660 to 13,000 feet).

ba·thym·e·try (bə-thĭm′ĭ-trē) *n.* Measurement of the depth of bodies of water. —**bath′y·met′ric** (băth′ə-mĕt′rĭk), **bath′y·met′ri·cal** *adj.* —**bath′y·met′ri·cal·ly** *adv.*

bath·y·pe·lag·ic (băth′ə-pə-lăj′ĭk) *adj.* Of, relating to, or living in the depths of the ocean, esp. between about 600 and 3,000 meters (2,000 and 10,000 feet).

bath·y·scaphe (băth′ĭ-skăf′, -skăf′) also **bath·y·scaph** (-skăf′) *n.* A free-diving deep-sea research vessel having a large flotation hull and an observation capsule, usu. capable of reaching full ocean depths. [BATHY- + Gk. *skaphos*, boat.]

bath·y·sphere (băth′ĭ-sfîr′) *n.* A spherical deep-diving chamber in which persons study the oceans.

bath·y·ther·mo·graph (băth′ĭ-thûr′mə-grăf′) *n.* An instrument that records water temperature in relation to ocean depth.

ba·tik (bə-tēk′, băt′ĭk) *n.* **1a.** A dyeing method by which the parts of fabric not dyed are covered with removable wax. **b.** A design created by this method. **2.** Fabric dyed by this method. [Malay *batek*, of Javanese orig. < Proto-Austronesian *beCik,* tattoo (< the fact that the original process was similar to tattooing).] —**ba·tik′** *v.*

Ba·tis·ta y Zal·dí·var (bə-tēs′tä ē zäl-dē′vär′, bä-tē′stä), **Fulgencio** 1901–73. Cuban dictator (1933–40) and president (1940–44 and 1954–58); overthrown by Fidel Castro (1959).

ba·tiste (bə-tēst′, bă-) *n.* A fine plain-woven fabric made from various fibers and used esp. for clothing. [Fr. < OFr., perhaps after *Baptiste* of Cambrai, 13th-cent. textile maker.]

bat·man (băt′mən) *n.* A British military officer's orderly. [Obs. *bat*, packsaddle (< Fr. *bât* < OFr. *bast* < LLat. *bastum*) + MAN.]

bat mitz·vah or **bat miz·vah** (băt mĭts′və) or **bas mitz·vah** or **bas miz·vah** (bäs) *n. Judaism* **1.** The ceremony that initiates and recognizes a 12- to 14-year-old Jewish girl as an adult responsible for her moral and religious duties. **2.** A girl so recognized. ❖ *tr.v.* **-vahed, -vah·ing, -vahs** To confirm in the ceremony of bat

mitzvah. [Heb. *bat miṣwâ* : *bat*, daughter + *miṣwâ*, commandment; see MITZVAH.]

ba·ton (bə-tŏn′, bă-, băt′n) *n.* **1.** *Music* A wooden stick or rod used to conduct an orchestra or band. **2.** A hollow metal rod with a heavy rubber tip or tips wielded and twirled by a drum major or drum majorette. **3.** A short staff carried by certain public officials as a symbol of office. **4.** *Sports* The hollow cylinder carried by each member of a relay team in a running race. **5.** A short stick carried by police; a billy club. **6.** *Heraldry* A shortened narrow bend, often signifying bastardy. [Fr. *bâton* < OFr. *baston,* stick < VLat. **bastō, *bastōn-.*]

Bat·on Rouge (băt′n rōōzh′) The cap. of LA, in the SE-central part on a bluff above the Mississippi R. Pop. 227,818.

ba·tra·chi·an (bə-trā′kē-ən) *adj.* Of or relating to vertebrate amphibians without tails. [< Gk. *batrakhos,* frog.] —**ba·tra′chi·an** *n.*

bats (băts) *adj. Slang* Crazy; insane. [< *bats in the belfry.*]

bats·man (băts′mən) *n. Sports* The player at bat in cricket and baseball.

Bat·swa·na (bŏt-swä′nə) *n., pl.* **Batswana** or **-nas** See Tswana 1. [Tswana : *ba-*, pl. n. pref. + *-tswana,* Tswana.]

batt (băt) *n.* Pieces of fabric used for stuffing; batting. [Variant of BAT[1], cotton or wool fiber wadded into rolls or sheets.]

bat·tal·ion (bə-tăl′yən) *n.* **1a.** An army unit typically having a headquarters and two or more companies, batteries, or similar subdivisions. **b.** A large body of organized troops. **2.** A great number. [Fr. *bataillon* < OFr. < Ital. *battaglione,* augmentative of *battaglia* < VLat. **battalia.* See BATTLE.]

Bat·ta·ni (bə-tä′nē), **al-** 858?–929. Arab astronomer and mathematician who proved the possibility of annular eclipses and introduced an organized table of sines.

bat·ten[1] (băt′n) *v.* **-tened, -ten·ing, -tens** —*intr.* **1.** To become fat. **2.** To thrive and prosper, esp. at another's expense. —*tr.* To fatten; overfeed. [Ult. < ON *batna,* to improve.]

bat·ten[2] (băt′n) *n.* **1.** *Nautical* **a.** One of several flexible strips of wood or plastic placed in pockets at the outer edge of a sail to keep it flat. **b.** A strip of wood used to fasten the edges of the material that covers hatches. **2.** *Chiefly British* A narrow strip of wood used esp. for flooring. ❖ *tr.v.* **-tened, -ten·ing, -tens** *Nautical* To furnish, fasten, or secure with battens. —*idiom:* **batten down the hatches** To prepare for an imminent disaster or emergency. [ME *batent* < OFr. *bataunt,* wooden strip, clapper < pr. part. of *batre,* to beat. See BATTER[1].]

Batten, Jean 1909–82. New Zealand aviator who was the first woman to fly a solo round trip between England and Australia (1935).

bat·ter[1] (băt′ər) *v.* **-tered, -ter·ing, -ters** —*tr.* **1.** To hit repeatedly with violent blows. **2.** To damage, as by heavy wear. **3.** To subject to repeated beatings or physical abuse. —*intr.* To pound repeatedly with heavy blows. ❖ *n. Printing* A damaged area on the face of type or on a plate. [ME *bateren* < OFr. *batre* < LLat. *battere* < Lat. *battuere.*]

bat·ter[2] (băt′ər) *n. Sports* The player at bat in baseball and cricket.

bat·ter[3] (băt′ər) *n.* A liquid or semiliquid mixture, as of flour, milk, and eggs, used in cooking. ❖ *tr.v.* **-tered, -ter·ring, -ters** To coat in batter. [ME *bater,* prob. < OFr. *bateure,* a beating < *batre,* to beat. See BATTER[1].]

bat·ter[4] (băt′ər) *n.* A slope, as of the outer face of a wall, that recedes from bottom to top. ❖ *tr.v.* **-tered, -ter·ing, -ters** To construct so as to create an upwardly receding slope. [?]

batter bread *n. Virginia* See johnnycake. See Regional Note at johnnycake.

bat·ter·cake (băt′ər-kāk′) *n. Chiefly Southern US* **1.** See pancake. **2.** See johnnycake. See Regional Note at johnnycake.

bat·ter·ing ram (băt′ər-ĭng) *n.* **1.** A heavy metal bar used to break down walls and doors. **2.** A heavy beam used in ancient and medieval warfare to batter down the walls and gates of a place under siege.

bat·ter·y (băt′ə-rē) *n., pl.* **-ies 1a.** The act of beating or pounding. **b.** *Law* The unlawful and unwanted touching or striking of one person by another, with the intention of bringing about a harmful or offensive contact. **2a.** An emplacement for one or more pieces of artillery. **b.** A set of guns or other heavy artillery. **c.** An army artillery unit, corresponding to a company in the infantry. **3a.** An array of similar things intended for use together. **b.** An impressive body or group. **4.** *Baseball* The pitcher and catcher. **5.** *Music* The percussion section of an orchestra. **6.** *Electricity* **a.** Two or more connected cells that produce a direct current by converting chemical energy to electrical energy. **b.** A single cell that produces an electric current. [ME *batri,* forged metal ware < OFr. *baterie,* a beating < *batre,* to batter. See BATTER[1].]

bat·ting (băt′ĭng) *n.* **1.** The act of a batter. **2.** Cotton, wool, or synthetic fiber wadded into rolls or sheets, used for stuffing furniture and mattresses and for lining quilts. [Sense 2 < the beating of raw cotton to clean it.]

batting average *n. Baseball* A measure of a batter's performance obtained by dividing the total of base hits by the number of times at bat, not including walks.

bat·tle (băt′l) *n.* **1a.** An encounter between opposing forces. **b.** Armed fighting; combat. **2.** A match between two combatants.

3a. A protracted controversy or struggle. **b.** An intense competition. ❖ *v.* **-tled, -tling, -tles** —*intr.* To engage in or as if in battle. —*tr.* To fight against. [ME *batel* < OFr. *bataille* < VLat. **battālia* < LLat. *battuālia*, fighting and fencing exercises < Lat. *battuere*, to beat.] —**bat′tler** *n.*

Battle A town of SE England; site of the Battle of Hastings (1066). Pop. 4,987.

bat•tle-ax or **bat•tle-axe** (băt′l-ăks′) *n.* **1.** A heavy broad-headed ax formerly used as a weapon. **2.** *Slang* A woman held to be antagonistic or overbearing.

battle cry *n.* **1.** A rallying cry uttered in combat, esp. while attacking. **2.** A slogan used by the proponents of a cause.

bat•tle•dore (băt′l-dôr′) *n.* **1a.** An early form of badminton played with a flat wooden paddle and a shuttlecock. **b.** The paddle used in this game. **2.** A badminton racket. [ME *batildore*, perh. blend of *betel*, bat; see BEETLE³, and O Provençal *batedor*, bat (< *battre*, to beat < LLat. *battere*; see BATTER¹).]

battle fatigue *n.* See **combat fatigue**.

bat•tle•field (băt′l-fēld′) *n.* **1.** An area where a battle is fought. **2.** A sphere of contention.

bat•tle•front (băt′l-frŭnt′) *n.* **1.** The sector in which armed forces engage in combat. **2.** The area where opponents meet.

bat•tle•ground (băt′l-ground′) *n.* See **battlefield**.

battle group *n.* **1.** A US army unit usu. composed of five companies. **2.** A naval force composed of a variable number of warships, escorts, and supply vessels. **3.** An improvised force drawn from different units for a particular operation. **4.** *Chiefly British* A tactical force formed by attaching infantry and armored companies.

bat•tle•ment (băt′l-mənt) *n.* A notched parapet built on top of a wall, with alternating merlons and crenels for decoration or defense. [ME *batelment*, alteration (influenced by *batel*, battle) of OFr. *batillement*, tower, turret < *bastille*. See BASTILLE.] —**bat′tle•ment′ed** (-měn′tĭd) *adj.*

battle royal *n., pl.* **battles royal** **1.** An intense altercation. **2.** A battle involving many combatants. **3.** A fight to the finish. [BATTLE + ROYAL, grand in scale.]

bat•tle•ship (băt′l-shĭp′) *n.* Any one of a class of warships of the largest size, carrying the greatest number of weapons and clad with the heaviest armor. [Short for *line-of-battle ship*.]

bat•tle•wag•on (băt′l-wăg′ən) *n.* See **battleship**.

bat•ty (băt′ē) *adj.* **-ti•er, -ti•est** *Slang* Crazy; insane. [< *bats in the belfry*.] —**bat′ti•ness** *n.*

Ba•tu•mi (bə-tōō′mē) also **Ba•tum** (-tōōm′) A city of SW Georgia on the Black Sea near Turkey. Pop. 137,000.

Bat Yam (băt′ yäm′) A city of W-central Israel on the Mediterranean near Tel Aviv–Yafo. Pop. 144,200.

bau•ble (bô′bəl) *n.* **1.** A small showy ornament of little value; a trinket. **2.** *Archaic* A mock scepter carried by a court jester. [ME *babel* < OFr., plaything.]

Bau•cis (bô′sĭs) *n. Greek Mythology* A peasant woman of Phrygia who with her husband Philemon was honored for their hospitality to Zeus and Hermes disguised as men.

baud (bôd) *n. Computer Science* A unit of speed in data transmission equal to one bit per second. [After Jean Maurice Emile *Baudot* (1845–1903), French engineer.]

Baude•laire (bōd-lâr′), **Charles Pierre** 1821–67. French writer, translator, and critic known for his only volume of poetry, *Les Fleurs du Mal* (1857, expanded 1861).

Bau•douin I (bō-dwăn′) 1930–93. King of Belgium (1951–93).

Bau•haus (bou′hous′) *adj.* Of or relating to a 20th-century school of design influenced by and derived from techniques and materials esp. of industrial manufacture. [Ger., an architecture school founded by Walter Gropius : *Bau*, construction, architecture (< MHGer. *bū*, building < *būan*, to dwell; see **bheuə-** in App.) + *Haus*, house (< MHGer. *hūs* < OHGer.).]

bau•hin•i•a (bô-hĭn′ē-ə, bō-ĭn′-) *n.* Any of various tropical or subtropical trees, shrubs, or woody vines of the genus *Bauhinia* in the pea family. [NLat., after Jean *Bauhin* (1541–1612) and Gaspard *Bauhin* (1560–1624), Swiss botanists.]

baulk (bôk) *v. & n. Chiefly British* Variant of **balk**.

Baum (bôm, bäm), **Lyman Frank** 1856–1919. Amer. writer known esp. for *The Wonderful Wizard of Oz* (1900).

Bau•mé (bō-mā′), **Antoine** 1728–1804. French pharmacist who in 1768 devised an improved hydrometer using the scale that now bears his name.

Baumé scale *n.* A hydrometer scale used to measure the specific gravity of liquids. [After Antoine BAUMÉ.]

Bau•ru (bou-rōō′) A city of SE Brazil NW of São Paulo. Pop. 260,767.

baux•ite (bôk′sīt′) *n.* The principal ore of aluminum, composed mainly of hydrous aluminum oxides and aluminum hydroxides. [After Les *Baux*, a village of southeast France.] —**baux•it′ic** (-sĭt′ĭk) *adj.*

Ba•var•i•a (bə-vâr′ē-ə) A region and former duchy of S Germany.

Ba•var•i•an (bə-vâr′ē-ən) *n.* **1.** A native or inhabitant of Bavaria. **2.** The High German dialect of Bavaria and Austria. —**Ba•var′i•an** *adj.*

Bavarian Alps A range of the Alps between S Bavaria in Germany and the Tyrol in W Austria rising to 2,964.9 m (9,721 ft) in S Germany.

bawd (bôd) *n.* **1.** A woman who keeps a brothel. **2.** A woman prostitute. [ME, prob. < OFr. *baud*, merry, licentious < O Saxon *bald*, bold, merry.]

bawd•ry (bô′drē) *n.* Risqué, coarse, or obscene language. [ME *bawdery*, pandering < *bawd*, bawd. See BAWD.]

bawd•y (bô′dē) *adj.* **-i•er, -i•est** **1.** Humorously coarse; risqué. **2.** Vulgar; lewd. —**bawd′i•ly** *adv.* —**bawd′i•ness** *n.*

bawd•y•house (bô′dē-hous′) *n.* A house of prostitution.

bawl (bôl) *v.* **bawled, bawl•ing, bawls** —*intr.* **1.** To cry or sob loudly; wail. **2.** To cry out loudly and vehemently; shout. —*tr.* To utter in a loud, vehement voice. See Syns at **shout**. ❖ *n.* A loud, bellowing cry; a wail. —*phrasal verb:* **bawl out** *Informal* To reprimand loudly or harshly. [ME *bawlen*, to bark < Med.Lat. *baulāre*, to bark (prob. of Scand. orig.), or < ON *baula*, to low (of imit. orig.).] —**bawl′er** *n.*

bay¹ (bā) *n.* **1.** A body of water partially enclosed by land but with a wide mouth, affording access to the sea. **2.** An area of land that resembles a bay of the sea. [ME < OFr. *baie*, perh. < *baer*, to open out, gape. See BAY².]

bay² (bā) *n.* **1.** A part of a building marked off by vertical elements, such as columns. **2a.** A bay window. **b.** An opening or a recess in a wall. **3.** A section or compartment that is set off for a specific purpose: *a cargo bay.* **4.** A sickbay. **5.** *Computer Science* A drive bay. [ME < OFr. *baee*, an opening < *baer*, to gape < VLat. **badāre*.]

bay³ (bā) *adj.* Reddish-brown. ❖ *n.* **1.** A reddish brown. **2.** A reddish-brown animal, esp. a horse having a black mane and tail. [ME < OFr. *bai* < Lat. *badius*.]

bay⁴ (bā) *n.* **1.** A deep prolonged bark, such as the sound made by hounds. **2.** The position of one cornered by pursuers and forced to turn and fight at close quarters. **3.** The position of having been checked or held at a distance. ❖ *v.* **bayed, bay•ing, bays** —*intr.* To utter a deep, prolonged bark. —*tr.* **1.** To pursue or challenge with barking. **2.** To express by barking or howling. **3.** To bring to bay. [ME < *abai*, cornering a hunted animal < OFr. < *abaiier*, to bark, perh. < VLat. **abbaiāre* : Lat. *ad-*, ad- + VLat. **badāre*, to gape, yawn. V., ME *baien*, to bark < *abaien* < OFr. *abaiier*.]

bay⁵ (bā) *n.* **1.** See **laurel** 1. **2.** Any of certain other trees or shrubs with aromatic foliage, such as the California laurel. **3.** A crown or wreath made esp. of the leaves and branches of the laurel and given as a sign of honor or victory. **4.** Honor; renown. Often used in the plural. [ME < OFr. *baie*, berry < Lat. *bāca*.]

ba•ya•dere (bī′ə-dîr′, -dâr′) *n.* A fabric with contrasting horizontal stripes. [Fr. *bayadère* < Port. *bailadeira*, dancer < *bailar*, to dance < LLat. *ballāre*. See BALL².]

Ba•ya•món (bä′yä-mōn′) A town of NE Puerto Rico, a suburb of San Juan. Pop. 203,499.

Bay•ard (bā′ərd, bī′-, bä-yär′), **Seigneur de.** Orig. Pierre Terrail. 1473–1524. French military hero active in the Italian campaigns of Charles VII, Louis XII, and Francis I.

bay•ber•ry (bā′běr′ē) *n.* **1.** A deciduous eastern North American shrub (*Myrica pensylvanica*) having aromatic foliage and small waxy fruits. **2.** The fruit of this shrub. [BAY⁵ + BERRY.]

Ba•yeux (bī-yōō′, bä-, bä-yœ′) A town of NW France near the English Channel. The Bayeux tapestry depicts incidents in the Norman Conquest (1066). Pop. 14,721.

Bay•kal (bī-kôl′, -kôl′), **Lake** See **Lake Baikal**.

bay laurel *n.* See **laurel** 1.

Bayle (bāl, běl), **Pierre** 1647–1706. French philosopher who compiled the *Dictionnaire historique et critique* (1697).

bay leaf *n.* The dried aromatic leaf of the laurel or bay (*Laurus nobilis*) used as a seasoning in cooking.

bay lynx *n.* See **bobcat**.

Bay of For names of actual bays, see the specific element of the name; for example, **Biscay, Bay of**.

bay•o•net (bā′ə-nĭt, -nět′, bā′ə-nět′) *n.* A blade adapted to fit the muzzle end of a rifle, used as a weapon. ❖ *tr.v.* **-net•ed, -net•ing, -nets** or **-net•ted, -net•ting, -nets** To prod, stab, or kill with this weapon. [Fr. *baïonnette*, after *Bayonne*, a town of SW France.]

bay•ou (bī′ōō, bī′ō) *n.* **1.** A body of water that is a tributary of a larger body of water. **2.** A sluggish stream that meanders through lowlands, marshes, or plantation grounds. [Louisiana Fr. *bayouque, bayou*, poss. < Choctaw *bayuk*.]

Bay•reuth (bī-roit′, bī′roit) A city of E-central Germany NE of Nuremberg; home of Richard Wagner from 1872 to 1883. Pop. 71,811.

bay rum *n.* An aromatic liquid originally prepared by distilling the leaves of the bay rum tree in rum and water but now usu. made by mixing the oil from those leaves with other solvents.

bay rum tree *n.* A tropical American evergreen tree (*Pimenta racemosa*) having leathery leaves that yield a fragrant oil.

bay window *n.* **1.** A large window or series of windows projecting from the outer wall of a building and forming a recess within. **2.** *Slang* A protruding belly; a paunch.

ba•zaar also **ba•zar** (bə-zär′) *n.* **1.** A market consisting of a street lined with shops and stalls, esp. one in the Middle East. **2.** A shop or a part of a store in which miscellaneous articles are sold. **3.** A fair or sale at which miscellaneous articles are sold, often for charitable purposes. [Ital. *bazarro* and Urdu *bāzār*, both < Pers. *bāzār*. See **wes-³** in App.]

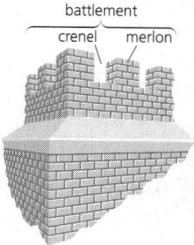

battlement

crenel   merlon

battlement

Bauhaus
The Gropius House, in Lincoln, Massachusetts, was designed by Walter Gropius in 1937.

bay window

ă pat	oi boy
ā pay	ou out
âr care	ŏŏ took
ä father	ōō boot
ĕ pet	ŭ cut
ē be	ûr urge
ĭ pit	th thin
ī pie	th this
îr pier	hw which
ŏ pot	zh vision
ō toe	ə about,
ô paw	item

Stress marks:
′ (primary);
′ (secondary), as in
lexicon (lĕk′sĭ-kŏn′)

ba·zoo·ka (bə-zōō′kə) *n.* A weapon consisting of a metal smoothbore tube for firing rockets at short range. [After the *bazooka,* a crude wind instrument made of pipes, invented and named by Bob Burns (1896–1956), American comedian, prob. < *bazoo,* kazoo.]

bb *abbr.* ball bearing

BB[1] (bē′bē) *n.* A standard size of lead pellet that measures 7/40 of an inch (0.44 centimeter) in diameter, used in air rifles.

BB[2] *abbr.* base on balls

BBA *abbr.* Bachelor of Business Administration

BBB *abbr.* Better Business Bureau

BBC *abbr.* British Broadcasting Corporation

BBC English (bē′bē-sē′) *n.* A pronunciation of British English based on upper-class speech of southeastern England, formerly used as a broadcast standard.

bbl *abbr.* barrel

b-boy·ing (bē′boi′ing) *n.* A style of urban dance that combines energetic footwork with tumbling and spins, usu. performed to funk music. [Prob. < *b(reak)-boy,* one who dances in this style.]

BBS *abbr. Computer Science* bulletin board system

BC *abbr.* **1.** Bachelor of Chemistry **2.** also **B.C.** British Columbia

B.C. *abbr.* also **b.c.** before Christ

BCE *abbr.* **1.** Bachelor of Chemical Engineering **2.** Bachelor of Civil Engineering

B.C.E. or **b.c.e.** *abbr.* before the Common Era

B cell *n.* Any of the lymphocytes that mature in the bone marrow and, when stimulated by a particular antigen, differentiate into plasma cells. [*b(ursa-dependent) cell,* after the *bursa* of Fabricius, gland in birds where the cells mature.]

BCG vaccine (bē′sē-jē′) *n.* A vaccine made from attenuated human tubercle bacilli, used to immunize against tuberculosis. [*B(acillus) C(almette-)G(uérin) vaccine,* after Albert L.C. Calmette (1863–1933) and Camille Guérin (1872–1961), French bacteriologists.]

BChE *abbr.* Bachelor of Chemical Engineering

BCL *abbr.* **1.** Bachelor of Canon Law **2.** Bachelor of Civil Law

B complex *n.* See **vitamin B complex.**

BD *abbr.* **1.** Bachelor of Divinity **2.** bank draft **3.** bomb disposal

bd. *abbr.* **1.** bond **2.** bound **3.** bundle

b/d *abbr.* barrels per day

bdel·li·um (dĕl′ē-əm) *n.* An aromatic gum resin produced by certain Asian and African shrubs or trees of the genus *Commiphora.* [ME < Lat. < Gk. *bdellion,* var. of *bdolkhon,* of Semitic orig.; akin to Akkadian *budulḫu.*]

bd. ft. *abbr.* board foot

bdl. *abbr.* bundle

bdrm. *abbr.* bedroom

BDS *abbr.* Bachelor of Dental Surgery

beagle

be (bē) *v.* First and third person singular past indicative **was** (wŭz; wŏz; waz *when unstressed*), second person singular and plural and first and third person plural past indicative **were** (wûr), past subjunctive **were,** past participle **been** (bĭn), present participle **be·ing** (bē′ing), first person singular present indicative **am** (ăm), second person singular and plural and first and third person plural present indicative **are** (är), third person singular present indicative **is** (ĭz), present subjunctive **be** —*intr.* **1.** To exist in actuality; have life or reality: *I think, therefore I am.* **2a.** To occupy a specified position: *The food is on the table.* **b.** To remain in a certain state or situation undisturbed, untouched, or unmolested: *Let the children be.* **3.** To take place; occur: *The test was yesterday.* **4.** To go or come: *Have you been home?* **5.** Used as a copula in such senses as: **a.** To equal in identity: *"To be a Christian was to be a Roman"* (James Bryce). **b.** To have a specified significance: *A is excellent.* **c.** To belong to a specified class or group: *The human being is a primate.* **d.** To have or show a specified quality or characteristic: *She is witty.* **e.** To seem to consist or be made of: *The yard is all snow.* **6.** To belong; befall: *Woe is me.* —*aux.* **1.** Used with the past participle of a transitive verb to form the passive voice: *The election is held annually.* **2.** Used with the present participle of a verb to express a continuing action: *We are trying to improve.* **3.** Used with the infinitive of a verb to express intention, obligation, or future action: *She was to call.* **4.** *Archaic* Used with the past participle of certain intransitive verbs to form the perfect tense: *"Where be those roses gone?"* (Philip Sidney). [ME *ben* < OE *bēon.* See **bheuə-** in App. See **AM, IS,** etc. for links to other IE roots.]

USAGE NOTE Traditional grammar requires the nominative form of the pronoun in the predicate of the verb *be: It is I* (not *me*). The stigmatization of *It is me* is by now so deeply lodged among the canons of correctness that there is little likelihood that the construction will ever be entirely acceptable in formal writing. Adherence to the traditional rule in informal speech, however, has come to sound increasingly pedantic. • The traditional rule creates particular problems when the pronoun following *be* is the antecedent of a relative pronoun that functions as the object of a verb or preposition in its clause, as in *It is not them/they that we have in mind,* where the plural pronoun is attracted to the case of the following relative pronoun. Writers can usually find a way to avoid this problem: *We have someone else in mind.* See Usage Notes at **I**[1], **we.**

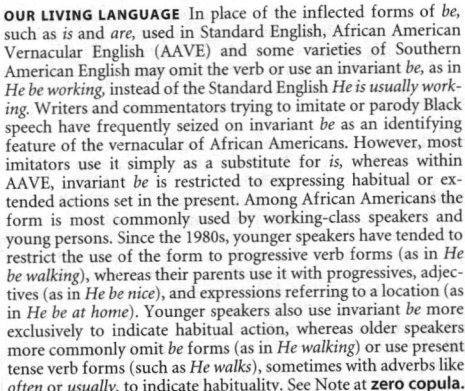

OUR LIVING LANGUAGE In place of the inflected forms of *be,* such as *is* and *are,* used in Standard English, African American Vernacular English (AAVE) and some varieties of Southern American English may omit the verb or use an invariant *be,* as in *He be working,* instead of the Standard English *He is usually working.* Writers and commentators trying to imitate or parody Black speech have frequently seized on invariant *be* as an identifying feature of the vernacular of African Americans. However, most imitators use it simply as a substitute for *is,* whereas within AAVE, invariant *be* is restricted to expressing habitual or extended actions set in the present. Among African Americans the form is most commonly used by working-class speakers and young persons. Since the 1980s, younger speakers have tended to restrict the use of the form to progressive verb forms (as in *He be walking*), whereas their parents use it with progressives, adjectives (as in *He be nice*), and expressions referring to a location (as in *He be at home*). Younger speakers also use invariant *be* more exclusively to indicate habitual action, whereas older speakers more commonly omit *be* forms (as in *He walking*) or use present tense verb forms (such as *He walks*), sometimes with adverbs like *often* or *usually,* to indicate habituality. See Note at **zero copula.**

Be The symbol for the element **beryllium.**

BE *abbr.* **1.** Bachelor of Education **2.** Bachelor of Engineering **3.** Board of Education

B/E *abbr.* **1.** bill of entry **2.** bill of exchange

be– *pref.* **1.** Completely; thoroughly; excessively. Used as an intensive: *bemuse.* **2.** On; around; over: *besmear.* **3.** About; to: *bespeak.* **4.** Used to form transitive verbs from nouns, adjectives, and intransitive verbs, as: **a.** To make; cause to become: *bedim.* **b.** To affect, cover, or provide: *bespectacled.* [ME *bi-, be-* < OE *be-, bi-.* See **ambhi** in App.]

Bé *abbr.* Baumé scale

beach (bēch) *n.* **1.** The shore of a body of water, esp. when sandy or pebbly. **2.** The sand or pebbles on a shore. **3.** The zone above the low water line at the shore of a body of water, marked by an accumulation of sand, stone, or gravel that has been deposited by the tide or waves. ❖ *tr.v.* **beached, beach·ing, beach·es 1.** To haul or run ashore: *beached the rowboat.* **2.** To leave stranded or helpless. [Perh. ME *beche,* stream < OE *bece.*]

Beach, Alfred Ely 1826–96. Amer. editor and inventor who built (1870) a demonstration pneumatic subway under Broadway in New York City.

Beach, Moses Yale 1800–68. Amer. publisher who established the *New York Sun* as a leading daily newspaper.

Beach, Sylvia Woodbridge 1887–1962. Amer. bookseller in Paris who published the first edition of James Joyce's *Ulysses* in 1922.

beach ball *n.* A large inflatable ball used for games, esp. at a beach or swimming pool.

beach buggy *n.* See **dune buggy.**

beach bum *n. Informal* A person who habitually loafs or idles on beaches.

beach·comb·er (bēch′kō′mər) *n.* **1.** A person who scavenges along beaches or in wharf areas. **2.** A seaside vacationer. —**beach′comb′** *v.*

beach flea *n.* Any of various small, jumping crustaceans of the family Orchestiidae, living on sandy beaches.

beach·front (bēch′frŭnt′) *n.* A strip of land facing or running along a beach. —**beach′front′** *adj.*

beach grass *n.* A perennial grass of the genus *Ammophila,* esp. *A. breviligulata,* native to sandy shores of eastern and central North America and having spikelets in long, erect, crowded clusters.

beach·head (bēch′hĕd′) *n.* **1.** A position on an enemy shoreline captured by troops in advance of an invading force. **2.** A first achievement that opens the way for further developments.

Beach-la-Mar (bēch′lə-mär′) *n.* See **Bislama.**

beach pea or **beach-pea** (bēch′pē′) *n.* Any of certain perennial herbs of the genus *Lathyrus* in the pea family, esp. *L. japonicus,* native to shores in the Northern Hemisphere.

beach plum *n.* A seacoast shrub (*Prunus maritima*) in the rose family, native to northeast North America and having edible plumlike fruits.

beach·wear (bēch′wâr′) *n.* Clothing appropriate for swimming, boating, or sunning.

beach wormwood *n.* An Asian perennial seacoast plant (*Artemisia stelleriana*) in the composite family, densely covered with felty hairs.

bea·con (bē′kən) *n.* **1.** A signaling or guiding device, such as a lighthouse, located on a coast. **2.** A radio transmitter that emits a characteristic guidance signal for aircraft. **3.** A source of guidance or inspiration. **4.** A signal fire, esp. one used to warn of an enemy's approach. ❖ *tr. & intr.v.* **-coned, -con·ing, -cons** To provide with or shine as a beacon. [ME *beken* < OE *bēacen.*]

Beacon Hill An area of Boston MA noted for its historic residences, brick sidewalks, and picturesque mews.

bead (bēd) *n.* **1a.** A small, often round piece of material, such as glass, plastic, or wood, that is pierced for stringing or threading. **b. beads** A necklace made of such pieces. **c. beads** *Roman Catholic Church* A rosary. **d.** *Obsolete* A prayer. Often used in the plural. **2.** A small, round object, esp.: **a.** A drop of moisture: *beads of sweat.* **b.** A bubble of gas in a liquid. **c.** A small metal knob on the muzzle of a firearm used for sighting. **3.** A strip of material, usu. wood, with one molded edge placed flush against the inner part of a door or window frame. **4.** *Architecture* **a.** A decoration consisting of a usu. continuous series of small spherical shapes, as on a convex molding. **b.** Beading. **5.** A projecting rim or lip, as on a pneumatic tire. **6.** A line of continuously applied ductile material, such as solder or caulking compound. **7.** *Chemistry* A globule of fused borax or other flux covered with a mineral to be analyzed, heated in a flame as a test for the presence of metals. ❖ *tr. & intr.v.* **bead•ed, bead•ing, beads** To furnish with or collect into beads. ***—idiom:* draw** (or **get**) **a bead on** To take careful aim at. [ME *bede,* rosary bead, prayer < OE *bed, bedu, gebed,* prayer.]

bead•ing (bē′dĭng) *n.* **1.** Beads or the material used for making them. **2.** Ornamentation with beads. **3.** *Architecture* A narrow, half-rounded molding; a bead. **4.** A narrow piece of openwork lace through which ribbon may be run. **5.** Tiny drops of condensation, as on the outside of a glass.

bea•dle (bēd′l) *n.* A minor parish official formerly employed in an English church to usher and keep order during services. [ME *bedel,* herald (< OE *bydel*) and OFr. *bedel* (< Med.Lat. *bedellus* < OHGer. *butil;* see **bheudh-** in App.).]

bead plant *n.* An evergreen plant *(Nertera granadensis)* chiefly of the Southern Hemisphere, grown esp. as a houseplant for its orange drupes.

bead•work (bēd′wûrk′) *n.* **1.** See **beading** 2. **2.** *Architecture* Beaded molding.

bead•y (bē′dē) *adj.* **-i•er, -i•est 1.** Small, round, and shiny: *beady eyes.* **2.** Decorated or covered with beads.

bea•gle (bē′gəl) *n.* One of a breed of hounds having short legs, drooping ears, and white, black, and tan markings. [ME *begle,* poss. < OFr. *bee gueule,* loudmouth : *beer,* to gape (var. of *baer;* see BAY[2]) + *gueule,* gullet (< Lat. *gula*).]

beak (bēk) *n.* **1a.** The horny projecting structure forming the mandibles of a bird, esp. one that is useful in striking and tearing; a bill. **b.** A similar structure in other animals, such as turtles. **2.** A usu. firm, tapering tip on certain plant structures. **3.** A beaklike structure or part, as: **a.** The spout of a pitcher. **b.** A metal or metal-clad ram projecting from the bow of an ancient warship. **4.** *Informal* The human nose. **5.** *Chiefly British Slang* **a.** A schoolmaster. **b.** A judge. [ME *bek* < OFr. *bec* < Lat. *beccus,* of Celt. orig.] **—beaked** (bēkt) *adj.*

beaked salmon *n.* See **sandfish** 2.

beak•er (bē′kər) *n.* **1.** A wide cylindrical glass vessel with a pouring lip, used as a laboratory container and mixing jar. **2.** A large drinking cup with a wide mouth. **3.** The quantity that a beaker holds. [ME *biker* and MDu. *bēker,* drinking vessel, both < Med.Lat. *bicārius, bicārium.* See PITCHER[2].]

be all and end all or **be-all and end-all** (bē′ôl′ ənd ĕnd′ôl′) *n.* The quintessential or all-important element.

beam (bēm) *n.* **1.** A squared-off log or a large oblong piece of timber, metal, or stone used esp. as a horizontal support in construction. **2.** *Nautical* **a.** A transverse structural member of a ship's frame, used to support a deck and brace the sides against stress. **b.** The breadth of a ship at the widest point. **c.** The side of a ship. **3.** *Informal* The widest part of a person's hips. **4.** A steel tube or wooden roller on which the warp is wound in a loom. **5.** An oscillating lever connected to an engine piston rod and used to transmit power to the crankshaft. **6a.** The bar of a balance from which weighing pans are suspended. **b.** *Sports* A balance beam. **7.** The main horizontal bar on a plow to which the share, colter, and handles are attached. **8.** One of the main stems of a deer's antlers. **9a.** A ray or shaft of light. **b.** A concentrated stream of particles or a similar propagation of waves: *a beam of light.* **10.** A radio beam. ❖ *v.* **beamed, beam•ing, beams** *—intr.* **1.** To radiate light; shine. **2.** To smile expansively. *—tr.* **1.** To emit or transmit: *beam a message via satellite.* **2.** To express by means of a radiant smile. ***—idiom:* on the beam 1.** Following a radio beam. Used of aircraft. **2.** On the right track; operating correctly. [ME *bem* < OE *bēam.* See **bheuə-** in App.]

beam•ish (bē′mĭsh) *adj.* Smiling, as with happiness or optimism. **—beam′ish•ly** *adv.*

beam•y (bē′mē) *adj.* **-i•er, -i•est 1.** Broad in the beam, as a ship. **2.** Emitting beams, as of light; radiant.

bean (bēn) *n.* **1a.** Any of various New World herbs of the genus *Phaseolus* in the pea family, having leaves with three leaflets and edible pods and seeds. **b.** A seed or pod of any of these plants. **2.** Any of several related plants or their seeds or pods, such as the adzuki bean. **3.** Any of various other plants or their seeds or fruits, esp. those suggestive of beans, such as the coffee bean. **4.** *Slang* A person's head. **5. beans** *Slang* A small amount. **6.** *Chiefly British* A fellow; a chap. ❖ *tr.v.* **beaned, bean•ing, beans** *Slang* To hit (another) on the head with a thrown object, esp. a pitched baseball. ***—idioms:* full of beans 1.** Energetic; frisky. **2.** Badly mistaken. **spill the beans** To disclose a secret. [ME *ben,* broad bean < OE *bēan.* See **bha-bhā-** in App.]

bean•bag (bēn′băg′) *n.* **1.** A small bag filled with pellets or dried beans and used for throwing in games. **2.** An article, such as a chair, that is constructed as a bag filled with small pellets.

bean ball *n. Baseball* A pitch aimed at the batter's head.

bean counter *n. Slang* A person, such as a financial officer, who is concerned with quantification, esp. to the exclusion of other matters.

bean curd *n.* Tofu.

bean•er•y (bē′nə-rē) *n., pl.* **-ies** *Informal* An inexpensive restaurant or café.

bean family *n.* The pea family.

bean•ie (bē′nē) *n.* A small brimless cap. [Prob. < BEAN, head.]

bean•o (bē′nō) *n., pl.* **-os** A form of bingo, esp. one using beans as markers. [Blend of BEAN and (BING)O.]

bean•pole (bēn′pōl′) *n.* **1.** A thin pole used to support bean vines. **2.** *Informal* A very tall, thin person.

bean sprouts *pl.n.* The tender edible seedlings of certain bean plants, esp. those of the mung bean.

bean•stalk (bēn′stôk′) *n.* The stem of a bean plant.

bear[1] (bâr) *v.* **bore** (bôr, bōr), **borne** (bôrn, bōrn) or **born** (bôrn), **bear•ing, bears** *—tr.* **1.** To hold up; support. **2.** To carry on one's person; convey. **3.** To carry in the mind; harbor: *bear a grudge.* **4.** To transmit at large; relate: *bearing glad tidings.* **5.** To have as a visible characteristic: *bore a scar.* **6.** To have as a quality; exhibit: *"A thousand different shapes it bears"* (Abraham Cowley). **7.** To carry (oneself) in a specified way; conduct: *She bore herself with dignity.* **8.** To be accountable for; assume: *bore heavy responsibilities.* **9.** To have a tolerance for; endure: *couldn't bear lying.* **10.** To call for; warrant: *This case bears investigation.* **11.** To give birth to: *bore four children.* **12.** To produce; yield: *plants bearing flowers.* **13.** To offer; render: *I will bear witness to the deed.* **14.** To move by or as if by steady pressure; push: *"boats against the current, borne back ceaselessly into the past"* (F. Scott Fitzgerald). *—intr.* **1.** To yield fruit; produce: *peach trees that bear every summer.* **2.** To have relevance; apply: *news bearing on the trial.* **3.** To exert pressure, force, or influence. **4a.** To force oneself along; forge. **b.** To endure something with tolerance and patience: *Bear with me.* **5.** To extend or proceed in a specified direction: *bears to the right.* ***—phrasal verbs:* bear down 1.** To overwhelm; vanquish. **2.** To apply maximum effort and concentration. **bear out** To prove right or justified; confirm. **bear up** To withstand stress, difficulty, or attrition. ***—idioms:* bear down on** To effect in a harmful or adverse way. **bear fruit** To come to a satisfactory conclusion or to fruition. **bear in mind** To hold in one's mind; remember. [ME *beren* < OE *beran.* See **bher-**[1] in App.]

SYNONYMS *bear, endure, stand, abide, suffer, tolerate* These verbs mean to experience something difficult or painful in a patient way: *Bear* pertains broadly to capacity to withstand: *"Those best can bear reproof who merit praise"* (Alexander Pope). *Endure* specifies a continuing capacity to face pain or hardship: *"Human life is everywhere a state in which much is to be endured and little to be enjoyed"* (Samuel Johnson). *Stand* implies resoluteness: *He can't stand criticism. Abide* and *suffer* suggest the capacity to withstand patiently: *She couldn't abide fools. He suffered their insults in silence. Tolerate,* when applied to something other than pain, connotes reluctant acceptance: *He tolerated the noise.* See also Syns at **produce.**

bear[2] (bâr) *n.* **1a.** Any of various usu. omnivorous mammals of the family Ursidae, having a shaggy coat and a short tail. **b.** Any of various other animals, such as the koala, that resemble a true bear. **2.** A large, clumsy, or ill-mannered person. **3a.** One that sells securities or commodities in expectation of falling prices. **b.** A pessimist, esp. regarding business conditions. **4.** *Slang* Something that is difficult or unpleasant. ❖ *adj.* Characterized by falling prices: *a bear market.* [ME *bere* < OE *bera.* See **bher-**[2] in App. Sense 3, prob. < proverb *To sell the bear's skin before catching the bear.*]

Bear, Mount A peak, 4,523.5 m (14,831 ft), in the Wrangell Mts. of S AK near the British Columbia border.

bear•a•ble (bâr′ə-bəl) *adj.* That can be endured: *a bearable schedule.* **—bear′a•bil′i•ty** *n.* **—bear′a•bly** *adv.*

bear•bait•ing (bâr′bā′tĭng) *n.* The practice of setting dogs on a chained bear.

bear•ber•ry (bâr′bĕr′ē) *n.* Any of certain shrubs of the genus *Arctostaphylos,* esp. *A. uva-ursi,* native to North America and Eurasia and having leathery leaves and red fruits.

bear•cat (bâr′kăt′) *n.* See **binturong.**

beard (bîrd) *n.* **1.** The hair on a man's chin, cheeks, and throat. **2.** A hairy or hairlike growth such as that on or near the face of certain mammals. **3.** A tuft or group of hairs or bristles on certain plants, such as barley and wheat. **4.** One who serves to divert suspicion or attention from another. **5.** *Printing* The raised slope on a piece of type between the shoulder and face. ❖ *tr.v.* **beard•ed, beard•ing, beards 1.** To furnish with a beard. **2.** To confront boldly. [ME *berd* < OE *beard.* See **bhardh-ā-** in App.]

Beard, Charles Austin 1874–1948. Amer. historian who explored the economic aspects of history in works such as *An Economic Interpretation of the Constitution* (1913).

Beard, Daniel Carter Known as "Dan." 1850–1941. Amer. writer and illustrator who founded the first Boy Scout organization in the US (1910).

Beard, Mary Ritter 1876–1958. Amer. historian who collaborated with her husband, Charles, on *The Rise of American Civilization* (first volume 1927).

beard•ed iris (bîr′dĭd) *n.* Any of various irises having hairs or

beak
top to bottom: black skimmer, male pileated woodpecker, and male American goldfinch

bearded iris

ă	pat	oi	boy
ā	pay	ou	out
âr	care	ŏŏ	took
ä	father	ōō	boot
ĕ	pet	ŭ	cut
ē	be	ûr	urge
ĭ	pit	th	thin
ī	pie	*th*	this
îr	pier	hw	which
ŏ	pot	zh	vision
ō	toe	ə	about, item
ô	paw		

Stress marks:
′ (primary);
′ (secondary), as in
lexicon (lĕk′sĭ-kŏn′)

hairlike structures on the lower parts of the three outer perianth segments.

bearded vulture *n.* See **lammergeier.**

Bear·den (bîr′dn), **Romare Howard** 1912–88. Amer. painter and collagist whose subjects often are drawn from the African-American community.

Beards·ley (bîrdz′lē), **Aubrey Vincent** 1872–98. British illustrator whose black and white drawings were typical of the art nouveau style.

beard·tongue or **beard-tongue** (bîrd′tŭng′) *n.* See **penstemon.** [After its bearded, tonguelike stamen.]

bear·er (bâr′ər) *n.* **1.** One that carries or supports, as: **a.** A porter. **b.** A pallbearer. **2.** One that holds a redeemable note for payment. **3.** A fruit- or flower-bearing plant.

bear grass *n.* **1.** A western North American perennial herb (*Xerophyllum tenax*) in the lily family, having a dense clump of grasslike leaves and a tall stalk. **2.** Any of several similar North American plants.

bear hug *n.* A rough, tight hug.

bear·ing (bâr′ĭng) *n.* **1.** The manner in which one carries or conducts oneself: *regal bearing.* **2a.** A machine or structural part that supports another part. **b.** A device that supports, guides, and reduces the friction of motion between fixed and moving machine parts. **3.** Something that supports weight. **4.** The part of an arch or beam that rests on a support. **5a.** The act, power, or period of producing fruit or offspring. **b.** The quantity produced; yield. **6.** Direction, esp. angular direction measured from one position to another using geographical or celestial reference lines. **7.** Awareness of one's position or situation relative to one's surroundings. Often used in the plural. **8.** Relevant relationship or interconnection. **9.** *Heraldry* A charge or device on a field. ❖ *adj. Architecture* Designed to support structural weight.

bearing rein *n.* A rein for a horse; a checkrein.

bear·ish (bâr′ĭsh) *adj.* **1.** Clumsy, boorish, and surly. **2a.** Causing, expecting, or characterized by falling stock market prices. **b.** Pessimistic. —**bear′ish·ly** *adv.* —**bear′ish·ness** *n.*

Bé·arn (bā-ärn′) A historical region and former province of SW France in the W Pyrenees; autonomous until 1620.

béar·naise sauce (bâr-nāz′, bā′ār-, -əz-) *n.* A sauce of butter and egg yolks flavored with vinegar, wine, shallots, tarragon, and chervil. [Fr. *béarnaise,* fem. of *béarnais,* of Béarn.]

Bear River A river rising in NE UT and flowing c. 563 km (350 mi) in a U-shaped course.

bear's breech (bârz) *n.* See **acanthus** 1.

bear's ear *n.* See **auricula** 1.

bear·skin (bâr′skĭn′) *n.* **1.** Something made from the skin of a bear. **2.** A tall military hat made of black fur.

Be·as (bē′äs′) A river, c. 402 km (250 mi), of N India rising in the Himalaya Mts.; one of the five rivers of the Punjab.

beast (bēst) *n.* **1a.** An animal other than a human, esp. a large four-footed mammal. **b.** *New England & Southern US* A large domestic animal, esp. a horse or bull. **2.** Animal nature as opposed to intellect or spirit. **3.** A brutal, contemptible person. [ME *beste* < OFr. < Lat. *bēstia.*]

beast·ings (bē′stĭngz) *pl.n.* (*used with a sing. or pl. verb*) Variant of **beestings.**

beast·ly (bēst′lē) *adj.* **-li·er, -li·est 1.** Of or resembling a beast; bestial. **2.** Very disagreeable; unpleasant. ❖ *adv. Chiefly British* To an extreme degree; very. —**beast′li·ness** *n.*

beast of burden *n., pl.* **beasts of burden** An animal, such as a donkey, used to transport loads or do other heavy work.

beat (bēt) *v.* **beat, beat·en** (bēt′n) or **beat, beat·ing, beats** —*tr.* **1a.** To strike repeatedly. **b.** To punish by hitting or whipping; flog. **2a.** To strike against repeatedly and with force; pound: *waves beating the shore.* **b.** To flap, esp. wings. **c.** To strike so as to produce music or a signal: *beat a drum.* **d.** *Music* To mark or count (time or rhythm) with the hands or with a baton. **3a.** To shape or break by repeated blows; forge: *beat the glowing metal into a dagger.* **b.** To make by pounding or trampling: *beat a path.* **4.** To mix rapidly with a utensil: *beat two eggs.* **5a.** To defeat or subdue, as in a contest. See Syns at **defeat. b.** To force to withdraw or retreat: *beat back the enemy.* **c.** To dislodge from a position: *I beat him down to a lower price.* **6.** *Informal* To be superior to or better than: *Riding beats walking.* **7.** *Slang* To perplex or baffle: *It beats me; I don't know the answer.* **8.** *Informal* **a.** To avoid or counter the effects of; circumvent: *beat the traffic.* **b.** To arrive or finish before (another): *We beat you home.* **c.** To deprive, as by craft or ability: *beat me out of 20 dollars.* —*intr.* **1.** To inflict repeated blows. **2.** To pulsate; throb. **3a.** To emit sound when struck. **b.** To strike a drum. **4.** To flap repeatedly. **5.** To shine or glare intensely: *The sun beat down all day.* **6.** To fall in torrents: *The rain beat down for hours.* **7.** To be victorious or successful; win. **8.** To hunt through woods or underbrush in search of game. **9.** *Nautical* To sail in the direction from which the wind blows. ❖ *n.* **1.** A stroke or blow, esp. one that produces a sound or serves as a signal. **2.** A pulsation or throb. **3.** *Physics* A variation in wave amplitude produced by beating. Often used in the plural. **4.** *Music* **a.** A steady succession of units of rhythm. **b.** A gesture used by a conductor to indicate a beat. **5.** A pattern of stress that produces the rhythm of verse. **6.** A variable unit of time measuring a pause taken by an actor, as for dramatic effect. **7a.** The area reg-

bearskin

ularly covered by a reporter, a police officer, or a sentry. **b.** The reporting of a news item obtained ahead of one's competitors. **8.** also **Beat** A member of the Beat Generation. ❖ *adj.* **1.** *Informal* Worn-out; fatigued. **2.** Of or relating to the Beat Generation. —*phrasal verbs:* **beat off 1.** To drive away. **2.** *Vulgar Slang* To masturbate. **beat out** *Baseball* To reach base safely on (a bunt or ground ball) when a putout is attempted. —*idioms:* **beat a retreat** To make a hasty withdrawal. **beat around** (or **about**) **the bush** To fail to confront a subject directly. **beat it** *Slang* To leave hurriedly. **beat the bushes** To make an exhaustive search. **beat the drum** (or **drums**) To give enthusiastic public support or promotion. **to beat the band** With great vigor; in a fast and furious manner. [ME *beten* < OE *bēatan.*]

beat·en (bēt′n) *adj.* **1.** Formed or made thin by hammering: *beaten gold.* **2.** Worn by continuous use; familiar and much traveled. **3.** Totally worn-out; exhausted.

beat·er (bē′tər) *n.* **1.** One that beats, esp. a device for beating. **2.** A person who drives game from under cover for a hunter.

Beat Generation *n.* A group of American writers and artists popular in the 1950s and early 1960s, known esp. for their use of nontraditional forms and their rejection of conventional social values. [< BEAT, weary, or short for BEATITUDE.]

be·a·tif·ic (bē′ə-tĭf′ĭk) *adj.* Showing or producing exalted joy or blessedness: *a beatific smile.* [Lat. *beātificus : beātus,* happy < p. part. of *beāre,* to bless; see **deu-²** in App. + *-ficus, -fic.*] —**be′a·tif′i·cal·ly** *adv.*

be·at·i·fy (bē-ăt′ə-fī′) *tr.v.* **-fied, -fy·ing, -fies 1.** To make blessedly happy. **2.** *Roman Catholic Church* To proclaim (a deceased person) to be one of the blessed and thus worthy of public veneration in a particular region or congregation. **3.** To exalt above all others. [Fr. *beatifier* < LLat. *beātificāre :* Lat. *beātus,* happy; see BEATIFIC + Lat. *-ficāre, -fy.*] —**be·at′i·fi·ca′tion** (-fĭ-kā′shən) *n.*

beat·ing (bē′tĭng) *n.* **1.** Punishment by whipping or flogging. **2.** A sound defeat. **3.** A throbbing or pulsation. **4.** *Physics* The periodic variation in the amplitude of a wave produced by the superposition of two waves of different frequencies.

be·at·i·tude (bē-ăt′ĭ-tōōd′, -tyōōd′) *n.* **1.** Supreme blessedness or happiness. **2. Beatitude** Any of the declarations of blessedness made by Jesus in the Sermon on the Mount. [ME < OFr. < Lat. *beātitūdō < beātus,* happy. See BEATIFIC.]

beat·nik (bēt′nĭk) *n.* A person, esp. a member or follower of the Beat Generation, whose behavior, views, and often style of dress are pointedly unconventional. [BEAT (GENERATION) + -NIK.]

Bea·ton (bēt′n), **Cecil Walter Hardy** 1904–80. British photographer, diarist, and theatrical designer.

Be·a·trix (bā′ə-trĭks′, bē′-) b. 1938. Queen of the Netherlands who ascended the throne (1980) after the abdication of her mother, Juliana.

beat-up (bēt′ŭp′) *adj. Slang* Damaged or worn because of neglect or heavy use.

beat wave *n.* A wave whose amplitude varies periodically, produced by the superposition of two waves of different frequencies.

beau (bō) *n., pl.* **beaus** or **beaux** (bōz) **1.** The boyfriend of a woman or girl. **2.** A dandy; a fop. [Fr. < *beau, bel,* handsome < Lat. *bellus.* See **deu-²** in App.]

Beau Brum·mell (bō brŭm′əl) *n.* A dandy; a fop. [After George Bryan ("Beau") BRUMMELL.]

beau·coup (bō′kōō′, bōō′-, bō-kōō′) also **boo·coo** or **boo·koo** (bōō′-) *Chiefly Southern US adj.* Many; much: *beaucoup money.* ❖ *n., pl.* **-coups** also **-coos** or **-koos** An abundance; a lot. ❖ *adv.* In abundance; galore. [Fr.: *beau, bel,* fine, handsome; see BEAU + *coup,* stroke; see COUP.]

Beaufort scale (bō′fərt) *n.* A scale of wind force ranging from 0 (calm) to 12 (hurricane). [After Sir Francis *Beaufort* (1774–1857), British naval officer.]

Beaufort Sea A part of the Arctic Ocean N of NE AK and NW Canada extending from Point Barrow to the Canadian Arctic Archipelago.

beau geste (bō zhĕst′) *n., pl.* **beaux gestes** or **beau gestes** (bō zhĕst′) **1.** A gracious gesture. **2.** A gesture noble in form but meaningless in substance. [Fr. : *beau, bel* + *geste,* gesture.]

Beau·har·nais (bō-är-nā′), **Eugène de** 1781–1824. French soldier who was adopted by Napoleon I and became heir apparent to the throne of Italy (1806).

Beauharnais, Josephine de 1763–1814. Empress of the French (1804–09) as the wife of Napoleon I.

beau i·de·al (bō′ ī-dē′əl) *n., pl.* **beau ideals 1.** The concept of perfect beauty. **2.** An idealized type or model. [Fr. *beau idéal : beau,* perfect + *idéal,* ideal.]

Beau·jo·lais¹ (bō′zhə-lā′) A hilly region of E-central France W of the Saône R. between Mâcon and Lyons.

Beau·jo·lais² (bō′zhə-lā′) *n.* A light red table wine made from the gamay grape. [After BEAUJOLAIS¹.]

Beau·mar·chais (bō-mär-shā′), **Pierre Augustin Caron de** 1732–99. French writer whose comic plays *Le Barbier de Séville* (1775) and *Le Mariage de Figaro* (1784) inspired operas by Rossini and Mozart.

beau monde (bō mŏnd′, môNd′) *n., pl.* **beaux mondes** (bō mônd′) or **beau mondes** (bō mŏndz′) The world of fashionable society. [Fr. : *beau*, good + *monde*, world, society.]

Beau·mont (bō′mŏnt′) A city of SE TX NNE of Houston. Pop. 113,866.

Beau·mont (bō′mŏnt′, -mənt), **Francis** 1584–1616. English poet and playwright whose major works, including *The Maid's Tragedy* (1611), were written with John Fletcher.

Beau·re·gard (bō′rĭ-gärd′, bō-rə-gär′), **Pierre Gustave Toutant** 1818–93. Amer. Confederate general who ordered the bombardment of Fort Sumter (1861).

beaut (byo͞ot) *n. Slang* Something outstanding of its kind. [Short for BEAUTY.]

beau·te·ous (byo͞o′tē-əs) *adj.* Beautiful, esp. to the sight. —**beau′te·ous·ly** *adv.* —**beau′te·ous·ness** *n.*

beau·ti·cian (byo͞o-tĭsh′ən) *n.* A cosmetician.

beau·ti·ful (byo͞o′tə-fəl) *adj.* **1.** Having qualities that delight the senses, esp. sight. **2.** Excellent; wonderful. —**beau′ti·ful·ly** *adv.* —**beau′ti·ful·ness** *n.*

beautiful people also **Beautiful People** *pl.n.* Wealthy, prominent people, esp. those in international society.

beau·ti·fy (byo͞o′tə-fī′) *tr. & intr.v.* **-fied, -fy·ing, -fies** To make or become beautiful. —**beau′ti·fi·ca′tion** (-fĭ-kā′shən) *n.* —**beau′ti·fi′er** *n.*

beau·ty (byo͞o′tē) *n., pl.* **-ties 1.** The quality that gives pleasure to the mind or senses and is associated with such properties as harmony of form or color, excellence of artistry, truthfulness, and originality. **2.** One that is beautiful. **3.** A quality or feature that is most effective, gratifying, or telling. **4.** An outstanding or conspicuous example. [ME *beaute* < OFr. *biaute* < VLat. **bellitās* < Lat. *bellus*, pretty. See **deu-²** in App.]

beau·ty·ber·ry (byo͞o′tē-bĕr′ē) *n.* Any of various shrubs of the genus *Callicarpa* cultivated for their berrylike fruits.

beau·ty·bush (byo͞o′tē-bo͞osh′) *n.* A deciduous Chinese ornamental shrub (*Kolkwitzia amabilis*) cultivated for its pink flowers.

beauty mark *n.* See **beauty spot.**

beauty parlor *n.* An establishment providing services that include hair treatment, manicures, and facials.

beauty quark *n.* See **bottom quark.**

beauty salon *n.* See **beauty parlor.**

beauty shop *n.* See **beauty parlor.**

beauty spot *n.* **1.** A mole or birthmark. **2.** A small black mark penciled or glued on the face or shoulders to accentuate fairness of skin or to conceal a blemish.

Beau·voir (bō-vwär′), **Simone de** 1908–86. French writer and existentialist whose works include *The Second Sex* (1949).

beaux (bōz) *n.* A plural of **beau.**

beaux arts (bō-zär′, -zärt′) *pl.n.* The fine arts. [Fr. : *beaux*, pl. of *beau*, fine + *arts*, pl. of *art*, art.]

Beaux Arts *adj.* Of or relating to an architectural style originating in France in the late 19th century and characterized by classical forms, symmetry, rich ornamentation, and a grand scale. [After the *École des Beaux Arts*, School of Fine Arts, in Paris.]

beaux es·prits (bō′zĕ-sprē′) *n.* Plural of **bel esprit.**

beaux gestes (bō zhĕst′) *n.* A plural of **beau geste.**

beaux mondes (bō mônd′) *n.* A plural of **beau monde.**

bea·ver¹ (bē′vər) *n.* **1a.** A large aquatic rodent of the genus *Castor*, having thick brown fur, webbed hind feet, a broad flat tail, and sharp incisors adapted for gnawing bark, felling trees, and constructing dams and underwater lodges. **b.** The fur of this rodent. **c.** A top hat originally made of the fur of this rodent. **2.** A napped wool fabric, similar to felt, used for outer garments. **3.** *Vulgar Slang* The female genitals. ❖ *intr.v.* **-vered, -ver·ing, -vers** To work diligently and energetically. [ME *bever* < OE *beofor*. See **bher-²** in App.]

bea·ver² (bē′vər) *n.* **1.** A piece of armor on a helmet or breastplate to protect the mouth and chin. **2.** The visor on a helmet. [ME *bavier* < OFr. *baviere*, child's bib, beaver < *bave*, saliva.]

bea·ver·board (bē′vər-bôrd′, -bōrd′) *n.* A light building material of compressed wood pulp. [Orig. a trademark.]

Bea·ver·brook (bē′vər-bro͝ok′), **1st Baron.** Orig. William Maxwell Aitken. 1879–1964. Canadian-born British publisher, financier, and politician.

Beaver River 1. A river rising in central Alberta, Canada, and flowing c. 491 km (305 mi) to the headwaters of the Churchill R. **2.** A name for the North Canadian R. as it flows c. 450 km (280 mi) through NW OK.

be·bop (bē′bŏp′) *n. Music* Bop. [Imitation of a two-note phrase in this music.] —**be′bop′per** *n.*

be·calm (bĭ-käm′) *tr.v.* **-calmed, -calm·ing, -calms 1.** To render motionless for lack of wind. **2.** To make calm or still.

be·came (bĭ-kām′) *v.* Past tense of **become.**

be·cause (bĭ-kôz′, -kŭz′) *conj.* For the reason that; since. [ME, short for *bi cause of.* See BECAUSE OF.]

because of *prep.* On account of; by reason of. [ME *bi cause of*, by reason of : *bi*, by; see BY¹ + *cause*, reason; see CAUSE + *of*, of; see OF.]

bec·ca·fi·co (bĕk′ə-fē′kō) *n., pl.* **-cos** A small songbird or warbler of various genera, esp. the European garden warbler (*Sylvia hortensis*). [Ital. *beccafico* : *beccare*, to peck (< *becco*, beak < Lat. *beccus*; see BEAK) + *fico*, fig (< Lat. *ficus*).]

bé·cha·mel sauce (bā′shə-mĕl′) *n.* A white sauce of butter, flour, and milk or cream. [Fr. *sauce béchamel*, after Louis de Béchamel (1603–1703), chief steward of Louis XIV.]

be·chance (bĭ-chăns′) *intr. & tr.v.* **-chanced, -chanc·ing, -chanc·es** *Archaic* To happen or happen to.

bêche-de-mer (bĕsh′də-mâr′) *n., pl.* **bêches-de-mer** (bĕsh′-) See **trepang.** [Fr., alteration (influenced by *bêche*, grub) of *biche-de-mer* < Port. *bicho do mar* : *bicho*, worm (< LLat. *bēstulus*, dim. of Lat. *bēstia*, beast) + *do*, of the + *mar*, sea (< Lat. *mare*; see **mori-** in App.).]

Bêche-de-Mer *n.* See **Bislama.** [From the commercial importance of BÊCHE-DE-MER where the language is spoken.]

Bech·u·a·na (bĕch′o͞o-ä′nə) *n., pl.* **Bechuana** or **-nas** See **Tswana 1.**

Bech·u·a·na·land (bĕch′wä-nə-lănd′, bĕch′o͞o-ä′-) See **Botswana.**

beck¹ (bĕk) *n.* A gesture of beckoning or summons. —*idiom:* **at (someone's) beck and call** Ready to fulfill any wish or order. [ME *bek* < *bekken*, to beckon, alteration of *bekenen*. See BECKON.]

beck² (bĕk) *n. Chiefly British* A small brook; a creek. [ME < ON *bekkr*.]

Beck·et (bĕk′ĭt), **Saint Thomas à** 1118?–70. English Roman Catholic martyr who was appointed archbishop of Canterbury (1162) but fell into disfavor with Henry II over religious matters and was later murdered.

Beck·ett (bĕk′ĭt), **Samuel** 1906–89. Irish-born writer known esp. for his absurdist plays, such as *Waiting for Godot* (1952). He won the 1969 Nobel Prize for literature.

Beck·mann (bĕk′män), **Max** 1884–1950. German painter whose works include *Night* (1919).

beck·on (bĕk′ən) *v.* **-oned, -on·ing, -ons** —*tr.* **1.** To signal or summon, as by nodding or waving. **2.** To attract because of an inviting or enticing appearance. —*intr.* **1.** To make a signaling or summoning gesture. **2.** To be inviting or enticing. ❖ *n.* A gesture of summons. [ME *bekenen* < OE *bīecnan*, *bēcnan*.] —**beck′on·er** *n.* —**beck′on·ing·ly** *adv.*

be·cloud (bĭ-kloud′) *tr.v.* **-cloud·ed, -cloud·ing, -clouds** To darken with or as if with clouds; obscure.

be·come (bĭ-kŭm′) *v.* **-came** (-kām′), **-come, -com·ing, -comes** —*intr.* To grow or come to be: *became brighter; will become clearer in the morning.* —*tr.* **1.** To be appropriate or suitable to: *"It would not become me . . . to interfere with parties"* (Jonathan Swift). **2.** To show to advantage; look good with: *The new suit becomes you.* —*phrasal verb:* **become of** To be the fate of; happen to: [ME *bicomen* < OE *becuman*. See **gʷā-** in App.]

be·com·ing (bĭ-kŭm′ĭng) *adj.* **1.** Appropriate, suitable, or proper. **2.** Pleasing or attractive to the eye. —**be·com′ing·ly** *adv.* —**be·com′ing·ness** *n.*

bec·que·rel (bĕ-krĕl′, bĕk′ə-rĕl′) *n.* The International System unit of radioactivity, equal to one nuclear decay or other nuclear transformation per second. [After Antoine Henri *Becquerel* (1852–1908), French physicist.]

Becquerel Family of French physicists, including **Antoine César** (1788–1878), one of the first investigators of electrochemistry; his son **Alexandre Edmond** (1820–91), noted for his research on phosphorescence; and his grandson **Antoine Henri** (1852–1908), who shared a 1903 Nobel Prize.

bed (bĕd) *n.* **1a.** A piece of furniture for reclining and sleeping, typically consisting of a flat rectangular frame and a mattress on springs. **b.** A bedstead. **c.** A mattress. **2.** A place where one may sleep; lodging. **b.** Accommodations for a single person at a hospital or institution. **3.** A time at which one goes to sleep. **4.** A place for lovemaking. **5.** A marital relationship with its rights and intimacies. **6a.** A small plot of cultivated or planted land: *a flower bed.* **b.** An underwater or intertidal area in which a particular organism is established in large numbers: *an oyster bed.* **7.** The bottom of a body of water. **8.** A supporting, underlying, or securing part, esp.: **a.** A layer of food surmounted by another kind of food. **b.** A foundation of crushed rock or a similar substance for a road or railroad; a roadbed. **c.** A layer of mortar upon which stones or bricks are laid. **9.** *Printing* The heavy table of a printing press in which the type form is placed. **10.** The part of a truck, trailer, or freight car designed to carry loads. **11.** *Geology* **a.** A rock mass of large horizontal extent bounded, esp. above, by physically different material. **b.** A deposit, as of ore, parallel to local stratification. **12.** A heap of material. ❖ *v.* **bed·ded, bed·ding, beds** —*tr.* **1.** To furnish with a bed or sleeping quarters. **2.** To put or send to bed. **3.** To have sexual relations with. **4.** To plant in a prepared plot of soil. **5.** To lay flat or arrange in layers. **6a.** To embed. **b.** To establish; base. —*intr.* **1.** To go to bed. **2.** To form layers or strata. [ME < OE.]

BEd *abbr.* Bachelor of Education

bed-and-break·fast or **bed and breakfast** (bĕd′n-brĕk′fəst) *n.* A private home that provides rooms and breakfast for paying guests.

be·daub (bĭ-dôb′) *tr.v.* **-daubed, -daub·ing, -daubs 1.** To smear; soil. **2.** To ornament in a vulgar, showy fashion.

be·daz·zle (bĭ-dăz′əl) *tr.v.* **-zled, -zling, -zles 1.** To dazzle so completely as to make blind. **2.** To please irresistibly; enchant. —**be·daz′zle·ment** *n.*

bed·bug also **bed bug** (bĕd′bŭg′) *n.* A wingless odorous insect (*Cimex lectularius*) with a flat reddish body that infests dwellings

Pierre G.T. Beauregard

and bedding and feeds on human blood.

bed·cham·ber (bĕd′chām′bər) *n.* A bedroom.

bed·clothes (bĕd′klōz′, -klōthz′) *pl.n.* Coverings, such as sheets and blankets, that are ordinarily used on a bed.

bed·ding (bĕd′ĭng) *n.* **1.** Bedclothes. **2.** Material, esp. straw, on which animals sleep. **3.** A bottom layer; a foundation. **4.** *Geology* Stratification of rocks into beds.

Bede (bēd) *also* **Bae·da** *or* **Be·da** (bē′də) Known as "the Venerable Bede." 673?–735. Anglo-Saxon historian who introduced the method of dating events from the birth of Christ.

be·deck (bĭ-dĕk′) *tr.v.* **-decked, -deck·ing, -decks** To adorn or ornament in a showy fashion.

be·dev·il (bĭ-dĕv′əl) *tr.v.* **-iled, -il·ing, -ils** *or* **-illed, -il·ling, -ils 1.** To torment mercilessly; plague. **2.** To worry, annoy, or frustrate. **3.** To possess with or as if with a devil; bewitch. **4.** To spoil; ruin. **—be·dev′il·ment** *n.*

be·dew (bĭ-dōo′, -dyōo′) *tr.v.* **-dewed, -dew·ing, -dews** To wet with or as if with dew.

bed·fast (bĕd′făst′) *adj.* Confined to bed; bedridden.

bed·fel·low (bĕd′fĕl′ō) *n.* **1.** A bedmate. **2.** One that is closely associated or allied with another.

Bed·ford (bĕd′fərd), Duke of. See **John of Lancaster**.

Bedford cord *n.* A heavy fabric with a lengthwise ribbed weave that resembles corduroy. [After BEDFORD, England.]

be·dight (bĭ-dīt′) *tr.v.* **-dight** *or* **-dight·ed, -dight·ing, -dights** *Archaic* To dress or array.

be·dim (bĭ-dĭm′) *tr.v.* **-dimmed, -dim·ming, -dims** To dim.

be·di·zen (bĭ-dī′zən, -dĭz′ən) *tr.v.* **-zened, -zen·ing, -zens** To ornament or dress in a showy or gaudy manner. [BE- + DIZEN.] **—be·di′zen·ment** *n.*

bed·lam (bĕd′ləm) *n.* **1.** A place or situation of noisy uproar and confusion. **2.** *often* **Bedlam** *Archaic* An insane asylum. [ME *Bedlem,* Hospital of St. Mary of *Bethlehem,* an insane asylum in London.] **—bed′lam·ite′** (-lə-mīt′) *n.*

Bed·ling·ton terrier (bĕd′lĭng-tən) *n.* A gray- or brown-haired terrier of a breed developed in England. [After *Bedlington,* a town of northeast England.]

Bed·loe's Island (bĕd′lōz) See **Liberty Island.**

bed·mate (bĕd′māt′) *n.* One with whom a bed is shared.

bed molding *n.* **1.** The molding between the corona and frieze of an entablature. **2.** A molding below a projecting part.

bed of roses *n.* A state of great comfort or luxury.

Bed·ou·in *also* **Bed·u·in** (bĕd′ōo-ĭn, bĕd′wĭn) *n., pl.* **Bedouin** *or* **-ins** *also* **Beduin** *or* **-ins** An Arab of any of various nomadic desert tribes. [ME *Bedoin* < OFr. *beduin* < Ar. *badawīyīn,* pl. of *badawī,* nomadic < *badw,* desert nomads, Bedouins.]

bed·pan (bĕd′păn′) *n.* A metal, glass, or plastic receptacle for the urinary and fecal discharges of persons confined to bed.

bed·plate (bĕd′plāt′) *n.* A plate, frame, or platform serving as a base or support for a machine.

bed·post (bĕd′pōst′) *n.* A vertical post at the corner of a bed.

be·drag·gle (bĭ-drăg′əl) *tr.v.* **-gled, -gling, -gles** To make wet and limp. [BE- + DRAGGLE.]

be·drag·gled (bĭ-drăg′əld) *adj.* **1a.** Wet; limp. **b.** Soiled by or as if by having been dragged through mud. **2.** Being in a condition of deterioration; dilapidated.

bed·rid·den (bĕd′rĭd′n) *also* **bed·rid** (-rĭd′) *adj.* Confined to bed because of infirmity.

bed·rock (bĕd′rŏk′) *n.* **1.** The solid rock that underlies loose material, such as soil, sand, clay, or gravel. **2a.** The very basis; the foundation. **b.** The lowest point.

bed·roll (bĕd′rōl′) *n.* A portable roll of bedding used esp. by campers and others who sleep outdoors.

bed·room (bĕd′rōom′, -rŏom′) *n.* A room in which to sleep. ❖ *adj.* **1.** Sexually suggestive. **2.** Relating to commuters.

bed·side (bĕd′sīd′) *n.* The side of a bed or the space alongside it. ❖ *adj.* At or near the side of a bed.

bedside manner *n.* The attitude and conduct of a physician in the presence of a patient.

bed·sit·ter (bĕd′sĭt′ər) *n. Chiefly British* A one-room apartment that serves as a bedroom and a living room. [< BED + SITTING ROOM.]

bed·sore (bĕd′sôr′, -sōr′) *n.* A pressure-induced ulceration of the skin of persons confined to bed for long periods of time.

bed·spread (bĕd′sprĕd′) *n.* A usu. decorative bed covering.

bed·spring (bĕd′sprĭng′) *n.* One of the springs supporting the mattress of a bed. Often used in the plural.

bed·stead (bĕd′stĕd′) *n.* The frame supporting a bed.

bed·straw (bĕd′strô′) *n.* Any of several plants of the genus *Galium,* having whorled leaves, small flower clusters, and prickly stems. [Short for *Our Lady's Bedstraw,* a plant whose foliage was once used in mattresses.]

bed·time (bĕd′tīm′) *n.* The time at which one goes to bed.

Bed·u·in (bĕd′ōo-ĭn, bĕd′wĭn) *n.* Variant of **Bedouin.**

bed·warm·er (bĕd′wôr′mər) *n.* See **warming pan.**

bed·wet·ting (bĕd′wĕt′ĭng) *n.* Enuresis, esp. during sleep.

bee¹ (bē) *n.* **1a.** Any of several winged, hairy-bodied, usu. stinging insects of the superfamily Apoidea in the order Hymenoptera, marked by sucking and chewing mouthparts for gathering nectar and pollen. **b.** A bumblebee. **c.** A honeybee. **2.** A social gathering where people also work in competition. **—idiom:** a

beech
American beech
Fagus grandifolia

beefeater
Yeoman Warder at the
Tower of London

bee in (one's) bonnet 1. An impulsive, often eccentric turn of mind; a notion. **2.** An obsession. [ME < OE *bēo;* see **bhei-** in App. Sense 2, perh. alteration of dialectal *bean,* neighborly help to a farmer < ME *bene,* extra service by a tenant < OE *bēn,* prayer; see **bhā-** in App.]

bee² (bē) *n. Nautical* A bee block. [ME *be,* a ring < OE *bēag.*]

bee³ (bē) *n.* The letter *b.*

bee balm *n.* An aromatic eastern North American herb (*Monarda didyma*) in the mint family, having variously colored, tubular bilabiate flowers grouped in dense showy heads.

Bee·be (bē′bē), **(Charles) William** 1877–1962. Amer. naturalist and explorer who helped design the bathysphere.

bee block *n. Nautical* A piece of hardwood on either side of a bowsprit through which forestays are reeved.

bee·bread (bē′brĕd′) *n.* A brownish substance consisting of a mixture of pollen and honey and used by bees as food.

beech (bēch) *n.* **1.** A deciduous tree of the genus *Fagus* having smooth gray bark, alternate simple leaves, and three-angled nuts enclosed in prickly burs. **2.** The wood of a beech. [ME *beche* < OE *bēce.* See **bhāgo-** in App.]

Bee·cham (bē′chəm), Sir **Thomas** 1879–1961. British conductor who founded the London Philharmonic (1932) and the Royal Philharmonic (1947) orchestras.

beech·drops *or* **beech-drops** (bēch′drŏps′) *pl.n.* (*used with a sing. or pl. verb*) A brownish eastern North American annual plant (*Epifagus virginiana*) having scalelike leaves and whitish tubular flowers with brown-purple stripes.

Bee·cher (bē′chər), **Lyman** 1775–1863. Amer. cleric and father of the abolitionist editor **Henry Ward Beecher** (1813–87) and the novelist Harriet Beecher Stowe.

beech mast *n.* The nuts of the beech tree; beechnuts.

beech·nut (bēch′nŭt′) *n.* The three-angled beech tree nut.

bee·di (bē′dē) *n.* Variant of **bidi.**

bee-eat·er (bē′ē′tər) *n.* Any of various chiefly tropical Old World birds of the family Meropidae that have brightly colored plumage and feed on bees and wasps.

beef (bēf) *n., pl.* **beeves** (bēvz) *or* **beef 1a.** A full-grown steer, bull, ox, or cow, esp. one intended for use as meat. **b.** The flesh of slaughtered full-grown cattle. **2.** *Informal* Human muscle; brawn. **3.** *pl.* **beefs** *Slang* A complaint. ❖ *intr.v.* **beefed, beef·ing, beefs** *Slang* To complain. **—phrasal verb: beef up** *Informal* To make or become greater or stronger. [ME < OFr. *buef* < Lat. *bōs, bov-.* See **g^wou-** in App.]

WORD HISTORY Farmers raise cows for their beef, and hunters hunt deer for their venison. This distinction between the word for the animal and the word for its meat comes from the French nobles who ruled England after the Norman Conquest. They of course used French words for the food served to them; so the animal called *cū* by the Anglo-Saxon peasants working in the fields was called *buef* by the French nobles when it was brought to them cooked as dinner. In this way the word-pair *cow/beef* arose, as well as others such as *swine/pork, sheep/mutton,* and *deer/venison.* • Interestingly, both *cow* and Old French *buef* are descendants of the Indo-European root *g^wou-,* and thus are the same word, etymologically speaking.

beef·a·lo (bē′fə-lō′) *n., pl.* **beefalo** *or* **-los** *or* **-loes** A hybrid from a cross between the American buffalo, or bison, and beef cattle. [Blend of BEEF and (BUFF)ALO.]

beef bour·gui·gnon (bōor′gēn-yôn′, -yôN′) *n.* Braised beef cubes simmered in a seasoned red wine sauce with mushrooms, carrots, and onions. [Fr. *boeuf bourguignon* < *Bourgogne,* Burgundy, a region of E France.]

beef·cake (bēf′kāk′) *n. Informal* Photographs of minimally attired men with muscular physiques. [BEEF + (CHEESE)CAKE.]

beef·eat·er (bēf′ē′tər) *n.* A yeoman of the British monarch's royal guard. [Earlier, well-fed servant.]

bee fly *n.* Any of various beelike flies of the family Bombyliidae that feed on nectar and pollen and have parasitic larvae.

beef·steak (bēf′stāk′) *n.* A slice of beef, such as one taken from the loin, suitable for broiling or frying.

beefsteak fungus *n.* An edible fungus (*Fistulina hepatica*), growing on living tree trunks, such as oak and ash, and having a large, irregularly shaped reddish cap.

beefsteak tomato *n.* Any of several varieties of tomato having large fruit with thick flesh.

beef stro·ga·noff (strô′gə-nôf′, -nŏf′) *n.* Thinly sliced sautéed beef with onions, mushrooms, sour cream, and herbs. [After Count Pavel Alexandrovich Stroganov (1774–1817), Russian diplomat.]

beef Wellington *n.* A beef fillet covered with pâté de foie gras and encased in pastry. [Prob. < the name *Wellington.*]

beef·y (bē′fē) *adj.* **-i·er, -i·est 1a.** Muscular in build; brawny. **b.** Substantial; filling. **2.** Filled with beef. **—beef′i·ness** *n.*

bee gum *n. Chiefly Southern US* **1.** A beehive located in a hollow tree or log. **2.** Any beehive. [BEE¹ + *gum,* a hollowed-out log (< GUM¹).]

bee·hive (bē′hīv′) *n.* A hive for bees.

bee·keep·er (bē′kē′pər) *n.* One who keeps bees, specifically one who cares for and raises bees for commercial or agricultural purposes. **—bee′keep′ing** *n.*

bee·line (bē′līn′) n. A direct straight course. [< the belief that a bee returns to its hive in a straight course.]

Be·el·ze·bub (bē-ĕl′zə-bŭb′) n. **1.** The Devil; Satan. **2.** One of the fallen angels in Milton's *Paradise Lost.* **3.** An evil spirit; a demon. [Heb. *ba'al zəbûb,* lord (of the) fly, pejorative alteration of *ba'al zəbûl,* lord prince (a Philistine god) : *ba'al,* lord, Baal + *zəbûl,* exalted.]

bee moth n. A moth (*Galleria mellonella*) that lays its eggs in beehives, where the larvae feed on wax and debris.

been (bĭn) v. Past participle of **be.**

beep (bēp) n. A sound or a signal, as from a horn. ❖ v. **beeped, beep·ing, beeps** —*intr.* **1.** To make a beep. —*tr.* **1.** To cause to make a beep. **2.** To call or warn with a beeper. [Imit.]

beep·er (bē′pər) n. **1.** One that beeps. **2.** A portable electronic device that beeps when the person carrying it is being paged.

bee plant n. Any of numerous plants that attract bees.

beer (bîr) n. **1.** A fermented alcoholic beverage brewed from malt and flavored with hops. **2.** A beverage made from extracts of roots and plants. **3.** A serving of one of these beverages. [ME *ber* < OE *bēor* < West Gmc., prob. < Lat. *bibere,* to drink. See **pō(i)-** in App.]

Beer·bohm (bîr′bōm′), Sir **Henry Maximilian** ("**Max**") 1872–1956. British caricaturist, writer, and wit.

beer garden n. An outdoor tavern or an outdoor area adjoining a tavern where alcohol is served. [Transl. of Ger. *Biergarten* : *Bier,* beer + *Garten,* garden.]

Beer·she·ba (bîr-shē′bə, bĕr-shĕv′ə) A city of S Israel SW of Jerusalem; the S boundary of Palestine in biblical times. Pop. 138,100.

beer·y (bîr′ē) adj. **-i·er, -i·est 1.** Smelling or tasting of beer: *beery breath.* **2.** Affected or produced by beer: *beery humor.*

beest·ings also **beast·ings** (bē′stĭngz) pl.n. (*used with a sing. or pl. verb*) The first milk secreted by a mammal, esp. a cow, after parturition; colostrum. [ME *bestinggis,* pl. of *besting* < OE *bȳsting* < *bēost,* beestings.]

bee-stung (bē′stŭng′) adj. Full and sensuous. Used of lips.

bees·wax (bēz′wăks′) n. **1.** The wax secreted by the honeybee for constructing honeycombs. **2.** Commercial wax obtained by processing and purifying the crude wax of the honeybee.

beet (bēt) n. **1.** A biennial Eurasian plant (*Beta vulgaris*) grown as a crop plant for its edible roots and leaves. **2.** The swollen root of this plant eaten as a vegetable. **3.** The sugar beet. [ME *bete* < OE *bēte* < Lat. *bēta.*]

beet armyworm n. An armyworm (*Spodoptera exigua*) that feeds primarily on the foliage of beets and other crops.

Bee·tho·ven (bā′tō′vən), **Ludwig van** 1770–1827. German composer and pianist whose music formed a transition from classical to romantic composition.

bee·tle¹ (bēt′l) n. **1.** Any of numerous insects of the order Coleoptera, having biting mouthparts and forewings that form horny coverings to protect the underlying hind wings when at rest. **2.** An insect resembling a beetle. ❖ *intr.v.* **-tled, -tling, -tles** To make one's way or move like a beetle. [ME *betil* < OE *bitela* < *bītan,* to bite. See **bheid-** in App.]

bee·tle² (bēt′l) adj. Jutting; overhanging. ❖ *intr.v.* **-tled, -tling, -tles** To jut; overhang. [< ME *bitel-brouwed,* grim-browed : *bitel,* sharp (prob. < OE **bitol,* biting < OE *bite,* bite; see **BIT**²) + *brouwed* (< *brow,* brow; see **BROW**).]

bee·tle³ (bēt′l) n. **1.** A heavy mallet with a large wooden head. **2.** A small wooden household mallet. **3.** A machine with revolving wooden hammers that gives fabrics a lustrous sheen. [ME *betel* < OE *bȳtl.*]

beet leafhopper n. A small insect (*Eutettix tenellus*) that transmits a destructive viral disease to plants, esp. sugar beets, in the western United States.

bee tree n. **1.** Any of various trees having nectar-rich flowers attractive to bees. **2.** A hollow tree in which bees form nests.

beeves (bēvz) n. A plural of **beef.**

bef. *abbr.* before

be·fall (bĭ-fôl′) v. **-fell** (-fĕl′), **-fall·en** (-fô′lən), **-fall·ing, -falls** —*intr.* To come to pass; happen. —*tr.* To happen to. [ME *bifallen* < OE *befeallan,* to fall.]

be·fit (bĭ-fĭt′) tr.v. **-fit·ted, -fit·ting, -fits** To be suited to.

be·fit·ting (bĭ-fĭt′ĭng) adj. Appropriate; suitable; proper. —**be·fit′ting·ly** adv.

be·fog (bĭ-fôg′, -fŏg′) tr.v. **-fogged, -fog·ging, -fogs 1.** To cover or obscure with or as if with fog. **2.** To cause confusion in; muddle.

be·fool (bĭ-fool′) tr.v. **-fooled, -fool·ing, -fools 1.** To make a fool of. **2.** To hoodwink; deceive.

be·fore (bĭ-fôr′, -fōr′) adv. **1.** Earlier in time. **2.** In front; ahead. ❖ *prep.* **1.** Previous to in time. **2.** In front of. **3.** In store for; awaiting. **4.** Into or in the presence of. **5.** Under the consideration or jurisdiction of. **6.** In a position superior to. ❖ *conj.* **1.** In advance of the time when. **2.** Rather than; sooner than. [ME *bifore* < OE *beforan.* See **per**¹ in App.]

before Christ adv. In a given year of the pre-Christian era.

be·fore·hand (bĭ-fôr′hănd′, -fōr′-) adv. & adj. **1.** In anticipation. **2.** In advance; early.

be·fore·time (bĭ-fôr′tīm′, -fōr′-) adv. *Archaic* Formerly.

be·foul (bĭ-foul′) tr.v. **-fouled, -foul·ing, -fouls 1.** To make dirty; soil. **2.** To cast aspersions upon; speak badly of.

be·friend (bĭ-frĕnd′) tr.v. **-friend·ed, -friend·ing, -friends** To behave as a friend to.

be·fud·dle (bĭ-fŭd′l) tr.v. **-dled, -dling, -dles 1.** To confuse; perplex. See Syns at **confuse. 2.** To stupefy with or as if with alcoholic drink.

beg (bĕg) v. **begged, beg·ging, begs** —*tr.* **1.** To ask for as charity. **2.** To ask earnestly for or of; entreat. **3a.** To evade; dodge: *a speech that begged the real issues.* **b.** To take for granted without proof: *beg the point in a dispute.* —*intr.* **1.** To solicit alms. **2.** To make a humble or urgent plea. —*phrasal verb:* **beg off** To ask to be released from something, such as an obligation. [ME *beggen,* poss. < AN *begger* < OFr. *begart,* lay brother, one who prays. See **BEGGAR.**]

be·get (bĭ-gĕt′) tr.v. **-got** (-gŏt′), **-got·ten** (-gŏt′n) or **-got, -get·ting, -gets 1.** To father; sire. **2.** To cause to exist or occur; produce: *Violence begets violence.* [ME *biyeten, bigeten* < OE *begetan.* See **ghend-** in App.] —**be·get′ter** n.

beg·gar (bĕg′ər) n. **1.** One who solicits alms for a living. **2.** An impoverished person; a pauper. **3.** *Informal* A man or a boy. ❖ *tr.v.* **-gared, -gar·ing, -gars 1.** To make a beggar of; impoverish. **2.** To exceed the limits, resources, or capabilities of. [ME < OFr. *begart,* ult. < MDu. *beggaert,* one who rattles off prayers.]

beg·gar·ly (bĕg′ər-lē) adj. **1.** Of, relating to, or befitting a beggar; very poor. **2.** So mean, petty, or paltry as to deserve contempt. —**beg′gar·li·ness** n.

beg·gar's lice (bĕg′ərz) n. (*used with a sing. or pl. verb*) **1.** Any of several plants having small, often prickly fruits that cling to clothing or animal fur. **2.** The fruit of any of these plants.

beggar ticks also **beggar's ticks** pl.n. (*used with a sing. or pl. verb*) **1a.** Any of various weeds of the genus *Bidens* in the composite family. **b.** The small barbed achenes of any of these plants, clinging readily to clothing and animal fur. **2.** Any of certain other plants or their clinging fruits.

beg·gar·weed (bĕg′ər-wēd′) n. Any of several tick trefoils, esp. *Desmodium tortuosum* or *D. purpureum,* grown for forage or as a cover crop in subtropical and tropical regions.

beg·gar·y (bĕg′ə-rē) n. **1.** Extreme poverty; penury. **2.** The state of being a beggar. **3.** Beggars considered as a group.

be·gin (bĭ-gĭn′) v. **-gan** (-găn′), **-gun** (-gŭn′), **-gin·ning, -gins** —*intr.* **1.** To take the first step in performing an action; start. **2.** To come into being. **3.** To do or accomplish in the least degree: *That does not even begin to address the problem.* —*tr.* **1.** To take the first step in doing; start. **2.** To cause to come into being; originate. **3.** To come first in: *1 begins the sequence.* [ME *biginnen* < OE *beginnan.*]

Be·gin (bā′gĭn), **Menachem** 1913–92. Russian-born Israeli politician who shared the 1978 Nobel Peace Prize.

be·gin·ner (bĭ-gĭn′ər) n. **1.** One that begins. **2.** One who is just starting to learn or do something; a novice.

be·gin·ning (bĭ-gĭn′ĭng) n. **1.** The act or process of bringing or being brought into being; a start. **2.** The time when something begins or is begun. **3.** The place where something begins or is begun. **4.** A source; an origin. **5.** The first part. **6.** An early or rudimentary phase. Often used in the plural.

Menachem Begin

SYNONYMS *beginning, birth, dawn, genesis, nascence, rise* These nouns denote the initial stage of a developmental process: *the beginning of a new era; the birth of generative grammar; the dawn of civilization; the genesis of algebra; the nascence of classical sculpture; the rise of an ancient city-state.* **ANTONYM** end

beginning rhyme n. Rhyme at the beginning of consecutive lines of verse.

be·gird (bĭ-gûrd′) tr.v. **-girt** (-gûrt′) or **-gird·ed, -girt, -gird·ing, -girds** To encircle with or as if with a band.

be·gone (bĭ-gôn′, -gŏn′) v. Used chiefly in the imperative to express an order of dismissal.

be·go·nia (bĭ-gōn′yə) n. Any of various tropical or subtropical plants of the genus *Begonia,* having usu. asymmetrical, brightly colored leaves. [NLat. *Begonia,* genus name, after Michel *Bégon* (1638–1710), French governor in the West Indies.]

be·gor·ra (bĭ-gôr′ə, -gŏr′ə) interj. *Irish* Used as a mild oath. [Alteration of *by God.*]

be·got (bĭ-gŏt′) v. Past tense and past participle of **beget.**

be·got·ten (bĭ-gŏt′n) v. A past participle of **beget.**

be·grime (bĭ-grīm′) tr.v. **-grimed, -grim·ing, -grimes** To smear or soil with or as if with dirt.

be·grudge (bĭ-grŭj′) tr.v. **-grudged, -grudg·ing, -grudg·es 1.** To envy the possession or enjoyment of. See Syns at **envy. 2.** To give or expend with reluctance. —**be·grudg′ing·ly** adv.

be·guile (bĭ-gīl′) tr.v. **-guiled, -guil·ing, -guiles 1.** To deceive by guile; delude. See Syns at **deceive. 2.** To take away from by or as if by guile; cheat. **3.** To distract the attention of; divert: *"to beguile you from the grief of a loss so overwhelming"* (Abraham Lincoln). **4.** To pass (time) pleasantly. **5.** To amuse or charm; delight. See Syns at **charm.** —**be·guile′ment** n. —**be·guil′er** n. —**be·guil′ing·ly** adv.

be·guine (bĭ-gēn′) n. A ballroom dance similar to the rumba, based on a dance of Martinique and St. Lucia. [Fr. (West Indies) *béguine* < Fr. *béguin,* hood, flirtation < *beguine,* Beguine. See **BEG-UINE.**]

begonia

ă	pat	oi	boy
ā	pay	ou	out
âr	care	oŏ	took
ä	father	oō	boot
ĕ	pet	ŭ	cut
ē	be	ûr	urge
ĭ	pit	th	thin
ī	pie	*th*	this
îr	pier	hw	which
ŏ	pot	zh	vision
ō	toe	ə	about,
ô	paw		item

Stress marks:
′ (primary);
′ (secondary), as in
lexicon (lĕk′sĭ-kŏn′)

Beg·uine (bā′gēn′, bă-gēn′) *n. Roman Catholic Church* A member of any of several lay sisterhoods founded in the Netherlands in the 13th century. [ME *begine* < OFr. *beguine* < MDu. *beg-*, root of *beggaert*, one who rattles off prayers.]

be·gum (bā′gəm, bē′-) *n.* **1.** A Muslim woman of rank. **2.** Used as a form of address for such a woman. [Urdu *begam* < East Turkic *begüm*, first pers. sing. possessive of *beg*, master, mistress. See BEY.]

be·gun (bĭ-gŭn′) *v.* Past participle of **begin**.

be·half (bĭ-hăf′, -häf′) *n.* Interest, support, or benefit. —*idioms:* **in behalf of** For the benefit of; in the interest of. **on behalf of** As the agent of; on the part of. [ME *be healfe*, by (his) side : *be*, by, at; see BY¹ + *healf*, side, half; see HALF.]

> **USAGE NOTE** Traditionally, *in behalf of* and *on behalf of* have distinct meanings. *In behalf of* means "for the benefit of," as in *We raised money in behalf of the earthquake victims. On behalf of* means "as the agent of, on the part of," as in *The guardian signed the contract on behalf of the minor child.* The two senses are quite close, however, and are often used interchangeably, even by reputable writers.

Be·han (bē′ən), **Brendan Francis** 1923–64. Irish writer whose works include *The Quare Fellow* (1954) and the autobiographical *Borstal Boy* (1958).

be·have (bĭ-hāv′) *v.* **-haved, -hav·ing, -haves** —*intr.* **1a.** To conduct oneself in a specified way: *behave well.* **b.** To conduct oneself in a proper way: *I told the child to behave.* **2.** To act, react, function, or perform in a particular way. —*tr.* **1.** To conduct (oneself) properly. **2.** To conduct (oneself) in a specified way. [ME *behaven* : *be-*, be- + *haven*, to have; see HAVE.]

be·hav·ior (bĭ-hāv′yər) *n.* **1.** The manner in which one behaves. **2a.** The actions or reactions of persons or things in response to external or internal stimuli. **b.** One of these actions or reactions: *mating behaviors.* **3.** The manner in which something functions or operates. [ME *behavour* < *behaven*, to behave (on the model of *havour*, behavior < OFr. *avoir* < *avoir*, to have). See BEHAVE.] —**be·hav′ior·al** *adj.* —**be·hav′ior·al·ly** *adv.*

Belarus

SYNONYMS *behavior, conduct, deportment* These nouns all pertain to a person's actions as they constitute a means of evaluation by others. *Behavior* is the most general: *guilty of contemptible behavior. Conduct* applies to actions considered from the standpoint of morality and ethics: *"Life, not the person, teaches conduct"* (Oliver Wendell Holmes, Jr.). *Deportment* more narrowly pertains to actions measured by a prevailing code of social behavior: *"[Old Mr. Turveydrop] was not like anything in the world but a model of Deportment"* (Charles Dickens).

behavioral genetics *n.* The study of the genetic factors that determine behavioral phenotypes, such as eating or mating.

behavioral medicine *n.* The study, prevention, and treatment of medical and psychosomatic disorders and of undesirable behaviors by the application of behavior therapy.

behavioral science *n.* A scientific discipline that studies the actions and reactions of humans and animals through scientific procedures. —**behavioral scientist** *n.*

behavioral therapy *n.* See **behavior therapy.**

be·hav·ior·ism (bĭ-hāv′yə-rĭz′əm) *n.* A school of psychology that confines itself to the study of observable and quantifiable aspects of behavior and excludes subjective phenomena. —**be·hav′ior·ist** *n.* —**be·hav′ior·is′tic** *adj.*

behavior modification *n.* **1.** The use of basic learning techniques, such as conditioning, biofeedback, reinforcement, or aversion therapy, to alter human behavior. **2.** See **behavior therapy.** —**behavior modifier** *n.*

behavior therapy *n.* A form of psychotherapy that seeks to modify maladaptive behavior by substituting new responses to given stimuli. —**behavior therapist** *n.*

be·hav·iour (bĭ-hāv′yər) *n. Chiefly British* Variant of **behavior.**

be·head (bĭ-hĕd′) *tr.v.* **-head·ed, -head·ing, -heads** To separate the head from; decapitate. [ME *biheden* < OE *behēafdian* : *be-*, away from; see BE- + *hēafod*, head; see HEAD.]

belfry
Mission San Carlos
Borromeo de Carmelo,
Carmel, California

be·he·moth (bĭ-hē′məth, bē′ə-math) *n.* **1.** Something enormous in size or power. **2.** often **Behemoth** A huge animal, possibly the hippopotamus, described in the Bible. [ME *behemoth, behemoth* < Heb. *bəhēmôt*, pl. of *bəhēmâ*, beast.]

be·hest (bĭ-hĕst′) *n.* **1.** An authoritative command. **2.** An urgent request. [ME *bihest*, vow < OE *behǣs.* See kei-² in App.]

be·hind (bĭ-hīnd′) *adv.* **1.** In, to, or toward the rear. **2.** In a place or condition that has been passed or left. **3.** In arrears; late. **4.** Below the standard level; in or into an inferior position: *behind in class.* **5.** Slow: *My watch is running behind.* **6.** *Archaic* Yet to come. ❖ *prep.* **1.** At the back of or in the rear of. **2.** On the farther side or other side of; beyond: *behind the door.* **3.** In a place or time that has been passed or left by: *Their worries are behind them.* **4a.** Later than. **b.** Used to indicate deficiency in performance: *behind us in technology.* **5a.** Hidden or concealed by. **b.** In the background of; underlying. **6.** In a position or attitude of support. **7.** In pursuit of. ❖ *n. Informal* The buttocks. [ME *bihinde* < OE *behindan.* See ko- in App.]

be·hind·hand (bĭ-hīnd′hănd′) *adj.* **1.** Being in arrears. **2.** Being behind time; slow. —**be·hind′hand′** *adv.*

be·hind-the-scenes (bĭ-hīnd′thə-sēnz′) *adj.* **1.** Done, maintained, or held in secret. **2.** Revealing what is done out of public view.

be·hold (bĭ-hōld′) *v.* **-held** (-hĕld′), **-hold·ing, -holds** —*tr.* **1a.** To perceive by the visual faculty; see. **b.** To perceive through use of the mental faculty; comprehend. **2.** To look upon; gaze at. See Syns at see¹. —*intr.* Used in the imperative in order to call attention. [ME *biholden* < OE *behaldan* : *be-*, be- + *healdan*, to hold.] —**be·hold′er** *n.*

be·hold·en (bĭ-hōl′dən) *adj.* Owing something to another; indebted. [ME *biholden*, p. part. of *biholden*, to observe < OE *behaldan* : *be-*, bi- + *haldan*, to hold; see HOLD¹.]

be·hoof (bĭ-hoof′) *n.* Benefit; advantage. [ME *bihove* < OE *behōf.* See kap- in App.]

be·hoove (bĭ-hoov′) *v.* **-hooved, -hoov·ing, -hooves** —*tr.* To be necessary or proper for: *It behooves you to try.* —*intr.* To be necessary or proper. [ME *behoven* < OE *behōfian.* See kap- in App.]

Behr·man (bâr′mən), **S(amuel) N(athaniel)** 1893–1973. Amer. playwright whose works include *The Second Man* (1927).

Bei·der·becke (bī′dər-bĕk′), **Leon Bismark** Known as "Bix." 1903–31. Amer. jazz composer and musician.

beige (bāzh) *n.* **1.** A light grayish brown or yellowish brown to grayish yellow. **2.** A soft fabric of undyed, unbleached wool. [Fr., fine woolen fabric left in its natural color < OFr. *bege*, perh. < OItal. *bambagia*, cotton wool, ult. < Med.Lat. *bombax.* See BOMBAZINE.] —**beige** *adj.*

beig·net also **bei·gné** (bĕn-yā′, bĕn′yā′) *n. Southern Louisiana* **1.** A square doughnut with no hole. **2.** A fritter. [Fr., fritter, of Celt. orig.]

> **REGIONAL NOTE** New Orleans, Louisiana, has been a rich contributor of French loan words and local expressions to American English. Many of the words, such as *beignet, café au lait, faubourg, lagniappe,* and *krewe,* reflect the New World French cuisine and culture characterizing this region. Other words, such as *banquette, camelback,* and *shotgun,* reflect distinctive physical characteristics and architectural styles found in the city.

Bei·jing (bā′jĭng′) also **Pe·king** (pē′kĭng′, pā′-) Formerly (1928–49) **Pei·ping** (pā′pĭng′) The cap. of China, in the NE part; founded c. 700 B.C. Pop. 7,362,426.

be·ing (bē′ĭng) *n.* **1.** The state or quality of having existence. **2a.** Something that exists, is thought to exist, or is represented as existing. **b.** The totality of all things that exist. **3a.** A person: *"The artist after all is a solitary being"* (Virginia Woolf). **b.** All the qualities constituting one that exists; the essence. **c.** One's basic or essential nature; personality. ❖ *conj. Chiefly Southern US, Upper Southern US, & New England* Because; since. Often used with *as* or *that.*

Bei·ra (bā′rə) A city of E-central Mozambique on the Mozambique Channel. Pop. 264,202.

Bei·rut (bā-root′) The cap. of Lebanon, in the W part on the Mediterranean Sea. Pop. 474,870.

Be·ja (bā′jə) *n., pl.* **Beja** **1.** A member of a people living primarily as pastoral nomads in the area between the Nile River and the Red Sea. **2.** The Cushitic language of the Beja.

be·je·sus (bĭ-jē′zəs, -jā′-) *n. Slang* Used as an intensive: *The bear scared the bejesus out of us.* [Alteration of *by Jesus.*]

be·jew·eled or **be·jew·elled** (bĭ-joo′əld) *adj.* Decorated with or as if with jewels.

bel (bĕl) *n.* Ten decibels. [After Alexander Graham BELL.]

be·la·bor (bĭ-lā′bər) *tr.v.* **-bored, -bor·ing, -bors** **1.** To attack with blows; hit, beat, or whip. **2.** To assail verbally. **3.** To discuss repeatedly or at length; harp on.

be·la·bour (bĭ-lā′bər) *v. Chiefly British* Variant of **belabor.**

Bel·a·rus (bĕl′ə-roos′, bĕl′ə-roos′, byĕl′-) Formerly **Be·lo·rus·sia** (bĕl′ō-rŭsh′ə, byĕl′-) also **Bye·lo·rus·sia** (byĕl′ō-) A republic of E Europe E of Poland; a constituent republic of the USSR from 1922–91. Cap. Minsk. Pop. 10,355,000.

Be·la·rus·ian (bĕl′ə-roo′sē-ən, -rŭsh′ən, byĕl′-) also **Be·la·rus·sian** (-rŭsh′ən) *adj.* Of or relating to Belarus or its people, language, or culture. ❖ *n.* **1.** A native or inhabitant of Belarus. **2.** also **Be·lo·rus·sian** (bĕl′ō-rŭsh′ən, byĕl′-) The Slavic language of the Belarusians.

Be·las·co (bə-lăs′kō), **David** 1853–1931. Amer. playwright and theatrical producer known for his realistic stage settings and innovative lighting effects.

be·lat·ed (bĭ-lā′tĭd) *adj.* Having been delayed; done or sent too late: *a belated birthday card.* [BE- + LATED.] —**be·lat′ed·ly** *adv.* —**be·lat′ed·ness** *n.*

Be·lau (bə-lou′) See **Palau.**

be·lay (bĭ-lā′) *v.* **-layed, -lay·ing, -lays** —*tr.* **1.** *Nautical* To secure or make fast (a line, for example) by winding on a cleat or pin. **2.** To secure (a mountain climber, for example) at the end of a length of rope. **3.** To cause to stop. —*intr.* **1.** To be made secure. **2.** Used in the imperative as an order to stop. ❖ *n.* **1.** The securing of a rope on a rock or other projection during mountain climbing. **2.** An object thus used. [ME *bileggen*, to surround < OE *belecgan.* See legh- in App.]

Be·la·ya (bĕl′ə-yə) A river of SW Russia rising in the Ural Mts. and flowing c. 1,416 km (880 mi) to the Kama R.

Belgium

Belize

Alexander Graham Bell

be·lay·ing pin (bĭ-lā′ĭng) *n.* A short, removable wooden or metal pin fitted in a rail of a ship and used for securing rigging.

bel can·to (bĕl kän′tō) *n.* A style of operatic singing characterized by full, even tones and a brilliant display of vocal technique. [Ital. : *bel, bello,* beautiful + *canto,* singing.]

belch (bĕlch) *v.* **belched, belch·ing, belch·es** —*intr.* **1.** To expel stomach gas noisily through the mouth. **2.** To erupt or explode. **3.** To gush forth. —*tr.* **1.** To expel (stomach gas) noisily through the mouth. **2.** To eject violently. [ME *belchen* < OE *bealcettan* or < *bealcian.*] —**belch** *n.*

bel·dam or **bel·dame** (bĕl′dəm, -dăm) *n.* An old woman, esp. one who is considered ugly. [ME, grandmother : *bel,* indicating respect (< OFr. *bel,* fine < Lat. *bellus*; see **deu-²** in App.) + *dame,* lady; see DAME.]

be·lea·guer (bĭ-lē′gər) *tr.v.* **-guered, -guer·ing, -guers 1.** To harass; beset: *We were beleaguered by many serious problems.* **2.** To surround with troops; besiege. [Prob. Du. *belegeren* : *be-,* around (< MDu. *bie,* near; see **ambhi** in App.) + *leger,* camp; see **legh-** in App.] —**be·lea′guer·ment** *n.*

Be·lém (bə-lĕm′, -lĕN′) Formerly **Pa·rá** (pə-rä′) A city of N Brazil on the Pará R. Pop. 1,244,688.

bel·em·nite (bĕl′əm-nīt′) *n.* A cone-shaped, fossilized internal shell of any of an extinct genus of cephalopods related to the cuttlefish. [NLat. *belemnītēs* < Gk. *belemnon,* dart. See **gʷelə-** in App.]

bel es·prit (bĕl′ ĕ-sprē′) *n., pl.* **beaux es·prits** (bō′zĕ-sprē′) A cultivated, intelligent person. [Fr. : *bel,* fine + *esprit,* mind.]

Bel·fast (bĕl′făst′, bĕl-făst′) The cap. of Northern Ireland, in the E part on **Belfast Lough,** an inlet of the Irish Sea. Pop. 296,700.

Bel·fort (bĕl-fôr′) A city of NE France commanding the **Belfort Gap** between the Vosges and the Jura Mts. Pop. 51,206.

bel·fry (bĕl′frē) *n., pl.* **-fries 1.** A bell tower, esp. one attached to a building. **2.** The part of a tower or steeple in which bells are hung. [ME *belfrei* < ONFr. *belfroi,* alteration of OFr. *berfrei, berfroi.* See **bhergh-** in App.] —**bel′fried** *adj.*

Belg. *abbr.* Belgium

Bel·gae (bĕl′jī, -jē′) *pl.n.* A people who formerly inhabited northeast Gaul and areas of southeast England. [Lat.]

Bel·gian (bĕl′jən) *adj.* Of or relating to Belgium or its people or culture. ❖ *n.* **1a.** A native or inhabitant of Belgium. **b.** A person of Belgian descent. **2.** Any of a breed of typically large draft horses.

Belgian Congo See **Congo.**

Belgian East Africa The former Belgian trust territory of Ruanda-Urundi, now divided into the independent countries of Rwanda and Burundi.

Belgian hare *n.* A large reddish-brown rabbit of a domestic breed developed in England from Belgian stock.

Belgian Mal·in·ois (măl′ən-wä′) *n.* See **Belgian sheep dog** 2.

Belgian sheep dog *n.* **1.** Any of a breed of hardy sheep dogs developed in Belgium. **2.** Any of a breed of working dogs closely related to the Belgian sheep dog.

Belgian Ter·vu·ren (tĕr-vyŏor′ən, tər-) *n.* See **Belgian sheep dog** 2.

Bel·gic (bĕl′jĭk) *adj.* **1.** Of or relating to Belgium or the Belgians. **2.** Of or relating to the Belgae.

Bel·gium (bĕl′jəm) A country of NW Europe on the North Sea; culturally divided into Dutch-speaking Flanders in the N and French-speaking Wallonia in the S. Cap. Brussels. Pop. 10,080,000.

Bel·go·rod (bĕl′gə-rŏd′, byĕl′gə-rət) A city of SW Russia on the Donets R. Pop. 314,425.

Bel·grade (bĕl′grād′, -grād′, bĕl-grād′) also **Be·o·grad** (bĕ′ô-gräd) The cap. of Serbia and of Yugoslavia, in the N-central part of Serbia at the confluence of the Danube and Sava rivers; founded in the 3rd cent. B.C. Pop. 1,136,786.

Bel·gra·vi·a (bĕl-grā′vē-ə) A fashionable residential district of SW London, England, centered on Belgrave Square.

Be·li·al (bē′lē-əl, bēl′yəl) *n.* **1.** *Bible* A personification of wickedness and ungodliness. **2.** One of the fallen angels who rebelled against God in Milton's *Paradise Lost.*

be·lie (bĭ-lī′) *tr.v.* **-lied, -ly·ing, -lies 1.** To picture falsely; misrepresent: *"He spoke roughly in order to belie his air of gentility"* (James Joyce). **2.** To show to be false: *His smile belied his ire.* **3.** To be counter to; contradict. [ME *bilien* < OE *belēogan,* to deceive with lies. See **leugh-** in App.] —**be·li′er** *n.*

be·lief (bĭ-lēf′) *n.* **1.** The mental act, condition, or habit of placing trust or confidence in another. **2.** Mental acceptance of and conviction in the truth, actuality, or validity of something. **3.** Something believed or accepted as true, esp. a particular tenet or a body of tenets accepted by a group of persons. [ME *bileve,* alteration (influenced by *bileven,* to believe) of OE *gelēafa.*]

be·liev·a·ble (bĭ-lē′və-bəl) *adj.* Capable of eliciting belief or trust. See Syns at **plausible.** —**be·liev′a·bil′i·ty** *n.* —**be·liev′a·bly** *adv.*

be·lieve (bĭ-lēv′) *v.* **-lieved, -liev·ing, -lieves** —*tr.* **1.** To accept as true or real. **2.** To credit with veracity: *I believe you.* **3.** To expect or suppose; think. —*intr.* **1.** To have firm faith, esp. religious faith. **2.** To have faith, confidence, or trust. **3.** To have confidence in the truth or value of something. **4.** To have an opinion; think. —*idioms:* **believe (one's) ears** To trust what one has

heard. **believe (one's) eyes** To trust what one has seen. [ME *bileven* < OE *belȳfan, belēfan, gelēfan.*] —**be·liev′er** *n.*

be·like (bĭ-līk′) *adv. Archaic* Probably; perhaps. [Prob. *be-* (< BY¹) + LIKE², what is likely.]

Be·lin·da (bə-lĭn′də) *n.* A satellite of Uranus. [After *Belinda,* heroine of *The Rape of the Lock* by Alexander Pope.]

Bel·i·sar·i·us (bĕl′ĭ-sâr′ē-əs) 505?–565. Byzantine general who led campaigns against the barbarians in North Africa and Italy.

be·lit·tle (bĭ-lĭt′l) *tr.v.* **-tled, -tling, -tles 1.** To represent or speak of as contemptibly small or unimportant; disparage. **2.** To cause to seem less than another or little. —**be·lit′tle·ment** *n.* —**be·lit′tler** *n.*

Be·li·tung (bə-lē′tŏong) also **Bil·li·ton** (bə-lē′tŏn′) An island of W Indonesia in the Java Sea between Sumatra and Borneo.

Be·lize (bə-lēz′) **1.** Formerly **British Honduras.** A country of Central America on the Caribbean Sea; achieved independence in 1981. Cap. Belmopan. Pop. 211,000. **2.** also **Belize City** The former cap. (until 1970) of Belize, in the E part at the mouth of the **Belize River.** Pop. 39,771.

bell¹ (bĕl) *n.* **1.** A hollow metal musical instrument, usu. cup-shaped with a flared opening, that emits a metallic tone when struck. **2.** Something resembling a bell in shape or sound, as: **a.** The round, flared opening of a wind instrument at the opposite end from the mouthpiece. **b. bells** A percussion instrument consisting of metal tubes or bars that emit tones when struck. **c.** A hollow, usu. inverted vessel. **d.** The corolla of a flower. **3.** *Nautical* **a.** A stroke on a bell to mark the hour. **b.** The time indicated by these strokes, divided into half hours. ❖ *v.* **belled, bell·ing, bells** —*tr.* **1.** To put a bell on. **2.** To cause to flare like a bell. —*intr.* To assume the form of a bell; flare. —*idiom:* **bell the cat** To perform a daring act. [ME *belle* < OE.]

bell² (bĕl) *n.* The bellowing or baying cry of certain animals. ❖ *intr.v.* **belled, bell·ing, bells** To utter long, deep, resonant sounds; bellow. [< ME *bellen,* to bellow < OE *bellan.*]

Bell, Alexander Graham 1847–1922. Scottish-born Amer. inventor of the telephone (first demonstrated 1876).

Bell, (Arthur) Clive (Howard) 1881–1964. British critic who proposed his aesthetic theories in *Art* (1914).

Bel·la Coo·la (bĕl′ə kŏo′lə) *n., pl.* **Bella Coola** or **-las 1.** A member of a Native American people inhabiting the coast of British Columbia along the Bella Coola River, a stream flowing into a channel of Queen Charlotte Sound. **2.** The Salishan language of the Bella Coola.

bel·la·don·na (bĕl′ə-dŏn′ə) *n.* **1.** A poisonous Eurasian perennial herb (*Atropa belladonna*) having usu. solitary, nodding, bell-shaped flowers and glossy black berries. **2.** A medicinal alkaloidal extract or tincture derived from this plant. [Ital. : *bella,* fem. of *bello,* beautiful (< Lat. *bellus*; see **deu-²** in App.) + *donna,* lady; see DONNA.]

belladonna alkaloids *pl.n.* A group of alkaloids found in plants such as belladonna and used in medicine.

belladonna lily *n.* A bulbous, perennial southern African herb (*Amaryllis belladonna*) with trumpet-shaped flowers.

Bel·la·my (bĕl′ə-mē), **Edward** 1850–98. Amer. writer and utopian socialist noted for *Looking Backward* (1888).

Bel·lay (bə-lā′, bĕ-lā′), **Joachim du** 1522?–60. French poet who was a founder of a group of poets known as the Pléiade.

bell·bird (bĕl′bûrd′) *n.* Any of various tropical American birds of the family Cotingidae, having a bell-like call.

bell-bot·tom (bĕl′bŏt′əm) *adj.* Having legs that flare out at the bottom: *bell-bottom trousers.* —**bell-bottoms** *pl.n.*

bell·boy (bĕl′boi′) *n.* A bellhop.

bell buoy *n. Nautical* A buoy fitted with a warning bell that is activated by the movement of the waves.

bell captain *n.* The supervisor of a group of bellhops.

bell curve *n. Mathematics* The symmetrical curve of a normal distribution.

belle (bĕl) *n.* A popular, attractive girl or woman, esp. the most attractive in a group: *the belle of the ball.* [Fr., beautiful, belle < Lat. *bella,* fem. of *bellus.* See **deu-²** in App.]

Bel·leau Wood (bĕ-lō′, bĕl′ō) A forested area of N France E of Château-Thierry; site of a major World War I battle (Jun. 1918).

belle é·poque (ā-pŭk′) *n.* An era of artistic and cultural refinement in a society, esp. in France at the beginning of the 20th century. [Fr. : *belle,* beautiful + *époque,* era.]

Belle Fourche (fŏosh′) A river rising in NE WY and flowing c. 467 km (290 mi) to the Cheyenne R. in W SD.

Belle Isle, Strait of A channel between SE Labrador and NW Newfoundland, Canada.

Bel·ler·o·phon (bə-lĕr′ə-fən, -fŏn′) *n. Greek Mythology* The Corinthian hero who with the aid of Pegasus slew the Chimera.

belles-let·tres (bĕl-lĕt′rə) *pl.n.* (used with a sing. verb) **1.** Literature regarded for its aesthetic value rather than its didactic or informative content. **2.** Light, stylish writings, usu. on literary or intellectual subjects. [Fr. : *belles,* fine + *lettres,* letters, literature.]

bel·let·rist (bĕl-lĕt′rĭst) *n.* A writer of belles-lettres. —**bel·let′rism** *n.* —**bel·let·ris′tic** (bĕl′ĭ-trĭs′tĭk) *adj.*

Belle·vue (bĕl′vyŏo′) A city of W-central WA on Lake Washington opposite Seattle. Pop. 109,569.

bell·flow·er (bĕl′flou′ər) *n.* **1.** Any of various herbs of the genus *Campanula,* native chiefly to the Northern Hemisphere and often having showy, bell-shaped, violet or blue flowers. **2.** Any of several other plants, esp. one with bell-shaped flowers.

bell·hop (bĕl′hŏp′) *n.* A person employed by a hotel to assist guests, as by carrying luggage. [Prob. short for *bell-hopper*.]

bel·li·cose (bĕl′ĭ-kōs′) *adj.* Warlike in manner or temperament; pugnacious. [ME < Lat. *bellicōsus* < *bellicus*, of war < *bellum*, war.] —**bel′li·cose′ly** *adv.* —**bel′li·cos′i·ty** (-kŏs′ĭ-tē) *n.*

bel·lig·er·ence (bə-lĭj′ər-əns) *n.* A hostile or warlike attitude, nature, or inclination.

bel·lig·er·en·cy (bə-lĭj′ər-ən-sē) *n.* **1.** The state of being at war or being engaged in a warlike conflict. **2.** Belligerence.

bel·lig·er·ent (bə-lĭj′ər-ənt) *adj.* **1.** Inclined or eager to fight; hostile or aggressive. **2.** Of, relating to, or engaged in warfare. ❖ *n.* One that is hostile or aggressive, esp. one engaged in war. [Lat. *belligerāns, belligerant-*, pr. part. of *belligerāre*, to wage war < *belliger*, warlike : *bellum*, war + *gerere*, to make.] —**bel·lig′er·ent·ly** *adv.*

bell·ing (bĕl′ĭng) *n.* *Pennsylvania, West Virginia, Ohio, Indiana,* & *Michigan* See **shivaree.** [< BELL[1].]

Bel·ling·ham (bĕl′ĭng-hăm′) A city of NW WA on Bellingham Bay S of the Canadian border. Pop. 67,171.

Bel·lings·hau·sen Sea (bĕl′ĭngz-hou′zən) An arm of the S Pacific Ocean off the coast of Antarctica.

Bel·li·ni (bə-lē′nē) Family of Venetian painters, including **Jacopo** (1400?–70?) and his two sons, **Gentile** (1429?–1507) and **Giovanni** (1430?–1516).

Bellini, Vincenzo 1801–35. Italian composer whose operas include *La Sonnambula* and *Norma* (both 1831).

bell jar *n.* A cylindrical glass vessel with a rounded top and an open base, used to protect and display fragile objects or establish a controlled atmosphere in scientific experiments.

bell lap *n.* The final lap of a race, as at a track meet, signaled by the ringing of a bell as the leader begins the lap.

bell·man (bĕl′mən) *n.* **1.** A bellhop. **2.** A town crier.

bell metal *n.* An alloy of tin and copper used to make bells.

Bel·loc (bĕl′ŏk′, -ək), **Hilaire** 1870–1953. French-born British writer.

Bel·lo·na (bə-lō′nə) *n. Roman Mythology* The goddess of war.

bel·low (bĕl′ō) *v.* **-lowed, -low·ing, -lows** —*intr.* **1.** To roar deeply, as does a bull. **2.** To shout in a deep voice. —*tr.* To utter in a loud, powerful voice. See Syns at **shout.** ❖ *n.* **1.** The roar of a large animal, such as a bull. **2.** A very loud utterance or other sound. [ME *belwen*, perh. < OE *belgan*, to be enraged, and *bylgan*, to bellow.] —**bel′low·er** *n.*

Bellow, Saul b. 1915. Canadian-born Amer. writer who won the 1976 Nobel Prize for literature.

bel·lows (bĕl′ōz, -əz) *pl.n.* (*used with a sing. or pl. verb*) **1a.** An apparatus for making a strong current of air, made of a flexible valved air chamber that is contracted and expanded by pumping to force the air through a nozzle. **b.** Something that resembles a bellows. **2.** The lungs. [ME *belowes* < OE *belgas*, pl. of *belg*.]

Bel·lows (bĕl′ōz), **George Wesley** 1882–1925. Amer. artist noted for his energetic paintings of sporting scenes.

bell pepper *n.* **1.** A variety of sweet pepper widely cultivated for its edible fruit. **2.** The large, crisp, bell-shaped fruit of this plant.

bells and whistles *pl.n.* Nonessential features or enhancements intended esp. to add commercial appeal.

Bell's Law (bĕlz) *n. Anatomy* **1.** An axiom stating that the anterior or ventral roots of the spinal nerves are motor and the posterior or dorsal roots sensory. **2.** The neurological law that, in any reflex arc, nerve impulses are conducted in only one direction. [After Sir Charles *Bell* (1774–1842), Scottish anatomist.]

bells of Ireland *n.* An annual western Asian plant (*Moluccella laevis*) in the mint family, having long stems covered with shell-shaped calyxes.

Bell's palsy *n.* A unilateral facial muscle paralysis of sudden onset, resulting from trauma, compression, or infection of the facial nerve and characterized by a distorted facial expression. [After Sir Charles *Bell* (1774–1842), Scottish anatomist.]

bell·weth·er (bĕl′wĕth′ər) *n.* One that serves as a leader or as a leading indicator of future trends. [ME *bellewether*, wether with a bell hung from its neck, leader of the flock : *belle*, bell; see BELL[1] + *wether*, wether; see WETHER.]

bell·wort (bĕl′wûrt′, -wôrt′) *n.* Any of various perennial plants of the genus *Uvularia* in the lily family, native to eastern North America and having yellow bell-shaped flowers.

bel·ly (bĕl′ē) *n., pl.* **-lies 1.** See **abdomen** 1. **2.** The underside of the body of certain vertebrates, such as fish. **3.** *Informal* **a.** The stomach. **b.** An appetite for food. **4.** The womb; the uterus. **5a.** A part that bulges or protrudes. **b.** *Anatomy* The bulging central part of a muscle. **6.** A deep, hollow interior. ❖ *v.* **-lied, -ly·ing, -lies** To bulge or cause to bulge. —*phrasal verb:* **belly up** To approach closely. [ME *beli* < OE *belg*, bag.]

bel·ly·ache (bĕl′ē-āk′) *n.* **1.** Stomach pain; colic. **2.** *Slang* A whining complaint. ❖ *intr.v.* **-ached, -ach·ing, -aches** *Slang* To complain, esp. by whining. —**bel′ly·ach′er** *n.*

bel·ly·band (bĕl′ē-bănd′) *n.* **1.** A band passed around the belly of an animal to secure something. **2.** An encircling band for holding in a baby's protruding navel.

bel·ly·but·ton (bĕl′ē-bŭt′n) *n. Informal* The navel; the umbilicus.

belly dance *n.* A solo dance in which a woman makes sinuous hip and abdominal movements. —**bel′ly-dance′** (bĕl′ē-dăns′) *v.* —**belly dancer** *n.*

belly flop *n. Informal* A dive in which the front of the body hits flat against a surface. —**bel′ly-flop′** (bĕl′ē-flŏp′) *v.*

bel·ly·ful (bĕl′ē-fōol′) *n. Informal* An undesirable or unendurable amount: *a bellyful of criticism.*

bel·ly-land (bĕl′ē-lănd′) *intr.v.* **-land·ed, -land·ing, -lands** To land an aircraft on its underside without aid of landing gear.

belly laugh *n.* A deep laugh.

Bel·mo·pan (bĕl′mō-păn′) The cap. of Belize, in the N-central part. Pop. 44,087.

Be·lo (bĕl′ō, bĕ′lōō), **Carlos Felipe Ximenes** b. 1948. East Timorese Roman Catholic bishop who shared the 1996 Nobel Peace Prize.

Belo Ho·ri·zon·te (hôr′ĭ-zŏn′tē, ô′rĭ-zŏn′thĭ) A city of E Brazil N of Rio de Janeiro; built (1895–97) as the first of Brazil's planned communities. Pop. 2,017,127.

be·long (bĭ-lông′, -lŏng′) *intr.v.* **-longed, -long·ing, -longs 1a.** To be proper or suitable. **b.** To be in an appropriate situation or environment. **2a.** To be a member of a group. **b.** To fit into a group naturally. **3.** To have in one's possession. Often used with *to.* **4.** To be a part of something else. [ME *bilongen* : prob. *bi-*, be- + *longen*, to belong (prob. < *long*, dependent < OE *gelang*, along, depending; see **del-** in App.).]

be·long·ing (bĭ-lông′ĭng, -lŏng′-) *n.* **1.** A personal item that one owns; a possession. Often used in the plural. **2.** Acceptance as a natural member or part: *a sense of belonging.*

Be·lo·rus·sia (bĕl′ō-rŭsh′ə, byĕl′-) also **Bye·lo·rus·sia** (byĕl′-) Popularly known as **White Russia.** **1.** A region of E Europe in present-day Belarus and Poland. In 1921 the W part of the region was ceded to Poland, and the E part became the Belorussian Soviet Socialist Republic, now Belarus. **2.** See **Belarus.**

Be·lo·rus·sian (bĕl′ō-rŭsh′ən, byĕl′-) *adj.* Of or relating to the region or former Soviet Socialist Republic of Belorussia. ❖ *n.* **1.** A native or inhabitant of Belorussia. **2.** Variant of **Belarusian** 2.

be·lov·ed (bĭ-lŭv′ĭd, -lŭvd′) *adj.* Dearly loved. —**be·lov′ed** *n.*

be·low (bĭ-lō′) *adv.* **1.** In or to a lower place; beneath. **2a.** On or to a lower floor; downstairs. **b.** *Nautical* On to a lower deck. **3.** In a later part of a given text. **4.** Farther down, as along a slope or valley. **5.** In or to hell or Hades. **6.** On earth. **7a.** In a lower rank or class. **b.** Below zero in temperature: *40° below.* ❖ *prep.* **1.** Underneath; beneath. **2.** Lower than, as on a graduated scale. **3.** Downstream of: *below the rapids.* **4.** South of: *Arizona is below Utah.* **5.** Unsuitable to the rank or dignity of. [ME *bilooghe* : *bi*, by; see BY[1] + *loghe*, low; see LOW[1].]

be·low·ground (bĭ-lō′ground′) *adv.* & *adj.* Situated or occurring below the surface of the ground.

Bel·sen (bĕl′zən) In full **Ber·gen-Bel·sen** (bûr′gən-bĕl′sən, bĕr′gən-bĕl′zən) A village of N Germany N of Hanover; site of a Nazi concentration camp during World War II.

Bel·shaz·zar (bĕl-shăz′ər) Son of Nebuchadnezzar II and last king of Babylon, who in the Bible was warned of his doom by handwriting on the wall that was interpreted by Daniel.

belt (bĕlt) *n.* **1a.** A flexible band worn around the waist to support clothing, secure tools, or serve as decoration. **b.** Something resembling a belt, as a number of machine-gun rounds attached together in a strip. **2.** An encircling route. **3.** A seat belt or safety belt. **4.** A continuous band or chain for transferring motion or power or conveying materials. **5.** A band of tough reinforcing material beneath the tread of a tire. **6.** A geographic region that is distinctive in a specific respect. **7.** *Slang* A powerful blow; a wallop. **8.** *Slang* A strong emotional reaction. **9.** *Slang* A drink of hard liquor. ❖ *tr.v.* **belt·ed, belt·ing, belts 1.** To encircle; gird. **2.** To support or attach with or as if with a belt. **3.** To mark with or as if with a belt. **4.** *Slang* To strike forcefully; hit. **5.** *Slang* To sing in a loud and forceful manner: *belt out a song.* **6.** *Slang* To swig (an alcoholic beverage). —*idioms:* **below the belt** Not according to the rules; unfairly. **tighten (one's) belt** To begin to exercise thrift and frugality. **under (one's) belt** In one's possession or experience. [ME < OE, ult. < Lat. *balteus.*]

Bel·tane (bĕl′tān, -tən) *n.* An ancient Celtic feast marked by bonfires and various rites of purification, usu. observed on May 1. [ME < Sc. Gael. *bealltainn* < OIr. *beltaine*, fire of Bel : *Bel*, Bel (name of a Celt. god) + *ten*, fire.]

belt highway *n.* See **beltway.**

belt·ing (bĕl′tĭng) *n.* **1.** Belts considered as a group. **2.** The material used to make belts. **3.** A beating or thrashing.

belt·way (bĕlt′wā′) *n.* A high-speed highway that encircles or skirts an urban area.

Beltway *n.* **1.** The beltway surrounding Washington, DC. **2.** The political establishment of Washington, DC.

be·lu·ga (bə-lōō′gə) *n.* **1.** See **white whale.** **2.** A large white sturgeon (*Huso huso*) of the Black and Caspian seas, whose roe is processed into caviar. [Russ. *belukha*, white whale, *beluga*, sturgeon, both < *belyĭ*, white.]

bel·ve·dere (bĕl′vĭ-dîr′) *n.* A roofed structure, such as a gazebo or turret, situated so as to command a wide view. [Ital. : *bel, bello,* beautiful (< Lat. *bellus*; see **deu-[2]** in App.) + *vedere*, to see, view (< Lat. *vidēre*; see **weid-** in App.).]

be·ma (bē′mə) *n., pl.* **-ma·ta** (-mə-tə) **1.** *Judaism* The platform

bellows

for services in a synagogue. **2.** *Eastern Orthodox Church* The area of a church in which the altar is located; the sanctuary. [Ult. < Gk. *bēma*, step, platform. See **gʷā-** in App.]

Bem·ba (bĕm′bə) *n.* **1.** A member of a people centered in northeast Zambia. **2.** Their Bantu language.

be·med·aled or **be·med·alled** (bĭ-mĕd′ld) *adj.* Decorated with or wearing medals.

Be·mel·mans (bē′məl-mənz, bĕm′əl-), **Ludwig** 1898–1962. Austrian-born Amer. illustrator and writer whose children's books include *Madeleine* (1939).

be·mire (bĭ-mīr′) *tr.v.* **-mired, -mir·ing, -mires 1.** To soil with mud. **2.** To cause to sink into mud.

be·moan (bĭ-mōn′) *tr.v.* **-moaned, -moan·ing, -moans 1.** To express grief over; lament. **2.** To express disapproval of or regret for; deplore. [ME *bimonen*, alteration (influenced by *mone*, moan) of *bimenen* < OE *bemǣnan* : *be-*, be- + *mǣnan*, to complain of.]

be·muse (bĭ-myōōz′) *tr.v.* **-mused, -mus·ing, -mus·es 1.** To cause to be bewildered; confuse. **2.** To cause to be engrossed in thought. **—be·mus′ed·ly** (-myōō′zĭd-lē) *adv.* **—be·muse′-ment** *n.*

ben (bĕn) *Scots n.* The inner room or parlor of a house with two rooms. ❖ *adv.* Inside; within. ❖ *prep.* Within. [ME, var. of *binne*, within < OE *binnan*. See **en** in App.]

Be·na·res (bə-när′əs, -ēz) See **Varanasi.**

Be·na·ven·te y Mar·tí·nez (bĕn′ə-vĕn′tĕ ē mär-tē′nəs, bĕ′nä-vĕn′tĕ ē mär-tē′nĕth), **Jacinto** 1866–1954. Spanish playwright who won the 1922 Nobel Prize for literature.

Ben Bel·la (bĕn bĕl′ə), **Ahmed** b. 1919. Algerian revolutionary leader.

Bence-Jones protein (bĕns′jōnz′) *n.* A protein occurring in the serum and urine of patients with certain diseases, esp. multiple myeloma. [After Henry *Bence-Jones* (1813–73), British physician.]

bench (bĕnch) *n.* **1.** A long seat for two or more persons. **2.** *Law* **a.** A judge's seat in a courtroom. **b.** A judge's office or position. **c.** often **Bench** The judge or judges composing a court. **3a.** A seat occupied by a person in an official capacity. **b.** The office of such a person. **4.** A strong worktable. **5.** A platform on which animals, esp. dogs, are exhibited. **6.** *Sports* **a.** The place where the players on a team sit when not playing. **b.** The reserve players on a team. **7a.** A level, narrow stretch of land interrupting a declivity. **b.** A level elevation of land along a shore or coast, esp. one marking a former shoreline. ❖ *tr.v.* **benched, bench·ing, bench·es 1.** To furnish with benches. **2.** To seat on a bench. **3.** *Sports* To keep out of or remove from a game: *benched the goalie for fighting.* [ME < OE *benc*.]

bench·er (bĕn′chər) *n.* **1.** One that sits on a bench. **2.** *Chiefly British* A member of the inner or higher bar who acts as a governor of one of the Inns of Court. **3.** An official who occupies a bench.

Bench·ley (bĕnch′lē), **Robert Charles** 1889–1945. Amer. humorist, critic, and actor whose works include the book *My Ten Years in a Quandary* (1936).

bench·mark (bĕnch′märk′) *n.* **1.** A standard by which something can be measured or judged. **2.** often **bench mark** A surveyor's mark made on a stationary object of previously determined position and elevation and used as a reference point in tidal observations and surveys. [< the use of the mark as a place to insert an angle iron that serves as a support for a leveling rod.]

bench press *n.* A lift in weightlifting executed from a horizontal position on a bench, in which the weight is lifted from the chest to arm's length and then lowered back to the chest. **—bench′-press′** (bĕnch′prĕs′) *v.*

bench warrant *n.* A warrant issued by a judge or court ordering the apprehension of an offender.

bend[1] (bĕnd) *v.* **bent** (bĕnt), **bend·ing, bends** **—***tr.* **1.** To bring (something) into a state of tension: *bend a bow.* **2a.** To cause to assume a curved or angular shape: *bend a piece of iron into a horseshoe.* **b.** To force to assume a different direction or shape, according to one's own purpose: *bend the course of events.* **c.** To misrepresent: *bent the truth.* **d.** To make an exception to: *bent the rules.* **3.** To cause to swerve from a straight line; deflect. **4.** To render submissive; subdue. **5.** To apply (the mind) closely. **6.** *Nautical* To fasten: *bend a mainsail onto the boom.* **—***intr.* **1a.** To deviate from a straight line or position: *The lane bends to the right at the bridge.* **b.** To assume a curved, crooked, or angular form or direction: *The saplings bent in the wind.* **2.** To incline the body; stoop. **3.** To make a concession; yield. **4.** To apply oneself closely; concentrate. ❖ *n.* **1a.** The act or fact of bending. **b.** The state of being bent. **2.** Something bent: *a bend in the road.* **3. bends** (used *with a sing.* or *pl. verb*) Decompression sickness. Used with *the.* **—idioms: around the bend** *Slang* Insane; crazy. **bend (or lean) over backward** To make an effort greater than is required. **bend (someone's) ear** *Slang* To talk to at length, usu. excessively. [ME *benden* < OE *bendan*. See **bhendh-** in App.]

SYNONYMS *bend, crook, curve, round* These verbs mean to swerve or cause to swerve from a straight line: *bent his knees and knelt; crooked an arm around the package; claws that curve under; rounding the lips to articulate an "o."* **ANTONYM** *straighten*

---

bend[2] (bĕnd) *n.* **1.** *Heraldry* A band passing from the upper dexter corner of an escutcheon to the lower sinister corner. **2.** *Nautical* A knot that joins a rope to a rope or another object. [ME < OE *bend*, band, and < OFr. *bende, bande*, band (of Gmc. orig.; see **bhendh-** in App.).]

Ben Day also **ben·day** or **Ben·day** (bĕn-dā′) *n.* A method of adding a tone to a printed image by imposing a transparent sheet of dots or other patterns on the image at some stage of a photographic reproduction process. [After *Ben(jamin) Day* (1838–1916), American printer.]

bend·ed (bĕn′dĭd) *v. Archaic* A past participle of **bend**[1]. **—idiom: on bended knee** On one's knee or knees.

bend·er (bĕn′dər) *n.* **1.** One that bends: *a bender of iron bars; a bender of the truth.* **2.** *Slang* A spree, esp. a drinking spree.

bend sinister *n. Heraldry* A band passing from the upper sinister corner of an escutcheon to the lower dexter corner.

be·neath (bĭ-nēth′) *adv.* **1.** In a lower place; below. **2.** Underneath. ❖ *prep.* **1a.** Lower than; below. **b.** To or into a lower position than. **2.** Covered or concealed by. **3.** Under the force, control, or influence of. **4a.** Lower than, as in rank or station. **b.** Unworthy of; unbefitting. [ME *binethe* < OE *beneothan* : *be*, by; see **BY**[1] + *neothan*, below.]

ben·e·dict (bĕn′ĭ-dĭkt′) *n.* A newly married man who was previously considered a confirmed bachelor. [After *Benedick*, a character in *Much Ado About Nothing* by William Shakespeare.]

Benedict XIV 1675–1758. Pope (1740–58) who enlarged the Vatican Library.

Benedict XV 1854–1922. Pope (1914–22) who sponsored World War I relief efforts.

Benedict, Ruth Fulton 1887–1948. Amer. anthropologist noted for her study of Native American and Japanese cultures.

Ben·e·dic·tine (bĕn′ĭ-dĭk′tĭn, -tēn′) *n. Roman Catholic Church* A monk or nun of the order founded by Saint Benedict of Nursia. **—Ben′e·dic′tine** *adj.*

ben·e·dic·tion (bĕn′ĭ-dĭk′shən) *n.* **1.** A blessing. **2.** An invocation of divine blessing. **3.** often **Benediction** A short Christian service consisting of prayers, the singing of a Eucharistic hymn, and the blessing of the congregation with the host. **4.** An expression of good wishes. [ME *benediccioun* < OFr. *benedicion* < Lat. *benedictiō, benedictiōn-* < *benedictus*, p. part. of *benedīcere*, to bless : *bene*, well; see **deu-**[2] in App. + *dīcere*, to speak; see **deik-** in App.] **—ben′e·dic′tive, ben′e·dic′to·ry** (-dĭk′tə-rē) *adj.*

Benedict of Nur·si·a (nûr′shē-ə, -shə), **Saint.** A.D. 480?–547? Italian monk who founded the Benedictine order (c. 529).

Ben·e·dict's solution (bĕn′ĭ-dĭkts) *n.* A solution of sodium citrate, sodium carbonate, and copper sulfate that is changed from blue to yellow or red by reducing sugars. [After Stanley Rossiter *Benedict* (1884–1936), American chemist.]

Ben·e·dic·tus (bĕn′ĭ-dĭk′təs) *n.* **1.** A canticle that begins "Blessed is he that cometh in the name of the Lord" (Matthew 21:9). **2.** A canticle that begins "Blessed be the Lord God of Israel" (Luke 1:68). [Lat., p. part. of *benedīcere*, to bless. See BENEDICTION.]

ben·e·fac·tion (bĕn′ə-făk′shən, bĕn′ə-făk′-) *n.* **1.** The act of conferring aid. **2.** A charitable gift or deed. [LLat. *benefactiō, benefactiōn-* < Lat. *benefactus*, p. part. of *benefacere*, to do a service : *bene*, well; see **deu-**[2] in App. + *facere*, to do; see **dhē-** in App.] **—ben′e·fac′tive** (-tĭv) *adj.*

ben·e·fac·tor (bĕn′ə-făk′tər) *n.* One that gives aid, esp. financial aid. [ME < LLat. < Lat. *benefacere*, to do a service. See BENEFACTION.]

ben·e·fac·tress (bĕn′ə-făk′trĭs) *n.* A woman who gives aid, esp. financial aid.

be·nef·ic (bə-nĕf′ĭk) *adj.* Beneficent. [Lat. *beneficus* : *bene*, well; see BENEFACTION + *-ficus*, -fic.]

ben·e·fice (bĕn′ə-fĭs) *n.* **1.** *Ecclesiastical* **a.** A church office endowed with assets that provide a living. **b.** The revenue from such assets. **2.** A landed estate granted in feudal tenure. [ME < OFr. < Lat. *beneficium*, benefit < *beneficus*, benefic. See BENEFIC.] **—ben′e·fice** *v.*

be·nef·i·cence (bə-nĕf′ĭ-səns) *n.* **1.** The state or quality of being kind, charitable, or beneficial. **2.** A charitable act or gift. [Lat. *beneficentia* < *beneficus, beneficent-*, benefic. See BENEFIC.]

be·nef·i·cent (bə-nĕf′ĭ-sənt) *adj.* **1.** Characterized by or performing acts of kindness or charity. **2.** Producing benefit; beneficial. [Prob. < BENEFICENCE, on the model of such pairs as *benevolent, benevolence.*] **—be·nef′i·cent·ly** *adv.*

ben·e·fi·cial (bĕn′ə-fĭsh′əl) *adj.* **1.** Producing or promoting a favorable result; advantageous. **2.** *Law* Receiving or having the right to receive proceeds or other advantages. [ME < OFr. *beneficial* < LLat. *beneficiālis* < Lat. *beneficium*, benefit. See BENEFICE.] **—ben′e·fi′cial·ly** *adv.* **—ben′e·fi′cial·ness** *n.*

SYNONYMS *beneficial, profitable, advantageous* These adjectives apply to what promotes a favorable result or gain. *Beneficial* is said of what enhances well-being: *a beneficial trade agreement. Profitable* refers to what yields material gain or useful compensation: *profitable speculation on the stock market.* Something *advantageous* affords improvement in relative position or in chances of success: *socially advantageous.*

ă	pat	oi	boy
ā	pay	ou	out
âr	care	ŏŏ	took
ä	father	ōō	boot
ĕ	pet	ŭ	cut
ē	be	ûr	urge
ĭ	pit	th	thin
ī	pie	*th*	this
îr	pier	hw	which
ŏ	pot	zh	vision
ō	toe	ə	about,
ô	paw		item

Stress marks:
′ (primary);
′ (secondary), as in
lexicon (lĕk′sĭ-kŏn′)

ben·e·fi·ci·ar·y (bĕn′ə-fĭsh′ē-ĕr′ē, -fĭsh′ə-rē) *n., pl.* **-ies 1.** One that receives a benefit. **2.** The recipient of funds, property, or other benefits, as from an insurance policy or will. **3.** *Ecclesiastical* The holder of a benefice. [Med.Lat. *beneficiārius*, holder of a feudal benefice < Lat., soldier granted privileges < *beneficium*, benefit. See BENEFICE.] —**ben′e·fi′ci·ar′y** *adj.*

ben·e·fit (bĕn′ə-fĭt) *n.* **1a.** Something that promotes or enhances well-being; an advantage. **b.** Help; aid. **2.** A payment made or an entitlement available in accordance with a wage agreement, an insurance policy, or a public assistance program. **3.** A public entertainment or social event held to raise funds for a cause. **4.** *Archaic* A kindly deed. ❖ *v.* **-fit·ed, -fit·ing, -fits** also **-fit·ted, -fit·ting, -fits** —*tr.* To be helpful or useful to. —*intr.* To derive benefit. —*idiom:* **benefit of the doubt** A favorable judgment granted in the absence of full evidence. [ME < OFr. *bienfait*, good deed < Lat. *benefactum* < *benefacere*, to do a service. See BENEFACTION.]

benefit of clergy *n.* **1.** The authorized sanction of a religious rite. **2.** Exemption from trial or punishment in a civil court, given to the clergy in the Middle Ages.

Be·ne·lux (bĕn′ə-lŭks′) An economic union of Belgium, the Netherlands, and Luxembourg.

Be·neš (bĕn′ĕsh′), **Eduard** 1884–1948. Czechoslovakian politician who served as president (1935–38 and 1946–48).

Be·nét (bĭ-nā′), **William Rose** 1886–1950. Amer. writer and editor whose works include *The Reader's Encyclopedia* (1948). His brother **Stephen Vincent Benét** (1898–1943) is best known for his Civil War narrative poem *John Brown's Body* (1928).

be·nev·o·lence (bə-nĕv′ə-ləns) *n.* **1.** An inclination to perform generous acts. **2.** An act of generosity. **3.** A compulsory payment exacted by an English monarch without parliamentary consent.

be·nev·o·lent (bə-nĕv′ə-lənt) *adj.* **1.** Characterized by or suggestive of doing good. **2.** Of, concerned with, or organized for the benefit of charity. [ME < OFr. < Lat. *benevolēns, benevolent-* : *bene*, well; see **deu-**² in App. + *volēns*, pr. part. of *velle*, to wish.] —**be·nev′o·lent·ly** *adv.*

BEng *abbr.* Bachelor of Engineering

Ben·gal (bĕn-gôl′, bĕng-, bĕn′gəl, bĕng′-) A region of E India and Bangladesh. —**Ben′ga·lese′** (bĕn′gə-lēz′, -lēs′, bĕng′-) *adj. & n.*

Bengal, Bay of An arm of the Indian Ocean bordered by Sri Lanka and India on the W, Bangladesh on the N, and Myanmar (Burma) and Thailand on the E.

Ben·ga·li (bĕn-gô′lē, bĕng-) *adj.* Of or relating to Bengal or its people, language, or culture. ❖ *n., pl.* **Bengali** or **-lis 1.** A native or inhabitant of Bengal. **2.** The modern Indic language of Bangladesh and West Bengal, a state of eastern India.

ben·ga·line (bĕng′gə-lēn′) *n.* A fabric of silk, wool, or synthetic fibers having a crosswise ribbed effect. [Fr. < *Bengale*, Bengal.]

Bengal light *n.* **1.** A colored flare or light. **2.** A blue light, formerly used for signaling.

Bengal tiger *n.* A tiger (*Panthera tigris*) of India, Bhutan, Bangladesh, and Myanmar.

Beng·bu (bŭng′bōō′) also **Peng·pu** (pŭng′pōō′) A city of E China NW of Nanjing. Pop. 695,040.

Ben·gha·zi also **Ben·ga·si** (bən-gä′zē, bĕng-) A city of NE Libya on the Gulf of Sidra; formerly cap. of Libya (1951–72). Pop. 367,600.

BEngr *abbr.* Bachelor of Engineering

Ben Gur·i·on (bĕn gŏŏr′ē-ən), **David** 1886–1973. Polish-born Israeli prime minister (1948–53 and 1955–63).

Be·ni (bē′nē) A river of central and NW Bolivia rising in the Andes and flowing c. 1,599 km (994 mi) to the Mamoré R.

be·night·ed (bĭ-nī′tĭd) *adj.* **1.** Overtaken by night or darkness. **2.** Being in a state of moral or intellectual darkness. —**be·night′ed·ly** *adv.* —**be·night′ed·ness** *n.*

be·nign (bĭ-nīn′) *adj.* **1.** Of a kind and gentle disposition. **2.** Showing gentleness and mildness. **3.** Tending to exert a beneficial influence; favorable. See Syns at **favorable. 4.** Having little or no detrimental effect; harmless. **5.** *Medicine* Not recurrent, progressive, or malignant: *a benign tumor*. [ME *benigne* < OFr. < Lat. *benignus*. See **genə-** in App.] —**be·nign′ly** *adv.*

be·nig·nan·cy (bĭ-nĭg′nən-sē) *n., pl.* **-cies** Benignity.

be·nig·nant (bĭ-nĭg′nənt) *adj.* **1.** Favorable; beneficial. **2.** Kind and gracious. —**be·nig′nant·ly** *adv.*

be·nig·ni·ty (bĭ-nĭg′nĭ-tē) *n., pl.* **-ties 1.** The quality or condition of being kind and gentle. **2.** A kindly or gracious act.

benign neglect *n.* A policy or attitude of ignoring a situation instead of assuming responsibility for managing or improving it.

benign prostatic hyperplasia *n.* Nonmalignant enlargement of the prostate gland usu. seen in older men and marked by compression of the urethra.

Be·nin (bə-nĭn′, bĕ-nēn′) **1.** A former kingdom of W Africa, now part of Nigeria. **2.** Formerly **Da·ho·mey** (də-hō′mē, dä-ō-mā′) A country of W Africa; achieved independence in 1960. Cap. Porto-Novo. Pop. 5,387,000. **3.** also **Benin City** A city of S Nigeria on the **Benin River,** c. 161 km (100 mi) long. Pop. 136,000.

Benin, Bight of A wide indentation of the Gulf of Guinea in W Africa.

ben·i·son (bĕn′ĭ-zən, -sən) *n.* A blessing; a benediction. [ME < OFr. *beneison* < Lat. *benedictiō, benedictiōn-*, praising. See BENEDICTION.]

ben·ja·min (bĕn′jə-mən) *n.* See **benzoin** 1. [Alteration (influenced by the name *Benjamin*) of *benjoin*, benzoin; see BENZOIN.]

Benjamin In the Bible, the younger son of Jacob and Rachel and the forebear of one of the tribes of Israel.

Benjamin, Judah Philip 1811–84. British-born Amer. politician who served as Confederate secretary of war (1861–62).

Ben Lo·mond (lō′mənd) A mountain, 973.6 m (3,192 ft), of S-central Scotland on the E shore of Loch Lomond.

ben·net (bĕn′ĭt) *n.* Herb bennet.

Ben·nett (bĕn′ĭt), **(Enoch) Arnold** 1867–1931. British writer whose plays and novels were influenced by the French realists.

Bennett, James Gordon 1795–1872. Amer. journalist who founded and edited (1835–67) the *New York Herald.*

Bennett, Richard Bedford. Viscount Bennett. 1870–1947. Canadian prime minister (1930–35) who convened the 1932 economic conference in Ottawa.

Ben Ne·vis (nĕ′vĭs, nĕv′ĭs) The highest mountain of Great Britain, rising to 1,343.8 m (4,406 ft) in the Grampian Mts. of W Scotland.

ben·ny (bĕn′ē) *n., pl.* **-nies** *Slang* An amphetamine tablet taken as a stimulant. [< BENZEDRINE.]

Benny, Jack 1894–1974. Amer. comedian known for his shows on radio (1932–55) and television (1950–65).

Be·noît de Sainte-Maure (bən-wä′ də sănt-môr′) fl. 12th cent. French trouvère whose *Roman de Troie* was a source for works such as Chaucer's *Troilus and Criseyde.*

bent¹ (bĕnt) *v.* Past tense and past participle of **bend**¹. ❖ *adj.* **1.** Altered from a straight or even condition. **2.** Set on a course of action: *I was bent on going to the movies.* **3.** *Chiefly British* Corrupt; venal. ❖ *n.* **1.** A tendency, disposition, or inclination. **2.** A transverse structural member or framework for strengthening a bridge or trestle.

bent² (bĕnt) *n.* **1.** Bent grass. **2.** The stiff stalk of various grasses. **3.** An area of grassland unbounded by hedges or fences. [ME < OE *beonet* (attested only in place names).]

bent grass also **bent·grass** (bĕnt′grăs′) *n.* Any of various grasses of the genus *Agrostis*, native to chiefly temperate regions.

Ben·tham (bĕn′thəm), **Jeremy** 1748–1832. British writer and philosopher whose systematic analysis of law and legislation laid the foundations of utilitarianism.

Ben·tham·ism (bĕn′thə-mĭz′əm) *n.* The utilitarian philosophy of Jeremy Bentham, holding that pleasure is the only good. —**Ben′tham·ite′** (-mīt′) *n.*

ben·thos (bĕn′thŏs′) *n.* **1.** The collection of organisms living on or in sea or lake bottoms. **2.** The bottom of a sea or lake. [Gk.] —**ben′thic** (-thĭk), **ben·thon·ic** (bĕn-thŏn′ĭk) *adj.*

ben·to (bĕn′tō) *n.* Variant of **obento.**

Ben·ton¹ (bĕn′tən), **Thomas Hart** Called "Old Bullion." 1782–1858. Amer. legislator who staunchly opposed the use of paper currency.

Benton², **Thomas Hart** 1889–1975. Amer. artist whose paintings and murals, such as *The History of Missouri,* were executed in a flat, realistic style known as regionalism.

ben·ton·ite (bĕn′tə-nīt′) *n.* A silicate clay formed from volcanic ash and used in various adhesives and cements. [After *Benton* Formation (formerly Fort Benton Formation) of the Rock Creek district in eastern Wyoming.] —**ben′ton·it′ic** (-nĭt′ĭk) *adj.*

bent·wood (bĕnt′wŏŏd′) *n.* Wood that has been steamed until pliable and then bent into shape.

Be·nue (bān′wā) A river of W Africa rising in Cameroon and flowing c. 1,078 km (670 mi) to the Niger R. in central Nigeria.

Be·nue-Con·go (bān′wā-kŏng′gō) *n.* The branch of the Niger-Congo language family that contains the Bantu languages.

be·numb (bĭ-nŭm′) *tr.v.* **-numbed, -numb·ing, -numbs 1.** To make numb, esp. by cold. **2.** To make inactive; dull. [ME *binomen*, p. part. of *binimen*, to take away < OE *beniman* : *be-*, away; see BE- + *niman*, to take; see NUMB.] —**be·numb′ment** *n.*

Ben·xi (bŭn′shē′) also **Pen·ki** (-jē′) A city of NE China SSE of Shenyang. Pop. 937,805.

benz·al·de·hyde (bĕn-zăl′də-hīd′) *n.* An aromatic oil, C_6H_5CHO, obtained from the bitter almond or made synthetically and used in perfumes and flavorings.

ben·zal·ko·ni·um chloride (bĕn′zăl-kō′nē-əm) *n.* A water-soluble powder used as a detergent, fungicide, bactericide, and spermicide. [BENZ(O)- + ALK(YL) + (AMM)ONIUM.]

Ben·ze·drine (bĕn′zĭ-drēn′) A trademark formerly used for a preparation of amphetamine.

ben·zene (bĕn′zēn′, bĕn-zēn′) *n.* A clear, flammable, liquid aromatic hydrocarbon, C_6H_6, derived from petroleum and used in detergents, insecticides, and motor fuels.

benzene hexachloride *n.* A musty-smelling crystalline substance, $C_6H_6Cl_6$, prepared by the chlorination of benzene and used as a powerful insecticide.

benzene ring *n.* A hexagonal ring arrangement found in benzene and other aromatic compounds, consisting of six carbon atoms, each bonded to hydrogen or derivatives of benzene.

ben·zi·dine (bĕn′zĭ-dēn′) *n.* A crystalline powder, $NH_2C_6H_4C_6H_4NH_2$, used in the detection of blood stains,

David Ben Gurion
photographed in 1946

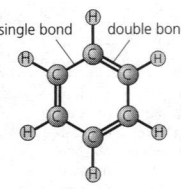

Benin

single bond   double bond

benzene ring

[BENZ(ENE) + –ID(E) + –INE².]

ben·zim·id·az·ole (běn′zə-mĭ-dăz′ōl′, -mĭd′ə-zōl′) *n.* A crystalline compound, $C_7H_4N_2$, that is used in organic synthesis and inhibits the growth of certain microorganisms.

ben·zine (běn′zēn′, běn-zēn′) also **ben·zin** (běn′zĭn) *n.* **1.** A liquid mixture of hydrocarbons obtained in distilling petroleum, used in cleaning and dyeing. **2.** See **benzene.**

benzo– or **benz–** *pref.* Benzene; benzoic acid: *benzophenone.* [< BENZOIN.]

ben·zo·ate (běn′zō-āt′) *n.* A salt or ester of benzoic acid.

benzoate of soda *n.* See **sodium benzoate.**

ben·zo·caine (běn′zə-kān′) *n.* A white, odorless, crystalline ester, $C_6H_4NH_2CO_2C_2H_5$, used as a local anesthetic.

ben·zo·di·az·e·pine (běn′zō-dī-ăz′ə-pēn′, -pĭn) *n.* Any of a group of chemical compounds with a common structure and similar pharmacologic effects, used esp. as antianxiety agents, muscle relaxants, and sedatives. [BENZO– + DIAZEP(AM) + –INE².]

ben·zo·fu·ran (běn′zō-fyŏŏr′ăn′, -fyŏŏ-răn′) *n.* A colorless liquid, C_8H_6O, found in coal tar and used in paints and varnishes.

ben·zo·ic acid (běn-zō′ĭk) *n.* An aromatic white crystalline acid, C_6H_5COOH, used to season tobacco and in perfumes, dentifrices, and germicides. [< BENZOIN.]

ben·zo·in (běn′zō-ĭn, -zoin′) *n.* **1.** A balsamic resin obtained from certain tropical Asian trees of the genus *Styrax* and used in perfumery and medicine. **2.** A crystalline compound, $C_{14}H_{12}O_2$, derived from benzaldehyde. [Earlier *benjoin,* Fr. *benjoin* and Ital. *benzoino,* both < Ar. *lubān jāwī,* frankincense of Java.]

ben·zol (běn′zōl′, -zōl′, -zôl′) *n.* See **benzene.** [BENZ(O)– + –OL¹.]

ben·zo·phe·none (běn′zō-fĭ-nōn′, -fē′nōn) *n.* A crystalline compound, $C_6H_5COC_6H_6$, used in perfumery.

ben·zo·py·rene (běn′zō-pī′rēn′, -pī-rēn′) *n.* A carcinogenic aromatic hydrocarbon, $C_{20}H_{12}$, found in cigarette smoke.

ben·zo·yl (běn′zō-ĭl′, -zoil′) *n.* The univalent radical $C_6H_5CO^-$, derived from benzoic acid.

benzoyl peroxide *n.* A granular solid, $(C_6H_5CO)_2O_2$, used as a bleaching agent for flour, fats, waxes, and oils, as a polymerization catalyst, and in pharmaceuticals.

ben·zyl (běn′zĭl, -zēl′) *n.* The univalent radical $C_6H_5CH_2^-$, derived from toluene.

Be·o·grad (bě′ô-gräd) See **Belgrade.**

Be·o·wulf (bā′ə-wŏŏlf′) *n.* **1.** An Old English epic poem probably composed in the early eighth century. **2.** The hero of this poem.

be·queath (bĭ-kwē*th*′, -kwēth′) *tr.v.* **-queathed, -queath·ing, -queaths** **1.** *Law* To leave or give (personal property) by will. **2.** To pass (something) on to another; hand down. [ME *biquethen* < OE *becwethan* : *be-,* be- + *cwethan,* to say.] —**be·queath′al, be·queath′ment** *n.* —**be·queath′er** *n.*

be·quest (bĭ-kwěst′) *n.* **1.** The act of giving, leaving by will, or passing on to another. **2.** Something that is bequeathed; a legacy. [ME *biquest* (influenced by *biquethen,* to bequeath) : *bi-,* be- + *quist,* will (< OE *-cwis,* as in *andcwis,* answer).]

Be·rar (bā-rär′, bə-) A region of W-central India, one of the early kingdoms of the Deccan.

be·rate (bĭ-rāt′) *tr.v.* **-rat·ed, -rat·ing, -rates** To rebuke or scold angrily and at length. [BE– + RATE².]

Ber·ber (bûr′bər) *n.* **1.** A member of a North African, primarily Muslim people living in settled or nomadic tribes from Morocco to Egypt. **2.** Any of the Afro-Asiatic languages of the Berbers. [Ar. *Barbar.*] —**Ber′ber** *adj.*

ber·ber·ine (bûr′bə-rēn′) *n.* An alkaloid, $C_{20}H_{19}NO_5$, obtained from plants such as goldenseal and used as an antipyretic and antibacterial agent. [NLat. *Berberis,* barberry genus (< Med.Lat. *berberis,* barberry) + –INE².]

ber·ceuse (běr-sœz′) *n., pl.* **-ceuses** (-sœz′) **1.** A lullaby. **2.** A soothing musical composition, usu. in 6/8 time. [Fr., fem. of *berceur,* cradle rocker < *bercer,* to rock < VLat. *bertiāre.*]

Berch·tes·ga·den (běrk′təs-gäd′n, běrкн′-) A town of SE Germany in the Bavarian Alps. The site of Adolf Hitler's wartime villa is on a peak overlooking the town. Pop. 8,126.

ber·dache (bər-dăsh′) *n.* Among certain Native American peoples, a person, usu. a male, who assumes the gender identity and social roles of the opposite sex. [N.Amer.Fr. < Fr. *bardache,* catamite < Ital. dialectal *bardascia* < Ar. *bardaj,* slave < Pers. *bardah,* prisoner < MPers. *vartak* < OIran. **varta-.* See **weļə-** in App.] —**ber·dach′ism** *n.*

USAGE NOTE Due to the derogatory implications implicit in the etymology of *berdache,* contemporary Native Americans have suggested that its scholarly use be discontinued. Among the alternatives in current use, the most widely employed is *two-spirit.* Other scholars use specific native terms, such as *winkte* (from Lakota) or *nadle* (from Navajo).

be·reave (bĭ-rēv′) *tr.v.* **-reaved** or **-reft** (-rěft′), **-reav·ing, -reaves** **1.** To leave desolate or alone, esp. by death. **2.** *Archaic* To take (something valuable or necessary), esp. by force. [ME *bireven,* to deprive < OE *berēafian.* See **reup–** in App.] —**be·reave′ment** *n.* —**be·reav′er** *n.*

be·reaved (bĭ-rēvd′) *adj.* Suffering the loss of a loved one. ❖ *n.* One or those bereaved.

be·reft (bĭ-rěft′) *adj.* **1a.** Deprived of something: *They are bereft of dignity.* **b.** Lacking something needed or expected. **2.** Suffering the death of a loved one; bereaved.

Ber·e·ni·ce's Hair (běr′ə-nī′sēz) *n.* See **Coma Berenices.**

Ber·en·son (běr′ĭn-sən), **Bernard** also **Bernhard** 1865–1959. Lithuanian-born Amer. art critic and historian noted for his writings on the Italian Renaissance.

be·ret (bə-rā′) *n.* A round, soft, brimless cap that fits snugly and is often worn angled to one side. [Fr. *béret* < Fr. dialectal *berret* and < O Provençal *berret,* cap, both < LLat. *birrus,* hooded cloak. See BIRETTA.]

be·ret·ta or **ber·ret·ta** (bə-rět′ə) *n.* Variants of **biretta.**

Be·re·zi·na (bə-rĕz′ĭ-nə, byə-ryĕ-zyĭ-nä′) A river rising in NW Belarus flowing c. 611 km (380 mi) to the Dnieper R.

berg (bûrg) *n.* A mass of floating or stationary ice; an iceberg. [Short for ICEBERG.]

Berg (běrg, běrk), **Alban** 1885–1935. Austrian composer who blended classical forms and an atonal style, as in his opera *Wozzeck* (1925).

Berg (bûrg), **Patricia Jane** Known as "Patty." b. 1918. Amer. golfer who won 57 professional tournament titles.

Ber·ga·ma (bər-gä′mə, bûr′gə-) A town of W Turkey N of Izmir on the site of ancient Pergamum. Pop. 34,716.

ber·ga·mot (bûr′gə-mŏt′) *n.* **1a.** A tree (*Citrus aurantium* subsp. *bergamia*) grown chiefly in southern Italy for its fruits, the rinds of which yield an aromatic oil. **b.** The oil itself, used extensively in perfumery. **2.** See **bee balm.** [Fr. *bergamote* < Ital. *bergamotta* < Turk. dialectal *beg-armudu,* bey's pear : *beg,* bey; see BEY + *armud,* pear + *-u,* possessive suff.]

Ber·gen (bûr′gən, běr′-) A city of SW Norway on inlets of the North Sea; founded c. 1070. Pop. 218,144.

Ber·gen-Bel·sen (bûr′gən-běl′sən, běr′gən-běl′zən) See **Belsen.**

Bergh (bûrg), **Henry** 1811–88. Amer. reformer who founded the American Society for the Prevention of Cruelty to Animals (1866).

Berg·man (bûrg′mən), **Ingmar** b. 1918. Swedish director whose films include *The Silence* (1963).

Bergman, Ingrid 1915–82. Swedish actress whose films include *Gaslight* (1944) and *Anastasia* (1956).

Berg·mann's rule (bûrg′mənz) *n.* The principle holding that in a warm-blooded, polytypic, wide-ranging animal species, the body size of the members of each geographic group varies inversely with the average environmental temperature. [After Karl *Bergmann* (died 1865), German biologist.]

Berg·son (běrg′sən, běrg-sôn′), **Henri Louis** 1859–1941. French philosopher and writer who won the 1927 Nobel Prize for literature. —**Berg·so′ni·an** (-sô′ne-ən) *adj. & n.*

Berg·son·ism (běrg′sə-nĭz′əm) *n.* The philosophy of Henri Bergson, which asserts that all living forms arise from a persisting natural force, the élan vital.

Ber·i·a (běr′ē-ə), **Lavrenti Pavlovich** 1899–1953. Soviet secret police chief (1938–53) during the regime of Joseph Stalin; convicted of conspiracy and executed.

ber·i·ber·i (běr′ē-běr′ē) *n.* A disease caused by a deficiency of thiamine, characterized by neuropathy, heart abnormalities, and edema. [Sinhalese, redup. of *beri,* weakness.]

be·rim·bau (bə-rēnm′bou) *n.* A musical instrument with a gourd resonator and a single steel wire stretched across a long pole or stick. [Port. < Kimbundu *mbi-rimbau* : *mbi-,* n. pref. + *-rimbau,* berimbau.]

Ber·ing (bîr′ĭng, bâr′-, băr′- bā′rĭng), **Vitus** 1681–1741. Danish navigator and explorer who in 1728 sailed through the Bering Strait.

Bering Sea A northward extension of the Pacific Ocean between Siberia and AK, lying N of the Aleutian Is. and connected with the Arctic Ocean by the Bering Strait.

Bering Standard Time *n.* Standard time in the 11th time zone west of Greenwich, England, reckoned at 165° west and used, for example, in the Midway Islands. [After the BERING (SEA) or BERING (STRAIT).]

Bering Strait A narrow stretch of water separating AK from Siberia and connecting the Arctic Ocean with the Bering Sea. It is believed that during prehistoric times the strait formed a land bridge by which the original inhabitants of North America arrived from Asia.

Bering Time *n.* See Bering Standard Time.

Berke·le·ian·ism (bärk′lē-ə-nĭz′əm, bûr′-) *n.* George Berkeley's philosophy of subjective idealism, which holds that material objects exist as concepts in God's mind and as perceptions of these concepts in other minds.

Berke·ley (bûrk′lē) A city of W CA on San Francisco Bay N of Oakland. Pop. 102,743.

Berkeley, Busby 1895–1976. Amer. choreographer and film director noted for lavish dance routines in films such as *42nd Street* (1933).

Berke·ley (bärk′lē, bûrk′-), **George** 1685–1753. Irish philosopher who wrote *Treatise Concerning the Principles of Human Knowledge* (1710). —**Berke′le·ian** *adj. & n.*

Berke·ley (bûrk′lē, bärk′-), **Sir William** 1606–77. English colonial governor of Virginia (1641–49 and 1660–77).

ă	pat	oi	boy
ā	pay	ou	out
âr	care	ŏŏ	took
ä	father	ōō	boot
ĕ	pet	ŭ	cut
ē	be	ûr	urge
ĭ	pit	th	thin
ī	pie	*th*	this
îr	pier	hw	which
ŏ	pot	zh	vision
ō	toe	ə	about,
ô	paw		item

Stress marks:
′ (primary);
′ (secondary), as in
lexicon (lĕk′sĭ-kŏn′)

ber·ke·li·um (bər-kē′lē-əm, bûrk′lē-əm) *n. Symbol* **Bk** A synthetic radioactive element. Its most stable isotope is Bk 247, with a half-life of 1,380 years. Atomic number 97; melting point 986°C; valence 3, 4. See table at **element.** [After BERKELEY.]

Berk·shire (bûrk′shîr′, -shər) *n.* One of a domestic breed of medium-sized black swine with white markings. [After *Berkshire*, a county of south-central England.]

Berkshire Hills also **Berk·shires** (bûrk′shîrz′, -shərz) A region of wooded hills in W MA rising to 1,064.8 m (3,491 ft).

Berle (bûrl), **Milton** b. 1908. American entertainer and comedian often called "Mr. Television."

Ber·lin (bûr-lĭn′) The cap. of Germany, in the NE part; divided (1945–90) into **East Berlin** and **West Berlin.** The **Berlin Wall,** a wire and concrete barrier, was erected by the East German government in 1961 and dismantled in 1989. Pop. 3,475,392. —**Ber·lin′er** *n.*

Berlin, Irving 1888–1989. Russian-born Amer. songwriter whose musical comedies include *Annie Get Your Gun* (1946).

Ber·lin·er (bûr′lə-nər), **Emile** 1851–1929. German-born Amer. inventor of the gramophone (1887).

Ber·li·oz (bĕr′lē-ōz′, -ōs′), **(Louis) Hector** 1803–69. French composer whose works include *Symphonie fantastique* (1830).

berm also **berme** (bûrm) *n.* **1a.** A narrow ledge or shelf, as along the top or bottom of a slope. **b.** *Pennsylvania, Ohio, Indiana, & West Virginia* The shoulder of a road. **c.** A raised bank or path, such as one along a canal. **2.** A terrace formed by wave action along the backshore of a beach. **3.** A mound or bank of earth, used esp. as a barrier or to provide insulation. ❖ *tr.v.* **bermed, berm·ing, berms** To provide with a berm or berms. [Fr. *berme* < Du. *berm* < MDu. *barm, berme.*]

Ber·me·jo (bər-mā′hō, bĕr-) A river of N Argentina rising near the Bolivian border and flowing c. 1,046 km (650 mi) to the Paraguay R. at the Paraguay border.

Ber·mu·da (bər-myōo′də) A self-governing British colony comprising c. 300 coral islands in the Atlantic Ocean SE of Cape Hatteras. Cap. Hamilton, on **Bermuda Island.** Pop. 63,000. —**Ber·mu′di·an, Ber·mu′dan** *adj. & n.*

Bermuda grass *n.* A mat-forming perennial grass (*Cynodon dactylon*) widespread in warm regions and important as a lawn and pasturage grass in the southern United States.

Bermuda lily *n.* See **Easter lily.**

Bermuda onion *n.* Any of several varieties of mild-flavored onions shaped like a flattened sphere.

Bermuda petrel *n.* See **cahow.**

Bermuda rig *n. Nautical* A fore-and-aft rig with a tall triangular mainsail and jib, used on cruising and racing vessels.

Bermuda shorts *pl.n.* Short pants that end slightly above the knee.

Bermuda Triangle A triangular area of the Atlantic Ocean bounded by Bermuda, Puerto Rico, and Florida, in which numerous watercraft and aircraft are said to have mysteriously disappeared.

Bern or **Berne** (bûrn, bĕrn) The cap. of Switzerland, in the W-central part on the Aare R.; founded as a military post in 1191. Pop. 129,692.

Ber·na·dette of Lourdes (bûr′nə-dĕt′; lŏord, lŏordz), Saint. 1844–79. French peasant girl whose visions of the Virgin Mary led to the establishment of the shrine at Lourdes.

Ber·na·dotte (bûr′nə-dŏt′), Count **Folke** 1895–1948. Swedish diplomat who was a leader of the Swedish Red Cross (1943–48).

Ber·nard (bĕr-när′), **Claude** 1813–78. French physiologist noted for his study of the digestive and nervous systems.

Ber·nard of Clair·vaux (bər-närd′, bĕr-när′; klâr-vō′), Saint. 1090–1153. French monastic reformer who rallied support for the Second Crusade.

Ber·nese Alps (bûr′nēz, -nēs, bûr-nēz′, -nĕs′) A range of the Alps in S-central Switzerland rising to 4,276.7 m (14,022 ft).

Bernese mountain dog *n.* Any of a Swiss breed of large muscular dogs having a black coat with russet or tan markings and a white chest.

Bern·hardt (bûrn′härt′, bĕr-när′), **Sarah** Orig. Henrietta Rosine Bernard. Known as "the Divine Sarah." 1844–1923. French actress who first achieved fame for her performance in *Phèdre* (1874).

Ber·ni·na Alps (bər-nē′nə, bĕr-) A mountain group of SE Switzerland in the Rhaetian Alps on the Swiss-Italian border, rising to 4,051.6 m (13,284 ft).

Ber·ni·ni (bər-nē′nē, bĕr-), **Giovanni Lorenzo** or **Gianlorenzo** 1598–1680. Italian sculptor, painter, and architect whose sculptures include *Apollo and Daphne* (1622–24).

Ber·noul·li (bər-nōō′lē) Family of Swiss mathematicians and scientists, including **Jakob** or **Jacques** (1654–1705), an important theorist of the calculus of variations. His brother **Johann** or **Jean** (1667–1748) developed integral and exponential calculus. Johann's son **Daniel** (1700–82) did pioneering work in the molecular theory of gases.

Bernoulli distribution *n.* See **binomial distribution.** [After Jakob BERNOULLI.]

Bernoulli effect *n.* The phenomenon of internal pressure reduction with increased stream velocity in a fluid. [After Daniel BERNOULLI.]

Bermuda shorts

Bernese mountain dog

Sarah Bernhardt

Ber·noul·li's law (bər-nōō′lēz) *n.* See **law of large numbers.** [After Jakob BERNOULLI.]

Bern·stein (bûrn′stīn′, -stēn′), **Leonard** 1918–90. Amer. conductor and composer whose works include *West Side Story* (1957).

Ber·ra (bĕr′ə), **Lawrence Peter** Known as "Yogi." b. 1925. Amer. athlete considered among the best catchers in baseball history.

ber·ried (bĕr′ēd) *adj.* **1.** Having or bearing berries. **2.** Resembling a berry or berries. **3.** Bearing eggs. Used esp. of crustaceans or fishes.

ber·ry (bĕr′ē) *n., pl.* **-ries 1.** *Botany* An indehiscent fruit derived from a single ovary and having the whole wall fleshy, such as the grape. **2.** A small, juicy, fleshy fruit, such as a raspberry, regardless of its botanical structure. **3.** Any of various seeds or dried kernels, as of wheat. **4.** The small dark egg of certain crustaceans or fishes. ❖ *intr.v.* **-ried, -ry·ing, -ries 1.** To hunt for or gather berries. **2.** To bear or produce berries. [ME *berye* < OE *berie.*]

Ber·ry (bĕ-rē′) A historical region and former province of central France.

Ber·ry (bĕr′ē), **Charles Edward Anderson** Known as "Chuck." b. 1926. Amer. musician considered among the earliest and most influential rock 'n' roll performers.

Ber·ry·man (bĕr′ē-mən), **John** 1914–72. Amer. poet whose works include *Homage to Mistress Bradstreet* (1956).

ber·seem (bər-sēm′) *n.* A yellowish-flowered annual clover (*Trifolium alexandrinum*) grown for forage in warm areas. [Ar. *birsīm* < Coptic *bersīm.*]

ber·serk (bər-sûrk′, -zûrk′, bə-) *adj.* **1.** Destructively or frenetically violent. **2.** Mentally or emotionally upset; deranged. **3.** *Informal* Unrestrained, as with enthusiasm; wild. ❖ *n.* **1.** One that is violent, upset, or unrestrained. **2.** A berserker. [Back-formation < BERSERKER.] —**ber·serk′** *adv.* —**ber·serk′ly** *adv.*

WORD HISTORY When we say that we are going berserk, we may not realize how extreme a state this might be. Our adjective comes from the noun *berserker*, or *berserk,* which is from the Old Norse word *berserkr,* "a wild warrior or champion." Such warriors wore hides of bears, which explains the probable origin of *berserkr* as a compound of *bera,* "bear," and *serkr,* "shirt, coat." These *berserkers* became frenzied in battle, howling like animals, foaming at the mouth, and biting the edges of their iron shields. *Berserker* is first recorded in English in the early 19th century, long after these wild warriors ceased to exist.

ber·serk·er (bər-sûr′kər, -zûr′-) *n.* One of a band of ancient Norse warriors legendary for their savagery and reckless frenzy in battle. [ON *berserkr*: *bera,* fem. of *björn,* bear; see **bher-²** in App. + *serkr,* shirt.]

berth (bûrth) *n.* **1.** Sufficient space for a ship to maneuver; sea room. **2.** A space for a ship to dock or anchor. **3a.** Employment on a ship. **b.** A job. **4a.** A built-in bed or bunk, as on a ship or train. **b.** A place to sleep or stay; accommodations. **5.** A space where a vehicle can be parked, as for loading. ❖ *v.* **berthed, berth·ing, berths** —*tr.* **1.** To bring (a ship) to a berth. **2.** To provide with a berth. —*intr.* To come to a berth; dock. —*idiom:* **wide berth** Ample space or distance to avoid an unwanted consequence. [ME *birth;* perh. akin to *beren,* to bear. See BEAR¹.]

ber·tha (bûr′thə) *n.* A wide deep collar, often of lace, that covers the shoulders of a dress. [Fr. *berthe,* after *Bertha* (died 783), Carolingian queen as the wife of Pepin the Short.]

Ber·til·lon (bûr′tl-ŏn′, bĕr-tē-yôn′), **Alphonse** 1853–1914. French criminologist who devised the Bertillon system (1880).

Bertillon system *n.* A former system used for identifying persons by means of body measurements, physical description, and photographs. [After Alphonse BERTILLON.]

ber·yl (bĕr′əl) *n.* A transparent to translucent glassy mineral, Be₃Al₂Si₆O₁₈, constituting the chief source of beryllium and in its transparent varieties valued as gems. [ME < OFr. < Lat. *bēryllus* < Gk. *bērullos* < *bērullion* < Prakrit *veruliya* < Pali *veḷuriya.*]

be·ryl·li·um (bə-rĭl′ē-əm) *n. Symbol* **Be** A lightweight, corrosion-resistant metallic element used as an aerospace structural material, in nuclear reactors, and in a copper alloy for springs and electrical contacts. Atomic number 4; atomic weight 9.0122; melting point 1,278°C; boiling point 2,970°C; specific gravity 1.848; valence 2. See table at **element.** [< BERYL.]

Ber·ze·li·us (bər-zēl′ē-əs, bĕr-sā′lē-ōōs′), Baron **Jöns Jakob** 1779–1848. Swedish chemist who published a table of atomic weights (1828).

Bes (bĕs) *n. Mythology* The Egyptian god of music and revelry and the guardian deity of women in labor.

Bes·ant (bĕz′ənt), **Annie Wood** 1847–1933. English theosophist, philosopher, and political figure who advocated home rule and educational reforms in India.

be·seech (bĭ-sēch′) *tr.v.* **-sought** (-sôt′) or **-seeched, -seech·ing, -seech·es 1.** To address an earnest or urgent request to; implore: *beseech him for help.* **2.** To request earnestly; beg for: *beseech help.* [ME *bisechen* < OE *besēcan : be-,* be- + *sēcan,* to seek; see SEEK.] —**be·seech′er** *n.*

be·seem (bĭ-sēm′) *tr.v.* **-seemed, -seem·ing, -seems** *Archaic* To be appropriate for; befit. [ME *bisemen : bi-,* be- + *semen,* to seem; see SEEM.]

be·set (bĭ-sĕt′) *tr.v.* **-set, -set·ting, -sets 1.** To attack from all sides. **2.** To trouble persistently; harass; beleaguer. **3.** To hem in; surround. **4.** To stud, as with jewels. [ME *bisetten* < OE *besettan.* See sed- in App.] **—be·set′ment** *n.*

be·set·ting (bĭ-sĕt′ĭng) *adj.* Constantly troubling or attacking.

be·shrew (bĭ-shrōō′) *tr.v.* **-shrewed, -shrew·ing, -shrews** *Archaic* To invoke evil upon; curse.

be·side (bĭ-sīd′) *prep.* **1.** At the side of; next to. **2a.** In comparison with. **b.** On an equal footing with. **3.** In addition to. See Usage Note at **besides. 4.** Except for. See Usage Note at **besides. 5.** Not relevant to. ❖ *adv. Archaic* **1.** In addition. **2.** Nearby. **—idiom: beside (oneself)** In a state of extreme excitement or agitation. [ME *biside* < OE *be sīdan* : *be,* by; see BY[1] + *sīde,* side.]

be·sides (bĭ-sīdz′) *adv.* **1.** In addition; also. **2.** Moreover; furthermore. **3.** Otherwise; else. ❖ *prep.* **1.** In addition to. **2.** Except for; other than. [ME : *biside,* at the side; see BESIDE + *-es,* adv. suff.; see –S[3].]

USAGE NOTE While some critics argue that *beside* and *besides* should not be used interchangeably as prepositions meaning "in addition to" or "except for," this distinction is often ignored, even by reputable writers. *Beside* regularly appears in print in place of *besides,* although the reverse is not true—*besides* can never mean "at the side of." Using *beside* in this way can lead to ambiguity, however: *There was no one beside him at the table* could mean that he had the table to himself or that the seats next to him were unoccupied. See Usage Note at **together.**

be·siege (bĭ-sēj′) *tr.v.* **-sieged, -sieg·ing, -sieg·es 1.** To surround with hostile forces. **2.** To crowd around; hem in. **3.** To harass or importune, as with requests. **4.** To cause to feel distressed or worried. [ME *besegen,* prob. alteration of *assegen* < OFr. *assegier* < VLat. *assedicāre* : Lat. *ad-, ad-* + VLat. *sedicāre,* to sit; see SIEGE.] **—be·sieg′ment** *n.* **—be·sieg′er** *n.*

Bes·kids (bĕs′kĭdz′, bĕs-kēdz′) A mountain range of the W Carpathians extending c. 322 km (200 mi) along the Polish-Slovak border and rising to 1,726 m (5,659 ft). The range is divided into the **East Beskids** and the **West Beskids.**

be·smear (bĭ-smîr′) *tr.v.* **-smeared, -smear·ing, -smears** To smear.

be·smirch (bĭ-smûrch′) *tr.v.* **-smirched, -smirch·ing, -smirch·es 1.** To stain; sully: *besmirched by slander.* **2.** To make dirty; soil. **—be·smirch′er** *n.* **—be·smirch′ment** *n.*

be·som (bē′zəm) *n.* **1.** A bundle of twigs attached to a handle and used as a broom. **2.** *Sports* The broom used to sweep the ice in curling. [ME < OE *besma.*]

besom pocket *n.* A pocket trimmed with welting or reinforced stitching. [*besom,* reinforcement around pocket opening.]

be·sot (bĭ-sŏt′) *tr.v.* **-sot·ted, -sot·ting, -sots** To muddle or stupefy, as with alcohol. [BE– + *sot,* to stupefy (< *sot,* fool; see SOT) or < *assot,* to befool (< OFr. *assoter* < *sot,* foolish).]

be·sought (bĭ-sôt′) *v.* A past tense and a past participle of **beseech.**

be·spake (bĭ-spāk′) *v. Archaic* A past tense of **bespeak.**

be·spat·ter (bĭ-spăt′ər) *tr.v.* **-tered, -ter·ing, -ters** To spatter with or as if with mud.

be·speak (bĭ-spēk′) *tr.v.* **-spoke** (-spōk′), **-spo·ken** (-spō′kən) or **-spoke, -speak·ing, -speaks 1.** To be or give a sign of; indicate. **2a.** To engage, hire, or order in advance. **b.** To request. **3.** To foretell; portend. **4.** *Archaic* To speak to; address. [ME *bispeken,* to speak of < OE *besprecan,* to speak about.]

be·spec·ta·cled (bĭ-spĕk′tə-kəld) *adj.* Wearing eyeglasses.

be·sprent (bĭ-sprĕnt′) *adj. Archaic* Sprinkled over. [ME *bisprent,* p. part. of *bisprengen,* to besprinkle. See BESPRINKLE.]

be·sprin·kle (bĭ-sprĭng′kəl) *tr.v.* **-kled, -kling, -kles** To sprinkle. [Prob. < ME *bisprenklen* < OE *besprengen* : *be-,* be- + *sprengan,* to sprinkle.]

Bes·sa·ra·bi·a (bĕs′ə-rā′bē-ə) A region of Moldova and W Ukraine; became part of Russia in 1812 but declared itself independent in 1918 and later voted for union with Romania, which was forced to cede it to the USSR in 1940. **—Bes′sa·ra′bi·an** *adj. & n.*

Bes·se·mer (bĕs′ə-mər), Sir **Henry** 1813–98. British inventor and metallurgist who patented the Bessemer process.

Bessemer process *n.* A method for making steel by blasting compressed air through molten iron to burn out excess carbon and impurities. [After Sir Henry BESSEMER.]

best (bĕst) *adj.* Superlative of **good. 1.** Surpassing all others in excellence, achievement, or quality; most excellent. **2.** Most satisfactory, suitable, or useful; most desirable. **3.** Greatest; most: *for the best part of an hour.* **4.** Most highly skilled. ❖ *adv.* Superlative of **well[2]. 1.** In a most excellent way; most creditably or advantageously. **2.** To the greatest degree or extent; most. ❖ *n.* **1.** One that surpasses all others. **2.** The best part, moment, or value: *The best is still to come.* **3.** The optimum condition or quality: *look your best.* **4.** One's nicest or most formal clothing. **5.** The supreme effort one can make: *doing our best.* **6.** One's warmest wishes or regards. ❖ *v.* **best·ed, best·ing, bests** To get the better of; beat. **—idioms: at best 1.** Interpreted most favorably; at the most. **2.** Under the most favorable conditions. **for the best** With an ultimately positive or preferable result. **get (or have) the best of** To outdo or outwit; defeat. [ME < OE *betst.*]

USAGE NOTE According to a traditional rule of grammar, *better* should be used in comparisons between two things: *Which house of Congress has the better* (not *best*) *attendance record?* In certain fixed expressions, however, *best* is used idiomatically for comparisons between two: *Put your best foot forward.* See Usage Notes at **have, rather.**

Best, Charles Herbert 1899–1978. Amer.-born Canadian physiologist noted for his work on insulin.

best-ball (bĕst′bôl′) *n.* A form of team competition in golf in which the best individual score on a hole is recorded as the team's score.

best boy *n.* The chief assistant to the gaffer on a movie or television set.

best-case (bĕst′kās′) *adj.* Most favorable; optimum.

be·stead (bĭ-stĕd′) *Archaic tr.v.* **-stead·ed** or **-stead, -stead·ing, -steads 1.** To be of service to; aid. **2.** To be of use to; avail. ❖ *adj.* Having been placed; located. [Prob. BE- + STEAD, to help. Adj., ME *bistad,* placed : *bi-,* be- + *-stad* (ult. < ON *staddr,* placed, p. part. of *stedhja,* to stop < *stadhr,* place; see stā- in App.).]

bes·tial (bĕs′chəl, bēs′-) *adj.* **1.** Beastly. **2.** Marked by brutality or depravity. **3.** Lacking in intelligence or reason; subhuman. [ME < OFr. < LLat. *bēstiālis* < Lat. *bēstia,* beast.] **—bes′tial·ly** *adv.*

bes·ti·al·i·ty (bĕs′chē-ăl′ĭ-tē, bēs′-) *n., pl.* **-ties 1.** The quality or condition of being an animal or like an animal. **2.** Conduct or an action marked by depravity or brutality. **3.** Sexual relations between a human and an animal.

bes·ti·ar·y (bĕs′chē-ĕr′ē, bēs′-) *n., pl.* **-ies** A collection of stories providing descriptions of real and imaginary animals along with moral interpretations of their behavior. [Med.Lat. *bēstiārium* < Lat. *bēstia,* beast.]

be·stir (bĭ-stûr′) *tr.v.* **-stirred, -stir·ring, -stirs** To cause to become active; rouse: *bestirred himself to look for work.* [ME *bistiren* : prob. *bi-,* be- + *stiren,* to rouse; see STIR[1].]

best man *n.* The bridegroom's chief attendant at a wedding.

be·stow (bĭ-stō′) *tr.v.* **-stowed, -stow·ing, -stows 1.** To present as a gift or an honor; confer: *bestowed praise on the winners.* **2.** To apply; use. **3.** To place or store. **4.** To house. **—be·stow′a·ble** *adj.* **—be·stow′al, be·stow′ment** *n.*

be·strew (bĭ-strōō′) *tr.v.* **-strewed, -strewed** or **-strewn** (-strōōn′), **-strew·ing, -strews 1.** To strew (a surface) with things so as to cover it. **2.** To lie scattered over or about.

be·stride (bĭ-strīd′) *tr.v.* **-strode** (-strōd′), **-strid·den** (-strĭd′n), **-strid·ing, -strides 1.** To sit or stand on with the legs astride; straddle. **2.** To dominate by position; tower over. **3.** *Archaic* To step or stride across.

best-sell·er also **best seller** (bĕst′sĕl′ər) *n.* A product, such as a book, that is among those sold in the largest numbers. **—best′-sell′er·dom** *n.* **—best′-sell′ing** *adj.*

bet (bĕt) *n.* **1.** An agreement that one who has made an incorrect prediction about an uncertain outcome will forfeit something stipulated to another; a wager. **2.** An amount or object risked in a wager; a stake. **3.** One on which a stake is or can be placed: *Our team is a sure bet to win the game.* **4a.** A plan or option considered with regard to its probable consequence. **b.** *Informal* A view or opinion, esp. about something that cannot be known at the present time. ❖ *v.* **bet** or **bet·ted, bet·ting, bets** *—tr.* **1.** To stake (an amount, for example) in a bet. **2.** To make a bet with. **3.** To make a bet on (a contestant or an outcome). **4.** To maintain confidently, as if making a bet: *I bet they were surprised.* *—intr.* To make or place a bet. **—idiom: you bet** *Informal* Of course; surely. [?]

SYNONYMS *bet, ante, pot, stake, wager* These nouns denote something valuable risked on an uncertain outcome: *placed a 50-dollar bet in the first race; raising the ante in a poker game; won the whole pot at cards; played for high stakes; laid a wager on who would win.*

Chuck Berry

be·ta (bā′tə, bē′-) *n.* **1.** The second letter of the Greek alphabet. **2.** The second item in a series or system of classification. **3.** A mathematical measure of the sensitivity of rates of return on a portfolio or a given stock compared with rates of return on the market as a whole. **4.** *Physics* A beta particle. **5.** *Chemistry* **a.** The second position from a designated carbon atom in an organic molecule at which an atom or a radical may be substituted. **b.** An isomeric variation of a chemical compound. Used in combination: *beta-estradiol.* **6.** *Computer Science* The version of a software product used in a beta test. [Gk. *bēta* < Phoenician **bēt,* house, second letter of the Phoenician alphabet.]

be·ta-ad·re·ner·gic (bā′tə-ăd′rə-nûr′jĭk, bē′-) *adj.* Of, relating to, or being a beta-receptor.

beta-adrenergic blocking agent *n.* See **beta-blocker.**

beta-adrenergic receptor *n.* See **beta-receptor.**

be·ta-ag·o·nist (bā′tə-ăg′ə-nĭst, bē′-) *n.* An agent, such as albuterol, that stimulates beta-receptors.

be·ta-block·er (bā′tə-blŏk′ər, bē′-) *n.* A drug that opposes the excitatory effects of norepinephrine released from sympathetic nerve endings at beta-receptors, used to treat angina, hypertension, arrhythmia, and migraine.

be·ta car·o·tene also **be·ta-car·o·tene** (bā′tə-kăr′ə-tēn′,

ă	pat	oi	boy
ā	pay	ou	out
âr	care	ŏŏ	took
ä	father	ōō	boot
ĕ	pet	ŭ	cut
ē	be	ûr	urge
ĭ	pit	th	thin
ī	pie	*th*	this
îr	pier	hw	which
ŏ	pot	zh	vision
ō	toe	ə	about,
ô	paw		item

Stress marks:
′ (primary);
′ (secondary), as in
lexicon (lĕk′sĭ-kŏn′)

bē'-) *n.* The isomeric form of carotene that is widely distributed in nature and most efficiently converted to vitamin A.

beta cell *n.* **1.** Any of the insulin-producing cells of the islets of Langerhans in the pancreas. **2.** Any of the basophilic chromophil cells located in the anterior lobe of the pituitary gland.

beta decay *n.* Radioactive decay in which a beta particle is emitted by an atomic nucleus.

be·ta·ine (bē'tə-ēn', -ĭn) *n.* **1.** An alkaloid, $C_5H_{11}NO_2$, found esp. in sugar beets and used to treat certain metabolic disorders. **2.** Any of several similar alkaloids. [Lat. *bēta,* beet + -INE².]

be·take (bĭ-tāk') *tr.v.* **-took** (-tŏok'), **-tak·en** (-tā'kən), **-tak·ing, -takes 1.** To make (oneself) move. **2.** *Archaic* To commit.

be·ta·meth·a·sone (bā'tə-mĕth'ə-sōn', bĕ'-) *n.* A synthetic glucocorticoid, $C_{22}H_{29}FO_5$, used as a topical anti-inflammatory agent. [BETA + METH(YL) + (PREDNI)S(OL)ONE.]

beta particle *n.* A high-speed electron or positron, esp. one emitted in radioactive decay.

beta ray *n.* A stream of beta particles, esp. of electrons.

be·ta-re·cep·tor (bā'tə-rĭ-sĕp'tər, bĕ'-) *n.* A site on a cell in the autonomic nervous system in which inhibitory responses occur when adrenergic agents, such as epinephrine and norepinephrine, are released.

beta rhythm *n.* See **beta wave.**

beta test *n.* The final stage in the testing of new software before its commercial release. **—be'ta-test'** (bā'tə-tĕst', bĕ'-) *v.*

be·ta·tron (bā'tə-trŏn', bĕ'-) *n.* A magnetic induction particle accelerator capable of producing high-energy electrons.

beta wave *n.* A waveform in electroencephalograms of the adult brain, characteristically of a frequency from 13 to 30 hertz and accompanying an alert or anxious waking state.

be·tel (bēt'l) *n.* An evergreen Indo-Malayan climbing or trailing shrub *(Piper betle)* having leaves used to wrap betel nuts. [Port. < Malayalam *vettila, veṟṟila* < Tamil *veṟṟilai.*]

Be·tel·geuse (bēt'l-jōoz', bĕt'l-jœz') *n.* A bright-red intrinsic variable star in the constellation Orion. [Fr. *Bételgeuse,* ult. < Ar. *yad al-jawzā' : yad,* hand + *al-,* the + *jawzā',* Gemini (later also Orion).]

betel nut also **be·tel·nut** (bēt'l-nŭt') *n.* The seed of the betel palm, chewed with betel leaves and lime as a mild stimulant.

betel palm *n.* A tropical Asian feather-leaved palm *(Areca catechu)* cultivated for its seeds.

bête noire (bĕt nwär') *n.* One that is particularly disliked or that is to be avoided. [Fr. : *bête,* beast + *noire,* black.]

beth (bĕt) *n.* The second letter of the Hebrew alphabet. [Heb. *bêt* < Phoenician **bēt,* house, second letter of the Phoenician alphabet.]

Beth·a·ny (bĕth'ə-nē) A village of ancient Palestine at the foot of the Mount of Olives near Jerusalem. According to the Bible, it was the site of the resurrection of Lazarus.

Be·the (bā'tə), **Hans Albrecht** b. 1906. German-born Amer. physicist who won a 1967 Nobel Prize.

beth·el (bĕth'əl) *n.* **1.** A hallowed or holy place. **2a.** A chapel for seafarers. **b.** *Chiefly British* A Nonconformist chapel, esp. a Baptist or Methodist one. [Heb. *bêt 'ēl,* house of God : *bayit,* house + *'ēl,* God.]

Beth·el (bĕth'əl, bĕth'ĕl') A town of ancient Palestine N of Jerusalem; now a major archaeological site.

Be·thes·da (bə-thĕz'də) An unincorporated city of W-central MD, a suburb of Washington DC. Pop. 55,277.

be·think (bĭ-thĭngk') *v.* **-thought** (-thôt'), **-think·ing, -thinks** **—***tr.* **1.** To make (oneself) consider. **2.** To remind (oneself); remember. **—***intr. Archaic* To meditate. [ME *bithinken* < OE *bethencan.*]

Beth·le·hem (bĕth'lĭ-hĕm', -lē-əm) **1.** A town in the West Bank S of Jerusalem; traditional birthplace of Jesus. Pop. 25,000. **2.** A city of E PA on the Lehigh R. NNW of Philadelphia. Pop. 71,329.

Be·thune (bə-thōon', -thyōon') **Mary McLeod** 1875–1955. Amer. educator who sought improved racial relations and educational opportunities for African Americans.

be·tide (bĭ-tīd') *v.* **-tid·ed, -tid·ing, -tides** **—***tr.* To happen to. **—***intr.* To take place; befall. [ME *bitiden* : *bi-,* be- + *tiden,* to happen (< OE *tīdan;* see TIDE².).]

be·times (bĭ-tīmz') *adv.* **1.** In good time; early. **2.** Once in a while; on occasion. **3.** *Archaic* Quickly; soon. [ME *bitimes* : *bi,* by; see BY¹ + *time,* TIME + *-es,* adv. suffix; see -S³.]

bê·tise (bā-tēz') *n., pl.* **-tises** (-tēz') **1.** Stupidity; folly. **2.** A stupid or foolish act or remark. [Fr. < *bête,* beast, fool, foolish < OFr. *beste,* beast. See BEAST.]

Bet·je·man (bĕch'ə-mən), **Sir John** 1906–84. British writer and poet laureate (1972–84) whose works include *A Few Late Chrysanthemums* (1955).

be·to·ken (bĭ-tō'kən) *tr.v.* **-kened, -ken·ing, -kens** To be or give a sign or portent of. [ME *bitoknen* : *bi-,* be- + *toknen,* to signify (< OE *tācnian;* see deik- in App.).]

bet·o·ny (bĕt'n-ē) *n., pl.* **-nies 1.** Any of several plants of the widespread genus *Stachys* in the mint family, esp. *S. officinalis,* native chiefly to Europe and once used in medicine. **2.** The lousewort. [ME < OFr. *betoine* < Med.Lat. *betōnia,* both < Lat. *vettōnica,* prob. < *Vettōnēs,* an ancient Iberian tribe.]

be·took (bĭ-tŏok') *v.* Past tense of **betake.**

be·tray (bĭ-trā') *tr.v.* **-trayed, -tray·ing, -trays 1a.** To give aid or information to an enemy of; commit treason against. **b.** To deliver into the hands of an enemy in violation of a trust or allegiance. **2.** To be false or disloyal to. **3.** To divulge in a breach of confidence. **4.** To make known unintentionally. **5.** *To reveal against one's desire or will. **6.** To lead astray; deceive. See Syns at **deceive.** [ME *bitrayen* : *bi-,* be- + *trayen,* to betray (< OFr. *trair* < Lat. *trādere,* to hand over; see TRADITION).] **—be·tray'al** *n.* **—be·tray'er** *n.*

be·troth (bĭ-trōth', -trôth') *tr.v.* **-trothed, -troth·ing, -troths 1.** To promise to give in marriage. **2.** *Archaic* To promise to marry. [ME *bitrouthen* : *bi-,* be- + *trouth,* troth (< OE *trēowth;* see **deru-** in App.).] **—be·trothed'** (-trōthd', -trôtht') *adj. & n.*

be·troth·al (bĭ-trō'thəl, -trô'thəl) *n.* **1.** The act of betrothing or the fact of being betrothed. **2.** A mutual promise to marry.

bet·ta (bĕt'ə) *n.* Any of various species of small, brightly colored, long-finned freshwater fishes of the genus *Betta,* found in southeast Asia. [NLat. *Betta,* genus name.]

bet·ter¹ (bĕt'ər) *adj.* Comparative of **good. 1.** Greater in excellence or higher in quality than another or others. **2.** More useful, suitable, or desirable than another or others. **3.** More highly skilled or adept than another or others. **4.** Greater or larger: *the better part of an hour.* **5.** More advantageous or favorable; improved. **6.** Healthier or more fit than before. ❖ *adv.* Comparative of **well². 1.** In a more excellent way. **2a.** To a greater extent or degree. **b.** To greater advantage; preferably: *better left undone.* See Usage Notes at **best, have, rather. 3.** More: *better than a year.* ❖ *n.* **1.** One that is greater in excellence or higher in quality. **2.** A superior, as in standing, competence, or intelligence. Often used in the plural. ❖ *v.* **-tered, -ter·ing, -ters** **—***tr.* **1.** To make better; improve. **2.** To surpass or exceed. **—***intr.* To become better. **—idioms: better off** In a better or more prosperous condition. **for the better** Resulting in or aiming at an improvement. **think better of** To change one's mind about (a course of action) after reconsideration. [ME < OE *betera.*]

bet·ter² (bĕt'ər) *n.* Variant of **bettor.**

better half *n. Informal* One's spouse. [< *my better half,* the larger part of me, a close friend.]

bet·ter·ment (bĕt'ər-mənt) *n.* **1.** An improvement over what has been the case. **2.** *Law* An improvement beyond normal upkeep that adds to the value of real property.

bet·ter-off (bĕt'ər-ôf', -ŏf') *adj.* Being in a better or more prosperous condition: *a visit to her better-off relatives.*

bet·tor also **bet·ter** (bĕt'ər) *n.* One that bets or places a bet.

be·tween (bĭ-twēn') *prep.* **1a.** In or through the position or interval separating. **b.** Intermediate to, as in quantity, amount, or degree: *between 15 and 20 dollars.* **2.** Connecting spatially. **3.** Associating or uniting in a reciprocal action or relationship. **4.** In confidence restricted to: *Between you and me, he is not qualified.* **5a.** By the combined effort or effect of. **b.** In the combined ownership of: *a few dollars between them.* **6.** As measured against. Often used to express a reciprocal relationship: *choose between riding and walking.* ❖ *adv.* In an intermediate space, position, or time; in the interim. **—idioms: in between** In an intermediate situation. **in between times** During an intervening period; in the meantime. [ME *bitwene* < OE *betwēonum.* See **dwo-** in App.] **—between'ness** *n.*

be·tween·brain (bĭ-twēn'brān') *n.* See **diencephalon.**

be·tween·times (bĭ-twēn'tīmz') *adv.* At or during pauses.

be·twixt (bĭ-twĭkst') *adv. & prep.* Between. **—idiom: betwixt and between** In an intermediate position. [ME *bitwixt* < OE *betwix.* See **dwo-** in App.]

Beu·lah (byōo'lə) *n.* **1.** The land of Israel in the Bible **2.** The land of peace promised in John Bunyan's *Pilgrim's Progress.*

beurre blanc (bûr' blängk', bœr blän') *n.* A sauce made with butter, shallots, and vinegar or lemon juice. [Fr. : *beurre,* butter + *blanc,* white, not browned.]

Beuys (boiz, bois), **Joseph** 1921–86. German sculptor and performance artist also known for his political activism.

BeV *abbr.* billion electron volts

BEV *abbr.* Black English Vernacular

Bev·an (bĕv'ən), **Aneurin** 1897–1960. Welsh-born British politician who as minister of health (1945–51) was the chief architect of the National Health Service.

Mary McLeod Bethune
c. 1943 portrait by Betsy
Graves Reyneau
(1888–1964)

bev·el (bĕv′əl) *n.* **1.** The angle or inclination of a line or surface that meets another at any angle but 90°. **2.** Two rules joined together as adjustable arms used to measure or draw angles of any size or to fix a surface at an angle. ❖ *v.* **-eled, -el·ing, -els** or **-elled, -el·ling, -els** —*tr.* To cut at an inclination that forms an angle other than a right angle. —*intr.* To be inclined; slant. [Poss. < OFr. **bevel,* perh. < *baif,* open-mouthed < *baer,* to gape < VLat. **badāre.*]

bevel gear *n.* Either of a pair of gears with teeth surfaces cut so that they can connect unparallel gear shafts.

bevel square *n.* See **bevel** 2.

bev·er·age (bĕv′ər-ĭj, bĕv′rĭj) *n.* Any one of various liquids for drinking, usu. excluding water. [ME < OFr. *bevrage* < *beivre,* to drink < Lat. *bibere.* See **pō(i)-** in App.]

Bev·er·ly Hills (bĕv′ər-lē) A city of S CA surrounded by Los Angeles. Pop. 33,784.

Bev·in (bĕv′ĭn), **Ernest** 1884–1951. British labor leader and politician who helped draft the NATO treaty of 1949.

bev·y (bĕv′ē) *n., pl.* **-ies 1.** A group of animals or birds, esp. larks or quail. **2.** A group or assemblage. [ME < AN *bevee.*]

be·wail (bĭ-wāl′) *tr.v.* **-wailed, -wail·ing, -wails 1.** To cry over; lament: *bewail the dead.* **2.** To express sorrow or unhappiness over: *"bewailing the possible effects of double-digit unemployment"* (Washington Post). —*intr.* —**be·wail′er** *n.* —**be·wail′ment** *n.*

be·ware (bĭ-wâr′) *v.* **-wared, -war·ing, -wares** —*tr.* To be on guard against; be cautious of: *"Beware the ides of March"* (Shakespeare). —*intr.* To be cautious; exert caution: *We had to beware of the icy patches on the road. Beware of the dog.* [ME *ben war : ben,* to be; see BE + *war,* on one's guard; see WARE².]

be·whisk·ered (bĭ-wĭs′kərd, -wĭs′-) *adj.* Having whiskers.

be·wigged (bĭ-wĭgd′) *adj.* Wearing a wig.

be·wil·der (bĭ-wĭl′dər) *tr.v.* **-dered, -der·ing, -ders 1.** To confuse or befuddle, esp. with numerous conflicting situations, objects, or statements. **2.** To cause to lose one's bearings; disorient. —**be·wil′dered·ly** *adv.* —**be·wil′der·ing·ly** *adv.*

be·wil·der·ment (bĭ-wĭl′dər-mənt) *n.* **1a.** The condition of being confused. **b.** A situation of confusion; a tangle.

be·witch (bĭ-wĭch′) *tr.v.* **-witched, -witch·ing, -witch·es 1.** To place under one's power by magic; cast a spell over. **2.** To captivate completely; entrance. See Syns at **charm.** [ME *biwicchen* : prob. *bi-, be-* + *wicchen* (< OE *wiccian* < *wicce,* witch, or *wicca,* sorcerer).] —**be·witch′er** *n.* —**be·witch′er·y** *n.* —**be·witch′ing·ly** *adv.*

be·witch·ment (bĭ-wĭch′mənt) *n.* **1a.** The act of bewitching. **b.** The power to bewitch. **c.** The state of being bewitched. **2.** A bewitching spell.

be·wray (bĭ-rā′) *tr.v.* **-wrayed, -wray·ing, -wrays** *Archaic* To disclose or betray. [ME *biwreien* : *bi-, be-* + *wreien,* to accuse (< OE *wrēgan*).]

bey (bā) *n.* **1.** A provincial governor in the Ottoman Empire. **2.** A ruler of the former kingdom of Tunis. **3.** Used formerly as a title for various Turkish and Egyptian dignitaries. [Turk. < O Turkic *beg,* ruler, prince.]

be·yond (bē-ŏnd′, bĭ-yŏnd′) *prep.* **1.** On the far side of; past: *Just beyond the fence.* **2.** Later than; after: *beyond midnight.* **3.** To a degree that is past the understanding, reach, or scope of: *beyond remedy.* **4.** To a degree or amount greater than. **5.** In addition to. ❖ *adv.* **1.** Farther along or away. **2.** In addition; more. ❖ *n.* **1.** That which is unknown or unexplored. **2.** The afterlife; the hereafter. [ME *biyonde* < OE *begeondan* : *be,* by; see BY¹ + *geondan,* on the far side of; see **i-** in App.]

bez·ant (bĕz′ənt, bə-zănt′) *n.* **1.** See **solidus** 1. **2.** *Architecture* A flat disk used as an ornament. [ME *besant* < OFr. < Med.Lat. *Bȳzantius* < Lat., of Byzantium.]

bez·el (bĕz′əl) *n.* **1.** A slanting surface or bevel on the edge of a cutting tool. **2.** The upper, faceted portion of a cut gem. **3.** A groove or flange designed to hold a beveled edge, as of a watch crystal or a gem. [Prob. Fr. dialectal; akin to Fr. *biseau* < *bis,* two times < Lat. See **dwo-** in App.]

be·zique (bə-zēk′) *n.* A card game similar to pinochle that is played with a deck of 64 cards. [Fr. *bésigue,* poss. < Ital. *bazzica,* a kind of card game.]

be·zoar (bē′zôr′, -zōr′) *n.* A hard mass of indigestible material found in the stomachs or intestines of humans and animals, once considered a poison antidote. [ME *bezear,* stone poison antidote, prob. < OFr. *bezahar,* gastric or intestinal mass used as poison antidote < Ar. *bāzahr* < Pers. *pādzahr :* *pād-,* protector (< Avestan *pātar-;* see **pā-** in App.) + *zahr,* poison (< MPers.; see **gʷhen-** in App.]

Bez·wa·da (bĕz-wä′də) See **Vijayawada.**

bf *abbr.* boldface

BF *abbr.* **1.** board-foot **2.** also **B/F** *Accounting* brought forward

BFA *abbr.* Bachelor of Fine Arts

BG or **BGen** *abbr.* brigadier general

BGH *abbr.* bovine growth hormone

B-girl (bē′gûrl′) *n.* A woman employed by a bar to encourage customers to spend money freely. [B(AR)¹ + GIRL.]

Bh The symbol for the element **bohrium.**

B/H *abbr.* bill of health

BHA (bē′āch-ā′) *n.* A white, waxy phenolic antioxidant, $C_{11}H_{16}O_2$, used to preserve fats and oils, esp. in foods. [*b(utylated) h(ydroxy)a(nisole).*]

Bha·ga·vad-Gi·ta (bä′gə-väd-gē′tə) *n.* A sacred Hindu text, incorporated into the *Mahabharata,* in which Krishna instructs the prince Arjuna in ethical matters. [Skt. *bhagavad-gītā,* song of the Blessed One (Krishna) : *bhagavat-,* fortunate, blessed (< *bhagaḥ,* good fortune; see **bhag-** in App.) + *gītā,* song (< *gāyati,* he sings).]

bhak·ti (bŭk′tē) *n.* *Hinduism* The devotional way of achieving salvation, emphasizing loving faith for a deity and open to all. [Skt. *bhaktiḥ,* devotion < *bhajati,* he apportions. See **bhag-** in App.]

bhang also **bang** (băng, bäng) *n.* A preparation from the leaves and seed capsules of the cannabis plant, smoked or ingested to obtain mild euphoria. [Ult. < Skt. *bhaṅgā.*]

bhan·gra (bŭng′grä′) *n.* **1.** A Punjabi dance music traditionally performed during harvest festivals and weddings, characterized by the beating of a large, two-headed drum. **2.** A style of Western popular music incorporating such drumming. [Punjabi *bhāṅgrā.*]

Bhat·pa·ra (bät-pä′rə) A city of NE India on the Hugli R. N of Calcutta. Pop. 304,952.

Bhav·na·gar (bou-nŭg′ər, bäv-) A city of W India on the Gulf of Khambhat S of Ahmadabad. Pop. 402,338.

BHC *abbr.* benzene hexachloride

Bhn *abbr.* Brinell hardness number

Bho·lan Pass (bō-län′) See **Bolan Pass.**

Bho·pal (bō-päl′) A city of central India NNW of Nagpur; site of a 1984 toxic gas leak that killed more than 2,000 people. Pop. 1,062,771.

B horizon *n.* In ABC soil, the second or subsurface zone of soil made of clay and oxidized materials and organic matter leached from the A-horizon; subsoil.

bhp or **b.hp.** *abbr.* brake horsepower

BHT (bē′āch-tē′) *n.* A crystalline phenolic antioxidant, $C_{15}H_{24}O$, used to preserve fats and oils, esp. in foods. [B(UTYLATED) H(YDROXY)T(OLUENE).]

Bhu. *abbr.* Bhutan

Bhu·ba·nes·war (boō′bə-nĕsh′wər) A city of E-central India SW of Calcutta; known for its Hindu and Buddhist shrines. Pop. 411,542.

Bhu·tan (boō-tän′, -tän′) An isolated country of central Asia in the E Himalaya Mts. Cap. Thimbu. Pop. 1,614,000.

Bhu·tan·ese (boō′tə-nēz′, -nēs′) *adj.* Of or relating to Bhutan or its people, language, or culture. ❖ *n., pl.* **Bhutanese 1.** A native or inhabitant of Bhutan. **2.** The Sino-Tibetan language of Bhutan.

Bhut·to (boō′tō), **Benazir** b. 1953. Pakistani politician who served as prime minister (1988–90 and 1993–96).

Bhutto, Zulfikar Ali 1928–79. Pakistani prime minister (1973–77); deposed by a coup d'état and later executed.

bi (bī) *Slang n., pl.* **bis** or **bi's** A bisexual person. ❖ *adj.* Bisexual.

Bi The symbol for the element **bismuth.**

bi-¹ or **bin-** *pref.* **1a.** Two: *biform.* **b.** Both: *binaural.* **c.** Both sides, parts, or directions: *biconcave.* **2a.** Occurring at intervals of two: *bicentennial.* **b.** *Usage Problem* Occurring twice during: *biweekly.* **3a.** Containing twice the proportion of a specified chemical element or group necessary for stability: *bicarbonate.* **b.** Containing two chemical atoms, radicals, or groups: *biphenyl.* [Lat. *bis, bi-,* twice, and *bīnī,* two by two; see App.]

USAGE NOTE *Bimonthly* and *biweekly* mean "once every two months" and "once every two weeks." For "twice a month" and "twice a week," the words *semimonthly* and *semiweekly* should be used. Because of this potential confusion, a writer is well advised to substitute expressions like *twice a month* where possible. However, each noun form has only one sense in the publishing world. Thus, a *bimonthly* is published every two months, and a *biweekly* every two weeks.

bi-² *pref.* Variant of **bio-.**

BIA *abbr.* Bureau of Indian Affairs

Bi·a·fra (bē-ăf′rə, -äf′rə) A region of E Nigeria on the **Bight of Biafra,** an arm of the Gulf of Guinea stretching from the Niger R. delta to N Gabon. It formed a secessionist state from May 1967 to Jan. 1970. —**Bi·a′fran** *adj. & n.*

Bi·ak (bē-yäk′) The largest of the Schouten Is. of Indonesia off

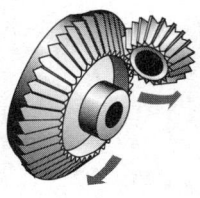

bevel gear

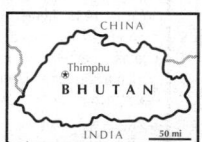

Bhutan

---

bi·ax′i·al *adj.*	bi′col·ored *adj.*	bi·lob′u·lar *adj.*	bi·mor′phe′mic *adj.*
bi·ax′i·al·ly *adv.*	bi·cul′tur·al *adj.*	bi·loc′u·lar *adj.*	bi·na′tion·al *adj.*
bi·cel′lu·lar *adj.*	bi·cul′tur·al·ism *n.*	bi·loc′u·late *adj.*	bi·pa′ren·tal *adj.*
bi·cen′tric *adj.*	bi·di′a·lec′tal *adj.*	bi·man′u·al *adj.*	bi·ra′mous *adj.*
bi·cen′tric·i·ty *n.*	bi·flag′el·late *adj.*	bi·max′il·lar′y *adj.*	bi·se′ri·ate *adj.*
bi′col·or *adj.*	bi·lo′bate *adj.*	bi·mo′lec·u·lar *adj.*	bi′state′ *adj.*

the NW coast of New Guinea.

bi·a·ly (bē-ä′lē) *n., pl.* **-lys** A flat, round baked roll topped with onion flakes. [After BIAŁYSTOK.]

Bia·ły·stok (bē-ä′lĭ-stôk′, byä′wĭ-) A city of NE Poland near the border of Belarus. About half the city's population was killed by Nazi occupation forces (1941–44). Pop. 272,137.

Bi·an·ca (byăng′kä, bē-äng′kə) *n.* A satellite of Uranus. [After *Bianca*, sister of Katherine in *The Taming of the Shrew* by William Shakespeare.]

bi·an·nu·al (bī-ăn′yōō-əl) *adj.* **1.** Happening twice each year; semiannual. **2.** Occurring every two years; biennial. See Usage Note at **bi-**[1]. **—bi·an′nu·al·ly** *adv.*

Biar·ritz (bē′ə-rĭts′, bē′ə-rĭts′) A city of SW France on the Bay of Biscay near the Spanish border. Pop. 26,598.

bi·as (bī′əs) *n.* **1.** A line going diagonally across the grain of fabric. **2a.** A preference or an inclination, esp. one that inhibits impartial judgment. See Syns at **predilection**. **b.** An unfair act or policy stemming from prejudice. **3.** A statistical sampling or testing error caused by systematically favoring some outcomes over others. **4.** *Sports* **a.** A weight or irregularity in a ball that causes it to swerve. **b.** The tendency of such a ball to swerve. **5.** The fixed voltage applied to an electrode. ❖ *adj.* Slanting or diagonal; oblique: *a bias fold.* ❖ *tr.v.* **-ased, -as·ing, -as·es** or **-assed, -as·sing, -as·ses** **1.** To influence in a particular, typically unfair direction; prejudice. See Syns at **incline**. **2.** To apply a small voltage to (a grid). [Fr. *biais*, slant < Provençal, perh. ult. < Gk. *epikarsios*, slanted. See **sker-**[1] in App.]

bias crime *n.* A hate crime.

bi·ased also **bi·assed** (bī′əst) *adj.* Marked by bias.

bi·as-ply tire (bī′əs-plī′) *n.* A pneumatic tire having crossed layers of ply cord running diagonally to the tread.

bi·ath·lon (bī-ăth′lŏn, -lŏn′) *n.* **1.** A competition that combines events in cross-country skiing and rifle shooting. **2.** An athletic contest in which participants compete in two successive events, such as long-distance swimming and running. [BI-[1] + Gk. *āthlon*, prize of contest.] **—bi·ath′lete** (-lēt) *n.*

bib (bĭb) *n.* **1.** A piece of cloth or plastic secured under the chin and worn to protect the clothing while eating. **2a.** The part of an apron or pair of overalls worn over the chest. **b.** Bibbed overalls worn while skiing. ❖ *tr. & intr.v.* **bibbed, bib·bing, bibs** To drink or to indulge in drinking. [Prob. < ME *bibben*, to drink heartily < Lat. *bibere.* See **pō(i)-** in App.]

Bib. *abbr.* **1.** Bible **2.** also **bib.** biblical

bib and tucker *n. Informal* Clothing.

bibb (bĭb) *n.* A bibcock. [Alteration of BIB.]

bibbed (bĭbd) *adj.* Having a bib: *bibbed overalls.*

bib·ber (bĭb′ər) *n.* A tippler; a drinker. [< BIB.]

Bibb lettuce *n.* A kind of lettuce forming a small, loose head and having tender, dark green leaves. [After Jack *Bibb*, 19th-cent. American vegetable grower.]

bib·cock (bĭb′kŏk′) *n.* A faucet with a nozzle that is bent downward. [Prob. BIB + COCK[1].]

bi·be·lot (bē′bə-lō′, bē-blō′) *n.* **1.** A small decorative object; a trinket. **2.** A miniature book, esp. one that is finely crafted. [Fr. < OFr. *beubelet* < a redup. of *bel*, beautiful < Lat. *bellus*, handsome. See BELLE.]

Bi·ble (bī′bəl) *n.* **1a.** The sacred book of Christianity, a collection of ancient writings including both the Old Testament and the New Testament. **b.** The Hebrew Scriptures, the sacred book of Judaism. **c.** A particular copy of a Bible. **d.** A book or collection of writings constituting the sacred text of a religion. **2.** often **bible** A book considered authoritative in its field. [ME < OFr. < LLat. *biblia* < Gk., pl. of *biblion*, book, dim. of *biblos*, papyrus, book < *Bublos*, Byblos.]

Bible belt *n.* Those sections of the US, esp. in the South and Midwest, where Protestant fundamentalism is widely practiced.

Bible paper *n.* A thin, strong, opaque printing paper used for Bibles and reference books.

bib·li·cal also **Bib·li·cal** (bĭb′lĭ-kəl) *adj.* **1.** Of, relating to, or contained in the Bible. **2.** Being in keeping with the nature of the Bible. **3.** Very great in extent; enormous: *a disaster of near biblical proportions.* [< Med.Lat. *biblicus* < LLat. *biblia*, Bible. See BIBLE.] **—Bib′li·cal·ly** *adv.*

Bib·li·cist (bĭb′lĭ-sĭst) *n.* **1.** An expert on the Bible. **2.** One who interprets the Bible literally. **—Bib′li·cism** *n.*

biblio– *pref.* Book: *bibliophile.* [< Gk. *biblion*, book. See BIBLE.]

bib·li·og·ra·pher (bĭb′lē-ŏg′rə-fər) *n.* **1.** One trained in the description and cataloging of printed matter. **2.** One who compiles a bibliography.

bib·li·og·ra·phy (bĭb′lē-ŏg′rə-fē) *n., pl.* **-phies** **1.** A list of the works of a specific author or publisher. **2a.** A list of writings relating to a given subject. **b.** A list of writings used or considered by an author in preparing a particular work. **3a.** The description and identification of the editions, dates of issue, authorship, and typography of books or other written material. **b.** A compilation of such information. **—bib′li·o·graph′i·cal** (-ə-grăf′ĭ-kəl), **bib′li·o·graph′ic** (-ĭk) *adj.* **—bib′li·o·graph′i·cal·ly** *adv.*

bib·li·o·la·try (bĭb′lē-ŏl′ə-trē) *n.* **1.** Excessive adherence to a literal interpretation of the Bible. **2.** Extreme devotion to books. **—bib′li·o·la′ter** *n.* **—bib′li·o·la′trous** *adj.*

bib·li·o·man·cy (bĭb′lē-ə-măn′sē) *n., pl.* **-cies** Divination by interpretation of a passage chosen at random from a book.

bib·li·o·ma·ni·a (bĭb′lē-ə-mā′nē-ə, -mān′yə) *n.* An exaggerated preoccupation with owning books. **—bib′li·o·ma′ni·ac′** (-ăk′) *n.* **—bib′li·o·ma·ni′a·cal** (-mə-nī′ə-kəl) *adj.*

bib·li·o·phile (bĭb′lē-ə-fīl′) also **bib·li·o·phil** (-fĭl′) *n.* **1.** A lover of books. **2.** A collector of books. **—bib′li·oph′i·lism** *n.* **—bib′li·oph′i·lis′tic** *adj.*

bib·li·o·pole (bĭb′lē-ə-pōl′) also **bib·li·op·o·list** (bĭb′lē-ŏp′ə-lĭst) *n.* A dealer in rare books. [Lat. *bibliopōla*, bookseller < Gk. *bibliopōlēs* : *biblio-*, biblio- + *pōlein*, to sell.] **—bib′li·o·pol′ic** (-pŏl′ĭk), **bib′li·o·pol′i·cal** *adj.*

bib·li·o·the·ca (bĭb′lē-ə-thē′kə) *n.* **1.** A collection of books; a library. **2.** A catalog of books. [Lat. *bibliothēca* < Gk. *bibliothēkē* : *biblio-*, biblio- + *thēkē*, case; see **dhē-** in App.]

bib·li·o·ther·a·py (bĭb′lē-ō-thĕr′ə-pē) *n.* The use of selected reading materials as a form of supportive psychotherapy.

bib·li·ot·ics (bĭb′lē-ŏt′ĭks) *n.* (used with a sing. verb) Examination of written documents to determine authorship or authenticity.

bib·u·lous (bĭb′yə-ləs) *adj.* **1.** Given to or marked by the consumption of alcoholic drink: *a bibulous evening.* **2.** Very absorbent, as paper or soil. [< Lat. *bibulus* < *bibere*, to drink. See **pō(i)-** in App.] **—bib′u·lous·ly** *adv.* **—bib′u·lous·ness** *n.*

bi·cam·er·al (bī-kăm′ər-əl) *adj.* Composed of two chambers or branches, as a legislature. [BI-[1] + Lat. *camera*, chamber; see CHAMBER + –AL[1].] **—bi·cam′er·al·ism** *n.*

bi·car·bon·ate (bī-kär′bə-nāt′, -nĭt) *n.* The radical group HCO₃ or a compound containing it.

bicarbonate of soda *n.* See baking soda.

bi·cau·dal (bī-kôd′l) *adj. Zoology* Having two tails.

bice blue (bīs) *n.* A moderate blue. [ME *bis*, blue-gray (sense uncertain) < OFr. *bis*, dark.]

bice green *n.* A moderate yellow green. [BICE (BLUE) + GREEN.]

bi·cen·ten·a·ry (bī′sĕn-tĕn′ə-rē, bī-sĕn′tə-nĕr′ē) *n., pl.* **-ries** See bicentennial. **—bi′cen·ten′a·ry** *adj.*

bi·cen·ten·ni·al (bī′sĕn-tĕn′ē-əl) *adj.* **1.** Happening once every 200 years. **2.** Lasting for 200 years. **3.** Relating to a 200th anniversary. **—bi′cen·ten′ni·al** *n.*

bi·ceph·a·lous (bī-sĕf′ə-ləs) *adj. Zoology* Having two heads.

bi·ceps (bī′sĕps′) *n., pl.* **biceps** or **-ceps·es** (-sĕp′sĭz) **1.** A muscle with two heads or points of origin. **2a.** The large muscle at the front of the upper arm that flexes the forearm. **b.** The large mus-

---

BOOKS OF THE BIBLE

Books of the Hebrew Scriptures appear as listed in the translation by the Jewish Publication Society of America. Books of the Christian Bible appear as listed in the Jerusalem Bible, a 1966 translation of the 1956 French Roman Catholic version. The Old Testament books shown in italic are considered apocryphal in many Christian churches, but they are accepted as canonical in the Roman Catholic Church, the Eastern Orthodox Church, and the Armenian and the Ethiopian Oriental Orthodox Church. The Christian Old Testament parallels the Hebrew Scriptures with the exception of these books.

HEBREW SCRIPTURES		CHRISTIAN BIBLE		
The Torah		**Old Testament**		**New Testament**
Genesis		Genesis	*Wisdom of Solomon*	Matthew
Exodus		Exodus	*Ecclesiasticus*	Mark
Leviticus		Leviticus	Isaiah	Luke
Numbers		Numbers	Jeremiah	John
Deuteronomy		Deuteronomy	Lamentations	Acts of the Apostles
		Joshua	*Baruch*	Romans
The Prophets		Judges	Ezekiel	I Corinthians
		Ruth	Daniel	II Corinthians
Joshua	Amos	I Samuel	Hosea	Galatians
Judges	Obadiah	II Samuel	Joel	Ephesians
I Samuel	Jonah	I Kings	Amos	Philippians
II Samuel	Micah	II Kings	Obadiah	Colossians
I Kings	Nahum	I Chronicles	Jonah	I Thessalonians
II Kings	Habakkuk	II Chronicles	Micah	II Thessalonians
Isaiah	Zephaniah	Ezra	Nahum	I Timothy
Jeremiah	Haggai	Nehemiah	Habakkuk	II Timothy
Ezekiel	Zechariah	*Tobit*	Zephaniah	Titus
Hosea	Malachi	*Judith*	Haggai	Philemon
Joel		Esther	Zechariah	Hebrews
		I Maccabees	Malachi	James
The Writings		*II Maccabees*		I Peter
		Job		II Peter
Psalms	Esther	Psalms		I John
Proverbs	Daniel	Proverbs		II John
Job	Ezra	Ecclesiastes		III John
Song of Songs	Nehemiah	Song of Songs		Jude
Ruth	I Chronicles	(Song of Solomon)		Revelation
Lamentations	II Chronicles			
Ecclesiastes				

cle at the back of the thigh that flexes the knee joint. [< Lat., two-headed : *bi-*, two; see BI–[1] + *caput*, head; see **kaput-** in App.]

bi•chlo•ride (bī-klôr′īd, -klōr′-) *n.* See **dichloride.**

bi•chon fri•sé (bē-shŏn′ frē-zā′, frēz, bē′shŏn) *n., pl.* **bi•chons fri•sés** (bē-shŏn′ frē-zā′, frēz, bē′shŏn) Any of a European breed of small dogs having a wavy white coat, drooping ears, and a curved tail. [Fr. : *bichon*, lapdog + *frisé*, curly.]

bi•chro•mate (bī-krō′māt′, -mĭt) *n.* See **dichromate.**

bi•cip•i•tal (bī-sĭp′ĭ-tl) *adj.* **1.** Having two heads or points of origin, as a muscle. **2.** Of or relating to a biceps. [< Lat. *biceps, bicipit-*, two-headed. See BICEPS.]

bick•er (bĭk′ər) *intr.v.* **-ered, -er•ing, -ers 1.** To engage in a petty, bad-tempered quarrel; squabble. **2.** To flicker; quiver. ❖ *n.* A petty quarrel; a squabble. [ME *bikeren*, to attack.] **—bick′er•er** *n.*

bi•coas•tal (bī-kō′stəl) *adj.* Relating to or occurring on the east and west coasts of the United States.

bi•con•cave (bī′kŏn-kāv′, bī-kŏn′kāv′) *adj.* Concave on both sides or surfaces. **—bi′con•cav′i•ty** (-kăv′ĭ-tē) *n.*

bi•con•vex (bī′kŏn-vĕks′, bī-kŏn′vĕks′) *adj.* Convex on both sides or surfaces. **—bi′con•vex′i•ty** (-vĕk′sĭ-tē) *n.*

bi•cor•nu•ate (bī-kôr′nyo͞o-ĭt, -āt′) also **bi•corn** (bī′kôrn′) *adj.* **1.** Having two horns or horn-shaped parts. **2.** Shaped like a crescent. [< BI–[1] + Lat. *cornū*, horn; see **ker-**[1] in App.]

bi•cus•pid (bī-kŭs′pĭd) *adj.* Having two points or cusps, as the crescent moon. ❖ *n.* A bicuspid tooth, esp. a premolar. [NLat. *bicuspis, bicuspid-* : Lat. *bi-*, two; see BI–[1] + Lat. *cuspis*, sharp point.]

bicuspid valve *n.* See **mitral valve.**

bi•cy•cle (bī′sĭk′əl, -sĭ-kəl, -sī′kəl) *n.* **1.** A vehicle consisting of a light frame mounted on two wheels one behind the other and having a seat, handlebars for steering, brakes, and two pedals or a small motor by which it is driven. **2.** An exercise bicycle. ❖ *intr.v.* **-cled, -cling, -cles** To ride or travel on a bicycle. [Prob. BI–[1] + *-cycle* (on the model of TRICYCLE, three-wheeled coach).] **—bi′cy•cler** (-klər), **bi′cy•clist** (-klĭst) *n.*

bi•cy•clic (bī-sī′klĭk, -sĭk′lĭk) also **bi•cy•cli•cal** (-sī′klĭ-kəl, -sĭk′lĭ-) *adj.* **1.** Consisting of or having two cycles. **2.** *Botany* Composed of or arranged in two distinct whorls. **3.** *Chemistry* Containing molecules consisting of two fused rings.

bid (bĭd) *v.* **bade** (băd, bād) or **bid, bid•den** (bĭd′n) or **bid, bid•ding, bids —***tr.* **1.** To issue a command to; direct. **2.** To utter (a greeting or salutation). **3.** To invite to attend; summon. **4.** *past tense and past participle* **bid** *Games* To state one's intention to take (tricks in cards). **5.** *past tense and past participle* **bid a.** To offer or propose (an amount) as a price. **b.** To offer (someone) membership, as in a club. —*intr. past tense and past participle* **bid 1.** To make an offer to pay or accept a specified price. **2.** To seek to win or attain something; strive. ❖ *n.* **1a.** An offer or proposal of a price. **b.** The amount offered or proposed. **2.** An invitation, esp. one offering membership in a group or club. **3.** *Games* **a.** The act of bidding in cards. **b.** The number of tricks or points declared. **c.** The trump or no-trump declared. **d.** The turn of a player to bid. **4.** An earnest effort to win or attain something. ***—phrasal verbs:* bid in** To outbid on one's own property at an auction in order to raise the final selling price. **bid out** To offer (work) for bids from outside contractors. **bid up** To cause (a price) to rise by increasing the amount bid. ***—idiom:* bid fair** To appear likely. [ME *bidden*, to ask, command (< OE *biddan*) and ME *beden*, to offer, proclaim (< OE *bēodan*; see **bheudh-** in App.).] **—bid′der** *n.*

b.i.d. *abbr. Latin* bis in die (twice a day)

bid•da•ble (bĭd′ə-bəl) *adj.* **1.** *Games* Strong enough to be bid. Used of a hand of cards. **2.** Following directions or obeying commands; docile.

bid•ding (bĭd′ĭng) *n.* **1.** A demand that something be done; a command. **2.** A request to appear; a summons. **3.** Bids considered as a group, as at an auction or in card games.

Bid•dle (bĭd′l), **John** 1615–62. English theologian and founder of English Unitarianism.

bid•dy[1] (bĭd′ē) *n., pl.* **-dies** A hen; a fowl. [?]

bid•dy[2] (bĭd′ē) *n., pl.* **-dies** *Slang* A woman, esp. a garrulous old one. [Nickname for *Bridget.*]

bide (bīd) *v.* **bid•ed** or **bode** (bōd), **bid•ed, bid•ing, bides** —*intr.* **1.** To remain in a condition or state. **2a.** To wait; tarry. **b.** To stay; dwell. —*tr.* Past tense **bided** To await; wait for. ***—idiom:* bide (one's) time** To wait for further developments. [ME *biden* < OE *bīdan*. See **bheidh-** in App.]

bi•den•tate (bī-dĕn′tāt′) *adj.* Having two teeth or toothlike parts.

bi•det (bē-dā′) *n.* A fixture similar in design to a toilet that is straddled for bathing the genitals and the posterior parts. [Fr., pony, bidet, prob. < OFr. *bider*, to trot.]

bi•di also **bee•di** (bē′dē) *n., pl.* **bi•dis** also **bee•dies** A thin, often flavored Indian cigarette made of tobacco wrapped in a tendu leaf. [Hindi *bīṛī* < Skt. *vīṭakam, vīṭikam*, areca nut and spices rolled up in a betel leaf.]

bi•di•rec•tion•al (bī′dī-rĕk′shə-nəl, -dī-) *adj.* Moving or operating in two usu. opposite directions: *bidirectional data flow.*

bi•don•ville (bē′dôN-vēl′) *n.* A shantytown on the outskirts of a city, esp. in France or North Africa. [Fr. : *bidon*, gas can, oildrum (< OFr., bottle, tankard, prob. of Scand. orig.) + *ville*, town; see VILLAGE.]

Bie•der•mei•er (bē′dər-mī′ər) *adj.* Of or relating to a type of furniture developed in Germany during the first half of the 19th century and modeled after French Empire styles. [After Gottlieb *Biedermeier*, the unsophisticated imaginary author of poems written by Ludwig Eichrodt (1827–92) and others.]

Biel (bēl) also **Bi•enne** (bē-ĕn′) A city of NW Switzerland at the NE end of the **Lake of Biel** at the foot of the Jura Mts. Pop. 52,600.

Bie•le•feld (bē′lə-fĕlt′) A city of NW Germany E of Münster. Pop. 324,674.

Biel•sko-Bia•ła (byĕl′skô-byä′lä, -byä′wä) A city of S Poland S of Katowice; passed to Austria in 1772 and was returned to Poland in 1919. Pop. 184,108.

bi•en•ni•al (bī-ĕn′ē-əl) *adj.* **1.** Lasting or living for two years. **2.** Happening every second year. **3.** *Botany* Having a life cycle normally of two growing seasons. ❖ *n.* **1.** An event that occurs every two years. **2.** *Botany* **a.** A biennial plant. **b.** A perennial plant cultivated as a biennial. **—bi•en′ni•al•ly** *adv.*

bi•en•ni•um (bī-ĕn′ē-əm) *n., pl.* **-en•ni•ums** or **-en•ni•a** (-ĕn′ē-ə) A two-year period. [Lat. : *bi-*, two; see BI–[1] + *annus*, year.]

Bien•ville (byĕn′vĭl′, byăN-vēl′), Sieur **Jean Baptiste Lemoyne de** 1680–1768. French colonial administrator who as governor of Louisiana founded New Orleans (1718).

bier (bîr) *n.* **1.** A stand on which a corpse or a coffin is placed before burial. **2.** A coffin along with its stand. [Alteration (influenced by Fr. *bière*, coffin) of ME *ber* < OE *bēr*. See **bher-**[1] in App.]

Bierce (bîrs), **Ambrose Gwinett** 1842–1914? Amer. writer whose satiric works include *The Devil's Dictionary* (1906).

Bier•stadt (bîr′stăt′, -shtăt′), **Albert** 1830–1902. German-born Amer. landscape painter noted for his romanticized works, including *Domes of the Yosemite* (1864).

Bierstadt, Mount A peak, 4,288.3 m (14,000 ft), of N-central CO in the Front Range of the Rocky Mts.

bi•face (bī′fās′) *n. Archaeology* A bifacial stone tool.

bi•fa•cial (bī-fā′shəl) *adj.* **1.** Having two faces, fronts, or façades. **2.** Having two opposing surfaces that are alike. **3.** *Archaeology* Of or being a stone tool having a flaked edge that is sharp on both sides. **—bi•fa′cial•ly** *adv.*

biff[1] (bĭf) *Informal tr.v.* **biffed, biff•ing, biffs** To strike or punch. ❖ *n.* A blow or punch. [< E. *biff*, interj., prob. of imit. orig.]

biff[2] (bĭf) *n. Upper Midwest* Variant of **biffy.**

bif•fy (bĭf′ē) also **biff** (bĭf) *n., pl.* **-fies** also **biffs** *Upper Midwest* **1.** An outdoor toilet; an outhouse. **2.** An indoor toilet. [Perh. alteration of PRIVY.]

bi•fid (bī′fĭd) *adj.* Forked or cleft into two parts: *a bifid petal.* **—bi•fid′i•ty** (-fĭd′ĭ-tē) *n.* **—bi′fid•ly** *adv.*

bi•fi•lar (bī-fī′lər) *adj.* Fitted with or involving the use of two threads or wires. **—bi•fi′lar•ly** *adv.*

bi•fo•cal (bī-fō′kəl, bī′fō′-) *adj.* **1.** Having two focal lengths. **2.** Having one section that corrects for distant vision and another that corrects for near vision, as an eyeglass lens. ❖ *pl.n.* **bi•fo•cals** (bī-fō′kəlz, bī′fō′-) Eyeglasses with bifocal lenses. **—bi•fo′cal•ism** *n.*

bi•fo•caled (bī-fō′kəld) *adj.* Wearing bifocals.

bi•fo•li•o•late (bī-fō′lē-ə-lāt′, -lĭt) *adj. Botany* Having two leaflets.

bi•form (bī′fôrm′) *adj.* Having a combination of features or qualities of two distinct forms. [Lat. *bifōrmis* : *bi-*, two; see BI–[1] + *fōrma*, form; see FORM.]

bi•func•tion•al (bī-fŭngk′shə-nəl) *adj.* **1.** Having two functions: *bifunctional neurons.* **2.** *Chemistry* Having or involving two functional groups or binding sites: *bifunctional reagents.*

bi•fur•cate (bī′fər-kāt′, bī-fûr′-) *tr. & intr.v.* **-cat•ed, -cat•ing, -cates** To divide or be divided into two parts or branches. ❖ *adj.* (-kāt′, -kĭt) Forked or divided into two parts or branches. [Med. Lat. *bifurcāre, bifurcāt-*, to divide < Lat. *bifurcus*, two-pronged : *bi-*, two; see BI–[1] + *furca*, fork.] **—bi′fur•cate′ly** *adv.* **—bi′fur•ca′tion** *n.*

big (bĭg) *adj.* **big•ger, big•gest 1.** Of considerable size, number, quantity, magnitude, or extent; large. See Syns at **large. 2a.** Of great force; strong: *a big wind.* **b.** *Obsolete* Of great strength. **3a.** Mature or grown-up. **b.** Older or eldest. Used esp. of a sibling. **4.** Pregnant: *big with child.* **5.** Filled up; brimming over. **6.** Having or exercising considerable authority, control, or influence: *a big official.* **7.** Conspicuous in position, wealth, or importance; prominent. **8.** Of great significance; momentous: *a big decision.* **9.** Widely liked, used, or practiced; popular. **10.** *Informal* Self-important; cocky. **11.** Loud and firm; resounding: *a big voice.* **12.** Bountiful; generous: *a big heart.* ❖ *adv.* **1.** In a pretentious or boastful way. **2.** *Informal* **a.** With considerable success: *made it big.* **b.** In a thorough or unmistakable way; emphatically. ***—idiom:* big on** Enthusiastic about; partial to. [ME, perh. of Scand. orig.] **—big′gish** *adj.* **—big′ly** *adv.* **—big′ness** *n.*

big•a•mous (bĭg′ə-məs) *adj.* **1.** Involving bigamy. **2.** Guilty of bigamy. **—big′a•mous•ly** *adv.*

big•a•my (bĭg′ə-mē) *n.* The criminal offense of marrying one person while still legally married to another. [ME *bigamie* < OFr.

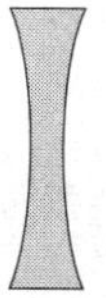

biconcave
biconcave lens

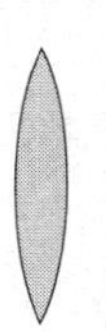

biconvex
biconvex lens

ă pat	oi boy
ā pay	ou out
âr care	o͝o took
ä father	o͞o boot
ĕ pet	ŭ cut
ē be	ûr urge
ĭ pit	th thin
ī pie	*th* this
îr pier	hw which
ŏ pot	zh vision
ō toe	ə about, item
ô paw	

Stress marks:
′ (primary);
′ (secondary), as in
lexicon (lĕk′sĭ-kŏn′)

< Med.Lat. *bigamia* < LLat. *bigamus*, twice married : Lat. *bi-*, two; see BI-[1] + Gk. *gamos*, marriage; see –GAMOUS.] —**big′a·mist** *n.*

bi·ga·rade (bē′gä-räd′) *n.* **1.** See **sour orange. 2.** A rich sauce served with duck, consisting of stock and flavorings. [Fr. < Provençal *bigarrado* < p. part. of *bigarrar*, to variegate < OFr. *bigarrer* : *bi-*, two (< Lat.; see BI-[1]) + *garrer*, to variegate (< *garre*, of two colors).]

big band or **Big Band** *n.* A large dance or jazz band.

big bang *n.* The cosmic explosion that marked the origin of the universe according to the big bang theory.

big bang theory *n.* A cosmological theory holding that the universe originated approx. 10 to 15 billion years ago from the explosion of a very small agglomeration of hot, dense matter.

Big Bend A region of SW TX on the Mexican border in a triangle formed by a bend in the Rio Grande.

Big Black River A river rising in N-central MS and flowing c. 531 km (330 mi) to the Mississippi R.

Big Blue River A river rising in SE NE and flowing c. 483 km (300 mi) to the Kansas R. in NE KS.

big brother *n.* **1.** An older brother. **2.** A man who assumes this role. **3.** also **Big Brother** A ruthlessly oppressive or authoritarian state, organization, or leader. [Sense 3, after *Big Brother*, a character in the novel *1984* by George Orwell.]

big bucks *pl.n. Slang* A large amount of money.

big business *n.* Commercial operations organized and financed on a large scale.

big C *n. Slang* The disease cancer. Used with *the.*

big daddy or **Big Daddy** *n. Slang* **1.** One that is predominant or big, as in size, influence, or priority. **2.** One that exercises a paternalistic authority or control.

big deal *n. Slang* **1.** Something of great importance: *made a big deal out of getting there on time.* **2.** An important person. ❖ *interj.* Used ironically to indicate that something is unimportant or unimpressive. —**big′-deal′** (bĭg′dēl′) *adj.*

Big Diomede Island See **Diomede Islands.**

Big Dipper *n.* A cluster of seven stars in the constellation Ursa Major, forming a dipper-shaped configuration.

bi·gem·i·nal (bī-jĕm′ə-nəl) *adj.* Occurring in pairs; doubled or twinned: *a bigeminal pulse.* [Poss. < LLat. *bigeminus*, doubled : Lat. *bi-*, two; see BI-[1] + Lat. *geminus*, double.]

bi·gem·i·ny (bī-jĕm′ə-nē) *n. Medicine* **1.** An association in pairs. **2.** An abnormal pulse characterized by two beats in rapid succession followed by a pause.

big enchilada or **Big Enchilada** *n. Slang* **1.** One who is in charge. **2.** Something of the highest value or importance. [On the model of such expressions as *big cheese.*]

bi·ge·ner·ic (bī′jə-nĕr′ĭk) *adj.* **1.** Relating to a hybrid that results from a cross between plants of different genera. **2.** Having the characteristics of two different genera.

big·eye (bĭg′ī′) *n.* Any of several small tropical marine fishes of the family Priacanthidae, having large eyes and reddish scales.

Big·foot (bĭg′fŏot′) *n.* A very large, hairy, humanlike creature purported to inhabit the Pacific Northwest and Canada.

big game *n.* **1.** Large animals or fish hunted or caught for sport. **2.** *Informal* An important objective. —**big′-game′** (bĭg′gām′) *adj.*

big·gie (bĭg′ē) *n. Slang* **1.** A very important person. **2.** Something that is considered big or important.

big·gi·ty also **big·ge·ty** (bĭg′ĭ-tē) *adj. Informal* Self-important; conceited. [< BIG.]

big gun *n. Slang* One that is powerful or influential.

big·head (bĭg′hĕd′) *n.* **1.** *Informal* Conceit; egotism. **2.** also **big head** Any of various diseases of animals, esp. rams, characterized by swelling of the head, face, or neck. —**big′head′ed** *adj.* —**big′head′ed·ness** *n.*

big·heart·ed (bĭg′här′tĭd) *adj.* Generous; kind. —**big′-heart′ed·ly** *adv.* —**big′heart′ed·ness** *n.*

big·horn (bĭg′hôrn′) *n., pl.* **bighorn** or **-horns** A wild sheep (*Ovis canadensis*) of the mountains of western North America, the male of which has massive curved horns.

bighorn
bighorn ram
Ovis canadensis

Bighorn Mountains A section of the Rocky Mts. of N WY and S MT rising to 4,018.4 m (13,175 ft).

Bighorn River A river rising in W-central WY and flowing c. 742 km (461 mi) to join the Yellowstone R. in S MT.

big house *n. Slang* A penitentiary.

bight (bīt) *n.* **1a.** A loop in a rope. **b.** The middle or slack part of an extended rope. **2a.** A bend or curve, esp. in a shoreline. **b.** A wide bay formed by such a bend or curve. [ME, bend, angle < OE *byht*.]

big league *n.* **1.** *Sports* A major league. **2.** *Informal* The most prestigious level of accomplishment. —**big′-league′** (bĭg′lēg′) *adj.* —**big leaguer** *n.*

big lie *n.* Intentional distortion of the truth, esp. for political purposes.

big money *n. Slang* **1.** A large amount of money, as in profits or salary: *made big money on the transaction.* **2.** A large-scale commercial enterprise. —**big′-mon′ey** (bĭg′mŭn′ē) *adj.*

big·mouth (bĭg′mouth′) *n.* **1.** *Slang* A loudmouthed or gossipy person. **2.** Any of various fishes having unusually large mouths.

big·mouthed (bĭg′mouthd′, -moutht′) *adj.* **1.** *Slang* Speaking loudly and indiscreetly. **2.** Having a large mouth.

Big Muddy River A river of SW IL flowing c. 217 km (135 mi) to the Mississippi R.

big·no·ni·a (bĭg-nō′nē-ə) *n.* An evergreen woody vine (*Bignonia capreolata*) native chiefly to the southeast United States and having trumpet-shaped flowers. [NLat. *Bignonia*, genus name, after Jean Paul *Bignon* (1662–1743), French royal librarian.]

bi·gos (bē′gōs) *n.* A Polish stew made with meat and cabbage, traditionally simmered for several days before serving. [Pol.]

big·ot (bĭg′ət) *n.* One who is strongly partial to one's own group, religion, race, or politics and is intolerant of those who differ. [Fr. < OFr.]

big·ot·ed (bĭg′ə-tĭd) *adj.* Being or characteristic of a bigot. —**big′ot·ed·ly** *adv.*

big·ot·ry (bĭg′ə-trē) *n.* The attitude, state of mind, or behavior characteristic of a bigot; intolerance.

big science *n.* Scientific research involving large amounts of money and often large teams of researchers.

big shot *n. Slang* An important or influential person.

Big Sioux River A river rising in NE SD and flowing c. 676 km (420 mi) to the Missouri R. at Sioux City IA.

big sister *n.* **1.** An older sister. **2.** A woman who assumes this role.

big stick *n.* A display or threat, esp. of military force: *a policy that relied on the big stick.* —**big′stick′** (bĭg′stĭk′) *adj.*

Big Sur (sûr′) A rugged, picturesque resort region along the Pacific coast of CA S of Carmel and Monterey.

big-tick·et (bĭg′tĭk′ĭt) *adj. Informal* Having a high price.

big·time or **big-time** (bĭg′tīm′) *Informal adj.* Significant or important; major. ❖ *adv.* To an extreme degree; very much: *Sales are expanding, big-time.*

big time *n. Informal* The most prestigious level of attainment in a competitive field. —**big′-tim′er** *n.*

big toe *n.* The largest and innermost toe of the human foot.

big top *n.* **1.** The main tent of a circus. **2.** The circus.

big tree *n.* See **giant sequoia.**

big wheel *n. Slang* A very important person.

big·wig (bĭg′wĭg′) *n. Slang* A very important person.

Bi·har (bē-här′) A region of E-central India crossed by the Ganges R. Buddha spent his early days in the area.

Bi·ha·ri (bĭ-hä′rē) *n., pl.* **Bihari** or **-ris 1.** A native or inhabitant of Bihar. **2.** The Indic language of the Bihari.

bi·jou (bē′zhōō) *n., pl.* **-joux** (-zhōō′, -zhōōz′) A small, exquisitely wrought trinket. [Fr. < Breton *bizou*, jeweled ring < *biz*, finger.]

bi·jou·te·rie (bē-zhōō′tə-rē) *n.* **1.** A collection of trinkets or jewelry. **2.** Decoration.

bi·ju·gate (bĭ′jə-gāt′, -gĭt, bī-jōō′-) also **bi·ju·gous** (bĭ′jə-gəs, bī-jōō′-) *adj. Botany* Relating to a pinnate leaf with two pairs of leaflets.

Bi·ka·ner (bē′kə-nîr′, -nâr′) A city of NW India in the Thar Desert near the Pakistan border WSW of Delhi. Pop. 416,289.

bike (bīk) *n.* **1.** A bicycle. **2.** A motorcycle. **3.** A motorbike. ❖ *intr.v.* **biked, bik·ing, bikes** To ride a bike. [Shortening and alteration of BICYCLE.]

bik·er (bī′kər) *n.* **1.** One who rides a bicycle or a motorbike. **2.** A motorcyclist, esp. a member of a motorcycle gang.

bike·way (bīk′wā′) *n.* A bicycle lane or path.

bi·ki·ni (bĭ-kē′nē) *n.* **1.** A very brief, close-fitting bathing suit. **2.** Brief underpants that reach only to the hips. Often used in the plural. [Fr., after BIKINI.] —**bi·ki′nied** (-nēd) *adj.*

Bikini An atoll in the Ralik Chain of the Marshall Is. in the W-central Pacific Ocean; site of US nuclear tests (1946–58).

bikini scar *n.* A horizontal scar across the center of the lower abdomen, esp. one resulting from a cesarean section.

Bi·ko (bē′kō), **Steven Bantu** 1946–77. South African political activist and leader of an antiapartheid movement.

bi·la·bi·al (bī-lā′bē-əl) *adj.* **1.** Pronounced with both lips, as the consonants *b, p, m,* and *w.* **2.** Relating to both lips. ❖ *n.* A bilabial sound or consonant.

bi·la·bi·ate (bī-lā′bē-ĭt, -āt′) *adj. Botany* Having two lips.

bi·lat·er·al (bī-lăt′ər-əl) *adj.* **1.** Having or formed of two sides; two-sided. **2.** Affecting or undertaken by two sides equally; binding on both parties: *a bilateral pact.* **3.** Relating to the right and left sides of the body. **4.** Having or marked by bilateral symmetry. —**bi·lat′er·al·ism, bi·lat′er·al·ness** *n.* —**bi·lat′er·al·ly** *adv.*

bilateral symmetry *n.* Symmetry along a central axis, so that a body is divided into right and left halves by only one plane.

bi·lay·er (bī′lā′ər) *n.* A structure, such as a film or membrane, consisting of two molecular layers.

Bil·ba·o (bĭl-bä′ō, -bou′) A city of N Spain near the Bay of Biscay; founded c. 1300. Pop. 365,269.

bil·ber·ry (bĭl′bĕr′ē) *n.* See **blueberry.** [*bil-*, prob. of Scand. orig. + BERRY.]

bil·bo[1] (bĭl′bō) *n., pl.* **-boes** An iron bar with sliding fetters, formerly used to shackle the feet of prisoners. [?]

bil·bo[2] (bĭl′bō) *n., pl.* **-boes** *Archaic* A sword, esp. one having a well-tempered blade. [After BILBAO.]

bil·dungs·ro·man or **Bil·dungs·ro·man** (bĭl′dŏōngz-rō-män′, -dŏōngks-) *n.* A novel whose subject is the moral, psychological, and intellectual development of a usu. youthful main character. [Ger. : *Bildung*, formation (< MHGer. *bildunge* < OHGer. *bildunga* < *bilidōn*, to shape < *bilōdi*, form, shape) +

Roman, novel (< Fr., a story in the vernacular, novel; see ROMAN).]

bile (bīl) *n.* **1.** A bitter, alkaline, yellowish fluid that is secreted by the liver, stored in the gallbladder, and discharged into the duodenum to aid in the digestion of fats. **2.** Bitterness of temper; ill humor. **3.** Either of two bodily humors, black bile or yellow bile, in medieval physiology. [Fr. < Lat. *bīlis.*]

bile acid *n.* Any of the liver-generated steroid acids that occur in the bile with glycine and taurine as sodium salts.

bile duct *n.* Any of the excretory passages in the liver that carry bile to the hepatic duct.

bile salt *n.* **1.** Any of the sodium salts of the bile acids occurring in bile. **2.** A mixture, such as that derived from the bile of the ox, used medicinally as a hepatic stimulant or laxative.

bi•lev•el or **bi•lev•el** (bī′lĕv′əl) *adj.* **1.** Having or existing on two levels: *a bi-level passenger coach.* **2.** Divided vertically into two ground-floor levels. ❖ *n.* A bi-level dwelling.

bilge (bĭlj) *n.* **1.** *Nautical* The lowest inner part of a ship's hull. **2.** Bilge water. **3.** *Slang* Stupid talk or writing; nonsense. **4.** The bulging part of a barrel or cask. ❖ *v.* **bilged, bilg•ing, bilg•es** —*intr. Nautical* To bulge or swell. [Prob. alteration of BULGE.] —**bilg′y** *adj.*

bilge water *n.* **1.** Stagnant water that collects in a ship's bilge. **2.** *Slang* Nonsense.

bil•har•zi•a (bĭl-här′zē-ə) *n.* See **schistosome.** [NLat. *Bilharzia,* genus name, after Theodor *Bilharz* (1825–62), German physician.]

bil•har•zi•a•sis (bĭl′här-zī′ə-sĭs) *n.* See **schistosomiasis.** [BILHARZ(IA) + -IASIS.]

bil•i•ar•y (bĭl′ē-ĕr′ē) *adj.* **1.** Of or relating to bile, the bile ducts, or the gallbladder. **2.** Transporting bile.

bi•lin•e•ar (bī-lĭn′ē-ər) *adj.* Linear with respect to each of two variables or positions.

bi•lin•gual (bī-lĭng′gwəl) *adj.* **1a.** Using or able to use two languages, esp. with nearly equal fluency. **b.** Using two languages to facilitate learning by students who have a proficiency in one language and are acquiring proficiency in the other: *bilingual education.* **2.** Of, relating to, or expressed in two languages: *a bilingual dictionary.* ❖ *n.* A person who uses or is able to use two languages, esp. with equal fluency. —**bi•lin′gual•ism** *n.* —**bi•lin′gual•ly** *adv.*

bil•ious (bĭl′yəs) *adj.* **1.** Of, relating to, or containing bile. **2a.** Characterized by an excess secretion of bile. **b.** Of or relating to gastric distress caused by a disorder of the liver or gallbladder. **c.** Appearing as if affected by such a disorder; sickly. **3.** Resembling bile, esp. in color. **4.** Having a peevish disposition. —**bil′ious•ly** *adv.* —**bil′ious•ness** *n.*

bil•i•ru•bin (bĭl′ĭ-roo′bĭn, bĭl′ĭ-roo′-) *n.* A reddish-yellow bile pigment, $C_{33}H_{36}N_4O_6$, derived from the breakdown of heme. [Lat. *bīlis,* bile + *ruber,* red; see **reudh-** in App. + -IN.]

bil•i•ver•din (bĭl′ĭ-vûr′dĭn, bĭl′ĭ-vûr′-) *n.* A green pigment, $C_{33}H_{34}N_4O_6$, occurring in bile and sometimes formed by oxidation of bilirubin. [Ger. : Lat. *bīlis,* bile + Fr. *verdir,* to make green; see VERDANT.]

bilk (bĭlk) *tr.v.* **bilked, bilk•ing, bilks 1a.** To defraud or swindle. **b.** To evade payment of. **2.** To thwart or frustrate. **3.** To elude. ❖ *n.* **1.** One who cheats. **2.** *Obsolete* A hoax or swindle. [Perh. alteration of BALK.] —**bilk′er** *n.*

bill¹ (bĭl) *n.* **1.** An itemized list or statement of fees or charges. **2.** A statement or list of particulars, such as a menu. **3.** The entertainment offered by a theater. **4.** A public notice, such as a poster. **5a.** A piece of legal paper money. **b.** *Slang* One hundred dollars. **6a.** A bill of exchange. **b.** *Obsolete* A promissory note. **7a.** A draft of a proposed law presented for approval to a legislative body. **b.** The law enacted from such a draft. **8.** *Law* A document presented to a court and containing a formal statement of a case, complaint, or petition. ❖ *tr.v.* **billed, bill•ing, bills 1.** To present a statement of costs or charges to. **2.** To enter on a statement of costs or on a particularized list. **3a.** To advertise or schedule by public notice or as part of a program. **b.** To declare or describe officially; proclaim. [ME *bille* < Norman Fr. < Med.Lat. *billa,* alteration of *bulla,* seal on a document < Lat., bubble.] —**bill′a•ble** *adj.*

bill² (bĭl) *n.* **1.** The horny part of the jaws of a bird; a beak. **2.** A beaklike mouth part, such as that of a turtle. **3.** The visor of a cap. ❖ *intr.v.* **billed, bill•ing, bills** To touch beaks together. —*idiom:* **bill and coo** To kiss or caress and murmur endearments. [ME < OE *bile.*]

bill³ (bĭl) *n.* **1.** A billhook. **2.** A halberd or similar weapon with a hooked blade. [ME *bil* < OE *bill.*]

bil•la•bong (bĭl′ə-bông′, -bŏng′) *n. Australian* A stagnant pool or backwater filled with water only in the rainy season. [Wiradhuri (Aboriginal language of SE Australia) *bilabaŋ,* watercourse filled only after rain.]

bill•board¹ (bĭl′bôrd′, -bōrd′) *n.* **1.** A panel for the display of advertisements in public places, as alongside highways. **2.** The advertisement or message on a billboard. **3.** An introductory list of highlights from the program or text that follows. ❖ *tr.v.* **-board•ed, -board•ing, -boards** To advertise or proclaim on or as if on a billboard. [BILL¹ + BOARD.]

bill•board² (bĭl′bôrd′, -bōrd′) *n.* A ledge on the bow of a ship

on which the bill of an anchor rests when the anchor is secured to the cathead. [BILL² + BOARD.]

bill•bug (bĭl′bŭg′) *n.* Any of several weevils, esp. of the genera *Calendra* and *Sitophilus,* whose larvae feed on cereal grasses. [BILL² + BUG.]

bill•er (bĭl′ər) *n.* One that bills, as: **a.** A clerk who prepares bills. **b.** A machine used in preparing bills.

bil•let¹ (bĭl′ĭt) *n.* **1a.** Lodging for troops. **b.** A written order directing that such lodging be provided. **2.** A position of employment; a job. **3.** *Archaic* A short letter; a note. ❖ *v.* **-let•ed, -let•ing, -lets** —*tr.* **1a.** To lodge (soldiers). **b.** To serve (a person) with a written order to provide lodging for soldiers. **2.** To assign lodging to. —*intr.* To be quartered; lodge. [ME, official register < OFr. *billette* < *bullette,* dim. of *bulle,* document < Med.Lat. *bulla,* document, seal. See BILL¹.]

bil•let² (bĭl′ĭt) *n.* **1.** A short, thick piece of wood, esp. one used as firewood. **2.** One of a series of regularly spaced, log-shaped segments used in the moldings of Norman architecture. **3a.** A small, usu. rectangular bar of iron or steel in an intermediate stage of manufacture. **b.** A small ingot of nonferrous metal. **4a.** The part of a harness strap that passes through a buckle. **b.** A loop or pocket for securing the end of a buckled harness strap. [ME < OFr. *billette,* dim. of *bille,* log < VLat. **bilia,* poss. of Celt. orig.]

bil•let-doux (bĭl′ā-doo′) *n., pl.* **bil•lets-doux** (bĭl′ā-dooz′) A love letter. [Fr. : *billet,* short note; see BILLET¹ + *doux,* sweet (< Lat. *dulcis*).]

bill•fish (bĭl′fĭsh′) *n., pl.* **billfish** or **-fish•es 1.** Any of various fishes of the family Istiophoridae, such as a marlin, having an elongated swordlike or spearlike snout and upper jaw. **2.** Any of various other fishes having long pointed jaws.

bill•fold (bĭl′fōld′) *n.* A folding, pocket-sized case for carrying paper money, small personal documents, and change.

bill•head (bĭl′hĕd′) *n.* A letterhead used for billing.

bill•hook (bĭl′hook′) *n.* An implement with a curved blade on a handle, used esp. for pruning and clearing brush. [BILL³ + HOOK.]

bil•liard (bĭl′yərd) *adj.* Relating to or used in billiards. ❖ *n.* See **carom** 2.

bil•liards (bĭl′yərdz) *pl.n. (used with a sing. verb)* **1.** A game on a rectangular table, in which a cue is used to hit three small, hard balls against one another or the sides of the table. **2.** One of several similar games, sometimes using a table with pockets. [Fr. *billard* < *bille,* log. See BILLET².]

bill•ing (bĭl′ĭng) *n.* **1.** The relative importance of performers as indicated by the position and type size in which their names are listed. **2.** Advertising; promotion. **3.** The amount of business done in a period, as by an advertising agency. Often used in the plural.

Bil•lings (bĭl′ĭngz) A city of S MT on the Yellowstone R. ESE of Helena. Pop. 89,847.

Billings, Josh See **Henry Wheeler Shaw.**

bil•lings•gate (bĭl′ĭngz-gāt′, -gĭt) *n.* Foul, abusive language. [After *Billingsgate,* a former fish market in London, England.]

bil•lion (bĭl′yən) *n.* **1.** The cardinal number equal to 10^9. **2.** *Chiefly British* The cardinal number equal to 10^{12}. **3.** An indefinitely large number. [Fr., a million million : blend of *bi-,* second power; see BI-¹ and MILLION.] —**bil′lion** *adj.*

bil•lion•aire (bĭl′yə-nâr′, bĭl′yə-nâr′) *n.* A person whose wealth amounts to at least a billion dollars, pounds, or the equivalent in other currency. [BILLION + (MILLION)AIRE.]

bil•lionth (bĭl′yənth) *n.* **1.** The ordinal number matching the number one billion in a series. **2.** One of a billion equal parts. —**bil′lionth** *adj. & adv.*

Bil•li•ton (bə-lē′tŏn′) See **Belitung.**

bill of attainder *n., pl.* **bills of attainder** A legislative act pronouncing a person guilty of a crime, usu. treason, without trial and subject to capital punishment and attainder.

bill of entry *n., pl.* **bills of entry** A listing of goods received at a customhouse as imports or for export.

bill of exchange *n., pl.* **bills of exchange** A written order directing that a sum of money be paid to a specified person.

bill of fare *n., pl.* **bills of fare 1.** A list of dishes offered; a menu. **2.** A list of items in a presentation; a program.

bill of goods *n., pl.* **bills of goods 1.** A consignment of items for sale. **2.** *Informal* A plan, promise, or offer, esp. one that is dishonest or misleading.

bill of health *n., pl.* **bills of health 1.** A certificate stating whether there is infectious disease aboard a ship or in a port of departure, to be presented at the next port of arrival. **2.** *Informal* An attestation as to condition, esp. a favorable one.

bill of lading *n., pl.* **bills of lading** A document issued by a carrier to a shipper, listing and acknowledging receipt of goods and specifying terms of delivery.

bill of particulars *n., pl.* **bills of particulars** *Law* An itemization of charges, claims, or counterclaims in an action.

bill of rights *n., pl.* **bills of rights 1.** A summary of those rights considered essential to a group of people. **2.** Bill of Rights The first ten amendments to the US Constitution, added in 1791. **3.** Bill of Rights A declaration of certain rights of subjects, enacted by the English Parliament in 1689.

bill of sale *n., pl.* **bills of sale** A document that attests a transfer of the ownership of personal property.

ă pat   oi boy
ā pay   ou out
âr care   oo took
ä father   oo boot
ĕ pet   ŭ cut
ē be   ûr urge
ĭ pit   th thin
ī pie   th this
îr pier   hw which
ŏ pot   zh vision
ō toe   ə about,
ô paw   item

Stress marks:
′ (primary);
′ (secondary), as in
lexicon (lĕk′sĭ-kŏn′)

bil·lon (bĭl′ən) *n.* **1.** An alloy of gold or silver with a greater proportion of another metal, such as copper, used in making coins. **2.** An alloy of silver with a high percentage of copper, used in making medals and tokens. [Fr. < OFr., ingot < *bille*, log. See BILLET².]

bil·low (bĭl′ō) *n.* **1.** A large wave or swell of water. **2.** A great swell, surge, or undulating mass. ❖ *v.* **-lowed, -low·ing, -lows** —*intr.* **1.** To surge or roll in billows. **2.** To swell out or bulge. —*tr.* To cause to billow. [< ON *bylgja*, a wave.] —**bil′low·i·ness** *n.* —**bil′low·y** *adj.*

bill·post·er (bĭl′pō′stər) *n.* One that posts notices, posters, or advertisements. —**bill′post′ing** *n.*

bil·ly¹ (bĭl′ē) *n., pl.* **-lies** A billy club.

bil·ly² (bĭl′ē) *n., pl.* **-lies** *Australian* A metal pot or kettle used in camp cooking. [Prob. short for *billypot* < *Billy*, nickname for *William.*]

billy club *n.* A short stick or club, esp. a police officer's club. [Perh. alteration of *bully club*; see BULLY¹, or < BILLET².]

bil·ly·cock (bĭl′ē-kŏk′) *n. Chiefly British* A felt hat with a low rounded crown, similar to a derby. [Perh. < earlier *bullycocked*, cocked in the fashion of a swashbuckler : BULLY¹, gallant figure + COCK¹.]

billy goat *n. Informal* A male goat.

Billy the Kid See William H. **Bonney.**

bi·lo·ca·tion (bī′lō-kā′shən) *n.* Existence or the ability to exist simultaneously in two places.

Bi·lox·i¹ (bə-lŭk′sē, -lŏk′-) *n., pl.* **Biloxi** or **-is 1.** A member of an extinct Native American people of southeast Mississippi. **2.** Their extinct Siouan language. [Alteration of Biloxi *taneks aʸya,* first people.]

Bi·lox·i² (bə-lŭk′sē, -lŏk′-) A city of SE MS on a peninsula between **Biloxi Bay** and Mississippi Sound on the Gulf of Mexico. Pop. 50,644.

bil·tong (bĭl′tŏng′, -tông) *n. South African* Narrow strips of meat dried in the sun. [Afr. : *bil,* buttock (< MDu. *bille;* see **bhel-²** in App.) + *tong,* tongue (< MDu. *tonghe;* see **dn̥ghū-** in App.).]

bim·bo (bĭm′bō) *n., pl.* **-bos** *Slang* **1.** A woman regarded as vacuous or as having an exaggerated interest in her sexual appeal. **2.** A vacuous person. [Perh. < Ital. *bimbo,* baby.]

bi·mes·tri·al (bī-mĕs′trē-əl) *adj.* **1.** Occurring every two months; bimonthly. **2.** Lasting two months. [< Lat. *bimēstris : bi-,* two; see BI-¹ + *mēnsis,* month; see **mē-¹** in App.]

bi·me·tal·lic (bī′mə-tăl′ĭk) *adj.* **1.** Consisting of two metals, often bonded together and having different rates of thermal expansion. **2.** Of or based on bimetallism.

bi·met·al·lism (bī-mĕt′l-ĭz′əm) *n.* **1.** The use of a monetary standard consisting of two metals, esp. gold and silver, in a fixed ratio of value. **2.** The doctrine advocating bimetallism. —**bi·met′al·list** *n.* —**bi·met′al·lis′tic** *adj.*

bi·mil·le·nar·y (bī-mĭl′ə-nĕr′ē, bī′mə-lĕn′ə-rē) *n., pl.* **-ies** A bimillennium. —**bi·mil′le·nar′y** *adj.*

bi·mil·len·ni·um (bī′mə-lĕn′ē-əm) *n., pl.* **-len·ni·ums** or **-len·ni·a** (-lĕn′ē-ə) **1.** A 2,000-year span. **2.** A 2,000th anniversary. —**bi·mil′len′ni·al** *adj.* —**bi·mil′len′ni·al·ly** *adv.*

Bim·i·nis (bĭm′ə-nēz) A group of small islands in the W Bahamas in the Straits of Florida; legendary site of the Fountain of Youth sought by Juan Ponce de León.

bi·mod·al (bī-mōd′l) *adj.* **1.** Having or exhibiting two contrasting modes or forms. **2.** *Statistics* Having two modes of distribution. **3.** Designed for operation on either railroads or highways. Used of vehicles. —**bi′mo·dal′i·ty** (bī′mō-dăl′ĭ-tē) *n.*

bi·month·ly (bī-mŭnth′lē) *adj.* **1.** Happening every two months. **2.** Happening twice a month; semimonthly. See Usage Note at **bi-¹.** ❖ *n., pl.* **-lies** A bimonthly publication. —**bi·month′ly** *adv.*

bin (bĭn) *n.* A container or enclosed space for storage. ❖ *tr.v.* **binned, bin·ning, bins** To place or store in a bin. [ME *binne* < OE, prob. of Celt. orig.]

bin- *pref.* Variant of bi-¹.

bi·nal (bī′nəl) *adj.* Twofold; double. [NLat. *bīnālis,* twin < Lat. *bīnī,* two by two. See **dwo-** in App.]

bi·na·ry (bī′nə-rē) *adj.* **1.** Characterized by or consisting of two parts or components; twofold. **2.** Of or relating to a method of representing numbers having two as its base and using the digits 0 and 1. **3.** *Chemistry* Consisting of or containing only molecules consisting of two kinds of atoms. **4.** Of or employing two comparatively nontoxic chemicals that combine to produce a deadly poison: *binary weapons.* **5.** *Music* Having two sections or subjects. ❖ *n., pl.* **-ries** Something that is binary, esp. a binary star. [ME *binarie* < LLat. *bīnārius* < Lat. *bīnī,* two by two. See **dwo-** in App.]

binary digit *n.* Either of the digits 0 or 1, used in the binary number system.

binary fission *n.* A method of asexual reproduction that involves the splitting of a parent cell into two approximately equal parts.

binary star *n.* A stellar system consisting of two stars orbiting about a common center of mass and often appearing as a single visual or telescopic object.

bin·au·ral (bī-ôr′əl, bĭn-ôr′-) *adj.* **1a.** Having or relating to two ears. **b.** Having to do with the perception of sound with both ears: *binaural hearing.* **2.** Of or relating to sound transmission from two sources, which may vary acoustically to give a stereophonic effect. —**bin·au′ral·ly** *adv.*

bind (bīnd) *v.* **bound** (bound), **bind·ing, binds** —*tr.* **1.** To tie or secure, as with a rope. **2.** To fasten or wrap by encircling, as with a belt. **3.** To bandage: *bound up their wounds.* **4.** To hold or restrain with or as if with bonds. **5.** To compel, obligate, or unite. **6.** *Law* To place under legal obligation by contract or oath. **7.** To make certain or irrevocable. **8.** To apprentice or indenture: *was bound out as a servant.* **9.** To cause to cohere or stick together in a mass. **10.** To enclose and fasten (a book or other printed material) between covers. **11.** To furnish with an edge or border, as for protection. **12.** To constipate. **13.** To form a chemical bond with or be taken up by: *an enzyme binding with its substrate.* —*intr.* **1.** To tie up or fasten something. **2.** To stick or become stuck. **3.** To be uncomfortably tight or restricting, as clothes. **4.** To become compact or solid; cohere. **5.** To be compelling or unifying: *the ties that bind.* **6.** To combine chemically or form a chemical bond. ❖ *n.* **1a.** The act of binding. **b.** The state of being bound. **c.** Something that binds. **d.** A place where something binds: *a bind in the seam.* **2.** *Informal* A difficult, restrictive, or unresolvable situation: *in a bind.* **3.** *Music* A tie, slur, or brace. —**phrasal verbs: bind off** To cast off in knitting. **bind over** *Law* To hold on bail or place under bond. [ME *binden* < OE *bindan.* See **bhendh-** in App.]

bind·er (bīn′dər) *n.* **1.** One that binds, esp. a bookbinder. **2.** Something used to bind. **3.** A notebook cover with rings or clamps for holding paper. **4.** Something, such as the latex in certain paints, that creates uniform consistency, solidification, or cohesion. **5a.** A machine that reaps and ties grain. **b.** An attachment on a reaping machine that ties grain in bundles. **6.** *Law* A payment or written statement making an agreement legally binding until the completion of a contract, esp. an insurance contract. **7.** A plant, such as a ground cover, whose growth retards erosion.

bind·er·y (bīn′də-rē) *n., pl.* **-ies** A place where books are bound.

bind·ing (bīn′dĭng) *n.* **1.** The action of one that binds. **2.** Something that binds or is used as a binder. **3.** The cover that holds together the pages of a book. **4.** A strip sewn or attached over or along an edge, as for protection. **5.** *Sports* A fastening on a ski for securing the boot. ❖ *adj.* **1.** Serving to bind. **2.** Uncomfortably tight and confining. **3.** Imposing or commanding adherence to a commitment, obligation, or duty: *a binding agreement.* —**bind′ing·ly** *adv.* —**bind′ing·ness** *n.*

binding energy *n.* **1.** The net energy required to decompose a molecule, atom, or nucleus into its components. **2.** The net energy required to remove an atomic electron to an infinitely remote position from its orbit.

bin·dle·stiff (bĭn′dl-stĭf′) *n.* A hobo, esp. one who carries a bedroll. [E. *bindle,* bundle (prob. < Ger. dialectal *bindel* < MHGer. *bündel* < *binden,* to bind < OHGer. *binten;* see **bhendh-** in App.) + STIFF.]

bind·weed (bīnd′wēd′) *n.* **1.** Any of various trailing or twining plants of the genera *Calystegia* and *Convolvulus,* having bell-shaped or funnel-shaped flowers. **2.** Any of various similar trailing or twining plants, such as the black bindweed.

bine (bīn) *n.* The flexible twining or climbing stem of certain plants, such as the hop or woodbine. [Alteration of BIND, vine.]

Bi·net-Si·mon scale (bī-nā′sē-mōN′, -sī′mən) *n.* An evaluation of the relative mental development of a person by psychological tests of intellectual ability. [After Alfred *Binet* (1857–1911) and Théodore *Simon* (1873–1961), French psychologists.]

Bing cherry (bĭng) *n.* A variety of cherry with sweet, red to nearly black fruit.

binge (bĭnj) *n.* **1.** A drunken spree or revel. **2a.** A period of unrestrained, immoderate self-indulgence. **b.** A period of excessive indulgence in food or drink. ❖ *intr.v.* **binged, bing·ing** or **binge·ing, bing·es 1.** To be immoderately self-indulgent and unrestrained. **2.** To indulge excessively in food or drink. [< dialectal *binge,* to soak.] —**bing′er** *n.*

SYNONYMS binge, fling, jag, orgy, spree These nouns denote a period of uncontrolled self-indulgence: *a gambling binge; a fling before starting the new job; a crying jag; an eating orgy; a shopping spree.*

binge eating *n.* Consumption of large amounts of food in a short period, esp. as a symptom of bulimia.

Bing·en (bĭng′ən), Hildegard von See **Hildegard von Bingen.**

Bing·ham (bĭng′əm), George Caleb 1811–79. Amer. painter noted for his portraits and genre paintings of the frontier.

Bing·ham·ton (bĭng′əm-tən) A city of S-central NY near the PA border SSE of Syracuse; settled in 1787. Pop. 47,380.

bin·go (bĭng′gō) *n., pl.* **-goes** A game in which each player has one or more cards printed with differently numbered squares on which to place markers when the respective numbers are drawn and announced, the winner being the first player to mark a complete row of numbers. ❖ *interj.* Used to express the sudden completion of an event, occurrence of an idea, or confirmation of a guess. [?]

bin·na·cle (bĭn′ə-kəl) *n.* A case that supports and protects a ship's compass, located near the helm. [Alteration of ME *bitakille* < OSpan. *bitácula* or < OPort. *bitácola,* both < Lat. *habitāculum,*

binnacle
deck mount model

habitation < *habitāre*, to inhabit. See **ghabh-** in App.]

bin·oc·u·lar (bə-nŏk′yə-lər, bī-) *adj.* **1.** Relating to, used by, or involving both eyes at the same time. **2.** Having two eyes arranged to produce stereoscopic vision. ❖ *n.* An optical device consisting of two small telescopes joined with a single focusing device. Often used in the plural. —**bin·oc′u·lar′i·ty** (-lăr′ĭ-tē) *n.* —**bin·oc′u·lar·ly** *adv.*

bi·no·mi·al (bī-nō′mē-əl) *adj.* Consisting of or relating to two names or terms. ❖ *n.* **1.** *Mathematics* A polynomial with two terms. **2.** *Biology* A taxonomic name in binomial nomenclature. [< NLat. *binōmius,* having two names : BI-¹ + Fr. *nom,* name (< Lat. *nōmen;* see NOMINAL).] —**bi·no′mi·al·ly** *adv.*

binomial distribution *n.* The frequency distribution of the probability of a possible number of specified outcomes in an arbitrary number of repeated independent trials.

binomial nomenclature *n.* The scientific naming of species whereby each species receives a Latin or Latinized name of two parts, the first indicating the genus and the second being the specific epithet.

binomial theorem *n. Mathematics* A theorem that specifies the expansion of a binomial to any power without requiring the explicit multiplication of the binomial terms.

bint (bĭnt) *n. Chiefly British & Offensive* A woman or girl. [Ar., daughter.]

bin·tu·rong (bĭn-toor′ŏng, -ŏng) *n.* A civet (*Arctictis binturong*) of southeast Asia with a long prehensile tail. [Malay *benturong, binturong.*]

bi·nu·cle·ate (bī-noo′klē-ĭt, -āt′, -nyoo′-) also **bi·nu·cle·at·ed** (-ā′tĭd) or **bi·nu·cle·ar** (-klē-ər, -nyoo′-) *adj.* Having two nuclei.

bi·o (bī′ō) *n., pl.* **-os** *Informal* **1.** A biography. **2.** A biographical sketch or outline.

bio- or **bi-** *pref.* **1.** Life; living organism: *biome.* **2.** Biology; biological: *biophysics.* [Gk. < *bios,* life. See **g**ʷ**eiə-** in App.]

bi·o·a·cous·tics (bī′ō-ə-koo′stĭks) *n. (used with a sing. verb)* The study of sounds produced by or affecting living organisms, esp. those sounds involved in communication.

bi·o·ac·tive (bī′ō-ăk′tĭv) *adj.* Of or relating to a substance that affects living tissue. —**bi′o·ac·tiv′i·ty** *n.*

bi·o·as·say (bī′ō-ăs′ā′, -ă-sā′) *n.* **1.** Determination of the strength or biological activity of a substance, such as a drug, by comparing its effects with those of a standard preparation on a test organism. **2.** A test used to determine such strength or activity. ❖ *tr.v.* **-sayed, -say·ing, -says** To cause to undergo a bioassay.

bi·o·as·tro·nau·tics (bī′ō-ăs′trə-nô′tĭks) *n. (used with a sing. verb)* The study of the biological and medical effects of space flight on living organisms. —**bi′o·as′tro·nau′ti·cal** *adj.*

bi·o·a·vail·a·bil·i·ty (bī′ō-ə-vā′lə-bĭl′ĭ-tē) *n.* The degree to which a drug or other substance is absorbed or becomes available at the site of activity after administration.

Bí·o-Bí·o (bē′ō-bē′ō) A river of central Chile flowing c. 386 km (240 mi) from the Andes to the Pacific Ocean near Concepción.

bi·o·ce·no·sis also **bi·o·coe·no·sis** (bī′ō-sĭ-nō′sĭs) or **bi·o·ce·nose** (-sē′nōs) *n., pl.* **-ses** (-sēz) A group of interacting organisms that live in a habitat and form an ecological community.

biochemical oxygen demand *n.* The amount of oxygen required by aerobic microorganisms to decompose the organic matter in a sample of water, used as a measure of the degree of water pollution.

bi·o·chem·is·try (bī′ō-kĕm′ĭ-strē) *n.* **1.** The study of the chemical substances and vital processes occurring in living organisms; biological chemistry; physiological chemistry. **2.** The chemical composition of a particular living system or biological substance. —**bi′o·chem′i·cal** (-ĭ-kəl) *adj. & n.* —**bi′o·chem′i·cal·ly** *adv.* —**bi′o·chem′ist** *n.*

bi·o·chip (bī′ō-chĭp′) *n.* A computer chip made from organic molecules rather than silicon or germanium.

bi·o·cide (bī′ə-sīd′) *n.* A chemical substance capable of destroying living organisms. —**bi′o·cid′al** (-sīd′l) *adj.*

bi·o·com·pat·i·bil·i·ty (bī′ō-kəm-păt′ə-bĭl′ĭ-tē) *n.* The property of being biologically compatible by not producing a toxic, injurious, or immunological response in living tissue. —**bi′o·com·pat′i·ble** *adj.*

bi·o·con·trol (bī′ō-kən-trōl′) *n.* See **biological control.**

bi·o·con·ver·sion (bī′ō-kən-vûr′zhən, -shən) *n.* The conversion of organic materials, such as plant waste, into usable products or energy sources by biological processes or agents.

bi·o·de·grad·a·ble (bī′ō-dĭ-grā′də-bəl) *adj.* Capable of being decomposed by biological agents, esp. bacteria: *a biodegradable detergent.* —**bi′o·de·grad′a·bil′i·ty** *n.* —**bi′o·deg′ra·da′tion** (-dĕg′rə-dā′shən) *n.* —**bi′o·de·grade′** *v.*

bi·o·di·ver·si·fi·ca·tion (bī′ō-dĭ-vûr′sə-fĭ-kā′shən, -dī-) *n.* The process by which biodiversity develops or is increased within a region or a group of organisms. —**bi′o·di·ver′si·fied** *v.*

bi·o·di·ver·si·ty (bī′ō-dĭ-vûr′sĭ-tē) *n.* **1.** The variety of organisms found within a specified geographic region. **2.** The degree to which living organisms vary, as within and between species or within and between ecosystems.

bi·o·dy·nam·ic (bī′ō-dī-năm′ĭk, -dī-) *adj.* **1.** Of or relating to the study of the effects of dynamic processes on living organisms.

2. Of or relating to a system of organic crop cultivation.

bi·o·dy·nam·ics (bī′ō-dī-năm′ĭks, -dī-) *n. (used with a sing. verb)* **1.** The study of the effects of dynamic processes on living organisms. **2.** The science of the force or energy of living matter and physiological processes.

bi·o·e·lec·tric (bī′ō-ĭ-lĕk′trĭk) also **bi·o·e·lec·tri·cal** (-trĭ-kəl) *adj.* **1.** Of or having to do with the electric current generated by living tissue. **2.** Of or relating to the effects of electricity on living tissue.

bi·o·e·lec·tric·i·ty (bī′ō-ĭ-lĕk-trĭs′ĭ-tē, -ē′lĕk-) *n.* An electric current that is generated by living tissue, such as nerve.

bi·o·e·lec·tron·ics (bī′ō-ĭ-lĕk-trŏn′ĭks, -ē-lĕk-) *n. (used with a sing. verb)* **1.** The application of the principles of electronics to biology and medicine. **2.** The study of the role of intermolecular electron transfer in physiological processes. —**bi′o·e·lec·tron′ic** *adj.*

bi·o·en·er·get·ics (bī′ō-ĕn′ər-jĕt′ĭks) *n. (used with a sing. verb)* **1.** *Biochemistry* The study of the flow and transformation of energy in and between living organisms and between living organisms and their environment. **2.** A mind-body therapy involving the use of movement, breathing, and free expression of feelings to relieve tension and promote well-being. —**bi′o·en·er·get′ic** *adj.*

bi·o·en·gi·neer·ing (bī′ō-ĕn′jə-nîr′ĭng) *n.* **1.** The application of engineering principles to the fields of biology and medicine. **2.** Genetic engineering. —**bi′o·en′gi·neer′** *n.*

bi·o·e·quiv·a·lence (bī′ō-ĭ-kwĭv′ə-ləns) *n.* Equivalence of potency and bioavailability among different formulations of a drug administered in equal dosages. —**bi′o·e·quiv′a·lent** *adj.*

bi·o·eth·ics (bī′ō-ĕth′ĭks) *n. (used with a sing. verb)* The study of the ethical and moral implications of discoveries and advances, as in the fields of genetic engineering. —**bi′o·eth′i·cal** *adj.* —**bi′o·eth′i·cist** (-ĭ-sĭst) *n.*

bi·o·feed·back (bī′ō-fēd′băk′) *n.* The technique of using monitoring devices to gain some voluntary control over autonomic bodily functions, such as heart rate.

bi·o·fla·vo·noid (bī′ō-flā′və-noid′) *n.* Any of a group of biologically active substances found in plants and functioning in the maintenance of the walls of small blood vessels in mammals.

bi·o·foul·ing (bī′ō-fou′lĭng) *n.* The impairment or degradation of something, such as a ship's hull, resulting from the growth or activity of living organisms. —**bi′o·foul′er** *n.*

bi·o·fuel (bī′ō-fyoo′əl) *n.* Fuel such as methane produced from renewable resources, esp. plant biomass and treated municipal and industrial wastes. —**bi′o·fuel′ed** (-əld) *adj.*

bi·o·gas (bī′ō-găs′) *n.* A mixture of methane and carbon dioxide produced by bacterial degradation of organic matter and used as a fuel.

bi·o·gen·e·sis (bī′ō-jĕn′ĭ-sĭs) also **bi·og·e·ny** (bī-ŏj′ə-nē) *n.* **1.** The principle that living organisms develop only from other living organisms and not from nonliving matter. **2.** Generation of living organisms from other living organisms. **3.** See **biosynthesis. 4.** The supposed recurrence of the evolutionary stages of a species during ontogeny. —**bi′o·ge·net′ic** (-jə-nĕt′ĭk), **bi′o·ge·net′i·cal** (-ĭ-kəl) *adj.* —**bi′o·ge·net′i·cal·ly** *adv.*

biogenetic law *n.* The theory that ontogeny recapitulates phylogeny.

bi·o·gen·ic (bī′ō-jĕn′ĭk) *adj.* Produced by or necessary for the maintenance of living organisms or biological processes.

bi·o·ge·o·chem·is·try (bī′ō-jē′ō-kĕm′ĭ-strē) *n.* The study of the relationship between regional geochemistry and animal and plant life. —**bi′o·ge′o·chem′i·cal** (-ĭ-kəl) *adj.*

bi·o·ge·og·ra·phy (bī′ō-jē-ŏg′rə-fē) *n.* The study of the geographic distribution of organisms. —**bi′o·ge·og′ra·pher** *n.* —**bi′o·ge′o·graph′ic** (-jē′ə-grăf′ĭk), **bi′o·ge′o·graph′i·cal** (-ĭ-kəl) *adj.*

bi·og·ra·phee (bī-ŏg′rə-fē′) *n.* The subject of a biography.

bi·og·ra·pher (bī-ŏg′rə-fər) *n.* One who writes, composes, or produces biography.

bi·o·graph·i·cal (bī′ə-grăf′ĭ-kəl) also **bi·o·graph·ic** (-grăf′ĭk) *adj.* **1.** Containing, consisting of, or relating to the facts or events in a person's life. **2.** Of or relating to biography as a literary form. —**bi′o·graph′i·cal·ly** *adv.*

bi·og·ra·phy (bī-ŏg′rə-fē) *n., pl.* **-phies 1.** An account of a person's life written, composed, or produced by another. **2.** Biographies considered as a group, esp. as a genre. **3.** The writing, composition, or production of biographies. [LGk. *biographia* : Gk. *bio-, bio-* + Gk. *-graphiā, -graphy.*]

bi·o·haz·ard (bī′ō-hăz′ərd) *n.* **1.** A biological agent, such as an infectious microorganism, or a condition that constitutes a threat to humans, esp. in biological research. **2.** The potential danger from a biohazard.

bi·o·in·for·mat·ics (bī′ō-ĭn′fər-măt′ĭks) *n. (used with a sing. verb)* Information technology as applied to the life sciences, esp. the technology used for the collection, storage, and retrieval of genomic data.

bi·o·in·stru·men·ta·tion (bī′ō-ĭn′strə-mĕn-tā′shən) *n.* **1.** Use of instruments for the recording or transmission of physiological information, such as heart rate. **2.** The instruments so used.

Bi·o·ko (bē-ō′kō) Formerly **Fer·nan·do Po** (fər-năn′dō pō′)

An island of Equatorial Guinea in the Gulf of Guinea.

bi·o·log·i·cal (bī'ə-lŏj'ĭ-kəl) also **bi·o·log·ic** (-lŏj'ĭk) *adj.* **1.** Of, relating to, caused by, or affecting life or living organisms. **2.** Having to do with biology. **3.** Related by blood: *his biological sister.* ❖ *n.* A preparation synthesized from living organisms and used medically. —**bi'o·log'i·cal·ly** *adv.*

biological clock *n.* **1.** An internal mechanism in organisms that controls the periodicity of various functions or activities, such as metabolic changes, sleep cycles, or photosynthesis. **2.** The progression in women from puberty to menopause; child-bearing age.

biological control *n.* Control of pests by disrupting their ecological status, as through the use of organisms that are natural predators or pathogens.

biological half-life *n.* See **half-life** 2a.

biological oxygen demand *n.* See **biochemical oxygen demand.**

biological warfare *n.* The use of disease-producing microorganisms, toxic biological products, or organic biocides to cause death or injury to humans, animals, or plants.

bi·ol·o·gy (bī-ŏl'ə-jē) *n.* **1.** The science of life and of living organisms, including their structure, function, growth, origin, evolution, and distribution. **2.** The life processes or characteristic phenomena of a group or category of living organisms. **3.** The plant and animal life of a specific area. [Ger. *Biologie* : Gk. *bio-*, bio- + Gk. *-logiā, -logy.*] —**bi·ol'o·gist** *n.*

bi·o·lu·mi·nes·cence (bī'ō-lōō'mə-nĕs'əns) *n.* Emission of visible light by living organisms. —**bi'o·lu'mi·nes'cent** *adj.*

bi·ol·y·sis (bī-ŏl'ĭ-sĭs) *n.* **1.** Death of a living organism or tissue caused or accompanied by lysis. **2.** The decomposition of organic material by living organisms, such as microorganisms. —**bi'o·lyt'ic** (bī'ə-lĭt'ĭk) *adj.*

bi·o·mark·er (bī'ō-mär'kər) *n. Medicine* **1.** See **marker** 9. **2.** A specific physical trait used to measure or indicate the effects or progress of a disease or condition.

bi·o·mass (bī'ō-măs') *n.* **1.** The total mass of living matter within a given unit of environmental area. **2.** Plant material, vegetation, or agricultural waste used as an energy source.

bi·o·ma·te·ri·al (bī'ō-mə-tîr'ē-əl) *n.* A biocompatible material used in the replacement of body organs or tissues and in prosthetics. [BIO(COMPATIBLE) + MATERIAL.]

bi·o·math·e·mat·ics (bī'ō-măth'ə-măt'ĭks) *n.* (*used with a sing. verb*) The application of mathematical principles to biological processes. —**bi'o·math'e·mat'i·cal** *adj.* —**bi'o·math'e·ma·ti'cian** (-mə-tĭsh'ən) *n.*

bi·ome (bī'ōm') *n.* A major regional or global biotic community, such as a desert, characterized chiefly by the dominant forms of plant life and the prevailing climate.

bi·o·me·chan·ics (bī'ō-mĭ-kăn'ĭks) *n.* **1.** (*used with a sing. verb*) The study of the mechanics of a living body. **2.** (*used with a pl. verb*) The mechanics of a part or function of a living body. —**bi'o·me·chan'i·cal** *adj.* —**bi'o·me·chan'i·cal·ly** *adv.*

biomedical engineering *n.* See **bioengineering.**

bi·o·med·i·cine (bī'ō-mĕd'ĭ-sĭn) *n.* **1.** The branch of medical science that deals with the ability of humans to tolerate environmental stresses and variations, as in space travel. **2.** The application of the principles of the natural sciences to clinical medicine. —**bi'o·med'i·cal** (-ĭ-kəl) *adj.*

bi·o·me·te·or·ol·o·gy (bī'ō-mē'tē-ə-rŏl'ə-jē) *n.* The study of the relationship between atmospheric conditions, such as temperature and humidity, and living organisms.

bi·o·met·rics (bī'ō-mĕt'rĭks) *n.* (*used with a sing. verb*) The statistical study of biological phenomena. —**bi'o·met'ric, bi'o·met'ri·cal** *adj.* —**bi'o·met'ri·cal·ly** *adv.*

bi·om·e·try (bī-ŏm'ĭ-trē) *n.* Biometrics.

bi·o·mi·met·ics (bī'ō-mĭ-mĕt'ĭks, -mī-) *n.* (*used with a sing. verb*) The study of the structure and function of biological systems as models for the design and engineering of materials. —**bi'o·mi·met'ic** *adj.*

bi·o·morph (bī'ō-môrf') *n.* A nonrepresentational form or pattern that resembles a living organism in shape or appearance. —**bi'o·mor'phic** *adj.* —**bi'o·mor'phism** *n.*

bi·on·ic (bī-ŏn'ĭk) *adj.* **1.** Of or relating to bionics. **2.** Having electronically or mechanically enhanced or replaced anatomical structures or physiological processes. **3.** Having extraordinary strength, powers, or capabilities. [BI(O)- + (ELECTR)ONIC.]

bi·on·ics (bī-ŏn'ĭks) *n.* (*used with a sing. verb*) Application of biological principles to the study and design of engineering systems, esp. electronic systems. [BI(O)- + (ELECTR)ONICS.]

bi·o·nom·ics (bī'ə-nŏm'ĭks) *n.* (*used with a sing. verb*) See **ecology** 1a. [< Fr. *bionomique*, pertaining to ecology < *bionomie*, ecology : Gk. *bio-*, bio- + Gk. *-nomiā, -nomy.*] —**bi'o·nom'ic, bi'o·nom'i·cal** *adj.* —**bi'o·nom'i·cal·ly** *adv.*

–bi·ont (bī'ŏnt') *suff.* Living organism; mode of living: *symbiont.* [BI(O)- + -ONT.]

bi·o·or·gan·ic (bī'ō-ôr-găn'ĭk) *adj.* Of or having to do with organic compounds and their role in biochemical processes.

bi·o·phys·ics (bī'ō-fĭz'ĭks) *n.* (*used with a sing. verb*) The science that deals with the application of physics to biological processes and phenomena. —**bi'o·phys'i·cal** *adj.* —**bi'o·phys'i·cal·ly** *adv.* —**bi'o·phys'i·cist** *n.*

bi·o·pic (bī'ō-pĭk') *n.* A film or television biography, often with fictionalized episodes.

bi·o·pi·ra·cy (bī'ō-pī'rə-sē) *n.* The commercial development of naturally occurring biological materials, such as plant substances, without fair compensation to the people or nation in whose territory the materials were discovered. —**bi'o·pi'rate** (bī'ō-pī'rĭt) *n.*

bi·o·pol·y·mer (bī'ō-pŏl'ə-mər) *n.* A macromolecule in a living organism that is formed by linking together several smaller molecules, as a protein from amino acids.

bi·o·proc·ess (bī'ō-prŏs'ĕs, -ə-sĕs) *n.* **1.** A technique that produces a biological material for commercial use. **2.** Production of a commercially useful chemical or fuel by a biological process. —**bi'o·proc'ess** *v.*

bi·op·sy (bī'ŏp'sē) *n., pl.* **-sies 1.** The removal and examination of a sample of tissue from a living body for diagnostic purposes. **2.** A sample so obtained. ❖ *tr.v.* **-sied, -sy·ing, -sies** To remove (tissue) from a living body for diagnostic purposes. —**bi·op'tic** (bī-ŏp'tĭk) *adj.*

bi·o·psy·chol·o·gy (bī'ō-sī-kŏl'ə-jē) *n.* The branch of psychology that deals with the biological foundations of behavior and emotion.

bi·o·re·ac·tor (bī'ō-rē-ăk'tər) *n.* An apparatus, such as a large fermentation chamber, used to grow organisms for use in biotechnology.

bi·o·re·me·di·a·tion (bī'ō-rĭ-mē'dē-ā'shən) *n.* The use of biological agents, such as bacteria or plants, to remove or neutralize contaminants, as in polluted soil or water.

bi·o·re·search (bī'ō-rĭ-sûrch', -rē'sûrch) *n.* Research in the biological sciences.

bi·o·re·serve (bī'ō-rĭ-zûrv') *n.* An area containing a wildlife preserve bordered by a buffer zone that is less restricted for human use, established to integrate habitat conservation with community interests.

bi·o·rhythm (bī'ō-rĭth'əm) *n.* An innate, cyclical biological process or function. —**bi'o·rhyth'mic** (-rĭth'mĭk) *adj.*

BIOS (bī'ōs) *n.* The set of routines stored in ROM that enable a computer to start the operating system and to communicate with system hardware. [*b*(*asic*) *i*(*nput*)/*o*(*utput*) *s*(*ystem*).]

bi·o·sat·el·lite (bī'ō-săt'l-īt') *n.* An artificial, recoverable satellite designed to carry humans, animals, or other life.

bi·o·sci·ence (bī'ō-sī'əns) *n.* See **life science.** —**bi'o·sci'en·tif'ic** (-sī'ən-tĭf'ĭk) *adj.* —**bi'o·sci'en·tist** *n.*

bi·os·co·py (bī-ŏs'kə-pē) *n., pl.* **-pies** Medical examination of a body to determine the presence or absence of life.

–biosis *suff.* A way of living: *parabiosis.* [< Gk. *biōsis*, way of life < *bioun*, to live < *bios*, life. See BIO–.]

bi·o·so·cial (bī'ō-sō'shəl) *adj.* Of or relating to the interaction of biological and social forces. —**bi'o·so'cial·ly** *adv.*

bi·o·sol·ids (bī'ō-sŏl'ĭdz) *pl.n.* Solid or semisolid material obtained from treated wastewater, often used as fertilizer.

bi·o·sphere (bī'ə-sfîr') *n.* **1.** The part of the earth and its atmosphere capable of supporting life. **2.** The collection of living organisms together with their environment. —**bi'o·spher'ic** (-sfîr'ĭk, -sfĕr'-) *adj.*

bi·o·sta·tis·tics (bī'ō-stə-tĭs'tĭks) *n.* (*used with a sing. verb*) Application of statistics to biological and medical data.

bi·o·stra·tig·ra·phy (bī'ō-strə-tĭg'rə-fē) *n.* The study of the spatial and temporal distribution of fossil organisms, often as a means of dating rock strata.

bi·o·syn·the·sis (bī'ō-sĭn'thĭ-sĭs) *n.* Formation of a chemical compound by a living organism. —**bi'o·syn·thet'ic** (-thĕt'ĭk) *adj.* —**bi'o·syn·thet'i·cal·ly** *adv.*

bi·o·sys·tem·at·ics (bī'ō-sĭs'tə-măt'ĭks) *n.* (*used with a sing. verb*) The statistical analysis of data obtained from genetic, biochemical, and other studies to assess the taxonomic relationships of organisms or populations. —**bi'o·sys'tem·at'ic** *adj.*

bi·o·ta (bī-ō'tə) *n.* The combined flora and fauna of a region. [NLat. < Gk. *biotē*, way of life < *bios*, life. See gʷei·ə- in App.]

bi·o·tech·nol·o·gy (bī'ō-tĕk-nŏl'ə-jē) *n.* **1.** The use of microorganisms or biological substances to perform specific industrial or manufacturing processes. **2a.** The application of engineering and technology to the life sciences; bioengineering. **b.** See **ergonomics** 1. —**bi'o·tech'ni·cal** (-nĭ-kəl) *adj.* —**bi'o·tech'no·log'i·cal** (-nə-lŏj'ĭ-kəl) *adj.*

bi·o·te·lem·e·try (bī'ō-tə-lĕm'ĭ-trē) *n.* The monitoring, recording, and measuring of a living organism's physiological functions, such as heart rate, by telemetry.

bi·o·ter·ror·ism (bī'ō-tĕr'ə-rĭz'əm) *n.* The use of biological agents, such as pathogenic organisms, for terrorist purposes. —**bi'o·ter'ror·ist** *adj. & n.*

bi·o·ther·a·py (bī'ō-thĕr'ə-pē) *n., pl.* **-pies** Treatment of disease with biologicals, such as certain drugs or antitoxins.

bi·ot·ic (bī-ŏt'ĭk) *adj.* **1.** Of or having to do with life or living organisms. **2.** Produced or caused by living organisms. [Prob. Gk. *biōtikos* < *biotos*, life < *bioun*, to live < *bios*, life. See gʷei·ə- in App.]

–biotic *suff.* A mode of living: *endobiotic.* [Prob. NLat. *-bioticus* < Gk. *biōtikos*. See BIOTIC.]

bi·o·tin (bī'ə-tĭn) *n.* A colorless crystalline vitamin, $C_{10}H_{16}N_2O_3S$, of the vitamin B complex, essential for the activity

biplane

of many enzyme systems. [Gk. *biōtos,* life; see BIOTIC + –IN.]

bi•o•tite (bī′ə-tīt′) *n.* A dark-brown to black mica, $K_2(Mg,Fe,Al)_6(Si,Al)_8O_{20}(OH)_4$, found in igneous and metamorphic rocks. [After Jean Baptiste *Biot* (1774–1862), French physicist.] **—bi′o•tit′ic** (-tĭt′ĭk) *adj.*

bi•o•tope (bī′ə-tōp′) *n.* An area that is uniform in environmental conditions and in its distribution of animal and plant life. [BIO– + Gk. *topos,* place.]

bi•o•trans•for•ma•tion (bī′ō-trăns′fər-mā′shən) *n.* Chemical alteration of a substance within the body.

bi•o•tron (bī′ə-trŏn′) *n.* A climate-control chamber for studying a living organism's response to environmental conditions.

bi•o•tur•ba•tion (bī′ō-tər-bā′shən) *n.* The stirring or mixing of sediment or soil by organisms, esp. by burrowing or boring. [Ger. : *bio-,* bio- + Lat. *turbātiō, turbātiōn-,* disturbance (< *turbātus,* p. part. of *turbāre,* to stir up; see DISTURB).] **—bi′o•turbed′** (-tûrbd′) *adj.*

bi•o•type (bī′ə-tīp′) *n.* A group of organisms having the same genotype. **—bi′o•typ′ic** (-tĭp′ĭk) *adj.*

bip•a•rous (bĭp′ər-əs) *adj. Zoology* Producing two offspring in a single birth.

bi•par•ti•san (bī-pär′tĭ-zən, -sən) *adj.* Of, consisting of, or supported by members of two parties, esp. two major political parties. **—bi•par′ti•san•ism** *n.* **—bi•par′ti•san•ship′** *n.*

bi•par•tite (bī-pär′tīt′) *adj.* **1.** Having or consisting of two parts. **2a.** Having two corresponding parts, one for each party. **b.** Having two participants; joint. **3.** *Botany* Divided into two portions almost to the base, as certain leaves. [Lat. *bipartītus,* p. part. of *bipartīre,* to divide into two parts : *bi-,* two; see BI–[1] + *partīre,* to part (< *pars, part-,* a share; see **perə-** in App.).] **—bi•par′tite′ly** *adv.* **—bi′par•ti′tion** (-tĭsh′ən) *n.*

bi•ped (bī′pĕd′) *n.* An animal with two feet. ❖ *adj.* also **bi•ped•al** (bī-pĕd′l) Having two feet. [Lat. *bipēs, biped-,* two-footed : *bi-,* two; see BI–[1] + *pēs,* foot; see PEDESTRIAN.]

bi•pha•sic (bī′fā′zĭk) *adj.* Having two distinct phases: *a biphasic waveform; a biphasic response to a stimulus.*

bi•phen•yl (bī-fĕn′əl, -fē′nəl) *n.* A colorless crystalline compound, $C_{12}H_{10}$, used as a heat-transfer agent, in fungicides, and in organic synthesis.

bi•pin•nate (bī-pĭn′āt′) *adj. Botany* Decompound. **—bi•pin′nate′ly** *adv.*

bi•plane (bī′plān′) *n.* An airplane having two pairs of wings at different levels, esp. one above and one below the fuselage.

bi•pod (bī′pŏd′) *n.* A stand having two legs.

bi•po•lar (bī-pō′lər) *adj.* **1.** Relating to or having two poles or charges. **2.** *Electronics* Relating to a device, such as a transistor, capable of using two polarizations. **3.** Relating to or involving both of the earth's polar regions. **4.** Having two opposite or contradictory ideas or natures. **5.** *Biology* Having two poles or opposite extremities. **6.** *Psychology* Of or relating to bipolar disorder. **—bi′po•lar′i•ty** (-lăr′ĭ-tē) *n.*

bipolar disorder *n.* A major affective disorder marked by alternating episodes of mania and depression.

bi•pro•pel•lant (bī′prə-pĕl′ənt) *n.* A two-component rocket propellant, such as liquid hydrogen and liquid oxygen, fed separately to the combustion chamber as fuel and oxidizer.

bi•quad•rat•ic (bī′kwŏ-drăt′ĭk) *Mathematics adj.* Of or relating to the fourth degree. ❖ *n.* A biquadratic algebraic equation.

bi•quar•ter•ly (bī-kwôr′tər-lē) *adj.* Happening or appearing twice quarterly. **—bi•quar′ter•ly** *adv.*

bi•ra•cial (bī-rā′shəl) *adj.* **1.** Of, for, relating to, or consisting of members of two races. **2.** Having parents of two different races. **—bi•ra′cial•ism** *n.*

birch (bûrch) *n.* **1a.** Any of various deciduous trees or shrubs of the genus *Betula,* native to the Northern Hemisphere and having toothed leaves and bark that often peels in thin papery layers. **b.** The hard close-grained wood of any of these trees. **2.** A rod from a birch, used to administer a whipping. ❖ *tr.v.* **birched, birch•ing, birch•es** To whip with or as if with a birch. [ME < OE *birce.*]

Birch•er (bûr′chər) also **Birch•ist** (-chĭst) or **Birch•ite** (-chīt′) *n.* A member or supporter of the John Birch Society, an anti-Communist organization founded in 1958. [After John *Birch* (1918–45), Indian-born American missionary and intelligence officer.] **—Birch′ism** *n.* **—Birch′ist, Birch′ite** *adj.*

birch partridge *n.* See **ruffed grouse.**

bird (bûrd) *n.* **1a.** Any of various warm-blooded egg-laying feathered vertebrates of the class Aves, having forelimbs modified to form wings. **b.** Such an animal hunted as game. **c.** Such an animal, esp. a chicken or turkey, used as food: *put the bird in the oven.* **2.** See **clay pigeon. 3.** *Sports* See **shuttlecock. 4.** *Slang* A rocket, guided missile, satellite, or airplane. **5.** *Slang* A person, esp. one who is odd or remarkable. **6.** *Chiefly British Slang* A young woman. **7.** *Slang* **a.** A loud sound expressing disapproval; a raspberry. **b.** Discharge from employment. **8.** An obscene gesture, as of anger, made by pointing the middle finger upward. ❖ *intr.v.* **bird•ed, bird•ing, birds 1.** To observe and identify birds in their natural surroundings. **2.** To trap, shoot, or catch birds. ***—idiom:* for the birds** Objectionable or worthless. [ME < OE *brid,* young bird.] **—bird′ing** *n.*

bird•bath (bûrd′băth′, -bäth′) *n.* A basin filled with water for birds to drink and bathe in.

bird•brain (bûrd′brān′) *n. Slang* A person regarded as silly or stupid. **—bird′brained′** *adj.*

bird•cage (bûrd′kāj′) *n.* A cage for birds.

bird•call (bûrd′kôl′) *n.* **1.** The song or cry of a bird. **2a.** An imitation of a birdcall. **b.** A small device for producing a birdcall.

bird cherry *n.* Any of several cherry trees, esp. the Eurasian *Prunus padus,* having white flowers and small black fruits.

bird dog *n.* **1.** A dog used to hunt game birds; a gun dog. **2.** *Informal* One that bird-dogs.

bird-dog also **bird•dog** (bûrd′dôg′, -dŏg′) *v.* **-dogged, -dog•ging, -dogs** *Informal —intr.* To follow a subject of interest, such as a person or trend, with persistent attention. *—tr.* **1.** To observe or follow closely; monitor: *bird-dogged the suspect's movements.* **2.** To seek out (talent or clients, for example).

bird•er (bûr′dər) *n.* **1.** A bird watcher. **2a.** A breeder of birds. **b.** A hunter of birds.

bird feed or **bird•feed** (bûrd′fēd′) *n.* Birdseed.

bird-foot violet (bûrd′fo͝ot′) *n.* Variant of **bird's-foot violet.**

bird•house (bûrd′hous′) *n.* **1.** A box with one or more small entry holes, made as a nesting place for birds. **2.** An aviary.

bird•ie (bûr′dē) *n.* **1.** *Informal* A small bird. **2a.** One stroke under par for a hole in golf. **b.** See **shuttlecock.** ❖ *tr.v.* **-ied, -ie•ing, -ies** To shoot (a hole in golf) in one stroke under par.

bird•lime (bûrd′līm′) *n.* **1.** A sticky substance that is smeared on branches or twigs to capture small birds. **2.** Something that captures or ensnares. ❖ *tr.v.* **-limed, -lim•ing, -limes 1.** To smear with birdlime. **2.** To catch with or as if with birdlime.

bird louse *n.* See **biting louse.**

bird•man (bûrd′mən) *n.* **1.** (*also* -măn′) One, such as an ornithologist, who works with birds. **2.** *Slang* An aviator.

bird of paradise *n., pl.* **birds of paradise 1.** Any of various birds of the family Paradisaeidae, native to New Guinea and adjacent islands and usu. having brilliant plumage and long tail feathers in the male. **2.** Any of several southern African herbs of the genus *Strelitzia,* esp. *S. reginae,* having orange and blue flowers.

bird of passage *n., pl.* **birds of passage 1.** A migratory bird. **2.** A person who moves from place to place frequently.

bird of prey *n., pl.* **birds of prey** Any of various predatory carnivorous birds such as the eagle or hawk.

bird pepper *n.* **1.** A variety of pepper *(Capsicum annum* var. *glabriusculum)* that includes the wild forms native to the southern United States and from Mexico south to Colombia. **2.** The small pungent fruit of this plant.

bird•seed (bûrd′sēd′) *n.* A mixture of various kinds of seeds used for feeding birds.

Birds•eye (bûrd′zī′), **Clarence** 1886–1956. Amer. inventor who received more than 300 patents, most notably for methods of quick-freezing food.

bird's-eye (bûrdz′ī′) *n.* **1.** A fabric woven with a pattern of small diamonds, each having a dot in the center. **2.** The pattern of such a fabric. ❖ *adj.* **1.** Marked with a spot or spots resembling a bird's eye or eyes, as the bird's-eye maple. **2.** Derived from or as if from an altitude or distance.

bird's-eye maple *n.* A form of wood, chiefly of the sugar maple, that is patterned with small rounded figures.

bird's-foot trefoil (bûrdz′fo͝ot′) *n.* A perennial Old World herb *(Lotus corniculata)* in the pea family, having golden-yellow flowers and clusters of pods arranged like bird claws.

bird's-foot violet also **bird-foot violet** (bûrd′fo͝ot′) *n.* An eastern North American violet *(Viola pedata)* having large flowers and leaves shaped somewhat like a bird's foot.

bird's-nest fern (bûrdz′nĕst′) *n.* An Old World tropical fern *(Asplenium nidus)* having leaves resembling a bird's nest.

bird's-nest fungus *n.* Any of various fungi having a cuplike body containing round egglike structures that enclose the spores.

bird watcher or **bird•watch•er** also **bird-watch•er** (bûrd′wŏch′ər) *n.* A person who observes and identifies birds in their natural surroundings. **—bird watching** *n.*

bi•re•frin•gence (bī′rĭ-frĭn′jəns) *n.* The resolution or splitting of a light wave into two unequally reflected or transmitted waves by an optically anisotropic medium such as calcite. **—bi′re•frin′gent** *adj.*

bi•reme (bī′rēm′) *n.* An ancient galley equipped with two tiers of oars on each side. [Lat. *birēmis* : *bi-,* two; see BI–[1] + *rēmus,* oar.]

bi•ret•ta also **be•ret•ta** or **ber•ret•ta** (bə-rĕt′ə) *n.* A stiff square cap with three or four ridges across the crown, worn esp. by Roman Catholic clergy. [Ital. *berretta* < O Provençal *berret,* cap < LLat. *birrus,* hooded cloak, prob. of Celt. orig.]

bi•ri•a•ni (bĭr′ē-ä′nē) *n.* Variant of **biryani.**

birk (bûrk) *n. Scots* Birch. [ME < OE *birce.*]

Bir•ken•head (bûr′kən-hĕd′) A borough of NW England at the mouth of the Mersey R. near Liverpool. Pop. 124,000.

birl (bûrl) *v.* **birled, birl•ing, birls** *—tr.* To cause (a floating log) to spin rapidly by rotating with the feet. *—intr.* **1.** To participate in birling. **2.** To spin. ❖ *n.* A whirring noise; a hum. [Blend of BIRR[1] and WHIRL.] **—birl′er** *n.*

birl•ing (bûr′lĭng) *n.* A game, esp. among loggers, in which two competitors try to birl a floating log.

Bir•ming•ham (bûr′mĭng-hăm′) **1.** (*also* -əm) A city of central England NW of London. Pop. 1,012,351. **2.** A city of N-central AL NE of Tuscaloosa. Pop. 242,820.

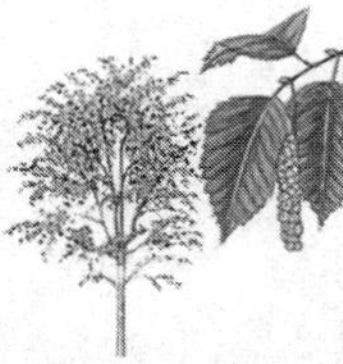

birch
paper birch
Betula papyrifera

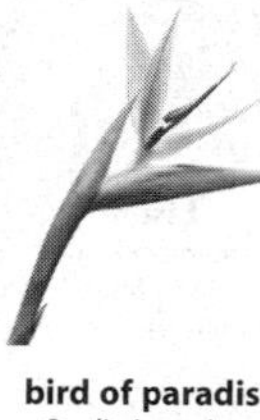

bird of paradise
Strelitzia reginae

ă	pat	oi	boy
ā	pay	ou	out
âr	care	o͝o	took
ä	father	o͞o	boot
ĕ	pet	ŭ	cut
ē	be	ûr	urge
ĭ	pit	th	thin
ī	pie	*th*	this
îr	pier	hw	which
ŏ	pot	zh	vision
ō	toe	ə	about, item
ô	paw		

Stress marks:
′ (primary);
′ (secondary), as in
lexicon (lĕk′sĭ-kŏn′)

birr¹ (bûr) *n.* **1.** A whirring sound. **2.** Strong forward momentum; driving force. ❖ *intr.v.* **birred, birr•ing, birrs** To make a whirring sound. [ME *bir,* favorable wind < ON *byrr.* See **bher-¹** in App.]

birr² (bîr) *n., pl.* **birr** or **birrs** See table at **currency.** [Amharic *bərr* < *brr,* to be white.]

birth (bûrth) *n.* **1a.** The emergence and separation of offspring from the body of the mother. **b.** The act or process of bearing young; parturition. **c.** The circumstances or conditions relating to this event: *a Bostonian by birth.* **2a.** The set of characteristics or circumstances received from one's ancestors; inheritance. **b.** Origin; extraction: *of humble birth.* **c.** Noble or high status. **3.** A beginning or commencement. See Syns at **beginning.** ❖ *tr.v.* **birthed, birth•ing, births** *Chiefly Southern US* **1.** To deliver (a baby). **2.** To bear (a child). [ME, prob. of Scand. orig. See **bher-¹** in App.]

birth canal *n.* The passageway through which the fetus is expelled during parturition, leading from the uterus through the cervix, vagina, and vulva.

birth certificate *n.* An official record of the date and place of a person's birth, usu. including the names of the parents.

birth control *n.* **1.** Limitation or control of the number of children conceived, as by the use of contraception. **2.** A contraceptive device or technique.

birth control pill *n.* See **oral contraceptive.**

birth•day (bûrth′dā′) *n.* **1.** The day of one's birth. **2.** The anniversary of one's birth.

birthday suit *n.* The state of being nude; nakedness.

birth defect *n.* A physiological or structural abnormality that develops at or before birth and is present at birth, esp. as a result of faulty development, infection, heredity, or injury.

birth•ing (bûr′thĭng) *adj.* Having to do with or used during birth: *a birthing counselor.* ❖ *n.* The act of giving birth.

birth•mark (bûrth′märk′) *n.* A mole or blemish present on the skin from birth; a nevus.

birth name also **birth•name** (bûrth′nām′) *n.* **1.** The name given to a person at birth, esp. that of an adoptee before he or she is renamed. **2.** See **maiden name.**

birth pang *n.* **1.** One of the repetitive pains occurring in childbirth. Often used in the plural. **2. birth pangs** Difficulty or turmoil associated with a development or transition.

birth parent also **birth•par•ent** (bûrth′pâr′ənt, -pär′-) *n.* A biological parent.

birth•place (bûrth′plās′) *n.* The place where someone is born or where something originates.

birth•rate also **birth rate** (bûrth′rāt′) *n.* The ratio of total live births to total population in a specified community or area over a specified period of time.

birth•right (bûrth′rīt′) *n.* **1.** A right, possession, or privilege that is one's due by birth. See Syns at **right.** **2.** A special privilege accorded a first-born.

birth•root (bûrth′rōōt′, -rŏŏt′) *n.* See **trillium.**

birth•stone (bûrth′stōn′) *n.* A gemstone associated with a month and customarily worn by persons born in that month.

birth weight or **birth•weight** (bûrth′wāt′) *n.* The weight of an infant at birth.

birth•wort (bûrth′wûrt′, -wôrt′) *n.* Any of several herbs or woody vines of the genus *Aristolochia,* having malodorous flowers with unusual shapes.

bi•ry•a•ni also **bi•ri•a•ni** (bĭ′rē-ä′nē) *n., pl.* **-nis** An Indian dish containing meat, fish, or vegetables and rice flavored with saffron or turmeric. [Hindi or Urdu *biryānī* < Pers. *beryā,* roasted, grilled < *berīdan, berī-,* to roast.]

bis (bĭs) *adv. Music* Again; twice. ❖ *interj.* Used to request an additional performance. [Fr. or Ital., both < Lat. See **dwo-** in App.]

Bi•sa•yan (bĭ-sī′ən) *n.* Variant of **Visayan.** —**Bi•sa′yan** *adj.*

Bis•cay (bĭs′kā), **Bay of** An arm of the Atlantic Ocean indenting the W coast of Europe from Brittany in NW France to NW Spain.

Bis•cayne Bay (bĭs-kān′, bĭs′kān′) A narrow inlet of the Atlantic Ocean in SE FL.

bi•scot•to (bĭ-skŏt′ō) *n., pl.* **-scot•ti** (-skŏt′ē) A crisp Italian cookie traditionally flavored with anise and often containing almonds or filberts. [Ital. < Med.Lat. *bis coctus,* twice cooked. See BISCUIT.]

bis•cuit (bĭs′kĭt) *n., pl.* **-cuits 1.** A small cake of shortened bread leavened with baking powder or soda. **2.** *Chiefly British* **a.** A thin, crisp cracker. **b.** A cookie. **3.** A pale brown. **4.** *pl.* **biscuit** Clay that has been fired once but not glazed. [M English *bisquit* < OFr. *biscuit* < Med.Lat. *bis coctus* : Lat. *bis,* twice; see **dwo-** in App. + Lat. *coctus,* p. part. of *coquere,* to cook; see **pekʷ-** in App.]

bise (bēz) *n.* A cold north wind of the Swiss Alps and nearby regions of France and Italy. [ME < OFr., of Gmc. orig.]

bi•sect (bī′sĕkt′, bī-sĕkt′) *v.* **-sect•ed, -sect•ing, -sects** —*tr.* To cut or divide into two parts, esp. two equal parts. —*intr.* To split; fork. —**bi•sec′tion** *n.* —**bi•sec′tion•al** *adj.* —**bi•sec′tion•al•ly** *adv.*

bi•sec•tor (bī′sĕk′tər, bī-sĕk′-) *n.* Something that bisects, esp. a ray that bisects an angle.

bi•ser•rate (bī-sĕr′āt′) *adj.* **1.** *Botany* Having serrations that are themselves serrated. **2.** *Zoology* Serrated on both sides.

bi•sex•u•al (bī-sĕk′shōō-əl) *adj.* **1.** Of or relating to both sexes.

2a. Having both male and female reproductive organs; hermaphroditic. **b.** *Botany* Of or relating to a single flower that contains functional staminate and pistillate structures. **3.** Of, relating to, or having a sexual orientation to persons of either sex. ❖ *n.* **1.** A bisexual organism; a hermaphrodite. **2.** A bisexual person. —**bi′sex•u•al′i•ty** (-ăl′ĭ-tē) *n.* —**bi•sex′u•al•ly** *adv.*

Bish•kek (bĭsh′kĕk, bĕsh′-) Formerly **Frun•ze** (frŏŏn′zə) The cap. of Kyrgyzstan, in the N-central part on the Chu R. Pop. 627,800.

bish•op (bĭsh′əp) *n.* **1.** A high-ranking Christian cleric, in modern churches usu. in charge of a diocese. **2.** *Games* A usu. mitershaped chess piece that can move diagonally across any number of unoccupied spaces. **3.** Mulled port spiced with oranges, sugar, and cloves. [ME < OE *bisceope* < VLat. **ebiscopus* < LLat. *episcopus* < L.Gk. *episkopos* < Gk., overseer : *epi-,* epi- + *skopos,* watcher; see **spek-** in App.]

Bishop, Elizabeth 1911–79. Amer. poet whose works include *Questions of Travel* (1965).

bish•op•ric (bĭsh′ə-prĭk) *n.* **1.** The office or rank of a bishop. **2.** The diocese of a bishop. [ME *bishoprik* < OE *bisceoprīce,* the diocese of a bishop : *bisceop,* bishop; see BISHOP + *rīce,* realm; see **reg-** in App.]

bish•op's cap (bĭsh′əps) *n.* See **miterwort.**

Bisk (bĭsk, bĕsk) See **Biysk.**

Bis•la•ma (bĭs-lä′mə) *n.* A lingua franca based on Malay and English, spoken in the southwest Pacific. [Pidgin or native var. of BÊCHE-DE-MER.]

Bis•marck (bĭz′märk′) The cap. of ND, in the S-central part on hills overlooking the Missouri R. Pop. 55,532.

Bismarck, Prince Otto Eduard Leopold von Called "the Iron Chancellor." 1815–98. Creator and first chancellor of the German Empire (1871–90). —**Bis•marck′i•an** *adj.*

Bismarck Archipelago A group of volcanic islands and islets of Papua New Guinea in the SW Pacific.

Bismarck Sea A section of the SW Pacific NE of New Guinea and NW of New Britain; site of a major World War II naval battle (1943).

bis•muth (bĭz′məth) *n. Symbol* **Bi** A highly diamagnetic metallic element used in various low-melting alloys in castings, solders, and fire-safety devices. Atomic number 83; atomic weight 208.98; melting point 271.3°C; boiling point 1,560°C; specific gravity 9.747; valence 3, 5. See table at **element.** [Obsolete Ger. *Bismuth, Wismuth*; perh. akin to OHGer. *wiz,* white.] —**bis′muth•al** *adj.*

bi•son (bī′sən, -zən) *n., pl.* **bison 1.** A bovine mammal (*Bison bison*) of western North America, having large forequarters, a shaggy mane, and a massive head with short curved horns; a buffalo. **2.** An animal (*B. bonasus*) of Europe, similar to but somewhat smaller than the bison; a wisent. [Lat. *bisōn,* of Gmc. orig.; akin to OHGer. *wisunt.*]

bisque¹ (bĭsk) *n.* **1a.** A rich creamy soup made from meat, fish, or shellfish. **b.** A thick cream soup made of puréed vegetables. **2.** Ice cream mixed with crushed macaroons or nuts. [Perh. < Fr. dialectal, sour soup < *Biscaye,* Bay of Biscay.]

bisque² (bĭsk) *n.* **1.** See **biscuit** 4. **2a.** A pale orange-yellow to yellowish gray. **b.** A color ranging from moderate yellowish pink to grayish yellow. [< BISCUIT.]

bisque³ (bĭsk) *n.* An advantage allowed an inferior player in certain games, as in tennis or croquet. [Fr.]

Bis•sau (bĭ-sou′) The cap. of Guinea-Bissau, on an estuary of the Atlantic Ocean; founded 1687. Pop. 109,486.

bis•sex•tile (bĭ-sĕk′stĭl, -stĭl′, bī-) *adj.* **1.** Of or relating to a leap year. **2.** Of or relating to the extra day falling in a leap year. ❖ *n.* A leap year. [LLat. *bissextīlis,* containing an intercalary day < *bisextus* (*diēs*), *bis sextus* (*diēs*) and Lat. *bisextum,* intercalary day : *bis,* twice; see BIS + *sextus,* sixth (because the sixth day before the Calends of March on February 24 occurred twice every leap year); see SEXT.]

bis•ter or **bis•tre** (bĭs′tər) *n.* **1.** A water-soluble yellowish-brown pigment. **2.** A grayish to yellowish brown. [Fr. *bistre.*] —**bis′tered** *adj.*

bis•tort (bĭs′tôrt′) *n.* **1.** A Eurasian perennial herb (*Polygonum bistorta*) having cylindrical flower spikes and a rhizome used as an astringent in folk medicine. **2.** Any of related plants of the genus *Polygonum.* [Fr. *bistorte* < OFr. < Med.Lat. **bistorta* : Lat. *bis,* twice; see BIS + *torta,* p. part. of *torquēre,* to twist; see TORQUE¹.]

bis•tro (bē′strō, bĭs′trō) *n., pl.* **-tros 1.** A small bar, tavern, or nightclub. **2.** A small informal restaurant serving wine. [Fr. *bistro* or *bistrot,* tavern owner, tavern.]

bi•sul•cate (bī-sŭl′kāt′) *adj.* Cleft or cloven, as a hoof.

bi•sul•fate (bī-sŭl′fāt′) *n.* The univalent inorganic acid group HSO₄ or a salt of sulfuric acid containing it.

bi•sul•fide (bī-sŭl′fīd′) *n.* See **disulfide.**

bi•sul•fite (bī-sŭl′fīt′) *n.* The univalent inorganic acid group HSO₃ or a salt of sulfurous acid containing it.

bit¹ (bĭt) *n.* **1.** A small portion, degree, or amount. **2.** A brief amount of time; a moment. **3a.** A short scene or episode in a theatrical performance. **b.** A bit part. **4.** An entertainment routine given regularly by a performer; an act. **5.** *Informal* **a.** A particular kind of action, situation, or behavior. **b.** A matter being considered. **6.** *Informal* An amount equal to one eighth of a dollar: *two*

Otto von Bismarck

bison
American bison
Bison bison
with newborn calf

bits. **7.** *Chiefly British* A small coin: *a threepenny bit.* —**idioms: a bit** To a small degree; somewhat: *a bit warm.* **bit by bit** Little by little; gradually. [ME *bite*, morsel < OE *bita.* See **bheid-** in App.]
bit² (bĭt) *n.* **1.** The sharp part of a tool, such as the cutting edge of an ax. **2.** A pointed and threaded tool for drilling and boring that is secured in a brace, bitstock, or drill press. **3.** The part of a key that engages the bolt and tumblers of a lock. **4.** The tip of the mouthpiece on a pipe or a cigarette or cigar holder. **5.** The metal mouthpiece of a bridle, serving to control, curb, and direct an animal. **6.** Something that controls, guides, or curbs. ❖ *tr.v.* **bit·ted, bit·ting, bits 1.** To place a bit in the mouth of (a horse, for example). **2.** To check or control with or as if with a bit. **3.** To make or grind a bit on (a key). —**idiom: have (or take) the bit in one's teeth** To be uncontrollable; to cast off or refuse restraint. [ME *bite* < OE, act of biting. See **bheid-** in App.]
bit³ (bĭt) *n. Computer Science* A fundamental unit of information having just two possible values, as either of the binary digits 0 or 1. [Blend of B(INARY) and (DIG)IT.]
bit⁴ (bĭt) *v.* Past tense and a past participle of **bite.**
bi·tar·trate (bī-tär′trāt′) *n.* The group C₄H₅O₆ or a salt of tartaric acid containing it.
bitch (bĭch) *n.* **1.** A female canine animal, esp. a dog. **2.** *Offensive* **a.** A woman considered to be spiteful or overbearing. **b.** A woman considered to be lewd. **3.** *Slang* A complaint. **4.** *Slang* Something very unpleasant or difficult. ❖ *v.* **bitched, bitch·ing, bitch·es** *Slang* —*intr.* To complain; grumble. —*tr.* To botch; bungle. Often used with *up.* [ME *bicche* < OE *bicce.*]
bitch·er·y (bĭch′ə-rē) *n.* Mean remarks or spiteful behavior.
bitch·in' or **bitch·en** (bĭch′ən) *adj. Slang* Excellent; first-rate. [Alteration of *bitching* < (SON OF A) BITCH.]
bitch·y (bĭch′ē) *adj.* **-i·er, -i·est** *Slang* **1.** Malicious, spiteful, or overbearing. **2.** In a bad mood; irritable. —**bitch′i·ly** *adv.* —**bitch′i·ness** *n.*
bite (bīt) *v.* **bit** (bĭt), **bit·ten** (bĭt′n) or **bit, bit·ing, bites** —*tr.* **1.** To cut, grip, or tear with or as if with the teeth. **2a.** To pierce the skin or with the teeth, fangs, or mouthparts. **b.** To sting with a stinger. **3.** To cut into with or as if with a sharp instrument. **4.** To grip, grab, or seize: *bitten by a sudden desire to travel.* **5.** To eat into; corrode. **6.** To cause to sting or be painful: *cold that bites the skin.* —*intr.* **1.** To grip, cut into, or injure something with or as if with the teeth. **2.** To have a stinging effect. **3.** To have a sharp taste. **4.** To take or swallow bait. **5.** To be taken in by a ploy or deception. **6.** *Vulgar Slang* To be highly disagreeable or annoying. ❖ *n.* **1.** The act of biting. **2.** A skin wound or puncture produced by an animal's teeth or mouthparts. **3a.** A stinging or smarting sensation. **b.** An incisive, penetrating quality. **4.** An amount removed by or as if by an act of biting. **5.** An excerpt taken from something larger, such as a recording. **6a.** An amount of food taken into the mouth at one time; a mouthful. **b.** *Informal* A light meal or snack. **7.** The act or an instance of taking bait. **8a.** A secure grip or hold applied by a tool or machine upon a working surface. **b.** The part of a tool or machine that presses against and maintains a firm hold on a working surface. **9.** *Dentistry* The angle at which the upper and lower teeth meet; occlusion. **10.** The corrosive action of acid upon an etcher's metal plate. **11.** *Slang* An amount of money appropriated or withheld. —**idioms: bite off more than (one) can chew** To decide or agree to do more than one can finally accomplish. **bite the bullet** *Slang* To face a painful situation bravely and stoically. **bite the dust** *Slang* **1.** To fall dead, esp. in combat. **2.** To be defeated. **3.** To come to an end. **bite the hand that feeds (one)** To repay generosity or kindness with ingratitude and injury. [ME *biten* < OE *bītan.* See **bheid-** in App.] —**bit′a·ble, bite′a·ble** *adj.* —**bit′er** *n.*
bite·plate also **bite plate** (bīt′plāt′) *n.* A removable dental appliance that is fitted to the palate and used as a diagnostic or therapeutic aid, esp. in orthodontics.
bite·wing (bīt′wĭng′) *n.* A dental x-ray film with a central projection on which the teeth can close.
Bi·thyn·i·a (bī-thĭn′ē-ə) An ancient country of NW Asia Minor in present-day Turkey; orig. inhabited by Thracians and absorbed into the Roman Empire by the end of the 1st cent. B.C. —**Bi·thyn′i·an** *adj. & n.*
bit·ing (bī′tĭng) *adj.* **1a.** Capable of wounding with a sting, mouthparts, or fangs. **b.** Causing a stinging sensation. **2.** Injuring or capable of injuring the feelings: *biting sarcasm.* —**bit′ing·ly** *adv.*
biting louse *n.* Any of several small, wingless, biting insects of the order Mallophaga that are external parasites on birds.
biting midge *n.* See **punkie.**
bit map or **bit·map** (bĭt′măp′) *n. Computer Science* A set of bits that represents a graphic image, with each bit or group of bits corresponding to a pixel in the image. —**bit′-mapped′** (-măpt′) *adj.*
bit part *n.* A small or insignificant role, as in a play or movie, usu. having a few spoken lines.
bit·stock (bĭt′stŏk′) *n.* A handle used to secure and turn a drilling or boring bit; a brace.
bit stream or **bit·stream** (bĭt′strēm′) *n. Computer Science* The transmission of binary digits as a simple, unstructured sequence of bits.
bit·sy (bĭt′sē) *adj.* **-si·er, -si·est** Bitty. [Alteration of BITTY.]

bitt (bĭt) *n.* A vertical post, usu. one of a pair, set on the deck of a ship and used to secure lines or cables. ❖ *tr.v.* **bitt·ed, bitt·ing, bitts** To wind (a cable) around a bitt. [Perh. of Du. or LGer. orig.; akin to ON *biti*, crossbeam.]
bit·ten (bĭt′n) *v.* A past participle of **bite.**
bit·ter (bĭt′ər) *adj.* **-er, -est 1.** Having or being a taste that is sharp, acrid, and unpleasant. **2.** Causing a sharply unpleasant, painful, or stinging sensation; harsh. **3.** Difficult or distasteful to accept, admit, or bear. **4.** Proceeding from or exhibiting strong animosity: *bitter foes.* **5.** Resulting from or expressive of severe grief, anguish, or disappointment. **6.** Marked by resentment or cynicism. ❖ *adv.* In an intense or harsh way; bitterly. ❖ *tr.v.* **-tered, -ter·ing, -ters** To make bitter. ❖ *n.* **1.** That which is bitter. **2. bitters** A bitter, usu. alcoholic liquid made with herbs or roots and used in cocktails or as a tonic. **3.** *Chiefly British* A sharp-tasting beer made with hops. [ME < OE. See **bheid-** in App.] —**bit′ter·ly** *adv.* —**bit′ter·ness** *n.*
bitter almond *n.* A variety of almond (*Prunus dulcis* var. *amara*) having kernels that yield an oil used for flavoring.
bitter aloes *pl.n.* (*used with a sing. verb*) See **aloe** 3.
bitter apple *n.* See **colocynth.**
bit·ter·brush (bĭt′ər-brŭsh′) *n.* A shrub of the genus *Purshia*, esp. *P. tridentata* of western North America, having bitter-tasting leaves with fuzzy undersides.
bitter cress *n.* Any of several herbs of the genus *Cardamine* in the mustard family, having usu. divided leaves and pods that dehisce explosively.
bitter end *n.* **1.** A final, painful, or disastrous extremity. **2.** *Nautical* The inboard end of a chain, line, or cable, esp. the end of a rope or cable that is wound around a bitt. [*bitter*, bitt (BITT + -ER¹) + END. Sense 1 influenced by BITTER.]
bit·ter·end·er or **bit·ter-end·er** (bĭt′ər-ĕn′dər) *n.* One who persists until it becomes impossible to continue.
bit·tern¹ (bĭt′ərn) *n.* Any of several wading birds of the genera *Botaurus* and *Ixobrychus*, having brownish plumage and a deep cry in the male. [Alteration (perh. influenced by TERN¹) of ME *bitour* < OFr. *butor*, poss. < VLat. *buti-taurus* : Lat. *būtiō*, buzzard + Lat. *taurus*, bull (after its cry); see **tauro-** in App.]
bit·tern² (bĭt′ərn) *n.* The bitter water solution of bromides, magnesium, and calcium salts remaining after sodium chloride is crystallized out of seawater. [< BITTER.]
bit·ter·nut (bĭt′ər-nŭt′) *n.* A hickory tree (*Carya cordiformis*) of eastern North America having bitter thin-shelled nuts.
bitter orange *n.* See **sour orange.**
bit·ter·root (bĭt′ər-rōōt′, -rŏŏt′) *n.* A perennial herb (*Lewisia rediviva*) of western North America having an edible root.
Bitterroot Range A chain of the Rocky Mts. along the ID–MT border rising to 3,474.9 m (11,393 ft).
bit·ter·sweet (bĭt′ər-swēt′) *n.* **1.** A vine of the genus *Celastrus*, esp. the North American species *C. scandens* and the eastern Asian species *C. orbiculata*, having yellow-orange fruits that open at maturity to expose red seeds. **2.** See **bittersweet nightshade. 3.** A dark to deep reddish orange. ❖ *adj.* **1.** Bitter and sweet at the same time: *bittersweet chocolate.* **2.** Producing or expressing a mixture of pain and pleasure. **3.** Dark to deep reddish-orange. [After its roots, which are said to taste bitter, then sweet when chewed.]
bittersweet nightshade *n.* A poisonous climbing or trailing plant (*Solanum dulcamara*) native to Eurasia and having violet flowers and red berries. [After its roots, which are said to taste bitter, then sweet when chewed.]
bit·ty (bĭt′ē) *adj.* **-ti·er, -ti·est 1.** *Informal* Tiny. **2.** *Chiefly British* Composed of small segments lacking cohesion; fragmented. —**bit′ti·ness** *n.*
bi·tu·men (bĭ-tōō′mən, -tyōō′-, bī-) *n.* Any of various flammable mixtures of hydrocarbons and other substances, occurring naturally or obtained by distillation from coal or petroleum, that are a component of asphalt and tar. [ME *bithumen*, a mineral pitch < Lat. *bitūmen*, perh. of Celt. orig.] —**bi·tu′mi·noid′** (-mə-noid′) *adj.* —**bi·tu′mi·nize′** *v.* —**bi·tu′mi·ni·za′tion** (-nĭzā′shən) *n.*
bi·tu·mi·nous (bĭ-tōō′mə-nəs, -tyōō′-, bī-) *adj.* **1.** Like or containing bitumen. **2.** Of or relating to bituminous coal.
bituminous coal *n.* A type of coal with a high percentage of volatile matter that burns with a smoky yellow flame.
bi·va·lent (bī-vā′lənt) *adj.* **1.** *Chemistry* Divalent. **2.** *Biology* Consisting of a pair of homologous synapsed chromosomes, associated together during meiosis; double. ❖ *n. Biology* A pair of bivalent chromosomes. —**bi·va′lence, bi·va′len·cy** *n.*
bi·valve (bī′vălv′) *n.* A mollusk, such as an oyster or clam, that has a shell consisting of two hinged valves. ❖ *adj.* **1.** Having a shell consisting of two hinged valves. **2.** Consisting of two similar separable parts. —**bi′valved′** *adj.*
biv·ou·ac (bĭv′ōō-ăk′, bĭv′wăk′) *n.* A temporary encampment often in an unsheltered area. ❖ *intr.v.* **-acked, -ack·ing, -acs** also **-acks** To camp in a bivouac. [Fr. < Ger. dialectal *beiwacht*, supplementary night watch : *bei-*, beside (< MHGer. *bi-* < OHGer.; see **ambhi** in App.) + *Wacht*, watch, vigil (< MHGer. *wahte* < OHGer. *wahta*).]
Bi·wa (bē′wä) A lake of S Honshu, Japan, W of Nagoya.
bi·week·ly (bī-wēk′lē) *adj.* **1.** Happening every two weeks. **2.**

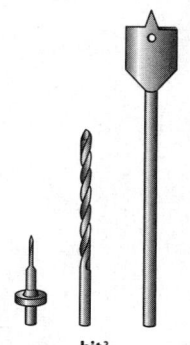

bit²
left to right: pilot, twist, and spade bits

Happening twice a week; semiweekly. See Usage Note at **bi-¹**. ❖ *n., pl.* **-lies** A publication issued every two weeks. —**bi·week′ly** *adv.*

bi·year·ly (bī-yîr′lē) *adj.* **1.** Happening every two years. **2.** Happening twice a year; semiyearly. See Usage Note at **bi-¹**. —**bi·year′ly** *adv.*

Bi·ysk (bē′ĭsk, bēsk) or **Bisk** (bĭsk, bēsk) A city of S-central Russia ESE of Barnaul; founded 1709. Pop. 232,529.

biz (bĭz) *n. Informal* Business.

bi·zarre (bĭ-zär′) *adj.* Strikingly unconventional and far-fetched in style or appearance; odd. See Syns at **fantastic.** [Fr. < Sp. *bizarro,* brave, prob. < Basque *bizar,* beard.] —**bi·zarre′ly** *adv.* —**bi·zarre′ness** *n.*

Bi·zet (bē-zā′), **Alexandre César Léopold** Known as "Georges." 1838–75. French composer whose best-known work is the opera *Carmen* (1875).

BJ *abbr.* Bachelor of Journalism

Björn·son (byûrn′sən), **Björnstjerne** 1832–1910. Norwegian writer who won the 1903 Nobel Prize for literature.

Bk The symbol for the element **berkelium.**

bkpt. *abbr.* bankrupt

BL *abbr.* **1.** Bachelor of Laws **2.** Bachelor of Letters **3.** Bachelor of Literature

bl. *abbr.* barrel

B/L *abbr.* bill of lading

BLA *abbr.* Bachelor of Liberal Arts

blab (blăb) *v.* **blabbed, blab·bing, blabs** —*tr.* To reveal (secret matters) esp. through indiscreet or unreserved talk. —*intr.* **1.** To reveal secret matters. **2.** To chatter thoughtlessly or indiscreetly. ❖ *n.* **1.** An incessant or indiscreet talker. **2.** Lengthy chatter. [ME *blabben,* to talk foolishly, back-formation < *blaberen.*] —**blab′by** *adj.*

blab·ber (blăb′ər) *intr.v.* **-bered, -ber·ing, -bers** To chatter; babble. ❖ *n.* **1.** Idle chatter. **2.** A blabbermouth. [ME *blaberen.*]

blab·ber·mouth (blăb′ər-mouth′) *n. Informal* One who talks indiscreetly or incessantly.

black (blăk) *adj.* **black·er, black·est 1.** Being of the color black, producing or reflecting comparatively little light and having no predominant hue. **2.** Having little or no light: *a black, moonless night.* **3.** often **Black a.** Of, relating to, or belonging to a racial group having brown to black skin, esp. one of African origin. **b.** Of, relating to, or belonging to an American ethnic group descended from African peoples having dark skin; African-American. **4.** Very dark in color: *rich black soil.* **5.** Soiled, as from soot. **6.** Evil; wicked. **7.** Cheerless and depressing; gloomy: *black thoughts.* **8.** Being or characterized by morbid or grimly satiric humor. **9.** Marked by anger or sullenness: *a black look.* **10.** Attended with disaster; calamitous. **11.** Deserving of, indicating, or incurring censure or dishonor: *"Man . . . has written one of his blackest records as a destroyer on the oceanic islands"* (Rachel Carson). **12.** Wearing clothing of the darkest visual hue: *the black knight.* **13.** Served without milk or cream. **14.** *Chiefly British* Boycotted as part of a labor union action. ❖ *n.* **1a.** The achromatic color value of minimum lightness or maximum darkness; the color of objects that absorb nearly all light of all visible wavelengths; one extreme of the neutral gray series, the opposite being white. **b.** A pigment or dye having this color value. **2.** Complete or almost complete absence of light; darkness. **3.** Clothing of the darkest hue, esp. such clothing worn for mourning. **4.** often **Black a.** A member of a racial group having brown to black skin, esp. one of African origin. **b.** An American descended from peoples of African origin having brown to black skin; an African American. **5.** Something that is colored black. **6.** *Games* **a.** The black-colored pieces, as in chess or checkers. **b.** The player using these pieces. ❖ *v.* **blacked, black·ing, blacks** —*tr.* **1.** To make black. **2.** To apply blacking to. **3.** *Chiefly British* To boycott as part of a labor union action. —*intr.* To become black. —*phrasal verb:* **black out 1a.** To lose consciousness or memory temporarily. **b.** To suppress (a fact or memory, for example) from conscious recognition. **2.** To prohibit the dissemination of, esp. by censorship. **3.** To extinguish or conceal all lights that might help enemy aircraft find a target during an air raid. **4.** To extinguish all the lights on (a stage). **5.** To cause a failure of electrical power in. **6a.** To withhold (a televised event or program) from a broadcast area. **b.** To withhold a televised event or program from. —*idiom:* in the black On the credit side of a ledger; prosperous. [ME *blak* < OE *blæc.*] —**black′ish** *adj.* —**black′ly** *adv.* —**black′ness** *n.*

Black Hawk
c. 1837–44 lithograph from
McKenney and Hall's *History
of the Indian Tribes of North
America*

USAGE NOTE *Black* is sometimes capitalized in its racial sense, especially in the African-American press, though the lowercase form is still widely used by authors of all races. The capitalization of *Black* does raise ancillary problems for the treatment of the term *white.* Orthographic evenhandedness would seem to require the use of uppercase *White,* but this form might be taken to imply that whites constitute a single ethnic group, an issue that is certainly debatable. Uppercase *White* is also sometimes associated with the writings of white supremacist groups, a sufficient reason of itself for many to dismiss it. On the other hand, the use of lowercase *white* in the same context as uppercase *Black* will obviously raise questions as to how and why the writer has distinguished between the two groups. There is no entirely happy solution to this problem. In all likelihood, uncertainty as to the mode of styling of *white* has dissuaded many publications from adopting the capitalized form *Black.* See Usage Notes at **color, colored.**

Black, Hugo La Fayette 1886–1971. Amer. jurist; associate justice of the US Supreme Court (1937–71).

Black, Joseph 1728–99. British chemist who rediscovered carbon dioxide (1756).

Black, Shirley Temple b. 1928. Amer. actress and public official. As Shirley Temple she was an immensely popular child actress of the 1930s.

black alder *n.* **1.** A widespread North American deciduous shrub or small tree *(Ilex verticillata)* of the holly family. **2.** A Eurasian alder tree *(Alnus glutinosa).*

black·a·moor (blăk′ə-mŏŏr′) *n. Offensive* A dark-skinned person, esp. a person from northern Africa. [BLACK + *-a-,* of unknown orig. + MOOR.]

black-and-blue (blăk′ən-blōō′) *adj.* Discolored from coagulation of blood below the surface of the skin.

black-and-tan (blăk′ən-tăn′) *adj.* **1.** Having a black coat with tannish markings. Used of a dog. **2.** Involving, recognizing, or admitting Black and white people equally.

Black and Tan *n., pl.* **Black and Tans** A member of a paramilitary force recruited in Britain and sent to Ireland as part of the Royal Irish Constabulary to suppress the Sinn Fein rebellion of 1919 to 1921. [< the color of their uniform.]

black-and-tan terrier *n.* See **Manchester terrier.**

black and white *n.* **1.** Writing or print. **2.** A visual medium, as in photography, employing only black and white or black, white, and values of gray.

black-and-white (blăk′ən-hwīt′, -wīt′) *adj.* **1.** Partially black and partially white. **2.** Being in writing or print. **3a.** Rendered in black and white or in achromatic colors. **b.** Of or relating to the reproduction or presentation of visual images in black and white. **4.** Expressing, recognizing, or based on two mutually exclusive sets of ideas or values.

Black Ang·us (ăng′gəs) *n.* See **Aberdeen Angus.**

black art *n.* Sorcery; witchcraft.

black·ball (blăk′bôl′) *n.* **1.** A negative vote, esp. one that blocks the admission of an applicant to an organization. **2.** A small black ball used as a negative ballot. ❖ *tr.v.* **-balled, -ball·ing, -balls 1.** To vote against, esp. to veto the admission of. **2.** To shut out from social or commercial participation; ostracize or boycott. —**black′ball′er** *n.*

black bass (băs) *n.* Any of several North American freshwater game fishes of the genus *Micropterus.*

black bean *n.* Any of various black-colored beans, esp.: **a.** A small black bean having cream-colored flesh, used in southern and Latin-American cuisine. **b.** A fermented black soybean having a pungent flavor, preserved in salt and used in Asian cuisine.

black bear *n.* **1.** The common North American bear *(Euarctos* or *Ursus americanus)* that lives in forests, is omnivorous, and has a black or dark brown coat. **2.** Any of several black or dark brown Asiatic bears, esp. *Selenarctos thibetanus,* with a pointed snout and a white V-shaped mark on the chest.

Black·beard (blăk′bîrd′) See Edward **Teach.**

black belt *n.* **1a.** The black sash that symbolizes the rank of expert in a martial art such as judo or karate. **b.** A person who has attained this rank. **2.** A region of rich, black soil.

black·ber·ry (blăk′bĕr′ē) *n.* **1.** Any of various shrubs of the genus *Rubus,* having usu. prickly stems and an aggregate fruit of drupelets. **2.** The edible fruit of these plants.

black bile *n.* One of the four humors of ancient and medieval physiology, supposed to cause melancholy when present in excess.

black birch *n.* See **sweet birch.**

black·bird (blăk′bûrd′) *n.* **1.** Any of various New World birds of the family Icteridae, the male of which has black or predominantly black plumage. **2.** An Old World songbird *(Turdus merula),* the male of which is black with a yellow bill.

black·board (blăk′bôrd′, -bōrd′) *n.* A smooth, hard, dark-colored panel for writing on with chalk.

black·bod·y (blăk′bŏd′ē) *n., pl.* **-ies** A theoretically perfect absorber of all incident radiation.

black book *n.* A book containing names of people or organizations to blacklist.

black box *n.* **1a.** A device or theoretical construct whose function is known but whose parts and method of operation are unknown. **b.** Something that is mysterious, esp. as to function. **2.** See **flight recorder.**

black bryony *n.* A poisonous perennial twining herb *(Tamus communis)* native to Eurasia and having red berries.

black·buck (blăk′bŭk′) *n.* An antelope *(Antilope cervicapra)* of India that inhabits open grasslands and in the male has long spiraled horns and a black coat with white underparts.

Black·burn (blăk′bûrn′), **Mount** A peak, 5,039.5 m (16,523 ft), of the Wrangell Mts. in S AK.

black·cap (blăk′kăp′) *n.* **1.** See **black raspberry 1. 2a.** A small European warbler *(Sylvia atricapilla),* the male of which is gray with a black crown. **b.** Any of various other black-crowned birds, such as the chickadee.

black cherry *n.* **1a.** A deciduous North American tree (*Prunus serotina*) having drooping elongate clusters of white flowers and blackish fruits. **b.** The reddish-brown wood of this tree. **2.** Any of various dark-fruited kinds of cherry.

black·cock (blăk′kŏk′) *n.* The male of the black grouse.

black cod *n.* See **sablefish.**

black cohosh *n.* An eastern North American perennial herb (*Cimicifuga racemosa*) having large, pinnately compound leaves and racemes of small white flowers.

black cow *n.* **1.** Chocolate milk. **2.** *Chicago* A float made with root beer and vanilla ice cream. [BLACK + COW¹ (< the ice cream).]

black crappie *n.* An edible North American sunfish (*Pomoxis nigromaculatus*) having dark mottled coloring.

black cumin *n.* An annual Eurasian herb (*Nigella sativa*) having bluish-white flowers and pungent black seeds used as a seasoning in Asian cuisines.

black·damp (blăk′dămp′) *n.* A suffocating gas that consists of a mixture of carbon dioxide and nitrogen, found in mines after fires or explosions. [BLACK + DAMP, gas.]

Black Death *n.* An outbreak of bubonic plague that was pandemic throughout Europe and much of Asia in the 14th century. [< the dark splotches it causes on its victims.]

black diamond *n.* **1.** See **carbonado².** **2. black diamonds** Coal.

black duck *n.* A common duck (*Anas rubripes*) of the northeast United States and Canada, characterized by dark plumage.

black dwarf star *n.* The remains of a white dwarf star after it has expended all of its energy and is no longer emitting detectable radiation.

black·en (blăk′ən) *v.* **-ened, -en·ing, -ens** —*tr.* **1.** To make black. **2.** To sully or defame: *a scandal that blackened his name.* **3.** To sear in a hot skillet until black. —*intr.* To become dark or black. —**black′en·er** *n.*

Black English *n.* **1.** See **African American Vernacular English. 2.** Any of the nonstandard varieties of English spoken by Black people throughout the world.

USAGE NOTE In the United States, *Black English* usually refers to the everyday spoken varieties of English used by African Americans, especially of the working class in urban neighborhoods or rural communities. Linguists generally prefer the term *African American Vernacular English,* although some use the term *Ebonics,* which saw widespread use in the late 1990s.

Black English Vernacular *n.* See **African American Vernacular English.**

black eye *n.* **1.** A bruised discoloration of the flesh surrounding the eye, often resulting from a blow. **2.** A dishonored reputation; a bad name.

black-eyed pea (blăk′īd′) *n.* See **cowpea.**

black-eyed Su·san (sōō′zən) *n.* Any of several North American herbs of the genus *Rudbeckia* in the composite family, having flower heads with yellow rays and dark centers.

black·face (blăk′fās′) *n.* **1.** Makeup for a comic travesty of Black people, esp. in a minstrel show. **2.** An actor wearing such makeup in a minstrel show.

black·fish (blăk′fĭsh′) *n., pl.* **blackfish** or **-fish·es 1.** Any of various dark-colored fishes, such as: **a.** A small, edible freshwater fish (*Dallia pectoralis*) of Alaska and Siberia, noted for its ability to withstand freezing. **b.** See **tautog. 2.** See **pilot whale.**

black flag *n.* A Jolly Roger.

black fly *n.* Any of various small, dark-colored biting flies of the family Simuliidae, the larvae of which attach to rocks in running streams.

Black·foot (blăk′fŏot′) *n., pl.* **Blackfoot** or **-feet** (-fēt′) **1.** A member of a Native American confederacy located on the northern Great Plains, composed of the Blackfoot, Blood, and Piegan tribes. **2.** A member of the northernmost tribe of the Blackfoot confederacy, inhabiting central Alberta. **3.** The Algonquian language of the Blackfoot, Blood, and Piegan. **4.** See **Sihasapa.** [Transl. of Blackfoot *siksiká* (perh. < the blackening of their moccasins from painting them or from walking near prairie fires) : *sik,* black + *ika,* foot.] —**black′foot′** *adj.*

black-foot·ed albatross (blăk′fŏot′ĭd) *n.* An albatross (*Diomedea nigripes*) of the Pacific coastal islands that is blackish and dusky with black feet and a whitish head.

black-footed ferret *n.* A North American weasel (*Mustela nigripes*) that has a blackish mask and feet.

Blackfoot Sioux *n., pl.* **Blackfoot Sioux** See **Sihasapa.**

Black Forest A mountainous region of SW Germany between the Rhine and Neckar rivers.

black frost *n.* A dry freeze that results in the internal freezing and death of vegetation.

black gold *n. Informal* Petroleum.

black grouse *n.* A Eurasian game bird (*Lyrurus tetrix*) with black plumage in the male.

black·guard (blăg′ərd, -ärd′) *n.* **1.** An unprincipled person; a scoundrel. **2.** A foul-mouthed person. ❖ *tr.v.* **-guard·ed, -guard·ing, -guards** To abuse verbally; revile. —**black′guard·ism** *n.* —**black′guard·ly** *adj. & adv.*

black gum *n.* See **sour gum.**

Black Hand *n.* A secret society organized for acts of terrorism and blackmail that was active in the United States in the early 20th century.

black haw *n.* Either of two deciduous plants (*Viburnum lentago* or *V. prunifolium*) native to the eastern United States and having white flowers and blue-black berrylike fruits.

Black Hawk 1767–1838. Sauk leader. Resenting an 1804 treaty that ceded all Sauk and Fox lands E of the Mississippi R. to the US, he led 1,000 Sauk and Fox warriors in the Black Hawk War (1832).

black·head (blăk′hĕd′) *n.* **1.** *Medicine* A plug of keratin and sebum within a hair follicle that is blackened at the surface. **2.** An infectious disease of turkeys and some wildfowl that is caused by a protozoan (*Histomonas meleagridis*) and results in lesions of the intestine and liver. **3.** Any of various birds, such as the scaup, with dark head markings.

Black Hills A group of rugged mountains of SW SD and NE WY rising to 2,208.8 m (7,242 ft).

black hole *n.* **1.** An extremely small region of space-time with a gravitational field so intense that nothing can escape, not even light. **2.** A great void; an abyss.

black ice *n.* A thin, nearly invisible coating of ice that forms on paved surfaces.

black·ing (blăk′ĭng) *n.* **1.** See **lampblack. 2.** A preparation, such as a shoe or stove polish, used to impart a black color.

black·jack (blăk′jăk′) *n.* **1.** A leather-covered bludgeon with a short shaft or strap, used as a hand weapon. **2.** The blackjack oak. **3.** *Games* A card game in which the object is to accumulate cards with a higher count than that of the dealer but not exceeding 21. **4.** Sphalerite. ❖ *tr.v.* **-jacked, -jack·ing, -jacks 1.** To hit or beat with a blackjack. **2.** To coerce by threats.

blackjack oak *n.* A deciduous oak tree (*Quercus marilandica*) native mostly to the southeastern United States and having blackish bark.

black knot *n.* A disease of the plum, the cherry, and related plants caused by the fungus *Apiosporina morbosa* and resulting in black knotlike swellings on the branches.

black lead (lĕd) *n.* See **graphite.**

black·leg (blăk′lĕg′) *n.* **1.** An infectious, usu. fatal bacterial disease of cattle and other animals, characterized by gas-filled swellings in the musculature. **2.** A bacterial or fungal disease of certain plants that turns the stems black at the soil line. **3.** One who cheats at cards; a cardsharp. **4.** *Chiefly British* A worker opposed to trade unions; a scab.

black letter *n.* A heavy typeface with very broad counters and thick ornamental serifs.

black light *n.* Invisible ultraviolet or infrared radiation that is used to take pictures in the dark.

black·light trap (blăk′līt′) *n.* An insect trap that attracts a wide variety of insects by the use of a form of black light.

black·list (blăk′lĭst′) *n.* A list of persons or organizations that have incurred disapproval or suspicion or are to be boycotted or otherwise penalized. ❖ *tr.v.* **-list·ed, -list·ing, -lists** To place on or as if on a blacklist. —**black′list′er** *n.*

black locust *n.* A deciduous tree (*Robinia pseudoacacia*) in the pea family, native to the United States and having alternate, pinnately compound leaves and fragrant white flowers.

black lung *n.* Pneumoconiosis caused by the long-term inhalation of coal dust.

black magic *n.* Magic practiced for evil purposes or in league with supposed evil spirits; witchcraft.

black·mail (blăk′māl′) *n.* **1a.** Extortion, as of money, from a person by the threat of exposing a criminal act or discreditable information. **b.** Something of value extorted in this manner. **2.** Tribute formerly paid to freebooters along the Scottish border for protection from pillage. [BLACK + MAIL³.] —**black′mail′** *v.* —**black′mail′er** *n.*

Black Ma·ri·a (mə-rī′ə) *n.* A patrol wagon. [?]

black market *n.* **1.** The illegal business of buying or selling goods or currency in violation of restrictions such as price controls or rationing. **2.** A place where these illegal operations are carried on. —**black′-mar′ket** (blăk′mär′kĭt) *adj.*

black-mar·ket (blăk′mär′kĭt) *tr.v.* **-ket·ed, -ket·ing, -kets** To trade (something) in the black market. —**black′-mar′ket·er** (-kĭ-tər), **black′-mar′ket·eer** (-tîr′) *n.* —**black′-mar′ket·eer′ing** *n.*

black mass *n.* **1.** A travesty of the Roman Catholic Mass, ascribed to worshipers of Satanism. **2. Black Mass** *Informal* A Requiem Mass.

black measles *n.* (used with a sing. or pl. verb) A severe form of measles characterized by dark, hemorrhagic skin eruptions.

black medic or **black medick** *n.* A cloverlike Eurasian plant (*Medicago lupulina*) in the pea family, having dense clusters of small yellow flowers and black pods. [BLACK + MEDIC¹.]

black money *n.* Income, as from illegal activities, that is not reported to the government for tax purposes.

Black Mountains A range of the Blue Ridge in W NC rising to 2,038.6 km (6,684 ft).

Black·mun (blăk′mən), **Harry Andrew** 1908–99. Amer. jurist; associate justice of the US Supreme Court (1970–94).

Black Muslim *n.* A member of the Nation of Islam.

black knot
Apiosporina morbosa

black letter

ă	pat	oi	boy
ā	pay	ou	out
âr	care	ŏŏ	took
ä	father	ōō	boot
ĕ	pet	ŭ	cut
ē	be	ûr	urge
ĭ	pit	th	thin
ī	pie	th	this
îr	pier	hw	which
ŏ	pot	zh	vision
ō	toe	ə	about,
ô	paw		item

Stress marks:
′ (primary);
′ (secondary), as in
lexicon (lĕk′sĭ-kŏn′)

black mustard *n.* A weedy, annual Eurasian plant (*Brassica nigra*) in the mustard family, having racemes of yellow flowers and pungent seeds.

Black Nationalist *n.* A member of a group of militant Black people who urge separatism from white people and self-government for Black communities. —**Black Nationalism** *n.*

black nightshade *n.* A poisonous annual Eurasian plant (*Solanum nigrum*) widespread as a weed and having clusters of white star-shaped flowers and usu. blackish berries.

black oak *n.* A deciduous North American tree (*Quercus velutina*) having a blackish bark and durable wood.

black·out (blăk′out′) *n.* **1.** A cutoff of electrical power, esp. as a result of a shortage, a mechanical failure, or overuse by consumers. **2.** The concealment or extinguishment of lights that might be visible during an air raid. **3a.** The extinguishing of all stage lights in a theater to indicate the passage of time or mark the end of a scene. **b.** A short, comic vaudeville skit that ends with lights off. **4.** A temporary loss of memory or consciousness. **5a.** A suppression, as of news, by censorship. **b.** Restriction or prohibition of telecasting a sports event to ensure ticket sales.

Black Panther *n.* A member of a militant Black American organization.

black pepper *n.* The small, dark, unripe fruit of the pepper plant (*Piper nigrum*), used whole or ground as a spice.

black·poll (blăk′pōl′) *n.* A North American warbler (*Dendroica striata*), the male of which has a black cap. [BLACK + POLL, head.]

Black·pool (blăk′pōol′) A borough of NW England on the Irish Sea N of Liverpool. Pop. 153,614.

black poplar *n.* A Eurasian shade tree (*Populus nigra*) with spreading branches.

black powder *n.* An explosive mixture of saltpeter, charcoal, and sulfur, formerly used in firearms.

Black Power *n.* A movement among Black Americans emphasizing racial pride and social equality.

black pudding *n.* A French black sausage made of pork and seasoned pig's blood.

black racer *n.* A North American blacksnake (*Coluber constrictor*) commonly found in the eastern United States.

black raspberry *n.* **1.** A prickly eastern North American shrub (*Rubus occidentalis*) having an aggregate, edible, juicy purple-black fruit. **2.** The fruit of this plant.

Black River 1. In China **Ba·bian Jiang** (bä′byän′ jyäng′) and in Vietnam **Song Da** (sông′ dä′) A river of SE Asia rising in S China and flowing c. 805 km (500 mi) to the Red R. in N Vietnam. **2.** A river rising in SE MO and flowing c. 483 km (300 mi) to the White R. in NE AR.

Black Rod *n.* The chief usher of the British House of Lords. [After the rod carried as symbol of the office.]

black rot *n.* Any of several fungal or bacterial plant diseases resulting in dark discoloration and decay of affected parts.

black salsify *n.* A European plant (*Scorzonera hispanica*) in the composite family, having heads of yellow ray flowers and a large, edible, fleshy root.

black sapote *n.* **1.** A tropical American tree (*Diospyros digyna*) related to the persimmon, with fruit that blackens when ripe. **2.** The fruit of this plant. [BLACK + Am.Sp. *zapote*, persimmonlike fruit (< Nahuatl *tzapotl*).]

Black Sea An inland sea between Europe and Asia connected with the Aegean by the Bosporus, Sea of Marmara, and Dardanelles.

black sheep *n.* **1.** A sheep with black fleece. **2.** A member of a family or other group who is considered undesirable or disreputable.

Black Shirt also **Black·shirt** (blăk′shûrt′) *n.* A member of a fascist party organization having a black shirt as part of its uniform, esp. an Italian fascist.

black skimmer *n.* A skimmer (*Rynchops niger*) of North and South America that is black above and white below.

black·smith (blăk′smĭth′) *n.* **1.** One that forges and shapes iron with an anvil and hammer. **2.** One that makes, repairs, and fits horseshoes. [< the color of iron.] —**black′smith′ing** *n.*

black·snake (blăk′snāk′) *n.* **1.** Any of various dark-colored, chiefly nonvenomous snakes, such as the black racer of North America. **2.** A long braided rawhide or leather whip.

black snakeroot *n.* See **black cohosh.**

black spot *n.* Any of various fungal or bacterial diseases of plants, resulting in small black spots, as on the leaves.

black spruce *n.* A northern North American spruce (*Picea mariana*) having blue-green needles and small egg-shaped cones.

Black·stone (blăk′stōn′, -stən), Sir **William** 1723–80. British jurist and educator who wrote *Commentaries on the Laws of England* (1765–69).

black·strap (blăk′străp′) *n.* A dark, thick molasses, esp. a residual product of sugar refining. [< its color and texture.]

black studies *pl.n.* (*used with a sing. or pl. verb*) An academic curriculum focusing on the history and culture of Black people.

black-tailed deer (blăk′tāld′) also **black·tail deer** (-tāl′) *n.* See **mule deer.**

black tea *n.* A dark tea prepared from fresh tea leaves that have been fully fermented before being dried.

black·thorn (blăk′thôrn′) *n.* A thorny, deciduous Eurasian shrub (*Prunus spinosa*) having white flowers and small bluish-black fruits used for flavoring alcoholic beverages.

black tie *n.* **1.** A black bow tie worn with a dinner jacket. **2.** Semi-formal evening wear typically for men, usu. requiring a dinner jacket. —**black′-tie′** (blăk′tī′) *adj.*

black·top (blăk′tŏp′) *n.* A bituminous material, such as asphalt, used to pave roads. ❖ *tr.v.* **-topped, -top·ping, -tops** To pave with a bituminous material.

Black Vernacular English *n.* See **African American Vernacular English.**

Black Vol·ta (vŏl′tə, vōl′-, vôl′-) A river of W Africa rising in W Burkina Faso and flowing c. 1,352 km (840 mi) to the White Volta in Ghana.

black vomit *n.* **1.** Dark vomit consisting of digested blood and gastric contents. **2.** Severe yellow fever with regurgitation of dark matter.

black vulture *n.* A carrion-eating bird (*Coragyps atratus*) of central North America and South America, having black plumage and a bald black head.

black walnut *n.* **1.** An eastern North American tree (*Juglans nigra*) having dark brown wood and a deeply furrowed nut. **2.** The wood of this tree. **3.** The nut of this tree.

black·wa·ter fever (blăk′wô′tər, -wŏt′ər) *n.* A serious, often fatal complication of chronic malaria, characterized by the passage of bloody, dark red or black urine.

Black·well (blăk′wĕl′, -wəl), **Antoinette Louisa Brown** 1825–1921. Amer. social reformer who was the first formally appointed (1852) woman pastor in America.

Blackwell, Elizabeth 1821–1910. British-born Amer. physician who was the first woman to be awarded a medical doctorate in modern times (1849).

black widow *n.* A poisonous New World spider (*Latrodectus mactans*), the female of which has a shiny black body with red markings. [< the fact that the female eats its mate.]

Black·wood (blăk′wōod′), **William** 1776–1834. Scottish publisher and editor (1817–34) of *Blackwood's Magazine*, a Tory literary review.

blad·der (blăd′ər) *n.* **1a.** *Anatomy* Any of various distensible membranous sacs, such as the urinary bladder, that serve as receptacles for fluid or gas. **b.** An item resembling a bladder. **2.** *Botany* Any of various hollow or inflated saclike organs or structures. **3.** *Pathology* A blister, pustule, or cyst filled with fluid or air; a vesicle. [ME *bladdre* < OE *blǣdre.*]

bladder campion *n.* A weedy Eurasian perennial herb (*Silene vulgaris*) having white flowers and an inflated calyx.

bladder fern *n.* Any of various ferns of the widespread genus *Cystopteris*, having pinnately compound fronds and often growing in rocky areas. [After its bladderlike indusium.]

blad·der·nose (blăd′ər-nōz′) *n.* See **hooded seal.**

blad·der·nut (blăd′ər-nŭt′) *n.* **1.** Any of various deciduous shrubs or small trees of the genus *Staphylea*, native to northern temperate regions and having opposite compound leaves and bladderlike fruits. **2.** The fruit of such a plant.

bladder worm *n.* The bladderlike, encysted larva of the tapeworm that is characteristic of the cysticercus stage.

blad·der·wort (blăd′ər-wûrt′, -wôrt′) *n.* Any of various mostly aquatic carnivorous plants of the genus *Utricularia*, having bladders that trap minute insects and crustaceans.

bladder wrack *n.* Any of certain rockweeds, esp. *Fucus vesiculosus*, having forked brownish-green branches with gas-filled bladders.

blad·der·y (blăd′ə-rē) *adj.* **1.** Resembling or like a bladder. **2.** Possessing a bladder or bladders.

blade (blād) *n.* **1.** The flat cutting part of a sharpened weapon or tool. **2a.** A sword. **b.** A swordsman. **3.** *Archaeology* A slender, sharp-edged, relatively long flake. **4.** A dashing youth. **5.** A flat, thin part or section, esp. one that makes contact to perform a desired action: *the blade of an oar.* **6.** The metal runner of an ice skate. **7.** A wide flat bone or bony part. **8.** The flat upper surface of the tongue just behind the tip. **9.** *Botany* **a.** The expanded part of a leaf or petal. **b.** The leaf of grasses and similar plants. ❖ *intr.v.* **blad·ed, blad·ing, blades** To skate on in-line skates. [ME < OE *blæd.* See **bhel-** in App.] —**blad′ed** *adj.*

blaff (blăf) *n. Caribbean* A West Indian stew consisting of fish or pork, seasonings such as lime and garlic, and often fruits and vegetables. [Prob. < Dominican E. *braff* < BROTH.]

blag·ging (blăg′ĭng) *n. Caribbean* Informal talk, usu. among men, occurring in a public place. [< Fr. *blaguer*, to talk through one's hat < *blague*, bladder, pouch, of Gmc. orig., ult. < Lat. *bulga*, leather bag. See BULGE.]

Bla·go·vesh·chensk (blä′gə-vĕsh′chĕnsk, blə-gə-vyĕsh′-chĭnsk) A city of E Russia at the confluence of the Amur and Zeya rivers. Pop. 212,179.

blah (blä) *Informal n.* **1.** Worthless nonsense; drivel. **2. blahs** A general feeling of discomfort, dissatisfaction, or depression. ❖ *adj.* **1.** Dull and uninteresting. **2.** Low in spirit or health; down. [Imit. of meaningless talk or a feeling of malaise.] —**blah** *adv.*

blain (blān) *n.* A skin swelling or sore; a blister; a blotch. [ME < OE *blegen.*]

Blaine (blān), **James Gillespie** 1830–93. Amer. politician who served as US secretary of state (1881 and 1889–92) and lost the

1884 presidential election to Grover Cleveland.

Blair (blâr), **Anthony Charles Lynton** Known as "Tony." b. 1953. British lawyer, politician, and Labour Party leader who was elected prime minister in 1997.

Blair, John 1732–1800. Amer. jurist; associate justice of the US Supreme Court (1789–96).

Blake (blāk), **James Herbert** Known as "Eubie." 1883–1983. Amer. pianist and composer noted for his Broadway productions, such as *Shuffle Along* (1921).

Blake, Robert 1599–1657. English Parliamentarian admiral who defeated the Royalist fleet in the Mediterranean Sea (1650) during the English Civil War.

Blake, William 1757–1827. British poet and artist whose works include *Songs of Innocence* (1789).

Bla·key (blā′kē), **Art** 1919–90. Amer. jazz drummer who initiated the practice of cross-rhythm drumming.

blam·a·ble also **blame·a·ble** (blā′mə-bəl) *adj.* Deserving blame. —**blam′a·ble·ness** *n.* —**blam′a·bly** *adv.*

blame (blām) *tr.v.* **blamed, blam·ing, blames** 1. To hold responsible. 2. To find fault with; censure. 3. To place responsibility for: *blamed the crisis on poor planning.* ❖ *n.* 1. The state of being responsible for a fault or error; culpability. 2. Censure; condemnation. —*idiom:* **to blame** 1. Deserving censure; at fault. 2. Being the cause or source of something. [ME *blamen* < OFr. *blasmer, blamer* < VLat. **blastēmāre,* alteration of LLat. *blasphēmāre,* to reproach. See BLASPHEME.] —**blam′er** *n.*

SYNONYMS *blame, fault, guilt* These nouns denote a sense of responsibility for an offense. *Blame* stresses censure or punishment for something for which one is held accountable: *The police laid the blame for the accident on the driver. Fault* is culpability for wrongdoing or failure: *It is my own fault that I failed the exam. Guilt* applies to willful wrongdoing and stresses moral culpability: *The prosecution had evidence of the defendant's guilt.* See also Syns at **criticize.**

---

blamed (blāmd) *adv. & adj. Informal* Used as an intensive: *called me a blamed fool.*

blame·ful (blām′fəl) *adj.* Deserving of blame; blameworthy. —**blame′ful·ly** *adv.* —**blame′ful·ness** *n.*

blame·less (blām′lĭs) *adj.* Free of blame or guilt; innocent. —**blame′less·ly** *adv.* —**blame′less·ness** *n.*

blame·wor·thy (blām′wûr′thē) *adj.* -thi·er, -thi·est Deserving blame; reprehensible. —**blame′wor′thi·ness** *n.*

Blanc (blăngk), **Melvin Jerome ("Mel")** 1908–89. Amer. actor who gained fame as the voice of more than 400 cartoon characters.

Blanc (blăngk, bläɴ), **Mont** The highest peak of the Alps, rising to 4,810.2 m (15,771 ft) in the Savoy Alps of SE France.

Blan·ca Peak (blăng′kə) A mountain, 4,375.2 m (14,345 ft), in the Sangre de Cristo Mts. of S CO.

blanc fixe (blängk′ fĭks′, blăn fēks′) *n.* Powdered barium sulfate used as a base for watercolor pigments and as a filler in paper. [Fr. : *blanc,* white + *fixe,* fixed.]

blanch (blănch) also **blench** (blĕnch) *v.* **blanched, blanch·ing, blanch·es** also **blenched, blench·ing, blench·es** —*tr.* 1. To take the color from; bleach. 2. To whiten (a growing plant or plant part) by excluding light. 3. To whiten (a metal) by soaking in acid or by coating with tin. 4. To boil (food) briefly, as to loosen skin. 5. To cause to turn white or become pale. —*intr.* To turn white or become pale: *Their faces blanched in terror.* [ME *blaunchen,* to whiten < OFr. *blanchir < blanche,* fem. of *blanc,* white, of Gmc. orig.] —**blanch′er** *n.*

blanc·mange (blə-mänj′, -mänzh′) *n.* A flavored and sweetened milk pudding thickened with cornstarch. [ME *blankmanger,* a dish made with almond milk < OFr. *blanc mangier : blanc,* white (of Gmc. orig.) + *mangier,* to eat, food (< Lat. *manducāre;* see MANGER).]

bland (blănd) *adj.* **bland·er, bland·est** 1a. Pleasant in manner; smooth: *a bland smile.* b. Not irritating or stimulating; soothing: *a bland diet.* c. Exhibiting no embarrassment or concern: *bland lies.* 2a. Dull and insipid: *a bland drama.* b. Having little or no distinctive flavor: *bland cooking.* [Lat. *blandus,* caressing, flattering.] —**bland′ly** *adv.* —**bland′ness** *n.*

blan·dish (blăn′dĭsh) *tr.v.* **-dished, -dish·ing, -dish·es** To coax by flattery or wheedling; cajole. [ME *blandishen* < OFr. *blandir, blandiss- < Lat. blandīrī < blandus,* flattering. See mel-[1] in App.] —**blan′dish·er** *n.* —**blan′dish·ment** *n.*

blank (blăngk) *adj.* **blank·er, blank·est** 1a. Devoid of writing, images, or marks: *a blank page.* b. Containing no information; unrecorded or erased: *a blank tape.* 2. Not completed or filled in: *a blank questionnaire.* 3. Not having received final processing; unfinished: *a blank key.* 4a. Lacking expression; expressionless. b. Appearing or seeming to appear dazed or confused. 5. Devoid of thought or impression: *a blank mind.* 6. Devoid of activity, interest, or distinctive character; empty. 7. Absolute; complete: *a blank refusal.* ❖ *n.* 1. An empty space or place; a void: *My mind was a blank.* 2a. An empty space on a document to be filled in. b. A document with one or more such spaces. 3. A manufactured article of a standard shape or form that is ready for final processing: *a key blank.* 4. A gun cartridge with a charge of powder but no bullet. 5. Something worthless, such as a losing lottery ticket. 6.

A mark, usu. a dash (—), indicating the omission of a word or of a letter or letters. 7. The white circle in the center of a target; a bull's-eye. ❖ *v.* **blanked, blank·ing, blanks** —*tr.* 1. To remove, as from view; obliterate. 2. To block access to: *blank off a subway tunnel.* 3. *Sports* To prevent (an opponent) from scoring. 4. To punch or stamp from flat stock, esp. with a die. —*intr.* 1. To become abstracted: *My mind blanked out.* 2. To fade away: *The music gradually blanked out.* [ME, white, having spaces to be filled in < OFr. *blanc,* white, of Gmc. orig.] —**blank′ly** *adv.* —**blank′ness** *n.*

blank check *n.* 1. A signed check with no amount to be paid filled in. 2. Total freedom of action; carte blanche.

blank endorsement *n.* An endorsement on a check or note that names no payee, making it payable to the bearer.

blan·ket (blăng′kĭt) *n.* 1. A large piece of woven material used as a covering for warmth, esp. on a bed. 2. A layer that covers or encloses: *a thick blanket of snow.* ❖ *adj.* Applying to or covering all conditions, instances, or members of a class: *a blanket insurance policy.* ❖ *tr.v.* **-ket·ed, -ket·ing, -kets** 1. To cover with or as if with a blanket: *leaves that blanket the ground.* 2. To cover so as to inhibit, suppress, or extinguish: *blanketed the grease fire with sand.* 3. To apply to generally and uniformly without exception. [ME < OFr., an unbleached soft cloth < *blanc,* white, of Gmc. orig.]

blanket flower *n.* See **gaillardia.**

blanket stitch *n.* A buttonhole stitch used for edging around heavy material.

blan·ket-stitch (blăng′kĭt-stĭch′) *tr.v.* **-stitched, -stitch·ing, -stitch·es** To sew with a buttonhole stitch.

blank slate *n.* Something that has yet to be marked, determined, or developed: "*Neurobiologists have been arguing for decades over whether embryonic neurons are blank slates or prefabricated units destined for a particular fate*" (Natalie Angier).

blank verse *n.* Verse consisting of unrhymed lines, usu. of iambic pentameter.

Blan·tyre (blăn-tīr′) A city of S Malawi. Pop. 331,588.

blare (blâr) *v.* **blared, blar·ing, blares** —*intr.* To sound loudly and stridently. —*tr.* 1. To cause to blare. 2. To proclaim loudly and flamboyantly: *headlines blaring the scandal.* ❖ *n.* 1. A loud, strident noise. 2. Flamboyance. [ME *bleren.*]

blar·ney (blär′nē) *n.* 1. Smooth, flattering talk. 2. Deceptive nonsense. [After the BLARNEY Stone in Blarney Castle, Blarney, Ireland.] —**blar′ney** *v.*

Blarney A village of S Ireland near Cork. Blarney Castle (dating from the 15th cent.) is the site of the Blarney Stone, said to impart powers of eloquence and persuasion.

Blas·co I·bá·ñez (blä′skō ē-bän′yäs, ē-vän′yĕth), **Vicente** 1867–1928. Spanish novelist and journalist whose works include *The Cabin* (1898).

bla·sé (blä-zā′) *adj.* 1. Uninterested because of frequent exposure or indulgence. 2. Unconcerned; nonchalant. 3. Very sophisticated. [Fr. < *p.* part. of *blaser,* to cloy < Fr. dialectal, to be chronically hung over, prob. < MDu. *blāsen,* to blow up, swell.]

blas·pheme (blăs-fēm′, blăs′fēm′) *v.* **-phemed, -phem·ing, -phemes** —*tr.* 1. To speak of (God or a sacred entity) in an irreverent, impious manner. 2. To revile; execrate. —*intr.* To speak blasphemy. [ME *blasfemen* < OFr. *blasfemer* < LLat. *blasphēmāre* < Gk. *blasphēmein < blasphēmos,* evil-speaking, blasphemous. See bhā- in App.] —**blas·phem′er** (blăs-fē′mər, blăs′fə-) *n.*

blas·phe·mous (blăs′fə-məs) *adj.* Impiously irreverent. —**blas′phe·mous·ly** *adv.* —**blas′phe·mous·ness** *n.*

blas·phe·my (blăs′fə-mē) *n., pl.* **-mies** 1. A contemptuous or profane act, utterance, or writing concerning God or a sacred entity. 2. An irreverent or impious act, attitude, or utterance. [ME *blasfemie* < LLat. *blasphēmia* < Gk. *blasphēmia < blasphēmein,* to blaspheme. See BLASPHEME.]

blast (blăst) *n.* **1a.** A very strong gust of wind or air. **b.** The effect of such a gust. **2.** A forcible stream of air, gas, or steam from an opening, as in a blast furnace. **3.** A sudden loud sound. **4a.** A violent explosion, as of dynamite. **b.** The violent effect of such an explosion, consisting of a wave of increased atmospheric pressure followed by a wave of decreased pressure. **c.** An explosive charge. **5.** *Botany* Any of several plant diseases, resulting in sudden death of buds, flowers, foliage, or young fruits. **6.** A destructive or damaging influence. **7.** A powerful hit, blow, or shot. **8.** A violent assault or outburst. **9.** *Slang* A highly exciting event, such as a big party. ❖ *v.* **blast·ed, blast·ing, blasts** —*tr.* 1. To knock down or shatter by or as if by explosion; smash. 2. To play or sound loudly: *blasted his whistle.* **3a.** To hit with great force: *blasted the baseball to right field.* **b.** To kill or destroy by hitting or shooting. 4. To have a harmful or destructive effect on. 5. To cause to shrivel, wither, or mature imperfectly by or as if by blast or blight. 6. To make or open by or as if by explosion: *blast a tunnel through the mountains.* 7. To criticize or attack vigorously. —*intr.* 1. To use or detonate explosives. 2. To emit a loud, intense sound; blare: *speakers blasting at full volume.* 3. To wither or shrivel or mature imperfectly. 4. To criticize or attack with vigor. 5. To shoot. —*phrasal verb:* **blast off** To take off, as a rocket. —*idiom:* **full blast** At full speed, volume, or capacity. [ME < OE *blǣst.*] —**blast′er** *n.*

–blast *suff.* An immature, embryonic stage in the development of

Tony Blair

Mont Blanc

ă	pat	oi	boy
ā	pay	ou	out
âr	care	ŏŏ	took
ä	father	ōō	boot
ĕ	pet	ŭ	cut
ē	be	ûr	urge
ĭ	pit	th	thin
ī	pie	th	this
îr	pier	hw	which
ŏ	pot	zh	vision
ō	toe	ə	about,
ô	paw		item

Stress marks:
′ (primary);
′ (secondary); as in
lexicon (lĕk′sĭ-kŏn′)

cells or tissues: *erythroblast.* [< Gk. *blastos,* bud.]

blast cell *n.* **1.** A precursor of a human blood cell. **2.** An immature undifferentiated cell. [–BLAST + CELL.]

blast·ed (blăs′tĭd) *adj.* **1.** Used as an intensive: *I hate these blasted flies.* **2.** *Slang* Drunk or intoxicated. **3.** Blighted, withered, or shriveled.

blas·te·ma (blă-stē′mə) *n., pl.* **-mas** or **-ma·ta** (-mə-tə) **1.** The undifferentiated material from which cells are formed. **2.** A mass of embryonic cells from which a body part develops, either normally or in regeneration. [Gk. *blastēma,* offspring, sprout < *blastos,* bud.] —**blas·te′mal, blas·te·mat′ic** (blăs′tə-măt′ĭk), **blas·te′mic** (blă-stē′mĭk) *adj.*

blast furnace *n.* A furnace in which combustion is intensified by a blast of air.

–blastic *suff.* Having a specified number or kind of formative elements such as buds, germs, cells, or cell layers: *meroblastic.* [< –BLAST.]

blasto– or **blast–** *pref.* Bud; germ; budding; germination: *blastocyst.* [< Gk. *blastos,* bud.]

blas·to·coel or **blas·to·coele** (blăs′tə-sēl′) *n.* The fluid-filled central cavity of a blastula. —**blas′to·coe′lic** *adj.*

blas·to·cyst (blăs′tə-sĭst′) *n.* The modified blastula characteristic of placental mammals. —**blas′to·cys′tic** *adj.*

blas·to·derm (blăs′tə-dûrm′) *n.* **1.** The layer of cells that gives rise to the germinal disk from which an avian or reptilian embryo develops. **2.** The layer of cells formed by the cleavage of a fertilized mammalian egg. —**blas′to·der′mic, blas′to·der·mat′ic** (-dər-măt′ĭk) *adj.*

blas·to·disk or **blas·to·disc** (blăs′tə-dĭsk′) *n.* See **germinal disk.**

blast·off also **blast-off** (blăst′ôf′, -ŏf′) *n.* The launch, esp. of a rocket.

blas·to·gen·e·sis (blăs′tə-jĕn′ĭ-sĭs) *n.* **1.** The transformation of small lymphocytes into larger cells that are capable of undergoing mitosis. **2.** The theory that inherited characteristics are transmitted from parent to offspring by a germ cell's cytoplasm. **3.** Reproduction of an organism by budding. —**blas′to·ge·net′ic** (-jə-nĕt′ĭk), **blas′to·gen′ic** (-jĕn′ĭk) *adj.*

blas·to·ma (blă-stō′mə) *n., pl.* **-mas** or **-ma·ta** (-mə-tə) A neoplasm composed of immature and undifferentiated cells.

blas·to·mere (blăs′tə-mîr′) *n.* A cell resulting from the cleavage of a fertilized ovum during early embryonic development. —**blas′to·mer′ic** (-mîr′ĭk, -mĕr′-) *adj.*

blas·to·my·cete (blăs′tə-mī′sēt, -mī-sēt′) *n.* Any of various yeastlike budding fungi of the genus *Blastomyces* that cause diseases in humans and animals.

blas·to·my·co·sis (blăs′tō-mī-kō′sĭs) *n.* A fungal infection caused by a blastomycete and marked by multiple inflammatory lesions of the skin, mucous membranes, or internal organs.

blas·to·pore (blăs′tə-pôr′, -pōr′) *n. Embryology* The opening of the archenteron. [BLASTO– + PORE[2].] —**blas′to·por′ic, blas′to·por′al** (-pôr′əl, -pōr′-) *adj.*

blas·to·sphere (blăs′tə-sfîr′) *n.* See **blastula.**

blas·to·spore (blăs′tə-spôr′, -spōr′) *n.* A fungal spore produced by budding.

blas·tu·la (blăs′chə-lə) *n., pl.* **-las** or **-lae** (-lē′) An early embryonic form produced by cleavage of a fertilized ovum and consisting of a spherical layer of cells surrounding a fluid-filled cavity. [NLat. : Gk. *blastos,* bud + Lat. *-ula,* fem. dim. suff.] —**blas′tu·lar** *adj.* —**blas′tu·la′tion** (-lā′shən) *n.*

blat (blăt) *v.* **blat·ted, blat·ting, blats** —*tr.* To utter without thinking; blurt. —*intr.* **1.** To cry, esp. like a sheep; bleat. **2.** To make a harsh or raucous noise. [Imit.] —**blat** *n.*

bla·tant (blāt′nt) *adj.* **1.** Unpleasantly loud and noisy. **2.** *Usage Problem* Totally or offensively conspicuous or obtrusive: *a blatant lie.* [< Lat. *blatīre,* to blab (on the model of words such as RAMPANT).] —**bla′tan·cy** *n.* —**bla′tant·ly** *adv.*

USAGE NOTE It is natural that *blatant* and *flagrant* are often confused, since the words overlap in meaning. Both attribute conspicuousness and offensiveness to certain acts. *Blatant* emphasizes the failure to conceal the act: *blatant vanity. Flagrant,* on the other hand, tends to emphasize the serious wrongdoing inherent in the offense: *flagrant child abuse. Blatant* is sometimes used to mean simply "obvious," but this use has not been established and is widely considered an error.

blaze[2]

blazing star
Chamaelirium luteum

blath·er (blăth′ər) also **bleth·er** (blĕth′-) *intr.v.* **-ered, -er·ing, -ers** To talk nonsensically. ❖ *n.* Nonsensical talk. [ON *blathra.*] —**blath′er·er** *n.*

blath·er·skite (blăth′ər-skīt′) *n.* **1.** A babbling, foolish person. **2.** Blather. [BLATHER + dialectal *skite,* a contemptible person (< ME *skite,* diarrhea < ON *skītr,* excrement < *skīta,* to defecate).]

Bla·vat·sky (blə-văt′skē, -vät′-), **Helena Petrovna Hahn** 1831–91. Russian-born theosophist who founded (1875) the Theosophical Society in New York City.

blaze[1] (blāz) *n.* **1a.** A brilliant flame. **b.** A destructive fire. **2.** A bright or steady light or glare. **3.** A brilliant, striking display. **4.** A sudden outburst: *a blaze of anger.* **5. blazes** Used as an intensive: *Where in blazes are my keys?* ❖ *v.* **blazed, blaz·ing, blaz·es** —*intr.* **1.** To burn with a bright flame. **2.** To shine brightly. **3.** To be resplendent: *a garden blazing with flowers.* **4.** To flare up

suddenly: *My temper blazed.* **5.** To shoot rapidly and continuously: *eyes that blazed hatred.* [ME *blase* < OE *blæse.*] —**blaz′ing·ly** *adv.*

blaze[2] (blāz) *n.* **1.** A white or light-colored spot or stripe on the face of an animal, such as a horse. **2.** A mark cut or painted on a tree to indicate a trail. ❖ *tr.v.* **blazed, blaz·ing, blaz·es 1.** To mark (a tree) with or as if with blazes. **2.** To indicate (a trail) by marking trees with blazes. [Of Gmc. orig.; akin to BLAZE[1].]

blaze[3] (blāz) *tr.v.* **blazed, blaz·ing, blaz·es** To make known publicly; proclaim: *Headlines blazed the news.* [ME *blasen* < MDu. *blāsen,* to blow up, swell.]

blaz·er (blā′zər) *n.* A lightweight, often striped or brightly colored sports jacket having pockets and notched lapels.

blaz·ing star (blā′zĭng) *n.* **1.** A North American dioecious herb (*Chamaelirium luteum*) in the lily family, having long racemes of small flowers. **2.** Any of various North American plants of the genus *Liatris* in the composite family, having small discoid flower heads grouped in a dense raceme or panicle. **3.** A biennial plant (*Mentzelia laevicaulis*) of western North America, having large star-shaped flowers.

bla·zon (blā′zən) *tr.v.* **-zoned, -zon·ing, -zons 1.** *Heraldry* **a.** To describe (a coat of arms) in proper terms. **b.** To paint or depict (a coat of arms) with accurate detail. **2.** To adorn or embellish with or as if with a coat of arms. **3.** To proclaim widely. ❖ *n.* **1.** *Heraldry* **a.** A coat of arms. **b.** The description or representation of a coat of arms. **2.** An ostentatious display. [Prob. < ME *blasoun,* shield < OFr. *blason.*] —**bla′zon·er** *n.* —**bla′zon·ment** *n.*

bla·zon·ry (blā′zən-rē) *n., pl.* **-ries 1.** *Heraldry* **a.** The art of properly and accurately describing or representing armorial bearings. **b.** A coat of arms. **2.** An ostentatious display.

bld. *abbr.* **1.** blood **2.** boldface

bldg. *abbr.* building

bleach (blēch) *v.* **bleached, bleach·ing, bleach·es** —*tr.* **1.** To remove the color from, as by means of chemical agents or sunlight. **2.** To make white or colorless. —*intr.* To become white or colorless. ❖ *n.* **1.** A chemical agent used for bleaching. **2a.** The act of bleaching. **b.** The degree of bleaching obtained. [ME *blechen* < OE *blǣcan.*]

bleach·er (blē′chər) *n.* **1.** One that bleaches or is used in bleaching. **2.** Often unroofed outdoor grandstand for seating spectators. Often used in the plural.

bleach·ing powder (blē′chĭng) *n.* A powder containing calcium chloride and calcium hypochlorite, used as a bleach.

bleak[1] (blēk) *adj.* **bleak·er, bleak·est 1a.** Gloomy and somber; dreary. **b.** Providing no encouragement; depressing. **2.** Cold and cutting; raw: *bleak winds of the North Atlantic.* **3.** Exposed to the elements; unsheltered and barren. [ME *bleik,* pale < ON *bleikr,* white.] —**bleak′ly** *adv.* —**bleak′ness** *n.*

bleak[2] (blēk) *n., pl.* **bleak** or **bleaks** A small European freshwater fish of the genus *Alburnus,* having silvery scales used in making artificial pearls. [ME *bleke,* prob. alteration (influenced by *bleke,* pale) of *blay < OE *blǣge.*]

blear (blîr) *tr.v.* **bleared, blear·ing, blears 1.** To blur or redden (the eyes). **2.** To blur; dim. ❖ *adj.* Bleary. [ME *bleren.*]

blear·y (blîr′ē) *adj.* **-i·er, -i·est 1.** Blurred or dimmed by or as if by tears: *bleary eyes.* **2.** Vaguely outlined; indistinct. **3.** Exhausted; worn-out. —**blear′i·ly** *adv.* —**blear′i·ness** *n.*

blear·y-eyed (blîr′ē-īd′) also **blear-eyed** (blîr′īd′) *adj.* With eyes blurred or reddened, as from lack of sleep.

bleat (blēt) *n.* **1a.** The cry of a goat or sheep. **b.** A sound like this. **2.** A whining complaint. ❖ *v.* **bleat·ed, bleat·ing, bleats** —*intr.* **1.** To utter the cry of a goat or sheep. **2.** To utter a sound like this. **3.** To utter in a whining way. [ME *blet* < *bleten,* to bleat < OE *blǣtan.*] —**bleat′er** *n.*

bleb (blĕb) *n.* **1.** A small blister or pustule. **2.** An air bubble. [Prob. alteration of BLOB.]

bleed (blēd) *v.* **bled** (blĕd), **bleed·ing, bleeds** —*intr.* **1.** To emit or lose blood. **2.** To be wounded, esp. in battle. **3.** To feel sympathetic grief or anguish. **4.** To exude a fluid such as sap. **5.** To pay out money, esp. an exorbitant amount. **6a.** To run together or be diffused, as dyes in wet cloth. **b.** To undergo or be subject to such a diffusion of color. **7.** To show through a layer of paint. **8.** To be printed so as to go off the edge or edges of a page after trimming. —*tr.* **1a.** To take or remove blood from. **b.** To extract sap or juice from. **2a.** To draw liquid or gaseous contents from; drain. **b.** To draw off (liquid or gaseous matter) from a container. **3.** To obtain money from, esp. by improper means. **4a.** To cause (an illustration, for example) to bleed. **b.** To trim (a page, for example) so as to mutilate the printed matter. ❖ *n.* **1.** An instance of bleeding. **2.** Illustrative matter that bleeds. **3a.** A page trimmed so as to bleed. **b.** The part of the page that is trimmed off. [ME *bleden* < OE *blēdan* in App.]

bleed·er (blē′dər) *n.* **1.** A person, such as a hemophiliac, who bleeds freely or is subject to hemorrhages. **2.** A person who draws blood from another; a phlebotomist.

bleed·ing (blē′dĭng) *adv. Chiefly British Slang* Used as an intensive.

bleeding heart *n.* **1.** Any of various perennial herbs of the genus *Dicentra,* esp. *D. spectabilis,* having clusters of pink or red heart-shaped flowers. **2.** A person who is considered excessively sympathetic toward those who claim to be underprivileged.

—bleed′ing-heart′ (-härt′) *adj.*

bleep (blēp) *n.* A brief high-pitched sound, as from an electronic device. ❖ *v.* **bleeped, bleep•ing, bleeps** —*intr.* To emit a bleep or bleeps. —*tr.* To edit out (spoken material) from a broadcast or recording, esp. by replacing with a bleep. [Imit.] —**bleep′er** *n.*

blem•ish (blĕm′ĭsh) *tr.v.* **-ished, -ish•ing, -ish•es** To mar or impair by a flaw. ❖ *n.* An imperfection that mars or impairs. [ME *blemisshen* < OFr. *blesmir, blemir, blemiss-*, to make pale, of Gmc. orig.] —**blem′ish•er** *n.*

blench¹ (blĕnch) *intr.v.* **blenched, blench•ing, blench•es** To draw back or shy away, as from fear; flinch. [ME *blenchen* < OE *blencan*, to deceive.] —**blench′er** *n.*

blench² (blĕnch) *v.* Variant of **blanch.**

blend (blĕnd) *v.* **blend•ed** or **blent** (blĕnt), **blend•ing, blends** —*tr.* **1.** To combine or mix so that the constituent parts are indistinguishable from one another. **2.** To combine (varieties or grades) to obtain a mixture of a particular character or consistency. —*intr.* **1.** To form a uniform mixture. **2.** To become merged into one; unite. **3.** To create a harmonious effect or result: *The tie blended with the jacket.* ❖ *n.* **1a.** The act of blending. **b.** Something, such as an effect or a product, that is created by blending: *a blend of coffees.* See Syns at **mixture. 2.** *Linguistics* A word produced by combining parts of other words, as *smog* from *smoke* and *fog.* [ME *blenden*, prob. < ON *blanda, blend-.*]

blende (blĕnd) *n.* **1.** Any of various shiny minerals composed chiefly of metallic sulfides. **2.** See **sphalerite.** [Ger. < *blenden*, to deceive (because it resembles lead ore) < MHGer. *blenden* < OHGer. *blentan*, to blind, deceive.]

blend•ed family (blĕn′dĭd) *n.* A stepfamily.

blended whiskey *n.* Whiskey that is a blend of straight whiskeys or of whiskey and neutral spirits.

blend•er (blĕn′dər) *n.* One that blends, esp. an appliance with blades for chopping, mixing, or liquefying foods.

blend•ing inheritance (blĕn′dĭng) *n. Genetics* The inheritance pattern in which the inherited characters in the offspring are intermediate between those of the parents.

blen•ny (blĕn′ē) *n., pl.* **-nies** Any of several chiefly marine fishes that are primarily of the families Blenniidae and Clinidae and have small elongated bodies. [Lat. *blennius*, a kind of sea fish < Gk. *blennos*, slime, blenny.]

bleph•a•ri•tis (blĕf′ə-rī′tĭs) *n.* Inflammation of the eyelids.

blepharo– or **blephar–** *pref.* **1.** Eyelid; eyelids: *blepharospasm.* **2.** Cilium; flagellum: *blepharoplast.* [Gk. < *blepharon*, eyelid.]

bleph•a•ro•plast (blĕf′ər-ə-plăst′) *n.* A basal body in certain flagellated protozoans that consists of a minute mass of chromatin embedded in the cytoplasm at the base of the flagellum.

bleph•a•ro•plas•ty (blĕf′ər-ə-plăs′tē) *n.* Plastic surgery of the eyelids.

bleph•a•ro•spasm (blĕf′ə-rō-spăz′əm) *n.* Spasmodic winking caused by involuntary contraction of an eyelid muscle.

Blé•riot (blā′rē-ō, blā-ryō′), **Louis** 1872–1936. French inventor and aviator who was the first to cross the English Channel by airplane (1909).

bles•bok (blĕs′bŏk′) *n., pl.* **blesbok** or **-boks** A South African antelope (*Damaliscus albifrons*) having curved horns and a large white mark on its face. [Afr. : *bles*, white mark on an animal's face (< MDu.; see **bhel-¹** in App.) + *bok*, buck (< MDu. *boc*).]

bless (blĕs) *tr.v.* **blessed** or **blest** (blĕst), **bless•ing, bless•es 1.** To make holy by religious rite; sanctify. **2.** To make the sign of the cross over so as to sanctify. **3.** To invoke divine favor upon. **4.** To honor as holy; glorify. **5.** To confer well-being on. **6.** To endow, as with talent. [ME *blessen* < OE *blētsian*, to consecrate. See **bhel-¹** in App.] —**bless′er** *n.*

WORD HISTORY The verb *bless* comes from Old English *blǣdsian, blēdsian, blētsian*, "to bless, wish happiness, consecrate." Etymologically this verb can be shown to derive from the prehistoric Germanic noun **blōdan*, "blood." *Blǣdsian* therefore literally means "to consecrate with blood, sprinkle with blood." The Angles, Saxons, and Jutes, the early Germanic migrants to Britain, used *blǣdsian* for their pagan sacrifices. After they converted to Christianity, *blǣdsian* acquired new meanings as a result of its use in translations of the Latin Bible, but it kept its pagan Germanic senses as well.

bless•ed (blĕs′ĭd) *also* **blest** (blĕst) *adj.* **1a.** Worthy of worship; holy. **b.** Held in veneration; revered. **2. Blessed** *Roman Catholic Church* Used as a title before the name of one who has been beatified. **3.** Bringing happiness, pleasure, or contentment. **4. Blessed** Used as an intensive: *I don't have a blessed dime.* [Sense 4, euphemistic for CURSED or DAMNED.] —**bless′ed•ly** *adv.* —**bless′ed•ness** *n.*

Blessed Sacrament *n. Roman Catholic Church* The consecrated host.

Blessed Virgin Mary *n.* The Virgin Mary.

bless•ing (blĕs′ĭng) *n.* **1.** The act of one that blesses. **2.** A short prayer said before or after a meal; grace. **3.** Something promoting or contributing to happiness, well-being, or prosperity; a boon. **4.** Approbation; approval.

bleth•er (blĕth′ər) *v. & n.* Variant of **blather.**

bleu cheese (blōo) *n.* See **blue cheese.** [Fr., blue < OFr. BLUE.]

blew¹ (blōo) *v.* Past tense of **blow¹.**

blew² (blōo) *v.* Past tense of **blow³.**

Bligh (blī), **William** 1754–1817. British naval officer who as captain of the H.M.S. *Bounty* was set adrift by his mutinous crew during a voyage to Tahiti (1789).

blight (blīt) *n.* **1a.** Any of numerous plant diseases resulting in sudden conspicuous wilting and dying of affected parts. **b.** The causative agent, such as a fungus, that results in blight. **2.** An adverse environmental condition, such as air pollution. **3.** Something that frustrates hope or impedes progress and prosperity. ❖ *v.* **blight•ed, blight•ing, blights** —*tr.* **1.** To cause (a plant, for example) to undergo blight. **2.** To have a deleterious effect on; ruin. —*intr.* To suffer blight. [?]

blight•er (blī′tər) *n. Chiefly British Slang* A fellow, esp. one held in low esteem.

blimp (blĭmp) *n.* A nonrigid, buoyant airship. [Perh. < LIMP.]

Blimp *n. Chiefly British* A pompous ultranationalistic reactionary. [After Colonel *Blimp*, a cartoon character invented by David Low (1891–1963).] —**Blimp′ish** *adj.*

blind (blīnd) *adj.* **blind•er, blind•est 1a.** Unable to see; sightless. **b.** Of, relating to, or for sightless persons. **2a.** Performed or made without information that might prejudice the result: *blind tests of a new drug.* **b.** Performed without preparation or knowledge: *a blind stab at the question.* **c.** Performed solely by instruments: *blind navigation.* **3.** Unable or unwilling to perceive or understand: *blind to her faults.* **4.** Not based on reason or evidence; unquestioning. **5.** *Slang* Drunk. **6.** Lacking reason or purpose: *blind fate.* **7a.** Difficult to comprehend or see; illegible. **b.** Incompletely or illegibly addressed: *blind mail.* **c.** Hidden from sight: *a blind driveway.* **8.** Closed at one end: *a blind passage.* **9.** Having no opening: *a blind wall.* **10.** *Botany* Failing to produce flowers or fruits: *a blind bud.* ❖ *n.* **1.** (*used with a pl. verb*) Blind people considered as a group. Used with *the.* **2.** Something, such as a window shade, that hinders vision or shuts out light. **3.** A shelter for concealing hunters or observers of wildlife. **4.** Something intended to conceal the true nature, esp. of an activity; a subterfuge. ❖ *adv.* **1a.** Without seeing; blindly. **b.** Without the aid of visual reference: *flew blind.* **2.** Without forethought or provision; unawares: *entered into the scheme blind.* **3.** Without significant information, esp. that might affect an outcome or result: *"When you read blind, you see everything but the author"* (Margaret Atwood). **4.** *Informal* Into a stupor. **5.** Used as an intensive: *robbed us blind.* ❖ *tr.v.* **blind•ed, blind•ing, blinds 1.** To deprive of sight. **2.** To dazzle: *blinded by sunlight.* **3.** To deprive of perception or insight: *Prejudice blinded them.* **4.** To withhold light from. [ME < OE.] —**blind′ing•ly** *adv.* —**blind′ly** *adv.* —**blind′ness** *n.*

blind alley *n.* **1.** An alley or passage that is closed at one end. **2.** A mistaken, unproductive undertaking.

blind date *n.* **1.** A social engagement between two persons who have not previously met, usu. arranged by a mutual acquaintance. **2.** Either of the persons on a blind date.

blind•er (blīn′dər) *n.* **1. blinders** A pair of leather flaps attached to a horse's bridle to curtail side vision. **2.** Something that serves to obscure clear perception and discernment.

blind•fish (blīnd′fĭsh′) *n., pl.* **blindfish** or **-fish•es** Any of various small fishes with rudimentary nonfunctioning eyes, inhabiting cave waters and underground streams.

blind•fold (blīnd′fōld′) *tr.v.* **-fold•ed, -fold•ing, -folds 1.** To cover the eyes of with or as if with a bandage. **2.** To prevent from seeing and esp. from comprehending. ❖ *n.* **1.** A bandage to cover the eyes. **2.** Something that serves to obscure clear perception. [< ME *blindfolde*, p. part. of *blindfellen*, to strike blind, cover the eyes < OE *geblindfellan* : *blind*, blind + *fellan*, to strike down.] —**blind′fold′ed** *adj.*

blind gut *n.* **1.** A digestive cavity having only one opening. **2.** See **cecum** 2.

blind•man's bluff (blīnd′mănz′) *n.* A game in which a blindfolded player tries to catch and identify one of the other players. [Alteration of BLINDMAN'S BUFF.]

blindman's buff *n.* See **blindman's bluff.** [< *buff*, a blow, short for BUFFET².]

blind pig *n. Chiefly Upper Midwest & Western US* See **blind tiger.**

blind side *n.* **1.** The side on which one's vision is limited or obstructed. **2.** The side away from which one is looking.

blind-side or **blind•side** (blīnd′sīd′) *tr.v.* **-sid•ed, -sid•ing, -sides 1.** To hit or attack on or from the blind side. **2.** To catch or take unawares, esp. with harmful results.

blind•sight (blīnd′sīt′) *n.* The ability of a blind person to sense the presence of a light source.

blind spot *n.* **1.** *Anatomy* The small, circular, optically insensitive region in the retina where fibers of the optic nerve emerge from the eyeball. **2.** A part of an area that cannot be directly observed under existing circumstances. **3.** An area where radio reception is weak or nonexistent. **4.** A subject about which one is markedly ignorant or prejudiced.

blind staggers *pl.n.* (*used with a sing. verb*) See **stagger** 3.

blind tiger *n. Chiefly Southern & Midland US* A place where alcoholic beverages are sold illegally; a speakeasy. [After the early custom of exhibiting animal curiosities in speakeasies.]

blind trust *n.* An arrangement in which a person, such as a public official, relegates the management of certain financial assets to a

blinders

blind·worm (blīnd′wûrm′) *n.* See **slowworm**. [< its small eyes.]

blink (blĭngk) *v.* **blinked, blink·ing, blinks** —*intr.* **1.** To close and open one or both of the eyes rapidly. **2.** To look through half-closed eyes, as in a bright glare; squint. **3.** To shine with intermittent gleams; flash on and off. **4.** To be startled or dismayed. **5.** To look with feigned ignorance. —*tr.* **1.** To cause to blink. **2.** To hold back or remove (tears) by blinking. **3.** To refuse to recognize or face: *blink ugly facts.* **4.** To transmit (a message) with a flashing light. ❖ *n.* **1.** The act or an instance of rapidly closing and opening the eyes or an eye. **2.** An instant. **3.** *Scots* A quick look or glimpse; a glance. **4.** A flash of light; a twinkle. **5.** See **iceblink** 1. —*idiom:* **on the blink** Out of working order. [Prob. ME *blinken*, to move suddenly, var. of *blenchen*. See BLENCH[1].]

blink·er (blĭng′kər) *n.* **1.** One that blinks, esp. a light that blinks in order to convey a message. **2. blinkers** See **blinder** 1. ❖ *tr.v.* **-ered, -er·ing, -ers** To put blinders on.

blintz (blĭnts) also **blin·tze** (blĭn′tsə) *n.* A thin pancake, usu. filled with cottage cheese, that is folded and then sautéed or baked. [Yiddish *blintse* < Belarusian *blintsy*, pl. of *blinets*, dim. of *blin*, pancake < ORuss. *mlinŭ, blinŭ.* See **melə-** in App.]

blip (blĭp) *n.* **1.** A spot of light on a radar or sonar screen indicating the position of a detected object. **2.** A high-pitched electronic sound; a bleep. **3.** A transient sharp upward or downward movement, as on a graph. **4.** A brief departure from the normal. ❖ *tr.v.* **blipped, blip·ping, blips** To bleep. [Imit.]

bliss (blĭs) *n.* **1.** Extreme happiness; ecstasy. **2.** The ecstasy of salvation; spiritual joy. [ME *blisse* < OE *bliss < blīths < blīthe,* joyful. See BLITHE.] —**bliss′ful** *adj.* —**bliss′ful·ly** *adv.* —**bliss′ful·ness** *n.*

blis·ter (blĭs′tər) *n.* **1a.** A local swelling of the skin that contains watery fluid and is caused by burning or irritation. **b.** A similar swelling on a plant. **2a.** A raised bubble, as on a painted surface. **b.** A rounded, usu. transparent structure. ❖ *v.* **-tered, -ter·ing, -ters** —*tr.* **1.** To cause a blister to form on. **2.** To reprove harshly. —*intr.* To break out in or as if in blisters. [ME, prob. < OFr. *blestre,* of Gmc. orig.] —**blis′ter·y** *adj.*

blister beetle *n.* Any of various soft-bodied beetles of the family Meloidae, such as the cantharis, that secrete a substance capable of blistering the skin.

blister copper *n.* An almost pure copper produced in an intermediate stage of refining. [< its blistered appearance.]

blis·ter·ing (blĭs′tər-ĭng) *adj.* **1.** Intensely hot. **2.** Harsh; severe. **3.** Very rapid. **4.** Producing a blister or blisters. —**blis′ter·ing·ly** *adv.*

blister pack *n.* A transparent, molded piece of plastic, often sealed to a sheet of cardboard, used to package merchandise.

blister rust *n.* Any of several diseases of pine trees caused by certain fungi of the genus *Cronartium* and resulting in conspicuous blistering.

BLit or **BLitt** *abbr.* Latin Baccalaureus Litterarum (Bachelor of Literature)

blithe (blīth, blĭth) *adj.* **blith·er, blith·est** **1.** Carefree and lighthearted. **2.** Lacking due concern; casual. [ME < OE *blīthe.*] —**blithe′ly** *adv.* —**blithe′ness** *n.*

blith·er (blĭth′ər) *intr.v.* **-ered, -er·ing, -ers** To blather. [Poss. blend of BLATHER and DITHER.]

blithe·some (blīth′səm, blĭth′-) *adj.* Cheerful; merry; lighthearted. —**blithe′some·ly** *adv.* —**blithe′some·ness** *n.*

blitz (blĭts) *n.* **1a.** A blitzkrieg. **b.** A heavy aerial bombardment. **2.** An intense campaign: *a media blitz.* **3.** *Football* A sudden charge upon the quarterback by one or more of the linebackers or defensive backs when the ball is snapped. ❖ *v.* **blitzed, blitz·ing, blitz·es** —*tr.* **1.** To subject to a blitz. **2.** *Football* To rush (the quarterback) in a blitz. —*intr.* *Football* To carry out a blitz. [Short for BLITZKRIEG.]

blitzed (blĭtst) *adj.* *Slang* Drunk or intoxicated.

blitz·krieg (blĭts′krēg′) *n.* A swift, sudden military offensive, usu. by combined air and land forces. [Ger. : *Blitz,* lightning (< MHGer. *blitze < bliczen,* to flash < OHGer. *blekkazzen*) + *Krieg,* war (< MHGer. *kriec* < OHGer. *krēg,* stubbornness; see **gʷerə-** in App.).]

bliz·zard (blĭz′ərd) *n.* **1.** A very heavy snowstorm with high winds. **2.** A torrent; a superabundance. [Perh. of imit. orig.]

blk. *abbr.* **1.** block **2.** bulk

bloat (blōt) *v.* **bloat·ed, bloat·ing, bloats** —*tr.* **1.** To cause to swell up or inflate, as with gas. **2.** To cure (fish) by soaking in brine and half-drying in smoke. —*intr.* To become swollen or inflated. ❖ *n.* **1.** A swelling of the rumen or intestine of cattle and domestic animals caused by gas formation from eating watery legumes or green forage. **2.** An excess or surfeit, as of employees. [< ME *blout,* soft, puffed < ON *blautr,* soft, soaked.]

bloat·ed (blō′tĭd) *adj.* **1.** Much bigger than desired. **2.** *Medicine* Swollen or distended by fluid or gaseous material.

bloat·er[1] (blō′tər) *n.* A large mackerel or herring, lightly smoked and salted. [< obsolete dialectal *bloat,* a soft, moist cured fish, prob. < BLOAT.]

bloat·er[2] (blō′tər) *n.* A small whitefish (*Coregonus hoyi*) of the Great Lakes and the lakes of eastern Canada.

bloat·ware (blōt′wâr′) *n.* *Informal* Software with large, often

unused additional features.

blob (blŏb) *n.* **1.** A soft amorphous mass. **2.** A daub, as of color. ❖ *tr.v.* **blobbed, blob·bing, blobs** To splash or daub with blobs; splotch. [< ME *blober,* bubble, bubbling, prob. of imit. orig.]

bloc (blŏk) *n.* **1.** A group of nations, parties, or persons united for common action. **2.** A coalition of legislators acting for a common purpose. [Fr. < OFr., block. See BLOCK.]

Bloch (blŏk, blôk, blôкʜ), **Ernest** 1880–1959. Swiss-born Amer. composer noted for his chamber music.

Bloch, Konrad Emil 1912–2000. German-born Amer. biochemist who shared a 1964 Nobel Prize.

block (blŏk) *n.* **1a.** A solid piece of a hard substance, such as wood, having one or more flat sides. **b.** A block used in construction or as a support. **c.** A block upon which chopping or cutting is done. **d.** A block upon which persons are beheaded. **e.** One of a set of small wooden or plastic pieces, such as a cube or bar, used as a building toy. **f.** *Printing* A large amount of text. **g.** *Sports* A starting block. **2.** A stand from which articles are displayed and sold at an auction. **3.** A mold or form on which an item is shaped or displayed. **4.** A substance, such as wood or stone, that has been prepared for engraving. **5a.** A pulley or a system of pulleys set in a casing. **b.** An engine block. **6.** A bloc. **7.** A set of like items, such as shares of stock, sold or handled as a unit. **8.** A group of four or more unseparated postage stamps forming a rectangle. **9.** *Canadian* A group of townships in an unsurveyed area. **10a.** A usu. rectangular section of a city or town bounded on each side by consecutive streets. **b.** A segment of a street bounded by cross streets and including its buildings and inhabitants. **11.** A large building divided into separate units, such as apartments. **12.** A length of railroad track controlled by signals. **13.** The act of obstructing. **14.** Something that obstructs; an obstacle. **15.** *Sports* An act of bodily obstruction, as of a player or ball. **16.** *Medicine* Interruption, esp. obstruction, of a normal physiological function. **17.** *Psychology* A mental block. **18.** *Slang* The human head. **19.** A blockhead. ❖ *v.* **blocked, block·ing, blocks** —*tr.* **1.** To shape into a block or blocks. **2.** To support, strengthen, or retain in place by means of a block. **3.** To shape, mold, or form with or on a block: *block a hat.* **4a.** To stop or impede the passage of or movement through; obstruct: *block traffic.* **b.** To shut out from view. **c.** To stop the passage of (a motion or bill) in a legislative assembly. **5.** To indicate broadly without great detail; sketch: *block out a plan.* **6.** *Sports* To impede the movement of (an opponent, for instance) by physical interference. **7.** *Medicine* To interrupt the proper functioning of (a physiological process), esp. by the use of anesthesia. **8.** *Psychology* To fail to remember. **9.** To run (trains) on a block system. —*intr.* **1.** *Sports* To obstruct the movement of an opponent. **2.** To suffer a mental block. Often used with *on: I blocked on his name.* [ME *blok* < OFr. *bloc* < MDu.] —**block′er** *n.*

SYNONYMS block, hide, obscure, obstruct, screen, shroud These verbs mean to cut off from sight: *trees that block the view; a road hidden by brush; mist that obscures the mountain peak; skyscrapers obstructing the sky; a fence that screens the alley; a face shrouded by a veil.*

block·ade (blŏ-kād′) *n.* **1.** The isolation of a nation, area, city, or harbor by hostile ships or forces to prevent the passage of traffic and commerce. **2.** The forces used to effect this isolation. ❖ *tr.v.* **-ad·ed, -ad·ing, -ades** To set up a blockade against. [Prob. BLOCK + -ade (as in BARRICADE).] —**block·ad′er** *n.*

block·ade-run·ner (blŏ-kād′rŭn′ər) *n.* One that penetrates or evades a blockade. —**block·ade′-run′ning** *n.*

block·age (blŏk′ĭj) *n.* **1.** The act of obstructing. **2.** An obstruction.

block and tackle *n.* An apparatus of pulley blocks and ropes or cables used for hauling and hoisting heavy objects.

block·bust·er (blŏk′bŭs′tər) *n.* **1.** Something that sustains widespread popularity and achieves enormous sales. **2.** A high-explosive bomb used for demolition purposes. **3.** One that engages in the practice of blockbusting. [< BLOCKBUSTING.]

block·bust·ing (blŏk′bŭs′tĭng) *n.* *Informal* The practice of persuading homeowners to sell by appealing to the fear that incoming minority groups will lower property values.

block grant *n.* An unrestricted federal grant, as to a locality.

block·head (blŏk′hĕd′) *n.* A person regarded as very stupid.

block·house (blŏk′hous′) *n.* **1.** A military fortification constructed of sturdy material, such as concrete, and designed for firing or observation. **2.** A heavily reinforced building used for launch operations of missiles and space launch vehicles. **3.** A fort made of squared timbers with a projecting upper story.

block·ish (blŏk′ĭsh) *adj.* Resembling a block, as in shape. —**block′ish·ly** *adv.* —**block′ish·ness** *n.*

Block Island An island of S RI at the E entrance to Long Island Sound; settled in 1661.

block letter *n.* **1.** A plain capital letter written or printed unjoined to a following or preceding letter. **2.** A letter printed or written sans serif. **3.** A sans-serif style of type.

block plane *n.* A small plane used by carpenters for cutting across the grain of wood.

block signal *n.* A fixed signal at the entrance to a railroad block,

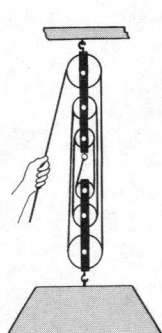

block and tackle
multiple block and tackle

blockhouse
reconstructed blockhouse
at Ft. Abraham Lincoln State
Park, Mandan, North Dakota

indicating whether or not trains may enter.

block system *n.* A system for controlling and safeguarding the flow of railway trains in which track is divided into blocks, each controlled by automatic signals.

block•y (blŏk′ē) *adj.* **-i•er, -i•est** Blockish.

Bloem•fon•tein (bloom′fŏn-tān′) A city of central South Africa W of Durban. Pop. 104,381.

bloke (blōk) *n. Chiefly British Slang* A fellow; a man. [?]

blond also **blonde** (blŏnd) *adj.* **blond•er, blond•est 1.** Having fair hair and skin and usu. light eyes. **2.** Of a light color, such as auburn or yellowish brown. **3.** Light-colored through bleaching. ❖ *n.* **1.** A blond person. **2.** A light yellowish brown to dark grayish yellow. [ME *blounde* < OFr. *blonde,* of Gmc. orig.] —**blond′ish** *adj.* —**blond′ness** *n.*

blood (blŭd) *n.* **1a.** The fluid consisting of plasma, blood cells, and platelets that is circulated by the heart through the vertebrate vascular system, carrying oxygen and nutrients to and waste materials away from all body tissues. **b.** A functionally similar fluid in animals other than vertebrates. **c.** The juice or sap of certain plants. **2.** A vital or animating force; lifeblood. **3.** One of the four humors of ancient and medieval physiology, identified with the blood found in blood vessels, and thought to cause cheerfulness. **4.** Bloodshed; murder. **5.** Temperament or disposition: *a person of hot blood.* **6a.** Descent from a common ancestor; parental lineage. **b.** Family relationship; kinship. **c.** Descent from noble or royal lineage. **d.** Recorded descent from purebred stock. **e.** National or racial ancestry. **7a.** A dandy. **b.** *Slang* A youth who is a gang member. ❖ *tr.v.* **blood•ed, blood•ing, bloods 1.** To give (a hunting dog) its first taste of blood. **2a.** To subject (troops) to experience under fire. **b.** To initiate by subjecting to an unpleasant or difficult experience. —*idioms:* **in cold blood** Deliberately, coldly, and dispassionately. **in (one's) blood** So characteristic as to seem inherited or passed down by family tradition. [ME *blod* < OE *blōd.* See **bhel-** in App.]

Blood *n., pl.* **Blood** or **Bloods** A member of a tribe of the Blackfoot confederacy inhabiting southern Alberta.

blood bank *n.* **1.** A place where whole blood or plasma is typed, processed, and stored for future use in transfusion. **2.** Blood or plasma stored in such a place.

blood•bath also **blood bath** (blŭd′băth′, -bäth′) *n.* Savage indiscriminate killing; a massacre.

blood-brain barrier (blŭd′brān′) *n.* A physiological mechanism that alters the permeability of brain capillaries and prevents some substances, such as certain drugs, from entering brain tissue.

blood brother *n.* **1.** A brother by birth. **2.** One of two individuals who vow mutual fidelity by a ceremony involving the mingling of each other's blood. —**blood brotherhood** *n.*

blood cell *n.* Any of the cells contained in blood; an erythrocyte or leukocyte; a blood corpuscle.

blood clot *n.* A mass of coagulated blood that consists of red blood cells, white blood cells, and platelets in a fibrin network.

blood count *n.* **1.** The number of red blood cells, white blood cells, and platelets in a definite volume of blood. **2.** The determination of such a count. **3.** Complete blood count.

blood•cur•dling (blŭd′kûrd′lĭng) *adj.* Causing great horror; terrifying. —**blood′cur′dling•ly** *adv.*

blood doping *n.* The process of increasing the number of circulating red blood cells as a means of improving athletic endurance, either by the intravenous infusion of previously removed and centrifuged red blood cells or by the administration of erythropoietin.

blood•ed (blŭd′ĭd) *adj.* **1.** Having blood or a temperament of a specified kind. Used only in combination: *a cold-blooded reptile.* **2.** Thoroughbred.

blood feud *n.* A feud involving the members of a family or clan.

blood fluke *n.* See **schistosome.**

blood gas *n.* **1.** An analysis of the dissolved gases in blood plasma, such as oxygen and carbon dioxide. **2.** Any of the dissolved gases in blood plasma.

blood group *n.* Any of several immunologically distinct classes of human blood that are based on the presence or absence of certain antigens and are identified by characteristic agglutination reactions.

blood•guilt (blŭd′gĭlt′) *n.* The fact or state of being guilty of murder or bloodshed.

blood heat *n.* The normal temperature (about 37.0°C or 98.6°F) of human blood.

blood•hound (blŭd′hound′) *n.* **1.** One of a breed of hounds with a smooth coat, drooping ears, sagging jowls, and a keen sense of smell. **2.** *Informal* A relentless pursuer.

blood•less (blŭd′lĭs) *adj.* **1.** Deficient in or lacking blood. **2.** Pale and anemic in color: *bloodless lips.* **3.** Achieved without bloodshed: *a bloodless coup.* **4.** Lacking vivacity or spirit: *a long, bloodless speech.* **5.** Devoid of human emotion or feeling. —**blood′less•ly** *adv.* —**blood′less•ness** *n.*

blood•let•ting (blŭd′lĕt′ĭng) *n.* **1.** Bloodshed. **2.** The removal of blood, usu. from a vein, as a therapeutic measure. **3.** A sharp reduction or elimination. —**blood′let′ter** *n.*

blood•line (blŭd′līn′) *n.* Direct line of descent; pedigree.

blood meal *n.* The dried and powdered blood of animals, used in animal feeds and as a nitrogen-rich fertilizer for plants.

blood•mo•bile (blŭd′mə-bēl′) *n.* A motor vehicle equipped for collecting blood from donors. [BLOOD + (AUTO)MOBILE.]

blood money *n.* **1.** Money paid by a killer as compensation to the next of kin of a murder victim. **2.** Money gained at the cost of another's life or livelihood.

blood orange *n.* A sweet orange having pulp that is red or streaked with red.

blood plasma *n.* The fluid portion of the blood in which the blood cells and platelets are normally suspended.

blood platelet *n.* A disklike, nonnucleated, cytoplasmic body in the blood plasma of mammals that promotes blood clotting.

blood poisoning *n.* **1.** See **septicemia. 2.** See **toxemia.**

blood pressure *n.* The pressure exerted by the blood against the walls of the blood vessels, esp. the arteries.

blood profile *n.* See **complete blood count.**

blood pudding *n.* See **blood sausage.**

blood red *n.* A moderate to vivid red. —**blood′-red′** (blŭd′rĕd′) *adj.*

blood relation *n.* A person who is related to another by birth rather than by marriage. —**blood relationship** *n.*

blood•root (blŭd′root′, -rŏot′) *n.* A perennial wildflower (*Sanguinaria canadensis*) native to forests in eastern North America and having a fleshy rootstock, a single lobed leaf, and a solitary white flower.

blood sausage *n.* A link sausage made of pig's blood, diced pork fat, and other ingredients.

blood serum *n.* See **serum** 1.

blood•shed (blŭd′shĕd′) *n.* The shedding of blood, esp. the injury or killing of people.

blood•shot (blŭd′shŏt′) *adj.* Red and inflamed as a result of congested blood vessels: *bloodshot eyes.* [< obsolete *bloodshotten* : BLOOD + *shotten,* suffused, p. part. of SHOOT.]

blood•stain (blŭd′stān′) *n.* A stain caused by blood. ❖ *tr.v.* **-stained, -stain•ing, -stains** To stain with blood. [V., back-formation < *bloodstained.*]

blood•stone (blŭd′stōn′) *n.* A variety of deep-green chalcedony flecked with red jasper.

blood•stream also **blood stream** (blŭd′strēm′) *n.* The flow of blood through the circulatory system of an organism.

blood•suck•er (blŭd′sŭk′ər) *n.* **1.** An animal, such as a leech, that sucks blood. **2.** An extortionist or blackmailer. —**blood′suck′ing** *adj.*

blood sugar *n.* **1.** Sugar in the form of glucose in the blood. **2.** The concentration of glucose in the blood.

blood test *n.* **1.** An examination of a sample of blood to determine its chemical, physical, or serologic characteristics. **2.** A serologic test for certain diseases, such as AIDS.

blood•thirst•y (blŭd′thûr′stē) *adj.* **1.** Eager to shed blood. **2.** Characterized by great carnage. —**blood′thirst′i•ly** *adv.* —**blood′thirst′i•ness** *n.*

blood type *n.* See **blood group.**

blood typing or **blood-typ•ing** (blŭd′tī′pĭng) *n.* The process of identifying a person's blood group by serologic testing.

blood vessel *n.* An elastic tubular channel, such as an artery, vein, or capillary, through which the blood circulates.

blood•worm (blŭd′wûrm′) *n.* **1.** Any of various red, segmented marine worms of the genera *Polycirrus* and *Enoplobranchus.* **2.** The red freshwater larvae of certain midges.

blood•y (blŭd′ē) *adj.* **-i•er, -i•est 1.** Stained with blood. **2.** Of, characteristic of, or containing blood. **3.** Accompanied by or giving rise to bloodshed: *a bloody fight.* **4.** Bloodthirsty. **5.** Suggesting the color of blood; blood-red. **6.** *Chiefly British Slang* Used as an intensive: *Your desk is a bloody mess.* ❖ *adv. Chiefly British Slang* Used as an intensive: *bloody well right.* ❖ *tr.v.* **-ied, -y•ing, -ies 1.** To stain, spot, or color with or as if with blood. **2.** To make bleed. —**blood′i•ly** *adv.* —**blood′i•ness** *n.*

bloody mary also **Bloody Mary** *n., pl.* **bloody marys** A cocktail usu. made of vodka, tomato juice, and seasonings. [After MARY I.]

blood•y-mind•ed (blŭd′ē-mīn′dĭd) *adj.* **1.** Ready and willing to accept bloodshed or to resort to violence. **2.** *Chiefly British* Perversely cantankerous. —**blood′y-mind′ed•ness** *n.*

bloom[1] (bloom) *n.* **1.** The flower of a plant. **2a.** The condition of being in flower. **b.** A condition or time of vigor and beauty; prime: *"the radiant bloom of Greek genius"* (Edith Hamilton). **3.** A fresh, rosy complexion: *"She was short, plump, and fair, with a fine bloom"* (Jane Austen). **4a.** A waxy or powdery bluish coating on the surface of certain plant parts, as on plums or cabbage leaves, that forms naturally to prevent the loss of fluids. **b.** A similar coating, as on newly minted coins. **c.** Grayish marks on the surface of chocolate produced by the formation of cocoa butter crystals. **d.** *Chemistry* See **efflorescence** 3a. **5.** Glare that is caused by a shiny object reflecting too much light into a television camera. **6.** A colored area on the surface of water caused by planktonic growth. ❖ *v.* **bloomed, bloom•ing, blooms** —*intr.* **1a.** To bear a flower or flowers. **b.** To support plant life in abundance. **2.** To shine; glow. **3.** To grow or flourish with youth and vigor. **4.** To appear or expand suddenly. —*tr.* **1.** To cause to flourish. **2.** *Obsolete* To cause to flower. [ME *blom* < ON *blōm.* See **bhel-** in App.] —**bloom′y** *adj.*

bloom[2] (bloom) *n.* **1.** A bar of steel prepared for rolling. **2.** A

ă	pat	oi	boy
ā	pay	ou	out
âr	care	ŏŏ	took
ä	father	ōō	boot
ĕ	pet	ŭ	cut
ē	be	ûr	urge
ĭ	pit	th	thin
ī	pie	*th*	this
îr	pier	hw	which
ŏ	pot	zh	vision
ō	toe	ə	about,
ô	paw		item

Stress marks:
′ (primary);
′ (secondary), as in
lexicon (lĕk′sĭ-kŏn′)

mass of wrought iron ready for further working. [ME *blome,* lump of metal < OE *blōma.* See **bhel-** in App.]

Bloom, Harold b. 1930. Amer. literary theorist whose works include *The Anxiety of Influence* (1972).

bloom•er[1] (blo͞oʹmər) *n.* **1a.** A plant that blooms. **b.** A person who attains full maturity and competence: *a late bloomer.* **2.** *Slang* A blunder.

bloom•er[2] (blo͞oʹmər) *n.* **1.** A costume formerly worn by women and girls that was composed of loose trousers gathered about the ankles. **2. bloomers a.** Baggy trousers gathered at the knee and formerly worn by women and girls as an athletic costume. **b.** Girls' underpants of similar design. [After Amelia Jenks BLOOMER.]

Bloomer, Amelia Jenks 1818–94. Amer. social reformer who founded and edited the *Lily* (1849–55) and advocated a new style of dress for women.

Bloom•field (blo͞omʹfēldʹ), **Leonard** 1887–1949. Amer. linguist who introduced a behavioristic approach in his text *Language* (1933).

bloom•ing (blo͞oʹmĭng) *adv. & adj. Chiefly British Slang* Used as an intensive: *a blooming idiot.* [Prob. a euphemism for BLOODY.]

Bloo•ming•ton (blo͞oʹmĭng-tən) **1.** A city of S-central IN SSW of Indianapolis. Pop. 69,291. **2.** A city of E MN, a suburb of Minneapolis. Pop. 85,172.

Blooms•bur•y (blo͞omzʹbĕrʹē, -bə-rē, -brē) A residential district of N-central London, England, famous for its associations with members of the intelligentsia, including Virginia Woolf and John Maynard Keynes, in the early 20th cent.

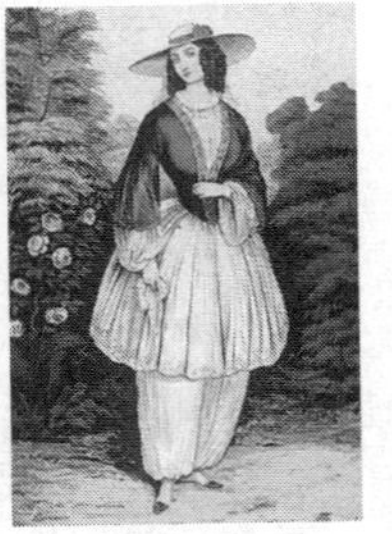

bloomer[2]
The Bloomer Costume, 1851 lithograph by Nathaniel Currier

bloop (blo͞op) *Baseball n.* A blooper. ❖ *tr.v.* **blooped, bloop•ing, bloops** To hit (a ball) into the air just beyond the infield. ❖ *adj.* Hit just beyond the infield.

bloop•er (blo͞oʹpər) *n.* **1.** *Informal* A clumsy mistake, esp. one made in public; a faux pas. **2.** *Baseball* **a.** A weakly hit ball that carries just beyond the infield. **b.** A high pitch that is lobbed to the batter. [< BLOOP, a high-pitched howl on the radio caused by interference (of imit. orig.), and imit. of the sound made by hitting a ball weakly.]

blos•som (blŏsʹəm) *n.* **1.** A flower or cluster of flowers. **2.** The condition or time of flowering: *peach trees in blossom.* **3.** A period or condition of maximum development. ❖ *intr.v.* **-somed, -som•ing, -soms 1.** To come into flower; bloom. **2.** To develop; flourish: *The child blossomed into a beauty.* [ME < OE *blōstm.* See **bhel-** in App.] **—blosʹsom•y** *adj.*

blot[1] (blŏt) *n.* **1.** A spot or stain caused by a discoloring substance. **2.** A stain on one's character or reputation; a disgrace. **3.** Any of several techniques for analyzing or identifying specific proteins or DNA sequences or their fragments that involve the transfer of molecules to be analyzed to nitrocellulose. ❖ *v.* **blot•ted, blot•ting, blots** —*tr.* **1.** To spot or stain, as with a discoloring substance. **2.** To bring moral disgrace to. **3.** To obliterate (writing, for example). **4.** To make obscure; hide. **5.** To destroy utterly; annihilate: *War blotted out their way of life.* **6.** To soak up or dry with absorbent material. —*intr.* **1.** To spill or spread in a spot or stain. **2.** To become blotted, soaked up, or absorbed. [ME.]

blot[2] (blŏt) *n.* **1.** *Games* An exposed piece in backgammon. **2.** *Archaic* A weak point. [Poss. < LGer. *blat,* naked, unprotected.]

blotch (blŏch) *n.* **1.** A spot or blot; a splotch. **2.** A discoloration on the skin; a blemish. **3.** Any of several plant diseases caused by fungi and resulting in dead areas on leaves or fruit. ❖ *tr. & intr.v.* **blotched, blotch•ing, blotch•es** To mark or become marked with blotches. [Prob. blend of BLOT[1] and BOTCH.] **—blotchʹi•ly** *adv.* **—blotchʹi•ness** *n.* **—blotchʹy** *adj.*

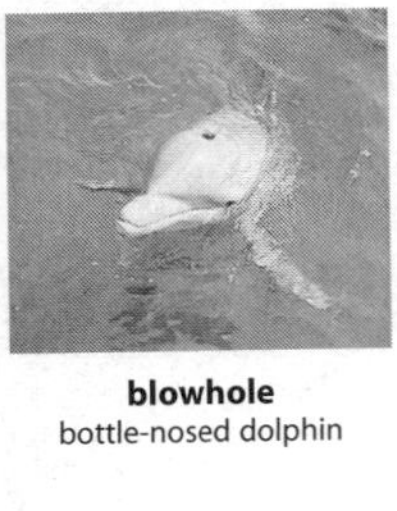

blowhole
bottle-nosed dolphin

blot•ter (blŏtʹər) *n.* **1.** A piece or pad of blotting paper. **2.** A book containing daily records of occurrences or transactions.

blot•ting paper (blŏtʹĭng) *n.* Absorbent paper used to blot a surface by soaking up excess ink.

blot•to (blŏtʹō) *adj. Slang* Intoxicated; drunk. [Perh. < BLOT[1].]

blouse (blous, blouz) *n.* **1.** A woman's or child's loosely fitting shirt that extends to the waist or slightly below. **2.** A loosely fitting garment resembling a long shirt. **3.** The service coat or tunic worn by the members of some branches of the US armed forces. ❖ *intr. & tr.v.* **bloused, blous•ing, blous•es** To hang or cause to hang loosely and fully. [Fr., poss. alteration (influenced by *blousse,* wool scraps) of obsolete Fr. *blaude* < OFr. *bliaut,* prob. of Gmc. orig.]

blou•son (blouʹsŏnʹ, blo͞oʹzŏnʹ) *n.* A garment, such as a dress or shirt, with a fitted waistband over which material blouses. [Fr., dim. of *blouse,* blouse. See BLOUSE.]

blo•vi•ate (blōʹvē-ātʹ) *intr.v.* **-at•ed, -at•ing, -ates** *Slang* To discourse pompously or boastfully at length: *"the rural Babbitt who bloviates about 'progress' and 'growth'"* (George Rebeck). [Mock-Latinate formation < BLOW[1].] **—bloʹvi•aʹtion** *n.*

blow[1] (blō) *v.* **blew** (blo͞o), **blown** (blōn), **blow•ing, blows** —*intr.* **1.** To be in a state of motion. Used of the air or of wind. **2.** To move along or be carried by or as if by the wind: *My hat blew away.* **3.** To expel a current of air, as from the mouth or from a bellows. **4.** To produce a sound by expelling a current of air, as in sounding a whistle. **5.** To breathe hard; pant. **6.** To storm. **7.** To release air or gas suddenly; burst or explode: *The tire blew.* **8a.** To fail or break down: *The furnace blew.* **b.** To melt or otherwise become disabled. Used of a fuse. **9.** To spout moist air from the blowhole. Used of a whale. **10.** *Informal* To boast. **11.** *Slang* To go away; depart. —*tr.* **1.** To cause to move by means of a current of air. **2.** To expel (air) from the mouth. **3.** To cause air to be expelled suddenly from: *blew a tire.* **4.** To drive a current of air on, in, or through: *blew my hair dry.* **5.** To clear out or make free of obstruction by forcing air through: *blew her nose.* **6.** To shape or form (glass, for example) by forcing air or gas through at the end of a pipe. **7.** *Music* **a.** To cause (a wind instrument) to sound. **b.** To sound: *a bugle blowing taps.* **8.** To cause to be out of breath. **9.** To demolish by the force of an explosion: *a bomb that blew the headquarters apart.* **10.** To lay or deposit eggs in. Used of certain insects. **11a.** To cause to fail or break down. **b.** To cause (a fuse) to melt or become disabled. **12.** *Slang* **a.** To spend (money) freely and rashly. **b.** To spend money freely on; treat: *blew me to a sumptuous dinner.* **13.** *Vulgar Slang* To perform fellatio on. **14a.** *Slang* To spoil or lose through ineptitude. See Syns at **botch. b.** To cause (a covert intelligence operation or operative) to be revealed. **15.** *Slang* To depart (a place) in a great hurry. ❖ *n.* **1.** The act or an instance of blowing. **2a.** A blast of air or wind. **b.** A storm. **3.** *Informal* An act of bragging. **4.** *Slang* Cocaine. ***—phrasal verbs:* blow away** *Slang* **1.** To kill by shooting. **2.** To defeat decisively. **3.** To affect intensely; overwhelm. **blow in** *Slang* To arrive, esp. when unexpected. **blow off 1.** To relieve or release (pressure); let off. **2.** *Slang* To choose not to attend or accompany. **blow out 1.** To extinguish or be extinguished by a gust of air. **2.** To fail, as an electrical apparatus. **3.** To erupt in an uncontrolled manner. Used of a gas or oil well. **blow over** To subside or pass over with little lasting effect. **blow up 1.** To come into being: *A storm blew up.* **2.** To fill with air; inflate. **3.** To enlarge (a photographic image or print). **4.** To explode. **5.** To lose one's temper. ***—idioms:* blow a fuse** (or **gasket**) *Slang* To explode with anger. **blow hot and cold** To change one's opinion often on a matter; vacillate. **blow off steam** To give vent to pent-up emotion. **blow (one's) cool** *Slang* To lose one's composure. **blow (one's) mind** *Slang* To affect with intense emotion. **blow (one's) top** (or **stack**) *Informal* To lose one's temper. [ME *blowen* < OE *blāwan.*]

blow[2] (blō) *n.* **1.** A sudden hard stroke or hit, as with the fist or an object. **2.** An unexpected shock or calamity. **3.** An unexpected attack; an assault. [ME *blaw.*]

blow[3] (blō) *n.* **1.** A mass of blossoms: *peach blow.* **2.** The state of blossoming. ❖ *intr. & tr.v.* **blew** (blo͞o), **blown** (blōn), **blow•ing, blows** To bloom or cause to bloom. [< ME *blowen,* to bloom < OE *blōwan.* See **bhel-** in App.]

blow-by-blow (blōʹbī-blōʹ) *adj.* Exhibiting great detail.

blow-dry (blōʹdrīʹ) *tr.v.* **-dried, -dry•ing, -dries** To dry and often style (hair) with a hand-held dryer. **—blow dryer** *n.*

blow•er (blōʹər) *n.* **1.** One that blows, esp. a mechanical device, such as a fan, that produces a current of air. **2.** *Slang* A braggart. **3.** *Chiefly British Slang* A telephone.

blow•fish (blōʹfĭshʹ) *n., pl.* **blowfish** or **-fish•es** See **puffer.**

blow•fly (blōʹflīʹ) *n.* Any of several flies of the family Calliphoridae that deposit their eggs in carcasses or carrion or in open sores and wounds.

blow•gun (blōʹgŭnʹ) *n.* A long narrow pipe through which darts or pellets may be blown.

blow•hard (blōʹhärdʹ) *n. Informal* A boaster or braggart.

blow•hole (blōʹhōlʹ) *n.* **1.** An opening or one of a pair of openings for breathing, on top of the head of cetaceans. **2.** A hole in ice to which aquatic mammals come to breathe. **3.** A vent to permit the escape of air or other gas.

blow•job (blōʹjŏbʹ) *n. Vulgar Slang* The act or an instance of fellatio.

blown[1] (blōn) *v.* Past participle of **blow**[1]. ❖ *adj.* **1.** Swollen or inflated; distended. **2.** Out of breath; panting. **3.** Flyblown. **4.** Formed by blowing: *blown glass.*

blown[2] (blōn) *v.* Past participle of **blow**[3].

blow•off (blōʹôfʹ, -ŏfʹ) *n.* **1.** Something, such as a gas, that is blown off. **2.** A device or channel for blowing off something.

blow•out (blōʹoutʹ) *n.* **1a.** A sudden rupture or bursting, as of an automobile tire. **b.** The hole made by such a rupture. **2.** A sudden escape of a confined gas or liquid, as from a well. **3.** *Slang* A large party or other social affair. **4.** A lopsided victory or thorough defeat.

blow•pipe (blōʹpīpʹ) *n.* **1.** A metal tube in which a flow of gas is mixed with a controlled flow of air to concentrate the heat of a flame, used esp. in the identification of minerals. **2.** See **blowgun. 3.** A long narrow pipe used to work molten glass.

blow•torch (blōʹtôrchʹ) *n.* A portable burner for mixing gas and oxygen to produce a very hot flame, used for soldering, welding, and glass blowing.

blow•up (blōʹŭpʹ) *n.* **1.** An explosion. **2.** An outburst of temper. **3.** A photographic enlargement.

blow•y (blōʹē) *adj.* **-i•er, -i•est** Windy or breezy.

blow•zy also **blow•sy** (blouʹzē) *adj.* **-zi•er, -zi•est** also **-si•er, -si•est 1.** Having a coarsely ruddy and bloated appearance. **2.** Disheveled and frowzy; unkempt: *blowzy hair.* [< obsolete *blowze,* beggar woman, slattern.] **—blowʹzi•ly** *adv.* **—blowʹzi•ness** *n.*

BLS *abbr.* **1.** Bachelor of Library Science **2.** Bureau of Labor Statistics

BLT (bēʹĕl-tēʹ) *n.* A bacon, lettuce, and tomato sandwich.

blub·ber¹ (blŭb′ər) v. -bered, -ber·ing, -bers —intr. To sob noisily. See Syns at **cry. 1.** To utter while crying and sobbing. **2.** To make wet and swollen by weeping. ❖ n. A loud sobbing. [ME *bluberen*, to bubble < *bluber*, foam.] —**blub′ber·er** n. —**blub′ber·ing·ly** adv.

blub·ber² (blŭb′ər) n. **1.** The thick layer of fat between the skin and the muscle layers of whales and other marine mammals. **2.** Excessive body fat. **3.** A large sea nettle or medusa. ❖ adj. Swollen and protruding: *blubber cheeks.* [ME *bluber*, foam.] —**blub′ber·y** adj.

blu·cher (bloo′chər, -kər) n. **1.** A high shoe or half boot. **2.** A shoe with the vamp and tongue of one piece and the quarters lapping over the vamp. [After Gebhard Leberecht von BLÜCHER.]

Blü·cher (bloo′kər, -chər, -кнər), Gebhard Leberecht von 1742–1819. Prussian field marshal who led the Prussian army in campaigns against Napoleon.

bludg·eon (blŭj′ən) n. A short heavy club, usu. of wood, that is thicker or loaded at one end. ❖ tr.v. -eoned, -eon·ing, -eons **1.** To hit with or as if with a heavy club. **2.** To overcome by or as if by using a heavy club. [?] —**bludg′eon·er, bludg′eon·eer** (-ə-nîr′) n.

blue (bloo) n. **1.** The hue of the portion of the visible spectrum between green and indigo, evoked in the human observer by radiant energy with wavelengths of approx. 420 to 490 nanometers; any of a group of colors whose hue is that of a clear daytime sky; one of the additive or light primaries; one of the psychological primary hues. **2a.** A pigment or dye imparting this hue. **b.** Bluing. **3a.** An object having this hue. **b.** Dress or clothing of this hue. **4a.** A person who wears a blue uniform. **b. blues** A dress blue uniform, esp. that of the US Army. **5.** often **Blue a.** A member of the Union Army in the Civil War. **b.** The Union Army. **6.** A bluefish. **7.** A small blue butterfly of the family Lycaenidae. **8a.** The sky. **b.** The sea. ❖ adj. **blu·er, blu·est 1.** Of the color blue. **2.** Bluish or having parts that are blue or bluish, as the blue whale. **3.** Having a gray or purplish color, as from cold or contusion. **4.** Wearing blue. **5a.** Gloomy; depressed. **b.** Dismal; dreary: *a blue day.* **6.** Puritanical; strict. **7.** Aristocratic; patrician. **8.** Indecent; risqué: *a blue movie.* ❖ tr. & intr.v. **blued, blu·ing, blues** To make or become blue. —**idioms: blue in the face** At the point of extreme exasperation. **out of the blue 1.** From an unexpected or unforeseen source: *criticism that came out of the blue.* **2.** At a completely unexpected time. [ME *blue, bleu* < OFr. *bleu,* of Gmc. orig.] —**blue′ly** adv. —**blue′ness** n.

blue angel n. *Slang* A blue devil.

blue baby n. An infant born with cyanosis as a result of a congenital cardiac or pulmonary defect.

blue·back salmon (bloo′băk′) n. See **sockeye salmon.**

blue·beard (bloo′bîrd′) n. A man who marries and murders one wife after another. [After *Blue Beard,* transl. of French *Barbe Bleue,* a character in a story by Charles Perrault (1628–1703).]

blue·bell (bloo′běl′) also **blue·bells** (-bělz′) n. **1.** Any of several bulbous plants of the genus *Hyacinthoides* in the lily family, having usu. blue to pink bell-shaped flowers. **2.** Any of numerous plants of the genus *Mertensia,* esp. the Virginia cowslip. **3.** See **harebell. 4.** Any of several other plants having bluish, usu. bell-shaped flowers.

blue·ber·ry (bloo′běr′ē) n. **1.** Any of numerous plants of the genus *Vaccinium,* having edible blue to blue-black berries. **2.** The fruit of any of these plants.

blue·bill (bloo′bĭl′) n. See **scaup.**

blue·bird (bloo′bûrd′) n. Any of several North American songbirds of the genus *Sialia,* having blue plumage and usu. a rust-colored breast in the male.

blue-black (bloo′blăk′) adj. Very dark blue.

blue blood also **blue·blood** (bloo′blŭd′) n. **1.** Noble or aristocratic descent. **2.** A member of the aristocracy. [Transl. of Sp. *sangre azul : sangre,* blood + *azul,* blue (prob. < the visible veins of fair-complexioned aristocrats).] —**blue′-blood′ed** adj.

blue·bon·net (bloo′bŏn′ĭt) n. **1.** Either of two annual lupines (*Lupinus texensis* and *L. subcarnosus*) native to Texas and having light blue flowers. **2a.** A broad, blue woolen cap worn in Scotland. **b.** A person wearing such a cap.

blue book also **blue·book** (bloo′book′) n. **1.** An official list of persons employed by the US government. **2.** A book listing socially prominent people. **3.** A blank notebook with blue covers in which to answer examination questions.

blue·bot·tle (bloo′bŏt′l) n. Any of several flies of the genus *Calliphora* that have a bright metallic-blue body.

blue catfish n. A large bluish freshwater catfish (*Ictalurus furcatus*) of the Mississippi River valley.

blue cheese n. Any of several types of semisoft cheeses having a greenish-blue mold and strong flavor.

blue chip also **blue-chip·per** (bloo′chĭp′ər) n. **1.** A stock that sells at a high price because of public confidence in its long record of steady earnings. **2.** A valuable asset or property. **3.** *Games* A blue poker chip of high value. —**blue′-chip′** adj.

blue·coat (bloo′kōt′) n. A person who wears a blue uniform, esp. a police officer. —**blue′coat′ed** adj.

blue cohosh n. A perennial herb (*Caulophyllum thalictroides*) of eastern North America, having blue berrylike seeds.

blue-col·lar (bloo′kŏl′ər) adj. Of or relating to wage earners whose jobs are performed in work clothes and often involve manual labor. —**blue′-col′lar** n.

blue crab n. An edible bluish swimming crab (*Callinectes sapidus*) that has a wide distribution along the Atlantic and Gulf coasts of North America.

blue-curls also **blue curls** (bloo′kûrlz′) pl.n. (*used with a sing. or pl. verb*) Any of several North American plants of the genus *Trichostema* in the mint family, having clusters of mostly bluish or purplish flowers with long curved stamens.

blue devil n. **1.** *Slang* A blue capsule or tablet containing barbiturate amobarbital or its sodium derivative. **2. blue devils** *Informal* A feeling of depression; despondency.

blue-eyed grass (bloo′īd′) n. Any of various New World perennial herbs of the genus *Sisyrinchium,* having grasslike leaves.

blue-eyed Mary n. An annual North American herb (*Collinsia verna*) having bicolored flowers with two lips.

blue·fin tuna (bloo′fĭn′) n. A very large tuna (*Thunnus thynnus*) of temperate waters.

blue·fish (bloo′fĭsh′) n., pl. bluefish or -fish·es **1.** A food and game fish (*Pomatomus saltatrix*) of the Atlantic and Indian oceans. **2.** Any of various predominantly blue fishes.

blue flag n. Any of several irises having blue or blue-violet flowers, esp. *Iris versicolor* of eastern North America.

blue flu n. A sickout, esp. by uniformed police officers. [< the blue color of most police officers' uniforms.]

blue fox n. **1.** An arctic fox whose fur is bluish gray during a color phase typically occurring in the summer or extending throughout the year. **2.** The fur of such a fox.

blue·gill (bloo′gĭl′) n., pl. bluegill or -gills A common edible sunfish (*Lepomis macrochirus*) of North American lakes and streams.

blue·grass (bloo′grăs′) n. **1.** also **blue grass** Any of various grasses of the genus *Poa,* including Kentucky bluegrass. **2.** *Music* A type of folk music that originated in the southern United States, typically played on banjos and guitars.

Bluegrass also **Bluegrass Country** or **Bluegrass Region** A region of central KY noted for the breeding of thoroughbred horses.

blue-green alga (bloo′grēn′) n. See **cyanobacterium.**

blue grouse n. A wildfowl (*Dendragapus obscurus*) of western North America having predominantly gray plumage.

blue gum n. A tall timber tree (*Eucalyptus globulus*) of Australia having smooth bluish bark and lance-shaped leaves.

blue heaven n. *Slang* A blue devil.

blue heron n. Any of several varieties of heron with blue or blue-gray plumage.

blue·ing (bloo′ĭng) n. Variant of **bluing.**

blue·ish (bloo′ĭsh) adj. Variant of **bluish.**

blue·jack·et (bloo′jăk′ĭt) n. An enlisted person in the US or British Navy; a sailor.

blue jay n. A North American bird (*Cyanocitta cristata*) having a crested head, predominantly blue plumage, and a harsh cry.

blue jeans also **blue·jeans** (bloo′jēnz′) pl.n. Clothes, esp. pants, made of blue denim.

blue law n. **1.** A law regulating commercial business on Sunday. **2.** One of a body of laws in colonial New England enforcing strict moral standards.

blue·line or **blue line** (bloo′līn′) n. Either of two blue lines running across an ice-hockey rink, dividing the rink into defensive, neutral, and offensive zones.

blue marlin n. A large marlin (*Makaira nigricans*) of warm Atlantic and Pacific waters, having dark blue to brownish upper parts and pale blue vertical bars on the sides.

blue moon n. **1a.** The third full moon in a three-month calendrical season that has four full moons. **b.** The second of two full moons in a single month. **2.** *Informal* A relatively long period of time. [Sense 2, prob. < the rare occurrence whereby the moon appears blue from high amounts of dust in the atmosphere.]

Blue Mountains 1. A range of NE OR and SE WA rising to 2,777.3 m (9,106 ft). **2.** A range of E Jamaica rising to 2,252 m (7,388 ft) at **Blue Mountain Peak.**

Blue Nile A river of NE Africa flowing c. 1,609 km (1,000 mi) from NW Ethiopia to Khartoum, where it merges with the White Nile.

blue·nose (bloo′nōz′) n. A puritanical person.

blue note n. *Music* A flatted note, esp. the third or seventh note of a scale, in place of an expected major interval. [< its use in blues music.]

blue pike n. A freshwater food and game fish (*Strizostedion vitreum glaucum*) found in the Great Lakes.

blue-plate (bloo′plāt′) adj. Being a main course of a restaurant meal usu. offered at a special price. [Perh. < the blue-patterned plate on which such meals were orig. served.]

blue·point also **blue point** (bloo′point′) n. A type of small oyster cultured chiefly in coastal waters of the eastern United States. [After *Blue Point,* a locality on Great South Bay, Long Island, New York.]

blue point n. A variety of a domestic cat, esp. the Siamese, with a bluish-white coat and darker bluish-gray points.

blue·print (bloo′prĭnt′) n. **1a.** A contact print of a drawing rendered as white lines on a blue background, esp. such a print of

ă	pat	oi	boy
ā	pay	ou	out
âr	care	oo	took
ä	father	oo	boot
ĕ	pet	ŭ	cut
ē	be	ûr	urge
ĭ	pit	th	thin
ī	pie	th	this
îr	pier	hw	which
ŏ	pot	zh	vision
ō	toe	ə	about,
ô	paw		item

Stress marks:
′ (primary);
′ (secondary); as in
lexicon (lĕk′sĭ-kŏn′)

an architectural plan or technical drawing. **b.** A whiteprint. **2.** A detailed plan of action. See Syns at **plan. 3.** A model or prototype. —**blue′print′** v.

blue racer n. A bluish-green harmless variety (Coluber constrictor subsp. flaviventris) of the blacksnake, found in the central United States.

blue ribbon n. **1.** An emblem, badge, or rosette of blue ribbon awarded as first prize in a competition. **2.** An award or honor for excellence. —**blue′-rib′bon** (blōō′rĭb′ən) adj.

blue-ribbon jury n. A jury whose members have been selected for their special qualifications, such as higher education, that enable them to deal with complex legal issues.

Blue Ridge also **Blue Ridge Mountains** A range of the Appalachian Mts. extending from S PA to N GA and rising to 2,038.6 m (6,684 ft).

blue runner n. See **runner** 15.

blues (blōōz) pl.n. (used with a sing. or pl. verb) **1.** A state of depression or melancholy. **2.** Music A style of music that evolved from southern African-American secular songs and usu. distinguished by a strong 4/4 rhythm and flatted thirds and sevenths. [Short for blue devils.] —**blues′man** n. —**blues′y** adj.

blue shark n. A pelagic shark (Prionace glauca) of tropical and temperate oceans that is a brilliant dark blue on top.

blue·shift (blōō′shĭft′) n. A decrease in the wavelength of radiation emitted by an approaching celestial body as a consequence of the Doppler effect. [< the fact that the shorter wavelengths of light are at the blue end of the visible spectrum.]

blue-sky (blōō′skī′) adj. **1.** Unrealistic and impractical. **2.** Having a cloudless sky; clear.

blue-sky law A law designed to protect the public from buying fraudulent securities.

blue spruce n. A Rocky Mountain tree (Picea pungens) having silvery-blue or blue-green, four-angled, needlelike leaves and cylindrical cones.

blues-rock (blōōz′rŏk′) n. A style of music that combines blues and rock 'n' roll.

blue·stem (blōō′stĕm′) n. Any of several chiefly North American grasses of the genera Andropogon, Bothriochloa, and Schizachyrium, some of which are important prairie grasses.

blue·stock·ing (blōō′stŏk′ĭng) n. A woman with strong scholarly or literary interests. [After the Blue Stocking Society, a nickname for a predominantly female literary club of 18th-cent. London.]

blue·stone (blōō′stōn′) n. **1.** A bluish-gray sandstone used for paving and building. **2.** A similar stone.

blue streak n. Informal **1.** Something moving very fast. **2.** A rapid and seemingly interminable stream of words: curse a blue streak. [Prob. in allusion to a bolt of lightning.]

blue·tongue (blōō′tŭng′) n. A viral disease of sheep and cattle transmitted by biting insects and characterized by cyanosis of the lips and tongue.

blu·ets (blōō′ĭts) pl.n. (used with a sing. or pl. verb) Any of several herbs of the genus Hedyotis, esp. the low-growing H. caerulea, of eastern North America that has blue flowers with yellow centers. [ME < bleu, blue. See BLUE.]

blue vitriol n. A blue crystalline hydrous solution of copper sulfate, $CuSO_4 \cdot 5H_2O$, used in fungicides, as a wood preservative, and in the processing of leather and textiles.

blue walleye n. See **blue pike**.

blue·weed (blōō′wēd′) n. A biennial Eurasian plant (Echium vulgare) having usu. blue flowers.

blue whale n. A large whalebone whale (Balaenoptera musculus) having a bluish-gray back, yellow underparts, and several ventral throat grooves, and sometimes reaching a length of 30.5 meters (100 feet).

bluff¹ (blŭf) v. **bluffed, bluff·ing, bluffs** —tr. **1.** To mislead or deceive. **2.** To impress or deter by a false display of confidence. **3.** Games To mislead (opponents) in a card game, as by heavy betting on a poor hand. —intr. To engage in a false display of strength or confidence. ❖ n. **1.** The act or practice of bluffing. **2.** One that bluffs. [Prob. < Du. bluffen < LGer.] —**bluff′a·ble** adj. —**bluff′er** n.

bluff² (blŭf) n. A steep headland, promontory, riverbank, or cliff. ❖ adj. **bluff·er, bluff·est 1.** Rough and blunt but not unkind in manner. **2.** Having a broad steep front. [Prob. < obsolete Du. blaf or MLGer. blaff, broad.] —**bluff′ly** adv. —**bluff′ness** n.

blu·ing also **blue·ing** (blōō′ĭng) n. **1.** Any of various coloring agents that counteract yellowing of laundered fabrics. **2.** A rinsing agent used to tint gray or graying hair silver.

blu·ish also **blue·ish** (blōō′ĭsh) adj. Somewhat blue. —**blu′ish·ness** n.

Blum (blōōm), **Léon** 1872–1950. French socialist politician who served as premier (1936–37, 1938, and 1946–47).

blun·der (blŭn′dər) n. A usu. serious mistake typically caused by ignorance or confusion. ❖ v. **-dered, -der·ing, -ders** —intr. **1.** To move clumsily or blindly. **2.** To make a blunder. —tr. **1.** To make a blunder in; botch. **2.** To utter (something) stupidly or thoughtlessly. [< ME blunderen, to go blindly, perh. < OSwed. blundra, have one's eyes closed < ON blunda.] —**blun′der·er** n. —**blun′der·ing·ly** adv.

blue whale
Balaenoptera musculus

blunder, bumble, flounder, lumber, lurch, stumble These verbs mean to move awkwardly or unsteadily: blundered into the room; flies bumbling against the screen; floundered up the muddy trail; a wagon lumbering along a dirt road; twisted her ankle and lurched home; stumbled but regained his balance.

blun·der·buss (blŭn′dər-bŭs′) n. **1.** A short musket of wide bore and flaring muzzle, formerly used to scatter shot at close range. **2.** A clumsy and stupid person. [Alteration of Du. donderbus : donder, thunder (< MDu. doner; see (s)tenə- in App.) + bus, gun (< MDu. busse, tube < Lat. buxis, box; see BOX¹).]

blunt (blŭnt) adj. **blunt·er, blunt·est 1.** Having a dull edge or end; not sharp. **2.** Abrupt and often disconcertingly frank in speech. **3.** Slow to understand or perceive; dull. **4.** Lacking in feeling; insensitive. ❖ v. **blunt·ed, blunt·ing, blunts** —tr. **1.** To dull the edge of. **2.** To make less effective; weaken. —intr. To become blunt. [ME.] —**blunt′ly** adv. —**blunt′ness** n.

blur (blûr) v. **blurred, blur·ring, blurs** —tr. **1.** To make indistinct and hazy in outline or appearance; obscure. **2.** To smear or stain; smudge. **3.** To lessen the perception of; dim. —intr. **1.** To become indistinct. **2.** To make smudges or stains by smearing. ❖ n. **1.** A smear or blot. **2.** Something hazy and indistinct to the sight or mind. [Prob. akin to ME bleren, to blear.] —**blur′ri·ness** n. —**blur′ry** adj.

blurb (blûrb) n. A brief publicity notice, as on a book jacket. [Coined by Gelett Burgess (1866–1951), American humorist.] —**blurb** v.

blurt (blûrt) tr.v. **blurt·ed, blurt·ing, blurts** To utter suddenly and impulsively. [Prob. imit.] —**blurt′er** n.

blush (blŭsh) intr.v. **blushed, blush·ing, blush·es 1.** To become red in the face, as from embarrassment; flush. **2.** To become red or rosy. **3.** To feel embarrassed or ashamed. ❖ n. **1.** A reddening of the face, esp. as from embarrassment. **2.** A red or rosy color: the blush of dawn. **3.** A glance, look, or view: seems so at first blush. **4.** Blusher. [ME blushen < OE blyscan.] —**blush′ful** adj. —**blush′ing·ly** adv.

blush·er (blŭsh′ər) n. Makeup used esp. on the cheekbones to give a usu. rosy tint.

blush wine n. Any of several wines having a pink tinge.

blus·ter (blŭs′tər) v. **-tered, -ter·ing, -ters** —intr. **1.** To blow in violent gusts, as the wind during a storm. **2a.** To speak in a loudly arrogant or bullying manner. **b.** To brag or make loud, empty threats. —tr. To force or bully with swaggering threats. ❖ n. **1.** A violent gusty wind. **2.** Turbulence or noisy confusion. **3.** Loud, arrogant speech, often full of empty threats. [ME blusteren < MLGer. blüsteren.] —**blus′ter·er** n. —**blus′ter·y, blus′ter·ous** adj.

Blvd. abbr. boulevard

Bly (blī), **Nellie** See Elizabeth Cochrane **Seaman**.

B lymphocyte also **B-lym·pho·cyte** (bē′lĭm′fə-sīt′) n. See **B cell**.

Blyth (blī, blĭth) A municipal borough of NE England on the North Sea at the mouth of the **Blyth River**. Pop. 78,200.

BM abbr. **1.** Bachelor of Medicine **2.** Bachelor of Music **3.** basal metabolism **4.** board measure **5.** bowel movement

BME abbr. **1.** Bachelor of Mechanical Engineering **2.** Bachelor of Mining Engineering **3.** Bachelor of Music Education

BMI abbr. body mass index

B movie n. See **B picture**.

BMR abbr. basal metabolic rate

BMS abbr. Bachelor of Marine Science

BMus abbr. Bachelor of Music

BMX abbr. bicycle motocross

Bn. abbr. baron

B'nai B'rith (bnā′ brĭth′) n. A Jewish international service organization. [Heb. bənê bərît, sons of (the) covenant : bənê, bound pl. of bēn, son + bərît, covenant.]

bo·a (bō′ə) n. **1.** Any of various large, nonvenomous, chiefly tropical snakes of the family Boidae, which coil around and suffocate their prey. **2.** A long fluffy scarf made of soft material, such as fur. [ME < Lat. boa, a large water snake.]

Bo·ab·dil (bō′ab-dēl′, -äb-thēl′) Orig. Abu Abdallah. d. c. 1527. Last Moorish king of Granada (1482–83 and 1486–92).

boa constrictor n. A large boa (Constrictor constrictor) of tropical America that kills its prey by constriction.

Bo·ad·i·ce·a (bō′ăd-ĭ-sē′ə) See **Boudicca**.

boar (bôr, bōr) n. **1a.** An uncastrated male pig. **b.** The adult male of any of several mammals, such as the beaver or raccoon. **2.** The wild boar. [ME bor < OE bār.]

board (bôrd, bōrd) n. **1.** A long flat slab of sawed lumber; a plank. **2.** A flat piece of wood or similarly rigid material adapted for a special use. **3.** Games A surface on which a game is played. **4.** The hard cover of a book. **5. boards** A theater stage. **6a.** A table, esp. one set for serving food. **b.** Food or meals considered as a whole. **7.** A table at which official meetings are held; a council table. **8.** An organized body of administrators or investigators. **9.** An electrical equipment panel. **10.** Computer Science A circuit board. **11.** A usu. large, vertically positioned flat surface used for writing or posting, esp. a blackboard. **12.** Sports **a.** A scoreboard. **b.** A tote board. **c. boards** The wooden structure enclosing an ice hockey rink. **d.** A diving board. **e.** A surfboard, snowboard, wakeboard, or similar item. **13.** *Basketball* **a.** A backboard. **b.** A rebound. **14.** *Nautical* **a.** The side of a ship. **b.** A centerboard. **15.** *Obsolete* A border or an edge. ❖ *v.* **board·ed, board·ing, boards** —*tr.* **1.** To cover or close with boards: *board up a window.* **2a.** To furnish with meals for pay. **b.** To house where board is furnished. **3.** To enter or go aboard (a vehicle or ship). **4.** To force (an opposing hockey player) into the boards with a body check. **5.** *Obsolete* To approach. —*intr.* To receive meals for pay. —*idioms:* **across the board** So as to affect or include all people, classes, or categories. **on board 1.** Aboard. **2.** On the job. [ME *bord* < OE.]

board·er[1] (bôr′dər, bōr′-) *n.* One who boards, esp. one who pays for regular meals or for meals and lodging.

board·er[2] (bôr′dər, bōr′-) *n.* **1.** One who skis. **2.** One who skateboards. **3.** One who snowboards.

board foot *n., pl.* **board feet** A unit of cubic measure for lumber, equal to one foot square by one inch thick.

board game *n.* A game of strategy, such as chess or backgammon, played by moving pieces on a board.

board·ing house also **board·ing·house** (bôr′dĭng-hous′, bōr′-) *n.* A house where paying guests are provided with meals and lodging.

boarding pass *n.* A pass that authorizes a passenger to board an aircraft.

boarding school *n.* A school where pupils are provided with meals and lodging.

board measure *n.* Measurement in board feet.

board of education *n., pl.* **boards of education** A school board.

board of trade *n., pl.* **boards of trade** An association of bankers and business people to promote common commercial interests.

board·room (bôrd′rōōm′, -rŏŏm′, bōrd′-) *n.* The room where the members of a board meet.

board rule *n.* A measuring stick for determining board feet.

board·sail·ing (bôrd′sā′lĭng, bōrd′-) *n.* See **windsurfing.** —**board sailor** *n.*

board·walk (bôrd′wôk′, bōrd′-) *n.* **1.** A walk made of wooden planks. **2.** A promenade, esp. of planks, along a beach or waterfront.

boar·fish (bôr′fĭsh, bōr′-) *n., pl.* **boarfish** or **-fish·es** Any of several marine fishes of the genus *Antigonia,* having a flattened body, a projecting snout, and red coloring.

boar·hound (bôr′hound′, bōr′-) *n.* A large dog, such as the Great Dane, used originally for hunting wild boars.

Bo·as (bō′ăz), Franz 1858–1942. German-born Amer. anthropologist who emphasized the systematic analysis of culture and language institutions.

boast[1] (bōst) *v.* **boast·ed, boast·ing, boasts** —*intr.* To glorify oneself in speech; talk in a self-admiring way. —*tr.* **1.** To speak of with excessive pride. **2.** To possess or own (a desirable feature). **3.** To contain; have. ❖ *n.* **1.** The act or an instance of bragging. **2.** A source of pride. [ME *bosten* < *bost,* a brag.] —**boast′er** *n.* —**boast′ful·ly** *adv.* —**boast′ful·ness** *n.*

boast[2] (bōst) *tr.v.* **boast·ed, boast·ing, boasts** To shape or form (stone) roughly with a broad chisel. [?]

boat (bōt) *n.* **1a.** A relatively small, usu. open craft of a size that might be carried aboard a ship. **b.** An inland vessel of any size. **c.** A ship or submarine. **2.** A dish shaped like a boat. ❖ *intr.v.* **boat·ed, boat·ing, boats 1.** To travel by boat. **2.** To ride a boat for pleasure. —*idiom:* **in the same boat** In the same situation as another or others. [ME *bot* < OE *bāt.* See **bheid-** in App.]

boat·bill (bōt′bĭl′) *n.* A tropical American wading bird (*Cochlearius cochlearius*) having a large bill shaped like an inverted boat.

boat-billed heron (bōt′bĭld′) *n.* See **boatbill.**

boat·er (bō′tər) *n.* **1.** One that drives or rides in a boat, esp. a pleasure craft. **2.** A stiff straw hat with a flat crown.

boat hook *n.* A pole with a point and hook at one end used esp. to maneuver logs, rafts, and boats.

boat·house (bōt′hous′) *n.* A building at the water's edge in which boats are kept.

boat·lift (bōt′lĭft′) *n.* An unofficial system of transporting supplies and people, esp. refugees, by boats or ships. [BOAT + (AIR)LIFT.] —**boat′lift′** *v.*

boat·load (bōt′lōd′) *n.* The number of passengers or the amount of cargo that a boat can hold.

boat·man (bōt′mən) *n.* One who works on or operates boats. —**boat′man·ship′** *n.*

boat·swain also **bo's'n** or **bos'n** or **bo·sun** (bō′sən) *n.* A warrant officer or petty officer in charge of a ship's rigging, anchors, cables, and deck crew. [ME *botswein* : *bot,* boat; see BOAT + *swein,* mate; see SWAIN.]

boat·swain's chair (bō′sənz) *n.* A short board secured by ropes and used as a seat by sailors when working aloft or over a ship's side.

boat train *n.* A train that regularly carries passengers between a city and a port.

Bo·az (bō′ăz) In the Bible, the husband of Ruth.

bob[1] (bŏb) *v.* **bobbed, bob·bing, bobs** —*tr.* **1.** To hit lightly and quickly; tap. **2.** To cause to move up and down. —*intr.* **1.** To move up and down: *a cork bobbing on the water.* **2.** To grab at floating or hanging objects with the teeth: *bobbed for apples.* **3.** To curtsy or bow. ❖ *n.* **1.** A tap or light blow. **2.** A quick, jerky move-

ment of the head or body. —*phrasal verb:* **bob up** To appear or arise unexpectedly or suddenly. [ME *bobben,* to move up and down, prob. ult. of imit. orig.]

bob[2] (bŏb) *n.* **1.** A small knoblike pendent object, such as a plumb bob. **2.** A fishing float or cork. **3.** A small lock or curl of hair. **4.** A woman's or child's short haircut. **5.** *Informal* Surgical shortening or reshaping of the nose. **6.** The docked tail of a horse. **7a.** A bobsled. **b.** A bob skate. ❖ *v.* **bobbed, bob·bing, bobs** —*intr.* To fish with a bob. —*tr.* To cut short or reshape. [ME *bobbe,* cluster of fruit.] —**bob′ber** *n.*

bob[3] (bŏb) *n., pl.* **bob** *Chiefly British* A shilling. [?]

bob·bin (bŏb′ĭn) *n.* **1.** A spool or reel that holds thread or yarn. **2.** Narrow braid formerly used as trimming. [Fr. *bobine.*]

bob·bi·net (bŏb′ə-nĕt′) *n.* A machine-woven net fabric with hexagonal meshes. [BOBBI(N) + NET[1].]

bobbin lace *n.* A handmade lace made by interlacing thread around small notched pins or bobbins stuck into a pillow.

bob·ble (bŏb′əl) *v.* **-bled, -bling, -bles** —*intr.* To bob up and down. —*tr.* To lose one's grip on (a ball, for example) momentarily. ❖ *n.* A mistake or blunder. [< BOB[1].]

bob·by (bŏb′ē) *n., pl.* **-bies** *Chiefly British* A police officer. [After Sir Robert PEEL, home secretary of England when the Metropolitan Police Force was created in 1829.]

bobby pin *n.* A small metal hair clip with the ends pressed tightly together. [< BOB[2].]

bobby socks also **bobby sox** *pl.n. Informal* Ankle socks worn by girls or women. [Poss. < BOB[2] (influenced by BOBBY PIN).]

bob·by·sox·er also **bobby sox·er** (bŏb′ē-sŏk′sər) *n. Informal* A teenage girl.

bob·cat (bŏb′kăt′) *n.* A wild cat (*Lynx rufus*) of North America having spotted reddish-brown fur, tufted ears, and a short tail. [BOB(TAIL) + CAT.]

bob·o·link (bŏb′ə-lĭngk′) *n.* An American migratory songbird (*Dolichonyx oryzivorus*), the male of which has black, white, and yellowish plumage. [Imit. of its song.]

Bo·bruysk (bə-brōō′ĭsk) See **Babrusk.**

bob skate *n.* An ice skate with two parallel bearing edges. [Poss. BOB(SLED) + SKATE[1].]

bob·sled (bŏb′slĕd′) *n.* **1.** A long racing sled with a steering mechanism controlling the front runners. **2a.** A long sled made of two shorter sleds joined in tandem. **b.** Either of these two smaller sleds. [BOB[2] + SLED.] —**bob′sled′** *v.* —**bob′sled·der** *n.*

bob·stay (bŏb′stā′) *n.* A rope or chain used to steady the bowsprit of a ship.

bob·tail (bŏb′tāl′) *n.* **1.** A short or shortened tail. **2.** An animal, such as a horse, having a short or abbreviated tail. **3.** Something that has been cut short or abbreviated. —**bob′tailed′** *adj.*

bob·white (bŏb-hwīt′, -wīt′) *n.* A small North American quail (*Colinus virginianus*) having brown plumage with white markings. [Imit. of its call.]

bo·cac·cio (bə-kä′chō, -chē-ō′) *n., pl.* **-cios** A large rockfish (*Sebastes paucispinis*) of American Pacific waters. [Alteration (perh. influenced by Ital. *boccaccia,* ugly mouth, or the name BOCCACCIO) of Am.Sp. *bocacho* < Sp. *bocacha,* big mouth < *boca,* mouth < OSpan. < Lat. *bucca.*]

Bo·ca Ra·ton (bō′kə rə-tōn′) A city of SE FL on the Atlantic Ocean S of Palm Beach. Pop. 74,764.

Boc·cac·cio (bō-kä′chē-ō′, -chō′), Giovanni 1313–75. French-born Italian poet and writer best known for the *Decameron* (1351–53).

boc·ce or **boc·ci** or **boc·cie** (bŏch′ē) *n.* A game of Italian origin similar to lawn bowling that is played with wooden balls on a long, narrow court covered with fine gravel. [Ital. *bocce,* pl. of *boccia,* ball.]

Boc·che·ri·ni (bō′kə-rē′nē, bŏk′ə-, bōk′kĕ-), Luigi 1743–1805. Italian composer noted for his concertos.

Boc·cio·ni (bŏ-chō′nē, bōt-chō′-), Umberto 1882–1916. Italian artist whose works embodied futurism.

Boche also **boche** (bōsh, bôsh) *n. Offensive Slang* Used as a disparaging term for a German. [Fr., alteration of *Alboche,* blend of *Allemand,* German; see ALLEMANDE, and Fr. dialectal *caboche,* cabbage, blockhead; see CABBAGE.]

Bo·chum (bō′kəm, -кнŏōm) A city of W-central Germany in the Ruhr Valley E of Essen; chartered 1321. Pop. 401,058.

bock beer (bŏk) *n.* A strong dark beer drawn first from the vats, esp. in spring. [Partial transl. of Ger. *Bockbier* : *Bock* (shortening and transl. of *Einbeck,* town of NW Germany in which the beer originated + perh. influenced by *Bock,* goat), *Bier,* beer.]

BOD *abbr.* biochemical oxygen demand

bo·da·cious also **bow·da·cious** (bō-dā′shəs) or **bar·da·cious** (bär-) *Southern & South Midland US adj.* **1.** Remarkable; prodigious. **2.** Audacious; gutsy. ❖ *adv.* **1.** Completely; extremely. **2.** Audaciously; boldly. [Prob. < dialectal *boldacious,* blend of BOLD and AUDACIOUS.]

REGIONAL NOTE *Bodacious* is probably a blend of the words *bold* and *audacious,* whose combined senses are evident in the following description of Sevier County, Tennessee, as "*the most bodacious display of tourism this side of Anaheim*" (Los Angeles Times). African-American speech in New York City retains this Southernism as *bardacious.* The English dialect form *boldacious,*

bobbin lace

bobcat
Lynx rufus

bobsled

ă	pat	oi	boy
ā	pay	ou	out
âr	care	ŏŏ	took
ä	father	ōō	boot
ĕ	pet	ŭ	cut
ē	be	ûr	urge
ĭ	pit	th	thin
ī	pie	th	this
îr	pier	hw	which
ŏ	pot	zh	vision
ō	toe	ə	about,
ô	paw		item

Stress marks:
′ (primary);
′ (secondary), as in
lexicon (lĕk′sĭ-kŏn′)

the likely source for *bodacious*, strengthens the theory that the speech of the American South preserves some archaic British expressions.

bode¹ (bōd) *v.* **bod·ed, bod·ing, bodes** —*tr.* **1.** To be an omen of: *a frown that boded trouble.* **2.** *Archaic* To predict; foretell. —*intr.* To be an omen; portend: *an accord that bodes well.* [ME *boden* < OE *bodian,* to announce. See **bheudh-** in App.]

bode² (bōd) *v.* A past tense of **bide.**

bo·de·ga (bō-dā′gə) *n.* **1.** A small grocery store that specializes in Caribbean and Latin American products. **2.** A warehouse for storing wine. [Sp. < Lat. *apothēca,* storehouse. See APOTHECARY.]

Bo·den·see (bōd′n-zā′) See Lake of **Constance.**

bo·dhi·satt·va (bō′dĭ-sŭt′və) *n.* A future Buddha who, out of compassion, forgoes nirvana in order to save others. [Skt. *bodhi-sattvaḥ,* one whose essence is enlightenment : *bodhiḥ,* perfect knowledge; see **bheudh-** in App. + *sattvam,* essence, being (< *sat-,* existing; see **es-** in App.).]

bodh·ran (bō′rän′, bou′-) *n.* A hand-held goatskin drum used in traditional Irish music and often played with a stick. [Ir.Gael. *bodhrán* < MIr. *bodrán* < OIr. < *bodar,* deaf, deafening.]

bod·ice (bŏd′ĭs) *n.* **1.** The fitted part of a dress that extends from the waist to the shoulder. **2.** A woman's laced outer garment, worn like a vest over a blouse. **3.** *Obsolete* A corset. [Alteration of *bodies,* pl. of BODY.]

bodice ripper *n.* *Slang* A work of popular fiction characterized by scenes of unrestrained romantic passion.

bod·ied (bŏd′ēd) *adj.* Having a body, esp. of a specified kind. Often used in combination: *strong-bodied; weak-bodied.*

bod·i·less (bŏd′ē-lĭs) *adj.* Having no body, form, or substance; incorporeal.

bod·i·ly (bŏd′l-ē) *adj.* **1.** Of, relating to, or belonging to the body. **2.** Physical as opposed to mental or spiritual: *bodily welfare.* ❖ *adv.* **1.** In the flesh; in person: *bodily but not mentally present.* **2.** As a complete physical entity.

SYNONYMS *bodily, corporal, corporeal, fleshly, physical, somatic* These adjectives mean of or relating to the human body: *a bodily organ; a corporal defect; corporeal suffering; fleshly frailty; physical robustness; a somatic symptom.*

bod·ing (bō′dĭng) *n.* An omen or foreboding, esp. of evil.

bod·kin (bŏd′kĭn) *n.* **1.** A small, sharply pointed instrument for making holes in fabric or leather. **2.** A blunt needle for pulling tape or ribbon through a series of loops or a hem. **3.** A long hairpin, usu. with an ornamental head. **4.** *Printing* An awl or pick for extracting letters from set type. **5.** A dagger or stiletto. [ME *boide-kin.*]

Bo·do·ni (bō-dō′nē, bə-), Gianbattista 1740–1813. Italian printer and designer of the Bodoni typeface.

bod·y (bŏd′ē) *n., pl.* **-ies 1a.** The entire material or physical structure of an organism, esp. of a human or animal. **b.** The physical part of a person. **c.** A corpse or carcass. **2a.** The trunk or torso of a human or animal. **b.** The part of a garment covering the torso. **3a.** A human; a person. **b.** A group of individuals regarded as an entity; a corporation. **4.** A number of persons, concepts, or things regarded as a group. **5.** The main or central part, as: **a.** *Anatomy* The largest or principal part of an organ; corpus. **b.** The nave of a church. **c.** The content of a book or document exclusive of prefatory matter, codicils, indexes, or appendixes. **d.** The passenger- and cargo-carrying part of an aircraft, ship, or other vehicle. **e.** *Music* The sound box of an instrument. **6.** A mass of matter that is distinct from other masses: *a body of water.* **7.** A collection or quantity, as of information. **8.** Consistency of substance, as in paint: *a sauce with body.* **9.** *Printing* The part of a block of type underlying the impression surface. ❖ *tr.v.* **-ied, -y·ing, -ies 1.** To furnish with a body. **2.** To give shape to. [ME *bodi* < OE *bodig.*]

body bag *n.* A zippered bag, usu. of rubber, for transporting a human corpse.

body blow *n.* **1.** *Sports* A blow delivered to the front of the torso above the waist in boxing. **2.** A serious setback.

bod·y·board also **bod·y-board** (bŏd′ē-bôrd′, -bōrd′) *n.* A very short surfboard with one straight end, ridden usu. by lying on one's chest. ❖ *intr.v.* **-board·ed, -board·ing, -boards** To surf on a bodyboard. —**bod′y·board′er** *n.*

bod·y·build·ing (bŏd′ē-bĭl′dĭng) *n.* The process of developing muscles through specific types of diet and physical exercise, such as weightlifting. —**bod′y·build′er** *n.*

body cavity *n.* See **coelom.**

body cell *n.* See **somatic cell.**

body check *n.* A check, as in ice hockey, in which a player impedes another with the body. —**bod′y-check′** (bŏd′ē-chĕk′) *v.*

body clock *n.* A physiological mechanism that is thought to regulate circadian rhythm.

body corporate *n.* See **corporation** 2.

body count *n.* A count of individual bodies.

body double *n.* A movie actor who substitutes for a leading performer, esp. in distance shots or scenes not involving the face.

body English *n.* Bodily movement in a usu. unconscious attempt to influence the movement of a propelled object, such as a ball.

body fluid *n.* **1.** A natural bodily fluid or secretion of fluid. **2.**

Humphrey Bogart

Total body water, contained principally in blood plasma and in intracellular and interstitial fluids.

bod·y·guard (bŏd′ē-gärd′) *n.* A person or group of persons responsible for the safety of someone else.

body language *n.* The gestures, postures, and facial expressions of nonverbal communication.

body louse *n.* A parasitic louse (*Pediculus humanus corporis*) that infests the body and clothes of humans.

body mass index *n.* A measurement of the relative percentages of fat and muscle mass in the human body.

body mechanics *n.* (used with a sing. or pl. verb) The application of kinesiology to help develop proper body movement, coordination, and endurance and to assist with posture problems.

body mike *n.* A small wireless microphone worn inconspicuously, as by a performer.

body politic *n.* The people of a politically organized nation or state considered as a group.

body shirt *n.* **1.** A woman's garment for the torso with a sewn-in or snapped crotch. **2.** A tight-fitting shirt or blouse.

body shop *n.* A shop or garage where the bodies of automotive vehicles are repaired.

body snatcher *n.* **1.** A person who steals corpses from graves for sale, usu. for purposes of dissection. **2.** *Slang* A corporate recruiter. —**bod′y·snatch′ing** (bŏd′ē-snăch′ĭng) *n.*

body stocking *n.* A tight-fitting, usu. one-piece garment that covers the torso and sometimes has sleeves and legs.

body suit *n.* A tight-fitting one-piece garment for the torso.

bod·y·surf (bŏd′ē-sûrf′) *intr.v.* **-surfed, -surf·ing, -surfs** To ride the waves to shore without a surfboard. —**bod′y·surf′er** *n.*

body wall *n.* The portion of an animal body that consists of ectoderm and mesoderm, forms the external body surface, and encloses the body cavity.

bod·y·work (bŏd′ē-wûrk′) *n.* **1.** The external structure of a motor vehicle. **2.** The repairing of motor vehicle bodies. **3.** The application of physical therapy methods such as massage and relaxation techniques to promote physical and emotional well-being. —**bod′y·work′er** *n.*

Boeh·me (bœ′mə) *or* **Boehm** (bœm), Jakob See Jakob **Böhme.**

Boe·o·tia (bē-ō′shə, -shē-ə) An ancient region of Greece N of Attica and the Gulf of Corinth whose cities formed the **Boeotian League** in the 7th cent. B.C. —**Boe·o′tian** *adj. & n.*

Boer (bôr, bōr, boor) *n.* A Dutch colonist or descendant of a Dutch colonist in South Africa. [Afr. < Du., farmer < MDu. *ghe-boer,* peasant. See **bheuə-** in App.]

Boer War *n.* A war fought from 1899 to 1902 between an alliance of the Boer governments of the Transvaal and the Orange Free State on the one hand and Great Britain on the other, over the sovereignty and commercial rights in these lands. The war ended with British victory.

Bo·e·thi·us (bō-ē′thē-əs), Anicius Manlius Severinus A.D. 480?–524? Roman philosopher and mathematician who wrote *The Consolation of Philosophy.*

boff¹ (bŏf) *n.* *Slang* **1.** A line in a play or film, for example, that elicits a big laugh. **2.** A big laugh. **3.** A conspicuous success. [Prob. < B(OX) OFF(ICE).]

boff² (bŏf) *Vulgar Slang v.* **boffed, boff·ing, boffs** —*tr.* To have sexual intercourse with. —*intr.* To engage in sexual intercourse. [< *boff,* to hit, var. of *buff* < ME *buffe,* a blow < OFr., of imit. orig.]

bof·fin (bŏf′ĭn) *n. Chiefly British Slang* A scientist. [?]

bof·fo (bŏf′ō) *Slang adj.* Extremely successful; great. ❖ *n., pl.* **-fos** See **boff¹** 3. [Alteration of BOFF¹.]

bof·fo·la (bŏf-ō′lə) *n. Slang* See **boff¹** 3. [< BOFF¹.]

Bo·fors gun (bō′fôrz′, boō′-) *n.* An automatic antiaircraft gun having a caliber of 37 or 44 millimeters. [After *Bofors,* a city of south-central Sweden.]

bog (bŏg, bôg) *n.* **1a.** An area having a wet, spongy, acidic substrate composed chiefly of sphagnum moss and peat in which characteristic shrubs and herbs and sometimes trees usu. grow. **b.** Any of certain other wetland areas, such as a fen, having a peat substrate. **2.** An area of soft, naturally waterlogged ground. ❖ *v.* **bogged, bog·ging, bogs** —*tr.* To cause to sink in or as if in a bog. —*intr.* To be hindered and slowed. [Ir.Gael. *bogach* < *bog,* soft.] —**bog′gi·ness** *n.* —**bog′gy** *adj.*

Bo·gart (bō′gärt), Humphrey DeForest 1899–1957. Amer. actor who starred in *Casablanca* (1942) and *The African Queen* (1951).

bog asphodel *or* **bog-as·pho·del** (bŏg′ăs′fə-dĕl′, bôg′-) *n.* Any of several perennial herbs of the genus *Narthecium* in the lily family, native to boggy areas in northern temperate regions.

bo·gey (bō′gē) *n.* also **bo·gy** *or* **bo·gie** (bō′gē) *pl.* **-geys** also **-gies 1.** (*also* boōg′ē, boō′gē) An evil or mischievous spirit; a hobgoblin. **2.** (*also* boōg′ē, boō′gē) A cause of annoyance or harassment. **3.** *Sports* **a.** The number of strokes that a good player is likely to need to finish a golf hole or course. **b.** A golf score of one stroke over par. **4.** *Slang* An unidentified flying aircraft. **5.** *Slang* A detective or a police officer. ❖ *tr.v.* **-geyed, -gey·ing, -geys** *Sports* To play (a hole in golf) scoring one stroke over par. [Poss. var. of BOGLE.]

bog·ey·man also **boog·ey·man** *or* **boog·y·man** *or* **boog·ie·man** (boōg′ē-măn′, bō′gē-, boō′gē-) *n.* A terrifying specter; a hobgoblin.

bog·gle (bŏg′əl) v. **bog·gled, bog·gling, bog·gles** —intr. **1.** To hesitate as if in fear or doubt. **2.** To shy away or be overcome with fright or astonishment. **3.** To act ineptly or inefficiently; bungle. —tr. **1.** To cause to be overcome, as with fright or astonishment. **2.** To botch; bungle. [Prob. < boggle, dialectal var. of BOGLE.] —**bog′gle** n. —**bog′gler** n.

bog hole n. A hole containing soft mud or quicksand.

bo·gie[1] also **bo·gy** (bō′gē) n., pl. **-gies 1.** One of several wheels or supporting and aligning rollers inside the tread of a tractor or tank. **2.** Chiefly British A railroad car or locomotive undercarriage having pairs of wheels that swivel so that curves can be negotiated. [?]

bo·gie[2] (bō′gē, bōōg′ē, bōō′gē) n. Variant of **bogey**.

bo·gle (bō′gəl) n. A hobgoblin; a bogey. [Sc. bogill, perh. ult. < Welsh bwg, ghost, hobgoblin.]

Bo·go·tá (bō′gə-tä′) The cap. of Colombia, in the central part on a high plain in the E Andes; settled by the Spanish in 1538. Pop. 5,025,989.

bog rosemary n. Any of several evergreen shrubs of the genus Andromeda, having pink or white urn-shaped flowers.

bog·trot·ter (bŏg′trŏt′ər, bôg′-) n. **1.** A person who lives in or frequents bogs. **2.** Offensive Slang Used as a disparaging term for an Irish person.

bo·gus (bō′gəs) adj. Counterfeit or fake; not genuine. [< obsolete bogus, a device for making counterfeit money.]

bog·wood (bŏg′wŏŏd′, bôg′-) n. Wood that has been preserved in a peat bog.

bo·gy[1] (bō′gē, bōōg′ē, bōō′gē) n. Variant of **bogey**.

bo·gy[2] (bō′gē) n. Variant of **bogie**[1].

Bo Hai also **Po Hai** (bō′ hī′) An inlet of the Yellow Sea on the NE coast of China.

bo·hea (bō-hē′) n. A black Chinese tea. [After the Fujian pronunciation of Chin. (Mandarin) wǔ yí (shān), the Wuyi mountain range on the border of Jiangxi and Fujian provinces.]

bo·he·mi·a (bō-hē′mē-ə) n. **1.** A community of persons with artistic or literary tastes who adopt unconventional manners and mores. **2.** The district in which bohemians live. [Back-formation < BOHEMIAN.]

Bohemia A historical region and former kingdom of present-day W Czech Republic, settled by Czechs between the 1st and 5th cent. A.D.

bo·he·mi·an (bō-hē′mē-ən) n. A person with artistic or literary interests who disregards conventional standards of behavior. [Fr. bohémien < Bohème, Bohemia (< the unconventional lifestyle of Gypsies, erroneously supposed to have come from there).] —**bo·he′mi·an·ism** n.

Bohemian n. **1.** A native or inhabitant of Bohemia. **2.** The Czech dialects of Bohemia. **3a.** A Gypsy. **b.** An itinerant person; a vagabond. [Sense 3, transl. of Fr. bohémien. See BOHEMIAN.] —**Bo·he′mi·an** adj.

Bohemian Brethren n. A religious society organized in the 15th century by the Hussites.

Böh·me also **Boeh·me** (bœ′mə) or **Boehm** (bœm), **Jakob** 1575–1624. German mystic considered the founder of modern theosophy.

Bo·hol (bō-hôl′) An island in the Visayan Is. of central Philippines N of Mindanao in the **Bohol Sea.**

Bohr (bôr, bōr), **Niels Henrik David** 1885–1962. Danish physicist who won a 1922 Nobel Prize. His son **Aage Niels Bohr** (b. 1922), also a physicist, shared a 1975 Nobel Prize.

bohr·i·um (bôr′ē-əm, bōr′-) n. Symbol **Bh** An artificially produced radioactive element with atomic number 107 whose most long-lived isotopes have mass numbers of 261, 262, and 264 with half-lives of 11.8 milliseconds, 0.1 second, and 0.44 second, respectively. See table at **element.** [After Niels Henrik David BOHR.]

Bohr theory n. An early model of atomic structure in which electrons travel around the nucleus in a number of discrete stable orbits determined by quantum conditions. [After Niels Henrik David BOHR.]

bo·hunk (bō′hŭngk′) n. Offensive Slang Used as a disparaging term for a person from east-central Europe, esp. a laborer. [Blend of BO(HEMIAN) and HUN(GARIAN).]

Bo·iar·do (boi-är′dō, bô-yär′-), **Matteo Maria** 1440?–94. Italian lyric poet known for his unfinished romantic epic Orlando Innamorato (1487).

boil[1] (boil) v. **boiled, boil·ing, boils** —intr. **1a.** To change from a liquid to a vapor by the application of heat. **b.** To reach the boiling point. **c.** To undergo the action of boiling, esp. in being cooked. **2.** To be in a state of agitation; seethe: a boiling river. **3.** To be stirred up or greatly excited. —tr. **1a.** To vaporize (a liquid) by the application of heat. **b.** To heat to the boiling point. **2.** To cook or clean by boiling. **3.** To separate by evaporation in the process of boiling. ❖ n. **1.** The condition or act of boiling. **2.** Lower Southern US A picnic featuring shrimp, crab, or crayfish boiled in large pots with spices and then shelled and eaten. **3.** An agitated, swirling, roiling mass of liquid. —**phrasal verbs: boil down 1.** To reduce in bulk or size by boiling. **2.** To condense; summarize. **3.** To constitute the equivalent of in summary. **boil over 1.** To overflow while boiling. **2.** To lose one's temper. [ME boillen < OFr. boillir < Lat. bullīre < bulla, bubble.]

SYNONYMS boil, simmer, seethe, stew To boil is to cook in a heated liquid that bubbles up and gives off vapor. Figuratively boil pertains to intense agitation: She boiled with anger. Simmer denotes gentle cooking just at or below the boiling point; figuratively it refers to a state of gentle ferment: plans simmering in his mind. Seethe emphasizes in both senses the turbulence of steady boiling: "The city had . . . been seething with discontent" (John R. Green). Stew refers literally to slow boiling and figuratively to a persistent but not violent state of agitation: "They don't want a man to fret and stew about his work" (William H. Whyte, Jr.).

boil[2] (boil) n. A painful, circumscribed, pus-filled inflammation of the skin and subcutaneous tissue usu. caused by a local staphylococcal infection. [ME bile < OE bȳle.]

Boi·leau-Des·pré·aux (bwä-lō′dĕ-prä-ō′), **Nicolas** 1636–1711. French critic who wrote Art of Poetry (1674).

boil·er (boi′lər) n. **1.** An enclosed vessel in which water is heated and circulated, either as hot water or as steam, for heating or power. **2.** A container, such as a kettle, for boiling liquids. **3.** A storage tank for hot water.

boil·er·mak·er (boi′lər-mā′kər) n. **1.** One that makes or repairs boilers. **2.** Slang A drink of whiskey with a beer chaser.

boil·er·plate (boi′lər-plāt′) n. **1.** A steel plate used in making the shells of steam boilers. **2.** Journalistic material, such as syndicated features, available in plate or mat form. **3.** Inconsequential, formulaic, or stereotypical language.

boil·ing point (boi′lĭng) n. **1.** The temperature at which a liquid boils at a fixed pressure, esp. under standard atmospheric conditions. **2.** Informal **a.** The point at which one loses one's temper. **b.** The point of crisis; the turning point.

boil·off (boil′ôf′, -ŏf′) n. The vaporization of liquid.

Bois de Bou·logne (bwä′ də bōō-lōn′, -lôn′yə) A park in Paris, France, bordering on Neuilly-sur-Seine; a popular recreation area since the 17th cent.

bois de rose (bwä′ də rōz′) n. A grayish red. [Fr., rosewood : bois, wood + de, of + rose, rose.]

Boi·se (boi′sē, -zē) The cap. of ID, in the SW part on the **Boise River,** c. 257 km (160 mi); founded 1863. Pop. 185,787.

bois·ter·ous (boi′stər-əs, -strəs) adj. **1.** Rough and stormy; violent. **2.** Noisy and lacking in restraint or discipline. [ME boisterous, var. of boistous, rude, rough, perh. < OFr. boisteus, lame, limping < boiste, knee joint.] —**bois′ter·ous·ly** adv. —**bois′ter·ous·ness** n.

boîte (bwät) n. A small restaurant or nightclub. [Fr. < OFr. boiste, box < LLat. buxida < buxis. See BOX[1].]

bok choy also **pak choi** (bŏk′ choi′) n. A Chinese vegetable (Brassica rapa subsp. chinensis) in the mustard family, having a loose head of dark green leaves with thick white stems. [Chin. (Cantonese) paak ts'oi, equivalent to Chin. (Mandarin) báicài : bái, white + cài, vegetable.]

Bok·mål (bōōk′môl′, bôk′-) n. See **Dano-Norwegian.** [Norw. : bok, book; see bhāgo- in App. + mål, language.]

Bol. abbr. **1.** Bolivia **2.** Bolivian

bo·la (bō′lə) also **bo·las** (-ləs) n. A rope with weights attached, used esp. in South America to catch cattle or game by entangling their legs. [< Am.Sp. bolas, pl. of Sp. bola, ball, prob. < Lat. bulla.]

Bo·lan Pass also **Bho·lan Pass** (bō-län′) A mountain pass of W Pakistan at an altitude of 1,793.4 m (5,880 ft).

bola tie n. Variant of **bolo tie.**

bold (bōld) adj. **bold·er, bold·est 1.** Fearless and daring; courageous. **2.** Requiring or exhibiting courage and bravery. See Syns at **brave. 3.** Unduly forward and brazen; impudent. **4.** Clear and distinct to the eye; conspicuous. **5.** Steep or abrupt in grade or terrain. **6.** Printing Boldface. [ME < OE bald.] —**bold′ly** adv. —**bold′ness** n.

bold·face (bōld′fās′) Printing n. Type with thick heavy lines. ❖ adj. Printed in thick heavy type. ❖ tr.v. **-faced, -fac·ing, -fac·es 1.** To mark (copy) for printing in this type. **2.** To set or print in this type.

bold-faced (bōld′fāst′) adj. **1.** Impudent; brazen. **2.** Printed in thick, heavy type.

bole[1] (bōl) n. The trunk of a tree. [ME < ON bolr.]

bole[2] (bōl) n. **1.** Any of various soft fine clays, esp. a reddish-brown variety used as a pigment. **2.** A moderate reddish brown. [ME < Med.Lat. bōlus. See BOLUS.] —**bole** adj.

bo·lec·tion (bō-lĕk′shən) n. Architecture A molding that projects from the surface of a panel. [?]

bo·le·ro (bō-lâr′ō, bə-) n., pl. **-ros 1.** A very short jacket worn open in the front. **2a.** A lively Spanish dance in triple meter. **b.** The music for this dance. **3a.** A slow Latin American dance, often in duple meter. **b.** The music for this dance. [Sp. < bola, ball. See BOLA.]

bo·le·tus (bō-lē′təs) n., pl. **-tus·es** or **-ti** (-tī′) A fungus of the genus Boletus, having an umbrella-shaped cap with spore-bearing tubules on the underside. [Lat. bōlētus, mushroom.]

Bol·eyn (bōōl′ĭn, bōō-lĭn′), **Anne** 1507–36. Queen of England (1533–36) as the second wife of Henry VIII; accused of adultery and beheaded.

bo·lide (bō′līd, -lĭd) n. A meteoric fireball. [Fr. < Lat. bolis, bolid-, kind of meteor < Gk. bolis, missile, flash (of lightning) < ballein, to throw. See gʷelǝ- in App.]

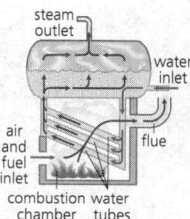

boiler
water-tube boiler

bok choy
Brassica rapa subsp.
chinensis

ă	pat	oi	boy
ā	pay	ou	out
âr	care	ōō	took
ä	father	ōō	boot
ĕ	pet	ŭ	cut
ē	be	ûr	urge
ĭ	pit	th	thin
ī	pie	th	this
îr	pier	hw	which
ŏ	pot	zh	vision
ō	toe	ə	about,
ô	paw		item

Stress marks:
′ (primary);
′ (secondary), as in
lexicon (lĕk′sĭ-kŏn′)

Bol·ing·broke (bŏl′ĭng-brŏŏk′, bŏŏl′-, bō′lĭng-), 1st Viscount. See Henry **Saint John**.

bo·li·var (bō-lē′vär, bŏl′ə-vər) *n.*, *pl.* **-vars** or **bo·li·va·res** (bō-lē′vä-rĕs′) See table at **currency**. [Am.Sp. *bolívar*, after Simón **Bolívar**.]

Bo·lí·var (bō-lē′vär), **Pico** A mountain, 5,005.4 m (16,411 ft), of W Venezuela in the Cordillera Mérida S of Lake Maracaibo.

Bolívar, Simón Known as "the Liberator." 1783–1830. South American revolutionary leader who defeated the Spanish in 1819 and helped liberate (1823–34) Peru and Bolivia.

Bo·liv·i·a (bə-lĭv′ē-ə, bō-) A landlocked country of W South America; named after Simón Bolívar, who helped win its independence from Spain in 1825. Caps. Sucre and La Paz. Pop. 7,237,000. —**Bo·liv′i·an** *adj. & n.*

bo·li·vi·a·no (bə-lĭv′ē-ä′nō, bō-) *n.*, *pl.* **-nos** See table at **currency**. [Sp., Bolivian, *boliviano* < **BOLIVIA**.]

boll (bōl) *n.* The seed-bearing capsule of certain plants, esp. cotton and flax. [ME < MDu. *bolle*, round object.]

Böll (bœl), **Heinrich** 1917–85. German writer who won the 1972 Nobel Prize for literature.

bol·lard (bŏl′ərd) *n.* **1.** A thick post on a ship or wharf, used for securing lines and hawsers. **2.** *Chiefly British* One of a series of posts preventing vehicles from entering an area. [ME, prob. < *bole*, tree trunk. See BOLE¹.]

bol·li·to mis·to (bō-lē′tō mĭs′tō) *n.*, *pl.* **bol·li·ti mis·ti** (bō-lē′tē mĭs′tē) A dish of vegetables and various meats simmered together and usu. served with an anchovy-garlic sauce. [Ital., mixed stew : *bollito*, stew + *misto*, mixed.]

bol·lix also **bol·lox** (bŏl′ĭks) *tr.v.* **-lixed, -lix·ing, -lix·es** also **-loxed, -lox·ing, -lox·es** *Informal* To throw into confusion; botch or bungle: *bollixed it up*. [Prob. < ME *ballocks*, testicles < ME *ballokes* < OE *beallucas*.] —**bol′lix** *n.*

boll weevil *n.* **1.** A small, grayish, long-snouted beetle (*Anthonomus grandis*) of Mexico and the southern United States that damages cotton. **2.** *Informal* A conservative white Southern Democrat in the US House of Representatives.

boll·worm (bōl′wûrm′) *n.* **1.** The pink bollworm. **2.** See **corn earworm**.

bo·lo (bō′lō) *n.*, *pl.* **-los** A long, heavy, single-edged machete originally used in the Philippines. [Sp. of Philippine orig.]

bo·lo·gna (bə-lō′nē, -nə, -nyə) also **ba·lo·ney** or **bo·lo·ney** (-nē) *n.* A seasoned smoked sausage made of mixed meats, such as beef, pork, and veal. [After BOLOGNA.]

Bo·lo·gna (bə-lōn′yə) A city of N-central Italy at the foot of the Apennines NNE of Florence; orig. an Etruscan town. Pop. 404,322. —**Bo·lo′gnan, Bo′lo·gnese′** (bō′lə-nēz′, -nēs′, -lən-yēz′, -yēs′) *adj. & n.*

bo·lom·e·ter (bō-lŏm′ĭ-tər) *n.* An instrument that measures radiant energy by correlating the change in resistance of an electrical element with the amount of radiation absorbed. [Gk. *bolē*, ray; see gʷelə- in App. + –METER.] —**bo′lo·met′ric** (bō′lə-mĕt′rĭk) *adj.*

bo·lo·ney (bə-lō′nē) *n.* **1.** Variant of **bologna**. **2.** Variant of **baloney²**.

bolo tie also **bola tie** *n.* A necktie consisting of a piece of cord fastened with an ornamental bar or clasp. [Alteration of BOLA + TIE.]

Bol·she·vik (bōl′shə-vĭk′, bŏl′-) *n.*, *pl.* **-viks** or **-vi·ki** (-vē′kē) **1a.** A member of the left-wing majority group of the Russian Social Democratic Workers' Party that adopted Lenin's theses on party organization (1903). **b.** A member of the Russian Social Democratic Workers' Party that seized power in November 1917. **c.** A member or a supporter of a Marxist-Leninist party; a Communist. **2.** often **bolshevik** A radical. [Russ. *Bol'shevik* < *bol'she*, comp. of *bol'shoĭ*, large. See **bel-** in App.] —**Bol′she·vik′** *adj.*

Bol·she·vism also **bol·she·vism** (bōl′shə-vĭz′əm, bŏl′-) *n.* **1.** The strategy developed by the Bolsheviks between 1903 and 1917 with a view to seizing state power and establishing a dictatorship of the proletariat. **2.** Soviet Communism. [BOLSHEV(IK) + –ISM.]

Bol·she·vist also **bol·she·vist** (bōl′shə-vĭst, bŏl′-) *n.* See **Bolshevik**. —**Bol′she·vist** *n.* **Bol′she·vis′tic** *adj.*

bol·son (bōl-sōn′) *n. Chiefly Southwestern US* A flat arid valley surrounded by mountains and draining into a shallow central lake. [Am.Sp. *bolsón*, augmentative of Sp. *bolsa*, purse, pouch < LLat. *bursa*. See BURSA.]

bol·ster (bōl′stər) *n.* A long narrow pillow or cushion. ❖ *tr.v.* **-stered, -ster·ing, -sters** **1.** To support or prop up with or as if with a long narrow pillow or cushion. **2.** To buoy up or hearten. [ME < OE.] —**bol′ster·er** *n.*

bolt¹ (bōlt) *n.* **1.** A bar made of wood or metal that slides into a socket and is used to fasten doors and gates. **2.** A metal bar or rod in the mechanism of a lock that is thrown or withdrawn by turning the key. **3.** A fastener consisting of a threaded pin or rod with a head at one end, designed to be inserted through holes in assembled parts and secured by a nut that is tightened by applying torque. **4a.** A sliding metal bar that positions the cartridge in breechloading rifles, closes the breech, and ejects the spent cartridge. **b.** A similar device in any breech mechanism. **5.** A short heavy arrow with a thick head, used esp. with a crossbow. **6.** A flash of lightning; a thunderbolt. **7.** A sudden or unexpected event. **8.** A sudden movement toward or away. **9.** A large roll of

cloth of a definite length, esp. as it comes from the loom. ❖ *v.* **bolt·ed, bolt·ing, bolts** —*tr.* **1.** To secure or lock with or as if with a bolt. **2.** To arrange or roll (lengths of cloth, for example) on or in a bolt. **3.** To eat (food) hurriedly. **4.** To desert or withdraw support from (a political party). **5.** To utter impulsively; blurt. **6.** *Archaic* To shoot or discharge (a missile). —*intr.* **1.** To move or spring suddenly. **2.** To start suddenly and run away. **3.** To break away from an affiliation, as from a political party. **4.** *Botany* To flower or produce seeds prematurely or develop a flowering stem from a rosette. —*idioms:* **bolt from the blue** A sudden, shocking surprise. **bolt upright** In a rigidly vertical position. [ME < OE, heavy arrow.]

bolt² (bōlt) *tr.v.* **bolt·ed, bolt·ing, bolts** To pass (flour, for example) through a sieve. [ME *bulten* < OFr. *buleter* < MHGer. *biuteln* < *biutel*, bag, purse.]

bolt-ac·tion (bōlt′ăk′shən) *adj.* Loaded by a manually operated bolt. Used of a firearm.

bolt·er¹ (bōl′tər) *n.* **1.** A horse given to bolting. **2.** One who withdraws support from a political party.

bolt·er² (bōl′tər) *n.* **1.** A machine used for sifting, esp. for sifting flour. **2.** One who operates a sifting machine.

bolt·hole (bōlt′hōl′) *n.* **1.** A hole through which to bolt. **2.** A place affording escape.

Bol·ton (bōl′tən) A borough of NW England NW of Manchester. Pop. 264,880.

bol·to·ni·a (bōl-tō′nē-ə) *n.* Any of several perennial herbs of the genus *Boltonia* in the composite family, having flower heads with white to purplish rays and yellow centers. [NLat., genus name, after James *Bolton*, 18th-cent. British botanist.]

bolt·rope (bōlt′rōp′) *n. Nautical* A rope sewn into the outer edge of a sail to prevent it from tearing.

bo·lus (bō′ləs) *n.*, *pl.* **-lus·es** **1.** A round mass. **2.** A relatively large quantity of a drug that is taken orally or administered intravenously. **3.** A soft mass of chewed food within the mouth or alimentary canal. [Med.Lat. *bōlus* < Gk. *bōlos*, lump of earth.]

bomb (bŏm) *n.* **1a.** An explosive weapon detonated by impact, a timing mechanism, or other means. **b.** An atomic or a nuclear bomb. **2.** Any of various weapons detonated to release destructive material, such as smoke. **3.** *Football* A long forward pass. **4a.** A container capable of withstanding high internal pressure. **b.** A vessel for storing compressed gas. **c.** A portable, manually operated container that ejects a spray, foam, or gas under pressure. **5.** *Slang* A dismal failure. **6.** *Slang* An old car. **7.** *Slang* One that is excellent or superior. Used with *the*. **8.** *Chiefly British Slang* **a.** A large amount of money. **b.** A great success. ❖ *v.* **bombed, bomb·ing, bombs** —*tr.* To attack, damage, or destroy with or as if with bombs. —*intr.* **1.** To drop bombs. **2.** *Slang* To fail miserably: *The movie bombed.* **3.** *Slang* To paint a graffito. [Fr. *bombe* < Ital. *bomba*, prob. < Lat. *bombus*, a booming sound < Gk. *bombos*, of imit. orig.]

bom·bard (bŏm-bärd′, bəm-) *tr.v.* **-bard·ed, -bard·ing, -bards** **1.** To attack with bombs, shells, or missiles. **2.** To assail persistently, as with requests. **3.** To irradiate (an atom). **4.** To attack with a cannon firing stone balls. ❖ *n.* (bŏm′bärd) An early form of cannon that fired stone balls. [ME, a bombard < OFr. *bombarde* < Med.Lat. *bombarda*, prob. < Lat. *bombus*, a booming sound. See BOMB.] —**bom·bard′er** *n.* —**bom·bard′ment** *n.*

bom·bar·dier (bŏm′bər-dîr′) *n.* **1.** The member of a combat aircraft crew who drops the bombs. **2.** *Chiefly British* A noncommissioned artillery officer. **3.** *Archaic* An artillery soldier. [Fr. < OFr. *bombarde*, bombard < *bombarde*.]

bombardier beetle *n.* Any of various beetles of the genus *Brachinus* and related genera that expel an acrid volatile secretion from the abdomen when disturbed.

bom·bar·don (bŏm′bər-dŏn′, bŏm-bär′dn) *n.* A bass or contrabass tuba. [Fr. < Ital. *bombardone*, augmentative of *bombardo*, alteration of *bombarda*, bombard < Med.Lat. See BOMBARD.]

bom·bast (bŏm′băst′) *n.* Grandiloquent, pompous speech or writing. [Alteration of obsolete *bombace*, cotton padding < OFr. < Med.Lat. *bambax, bombac-*, cotton < Lat. *bombax* < Gk. *bombyx*, silkworm, silk < Gk. See BOMBAZINE.] —**bom·bast′er** *n.* —**bom·bas′tic** *adj.* —**bom·bas′ti·cal·ly** *adv.*

Bom·bay (bŏm-bā′) See **Mumbai**.

Bombay duck *n.* **1.** A small edible lizardfish (*Harpodon nehereus*) of Asia having a thin, nearly transparent body. **2.** The dried salted flesh of this fish that is used in India as a relish. [Alteration of Marathi *bombīla, bombil.*]

bom·ba·zine (bŏm′bə-zēn′) *n.* A fine twilled fabric of silk and worsted or cotton, often used for mourning clothes. [Fr. *bombasin* < Med.Lat. *bambacīnum*, cotton fabric < *bombax, bombac-*, cotton < Lat. *bombyx*, silk, silkworm < Gk. *bombūx*, silkworm.]

bomb bay *n.* The compartment in the fuselage of a combat aircraft from which bombs are dropped.

bombe (bŏm, bônb) *n.* A dessert consisting of two or more layers of variously flavored ice cream frozen in a round or melon-shaped mold. [Fr. (< its shape). See BOMB.]

bom·bé (bŏm′bā′, bôn′-) *adj.* Curving or bulging outward. Used of furniture. [Fr. < *bombe*, bomb. See BOMB.]

bombed (bŏmd) *adj. Slang* Intoxicated by alcohol or a drug.

bomb·er (bŏm′ər) *n.* **1.** A combat aircraft designed to carry and drop bombs. **2.** One who makes and sets off bombs.

bomb·proof (bŏm′prŏŏf′) *adj.* Designed and constructed to re-

Simón Bolívar
full-length portrait by
Paulin-Jean-Baptiste Guérin
(1783–1855)

Bolivia

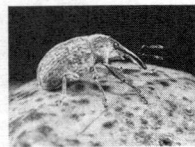

boll weevil
Anthonomus grandis

sist destruction by a bomb.

bomb·shell (bŏm′shĕl′) *n.* **1.** An explosive bomb. **2.** One that is shocking, surprising, or amazing.

bomb·sight (bŏm′sīt′) *n.* A device in a combat aircraft for determining the point at which to drop a bomb.

bom·by·cid (bŏm′bĭ-sĭd) *n.* A moth of the family Bombycidae, which includes the silkworms. [< NLat. *Bombýcidae,* family name < Lat. *bombýx, bombýc-,* silkworm. See BOMBAZINE.]

Bo·mu (bō′mōō) A river of central Africa rising in SE Central African Republic and flowing c. 805 km (500 mi) to join the Uele and form the Ubangi R.

Bo·na (bō′nə), Mount A peak, 5,032.5 m (16,500 ft), of S AK at the S end of the Wrangell Mts.

bo·na fide (bō′nə fīd′, fī′dē, bŏn′ə) *adj.* **1.** Made or carried out in good faith; sincere. **2.** Authentic; genuine. See Syns at **authentic.** [Lat. *bonā fidē : bonā,* fem. ablative of *bonus,* good + *fidē,* ablative of *fidēs,* faith.]

Bo·naire (bô-nâr′) An island of the Netherlands Antilles in the Caribbean Sea off the N coast of Venezuela.

Bo·nam·pak (bō-näm′päk) A ruined Mayan city near present-day Tuxtla Gutiérrez in S Mexico.

bo·nan·za (bə-năn′zə) *n.* **1.** A rich mine, vein, or pocket of ore. **2.** A source of great wealth or prosperity. [Sp. < Med.Lat. *bonacia,* calm sea, blend of Lat. *bonus,* good; see deu-² in App., and Med.Lat. *malacia,* calm sea (< Gk. *malakiā < malakos,* soft).]

Bo·na·parte (bō′nə-pärt′) Corsican family, all brothers of Napoleon I, including **Joseph** (1768–1844), king of Naples (1806–08) and Spain (1808–13); **Lucien** (1775–1840); **Louis** (1778–1846), king of Holland (1806–10); and **Jérôme** (1784–1860), king of Westphalia (1807–13). —**Bo′na·part′ism** *n.* —**Bo′na·part′ist** *n.*

Bon·a·ven·ture (bŏn′ə-vĕn′chər) also **Bon·a·ven·tu·ra** (bŏn′ə-vĕn-chōōr′ə, -tōōr′ə, -tyōōr′ə), Saint. Orig. Giovanni di Fidanza. 1217?–74. Italian theologian and philosopher who advocated direct contemplation of God as the highest goal.

bon·bon (bŏn′bŏn′) *n.* A candy that often has a center of fondant, fruit, or nuts and is coated with chocolate or fondant. [Fr., redup. of *bon,* good < Lat. *bonus.* See deu-² in App.]

bond (bŏnd) *n.* **1.** Something, such as a band, that binds, ties, or fastens things together. **2.** Confinement in prison; captivity. Often used in the plural. **3.** A uniting force or tie; a link: *the familial bond.* **4.** A binding agreement; a covenant. **5.** An obligation, such as a promise, by which one is bound. **6a.** A substance or an agent that causes two or more objects or parts to cohere. **b.** The union or cohesion brought about by such a substance or agent. **7.** A chemical bond. **8.** An overlapping or alternating arrangement of bricks or stones in a wall. **9.** *Law* **a.** A written and sealed obligation, esp. one requiring payment of a stipulated amount of money on or before a given day. **b.** A sum of money paid as bail or surety. **c.** A bail bondsman. **10.** A certificate of debt issued by a government or corporation guaranteeing payment of the original investment plus interest by a specified future date. **11.** The condition of taxable goods being stored in a warehouse until the taxes or duties owed on them are paid. **12.** An insurance contract in which an agency guarantees payment to an employer in the event of unforeseen financial loss through the actions of an employee. **13.** Bond paper. ❖ *v.* **bond·ed, bond·ing, bonds** —*tr.* **1.** To mortgage or place a guaranteed bond on. **2.** To furnish bond or surety for. **3.** To place (an employee, for example) under bond or guarantee. **4.** To join securely, as with glue or cement. **5.** To join (two or more individuals) in or as if in a nurturing relationship. **6.** To lay (bricks or stones) in an overlapping or alternating pattern. —*intr.* **1.** To cohere with or as if with a bond. **2.** To form a close personal relationship. [ME, var. of *band* < ON. See **bhendh-** in App.] —**bond′a·ble** *adj.* —**bond′er** *n.*

bond·age (bŏn′dĭj) *n.* **1.** The state of one who is bound as a slave or serf. **2.** A state of subjection to a force or influence. **3.** The practice of being physically restrained as a means of attaining sexual gratification. **4.** Villeinage. [ME < AN < ME *bonde,* serf < OE *bōnda,* husbandman < ON *bōndi,* pr. part. of *būa,* to live. See **bheua-** in App.]

bond·hold·er (bŏnd′hōl′dər) *n.* One that owns a bond certificate of a government or corporation.

bond·ing (bŏn′dĭng) *n.* **1a.** The emotional attachment that occurs between parent and offspring, usu. beginning at birth. **b.** The formation of a close human relationship, as between friends. **2.** A technique in dentistry or orthodontics for the attachment of a material such as porcelain, plastic, or metal to the surface of the teeth.

bond·maid (bŏnd′mād′) *n.* A woman bondservant. [BOND(WOMAN) + MAID.]

bond·man (bŏnd′mən) *n.* A male bondservant. [ME < *bonde,* serf. See BONDAGE.]

bond paper *n.* A superior grade of strong white paper made wholly or in part from rag pulp.

bond·ser·vant (bŏnd′sûr′vənt) *n.* **1.** A person obligated to service without wages. **2.** A slave or serf. [BOND(MAN) + SERVANT.]

bonds·man (bŏndz′mən) *n.* **1.** A person who provides bond or surety for another. **2.** A male bondservant.

bond·wom·an (bŏnd′wŏŏm′ən) *n.* A woman bondservant.

[ME *bondewomman < bonde,* serf. See BONDAGE.]

bone (bōn) *n.* **1a.** The dense, semirigid, porous, calcified connective tissue forming the major portion of the skeleton of most vertebrates. **b.** Any of numerous anatomically distinct structures making up the skeleton of a vertebrate animal. **c.** A piece of bone. **2. bones a.** The skeleton. **b.** The body. **c.** Mortal remains. **3.** An animal structure or material, such as ivory, resembling bone. **4.** Something made of bone or of material resembling bone, esp.: **a.** A piece of whalebone or similar material used as a corset stay. **b. bones** *Informal* Dice. **5. bones** The fundamental plan or design, as of the plot of a book. **6. bones** Flat clappers made of bone or wood. ❖ *tr.v.* **boned, bon·ing, bones 1.** To remove the bones from. **2.** To stiffen (a piece of clothing) with stays, as of whalebone. —*phrasal verb:* **bone up** *Informal* To study intensely, usu. at the last minute: *boned up for the final exam.* —*idioms:* **bone of contention** The subject of a dispute. **bone to pick** Grounds for a complaint or dispute. [ME *bon* < OE *bān.*]

bone ash *n.* The white, powdery calcium phosphate ash of burned bones, used as a fertilizer and in making ceramics.

bone·black also **bone black** (bōn′blăk′) *n.* A black pigment containing about 10 percent charcoal, made by roasting bones in an airtight container.

bone china *n.* Porcelain made of clay mixed with bone ash.

bone-dry (bōn′drī′) *adj.* Having no trace of moisture.

bone·fish (bōn′fĭsh′) *n., pl.* **bonefish** or **-fish·es** A marine game fish (*Albula vulpes*) of warm shallow waters, having silvery scales. [< its many small bones.]

bone·head (bōn′hĕd′) *n. Informal* A stupid person; a dunce. —**bone′head′ed** *adj.* —**bone′head′ed·ness** *n.*

bone marrow *n.* The soft, fatty, vascular tissue that fills most bone cavities and is the source of red blood cells and many white blood cells.

bone mass *n.* The mineral content of bone.

bone meal *n.* A substance made of crushed and coarsely ground bones, used as a fertilizer and in animal feed.

bone mineral density *n.* The mineral content in a given volume of bone, used as a measure of bony health and in the diagnosis of osteoporosis.

bon·er¹ (bō′nər) *n. Informal* A blunder or error. [BONE(HEAD) + —ER¹.]

bon·er² (bō′nər) *n. Vulgar Slang* An erection of the penis.

bone·set (bōn′sĕt′) *n.* Any of several plants of the genus *Eupatorium* in the composite family, esp. the eastern North American species *E. perfoliatum,* having clusters of small white flower heads. [< its use as a folk medicine.]

bon·ey (bō′nē) *adj.* Variant of **bony.**

bone·yard (bōn′yärd′) *n.* **1.** A cemetery. **2.** A place where the bones of wild animals accumulate. **3.** A place where refuse, esp. discarded cars, accumulates or is kept.

bon·fire (bŏn′fīr′) *n.* A large fire built outdoors. [ME *bonnefire : bon,* bone; see BONE + *fir,* fire; see FIRE.]

bong¹ (bŏng, bông) *n.* A deep ringing sound. ❖ *v.* **bonged, bong·ing, bongs** —*tr.* To cause to sound with a deep ringing noise. —*intr.* To make a deep ringing noise. [Imit.]

bong² (bŏng, bông) *n.* A water pipe that consists of a bottle or a vertical tube partially filled with liquid and a smaller tube ending in a bowl. [Thai *baung.*]

bon·go¹ (bŏng′gō, bông′-) *n., pl.* **-gos** A large antelope (*Boocercus eurycerus*) of central Africa having a reddish-brown coat with white stripes and spirally twisted horns. [Prob. of Bantu orig.; akin to Lingala *mongu,* antelope.]

bon·go² (bŏng′gō, bông′-) *n., pl.* **-gos** or **-goes** One of a pair of connected tuned drums that are played by beating with the hands. [Am.Sp. *bongó,* prob. of W African orig.]

bon·ho·mie (bŏn′ə-mē′) *n.* A pleasant and affable disposition; geniality. [Fr. < *bonhomme,* good-natured man : *bon,* good (< Lat. *bonus;* see deu-² in App.) + *homme,* man (< Lat. *homō;* see **dhghem-** in App.) —**bon′ho·mous** (-məs) *adj.*

Bon·i·face (bŏn′ə-fās′), Saint. 675?–754. English Roman Catholic missionary active in Germany.

Boniface VIII 1235?–1303. Pope (1294–1303) who struggled to assert authority over England, France, and Sicily.

bon·ing knife (bō′nĭng) *n.* A knife with a narrow blade and a sharp point, used for removing animal bones.

Bo·nin Islands (bō′nĭn) An archipelago of volcanic islands in the W Pacific Ocean S of Japan.

bo·ni·to (bə-nē′tō) *n., pl.* **bonito** or **-tos 1.** Any of several marine fishes of the genus *Sarda,* related to and resembling the tuna. **2.** Any of several similar fishes, such as the skipjack. [Sp., prob. < *bonito,* pretty, dim. of *bueno,* good < Lat. *bonus,* good. See deu-² in App.]

bonk (bŏngk) *v.* **bonked, bonk·ing, bonks** —*tr.* To strike or cause to come into contact. —*intr.* To collide with or against something. ❖ *n.* **1.** A blow to the head. **2.** A hollow thud. [Imit.]

bon·kers (bŏng′kərz) *adj. Informal* Crazy. [?]

bon mot (bôn mō′) *n., pl.* **bons mots** (bôn mō′, mōz′) A clever saying; a witticism. [Fr. : *bon,* good + *mot,* word.]

Bonn (bŏn, bôn) The former cap. of West Germany, in the W part on the Rhine R.; founded as a Roman garrison in the 1st cent. A.D. and from 1990–99 the seat of the reunified German government. Pop. 296,859.

bongo¹
Boocercus eurycerus

ă	pat	oi	boy
ā	pay	ou	out
âr	care	ŏŏ	took
ä	father	ōō	boot
ĕ	pet	ŭ	cut
ē	be	ûr	urge
ĭ	pit	th	thin
ī	pie	*th*	this
îr	pier	hw	which
ŏ	pot	zh	vision
ō	toe	ə	about,
ô	paw		item

Stress marks:
′ (primary);
′ (secondary), as in
lexicon (lĕk′sĭ-kŏn′)

Bon·nard (bô-när′), **Pierre** 1867–1947. French painter who adhered to an impressionistic style in works such as *The Bath.*

bon·net (bŏn′ĭt) *n.* **1a.** A cloth or straw hat held in place by ribbons tied under the chin and worn by women and children. **b.** *Scots* A brimless cap worn by men or boys. **2.** A removable metal plate over a machine part. **3.** *Chiefly British* The hood of an automobile. **4a.** A windscreen for a chimney. **b.** A cover for a fireplace. ❖ *tr.v.* **-net·ed, -net·ing, -nets** To put a bonnet on. [ME *bonet,* cap < OFr., material for a headdress, perh. < Med.Lat. *obbonis,* prob. of Gmc. orig.]

Bon·ne·ville Salt Flats (bŏn′ə-vĭl′) A plain of NW UT W of Great Salt Lake in the bed of prehistoric **Lake Bonneville.**

Bon·ney (bŏn′ē), **William H.** Known as "Billy the Kid." 1859–81. Amer. outlaw who murdered 21 men and was killed by Sheriff Pat Garrett (1850–1908).

bon·ny also **bon·nie** (bŏn′ē) *adj.* **-ni·er, -ni·est** *Scots* **1.** Physically attractive or appealing; pretty. **2.** Excellent. [Prob. ult. < Fr. *bon,* good < Lat. *bonus.* See **deu-**[2] in App.] —**bon′ni·ly** *adv.* —**bon′ni·ness** *n.*

bon·ny·clab·ber (bŏn′ē-klăb′ər) *n. New England & Central Atlantic US* Thick soured milk eaten with cream and sugar, honey, or molasses. [Ir.Gael. *bainne clabair : bainne,* milk (< MIr., drop, milk < OIr. *bannae,* drop) + prob. *clabair,* genitive of *clabar,* dasher of a churn.]

bo·no·bo (bə-nō′bō) *n., pl.* **-bos** An anthropoid ape (*Pan paniscus*) of central Congo (formerly Zaire), having more arboreal habits than the closely related chimpanzee. [Of central African orig.]

bon·sai (bŏn-sī′, bŏn′sī′, -zī′) *n., pl.* **bonsai 1.** The art of growing dwarfed ornamental trees or shrubs in shallow pots or trays. **2.** A tree or shrub so grown. [J., potted plant : *bon,* basin (< M Chin. *bán*) + *sai,* to plant (< Chin. *tsəj, tsaj*).]

bon·spiel (bŏn′spēl′) *n. Scots* A curling match or tournament. [Prob. Du. **bonspel,* league game : *bon,* league (perh. < *bonne,* precinct of a city) + *spel,* game < MDu.]

bon·te·bok (bŏn′tə-bŏk′) *n.* A rare South African antelope (*Damaliscus dorcas* or *D. pygargus*) having a dark reddish coat, a white rump, and a white mark on the face. [Afr. : *bont,* spotted (< MDu., prob. < Lat. *pūnctus;* see **POINT**) + *bok,* buck (< MDu. *boc*).]

Bon·temps (bôN-tän′), **Arna Wendell** 1902–73. Amer. writer whose works of poetry, history, and fiction established him as a leading figure of the Harlem Renaissance.

bon ton (bŏn tŏn′) *n.* **1a.** A sophisticated manner or style. **b.** The proper thing to do. **2.** High society. [Fr. : *bon,* good + *ton,* tone.]

bo·nus (bō′nəs) *n., pl.* **-nus·es 1.** Something given or paid beyond what is usual or expected. **2.** A sum of money or the equivalent given in addition to an employee's usual compensation. **3.** A government subsidy to an industry. **4.** A sum of money paid by a government to a war veteran. **5.** A premium given by a corporation to another party. **6.** A sum of money paid by a corporation in excess of interest or royalties charged for a privilege or a loan. **7.** *Basketball* An additional free throw awarded to a player who has been fouled when the opposing team has committed more than a specified number of fouls during a period of play. [< Lat., good. See **deu-**[2] in App.]

bon vi·vant (bôn′ vē-vän′) *n., pl.* **bons vi·vants** (bôn′ vē-vän′) One with refined taste, esp. for food and drink. [Fr. : *bon,* good + *vivant,* pr. part. of *vivre,* to live.]

bon voy·age (bôn′ vwä-yäzh′) *interj.* Used to express farewell and good wishes to a departing traveler. [Fr. : *bon,* good + *voyage,* journey.]

bon·y or **bon·ey** (bō′nē) *adj.* **-i·er, -i·est** or **-ey·er, -ey·est 1.** Of, resembling, or consisting of bone. **2.** Having an internal skeleton of bones. **3.** Full of bones. **4a.** Having prominent or protruding bones. **b.** Lean; scrawny. —**bon′i·ness** *n.*

bony fish *n.* A fish having a bony rather than cartilaginous skeleton; a teleost.

bonze (bŏnz) *n.* A Buddhist monk, esp. of Asia. [Fr. < Port. *bonzo* < J. *bonsō : bon,* ordinary (< M Chin. *buan, fhan*) + *sō,* monk (< M Chin. *səng* < Skt. *saṃghaḥ,* brotherhood of monks < *saṃhanti, saṃgha-,* he puts together : *sam,* together; see **sem-** in App. + *hanti,* he strikes; see **g^when-** in App.).]

boo (bo͞o) *n., pl.* **boos 1.** A sound uttered to show contempt or disapproval. **2.** *Informal* Any sound or word: *You never said boo to me about overtime.* ❖ *interj.* Used to express contempt or disapproval or to frighten or surprise another. ❖ *v.* **booed, boo·ing, boos** —*intr.* To utter a boo. —*tr.* To express contempt or disapproval of by booing. [Imit.]

boob[1] (bo͞ob) *n. Slang* A stupid or foolish person; a dolt. [Short for **BOOBY**[1].]

boob[2] (bo͞ob) *n. Vulgar Slang* A woman's breast. [Short for **BOOBY**[2].]

boo-boo also **boo·boo** (bo͞o′bo͞o) *n., pl.* **-boos** *Informal* **1.** A stupid mistake; a blunder. **2.** A slight physical injury, such as a scratch. [Perh. alteration of *boohoo,* to weep noisily.]

boob tube *n. Slang* Television. [**BOOB**[1] + TUBE, television set.]

boo·by[1] (bo͞o′bē) *n., pl.* **-bies 1.** A person regarded as stupid. **2.** Any of several tropical sea birds of the genus *Sula,* resembling and related to the gannets. [Prob. Sp. *bobo* < Lat. *balbus,* stammering.]

boo·by[2] (bo͞o′bē) *n., pl.* **-bies** *Vulgar Slang* A woman's breast. [Perh. alteration of obsolete E. *bubby.*]

booby hatch *n.* **1.** *Nautical* A raised covering over a small hatchway. **2.** *Offensive Slang* An institution for the mentally ill.

booby prize *n.* **1.** An award given to the one who performs worst in a game or contest. **2.** *Informal* Acknowledgment of great inferiority, as in ability.

booby trap *n.* **1.** An explosive device designed to be triggered when an unsuspecting victim touches or disturbs a seemingly harmless object. **2.** A situation that catches one off guard; a pitfall. —**boo′by-trap′** (bo͞o′bē-trăp′) *v.*

boo·coo (bo͞o′ko͞o′) *adj., n., & adv. Chiefly Southern US* Variant of **beaucoup.**

boo·dle (bo͞od′l) *n. Slang* **1a.** Money, esp. counterfeit money. **b.** Money accepted as a bribe. **2.** Stolen goods; swag. **3.** A crowd of people; caboodle. [Du. *boedel,* estate < MDu. *bōdel.* See **bheuə-** in App.]

boo·dy (bo͞o′dē) *n., pl.* **-dies** *Vulgar Slang* Variant of **booty**[2].

boog·er (bo͝og′ər) *n.* **1.** A bogeyman. **2.** *Slang* Dried nasal mucus. **3.** *Slang* An unnamed or unnameable item. **4.** *Slang* **a.** A worthless, despicable person. **b.** A person. [?]

boog·ey·man (bo͝og′ē-măn′, bo′gē-, bo͞o′gē-) *n.* Variant of **bogeyman.**

boog·ie (bo͝og′ē, bo͞o′gē) *Slang intr.v.* **-ied, -y·ing, -ies 1.** To dance to rock music. **2a.** To get going; leave. **b.** To move quickly. ❖ *n.* **1.** Strongly rhythmic rock music. **2.** Boogie-woogie. [< BOOGIE-WOOGIE.]

boog·ie·man (bo͝og′ē-măn′, bo′gē-, bo͞o′gē-) *n.* Variant of **bogeyman.**

boog·ie·woog·ie (bo͝og′ē-wo͝og′ē, bo͞o′gē-wo͞o′gē) *n.* A style of blues piano playing characterized by an up-tempo rhythm, a repeated melodic pattern in the bass, and a series of improvised variations in the treble. [Poss. < Black W African E. (Sierra Leone) *bogi(-bogi),* to dance.]

boog·y·man (bo͝og′ē-măn′, bo′gē-, bo͞o′gē-) *n.* Variant of **bogeyman.**

boo·jum tree (bo͞o′jəm) *n.* A deciduous tree (*Idria columnaris*) native to Baja California and having a tapering trunk and spiny branches. [After the *boojum,* an imaginary character in the poem *The Hunting of the Snark* by Lewis Carroll.]

book (bo͝ok) *n.* **1.** A set of pages fastened along one side and encased between protective covers. **2a.** A printed or written literary work. **b.** A main division of a larger printed or written work: *a book of the Iliad.* **3a.** A volume in which financial or business transactions are recorded. **b. books** Financial or business records considered as a group: *checked the expenditures on the books.* **4a.** A libretto. **b.** The script of a play. **5.** Book **a.** The Bible. **b.** The Koran. **6a.** A set of prescribed standards or rules on which decisions are based: *runs the company by the book.* **b.** Something regarded as a source of knowledge or understanding. **7.** A packet of like or similar items bound together: *a book of matches.* **8.** A record of bets placed on a race. **9.** *Games* The number of card tricks needed before any tricks can have scoring value, as the first six tricks taken by the declaring side in bridge. ❖ *v.* **booked, book·ing, books** —*tr.* **1.** To list or register in or as if in a book. **2.** To record charges against (a person) on a police blotter. **3.** To arrange for (lodgings, for example) in advance; reserve. **4.** To hire or engage: *The manager booked a magic show for Sunday evening.* **5.** To allocate for. —*intr. Slang* To move rapidly in a vehicle. ❖ *adj.* **1.** Of or relating to knowledge learned from books rather than actual experience. **2.** Appearing in a company's financial records: *book profits.* —**idioms: bring to book** To demand an explanation from; call to account. **in (one's) book** In one's opinion. **like a book** Thoroughly; completely: *I know my child like a book.* **one for the books** A noteworthy act or occurrence. **throw the book at 1.** To make all possible charges against (a lawbreaker, for example). **2.** To reprimand or punish severely. [ME *bok* < OE *bōc.* See **bhāgo-** in App.] —**book′er** *n.*

book·bind·er·y (bo͝ok′bīn′də-rē) *n., pl.* **-ies** An establishment where books are bound.

book·bind·ing (bo͝ok′bīn′dĭng) *n.* The art, trade, or profession of binding books. —**book′bind′er** *n.*

book·case (bo͝ok′kās′) *n.* A cabinet with bookshelves.

book club *n.* A commercial organization that sells books to its members on a regular basis and typically at a discount.

book·end (bo͝ok′ĕnd′) *n.* A prop to keep books upright.

book·er (bo͝ok′ər) *n.* See **bookmaker** 2.

book·ing (bo͝ok′ĭng) *n.* **1.** An engagement, as for a performance. **2.** A reservation, as for accommodations at a hotel.

book·ish (bo͝ok′ĭsh) *adj.* **1.** Of or resembling a book. **2.** Fond of books; studious. **3.** Relying chiefly on book learning. **4.** Pedantic; dull. **5.** Literary and formal in tone. Used of words. —**book′ish·ly** *adv.* —**book′ish·ness** *n.*

book·keep·ing (bo͝ok′kē′pĭng) *n.* The practice or profession of recording the accounts and transactions of a business. —**book′keep′er** *n.*

book·let (bo͝ok′lĭt) *n.* A small bound book or pamphlet.

book·lore (bo͝ok′lôr′, -lōr′) *n.* Knowledge gained from books.

book·louse or **book louse** (bo͝ok′lous′) *n.* Any of various insects of the order Psocoptera (or Corrodentia), some of which eat stored flour products, paper, or bookbindings.

bonsai
juniper tree

boom[2]

book lung *n.* A sacculate respiratory organ found in some arachnids, such as scorpions and spiders, consisting of several parallel membranous folds arranged like the pages in a book.

book·mak·er (book′mā′kər) *n.* **1.** One that edits, prints, publishes, or binds books. **2.** One who accepts and pays off bets, as on a horserace. —**book′mak′ing** *n.*

book·mark (book′märk′) *n.* A strip of material or a metal clamp inserted between the pages of a book to mark a place.

book·mo·bile (book′mō-bēl′) *n.* A truck, trailer, or van serving as a mobile lending library. [BOOK + (AUTO)MOBILE.]

Book of Changes *n.* See **I Ching.**

Book of Common Prayer *n.* The book of services and prayers used in the Anglican Church.

Book of Mormon *n.* One of the sacred books of the Mormon Church, published in 1830 by Joseph Smith, and believed by Mormons to contain the sacred history of the lost tribes of Israel in the Americas.

Book of the Dead *n.* A collection of ancient Egyptian funerary texts containing prayers, magic formulas, and hymns to be used by the soul of the deceased for guidance and protection on its journey to the afterlife.

boo·koo (boo′koo′) *adj., n., & adv. Chiefly Southern US* Variant of **beaucoup.**

book·plate (book′plāt′) *n.* A label with the owner's name or other identification, pasted usu. on a book's inside cover.

book·rack (book′răk′) *n.* A rack for books or a book.

book·sell·er (book′sĕl′ər) *n.* One that sells books, esp. the owner of a bookstore.

book·shelf (book′shĕlf′) *n., pl.* **-shelves** A shelf or set of shelves for books.

book·shop (book′shŏp′) *n.* A bookstore.

book·stall (book′stôl′) *n.* A stall where books are sold.

book·stand (book′stănd′) *n.* **1.** A small counter where books are sold. **2.** A bookrack.

book·store (book′stôr′, -stōr′) *n.* A store that sells books.

book value *n.* The monetary amount, not necessarily the open market price, by which an asset is valued in business records.

book·worm (book′wûrm′) *n.* **1.** One who spends much time reading or studying. **2.** Any of various insects that infest books and feed on the paste in the bindings.

Boole (bool), **George** 1815–64. British mathematician and logician who developed a calculus of symbolic logic.

Bool·e·an (boo′lē-ən) *adj.* Of or relating to Boolean algebra. [After George BOOLE.]

Boolean algebra *n.* An algebra in which elements have one of two values and the algebraic operations defined on the set are logical OR, a type of addition, and logical AND, a type of multiplication.

boom¹ (boom) *v.* **boomed, boom·ing, booms** —*intr.* **1.** To make a deep resonant sound. **2.** To grow, develop, or progress rapidly; flourish. —*tr.* **1.** To utter or give forth a boom. **2.** To cause to boom; boost. ❖ *n.* **1.** A deep resonant sound, as of an explosion. **2.** A time of economic prosperity. **3.** A sudden increase. [ME *bomben,* imit. of a loud noise.]

boom² (boom) *n.* **1.** *Nautical* A spar extending from a mast to hold or extend the foot of a sail. **2.** A long pole extending upward from the mast of a derrick to support or guide objects being lifted or suspended. **3a.** A barrier composed of a chain of floating logs enclosing other free-floating logs. **b.** A floating barrier serving to contain an oil spill. **4.** A long movable arm used to support a microphone. **5a.** A spar that controls the tail surfaces and the main structure of an airplane. **b.** A long tube attached to a tanker aircraft, used to fuel another aircraft in flight. —*idiom:* **drop (or lower) the boom** To act suddenly and forcefully to repress a practice or reprimand an offender. [Du., tree, pole < MDu. See **bheuə-** in App.]

boom box *n. Informal* A portable audio system, usu. consisting of a radio and a cassette or CD player, and loudspeakers.

boom·er (boo′mər) *n.* **1.** A transient worker, esp. in bridge construction. **2.** *Informal* A baby boomer.

boo·mer·ang (boo′mə-răng′) *n.* **1.** A flat curved missile that returns to the thrower when hurled. **2.** A statement or course of action that backfires. ❖ *intr.v.* **-anged, -ang·ing, -angs** To have the opposite effect from that intended. [Dharuk (Aboriginal language of SE Australia) *bumarin′.*]

boom·let (boom′lĭt) *n.* A small boom, as in the birth rate.

boom·town (boom′toun′) *n.* A town experiencing an economic or a population boom.

boon¹ (boon) *n.* **1.** A benefit bestowed, esp. in response to a request. **2.** A timely blessing or benefit. [ME *bone* < ON *bōn,* prayer. See **bhā-** in App.]

boon² (boon) *adj.* **1.** Convivial; jolly. **2.** *Archaic* Favorable. [ME *bon,* good < OFr. < Lat. *bonus.* See **deu-²** in App.]

boon·docks (boon′dŏks′) *pl.n. Slang* **1.** Wild and dense brush; jungle. **2.** Rural country; the backwoods. [< Tagalog *bundok,* mountain.]

boon·dog·gle (boon′dô′gəl, -dŏg′əl) *Informal n.* Unnecessary, wasteful, and often counterproductive work. ❖ *v.* **-gled, -gling, -gles** **1.** To waste time or money on unnecessary and often counterproductive work. **2a.** A braided leather cord worn as a decoration esp. by Boy Scouts. **b.** A cord of braided leather,

fabric, or plastic strips made by a child as a project to keep busy. [Coined by Robert H. Link (died 1957), American scoutmaster.] —**boon′dog′gler** *n.*

Boone (boon), **Daniel** 1734–1820. Amer. pioneer, folk hero, and central figure in the settlement of Kentucky.

boon·ies (boo′nēz) *pl.n. Slang* Rural country or a jungle. [Shortening and alteration of BOONDOCKS.]

boor (boor) *n.* **1.** A rude, clumsy person with little refinement. **2.** A peasant. [Du. *boer* < MDu. *gheboer.* See **bheua-** in App.] —**boor′ish** *adj.* —**boor′ish·ly** *adv.* —**boor′ish·ness** *n.*

boost (boost) *v.* **boost·ed, boost·ing, boosts** —*tr.* **1.** To raise or lift by pushing up from behind or below. See Syns at **lift. 2a.** To increase; raise: *boost prices.* **b.** To assist in further development or progress. **3.** To stir up enthusiasm for; promote vigorously. **4.** *Electricity* To increase the voltage of (a circuit). **5.** *Slang* To steal or rob, esp. by shoplifting or pickpocketing. —*intr. Slang* To engage in stealing, esp. shoplifting or pickpocketing. ❖ *n.* **1.** A push upward or ahead. **2.** An encouraging act or comment. **3.** An increase. [Perh. < dialectal *boostering,* bustling, active.]

boost·er (boo′stər) *n.* **1.** One that boosts, as: **a.** A device for increasing power or effectiveness. **b.** An enthusiastic promoter. **c.** The primary stage of a multistage rocket that provides the main thrust for launch, liftoff, and initial flight. **2.** A booster shot. **3.** *Slang* One who shoplifts.

booster cable *n.* An electric cable used to connect a discharged battery to a power source for charging.

booster dose *n.* See **booster shot.**

boost·er·ism (boo′stə-rĭz′əm) *n.* The highly supportive attitudes and activities of boosters.

booster shot *n.* An additional dose of an immunizing agent given at a time after the initial dose to sustain the immune response elicited by the previous dose.

boot¹ (boot) *n.* **1.** Protective footgear, as of leather or rubber, covering part or all of the leg. **2.** A protective covering, esp. a sheath for the base of a floor-mounted gear shift lever in a car or truck. **3.** *Chiefly British* A car trunk. **4a.** A kick. **b.** *Slang* A dismissal from employment. **c.** *Slang* A swift, pleasurable feeling; a thrill. **5.** A Denver boot. **6.** A marine or navy recruit in basic training. **7.** The process of starting or restarting a computer. **8.** *boots* A torture instrument, used to crush the foot and leg. ❖ *tr.v.* **boot·ed, boot·ing, boots** **1.** To put boots on. **2.** To kick. **3.** *Slang* To dismiss from employment. **4.** *Computer Science* To start (a computer) by loading an operating system from a disk. **5.** *Baseball* To misplay (a ground ball). [ME *bote* < OFr.]

boot² (boot) *intr.v.* **boot·ed, boot·ing, boots** To be of help or advantage; avail. ❖ *n.* **1.** *Chiefly Southern & Midland US* See **lagniappe. 2.** *Archaic* Advantage; avail. —*idiom:* **to boot** In addition; besides. [ME *boten,* to be of help < OE *bōtian < bōt,* help.]

boot·black (boot′blăk′) *n.* A person who cleans and polishes shoes for a living.

boot camp *n.* **1.** A training camp for military recruits. **2.** A correctional facility that uses training techniques applied to military recruits to teach socially acceptable behavior.

boot·ed (boo′tĭd) *adj.* Wearing boots.

boo·tee also **boo·tie** (boo′tē) *n.* **1.** A soft, usu. knitted shoe for a baby. **2.** An ankle-length disposable foot covering, used by medical personnel and others in sterile environments.

Bo·ö·tes (bō-ō′tēz) *n.* A constellation in the Northern Hemisphere near Virgo and Canes Venatici, containing the bright star Arcturus. [Lat. *Boōtēs* < Gk. *boōtēs,* plowman, Boōtes < *boōtein,* to plow < *bous,* ox. See **gʷou-** in App.]

booth (booth) *n., pl.* **booths** (boothz, booths) **1a.** A small, often enclosed compartment, usu. accommodating only one person. **b.** A small enclosed compartment with a window, used to separate the occupant from others. **2.** A seating area in a restaurant that has a table and seats whose high backs serve as partitions. **3.** A small stall for the display and sale of goods. [ME *bothe,* of Scand. orig. See **bheuə-** in App.]

Booth¹ Family of Amer. Shakespearean actors, including **Junius Brutus** (1796–1852), born in Great Britain, and his sons **Edwin Thomas** (1833–93), noted for his portrayal of Hamlet, and **John Wilkes** (1838–65), the assassin of Abraham Lincoln.

Booth² Family of reformers, including **William** (1829–1912), a British religious leader who founded the Salvation Army (1878) with his wife, **Catherine Mumford Booth** (1829–90). Their children **William Bramwell** (1856–1929); **Ballington** (1857–1940), who with his wife, **Maud Ballington Booth** (1865–1948), founded the Volunteers of America (1896); and **Evangeline Cory** (1865–1950) were active in the Salvation Army.

Boo·thi·a Peninsula (boo′thē-ə) The northernmost tip of the North American mainland, in central Nunavut, Canada; separated from Baffin I. by the **Gulf of Boothia,** an arm of the Arctic Ocean.

boot·jack (boot′jăk′) *n.* A forked device for holding a boot secure while the foot is being withdrawn.

boot·leg (boot′lĕg′) *v.* **-legged, -leg·ging, -legs** —*tr.* **1.** To make, sell, or transport (alcoholic liquor) for illegal sale. **2.** To produce, distribute, or sell without permission or illegally: *bootlegged compact discs from abroad.* —*intr.* To engage in bootlegging. ❖ *n.* **1.** A product, esp. alcoholic liquor, that is bootlegged. **2.** The part of a boot above the instep. [< a smuggler's practice of

Daniel Boone
portrait by Chester Harding
(1792–1866)

John Wilkes Booth

ă	pat	oi	boy
ā	pay	ou	out
âr	care	oo	took
ä	father	oo	boot
ĕ	pet	ŭ	cut
ē	be	ûr	urge
ĭ	pit	th	thin
ī	pie	th	this
îr	pier	hw	which
ŏ	pot	zh	vision
ō	toe	ə	about,
ô	paw		item

Stress marks:
′ (primary);
′ (secondary), as in
lexicon (lĕk′sĭ-kŏn′)

carrying liquor in the legs of boots.] —**boot′leg′ger** *n.*
boot·less (bo͞ot′lĭs) *adj.* Without advantage or benefit; useless.
See Syns at **futile.** [BOOT² + -LESS.] —**boot′less·ly** *adv.*
boot·lick (bo͞ot′lĭk′) *v.* **-licked, -lick·ing, -licks** —*tr.* To behave
toward in a servile or obsequious manner. —*intr.* To behave in a
servile or obsequious manner. —**boot′lick′er** *n.*
boot·strap (bo͞ot′străp′) *n.* **1.** A loop that is sewn at the side or
the top rear of a boot to help in pulling the boot on. **2.** An instance of starting of a computer; a boot. ❖ *tr.v.* **-strapped,
-strap·ping, -straps 1.** To promote and develop by use of one's
own initiative and work without outside help. **2.** *Computer Science* To boot (a computer). ❖ *adj.* **1.** Undertaken or accomplished with little or no outside help. **2.** Being or relating to a self-
initiating or self-sustaining process. —*idiom:* **by (one's) (own)
bootstraps** By one's own efforts.
boo·ty¹ (bo͞o′tē) *n., pl.* **-ties 1.** Plunder taken from an enemy in
time of war. **2.** Goods or property seized by force. **3.** A valuable
prize, award, or gain. [ME *botye* (influenced by *bote,* advantage),
prob. < MLGer. *būte,* exchange.]
boo·ty² (bo͞o′tē) also **boo·dy** (-dē) *n., pl.* **-ties** also **-dies 1.**
Slang The buttocks. **2.** *Vulgar Slang* **a.** The vulva or vagina. **b.** Sexual intercourse. [African American Vernacular E. < obsolete
Black E. *booty,* body, perh. alteration of BODY.]
booze (bo͞oz) *Slang n.* **1a.** Hard liquor. **b.** An alcoholic beverage.
2. A drinking spree. ❖ *intr.v.* **boozed, booz·ing, booz·es** To
drink liquor to excess. [Alteration of obsolete *bouse* < ME *bousen,*
to drink to excess < MDu. *būsen.*] —**booz′er** *n.* —**booz′y** *adj.*
bop¹ (bŏp) *Informal tr.v.* **bopped, bop·ping, bops** To hit or
strike. ❖ *n.* A blow; a punch. [Imit.]
bop² (bŏp) *n.* A style of jazz characterized by rhythmic and harmonic complexity, improvised solo performances, and brilliant
execution. ❖ *intr.v.* **bopped, bop·ping, bops 1.** To dance or
move to the beat of this music. **2.** *Slang* To go: *bopped off to the
movies.* [Short for BEBOP.] —**bop′per** *n.*
Bo·phu·tha·tswa·na (bō-po͞o′tät-swä′nə) An former autonomous Black homeland within South Africa; reintegrated into
South Africa under the 1994 constitution.
Bopp (bŏp), **Franz** 1791–1867. German philologist who illustrated the similarities among Indo-European languages.
BOQ *abbr.* Bachelor Officers' Quarters
Bor. *abbr.* borough
bor– *pref.* Variant of **boro–.**
bo·ra (bôr′ə, bōr′ə) *n.* A violent, cold, northeasterly winter wind
on the Adriatic Sea. [Ital. dialectal < Lat. *Boreās,* Boreas. See BO-
REAS.]
Bo·ra Bo·ra (bôr′ə bôr′ə, bōr′ə bōr′ə) A volcanic island of
French Polynesia in the Society Is. of the S Pacific Ocean.
bo·rac·ic (bə-răs′ĭk) *adj.* Variant of **boric.** [< Med.Lat. *bōrāx,
bōrāc-,* borax. See BORAX¹.]
bor·age (bôr′ĭj, bŏr′-) *n.* An annual, bristly European herb (*Bo-
rago officinalis*) having blue or purplish star-shaped flowers. [ME
< OFr. *bourage* < Med.Lat. *borāgō,* prob. < Ar. *bū'araq* < *'abū
'araq,* source of sweat (< its use as a sudorific) : *'ab,* father, source
+ *'araq,* sweat.]
bo·rane (bôr′ān′, bōr′-) *n.* Any of a series of boron-hydrogen
compounds or a derivative of such a compound.
bo·rate (bôr′āt′, bōr′-) *n.* A salt or ester of boric acid.
bo·rat·ed (bôr′ā-tĭd, bōr′-) *adj.* Combined with or containing
borax or boric acid.
bo·rax¹ (bôr′ăks′, -əks, bōr′-) *n.* **1.** A hydrated sodium borate,
$Na_2B_4O_7·10H_2O$, an ore of boron, used as a cleaning compound.
2. An anhydrous sodium borate used in the manufacture of glass
and various ceramics. [ME < Med.Lat. *bōrāx* < Ar. *būraq*
< MPers. *būrak.*]
bo·rax² (bôr′ăks′, bōr′-) *n.* Cheap merchandise, esp. tasteless
furnishings.
bor·bo·ryg·mus (bôr′bə-rĭg′məs) *n., pl.* **-mi** (-mī′) The rumbling noise of gas moving through the intestines. [NLat. < Gk.
borborugmos, of imit. orig.]
Bor·deaux¹ (bôr-dō′) A city of SW France on the Garonne R.
Pop. 210,467.
Bor·deaux² (bôr-dō′) *n., pl.* **Bor·deaux** (bôr-dō′, -dōz′) A wine
produced in the region of Bordeaux, France.
Bordeaux mixture *n.* A fungicide mixture of copper sulfate,
lime, and water. [Transl. of Fr. *bouillie bordelaise* : *bouillie,* gruel,
mixture + *bordelaise,* of Bordeaux.]
bor·del·lo (bôr-dĕl′ō) *n., pl.* **-los** A house of prostitution. [Ital.
< OFr. *bordel* < *borde,* wooden hut, of Gmc. orig.]
Bor·den (bôr′dn), **Lizzie Andrew** 1860–1927. Amer. woman accused and acquitted of the ax murder of her parents (1892).
Borden, Sir Robert Laird 1854–1937. Canadian politician who
served as prime minister (1911–20).
bor·der (bôr′dər) *n.* **1.** A part that forms the outer edge of something. **2.** A decorative strip around the edge of something, such
as fabric. **3.** A strip of ground, as at the edge of a walk, for ornamental plants. **4.** The line or frontier area separating political divisions or geographic regions. ❖ *v.* **-dered, -der·ing, -ders** —*tr.*
1. To put a border on. **2.** To lie along or adjacent to the border
of. —*intr.* **1.** To lie adjacent to another. **2.** To be almost like another in character. [ME *bordure* < OFr. *bordeure* < *border,* to border < *bort,* border, of Gmc. orig.] —**bor′der·er** *n.*

SYNONYMS *border, margin, edge, verge, brink, rim, brim* These
nouns refer to the line or narrow area that marks the outside
limit of something such as a surface. *Border* refers either to the
boundary line (*a fence along the border of the property*) or to the
area immediately inside it (*a frame with a wide border*). *Margin*
is a border of more or less precisely definable width: *the margin
of the page. Edge* refers to the bounding line formed by the continuous convergence of two surfaces: *sat on the chair's edge. Verge*
is an extreme terminating line or edge: *the sun's afterglow on the
verge of the horizon. Brink* denotes the edge of a steep place: *the
brink of the cliff. Rim* most often denotes the edge of something
circular or curved: *a crack in the rim of the lens. Brim* applies to
the upper edge or inner side of the rim of something shaped like
a basin: *lava issuing from the brim of the crater.*

Border collie *n.* A British sheepdog used for herding. [< the border country of England and Scotland.]
bor·de·reau (bôr′də-rō′) *n., pl.* **-reaux** (-rō′) A detailed memorandum, esp. one that lists documents or accounts. [Fr., prob.
< *bord,* edge, margin < OFr. *bort,* of Gmc. orig.]
bor·der·land (bôr′dər-lănd′) *n.* **1a.** Land located on or near a
frontier. **b.** The fringe. **2.** An indeterminate area, situation, or
condition: *the borderland between sanity and insanity.*
bor·der·line (bôr′dər-līn′) *n.* **1.** A line that establishes or marks
a border. **2.** An indefinite area intermediate between two qualities
or conditions. ❖ *adj.* **1a.** Verging on a given quality or condition.
b. Of a questionable nature or quality; dubious. **2a.** *Psychology*
Relating to any phenomenon that is intermediate between two
groups and therefore not clearly categorized. **b.** Relating to a condition characterized by instability, as in mood, and manifested by
self-destructive, impulsive, and inconsistent behavior.
Border States The slave states of DE, MD, VA, KY, and MO that
were adjacent to the free states of the North during the Civil War.
Border terrier *n.* A small, hardy, rough-coated terrier bred to
hunt foxes in the border country of England and Scotland.
bor·de·tel·la (bôr′də-tĕl′ə) *n.* Any of various small gram-negative bacteria of the genus *Bordetella,* some of which are pathogenic in the human respiratory tract. [NLat. *Bordetella,* genus
name, after Jules Jean Baptiste Vincent *Bordet* (1870–1961), Belgian bacteriologist.]
bor·dure (bôr′jər) *n. Heraldry* A border around a shield. [ME.
See BORDER.]
bore¹ (bôr, bōr) *v.* **bored, bor·ing, bores** —*tr.* **1.** To make a hole
in or through, with or as if with a drill. **2.** To form (a tunnel, for
example) by drilling, digging, or burrowing. —*intr.* **1.** To make a
hole in or through something by boring. **2.** To proceed or advance steadily or laboriously. ❖ *n.* **1.** A hole or passage made by
or as if by boring. **2.** A hollow, usu. cylindrical chamber or barrel,
as of a firearm. **3.** The interior diameter of a hole, tube, or cylinder. **4.** The caliber of a firearm. **5.** A drilling tool. [ME *boren*
< OE *borian.*]
bore² (bôr, bōr) *tr.v.* **bored, bor·ing, bores** To make weary by
being dull or repetitive. ❖ *n.* One that is wearingly dull or repetitive. [?]
bore³ (bôr, bōr) *n.* A high, often dangerous wave caused by the
surge of a flood tide up a narrowing estuary or by colliding tidal
currents. [ME *bare,* wave < ON *bāra.* See bher-¹ in App.]
bore⁴ (bôr, bōr) *v.* Past tense of **bear¹.**
bo·re·al (bôr′ē-əl, bōr′-) *adj.* **1.** Of or relating to the north;
northern. **2.** Of or concerning the north wind. **3.** **Boreal** Of or
relating to the forest areas of the northern North Temperate
Zone, dominated by coniferous trees. [ME < LLat. *Boreālis* < Lat.
Boreās, Boreas. See BOREAS.]
Bo·re·as (bôr′ē-əs, bōr′-) *n.* **1.** *Greek Mythology* The god of the
north wind. **2.** **boreas** The north wind. [ME < Lat. *Boreās* < Gk.
< *boreios,* coming from the north.]
bore·cole (bôr′kōl′, bōr′-) *n.* See **kale 1.** [Du. *boerenkool* : *boer,*
farmer, peasant; see BOOR + *kool,* cabbage < MDu. *cōle* < Lat. *caulis,* stalk.]
bore·dom (bôr′dəm, bōr′-) *n.* The condition of being bored.
bore·hole (bôr′hōl′, bōr′-) *n.* A hole drilled into the earth, as in
exploratory well drilling.
bor·er (bôr′ər, bōr′-) *n.* **1.** A tool used for drilling. **2.** An insect
or insect larva that bores into woody plant parts. **3.** Any of various mollusks that bore into soft rock or wood.
Borg (bôrg), **Bjorn** b. 1956. Swedish tennis player who won five
consecutive Wimbledon championships (1976–80).
Bor·ges (bôr′hĕs), **Jorge Luis** 1899–1986. Argentinian writer
particularly known for his short stories. —**Bor·ges′i·an** (-hä′sē-
ən, -hĕs′ē-) *adj.*
Bor·gia (bôr′jə, -zhə) Italian family, influential from the 14th to
the 16th cent., that included the son and daughter of Pope Alexander VI. **Cesare** (1475?–1507), a religious, military, and political
leader, was the model for Machiavelli's *The Prince.* **Lucrezia**
(1489–1519), the Duchess of Ferrara, was a patron of learning
and the arts.
Bor·glum (bôr′gləm), **Gutzon** 1867–1941. Amer. sculptor noted
for the busts of four US Presidents on Mt. Rushmore.
bo·ric (bôr′ĭk, bōr′-) also **bo·rac·ic** (bə-răs′ĭk) *adj.* Of, relating
to, derived from, or containing boron.
boric acid *n.* A water-soluble crystalline compound, H_3BO_3, used

as an antiseptic and a preservative and in detergents.

bo•ride (bôr′īd′, bōr′-) *n.* A binary compound of boron with a more electropositive element or radical.

bor•ing (bôr′ĭng, bōr′-) *adj.* Not interesting; tiresome; dull. **—bor′ing•ly** *adv.* **—bor′ing•ness** *n.*

SYNONYMS *boring, monotonous, tedious, irksome, tiresome, humdrum* These adjectives refer to what is so uninteresting as to cause mental weariness. *Boring* implies feelings of listlessness and discontent: *a boring book.* What is *monotonous* bores because of lack of variety: *a monotonous day. Tedious* suggests dull slowness or long-windedness: *spent tedious hours on the train. Irksome* describes what is demanding of time and effort and yet is dull and often unrewarding: "*I know and feel what an irksome task the writing of long letters is*" (Edmund Burke). Something *tiresome* fatigues because it seems to be interminable or marked by unremitting sameness: "*What a tiresome being is a man who is fond of talking*" (Benjamin Jowett). *Humdrum* refers to what is commonplace, trivial, or unexcitingly routine: *led a humdrum existence.*

Bor•laug (bôr′lôg′), **Norman Ernest** b. 1914. Amer. agronomist who won the 1970 Nobel Peace Prize for his attempts to overcome world hunger through advances in agriculture.

Bor•mann (bôr′män′), **Martin Ludwig** 1900–45? German Nazi official who served as Hitler's secretary (1941–45).

born (bôrn) *v.* A past participle of **bear**[1]. ❖ *adj.* **1a.** Brought into life by birth. **b.** Brought into existence; created. **2a.** Having from birth a particular quality or talent: *a born artist.* **b.** Destined, or seemingly destined, from birth. **3.** Resulting or arising. **4.** Native to a particular place. Often used in combination: *Irish-born.* **—idiom: born yesterday** Naive or ignorant. Used in negative constructions: *Of course I can use a computer; I wasn't born yesterday.*

Born, Max 1882–1970. German-born physicist who shared a 1954 Nobel Prize.

born-a•gain (bôrn′ə-gĕn′) *adj.* **1a.** Of, relating to, or being one who has converted to or renewed faith in Christianity. **b.** Of or relating to evangelical Christianity. **2.** Characterized by fervent renewal, resurgence, or return. [From *born again* in John 3:3 and 3:7.]

borne (bôrn, bōrn) *v.* A past participle of **bear**[1].

Bor•ne•o (bôr′nē-ō′) An island of the W Pacific Ocean in the Malay Archipelago between the Sulu and Java seas SW of the Philippines. The sultanate of Brunei is on the NW coast; the rest of the island is divided between Indonesia and Malaysia. **—Bor′ne•an** *adj. & n.*

Born•holm (bôrn′hōlm′, -hōm′) An island of E Denmark in the Baltic Sea near Sweden.

born•ite (bôr′nīt′) *n.* A brownish-bronze, lustrous copper ore, Cu₅FeS₄, that tarnishes to purple when exposed to air. [After Ignaz von Born (1742–91), Austrian mineralogist.]

Bor•nu (bôr′nōō) A region and former Muslim kingdom of W Africa that became part of Nigeria in 1902.

boro– or **bor–** *pref.* Boron: *borosilicate.* [< BORON.]

Bo•ro•bu•dur (bôr′ə-bə-dōōr′, bōr′-) A ruined Buddhist shrine in central Java; dating probably from the 9th cent.

Bo•ro•din (bôr′ə-dēn′, bär′-, bə-rə-dēn′), **Aleksandr Porfirevich** 1833–87. Russian composer whose works are based on folk themes.

Bo•ro•di•no (bôr′ə-dē′nō, bôr′-, bə-rə-dyē-nô′) A village of W Russia W of Moscow. Nearby, Napoleon defeated the Russian troops defending Moscow in 1812.

bo•ron (bôr′ŏn′, bōr′-) *n. Symbol* **B** A soft, amorphous or crystalline nonmetallic element, used in flares and nuclear reactor control rods. Atomic number 5; atomic weight 10.811; melting point 2,300°C; sublimation point 2,550°C; specific gravity (crystal) 2.34; valence 3. See table at **element**. [BOR(AX)[1] + (CARB)ON.] **—bo•ron′ic** (bə-rŏn′ĭk, bō-) *adj.*

boron carbide *n.* A compound of boron and carbon, esp. B₄C, an extremely hard crystalline compound used as an abrasive and a neutron absorber.

bo•ro•sil•i•cate (bôr′ō-sĭl′ĭ-kĭt, -kāt′, bōr′-, bôr′-) *n.* A salt that is derived from both boric acid and silicic acid and occurs naturally in dumortierite.

borosilicate glass *n.* A strong heat-resistant glass that contains a minimum of 5 percent boric oxide.

bor•ough (bûr′ō, bŭr′ō) *n.* **1.** A self-governing incorporated town in some US states. **2.** One of the five administrative units of New York City. **3.** A civil division of Alaska that is the equivalent of a county in most other US states. **4.** *Chiefly British* **a.** A town having a municipal corporation and certain rights. **b.** A town that sends a representative to Parliament. **5.** A medieval group of fortified houses that formed a town with special privileges and rights. [ME *burgh*, city < OE *burg*, fortified town. See **bhergh-** in App.]

bor•ough-Eng•lish (bûr′ō-ĭng′glĭsh, bŭr′-) *n.* An old custom in certain English boroughs whereby the right to inherit an estate intestate went to the youngest son or, in default of male issue, to the youngest brother. [Partial transl. of AN *tenure en burgh Engloys,* tenure in an English borough. See BOROUGH.]

bor•rel•i•a (bə-rĕl′ē-ə, -rē′lē-ə) *n.* Any of various irregularly coiled helical spirochetes of the genus *Borrelia,* some of which cause relapsing fever. [NLat., after Amédée *Borrel* (1867–1936), French bacteriologist.]

bor•row (bôr′ō, bōr′ō) *v.* **-rowed, -row•ing, -rows** **—tr.** **1.** To obtain or receive (something) on loan with the promise or understanding of returning it or its equivalent. **2.** To adopt or use as one's own. **3.** In subtraction, to take a unit from the next larger denomination in the minuend so as to make a number larger than the number to be subtracted. **—intr.** **1.** To obtain or receive something. **2.** *Linguistics* To adopt words from one language for use in another. **—idiom: borrow trouble** To take an unnecessary action that will probably have adverse effects. [ME *borwen* < OE *borgian.*] **—bor′row•er** *n.*

bor•rowed time (bôr′ōd, bōr′-) *n.* A period of uncertainty during which the inevitable consequences of a current situation are postponed or avoided.

bor•row•ing (bôr′ō-ĭng, bōr′-) *n.* Something that is borrowed, esp. a word borrowed from one language to another.

borscht also **borsht** (bôrsht) or **borsch** (bôrsh) *n.* A beet soup usu. served with sour cream. [Yiddish *borsht* < Russ. *borshch,* cow parsnip (the original soup base), borscht.]

borscht belt or **Borscht Belt** *n. Informal* The predominantly Jewish hotels of the Catskill Mountains, known for their vaudeville-type entertainment. [< the popularity of borscht in the cuisine.]

bort (bôrt) *n.* **1.** Poorly crystallized diamonds used for industrial cutting and abrasion. **2.** A carbonado. [Prob. < Du. *boort.*] **—bort′y** *adj.*

bor•zoi (bôr′zoi′) *n., pl.* **-zois** Any of a breed of tall slender dogs with a narrow pointed head and a silky coat, originally developed in Russia for hunting wolves. [< Russ. *borzoĭ,* swift, var. of *borzyĭ.*]

Bosc (bŏsk) *n.* A variety of pear with greenish-yellow skin overlaid with reddish-brown and juicy sweet flesh. [After Louis Auguste Guillaume *Bosc* (1759–1828), Belgian horticulturist.]

bos•cage also **bos•kage** (bŏs′kĭj) *n.* A mass of trees or shrubs; a thicket. [ME *boskage* < OFr. *boscage* < *bosc,* forest, of Gmc. orig.]

Bosch (bŏsh, bôsh, bōs), **Hieronymus** 1450?–1516. Dutch painter whose largely religious works are characterized by grotesque, fantastic creatures mingling with human figures.

Bose (bōs), **Satyendra Nath** 1894–1974. Indian physicist noted for his work in quantum mechanics.

Bose-Ein•stein condensate (bōs′īn′stīn′) *n.* A state of matter that forms below a critical temperature in which all bosons that comprise the matter fall into the same quantum state. [After Satyendra Nath BOSE and Albert EINSTEIN.]

bosh (bŏsh) *Informal n.* Nonsense. ❖ *interj.* Used to express disbelief or annoyance. [< Turk. *boş,* empty.]

bosk (bŏsk) *n.* A small wooded area. [Back-formation < BOSKY.]

bosk•y (bŏs′kē) *adj.* **-i•er, -i•est** **1.** Having many bushes, shrubs, or trees. **2.** Of or relating to woods. [< ME *bosk,* bush < Med.Lat. *bosca,* of Gmc. orig.] **—bosk′i•ness** *n.*

bo's'n or **bos'n** (bō′sən) *n.* Variants of boatswain.

Bos•ni•a (bŏz′nē-ə) **1.** A region constituting the N section of Bosnia and Herzegovina; settled by Serbs in the 7th cent. **2.** Bosnia and Herzegovina. **—Bos′ni•an** *adj. & n.*

Bosnia and Her•ze•go•vi•na (hĕrt′sə-gō′vē-nə, -gō-vē′-, hûrt′-) also **Bosnia-Herzegovina** Commonly known as **Bosnia.** A country of the NW Balkan Peninsula W of Serbia; a constituent republic of Yugoslavia from 1946 to 1991. Cap. Sarajevo. Pop. 3,527,000.

bos•om (bōōz′əm, bōō′zəm) *n.* **1a.** The chest of a human. **b.** A woman's breast or breasts. **2.** The part of a garment covering the chest or breasts. **3.** Security and closeness relating to being held in a warm familial embrace. **4.** The chest considered as the source of emotion. ❖ *adj.* Beloved; intimate. [ME < OE *bōsm.*]

bo•son (bō′sŏn) *n.* Any of a class of particles that have zero or integral spin and obey statistical rules permitting any number of identical particles to occupy the same quantum state. [After Satyendra Nath BOSE.]

Bos•po•rus (bŏs′pər-əs) A narrow strait separating European and Asian Turkey and joining the Black Sea with the Sea of Marmara; an important trade route since ancient times.

bos•quet (bŏs′kĭt) *n.* A small grove; a thicket. [Fr. < Ital. *boschetto,* dim. of *bosco,* forest, of Gmc. orig.]

boss[1] (bôs) *n.* **1a.** An employer or a supervisor. **b.** One who makes decisions or exercises authority. **2.** A politician who controls a party or a political machine. ❖ *v.* **bossed, boss•ing, boss•es** **—tr.** **1.** To supervise or control. **2.** To give orders to, esp. arrogantly or domineeringly. **—intr.** To be or act as a supervisor or controlling element. ❖ *adj. Slang* First-rate; top-notch. [Du. *baas,* master.]

boss[2] (bôs, bŏs) *n.* **1.** A circular protuberance or knoblike swelling, as on animal horns. **2.** A raised area used as ornamentation. **3.** *Architecture* A raised ornament. **4a.** An enlarged part of a shaft to which another shaft is coupled or to which a wheel or gear is keyed. **b.** A hub, esp. of a propeller. ❖ *tr.v.* **bossed, boss•ing, boss•es** To emboss. [ME *boce* < OFr.]

boss[3] (bôs, bŏs) *n.* A cow or calf. [Perh. ult. < Lat. *bōs.* See BO-VINE.]

bos•sa no•va (bŏs′ə nō′və, bô′sə) *n.* **1.** A style of popular Bra-

borzoi

BOSNIA AND HERZEGOVINA
Sarajevo
CROATIA
YUGOSLAVIA
Adriatic Sea
50 mi

Bosnia and Herzegovina

boss[2]

ă	pat	oi	boy
ā	pay	ou	out
âr	care	ōō	took
ä	father	ōō	boot
ĕ	pet	ŭ	cut
ē	be	ûr	urge
ĭ	pit	th	thin
ī	pie	th	this
îr	pier	hw	which
ŏ	pot	zh	vision
ō	toe	ə	about,
ô	paw		item

Stress marks:
′ (primary)
′ (secondary), as in
lexicon (lĕk′sĭ-kŏn′)

zilian music derived from the samba but with more harmonic complexity. **2.** A lively Brazilian dance similar to the samba. [Port. : *bossa,* trend + *nova,* new.]

boss·ism (bô′sĭz′əm, bŏs′ĭz′-) *n.* The domination of a political organization by a boss.

Bos·suet (bôs-wā′), **Jacques Bénigne** 1627–1704. French prelate and historian noted for his philosophical treatise on history.

boss·y[1] (bô′sē, bŏs′ē) *adj.* **-i·er, -i·est** Given to ordering others around. **—boss′i·ly** *adv.* **—boss′i·ness** *n.*

boss·y[2] (bô′sē, bŏs′ē) *adj.* Decorated with raised ornaments.

boss·y[3] (bô′sē, bŏs′ē) *n., pl.* **-ies** *Informal* A cow or calf. [< BOSS[3].]

Bos·ton (bô′stən, bŏs′tən) The cap. of MA, in the E part on **Boston Bay,** an arm of Massachusetts Bay; founded in the 17th cent. Pop. 589,141. **—Bos′to′ni·an** (bô-stō′nē-ən, bŏs-) *adj. & n.*

Boston bull *n.* See **Boston terrier.**

Boston cream pie *n.* A round cake with a custard or cream filling, often with a chocolate glaze.

Boston fern *n.* **1.** A cultivar of sword fern (*Nephrolepis exaltata* cv. *Bostoniensis*) having arching or drooping pinnate fronds. **2.** Any of numerous ferns derived from the sword fern.

Boston ivy *n.* A high-climbing woody vine (*Parthenocissus tricuspidata*) from eastern Asia, with three-lobed deciduous leaves.

Boston lettuce *n.* A type of cultivated lettuce forming a rounded head and having soft, yellow-green inner leaves.

Boston marriage *n.* A long-term, intimate sexual relationship between two women. [Perh. after the devoted women pairs from Boston depicted in *The Bostonians* by Henry James.]

Boston rocker *n.* A rocking chair having a high back with spindles, a decorative panel at the top, and a seat and arms that curve downward in front.

Boston terrier *n.* Any of a breed of small dogs originating in New England as a cross between a bull terrier and a bulldog and having a brindled or black coat with white markings.

bo·sun (bô′sən) *n.* Variant of **boatswain.**

Bos·well (bŏz′wĕl′, -wəl), **James** 1740–95. Scottish lawyer, diarist, and writer renowned as the biographer of Samuel Johnson. **—Bos·well′i·an** *adj. & n.*

Bos·worth Field (bŏz′wərth) A locality in central England near Leicester; site of the final battle (1485) of the Wars of the Roses.

bot[1] also **bott** (bŏt) *n.* **1.** The parasitic larva of a botfly. **2. bots** (*used with a sing. or pl. verb*) A disease of mammals caused by infestation of the stomach or intestines with botfly larvae. [ME, prob. of LGer. orig.]

bot[2] (bŏt) *n.* A software program that imitates the behavior of a human, as by querying search engines or participating in chatroom discussions. [Short for ROBOT.]

bo·tan·i·ca (bə-tăn′ĭ-kə) *n.* A shop that sells herbs, charms, and spiritual items, esp. those associated with Santeria. [Am.Sp. *botánica* < Gk. *botanikē,* fem. of *botanikos,* herbal. See BOTANICAL.]

bo·tan·i·cal (bə-tăn′ĭ-kəl) also **bo·tan·ic** (-tăn′ĭk) *adj.* **1.** Of or relating to plants or plant life. **2.** Of or relating to botany. ❖ *n.* A drug or similar substance obtained from a plant or plants. [< LLat. *botanicus* < Gk. *botanikos < botanē,* fodder, plants.] **—bo·tan′i·cal·ly** *adv.*

botanical garden *n.* A place where a wide variety of plants are cultivated for scientific, educational, and ornamental purposes.

bot·a·nist (bŏt′n-ĭst) *n.* One who specializes in botany.

bot·a·nize (bŏt′n-īz′) *v.* **-nized, -niz·ing, -niz·es** *—intr.* **1.** To collect plants for scientific study. **2.** To investigate or study plants scientifically. *—tr.* To investigate or explore the plant life of (a region). **—bot′a·niz′er** *n.*

bot·a·ny (bŏt′n-ē) *n., pl.* **-nies 1a.** The science or study of plants. **b.** A book or scholarly work on this subject. **2.** The plant life of a particular area. **3.** The characteristic features and biology of a particular plant or plant group. [Back-formation < earlier *botanic,* botanical < LLat. *botanicus.* See BOTANICAL.]

Botany Bay An inlet of the Tasman Sea in SE Australia.

botch (bŏch) *tr.v.* **botched, botch·ing, botch·es 1.** To ruin through clumsiness. **2.** To make or perform clumsily; bungle. **3.** To repair or mend clumsily. ❖ *n.* **1.** A ruined or defective piece of work: *"I have made a miserable botch of this description"* (Nathaniel Hawthorne). **2.** A hodgepodge. [ME *bocchen,* to mend.] **—botch′er** *n.* **—botch′y** *adj.*

SYNONYMS *botch, blow, bungle, fumble, muff* These verbs mean to harm or spoil through inept or clumsy handling: *botch a repair; blow an opportunity; bungle an interview; fumbled my chance; muffed the painting job.*

bot·fly also **bot fly** (bŏt′flī′) *n.* Any of various stout two-winged flies, chiefly of the genera *Gasterophilus* and *Oestrus,* having larvae that are parasitic on various animals.

both (bōth) *adj.* One and the other; relating to or being two in conjunction: *Both guests came.* ❖ *pron.* The one and the other: *Both are mad.* ❖ *conj.* Used with *and* to link two things in a coordinated phrase or clause: *both he and I.* [ME *bothe* < ON *bāthar.* See **to-** in App.]

USAGE NOTE *Both* is used to indicate that the action or state denoted by the verb applies individually to each of two entities.

Botswana

Both books weigh more than five pounds, for example, means that each book weighs more than five pounds by itself, not that the two books weighed together come to more than five pounds. • In possessive constructions of *both* is usually preferred: *the mothers of both* (rather than *both their mothers*). • When *both* is used with *and* to link parallel elements in a sentence, the words or phrases that follow them should correspond grammatically: *in both India and China* or *both in India and in China* (not *both in India and China*).

Bo·tha (bō′tə, -tä′), **Louis** 1862–1919. South African general and first prime minister of South Africa (1910–19).

Botha, Pieter Willem b. 1916. South African prime minister (1978–89) who upheld apartheid.

both·er (bŏth′ər) *v.* **-ered, -er·ing, -ers** *—tr.* **1.** To disturb or anger, esp. by minor irritations; annoy. **2a.** To make agitated or nervous; fluster. **b.** To make confused or perplexed; puzzle. **3.** To intrude on without warrant; disturb. **4.** To give trouble to. *—intr.* **1.** To take the trouble; concern oneself. **2.** To cause trouble. ❖ *n.* A cause or state of disturbance. ❖ *interj.* Used to express annoyance or mild irritation. [Prob. < dialectal *bodder,* poss. of Celt. orig.]

both·er·a·tion (bŏth′ə-rā′shən) *n.* The act of bothering or the state of being bothered. ❖ *interj.* Used to express annoyance or irritation.

both·er·some (bŏth′ər-səm) *adj.* Causing bother.

Both·ni·a (bŏth′nē-ə), **Gulf of** An arm of the Baltic Sea between Sweden and Finland.

Both·well (bŏth′wĕl′, -wəl, bŏth′-), **4th Earl of.** Title of James Hepburn. 1536?–78. Scottish noble and third husband of Mary Queen of Scots, whose second husband, Lord Darnley, he murdered (1567).

bo tree (bō) *n.* See **pipal.** [Partial transl. of Sinhalese *bo-gaha,* tree of wisdom (because it was the tree under which the Buddha was enlightened) : *bo,* wisdom (< Pali *bodhi* < Skt. *bodhiḥ,* enlightenment; see **bheudh-** in App.) + *gaha,* tree.]

bot·ry·oi·dal (bŏt′rē-oid′l) also **bot·ry·oid** (bŏt′rē-oid′) *adj.* Shaped like a bunch of grapes. Used esp. of mineral formations: *botryoidal hematite.* [< Gk. *botruoeidēs : botrus,* bunch of grapes + *-oeidēs,* -oid.] **—bot′ry·oi′dal·ly** *adv.*

bo·try·tis (bō-trī′tĭs) *n.* **1.** Any of various fungi of the genus *Botrytis* responsible for numerous fruit and vegetable diseases. **2.** Noble rot. [NLat., genus name < Gk. *botrus,* bunch of grapes.]

Bot·swa·na (bŏt-swä′nə) Formerly **Bech·u·a·na·land** (bĕch-wä′nə-lănd′, bĕch′oo-ä′-) A country of S-central Africa; gained independence from Great Britain in 1966. Cap. Gaborone. Pop. 1,443,000. **—Bot·swa′nan** *adj. & n.*

bott (bŏt) *n.* Variant of **bot**[1].

Bot·ti·cel·li (bŏt′ĭ-chĕl′ē), **Sandro** 1444?–1510. Italian painter whose works include *Birth of Venus* (c. 1485).

bot·tle (bŏt′l) *n.* **1.** A receptacle having a narrow neck, usu. no handles, and a mouth that can be stopped. **2.** The quantity that a bottle holds. **3.** A receptacle filled with milk or formula that is fed to babies in place of breast milk. **4.** *Informal* **a.** Intoxicating liquor: *Don't take to the bottle.* **b.** The practice of drinking large quantities of intoxicating liquor. ❖ *tr.v.* **-tled, -tling, -tles 1.** To place in a bottle. **2.** To hold in; restrain: *bottled up my emotions.* [ME *botel* < OFr. *botele* < Med.Lat. *butticula,* dim. of LLat. *buttis,* cask.] **—bot′tler** *n.*

bot·tle·brush (bŏt′l-brŭsh′) *n.* Any of various Australian shrubs or trees of the genera *Callistemon* and *Melaleuca,* having densely flowered cylindrical spikes with numerous protruding stamens that suggest a brush used to clean bottles.

bot·tled gas (bŏt′ld) *n.* Gas, such as butane or propane, stored under pressure in portable tanks.

bot·tle-feed (bŏt′l-fēd′) *tr.v.* **-fed (-fĕd′), -feed·ing, -feeds** To feed (a baby, for example) with a bottle.

bottle gourd *n.* See **calabash** 1.

bottle green *n.* A dark to moderate or grayish green.

bot·tle·neck (bŏt′l-nĕk′) *n.* **1a.** A narrow or obstructed section. **b.** A point or area of traffic congestion. **2.** A hindrance to progress or production. **3.** The narrow part of a bottle near the top. **4.** *Music* A style of guitar playing in which an object is passed across the strings to achieve a gliding sound. ❖ *tr.v.* **-necked, -necking, -necks** To obstruct.

bot·tle·nose (bŏt′l-nōz′) *n.* See **bottle-nosed dolphin.**

bot·tle-nosed dolphin (bŏt′l-nōzd′) *n.* Any of several marine mammals of the genus *Tursiops,* esp. *T. truncatus,* of temperate and tropical waters and characterized by a short protruding beak, a large stocky body, and a falcate dorsal fin.

bottle tree *n.* Any of certain Australian trees of the genus *Brachychiton,* having a sometimes bottle-shaped trunk.

bot·tom (bŏt′əm) *n.* **1.** The deepest or lowest part. **2.** The part closest to a reference point: *scored a basket from the bottom of the key.* **3.** The underside. **4.** The supporting part; the base. **5.** The far end or part: *the bottom of the bed.* **6a.** The last place, as on a list. **b.** The lowest or least favorable position. **7.** The basic underlying quality; the source. **8.** The solid surface under a body of water. **9.** Low-lying alluvial land adjacent to a river. Often used in the plural. **10a.** *Nautical* The part of a ship's hull below the water line. **b.** A ship; a boat. **11.** Pajama pants. Often used in the plural. **12.**

Informal The buttocks. **13.** The seat of a chair. **14.** *Baseball* The second or last half of an inning. **15.** Staying power; stamina. Used of a horse. ❖ *adj.* **1.** Situated at the bottom: *the bottom shelf.* **2.** Of the lowest degree, quality, rank, or amount. ❖ *v.* **-tomed, -tom•ing, -toms** —*tr.* **1.** To provide with an underside. **2.** To provide with a foundation. **3.** To get to the bottom of; fathom. —*intr.* **1.** To be or become based or grounded. **2.** To rest on or touch the bottom. —*phrasal verb:* **bottom out** To descend to the lowest point possible, after which only a rise may occur. —*idiom:* **at bottom** Basically. [ME *botme* < OE *botm.*] —**bot′tom•er** *n.*

bottom break *n.* A branch arising from a plant stem base. [BOTTOM + BREAK, branch formed by pinching or disbudding.]

bottom feeder *n.* **1.** A fish or other animal that feeds on the bottom of a body of water. **2.** One that feeds low on the food chain; a scavenger. **3.** *Slang* **a.** An opportunist who profits from the misfortunes of others: *"The frazzled, adrenaline-pumped tabloid newshounds* [in the movie] *are the bottom feeders of contemporary journalism"* (Entertainment Weekly). **b.** A low or despicable person. —**bottom feeding** *n.* —**bot′tom-feed′ing** (bŏt′əm-fē′dĭng) *adj.*

bottom fish *n.* A fish, such as a catfish, carp, or flounder, that lives on or near the bottom of a body of water.

bottom fishing *n.* **1.** The activity of fishing for bottom feeders. **2.** Researching or investing in securities at what is believed to be the low point of a market after a decline.

bot•tom•land (bŏt′əm-lănd′) *n.* See **bottom** 9.

bot•tom•less (bŏt′əm-lĭs) *adj.* **1.** Having no bottom. **2.** Too deep to be measured. **3.** Difficult or impossible to understand. **4.** Having no limitations or bounds. —**bot′tom•less•ly** *adv.*

bottom line *n.* **1.** The line in a financial statement for net income or loss. **2.** Financial matters, esp. profit or loss. **3.** The final result. **4.** The main point.

bot•tom•most (bŏt′əm-mōst′) *adj.* **1.** Sited at the very bottom. **2.** Coming after all others. **3.** Forming the basis.

bottom quark *n.* A quark with a charge of −⅓ and a mass about 10,000 times that of the electron.

bottom round *n.* A cut of meat from the outer section of a round of beef.

bot•u•lin (bŏch′ə-lĭn) *n.* Any of several potent neurotoxins produced by botulinum and resistant to proteolytic digestion. [Lat. *botulus,* sausage (a common source of contamination) + –IN.]

bot•u•li•num (bŏch′ə-lī′nəm) also **bot•u•li•nus** (-nəs) *n.* An anaerobic rod-shaped bacterium (*Clostridium botulinum*) that secretes botulin and inhabits soils. [NLat. *botulīnum,* specific epithet < Lat. *botulus,* sausage.] —**bot′u•li′nal** *adj.*

bot•u•lism (bŏch′ə-lĭz′əm) *n.* A severe, sometimes fatal food poisoning caused by ingestion of food containing botulin and characterized by nausea, vomiting, disturbed vision, and fatigue. [Ger. *Botulismus* < Lat. *botulus,* sausage.]

Bou•cher (boo-shā′), **François** 1703–70. French artist who painted in the rococo style.

bou•clé or **bou•cle** (boo-klā′) *n.* **1.** A type of yarn, usu. three-ply and having one thread looser than the others. **2.** Fabric made from this yarn. [Fr. < p. part. of *boucler,* to curl < OFr. < *boucle,* buckle, curl of hair. See BUCKLE.]

Bou•dain (boo-dăn′, -dăN′) *n.* Variant of **boudin.**

Bou•dic•ca (boo-dĭk′ə) also **Bo•ad•i•ce•a** (bō′ăd-ĭ-sē′ə) 1st cent. A.D. Queen of ancient Britain who led a revolt against the Roman army.

bou•din also **Bou•dain** (boo-dăn′, -dăN′) *n., pl.* **-dins** also **-dains** (-dăN′, -dănz′) A Louisiana Creole link sausage of pork, pork liver, and rice. [Fr. < OFr. *bodine,* intestines.]

boudin blanc (blăN) *n., pl.* **boudins blancs** (blăN) A French white sausage of pork, chicken, or veal. [Fr. : *boudin,* boudin + *blanc,* white.]

boudin noir *n., pl.* **boudins noirs** (nwär) See **black pudding.** [Fr. : *boudin,* boudin + *noir,* black.]

bou•doir (boo′dwär′, -dwôr′) *n.* A woman's private sitting room, dressing room, or bedroom. [Fr. < OFr. *bouder,* to sulk.]

bouf•fant (boo-fänt′) *adj.* Puffed-out; full. [Fr., pr. part. of *bouffer,* to puff up < OFr.]

bouffe (boof) *n.* See **comic opera.** [Short for OPÉRA BOUFFE.]

Bou•gain•ville (boo′gən-vĭl′, boo-găn-vēl′) A volcanic island of Papua New Guinea in the Solomon Is. of the SW Pacific Ocean.

Bougainville, Louis Antoine de 1729–1811. French explorer who circumnavigated the globe (1766–69).

bou•gain•vil•le•a also **bou•gain•vil•lae•a** (boo′gən-vĭl′ē-ə, -vĭl′yə, -vē′ə, bō′-) *n.* Any of several South American woody shrubs or vines of the genus *Bougainvillea,* having groups of three petallike, usually colored bracts attached to the flower. [NLat. *Bougainvillea,* genus name, after Louis Antoine de BOUGAINVILLE.]

bough (bou) *n.* A tree branch, esp. a large or main branch. [ME < OE *bōh.*]

bought (bôt) *v.* Past tense and past participle of **buy.**

bought•en (bôt′n) *Chiefly Northern US v.* A past participle of **buy.** ❖ *adj.* **1.** Commercially made; purchased: *boughten bread.* **2.** Artificial; false. Used of teeth.

bou•gie (boo′zhē, -jē) *n.* **1.** *Medicine* **a.** A slender, flexible, cylin-

drical instrument that is inserted into a body canal, such as the urethra. **b.** See **suppository.** **2.** A wax candle. [Fr. < OFr., a fine wax, after *Bougie* (Bejaïa), a city of northern Algeria.]

bouil•la•baisse (boo′yə-bās′, bool′yə-bās′) *n.* **1.** A highly seasoned stew made of several kinds of fish and shellfish. **2.** A combination of various different, often incongruous elements. [Fr. < Provençal *bouiabaisso* : *boui,* imper. of *bouie,* to boil (< Lat. *bullīre* < *bulla,* bubble) + *abaisso,* to lower (< VLat. *abbassiāre* : Lat. *ad-,* ad- + Med.Lat. *bassus,* low).]

bouil•lon (bool′yŏn′, -yən, boo′yŏn′) *n.* A clear thin broth made typically by simmering beef or chicken in water with seasonings. [Fr. < OFr. < *boulir,* to boil < Lat. *bullīre* < *bulla,* bubble.]

bouillon cube *n.* A small cube of evaporated seasoned meat, poultry, or vegetable stock, used in broths for flavor.

Boul. *abbr.* boulevard

Bou•lan•ger (boo-län-zhā′), **Nadia Juliette** 1887–1979. French music teacher whose students included Virgil Thomson and Aaron Copland.

boul•der also **bowl•der** (bōl′dər) *n.* A large rounded mass of rock lying on the surface of the ground or embedded in the soil. [ME *bulder,* of Scand. orig.]

Boulder A city of N-central CO NW of Denver. Pop. 94,673.

bou•le¹ (boo′lē, boo-lā′) *n.* **1.** The lower house of the modern Greek legislature. **2a.** The senate of 400 founded by Solon in ancient Athens. **b.** A legislative assembly in any one of the ancient Greek states. [Gk. *boulē,* assembly. See **gʷelə-** in App.]

boule² (bool) *n.* **1.** A pear-shaped synthetic gem, produced by fusing and tinting alumina. **2.** A round loaf of white bread. [Fr., ball < OFr., bubble < Lat. *bulla.*]

boul•e•vard (bool′ə-värd′, boo′lə-) *n.* **1.** A broad city street, often tree-lined and landscaped. **2.** *Upper Midwest* See **parking** 3. **3.** *Chiefly Midwestern US* See **median strip.** See Regional Note at **neutral ground.** [Fr. < OFr. *bollevart,* rampart converted to a promenade < MDu. *bolwerc,* bulwark. See BULWARK.]

boul•e•vard•ier (boo′lə-vär-dyā′, -dîr′) *n.* A man about town. [Obsolete Fr. < *boulevard,* boulevard. See BOULEVARD.]

boulevard strip *n.* *Upper Midwest* See **parking** 3. See Regional Note at **parking.**

bou•le•ver•se•ment (boo′lə-věr′sə-mäN′) *n.* **1.** A violent uproar; a tumult. **2.** A reversal. [Fr. < OFr. *bouleverser,* to overturn : *boule,* ball (< Lat. *bulla*) + *verser,* to overturn < OFr. < Lat. *versāre,* freq. of *vertere,* to turn; see **wer-²** in App.).]

Bou•lez (boo-lěz′), **Pierre** b. 1925. French conductor and composer of works such as *Le Marteau sans Maître* (1955).

boulle (bool) *n.* Variant of **buhl.**

Bou•logne (boo-lōn′, -lôN′yə) also **Bou•logne-sur-Mer** (-sûr-mêr′) A city of N France on the English Channel NNW of Amiens; of Celtic origin. Pop. 47,653.

bounce (bouns) *v.* **bounced, bounc•ing, bounc•es** —*intr.* **1.** To rebound after having struck an object or a surface. **2.** To move jerkily; bump. **3.** To recover quickly, as from a setback. **4.** To bound. **5.** To be sent back by a bank as valueless: *a check that bounced.* **6.** *Baseball* To hit a ground ball that rebounds before reaching an infielder. —*tr.* **1.** To cause to strike an object or a surface and rebound. **2.** To present or propose for comment or approval. Often used with *off: bounced an idea off my boss.* **3.** *Slang* **a.** To expel by force. **b.** To dismiss from employment. **4.** To write (a check) on an overdrawn bank account. ❖ *n.* **1.** A rebound. **2.** A sudden bound, spring, or leap. **3.** The capacity to rebound; spring. **4.** Spirit; liveliness. **5.** *Slang* Expulsion; dismissal. **6.** *Chiefly British* Loud, arrogant speech; bluster. [Prob. < ME *bounsen,* to beat.]

bounc•er (boun′sər) *n.* **1.** *Slang* A person employed to expel disorderly persons from a public place, esp. a bar. **2.** *Baseball* A ground ball hit in such a way that it bounces.

bounc•ing (boun′sĭng) *adj.* **1.** Vigorous; healthy. **2.** Spirited; lively: *a bouncing gait.* —**bounc′ing•ly** *adv.*

bouncing Bet *n.* A perennial Eurasian herb (*Saponaria officinalis*) having dense clusters of pink to whitish flowers. [< *Bet,* nickname for Elizabeth.]

bounc•y (boun′sē) *adj.* **-i•er, -i•est** **1.** Tending to bounce. **2.** Springy; elastic. **3.** Lively; energetic. —**bounc′i•ly** *adv.* —**bounc′i•ness** *n.*

bound¹ (bound) *intr.v.* **bound•ed, bound•ing, bounds** **1.** To leap forward or upward; spring. **2.** To progress by forward leaps or springs. **3.** To bounce; rebound. ❖ *n.* **1.** A leap; a jump. **2.** A rebound; a bounce. [Fr. *bondir,* to bounce < OFr., to resound, perh. ult. < Lat. *bombus,* a humming sound < Gk. *bombos.*]

bound² (bound) *n.* **1.** A boundary; a limit. Often used in the plural: *Our joy knew no bounds.* **2. bounds** The territory on, within, or near limiting lines. ❖ *v.* **bound•ed, bound•ing, bounds** —*tr.* **1.** To set a limit to; confine. **2.** To constitute the boundary or limit of. **3.** To identify the boundaries of; demarcate. —*intr.* To border on another place, state, or country. [ME < OFr. *bodne, bonde* and AN *bunde,* both < Med.Lat. *bodina,* of Celt. orig.]

bound³ (bound) *v.* Past tense and past participle of **bind.** ❖ *adj.* **1.** Confined by bonds; tied. **2.** Being under legal or moral obligation. **3.** Equipped with a cover or binding. **4.** Predetermined; certain: *bound to be late.* **5.** Determined; resolved: *She's bound to be mayor.* **6.** *Linguistics* Being a form that cannot stand as an independent word, such as an affix. **7.** Constipated.

bound⁴ (bound) *adj.* Headed or intending to head in a specified direction: *south-bound.* [Alteration of ME *boun,* ready < ON *būinn,* p. part. of *būa,* to get ready. See **bheua-** in App.]

bound•a•ry (boun′də-rē, -drē) *n., pl.* **-ries 1.** Something indicating a border or limit. **2.** A border or limit so indicated.

boundary layer *n.* The layer of reduced velocity in fluids that is adjacent to the solid surface past which the fluid flows.

bound•en (boun′dən) *adj.* **1.** Obligatory: *their bounden duty.* **2.** *Archaic* Being under obligation; obliged. [ME, p. part. of *binden,* to bind < OE *bindan.* See BIND.]

bound•er (boun′dər) *n. Chiefly British* A cad.

bound•less (bound′lĭs) *adj.* Being without boundaries or limits; infinite. See Syns at **infinite.** —**bound′less•ly** *adv.* —**bound′-less•ness** *n.*

boun•te•ous (boun′tē-əs) *adj.* **1.** Giving or inclined to give generously. **2.** Generously and copiously given. See Syns at **liberal.** [ME *bountevous* < OFr. *bontive,* benevolent < *bonte,* bounty. See BOUNTY.] —**boun′te•ous•ly** *adv.* —**boun′te•ous•ness** *n.*

boun•ti•ful (boun′tĭ-fəl) *adj.* **1.** Giving freely and generously; liberal. **2.** Marked by abundance; plentiful. See Syns at **liberal.** —**boun′ti•ful•ly** *adv.* —**boun′ti•ful•ness** *n.*

boun•ty (boun′tē) *n., pl.* **-ties 1.** Liberality in giving. **2.** Something given liberally. **3.** A reward, inducement, or payment, esp. from a government for acts deemed beneficial to the state. [ME *bounte* < OFr. *bonte* < Lat. *bonitās,* goodness < *bonus,* good. See **deu-²** in App.]

bounty hunter *n.* **1.** One who hunts predatory animals in order to collect a bounty. **2.** One who pursues a criminal or fugitive for whom a reward is offered.

bou•quet (bō-kā′, boō-) *n.* **1.** A cluster of flowers; a nosegay. **2.** The fragrance typical of a wine or liqueur. [Fr. < OFr. *bosquet,* thicket, dim. of *bosc,* forest, of Gmc. orig.]

bouquet gar•ni (gär-nē′) *n., pl.* **bou•quets gar•nis** (bō-kāz′ gär-nē′, boō-) A bunch of herbs tied together for cooking, wrapped in cheesecloth or enclosed in a small cloth sack. [Fr. : *bouquet,* bunch + *garni,* p. part. of *garnir,* to garnish.]

bour•bon (bûr′bən) *n.* A whiskey distilled from a fermented mash containing not less than 51 percent corn in addition to malt and rye. [After *Bourbon* County in northeast Kentucky.]

Bour•bon¹ (boōr′bən, boōr-bôN′) French royal family descended from Louis I, Duke of Bourbon (1270?–1342), whose members have ruled in France, Spain, Naples, and Sicily.

Bour•bon² (bûr′bən) *n.* A sociopolitical reactionary. [After BOURBON¹ family.]

Bour•bon (boōr′bən, boōr-bôN′), Duc **Charles de** 1490–1527. French general who led a failed invasion of France (1524).

Bour•bon•nais (boōr-bôN-nā′) A historical region and former province of central France in the Massif Central; held by the Bourbons until 1527.

bour•don (boōr′dn) *n.* **1.** The drone pipe of a bagpipe. **2.** The bass string, as of a violin. [ME *burdoun,* bass < OFr. *bourdon.*]

bourg (boōrg) *n.* **1.** A market town. **2.** A medieval village, esp. one near a castle. [Fr. < OFr. < LLat. *burgus,* fortress, of Gmc. orig. See **bhergh-** in App.]

bour•geois (boōr-zhwä′, boōr′zhwä′) *n., pl.* **bourgeois 1.** A member of the middle class. **2.** A person whose attitudes and behavior conform to that of the middle class. **3.** In Marxist theory, a member of the property-owning class; a capitalist. ❖ *adj.* **1.** Of, relating to, or typical of the middle class. **2.** Preoccupied with respectability and material values. [Fr. < OFr. *burgeis,* citizen < *bourg,* bourg. See BOURG.]

Bour•geois (boōr-zhwä′), **Léon Victor Auguste** 1851–1925. French politician who won the 1920 Nobel Peace Prize.

Bourgeois, Louise b. 1911. French-born Amer. sculptor whose works are characterized by elongated figures and abstract shapes.

bour•geoise (boōr-zhwäz′, boōr′zhwäz′) *n., pl.* **-geois•es** (-zhwä′zĭz) A middle-class woman. [Fr., fem. of *bourgeois,* bourgeois. See BOURGEOIS.] —**bour•geoise′** *adj.*

bour•geoi•sie (boōr′zhwä-zē′) *n.* **1.** The middle class. **2.** In Marxist theory, the social group opposed to the proletariat in the class struggle. [Fr. < *bourgeois,* bourgeois. See BOURGEOIS.]

bour•geoi•si•fy (boōr-zhwä′zə-fī′) *tr.v.* **-fied, -fy•ing, -fies** To cause to adopt the characteristics attributed to the bourgeoisie. —**bourg′eoi′si•fi•ca′tion** (-zə-fĭ-kā′shən) *n.*

bour•geon (bûr′jən) *v.* Variant of **burgeon.**

Bourges (boōrzh) A city of central France SSE of Orléans; a Roman provincial cap. under Augustus. Pop. 76,432.

Bour•gogne (boōr-gôN′yə) See **Burgundy².**

Bourke-White (bûrk′hwīt′, -wīt′), **Margaret** 1906–71. Amer. photographer and writer who was an editor of *Life* magazine (1936–69).

Margaret Bourke-White
photographed in 1940

bourn¹ also **bourne** (bôrn, bōrn, boōrn) *n.* A small stream; a brook. [ME < OE *burna.*]

bourn² also **bourne** (bôrn, bōrn, boōrn) *n. Archaic* **1.** A destination; a goal. **2.** A boundary; a limit. [Fr. *bourne* < Fr. dialectal *bosne, borne* < OFr. *bodne,* limit, boundary marker < Med.Lat. *bodina,* of Celt. orig.]

Bourne•mouth (bôrn′məth, bōrn′-, boōrn′-) A borough of S England SW of Southampton. Pop. 159,876.

bour•rée (boō-rā′, boō-) *n.* **1a.** An old French dance resembling the gavotte. **b.** The music for this dance. **2.** A pas de bourrée. [Fr.

< *bourrer,* to stuff < *bourre,* hair, fluff < LLat. *burra,* a shaggy garment.]

bourse (boōrs) *n.* A stock exchange, esp. one in a continental European city. [Fr. < LLat. *bursa,* purse < Lat. BURSA.]

bou•stro•phe•don (boō′strə-fēd′n, -fē′dŏn′) *n.* An ancient method of writing in which the lines are inscribed alternately from right to left and from left to right. [< Gk. *boustrophēdon,* turning like an ox while plowing : *bous,* ox; see **gʷou-** in App. + *strophē,* a turning (< *strephein,* to turn).] —**bou•stroph′e•don′ic** (-strŏf′ĭ-dŏn′ĭk) *adj.*

bout (bout) *n.* **1.** A contest between antagonists; a match. **2.** A period of time spent in a particular way; a spell: *a drinking bout.* [< obsolete *bought,* a turning (influenced by ABOUT) < ME < *bowen,* to bend, turn. See BOW².]

bou•tique (boō-tēk′) *n.* **1a.** A small retail shop that specializes in items such as gifts. **b.** A small shop located within a large department store or supermarket. **2.** A small business offering specialized products and services: *an investment boutique.* [Fr. < OFr. *botique,* shop < O Provençal *botica* < Lat. *apothēca,* storehouse. See APOTHECARY.]

bou•ton (boō-tôN′) *n.* A knoblike enlargement at the end of an axon, where it forms a synapse with other neurons. [Fr., button < OFr. See BUTTON.]

bou•ton•niere also **bou•ton•nière** (boō′tə-nîr′, -tən-yâr′) *n.* A flower or nosegay worn in a buttonhole. [Fr. *boutonnière* < OFr., buttonhole < *bouton,* button. See BUTTON.]

Bou•tros-Gha•li (boō′trŏs-gä′lē), **Boutros** b. 1922. Egyptian diplomat who served as secretary-general of the United Nations (1992–96).

bou•var•di•a (boō-vär′dē-ə) *n.* Any of several Mexican and Central American shrubs or herbs of the genus *Bouvardia,* having showy, narrowly tubular flowers. [NLat. *Bouvardia,* genus name, after Charles *Bouvard* (1572–1658), French physician.]

Bou•vier des Flan•dres (boō-vyä′ dā flän′dərz, dā flän′drə) *n.* Any of a breed of large, shaggy dogs developed in Belgium, originally used for herding and guarding cattle. [Fr. : *bouvier,* cowherd + *des,* of + *Flandres,* Flanders.]

bou•zou•ki (boō-zoō′kē, bə-) *n.* A Greek stringed instrument having a long fretted neck and usu. pear-shaped body. [Mod.Gk. *mpouzouki,* prob. of Turk. orig.]

Bo•vet (bō-vā′, -vĕt′), **Daniel** 1907–92. Swiss-born Italian physiologist who won a 1957 Nobel Prize.

bo•vid (bō′vĭd) *adj.* Of or belonging to the family Bovidae, which includes hoofed, hollow-horned ruminants such as cattle and sheep. [< NLat. *Bovidae,* family name < Lat. *bōs, bov-,* cow. See BOVINE.] —**bo′vid** *n.*

bo•vine (bō′vīn′, -vēn′) *adj.* **1.** Of, relating to, or resembling a ruminant mammal of the genus *Bos,* such as a cow. **2.** Sluggish, dull, and stolid. ❖ *n.* An animal of the genus *Bos.* [LLat. *bovīnus* < Lat. *bōs, bov-,* cow. See **gʷou-** in App.]

bovine growth hormone *n.* **1.** A hormone of cattle that regulates growth and milk production. **2.** A genetically engineered hormone with similar structure and function.

bovine somatotropin *n.* See **bovine growth hormone.**

bovine spongiform encephalopathy *n.* An infectious degenerative brain disease occurring in cattle.

bow¹ (bou) *n. Nautical* **1.** The front section of a ship or boat. **2.** The oar or the person wielding the oar closest to the bow. [ME *boue,* prob. of LGer. orig.]

bow² (bou) *v.* **bowed, bow•ing, bows** —*intr.* **1.** To bend or curve downward; stoop. **2.** To incline the body or head or bend the knee, as in greeting, consent, or courtesy. **3.** To yield in defeat or out of courtesy; submit. See Syns at **yield.** —*tr.* **1.** To bend (the head, knee, or body), as in greeting. **2.** To convey (greeting, for example) by bending the body. **3.** To escort deferentially. **4.** To cause to acquiesce; submit. **5.** To overburden. ❖ *n.* An inclination of the head or body, as in greeting. —*phrasal verb:* **bow out** To remove oneself; withdraw. —*idiom:* **bow and scrape** To behave obsequiously. [ME *bowen* < OE *būgan.*]

bow³ (bō) *n.* **1.** A bent, curved, or arched object. **2.** A weapon made of a curved flexible strip of material, esp. wood, strung taut and used to launch arrows. **3a.** An archer. **b.** Archers considered as a group. **4a.** *Music* A rod having horsehair drawn tightly between its two raised ends, used in playing instruments of the violin and viol families. **b.** A stroke made by this rod. **5.** A knot usu. having two loops and two ends; a bowknot. **6a.** A frame for eyeglass lenses. **b.** The part of such a frame passing over the ear. **7.** A rainbow. **8.** An oxbow. ❖ *v.* **bowed, bow•ing, bows** —*tr.* **1.** To bend (something) into the shape of a bow. **2.** *Music* To play (a stringed instrument) with a bow. —*intr.* **1.** To bend into a curve or bow. **2.** *Music* To play a stringed instrument with a bow. [ME *bowe* < OE *boga.*]

Bow (bō), **Clara** 1905–65. Amer. actress known for silent films such as *It* (1927).

bow compass (bō) *n.* A drawing compass with legs that are connected by an adjustable metal spring band.

bow•da•cious (bō′dā′shəs) *adj. & adv. Southern & South Midland US* Variant of **bodacious.**

Bow•ditch (bou′dĭch), **Nathaniel** 1773–1838. Amer. mathematician and astronomer noted for his works on navigation.

bowd•ler•ize (bōd′lə-rīz′, boud′-) *tr.v.* **-ized, -iz•ing, -iz•es** I

bouzouki

To expurgate (a book, for example) prudishly. **2.** To modify, as by shortening or simplifying or by skewing content. [After Thomas *Bowdler* (1754–1825), who expurgated Shakespeare.] **—bowd′ler•ism** *n.* **—bowd′ler•i•za′tion** (-lər-ĭ-zā′shən) *n.* **—bowd′ler•iz′er** *n.*

bow•el (bou′əl, boul) *n.* **1a.** The intestine. Often used in the plural. **b.** A part or division of the intestine. **2. bowels** The interior of something. **3. bowels** *Archaic* The seat of pity or the gentler emotions. [ME < OFr. *boel* < Lat. *botellus*, small intestine, dim. of *botulus*, sausage.]

Bow•ell (bō′əl), Sir **Mackenzie** 1823–1917. British-born Canadian politician who served as prime minister (1894–96).

bowel movement *n.* **1.** The discharge of waste matter from the large intestine; defecation. **2.** The waste matter discharged from the large intestine; feces.

bow•er[1] (bou′ər) *n.* **1.** A shaded leafy recess; an arbor. **2.** A woman's private room in a medieval castle; a boudoir. **3.** A rustic cottage; a country retreat. ❖ *tr.v.* **-ered, -er•ing, -ers** To enclose in or as if in a bower; embower. [ME *bour*, a dwelling < OE *būr*. See **bheuə-** in App.] **—bow′er•y** *adj.*

bow•er[2] (bou′ər) *n. Nautical* An anchor carried at the bow.

bow•er•bird (bou′ər-bûrd′) *n.* Any of various birds of the family Ptilonorhynchidae of Australia and New Guinea, the males of which build large elaborate structures.

Bow•er•y (bou′ə-rē, bou′rē) A section of lower Manhattan in New York City. The street that gives the area its name was once the road to Peter Stuyvesant's *bouwerij*, or farm.

bow•fin (bō′fĭn′) *n.* A primitive bony freshwater fish *(Amia calva)* of central and eastern North America, with a long spineless dorsal fin.

bow•front (bō′frŭnt′) *adj.* **1.** Having an outward-curving front. **2.** Designed with a bow window in front.

bow•head (bō′hĕd′) *n.* A whalebone whale *(Balaena mysticetus)* of Arctic seas, having a large head and an arched upper jaw.

Bow•ie (bo͞o′ē, bō′ē), **James** 1796–1836. Amer.-born Mexican colonist who died during the defense of the Alamo.

bow•ie knife (bō′ē, bo͞o′ē) *n.* A single-edged steel hunting knife, about 15 inches (38 centimeters) in length, having a hilt and a crosspiece. [After James BOWIE.]

bow•knot (bō′nŏt′) *n.* A knot with large decorative loops.

bowl[1] (bōl) *n.* **1a.** A wide hemispherical vessel for holding food or fluids. **b.** The contents of such a vessel. **2.** A drinking goblet. **3.** A bowl-shaped part, as of a spoon or pipe. **4a.** A bowl-shaped topographic depression. **b.** A bowl-shaped stadium or outdoor theater. **5.** *Football* Any of various postseason games played between specially selected teams. [ME *bowle* < OE *bolla*.]

bowl[2] (bōl) *n.* **1.** A large wooden ball weighted or slightly flattened so as to roll with a bias. **2.** A roll or throw of the ball, as in bowling. **3. bowls** *(used with a sing. verb)* See **lawn bowling. 4.** A revolving cylinder or drum in a machine. ❖ *v.* **bowled, bowl•ing, bowls** *—intr.* **1a.** To participate in a game of bowling. **b.** To throw or roll a ball in bowling. **c.** To hurl a cricket ball toward the batsman. **2.** To move quickly and smoothly, esp. by rolling. *—tr.* **1.** To throw or roll (a ball). **2.** To achieve (a score) or complete (a game, for example) in bowling. **3.** To move quickly and smoothly by or as if by rolling. ***—phrasal verbs:* bowl out** To retire (a batsman in cricket) with a bowled ball that knocks the bails off the wicket. **bowl over 1.** To take by surprise. **2.** To make a powerful impression on; overwhelm. [ME *boule* < OFr. < Lat. *bulla*, round object.]

bowl•der (bōl′dər) *n.* Variant of **boulder.**

bow•leg (bō′lĕg′) *n.* **1.** A leg having an outward curvature in the knee region. **2.** The condition of such a curvature.

bow•leg•ged (bō′lĕg′ĭd, -lĕgd′) *adj.* Having bowlegs.

bowl•er[1] (bō′lər) *n.* One that bowls, as in bowling.

bowl•er[2] (bō′lər) *n.* A derby hat. [Prob. < BOWL[2].]

bow•line (bō′lĭn, -līn′) *n. Nautical* A rope attached to the weather leech of a square sail to hold the leech forward when sailing close-hauled. [ME *bouline*, prob. < M Dan. *bovline* or MLGer. *bōlīne*, both < MLGer. *bōch līne* : *bōch*, bow + *līne*, line (< Lat. *līnea*; see LINE[1]).]

bowl•ing (bō′lĭng) *n.* **1a.** A game played by rolling a ball down a wooden alley in order to knock down ten pins. **b.** A similar game, such as duckpins or ninepins. **2.** Lawn bowling. **3.** The playing of one of these games.

bowling alley *n.* **1.** A level wooden lane used in bowling. **2.** A building or room containing lanes for bowling.

bowling green *n.* A level grassy area for lawn bowling.

bow•man[1] (bō′mən) *n.* An archer.

bow•man[2] (bou′mən) *n.* A person who oars, rows, or paddles at the bow of a boat.

Bow•man's capsule (bō′mənz) *n.* A double-walled, cup-shaped structure around the glomerulus of each nephron of the kidney that filters out wastes, excess salts, and water. [After Sir William *Bowman* (1816–92), British surgeon.]

bow pen (bō) *n.* A bow compass with a pen at one leg end.

bow saw (bō) *n.* A slender-bladed saw with a narrow handle at each end curved outward like an archer's bow.

bowse (bouz) *v.* Variant of **bouse.**

bow•shot (bō′shŏt′) *n.* The distance of an arrow shot.

bow•sprit (bou′sprĭt′, bō′-) *n.* A spar, extending forward from the stem of a ship, to which the stays of the foremast are fastened. [ME *bouspret*, poss. < MLGer. *bōchsprēt* : *bōch*, bow + *sprēt*, sprit.]

bow•string (bō′strĭng′) *n.* The cord attached to both ends of an archer's bow.

bowstring hemp *n.* **1.** Any of several tropical African and Asian perennial plants of the genus *Sansevieria*, having thick swordlike leaves. **2.** The fibers of any of these plants, used for bowstrings, cordage, mats, and nets.

bow tie (bō) *n.* A short necktie fashioned into a bowknot close to the throat.

bow window (bō) *n.* A bay window built in a curve.

bow-wow or **bow•wow** (bou′wou′) *n.* **1.** The bark of a dog. **2.** *Informal* A dog. [Imit.]

bow•yer (bō′yər) *n.* **1.** One who makes or sells bows for archery. **2.** *Archaic* An archer.

box[1] (bŏks) *n.* **1a.** A container typically constructed with four sides perpendicular to the base and often having a lid or cover. **b.** The amount or quantity that such a container can hold. **2.** A square or rectangle: *Draw a box around your answer.* **3a.** A compartment in a place of entertainment, such as a theater or stadium, for the accommodation of a small group. **b.** An area of a public place, such as a courtroom or stadium, marked off for a specific function: *a jury box.* **4.** A small structure serving as a shelter: *a sentry box.* **5.** *Chiefly British* A small country house used as a sporting lodge: *a shooting box.* **6.** A box stall. **7.** The raised seat for the driver of a coach or carriage. **8.** *Baseball* One of various areas on a diamond marked by lines designating where the batter, catcher, or other team members may stand. **9.** *Sports* A penalty box. **10.** *Printing* Featured printed matter enclosed by borders and placed within or between text columns. **11.** A hollow made in the side of a tree for the collection of sap. **12.** A post office box. **13a.** An insulating, enclosing, or protective casing or part in a machine. **b.** A signaling device enclosed in a casing: *an alarm box.* **14a.** *Informal* A television. **b.** A very large portable radio. **15.** *Chiefly British* A gift or gratuity, esp. one given at Christmas. **16.** An awkward or perplexing situation; a predicament. **17.** *Vulgar Slang* The vulva and the vagina. ❖ *tr.v.* **boxed, box•ing, box•es 1.** To pack in a box. **2.** To confine or enclose in or as if in a box. **3.** *Sports* To block (a competitor or opponent) from advancing and esp. from getting a rebound in basketball. **4.** To cut a hole in (a tree) for the collection of sap. **5.** To blend (paint) by pouring alternately between two containers. **6.** To change the shape of (a structure) by applying lath and plaster or boarding. ***—idiom:* box the compass 1.** To name the 32 points of the compass in proper order. **2.** To make a complete revolution or reversal. [ME < OE < LLat. *buxis* < Gk. *puxis* < *puxos*, box tree.]

box[2] (bŏks) *n.* A slap or blow with the hand or fist. ❖ *v.* **boxed, box•ing, box•es** *—tr.* **1.** To hit with the hand or fist. **2.** *Sports* To take part in a boxing match with. *—intr.* To fight with the fists or in a boxing match. [ME.]

box[3] (bŏks) *n., pl.* **box** or **box•es 1a.** Any of several evergreen shrubs or trees of the genus *Buxus*, esp. *B. sempervirens*, having opposite leathery leaves and widely grown as a hedge plant. **b.** The hard yellow wood of these plants. **2.** Any of several other shrubs or trees with similar foliage or timber. [ME < OE < Lat. *buxus* < Gk. *puxos*.]

box•board (bŏks′bôrd′, -bōrd′) *n.* A firm cardboard used for making boxes.

box camera *n.* A simple camera shaped like a box and usu. having a fixed focus and a single shutter speed.

box•car (bŏks′kär′) *n.* **1.** A fully enclosed railroad car, typically having sliding side doors and used for freight. **2. boxcars** *Games* A pair of sixes on the first throw in craps.

box coat *n.* **1.** A coat designed to hang loosely from the shoulders. **2.** A heavy overcoat formerly worn by coachmen. [BOX[1] + COAT.]

box elder *n.* A North American maple tree *(Acer negundo)* having pinnately compound leaves with lobed leaflets.

box•er[1] (bŏk′sər) *n.* **1.** One who boxes as a sport. **2. boxers** Boxer shorts.

box•er[2] (bŏk′sər) *n.* One that packs items in boxes.

box•er[3] (bŏk′sər) *n.* A medium-sized, short-haired dog of a breed developed in Germany, having a brownish coat and a short square-jawed muzzle. [Ger. < E. BOXER[1].]

Boxer *n.* A member of a secret society in China that unsuccessfully attempted in 1900 to drive foreigners from the country by violence and to force Chinese Christians to renounce their religion. [Approximate transl. of Chin. (Mandarin) *(yìhé) quán*, (righteous harmonious) fists, name of a secret political organization, alteration of *yìhétuán*, righteous harmonious society.]

boxer shorts *pl.n.* Men's full-cut undershorts.

box•fish (bŏks′fĭsh′) *n., pl.* **boxfish** or **-fish•es** See **trunkfish.**

box•haul (bŏks′hôl′) *tr.v.* **-hauled, -haul•ing, -hauls** *Nautical* To turn (a square-rigged ship) about on the heel by bracing the sails aback. [BOX[1], to confine, reverse + HAUL.]

box•ing[1] (bŏk′sĭng) *n.* **1.** Material used for boxes. **2.** A boxlike covering or enclosure. **3.** The act of enclosing in a box.

box•ing[2] (bŏk′sĭng) *n.* The act, activity, or sport of fighting with the fists.

Boxing Day *n.* The first weekday after Christmas, celebrated as a holiday in parts of the British Commonwealth, when Christmas

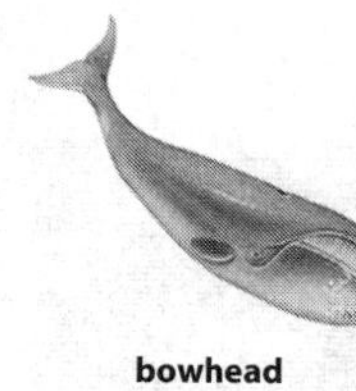

bowhead
bowhead whale
Balaena mysticetus

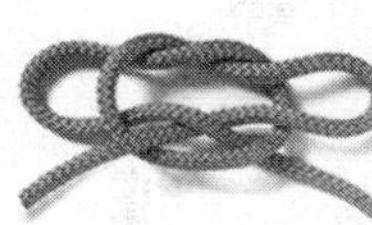

bowknot

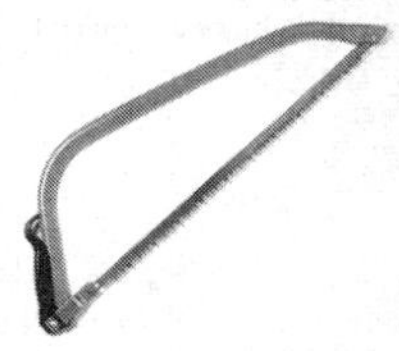

bow saw

ă	pat	oi	boy
ā	pay	ou	out
âr	care	o͝o	took
ä	father	o͞o	boot
ĕ	pet	ŭ	cut
ē	be	ûr	urge
ĭ	pit	th	thin
ī	pie	*th*	this
îr	pier	hw	which
ŏ	pot	zh	vision
ō	toe	ə	about, item
ô	paw		

Stress marks:
′ (primary);
′ (secondary), as in
lexicon (lĕk′sĭ-kŏn′)

gifts are given to service workers.

boxing glove *n.* A heavily padded leather mitten worn for boxing.

box kite *n.* A tailless kite formed in the shape of open-ended boxes connected by shafts spanning an interval of open space.

box lunch *n.* An individually portioned lunch in a small box.

box office *n.* **1.** A booth, as in a theater, where tickets are sold. **2a.** The drawing power of a theatrical entertainment or of a performer. **b.** A factor influencing this power. **3.** Total attendance or receipts for an entertainment. [Orig. an office for the booking of boxes in a theater.] —**box′-of′fice** (bŏks′ô′fĭs, -ŏf′ĭs) *adj.*

box pleat *n.* A double pleat with two upper folds facing in opposite directions and two under folds pressed toward each other.

box score *n.* A tabular printed summary of a game, esp. in baseball, recording individual performance.

box seat *n.* **1.** A seat in a box at a public place of entertainment, such as a theater or stadium. **2.** A storage box on a coach, the lid of which serves as a seat for the driver.

box social *n.* A fund-raising event in which donated box lunches are auctioned off.

box spring *n.* A bedspring consisting of a cloth-covered frame containing rows of coil springs.

box stall *n.* A large enclosed stall for a single animal.

box·thorn (bŏks′thôrn′) *n.* See **matrimony vine.**

box turtle *n.* Any of several North American land turtles of the genus *Terrapene,* having a hinged plastron that pulls up against the carapace, completely closing the shell.

box·wood (bŏks′wo͝od′) *n.* **1.** The box plant. **2.** Its wood.

box·y (bŏk′sē) *adj.* **-i·er, -i·est** Resembling a box, esp. in simplicity or rectangularity. —**box′i·ness** *n.*

boy (boi) *n.* **1.** A male child. **2.** An immature or inexperienced man, esp. a young man. **3.** A son. **4.** *Informal* A grown man; a fellow. **5.** A male who comes from or belongs to a particular place: *a city boy.* **6.** *Offensive* A male servant, such as a valet. ❖ *interj.* Used to express mild astonishment, elation, or disgust: *Oh boy!* [ME *boi,* poss. < OFr. *embuié,* servant, p. part. of *embuier,* to fetter.] —**boy′hood′** *n.*

bo·yar (bō-yär′, boi′ər) *n.* A member of a class of higher Russian nobility that until the time of Peter I headed the civil and military administration. [< *boiaren* < Russ. *boyarin* < ORuss. *boljarin* < Turkic *baylar,* pl. of *bay,* rich; akin to Turk. *bay,* rich, gentleman.]

boy·cott (boi′kŏt′) *tr.v.* **-cott·ed, -cott·ing, -cotts** To act together in abstaining from using, buying, or dealing with as an expression of protest or disfavor or as a means of coercion. ❖ *n.* The act or an instance of boycotting. [After Charles C. *Boycott* (1832–97), English land agent in Ireland.] —**boy′cott′er** *n.*

WORD HISTORY Charles C. Boycott seems to have become a household word because of his strong sense of duty to his employer. An Englishman and former British soldier, Boycott was the estate agent of the Earl of Erne in County Mayo, Ireland. The earl was one of the absentee landowners who as a group held most of the land in Ireland. Boycott was chosen in the fall of 1880 to be the test case for a new policy advocated by Charles Parnell, an Irish politician who wanted land reform. Parnell urged that any landlord who would not charge lower rents or any tenant who took over the farm of an evicted tenant should be given the complete cold shoulder. Boycott, a former British soldier, refused to charge lower rents and ejected his tenants. Boycott and his family found themselves without servants, farmhands, service in stores, or mail delivery. Boycott's name was quickly adopted as the term for this treatment, not just in English but in French, Dutch, German, and Russian as well.

Boyd Orr (boid′ ôr′, ōr′), Lord **John** 1880–1971. British nutritionist who won the 1949 Nobel Peace Prize for his efforts to alleviate world hunger.

boy·friend (boi′frĕnd′) *n.* **1.** A favored male companion or sweetheart. **2.** A male friend.

boy·ish (boi′ĭsh) *adj.* Characteristic of or befitting a boy: *boyish charm.* —**boy′ish·ly** *adv.* —**boy′ish·ness** *n.*

Boyle (boil), **Robert** 1627–91. Irish-born British physicist and chemist who formulated Boyle's law (1622).

Boyle's law (boilz) *n.* The principle that at a constant temperature the volume of a confined ideal gas varies inversely with its pressure. [After Robert BOYLE.]

Boyne (boin) A river of E Ireland flowing c. 113 km (70 mi) to the Irish Sea; site of the Battle of the Boyne (1690).

Boy Scout *n.* A member of a worldwide organization of young men and boys, founded in England in 1908, for character development and citizenship training.

boy·sen·ber·ry (boi′zən-bĕr′ē) *n.* **1.** A prickly bramble derived from a western North American blackberry (*Rubus ursinus*). **2.** The edible dark red to nearly black fruit of this plant. [After Rudolph *Boysen* (died 1950), American botanist.]

boy toy *n. Slang* A young man who is the lover of an often older, more prosperous person.

boy wonder *n.* A very talented, accomplished young man.

Boz·ca·a·da (bŏz′jä-ä-dä′) An island of Turkey in the NE Aegean Sea S of the Dardanelles; traditional site of a Greek naval station during the Trojan War.

brace
top: orthodontic braces
bottom: brace and drill bit

bracer²

Boze·man (bōz′mən) A city of SW MT ESE of Butte; settled in the 1860s. Pop. 27,509.

bo·zo (bō′zō) *n., pl.* **-zos** *Slang* **1.** A fellow; a guy. **2.** A dunce; a fool. [?]

bp *abbr.* boiling point

BP *abbr.* **1.** Bachelor of Pharmacy **2.** Bachelor of Philosophy **3.** basis point **4.** before present **5.** or **B/P** bills payable **6.** blood pressure

bp. *abbr.* birthplace

B particle *n.* Either of two subatomic particles in the meson family, one neutral and one positively charged, having masses 10,331 times that of an electron and average lifetimes of 1.6×10^{-12} seconds.

bpd *abbr.* barrels per day

BPd *abbr.* Bachelor of Pedagogy

BPE *abbr.* Bachelor of Physical Education

BPh or **BPhil** *abbr.* Bachelor of Philosophy

B picture *n.* A movie produced on a low budget, originally made to accompany the main feature in a double billing.

bpl. *abbr.* birthplace

bpm *abbr. Music* beats per minute

BPOE *abbr.* Benevolent and Protective Order of Elks

bps *abbr. Computer Science* bits per second

Bq *abbr.* becquerel

Br The symbol for the element **bromine.**

BR *abbr.* **1.** bedroom **2.** or **B/R** bills receivable

br. *abbr. Law* brief

Br. *abbr.* **1a.** Britain **b.** British **2.** *Ecclesiastical* brother (title)

bra (brä) *n.* A brassiere.

Bra·bant (brə-bănt′, -bänt′, brä′bənt, -bänt′) A region and former duchy of the Netherlands now divided between the S Netherlands and N-central Belgium.

brace (brās) *n.* **1.** A device that holds or fastens two or more parts together or in place; a clamp. **2.** A device, such as a supporting beam in a building, that steadies or holds something else erect. **3.** **braces** *Chiefly British* Suspenders. **4.** An orthopedic appliance used to support or align a body part. **5.** A dental appliance constructed of bands and wires that is fixed to the teeth to correct irregular alignment. Often used in the plural. **6.** An extremely stiff, erect posture. **7.** A cause or source of renewed physical or spiritual vigor. **8.** A protective pad strapped to the bow arm of an archer. **9.** *Nautical* A rope by which a yard is swung and secured on a square-rigged ship. **10.** A tool with an adjustable aperture for securing and turning a bit. **11.** *Music* A leather loop that slides to change the tension on the cord of a drum. **12.** *Music* **a.** A vertical line, usu. accompanied by the symbol {, connecting two or more staffs. **b.** A set of staffs connected in this way. **13.** A symbol, { or }, enclosing lines of text, listed items, or mathematical expressions that are considered as a unit. **14.** *Mathematics* Either of a pair of symbols, { }, used to indicate aggregation or to clarify the grouping of quantities when parentheses and square brackets have already been used. **15.** *pl.* **brace** A pair of like things: *three brace of partridges.* ❖ *v.* **braced, brac·ing, brac·es** —*tr.* **1.** To furnish with a brace. **2.** To support or hold steady with or as if with a brace; reinforce. **3.** To prepare or position for impact or danger: *braced themselves for a confrontation.* **4.** To confront with questions or requests. **5.** To increase the tension of. **6.** To invigorate; stimulate. **7.** *Nautical* To turn (the yards of a ship) by the braces. —*intr.* To get ready; make preparations. —*phrasal verb:* **brace up** To summon one's strength or endurance. [ME < OFr., the two arms < VLat. **bracia* < Lat. *brācchia,* pl. of *brācchium,* arm. See BRACHIUM.]

brace·let (brās′lĭt) *n.* **1.** An ornamental band or chain encircling the wrist or arm. **2.** Something, such as a handcuff, that resembles a wrist ornament. [ME < OFr., dim. of *bracel,* armlet < Lat. *brācchiāle* < *brācchium,* arm. See BRACE.] —**brace′let·ed** *adj.*

brac·er¹ (brā′sər) *n.* **1.** One that braces, esp. one that supports. **2.** *Informal* A stimulating, usu. alcoholic drink.

brac·er² (brā′sər) *n.* An arm or wrist guard worn by archers and fencers. [ME, prob. < AN < OFr. *braceure < bras,* arm < Lat. *brācchium.* See BRACE.]

bra·ce·ro (brə-sâr′ō) *n., pl.* **-ros** A Mexican laborer permitted to work in the United States for a limited period, esp. in agriculture. [Sp., laborer < *brazo,* arm < Lat. *brācchium.* See BRACHIUM.]

bra·chi·al (brā′kē-əl, brăk′ē-) *adj.* Of, relating to, or resembling the arm or a similar or homologous part. [< Lat. *brācchiālis* < *brācchium,* arm. See BRACHIUM.]

bra·chi·ate (brā′kē-ĭt, -āt′, brăk′ē-) *adj. Zoology* Having arms or armlike appendages. ❖ *intr.v.* (-āt′) **-at·ed, -at·ing, -ates** To move by swinging with the arms from one hold to another, as certain apes do. [Lat. *brācchiātus < brācchium,* arm. See BRACHIUM.] —**bra′chi·a′tion** *n.*

bra·chi·o·pod (brā′kē-ə-pŏd′, brăk′ē-) *n.* Any of various marine invertebrates of the phylum Brachiopoda, having bivalve dorsal and ventral shells enclosing a pair of armlike structures that sweep food particles into the mouth. [< NLat. *Brāchiopoda,* phylum name : Lat. *brācchium,* arm; see BRACHIUM + NLat. *-poda,* -pod.] —**brach′i·o′pod′** *adj.*

bra·chi·o·saur (brā′kē-ə-sôr′, brăk′ē-) or **bra·chi·o·sau·rus** (brā′kē-ə-sôr′əs, brăk′ē-) *n.* Any of various massive, herbivorous sauropod dinosaurs of the genus *Brachiosaurus* of the Jurassic and Cretaceous Periods, having forelegs that were longer than the hind legs. [NLat. *Brāchiosaurus*, genus name : Lat. *brācchium*, arm; see BRACHIUM + Gk. *sauros*, lizard.]

bra·chi·um (brā′kē-əm, brăk′ē-) *n., pl.* **bra·chi·a** (brā′kē-ə, brăk′ē-ə) **1.** The part of the upper arm or forelimb extending from the shoulder to the elbow. **2.** An arm or a homologous anatomical structure, such as a flipper or wing. **3.** The part of a limb or process corresponding to an arm. [Lat. *brācchium*, arm < Gk. *brakhīōn*, upper arm.]

brachy– *pref.* Short: *brachycephalic*. [Gk. *brakhu-* < *brakhus*, short.]

brach·y·ce·phal·ic (brăk′ĭ-sə-făl′ĭk) also **brach·y·ceph·a·lous** (-sĕf′ə-ləs) *adj.* Having a short, broad head with a cephalic index over 80. —**brach′y·ceph·a·ly** (-sĕf′ə-lē), **brach′y·ceph′a·lism** *n.*

bra·chyl·o·gy (brā-kĭl′ə-jē) *n., pl.* **-gies 1.** Brevity of speech; conciseness. **2.** A shortened expression. [Med.Lat. *brachylogia* < Gk. *brakhulogiā* : *brakhu-*, brachy- + *logos*, speech; see –LOGY.]

bra·chyp·ter·ous (brā-kĭp′tər-əs) *adj.* Having very short or rudimentary wings, as certain insects. [< Gk. *brakhupteros* : *brakhu-*, brachy- + *pteron*, wing; see –PTER.] —**bra·chyp′ter·ism** (-tə-rĭz′əm) *n.*

brach·y·u·ran (brăk′ē-yŏŏr′ən) also **brach·y·u·ral** (-yŏŏr′əl) or **brach·y·u·rous** (-yŏŏr′əs) *adj.* Of or belonging to the Brachyura, a group of crustaceans including the true crabs, characterized by a short abdomen concealed under the cephalothorax. ❖ *n.* A member of the Brachyura. [< NLat. *Brachyūra*, suborder name : Gk. *brakhu-*, brachy- + Gk. *ourā*, tail; see –UROUS.]

brac·ing (brā′sĭng) *adj.* Invigorating or refreshing; strengthening: *a bracing tonic.* ❖ *n.* **1.** A support; a brace. **2.** Braces considered as a group. —**brac′ing·ly** *adv.*

bra·ci·o·la (brä′chē-ō′lä, brä-chō′-) or **bra·ci·o·le** (-lä′, -lē′) *n.* A thin slice of meat, usu. wrapped around a stuffing and cooked with wine. [Ital., prob. < dialectal *brasola* < *brasa*, glowing ember, of Gmc. orig.]

brack·en (brăk′ən) *n.* **1.** A widespread fern (*Pteridium aquilinum*) having large, triangular, pinnately compound fronds. **2.** An area overgrown with this fern. [ME *braken*, prob. of Scand. orig. See **bhreg-** in App.]

brack·et (brăk′ĭt) *n.* **1a.** A rigid structure in the shape of an L, used to support a shelf or other weight. **b.** A shelf or shelves supported by such structures. **2.** *Architecture* A right-angled, decorative or weight-bearing structural unit set flush beneath a projecting surface, such as eaves or a bay window. **3.** A wall fixture for gas or electricity. **4a.** A square bracket. **b.** An angle bracket. **c.** *Mathematics* See **brace** 14. **5.** *Chiefly British* One of a pair of parentheses. **6.** A classification or grouping, such as a category of incomes sharing the same tax rate. **7a.** The distance between two impacting artillery shells, the first aimed beyond a target and the second aimed short of it, used to determine range. **b.** The shells fired in such a manner. ❖ *tr.v.* **-et·ed, -et·ing, -ets 1.** To furnish or support with a bracket or brackets. **2.** To place within or as if within brackets. **3.** To classify or group together. **4.** To include or exclude by establishing specific boundaries. **5.** To fire beyond and short of (a target) in order to determine artillery range. [Poss. Fr. *braguette*, codpiece, dim. of *brague*, breeches < O Provençal *braga* < Lat. *brāca* < Gaulish *brāca*, leg covering.]

bracket creep *n. Informal* A shift of personal income into a higher tax bracket when the taxable income increases.

bracket fungus *n.* Any of various fungi that form shelflike growths on tree trunks and wood structures.

brack·ish (brăk′ĭsh) *adj.* **1.** Having a somewhat salty taste, esp. from containing seawater. **2.** Distasteful; unpalatable: *brackish gruel.* [< Du. *brak*.] —**brack′ish·ness** *n.*

bract (brăkt) *n.* A leaflike or scalelike plant part, usu. small, sometimes brightly colored, and located just below a flower, a flower stalk, or an inflorescence. [< Lat. *bractea*, gold leaf, perh. < Gk. *brakhein*, to rattle.] —**brac′te·al** (brăk′tē-əl) *adj.*

brac·te·ate (brăk′tē-ĭt, -āt′) *adj.* Bearing bracts. [NLat. *bracteātus* < Lat. *bractea*, gold leaf. See BRACT.]

brac·te·o·late (brăk′tē-ə-lĭt, -lāt′) *adj.* Bearing bracteoles.

brac·te·ole (brăk′tē-ōl′) *n.* A small bract. [Lat. *bracteola*, gold leaf, dim. of *bractea*. See BRACT.]

brad (brăd) *n.* A thin wire nail with a small head or a slight side projection instead of a head. [ME < ON *broddr*, spike.] —**brad** *v.*

brad·awl (brăd′ôl′) *n.* An awl with a beveled tip, used to make holes in wood for brads or screws.

Brad·bur·y (brăd′bĕr′ē, -bə-rē), **Ray Douglas** b. 1920. Amer. writer whose works include *The Martian Chronicles* (1950).

Brad·dock (brăd′ək), **Edward** 1695–1755. British general in America during the French and Indian War.

Brad·ford (brăd′fərd) A borough of N-central England W of Leeds. Pop. 479,996.

Bradford, Roark 1896–1948. Amer. writer whose works, including *John Henry* (1931), reflect African-American folklore.

Bradford¹, William 1590–1657. English Puritan colonist in America; a signer of the Mayflower Compact and governor of Plymouth Plantation for 30 one-year terms.

Bradford², William 1663–1752. English-born Amer. colonial printer who produced the first American Book of Common Prayer (1710).

Brad·ley (brăd′lē), **Omar Nelson** 1893–1981. Amer. general who played a major part in the Allied victory in World War II.

Bradley, Thomas 1917–98. Amer. politician who became the first African-American mayor of Los Angeles in 1973.

Brad·street (brăd′strēt′), **Anne Dudley** 1612–72. English-born colonial poet who wrote several collections of verse, including *The Tenth Muse Lately Sprung Up in America* (1650).

Bra·dy (brā′dē), **James Buchanan** Known as "Diamond Jim." 1856–1917. Amer. financier and philanthropist known for his extravagant lifestyle.

Brady, Mathew B. 1823–96. Amer. pioneer photographer who was appointed official Union photographer of the Civil War in 1861.

brady– *pref.* Slow: *bradycardia*. [Gk. *bradu-* < *bradus*, slow.]

brad·y·car·di·a (brăd′ĭ-kär′dē-ə) *n.* Slowness of the heart rate, usu. fewer than 60 beats per minute in an adult human. [BRADY– + Gk. *kardiā*, heart; see CARDIA.] —**brad′y·car′dic** (-dĭk) *adj.*

brad·y·ki·nin (brăd′ĭ-kī′nĭn, -kĭn′ĭn) *n.* A polypeptide that forms from a blood plasma globulin and stimulates pain receptors, increases vasodilation, and causes contraction of smooth muscle. [BRADY– + Gk. *kīnein*, to move; see **kei-²** in App. + –IN.]

brae (brā) *n. Scots* A hillside; a slope. [ME *bra* < ON *brā*, eyebrow (unattested sense), eyelash.]

brag (brăg) *v.* **bragged, brag·ging, brags** —*intr.* To talk boastfully. —*tr.* To assert boastfully. ❖ *n.* **1.** A boast. **2.** Arrogant or boastful speech or manner. **3.** Something boasted of. **4.** A braggart. **5.** *Games* A card game similar to poker. ❖ *adj.* **brag·ger, brag·gest** Exceptionally fine. [ME *braggen* < *brag*, ostentatious.] —**brag′ger** *n.*

Bra·gan·za (brə-găn′zə) also **Bra·gan·ça** (-gän′sä) A dynasty of Portuguese rulers (1640–1910) who also controlled Brazil (1822–89).

Bragg (brăg), **Braxton** 1817–76. Amer. Confederate general in the Civil War who was defeated in the Chattanooga campaign (1863).

Bragg, Sir William Henry 1862–1942. British physicist who shared a 1915 Nobel Prize with his son Sir **William Lawrence Bragg** (1890–1971).

brag·ga·do·ci·o (brăg′ə-dō′sē-ō′, -shē-ō′, -shō) *n., pl.* **-os 1.** A braggart. **2.** Empty or pretentious bragging. [Alteration of *Braggadocchio*, the personification of vainglory in *The Faerie Queene* by Edmund Spenser < BRAG.]

brag·gart (brăg′ərt) *n.* One given to loud, empty boasting; a bragger. ❖ *adj.* Boastful. [Fr. *bragard* < *braguer*, to brag, perh. < ME *braggen*. See BRAG.]

Brahe (brä, brä′hē, brä′ə), **Tycho** 1546–1601. Danish astronomer whose astronomical observations formed the basis for Kepler's laws of planetary motion.

Brah·ma¹ (brä′mə) *n.* **1.** *Hinduism* **a.** The creator god, conceived chiefly as a member of the triad including also Vishnu and Shiva. **b.** Variant of **Brahman** 1. **2.** Variant of **Brahman** 3. [Skt. *brahmā* < *brahma*, prayer.]

Brah·ma² also **brah·ma** (brä′mə, brä′-) *n.* A large domestic fowl of a breed originating in Asia and having feathered legs and small wings and tail. [After BRAHMAPUTRA.]

Brah·man (brä′mən) *n.* **1.** also **Brah·ma** (-mə) *Hinduism* The single absolute being pervading the universe and found within the individual; atman. **2.** also **Brah·min** (-mĭn) *Hinduism* A member of the highest of the four major castes of traditional Indian society, responsible for officiating at religious rites and studying and teaching the Vedas. **3.** also **Brahma** or **Brahmin** One of a breed of domestic cattle developed in the southern United States from stock originating in India and having a hump between the shoulders and a pendulous dewlap. [Skt. *brahma*, *brahmaṇ-*. Senses 2 and 3, Skt. *brāhmaṇa-*, Brahmanic < *brahma*, *brahmaṇ-*. Brahman. See BRAHMA¹.] —**Brah·man′ic** (-măn′ĭk), **Brah·man′i·cal** *adj.*

Brah·ma·na (brä′mə-nə) *n.* Any of several ancient Hindu religious prose texts that relate the Vedas to sacrificial ceremonies. [Skt. *Brāhmaṇam* < neut. of *brāhmaṇa-*, brahminical. See BRAHMAN.]

Brah·man·ism (brä′mə-nĭz′əm) also **Brah·min·ism** (brä′mĭ-) *n. Hinduism* **1.** The religious practices and beliefs of ancient India as reflected in the Vedas. **2.** The social and religious system of orthodox Hindus, esp. of the Brahmins, based on a caste structure and various forms of pantheism. —**Brah′man·ist** *n.*

Brah·ma·pu·tra (brä′mə-pōō′trə) A river of S Asia rising in the Himalaya Mts. and flowing c. 2,896 km (1,800 mi) to the Ganges R. in central Bangladesh.

Brah·min (brä′mĭn) *n.* **1.** *Hinduism* Variant of **Brahman** 2. **2.** A member of a cultural and social elite: *a Boston Brahmin.* **3.** Variant of **Brahman** 3. [Prob. alteration of Skt. *brāhmaṇaḥ* < *brāhmaṇa-*, brahminic. See BRAHMAN.] —**Brah·min′ic** (-mĭn′ĭk), **Brah·min′i·cal** *adj.*

Brah·min·ism (brä′mə-nĭz′əm) *n.* **1.** The attitude or conduct of a social or cultural elite. **2.** *Hinduism* Variant of **Brahmanism**.

Brahms (brämz), **Johannes** 1833–97. German composer whose works blend classical tradition with romanticism. —**Brahms′i·an** *adj.*

braid (brād) *v.* **braid·ed, braid·ing, braids** —*tr.* **1a.** To interweave three or more lengths of: *braided the rags into a rope.* **b.** To

Mathew Brady

ă	pat	oi	boy
ā	pay	ou	out
âr	care	ŏŏ	took
ä	father	ōō	boot
ĕ	pet	ŭ	cut
ē	be	ûr	urge
ĭ	pit	th	thin
ī	pie	th	this
îr	pier	hw	which
ŏ	pot	zh	vision
ō	toe	ə	about,
ô	paw		item

Stress marks:
′ (primary);
′ (secondary), as in
lexicon (lĕk′sĭ-kŏn′)

create (something) by such interweaving: *braid a rug.* **c.** To style (the hair) by such interweaving. **2.** To decorate or edge (something) with a trim of interwoven strands. **3.** To fasten or decorate (hair) with a band or ribbon. —*intr.* To flow, twist, or wind as if interwoven. ❖ *n.* **1.** A braided segment or length, as of hair, fabric, or fiber. **2.** Ornamental cord or ribbon, used esp. for decorating fabrics. **3.** A ribbon or band used to fasten the hair. [ME *braiden* < OE *bregdan,* to weave.] —**braid′er** *n.*

braid·ed (brā′dĭd) *adj.* **1a.** Produced by or as if by braiding. **b.** Having braids. **2.** Decorated with braid. **3.** Flowing as if interwoven: *a braided stream.*

braid·ing (brā′dĭng) *n.* **1.** Braided embroidery or trim. **2.** Braids considered as a group.

brail (brāl) *Nautical n.* **1.** One of several small lines attached to the leech of a sail for drawing the sail in or up. **2.** A small net for drawing fish from a trap or a larger net into a boat. ❖ *tr.v.* **brailed, brail·ing, brails 1.** To gather in (a sail) with brails. **2.** To haul in (fish) with a brail. [ME *braile* < OFr. *brail,* belt < Med.Lat. *brācāle* < Lat. *brācae,* breeches. See BRACKET.]

Brā·i·la (brə-ē′lə) A city of SE Romania on the Danube R. near the Moldavian and Ukrainian borders. Pop. 236,344.

Braille or **braille** (brāl) *n.* A system of writing and printing for blind or visually impaired people, in which varied arrangements of raised dots representing letters and numerals are identified by touch. ❖ *tr.v.* **Brailled, Braill·ing, Brailles** or **brailled, braill·ing, brailles** To print or transliterate using this system. [After Louis BRAILLE.]

Braille, Louis 1809–52. French inventor of the Braille system of writing and printing (1829).

Braill·er or **braill·er** (brā′lər) *n.* A machine analogous to a typewriter, used for printing in Braille.

Braille·writ·er or **braille·writ·er** (brāl′rī′tər) *n.* See **Brailler.**

brain (brān) *n.* **1a.** The portion of the vertebrate central nervous system that is enclosed within the cranium, continuous with the spinal cord, and composed of gray matter and white matter. It regulates and controls many bodily activities and is the seat of consciousness, memory, and emotion. **b.** A functionally similar portion of the invertebrate nervous system. **2a.** Intellectual ability; mind: *a dull brain.* **b.** Intellectual power; intelligence. Often used in the plural. **3.** A highly intelligent person. **4.** The primary director or planner, as of an organization. Often used in the plural. **5.** The control center, as of a ship. ❖ *tr.v.* **brained, brain·ing, brains** *Slang* **1.** To smash in the skull of. **2.** To hit on the head. —*idioms:* **beat (one's brains (out)** *Informal* To exert or expend great mental effort. **on the brain** Obsessively in mind. **pick (someone's) brain (or brains)** To explore another's ideas through questioning. **rack (one's) brain** *Informal* To think long and hard. [ME < OE *brægen.*]

brain·case also **brain case** (brān′kās′) *n.* The part of the skull that encloses the brain; the cranium.

brain·child (brān′chīld′) *n.* An original idea or plan attributed to a person or group.

brain coral *n.* Any of several reef-building corals of the genus *Meandrina,* forming rounded colonies that resemble the convolutions of the human brain.

brain death *n.* Irreversible brain damage and loss of brain function, as evidenced by cessation of breathing and other vital reflexes, unresponsiveness to stimuli, absence of muscle activity, and a flat electroencephalogram for a specific length of time. —**brain′-dead′** (brān′dĕd′) *adj.*

brain drain *n.* The loss of intellectual and technical labor, esp. through emigration to more appealing countries. —**brain′drain′** (brān′drān′) *v.*

Braine (brān), **John** 1922–86. British writer noted for his novel *Room at the Top* (1957).

brained (brānd) *adj.* Having a brain. Often used in combination: *small-brained reptiles.*

brain fever *n.* Inflammation of the brain or meninges, as in encephalitis or meningitis.

brain·i·ac (brā′nē-ăk′) *n. Slang* A highly intelligent person. [Prob. < *Braniac,* a highly intelligent villain in DC Comics, blend of BRAIN and MANIAC.]

brain·less (brān′lĭs) *adj.* Unintelligent; stupid. —**brain′less·ly** *adv.* —**brain′less·ness** *n.*

brain·pan (brān′păn′) *n.* See **braincase.**

brain·pow·er (brān′pou′ər) *n.* **1.** Intellectual capacity. **2.** People of well-developed mental abilities.

brain·sick (brān′sĭk′) *adj.* Of, relating to, or induced by a mental disorder; insane or mad. —**brain′sick·ly** *adv.* —**brain′sick′ness** *n.*

brain stem or **brain·stem** (brān′stĕm′) *n.* The portion of the brain, consisting of the medulla oblongata, pons Varolii, and midbrain, that connects the spinal cord to the forebrain and cerebrum.

brain·storm (brān′stôrm′) *n.* **1.** A sudden clever plan or idea. **2.** A sudden, violent disturbance of the mind. ❖ *v.* **-stormed, -storm·ing, -storms** —*intr.* To engage in or organize shared problem solving. —*tr.* To produce or consider by brainstorming. —**brain′storm′er** *n.* —**brain′storm′ing** *n.*

brain·teas·er (brān′tē′zər) *n.* A mentally challenging problem or puzzle.

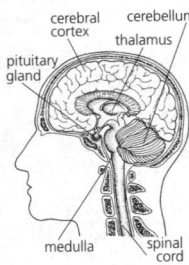

Braille
Braille alphabet and numerals

brain

brain coral

brain trust *n.* A group of experts who serve as unofficial advisers and policy planners, esp. in a government. —**brain truster** *n.*

brain·wash (brān′wŏsh′, -wôsh′) *tr.v.* **-washed, -wash·ing, -wash·es** To subject to brainwashing. ❖ *n.* The process or an instance of brainwashing.

brain·wash·ing (brān′wŏsh′ĭng, -wô′shĭng) *n.* **1.** Intensive, forcible indoctrination aimed at replacing a person's basic convictions with an alternative set of beliefs. **2.** The application of a concentrated means of persuasion in order to develop a specific belief or motivation. [Transl. of Chin. (Mandarin) *xĭ năo : xĭ,* to wash + *năo,* brain.]

brain wave *n.* **1.** A rhythmic fluctuation of electric potential between parts of the brain, as seen on an electroencephalogram. **2.** *Informal* A sudden inspiration.

brain·y (brā′nē) *adj.* **-i·er, -i·est** *Informal* Intelligent; smart. —**brain′i·ly** *adv.* —**brain′i·ness** *n.*

braise (brāz) *tr.v.* **braised, brais·ing, brais·es** To cook (meat or vegetables) by browning in fat, then simmering in a small quantity of liquid in a covered container. [Fr. *braiser* < *braise,* hot charcoal < OFr. *brese,* of Gmc. orig.]

brake¹ (brāk) *n.* **1.** A device for slowing or stopping motion, as of a vehicle, esp. by contact friction. **2.** Something that slows or stops action. ❖ *v.* **braked, brak·ing, brakes** —*tr.* To reduce the speed of with or as if with a brake. —*intr.* **1.** To operate or apply a brake. **2.** To be slowed or stopped by or as if by a brake. [Prob. *brake,* bridle, curb < MDu. or MLGer., nose ring, curb, flax brake; see BRAKE².]

brake² (brāk) *n.* **1.** A toothed device for crushing and beating flax or hemp. **2.** A heavy harrow for breaking clods of earth. **3.** An apparatus for kneading large amounts of dough. **4.** A machine for bending and folding sheet metal. ❖ *tr.v.* **braked, brak·ing, brakes 1.** To crush (flax or hemp) in a toothed device. **2.** To break up (clods of earth) with a harrow. [ME < MDu. < MLGer. See **bhreg-** in App.]

brake³ (brāk) *n.* A lever or handle on a machine such as a pump. [ME < OFr. *brac* < oblique form of *bras,* arm. See BRACER².]

brake⁴ (brāk) *n.* **1.** Any of various ferns of the genus *Pteris,* having pinnately compound leaves and including several popular houseplants. **2.** Any of certain other ferns, such as bracken. [ME, prob. back-formation < *braken.* See BRACKEN.]

brake⁵ (brāk) *n.* An area overgrown with dense brushwood, briers, and undergrowth; a thicket. [ME < MLGer. See **bhreg-** in App.]

brake⁶ (brāk) *n.* Variant of **break** 25. ❖ *v. Archaic* A past tense of **break.**

brake drum *n.* A metal cylinder to which pressure is applied by a braking mechanism in order to arrest rotation of the wheel or shaft to which the cylinder is attached.

brake horsepower *n.* The actual horsepower of an engine, usu. determined from the force exerted on a friction brake or dynamometer connected to the drive shaft.

brake lining *n.* The covering of a brake shoe.

brake·man (brāk′mən) *n.* One who operates, inspects, or repairs brakes, esp. on a train.

brake pad *n.* A flat block that presses against the disk of a disc brake.

brake shoe *n.* A curved metal block that presses against and arrests the rotation of a wheel or brake drum.

Bra·man·te (brə-män′tā, brä-män′tĕ), **Donato** 1444–1514. Italian architect who evolved the High Renaissance style.

bram·ble (brăm′bəl) *n.* **1.** A prickly shrub of the genus *Rubus,* including the blackberry and the raspberry. **2.** A prickly shrub or bush. [ME *brembel* < OE *bræmbel.*] —**bram′bly** *adj.*

bram·ble·ber·ry (brăm′bəl-bĕr′ē) *n.* The fruit of a bramble.

bram·bling (brăm′blĭng) *n.* A finch (*Fringilla montifringilla*) of northern Eurasia having black, white, and rust-brown plumage. [Prob. < OE **bræmbling : bræmbel,* bramble + *-ling,* one connected with; see -LING¹.]

Bramp·ton (brămp′tən) A city of S Ontario, Canada, a suburb of Toronto. Pop. 268,251.

bran (brăn) *n.* The outer layers of the grain of cereals, removed during the process of milling and used as a source of dietary fiber. [ME < OFr., of Celt. orig.] —**bran′ny** *adj.*

Bran (brăn) *n. Mythology* A gigantic Celtic god and ruler of Britain. [Welsh *Brân* < *brân,* raven.]

branch (brănch) *n.* **1a.** A secondary woody stem or limb growing from the trunk of a tree or shrub or from another secondary limb. **b.** A lateral division or subdivision of certain other plant parts, such as a root. **2.** Something that resembles a branch of a tree, as in form or function, as: **a.** A secondary outgrowth or subdivision of a main axis, such as the tine of a deer's antlers. **b.** *Anatomy* An offshoot or a division of the main portion of a structure, such as a nerve or blood vessel. **3.** A limited part of a larger or more complex system, esp.: **a.** An area of skill or knowledge that is related to but separate from other areas. **b.** A division of a business or other organization. **c.** A division of a family, categorized by descent from a particular ancestor. **d.** *Linguistics* A subdivision of a family of languages. **4a.** A tributary of a river. **b.** *Chiefly Southern US* See **creek** 1. See Regional Note at **run. c.** A divergent section of a river, esp. near the mouth. **5.** *Mathematics* A part of a curve that is separated, as by discontinuities. **6.** *Com-*

cerebral cortex · cerebellum · thalamus · pituitary gland · medulla · spinal cord

Joseph Brant
c. 1807 portrait by William
Berczy (1744–1813)

puter Science A sequence of program instructions to which the normal sequence of instructions relinquishes control, depending on the value of certain variables. ❖ v. **branched, branch•ing, branch•es** —intr. **1.** To put forth a branch or branches; spread by dividing. **2a.** To come forth as a branch or subdivision; develop or diverge from. **b.** To enlarge the scope of one's interests or activities: branch out into related fields. **3.** Computer Science To relinquish control to another set of instructions or another routine as a result of the presence of a branch. —tr. **1.** To separate (something) into or as if into branches. **2.** To embroider (something) with a design of foliage or flowers. [ME < OFr. branche < LLat. branca, paw, perh. of Celt. orig.] —**branch′less** adj. —**branch′y** adj.

bran•chi•a (brăng′kē-ə) n., pl. **-chi•ae** (-kē-ē) A gill or similar organ of respiration. [Lat. < Gk. brankhia, gills.] —**bran′chi•al** (-kē-əl) adj.

branchial arch n. See **gill arch.**

branchial cleft n. See **gill slit** 1.

branchial groove n. See **gill slit** 2.

bran•chi•o•pod (brăng′kē-ə-pŏd′) n. Any of various aquatic crustaceans of the subclass Branchiopoda, such as the fairy shrimp and water flea, characterized by a segmented body and flattened, leaflike thoracic appendages. [< NLat. Branchiopoda, subclass name : Lat. branchia, gills; see BRANCHIA + NLat. -poda, -pod; see -POD.] —**bran′chi•o•pod′, bran′chi•op′o•dan** (-ŏp′ə-dən), **bran′chi•op′a•dous** (-dəs) adj.

branch•let (brănch′lĭt) n. A small branch or the terminal or ultimate subdivision of a branch.

branch water n. **1.** Plain water, esp. when mixed with a liquor such as whiskey. **2.** Chiefly Southern US Water from a stream. [BRANCH, stream + WATER.]

Bran•cu•si (brän-ko̅o̅′zē, bräng-ko̅o̅sh′), **Constantin** 1876–1957. Romanian-born sculptor of abstract metal and stone sculptures of great simplicity.

brand (brănd) n. **1a.** A trademark or distinctive name identifying a product or a manufacturer. **b.** A product line so identified. **c.** A distinctive category; a particular kind. **2.** A mark indicating ownership, burned on the hide of an animal with a hot iron. **3.** A mark burned into the flesh of criminals. **4.** A mark of disgrace or notoriety; a stigma. **5.** A branding iron. **6.** A piece of burning or charred wood. **7.** A sword. ❖ tr.v. **brand•ed, brand•ing, brands 1.** To mark with or as if with a hot iron. **2a.** To mark to show ownership. **b.** To provide with or publicize using a brand name. **3.** To mark with disgrace or infamy; stigmatize. **4.** To impress firmly; fix ineradicably. [ME, torch < OE. See gʷher- in App.] —**brand′er** n.

Bran•deis (brăn′dīs′, -dīz′), **Louis Dembitz** 1856–1941. Amer. jurist; associate justice of the US Supreme Court (1916–39).

Bran•den•burg (brăn′dən-bûrg′, brän′dən-bo̅o̅rk′) **1.** A historical region and former duchy of N-central Germany now divided between Poland and Germany. **2.** A city of NE Germany on the Havel R. WSW of Berlin. Pop. 95,133.

brand•ing iron (brăn′dĭng) n. An iron that is heated and used for indicating ownership.

bran•dish (brăn′dĭsh) tr.v. **-dished, -dish•ing, -dish•es 1.** To wave or flourish (a weapon, for example) menacingly. **2.** To display ostentatiously. ❖ n. A menacing or defiant wave or flourish. [ME brandissen < OFr. brandir, brandiss- < brand, sword, of Gmc. orig. See gʷher- in App.] —**bran′dish•er** n.

brand•ling (brănd′lĭng) n. A common reddish-brown earthworm (Eisenia foetida) often used as fish bait. [BRAND (< its markings) + -LING¹.]

brand name n. **1.** See **trade name** 1. **2.** A commodity, service, or process having a trade name. —**brand′-name′** (brănd′nām′) adj.

brand-new (brănd′no̅o̅′, -nyo̅o̅′) adj. Being in a fresh and unused condition; completely new.

Bran•do (brăn′dō), **Marlon** b. 1924. Amer. actor whose films include A Streetcar Named Desire (1951).

Brandt (brănt, bränt), **Willy** 1913–92. German political leader who served as chancellor of West Germany (1969–74) and won the 1971 Nobel Peace Prize.

bran•dy (brăn′dē) n., pl. **-dies** An alcoholic liquor distilled from wine or fermented fruit juice. ❖ tr.v. **-died, -dy•ing, -dies** To preserve, flavor, or mix with brandy. [Short for brandy-wine < Du. brandewijn : brandende, pr. part. of branden, to burn; see gʷher- in App. + wijn, wine; see WINE.]

Bran•dy•wine (brăn′dē-wīn′) A creek of SE PA and N DE; site of a major defeat of the Continental Army (1777) in the American Revolution.

brank (brăngk) n. A device consisting of a metal frame for the head and a bit to restrain the tongue, formerly used to punish scolds. Often used in the plural. [Poss. < Du. branken, legs (of a compass, scissors, etc.), pl. of branke, branch < LLat. branca, paw. See BRANCH.]

bran•ni•gan (brăn′ĭ-gən) n. **1.** A noisy or confused quarrel. **2.** A drinking spree. [Prob. < the name Brannigan.]

brant (brănt) n., pl. **brant** or **brants** Any of several small dark wild geese of the genus Branta that breed in Arctic regions, esp. B. bernicla having a black neck and head. [Variant of brent(-goose), poss. < ME brende, brindled. See BRINDLED.]

Brant, Joseph 1742–1807. Mohawk leader who supported the British in the French and Indian War and the American Revolution.

Brant•ford (brănt′fərd) A city of S Ontario, Canada, SW of Toronto; named for Joseph Brant. Pop. 84,764.

Bran•ting (brän′tĭng, brän′-), **Karl Hjalmar** 1860–1925. Swedish politician who shared the 1921 Nobel Peace Prize.

Braque (bräk, bräk), **Georges** 1882–1963. French painter who was a leading exponent of the cubist movement.

brash¹ (brăsh) adj. **brash•er, brash•est 1a.** Hasty and unthinking; impetuous. **b.** Rash. **2.** Lacking in sensitivity or tact. **3.** Presumptuously forward; impudent. **4.** Brittle: brash timbers. [Poss. imit. (influenced by RASH¹), or < brash, attack.] —**brash′ly** adv. —**brash′ness** n.

brash² (brăsh) n. A mass or pile of fragments, as of stone or ice. [Perh. an alteration of Fr. brèche, breach in a wall < Ital. breccia. See BRECCIA.]

bra•sier¹ (brā′zhər) n. Variant of **brazier¹.**

bra•sier² (brā′zhər) n. Variant of **brazier².**

Bra•sí•lia (brə-zēl′yə) The cap. of Brazil (since 1960), in the central plateau NW of Rio de Janeiro. Pop. 1,598,415.

Bra•şov (brä-shôv′) A city of central Romania NNW of Bucharest; founded 1211. Pop. 324,104.

brass (brăs) n. **1a.** A yellowish alloy of copper and zinc, sometimes including small amounts of other metals. **b.** Ornaments, objects, or utensils made of this alloy. **2.** Music **a.** The section of a band or an orchestra composed of brass instruments. Often used in the plural. **b.** Brass instruments or their players considered as a group. Often used in the plural. **3.** A memorial plaque or tablet made of brass. **4.** A bushing or similar lining for a bearing, made from a copper alloy. **5.** Informal Bold self-assurance; effrontery. **6.** Slang High-ranking military officers or other high officials. [ME bras < OE bræs.] —**brass** adj.

bras•sard (brə-särd′, brăs′ärd′) n. **1.** A band or badge worn around the upper arm. **2.** also **bras•sart** (brə-särt′, brăs′ärt′) A piece of armor covering the arm. [Fr. < OFr. bras, arm < Lat. brācchium. See BRACHIUM.]

brass band n. Music A band composed of brass and sometimes percussion instruments.

brass•bound (brăs′bound′) adj. **1.** Banded or trimmed with brass or a similar metal, such as bronze. **2.** Inflexible; rigid: brass-bound party loyalists. **3.** Bold and impudent; brazen.

brass-col•lar (brăs′kŏl′ər) adj. Unwavering in political allegiance; consistently voting a straight party ticket.

bras•se•rie (brăs′ə-rē′, brăs-rē′) n. A restaurant serving alcoholic beverages, esp. beer, and simple food. [Fr. < brasser, to malt, brew < OFr. bracier < VLat. *braciāre < Lat. brace, malt, of Celt. orig.]

brass hat n. Slang A high-ranking military officer or civilian official. [< the gold braid on the hat.]

bras•si•ca (brăs′ĭ-kə) n. Any of various plants of the genus Brassica of the mustard family, including cabbage, broccoli, and turnip. [NLat. Brassica, genus name < Lat. brassica, cabbage.]

brass•ie also **brass•y** (brăs′ē) n., pl. **-ies** A two wood used in golf.

bras•siere (brə-zîr′) n. A woman's undergarment worn to support and give contour to the breasts. [Fr. brassière, child's jacket with sleeves, brassiere : OFr. bras, arm < Lat. brācchium; see BRACHIUM) + OFr. -iere, one associated with; see -ER¹.]

brass instrument n. A wind instrument, such as the trombone, made of brass or other metal.

brass knuckles pl.n. (used with a sing. or pl. verb) A metal chain or a set of rings attached to a bar that can be fitted over the fingers to increase the impact of a blow with the fist.

brass tacks pl.n. Informal Essential facts; basics.

brass•ware (brăs′wâr′) n. Articles made from brass.

brass•y¹ (brăs′ē) adj. **-i•er, -i•est 1.** Made of or decorated with brass. **2.** Resembling brass, as in color. **3.** Music Resembling or characterized by the sound of brass instruments. **4.** Cheap and showy; flashy. **5.** Informal Brazen; insolent. —**brass′i•ly** adv. —**brass′i•ness** n.

brass•y² (brăs′ē) n. Variant of **brassie.**

brat¹ (brăt) n. **1.** A child, esp. a spoiled or ill-mannered one. **2.** A child of a career military person. [Poss. < brat, coarse garment < ME < OE bratt, of Celt. orig.] —**brat′tish** adj. —**brat′tish•ness** n. —**brat′ty** adj.

brat² (brăt) n. Bratwurst.

Bra•ti•sla•va (brăt′ĭ-slä′və, brä′tĭ-) The cap. and largest city of Slovakia, on the Danube R. near the Austrian and Hungarian borders; cap. of Hungary (1541–1784). Pop. 445,089.

Bratsk (brätsk) A city of S-central Russia NNW of Irkutsk. Pop. 260,201.

brat•tice (brăt′ĭs) n. **1.** A partition, usually of wood or cloth, erected in a mine for ventilation. **2.** A breastwork erected during a siege. [ME bretice, defensive structure < OFr. bretesche < Med.Lat. bretescha (turris), British-style (tower), prob. < OE bryttisc, British.] —**brat′tice** v.

brat•tle (brăt′l) Scots n. **1.** A rattling or clattering sound. **2.** A movement that produces such a sound. ❖ intr.v. **-tled, -tling, -tles** To make a rattling or clattering sound. [Imit.]

brat•wurst (brăt′wûrst′, -vo̅o̅rst′) n. A sausage of highly seasoned fresh pork. [Ger. < MHGer. *brātwurst* < OHGer. : *brāto*, meat + *wurst*, sausage; see WURST.]

Braun (brôn, broun), *Eva* 1912–45. German lover and later wife of Adolf Hitler.

Braun, Wernher Magnus Maximilian von 1912–77. German-born Amer. rocket engineer who directed the development and launch of *Explorer I* (1958).

Braun•schwei•ger (broun′shwī′gər) *n.* A smoked liver sausage. [Ger., after *Braunschweig* (Brunswick), Germany.]

bra•va (brä′vä, brä-vä′) *interj.* Used to express approval of a woman, esp. for a performance. ❖ *n.* A shout or cry of "brava." [Ital., fem. of *bravo*, bravo. See BRAVO[1].]

bra•va•do (brə-vä′dō) *n., pl.* **-dos** or **-does** 1. Defiant or swaggering behavior. 2. A false show of bravery. [Fr. *bravade* and OSpan. *bravada*, swagger, bravery, both ult. < VLat. **brabus*, brave. See BRAVE.]

brave (brāv) *adj.* **brav•er, brav•est** 1. Possessing or displaying courage; valiant. 2. Making a fine display; impressive or showy. 3. Excellent; great. ❖ *n.* 1. A Native American warrior. 2. A courageous person. 3. *Archaic* A bully. ❖ *v.* **braved, brav•ing, braves** —*tr.* 1. To undergo or face courageously. 2. To challenge; dare. 3. *Obsolete* To make showy or splendid. —*intr. Archaic* To make a courageous show. [ME < OFr. < OItal. or OSpan. *bravo*, wild, brave, excellent, prob. < VLat. **brabus* < Lat. *barbarus*. See BARBAROUS.] —**brave′ly** *adv.* —**brave′ness** *n.*

SYNONYMS *brave, courageous, fearless, intrepid, bold, audacious, valiant, plucky, undaunted* These adjectives mean having or showing courage under difficult or dangerous conditions. *Brave,* the least specific, is frequently associated with an innate quality: *"Familiarity with danger makes a brave man braver"* (Herman Melville). *Courageous* implies consciously rising to a specific test by drawing on a reserve of inner strength: *a courageous battle with cancer. Fearless* emphasizes absence of fear and resolute self-possession: *"world-class* [boating] *races for fearless loners"* (Jo Ann Morse Ridley). *Intrepid* sometimes suggests invulnerability to fear: *Intrepid pioneers settled the American West. Bold* stresses readiness to meet danger or difficulty and often a tendency to seek it out: *"If we shrink from the hard contests . . . then bolder and stronger peoples will pass us by"* (Theodore Roosevelt). *Audacious* implies extreme confidence and boldness: *"To demand these God-given rights is to seek black power—what I call audacious power"* (Adam Clayton Powell, Jr.). *Valiant* suggests the bravery of a hero or a heroine: *"a . . . biography that sees Hemingway as a valiant and moral man"* (New York Times). *Plucky* emphasizes spirit and heart in the face of unfavorable odds: *"Everybody was . . . anxious to show these Belgians what England thought of their plucky little country"* (H.G. Wells). *Undaunted* suggests persistent courage and resolve: *"We must be united, we must be undaunted, we must be inflexible"* (Winston S. Churchill).

brav•er•y (brā′və-rē, brāv′rē) *n., pl.* **-ies** 1. The condition or quality of being brave; courage. 2. Splendor or magnificence; show.

bra•vis•si•mo (brä-vīs′ə-mō′) *interj.* Used to express great approval, esp. of a performance. [Ital., superl. of *bravo*, fine. See BRAVO[1].]

bra•vo[1] (brä′vō, brä-vō′) *interj.* Used to express approval, esp. of a performance. ❖ *n., pl.* **-vos** A shout or cry of "bravo." [Ital. See BRAVE.] —**bra′vo** *v.*

bra•vo[2] (brä′vō) *n., pl.* **-voes** or **bra•vos** A villain, esp. a hired killer. [Ital. < *bravo*, wild, excellent. See BRAVE.]

bra•vu•ra (brə-vŏŏr′ə, -vyŏŏr′ə) *n.* 1. *Music* **a.** Brilliant technique or style in performance. **b.** A piece or passage that emphasizes a performer's virtuosity. 2. A showy manner or display. [Ital. < *bravo*, excellent. See BRAVE.]

braw (brô) *adj.* **-er, -est** *Scots* 1. Fine; splendid. 2. Dressed in a fine or showy manner. [Sc., var. of BRAVE.]

brawl (brôl) *n.* 1. A noisy quarrel or fight. 2. A loud party. 3. A loud, roaring noise. ❖ *intr.v.* **brawled, brawl•ing, brawls** 1. To quarrel or fight noisily. 2. To flow noisily, as water. [ME *braul* < *braullen*, to quarrel.] —**brawl′er** *n.* —**brawl′y** *adj.*

brawn (brôn) *n.* 1. Solid and well-developed muscles. 2. Muscular strength and power. 3. *Chiefly British* The meat of a boar. 4. Headcheese. [ME, muscle < OFr. *braon*, meat, of Gmc. orig.]

brawn•y (brô′nē) *adj.* **-i•er, -i•est** 1. Strong and muscular. See Syns at **muscular.** 2. Hardened; calloused. —**brawn′i•ly** *adv.* —**brawn′i•ness** *n.*

bray[1] (brā) *v.* **brayed, bray•ing, brays** —*intr.* 1. To utter the bray of a donkey. 2. To sound loudly and harshly. —*tr.* 1. To emit (an utterance or a sound) loudly and harshly. ❖ *n.* 1. The loud, harsh cry of a donkey. 2. A sound resembling a bray. [ME *braien* < OFr. *braire* < VLat. **bragere*, of Celt. orig.]

bray[2] (brā) *tr.v.* **brayed, bray•ing, brays** 1. To crush and pound to a fine consistency, as in a mortar. 2. To spread (ink) thinly over a surface. [ME *braien* < OFr. *breier*, of Gmc. orig. See bhreg- in App.]

bray•er[1] (brā′ər) *n.* One that brays, esp. a donkey.

bray•er[2] (brā′ər) *n. Printing* A small hand roller used to spread ink thinly and evenly.

Braz. *abbr.* 1. Brazil 2. Brazilian

braze[1] (brāz) *tr.v.* **brazed, braz•ing, braz•es** 1. To make of or

---

decorate with brass. 2. To make hard like brass. [ME *brasen* < OE *brasian* < *bræs*, brass.]

braze[2] (brāz) *tr.v.* **brazed, braz•ing, braz•es** To solder (two pieces of metal) together using a hard solder with a high melting point. [Prob. < Fr. *braser* < OFr., to burn < *brese*, hot coal, of Gmc. orig.] —**braz′er** *n.*

bra•zen (brā′zən) *adj.* 1. Marked by flagrant and insolent audacity. 2. Having a loud, usu. harsh resonant sound. 3. Made of brass. 4. Resembling brass, as in color or strength. ❖ *tr.v.* **-zened, -zen•ing, -zens** To face or undergo with bold self-assurance. [ME *brasen*, made of brass < OE *bræsen* < *bræs*, brass.] —**bra′zen•ly** *adv.* —**bra′zen•ness** *n.*

bra•zen•faced (brā′zən-fāst′) *adj.* Flagrantly and insolently audacious.

bra•zier[1] also **bra•sier** (brā′zhər) *n.* One who makes brass articles. [ME *brasier* < *bras*, brass. See BRASS.]

bra•zier[2] also **bra•sier** (brā′zhər) *n.* 1. A metal pan for holding burning coals or charcoal. 2. A cooking device consisting of a charcoal or electric heating source over which food is grilled. [Fr. *brasier* < *braise*, hot coals. See BRAISE.]

Bra•zil (brə-zĭl′) A country of E South America; achieved independence from Portugal in 1822. Cap. Brasília. Pop. 153,725,000. —**Bra•zil′i•an** *adj. & n.*

Brazilian pepper tree *n.* An evergreen Brazilian tree (*Schinus terebinthifolius*) having aromatic foliage and clusters of red berrylike fruits used for Christmas decorations.

Brazil nut *n.* 1. A tropical South American evergreen tree (*Bertholletia excelsa*) having edible dark brown seeds. 2. The seed of this tree. [After BRAZIL.]

bra•zil•wood (brə-zĭl′wŏŏd′) *n.* The reddish wood of certain tropical trees or shrubs in the pea family, esp. the Brazilian tree *Caesalpinia echinata* whose wood is used for violin bows and as a source of a red or purplish dye. [Obsolete *brazil*, brazilwood (< ME *brasile* < OSpan. or Port. *brasil*, prob. of E Indian orig.) + WOOD[1].]

Braz•os (brāz′əs) A river rising in E NM and flowing c. 1,400 km (870 mi) to the Gulf of Mexico SW of Galveston TX.

Braz•za•ville (brāz′ə-vĭl′, brä-zä-vēl′) The cap. of the Republic of the Congo, in the S part on the Congo R.; founded in the 1880s. Pop. 596,200.

BRE *abbr.* Bachelor of Religious Education

breach (brēch) *n.* **1a.** An opening, tear, or rupture. **b.** A gap or rift, as in a dike or fortification. 2. A violation or infraction, as of a law or promise. 3. A breaking up or disruption of friendly relations; an estrangement. 4. A leap of a whale from the water. 5. The breaking of waves or surf. ❖ *v.* **breached, breach•ing, breach•es** —*tr.* 1. To make a hole or gap in; break through. 2. To break or violate (an agreement, for example). —*intr.* To leap from the water. [ME *breche* < OE *brēc.* See bhreg- in App.]

SYNONYMS *breach, infraction, violation, transgression, trespass, infringement* These nouns denote an act or instance of breaking a law or regulation or failing to fulfill a duty, obligation, or promise. *Breach* and *infraction* are the least specific: *a breach of trust; infractions of the rules.* A *violation* is committed willfully and with complete lack of regard for legal, moral, or ethical considerations: *a violation of her contract. Transgression* most often applies to divine or moral law: *"The children shall not be punished for the father's transgression"* (Daniel Defoe). *Trespass* implies willful intrusion on another's rights, possessions, or person: *committed trespass when hunting. Infringement* is most frequently used to denote encroachment on another's rights: *"Necessity is the plea for every infringement of human freedom"* (William Pitt the Younger).

breach of promise *n.* Failure to fulfill a promise, esp. a promise to marry.

bread (brĕd) *n.* 1. A staple food made from flour or meal mixed with other ingredients, usu. combined with a leavening agent, and baked. 2. Food in general, regarded as necessary for sustaining life. **3a.** Means of support; livelihood: *earn one's bread.* **b.** *Slang* Money. ❖ *tr.v.* **bread•ed, bread•ing, breads** To coat with bread crumbs, as before cooking: *breaded the fillets.* [ME < OE *brēad.*]

bread and butter *n.* 1. Means of support; livelihood. 2. The essential sustaining element or elements; the mainstay.

bread-and-but•ter (brĕd′n-bŭt′ər) *adj.* **1a.** Influenced by or undertaken out of necessity: *a bread-and-butter job.* **b.** Reliable, esp. for producing income; basic. 2. Expressive of gratitude for hospitality.

bread and circuses *pl.n.* Offerings, such as benefits or entertainments, intended to placate discontent or distract attention from a policy or situation. [Transl. of Lat. *pānem et circēnsēs* : *pānem*, accusative sing. of *pānis*, bread + *et*, and + *circēnsēs*, circus games.]

bread•bas•ket (brĕd′bās′kĭt) *n.* 1. A basket for serving bread. 2. A geographic region serving as a principal source of grain supply. 3. *Slang* The stomach.

bread•board (brĕd′bôrd′, -bōrd′) *n.* 1. A board on which bread is sliced or dough is kneaded. 2. An experimental model, esp. of an electric circuit; a prototype. 3. A thin blank board on which a prototype circuit with connections for circuit elements is con-

Brazil

structed. ❖ *tr.v.* **-board•ed, -board•ing, -boards** To construct an experimental model of.

bread•box (brĕd′bŏks′) *n.* A container in which baked goods are stored to maintain their freshness.

bread•fruit (brĕd′fro͞ot′) *n.* **1.** A Malaysian evergreen timber tree *(Artocarpus altilis)* having large, round, yellowish edible fruits. **2.** The fruit of this tree.

bread•line also **bread line** (brĕd′līn′) *n.* A line of people waiting to receive food from a charitable organization or public agency.

bread mold *n.* Any of various fungi of the genus *Rhizopus* forming a dense cottony growth on bread and other foods.

bread•nut (brĕd′nŭt′) *n.* **1.** A large tree *(Brosimum alicastrum)* native to Mexico, Central America, and the West Indies and having yellow fruits, each with a large edible seed. **2.** The seed of this tree.

bread•root (brĕd′ro͞ot′, -ro͝ot′) *n.* A perennial herb *(Psoralea esculenta)* in the pea family, native to prairies and plains in central North America and having a tuberous starchy root.

bread•stuff (brĕd′stŭf′) *n.* **1.** Bread in any form or shape. **2.** Flour, meal, or grain used in the baking of bread.

breadth (brĕdth) *n.* **1.** The measure or dimension from side to side; width. **2.** A piece usu. produced in a standard width: *a breadth of canvas.* **3a.** Wide range or scope: *breadth of knowledge.* **b.** Tolerance; broadmindedness. **4.** An effect of unified, encompassing vision in an artistic composition. [ME *breth* < *brede* (on the model of *length,* length) < OE *brǣd.*]

breadth•ways (brĕdth′wāz′) or **breadth•wise** (-wīz′) *adv. & adj.* In the direction of the breadth.

bread•win•ner (brĕd′wĭn′ər) *n.* One whose earnings are the primary source of support for one's dependents.

break (brāk) *v.* **broke** (brōk), **bro•ken** (brō′kən), **break•ing, breaks** —*tr.* **1.** To cause to separate into pieces suddenly or violently; smash. **2a.** To divide into pieces, as by bending or cutting. **b.** To separate into components or parts: *broke the job into discrete tasks.* **3.** To snap off or detach: *broke a twig from the tree.* **4a.** To fracture a bone of: *I broke my leg.* **b.** To fracture (a bone): *I broke my femur.* **5.** To crack without separating into pieces. **6a.** To destroy the completeness of (a set or collection): *broke the set of books by giving some away.* **b.** To exchange for smaller monetary units: *break a dollar.* **7.** To disrupt the uniformity or continuity of: *a plain broken by low hills.* **8.** *Electricity* To render (a circuit) inoperative by disruption; open. **9a.** To puncture or penetrate: *The blade broke the skin.* **b.** To part or pierce the surface of: *a dolphin breaking water.* **10.** To produce (a sweat) copiously on the skin, as from exercise. **11.** To force one's way out of; escape from: *break jail.* **12.** To make or bring about by cutting or forcing: *break a trail.* **13a.** To prove false: *They broke my alibi.* **b.** To uncover the basic elements and arrangement of: *break a code.* **14.** To make known, as news: *break a story.* **15.** To surpass or outdo: *broke the record.* **16.** To overcome or put an end to: *break a strike.* **17.** To lessen in force or effect: *break a fall.* **18.** To render useless or inoperative: *We broke the radio.* **19.** To weaken or destroy, as in spirit or health: *"For a hero loves the world till it breaks him"* (William Butler Yeats). **20.** To cause the ruin or failure of (an enterprise, for example). **21.** To reduce in rank; demote. **22.** To cause to be without money or go into bankruptcy. **23.** To fail to fulfill; cancel: *break one's plans.* **24.** To fail to conform to; violate: *break the law.* **25.** *Law* To invalidate (a will) by judicial action. **26a.** To give up (a habit). **b.** To cause to give up a habit. **27.** To train to obey; tame. —*intr.* **1.** To become separated into pieces or fragments. **2.** To become cracked or split. **3.** To become fractured: *His arm broke from the fall.* **4.** To become unusable or inoperative: *The television broke.* **5.** To give way; collapse: *The scaffolding broke during the storm.* **6.** To burst: *The balloon broke.* **7.** To intrude on: *broke in on the conversation.* **8.** To scatter or disperse; part: *The clouds broke.* **9.** *Games* To make the opening shot that scatters the grouped balls in billiards or pool. **10.** *Sports* To separate from a clinch in boxing. **11.** To move away or escape suddenly. **12.** To come forth or begin from a state of latency: *A storm was breaking over Miami.* **13.** To emerge above the surface of water. **14.** To become known or noticed: *The story broke on Friday.* **15.** To change direction suddenly. **16.** *Baseball* To curve near or over the plate. **17.** To change suddenly, as in tone: *My voice broke to a whisper.* **18.** *Linguistics* To undergo breaking. **19.** To change to a gait different from the one set. Used of a horse. **20.** To interrupt or cease an activity. **21.** To discontinue an association, an agreement, or a relationship. **22.** To diminish or discontinue abruptly: *The fever is breaking.* **23.** To lose physical or spiritual strength. **24.** To decrease sharply in value or quantity. **25.** To collapse or crash into surf or spray. **26.** *Informal* To take place or happen; proceed. **27.** To engage in breaking; break dance. ❖ *n.* **1.** The act or an occurrence of breaking. **2.** The result of breaking, as a crack or separation. **3.** The beginning or emergence of something: *the break of day.* **4.** A sudden movement; a dash. **5.** An escape: *a prison break.* **6.** An interruption or a disruption in continuity or regularity: *commercial breaks.* **7.** A pause or an interval, as from work: *a coffee break.* **8.** A sudden or marked change. **9.** A violation: *a security break.* **10.** An often sudden piece of luck: *finally got a break.* **11.** *Informal* **a.** An allowance or indulgence; accommodating treatment. **b.** A favorable price or reduction: *a tax break.* **12.** A severing of ties: *a break between families.* **13.** *Informal* A faux pas. **14.** A sudden decline in prices. **15.** A caesura. **16.** *Printing* **a.** The space between two paragraphs. **b.** A series of three dots (. . .) used to indicate an omission in a text. **c.** The place where a word is or should be divided at the end of a line. **17.** *Electricity* Interruption of a flow of current. **18.** *Geology* A marked change in topography, such as a fault or deep valley. **19.** *Music* **a.** The point at which one register or tonal quality changes to another. **b.** The change itself. **c.** A solo jazz cadenza played between the regular phrases or choruses of a melody or that serves as an introduction to a more extended solo. **20.** A change in a horse's gait to one different from that set by the rider. **21.** *Sports* The swerving of a ball from a straight path of flight, as in baseball. **22.** *Sports* **a.** The beginning of a race. **b.** A rush toward the goal, as in hockey, by offensive players. **c.** The separation after a clinch in boxing. **23.** *Games* **a.** The opening shot that scatters the grouped balls in billiards or pool. **b.** An unbroken series of successful shots, as in billiards. **24.** *Sports* Failure to score a strike or a spare in a given bowling frame. **25.** also **brake** A high horse-drawn carriage with four wheels. ***—phrasal verbs:*** **break down 1.** To cause to collapse; destroy. **2a.** To become or cause to become distressed or upset. **b.** To have a physical or mental collapse. **3.** To give up resistance; give way. **4.** To fail to function; cease to be useful or effective. **5.** To render weak or ineffective. **6a.** To divide into or consider in parts; analyze. **b.** To be divisible; admit of analysis. **7.** To decompose or cause to decompose chemically. **8.** *Electricity* To undergo a breakdown. **break in 1.** To train or adapt for a purpose. **2.** To loosen or soften with use: *break in new shoes.* **3.** To enter premises forcibly or illegally. **4a.** To interrupt a conversation or discussion. **b.** To intrude. **break into 1.** To interrupt. **2.** To begin suddenly: *The child broke into tears.* **3.** To enter (a field of activity): *broke into journalism.* **break off 1.** To separate or become separated, as by twisting or tearing. **2.** To stop suddenly, as in speaking. **3a.** To discontinue (a relationship). **b.** To cease to be friendly. **break out 1.** To become affected with a skin eruption, such as pimples. **2.** To develop suddenly and forcefully: *Measles broke out.* **3a.** To ready for action or use: *Break out the rifles!* **b.** To bring forth for consumption: *break out the champagne.* **4.** To emerge or escape. **5.** To separate or be separable into categories, as data. **break through** To make a sudden, quick advance, as through obstruction or opposition. **break up 1a.** To separate into pieces; divide. **b.** To interrupt the uniformity or continuity of: *His visit broke up the afternoon.* **2.** To scatter; disperse: *The crowd broke up.* **3.** To bring or come to an end: *Their friendship broke up.* **4.** *Informal* To burst or cause to burst into laughter. ***—idioms:*** **break a leg** Used to wish someone success in a performance. **break camp** To pack up equipment and leave a campsite. **break even** To gain an amount equal to that risked or invested. **break rank** (or **ranks**) **1.** To fall into disorder, as a formation of soldiers. **2.** To fail to conform to a prevailing or expected pattern or order. **break (someone's) service** *Sports* To win a game, as in tennis, served by one's opponent. **break the ice 1.** To make a start. **2.** To relax a tense or formal social situation. **break wind** To expel intestinal gas. [ME *breken* < OE *brecan.* See **bhreg-** in App.]

SYNONYMS *break, crack, fracture, burst, split, splinter, shatter, smash* These verbs mean to separate or cause to separate into parts or pieces, either by the sudden application of force or by the pressure of internal stress. *Break* is the most general: *vandals breaking windows.* To *crack* is to break, often with a sharp snapping sound, without dividing into parts: *I cracked the plate.* *Fracture* applies to a break or crack in a rigid body: *bones that fractured in the fall.* *Burst* implies a sudden coming apart, esp. from internal pressure, and the dispersion of contents: *burst the balloon with a pin.* *Split* refers to a division longitudinally or with the grain: *split the log with an ax.* *Splinter* implies splitting into long, thin, sharp pieces: *Repeated blows splintered the door.* To *shatter* is to break into many scattered pieces: *The bottle shattered.* *Smash* stresses force of blow or impact and suggests complete destruction: *angrily smashed the vase against the wall.*

break•a•ble (brā′kə-bəl) *adj.* Liable to break or to be broken. See Syns at **fragile.** ❖ *n.* An article that can be broken easily. —**break′a•ble•ness** *n.*

break•age (brā′kĭj) *n.* **1.** The act of breaking. **2.** A quantity broken. **3.** Loss or damage as a result of breaking. **4.** A commercial allowance for loss or damage.

break•a•way (brāk′ə-wā′) *adj.* **1.** Designed to break, bend, or fall apart easily upon impact. **2.** Severing or having severed alliance with another entity, policy, or attitude. ❖ *n.* **1.** One that breaks away. **2.** The act of breaking away, esp. an offensive play in a team sport in which a player with the ball or puck advances past the defenders toward the goal. **3.** An object designed to break away.

break•bone fever (brāk′bōn′) *n.* See **dengue.**

break dancing also **break•danc•ing** (brāk′dăn′sĭng) *n.* See **breaking².** —**break dance** *n. & v.* —**break dancer** *n.*

break•down (brāk′doun′) *n.* **1a.** The act or process of failing to function or continue. **b.** The condition resulting from this. **2.** *Electricity* The abrupt failure of an insulator or insulating medium to restrict the flow of current. **3.** A typically sudden collapse in physical or mental health. **4.** An analysis, an outline, or a sum-

breadfruit
Artocarpus altilis

ă	pat	oi	boy
ā	pay	ou	out
âr	care	o͝o	took
ä	father	o͞o	boot
ĕ	pet	ŭ	cut
ē	be	ûr	urge
ĭ	pit	th	thin
ī	pie	*th*	this
îr	pier	hw	which
ŏ	pot	zh	vision
ō	toe	ə	about, item
ô	paw		

Stress marks:
′ (primary);
′ (secondary), as in
lexicon (lĕk′sĭ-kŏn′)

mary consisting of itemized data or essentials. **5.** Disintegration or decomposition into parts or elements. **6.** An energetic American country dance.

break·er¹ (brāʹkər) *n.* **1.** One that breaks, as a machine for crushing rock. **2.** A circuit breaker. **3.** A wave that crests or breaks into foam.

brea·ker² (brāʹkər) *n. Nautical* A small water cask, often used in lifeboats. [Alteration of Sp. *barrica*. See BARRICADE.]

breaker zone *n.* The nearshore zone between the outermost breakers and the area of the wave uprush.

break·e·ven or **break-e·ven** (brākʹēʹvən) *adj.* Marked by or indicating a balance, esp. of investment and return. ❖ *n.* **1.** The point, esp. the level of sales of a good or service, at which the return on investment is exactly equal to the amount invested. **2.** The point at which the energy produced by a system is equal to that put into it, thereby rendering the system self-sustaining.

break·fast (brĕkʹfəst) *n.* The first meal of the day, usu. eaten in the morning. ❖ *v.* **-fast·ed, -fast·ing, -fasts** —*intr.* To eat breakfast. —*tr.* To provide breakfast for. [ME *brekfast* : *breken*, to break; see BREAK + *faste*, a fast (< ON *fasta*, to fast).] —**breakʹfast·er** *n.*

break·front (brākʹfrŭntʹ) *n.* A piece of furniture, such as a cabinet or bookcase, with a central section that projects beyond the sections to either side.

break-in (brākʹĭnʹ) *n.* **1.** A forcible entry, as into a building or room, for an illegal purpose. **2.** An initial, evaluative period of employment or operation.

break·ing¹ (brāʹkĭng) *n.* The change of a simple vowel to a diphthong, often caused by the influence of neighboring consonants. [Transl. of Ger. *Brechung*.]

break·ing² (brāʹkĭng) *n.* A form of urban dance usu. performed to funk music.

breaking and entering *n.* The gaining of unauthorized illegal access to another's premises.

breaking point *n.* **1.** The point at which physical, mental, or emotional strength gives way under stress. **2.** The point at which a condition or situation becomes critical.

break·neck (brākʹnĕkʹ) *adj.* **1.** Dangerously fast: *a breakneck pace.* **2.** Likely to cause an accident: *a breakneck curve.*

break·out (brākʹoutʹ) *n.* **1.** A forceful emergence from a restrictive condition or situation. **2.** A sudden manifestation or increase, as of a disease; an outbreak.

break·point (brākʹpointʹ) *n.* **1.** or **break point** A point of discontinuity, change, or cessation. **2.** *Computer Science* A point in a program at which operation may be interrupted for manual intervention. **3.** or **break point** *Sports* **a.** A situation in tennis in which one more point is needed to break the opponent's serve. **b.** The point awarded in such a situation.

break·through (brākʹthro̅o̅ʹ) *n.* **1.** An act of overcoming or penetrating an obstacle or restriction. **2.** A military offensive that penetrates an enemy's lines of defense. **3.** A major achievement or success that permits further progress.

break·up (brākʹŭpʹ) *n.* **1.** The act or an instance of breaking up. **2.** The discontinuance of a relationship, as a marriage or a friendship. **3.** The cracking and shifting of ice in rivers or harbors during the spring. **4.** A loss of control or composure.

break·wa·ter (brākʹwôʹtər, -wŏtʹər) *n.* A barrier that protects a harbor or shore from the full impact of waves.

bream¹ (brēm, brĭm) *n., pl.* **bream** or **breams** **1.** Any of several European freshwater fishes of the genus *Abramis*, esp. *A. brama*, having a flattened body. **2a.** Any of various saltwater fishes in the family Sparidae. **b.** Any of various freshwater sunfishes of the genus *Lepomis* and related genera. [ME *breme* < OFr., of Gmc. orig.]

bream² (brēm) *tr.v.* **breamed, bream·ing, breams** *Nautical* To clean (a wooden ship's hull) by applying heat to soften the pitch and then scraping. [< MDu. *brem(e)*, furze, broom.]

breast (brĕst) *n.* **1a.** Either of two milk-secreting glandular organs on the chest of a woman; the human mammary gland. **b.** A corresponding organ in other mammals. **c.** A corresponding rudimentary gland in the male. **2a.** The surface of the human body extending from the neck to the abdomen. **b.** A corresponding part in other animals. **3.** The part of a garment that covers the chest. **4.** The seat of affection and emotion. **5.** A source of nourishment. **6.** Something likened to the human breast: *the breast of a hill.* **7.** The face of a mine or tunnel. ❖ *v.* **breast·ed, breast·ing, breasts 1.** To rise over; climb. **2.** To encounter or advance against resolutely; confront boldly. [ME *brest* < OE *brēost*.]

breast-beat·ing (brĕstʹbēʹtĭng) *n.* A loud demonstration of emotion, esp. of remorse. —**breastʹ-beatʹing** *adj.*

breast·bone (brĕstʹbōnʹ) *n.* See sternum.

breast·feed or **breast-feed** (brĕstʹfēdʹ) *tr.v.* **-fed** (-fĕdʹ), **-feed·ing, -feeds** —*tr.* To feed (a baby) mother's milk from the breast; suckle. —*intr.* To breastfeed a baby.

breast·plate (brĕstʹplātʹ) *n.* **1.** A piece of armor that covers the breast. **2.** *Judaism* A square cloth set with 12 precious stones representing the 12 tribes of Israel, worn over the breast by ancient high priests.

breast·stroke (brĕstʹstrōkʹ) *n.* A swimming stroke in which a person lies face down and extends the arms in front of the head, then sweeps them back laterally under the surface of the water

while performing a frog kick. —**breastʹstrokeʹ** *v.* —**breastʹstrokʹer** *n.*

breast·work (brĕstʹwûrkʹ) *n.* A temporary, quickly constructed fortification, usu. breast-high.

breath (brĕth) *n.* **1.** The air inhaled and exhaled in respiration. **2.** The act or process of breathing; respiration. **3.** The capacity to breathe, esp. in an unlabored manner: *shortness of breath.* **4.** Spirit or vitality; life. **5.** A single respiration: *a deep breath.* **6.** Exhaled air, as evidenced by vapor, odor, or heat. **7.** A momentary pause or rest. **8a.** A momentary stirring of air. **b.** A slight gust of fragrant air. **9.** A trace or suggestion. **10.** A softly spoken sound; a whisper. **11.** *Linguistics* Exhalation of air without vibration of the vocal cords, as in the articulation of *p* and *s.* —*idioms:* **in one (or the same) breath** At or almost at the same time. **out of breath** Breathing with difficulty, as from exertion; gasping. **under (one's) breath** In a muted voice or whisper. [ME *breth* < OE *brǣth*.]

breath·a·ble (brēʹthə-bəl) *adj.* **1.** Suitable or pleasant for breathing: *breathable air.* **2.** Permitting air to pass through: *a breathable fabric.* —**breathʹa·bilʹi·ty** *n.*

Breath·a·lyz·er (brĕthʹə-līʹzər) A trademark used for a device that measures alcohol in a person's breath to determine the concentration of alcohol in the blood.

breathe (brēth) *v.* **breathed, breath·ing, breathes** —*intr.* **1.** To inhale and exhale air. **2.** To be alive; live. **3.** To pause to rest or regain breath. **4.** To move or blow gently, as air. **5.** To allow air to pass through: *a fabric that breathes.* **6.** To be exhaled or emanated, as a fragrance. **7.** To be manifested or suggested, as a feeling. **8.** To reach fullness of flavor and aroma through exposure to air. Used chiefly of wine. **9.** To require air in the combustion process. Used of an internal-combustion engine. —*tr.* **1.** To inhale and exhale (air, for example) during respiration. **2.** To inhale (an aroma, for example). **3.** To impart as if by breathing; instill. **4.** To exhale (something); emit. **5.** To utter, esp. quietly; whisper: *Don't breathe a word of this.* **6.** To make apparent or manifest; suggest. **7.** To allow (a person or animal) to rest or regain breath. **8.** *Linguistics* To utter with a voiceless exhalation of air. **9.** To draw in (air) for the combustion process. Used of an internal-combustion engine. —*idioms:* **breathe down (someone's) neck 1.** To threaten by proximity, esp. by pursuing closely. **2.** To watch or monitor closely, often annoyingly. **breathe (one's) last** To die. [ME *brethen* < *breth*, breath. See BREATH.]

OUR LIVING LANGUAGE The euphemistic expression *breathe one's last* illustrates a widespread linguistic and cultural phenomenon known as *taboo avoidance.* There are certain concepts that few people like to talk or think about, and death is certainly one of them. Such concepts are often expressed with circumlocutions or other substitutions for the word that expresses the concept directly (in this case, the verb *to die*), probably as a way of minimizing the power of the basic word for the concept. It is interesting to compare how two different styles of language, formal and slang, avoid saying "die." More formal or elevated speech is full of euphemistic expressions such as *breathe one's last, pass away, depart, expire, go to one's eternal reward, go the way of all flesh,* and *go to a better place.* Many of these expressions try to cast death in a positive light, often with religious overtones. Speakers of slang are just as interested in avoiding the word *die,* partly for the same taboo-avoidance reasons and partly because of the general striving on the part of slang speakers to come up with novel expressions for old concepts. The result is a raft of irreverent expressions that are much more direct than the elevated ones—but not so direct as to actually say "die." These expressions often concentrate on a particular physical aspect of dying, lending them an unusually vivid quality: *croak, go belly up, kick the bucket, cash in one's chips, bite the dust.*

breathed (brĕtht) *adj.* **1.** (also brēthd) *Linguistics* Voiceless. **2.** Having breath of a specified kind. Often used in combination: *sour-breathed.*

breath·er (brēʹthər) *n.* **1.** One that breathes, esp. in a specified manner: *a shallow breather.* **2.** *Informal* A short rest period: *took a breather.* **3.** *Informal* An activity, such as exercise, that causes difficult breathing. **4.** A small vent allowing the passage of gas or liquid to or from an enclosed area.

breath·ing (brēʹthĭng) *n.* **1a.** The act or process of respiration. **b.** A single breath. **2.** The time required to take one's breath. **3a.** Either of two marks, the rough breathing (ʽ) and the smooth breathing (ʼ), used in Greek to indicate presence or absence of aspiration. **b.** The presence or absence of aspiration indicated by either of these marks.

breathing room *n.* Sufficient room to permit ease of breathing or movement: *no breathing room on the crowded bus.*

breathing space *n.* **1.** Breathing room. **2.** A breathing spell.

breathing spell *n.* An opportunity for rest or thought.

breath·less (brĕthʹlĭs) *adj.* **1.** Breathing with difficulty; gasping. **2.** Marked by the suspension of regular breathing, as from tension. **3.** Causing the suspension of regular breathing; tense or exciting. **4a.** Not breathing; without breath. **b.** Dead. **5.** Having no air or breeze; still. —**breathʹless·ly** *adv.* —**breathʹless·ness** *n.*

breath·tak·ing (brĕthʹtāʹkĭng) *adj.* **1.** Inspiring or exciting: *a breathtaking view.* **2.** Astonishing; astounding: *breathtaking stu-*

pidity. —**breath′tak′ing•ly** adv.

breath•y (brĕth′ē) adj. **-i•er, -i•est** Marked by audible or noisy breathing. —**breath′i•ly** adv. —**breath′i•ness** n.

brec•ci•a (brĕch′ē-ə, brĕsh′-) n. Rock composed of sharp-angled fragments embedded in a fine-grained matrix. [Ital., of Gmc. orig. See **bhreg-** in App.]

brec•ci•ate (brĕch′ē-āt′, brĕsh′-) tr.v. **-at•ed, -at•ing, -ates** To form (rock) into breccia. —**brec′ci•a′tion** n.

Brecht (brĕkt, brĕкнt), **Bertolt** 1898–1956. German poet and playwright whose works include *The Threepenny Opera* (1928). —**Brecht′i•an** adj.

bred (brĕd) v. Past tense and past participle of **breed.**

brede (brēd) n. Archaic Ornamental embroidery or braiding. [Variant of BRAID.]

bred-in-the-bone (brĕd′n-thə-bōn′) adj. **1.** Deeply instilled; firmly established. **2.** Persistent; habitual.

breech (brēch) n. **1.** The lower rear portion of the human trunk; the buttocks. **2. breeches** (brĭch′ĭz, brē′chĭz) **a.** Knee breeches. **b.** Informal Trousers. **3.** The part of a firearm behind the barrel. **4.** The lower part of a pulley block. [ME brech < OE brēc, pl. of brōc, leg covering; akin to Gaulish brāca, hose, trousers.]

breech birth n. See **breech delivery.**

breech•block (brēch′blŏk′) n. The metal part that closes the breech end of the barrel of a breechloading gun.

breech•cloth (brēch′klôth′, -klŏth′) also **breech•clout** (-klout′) n. A cloth worn to cover the loins; a loincloth.

breech delivery n. Delivery of a fetus with the buttocks or feet appearing first.

breech•ing (brē′chĭng, brĭch′ĭng) n. **1.** The strap of a harness that passes behind a draft animal's haunches. **2.** The short wool or hair on the rump and hind legs of a sheep, goat, or dog.

breech•load•er (brēch′lō′dər) n. A gun or other firearm loaded at the breech. —**breech′load′ing** (-lō′dĭng) adj.

breech presentation n. The position of a fetus during labor in which the buttocks or feet appear first.

breed (brēd) v. **bred** (brĕd), **breed•ing, breeds** —tr. **1.** To produce; give birth to or hatch. **2.** To bring about; engender. **3a.** To cause to reproduce, esp. by controlled mating. **b.** To inseminate or impregnate; mate with. **4.** To rear or train; bring up: *a writer bred in a seafaring culture.* **5.** To be the place of origin of: *Austria breeds great skiers.* **6.** To produce (fissionable material) in a breeder reactor. —intr. **1.** To produce offspring. **2.** To copulate; mate. **3.** To originate and thrive. ❖ n. **1.** A group of organisms having common ancestors and certain distinguishable characteristics, esp. when developed and maintained by controlled propagation. **2.** A kind; a sort. **3.** Offensive A person of mixed racial descent; a half-breed. —**idiom: breed up a storm** New England To become cloudy. [ME breden < OE brēdan.] —**breed′er** n.

breeder reactor n. A nuclear reactor that produces more fissionable material than it consumes.

breed•ing (brē′dĭng) n. **1.** One's line of descent; ancestry. **2.** Training in the proper forms of social and personal conduct. **3.** Production of offspring or young. **4.** The propagation of animals or plants.

breeding ground n. **1.** A place where animals breed. **2.** A place or set of circumstances that encourages the development of certain ideas or conditions.

breeks (brēks) pl.n. Scots Breeches. [ME, pl. of brek < OE brēc. See BREECH.]

breeze¹ (brēz) n. **1.** A light current of air; a gentle wind. **2.** A wind speed of from 4 to 31 miles (6 to 50 kilometers) per hour, according to the Beaufort scale. **3.** Informal Something that is easy to do. ❖ intr.v. **breezed, breez•ing, breez•es 1.** To blow lightly. **2.** Informal To progress swiftly and effortlessly: *We breezed through the test.* **3.** To sprint around a racetrack as a means of exercise. Used of a racehorse. [Perh. < OSpan. briza, northeast wind.]

breeze² (brēz) n. The refuse left when coke or charcoal is made. [Prob. < Fr. braise, hot coals < OFr. brese, of Gmc. orig.]

breeze•way (brēz′wā′) n. A roofed, open-sided passageway connecting two structures, such as a house and a garage.

breez•y (brē′zē) adj. **-i•er, -i•est 1.** Exposed to breezes; windy. **2.** Fresh and animated; lively: *a breezy prose style.* —**breez′i•ly** adv. —**breez′i•ness** n.

breg•ma (brĕg′mə) n., pl. **-ma•ta** (-mə-tə) The junction of the sagittal and coronal sutures at the top of the skull. [Lat., top of the head < Gk.] —**breg•mat′ic** (-măt′ĭk) adj.

Bre•men (brĕm′ən, brā′mən) A city of NW Germany on the Weser R. SW of Hamburg. Pop. 551,604.

brems•strah•lung (brĕm′shträ′lʊng) n. The electromagnetic radiation produced by a change in the velocity of a charged subatomic particle, as when it is scattered or deflected in the electric field of an atom or molecule. [Ger. : Bremse, brake (< MLGer. premse < pramen, to press) + Strahlung, radiation (< strahlen, to radiate < Strahl, ray < MHGer. strāle < OHGer. strāla, arrow, stripe).]

Bren gun (brĕn) n. A .303-caliber, gas-operated, magazine-fed light machine gun. [BR(NO) + En(field), a borough of London in southeast England.]

Bren•nan (brĕn′ən), **William Joseph, Jr.** 1906–97. Amer. jurist;

associate justice of the US Supreme Court (1956–90).

Bren•ner Pass (brĕn′ər) An Alpine pass, 1,371 m (4,495 ft) high, connecting Innsbruck, Austria, with Bolzano, Italy.

brent (brĕnt) n. Chiefly British Variant of **brant.**

Brent, Margaret 1600–71? English-born colonist; the first woman to obtain a land grant in the colony of Maryland.

Bre•scia (brĕsh′ə) A city of N Italy E of Milan; a free city from 936 to 1426. Pop. 200,722.

Bres•lau (brĕs′lou) See Wrocław.

Brest (brĕst) **1.** A city of NW France on an inlet of the Atlantic Ocean. Pop. 147,888. **2.** Formerly **Brest-Li•tovsk** (-lĭ-tôfsk′) A city of SW Belarus on the Bug R.; site of signing of the Treaty of Brest-Litovsk (1918). Pop. 287,200.

Bre•tagne (brə-tän′yə) See Brittany.

breth•ren (brĕth′rən) n. A plural of **brother** 2, 3, 4c.

Bret•on (brĕt′n) adj. Of or relating to Brittany or its people, language, or culture. ❖ n. **1.** A native or inhabitant of Brittany. **2.** The Celtic language of Brittany. [ME < OFr. See BRITON.]

Bre•ton (brĭ-tôn′), **André** 1896–1966. French poet who wrote the first manifesto of surrealism (1924).

Breu•er (broi′ər), **Marcel Lajos** 1902–81. Hungarian-born Amer. architect and furniture designer who was associated with the Bauhaus in the 1920s.

Breu•ghel (broi′gəl, brōō′-, brœ′-) See Brueghel.

breve (brēv, brĕv) n. **1.** A symbol (˘) placed over a vowel to show that it has a short sound, as the a in bat. **2.** A curved mark used to indicate a short or unstressed syllable of verse. **3.** Music A note equivalent to two whole notes. [ME, written communication < OFr. < Med.Lat., short syllable < Lat., neut. of brevis, short. See BRIEF.]

bre•vet (brə-vĕt′, brĕv′ĭt) n. A commission promoting a military officer in rank without an increase in pay. ❖ tr.v. **-vet•ted, -vet•ting, -vets** or **-vet•ed, -vet•ing, -vets** To promote by brevet. [ME, official letter < AN, dim. of bref, letter < Lat. brevis, short. See BRIEF.] —**bre•vet′cy** (brə-vĕt′sē) n.

bre•vi•ar•y (brē′vē-ĕr′ē, brĕv′ē-) n., pl. **-ies** Ecclesiastical A book containing the hymns, offices, and prayers for the canonical hours. [ME breviarie < OFr. breviaire < Med.Lat. breviārium < Lat., summary < brevis, short. See BRIEF.]

brev•i•ty (brĕv′ĭ-tē) n. **1.** The quality or state of being brief in duration. **2.** Concise expression; terseness. [Lat. brevitās < brevis, short. See BRIEF.]

brew (broō) v. **brewed, brew•ing, brews** —tr. **1.** To make (ale or beer) from malt and hops by infusion, boiling, and fermentation. **2.** To make (a beverage) by boiling, steeping, or mixing various ingredients. **3.** To concoct; devise. —intr. **1.** To make ale or beer as an occupation. **2.** To be made by boiling or steeping. **3.** To be imminent; impend. ❖ n. **1a.** A beverage made by brewing. **b.** A serving of such a beverage. **2.** Something produced as if by brewing; a mix. [ME brewen < OE brēowan.] —**brew′age** n. —**brew′er** n.

brew•er's yeast (broō′ərz) n. A yeast of the genus Saccharomyces, used as a ferment and a source of B vitamins.

brew•er•y (broō′ə-rē, broōr′ē) n., pl. **-ies** An establishment for the manufacture of malt liquors, such as beer and ale.

brew•is (broō′ĭs, broōz) n. New England Bread soaked in liquid, usu. milk, and eaten as a pudding or a side dish. [ME brewes < OFr. broez, pl. of broet, dim. of breu, broth < VLat. *brodum, of Gmc. orig.]

brew•ski (broō′skē) n., pl. **-skies** or **-skis** Slang **1.** Beer. **2.** A serving of beer. [BREW + -ski, -sky, n. suff. (< Russ. -skiĭ, perh. modeled on RUSSKY).]

Brew•ster (broō′stər), **William** 1567–1644. English Pilgrim colonist who was the religious leader of Plymouth Colony.

Brey•er (brī′ər), **Stephen Gerald** b. 1939. Amer. jurist who was appointed an associate justice of the US Supreme Court in 1994.

Brezh•nev (brĕzh′nĕf, -nyĭf), **Leonid Ilyich** 1906–82. Soviet leader; president of the USSR (1960–64 and 1977–82) and secretary of the Communist Party (1964–82).

Bri•an Bo•ru (brī′ən bə-roō′, bô-rō′, brĕn) 926–1014. Irish king (1002–14) who defeated the Danes and the Norse.

Bri•and (brē-änd′, -än′), **Aristide** 1862–1932. French politician who shared the 1926 Nobel Peace Prize.

Bri•ansk (brē-änsk′) See Bryansk.

bri•ar¹ (brī′ər) also **bri•er** (brī′ər) n. **1.** A Mediterranean shrub or small tree (Erica arborea). **2.** A tobacco pipe made from the hard, woody root of this plant or from a similar wood. [Fr. bruyère, heath < OFr. < VLat. *brūcāria < LLat. brūcus, heather, of Celt. orig. See wer-² in App.]

bri•ar² (brī′ər) n. Variant of **brier¹.**

bri•ard (brē-ärd′) n. Any of an ancient French breed of sturdily built dogs. [Fr. < Brie, a region of N France.]

bri•ar•root (brī′ər-roōt′, -roŏt′) n. The hard, woody root of the briar.

bri•ar•wood (brī′ər-woŏd′) n. Wood from the briarroot.

bribe (brīb) n. **1.** Something offered or given to a person in a position of trust to influence that person's views or conduct. **2.** Something serving to influence or persuade. ❖ v. **bribed, brib•ing, bribes** —tr. To give, offer, or promise a bribe to. —intr. To give, offer, or promise bribes. [ME < OFr., piece of bread given as alms.] —**brib′a•ble** adj. —**brib′er** n.

ă pat   oi boy
ā pay   ou out
âr care   oŏ took
ä father   oō boot
ĕ pet   ŭ cut
ē be   ûr urge
ĭ pit   th thin
ī pie   th this
îr pier   hw which
ŏ pot   zh vision
ō toe   ə about,
ô paw   item

Stress marks:
′ (primary);
′ (secondary), as in
lexicon (lĕk′sĭ-kŏn′)

brib•er•y (brī′bə-rē) *n., pl.* **-ies** The act or practice of offering, giving, or taking a bribe.

bric-a-brac (brĭk′ə-brăk′) *n.* Small, usu. ornamental objects valued for their antiquity, rarity, originality, or sentimental associations. [Fr. *bric-à-brac,* expressive of confusion.]

Brice (brīs), **Fannie** 1891–1951. Amer. entertainer known for her work in films, radio, and the Ziegfeld Follies.

brick (brĭk) *n.* **1.** *pl.* **bricks** or **brick** A molded rectangular block of clay baked by the sun or in a kiln until hard and used as a building and paving material. **2.** An object shaped like such a block: *a brick of cheese.* **3.** *Informal* A helpful, reliable person. ❖ *tr.v.* **bricked, brick•ing, bricks 1.** To construct, line, or pave with bricks. **2.** To close or wall with brick. [ME *brike* < MDu. *bricke.*] —**brick′y** *adj.*

brick-and-mor•tar (brĭk′ənd-môr′tər) *adj.* Located or serving consumers in a physical facility as distinct from providing remote, esp. online, services.

brick•bat (brĭk′băt′) *n.* **1.** A piece, esp. of brick, used as a weapon or missile. **2.** An unfavorable remark; a criticism. [BRICK + BAT[1], piece of brick.]

brick•lay•er (brĭk′lā′ər) *n.* A person skilled in building with bricks. —**brick′lay′ing** *n.*

brick red *n.* A moderate to strong reddish brown. —**brick′-red′** (brĭk′rĕd′) *adj.*

brick•work (brĭk′wûrk′) *n.* **1.** The technique or work of constructing with bricks and mortar. **2.** A brick structure.

brick•yard (brĭk′yärd′) *n.* A place where bricks are made.

bri•co•lage (brē′kō-läzh′, brĭk′ō-) *n.* Something made or put together using whatever materials happen to be available. [Fr. < *bricole,* trifle < OFr., catapult < OItal. *briccola,* of Gmc. orig.]

bri•dal (brīd′l) *n.* A marriage ceremony; a wedding. ❖ *adj.* **1.** Of or relating to a bride or a marriage ceremony; nuptial. **2.** Designed for a bride or a newly married couple: *a bridal shop.* [ME *bridale,* wedding, wedding feast < OE *brȳdealo* : *brȳd,* bride; see BRIDE + *ealu,* ale; see ALE.]

bridal wreath or **bri•dal-wreath** (brīd′l-rēth) *n.* Any of various shrubs of the genus *Spiraea,* having arching branches covered with white bloom and popular as an ornamental.

bride (brīd) *n.* A woman who is about to be married or has recently been married. [ME < OE *brȳd.*]

bride•groom (brīd′grōōm′, -grŏŏm′) *n.* A man who is about to be married or has recently been married. [Alteration (influenced by GROOM) of ME *bridegome* < OE *brȳdguma* : *brȳd,* bride + *guma,* man; see dhghem- in App.]

bride price *n.* See **bride wealth.**

brides•maid (brīdz′mād′) *n.* A woman who attends the bride at a wedding.

bride wealth *n.* A payment, as of money or property, made by or on behalf of a prospective husband to the bride's family in certain cultures or societies.

bridge[1] (brĭj) *n.* **1.** A structure spanning and providing passage over a gap or barrier. **2.** Something resembling or analogous to this structure in form or function. **3a.** The upper bony ridge of the human nose. **b.** The part of a pair of eyeglasses that rests against this ridge. **4.** A fixed or removable replacement for one or several of the natural teeth. **5.** *Music* **a.** A thin upright piece of wood in some stringed instruments that supports the strings above the soundboard. **b.** A transitional passage connecting two subjects or movements. **6.** *Nautical* A crosswise platform or enclosed area above the main deck of a ship from which the ship is controlled. **7.** *Games* **a.** A long stick with a notched platform at one end, used to steady the cue in billiards. **b.** The hand used as a support to steady the cue. **8.** *Electricity* **a.** Any of various instruments for measuring the characteristics, such as impedance, of a conductor. **b.** An electrical shunt. **9.** *Chemistry* An intramolecular connection that spans atoms or groups of atoms. ❖ *tr.v.* **bridged, bridg•ing, bridg•es 1.** To build a bridge over. **2.** To cross by or as if by a bridge. [ME *brigge* < OE *brycg.* See bhrū- in App.] —**bridge′a•ble** *adj.*

bridge[2] (brĭj) *n.* Any of several card games derived from whist, usu. for two pairs of players. [< earlier *biritch* (influenced by BRIDGE[1]) < Russ. *birich,* a call < ORuss. *birichĭ.*]

bridge•board (brĭj′bôrd′, -bōrd′) *n.* A notched board at either side of a staircase that supports the treads and risers.

bridge•head (brĭj′hĕd′) *n.* **1a.** A fortified position from which troops defend the end of a bridge nearest the enemy. **b.** A forward position seized by advancing troops in enemy territory as a foothold for further advance. **2.** The area immediately adjacent to the end of a bridge.

bridge[1]
top: at Lake Travis,
Austin, Texas
bottom: on a viola da
gamba

bridge loan *n.* A short-term loan intended to provide or extend financing until a more permanent arrangement is made.

Bridge•port (brĭj′pôrt′, -pōrt′) A city of SW CT on Long Island Sound; settled in 1639. Pop. 139,529.

Bridg•es (brĭj′ĭz), **Robert Seymour** 1844–1930. British poet and essayist who was appointed poet laureate in 1913.

Bridge•town (brĭj′toun′) The cap. of Barbados; founded by the British in 1628. Pop. 7,466.

bridge•work (brĭj′wûrk′) *n.* **1.** A dental bridge. **2.** Dental prosthetics involving a bridge or bridges.

bri•dle (brīd′l) *n.* **1.** A harness, consisting of a headstall, bit, and reins, fitted about a horse's head and used to restrain or guide the

animal. **2.** A curb or check. ❖ *v.* **-dled, -dling, -dles** —*tr.* **1.** To put a bridle on. **2.** To control or restrain with or as if with a bridle. —*intr.* **1.** To lift the head and draw in the chin as an expression of scorn or resentment. **2.** To show anger or resentment; take offense: *bridling at the criticism.* [ME *bridel* < OE *brīdel.*] —**bri′dler** *n.*

bridle path *n.* A trail for horseback riding.

Brie (brē) *n.* A mold-ripened cheese with a whitish rind and a soft, light yellow center. [After *Brie,* a region of northern France.]

brief (brēf) *adj.* **brief•er, brief•est 1.** Short in time, duration, length, or extent. **2.** Succinct; concise: *a brief account of the incident.* **3.** Curt; abrupt. ❖ *n.* **1.** A short, succinct statement. **2.** A condensation or an abstract of a larger document or series of documents. **3.** *Law* **a.** A formal outline listing main contentions along with supporting evidence. **b.** A document containing all the facts and points of law pertinent to a specific case, filed by an attorney before arguing the case in court. **4.** *Roman Catholic Church* A papal letter that is not as formal as a bull. **5.** A briefing. **6. briefs** Short, tight-fitting underpants. ❖ *tr.v.* **briefed, brief•ing, briefs 1.** To summarize. **2.** To give instructions or preparatory information to: *briefed the astronauts before the mission.* —**idiom:** **in brief** In short. [ME *bref* < OFr. < Lat. *brevis.*] —**brief′er** *n.* —**brief′ly** *adv.* —**brief′ness** *n.*

brief•case (brēf′kās′) *n.* A portable case with a handle, used for carrying papers or books. [BRIEF, document + CASE[2].]

brief•ing (brē′fĭng) *n.* **1.** The act or an instance of giving instructions or preparatory information to someone. **2.** A meeting at which such information is presented. **3.** The information conveyed at such a meeting.

Bri•enz (brē-ĕnts′), **Lake of** A scenic lake of central Switzerland near Interlaken.

bri•er[1] also **bri•ar** (brī′ər) *n.* Any of several prickly plants, such as certain rosebushes or the greenbrier. [ME *brer* < OE *brēr.*] —**bri′er•y** *adj.*

bri•er[2] (brī′ər) *n.* Variant of **briar**[1].

brig (brĭg) *n.* **1.** A two-masted sailing ship, square-rigged on both masts. **2.** A jail or prison on board a US Navy or Coast Guard vessel. **3.** A jail or guardhouse, esp. at a US military installation. [Short for BRIGANTINE. Senses 2 and 3 < the use of ships as prisons.]

bri•gade (brĭ-gād′) *n.* **1a.** A military unit consisting of a variable number of combat battalions or regiments. **b.** A US Army administrative and tactical unit composed of headquarters, infantry, armor, and designated support units. **2.** A group of persons organized for a specific purpose: *a bucket brigade.* ❖ *tr.v.* **-gad•ed, -gad•ing, -gades** To form into a brigade. [Fr. < OFr., company < OItal. *brigata* < *brigare,* to fight < *briga,* strife, of Celt. orig. See gʷerə- in App.]

brig•a•dier (brĭg′ə-dîr′) *n.* A brigadier general. [Fr. < *brigade,* brigade. See BRIGADE.]

brigadier general *n.* A commissioned officer in the US Army, Air Force, or Marine Corps ranking above colonel and below major general.

brig•and (brĭg′ənd) *n.* A robber or bandit, esp. one of an outlaw band. [ME *brigaunt* < OFr. < OItal. *brigante,* pr. part. of *brigare,* to fight. See BRIGADE.] —**brig′and•age** (-ə-dĭj) *n.* **brig′and•ism** *n.*

brig•an•dine (brĭg′ən-dēn′, -dīn′) *n.* Flexible body armor of small metal plates or rings, often covered with cloth. [ME < OFr., armor for a skirmisher < *brigand,* skirmisher. See BRIGAND.]

brig•an•tine (brĭg′ən-tēn′) *n.* A two-masted sailing ship, square-rigged on the foremast and having a fore-and-aft mainsail with square main topsails. [Fr. *brigantin* < OFr. *brigandin* < OItal. *brigantino,* skirmishing ship < *brigante,* skirmisher. See BRIGAND.]

Brig Gen *abbr.* brigadier general

Briggs (brĭgz), **Henry** 1561–1630. English mathematician who devised the decimal-based system of logarithms.

bright (brīt) *adj.* **bright•er, bright•est 1a.** Emitting or reflecting light readily or in large amounts; shining. **b.** Comparatively high on the scale of brightness. **c.** Full of light or illumination. **2.** Characterizing a dyestuff that produces a highly saturated color; brilliant. **3.** Glorious; splendid: *a bright moment in history.* **4.** Full of promise and hope; auspicious: *a bright future.* **5.** Happy; cheerful: *bright faces.* **6.** Animatedly clever; intelligent. **7.** High and clear: *the bright sound of trumpets.* [ME < OE *beorht.*] —**bright, bright′ly** *adv.*

SYNONYMS *bright, brilliant, radiant, lustrous, lambent, luminous, incandescent, effulgent* These adjectives refer to what emits or reflects light. *Bright* is the most general: *bright sunshine. Brilliant* implies intense brightness and often suggests sparkling or gleaming light: *a brilliant gemstone.* Something *radiant* emits or seems to emit light in rays: *a radiant smile.* A *lustrous* object reflects an agreeable sheen: *thick, lustrous auburn hair. Lambent* applies to a soft, flickering light: *"its tranquil streets, bathed in the lambent green of budding trees"* (James C. McKinley). *Luminous* especially refers to something that glows in the dark: *a luminous watch dial. Incandescent* stresses burning brilliance: *Flames consist of incandescent gases. Effulgent* suggests splendid radiance: *"The crocus, the snowdrop, and the effulgent daffodil are considered* bright harbingers of spring" (John Gould). See also Syns at **intelligent.**

bright•en (brīt'n) tr. & intr.v. **-ened, -en•ing, -ens** To make or become bright or brighter. —**bright'en•er** n.

bright•ness (brīt'nĭs) n. **1.** The state or quality of being bright. **2.** The effect or sensation by which an observer can distinguish differences in luminance. **3.** The dimension of a color that represents its similarity to one of a series of achromatic colors ranging from very dim (dark) to very bright (dazzling).

Brigh•ton (brīt'n) A resort borough of SE England on the English Channel S of London. Pop. 154,370.

Bright's disease (brīts) n. Any of several diseases of the kidney marked by the presence of albumin in the urine. [After Richard Bright (1789–1858), British physician.]

bright•work (brīt'wûrk') n. Metal parts or fixtures made bright by polishing.

brill (brĭl) n., pl. **brill** or **brills** An edible flatfish (Bothas rhombus) of European waters. [?]

Bril•lat-Sa•va•rin (brē-yä' sä-vä-răn'), Anthelme 1755–1826. French politician and gourmet who wrote Physiologie de Goût (1825).

bril•liance (brĭl'yəns) n. **1.** The state or quality of being brilliant, as: **a.** Extreme brightness. **b.** Exceptional clarity and agility of intellect or invention. **2.** Splendor; magnificence. **3.** Music Sharpness and clarity of tone.

bril•lian•cy (brĭl'yən-sē) n. Brilliance, as of intellect.

bril•liant (brĭl'yənt) adj. **1.** Full of light; shining. See Syns at **bright. 2.** Relating to or being a hue that has a combination of high lightness and strong saturation. **3.** Sharp and clear in tone. **4.** Glorious; magnificent. **5.** Superb; wonderful. **6.** Marked by unusual and impressive intellectual acuteness. See Syns at **intelligent.** ❖ n. A precious gem finely cut with numerous facets. [Fr. brillant, pr. part. of briller, to shine < Ital. brillare, perh. < brillo, beryl < Lat. bēryllus. See BERYL.] —**bril'liant•ly** adv. —**bril'liant•ness** n.

bril•lian•tine (brĭl'yən-tēn') n. **1.** An oily perfumed hairdressing. **2.** A glossy fabric made from cotton and worsted or cotton and mohair. [Fr. brillantine < brillant, brilliant. See BRILLIANT.]

brim (brĭm) n. **1.** The rim or uppermost edge of a hollow container or natural basin. **2.** A projecting rim or edge: the brim of a hat. **3.** A border or edge. See Syns at **border. 4.** Full capacity: a room full to the brim with people. ❖ v. **brimmed, brim•ming, brims** —intr. **1.** To be full to the brim, often to overflowing. **2.** To overflow. —tr. To fill to the brim. [ME brimme.]

brim•ful (brĭm'fŏŏl') adj. Full to overflowing.

brim•stone (brĭm'stōn') n. **1.** Sulfur. **2a.** Damnation to hell. **b.** Fiery or passionate rhetoric. [ME brimstone < OE brynstān. See gʷher- in App.]

brin•dle (brĭn'dl) n. **1.** A brindled color. **2.** A brindled animal. [Back-formation < BRINDLED.]

brin•dled (brĭn'dld) adj. Tawny or grayish with streaks or spots of a darker color. [Alteration of ME brended, prob. < brende, p. part. of brennen, to burn < ON brenna. See gʷher- in App.]

brine (brīn) n. **1.** Water saturated with or containing large amounts of a salt, esp. sodium chloride. **2a.** The water of a sea or an ocean. **b.** A large body of salt water. **3.** Salt water used for preserving and pickling foods. ❖ tr.v. **brined, brin•ing, brines** To immerse, preserve, or pickle in salt water. [ME < OE brīne.] —**brin'er** n.

Bri•nell hardness (brĭ-nĕl') n. The relative hardness of metals and alloys, determined by forcing a steel ball into a test piece. [After Johan August Brinell (1849–1925), Swedish engineer.]

Brinell hardness number n. The numerical value assigned to the Brinell hardness of metals and alloys.

brine shrimp n. Any of various small crustaceans of the genus Artemia.

bring (brĭng) tr.v. **brought** (brôt), **bring•ing, brings 1.** To carry, convey, lead, or cause to go along to another place. **2.** To carry as an attribute or contribution: brought much experience to the post. **3.** To lead or force into a specified state, situation, or location: bring the water to a boil. **4a.** To persuade; induce. **b.** To get the attention of; attract: The smoke brought the neighbors. **5.** To cause to occur as a consequence or concomitant: Floods brought destruction to the valley. **6.** To cause to become apparent to the mind; recall: brings back memories. **7.** Law To advance or set forth (charges) in a court. **8.** To sell for: The portrait brought a million dollars. —**phrasal verbs: bring around** (or **round**) **1.** To cause to adopt an opinion or take a certain course of action. **2.** To cause to recover consciousness. **bring down 1.** To cause to fall or collapse. **2.** To kill. **3** To disappoint; let down. **bring forth 1.** To give rise to; produce. **2.** To give birth to (young). **bring forward 1.** To present; produce: bring forward proof. **2.** Accounting To carry (a sum) from one page or column to another. **bring in** To produce, yield, or earn (profits or income). **bring off** To accomplish: bring off a successful campaign. **bring on** To cause to appear: brought on the dessert. **bring out 1a.** To reveal or expose. **b.** To introduce (a debutante) to society. **2.** To produce or publish. **3.** To nurture and develop to best advantage: bring out the best. **bring to** To cause to recover consciousness. **bring up 1.** To take care of and educate (a child); rear. **2.** To introduce into discussion; mention.

3. To vomit. **4.** To cause to come to a sudden stop. —**idioms: bring down the house** To win overwhelming approval from an audience. **bring home** To make perfectly clear. **bring to bear 1.** To exert; apply: bring pressure to bear. **2.** To put (something) to good use. **bring to light** To reveal or disclose. **bring to mind** To cause to be remembered. **bring to terms** To force (another) to agree. **bring up the rear** To be the last in a line or sequence. [ME bringen < OE bringan. See bher-1 in App.] —**bring'er** n.

bring•down (brĭng'doun') n. Something disappointing; a letdown.

brink (brĭngk) n. **1a.** The upper edge of a steep or vertical slope. **b.** The margin of land bordering a body of water. **2.** The point at which something is likely to begin; the verge. See Syns at **border.** [ME, prob. of Scandinavian orig.]

Brin•kley (brĭng'klē), David b. 1920. Amer. radio and television news broadcaster and political commentator.

brink•man•ship (brĭngk'mən-shĭp') also **brinks•man•ship** (brĭngks'-) n. The practice of seeking advantage by pushing a highly dangerous situation to the limit.

Brin•ton (brĭn'tən), Daniel Garrison 1837–99. Amer. anthropologist who first classified Native American languages.

brin•y (brī'nē) adj. **-i•er, -i•est** Of, relating to, or resembling brine; salty. —**brin'i•ness** n.

bri•o (brē'ō) n. Vigor; vivacity: "She tells their story with brio and a mixture of sympathy and tart insight" (Michiko Kakutani). [Ital. < Sp. brio or Provençal briu, both of Celt. orig. See gʷerə- in App.]

bri•oche (brē-ôsh', -ōsh') n. A soft light-textured bread formed into a roll or bun. [Fr. < OFr. < broyer, brier, to knead, of Gmc. orig. See bhreg- in App.]

bri•o•lette (brē'ō-lĕt') n. A pear-shaped or oval gem cut in triangular facets. [Fr., perh. alteration (influenced by brillant, brilliant) of brignolette, dim. of brignole, dried plum < Brignoles, a town of SE France.]

bri•quette also **bri•quet** (brĭ-kĕt') n. A block of compressed coal dust, charcoal, or sawdust and wood chips, used for fuel. [Fr., dim. of brique, brick < MDu. bricke.]

bris (brĭs) n., pl. **bris•es** Judaism The rite or ceremony of male circumcision, usu. performed on the eighth day of life. [Ashkenazi Heb. brīs < Heb. bərît (mīlâh), covenant (of circumcision).]

bri•sance (brĭ-zäns', -zäns') n. The shattering effect of the sudden release of energy in an explosion. [Fr. < brisant, pr. part. of briser, to break < OFr. brisier < VLat. *brisiāre, perh. of Celt. orig.] —**bri•sant'** (-zänt', -zänt') adj.

Bris•bane (brĭz'bən, -bān') A city of E Australia on the **Brisbane River,** c. 346 km (215 mi), near its mouth on Moreton Bay; settled in 1824 as a penal colony. Pop. 1,421,600.

brisk (brĭsk) adj. **brisk•er, brisk•est 1.** Marked by speed, liveliness, and vigor; energetic. **2.** Keen or sharp in speech or manner. **3.** Stimulating and invigorating: a brisk wind. **4.** Pleasantly zestful: a brisk tea. [Prob. of Scand. orig.] —**brisk'ly** adv. —**brisk'ness** n.

bris•ket (brĭs'kĭt) n. **1.** The chest of an animal. **2.** The ribs and meat taken from the chest of an animal. [ME brusket, perh. of Scand. orig.]

bris•ling (brĭz'lĭng, brĭs'-) n. See **sprat** 1. [Norw., alteration (influenced by brisa, to flash) of LGer. bretling < bret, broad.]

bris•tle (brĭs'əl) n. **1.** A stiff hair. **2.** A stiff hairlike structure: the bristles of a wire brush. ❖ v. **-tled, -tling, -tles** —intr. **1.** To stand stiffly on end like bristles: The cat bristled. **2.** To raise the bristles. **3.** To react in an angry or offended manner. **4.** To be covered or thick with or as if with bristles. —tr. **1.** To cause to stand erect like bristles; stiffen. **2.** To furnish or supply with bristles. **3.** To make bristly; ruffle. [ME bristel, prob. < OE *byrstel < byrst, bristle.]

bris•tle•cone pine (brĭs'əl-kōn') n. Either of two small, long-lived pines (Pinus aristata or P. longaeva) native to the western United States.

bris•tle•tail (brĭs'əl-tāl') n. Any of various wingless insects of the order Thysanura, having bristlelike posterior appendages.

bris•tly (brĭs'lē) adj. **-tli•er, -tli•est 1a.** Consisting of or similar to bristles. **b.** Thick with bristles. **2.** Exhibiting or tending to exhibit agitation or anger.

Bris•tol (brĭs'təl) A city of SW England W of London. Pop. 397,585.

Bristol Bay An arm of the Bering Sea in SW AK.

Bristol board n. A smooth, heavy pasteboard of fine quality. [After BRISTOL, England.]

Bristol Channel An inlet of the Atlantic Ocean stretching W from the Severn R. and separating Wales from SW England.

brit also **britt** (brĭt) n. **1.** The young of herring and similar fish. **2.** Minute marine organisms that are a major source of food for right whales. [Perh. < Cornish brythel, mackerel (< O Cornish breithil < *breith, speckled), or < Welsh brithyll, trout (< brith, speckled).]

Brit n. Informal A British person.

Brit. abbr. **1.** Britain **2.** British

Brit•ain¹ (brĭt'n) The island of Great Britain during pre-Roman, Roman, and early Anglo-Saxon times.

Brit•ain² (brĭt'n) See **United Kingdom.**

Bri•tan•nia (brĭ-tăn'yə, -tăn'ē-ə) n. **1.** A female personification

brisket

bristlecone pine
Great Basin bristlecone pine
Pinus longaeva

of Great Britain or the British Empire. **2.** also **britannia** Britannia metal. [Lat., Britain < *Britannī*, the Britons.]

britannia metal *n.* An alloy of tin, copper, and antimony used in utensils and tableware.

Bri·tan·nic (brĭ-tănʹĭk) *adj.* British.

britch·es (brĭchʹĭz) *pl.n.* Breeches. —**idiom: too big for (one's) britches** Overconfident; cocky. [Alteration of *breeches*, pl. of BREECH.]

Brit·i·cism (brĭtʹĭ-sĭzʹəm) also **Brit·ish·ism** (-shĭzʹəm) *n.* A word, phrase, or idiom characteristic of or peculiar to English as it is spoken in Great Britain. [< BRITI(SH), on the model of words such as GALLICISM.]

Brit·ish (brĭtʹĭsh) *adj.* **1a.** Of or relating to Great Britain or its people, language, or culture. **b.** Of or relating to the United Kingdom or the Commonwealth of Nations. **2.** Of or relating to the ancient Britons. ❖ *n.* **1.** (*used with a pl. verb*) The people of Great Britain. **2.** British English. **3.** The Celtic language of the ancient Britons. [ME *Brittish* < OE *Bryttisc*, relating to the ancient Britons < *Bryttas*, Britons, of Celt. orig.]

British Antarctic Territory A British territory of the extreme Southern Hemisphere.

British an·ti·lew·is·ite (ănʹtē-lōōʹĭ-sītʹ, ănʹtī-) *n.* See **dimercaprol.**

British Cameroons A former territory of W Africa, divided in 1961 between Nigeria and Cameroon.

British Columbia A province of W Canada bordering on the Pacific Ocean; joined the confederation in 1871. Cap. Victoria. Pop. 3,724,500.

British Commonwealth See **Commonwealth of Nations.**

British Empire The geographic and political units formerly under British control; at the height of its power in the late 19th and early 20th cent.

British English *n.* The English language as used in England.

Brit·ish·er (brĭtʹĭ-shər) *n. Informal* A native or inhabitant of Great Britain.

British Guiana See **Guyana.**

British Honduras See **Belize** 1.

British India The part of the Indian subcontinent under British administration until India's independence in 1947.

British Indian Ocean Territory A British island colony in the W Indian Ocean; formed in 1965.

British Isles A group of islands off the NW coast of Europe comprising Great Britain, Ireland, and adjacent islands.

Brit·ish·ism (brĭtʹĭ-shĭzʹəm) *n.* Variant of **Briticism.**

British Somaliland A former protectorate of E Africa on the Gulf of Aden; part of Somaliland since 1960.

British thermal unit *n.* The heat equal to $\frac{1}{180}$ of the heat required to raise the temperature of one pound of water from 32° to 212°F at a constant pressure of one atmosphere.

British Virgin Islands A British colony in the E Caribbean. Cap. Road Town, on Tortola I. Pop. 12,034.

British West Indies The islands of the West Indies formerly under British control.

Brit·on (brĭtʹn) *n.* **1.** A native or inhabitant of Great Britain. **2.** One of a Celtic people inhabiting Britain at the time of the Roman invasion. **3.** A member of a Brittonic-speaking people. [ME *Britoun*, Celt, Briton < AN *Britun* < Lat. *Brittonēs*, Britons, of Celt. orig.]

britt (brĭt) *n.* Variant of **brit.**

Brit·ta·ny (brĭtʹn-ē) also **Bre·tagne** (brə-tänʹyə) A historical region and former province of NW France on a peninsula between the English Channel and the Bay of Biscay; settled c. 500 by Britons and incorporated into France in 1532.

Brittany spaniel *n.* A large pointing spaniel of a breed originating in France.

Brit·ten (brĭtʹn), **(Edward) Benjamin** 1913–76. British composer known for his song cycles and operas.

brit·tle (brĭtʹl) *adj.* **-tler, -tlest 1a.** Likely to break, snap, or crack. **b.** Easily damaged or disrupted: *a brittle friendship.* See Syns at **fragile. 2a.** Difficult to deal with; snappish. **b.** Lacking warmth of feeling; cold. **3.** Brilliantly sharp, as in percussive sound. ❖ *n.* A confection of caramelized sugar and nuts. [ME *britel*, prob. < OE **brytel* < *bryttian*, to shatter.] —**britʹtle·ly** (brĭtʹl-ē) *adv.* —**britʹtle·ness** *n.*

brit·tle·bush (brĭtʹl-bŏōshʹ) *n.* A shrub (*Encelia farinosa*) in the composite family, native to Mexico and the southwest United States and having grayish foliage and flowers with yellow rays.

brittle star *n.* Any of various marine organisms of the class Ophiuroidea, related to and resembling the starfish but having long slender arms.

Brit·ton·ic (brĭ-tŏnʹĭk) also **Bry·thon·ic** (-thŏnʹ-) *n.* The subdivision of the Insular Celtic languages that includes Welsh, Breton, and Cornish. [Ult. < Lat. *Brittonēs*, Britons. See BRITON.]

Brix scale (brĭks) *n.* A hydrometer scale for measuring the sugar content of a solution at a given temperature. [After Adolf F. *Brix* (1798–1870), German scientist.]

Br·no (bûrʹnō) A city of SE Czech Republic SE of Prague; founded in the 10th cent. Pop. 389,762.

bro (brō) *n., pl.* **bros** *Slang* **1.** A brother. **2.** Friend; pal. Used as a form of familiar address for a man or boy: *So long, bro.* [African American Vernacular E.]

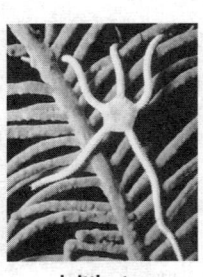
brittle star

Bro. *abbr. Ecclesiastical* brother (title)

broach¹ (brōch) *tr.v.* **broached, broach·ing, broach·es 1a.** To bring up (a subject) for discussion or debate. **b.** To announce. **2.** To pierce in order to draw off liquid. **3.** To draw off (a liquid) by piercing a hole in a container. **4.** To shape or enlarge (a hole) with a tapered, serrated tool. ❖ *n.* **1a.** A tapered, serrated tool used to broach a hole. **b.** The hole made by such a tool. **2.** A spit for roasting meat. **3.** A mason's narrow chisel. **4.** A gimlet for tapping or broaching casks. **5.** Variant of **brooch.** [ME *brochen*, to pierce, prob. < *broche*, pointed weapon or implement < OFr. < VLat. **brocca* < Lat. *broccus*, projecting.] —**broachʹer** *n.*

broach² (brōch) *intr. & tr.v.* **broached, broach·ing, broach·es** *Nautical* To veer or cause to veer broadside to the wind and waves. [Prob. < BROACH¹.]

broad (brôd) *adj.* **broad·er, broad·est 1.** Wide in extent from side to side: *a broad river.* **2.** Large in expanse; spacious: *a broad lawn.* **3.** Having a certain width from side to side: *three feet broad.* **4.** Full; open: *broad daylight.* **5.** Covering a wide scope; general: *a broad rule.* **6.** Liberal; tolerant. See Syns at **broad-minded. 7.** Relating to or covering the main facts or the essential points. **8.** Plain and clear; obvious. **9.** *Obsolete* Outspoken. **10.** Vulgar; ribald: *a broad joke.* **11.** Strikingly regional or dialectal: *a broad Southern accent.* **12.** *Linguistics* Pronounced with the tongue placed low and flat and with the mouth wide open, like the *a* in *father.* ❖ *n.* **1.** A wide flat part, as of one's hand. **2.** *Often Offensive Slang* A woman or girl. ❖ *adv.* Fully; completely. [ME *brod* < OE *brād*.] —**broadʹly** *adv.* —**broadʹness** *n.*

broad arrow *n.* **1.** An arrow with a wide barbed head. **2.** *Chiefly British* A wide arrowhead mark identifying government property.

broad·ax also **broad·axe** (brôdʹăksʹ) *n.* An ax with a wide flat head and a short handle; a battle-ax.

broad·band (brôdʹbăndʹ) *adj.* Of, relating to, or having a wide band of electromagnetic frequencies. —**broadʹbandʹ** *n.*

broad bean also **broad·bean** (brôdʹbēnʹ) *n.* **1.** An annual Old World plant (*Vicia faba*) in the pea family, having pinnately compound leaves and long thick pods. **2.** The edible seed or green pod of this plant.

broad-brush (brôdʹbrŭshʹ) *adj.* Sweepingly general in scope.

broad·cast (brôdʹkăstʹ) *v.* **-cast** or **-cast·ed, -cast·ing, -casts** —*tr.* **1.** To transmit (a radio or television program) for public or general use. **2.** To send out or communicate, esp. by radio or television. **3.** To make known over a wide area: *broadcast rumors.* **4.** To sow (seed) over a wide area, esp. by hand. —*intr.* **1a.** To transmit a radio or television program for public or general use. **b.** To be on the air. **2.** To participate in a radio or television program. **3.** To send a transmission or signal; transmit. ❖ *n.* **1.** Transmission of a radio or television program or signal for public use. **2a.** A radio or television program. **b.** The duration of such a program. **3.** The act of scattering seed. ❖ *adj.* **1a.** Communicated by means of television or radio. **b.** Of or relating to television or radio communications. **2.** Widely known. **3.** Scattered over a wide area. ❖ *adv.* In a scattered manner. —**broadʹcastʹer** *n.*

Broad-Church (brôdʹchûrchʹ) *adj.* Of or relating to members of the Anglican Communion in the late 19th century who favored liberalization of ritual and doctrine.

broad·cloth (brôdʹklôthʹ, -klŏthʹ) *n.* **1.** A densely textured woolen cloth with a plain or twill weave and a lustrous finish. **2.** A closely woven silk, cotton, or synthetic fabric with a narrow crosswise rib.

broad·en (brôdʹn) *tr. & intr.v.* **-ened, -en·ing, -ens** To make or become broad or broader. —**broadʹen·er** *n.*

broad gauge *n.* **1.** A distance between the rails of a railroad track that is greater than the standard width of 56½ inches (143.5 centimeters). **2.** A locomotive, car, or railway line of this gauge.

broad-gauge (brôdʹgājʹ) *adj.* **1.** Having a broad gauge. Used of a railroad track. **2.** *Informal* Having a wide scope.

broad jump *n. Sports* The long jump.

broad-leaf (brôdʹlēfʹ) *adj.* Broad-leaved.

broad-leaved (brôdʹlēvdʹ) also **broad-leafed** (-lēftʹ) *adj.* Having broad leaves rather than needlelike or scalelike leaves.

broad·loom (brôdʹlōōmʹ) *adj.* Woven on a wide loom: *a broadloom carpet.* —**broadʹloomʹ** *n.*

broad-mind·ed (brôdʹmīnʹdĭd) *adj.* Having or characterized by tolerant or liberal views. —**broadʹ-mindʹed·ly** *adv.* —**broadʹ-mindʹed·ness** *n.*

SYNONYMS *broad-minded, broad, liberal, open-minded, tolerant* These adjectives mean having or showing an inclination to respect views and beliefs that differ from one's own: *a broad-minded judge; showed broad sympathies; a liberal cleric; open-minded impartiality; a tolerant attitude.* **ANTONYM** *narrow-minded*

Broads (brôdz) A low-lying region of E England with wide shallow lakes interconnected by rivers and small streams.

broad·sheet (brôdʹshētʹ) *n.* See **broadside** 4.

broad·side (brôdʹsīdʹ) *n.* **1.** The side of a ship above the water line. **2a.** All the guns on one side of a warship. **b.** The simultaneous discharge of these guns. **3.** A forceful verbal attack. **4a.** A large sheet of paper usu. printed on one side. **b.** Something, such as an advertisement, that is printed on a broadside. **5.** A broad unbroken surface. ❖ *adv.* With the side turned to a given point or object: *The wave caught the canoe broadside.* ❖ *tr.v.* **-sid·ed, -sid·ing, -sides** To strike or collide with full on the side.

broad-spec·trum (brôd′spĕk′trəm) *adj.* Widely applicable or effective: *a broad-spectrum antibiotic.*

broad·sword (brôd′sôrd′, -sōrd′) *n.* A sword with a wide, usu. two-edged blade for slashing rather than thrusting.

broad·tail (brôd′tāl′) *n.* **1.** See **karakul. 2.** The black pelt of a prematurely born karakul sheep.

Broad·way (brôd′wā′) **1.** A thoroughfare of NY, the longest street in the world. It begins at the S tip of Manhattan and extends c. 241 km (150 mi) N to Albany. **2.** The principal theater and amusement district of New York City.

broad-winged hawk (brôd′wĭngd′) *n.* A crow-sized forest hawk (*Buteo platypterous*) of eastern North America.

Brob·ding·nag·i·an (brŏb′dĭng-năg′ē-ən) *adj.* Immense; enormous. [After *Brobdingnag,* a country in *Gulliver's Travels* by Jonathan Swift, where everything was enormous.]

bro·cade (brō-kād′) *n.* A heavy fabric interwoven with a rich, raised design. [Sp. or Port. *brocado* < Ital. *brocato* < *brocco,* twisted thread < VLat. **brocca,* spike < Lat. *brocchus,* projecting, of Celt. orig.] **—bro·cade′** *v.*

Bro·ca's area (brō′kəz) *n.* An area of the frontal lobe associated with the motor control of speech. [After Paul Broca (1824–80), French surgeon and physical anthropologist.]

broc·a·tel also **broc·a·telle** (brŏk′ə-tĕl′) *n.* A heavy fabric with highly raised designs. [Fr. *brocatelle* < Ital. *broccatello,* dim. of *broccato,* brocade. See BROCADE.]

broc·co·li (brŏk′ə-lē) *n.* **1.** A vegetable (*Brassica oleracea* var. *italica*) in the mustard family, related to the cauliflower and having clusters of green flower buds. **2.** The flower clusters of this plant, eaten as a vegetable before the buds open. [Ital., pl. of *broccolo,* flowering sprout of a turnip, dim. of *brocco,* shoot, sprout < VLat. **brocca,* spike. See BROCADE.]

broccoli raab or **broccoli rabe** (räb) *n.* A vegetable plant (*Brassica rapa*) related to the turnip. [Ital. *broccoli di rapa : broccoli,* pl. of *brocco,* sprout, shoot; see BROCCOLI + *di,* of (< Lat. *dē*; see DE–) + *rapa,* turnip; see RAPE².]

bro·chette (brō-shĕt′) *n.* **1.** A small skewer or spit used to broil or roast meat, fish, or vegetables. **2.** Food broiled or roasted on a brochette. [Fr. < OFr., dim. of *broche,* spit. See BROACH¹.]

bro·chure (brō-shoor′) *n.* A small booklet or pamphlet. [Fr. < *brocher,* to stitch < *broche,* knitting needle < OFr., spit, needle. See BROACH¹.]

brock (brŏk) *n. Chiefly British* A badger. [ME *brok* < OE *broc,* of Celt. orig.]

Brock·en (brŏk′ən) A granite peak, 1,142.8 m (3,747 ft), of the Harz Mts. in central Germany.

brock·et (brŏk′ĭt) *n.* **1.** A two-year-old red deer with its first horns. **2.** Any of several small South American deer of the genus *Mazama,* having short unbranched horns. [ME *broket* < OFr. *brocard* < *broque,* animal's horn, dialectal var. of *broche,* spit. See BROACH¹.]

Brock·house (brŏk′hous′), **Bertram Neville** b. 1918. Canadian physicist who shared a 1994 Nobel Prize.

Brock·ton (brŏk′tən) A city of E MA S of Boston; settled in 1700. Pop. 94,304.

Brod·sky (brôd′skē), **Joseph** 1940–96. Russian poet and essayist who won the 1987 Nobel Prize for literature.

bro·gan (brō′gən) *n.* A heavy, ankle-high work shoe. [Ir.Gael. *brógan,* dim. of *bróg,* brogue. See BROGUE¹.]

Bro·glie (brō-glē′), **Louis Victor de** 1892–1987. French physicist who won a 1929 Nobel Prize.

brogue¹ (brōg) *n.* **1.** A heavy shoe of untanned leather, formerly worn in Scotland and Ireland. **2.** A strong oxford shoe, usu. with ornamental perforations and wing tips. [Ir. and Sc. Gael. *bróg* < OIr. *bróc,* shoe, poss. < ON *brók,* legging, or < OE *brōc.* See BREECH.]

brogue² (brōg) *n.* A strong dialectal accent, esp. a strong Irish accent. [Poss. < the brogues worn by peasants.]

broi·der (broi′dər) *tr.v.* **-dered, -der·ing, -ders** To ornament with needlework; embroider. [Alteration (influenced by ME *broiden,* braided) of ME *brouderen* < OFr. *brosder, brouder.* See EMBROIDER.] **—broi′der·y** *n.*

broil¹ (broil) *v.* **broiled, broil·ing, broils** —*tr.* **1.** To cook by direct radiant heat, as over a grill. **2.** To expose to great heat. —*intr.* To be exposed to great heat. ❖ *n.* **1.** The act of broiling or the condition of being broiled. **2.** Food, esp. meat, that is broiled. [ME *broilen* < OFr. *brusler, bruler,* perh. < *usler,* to burn (with *br-* < *bruir,* to burn) < Lat. *ustulâre,* to scorch < *ustus,* p. part. of *ûrere,* to burn.]

broil² (broil) *n.* A rowdy argument; a brawl. ❖ *intr.v.* **broiled, broil·ing, broils** To engage in a rowdy argument. [ME *broilen* < AN *broiller,* to mix up, confuse < OFr. *brouiller* < *breu,* broth, brew < VLat. **brodum* < Gmc. orig.]

broil·er (broi′lər) *n.* **1.** One that broils, esp. a small oven or the part of a stove used for broiling food. **2.** A tender young chicken suitable for broiling.

broke (brōk) *v.* **1.** Past tense of **break. 2.** *Nonstandard* A past participle of **break.** ❖ *adj. Informal* **1.** Bankrupt. **2.** Lacking funds.

bro·ken (brō′kən) *v.* Past participle of **break.** ❖ *adj.* **1a.** Forcibly

---

separated into two or more pieces; fractured. **b.** Sundered by divorce, separation, or desertion. **2.** Having been violated: *a broken promise.* **3a.** Incomplete: *a broken set of books.* **b.** Being in a state of disarray; disordered. **4a.** Intermittently stopping and starting; discontinuous. **b.** Varying abruptly, as in pitch: *broken sobs.* **c.** Spoken with gaps and errors: *broken English.* **5.** Topographically rough; uneven. **6a.** Subdued totally; humbled. **b.** Weakened and infirm. **7.** Crushed by grief: *a broken heart.* **8.** Financially ruined; bankrupt. **9.** Not functioning; out of order. **—bro′ken·ly** *adv.* **—bro′ken·ness** *n.*

bro·ken-down (brō′kən-doun′) *adj.* **1.** Not in working order. **2.** In poor condition, as from old age; infirm.

bro·ken·heart·ed (brō′kən-här′tĭd) *adj.* Grievously sad.

broken wind *n.* A pulmonary disease of horses; the heaves. **—bro′ken-wind′ed** (brō′kən-wĭn′dĭd) *adj.*

bro·ker (brō′kər) *n.* **1.** One that acts as an agent for others, as in negotiating contracts, purchases, or sales, in return for a fee or commission. **2.** A stockbroker. **3.** A power broker. ❖ *tr.v.* **-kered, -ker·ing, -kers** To arrange or manage as a broker. [ME < AN *brocour, abrocour;* akin to Sp. *alboroque,* ceremonial gift at conclusion of business deal < Ar. *al-baraka,* the blessing, colloquial var. of *al-baraka : al-,* the + *baraka,* blessing, divine favor (< *bāraka,* to bless).]

bro·ker·age (brō′kər-ĭj) *n.* **1.** The business of a broker. **2.** A fee or commission paid to a broker. **3.** A firm engaged in buying and selling stocks and bonds for clients.

brol·ly (brŏl′ē) *n., pl.* **-lies** *Chiefly British* An umbrella. [Shortening and alteration of UMBRELLA.]

bro·mate (brō′māt′) *n.* **1.** A salt of bromic acid. **2.** An ion of bromic acid, BrO₃. ❖ *tr.v.* **-mat·ed, -mat·ing, -mates** To treat (a substance) chemically with a bromate.

brome (brōm) *n.* Any of various grasses of the genus *Bromus,* native to temperate regions and including weed, ornamental, and forage species. [NLat. *Bromus,* genus name < Gk. *bromos,* oats.]

bro·me·lain (brō′mə-lən, -lān′) *n.* A proteolytic enzyme obtained from pineapples. [NLat. *Bromel(ia),* former pineapple genus; see BROMELIAD + (PAP)AIN.]

bro·me·li·ad (brō-mē′lē-ăd′) *n.* Any of various mostly epiphytic tropical American plants of the family Bromeliaceae, usu. having long stiff leaves, colorful flowers, and showy bracts. [< NLat. *Bromelia,* type genus, after Olaf *Bromelius* (1639–1705), Swedish botanist.]

bro·mic acid (brō′mĭk) *n.* A corrosive colorless liquid, HBrO₃, used in making dyes and pharmaceuticals.

bro·mide (brō′mīd′) *n.* **1a.** A binary compound of bromine with another element. **b.** Potassium bromide. **2a.** A commonplace remark or notion; a platitude. **b.** A tiresome person; a bore.

bro·mi·nate (brō′mə-nāt′) *tr.v.* **-nat·ed, -nat·ing, -nates** To combine (a substance) with bromine or a bromine compound. **—bro′mi·na′tion** *n.*

bro·mine (brō′mēn) *n.* *Symbol* **Br** A volatile nonmetallic liquid element, having a highly irritating vapor. It is used in gasoline antiknock mixtures and photographic chemicals. Atomic weight 79.904; atomic number 35; melting point 7.2°C; boiling point 58.78°C; specific gravity 3.12; valence 1, 3, 5, 7. See table at **element.** [Fr. *brome* (< Gk. *brōmos,* stench) + −INE².]

bro·mism (brō′mĭz′əm) also **bro·min·ism** (brō′mə-nĭz′əm) *n.* A toxic condition caused by the chronic overuse of bromides, characterized by mental dullness, loss of muscular coordination, and sometimes skin eruptions.

bromo- or **brom-** *pref.* Bromine: *bromide.* [< BROMINE and BROMIDE.]

bron·chi (brŏng′kī′, -kē′) *n.* Plural of **bronchus.**

bron·chi·al (brŏng′kē-al) *adj.* Of or relating to the bronchi, the bronchia, or the bronchioles. **—bron′chi·al·ly** *adv.*

bronchial asthma *n.* Asthma that is caused by spasmodic contraction of the muscular walls of the bronchial tubes.

bronchial tube *n.* A bronchus or any of its branches.

bron·chi·ec·ta·sis (brŏng′kē-ĕk′tə-sĭs) *n.* Chronic dilatation of the bronchial tubes. [Gk. *bronkhia,* bronchial tubes (< *bronkhos,* windpipe) + Gk. *ektasis,* extension (*ek-,* out; see ECTO– + *tasis,* a stretching < *teinein, ta-,* to stretch; see ten- in App.).]

bron·chi·ole (brŏng′kē-ōl′) *n.* Any of the fine, thin-walled, tubular extensions of a bronchus. [Fr. < NLat. *bronchiola,* dim. of Lat. *bronchus.* See BRONCHUS.] **—bron′chi·o′lar** (-ō′lər) *adj.*

bron·chi·tis (brŏn-kī′tĭs, brŏng-) *n.* **1.** Inflammation of the mucous membrane of the bronchial tubes. **2.** A disease marked by this inflammation. **—bron·chit′ic** (-kĭt′ĭk) *adj.*

bron·chi·um (brŏng′kē-əm) *n., pl.* **-chi·a** (-kē-ə) A bronchial tube that is smaller than a bronchus and larger than a bronchiole. [NLat., sing. of LLat. *bronchia,* bronchial tubes < Gk. *bronkhia* < *bronkhos,* windpipe.]

broncho- or **bronch-** *pref.* Bronchus; bronchial: *bronchoscope.* [LLat. *bronchus* < Gk. *bronkhos,* windpipe.]

bron·cho·di·la·tor (brŏng′kō-dī-lā′tər, -dī′-, -dī′lā-) *n.* A drug that relaxes bronchial smooth muscle to ease breathing.

bron·cho·pneu·mo·ni·a (brŏng′kō-nŏo-mōn′yə, -nyōo-) *n.* A pneumonia involving inflammation of the lungs that spreads from the bronchi.

bron·cho·pul·mo·nar·y (brŏng′kō-pŏol′mə-nĕr′ē, -pŭl′-)

brocade

bromeliad

ă	pat	oi	boy
ā	pay	ou	out
âr	care	ŏŏ	took
ä	father	ōō	boot
ĕ	pet	ŭ	cut
ē	be	ûr	urge
ĭ	pit	th	thin
ī	pie	*th*	this
îr	pier	hw	which
ŏ	pot	zh	vision
ō	toe	ə	about,
ô	paw		item

Stress marks:
′ (primary);
′ (secondary); as in
lexicon (lĕk′sĭ-kŏn′)

adj. Relating to the bronchial tubes and the lungs.

bron·cho·scope (brŏng′kə-skōp′) *n.* A slender tubular instrument with a small light on the end for inspection of the interior of the bronchi. —**bron′cho·scop′ic** (-skŏp′ĭk) *adj.* —**bron·chos′co·pist** (brŏn-kŏs′kə-pĭst, brŏng-) *n.* —**bron·chos′co·py** (-kə-pē) *n.*

bron·chus (brŏng′kəs) *n., pl.* **-chi** (-kī′, -kē′) Either of two main branches of the trachea, leading directly to the lungs. [NLat. < Gk. *bronkhos,* windpipe.]

bron·co (brŏng′kō) *n., pl.* **-cos** A wild or semiwild horse or pony of western North America. [Am.Sp. < Sp., wild, perh. < VLat. **bruncus,* knot in a tree, perh. < Lat. *broccus,* projecting (influenced by *truncus,* stump).]

bron·co·bust·er (brŏng′kō-bŭs′tər) *n.* One who breaks wild horses to the saddle.

Bron·të (brŏn′tē) Family of British novelists and poets, including **Charlotte** (1816–55), known for *Jane Eyre* (1847); **Emily** (1818–48), known for *Wuthering Heights* (1847); and **Anne** (1820–49), known for *Agnes Gray* (1847).

bron·to·saur (brŏn′tə-sôr′) or **bron·to·sau·rus** (brŏn′tə-sôr′əs) *n.* An apatosaur. [NLat. *Brontosaurus,* former genus name : Gk. *brontē,* thunder + Gk. *sauros,* lizard.]

Bronx (brŏngks) A borough of New York City in SE NY on the mainland N of Manhattan. Pop. 1,332,650.

Bronx cheer *n. Slang* A loud sound expressing disapproval; a raspberry. [After the Bronx.]

bronze (brŏnz) *n.* **1a.** Any of various alloys of copper and tin, sometimes with traces of other metals. **b.** Any of various alloys of copper, with or without tin, and antimony, phosphorus, or other components. **2.** A work of art made of one of these alloys. **3.** A medal made of bronze, awarded for third place in a competition. **4a.** A moderate yellowish to olive brown. **b.** A pigment of this color. ❖ *adj.* **1.** Made of or consisting of bronze. **2.** Of the color bronze. ❖ *tr.v.* **bronzed, bronz·ing, bronz·es** **1.** To give the color or appearance of bronze to. **2.** To make brown by exposure to the sun; tan. [Fr. < Ital. *bronzo.*] —**bronz′er** *n.* —**bronz′y** *adj.*

Bronze Age *n.* A period of human culture between the Stone Age and the Iron Age, characterized by weapons and implements made of bronze.

bronze grackle *n.* A type of common grackle distinguished by its deep bronze back, having a more westerly range than other common grackles.

Bronze Star *n.* A US military decoration awarded either for heroism or for meritorious achievement in ground combat.

brooch (brōch, brooch) also **broach** (brōch) *n.* A relatively large decorative pin or clasp. [ME *broche,* pointed tool, brooch, pin. See BROACH[1].]

brood (brood) *n.* **1.** The young of certain animals, esp. a group of young birds or fowl. **2.** The children in one family. ❖ *v.* **brood·ed, brood·ing, broods** —*tr.* **1.** To sit on or hatch (eggs). **2.** To protect (young) by or as if by covering with the wings. —*intr.* **1.** To sit on or hatch eggs. **2.** To hover enveilopingly; loom. **3a.** To be deep in thought; meditate. **b.** To focus the attention on a subject persistently and moodily; worry. **c.** To be depressed. ❖ *adj.* Kept for breeding: *a brood hen.* [ME < OE *brōd.*] —**brood′·ing·ly** *adv.*

SYNONYMS *brood, dwell, fret, mope, stew, worry* These verbs mean to turn over in the mind moodily and at length: *brooding about life; dwelled on defeat; fretting over the job; moping about his illness; stewing over her upcoming trial; worrying about bills.*

brood·er (broo′dər) *n.* **1.** One that broods. **2.** A heated enclosure in which fowls are raised.

brood·mare (brood′mâr′) *n.* A mare used for breeding.

brood·y (broo′dē) *adj.* **-i·er, -i·est** **1a.** Meditative; contemplative. **b.** Oppressive. **2.** Disposed to sit on eggs to hatch them. —**brood′i·ness** *n.*

brook[1] (brook) *n. Chiefly Northeastern US* See CREEK 1. See Regional Note at **run.** [ME < OE *brōc.*]

brook[2] (brook) *tr.v.* **brooked, brook·ing, brooks** To put up with; tolerate. [ME *brouken* < OE *brūcan,* to use, enjoy.]

Brooke (brook), **Rupert** 1887–1915. British poet known esp. for his romantic war poetry.

brook·ite (brook′īt′) *n.* A mineral form of titanium dioxide, TiO₂. [After Henry James *Brooke* (1771–1857), British mineralogist.]

brook·let (brook′lĭt) *n.* A small brook.

brook·lime (brook′līm′) *n.* Either of two trailing plants, *Veronica americana* of North America and *V. beccabunga* of Eurasia, having clusters of small blue or purplish flowers. [Alteration of ME *brokelemok* : *broke,* brook; see BROOK[1] + *lemok,* a kind of brooklime (< OE *hleomoc*).]

Brook·lyn (brook′lĭn) A borough of New York City in SE NY on W Long I.; settled by Dutch colonists in 1645. Pop. 2,465,326.

Brooks (brooks), **Gwendolyn Elizabeth** 1917–2000. Amer. poet known for her verses detailing the dreams and struggles of African Americans.

Brooks, Van Wyck 1886–1963. Amer. literary historian whose works include *The Flowering of New England* (1936).

Brooks Range A section of the Rocky Mts. in N AK within the Arctic Circle and rising to c. 2,763 m (9,060 ft).

brook trout *n.* A freshwater game fish (*Salvelinus fontinalis*) of eastern North America.

broom (broom, broom) *n.* **1.** An implement used for sweeping, usu. consisting of a bunch of twigs, straw, or bristles bound together and attached to a stick or handle. **2a.** Any of various Mediterranean shrubs of the genus *Cytisus* in the pea family, esp. *C. scoparius,* having compound leaves with bright yellow flowers. **b.** Any of several similar shrubs, esp. in the genera *Genista* and *Spartium.* ❖ *tr.v.* **broomed, broom·ing, brooms** To sweep with or as if with a broom. [ME < OE *brōm.*] —**broom′y** *adj.*

broom·corn (broom′kôrn′, broom′-) *n.* A variety of sorghum (*Sorghum bicolor*), the stalks of which are used to make brooms.

broom·rape (broom′rāp′, broom′-) *n.* Any of various parasitic herbs of the genus *Orobanche,* having purplish or yellowish flowers and small scalelike leaves that lack chlorophyll. [Transl. of Med.Lat. *rāpum genistae* : Lat. *rāpum,* underground stock of a tree + Lat. *genistae,* genitive of *genista,* broom (< growth of these tubers on broom roots.).]

broom·stick (broom′stĭk′, broom′-) *n.* The handle of a broom.

bros. *abbr.* brothers

broth (brôth, brŏth) *n., pl.* **broths** (brôths, brŏths, brôthz, brŏthz) **1.** The water in which meat, fish, or vegetables have been boiled; stock. **2.** A thin clear soup based on stock. **3.** A liquid containing nutrients for culturing microorganisms. [ME < OE.]

broth·el (brŏth′əl, brô′thəl) *n.* A house of prostitution. [Short for *brothel-house* < ME *brothel,* prostitute < *brothen,* p. part. of *brethen,* to go to ruin < OE *brēothan,* to decay.]

broth·er (brŭth′ər) *n., pl.* **-ers** **1.** A male having the same parents as another or one parent in common with another. **2.** *pl.* often **breth·ren** (brĕth′rən) One who shares a common ancestry, allegiance, character, or purpose with another or others; esp.: **a.** A kinsman. **b.** A fellow man. **c.** A fellow member, as of a fraternity or trade union. **d.** A close male friend. **e.** A fellow African-American man or boy. **3.** *pl.* often **brethren** Something, such as a corporation or institution, that is regarded as a member of a class. **4.** *Ecclesiastical* **a.** A member of a men's religious order who is not in holy orders but engages in the work of the order. **b.** A lay member of a religious order of men. **c.** *pl.* often **brethren** A fellow member of the Christian church. [ME < OE *brōthor.* See **bhrāter-** in App.]

broth·er·hood (brŭth′ər-hood′) *n.* **1.** The state or relationship of being brothers. **2.** Fellowship. **3.** An association of men, such as a fraternity or union, united for common purposes. **4.** All the members of a profession or trade.

broth·er-in-law (brŭth′ər-ĭn-lô′) *n., pl.* **broth·ers-in-law** (-ərz-) **1.** The brother of one's spouse. **2.** The husband of one's sister. **3.** The husband of the sister of one's spouse.

broth·er·ly (brŭth′ər-lē) *adj.* Characteristic of or befitting brothers. —**broth′er·li·ness** *n.* —**broth′er·ly** *adv.*

broug·ham (broom, broo′əm, brōm, brō′əm) *n.* **1.** A closed four-wheeled carriage with an open driver's seat. **2.** An automobile with an open driver's seat. **3.** An electrically powered automobile resembling a coupé. [After Henry Peter *Brougham,* 1st Baron Brougham and Vaux (1778–1868), Scottish-born jurist.]

brought (brôt) *v.* Past tense and past participle of **bring.**

brou·ha·ha (broo′hä-hä′) *n.* An uproar; a hubbub. [Fr., of imit. orig.]

brow (brou) *n.* **1a.** The superciliary ridge over the eyes. **b.** The eyebrow. **c.** The forehead. **2.** A facial expression; countenance. **3.** The projecting upper edge of a steep place: *the brow of a hill.* [ME < OE *brū.* See **bhrū-** in App.]

brow·beat (brou′bēt′) *tr.v.* **-beat, -beat·en** (-bēt′n), **-beat·ing, -beats** To intimidate or subjugate by an overbearing manner or domineering speech; bully. —**brow′beat′er** *n.*

brown (broun) *n.* Any of a group of colors between red and yellow in hue that are medium to low in lightness and low to moderate in saturation. ❖ *adj.* **brown·er, brown·est** **1.** Of the color brown. **2a.** Having a brownish or dark skin color. **b.** *Often Offensive* Of or being a person of nonwhite origin. **3.** Deeply suntanned. ❖ *tr. & intr.v.* **browned, brown·ing, browns** **1.** To make or become brown. **2.** To cook until brown. [ME < OE *brūn.* See **bher-[2]** in App.] —**brown′ish** *adj.* —**brown′ness** *n.*

Brown, Charles Brockden 1771–1810. Amer. writer and editor considered America's first professional novelist.

Brown, Clifford Known as "Brownie." 1930–56. Amer. jazz trumpeter whose work influenced jazz improvisation and bop styles.

Brown, Herbert Charles b. 1912. British-born Amer. chemist who shared a 1979 Nobel Prize.

Brown, James b. 1933. Amer. singer often called the "Godfather of Soul."

Brown, James Nathaniel Known as "Jim." b. 1936. Amer. football player who was a running back with the Cleveland Browns (1957–71) and is one of the NFL all-time rushing leaders.

Brown, John 1800–59. Amer. abolitionist who captured the US arsenal at Harper's Ferry as part of an effort to liberate Southern slaves (1859).

Brown, Margaret Wise 1910–52. Amer. author of children's picture books, including *Goodnight Moon* (1947).

Brown, Olympia 1835–1926. Amer. minister and suffragist who was the first woman in the US to be ordained in the ministry of an established denomination (1863).

Brontë
detail of a portrait of Anne, Emily, and Charlotte, painted by Patrick Branwell Brontë (1817–48), who obliterated his own image from the painting

brooch

John Brown

Brown, Robert 1773–1858. Scottish botanist known for his discovery of the irregular movement of pollen grains.

brown alga *n.* Any of a group of chiefly marine algae of the division Phaeophyta, including rockweed and kelp, having brown and yellow pigments that mask the chlorophyll.

brown-bag (broun′băg′) *tr.v.* **-bagged, -bag•ging, -bags 1.** To take (lunch) to work, typically in a brown paper bag. **2.** To take (liquor) into a public establishment, such as a restaurant, that does not serve alcohol. —**brown bagger** *n.*

brown bear *n.* Any of several large bears of the genus *Ursus*, such as the grizzly and Kodiak bears, inhabiting western North America and northern Eurasia and having brown to yellowish fur.

brown Bet•ty (bĕt′ē) *n.* A baked pudding of chopped or sliced apples, bread crumbs, raisins, sugar, butter, and spices.

brown bread *n.* **1.** A bread made of a dark flour, such as graham or whole-wheat flour. **2.** A steamed bread usu. made of cornmeal, flour, and molasses.

brown coal *n.* See **lignite**.

brown dwarf *n.* A celestial body that resembles a star but does not emit light because it is too small to ignite internal nuclear fusion.

Browne (broun), **Charles Farrar** Pen name **Artemus Ward**. 1834–67. Amer. humorist who used backwoods characters and local dialect to comment on current events.

Browne, Sir Thomas 1605–82. English physician and writer whose works include *Religio Medici* (1642).

brown fat *n.* A dark-colored, mitochondrion-rich adipose tissue in many mammals that generates heat to regulate body temperature, esp. in hibernating animals.

brown•field (broun′fēld′) *n.* An abandoned, usu. contaminated commercial property that has potential for redevelopment.

Brown•i•an movement (brou′nē-ən) *n.* The random movement of microscopic particles suspended in a liquid or gas, caused by collisions with molecules of the surrounding medium. [After Robert BROWN.]

brown•ie (brou′nē) *n.* **1. Brownie** A member of the Girl Scouts from six through eight years of age. **2.** A bar of moist, usu. chocolate cake, often with nuts. **3.** A small sprite thought to do helpful work at night. [Sense 3 < the notion of the sprite as a tiny brown man.]

Brownie point also **brownie point** *n.* An amount of credit considered as earned, esp. by favorably impressing a superior.

Brown•ing (brou′nĭng), **Elizabeth Barrett** 1806–61. British poet best known for *Sonnets from the Portuguese* (1850).

Browning, John Moses 1855–1926. Amer. firearms inventor whose designs include repeating rifles, automatic pistols, and a machine gun dubbed "the Peacemaker."

Browning, Robert 1812–89. British poet best known for dramatic monologues such as "My Last Duchess" (1846).

Browning automatic rifle *n.* A .30-caliber automatic or semiautomatic, gas-operated, magazine-fed rifle used by US troops in World Wars I and II and the Korean War. [After John Moses BROWNING.]

Browning machine gun *n.* A .30- or .50-caliber automatic belt-fed machine gun capable of firing more than 500 rounds per minute, used by US troops in World War II and the Korean War. [After John Moses BROWNING.]

brown lung *n.* See **byssinosis**.

brown mustard *n.* **1.** See **Indian mustard. 2.** The black mustard.

brown•nose or **brown-nose** (broun′nōz′) *tr.v.* **-nosed, -nos•ing, -nos•es** *Informal* To curry favor with; fawn on. [< the image of an obsequious person whose nose becomes soiled in kissing the rump of someone from whom favor is sought.] —**brown′nose′** *n.* —**brown′nos′er** *n.*

brown•out (broun′out′) *n.* A reduction or cutback in electric power, esp. as a result of a shortage, a mechanical failure, or overuse by consumers. [BROWN + (BLACK)OUT.]

brown rat *n.* See **Norway rat**.

brown recluse spider *n.* A venomous spider (*Loxosceles reclusa*) having a violin-shaped mark on the cephalothorax.

brown rice *n.* The whole grain of rice, including the germ and outer layers containing the bran; unpolished rice.

brown rot *n.* Any of several plant diseases, esp. a disease of peach, plum, and related plants, characterized by wilting and browning of the flowers and leaves and rotting of the fruits.

brown sauce *n.* A sauce made from butter and flour browned together and stock.

Brown Shirt or **brown•shirt** (broun′shûrt′) *n.* **1.** A Nazi, esp. a storm trooper. **2.** A racist, violent right-wing one. [Transl. of Ger. *Braunhemd* : *braun*, brown + *Hemd*, shirt.]

brown•stone (broun′stōn′) *n.* **1.** A brownish-red sandstone used as a building material. **2.** A house built or faced with brownish-red sandstone.

brown study *n.* A state of deep thought. [BROWN, gloomy + STUDY, mental state.]

brown sugar *n.* **1.** Unrefined or incompletely refined sugar that retains some molasses, which gives it a brownish color. **2.** A product made by the addition of molasses to white sugar.

Browns•ville (brounz′vĭl′, -vəl) *n.* A city of S TX on the Rio Grande near its mouth on the Gulf of Mexico. Pop. 139,722.

Brown Swiss *n.* One of a hardy breed of large brown dairy cattle

that originated in Switzerland.

brown-tail moth (broun′tāl′) *n.* A small tussock moth (*Euproctis phaeorrhoea*) whose caterpillars defoliate shade trees and produce a poison capable of causing a skin rash on contact.

brown thrasher *n.* A North American bird (*Toxostoma rufum*) having a reddish-brown back and a dark-streaked breast.

brown trout *n.* A freshwater game fish (*Salmo trutta*).

browse (brouz) *v.* **browsed, brows•ing, brows•es** —*intr.* **1a.** To inspect something in a leisurely and casual way: *browsed through the map collection for items of interest.* **b.** To read something superficially by selecting passages at random: *browsed through the report during lunch.* **2.** To look for information on the Internet. **3.** To feed on leaves, young shoots, and other vegetation; graze. —*tr.* **1.** To look through or over (something) casually: *browsed the newspaper.* **2.** To read (websites) casually on the Internet. **3a.** To nibble; crop. **b.** To graze on. ❖ *n.* **1.** Young twigs, leaves, and shoots fit for animals to eat. **2.** An act of browsing. [Prob. < obsolete Fr. *broust*, young shoot < OFr. *brost*, of Gmc. orig.] —**brows′a•ble** (-zə-bəl) *n.*

brows•er (brou′zər) *n.* **1.** One that browses. **2.** *Computer Science* A program that accesses and displays files and other data available on the Internet and other networks.

Broz (brōz, brôz), **Josip** See Marshal **Tito**.

Bru•beck (broo′bĕk), **David Warren** Known as "Dave." b. 1920. Amer. jazz pianist and composer considered one of the foremost exponents of progressive jazz.

Bruce (broos), **Blanche Kelso** 1841–98. Amer. politician who was the first African-American US senator to serve a full term (1875–81).

Bruce, Sir David 1855–1931. Australian physician and bacteriologist known for his description (1887) of the bacterium that causes brucellosis.

Bruce, Robert the See **Robert I²**.

Bruce, Stanley Melbourne. 1st Viscount Bruce of Melbourne. 1883–1967. Australian politician who served as prime minister (1923–29).

bru•cel•la (broo-sĕl′ə) *n., pl.* **-cel•lae** (-sĕl′ē) or **-cel•las** Any of various pathogenic aerobic bacteria of the genus *Brucella*. [After Sir David BRUCE.]

bru•cel•lo•sis (broo′sə-lō′sĭs) *n.* **1.** An infectious disease of humans caused by brucellae, transmitted by contact with infected animals and characterized by fever, malaise, and headache. **2.** A disease of domestic animals caused by brucellae and sometimes resulting in spontaneous abortions in newly infected animals. [BRUCELL(A) + -OSIS.]

bru•cine (broo′sēn′, -sĭn) *n.* A poisonous alkaloid, $C_{23}H_{26}N_2O_4$, derived from the seeds of nux vomica and used to denature alcohol. [After James Bruce (1730–94), Scottish explorer.]

Bruck•ner (brook′nər), **Anton** 1824–96. Austrian organist and composer whose works include Requiem in D minor (1848–49).

Brue•ghel or **Brue•gel** also **Breu•ghel** (broi′gəl, broo′-, broe′-), **Pieter** Known as "the Elder." 1525?–69. Flemish painter noted for his landscapes and genre scenes, including *Peasant Wedding* (c. 1567). His son **Pieter** (1564–1638?), "the Younger," is primarily remembered for copies of his father's works; another son, **Jan** (1568–1625), is known for his still-life paintings.

Bruges (broozh) A city of NW Belgium connected by canal with the North Sea; founded in the 9th cent. Pop. 117,100.

bru•in (broo′ĭn) *n.* A bear. [ME, name of the bear in *History of Reynard the Fox*, translated by William Caxton < MDu. *bruun*, *bruin*, brown, name of the bear in the MDu. version of the fable. See **bher-²** in App.]

bruise (brooz) *v.* **bruised, bruis•ing, bruis•es** —*tr.* **1a.** To injure the underlying soft tissue or bone of (part of the body) without breaking the skin. **b.** To damage (plant tissue), as by abrasion or pressure. **2.** To dent or mar. **3.** To pound (berries, for example) into fragments; crush. **4.** To hurt, esp. psychologically. —*intr.* To experience or undergo bruising. ❖ *n.* **1.** An injury to underlying tissues or bone in which the skin is not broken, often characterized by ruptured blood vessels and discolorations. **2.** A similar injury to plant tissue, often resulting in discoloration or spoilage. **3.** An injury, esp. to one's feelings. [ME *bruisen* < OE *brȳsan*, to crush, and < OFr. *bruisier* (of Celt. orig.).]

bruis•er (broo′zər) *n. Informal* A large, heavyset man.

bruit (broot) *tr.v.* **bruit•ed, bruit•ing, bruits** To spread news of; repeat. ❖ *n.* **1.** (also broo′ē) *Medicine* An abnormal sound heard in auscultation. **2.** *Archaic* **a.** A rumor. **b.** A din; a clamor. [< ME, noise < OFr., p. part. of *bruire*, to roar < VLat. *brūgīre*, blend of Lat. *rūgīre* and VLat. *bragere*, to bray (of Celt. orig.).]

Bru•lé (broo-lā′) *n., pl.* **Brulé** or **-lés** A member of a Native American people constituting a subdivision of the Teton Sioux, inhabiting Nebraska and South Dakota. [Fr. *brûlé*, burnt (partial transl. of their own name).]

bru•mal (broo′məl) *adj.* Of, relating to, or occurring in winter. [Lat. *brūmālis* < *brūma*, winter < *brevima* (*diēs*), the shortest (day), archaic superl. of *brevis*, short.]

brume (broom) *n.* Fog or mist. [Fr. < OFr., perh. < Provençal < Lat. *brūma*. See BRUMAL.] —**bru′mous** (broo′məs) *adj.*

brum•ma•gem (brŭm′ə-jəm) *adj.* Cheap and showy; meretricious. [Alteration of BIRMINGHAM, England (< 17th-cent. counterfeit coins made there).] —**brum′ma•gem** *n.*

Brown Swiss

Blanche Kelso Bruce

ă	pat	oi	boy
ā	pay	ou	out
âr	care	oo	took
ä	father	oo	boot
ĕ	pet	ŭ	cut
ē	be	ûr	urge
ĭ	pit	th	thin
ī	pie	th	this
îr	pier	hw	which
ŏ	pot	zh	vision
ō	toe	ə	about,
ô	paw		item

Stress marks:
′ (primary);
′ (secondary); as in
lexicon (lĕk′sĭ-kŏn′)

Brum·mell (brŭm′əl), **George Bryan** Known as "Beau Brummell." 1778–1840. British dandy who popularized new men's fashions, including trousers.

brunch (brŭnch) *n.* A meal typically eaten late in the morning as a combination of a late breakfast and an early lunch. [BR(EAKFAST) + (L)UNCH.]

Bru·nei (broo-nī′) A sultanate of NW Borneo on the South China Sea; gained independence from Great Britain in 1984. Cap. Bandar Seri Begawan. Pop. 280,000. **—Bru·nei′an** *adj. & n.*

Bru·nel·le·schi (broo′nə-lĕs′kē), **Filippo** 1377–1446. Italian architect celebrated for his work during the Florentine Renaissance.

bru·net (broo-nĕt′) *adj.* **1.** Of a dark complexion or coloring. **2.** Having dark brown or black hair or eyes. ❖ *n.* A person with dark brown hair. [Fr. < OFr., dim. of *brun,* brown, of Gmc. orig. See **bher-²** in App.]

bru·nette (broo-nĕt′) *adj.* Having dark or brown hair. ❖ *n.* A girl or woman with dark or brown hair. [Fr., fem. of *brunet.* See BRUNET.]

brung (brŭng) *v. Nonstandard* A past tense and a past participle of **bring.**

Brun·hild (broon′hĭlt′) *n.* A queen in the *Nibelungenlied* who is won as a bride by Gunther.

Bru·no (broo′nō), **Giordano** 1548?–1600. Italian philosopher who formulated a cosmic theory of an infinite universe.

Bruno of Cologne, Saint. 1030?–1101. German monk who founded a monastery at Chartreuse in S France (1084) and founded the Carthusian order.

Bruns·wick (brŭnz′wĭk) **1.** A region and former duchy of N-central Germany; est. in the 13th cent. **2.** A city of N-central Germany ESE of Hanover; founded 861. Pop. 256,267.

Brunswick stew *n.* A stew that usu. contains chicken and rabbit or squirrel meat. [After *Brunswick,* a county of southern Virginia.]

brunt (brŭnt) *n.* **1.** The main impact or force, as of an attack. **2.** The main burden. [ME, perh. of Scand. orig.]

brush¹ (brŭsh) *n.* **1a.** A device consisting of bristles fastened into a handle, used in scrubbing, polishing, or painting. **b.** The act of using this device. **2.** A light touch in passing; a graze. **3.** An instance of contact with something undesirable or dangerous: *a brush with the law.* **4.** A bushy tail. **5.** A sliding contact between a fixed and a moving conductor. **6.** A snub; a brushoff. ❖ *v.* **brushed, brush·ing, brush·es** —*tr.* **1a.** To clean, polish, or groom with a brush. **b.** To apply with or as if with motions of a brush. **c.** To remove with or as if with motions of a brush. **2.** To dismiss abruptly or curtly: *brushed the matter aside.* **3.** To touch lightly in passing; graze against. —*intr.* **1.** To use or apply a brush. **2.** To move past something so as to touch it lightly. —*phrasal verbs:* **brush back** *Baseball* To force (a batter) to move away from the plate by throwing an inside pitch. **brush up 1.** To refresh one's memory. **2.** To renew a skill. [ME *brusshe* < OFr. *brosse,* brushwood, brush. See BRUSH².] **—brush′er** *n.* **—brush′y** *adj.*

brush² (brŭsh) *n.* **1a.** A dense growth of bushes or shrubs. **b.** Land covered by such a growth. **2.** Cut or broken branches. [ME *brusshe* < OFr. *brosse,* brushwood < VLat. **bruscia,* perh. < Lat. *bruscum,* knot on a maple.] **—brush′y** *adj.*

brush cut *n.* A short haircut in which the hair stands up on top, resembling a brush.

brush discharge *n.* A faintly visible, relatively slow crackling discharge of electricity without sparking.

brushed (brŭsht) *adj.* Having a nap produced by brushing.

brush·fire also **brush fire** (brŭsh′fīr′) *n.* **1.** A fire in low-growing scrubby trees and brush. **2.** A relatively minor crisis.

brush·off also **brush-off** (brŭsh′ôf′, -ŏf′) *n.* An abrupt dismissal or snub.

brush·wood (brŭsh′wood′) *n.* **1.** Branches that have been cut or broken off. **2a.** Dense undergrowth. **b.** An area covered by such growth.

brush·work (brŭsh′wûrk′) *n.* **1.** Work done with a brush. **2.** The manner in which a painter applies paint with a brush.

brusque also **brusk** (brŭsk) *adj.* Abrupt and curt in manner or speech; discourteously blunt. [Fr., lively, fierce < Ital. *brusco,* coarse, rough < LLat. *bruscum,* perh. blend of Lat. *ruscus,* butcher's broom, and LLat. *brucus,* heather; see BRIAR¹.] **—brusque′ly** *adv.* **—brusque′ness** *n.*

brus·que·rie (brüs′kə-rē′) *n.* Curtness or bluntness of manner. [Fr. < *brusque,* brusque. See BRUSQUE.]

Brus·sels (brŭs′əlz) The cap. of Belgium, in the central part; officially bilingual (Flemish and French). Pop. 136,488.

Brussels carpet *n.* A machine-made carpet consisting of small, colored woolen loops that form a heavy patterned pile.

Brussels griffon *n.* See **griffon** 1.

Brussels lace *n.* Net lace with an appliqué design, formerly made by hand but now usu. made by machine.

Brussels sprouts *pl.n.* (*used with a sing. or pl. verb*) **1.** A vegetable (*Brassica oleracea* var. *gemmifera*) in the mustard family, having cabbagelike buds. **2.** The edible buds of this plant.

brut (broot) *adj.* Very dry. Used of champagne. [Fr. < OFr., rough < Lat. *brutus,* heavy. See **gwera-** in App.]

bru·tal (broot′l) *adj.* **1.** Extremely ruthless or cruel. **2.** Crude or

South China Sea · Bandar Seri Begawan · BRUNEI · MALAYSIA · INDONESIA · 100 mi

Brunei

unfeeling in manner or speech. **3.** Harsh; unrelenting. **4.** Disagreeably precise or penetrating. **—Bru′tal·ly** *adv.*

Bru·tal·ism (broot′l-ĭz′əm) *n.* An architectural style of the mid-20th century characterized by massive forms, usu. of poured concrete and unrelieved by exterior decoration. **—Bru′tal·ist** *n.*

bru·tal·i·ty (broo-tăl′ĭ-tē) *n., pl.* **-ties 1.** The state or quality of being ruthless, cruel, harsh, or unrelenting. **2.** A ruthless, cruel, harsh, or unrelenting act.

bru·tal·ize (broot′l-īz′) *tr.v.* **-ized, -iz·ing, -iz·es 1.** To make cruel, harsh, or unfeeling. **2.** To treat cruelly or harshly. **—bru′-tal·i·za′tion** (-ĭ-zā′shən) *n.*

brute (broot) *n.* **1.** An animal; a beast. **2.** A brutal, crude, or insensitive person. ❖ *adj.* **1.** Of or relating to beasts; animal. **2.** Characteristic of a brute, esp.: **a.** Entirely physical. **b.** Lacking or showing a lack of reason or intelligence. **c.** Savage; cruel: *brute coercion.* **d.** Unremittingly severe: *brute necessity.* **3.** Coarse; brutish. [< ME, nonhuman < OFr. *brut* < Lat. *brutus,* stupid. See **gwera-** in App.] **—brut′ism** *n.*

brut·ish (broot′ĭsh) *adj.* **1.** Of or characteristic of a brute. **2.** Crude in feeling or manner. **3.** Sensual; carnal. **4.** Rough; uncivilized. **—brut′ish·ly** *adv.* **—brut′ish·ness** *n.*

Brut·ti·um (broot′ē-əm, brŭt′-) An ancient region of S Italy roughly occupying present-day Calabria.

Bru·tus (broo′təs), **Marcus Junius** 85?–42 B.C. Roman politician and general who conspired to assassinate Julius Caesar.

brux·ism (brŭk′sĭz′əm) *n.* The habitual, involuntary grinding or clenching of the teeth, usu. during sleep, as from tension. [< NLat. *bruxis,* a gnashing < Gk. *brukein,* to gnash.]

Bry·an (brī′ən), **William Jennings** Called "the Great Commoner." 1860–1925. Amer. lawyer and politician famous for his "Cross of Gold" speech (1896).

Bry·ansk also **Bri·ansk** (brē-änsk′) A city of W Russia SW of Moscow; part of Lithuania until the 16th cent. Pop. 456,202.

Bry·ant (brī′ənt), **William Cullen** 1794–1878. Amer. poet, critic, and editor known esp. for his poem "Thanatopsis" (1817).

Bryn·hild (brĭn′hĭld′) *n.* A Valkyrie who is revived from an enchanted sleep by Sigurd.

bryo- *pref.* Moss: bryology. [NLat. < Gk. *bruon,* moss < *bruein,* to swell, teem.]

bry·ol·o·gy (brī-ŏl′ə-jē) *n.* The study of bryophytes. **—bry′o·log′i·cal** (-ə-lŏj′ĭ-kəl) *adj.* **—bry·ol′o·gist** *n.*

bry·o·ny (brī′ə-nē) *n., pl.* **-nies 1.** Any of various Eurasian vines of the genus *Bryonia,* having red or black berries and tuberous roots formerly used as medicine. **2.** The black bryony. [Lat. *bryōnia* < Gk. *bruōnia* < *bruein,* to swell, teem.]

bry·o·phyte (brī′ə-fīt′) *n.* A plant of the Bryophyta, a division of photosynthetic, chiefly terrestrial nonvascular plants, including the mosses. **—bry′o·phyt′ic** (-fĭt′ĭk) *adj.*

bry·o·zo·an (brī′ə-zō′ən) *n.* Any of various small aquatic animals of the phylum Bryozoa that reproduce by budding and form colonies attached to stones or seaweed. [< NLat. *Bryozōa,* phylum name : BRYO- + Gk. *zōia,* pl. of *zōion,* animal; see -ZOON.] **—bry′o·zo′an** *adj.*

Bryth·on (brĭth′ən, -ŏn′) *n.* **1.** An ancient Celtic Briton. No longer in scholarly use. **2.** A member of a Brittonic-speaking people. No longer in scholarly use. [Welsh < Lat. *Brittonēs,* Britons. See BRITON.]

Bry·thon·ic (brĭ-thŏn′ĭk) *adj.* Of or relating to the Brythons or their language or culture. ❖ *n.* Variant of **Brittonic.**

BS *abbr.* **1.** Bachelor of Science **2.** balance sheet **3.** or **B/S** bill of sale **4.** *Vulgar Slang* bullshit

BSA *abbr.* Boy Scouts of America

BSc *abbr.* Bachelor of Science

B school *n. Informal* A business school.

BSEd *abbr.* Bachelor of Science in Education

bsh. *abbr.* bushel

BSI *abbr.* British Standards Institution

B-side (bē′sīd′) *n.* The reverse side of a phonograph record, esp. a single. [< the *B* on the record's label.]

B-s particle (bē′ĕs′) *n.* An electrically neutral meson having a mass 10,507 times that of the electron and a mean lifetime of approx. 1.6×10^{-12} seconds.

BST or **bST** *abbr.* bovine somatotropin

BT or **BTh** *abbr.* Bachelor of Theology

Btu *abbr.* British thermal unit

BTW *abbr.* by the way

bu. *abbr.* **1.** bureau **2.** bushel

bub (bŭb) *n. Slang* Used as a term of familiar address, esp. for a man or boy. [Prob. shortening and alteration of BROTHER.]

Bu·bas·tis (byoo-băs′tĭs) An ancient city of NE Egypt in the Nile delta.

bub·ba (bŭb′ə) *n. Slang* **1.** *Chiefly Southern US* Brother. **2.** A white working-class man of the southern United States, stereotypically regarded as uneducated and gregarious with his peers. [Alteration of BUB.]

bub·ble (bŭb′əl) *n.* **1.** A thin, usu. spherical or hemispherical film of liquid filled with air or gas. **2.** A globular body of air or gas formed within a liquid. **3.** A pocket formed in a solid by trapped air or gas, as during cooling. **4a.** The act or process of forming bubbles. **b.** A sound made by or as if by the forming and bursting of bubbles. **5.** Something insubstantial, groundless, or ephemeral, esp.: **a.** A fantastic or impracticable idea or belief; an illusion. **b.** A speculative scheme that comes to nothing. **6.** Something light or effervescent. **7.** A usu. transparent glass or plastic dome. **8.** A protective, often isolating envelope or cover. ❖ *v.* **-bled, -bling, -bles** —*intr.* **1.** To form or give off bubbles. **2.** To move or flow with a gurgling sound. **3.** To rise to or as if to the surface; emerge. **4.** To display irrepressible activity or emotion. —*tr.* To cause to form bubbles. [< ME *bubelen,* to bubble.]

bubble and squeak *n. Chiefly British* Cabbage and potatoes fried together. [Imit. of the sounds made as it cooks.]

bubble bath *n.* **1.** A perfumed preparation added to bath water to make it foam. **2.** A bath containing such a preparation.

bubble chamber *n.* An apparatus in which the movement and collision of ionizing particles is seen as trails of gas bubbles that form as the particles move through a superheated liquid.

bub•ble•gum (bŭb′əl-gŭm′) *n.* **1.** also **bubble gum** Chewing gum that can be blown into bubbles. **2.** A style of popular music designed to appeal to adolescents, characterized by bouncy rhythms and a cheerful tone.

bubble memory *n.* Magnetic bubble memory.

bubble pack *n.* **1.** Flexible plastic sheeting containing small air pockets, used to cushion items during shipment. **2.** See **blister pack.**

bub•bler (bŭb′lər) *n. Northern US* A drinking fountain.

bubble top *n.* A transparent, often bulletproof enclosure forming the top of an automobile.

bubble wrap *n.* See **bubble pack** 1.

bub•bly (bŭb′lē) *adj.* **1.** Full of or producing bubbles. **2.** Resembling bubbles. **3.** Full of high spirits; effervescent. ❖ *n., pl.* **-blies** *Informal* Champagne.

Bu•ber (bo͞o′bər), **Martin** 1878–1965. Austrian-born Judaic scholar and philosopher who wrote *I and Thou* (1923).

bu•bo (bo͞o′bō, byo͞o′-) *n., pl.* **-boes** An inflamed tender swelling of a lymph node, esp. of the armpit or groin, that is characteristic of certain infections such as bubonic plague. [ME < LLat. *būbō, būbōn-* < Gk. *boubōn,* groin, swelling.]

bu•bon•ic plague (bo͞o-bŏn′ĭk, byo͞o-) *n.* A contagious, often fatal epidemic disease caused by the bacterium *Yersinia* (syn. *Pasteurella*) *pestis,* transmitted from person to person or by the bite of fleas from an infected host, esp. a rat, and characterized by chills, fever, vomiting, diarrhea, and the formation of buboes.

Bu•ca•ra•man•ga (bo͞o′kə-rə-mäng′gə, -kä-rä-mäng′gä) A city of N-central Colombia; founded 1622. Pop. 351,687.

buc•cal (bŭk′əl) *adj.* Of or relating to the cheeks or the mouth cavity. [< Lat. *bucca,* cheek.]

buc•ca•neer (bŭk′ə-nîr′) *n.* **1.** A pirate, esp. one who preyed on Spanish shipping in the West Indies during the 17th century. **2.** A ruthless speculator or adventurer. [Fr. *boucanier* < *boucaner,* to cure meat < *boucan,* barbecue frame, of Tupian orig.; akin to Tupi *mukém,* rack.] —**buc′ca•neer′** *v.*

buc•ci•na•tor (bŭk′sĭ-nā′tər) *n.* The thin, flat muscle forming the wall of the cheek. [Lat. *buccinātor,* trumpeter (< its being the chief muscle used in blowing) < *buccinātus,* p. part. of *buccināre,* to blow a horn < *būcina, buccina,* horn, trumpet. See **gʷou-** in App.]

Bu•ceph•a•lus (byo͞o-sĕf′ə-ləs) *n.* Alexander the Great's war horse.

Buch•an (bŭk′ən, bŭKH′-), Sir **John.** 1st Baron Tweedsmuir. 1875–1940. Scottish writer and politician whose adventure novels include *The Thirty-Nine Steps* (1915).

Bu•chan•an (byo͞o-kăn′ən, bə-), **James** 1791–1868. The 15th President of the US (1857–61). He tried to maintain a balance between proslavery and antislavery factions but was unable to forestall the secession of South Carolina on December 20, 1860.

Bu•cha•rest (bo͞o′kə-rĕst′, byo͞o′-) The cap. of Romania, in the SE part on a tributary of the Danube R. Pop. 2,343,824.

Bu•chen•wald (bo͞o′kən-wôld′, -KHən-vält′) A village of central Germany near Weimar; site of a Nazi concentration camp during World War II.

buck[1] (bŭk) *n.* **1a.** The adult male of some animals, such as the deer, antelope, or rabbit. **b.** Antelope considered as a group. **2a.** A robust or high-spirited young man. **b.** A fop. **3.** *Offensive* A Native American or Black man. **4.** An act or instance of bucking. **5a.** Buckskin. **b. bucks** Buckskin breeches or shoes. ❖ *v.* **bucked, buck•ing, bucks** —*intr.* **1.** To leap upward arching the back. **2.** To charge with the head lowered; butt. **3.** To make sudden jerky movements; jolt. **4.** To resist stubbornly and obstinately; balk. **5.** *Informal* To strive with determination. —*tr.* **1.** To throw or toss by bucking: *buck off a rider.* **2.** To oppose directly and stubbornly; go against. **3.** *Football* To charge into (an opponent's line) carrying the ball. **4.** *Archaic* To butt against with the head. ❖ *adj.* Of the lowest rank in a specified military category. ***—phrasal verb:*** **buck up** To summon one's courage or spirits; hearten. [ME *bukke* < OE *buc,* male deer, and *bucca,* male goat.] —**buck′er** *n.*

buck[2] (bŭk) *n.* **1.** A sawhorse or sawbuck. **2.** A leather-covered frame used for gymnastic vaulting. [Alteration (influenced by BUCK[1]) of Du. *bok,* male goat, trestle < MDu. *boc.*]

buck[3] (bŭk) *n. Informal* **1.** A dollar. **2.** An amount of money. [Short for BUCKSKIN (< its use in trade).]

buck[4] (bŭk) *n.* A counter or marker formerly passed from one poker player to another to indicate an obligation, esp. one's turn to deal. ❖ *tr.v.* **bucked, buck•ing, bucks** To pass (a task or duty) to another, esp. so as to avoid responsibility. ***—idiom:*** **the buck stops here** *Informal* The ultimate responsibility rests here. [Short for *buckhorn knife* (< its use as a marker in poker).]

Buck, Pearl Sydenstricker 1892–1973. Amer. writer who won the 1938 Nobel Prize for literature.

buck•a•roo also **buck•er•oo** (bŭk′ə-ro͞o′) *n., pl.* **-a•roos** also **-er•oos** *Western US* See **cowboy** 1. [Alteration (perh. influenced by BUCK[1]) of Sp. *vaquero* < *vaca,* cow < Lat. *vacca.*]

buck•bean (bŭk′bēn′) *n.* A perennial herb *(Menyanthes trifoliata)* of the Northern Hemisphere having trifoliate leaves and white, pink, or purplish flowers. [Transl. of Flem. *bocks boonen,* goat's beans : *bocks,* genitive of *bock,* goat + *boonen,* pl. of *boon,* bean.]

buck•board (bŭk′bôrd′, -bōrd′) *n.* A four-wheeled open carriage with the seat or seats attached to a flexible board running between the front and rear axles. [Obsolete *buck,* body of a wagon (< ME *bouk,* belly < OE *būc*) + BOARD.]

buck•et (bŭk′ĭt) *n.* **1a.** A cylindrical vessel used for holding or carrying liquids or solids; a pail. **b.** The amount that a bucket can hold. **2.** A unit of dry measure in the US Customary System equal to 2 pecks (17.6 liters). See table at **measurement. 3.** A receptacle on various machines, such as the scoop of a power shovel, used to gather and convey material. **4.** *Basketball* A basket. ❖ *v.* **-et•ed, -et•ing, -ets** —*tr.* **1.** To hold, carry, or put in a bucket. **2.** To ride (a horse) long and hard. —*intr.* **1.** To move or proceed rapidly and jerkily. **2.** To make haste; hustle. ***—idiom:*** **a drop in the bucket** An insufficient or inconsequential amount in comparison with what is required. [ME < OFr. *buket,* of Gmc. orig.]

bucket brigade *n.* A line of people formed to fight a fire by passing buckets of water from a source to the fire.

bucket seat *n.* A single, usu. low seat with a contoured back, typically used in some automobiles.

bucket shop *n.* **1.** A fraudulent brokerage operation in which orders to buy and sell are accepted but no executions take place. **2.** A business, such as a travel agency, that buys unsold tickets and resells them at a discount. [< *bucket shop,* a saloon selling small amounts of liquor in buckets.]

bucket truck *n.* A truck equipped with a cherry picker.

buck•eye (bŭk′ī′) *n.* **1.** Any of various North American poisonous trees or shrubs of the genus *Aesculus,* having palmately compound opposite leaves and large shiny seeds. **2.** The fruit of any of these plants. **3.** The brown seed of such a fruit. [BUCK[1] + EYE.]

buck•hound (bŭk′hound′) *n.* A hound used for coursing deer.

Buck•ing•ham (bŭk′ĭng-əm, -hăm′), 1st Duke of. Orig. George Villiers. 1592–1628. English courtier and politician whose military and political policies caused continual friction with Parliament.

Buckingham, 2nd Duke of. Orig. George Villiers. 1628–87. English courtier who was a prominent member of the group known as the Cabal that formed the ministry of Charles II after the Restoration.

buck•le (bŭk′əl) *n.* **1.** A clasp for fastening two ends, as of a belt, in which a device attached to one of the ends is fitted or coupled to the other. **2.** An ornament that resembles a buckle, such as a metal square on a hat. **3.** An instance of bending, warping, or crumpling; a bend or bulge. ❖ *v.* **-led, -ling, -les** —*tr.* **1.** To fasten with a buckle. **2.** To cause to bend, warp, or crumple. —*intr.* **1.** To become fastened with a buckle. **2.** To bend, warp, or crumple, as under pressure. **3.** To give way; collapse. **4.** To succumb, as to exhaustion or authority; give in. ***—phrasal verbs:*** **buckle down** To apply oneself with determination. **buckle up** To use a safety belt, esp. in an automobile. [ME *bokel* < OFr. *boucle* < Lat. *buccula,* cheek strap of a helmet, dim. of *bucca,* cheek.]

buck•ler (bŭk′lər) *n.* **1.** A small, round shield either carried or worn on the arm. **2.** A means of protection; a defense. ❖ *tr.v.* **-lered, -ler•ing, -lers** To shield; protect. [ME *bokeler* < OFr. *bouclier* < *boucle,* boss on a shield < Lat. *buccula,* dim. of *bucca,* cheek.]

buck•min•ster•ful•ler•ene (bŭk′mĭn-stər-fo͝ol′ə-rēn′) *n.* An extremely stable, ball-shaped carbon molecule, C_{60}, reminiscent of a geodesic dome, and believed to occur naturally in soot. [After Richard *Buckminster* FULLER.]

buck-na•ked (bŭk′nĕk′ĭd) *adv. & adj. Chiefly Southern US* Bare-naked. See Regional Note at **bare-naked.** [*buck-* (perh. alteration of BUTT[4]) + NAKED.]

buck•o (bŭk′ō) *n., pl.* **-oes** or **-os 1.** A blustering or bossy person. **2.** *Irish* A young man; a lad. [Alteration of BUCK[1].]

buck•ram (bŭk′rəm) *n.* **1.** A coarse cotton fabric heavily sized with glue, used for stiffening garments and in bookbinding. **2.** *Archaic* Rigid formality. ❖ *tr.v.* **-ramed, -ram•ing, -rams** To stiffen with or as if with buckram. [ME *bukeram,* fine linen < OFr. *boquerant* and < OItal. *bucherame,* both after *Bukhara* (Bukhoro), from which fine linen was once imported.] —**buck′ram** *adj.*

buck•saw (bŭk′sô′) *n.* A woodcutting saw, usu. set in an H-shaped frame. [< BUCK[2].]

buck•shee (bŭk′shē) *Chiefly British n.* **1.** Something extra or left over that is obtained free. **2.** An extra ration. ❖ *adj.* **1.** Free of charge; gratis. **2.** Unsolicited; gratuitous. [Variant of BAKSHEESH.]

buck•shot (bŭk′shŏt′) *n.* A large lead shot for shotgun shells

James Buchanan
portrait by Alonzo Chappell (1828–87)

Pearl S. Buck

ă pat	oi boy
ā pay	ou out
âr care	o͝o took
ä father	o͞o boot
ĕ pet	ŭ cut
ē be	ûr urge
ĭ pit	th thin
ī pie	*th* this
îr pier	hw which
ŏ pot	zh vision
ō toe	ə about, item
ô paw	

Stress marks:
′ (primary);
′ (secondary), as in **lexicon** (lĕk′sĭ-kŏn′)

that is used esp. in hunting big game.

buck·skin (bŭk'skĭn') n. **1a.** The skin of a male deer. **b.** A soft, grayish-yellow leather usu. having a suede finish. **2. buckskins** Clothing, esp. breeches or shoes, made from buckskin. **3.** A person who wears buckskins. **4.** A grayish-yellow horse. —**buck'skin'** adj.

buck·thorn (bŭk'thôrn') n. **1.** Any of various shrubs or small trees of the genus *Rhamnus*, including ornamentals and medicinal species. See **bumelia**. [Transl. of NLat. *cervī spīna* : *cervī*, genitive of *cervus*, deer, buck + *spīna*, thorn.]

buck·tooth (bŭk'tooth') n. A projecting upper front tooth. [BUCK¹ + TOOTH.] —**buck'toothed'** (-tootht') adj.

buck·wheat (bŭk'hwēt', -wēt') n. **1a.** An annual Asian plant (*Fagopyrum esculentum*) having small, seedlike triangular fruits. **b.** The edible fruits of this plant, used whole or ground into flour. **2.** Any of several similar or related plants. [Prob. partial transl. of MDu. *boecweite* : *boek*, beech; see **bhāgo-** in App. + *weite*, wheat.]

buck·y·ball (bŭk'ē-bôl') n. A molecule of buckminsterfullerene. [Shortening and alteration of BUCKMINSTERFULLERENE + BALL¹.]

bu·col·ic (byoo-kŏl'ĭk) adj. **1.** Of or characteristic of the countryside or its people; rustic. **2.** Of or characteristic of shepherds or flocks; pastoral. ❖ n. **1.** A pastoral poem. **2.** A farmer or shepherd; a rustic. [Lat. *būcolicus*, pastoral < Gk. *boukolikos* < *boukolos*, cowherd : *bous*, cow; see **gʷou-** in App. + *-kolos*, herdsman; see **kʷel-** in App.] —**bu·col'i·cal·ly** adv.

Bu·co·vi·na (boō'kə-vē'nə) See **Bukovina**.

bud¹ (bŭd) n. **1.** *Botany* **a.** A small protuberance on a stem or branch, containing an undeveloped shoot, leaf, or flower. **b.** The stage or condition of having buds. **2.** *Biology* **a.** An asexual reproductive structure, as in yeast, that consists of an outgrowth capable of developing into a new individual. **b.** A small rounded organic part, such as a taste bud, that resembles a plant bud. **3.** One that is not yet fully developed. ❖ v. **bud·ded, bud·ding, buds** —*intr.* **1.** To put forth or produce buds. **2.** To develop or grow from or as if from a bud. **3.** To be in an undeveloped stage or condition. **4.** To reproduce asexually by forming a bud. —*tr.* **1.** To cause to put forth buds. **2.** To graft a bud onto (a plant). [ME *budde*.] —**bud'der** n.

bud² (bŭd) n. *Informal* Friend; chum. Used as a form of familiar address, esp. for a man or boy. [Short for BUDDY.]

Bu·da·pest (boō'də-pĕst', -pĕsht') The cap. of Hungary, in the N-central part on the Danube R.; formed (1873) by the union of Buda on the right bank of the river with Pest on the left bank. Pop. 2,002,121.

Bud·dha¹ (boō'də, bood'ə) Orig. Siddhartha Gautama. 563?–483? B.C. Indian mystic and founder of Buddhism who began preaching after achieving supreme enlightenment at the age of 35.

Bud·dha² (boō'də, bood'ə) n. **1.** One who has achieved a state of perfect spiritual enlightenment in accordance with the teachings of Buddha. **2.** A representation or likeness of Buddha. [Skt. *buddha-*, enlightened, p. part. of *bodhati*, he awakes. See **bheudh-** in App.]

Bud·dhism (boō'dĭz'əm, bood'ĭz'-) n. **1.** The teaching of Buddha that life is permeated with suffering caused by desire, that suffering ceases when desire ceases, and that enlightenment obtained through right conduct, wisdom, and meditation releases one from desire, suffering, and rebirth. **2.** The religion of the many groups that profess varying forms of this doctrine and that venerate Buddha. —**Bud'dhist** adj. & n. —**Bud·dhis'tic** adj.

bud·dle (bŭd'l) n. An inclined trough in which crushed ore is washed. [Prob. < LGer. *buddeln*, to agitate.]

bud·dle·ia (bŭd'lē-ə, bŭd-lē'ə) n. See **butterfly bush**. [NLat., after Adam *Buddle* (died 1715), British botanist.]

bud·dy (bŭd'ē) *Informal* n., pl. **-dies 1.** A good friend. **2.** A partner, esp. one of a pair or team associated under the buddy system. **3.** Friend or comrade; chum. Used as a form of familiar address, esp. for a man or boy. ❖ *intr.v.* **-died, -dy·ing, -dies** To associate as a buddy or buddies. —*phrasal verb*: **buddy up** To ingratiate oneself, as by presuming friendship: *buddied up to the coach.* [Prob. alteration of BROTHER.]

bud·dy-bud·dy (bŭd'ē-bŭd'ē) adj. *Informal* Showing or marked by great outward friendship.

buddy system n. An arrangement in which persons are paired, as for mutual safety or assistance.

budge¹ (bŭj) v. **budged, budg·ing, budg·es** —*intr.* **1.** To move or stir slightly. **2.** To alter a position or attitude. —*tr.* **1.** To cause to move slightly. **2.** To cause to alter a position or attitude. [OFr. *bouger* < VLat. *bullicāre*, to bubble < Lat. *bullīre*, to boil.]

budge² (bŭj) n. Fur made from lambskin dressed with the wool outside, formerly used to trim academic robes. ❖ adj. *Archaic* Overformal; pompous. [ME *bouge* < AN < Med.Lat. *bugia*, prob. < Lat. *bulga*, leather bag. See BUDGET.]

budg·er·i·gar (bŭj'ə-rē-gär', bŭj'ə-rē-gär') n. A parakeet (*Melopsittacus undulatus*) of Australia having green, yellow, or blue plumage. [Prob. alteration of Kamilaroi (Aboriginal language of SE Australia) *gijirrigaa*.]

budg·et (bŭj'ĭt) n. **1a.** An itemized summary of expenditures for a given period along with proposals for financing them. **b.** A plan for the expenditure of a usu. fixed resource, such as money or

time, during a given period. **c.** The total sum of money allocated for a particular purpose or period of time. **2.** A stock or collection with definite limits. ❖ v. **-et·ed, -et·ing, -ets** —*tr.* **1.** To plan in advance the expenditure of. **2.** To enter or account for in a budget. —*intr.* To make or use a budget. ❖ adj. **1.** Of or relating to a budget: *budget items.* **2.** Appropriate to a budget; inexpensive: *budget meals.* [ME *bouget*, wallet < OFr. *bougette*, dim. of *bouge*, leather bag < Lat. *bulga*, of Celt. orig.] —**budg'et·ar'y** (bŭj'ĭ-tĕr'ē) adj. —**budg'et·er, budg'et·eer'** (-ĭ-tîr') n.

budg·ie (bŭj'ē) n. *Informal* A budgerigar.

bud·worm (bŭd'wûrm') n. A larva of several tortricid moths, esp. the spruce budworm, that devours plant buds.

Bue·na·ven·tu·ra (bwā'nə-věn-toor'ə, -tyoor'-, bwĕ'nä-věn-toor'rä) A city of W Colombia on **Buenaventura Bay**, an inlet of the Pacific Ocean. Pop. 165,829.

Bue·na Vis·ta (bwā'nə vĭs'tə, bwĕ'nä vēs'tä) A locality in N Mexico just S of Saltillo; site of a US victory (1847) in the Mexican War.

Bue·nos Ai·res (bwā'nəs âr'ēz, ī'rĭz, bwĕ'nōs ī'rĕs) The cap. of Argentina, in the E part on the Río de la Plata; founded 1536. Pop. 2,960,976.

buff¹ (bŭf) n. **1.** A soft, thick, undyed leather made chiefly from the skins of buffalo, elk, or oxen. **2.** A military uniform coat made of such leather. **3.** A pale, light, or moderate yellowish pink to yellow, including moderate orange-yellow to light yellowish brown. **4.** *Informal* Bare skin. **5.** A piece of soft material, such as leather, often mounted on a block and used for polishing. ❖ adj. **1.** Made or formed of buff. **2.** Of the color buff. **3. buff·er buff·est** *Slang* Physically fit and trim. ❖ *tr.v.* **buffed, buff·ing, buffs 1.** To polish or shine with a piece of soft material. **2.** To soften the surface of (leather) by raising a nap. **3.** To make the color of buff. [< obsolete *buffle*, buffalo < Fr. *buffle* < Ital. *bufalo.* See BUFFALO.]

buff² (bŭf) n. *Informal* One who is enthusiastic and knowledgeable about a subject: *a Civil War buff.* [Orig. an enthusiast of fires and firefighting < the buff-colored uniform worn by New York volunteer firemen in the 19th cent.]

buf·fa·lo (bŭf'ə-lō') n., pl. **buffalo** or **-loes** or **-los 1a.** Any of several oxlike Old World mammals of the family Bovidae, such as the water buffalo and African buffalo. **b.** The North American bison, *Bison bison.* **2.** The buffalo fish. ❖ *tr.v.* **-loed, -lo·ing, -loes 1.** To intimidate. **2.** To deceive; hoodwink. **3.** To confuse; bewilder. [Ital. *bufalo* or Port. or Sp. *búfalo* < LLat. *būfalus* < Lat. *būbalus*, antelope, buffalo < Gk. *boubalos*, perh. < *bous*, cow. See **gʷou-** in App.]

Buffalo A city of W NY at the E end of Lake Erie on the Canadian border. Pop. 292,648.

buffalo berry n. **1.** Any of three North American shrubs or small trees of the genus *Shepherdia*, having yellowish flowers, drupelike fruits, and silvery foliage. **2.** The berry of any of these plants.

Buffalo Bill See William Frederick **Cody**.

buffalo bug n. See **carpet beetle**.

buffalo fish n. Any of several sucker fishes of the genus *Ictiobus*, mostly of the Mississippi Valley and having a humped back.

buffalo gnat n. See **black fly**.

buffalo grass n. A perennial grass (*Buchloe dactyloides*) of central North America, used for grazing and sometimes for lawns.

buffalo robe n. The dressed skin of the North American bison, used as a lap robe, cape, or blanket.

buffalo soldier n. A member of one of the African-American regiments within the US Army after the Civil War, serving primarily in the Indian wars of the late 1860s. [Transl. of a Kiowa term < the perceived similarity between the soldiers' hair and the hair on a buffalo's head.]

Buffalo wing n. A fried chicken wing, usu. served with hot sauce and blue cheese dressing. [After BUFFALO, where such wings were first served.]

buff·er¹ (bŭf'ər) n. **1.** One that buffs, esp. a piece of soft leather or cloth used to shine or polish. **2.** A buffing wheel.

buff·er² (bŭf'ər) n. **1.** Something that lessens or absorbs the shock of an impact. **2.** One that protects by intercepting or moderating adverse pressures or influences. **3.** Something that separates potentially antagonistic entities. **4.** *Chemistry* A substance that minimizes change in the acidity of a solution when an acid or base is added to the solution. **5.** *Computer Science* A device or area used to store data temporarily. ❖ *tr.v.* **-ered, -er·ing, -ers 1.** To act as a buffer for or between. **2.** *Chemistry* To treat (a solution) with a buffer. **3.** *Computer Science* To hold or collect (data) in a buffer. [Prob. < obsolete *buff*, to make a sound like a soft body being hit, of imit. orig.]

buffer state n. A neutral state between two rival or potentially hostile states that serves to prevent conflict.

buffer zone n. A neutral area between hostile or belligerent forces that serves to prevent conflict.

buf·fet¹ (bə-fā', boo-) n. **1.** A large sideboard with drawers and cupboards. **2a.** A counter or table from which meals or refreshments are served. **b.** A restaurant having such a counter. **3.** A meal at which guests serve themselves from various dishes on a table or sideboard. ❖ adj. Informally served. [Fr.]

buf·fet² (bŭf'ĭt) n. A blow or cuff with or as if with the hand. ❖ v. **-fet·ed, -fet·ing, -fets** —*tr.* **1.** To hit or beat, esp. repeatedly.

Buddha¹

2. To strike against forcefully; batter. **3.** To drive or force with or as if with repeated blows. **4.** To force (one's way) with difficulty. —*intr.* To buffet one's way. [ME < OFr., dim. of *buffe*, blow.] —**buf′fet·er** *n.*

buff·ing wheel (bŭf′ĭng) *n.* A wheel covered with a soft material, such as velvet, for shining and polishing.

buf·fle·head (bŭf′əl-hĕd′) *n.* A small North American diving duck (*Bucephala albeola*) having black and white plumage and a densely feathered, rounded head. [Obsolete *buffle*, buffalo (< Fr. < LLat. *būfalus*; see BUFFALO) + HEAD.]

buf·fo (bōō′fō) *n., pl.* **-fi** (-fē) or **-fos** A man who sings comic opera roles. [Ital. < *buffare*, to puff, of imit. orig.]

Buf·fon (bōō-fôN′), Comte **Georges Louis Leclerc de** 1707–88. French naturalist noted for his monumental *Histoire Naturelle* (1749–88 and 1804).

buf·foon (bə-fōōn′) *n.* **1.** A clown; a jester. **2.** A person given to clowning and joking. **3.** A ludicrous or bumbling person. [Fr. *bouffon* < OItal. *buffone* < *buffa*, jest < *buffare*, to puff, of imit. orig.] —**buf·foon′er·y** (bə-fōō′nə-rē) *n.*

bug (bŭg) *n.* **1.** A true bug. **2.** An insect or similar organism, such as a centipede or an earwig. **3a.** A disease-producing microorganism: *a flu bug.* **b.** The illness or disease so produced. **4a.** A defect or difficulty, as in a system or design. **b.** *Computer Science* A defect in the code or routine of a program. **5.** An enthusiasm or obsession. **6.** An enthusiast or devotee; a buff. **7.** An electronic listening device used in surveillance. ❖ *v.* **bugged**, **bug·ging**, **bugs** —*intr.* To grow large; bulge: *My eyes bugged when I saw the mess.* —*tr.* **1a.** To annoy; pester. **b.** To prey on; worry. **2.** To equip (a room, for example) with a concealed electronic listening device. **3.** To make (the eyes) bulge or grow large. —*phrasal verbs:* **bug off** *Slang* To leave someone alone; go away. **bug out** *Slang* **1.** To leave or quit, usu. in a hurry. **2.** To avoid a responsibility or duty. Often used with *on* or *of.* —*idiom:* **put a bug in (someone's) ear** *Informal* To impart useful information to (another) in a subtle, discreet way. [?] —**bug′ger** *n.*

WORD HISTORY It is often thought that a defect in a system, design, or computer program was named a *bug* after a moth found in an early computer in 1947 and now preserved at the Smithsonian Institute. There was indeed a moth discovered in a computer in 1947 by the computer scientist Grace Murray, but the entry in her log is telling: "First actual case of bug being found." This implies that computer glitches were already called *bugs* before then, and in fact Murray herself had used the term in writing by 1945. But its history is even older than that, for *bug* in the meaning "glitch in a machine" is known from as early as 1889. In that year, one of Thomas Edison's associates reported it as a term used by the great inventor. Whether he was responsible for this linguistic invention is not known; but the myth that *bug* originally referred to Murray's unfortunate moth stems probably from the repeated tellings of the moth story by Murray herself in subsequent lectures around the country.

Bug (bōōg, bōōk) **1.** also **Western Bug** A river of E Europe rising in SW Ukraine and flowing c. 772 km (480 mi) through Poland to the Vistula R. **2.** also **Southern Bug** A river rising in the SW Ukraine and flowing c. 853 km (530 mi) to the Black Sea.

bug·a·boo (bŭg′ə-bōō′) *n., pl.* **-boos 1.** An object of obsessive, usu. exaggerated fear or anxiety. **2.** A recurring or persistent problem. [Perh. of Celt. orig.]

Bu·gan·da (bōō-gän′də, byōō-) A region and former kingdom of E Africa on the N shore of Lake Victoria in present-day Uganda; a British protectorate (1900–62).

bug·bane (bŭg′bān′) *n.* Any of several plants of the genus *Cimicifuga* of northern temperate regions, including the black cohosh.

bug·bear (bŭg′bâr′) *n.* **1.** A bugaboo. **2.** A fearsome imaginary creature, esp. one evoked to frighten children. [Obsolete *bug*, hobgoblin (< ME *bugge*, perh. < Welsh *bwg*) + BEAR².]

bug-eyed (bŭg′īd′) *adj.* **1.** Having protruding eyes. **2.** Wide-eyed, as with astonishment or curiosity; agog.

bug·ger¹ (bŭg′ər, bōōg′-) *n.* **1.** *Vulgar Slang* A sodomite. **2.** *Slang* A contemptible or disreputable person. **3.** *Slang* A fellow; a chap. ❖ *v.* **-gered**, **-ger·ing**, **-gers** *Vulgar Slang* —*intr.* To practice sodomy. —*tr.* **1.** To practice sodomy with. **2.** To damn. —*phrasal verb:* **bugger off** *Chiefly British Slang* To leave someone alone; go away. [ME *bougre*, heretic < OFr. *boulgre* < Med.Lat. *Bulgarus*. See BULGAR.]

bug·ger² (bŭg′ər) *n.* One who installs electronic bugs.

bug·ger·y (bŭg′ə-rē, bōōg′-) *n. Vulgar* Sodomy.

bug·gy¹ (bŭg′ē) *n., pl.* **-gies 1.** A small, light, one-horse carriage usu. having four wheels or two wheels. **2.** A baby carriage. **3.** A motor vehicle, usu. with oversized tires, designed for off-road use. **4.** *Informal* An automobile. **5.** *Chiefly Southern US* A shopping cart, esp. for groceries. [?]

bug·gy² (bŭg′ē) *adj.* **-gi·er**, **-gi·est 1.** Infested with bugs. **2.** *Slang* Crazy. —**bug′gi·ness** *n.*

bug·house (bŭg′hous′) *Offensive Slang n.* An institution for the mentally ill. ❖ *adj.* Insane; crazy. [Prob. < BUG, enthusiast.]

bug juice *n. Slang* **1.** A sweet, flavored, usu. uncarbonated drink. **2.** A liquid insect repellent. **3.** Inferior liquor. [Sense 1 < name given to instant drinks in the military < earlier name for bad whiskey.]

bu·gle¹ (byōō′gəl) *n. Music* A brass wind instrument somewhat shorter than a trumpet and lacking keys or valves. ❖ *intr.v.* **-gled**, **-gling**, **-gles 1.** *Music* To sound a bugle. **2.** To make a deep prolonged sound similar to the bay of a hound. [ME < OFr. < Lat. *būculus*, steer, dim. of *bōs*, ox. See **gʷou-** in App.] —**bu′gler** *n.*

bu·gle² (byōō′gəl) *n.* A tubular glass or plastic bead that is used to trim clothing. [?]

bu·gle³ (byōō′gəl) *n.* Any of several creeping Old World herbs of the genus *Ajuga* in the mint family, having square stems and purplish flowers. [ME < OFr. < LLat. *būgula* (perh. influenced by *būglōssa*, bugloss) < Lat. *būgillō*.]

bu·gle·weed (byōō′gəl-wēd′) *n.* See bugle³. [ME *bugle*. See BUGLE³.]

bu·gloss (byōō′glôs′, -glŏs′) *n.* Any of several usu. hairy Old World plants, esp. in the genera *Anchusa*, *Brunnera*, and *Echium*, having blue or violet flowers. [ME *buglosse* < OFr. < LLat. *būglōssa* < Lat. *būglōssos* < Gk. *bouglōssos* : *bous*, ox; see **gʷou-** in App. + *glōssa*, tongue.]

buhl or **boulle** (bōōl) *n.* An inlay of tortoiseshell, ivory, and metal, used esp. in decorating furniture. [After André Charles Boulle (1642–1732), French woodcarver.]

buhr·stone also **burr·stone** (bûr′stōn′) *n.* A tough silicified limestone used for millstones. [Variant of BURR¹ + STONE.]

build (bĭld) *v.* **built** (bĭlt), **build·ing**, **builds** —*tr.* **1.** To form by combining materials or parts; construct. **2.** To order, finance, or supervise the construction of. **3.** To develop or give form to according to a plan or process; create: *build a nation.* **4.** To increase or strengthen by adding gradually to: *build support.* **5.** To establish a basis for; found or ground: *build an argument.* —*intr.* **1.** To make something by combining materials or parts. **2.** To engage in the construction or design of buildings. **3.** To develop in magnitude or extent: *clouds building.* **4.** To progress toward a maximum, as of intensity: *suspense building.* ❖ *n.* **1.** The physical makeup of a person or thing: *an athletic build.* **2.** *Computer Science* Any of various versions of a software product as it is being developed for release to users. —*phrasal verbs:* **build in (or into)** To construct or include as an integral part of. **build on (or upon)** To use as a basis or foundation. **build up 1.** To develop or increase in stages or by degrees. **2.** To accumulate or collect. **3.** To bolster: *built up my hopes.* **4.** To fill up (an area) with buildings. [ME *bilden* < OE *byldan*. See **bheuə-** in App.] —**build′a·ble** *adj.*

build·down also **build-down** (bĭld′doun′) *n.* A systematic numerical reduction, esp. of nuclear weapons, in which more than one weapon or warhead is destroyed for every new one built. [On the model of BUILDUP.] —**build′-down′** *adj.*

build·er (bĭl′dər) *n.* **1.** One that builds, esp. a person who contracts for and supervises the construction of a building. **2.** An abrasive or filler used in a soap or detergent.

build·ing (bĭl′dĭng) *n.* **1.** Something that is built, as for human habitation; a structure. **2.** The act, process, art, or occupation of constructing.

building sickness *n.* See sick building syndrome.

building society *n. Chiefly British* A savings and loan association.

build·up also **build-up** (bĭld′ŭp′) *n.* **1.** The act or process of amassing or increasing: *a buildup of tension.* **2.** The result of building up. **3a.** Widely favorable publicity, esp. by a systematic campaign. **b.** Extravagant praise.

built (bĭlt) *v.* Past tense and past participle of **build**. ❖ *adj.* **1.** Having a specified physique: *a heavily built boxer.* **2.** *Informal* Having a well-developed or attractive body.

built-in (bĭlt′ĭn′) *adj.* **1.** Constructed as part of a larger unit; not detachable: *a built-in cabinet.* **2.** Forming a permanent or essential element or quality. —**built′-in′** *n.*

built-up (bĭlt′ŭp′) *adj.* **1.** Made by fastening several layers or sections one on top of the other: *a built-up roof.* **2.** Filled with buildings; developed: *a built-up neighborhood.*

Buis·son (bwē-sôN′), **Ferdinand Édouard** 1841–1932. French educator who shared the 1927 Nobel Peace Prize.

Bu·jum·bu·ra (bōō′jəm-bŏŏr′ə) The cap. of Burundi, in the W part on Lake Tanganyika. Pop. 235,440.

Bu·kha·rin (bōō-kär′ĭn, -Ḥär′-), **Nikolai Ivanovich** 1888–1938. Bolshevik revolutionary and Soviet politician who advocated gradual agricultural collectivization.

Bu·kho·ro (bōō-kôr′ō, -Ḥôr′ō) or **Bu·kha·ra** (-kär′ə, -Ḥär′ə) A city of S Uzbekistan W of Samarkand; cap. of the former emirate of **Bukhara** from the 16th to the 19th cent. Pop. 228,000.

Bu·ko·vi·na also **Bu·co·vi·na** (bōō′kə-vē′nə) A historical region of E Europe in W Ukraine and NE Romania.

bul. *abbr.* bulletin

Bu·la·wa·yo (bōō′lə-wä′yō, -wä′-) A city of SW Zimbabwe SW of Harare; founded 1893. Pop. 621,742.

bulb (bŭlb) *n.* **1.** *Botany* **a.** A short, modified underground stem surrounded by usu. fleshy, modified leaves that contain stored food for the shoot within: *an onion bulb.* **b.** A similar underground stem or root, such as a corm, rhizome, or tuber. **c.** A plant that grows from a bulb. **2.** A rounded projection or part: *the bulb of a syringe.* **3.** An incandescent lamp or its glass housing. **4.** *Anatomy* A rounded dilation or expansion of a canal, vessel, or organ.

bugle¹

[Lat. *bulbus* < Gk. *bolbos*, bulbous plant.]

bul•bar (bŭl′bər, -bär′) *adj.* Of, relating to, or characteristic of a bulb, esp. of the medulla oblongata: *bulbar poliomyelitis.*

bul•bel (bŭl′bəl, -bĕl′) *n.* **1.** A smaller bulb produced from a larger bulb. **2.** A bulblet. [Fr. *bulbille.* See BULBIL.]

bul•bif•er•ous (bŭl-bĭf′ər-əs) *adj.* Bearing or producing bulbs or bulbils.

bul•bil (bŭl′bəl, -bĭl′) *n.* **1.** A small bulb or bulblike structure in the place of a flower or in a leaf axil. **2.** A bulblet. [Fr. *bulbille,* dim. of *bulbe,* bulb < Lat. *bulbus.* See BULB.]

bulb•let (bŭlb′lĭt) *n.* A small bulb.

bul•bo•u•re•thral gland (bŭl′bō-yo͝o-rē′thrəl) *n.* Either of two small glands below the prostate that discharge a component of the seminal fluid into the urethra. [BULBO(US) + URETHRAL + GLAND[1].]

bul•bous (bŭl′bəs) *adj.* **1.** Resembling a bulb in shape; rounded or swollen: *a bulbous stem base.* **2.** *Botany* Bearing bulbs or growing from a bulb. **—bul′bous•ly** *adv.*

bul•bul (bo͝ol′bo͝ol′) *n.* **1.** Any of various passerine, chiefly tropical Old World songbirds of the family Pycnonotidae, having grayish or brownish plumage. **2.** A songbird mentioned in Persian poetry and thought to be a nightingale. [Pers. < Ar.]

Bul•finch (bo͝ol′fĭnch′), **Charles** 1763–1844. Amer. architect who completed work on the US Capitol (1830).

Bulfinch, Thomas 1796–1867. Amer. writer best known for his books popularizing mythology.

Bulg. *abbr.* **1.** Bulgaria **2.** Bulgarian

Bulgaria

Bul•ga•nin (bo͝ol-găn′ĭn, -gä′nyĭn), **Nikolai Aleksandrovich** 1895–1975. Soviet politician who was premier from 1955–58.

Bul•gar (bŭl′gär′, bo͝ol′-) *n.* See **Bulgarian** 1. [Med.Lat. *Bulgarus* < Gk. *Boulgaros* < Turkic *bulghar,* of mixed orig., promiscuous < *bulgamaq,* to mix.]

Bul•gar•i•a (bŭl-gâr′ē-ə, bo͝ol-) A country of SE Europe on the Black Sea; settled in the 6th cent. A.D. by Slavic tribes. Cap. Sofia. Pop. 8,443,000.

Bul•gar•i•an (bŭl-gâr′ē-ən, bo͝ol-) *adj.* Of or relating to Bulgaria or its people, language, or culture. ❖ *n.* **1.** A native or inhabitant of Bulgaria. **2.** The Slavic language of the Bulgarians.

bulge (bŭlj) *n.* **1.** A protruding part; an outward curve or swelling. **2.** A sudden, usu. temporary increase in number or quantity: *a bulge in school enrollment.* **3.** An advantage. ❖ *v.* **bulged, bulg•ing, bulg•es** *—tr.* To cause to curve outward. *—intr.* **1.** To curve outward. **2.** To swell up. **3.** To stick out; protrude. **4.** To be filled or overfilled: *pockets bulging with coins.* [ME, pouch < OFr. *bulge, bouge* < Lat. *bulga,* bag, of Celt. orig.] **—bulg′i•ness** *n.* **—bulg′y** *adj.*

bul•gur also **bul•ghur** (bo͝ol-go͝or′, bŭl′gər) *n.* Cracked wheat grains, often used in Middle Eastern dishes. [Ottoman Turk. *bulğūr* < Ar. *burğul, burğul* < Pers. *barghūl.*]

bullfinch
male bullfinch
Pyrrhula pyrrhula

bu•lim•a•rex•i•a (byo͞o-lĭm′ə-rĕk′sē-ə, -lē′mə-, bo͞o-) *n.* See **bulimia** 1. [BULIM(IA) + (AN)OREXIA.] **—bu•lim′a•rex′ic** *adj.* & *n.*

bu•li•mi•a (bo͞o-lē′mē-ə, -lĭm′ē-ə, byo͞o-) *n.* **1.** An eating disorder characterized by episodic binge eating and often associated with measures to prevent weight gain, such as self-induced vomiting, dieting, or fasting. **2.** Insatiable appetite. [NLat. *būlīmia* < Gk. *boulīmiā* : *bous,* ox; see **gʷou-** in App. + *līmos,* hunger.] **—bu•li′mic** *adj.* & *n.*

bulimia ner•vo•sa (nûr-vō′sə) *n.* See **bulimia** 1. [NLat. *būlīmia nervōsa* : *būlīmia,* bulimia + *nervōsa,* fem. of *nervōsus,* nervous.]

bulk (bŭlk) *n.* **1.** Size, mass, or volume, esp. when very large. **2a.** A distinct mass or portion of matter, esp. a large one. **b.** The body of a human, esp. when large or muscular. **3.** The major portion or greater part: *"The great bulk of necessary work can never be anything but painful"* (Bertrand Russell). **4.** See **fiber** 6. **5.** Thickness of paper or cardboard in relation to weight. **6.** A ship's cargo. ❖ *v.* **bulked, bulk•ing, bulks** *—intr.* **1.** To be or appear to be massive in terms of size, volume, or importance; loom. **2.** To grow or increase in size or importance. **3.** To cohere or form a mass: *Certain paper bulks well.* *—tr.* **1.** To cause to swell or expand. **2.** To cause to cohere or form a mass. ❖ *adj.* Being large in mass, quantity, or volume: *a bulk mailing.* ***—idiom:*** **in bulk 1.** Unpackaged; loose. **2.** In large numbers, amounts, or volume. [ME, perh. partly alteration of *bouk,* belly, trunk of the body (< OE *būc*) and partly < ON *bulki,* cargo, heap.]

bullfrog
Rana catesbeiana

bulk•head (bŭlk′hĕd′) *n.* **1a.** One of the upright partitions dividing a ship into compartments and serving to add structural rigidity and prevent the spread of leakage or fire. **b.** A partition or wall serving a similar purpose in a vehicle, such as an aircraft. **2.** A wall or an embankment, as in a mine, that acts as a protective barrier. **3.** *Chiefly New England* A horizontal or sloping structure providing access to a cellar stairway. [*bulk,* stall, partition (perh. of Scand. orig.) + HEAD.]

bulk•y (bŭl′kē) *adj.* **-i•er, -i•est 1.** Having considerable bulk; massive. **2.** Of large size for its weight. **3.** Clumsy to manage; unwieldy. **—bulk′i•ly** *adv.* **—bulk′i•ness** *n.*

bull[1] (bo͝ol) *n.* **1a.** An adult male bovine mammal. **b.** The uncastrated adult male of domestic cattle. **c.** The male of certain other large animals, such as the alligator. **2.** An exceptionally large, strong, and aggressive person. **3a.** An optimist, esp. regarding business conditions. **b.** A person who buys commodities or securities in anticipation of a rise in prices or who tries by speculative purchases to effect such a rise. **4.** *Slang* A police officer or detective. **5.** *Slang* **a.** Foolish, deceitful, or boastful language. **b.** Insolent talk or behavior. **6. Bull** See **Taurus.** ❖ *v.* **bulled, bull•ing, bulls** *—tr.* To push; force. *—intr.* To push ahead or through forcefully. ❖ *adj.* **1.** Male. **2.** Large and strong like a bull. **3.** Characterized by rising prices. ***—idiom:*** **grab** (or **take**) **the bull by the horns** To deal with a problem directly and resolutely. [ME *bule* < OE *bula,* prob. < ON *boli.* N., sense 5, short for BULLSHIT.]

bull[2] (bo͝ol) *n.* **1.** An official document issued by the pope and sealed with a bulla. **2.** The bulla used to seal such a document. [ME *bulle* < OFr. < Med.Lat. *bulla.* See BULLA.]

bull[3] (bo͝ol) *n.* A gross blunder in logical speech or expression. [?]

bull. *abbr.* bulletin

bul•la (bo͝ol′ə) *n., pl.* **bul•lae** (bo͝ol′ē) **1.** A round seal affixed to a papal bull. **2.** *Pathology* A large blister or vesicle. [Med.Lat. < Lat., bubble, seal.]

bul•lace (bo͝ol′ĭs) *n.* See **damson.** [ME *bolas* < AN *bullace* < Med.Lat. *bolluca.*]

bul•late (bo͝ol′āt′, bŭl′-) *adj.* Having a puckered or blistered appearance: *bullate leaves.* [Lat. *bullātus* < *bulla,* bubble.]

bull•bait•ing (bo͝ol′bā′tĭng) *n.* The formerly popular sport of setting dogs to attack a chained bull, esp. its nose.

bull•bat (bo͝ol′băt′) *n.* See **nighthawk** 1a. [< its roaring sound in flight.]

bull•dog (bo͝ol′dôg′, -dŏg′) *n.* **1.** Any of a breed of short-haired dog characterized by a large head, strong square jaws with dewlaps, and a stocky body, originally bred for bullbaiting. **2.** A short-barreled, large-caliber revolver or pistol. **3.** A heat-resistant material used to line puddling furnaces. **4.** *Chiefly British* A proctor's assistant at Oxford University or Cambridge University. ❖ *adj.* Stubborn. ❖ *tr.v.* **-dogged, -dog•ging, -dogs** *Western US* To throw (a calf or steer) by seizing its horns and twisting its neck until the animal falls. **—bull′dog′ger** *n.*

bull•doze (bo͝ol′dōz′) *v.* **-dozed, -doz•ing, -doz•es** *—tr.* **1.** To clear, dig up, or move with a bulldozer. **2.** To treat in an abusive manner; bully. **3.** To coerce in an unsympathetic or cruel way. **4.** To do away with; demolish. *—intr.* **1.** To operate a bulldozer. **2.** To proceed forcefully or insensitively. [Perh. alteration of obsolete *bulldose,* severe beating : BULL[1] + DOSE.]

bull•doz•er (bo͝ol′dō′zər) *n.* **1.** A heavy machine for clearing and grading land, usu. having continuous treads and a broad hydraulic blade in front. **2.** An overbearing person; a bully.

bul•let (bo͝ol′ĭt) *n.* **1a.** A usu. metal projectile in the shape of a pointed cylinder or a ball that is expelled from a firearm, esp. a rifle or handgun. **b.** Such a projectile in a metal casing; a cartridge. **2.** An object resembling a projectile in shape, action, or effect. **3.** *Printing* A heavy dot (•) used to highlight a particular passage. [Fr. *boulette,* dim. of *boule,* ball < OFr. < Lat. *bulla.*]

bul•le•tin (bo͝ol′ĭ-tn, -tĭn) *n.* **1.** A brief report, esp. an official statement on a matter of public interest issued for immediate publication or broadcast. **2.** A brief update or summary of current news, as on television or in a newspaper. **3.** A periodical, esp. one published by an organization or society. **4.** A printed program, esp. one listing the order of worship for a religious service. ❖ *tr.v.* **-tined, -tin•ing, -tins** To announce or make known by bulletin. [Fr., prob. < Ital. *bullettino,* dim. of *bolletta,* bill, dim. of *bolla,* bubble, bull < Med.Lat. *bulla.* See BULL[2].]

bulletin board *n.* **1.** A board on which notices are posted. **2.** *Computer Science* A system that enables users to send or read messages or files that are of general public interest.

bul•let•proof (bo͝ol′ĭt-pro͞of′) *adj.* Impenetrable by bullets. ❖ *tr.v.* **-proofed, -proof•ing, -proofs** To make bulletproof.

bullet train *n.* A high-speed passenger train.

bull fiddle *n.* See **double bass.**

bull•fight (bo͝ol′fīt′) *n.* A public spectacle, esp. in Spain, Portugal, and parts of Latin America, in which a bull, after being engaged in a series of traditional maneuvers, is usu. killed. **—bull′fight′er** *n.* **—bull′fight′ing** *n.*

bull•finch (bo͝ol′fĭnch′) *n.* **1.** A European bird *(Pyrrhula pyrrhula)* having a short thick bill and in the male a red breast, blue-gray back, and black head, wings, and tail. **2.** Any of several similar finches.

bull•frog (bo͝ol′frôg′, -frŏg′) *n.* Any of several large frogs, chiefly of the genus *Rana* and esp. *R. catesbeiana,* native to North America and having a deep resonant croak.

bull•head (bo͝ol′hĕd′) *n.* **1.** Any of several large-headed North American freshwater catfishes of the genus *Ictalurus.* **2.** Any of several fishes of the family Cottidae, such as the sculpin and the miller's thumb. **3.** *Upper Northern US* See **catfish.**

bull•head•ed (bo͝ol′hĕd′ĭd) *adj.* Foolishly or irrationally stubborn; headstrong. See Syns at **obstinate.** **—bull′head′ed•ly** *adv.* **—bull′head′ed•ness** *n.*

bull•horn (bo͝ol′hôrn′) *n.* A portable device consisting of a microphone and a loudspeaker, used esp. to amplify the voice.

bul•lion (bo͝ol′yən) *n.* **1a.** Gold or silver considered with respect to quantity rather than value. **b.** Gold or silver in the form of bars, ingots, or plates. **2.** A heavy lace trimming made of twisted gold or silver threads. [ME, ingot of precious metal < AN < OFr. *billon* (< *bille,* stick; see BILLON) and < OFr. *bouillon,* bubble (< *boilir,* to boil; see BOIL[1]).]

bull·ish (bŏŏl′ĭsh) *adj.* **1a.** Having a heavy muscular physique. **b.** Bullheaded. **2a.** Causing, expecting, or characterized by rising stock market prices. **b.** Optimistic or confident. —**bull′ish·ly** *adv.* —**bull′ish·ness** *n.*

bull·mas·tiff (bŏŏl′măs′tĭf) *n.* A large, heavy-set, powerful dog of a breed developed from the bulldog and the mastiff.

Bull Moose Party *n.* See **Progressive Party** 1.

bull·necked (bŏŏl′nĕkt′) *adj.* Having a short thick neck: *a bull-necked wrestler.* —**bull′neck′** *n.*

bull·nose (bŏŏl′nōz′) *n.* A rounded edge, corner, or projection, as on a stairstep.

bul·lock (bŏŏl′ək) *n.* **1.** A castrated bull; a steer. **2.** A young bull. [ME *bullok* < OE *bulluc.*]

bul·lock's heart (bŏŏl′əks) *n.* See **custard apple.**

Bullock's oriole A subspecies of the northern oriole in its western range, the male of which has orange cheeks and large white wing patches. [After William *Bullock,* 19th-cent. British naturalist.]

bull·pen (bŏŏl′pĕn′) *n.* **1.** *Baseball* **a.** An area where relief pitchers warm up during a game. **b.** The relief pitchers of a team considered as a group. **2.** A temporary holding area for prisoners, as in a courthouse. **3.** An open area in an office with workspace for a number of employees. [Earlier, stockade, exercise area for prisoners.]

bull·ring (bŏŏl′rĭng′) *n.* A circular arena for bullfights.

bull·roar·er (bŏŏl′rôr′ər, -rōr′-) *n.* A small wooden slat attached to a string that makes a roaring noise when whirled.

Bull Run A small stream of NE VA SW of Washington DC near Manassas; site of two important Civil War battles (Jul. 1861 and Aug. 1862).

bull session *n. Informal* An informal group discussion.

bull's-eye or **bull's eye** (bŏŏlz′ī′) *n.* **1a.** The small central circle on a target. **b.** A shot that hits this circle. **2a.** A direct hit: *scored a bull's-eye.* **b.** The precise accomplishment of a goal. **3.** A thick, circular piece of glass set, as in a ship's deck, to admit light. **4.** A circular opening or window. **5a.** A planoconvex lens used to concentrate light. **b.** A lantern or lamp having such a lens. **6.** A piece of round hard candy.

bull·shit (bŏŏl′shĭt′) *Vulgar Slang n.* **1.** Foolish, deceitful, boastful, or insolent language. **2.** Something worthless, deceptive, or insincere. ❖ *v.* -**shit** also -**shat** (-shăt) or -**shit·ted** (-shĭt′ĭd), -**shit·ting**, -**shits** —*intr.* **1.** To speak foolishly or insolently. **2.** To engage in idle conversation. —*tr.* To attempt to mislead or deceive by talking nonsense. ❖ *adj.* Very angry; incensed. ❖ *interj.* Used to express extreme displeasure or exasperation. —**bull′shit′ter** *n.*

bull snake *n.* Any of several large, nonvenomous North American snakes of the genus *Pituophis,* having yellow and brown or black markings and feeding chiefly on rodents.

bull terrier *n.* Any of a breed of dog having a short, usu. white coat and a tapering muzzle, developed by crossing a bulldog with a now extinct breed of terrier.

bull thistle *n.* A biennial Eurasian thistle (*Cirsium vulgare*) in the composite family, having heads of purplish flowers and spiny stems and leaves. [< its large head.]

bull tongue *n.* A large detachable plowshare with a single blade, used chiefly for breaking or clearing heavy soil.

bull·whip (bŏŏl′hwĭp′, -wĭp′) *n.* A long plaited rawhide whip with a knotted end. ❖ *tr.v.* -**whipped**, -**whip·ping**, -**whips** To whip or beat with a bullwhip.

bul·ly[1] (bŏŏl′ē) *n., pl.* -**lies 1.** A person who is habitually cruel or overbearing, esp. to smaller or weaker people. **2.** A hired ruffian; a thug. **3.** A pimp. **4.** *Archaic* A fine person. **5.** *Archaic* A sweetheart. ❖ *v.* -**lied**, -**ly·ing**, -**lies** —*tr.* **1.** To treat in an overbearing or intimidating manner. **2.** To make (one's way) aggressively. —*intr.* **1.** To behave like a bully. **2.** To force one's way aggressively or by intimidation. ❖ *adj.* Excellent; splendid. ❖ *interj.* Used to express approval: *Bully for you!* [Poss. < MDu. *boele,* sweetheart, prob. alteration of *broeder,* brother. See **bhrāter-** in App.]

bul·ly[2] (bŏŏl′ē) *n.* Canned or pickled beef. [Perh. Fr. *bouilli,* boiled meat, label on canned beef < p. part. of *bouillir,* to boil < OFr. *boilir.* See **BOIL[1].**]

bul·ly·boy (bŏŏl′ē-boi′) *n.* A hired thug or ruffian.

bul·ly·rag (bŏŏl′ē-răg′) also **bal·ly·rag** (băl′ē-) *tr.v.* -**ragged**, -**rag·ging**, -**rags** To mistreat or intimidate by bullying. [< dialectal *ballarag.*]

Bü·low (byōō′lō), Prince **Bernhard Heinrich Martin Karl von** 1849–1929. German politician and diplomat who served as chancellor (1900–09).

bul·rush (bŏŏl′rŭsh′) *n.* **1.** Any of various aquatic or wetland herbs of the genus *Scirpus,* having grasslike leaves and usu. small, often brown spikelets. **2.** Any of several similar wetland plants, such as the papyrus. [ME *bulrish* : perh. alteration (influenced by *bule,* bull) of *bole,* stem; see **BOLE[1]** + *rish,* rush; see **RUSH[2].**]

bul·wark (bŏŏl′wərk, -wôrk′, bŭl′-) *n.* **1.** A wall or embankment raised as a defensive fortification; a rampart. **2.** Something serving as a defense or safeguard. **3.** A breakwater. **4.** The part of a ship's side that is above the upper deck. Often used in the plural. ❖ *tr.v.* -**warked**, -**wark·ing**, -**warks 1.** To fortify with a wall, embankment, or rampart. **2.** To provide defense or protection

for. [ME *bulwerk* < MDu. *bolwerk* < MHGer. *bolwerc* : *bole,* plank + *werc,* work (< OHGer.; see **werg-** in App.).]

Bul·wer (bŏŏl′wər), **William Henry Lytton Earle.** Baron Dalling and Bulwer. 1801–72. British politician and diplomat who negotiated the Clayton-Bulwer Treaty (1850).

Bul·wer-Lyt·ton (bŏŏl′wər-lĭt′n), **Edward George Earle Lytton.** 1st Baron Lytton. 1803–73. British writer known for his historical novels, esp. *The Last Days of Pompeii* (1834).

bum[1] (bŭm) *n.* **1.** A tramp; a vagrant. **2.** A lazy or shiftless person, esp. one who seeks to live solely by others' support. **3.** An incompetent, insignificant, or obnoxious person. **4.** One who is devoted to a particular activity or milieu. ❖ *v.* **bummed, bum·ming, bums** —*intr.* **1.** To live by begging and scavenging from place to place. Often used with *around.* **2.** To loaf. —*tr.* **1.** To acquire by begging; cadge. **2.** *Slang* To depress, dishearten, or dismay. Often used with *out.* ❖ *adj.* **1.** Inferior; worthless. **2.** Disabled; malfunctioning: *a bum shoulder.* **3.** Unfavorable or unfair. **4.** Unpleasant; lousy. —*idiom:* **on the bum 1.** Living as a vagrant or tramp. **2.** Out of order; broken. [Back-formation < BUMMER.]

bum[2] (bŭm) *n. Chiefly British Slang* The buttocks. [ME *bom.*]

bum·ber·shoot (bŭm′bər-shōōt′) *n.* An umbrella. [Alteration of UMBRELLA + alteration of (PARA)CHUTE.]

bum·ble[1] (bŭm′bəl) *v.* -**bled**, -**bling**, -**bles** —*intr.* **1.** To speak in a faltering manner. **2.** To move or proceed clumsily. See Syns at **blunder.** —*tr.* To bungle; botch. [Perh. blend of BUNGLE and STUMBLE.] —**bum′bler** *n.*

bum·ble[2] (bŭm′bəl) *intr.v.* -**bled**, -**bling**, -**bles** To make a humming or droning sound; buzz. ❖ *n.* A humming or droning sound; a buzz. [ME *bomblen,* of imit. orig.]

bum·ble·bee (bŭm′bəl-bē′) *n.* Any of various large, hairy, social bees of the genus *Bombus* that nest underground. [BUMBLE[2] + BEE[1].]

bu·mel·ia (byōō-mē′lē-ə) *n.* Any of various often thorny North American trees or shrubs of the genus *Bumelia,* esp. *B. lanuginosa* or *B. lycioides* of the southern United States, having hard wood and black fleshy fruit. [NLat. *Bumelia,* genus name < Lat. *būmelia,* ash tree < Gk. *boumeliā* : *bous,* cow; see **gʷou-** in App. : *meliā,* ash.]

bumf or **bumph** (bŭmf) *n. Chiefly British Slang* **1.** Printed matter, such as pamphlets or forms, esp. that deemed of little interest or importance. **2.** Toilet paper. [Short for *bum fodder* : BUM[2] + FODDER.]

bum·fuz·zle (bŭm′fŭz′əl) *tr.v.* -**zled**, -**zling**, -**zles** *Chiefly Southern US* To confuse. [Prob. *bum-* (prob. alteration of BAMBOOZLE) + *fuzzle* (perh. blend of FUDDLE and FUZZY).]

bum·ma·lo (bŭm′ə-lō) *n., pl.* -**los** See **Bombay duck** 2. [Marathi *bombīla.*]

bum·mer (bŭm′ər) *n. Slang* **1a.** An adverse reaction to a hallucinogenic drug. **b.** A disagreeable person, experience, or situation. **2.** *Slang* One that depresses, frustrates, or disappoints. **3.** A loafer, idler, or beggar. [< BUM[1], *adj.* Sense 3, prob. < Ger. *Bummler,* loafer < *bummeln,* to loaf.]

bump (bŭmp) *v.* **bumped, bump·ing, bumps** —*tr.* **1.** To strike or collide with. **2.** To cause to knock against an obstacle. **3a.** To knock to a new position; shift: *bumped the crate out of the way.* **b.** To shake up and down; jolt. **4a.** To displace from a position within a group or organization. **b.** To deprive (a passenger) of a reserved seat because of overbooking. **5.** To raise; boost: *bump up the price.* —*intr.* **1.** To hit or knock against something. **2.** To proceed with jerks and jolts. ❖ *n.* **1a.** A blow, collision, or jolt. **b.** The sound of something bumping. **2a.** A raised or rounded spot; a bulge. **b.** A slight swelling or lump. **c.** Something, such as a hole in a road, that causes a bump. **3.** A rise or increase, as in prices. **4.** One of the natural protuberances on the human skull, considered significant in phrenology. **5.** A forward thrust of the pelvis, as in an erotic dance. **6.** *Slang* A shot of hard liquor, sometimes accompanied by a beer chaser. —*phrasal verbs:* **bump into** To meet by chance. **bump off** *Slang* To murder. [Imit.]

bump·er[1] (bŭm′pər) *n.* **1.** A usu. metal or rubber bar attached to either end of a motor vehicle to absorb impact in a collision. **2.** A device for absorbing shocks or impeding contact.

bump·er[2] (bŭm′pər) *n.* **1.** A drinking vessel filled to the brim. **2.** Something extraordinarily large. ❖ *adj.* Extraordinarily abundant or full: *a bumper crop of corn.* [Perh. < BUMP.]

bumper sticker *n.* A sticker bearing a printed message for display on a vehicle's bumper.

bump·kin[1] (bŭmp′kĭn, bŭm′-) *n.* An awkward unsophisticated person; a yokel. [Perh. < Flem. *boomken,* shrub, dim. of *boom,* tree; see **bheuə-** in App., or < MDu. *bommekijn,* dim. of *bomme,* barrel.]

bump·kin[2] (bŭmp′kĭn, bŭm′-) *n.* A short spar projecting from the deck of a ship, used to extend a sail or secure a block or stay. [Prob. < Du. *boomken,* dim. of *boom,* tree. See **BOOM[2].**]

bump·tious (bŭmp′shəs) *adj.* Crudely or loudly assertive; pushy. [Perh. blend of BUMP and PRESUMPTUOUS.] —**bump′tious·ly** *adv.* —**bump′tious·ness** *n.*

bump·y (bŭm′pē) *adj.* -**i·er**, -**i·est 1.** Covered with or full of bumps: *a bumpy country road.* **2.** Marked by bumps and jolts; rough. —**bump′i·ly** *adv.* —**bump′i·ness** *n.*

bun[1] (bŭn) *n.* **1.** A small bread roll, often sweetened or spiced and sometimes containing dried fruit. **2.** A tight roll of hair worn at the back of the head. [ME *bunne,* prob. < OFr. *bugne,* boil, of Celt. orig.]

bun² (bŭn) *n. Slang* A drunken spree. [?]

bun³ (bŭn) *n. Slang* One of the buttocks. Often used in the plural. [Dialectal, hind part of a rabbit or squirrel < Sc. Gael., stump, bottom < OIr.]

bu•na (boo͞o′nə, byoo͞o′-) *n.* A synthetic rubber made from the polymerization of butadiene and sodium. [Orig. a trademark.]

bunch (bŭnch) *n.* **1a.** A group of things growing close together; a cluster or clump. **b.** A group of like items or individuals gathered or placed together. **2.** *Informal* A group of people usu. having a common interest or association. **3.** *Informal* A considerable number or amount; a lot. **4.** A small lump or swelling; a bump. ❖ *v.* **bunched, bunch•ing, bunch•es** —*tr.* **1.** To gather or form into a cluster. **2.** To gather together into a group. **3.** To gather (fabric) into folds. —*intr.* **1.** To form a cluster or group. **2.** To be gathered together in folds, as fabric. **3.** To swell; protrude. [ME *bonche,* prob. < Flem. *bondje,* dim. of *bont,* bundle < MDu. See BUNDLE.] —**bunch′i•ness** *n.* —**bunch′y** *adj.*

bunch•ber•ry (bŭnch′bĕr′ē) *n.* See dwarf cornel.

Bunche (bŭnch), **Ralph Johnson** 1904–71. Amer. diplomat who won the 1950 Nobel Peace Prize.

bunch•flow•er (bŭnch′flou′ər) *n.* A perennial herb (*Melanthium virginicum*) in the lily family, native to the eastern United States and having a cluster of cream-colored or greenish flowers.

bunch grass or **bunch•grass** (bŭnch′grăs′) *n.* Any of various grasses in different genera that grow in clumplike fashion.

bunch•ing onion (bŭn′chĭng) *n.* Any of certain kinds of onion plants, such as the Welsh onion, grown for their multiple stems, which are used as scallions.

bun•co also **bun•ko** (bŭng′kō) *Informal n., pl.* **-cos** also **-kos** A swindle in which an unsuspecting person is cheated; a confidence game. ❖ *tr.v.* **-coed, -co•ing, -cos** also **-koed, -ko•ing, -kos** To swindle. [Prob. alteration of Sp. *banca,* card game < Ital. *banca,* bank, of Gmc. orig. See BANK².]

bun•combe (bŭng′kəm) *n.* Variant of bunkum.

bund¹ (bŭnd) *n.* **1.** An embankment or dike, esp. in India. **2.** A street running along a harbor or waterway, esp. in the Far East. [Hindi *band* < Pers. < MPers. < Avestan **banda-.* See bhendh- in App.]

bundt cake
frosting a bundt cake

bund² (boo͞ond, bŭnd) *n.* **1.** An association, esp. a political association. **2.** often **Bund** A pro-Nazi German-American organization of the 1930s. **3.** often **Bund** A European Jewish socialist movement founded in Russia in 1897. [Ger. < MHGer. *bunt.* See bhendh- in App.] —**bund′ist** *n.*

bun•dle (bŭn′dl) *n.* **1.** A group of objects held together, as by tying or wrapping. **2.** Something wrapped or tied up for carrying; a package. **3.** *Biology* A cluster or strand of closely bound muscle or nerve fibers. **4.** *Botany* A vascular bundle. **5.** *Informal* **a.** A large amount; a lot. **b.** A large sum of money. ❖ *v.* **-dled, -dling, -dles** —*tr.* **1.** To tie, wrap, or gather together. **2.** To dispatch or dispense of quickly and with little fuss; hustle. **3.** To dress (a person) warmly: *bundled them up in winter clothes.* —*intr.* **1.** To hurry; hasten. **2.** To dress oneself warmly. **3.** To sleep in the same bed with another while fully clothed. [ME *bundel,* prob. < MDu. *bondel.* See bhendh- in App.] —**bun′dler** *n.*

bundt cake (bŭnt, boo͞ont) *n.* A ring-shaped cake baked in a tube pan that has fluted sides. [Orig. a trademark.]

bung (bŭng) *n.* **1.** A stopper esp. for the hole through which a cask, keg, or barrel is filled or emptied. **2.** A bunghole. ❖ *tr.v.* **bunged, bung•ing, bungs 1.** To close with or as if with a cork or stopper. **2.** *Informal* To injure or damage. **3.** *Chiefly British* To fling; toss. [ME *bunge* < MDu. *bonge* < LLat. *pūncta,* hole < Lat. fem. p. part. of *pungere,* to prick.]

bun•ga•low (bŭng′gə-lō′) *n.* **1.** A small house or cottage usu. having a single story and sometimes an attic story. **2.** A thatched or tiled one-story house in India surrounded by a wide veranda. [Hindi *banglā,* Bengali, bungalow.]

bungee jumping

bun•gee cord (bŭn′jē′) *n.* An elasticized rubber cord used to fasten, bear weight, or absorb shock. [Alteration of *bunjie,* rubber.]

bungee jumping *n.* The sport of jumping usu. headfirst from a great height while attached to a secured bungee cord. —**bungee jumper** *n.*

bung•hole (bŭng′hōl′) *n.* **1.** The hole in a cask, keg, or barrel through which liquid is poured in or drained out. **2.** *Vulgar Slang* The anus.

bun•gle (bŭng′gəl) *v.* **-gled, -gling, -gles** —*intr.* To work or act ineptly or inefficiently. —*tr.* To handle badly; botch. See Syns at **botch.** ❖ *n.* A clumsy or inept performance; a botch. [Perh. of Scand. orig.] —**bun′gler** *n.* —**bun′gling•ly** *adv.*

Bu•nin (boo͞o′nĭn, -nyĭn), **Ivan Alekseevich** 1870–1953. Russian writer who won the 1933 Nobel Prize for literature.

bun•ion (bŭn′yən) *n.* A painful inflamed swelling of the bursa at the first joint of the big toe, characterized by enlargement of the joint and lateral displacement of the toe. [Prob. alteration of obsolete *bunny,* swelling < ME *bony,* perh. < OFr. *bugne.* See BUN¹.]

bunk¹ (bŭngk) *n.* **1.** A narrow bed built like a shelf into or against a wall, as in a ship's cabin. **2.** A bunk bed. **3.** A place for sleeping. ❖ *v.* **bunked, bunk•ing, bunks** —*intr.* **1a.** To sleep in a bunk or bed. **b.** To stay the night; sleep. **2.** To go to bed: *bunked down*

Bunraku

early. —*tr.* To provide with sleeping quarters. [Perh. short for BUNKER.]

bunk² (bŭngk) *n.* Empty talk; nonsense. [Short for BUNKUM.]

bunk bed *n.* Either of a pair of narrow beds stacked one on top of the other.

bun•ker (bŭng′kər) *n.* **1.** A bin or tank esp. for fuel storage, as on a ship. **2a.** An underground defensive position with a fortified projection above ground level for gun emplacements. **b.** A protective chamber. **3.** *Sports* A sand trap serving as an obstacle on a golf course. ❖ *tr.v.* **-kered, -ker•ing, -kers 1.** To store or place (fuel) in a bunker. **2.** *Sports* To hit (a golf ball) into a bunker. [Sc. *bonker,* chest, perh. of Scand. orig.] —**bun′ker** *adj.*

Bunker Hill A section of Charlestown MA. The first major Revolutionary War battle took place nearby (Jun. 17, 1775).

bunk•house (bŭngk′hous′) *n.* A building providing sleeping quarters on a ranch or in a camp.

bunk•mate (bŭngk′māt′) *n.* A person with whom one shares sleeping quarters.

bun•ko (bŭng′kō) *n. & v.* Variant of bunco.

bun•kum also **bun•combe** (bŭng′kəm) *n.* Empty or insincere talk; claptrap. [After *Buncombe,* a county of western North Carolina, from a remark made around 1820 by its congressman, who felt obligated to give a dull speech "for Buncombe."]

bun•ny (bŭn′ē) *n., pl.* **-nies** A rabbit, esp. a young one. [< dialectal *bun,* tail of a rabbit. See BUN³.]

Bun•ra•ku (boo͞on-rä′koo, boo͞on′rä′-) *n.* A traditional Japanese puppet theater featuring large puppets and a narrative recited from offstage. [J., after the *Bunraku-za* theater built in the early 19th cent. by Bunraku-ken Oemurea (died 1810).]

Bun•sen (bŭn′sən), **Robert Wilhelm** 1811–99. German chemist who pioneered in spectrum analysis.

Bunsen burner *n.* A small laboratory burner consisting of a vertical metal tube connected to a gas source and producing a very hot flame from a mixture of gas and air let in through adjustable holes at the base. [After Robert Wilhelm BUNSEN.]

bunt¹ (bŭnt) *v.* **bunt•ed, bunt•ing, bunts** —*tr.* **1.** *Baseball* To bat (a pitched ball) by tapping it lightly so that the ball rolls slowly in front of the infielders. **2.** To push or strike with or as if with the head; butt. —*intr.* **1.** *Baseball* To bunt a pitched ball: *The batter squared away to bunt.* **2.** To butt. ❖ *n.* **1.** *Baseball* **a.** The act of bunting. **b.** A bunted ball. **2.** A butt with or as if with the head. [Dialectal, to push, strike.] —**bunt′er** *n.*

bunt² (bŭnt) *n.* The middle portion of a sail, esp. a square one, that is shaped like a pouch to increase the effect of the wind. **2.** The pouchlike midsection of a fishing net in which the catch is concentrated. [Perh. < Swed. *bunt* or Dan. *bundt,* both of LGer. orig.]

bunt³ (bŭnt) *n.* A smut disease of wheat and other cereal grasses, caused by fungi of the genus *Tilletia* and resulting in grains filled with foul-smelling, sooty black spores. [?]

bunt•ing¹ (bŭn′tĭng) *n.* **1.** A light cotton or woolen cloth used for making flags. **2.** Flags considered as a group. **3.** Strips of cloth or material usu. in the colors of the national flag, used esp. as drapery or streamers for festive decoration. [Perh. < Ger. *bunt,* colored.]

bunt•ing² (bŭn′tĭng) *n.* Any of various birds of the family Fringillidae, having short cone-shaped bills and brownish or grayish plumage. [ME.]

bunt•ing³ (bŭn′tĭng) *n.* A snug-fitting, hooded sleeping bag for infants. [Perh. < Sc. *buntin,* plump, short.]

Bunt•line (bŭnt′lĭn, -lĭn′), **Ned** See Edward Zane Carroll Judson.

Bu•ñu•el (boo͞o-nyoo͞o-ĕl′), **Luis** 1900–83. Spanish director known for films such as *The Discreet Charm of the Bourgeoisie* (1972).

bun•ya-bun•ya (bŭn′yə-bŭn′yə) also **bun•ya-bun•ya** *n.* An Australian evergreen tree (*Araucaria bidwilli*) having tiers of nearly whorled branches and large cones. [Yagara (Aboriginal language of E Australia).]

Bun•yan (bŭn′yən), **John** 1628–88. English preacher and writer celebrated for his *Pilgrim's Progress* (two parts, 1678 and 1684).

Bun•yan•esque (bŭn′yə-nĕsk′) *adj.* **1.** Of or relating to the allegorical writings of John Bunyan. **2a.** Of or relating to the legend of Paul Bunyan. **b.** Of very large size.

bun•ya pine (bŭn′yə) *n.* See bunya-bunya.

buoy (boo͞o′ē, boi) *n.* **1.** *Nautical* A float moored in water to mark a location, warn of danger, or indicate a channel. **2.** A life buoy. ❖ *tr.v.* **buoyed, buoy•ing, buoys 1.** To keep afloat or aloft. **2a.** To maintain at a high level; support. **b.** To hearten or inspire; uplift. **3.** To mark with or as if with a buoy. [ME *boie* < OFr. *boue,* prob. of Gmc. orig.]

buoy•ance (boi′əns, boo͞o′yəns) *n.* Buoyancy.

buoy•an•cy (boi′ən-sē, boo͞o′yən-) *n.* **1a.** The tendency or capacity to remain afloat in a liquid or rise in air or gas. **b.** The upward force that a fluid exerts on an object less dense than itself. **2.** Ability to recover quickly from setbacks; resilience. **3.** Lightness of spirit; cheerfulness.

buoy•ant (boi′ənt, boo͞o′yənt) *adj.* **1.** Having or marked by buoyancy. **2.** Lighthearted; gay: *in a buoyant mood.* [Sp. *boyante,* pr. part. of *boyar,* to refloat a boat < *boya,* buoy < OFr. *boue.* See BUOY.] —**buoy′ant•ly** *adv.*

bup•pie (bŭp′ē) *n. Informal* A young Black city or suburban resident with a well-paid professional job and an affluent lifestyle. [B(LACK) + (Y)UPPIE.]

bu·pres·tid (byoō-prĕs′tĭd) *n.* Any of various beetles of the family Buprestidae, which are destructive wood borers as larvae. [< NLat. *Būprēstidae*, family name < *Būprēstis*, type genus < Lat. *būprēstis*, beetle harmful to cattle < Gk. *bouprēstis* : *bous*, ox; see g^wou- in App. + *prēthein*, to swell up.]

bur[1] also **burr** (bûr) *n.* **1a.** A rough husk or covering surrounding the seeds or fruits of plants. **b.** A plant producing such husks or coverings. **2.** A persistently clinging or nettlesome person or thing. **3.** A rough protuberance, esp. a burl on a tree. **4.** Any of various rotary cutting tools designed to be attached to a drill. [ME *burre*, of Scand. orig.]

bur[2] (bûr) *n. & v.* Variant of **burr**[2].

bur[3] (bûr) *n.* Variant of **burr**[3].

bur. *abbr.* bureau

bu·ran (boō-rän′) *n.* A violent windstorm of the Eurasian steppes. [Russ., prob. < Tatar.]

Bur·bage (bûr′bĭj), **Richard** 1567?–1619. English actor and theater manager who was the first to play the title roles in Shakespeare's *Hamlet, King Lear, Othello,* and *Richard III.*

Bur·bank (bûr′băngk′) A city of S CA near Los Angeles. Pop. 100,316.

Burbank, Luther 1849–1926. Amer. horticulturist who developed new varieties of fruits, vegetables, and flowers.

Bur·bidge (bûr′bĭj), **(Eleanor) Margaret** b. 1919. British-born Amer. astronomer who directed the Royal Greenwich Observatory (1972–73).

bur·ble (bûr′bəl) *n.* **1.** A gurgling or bubbling sound, as of running water. **2.** A rapid, excited flow of speech. **3.** A breakdown in the smooth flow of fluid past a moving streamlined body, such as an airplane wing, resulting in turbulence. ❖ *intr.v.* **-bled, -bling, -bles 1.** To bubble; gurgle. **2.** To speak quickly and excitedly; gush. [ME *burblen*, to bubble.] —**bur′bler** *n.* —**bur′bly** *adj.*

bur·bot (bûr′bət) *n., pl.* **burbot** or **-bots** A freshwater food fish *(Lota lota)* of the Northern Hemisphere, having barbels on the nose and chin. [ME < OFr. *borbote* < *borbeter*, to move about in mud.]

Burch·field (bûrch′fēld′), **Charles Ephraim** 1893–1967. Amer. painter whose works include somber urban scenes.

bur cucumber *n.* **1.** A weedy annual vine *(Sicyos angulatus)* of North America having whitish flowers and small fruits with long slender prickles. **2.** The fruit of this vine.

bur·den[1] (bûr′dn) *n.* **1.** Something that is carried. **2a.** Something that is emotionally difficult to bear. **b.** A source of great worry or stress; weight. **3.** A responsibility or duty. **4.** *Nautical* **a.** The amount of cargo that a vessel can carry. **b.** The weight of the cargo carried by a vessel at one time. **5.** The incidence or concentration, as in a population, of a disease-producing organism or of a disease itself. ❖ *tr.v.* **-dened, -den·ing, -dens 1.** To weigh down; oppress. **2.** To load or overload. [ME < OE *byrthen*. See **bher-**[1] in App.]

bur·den[2] (bûr′dn) *n.* **1.** A principal or recurring idea; a theme. **2.** *Music* **a.** The chorus or refrain of a composition, esp. of a 15th-century carol. **b.** A drone, as of a bagpipe. **c.** *Archaic* The bass accompaniment to a song. [Variant of BOURDON.]

burden of proof *n. Law* The responsibility of proving a disputed charge or allegation.

bur·den·some (bûr′dn-səm) *adj.* Of or like a burden; onerous.

bur·dock (bûr′dŏk′) *n.* Any of several weedy, chiefly biennial plants of the genus *Arctium* in the composite family, having pink or purplish flower heads surrounded by prickly bracts and forming a bur in fruit. [BUR[1] + DOCK[1].]

bu·reau (byoŏr′ō) *n., pl.* **-reaus** or **-reaux** (-ōz) **1.** A chest of drawers, esp. a dresser for holding clothes. **2.** *Chiefly British* A writing desk or writing table with drawers. **3a.** A government department or a subdivision of a department. **b.** An office, usu. of a large organization, that is responsible for a specific duty: *a news bureau.* **4.** A business that offers information of a specified kind: *a travel bureau.* [Fr., cloth cover for desks, desk, office < OFr. *burel*, woolen cloth, prob. < VLat. *būra* < LLat. *burra*, shaggy garment.]

bu·reauc·ra·cy (byoŏ-rŏk′rə-sē) *n., pl.* **-cies 1a.** Administration of a government chiefly through bureaus or departments staffed with nonelected officials. **b.** The departments and their officials as a group. **2a.** Management or administration marked by hierarchical authority among numerous offices and by fixed procedures. **b.** The administrative structure of a large or complex organization. **3.** An administrative system in which the need or inclination to follow complex procedures impedes effective action. [Fr. *bureaucratie* : *bureau*, office; see BUREAU + *-cratie*, rule (< OFr.; see -CRACY].

bu·reau·crat (byoŏr′ə-krăt′) *n.* **1.** An official of a bureaucracy. **2.** One who is rigidly devoted to the details of administrative procedure. —**bu′reau·crat′ic** *adj.* —**bu′reau·crat′i·cal·ly** *adv.*

—**bu·reauc·ra·ti·za·tion** (-tĭ-zā′shən) *n.* —**bu·reauc′ra·tize**′ (byoŏ-rŏk′rə-tīz′) *v.*

bu·rette also **bu·ret** (byoŏ-rĕt′) *n.* A uniform-bore glass tube with fine gradations and a stopcock at the bottom, used esp. in laboratory procedures. [Fr., dim. of *buire*, vase for liquors < OFr., prob. of Gmc. orig.]

burg (bûrg) *n.* **1.** *Informal* A city or town. **2.** A fortified or walled town in early or medieval Europe. [Probably from *-burg* (in place names such as HARRISBURG) < ME *burgh*, town < OE *burg.* See **bhergh-** in App. Sense 2, ult. < Gmc. **burgs*, hill fort; see **bhergh-** in App.]

bur·gage (bûr′gĭj) *n.* A tenure in England and Scotland under which property of the king or a lord in a town was held in return for a yearly rent or the rendering of a service. [ME < OFr. *bourgage* < Med.Lat. *burgāgium* < LLat. *burgus*, fortified town, of Gmc. orig. See BURGESS.]

Bur·gas (boŏr-gäs′) A city of SE Bulgaria on the Black Sea. Pop. 195,986.

bur·gee (bər-jē′, bûr′jē) *n.* A small distinguishing flag displayed by a yacht. [Perh. < Fr. dialectal *bourgeais*, shipowner < OFr. *burgeis*, citizen < *bourg*, bourg. See BOURG.]

bur·geon also **bour·geon** (bûr′jən) *intr.v.* **-geoned, -geon·ing, -geons 1a.** To put forth new buds, leaves, or greenery. **b.** To begin to grow or blossom. **2.** To grow and flourish. [ME *burgeonen* < OFr. *borjoner* < *burjon*, a bud < VLat. **burriōnem, burriōn-* < LLat. *burra*, a shaggy garment.]

burg·er (bûr′gər) *n.* **1.** A sandwich consisting of a bun, cooked beef patty, and often other ingredients such as cheese. Often used in combination: *a cheeseburger.* **2.** A similar sandwich with a non-beef filling. Often used in combination: *a crab burger.* [Short for HAMBURGER.]

Burger, Warren Earl 1907–95. Amer. jurist; chief justice of the US Supreme Court (1969–86).

bur·gess (bûr′jĭs) *n.* **1.** A freeman or citizen of an English borough. **2.** A member of the English Parliament who once represented a town, borough, or university. **3.** A member of the lower house of the legislature of colonial Virginia or Maryland. [ME *burgeis* < OFr. < LLat. *burgēnsis* < *burgus*, fortified town. See **bhergh-** in App.]

Burgess, Anthony 1917–93. British writer and critic whose novels include *A Clockwork Orange* (1962).

Burgess Shale *n.* A rock formation in the western Canadian Rockies containing a wealth of fossilized invertebrates of the early Cambrian Period and providing valuable information about the evolution of early life. [After nearby Mount *Burgess.*]

burgh (bûrg) *n.* A chartered town or borough in Scotland. [Sc., var. of BOROUGH.]

burgh·er (bûr′gər) *n.* **1.** A citizen of a town or borough. **2.** A comfortable or complacent member of the middle class. **3a.** A member of the mercantile class of a medieval European city. **b.** A citizen of a medieval European city. [Ger. *Bürger* or Du. *burger,* both < MHGer. *burgaere* < OHGer. *burgāri* < *burg,* city. See **bhergh-** in App.]

Burgh·ley (bûr′lē), 1st Baron. See William **Cecil.**

bur·glar (bûr′glər) *n.* One who burglarizes. [AN *burgler* (alteration of *burgesur,* prob. < OFr. *burg,* borough) and Med.Lat. *burgulātor* (alteration of *burgātor* < *burgāre,* to commit burglary in < LLat. *burgus,* fortified town), both of Gmc. orig. See **bhergh-** in App.]

bur·glar·i·ous (bər-glâr′ē-əs) *adj.* Of or relating to burglary. —**bur·glar′i·ous·ly** *adv.*

bur·glar·ize (bûr′glə-rīz′) *v.* **-ized, -iz·ing, -iz·es** —*tr.* **1.** To enter and steal from (a building or other premises). **2.** To commit burglary against. —*intr.* To commit burglary.

bur·gla·ry (bûr′glə-rē) *n., pl.* **-ries** The act of entering a building or other premises with the intent to steal.

bur·gle (bûr′gəl) *tr. & intr.v.* **-gled, -gling, -gles** To burglarize. [Back-formation < BURGLAR.]

bur·go·mas·ter (bûr′gə-măs′tər) *n.* The principal magistrate of a city or town in the Netherlands, Flanders, Austria, or Germany. [Partial transl. of Du. *burgemeester* : *burg,* town (< MDu. *burch*; see **bhergh-** in App.) + *meester,* master.]

bur·go·net (bûr′gə-nĭt, bûr′gə-nĕt′) *n.* A light steel helmet with a peak and hinged flaps covering the cheeks, worn in the 16th century. [Fr. *bourguignotte,* prob. < *Bourgogne,* Burgundy, a region of E France.]

bur·goo (bûr′goō, bər-goō′) *n., pl.* **-goos 1.** *New England* Any of several thick stews, originally an oatmeal porridge. **2.** *Chiefly Kentucky & Southern Illinois* **a.** A spicy stew made of poultry, game, other meats, and vegetables, usu. cooked outdoors. **b.** A picnic featuring such a stew. [Perh. alteration of RAGOUT.]

Bur·gos (boŏr′gōs′) A city of N Spain on a high plateau SSW of Bilbao; founded c. 884. Pop. 161,700.

Bur·goyne (bûr-goin′, bûr′goin′), **John** Known as "Gentleman Johnny." 1722–92. British general and playwright who captured Fort Ticonderoga (Jul. 6, 1777).

Bur·gun·dy[1] (bûr′gən-dē) **1.** A ducal house of Burgundy split into the Capetian line (1032–1361) and the Cadet, or Valois, line (1363–1477). **2.** A Portuguese dynasty (1139–1383) beginning with Alfonso I, who made Portugal an independent kingdom.

Bur·gun·dy[2] (bûr′gən-dē) also **Bour·gogne** (boŏr-gôn′yə) A

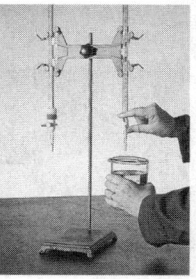

burette
liquid being dispensed from a burette into a beaker

ă	pat	oi	boy
ā	pay	ou	out
âr	care	oŏ	took
ä	father	oō	boot
ĕ	pet	ŭ	cut
ē	be	ûr	urge
ĭ	pit	th	thin
ī	pie	th	this
îr	pier	hw	which
ŏ	pot	zh	vision
ō	toe	ə	about,
ô	paw		item

Stress marks:
′ (primary);
′ (secondary), as in
lexicon (lĕk′sĭ-kŏn′)

historical region and former province of E France; incorporated into the French crown lands by Louis XI in 1477. **—Bur•gun′di•an** (bər-gŭn′dē-ən) *adj. & n.*

Bur•gun•dy[3] (bûr′gən-dē) *n., pl.* **-dies 1a.** Any of various wines produced in Burgundy, France. **b.** Any of various similar wines produced elsewhere. **2. burgundy** A dark grayish or blackish red to dark purplish red or reddish brown.

bur•i•al (bĕr′ē-əl) *n.* The act or process of burying. [ME *buriel,* back-formation < *buriels* (taken as pl.) < OE *byrgels.*] **—bur′i•al** *adj.*

bu•rin (byo͝or′ĭn, bûr′-) *n.* **1.** A steel cutting tool with a sharp beveled point, used in engraving or carving stone. **2.** The style or technique of an engraver's work. **3.** *Archaeology* A stone tool with a chisellike head. [Fr., prob. < obsolete Ital. *burino,* of Gmc. orig.]

Burk or **Burke** (bûrk), **Martha Jane** Known as "Calamity Jane." 1852?–1903. Amer. frontierswoman and legendary figure of the Wild West; reputed to be a crack shot and an expert rider.

burke (bûrk) *tr.v.* **burked, burk•ing, burkes 1.** To suppress or extinguish quietly; stifle. **2.** To avoid; disregard. **3.** To execute (someone) by suffocation so as to leave the body intact and suitable for dissection. [After William *Burke* (1792–1829), Irish-born grave robber and murderer.]

Burke, Edmund 1729–97. Irish-born British politician and writer who was instrumental in developing the notion of a loyal opposition within the parliamentary system.

Burkina Faso

Bur•ki•na Fa•so (bər-kē′nə fä′sō) Formerly **Upper Vol•ta** (vŏl′tə, vōl′-, vôl′-) A landlocked country of W Africa; gained independence from France in 1960. Cap. Ouagadougou. Pop. 9,889,000.

Bur•kitt's lymphoma (bûr′kĭts) *n.* A malignant lymphoma usu. occurring among children in central Africa, associated with the Epstein-Barr virus. [After Denis Parsons *Burkitt* (1911–93), Ugandan physician.]

burl (bûrl) *n.* **1.** A knot, lump, or slub in yarn or cloth. **2a.** A large rounded outgrowth on a tree. **b.** The wood cut from a burl. ❖ *tr.v.* **burled, burl•ing, burls** To dress or finish (cloth) by removing burls. [ME *burle* < OFr. *bourle,* tuft of wool, dim. of *bourre,* coarse wool < LLat. *burra,* shaggy garment.] **—burl′er** *n.*

burl

bur•lap (bûr′lăp′) *n.* A strong, coarsely woven cloth made of fibers of jute, flax, or hemp and used to make bags, to reinforce linoleum, and in interior decoration. [?]

Bur•leigh (bûr′lē), 1st Baron. See William **Cecil.**

bur•lesque (bər-lĕsk′) *n.* **1.** A literary or dramatic work that ridicules a subject by presenting either a solemn subject in an undignified style or an inconsequential subject in a dignified style. **2.** A ludicrous or mocking imitation; a travesty. **3.** A variety show characterized by broad ribald comedy, dancing, and striptease. ❖ *v.* **-lesqued, -lesqu•ing, -lesques** *—tr.* To imitate mockingly or humorously: *"always bringing junk . . . home, as if he were burlesquing his role as provider"* (John Updike). *—intr.* To use the methods or techniques of burlesque. [< Fr., comical < Ital. *burlesco* < *burla,* joke, prob. < Sp. < VLat. **burrula,* dim. of LLat. *burrae,* nonsense < *burra,* wool.] **—bur•lesque′** *adj.* **—bur•lesque′ly** *adv.* **—bur•lesqu′er** *n.*

bur•ley (bûr′lē) *n., pl.* **-leys** A light-colored tobacco grown chiefly in Kentucky and used esp. in making cigarettes. [Prob. < the name *Burley.*]

Burundi

Bur•ling•ton (bûr′lĭng-tən) **1.** A city of S Ontario, Canada, a suburb of Hamilton on Lake Ontario. Pop. 136,976. **2.** A city of NW VT on Lake Champlain WNW of Montpelier. Pop. 38,889.

bur•ly (bûr′lē) *adj.* **-li•er, -li•est** Heavy, strong, and muscular; husky. See Syns at **muscular.** [ME *burlich* < OE **borlic,* excellent. See **bher-[1]** in App.] **—bur′li•ly** *adv.* **—bur′li•ness** *n.*

Bur•ma (bûr′mə) See **Myanmar.**

Bur•man (bûr′mən) *n.* **1.** Of or relating to the principal, Burmese-speaking ethnic group of Myanmar. **2.** Of or relating to Myanmar; Burmese. ❖ *adj.* **1.** A member of the principal, Burmese-speaking ethnic group of Myanmar, esp. as distinguished from the Shan, Karen, and other minority peoples. **2.** A native or inhabitant of Myanmar; a Burmese.

bur marigold *n.* Any of several weeds of the genus *Bidens* of the composite family, having yellow flowers and barbed achenes that stick to clothing or fur.

Burma Road A former highway extending c. 1,126 km (700 mi) NE through mountainous country from NE Myanmar (Burma) to Kunming, China. It was a vital transportation route for wartime supplies to the Chinese government from 1938 to 1946.

Barbara Bush

Bur•mese (bər-mēz′, -mēs′) *adj.* Of or relating to Myanmar (formerly Burma) or its people, language, or culture. ❖ *n., pl.* **Burmese 1.** A native or inhabitant of Myanmar. **2.** The Sino-Tibetan language of Myanmar.

burn[1] (bûrn) *v.* **burned** or **burnt** (bûrnt), **burn•ing, burns** *—tr.* **1a.** To cause to undergo combustion. **b.** To destroy with fire. **c.** To consume (fuel or energy, for example). **2.** *Physics* To cause to undergo nuclear fission or fusion. **3.** To damage or injure by fire, heat, radiation, electricity, or a caustic agent. **4a.** To execute or kill with fire. **b.** To execute by electrocution. **5a.** To make or produce by fire or heat: *burn a hole in the rug.* **b.** To dispel; dissipate: *The sun burned off the fog.* **6a.** To use as a fuel. **b.** To metabolize (glucose, for example) in the body. **7.** To impart a sensation of intense heat to: *The chili burned my mouth.* **8a.** To irritate or inflame, as by chafing or sunburn. **b.** To let (oneself or a part of one's body) become sunburned. **9.** To brand (an animal). **10.** To engrave or make indelible by as or as if by burning: *a scene that was burned in his memory.* **11.** To harden or impart a finish to by subjecting to intense heat; fire. **12.** To make angry. **13a.** To defeat in a contest, esp. by a narrow margin. **b.** To inflict harm or hardship on; hurt. **c.** To swindle or deceive; cheat. **14.** To record data on (a compact disk). *—intr.* **1a.** To undergo combustion. **b.** To admit of burning: *Wood burns easily.* **2.** To consume fuel. **3.** *Physics* To undergo nuclear fission or fusion. **4a.** To emit heat or light by or as if by fire. **b.** To become dissipated or to be dispelled by or as if by heat. **5.** To give off light; shine. **6.** To be destroyed, injured, damaged, or changed by or as if by fire. **7a.** To be very hot; bake. **b.** To feel or look hot: *a child burning with fever.* **c.** To impart a sensation of heat. **8a.** To become irritated or painful, as by chafing or inflammation. **b.** To become sunburned or windburned. **9.** To be consumed with strong emotion, esp.: **a.** To be or become angry. **b.** To be very eager. **10.** To penetrate by or as if by intense heat or flames. **11.** To be vividly or painfully present: *shame burning in my heart.* **12a.** To suffer punishment or death by or as if by fire. **b.** To be electrocuted. ❖ *n.* **1.** An injury produced by fire, heat, radiation, electricity, or a caustic agent. **2.** A burned place or area. **3.** An act, process, or result of burning. **4.** A sensation of intense heat or stinging pain. **5.** A sunburn or windburn. **6.** *Aerospace* A firing of a rocket. **7.** A swindle. ***—phrasal verbs:* burn out 1.** To stop burning from lack of fuel. **2.** To wear out or make or become inoperative as a result of heat or friction. **3.** To cause (a property owner or a resident) to have to evacuate the premises because of fire. **4.** To make or become exhausted, esp. as a result of long-term stress. **burn up 1.** To make angry. **2.** To travel over or through at high speed: *burning up the track.* ***—idioms:* burn (one's) bridges** To eliminate the possibility of return or retreat. **burn the (or one's) candle at both ends** To exhaust oneself or one's resources by leading a hectic or extravagant life. **burn the midnight oil** To work or study very late at night. **to burn** In great amounts: *money to burn.* [ME *burnen* < OE *beornan,* to be on fire, and < *bærnan,* to set on fire; see **gʷher-** in App.]

burn[2] (bûrn) *n. Scots* A small stream; a brook. [ME < OE *burna.*]

Bur•na•by (bûr′nə-bē) A city of SW British Columbia, Canada, a suburb of Vancouver. Pop. 179,209.

burned-out (bûrnd′out′) or **burnt-out** (bûrnt′-) *adj.* Worn out or exhausted, esp. as a result of long-term stress.

Burne-Jones (bûrn′jōnz′), Sir **Edward Coley** 1833–98. British painter known for the mystical dreamlike settings of his paintings and stained-glass designs.

burn•er (bûr′nər) *n.* **1.** One that burns, esp.: **a.** A device, as in a stove, that is lighted to produce a flame. **b.** A device on a stovetop that produces heat. **2a.** A unit, such as a furnace, in which something is burned. **b.** An incinerator. ***—idioms:* on the back burner** As a low priority: *a trivial project left on the back burner.* **on the front burner** As a high priority.

bur•net (bər-nĕt′, bûr′nĭt) *n.* A perennial plant of the genus *Sanguisorba,* having pinnately compound leaves and apetalous flowers. [ME < Med.Lat. *burneta* < OFr. *brunete,* dark brown, dim. of *brun,* brown, of Gmc. orig. See **bher-[2]** in App.]

Bur•nett (bûr-nĕt′, bûr′nĭt), **Frances Eliza Hodgson** 1849–1924. British-born Amer. writer famous for her popular children's books, including *Little Lord Fauntleroy* (1886).

Bur•ney (bûr′nē), **Frances** Known as "Fanny." 1752–1840. British writer best known for her witty letters and diaries.

burn•ing (bûr′nĭng) *adj.* **1.** Marked by flames or intense heat: *a burning sun.* **2.** Characterized by intense emotion; passionate. **3.** Of immediate import; urgent. **—burn′ing•ly** *adv.*

burning bush also **burn•ing-bush** (bûr′nĭng-bo͝osh′) *n.* **1.** Any of several shrubs or shrubby plants having foliage that turns bright red in autumn. **2.** See **gas plant.**

bur•nish (bûr′nĭsh) *tr.v.* **-nished, -nish•ing, -nish•es 1.** To make smooth or glossy by or as if by rubbing; polish. **2.** To rub with a tool that serves esp. to smooth or polish. ❖ *n.* A smooth glossy finish or appearance; luster. [ME *burnishen* < OFr. *burnir, burniss-,* var. of *brunir* < *brun,* shining, of Gmc. orig. See **bher-[2]** in App.] **—bur′nish•er** *n.*

bur•noose also **bur•nous** (bər-no͞os′) *n.* A hooded cloak worn esp. by Arabs and Berbers. [Fr. *burnous* < Ar. *burnus* < Gk. *birros,* hooded cloak < LLat. *birrus.*]

burn•out (bûrn′out′) *n.* **1.** A failure in a device due to burning, excessive heat, or friction. **2.** *Aerospace* **a.** The termination of rocket or jet-engine operation because of fuel exhaustion or shutoff. **b.** The point at which this termination occurs. **3a.** Physical or emotional exhaustion, esp. as a result of long-term stress or dissipation. **b.** One who is burned out.

Burns (bûrnz), **George** 1896–1996. Amer. comedian and actor known for his comedy act (1922–64) with Gracie Allen and his later work in films.

Burns, Robert 1759–96. Scottish poet renowned for his use of dialect and humor. **—Burns′i•an** *adj.*

Burn•side (bûrn′sīd′), **Ambrose Everett** 1824–81. Amer. Union Army general; defeated at Fredericksburg (1862) and Petersburg (1864).

burn•sides (bûrn′sīdz′) *pl.n.* Heavy side-whiskers worn with the

chin clean-shaven. [After Ambrose Everett BURNSIDE.]

burnt (bûrnt) *v.* A past tense and a past participle of **burn[1]**.

burnt offering *n.* A slaughtered animal or other offering burned on an altar as a religious sacrifice.

burnt-out (bûrnt′out′) *adj.* Variant of **burned-out.**

burnt sienna *n.* **1.** A reddish-brown pigment prepared by calcining raw sienna. **2.** A dark reddish orange.

bur oak *n.* An oak tree *(Quercus macrocarpa)* of eastern North America, having pinnately lobed leaves, acorns enclosed within a deep fringed cup, and hard durable wood.

burp (bûrp) *n.* A belch. ❖ *v.* **burped, burp•ing, burps** *—intr.* To belch. *—tr.* To cause (a baby) to expel gas from the stomach, as by patting the back after feeding. [Imit.]

burp gun *n.* A lightweight portable submachine gun.

bur•qa (bo͝or′kə) *n.* A loose, usu. black or light blue robe worn by Muslim women, esp. in Afghanistan, that covers the body from head to toe. [Hindi *burqā* < Ar. *burqa*ʿ, veil, var. of *burqu*ʿ < *barqa*ʿ*a*, to veil.]

burr[1] (bûr) *n.* **1.** A rough edge or area remaining on material, such as metal, after it has been cast, cut, or drilled. **2.** Variant of **bur[1]**. ❖ *tr.v.* **burred, burr•ing, burrs 1.** To form a burr on. **2.** To remove burrs from. [Variant of BUR[1].]

burr[2] also **bur** (bûr) *n.* **1.** A trilling of the letter *r* characteristic of Scottish speech. **2.** A buzzing or whirring sound. ❖ *v.* **burred, burr•ing, burrs** also **burs** *—tr.* To pronounce with a burr. *—intr.* **1.** To speak with a burr. **2.** To make a buzzing or whirring sound. [Imit.]

burr[3] also **bur** (bûr) *n.* A washer that fits around the smaller end of a rivet. [ME *burre,* ring, disk, alteration of *burwhe,* circle, disk.]

Burr, Aaron 1756–1836. Vice President of the US (1801–05) who mortally wounded Alexander Hamilton in a duel (1804).

bur reed or **bur-reed** (bûr′rēd′) *n.* Any of various aquatic or wetland plants of the genus *Sparganium,* having elongated leaves and ball-like clusters of tiny beaked fruits.

bur•ri•to (bo͞o-rē′tō, bə-) *n., pl.* **-tos** A dish consisting of a flour tortilla wrapped around a filling, as of beef, beans, or cheese. [Am.Sp. < Sp., dim. of *burro,* burro. See BURRO.]

bur•ro (bûr′ō, bo͝or′ō, bŭr′ō) *n., pl.* **-ros** A small donkey, esp. one used as a pack animal. [Sp., back-formation < *borrico,* donkey < LLat. *burrīcus,* small horse.]

Bur•roughs (bûr′ōz, bŭr′-), **Edgar Rice** 1875–1950. Amer. writer best known for his novel *Tarzan of the Apes* (1914).

Burroughs[1], William Seward 1855–98. Amer. inventor who patented the first practical adding machine.

Burroughs[2], William Seward 1914–97. Amer. writer noted for *Naked Lunch* (1959).

bur•row (bûr′ō, bŭr′ō) *n.* **1.** A hole or tunnel dug in the ground by a small animal for habitation or refuge. **2.** A narrow or snug place. ❖ *v.* **-rowed, -row•ing, -rows** *—intr.* **1a.** To dig a burrow. **b.** To live or hide in a burrow. **2.** To move or progress by or as if by digging or tunneling. *—tr.* **1.** To make by or as if by tunneling. **2.** To dig a hole or tunnel in or through. **3.** *Archaic* To hide in or as if in a burrow. [ME *borow.*] **—bur′row•er** *n.*

burr•stone (bûr′stōn′) *n.* Variant of **buhrstone.**

bur•ry (bûr′ē) *adj.* **-ri•er, -ri•est** Having burs; prickly.

bur•sa (bûr′sə) *n., pl.* **-sae** (-sē) or **-sas** A sac or saclike body cavity, esp. one containing a viscous lubricating fluid and located between a tendon and a bone or at points of friction between moving structures. [LLat., purse, pouch < Gk., skin, wineskin.] **—bur′sal** *adj.*

Bur•sa (bûr′sə, bo͝or-sä′) A city of NW Turkey W of Ankara; est. in the 3rd cent. B.C. Pop. 996,600.

bursa of Fa•bri•ci•us (fə-brĭsh′ē-əs, -brĭsh′əs) *n.* A thymuslike lymphoid gland in birds that is an outgrowth of the cloaca and the site of B cell maturation. [After Hieronymus *Fabricius* (1537–1619), Italian anatomist.]

bur•sar (bûr′sər, -sär′) *n.* An official in charge of funds, as at a college or university; a treasurer. [ME *burser* < Med.Lat. *bursārius* < LLat. *bursa,* purse. See BURSA.]

bur•sa•ry (bûr′sə-rē) *n., pl.* **-ries 1.** A treasury, esp. of a public institution or religious order. **2.** *Chiefly British* A university scholarship based on need. [Med.Lat. *bursāria* < *bursa,* purse. See BURSA.] **—bur•sar′i•al** (bər-sâr′ē-əl) *adj.*

burse (bûrs) *n.* **1.** A purse. **2.** *Ecclesiastical* A flat cloth case for carrying the corporal. [LLat. *bursa.* See BURSA.]

bur•si•tis (bər-sī′tĭs) *n.* Inflammation of a bursa.

burst (bûrst) *v.* **burst, burst•ing, bursts** *—intr.* **1a.** To come open or fly apart suddenly or violently, esp. from internal pressure. **b.** To explode. **2.** To be or seem to be full to the point of breaking open. **3.** To emerge, come forth, or arrive suddenly. **4.** To come apart or seem to come apart because of overwhelming emotion. **5.** To give sudden expression: *burst out laughing. —tr.* **1.** To cause to burst. See Syns at **break. 2.** To exert strong pressure in order to force (something) open. **3.** To separate (a continuous form or printout) into individual sheets. ❖ *n.* **1.** A sudden outbreak or outburst; an explosion. **2.** The result of bursting, esp. the explosion of a projectile or bomb. **3a.** The number of bullets fired from an automatic weapon by one pull of the trigger. **b.** A volley of bullets from an automatic weapon. **4.** An abrupt, intense increase; a rush. **5.** A period of intense activity: *a novel written in short bursts.* [ME *bursten* < OE *berstan.*]

bur•then (bûr′thən) *n.* A burden.

bur•ton (bûr′tn) *n. Nautical* A light tackle having double or single blocks, used to hoist or tighten rigging. [?]

Burton, Sir Richard Francis 1821–90. British explorer and Orientalist whose best-known work is a translation of *The Arabian Nights* (1855–88).

Burton, Robert 1577–1640. English cleric and writer known chiefly for his *Anatomy of Melancholy* (1621).

Bu•ru (bo͝or′o͞o) An island of E Indonesia in the Moluccas.

Bu•run•di (bo͞o-ro͞on′dē, -ro͝on′-) A country of E-central Africa with a coastline on Lake Tanganyika; gained independence in 1962. Cap. Bujumbura. Pop. 6,134,000. **—Bu•run′di•an** *adj. & n.*

bur•y (bĕr′ē) *tr.v.* **-ied, -y•ing, -ies 1.** To place in the ground: *bury a bone.* **2a.** To place (a corpse) in a grave, a tomb, or the sea; inter. **b.** To dispose of (a corpse) ritualistically by means other than interment or cremation. **3.** To conceal by or as if by covering over with earth; hide. **4.** To occupy (oneself) with deep concentration; absorb: *buried myself in my studies.* **5.** To put an end to; abandon. ***—idiom:* bury the hatchet** To stop fighting. [ME *burien* < OE *byrgan.*] **—bur′i•er** *n.*

Bury A borough of NW England NNW of Manchester; founded on the site of a Saxon settlement. Pop. 181,390.

bur•y•ing beetle (bĕr′ē-ĭng) *n.* Any of various beetles of the genus *Nicrophorus* that bury small animals on which they feed and lay their eggs.

Bury Saint Ed•munds (ĕd′məndz) A municipal borough of E-central England E of Cambridge; chartered 1606. Pop. 28,914.

bus (bŭs) *n., pl.* **bus•es** or **bus•ses 1.** A long motor vehicle for carrying passengers, usu. along a fixed route. **2.** *Informal* A large or ungainly automobile. **3.** A four-wheeled cart for carrying dishes in a restaurant. **4.** *Electricity* A bus bar. **5.** *Computer Science* A parallel circuit that connects the major components of a computer, allowing the transfer of electric impulses from one connected component to any other. ❖ *v.* **bused, bus•ing, bus•es** or **bussed, bus•sing, bus•ses** *—tr.* **1.** To transport in a bus. **2.** To transport (schoolchildren) by bus to schools outside their neighborhoods, esp. for racial integration. **3a.** To carry or clear (dishes) in a restaurant. **b.** To clear dishes from (a table). *—intr.* **1.** To travel in a bus. **2.** To work busing tables. [Short for OMNIBUS.]

bus. *abbr.* business

bus bar *n. Electricity* A conducting bar that carries heavy currents to supply several electric circuits.

bus•boy also **bus boy** (bŭs′boi′) *n.* A male employee who assists in a restaurant, as by busing tables. [(OMNI)BUS + BOY.]

bus•by (bŭz′bē) *n., pl.* **-bies** A full-dress fur hat of varying shape, worn by hussars in the 19th century and by certain guard regiments of the British army. [Poss. < the name *Busby.*]

bush[1] (bo͝osh) *n.* **1.** A low shrub with many branches. **2.** A thick growth of shrubs; a thicket. **3a.** Land covered with dense vegetation or undergrowth. **b.** Land remote from settlement. **4.** A shaggy mass, as of hair. **5.** A fox's tail. **6a.** *Archaic* A clump of ivy hung outside a tavern to indicate the availability of wine inside. **b.** *Obsolete* A tavern. ❖ *v.* **bushed, bush•ing, bushes** *—intr.* **1.** To grow or branch out like a bush. **2.** To extend in a bushy growth. *—tr.* To decorate, protect, or support with bushes. ❖ *adj. Slang* Bush-league; second-rate. [ME, partly < OE *busc,* partly < OFr. *bois,* wood (of Gmc. orig.), and partly of Scand. orig.; akin to Dan. *busk.* N., sense 3, poss. < Du. *bosch.*]

bush[2] (bo͝osh) *tr.v.* **bushed, bush•ing, bush•es** To furnish or line with a bushing. [< *bush,* bushing, poss. alteration of Du. *bus,* box.]

Bush, Barbara b. 1925. First Lady of the US (1989–93); active in promoting literacy.

Bush, George Herbert Walker b. 1924. The 41st President of the US (1989–93); previously Vice President (1981–89).

Bush, George Walker b. 1946. The 43rd President of the US (since 2001); previously governor of TX (1994–2000).

Bush, Laura b. 1946. First Lady of the US (since 2001) as the wife of President George W. Bush.

bush baby *n.* Any of several small nocturnal African primates of the genera *Galago* and *Euoticus,* having dense woolly fur, large round eyes, prominent ears, and a long tail.

bush bean *n.* **1.** A shrubby variety of the snap bean. **2.** Any upright bean plant not requiring an artificial support.

bush•buck (bo͝osh′bŭk′) *n.* An African antelope *(Tragelaphus scriptus)* having a brownish coat with white spots and twisted horns. [Transl. of Afr. *bosbok* : *bos,* bush + *bok,* buck.]

bush clover *n.* Any of various plants of the genus *Lespedeza* in the pea family, having compound leaves with three leaflets and various colored flowers.

bushed (bo͝osht) *adj. Informal* Extremely tired; exhausted. [Poss. < Australian slang, lost in the bush.]

bush•el[1] (bo͝osh′əl) *n.* **1a.** A unit of volume or capacity in the US Customary System, used in dry measure and equal to 4 pecks, 2,150.42 cubic inches, or 35.24 liters. **b.** A unit of volume or capacity in the British Imperial System, used in dry and liquid measure and equal to 2,219.36 cubic inches or 36.37 liters. See table at **measurement. 2.** A container with the capacity of a bushel. **3.** *Informal* A large amount; a great deal. [ME < AN *bus-*

George Bush

George W. Bush

Laura Bush

ă	pat	oi	boy
ā	pay	ou	out
âr	care	o͝o	took
ä	father	o͞o	boot
ĕ	pet	ŭ	cut
ē	be	ûr	urge
ĭ	pit	th	thin
ī	pie	*th*	this
îr	pier	hw	which
ŏ	pot	zh	vision
ō	toe	ə	about, item
ô	paw		

Stress marks:
′ (primary);
′ (secondary), as in
lexicon (lĕk′sĭ-kŏn′)

sel, var. of OFr. *boissiel < boisse,* one sixth of a bushel, of Celt. orig.]

bush•el² (bŏŏsh′əl) *tr.v.* **-eled, -el•ing, -els** or **-elled, -el•ling, -els** To alter or mend (clothing). [Prob. < Ger. *bosseln,* to do odd jobs, alteration (perh. influenced by *bosseln,* to emboss) of *basteln,* to putter.] —**bush′el•er, bush′el•ler** *n.* —**bush′el•man** (-mən) *n.*

bush honeysuckle *n.* **1.** Any of three eastern North American shrubs of the genus *Diervilla,* having opposite deciduous leaves and clusters of yellow flowers. **2.** Any of several shrubby honeysuckle plants of the genus *Lonicera.*

Bu•shi•do also **bu•shi•do** (bōō′shĭ-dō′, bōō′shĭ-) *n.* The traditional code of the Japanese samurai, stressing honor, self-discipline, bravery, and simple living. [J. *bushidō : bushi,* warrior (< M Chin. *wushi,* knight, warrior : *wə, wu,* military + *shi,* brave warrior) + *dō,* way; see AIKIDO.]

bush•ing (bŏŏsh′ĭng) *n.* **1.** A fixed or removable cylindrical metal lining used to constrain, guide, or reduce friction. **2.** *Electricity* An insulating lining for an aperture through which a conductor passes. **3.** An adapter threaded to permit joining of pipes with different diameters. [< BUSH².]

bush jacket *n.* A long, cotton, shirtlike jacket usu. with four flat pockets and a belt.

bush league *n. Sports* A minor league. —**bush leaguer** *n.*

bush-league (bŏŏsh′lēg′) *adj.* **1.** *Baseball* Of or belonging to a minor league. **2.** *Slang* Inferior or unprofessional.

Bush•man (bŏŏsh′mən) *n.* **1.** See **San. 2. bushman** *Australian* One who lives or travels in the wilderness, esp. in the outback. [Transl. of Afr. *boschjeman.*]

bush•mas•ter (bŏŏsh′măs′tər) *n.* A large venomous snake (*Lachesis mutus*) of tropical America having brown and grayish markings.

Bush•nell (bŏŏsh′nəl), **David** 1742–1824. Amer. inventor who designed (1775) a self-propelled submarine.

bush pilot *n.* A person who flies a small airplane to and from areas inaccessible by other means of transportation.

bush•rang•er (bŏŏsh′rān′jər) *n.* **1.** One who lives in the wilderness. **2.** *Australian* An outlaw living in the bush.

bush•tit (bŏŏsh′tĭt′) *n.* Either of two small long-tailed birds (*Psaltriparus minimus* or *P. melanotis*) of western North America having predominantly gray plumage.

bush•whack (bŏŏsh′hwăk′, -wăk′) *v.* **-whacked, -whack•ing, -whacks** —*intr.* **1.** To make one's way through thick woods by cutting away bushes and branches. **2.** To travel through or live in the woods. **3.** To fight as a guerrilla in the woods. —*tr.* To ambush. —**bush′whack′er** *n.*

bush•y (bŏŏsh′ē) *adj.* **-i•er, -i•est 1.** Overgrown with bushes. **2.** Thick and shaggy. —**bush′i•ly** *adv.* —**bush′i•ness** *n.*

busi•ness (bĭz′nĭs) *n.* **1a.** The occupation, work, or trade in which a person is engaged. **b.** A specific occupation or pursuit. **2.** Commercial, industrial, or professional dealings. **3.** A commercial enterprise or establishment. **4.** Volume or amount of commercial trade. **5.** Commercial dealings; patronage. **6a.** One's rightful or proper concern or interest. **b.** Something involving one personally. **7.** Serious work or endeavor: *down to business.* **8.** An affair or matter. **9.** An incidental action performed on the stage to fill a pause between lines or to provide detail. **10.** *Informal* Verbal abuse; scolding. **11.** *Obsolete* The condition of being busy. [ME *businesse < bisi,* busy. See BUSY.]

SYNONYMS *business, industry, commerce, trade, traffic* These nouns apply to forms of activity that have the objective of supplying commodities. *Business* pertains broadly to commercial, financial, and industrial activity: *decided to go into business. Industry* entails the production and manufacture of goods or commodities, especially on a large scale: *the computer industry. Commerce* and *trade* refer to the exchange and distribution of goods or commodities: *interstate commerce; domestic trade. Traffic* pertains in particular to businesses engaged in the transportation of goods or passengers: *shipping traffic.* The word may also suggest illegal trade: *Traffic in stolen goods.*

business administration *n.* A college or university course of studies that offers instruction in business.

business card *n.* A small card printed or engraved with a person's name and business affiliation.

business cycle *n.* A sequence of economic activity typically marked by recession, recovery, growth, and decline.

business end *n.* The part of a weapon or tool that inflicts damage or performs work.

busi•ness•like (bĭz′nĭs-līk′) *adj.* **1.** Showing or having characteristics useful in business; methodical and systematic. **2.** Purposeful; earnest. **3.** Practical; unemotional.

busi•ness•man (bĭz′nĭs-măn′) *n.* A man engaged in business. See Usage Note at **man.**

busi•ness•per•son (bĭz′nĭs-pûr′sən) *n.* One engaged in business. See Usage Note at **man.**

busi•ness•wom•an (bĭz′nĭs-wŏŏm′ən) *n.* A woman engaged in business. See Usage Note at **man.**

busk (bŭsk) *intr.v.* **busked, busk•ing, busks** To play music or perform entertainment in public, usu. while soliciting money. [Earlier, to be an itinerant performer, prob. < *busk,* to go about

seeking, cruise as a pirate, perh. < obsolete Fr. *busquer,* to prowl < Ital. *buscare,* to prowl, or Sp. *buscar,* to seek < OSpan. *boscar.*] —**busk′er** *n.*

bus•kin (bŭs′kĭn) *n.* **1.** A usu. laced half boot. **2a.** A thick-soled, laced half boot worn by actors of Greek and Roman tragedies. **b.** Tragedy, esp. that which resembles a Greek tragedy. [Perh. alteration (influenced by BUCKSKIN) of obsolete Fr. *broisequin,* small leather boot.]

bus•load (bŭs′lōd′) *n.* The number of passengers or the quantity of cargo that a bus can carry.

bus•man (bŭs′mən) *n.* One who drives a bus.

bus•man's holiday (bŭs′mənz) *n. Informal* A vacation during which one engages in activity similar to one's usual work.

Bu•so•ni (bōō-zō′nē, byōō-), **Ferruccio Benvenuto** 1866–1924. Italian pianist, conductor, and composer.

buss (bŭs) *tr. & intr.v.* **bussed, buss•ing, buss•es** To kiss. ❖ *n.* A kiss. [Poss. blend of obsolete *bass* (akin to Fr. *baiser*) and obsolete *cuss* (akin to ME *kissen,* to kiss; see KISS), or < Sc. Gael. *bus,* lips, mouth. See PUSS².]

bus•ses (bŭs′ĭz) *n.* A plural of **bus.**

bust¹ (bŭst) *n.* **1.** A sculpture representing a person's head, shoulders, and upper chest. **2a.** A woman's bosom. **b.** The human chest. [Fr. *buste < Ital. busto,* poss. < Lat. *bustum,* sepulchral monument.]

bust² (bŭst) *v.* **bust•ed, bust•ing, busts** —*tr.* **1.** *Slang* **a.** To smash or break, esp. forcefully. **b.** To render inoperable or unusable. **2.** To cause to come to an end; break up. **3.** To break or tame (a horse). **4.** To cause to become bankrupt or short of money. **5.** *Slang* To reduce in rank. **6.** To hit; punch. **7.** *Slang* **a.** To place under arrest. **b.** To make a police raid on. —*intr.* **1. a.** To undergo breakage. **b.** To burst; break. **2.** To become bankrupt or short of money. **3.** *Games* To lose at blackjack by exceeding a score of 21. ❖ *n.* **1.** A failure. **2.** A state of bankruptcy. **3.** A time of widespread financial depression. **4.** A punch; a blow. **5.** A spree. **6.** *Slang* **a.** An arrest. **b.** A raid. ❖ *adj.* Variant of **busted** 1. [Variant of BURST.]

bus•tard (bŭs′tərd) *n.* Any of various large long-legged Old World game birds of the family Otididae that frequent dry grassy plains. [ME < blend of OFr. *bistarde* and *oustarde,* both < Lat. *avis tarda : avis,* bird; see awi- in App. + *tarda,* fem. of *tardus,* slow.]

bust•ed (bŭs′tĭd) *adj.* **1.** also **bust** (bŭst) **a.** Smashed or broken. **b.** Out of order; inoperable. **c.** Bankrupt or out of funds. **2.** Tamed or broken. **3.** *Slang* **a.** Placed under arrest. **b.** Discovered to have done something unpermitted or immoral.

bust•er (bŭs′tər) *n.* **1.** One that breaks up something: *a crime buster.* **2.** A broncobuster. **3.** A particularly robust child. **4.** *Informal* Fellow. Used in addressing a man or boy, esp. out of annoyance.

bus•ti•cate (bŭs′tĭ-kāt′) *tr.v.* **-cat•ed, -cat•ing, -cates** *Northern US* To break into pieces. See Regional Note at **absquatulate.** [BUST² + -*icate* (as in MEDICATE).]

bus•tier (bōōs-tyā′, bŭs-) *n.* A formfitting sleeveless and usu. strapless woman's top, worn as lingerie and often as evening attire. [Fr. < *buste,* bust. See BUST¹.]

bus•tle¹ (bŭs′əl) *intr. & tr.v.* **-tled, -tling, -tles** To move or cause to move energetically and busily. ❖ *n.* Excited and often noisy activity; a stir. [Poss. var. of obsolete *buskle,* freq. of *busk,* to prepare oneself < ON *būask,* reflexive of *būa,* to prepare. See bheuə- in App.]

bus•tle² (bŭs′əl) *n.* A frame or pad formerly worn to expand the back of a woman's skirt. [?]

bus topology *n. Computer Science* A topology for a LAN in which all nodes are connected to a central cable.

bust•y (bŭs′tē) *adj.* **-i•er, -i•est** Having large breasts.

bu•sul•fan (byōō-sŭl′fən) *n.* An alkylating agent, $C_6H_{14}O_6S_2$, used as an antineoplastic drug in the treatment of chronic myelocytic leukemia. [BU(TANE) + alteration of SULFON(ATE).]

bus•y (bĭz′ē) *adj.* **-i•er, -i•est 1.** Engaged in activity; occupied. **2.** Sustaining much activity: *a busy street.* **3.** Meddlesome; prying. **4.** Being in use, as a telephone line. **5.** Cluttered with detail to the point of being distracting. ❖ *tr.v.* **-ied, -y•ing, -ies** To make busy; occupy. [ME *bisi, busi < OE bysig.*] —**bus′i•ly** *adv.* —**bus′y•ness** *n.*

bus•y•bod•y (bĭz′ē-bŏd′ē) *n., pl.* **-ies** A person who meddles or pries.

busy signal *n.* A series of sharp buzzing tones heard over a telephone when the line dialed is already in use.

bus•y•work (bĭz′ē-wûrk′) *n.* Activity meant to take up time but not necessarily yield productive results.

but (bŭt; bət *when unstressed*) *conj.* **1.** On the contrary: *caused not gain but loss.* **2.** Contrary to expectation; yet: *tired but happy.* **3.** *Usage Problem* Used to indicate an exception: *No one but she.* **4.** With the exception that; except that. Often used with *that: would have acted but that he fainted.* **5.** *Informal* Without the result that: *It never rains but it pours.* **6.** *Informal* That. Often used after a negative: *no doubt but right will prevail.* **7.** That . . . not. Used after a negative or question: *There never is a law but someone will oppose it.* **8.** If not; unless. **9.** *Informal* Than. ❖ *prep. Usage Problem* Except. ❖ *adv.* **1.** Merely; just; only: *lasted but a moment.* **2.** Used as an intensive: *Move but fast!* —**idiom: but for** Were it not for:

bustard
black korhaan
Eupodotis afra

We would have gone but for the weather. [ME < OE *būtan.* See **ud-** in App.]

USAGE NOTE Some traditional grammarians have argued that *but* is a conjunction in sentences such as *No one but I has read it* and therefore should be followed by the nominative form *I.* If *but* were truly a conjunction here, however, the verb would agree in person and number with the noun or pronoun following *but:* *No one but I have read it.* Furthermore, we would not expect that it could be moved to the end of a clause, as in *No one has read it but I.* These observations suggest that *but* is best considered as a preposition here and followed by accusative forms such as *me* and *them* in all positions: *No one but me has read it. No one has read it but me.* These recommendations are supported by 73 percent of the Usage Panel when the *but* phrase precedes the verb and by 93 percent when the *but* phrase follows the verb. • *But* is redundant when used together with *however,* as in *But the army, however, proceeded.* • *But* is generally not followed by a comma. Correct written style requires *Kim wanted to go, but because it started to rain, we stayed.* • *But* may be used to begin a sentence at all levels of style. See Usage Notes at **and, cannot, doubt, however, I**[1].

but– *pref.* Containing a group of four carbon atoms: *butyl.* [< BUTYRIC.]

bu·ta·di·ene (byōō′tə-dī′ēn′, -dī-ēn′) *n.* A colorless, highly flammable hydrocarbon, C_4H_6, distilled from petroleum and used to make synthetic rubber. [BUTA(NE) + DI-[1] + -ENE.]

bu·tane (byōō′tān′) *n.* Either of two isomers of a gaseous hydrocarbon, C_4H_{10}, synthesized from petroleum and used as a fuel. [BUT(YL) + -ANE.]

bu·ta·no·ic acid (byōō′tə-nō′ĭk) *n.* See **butyric acid.** [BUTAN(E) + -OIC.]

bu·ta·nol (byōō′tə-nôl′, -nŏl′, nōl′) *n.* Either of two butyl alcohols derived from butane and used as solvents and in organic synthesis. [BUTAN(E) + -OL[1].]

bu·ta·none (byōō′tə-nōn′) *n.* A colorless flammable ketone, $CH_3COCH_2CH_3$, used as a solvent. [BUTAN(E) + -ONE.]

butch (bōōch) *adj. Slang* Exhibiting stereotypically or exaggeratedly masculine traits or appearance. Used esp. of lesbians and gay men. —*n.* A haircut in which the hair is cropped close. [Prob. < the male nickname *Butch.*] —**butch** *adj.*

butch·er (bōōch′ər) *n.* **1a.** One who slaughters and dresses animals for food or market. **b.** One who sells meats. **2.** One that kills brutally or indiscriminately. **3.** A vendor, esp. one on a train or in a theater. **4.** One who bungles something. ❖ *tr.v.* **-ered, -er·ing, -ers 1.** To slaughter or prepare (animals) for market. **2.** To kill brutally or indiscriminately. **3.** To botch; bungle. [ME *bucher* < OFr. *bouchier* < *bouc, boc,* he-goat, prob. of Celt. orig.] —**butch′er·er** *n.*

butch·er·bird (bōōch′ər-bûrd′) *n.* Any of various birds, esp. the shrike, that impale their prey on thorns.

butch·er·block (bōōch′ər-blŏk′) *adj.* Made of or resembling a board of thick strips of hardwood like that on which butchers chop meat.

butcher knife *n.* A heavy-duty knife with a broad sharp blade used for cutting meat.

butch·er's broom (bōōch′ərz) *n.* An evergreen shrub (*Ruscus aculeatus*) native to Europe and the Mediterranean region, with leaflike stems, greenish flowers, and usu. red berries.

butch·er·y (bōōch′ə-rē) *n., pl.* **-ies 1.** Wanton or cruel killing; carnage. **2.** Something botched; a bungle. **3.** The trade of a butcher. **4.** *Chiefly British* A slaughterhouse.

Bute (byōōt) An island of SW Scotland in the Firth of Clyde.

Bu·te·nandt (bōōt′n-änt′), **Adolf Friedrich** 1903–95. German chemist who shared a 1939 Nobel Prize.

bu·tene (byōō′tēn′) *n.* Any of several forms of butylene.

bu·te·o (byōō′tē-ō′) *n., pl.* **-os** Any of various broad-winged, soaring hawks of the genus *Buteo.* [Lat. *būteō,* a kind of hawk or falcon.]

but·ler (bŭt′lər) *n.* A household head servant who is usu. in charge of food service and the deportment of the other servants. [ME < OFr. *bouteillier,* bottle bearer < *bouteille, botele,* bottle. See BOTTLE.]

Butler, Benjamin Franklin 1818–93. Amer. army officer and politician; military governor of New Orleans (May–Dec. 1862).

Butler, Nicholas Murray 1862–1947. Amer. educator who shared the 1931 Nobel Peace Prize.

Butler[1], **Samuel** 1612–80. English poet remembered primarily for his three-part work *Hudibras* (1663–78).

Butler[2], **Samuel** 1835–1902. British writer best known for his semiautobiographical novel *The Way of All Flesh* (1903).

but·ler's pantry (bŭt′lərz) *n.* A serving and storage room between a kitchen and dining room.

butt[1] (bŭt) *v.* **butt·ed, butt·ing, butts** —*tr.* To hit or push against with the head or horns; ram. —*intr.* **1.** To hit or push something with the head or horns. **2.** To project forward or out. ❖ *n.* A push or blow with the head or horns. —*phrasal verbs:* **butt in** To interfere or meddle in other people's affairs. **butt out 1.** To leave someone alone. **2.** To leave; depart. [ME *butten* < OFr. *bouter,* to strike, of Gmc. orig.] —**butt′er** *n.*

butt[2] (bŭt) *tr. & intr.v.* **butt·ed, butt·ing, butts** To join or be

joined end to end; abut. ❖ *n.* **1.** A butt joint. **2.** A butt hinge. [ME *butten* < AN *butter* (var. of OFr. *bouter;* see BUTT[1]) and < *but,* end; see BUTT[4].]

butt[3] (bŭt) *n.* **1.** One that serves as an object of ridicule or contempt. **2a.** A target, as in archery or riflery. **b. butts** A target range. **c.** An obstacle behind a target for stopping the shot. **3.** An embankment or hollow used as a blind by hunters of wildfowl. **4a.** *Archaic* A goal. **b.** *Obsolete* A bound; a limit. [ME *butte,* target < OFr. < *but,* goal, end, target. See BUTT[4].]

butt[4] (bŭt) *n.* **1.** The larger or thicker end of an object. **2a.** An unburned end, as of a cigarette. **b.** *Informal* A cigarette. **3.** A short or broken remnant; a stub. **4.** *Informal* The buttocks; the rear end. [ME *butte* < OFr. *but,* end, of Gmc. orig.]

butt[5] (bŭt) *n.* **1.** A large cask. **2.** A unit of volume equal to two hogsheads, usu. the equivalent of 126 US gallons (about 477 liters). [ME < OFr. *boute* < LLat. **buttia,* var. of *buttis.*]

butte (byōōt) *n. Chiefly Western US* A hill that rises abruptly from the surrounding area and has sloping sides and a flat top. [Fr. < OFr., mound behind targets. See BUTT[3].]

Butte A city of SW MT SSW of Helena; settled in the 1860s. Pop. 34,606.

but·ter (bŭt′ər) *n.* **1.** A soft yellowish or whitish emulsion of butterfat, water, air, and sometimes salt, churned from milk or cream and processed for culinary use. **2.** Any of various substances similar to butter, esp.: **a.** A spread made from fruit, nuts, or other foods: *apple butter.* **b.** A vegetable fat having a nearly solid consistency at ordinary temperatures. **3.** Flattery. ❖ *tr.v.* **-tered, -ter·ing, -ters** To put butter on or in. —*phrasal verb:* **butter up** To praise or flatter excessively. [ME *butere* < Lat. *būtyrum* < Gk. *boutūron* : *bous,* cow; see g*w*ou- in App. + *tūros,* cheese.]

but·ter-and-eggs (bŭt′ər-ən-ĕgz′) *pl.n. (used with a sing. or pl. verb)* A weedy perennial herb (*Linaria vulgaris*) native to Eurasia and having narrow leaves and racemes of showy, long-spurred yellow and orange flowers.

but·ter·ball (bŭt′ər-bôl′) *n.* **1.** *Informal* A chubby or fat person. **2.** See **bufflehead.**

butter bean *n.* **1.** *Chiefly Southern & Midland US* See **lima bean. 2.** *New England* See **wax bean.**

but·ter·bur (bŭt′ər-bûr′) *n.* Any of several perennial herbs of the genus *Petasites* in the composite family, native to northern temperate regions and having large basal leaves.

butter clam *n.* A large clam of the genus *Saxidomus,* found on the Pacific coast of North America and having a distinctive shell formerly used as money by Native Americans.

but·ter·cup (bŭt′ər-kŭp′) *n.* Any of numerous herbs of the genus *Ranunculus,* native chiefly to temperate and cold regions and having usu. yellow or white flowers.

buttercup squash *n.* A round winter squash (*Cucurbita maxima*) shaped somewhat like a drum and having a dark green rind marked with silver or gray and yellowish to orange flesh.

but·ter·fat (bŭt′ər-făt′) *n.* The natural fat of milk from which butter is made, consisting largely of the glycerides of oleic, stearic, and palmitic acids.

but·ter·fin·gers (bŭt′ər-fĭng′gərz) *pl.n. (used with a sing. verb)* A person who drops things. —**but′ter·fin′gered** *adj.*

but·ter·fish (bŭt′ər-fĭsh′) *n., pl.* **butterfish** or **-fish·es 1.** A marine food fish (*Poronotus triacanthus*) of the North American Atlantic coast, having a flattened body. **2.** Any of various similar or related fishes. [< its slippery mucous coating.]

but·ter·fly (bŭt′ər-flī′) *n.* **1.** Any of various insects of the order Lepidoptera, characteristically having slender bodies, knobbed antennae, and four broad, usu. colorful wings. **2.** A person interested principally in frivolous pleasure. **3.** *Sports* A swimming stroke in which both arms are drawn upward out of the water and forward with a dolphin kick. **4. butterflies** A feeling of unease or mild nausea caused esp. by fearful anticipation. ❖ *tr.v.* **-flied, -fly·ing, -flies** To cut and spread open and flat. [ME *butterflye* < OE *butorflēoge* : *butere,* butter; see BUTTER + *flēoge,* fly; see FLY[2].]

butterfly bush *n.* Any of various shrubs of the genus *Buddleja,* native chiefly to warm regions and cultivated for their clusters of small, variously colored flowers.

butterfly fish *n.* **1.** Any of various small, brightly colored tropical marine fishes of the family Chaetodontidae, having flattened bodies and a single dorsal fin. **2.** Any of various fishes with broad winglike fins.

butterfly orchid *n.* Any of certain orchids having showy, brightly colored flowers.

butterfly pea *n.* Any of several plants of the genera *Centrosema* and *Clitoria* in the pea family, having flat pea pods.

butterfly valve *n.* **1.** A disk turning on a diametrical axis inside a pipe, used as a throttle valve or damper. **2.** A valve composed of two semicircular plates hinged on a common spindle to permit flow in one direction only.

butterfly weed *n.* A North American milkweed (*Asclepias tuberosa*) having clusters of usu. bright orange flowers.

but·ter·milk (bŭt′ər-mĭlk′) *n.* **1.** The sour liquid that remains after the butterfat has been removed from whole milk or cream by churning. **2.** A cultured sour milk made by adding certain microorganisms to sweet milk.

buttermilk sky *n. Chiefly Inland Northern & Inland Southern US*

butte
Monument Valley, Arizona

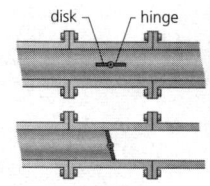

butterfly valve
top: open valve
bottom: closed valve

ă	pat	oi	**boy**
ā	pay	ou	**out**
âr	care	ŏŏ	**took**
ä	father	ōō	**boot**
ĕ	pet	ŭ	**cut**
ē	be	ûr	**urge**
ĭ	pit	th	**thin**
ī	pie	th	**this**
îr	pier	hw	**which**
ŏ	pot	zh	**vision**
ō	toe	ə	**about,**
ô	paw		**item**

Stress marks:
′ (primary);
′ (secondary), as in
lexicon (lĕk′sĭ-kŏn′)

See **mackerel sky**. [< resemblance of clouds to texture of cultured milk.]

but·ter·nut (bŭt′ər-nŭt′) n. **1a.** An eastern North American walnut (*Juglans cinerea*) having light brown wood, pinnately compound leaves, and a furrowed nut. **b.** The nut of this tree. **c.** The wood of this tree. **d.** The bark of this tree. **e.** A brownish dye from the husks of the fruits of this tree. **2a. butternuts** Clothing dyed with butternut extract, esp. Confederate uniforms. **b.** *Informal* A Confederate soldier or partisan. **3.** See **souari nut**. [< the nut's oiliness.]

butternut squash n. A bell-shaped winter squash (*Cucurbita moschata*) with a tan rind and yellowish to orange flesh.

but·ter·scotch (bŭt′ər-skŏch′) n. **1.** A syrup, sauce, candy, or flavoring made by melting butter and brown sugar together. **2.** A golden or tawny brown. [Alteration of *butterscot* : BUTTER + *scot*, of unknown orig.]

but·ter·weed (bŭt′ər-wēd′) n. **1.** A succulent annual or biennial plant (*Senecio glabellus*) native to the eastern United States and having pinnately divided leaves and bright yellow radiate flower heads. **2.** The horseweed.

but·ter·wort (bŭt′ər-wûrt′, -wôrt′) n. Any of numerous carnivorous plants of the genus *Pinguicula*, having basal leaves coated with a sticky secretion that traps small insects.

but·ter·y¹ (bŭt′ə-rē) adj. **1.** Containing or spread with butter. **2.** Like or resembling butter. **3.** Marked by effusive and insincere flattery. —**but′ter·i·ness** n.

but·ter·y² (bŭt′ə-rē, bŭt′rē) n., pl. **-ies 1.** A room for storing liquors. **2.** *Chiefly British* A store for provisions in colleges and universities. [ME *buttrie* < AN *buterie*, alteration of *botelerie* < OFr. *botele*, bottle. See BOTTLE.]

butt·head (bŭt′hĕd′) n. *Slang* A person regarded as stupid or inept.

butt hinge n. A hinge of two plates attached to abutting surfaces of a door and door jamb and joined by a pin. [< BUTT².]

butt·in·sky (bŭt-ĭn′skē) n., pl. **-skies** *Slang* One who butts in; a meddler. [*butt in* + *-sky*, last syllable in many Slav. surnames.]

butt joint n. A joint formed by two abutting surfaces placed squarely together. [< BUTT².]

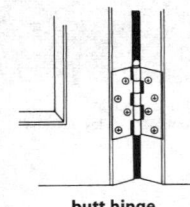

butt hinge

but·tock (bŭt′ək) n. **1.** Either of the two rounded prominences of the rear pelvic area. **2. buttocks** The rear pelvic area of the human body. [ME < OE *buttuc*, strip of land, end.]

but·ton (bŭt′n) n. **1a.** A generally disk-shaped fastener used to join two parts of a garment by fitting through a buttonhole or loop. **b.** Such an object used for decoration. **2.** Any of various objects resembling a button, esp.: **a.** A push-button switch. **b.** The blunt tip of a fencing foil. **c.** A fused metal or glass globule. **3.** *Computer Science* **a.** A well-defined area within a graphical user interface that is clicked to select a command. **b.** In a hypertext database, an icon whose selection allows a user to view an associated object. **4.** Any of various knoblike structures of a plant or animal, esp.: **a.** An immature, unexpanded mushroom. **b.** The tip of a rattlesnake's rattle. **5.** A usu. round, flat pin that bears a design or printed information: *a campaign button.* **6.** *Informal* The end of the chin, regarded as the point of impact for a punch. ❖ v. **-toned, -ton·ing, -tons** —*tr.* **1.** To fasten with buttons. **2.** To decorate or furnish with buttons. **3.** *Informal* To close (the lips or mouth). —*intr.* To be or be capable of being fastened with buttons. —*phrasal verb:* **button up 1.** To fasten one's clothing tightly, as against cold weather. **2.** To close or seal securely. **3.** To complete the final details of. —*idiom:* **on the button** Exactly; precisely. [ME < OFr. *bouton* < *bouter*, to thrust, of Gmc. orig.] —**but′ton·er** n. —**but′ton·y** adj.

but·ton·ball (bŭt′n-bôl′) n. See **sycamore** 1. [< its button-shaped fruit.]

but·ton·bush (bŭt′n-bŏosh′) n. A deciduous North American shrub (*Cephalanthus occidentalis*) having opposite leaves and spherical clusters of small white flowers.

but·ton-down (bŭt′n-doun′) adj. **1.** Having the ends of the collar fastened down by buttons. **2.** also **but·toned-down** (bŭt′nd-) Conservative, conventional, or unimaginative.

button fern n. A New Zealand fern (*Pellaea rotundifolia*) with round, dark green, buttonlike leaflets.

but·ton·hole (bŭt′n-hōl′) n. **1.** A small slit in a garment or piece of fabric for fastening a button. **2.** *Chiefly British* A boutonniere. ❖ tr.v. **-holed, -hol·ing, -holes 1.** To make a buttonhole in. **2.** To sew with a buttonhole stitch. **3.** To accost and detain (a person) in conversation by or as if by grasping the person's outer garments. —**but′ton·hol′er** n.

buttonhole stitch n. A loop stitch that forms a reinforced edge, as around a buttonhole.

but·ton·hook (bŭt′n-hŏok′) n. **1.** A small hook for fastening a button on shoes or gloves. **2.** *Football* A pass pattern in which the receiver runs straight downfield and then turns abruptly back toward the line of scrimmage to catch the ball.

button man n. A low-ranking member of an organized crime syndicate. [< a comparison between such a man and a soldier (wearing a uniform with buttons).]

button mangrove n. See **buttonwood** 2.

but·ton·mold (bŭt′n-mōld′) n. A piece of wood, plastic, or metal that is covered with fabric to form a button.

but·ton-quail (bŭt′n-kwāl′) n. Any of various small quaillike

Old World birds of the family Turnicidae, lacking a hind toe.

button snakeroot n. See **blazing star** 2.

but·ton·wood (bŭt′n-wŏod′) n. **1.** See **sycamore** 1. **2.** An evergreen shrub or tree (*Conocarpus erectus*) growing in tropical America and western Africa and having alternate leathery leaves and small heads of greenish flowers.

butt pack n. *Informal* A fanny pack.

but·tress (bŭt′rĭs) n. **1.** A structure, usu. brick or stone, built against a wall for support or reinforcement. **2.** Something resembling a buttress, as: **a.** The flared base of certain tree trunks. **b.** A horny growth on the heel of a horse's hoof. **3.** Something that serves to support, prop, or reinforce. ❖ tr.v. **-tressed, -tress·ing, -tress·es 1.** To support or reinforce with a buttress. **2.** To sustain, prop, or bolster. [ME *buteras* < OFr. *bouterez* < *bouter*, to strike against, of Gmc. orig.]

butt weld n. A welded butt joint. —**butt′-weld′** (bŭt′wĕld′) v.

bu·tyl (byōōt′l) n. A hydrocarbon radical, C_4H_9, with the structure of butane and valence 1.

butyl alcohol n. Any of four isomeric alcohols, C_4H_9OH, widely used as solvents and in organic synthesis.

bu·tyl·ate (byōōt′l-āt′) tr.v. **-at·ed, -at·ing, -ates** To bring a butyl group into (a compound). —**bu′tyl·a′tion** n.

bu·tyl·at·ed hy·drox·y·an·i·sole (byōōt′l-ā′tĭd hī-drŏk′sē-ăn′ĭ-sōl′) n. BHA.

butylated hy·drox·y·tol·u·ene (hī-drŏk′sē-tŏl′yōō-ēn′) n. BHT.

bu·tyl·ene (byōōt′l-ēn′) n. Any of three gaseous isomeric ethylene hydrocarbons, C_4H_8, used principally in making synthetic rubbers.

butyl rubber n. A synthetic rubber produced by copolymerization of a butylene with isoprene.

bu·ty·ra·ceous (byōō′tə-rā′shəs) adj. Resembling butter in appearance, consistency, or chemical properties. [Lat. *būtyrum*, butter; see BUTTER + –ACEOUS.]

bu·tyr·al·de·hyde (byōō′tə-răl′də-hīd′) n. A transparent, highly flammable liquid, C_4H_8O, used in synthesizing resins. [BUTYR(IC) + ALDEHYDE.]

bu·ty·rate (byōō′tə-rāt′) n. A salt or ester of butyric acid. [BUTYR(IC) + –ATE².]

bu·tyr·ic (byōō-tîr′ĭk) adj. **1.** Relating to, containing, or derived from butter. **2.** Relating to or derived from butyric acid. [< Lat. *būtyrum*, butter. See BUTTER.]

butyric acid n. Either of two colorless isomeric acids, C_3H_7COOH, occurring in animal milk fats and used in disinfectants, emulsifying agents, and pharmaceuticals.

bu·ty·rin (byōō′tə-rĭn) n. Any of three isomeric glyceryl esters of butyric acid, naturally present in butter. [Fr. *butyrine* < Lat. *būtyrum*, butter. See BUTTER.]

bu·ty·ro·phe·none (byōō-tîr′ō-fə-nōn′, byōō′tə-rō-) n. Any of a group of neuroleptic drugs, such as haloperidol, used to treat psychiatric disorders. [BUTYR(IC) + PHEN(O)– + –ONE.]

bux·om (bŭk′səm) adj. **1a.** Healthily plump and ample of figure. **b.** Having large breasts. **2.** *Archaic* Lively, vivacious, and gay. **3.** *Obsolete* Obedient; yielding; pliant. [ME, obedient < OE *būhsum* < *būgan*, to bend, submit.] —**bux′om·ly** adv. —**bux′om·ness** n.

Bux·te·hu·de (bŏok′stə-hōo′də), **Dietrich** 1637–1707. Swedish-born organist and composer in Germany.

buy (bī) v. **bought** (bôt), **buy·ing, buys** —*tr.* **1.** To acquire in exchange for money or its equivalent; purchase. **2.** To be capable of purchasing. Used of money, objects, and time. **3.** To acquire by sacrifice, exchange, or trade. **4.** To bribe. **5.** *Informal* To accept the truth or feasibility of. —*intr.* **1.** To purchase goods; act as a purchaser. **2.** To believe in a person or movement or subscribe to an idea or theory. ❖ n. **1.** Something bought or for sale; purchase. **2.** An act of purchasing. **3.** Something that is underpriced; a bargain. —*phrasal verbs:* **buy into 1.** To acquire a stake or interest in. **2.** To believe in, esp. wholeheartedly. **buy off** To bribe (an official, for example) in order to secure improper cooperation or gain exemption from a regulation or legal consequence. **buy out** To purchase the entire stock, business rights, or interests of. **buy up** To purchase all that is available of. —*idioms:* **buy time** To increase the time available for a specific purpose. **buy the farm** *Slang* To die, esp. suddenly or violently. [ME < OE *bycgan*.] —**buy′a·ble** adj.

buy·back (bī′băk′) n. **1.** An act of buying something that one previously sold or owned. **2.** The repurchase of stock by the company that issued it, as to reduce holdings of a single investor or increase the value of shares by reducing their number.

buy·er (bī′ər) n. One that buys, esp. for a retail store.

buyer's market also **buy·ers′ market** (bī′ərz) n. A market marked by low prices and a supply exceeding demand.

buy·out also **buy-out** (bī′out′) n. **1.** The purchase of the entire holdings or interests of an owner or investor. **2.** The purchase of a company or business.

Bu·zău (bə-zou′, bŏo-zŭ′ŏō) A city of SE Romania NE of Bucharest. Pop. 149,032.

buzz (bŭz) v. **buzzed, buzz·ing, buzz·es** —*intr.* **1.** To make a low droning or vibrating sound like that of a bee. **2a.** To talk, often excitedly, in low tones. **b.** To be abuzz; hum: *buzzing with rumors.* **3.** To move quickly and busily; bustle. **4.** To make a signal with a buzzer. —*tr.* **1.** To cause to buzz. **2.** To utter in a rapid, low voice. **3.** *Informal* To fly low over. **4.** To signal with a buzzer. **5.** To make a telephone call to. ❖ *n.* **1.** A vibrating, humming, or droning sound. **2.** A low murmur. **3.** A telephone call. **4.** *Slang* Pleasant intoxication, as from alcohol. —*phrasal verb:* **buzz off** *Informal* To leave quickly; go away. [ME *bussen,* of imit. orig.]

buz·zard (bŭz′ərd) *n.* **1.** Any of various North American vultures, such as the turkey vulture. **2.** *Chiefly British* A hawk of the genus *Buteo,* having broad wings and a broad tail. **3.** An avaricious or otherwise unpleasant person. [ME *busard,* hawk of the genus *Buteo* < OFr. < Lat. *būteō.*]

Buz·zards Bay (bŭz′ərdz) An inlet of the Atlantic Ocean in SE MA connected with Cape Cod Bay by the Cape Cod Canal.

buzz bomb *n.* See **robot bomb.**

buzz·cut or **buzz cut** (bŭz′kŭt′) *n.* A closely cropped haircut. [< the use of electric clippers instead of scissors.]

buzz·er (bŭz′ər) *n.* An electric signaling device, such as a doorbell, that makes a buzzing sound.

buzz saw *n.* See **circular saw.**

buzz·word (bŭz′wûrd′) *n.* **1.** A word or phrase of a specialized field or group used primarily to impress laypersons. **2.** A trendy word or phrase.

BVE *abbr.* Black Vernacular English

B vitamin *n.* A member of the vitamin B complex group.

BW *abbr.* **1.** biological warfare **2.** also **b/w** black and white

bwa·na (bwä′nə) *n.* Used as a form of respectful address in parts of Africa. [Swahili < Ar. *abūnā,* our father : *abū,* bound form of *'ab,* father + *-nā,* our.]

BWI *abbr.* British West Indies

by[1] (bī) *prep.* **1.** Close to; next to. **2.** With the use or help of; through: *by sea.* **3.** Up to and beyond; past: *drove by the house.* **4.** At or to: *stopped by the bakery; came by the house.* **5.** In the period of; during: *by day.* **6.** Not later than: *by 5:30 P.M.* **7a.** In the amount of: *by the thousands.* **b.** To the extent of: *by two inches.* **8a.** According to: *by the rules.* **b.** With respect to: *siblings by blood.* **9.** In the name of. **10.** Through the agency or action of. **11.** Used to indicate a succession of specified individuals, groups, or quantities: *little by little.* **12a.** Used in multiplication and division: *Multiply 6 by 6.* **b.** Used with measurements: *12 by 18 feet.* **c.** Used to express direction with points of the compass: *south by east.* ❖ *adv.* **1.** On hand; nearby: *Stand by.* **2.** Aside; away: *We put it by.* **3.** Up to, alongside, and past: *racing by.* **4.** At or to one's home or location: *Stop by later on.* **5.** Into the past: *as days go by.* [ME < OE *bī, be.* See **ambhi** in App.]

by[2] (bī) *n.* Variant of **bye**[1].

b.y. *abbr.* billion years

by– or **bye–** *pref.* **1.** By: *bygone.* **2.** Secondary; incidental: *byway.*

by and by *adv.* After a while; soon.

by-and-by (bī′ən-bī′) *n.* Some future time or occasion.

by and large *adv.* For the most part; generally. [Earlier, as to (the wind) and off it, in one direction and another (said of the manner of handling a sailing vessel) : BY[1], toward + LARGE, with the wind abaft the beam.]

Byb·los (bĭb′ləs, -lōs′) An ancient city of Phoenicia NNE of present-day Beirut, Lebanon; chief city of Phoenicia in the 2nd millennium B.C.

by-blow (bī′blō′) *n.* **1.** An indirect or chance blow. **2.** A child born out of wedlock.

by-catch (bī′kăch′, -kĕch′) *n.* The portion of a fishing catch that is discarded as unwanted or commercially unusable.

Byd·goszcz (bĭd′gôsh, -gôshch) A city of N-central Poland NE of Poznań; chartered 1346. Pop. 382,004.

bye[1] also **by** (bī) *n.* **1.** A secondary matter; a side issue. **2.** *Sports* The position of one who draws no opponent for a round in a tournament and so advances to the next round. —**idiom:** by the **bye** By the way; incidentally. [< BY[1].]

bye[2] (bī) *interj.* Used to express farewell. [Short for GOODBYE.]

bye-bye (bī′bī′, bī-bī′) *interj.* Used to express farewell. ❖ *adv. Informal* **1.** Away. **2.** To bed; to sleep. [Reduplication of BYE[2].]

by-e·lec·tion also **bye-e·lec·tion** (bī′ĭ-lĕk′shən) *n.* A special election held between general elections to fill a vacancy.

Bye·lo·rus·sia (byĕl′ō-rŭsh′ə) See **Belarus.** —**Bye·lo·rus′sian** *adj. & n.*

by·gone (bī′gôn′, -gŏn′) *adj.* Gone by; past. ❖ *n.* One, esp. a grievance, that is past: *Let bygones be bygones.*

by·law (bī′lô′) *n.* **1.** A law or rule governing the internal affairs of an organization. **2.** A secondary law. [ME *bilawe,* body of local regulations; akin to Dan. *by-lag,* township ordinance : ON *byr,* settlement; see **bheuə-** in App. + ON **lagu,* law; see **legh-** in App.]

by·line (bī′līn′) *n.* A line at the head of a newspaper or magazine article carrying the writer's name. ❖ *tr.v.* **-lined, -lin·ing, -lines** To publish (a newspaper or magazine article) under a byline. —**by′lin·er** *n.*

by-name (bī′nām′) *n.* **1.** A surname. **2.** A nickname.

by·pass also **by-pass** (bī′păs′) *n.* **1.** A highway or section of a highway that passes around an obstructed or congested area. **2.** A pipe or channel used to conduct gas or liquid around another pipe or a fixture. **3.** A means of circumvention. **4.** *Electricity* See **shunt** 3. **5.** *Medicine* **a.** An alternative passage created surgically to divert a body fluid or circumvent an obstructed or diseased organ. **b.** A surgical procedure to create a bypass. ❖ *tr.v.* **-passed, -pass·ing, -pass·es** **1.** To avoid (an obstacle) by using a bypass. **2.** To be heedless of; ignore. **3.** To channel (piped liquid, for example) through a bypass.

by·past (bī′păst′) *adj.* Past; bygone.

by-path (bī′păth′, -päth′) *n.* An indirect or rarely used path; a byway.

by-play (bī′plā′) *n.* Secondary action or speech taking place while the main action proceeds, as during a play.

by·prod·uct or **by-prod·uct** (bī′prŏd′əkt) *n.* **1.** Something produced in the making of something else. **2.** A secondary result; a side effect.

Byrd (bûrd), **Richard Evelyn** 1888–1957. Amer. naval officer and explorer; first to fly over the North Pole (1926) and leader of five expeditions to Antarctica (1929–56).

Byrd, William 1674–1744. Amer. planter and colonial official whose diaries depict daily life in Virginia.

byre (bīr) *n. Chiefly British* A barn for cows. [ME < OE *bȳre.* See **bheuə-** in App.]

Byrnes (bûrnz), **James Francis** 1879–1972. Amer. politician; associate justice of the US Supreme Court (1941–42) and secretary of state (1945–47).

by·road (bī′rōd′) *n.* See **byway** 1.

By·ron (bī′rən), **George Gordon.** 6th Baron Byron of Rochdale. 1788–1824. British poet whose works include *Childe Harold* (1812–18) and *Don Juan* (1819–24). —**By·ron′ic** (bī-rŏn′ĭk) *adj.*

bys·si·no·sis (bĭs′ĭ-nō′sĭs) *n.* A respiratory disease caused by the long-term inhalation of cotton, flax, or hemp dust and marked by shortness of breath, coughing, and wheezing. [LLat. *byssinum,* linen garment (< Lat. *byssus,* linen cloth; see BYSSUS) + *-OSIS.*]

bys·sus (bĭs′əs) *n., pl.* **bys·sus·es** or **bys·si** (bĭs′ī′) **1.** *Zoology* A mass of strong silky filaments by which certain bivalve mollusks attach themselves to fixed surfaces. **2.** A fine-textured linen of ancient times, used by the Egyptians for wrapping mummies. [ME *bissus,* linen cloth < Lat. < Gk. *bussos,* linen; akin to Skt. *picuh,* cotton, of Dravidian orig. or ult. < Egypt. *w'ḏ,* linen.] —**bys′sal** (bĭs′əl) *adj.*

by·stand·er (bī′stăn′dər) *n.* A person who is present at an event without participating in it.

by·street (bī′strēt′) *n.* A side street.

byte (bīt) *n.* A sequence of adjacent bits, usu. eight, operated on as a unit by a computer. [Alteration and blend of BIT[3] and BITE.]

By·tom (bĕ′tôm′, bī′-) A city of SW Poland NW of Katowice; assigned to Poland in 1945. Pop. 231,848.

by·way (bī′wā′) *n.* **1.** A side road. **2.** A secondary or arcane field of study.

by·word also **by-word** (bī′wûrd′) *n.* **1a.** A proverbial expression; a proverb. **b.** An often-used word or phrase. **2.** One that represents a type, class, or quality. **3.** An object of notoriety or interest. **4.** An epithet. [ME *byworde* < OE *bīword,* transl. of Lat. *prōverbium.*]

Byz·an·tine (bĭz′ən-tēn′, -tīn′, bĭ-zăn′tīn) *adj.* **1a.** Of or relating to the ancient city or the Byzantine Empire. **b.** Of or relating to the Byzantine Empire. **2.** Of or belonging to the architecture developed from the fifth century A.D. in the Byzantine Empire, characterized esp. by a central dome resting on a cube and by the extensive use of surface decoration. **3.** Of the painting and decorative style developed in the Byzantine Empire, marked by frontal stylized figures, rich use of color, and religious subject matter. **4.** Of the Eastern Orthodox Church or its rites. **5.** often **byzantine a.** Of or relating to intrigue; scheming. **b.** Highly complicated. ❖ *n.* A native or inhabitant of Byzantium or the Byzantine Empire.

Byzantine Empire The E part of the later Roman Empire, dating from A.D. 330 to the fall of Constantinople in 1453.

By·zan·ti·um (bĭ-zăn′shē-əm, -tē-əm) **1.** The Byzantine Empire. **2.** An ancient city of Thrace on the site of present-day Istanbul, Turkey; founded by the Greeks in the 7th cent. B.C. and rebuilt by Constantine I in A.D. 330.

Byzantine
13th-century Russian icon depicting St. Nicholas

Cc

c¹ or **C** (sē) *n.*, *pl.* **c's** or **C's** also **cs** or **Cs 1.** The third letter of the modern English alphabet. **2.** Any of the speech sounds represented by the letter *c.* **3.** The third in a series. **4.** Something shaped like the letter C. **5. C** The third best or third highest in quality or rank. **6.** *Music* **a.** The first tone in the scale of C major or the third tone in the relative minor scale. **b.** A key or scale in which the tone of C is the tonic.

c² *abbr.* **1.** *Physics* candle **2.** carat **3.** charm quark **4.** also **C** *Mathematics* constant **5.** cubic

C¹ *n.* A programming language widely used for developing programs that are a part of an operating system.

C² 1. The symbol for the element **carbon** 1. **2.** also **c** The symbol for the Roman numeral one hundred. **3. c** The symbol for the speed of light in a vacuum. **4.** The symbol for **capacitance** 1, 2. **5.** The symbol for **charge conjugation.**

C³ *abbr.* **1.** Celsius **2.** centigrade **3.** cold **4.** consonant **5.** coulomb **6.** cytosine

c. *abbr.* **1.** capacity **2.** cent **3.** centavo **4.** centime **5.** centimo **6.** chapter **7.** circa **8.** *Pharmacology* congius (gallon) **9.** copy **10.** copyright **11.** cup

C. *abbr.* **1.** cape **2.** Celtic **3.** or **c.** century **4.** chancellor

ca *abbr.* circa

Ca The symbol for the element **calcium.**

CA *abbr.* **1.** California **2.** Central America **3.** chartered accountant **4.** chronological age

CAA *abbr.* Civil Aeronautics Administration

cab¹ (kăb) *n.* **1.** A taxicab. **2.** The covered compartment for the operator or driver of a heavy vehicle or machine. **3.** A one-horse vehicle for public hire. ❖ *intr.v.* **cabbed, cab·bing, cabs 1.** To travel in a taxicab. **2.** To drive a taxicab. [Short for CABRIOLET.]

cab² also **kab** (kăb) *n.* An ancient Hebrew unit of measure equal to about 2 liters (2.1 quarts). [Heb. *qab.*]

CAB *abbr.* Civil Aeronautics Board

ca·bal (kə-băl′, -bäl′) *n.* **1.** A conspiratorial group. **2.** A secret scheme. ❖ *intr.v.* **-balled, -bal·ling, -bals** To form a cabal. [Fr. *cabale* < Med.Lat. *cabala*. See KABBALAH.]

cab·a·la (kăb′ə-lə, kə-bä′-) *n.* Variant of kabbalah. **—cab′a·lism** *n.* **—cab′a·list** *n.*

cab·a·let·ta (kăb′ə-lĕt′ə, kä′bə-) *n.*, *pl.* **-let·tas** or **-let·te** (-lĕt′ē) **1.** A short aria that has a repetitive rhythm and a simple style. **2.** The final section of an aria or duet in a quick uniform rhythm. [Ital., alteration of *coboletta*, stanza, dim. of *cobola* < O Provençal *cobla* < Lat. *cōpula*, link.]

cab·a·lis·tic (kăb′ə-lĭs′tĭk) *adj.* **1.** Having a secret or hidden meaning; occult. **2.** Variant of kabbalistic. **—cab′a·lis′ti·cal·ly** *adv.*

cab·al·le·ro (kăb′ə-lâr′ō, -əl-yâr′ō, kä′bä-yĕ′rō) *n.*, *pl.* **-ros 1.** A Spanish gentleman; a cavalier. **2.** A man skilled in riding and managing horses. [Sp. < LLat. *caballārius*, horse groom < Lat. *caballus*, horse.]

ca·ban·a also **ca·ba·ña** (kə-băn′ə, -băn′yə) *n.* **1.** A shelter on a beach or at a swimming pool used as a bathhouse. **2.** A cabin or hut. [Sp. *cabaña* < LLat. *capanna*, hut.]

cab·a·ret (kăb′ə-rā′) *n.* **1.** A restaurant or nightclub providing short programs of live entertainment. **2.** The entertainment so provided. [Fr., taproom < MDu. *cabret* < ONFr. *camberette* < LLat. *camera*, room. See CHAMBER.]

cab·bage (kăb′ĭj) *n.* **1.** Any of several forms of a European vegetable (*Brassica oleracea* var. *capitata*) of the mustard family, having a globose head consisting of a short stem and tightly overlapping leaves. **2.** Any of several similar or related plants, such as Chinese cabbage. **3.** The terminal bud of several species of palm, eaten as a vegetable. **4.** *Slang* Money, esp. bills. [ME *caboche* < ONFr., head, poss. < alteration of Lat. *caput*. See CAPITAL¹.] **—cab′bag·y** *adj.*

cabbage butterfly *n.* Any of several white butterflies of the genus *Pieris*, having larvae that feed on cabbage.

cabbage palm *n.* Any of several palms, such as the assai, with edible terminal buds. **2.** See cabbage palmetto.

cabbage palmetto *n.* A species of palmetto (*Sabal palmetto*) native to southeast North America and having an edible terminal bud.

cabbage rose *n.* A prickly shrub (*Rosa centifolia*) native to the Caucasus and having fragrant pink double-petaled flowers.

cab·bage·worm (kăb′ĭj-wûrm′) *n.* A larva that feeds on cabbage, esp. the bright green larva of the cabbage butterfly.

cab·by or **cab·bie** (kăb′ē) *n.*, *pl.* **-bies** A cabdriver.

cab·driv·er also **cab driver** (kăb′drī′vər) *n.* One who drives a taxicab for hire.

cable car
San Francisco, California

cable stitch

Cab·ell (kăb′əl), **James Branch** 1879–1958. Amer. writer best known for his satirical novels, including *Jurgen* (1919).

ca·ber (kä′bər) *n.* A long heavy wooden pole tossed end over end as a demonstration of strength in Scottish highland games. [Sc. Gael. *cabar*, pole, beam, rafter < VLat. **capriō* < Lat. *capra*, she-goat. See CHEVRON.]

Cab·er·net Sau·vi·gnon (kăb′ər-nā′ sō-vē-nyôn′) *n.* **1.** A variety of black grape used to make red wine. **2.** A dry red wine made from this grape. [Fr.]

Ca·be·za de Va·ca (kə-bā′zə də vä′kə, kä-vĕ′thä thĕ vä′kä), **Álvar Núñez** 1490?–1557? Spanish colonial administrator who explored parts of present-day FL, TX, and Mexico.

cab·in (kăb′ĭn) *n.* **1.** A small, roughly built house. **2.** *Nautical* **a.** A room in a ship used as living quarters. **b.** An enclosed compartment in a boat serving as a shelter or living quarters. **3.** The enclosed space in an aircraft or spacecraft for the crew, passengers, or cargo. ❖ *tr. & intr.v.* **-ined, -in·ing, -ins** To confine or live in or as if in a small space. [ME *caban* < OFr. *cabane* < O Provençal *cabana* < LLat. *capanna.*]

cabin boy *n.* A boy servant aboard a ship.

cabin class *n.* A class of accommodations on passenger ships, below first class and above tourist class.

cabin cruiser *n.* A powerboat with a cabin that has living accommodations.

Ca·bin·da (kə-bĭn′də) A territory of Angola forming an exclave on the Atlantic Ocean between the Republic of the Congo and the Democratic Republic of the Congo (formerly Zaire).

cab·i·net (kăb′ə-nĭt) *n.* **1.** An upright cupboardlike repository with shelves, drawers, or compartments. **2.** *Computer Science* The box that houses the main components of a computer. **3.** often **Cabinet** A body of persons appointed by a chief of state or prime minister to head the executive departments of the government and act as official advisers. **4.** *Archaic* A small or private room set aside for a specific activity. **5.** *Rhode Island & Southeastern Massachusetts* See milk shake 1. See Regional Note at milk shake. [Fr., partly < dim. of ONFr. *cabine*, gambling room (perh. alteration of OFr. *cabane*, small house; see CABIN) and partly < Ital. *gabinetto*, closet, chest of drawers; akin to ONFr. *cabine*. N., sense 5, poss. < the square wooden container in which the mixer was encased.] **—cab′i·net** *adj.* **—cab′i·net·ful** *n.*

cab·i·net·mak·er (kăb′ə-nĭt-mā′kər) *n.* An artisan specializing in making fine articles of wooden furniture. **—cab′i·net·mak′ing** *n.*

cab·i·net·ry (kăb′ĭ-nĭ-trē) *n.* Cabinetwork.

cab·i·net·work (kăb′ə-nĭt-wûrk′) *n.* Finished woodwork fashioned by a cabinetmaker.

cabin fever *n.* Uneasiness or distress that results from a prolonged stay in a remote region or in a small enclosed space.

ca·ble (kā′bəl) *n.* **1a.** A strong, heavy steel or fiber rope. **b.** Something that resembles such rope. **2.** *Electricity* A bound or sheathed group of insulated conductors. **3.** *Nautical* **a.** A heavy rope or chain for mooring or anchoring a ship. **b.** A cable length. **4.** A cablegram. **5.** Cable television. ❖ *v.* **-bled, -bling, -bles** —*tr.* **1a.** To send a cablegram to. **b.** To transmit (a message) by telegraph. **2.** To supply or fasten with a cable. —*intr.* To send a cablegram. [ME < ONFr. < LLat. *capulum*, lasso < Lat. *capere*, to seize. See **kap-** in App.] **—ca′bler** *n.*

Cable, George Washington 1844–1925. Amer. writer whose works include *Grandissimes* (1880).

cable box *n.* An electronic tuning device, often including a descrambler, that allows channels transmitted by cable to be selected for viewing on a television.

cable car *n.* A car designed to operate on a cableway or cable railway.

ca·ble·cast (kā′bəl-kăst′) *n.* A telecast by cable television. [CABLE + (BROAD)CAST.] **—ca′ble·cast′** *v.* **—ca′ble·cast′er** *n.*

ca·ble·gram (kā′bəl-grăm′) *n.* A telegram sent by submarine cable. [CABLE + (TELE)GRAM.]

ca·ble-laid (kā′bəl-lād′) *adj.* Made of three ropes of three strands each, twisted together counterclockwise.

cable length *n.* *Nautical* A unit of length equal to 720 feet (220 meters) in the United States and 608 feet (185 meters) in England.

cable railway *n.* A railroad on which the cars are moved by an endless cable driven by a stationary engine.

cable stitch *n.* A stitch in knitting that produces a twisted rope-like design.

ca·blet (kā′blĭt) *n.* A cable-laid rope with a circumference of less than 10 inches (25 centimeters).

cable television *n.* A television distribution system in which station signals are delivered by cable to subscribers.

ca·ble·way (kā′bəl-wā′) *n.* A suspended cable used as a track typically for a cable car.

cab·man (kăb′mən) *n.* A man who drives a taxicab.

cab·o·chon (kăb′ə-shŏn′) *n.* **1.** A highly polished, convex-cut, unfaceted gem. **2.** A convex style of cutting gems. [Fr. < ONFr., augmentative of *caboche,* head. See CABBAGE.] —**cab′o·chon′** *adv.*

ca·bom·ba (kə-bŏm′bə) *n.* See fanwort. [Am.Sp.]

ca·boo·dle (kə-bōod′l) *n. Informal* **1.** The lot or bunch: *donated the whole caboodle.* **2.** A crowd or collection of people. [Alteration of BOODLE.]

ca·boose (kə-bōōs′) *n.* **1.** The last car on a freight train, having kitchen and sleeping facilities for the train crew. **2.** *Obsolete* **a.** A ship's galley. **b.** A cast-iron cooking range used in such galleys. **c.** An outdoor oven or fireplace. [Poss. < obsolete Du. *cabuse,* ship's galley < MLGer. *kabūse* : perh. *kab-,* cabin; akin to OFr. *cabane;* see CABIN + MHGer. *hūs,* house.]

Cab·ot (kăb′ət), **John** Orig. Giovanni Caboto. 1450?–98? Italian-born explorer who commanded the English expedition that explored the North American mainland (1497).

Cabot, Sebastian 1476?–1557. Italian-born explorer who led an English expedition in search of the Northwest Passage (1509).

cab·o·tage (kăb′ə-täzh′) *n.* **1.** Trade or navigation in coastal waters. **2.** The exclusive right of a country to operate the air traffic within its territory. [Fr. < *caboter,* to sail along a coast, perh. < Sp. *cabo,* cape < Lat. *caput,* head. See CAPE².]

ca·bret·ta (kə-brĕt′ə) *n.* A soft kidlike leather made from sheepskin having coarse hairlike wool. [Sp. and Port. *cabra,* she-goat (both < Lat. *capra,* fem. of *caper,* goat) + Ital. *-etta,* dim. suff.]

ca·bril·la (kə-brē′yə, -brēl′ə) *n.* Any of various sea basses, esp. *Epinephelus guttatus,* of tropical waters. [Sp., dim. of *cabra,* she-goat. See CABRETTA.]

Ca·bri·ni (kə-brē′nē), **Saint Frances Xavier** Known as "Mother Cabrini." 1850–1917. Italian-born religious leader who was the first American to be canonized (1946).

cab·ri·ole (kăb′rē-ōl′) *n.* A form of furniture leg that curves outward and then narrows downward into an ornamental foot. [Fr., caper. See CABRIOLET.]

cab·ri·o·let (kăb′rē-ə-lā′) *n.* **1.** A two-wheeled one-horse carriage that has two seats and a folding top. **2.** An automobile with a folding top; a convertible coupe. [Fr., dim. of *cabriole,* caper < obsolete *capriole* < Ital. *capriola* < *capriolo,* roebuck < Lat. *capreolus,* masc. dim. of *caprea,* roe deer < *caper,* he-goat.]

cab·stand (kăb′stănd′) *n.* A place for taxicabs to wait.

cac– *pref.* Variant of caco–.

ca·ca·o (kə-kā′ō, -kä′ō) *n., pl.* **-os** **1.** An evergreen tropical American tree (*Theobroma cacao*) having leathery, ellipsoid ten-ribbed fruits. **2.** The cacao seed, used in making chocolate, cocoa, and cocoa butter. [Sp. < Nahuatl *cacahuatl.*]

cacao butter *n.* See cocoa butter.

cac·cia·to·re (kăch′ə-tôr′ē, -tōr′ē) *adj.* Prepared with tomatoes, onions, mushrooms, herbs, and sometimes wine: *chicken cacciatore.* [Ital., hunter < *cacciare,* to hunt < VLat. *captiāre.* See CHASE¹.]

cach·a·lot (kăsh′ə-lŏt′, -lō′) *n.* See sperm whale. [Fr. < Sp. or Port. *cachalote,* augmentative of *cachola,* big head.]

cache (kăsh) *n.* **1a.** A hiding place used for storing provisions. **b.** A place for concealment and safekeeping, as of valuables. **c.** The store of goods in a hiding place. **2.** A fast storage buffer in the central processing unit of a computer. ❖ *tr.v.* **cached, cach·ing, cach·es** To hide or store in a cache. See Syns at **hide¹.** [Fr. < *cacher,* to hide < OFr., to press, hide < VLat. *coācticāre,* to store, pack together, freq. of Lat. *coāctāre,* to constrain < *coāctus,* p. part. of *cōgere,* to force. See COGENT.]

cache·pot (kăsh′pŏt′, -pō′) *n.* An ornamental container for a flowerpot. [Fr. : *cacher,* to hide; see CACHE + *pot,* pot (< OFr. < VLat. *pottus.*)]

ca·chet (kă-shā′) *n.* **1.** A mark or quality, as of distinction or authenticity. **2.** A seal on a document, such as a letter. **3a.** A commemorative design stamped on an envelope. **b.** A motto or postal cancellation. **4.** A wafer capsule formerly used by pharmacists to present an unpleasant-tasting drug. [Fr. < OFr. < *cacher,* to press. See CACHE.]

ca·chex·i·a (kə-kĕk′sē-ə) *n.* Weight loss, wasting of muscle, and debility that can occur during a chronic illness. [LLat. < Gk. *kakhexiā* : *kako-, caco-* + *hexis,* condition (< *ekhein,* to have; see **segh–** in App.).] —**ca·chec′tic** (kə-kĕk′tĭk) *adj.*

cach·in·nate (kăk′ə-nāt′) *intr.v.* **-nat·ed, -nat·ing, -nates** To laugh hard, loudly, or convulsively; guffaw. [Lat. *cachinnāre, cachinnāt-,* of imit. orig.] —**cach′in·na′tion** *n.* —**cach′in·na′tor** *n.*

ca·chou (kă-shōo′, kăsh′ōo) *n.* A pastille used to sweeten the breath. [Fr. < Port. *cachu* < Malayalam *kāccu* < Tamil *kāyccu.*]

ca·chu·cha (kə-chōo′chə) *n.* An Andalusian solo dance in 3/4 time. [Sp., small boat, cachucha, poss. < dim. of *cacho,* shard, saucepan, prob. < VLat. **caccula,* alteration of Lat. *caccabus,* pot < Gk. *kakkabos,* prob. < of Semitic orig.; akin to Akkadian *kukkubu,* a small container.]

ca·cique (kə-sēk′) *n.* **1.** An American Indian chief, esp. in Latin America during colonial and postcolonial times. **2.** A local political boss in Spain or Latin America. [Am.Sp. < Arawak *kassequa,* chieftain.]

cack·le (kăk′əl) *v.* **-led, -ling, -les** —*intr.* **1.** To make the shrill cry characteristic of a hen after laying an egg. **2.** To laugh or talk in a shrill manner. —*tr.* To utter in cackles. ❖ *n.* **1.** The act or sound of cackling. **2.** Shrill laughter. **3.** Foolish chatter. [ME *cakelen,* prob. < MLGer. *kākeln,* of imit. orig.] —**cack′ler** *n.*

caco– or **cac–** *pref.* Bad: *cacography.* [Gk. *kako-* < *kakos,* bad. See **kakka–** in App.]

cac·o·dyl (kăk′ə-dĭl′) *n.* **1.** The arsenic group (CH₃)₂As⁻. **2.** A foul-smelling poisonous oil, As₂(CH₃)₄. [Gk. *kakōdēs,* bad-smelling (*kakos,* bad; see **kakka–** in App. + *-ōdēs,* -smelling < *ozein, od-,* to smell) + -YL.] —**cac′o·dyl′ic** *adj.*

cac·o·ë·thes (kăk′ō-ē′thēz) *n.* An irresistible compulsion; a mania. [Lat. *cacoēthes* < neut. of Gk. *kakoēthēs,* ill-disposed : *kakos,* bad + *ēthos,* disposition; see **s(w)e–** in App.]

ca·cog·ra·phy (kə-kŏg′rə-fē) *n.* **1.** Bad handwriting. **2.** Bad spelling.

cac·o·mis·tle (kăk′ə-mĭs′əl) *n.* A small carnivorous raccoonlike mammal (*Bassariscus sumichrasti*) of Central America, having a black-banded tail. [Am.Sp. *cacomiztle* < Nahuatl *tlacomiztli* : *tlaco,* half, part + *miztli,* mountain lion.]

cac·o·nym (kăk′ə-nĭm) *n.* An erroneous name, esp. in taxonomy; a misnomer. —**ca·con′y·my** (kə-kŏn′ə-mē) *n.*

ca·coph·o·nous (kə-kŏf′ə-nəs) *adj.* Having a harsh unpleasant sound. [< Gk. *kakophōnos* : *kakos,* bad + *phōnē,* sound; see **bhā–** in App.] —**ca·coph′o·nous·ly** *adv.*

ca·coph·o·ny (kə-kŏf′ə-nē) *n., pl.* **-nies** **1.** Jarring, discordant sound; dissonance. **2.** The use of harsh or discordant sounds in literary composition. [Fr. *cacophonie* < Gk. *kakophōniā* < *kakophōnos,* cacophonous. See CACOPHONOUS.]

cac·tus (kăk′təs) *n., pl.* **-ti** (-tī′) or **-tus·es** **1.** Any of various succulent spiny plants native mostly to arid regions of the New World, often having showy flowers. **2.** Any of several similar plants. [Lat., cardoon < Gk. *kaktos.*]

cactus pear *n.* See tuna².

ca·cu·mi·nal (kə-kyōō′mə-nəl) *adj.* Articulated with the tip of the tongue turned back and up toward the roof of the mouth; retroflex. [< Lat. *cacūmen, cacūmin-,* summit, point.]

cad (kăd) *n.* An unprincipled or dishonorable man. [Short for CADDIE.] —**cad′dish** *adj.* —**cad′dish·ly** *adv.*

CAD *abbr.* computer-aided design

ca·das·tre also **ca·das·ter** (kə-dăs′tər) *n.* A public record, survey, or map of the value, extent, and ownership of land as a basis of taxation. [Fr. < Provençal *cadastro* < Ital. *catastro,* alteration of OItal. *catastico* < L.Gk. *katastikhon,* register : *kata-,* down; see CATA– + Gk. *stikhos,* line; see **steigh–** in App.] —**ca·das′tral** *adj.*

ca·dav·er (kə-dăv′ər) *n.* A dead body, esp. one intended for dissection. [ME < Lat. *cadāver < cadere,* to fall, die.] —**ca·dav′er·ic** (-ər-ĭk) *adj.*

ca·dav·er·ine (kə-dăv′ə-rēn′) *n.* A syrupy, colorless, fuming ptomaine, C₅H₁₄N₂, formed by the carboxylation of lysine by bacteria in decaying animal flesh.

ca·dav·er·ous (kə-dăv′ər-əs) *adj.* **1.** Suggestive of death; corpselike. **2a.** Of corpselike pallor; pallid. **b.** Emaciated; gaunt. —**ca·dav′er·ous·ly** *adv.* —**ca·dav′er·ous·ness** *n.*

cad·die also **cad·dy** (kăd′ē) *n., pl.* **-dies** **1.** One hired to assist a golfer, esp. to carry golf clubs. **2.** *Scots* A boy who does odd jobs. **3.** Any of various devices for moving, carrying, or holding an item or collection of items, such as a wheeled cart fitted with shelves or racks. ❖ *intr.v.* **-died, -dy·ing, -dies** To serve as a caddie. [Sc. < Fr. *cadet,* cadet, caddie. See CADET.]

cad·dis also **cad·dice** (kăd′ĭs) *n.* A coarse woolen fabric, yarn, or ribbon binding. [Prob. < ME *cadace,* cotton wool (< AN < O Provençal *cadarz*) and < Fr. *cadis,* woolen cloth (< O Provençal).]

caddis fly also **caddice fly** *n.* Any of various four-winged insects of the order Trichoptera, found near lakes and streams. [Perh. < obsolete *cad* (influenced by CADDIS), var. of COD².]

caddis worm also **caddice worm** *n.* The aquatic wormlike larva of the caddis fly, enclosed in a cylindrical case.

Cad·do (kăd′ō) *n., pl.* **Caddo** or **-dos** **1.** A member of a Native American confederacy formerly inhabiting the Red River area of Louisiana, Arkansas, and eastern Texas and now located in central Oklahoma. **2.** The Caddoan language of the Caddo. [Fr. < Caddo *kaduhdá·čuʔ,* a Caddo tribe.]

Cad·do·an (kăd′ō-ən) *n.* A family of North American Indian languages spoken formerly in the Dakotas, Kansas, Nebraska, Texas, Oklahoma, Arkansas, and Louisiana and presently in North Dakota and Oklahoma.

cad·dy¹ (kăd′ē) *n., pl.* **-dies** **1.** A small container, such as a box, used esp. for holding tea. **2.** A container for storing a group of items not in use. **3.** A protective case used to load a CD-ROM into a disk drive. [Alteration of CATTY¹.]

cad·dy² (kăd′ē) *n. & v.* Variant of **caddie.**

cade (kăd) *adj.* Left by its mother and reared by hand: *a cade calf.* ❖ *n.* A bushy juniper (*Juniperus oxycedrus*) of the Mediterranean region, whose wood yields juniper tar. [ME, pet lamb.]

Cade, Jack d. 1450. English rebel who led an unsuccessful rebellion against Henry VI.

–cade *suff.* Procession: *motorcade.* [< CAVALCADE.]

cabochon
cabochon emerald pendant

Mother Cabrini

ă	pat	oi	boy
ā	pay	ou	out
âr	care	ōo	took
ä	father	ōō	boot
ĕ	pet	ŭ	cut
ē	be	ûr	urge
ĭ	pit	th	thin
ī	pie	th	this
îr	pier	hw	which
ŏ	pot	zh	vision
ō	toe	ə	about,
ô	paw		item

Stress marks:
′ (primary);
′ (secondary), as in
lexicon (lĕk′sĭ-kŏn′)

ca·delle (kə-dĕl′) *n.* A small blackish beetle (*Tenebroides mauritanicus*), both the larval and adult forms of which damage stored grain. [Fr. < Provençal *cadello* < Lat. *catella*, fem. of *catellus*, puppy < *catulus*, the young of animals.]

ca·dence (kād′ns) *n., pl.* **-denc·es** **1.** Balanced, rhythmic flow, as of poetry. **2.** The measure or beat of movement, as in dancing. **3a.** A falling inflection of the voice. **b.** General inflection or modulation of the voice. **4.** *Music* A progression of chords moving to a harmonic close, point of rest, or sense of resolution. [ME < OFr. *cadence* < OItal. *cadenza* < VLat. *cadentia*, a falling < Lat. *cadēns, cadent-*, pr. part. of *cadere*, to fall.] —**ca′denced** *adj.*

ca·den·cy (kād′n-sē) *n., pl.* **-cies** Cadence.

ca·dent (kād′nt) *adj.* **1.** Having cadence or rhythm. **2.** *Archaic* Falling, as water or tears. [Lat. *cadēns, cadent-*, pr. part. of *cadere*, to fall.]

ca·den·tial (kə-dĕn′shəl) *adj.* **1.** Of or relating to a cadence. **2.** Of or having to do with a cadenza.

ca·den·za (kə-dĕn′zə) *n.* **1.** An elaborate melodic flourish interpolated into an aria or other vocal piece. **2.** An extended virtuosic section for the soloist usu. near the end of a movement of a concerto. [Ital. < OItal., cadence. See CADENCE.]

ca·det (kə-dĕt′) *n.* **1.** A student at a military school who is training to be an officer. **2a.** A younger son or brother. **b.** A youngest son. **3.** *Slang* A pimp. [Fr. < dialectal *capdet*, captain < LLat. *capitellum*, dim. of Lat. *caput, capit-*, head. See **kaput** in App.] —**ca·det′ship′** *n.*

cadge (kăj) *intr. & tr.v.* **cadged, cadg·ing, cadg·es** To beg or get by begging. [Perh. back-formation < obsolete *cadger*, peddler < ME *cadgear*.] —**cadg′er** *n.*

Cad·il·lac (kăd′l-ăk′, kä-dē-yäk′), Sieur **Antoine de la Mothe** 1658–1730. French explorer and colonial administrator who founded Detroit MI (1701).

Cá·diz (kə-dĭz′, kā′dĭz, kăf-, kä′thĕth, -thĕs) A city of SW Spain NW of Gibraltar on the **Gulf of Cádiz**, an inlet of the Atlantic Ocean; founded c. 1100 B.C. Pop. 152,187.

cad·mi·um (kăd′mē-əm) *n. Symbol* **Cd** A soft metallic element occurring primarily in zinc, copper, and lead ores that is used in low-friction fatigue-resistant alloys, solders, batteries, nuclear reactor shields, and electroplating. Atomic number 48; atomic weight 112.41; melting point 320.9°C; boiling point 765°C; specific gravity 8.65; valence 2. See table at **element**. [Lat. *cadmīa*, calamine (< its being found with calamine in zinc ore) (< Gk. *kadmeia (gē)*, Theban (earth) < *Kadmos*, Cadmus; see CADMUS) + –IUM.] —**cad′mic** (-mĭk) *adj.*

Cad·mus (kăd′məs) *n. Greek Mythology* A Phoenician prince who founded Thebes and introduced writing to the Greeks. [Gk. *Kadmos* < Phoenician *qadm*, east.]

cad·re (kä′drā, -drə, kăd′rē) *n.* **1.** A nucleus of trained personnel around which a larger organization can be built. **2a.** A tightly knit group of zealots in a revolutionary party. **b.** A member of a cadre. **3.** A framework. [Fr. < Ital. *quadro*, frame < Lat. *quadrum*, a square. See kʷetwer- in App.]

ca·du·ce·us (kə-dōō′sē-əs, -shəs, -dyōō′-) *n., pl.* **-ce·i** (-sē-ī′) **1a.** A herald's wand or staff. **b.** *Greek Mythology* A winged staff with two serpents twined around it, carried by Hermes. **2.** An insignia modeled on Hermes's staff, used as the symbol of the medical profession. [Lat. *cādūceus*, alteration of Gk. dialectal *kārūkeion* < *kārūx*, herald.] —**ca·du′ce·an** (-sē-ən, -shən) *adj.*

ca·du·ci·ty (kə-dōō′sĭ-tē, -dyōō′-) *n.* **1.** The frailty of old age; senility. **2.** The quality or state of being perishable; impermanence. [Fr. *caducité* < *caduc*, frail, falling < Lat. *cadūcus*. See CA-DUCOUS.]

ca·du·cous (kə-dōō′kəs, -dyōō′-) *adj.* Dropping off or shedding at an early stage of development, as some sepals. [< Lat. *cadūcus*, falling < *cadere*, to fall.]

cae·cil·ian (sə-sĭl′yən, -sĭl′ē-ən, -sēl′-) *n.* Any of various legless, burrowing, wormlike amphibians of the order Gymnophiona, of tropical regions. [< Lat. *caecilia*, a kind of lizard < *caecus*, blind (< its small eyes).]

cae·cum (sē′kəm) *n.* Variant of **cecum**.

Caed·mon (kăd′mən) d. c. 680. The earliest English poet, who supposedly received the power of song in a vision.

Cae·li·an (sē′lē-ən) One of the seven hills of ancient Rome; devastated by fire in A.D. 27. —**Cae′li·an** *adj.*

Cae·lum (sē′ləm) *n.* A constellation in the Southern Hemisphere near Columba and Eridanus. [Lat. *caelum*, sculptor's chisel.]

Caen (käN) A city of N France SW of Le Havre; a Huguenot stronghold in the 16th and 17th cent. Pop. 112,872.

caer·phil·ly (kär-fĭl′ē) *n.* A mild white Welsh cheese. [After *Caerphilly*, a district of southeast Wales.]

cae·sar also **Cae·sar** (sē′zər) *n.* **1.** Used as a title and form of address for Roman emperors. **2.** A dictator or autocrat. [ME *cesar* < Lat. *Caesar*, after Julius CAESAR.]

Caesar, Gaius Julius 100–44 B.C. Roman general, statesman, and historian who invaded Britain (55), crushed the army of his political enemy Pompey (48), and was given a mandate by the people to rule as dictator for life (45). He was murdered by a group of republicans led by Cassius and Brutus. —**Cae·sar′e·an, Cae·sar′i·an** (sĭ-zâr′ē-ən) *adj.*

Caesar, Sidney Known as "Sid." b. 1922. Amer. comedian who

caduceus

Julius Caesar

pioneered the comedy sketch show.

Cae·sa·re·a (sē′zə-rē′ə, sĕs′ə-, sĕz′ə-) **1.** also **Caesarea Pal·e·sti·nae** (păl′ĭ-stī′nē) An ancient seaport of Palestine S of present-day Haifa, Israel; founded 30 B.C. by Herod the Great. **2.** also **Caesarea Phil·ip·pi** (fĭl′ĭ-pī, fĭ-lĭp′ī) An ancient city of N Palestine near Mt. Hermon in present-day SW Syria. **3.** also **Caesarea Maz·a·ca** (măz′ə-kə) An ancient city of Cappadocia on the site of Kayseri, in central Turkey.

cae·sar·e·an (sĭ-zâr′ē-ən) *adj. & n.* Variant of **cesarean**.

cae·sar·i·an (sĭ-zâr′ē-ən) *adj. & n.* Variant of **cesarean**.

cae·sar·ism (sē′zə-rĭz′əm) *n.* Military or imperial dictatorship; political authoritarianism. —**Cae′sar·ist** *n.* —**Cae′sar·is′tic** *adj.*

caesar salad *n.* A tossed salad of greens, anchovies, croutons, and grated cheese with a dressing of olive oil, lemon juice, and a raw or coddled egg. [Possibly after *Caesar's*, a restaurant in Tijuana, Mexico.]

cae·si·um (sē′zē-əm) *n.* Variant of **cesium**.

cae·su·ra also **ce·su·ra** (sĭ-zhŏŏr′ə, -zŏŏr′ə) *n., pl.* **-su·ras** or **-su·rae** (-zhŏŏr′ē, -zŏŏr′ē) **1.** A pause in a line of verse, esp. at a sense division. **2.** A pause or interruption, as in conversation. **3.** In Latin and Greek prosody, a word ending within a foot. **4.** *Music* A pause or breathing at a point of rhythmic division in a melody. [Lat. *caesūra*, a cutting < *caesus*, p. part. of *caedere*, to cut off.] —**cae·su′ral, cae·su′ric** *adj.*

ca·fé also **ca·fe** (kă-fā′, kə-) *n.* A coffeehouse, restaurant, or bar. [Fr., coffee, café < Ital. *caffè*, coffee < Ottoman Turk. *qahveh*. See COFFEE.]

ca·fé au lait (kă-fā′ ō lā′) *n.* **1.** Coffee served with hot milk. See Regional Note at **beignet**. **2.** A light coffee hue. [Fr. : *café*, coffee + *à*, with + *lait*, milk.]

café noir *n.* Coffee served without cream or milk. [Fr. : *café*, coffee + *noir*, black.]

caf·e·te·ri·a (kăf′ĭ-tîr′ē-ə) *n.* **1.** A restaurant in which the customers are served at a counter and carry their meals on trays to tables. **2.** A dining area, as at a school, where meals may be purchased or brought from home and eaten. [Sp. *cafeteria*, coffee shop, cafeteria < *café*, coffee < Ottoman Turk. *qahveh*. See COFFEE.]

caf·e·to·ri·um (kăf′ĭ-tôr′ē-əm, -tōr′-) *n., pl.* **-to·ri·ums** or **-to·ri·a** (-tôr′ē-ə, -tōr′-) A room, usu. in a school, doubling as cafeteria and auditorium. [CAFE(TERIA) + (AUDI)TORIUM.]

caf·feine also **caf·fein** (kă-fēn′, kăf′ēn′, kăf′ē-ĭn) *n.* A bitter white alkaloid, $C_8H_{10}N_4O_2$, often derived from tea or coffee and used in medicine chiefly as a mild stimulant. [Ger. *Kaffein* (< *Kaffee*, coffee) or Fr. *caféine*, both < Fr. *café*, coffee. See CAFÉ.] —**caf′fein·at′ed** (kăf′ə-nā′tĭd) *adj.*

caf·fe lat·te (kăf′ā lä′tā, käf·fā′ lät′tĕ) *n.* A strong espresso coffee topped with steamed frothed milk. [Ital. *caffè (e) latte*, coffee (and) milk.]

caf·tan or **kaf·tan** (kăf′tăn′, -tən, kăf-tăn′) *n.* **1.** A full-length garment with elbow-length or long sleeves, worn chiefly in eastern Mediterranean countries. **2.** A westernized version of this garment consisting of a loose, usu. brightly colored tunic. [Russ. *kaftan* < Ottoman Turk. *qaftān*.]

cage (kāj) *n.* **1.** A structure for confining animals, built in part with wires or bars. **2.** An enclosure for prisoners. **3.** An enclosing openwork structure. **4.** A skeletal support, as for a building; a framework. **5.** An elevator car. **6a.** *Baseball* A wire screen placed behind home plate to stop batting practice balls. **b.** *Sports* A goal, as in hockey or soccer, made of a net attached to a frame. ❖ *tr.v.* **caged, cag·ing, cag·es** To put in or as if in a cage. [ME < OFr. < Lat. *cavea*.]

Cage, John Milton, Jr. 1912–92. Amer. composer of avant-garde works, such as *Sonatas and Interludes* (1946–48).

cage·ling (kāj′lĭng) *n.* A bird kept as a pet in a cage.

ca·gey also **ca·gy** (kā′jē) *adj.* **-gi·er, -gi·est 1.** Wary; careful. **2.** Crafty; shrewd: *a cagey lawyer.* [?] —**ca′gi·ly** *adv.* —**ca′gi·ness** *n.*

Ca·glia·ri (käl′yə-rē′) A city of Sardinia, Italy, on the S coast on the **Gulf of Cagliari**, an inlet of the Mediterranean. Pop. 203,254.

Cag·ney (kăg′nē), **James** ("Jimmy") 1899–1986. Amer. actor whose films include *Public Enemy* (1931).

CAGS *abbr.* Certificate of Advanced Graduate Study

Ca·guas (kä′gwäs′) A city of E-central Puerto Rico SSE of San Juan. Pop. 88,680.

ca·hier (kä-yā′) *n.* A report, esp. on parliamentary matters. [Fr., notebook < OFr. *quaier* < VLat. *quaternum* < Lat. *quaternī*, foursome < *quater*, four times. See kʷetwer- in App.]

Ca·ho·ki·a (kə-hō′kē-ə) A village of SW IL, a suburb of East St. Louis near the **Cahokia Mounds**, a group of prehistoric earthworks. Pop. 16,391.

ca·hoots (kə-hōōts′) *pl.n. Informal* Questionable collaboration; secret partnership. [Perh. < Fr. *cahute*, cabin < OFr., poss. blend of *cabane*; see CABIN, and *hutte*; see HUT.]

ca·how (kə-hou′) *n.* An earth-burrowing nocturnal bird (*Pterodroma cahow*), once abundant in Bermuda but now nearly extinct. [Imit. of its cry.]

Ca·huil·la (kə-wē′ə) *n., pl.* **Cahuilla** or **-las 1.** A member of a Native American people inhabiting parts of southeast California. **2.** The Uto-Aztecan language of the Cahuilla. [Am.Sp.]

CAI *abbr.* computer-aided instruction

Cai·a·phas (kā′ə-fəs, kī′-), **Joseph** fl. 1st cent. A.D. Jewish high priest who presided over the counsel that condemned Jesus.

Cai·cos Islands (kā′kəs, -kōs) One of the island groups constituting the Turks and Caicos Is. in the Atlantic Ocean.

cai·man also **cay·man** (kā′mən) *n., pl.* **-mans** Any of various tropical American crocodilians of the genus *Caiman* and related genera, resembling and closely related to the alligators. [Sp. *caimán* < Carib *acayuman.*]

Cain (kān) The eldest son of Adam and Eve, who murdered his brother Abel and was condemned to be a fugitive.

–caine *suff.* A synthetic alkaloid anesthetic: *eucaine.* [< COCAINE.]

cai·no·to·pho·bi·a (kā-nō′tə-fō′bē-ə) *n.* An abnormal fear of newness. [Gk. *kainotēs,* newness (< *kainos,* new) + –PHOBIA.]

ca·ïque (kä-ēk′) *n.* **1.** A long narrow rowboat used in the Middle East. **2.** A small sailing vessel used in the eastern Mediterranean. [Fr. < Ital. *caicco* < Ottoman Turk. *qayïq* < O Turkic *qayghuq.*]

caird (kârd) *n. Scots* An itinerant tinker. [Sc. Gael. *ceard,* tinker, smith < OIr. *cerd,* artisan, skill.]

cairn (kârn) *n.* A mound of stones erected as a memorial or marker. [ME *carne* < Sc. Gael. *carn* < OIr.] —**cairned** *adj.*

cairn·gorm (kârn′gôrm′) *n.* See **smoky quartz.**

Cairngorm Mountains A range of the Grampian Mts. in central Scotland rising to 1,310.3 m (4,296 ft).

Cairn terrier (kârn) *n.* A small dog of a breed developed in Scotland, having a broad head and a rough shaggy coat.

Cai·ro (kī′rō) The cap. of Egypt, in the NE part on the Nile R. Old Cairo was built c. 642; the new city was founded c. 968. Pop. 6,663,000. —**Cai′rene** *adj. & n.*

cais·son (kā′sŏn′, -sən) *n.* **1.** A watertight structure within which construction work is carried on under water. **2.** See **camel** 2. **3.** A large open box designed to fit against the side of a ship and used to repair damaged hulls under water. **4.** A floating structure used to close off the entrance to a dock or canal lock. **5a.** A horse-drawn vehicle used to carry artillery ammunition and coffins at military funerals. **b.** A large box for ammunition. [Fr. < OFr., large box, alteration (influenced by *caisse,* chest) of *casson* < Ital. *cassone,* augmentative of *cassa,* box < Lat. *capsa.*]

caisson disease *n.* Decompression sickness.

Caith·ness (kāth′nĕs, kăth-nĕs′) A historical region and former county of NE Scotland; settled by the Picts.

cai·tiff (kā′tĭf) *n.* A despicable coward; a wretch. ❖ *adj.* Despicable and cowardly. [ME *caitif* < Norman Fr. < Lat. *captīvus,* prisoner. See CAPTIVE.]

Ca·ius (kā′əs, kī′-) See **Gaius.**

ca·jan pea (kā′jən) *n.* See **pigeon pea.** [Malay *kachang,* bean, pea.]

ca·jole (kə-jōl′) *tr.v.* **-joled, -jol·ing, -joles** To urge with gentle and repeated appeals, teasing, or flattery; wheedle. [Fr. *cajoler,* poss. blend of OFr. *cageoler,* to chatter like a jay (< *geai, jai,* jay; see JAY²) and OFr. *gaioler,* to lure into a cage (< *gaiole, jaiole,* cage; see JAIL).] —**ca·jol′er** *n.* —**ca·jol′er·y** (-jō′lə-rē) *n.*

Ca·jun also **Ca·jan** (kā′jən) *n.* **1.** A member of a group of people in southern Louisiana descended from French colonists exiled from Acadia in the 18th century. **2.** often **Cajan** A member of a group living in southern Alabama and southeast Mississippi, of mixed white, Black, and Native American ancestry. [Alteration of ACADIAN.] —**Ca′jun** *adj.*

cake (kāk) *n.* **1.** A sweet baked food made of flour, liquid, eggs, and other ingredients. **2.** A flat rounded mass of dough or batter that is baked or fried. **3.** A flat rounded mass of hashed or chopped food that is baked or fried; a patty. **4.** A shaped or molded piece, as of soap or ice. **5.** A layer or deposit of compacted matter. ❖ *v.* **caked, cak·ing, cakes** —*tr.* To cover or fill with a thick layer, as of compacted matter. —*intr.* To become formed into a compact or crusty mass. [ME < ON *kaka.*]

cake·walk (kāk′wôk′) *n.* **1.** Something easily accomplished. **2.** A 19th-century entertainment among African Americans in which walkers performing the most accomplished or amusing steps won cakes. —**cake′walk′er** *n.*

cal *abbr.* **1.** calorie (mean calorie) **2.** calorie (small calorie)

Cal *abbr.* calorie (large calorie)

cal. *abbr.* **1.** calendar **2.** caliber

Cal. *abbr.* California

Cal·a·bar bean (kăl′ə-bär) *n.* The poisonous seed of a tropical western African woody vine (*Physostigma venenosum*) in the pea family, which is the source of the drug physostigmine. [After *Calabar,* a town of southeast Nigeria.]

cal·a·bash (kăl′ə-băsh′) *n.* **1.** An annual vine (*Lagenaria siceraria*) having white flowers and smooth, large, hard-shelled gourds. **2.** A tropical American tree (*Crescentia cujete*) bearing hard-shelled, gourdlike fruits. **3.** Any of certain similar or related plants. **4.** The fruit of a calabash. **5.** A utensil or container made from a calabash shell. **6.** A smoking pipe with a large bowl made from a gourd. [Fr. *calebasse,* gourd < Sp. *calabaza* < Catalan *carabaça,* perh. < Ar. *qar'a yābisa,* dried gourd : *qar'a,* gourd + *yābisa,* fem. of *yābis,* dried, part. of *yabisa,* to become dry.]

cal·a·boose (kăl′ə-bōōs′) *n. Chiefly Southern & Western US* A jail. [Louisiana Fr. *calabouse* < Sp. *calabozo,* dungeon.]

Ca·la·bri·a (kə-lā′brē-ə, kä-lä′brē-ä) A region of S Italy forming the toe of the Italian "boot."

ca·la·di·um (kə-lā′dē-əm) *n.* Any of various tropical American plants of the genus *Caladium,* cultivated for their ornamental foliage. [NLat. *Caladium,* genus name < Malay *keladi,* an aroid.]

Ca·lah (kā′lə) also **Ka·lakh** (kā′läкн) An ancient city of Assyria on the Tigris R. S of present-day Mosul, Iraq; probably founded in the 13th cent. B.C.

Ca·lais (kă-lā′, kăl′ā) A city of N France on the Strait of Dover opposite Dover, England. Pop. 76,527.

cal·a·man·co (kăl′ə-măng′kō) *n., pl.* **-coes** A glossy woolen fabric with a checked pattern on one side. [Perh. < Sp. *calamaco* < LLat. *calamaucus,* felt cap.]

cal·a·man·der (kăl′ə-măn′dər) *n.* The hard, black-and-brown-striped wood of certain tropical Asian trees of the genus *Diospyros,* esp. *D. quaesita* of Sri Lanka. [Prob. < Du. *kalamanderhout,* calamander wood, perh. < alteration of COROMANDEL (COAST).]

cal·a·mar·i (kăl′ə-mär′ē, käl′ə-) *n.* Squid as food. [Ital., pl. of *calamaro* < LLat. *calamārium,* pen-case < Lat. *calamārius,* of a reed pen < *calamus,* reed pen (perh. < squid "ink"). See CALAMUS.]

ca·la·ma·ta olive (kä′lə-mä′tə, kăl′ə-) *n.* Variant of **kalamata olive.**

cal·a·mine (kăl′ə-mīn′, -mīn) *n.* **1.** See **hemimorphite. 2.** A pink, odorless, tasteless powder of zinc oxide with a small amount of ferric oxide, dissolved in mineral oils and used in skin lotions. **3.** An alloy composed of lead, tin, and zinc. [Fr. < Med.Lat. *calamīna,* alteration of Lat. *cadmīa.* See CADMIUM.]

cal·a·mint (kăl′ə-mĭnt′) *n.* Any of several plants of the genera *Calamintha* and *Satureja* in the mint family, cultivated for their aromatic foliage and flower clusters. [ME *calaminte* < OFr. *calamente* < Med.Lat. *calamentum* < Lat. *calaminthē* < Gk. *kalaminthē.*]

cal·a·mite (kăl′ə-mīt′) *n.* Any of various extinct, chiefly carboniferous trees of the genus *Calamites,* related to herbaceous horsetails (*Equisetum*). [NLat. *Calamītēs,* genus name < L.Gk. *kalamītēs,* reedlike < Gk. *kalamos,* reed.]

ca·lam·i·tous (kə-lăm′ĭ-təs) *adj.* Causing or involving calamity. —**ca·lam′i·tous·ly** *adv.* —**ca·lam′i·tous·ness** *n.*

ca·lam·i·ty (kə-lăm′ĭ-tē) *n., pl.* **-ties 1.** An event that brings terrible loss, lasting distress, or severe affliction; a disaster. **2.** Dire distress due to loss or tragedy. [ME *calamite* < OFr. < Lat. *calamitās.*]

Calamity Jane See Martha Jane **Burk.**

cal·a·mon·din (kăl′ə-mŏn′dĭn) *n.* **1.** A small evergreen citrus tree (×*Citrofortunella mitis*) having glossy foliage and ornamental fruits. **2.** Its sour fruit. [Tagalog *kalamunding.*]

cal·a·mus (kăl′ə-məs) *n., pl.* **-mi** (-mī′) **1a.** See **sweet flag. b.** The aromatic underground stem of the sweet flag, yielding an oil used in perfumery. **2.** Any of various chiefly tropical Asian climbing palms of the genus *Calamus,* having strong flexible stems used as a source of rattan. **3.** See **quill** 1. [Lat., reed < Gk. *kalamos.*]

ca·lan·do (kə-län′dō) *adv. & adj. Music* With a gradual decrease in volume and often tempo. [Ital., pr. part. of *calare,* to slacken < Lat. *calāre* < Gk. *khalān.*]

ca·lash (kə-lăsh′) also **ca·lèche** (-lĕsh′) *n.* **1a.** A light carriage with low wheels and a collapsible top. **b.** A top for this or a similar carriage. **2.** A woman's folding bonnet of the late 18th century. [Fr. *calèche* < Ger. *Kalesche* < Czech *kolesa* < pl. of *kolo,* wheel < O Church Slavonic. See kʷel- in App.]

cal·a·thus (kăl′ə-thəs) *n., pl.* **-thi** (-thī′) A vase-shaped basket represented in Greek art. [Lat. < Gk. *kalathos.*]

calc- *pref.* Variant of **calci-.**

cal·ca·ne·us (kăl-kā′nē-əs) also **cal·ca·ne·um** (-nē-əm) *n., pl.* **-ne·i** (-nē-ī′) also **-ne·a** (-nē-ə) The quadrangular bone at the back of the tarsus that forms the bony protuberance of the heel. [LLat. *calcāneus,* heel < Lat. *calcāneum* < *calx, calc-.*] —**cal·ca′ne·al** *adj.*

cal·car¹ (kăl′kär′) *n., pl.* **cal·car·i·a** (kăl-kâr′ē-ə) A spur or spurlike projection, as on the wing or leg of a bird. [Lat., spur < *calx, calc-,* heel.]

cal·car² (kăl′kär′) *n.* A furnace formerly used in glassmaking for calcination of materials into frit. [Ital. *calcara* < LLat. *calcāria* (*fornax*), lime(-kiln) < Lat., fem. of *calcārius,* of lime. See CALCAREOUS.]

cal·car·e·ous (kăl-kâr′ē-əs) *adj.* Composed of, containing, or characteristic of calcium carbonate, calcium, or limestone; chalky. [< Lat. *calcārius* < *calx, calc-,* lime. See CALX.] —**cal·car′e·ous·ly** *adv.*

cal·ced·o·ny (kăl-sĕd′n-ē) *n.* Variant of **chalcedony.**

cal·ce·o·lar·i·a (kăl′sē-ə-lâr′ē-ə) *n.* Any of various plants of the genus *Calceolaria,* native from Mexico to South America and having speckled, slipper-shaped flowers. [NLat. *Calceolāria,* genus name < Lat. *calceolus,* small shoe. See CALCEOLATE.]

cal·ce·o·late (kăl′sē-ə-lāt′) *adj.* Shaped like a slipper, as the pouchlike petal of the flower of the lady's slipper. [< Lat. *calceolus,* dim. of *calceus,* shoe < *calx, calc-,* heel.]

cal·ces (kăl′sēz′) *n.* A plural of **calx.**

calci– or **calc–** *pref.* Calcium; calcium salt; lime: *calciferous.* [< Lat. *calx, calc-,* lime. See CALX.]

cal·cic (kăl′sĭk) *adj.* Composed of, containing, derived from, or

cairn
the Nire Valley,
Waterford, Ireland

ă	pat	oi	boy
ā	pay	ou	out
âr	care	ŏŏ	took
ä	father	ōō	boot
ĕ	pet	ŭ	cut
ē	be	ûr	urge
ĭ	pit	th	thin
ī	pie	th	this
îr	pier	hw	which
ŏ	pot	zh	vision
ō	toe	ə	about,
ô	paw		item

Stress marks:
′ (primary);
′ (secondary); as in
lexicon (lĕk′sĭ-kŏn′)

relating to calcium or lime.

cal·ci·cole (kăl′sĭ-kōl′) *n.* A plant that thrives in soil rich in lime. [Fr. : *calci-*, calcium (< Lat. *calx, calc-*, lime; see CALX) + *-cole*, -dwelling (< Lat. *-cola*; see -COLOUS).] —**cal·cic′o·lous** (-sĭk′ə-ləs) *adj.*

cal·cif·er·ol (kăl-sĭf′ə-rôl′, -rōl′, -rŏl′) *n.* See **vitamin D₂**. [CALCIFER(OUS) + -OL¹.]

cal·cif·er·ous (kăl-sĭf′ər-əs) *adj.* Of, forming, or containing calcium or calcium carbonate.

cal·cif·ic (kăl-sĭf′ĭk) *adj.* Producing salts of lime.

cal·ci·fi·ca·tion (kăl′sə-fĭ-kā′shən) *n.* **1a.** Impregnation with calcium or calcium salts, as with calcium carbonate. **b.** Hardening, as of tissue, by such impregnation. **2.** A calcified substance or part. **3.** An inflexible, unchanging state.

cal·ci·fuge (kăl′sə-fyōōj′) *n.* A plant that does not grow well in lime-rich soil. —**cal·cif′u·gal** (-sĭf′yə-gəl), **cal·cif′u·gous** (-yə-gəs) *adj.*

cal·ci·fy (kăl′sə-fī′) *tr. & intr.v.* **-fied, -fy·ing, -fies** **1.** To make or become stony or chalky by deposition of calcium salts. **2.** To make or become inflexible and unchanging.

cal·ci·mine also **kal·so·mine** (kăl′sə-mīn′) *n.* A white or tinted liquid containing zinc oxide, water, and glue, used as a wash for walls and ceilings. [Orig. a trademark.] —**cal′ci·mine′** *v.*

cal·cine (kăl-sīn′, kăl′sīn′) *v.* **-cined, -cin·ing, -cines** —*tr.* To heat (a substance) to a high temperature but below the melting or fusing point, causing loss of moisture, reduction or oxidation, and the decomposition of carbonates and other compounds. —*intr.* To undergo calcination. [ME *calcinen* < OFr. *calciner* < Med.Lat. *calcīnāre* < LLat. *calcīna*, quicklime < Lat. *calx, calc-*, lime. See CALX.] —**cal′ci·na′tion** (-sə-nā′shən) *n.*

cal·ci·no·sis (kăl′sə-nō′sĭs) *n.* An abnormal condition in which calcium salts are deposited in a part or tissue of the body. [CALC(I)– (influenced by CALCINE) + -OSIS.]

cal·cite (kăl′sīt′) *n.* A common crystalline form of natural calcium carbonate, CaCO₃, that is the basic constituent of limestone, marble, and chalk. —**cal·cit′ic** (-sĭt′ĭk) *adj.*

cal·ci·to·nin (kăl′sĭ-tō′nĭn) *n.* A peptide hormone that lowers plasma calcium and phosphate levels without augmenting calcium accretion. [CALCI– + TON(E) + -IN.]

cal·ci·um (kăl′sē-əm) *n. Symbol* **Ca** A soft metallic element that is a basic component of animals and plants and constitutes approx. 3 percent of Earth's crust. It occurs naturally in limestone, gypsum, and fluorite. Atomic number 20; atomic weight 40.08; melting point 842 to 848°C; boiling point 1,487°C; specific gravity 1.55; valence 2. See table at **element**. [Lat. *calx, calc-*, lime; see CALX + -IUM.]

calcium carbide *n.* A crystalline compound, CaC₂, obtained by heating pulverized limestone or quicklime with carbon and used to generate acetylene gas.

calcium carbonate *n.* A crystalline compound, CaCO₃, occurring naturally as chalk, limestone, marble, and other forms and used in commercial chalk, medicines, and dentifrices.

calcium chloride *n.* A deliquescent compound, CaCl₂, used as a drying agent, refrigerant, and deicer and to control dust.

calcium cyanamide *n.* A gray-black compound, CaCN₂, used as a fertilizer.

calcium cyclamate *n.* An artificial salt of cyclamic acid, C₁₂H₂₄O₆N₂S₂Ca₂H₂O, formerly used as a low-calorie sweetener.

calcium fluoride *n.* A colorless powder, CaF₂, used in emery wheels, carbon electrodes, and cements.

calcium hydroxide *n.* A soft white powder, Ca(OH)₂, used in making mortar cements, paints, and petrochemicals.

calcium hypochlorite *n.* A crystalline solid, Ca(OCl)₂·4H₂O, used as a bactericide, fungicide, and bleaching agent.

calcium light *n.* See **limelight** 2.

calcium oxide *n.* A caustic lumpy powder, CaO, used as a flux, in manufacturing steel and paper, and in glassmaking.

calcium phosphate *n.* **1.** A deliquescent powder, Ca(H₂PO₄)₂, used in baking powders and as a plant food. **2.** A crystalline powder, CaHPO₄, used in animal feed, glass, and toothpaste. **3.** An amorphous powder, Ca₃(PO₄)₂, used in fertilizers and as a nutritional supplement.

calc·spar or **calc-spar** (kălk′spär′) *n.* See **calcite**. [Partial transl. of Swed. *kalkspat* : *kalk*, lime (< OSwed. *kalker* < MLGer. *kalk* < Lat. *calx, calc-*, lime; see CALX) + *spat*, spar (mineral).]

cal·cu·la·ble (kăl′kyə-lə-bəl) *adj.* **1.** That can be calculated or estimated: *calculable odds.* **2.** Readily relied on; dependable: *a calculable assistant.* —**cal′cu·la·bil′i·ty** *n.*

cal·cu·late (kăl′kyə-lāt′) *v.* **-lat·ed, -lat·ing, -lates** —*tr.* **1.** To ascertain by computation; reckon. **2.** To make an estimate of; evaluate. **3.** To make for a deliberate purpose; design. **4.** also **cal′late** (kăl′āt′, -lāt′) *Chiefly New England* **a.** To suppose: *"I cal'late she's a right smart cook"* (Dialect Notes). **b.** To plan, intend, or count on. —*intr.* **1.** To perform a mathematical process; figure. **2.** To predict consequences. **3.** *Chiefly New England* **a.** To suppose; guess. **b.** To count, depend, or rely on someone or something. [LLat. *calculāre, calculāt-* < Lat. *calculus*, small stone used in reckoning, dim. of *calx, calc-*, small stone for gaming. See CALX.] —**cal′cu·la′tive** *adj.*

cal·cu·lat·ed (kăl′kyə-lā′tĭd) *adj.* **1.** Determined by mathematical calculation. **2.** Undertaken after careful estimation of the

likely outcome. **3.** Made or planned to accomplish a certain purpose; deliberate: *insincere, calculated modesty.* **4.** Likely; apt. —**cal′cu·lat′ed·ly** *adv.*

cal·cu·lat·ing (kăl′kyə-lā′tĭng) *adj.* **1.** Capable of performing calculations: *a calculating machine.* **2a.** Shrewd; crafty. **b.** Coldly scheming or conniving. —**cal′cu·lat′ing·ly** *adv.*

cal·cu·la·tion (kăl′kyə-lā′shən) *n.* **1a.** The act, process, or result of calculating. **b.** An estimate based on probabilities. **2.** Careful, often cunning estimation and planning of outcomes, esp. to advance one's own interests.

cal·cu·la·tor (kăl′kyə-lā′tər) *n.* **1.** One that calculates, as: **a.** An electronic or mechanical device for the performance of mathematical computations. **b.** A person who operates such a machine or otherwise makes calculations. **2.** A set of mathematical tables used to aid in calculating.

cal·cu·lous (kăl′kyə-ləs) *adj.* Relating to, caused by, or having a calculus or calculi.

cal·cu·lus (kăl′kyə-ləs) *n., pl.* **-li** (-lī′) or **-lus·es** **1.** *Pathology* An abnormal concretion in the body, usu. formed of mineral salts, as in the kidney. **2.** *Dentistry* See **tartar** 1. **3.** *Mathematics* **a.** The branch of mathematics that deals with limits and the differentiation and integration of functions of one or more variables. **b.** A method of analysis or calculation using a special symbolic notation. **4.** A system or method of calculation. [Lat., small stone used in reckoning. See CALCULATE.]

calculus of variations *n.* The study of maxima and minima of definite integrals whose integrands are functions of independent variables and dependent variables and their derivatives.

Cal·cut·ta (kăl-kŭt′ə) A city of E India on the Hugli R. in the Ganges delta; founded c. 1690. Pop. 4,399,819.

Cal·der (kôl′dər, kŏl′-), **Alexander** 1898–1976. Amer. sculptor who created the mobile in Paris in the early 1930s.

cal·de·ra (kăl-dâr′ə, -dîr′ə, kăl-) *n.* A large crater formed by volcanic explosion or by collapse of a volcanic cone. [Sp., cauldron, caldera < LLat. *caldāria*. See CAULDRON.]

Cal·de·rón de la Bar·ca (kăl′də-rōn′ dä lä bär′kə, käl′thĕ-rōn′ thĕ lä bär′kä), **Pedro** 1600–81. Spanish playwright whose plays include *Life Is a Dream* (1635).

cal·dron (kôl′drən) *n.* Variant of **cauldron**.

Cald·well (kôld′wĕl′, -wəl, kŏld′-), **Erskine Preston** 1903–87. Amer. writer best known for *Tobacco Road* (1932).

Caldwell, Sarah b. 1928. Amer. conductor and opera producer noted for her staging of classical and modern works.

ca·lèche (kə-lĕsh′) *n.* Variant of **calash**.

Cal·e·do·ni·a (kăl′ĭ-dō′nē-ə, -dōn′yə) **1.** Roman Britain N of the Antonine Wall, stretching from the Firth of Forth to the Firth of Clyde. **2.** Scotland. —**Cal′e·do′ni·an** *adj. & n.*

Caledonian Canal A waterway, c. 97 km (60 mi), of N Scotland from Loch Linnhe to Moray Firth.

cal·en·dar (kăl′ən-dər) *n.* **1.** Any of various systems of reckoning time in which the beginning, length, and divisions of a year are defined. See table on page 6. **2.** A table of the months, weeks, and days in at least one year. **3.** A schedule of events. **4.** An ordered list of matters to be considered. **5.** *Chiefly British* A university catalog. ❖ *tr.v.* **-dared, -dar·ing, -dars** To enter in a calendar; schedule. [ME *calender* < OFr. *calendier* < LLat. *kalendārium* < Lat., account book < *kalendae*, calends (interest being due on the calends). See kelə- in App.]

calendar month *n.* See **month** 2.

calendar year *n.* See **year** 1a.

cal·en·der (kăl′ən-dər) *n.* A machine in which paper or cloth is made smooth and glossy by being pressed through rollers. ❖ *tr.v.* **-dered, -der·ing, -ders** To press (paper or cloth) in such a machine. [Fr. *calandre* < VLat. **colendra*, alteration (poss. influenced by CYLINDER) of Lat. *cylindrus*, roller; see CYLINDER.] —**cal′en·der·er** *n.*

ca·len·dri·cal (kə-lĕn′drĭ-kəl) also **ca·len·dric** (-drĭk) *adj.* Of, relating to, or used in a calendar.

cal·ends also **kal·ends** (kăl′əndz, kā′ləndz) *n., pl.* **calends** also **kalends** The day of the new moon and the first day of the month in the ancient Roman calendar. [ME *kalendes* < Lat. *kalendae*. See kelə- in App.] —**ca·len′dal** (kə-lĕn′dəl) *adj.*

ca·len·du·la (kə-lĕn′jə-lə) *n.* A Mediterranean annual plant (*Calendula officinalis*) in the composite family, cultivated for its yellow or orange, rayed flower heads. [Med.Lat., marigold < Lat. *kalendae*, calends. See CALENDS.]

cal·en·ture (kăl′ən-choor′) *n.* A tropical fever once attributed to heat. [Sp. *calentura* < *calentar*, to heat < Lat. *calēns, calent-*, pr. part. of *calēre*, to be warm.]

calf¹ (kăf, käf) *n., pl.* **calves** (kăvz, kävz) **1a.** A young cow or bull. **b.** The young of certain other mammals, such as the elephant or whale. **2.** Calfskin leather. **3.** A large floating chunk of ice split off from a glacier, iceberg, or floe. **4.** An awkward, callow youth. [ME < OE *cealf*.]

calf² (kăf, käf) *n., pl.* **calves** (kăvz, kävz) The muscular back part of the human leg between the knee and ankle. [ME < ON *kálfi*; poss. akin to CALF¹ (< its shape).]

calf·skin (kăf′skĭn′, käf′-) *n.* **1.** The hide of a calf. **2.** Fine leather made from the hide of a calf.

Cal·ga·ry (kăl′gə-rē) A city of S Alberta, Canada, S of Edmonton; site of the annual Calgary Stampede, dating from 1912. Pop.

Sarah Caldwell

The Gregorian calendar is now in use as the civil calendar throughout most of the world. The Jewish calendar is the official calendar of the Jewish religious community. The Islamic calendar is the official calendar in many Muslim countries. Each calendar listed below begins with the first month of the year and includes the number of days each month contains. Many months have a variable number of days, as described below.

GREGORIAN		JEWISH			ISLAMIC		
The Gregorian calendar, introduced in 1582 by Pope Gregory XIII, is a corrected form of the Julian calendar. It is based on a solar year of 365 days. Every fourth year is a leap year of 366 days except for centenary years not evenly divisible by 400.		The Jewish calendar is based on both the solar and lunar cycles. The lunar year of 354 days is adjusted to the solar year with the intercalary month Adar Sheni in leap years. This ensures that the major religious festivals fall in their proper season.			The Islamic calendar is based on the lunar year and contains 354 or 355 days. The number of days in each month varies with the lunar cycle. The beginning of the year retrogresses through the solar year, completing a full cycle every 32.5 years.		
Months	**Number of Days**	**Months**		**Number of Days**	**Months**	**Number of Days**	
January	31	Tishri	(Sep-Oct)	30	Muharram	29 or 30	
February	28 or 29	Heshvan	(Oct-Nov)	29 or 30	Safar	29 or 30	
March	31	Kislev	(Nov-Dec)	29 or 30	Rabi I	29 or 30	
April	30	Tevet	(Dec-Jan)	30	Rabi II	29 or 30	
May	31	Shevat	(Jan-Feb)	30	Jumada I	29 or 30	
June	30	Adar	(Feb-Mar)	29 or 30	Jumada II	29 or 30	
July	31	Adar Sheni	(leap year only)	29	Rajab	29 or 30	
August	31	Nisan	(Mar-Apr)	30	Sha'ban	29 or 30	
September	30	Iyar	(Apr-May)	29	Ramadan	29 or 30	
October	31	Sivan	(May-Jun)	30	Shawwal	29 or 30	
November	30	Tammuz	(Jun-Jul)	29	Dhu'l-Qa'dah	29 or 30	
December	31	Av	(Jul-Aug)	30	Dhu'l-Hijjah	29 or 30	
		Elul	(Aug-Sep)	29			

calico
a calico cat

768,082. —**Cal·gar′i·an** (-gâr′ē-ən, -gär′-) *n.*
Cal·houn (kăl-hōōn′), John Caldwell 1782–1850. Vice President of the US (1825–32) who maintained that states had the right to nullify federal legislation.
Ca·li (kä′lē) A city of W Colombia on the **Cali River** SW of Bogotá; founded 1536. Pop. 1,369,331.
Cal·i·ban (kăl′ə-băn′) *n.* The satellite of Uranus that is 16th in distance from the planet. [After *Caliban*, the slave in *The Tempest* by William Shakespeare.]
cal·i·ber (kăl′ə-bər) *n.* **1a.** The diameter of the inside of a cylinder. **b.** The diameter of the bore of a firearm, usu. in hundredths or thousandths of an inch and written as a decimal fraction. **c.** The diameter of a large projectile in millimeters or inches. **2.** Degree of worth; quality. [Fr. *calibre* < Ital. *calibro* < Ar. *qālib, qālab,* mold, shoe tree < Gk. *kălapous,* shoemaker's last : *kălon,* wood + *pous,* foot; see **ped-** in App.]
cal·i·brate (kăl′ə-brāt′) *tr.v.* **-brat·ed, -brat·ing, -brates 1.** To check, adjust, or determine the graduations of (a quantitative measuring instrument). **2.** To determine the caliber of (a tube). **3.** To correct; adjust. —**cal′i·bra′tor** *n.*
cal·i·bra·tion (kăl′ə-brā′shən) *n.* **1.** The act or process of calibrating; the state of being calibrated. **2.** Gradations showing positions or values. Often used in the plural.
cal·i·bre (kăl′ə-bər) *n. Chiefly British* Variant of **caliber.**
ca·li·ces (kā′lĭ-sēz′, kăl′ĭ-) *n.* Plural of **calix.**
ca·li·che (kə-lē′chē) *n.* **1a.** A crude sodium nitrate occurring naturally in Chile, Peru, and the southwest United States, used as fertilizer. **b.** See **sodium nitrate. 2.** See **hardpan** 1. [Am.Sp. < Sp., pebble in a brick, flake of lime < *cal,* lime < Lat. *calx, calc-,* lime. See CALX.]
cal·i·co (kăl′ĭ-kō′) *n., pl.* **-coes** or **-cos 1a.** A coarse, brightly printed cloth. **b.** *Chiefly British* A white cotton cloth, heavier than muslin. **2.** An animal with a mottled coat in white tones with red and black. [After CALICUT.] —**cal′i·co** *adj.*
cal·i·co·back (kăl′ĭ-kō-băk′) *n.* See **harlequin bug.**
calico bass *n.* See **black crappie.** [< its colored spots.]
calico bush *n.* See **mountain laurel.**
Cal·i·cut (kăl′ĭ-kŭt′) also **Ko·zhi·kode** (kō′zhĭ-kōd′) A city of SW India on the Malabar Coast SW of Bangalore; site of Vasco da Gama's first landfall in India (1498). Pop. 419,831.
ca·lif (kā′lĭf, kăl′ĭf) *n.* Variant of **caliph.**
Calif. *abbr.* California
Cal·i·for·nia (kăl′ĭ-fôr′nyə, -fôr′nē-ə) A state of the W US on the Pacific Ocean; admitted as the 31st state in 1850. The area was colonized by the Spanish and formally ceded to the US in 1848. Cap. Sacramento. Pop. 33,871,648. —**Cal′i·for′nian** *adj. & n.*
California, Gulf of An arm of the Pacific Ocean in NW Mexico separating Baja California from the mainland.
California condor *n.* A very large vulture (*Gymnogyps*

californianus) that is nearly extinct.
California laurel *n.* An aromatic evergreen tree (*Umbellularia californica*) native to California and southern Oregon and having clusters of yellowish-green flowers, olivelike fruits, and light brown wood.
California pepper tree *n.* See **pepper tree.**
California poppy *n.* An herb(*Eschscholzia californica*) native to western North America and having finely divided leaves and showy, often orange or yellow flowers.
cal·i·for·ni·um (kăl′ə-fôr′nē-əm) *n. Symbol* **Cf** A synthetic radioactive element produced in trace quantities by neutron bombardment of curium. Atomic number 98; mass numbers 244 to 254; half-lives varying from 25 minutes to 800 years. See table at **element.** [After CALIFORNIA.]
ca·lig·i·nous (kə-lĭj′ə-nəs) *adj.* Dark, misty, and gloomy. [< Lat. *cālīginōsus* < *cālīgō, cālīgin-,* darkness.]
Ca·lig·u·la (kə-lĭg′yə-lə) Orig. Gaius Claudius Caesar Germanicus. A.D. 12–41. Emperor of Rome (37–41) who succeeded his adoptive father, Tiberius.
Ca·li·na·go (kăl′ĭ-nä′gō, kä′lĭ-) *n., pl.* **Calinago** or **-gos 1.** A member of a Caribbean Indian people inhabiting the Lesser Antilles. **2.** The language of the Calinago. [Sp. *calinago,* alteration of *karinako* < Carib *kari'na-ko,* Caribs : *kari'na,* Carib + *-ko,* var. of *-koŋ,* pl. suff.]
cal·i·per also **cal·li·per** (kăl′ə-pər) *n.* **1.** An instrument consisting of two curved hinged legs, used to measure thickness and distances. Often used in the plural. **2.** A large instrument with a fixed and a movable arm, used to measure diameters. **3.** A vernier caliper. [Alteration of CALIBER.] —**cal′i·per** *v.*
ca·liph also **ca·lif** or **kha·lif** (kā′lĭf, kăl′ĭf) *n.* A leader of an Islamic polity, by tradition always male. [ME *calife* < OFr. < Ar. *ḥalīfa,* successor (to Muhammad), (caliph < *ḥalafa,* to succeed.]
ca·liph·ate (kā′lĭ-fāt′, -fĭt, kăl′ĭ-) *n.* The office or jurisdiction of a caliph. The last caliphate was abolished in Turkey in 1924.
cal·is·then·ics (kăl′ĭs-thĕn′ĭks) *n.* **1.** (*used with a pl. verb*) Gymnastic exercises designed to develop muscular tone and promote physical well-being. **2.** (*used with a sing. verb*) The practice or art of such exercises. [< Gk. *kalli-,* beautiful (< *kallos,* beauty) + *sthenos,* strength; see **segh-** in App.] —**cal′is·then′ic** *adj.*
ca·lix (kā′lĭks, kăl′ĭks) *n., pl.* **ca·li·ces** (kā′lĭ-sēz′, kăl′ĭ-) *Ecclesiastical* A chalice. [Lat. *calix, calic-,* cup.]
Ca·lix·tus III (kə-lĭk′stəs) or **Cal·lis·tus III** (-lĭs′təs) Orig. Alfonso Borgia. 1378–1458. Pope (1455–58) whose nepotism empowered the Borgia family in Italy.
calk[1] (kôk) *n.* **1.** A pointed extension on a horseshoe to prevent slipping. **2.** A similar extension on the toe or heel of a shoe. [Prob. back-formation < obsolete *calkin* < ME *kakun,* poss. < MDu. *kalkoen,* hoof, or < OFr. *calcain,* heel < Lat. *calcāneum,* heel bone. See CALCANEUS.] —**calk** *v.*

California condor
Gymnogyps californianus

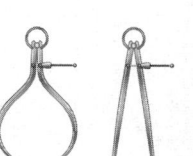

caliper
left to right: spring and
inside calipers

ă	pat	oi	boy
ā	pay	ou	out
âr	care	ŏŏ	took
ä	father	ōō	boot
ĕ	pet	ŭ	cut
ē	be	ûr	urge
ĭ	pit	th	thin
ī	pie	th	this
îr	pier	hw	which
ŏ	pot	zh	vision
ō	toe	ə	about,
ô	paw		item

Stress marks:
′ (primary);
′ (secondary), as in
lexicon (lĕk′sĭ-kŏn′)

calk² (kôk) *v.* Variant of **caulk.**

call (kôl) *v.* **called, call·ing, calls** —*tr.* **1.** To say in a loud voice; announce. **2.** To demand or ask for the presence of. **3.** To demand or ask for a meeting of; convene or convoke. **4.** To order or request to undertake a particular activity or work; summon: *called for jury duty.* **5.** To give the command for; order: *call a halt.* **6a.** To communicate or try to communicate with by telephone. **b.** To dial (a telephone number). **7.** To lure (prey) by imitating the characteristic cry of an animal. **8.** To cause to come to the mind or to attention. **9.** To name. **10.** To regard as being of a particular type; characterize: *Let's call it a draw.* **11.** To designate; label. **12a.** To demand payment of: *call a loan.* **b.** To require the presentation of (a bond) for redemption before maturity. **c.** To force the sale of (a stock or commodity) by exercising a call option. **13.** *Sports* **a.** To stop or postpone (a game) because of bad weather or other adverse conditions. **b.** To declare in the capacity of an umpire or referee. **c.** To indicate a decision in regard to: *called a close play.* **d.** To give the orders or signals for. **14.** *Games* **a.** To describe the intended outcome of (one's billiard shot) before playing. **b.** To equal the bet of (the preceding bet or bettor) in poker. **15.** To indicate or characterize accurately in advance; predict. **16.** To challenge the truthfulness or genuineness of: *called her on that.* **17.** To shout directions in rhythm for (a square dance). —*intr.* **1a.** To speak loudly; shout. **b.** To utter a characteristic cry. Used of an animal. **2.** To communicate or try to communicate with someone by telephone. **3.** To pay a short visit. ❖ *n.* **1.** A loud cry; a shout. **2a.** The characteristic cry of an animal. **b.** A sound or an instrument made to imitate such a cry, used as a lure. **3.** A telephone communication or connection. **4.** Need or occasion: *call for an apology.* **5.** A claim on a person's time or life. **6.** A short visit, esp. a formal one. **7.** A summons or invitation. **8.** A signal, such as that made by a horn. **9a.** A strong inner urge or prompting; a vocation. **b.** Strong attraction or appeal. **10.** A roll call. **11.** A notice of rehearsal times posted in a theater. **12.** *Sports* A decision made by an umpire or a referee. **13.** A direction or series of directions rhythmically called out to square dancers. **14a.** A demand for payment of a debt. **b.** A demand to submit bonds to the issuer for redemption before maturity. **c.** An option to buy a certain quantity of a stock or commodity for a specified price within a specified time. **d.** A demand for payment due on stock bought on margin when the value has shrunk. —*phrasal verbs:* **call back 1.** To communicate the need for (someone) to return from one situation or location to a previous one. **2.** To telephone or radio (a person) who has called previously. **3.** To recall (a defective product) for repair. **call down 1.** To find fault with; reprimand. **2.** To invoke, as from heaven. **call for 1.** To appear, as on someone else's premises, in order to get. **2.** To be an appropriate occasion for. **3.** To require; demand. **call forth** To evoke; elicit. **call in 1.** To take out of circulation: *calling in silver dollars.* **2.** To summon for assistance or consultation. **3.** To communicate with another by telephone. **call off 1.** To cancel or postpone. **2.** To restrain or recall. **call out 1.** To cause to assemble; summon. **2.** To challenge to a duel. **call up 1.** To summon to active military service. **2.** To cause one to remember; bring to mind. **3.** To bring forth for action or discussion; raise. **call upon 1.** To order or require (a person). **2.** To make a demand or a series of demands on. —*idioms:* **call a spade a spade** To speak precisely and forthrightly. **call it a day** *Informal* To stop whatever one has been doing. **call it quits** *Informal* To stop working or trying; quit. **call the shots** (or **tune**) *Informal* To exercise authority; be in charge. **on call 1.** Available when summoned for service or use. **2.** Subject to payment on demand. **within call** Close enough to come if summoned. [ME *callen,* prob. < ON *kalla.*]

cal·la (kăl′ə) *n.* **1.** A calla lily. **2.** A marsh plant *(Calla palustris)* of the North Temperate Zone having small, densely clustered flowers in a spreading white spathe. [NLat. *Calla,* genus name < Gk. *kallaia,* wattle of a cock, perh. < *kallos,* beauty.]

calla lily

Cal·la·ghan (kăl′ə-hən, -hăn′), **(Leonard) James** b. 1912. British politician who served as prime minister (1976–79).

calla lily *n.* Any of several southern African plants of the genus *Zantedeschia,* having white, yellow, pink, or purple spathes.

cal·la·loo (kăl′ə-lōō′, kăl′ə-lōō′) *n.* **1.** The edible spinachlike leaves of the dasheen. **2.** A soup or stew made of these leaves or other greens, okra, crabmeat, and seasonings. [Am.Sp. *calulú,* plant whose leaves are used as greens, perh. < Tupi *caárurú,* thick leaf.]

call-and-re·sponse or **call and response** (kôl′ənd-rĭ-spŏns′) *n.* A style of singing in which the melody sung by one singer is responded to or echoed by another or others. —**call′-and-re·sponse′** *adj.*

Cal·la·o (kə-yä′ō, kä-you′) A city of W-central Peru on the Pacific Ocean near Lima; founded 1537. Pop. 515,200.

Cal·las (kăl′əs, käl′əs), **Maria** Orig. Maria Anna Sophia Cecilia Kalogeropoulos. 1923–77. Amer. coloratura soprano known for her dramatic intensity.

cal′late (kăl′āt′, -lāt′) *v. Chiefly New England* Variant of **calculate** 4.

call·back (kôl′băk′) *n.* **1.** The act or an instance of calling back from one location or situation to the previous one. **2.** A return telephone or radio call. **3.** A recall of a product by the manufacturer to correct a defect.

call·board (kôl′bôrd′, -bōrd′) *n.* A bulletin board backstage in a theater for posting instructions and notices.

call box *n.* **1.** A roadside telephone used for reporting motorists' emergencies. **2.** *Chiefly British* A public telephone booth.

call·boy (kôl′boi′) *n.* **1.** One who prompts performers to go on stage. **2.** A bellhop. **3.** A male prostitute hired by telephone.

called strike *n. Baseball* A pitch judged by the umpire to be a strike and not swung at by the batter.

call·er¹ (kô′lər) *n.* **1.** One that calls, esp. a party placing a telephone call. **2.** A person paying a short social visit. **3.** A person who calls out numbers or directions, as at bingo.

cal·ler² (kăl′ər) *adj. Scots* **1.** Fresh. **2.** Cool and refreshing. [ME *calour,* alteration of *calver.*]

call·er ID (kô′lər) *n.* A telephone service that displays the name and telephone number of a caller as the call is being received.

call forwarding *n.* A telephone service that automatically reroutes incoming calls to another extension.

call girl *n.* A female prostitute hired by telephone.

cal·lig·ra·phy (kə-lĭg′rə-fē) *n.* **1a.** The art of fine handwriting. **b.** Works in fine handwriting considered as a group. **2.** Handwriting. [Fr. *calligraphie* < Gk. *kalligraphiā,* beautiful writing : *kalli-,* beautiful (< *kallos,* beauty) + *-graphiā,* -graphy.] —**cal·lig′ra·pher, cal·lig′ra·phist** *n.* —**cal′li·graph′ic** (kăl′ĭ-grăf′ĭk) *adj.*

Cal·lim·a·chus¹ (kə-lĭm′ə-kəs) 5th cent. B.C. Greek sculptor who reputedly designed the Corinthian column.

Cal·lim·a·chus² (kə-lĭm′ə-kəs) 3rd cent. B.C. Greek poet and scholar whose extant works include 64 epigrams.

call-in (kôl′ĭn′) *adj.* Being in a format such that listeners or viewers of a show are invited to have their telephone calls broadcast to other listeners. ❖ *n.* **1.** A viewer or listener's telephone call to such a show. **2.** One making such a call.

call·ing (kô′lĭng) *n.* **1.** An inner urge or a strong impulse, esp. one believed to be divinely inspired. **2.** An occupation, profession, or career.

calling card *n.* **1.** An engraved card bearing one's full name. **2.** See **phone card.**

cal·li·o·pe (kə-lī′ə-pē′, kăl′ē-ōp′) *n.* A musical instrument fitted with steam whistles, played by a keyboard. [< CALLIOPE.]

Cal·li·o·pe (kə-lī′ə-pē′) *n. Greek Mythology* The Muse of epic poetry. [Lat. *Calliopē* < Gk. *Kalliopē* : *kalli-,* beautiful (< *kallos,* beauty) + *ops, op-,* voice; see wekʷ- in App.]

cal·li·op·sis (kăl′ē-ŏp′sĭs) *n.* A North American annual plant *(Coreopsis tinctoria)* having flower heads with yellow rays and dark centers. [NLat. : Gk. *kalli-,* beautiful (< *kallos,* beauty) + Gk. *opsis,* appearance; see —OPSIS.]

cal·li·per (kăl′ə-pər) *n.* Variant of **caliper.**

cal·li·pyg·i·an (kăl′ə-pĭj′ē-ən) also **cal·li·py·gous** (-pī′gəs) *adj.* Having beautiful buttocks. [< Gk. *kallipugos: kalli-,* beautiful (< *kallos,* beauty) + *pugē,* buttocks.]

Cal·lis·to (kə-lĭs′tō) *n.* **1.** *Greek Mythology* A nymph beloved by Zeus whom Hera changed into a bear and Zeus then placed in the sky as the constellation Ursa Major. **2.** One of the four brightest satellites of Jupiter. [Lat. < Gk. *Kallistō,* perh. < *kallistos,* superl. of *kalos,* beautiful.]

Cal·lis·tus III (kə-lĭs′təs) See **Calixtus III.**

call letters *pl.n.* The code letters or numbers of a radio or television transmitting station, assigned by a regulatory body.

call loan *n.* A loan repayable on demand at any time.

call number *n.* A number used in libraries to classify a book and indicate its location on the shelves.

cal·lose (kăl′ōs′) *n. Botany* A complex branched carbohydrate commonly associated with sieve tube cells. [< Lat. *callōsus,* callous. See CALLOUS.]

cal·los·i·ty (kə-lŏs′ĭ-tē) *n., pl.* **-ties 1.** The condition of being calloused. **2.** Hardheartedness; insensitivity. **3.** See **callus** 1a. [ME *callosite* < OFr. < LLat. *callōsitās* < Lat. *callōsus,* callous. See CALLOUS.]

cal·lous (kăl′əs) *adj.* **1.** Having calluses; toughened. **2.** Emotionally hardened; unfeeling. ❖ *tr. & intr.v.* **-loused, -lous·ing, -lous·es** To make or become callous. [ME < OFr. *cailleux* < Lat. *callōsus* < *callum,* hard skin.] —**cal′lous·ly** *adv.* —**cal′lous·ness** *n.*

> **USAGE NOTE** Do not confuse the adjective *callous,* as in *the callous criminal,* with the noun *callus,* as in *a callus on my thumb.*

cal·low (kăl′ō) *adj.* Lacking adult maturity or experience; immature. [ME *calwe,* bald < OE *calu.*] —**cal′low·ness** *n.*

Cal·lo·way (kăl′ə-wā′), **Cabell** Known as "Cab." 1907–94. Amer. jazz musician and bandleader noted for his scat singing.

call sign *n.* See **call letters.**

call-up (kôl′ŭp′) *n.* The summoning of reservists to active service.

cal·lus (kăl′əs) *n., pl.* **-lus·es 1a.** A localized thickening and enlargement of the horny layer of the skin. **b.** The hard bony tissue that develops around the ends of a fractured bone during healing. **2.** *Botany* **a.** Undifferentiated tissue that develops on or around an injured or cut plant surface or in tissue culture. **b.** The hardened, sometimes sharp base of the floret of certain grasses. ❖ *intr.v.* **-lused, -lus·ing, -lus·es** To form or develop such hardened tissue. See Usage Note at **callous.** [Lat., masc. of *callum.*]

calligraphy
Chinese calligraphy
characters

call waiting *n.* A telephone service that alerts someone using the phone to an incoming call and allows switching between calls.

calm (käm) *adj.* **calm·er, calm·est 1.** Nearly or completely motionless; undisturbed. **2.** Not excited or agitated; composed. ❖ *n.* **1.** An absence or cessation of motion; stillness. **2.** Serenity; tranquillity; peace. ❖ *tr. & intr.v.* **calmed, calm·ing, calms** To make or become calm or quiet. [ME *calme* < OFr. < OItal. *calmo* < LLat. *cauma,* resting place in the heat of the day < Gk. *kauma,* burning heat < *kaiein,* to burn.] —**calm′ly** *adv.* —**calm′ness** *n.*

SYNONYMS calm, tranquil, placid, serene, peaceful These adjectives denote absence of excitement or disturbance: *calm acceptance of the inevitable; a tranquil country life; a soothing, placid temperament; a serene, restful weekend at the lake; a peaceful hike through the hills.*

calm·a·tive (kä′mə-tīv, käl′mə-) *adj.* Having relaxing or pacifying properties; sedative. ❖ *n.* A sedative.

cal·mod·u·lin (kăl-mŏj′ə-lĭn) *n.* A calcium-binding protein found in all nucleated cells that affects the activity of many calcium-sensitive enzymes, including those involved in muscular contraction. [CAL(CIUM) + MODUL(ATE) + −IN.]

cal·o·mel (kăl′ə-mĕl′, -məl) *n.* A tasteless compound, Hg_2Cl_2, used as a purgative and insecticide. [Prob. < NLat. *calomelas* : Gk. *kalos,* beautiful + *melās,* black.]

cal·o·re·cep·tor (kăl′ə-rĭ-sĕp′tər) *n.* A sensory receptor that detects warmth. [Lat. *calor,* heat + RECEPTOR.]

ca·lor·ic (kə-lôr′ĭk, -lŏr′-) *adj.* **1.** Of or relating to heat. **2.** Of or relating to calories. ❖ *n.* A hypothetical thought responsible for the phenomena of heat until Joule proved that heat is a form of energy. [Fr. *calorique* < Lat. *calor,* heat.] —**ca·lor′i·cal·ly** *adv.*

cal·o·rie (kăl′ə-rē) *n.* **1.** Any of several approx. equal units of heat, each measured as the quantity of heat required to raise the temperature of 1 gram of water by 1°C from a standard initial temperature, esp. from 3.98°C, 14.5°C, or 19.5°C, at 1 atmosphere pressure. **2.** The unit of heat equal to 1⁄100 the quantity of heat required to raise the temperature of 1 gram of water from 0 to 100°C at 1 atmosphere pressure. **3a.** The unit of heat equal to the amount of heat required to raise the temperature of 1 kilogram of water by 1°C at 1 atmosphere pressure. **b.** A unit of energy-producing potential equal to this amount of heat that is contained in food and released upon oxidation by the body. [Fr. < Lat. *calor,* heat.]

cal·o·rif·ic (kăl′ə-rĭf′ĭk) *adj.* Relating to or generating heat or calories. [Fr. *calorifique* < Lat. *calōrificus* : *calor,* heat + -*ficus,* -fic.]

calorific value *n.* The calories or thermal units contained in one unit of a substance and released by burning.

cal·o·rim·e·ter (kăl′ə-rĭm′ĭ-tər) *n.* **1.** An apparatus for calorimetry. **2.** The part of this apparatus in which the heat measured causes a change of state. [Lat. *calor,* heat + −METER.] —**ca·lor′i·met′ric** (kə-lôr′ə-mĕt′rĭk, -lôr′-) —**ca·lor′i·met′ri·cal·ly** *adv.*

cal·o·rim·e·try (kăl′ə-rĭm′ĭ-trē) *n.* Measurement of the amount of heat evolved or absorbed in a chemical reaction, change of state, or formation of a solution. [Lat. *calor,* heat + −METRY.]

ca·lotte (kə-lŏt′) *n. Ecclesiastical* A skullcap, esp. one worn by Roman Catholic priests. [Fr. < Provençal *calota* or Ital. *callotta.*]

cal·pac or **cal·pack** also **kal·pac** (kăl′păk′, kăl-păk′) *n.* A large black cap, usu. of sheepskin or felt, worn in Turkey, the Caucasus, Iran, and neighboring regions. [Ottoman Turk. *qalpāq* < O Turkic, prob. ult. < MPers. *kulāfak,* cap, dim. of *kulāf,* hat.]

cal·pain (kăl′pān′) *n.* A proteolytic enzyme that is regulated by the concentration of calcium ions. [Prob. CAL(CIUM) + P(ROTE)A(SE) + −IN.]

Cal·pe (kăl′pē) Ancient Gibraltar, one of the Pillars of Hercules at the entrance to the Mediterranean Sea.

calque (kălk) *n.* See **loan translation.** [Fr. < *calquer,* to trace, copy < Ital. *calcare,* to press < Lat. *calcāre,* to tread on < *calx,* heel.]

cal·trop (kăl′trəp, kôl′-) *n.* **1.** Any of various plants of the genera *Tribulus* and *Kallstroemia,* having spiny or tuberculate fruits. **2.** A Mediterranean species of star thistle (*Centaurea calcitrapa*). See **water chestnut 1. 4.** A metal device with four spikes so arranged that when three are on the ground, the fourth points upward, used as a hazard to pneumatic tires or horses. [ME *calketrappe* < Norman Fr. and < OE *calcatrippe,* thistle, both < Med. Lat. *calcatrippa.*]

cal·u·met (kăl′yə-mĕt′, -mĭt, kăl′yə-mĕt′) *n.* A long-stemmed ceremonial tobacco pipe used by certain Native American peoples. [Canadian Fr. < Fr. dialectal, straw < LLat. *calamellus,* dim. of *calamus,* reed < Gk. *kalamos.*]

ca·lum·ni·ate (kə-lŭm′nē-āt′) *tr.v.* -**at·ed, -at·ing, -ates** To make maliciously or knowingly false statements about. [Lat. *calumniārī, calumniāt-* < *calumnia,* calumny. See CALUMNY.] —**ca·lum′ni·a′tion** *n.* —**ca·lum′ni·a′tor** *n.*

ca·lum·ni·ous (kə-lŭm′nē-əs) *adj.* Containing or implying calumny; slanderous. —**ca·lum′ni·ous·ly** *adv.*

cal·um·ny (kăl′əm-nē) *n., pl.* -**nies 1.** A false statement maliciously made to injure another's reputation. **2.** The utterance of malicious falsehoods; slander. [ME *calumnie* < OFr. *calomnie*

< Lat. *calumnia* < *calvī,* to deceive.]

Ca·lu·sa (kə-loo′sə) *n., pl.* **Calusa** or -**sas 1.** A member of an extinct Native American people of the southwest coast of Florida. **2.** Their extinct language, of unknown linguistic affiliation. [Calusa, fierce people (sense uncertain); perh. akin to Choctaw *kallo,* strong.]

cal·va·dos (kăl′və-dōs′, kăl′və-dōs′) *n.* A French brandy made from apples. [Fr., after *Calvados,* a department of northwest France.]

cal·var·i·um (kăl-vâr′ē-əm) *n., pl.* -**i·ums** or -**i·a** (-ē-ə) A skull that lacks the lower jaw and sometimes the facial parts. [Lat. *calvāria,* skull < *calva,* scalp < *calvus,* bald.]

Cal·va·ry¹ (kăl′və-rē, kăl′vrē) also **Gol·go·tha** (gŏl′gə-thə, gŏl-gŏth′ə) A hill outside ancient Jerusalem where Jesus was crucified.

cal·va·ry² also **cal·va·ry** (kăl′və-rē) *n., pl.* -**ries 1.** A sculptured depiction of the Crucifixion. **2. calvary** A great ordeal. [Fr. *calvaire,* from *Calvaire,* Calvary (hill). Sense 2 < CALVARY¹.]

Calvary cross *n. Heraldry* A Latin cross set on three steps.

calve (kăv, käv) *v.* **calved, calv·ing, calves** —*intr.* **1.** To give birth to a calf. **2.** To break at an edge, so that a portion separates. Used of a glacier or iceberg. —*tr.* **1.** To give birth to (a calf). **2.** To set loose (a mass of ice). Used of a glacier or iceberg. [ME *calven* < OE **calfian* < *calf,* calf.]

Cal·vert (kăl′vərt) Family of English colonists in America, including George (1580?–1632), 1st Baron Baltimore, and his son Leonard (1606–47), who served as governor of Maryland (1634–47).

calves¹ (kăvz, kävz) *n.* Plural of **calf¹.**

calves² (kăvz, kävz) *n.* Plural of **calf².**

Cal·vin (kăl′vĭn), **John** 1509–64. French-born Swiss Protestant theologian who founded Presbyterianism (1536).

Calvin, Melvin 1911–97. Amer. chemist who won a 1961 Nobel Prize.

Cal·vin·ism (kăl′vĭ-nĭz′əm) *n.* The doctrines of John Calvin, emphasizing salvation by grace alone. —**Cal′vin·ist** *adj. & n.* —**Cal′vin·is′tic** *adj.* —**Cal′vin·is′ti·cal·ly** *adv.*

calx (kălks) *n., pl.* **calx·es** or **cal·ces** (kăl′sēz′) The residue left after a mineral or metal has been calcined or roasted. [ME < Lat., limestone, pebble < Gk. *khalix,* pebble.]

ca·ly·cine (kă′lĭ-sīn′, -sĭn, kăl′ĭ-) *adj.* Of, relating to, or resembling a calyx.

ca·ly·cu·lus (kə-lĭk′yə-ləs) *n., pl.* -**li** (-lī′) **1.** *Biology* A small cup-shaped structure. **2.** *Botany* A group of small bracts resembling a calyx. [Lat., dim. of *calyx, calyc-,* calyx. See CALYX.] —**ca·lyc′u·lar** *adj.* —**ca·lyc′u·late** (-lĭt, lāt′) *adj.*

Cal·y·don (kăl′ĭ-dŏn′, -dən) An ancient city of W-central Greece N of the Gulf of Patras. —**Cal′y·do′ni·an** (-dō′nē-ən, -dōn′yən) *adj. & n.*

ca·lyp·so (kə-lĭp′sō) *n., pl.* -**sos** A terrestrial orchid (*Calypso bulbosa*) native to northern and temperate regions and having a rose-pink flower with an inflated pouchlike lip. [Prob. Lat. *Calypsō,* Calypso. See CALYPSO¹.]

Calypso¹ *n.* **1.** *Greek Mythology* A sea nymph who delayed Odysseus for seven years. **2.** A satellite of Saturn. [Lat. *Calypsō* < Gk. *Kalupsō* < *kaluptein,* to conceal. See **kel-** in App.]

Calypso² or **calypso** *n., pl.* -**sos** also -**soes** A type of music that originated in Trinidad and is marked by improvised topical or humorous lyrics. [?] —**Ca·lyp′so′ni·an** (kə-lĭp-sō′nē-ən, kăl′ĭp-) *n.*

ca·lyp·tra (kə-lĭp′trə) *n.* **1.** The protective cap or hood covering the spore case of a moss or related plant. **2.** A similar hoodlike, lidlike, or caplike structure, such as a root cap. [Med.Lat. < Gk. *kaluptra,* veil < *kaluptein,* to cover. See **kel-** in App.] —**ca·lyp′trate′** (-trāt′) *adj.*

ca·lyx (kā′lĭks, kăl′ĭks) *n., pl.* **ca·lyx·es** or **ca·ly·ces** (kā′lĭ-sēz′, kăl′ĭ-) **1.** The sepals of a flower considered as a group. **2.** A cuplike structure or organ. **3.** A collecting structure in the kidney. [Lat. *calyx, calyc-* < Gk. *kalux.*]

cal·zo·ne (kăl-zō′nē, -zōn′) *n.* A baked or fried Italian turnover of pizza dough filled with vegetables, meat, or cheese. [Ital., pant leg, calzone < *calza,* sock < VLat. **calcea* < Lat. *calceus,* shoe. See DISCALCED.]

cam (kăm) *n.* An eccentric or multiply curved wheel mounted on a rotating shaft, used to produce variable or reciprocating motion in another part. [Du. *kam,* cog, comb. See **gembh-** in App.]

Cam A river, c. 64 km (40 mi), of E-central England flowing past Cambridge to join the Ouse R. S of Ely.

CAM *abbr.* computer-aided manufacturing

Ca·ma·güey (kăm′ə-gwā′, kä′mä-) A city of E-central Cuba; founded 1514. Pop. 291,426.

ca·ma·ra·der·ie (kä′mə-rä′də-rē, kăm′ə-răd′ə-) *n.* Goodwill and lighthearted rapport between or among friends. [Fr. < *camarade,* comrade < OFr., roommate. See COMRADE.]

cam·a·ril·la (kăm′ə-rĭl′ə, -rē′yə) *n.* A group of confidential, often scheming advisers; a cabal. [Sp., dim. of *cámara,* room < LLat. *camera.* See CHAMBER.]

cam·as or **cam·ass** (kăm′əs) *n.* **1.** Any of several plants of the genus *Camassia* in the lily family, esp. *C. quamash* of western North America, having blue flowers and an edible bulb. **2.** Death camas. [Chinook Jargon, perh. of Nootka orig.]

ă	pat	oi	boy
ā	pay	ou	out
âr	care	ŏŏ	took
ä	father	ōō	boot
ĕ	pet	ŭ	cut
ē	be	ûr	urge
ĭ	pit	th	thin
ī	pie	th	this
îr	pier	hw	which
ŏ	pot	zh	vision
ō	toe	ə	about,
ô	paw		item

Stress marks:
′ (primary);
′ (secondary); as in
lexicon (lĕk′sĭ-kŏn′)

Cam·bay (kăm-bā′), **Gulf of** See **Khambhat.**

cam·ber (kăm′bər) *n.* **1a.** A slightly arched surface, as of a road or snow ski. **b.** The condition of having an arched surface. **2.** A setting of automobile wheels in which they are closer together at the bottom than at the top. ❖ *intr. & tr.v.* **-bered, -ber·ing, -bers** To arch or cause to arch slightly. [< ME *cauber,* curved < ONFr. dialectal *caumbre* < Lat. *camur,* perh. < Gk. *kamara,* vault.]

cam·bi·um (kăm′bē-əm) *n., pl.* **-bi·ums** or **-bi·a** (-bē-ə) A lateral meristem in most vascular plants that forms parallel rows of cells resulting in secondary tissues. [Med.Lat., exchange < LLat. *cambīre, cambiāre,* to exchange, of Celt. orig.] —**cam′bi·al** *adj.*

Cam·bo·di·a (kăm-bō′dē-ə) or **Kam·pu·che·a** (kăm′pōō-chē′ə) A country of SE Asia on the Gulf of Siam. Part of French Indochina in the 19th cent., it proclaimed its independence 1953. Cap. Phnom Penh. Pop. 9,568,000. —**Cam·bo′di·an** *adj. & n.*

Cam·bri·a (kăm′brē-ə) Wales during Roman times.

Cam·bri·an (kăm′brē-ən, kăm′-) *adj.* **1.** Of or relating to Wales; Welsh. **2.** Of or belonging to the geologic time of the first period of the Paleozoic Era, characterized by warm seas and desert land areas, and the rise of almost all modern animal phyla. See table at **geologic time.** ❖ *n.* **1.** A native of Wales. **2.** The Cambrian Period or its deposits. [< Med.Lat. *Cambria,* Wales, alteration of *Cumbria* < Welsh *Cymry.*]

Cambrian Explosion *n.* The rapid diversification of multicellular animal life around the beginning of the Cambrian Period, resulting in the appearance of almost all modern animal phyla.

cam·bric (kām′brĭk) *n.* A finely woven white linen or cotton fabric. [Obsolete Flem. *kameryk* < *Kameryk,* Cambrai, a city of N France.]

cambric tea *n.* A drink for children, made of hot water, milk, sugar, and usu. a small amount of tea. [So called because it is thin and white like cambric.]

Cam·bridge (kām′brĭj) **1.** A municipal borough of E-central England on the Cam R. NNE of London; site of Cambridge University (est. c. 13th cent.). Pop. 100,200. **2.** A city of E MA on the Charles R. opposite Boston; known for its universities and research facilities. Pop. 101,355.

Cam·by·ses (kăm-bī′sēz) d. 522 B.C. King of Persia (529–522) who extended Persian rule throughout the Nile Valley.

cam·cord·er (kăm′kôr′dər) *n.* A self-contained unit of communications equipment made up of a hand-held television camera and a videocassette recorder. [CAM(ERA) + (RE)CORDER.]

Cam·den (kăm′dən) A city of W NJ on the Delaware R. opposite Philadelphia. Pop. 79,904.

came¹ (kām) *n.* A grooved lead bar used to hold together windowpanes. [Poss. dialectal *kame,* ridge. See KAME.]

came² (kām) *v.* Past tense of **come.**

cam·el (kăm′əl) *n.* **1.** A humped, long-necked ruminant mammal of the genus *Camelus,* domesticated in Old World desert regions as a beast of burden. **2.** A device used to raise sunken objects, consisting of a hollow structure that is submerged, attached to the object, and pumped free of water. **3.** *Sports* An arabesque spin in figure skating. [ME < OE and < AN *cameil,* both < Lat. *camēlus* < Gk. *kamēlos,* of Semitic orig.; akin to Heb. *gāmāl.*]

cam·el·back (kăm′əl-băk′) *adj.* Shaped like a hump or an arching curve. ❖ *n. New Orleans* A narrow house with one story in front and two in the rear. See Regional Note at **beignet.**

cam·el·eer (kăm′ə-lîr′) *n.* One who drives or rides a camel.

cam·el·hair (kăm′əl-hâr′) also **camel's hair** (kăm′əlz) *n.* **1.** The soft, fine hair of the camel or a substitute for it. **2.** A soft, heavy, usu. light tan cloth, made chiefly of the hair of camel.

ca·mel·lia (kə-mēl′yə) *n.* Any of several evergreen shrubs or small trees of the genus *Camellia,* esp. *C. japonica,* native to eastern Asia and having shiny leaves and roselike flowers. [NLat. *Camellia,* genus name, after Georg Josef *Kamel* (1661–1706), Moravian Jesuit missionary.]

ca·mel·o·pard (kə-mĕl′ə-pärd) *n.* **1.** A giraffe. **2.** *Heraldry* A bearing resembling a giraffe but represented with long curved horns. [ME < Med.Lat. *camēlopardus* < Lat. *camēlopardalis* < Gk. *kamēlopardalis : kamēlos,* camel; see CAMEL + *pardalis,* pard.]

Ca·mel·o·par·da·lis (kə-mĕl′ō-pär′dl-ĭs) *n.* A constellation in the Northern Hemisphere in the large space between Ursa Major, Ursa Minor, and Perseus. [Lat. *camēlopardalis,* camelopard. See CAMELOPARD.]

Cam·e·lot (kăm′ə-lŏt′) *n.* **1.** In Arthurian legend, the site of King Arthur's court. **2.** An idealized place or time.

Cam·em·bert (kăm′əm-bâr′) *n.* A creamy mold-ripened cheese that softens on the inside as it matures. [Fr., after *Camembert,* a village of NW France.]

cam·e·o (kăm′ē-ō′) *n., pl.* **-os 1a.** A gem or shell carved in relief, esp. one in which the raised design and the background consist of layers of contrasting colors. **b.** The technique of carving in this way. **c.** A medallion with a profile in raised relief. **2.** A brief vivid portrayal or depiction. **3.** A brief appearance of a prominent actor, as in a motion picture. [Ital. *cameo* and ME *cameu* (< OFr. *camaieu* and Med.Lat. *camahūtus.*]

cam·er·a (kăm′ər-ə, kăm′rə) *n.* An apparatus for taking photographs, consisting of a lightproof enclosure having an aperture through which the image of an object is recorded on a photosensitive film or plate. **2.** The part of a television transmitter that re-

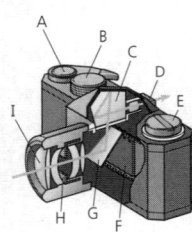

Cambodia

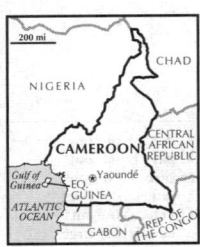

camera
A. film advance lever
B. shutter speed dial
C. prism
D. viewfinder
E. rewind lever
F. film
G. mirror
H. diaphragm
I. lens

ceives the primary image on a light-sensitive cathode-ray tube and transforms it into electrical impulses. **3.** Camera obscura. **4.** *pl.* **-er·ae** (-ə-rē) A judge's private chamber. —*idiom:* **in camera** In private. [LLat., room. See CHAMBER.]

camera lu·ci·da (lōō′sĭ-də) *n., pl.* **camera lu·ci·das** An optical device that projects an image of an object onto a plane surface, esp. for tracing. [NLat. *camera lūcida :* Lat. *camera,* chamber + Lat. *lūcida,* fem. of *lūcidus,* light.]

cam·er·a·man (kăm′ər-ə-măn′, kăm′rə-) *n.* A man who operates a movie or television camera.

camera ob·scu·ra (əb-skyŏŏr′ə) *n., pl.* **camera ob·scu·ras** A darkened chamber in which the image of an object is received through a small aperture and focused onto a facing surface. [NLat. *camera obscūra :* Lat. *camera,* chamber + Lat. *obscūra,* fem. of *obscūrus,* dark.]

cam·er·a·per·son (kăm′ər-ə-pûr′sən, kăm′rə-) *n.* One who operates a movie or television camera.

cam·er·a·read·y (kăm′ər-ə-rĕd′ē, kăm′rə-) *adj.* Prepared in such a way as to be appropriate for photographing prior to being made into a printing plate: *camera-ready art.*

cam·er·a·wom·an (kăm′ər-ə-wŏŏm′ən, kăm′rə-) *n.* A woman who operates a movie or television camera.

cam·er·len·go (kăm′ər-lĕng′gō) also **cam·er·lin·go** (-lĭng′gō) *n., pl.* **-gos** The cardinal who manages the pope's secular affairs. [Ital. *camerlengo;* akin to OFr. *chamberlenc.* See CHAMBERLAIN.]

Cam·er·on (kăm′ər-ən, kăm′rən), **Mount** A peak, 4,342.6 m (14,238 ft), in the Rocky Mts. of central CO.

Cam·e·roon (kăm′ə-rōōn′) also **Came·roun** (kăm-rōōn′) A country of W-central Africa on the Bight of Biafra; gained independence from France and Great Britain in 1960. Cap. Yaoundé. Pop. 12,871,000.

Cam·e·roons (kăm′ə-rōōnz′) A region and former German protectorate of W-central Africa.

cam·i·on (kăm′ē-ən, kăm-yôn′) *n.* **1.** A truck. **2.** A bus. [Fr. < OFr. *chamion,* three-wheeled cart.]

ca·mise (kə-mēz′, -mēs′) *n.* A loose shirt, shift, or tunic. [Ar. *qamīṣ.*]

cam·i·sole (kăm′ĭ-sōl′) *n.* **1.** A woman's sleeveless undergarment. **2.** A short negligee. [Fr. (< Ital. *camiciola,* dim. of *camicia,* shirt) or < O Provençal *camisola,* dim. of *camisa,* shirt, both < LLat. *camisia, camīsa.* See CHEMISE.]

cam·let (kăm′lĭt) *n.* **1.** A rich cloth of Asian origin, generally made of camel's hair or goat's hair and silk. **2.** A garment made from this cloth. [ME *chamelet* < OFr. *chamelot,* perh. < Ar. *ḥamla,* fibers.]

cam·o (kăm′ō) *n., pl.* **-os** *Informal* Camouflage fabric or a garment made of it. [Short for CAMOUFLAGE.]

Ca·mões (kə-moinsh′) also **Ca·mo·ens** (kăm′ō-ənz, kə-mō′-), **Luiz Vaz de** 1524?–80. Portuguese writer noted for his epic poem *Os Lusíadas* (1572).

cam·o·mile (kăm′ə-mīl′, -mēl′) *n.* Variant of **chamomile.**

Ca·mor·ra (kə-môr′ə, -mōr′ə) *n.* **1.** A Neapolitan secret society organized about 1820, notorious for its violence and blackmail. **2. camorra** An unscrupulous, clandestine group. [Ital., perh. < *camorra,* a kind of smock.]

cam·ou·flage (kăm′ə-fläzh′, -fläj′) *n.* **1.** The method or result of concealing personnel or equipment from an enemy by making them appear to be part of the natural surroundings. **2.** Concealment by disguise or protective coloring. **3.** Fabric or a garment dyed so as to make the wearer indistinguishable from the surrounding environment. ❖ *v.* **-flaged, -flag·ing, -flag·es** —*tr.* **1.** To conceal by the use of disguise or by protective coloring. **2.** To conceal, usu. through misrepresentation or other artifice. —*intr.* To use protective coloring or garments for concealment. [Fr. < *camoufler,* to disguise, alteration (influenced by *camouflet,* snub, smoke blown in one's face) of Ital. *camuffare.*] —**cam′ou·flag′er** *n.*

camp¹ (kămp) *n.* **1a.** A place where tents, huts, or other temporary shelters are set up. **b.** A cabin or shelter or group of such buildings. **c.** The people using such shelters. **2a.** A place in the country that offers simple group accommodations and organized recreation or instruction. **b.** *Sports* A place where athletes share in intensive training. **c.** The people attending a camp. **3.** Military service; army life. **4.** A group of people who think alike or share a cause; settle. ❖ *v.* **camped, camp·ing, camps** —*intr.* **1.** To pitch or set up a camp. **2.** To live in or as if in a camp; settle. —*tr.* To shelter or lodge in a camp; encamp. [Obsolete Fr., perh. < Ital. or Sp. *campo,* all < Lat. *campus,* field.]

camp² (kămp) *n.* **1.** An affectation or appreciation of manners and tastes commonly thought artificial, vulgar, or banal. **2.** Banality, vulgarity, or artificiality when deliberately affected or appreciated for its humor. [?] —**camp** *adj. & v.* —**camp′y** *adj.*

Camp, Walter Chauncey 1859–1925. Amer. football coach who developed many of the sport's basic rules.

Cam·pa·gna di Ro·ma (kăm-pän′yə dē rō′mə, -mä, kăm-) A low-lying residential region surrounding Rome, Italy.

cam·paign (kăm-pān′) *n.* **1.** A series of military operations undertaken to achieve a large-scale objective during a war. **2.** An operation energetically pursued to accomplish a purpose: *an advertising campaign.* ❖ *intr.v.* **-paigned, -paign·ing, -paigns** To engage in a campaign. [Fr. *campagne* < Ital. *campagna*, field, military operation < LLat. *campānia*, open country, battlefield < Lat. *campus*, field.] —**cam·paign′er** *n.*

Cam·pa·ni·a (kăm-pā′nē-ə, -pān′yə, käm-pä′nyä) A region of S Italy on the Tyrrhenian Sea.

cam·pa·ni·le (kăm′pə-nē′lē) *n., pl.* **-les** (-lēz) or **-li** (-lē) A bell tower, esp. one near but not attached to a church or other public building. [Fr. < Ital. < *campana*, bell < LLat. *campāna*, bell (made of metal produced in Campania) < Lat. *campānus*, of Campania < *Campānia*, Campania.]

cam·pa·nol·o·gy (kăm′pə-nŏl′ə-jē) *n.* The art or study of bell casting and ringing. [LLat. *campāna*, bell; see CAMPANILE + -LOGY.] —**cam′pa·nol′o·gist** *n.*

cam·pan·u·la (kăm-păn′yə-lə) *n.* Any of various plants of the genus *Campanula*, which includes the harebell and bellflower. [NLat. *Campanula*, genus name, dim. of LLat. *campāna*, bell. See CAMPANILE.]

cam·pan·u·late (kăm-păn′yə-lĭt, -lāt′) *adj. Botany* Bell-shaped.

Camp·bell (kăm′bəl), **Avril Phaedra** Known as "Kim." b. 1947. Canadian lawyer and politician who was the first woman prime minister of Canada (1993).

Campbell, Joseph 1904–87. Amer. mythologist whose works include *Masks of God* (1959–67).

Camp·bell-Ban·ner·man (kăm′bəl-băn′ər-mən, kăm′əl-), Sir **Henry** 1836–1908. British prime minister (1905–08).

Camp Da·vid (dā′vĭd) A presidential retreat in the Catoctin Mts. of N MD NNW of Washington DC.

Cam·pe·che (kăm-pĕ′chē, käm-pĕ′chĕ) A city of SE Mexico on the **Bay of Campeche,** a section of the Gulf of Mexico W of Yucatán. Pop. 128,434.

camp·er (kăm′pər) *n.* **1.** One that camps, as in a tent. **2a.** A motor vehicle used for camping and recreational travel. **b.** The rear compartment or attached trailer of such a vehicle.

cam·pe·si·no (kăm′pĭ-sē′nō, käm′-) *n., pl.* **-nos** A Latin-American farmer or farm worker. [Sp. < *campo*, field < Lat. *campus*.]

cam·pes·tral (kăm-pĕs′trəl) *adj.* Of, relating to, or growing in uncultivated land or open fields. [< Lat. *campester,* of a field < *campus*, field.]

camp·fire (kămp′fīr′) *n.* **1.** An outdoor fire in a camp, used for cooking or warmth. **2.** A meeting held around such a fire.

camp follower *n.* A civilian who follows a military unit from place to place, esp. as a vendor or a prostitute.

camp·ground (kămp′ground′) *n.* An area used for setting up a camp or holding a camp meeting.

cam·phene (kăm′fēn′) *n.* A crystalline terpene, $C_{10}H_{16}$, used to make synthetic camphor and insecticides. [CAMPH(OR) + -ENE.]

cam·phor (kăm′fər) *n.* An aromatic crystalline compound, $C_{10}H_{16}O$, obtained naturally from the camphor tree or synthesized and used in the manufacture of film and plastics and in medicine for mild pain and itching. [ME *caumfre* < AN < Med.Lat. *camphora* < Ar. *kāfūr*, poss. < Malay *kapur*; akin to Skt. *karpūraḥ*.] —**cam′phor·a′ceous** (kăm′fə-rā′shəs) *adj.* —**cam·phor′ic** (kăm-fôr′ĭk, -fŏr′-) *adj.*

cam·phor·ate (kăm′fə-rāt′) *tr.v.* **-at·ed, -at·ing, -ates** To treat or impregnate with camphor.

camphor oil *n.* The oil obtained by steam distillation from the wood of the camphor tree and used to produce natural camphor.

camphor tree *n.* An east Asian evergreen tree (*Cinnamomum camphora*) having wood and leathery leaves that are a source of camphor.

Cam·pi·na Gran·de (kăm′pē-nə grän′də, -dē, kän-pē′nə grän′də) A city of extreme E Brazil NW of Recife. Pop. 326,106.

Cam·pi·nas (kăm-pē′nəs, kän-) A city of SE Brazil NNW of São Paulo. Pop. 846,434.

cam·pi·on (kăm′pē-ən) *n.* Any of several plants of the genera *Lychnis* and *Silene*, native chiefly to the Northern Hemisphere and having notched or fringed flower petals. [?]

Campion, Thomas 1567–1620. English poet and composer of songs for voice and lute.

camp meeting *n.* An evangelistic gathering held in a tent or outdoors and often lasting several days.

cam·po (kăm′pō, käm′-) *n., pl.* **-pos** A large grassy plain in South America, with scattered bushes and small trees. [Sp., field < Lat. *campus*.]

Cam·po·bel·lo Island (kăm′pə-bĕl′ō) An island of SW New Brunswick, Canada, off the coast of ME.

Cam·po Gran·de (kăm′pō grän′də, -dē, kän′pōō grän′də) A city of SW Brazil WNW of São Paulo. Pop. 525,463.

camp·o·ree (kăm′pə-rē′) *n.* A local gathering of Boy Scouts or Girl Scouts. [CAMP[1] + (JAMB)OREE.]

camp robber *n.* See gray jay.

camp·site (kămp′sīt′) *n.* An area for camping.

cam·pus (kăm′pəs) *n., pl.* **-pus·es 1.** The grounds of a school, college, university, or hospital. **2.** A college or university. [Lat., field.]

cam·py·lo·bac·te·ri·o·sis (kăm′pə-lō-băk-tîr′ē-ō′sĭs) *n.* A gastrointestinal disorder caused by consuming foods contaminated with *Campylobacter jejuni*. [NLat. *Campylobacter*, genus name (Gk. *kampulos*, curved + BACTER(IUM)) + -OSIS.]

cam·py·lot·ro·pous (kăm′pə-lŏt′rə-pəs) *adj. Botany* Having a

partially inverted ovule such that the micropyle nearly meets the funiculus. [Gk. *kampulos,* curved + -TROPOUS.]

cam·shaft (kăm′shăft′) *n.* An engine shaft fitted with a cam or cams.

Ca·mus (kä-mōō′, -mü′), **Albert** 1913–60. French existentialist who won the 1957 Nobel Prize for literature.

can[1] (kăn; kən *when unstressed*) *aux.v.* Past tense **could** (kŏŏd) **1a.** Used to indicate physical or mental ability: *I can lift it.* **b.** Used to indicate possession of a specified power, right, or privilege: *We can vote.* **c.** Used to indicate possession of a specified capability or skill: *I can sing. This room can hold 20 people.* **2a.** Used to indicate possibility or probability: *Such things can happen.* **b.** Used to indicate that which is permitted, as by conscience or feelings: *One can hardly blame you.* **c.** Used to indicate probability or possibility under the specified circumstances: *They can hardly have intended that.* **3.** *Usage Problem* Used to request or grant permission: *Can I be excused?* [ME, first and third pers. sing. pr. t. of *connen,* to know how < OE *cunnan.* See **gnō-** in App.]

USAGE NOTE Generations of grammarians and schoolteachers have insisted that *can* should be used only to express the capacity to do something and that *may* must be used to express permission. In idiomatic spoken English, it is perfectly acceptable to use *can* to express permission: *Yes, you can go outside and play.* But in more formal contexts, correct usage technically requires *may* in this sense: *May* (not *can*) *I take another week to submit the application?* Only 21 percent of the Usage Panel accepts *can* in this sentence. *Can* does have a long history of use by educated speakers to express permission, particularly in British English. But observance of the distinction is often advisable in the interests of clarity.

---

can[2] (kăn) *n.* **1.** A usu. cylindrical metal container. **2a.** An airtight container, usu. made of tin-coated iron, in which foods or beverages are preserved. **b.** The contents of such a container. **3.** *Slang* A jail or prison. **4.** *Slang* A toilet or restroom. **5.** *Slang* The buttocks. ❖ *tr.v.* **canned, can·ning, cans 1.** To seal (food) in an airtight container for future use; preserve. **2.** *Slang* To make a recording of. **3.** *Slang* To dismiss from employment or school. **4.** *Slang* To put a stop to; quit: *Let's can the chatter.* [ME *canne,* a water container < OE.] —**can′ner** *n.*

can. *abbr.* **1a.** canceled **b.** cancellation **2.** canon **3.** canto

Can. *abbr.* **1.** Canada **2.** Canadian

Ca·na (kā′nə) A village of N Palestine near Nazareth where Jesus performed his first miracle, changing water into wine.

Ca·naan (kā′nən) An ancient region made up of Palestine or the part of it between the Jordan R. and the Mediterranean.

Ca·naan·ite (kā′nə-nīt′) *n.* **1.** A member of a Semitic people who inhabited Canaan from late prehistoric times and were conquered by the Israelites around 1000 B.C. **2.** The Semitic language of the Canaanites. —**Ca′naan·ite** *adj.*

Can·a·da (kăn′ə-də) A country of N North America; settled by English and French colonists and ceded to England in 1763. The Dominion of Canada was formed in 1867. Cap. Ottawa. Pop. 28,846,761. —**Ca·na′di·an** (kə-nā′dē-ən) *adj. & n.*

Canada balsam *n.* A viscous transparent resin obtained from the balsam fir and used as a cement for glass lenses and for mounting specimens on microscopic slides.

Canada goose or **Canadian goose** *n.* A common wild goose (*Branta canadensis*) of North America having grayish plumage, a black neck and head, and a white throat patch.

Canada jay *n.* See gray jay.

Canada thistle *n.* A perennial herb (*Cirsium arvense*) in the composite family, native to Europe and naturalized as a noxious weed in North America, having spiny-margined leaves.

Canadian bacon *n.* Cured rolled bacon from the loin of a pig.

Canadian Falls also **Horseshoe Falls** A section, c. 48 m (158 ft) high, of Niagara Falls within Ontario, Canada.

Canadian French *n.* The French language as used in Canada.

Canadian hemlock *n.* A coniferous evergreen monoecious tree (*Tsuga canadensis*) native from Nova Scotia to Alaska and valuable for its timber, as a pulpwood, and for tanning.

Canadian River A river rising in NE NM and flowing c. 1,458 km (906 mi) E to the Arkansas R.

Canadian Shield See Laurentian Plateau.

ca·naille (kə-nī′, -nāl′) *n.* **1.** The masses of the people; the proletariat. **2.** Rabble; riffraff. [Fr. < Ital. *canaglia*, pack of dogs, rabble < *cane*, dog < Lat. *canis.* See **kwon-** in App.]

ca·nal (kə-năl′) *n.* **1.** An artificial waterway or artificially improved river used for travel, shipping, or irrigation. **2.** *Anatomy* A tube, duct, or passageway. **3.** *Astronomy* One of the faint hazy markings resembling straight lines on early telescopic images of the surface of Mars. ❖ *tr.v.* **-nalled, -nal·ling, -nals** or **-naled, -nal·ing, -nals 1.** To dig a canal through. **2.** To provide with a canal. [Partly Fr., channel, and partly ME, tube (< Med.Lat. *canālis*), both < Lat. *canālis*, prob. < *canna*, small reed. See CANE.]

Ca·na·let·to (kän′ə-lĕt′ō) Orig. Giovanni Antonio Canal. 1697–1768. Italian painter noted for his detailed views of Venice.

can·a·lic·u·late (kăn′ə-lĭk′yə-lĭt, -lāt′) *adj.* Having one or more longitudinal grooves or channels. [Lat. *canāliculātus* < *canāliculus,* dim. of *canālis,* channel. See CANAL.]

can·a·lic·u·lus (kăn′ə-lĭk′yə-ləs) *n., pl.* **-li** (-lī′) A small canal

campanile
campanile of the 14th-century Mother Church, Erice, Sicily

Canada

canal
Corinth Canal, Greece

ă	pat	oi	boy
ā	pay	ou	out
âr	care	ŏŏ	took
ä	father	ōō	boot
ĕ	pet	ŭ	cut
ē	be	ûr	urge
ĭ	pit	th	thin
ī	pie	th	this
îr	pier	hw	which
ŏ	pot	zh	vision
ō	toe	ə	about,
ô	paw		item

Stress marks:
′ (primary);
′ (secondary), as in
lexicon (lĕk′sĭ-kŏn′)

or duct in the body. [Lat. *canāliculus*, dim. of *canālis*, conduit. See CANAL.] —**can'a·lic'u·lar** (-lər) *adj.*

can·al·i·za·tion (kăn'ə-lĭ-zā'shən) *n.* **1.** The act or an instance of canalizing. **2.** A system of canals.

can·al·ize (kăn'ə-līz') *tr.v.* **-ized, -iz·ing, -iz·es** **1.** To furnish with or convert into a canal or canals. **2.** To provide an outlet for; channel.

Canal Zone also **Panama Canal Zone** A strip of land, c. 16 km (10 mi) wide, across the Isthmus of Panama; formerly administered by the US and turned over to Panama in 1979.

can·a·pé (kăn'ə-pā', -pē) *n.* A cracker or a small piece of bread served with a spread as an appetizer. [Fr. < *canapé*, couch < Med.Lat. *canāpēum*, mosquito net. See CANOPY.]

ca·nard (kə-närd') *n.* **1.** An unfounded or false, deliberately misleading story. **2a.** A short winglike control surface projecting from the fuselage of an aircraft, mounted forward of the main wing and serving as a horizontal stabilizer. **b.** An aircraft with canards. [Fr., duck, canard, prob. < the phrase *vendre un canard à moitié*, to sell half a duck, to swindle < OFr. *quanart*, duck < *caner*, to cackle, of imit. orig.]

ca·nar·y (kə-nâr'ē) *n., pl.* **-ies** **1.** A small, greenish to yellow finch (*Serinus canaria*) native to the Canary Islands. **2.** *Slang* An informer; a stool pigeon. **3.** A sweet white wine from the Canary Islands, similar to Madeira. **4.** A light to vivid yellow. [Fr. *canari* < Sp. *canario*, of the Canary Islands < (*Islas*) *Canarias*, Canary (Islands) < LLat. *Canāriae* (*Insulae*), (islands) of dogs < Lat. *canārius*, canine < *canis*, dog. See **kwon-** in App.]

ca·nar·y-bird flower (kə-nâr'ē-bûrd') *n.* A Peruvian climbing plant (*Tropaeolum peregrinum*) with yellow flowers.

canary grass *n.* **1.** An annual Mediterranean grass (*Phalaris canariensis*) having grains used as food for caged birds, such as canaries. **2.** Any of several related grasses.

Canary Islands A group of Spanish islands in the Atlantic Ocean off the NW coast of Africa; part of Spain since 1479.

ca·nas·ta (kə-năs'tə) *n.* A card game for two to six players, related to rummy and requiring two decks. [Sp. < *canasto*, basket < Lat. *canistrum*. See CANISTER.]

Ca·nav·er·al (kə-năv'ər-əl, -năv'rəl), **Cape** Formerly (1963–73) **Cape Kennedy.** A promontory extending into the Atlantic Ocean from a barrier island on the E-central coast of FL; launching area for US space missions.

Can·ber·ra (kăn'bər-ə, -bĕr'ə) The cap. of Australia, in the SE part; settled in 1824. Pop. 298,200.

can·can (kăn'kăn') *n.* A dance that originated in France, performed by women and marked by high kicking. [Fr.]

can·cel (kăn'səl) *v.* **-celed, -cel·ing, -cels** also **-celled, -cel·ling, -cels** —*tr.* **1.** To cross out with lines or other markings. See Syns at **erase. 2.** To annul or invalidate. **3.** To mark or perforate (a check, for example) to indicate that it need not be used again. **4.** To equalize or make up for; offset. **5.** *Mathematics* **a.** To remove (a common factor) from the numerator and denominator of a fractional expression. **b.** To remove (a common factor or term) from both sides of an equation or inequality. **6.** *Printing* To omit or delete. —*intr.* To neutralize one another; counterbalance. ❖ *n.* **1.** The act or an instance of canceling; a cancellation. **2.** *Printing* **a.** Deletion of typed or printed matter. **b.** The matter deleted. **c.** A replacement for deleted matter. [ME *cancellen* < OFr. *canceler* < Lat. *cancellāre*, to cross out < *cancellus*, lattice, dim. of *cancer*, lattice.] —**can'cel·a·ble** *adj.* —**can'cel·er** *n.*

can·cel·late (kăn-sĕl'ĭt, kăn'sə-lāt') also **can·cel·lat·ed** (-lā'tĭd) *adj.* Cancellous. [Lat. *cancellātus*, p. part. of *cancellāre*, to make in a crisscross pattern. See CANCEL.]

can·cel·la·tion also **can·ce·la·tion** (kăn'sə-lā'shən) *n.* **1.** The act or an instance of canceling. **2.** A mark or a perforation indicating canceling. **3.** Something canceled.

can·cel·lous (kăn-sĕl'əs, kăn'sə-ləs) *adj. Anatomy* Having an open, latticed, or porous structure. Used esp. of bone. [< Lat. *cancellus*, lattice. See CANCEL.]

can·cer (kăn'sər) *n.* **1a.** Any of various malignant neoplasms marked by the proliferation of anaplastic cells that tend to invade surrounding tissue and metastasize to new body sites. **b.** The pathological condition characterized by such growths. **2.** A pernicious, spreading evil. [ME. See CANKER.] —**can'cer·ous** (kăn'sər-əs) *adj.*

Cancer *n.* **1.** A constellation in the Northern Hemisphere near Leo and Gemini. **2a.** The fourth sign of the zodiac in astrology. **b.** One born under this sign. [ME < Lat. See CANKER.]

Can·cún (kän-kōōn', käng-) An island resort community of SE Mexico off NE Yucatán. Pop. 33,273.

can·del·a (kăn-dĕl'ə) *n.* A unit of luminous intensity equal to ¹⁄₆₀ of the luminous intensity per square centimeter of a blackbody radiating at the temperature of solidification of platinum (2,046°K). See table at **measurement.** [Lat. *candēla*, candle. See CANDLE.]

can·de·la·bra (kăn'dl-ä'brə, -äb'rə, -ä'brə) *n.* A candelabrum. [< Lat. *candēlābra*, pl. of *candēlābrum*. See CANDELABRUM.]

can·de·la·brum (kăn'dl-ä'brəm, -äb'rəm, -ä'brəm) *n., pl.* **-bra** (-brə) or **-brums** A large branched candlestick with several arms or branches. [Lat. *candēlābrum*, candlestick < *candēla*, candle. See CANDLE.]

can·de·lil·la (kăn'dl-ē'ə) *n.* A shrubby spurge (*Euphorbia antisyphilitica*) native to southwest Texas and Mexico and having

candelabrum

leafless stems that yield a multipurpose wax. [Am.Sp., dim. of Sp. *candela*, candle < Lat. *candēla*. See CANDLE.]

can·dent (kăn'dənt) *adj.* Having a white-hot glow; incandescent. [Lat. *candēns, candent-,* pr. part. of *candēre,* to shine.]

can·des·cence (kăn-dĕs'əns) *n.* The state of being white hot; incandescence. [< Lat. *candēscēns, candēscent-,* pr. part. of *candēscere,* inchoative of *candēre,* to shine.] —**can·des'cent** *adj.* —**can·des'cent·ly** *adv.*

Can·di·a (kăn'dē-ə) **1.** The island of Crete. **2.** See **Iráklion.**

can·did (kăn'dĭd) *adj.* **1.** Unprejudiced; impartial. **2.** Open and sincere, esp. in expression. See Syns at **frank**[1]. **3.** Not posed or rehearsed. ❖ *n.* A candid photograph. [Lat. *candidus,* guileless < *candēre,* to shine.] —**can'did·ly** *adv.* —**can'did·ness** *n.*

can·di·da (kăn'dĭ-də) *n.* Any of the yeastlike imperfect fungi of the genus *Candida,* capable of becoming parasitic and normally present on the skin and in the mouth, intestinal tract, and vagina. [Lat., fem. of *candidus,* white. See CANDID.]

can·di·date (kăn'dĭ-dāt', -dĭt) *n.* **1.** A person seeking an office, prize, or honor. **2.** A student who has nearly completed the requirements for a degree. **3.** One likely to gain a position or come to a certain fate. [Lat. *candidātus,* clothed in white, candidate < *candidus,* white. See CANDID.] —**can'di·da·cy** (-də-sē), **can'di·da·ture'** (-də-chōōr', -chər) *n.*

candid camera *n.* A small simple camera with a fast lens for taking unposed photographs.

can·di·di·a·sis (kăn'dĭ-dī'ə-sĭs) *n.* Infection with a fungus of the genus *Candida,* esp. *C. albicans,* usu. occurring in the mouth, respiratory tract, or vagina.

can·died (kăn'dēd) *adj.* Covered or cooked with sugar.

can·dle (kăn'dl) *n.* **1a.** A solid, usu. cylindrical mass of tallow, wax, or other fatty substance with an embedded wick, burned to provide light. **b.** Something resembling this. **2.** *Physics* **a.** An obsolete unit of luminous intensity, originally defined in terms of a standard wax candle and equal to 1.02 candelas. **b.** See **candela.** ❖ *tr.v.* **-dled, -dling, -dles** To examine (an egg) for freshness or fertility before a bright light. [ME *candel* < OE and < AN *candele,* both < Lat. *candēla* < *candēre,* to shine.] —**can'dler** *n.*

can·dle·ber·ry (kăn'dl-bĕr'ē) *n.* **1.** Any of certain bayberries, the wax myrtle, or the fruit of these plants. **2.** See **candlenut.**

can·dle·fish (kăn'dl-fĭsh') *n., pl.* **-fish** or **-fish·es** An oily edible fish (*Thaleichthys pacificus*) of northern Pacific waters, formerly used as a torch by Native Americans.

can·dle·light (kăn'dl-līt') *n.* **1.** Illumination from a candle or candles. **2.** Dusk; twilight.

can·dle·lit (kăn'dl-lĭt') *adj.* Illuminated by candles.

Can·dle·mas (kăn'dl-məs) *n.* A Christian feast commemorating the purification of the Virgin Mary and the presentation of the infant Jesus in the Temple, traditionally observed on February 2. [ME *candelmasse* < OE *candelmæsse :* *candel,* candle; see CANDLE + *mæsse,* mass; see MASS.]

can·dle·nut (kăn'dl-nŭt') *n.* **1.** A tropical southeast Asian tree (*Aleurites moluccana*) bearing seeds used to make candles and whose oil is used in paints, varnishes, lacquer, and soft soap. **2.** The seed of this tree.

can·dle·pin (kăn'dl-pĭn') *n.* **1.** A slender bowling pin used in a variation of the game of tenpins. **2.** also **candlepins** (*used with a sing. verb*) A bowling game using candlepins.

can·dle·pow·er (kăn'dl-pou'ər) *n.* Luminous intensity expressed in candelas.

can·dle·snuff·er (kăn'dl-snŭf'ər) *n.* An implement with a bell-shaped cup used to extinguish the flame of a candle.

can·dle·stick (kăn'dl-stĭk') *n.* A holder with a cup or spike for a candle.

can·dle·wick (kăn'dl-wĭk') *n.* **1.** The wick of a candle. **2a.** A soft, heavy cotton thread similar to that used to make wicks for candles. **b.** Embroidery made of tufts of this thread.

can·dle·wood (kăn'dl-wood') *n.* **1.** Any of several trees or shrubs yielding a usu. resinous wood. **2.** The wood of such a plant, burned for light or fuel. **3.** The ocotillo.

can-do (kăn'dōō') *adj. Informal* Marked by a willingness to tackle a job and get it done.

Can·dom·ble or **Can·dom·blé** (kän-dōōm-blĕ') *n.* A religion based on African traditions with elements derived from Christianity, practiced chiefly in Brazil. [Port. *Candomblé,* ritual drum music, of Bantu orig. (perh. imit.).]

can·dor (kăn'dər) *n.* **1.** Frankness or sincerity of expression; openness. **2.** Freedom from prejudice; impartiality. [ME < OFr. < Lat. < *candēre,* to shine.]

C & W *abbr.* country and western

can·dy (kăn'dē) *n., pl.* **-dies** **1.** A rich sweet confection made with sugar, often combined with fruits or nuts. **2.** A piece of candy. ❖ *v.* **-died, -dy·ing, -dies** —*tr.* **1.** To reduce to sugar crystals. **2.** To cook, preserve, saturate, or coat with sugar or syrup. **3.** To make pleasant or agreeable; sweeten. —*intr.* To become candied. [ME *candi,* crystallized cane sugar, short for *sugrecandi,* ult. < Ar. *sukkar qandī :* *sukkar,* sugar + *qandī,* candied (< *qand,* cane sugar, prob. < Dravidian *kaṇṭu,* lump.)]

can·dy-ass or **candy ass** (kăn'dē-ăs') *n. Vulgar Slang* A sissy; a wimp. —**can'dy-ass'** *adj.*

candy cane *n.* A usu. striped stick of peppermint candy with the top curved to resemble a walking cane.

candy corn *n.* Candy shaped like kernels of corn.

can•dy•gram (kăn′dē-grăm′) *n.* A delivery of candy or other sweets along with a personalized message.

candy striper *n.* A volunteer worker in a hospital. [< the red and white striped uniform.]

can•dy•tuft (kăn′dē-tŭft′) *n.* Any of several plants of the genus *Iberis* in the mustard family, native to Europe and the Mediterranean region and widely cultivated for their showy flowers. [Obsolete *Candy* (var. of CANDIA) + TUFT.]

cane (kān) *n.* **1a.** A slender, strong but often flexible stem, as of certain reeds. **b.** A plant having such a stem. **c.** Cane used for wickerwork or baskets. **2.** A bamboo *(Arundinaria gigantea)* native to the southeast United States, having stiff stems and often forming canebrakes. **3.** The stem of a raspberry, blackberry, certain roses, or similar plants. **4.** Sugar cane. **5.** A stick used as an aid in walking or carried as an accessory. **6.** A rod used for flogging. ❖ *tr.v.* **caned, can•ing, canes 1.** To make, supply, or repair with flexible woody material. **2.** To hit or beat with a rod. [ME < OFr. < Lat. *canna*, small reed < Gk. *kanna*, of Semitic orig.; akin to Akkadian *qanû*.] **—can′er** *n.*

cane•brake (kān′brāk′) *n.* A dense thicket of cane.

ca•nes•cent (kə-nĕs′ənt) *adj.* **1.** *Biology* Covered with short, fine whitish or grayish hairs or down; hoary. **2.** Turning white or grayish. [Lat. *cānēscēns, cānēscent-*, pr. part. of *cānēscere*, inchoative of *cānēre*, to be white < *cānus*, white.] **—ca•nes′cence** *n.*

cane sugar *n.* Sucrose obtained from sugar cane.

Ca•nes Ve•nat•i•ci (kā′nēz vĭ-năt′ĭ-sī′) *n.* A constellation in the Northern Hemisphere near Ursa Major and Boötes. [Lat. *Canēs Vēnāticī* : *canēs*, pl. of *canis*, dog + *vēnāticī*, pl. of *vēnāticus*, hunting.]

cane toad *n.* A large poisonous toad, *Bufo marinus*, native to Central and South America and widely exported in the 1930s to control sugar cane beetles.

Ca•net•ti (kä-nĕt′ē), **Elias** 1905–94. Bulgarian-born writer who won the 1981 Nobel Prize for literature.

can•field (kăn′fēld′) *n.* *Games* A form of solitaire. [After Richard Albert *Canfield* (1855–1914), American gambler.]

Can•i•a•pis•cau also **Kan•i•a•pis•kau** (kăn′ē-ə-pĭs′kō, -kou) A river of N Quebec, Canada, rising in **Lake Caniapiscau** (or **Lake Kaniapiskau**) and flowing c. 925 km (575 mi) to the Larch R.

ca•nic•u•lar (kə-nĭk′yə-lər) *adj.* **1.** Relating to Sirius or Procyon. **2.** Relating to the dog days. [LLat. *canīculāris*, of Sirius < Lat. *Canīcula*, Sirius, dim. of *canis*, dog. See **kwon-** in App.]

ca•nid (kā′nĭd, kăn′ĭd) *n.* Any of various widely distributed carnivorous mammals of the dog family Canidae. [< NLat. *Canidae*, family name < *Canis*, type genus < Lat. *canis, dog*. See **kwon-** in App.]

ca•nine (kā′nīn) *adj.* **1.** Of, relating to, or characteristic of the canids. **2.** Of, relating to, or being one of the pointed, conical teeth located between the incisors and the first bicuspids. ❖ *n.* **1.** An animal of the family Canidae, esp. a dog. **2.** One of the pointed, conical teeth located between the incisors and the first bicuspids. [Lat. *canīnus* < *canis*, dog. See **kwon-** in App.]

canine distemper *n.* See **distemper**[1] 1a.

Ca•nis Major (kā′nĭs, kăn′ĭs) *n.* A constellation in the Southern Hemisphere near Puppis and Lepus, containing the star Sirius. [Lat. *Canis Māior* : *canis*, dog + *māior*, larger.]

Canis Minor *n.* A constellation in the equatorial region of the Southern Hemisphere near Hydra and Monoceros, containing Procyon. [Lat. : *canis*, dog + *minor*, smaller.]

can•is•tel (kăn′ĭ-stĕl′) *n.* **1.** A tree *(Pouteria campechiana)* native to Mexico, Central America, and the Caribbean and having sweet fruit. **2.** The fruit of this tree. [Am.Sp. < dialectal var. of Sp. *canastillo*, small basket < Lat. *canistellum*, dim. of *canistrum*, basket. See CANISTER.]

can•is•ter (kăn′ĭ-stər) *n.* **1.** A usu. cylindrical storage container, such as a metal or plastic can, used for holding dry cooking ingredients. **2a.** A metallic cylinder packed with shot that scatters on firing. **b.** The shot in such a cylinder. **3.** The part of a gas mask containing the filter for removing toxic agents from the air. [Lat. *canistrum*, basket < Gk. *kanastron* < *kanna*, reed. See CANE.]

can•ker (kăng′kər) *n.* **1.** Ulceration of the mouth and lips. **2.** An inflammation or infection of the ear and auditory canal, esp. in dogs and cats. **3.** A condition in horses similar to but more advanced than thrush. **4a.** A localized diseased or necrotic area on a plant part, usu. caused by fungi or bacteria. **b.** Any of several diseases of plants characterized by the presence of such lesions. **5.** A source of spreading corruption or decay. ❖ *v.* **-kered, -ker•ing, -kers** *—tr.* **1.** To attack or infect with canker. **2.** To infect with corruption or decay. *—intr.* To become infected with or as if with canker. [ME < OE *cancer* and < OFr. *cancre*, both < Lat. *cancer*, crab, malignant disease.]

canker brake *n.* See **Christmas fern.**

can•ker•ous (kăng′kər-əs) *adj.* **1.** Marked by or infected with canker; ulcerous. **2.** Causing canker; ulcerating.

canker sore *n.* A small painful ulcer or sore, usu. of the mouth.

can•ker•worm (kăng′kər-wûrm′) *n.* The larva of either of two moths *(Paleacrita vernata* or *Alsophila pometaria)*, destructive to fruit and shade trees.

can•na (kăn′ə) *n.* Any of various perennial tropical herbs of the genus *Canna*, having clusters of large showy flowers and including an edible variety. [Lat. *canna*, cane. See CANE.]

can•na•bin (kăn′ə-bĭn) *n.* A resinous material extracted from cannabis. [CANNAB(IS) + –IN.]

can•nab•i•noid (kə-năb′ə-noid′) *n.* Any of various organic substances, such as THC, found in cannabis.

can•na•bis (kăn′ə-bĭs) *n.* **1.** An annual dioecious plant *(Cannabis sativa)* native to central Asia and having tough bast fibers. **2.** Any of several mildly euphoriant, intoxicating hallucinogenic drugs, such as marijuana, prepared from this plant. [Lat. < Gk. *kannabis*.] **—can′na•bic** (-bĭk) *adj.*

Can•nae (kăn′ē) An ancient town of SE Italy where Carthaginians defeated the Romans in 216 B.C.

canned (kănd) *adj.* **1.** Preserved and sealed in a can or jar. **2.** *Informal* Recorded or taped for repeated use on television or radio. **3.** *Informal* **a.** Used repeatedly with little or no change. **b.** Completely unoriginal.

can•nel (kăn′əl) *n.* A bituminous coal that burns brightly with much smoke. [Perh. short for *cannel coal*, dialectal var. of *candle coal* (< its bright flame).]

can•nel•li•ni bean (kăn′ə-lē′nē, kä′nə-) *n.* A large white variety of kidney bean. [Ital. *cannellini*, pl. of *cannellino*, dim. of *cannello*, little tube, dim. of *canna*, reed, stalk < Lat. See CANE.]

can•nel•lo•ni (kăn′ə-lō′nē, kä′nə-) *n.* **1.** Pasta in large-sized tubes. **2.** A dish consisting of such tubes stuffed with meat or cheese and baked in a tomato or cream sauce. [Ital., pl. of *cannellone*, tubular soup noodle < *cannello*, small tube, dim. of *canna*, reed < Lat. See CANE.]

can•ner•y (kăn′ə-rē) *n., pl.* **-ies** A factory where fish, vegetables, or other foods are canned.

Cannes (kăn, kănz, kän) A resort city of SE France on the Mediterranean Sea near Nice. Pop. 72,259.

can•ni•bal (kăn′ə-bəl) *n.* **1.** A person who eats the flesh of other humans. **2.** An animal that feeds on others of its own kind. [< Sp. *Caníbalis*, name (as recorded by Christopher Columbus) of the allegedly cannibalistic Caribs of Cuba and Haiti, var. of *caríbalis* < earlier Carib *karibna*, person, Carib.] **—can′ni•bal•ism** *n.* **—can′ni•bal•is′tic** *adj.*

can•ni•bal•ize (kăn′ə-bə-līz′) *v.* **-ized, -iz•ing, -iz•es** *—tr.* **1.** To remove parts from (damaged airplanes, for example) for use in repairing similar equipment. **2.** To deprive of vital elements or resources for use elsewhere. **3.** To draw on as a major source. **4.** To practice cannibalism on. *—intr.* To practice cannibalism. **—can′ni•bal•i•za′tion** (-bə-lĭ-zā′shən) *n.*

can•ni•kin (kăn′ĭ-kĭn) *n.* **1.** A small can or cup. **2.** A small wooden bucket. [Du. *kanneken* (< MDu. *cannekijn*, dim. of *canne*, can) and Flem. *cannikin*, dim. of *cann*, can.]

Can•ning (kăn′ĭng), **George** 1770–1827. British politician who served as foreign secretary (1807–09 and 1822–27) and prime minister (1827).

Can•nock (kăn′ək) An urban district of W-central England NNW of Birmingham; center of a mining area based at **Cannock Chase**, a nearby moorland. Pop. 84,900.

can•no•li (kə-nō′lē, kă-) *n., pl.* **-lis** A pastry roll with a creamy sweet filling. [Ital., pl. of *cannolo*, tube, dim. of *canna*, reed < Lat. See CANE.]

can•non (kăn′ən) *n., pl.* **cannon** or **-nons 1.** A large mounted weapon that fires heavy projectiles. **2.** The loop at the top of a bell by which it is hung. **3.** A round bit for a horse. **4.** *Zoology* The section of the lower leg in some hoofed mammals between the hock or knee and the fetlock, containing the cannon bone. **5.** *Chiefly British* A carom made in billiards. ❖ *v.* **-noned, -non•ing, -nons** *—tr.* **1.** To bombard with cannon. **2.** *Chiefly British* To cause to carom in billiards. *—intr.* **1.** To fire cannon. **2.** *Chiefly British* To make a carom in billiards. [ME *canon* < OFr. < OItal. *cannone*, augmentative of *canna*, tube < Lat., reed. See CANE.]

Cannon, Joseph Gurney 1836–1926. Amer. politician who was speaker of the US House of Representatives (1903–11).

can•non•ade (kăn′ə-nād′) *tr. & intr.v.* **-ad•ed, -ad•ing, -ades** To assault with or deliver heavy artillery fire. ❖ *n.* **1.** A long, usu. heavy discharge of artillery. **2.** A harsh verbal or physical attack. [< Fr. *canonade*, artillery discharge < Ital. *cannonata* < *cannone*, cannon < OItal. See CANNON.]

can•non•ball also **cannon ball** (kăn′ən-bôl′) *n.* **1.** A round projectile fired from a cannon. **2.** A jump into water made with the arms grasping the upraised knees. **3.** Something, such as a fast train, moving with great speed. **4.** *Sports* A fast low serve in tennis. ❖ *intr.v.* **-balled, -ball•ing, -balls 1.** To travel with great speed. **2.** To make a cannonball jump.

cannon bone *n.* A supporting bone of the leg in some hoofed mammals, analogous to the metatarsus in humans.

can•non•eer (kăn′ə-nîr′) *n.* A soldier in the artillery.

cannon fodder *n.* Soldiers, sailors, or other military personnel regarded as likely to be killed or wounded in combat.

can•non•ry (kăn′ən-rē) *n., pl.* **-ries 1.** A battery of cannons; artillery. **2.** Artillery fire.

can•not (kăn′ŏt, kə-nŏt′, kă-) *aux.v.* The negative form of **can**[1].

USAGE NOTE Several idiomatic phrases containing *cannot* have come under fire for being redundant or illogical; in truth, all are

cane toad
Bufo marinus

cannoli

ă	**pat**	oi	**boy**
ā	**pay**	ou	**out**
âr	**care**	ŏŏ	**took**
ä	**father**	ōō	**boot**
ĕ	**pet**	ŭ	**cut**
ē	**be**	ûr	**urge**
ĭ	**pit**	th	**thin**
ī	**pie**	*th*	**this**
îr	**pier**	hw	**which**
ŏ	**pot**	zh	**vision**
ō	**toe**	ə	**about,**
ô	**paw**		**item**

Stress marks:
′ (primary);
′ (secondary), as in
lexicon (lĕk′sĭ-kŏn′)

well established and have been used by respected writers. *Cannot but* has sometimes been criticized as a double negative, perhaps because it has been confused with the synonymous *can but*. In *cannot but,* however, *but* means "except" (as it also does in *no one but*), while in *can but* it means *only.* • The construction *cannot help* is used with a present participle to roughly the same effect as *cannot but* (as in *We cannot help admiring his courage*), usually implying that a person is unable to affect an outcome normally under his or her control. • The construction *cannot help but* probably arose as a blend of *cannot help* and *cannot but*; it has the meaning of the first and the syntax of the second: *We cannot help but admire his courage.* • The expression *cannot seem to* means "appear to be unable to" (as in *He can't seem to get angry*); it has been objected to because its syntax would seem to dictate that it should mean "be incapable of appearing to." But the syntax of English does not allow a logical equivalent such as *He seems to cannot get angry*, and *cannot seem to* is used so widely that objections on logical grounds are pedantic. See Usage Notes at **but, help.**

can·nu·la also **can·u·la** (kăn′yə-lə) *n., pl.* **-las** or **-lae** (-lē′) A flexible tube, usu. containing a trocar at one end, that is inserted into a body cavity, duct, or vessel to drain fluid or administer a substance. [Lat., dim. of *canna*, reed. See CANE.]

can·nu·lar also **can·u·lar** (kăn′yə-lər) *adj.* Of, relating to, or resembling a tube; tubular.

can·nu·late also **can·u·late** (kăn′yə-lāt′) *tr.v.* **-lat·ed, -lat·ing, -lates** To insert a cannula into (a body cavity, duct, or vessel). ❖ *adj.* Tubular; hollow. —**can′nu·la′tion** *n.*

can·ny (kăn′ē) *adj.* **-ni·er, -ni·est** 1. Careful and shrewd, esp. in regard to one's own interests. 2. Cautious with money; frugal. 3. *Scots* **a.** Steady, restrained, and gentle. **b.** Snug and quiet. [< CAN¹.] —**can′ni·ly** *adv.* —**can′ni·ness** *n.*

ca·noe (kə-nōō′) *n.* A light, open, slender boat that has pointed ends and is propelled by paddles. ❖ *v.* **-noed, -noe·ing, -noes** —*tr.* To carry or send by canoe. —*intr.* To travel in or propel a canoe. [Fr. *canoe* and Sp. *canoa* (Fr. < Sp.), of Cariban orig.] —**ca·noe′ist** *n.*

canoe birch *n.* See **paper birch.**

can of worms *n., pl.* **cans of worms** *Informal* A source of unforeseen and troublesome complexity.

ca·no·la (kə-nō′lə) *n.* A rapeseed oil that is low in erucic acid content and high in monounsaturated fatty acids. [*Can(ada) o(il,) l(ow) a(cid).*]

can·on¹ (kăn′ən) *n.* 1. A law or code of laws established by a church council. 2. A secular law, rule, or code of law. 3a. An established principle. **b.** A basis for judgment; a standard or criterion. 4. The books of the Bible officially accepted as Holy Scripture. 5a. A group of literary works generally accepted as representing a field. **b.** The works of a writer that have been accepted as authentic. 6. *Canon* The part of the Mass beginning after the Preface and Sanctus and ending just before the Lord's Prayer. 7. *Roman Catholic Church* The calendar of saints. 8. *Music* A composition or passage in which a melody is imitated by one or more voices at fixed intervals of pitch and time. [ME *canoun* < OE *canon* and < OFr., both < Lat. *canōn*, rule < Gk. *kanōn*, measuring rod, rule.]

can·on² (kăn′ən) *n.* 1. A member of a chapter of priests serving in a cathedral or collegiate church. 2. A member of certain religious communities living under a common rule and bound by vows. [ME *canoun* < Norman Fr. *canun* < LLat. *canōnicus*, one living under a rule < Lat. *canōn*, rule. See CANON¹.]

ca·ñon (kăn′yən) *n.* Variant of **canyon.**

can·on·ess (kăn′ə-nĭs) *n.* A member of a religious community of women under a common rule but not bound by vows.

ca·non·i·cal (kə-nŏn′ĭ-kəl) also **ca·non·ic** (-ĭk) *adj.* 1. Of, relating to, or required by canon law. 2. Of the biblical canon. 3. Conforming to orthodox or well-established rules or patterns. 4. Of or belonging to a cathedral chapter. 5. Of or relating to a literary canon. 6. *Music* Having the form of a canon. —**ca·non′i·cal·ly** *adv.* —**can′on·ic′i·ty** (kăn′ə-nĭs′ĭ-tē) *n.*

canonical hours *pl.n. Ecclesiastical* 1. The times of day at which canon law prescribes certain prayers to be said. 2. The prayers said at these times.

ca·non·i·cals (kə-nŏn′ĭ-kəlz) *pl.n. Ecclesiastical* The dress prescribed by canon for officiating clergy.

can·on·ist (kăn′ə-nĭst) *n.* A person specializing in canon law. —**can′on·is′tic, can′on·is′ti·cal** *adj.*

can·on·ize (kăn′ə-nīz′) *tr.v.* **-ized, -iz·ing, -iz·es** 1. To declare (a deceased person) to be a saint and entitled to full honor as such. 2. To include in the biblical canon. 3. To include in a literary canon. 4. To approve as within canon law. 5. To treat as sacred; glorify. —**can′on·i·za′tion** (-ĭ-zā′shən) *n.* —**can′on·iz′er** *n.*

canon law *n.* The body of rules for a Christian church.

can·on·ry (kăn′ən-rē) *n., pl.* **-ries** 1. The office or dignity of a canon. 2. Canons considered as a group.

Ca·no·pic or **Ca·no·pic** (kə-nō′pĭk, -nŏp′ĭk) *adj.* Of, relating to, or being an ancient Egyptian vase, urn, or jar used to hold the viscera of an embalmed body. [After CANOPUS¹.]

Ca·no·pus¹ (kə-nō′pəs) An ancient city of N Egypt E of Alexan-

canopy
canopy bed

cantaloupe
Cucumis melo var.
reticulatus

dria; site of a temple honoring Serapis.

Ca·no·pus² (kə-nō′pəs) *n.* A star in the constellation Carina. [Lat. *Canōpus* < Gk. *kanōpos*, perh. of Egypt. orig.]

can·o·py (kăn′ə-pē) *n., pl.* **-pies** 1. A covering, usu. of cloth, suspended over a throne or bed or held aloft on poles. 2. *Architecture* An ornamental rooflike projection over a niche, an altar, or a tomb. 3. A protective rooflike covering over a walkway or door. 4. A high, overarching covering, such as the sky. 5. The uppermost layer in a forest, formed by the crowns of the trees. 6. The transparent enclosure over the cockpit of an aircraft. 7. The part of a parachute that opens up to catch the air. ❖ *tr.v.* **-pied, -py·ing, -pies** To cover with or as if with a canopy. [ME *canape* < Med.Lat. *canāpēum*, mosquito net < Lat. *cōnōpēum* < Gk. *kōnōpeion*, bed with mosquito netting < *kōnōps, kōnōp-*, mosquito.]

ca·no·rous (kə-nôr′əs, -nōr′-, kăn′ər-əs) *adj.* Richly melodious; tuneful. [< Lat. *canōrus* < *canor*, tune < *canere*, to sing. See kanin App.] —**ca·no′rous·ly** *adv.* —**ca·no′rous·ness** *n.*

Ca·no·va (kə-nō′və), **Antonio** 1757–1822. Italian sculptor who was important in the development of neoclassicism.

Can·so (kăn′sō), **Strait of** A narrow channel between Cape Breton I. and the NE mainland of Nova Scotia, Canada.

canst (kănst) *aux.v. Archaic* A second person singular present tense of **can¹.**

cant¹ (kănt) *n.* 1. Angular deviation from a vertical or horizontal plane or surface; an inclination or a slope. 2. A slanted or oblique surface. 3a. A thrust or motion that tilts something. **b.** The tilt caused by such a thrust or motion. 4. An outer corner, as of a building. ❖ *v.* **cant·ed, cant·ing, cants** —*tr.* 1. To set at an oblique angle; tilt. 2. To give a slanting edge to; bevel. 3. To change the direction of suddenly. —*intr.* 1. To lean to one side; slant. 2. To take an oblique direction or course; swing around. [ME, side < ONFr. < VLat. **cantus*, corner < Lat. *canthus*, rim of wheel, tire, of Celt. orig.]

cant² (kănt) *n.* 1. Insincere speech full of platitudes or pious expressions. 2. The special vocabulary peculiar to the members of a group. 3. Whining or singsong speech, such as that of beggars. 4. *Cant* See **Shelta.** ❖ *intr.v.* **cant·ed, cant·ing, cants** 1. To speak tediously or sententiously; moralize. 2. To speak in argot or jargon. 3. To speak in a whining, pleading tone. [AN *cant*, song, singing < *canter*, to sing < Lat. *cantāre*. See kan- in App.]

Cant. *abbr. Bible* Canticle of Canticles

can't (kănt) Contraction of *cannot.*

can·ta·bi·le (kän-tä′bĭ-lā′) *Music adv. & adj.* In a smooth, lyrical, flowing style. ❖ *n.* A cantabile passage or movement. [Ital. < LLat. *cantābilis*, worthy to be sung < Lat. *cantāre*, to sing. See kan- in App.]

Can·ta·bri·an Mountains (kăn-tā′brē-ən) A range of N Spain extending c. 483 km (300 mi) along the coast of the Bay of Biscay.

Can·ta·brig·i·an (kăn′tə-brĭj′ē-ən) *adj.* 1. Of or relating to Cambridge, England, or Cambridge, Massachusetts. 2. Of or relating to Cambridge University. [< Med.Lat. *Cantabrigia*, Cambridge, England.] —**Can′ta·brig′i·an** *n.*

can·ta·la (kăn-tä′lə) *n.* 1. A species of agave (*Agave cantala*) cultivated chiefly in warm regions of the Old World. 2. The fiber of this plant, used for twine, rope, and nets. [NLat., specific epithet, perh. < Skt. *kaṇṭalah*, babul < *kaṇṭaḥ*, thorn.]

can·ta·loup also **can·ta·loupe** (kăn′tl-ōp′) *n.* 1. A variety of melon (*Cucumis melo* var. *reticulatus*) having a tan rind with netlike ridges and a sweet fragrant orange flesh. 2. Any of several other related or similar melons. [Fr. *cantaloup*, perh. < Ital. *cantalupo* (< Cantalupo, a former papal villa near Rome) or < Cantaloup, a village of S France.]

can·tan·ker·ous (kăn-tăng′kər-əs) *adj.* Ill-tempered and quarrelsome; disagreeable. [Perh. < ME *contek*, dissension (influenced by such words as RANCOROUS and CANKEROUS) < AN *contec*, poss. < Lat. *contāctus*, p. part. of *contingere*, to touch. See CONTACT.] —**can·tan′ker·ous·ly** *adv.* —**can·tan′ker·ous·ness** *n.*

can·ta·ta (kən-tä′tə) *n.* A musical composition, often using a sacred text, comprising recitatives, arias, and choruses. [Ital. (*aria*) *cantata*, sung (aria), fem. p. part. of *cantare*, to sing < Lat. *cantāre*. See kan- in App.]

can·teen (kăn-tēn′) *n.* 1a. A snack bar or small cafeteria, as on a military installation. **b.** A recreational facility, bar, or small general store formerly established for the patronage of soldiers. 2. A recreation hall or social club where refreshments are available. 3. A temporary or mobile eating place. 4. A flask for carrying drinking water, as on a hike. 5a. A box with compartments for carrying cooking gear and eating utensils. **b.** A soldier's mess kit. 6. *Chiefly British* A box used to store silverware. [Fr. *cantine* < Ital. *cantina*, wine cellar.]

can·ter (kăn′tər) *n.* A smooth gait, esp. of a horse, that is slower than a gallop but faster than a trot. ❖ *v.* **-tered, -ter·ing, -ters** —*intr.* 1. To ride a horse at a canter. 2. To go or move at a canter. —*tr.* To cause (a horse) to go at a canter. [Ult. < phrases such as *Canterbury gallop*, after CANTERBURY, toward which pilgrims rode at an easy pace.]

Can·ter·bur·y (kăn′tər-bĕr′ē, -brē, -tə-) A borough of SE England on the Stour R. ESE of London. Canterbury Cathedral (11th–16th cent.) is the seat of the archbishop and primate of the Anglican Communion. Pop. 36,000.

Canterbury bells *pl.n. (used with a sing. or pl. verb)* A European biennial herb *(Campanula medium)* widely cultivated for its showy flowers.

can•tha•ris (kăn′thər-ĭs) *n., pl.* **can•thar•i•des** (kăn-thăr′ĭ-dēz′) **1.** A green blister beetle *(Lytta vesicatoria* or *Cantharis vesicatoria)* of central and southern Europe. **2. cantharides** *(used with a sing. or pl. verb)* A toxic preparation of the crushed dried bodies of this beetle, formerly used as a counterirritant for skin blisters and as an aphrodisiac. [Lat. *cantharis, cantharid-* < Gk. *kantharis* < *kantharos.*]

can•thi•tis (kăn-thī′tĭs) *n.* Inflammation of the canthus.

cant hook *n.* A wooden lever with a movable metal hook near one end, used for handling logs. [< CANT[1].]

can•thus (kăn′thəs) *n., pl.* **-thi** (-thī′) The angle formed by the meeting of the upper and lower eyelids at either side of the eye. [LLat. < Gk. *kanthos.*]

can•ti•cle (kăn′tĭ-kəl) *n.* **1.** A song or chant based on a biblical text not in the Book of Psalms. **2. Canticles** *Bible* The Song of Songs. [ME < Lat. *canticulum,* dim. of *cantus,* song < p. part. of *canere,* to sing.]

Canticle of Canticles *n.* The Song of Songs.

Can•ti•gny (käɴ-tē-nyē′) A village of N France S of Amiens; site of the first US World War I offensive (May 1918).

can•ti•le•na (kăn′tl-ē′nə) *n.* A sustained, smooth-flowing melody. [Ital. < Lat. *cantilēna,* song < *cantus.* See CANTICLE.]

can•ti•le•ver (kăn′tl-ē′vər, -ĕv′ər) *n.* **1.** A projecting structure, such as a beam, that is supported at one end and carries a load at the other end or along its length. **2.** A member, such as a beam, that projects beyond a fulcrum and is supported by a balancing member or a downward force behind the fulcrum. **3.** A bracket or block supporting a balcony or cornice. ❖ *v.* **-vered, -ver•ing, -vers** *—tr.* To construct as or in the manner of a cantilever. *—intr.* To extend outward as or in the manner of a cantilever. [Perh. CANT[1] + LEVER.]

cantilever bridge *n.* A bridge formed by two projecting beams or trusses joined in the center by a connecting member and supported on piers and anchored by counterbalancing members.

can•til•late (kăn′tl-āt′) *tr. & intr.v.* **-lat•ed, -lat•ing, -lates** To chant or recite in a musical monotone. [Lat. *cantilāre, cantilāt-,* to sing < *cantāre.* See **kan-** in App.] **—can′til•la′tion** *n.*

can•ti•na (kăn-tē′nə) *n. Southwestern US* A bar; a tavern. [Sp., canteen < Ital., wine cellar.]

can•tle (kăn′tl) *n.* **1.** The raised rear part of a saddle. **2.** A corner, segment, or portion; a piece. [ME *cantel,* corner < OFr. < Med.Lat. *cantellus* < VLat. *cantus. See CANT[1].]

can•to (kăn′tō) *n., pl.* **-tos** One of the principal divisions of a long poem. [Ital. < Lat. *cantus,* song. See CANTICLE.]

can•ton (kăn′tən, -tŏn′) *n.* **1a.** A small territorial division of a country. **b.** A subdivision of an arrondissement in France. **2.** *Heraldry* A small, square division of a shield, usu. in the upper right corner. **3.** A usu. rectangular division of a flag in the upper corner next to the staff. [Fr. < OFr. < OItal. *cantone,* augmentative of *canto,* corner < VLat. *cantus. See CANT[1].] **—can′ton•al** (kăn′tə-nəl, kăn-tŏn′əl) *adj.*

Can•ton (kăn′tən) **1.** A city of NE OH SSE of Akron. Pop. 80,806. **2.** (kăn′tŏn′, kăn′tŏn′) See **Guangzhou.**

Can•ton crepe (kăn′tŏn′) *n.* A soft silk or rayon fabric with a crinkled texture. [After *Canton* (Guangzhou), China.]

Can•ton•ese (kăn′tə-nēz′, -nēs′) *n.* **1.** A native or inhabitant of Guangzhou (formerly Canton). **2.** The variety of Chinese spoken in and around Guangzhou. **—Can′ton•ese′** *adj.*

Can•ton flannel (kăn′tŏn′) *n.* Flannelette. [After *Canton* (Guangzhou), China.]

can•ton•ment (kăn-tōn′mənt, -tŏn′-) *n.* **1a.** A group of temporary billets for troops. **b.** Assignment of troops to temporary quarters. **2.** A permanent military installation in India. [< CANTON, to quarter soldiers.]

can•tor (kăn′tər) *n.* **1.** The religious official who leads the musical part of a Jewish service. **2.** The person who leads the singing in a church; a precentor. [Lat., singer < *canere,* to sing. See **kan-** in App.] **—can•to′ri•al** (kăn-tôr′ē-əl, -tōr′-) *adj.*

can•trip (kăn′trĭp) *n.* **1.** *Scots* A magic spell; a witch's trick. **2.** *Chiefly British* A deceptive move; a sham. [?]

can•tus fir•mus (kăn′təs fîr′məs, fûr′-) *n.* A preexisting melody used as the basis of a polyphonic composition. [Med.Lat. : Lat. *cantus,* song + Lat. *firmus,* fixed.]

Ca•nuck (kə-nŭk′) *n. Often Offensive Slang* A Canadian, esp. a French Canadian. [Prob. alteration of CANADIAN.]

can•u•la (kăn′yə-lə) *n.* Variant of **cannula.**

can•u•lar (kăn′yə-lər) *adj.* Variant of **cannular.**

can•u•late (kăn′yə-lāt′) *v. & adj.* Variant of **cannulate.**

Ca•nute also **Cnut** or **Knut** (kə-no͞ot′, -nyo͞ot′) Known as "the Great." 994?–1035. King of England (1016–35), Denmark (1018–35), and Norway (1028–35).

can•vas (kăn′vəs) *n.* **1.** A heavy, coarse fabric of cotton, hemp, or flax, used for tents and sails. **2a.** A piece of canvas on which a painting is created. **b.** A painting thus created. **3.** A fabric of coarse open weave, used as a foundation for needlework. **4.** The background of events. **5.** *Nautical* A sail or set of sails. **6a.** A tent or group of tents. **b.** A circus tent. **7.** *Sports* The floor of a boxing or wrestling ring. ***—idiom:* under canvas 1.** *Nautical* With sails spread. **2.** In a tent or tents. [ME *canevas* < OFr. and < Med.Lat. *canavāsium,* both ult. < Lat. *cannabis,* hemp. See CANNABIS.]

can•vas•back (kăn′vəs-băk′) *n.* A North American wild duck *(Aythya valisineria)* having a reddish-brown head and neck and a whitish back.

canvas duck *n.* A fabric made of lightweight cotton or linen.

can•vass (kăn′vəs) *v.* **-vassed, -vass•ing, -vass•es** *—tr.* **1.** To examine carefully or discuss thoroughly; scrutinize. **2a.** To go through (a region) or go to (persons) to solicit votes or orders. **b.** To survey (public opinion). *—intr.* **1.** To make or conduct a thorough canvass. **2.** To solicit voters, orders, or opinions. ❖ *n.* **1.** An examination or discussion. **2.** A solicitation of votes or orders. **3.** A survey of public opinion. [< obsolete *canvass,* to toss in a canvas sheet as punishment < CANVAS.] **—can′vass•er** *n.*

can•yon also **ca•ñon** (kăn′yən) *n.* A narrow chasm with steep cliff walls, cut into the earth by running water; a gorge. [Sp. *cañon,* augmentative of *caña,* tube, cane < Lat. *canna,* reed. See CANE.]

Canyon de Chel•ly (də shā′) A canyon in NE AZ containing the ruins of Anasazi cliff dwellings built between A.D. 350 and 1300.

can•zo•ne (kăn-zō′nē, kănt-sō′nĕ) *n., pl.* **-nes** (-nēz, -nāz) or **-ni** (-nē) **1.** A medieval Italian or Provençal lyric of varying stanzaic form. **2.** A polyphonic song evolving from this form of poetry. [Ital. < Lat. *cantiō, cantiōn-,* song < *cantus,* p. part. of *canere,* to sing. See **kan-** in App.]

can•zo•net (kăn′zə-nĕt′) *n.* A short lighthearted song. [< Ital. *canzonetta,* dim. of *canzone.* See CANZONE.]

caou•tchouc (kou′cho͝ok′, -cho͝ok′) *n.* See **rubber**[1] 1. [Fr., prob. < Sp. *caucho* < Tupi *cau-ucha.*]

cap[1] (kăp) *n.* **1.** A usu. soft and close-fitting head covering. **2a.** A head covering worn to indicate rank, occupation, or membership in a group. **b.** An academic mortarboard. **3a.** A protective cover or seal, esp. one that closes off an end or a tip. **b.** A crown for covering or sealing a tooth. **c.** A tread for a worn pneumatic tire. **d.** A fitted covering used to seal a well or large pipe. **4.** A summit or top, as of a mountain. **5.** An upper limit; a ceiling. **6.** *Architecture* The capital of a column. **7.** *Botany* **a.** The pileus of a mushroom. **b.** A calyptra. **8a.** A percussion cap. **b.** A small explosive charge enclosed in paper for use in a toy gun. **9.** Any of several sizes of writing paper, such as foolscap. **10.** *Sports* An appearance by a player in an international soccer game, traditionally rewarded with a hat. ❖ *tr.v.* **capped, cap•ping, caps 1.** To cover, protect, or seal with a cap. **2.** To award a special cap to as a sign of rank or achievement. **3.** To lie over or on top of; cover. **4.** To apply the finishing touch to; complete: *cap a meal with dessert.* **5.** To follow with something better; surpass or outdo. **6.** To set an upper limit on. ***—idioms:* cap in hand** Respectfully or humbly. **set (one's) cap for** To attempt to attract and win as a mate. [ME *cappe* < OE *cæppe* < LLat. *cappa.*]

cap[2] (kăp) *Informal n.* A capital letter. ❖ *tr.v.* **capped, cap•ping, caps** To capitalize. [Shortened form of CAPITAL[1].]

cap[3] (kăp) *n. Informal* **1.** Capital: *venture cap.* **2.** Capitalization: *market cap.*

CAP *abbr.* Civil Air Patrol

cap. *abbr.* **1.** capacity **2.** capital

ca•pa•bil•i•ty (kā′pə-bĭl′ĭ-tē) *n., pl.* **-ties 1.** The quality of being capable; ability. **2.** A talent or ability that has potential for development or use. Often used in the plural. **3.** The capacity to be used, treated, or developed for a specific purpose.

ca•pa•ble (kā′pə-bəl) *adj.* **1.** Having capacity or ability; efficient and able. **2.** Having the ability required for a specific task or accomplishment; qualified. **3.** Having the inclination or disposition. **4.** Permitting an action to be performed: *a camera capable of being used underwater.* [LLat. *capābilis* < *capere,* to take. See **kap-** in App.] **—ca′pa•ble•ness** *n.* **—ca′pa•bly** *adv.*

ca•pa•cious (kə-pā′shəs) *adj.* Capable of containing a large quantity; spacious. [< Lat. *capāx, capāc-* < *capere,* to take. See **kap-** in App.] **—ca•pa′cious•ly** *adv.* **—ca•pa′cious•ness** *n.*

ca•pac•i•tance (kə-păs′ĭ-təns) *n.* **1.** *Symbol* **C** The ratio of electric charge to potential on an isolated conductor. **2.** *Symbol* **C** The ratio of the electric charge on one of a pair of conductors to the potential difference between them. **3a.** The property of a circuit element that permits it to store charge. **b.** The part of the circuit exhibiting capacitance. [CAPACIT(Y) + -ANCE.] **—ca•pac′i•tive** (-tĭv) *adj.* **—ca•pac′i•tive•ly** *adv.*

ca•pac•i•tate (kə-păs′ĭ-tāt′) *tr.v.* **-tat•ed, -tat•ing, -tates 1.** To render fit or make qualified; enable. **2.** *Biology* To cause (spermatozoa) to undergo the physical changes needed to fertilize an egg. [CAPACIT(Y) + -ATE[1].] **—ca•pac′i•ta′tion** *n.*

ca•pac•i•tor (kə-păs′ĭ-tər) *n.* An electric circuit element used to store charge temporarily, consisting in general of two metallic plates separated and insulated from each other by a dielectric.

ca•pac•i•ty (kə-păs′ĭ-tē) *n., pl.* **-ties 1a.** The ability to receive, hold, or absorb. **b.** A measure of this ability; volume. **2.** The maximum amount that can be contained. **3a.** Ability to perform or produce; capability. **b.** The maximum or optimum amount that can be produced. **4.** The power to learn or retain knowledge; mental ability. **5.** Innate potential for development or accomplishment; faculty. **6.** The quality of being suitable for specified treatment. **7.** The position in which one functions; role. **8.** *Legal* qualification or authority. **9.** *Electricity* Capacitance. ❖ *adj.* Filling a space to capacity. [ME *capacite* < OFr. < Lat. *capācitās*

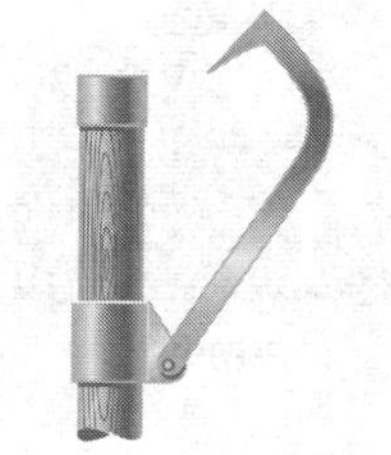

cant hook

canvasback
Aythya valisineria

ă pat	oi boy
ā pay	ou out
âr care	o͝o took
ä father	o͞o boot
ĕ pet	ŭ cut
ē be	ûr urge
ĭ pit	th thin
ī pie	*th* this
îr pier	hw which
ŏ pot	zh vision
ō toe	ə about,
ô paw	item

Stress marks:
′ (primary);
′ (secondary), as in
lexicon (lĕk′sĭ-kŏn′)

< *capāx, capāc-,* spacious. See CAPACIOUS.]

ca·par·i·son (kə-păr′ĭ-sən) *n.* **1.** An ornamental covering for a horse or for its saddle or harness; trappings. **2.** Richly ornamented clothing; finery. ❖ *tr.v.* **-soned, -son·ing, -sons 1.** To outfit (a horse) with an ornamental covering. **2.** To dress (another) in rich clothing. [Obsolete Fr. *caparasson* < OSpan. *caparazón* < Med.Lat. *cappa,* cloak. See CAPE¹.]

cape¹ (kāp) *n.* **1.** A sleeveless outer garment fastened at the throat and worn over the shoulders. **2.** A brightly colored cloth used in maneuvering the bull in a bullfight; a capote or muleta. [ME *cape,* partly < var. of *cope,* cope; see COPE¹, and partly < AN *cape* (< Med.Lat. *cāpa,* var. of LLat. *cappa*).]

cape² (kāp) *n.* A point or head of land projecting into a body of water. [ME *cap* < OFr. < O Provençal < Lat. *caput,* head. See **kaput-** in App.]

Cape *or* **Cape of** For names of actual capes, see the specific element of the names; for example, **Hatteras, Cape; Good Hope, Cape of.**

Cape Bret·on Island (brĕt′n, brĭt′n) An island forming the NE part of Nova Scotia, Canada.

Cape buffalo *n.* See **African buffalo.**

Cape Cod Canal A waterway, c. 28 km (17.5 mi), of SE MA connecting Buzzards Bay with **Cape Cod Bay,** the S part of Massachusetts Bay.

Cape Cod cottage *n.* A compact house of one or one-and-a-half stories with a gabled roof and a central chimney.

Cape Coral A city of SW FL on the estuary of the Caloosahatchee R. SW of Fort Myers. Pop. 102,286.

Cape Fear River A river rising in central NC and flowing c. 325 km (202 mi) SE to the Atlantic Ocean N of Cape Fear.

Cape gooseberry *n.* A tropical South American plant (*Physalis peruviana*) having an edible yellow berry.

Cape jasmine *n.* See **gardenia.**

Ča·pek (chä′pĕk′), **Karel** 1890–1938. Czech writer whose works include the play *R.U.R.* (1921).

cap·e·lin (kăp′ə-lĭn, kăp′lĭn) *also* **cap·lin** (kăp′lĭn) *n.* A small edible marine fish (*Mallotus villosus*) of northern Atlantic and Pacific waters. [Canadian Fr. *capelan* < Fr., codfish < O Provençal < Med.Lat. *cappelānus.* See CHAPLAIN.]

Ca·pel·la (kə-pĕl′ə) *n.* A double star in Auriga, the brightest star in the constellation. [Lat., dim. of *caper,* goat.]

Cape primrose *n.* Any of various chiefly African plants of the genus *Streptocarpus,* having clusters of showy flowers.

Cape Province Officially **Cape of Good Hope Province;** formerly (before 1910) **Cape Colony.** A province and historical region of S South Africa on the Atlantic and Indian oceans.

ca·per¹ (kā′pər) *n.* **1.** A playful leap or hop. **2.** A frivolous escapade or prank. **3.** *Slang* An illegal plot or enterprise, esp. one involving theft. ❖ *intr.v.* **-pered, -per·ing, -pers** To leap or frisk about; frolic. [Alteration of CAPRIOLE.]

ca·per² (kā′pər) *n.* **1.** A usu. spiny Mediterranean shrub (*Capparis spinosa*) having dehiscent fruits with reddish pulp. **2.** A pickled flower bud of this plant, used as a pungent condiment. [ME *caperis, capar* < Lat. *capparis* < Gk. *kapparis.*]

cap·er·cail·lie (kăp′ər-kāl′yē) *also* **cap·er·cail·zie** (-kāl′zē) *n.* A large grouse (*Tetrao urogallus*) native to northern Europe with dark plumage and a fanlike tail. [Sc. Gael. *capull coille* : *capull,* horse (ult. < Lat. *caballus,* of Celt. orig.) + *coille,* genitive of *coille,* forest (< OIr. *caill*).]

Ca·per·na·um (kə-pûr′nē-əm) A city of ancient Palestine on the NW shore of the Sea of Galilee.

cape·skin (kāp′skĭn′) *n.* Soft leather made from sheepskin, used esp. for gloves. [After the *Cape* of GOOD HOPE.]

Ca·pet (kā′pĭt, kăp′ĭt, kä-pā′) A dynasty of French kings (987–1328), including **Hugh Capet** (940?–996), who was elected king in 987. —**Ca·pe′tian** (kə-pē′shən) *adj. & n.*

Cape Town *or* **Cape·town** (kāp′toun′) The legislative cap. of South Africa, in the extreme SW part on the Atlantic Ocean; founded 1652. Pop. 854,616.

Cape Verde (vûrd) An island country of the Atlantic Ocean W of Senegal; gained independence from Portugal in 1975. Cap. Praia. Pop. 381,000.

Cape York Peninsula A peninsula of NE Australia between the Gulf of Carpentaria and the Coral Sea.

cap·ful (kăp′fŏŏl) *n., pl.* **-fuls** The amount a cap can hold.

Cap Hai·tien (kăp′ hā′shən) *or* **Cap-Ha·ï·tien** (kä-pä-ē-syăN′) A city of N Haiti on the Atlantic Ocean; founded c. 1670. Pop. 64,406.

ca·pi·as (kā′pē-əs) *n. Law* A warrant for arrest. [ME < Med.Lat. *capiās* < Lat., second pers. sing. pr. subjunctive of *capere,* to seize (the first word of the writ). See **kap-** in App.]

cap·il·lar·i·ty (kăp′ə-lăr′ĭ-tē) *n., pl.* **-ties** The interaction between contacting surfaces of a liquid and a solid that distorts the liquid surface from a planar shape.

cap·il·lar·y (kăp′ə-lĕr′ē) *adj.* **1.** Relating to or resembling a hair; fine and slender. **2.** Having a very small internal diameter. **3.** *Anatomy* Of or relating to the capillaries. **4.** *Physics* Of or relating to capillarity. ❖ *n., pl.* **-ies 1.** *Anatomy* One of the minute blood vessels that connect arterioles and venules. **2.** A capillary tube. [< Lat. *capillāris* < *capillus,* hair.]

capillary action *n.* See **capillary.**

caparison

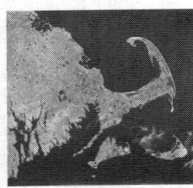
cape²
infrared image of Cape Cod, Massachusetts

Cape Cod cottage

capillary attraction *n.* The force that results from greater adhesion of a liquid to a solid surface than internal cohesion of the liquid itself and causes the liquid to be raised against a vertical surface.

cap·i·tal¹ (kăp′ĭ-tl) *n.* **1a.** A town or city that is the official seat of government in a political entity, such as a state or nation. **b.** A city that is the center of a specific activity or industry. **2a.** Wealth in the form of money or property, used or accumulated in a business by a person, partnership, or corporation. **b.** Material wealth used or available for use in the production of more wealth. **c.** Human resources considered in terms of their contributions to an economy. **3.** *Accounting* The remaining assets of a business after all liabilities have been deducted; net worth. **4.** Capital stock. **5.** Capitalists considered as a group or class. **6.** An asset or advantage. **7.** A capital letter. ❖ *adj.* **1.** First and foremost; principal. **2.** First-rate; excellent: *a capital idea.* **3.** Relating to or being a seat of government. **4.** Extremely serious. **5.** Involving death or calling for the death penalty. **6.** Of, relating to, or being financial assets, esp. those that add to the net worth of a business. **7.** Relating to or being a capital letter. [< ME, principal < OFr. < Lat. *capitālis* < *caput,* head, money laid out. See **kaput-** in App.]

USAGE NOTE The term for a town or city that serves as a seat of government is spelled *capital.* The term for the building in which a legislative assembly meets is spelled *capitol.*

cap·i·tal² (kăp′ĭ-tl) *n. Architecture* The top part of a pillar or column. [ME < AN < LLat. *capitellum,* dim. of Lat. *caput,* head. See **kaput-** in App.]

capital account *n.* **1.** An account stating the amount of funds and assets invested in a business by the owners or stockholders. **2.** A statement of the net worth of a business at a given time.

capital asset *n.* A long-term asset, such as land or a building.

capital expenditure *n.* Funds spent for the acquisition of a long-term asset.

capital gain *n.* The amount by which proceeds from the sale of a capital asset exceed the original cost.

capital goods *pl.n.* Producer goods.

cap·i·tal-in·ten·sive (kăp′ĭ-tl-ĭn-tĕn′sĭv) *adj.* Requiring a large expenditure of capital in comparison to labor.

cap·i·tal·ism (kăp′ĭ-tl-ĭz′əm) *n.* An economic system in which the means of production and distribution are privately or corporately owned and development is proportionate to the accumulation and reinvestment of profits gained in a free market.

cap·i·tal·ist (kăp′ĭ-tl-ĭst) *n.* **1.** A supporter of capitalism. **2.** An investor of capital in business, esp. one having a major financial interest in an important enterprise. **3.** A person of great wealth. ❖ *adj.* Capitalistic.

cap·i·tal·is·tic (kăp′ĭ-tl-ĭs′tĭk) *adj.* **1.** Of or relating to capitalism or capitalists. **2.** Favoring or practicing capitalism: *a capitalistic country.* —**cap′i·tal·is′ti·cal·ly** *adv.*

cap·i·tal·i·za·tion (kăp′ĭ-tl-ĭ-zā′shən) *n.* **1a.** The practice or act of capitalizing. **b.** The sum that results from capitalizing. **2a.** The amounts and types of long-term financing used by a firm. **b.** The total par value or stated value of no-par capital stock issues. **3.** The use of capital letters.

cap·i·tal·ize (kăp′ĭ-tl-īz′) *v.* **-ized, -iz·ing, -iz·es** —*tr.* **1.** To use as or convert into capital. **2.** To supply with capital or investment funds. **3.** To authorize the issue of a certain amount of capital stock of. **4.** To convert (debt) into capital stock or shares. **5.** To calculate the current value of (a future stream of earnings or cash flows). **6.** To include (expenditures) in business accounts as assets instead of expenses. **7a.** To write or print in capital letters. **b.** To begin a word with a capital letter. —*intr.* To turn something to one's advantage; benefit. —**cap′i·tal·iz′a·ble** *adj.*

capital letter *n.* A letter written or printed in a size larger than and often in a form differing from its lowercase form.

cap·i·tal·ly (kăp′ĭ-tl-ē) *adv.* Excellently; admirably.

capital stock *n.* **1.** The total amount of stock authorized for issue by a corporation. **2.** The total stated or par value of the permanently invested capital of a corporation.

cap·i·tate (kăp′ĭ-tāt′) *adj.* **1.** *Anatomy* Enlarged and globular at the tip. **2.** *Botany* Forming a headlike mass or dense cluster. [Lat. *capitātus,* having a head < *caput, capit-,* head. See **kaput-** in App.]

cap·i·ta·tion (kăp′ĭ-tā′shən) *n.* **1.** A poll tax. **2.** A fixed payment or fee per person. [LLat. *capitātiō, capitātiōn-* < Lat. *caput, capit-,* head. See **kaput-** in App.] —**cap′i·ta′tive** *adj.*

cap·i·tel·lum (kăp′ĭ-tĕl′əm) *n., pl.* **-tel·la** (-tĕl′ə) *Anatomy* The rounded protuberance at the lower end of the humerus that articulates with the radius. [LLat., dim. of Lat. *caput, capit-,* head. See **kaput-** in App.]

cap·i·tol (kăp′ĭ-tl) *n.* **1.** A building or complex of buildings in which a state legislature meets. **2. Capitol** The building in Washington DC where the US Congress meets. See Usage Note at **capital¹.** [ME *Capitol,* Jupiter's temple in Rome < OFr. *capitole* < Lat. *Capitōlium,* after *Capitōlīnus,* Capitoline; perh. akin to *caput, capit-,* head. See CAPITAL¹.]

Capitol Hill *n. Informal* The US Congress.

Cap·i·to·line (kăp′ĭ-tə-līn′) The highest of the seven hills of ancient Rome. —**Cap′i·to·line′** *adj.*

Capitol Peak A mountain, 4,309.7 m (14,130 ft), in the Rocky Mts. of W-central CO.

ca•pit•u•lar (kə-pĭch′ə-lər) *adj.* Of or relating to a chapter, esp. an ecclesiastical chapter. [Med.Lat. *capitulāris* < *capitulum*, chapter. See CHAPTER.] —**ca•pit′u•lar•ly** *adv.*

ca•pit•u•lar•y (kə-pĭch′ə-lĕr′ē) *n., pl.* **-ies 1.** A member of an ecclesiastical or a similar chapter. **2a.** An ecclesiastical or a civil ordinance. **b.** A set of such ordinances. [Med.Lat. *capitulārius* < *capitulum*, chapter. See CHAPTER.]

ca•pit•u•late (kə-pĭch′ə-lāt′) *intr.v.* **-lat•ed, -lat•ing, -lates 1.** To surrender under specified conditions; come to terms. **2.** To give up all resistance; acquiesce. [Med.Lat. *capitulāre, capitulāt-*, to draw up in chapters < *capitulum*, chapter. See CHAPTER.] —**ca•pit′u•lant, ca•pit′u•la′tor** *n.* —**ca•pit′u•la•to′ry** (-lə-tôr′ē, -tōr′ē) *adj.*

ca•pit•u•la•tion (kə-pĭch′ə-lā′shən) *n.* **1.** The act of surrendering. **2.** A document with the terms of surrender. **3.** An enumeration of the main parts of a subject; a summary.

ca•pit•u•lum (kə-pĭch′ə-ləm) *n., pl.* **-la** (-lə) **1.** *Botany* See **flower head** 1. **2.** *Biology* A small knob or head-shaped part. [Lat., dim. of *caput, capit-*, head. See **kaput-** in App.]

cap•let (kăp′lĭt) *n.* A smooth, coated, oval-shaped medicine tablet intended to be tamper-resistant. [CAP(SULE) + (TAB)LET.]

cap•lin (kăp′lĭn) *n.* Variant of **capelin.**

ca•po¹ (kā′pō) *n., pl.* **-pos** A small movable bar placed across the fingerboard of a guitar or similar instrument to raise the pitch of all the strings uniformly. [Ital. *capo (di tastiera)*, head (of the fingerboard) < Lat. *caput*. See **kaput-** in App.]

ca•po² (kä′pō, kăp′ō) *n., pl.* **-pos** The head of an organized crime syndicate branch. [Ital. < Lat. *caput*, head. See CAPO¹.]

cap•o•ei•ra (kăp′ō-ā′rə, kä′po͞o-ā′rä) *n.* An Afro-Brazilian dance form that incorporates self-defense maneuvers. [Port. < earlier **capon*, capon < VLat. **cappō*, **cappōn-* < Lat. *cāpō, cāpōn-*.]

ca•pon (kā′pŏn′, -pən) *n.* A male chicken castrated when young to improve the quality of its flesh for food. [ME *capoun* < OE *capūn* and < OFr. *capon*, both < Lat. *cāpō, cāpōn-*.]

ca•po•na•ta (kä′pə-nä′tə) *n.* A seasoned mixture of eggplant and other vegetables. [Ital., of Sicilian dialectal orig.]

Ca•pone (kə-pōn′), **Alphonse** Known as "Al." Also called "Scarface." 1899–1947. Italian-born Amer. gangster who ruthlessly ruled the Chicago underworld.

cap•o•ral (kăp′ər-əl, kăp′ə-răl′) *n.* A strong dark tobacco. [Fr., short for *(tabac de) caporal*, corporal('s tobacco) < Ital. *caporale* < *capo*, head. See CAPO¹.]

ca•pote (kə-pōt′) *n.* **1.** A long, usu. hooded cloak or coat. **2.** A usu. purple and yellow cape used in maneuvering the bull esp. during the initial stage of a bullfight. [Fr. < OFr. *capote, capette*, dim. of *cape*, cloak < Med.Lat. *cāpa*. See CAPE¹.]

Ca•po•te (kə-pō′tē), **Truman** 1924–84. Amer. writer whose works include *In Cold Blood* (1966).

Cap•pa•do•cia (kăp′ə-dō′shə, -shē-ə) An ancient region of Asia Minor in present-day E-central Turkey; center of a Hittite state and a Persian satrapy. —**Cap′pa•do′cian** *adj. & n.*

cap•per (kăp′ər) *n.* **1.** One that caps or makes caps. **2.** *Informal* Something that surpasses or completes; a finishing touch or finale. **3.** *Slang* One who acts as a decoy.

cap•puc•ci•no (kăp′ə-chē′nō, kä′pə-) *n., pl.* **-nos** Espresso coffee mixed or topped with steamed milk or cream. [Ital., Capuchin, cappuccino. See CAPUCHIN.]

WORD HISTORY The history of the word *cappuccino* shows how words can develop new senses because of resemblances that the original coiners of the terms might not have dreamed possible. The Italian name of the Capuchin order of friars, established after 1525, came from the long pointed cowl, or *cappuccino*, that was worn as part of the order's habit. In Italian *cappuccino* went on to develop another sense, "espresso coffee mixed or topped with steamed milk or cream," so called because the color of the coffee resembled the color of the habit of a Capuchin friar.

Cap•ra (kăp′rə), **Frank** 1897–1991. Amer. filmmaker whose works include *It Happened One Night* (1934).

Ca•pri (kə-prē′, kăp′rē, kä′prē) An island of S Italy on the S edge of the Bay of Naples; famous for its Blue Grotto.

cap•ric acid (kăp′rĭk) *n.* A fatty acid, $CH_3(CH_2)_8COOH$, obtained from animal fats and oils and used in the manufacture of perfumes and fruit flavors. [< Lat. *caper, capr-*, goat (< its smell).]

ca•pric•cio (kə-prē′chō, -chē-ō′) *n., pl.* **-cios 1.** *Music* An instrumental work with an improvisatory style and a free form. **2.** A prank; a caper. **3.** A whim. [Ital. See CAPRICE.]

ca•pric•cio•so (kə-prē′chē-ō′sō, kä′prē-chō′sō) *adj. Music* Lively and free. [Ital. < *capriccio*, caprice. See CAPRICE.]

ca•price (kə-prēs′) *n.* **1a.** An impulsive change of mind. **b.** An inclination to change one's mind impulsively. **c.** A sudden, unpredictable action, change, or series of actions or changes. **2.** *Music* A capriccio. [Fr. < Ital. *capriccio* < *caporiccio*, fright, sudden start : *capo*, head (< Lat. *caput*; see **kaput-** in App.) + *riccio*, curly (< Lat. *ēricius*, hedgehog < *ēr*).]

ca•pri•cious (kə-prĭsh′əs, -prē′shəs) *adj.* Characterized by or subject to whim. —**ca•pri′cious•ly** *adv.* —**ca•pri′cious•ness** *n.*

Cap•ri•corn (kăp′rĭ-kôrn′) also **Cap•ri•cor•nus** (kăp′rĭ-kôr′nəs) *n.* **1.** A constellation in the equatorial region of the Southern Hemisphere, near Aquarius and Sagittarius. **2a.** The tenth sign of the zodiac in astrology. **b.** One born under Capricorn. [ME *Capricorne* < Lat. *Capricornus* : *caper, capr-*, goat + *cornū*, horn; see **ker-¹** in App.]

cap•ri•fi•ca•tion (kăp′rə-fĭ-kā′shən) *n.* A method of pollination of edible figs in which wasps carry pollen from the flowers of the caprifig to those of the edible varieties. [Lat. *caprificātio, caprificātiōn-* < *caprificātus*, p. part. of *caprificāre*, to ripen figs by caprification < *caprifīcus*, caprifig. See CAPRIFIG.]

cap•ri•fig (kăp′rə-fĭg′) *n.* A wild fig *(Ficus carica* var. *sylvestris)* used in the caprification of edible figs. [ME < Lat. *caprifīcus* (influenced by ME *fig*, fig) : *caper, capr-*, goat + *fīcus*, fig; see FIG¹.]

cap•rine (kăp′rīn′) *adj.* Of, relating to, or characteristic of a goat. [Lat. *caprīnus* < *caper, capr-*, goat.]

cap•ri•ole (kăp′rē-ōl′) *n.* **1.** An upward leap made by a trained horse with a backward kick of the hind legs. **2.** A playful leap or jump; a caper. [Fr. < Ital. *capriola*, somersault < *capriolo*, roebuck, wild goat < Lat. *capreolus*, dim. of *caper, capr-*, goat.] —**cap′ri•ole′** *v.*

ca•pri pants (kə-prē′) *pl.n.* Tight-fitting, calf-length women's pants. [After CAPRI.]

ca•pro•ic acid (kə-prō′ĭk, kă-) *n.* A liquid fatty acid, $CH_3(CH_2)_4COOH$, found in animal fats and oils or synthesized and used in the manufacture of pharmaceuticals and flavorings. [< Lat. *caper, capr-*, goat.]

ca•pryl•ic acid (kə-prĭl′ĭk, kă-) *n.* A liquid fatty acid, $C_8H_{16}O_2$, found in butter and other fats and oils and having a rancid taste. [CAPR(IC ACID) + –YL + –IC.]

cap•sa•i•cin (kăp-sā′ĭ-sĭn) *n.* A colorless, pungent, crystalline compound, $C_{18}H_{27}NO_3$, that is derived from capsicum and is a strong irritant to skin and mucous membranes. [Alteration (perh. influenced by Lat. *capsa*, box) of earlier *capsicin* : CAPSIC(UM) + –IN.]

cap screw *n.* A long-threaded bolt, usu. with a square head, used in fastening machine parts.

Cap•si•an (kăp′sē-ən) *adj.* Of, relating to, or being a Paleolithic culture of northern Africa and southern Europe. [Fr. *capsien* < Lat. *Capsa*, Gafsa, a town of W-central Tunisia.]

cap•si•cum (kăp′sĭ-kəm) *n.* **1.** Any of various tropical American pepper plants of the genus *Capsicum*, esp. of the species *C. annuum* and *C. frutescens*. **2.** The fruit of any of these plants, esp. the dried pungent types used as a condiment and in medicine. [NLat. *Capsicum*, genus name, perh. < Lat. *capsa*, box (< its pod-like fruit).]

cap•sid (kăp′sĭd) *n.* The protein shell that surrounds a virus particle. [< Lat. *capsa*, box.]

cap•size (kăp′sīz′, kăp-sīz′) *intr. & tr.v.* **-sized, -siz•ing, -siz•es** To overturn or cause to overturn. [?]

cap•so•mere (kăp′sə-mîr′) *n.* One of the individual subunits that makes up a capsid. [CAPS(ID) + –MERE.]

cap•stan (kăp′stən, -stăn′) *n.* **1.** *Nautical* An apparatus used for hoisting weights, consisting of a vertical spool-shaped cylinder around which a cable is wound. **2.** A shaft used to drive magnetic tape at a constant speed in a tape recorder. [ME < Norman Fr. < O Provençal *cabestan* < *cabestre*, noose < Lat. *capistrum*, halter, prob. < *capere*, to seize. See **kap-** in App.]

cap•stone (kăp′stōn′) *n.* **1.** The top stone of a structure or wall. **2.** The crowning achievement or final stroke; the acme.

cap•su•late (kăp′sə-lāt′, -lĭt, -syo͞o-) also **cap•su•lat•ed** (-lā′tĭd) *adj.* Enclosed in or formed into a capsule. —**cap′su•la′tion** *n.*

cap•sule (kăp′səl, -so͞ol) *n.* **1.** A small soluble container, usu. made of gelatin, that encloses a dose of an oral medicine or vitamin. **2.** *Anatomy* A fibrous, membranous, or fatty sheath that encloses an organ or part. **3.** *Microbiology* A mucopolysaccharide outer shell enveloping certain bacteria. **4.** *Botany* **a.** A dry dehiscent fruit that develops from two or more united carpels. **b.** The thin-walled, spore-containing structure of mosses and related plants. **5.** A space capsule. **6.** A brief summary; a condensation. ❖ *adj.* **1.** Highly condensed; very brief. **2.** Very small; compact. ❖ *tr.v.* **-suled, -sul•ing, -sules 1.** To enclose in or furnish with a capsule. **2.** To condense or summarize. [Fr. < Lat. *capsula*, dim. of *capsa*, box.] —**cap′su•lar** (-sə-lər, -syo͞o-) *adj.*

cap•sul•ize (kăp′sə-līz′, -syo͞o-) *tr.v.* **-ized, -iz•ing, -iz•es** To capsule: *capsulized the news every 30 minutes.*

Capt. or **Capt** or **CAPT** *abbr.* captain

cap•tain (kăp′tən) *n.* **1.** One who commands, leads, or guides others, esp.: **a.** The officer in command of a ship, aircraft, or spacecraft. **b.** A precinct commander in a police or fire department, usu. ranking above a lieutenant and below a chief. **c.** The designated leader of a team or crew in sports. **2a.** A commissioned rank in the US Army, Air Force, or Marine Corps that is above first lieutenant and below major. **b.** A commissioned rank in the US Navy or Coast Guard that is above commander and below commodore. **c.** One who holds the rank of captain. **3.** A figure in the forefront; a leader. **4.** One who supervises or directs the work of others, esp.: **a.** A district official for a political party. **b.** A restaurant employee who is in charge of the servers and usu. attends to table seating. **c.** A bell captain. ❖ *tr.v.* **-tained, -tain•ing, -tains** To act as captain of; command or direct. [ME *capitain* < OFr. < LLat. *capitāneus*, chief < Lat. *caput, capit-*, head. See

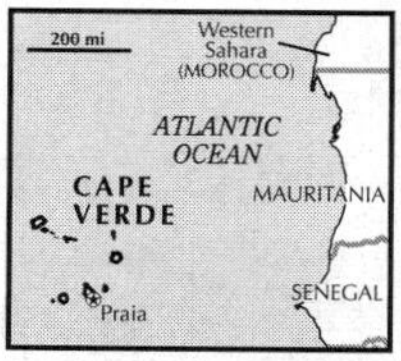

Cape Verde

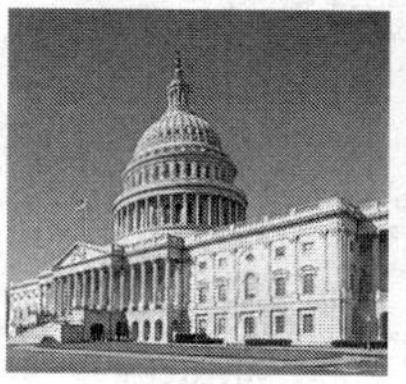

Capitol
US Capitol Building, Washington, DC

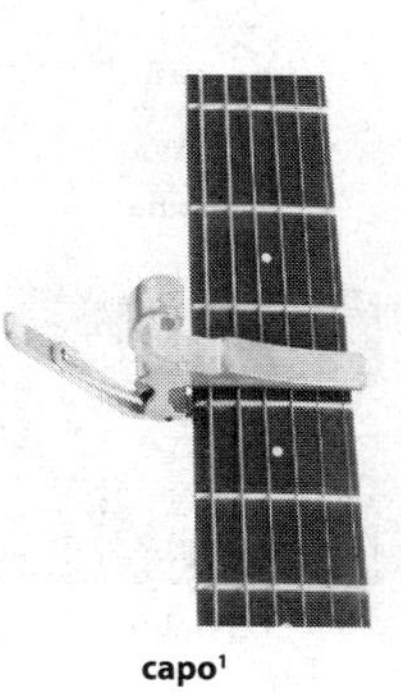

capo¹

ă	pat	oi	boy
ā	pay	ou	out
âr	care	o͝o	took
ä	father	o͞o	boot
ĕ	pet	ŭ	cut
ē	be	ûr	urge
ĭ	pit	th	thin
ī	pie	*th*	this
îr	pier	hw	which
ŏ	pot	zh	vision
ō	toe	ə	about, item
ô	paw		

Stress marks:
′ (primary);
′ (secondary), as in **lexicon** (lĕk′sĭ-kŏn′)

kaput- in App.] —**cap′tain•cy, cap′tain•ship′** *n.*

cap•tain's chair (kăp′tənz) *n.* A wooden chair having a low back with spindles that curve forward to provide armrests.

captain's mast *n.* A disciplinary hearing for enlisted personnel presided over by the commanding officer of a naval unit.

cap•tan (kăp′tən, -tăn′) *n.* A white solid agricultural fungicide, $C_9H_8O_2NSCl_3$. [Short for MERCAPTAN.]

cap•tion (kăp′shən) *n.* **1.** A title, short explanation, or description accompanying an illustration or photograph. **2.** Written dialogue superimposed on the bottom of television or motion picture frames. **3.** A title or heading, as of an article. **4.** *Law* The heading of a pleading or other document that identifies the parties, court, term, and number of the action. ❖ *tr.v.* **-tioned, -tion•ing, -tions** To furnish a caption for. [ME *capcioun*, arrest < OFr. *capcion* < Lat. *captiō, captiōn-* < *captus*, p. part. of *capere*, to seize. See **kap-** in App.]

cap•tious (kăp′shəs) *adj.* **1.** Marked by a disposition to find and point out trivial faults. **2.** Intended to entrap or confuse, as in an argument. [ME *capcious* < OFr. *captieux* < Lat. *captiōsus* < *captiō*, seizure, sophism < *captus*, p. part. of *capere*, to seize. See **kap-** in App.] —**cap′tious•ly** *adv.* —**cap′tious•ness** *n.*

cap•ti•vate (kăp′tə-vāt′) *tr.v.* **-vat•ed, -vat•ing, -vates 1.** To attract and hold by charm, beauty, or excellence. See Syns at **charm. 2.** *Archaic* To capture. [LLat. *captīvāre, captīvāt-*, to capture < Lat. *captīvus*, prisoner. See CAPTIVE.] —**cap′ti•va′tion** *n.* —**cap′ti•va′tor** *n.*

cap•tive (kăp′tĭv) *n.* **1.** One who is forcibly confined, subjugated, or enslaved. **2.** One in the grip of a strong emotion or passion. ❖ *adj.* **1.** Taken and held prisoner, as in war. **2.** Held in bondage; enslaved. **3.** Kept under restraint or control: *captive birds.* **4.** Restrained from free choice. **5.** Enraptured, as by beauty; captivated. [ME *captif* < OFr. < Lat. *captīvus* < *captus*, p. part. of *capere*, to seize. See **kap-** in App.]

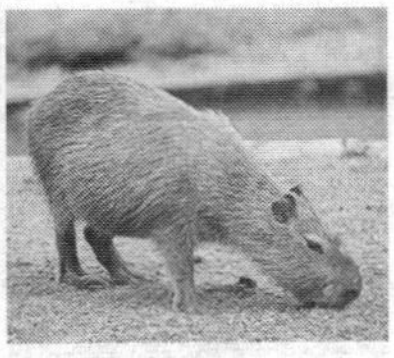
capybara
Hydrochoerus hydrochaeris

cap•tiv•i•ty (kăp-tĭv′ĭ-tē) *n., pl.* **-ties** The state or period of being imprisoned, confined, or enslaved.

cap•to•pril (kăp′tə-prĭl′) *n.* A cardiovascular drug, $C_9H_{15}NO_3S$, used esp. in the treatment of hypertension and heart failure. [(MER)CAPT(AN) + PR(OPANE) + alteration of –YL.]

cap•tor (kăp′tər, -tôr′) *n.* One that takes another as a captive. [LLat., hunter < Lat. *capere*, to seize. See **kap-** in App.]

cap•ture (kăp′chər) *tr.v.* **-tured, -tur•ing, -tures 1.** To take captive, as by force or craft; seize. **2.** To gain possession or control of, as in a game or contest. **3.** To attract and hold: *capture the imagination.* **4.** To succeed in preserving in lasting form: *capture a likeness.* ❖ *n.* **1.** The act of catching, taking, or winning, as by force or skill. **2.** One that has been seized, caught, or won. **3.** *Physics* The phenomenon in which an atom or nucleus absorbs a subatomic particle. [< Fr., capture < OFr. < Lat. *captūra* < *captus*, p. part. of *capere*, to seize. See **kap-** in App.]

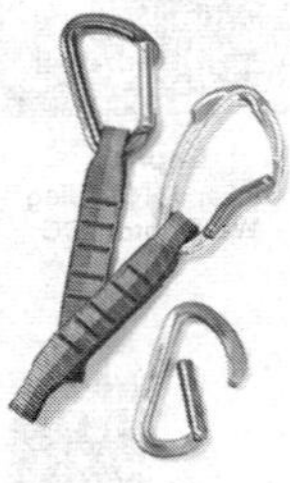
carabiner

Cap•u•a (kăp′yo͞o-ə, kä′pwä) A town of S Italy N of Naples near the site of the strategically important ancient Roman city of **Capua** on the Appian Way. Pop. 18,053.

ca•puche (kə-po͞och′, -po͞osh′) *n.* A hood on a cloak, esp. the long pointed cowl worn by a Capuchin monk. [Ital. *cappuccio* < *cappa*, hood < LLat., cloak.]

cap•u•chin (kăp′yə-chĭn, -shĭn, kə-pyo͞o′-) *n.* **1. Capuchin** A monk belonging to the Order of Friars Minor Capuchin. **2.** A hooded cloak worn by women. **3.** Any of several long-tailed monkeys of the genus *Cebus*, native to Central and South America and often having a hoodlike tuft of hair on the head. [Obsolete Fr. < Ital. *cappuccino*, pointed cowl, Capuchin < *cappuccio*, hood. See CAPUCHE.]

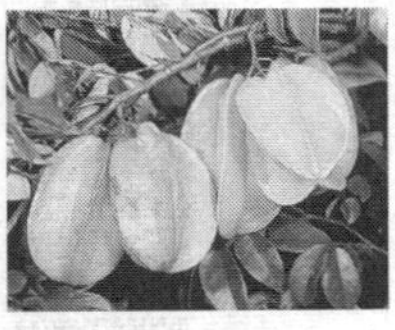
carambola

cap•y•ba•ra (kăp′ə-bär′ə, -băr′ə) *n.* A large rodent *(Hydrochoerus hydrochaeris)* of tropical South America having short limbs and a vestigial tail. [Port. *capybara* < Tupi *capivara, capibara* : *capii*, grass + *urara*, eater.]

car (kär) *n.* **1.** An automobile. **2.** A vehicle, such as a streetcar, that runs on rails. **3.** A boxlike enclosure for passengers and freight on a conveyance. **4.** The part of a balloon or airship that carries people and cargo. **5.** *Archaic* A chariot, carriage, or cart. [ME *carre*, cart < ONFr. < Lat. *carra*, pl. of *carrus, carrum*, a Gallic type of wagon < Gaulish *carros*.]

car. *abbr.* carat

car•a•bao (kăr′ə-bou′, kä′rə-) *n., pl.* **-baos** See **water buffalo.** [Sp. < Visayan *karabáw* < Malay *kerbau*.]

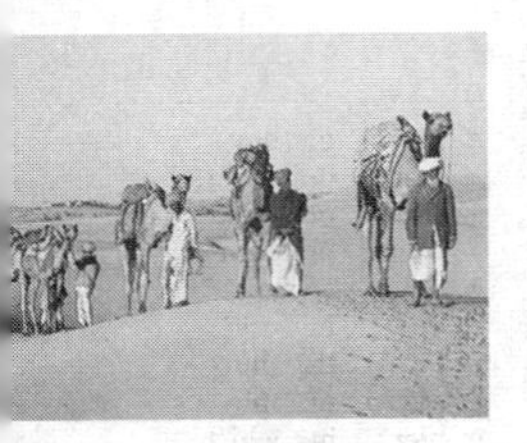
caravan
camel caravan, India

car•a•bid (kăr′ə-bĭd, kə-răb′ĭd) *n.* Any of a large family (Carabidae) of chiefly black beetles that feed on other insects. [< NLat. *Cārabidae*, family name < Lat. *cārabus*, crustacean < Gk. *kārabos*, horned beetle, crayfish.] —**car′a•bid** *adj.*

car•a•bi•neer also **car•a•bi•nier** (kăr′ə-bə-nîr′) or **car•bi•neer** (kär′bə-) *n.* A soldier armed with a carbine. [Fr. *carabinier* < *carabine*, carbine. See CARBINE.]

car•a•bi•ner also **kar•a•bi•ner** (kăr′ə-bē′nər) *n.* An oblong metal ring with a spring clip, used in mountaineering to attach a running rope to a piton or similar device. [Ger. *Karabiner*, short for *Karabinerhaken*, hook for a carbine < *Karabiner*, carbine < Fr. *carabine*. See CARBINE.]

ca•ra•bi•nie•re (kăr′ə-bĭn-yâr′ē, kä′rä-bē-nyĕ′rĕ) *n., pl.* **-bi•nie•ri** (-bĭn-yâr′ē, -bē-nyĕ′rē) A member of the Italian police force. [Ital. < Fr. *carabinier*. See CARABINEER.]

car•a•cal (kăr′ə-kăl′) *n.* A wildcat *(Felis caracal* syn. *Lynx caracal)* of Africa and southern Asia having short fur and long tufted ears. [Fr. < Ottoman Turk. *qaraqūlāq* : *qara*, black + *qūlāq*, ear.]

Car•a•cal•la (kăr′ə-kăl′ə) Real name Marcus Aurelius Antonius. A.D. 188–217. Emperor of Rome (211–217) whose brutal rule led to his assassination.

car•a•car•a (kăr′ə-kăr′ə, -kə-rä′) *n.* Any of several large carrion-eating or predatory hawks of the subfamily Caracarinae, native to South and Central America and the southern United States. [Sp. and Port. *caracará*, both < Tupi *caracara*.]

Ca•ra•cas (kə-rä′kəs) The cap. of Venezuela, in the N part near the Caribbean coast; founded by the Spanish in 1567. Pop. 1,964,846.

car•ack (kăr′ək) *n.* Variant of **carrack.**

car•a•cole (kăr′ə-kōl′) also **car•a•col** (-kŏl′) *n.* A half turn to right or left performed by a horse and rider. [Fr. < Sp. *caracol*, snail.] —**car′a•cole′** *v.*

car•a•cul (kăr′ə-kəl) *n.* Variant of **karakul.**

ca•rafe (kə-răf′) *n.* **1.** A glass or metal bottle, often with a flared lip, used for serving water or wine. **2.** A glass pot with a pouring spout, used in making coffee. [Fr. < Ital. *caraffa* < Sp. *garrafa*, prob. < Ar. *ġarrafa*, dipper, cup < *ġarafa*, to ladle, scoop.]

car•am•bo•la (kăr′əm-bō′lə) *n.* **1.** An ornamental evergreen tree *(Averrhoa carambola)* native to southeast Asia and having yellow to orange fruits that are star-shaped in cross section. **2.** The edible fruit of this plant. [Port., perh. < Marathi *karambal*.]

car•a•mel (kăr′ə-məl, -mĕl′, kär′məl) *n.* **1.** A smooth chewy candy made with sugar, butter, cream or milk, and flavoring. **2.** Burnt sugar, used for coloring and sweetening foods. **3.** A moderate yellow brown. [Fr. < OFr. < OSpan. *caramel, caramelo* < Port. *caramel* < LLat. *calamellus*, dim. of Lat. *calamus*, reed, cane < Gk. *kalamos*.]

car•a•mel•ize (kăr′ə-mə-līz′, kär′mə-) *tr. & intr.v.* **-ized, -iz•ing, -iz•es** To convert or be converted into caramel. —**car′a•mel•i•za′tion** (-mə-lĭ-zā′shən) *n.*

ca•ran•gid (kə-răn′jĭd, -răng′gĭd) *n.* Any of a family (Carangidae) of marine food and game fishes, such as the jacks. [< NLat. *Carangidae*, family name < Fr. *carangue*, mackerel < Sp. *caranga*, perh. ult. < Lat. *cancer*, crab.] —**ca•ran′gid** *adj.*

car•a•pace (kăr′ə-pās′) *n.* **1.** *Zoology* A hard bony or chitinous outer covering. **2.** A protective shell-like covering. [Fr. < Sp. *carapacho*.]

car•at (kăr′ət) *n.* **1.** A unit of weight for precious stones, equal to 200 milligrams. **2.** Variant of **karat.** [ME < OFr. < Med.Lat. *quarātus* < Ar. *qīrāṭ*, weight of four grains < Gk. *kerātion*, a weight, dim. of *keras, kerāt-*, horn. See **ker-**[1] in App.]

Ca•ra•vag•gio (kăr′ə-vä′jō, kä′rä-väd′jō), **Michelangelo Merisi da** 1573–1610. Italian painter of the baroque whose works include *Deposition of Christ* (1604).

car•a•van (kăr′ə-văn′) *n.* **1.** A company of travelers journeying together, as across a desert. **2.** A single file of vehicles or pack animals. **3.** A large covered vehicle; a van. **4.** *Chiefly British* A trailer or dwelling place on wheels. [Fr. *caravane* or Ital. *carovana*, both < Pers. *kārvān*.]

car•a•van•sa•ry (kăr′ə-văn′sə-rē) also **car•a•van•se•rai** (-rī′) *n., pl.* **-ries** also **-rais 1.** An inn built around a large court for accommodating caravans in central and western Asia. **2.** A large inn or hostelry. [Fr. *caravanserai* < Pers. *kārvānsarāy* : *kārvān*, caravan + *sarāy*, camp, palace; see **terə-**[2] in App.]

car•a•vel or **car•a•velle** (kăr′ə-vĕl′) also **car•vel** (kär′vəl, -vĕl′) *n.* Any of several types of small light sailing ships, esp. one with two or three masts and lateen sails used by the Spanish and Portuguese in the 15th and 16th centuries. [Fr. *caravelle* < OFr. < OPort. *caravela*, dim. of *cáravo*, ship < LLat. *cārabus*, a small wicker boat < L.Gk. *karabos*, light ship < Gk., horned beetle.]

car•a•way (kăr′ə-wā′) *n.* **1.** A biennial Eurasian herb *(Carum carvi)* in the parsley family, having finely divided leaves and white or pinkish flowers. **2.** The seedlike fruit of this plant, used as a flavoring and seasoning. [ME *carewei* < OFr. *carvi, caroi*, prob. < Med.Lat. *carvi, carwi*, ult. < Ar. *karawyā* < Gk. *karō*.]

carb[1] (kärb) *n.* *Informal* A carburetor.

carb[2] (kärb) *n.* *Informal* A carbohydrate.

car•ba•mate (kär′bə-māt′, kär-băm′āt′) *n.* A salt or ester of carbamic acid, esp. one used as an insecticide. [CARBAM(IC ACID) + –ATE[2].]

car•bam•ic acid (kär-băm′ĭk) *n.* A hypothetical acid, NH_2COOH, that exists only in the form of its esters and salts. [CARBAM(IDE) + –IC.]

car•ba•mide (kär′bə-mīd′, kär-băm′ĭd) *n.* See **urea.**

car•bam•o•yl (kär-băm′ō-ĭl′) *n.* The radical NH_2CO. [CARBAM(IC ACID) + –YL.]

car•ban•i•on (kär-băn′ī′ən, -ī′ŏn′) *n.* An anion in which carbon carries a negative charge and an unshared pair of electrons.

car•ba•ryl (kär′bə-rĭl′) *n.* A carbamate, $C_{12}H_{11}NO_2$, used as an insecticide. [CARB(AMATE) + AR(OMATIC) + –YL.]

car•bide (kär′bīd′) *n.* **1.** A binary compound consisting of carbon and a more electropositive element, esp. calcium. **2.** A hard material made of compacted binary compounds of carbon and heavy metals, used to make tools that cut metal.

car•bine (kär′bēn′, -bīn′) *n.* A lightweight rifle with a short barrel. [Fr. *carabine* < OFr. *carabin*, soldier armed with a musket, perh. < *escarrabin*, gravedigger < *scarabee*, dung beetle. See SCARAB.]

car·bi·neer (kär'bə-nîr') *n.* Variant of **carabineer**.

car·bi·nol (kär'bə-nôl', -nōl', -nōl') *n.* **1.** See **methanol**. **2.** An alcohol derived from methanol.

carbo (kär'bō) *n., pl.* **-bos** *Informal* A carbohydrate.

carbo– or **carb–** *pref.* Carbon: *carbohydrate*. [Fr. < *carbone*, carbon. See CARBON.]

car·bo·cy·clic (kär'bō-sī'klĭk, -sĭk'lĭk) *adj.* Having a ring composed exclusively of carbon atoms, as benzene.

car·bo·hy·drase (kär'bō-hī'drās', -drāz') *n.* Any of various enzymes that catalyze the hydrolysis of a carbohydrate.

car·bo·hy·drate (kär'bō-hī'drāt') *n.* Any of a group of organic compounds produced by photosynthetic plants that includes sugars, starches, celluloses, and gums and serves as a major energy source in the diet of animals.

car·bo·lat·ed (kär'bə-lā'tĭd) *adj.* Containing or treated with carbolic acid.

car·bol·ic acid (kär-bŏl'ĭk) *n.* See **phenol** 1. [CARB(O)– + –OL¹ + –IC.]

car·bon (kär'bən) *n.* **1.** *Symbol* **C** A nonmetallic element that occurs in many inorganic and in all organic compounds, exists freely as graphite and diamond and as a constituent of coal, limestone, and petroleum, and is capable of chemical self-bonding to form an enormous number of important molecules. Atomic number 6; atomic weight 12.011; sublimation point above 3,500°C; boiling point 4,827°C; specific gravity of amorphous carbon 1.8 to 2.1, of diamond 3.15 to 3.53, of graphite 1.9 to 2.3; valence 2, 3, 4. See table at **element**. **2a.** A sheet of carbon paper. **b.** A carbon copy. **3.** *Electricity* **a.** Either of two rods through which current flows to form an arc, as in lighting. **b.** A carbonaceous electrode in an electric cell. [Fr. *carbone* < Lat. *carbō*, *carbōn*-, a coal, charcoal.] —**car'bo·na'ceous** (-bə-nā'shəs), **car'bon·ous** (-bə-nəs) *adj.*

carbon 14 *n.* A naturally radioactive carbon isotope with atomic mass 14 and half-life 5,730 years, used in radiocarbon dating.

car·bon-14 dating (kär'bən-fôr-tēn', -fōr-) *n.* See **radiocarbon dating**.

car·bo·na·do¹ (kär'bə-nā'dō, -nā'-) *Archaic n., pl.* **-does** or **-dos** A piece of scored and broiled fish, fowl, or meat. ❖ *tr.v.* **-doed, -do·ing, -dos** **1.** To score and broil (fish, fowl, or meat). **2.** To slice or cut. [< Sp. *carbonada* < *carbón*, charcoal < Lat. *carbō*, *carbōn*-. See CARBON.]

car·bo·na·do² (kär'bə-nā'dō, -nā'-) *n., pl.* **-does** A form of opaque or dark-colored diamond used for drills. [Port. < *carbone*, carbon < Fr. See CARBON.]

car·bo·na·ra (kär'bə-när'ə) *n.* A sauce for pasta containing eggs, minced bacon or ham, grated cheese, and seasonings. [Ital. *(alla) carbonara*, (from) a charcoal grill < *carbone*, charcoal < Lat. *carbō*, *carbōn*-. See CARBON.]

car·bon·ate (kär'bə-nāt') *tr.v.* **-at·ed, -at·ing, -ates** **1.** To charge (a beverage, for example) with carbon dioxide gas. **2.** To burn to carbon; carbonize. **3.** To change into a carbonate. ❖ *n.* (-nāt', -nĭt) A salt or ester of carbonic acid. —**car'bon·a'tion** *n.* —**car'bon·a'tor** *n.*

car·bon·at·ed water (kär'bə-nā'tĭd) *n.* Effervescent water, usu. containing salts, charged under pressure with purified carbon dioxide gas and used as a beverage or mixer.

carbon black *n.* Any of various forms of carbon derived from the incomplete combustion of natural gas or petroleum oil, used to reinforce rubber and in inks, paints, crayons, and polishes.

carbon copy *n.* **1.** A duplicate, as of a letter, made with carbon paper. **2.** A person or thing that closely resembles another.

carbon cycle *n.* **1.** *Physics* See **carbon-nitrogen cycle**. **2.** *Ecology* The combined processes, including photosynthesis, decomposition, and respiration, by which carbon as a component of various compounds cycles between its major reservoirs—the atmosphere, oceans, and living organisms.

carbon dating *n.* See **radiocarbon dating**. —**car'bon-date'** (kär'bən-dāt') *v.*

carbon dioxide *n.* A colorless, odorless, incombustible gas, CO_2, formed during respiration, combustion, and organic decomposition and used in food refrigeration, carbonated beverages, inert atmospheres, fire extinguishers, and aerosols.

carbon disulfide *n.* A clear flammable liquid, CS_2, used to make viscose rayon and cellophane, as a solvent, and in matches, fumigants, and pesticides.

car·bon·ic acid (kär-bŏn'ĭk) *n.* A weak unstable acid, H_2CO_3, present in solutions of carbon dioxide in water.

carbonic acid gas *n.* See **carbon dioxide**.

Car·bon·if·er·ous (kär'bə-nĭf'ər-əs) *adj.* **1.** Of or belonging to the geologic time comprising the Mississippian (Lower Carboniferous) and Pennsylvanian (Upper Carboniferous) periods of the Paleozoic Era, characterized by swamp formation and deposition of plant remains later hardened into coal. In Europe, the Carboniferous is considered as a single Period. **2.** **carboniferous** Producing or containing carbon or coal. ❖ *n.* The Carboniferous Period or its deposits. See table at **geologic time**.

car·bo·ni·um (kär-bō'nē-əm) *n.* An organic cation, such as H_3C, having one less electron than a corresponding free radical and with a positive charge localized on the carbon atom.

car·bon·i·za·tion (kär'bə-nĭ-zā'shən) *n.* **1.** The process of carbonizing. **2.** The destructive distillation of coal, done in the absence of air in order to obtain coke and other fractions having a greater percentage of carbon than the original material.

car·bon·ize (kär'bə-nīz') *tr.v.* **-ized, -iz·ing, -iz·es** **1.** To reduce or convert a carbon-containing substance to carbon. **2.** To coat or combine with carbon. —**car'bon·iz'er** *n.*

carbon monoxide *n.* A colorless, odorless, highly poisonous gas, CO, formed by the incomplete combustion of carbon or a carbonaceous material, such as gasoline.

carbon nanotube *n.* A fullerene having a cylindrical or toroidal configuration.

car·bon-ni·tro·gen cycle (kär'bən-nī'trə-jən) *n.* A chain of thermonuclear reactions, thought to generate large amounts of energy in the sun and stars, in which four hydrogen atoms are converted into one helium atom.

carbon paper *n.* A lightweight paper coated on one side with a dark waxy pigment, used between two sheets of paper to copy what is on the top sheet to the bottom sheet.

carbon process *n.* A photographic printing process using permanent pigments, such as carbon, contained in a sensitized tissue or film of gelatin.

carbon star *n.* Any of a class of stars with high carbon-to-hydrogen ratios and primarily low temperatures.

carbon tetrachloride *n.* A poisonous nonflammable liquid, CCl_4, used as an industrial solvent.

car·bon·yl (kär'bə-nĭl') *n.* **1.** The bivalent radical CO. **2.** A metal compound containing the CO group. —**car'bon·yl'ic** *adj.*

Car·bo·run·dum (kär'bə-rŭn'dəm) A trademark used for an abrasive of silicon carbide crystals.

carboxy– *pref.* Carboxyl: *carboxylase*. [< CARBOXYL.]

car·box·yl (kär-bŏk'səl) *n.* The univalent radical, COOH, the functional group characteristic of all organic acids. [CARB(O)– + OX(Y)– + –YL.] —**car'box·yl'ic** (-sĭl'ĭk) *adj.*

car·box·yl·ase (kär-bŏk'sə-lās', -lāz') *n.* An enzyme that catalyzes a carboxylation or decarboxylation reaction.

car·box·yl·a·tion (kär-bŏk'sə-lā'shən) *n.* The introduction of a carboxyl group into a compound or molecule.

car·box·yl·ic acid (kär-bŏk-sĭl'ĭk) *n.* An organic acid that contains one or more carboxyl groups.

car·box·y·meth·yl·cel·lu·lose (kär-bŏk'sē-mĕth'əl-sĕl'yə-lōs') *n.* A derivative of cellulose whose sodium salt is used in the manufacture of processed foods and as a laxative.

car·boy (kär'boi') *n.* A large glass or plastic bottle, usu. encased in a basket or crate and often used to hold corrosive liquids. [Pers. *qarābah* < Ar. *qarrāba*, big jug < *qarraba*, to bring near, derived stem of *qaruba*, to be near.]

car·bun·cle (kär'bŭng'kəl) *n.* **1.** A painful localized bacterial infection of the skin and subcutaneous tissue that usu. has several openings through which pus is discharged. **2a.** A deep red garnet, unfaceted and convex. **b.** *Obsolete* A red precious stone. [ME < OFr. < Lat. *carbunculus*, small glowing ember, carbuncle, dim. of *carbō*, *carbōn*-, coal.] —**car'bun'cled** *adj.* —**car'bun'cu·lar** (-kyə-lər) *adj.*

car·bu·ret (kär'bə-rāt', -rĕt', -byə-) *tr.v.* **-ret·ed, -ret·ing, -rets** or **-ret·ted, -ret·ting, -rets** To combine or mix (a gas, for example) with volatile hydrocarbons, so as to increase available fuel energy. [< *carburet*, carbide < Fr. *carbure* < Lat. *carbō*, carbon. See CARBON.] —**car'bu·re'tion** *n.*

car·bu·re·tor (kär'bə-rā'tər, -byə-) *n.* A device used in internal-combustion engines to produce an explosive mixture of vaporized fuel and air. [< CARBURET.]

car·bu·rize (kär'bə-rīz', -byə-) *tr.v.* **-rized, -riz·ing, -riz·es** **1.** To treat, combine, or impregnate with carbon, as when casehardening steel. **2.** To carburet. [CARBUR(ET) + –IZE.] —**car'bu·ri·za'tion** (-bər-ĭ-zā'shən, -byər-) *n.*

car·ca·jou (kär'kə-jōō', -zhōō') *n.* See **wolverine**. [Canadian Fr. < Montagnais *kuàkuàtsheu*.]

car·ca·net (kär'kə-nĕt', -nĭt) *n. Archaic* A jeweled necklace, collar, or headband. [< OFr. *carcan*, collar, perh. < Med.Lat. *carcannum*, perh. of Gmc. orig.]

car·cass (kär'kəs) *n.* **1.** The dead body of an animal, esp. one slaughtered for food. **2.** The body of a human. **3.** The remains of something, such as a ruined building. **4.** A framework or basic structure, as of a ship. [ME *carcas* < AN *carcais* and Med.Lat. *carcasium*.]

Car·cas·sonne (kär'kə-sôn', -sōn', -kä-) A city of S France SE of Toulouse. Pop. 41,153.

Car·che·mish (kär'kə-mĭsh', kär-kē'mĭsh) An ancient Hittite and Assyrian city on the Euphrates R. in S Turkey.

carcino– *pref.* Cancer; cancerous: *carcinogen*. [Gk. *karkino*– < *karkinos*, crab, cancer.]

car·cin·o·gen (kär-sĭn'ə-jən, kär'sə-nə-jĕn') *n.* A cancer-causing substance or agent. —**car'ci·no·gen'e·sis** (kär'sə-nə-jĕn'ĭ-sĭs) *n.* —**car'ci·no·gen'ic** (-jĕn'ĭk) *adj.* —**car'ci·no·ge·nic'i·ty** (-jə-nĭs'ĭ-tē) *n.*

car·ci·noid (kär'sə-noid') *n.* A small tumor, usu. found in the gastrointestinal tract, that secretes serotonin.

car·ci·no·ma (kär'sə-nō'mə) *n., pl.* **-mas** or **-ma·ta** (-mə-tə) An invasive malignant tumor derived from epithelial tissue that tends to metastasize to other areas of the body. [Lat., cancerous

ă	pat	oi	boy
ā	pay	ou	out
âr	care	ŏŏ	took
ä	father	ōō	boot
ĕ	pet	ŭ	cut
ē	be	ûr	urge
ĭ	pit	th	thin
ī	pie	th	this
îr	pier	hw	which
ŏ	pot	zh	vision
ō	toe	ə	about,
ô	paw		item

Stress marks:
' (primary);
' (secondary), as in
lexicon (lĕk'sĭ-kŏn')

ulcer < Gk. *karkinōma* < *karkinos*, cancer.] **—car′ci•no′ma•toid** (-nō′mə-toid′) *adj.* **—car′ci•nom′a•tous** (-nŏm′ə-təs, -nō′mə-) *adj.*

car•ci•no•ma•to•sis (kär′sə-nō′mə-tō′sĭs) *n.* A pathological condition characterized by the presence of carcinomas that have metastasized to many parts of the body. [Gk. *karkinōma, karkinōmat-,* cancerous ulcer; see CARCINOMA + –OSIS.]

car coat *n.* An overcoat extending to about midthigh.

card[1] (kärd) *n.* **1.** A flat, usu. rectangular piece of stiff paper, cardboard, or plastic, esp.: **a.** One of a set or pack bearing numbers, symbols, or figures, used in games and in divination. **b.** A greeting card. **c.** A post card. **d.** One bearing a person's name and other information, used for purposes of identification or classification. **e.** A business card. **f.** A credit card. **g.** A magnetic card. **h.** One used for recording information in a file. **2. cards** (*used with a sing. or pl. verb*) *Games* **a.** A game played with cards. **b.** The playing of cards. **3.** A program, esp. for a sports event. **4a.** A menu, as in a restaurant. **b.** A wine list. **5.** *Computer Science* **a.** A circuit board, esp. for use in a computer. **b.** A punch card. **6.** A compass card. **7.** *Informal* An eccentrically amusing person. **8a.** Something that can be used to help gain an objective: *negotiators with good cards.* **b.** An appeal to a specified issue or argument, usu. one involving strong emotions: *a lawyer who played the race card.* ❖ *tr.v.* **card•ed, card•ing, cards 1.** To furnish with or attach to a card. **2.** To list (something) on a card; catalog. **3.** To check the identification of. **4.** *Sports* To warn or eject (a soccer player who has committed a flagrant foul) by showing a yellow card or a red card. **—*idioms:* card up (one's) sleeve** A secret resource or plan held in reserve. **in the cards** Likely or certain to happen. **put (or lay) (one's) cards on the table** To reveal frankly one's thoughts, motives, or intentions. [ME *carde* < OFr. *carte* < Lat. *charta,* paper made from papyrus < Gk. *khartēs.*]

card[2] (kärd) *n.* **1.** A wire-toothed brush or a machine fitted with rows of wire teeth, used to disentangle fibers, as of wool, prior to spinning. **2.** A device used to raise a fabric's nap. ❖ *tr.v.* **card•ed, card•ing, cards** To comb out or brush with a card. [ME *carde* < Med.Lat. *cardus* < Lat. *carduus,* thistle.] **—card′er** *n.*

car•da•mom (kär′də-məm) or **car•da•mon** (-mən) *n.* **1a.** A rhizomatous Indian herb (*Elettaria cardamomum*) having aromatic seeds used as a spice or condiment. **b.** The seed of this plant. **2.** Any of several plants of the related genus *Amomum.* [ME *cardamome* < OFr. *cardemome* < Lat. *cardamōmum* < Gk. *kardamōmon : kardamon,* cress + *amōmon,* a spice.]

card•board (kärd′bôrd′, -bōrd′) *n.* A stiff material made of pressed paper pulp or pasted sheets of paper and used for making cartons, for example. ❖ *adj.* **1.** Made of or consisting of cardboard. **2a.** Flimsy; insubstantial. **b.** Superficial.

card-car•ry•ing (kärd′kär′ē-ĭng) *adj.* **1.** Being enrolled in an organization. **2.** Avidly devoted to a group or cause.

card catalog *n.* An alphabetical listing, esp. of books in a library, made with a separate card for each item.

Cár•de•nas (kär′dn-äs′, -dĕ-näs′) A city of N Cuba on the **Bay of Cárdenas,** an inlet of the Straits of Florida. Pop. 59,532.

card•hold•er (kärd′hōl′dər) *n.* One who holds a card, esp. a credit card. **—card′hold′ing** *adj.*

cardi– *pref.* Variant of **cardio–.**

car•di•a (kär′dē-ə) *n., pl.* **-di•ae** (-dē-ē′) or **-di•as 1.** The opening of the esophagus into the stomach. **2.** The upper stomach adjoining the cardia. [Gk. *kardiā,* heart, cardiac orifice of the stomach. See kerd- in App.]

car•di•ac (kär′dē-ăk′) *adj.* **1.** Of, near, or relating to the heart: *cardiac arteries.* **2.** Of or relating to the cardia. ❖ *n.* A person with a heart disorder. [ME < Lat. *cardiacus* < Gk. *kardiakos* < *kardiā,* heart. See kerd- in App.]

cardiac arrest *n.* Sudden cessation of heartbeat.

cardiac massage *n.* A resuscitating procedure using rhythmic compression of the chest to restore circulation.

car•di•al•gia (kär′dē-ăl′jə, -jē-ə) *n.* **1.** See **heartburn. 2.** Localized pain in the region of the heart. [Gk. *kardialgiā : kardiā,* heart; see CARDIA + *-algiā, -algia.*]

Car•diff (kär′dĭf) The cap. of Wales, in the SE part on Bristol Channel. Pop. 298,697.

car•di•gan (kär′dĭ-gən) *n.* A knitted sweater or jacket that opens down the full length of the front. [After the 7th Earl of *Cardigan,* James Thomas Brudenell (1797–1868), British army officer.]

car•di•nal (kär′dn-əl, kärd′nəl) *adj.* **1.** Of foremost importance; paramount: *a cardinal rule.* **2.** Dark to deep or vivid red. ❖ *n.* **1.** *Roman Catholic Church* A high church official, ranking just below the pope, who has been appointed by a pope to membership in the College of Cardinals. **2.** A dark to deep or vivid red. **3.** A North American finch (*Cardinalis cardinalis*) having a crested head and bright red plumage in the male. **4.** A short hooded cloak, originally of scarlet cloth, worn by women in the 18th century. **5.** A cardinal number. [ME < LLat. *cardinālis* < Lat., serving as a hinge < *cardō, cardin-,* hinge.] **—car′di•nal•ship′** *n.*

car•di•nal•ate (kär′dn-ə-lĭt, -lāt′, kärd′nə-) *n. Roman Catholic Church* **1.** The position, rank, dignity, or term of a cardinal. **2.** The College of Cardinals.

cardinal flower *n.* A perennial lobelia (*Lobelia cardinalis*) native to North America and having brilliant red flowers.

cardinal number *n.* A number, such as 3 or 11 or 412, used in

card[2]
carding wool

cardinal
male cardinal
Cardinalis cardinalis

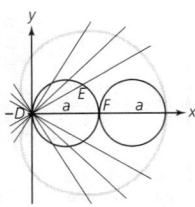

cardioid
constructed from circle *DEF*
and its secants through
fixed point *D*

counting to indicate quantity but not order.

cardinal point *n.* One of the four principal directions on a compass: north, south, east, or west.

cardinal virtue *n.* One of the four paramount virtues in classical philosophy: justice, prudence, fortitude, or temperance.

cardio– or **cardi–** *pref.* Heart: *cardiovascular.* [Gk. *kardio–* < *kardiā,* heart. See **kerd-** in App.]

car•di•o•gen•ic (kär′dē-ō-jĕn′ĭk, -jē′nĭk) *adj.* **1.** Originating in the heart. **2.** Resulting from a heart disease or disorder.

car•di•o•gram (kär′dē-ə-grăm′) *n.* **1.** The curve traced by a cardiograph, used to diagnose heart disorders. **2.** See **electrocardiogram.**

car•di•o•graph (kär′dē-ə-grăf′) *n.* **1.** An instrument used to record the mechanical movements of the heart. **2.** See **electrocardiograph. —car′di•og′ra•phy** (-ŏg′rə-fē) *n.*

car•di•oid (kär′dē-oid′) *n.* A heart-shaped plane curve, the locus of a fixed point on a circle that rolls on the circumference of another circle with the same radius.

car•di•ol•o•gy (kär′dē-ŏl′ə-jē) *n.* The medical study of the structure, function, and disorders of the heart. **—car′di•o•log′i•cal** (-ə-lŏj′ĭ-kəl) *adj.* **—car′di•ol′o•gist** *n.*

car•di•o•my•op•a•thy (kär′dē-ō-mī-ŏp′ə-thē) *n., pl.* **-thies** A disease or disorder of the heart muscle, esp. of unknown or obscure cause.

car•di•op•a•thy (kär′dē-ŏp′ə-thē) *n., pl.* **-thies** A disease or disorder of the heart.

car•di•o•pul•mo•nar•y (kär′dē-ō-pŏŏl′mə-nĕr′ē, -pŭl′-) *adj.* Of, relating to, or involving both the heart and the lungs.

cardiopulmonary bypass *n.* A procedure using a heart-lung machine to circulate and oxygenate the blood while surgery is performed on the heart.

cardiopulmonary resuscitation *n.* An emergency procedure in which cardiac massage, artificial respiration, and drugs are used to maintain the circulation of blood to the brain.

car•di•o•res•pi•ra•to•ry (kär′dē-ō-rĕs′pər-ə-tôr′ē, -tōr′-, -rĭ-spīr′ə-) *adj.* Of or relating to the heart and the respiratory system.

car•di•o•tho•rac•ic (kär′dē-ō-thə-răs′ĭk) *adj.* Of or relating to the heart and the chest.

car•di•o•vas•cu•lar (kär′dē-ō-văs′kyə-lər) *adj.* Of, relating to, or involving the heart and the blood vessels.

car•di•o•ver•sion (kär′dē-ō-vûr′zhən, -shən) *n.* The conversion of an abnormal cardiac rhythm to a normal one either by the use of medication or by the application of electric shock, as with a defibrillator. [CARDIO– + (CON)VERSION.]

car•di•tis (kär-dī′tĭs) *n.* Inflammation of the muscle tissue of the heart. [CARD(IO)– + –ITIS.]

car•doon (kär-dōōn′) *n.* A Mediterranean plant (*Cynara cardunculus*) cultivated for its edible leafstalks and roots. [ME *cardoun* < OFr. *cardon* < O Provençal < LLat. *cardō, cardōn-* < Lat. *carduus,* wild thistle.]

Car•do•zo (kär-dō′zō), Benjamin Nathan 1870–1938. Amer. jurist; associate justice of the US Supreme Court (1932–38).

card•sharp (kärd′shärp′) also **card•sharp•er** (-shär′pər) *n.* An expert in cheating at cards. **—card′sharp′ing** *n.*

Car•duc•ci (kär-dōō′chē), Giosuè 1835–1907. Italian poet who won the 1906 Nobel Prize for literature.

care (kâr) *n.* **1.** A burdened state of mind, as that arising from heavy responsibilities; worry. **2.** Mental suffering; grief. **3.** An object or source of worry or concern. **4.** Caution in avoiding harm or danger. **5a.** Close attention; painstaking application. **b.** Upkeep; maintenance: *lawn care.* **6.** Watchful oversight; charge or supervision. **7.** Attentive assistance or treatment to those in need. ❖ *v.* **cared, car•ing, cares** *—intr.* **1.** To be concerned or interested. **2.** To provide needed assistance or watchful supervision. **3.** To object or mind. **4a.** To have a liking or attachment. **b.** To have a wish; be inclined. *—tr.* **1.** To wish; desire. **2.** To be concerned to the degree of: *I don't care a bit.* [ME < OE *cearu.*]

SYNONYMS *care, charge, custody, keeping, supervision, trust* These nouns refer to the function of watching, guarding, or overseeing: *left the house keys in my care; had charge of these rare books; had custody of his children; left the canary in the neighbors' keeping; assumed supervision of the students; documents committed to the bank's trust.* See also Syns at **anxiety.**

CARE *abbr.* Cooperative for American Relief Everywhere

ca•reen (kə-rēn′) *v.* **-reened, -reen•ing, -reens** *—intr.* **1.** To lurch or swerve while in motion. **2.** To rush headlong or carelessly; career. **3.** To lean to one side, as a ship sailing in the wind. *—tr. Nautical* **1.** To cause (a ship) to careen; tilt. **2.** To lean (a ship) on one side for cleaning, caulking, or repairing. ❖ *n. Nautical* The position of a careened ship. [< Fr. *(en) carène,* (on) the keel < OFr. *carene* < OItal. *carena* < Lat. *carīna.*] **—ca•reen′er** *n.*

USAGE NOTE English has three similar-sounding verbs of motion—*careen, career,* and *carom,* that partly overlap in meaning. *Careen,* originally a nautical term meaning "to lean to one side," is now frequently used to mean "to lurch, swerve," especially with an implication of rapidity; in this it has been influenced by *career,* "to rush." *Carom* means "to collide and rebound," also implying speed.

ca·reer (kə-rîr′) n. **1a.** A chosen pursuit; a profession or occupation. **b.** The general course or progression of one's working life. **2.** A path or course, as of the sun through the heavens. **3.** Speed. ❖ *adj.* Doing what one does as a permanent occupation. ❖ *intr.v.* **-reered, -reer·ing, -reers** To move or run at full speed; rush. [Fr. *carrière* < OFr., racecourse < O Provençal *carriera*, street < Med.Lat. *(via) carrāria*, (road) for carts < Lat. *carrus*, a Gallic type of wagon. See CAR.]

ca·reer·ism (kə-rîr′ĭz′əm) n. Pursuit of professional advancement as one's chief or sole aim. **—ca·reer′ist** *adj. & n.*

care·free (kâr′frē′) *adj.* Free of worries and responsibilities.

care·ful (kâr′fəl) *adj.* **1.** Attentive to potential danger, error, or harm; cautious. **2.** Thorough and painstaking in action or execution; conscientious. **3.** Protective; solicitous. **4.** Full of cares or anxiety. **—care′ful·ly** *adv.* **—care′ful·ness** *n.*

SYNONYMS *careful, heedful, mindful, observant, watchful* These adjectives mean cautiously attentive: *was careful not to get her shoes muddy; heedful of the danger; mindful of his health; observant of the patient's symptoms; a watchful babysitter.*

care·giv·er (kâr′gĭv′ər) n. **1.** A person who assists a sick or disabled person. **2.** A person who attends to the needs of a child or dependent adult.

care·less (kâr′lĭs) *adj.* **1.** Taking insufficient care; negligent. **2.** Marked by or resulting from lack of forethought or thoroughness. **3.** Showing a lack of consideration. **4.** Unconcerned or indifferent; heedless. **5.** Unstudied or effortless. **6.** Free from cares; cheerful. **—care′less·ly** *adv.* **—care′less·ness** *n.*

ca·ress (kə-rĕs′) n. A gentle touch or gesture of tenderness or love. ❖ *tr.v.* **-ressed, -ress·ing, -ress·es 1.** To touch or stroke in an affectionate or loving manner. **2.** To touch or move as if with a caress. **3.** To treat fondly, kindly, or favorably; cherish. [Fr. *caresse* < Ital. *carezza* < *caro*, dear < Lat. *cārus*. See kā- in App.] **—ca·ress′er** *n.* **—ca·ress′ing·ly** *adv.* **—ca·res′sive** *adj.*

car·et (kâr′ĭt) n. A proofreading symbol (^) used to indicate an insertion in a line of printing or writing. [Lat., third pers. sing. pr. t. of *carēre*, to lack.]

care·tak·er (kâr′tā′kər) n. **1.** One that is employed to look after or take charge of property or a person; a custodian. **2.** One that temporarily performs the duties of an office.

care·worn (kâr′wôrn′, -wōrn′) *adj.* Showing worry.

car·fare (kär′fâr′) n. The fare a passenger pays, as on a bus.

car·go (kär′gō) n., pl. **-goes** or **-gos** The freight carried by a ship, an aircraft, or another vehicle. [Sp. < *cargar*, to load < LLat. *carricāre* < Lat. *carrus*, a Gallic type of wagon. See CAR.]

car·hop (kär′hŏp′) n. One who waits on customers at a drive-in restaurant.

Car·i·a (kâr′ē-ə) An ancient region of SW Asia Minor with a coastline on the Aegean Sea. **—Car′i·an** *adj. & n.*

Car·ib (kär′ĭb) n., pl. **Carib** or **-ibs** also **Car·i·ban** (kär′ə-bən, kə-rē′bən) **1.** A member of a group of American Indian peoples of northern South America, the Lesser Antilles, and the eastern coast of Central America. **2.** Any of the languages of the Carib. [Sp. *Caribe* < Carib *karibna*, person, Carib.] **—Car′ib** *adj.*

Car·i·ban (kär′ə-bən, kə-rē′bən) n., pl. **Cariban** or **-bans 1.** Variant of **Carib** 1. **2.** A language family comprising the Carib languages. **—Car′i·ban** *adj.*

Car·ib·be·an (kär′ə-bē′ən, kə-rĭb′ē-ən) *adj.* **1.** Of or relating to the Caribbean Sea, its islands, or its Central or South American coasts or to the peoples or cultures of this region. **2.** Of or relating to the Carib or their language or culture. ❖ *n.* A Carib.

Caribbean Sea An arm of the W Atlantic Ocean bounded by the coasts of Central and South America and the West Indies.

ca·ri·be (kə-rē′bē) n. See **piranha**. [Am.Sp. < Sp. *Caribe*, Carib. See CARIB.]

Car·i·boo Mountains (kär′ə-bōō′) A range of E British Columbia, Canada, parallel to and W of the Rocky Mts.

car·i·bou (kär′ə-bōō′) n., pl. **caribou** or **-bous** Any of several large reindeer native to northern North America. [Micmac *ĝalipu* (influenced by Canadian Fr. *caribou*, also < Micmac) < Proto-Algonquian **mekālixpowa* : **mekāl-*, to scrape + **-ixpo-*, snow.]

car·i·ca·ture (kär′ĭ-kə-chŏŏr′, -chər) n. **1a.** A representation in which the subject's distinctive features or peculiarities are exaggerated for comic or grotesque effect. **b.** The art of creating such representations. **2.** A grotesque imitation or misrepresentation: *The trial was a caricature of justice.* ❖ *tr.v.* **-tured, -tur·ing, -tures** To represent or imitate in an exaggerated, distorted manner. [Fr. < Ital. *caricatura* < *caricare*, to load, exaggerate < LLat. *carricāre* < Lat. *carrus*, a Gallic type of wagon. See CAR.] **—Car′i·ca·tur′ist** *n.*

car·ies (kâr′ēz) n., pl. **caries** Decay of a bone or tooth, esp. dental caries. [Lat. *cariēs*.]

car·il·lon (kär′ə-lŏn′, -lən) n. **1.** A stationary set of chromatically tuned bells in a tower, usu. played from a keyboard. **2.** A composition written or arranged for these bells. ❖ *intr.v.* **-lonned, -lon·ning, -lons** To play a carillon. [Fr., alteration of OFr. *quarregnon* < LLat. *quaterniō, quaterniōn-*, set of four. See QUATERNION.]

car·il·lon·neur (kär′ə-lə-nûr′) n. A person who plays a carillon. [Fr. < *carillon*, carillon. See CARILLON.]

ca·ri·na (kə-rī′nə, -rē′) n. **1.** pl. **-nae** (-nē) A keel-shaped ridge

or structure, such as that on the breastbone of a bird. **2. Carina** A constellation in the Southern Hemisphere near Volans and Vela. [Lat. *carīna*, keel.]

car·i·nate (kär′ə-nāt′, -nĭt) also **car·i·nat·ed** (-nā′tĭd) *adj.* Shaped like or having a carina or keel; ridged.

car·ing (kâr′ĭng) *adj.* Feeling and exhibiting concern and empathy for others.

Ca·rin·thi·a (kə-rĭn′thē-ə) A region and former duchy of central Europe in S Austria. **—Ca·rin′thi·an** *adj.*

Car·i·o·ca (kär′ē-ō′kə) n. **1.** A native or inhabitant of Rio de Janeiro, Brazil. **carioca** A dance similar to the samba. **b.** The music for this dance. [Port., of Tupian orig.] **—Car′i·o′can** *adj.*

car·i·ole also **car·ri·ole** (kär′ē-ōl′) n. **1.** A small, open, two- or four-wheeled carriage drawn by one horse. **2.** A light, often covered cart. [Fr. *carriole* < O Provençal *carriola*, dim. of *carri*, chariot < Lat. *carrus*, a Gallic type of wagon. See CAR.]

car·i·ous (kâr′ē-əs) *adj.* Having caries, esp. of the teeth; decayed. **—car′i·os′i·ty** (-ŏs′ĭ-tē), **car′i·ous·ness** *n.*

car·jack or **car-jack** (kär′jăk′) *tr.v.* **-jacked, -jack·ing, -jacks** To commit a forcible theft of (a vehicle) from its users. [CAR + (HI)JACK.]

cark (kärk) *tr. & intr.v.* **carked, cark·ing, carks** To burden or be burdened with trouble; worry. ❖ *n.* A worry; a trouble. [ME *carken* < Norman Fr. *carquier*, to burden, load < LLat. *carricāre*. See CARGO.]

Carl XVI Gus·tav (kärl gŭs′tăv, -täf, gŏŏs′-) b. 1946. King of Sweden (since 1973).

car·line or **car·lin** (kär′lĭn) n. Scots A woman, esp. an old one. [ME *kerling* < ON < *karl*, man.]

Car·list (kär′lĭst) n. A supporter of Don Carlos, the pretender to the Spanish throne, or his heirs. **—Car′list** *adj.*

car·load (kär′lōd′) n. **1.** The quantity that a car can hold. **2.** The minimum weight necessary to ship freight at a reduced rate.

Car·los (kär′ləs, -lōs), Don. Count of Molina. 1788–1855. Spanish pretender to the throne who claimed the title (1833) and waged an unsuccessful civil war until 1840.

Car·lo·ta (kär-lō′tə) 1840–1927. Belgian-born empress of Mexico (1864–67) as the wife of Maximilian of Austria.

Car·lo·vin·gian (kär′lə-vĭn′jən, -jē-ən) *adj. & n.* Variant of **Carolingian.**

Carls·bad Caverns (kärlz′băd′) A group of limestone caverns in the Guadalupe Mts. of SE NM.

Carls·ru·he (kärlz′rōō′ə, kärls′-) See **Karlsruhe.**

Car·lyle (kär-līl′, kär′līl), **Thomas** 1795–1881. British historian whose works include *The French Revolution* (1837).

car·mak·er (kär′mā′kər) n. An automobile manufacturer.

Car·me (kär′mā) n. A satellite of Jupiter. [< Gk. *Karmē*, mother by Zeus of Britomartis, a Cretan goddess.]

Car·mel (kär-mĕl′) also **Car·mel-by-the-Sea** (-bī-thə-sē′) A city of W CA on **Carmel Bay** at the S end of the Monterey Peninsula. Pop. 4,081.

Car·mel (kär′məl), **Mount** A limestone ridge of NW Israel extending from the Plain of Esdraelon to the Mediterranean Sea.

Car·mel·ite (kär′mə-līt′) n. **1.** A monk or mendicant friar belonging to the order of Our Lady of Mount Carmel, founded in 1155. **2.** A member of a community of nuns of this order, founded in 1452. **—Car′mel·ite′** *adj.*

Car·mi·chael (kär′mī-kəl), **Hoagland Howard** Known as "Hoagy." 1899–1981. Amer. songwriter whose popular works include "Stardust" (1929).

car·min·a·tive (kär-mĭn′ə-tĭv, kär′mə-nā′-) *adj.* Inducing the expulsion of gas from the stomach and intestines. ❖ *n.* A carminative drug or agent. [ME *carminatif* < OFr. < Lat. *carminātus*, p. part. of *carmināre*, to card wool < **carmen*, card for wool < *cārere*, to card.]

car·mine (kär′mĭn, -mīn′) n. **1.** A strong or vivid red. **2.** A crimson pigment derived from cochineal. ❖ *adj.* Strong to vivid red. [Fr. *carmin* < Med.Lat. *carminium*, prob. blend of Ar. *qirmiz*, kermes; see KERMES, and Lat. *minium*, cinnabar; see MINIUM.]

car·nage (kär′nĭj) n. **1.** Massive slaughter, as in war; a massacre. **2.** Corpses, esp. of those killed in battle. [Fr. < OFr. < OItal. *carnaggio* < Med.Lat. *carnāticum*, meat < Lat. *carō, carn-*, flesh. See **sker-¹** in App.]

car·nal (kär′nəl) *adj.* **1.** Relating to the physical and esp. sexual appetites. **2.** Worldly or earthly; temporal. **3.** Of or relating to the body or flesh. [ME < ONFr. *carnel* < Lat. *carnālis* < Lat. *carō, carn-*, flesh, see **sker-¹** in App.] **—car·nal′i·ty** (kär-năl′ĭ-tē) *n.* **—car′nal·ly** *adv.*

car·nal·lite (kär′nə-līt′) n. A white, brownish, or reddish mineral, $KMgCl_3 \cdot 6H_2O$, an ore of potassium, used to manufacture potash salts. [After Rudolf von *Carnall* (1804–74), German mining engineer.]

Car·nap (kär′năp′, -näp′), **Rudolf** 1891–1970. German-born Amer. philosopher who was central to the development of logical positivism.

car·nas·si·al (kär-năs′ē-əl) *adj.* Adapted for tearing apart flesh. ❖ *n.* A tooth adapted for tearing apart flesh. [< Fr. *carnassier*, carnivorous < Provençal < *carnasso*, meat in abundance < *carn*, flesh < Lat. *carō, carn-*, flesh. See **sker-¹** in App.]

car·na·tion (kär-nā′shən) n. **1a.** Any of numerous cultivated forms of a perennial plant (*Dianthus caryophyllus*) having showy

caricature
detail from a caricature of
Dwight Eisenhower by
Charles Dunn (1895–1978)

Carlsbad Caverns

ă	pat	oi	boy
ā	pay	ou	out
âr	care	ŏŏ	took
ä	father	ōō	boot
ĕ	pet	ŭ	cut
ē	be	ûr	urge
ĭ	pit	th	thin
ī	pie	*th*	this
îr	pier	hw	which
ŏ	pot	zh	vision
ō	toe	ə	about,
ô	paw		item

Stress marks:
′ (primary);
′ (secondary), as in
lexicon (lĕk′sĭ-kŏn′)

flowers with fringed petals. **b.** A flower of this plant. **2.** A pinkish tint once used in painting. [< obsolete Fr., flesh-colored < OFr. (< OItal. *carnagione*, skin, complexion < *carne*, flesh) or < LLat. *carnātiō*, *carnātiōn-*, flesh, both < Lat. *carō*, *carn-*. See **sker-**[1] in App.]

car·nau·ba (kär-nô′bə, -nou′-, -nōō′-) *n.* **1.** A Brazilian palm tree (*Copernicia prunifera*) having waxy fan-shaped leaves. **2.** A hard wax obtained from the leaves of this plant. [Port. < Tupi *carnaúba*.]

Car·ne·gie (kär′nə-gē, kär-nā′gē, -nĕg′ē), **Andrew** 1835–1919. Scottish-born Amer. industrialist and philanthropist who amassed a fortune in the steel industry.

car·nel·ian (kär-nēl′yən) also **cor·nel·ian** (kôr-) *n.* A pale to deep red or reddish-brown variety of clear chalcedony, used in jewelry. [ME *corneline* < OFr. < *cornel*, cornel < Lat. *cornus*.]

car·net (kär-nā′) *n.* **1.** An official pass or permit, esp. one for crossing national boundaries. **2.** A book of postage stamps. [Fr., notebook, carnet < OFr. *quernet*, pocket notebook < *quaer*, quire. See QUIRE[1].]

Car·nic Alps (kär′nĭk) A range of the E Alps in S Austria and NE Italy rising to c. 2,782 m (9,121 ft).

Car·ni·o·la (kär′nē-ō′lə, kärn-yō′-) A mountainous region of SW Slovenia; first settled by Celtic peoples. —**Car′ni·o′lan** *adj. & n.*

car·ni·tine (kär′nĭ-tēn′) *n.* A betaine commonly occurring in the liver and in skeletal muscle. [Ger. *Karnitin* < *Karnin*, a meat derivative < Lat. *carō*, *carn-*, flesh. See CARNAL.]

car·ni·val (kär′nə-vəl) *n.* **1.** often **Carnival** The period of merry-making and feasting celebrated just before Lent. **2.** A traveling amusement show usu. including rides, games, and sideshows. **3.** A festival or revel. [Ital. *carnevale* < OItal. *carnelevare*, Shrovetide : *carne*, meat (< Lat. *carō*, *carn-*; see **sker-**[1] in App.) + *levare*, to remove (< Lat. *levāre*, to raise).]

car·ni·vore (kär′nə-vôr′, -vōr′) *n.* **1.** A flesh-eating animal. **2.** Any of various predatory, flesh-eating mammals of the order Carnivora, including the dogs, cats, bears, weasels, hyenas, and raccoons. **3.** An insectivorous plant. [< Fr., meat-eating < Lat. *carnivorus*. See CARNIVOROUS.]

car·niv·o·rous (kär-nĭv′ər-əs) *adj.* **1.** Of or relating to carnivores. **2.** Flesh-eating or predatory: *a carnivorous bird.* **3.** *Botany* Capable of trapping insects or other small organisms and absorbing nutrients from them; insectivorous. [< Lat. *carnivorus* : *carō*, *carn-*, flesh; see **sker-**[1] in App. + *-vorus*, -vorous.] —**car·niv′o·rous·ly** *adv.* —**car·niv′o·rous·ness** *n.*

Car·not (kär-nō′), **Lazare Nicolas Marguerite** 1753–1823. French military strategist for the Republican armies during the French Revolution.

Carnot, Nicolas Léonard Sadi 1796–1832. French physicist and engineer who founded the science of thermodynamics.

car·no·tite (kär′nə-tīt′) *n.* A yellow ore of uranium and radium with composition $K(UO_2)_2(VO_4)_2 \cdot 3H_2O$. [Fr., after Marie Adolphe Carnot (1839–1920), French mining engineer.]

car·ny also **car·ney** (kär′nē) *n., pl.* **-nies** also **-neys** *Informal* **1.** A traveling amusement show; a carnival. **2.** A person who works with a carnival.

car·ob (kär′əb) *n.* **1a.** An eastern Mediterranean evergreen tree (*Ceratonia siliqua*) in the pea family, having pinnately compound leaves and large pods. **b.** The pod of this plant, containing an edible pulp and seeds that yield a gum used as a food stabilizer. **2.** An edible powder or flour made from the ground seeds and pods of this plant. [ME *carabe* < OFr. *carobe* < Med.Lat. *carrūbium* < Ar. *harrūba*, carob pod. See ALGARROBA.]

ca·roche (kə-rōch′, -rōsh′) *n.* A stately carriage of the late 16th and 17th centuries. [Obsolete Fr. *carroche* < OItal. *carrozza*, ult. < Lat. *carrus*, a Gallic type of wagon. See CAR.]

car·ol (kär′əl) *n.* **1.** A song of praise or joy, esp. for Christmas. **2.** An old round dance often with singing. ❖ *v.* **-oled**, **-ol·ing**, **-ols** also **-olled**, **-ol·ling**, **-ols** —*intr.* **1.** To sing in a loud, joyous manner. **2.** To go from house to house singing Christmas songs. —*tr.* **1.** To celebrate in or as if in song. **2.** To sing loudly and joyously. [ME *carole*, round dance with singing < OFr., prob. < LLat. *choraula*, choral song, ult. < Gk. *khoraulēs*, accompanist : *khoros*, choral dance; see **gher-** in App. + *aulos*, flute.] —**car′ol·er**, **car′ol·ler** *n.*

Car·o·le·an (kär′ə-lē′ən) *adj.* Relating to Charles I or II of England. [< Med.Lat. *Carolus*, Charles.]

Car·o·li·na[1] (kär′ə-lī′nə) An English colony of SE North America, first settled in 1653 and divided into North Carolina and South Carolina in 1729.

Ca·ro·li·na[2] (kä′rō-lē′nä) A city of NE Puerto Rico ESE of San Juan. Pop. 168,164.

Car·o·li·na allspice (kär′ə-lī′nə) *n.* A species of sweet shrub (*Calycanthus floridus*) native chiefly to the southeast United States.

Car·o·li·na jasmine also **Car·o·li·na jessamine** (kär′ə-lī′nə) *n.* Any of several poisonous woody evergreen vines of the genus *Gelsemium*, esp. *G. sempervirens*, of the southeast United States, having fragrant yellow funnel-shaped flowers.

Car·o·li·nas (kär′ə-lī′nəz) The colonies (after 1729) or present-day states of North Carolina and South Carolina.

Car·o·line (kär′ə-līn′, -lĭn) *adj.* Relating to Charles I or II of

England. [Med.Lat. *Carolīnus* < *Carolus*, Charles.]

Caroline Islands An archipelago of the W Pacific Ocean E of the Philippines; included in the US Trust Terr. of the Pacific Is. in 1947.

Car·o·lin·gian (kär′ə-lĭn′jən, -jē-ən) also **Car·lo·vin·gian** (kär′lə-vĭn′jən, -jē-ən) *adj.* Of or relating to the Frankish dynasty founded by Pepin the Short in 751 and lasting until 987 in France and 911 in Germany. ❖ *n.* A member of the Carolingian dynasty. [Fr. *Carolingien*, alteration of *Carlovingien*, blend of Med.Lat. *Carolus*, Charles, and Fr. *Mérovingien*, Merovingian.]

Car·o·lin·i·an (kär′ə-lĭn′ē-ən) *adj.* **1.** Caroline. **2.** Of or relating to Charlemagne and his times. **3.** Of or relating to Carolina or the Carolinas. ❖ *n.* A native or inhabitant of Carolina or the Carolinas.

car·om (kär′əm) *n.* **1.** A collision followed by a rebound. **2.** A shot, as in billiards, in which the cue ball successively strikes two other balls. ❖ *v.* **-omed**, **-om·ing**, **-oms** —*intr.* **1.** To collide and rebound; glance: *The car caromed off the guardrail.* **2.** To make a carom, as in billiards. —*tr.* To cause to carom. [Short for *carambole*, a stroke at billiards < Fr., a billiard ball < Sp. *carambola*, a stroke at billiards, perh. < Port., carambola. See CARAMBOLA.]

Ca·ro·ní (kär′ə-nē′) A river rising in SE Venezuela and flowing 885 km (550 mi) N to join the Orinoco R.

car·o·tene (kär′ə-tēn′) also **car·o·tin** (-tĭn) *n.* An orange-yellow to red crystalline pigment, $C_{40}H_{56}$, found in animal tissue and certain plants and converted to vitamin A in the liver. [Ger. *Karotin* < Lat. *carōta*, carrot. See CARROT.]

ca·rot·e·noid (kə-rŏt′n-oid′) *n.* Any of a class of yellow to red pigments, including the carotenes and the xanthophylls. ❖ *adj.* Of or relating to such a pigment.

Ca·roth·ers (kə-rŭth′ərz), **Wallace Hume** 1896–1937. Amer. chemist who developed the synthetic material nylon.

ca·rot·id (kə-rŏt′ĭd) *n.* Either of the two major arteries, one on each side of the neck, that carry blood to the head. ❖ *adj.* Of or relating to either of these arteries. [Fr. *carotide* < Gk. *karōtides*, carotid arteries < *karoun*, to stupefy (because compression of these arteries causes loss of consciousness). See **ker-**[1] in App.]

ca·rous·al (kə-rou′zəl) *n.* **1.** A riotous drinking party. **2.** Boisterous merrymaking; revelry.

ca·rouse (kə-rouz′) *intr.v.* **-roused**, **-rous·ing**, **-rous·es** **1.** To engage in carousal. **2.** To drink excessively. ❖ *n.* Carousal. [Ger. *garaus*, all out, drink up : *gar*, completely (< MHGer. < OHGer. *garo*) + *aus*, out, up; see AUSLANDER.] —**ca·rous′er** *n.*

car·ou·sel or **car·rou·sel** (kär′ə-sĕl′, -zĕl′) *n.* **1.** A merry-go-round. **2.** A circular conveyor to display or rotate objects. [Fr. *carrousel* < Ital. *carosello*, tilting match.]

carp[1] (kärp) *intr.v.* **carped**, **carp·ing**, **carps** To find fault in a disagreeable way; complain fretfully. ❖ *n.* A fretful complaint. [ME *carpen* < ON *karpa*, to boast.] —**carp′er** *n.*

carp[2] (kärp) *n., pl.* **carp** or **carps** **1.** An edible freshwater fish (*Cyprinus carpio*) of Europe and Asia. **2.** Any of various fishes of the family Cyprinidae. [ME *carpe* < OFr. *carpe* < Med.Lat. *carpa*, of Gmc. orig.]

–carp *suff.* Fruit; part of a fruit; fruitlike structure: *mesocarp.* [NLat. *-carpium* < Gk. *-karpion* < *karpos*, fruit. See **kerp-** in App.]

car·pac·cio (kär-pä′chō) *n.* Very thinly sliced raw beef or tuna garnished with a sauce. [Ital., after Vittore CARPACCIO.]

Car·pac·cio (kär-pä′chō, -chē-ō), **Vittore** 1460?–1525? Italian painter noted for his narrative series on religious subjects.

car·pal (kär′pəl) *adj.* Of, relating to, or near the carpus. ❖ *n.* A bone of the carpus. [NLat. *carpālis* < Gk. *karpos*, wrist.]

carpal tunnel *n.* A passageway in the wrist through which nerves and the long tendons of the flexor muscles of the wrist and fingers pass.

carpal tunnel syndrome *n.* A condition marked by pain and numbness or tingling in the hand, caused by compression of a nerve in the carpal tunnel of the wrist.

Car·pa·thi·an Mountains (kär-pā′thē-ən) A major mountain system of central Europe extending in an arc c. 2,253 km (1,400 mi) long through Slovakia, S Poland, W Ukraine, and NE Romania.

car·pe di·em (kär′pĕ dē′ĕm′, -əm, dī′-) *interj.* Used as an admonition to seize the pleasures of the moment without concern for the future. ❖ *n.* Such an admonition. [Lat. : *carpe*, sing. imper. of *carpere*, to seize + *diem*, accusative of *diēs*, day.]

car·pel (kär′pəl) *n.* One of the structural units of a pistil, representing a modified ovule-bearing leaf. [NLat. *carpellum* < Gk. *karpos*, fruit. See **kerp-** in App.] —**car′pel·lar′y** (-pə-lĕr′ē) *adj.*

car·pel·late (kär′pə-lāt′, -lĭt) *adj.* Having carpels; pistillate.

Car·pen·tar·i·a (kär′pən-târ′ē-ə), **Gulf of** A wide inlet of the Arafura Sea indenting the N coast of Australia.

car·pen·ter (kär′pən-tər) *n.* A worker who makes, finishes, and repairs wooden structures. ❖ *v.* **-tered**, **-ter·ing**, **-ters** —*tr.* To make, finish, or repair (wooden structures). —*intr.* To work as a carpenter. [ME < AN < Lat. *carpentārius* (*artifex*), (maker) of a carriage < *carpentum*, a two-wheeled carriage, ult. < Gaulish *carros*, type of wagon.] —**car′pen·try** (-trē) *n.*

carpenter ant *n.* Any of various large ants of the genus *Camponotus* that nest in and are destructive to wood.

carpenter bee *n.* Any of various solitary bees of the family Apidae that bore tunnels into wood to lay their eggs.

carnauba
Copernicia prunifera

Car•pen•tier (kär′pĕn-tyār′), **Alejo** 1904–80. Cuban writer whose novels include *The Kingdom of This World* (1942).

car•pet (kär′pĭt) *n.* **1a.** A thick heavy covering for a floor, usu. made of woven wool or synthetic fibers; a rug. **b.** The fabric used for this floor covering. **2.** A surface or surface covering that is similar to a rug: *a carpet of leaves.* ❖ *tr.v.* **-pet•ed, -pet•ing, -pets** To cover with or as if with a carpet. ***—idiom:* on the carpet 1.** In a position of being reprimanded by one in authority. **2.** Under discussion or consideration. [ME < OFr. *carpite* < Med.Lat. *carpīta* < OItal. *carpita* < *carpire,* to pluck < Lat. *carpere.* See **kerp-** in App.]

car•pet•bag (kär′pĭt-băg′) *n.* A traveling bag made of carpet fabric. ❖ *adj.* Carpetbagging.

car•pet•bag•ger (kär′pĭt-băg′ər) *n.* **1.** A Northerner who went to the South after the Civil War for political or financial advantage. **2.** An outsider who presumptuously seeks a position or success in a new locality. [So called because they carried their belongings in carpetbags.] **—car′pet•bag′ger•y** *n.*

car•pet•bag•ging (kär′pĭt-băg′ĭng) *adj.* Of or relating to carpetbaggers or their practices.

carpet beetle *n.* Any of various small beetles of the genera *Anthrenus* and *Attagenus,* having larvae that are injurious to fabrics and furs.

car•pet-bomb (kär′pĭt-bŏm′) *tr. & intr.v.* **-bombed, -bomb•ing, -bombs** To bomb in a systematic pattern, so as to devastate a large area. **—car′pet-bomb′ing** *n.*

car•pet•ing (kär′pĭ-tĭng) *n.* **1.** Material used for carpets. **2.** A carpet or carpets.

car•pet•weed (kär′pĭt-wēd′) *n.* A widespread North American annual plant *(Mollugo verticillata)* having whorled leaves and greenish-white flowers.

car phone *n.* A cellular telephone used or installed in a car.

carp•ing (kär′pĭng) *adj.* Naggingly critical or complaining. **—carp′ing•ly** *adv.*

carpo– *pref.* Fruit: *carpophore.* [Gk. *karpo-* < *karpos,* fruit. See **kerp-** in App.]

car•pool also **car pool** (kär′po͞ol′) *n.* **1.** An arrangement whereby several people travel in one vehicle, sharing costs and often taking turns as the driver. **2.** A group, as of commuters, participating in a carpool. **—car′pool′, car′-pool′** *v.* **—car′pool′er** *n.*

car•poph•a•gous (kär-pŏf′ə-gəs) *adj.* Feeding on fruit.

car•po•phore (kär′pə-fôr′, -fōr′) *n.* A slender stalk that supports each half of a dehisced fruit in many members of the parsley family.

car•port (kär′pôrt′, -pōrt′) *n.* An open-sided shelter for an automotive vehicle, usu. formed by a roof projecting from the side of a building.

–carpous or **–carpic** *suff.* A specified number or kind of carpel or fruit: *apocarpous.* [< NLat. *-carpus* < Gk. *karpos,* fruit. See **kerp-** in App.]

car•pus (kär′pəs) *n., pl.* **-pi** (-pī′) **1.** The group of eight bones forming the joint between the forearm and the hand. **2.** A joint in quadrupeds corresponding to the wrist. [NLat. < Gk. *karpos,* wrist.]

Car•rac•ci (kə-rä′chē, kä-rät′-) Family of Bolognese painters, including **Agostino** (1557–1602), his brother **Annibale** (1560–1609), and their cousin **Lodovico** (1555–1619), whose works provided a transition to the baroque style.

car•rack also **car•ack** (kăr′ək) *n.* A large galleon used in the 14th, 15th, and 16th centuries. [ME *carike* < Med.Lat. *carrica* and < OFr. *caraque* (< OSpan. *carraca*), both < Ar. *qarāqīr,* pl. of *qurqūr* < Gk. *kerkouros,* fast light vessel.]

car•ra•geen also **car•ra•gheen** (kăr′ə-gēn′) *n.* See **Irish moss.** [After *Carragheen,* a village of SE Ireland.]

car•ra•geen•an also **car•ra•geen•in** (kăr′ə-gē′nən) *n.* Any of a group of colloids derived from Irish moss and several other red algae, used esp. as a thickening, stabilizing, or emulsifying agent in food products.

car•re•four (kăr′ə-fo͝or′) *n.* **1.** A crossroads. **2.** A public square; a plaza. [Fr. < OFr. *carrefor* < Lat. *quadrifurcus,* four-forked : *quadri-,* quadri- + *furca,* fork.]

car•rel also **car•rell** (kăr′əl) *n.* A partitioned nook in or near the stacks in a library, used for private study. [ME *carole,* round dance ring, circle, stall for study. See CAROL.]

Car•rel (kə-rĕl′, kăr′əl), **Alexis** 1873–1944. French-born Amer. surgeon and biologist who won a 1912 Nobel Prize.

car•riage (kăr′ĭj) *n.* **1.** A wheeled vehicle, esp. a four-wheeled horse-drawn passenger vehicle. **2.** *Chiefly British* A railroad passenger car. **3.** A baby carriage. **4.** A wheeled support or frame for carrying a heavy object, such as a cannon. **5.** A moving part of a machine for holding or shifting another part. **6a.** The act or process of transporting or carrying. **b.** (kăr′ē-ĭj) The cost of or the charge for transporting. **7.** The manner of holding and moving one's head and body; bearing. **8.** *Archaic* Management; administration. [ME *cariage* < Norman Fr. < ONFr. *carier,* to carry. See CARRY.]

carriage dog *n.* See **Dalmatian** 2.

carriage trade *n.* Wealthy patrons or customers, as of a store.

car•rick bend (kăr′ĭk) *n. Nautical* A type of knot used to fasten two cables or hawsers together. [< obsolete *carrick,* var. of CARRACK.]

car•ri•er (kăr′ē-ər) *n.* **1.** One that transports or conveys: *baggage carriers.* **2.** One that deals in the transport of passengers or goods. **3.** A mechanism or device by which something is conveyed or conducted. **4.** *Medicine* A person or animal that shows no symptoms of a disease but harbors the infectious agent and is capable of transmitting it. **5.** *Genetics* An individual that carries one gene for a particular recessive trait and when mated with another carrier can produce offspring that express the trait. **6.** *Electronics* **a.** A carrier wave. **b.** A charge-carrying entity, esp. an electron or a hole in a semiconductor. **7.** An aircraft carrier. **8.** An insurance or underwriting organization. **9.** A telecommunications company.

carrier pigeon *n.* **1.** A homing pigeon, esp. one trained to carry messages. **2.** Any of various large domestic pigeons having a prominent wattle.

carrier wave *n.* An electromagnetic wave that can be modulated, as in frequency, amplitude, or phase, to transmit speech, music, images, or other signals.

car•ri•ole (kăr′ē-ōl′) *n.* Variant of **cariole.**

car•ri•on (kăr′ē-ən) *n.* Dead and decaying flesh. ❖ *adj.* **1.** Of or similar to carrion. **2.** Feeding on carrion. [ME *careine* < AN < VLat. **carōnia* < Lat. *carō,* flesh. See **sker-**[1] in App.]

carrion crow *n.* A common European crow *(Corvus corone)* having glossy black plumage.

carrion flower *n.* Any of several North American plants of the genus *Smilax,* esp. *S. herbacea,* an herbaceous tendril-bearing vine having clusters of small greenish flowers with the odor of decaying flesh.

Car•roll (kăr′əl), **Charles** 1737–1832. Amer. Revolutionary leader who signed the Declaration of Independence (1776).

Carroll, Lewis See Charles Lutwidge **Dodgson.**

Car•roll•ton (kăr′əl-tən) A city of N TX, a suburb of Dallas. Pop. 109,576.

car•rot (kăr′ət) *n.* **1.** A biennial Eurasian plant *(Daucus carota* subsp. *sativus)* in the parsley family, widely cultivated as an annual for its edible taproot. **2.** The fleshy orange root of this plant, eaten as a vegetable. **3.** Queen Anne's lace. **4.** A reward offered for desired behavior; an inducement. [Fr. *carotte* < OFr. *garroite* < Lat. *carōta* < Gk. *karōton.* See **ker-**[1] in App.]

car•rot-and-stick (kăr′ət-ən-stĭk′) *adj.* Combining a promised reward with a threatened penalty.

car•rot•top (kăr′ət-tŏp′) *n. Slang* A person with red hair; a redhead.

car•rot•y (kăr′ə-tē) *adj.* **1.** Bright orange in color. **2.** Having red hair; carrot-topped.

car•rou•sel (kăr′ə-sĕl′, -zĕl′) *n.* Variant of **carousel.**

car•ry (kăr′ē) *v.* **-ried, -ry•ing, -ries** *—tr.* **1.** To hold or support while moving; bear. **2a.** To take from one place to another; transport: *a train carrying freight.* **b.** *Chiefly Southern US* To escort or accompany. **3.** To serve as a means for the conveyance of; transmit: *pipes that carry water.* **4a.** To communicate; pass on: *news carried by word of mouth.* **b.** To express or contain: *Her words carried a threat.* **5.** To have (something) on the surface or skin; bear: *carried the scar ever after.* **6.** To hold or be capable of holding: *The tank carries 10 gallons.* **7.** To support the weight or responsibility of. **8.** To keep or have on one's person. **9.** To be pregnant with. **10a.** To hold and move (the body or a part of it) in a particular way. **b.** To behave or conduct (oneself) in a specified manner. **11.** To extend or continue in space, time, or degree: *carry a joke too far.* **12a.** To give impetus to; propel. **b.** To take further; advance: *carry a cause.* **13.** To take or seize, esp. by force; capture. **14a.** To be successful in; win. **b.** To gain victory, support, or acceptance for. **c.** To win a majority of the votes in: *carried ten states.* **d.** To gain the sympathy of; win over. **15.** To include or keep on a list: *carried six workers on the payroll.* **16a.** To have as an attribute or accompaniment: *The appliance carries a guarantee.* **b.** To involve as a condition, consequence, or effect: *The crime carried a five-year sentence.* **17.** To transfer from one place, as a column or page, to another. **18.** To keep in stock; offer for sale. **19.** To keep in one's accounts as a debtor. **20a.** To maintain or support (one that is less competent, for example). **b.** To compensate for (a weaker member or partner) by one's performance. **21.** To place before the public; print or broadcast. **22.** To produce as a crop. **23.** To provide forage for: *land that carries sheep.* **24.** To sing on key. **25.** *Nautical* To be equipped with (a mast or sail). **26.** *Sports* **a.** To cover (a distance) or advance beyond (a point or object) in one golf stroke. **b.** To control and advance (a ball or puck). **c.** *Basketball* To palm (the ball) in violation of the rules. *—intr.* **1.** To act as a bearer. **2.** To be transmitted or conveyed: *a voice that carries well.* **3.** To admit of being transported. **4.** To hold the neck and head in a certain way. Used of a horse. **5.** To be accepted or approved. ❖ *n., pl.* **-ries 1.** The act or process of carrying. **2.** A portage, as between two bodies of water. **3a.** The range of a gun or projectile. **b.** The distance traveled by a hurled or struck ball. **c.** Reach; projection: *a voice with great carry.* **4.** *Football* An act of rushing with the ball. ***—phrasal verbs:* carry away** To move or excite greatly. **carry forward** *Accounting* To transfer (an entry) to the next column, page, or book, or to another account. **carry off 1.** To cause the death of. **2.** To handle successfully. **carry on 1.** To conduct; maintain. **2.** To engage in. **3.** To continue without halting; persevere. **4.** To behave in an excited, improper, or silly

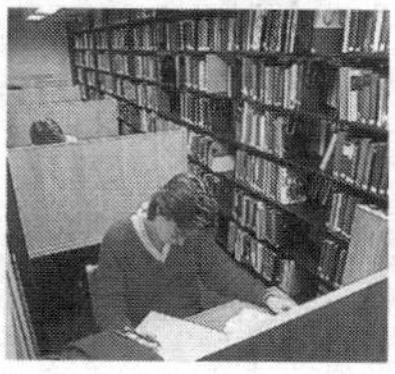

carrel

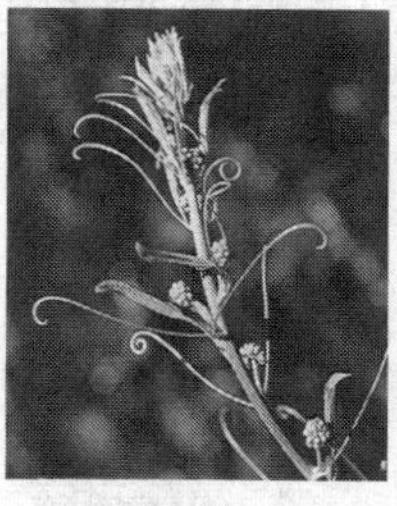

carrion flower
tendrils and flower buds
Smilax herbacea

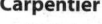

ă	pat	oi	boy
ā	pay	ou	out
âr	care	o͝o	took
ä	father	o͞o	boot
ĕ	pet	ŭ	cut
ē	be	ûr	urge
ĭ	pit	th	thin
ī	pie	*th*	this
îr	pier	hw	which
ŏ	pot	zh	vision
ō	toe	ə	about, item
ô	paw		

Stress marks:
′ (primary);
′ (secondary), as in
lexicon (lĕk′sĭ-kŏn′)

manner. **carry out 1.** To put into practice or effect. **2.** To follow or obey. **3.** To bring to a conclusion; accomplish. **carry over 1.** *Accounting* **a.** To transfer (an account) to the next column, page, or book relating to the same account. **b.** To retain (merchandise or other goods) for a subsequent season. **2.** To deduct (a loss, for example) in determining taxable income of a subsequent period. **3.** To persist to another time or situation. **carry through 1.** To accomplish; complete. **2.** To survive; persist. **3.** To enable to endure; sustain. ***—idioms:* carry a** (or **the**) **torch** To feel a painful unreciprocated love. **carry the day** To be victorious; win. [ME *carien* < ONFr. *carier* < *carre*, cart. See CAR.]

car•ry•all (kăr′ē-ôl′) *n.* **1.** A large receptacle, such as a bag, used to carry things around. **2.** A closed automobile with two lengthwise seats facing each other. **3.** A covered one-horse carriage with two seats. [Alteration of CARIOLE.]

car•ry•ing capacity (kăr′ē-ĭng) *n.* **1.** The maximum number of persons or things that a vehicle or a receptacle can carry. **2.** *Ecology* The maximum number of individuals that an environment can support without detrimental effects.

carrying charge *n.* The interest charged on the balance owed when paying in installments.

car•ry•ing-on (kăr′ē-ĭng-ŏn′, -ôn′) *n., pl.* **car•ry•ings-on** (-ĭngz-) **1.** Improper, irresponsible, or silly behavior. **2.** An instance of such behavior.

car•ry•on (kăr′ē-ŏn′) *adj.* Small or compact enough to be carried aboard and stowed on an airplane, train, or bus by a passenger. ❖ *n.* A piece of carryon luggage.

car•ry•out (kăr′ē-out′) *adj.* Intended to be consumed away from the place of sale; takeout. ❖ *n.* A carryout item of food.

car•ry•o•ver (kăr′ē-ō′vər) *n.* **1.** Something transferred or extended from an earlier time or another place. **2.** *Accounting* A sum transferred to a new column, page, or book relating to the same account.

car seat *n.* A small removable seat that is equipped with a restraining device or harness and can be fastened to the seat of a vehicle for securing young children.

car•sick (kär′sĭk′) *adj.* Suffering from motion sickness caused by travel in a motor vehicle. **—car′sick′ness** *n.*

Car•son (kär′sən) A city of S CA, a suburb of Los Angeles. Pop. 89,730.

Carson, Christopher Known as "Kit." 1809–68. Amer. pioneer who was a renowned guide and a Union general in the Civil War.

Carson, Johnny b. 1925. Amer. comedian and long-time host of television's *The Tonight Show* (1962–92).

Carson, Rachel Louise 1907–64. Amer. environmentalist whose works include *Silent Spring* (1962).

Carson City The cap. of NV, in the W part near the CA border; laid out in 1858. Pop. 52,457.

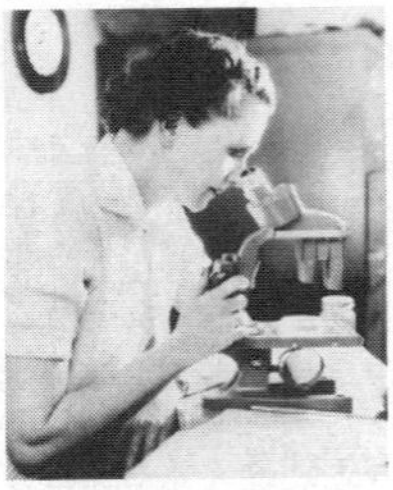

Rachel Carson

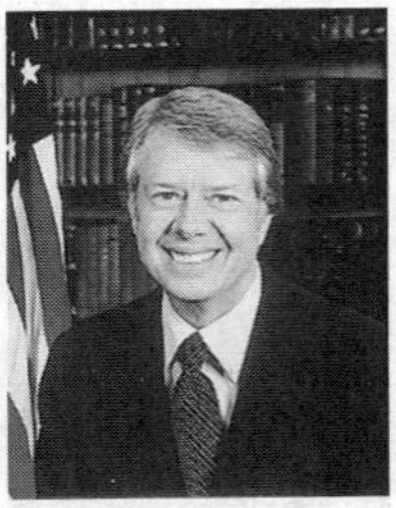

Jimmy Carter

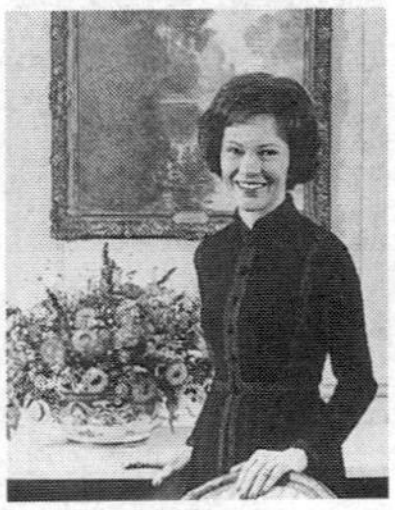

Rosalynn Carter

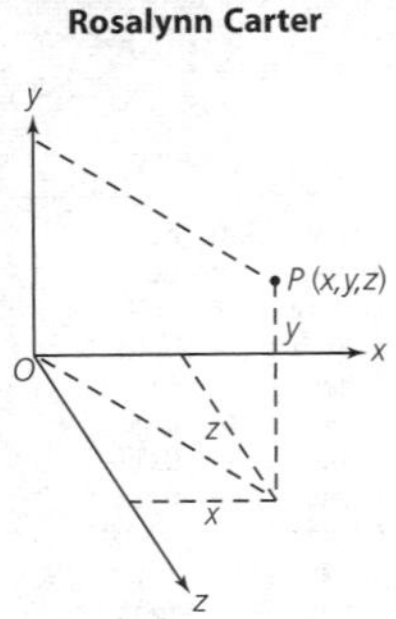

Cartesian coordinate system
three-dimensional coordinate system

cart (kärt) *n.* **1a.** A small wheeled vehicle typically pushed by hand. **b.** A two-wheeled vehicle drawn by an animal and used in farm work and for transporting goods. **c.** The quantity that a cart can hold. **2a.** An open two-wheeled carriage. **b.** A light motorized vehicle. ❖ *tr.v.* **cart•ed, cart•ing, carts 1.** To convey in a cart or truck: *cart away garbage.* **2.** To convey laboriously or unceremoniously; lug: *carted them off.* [ME, wagon < OE *cræt* and < ON *kartr.*] **—cart′a•ble** *adj.* **—cart′er** *n.*

cart•age (kär′tĭj) *n.* **1.** The act or process of carting. **2.** The cost of carting.

Car•ta•ge•na (kär′tä-hĕ′nä) **1.** A city of NW Colombia on the **Bay of Cartagena,** an inlet of the Caribbean Sea; founded 1533. Pop. 513,986. **2.** A city of SE Spain on the Mediterranean Sea SSE of Murcia; settled c. 225 B.C. Pop. 168,023.

Carte (kärt), **Richard D'Oyly** 1844–1901. British producer, esp. of the works of W.S. Gilbert and Arthur Sullivan.

carte blanche (kärt blänsh′, blänch′, blănch′) *n., pl.* **cartes blanches** (kärt blänsh′, kärts blänch′, blănch′) Unrestricted power or authority. [Fr. : *carte*, ticket + *blanche*, blank.]

car•tel (kär-tĕl′) *n.* **1.** A combination of independent business organizations formed to regulate production, pricing, and marketing of goods. **2.** An official agreement between governments at war, esp. one concerning the exchange of prisoners. **3.** A group of factions or nations united in a common cause; a bloc. [Ger. *Kartell* < Fr. *cartel* < Ital. *cartello*, placard < Med.Lat. *cartellus*, charter, dim. of Lat. *charta, carta*, paper made from papyrus. See CARD[1].]

car•tel•ize (kär′tə-līz′) *tr. & intr.v.* **-ized, -iz•ing, -iz•es** To form as or become a cartel. **—car′tel•i•za′tion** (-lĭ-zā′shən) *n.*

Car•ter (kär′tər), **Betty** Orig. Lillie Mae Jones. 1930–98. Amer. jazz singer known for her complex renditions of popular songs.

Carter, James Earl, Jr. Known as "Jimmy." b. 1924. The 39th President of the US (1977–81), who negotiated the Camp David accords between Egypt and Israel (1979).

Carter, Rosalynn Smith b. 1928. First Lady of the US (1977–81) who worked to improve care for the elderly and emotionally disadvantaged.

Car•te•sian (kär-tē′zhən) *adj.* Of or relating to the philosophy, mathematics, or methods of Descartes. [Fr. *cartésien* (< René DESCARTES) and NLat. *Cartesiānus* (< *Cartesius*, Lat. form of Descartes).] **—Car•te′sian•ism** *n.*

Cartesian coordinate system *n.* A coordinate system in which the coordinates of a point are its distances from a set of perpendicular lines that intersect at an origin, such as two lines in a plane or three in space.

Cartesian product *n.* A set of all pairs of elements (*x, y*) that can be constructed from given sets, *X* and *Y*, such that *x* belongs to *X* and *y* to *Y*.

Car•thage (kär′thĭj) An ancient city and state of N Africa on the Bay of Tunis NE of modern Tunis; founded by Phoenicians in the 9th cent. B.C. **—Car′tha•gin′i•an** (kär′thə-jĭn′ē-ən) *adj. & n.*

Car•thu•sian (kär-thōō′zhən) *Roman Catholic Church n.* A member of a contemplative order founded in the 11th century by Saint Bruno. ❖ *adj.* Of or relating to the Carthusian order. [Med. Lat. *Carthusiānus* < *Cartusius*.]

Car•tier (kär-tyā′, kär′tē-ā′), Sir **George Étienne** 1814–73. Prime minister of Canada (1858–62) who served jointly with Sir John Macdonald.

Cartier, Jacques 1491–1557. French explorer who navigated the St. Lawrence R. (1535) and claimed the region for France.

Car•tier-Bres•son (kär-tyā′brĕ-sôN′), **Henri** b. 1908. French photographer noted for his images of daily life.

car•ti•lage (kär′tl-ĭj) *n.* A tough, elastic, fibrous connective tissue found in body parts such as the joints, outer ear, and larynx. [ME < OFr. < Lat. *cartilāgō, cartilāgin-*.]

cartilage bone *n.* A bone developed from cartilage.

car•ti•lag•i•nous (kär′tl-ăj′ə-nəs) *adj.* **1.** Of, relating to, or consisting of cartilage. **2.** Having a skeleton consisting mainly of cartilage. **3.** Having the texture of cartilage.

cartilaginous fish *n.* A fish whose skeleton is mainly cartilage, esp. one of the class Chondrichthyes, such as a ray.

cart•load (kärt′lōd′) *n.* The amount that a cart can carry.

car•to•gram (kär′tə-grăm′) *n.* A presentation of statistical data in geographic distribution on a map. [Fr. *cartogramme* : *carte*, map (< OFr., card; see CARD[1]) + *-gramme*, a record (< LLat. *gramma*, something written; see -GRAM).]

car•tog•ra•phy (kär-tŏg′rə-fē) *n.* The art or technique of making maps or charts. [Fr. *cartographie* : *carte*, map (< OFr. < Lat. *charta, carta*, paper made from papyrus; see CARD[1]) + *-graphie*, writing (< Gk. *-graphiā*; see -GRAPHY).] **—car•tog′ra•pher** *n.* **—car′to•graph′ic** (kär′tə-grăf′ĭk), **car′to•graph′i•cal** *adj.*

car•ton (kär′tn) *n.* **1.** Any of various containers made from cardboard or coated paper. **2.** The contents of a carton. ❖ *tr.v.* **-toned, -ton•ing, -tons** To place (something) in a carton. [Fr. < Ital. *cartone*, pasteboard, augmentative of *carta*, card, paper < Lat. *charta, carta*, paper made from papyrus. See CARD[1].]

car•toon (kär-tōōn′) *n.* **1a.** A drawing depicting a humorous situation, often accompanied by a caption. **b.** A drawing representing current public figures or issues symbolically and often satirically. **2.** A preliminary sketch similar in size to the work, such as a fresco, that is to be copied from it. **3.** An animated cartoon. **4.** A comic strip. **5.** A ridiculously oversimplified representation. ❖ *v.* **-tooned, -toon•ing, -toons** *—tr.* To draw a humorous or satirical representation of; caricature. *—intr.* To make humorous or satirical drawings. [Fr. *carton*, drawing < Ital. *cartone*, pasteboard. See CARTON.] **—car•toon′ish** *adj.* **—car•toon′ist** *n.*

car•touche or **car•touch** (kär-tōōsh′) *n.* **1.** A scrolllike or oval tablet or figure, used as an ornament or to bear an inscription. **2.** An oval or oblong figure in ancient Egyptian hieroglyphics that encloses characters expressing the names of rulers or gods. **3.** A heavy paper cartridge case. [Fr. < Ital. *cartoccio*, paper cornet < *carta*, card, paper. See CARTON.]

car•tridge (kär′trĭj) *n.* **1a.** A cylindrical casing containing the primer and charge of ammunition for firearms. **b.** Such a casing fitted with a bullet. **2.** A case filled with high explosives, used in blasting. **3.** A modular unit designed to be inserted into a larger piece of equipment: *an ink cartridge.* **4.** A removable case containing the stylus and circuitry in a phonograph pickup. **5.** A case containing magnetic tape in a reel; a cassette. **6.** A lightproof case with photographic film that can be loaded directly into a camera. [Alteration of earlier *cartage*, alteration of Fr. *cartouche* < Ital. *cartuccio*, var. of *cartoccio*, roll of paper. See CARTOUCHE.]

cartridge belt *n.* A belt with loops or pockets for carrying ammunition or other kinds of equipment.

cartridge clip *n.* A metal container or frame for holding cartridges to be loaded into an automatic rifle or pistol.

car•tu•lar•y also **char•tu•lar•y** (kär′chə-lĕr′ē) *n., pl.* **-ies** A register of deeds or charters. [ME *cartularie*, collection of documents < Med.Lat. *cartulārium* < Lat. *cartula, chartula*, document. See CHARTER.]

cart•wheel (kärt′hwēl′, -wēl′) *n.* **1.** A handspring in which the body turns over sideways with the arms and legs spread like the spokes of a wheel. **2.** *Slang* A large coin.

Cart•wright (kärt′rīt′), **Edmund** 1743–1823. British cleric and inventor of the power loom (1785–90).

ca•run•cle (kə-rŭng′kəl, kăr′ŭng′-) *n.* **1.** *Biology* A fleshy naked outgrowth, such as a fowl's wattles. **2.** *Botany* An outgrowth or appendage at or near the hilum of certain seeds. [Obsolete Fr. *caruncule* < Lat. *caruncula*, dim. of *carō*, flesh. See **sker-**[1] in App.] **—ca•run′cu•lar** (-kyə-lər) *adj.* **—ca•run′cu•late** (-lĭt, -lāt′), **ca•run′cu•lat′ed** (-lā′tĭd) *adj.*

Ca•ru•so (kə-rōō′sō, -zō), **Enrico** 1873–1921. Italian operatic tenor who is considered one of the greatest singers ever.

car•va•crol (kär′və-krôl′, -krōl′) *n.* An aromatic phenolic compound, $C_{10}H_{14}O$, used in flavorings and fungicides. [NLat. *carvi* (specific epithet of *(Carum) carvi*, caraway < Med.Lat.; see CARAWAY) + Lat. *ăcer, ăcr-*, sharp; see **ak-** in App. + -OL[1].]

carve (kärv) *v.* **carved, carv•ing, carves** —*tr.* **1a.** To divide into pieces by cutting; slice. **b.** To divide by parceling out. **2.** To cut into a desired shape; fashion by cutting: *carve the wood into a figure.* **3.** To make or form by or as if by cutting: *carved out an empire.* **4.** To decorate by cutting and shaping carefully. —*intr.* **1.** To engrave or cut figures as an art, hobby, or trade. **2.** To slice and serve meat or poultry. [ME *kerven* < OE *ceorfan.* See **gerbh-** in App.] —**carv′er** *n.*

car•vel (kär′vəl, -vĕl′) *n.* Variant of **caravel.**

car•vel-built (kär′vəl-bĭlt′, -vĕl′-) *adj. Nautical* Built with the hull planks lying flush or edge to edge rather than overlapping: *a carvel-built ship.*

carv•en (kär′vən) *v. Archaic* A past tense and a past participle of **carve.** ❖ *adj.* Wrought or decorated by carving.

Car•ver (kär′vər), **George Washington** 1864?–1943. Amer. botanist, agricultural chemist, and educator who developed hundreds of uses for the peanut, soybean, and sweet potato.

Carver, John 1576?–1621. English-born Pilgrim colonist who was the first governor of Plymouth Colony (1620–21).

carv•ing (kär′vĭng) *n.* **1.** The cutting of material such as stone or wood to form a figure or design. **2.** A figure or design formed by this kind of cutting.

car wash *n.* A place or business equipped for washing cars and other motor vehicles.

car•y•at•id (kăr′ē-ăt′ĭd) *n., pl.* **-ids** or **-i•des** (-ĭ-dēz′) *Architecture* A supporting column sculptured in the form of a draped female figure. [< Lat. *Caryātides*, caryatids < Gk. *Karuătides*, priestesses of Artemis at Caryae, caryatids < *Karuai*, Caryae, a village of Laconia in S Greece.] —**car′y•at′i•dal** (-ĭ-dəl), **car′y•at′i•de′an** (-ĭ-dē′ən), **car′y•a•tid′ic** (-ə-tĭd′ĭk) *adj.*

caryo– *pref.* Variant of **karyo–.**

car•y•op•sis (kăr′ē-ŏp′sĭs) *n., pl.* **-op•ses** (-ŏp′sēz′) or **-op•si•des** (-ŏp′sĭ-dēz′) See **grain** 1a. [*cary(o)-*, var. of KARYO– + –OPSIS.]

ca•sa•ba also **cas•sa•ba** (kə-sä′bə) *n.* A variety of winter melon *(Cucumis melo* var. *Inodorus)* having a yellow rind and whitish flesh. [After *Kasaba* (Turgutlu), a city of western Turkey.]

Cas•a•blan•ca (kăs′ə-blăng′kə, kä′sə-bläng′kə) A city of NW Morocco on the Atlantic Ocean SSW of Tangier; a center of French influence in Africa after 1907. Pop. 2,943,000.

Ca•sals (kə-sälz′, -sälz′), **Pablo** 1876–1973. Spanish cellist considered the greatest of his time.

Cas•a•no•va (kăs′ə-nō′və, kăz′-) *n.* **1.** A man who is amorously and gallantly attentive to women. **2.** A promiscuous man. [After Giovanni Jacopo CASANOVA DE SEINGALT.]

Cas•a•no•va de Sein•galt (kăs′ə-nō′və də săN-gält′, kăz′-, kä′sä-nō′vä), **Giovanni Jacopo** 1725–98. Italian adventurer who established a legendary reputation as a lover.

Cas•bah also **Kas•bah** (kăz′bä′, käz′-) *n.* **1.** A castle or palace in northern Africa. **2.** often **casbah** The older section of a city in northern Africa or the Middle East. [Fr. < Ar. dialectal *qaṣba* < Ar. *qaṣaba*, to cut up.]

cas•cade (kăs-kād′) *n.* **1.** A waterfall or a series of small waterfalls over steep rocks. **2.** Something, such as lace, thought to resemble a cascade. **3.** A succession of stages, processes, or units. **4.** *Electronics* A series of components or networks, the output of each serving as the input for the next. **5.** *Biochemistry* A process that occurs in successive stages, usu. producing a cumulative effect: *an enzyme cascade.* ❖ *intr. & tr.v.* **-cad•ed, -cad•ing, -cades** To fall or cause to fall in or as if in a cascade. [Fr. < Ital. *cascata* < *cascare*, to fall < VLat. **casicāre* < Lat. *cadere.*]

cascade molecule *n.* See **dendrimer.**

Cascade Range A mountain chain of W Canada and the US extending c. 1,126 km (700 mi) S from British Columbia to N CA, where it joins the Sierra Nevada.

cas•car•a (kă-skăr′ə) *n.* A buckthorn *(Rhamnus purshiana)* native to northwest North America whose bark is the source of cascara sagrada. [Sp. *cáscara*, bark < *cascar*, to break off < VLat. **quassicāre* < Lat. *quassāre*, freq. of *quatere*, to shake.]

cascara sa•gra•da (sə-grä′də) *n.* The dried bark of the cascara buckthorn, used as a laxative. [Am.Sp. *cáscara sagrada* : Sp. *cáscara*, bark + Sp. *sagrada*, sacred.]

cas•ca•ril•la (kăs′kə-rĭl′ə, kăs′kə-rē′ə) *n.* **1.** A tropical shrub or tree *(Croton eluteria)* native to the West Indies and northern South America and having a bark that yields an aromatic oil used as a flavoring and fragrance. **2.** The bark of this plant. [Sp., dim. of *cáscara*, bark. See CASCARA.]

Cas•co Bay (kăs′kō) A deep inlet of the Atlantic Ocean in SW Maine.

case[1] (kās) *n.* **1.** An instance of something; an occurrence; an example. **2.** An occurrence of a disease or disorder. **3.** A set of circumstances or a state of affairs; a situation. **4.** Actual fact; reality: *It proved to be the case.* **5.** A question or problem; a matter: *It is a case of honor.* **6.** A situation that requires investigation, esp. by an official body. **7.** *Law* **a.** An action or a suit or just grounds for an action. **b.** The facts or evidence offered in support of a claim. **8.** A set of reasons or supporting facts; an argument. **9.** A person being assisted, treated, or studied, as by a physician or social worker. **10.** *Informal* A peculiar or eccentric person; a character. **11.** *Linguistics* In traditional grammar, a distinct form of a noun, pronoun, or modifier that is used to express one or more particular syntactic relationships to other words in a sentence. ***—idioms:*** **in any case** Regardless of what has occurred or will occur. **in case 1.** If it happens that; if. **2.** As a precaution. **in case of** If there should happen to be. **on (someone's) case** Persistently nagging or urging someone to do something. [ME *cas* < OFr. < Lat. *cāsus* < p. part. of *cadere*, to fall.]

case[2] (kās) *n.* **1.** A container; a receptacle. **2.** A container with its contents. **3.** A decorative or protective covering or cover. **4.** A set or pair: *a case of pistols.* **5.** The frame or framework, as of a door. **6.** The surface or outer layer of a metal alloy. **7.** *Printing* A shallow compartmented tray for storing type or type matrices. ❖ *tr.v.* **cased, cas•ing, cas•es 1.** To put into or cover with a case; encase. **2.** *Slang* To examine carefully, as in planning a crime. [ME < Norman Fr. *casse* < Lat. *capsa.*]

ca•se•ate (kā′sē-āt′) *intr.v.* **-at•ed, -at•ing, -ates** To undergo caseation. [Back-formation < CASEATION.]

ca•se•a•tion (kā′sē-ā′shən) *n.* Degeneration of body tissue into a soft cheeselike substance. [< Lat. *cāseus*, cheese.]

case•book (kās′bo͝ok′) *n.* A book containing source materials in a specific area, used as a reference and in teaching.

case goods *pl.n.* **1a.** Furniture, such as bookcases or chests of drawers, that provide interior storage space. **b.** Dining and bedroom furniture sold as sets. **2.** Food and beverage products sold by the case.

case•hard•en (kās′här′dn) *tr.v.* **-ened, -en•ing, -ens 1.** To harden the surface or case of (iron or steel) by high-temperature shallow infusion of carbon followed by quenching. **2.** To make callous or insensitive.

case history *n.* An account of the facts affecting the development or condition of a person or group under treatment or study.

ca•sein (kā′sēn′, -sē-ĭn) *n.* A protein precipitated from milk by rennin that is the basis of cheese and is used to make plastics, adhesives, paints, and foods. [Ult. < Lat. *cāseus*, cheese.]

case knife *n.* **1.** A knife kept in a sheath or case. **2.** A table knife.

case law *n.* Law based on judicial decision and precedent rather than on statutes.

case•load (kās′lōd′) *n.* The number of cases handled in a given period, as by a clinic or social services agency.

case•mate (kās′māt′) *n.* **1.** A fortified enclosure for artillery on a warship. **2.** An armored compartment for artillery on a rampart. [Fr. < Ital. *casamatta* : perh. *casa*, house (< Lat.) + *matto*, mad, crazy (< Lat. *mattus*, drunk, p. part. of *madēre*, to be drunk).] —**case′mat′ed** *adj.*

case•ment (kās′mənt) *n.* **1a.** A window sash that opens outward by means of hinges. **b.** A window with such sashes. **2.** A case or covering. [ME, a hollow molding, poss. < ME *case*, chest, frame. See CASE[2].] —**case′ment•ed** *adj.*

Casement, Sir **Roger David** 1864–1916. British diplomat who sought German assistance in the Irish nationalist cause during World War I and was executed for treason.

ca•se•ous (kā′sē-əs) *adj.* Resembling cheese. [< Lat. *cāseus*, cheese.]

ca•sern also **ca•serne** (kə-zûrn′) *n.* A military barracks or garrison. [Fr. *caserne* < OFr., small room for the night watch < O Provençal *cazerna*, group of four men < Lat. *quaterna*, four together < Lat. *quaternī*, by four. See QUATERNION.]

case shot *n.* **1.** A shot-packed metallic cylinder used as ammunition in a firearm; a canister. **2.** The shot in such a cylinder.

case study *n.* **1.** An analysis of a person or group, esp. as a medical or social model. **2a.** A study of a unit, such as a corporation, and causes of its success or failure. **b.** An exemplary or cautionary model; an instructive example.

case system *n.* A method of teaching law that emphasizes the study of selected cases rather than textbooks.

case•work (kās′wûrk′) *n.* Social work devoted to the needs of individual clients or cases. —**case′work′er** *n.*

cash[1] (kăsh) *n.* **1.** Money in the form of bills or coins; currency. **2.** Payment for goods or services in currency or by check. ❖ *tr.v.* **cashed, cash•ing, cash•es** To exchange for or convert into ready money. ***—phrasal verb:*** **cash in 1.** To withdraw from a venture by or as if by settling one's account. **2.** *Informal* To obtain an advantage by timely exploitation. **3.** *Slang* To die. [Obsolete Fr. *casse*, money box (< Norman Fr.; see CASE[2]) or < Ital. *cassa* (< Lat. *capsa*, case).]

cash[2] (kăsh) *n., pl.* **cash** Any of various Asian coins of small denomination. [Port. *caixa* < Tamil *kācu*, a small coin.]

Cash, John Known as "Johnny." b. 1932. Amer. country and western singer and songwriter whose songs include "Folsom Prison Blues" (1969).

cash-and-car•ry (kăsh′ən-kăr′ē) *adj.* Sold for cash, usu. without delivery service.

cash bar *n.* A bar, such as one at a large party, where drinks are sold by the glass.

cash•book (kăsh′bo͝ok′) *n.* A book in which a record of cash receipts and expenditures is kept.

cash cow *n. Slang* A steady dependable source of funds or income.

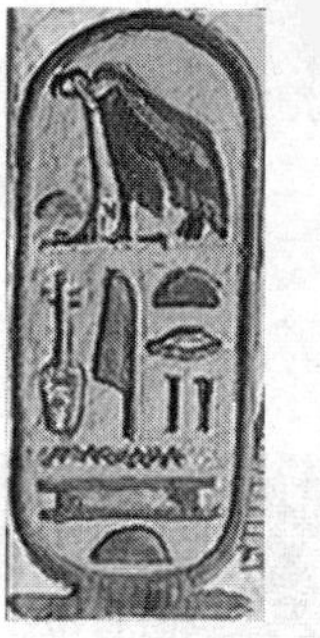

cartouche
from a wall painting in the tomb of Queen Nefertari

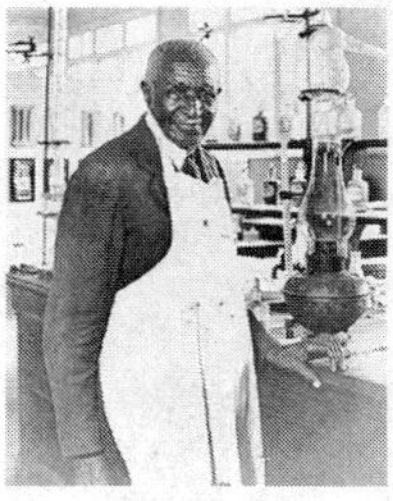

George Washington Carver

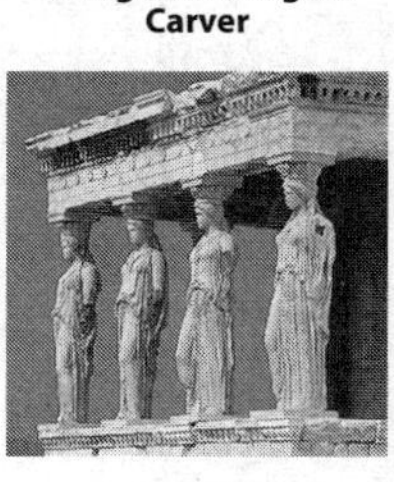

caryatid
Porch of the Maidens, Erechtheion, the Acropolis, Athens

ă	pat	oi	boy
ā	pay	ou	out
âr	care	o͝o	took
ä	father	o͞o	boot
ĕ	pet	ŭ	cut
ē	be	ûr	urge
ĭ	pit	th	thin
ī	pie	*th*	this
îr	pier	hw	which
ŏ	pot	zh	vision
ō	toe	ə	about, item
ô	paw		

Stress marks:
′ (primary);
′ (secondary), as in
lexicon (lĕk′sĭ-kŏn′)

cash crop *n.* A crop, such as tobacco, grown for direct sale rather than for livestock feed.

cash discount *n.* A discount allowed if payment is made within a stipulated period.

cash•ew (kăsh′ōō, kə-shōō′) *n.* **1.** A tropical American evergreen tree *(Anacardium occidentale)* having edible kernels. **2.** The kidney-shaped seed of this tree, eaten after roasting. [Prob. Port. *acajú* < Tupi < *cajú*, yellow fruit, acidic.]

cashew apple *n.* The soft, swollen, pear-shaped edible stalk of the fruit of the cashew.

cash flow *n.* **1.** The pattern of cash income and expenditures, as of a company or person, and the resulting availability of cash. **2.** The cash receipts from one or more assets for a given period, reckoned after taxes and other disbursements. —**cash′-flow′** (kăsh′flō′) *adj.*

cash•ier[1] (kă-shîr′) *n.* **1.** The officer of a bank or business concern in charge of paying and receiving money. **2.** A store employee who handles cash transactions with customers. [Du. *cassier* or Fr. *caissier*, both < Fr. *caisse*, money box < O Provençal *caisa* < VLat. **capsea* < Lat. *capsa*, case.]

ca•shier[2] (kă-shîr′) *tr.v.* **-shiered, -shier•ing, -shiers** To dismiss from a position of command or responsibility, esp. for disciplinary reasons. [Du. *casseren* < OFr. *casser*, to dismiss, annul. See QUASH[1].]

ca•shier's check (kă-shîrz′) *n.* A check drawn by a bank on its own funds and signed by the bank's cashier.

cash•mere (kăzh′mîr′, kăsh′-, kăzh-mîr′, kăsh-) *n.* **1.** Fine, downy wool growing beneath the outer hair of the Cashmere goat. **2.** A soft fabric made of this wool or of similar fibers. [After KASHMIR.]

Cashmere See **Kashmir.**

Cashmere goat also **Kashmir goat** *n.* A goat native to the Himalayan regions of India and Tibet and prized for its wool.

cash register *n.* A machine that tabulates the amount of sales transactions, makes a permanent record of them, and has a drawer in which cash can be kept.

cas•i•mere (kăz′ə-mîr′, kăs′-) *n.* Variant of **cassimere.**

cas•ing (kā′sĭng) *n.* **1.** An outer cover: *a shell casing.* **2.** The frame or framework for a window or door. **3.** A metal pipe or tube used as a lining for a well. **4.** A membranous case used to contain sausage or other processed meat. **5.** A narrow passage for a rod or cord, as in a curtain or waistband, made by folding and sewing a strip of fabric.

ca•si•no (kə-sē′nō) *n., pl.* **-nos 1.** A public room or building for gambling and other entertainment. **2.** also **cas•si•no** A card game for two to four players in which cards on the table are matched by cards in the hand. **3.** A summer or country house in Italy. [Ital., dim. of *casa*, house < Lat.]

cask (kăsk) *n.* **1.** A sturdy cylindrical container for storing liquids; a barrel. **2.** The quantity that such a container can hold. [ME *caske*, poss. < OSpan. *casco*, potsherd, helmet < *cascar*, to break. See CASCARA.]

cas•ket (kăs′kĭt) *n.* **1.** A coffin. **2.** A small case or chest. ❖ *tr.v.* **-ket•ed, -ket•ing, -kets** To enclose in a case, chest, or coffin. [ME, poss. alteration of OFr. *cassette.* See CASSETTE.]

Cas•lon (kăz′lən), **William** 1692–1766. English type designer whose typefaces were widely used in the 18th cent.

Cas•par (kăs′pär′, -pər) also **Gas•par** (găs′-) One of the three Magi.

Cas•per (kăs′pər) A city of E-central WY on the North Platte R. NW of Cheyenne; founded 1888. Pop. 49,644.

Cas•pi•an Sea (kăs′pē-ən) A saline lake between SE Europe and W Asia.

casque (kăsk) *n.* **1.** A helmet, esp. an ornate visorless headpiece of the 16th century. **2.** *Zoology* A helmetlike structure or protuberance. [Fr. < Sp. *casco.* See CASK.] —**casqued** (kăskt) *adj.*

Cass (kăs), **Lewis** 1782–1866. Amer. soldier and politician whose positions included US secretary of war (1831–36).

cas•sa•ba (kə-sä′bə) *n.* Variant of **casaba.**

Cas•san•dra (kə-săn′drə) *n.* **1.** *Greek Mythology* A daughter of Priam, the king of Troy, endowed with the gift of prophecy but fated by Apollo never to be believed. **2.** One that utters unheeded prophecies. [Lat. < Gk. *Kassandra.*]

cas•sa•tion (kă-sā′shən) *n.* Abrogation or annulment by a higher authority. [ME *cassatioun* < OFr. *cassation* < LLat. *cassātiō*, *cassātiōn-* < *cassātus*, p. part. of *cassāre*, to annul. See QUASH[1].]

Cas•satt (kə-săt′), **Mary Stevenson** 1844?–1926. Amer. painter whose works include *The Bath* (1891–92).

cas•sa•va (kə-sä′və) *n.* **1.** A shrubby tropical American plant *(Manihot esculenta)* widely grown for its large, tuberous, starchy roots. **2.** The root of this plant, eaten as a staple food in the tropics after leaching and drying to remove cyanide. [Ult. < Taino *casavi*, flour from manioc.]

Cas•sel (kăs′əl, kä′səl) See **Kassel.**

cas•se•role (kăs′ə-rōl′) *n.* **1a.** A dish, usu. of earthenware or glass, in which food is baked and served. **b.** Food prepared and served in such a dish. **2.** *Chemistry* A small-handled crucible used for heating and evaporating. [Fr., saucepan, dim. of OFr. *casse*, ladle, pan < O Provençal *cassa* < Med.Lat. *cattia*, dipper < Gk. *kuathion*, dim. of *kuathos*, ladle.]

cas•sette (kə-sĕt′, kă-) *n.* **1.** A small flat case containing two reels and a length of magnetic tape that winds between them, often used in audio and video recorders and players and as a medium for storing data in digital form. **2.** A lightproof cartridge containing photographic film or plates, used in specially designed cameras. [Fr., small box < OFr., dim. of Norman Fr. *casse*, case. See CASE[2].]

cas•sia (kăsh′ə) *n.* **1.** Any of various chiefly tropical or subtropical trees, shrubs, or herbs of the genus *Cassia* in the pea family, having pinnately compound leaves and long pods. **2a.** A tropical Asian evergreen tree *(Cinnamomum cassia)* having aromatic bark used as a substitute for cinnamon. **b.** The bark of this tree. [ME < Lat., a kind of plant < Gk. *kassia*, prob. ult. (via Semitic) of Chin. orig.]

cas•si•mere also **cas•i•mere** (kăz′ə-mîr′, kăs′-) *n.* A plain or twilled woolen cloth used for suits. [Variant of CASHMERE.]

cas•si•na also **cas•se•na** or **cas•se•ne** or **cas•si•ne** (kə-sē′nə) *n. Botany* **1.** See **dahoon. 2.** See **yaupon.** [Am.Sp., yaupon < Timucua *kasine.*]

Cas•si•ni division (kə-sē′nē) *n.* The large gap between the two most prominent of Saturn's rings, caused by the gravitational pull of the moon Mimas. [After Giovanni Domenico *Cassini* (1625–1712), Italian astronomer.]

cas•si•no (kə-sē′nō) *n.* Variant of **casino** 2.

Cas•si•no (kə-sē′nō, käs-) A town of central Italy in the Apennines NW of Naples. The town and nearby monastery of Monte Cassino were reduced to rubble during fierce German-Allied fighting (Feb.–May 1944). Pop. 26,300.

Cas•si•o•pe•ia (kăs′ē-ə-pē′ə) *n.* A W-shaped constellation in the Northern Hemisphere between Andromeda and Cepheus. [Lat. *Cassiepīa*, *Cassiopēa* < Gk. *Kassiepeia*, Cassiopeia, daughter of Cepheus and Andromeda, who was changed into a constellation.]

cas•sis (kə-sēs′) *n.* **1.** A Eurasian currant *(Ribes nigrum)* bearing black berries. **2.** A cordial made from the berries of this plant. [Fr. < Lat. *cassia*, a kind of plant. See CASSIA.]

cas•sit•er•ite (kə-sĭt′ə-rīt′) *n.* A light yellow, red-brown, or black mineral, SnO_2, that is an important tin ore. [Fr. *cassitérite* < Gk. *kassiteros*, tin.]

Cas•sius Lon•gi•nus (kăsh′əs lŏn-jī′nəs), **Gaius** d. 42 B.C. Roman general and politician who was a leading member of the conspiracy to assassinate Julius Caesar.

cas•sock (kăs′ək) *n. Ecclesiastical* A long garment with a close-fitting waist and sleeves, worn by the clergy and others assisting in church services. [Fr. *casaque*, long coat < OFr., perh. < Ital. *casacca* < Pers. *kazhāgand*, padded garment : *kazh*, raw silk + *āgand*, stuffed.]

cas•sou•let (kăs′ōō-lā′) *n.* A casserole of white beans, various meats, vegetables, and herbs, slowly simmered or baked. [Fr., stove dish, dim. of *cassolo*, earthenware vessel < *casso* < O Provençal *cassa.* See CASSEROLE.]

cas•so•war•y (kăs′ə-wĕr′ē) *n., pl.* **-ies** Any of several large flightless birds of the genus *Casuarius* of Australia, New Guinea, and adjacent areas, having a large bony projection on the top of the head and brightly colored wattles. [Malay *kesuari.*]

cast (kăst) *v.* **cast, cast•ing, casts** —*tr.* **1.** To throw; hurl. See Syns at **throw. 2.** To shed; molt. **3.** To throw on the ground, as in wrestling. **4.** To deposit or indicate (a ballot or vote). **5.** To turn or direct: *all eyes cast upon her.* **6.** To cause to fall onto or over something or in a certain direction, as if by throwing: *cast doubt.* **7.** To bestow; confer. **8.** To draw (lots). **9.** To give birth to prematurely. **10.** To cause (hounds) to scatter and circle in search of a lost scent. **11a.** To choose actors for (a play, for example). **b.** To assign a certain role to (an actor). **c.** To assign an actor to (a part). **12.** To form (liquid metal, for example) into a particular shape by pouring into a mold. **13.** To give a form to; arrange: *cast the book in three parts.* **14.** To contrive; devise: *cast a plan.* **15.** To calculate or compute; add up (a column of figures). **16.** To calculate astrologically. **17.** To warp; twist: *floorboards cast by age.* —*intr.* **1.** To throw something, esp. to throw out a baited fishing line. **2.** To add a column of figures; make calculations. **3.** To make a conjecture or a forecast. **4.** To receive form or shape in a mold. **5.** To search for a lost scent in hunting with hounds. **6.** To choose actors for parts, as in a play or movie. **7.** *Obsolete* To estimate; conjecture. ❖ *n.* **1a.** The act or an instance of casting or throwing. **b.** The distance thrown. **2a.** A throwing of a fishing line or net into the water. **b.** The line or net thrown. **3a.** A throw of dice. **b.** The number thrown. **4.** A stroke of fortune or fate; lot. **5a.** A direction or expression of the eyes. **b.** A slight squint. **6.** Something, such as molted skin, that is thrown off, out, or away. **7.** The addition of a column of figures; calculation. **8.** A conjecture; a forecast. **9a.** The act of pouring molten material into a mold. **b.** The amount of molten material poured into a mold at a single operation. **c.** Something formed by this means. **10.** An impression formed in a mold or matrix; a mold. **11.** A rigid dressing, usu. made of gauze and plaster of Paris, used to immobilize an injured body part. **12.** The form in which something is made or constructed; arrangement. **13.** Outward form or look; appearance: *a suit of stylish cast.* **14.** Sort; type. **15.** An inclination; tendency. **16.** The actors in a play, movie, or other theatrical presentation. **17.** A slight trace of color; a tinge. **18.** A distortion of shape. **19.** The circling of hounds to pick up a scent in hunting.

cashew
Anacardium occidentale

Mary Cassatt
watercolor self-portrait,
c. 1880

Cassini division

20. A pair of hawks released by a falconer at one time. **—phrasal verbs: cast about** (or **around**) **1.** To make a search; look. **2.** To devise means; contrive. **cast off 1.** To discard; reject. **2.** To let go; set loose. **3.** To make the last row of stitches in knitting. **4.** *Printing* To estimate the space a manuscript will occupy when set into type. **cast on** To make the first row of stitches in knitting. **cast out** To drive out by force; expel. **—idiom: cast (one's) lot with** To join or side with for better or worse. [ME *casten* < ON *kasta*.]

cas·ta·net (kās'tə-nĕt') *n.* A percussion instrument consisting of two concave shells of ivory or hardwood, held in the palm by a connecting cord over the thumb and clapped with the fingers. Often used in the plural. [Sp. *castañeta* < *castaña*, chestnut < Lat. *castanea*. See CHESTNUT.]

cast·a·way (kāst'ə-wā') *adj.* **1.** Cast adrift or ashore; shipwrecked. **2.** Discarded; thrown away. ❖ *n.* **1.** A shipwrecked person. **2.** A rejected or discarded person or thing.

caste (kāst) *n.* **1.** Any of the hereditary, endogamous social classes or subclasses of traditional Hindu society, stratified according to Hindu ritual purity, esp. the Brahman, Kshatriya, Vaisya, and Sudra castes. **2.** A social class separated from others by distinctions of hereditary rank, profession, or wealth. **3a.** A social system or the principle of grading society based on castes. **b.** The social position or status conferred by such a system. **4.** A level in a colony of social insects, such as ants, in which members carry out a specific function. [Sp. *casta*, race, and Port. *casta*, race, caste, both < fem. of *casto*, pure < Lat. *castus*.]

Cas·tel Gan·dol·fo (kä-stĕl' gän-dōl'fō) A town of central Italy SE of Rome; papal summer residence. Pop. 3,600.

cas·tel·lan (kās'tə-lən) *n.* The keeper or governor of a castle. [ME *castelain* < Norman Fr. < Med.Lat. *castellānus* < Lat., of a fortress < *castellum*, stronghold. See CASTLE.]

cas·tel·lat·ed (kās'tə-lā'tĭd) *adj.* **1.** Furnished with turrets and battlements in the style of a castle. **2.** Having a castle. [Med.Lat. *castellātus*, p. part. of *castellāre*, to fortify as a castle < Lat. *castellum*, fort. See CASTLE.] **—cas'tel·la'tion** *n.*

Cas·tel·lón de la Pla·na (kās'təl-yōn' də lä plä'nə, kä'stĕ-lyōn' dĕ lä plä'nä) A city of E Spain on the Mediterranean Sea NNE of Valencia. Pop. 136,816.

cast·er (kās'tər) *n.* **1.** One that casts: *a caster of nets.* **2.** also **cas·tor** (kās'tər) A small wheel on a swivel, attached under a heavy object to make it easier to move. **3.** also **castor a.** A small bottle, pot, or shaker for holding a condiment. **b.** A stand for a set of condiment containers.

cas·ti·gate (kās'tĭ-gāt') *tr.v.* **-gat·ed, -gat·ing, -gates 1.** To inflict severe punishment on. **2.** To criticize severely. [Lat. *castīgāre, castīgāt-* < *castus*, pure.] **—cas'ti·ga'tion** *n.* **—cas'ti·ga'tor** *n.*

Cas·ti·glio·ne (kä-stēl-yō'nā, -stē-lyō'nĕ), **Count Baldassare** 1478–1529. Italian diplomat and writer best known for *Il Cortegiano* (1528), which describes the perfect courtier.

Cas·tile (kās-tēl') A region and former kingdom of central and N Spain; joined with Aragon after the marriage of Isabella and Ferdinand in 1479.

Castile soap also **castile soap** *n.* A fine hard soap made with olive oil and sodium hydroxide. [After CASTILE.]

Cas·til·ian (kā-stĭl'yən) *n.* **1.** A native or inhabitant of Castile. **2a.** The Spanish dialect of Castile. **b.** The standard form of Spanish, based on this dialect. **—Cas·til'ian** *adj.*

cast·ing (kās'tĭng) *n.* **1a.** The act or process of making casts or molds. **b.** Something cast in a mold. **2.** The act of throwing a fishing line. **3.** Something cast off or out. **4.** The selection of actors or performers for the parts of a presentation.

casting vote *n.* The vote of a presiding officer in an assembly or council, given to break a tie.

cast iron *n.* A hard, brittle, nonmalleable iron alloy, containing 2 to 4.5 percent carbon and cast into shape.

cast-i·ron (kāst'ī'ərn) *adj.* **1.** Made of cast iron. **2.** Rigid; inflexible. **3.** Exceptionally strong or resistant.

cast-iron plant *n.* See aspidistra.

cas·tle (kās'əl) *n.* **1a.** A large fortified building or group of buildings with thick walls, usu. dominating the surrounding country. **b.** A building similar to a fortified stronghold. **2.** A place of privacy, security, or refuge. **3.** *Games* See rook[2]. ❖ *v.* **-tled, -tling, -tles** *—intr.* To move the king in chess from its own square two empty squares to one side and then, in the same move, bring the rook from that side to the square immediately past the new position of the king. *—tr.* **1.** To place in or as if in a castle. **2.** To move (the king in chess) by castling. [ME *castel* < OE and < Norman Fr., both < Lat. *castellum*, dim. of *castrum*.]

cas·tled (kās'əld) *adj.* Castellated.

Castle Peak A mountain, 4,350.8 m (14,265 ft), in the Elk Mts. of W-central CO.

Cas·tle·reagh (kās'əl-rā'), Viscount. Title of Robert Stewart, 2nd Marquis of Londonderry. 1769–1822. British politician who as chief secretary for Ireland (1798–1801) formed a political union between Ireland and Great Britain (1800).

cast·off (kāst'ôf', -ŏf') *n.* **1.** One that has been discarded. **2.** *Printing* A calculation of the amount of space a manuscript will occupy when set into type.

cas·tor¹ (kās'tər) *n.* **1.** An oily, brown, odorous substance obtained from glands in the groin of the beaver and used as a per-

fume fixative. **2.** A hat made of beaver fur or an imitation. **3.** A heavy wool fabric used esp. for overcoats. [ME < Lat., beaver < Gk. *kastōr.*]

cas·tor² (kās'tər) *n.* Variant of caster 2, 3.

Castor *n.* **1.** *Greek Mythology* One of the Dioscuri. **2.** A double star in Gemini. [Lat. < Gk. *Kastōr,* Castor.]

castor bean *n.* **1.** The castor-oil plant. **2.** The seed of this plant, from which castor oil is obtained. [CASTOR (OIL) + BEAN.]

castor oil *n.* An oil extracted from the seeds of the castor-oil plant, used as a laxative and skin softener and industrially as a lubricant.

cas·tor-oil plant (kās'tər-oil') *n.* A poisonous, ornamental tropical African herb or tree (*Ricinus communis*) having palmately lobed leaves and yielding castor oil.

cas·trate (kās'trāt') *tr.v.* **-trat·ed, -trat·ing, -trates 1.** To remove the testicles of (a male); geld. **2.** To remove the ovaries of (a female); spay. **3.** To deprive of virility or spirit. ❖ *n.* One who is sterile because of removal, destruction, or inactivation of the gonads. [Lat. *castrāre, castrāt-.*] **—cas'trat·er, cas'tra·tor** *n.* **—cas·tra'tion** *n.*

ca·stra·to (kä-strä'tō, kə-) *n., pl.* **-ti** (-tē) or **-tos** A male singer castrated before puberty so as to retain a high voice. [Ital. < Lat. *castrātus,* p. part. of *castrāre,* to castrate. See CASTRATE.]

Cas·tries (kās'trēz', -trēs') The cap. of St. Lucia, in the Windward Is. of the British West Indies. Pop. 51,994.

Cas·tro (kās'trō, kä'strō), **Fidel** b. 1927. Cuban revolutionary leader who overthrew Fulgencio Batista in 1959 and established a socialist state. **—Cas'tro·ism** *n.* **—Cas'tro·ist, Cas'tro·ite'** (-īt') *adj. & n.*

ca·su·al (kăzh'ōō-əl) *adj.* **1.** Occurring by chance. See Syns at chance. **2a.** Occurring at irregular or infrequent intervals; occasional. **b.** Unpremeditated; offhand. **3a.** Being without formality; relaxed. **b.** Suited for everyday wear or use; informal. **4.** Not serious or thorough; superficial. **5a.** Showing little interest; nonchalant. **b.** Lenient; permissive. **6.** Not close or intimate; passing. ❖ *n.* **1.** One that serves or appears irregularly, esp. a temporary worker. **2.** A soldier temporarily attached to a unit, awaiting permanent assignment. [ME *casuel* < OFr. < Lat. *cāsuālis* < *cāsus,* event. See CASE¹.] **—ca'su·al·ly** *adv.* **—ca'su·al·ness** *n.*

ca·su·al·ty (kăzh'ōō-əl-tē) *n., pl.* **-ties 1.** An accident, esp. one involving serious injury or loss of life. **2.** One injured or killed in an accident. **3.** One injured, killed, captured, or missing in action through engagement with an enemy. **4.** One harmed or eliminated as a result of a circumstance. [ME *casuelte* < OFr. < Med.Lat. *cāsuālitās,* chance, accident < Lat. *cāsuālis,* fortuitous. See CASUAL.]

ca·su·ist (kăzh'ōō-ĭst) *n.* One who is expert in or given to casuistry. [Fr. *casuiste* < Sp. *casuista* < Lat. *cāsus,* case. See CASE¹.] **—ca'su·is'tic, ca'su·is'ti·cal** *adj.* **—ca'su·is'ti·cal·ly** *adv.*

ca·su·ist·ry (kăzh'ōō-ĭ-strē) *n., pl.* **-ries 1.** Specious or overly subtle reasoning intended to rationalize or mislead. **2.** The determination of right and wrong by analyzing cases that illustrate general ethical principles. [< CASUIST.]

ca·sus bel·li (kā'səs bĕl'ī, kä'səs bĕl'ē) *n., pl.* **casus belli** An act or event that provokes or is used to justify war. [NLat. *cāsus bellī* : Lat. *cāsus,* occasion + Lat. *bellī,* of war.]

cat (kăt) *n.* **1a.** A small carnivorous mammal (*Felis catus* or *F. domesticus*) domesticated since early times as a catcher of rodents and as a pet and existing in several distinctive breeds and varieties. **b.** Any of various other carnivorous mammals of the family Felidae, such as the lion. **c.** The fur of a domestic cat. **2.** *Informal* A woman regarded as spiteful. **3.** *Slang* **a.** A person, esp. a man. **b.** A player or devotee of jazz music. **4.** A cat-o'-nine-tails. **5.** A catfish. **6.** *Nautical* **a.** A cathead. **b.** A device for raising an anchor to the cathead. **c.** A catboat. **d.** A catamaran. ❖ *v.* **cat·ted, cat·ting, cats** *—tr. Nautical* To hoist an anchor to (the cathead). *—intr. Slang* To look for sexual partners; have an affair or affairs. **—idiom: let the cat out of the bag** To let a secret be known. [ME < OE *catt* < Gmc. **kattuz,* perh. of African orig.]

CAT *abbr.* **1.** clear-air turbulence **2.** computerized axial tomography

cata– *pref.* **1.** Down: *catadromous.* **2.** Reverse; backward; degenerative: *cataplasia.* [Gk. *kata–* < *kata,* down, downward, thoroughly.]

ca·tab·o·lism (kə-tăb'ə-lĭz'əm) *n.* The metabolic breakdown of complex molecules into simpler ones, often resulting in a release of energy. [CATA– + (META)BOLISM.] **—cat'a·bol'ic** (kăt'ə-bŏl'ĭk) *adj.* **—cat'a·bol'i·cal·ly** *adv.*

ca·tab·o·lite (kə-tăb'ə-līt') *n.* A substance produced by the process of catabolism. [CATABOL(ISM) + –ITE².]

ca·tab·o·lize (kə-tăb'ə-līz') *intr. & tr.v.* **-lized, -liz·ing, -liz·es** To undergo or cause to undergo catabolism.

cat·a·chre·sis (kăt'ə-krē'sĭs) *n., pl.* **-ses** (-sēz) **1.** The misapplication of a word or phrase, as the use of *blatant* to mean "flagrant." **2.** The use of a strained figure of speech, such as a mixed metaphor. [Lat. *catachrēsis,* improper use of a word < Gk. *katakhrēsis,* excessive use < *katakhrēsthai,* to misuse : *kata–,* completely; see CATA– + *khrēsthai,* to use.] **—cat'a·chres'tic** (-krĕs'tĭk), **cat'a·chres'ti·cal** (-tĭ-kəl) *adj.* **—cat'a·chres'ti·cal·ly** *adv.*

cat·a·clysm (kăt'ə-klĭz'əm) *n.* **1.** A violent upheaval that causes great destruction or brings about a fundamental change. **2.** A vio-

Fidel Castro
photographed in 1984

lent sudden change in the earth's crust. **3.** A devastating flood. [Fr. *cataclysme* < Lat. *cataclysmos*, deluge < Gk. *kataklusmos* < *katakluzein*, to inundate : *kata-*, intensive pref.; see CATA– + *kluzein*, to wash away.] —**cat′a·clys′mic** (-klĭz′mĭk), **cat′a·clys′mal** (-klĭz′məl) *adj.* —**cat′a·clys′mi·cal·ly** *adv.*

cat·a·comb (kăt′ə-kōm′) *n.* **1.** An underground cemetery consisting of chambers or tunnels with recesses for graves. Often used in the plural. **2.** An underground, often labyrinthine passageway. [Prob. Fr. *catacombe* < OFr. < LLat. *catacumba*.]

cat·a·di·op·tric (kăt′ə-dī-ŏp′trĭk) *adj.* Of or relating to an optical system that uses both reflective and refractive optical devices.

ca·tad·ro·mous (kə-tăd′rə-məs) *adj.* Living in fresh water but migrating to marine waters to breed. Used of fish.

cat·a·falque (kăt′ə-fălk′, -fôlk′) *n.* **1.** A decorative structure on which a coffin rests in state during a funeral. **2.** A coffin-shaped structure used to represent the corpse at a requiem Mass after the burial. [Fr. < Ital. *catafalco*.]

Cat·a·lan (kăt′l-ăn′, -ən, kăt′l-ăn′) *adj.* Of or relating to Catalonia or its people, language, or culture. ❖ *n.* **1.** A native or inhabitant of Catalonia. **2.** The Romance language spoken esp. in Catalonia, the Balearic Islands, Andorra, and the Roussillon region of France.

cat·a·lase (kăt′l-ās′, -āz′) *n.* An enzyme in the blood and in most living cells that catalyzes the decomposition of hydrogen peroxide into water and oxygen. [CATAL(YSIS) + –ASE.]

cat·a·lec·tic (kăt′l-ĕk′tĭk) *adj.* Lacking one or more syllables, esp. in the final foot. Used of verse. [LLat. *catalēcticus* < Gk. *katalēktikos* < *katalēgein*, to leave off : *kata-*, intensive pref.; see CATA– + *lēgein*, to cease, terminate.]

cat·a·lep·sy (kăt′l-ĕp′sē) *n., pl.* **-sies** A condition characterized by muscular rigidity and occurring in a variety of physical and psychological disorders. [ME *catalempsi* < LLat. *catalēmpsia* < Gk. *katalēpsis* < *katalambanein*, to seize upon : *kata-*, intensive pref.; see CATA– + *lambanein*, *lēp-*, to seize.] —**cat′a·lep′tic** (kăt′l-ĕp′tĭk) *adj.*

cat·a·lex·is (kăt′l-ĕk′sĭs) *n., pl.* **-lex·es** (-sēz′) The absence of one or more syllables in a line of verse, esp. in the last foot. [Gk. *katalēxis* < *katalēgein*, to leave off. See CATALECTIC.]

Cat·a·li·na Island (kăt′l-ē′nə) See **Santa Catalina Island.**

cat·a·lo (kăt′l-ō′) *n.* Variant of **cattalo.**

cat·a·log or **cat·a·logue** (kăt′l-ôg′, -ŏg′) *n.* **1a.** A list or itemized display, as of titles or articles for sale, usu. including descriptive information or illustrations. **b.** A publication, such as a book or pamphlet, containing such a list or display: *a seed catalog.* **2.** A list or enumeration. **3.** A card catalog. ❖ *v.* **-loged, -log·ing, -logs** or **-logued, -logu·ing, -logues** —*tr.* **1.** To make an itemized list of: *catalog a record collection.* **2a.** To list or include in a catalog. **b.** To classify (a book, for example) according to a categorical system. —*intr.* To be listed in a catalog. [ME *cathaloge*, list, register < OFr. *catalogue* < LLat. *catalogus* < Gk. *katalogos* < *katalegein*, to list : *kata-*, down, off; see CATA– + *legein*, to count; see **leg-** in App.] —**cat′a·log′er** *n.*

ca·ta·logue rai·son·né (kăt′l-ôg′ rā′zə-nā′, -ŏg′, kä-tä-lôg′ rĕ-zô-nā′) *n., pl.* **ca·ta·logues rai·son·nés** (kăt′l-ôgz′ rā′zə-nā′, -ŏgz′, kä-tä-lôg′ rĕ-zô-nā′) A publication listing titles of articles or literary works, esp. of the contents of an exhibition, along with related descriptive or critical material. [Fr. : *catalogue*, catalog + *raisonné*, methodical, descriptive < p. part. of *raisonner*, to reason, analyze.]

Cat·a·lo·nia (kăt′l-ōn′yə, -ō′nē-ə) A region of NE Spain bordering on France and the Mediterranean Sea. —**Cat′a·lo′nian** *adj. & n.*

ca·tal·pa (kə-tăl′pə, -tôl′-) *n.* Any of various, usu. deciduous trees of the genus *Catalpa*, esp. *C. bignonioides* or *C. speciosa*, native to the United States and having heart-shaped leaves, white flowers, and long slender cylindrical pods. [Creek *katalpa* : *ka-*, head + *talpa*, wing (< the shape of its flowers).]

catalpa
Southern catalpa
Catalpa bignonioides

ca·tal·y·sis (kə-tăl′ĭ-sĭs) *n., pl.* **-ses** (-sēz′) The action of a catalyst, esp. an increase in the rate of a chemical reaction. [Gk. *katalusis*, dissolution < *kataluein*, to dissolve : *kata-*, intensive pref.; see CATA– + *lūein*, to loosen; see **leu-** in App.] —**cat′a·lyt′ic** (-lĭt′ĭk) *adj.* —**cat′a·lyt′i·cal·ly** *adv.*

cat·a·lyst (kăt′l-ĭst) *n.* **1.** *Chemistry* A substance that modifies and increases the rate of a reaction without being consumed in the process. **2.** One that precipitates a process or event, esp. without being involved in the consequences.

catalytic converter *n.* A device that uses a catalyst, such as platinum, to convert the pollutants of automotive exhaust into carbon dioxide and water.

catalytic cracker *n.* An oil refinery unit in which the cracking of petroleum takes place in the presence of a catalyst.

cat·a·lyze (kăt′l-īz′) *tr.v.* **-lyzed, -lyz·ing, -lyz·es 1.** To modify, esp. to increase, the rate of (a chemical reaction) by catalysis. **2.** To bring about; initiate. **3.** To produce fundamental change in; transform. [< CATALYSIS.] —**cat′a·lyz′er** *n.*

cat·a·ma·ran (kăt′ə-mə-răn′) *n.* **1.** A boat with two parallel hulls or floats, esp. a light sailboat with a frame joining the hulls. **2.** A raft of logs or floats lashed together and propelled by paddles or sails. [Tamil *kaṭṭumaram* : *kaṭṭu*, to tie + *maram*, wood, log.]

cat·a·me·ni·a (kăt′ə-mē′nē-ə) *n.* See **menses.** [Gk. *katamēnia* < neut. pl. of *katamēnios*, monthly : *kata-*, per; see CATA– + *mēn*, month; see **mē-¹** in App.] —**cat′a·me′ni·al** *adj.*

cat·a·mite (kăt′ə-mīt′) *n.* A boy who has a sexual relationship with a man. [Lat. *catamītus* < *Catamītus*, Ganymede < Etruscan *Catmite* < Gk. *Ganumēdēs*.]

cat·a·mount (kăt′ə-mount′) *n.* See **mountain lion.** [Short for CATAMOUNTAIN.]

cat·a·moun·tain (kăt′ə-moun′tən) *n.* Any of various wild felines. [Alteration of *cat of the mountain.*]

Ca·ta·nia (kə-tän′yə, -tä′nē-ə, kä-tä′nyä) A city of E Sicily, Italy, on the **Gulf of Catania,** an inlet of the Ionian Sea; founded in the 8th cent. B.C. Pop. 330,037.

ca·taph·o·ra (kə-tăf′ər-ə) *n.* The use of a linguistic unit, such as a pronoun, to refer ahead to another unit, such as a noun or noun phrase. [CATA– + (ANA)PHORA.] —**cat′a·phor′ic** (kăt′ə-fôr′ĭk, -fŏr′-) *adj.*

cat·a·pho·re·sis (kăt′ə-fə-rē′sĭs) *n.* See **electrophoresis** 1. —**cat′a·pho·ret′ic** (-rĕt′ĭk) *adj.* —**cat′a·pho·ret′i·cal·ly** *adv.*

cat·a·pla·sia (kăt′ə-plā′zhə, -zhē-ə) *n.* Degenerative reversion of cells or tissue to a less differentiated form. —**cat′a·plas′tic** (-plăs′tĭk) *adj.*

cat·a·plasm (kăt′ə-plăz′əm) *n.* See **poultice.** [ME *cathaplasma* and Fr. *cataplasme*, both < Lat. *cataplasma* < Gk. *kataplasma* < *kataplassein*, to plaster over : *kata-*, down, onto, over; see CATA– + *plassein*, to mold, form; see PLASMA.]

cat·a·pult (kăt′ə-pŭlt′, -pŏolt′) *n.* **1.** A military machine for hurling missiles, used in ancient and medieval times. **2.** A mechanism for launching aircraft at a speed sufficient for flight, as from a carrier deck. **3.** A slingshot. ❖ *v.* **-pult·ed, -pult·ing, -pults** —*tr.* To hurl or launch from or as if from a catapult. —*intr.* To become catapulted; spring or bolt. [Fr. *catapulte* < OFr. < Lat. *catapulta* < Gk. *katapaltēs* : *kata-*, cata- + *pallein*, to brandish.]

cat·a·ract (kăt′ə-răkt′) *n.* **1.** A large or high waterfall. **2.** A great downpour; a deluge. **3.** *Pathology* Opacity of the lens or capsule of the eye, causing impairment of vision or blindness. [ME *cataracte* < OFr. < Lat. *cataracta* < Gk. *katarraktēs, kataraktēs*, downrush, waterfull, portcullis, prob. < *katarassein*, to dash down (*kat-*, *kata-*, cata- + *arassein*, to strike). Sense 3 < a comparison to a portcullis or other falling impediment or covering.] —**cat′a·rac′tous** (-răk′təs) *adj.*

ca·tarrh (kə-tär′) *n.* Inflammation of mucous membranes, esp. of the nose and throat. [ME *catarre* < OFr. *catarrhe* < LLat. *catarrhus* < Gk. *katarrous* < *katarrein*, to flow down : *kata-*, cata- + *rhein*, to flow; see **sreu-** in App.] —**ca·tarrh′al, ca·tarrh′ous** *adj.* —**ca·tarrh′al·ly** *adv.*

cat·a·ta·sis (kə-tăs′tə-sĭs) *n., pl.* **-ses** (-sēz′) **1.** The intensified part of the action directly preceding the catastrophe in classical tragedy. **2.** The climax of a drama. [Gk. *katastasis*, settled state < *kathistanai*, to come into a certain state : *kat-, kata-*, cata- + *histanai*, to set; see **stā-** in App.]

ca·tas·tro·phe (kə-tăs′trə-fē) *n.* **1.** A great, often sudden calamity. **2.** A complete failure; a fiasco. **3.** The concluding action of a drama, esp. a classical tragedy, containing a resolution of the plot. **4.** A sudden violent change in the earth's surface; a cataclysm. [Gk. *katastrophē*, an overturning, ruin, conclusion < *katastrephein*, to ruin, undo : *kata-*, cata- + *strephein*, to turn.]

cat·a·stroph·ic (kăt′ə-strŏf′ĭk) *adj.* **1.** Of, relating to, or involving a catastrophe. **2.** Involving or resulting in substantial, often ruinous medical expense. —**cat′a·stroph′i·cal·ly** *adv.*

ca·tas·tro·phism (kə-tăs′trə-fĭz′əm) *n.* **1.** *Geology* The doctrine that major changes in the earth's crust result from catastrophes rather than gradual processes. **2.** The prediction of cataclysmic upheaval. —**ca·tas′tro·phist** *n.*

cat·a·to·ni·a (kăt′ə-tō′nē-ə) *n.* An abnormal condition variously characterized by stupor, stereotypy, mania, and either rigidity or extreme flexibility of the limbs. [NLat. < Ger. *Katatonie* < Gk. *katatonos*, stretching tight < *katateinein*, to stretch tight : *kata-*, intensive pref.; see CATA– + *teinein*, to stretch; see **ten-** in App.] —**cat′a·ton′ic** (-tŏn′ĭk) *adj. & n.* —**cat′a·ton′i·cal·ly** *adv.*

Ca·taw·ba¹ (kə-tô′bə) *n., pl.* **Catawba** or **-bas 1.** A member of a Native American people formerly inhabiting territory along the Catawba River in North and South Carolina and now located in western South Carolina. **2.** The Siouan language of the Catawba.

Ca·taw·ba² (kə-tô′bə) *n.* **1.** A reddish North American grape developed from the fox grape. **2.** Wine made from this grape. [After CATAWBA (RIVER).]

Catawba River A river rising in W NC and flowing c. 402 km (250 mi) into SC, where it is called the Wateree R.

cat·bird (kăt′bûrd′) *n.* A North American songbird (*Dumetella carolinensis*) having predominantly slate plumage.

catbird seat *n.* A position of power or prominence.

cat·boat (kăt′bōt′) *n.* A broad-beamed sailboat carrying a single, usu. gaff-headed sail on a mast stepped well forward and often fitted with a centerboard.

cat·bri·er (kăt′brī′ər) *n.* Any of several woody vines of the genus *Smilax*, having greenish flowers, heart-shaped leaves, and usu. bluish to black berries.

cat burglar *n.* A burglar esp. skilled at stealthy or undetected entry of a premises.

cat·call (kăt′kôl′) *n.* A harsh or shrill call or whistle expressing derision or disapproval. —**cat′call′** *v.*

catch (kăch, kĕch) *v.* **caught** (kôt), **catch·ing, catch·es** —*tr.* **1.** To capture or seize, esp. after a chase. **2.** To take by or as if by trapping or snaring. **3a.** To discover or come upon suddenly, unexpectedly, or accidentally: *He was caught in the act of stealing.* **b.** To become aware of suddenly: *caught her gazing out the window.* **4a.** To take hold of, esp. forcibly or suddenly; grasp: *caught me by the arm.* **b.** To grab so as to stop the motion of: *catch a ball.* **5a.** To overtake: *The red car caught me on the straightaway.* **b.** To reach just in time; take: *catch a wave.* **6a.** To hold, as by snagging or entangling. **b.** To cause to become suddenly or accidentally hooked, entangled, or fastened: *caught my hem on the stair.* **c.** To hold up; delay: *was caught in traffic for an hour.* **7.** To hit; strike: *a punch that caught me in the stomach.* **8.** To check (oneself) during an action: *I caught myself before replying.* **9.** To become subject to or to contract, as by exposure to a pathogen: *catch a cold.* **10a.** To become affected by or infused with: *caught the joyous mood of the festival.* **b.** To suffer from the receipt of: *caught hell.* **11a.** To take or get suddenly, momentarily, or quickly: *caught a glimpse.* **b.** To hear or listen to: *caught the news on TV.* **12a.** To grasp mentally; apprehend: *I don't catch your meaning.* **b.** To apprehend and reproduce accurately by or as if by artistic means. **13.** To attract and fix; arrest: *caught my eye.* **14.** To charm; captivate. **15.** To deceive: *failed to be caught by their fraudulent schemes.* **16a.** *Informal* To go to see (a performance, for example): *caught the midnight show.* **b.** To get (something required), usu. quickly or for a brief period: *catch some sleep.* —*intr.* **1.** To become held, entangled, or fastened: *My coat caught in the car door.* **2.** To act or move so as to hold or grab someone or something. **3.** To be communicable or infectious; spread. **4.** To ignite: *The fire caught.* **5.** *Baseball* To act as catcher. ❖ *n.* **1.** The act of catching; a taking and holding. **2.** Something that catches, esp. a device for fastening or for checking motion. **3a.** Something caught: *The mistake you found was a good catch.* **b.** *Informal* One that is worth having, esp. an admirable marital partner. **4.** *Sports* **a.** The grabbing and holding of a thrown, kicked, or batted ball before it hits the ground. **b.** A game of throwing and catching a ball. **5.** A quantity that is caught. **6.** A choking or stoppage of the breath or voice. **7.** A stop or break in the operation of a mechanism. **8.** *Informal* A tricky or previously unsuspected condition or drawback. **9.** A snatch; a fragment. **10.** *Music* A canonic, often rhythmically intricate composition for three or more voices. —*phrasal verbs:* **catch on 1.** To understand; perceive. **2.** To become popular: *Skateboarding caught on quickly.* **catch out** To detect (another) in wrongdoing or error. **catch up 1.** To move fast enough to attain the same progress as another; draw even. **2.** To become equal or on a par with another. **3.** To bring an activity to completion or to a state of currentness. **4.** To bring (another) up to date; brief. **5.** To seize or lift suddenly: *The wind caught up her hat.* **6a.** To involve, often unwillingly. **b.** To captivate; enthrall. **7a.** To bring up to date; brief. **b.** To bring an activity nearer to completion. —*idioms:* **catch fire 1.** To ignite. **2.** To become very enthusiastic. **3.** To become the subject of great interest and widespread enthusiasm. **catch it** *Informal* To receive a punishment or scolding. **catch (one's) breath** To rest so as to be able to continue an activity. [ME *cacchen* < ONFr. *cachier*, to chase < Lat. *captāre*, freq. of *capere*, to seize. See **kap-** in App.] —**catch′a·ble** *adj.*

Catch-22 also **catch-22** (kăch′twĕn-tē-tōō′, kĕch′-) *n.* A situation in which a desired outcome is impossible because of inherently illogical rules or conditions. [After *Catch-22*, a novel by Joseph Heller (1923–99), American writer.]

catch·all (kăch′ôl′, kĕch′-) *n.* **1.** A receptacle or storage area for odds and ends. **2.** Something that encompasses a wide variety of items or situations. —**catch′all′** *adj.*

catch-as-catch-can (kăch′əz-kăch-kăn′, kĕch′əz-kĕch-) *adv.* By whatever means possible.

catch basin *n.* **1.** A receptacle at the entrance to a sewer designed to keep out large or obstructive matter. **2.** A reservoir for collecting surface drainage or runoff.

catch colt *n. Western US* See **old-field colt**.

catch·er (kăch′ər, kĕch′-) *n.* One that catches, esp. the baseball player positioned behind home plate who receives pitches.

catch·fly (kăch′flī′, kĕch′-) *n.* Any of several plants of the genera *Silene* and *Lychnis*, native chiefly to the Northern Hemisphere and having sticky stems and calyxes on which small insects may become stuck.

catch·ing (kăch′ĭng, kĕch′-) *adj.* **1.** Infectious. **2.** Attractive.

catch·ment (kăch′mənt, kĕch′-) *n.* **1.** A catching or collecting of water, esp. rainwater. **2a.** A structure, such as a basin, used for collecting or draining water. **b.** The amount of water collected in

such a structure. **3.** A catchment area.

catchment area *n.* **1.** The area drained by a river or body of water. **2.** The surrounding area served by an institution.

catch·pen·ny (kăch′pĕn′ē, kĕch′-) *adj.* Designed and made to sell without concern for quality; cheap. ❖ *n.* A cheap item.

catch phrase *n.* A phrase in wide or popular use, esp. one serving as a slogan for a group or movement.

catch·pole also **catch·poll** (kăch′pōl′, kĕch′-) *n.* A sheriff's officer, esp. one who arrests debtors. [ME *cacchepol* < Norman Fr. *cachepol*, prob. < OFr. *chacepol* : *chacier*, to chase; see CHASE[1] + *poul*, rooster (< Lat. *pullus*, chicken).]

catch·up (kăch′əp, kĕch′-) *n.* Variant of **ketchup**.

catch-up (kăch′ŭp′, kĕch′-) *n.* **1.** An approach intended to overcome a disadvantage or lead. **2.** An increase intended to bring an amount or rate up to a standard.

catch·word (kăch′wûrd′, kĕch′-) *n.* **1a.** A well-known word or phrase, esp. one that exemplifies a notion, class, or quality. **b.** A catchy name or slogan. **2.** *Printing* **a.** A guideword. **b.** The first word of a page printed in the bottom right-hand corner of the preceding page.

catch·y (kăch′ē, kĕch′ē) *adj.* **-i·er, -i·est 1.** Attractive or appealing. **2.** Easily remembered. **3.** Tricky; deceptive. **4.** Fitful or spasmodic. —**catch′i·ness** *n.*

cate (kāt) *n. Archaic* A choice or dainty food; a delicacy. [Short for *acate* < ME *acat*, a purchase < Norman Fr. < *acater*, to buy. See CATER.]

cat·e·che·sis (kăt′ĭ-kē′sĭs) *n., pl.* **-ses** (-sēz) Oral instruction given to catechumens. [LLat. *catēchēsis* < Gk. *katēkhēsis*, oral instruction < *katēkhein*, to teach by word of mouth. See CATECHIZE.] —**cat′e·chet′i·cal** (-kĕt′ĭ-kəl) *adj.*

cat·e·chin (kăt′ĭ-kĭn′) *n.* A crystalline substance, $C_{15}H_{14}O_6$, derived from catechu and used in tanning and dyeing. [CATECH(U) + -IN.]

cat·e·chism (kăt′ĭ-kĭz′əm) *n.* **1.** A book giving a brief summary of the basic principles of Christianity in question-and-answer form. **2.** A manual giving basic instruction in a subject. **3.** A body of fundamental principles or beliefs, esp. when accepted uncritically. **4.** A close questioning or examination, as of a political figure.

cat·e·chist (kăt′ĭ-kĭst) *n.* One who catechizes, esp. one who instructs catechumens in preparation for admission into a Christian church. —**cat′e·chis′tic, cat′e·chis′ti·cal** *adj.*

cat·e·chize (kăt′ĭ-kīz′) *tr.v.* **-chized, -chiz·ing, -chiz·es 1.** To teach the principles of Christian dogma, discipline, and ethics by means of questions and answers. **2.** To question or examine closely or methodically. [ME *catecizen* < OFr. *catechiser* < Med.Lat. *catēchizāre* < L.Gk. *katēkhizein* < Gk. *katēkhein* : *kata-*, down, off, out; see CATA- + *ēkhein*, to sound (< *ēkhē*, sound).] —**cat′e·chi·za′tion** (-kĭ-zā′shən) *n.* —**cat′e·chiz′er** *n.*

cat·e·chol (kăt′ĭ-kôl′, -kōl′, -kŏl′) *n.* See **catechin**. **2.** A biologically important organic phenol, having two hydroxyl groups attached to the benzene ring. [CATECH(U) + -OL[1].]

cat·e·cho·la·mine (kăt′ĭ-kō′lə-mēn′, -kō′-) *n.* Any of a group of amines derived from catechol that have important physiological effects as neurotransmitters and hormones.

cat·e·chu (kăt′ə-chōō′) *n.* **1a.** A spiny Asian tree (*Acacia catechu*) having bipinnately compound leaves and dark heartwood. **b.** A raw material obtained from this heartwood, used in the preparation of tannins and brown dyes. **2.** See **betel palm**. [Prob. < Malay *kachu*, prob. < Dravidian *karaiyal, karaiccal*, that which is dissolved < *karai*, to melt.]

cat·e·chu·men (kăt′ĭ-kyōō′mən) *n.* **1.** One who is being taught the principles of Christianity. **2.** One who is being instructed in a subject at an elementary level. [ME *cathecumine* < OFr. *catechumene* < Lat. *catēchūmenus* < Gk. *katēkhoumenos*, pr. passive part. of *katēkhein*, to instruct. See CATECHIZE.]

cat·e·gor·i·cal (kăt′ĭ-gôr′ĭ-kəl, -gôr′-) also **cat·e·gor·ic** (-ĭk) *adj.* **1.** Being without exception or qualification; absolute. **2a.** Of or relating to a category or categories. **b.** According to or using categories. —**cat′e·gor′i·cal·ly** *adv.* —**cat′e·gor′i·cal·ness** *n.*

categorical imperative *n.* According to Immanuel Kant, an unconditional moral law that applies to all rational beings.

cat·e·go·rize (kăt′ĭ-gə-rīz′) *tr.v.* **-rized, -riz·ing, -riz·es** To put into a category or categories; classify. —**cat′e·go·riz′a·ble** *adj.* —**cat′e·go·ri·za′tion** (-gər-ĭ-zā′shən) *n.*

cat·e·go·ry (kăt′ĭ-gôr′ē, -gôr′ē) *n., pl.* **-ries 1.** A specifically defined division in a system of classification; a class. **2.** A general class of ideas, terms, or things that mark divisions or coordinations within a conceptual scheme, esp.: **a.** One of Aristotle's modes of objective being, such as quality or relation, that are inherent in everything. **b.** One of Kant's modes of subjective understanding, such as singularity, that organize perceptions into knowledge. **c.** A basic logical type of philosophical conception in post-Kantian philosophy. **3.** *Linguistics* **a.** A classificatory structural property of a language, such as a part of speech. **b.** A grammatical defining property of a linguistic unit, such as tense in the verb. [Fr. *catégorie* < OFr. < LLat. *catēgoria*, class of predicables < Gk. *katēgoriā*, accusation, charge < *katēgorein*, to accuse, predicate : *kat-, kata-*, down, against; see CATA- + *agoreuein, ēgor-*, to speak in public (< *agorā*, marketplace, assembly).]

ă	pat	oi	boy
ā	pay	ou	out
âr	care	ŏŏ	took
ä	father	ōō	boot
ĕ	be	ŭ	cut
ē	be	ûr	urge
ĭ	pit	th	thin
ī	pie	*th*	this
îr	pier	hw	which
ŏ	pot	zh	vision
ō	toe	ə	about,
ô	paw		item

Stress marks:
′ (primary);
′ (secondary), as in
lexicon (lĕk′sĭ-kŏn′)

ca·te·na (kə-tē′nə) *n., pl.* **-nae** (-nē) or **-nas** A closely linked series, esp. of excerpted writings. [Lat. *catēna*, chain.]

cat·e·nar·y (kăt′n-ĕr′ē, kə-tē′nə-rē) *n., pl.* **-ies** 1. The curve, identical to the graph of a hyperbolic cosine, theoretically formed by a perfectly flexible, uniformly dense, and inextensible cable suspended from its endpoints. 2. Something having the general shape of this curve. [NLat. *catēnāria* < Lat., fem. of *catēnārius*, relating to a chain < *catēna*, chain.] —**cat′e·nar′y** *adj.*

cat·e·nate (kăt′n-āt′) *tr.v.* **-nat·ed**, **-nat·ing**, **-nates** To connect in a series of ties or links; form into a chain. [Lat. *catēnāre*, *catēnāt-* < *catēna*, chain.]

ca·ter (kā′tər) *v.* **-tered**, **-ter·ing**, **-ters** —*intr.* 1. To provide food or entertainment. 2. To be particularly attentive or solicitous; minister. —*tr.* 1. To provide food service for. 2. To attend to the wants or needs of. [< obsolete *cater*, provisioner < ME *acatour*, short for *acatour* < Norman Fr. < *acater*, to buy < VLat. **accaptāre* : Lat. *ad-*, ad- + Lat. *captāre*, to chase; see CATCH.] —**ca′ter·er** *n.*

cat·er-cor·nered (kăt′ər-kôr′nərd, kăt′ē-) also **cat·er-cor·ner** (-nər) or **cat·ty-cor·nered** or **cat·ty-cor·ner** (kăt′ē-) or **kit·ty-cor·nered** or **kit·ty-cor·ner** (kĭt′ē-) *adj.* Diagonal. ❖ *adv.* In a diagonal position. [< obsolete *cater*, four at dice < ME < OFr. *catre*, four < Lat. *quattuor*. See kʷetwer- in App.]

cat·er·pil·lar (kăt′ər-pĭl′ər, kăt′ē-) *n.* 1. The wormlike larva of a butterfly or moth. 2. Any of various similar insect larvae. [ME *catirpel*, *catirpeller*, prob. alteration of ONFr. **catepelose*: *cate*, cat (< Lat. *cattus*, perh. of African orig.) + *pelose*, hairy (< Lat. *pilōsus*; see PILOSE).]

WORD HISTORY Larvae of moths and butterflies are popularly seen as resembling other, larger animals. Our word *caterpillar* appears to have come from the Old French term *chatepelose*, meaning "hairy cat." *Caterpillar* is first recorded in English in 1440 as *catyrpel*. *Catyr*, the first part of *catyrpel*, may indicate the existence of an English word **cater*, meaning "tomcat," otherwise attested only in *caterwaul*. The latter part of *catyrpel* seems to have become associated with the word *piller*, "plunderer." By giving the variant spelling *–ar*, Johnson's *Dictionary* set the spelling *caterpillar* with which we are familiar today.

Caterpillar A trademark used for a tractor equipped with continuous chain treads.

cat·er·waul (kăt′ər-wôl′) *intr.v.* **-wauled**, **-waul·ing**, **-wauls** 1. To cry or screech like a cat in heat. 2. To make a shrill, discordant sound. 3. To have a noisy argument. ❖ *n.* A shrill, discordant sound. [ME **caterwawlen* : **cater*, tomcat; akin to LGer. *kater* + *wawlen*, *wrawlen*, to yowl (ult. imit.).]

cat·fish (kăt′fĭsh′) *n., pl.* **catfish** or **-fish·es** Any of numerous scaleless, chiefly freshwater fishes of the order Siluriformes, with whiskerlike barbels extending from the upper jaw.

cat·gut (kăt′gŭt′) *n.* A tough thin cord made from the intestines of certain animals, esp. sheep, and used for stringing musical instruments and tennis rackets and for surgical ligatures.

ca·thar·sis (kə-thär′sĭs) *n., pl.* **-ses** (-sēz) 1. *Medicine* Purgation, esp. for the digestive system. 2. A purifying or figurative cleansing of the emotions, esp. as an effect of tragic drama. 3. *Psychology* The relief of tension and anxiety by bringing repressed feelings and fears to consciousness. [NLat. < Gk. *katharsis* < *kathairein*, to purge < *katharos*, pure.]

ca·thar·tic (kə-thär′tĭk) *n.* An agent for purging the bowels, esp. a laxative. [Lat. *catharticus* < Gk. *kathartikos* < *kathairein*, to purge. See CATHARSIS.] —**ca·thar′tic** *adj.*

Ca·thay (kă-thā′) A medieval name for China. The name was popularized by Marco Polo in accounts of his travels.

cat·head (kăt′hĕd′) *n.* A beam projecting outward from the bow of a ship and used as a support to lift the anchor. [Obsolete *cat*, catboat + HEAD.]

ca·thect (kə-thĕkt′, kă-) *tr.v.* **-thect·ed**, **-thect·ing**, **-thects** To invest emotional energy in (a person, object, or idea). [Back-formation < CATHEXIS.] —**ca·thec′tic** *adj.*

ca·the·dra (kə-thē′drə) *n., pl.* **-drae** (-drē) 1. A bishop's official chair or throne. 2. A bishop's office or see. 3. The official chair of an office or a position. [ME < Lat., chair < Gk. *kathedrā* : *kata-*, cata- + *hedrā*, seat; see sed- in App.]

ca·the·dral (kə-thē′drəl) *n.* 1. The principal church of a bishop's diocese. 2. A large church. 3. Something that resembles a cathedral, as in grandeur or authority. ❖ *adj.* 1. Of, relating to, or containing a bishop's throne: *a cathedral church*. 2. Relating to or issuing from a chair of office or authority; authoritative. 3. Of, relating to, or resembling a cathedral. [Short for *cathedral church* < ME *cathedral*, of a diocese < OFr. < Med.Lat. *cathedrālis*, of a bishop's see < Lat. *cathedra*, chair. See CATHEDRA.]

ca·thep·sin (kə-thĕp′sĭn) *n.* Any of various proteolytic enzymes found in animal tissue that catalyze the hydrolysis of proteins into polypeptides. [Ger. *Kathepsin* < Gk. *kathepsein*, to digest : *kat-*, *kata-*, cata- + *hepsein*, to boil.]

Cath·er (kăth′ər), **Willa Sibert** 1873–1947. Amer. writer whose works about frontier life include *One of Ours* (1922).

Cath·e·rine I (kăth′ər-ĭn, kăth′rĭn) 1684?–1727. Empress of Russia (1725–27) as successor to her husband, Peter I.

Catherine II Known as "Catherine the Great." 1729–96. Empress of Russia (1762–96) after her husband, Peter III (1728–62), was deposed by a group led by her lover.

Cath·e·rine de Mé·di·cis (kăth′ər-ĭn də mā-dē-sēs′, kăth′rĭn, kät-rēn′) 1519–89. Queen of France as the wife of Henry II and regent during the minority (1560–63) of her son Charles IX.

Cath·e·rine of Ar·a·gon (kăth′ər-ĭn, kăth′rĭn; ăr′ə-gŏn′) 1485–1536. The first wife of Henry VIII of England, whose divorce (1533) marked the start of the English Reformation.

cath·er·ine wheel (kăth′ər-ĭn, kăth′rĭn) *n.* See **pinwheel** 2. [After St. *Catherine* of Alexandria (died A.D. 307), who was condemned to be tortured on a wheel.]

cath·e·ter (kăth′ĭ-tər) *n.* A flexible tube inserted into a body cavity, duct, or vessel to allow fluids to pass or distend a passage. [LLat. < Gk. *kathetēr* < *kathīenai*, to send down : *kat-*, *kata-*, cata- + *hīenai*, *he-*, to send.]

cath·e·ter·ize (kăth′ĭ-tə-rīz′) *tr.v.* **-ized**, **-iz·ing**, **-iz·es** To put a catheter into. —**cath′e·ter·i·za′tion** (-rĭ-zā′shən) *n.*

ca·thex·is (kə-thĕk′sĭs) *n., pl.* **-thex·es** (-thĕk′sēz) *Psychology* Concentration of emotional energy on an object or idea. [Gk. *kathexis*, holding, retention < *katekhein*, to hold fast : *kat-*, *kata-*, intensive pref.; see CATA– + *ekhein*, to hold; see segh- in App.]

cath·ode (kăth′ōd′) *n.* 1. A negatively charged electrode, as of an electrolytic cell or a storage battery. 2. The positively charged terminal of a primary cell or a storage battery that is supplying current. [Gk. *kathodos*, descent : *kat-*, *kata-*, cata- + *hodos*, way, path.] —**ca·thod′ic** (kă-thŏd′ĭk) *adj.* —**ca·thod′i·cal·ly** *adv.*

cathode ray *n.* 1. A stream of electrons emitted by the cathode in electrical discharge tubes. 2. One of the electrons that is emitted in a stream from a cathode-ray tube.

cath·ode-ray tube (kăth′ōd-rā′) *n.* A vacuum tube in which a hot cathode emits electrons that are accelerated as a beam through an anode, then focused or deflected onto a phosphorescent screen.

cath·o·lic (kăth′ə-lĭk, kăth′lĭk) *adj.* 1. Of broad or liberal scope; comprehensive. 2. Including or concerning all humankind; universal. 3. **Catholic a.** Of or involving the Roman Catholic Church. **b.** Of or relating to the universal Christian church. **c.** Of or relating to the ancient undivided Christian church. **d.** Of or relating to those churches that have claimed to be representatives of the ancient undivided church. ❖ *n.* **Catholic** A member of a Catholic church, esp. a Roman Catholic. [ME *catholik*, universally accepted < OFr. *catholique* < Lat. *catholicus*, universal < Gk. *katholikos* < *katholou*, in general : *kat-*, *kata-*, down, along, according to; see CATA– + *holou* < neut. genitive of *holos*, whole; see sol- in App.] —**ca·thol′i·cal·ly** (kə-thŏl′ĭk-lē) *adv.*

Ca·thol·i·cism (kə-thŏl′ĭ-sĭz′əm) *n.* The faith, doctrine, and practice of a Catholic church, esp. the Roman Catholic Church.

cath·o·lic·i·ty (kăth′ə-lĭs′ĭ-tē) *n.* 1. The condition or quality of being catholic; inclusiveness. 2. General application or acceptance; universality. 3. **Catholicity** Roman Catholicism.

ca·thol·i·cize (kə-thŏl′ĭ-sīz′) *tr. & intr.v.* **-cized**, **-ciz·ing**, **-ciz·es** 1. To make or become catholic. 2. To convert or be converted to Catholicism.

ca·thol·i·con (kə-thŏl′ĭ-kŏn′) *n.* A universal remedy; a panacea. [ME < OFr. < Med.Lat. < Gk. *katholikon*, generic description < neut. of *katholikos*, universal. See CATHOLIC.]

cat·house (kăt′hous′) *n. Slang* A house of prostitution.

Cat·i·line (kăt′l-īn′) Orig. Lucius Sergius Catilina. 108?–62 B.C. Roman politician who led an unsuccessful revolt against the Roman Republic.

cat·i·on (kăt′ī′ən) *n.* An ion or group of ions having a positive charge and characteristically moving toward the negative electrode in electrolysis. [Gk. *kation*, something going down < neut. pr. part. of *katienai*, to go down : *kat-*, *kata-*, cata- + *ienai*, to go; see ei- in App.] —**cat′i·on′ic** (kăt′ī-ŏn′ĭk) *adj.*

cation exchange *n.* A chemical process in which cations of like charge are exchanged equally between a solid, such as zeolite, and a solution, such as water.

cat·jang (kăt′chăng′) *n.* 1. See pigeon pea. 2. See cowpea. [Du. *katjang* < Malay *kachang*, pea, bean.]

cat·kin (kăt′kĭn) *n.* A usu. dense cylindrical cluster of apetalous flowers found in willows, birches, and oaks. [< obsolete Du. *katteken*, kitten, dim. of *katte*, cat (< its resemblance to a kitten's tail) < Gmc. **kattuz*.]

cat·like (kăt′līk′) *adj.* Resembling a cat, esp. in being quiet or stealthy.

Cat·lin (kăt′lĭn), **George** 1796–1872. Amer. artist noted for his portraits of Native Americans.

cat·mint (kăt′mĭnt′) *n. Chiefly British* Catnip.

cat·nap (kăt′năp′) *n.* A short nap; a light sleep. ❖ *intr.v.* **-napped**, **-nap′ping**, **-naps** To take a short nap; doze.

cat·nip (kăt′nĭp′) *n.* 1. An aromatic perennial herb (*Nepeta cataria*) in the mint family, native to Eurasia and containing an aromatic oil to which cats are strongly attracted. 2. Any of various other mostly aromatic plants of the genus *Nepeta*, cultivated for their ornamental foliage and flowers. [CAT + *nip*, catnip (var. of *nep* < ME *nept*, *nep* < OE *nepte* < Lat. *nepeta*, aromatic herb, perh. of Etruscan orig.).]

Ca·to¹ (kā′tō), **Marcus Porcius** Known as "the Elder." 234–149 B.C. Roman politician, censor, and general who wrote the first history of Rome.

Ca·to² (kā′tō), **Marcus Porcius** Known as "the Younger." 95–46

Catherine the Great
detail of a portrait by
Dimitri Levitzkij
(1735–1822)

catkin
catkins of a Northern
red oak

catenary
The equation for this
catenary in rectangular
coordinates, with *a* as the
y-intercept, is:
$$y = \left(\frac{a}{2}\right)\left(e^{x/a} + e^{-x/a}\right)$$

B.C. Roman politician who supported Pompey against Caesar in the civil war and committed suicide after Caesar's victory.

Ca·toc·tin Mountains (kə-tŏk′tĭn) A section of the Blue Ridge in N MD extending from the PA border S to VA.

cat-o′-nine-tails (kăt′ə-nīn′tālz′) n., pl. **cat-o′-nine-tails** A whip consisting of nine knotted cords fastened to a handle, used in flogging. [< its cat scratch marks.]

ca·top·tric (kə-tŏp′trĭk) also **ca·top·tri·cal** (-trĭ-kəl) adj. Of or relating to mirrors and reflected images. [Gk. katoptrikos < katoptron, mirror. See **okʷ-** in App.] —**ca·top′trics** n.

cat rig n. The rig of a catboat. [< obsolete cat, catboat.]

CAT scan n. An image produced by a CAT scanner.

CAT scanner n. A device that produces cross-sectional views of a body structure using computerized axial tomography.

cat's cradle (kăts) n. A game in which a string is looped on the fingers to form an intricate pattern between a player's hands that can be varied or transferred to another player's hands.

cat scratch disease n. A disease thought to be transmitted to humans by the scratch or bite of a cat and characterized by fever and swollen lymph nodes.

cat's-eye (kăts′ī′) n., pl. **cat's-eyes** 1. Any of various semiprecious gems such as chrysoberyl, BeAl₂O₄, reflecting a band of light that shifts position as the gem is turned. 2. A glass or plastic reflector designed to glow in the beam of a headlight. 3. A marble having an eyelike design.

Cats·kill Mountains (kăts′kĭl′) A range of the Appalachian Mts. in SE NY rising to 1,282.2 m (4,204 ft).

cat's-paw also **cats·paw** (kăts′pô′) n., pl. **cat's-paws** also **cats·paws** 1. A person used by another as a dupe or tool. 2. A light breeze that ruffles small areas of a water surface. 3. Nautical A knot made by twisting a section of rope to form two adjacent eyes through which a hook is passed, used in hoisting. [< a fable about a monkey that used a cat's paw to pull chestnuts out of a fire.]

cat·sup (kăt′səp, kăch′əp, kĕch′-) n. Variant of **ketchup**.

Catt (kăt), **Carrie (Lane) Chapman** 1859–1947. Amer. suffragist who organized the League of Women Voters in 1919.

cat·tail (kăt′tāl′) n. Any of various perennial herbs of the genus Typha, widespread in marshy places and having a dense cylindrical cluster of minute flowers and fruits.

cat·ta·lo also **cat·a·lo** (kăt′l-ō′) n., pl. **-loes** or **-los** See **beefalo**. [CATT(LE) + (BUFF)ALO.]

cat·ter·y (kăt′ə-rē) n., pl. **-ies** An establishment where cats are kept and bred.

cat·tle (kăt′l) pl.n. 1. Any of various chiefly domesticated mammals of the genus Bos, including cows, steers, bulls, and oxen, often raised for meat and dairy products. 2. Humans, esp. when viewed contemptuously or as a mob. [ME catel, property, livestock < ONFr. < O Provençal capdal < Med.Lat. capitāle, funds < neut. of Lat. capitālis, principal < caput, head. See **kaput-** in App.]

cattle call n. Informal An audition in which a large number of often inexperienced actors or performers try out.

cattle egret n. A small egret (Bubulcus ibis) native to Africa and southern Eurasia that feeds among grazing cattle.

cattle grub n. The larva of a warble fly, esp. of the genus Hypoderma, that parasitizes cattle.

cat·tle·man (kăt′l-mən, -măn′) n. A man who raises cattle.

cattle tick n. A brown tick (Boophilus annulatus) whose bite transmits the causative agent of Texas fever in cattle.

cat·tle·ya (kăt′lē-ə) n. Any of various tropical American orchids of the genus Cattleya, cultivated for their showy flowers. [NLat. Cattleya, genus name, after William Cattley (died 1832), British patron of botany.]

Cat·ton (kăt′n), **(Charles) Bruce** 1899–1978. Amer. historian and editor who wrote extensively on the Civil War.

cat·ty¹ (kăt′ē) adj. **-ti·er, -ti·est** 1. Subtly cruel or malicious. 2. Catlike; stealthy. —**cat′ti·ly** adv. —**cat′ti·ness** n.

cat·ty² also **cat·tie** (kăt′ē) n., pl. **-ties** Any of various units of weight used in Southeast Asia, esp. a Chinese measure equal to 500 grams (approx. 1.1 pounds). [Malay kati.]

cat·ty-cor·nered (kăt′ē-kôr′nərd) or **cat·ty-cor·ner** (-nər) adj. & adv. Variants of **cater-cornered**.

Ca·tul·lus (kə-tŭl′əs), **Gaius Valerius** 84?–54? B.C. Roman lyric poet known for his love poems to "Lesbia."

CATV abbr. community antenna television

cat·walk (kăt′wôk′) n. A narrow, often elevated walkway, as on the sides of a bridge or in the flies above a theater stage.

Cau·ca (kou′kä) A river rising in W Colombia and flowing c. 965 km (600 mi) N to the Magdalena R.

Cau·ca·sian (kô-kā′zhən, -kăzh′ən) adj. 1. Anthropology Of or being a human racial classification distinguished esp. by very light to brown skin pigmentation and straight to wavy or curly hair and including peoples indigenous to Europe, northern Africa, western Asia, and India. Not in scientific use. 2. Of or relating to the Caucasus region or its peoples, languages, or cultures. 3. Of or relating to a group of three language families spoken in the region of the Caucasus mountains, including Chechen, Abkhaz, and the Kartvelian languages. ❖ n. 1. Anthropology A member of the Caucasian racial classification. Not in scientific use. 2. A native or inhabitant of the Caucasus. 3. The Caucasian language family.

Cau·ca·soid (kô′kə-soid′) adj. Anthropology Of or relating to the Caucasian racial classification. —**Cau′ca·soid′** n.

Cau·ca·sus (kô′kə-səs) also **Cau·ca·sia** (kô-kā′zhə, -shə) A region between the Black and Caspian seas that includes Georgia, Azerbaijan, Armenia, and part of SW Russia.

Caucasus Mountains A range in the Caucasus extending from the N to the SE and rising to 5,645.6 m (18,510 ft).

Cau·chy (kō-shē′), Baron **Augustin Louis** 1789–1857. French mathematician whose Cours d'Analyse (1821) introduced modern rigor into calculus.

cau·cus (kô′kəs) n., pl. **-cus·es** or **-cus·ses** 1a. A meeting of the local members of a political party esp. to select delegates to a convention or register preferences for political candidates. b. A closed meeting of party members within a legislative body. c. A group within a legislative or decision-making body seeking to represent a specific interest or influence a policy area. 2. Chiefly British A committee within a political party to determine policy. ❖ v. **-cused, -cus·ing, -cus·es** or **-cussed, -cus·sing, -cus·ses** —intr. To assemble in or hold a caucus. —tr. To assemble or canvass (members of a caucus). [After the Caucus Club of Boston (in the 1760s), poss. < Med.Lat. caucus, drinking vessel.]

cau·dad (kô′dăd′) adv. Toward the tail or posterior end of the body; caudally. [Lat. cauda, tail + –AD.]

cau·dal (kôd′l) adj. Anatomy 1a. Of, at, or near the tail or hind parts; posterior. b. Situated beneath or on the underside; inferior. 2. Similar to a tail in form or function. [NLat. caudālis < Lat. cauda, tail.] —**cau′dal·ly** adv.

cau·date (kô′dāt′) also **cau·dat·ed** (-dā′tĭd) adj. Having a tail or taillike appendage. [Med.Lat. caudātus < Lat. cauda, tail.] —**cau·da′tion** n.

cau·dex (kô′dĕks) n., pl. **-di·ces** (-dĭ-sēz′) or **-dex·es** 1. The thickened base of the stem of many perennial herbaceous plants, from which new leaves and flowering stems arise. 2. The trunk of a palm or tree fern. [Lat. caudex, tree trunk.]

cau·dil·lo (kô-dēl′yō, -dē′yō, kou-) n., pl. **-los** A leader or chief, esp. a military dictator. [Sp. < LLat. capitellum, dim. of Lat. caput, head. See **kaput-** in App.]

cau·dle (kôd′l) n. A warm drink of wine or ale mixed with sugar, eggs, bread, and various spices, sometimes given to ill persons. [ME caudel < ONFr. < Med.Lat. caldellus < Lat. caldum, hot drink < caldus, calidus, warm, hot.]

caught (kôt) v. Past tense and past participle of **catch**.

caul (kôl) n. 1. A portion of the amnion, esp. when it covers the head of a fetus at birth. 2. See **greater omentum**. [ME calle < OE cawl, basket.]

caul·dron also **cal·dron** (kôl′drən) n. 1. A large vessel used for boiling. 2. A state or situation of great distress or unrest. [ME, alteration of cauderon < Norman Fr., dim. of caudiere, cooking pot < LLat. caldāria < fem. of Lat. caldārius, suitable for warming < calidus, warm.]

cau·les·cent (kô-lĕs′ənt) adj. Botany Having a well-developed aboveground stem. [Lat. caulis, stem + –ESCENT.]

cau·li·flow·er (kô′lĭ-flou′ər, kŏl′ĭ-) n. An herb (Brassica oleracea var. botrytis) in the mustard family, related to the cabbage and broccoli and having a whitish undeveloped flower with a large edible head. [Prob. alteration (influenced by FLOWER) of NLat. cauliflōra : Lat. caulis, stem + Lat. flōs, flōr-, flower; see FLOWER.]

cauliflower ear n. An ear deformed by repeated blows.

cau·line (kô′līn′) adj. Of, having, or growing on a stem. [Lat. caulis, stem + –INE¹.]

caulk also **calk** (kôk) v. **caulked, caulk·ing, caulks** also **calked, calk·ing, calks** —tr. 1. To make watertight or airtight by filling or sealing: caulk a pipe joint. 2. Nautical To make (a boat) watertight by packing seams with a waterproof material, such as pitch. —intr. To apply caulking. ❖ n. Caulking. [ME cauken, to press < ONFr. cauquer < Lat. calcāre, to tread < calx, heel.] —**caulk′er** n.

caulk·ing (kô′kĭng) n. A usu. impermeable substance used for caulking.

caus·al (kô′zəl) adj. 1. Of, involving, or being a cause. 2. Indicative of a cause. ❖ n. A word or grammatical element expressing a cause or reason. —**caus′al·ly** adv.

cau·sal·i·ty (kô-zăl′ĭ-tē) n., pl. **-ties** 1. The principle of or relationship between cause and effect. 2. A causal agency, force, or quality.

causality paradox n. A hypothetical effect resulting if one were to travel back in time and cause changes to the circumstances that led to one's current actions.

cau·sa·tion (kô-zā′shən) n. 1. The act or process of causing. 2. A cause. 3. Causality.

caus·a·tive (kô′zə-tĭv) adj. 1. Functioning as an agent or cause. 2. Expressing causation. Used of a verb or verbal affix. —**caus′a·tive** n. —**caus′a·tive·ly** adv.

cause (kôz) n. 1a. The producer of an effect, result, or consequence. b. The one responsible for an action or result. 2. A basis for an action or response; a reason. 3. A goal or principle served with dedication: "the cause of freedom versus tyranny" (Hannah Arendt). 4. The interests of one engaged in a struggle: "The cause of America is in great measure the cause of all mankind" (Thomas Paine). 5. Law a. A ground for legal action. b. A lawsuit. 6. A subject under debate or discussion. ❖ tr.v. **caused, caus·ing, caus·**

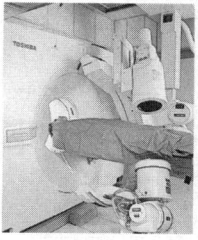

CAT scanner

Carrie Chapman Catt
detail from a 1927 portrait by Mary Foote (1872–1968)

cauldron

ă	pat	oi	boy
ā	pay	ou	out
âr	care	ŏŏ	took
ä	father	ōō	boot
ĕ	pet	ŭ	cut
ē	be	ûr	urge
ĭ	pit	th	thin
ī	pie	th	this
îr	pier	hw	which
ŏ	pot	zh	vision
ō	toe	ə	about,
ô	paw		item

Stress marks:
′ (primary);
′ (secondary), as in
lexicon (lĕk′sĭ-kŏn′)

es 1. To be the cause of or reason for. **2.** To bring about or compel by authority or force: *The moderator invoked a rule causing the debate to be ended.* [ME < OFr. < Lat. *causa*, reason, purpose.] **—caus′a·ble** *adj.* **—cause′less** *adj.* **—caus′er** *n.*

'cause (kôz, kŭz) *conj. Informal* Because.

cause cé·lè·bre (kôz′ sə-lĕb′, kôz′ sā-lĕb′rə) *n., pl.* **causes cé·lè·bres** (kôz′ sə-lĕb′, kôz′ sā-lĕb′rə) **1.** An issue arousing widespread controversy or heated public debate. **2.** A celebrated legal case. [Fr. : *cause*, case + *célèbre*, celebrated.]

cau·se·rie (kōz-rē′) *n.* **1.** An informal discussion or chat, esp. of an intellectual nature. **2.** A short conversational piece of writing or criticism. [Fr. < *causer*, to talk < Lat. *causārī*, to plead, discuss < *causa*, case, cause.]

cause·way (kôz′wā′) *n.* **1.** A raised roadway, as across water or marshland. **2.** A paved highway. [ME *caucewei* : *cauce*, raised road (< Norman Fr. *caucie* < Med.Lat. *calciāta (via)*, paved (road) < Lat. *calx, calc-*, limestone; see CALX) + *wei*, road (var. of *way*; see WAY).]

caus·tic (kô′stĭk) *adj.* **1.** Capable of burning, corroding, dissolving, or eating away by chemical action. **2.** Corrosive and bitingly trenchant; cutting. **3.** Causing a burning or stinging sensation, as from intense emotion. ❖ *n.* **1.** A caustic material or substance. **2.** A hydroxide of a light metal. **3.** The envelope of light rays reflecting or refracting from a curved surface. [ME *caustik* < Lat. *causticus* < Gk. *kaustikos* < *kaustos* < *kaiein, kau-*, to burn.] **—caus′ti·cal·ly** *adv.* **—caus·tic′i·ty** (kô-stĭs′ĭ-tē) *n.*

caustic potash *n.* See **potassium hydroxide.**

caustic soda *n.* See **sodium hydroxide.**

cau·ter·ize (kô′tə-rīz′) *tr.v.* **-ized, -iz·ing, -iz·es 1.** To burn or sear with a cautery. **2.** To deaden, as to feelings or moral scruples; callous. [ME *cauterizen* < LLat. *cautērizāre*, to cauterize, brand < Lat. *cautērium*, cautery. See CAUTERY.] **—cau′ter·i·za′tion** (-tər-ĭ-zā′shən) *n.*

cau·ter·y (kô′tə-rē) *n., pl.* **-ies 1.** An agent or instrument, such as a laser or an electric current, used to destroy abnormal tissue by burning, searing, or scarring. **2.** The act or process of cauterizing. [ME *cauterie* < Lat. *cautērium*, branding iron, cautery < Gk. *kautērion* < *kaiein, kau-*, to burn.]

cau·tion (kô′shən) *n.* **1a.** Careful forethought to avoid danger or harm. **b.** Close attention or vigilance to minimize risk: *went over the bridge with caution.* **2.** Prudence or restraint in action or decision. **3.** A warning or admonishment, esp. to take heed: *a caution about fat in my diet.* **4.** A cautious action; a precaution. **5.** *Informal* One that is striking or alarming. ❖ *tr.v.* **-tioned, -tion·ing, -tions** To advise to take heed; warn or admonish. [ME *caucioun* < OFr. *caution* < Lat. *cautiō, cautiōn-* < *cautus*, p. part. of *cavēre*, to take care.]

cau·tion·ar·y (kô′shə-nĕr′ē) *adj.* Admonitory; warning.

cau·tious (kô′shəs) *adj.* **1.** Showing or practicing caution; careful. **2.** Tentative or restrained; guarded: *a cautious optimism.* **—cau′tious·ly** *adv.* **—cau′tious·ness** *n.*

cav. *abbr.* cavalry

Ca·va·fy (kə-vä′fē), **Constantine Peter** Orig. Konstantínos Pétrou Kaváfis. 1863–1933. Greek poet whose works include "Waiting for the Barbarians."

cav·al·cade (kăv′əl-kād′, kăv′əl-kād′) *n.* **1.** A procession of riders or horse-drawn carriages. **2.** A ceremonial procession or display. **3.** A succession or series. [Fr. < OFr. < OItal. *cavalcata* < *cavalcare*, to ride on horseback < Med.Lat. *caballicāre* < Lat. *caballus*, horse.]

cav·a·lier (kăv′ə-lîr′) *n.* **1.** A chivalrous man, esp. one serving as escort to a woman of high social position; a gentleman. **2.** A mounted soldier; a knight. **3. Cavalier** A supporter of Charles I of England in his struggles with Parliament. ❖ *adj.* **1.** Showing arrogant or offhand disregard; dismissive: *a cavalier attitude.* **2.** Carefree and nonchalant; jaunty. **3. Cavalier** Of or relating to a group of English poets associated with the court of Charles I. [Fr., horseman < OItal. *cavaliere* < LLat. *caballārius* < Lat. *caballus*, horse.] **—cav′a·lier′ly** *adv.*

ca·val·la (kə-văl′ə) *n., pl.* **-las** or **cavalla 1.** Any of various tropical marine food fishes of the family Carangidae, which includes the jacks and pompanos. **2.** See **king mackerel.** [Sp. *caballa*, horse mackerel < LLat. < Lat. *caballus*, horse.]

cav·al·ry (kăv′əl-rē) *n., pl.* **-ries 1.** A highly mobile army unit using vehicular transport. **2.** Troops trained to fight on horseback. [Fr. *cavalerie* < Ital. *cavalleria* < *cavaliere*, cavalier < OItal. See CAVALIER.] **—cav′al·ry·man** *n.*

cave (kāv) *n.* **1.** A hollow or natural passage under or into the earth, esp. one with an opening to the surface. **2.** A storage cellar, esp. for wine. ❖ *v.* **caved, cav·ing, caves** —*tr.* **1.** To cause to collapse or fall: *The impact caved in the roof of the car.* —*intr.* **1.** To fall in; collapse. **2.** To give up all opposition: *caved in to our demands.* **3.** To explore caves. [ME < OFr. *cava* < neut. pl. of *cavus*, hollow.]

ca·ve·at (kăv′ē-ät′, kăv′ē-, kä′vē-ät′) *n.* **1.** A warning or caution. **2.** A qualification or explanation. [< Lat., let him beware, third pers. sing. pr. subjunctive of *cavēre*, to beware.]

caveat emp·tor (ĕmp′tôr′) *n.* The axiom or principle in commerce that the buyer alone is responsible for assessing the quality of a purchase before buying. [< Lat. *caveat ēmptor*, let the buyer beware : *caveat*, third pers. sing. pr. subjunctive of *cavēre*, to

beware + *ēmptor*, buyer.]

cave dweller *n.* One that dwells in a cave, esp. a prehistoric human. **—cave′-dwell′ing** (kāv′dwĕl′ĭng) *adj.*

cave·fish (kāv′fĭsh′) *n., pl.* **cavefish** or **-fish·es** Any of various freshwater fishes of the family Amblyopsidae, found in subterranean waters and having nonfunctioning eyes.

cave-in (kāv′ĭn′) *n.* **1a.** A collapse, as of a tunnel. **b.** A place of a cave-in. **2.** An act of yielding.

Cav·ell (kăv′əl, kə-vĕl′), **Edith Louisa** 1865–1915. British nurse who remained in Brussels after the German occupation (1915) to help smuggle Allied troops to the Dutch border.

cave·man also **cave man** (kāv′măn′) *n.* **1.** A prehistoric or primitive human living in caves. **2.** *Informal* A man who is crude or brutal, esp. toward women. **—cave′man′** *adj.*

Cav·en·dish (kăv′ən-dĭsh), **Henry** 1731–1810. British chemist and physicist who established that water is a compound of hydrogen and oxygen.

cav·er (kā′vər) *n.* **1.** One that caves. **2.** One who explores or studies caves.

cav·ern (kăv′ərn) *n.* **1.** A large cave. **2.** A large underground chamber, as in a cave. ❖ *tr.v.* **-erned, -ern·ing, -erns 1.** To enclose in or as if in a cavern. **2.** To hollow out. [ME *caverne* < OFr. < Lat. *caverna* < *cavus*, hollow.]

cav·ern·ous (kăv′ər-nəs) *adj.* **1.** Filled with caverns. **2.** Resembling a cavern, as in depth or vastness. **3.** *Anatomy* Filled with cavities or hollow areas. **—cav′ern·ous·ly** *adv.*

ca·vet·to (kə-vĕt′ō) *n., pl.* **-vet·ti** (-vĕt′ē) or **-vet·tos** A concave molding with a cross section that approximates a quarter circle. [Ital., dim. of *cavo*, hollow < Lat. *cavus.*]

cav·i·ar also **cav·i·are** (kăv′ē-är′, kä′vē-) *n.* The roe of a large fish, esp. sturgeon, eaten as a delicacy or relish. [Alteration of *caviarie* (prob. < obsolete Ital. *caviari*, pl. of *caviaro*), or < Fr. *caviare*, both < Turk. *havyar* < Pers. *khāvyār*; akin to *khāyah*, egg < MPers. *khāyak*. See **awi-** in App.]

cav·il (kăv′əl) *v.* **-iled, -il·ing, -ils** also **-illed, -il·ling, -ils** —*intr.* To find fault unnecessarily; raise trivial objections. —*tr.* To quibble about; detect petty flaws in. ❖ *n.* A carping or trivial objection. [Fr. *caviller* < OFr. < Lat. *cavillārī*, to jeer < *cavilla*, a jeering.] **—cav′il·er** *n.*

cav·i·ta·tion (kăv′ĭ-tā′shən) *n.* **1.** The sudden formation and collapse of low-pressure bubbles in liquids by means of mechanical forces, such as those resulting from rotation of a propeller. **2.** The pitting of a solid surface. **3.** *Medicine* The formation of cavities in a tissue or an organ, esp. those formed in the lung as a result of tuberculosis. [< CAVITY.] **—cav′i·tate′** *v.*

cav·i·ty (kăv′ĭ-tē) *n., pl.* **-ties 1.** A hollow; a hole. **2.** A hollow area within the body: *a sinus cavity.* **3.** A pitted area in a tooth caused by caries. [Fr. *cavité* < LLat. *cavitās* < Lat. *cavus*, hollow.]

ca·vort (kə-vôrt′) *intr.v.* **-vort·ed, -vort·ing, -vorts 1.** To bound or prance about in a sprightly manner; caper. **2.** To have lively fun; romp. [Poss. alteration of CURVET.]

Ca·vour (kə-voor′, kä-voor′), **Conte Camillo Benso di** 1810–61. Italian political leader who was premier of Sardinia (1852–59 and 1860–61) and helped unify Italy.

ca·vy (kā′vē) *n., pl.* **-vies 1.** Any of various tailless South American rodents of the family Caviidae, which includes the guinea pig. **2.** Any of various similar or related rodents, such as the coypu. [< NLat. *Cavia*, genus name, perh. < Galibi *cabiai.*]

caw (kô) *n.* The hoarse raucous sound that is characteristic of a crow or similar bird. [Imit.] **—caw** *v.*

Cawn·pore (kôn′pôr′, -pōr′) See **Kanpur.**

Ca·xi·as (kə-shē′əs), Duke of. Title of Luiz Alves de Lima y Silva. 1803–80. Brazilian general and politician who served as minister of war.

Caxias do Sul (də sool′) A city of S Brazil N of Pôrto Alegre. Pop. 290,969.

Cax·ton (kăk′stən), **William** 1422?–91. English printer of the first book in English, a history of Troy (c. 1475).

cay (kē, kā) *n.* A small low island composed largely of coral or sand. [Alteration (influenced by QUAY) of Sp. *cayo*, prob. < Taino.]

Cay·enne (kī-ĕn′, kā-) The cap. of French Guiana, on **Cayenne Island** at the mouth of the **Cayenne River;** founded by the French in 1664. Pop. 41,164.

cayenne pepper *n.* An orange-red to dark red condiment consisting of the ground ripe fruits of any of several pungent varieties of capsicum. [Alteration (by folk ety. < CAYENNE) of *kian, chian* < Tupi *quiínia*, hot pepper.]

cay·man (kā′mən) *n.* Variant of **caiman.**

Cayman Islands A British-administered island group in the Caribbean Sea NW of Jamaica, including **Grand Cayman, Little Cayman,** and **Cayman Brac.** Cap. Georgetown. Pop. 30,000.

Ca·yu·ga (kā-yōō′gə, kī-) *n., pl.* **Cayuga** or **-gas 1.** A member of a Native American people formerly inhabiting the shores of Cayuga Lake in west-central New York, with present-day populations in Ontario, western New York, Wisconsin, and Oklahoma. **2.** The Iroquoian language spoken by the Cayuga.

Cayuga Lake A lake of W-central NY, the longest of the Finger Lakes.

cay·use (kī-yōōs′, kī′yōōs′) *n. Pacific Northwest* A horse, esp. an Indian pony. [Short for *cayuse pony* < CAYUSE.]

causeway
crossing Pigeon Key, the
Florida Keys

REGIONAL NOTE The noun *cayuse* comes from the name of the Cayuse people in the Pacific Northwest. *Cayuse* is used chiefly in the territory of the word's origin—the states of Washington, Oregon, and Idaho—although its use has also spread into other Western states. A verb meaning "to buck," derived from the noun, is cited by Ramon F. Adams in *Old-Time Cowhand* (1961): "What cowboys in other sections called *buckin'*, the Texan called *pitchin'*, and a term used in South Texas, though seldom heard in other sections, was *cayusein'*."

Cayuse *n., pl.* **Cayuse** or **-us•es 1.** A member of a Native American people of northeast Oregon and southeast Washington. **2a.** Their extinct traditional language. **b.** The dialect of Nez Perce spoken by the Cayuse in the 19th and 20th centuries.
CB *abbr.* citizens band
CBC *abbr.* **1.** Canadian Broadcasting Corporation **2.** complete blood count
CBW *abbr.* chemical and biological warfare
cc *abbr.* **1.** carbon copy **2.** cubic centimeter
cc. *abbr.* chapters
CCA *abbr.* Circuit Court of Appeals
CCC *abbr.* **1.** Civilian Conservation Corps **2.** Commodity Credit Corporation
CCD *abbr.* Confraternity of Christian Doctrine
CCK *abbr.* cholecystokinin
C clef *n. Music* A symbol indicating which line of a staff represents the pitch of middle C. On the bottom line it becomes the soprano clef, on the middle line the alto clef, and on the third line above the bottom the tenor clef.
CCTV *abbr.* closed-circuit television
CCU *abbr.* coronary care unit
cd *abbr.* candela
Cd The symbol for the element **cadmium.**
CD *abbr.* **1.** also **C/D** certificate of deposit **2.** civil defense **3.** compact disk **4.** *French* corps diplomatique (diplomatic corps)
cd. *abbr.* cord
CD4 (sē′dē-fôr′, -fôr′) *n.* A glycoprotein on the surface of helper T cells that serves as a receptor for HIV. [*c(luster of) d(ifferentiation antigen) 4.*]
CD8 (sē′dē-āt′) *n.* A glycoprotein on the surface of killer cells that enhances binding with molecules of the major histocompatibility complex. [*c(luster of) d(ifferentiation antigen) 8.*]
CDC *abbr.* Centers for Disease Control and Prevention
CD-I *abbr.* compact disk–interactive
CDR *abbr.* commander
CD-R *abbr.* compact disk–recordable
CD-ROM (sē′dē-rŏm′) *n.* A compact disk that functions as read-only memory.
CD-RW *abbr.* compact disk–rewritable
CDT *abbr.* Central Daylight Time
Ce The symbol for the element **cerium.**
C.E. or **c.e.** *abbr.* Common Era
ce•a•no•thus (sē′ə-nô′thəs) *n.* Any of various shrubs or small trees of the genus *Ceanothus,* native to western North America and having showy clusters of usu. blue or whitish flowers. [NLat. *Ceanothus,* genus name < Gk. *keanothos,* corn thistle.]
cease (sēs) *v.* **ceased, ceas•ing, ceas•es** —*tr.* To put an end to; discontinue. See Syns at **stop.** —*intr.* **1.** To come to an end; stop. **2.** To stop performing; desist. ❖ *n.* Cessation; pause. [ME *cesen* < OFr. *cesser* < Lat. *cessāre,* to stop, freq. of *cēdere,* to yield.]
cease-fire or **cease•fire** (sēs′fīr′) *n.* **1.** An order to stop firing. **2.** Suspension of active hostilities; a truce.
cease•less (sēs′lĭs) *adj.* Without stop or pause. See Syns at **continual.** —**cease′less•ly** *adv.* —**cease′less•ness** *n.*
Ceau•ses•cu (chou-shĕs′kōō), **Nicolae** 1918–89. Romanian politician who ruled as dictator (1965–89).
Ce•bu (sĕ-bōō′) An island of the central Philippines in the Visayan Is. between Leyte and Negros. The city of **Cebu** is an important harbor on the E coast. Pop. 688,196.
Cech (chĕk), **Thomas Robert** b. 1947. Amer. biochemist who shared a 1989 Nobel Prize in chemistry.
Cec•il (sĕs′əl), **(Edgar Algernon) Robert.** 1st Viscount Cranborne and 1st Earl of Salisbury. 1864–1958. British public official who won the 1937 Nobel Peace Prize.
Cecil, Robert Arthur Talbot Gascoyne. 3rd Marquis of Salisbury. 1830–1903. British politician who served as prime minister (1885–92 and 1895–1902).
Cecil, William. 1st Baron Burghley *or* Burleigh. 1520–98. English politician and chief adviser to Elizabeth I.
ce•cro•pi•a moth (sĭ-krō′pē-ə) *n.* A large North American silkworm moth (*Hyalophora cecropia*) having wings with red, white, and black markings. [NLat. *cecropia,* specific epithet < Lat., fem. of *Cecropius,* Athenian < Gk. *Kekropios* < *Kekrops,* Cecrops, a legendary Athenian knight.]
ce•cum also **cae•cum** (sē′kəm) *n., pl.* **-ca** (-kə) **1.** A saclike cavity with only one opening. **2.** *Anatomy* The large blind pouch forming the beginning of the large intestine. [ME < Lat. *(intestīnum) caecum,* blind (intestine), neut. of *caecus,* blind.] —**ce′cal** *adj.* —**ce′cal•ly** *adv.*
ce•dar (sē′dər) *n.* **1.** Any of several Old World evergreen coniferous trees of the genus *Cedrus,* having stiff needles and large seed

cones. **2.** Any of several other evergreen coniferous trees or shrubs, such as the incense cedar or red cedar. **3.** The durable aromatic wood of any of these plants. [ME *cedre* < OFr. < Lat. *cedrus* < Gk. *kedros.*]
ce•dar•bird (sē′dər-bûrd′) *n.* See **cedar waxwing.**
cedar of Lebanon *n., pl.* **cedars of Lebanon** A large, long-lived cedar (*Cedrus libani*) native to Lebanon and Turkey.
Cedar Rapids A city of E-central IA on the Cedar R. WNW of Davenport. Pop. 120,758.
Cedar River A river rising in SE MN and flowing c. 531 km (330 mi) to the Iowa R. in SE IA.
cedar waxwing *n.* A North American bird (*Bombycilla cedrorum*) having a crested head, a yellow-tipped tail, and predominantly brown plumage.
cede (sēd) *tr.v.* **ced•ed, ced•ing, cedes 1.** To surrender possession of, esp. by treaty. See Syns at **relinquish. 2.** To yield; grant. [Fr. *céder* < OFr. < Lat. *cēdere.*]
ce•di (sā′dē) *n., pl.* **-dis** See table at **currency.** [Poss. < Akan (Fante) *sedī,* small shell, cowry.]
ce•dil•la (sĭ-dĭl′ə) *n.* A mark (̧) placed beneath the letter *c,* as in the French word *garçon,* to indicate that the letter is to be pronounced (s). [Obsolete Sp., dim. of *ceda,* the letter *z* (a small *z* having once been used after, and later below, a *c* to indicate that the hard *c* was pronounced like *s* or *z*) < LLat. *zeta,* zeta. See ZETA.]
cee (sē) *n.* The letter *c.*
cei•ba (sā′bə) *n.* The silk-cotton tree. [Sp., prob. of Arawakan orig.]
ceil (sēl) *tr.v.* **ceiled, ceil•ing, ceils** To provide or cover with a ceiling. [ME *celen,* prob. < OFr. **celer* < Lat. *caelāre,* to carve < *caelum,* chisel.]
ceil•ing (sē′lĭng) *n.* **1a.** The upper interior surface of a room. **b.** Material used to cover this surface. **2.** Something resembling a ceiling. **3.** An upper limit, esp. as set by regulation. **4a.** The highest altitude under particular weather conditions from which the ground is still visible. **b.** The altitude of the lowest layer of clouds. **c.** Absolute ceiling. **5.** *Nautical* The planking applied to the interior framework of a ship. [ME *celing* < *celen,* to ceil. See CEIL.] —**ceil′inged** *adj.*
ceil•om•e•ter (sē-lŏm′ĭ-tər) *n.* An instrument for ascertaining cloud heights. [CEIL(ING) + −METER.]
Ce•la (sā′lä, thä′-), **Camilo José** b. 1916. Spanish writer who won the 1989 Nobel Prize for literature.
cel•a•don (sĕl′ə-dŏn′) *n.* **1.** A pale to very pale green. **2.** A type of pottery having a pale green glaze. [Fr., after *Céladon,* a character of Honoré d'Urfé (1568–1625), French writer, after *Celadōn,* a character in Ovid's *Metamorphoses.*] —**cel′a•don′** *adj.*
cel•an•dine (sĕl′ən-dīn′, -dēn′) *n.* **1.** A perennial Eurasian herb (*Chelidonium majus*) having showy yellow flowers and yellow-orange latex. **2.** The lesser celandine. [ME *celidoine,* ult. < Gk. *khelīdonion* < *khelīdōn,* swallow (the blossoming of the plant being associated with the return of the swallows in spring).]
celandine poppy *n.* A perennial herb (*Stylophorum diphyllum*) native to midwest North America and similar to the celandine.
–cele[1] *suff.* Tumor; hernia: *cystocele.* [< Gk. *kēlē,* tumor.]
–cele[2] *suff.* Variant of −**coel.**
cel•eb (sə-lĕb′) *n. Informal* A celebrity.
Cel•e•bes (sĕl′ə-bēz′, sə-lē′bēz′, sē-lā′bĕs) See Sulawesi.
Celebes Sea A section of the W Pacific Ocean between Sulawesi and the S Philippines connected with the Java Sea by Makassar Strait.
cel•e•brant (sĕl′ə-brənt) *n.* **1a.** A person who participates in a religious ceremony or rite. **b.** A person who officiates at a religious or civil ceremony or rite, esp. a wedding. **c.** In some Christian churches, the cleric officiating at the celebration of the Eucharist. **2.** A participant in a celebration.

USAGE NOTE Strictly speaking, *celebrant* should be reserved for an official participant in a religious ceremony or rite. In an earlier survey, however, a majority of the Usage Panel accepted the use of *celebrant* to mean "a participant in a celebration" (as in *New Year's Eve celebrants*). In this more general sense, *celebrator* is an undisputed alternative.

cel•e•brate (sĕl′ə-brāt′) *v.* **-brat•ed, -brat•ing, -brates** —*tr.* **1.** To observe (a day or event) with ceremonies of respect, festivity, or rejoicing. **2.** To perform (a religious ceremony). **3.** To extol or praise. **4.** To make widely known; display. —*intr.* **1.** To observe an occasion with appropriate festivity. **2.** To perform a religious ceremony. **3.** To engage in festivities: *celebrated after the victory.* [ME *celebraten* < Lat. *celebrāre, celebrāt-,* to frequent, celebrate < *celeber, celebr-,* frequented, famous.] —**cel′e•bra′tion** *n.* —**cel′e•bra′tor** *n.* —**cel′e•bra•to′ry** (sĕl′ə-brə-tôr′ē, -tōr′ē, sə-lĕb′rə-) *adj.*
cel•e•brat•ed (sĕl′ə-brā′tĭd) *adj.* Known and praised widely; noted. See Syns at **noted.**
ce•leb•ri•ty (sə-lĕb′rĭ-tē) *n., pl.* **-ties 1.** A famous person. **2.** Renown; fame. [ME *celebrite,* fame < OFr. < Lat. *celebritās* < *celeber,* famous.] —**ce•leb′ri•ty•hood′** *n.*
ce•le•ri•ac (sə-lĭr′ē-ăk′, -lĕr′-) *n.* An edible variety of celery (*Apium graveolens* var. *rapaceum*) cultivated for its knobby root. [Alteration of CELERY.]
ce•ler•i•ty (sə-lĕr′ĭ-tē) *n.* Swiftness of action or motion; speed.

C clef

cecropia moth
Hyalophora cecropia

ă	pat	oi	boy
ā	pay	ou	out
âr	care	ōō	took
ä	father	ōō	boot
ĕ	be	ûr	urge
ĕ	pet	ŭ	cut
ē	be		
ĭ	pit	th	thin
ī	pie	th	this
îr	pier	hw	which
ŏ	pot	zh	vision
ō	toe	ə	about,
ô	paw		item

Stress marks:
′ (primary);
′ (secondary), as in
lexicon (lĕk′sĭ-kŏn′)

See Syns at **haste.** [Fr. *célérité* < OFr. < Lat. *celeritās* < *celer,* swift.]

cel·er·y (sĕl′ə-rē) *n., pl.* **-ies 1.** A biennial European plant (*Apium graveolens* var. *dulce*) in the parsley family, having edible roots, leafstalks, leaves, and fruits. **2.** The crisp thick leafstalks of this plant. **3.** The seedlike fruits of this plant used as a flavoring. [Fr. *céleri* < Ital. dialectal *seleri,* pl. of *selero,* alteration of LLat. *selīnon,* parsley < Gk.]

celery cabbage *n.* **1.** See **Chinese cabbage** 1. **2.** See **bok choy.**

celery root *n.* See **celeriac.**

ce·les·ta (sə-lĕs′tə) also **ce·leste** (-lĕst′) *n.* A musical instrument with a keyboard and metal plates struck by hammers that produce bell-like tones. [Fr. *célesta* < *céleste,* celestial < Lat. *caelestis.* See CELESTIAL.]

ce·les·tial (sə-lĕs′chəl) *adj.* **1.** Of or relating to the sky or the heavens. **2.** Of or relating to heaven; divine. **3.** Supremely good; sublime. **4. Celestial** Of or relating to the Chinese people or to the former Chinese Empire. ❖ *n.* A heavenly being; a god or angel. [ME < OFr. < Med.Lat. *celestiālis* < Lat. *caelestis* < *caelum,* sky.] —**ce·les′tial·ly** *adv.*

Celestial Empire An old name for China or the Chinese Empire.

celestial equator *n.* A great circle on the celestial sphere in the same plane as the earth's equator.

celestial globe *n.* A model of the celestial sphere showing the positions of the stars and other celestial bodies.

celestial horizon *n.* A great circle on the celestial sphere having a plane that passes through the center of the earth and is parallel to an observer's horizon.

celestial mechanics *n.* (*used with a sing. verb*) The science of the motion of celestial bodies under the influence of gravitational forces.

celestial navigation *n.* Navigation of a ship or aircraft based on the positions of celestial bodies.

celestial pole *n.* Either of two diametrically opposite points at which the extensions of the earth's axis intersect the celestial sphere.

celestial sphere *n.* An imaginary sphere of infinite extent with the earth at its center on which the stars, planets, and other heavenly bodies appear to be located.

cel·es·tine (sĕl′ĭ-stīn′, -stīn′, sə-lĕs′tīn, -tĭn) *n.* See **celestite.** [Ger. *Zölestin* < Lat. *caelestis,* celestial. See CELESTIAL.]

cel·es·tite (sĕl′ĭ-stīt′, sə-lĕs′tīt′) *n.* A white, red-brown, orange, or light blue strontium ore, essentially strontium sulfate, $SrSO_4$, found in sedimentary rock. [CELEST(INE) + -ITE.]

ce·li·ac also **coe·li·ac** (sē′lē-ăk′) *adj.* Of or relating to the abdomen or abdominal cavity. [Lat. *coeliacus* < Gk. *koiliakos* < *koiliā,* abdomen < *koilos,* hollow.]

celiac disease *n.* A chronic nutritional disturbance, usu. of young children, caused by the inability to metabolize gluten and resulting in malnutrition and a distended abdomen.

cel·i·ba·cy (sĕl′ə-bə-sē) *n.* **1.** Sexual abstinence, esp. for religious vows. **2.** The condition of being unmarried.

cel·i·bate (sĕl′ə-bĭt) *adj.* **1.** Practicing sexual abstinence, esp. for religious vows. **2.** Unmarried; unwed. [Lat. *caelibātus* < *caelebs,* *caelib-,* unmarried.] —**cel′i·bate** *n.*

> **USAGE NOTE** Historically, *celibate* means only "unmarried"; its use to mean "abstaining from sexual intercourse" is a 20th-century development. The more recent use of the word seems to have displaced the old, and the use of *celibate* in its older sense is almost sure to invite misinterpretation in other than narrowly ecclesiastical contexts. Sixty-eight percent of the Usage Panel rejected the older use in the sentence *He remained celibate* [unmarried], *although he engaged in sexual intercourse.*

cell (sĕl) *n.* **1.** A narrow confining room, as in a prison. **2.** A small enclosed cavity or space, as in a honeycomb. **3.** *Biology* The smallest structural unit of an organism that is capable of independent functioning, consisting of one or more nuclei, cytoplasm, and various organelles, all surrounded by a semipermeable cell membrane. **4.** *Architecture* See **web** 11. **5.** The smallest organizational unit of a centralized group or movement. **6.** *Electricity* **a.** A single unit for electrolysis or conversion of chemical into electric energy, usu. consisting of a container with electrodes and an electrolyte. **b.** A single unit that converts radiant energy into electric energy. **7.** *Computer Science* A basic unit of storage in a computer memory that can hold one unit of information. **8.** A geographic area or zone surrounding a transmitter in a cellular telephone system. **9.** A small humble abode, such as a hermit's hut. **10.** A small religious house dependent on a larger one. **11.** A box or other unit on a spreadsheet or similar array at the intersection of a column and a row. **12.** A storm cell. **13.** A fuel cell. ❖ *v.* **celled,** **cell·ing, cells** —*tr.* To store in a honeycomb. —*intr.* To live in or share a prison cell. [ME *celle* < OE *cell* and < OFr., both < Lat. *cella,* chamber. See kel- in App.]

cel·la (sĕl′ə) *n., pl.* **cel·lae** (sĕl′ē) The inner room or sanctuary of an ancient Greek or Roman temple. [Lat. See kel- in App.]

cel·lar (sĕl′ər) *n.* **1.** A room or enclosed space used for storage, usu. beneath the ground or under a building. **2.** A basement. **3.** An underground shelter, as from storms. **4.** A wine cellar. **5.** *Slang* The last place or lowest level. ❖ *tr.v.* **-lared, -lar·ing, -lars** To store in a cellar. [ME *celer* < OFr. < LLat. *cellārium,* pantry

< Lat. *cella,* storeroom. See kel- in App.]

cel·lar·age (sĕl′ər-ĭj) *n.* **1.** A fee charged for storage in a cellar. **2.** A cellar or several cellars.

cel·lar·er (sĕl′ər-ər) *n.* A person, as in a monastic community, responsible for maintaining the supply of food and drink. [ME *celerer* < OFr. < Lat. *cellārius,* steward < *cella,* storeroom. See kel- in App.]

cel·lar·ette also **cel·lar·et** (sĕl′ə-rĕt′) *n.* A cabinet for storing bottles of wine or liquor.

cell·block (sĕl′blŏk′) *n.* A group of cells that make up a section or unit of a prison.

cell body *n.* The portion of a nerve cell that contains the nucleus but does not incorporate the dendrites or axon.

cell cycle *n.* The series of events involving the growth, replication, and division of a eukaryotic cell.

cell division *n.* The process by which a cell divides to form two daughter cells, each of which contains the same genetic material as the original cell and roughly half of its cytoplasm.

Cel·li·ni (chə-lē′nē, chĕ-), **Benvenuto** 1500–71. Italian writer and sculptor known for his *Autobiography.*

cell·mate (sĕl′māt′) *n.* A person sharing a cell, esp. in prison.

cell-mediated immunity *n.* See **cellular immunity.**

cell membrane *n.* The semipermeable membrane that encloses the cytoplasm of a cell.

cel·lo[1] (chĕl′ō) *n., pl.* **-los** A four-stringed instrument of the violin family, lower than the viola but higher than the double bass. [Short for VIOLONCELLO.] —**cel′list** (chĕl′ĭst) *n.*

cel·lo[2] (sĕl′ō) *n.* Cellophane. —**cel·lo** *adj.*

cel·loi·din (sə-loid′n) *n.* A pure form of pyroxylin in which specimens for microscopic examination are embedded. [CELL(ULOSE) + -OID + -IN.]

cel·lo·phane (sĕl′ə-fān′) *n.* A thin, flexible, transparent cellulose material made from wood pulp and used as a moistureproof wrapping. [Orig. a trademark.] —**cel′lo·phane′** *adj.*

cellophane noodle *n.* A thin transparent noodle.

cell phone *n.* A cellular telephone.

cell plate *n.* A partition formed during cell division in plants and some algae that separates the two new daughter cells.

cell sap *n.* The liquid contained within a vacuole of a plant cell.

cel·lu·lar (sĕl′yə-lər) *adj.* **1.** Of, relating to, or resembling a cell. **2.** Consisting of or containing a cell or cells: *the cellular construction of a beehive.* **3.** Of or involving the cells of an organization or movement. [< Lat. *cellula,* cellule. See CELLULE.] —**cel′lu·lar′i·ty** (-lăr′ĭ-tē) *n.* —**cel′lu·lar·ly** *adv.*

cellular immunity *n.* Immunity resulting from the action of T cells on foreign antigens.

cellular respiration *n.* The series of metabolic processes by which living cells produce energy through the oxidation of organic substances.

cellular slime mold *n.* See **slime mold** 1.

cellular telephone also **cellular phone** *n.* A mobile radiotelephone that uses a network of short-range transmitters in overlapping cells and a central station making connections to telephone lines.

cel·lu·lase (sĕl′yə-lās′, -lāz′) *n.* Any of several enzymes produced chiefly by fungi, bacteria, and protozoans that catalyze the hydrolysis of cellulose. [CELLUL(OSE) + -ASE.]

cel·lule (sĕl′yōol) *n.* A small cell. [Fr. < Lat. *cellula,* dim. of *cella,* chamber. See CELLA.]

cel·lu·lite (sĕl′yə-līt′, -lēt′) *n.* A fatty deposit, as around the thighs. [Fr. : *cellule,* cellule; see CELLULE + -*ite,* disease (< NLat. -*ītis,* -itis).]

cel·lu·li·tis (sĕl′yə-lī′tĭs) *n.* A spreading inflammation of subcutaneous or connective tissue. [CELLUL(E) + -ITIS.]

cel·lu·loid (sĕl′yə-loid′) *n.* **1.** A colorless flammable material made from nitrocellulose and camphor and used to make photographic film. **2.** The cinema. ❖ *adj.* **1.** Made of or using celluloid. **2.** Of or portrayed on film or in motion pictures. **3.** Artificial; synthetic. [Orig. a trademark.]

cel·lu·lo·lyt·ic (sĕl′yə-lō-lĭt′ĭk) *adj.* Of, relating to, or causing the hydrolysis of cellulose. [CELLULO(SE) + -LYTIC.]

cel·lu·lose (sĕl′yə-lōs′, -lōz′) *n.* A complex carbohydrate, $(C_6H_{10}O_5)_n$, that is composed of glucose units, forms the main constituent of the cell wall in most plants, and is important in the manufacture of numerous products, such as paper and explosives. [Fr. < *cellule,* biological cell. See CELLULE.] —**cel′lu·lo′sic** (-lō′sĭk, -zĭk) *adj.*

cellulose acetate *n.* Any of several compounds obtained by treating cellulose with acetic anhydride, used in lacquers, photographic film, transparent sheeting, and cigarette filters.

cellulose nitrate *n.* See **nitrocellulose.**

cell wall *n.* The rigid outermost cell layer found in plants and certain algae, bacteria, and fungi but characteristically absent from animal cells.

ce·lom (sē′ləm) *n.* Variant of **coelom.**

ce·lo·sia (sə-lō′zhə, -zhē-) *n.* See **cockscomb** 3. [NLat. *Cēlosia,* genus name < Gk. *kēlos,* burnt < *kaiein,* to burn.]

Cel·si·us (sĕl′sē-əs, -shəs) *adj.* Of or relating to a temperature scale that registers the freezing point of water as 0° and the boiling point as 100° under normal atmospheric pressure. See table at **measurement.** [After Anders CELSIUS.]

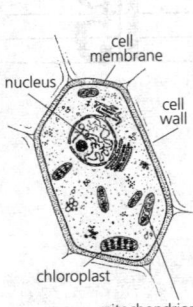

cell
membrane

nucleus

cell
wall

chloroplast

mitochondrion

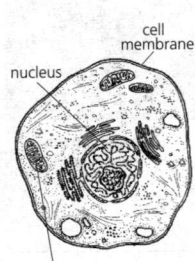

cell
membrane

nucleus

mitochondrion

cell
top: plant cell
bottom: animal cell

Celsius, Anders 1701–44. Swedish astronomer who devised (1742) the centigrade thermometer.

celt (sĕlt) *n.* A common prehistoric tool of stone or metal, shaped like a chisel or ax head. [Med.Lat. *celtis,* chisel.]

Celt (kĕlt, sĕlt) also **Kelt** (kĕlt) *n.* **1.** One of an Indo-European people originally of central Europe and spreading to western Europe and the British Isles and southeast to Galatia during pre-Roman times, esp. a Briton or Gaul. **2.** A native speaker of a modern Celtic language or a descendant of such a speaker. [Fr. *Celte,* sing. of *Celtes,* Celts < Lat. *Celtae* < Gk. *Keltoi.*]

Celt•i•ber•i•an (kĕl′tĭ-bĕr′ē-ən, sĕl′-) *n.* **1.** One of an ancient Celtic people of northern Spain. **2.** The language of this people. **—Celt′i•ber′i•an** *adj.*

Celt•ic (kĕl′tĭk, sĕl′-) also **Kelt•ic** (kĕl′-) *n.* A subfamily of the Indo-European language family comprising the Insular and Continental branches. ❖ *adj.* Of or relating to the Celtic people and languages.

Celtic cross *n.* A Latin cross with a circle superimposed on its center.

Celt•i•cism (kĕl′tĭ-sĭz′əm, sĕl′-) *n.* **1.** A Celtic custom. **2.** A Celtic idiom. **3.** A fondness for Celtic culture.

Celt•i•cist (kĕl′tĭ-sĭst, sĕl′-) *n.* A specialist in Celtic culture or Celtic languages.

cem•ba•lo (chĕm′bə-lō′) *n., pl.* **-los** A harpsichord. [Ital., short for *clavicembalo* < Med.Lat. *clāvicymbalum* : Lat. *clāvis,* key + Lat. *cymbalum,* cymbal; see CYMBAL.] **—cem′ba•list** (-bə-lĭst) *n.*

ce•ment (sĭ-mĕnt′) *n.* **1a.** A building material made by grinding calcined limestone and clay to a fine powder, which can be mixed with water and poured to set as a solid mass or used in making mortar or concrete. **b.** Portland cement. **c.** Concrete. **2.** A substance that hardens to act as an adhesive; glue. **3.** Something that binds or unites. **4.** *Geology* A chemically precipitated substance that binds particles of clastic rocks. **5.** *Dentistry* A substance used for filling cavities or anchoring restorations. **6.** Variant of **cementum.** ❖ *v.* **-ment•ed, -ment•ing, -ments** *—tr.* **1.** To bind with or as if with cement. **2.** To cover or coat with cement. *—intr.* To become cemented. ***—idiom:* in cement** Firmly settled; unalterable. [ME < OFr. *ciment* < Lat. *caementum,* rough-cut stone, rubble used in making concrete < *caedere,* to cut.] **—ce•ment′er** *n.*

ce•men•ta•tion (sē′mĕn-tā′shən) *n.* **1.** The act, process, or result of cementing. **2.** A metallurgical coating process in which iron or steel is immersed in a powder of another metal, such as zinc or chromium, and heated to a temperature below the melting point of either.

ce•ment•ite (sĭ-mĕn′tīt′) *n.* A hard brittle iron carbide, Fe_3C, found in steel with more than 0.85 percent carbon. [< CEMENT.]

ce•men•ti•tious (sē′mĕn-tĭsh′əs) *adj.* Of or relating to a chemical precipitate having the characteristics of cement. [< Lat. *caementīcius,* made of uncut stones or rubble < *caementum,* uncut stone. See CEMENT.]

cement mixer *n.* A machine having a revolving drum in which cement, sand, gravel, and water are combined into concrete.

ce•men•tum (sĭ-mĕn′təm) also **ce•ment** (-mĕnt′) *n.* A bonelike substance covering the root of a tooth. [NLat. < Lat. *caementum,* rough stone. See CEMENT.]

cem•e•ter•y (sĕm′ĭ-tĕr′ē) *n., pl.* **-ies** A place for burying the dead; a graveyard. [ME *cimiterie* < OFr. *cimitiere* < Med.Lat. *cimitērium* < LLat. *coemētērium* < Gk. *koimētērion* < *koimān,* to put to sleep. See **kei-**[1] in App.]

cen•a•cle (sĕn′ə-kəl) *n.* **1.** A clique or circle, esp. of writers. **2.** A small dining room, usu. on an upper floor. [Fr. *cénacle* < OFr., the room where the Last Supper took place < Lat. *cēnāculum,* dining room, garret < *cēna,* meal; see **sker-**[1] in App., Sense 2, ME < OFr. < Lat. *cēnāculum.*]

–cene *suff.* Recent. Used in names of geological periods: *Oligocene.* [< Gk. *kainos,* new.]

Ce•nis (sə-nē′), **Mont** A mountain pass, 2,083.5 m (6,831 ft), in the Alps on the French-Italian border.

ceno– *pref.* Variant of **coeno–.**

cen•o•bite also **coen•o•bite** (sĕn′ə-bīt′, sē′nə-) *n.* A member of a convent or other religious community. [ME < LLat. *coenobīta,* ult. < Gk. *koinobios,* living in community : *koinos,* common; see **kom** in App. + *bios,* life; see **gʷeiə-** in App.] **—cen′o•bit′ic** (-bĭt′ĭk), **cen′o•bit′i•cal** *adj.*

cen•o•taph (sĕn′ə-tăf′) *n.* A monument honoring a dead person whose remains lie elsewhere. [Fr. *cénotaphe* < OFr. < Lat. *cenotaphium* < Gk. *kenotaphion* : *kenos,* empty + *taphos,* tomb.]

ce•no•te (sə-nō′tē) *n.* A water-filled limestone sinkhole of the Yucatán. [Am.Sp. < Yucatec *ts'onot.*]

Cen•o•zo•ic (sĕn′ə-zō′ĭk, sē′nə-) *adj.* Of or belonging to the most recent era of geologic time, between approx. 65 million years ago and the present, characterized by the formation of modern continents and the diversification of animals and plants. See table at **geologic time.** ❖ *n.* The Cenozoic Era or its deposits. [Gk. *kainos,* new + –ZOIC.]

cense (sĕns) *tr.v.* **censed, cens•ing, cens•es 1.** To perfume with incense. **2.** To burn incense to. [ME *censen,* short for *encensen* < *encens,* incense. See INCENSE[2].]

cen•ser (sĕn′sər) *n.* A vessel in which incense is burned, esp. during religious services. [ME, short for *encenser* < AN *encensier* < *encens,* incense < OFr. See INCENSE[2].]

cen•sor (sĕn′sər) *n.* **1.** One authorized to examine books, films, or other material and suppress what is considered objectionable. **2.** An official who examines personal mail and official dispatches to remove information considered secret or a security risk. **3.** One that condemns or censures. **4.** One of two officials in ancient Rome responsible for the public census and public morals. **5.** *Psychology* The agent in the unconscious that is responsible for censorship. ❖ *tr.v.* **-sored, -sor•ing, -sors** To examine and expurgate. [Lat. *cēnsor,* Roman censor < *cēnsēre,* to assess.] **—cen′sor•a•ble** *adj.* **—cen•so′ri•al** (sĕn-sôr′ē-əl, -sōr′-) *adj.*

cen•so•ri•ous (sĕn-sôr′ē-əs, -sōr′-) *adj.* **1.** Tending to censure; highly critical. **2.** Expressing censure. **—cen•so′ri•ous•ly** *adv.* **—cen•so′ri•ous•ness** *n.*

cen•sor•ship (sĕn′sər-shĭp′) *n.* **1.** The act, process, or practice of censoring. **2.** The office or authority of a Roman censor. **3.** *Psychology* Prevention of disturbing thoughts or feelings from reaching consciousness except in a disguised form.

cen•sur•a•ble (sĕn′shər-ə-bəl) *adj.* Deserving of or open to censure. **—cen′sur•a•bly** *adv.*

cen•sure (sĕn′shər) *n.* **1.** An expression of strong disapproval or harsh criticism. **2.** An official rebuke, such as one by a legislature to a member. ❖ *tr.v.* **-sured, -sur•ing, -sures 1.** To criticize severely; blame. See Syns at **criticize. 2.** To express official disapproval of. [ME < Lat. *cēnsūra,* censorship < *cēnsor,* Roman censor. See CENSOR.] **—cen′sur•er** *n.*

cen•sus (sĕn′səs) *n.* **1.** An official count of a population, often including related demographic information. **2.** In ancient Rome, a count of the citizens and a property evaluation for taxation purposes. [Lat. *cēnsus,* registration of citizens < *cēnsēre,* to assess.]

cent (sĕnt) *n.* **1.** A monetary unit equal to 1/100 of a US dollar. **2.** A monetary unit equal to 1/100 of various standard monetary units. [ME < OFr., hundred < Lat. *centum.* See **dek̑m̥** in App.]

cent. *abbr.* **1.** centigrade **2.** *Latin* centum (hundred) **3.** century

cen•tal (sĕn′tl) *n.* See **hundredweight** 1. [< Lat. *centum,* hundred. See **dek̑m̥** in App.]

cen•taur (sĕn′tôr′) *n. Greek Mythology* One of a race of monsters with a human upper and an equine lower male body. [ME < Lat. *Centaurus* < Gk. *Kentauros.*]

Cen•tau•rus (sĕn-tôr′əs) *n.* A constellation in the Southern Hemisphere near Vela and Lupus. [Lat. *Centaurus,* centaur. See CENTAUR.]

cen•tau•ry (sĕn′tôr′ē) *n., pl.* **-ries** Any of several herbs of the genus *Centaurium,* esp. a Eurasian species *(C. erythraea)* long used in herbal medicine. [ME < OE *centaurie* < Lat. *centaurēum* < Gk. *kentaureion* < *Kentauros,* centaur.]

cen•ta•vo (sĕn-tä′vō) *n., pl.* **-vos 1.** A monetary unit equal to 1/100 of the Portuguese escudo. **2.** A similar unit used in various Central and South American countries. [Sp., hundredth < Lat. *centum,* hundred. See **dek̑m̥** in App.]

cen•te•nar•i•an (sĕn′tə-nâr′ē-ən) *n.* One who is 100 years old or older. [< Lat. *centēnārius,* of a hundred. See CENTENARY.] **—cen′te•nar′i•an** *adj.*

cen•ten•a•ry (sĕn-tĕn′ə-rē, sĕn′tə-nĕr′ē) *adj.* **1.** Of or relating to a 100-year period. **2.** Occurring once every 100 years. ❖ *n., pl.* **-ries 1.** A 100-year period. **2.** A centennial. [Lat. *centēnārius,* of a hundred < *centum,* hundred. See **dek̑m̥** in App.]

cen•ten•ni•al (sĕn-tĕn′ē-əl) *adj.* **1.** Of or relating to an age or period of 100 years. **2.** Occurring once every 100 years. **3.** Of or relating to a 100th anniversary. ❖ *n.* A 100th anniversary or a celebration of it. [Lat. *centum,* hundred; see **dek̑m̥** in App. + (BI)ENNIAL.] **—cen•ten′ni•al•ly** *adv.*

cen•ter (sĕn′tər) *n.* **1.** A point or place that is equally distant from the sides or outer boundaries of something; the middle: *the center of a stage.* **2a.** A point equidistant from the vertices of a regular polygon. **b.** A point equidistant from all points on the circumference of a circle or on the surface of a sphere. **3.** A point around which something rotates or revolves: *The sun is the center of our solar system.* **4.** A part of an object that is surrounded by the rest; a core: *chocolates with soft centers.* **5a.** A place where a particular activity or service is concentrated: *a medical center.* **b.** A point of origin, as of influence, ideas, or actions: *a center of power.* **c.** An area of dense population: *a metropolitan center.* **6.** A person or thing that is the chief object of attention, interest, activity, or emotion. **7.** A person, object, or group occupying a middle position. **8.** often **Center** A political group or a set of policies representing a moderate view. **9.** *Physiology* A group of neurons in the central nervous system that control a particular function. **10.** *Sports* A player who holds a middle position on the field, court, or forward line in some team sports. **11.** *Baseball* Center field. **12a.** A small conical hole made in a piece of work with a center punch so that a drill can be accurately positioned within it. **b.** A bar with a conical point used to support work, as during turning on a lathe. ❖ *v.* **-tered, -ter•ing, -ters** *—tr.* **1.** To place in or at the center: *centered the vase on the table.* **2.** To direct toward a center or central point; concentrate or focus. **3.** *Sports* To pass (a ball or puck) toward the center of a playing area. **4.** *Football* To pass (the ball) back between the legs to begin a down. *—intr.* **1.** To be concentrated; cluster: *The epidemic centered in the urban areas.* **2.** To have a central theme or concern; be focused: *Her novels center on the problems of adolescence.* [ME *centre* < OFr.

Celtic cross
County Tipperary, Ireland

ă	pat	oi	**boy**
ā	pay	ou	**out**
âr	**care**	ŏŏ	**took**
ä	father	ōō	**boot**
ĕ	pet	ŭ	cut
ē	be	ûr	urge
ĭ	pit	th	thin
ī	pie	*th*	this
îr	**pier**	hw	**which**
ŏ	pot	zh	vision
ō	toe	ə	about, item
ô	paw		

Stress marks:
′ (primary);
′ (secondary), as in
lexicon (lĕk′sĭ-kŏn′)

< Lat. *centrum* < Gk. *kentron*, center of a circle < *kentein*, to prick.]

SYNONYMS *center, focus, headquarters, heart, hub, seat* These nouns refer to a region, person, or thing around which some activity is concentrated: *a great cultural center; the focus of research efforts in biotechnology; the headquarters of a corporation; a town that is the heart of the colony; the hub of a steel empire; the seat of government.*

center bit *n.* A drill bit having a sharp center point, used in carpentry for boring holes.

cen·ter·board (sĕn′tər-bôrd′, -bōrd′) *n.* A keel in a sailboat that can be pivoted upward to reduce the boat's draft in shallow water.

cen·tered (sĕn′tərd) *adj.* **1.** Being at or placed in the center. **2.** Having a specified center. Often used in combination: *soft-centered.* **3.** Self-confident and well-balanced. —**cen′tered·ness** *n.*

center field *n. Baseball* **1.** The middle third of the outfield. **2.** The position played there. —**center fielder** *n.*

cen·ter·fold (sĕn′tər-fōld′) *n.* A magazine center spread, esp. a foldout of an oversize photograph or feature.

cen·ter·line (sĕn′tər-līn′) *n.* **1.** A line that bisects something into equal parts. **2.** A painted line dividing a road or highway into two sections.

center of gravity *n., pl.* **centers of gravity 1.** The point in or near a body through which the resultant of the gravitational forces on the component particles of the body acts. **2.** The point of greatest importance or interest.

center of mass *n., pl.* **centers of mass** The point in a system of bodies or an extended body at which the mass of the system may be considered to be concentrated and external forces may be considered to be applied.

cen·ter·piece (sĕn′tər-pēs′) *n.* **1.** Something in a central position, esp. a decorative object or arrangement placed at the center of a table. **2.** The central or most important feature.

center punch *n.* A tool with a sharp point used in metalworking to mark centers or centerlines on pieces to be drilled.

center spread *n.* **1.** The two facing pages in the center of a magazine or newspaper. **2.** A feature located there.

cen·tes·i·mal (sĕn-tĕs′ə-məl) *adj.* Relating to or divided into hundredths. [< Lat. *centēsimus* < *centum*, hundred. See **dekm̥** in App.] —**cen·tes′i·mal·ly** *adv.*

centi– *pref.* **1.** One hundredth (10^{-2}): *centiliter.* **2.** One hundred: *centipede.* [Fr. < Lat., hundred < *centum.* See **dekm̥** in App.]

cen·ti·grade (sĕn′tĭ-grād′) *adj.* Celsius. See table at **measurement.** [Fr. : *centi-*, centi- + *grade*, degree (< Ital. *grado*, rank, degree < Lat. *gradus*, step; see **ghredh-** in App.).]

cen·ti·gram (sĕn′tĭ-grăm′) *n.* A metric unit of mass equal to one hundredth (10^{-2}) of a gram.

cen·ti·li·ter (sĕn′tə-lē′tər) *n.* A metric unit of volume equal to one hundredth (10^{-2}) of a liter.

cen·til·lion (sĕn-tĭl′yən) *n.* **1.** The cardinal number equal to 10^{303}. **2.** *Chiefly British* The cardinal number equal to 10^{600}. [Lat. *centum*, hundred; see **dekm̥** in App. + (M)ILLION.] —**cen·til′lion** *adj.* —**cen·til′lionth** *adj., adv.* & *n.*

cen·time (sän′tēm′, săn-tēm′) *n.* A monetary unit equal to $\frac{1}{100}$ of the standard unit in France and various other countries. [Fr. < OFr. *centisme* < Lat. *centēsimus*, hundredth < *centum*, hundred. See **dekm̥** in App.]

cen·ti·me·ter (sĕn′tə-mē′tər) *n.* A unit of length equal to one hundredth (10^{-2}) of a meter. See table at **measurement.**

cen·ti·me·ter-gram-sec·ond system (sĕn′tə-mē′tər-grăm′sĕk′ənd) *n.* A system of measurement in which the base units of length, mass, and time are the centimeter, gram, and second.

cen·ti·mo (sĕn′tə-mō′) *n., pl.* **-mos** A monetary unit equal to $\frac{1}{100}$ of the standard unit in Spain and various other countries. [Sp. *céntimo* < Fr. *centime.* See CENTIME.]

cen·ti·pede (sĕn′tə-pēd′) *n.* Any of various wormlike arthropods of the class Chilopoda, with a flat body composed of segments, each bearing a pair of jointed appendages. [Lat. *centipeda* : *centi-*, centi- + *pēs, ped-*, foot; see –PED.]

centipede grass *n.* A low Southeast Asian perennial grass (*Eremochloa ophiuroides*) cultivated for lawns in warm regions.

cen·ti·poise (sĕn′tə-poiz′) *n.* A centimeter-gram-second unit of dynamic viscosity equal to one hundredth (10^{-2}) of a poise.

cen·tner (sĕnt′nər) *n.* **1a.** A unit of weight in Germany and Scandinavia equal to 50 kilograms (110.23 pounds). **b.** A unit of weight in parts of the former Soviet Union equal to 100 kilograms (220.46 pounds). **2.** An assaying unit equal to one dram. [Ger. *Zentner* < OHGer. *cëntenāri* < Lat. *centēnārius*, of a hundred. See CENTENARY.]

cen·to (sĕn′tō) *n., pl.* **-tos** A literary work pieced together from the works of several authors. [Lat. *centō*, patchwork.]

centr– *pref.* Variant of **centro–.**

cen·tra (sĕn′trə) *n.* A plural of **centrum.**

cen·tral (sĕn′trəl) *adj.* **1.** Situated at, in, or near the center. **2.** Forming the center. **3.** Having dominant or controlling power or influence. **4.** Of basic importance; essential or principal. **5.** Easily reached from various points. **6.** Of or constituting a single source controlling all components of a system. **7.** *Anatomy* **a.** Of, relat-

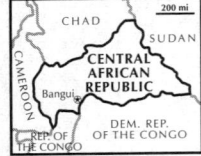

CHAD · SUDAN · CAMEROON · **CENTRAL AFRICAN REPUBLIC** · Bangui · DEM. REP. OF THE CONGO · REP. OF THE CONGO · 200 mi

Central African Republic

centrifuge

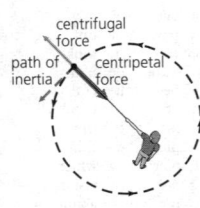

centrifugal force · path of inertia · centripetal force

centripetal force

ing to, or originating from the nervous system. **b.** Relating to a centrum. **8.** *Linguistics* Articulated in the middle of the oral cavity. Used of vowels, as the *u* in *cut.* ❖ *n.* **1a.** A telephone exchange. **b.** An operator at a telephone exchange. **2.** A coordinating office or agency at the center of a group of related activities. [Lat. *centrālis* < *centrum*, center. See CENTER.] —**cen′tral·ly** *adv.*

Central African Republic Formerly (1976–79) **Central African Empire.** A country of central Africa; gained independence from France in 1960. Cap. Bangui. Pop. 2,395,000.

Central America A region of S North America extending from the S border of Mexico to the N border of Colombia. —**Central American** *adj.* & *n.*

central angle *n.* An angle having its vertex at the center of a circle.

central bank *n.* A nation's principal monetary authority, which regulates the money supply and credit, issues currency, and manages the rate of exchange.

central casting *n.* A movie studio department responsible for hiring actors, esp. for nonstarring roles.

central city *n.* A heavily populated city at the core of a large metropolitan area.

cen·tral·ism (sĕn′trə-lĭz′əm) *n.* Concentration of power in a central organization. —**cen′tral·ist** *n.* —**cen′tral·is′tic** *adj.*

cen·tral·i·ty (sĕn-trăl′ĭ-tē) *n.* **1.** The state or quality of being central. **2.** A tendency to be or remain at the center.

cen·tral·ize (sĕn′trə-līz′) *v.* **-ized, -iz·ing, -iz·es** —*tr.* **1.** To draw into or toward a center; consolidate. **2.** To bring under a single, central authority. —*intr.* To come together at a center; concentrate. —**cen′tral·i·za′tion** (-trə-lĭ-zā′shən) *n.* —**cen′tral·iz′er** *n.*

central nervous system *n.* The portion of the vertebrate nervous system consisting of the brain and spinal cord.

Central Park An extensive recreational area of New York City in central Manhattan.

central processing unit *n.* The part of a computer that interprets and executes instructions.

Central Provinces The Canadian provinces of Ontario and Quebec.

Central Standard Time *n.* Standard time in the sixth time zone west of Greenwich, England, reckoned at 90° west and used in the central United States.

Central Valley A rich agricultural valley of central CA between the Sierra Nevada and the Coast Ranges.

cen·tre (sĕn′tər) *n.* & *v. Chiefly British* Variant of **center.**

centri– *pref.* Variant of **centro–.**

cen·tric (sĕn′trĭk) also **cen·tri·cal** (-trĭ-kəl) *adj.* **1.** Situated at or near the center; central. **2.** Having a center. **3.** Of or relating to diatoms of the class Centrales, distinguished by their radially symmetrical form. —**cen′tri·cal·ly** *adv.* —**cen·tric′i·ty** (sĕn-trĭs′ĭ-tē) *n.*

–centric *suff.* **1.** Having a specified kind or number of centers: *polycentric.* **2.** Having a specified object as the center: *geocentric.* **3.** Focused on or viewed in terms of a specified area, subject, or culture: *Afrocentric.*

cen·trif·u·gal (sĕn-trĭf′yə-gəl, -trĭf′ə-) *adj.* **1.** Moving or directed away from a center or axis. **2.** Operated by means of centrifugal force. **3.** *Physiology* Transmitting nerve impulses away from the central nervous system; efferent. **4.** *Botany* Developing or progressing outward from a center or axis. **5.** Tending or directed away from centralization, as of authority. [< NLat. *centrifugus* : Lat. *centrum*, center; see *centrum* + Lat. *fugere*, to flee.] —**cen·trif′u·gal·ism** *n.* —**cen·trif′u·gal·ly** *adv.*

centrifugal force *n.* The apparent force drawing a rotating body away from the center of rotation, caused by its inertia.

cen·tri·fuge (sĕn′trə-fyōōj′) *n.* **1.** An apparatus consisting of a compartment spun about a central axis to separate contained materials of different specific gravities or colloidal particles in a liquid. **2.** An apparatus in which humans or animals are enclosed and which is revolved to simulate spacecraft acceleration. ❖ *tr.v.* **-fuged, -fug·ing, -fug·es** To rotate (something) in a centrifuge or separate, dehydrate, or test by such means. [Fr., centrifugal < NLat. *centrifugus.* See CENTRIFUGAL.] —**cen·trif′u·ga′tion** (sĕn-trĭf′yə-gā′shən, -trĭf′ə-) *n.*

cen·tri·ole (sĕn′trē-ōl′) *n.* One of two cylindrical cellular structures that are composed of nine triplet microtubules and form the asters during mitosis. [NLat. *centriolum*, dim. of Lat. *centrum*, center. See CENTER.]

cen·trip·e·tal (sĕn-trĭp′ĭ-tl) *adj.* **1.** Moving or directed toward a center or axis. **2.** Operated by means of centripetal force. **3.** *Physiology* Transmitting nerve impulses toward the central nervous system; afferent. **4.** *Botany* Developing or progressing inward toward the center or axis. **5.** Tending or directed toward centralization. —**cen·trip′e·tal·ly** *adv.*

centripetal force *n.* The component of force acting on a body in curvilinear motion that is directed toward the center of curvature or axis of rotation.

cen·trism (sĕn′trĭz′əm) *n.* The centrist political philosophy.

cen·trist (sĕn′trĭst) *n.* One in the political center; a moderate. ❖ *adj.* Marked by or adhering to a moderate political view.

centro– or **centr–** or **centri–** *pref.* Center: *centroid.* [< Lat. *centrum* and Gk. *kentron*; see CENTER.]

cen·tro·bar·ic (sĕn′trə-băr′ĭk) *adj.* Of or relating to the center of gravity. [< Gk. *kentrobarikē*, theory of the center of gravity : *kentron*, center; see CENTER + *baros*, weight; see **gʷerə-** in App.]

cen·troid (sĕn′troid′) *n.* **1.** See **center of mass. 2.** The point in a system of masses each of whose coordinates is a mean value of the coordinates for each dimension of all points within the system.

cen·tro·lec·i·thal (sĕn′trə-lĕs′ə-thəl) *adj. Biology* Having the yolk in the center. [CENTRO- + LECITH(IN) + −AL[1].]

cen·tro·mere (sĕn′trə-mîr′) *n.* The most condensed and constricted region of a chromosome, to which the spindle fiber is attached during mitosis. **—cen′tro·mer′ic** (-mĕr′ĭk, -mîr′-) *adj.*

cen·tro·some (sĕn′trə-sōm′) *n.* A small region of cytoplasm adjacent to the nucleus that contains the centrioles and serves to organize microtubules. **—cen′tro·so′mic** (-sō′mĭk) *adj.*

cen·tro·sphere (sĕn′trə-sfîr′) *n.* **1.** The mass of cytoplasm surrounding the centriole. **2.** The central core of the earth.

cen·trum (sĕn′trəm) *n., pl.* **-trums** or **-tra** (-trə) The major part of a vertebra, exclusive of the bases of the neural arch. [Lat., center. See CENTER.]

cen·tum (kĕn′təm) *adj.* Designating those Indo-European languages that merged the palatal velar stops with the plain velars *k*, *g*, *gh* and maintained a distinction between them and the labiovelars *kʷ*, *gʷ*, *gʷh*. [Lat., hundred (a word whose initial sound in classical Latin is a plain velar *k* coming from an original IE palatal velar). See **dekṃ** in App.]

cen·tu·ri·on (sĕn-tŏŏr′ē-ən, -tyŏŏr′-) *n.* The commander of a century in the Roman army. [ME < OFr. < Lat. *centuriō*, *centuriōn-* < *centuria*, group of a hundred. See CENT.]

cen·tu·ry (sĕn′chə-rē) *n., pl.* **-ries 1a.** A period of 100 years. **b.** Each of the successive periods of 100 years before or since the advent of the Christian era. **2a.** A Roman army unit originally consisting of 100 men. **b.** One of the 193 Roman electoral divisions. **3.** A group of 100. [Lat. *centuria*, a group of a hundred < *centum*, hundred. See **dekṃ** in App.] **—cen·tu′ri·al** *adj.* **—cen′tu·ry long′** *adj.*

century plant *n.* See **agave.**

CEO *abbr.* chief executive officer

ce·orl (chā′ôrl) *n.* An Anglo-Saxon freeman of the lowest class. [OE.]

cep or **cèpe** (sĕp) *n.* See **porcino.** [Fr. *cèpe* < Gascon *cep*, tree trunk, cep < Lat. *cipus, cippus,* post, boundary marker.]

ceph·a·lad (sĕf′ə-lăd′) *adv. Biology* Toward the head or anterior section.

ceph·al·al·gia (sĕf′ə-lăl′jə, -jē-ə) *n.* A headache.

ce·phal·ic (sə-făl′ĭk) *adj.* **1.** Of or relating to the head. **2.** Located on, in, or near the head. [Fr. *céphalique* < Lat. *cephalicus* < Gk. *kephalikos* < *kephalē*, head. See **ghebh-el-** in App.] **—ce·phal′i·cal·ly** *adv.*

–cephalic *suff.* Having a specified kind or number of heads: *dolichocephalic.*

cephalic index *n.* The ratio of the maximum width of the head to its maximum length, multiplied by 100.

ceph·a·lin (sĕf′ə-lĭn) also **keph·a·lin** (kĕf′-) *n.* Any of a group of phospholipids having hemostatic properties and found esp. in the white matter of the brain and spinal cord.

ceph·a·li·za·tion (sĕf′ə-lĭ-zā′shən) *n.* An evolutionary trend in the animal kingdom toward centralization of neural and sensory organs in the head or anterior region of the body.

cephalo- or **cephal-** *pref.* Head: *cephalothorax.* [NLat. < Gk. *kephalo-* < *kephalē*, head. See **ghebh-el-** in App.]

ceph·a·lo·chor·date (sĕf′ə-lə-kôr′dāt′) *n.* Any of various primitive chordate animals of the subphylum Cephalochordata that lack a true vertebral column. [NLat. *Cephalochordāta*, subphylum name : CEPHALO- + *Chordāta*, chordate phylum; see CHORDATE.] **—ceph′a·lo·chor′date′** *adj.*

ceph·a·lo·me·ter (sĕf′ə-lŏm′ĭ-tər) *n.* A device for measuring the head.

ceph·a·lom·e·try (sĕf′ə-lŏm′ĭ-trē) *n.* Scientific measurement of the head. **—ceph′a·lo·met′ric** (-lō-mĕt′rĭk) *adj.*

Ceph·a·lo·ni·a (sĕf′ə-lō′nē-ə, -lōn′yə) also **Ke·fal·li·ní·a** (kĕ′fä-lē-nē′ä) The largest of the Ionian Is. off the W coast of Greece.

ceph·a·lo·pod (sĕf′ə-lə-pŏd′) *n.* Any of various marine mollusks of the class Cephalopoda, such as the squid, having a large head, large eyes, prehensile tentacles, and often an ink sac used for protection or defense. [< NLat. *Cephalopoda,* class name : CEPHALO- + *-poda,* -pod.] **—ceph′a·lo·pod′** *adj.* **—ceph′a·lop′o·dan** (sĕf′ə-lŏp′ə-dən) *n. & adj.*

ceph·a·lo·spo·rin (sĕf-ə-lə-spôr′ĭn, -spōr′-) *n.* Any of various broad-spectrum antibiotics originally derived from the fungus *Cephalosporium acremonium.* [NLat. *Cephalosporium,* genus name (CEPHALO- + *spora,* spore; see SPORE) + −IN.]

ceph·a·lo·tho·rax (sĕf′ə-lə-thôr′ăks′, -thōr′-) *n.* The anterior section of arachnids and many crustaceans, consisting of the fused head and thorax.

–cephalous *suff.* Having a specified kind or number of heads: *dicephalous.* [< Gk. *-kephalos* < *kephalē*, head. See **ghebh-el-** in App.]

–cephaly *suff.* A specified condition of the head: *microcephaly.*

Ce·phe·id (sē′fē-ĭd, sĕf′ē-) *n.* Any of a class of intrinsically vari-

able stars with exceptionally regular periods of light pulsation. [< CEPHEUS.]

Ce·pheus (sē′fyŏŏs′, -fē-əs, sĕf′ē-) *n.* A constellation in the Northern Hemisphere near Cassiopeia and Draco. [Lat. *Cēpheus* < Gk. *Kēpheus.*]

ce·ra·ceous (sə-rā′shəs) *adj.* Waxy or waxlike. [Lat. *cēra,* wax; see CERATE + −ACEOUS.]

Ce·ram (sā′răm′, sĕ-räm′) An island of E Indonesia in the Moluccas W of New Guinea bordering on the **Ceram Sea,** a section of the W Pacific Ocean.

ce·ram·al (sə-răm′əl) *n.* See **cermet.** [CERAM(IC) + AL(LOY).]

ce·ram·ic (sə-răm′ĭk) *n.* **1.** Any of various hard, brittle, heat- and corrosion-resistant materials made by shaping and then firing a nonmetallic mineral, such as clay, at a high temperature. **2a.** A ceramic object, such as earthenware. **b.** ceramics (*used with a sing. verb*) The art or technique of making ceramics, esp. from fired clay. [< Gk. *keramikos,* of pottery < *keramos,* potter's clay.] **—ce·ram′ic** *adj.* **—ce·ram′ist** (sə-răm′ĭst, sĕr′ə-mĭst) *n.*

ce·ras·tes (sə-răs′tēz) *n., pl.* **cerastes** Any of several venomous snakes of the genus *Cerastes,* having hornlike projections over each eye. [ME < Lat. *cerastēs* < Gk. *kerastēs,* horned serpent < *keras,* horn. See **ker-[1]** in App.]

cerat– *pref.* Variant of **kerato–.**

ce·rate (sîr′āt′) *n.* A hard, unctuous, fat- or wax-based solid, sometimes medicated, formerly applied to the skin. [Lat. *cērātum* < *cērātus,* p. part. of *cērāre,* to cover with wax < *cēra,* wax; akin to Gk. *kēros.*]

ce·rat·ed (sîr′ā′tĭd) *adj.* **1.** Coated with wax or resin. **2.** Having a cere: *a cerated beak.* See CERATE.]

cerato– *pref.* Variant of **kerato–.**

ce·rat·o·dus (sə-răt′ə-dəs) *n., pl.* **-dus·es 1.** Any of various extinct lungfishes of the genus *Ceratodus,* of the Triassic and Cretaceous periods. **2.** See **barramunda.** [NLat. *Cerātōdus,* genus name : Gk. *keras, kerāt-,* horn; see **ker-[1]** in App. + Gk. *odous,* tooth; see **dent–** in App.]

cer·a·toid (sĕr′ə-toid′) *adj.* Similar to a horn; hornlike.

cer·a·top·si·an (sĕr′ə-tŏp′sē-ən) *n.* Any of various herbivorous quadrupedal ornithischian dinosaurs of the suborder Ceratopsia of the late Jurassic and Cretaceous periods, having a bony frill covering the neck, a beaked mouth, and one or more horns on the head. [< NLat. *Cerātōpsia,* suborder name : Gk. *keras, kerāt-,* horn; see **ker-[1]** in App. + Gk. *ōps,* eye, face; see **okʷ-** in App.] **—cer′a·top′si·an** *adj.*

Cer·ber·us (sûr′bər-əs) *n. Greek & Roman Mythology* A three-headed dog guarding Hades. **—Cer′ber·e′an** (sûr′bə-rē′ən) *adj.*

cer·car·i·a (sər-kâr′ē-ə) *n., pl.* **-i·ae** (-ē-ē′) or **-i·as** The parasitic larva of a trematode worm, having a tail that disappears in the adult stage. [NLat. *cercāria* : Gk. *kerkos,* tail + *-āria,* fem. of Lat. *-ārius,* -ary.] **—cer·car′i·al** *adj.*

cer·cus (sûr′kəs, kĕr′-) *n., pl.* **cer·ci** (sûr′sī, -kī, kĕr′kē) Either of a pair of terminal, dorsolateral sensory appendages of certain insects. [NLat. < Gk. *kerkos,* tail.]

cere[1] (sîr) *tr.v.* **cered, cer·ing, ceres** To wrap in or as if in cerecloth. [ME *ceren, ciren* < OFr. *cirer,* to cover with wax < Lat. *cērāre.* See CERATE.]

cere[2] (sîr) *n.* A fleshy or waxlike swelling at the base of the upper part of the beak in certain birds. [ME *sere* < OFr. *cire* < Med.Lat. *cēra* < Lat., wax. See CERATE.] **—cered** *adj.*

ce·re·al (sîr′ē-əl) *n.* **1a.** A grass such as corn, the starchy grains of which are used as food. **b.** The grain of such a grass. **2.** Any of several other plants or their edible seed or fruit, such as grain amaranth. **3.** A food prepared from a cereal plant, esp. a breakfast food made from commercially processed grain. [< Lat. *cereālis,* of grain < *Cerēs,* Ceres. See **ker-[2]** in App.] **—ce′re·al** *adj.*

cereal leaf beetle *n.* An Old World beetle (*Oulema melanopus*) now found in the United States, where it is a grain pest.

cereal leaf beetle
cereal leaf beetle larva on a damaged wheat leaf

cer·e·bel·lum (sĕr′ə-bĕl′əm) *n., pl.* **-bel·lums** or **-bel·la** (-bĕl′ə) The trilobed structure of the brain, posterior to the pons and medulla oblongata and inferior to the occipital lobes of the cerebral hemispheres and responsible for the regulation and coordination of complex voluntary muscular movement and for posture and balance. [Med.Lat. < Lat., dim. of *cerebrum,* brain. See **ker-[1]** in App.] **—cer′e·bel′lar** (-bĕl′ər) *adj.*

cer·e·bra (sĕr′ə-brə, sə-rē′brə) *n.* A plural of **cerebrum.**

cer·e·bral (sĕr′ə-brəl, sə-rē′-) *adj.* **1.** Of or relating to the brain or cerebrum. **2.** Appealing to or requiring the use of the intellect; intellectual. **—cer′e·bral·ly** *adv.*

cerebral cortex *n.* The extensive outer layer of gray matter of the cerebral hemispheres, largely responsible for higher brain functions, including sensation, reasoning, and memory.

cerebral hemisphere *n.* Either of the two symmetrical halves of the cerebrum, as divided by the longitudinal cerebral fissure.

cerebral palsy *n.* A disorder usu. caused by brain damage occurring at or before birth and marked by muscular impairment. **—cer′e·bral-pal′sied** (sĕr′ə-brəl-pôl′zēd, sə-rē′-) *adj.*

cer·e·brate (sĕr′ə-brāt′) *intr.v.* **-brat·ed, -brat·ing, -brates** To use the power of reason; think. [Back-formation < *cerebration,* thinking < Lat. *cerebrum,* brain. See CEREBRUM.] **—cer′e·bra′tion** *n.*

cerebro– or **cerebr–** *pref.* Brain; cerebrum: *cerebroside.* [< CEREBRUM.]

ă pat   oi boy
ā pay   ou out
âr care   ŏŏ took
ä father   ōŏ boot
ĕ pet   ŭ cut
ē be   ûr urge
ĭ pit   th thin
ī pie   th this
îr pier   hw which
ŏ pot   zh vision
ō toe   ə about,
ô paw   item

Stress marks:
′ (primary);
′ (secondary), as in
lexicon (lĕk′sĭ-kŏn′)

cer·e·bro·side (sĕr′ə-brə-sīd′, sə-rē′-) *n.* Any of various lipid compounds containing glucose or galactose and glucose and found in nerve tissue. [CEREBR(O)- + -OS(E)² + -IDE.]

cer·e·bro·spi·nal (sĕr′ə-brō-spī′nəl, sə-rē′brō-) *adj.* Of or relating to the brain and spinal cord.

cerebrospinal fluid *n.* The serumlike fluid that circulates through the brain, the cavity of the spinal cord, and the subarachnoid space, functioning in shock absorption.

cerebrospinal meningitis *n.* Inflammation of the meninges of both the brain and the spinal cord.

cer·e·bro·vas·cu·lar (sĕr′ə-brō-văs′kyə-lər, sə-rē′brō-) *adj.* Of or relating to the blood vessels that supply the brain.

cer·e·brum (sĕr′ə-brəm, sə-rē′-) *n., pl.* **-brums** or **-bra** (-brə) The large rounded structure of the brain occupying most of the cranial cavity, divided into two cerebral hemispheres that are joined at the bottom by the corpus callosum and controlling and integrating motor, sensory, and higher mental functions. [Lat., brain. See **ker-¹** in App.]

cere·cloth (sîr′klôth′, -klŏth′) *n.* Cloth coated with wax, formerly used for wrapping the dead.

cer·e·ment (sĕr′ə-mənt, sîr′mənt) *n.* **1.** Cerecloth. **2.** A burial garment. Often used in the plural.

cer·e·mo·ni·al (sĕr′ə-mō′nē-əl) *adj.* **1.** Of, appropriate to, or marked by ceremony; formal or ritual. **2.** Involved or used in ceremonies. ❖ *n.* **1.** A set of ceremonies for an occasion; a ritual. **2.** A ceremony or rite. —**cer′e·mo′ni·al·ism** *n.* —**cer′e·mo′ni·al·ist** *n.* —**cer′e·mo′ni·al·ly** *adv.*

cer·e·mo·ni·ous (sĕr′ə-mō′nē-əs) *adj.* **1.** Strictly observant of or devoted to ceremony, ritual, or etiquette; punctilious. **2a.** Characterized by ceremony. **b.** In accord with prescribed or customary usage; rigidly formal. —**cer′e·mo′ni·ous·ly** *adv.* —**cer′e·mo′ni·ous·ness** *n.*

cer·e·mo·ny (sĕr′ə-mō′nē) *n., pl.* **-nies 1.** A formal act or set of acts performed as prescribed by ritual or custom. **2.** A conventional social gesture or act of courtesy. **3.** A formal act without intrinsic purpose; an empty form. **4.** Strict observance of formalities or etiquette. [ME *ceremonie* < Lat. *caerimōnia*, religious rite.]

Ce·ren·kov (chə-rĕng′kôf, -kəf, chĭ-ryĭn-kôf′), **Pavel Alekseevich** See Pavel Alekseevich **Cherenkov.**

Ce·ren·kov effect also **Che·ren·kov effect** (chə-rĕng′kôf, -kəf) *n.* The emission of light by a charged particle passing through a transparent nonconducting medium at a speed greater than the speed of light in that medium. [After Pavel Alekseevich CHERENKOV.]

Ce·res (sîr′ēz) *n.* **1.** *Roman Mythology* The goddess of agriculture. **2.** The largest asteroid and the first discovered, orbiting between Mars and Jupiter. [Lat. *Cerēs*. See **ker-²** in App.]

ce·re·us (sîr′ē-əs) *n.* Any of several cacti of the genus *Cereus* or closely related genera. [NLat. *Cēreus*, genus name < Lat. *cēreus*, candle (< its shape) < *cēra*, wax. See CERATE.]

ce·ric (sĭr′ĭk, sĕr′-) *adj.* Of, relating to, or containing cerium, esp. with valence 4. [CER(IUM) + -IC.]

ceric oxide *n.* A pale yellow-white powder, CeO_2, used in ceramics, to polish glass, and to sensitize photosensitive glass.

cer·iph (sĕr′ĭf) *n. Chiefly British* Variant of **serif.**

ce·rise (sə-rēs′, -rēz′) *n.* A deep to vivid purplish red. [Fr. < OFr., cherry. See CHERRY.] —**ce·rise′** *adj.*

ce·ri·um (sîr′ē-əm) *n. Symbol* **Ce** A lustrous, malleable metallic rare-earth element that occurs chiefly in the minerals monazite and bastnaesite, exists in four allotropic states, and is used in lighter flint alloys. Atomic number 58; atomic weight 140.12; melting point 795°C; boiling point 3,468°C; specific gravity 6.67 to 8.23; valence 3, 4. See table at **element.** [CER(ES) + -IUM.]

cer·met (sûr′mĕt′) *n.* A material consisting of processed ceramic particles bonded with metal and used in high-strength and high-temperature applications. [CER(AMIC) + MET(AL).]

cer·nu·ous (sûr′nyoo-əs) *adj. Botany* Nodding; drooping. [< Lat. *cernuus*, bowing forward.]

ce·ro (sîr′ō, sĕr′ō) *n., pl.* **ce·ros** or **cero** An edible fish (*Scomberomorus regalis*) of western Atlantic waters having silvery sides and a dark blue back. [Alteration of Sp. *sierra*, saw, sawfish. See SIERRA.]

ce·ro·tic acid (sə-rō′tĭk, -rŏt′ĭk) *n.* A fatty acid, $CH_3(CH_2)_{24}COOH$, occurring in waxes. [< Lat. *cērōtum*, wax plaster < Gk. *kērōton*, ult. < *kēros*, wax.]

ce·ro·type (sîr′ə-tīp′, sĕr′ə-) *n.* The process of preparing a printing surface for electrotyping by first engraving on a wax-coated metal plate. [Gk. *kēros*, wax + TYPE.]

ce·rous (sîr′əs) *adj.* Of, relating to, or containing cerium, esp. with valence 3. [CER(IUM) + -OUS.]

Cer·ro Gor·do (sĕr′ō gôr′dō) A mountain pass of SE Mexico between Veracruz and Mexico City; site of a US victory (1847) in the Mexican War.

cert. *abbr.* **1.** certificate **2.** certified

cer·tain (sûr′tn) *adj.* **1.** Definite; fixed. **2.** Sure to come or happen; inevitable. **3.** Established beyond doubt or question; indisputable. **4.** Capable of being relied on; dependable. **5.** Having or showing confidence; assured. **6a.** Not specified or identified but assumed to be known. **b.** Named but not known or previously mentioned. **7.** Perceptible; noticeable. **8.** Not great; calculable. ❖ *pron.* An indefinite but limited number; some. —*idiom:* for cer-

tain Without doubt; definitely. [ME < OFr. < VLat. **certānus* < Lat. *certus*, p. part. of *cernere*, to determine. See **krei-** in App.]

cer·tain·ly (sûr′tn-lē) *adv.* **1.** Undoubtedly; definitely. **2.** By all means; of course. **3.** Surely: *They certainly work hard.*

cer·tain·ty (sûr′tn-tē) *n., pl.* **-ties 1.** The fact, quality, or state of being certain: *the certainty of death.* **2.** Something that is clearly established or assured.

SYNONYMS certainty, certitude, assurance, conviction These nouns mean freedom from doubt. *Certainty* implies a thorough consideration of evidence: "*the emphasis of a certainty that is not impaired by any shade of doubt*" (Mark Twain). *Certitude* is based more on personal belief than on objective facts: "*Certitude is not the test of certainty*" (Oliver Wendell Holmes, Jr.). *Assurance* is a feeling of confidence resulting from subjective experience: *We had no assurance that the used car was in good condition.* *Conviction* arises from the vanquishing of doubt: "*His religion . . . was substantial and concrete, made up of good, hard convictions and opinions*" (Willa Cather).

cer·tes (sûr′tēz, sûrts) *adv. Archaic* Certainly; truly. [ME < OFr. *(a) certes*, perh. < Lat. *ad certās* or < VLat. **certānus*, both < Lat. *certus*, certain. See CERTAIN.]

cer·ti·fi·a·ble (sûr′tə-fī′ə-bəl) *adj.* **1.** That can be certified. **2.** Fit to be declared insane. —**cer′ti·fi′a·bly** *adv.*

cer·tif·i·cate (sər-tĭf′ĭ-kĭt) *n.* **1.** A document testifying to the truth of something. **2.** A document issued to a person completing a course of study not leading to a diploma. **3.** A document certifying that a person may officially practice in certain professions. **4.** A document certifying ownership. ❖ *tr.v.* (-kāt′) **-cat·ed, -cat·ing, -cates** To furnish with, testify to, or authorize by a certificate. [ME *certificat* < OFr. < Med.Lat. *certificātum*, something certified < neut. of LLat. *certificātus*, p. part. of *certificāre*, to certify. See CERTIFY.] —**cer·tif′i·ca·to·ry** (-kə-tôr′ē, -tōr′ē) *adj.*

certificate of deposit *n., pl.* **certificates of deposit** A certificate from a bank stating that the named party has a specified sum on deposit, usu. for a given period of time at a fixed rate of interest.

cer·ti·fi·ca·tion (sûr′tə-fĭ-kā′shən) *n.* **1a.** The act of certifying. **b.** The state of being certified. **2.** A certified statement.

cer·ti·fied check (sûr′tə-fīd′) *n.* A check guaranteed by a bank to be covered by sufficient funds on deposit.

certified mail *n.* Uninsured first-class mail for which proof of delivery is obtained.

certified public accountant *n.* A public accountant who has been certified by a state examining board.

cer·ti·fy (sûr′tə-fī′) *v.* **-fied, -fy·ing, -fies** —*tr.* **1a.** To confirm formally as true, accurate, or genuine. **b.** To guarantee as meeting a standard. See Syns at **approve. 2.** To acknowledge in writing on the face of (a check) that the signature of the maker is genuine and that sufficient funds are deposited for its payment. **3.** To issue a license or certificate to. **4.** To declare to be in need of psychiatric treatment or confinement. **5.** *Archaic* To inform positively; assure. —*intr.* To testify. [ME *certifien* < OFr. *certifier* < LLat. *certificāre* : Lat. *certus*, certain; see CERTAIN + Lat. *-ficāre*, *-fy*.] —**cer′ti·fi′er** *n.*

cer·ti·o·rar·i (sûr′shē-ə-râr′ē, -rä′rē) *n.* A writ from a higher court to a lower one requesting a transcript of the proceedings of a case for review. [ME < Lat. *certiōrārī (volumus)*, (we wish) to be informed (words in the writ), passive of *certiōrāre*, to inform < *certior*, comp. of *certus*, certain. See CERTAIN.]

cer·ti·tude (sûr′tĭ-tōōd′, -tyōōd′) *n.* **1.** The state of being certain; complete assurance. **2.** Sureness of occurrence; inevitability. **3.** Something assured. See Syns at **certainty.** [ME < LLat. *certitūdō* < Lat. *certus*, certain. See CERTAIN.]

ce·ru·le·an (sə-rōō′lē-ən) *adj.* Azure; sky blue. [< Lat. *caeruleus*, dark blue; akin to *caelum*, sky.]

ce·ru·lo·plas·min (sə-rōō′lō-plăz′mĭn) *n.* A blood glycoprotein to which copper is bound during transport and storage. [CERUL(EAN) + PLASM(A) + -IN.]

ce·ru·men (sə-rōō′mən) *n.* See **earwax.** [NLat. < Lat. *cēra*, wax. See CERATE.] —**ce·ru′mi·nous** (-mə-nəs) *adj.*

ce·ruse (sə-rōōs′, sîr′ōōs′) *n.* A white lead pigment, sometimes used in cosmetics. [ME < OFr. < Lat. *cērussa*.]

ce·rus·site (sə-rŭs′īt′) *n.* A colorless or white mineral, $PbCO_3$, that is an ore of lead; lead carbonate. [Ger. *Zerussit* < Lat. *cērussa*, ceruse.]

Cer·van·tes Sa·a·ve·dra (sər-văn′tēz sä′ə-vā′drə, thěr-bän′těs sä′ä-bĕth′rä), **Miguel de** 1547–1616. Spanish writer of the classic satirical novel *Don Quixote* (1605–15).

cer·vi·cal (sûr′vĭ-kəl) *adj.* Of or relating to a neck or a cervix. [< Lat. *cervīx, cervīc-,* neck. See CERVIX.]

cervical cap *n.* A small, rubber, cup-shaped contraceptive device that fits over the uterine cervix.

cer·vi·ci·tis (sûr′vĭ-sī′tĭs) *n.* Inflammation of the cervix of the uterus.

cer·vine (sûr′vīn′) *adj.* Of, like, or characteristic of deer. [Lat.

cervīnus < cervus, deer. See ker-¹ in App.]

cer·vix (sûr′vĭks) *n.*, *pl.* **cer·vix·es** or **cer·vi·ces** (sûr′vĭ-sēz′, sər-vī′sēz) **1.** The neck. **2.** A neck-shaped anatomical structure. [Lat. *cervīx*, neck. See ker-¹ in App.]

Cé·saire (sā-zâr′), **Aimé Fernand** b. 1913. Martinique-born poet, playwright, and politician who contributed to the development of the concept of negritude.

ce·sar·e·an also **cae·sar·e·an** or **cae·sar·i·an** or **ce·sar·i·an** (sĭ-zâr′ē-ən) *adj.* Of or relating to a cesarean section. ❖ *n.* A cesarean section.

cesarean section also **caesarean section** *n.* A surgical incision through the abdominal wall and uterus, performed to deliver a fetus. [From the traditional belief that Julius CAESAR (or his eponymous ancestor) was born by this operation.]

ce·si·um also **cae·si·um** (sē′zē-əm) *n. Symbol* **Cs** A soft ductile metal, liquid at room temperature, the most electropositive and alkaline of the elements, used in photoelectric cells. Atomic number 55; atomic weight 132.905; melting point 28.5°C; boiling point 690°C; specific gravity 1.87; valence 1. See table at **element.** [< Lat. *caesius*, bluish gray.]

ces·pi·tose (sĕs′pĭ-tōs′) *adj. Botany* Growing in tufts or clumps. [NLat. *caespītōsus* < Lat. *caespes, caespit-,* turf.] **—ces′pi·tose′ly** *adv.*

cess (sĕs) *n. Irish* Luck. [Poss. short for SUCCESS.]

ces·sa·tion (sĕ-sā′shən) *n.* A bringing or coming to an end; a ceasing. [ME *cessacioun* < OFr. *cessation* < Lat. *cessātiō, cessātiōn-* < *cessātus,* p. part. of *cessāre,* to stop. See CEASE.]

ces·sion (sĕsh′ən) *n.* **1.** A ceding or surrendering, as of territory. **2.** Something, such as territory, that is ceded. [ME < OFr. < Lat. *cessiō, cessiōn-* < *cessus,* p. part. of *cēdere,* to yield.]

cess·pit (sĕs′pĭt′) *n.* A refuse or sewage pit. [CESS(POOL) + PIT¹.]

cess·pool (sĕs′pōōl′) *n.* **1.** A covered hole or pit for drainage or sewage. **2.** A filthy, disgusting, or corrupt place. [Perh. alteration (influenced by POOL¹) of obsolete *cesperalle,* drainpipe < ME *suspiral,* vent < OFr. *sospirail,* breathing hole < *souspirer,* to breathe < Lat. *suspīrāre,* to sigh. See SUSPIRE.]

ces·ta (sĕs′tə) *n.* A scoop-shaped wicker basket that is worn over the hand and used to catch and throw the ball in jai alai. [Sp., basket < Lat. *cista,* chest. See CHEST.]

ces·tode (sĕs′tōd′) *n.* Any of various parasitic flatworms of the class Cestoda, having a long flat body with a specialized organ of attachment at one end. [< NLat. *Cestōda,* class name < alteration of *Cestoīdea* < Lat. *cestus,* belt < Gk. *kestos.* See CESTUS¹.] **—ces′tode′** *adj.*

ces·tus¹ (sĕs′təs) *n., pl.* **-ti** (-tī) A woman's belt or girdle, esp. in ancient Greece. [Lat., belt < Gk. *kestos.*]

ces·tus² (sĕs′təs) *n., pl.* **-tus·es** A hand covering made of weighted leather straps and worn by boxers in ancient Rome. [Lat. *caestus < caedere,* to strike.]

ce·su·ra (sĭ-zhōōr′ə, -zōōr′ə) *n.* Variant of **caesura.**

CETA *abbr.* Comprehensive Employment and Training Act

ce·ta·cean (sĭ-tā′shən) *n.* Any of various aquatic, chiefly marine mammals of the order Cetacea, including the whales, characterized by a nearly hairless body, broad flippers, vestigial posterior limbs, and a flat notched tail. [< NLat. *Cētācea,* order name < Lat. *cētus,* whale. See CETUS.] **—ce·ta′cean, ce·ta′ceous** (sĭ-tā′shəs) *adj.*

ce·tane (sē′tān′) *n.* A liquid, $C_{16}H_{34}$, used as a solvent and in standardized hydrocarbons. [Lat. *cētus,* whale (so called because it is found in sperm whale oil); see CETUS + -ANE.]

cetane number *n.* The performance rating of a diesel fuel, the percentage of cetane in a cetane-methylnaphthalene mixture with the same ignition performance.

cete (sēt) *n.* A company of badgers. [ME, poss. < Med.Lat. *cetus,* assembly < Lat. *coetus,* var. of *coitus.* See COITUS.]

ce·ter·is par·i·bus (kā′tər-ĭs pär′ə-bəs) *adv.* With all other factors or things remaining the same. [NLat. *cēterīs paribus,* with other things equal : Latin *cēterīs,* ablative pl. of *cēterus,* the other + Lat. *paribus,* ablative pl. of *pār,* equal.]

ce·tol·o·gy (sĭ-tŏl′ə-jē) *n.* The zoology of whales and related aquatic mammals. [Lat. *cētus,* whale. See CETUS + -LOGY.] **—ce′to·log′i·cal** (sēt′l-ŏj′ĭ-kəl) *adj.* **—ce·tol′o·gist** *n.*

cet. par. *abbr.* ceteris paribus

Ce·tus (sē′təs) *n.* A constellation in the Southern Hemisphere near Aquarius and Eridanus. [Lat. *cētus,* whale < Gk. *kētos.*]

ce·tyl alcohol (sēt′l) *n.* A waxy alcohol, $C_{15}H_{33}OH$, used in cosmetics and pharmaceuticals. [Lat. *cētus,* whale; see CETUS + -YL.]

Ceu·ta (syōō′tə, thĕ′ōō-tä, sĕ′-) A Spanish city of NW Africa, an enclave in Morocco on the Strait of Gibraltar. Pop. 68,882.

Cé·vennes (sā-vĕn′) A mountain range of S France W of the Rhone R. and rising to 1,754.7 m (5,753 ft).

ce·vi·che or **se·vi·che** (sə-vē′chā, sĕ-) *n.* Raw fish marinated in lime or lemon juice and served usu. as an appetizer. [Am.Sp. < Sp. *cebiche,* fish stew < *cebo,* bait < Lat. *cibus,* food.]

Cey·lon (sĭ-lŏn′, sā-) See **Sri Lanka.** **—Cey′lo·nese′** (-nēz′, -nēs′) *adj. & n.*

Cé·zanne (sā-zăn′, -zän′), **Paul** 1839–1906. French artist and leading postimpressionist whose paintings include *The Card Players* (1890–92). **—Cé·zan′nesque′** (-zän′ĕsk′) *adj.*

Cf The symbol for the element **californium.**

CF *abbr.* **1a.** center field **b.** center fielder **2.** conversion factor **3.** cost and freight **4.** cystic fibrosis

cf. *abbr. Latin* confer (compare)

CFA (sē′ĕf-ā′) A trademark for a credential of people certified as Chartered Financial Analysts.

CFC *abbr.* chlorofluorocarbon

CFIDS (sē′fĭdz′) *abbr.* chronic fatigue immune dysfunction syndrome

cfm *abbr.* cubic feet per minute

cfs *abbr.* cubic feet per second

CFS *abbr.* chronic fatigue syndrome

cg also **cgm.** *abbr.* centigram

CG *abbr.* **1.** center of gravity **2.** coast guard **3.** commanding general **4.** consul general

cgs *abbr.* centimeter-gram-second system

ch *abbr.* **1.** chain (measurement) **2.** check (chess)

CH *abbr.* **1.** courthouse **2.** customhouse

ch. *abbr.* **1.** chapter **2.** check (bank order) **3a.** child **b.** children

Ch. *abbr.* **1.** chaplain **2.** chief **3.** China **4.** church

Cha·blis (shă-blē′, shä-, shăb′lē) *n.* **1.** A dry white wine originally from east-central France. **2.** A blended white table wine of California. [After *Chablis,* a village of N-central France.]

cha-cha (chä′chä) *n.* A rhythmic ballroom dance that originated in Latin America. [Am.Sp. *chachachá,* of imit. orig.] **—cha′-cha** *v.*

chach·ka or **tchotch·ke** (chŏch′kə) also **tsats·ke** (tsäts′kə) *n. Slang* A cheap showy trinket. [Yiddish *tshatshke* < Pol. dialectal *czaczka.*]

chac·ma (chăk′mə) *n.* A grayish-black baboon *(Papio ursinus)* of southern and eastern Africa. [Poss. of Khokhoin orig.]

Cha·co (chä′kō) See **Gran Chaco.**

cha·conne (shä-kôn′, -kŏn′) *n.* **1.** A slow stately dance of the 18th century or the music for it. **2.** A form consisting of variations based on a reiterated harmonic pattern. [Fr. < Sp. *chacona,* a kind of dance.]

chad (chăd) *n.* **1.** Scraps or bits of paper, such as the tiny rectangles punched out from data cards. **2.** One of these scraps or bits of paper. [?]

Chad A country of N-central Africa; achieved independence from France in 1960. Cap. N'Djamena. Pop. 4,405,000. **—Chad′i·an** *adj. & n.*

Chad, Lake A shallow lake of N-central Africa in Chad, Cameroon, Niger, and Nigeria.

Chad·ic (chăd′ĭk) *n.* A branch of the Afro-Asiatic language family, spoken in west-central Africa and including Hausa.

cha·dor (chä-dôr′) *n.* A loose, usu. black robe worn by women, esp. Iranian Muslims, that covers the body from head to toe. [Urdu *chādar,* cover, cloth < Pers., screen, tent < Skt. *chattram,* screen, parasol. See CHUDDAR.]

Chad·wick (chăd′wĭk), **Sir James** 1891–1974. British physicist who won a 1935 Nobel Prize.

chae·bol (jĕ′bəl) *n., pl.* **chaebol** A conglomerate of businesses, usu. owned by a single family, esp. in Korea. [Korean *chaebŏl* : *chae,* wealth (< M Chin. *tshaj*) + *bŏl,* powerful family (< M Chin. *buat*).]

Chaer·o·ne·a (kĕr′ə-nē′ə, kîr′-) An ancient city of E Greece where Philip of Macedon defeated a confederation of Greek states in 338 B.C.

chae·ta (kē′tə) *n., pl.* **-tae** (-tē′) A bristle or seta, esp. of an annelid worm. [NLat. < Gk. *khaitē,* long hair.]

chae·tog·nath (kē′tŏg-năth′) *n.* Any of various marine worms of the phylum Chaetognatha. [< NLat. *Chaetognatha,* phylum name : *chaeta,* chaeta (see CHAETA + Gk. *gnathos,* jaw.] **—chae′tog·nath′, chae·tog′na·thous** (-nə-thəs) *adj.*

chafe (chāf) *v.* **chafed, chaf·ing, chafes** —*tr.* **1.** To wear away or irritate by rubbing. **2.** To annoy; vex. **3.** To warm by rubbing. —*intr.* **1.** To rub and cause irritation or friction. **2.** To become worn or sore from rubbing. **3.** To feel irritated or impatient. ❖ *n.* Warmth, wear, or soreness produced by friction. **2.** Annoyance; vexation. [ME *chafen* < OFr. *chaufer,* to warm < VLat. *calefāre,* alteration of Lat. *calefacere : calēre,* to be warm + *facere,* to make; see **dhē-** in App.]

cha·fer (chā′fər) *n.* Any of various beetles of the family Scarabaeidae. [ME, a kind of beetle < OE *ceafor.*]

chaff¹ (chăf) *n.* **1.** *Botany* Thin dry bracts or scales, esp.: **a.** The bracts enclosing mature grains of wheat and some other cereal grasses, removed during threshing. **b.** The scales or bracts borne on the receptacle among the flowers of many plants in the composite family. **2.** Finely cut straw or hay used as fodder. **3.** Trivial or worthless matter. **4.** Strips of metal, foil, or glass fiber with a metal content that are used to reflect electromagnetic energy as a radar countermeasure. [ME *chaf* < OE *ceaf.*] **—chaff′fy** *adj.*

chaff² (chăf) *v.* **chaffed, chaff·ing, chaffs** —*tr.* To make fun of in a good-natured way; tease. —*intr.* **1.** To tease playfully. [Poss. alteration of CHAFE or CHAFF¹.] **—chaff** *n.*

chaff·er¹ (chăf′ər) *n.* One who engages in banter or good-natured teasing.

chaf·fer² (chăf′ər) *v.* **-fered, -fer·ing, -fers** —*intr.* **1.** To bargain or haggle. **2.** *Chiefly British* To bandy words; engage in small talk. —*tr.* To bargain or haggle for. ❖ *n. Archaic* A bargaining. [ME *chaffaren,* to haggle < *chaffare, cheapfare,* bargaining : *chep,* purchase; see CHEAP + *fare,* journey, business (< OE *faru < faran,* to

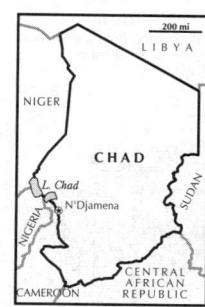

Chad

travel; see FARE).] —**chaf′fer·er** *n.*

chaf·finch (chăf′ĭnch) *n.* A small European songbird (*Fringilla coelebs*), the male of which has reddish-brown plumage. [ME *chaffinche* < OE *ceaffinc* : *ceaf*, chaff, husk + *finc*, finch.]

chaf·ing dish (chā′fĭng) *n.* A metal dish or pan mounted above a heating device and used to cook or warm food.

Cha·gall (shə-gäl′, -găl′, shä-), **Marc** 1887–1985. Russian-born painter noted for his dreamlike fanciful imagery.

Cha·gas′ disease (shä′gəs) *n.* A South American form of trypanosomiasis caused by the protozoan *Trypanosoma cruzi* and characterized by fever and enlargement of the spleen and lymph nodes. [After Carlos *Chagas* (1879–1934), Brazilian physician.]

Chag·a·tai (chăg′ə-tī′) See **Jagatai**.

Cha·gres (chä′grĕs) A river rising in central Panama and flowing SW to Gatún Lake then NW to the Caribbean Sea.

cha·grin (shə-grĭn′) *n.* A keen feeling of mental unease caused by failure, disappointment, or a disconcerting event. ❖ *tr.v.* **-grined**, **-grin·ing**, **-grins** To cause to feel chagrin; mortify or discomfit. [Fr., poss. < dialectal Fr. *chagraigner*, to distress < OFr. *graim*, gloomy, of Gmc. orig.]

chai (chī) *n.* A beverage made from spiced black tea, honey, and milk. [Ult. < Chin. (Mandarin) *chá*, tea.]

chain (chān) *n.* **1a.** A connected, flexible series of links, typically metal, used, for example, for binding or for transmitting mechanical power. **b.** Such a set of links, often of precious metal and with pendants attached, worn as an ornament or symbol of office. **2.** A restraining or confining agent or force. **3. chains a.** Bonds, fetters, or shackles. **b.** Captivity or oppression; bondage. **4.** A series of closely linked or connected things. **5.** A number of establishments under common ownership or management. **6.** A mountain range. **7.** *Chemistry* A group of atoms bonded in a spatial configuration like chain links. **8a.** A surveying instrument consisting of 100 linked pieces of iron or steel and measuring 66 feet (20.1 meters). **b.** A similar instrument used in engineering, measuring 100 feet (30.5 meters). **c.** A unit of measurement equal to the length of either of these instruments. ❖ *tr.v.* **chained**, **chain·ing**, **chains 1.** To bind or make fast with a chain or chains. **2.** To restrain or confine as if with chains. [ME *chaine* < OFr. < Lat. *catēna*.]

Chain, **Sir Ernst Boris** 1906–79. German-born British biochemist who shared a 1945 Nobel Prize.

chain·fall (chān′fôl′) *n.* A hoisting device consisting of a chain suspended from or laid over a fixed, raised structure such as a beam, used esp. to lift vehicle engines.

chain fern *n.* Any of various terrestrial ferns of the genus *Woodwardia*, native chiefly to the Northern Hemisphere and having leaves that bear chainlike rows of spore cases.

chain gang *n.* A group of convicts chained together.

chain letter *n.* A letter asking each recipient to send copies with the same request to a specified number of others.

chain·link fence (chān′lĭngk′) *n.* A fence made of thick steel wire interwoven in a diamond pattern.

chain mail *n.* Flexible armor made of metal links or scales.

chain·man (chān′mən) *n.* Either of the two persons who hold a surveyor's measuring chain.

chain pickerel *n.* A freshwater game and food fish (*Esox niger*) of eastern North America.

chain-re·act (chān′rē-ăkt′) *intr.v.* **-act·ed**, **-act·ing**, **-acts** To undergo a chain reaction.

chain reaction *n.* **1.** A series of events in which each induces or influences the next. **2.** *Physics* A multistage nuclear reaction, esp. a self-sustaining series of fissions in which the release of neutrons from the splitting of one atom leads to the splitting of others. **3.** *Chemistry* A series of reactions in which one product of a reacting set is a reactant in the following set.

chain saw *n.* A portable power saw with teeth linked in an endless chain. —**chain′-saw′** (chān′sô′) *v.*

chain-smoke (chān′smōk′) *v.* **-smoked**, **-smok·ing**, **-smokes** —*intr.* To smoke continually. —*tr.* To smoke (cigarettes, for example) in continuing succession. —**chain smoker** *n.*

chain stitch *n.* A decorative sewing stitch in which loops are connected like the links of a chain.

chain store *n.* A retail store that is part of a chain.

chair (châr) *n.* **1.** A piece of furniture consisting of a seat, legs, back, and often arms, holding one person. **2.** A seat of office, authority, or dignity. **3a.** An office or position of authority. **b.** A person who holds an office or a position of authority; a chairperson. **4.** The position of a player in an orchestra. **5.** *Slang* The electric chair. **6.** A seat carried about on poles; a sedan chair. **7.** Any of several objects that serve to support or secure. ❖ *tr.v.* **chaired**, **chair·ing**, **chairs 1.** To install in a position of authority, esp. as a presiding officer. **2.** To preside over as chairperson. [ME *chaiere* < OFr. < Lat. *cathedra*.]

chair car *n.* See **parlor car**.

chair·lift (châr′lĭft′) *n.* A mechanized, cable-suspended, aerial chair assembly used as transport along a mountain slope.

chair·man (châr′mən) *n.* **1.** A man who is a chairperson. **2.** A chairperson. See Usage Note at **man**. —**chair′man** *v.*

chair·man·ship (châr′mən-shĭp′) *n.* The office or term of a chairman.

chair·per·son (châr′pûr′sən) *n.* **1.** The presiding officer of an

assembly, a meeting, a committee, or a board. **2.** The administrative head of a department of instruction, as at a college. See Usage Note at **man**.

chair·wom·an (châr′wŏom′ən) *n.* A woman who is a chairperson. See Usage Note at **man**.

chaise (shāz) *n.* **1.** Any of various light open carriages, often with a collapsible hood, esp. a two-wheeled carriage drawn by one horse. **2.** A post chaise. **3.** A chaise longue. [Fr., chair, var. of OFr. *chaiere*. See CHAIR.]

chaise longue (shāz lông′) *n.*, *pl.* **chaise longues** or **chaises longues** (shāz lông′) A reclining chair with a long seat that supports the outstretched legs. [Fr. : *chaise*, chair + *longue*, long.]

chak·ra (chŭk′rə) *n.* One of the seven centers of spiritual energy in the human body according to yoga philosophy. [Skt. *cakram*, wheel, circle. See **kʷel-** in App.]

cha·lah (KHä′lə) *n.* Variant of **challah**.

cha·la·za (kə-lā′zə, -lăz′ə) *n.*, *pl.* **-zae** (-zē) or **-zas 1.** *Biology* One of two spiral bands of tissue in an egg that connect the yolk to the lining membrane at either end of the shell. **2.** *Botany* The region at the base of the nucellus of an ovule. [Gk. *khalaza*, hard lump, hailstone.] —**cha·la′zal** *adj.*

cha·la·zi·on (kə-lā′zē-ən, -ŏn′) *n.*, *pl.* **-zi·a** (-zē-ə) A cyst of a tarsal gland. [Gk. *khalazion*, dim. of *khalaza*, lump.]

Chal·ce·don (kăl′sĭ-dŏn′, kăl-sēd′n) An ancient Greek city of NW Asia Minor on the Bosporus; founded 685 B.C.

chal·ced·o·ny (kăl-sĕd′n-ē) *also* **cal·ced·o·ny** *n.*, *pl.* **-nies** A translucent to transparent milky or grayish quartz with distinctive microscopic crystals arranged in slender fibers in parallel bands. [LLat. *chalcēdonius* < Gk. *Khalkēdōn*, a mystical stone (Rev. 21:19), perh. < *Khalkēdōn*, Chalcedon.] —**chal′ce·don′ic** (kăl′sĭ-dŏn′ĭk) *adj.*

chal·cid (kăl′sĭd) *n.* Any of various minute wasps of the superfamily Chalcidoidea. [< NLat. *Chalcis*, type genus < Gk. *khalkos*, copper (< the wasp's metallic color).]

Chal·cid·i·ce (kăl-sĭd′ĭ-sē) *also* **Khal·ki·dhi·kí** (kăl-kē′thē-kē′, KHäl-) A mountainous peninsula of NE Greece projecting into the N Aegean Sea. —**Chal·cid′i·an** *adj. & n.*

Chal·cis (kăl′sĭs) *also* **Khal·kís** (kăl-kēs′, KHäl-) An ancient city of SE Greece on the W coast of Euboea.

chal·co·cite (kăl′kə-sīt′) *n.* A dark gray mineral, essentially Cu₂S, that is an important ore of copper. [Alteration of obsolete *chalcosine* < Gk. *khalkos*, copper.]

Chal·co·lith·ic (kăl′kə-lĭth′ĭk) *adj.* Of or relating to the period of human culture preliminary to the Bronze Age, characterized by the use of copper and stone tools. ❖ *n.* The Chalcolithic Period. [Gk. *khalkos*, copper + –LITH + –IC.]

chal·co·py·rite (kăl′kə-pī′rīt′) *n.* A yellow mineral, essentially CuFeS₂, that is an important ore of copper. [NLat. *chalcopyrites* : Gk. *khalkos*, copper + PYRITES.]

Chal·de·a *or* **Chal·dae·a** (kăl-dē′ə) An ancient region of S Mesopotamia; settled c. 1000 B.C.

Chal·de·an *also* **Chal·dae·an** (kăl-dē′ən) *or* **Chal·dee** (kăl′dē′) *adj.* Of or relating to Chaldea or its people, language, or culture. ❖ *n.* **1.** A member of an ancient Semitic people who ruled in Babylonia. **2.** See **Aramaic**. **3.** A person versed in occult learning. —**Chal·da′ic** (-dā′ĭk) *adj. & n.*

chal·dron (chôl′drən) *n.* A former unit of dry measure in England, equal to about 32 bushels for grain and 36 bushels for coal. [ME < OFr. *chauderon*, augmentative of *chaudiere*, kettle < LLat. *caldāria*. See CAULDRON.]

cha·let (shă-lā′, shăl′ā) *n.* **1a.** A wooden dwelling with a sloping roof and widely overhanging eaves, common in Alpine regions. **b.** A cottage or lodge built in this style. **2.** The hut of a herder in the Swiss Alps. [Fr. < Swiss Fr.]

Cha·leur Bay (shə-lŏor′, -lûr′) An inlet of the Gulf of St. Lawrence between E Quebec and N New Brunswick, Canada.

chal·ice (chăl′ĭs) *n.* **1.** A cup or goblet. **2.** A cup for the Eucharistic wine. [ME < OFr. < Lat. *calix*, calic-.]

chal·i·co·there (kăl′ĭ-kə-thîr′) *n.* Any of various extinct ungulate mammals of the Eocene to Pliocene epochs, having threeclawed, three-toed feet. [NLat. *Chalicotherium*, genus name : Gk. *khalix*, *khalik-*, pebble + Gk. *thērion*, dim. of *thēr*, beast; see **ghwer-** in App.]

chalk (chôk) *n.* **1.** A soft compact calcite, CaCO₃, with varying amounts of silica, quartz, feldspar, or other mineral impurities, generally gray-white or yellow-white and derived chiefly from fossil seashells. **2a.** A piece of chalk or chalklike substance in crayon form, used for marking on a surface. **b.** *Games* A small cube of chalk used in rubbing the tip of a billiard or pool cue to increase friction with the cue ball. **3.** A mark made with chalk. **4.** *Chiefly British* A score or tally. ❖ *tr.v.* **chalked**, **chalk·ing**, **chalks 1.** To mark, draw, or write with chalk. **2.** To rub or cover with chalk. **3.** To make pale; whiten. **4.** To treat (soil, for example) with chalk. —*phrasal verb:* **chalk up 1.** To earn or score. **2.** To credit or ascribe. [ME < OE *cealk* < Lat. *calx*, calc-, lime. See CALX.] —**chalk′i·ness** *n.* —**chalk′y** *adj.*

chalk·board (chôk′bôrd′, -bōrd′) *n.* A smooth hard panel, usu. green or black, for writing on with chalk; a blackboard.

chalk·stone (chôk′stōn′) *n.* See **tophus 1.**

chal·lah *also* **cha·lah** *or* **hal·lah** (KHä′lə, hä′-) *n.* A loaf of yeastleavened egg bread, usu. braided, traditionally eaten by Jews on

chain
left to right: figaro, sash, and stud links

chairlift

chalet
Zermatt, Switzerland

the Sabbath, holidays, and other ceremonial occasions. [Heb. *ḥallâ*, something perforated (unattested sense), challah < *ḥālal*, to pierce.]

chal•lenge (chăl′ənj) *n.* **1a.** A call to engage in a contest, fight, or competition. **b.** An act or statement of defiance; a call to confrontation. **2.** A demand for explanation or justification; a calling into question. **3.** A sentry's call to an unknown party for proper identification. **4.** A test of one's abilities or resources. **5.** A claim that a vote is invalid or that a voter is unqualified. **6.** *Law* A formal objection to the inclusion of a prospective juror in a jury. **7.** *Immunology* The challenging of an organism. ❖ *v.* **-lenged, -leng•ing, -leng•es** —*tr.* **1a.** To call to engage in a contest, fight, or competition. **b.** To invite with defiance; dare. **2.** To take exception to; dispute. **3.** To order to halt and be identified. **4.** *Law* To take formal objection to (a prospective juror). **5.** To question the qualifications of (a voter) or validity of (a vote). **6.** To have due claim to; call for. **7.** To summon to action, effort, or use; stimulate. **8.** *Immunology* To induce or evaluate an immune response in (an organism) by administering a specific antigen to which it has been sensitized. —*intr.* **1.** To make or give voice to a challenge. **2.** To begin barking upon picking up the scent. Used of hunting dogs. [ME *chalenge* < OFr. < Lat. *calumnia*, trickery, false accusation; see CALUMNY. V., ME *chalengen* < OFr. *chalangier* < Lat. *calumniāre* < *calumnia*.] —**chal′lenge•a•ble** *adj.*

chal•lenged (chăl′ənjd) *adj.* **1.** Having a disability or impairment: *developmentally challenged.* **2.** Deficient or lacking: *an ethically challenged politician.*

USAGE NOTE People who object to the terms *disabled* and *handicapped* as being too negative sometimes propose the substitution of *challenged* instead, as in referring to persons with physical disabilities as *physically challenged.* While this particular phrase is quite popular, similar usages such as *mentally challenged* are often taken to be condescending and so have failed to win equal acceptance. Indeed, the widespread parody of *challenged* in such expressions as *electronically challenged* for "inept at using computers" has effectively eliminated it as an all-purpose alternative to *disabled* or *handicapped.*

chal•leng•er (chăl′ən-jər) *n.* **1.** One that challenges. **2.** *Sports* One who competes against a champion.

chal•leng•ing (chăl′ən-jĭng) *adj.* **1.** Demanding all of one's abilities or resources in a stimulating way. **2.** Absorbing; intriguing.

chal•lis (shăl′ē) *n.* A soft, lightweight, usu. printed fabric made of wool, cotton, or rayon. [Poss. < the surname *Challis*.]

cha•lone (kā′lōn′, kăl′ōn′) *n.* Any of several polypeptides produced by a body tissue that cause the reversible inhibition of mitosis in the tissue cells. [< Gk. *khalōn*, pr. part. of *khalān*, to slacken.]

Châ•lons-sur-Marne (shä-lôN′sûr′märn′, -sür-) A city of NE France E of Paris. The Huns under Attila were defeated here in A.D. 451. Pop. 51,137.

cha•lyb•e•ate (kə-lĭb′ē-ĭt, -lē′bē-) *adj.* **1.** Impregnated with or containing salts of iron. **2.** Tasting like iron, as water from a mineral spring. ❖ *n.* Water or medicine containing iron in solution. [NLat. *chalybeātus* < Lat. *chalybs*, steel < Gk. *khalups*, *khalub-*, poss. < *Khalups*, sing. of *Khalubes*, Chalybes, people of Asia Minor famous for their steel.]

Cha•mae•leon also **Cha•me•leon** (kə-mēl′yən, -mē′lē-ən) *n.* A constellation in the southern polar region near Apus and Mensa. [Lat. *chamaeleōn*, chameleon. See CHAMELEON.]

cham•ae•phyte (kăm′ə-fīt′) *n.* A low-growing perennial plant with dormant overwintering buds borne near the ground. [Gk. *khamai*, on the ground; see **dhghem-** in App. + –PHYTE.]

cham•ber (chām′bər) *n.* **1.** A room in a house, esp. a bedroom. **2.** A room where a person of importance receives visitors. **3. chambers** A room in which a judge may consult privately with attorneys or hear cases not taken into court. **4. chambers** *Chiefly British* A suite of rooms, esp. one used by lawyers. **5.** A hall for the meetings of a legislative or other assembly. **6.** A legislative or judicial body. **7.** A board or council. **8.** A place where municipal or state funds are received and held; a treasury. **9a.** An enclosed space or compartment: *a compression chamber.* **b.** An enclosed space in the body of an organism; a cavity. **10a.** A compartment in a firearm that holds the cartridge in readiness for firing. **b.** An enclosed space in the bore of a gun that holds the charge. ❖ *tr.v.* **-bered, -ber•ing, -bers 1.** To put in or as if in a chamber; enclose or confine. **2.** To furnish with a chamber. **3.** To design or manufacture (a firearm) to hold a specific type of cartridge. [ME *chaumbre* < OFr. *chambre* < LLat. *camera*, chamber < Lat., vault < Gk. *kamarā*.]

cham•bered nautilus (chām′bərd) *n.* See **nautilus** 1.

cham•ber•lain (chām′bər-lĭn) *n.* **1a.** An officer who manages the household of a sovereign or noble; a chief steward. **b.** A high-ranking royal court official. **2.** An official who receives the rents and fees of a municipality; a treasurer. **3.** *Roman Catholic Church* An often honorary papal attendant. [ME *chaumberlein* < OFr. *chamberlenc* < Frankish **kamerling* : LLat. *camera*, chamber; see CHAMBER + Gmc. *-*linga-*, one connected with; see –LING[1].]

Chamberlain, (Arthur) Neville 1869–1940. British prime minister (1937–40) who advocated a policy of appeasement toward the fascist regimes of Europe.

Chamberlain, Sir **(Joseph) Austen** 1863–1937. British politician who shared the 1925 Nobel Peace Prize.

Chamberlain, Wilton Norman ("Wilt") 1936–99. Amer. basketball player who holds the record for most points (100) scored in a single NBA game.

cham•ber•maid (chām′bər-mād′) *n.* A woman who cleans and cares for bedrooms, as in a hotel.

chamber music *n.* Compositions traditionally intended for performance in a private room or small concert hall by an instrumental ensemble, with one player for each part.

chamber of commerce *n., pl.* **chambers of commerce** An association of businesspersons and merchants for the promotion of commercial interests in the community.

chamber pot *n.* A portable vessel used as a toilet.

chamber tomb *n.* A Neolithic tomb consisting of a chamber built out of large upright stones with one or more capstones, buried in an earthen mound.

cham•bray (shăm′brā′) *n.* A fine lightweight fabric woven with white threads across a colored warp. [Alteration of Fr. *cambrai*, cambric, after *Cambrai*, a city of northern France.]

cha•me•leon (kə-mēl′yən, -mē′lē-ən) *n.* **1.** Any of various tropical Old World lizards of the family Chamaeleonidae, marked by their ability to change color. **2.** See **anole. 3.** A changeable person. **4. Chameleon** Variant of **Chamaeleon.** [ME *camelioun* < Lat. *chamaeleōn* < Gk. *khamaileōn* : *khamai*, on the ground; see **dhghem-** in App. + *leōn*, lion (transl. of Akkadian *nēš qaqqari*, ground lion, lizard); see LION.] —**cha•me′le•on′ic** (-lē-ŏn′ĭk) *adj.*

cham•fer (chăm′fər) *tr.v.* **-fered, -fer•ing, -fers 1.** To cut off the edge or corner of; bevel. **2.** To cut a groove in; flute. ❖ *n.* **1.** A flat surface made by cutting off the edge or corner of a block of wood or other material. **2.** A furrow or groove, as in a column. [Prob. back-formation < *chamfering* < Fr. *chanfrein*, beveled edge < p. part. of OFr. *chanfreindre*, to bevel : *chant*, edge (< Lat. *canthus*, iron tire; see CANT[1]) + *fraindre*, to break (< Lat. *frangere*; see **bhreg-** in App.).]

cham•fron (chăm′frən) *n.* Armor used to protect the front of a war horse's head in medieval times. [ME *shamfron* < OFr. *chanfrein* : Lat. *cāmus*, horse muzzle, heavy necklace (< Gk. *kēmos*) + Lat. *frēnum*, bridle, bit; see FRENUM.]

cha•mi•se (chə-mēz′) also **cha•mi•so** (-mē′sō) *n., pl.* **-ses** also **-sos** An evergreen shrub *(Adenostoma fasciculatum)* in the rose family, native to California and having needlelike leaves in fascicles and small white flower clusters. [Sp. *chamisa* < Galician *chamiça*, dry brush, firewood < *chama*, flame < Lat. *flamma*.]

cham•ois (shăm′ē) *n., pl.* **cham•ois** (shăm′ēz) **1.** An extremely agile goat antelope *(Rupicapra rupicapra)* of mountainous regions of Europe, having upright horns with backward-hooked tips. **2.** also **cham•my** or **sham•my** (shăm′ē), *pl.* **-mies a.** A soft leather made from the hide of this animal or other animals such as deer. **b.** A piece of such leather, or a similar cotton fabric. **3.** A moderate to grayish yellow. [Fr. < OFr. < LLat. *camōx*.]

cham•o•mile or **cam•o•mile** (kăm′ə-mīl′, -mēl′) *n.* **1.** An aromatic perennial herb *(Chamaemelum nobile)* in the composite family, native to Europe and the Mediterranean and having feathery foliage and white and yellow flowers. **2.** A similar related Eurasian annual plant *(Matricaria recutita).* **3.** The dried flower heads of either one of these plants, used in herbal tea, commercial flavorings, and perfumery. [ME *camomille* < OFr. < LLat. *chamomilla*, alteration of Lat. *chamaemēlon* < Gk. *khamaimēlon* : *khamai*, on the ground; see **dhghem-** in App. + *mēlon*, apple.]

Cha•mor•ro (chə-môr′ō, chä-môr′rō) *n., pl.* **Chamorro** or **-ros 1.** A member of a people of Guam and the Northern Mariana Islands. **2.** The Austronesian language of the Chamorros.

champ[1] (chămp) *v.* **champed, champ•ing, champs** —*tr.* To bite or chew upon noisily. —*intr.* To work the jaws and teeth vigorously. —***idiom:* champ at the bit** To show impatience at being held back or delayed. [Prob. imit.]

champ[2] (chămp) *n. Informal* A champion.

cham•pagne (shăm-pān′) *n.* **1a.** A sparkling white wine made from a blend of grapes, produced in Champagne. **b.** A similar sparkling wine made elsewhere. **2.** A pale orange yellow to grayish yellow or yellowish gray. [Fr., short for *(vin de) Champagne*, (wine from) Champagne < LLat. *campānia*, flat open country. See CAMPAIGN.]

Cham•pagne (shăm-pān′, shäN-pän′yə) A historical region and former province of NE France; noted for its sparkling wine (first produced here c. 1700).

cham•paign (shăm-pān′) *n.* A stretch of level and open country; a plain. [ME *champain* < OFr. *champainge* < LLat. *campānia*. See CAMPAIGN.] —**cham•paign′** *adj.*

Champaign A city of E-central IL adjoining Urbana; founded 1855. Pop. 67,518.

cham•pak also **cham•pac** (chăm′păk, chŭm′pŭk) or **cham•pa•ca** (chăm′pə-kə, chŭm′-) *n.* An evergreen timber tree *(Michelia champaca)* native to India and having fragrant orange-yellow flowers that yield an oil used in perfumery. [Hindi *campak* < Skt. *campakaḥ*, of Dravidian orig.; akin to Tamil *caṇpakam*.]

cham•per•ty (chăm′pər-tē) *n., pl.* **-ties** A sharing in the proceeds of a lawsuit by an outside party who has promoted the litigation. [ME *champartie* < OFr. *champart*, the lord's share of the

chameleon
Meller's chameleon
Chamaeleo melleri

chamois
Rupicapra rupicapra

ă	pat	oi	boy
ā	pay	ou	out
âr	care	ŏŏ	took
ä	father	ōō	boot
ĕ	pet	ŭ	cut
ē	be	ûr	urge
ĭ	pit	th	thin
ī	pie	*th*	this
îr	pier	hw	which
ŏ	pot	zh	vision
ō	toe	ə	about, item
ô	paw		

Stress marks:
′ (primary);
′ (secondary), as in
lexicon (lĕk′sĭ-kŏn′)

tenant's crop < Med.Lat. *campars, campīpars* : Lat. *campī*, genitive of *campus*, field + Lat. *pars*, part; see PART.] —**cham′per•tous** (-təs) *adj.*

cham•pi•gnon (shăm-pǐn′yən) *n.* An edible mushroom, esp. *Agaricus bisporus.* [Fr., alteration of OFr. *champigneul*, prob. < VLat. *(fungus) campiniolus*, (fungus) growing in the fields < LLat. *campānia*, countryside. See CAMPAIGN.]

cham•pi•on (chăm′pē-ən) *n.* **1.** One that wins first place or first prize in a competition. **2.** One that is clearly superior or has the attributes of a winner. **3.** An ardent defender or supporter of a cause or another person. **4.** One who fights; a warrior. ❖ *tr.v.* **-oned, -on•ing, -ons** **1.** To fight for, defend, or support as a champion. See Syns at **support. 2.** *Obsolete* To defy or challenge. ❖ *adj.* **1.** Holding first place or prize. **2.** Superior to all others. [ME *champioun*, combatant, athlete < OFr. *champion* < Med.Lat. *campiō, campiōn-* < Lat. *campus*, field.]

cham•pi•on•ship (chăm′pē-ən-shǐp′) *n.* **1.** The position or title of a winner. **2.** Defense or support; advocacy. **3.** A competition or series of competitions held to determine a winner.

Cham•plain (shăm-plān′), **Lake** A lake of NE NY, NW VT, and S Quebec, Canada.

Cham•plain (shăm-plān′, shän-plăn′), **Samuel de** 1567?–1635. French explorer who founded a settlement (1608) on the site of present-day Quebec.

champ•le•vé (shän-lə-vā′) *n.* A technique of decorating metal in which hollowed-out areas are filled with colored enamel and fired. [Fr. : *champ*, field (< OFr. < Lat. *campus*) + *levé*, raised; see LEVEE[2].] —**champ′le•vé′** *adj.*

Cham•pol•lion (shän-pô-lyôn′), **Jean François** 1790–1832. French Egyptologist who first deciphered Egyptian hieroglyphics (1821).

Champs É•ly•sées (shän zā-lē-zā′) A tree-lined thoroughfare of Paris, France, leading from the Place de la Concorde to the Arc de Triomphe.

chance (chăns) *n.* **1a.** The unknown and unpredictable element in happenings that seems to have no assignable cause. **b.** A force assumed to cause events that cannot be foreseen or controlled; luck. **2.** The likelihood of something happening; possibility or probability. Often used in the plural. **3.** An accidental or unpredictable event. **4.** A favorable set of circumstances; an opportunity. **5.** A risk or hazard; a gamble. **6.** *Games* A raffle or lottery ticket. **7.** *Baseball* An opportunity to make a putout or assist that counts as an error if unsuccessful. ❖ *adj.* Caused by or ascribable to chance; unexpected, random, or casual. ❖ *v.* **chanced, chanc•ing, chanc•es** —*intr.* To come about by chance; occur. —*tr.* To take the risk or hazard of. —*phrasal verb:* **chance on (or upon)** To find or meet accidentally; happen upon. —*idioms:* **by chance 1.** Without plan; accidentally. **2.** Possibly; perchance. **on the off chance** In the slight hope or possibility. [ME, unexpected event < OFr. < VLat. **cadentia* < Lat. *cadēns, cadent-*, pr. part. of *cadere*, to fall, befall.]

SYNONYMS *chance, random, casual, haphazard, desultory* These adjectives apply to what is determined by accident. *Chance* stresses lack of premeditation: *a chance meeting. Random* implies the absence of a specific pattern or objective: *a random guess. Casual* often suggests an absence of due concern: *a casual query. Haphazard* implies a carelessness or a willful leaving to chance: *a haphazard plan. Desultory* suggests a shifting about from one thing to another without method: *a desultory conversation.*

chance•ful (chăns′fəl) *adj.* **1.** Eventful. **2.** *Archaic* Casual.

chan•cel (chăn′səl) *n.* The space around a church altar for the clergy and sometimes the choir, often enclosed by a lattice or railing. [ME *chauncel* < OFr. *chancel* < LLat. *cancellus*, latticework, sing. of Lat. *cancellī*. See CANCEL.]

chan•cel•ler•y or **chan•cel•lor•y** (chăn′sə-lə-rē, -slə-rē) *n., pl.* **-ies 1.** A chancellor's rank or position. **2a.** A chancellor's office or department. **b.** The building where such an office or department is located. **3.** The official place of business of an embassy or consulate. [ME *chancelrie* < OFr. *chancelerie* < *chancelier*, chancellor. See CHANCELLOR.]

chan•cel•lor (chăn′sə-lər, -slər) *n.* **1.** Any of various officials of high rank, esp.: **a.** A secretary to a monarch or noble. **b.** *Chiefly British* The chief secretary of an embassy. **c.** The chief minister of state in some European countries. **2a.** The president of certain American universities. **b.** *Chiefly British* The honorary or titular head of a university. **3.** *Law* The presiding judge of a court of chancery or equity in some states of the United States. [ME *chaunceler* < OFr. *chancelier* < LLat. *cancellārius*, doorkeeper < Lat. *cancellī*, bars, latticework. See CANCEL.] —**chan′cel•lor•ship′** *n.*

Chancellor of the Exchequer *n.* The senior finance minister in the British government and a member of the prime minister's cabinet.

Chan•cel•lors•ville (chăn′sə-lərz-vǐl′, -slərz-) A former town of NE VA W of Fredericksburg; site of a major Civil War battle (May 2–4, 1863).

chance-med•ley (chăns′měd′lē) *n.* A random, haphazard action or occurrence. [ME *chaunce medley*, manslaughter < Norman Fr. *chance medlee* : OFr. *chance*, accident; see CHANCE + OFr. *medlee*, mixed; see MEDLEY.]

chan•cer•y (chăn′sə-rē) *n., pl.* **-ies 1.** *Law* **a.** A court of chancery. **b.** The proceedings and practice of a court of chancery; equity. **c.** A court of public record; an office of archives. **d.** One of the five divisions of the British High Court of Justice, presided over by the Lord High Chancellor. **2.** A chancellor's office or department; a chancellery. [ME *chancerie*, alteration of *chancelrie.* See CHANCELLERY.]

Chan Chan (chän′ chän′) A ruined pre-Incan city of N Peru; probably built after A.D. 800.

Chan•chiang (jän′jyäng′) See **Zhanjiang.**

chan•cre (shăng′kər) *n.* **1.** A dull red, hard, insensitive lesion that is the first manifestation of syphilis. **2.** An ulcer at the initial point of entry of a pathogen. [Fr. < OFr. < Lat. *cancer*, tumor, crab.] —**chan′crous** (-krəs) *adj.*

chan•croid (shăng′kroid′) *n.* A soft, highly infectious, nonsyphilitic venereal ulcer of the genital region, caused by the bacillus *Hemophilus ducreyi.* [Fr. *chancroïde* < *chancre*, chancre. See CHANCRE.] —**chan′croi′dal** (-kroid′l) *adj.*

chanc•y (chăn′sē) *adj.* **-i•er, -i•est 1.** Uncertain as to outcome; risky; hazardous. **2.** Random; haphazard. **3.** *Scots* Lucky; propitious. —**chanc′i•ness** *n.*

chan•de•lier (shăn′də-lîr′) *n.* A branched decorative lighting fixture that holds a number of bulbs or candles and is suspended from a ceiling. [ME *chandeler* < OFr. *chandelier*, ult. < Lat. *candēlabrum*, candelabrum. See CANDELABRUM.]

chan•delle (shän-děl′) *n.* A sudden, steep climbing turn of an aircraft to alter flight direction while gaining altitude. [Fr. < *chandelle*, candle < OFr. < Lat. *candēla.* See CANDLE.]

Chan•di•garh (chŭn′dē-gər, chŭn′dĭ-gŭr′) A city of N India N of Delhi. Pop. 504,094.

chan•dler (chănd′lər) *n.* **1.** One that makes or sells candles. **2.** A retail dealer in specified goods or equipment. [ME *chaundeler* < OFr. *chandelier* < VLat. **candēlārius* < Lat. *candēla*, candle.] —**chan′dler•y** (chănd′lə-rē) *n.*

Chandler A city of S-central AZ SE of Phoenix. Pop. 176,581.

Chandler, Raymond Thornton 1888–1959. Amer. writer whose detective novels include *The Big Sleep* (1939).

Cha•nel (shə-něl′), **Gabrielle Bonheur** Known as "Coco." 1883–1971. French fashion designer famous for her tailored suits.

Chang•chow (chäng′jō′) See **Changzhou.**

Chang•chun (chäng′chōōn′) Formerly **Hsin•king** (shǐn′kǐng′, -gǐng′) A city of NE China SSW of Harbin; cap. of Jilin province. Pop. 2,980,870.

change (chānj) *v.* **changed, chang•ing, chang•es** —*tr.* **1a.** To cause to be different: *change the spelling of a word.* **b.** To give a completely different form or appearance to; transform: *changed the yard into a garden.* **2.** To give and receive reciprocally; interchange: *change places.* **3.** To exchange for or replace with another, usu. of the same kind or category: *a light that changes colors.* **4a.** To lay aside, abandon, or leave for another; switch: *change sides.* **b.** To transfer from (one conveyance) to another: *change planes.* **5.** To give or receive the equivalent of (money) in lower denominations or in foreign currency. **6.** To put a fresh covering on: *change a bed.* —*intr.* **1.** To become different or undergo alteration: *He changed as he matured.* **2.** To undergo transformation or transition: *The music changed to a slow waltz.* **3.** To go from one phase to another, as the moon. **4.** To make an exchange: *If you prefer this seat, I'll change with you.* **5.** To transfer from one conveyance to another: *She changed in Chicago on her way to the coast.* **6.** To put on other clothing: *We changed for dinner.* **7.** To become deeper in tone: *His voice began to change at 13.* ❖ *n.* **1.** The act, process, or result of altering or modifying: *a change in facial expression.* **2.** The replacing of one thing for another; substitution: *a change of ownership.* **3.** A transformation or transition from one state, condition, or phase to another: *the change of seasons.* **4.** Something different; variety: *ate early for a change.* **5.** A different or fresh set of clothing. **6a.** Money of smaller denomination given or received in exchange for money of higher denomination. **b.** The balance of money returned when an amount given is more than what is due. **c.** Coins: *had change jingling in his pocket.* **7.** *Music* **a.** A pattern or order in which bells are rung. **b.** In jazz, a change of harmony; a modulation. **8.** A market or exchange where business is transacted. —*phrasal verb:* **change off 1.** To alternate with another person in performing a task. **2.** To perform two tasks at once by alternating or a single task by alternate means. —*idioms:* **change hands** To pass from one owner to another. **change (one's) mind** To reverse a previously held opinion or an earlier decision. **change (one's) tune** To alter one's approach or attitude. [ME *changen* < Norman Fr. *chaunger* < Lat. *cambiāre, cambīre*, to exchange, prob. of Celt. orig.] —**chang′er** *n.*

change•a•ble (chān′jə-bəl) *adj.* **1.** Liable to change; capricious. **2.** Being such that alteration is possible. **3.** Varying in color or appearance from different viewpoints. —**change′a•bil′i•ty, change′a•ble•ness** *n.* —**change′a•bly** *adv.*

change•ful (chānj′fəl) *adj.* Having the tendency or ability to change. —**change′ful•ly** *adv.* —**change′ful•ness** *n.*

change•less (chānj′lĭs) *adj.* Unchanging; constant.

change•ling (chānj′lĭng) *n.* **1.** A child secretly exchanged for another. **2.** *Archaic* A changeable, fickle person. **3.** *Archaic* A person of deficient intelligence.

change of heart *n., pl.* **changes of heart** A reversal of one's opinion, attitude, or feelings.
change of life *n.* Menopause.
change•o•ver (chānj′ō′vər) *n.* A conversion to a different purpose or from one system to another, as in equipment.
change ringing *n.* The ringing of a set of chimes or bells, esp. in a belltower, with every possible unrepeated variation.
change•up (chānj′ŭp′) *n. Baseball* A pitch that looks like a fastball but actually moves more slowly, thereby prompting a premature swing. [Alteration of *change-of-pace.*]
Chang Jiang (chäng′ jyäng′) or **Yang•tze River** (yăng′sē′, -tsē′, yäng′dzə′) The longest river of China and of Asia, flowing c. 5,551 km (3,450 mi) from Xizang (Tibet) to the East China Sea.
Chang•sha (chäng′shä′) A city of S China on the Xiang Jiang WSW of Shanghai; cap. of Hunan province. Pop. 1,328,950.
Chang•zhou also **Chang•chow** (chäng′jō′) A city of E China on the Grand Canal WNW of Shanghai. Pop. 729,893.
Chan•kiang (chän′kyäng′, jän′jyäng′) See **Zhanjiang.**
chan•nel[1] (chăn′əl) *n.* **1.** The bed of a stream or river. **2.** The deeper part of a river or harbor, esp. a deep navigable passage. **3.** A broad strait, esp. one that connects two seas. **4.** A trench, furrow, or groove. **5.** A tubular passage for liquids; a conduit. **6.** A course or pathway through which information is transmitted: *channels of thought.* **7.** A route of communication or access. Often used in the plural. **8.** *Electronics* A specified frequency band for the transmission and reception of electromagnetic signals, as for television. **9.** *Computer Science* A site on a network, as on IRC, where people hold online conversations in real time. **10.** The medium through which a spirit guide purportedly communicates. **11.** A rolled metal bar with a bracket-shaped section. **12.** A temporary opening in a cell membrane for the passage of ions or molecules. ❖ *tr.v.* **-neled, -nel•ing, -nels** also **-nelled, -nel•ling, -nels 1.** To make or cut channels in. **2.** To form a groove or flute in. **3.** To direct or guide along some desired course. **4.** To serve as a medium for (a spirit guide). [ME *chanel* < OFr. < Lat. *canālis.* See CANAL.] **—chan′nel•er** *n.*
chan•nel[2] (chăn′əl) *n.* A ledge projecting from a sailing ship's sides to spread the shrouds and keep them clear of the gunwales. [Alteration of obsolete *chainwale* : CHAIN + WALE.]
channel bass *n.* See **red drum.**
channel black *n.* A type of carbon black formed by exposing an iron plate to a natural gas flame. [< CHANNEL[1].]
channel catfish *n.* A freshwater food fish *(Ictalurus punctatus)* common to the central United States.
chan•nel•ing (chăn′ə-lĭng) *n.* The act or practice of serving as a medium through which a spirit guide purportedly communicates with living persons.
Channel Islands A group of British islands in the English Channel off the coast of Normandy, France; orig. settled by Norse mariners.
chan•nel•ize (chăn′ə-līz′) *tr.v.* **-ized, -iz•ing, -iz•es 1.** To make, form, or cut channels in. **2.** To direct through a channel. **—chan′nel•i•za′tion** (chăn′ə-lĭ-zā′shən) *n.*
chan•nel-surf (chăn′əl-sûrf′) *intr.v.* **-surfed, -surf•ing, -surfs** To watch television stations in succession for short periods by using a remote control. **—channel surfer** *n.*
Chan•ning (chăn′ĭng), **William Ellery** 1780–1842. Amer. religious leader and a founder of Unitarianism.
cha•no•yu (chä′nô-yo͞o′) *n.* An ancient Japanese ritual for the preparation, serving, and drinking of tea. [J. : *cha,* tea (< M Chin.) + *no,* possessive particle + *yu,* hot water.]
chan•son (shäN-sôN′) *n., pl.* **-sons** (-sôN′, -sôNz′) A song, esp. a French one. [Fr. < OFr. < Lat. *cantiō, cantiōn-* < *cantus,* p. part. of *cantāre,* to sing. See CHANT.]
chanson de geste (də zhĕst′) *n., pl.* **chansons de geste** An Old French epic poem of the 11th to the 14th century celebrating the deeds of historical or legendary figures. [Fr. : *chanson,* song + *de,* of + *geste,* heroic exploit.]
chant (chănt) *n.* **1a.** A short simple melody in which syllables or words are sung on or intoned to the same note or a limited range of notes. **b.** A canticle or prayer sung or intoned in this manner. **c.** A song or melody. **2.** A monotonous rhythmic call or shout, as of a slogan. ❖ *v.* **chant•ed, chant•ing, chants** *—tr.* **1.** To sing or intone to a chant. **2.** To celebrate in song. **3.** To say in the manner of a chant. *—intr.* **1.** To sing, esp. in the manner of a chant. **2.** To speak monotonously. [Prob. < Fr., song < OFr. < Lat. *cantus* < p. part. of *canere,* to sing. V., ME *chaunten,* to sing < OFr. *chanter* < Lat. *cantāre,* freq. of *canere.* See **kan-** in App.] **—chant′ing•ly** *adv.*
chant•er (chăn′tər) *n.* **1.** A person who chants. **2.** The pipe of a bagpipe on which the melody is played. **3.** A priest who sings in a chantry.
chan•te•relle (shăn′tə-rĕl′, shän′-) *n.* **1.** A trumpet-shaped edible mushroom *(Cantharellus cibarius)* that is yellow to orange in color. **2.** Any of various similar mushrooms of the genera *Cantharellus, Polyozellus,* and *Gomphus,* several of which are inedible or poisonous. [Fr. < NLat. *cantharella,* fem. dim. of Lat. *cantharus,* cup (< its shape) < Gk. *kantharos.*]
chan•teuse (shäN-tœz′) *n.* A woman singer, esp. a nightclub singer. [Fr., fem. of *chanteur,* singer < *chanter,* to sing. See CHANT.]
chan•tey also **chan•ty** (shăn′tē, chăn′-) or **shan•tey** or **shan•ty** (shăn′tē) *n., pl.* **-teys** also **-ties** A sailors' song sung to the rhythm of their work movements. [Prob. < Fr. *chantez,* imper. pl. of *chanter,* to sing < OFr. See CHANT.]
chan•ti•cleer (chăn′tĭ-klîr′, shăn′-) *n.* A rooster. [ME *chaunteclere* < OFr. *chantecler,* the rooster in the tale of Reynard the Fox.]
chan•try (chăn′trē) *n., pl.* **-tries** *Ecclesiastical* **1.** An endowment to cover expenses for the saying of masses and prayers, usu. for the soul of the founder of the endowment. **2.** An altar or chapel endowed for the saying of such masses and prayers. [ME *chanterie* < OFr. < *chanter,* to sing. See CHANT.]
Cha•nu•kah (KHä′nə-kə, hä′-) *n.* Variant of **Hanukkah.**
Chao K'uang-yin (jou′ kwäng′yĭn′) See **Zhao Kuangyin.**
Chao Phra•ya (chou prä-yä′) A river of Thailand formed by the Nan and Ping rivers and flowing c. 225 km (140 mi) S to the Gulf of Thailand.
cha•os (kā′ŏs′) *n.* **1.** A condition or place of great disorder or confusion. **2.** A disorderly mass; a jumble. **3.** often **Chaos** The disordered state of unformed matter and infinite space supposed in some cosmogonic views to have existed before the ordered universe. **4.** *Mathematics* A dynamical system that has a sensitive dependence on its initial conditions. **5.** *Obsolete* An abyss; a chasm. [ME, formless primordial space < Lat. < Gk. *khaos.*] **—cha•ot′ic** (-ŏt′ĭk) *adj.* **—cha•ot′i•cal•ly** *adv.*
Chao Tzu-yang (jou′ dzo͞o-yäng′) See **Zhao Ziyang.**
chap[1] (chăp) *v.* **chapped, chap•ping, chaps** *—tr.* To cause (the skin) to chap. *—intr.* To split or become rough and sore. ❖ *n.* A chapping of the skin. [ME *chappen.*]
chap[2] (chăp) *n. Informal* A man or boy; a fellow. [Short for CHAPMAN.]
Cha•pa•la (chə-pä′lə) A lake of W-central Mexico SE of Guadalajara.
chap•ar•ral (shăp′ə-răl′) *n.* **1.** *Ecology* A biome characterized by hot dry summers and cool moist winters and dominated by a dense growth of mostly small-leaved evergreen shrubs. **2.** A dense thicket of shrubs and small trees. [Sp. < *chaparro,* evergreen oak < Basque *txapar,* dim. of *saphar,* thicket.]
chaparral bird *n.* See **roadrunner.**
chaparral cock *n.* See **roadrunner.**
cha•pa•ti also **cha•pat•ti** (chə-pä′tē) *n., pl.* **-tis** A flat, unleavened, disk-shaped bread of northern India, made of wheat flour, water, and salt. [Hindi *capātī.*]
chap•book (chăp′bo͝ok′) *n.* A small book or pamphlet of poems, ballads, stories, or religious tracts. [CHAP(MAN) + BOOK.]
chape (chāp, chăp) *n.* A metal tip or mounting on a scabbard or sheath. [ME < OFr., hood, head covering < LLat. *cappa,* hooded cloak.]
cha•peau (shă-pō′) *n., pl.* **-peaus** or **-peaux** (-pōz′) A hat. [Fr. < OFr. *chapel* < VLat. *cappellus,* dim. of LLat. *cappa,* hooded cloak.]
chap•el (chăp′əl) *n.* **1a.** A place of worship that is smaller than and subordinate to a church. **b.** A place of worship in an institution, such as a hospital. **c.** A recess or room in a church set apart for special or small services. **d.** A place of worship for those not belonging to an established church. **e.** The services held at a chapel. **2.** *Music* A choir or orchestra connected with a place of worship at a royal court. **3a.** A funeral home. **b.** A room in a funeral home for services. [ME *chapele* < OFr. < Med.Lat. *capella,* cape, canopy, chapel, dim. of *capa* < LLat. *cappa,* hooded cloak.]
Chapel Hill A town of N-central NC at the edge of the Piedmont WNW of Raleigh. Pop. 48,715.
chap•er•on or **chap•er•one** (shăp′ə-rōn′) *n.* **1.** A person, esp. an older or married woman, who accompanies a young unmarried woman in public. **2.** An older person who supervises a social gathering for young people. **3.** A guide or companion whose purpose is to ensure propriety or restrict activity. ❖ *tr.v.* **-oned, -on•ing, -ones** To act as chaperon to or for. See Syns at **accompany.** [Fr. < *chaperon,* hood < OFr., dim. of *chape,* cape, head covering. See CHAPE.] **—chap′er•on′age** (-rō′nĭj) *n.*
chap•fall•en (chăp′fô′lən) also **chop•fall•en** (chŏp′-) *adj.* Being in low spirits. [< obsolete *chaps,* alteration of CHOPS.]
chap•i•ter (chăp′ĭ-tər) *n. Architecture* The capital of a column. [ME *chapitre,* chapter, chapiter. See CHAPTER.]
chap•lain (chăp′lĭn) *n.* **1.** A member of the clergy attached to a chapel. **2a.** A member of the clergy who conducts religious services for an institution, such as a hospital. **b.** A member of the clergy who is connected with a royal court or an aristocratic household. **3.** A member of the clergy attached to a branch of the armed forces. [ME *chapelein* < OFr. *chapelain* < Med.Lat. *capellānus* < *capella,* chapel. See CHAPEL.] **—chap′lain•cy, chap′lain•ship′** *n.*
chap•let (chăp′lĭt) *n.* **1.** A wreath or garland for the head. **2.** *Roman Catholic Church* **a.** A rosary having beads for five decades of Hail Marys. **b.** The prayers counted on such a rosary. **3.** A string of beads. [ME *chapelet* < OFr., dim. of *chapel,* hat, wreath. See CHAPEAU.] **—chap′let•ed** *adj.*
Chap•lin (chăp′lĭn), Sir **Charles Spencer** Known as "Charlie." 1889–1977. British-born actor and filmmaker noted esp. for his role as a tramp in baggy trousers and a bowler hat.
chap•man (chăp′mən) *n.* **1.** *Chiefly British* A peddler. **2.** *Archaic*

chanoyu

chanterelle
Cantharellus cibarius

Charlie Chaplin

ă	pat	oi	boy
ā	pay	ou	out
âr	care	o͝o	took
ä	father	o͞o	boot
ĕ	pet	ŭ	cut
ē	be	ûr	urge
ĭ	pit	th	thin
ī	pie	*th*	this
îr	pier	hw	which
ŏ	pot	zh	vision
ō	toe	ə	about, item
ô	paw		

Stress marks:
′ (primary);
′ (secondary), as in
lexicon (lĕk′sĭ-kŏn′)

A dealer or merchant. [ME < OE *cēapman* : *cēap*, trade; see CHEAP + *man, mann*, man; see MAN.]

Chapman, George 1559?–1634. English writer and dramatist noted for his translations of Homer.

Chapman, John Known as "Johnny Appleseed." 1775?–1845. Amer. pioneer who was legendary for planting apple seeds in the Ohio R. Valley.

chaps (chăps, shăps) *pl.n.* Heavy leather trousers without a seat, worn over ordinary trousers by ranch hands to protect their legs. [Short for Am.Sp. *chaparreras* < Sp. *chaparro*, chaparral. See CHAPARRAL.]

Chap Stick A trademark used for a medicinal preparation for the prevention or treatment of chapped lips.

chap•ter (chăp′tər) *n.* **1.** One of the main divisions of a relatively lengthy piece of writing, such as a book, that is usu. numbered or titled. **2.** A distinct period or sequence of events. **3.** A local branch of an organization, such as a club or fraternity. **4a.** An assembly of the canons of a church or of the members of a religious residence. **b.** The canons of a church or the members of a religious residence considered as a group. **5.** A short scriptural passage read after the psalms in certain church services. [ME *chaptre*, var. of *chapitre*, chapter, chapiter < OFr. alteration of *chapitle* < Lat. *capitulum*, dim. of *caput*, head. See **kaput-** in App.]

chapter house *n.* **1.** A building in which the chapter of a church or religious residence assembles. **2.** A house in which a chapter of a fraternity or sorority lives and meets.

Cha•pul•te•pec (chə-pool′tə-pĕk′) A rocky hill S of Mexico City, Mexico; site of a major Amer. victory (Sep. 12–13, 1847) during the Mexican War.

char[1] (chär) *v.* **charred, char•ring, chars** —*tr.* **1.** To burn the surface of; scorch. **2.** To reduce to carbon or charcoal by incomplete combustion. —*intr.* **1.** To become scorched. **2.** To become reduced to carbon or charcoal. ❖ *n.* A charred substance. [Back-formation < CHARCOAL.]

char[2] *also* **charr** (chär) *n., pl.* **char** or **chars** *also* **charr** or **charrs** Any of several fishes of the genus *Salvelinus*, esp. the arctic char. [?]

char[3] (chär) *Chiefly British n.* A charwoman. ❖ *intr.v.* **charred, char•ring, chars** To work as a charwoman. [ME, a piece of work < OE *cierr*, a turning.]

char•a•banc (shăr′ə-băng′) *n. Chiefly British* A large sightseeing bus. [< Fr. *char à bancs* : *char*, coach, carriage + *à*, with + *bancs*, benches.]

char•a•cin (kăr′ə-sĭn) *also* **char•a•cid** (-sĭd) *n.* See **tetra.** [< NLat. Characinidae, former family name < Gk. *kharax, kharak-*, a kind of fish.]

char•ac•ter (kăr′ək-tər) *n.* **1.** The combination of qualities or features that distinguishes one person, group, or thing from another. **2.** A distinguishing feature or attribute, as of an individual, group, or category. **3.** *Genetics* A structure, function, or attribute determined by a gene or group of genes. **4.** Moral or ethical strength. **5.** A description of a person's attributes, traits, or abilities. **6.** A formal written statement as to competency and dependability, given by an employer to a former employee; a recommendation. **7.** Public estimation of someone; reputation. **8.** Status or role; capacity. **9a.** A notable or well-known person; a personage. **b.** A person, esp. one who is peculiar or eccentric. **10a.** A person portrayed in an artistic piece, such as a novel. **b.** Characterization in fiction or drama. **11.** A mark or symbol used in a writing system. **12.** *Computer Science* **a.** One of a set of symbols, such as letters or numbers, that are arranged to express information. **b.** The numerical code representing such a character. **13.** A style of printing or writing. **14.** A symbol used in secret writing; a cipher or code. ❖ *adj.* **1.** Of or relating to one's character. **2.** Of, relating to, or specializing in the interpretation of roles that emphasize fixed personality traits or specific physical characteristics. **3.** Dedicated to the portrayal of a person with regard to distinguishing psychological or physical features: *a character sketch.* **4.** *Law* Of or relating to one who testifies as to the morals and ethics of one engaged in a lawsuit. ❖ *tr.v.* **-tered, -ter•ing, -ters** *Archaic* **1.** To write, print, engrave, or inscribe. **2.** To portray or describe. —*idioms:* **in character** Consistent with someone's general character or behavior. **out of character** Inconsistent with someone's general character or behavior. [ME *carecter*, distinctive mark, imprint on the soul < OFr. *caractere* < Lat. *charactēr* < Gk. *kharaktēr* < *kharassein*, to inscribe < *kharax, kharak-*, pointed stick.] —**char′ac•ter•less** *adj.*

character assassination *n.* A vicious personal verbal attack, esp. one intended to damage a public figure's reputation.

char•ac•ter•is•tic (kăr′ək-tə-rĭs′tĭk) *adj.* Being a feature that helps to distinguish a person or thing; distinctive. ❖ *n.* **1.** A characteristic feature. **2.** *Mathematics* The integral part of a logarithm as distinguished from the mantissa: *The characteristic of the logarithm 6.3214 is 6.* —**char′ac•ter•is′ti•cal•ly** *adv.*

char•ac•ter•i•za•tion (kăr′ək-tər-ĭ-zā′shən) *n.* **1.** The act or an instance of characterizing. **2.** A description of qualities or peculiarities. **3.** Representation of a character or characters on the stage or in writing.

char•ac•ter•ize (kăr′ək-tə-rīz′) *tr.v.* **-ized, -iz•ing, -iz•es** **1.** To describe the qualities or peculiarities of. **2.** To be a distinctive mark of; distinguish. —**char′ac•ter•iz′er** *n.*

char•ac•ter•y (kăr′ək-tə-rē, kə-răk′-) *n., pl.* **-ies** A system of characters or symbols used to express thought and meaning.

cha•rade (shə-rād′) *n.* **1.** *Games* **a. charades** (*used with a sing. or pl. verb*) A game in which words or phrases are represented in pantomime until guessed. **b.** An episode in this game or a word or phrase so represented. **2.** A readily perceived pretense; a travesty. [Fr., prob. < Provençal *charrado*, chat < *charra*, perh. < Ital. *ciarlare*.]

char•broil (chär′broil′) *tr.v.* **-broiled, -broil•ing, -broils** To broil over charcoal. [CHAR[1] + BROIL[1].]

char•coal (chär′kōl′) *n.* **1.** A black, porous, carbonaceous material produced by the destructive distillation of wood and used as a fuel, filter, and absorbent. **2a.** A drawing pencil or crayon made from charcoal. **b.** A drawing executed with a charcoal. **3.** A dark grayish brown to black or dark purplish gray. ❖ *tr.v.* **-coaled, -coal•ing, -coals** **1.** To draw, write, or blacken with charcoal. **2.** To charbroil. [ME *charcol* : *char* (perh. < OFr. *charbon* < Lat. *carbō*; see CARBON) + *col*, charcoal, coal; see COAL.]

char•cu•ter•ie (shär-kōō′tə-rē′, -kōō′tə-rē) *n.* **1.** Sausages and other cooked or processed meat foods. **2.** A delicatessen specializing in such foods. [Fr. < *chaircuicterie* : *chair*, meat (< Lat. *carō*, flesh; see CARNAGE) + *cuict, cuit*, cooked (< Lat. *coctus*, p. part. of *coquere*; see COOK).]

chard (chärd) *n.* Swiss chard. [Alteration (poss. influenced by Fr. *chardon*, thistle) of Fr. *carde* < Provençal *cardon*, cardoon. See CARDOON.]

Char•don•nay *also* **char•don•nay** (shär′dn-ā′, shär′dn-ā′) *n.* **1.** A variety of grape used to make white wine. **2.** A dry white table wine made from this grape.

Cha•rente (shə-ränt′, shä-räNt′) A river of W France flowing c. 354 km (220 mi) to the Bay of Biscay.

charge (chärj) *v.* **charged, charg•ing, charg•es** —*tr.* **1.** To impose a duty, responsibility, or obligation on. **2.** To set or ask (a given amount) as a price. **3.** To hold financially liable; demand payment from. **4.** To postpone payment on (a purchase) by recording as a debt. **5a.** To load to capacity; fill. **b.** To saturate; impregnate. **6.** To load (a gun or other firearm) with a quantity of explosive. **7.** To instruct or urge authoritatively; command. **8.** *Law* To instruct (a jury) about the law, its application, and the weighing of evidence. **9.** To make a claim of wrongdoing against; accuse or blame. **10.** To put the blame for; attribute or impute. **11.** To attack violently. **12.** *Sports* To bump or rush into (an opposing player) illegally. **13.** *Electricity* **a.** To cause formation of a net electric charge on or in (a conductor, for example). **b.** To energize (a storage battery) by passing current through it in the direction opposite to discharge. **14.** To excite; rouse: *charged up the crowd.* **15.** To direct or put (a weapon) into position for use; level. **16.** *Heraldry* To place a charge on (an escutcheon). —*intr.* **1.** To rush forward in or as if in a violent attack. **2.** To demand or ask payment. **3.** To postpone payment for a purchase. **4.** *Accounting* To consider or record as a loss. Often used with *off.* ❖ *n.* **1a.** Expense; cost. **b.** The price asked for something. **2a.** A weight or burden; a load. **b.** The quantity that a container or apparatus can hold. **3.** A quantity of explosive to be set off at one time. **4.** An assigned duty or task; a responsibility. **5.** One that is entrusted to another's care or management. **6a.** Supervision; management. **b.** Care; custody. See Syns at **care. 7.** An order, command, or injunction. **8.** *Law* Instruction given by a judge to a jury about the law. **9.** A claim of wrongdoing; an accusation. **10a.** A rushing, forceful attack. **b.** The command to attack. **11.** A debt or an entry in an account recording a debt. **12.** A financial burden, such as a tax or lien. **13.** *Symbol* **q** *Physics* **a.** The intrinsic property of matter responsible for all electric phenomena, in particular for the force of the electromagnetic interaction, occurring in two forms arbitrarily designated *negative* and *positive.* **b.** A measure of this property. **c.** The net measure of this property possessed by a body or contained in a bounded region of space. **14.** *Informal* A feeling of pleasant excitement; a thrill. **15.** *Heraldry* Any figure or device represented on the field of an escutcheon. —*idiom:* **in charge 1.** In a position of leadership or supervision. **2.** *Chiefly British* Under arrest. [ME *chargen*, to load < OFr. *chargier* < LLat. *carricāre* < Lat. *carrus*, a Gallic type of wagon. See CAR.]

charge•a•ble (chär′jə-bəl) *adj.* **1.** Suitable to be charged, as to an account: *chargeable expenses.* **2.** Liable to be accused or indicted. —**charge′a•ble•ness** *n.*

charge account *n.* A credit arrangement in which a customer receives purchased goods or services before paying for them.

charge card *n.* See **credit card.**

charge conjugation *n. Symbol* **C** **1.** A mathematical operator that changes the sign of the charge and of the magnetic moment of every particle in the system to which it is applied. **2.** The theoretical conversion of matter to antimatter or of antimatter to matter.

char•gé d'af•faires (shär-zhā′ də-fâr′, dā-) *n., pl.* **char•gés d'affaires** (-zhā′, -zhāz′) **1.** A diplomat who temporarily substitutes for an absent ambassador or minister. **2.** A diplomat of the lowest rank, accredited by one government to the minister of foreign affairs of another. [Fr. : *chargé*, in charge, p. part. of *charger*, to charge + *de*, with, of + *affaires*, affairs.]

charge density *n.* The electric charge per unit area or per unit volume of a body or of a region of space.

charg·er[1] (chär′jər) *n.* **1.** One that charges, such as an instrument that charges or replenishes storage batteries. **2.** A horse trained for battle; a cavalry horse.

charg·er[2] (chär′jər) *n.* A large shallow dish; a platter. [ME *chargeour* < OFr. *chargeor* < *chargier*, to load. See CHARGE.]

Cha·ri or **Sha·ri** (shä′rē) A river of N-central Africa rising in the Central African Republic and flowing c. 2,253 km (1,400 mi) to Lake Chad.

char·i·ot (chăr′ē-ət) *n.* **1.** An ancient horse-drawn two-wheeled vehicle. **2.** A light four-wheeled carriage used for ceremony or pleasure. [ME, vehicle < OFr. < *char*, cart < Lat. *carrus*, a Gallic type of wagon. See CAR.] —**char′i·ot** *v.*

char·i·o·teer (chăr′ē-ə-tîr′) *n.* **1.** The driver of a chariot. **2.** Charioteer See **Auriga**.

char·ism (kăr′ĭz′əm) *n. Christianity* Charisma.

cha·ris·ma (kə-rĭz′mə) *n., pl.* **-ma·ta** (-mə-tə) **1a.** A rare personal quality of leaders who arouse fervent popular devotion and enthusiasm. **b.** Personal magnetism or charm. **2.** *Christianity* An extraordinary power, such as the ability to work miracles, granted by the Holy Spirit. [Gk. *kharisma*, divine favor < *kharizesthai*, to favor < *kharis*, favor.]

char·is·mat·ic (kăr′ĭz-măt′ĭk) *adj.* **1.** Of, relating to, or characterized by charisma. **2.** Of, relating to, or being a type of Christianity that emphasizes personal religious experience and divinely inspired powers. ❖ *n.* A member of a Christian charismatic group or movement.

char·i·ta·ble (chăr′ĭ-tə-bəl) *adj.* **1.** Generous in giving money or other help to the needy. **2.** Mild or tolerant in judging others; lenient. **3.** Of, for, or concerned with charity. —**char′i·ta·ble·ness** *n.* —**char′i·ta·bly** *adv.*

Char·i·ton (shăr′ĭ-tn) A river rising in S IA and flowing c. 451 km (280 mi) to the Missouri R. in N MO.

char·i·ty (chăr′ĭ-tē) *n., pl.* **-ties** **1.** Provision of help or relief to the poor; almsgiving. **2.** Something given to help the needy; alms. **3.** A charitable institution, organization, or fund. **4.** Benevolence or generosity toward others. **5.** Indulgence or forbearance in judging others. See Syns at **mercy.** **6.** often **Charity** *Christianity* The theological virtue defined as love directed first toward God but also toward oneself and one's neighbors as objects of God's love. [ME *charite* < OFr., Christian love < Lat. *cāritās*, affection < *cārus*, dear. See **kā-** in App.]

cha·ri·va·ri (shĭv′ə-rē′, shĭv′ə-rē′) *n., pl.* **-ris** *Regional* See **shivaree.** [Fr. < OFr., perh. < LLat. *caribaria*, headache < Gk. *karēbariā* : *karē*, head; see **ker-**[1] in App. + *barus*, heavy; see **gʷerə-** in App.]

char·kha also **char·ka** (chûr′kə, chär′-) *n.* A spinning wheel used in India for spinning cotton. [Hindi *carkhā* < Pers. *charkha*, dim. of *charkh*, wheel < OPers. *carka-. See **kʷel-** in App.]

char·la·tan (shär′lə-tn) *n.* A person who makes elaborate, fraudulent, and often voluble claims to skill or knowledge; a quack or fraud. [Fr. < Ital. *ciarlatano*, prob. alteration (influenced by *ciarlare*, to prattle) of *cerretano*, inhabitant of *Cerreto*, a city of Italy once famous for its quacks.] —**char′la·tan′ic** (-tăn′ĭk), **char′la·tan′i·cal** *adj.* —**char′la·tan·ism, char′la·tan·ry** *n.*

Char·le·magne (shär′lə-mān′) Also called **Charles I** or "**Charles the Great.**" 742?–814. King of the Franks (768–814) and founder of the first empire in W Europe after the fall of Rome.

Char·le·roi (shär′lə-roi′, shär-lə-rwä′) A city of S Belgium S of Brussels; founded 1666. Pop. 206,928.

Charles (chärlz) Prince of Wales. b. 1948. The eldest son of Elizabeth II and heir to the British throne.

Charles I[1] 1600–49. King of England, Scotland, and Ireland (1625–49) who was defeated in the English Civil War (1642–48), tried for treason, and beheaded.

Charles I[2] 1887–1922. Emperor of Austria (1916–18) and king of Hungary as Charles IV (1916–18); deposed.

Charles II 1630–85. King of England, Scotland, and Ireland (1660–85) who reigned during the Restoration.

Charles V 1500–58. Holy Roman emperor (1519–58) and king of Spain as Charles I (1516–56); summoned the Diet of Worms (1521) and the Council of Trent (1545–63).

Charles VII 1403–61. King of France (1422–61) who ended the Hundred Years' War (1453).

Charles IX 1550–74. King of France (1560–74) who ordered the Saint Bartholomew's Day Massacre (1572).

Charles X 1757–1836. King of France (1824–30) who attempted to restore absolutism by abolishing the Chamber of Deputies and freedom of the press.

Charles XIV Orig. Jean Baptiste Jules Bernadotte. 1763–1844. King of Sweden and Norway (1818–44) who founded the present Swedish royal dynasty.

Charles, Ray b. 1930. Amer. musician and composer whose songs are rooted in gospel music, blues, and jazz.

Charles·bourg (shärl-bûrg′, shärl-bōōr′) A city of S Quebec, Canada, near Quebec City; settled in 1659. Pop. 70,942.

Charles Mar·tel (mär-tĕl′) Known as "the Hammer." 688?–741. Frankish ruler of Austrasia (715–741) who in 732 halted the European invasion of the Moors.

Charles River A river, c. 97 km (60 mi), of E MA flowing into Boston harbor.

Charles's law (chärl′zĭz) *n.* The physical law that the volume of a fixed mass of gas held at a constant pressure varies directly with the absolute temperature. [After Jacques Alexandre César *Charles* (1746–1823), French physicist.]

Charles's Wain *n.* See **Big Dipper.** [ME *charleswen*, Charles's (Charlemagne's) wain.]

Charles·ton[1] (chärl′stən) **1.** A city of SE SC NE of Savannah. Pop. 96,650. **2.** The cap. of WV, in the W-central part. Pop. 53,421.

Charles·ton[2] (chärl′stən) *n.* A fast ballroom dance popular during the 1920s and characterized by lively leg kicking and arm swinging. [After CHARLESTON[1], SC.]

Charles·town (chärlz′toun′) A former city of E MA, the oldest part of present-day Boston; settled c. 1629.

char·ley horse (chär′lē) *n. Informal* A cramp or stiffness in a muscle, esp. of the upper leg, caused by strain. [?]

char·lock (chär′lŏk, -lŏk′) *n.* An annual weed (*Sinapis arvensis*) in the mustard family, native to Eurasia and having racemes of yellow flowers and hairy stems and foliage. [ME *cherlok* < OE *cerlic.*]

char·lotte (shär′lət) *n.* A dessert consisting of a mold of sponge cake or bread with a filling, as of fruits, whipped cream, or custard. [Fr. < the personal name *Charlotte.*]

Char·lotte[2] (shär′lət) A city of S NC near the SC border SSW of Winston-Salem; settled c. 1750. Pop. 540,828.

Charlotte A·ma·lie (ə-mäl′yə) The cap. of the US Virgin Islands, on St. Thomas I. in the West Indies. Pop. 11,842.

charlotte russe (rōōs′) *n.* A cold dessert of Bavarian cream set in a mold lined with ladyfingers. [Fr. : *charlotte,* charlotte + *russe,* Russian.]

Char·lotte·town (shär′lət-toun′) The cap. of Prince Edward I., Canada, on the S coast; founded c. 1720. Pop. 32,531.

charm (chärm) *n.* **1.** The power or quality of pleasing or delighting. **2.** A particular quality that attracts; a delightful characteristic. **3.** A small ornament, such as one worn on a bracelet. **4.** An item worn for its supposed magical benefit; an amulet. **5.** An action or formula thought to have magical power. **6.** The chanting of a magic word or verse; incantation. **7.** *Physics* A quantum property of the charm quark whose conservation explains the absence of certain strange-particle decay modes. ❖ *v.* **charmed, charm·ing, charms** —*tr.* **1.** To attract or delight greatly. **2.** To induce by using strong personal attractiveness. **3.** To cast or seem to cast a spell on; bewitch. —*intr.* **1.** To be alluring or pleasing. **2.** To function as an amulet or charm. **3.** To use magic spells. [ME *charme,* magic spell < OFr. < Lat. *carmen,* incantation. See **kan-** in App.] —**charm′ing·ly** *adv.* —**charm′less** *adj.*

SYNONYMS *charm, beguile, bewitch, captivate, enchant, entrance, fascinate* These verbs mean to attract strongly or irresistibly: *manners that charmed us all; delicacies that beguile the gourmet; a performance that bewitched the audience; a novel that captivates its readers; an evening that enchanted the guests; music that entrances listeners; a host who fascinated his guests.* **ANTONYM** *repel*

charmed life (chärmd) *n.* A life that seems to have been protected by a charm or spell.

charmed particle *n. Physics* A particle with nonzero total charm.

charm·er (chär′mər) *n.* **1.** One that charms, esp. a disarmingly attractive person. **2.** One who casts spells; an enchanter.

char·meuse (shär-mōōz′, -mōōs′, -mœz′) *n.* A satin-finished silk fabric. [Fr., trade name.]

char·mo·ni·um (chär-mō′nē-əm) *n.* Any of various elementary particles consisting of a charm quark and an antiquark. [< CHARM.]

charm quark *n.* A quark with a charge of +⅔, a mass about 2,900 times that of the electron, and a charm of +1.

char·nel (chär′nəl) *n.* A repository for the bones or bodies of the dead; a charnel house. ❖ *adj.* Resembling, suggesting, or suitable for receiving the dead. [ME < OFr. < LLat. *carnāle* < neut. of Lat. *carnālis,* of the flesh < *carō, carn-,* flesh. See **sker-**[1] in App.]

charnel house *n.* A building, room, or vault in which the bones or bodies of the dead are placed; a charnel.

Char·on (kâr′ən) *n. Greek Mythology* **1.** The ferryman who conveyed the dead to Hades over the river Styx. **2.** The only satellite of Pluto.

Char·pak (shär-päk′), **Georges** b. 1924. Polish-born French physicist who won a 1992 Nobel Prize.

char·qui (chär′kē) *n.* See **jerky**[2]. [Am.Sp. < Quechua *ch'arki.*]

charr (chär) *n.* Variant of **char**[2].

chart (chärt) *n.* **1.** A map showing coastlines, water depths, or other information of use to navigators. **2.** An outline map on which specific information, such as scientific data, can be plotted. **3.** A sheet presenting information in the form of graphs or tables. **4.** See **graph**[1] 2. **5.** A listing of best-selling recorded music or other items. Often used in the plural. ❖ *v.* **chart·ed, chart·ing, charts** —*tr.* **1.** To make a chart of. **2.** To plan (something) in detail. —*intr.* To be ranked on a chart of best-selling items. [Obsolete Fr. *charte* < Lat. *charta,* sheet of paper made from papyrus. See CARD[1].]

char·ter (chär′tər) *n.* **1.** A document issued by a sovereign, legislature, or other authority, creating a public or private corporation, such as a city, college, or bank, and defining its privileges

Charlemagne
with a model of his church
at Aachen

ă	pat	oi	boy
ā	pay	ou	out
âr	care	ŏŏ	took
ä	father	ōō	boot
ĕ	pet	ŭ	cut
ē	be	ûr	urge
ĭ	pit	th	thin
ī	pie	*th*	this
îr	pier	hw	which
ŏ	pot	zh	vision
ō	toe	ə	about,
ô	paw		item

Stress marks:
′ (primary);
′ (secondary); as in
lexicon (lĕk′sĭ-kŏn′)

and purposes. **2.** A written grant from the sovereign power of a country conferring certain rights and privileges on a person, a corporation, or the people. **3.** A document outlining the principles, functions, and organization of a corporate body; a constitution. **4.** An authorization from a central organization to establish a local branch or chapter. **5.** Special privilege or immunity. **6a.** A contract for the commercial leasing of a vessel or space on a vessel. **b.** The hiring or leasing of a vehicle, esp. for the exclusive, temporary use of a group of travelers. **7.** A written instrument given as evidence of agreement, transfer, or contract; a deed. ❖ *adj.* Of or relating to an arrangement in which transportation is leased by a group of travelers for their exclusive, temporary use. ❖ *tr.v.* **-tered, -ter·ing, -ters 1.** To grant a charter to; establish by charter. **2.** To hire or lease by charter. **3.** To hire (a bus or airplane, for example) for the exclusive, temporary use of a group of travelers. [ME *chartre* < OFr. < Lat. *chartula,* dim. of *charta,* paper made < papyrus. See CARD¹.] —**char′ter·er** *n.*

char·tered accountant (chär′tərd) *n. Chiefly British* A member of one of the institutes of accountants granted a royal charter.

char·ter·house (chär′tər-hous′) *n.* A Carthusian monastery. [ME *charterhous,* by folk ety. < AN *chartrouse* < OFr. *(maison) chartreuse,* Carthusian (house), fem. of *chartreus,* Carthusian, var. of *charteus* < Med.Lat. *cartusius.*]

charter member *n.* An original member or a founder of an organization.

charter school *n.* A public school operated independently of the local school board.

Chart·ism (chär′tĭz′əm) *n.* The principles and practices of a party of political reformers active in England from 1838 to 1848. [< Med.Lat. *charta,* charter (referring to the "People's Charter" of 1837) < Lat., paper, document. See CARD¹.] —**Chart′ist** *adj. & n.*

chart·ist (chär′tĭst) *n.* A stock-market analyst who attempts to determine future price movements by using charts and graphs showing past price movements.

Char·tres (shärt, shär′trə) A city of N France SW of Paris; noted for its 13th-cent. Gothic cathedral. Pop. 37,119.

char·treuse (shär-trooz′, -troos′, -trœz′) *n.* A strong to brilliant greenish yellow to moderate or strong yellow green. [After CHARTREUSE.] —**char′treuse′** *adj.*

Chartreuse A trademark used for a usu. yellow or green liqueur.

char·tu·lar·y (kär′chə-lĕr′ē) *n.* Variant of **cartulary.**

char·wom·an (chär′woom′ən) *n.* A woman hired to do cleaning or similar work, usu. in a large building.

char·y (châr′ē) *adj.* **-i·er, -i·est 1.** Very cautious; wary. **2.** Not giving or expending freely; sparing. [ME *chari,* careful, sorrowful < OE *cearig,* sorrowful < *cearu,* sorrow. See CARE.] —**char′i·ly** *adv.* —**char′i·ness** *n.*

Cha·ryb·dis (kə-rĭb′dĭs) *n. Greek Mythology* A whirlpool off the Sicilian coast, opposite the cave of Scylla.

chase¹ (chās) *v.* **chased, chas·ing, chas·es** —*tr.* **1.** To follow rapidly in order to catch or overtake; pursue. **2.** To follow (game) in order to capture or kill; hunt. **3.** *Informal* To seek the favor or company of persistently. **4.** To put to flight; drive. —*intr.* **1.** To go or follow in pursuit. **2.** *Informal* To go hurriedly; rush. ❖ *n.* **1.** The act of chasing; pursuit. **2a.** The hunting of game. **b.** Something that is hunted or pursued; quarry. **3.** *Chiefly British* **a.** A privately owned, unenclosed game preserve. **b.** The right to hunt or keep game on the land of others. —*idiom:* **give chase** To engage in pursuit of a quarry. [ME *chasen,* to hunt < OFr. *chacier* < VLat. **captiāre* < Lat. *captāre,* to catch. See CATCH.]

chase² (chās) *n. Printing* A rectangular frame into which pages or columns of type are locked for printing or plate making. [Perh. < Fr. *châsse,* case < OFr. *chasse* < Lat. *capsa.*]

chase³ (chās) *n.* **1a.** A groove cut in an object; a slot. **b.** A trench or channel for drainpipes or wiring. **2.** The part of a gun in front of the trunnions. **3.** The cavity of a mold. ❖ *tr.v.* **chased, chas·ing, chas·es 1.** To groove; indent. **2.** To cut (the thread of a screw). **3.** To decorate (metal) by engraving or embossing. [Poss. < obsolete Fr. *chas,* groove, enclosure < OFr. < Lat. *capsa,* box. V., var. of ENCHASE.]

Chase, Salmon Portland 1808–73. Amer. jurist; chief justice of the US Supreme Court (1864–73).

Chase, Samuel 1741–1811. Amer. jurist; associate justice of the US Supreme Court (1796–1811).

chas·er¹ (chā′sər) *n.* **1.** One that chases or pursues another. **2.** *Informal* A drink, as of beer, taken after hard liquor.

chas·er² (chā′sər) *n.* **1.** One who decorates metal by engraving or embossing. **2.** A steel tool for cutting or finishing screw threads.

chasm (kăz′əm) *n.* **1.** A deep, steep-sided opening in the earth's surface; an abyss or gorge. **2.** A sudden interruption of continuity; a gap. **3.** A pronounced difference of opinion, interests, or loyalty. [Lat. *chasma* < Gk. *khasma.*] —**chas′mal** (kăz′məl) *adj.*

chas·sé (shă-sā′) *n.* A ballet movement consisting of one or more quick galloping steps with the same foot always leading. [Fr. < p. part. of *chasser,* to chase < OFr. *chacier.* See CHASE¹.] —**chas·sé′** *v.*

chasse·pot (shăs′pō′) *n.* A breechloading rifle introduced into the French army in 1866. [Fr., after Antoine Alphonse *Chassepot* (1833–1905), French gunsmith.]

chas·seur (shă-sûr′) *n.* **1.** Any of certain light cavalry or infantry

chasuble

troops trained for rapid maneuvers. **2.** A hunter. **3.** A uniformed footman. [Fr. < OFr. *chaceor* < *chacier,* to pursue. See CHASE¹.]

Chas·sid (кнä′sĭd, кнô′-, hä′-) *n.* Variant of **Hasid.** —**Chas·si′dic** *adj.* —**Chas·si′dism** *n.*

chas·sis (shăs′ē, chăs′ē) *n., pl.* **chas·sis** (-ēz) **1.** The rectangular, usu. steel frame that holds the body and motor of an automotive vehicle. **2.** The landing gear of an aircraft. **3.** The frame on which a gun carriage moves forward and backward. **4.** The framework to which the components of a radio, television, or other electronic equipment are attached. [Fr. *châssis,* frame < OFr. < VLat. **capsīcium* < Lat. *capsa,* box.]

chaste (chāst) *adj.* **chast·er, chast·est 1.** Morally pure in thought or conduct; decent and modest. **2a.** Not having experienced sexual intercourse; virginal. **b.** Abstaining from all sexual intercourse; celibate. **3.** Pure or simple in design or style; austere. [ME < OFr. < Lat. *castus.*] —**chaste′ly** *adv.* —**chaste′ness** *n.*

chas·ten (chā′sən) *tr.v.* **-tened, -ten·ing, -tens 1.** To correct by punishment or reproof; take to task. **2.** To restrain; subdue. **3.** To rid of excess; refine or purify. [Alteration of obsolete *chaste* < ME *chasten, chastien* < OFr. *chastiier* < Lat. *castigāre.* See CASTIGATE.] —**chas′ten·er** *n.*

chas·tise (chăs-tīz′, chăs′tīz′) *tr.v.* **-tised, -tis·ing, -tis·es 1.** To punish, as by beating. **2.** To criticize severely; rebuke. **3.** *Archaic* To purify. [ME *chastisen,* alteration of *chasten.* See CHASTEN.] —**chas′tis·a·ble** *adj.* —**chas·tise′ment** (chăs-tīz′mənt, chăs′tĭz-mənt) *n.* —**chas·tis′er** *n.*

chas·ti·ty (chăs′tĭ-tē) *n.* **1.** The condition or quality of being pure or chaste. **2a.** Virginity. **b.** Virtuous character. **c.** Celibacy. [ME *chastite* < OFr. *chastete* < Lat. *castitās* < *castus,* pure. See CHASTE.]

chastity belt *n.* A beltlike device of medieval times designed to prevent the woman wearing it from having sexual intercourse.

chas·u·ble (chăz′ə-bəl, chăzh′ə-, chăs′ə-) *n.* A long sleeveless vestment worn over the alb by a priest during services. [Fr. < OFr. < LLat. *casubla,* hooded garment < **casupula,* dim. of *casa,* house.]

chat (chăt) *intr.v.* **chat·ted, chat·ting, chats 1.** To converse in an easy, familiar manner; talk lightly and casually. **2.** *Computer Science* To participate in a synchronous exchange of remarks over a computer network. ❖ *n.* **1.** An informal, light conversation. **2.** *Computer Science* A synchronous exchange of remarks over a computer network. **3.** Any of several birds known for their chattering call, as of the genera *Saxicola* or *Icteria.* [ME *chatten,* to jabber, alteration of *chateren.* See CHATTER.]

cha·teau also **châ·teau** (shă-tō′) *n., pl.* **-teaus** or **-teaux** (-tōz′) **1a.** A French castle. **b.** A French manor house. **2.** An estate where wine is produced and bottled. **3.** A large country house. [Fr. *château* < OFr. *chastel* < Lat. *castellum,* castle. See CASTLE.]

Cha·teau·bri·and also **châ·teau·bri·and** (shă-tō′brē-än′) *n.* A double-thick, tender center cut of beef tenderloin, sometimes stuffed with seasonings before grilling. [After Vicomte François René de CHATEAUBRIAND.]

Cha·teau·bri·and (shă-tō′brē-än′, shă-), Vicomte **François René de** 1768–1848. French politician and writer whose works include *Atala* (1801).

Châ·teau-Thier·ry (shă-tō-tyĕ-rē′) A town of N France on the Marne R. ENE of Paris; site of the second Battle of the Marne (Jun. 3–4, 1918). Pop. 14,557.

chat·e·lain (shăt′l-ān′) *n.* The master of a castle; a castellan. [ME *chatelein* < OFr. *chastelain* < Lat. *castellānus* < *castellum,* castle. See CASTLE.]

chat·e·laine (shăt′l-ān′) *n.* **1a.** The mistress of a castle. **b.** The mistress of a large, fashionable household. **2.** A clasp or chain worn at the waist for holding keys, a purse, or a watch. [Fr. *châtelaine,* fem. of *châtelain,* chatelain < OFr. *chastelain.* See CHATELAIN.]

Chat·ham (chăt′əm), 1st Earl of. See William **Pitt¹.**

Chatham Islands An island group of New Zealand in the SW Pacific Ocean E of South I.

cha·toy·ant (shə-toi′ənt) *adj.* Having a changeable luster. ❖ *n.* A chatoyant stone or gemstone, such as the cat's-eye. [Fr., pr. part. of *chatoyer,* to shimmer like cats' eyes < *chat,* cat < Lat. *cattus,* perh. of African orig.] —**cha·toy′an·cy** *n.*

chat·room (chăt′room′, -room′) *n.* A site on a computer network where online conversations are held in real time by a number of users.

Chat·ta·hoo·chee (chăt′ə-hoo′chē) A river rising in N GA and flowing c. 702 km (436 mi) generally S to the Flint R.

Chat·ta·noo·ga (chăt′ə-noo′gə) A city of SE TN on the Tennessee R. and the GA border SE of Nashville. Pop. 155,554.

chat·tel (chăt′l) *n.* **1.** *Law* An article of movable personal property. **2.** A slave. [ME *chatel,* movable property < OFr. < Med.Lat. *capitāle.* See CATTLE.]

chat·ter (chăt′ər) *v.* **-tered, -ter·ing, -ters** —*intr.* **1.** To talk rapidly, incessantly, and on trivial subjects; jabber. **2.** To utter a rapid series of short, inarticulate, speechlike sounds. **3.** To click quickly and repeatedly. **4.** To vibrate or rattle while in operation. —*tr.* To utter in a rapid, usu. thoughtless way. ❖ *n.* **1.** Idle, trivial talk. **2.** The sharp rapid sounds made by some birds and animals. **3.** A series of quick rattling or clicking sounds. [ME *chateren,* of imit. orig.] —**chat′ter·er** *n.*

chat·ter·box (chăt'ər-bŏks') *n.* A very talkative person.

chatter mark also **chat·ter·mark** (chăt'ər-märk') *n.* **1.** A riblike marking on wood or metal, caused by vibration of a cutting tool. **2.** *Geology* One of a series of short scars made by glacial drift on a surface of bedrock.

Chat·ter·ton (chăt'ər-tən), **Thomas** 1752–70. British poet whose work influenced the romantic poets.

chat·ty (chăt'ē) *adj.* **-ti·er, -ti·est** **1.** Inclined to chat; friendly and talkative. **2.** Full of or in the style of light informal talk: *a chatty letter.* —**chat'ti·ly** *adv.* —**chat'ti·ness** *n.*

Chau·cer (chô'sər), **Geoffrey** 1340?–1400. English poet regarded as the greatest literary figure of medieval England. His works include *The Canterbury Tales* (1387–1400). —**Chau·cer'i·an** (chô-sîr'ē-ən) *adj. & n.*

chauf·feur (shō'fər, shō-fûr') *n.* One employed to drive a private automobile. ❖ *v.* **-feured, -feur·ing, -feurs** —*tr.* **1.** To serve as a chauffeur for (another). **2.** To transport in (a motor vehicle); drive. —*intr.* To serve as a chauffeur. [Fr., stoker < *chauffer*, to heat, stoke < OFr. *chaufer.* See CHAFE.]

chaul·moo·gra (chôl-mōō'grə) *n.* Any of several tropical Asian trees of the genus *Hydnocarpus*, whose seeds contain an oil formerly used to treat leprosy. [Bengali *cāulmugrā*.]

chaunt (chônt, chänt) *n. & v. Archaic* Variant of **chant**.

Chau·tau·qua Lake (shə-tô'kwə, chə-) A lake of SW NY.

chau·vin·ism (shō'və-nĭz'əm) *n.* **1.** Militant devotion to and glorification of one's country; fanatical patriotism. **2.** Prejudiced belief in the superiority of one's own gender, group, or kind. [Fr. *chauvinisme*, after Nicolas *Chauvin*, a legendary French soldier devoted to Napoleon.] —**chau'vin·ist** *n.* —**chau'vin·is'tic** *adj.* —**chau'vin·is'ti·cal·ly** *adv.*

Cha·vannes (shä-vän'), **Pierre Puvis de** See Pierre **Puvis de Chavannes**.

Chá·vez (chä'věz', shä'-), **César Estrada** 1927–93. Amer. labor organizer who founded the National Farm Workers Association (1962).

Cha·vin or **Cha·vín** (chä-vēn') *n.* An early pre-Incan civilization that flourished in northern and central Peru from about 900 to 200 B.C. [After *Chavín de Huántar*, the civilization's cultural center, in N Peru.]

chaw (chô) *Regional intr. & tr.v.* **chawed, chaw·ing, chaws** To chew. ❖ *n.* A chew, esp. of tobacco. [Variant of CHEW.]

cha·yo·te (chä-yō'tā, -tě) *n.* **1.** A tropical American perennial herbaceous vine (*Sechium edule*) having tendrils, tuberous roots, and an edible pear-shaped fruit. **2.** The fruit of this plant. [Sp. < Nahuatl *chayotli*.]

cha·zan or **haz·zan** also **chaz·zan** (KHÄ'zən) *n.* A cantor in a synagogue. [Mishnaic Heb. and Jewish Aram. *ḥazzān* < Akkadian *ḥazannu*, administrator, mayor.]

ChE *abbr.* chemical engineer

cheap (chēp) *adj.* **cheap·er, cheap·est** **1a.** Relatively low in cost. **b.** Charging low prices. **2a.** Obtainable at a low rate of interest. Used of money. **b.** Devalued, as in buying power. **3.** Achieved with little effort. **4.** Of or considered of small value. **5.** Of poor quality; inferior. **6.** Worthy of no respect; vulgar or contemptible. **7.** Stingy; miserly. ❖ *adv.* **cheaper, cheapest** Inexpensively. —**idioms: cheap at twice the price** Extremely inexpensive. **on the cheap** By inexpensive means; cheaply. [< ME (*god*) *chep*, (good) price, purchase, bargain < OE *cēap*, trade < Lat. *caupō*, shopkeeper.] —**cheap'ly** *adv.* —**cheap'ness** *n.*

cheap·en (chē'pən) *v.* **-ened, -en·ing, -ens** —*tr.* **1.** To make cheap or cheaper. **2.** To lower in public estimation; debase. —*intr.* To become cheap or cheaper. —**cheap'en·er** *n.*

cheap·ie (chē'pē) *n. Slang* **1.** A cheap item. **2.** A stingy person.

cheap·jack (chēp'jăk') *n.* A peddler or dealer of cheap goods. ❖ *adj.* Inferior in quality or value; tawdry.

cheap shot *n.* An unfair or unsporting verbal attack on a vulnerable target.

Cheap·side (chēp'sīd') A street and district in the City of London, England; the market center of medieval London.

cheap·skate (chēp'skāt') *n. Slang* A stingy person; a miser. [CHEAP + SKATE[3].]

cheat (chēt) *v.* **cheat·ed, cheat·ing, cheats** —*tr.* **1.** To deceive by trickery; swindle. **2.** To deprive by trickery; defraud. **3.** To mislead; fool. **4.** To elude; escape: *cheat death.* —*intr.* **1.** To act dishonestly; practice fraud. **2.** To violate rules deliberately, as in a game. **3.** *Informal* To be sexually unfaithful. ❖ *n.* **1.** An act of cheating; a fraud or swindle. **2.** One who cheats; a swindler. **3.** *Law* Fraudulent acquisition of another's property. **4.** *Botany* An annual European species of brome grass (*Bromus secalinus*) widely naturalized in temperate regions. [ME *cheten*, to confiscate, short for *acheten*, var. of *escheten* < *eschete*, escheat. See ESCHEAT.]

cheat·grass (chēt'grăs') *n.* Either of two Eurasian grasses, *Bromus secalinus* or *B. tectorum*, now widespread in grasslands of the western United States. [Perh. akin to *cheat*, bread made of inferior-quality wheat (< ME *chet* < OFr.) + GRASS.]

Che·bok·sa·ry (chĭ-bŏk-sär'ē) A city of W-central Russia on the Volga R. W of Kazan. Pop. 445,707.

Chech·en (chěch'ən) *n.* **1a.** A native or inhabitant of Chechnya. **b.** A member of the predominant, traditionally Muslim ethnic group of Chechnya. **2.** The Caucasian language of the Chechens.

[Obsolete Russ. < Kabardian (Caucasian language of SW Russia and Turkey) *šešen*.] —**Chech'en** *adj.*

Chech·nya (chěch'nē-ə, chěch-nyä') A region of SW Russia in the N Caucasus bordering on Georgia. Chechnya declared its independence from the USSR in 1991; its status as part of Russia is being negotiated.

check (chěk) *n.* **1.** An action or influence that stops motion or expression; a restraint. **2.** The condition of being stopped or held back; restraint. **3.** An abrupt stop in forward movement or progress; a halt. **4.** The act or an instance of inspecting or testing, as for accuracy; examination. **5.** A standard for inspecting or evaluating; a test. **6.** A check mark. **7.** A ticket or slip of identification. **8.** A bill at a restaurant or bar. **9.** *Games* A chip or counter used in gambling. **10.** A written order to a bank to pay the amount specified from funds on deposit; a draft. **11.** A small crack; a chink. **12a.** A pattern of small squares, as on a chessboard. **b.** One of the squares of such a pattern. **c.** A fabric patterned with squares. **13.** *Games* **a.** A move in chess that directly attacks an opponent's king but does not constitute a checkmate. **b.** The position or condition of a king so attacked. **14.** *Sports* The act of checking an opponent in ice hockey. ❖ *interj.* **1.** *Games* Used to declare that a chess opponent's king is in check. **2.** *Informal* Used to express agreement or understanding. ❖ *v.* **checked, check·ing, checks** —*tr.* **1.** To arrest the motion of abruptly; halt. **2.** To hold in restraint; curb. **3.** To slow the growth of; retard. **4.** To rebuke; rebuff. **5.** To inspect so as to determine accuracy, quality, or other condition; test. **6.** To verify by consulting a source or authority. **7.** To put a check mark on or next to. **8.** To deposit for temporary safekeeping: *checked his coat.* **9.** To consign (luggage, for example) for shipment on a transportation vehicle. **10.** To make cracks or chinks in. **11.** *Games* To move in chess so as to put (an opponent's king) under direct attack. **12.** *Sports* To block or impede (an opposing player with the puck) in ice hockey by using one's body or one's stick. —*intr.* **1.** To come to an abrupt halt; stop. **2.** To agree point for point; correspond. **3.** To be verified or confirmed; pass inspection: *The story checked out.* **4.** To make an examination or investigation; inquire. **5.** To write a check on a bank account. **6.** To undergo cracking in a pattern of checks, as paint does. **7.** *Games* To place a chess opponent's king in check. **8a.** To pause to relocate a scent. Used of hunting dogs. **b.** To abandon the proper game and follow baser prey. Used of trained falcons. **9.** *Sports* To check an opposing player in ice hockey. —*phrasal verbs:* **check in** To register, as at a hotel. **check out** **1.** To settle one's bill and leave a hotel or other place of lodging. **2.** To withdraw (an item) after recording the withdrawal: *check out books.* **3.** To record and total up the prices of and receive payment for (items being purchased) at a retail store. **check over** To look over; examine. [ME *chek*, check in chess < OFr. *eschec* < Ar. *šāh* < Pers. *šāh*, king, check. See SHAH.] —**check'a·ble** *adj.*

WORD HISTORY The words *check*, *chess*, and *shah* are all related. *Shah* is a borrowing into English of the Persian title for the monarch of that country. The Persian word *shāh* was also a term used in chess, a game played in Persia long before it was introduced to Europe. One said *shāh* as a warning when the opponent's king was under attack. The Persian word in this sense, after passing through Arabic, probably Old Spanish, and then Old French, came into Middle English as *chek* about seven hundred years ago. *Chess* itself comes from a plural form of the Old French word that gave us the word *check*.

check·book (chěk'bŏŏk') *n.* A book containing blank checks issued by a bank. ❖ *adj.* Involving the payment of money to another in exchange for influence or knowledge: *checkbook politics.*

check card *n.* A debit card that enables the user to withdraw funds from a checking account.

checked (chěkt) *adj.* **1.** Having a pattern of checks or squares: *checked cloth.* **2.** Held in check; restrained. **3.** *Linguistics* Situated in a stopped or closed syllable: *a checked vowel.*

check·er (chěk'ər) *n.* **1a.** One, such as an inspector or examiner, that checks. **b.** One that receives items for temporary safekeeping or for shipment: *a baggage checker.* **2a. checkers** (*used with a sing. verb*) A game played on a checkerboard by two players, each using 12 pieces. **b.** One of the round flat pieces used in this game. **3a.** A pattern of checks or squares. **b.** One of the squares in such a pattern. **4.** A cashier. ❖ *tr.v.* **-ered, -er·ing, -ers** **1.** To mark with a checked or squared pattern. **2.** To diversify (something) in color, shading, or character; variegate. [ME *cheker*, chessboard, alteration of *escheker* < OFr. *eschequier* < *eschec*, check in chess. See CHECK.]

check·er·ber·ry (chěk'ər-běr'ē) *n.* See **wintergreen** 1a. [CHECKER(BOARD) + BERRY.]

check·er·bloom (chěk'ər-blōōm') *n.* An ornamental herb (*Sidalcea malviflora*) native to the western coast of North America and having pink to purple flowers. [CHECKER(BOARD) + BLOOM[1].]

check·er·board (chěk'ər-bôrd', -bōrd') *n.* A board on which chess and checkers are played, divided into 64 squares of two alternating colors.

check·ered (chěk'ərd) *adj.* **1.** Divided into squares. **2.** Marked by light and dark patches; diversified in color. **3.** Marked by great changes or shifts in fortune: *a checkered career.*

César Chávez

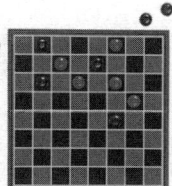

checkers

check•ing account (chĕk′ĭng) *n.* A bank account in which checks may be written against amounts on deposit.

check•list (chĕk′lĭst′) *n.* A list of items to be noted, checked, or remembered.

check mark *n.* A mark placed next to an item to show that it has been noted, verified, or approved.

check•mate (chĕk′māt′) *tr.v.* **-mat•ed, -mat•ing, -mates** **1.** To attack (a chess opponent's king) in such a manner that no escape or defense is possible, thus ending the game. **2.** To defeat completely. ❖ *n.* **1a.** A move that checkmates a chess opponent's king. **b.** The position or condition of a king so attacked. **2.** Utter defeat. ❖ *interj.* Used to checkmate. [ME *chekmat* < OFr. *eschec mat* < Ar. *šāh māt*, the king is dead : *šāh*, king (< Pers. *shāh*; see SHAH) + *māt*, died (< earlier *māta*, to die).]

check•off (chĕk′ôf′, -ŏf′) *n.* Collection of dues from members of a union by authorized deduction from their wages.

check•out (chĕk′out′) *n.* **1.** The act, time, or place of checking out, as at a hotel. **2.** A test, as of a machine, for proper functioning. **3.** An investigation; an inspection.

check•point (chĕk′point′) *n.* A point where a check is made.

check•rein (chĕk′rān′) *n.* **1.** A short rein that extends from a horse's bit to the saddle to keep the horse's head up. **2.** A rein joining the bit of one of a span of horses to the other's driving rein.

check•room (chĕk′rōōm′, -rōōm′) *n.* A place where hats, coats, packages, or other items can be stored temporarily.

check•up (chĕk′ŭp′) *n.* **1.** An examination or inspection. **2.** A general physical examination.

Ched•dar also **ched•dar** (chĕd′ər) *n.* Any of several types of smooth hard cheese varying in flavor from mild to extra sharp. [After *Cheddar*, a village of SW England.]

cheek (chēk) *n.* **1.** The fleshy part on either side of the face below the eye and between the nose and ear. **2.** Something resembling the cheek in shape or position. **3.** Either of the buttocks. **4.** Impertinent boldness. ❖ *tr.v.* **cheeked, cheek•ing, cheeks** *Informal* To speak impudently to. —***idiom:* cheek by jowl** Side by side. [ME *cheke* < OE *cēace*.]

cheek•bone (chēk′bōn′) *n.* See **zygomatic bone.**

cheek pouch *n.* A pocketlike fold of skin in the cheeks of various animals in which food is carried.

cheek•y (chē′kē) *adj.* **-i•er, -i•est** Impertinently bold; impudent and saucy. —**cheek′i•ly** *adv.* —**cheek′i•ness** *n.*

cheep (chēp) *n.* A faint shrill sound like that of a young bird; a chirp. ❖ *intr.v.* **cheeped, cheep•ing, cheeps** To make a faint shrill sound or sounds; chirp. [Imit.] —**cheep′er** *n.*

cheer (chîr) *n.* **1.** Lightness of spirits or mood; gaiety or joy. **2.** A source of joy or happiness; a comfort. **3a.** A shout of approval, encouragement, or congratulation. **b.** A short rehearsed jingle or phrase, shouted in unison by a squad of cheerleaders. **4.** Festive food and drink; refreshment. ❖ *v.* **cheered, cheer•ing, cheers** —*tr.* **1.** To make happier or more cheerful. **2.** To encourage with or as if with cheers; urge: *cheered us on.* **3.** To salute or acclaim with cheers; applaud. —*intr.* **1.** To shout cheers. **2.** To become cheerful: *I cheered up.* [ME *chere*, expression, mood < OFr. *chiere*, face < LLat. *cara* < Gk. *kara*, head. See ker-[1] in App.] —**cheer′er** *n.* —**cheer′ing•ly** *adv.*

cheer•ful (chîr′fəl) *adj.* **1.** Being in good spirits; merry. See Syns at **glad**[1]. **2.** Promoting a feeling of cheer; pleasant: *a cozy, cheerful room.* **3.** Reflecting willingness or good humor: *cheerful acceptance of one's duty.* —**cheer′ful•ly** *adv.* —**cheer′ful•ness** *n.*

cheer•i•o (chîr′ē-ō′) *interj.* *Chiefly British* Used in greeting or parting. [Alteration of CHEER.]

cheer•lead (chîr′lēd′) *intr.v.* **-led** (-lĕd′), **-lead•ing, -leads** To lead organized cheering, as at sports events.

cheer•lead•er (chîr′lē′dər) *n.* One who leads the cheering of spectators, as at a sports contest.

cheer•less (chîr′lĭs) *adj.* Lacking cheer; depressing. —**cheer′less•ly** *adv.* —**cheer′less•ness** *n.*

cheers (chîrz) *interj.* Used as a toast or valediction.

cheer•y (chîr′ē) *adj.* **-i•er, -i•est** Showing or suggesting good spirits; cheerful. —**cheer′i•ly** *adv.* —**cheer′i•ness** *n.*

cheese[1] (chēz) *n.* **1a.** A solid food made from the pressed curd of milk, often seasoned and aged. **b.** A molded mass of this substance. **2.** Something resembling this substance. [ME *chese* < OE *cȳse* < Gmc. **kasjus* < Lat. *cāseus.*]

cheese[2] (chēz) *tr.v.* **cheesed, chees•ing, chees•es** *Slang* To stop. —***idiom:* cheese it** *Slang* **1.** To look out. **2.** To get away fast; get going. [?]

cheese[3] (chēz) *n.* *Slang* An important person. Often used in the phrase *big cheese.* [Perh. < Urdu *chīz*, thing < Pers. < OPers. **cišciy*, something. See k*ʷ*o- in App.]

cheese•burg•er (chēz′bûr′gər) *n.* A hamburger topped with melted cheese.

cheese•cake (chēz′kāk′) *n.* **1.** A cake made of sweetened cottage cheese or cream cheese, eggs, milk, sugar, and flavorings. **2.** *Informal* Photographs of minimally attired women.

cheese•cloth (chēz′klôth′, -klŏth′) *n.* A coarse, loosely woven cotton gauze, originally used for wrapping cheese.

cheese-par•ing (chēz′pâr′ĭng) *adj.* Miserly; stingy. ❖ *n.* **1.** Something of little or no value. **2.** Stinginess; parsimony.

chees•y (chē′zē) *adj.* **-i•er, -i•est** **1.** Containing or resembling

cheetah
Acinonyx jubatus

cheese. **2.** *Informal* **a.** Tasteless and showy, often in a vulgar manner. **b.** Having an appreciation for what is tasteless and showy. **3.** *Informal* Of poor quality; shoddy. [Sense 2 and 3, poss. < CHEESE[3].] —**chees′i•ly** *adv.* —**chees′i•ness** *n.*

chee•tah also **che•tah** (chē′tə) *n.* A long-legged, swift-running wild cat (*Acinonyx jubatus*) of Africa and southwest Asia having black-spotted, tawny fur and nonretractile claws. [Hindi *cītā* < Skt. *citrakāyaḥ*, tiger, leopard : *citra-*, variegated + *kāyaḥ*, body.]

Chee•ver (chē′vər), **John** 1912–82. Amer. writer who depicted suburban life with humor and compassion.

chef (shĕf) *n.* A cook, esp. the head of a large kitchen staff. [Fr., short for *chef de cuisine*, head of the kitchen. See CHIEF.]

chef-d'oeu•vre (shā-dœ′vrə, -dûrv′) *n.*, *pl.* **chefs-d'oeuvre** (shā-) A masterpiece, esp. in literature or art. [Fr. *chef d'œuvre* : *chef*, head, beginning + *de*, of + *œuvre*, work.]

cheiro– *pref.* Variant of **chiro–**.

Che•ju (chē′jōō′) An island of South Korea separated from the SW coast of the mainland by **Cheju Strait,** a channel linking the Yellow Sea and Korea Strait.

Che•khov also **Che•kov** (chĕk′ôf, -ŏf, -ŏv, chyĕ′KHəf), **Anton Pavlovich** 1860–1904. Russian writer whose works include *The Seagull* (1896). —**Che•kho′vi•an** (chĕ-kō′vē-ən) *adj.*

Che•kiang (chŭ′kyäng′, jŭ′gyäng′) See **Zhejiang.**

che•la (kē′lə) *n., pl.* **-lae** (-lē) A pincerlike claw of a crustacean or arachnid. [NLat. *chēla* < Gk. *khēlē*, claw.]

che•late (kē′lāt′) *adj.* *Zoology* Having chelae or resembling a chela. ❖ *n.* *Chemistry* A chemical compound in the form of a heterocyclic ring, containing a metal ion attached by coordinate bonds to at least two nonmetal ions. ❖ *tr.v.* **-lat•ed, -lat•ing, -lates** **1.** *Chemistry* To combine (a metal ion) with a chemical compound to form a ring. **2.** *Medicine* To remove (a heavy metal, such as lead or mercury) from the bloodstream by means of a chelate, such as EDTA. —**che′lat•a•ble** *adj.* —**che•la′tion** *n.* —**che′la′tor** *n.*

che•lic•er•a (kĭ-lĭs′ər-ə) *n., pl.* **-er•ae** (-ə-rē′) Either of the first pair of fanglike appendages near the mouth of an arachnid. [NLat. : CHELA + Gk. *keras*, horn; see ker-[1] in App.]

che•li•form (kē′lə-fôrm′) *adj.* Having the shape of a chela.

Chel•li•an or **Chel•le•an** (shĕl′ē-ən) *adj.* Abbevillian. [After *Chelles*, a city of N-central France.]

che•loid (kē′loid′) *n.* Variant of **keloid.**

che•lo•ni•an (kĭ-lō′nē-ən) *adj.* Of, relating to, or belonging to the order Chelonia, which includes the turtles and tortoises. [< NLat. *Chelōnia*, order name < Gk. *khelōnē*, tortoise.] —**che•lo′ni•an** *n.*

Chel•sea (chĕl′sē) A district of W London, England, on the N bank of the Thames R.

Chel•ten•ham (chĕlt′nəm, chĕl′tən-əm) A municipal borough of W-central England S of Birmingham. Pop. 106,708.

Che•lya•binsk (chĕl-yä′bĭnsk, chĭ-lyä′-) A city of S-central Russia S of Sverdlovsk. Founded 1736. Pop. 1,129,661.

Che•lyus•kin (chĕl-yōō′skĭn, chĭ-lyōō′-), **Cape** A cape of N-central Russia on the Taymyr Peninsula.

chem– or **chemi–** *pref.* Variant of **chemo–**.

chem•ic (kĕm′ĭk) *adj.* **1.** Chemical. **2.** *Archaic* Alchemic. ❖ *n.* *Obsolete* An alchemist.

chem•i•cal (kĕm′ĭ-kəl) *adj.* **1.** Of or relating to chemistry. **2.** Of or relating to the properties or actions of chemicals. ❖ *n.* **1.** A substance with a distinct molecular composition that is produced by or used in a chemical process. **2.** A drug, esp. an illicit or addictive one. [Obsolete *chimical* < *chimic*, alchemist < NLat. *chimicus* < Med.Lat. *alchimicus* < *alchymia*, alchemy. See ALCHEMY.] —**chem′i•cal•ly** *adv.*

chemical abuse *n.* See **substance abuse.**

chemical bond *n.* Any of several forces or mechanisms by which atoms or ions are bound in a molecule or crystal.

chemical dependency *n.* A physical and psychological habituation to a mood- or mind-altering drug.

chemical engineering *n.* The branch of engineering that deals with the manufacture of products through chemical processes. —**chemical engineer** *n.*

chemical fingerprint *n.* A unique pattern produced by an analytical instrument, such as an x-ray spectrometer, indicating the presence of a particular molecule in a test sample, used esp. to detect pollutants.

chemical peel *n.* **1.** The removal of skin blemishes or wrinkles by applying a caustic chemical, such as an acid, that produces a mild, superficial burn. **2.** Any of various treatments used in such removal.

chemical pregnancy *n.* Pregnancy resulting from in vitro fertilization or other reproductive technology, characterized by low levels of HCG and usu. miscarriage prior to implantation.

chemical toilet *n.* A toilet consisting of a seat or bowl attached to a container holding a chemical solution that changes waste into sludge.

chemical warfare *n.* Warfare involving lethal and incapacitating munitions and agents, such as poisons.

chem•i•lu•mi•nes•cence (kĕm′ə-lōō′mə-nĕs′əns) *n.* Emission of light as a result of a chemical reaction at environmental temperatures. —**chem′i•lu•mi•nes′cent** *adj.*

che·min de fer (shə-măn′ də fâr′) *n.* A variation of baccarat. [Fr., railroad : *chemin,* way + *de,* of + *fer,* iron.]

che·mise (shə-mēz′) *n.* **1.** A woman's loose, shirtlike undergarment. **2.** A loosely fitting dress that hangs straight; a shift. [ME < OFr., shirt < LLat. *camisia* < L.Gk. *kamision,* prob. of Semitic orig.; akin to Ar. *qamīṣ,* shirt.]

chem·i·sette (shĕm′ĭ-zĕt′) *n.* **1.** A short sleeveless bodice. **2.** A blouse front; a dickey. [Fr., dim. of *chemise,* shirt < OFr. See CHEMISE.]

chem·i·sorb (kĕm′ĭ-sôrb′) also **chem·o·sorb** (-ə-sôrb′) *tr.v.* **-sorbed, -sorb·ing, -sorbs** To take up and chemically bind (a substance) onto the surface of another substance. [Alteration of CHEMO- + (AB)SORB.] —**chem′i·sorp′tion** (-sôrp′shən) *n.*

chem·ist (kĕm′ĭst) *n.* **1.** A scientist specializing in chemistry. **2.** *Chiefly British* A pharmacist. **3.** *Obsolete* An alchemist. [Obsolete *chimist* < NLat. *chimista* < Med.Lat. *alchymista,* alchemist < *alchymia,* alchemy. See ALCHEMY.]

chem·is·try (kĕm′ĭ-strē) *n., pl.* **-tries 1.** The science of the composition, structure, properties, and reactions of matter, esp. of atomic and molecular systems. **2.** The composition, structure, properties, and reactions of a substance. **3.** The elements of a complex entity and their dynamic interrelation. **4.** Mutual attraction or sympathy; rapport.

Chem·nitz (kĕm′nĭts) Formerly **Karl-Marx-Stadt** (kärl′märks-shtät′) A city of E-central Germany SE of Leipzig. Pop. 279,520.

che·mo (kē′mō, kĕm′ō) *n. Informal* Chemotherapy or a chemotherapeutic treatment.

chemo– or **chemi–** or **chem–** *pref.* Chemicals; chemical: *chemotherapy.* [< CHEMICAL.]

che·mo·au·to·troph (kē′mō-ô′tə-trŏf′, -trŏf′, kĕm′ō-) *n.* An organism that obtains its nourishment by oxidation of inorganic chemical compounds as opposed to photosynthesis. —**che′mo·au′to·troph′ic** (-trŏf′ĭk, -trŏf′ĭk) *adj.* —**che′mo·au·tot′ro·phy** (-ô-tŏt′rə-fē) *n.*

che·mo·kine (kē′mō-kīn′, kĕm′ō-) *n.* Any of various cytokines produced in inflammation that mobilize and activate white blood cells. [CHEMO- + (CYTO)KINE.]

che·mo·pre·ven·tion (kē′mō-prĭ-vĕn′shən, kĕm′ō-) *n.* The use of chemical agents, drugs, or food supplements to prevent disease. —**che′mo·pre·ven′tive** *adj. & n.*

che·mo·pro·phy·lax·is (kē′mō-prō′fə-lăk′sĭs, kĕm′ō-) *n.* See **chemoprevention.** —**che′mo·pro·phy·lac′tic** (-lăk′tĭk) *adj. & n.*

che·mo·re·cep·tion (kē′mō-rĭ-sĕp′shən, kĕm′ō-) *n.* The physiological response of a sense organ to a chemical stimulus. —**che′mo·re·cep′tive** *adj.* —**che′mo·re·cep·tiv′i·ty** (-rē′sĕp-tĭv′ĭ-tē) *n.*

che·mo·re·cep·tor (kē′mō-rĭ-sĕp′tər, kĕm′ō-) *n.* A sensory nerve cell or sense organ that responds to chemical stimuli.

che·mo·sen·so·ry (kē′mō-sĕn′sə-rē, kĕm′ō-) *adj.* Relating to the perception of a chemical stimulus by sensory means.

chem·o·sorb (kĕm′ə-sôrb′) *v.* Variant of **chemisorb.**

che·mo·sphere (kē′mə-sfîr′, kĕm′ə-) *n.* The region of the atmosphere from 30 to 190 kilometers (20 to 120 miles) above the earth's surface, in which photochemical reactions initiated by solar radiation occur.

che·mo·sur·ger·y (kē′mō-sûr′jə-rē, kĕm′ō-) *n.* Selective destruction of tissue by use of chemicals, as for removing malignant skin lesions. —**che′mo·sur′gi·cal** (-jĭ-kəl) *adj.*

che·mo·syn·the·sis (kē′mō-sĭn′thĭ-sĭs, kĕm′ō-) *n.* Synthesis of carbohydrate from carbon dioxide and water using energy obtained from the chemical oxidation of simple inorganic compounds. —**che′mo·syn·thet′ic** (-sĭn-thĕt′ĭk) *adj.* —**che′mo·syn·thet′i·cal·ly** *adv.*

che·mo·sys·tem·at·ics (kē′mō-sĭs′tə-măt′ĭks, kĕm′ō-) *n.* (*used with a sing. or pl. verb*) See **chemotaxonomy.**

che·mo·tax·is (kē′mō-tăk′sĭs, kĕm′ō-) *n.* The characteristic movement or orientation of an organism or cell along a chemical concentration gradient either toward or away from the chemical stimulus. —**che′mo·tac′tic** (-tăk′tĭk) *adj.* —**che′mo·tac′ti·cal·ly** *adv.*

che·mo·tax·on·o·my (kē′mō-tăk-sŏn′ə-mē, kĕm′ō-) *n.* Classification of organisms based on differences that occur at the biochemical level. —**che′mo·tax′o·nom′ic** (-tăk′sə-nŏm′ĭk) *adj.* —**che′mo·tax′o·nom′i·cal·ly** *adv.* —**che′mo·tax·on′o·mist** *n.*

che·mo·ther·a·py (kē′mō-thĕr′ə-pē, kĕm′ō-) *n.* **1.** The treatment of cancer using specific chemical agents or drugs that are selectively destructive to malignant cells and tissues. **2.** The treatment of disease using chemical agents or drugs that are selectively toxic to the causative agent of the disease. —**che′mo·ther′a·peu′tic** (-pyoo′tĭk) *adj.* —**che′mo·ther′a·peu′ti·cal·ly** *adv.* —**che′mo·ther′a·pist** *n.*

che·mot·ro·pism (kē-mŏt′rə-pĭz′əm) *n.* Movement or growth of an organism in response to a chemical stimulus. —**che′mo·trop′ic** (kē′mō-trŏp′ĭk, kĕm′ō-) *adj.*

chem·ur·gy (kĕm′ər-jē, kĭ-mûr′-) *n.* The development of industrial chemical products from organic raw materials. —**che·mur′gic** (kĭ-mûr′jĭk), **chem·ur′gi·cal** *adj.*

Chen also **Ch′ên** (chŭn) A Chinese dynasty (557–589).

Che·nab (chə-näb′) A river, c. 1,086 km (675 mi), of N India and E Pakistan; one of the five rivers of the Punjab.

Che·ney (chā′nē, chē′), **Richard** b. 1941. Vice President of the US (since 2001).

Cheng·chow (jŭng′jō′) See **Zhengzhou.**

Cheng·du also **Cheng·tu** (chŭng′doō′) A city of S-central China WNW of Chongqing; founded before 770 B.C. Pop. 3,483,834.

che·nille (shə-nēl′) *n.* **1.** A soft tufted cord of silk, cotton, or worsted used in embroidery or for fringing. **2.** Fabric made of this cord. [Fr. *chenille,* caterpillar, chenille < Lat. *canícula,* dim. of *canis,* dog. See **kwon-** in App.]

Che·nin Blanc (shĕn′ĭn blängk′) *n.* **1.** A variety of grape originating in the Loire Valley. **2.** A white wine made from this grape.

Chen·nai (chə-nī′) Formerly **Ma·dras** (mə-drăs′, -dräs′) A city of SE India on the Coromandel Coast of the Bay of Bengal; founded by the British East India Company in 1639. Pop. 3,841,396.

che·no·pod (kē′nə-pŏd′, kĕn′ə-) *n.* Any plant of the goosefoot family, which includes spinach, beets, and pigweed. [< NLat. *Chēnopodiāceae,* family name < *Chēnopodium,* type genus : Gk. *khēn,* goose; see **ghans-** in App. + *-podium,* neut. of *-podius,* -pod.]

cheong·sam (chông′säm′) *n.* A long dress with a high collar and slit skirt, traditionally worn by Chinese women. [Chin. (Cantonese) *ch'eūng shaam,* long gown, equivalent to Chin. (Mandarin) *cháng,* long + Chin. (Mandarin) *shān,* gown.]

Che·ops (kē′ŏps) Orig. Khufu. 2590–2567 B.C. King of the IV Dynasty of Egypt; builder of the Great Pyramid at Giza.

cheque (chĕk) *n. Chiefly British* Variant of **check** 10.

chequ·er (chĕk′ər) *n. Chiefly British* Variant of **checker.**

Cher (shĕr) A river of central France flowing c. 354 km (220 mi) to the Loire R. near Tours.

Che·ren·kov (chə-rĕng′kôf, -kəf, chĭ-ryĭn-kôf′), **Pavel Alekseevich** 1904–90. Russian physicist who shared a 1958 Nobel Prize.

Che·ren·kov effect (chə-rĕng′kôf, -kəf) *n.* Variant of **Cerenkov effect.**

Che·re·po·vets (chĕr′ə-pə-vĕts′, chĭ-rĭ-pŭ-vyĕts′) A city of E-central Russia N of Moscow. Pop. 318,216.

cher·i·moy·a (chĕr′ə-moi′ə) *n.* **1.** A tropical American tree (*Annona cherimola*) having heart-shaped edible fruits with green skin and white aromatic flesh. **2.** The fruit of this plant. [Am.Sp. < Quechua *chirimuya.*]

cher·ish (chĕr′ĭsh) *tr.v.* **-ished, -ish·ing, -ish·es 1.** To treat with affection and tenderness. **2.** To keep fondly in mind; entertain. See Syns at **appreciate.** [ME *cherishen* < OFr. *cherir, cheriss- < cher,* dear < Lat. *cārus.* See **kā-** in App.] —**cher′ish·a·ble** *n.* —**cher′ish·er** *n.*

Cher·ka·sy (chər-kä′sē) A city of central Ukraine on the Dnieper R. SSE of Kiev. Pop. 307,600.

Cher·ni·hiv (chər-nē′həv) or **Cher·ni·gov** (-gəf) A city of N-central Ukraine NNE of Kiev. Pop. 310,500.

Cher·niv·tsi (chər-nēv′tsē) A city of SW Ukraine near the Romanian border. Pop. 261,200.

Cher·no·byl (chər-nō′bəl, -bĭl) A city of N-central Ukraine NNW of Kiev; site of a major nuclear power plant accident in 1986.

cher·no·zem (chĕr′nə-zĕm′, chîr′nə-zyôm′) *n.* A very black topsoil, rich in humus, typical of cool to temperate semiarid regions. [Russ. *chernozëm : chërnyĭ,* black + ORuss. *zemĭ,* earth; see **dhghem-** in App.] —**cher′no·zem′ic** *adj.*

Cher·o·kee (chĕr′ə-kē′, chĕr′ə-kē′) *n., pl.* **Cherokee** or **-kees 1.** A member of a Native American people formerly inhabiting the southern Appalachian Mountains from the western Carolinas and eastern Tennessee to northern Georgia, with present-day populations in northeast Oklahoma and western North Carolina. **2.** The Iroquoian language of the Cherokee. [< Cherokee *tsalaki.*] —**Cher′o·kee′** *adj.*

Cherokee rose *n.* A prickly climbing evergreen rose (*Rosa laevigata*) native to China, with white fragrant flowers.

che·root also **she·root** (shə-root′) *n.* A cigar with square-cut ends. [Fr. *cheroute,* ult. < Tamil *curuṭṭu* < *curuḷ,* to be spiral.]

cher·ry (chĕr′ē) *n., pl.* **-ries 1a.** Any of several trees or shrubs of the genus *Prunus,* esp. *P. avium* or *P. cerasus,* native chiefly to northern temperate regions and having small juicy drupes. **b.** The fruit of any of these plants. **c.** The wood of any of these plants, esp. black cherry. **d.** Any of various plants, such as the Barbados cherry, having fruits resembling a cherry. **2.** A moderate or strong red to purplish red. **3.** *Vulgar Slang* The hymen considered as a symbol of virginity. ❖ *adj.* **1.** Containing or having the flavor of cherries. **2.** Made of the wood of a cherry tree. **3.** Of the color cherry. [ME *cheri* < AN *cherise,* var. of OFr. *cerise* < VLat. **ceresia* < **cerasia* < Gk. *kerasiā,* cherry tree < *kerasos.*]

cherry birch *n.* See **sweet birch.**

cherry bomb *n.* A loud, red, ball-shaped firecracker.

cherry laurel *n.* A frequently cultivated Eurasian evergreen shrub or small tree (*Prunus laurocerasus*) in the rose family, having showy clusters of white flowers and glossy foliage.

cherry picker *n.* **1.** A maneuverable vertical boom with an open bucket or cage at the end from which a worker can perform aerial

cheongsam

cherry picker

ă	pat	oi	boy
ā	pay	ou	out
âr	care	ŏŏ	took
ä	father	ōō	boot
ĕ	pet	ŭ	cut
ē	be	ûr	urge
ĭ	pit	th	thin
ī	pie	th	this
îr	pier	hw	which
ŏ	pot	zh	vision
ō	toe	ə	about,
ô	paw		item

Stress marks:
′ (primary);
′ (secondary), as in
lexicon (lĕk′sĭ-kŏn′)

work such as pruning trees. **2.** A vehicle equipped with such a boom.

cherry plum *n.* A deciduous ornamental Eurasian shrub or small tree (*Prunus cerasifera*) in the rose family, having white flowers and small red to yellow edible fruits.

cher·ry·stone (chĕr′ē-stōn′) *n.* The quahog clam when half-grown and of comparatively small size.

cherry tomato *n.* A variety of tomato (*Lycopersicon esculentum* var. *cerasiforme*) having small red to yellow fruits.

cher·so·nese (kûr′sə-nēz′, -nēs′) *n.* A peninsula. [Lat. *chersonēsus* < Gk. *khersonēsos* : *khersos*, dry land + *nēsos*, island; see **snā-** in App.]

chert (chûrt) *n.* **1.** A variety of silica that contains microcrystalline quartz. **2.** A siliceous rock of chalcedonic or opaline silica occurring in limestone. [?] —**chert′y** *adj.*

cher·ub (chĕr′əb) *n.* **1.** *pl.* **cher·u·bim** (chĕr′ə-bĭm′, -yə-bĭm′) **a.** A winged celestial being. **b. cherubim** The second order of angels. **2.** *pl.* **cher·ubs a.** A representation of a small angel, portrayed as a child with a chubby rosy face. **b.** A person, esp. a child, with an innocent or chubby face. [ME < LLat. < Heb. *kərûb*; akin to Akkadian *karābu*, to praise, bless.] —**che·ru′bic** (chə-rōō′bĭk) *adj.* —**che·ru′bi·cal·ly** *adv.*

Che·ru·bi·ni (kĕr′ə-bē′nē, kĕ′rōō-), (Maria) Luigi Carlo Zenobio Salvatore 1760–1842. Italian composer whose operas include *Les Deux Journées* (1800).

cher·vil (chûr′vəl) *n.* **1.** An annual Eurasian herb (*Anthriscus cerefolium*) in the parsley family, having aromatic parsleylike leaves. **2.** Any of several related plants, such as those of the genus *Chaerophyllum*. [ME < OE *cerfille* < Lat. *chaerephyllum* < Gk. *khairephullon* : *khairein*, to greet, delight in + *phullon*, leaf; see **bhel-** in App.]

Ches·a·peake (chĕs′ə-pēk′) An independent city of SE VA S of Norfolk. Pop. 199,184.

Chesapeake Bay An inlet of the Atlantic Ocean separating the Delmarva Peninsula from mainland MD and VA.

Chesapeake Bay retriever *n.* A hunting dog of a breed developed in the United States, having a short wavy coat ranging from dark brown to tan.

Chesh·ire also **chesh·ire** (chĕsh′ər) *n.* A hard yellow English cheese made from cow's milk. [After *Cheshire*, a county of W-central England.]

chess¹ (chĕs) *n.* A board game for two players, each beginning with 16 pieces of six kinds that are moved according to individual rules, with the objective of checkmating the opposing king. [ME *ches*, short for OFr. *esches*, pl. of *eschec*, check in chess. See **CHECK.**]

chess² (chĕs) *n.* Any of several species of brome grass, esp. the cheat. [?]

chess³ (chĕs) *n., pl.* **chess** or **chess·es** One of the floorboards of a pontoon bridge. [ME *ches*, tier, perh. < OFr. *chasse*, frame < Lat. *capsa*, box.]

chess·board (chĕs′bôrd′, -bōrd′) *n.* A game board marked with 64 squares, used in playing chess.

chess·man (chĕs′măn′, -mən) *n.* A chess piece.

ches·sy·lite (chĕs′ə-līt′, chĕs′-) *n.* See **azurite.** [After *Chessy*, a town of E-central France.]

chest (chĕst) *n.* **1.** The part of the body between the neck and the abdomen, enclosed by the ribs and the breastbone; the thorax. **2a.** A sturdy box with a lid and often a lock, used esp. for storage. **b.** A small closet or cabinet with shelves for storing supplies. **3a.** The treasury of a public institution. **b.** The funds kept there. **4a.** A box for the shipping of certain goods, such as tea. **b.** The quantity packed in such a box. **5.** A sealed receptacle for liquid, gas, or steam. **6.** A bureau; a dresser. —**idiom: get (something) off (one's) chest** To vent one's pent-up feelings. [ME < OE *cest*, box < West Gmc. **kista* < Lat. *cista* < Gk. *kistē*.]

chest·ed (chĕs′tĭd) *adj.* Having a specified kind of chest. Often used in combination: *a white-chested horse.*

ches·ter·field (chĕs′tər-fēld′) *n.* **1.** A single- or double-breasted overcoat, usu. with concealed buttons and a velvet collar. **2.** *Chiefly Northern California & Canada* A sofa. [After a 19th-cent. earl of *Chesterfield*.]

REGIONAL NOTE *Chesterfield*, a term for a sofa, especially a large one with upholstered arms, was probably brought down from Canada, where it is common. In the United States, it was largely limited to the trade region of San Francisco in northern California. According to Craig M. Carver in *American Regional Dialects*, the word probably comes from the name of a 19th-century earl of Chesterfield and originally referred "specifically to a couch with upright armrests at either end." It appears to have come into use in Canada around 1903 and in northern California at about the same time.

Chesterfield, 4th Earl of. Title of Philip Dormer Stanhope. 1694–1773. English politician known for *Letters to His Son* (1774).

Ches·ter·ton (chĕs′tər-tən), **Gilbert Keith** 1874–1936. British writer whose works include a series of detective novels.

Chester White *n.* Any of a breed of large white hogs with drooping ears, originally bred in Pennsylvania.

chest·nut (chĕs′nŭt′, -nət) *n.* **1a.** Any of several deciduous trees

of the genus *Castanea*, native to northern temperate regions and having alternate simple toothed leaves and nuts enclosed in a prickly husk. **b.** The often edible nut of any of these trees. **c.** The wood of any of these trees. **2.** Any of several other plants, such as the horse chestnut. **3.** A moderate to deep reddish brown. **4.** A reddish-brown horse. **5.** A small hard callus on the inner surface of a horse's foreleg. **6.** An old, frequently repeated joke, story, or song. ❖ *adj.* Of the color chestnut. [Earlier *chesten* (< ME *chesteine* < OFr. *chastaigne* < Lat. *castanea* < Gk. *kastaneā*, chestnut tree < *kastana*, sweet chestnuts) + NUT.]

chestnut blight *n.* A disease of chestnut trees caused by a fungus (*Cryphonectria parasitica*) and characterized by destructive cankers.

chestnut oak *n.* Either of two eastern North American deciduous oak trees (*Quercus prinus* and *Q. muehlenbergii*) having leaves that resemble those of the American chestnut.

chest of drawers *n., pl.* **chests of drawers** A piece of furniture consisting of a set of drawers that fit within a frame.

chest·y (chĕs′tē) *adj.* **-i·er, -i·est** *Informal* **1.** Having a large or well-developed chest or bust. **2.** Arrogant or proud; conceited. —**chest′i·ness** *n.*

che·tah (chē′tə) *n.* Variant of **cheetah.**

che·val-de-frise (shə-văl′də-frēz′) *n., pl.* **che·vaux-de-frise** (shə-vō′-) **1.** An obstacle of barbed wire or spikes on a wooden frame, used to block enemy advancement. **2.** An obstacle of jagged glass or spikes set into masonry on top of a wall. [Fr., Frisian horse : *cheval*, horse + *de*, of + *Frise*, Friesland.]

che·val·et (shə-văl′ĕ, shə-vă-lā′) *n.* The bridge of a stringed instrument. [Fr. < dim. of *cheval*, horse < Lat. *caballus*.]

che·val glass (shə-văl′) *n.* A long mirror mounted on swivels in a frame. [Fr. *cheval*, support, horse. See **CHEVAL.**]

chev·a·lier (shĕv′ə-lîr′) *n.* **1.** A member of certain orders of knighthood or merit. **2a.** A French nobleman of the lowest rank. **b.** Used as a title for such a nobleman. **3.** A knight. **4.** A chivalrous man. [ME *chevaler* < OFr. *chevalier* < LLat. *caballārius*, horseman. See **CAVALIER.**]

che·ve·lure (shəv-lür′) *n.* A head of hair. [ME *cheveler* < OFr. *cheveleure* < Lat. *capillātūra* < *capillus*, hair.]

Chev·i·ot (shĕv′ē-ət, chĕv′-) *n.* **1.** Any of a breed of hornless sheep with short thick wool, originally raised in the Cheviot Hills. **2.** also **cheviot** A woolen fabric with a coarse twill weave originally made from Cheviot wool.

Chev·i·ot Hills (chĕv′ē-ət, shĕv′-, chē′vē-) A range of hills extending along the border of England and Scotland.

chèv·re (shĕv′rə) *n.* Cheese made from goat's milk. [Fr. < OFr. < Lat. *capra*, she-goat, fem. of *caper*, goat.]

chev·ron (shĕv′rən) *n.* **1.** A badge or insignia consisting of stripes meeting at an angle, worn on the sleeve of a military or police uniform to indicate rank, merit, or length of service. **2.** *Heraldry* A device shaped like an inverted V. **3.** A V-shaped pattern, esp. a kind of fret used in architecture. [ME *cheveron* < OFr. *chevron*, rafter (< the meeting of rafters at an angle), prob. < VLat. **capriō, *capriōn-* < Lat. *caper, capr-*, goat.]

chev·ro·tain (shĕv′rə-tān′) *n.* Any of several small deerlike hornless ruminants of the genera *Hyemoschus* and *Tragulus* native to the rainforests of central Africa, India, and southeast Asia. [Fr. *chevrotin* < OFr., dim. of *chevrot*, kid, dim. of *chevre*, goat < Lat. *capra*, she-goat, fem. of *caper*, goat.]

chew (chōō) *v.* **chewed, chew·ing, chews** —*tr.* **1.** To bite and grind with the teeth. **2.** To meditate on. —*intr.* **1.** To make a crushing and grinding motion with the teeth. **2.** To meditate. **3.** *Informal* To use chewing tobacco. ❖ *n.* **1.** The act of chewing. **2.** Something held in the mouth and chewed, esp. a plug of tobacco. —**phrasal verb: chew out** *Slang* To reprimand; scold. —**idioms: chew the cud** *Slang* To ponder over. **chew the fat (or rag)** *Slang* To talk together in a friendly, leisurely way; chat at length. [ME *cheuen* < OE *cēowan*.] —**chew′a·ble** *adj.* —**chew′er** *n.*

Che·wa (chā′wä) *n.* A Bantu language spoken in Malawi.

chew·ing gum (chōō′ĭng) *n.* A sweetened flavored preparation for chewing, usu. made of chicle.

che·wink (chĭ-wĭngk′) *n.* See **towhee** 1. [Imit. of its call.]

chew·y (chōō′ē) *adj.* **-i·er, -i·est** Needing much chewing: *chewy candy.* —**chew′i·ness** *n.*

Chey·enne¹ (shī-ĕn′, -ăn′) *n., pl.* **Cheyenne** or **-ennes 1.** A member of a Native American people, divided after 1832 into the Northern and Southern Cheyenne, inhabiting respectively southeast Montana and southern Colorado, with present-day populations in Montana and Oklahoma. **2.** The Algonquian language of the Cheyenne. [Canadian Fr. < Dakota *šahíyela*.] —**Chey·enne′** *adj.*

Chey·enne² (shī-ăn′, -ĕn′) The cap. of WY, in the SE part near the NE and CO borders; founded 1867. Pop. 53,011.

Cheyenne River (shī-ăn′, -ĕn′) A river rising in E WY and flowing c. 848 km (527 mi) to the Missouri R. in central SD.

chez (shā) *prep.* At the home of; at or by. [Fr. < OFr. < Lat. *casa*, cottage, hut.]

chi¹ also **khi** (kī, kē) *n.* The 22nd letter of the Greek alphabet. [L.Gk. *khî* < earlier *khei*.]

chi² also **ch'i** or **Qi** or **qi** (chē) *n.* In Taoism and other Chinese thought, the vital force inherent in all things, whose unimpeded circulation is held to be essential to good health in traditional

Chiang Kai-shek

Chinese medicine. [Chin. (Mandarin) *qì*, air, spirit, energy of life.]

Chia-ling (jyä′lĭng′) See **Jialing.**

Chia·mus·su (jyä′mŏo′sŏo′) See **Jiamusi.**

Chiang Kai-shek (chăng′ kī′shĕk′, jyäng′) 1887–1975. Chinese military and political figure who led the Nationalists against the Communist forces and was driven to Taiwan (1949), where he became president of Nationalist China.

Chi·an·ti (kē-än′tē, -än′-) *n.* A dry red table wine made from a blend of different varieties of grapes, originally produced in northwest Italy. [After the *Chianti* Mountains, a range of the Apennines in central Italy.]

chi·a·ro·scu·ro (kē-är′ə-skōor′ō, -skyōor′ō) *n., pl.* **-ros 1.** The technique of using light and shade in pictorial representation. **2.** The arrangement of light and dark elements in a pictorial work of art. [Ital. : *chiaro*, bright, light (< Lat. *clārus*, clear; see **kelə-** in App.) + *oscuro*, dark (< Lat. *obscūrus*; see **(s)keu-** in App.).] —**chi·a′ro·scu′rist** *n.*

chi·as·ma (kī-ăz′mə) also **chi·asm** (kī′ăz′əm) *n., pl.* **-ma·ta** (-mə-tə) or **-mas** also **-asms 1.** *Anatomy* A crossing or intersection of two tracts. **2.** *Genetics* The point of contact between paired chromatids during meiosis, resulting in a cross-shaped configuration and representing the cytological manifestation of crossing over. [Gk. *khiasma*, cross-piece < *khiazein*, to mark with an X < *khei*, *khī*, chi (< the letter's shape).] —**chi·as′mal, chi·as′mic, chi′as·mat′ic** (-măt′ĭk) *adj.*

chi·as·mus (kī-ăz′məs) *n., pl.* **-mi** (-mī′) A rhetorical inversion of the second of two parallel structures, as in "*Each throat/Was parched, and glazed each eye*" (Samuel Taylor Coleridge). [NLat. *chīasmus* < Gk. *khīasmos*, syntactic inversion < *khiazein*, to invert or mark with an X. See CHIASMA.]

chi·as·to·lite (kī-ăs′tə-līt′) *n.* A mineral variety of andalusite with carbonaceous impurities regularly arranged along the longer axis of the crystal. [< Gk. *khīastos*, crossed, p. part. of *khiazein*, to mark with an X. See CHIASMA.]

chiaus (chous, choush) *n.* An official Turkish messenger, emissary, or sergeant. [Turk. *çavuş* < O Turkic *chāv*, announcement.]

Chi·ba (chē′bä′) A city of E-central Honshu, Japan, on the NE shore of Tokyo Bay. Pop. 850,631.

Chib·cha (chĭb′chə) *n., pl.* **Chibcha** or **-chas 1.** A member of an extinct Indian people formerly inhabiting central Colombia. **2.** Their extinct Chibchan language.

Chib·chan (chĭb′chən) *n.* **1.** A member of any of various widely scattered Indian peoples of Colombia and Central America. **2.** A language family comprising these peoples' languages, including Chibcha.

Chi·bem·ba (chĭ-bĕm′bə) *n.* See **Bemba.**

chi·bouk also **chi·bouque** (chĭ-book′, shĭ-) *n.* A Turkish tobacco pipe with a long stem and a red clay bowl. [Turk. dialectal *çibuk* < *çubuk*, shoot, twig, staff < O Turkic *chubuq, chībīq*, dim. of *chīp, chīb-*, branch.]

chic (shēk) *adj.* **chic·er, chic·est 1.** Conforming to the current fashion; stylish. **2.** Adopting or setting current fashions and styles; sophisticated. ❖ *n.* **1.** The quality or state of being stylish; fashionableness. **2.** Sophistication in dress and manner; elegance. [Fr., prob. < Ger. *Schick*, skill, fitness, elegance < MHGer. *(sich) schicken*, to outfit (oneself), fit.] —**chic′ly** *adv.* —**chic′ness** *n.*

Chi·ca·go (shĭ-kä′gō, -kô′-) A city of NE IL on Lake Michigan; nearly destroyed by a disastrous fire in 1871. Pop. 2,896,016. —**Chi·ca′go·an** *n.*

Chicago River A river formed at Chicago by the junction of N and S branches that total c. 55 km (34 mi) in length.

Chicago School *n.* A group of US architects of the late 19th to early 20th century noted for their utilitarian designs and their use of steel framing as a skeleton for multistory buildings. [< the core of the group being located at the University of *Chicago.*]

Chi·ca·na (chĭ-kä′nə, shĭ-) *n.* A Mexican-American woman or girl. See Usage Notes at **Chicano, Latina.** [Am.Sp. *chicana*, fem. of *chicano*, chicano. See CHICANO.] —**Chi·ca′na** *adj.*

chi·cane (shĭ-kān′, chĭ-) *v.* **-caned, -can·ing, -canes** —*intr.* To use chicanery. —*tr.* To trick; deceive. ❖ *n.* Chicanery. [Fr. *chicaner* < OFr., to quibble.] —**chi·can′er** *n.*

chi·can·er·y (shĭ-kā′nə-rē, chĭ-) *n., pl.* **-ies 1.** Deception by trickery or sophistry. **2.** A trick; a subterfuge.

Chi·ca·no (chĭ-kä′nō, shĭ-) *n., pl.* **-nos** A Mexican-American, esp. a man or boy. [Am.Sp. *chicano*, dialectal var. of *mexicano*, Mexican < *México*, Mexico.] —**Chi·ca′no** *adj.*

> **USAGE NOTE** While *Chicano* is a term of pride for many Mexican Americans, it remains a word with strong political associations. Since these politics are not necessarily espoused by all Mexican Americans, and since usage and acceptance of this word can vary from one region to another, an outsider who is unfamiliar with his or her audience may do well to use *Mexican American* instead. See Usage Note at **Hispanic.**

Chi·chén It·zá (chē-chĕn′ ē-tsä′, ĕt′sə) An ancient Mayan city of central Yucatán in Mexico; founded c. A.D. 514 and abandoned in 1194.

chi·chi (shē′shē) *adj.* **-chi·er, -chi·est** Ostentatiously stylish; deliberately chic. [Fr.] —**chi′chi** *n.*

chick (chĭk) *n.* **1a.** A young chicken. **b.** The young of any bird. **2.**

A child. **3.** *Slang* A girl or young woman. [ME *chike*, var. of *chiken*, chicken. See CHICKEN.]

chick·a·dee (chĭk′ə-dē′) *n.* Any of several small, plump North American birds of the genus *Parus*, having predominantly gray plumage and a dark-crowned head. [Imit. of its call.]

Chick·a·mau·ga (chĭk′ə-mô′gə) A city of extreme NW GA S of Chattanooga TN; site of a Union defeat (Sep. 19–20, 1863). Pop. 2,245.

chick·a·ree (chĭk′ə-rē′) *n.* A small squirrel (*Tamiasciurus douglasi*) of the evergreen forests of northwest North America, resembling and closely related to the red squirrel. [Imit.]

Chick·a·saw (chĭk′ə-sô′) *n., pl.* **Chick·a·saw** or **-saws 1.** A member of a Native American people formerly inhabiting northeast Mississippi and northwest Alabama, now located in south-central Oklahoma. **2.** The Muskogean language of the Chickasaw. —**Chick·a·saw′** *adj.*

Chick·a·sa·whay (chĭk-sô′wä) A river, c. 338 km (210 mi), of SE MS.

chick·en (chĭk′ən) *n.* **1a.** The common domestic fowl (*Gallus domesticus*) or its young. **b.** Any of various similar or related birds. **c.** The flesh of the common domestic fowl. **2.** *Slang* A coward. **3.** Any of various competitions in which the participants persist in a dangerous course of action until one loses nerve and stops. ❖ *adj. Slang* Afraid; cowardly. ❖ *intr.v.* **-ened, -en·ing, -ens** *Slang* To act in a cowardly manner; lose one's nerve: *I chickened out.* [ME *chiken* < OE *cīcen.*]

chicken feed *n. Slang* A trifling amount of money.

chick·en-fried (chĭk′ən-frīd′) *adj.* Coated with batter and seasoned flour and fried.

chicken hawk *n.* Any of various hawks that prey on or have the reputation of preying on chickens.

chick·en-heart·ed (chĭk′ən-här′tĭd) *adj.* Lacking courage; cowardly. —**chick′en·heart′ed·ness** *n.*

chick·en-liv·ered (chĭk′ən-lĭv′ərd) *adj.* Cowardly.

chick·en·pox or **chicken pox** (chĭk′ən-pŏks′) *n.* An acute contagious disease, chiefly of children, caused by the varicella-zoster virus and marked by skin eruptions and slight fever. [Perh. in allusion to the mildness of the disease as contrasted with smallpox.]

chick·en·shit (chĭk′ən-shĭt′) *Vulgar Slang n.* Contemptibly petty nonsense. ❖ *adj.* **1.** Contemptibly petty. **2.** Cowardly; afraid.

chicken snake *n.* See **rat snake.**

chicken wire *n.* A light-gauge galvanized wire fencing usu. made with hexagonal mesh.

chick·pea (chĭk′pē′) *n.* **1.** An annual Asian plant (*Cicer arietinum*) in the pea family, widely cultivated for its edible seeds. **2.** A seed of this plant. [Obsolete *chichpease* : ME *chiche*, chickpea (< OFr. < Lat. *cicer*) + *pease*, pea; see PEA.]

chick·weed (chĭk′wēd′) *n.* Any of various herbs of the genera *Cerastium* and *Stellaria*, esp. *S. media*, a European weed with small white flowers and opposite leaves.

Chi·cla·yo (chĭ-klä′yō, chē-) A city of NW Peru NNW of Lima. Pop. 448,400.

chic·le (chĭk′əl, chē′klĕ) *n.* The coagulated milky juice of the sapodilla, used as the principal ingredient of chewing gum. [Sp. < Nahuatl *chictli.*]

chic·o·ry (chĭk′ə-rē) *n., pl.* **-ries 1.** A perennial herb (*Cichorium intybus*) of the composite family, native to the Old World and having usu. blue florets. **2.** Any of various forms of this plant having edible leaves, such as radicchio. **3.** The dried, roasted, and ground roots of this plant, used as an adulterant of or substitute for coffee. [ME *cicoree* and Fr. *chicorée*, both ult. < Gk. *kikhoreia*, pl. dim. of *kikhorē.*]

chide (chīd) *v.* **chid·ed** or **chid** (chĭd), **chid·ed** or **chid** or **chid·den** (chĭd′n), **chid·ing, chides** —*tr.* To scold mildly so as to correct or improve; reprimand: *chided the boy.* —*intr.* To express disapproval. [ME *chiden* < OE *cīdan* < *cīd*, strife, contention.] —**chid′er** *n.* —**chid′ing·ly** *adv.*

chief (chēf) *n.* **1.** One who is highest in rank or authority; a leader. **2.** often **Chief a.** A chief petty officer. **b.** *Nautical* The chief engineer of a ship. **3.** *Slang* A boss. **4.** *Heraldry* The upper section of a shield. **5.** The most important or valuable part. ❖ *adj.* **1.** Highest in rank, authority, or office. **2.** Most important or influential. ❖ *adv. Archaic* Chiefly. [ME *chef* < OFr. < Lat. *caput*, head. See **kaput-** in App.] —**chief′dom** *n.* —**chief′ship** *n.*

chief executive *n.* **1. Chief Executive** The President of the United States. **2.** A principal executive official.

chief executive officer *n.* The highest-ranking executive in a company or organization.

chief justice also **Chief Justice** *n.* The presiding judge of a high court having several judges, esp. the US Supreme Court.

chief·ly (chēf′lē) *adv.* **1.** Above all; especially. **2.** Almost entirely; mainly. ❖ *adj.* Of or relating to a chief.

chief master sergeant *n.* A noncommissioned officer in the US Air Force, ranking above senior master sergeant.

chief of naval operations *n., pl.* **chiefs of naval operations** The ranking officer of the US Navy, responsible to the secretary of the Navy and the President.

chief of staff *n., pl.* **chiefs of staff 1.** The ranking officer of the US Army, Navy, or Air Force, responsible to the secretary of the

Chicago School
the Bayard-Condict Building
in New York City, designed
c. 1898 by Louis Sullivan

Chichén Itzá
the Castillo, with the
Temple of a Thousand
Columns in the foreground

ă	pat	oi	boy
ā	pay	ou	out
âr	care	ŏŏ	took
ä	father	ōō	boot
ĕ	pet	ŭ	cut
ē	be	ûr	urge
ĭ	pit	th	thin
ī	pie	*th*	this
îr	pier	hw	which
ŏ	pot	zh	vision
ō	toe	ə	about,
ô	paw		item

Stress marks:
′ (primary);
′ (secondary), as in
lexicon (lĕk′sĭ-kŏn′)

branch and the President. **2.** The senior military staff officer at the division level or higher.

chief of state *n., pl.* **chiefs of state** The formal head of a nation, distinct from the head of the government.

chief petty officer *n.* An enlisted officer in the US Navy, ranking above petty officer first class and below senior chief petty officer.

chief·tain (chēf′tən) *n.* The leader or head of a group, esp. of a clan or tribe. [ME *cheftain* < OFr. *chevetain* < LLat. *capitāneus* < Lat. *caput,* head. See **kaput-** in App.] —**chief′tain·cy** *n.* —**chief′tain·ship′** *n.*

chief warrant officer *n.* A military officer holding the highest rank of warrant officer.

Ch'ien-lung (chyĕn′lōong′) See **Qianlong.**

chiff·chaff (chĭf′chăf′) *n.* A European warbler (*Phylloscopus collybita*) with yellowish-green plumage. [Imit. of its song.]

chif·fon (shĭ-fŏn′, shĭf′ŏn′) *n.* A fabric of sheer silk or rayon. **2.** Ornamental accessories, such as ribbons or laces, for women's clothing. ❖ *adj.* **1.** Of, relating to, or resembling the fabric chiffon. **2.** Made light and fluffy by beaten egg whites or gelatin: *a lemon chiffon pie.* [Fr., rag, chiffon < *chiffe,* old rag, perh. var. of OFr. *chipe,* of Gmc. orig.]

chif·fo·nier (shĭf′ə-nîr′) *n.* A tall narrow chest of drawers or bureau, often with a mirror attached. [Fr. < *chiffon,* rag. See CHIFFON.]

chif·fo·robe (shĭf′ə-rōb′, shĭf′rōb′) *n. Chiefly Southern US* A tall piece of furniture typically having drawers on one side and space for hanging clothes on the other. [CHIFFO(NIER) + (WARD)ROBE.]

chig·ger (chĭg′ər) *n.* **1.** Any of various small, six-legged mite larvae of the family Trombiculidae, parasitic on insects and vertebrates. **2.** See **chigoe** 1. [Alteration of CHIGOE.]

chi·gnon (shēn′yŏn′, shēn′yŏn′) *n.* A roll or knot of hair worn esp. at the nape of the neck. [Fr. < OFr. *chaignon,* chain, collar, nape < VLat. **catēnio* < Lat. *catēna,* chain.]

chig·oe (chĭg′ō, chē′gō) *n.* **1.** A small tropical flea (*Tunga penetrans*), the fertilized female of which burrows under the skin of animals and humans. **2.** See **chigger** 1. [Poss. < Galibi *chico,* or of African orig. See JIGGER².]

Chi·hua·hua¹ (chə-wä′wä, chē-) A city of N Mexico S of Ciudad Juárez. Pop. 385,603.

Chi·hua·hua² (chĭ-wä′wä, -wə) *n.* A very small dog of a breed originating in Mexico, having pointed ears and a smooth coat. [After *Chihuahua,* a city and state of northern Mexico.]

chil·blain (chĭl′blān′) *n.* An inflammation followed by itchy irritation on the hands, feet, or ears, resulting from exposure to moist cold. [CHIL(L) + BLAIN.] —**chil′blained′** *adj.*

child (chīld) *n., pl.* **chil·dren** (chĭl′drən) **1.** A person between birth and puberty. **2a.** A human fetus. **b.** An infant; a baby. **3.** One who is childish or immature. **4.** A son or daughter; an offspring. **5.** A member of a tribe; descendant. **6.** One regarded as strongly affected by or as the product or result of something specified: *a child of nature; a child of the Sixties.* —*idiom:* **with child** Pregnant. [ME < OE *cild.*] —**child′less** *adj.* —**child′less·ness** *n.*

Child, Lydia Maria Francis 1802–80. Amer. abolitionist and writer of novels and children's books.

child·bear·ing (chīld′bâr′ĭng) *n.* The human act or process of giving birth; parturition. —**child′bear′ing** *adj.*

child·bed (chīld′bĕd′) *n.* The condition of a woman in the process of giving birth.

childbed fever *n.* See **puerperal fever.**

child·birth (chīld′bûrth′) *n.* The human act or process of giving birth; parturition.

child-care or **child·care** (chīld′kâr′) *adj.* Of or providing care for children, esp. preschoolers. —**child′care′** *n.*

childe (chīld) *n. Archaic* A child of noble birth. [ME.]

child·hood (chīld′hood′) *n.* **1.** The time or state of being a child. **2.** The early stage in existence or development.

child·ish (chīl′dĭsh) *adj.* **1.** Of or suitable for a child or childhood. **2a.** Marked by or indicating a lack of maturity. **b.** Not complicated; simple. **c.** Affected mentally by old age; senile. —**child′ish·ly** *adv.* —**child′ish·ness** *n.*

child labor *n.* The full-time employment of children under a minimum legal age.

child·like (chīld′līk′) *adj.* Like or befitting a child, as in innocence, trustfulness, or candor.

child·proof (chīld′proof′) *adj.* **1.** Designed to resist tampering by young children: *a childproof bottle.* **2.** Made safe for young children. —**child′proof′** *v.*

chil·dren (chĭl′drən) *n.* Plural of **child.**

child's play (chīldz) *n.* **1.** An easy task. **2.** A trivial matter.

Chil·e (chĭl′ē, chē′lě) A country of SW South America on the Pacific Ocean; declared independence from Spain in 1818. Cap. Santiago. Pop. 13,994,000. —**Chil′e·an** (chĭl′ē-ən, chĭ-lā′-) *adj. & n.*

Chile saltpeter (chĭl′ē) *n.* See **sodium nitrate.**

chil·i also **chil·e** or **chil·li** (chĭl′ē) *n., pl.* **chil·ies** also **chil·es** or **chil·lies 1.** The pungent fruit of any of several cultivated varieties of capsicum, used esp. as a flavoring. **2.** Chili con carne. [Sp. *chile* < Nahuatl *chilli.*]

chil·i·ad (kĭl′ē-ăd′, -əd) *n.* **1.** A group that contains 1,000

Chile

Chimera

elements. **2.** One thousand years; a millennium. [LLat. *chīlias, chīliad-* < Gk. *khīlias* < *khīlioi,* thousand.]

chil·i·asm (kĭl′ē-ăz′əm) *n.* The doctrine stating that Jesus will reign on earth for 1,000 years. [NLat. *chīliasmus* < LLat. *chīlias, chiliad.* See CHILIAD.] —**chil′i·ast′** (-ăst′, -əst) *n.*

chili con car·ne (kŏn kär′nē) *n.* A highly spiced dish made of red peppers, meat, and often beans. [Sp. : *chile, chili* + *con,* with + *carne,* meat.]

chil·i·dog (chĭl′ē-dôg′, -dŏg′) *n.* A hot dog covered with chili con carne, served in a long roll.

Chi·lin (jē′lĭn′) See **Jilin.**

chili pepper *n.* See **chili** 1.

chili powder *n.* A seasoning consisting of ground chilies mixed with other spices, such as cumin and oregano.

chili sauce *n.* A spiced sauce made with chilies and tomatoes.

chill (chĭl) *n.* **1.** A moderate but penetrating coldness. **2.** A sensation of coldness, often accompanied by shivering and pallor of the skin. **3.** A checking or dampening of enthusiasm, spirit, or joy. **4.** A sudden numbing fear or dread. ❖ *adj.* **1.** Moderately cold; chilly. **2.** Not warm and friendly; distant: *a chill greeting.* **3.** Discouraging; dispiriting. ❖ *v.* **chilled, chill·ing, chills** —*tr.* **1.** To affect with or as if with cold. **2.** To lower in temperature; cool. **3.** To make discouraged; dispirit. **4.** *Metallurgy* To harden (a metallic surface) by rapid cooling. —*intr.* **1.** To be seized with cold. **2.** To become cold or set. **3.** *Metallurgy* To become hard by rapid cooling. **4.** *Slang* **a.** To calm down or relax. **b.** To pass time idly; loiter. **c.** To keep company; see socially. [ME *chile* < OE *cele.* See **gel-** in App.] —**chill′ing·ly** *adv.* —**chill′ness** *n.*

chill·er (chĭl′ər) *n.* **1.** One that chills. **2.** A frightening story, esp. one involving violence, evil, or the supernatural.

chill factor *n.* Wind-chill factor.

chil·li (chĭl′ē) *n.* Variant of **chili.**

chill pill *n. Slang* Something that calms nerves or induces relaxation. —*idiom:* **take a chill pill** To calm down; relax.

chill·y (chĭl′ē) *adj.* **-i·er, -i·est 1.** Cool or cold enough to cause shivering. See Syns at **cold.** **2.** Seized with or feeling cold; shivering. **3.** Distant and cool; unfriendly: *a chilly look.* —**chill′i·ly** *adv.* —**chill′i·ness** *n.*

Chi·lo·é (chĭl′ō-ā′, chē′lō-ĕ′) An island off S-central Chile.

chi·lo·pod (kī′lə-pŏd′) *n.* Any of various arthropods of the class Chilopoda, which includes the centipedes. [< NLat. *Chīlopoda,* class name : Gk. *kheilos,* lip + *-poda,* -pod.]

Chil·tern Hundreds (chĭl′tərn) *n. (used with a sing. verb) Chiefly British* A merely formal office applied for by members of Parliament when they wish to resign from the House of Commons. [Short for *Stewardship of the Chiltern Hundreds,* tracts of crown lands in S-central England.]

Chi·lung (jē′lōong′, chē′-) A city of N Taiwan on the East China Sea. Pop. 349,686.

chi·mae·ra (kī-mîr′ə, kĭ-) *n.* **1.** A deep-sea cartilaginous fish of the family Chimaeridae, having a tapering body and a whiplike tail. **2.** Variant of **chimera.** [NLat. *Chimaera,* type genus < Lat. *chimaera,* chimera. See CHIMERA.]

Chim·bo·ra·zo (chĭm′bə-rä′zō, -rä′-, chēm′bō-rä′sō) An inactive volcano, 6,271.1 m (20,561 ft), in central Ecuador.

Chim·bo·te (chĭm-bō′tē, chēm-bō′tě) A city of W Peru on the Pacific Ocean NNW of Callao. Pop. 314,700.

chime¹ (chīm) *n.* **1.** An apparatus for striking a bell or set of bells to produce a musical sound. **2.** *Music* A set of tuned bells used as an orchestral instrument. Often used in the plural. **3.** A single bell, as in a clock mechanism. **4.** The sound produced by or as if by a bell or bells. **5.** Agreement; accord. ❖ *v.* **chimed, chim·ing, chimes** —*intr.* **1a.** To sound with a harmonious ring when struck. **b.** To make a musical sound by striking a bell or set of bells. **2.** To be in agreement or accord; harmonize. —*tr.* **1.** To produce (music) by striking bells. **2.** To strike (a bell) to produce music. **3a.** To signal or make known by chiming. **b.** To call, send, or welcome by chiming. **4.** To repeat insistently. —*phrasal verb:* **chime in 1.** To interrupt the speech of others, esp. with an unwanted opinion. **2.** To join in harmoniously. **3.** To go together harmoniously; agree. [< ME *chimbe (belle)* < OFr., var. of *cimble,* cymbal < Lat. *cymbalum.* See CYMBAL.] —**chim′er** *n.*

chime² (chīm) *n.* The rim of a cask. [ME *chimb* < OE *cim-, cimb-* (in *cimstānas,* bases of a pillar, and *cimbing,* jointing). See **gembh-** in App.]

chi·me·ra (kī-mîr′ə, kĭ-) also **chi·mae·ra** (kī-mîr′ə, kĭ-) *n.* **1a.** An organism, organ, or part consisting of two or more tissues of different genetic composition, produced as a result of organ transplant, grafting, or genetic engineering. **b.** A substance created from the proteins or genes of two different species. **2.** A fanciful mental illusion or fabrication. [ME *chimere,* Chimera < OFr. < Lat. *chimaera* < Gk. *khimaira,* chimera, she-goat. See **ghei-** in App.]

Chimera also **Chimaera** *n.* **1.** *Greek Mythology* A fire-breathing female monster usu. represented as a composite of a lion, goat, and serpent. **2.** An imaginary monster made up of grotesquely disparate parts.

chi·mere (chə-mîr′, shə-) *n.* A loose sleeveless robe worn esp. by Anglican bishops. [ME *chimer,* perh. < Anglo-Lat. *chimēra;* prob. akin to Sp. *chamarra, zamarra,* type of garment, of Basque orig.]

chi·mer·i·cal (kī-mĕr′ĭ-kəl, -mîr′-, kĭ-) also **chi·mer·ic** (-mĕr′ĭk, -mîr′-) *adj.* **1.** Created by or as if by a wildly fanciful imagination; highly improbable. **2.** Given to unrealistic fantasies; fanciful. **3.** often **chimeric** Of, related to, or being a chimera. —**chi·mer′i·cal·ly** *adv.*

chim·i·chur·ri (chĭm′ē-cho͝or′ē) *n.* A sauce made of chopped fresh herbs, garlic, and pepper and bound with oil and vinegar. [Am.Sp.]

Chim·kent (chĭm-kĕnt′) See **Shymkent.**

chim·ney (chĭm′nē) *n., pl.* **-neys 1a.** A passage through which smoke and gases escape from a fire or furnace; a flue. **b.** The usu. vertical structure containing a chimney. **c.** The part of such a structure that rises above a roof. **2.** *Chiefly British* A smokestack, as of a ship. **3.** A glass tube for enclosing the flame of a lamp. **4.** Something resembling a chimney. [ME *chimenei* < OFr. *cheminee* < LLat. *camīnāta*, fireplace < Lat. *camīnus*, furnace < Gk. *kamīnos*.]

chim·ney·piece (chĭm′nē-pēs′) *n.* **1.** The mantel of a fireplace. **2.** A decoration over a fireplace.

chimney pot *n.* A short, usu. earthenware pipe placed on the top of a chimney to improve the draft.

chimney sweep or **chimney sweeper** *n.* A worker who cleans chimneys.

chimney swift *n.* A small, dark, swallowlike New World bird (*Chaetura pelagica*) that frequently nests in chimneys.

chimp (chĭmp) *n. Informal* A chimpanzee.

chim·pan·zee (chĭm′păn-zē′, -pən-, chĭm-păn′zē) *n.* A gregarious anthropoid ape (*Pan troglodytes*) of tropical Africa having dark hair, somewhat arboreal habits, and a high degree of intelligence. [Port. < Vili (Bantu language of Congo) *ci-mpenzi*.]

chin (chĭn) *n.* The central forward portion of the lower jaw. ❖ *v.* **chinned, chin·ning, chins** —*tr.* **1.** To pull (oneself) up with the arms on an overhead horizontal bar until the chin tops the bar. **2.** *Music* To place (a violin) under the chin before playing. —*intr.* **1.** To chin oneself. **2.** *Informal* To chatter. [ME < OE *cin*.] —**chin′less** *adj.*

Chin (jĭn) See **Jin.**

Chin. *abbr.* Chinese

Ch'in (chĭn) See **Qin.**

chi·na (chī′nə) *n.* **1.** High-quality porcelain or ceramic ware, originally made in China. **2.** Porcelain or earthenware used for the table. [Pers. *chīnī*, ult. < Chin. (Mandarin) *Qín*, Qin. See **Qin.**]

China A country of E Asia whose civilization traditionally dates to c. 2700 B.C. After a bitter civil war (1946–49) a people's republic was established on the mainland, and the Nationalists fled to Taiwan. Cap. Beijing. Pop. 1,237,000,000.

China, Republic of See **Taiwan.**

China aster *n.* An annual Chinese plant (*Callistephus chinensis*) in the composite family, grown for its showy flower heads.

chi·na·ber·ry (chī′nə-bĕr′ē) *n.* A deciduous Asian tree (*Melia azedarach*) having bipinnately compound leaves and yellow poisonous fruits.

Chi·na·man (chī′nə-mən) *n. Offensive* A Chinese man.

China rose *n.* A Chinese rose (*Rosa chinensis*) having mostly red, pink, or white flowers.

China Sea The W part of the Pacific Ocean extending along the E coast of Asia and divided by Taiwan into the **East China Sea** and the **South China Sea.**

Chi·na·town (chī′nə-toun′) *n.* A neighborhood or section of a city that is inhabited chiefly by Chinese people.

China tree *n.* See **chinaberry.**

chi·na·ware (chī′nə-wâr′) *n.* Tableware made of china.

chi·na·wood oil (chī′nə-wo͝od′) *n.* See **tung oil.**

chinch (chĭnch) *n. Chiefly Southern & Midland US* See **bedbug.** [Sp. *chinche* < Lat. *cīmex, cīmic-*, bug.]

chinch bug also **cinch bug** *n. Chiefly Southern & Midland US* **1.** A small black and white insect (*Blissus leucopterus*) that is very destructive to grains and grasses. **2.** See **bedbug.**

chin·che·rin·chee (chĭn′chə-rĭn-chē′, chĭng′kə-) *n.* A southern African plant (*Ornithogalum thyrsoides*) in the lily family whose blossom is popular as a cut flower. [Afr. *tjienkerientjee* < *tjienker-*, imit. of a tinkling sound (< the sound the stems make when rubbed together) + *uintjie*, bulb, dim. of *ui*, onion (< MDu. *uyen*, ult. < Lat. *uniō*, a kind of onion).]

chin·chil·la (chĭn-chĭl′ə) *n.* **1a.** A squirrellike rodent (*Chinchilla laniger*) of South America widely raised in captivity for its soft, pale gray fur. **b.** The fur of this animal. **2.** A thick twilled cloth of wool and cotton used for overcoats. [Sp., prob. of Aymara orig.]

Chin·chow (jĭn′jō′) See **Jinzhou.**

chinch·y (chĭn′chē) *adj.* **-i·er, -i·est** *Chiefly Southern US* Stingy; tightfisted; cheap. [Alteration of CHINTZY.]

Chin·co·teague Bay (shĭng′kə-tēg′, chĭng′-) A long narrow bay off NE VA and SE MD including **Chincoteague Island.**

Chincoteague pony *n.* A type of small, inbred North American horse. [After CHINCOTEAGUE ISLAND.]

Chin·dwin (chĭn′dwĭn′) A river rising in N Myanmar (Burma) and flowing c. 1,158 km (720 mi) S to the Irrawaddy R.

chine (chīn) *n.* **1a.** The backbone or spine, esp. of an animal. **b.** A cut of meat containing part of the backbone. **2.** A ridge or crest. **3.** *Nautical* The line of intersection between the side and bottom of a flatbottom or V-bottom boat. ❖ *tr.v.* **chined, chin·ing, chines** To cut (a carcass) through the spine, as when butchering

meat. [ME < OFr. *eschine*, of Gmc. orig.]

Chi·nese (chī-nēz′, -nēs′) *adj.* Of or relating to China or its peoples, languages, or cultures. ❖ *n., pl.* **Chinese 1a.** A native or inhabitant of China. **b.** A person of Chinese ancestry. **c.** See **Han 2. 2a.** The sole member of the Sinitic branch of the Sino-Tibetan language family, consisting of numerous languages and dialects such as Mandarin, Cantonese, and Taiwanese. **b.** Any of these languages or dialects. **c.** The official national language of China; Mandarin. **3.** *Informal* Chinese food.

Chinese anise *n.* An evergreen tree (*Illicium anisatum*) native to Japan and Korea having aromatic leaves and fragrant white or yellow flowers.

Chinese artichoke *n.* A perennial Chinese herb (*Stachys affinis*) in the mint family, cultivated for its edible stems.

Chinese black mushroom *n.* See **shiitake.**

Chinese boxes *pl.n.* A set of boxes of graduated size, each fitting inside the next larger one.

Chinese cabbage *n.* **1.** A plant (*Brassica rapa* subsp. *pekinensis*) of the mustard family, having an edible elongated head of overlapping, crinkled, broad-stalked leaves. **2.** See **bok choy.**

Chinese calendar *n.* The traditional lunisolar calendar of the Chinese people, based on 24 seasonal segments each about 15 days long and an occasional intercalary month.

Chinese checkers *pl.n.* (used with a sing. or pl. verb) A board game in which each player tries to move a set of marbles arranged in holes from one point of a six-pointed star to the opposite point by means of single moves or jumps.

Chinese chestnut *n.* A chestnut (*Castanea mollissima*) native to China and Korea cultivated as an ornamental and for its edible nuts.

Chinese chive *n.* An eastern Asian herb (*Allium tuberosum*) having flat leaves, small white flowers, and elongated bulbs. Often used in the plural.

Chinese date *n.* See **jujube 1.**

Chinese evergreen *n.* A Chinese evergreen plant (*Aglaonena modestum*) with often dark green foliage.

Chinese gooseberry *n.* See **kiwi 2.**

Chinese houses *pl.n.* (used with a sing. or pl. verb) Any of several chiefly Californian plants of the genus *Collinsia*, esp. *C. heterophylla*, having whorls of flowers resembling a pagoda.

Chinese ink *n.* See **India ink 2.**

Chinese kale *n.* A Chinese vegetable (*Brassica oleracea* var. *alboglabra*) of the mustard family.

Chinese lantern *n.* A decorative collapsible lantern of thin, brightly colored paper.

Chinese mustard *n.* Any of several cultivated varieties of the Indian mustard, eaten as a vegetable.

Chinese parsley *n.* See **coriander 1.**

Chinese pear *n.* See **sand pear.**

Chinese puzzle *n.* **1.** An intricate puzzle. **2.** Something complex.

Chinese radish *n.* See **daikon.**

Chinese red *n.* See **vermilion 2.**

Chinese Shar-Pei *n.* See **Shar-Pei.**

Chinese tallow tree *n.* An ornamental tree (*Sapium sebiferum*), native to China and Japan and having a waxy seed coat used in making candles and soap.

Chinese water chestnut *n.* See **water chestnut 2.**

Chinese white *n.* See **zinc oxide.**

Chinese windlass *n.* See **differential windlass.**

Ch'ing (chĭng) See **Qing.**

Ching·hai (chĭng′hī′) See **Qinghai.**

Chin Hills (chĭn) A range of hills in W Myanmar (Burma) rising to 3,055.5 m (10,018 ft).

chink[1] (chĭngk) *n.* A narrow opening, such as a crack or fissure. ❖ *tr.v.* **chinked, chink·ing, chinks 1.** To make narrow openings in. **2.** To fill narrow openings in. [Prob. alteration of obsolete *chine* < ME, crack < OE *cine*.] —**chink′y** *adj.*

chink[2] (chĭngk) *n.* A slight, metallic sound. [Imit.] —**chink** *v.*

Chink *n. Offensive Slang* Used as a disparaging term for a person of Chinese birth or descent. [Prob. alteration of CHINESE.]

Chin·kiang (chĭn′kyăng′, jĭn′gyäng′) See **Zhenjiang.**

chi·no (chē′nō, shē′-) *n., pl.* **-nos 1.** A coarse twilled cotton fabric used for uniforms and sometimes work or sports clothes. **2.** Trousers of a coarse twilled cotton. Often used in the plural. [Am.Sp., mestizo, yellowish (< its original tan color), prob. < Sp. *chino*, Chin. < China, China.]

chi·noi·se·rie or **Chi·noi·se·rie** (shēn′wäz-rē′) *n.* **1.** A style in Western art reflecting Chinese influence through use of elaborate decoration and intricate patterns. **2.** An object reflecting Chinese artistic influence. [Fr. < *chinois*, Chin. < *Chine*, China.]

chi·nook (shĭ-no͝ok′, chĭ-) *n.* **1.** A moist warm wind blowing from the sea in coastal regions of the Pacific Northwest. **2.** A warm dry wind that descends from the eastern slopes of the Rocky Mountains. [Short for *Chinook wind*.]

Chinook *n., pl.* **Chinook** or **-nooks 1a.** A member of a Native American people formerly inhabiting the lower Columbia River valley and adjoining coastal regions of Washington and Oregon, now located in western Washington. **b.** The Chinookan language of the Chinook. **2.** A member of any of various Chinookan-speaking peoples formerly inhabiting the Columbia River valley eastward to The Dalles and now located in southern Washington

China

Chincoteague pony

Chinese lantern

ă pat	oi boy	
ā pay	ou out	
âr care	o͝o took	
ä father	o͞o boot	
ĕ pet	ŭ cut	
ē be	ûr urge	
ĭ pit	th thin	
ī pie	th this	
îr pier	hw which	
ŏ pot	zh vision	
ō toe	ə about,	
ô paw	item	

Stress marks:
′ (primary);
′ (secondary), as in
lexicon (lĕk′sĭ-kŏn′)

and northern Oregon. [Chehalis (Salishan language of W Washington) c'inúk.]

Chi·nook·an (shĭ-nōōk'ən, chĭ-) *n.* A North American Indian language family of Washington and Oregon.

Chinook Jargon *n.* A pidgin language combining words from Nootka, Chinook, Salishan languages, French, and English.

Chinook salmon *n.* A very large, commercially valuable salmon (*Oncorhynchus tshawytscha*) of northern Pacific waters, characterized by irregular black spots on its back.

chin·qua·pin (chĭng'kə-pĭn') *n.* **1.** Any of several deciduous shrubs or small trees related to the chestnut, esp. *Castanea pumila* of the eastern United States. **2.** A large evergreen tree (*Castanopsis chrysophylla*) of the Pacific coast of North America. **3.** The chinquapin nut. [Of Algonquian orig.]

chintz (chĭnts) *n.* A printed and glazed cotton fabric, usu. of bright colors. [Obsolete *chints,* pl. of *chint,* calico cloth < Hindi *cīṇṭ* < Skt. *citra-,* shiny, variegated.]

chintz·y (chĭnt'sē) *adj.* **-i·er, -i·est** **1.** Of, relating to, or decorated with chintz. **2a.** Gaudy and cheaply made. **b.** Stingy.

chin-up (chĭn'ŭp') *n.* The act of chinning oneself.

Chin·wang·tao (chĭn'wäng'tou') See **Qinhuangdao.**

Chi·os (kī'ōs, kē'-, kē'-, KHē'ōs, KHē'-) also **Khí·os** (kē'ōs, KHē'-) An island of E Greece in the Aegean Sea off the W coast of Turkey; noted in antiquity for its school of epic poets.

chip¹ (chĭp) *n.* **1.** A small broken or cut off piece, as of wood or glass. **2.** A crack or flaw caused by the removal of a small piece. **3a.** A small disk or counter used in poker and other games to represent money. **b. chips** *Slang* Money. **4a.** *Electronics* A minute slice of a semiconducting material, such as silicon or germanium, processed to have specified electrical characteristics. **b.** An integrated circuit. **5a.** A thin, usu. fried slice of food, esp. a potato chip. Often used in the plural. **b.** A very small piece of food or candy. Often used in the plural. **c. chips** *Chiefly British* French fries. **6.** Wood, palm leaves, straw, or similar material cut and dried for weaving. **7.** A fragment of dried animal dung used as fuel. **8.** Something worthless. **9.** *Sports* A chip shot. ❖ *v.* **chipped, chip·ping, chips** —*tr.* **1.** To chop or cut, as with an ax. **2a.** To break a small piece from. **b.** To break or cut off (a small piece). **3.** To shape or carve by cutting or chopping. —*intr.* **1.** To become broken off into small pieces. **2.** *Sports* To make a chip shot in golf. —*phrasal verbs:* **chip away** To make progress incrementally. **chip in 1.** To contribute money or labor. **2.** To interrupt with comments; interject. **3.** To put up chips or money as one's bet in poker and other games. —*idioms:* **chip off the old block** A child who closely resembles a parent. **chip on (one's) shoulder** A habitually hostile or combative attitude. [ME < OE *cyp,* beam < Lat. *cippus.*]

chip² (chĭp) *intr.v.* **chipped, chip·ping, chips** To cheep, as a bird. [Imit.] —**chip** *n.*

chip³ (chĭp) *n. Sports* A trick method of throwing one's opponent in wrestling. [?]

chi particle (kī, kē) *n.* An electrically neutral meson having a mass 6,687 times that of the electron and a mean lifetime of approx. 1.5 ×10⁻²⁰ seconds.

chip·board (chĭp'bôrd', -bōrd') *n.* A pasteboard made from discarded paper.

Chip·e·wy·an (chĭp'ə-wī'ən) *n., pl.* **Chipewyan** or **-ans** **1.** A member of a Native American people inhabiting a large area of northern Canada north of the Churchill River. **2.** The Athabaskan language of the Chipewyan. [Cree *čīpwayān,* parka wearer : *čīpw-,* pointed + *ayān,* skin.]

chip·munk (chĭp'mŭngk') *n.* Any of several small striped squirrels of the genera *Tamias* and *Eutamias,* esp. *T. striatus* of eastern North America. [Alteration of obsolete *chitmunk,* perh. < Ojibwa *ajidamoon²,* red squirrel.]

chi·pot·le (chə-pōt'lā) *n.* A ripe jalapeño pepper that has been dried and smoked for use in cooking. [Am.Sp. < Nahuatl *xipotli.*]

chipped beef (chĭpt) *n.* Thinly sliced smoked dried beef.

Chip·pen·dale (chĭp'ən-dāl') *adj.* Of an 18th-century English furniture style marked by flowing lines and often rococo ornamentation. [After Thomas CHIPPENDALE.]

Chippendale, Thomas 1718–79. British cabinetmaker noted for his graceful neoclassical furniture.

chip·per¹ (chĭp'ər) *n.* One that chips or cuts: *a wood chipper.*

chip·per² (chĭp'ər) *intr.v.* **-pered, -per·ing, -pers** **1.** To chirp or twitter, as a bird. **2.** To babble. [Frequentative of CHIP².]

chip·per³ (chĭp'ər) *adj.* In lively spirits; cheerful. [Poss. alteration of Brit. dialectal *kipper,* lively.]

Chip·pe·wa (chĭp'ə-wô', -wä', -wā', -wə) *n., pl.* **Chippewa** or **-was** See **Ojibwa.**

chipping sparrow (chĭp'ĭng) *n.* A small North American sparrow (*Spizella passerina*) having a reddish-brown crown.

chip·py or **chip·pie** (chĭp'ē) *n., pl.* **-pies** **1.** A chipping sparrow. **2.** *Slang* A woman prostitute. [< CHIP².]

chip shot *n.* A short lofted golf stroke.

Chi·rac (shē-räk'), **Jacques** b. 1932. French politician who was elected president in 1995.

chi·ral (kī'rəl) *adj.* Of or relating to the structural characteristic of a molecule that is impossible to superimpose on its own mirror image. [CHIR(O)– + –AL¹.] —**chi·ral'i·ty** (kī-rǎl'ĭ-tē) *n.*

Chi-Rho (kī'rō', kē'-) *n., pl.* **-Rhos** A monogram and symbol for

Jacques Chirac

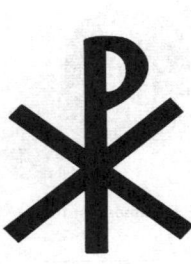

Chi-Rho

Christ, consisting of the superimposed Greek letters *chi* (X) and *rho* (P). [CHI¹ + RHO, first two letters of Gk. *Khrīstos,* Christ.]

Chir·i·ca·hua (chĭr'ĭ-kä'wə) *n., pl.* **Chiricahua** or **-huas** A member of a formerly nomadic Apache tribe inhabiting southern New Mexico, southeast Arizona, and northern Mexico, with present-day populations in Oklahoma and New Mexico.

Chi·ri·co (kîr'ĭ-kō', kē'rē-), **Giorgio de** 1888–1978. Italian painter whose works are characterized by barren landscapes and elements of classical architecture and sculpture.

chirk (chûrk) *tr. & intr.v.* **chirked, chirk·ing, chirks** To make or become cheerful. [ME *chirken,* to chirp < OE *cearcian,* to chatter, alteration of *cracian,* to resound. See CRACK.]

chiro– or **cheiro–** *pref. Hand: chiropractic.* [Lat. *chīro-* < Gk. *kheir,* hand. See ghes- in App.]

chi·rog·ra·phy (kī-rŏg'rə-fē) *n.* Penmanship. —**chi·rog'ra·pher** *n.* —**chi·ro·graph·ic** (kī'rə-grăf'ĭk), **chi'ro·graph·i·cal** *adj.*

chi·ro·man·cy (kī'rə-măn'sē) *n.* Palmistry. —**chi'ro·man'cer** *n.*

Chi·ron (kī'rŏn') *n. Greek Mythology* The wise centaur who tutored Achilles, Hercules, and Asclepius.

chi·rop·o·dy (kī-rŏp'ə-dē, shĭ-) *n.* See **podiatry.** [CHIRO– + –POD– + –Y².] —**chi·rop'o·dist** *n.*

chi·ro·prac·tic (kī'rə-prăk'tĭk) *n.* A system of therapy usu. involving manipulation of the spinal column and other body structures. [CHIRO– + Gk. *prāktikos,* practical; see PRACTICAL.] —**chi'ro·prac'tor** *n.*

chi·rop·ter·an (kī-rŏp'tər-ən) also **chi·rop·ter** (-rŏp'tər) *n.* A mammal, such as the bat, that is a member of the order Chiroptera and has forelimbs modified as wings. [< NLat. *Chīroptera,* order name : CHIRO– + –PTER.] —**chi·rop'ter·an** *adj.*

chirp (chûrp) *n.* A short high-pitched sound, such as that made by a small bird. [ME **chirpen,* of imit. orig.] —**chirp** *v.*

chirr (chûr) *n.* A harsh trilling sound, such as that made by crickets. [Imit.] —**chirr** *v.*

chir·ren (chĭr'ən) *pl.n. Chiefly Southern US* Children.

REGIONAL NOTE The linguistic process of ellipsis allows for the deletion within words of some internal sounds, such as weakly stressed syllables and less prominent consonants. This process is still active in American regional dialects. For example, in *chirren* both the (l) and the (d) of *children* are omitted in favor of the more conspicuous (r).

---

chir·rup (chûr'əp, chĭr'-) *v.* **-ruped, -rup·ing, -rups** —*intr.* **1.** To utter a series of chirps. **2.** To make clucking or clicking sounds with the lips, as in urging on a horse. —*tr.* **1.** To sound with chirps. **2.** To make clucking sounds to. [Variant of CHIRP.] —**chir'rup** *n.*

chi·rur·geon (kī-rûr'jən) *n. Archaic* A surgeon. [ME *cirurgien* < OFr. < Lat. *chīrurgia,* surgery. See SURGERY.]

chis·el (chĭz'əl) *n.* A metal tool with a sharp beveled edge, used to cut and shape stone, wood, or metal. ❖ *v.* **-eled, -el·ing, -els** or **-elled, -el·ling, -els** —*tr.* **1.** To shape or cut with a chisel. **2.** *Informal* **a.** To cheat or swindle. **b.** To obtain by deception. —*intr.* **1.** To use a chisel. **2.** *Informal* **a.** To use unethical methods; cheat. **b.** To intrude oneself without welcome: *always tries to chisel in.* [ME < OFr. *cisel < *cīsellus,* cutting tool < dim. of Lat. *caesus,* p. part. of *caedere,* to cut.] —**chis'el·er** *n.*

chis·eled or **chis·elled** (chĭz'əld) *adj.* Made or shaped with or as if with a chisel: *a finely chiseled nose.*

Chis·holm (chĭz'əm), **Shirley Anita Saint Hill** b. 1924. Amer. politician who was a US representative from NY (1969–83).

Chisholm Trail A former cattle trail from San Antonio TX north to Abilene KS.

Chi·și·năŭ (kĭsh'ə-nou') or **Ki·shi·nev** (kĭsh'ə-nĕf', -nôf') The cap. and largest city of Moldova, near the Romanian border NW of Odessa. Pop. 624,000.

chi-square test (kī'skwâr') *n.* A statistical test for the degree to which a theoretical frequency distribution corresponds to a frequency distribution of observed data.

chit¹ (chĭt) *n.* **1.** A statement of an amount owed for food and drink; a check. **2.** A short letter; a note. [Obsolete *chitty* < Hindi *ciṭṭhī,* note, letter < Skt. **citrikā, *citritā,* note.]

chit² (chĭt) *n.* **1.** A child. **2.** A girl or young woman considered saucy. [ME, young animal.]

Chi·ta (chĭ-tä') A city of SE Russia E of Irkutsk; founded 1653. Pop. 364,903.

chit·chat (chĭt'chăt') *n.* **1.** Casual conversation; small talk. **2.** Gossip. [Reduplication of CHAT.] —**chit'chat'** *v.*

chi·tin (kīt'n) *n.* A tough semitransparent substance forming the principal component of arthropod exoskeletons and the cell walls of certain fungi. [Fr. *chitine* : NLat. *chitōn,* mollusk (< Gk. *khitōn,* chiton; see CHITON) + –INE².] —**chi'tin·ous** *adj.*

chi·ton (kīt'n, kī'tŏn') *n.* **1.** Any of various marine mollusks of the class Polyplacophora that live on rocks and have shells consisting of eight overlapping calcareous plates. **2.** A tunic worn in ancient Greece. [Gk. *khitōn,* tunic < Central Semitic **kittān* < Akkadian *kitû, kita'um,* flax, linen < Sumerian *gada, gida.*]

Chit·ta·gong (chĭt'ə-gông', -gŏng') A city of SE Bangladesh near the Bay of Bengal. Pop. 1,363,998.

chit·ter (chĭt'ər) *intr.v.* **-tered, -ter·ing, -ters** To twitter or chatter, as a bird. [ME *chiteren,* of imit. orig.]

chit•ter•lings also **chit•lins** or **chit•lings** (chĭt′lĭnz) *pl.n.* The small intestines of pigs, esp. when cooked and eaten as food. [< ME *chiterling,* prob. dim. of OE **cieter,* intestines.]

chiv•al•rous (shĭv′əl-rəs) *adj.* **1.** Having the qualities attributed to an ideal knight. **2.** Of or relating to chivalry. **3.** Characterized by consideration and courtesy, esp. toward women. —**chiv′al•rous•ly** *adv.* —**chiv′al•rous•ness** *n.*

chiv•al•ry (shĭv′əl-rē) *n., pl.* **-ries** **1.** The medieval system, principles, and customs of knighthood. **2a.** The qualities idealized by knighthood, such as bravery, courtesy, honor, and gallantry toward women. **b.** A manifestation of any of these qualities. **3.** A group of knights or gallant gentlemen. [ME *chivalrie* < OFr. *chevalerie* < *chevalier,* knight. See CHEVALIER.] —**chi•val′ric** (shĭ-văl′rĭk, shĭv′əl-) *adj.*

chive (chīv) *n.* A Eurasian bulbous herb (*Allium schoenoprasum*) in the lily family, cultivated for its long hollow leaves used as a mild onion-flavored seasoning. Often used in the plural. [ME *chive* < AN < Lat. *cēpa,* onion.]

chiv•vy or **chiv•y** (chĭv′ē) *v.* **-vied, -vy•ing, -vies** or **-ied, -y•ing, -ies** —*tr.* **1.** To vex or harass with petty attacks. **2.** To maneuver or secure gradually. —*intr.* To scurry. ❖ *n., pl.* **-vies** or **-ies** **1.** A hunt or chase. **2.** A hunting cry. [Variant of *chevy,* a hunt, hunting cry < *Chevy Chase,* title of a ballad about a border skirmish.]

Chka•lov (chə-kä′ləf, chkä′-) See **Orenburg.**

chlam•y•date (klăm′ĭ-dāt′) *adj.* Having a mantle. Used of mollusks. [Lat. *chlamydātus,* cloaked < *chlamys, chlamyd-,* mantle. See CHLAMYS.]

chla•myd•e•ous (klə-mĭd′ē-əs) *adj. Botany* Having a perianth. [Lat. *chlamys, chlamyd-,* mantle; see CHLAMYS + -EOUS.]

chla•myd•i•a (klə-mĭd′ē-ə) *n., pl.* **-i•ae** (-ē-ē′) **1.** Any of various gram-negative coccoid microorganisms of the genus *Chlamydia,* esp. *C. psittaci* and *C. trachomatis,* that are pathogenic to humans and animals. **2.** Any of several common, often asymptomatic, sexually transmitted diseases caused by the microorganism *Chlamydia trachomatis.* [NLat. *Chlamydia,* genus name < Lat. *chlamys, chlamyd-,* mantle. See CHLAMYS.] —**chla•myd′i•al** *adj.*

chla•myd•o•spore (klə-mĭd′ə-spôr′, -spōr′) *n.* A thick-walled asexual fungal spore that can function as a resting spore. [Lat. *chlamys, chlamyd-,* mantle; see CHLAMYS + SPORE.]

chla•mys (klăm′ĭs, klā′mĭs) *n., pl.* **chlam•ys•es** or **chlam•y•des** (klăm′ĭ-dēz′) A short mantle fastened at the shoulder, worn by men in ancient Greece. [Lat. < Gk. *khlamus.*]

chlo•as•ma (klō-ăz′mə) *n., pl.* **-ma•ta** (-mə-tə) A patchy brown or dark brown skin discoloration that usu. occurs on a woman's face and may result from hormonal changes. [NLat. < Gk. *khloasma,* greenness < *khloazein,* to be green < *khloos,* greenish color. See **ghel-** in App.]

chlor– *pref.* Variant of **chloro–.**

chlor•ac•ne (klôr-ăk′nē, klōr-) *n.* An acnelike skin disorder caused by prolonged exposure to chlorinated hydrocarbons.

chlo•ral (klôr′əl, klōr′-) *n.* A colorless, mobile, oily aldehyde, CCl_3CHO, a penetrating lung irritant used to manufacture DDT and chloral hydrate. [CHLOR(INE) + AL(COHOL).]

chloral hydrate *n.* A colorless crystalline compound, $CCl_3CH(OH)_2$, used medicinally as a sedative and hypnotic.

chlo•ra•mine (klôr′ə-mēn′, klōr′-) *n.* Any of several compounds containing nitrogen and chlorine, esp. an unstable colorless liquid, NH_2Cl, used to make hydrazine.

chlor•am•phen•i•col (klôr′ăm-fĕn′ĭ-kôl′, -kŏl′, -kōl′, klōr′-) *n.* A broad-spectrum antibiotic, $C_{11}H_{12}Cl_2N_2O_5$, derived from the bacterium *Streptomyces venezuelae.* [CHLOR(O)– + AM(IDE) + PHE(NO)– + NI(TRO)– + (GLY)COL.]

chlo•rate (klôr′āt′, klōr′-) *n.* The inorganic group ClO_3 or a compound containing it.

chlor•dane (klôr′dān′, klōr′-) also **chlor•dan** (-dăn′) *n.* A toxic, odorless, viscous liquid, $C_{10}H_6Cl_8,$ used as an insecticide. [CHLOR(O)– + (IN)D(ENE) + –ANE.]

chlor•di•az•e•pox•ide (klôr′dī-ăz′ə-pŏk′sīd′, klōr′-) *n.* A benzodiazepine drug, $C_{16}H_{14}ClN_3O,$ used to treat anxiety, chronic alcoholism, and alcohol withdrawal. [CHLOR(O)– + (BENZO)DIAZEP(INE) + OXIDE.]

chlo•rel•la (klə-rĕl′ə) *n.* Any of various unicellular green algae of the genus *Chlorella,* often used in experiments. [NLat. *Chlōrella,* genus name < Gk. *khlōros,* green. See CHLORO–.]

chlo•ren•chy•ma (klə-rĕng′kə-mə) *n.* Plant tissue consisting of parenchyma cells that contain chloroplasts. [CHLOR(OPHYLL) + –ENCHYMA.]

chlo•ric (klôr′ĭk, klōr′-) *adj.* Of or containing chlorine.

chloric acid *n.* A strongly oxidizing unstable acid, $HClO_3 \cdot 7H_2O.$

chlo•ride (klôr′īd′, klōr′-) *n.* A binary compound of chlorine. —**chlo•rid′ic** (klə-rĭd′ĭk) *adj.*

chloride of lime *n.* See **bleaching powder.**

chlo•ri•nate (klôr′ə-nāt′, klōr′-) *tr.v.* **-nat•ed, -nat•ing, -nates** To treat or combine with chlorine or a chlorine compound. —**chlo′ri•na′tion** *n.* —**chlo′ri•na′tor** *n.*

chlo•ri•nat•ed lime (klôr′ə-nā′tĭd, klōr′-) *n.* See **bleaching powder.**

chlo•rine (klôr′ēn′, -ĭn, klōr′-) *n. Symbol* **Cl** A highly irritating poisonous halogen, capable of combining with nearly all other elements, produced principally by electrolysis of sodium chloride and used widely to purify water, as a disinfectant and bleaching agent, and in the manufacture of many important compounds. Atomic number 17; atomic weight 35.453; freezing point –100.98°C; boiling point –34.6°C; specific gravity 1.56 (–33.6°C); valence 1, 3, 5, 7. See table at **element.**

chlo•rin•i•ty (klôr-ĭn′ĭ-tē, klōr-) *n.* A measure of the amount of chlorine or other halides in water, esp. seawater.

chlo•rite[1] (klôr′īt′, klōr′-) *n.* A generally green or black secondary mineral, $(Mg,Fe,Al)_6(Si,Al)_4O_{10}(OH)_8,$ often formed by metamorphic alteration of primary dark rock minerals. [Lat. *chlōrītis,* a green precious stone < Gk. *khlōrītis* < *khlōros,* green. See **ghel-** in App.] —**chlo•rit′ic** (klô-rĭt′ĭk, klōr-) *adj.*

chlo•rite[2] (klôr′īt′, klōr′-) *n.* The inorganic group ClO_2 or a salt containing it.

chloro– or **chlor–** *pref.* **1.** Green: *chlorosis.* **2.** Chlorine: *chloroform.* [< Gk. *khlōros,* green. See **ghel-** in App.]

chlo•ro•ben•zene (klôr′ō-bĕn′zēn′, -bĕn-zēn′, klōr′-) *n.* A colorless volatile flammable liquid, $C_6H_5Cl,$ used to prepare phenol, DDT, and aniline and as a general solvent.

chlo•ro•car•bon (klôr′ō-kär′bən, klōr′-) *n.* A compound that consists of chlorine and halocarbon.

chlo•ro•fluor•o•car•bon (klôr′ō-floor′ō-kär′bən, -flôr′-, -flōr′-, klōr′-) *n.* Any of various halocarbon compounds consisting of carbon, hydrogen, chlorine, and fluorine, once used widely as aerosol propellants and refrigerants and now believed to cause depletion of the atmospheric ozone layer.

chlo•ro•form (klôr′ə-fôrm′, klōr′-) *n.* A clear, colorless, heavy, sweet-smelling liquid, $CHCl_3,$ used in refrigerants, propellants, and resins, as a solvent, and sometimes as an anesthetic. ❖ *tr.v.* **-formed, -form•ing, -forms** **1.** To treat with chloroform to anesthetize, render unconscious, or kill. **2.** To apply chloroform to. [CHLORO– + FORM(YL).]

chlo•ro•hy•drin (klôr′ō-hī′drĭn, klōr′-) *n.* Any of a group of aliphatic chemical compounds that are both alkyl chlorides and alcohols.

chlo•ro•phyll also **chlo•ro•phyl** (klôr′ə-fĭl, klōr′-) *n.* Any of a group of green pigments found in photosynthetic organisms, esp.: **a.** A waxy blue-black microcrystalline green-plant pigment, $C_{55}H_{72}MgN_4O_5.$ **b.** A similar green-plant pigment, $C_{55}H_{70}MgN_4O_6.$ —**chlo′ro•phyl′lous** *adj.*

chlo•ro•pic•rin (klôr′ə-pĭk′rĭn, klōr′-) *n.* An oily colorless liquid, $CCl_3NO_2,$ used in tear gas, dyestuffs, disinfectants, insecticides, and soil fumigants. [CHLORO– + PICR(O)– + –IN.]

chlo•ro•plast (klôr′ə-plăst′, klōr′-) also **chlo•ro•plas•tid** (klôr′ə-plăs′tĭd, klōr′-) *n.* A chlorophyll-containing plastid in algal and green plant cells. [CHLORO– + PLAST(ID).] —**chlo′ro•plas′tic** *adj.*

chlo•ro•prene (klôr′ə-prēn′, klōr′-) *n.* A liquid, $C_4H_5Cl,$ that polymerizes to neoprene. [CHLORO– + (ISO)PRENE.]

chlo•ro•quine (klôr′ə-kwīn′, -kwēn′, klōr′-) *n.* A drug, $C_{18}H_{26}ClN_3,$ used to treat and prevent malaria. [CHLORO– + QUIN(OLIN)E.]

chlo•ro•sis (klə-rō′sĭs) *n.* **1.** *Botany* The yellowing or whitening of normally green plant tissue because of a decreased amount of chlorophyll. **2.** *Pathology* Iron-deficiency anemia seen chiefly in young women. Not in scientific use. —**chlo•rot′ic** (-rŏt′ĭk) *adj.* —**chlo•rot′i•cal•ly** *adv.*

chlo•ro•thi•a•zide (klôr′ō-thī′ə-zīd′, klōr′-) *n.* A thiazide diuretic used to treat hypertension, heart failure, and edema.

chlor•prom•a•zine (klôr-prŏm′ə-zēn′, -prō′mə-, klōr-) *n.* A drug, $C_{17}H_{19}ClN_2S,$ derived from phenothiazine and used to suppress vomiting and as a sedative and tranquilizer. [CHLOR(O)– + PRO(PYL) + M(ETHYL) + AZINE.]

chlor•tet•ra•cy•cline (klôr′tĕt-rə-sī′klēn′, -klĭn, klōr′-) *n.* A broad-spectrum antibiotic, $C_{22}H_{23}ClN_2O_8,$ obtained from the soil bacterium *Streptomyces aureofaciens.*

chm. or **chmn** *abbr.* chairman

cho•an•o•cyte (kō-ăn′ə-sīt′) *n.* One of a layer of flagellated cells lining the body cavity of a sponge and characterized by a collar of cytoplasm surrounding the flagellum. [Gk. *khoanē,* funnel (< *khein,* to pour; see **gheu-** in App.) + –CYTE.]

chock (chŏk) *n.* **1.** A block or wedge placed under something else to keep it from moving. **2.** *Nautical* A heavy fitting of metal or wood with two jaws curving inward, through which a rope or cable may be run. ❖ *tr.v.* **chocked, chock•ing, chocks** To fit with or secure by a chock. ❖ *adv.* As close as possible. [Poss. < ONFr. *choque,* log < Gaulish **tsukka,* stump, of Gmc. orig.]

chock-a-block or **chock•a•block** (chŏk′ə-blŏk′) *adj.* **1.** Squeezed together; jammed. **2.** Completely filled; stuffed. **3.** *Nautical* Drawn so close as to have the blocks touching. Used of a ship's hoisting tackle. ❖ *adv.* Chock. [Alteration (influenced by CHOCK) of *chock-a-block* : BLOCK + A–[2] + BLOCK.]

chock-full or **chock•full** (chŏk′fool′) *adj.* Full to the limit; as full as possible.

choc•o•late (chô′kə-lĭt, chŏk′lĭt, chŏk′-) *n.* **1.** Fermented, roasted, shelled, and ground cacao seeds, often combined with a sweetener or flavoring agent. **2.** A beverage of water or milk and chocolate. **3.** A small chocolate-covered candy with a hard or soft center. **4.** A grayish to deep reddish brown to deep grayish brown. ❖ *adj.* **1.** Made or flavored with chocolate. **2.** Of the color of

ă	pat	oi	boy
ā	pay	ou	out
âr	care	ŏŏ	took
ä	father	ōō	boot
ĕ	pet	ŭ	cut
ē	be	ûr	urge
ĭ	pit	th	thin
ī	pie	th	this
îr	pier	hw	which
ŏ	pot	zh	vision
ō	toe	ə	about,
ô	paw		item

Stress marks:
′ (primary);
′ (secondary), as in
lexicon (lĕk′sĭ-kŏn′)

chocolate. [Sp. < Nahuatl *xocolatl* : *xococ*, bitter + *atl*, water.]
—**choc·o·lat·ey, choc·o·lat·y** (-lĭ-tē) *adj.*

chocolate tree *n.* See **cacao** 1.

choc·o·la·tier (chŏk′kə-lĭ-tîr′, chôk′lĭ-tî′, chŏk′-) *n.* **1.** One who makes or sells chocolate. **2.** A place where chocolate is made or sold. [Fr. < *chocolat*, chocolate < Sp. *chocolate*. See CHOCOLATE.]

Choc·taw (chŏk′tô) *n., pl.* **Choctaw** or **-taws** **1.** A member of a Native American people formerly inhabiting Mississippi and Alabama, with present-day populations in Mississippi and southeast Oklahoma. **2.** The Muskogean language of the Choctaw. [Choctaw *Chahta*.]

choice (chois) *n.* **1.** The act of choosing; selection. **2.** The power, right, or liberty to choose; option. **3.** One that is chosen. **4.** A number or variety from which to choose. **5.** The best or most preferable part. **6.** Care in choosing. ❖ *adj.* **choic·er, choic·est** **1a.** Of very fine quality. **b.** Appealing to refined taste. **2.** Selected with care. **3.** Of the US Government grade of meat higher than good and lower than prime. —**idiom: of choice** Preferred above others of the same kind or set. [ME *chois* < OFr. < *choisir*, to choose < VLat. *causīre*, of Gmc. orig. See **geus-** in App.] —**choice′ly** *adv.* —**choice′ness** *n.*

SYNONYMS *choice, alternative, option, preference, selection, election* These nouns denote the act, power, or right of choosing. *Choice* implies broadly the freedom to choose from a set: *a wide choice of fruits. Alternative* emphasizes choice between only two possibilities: "*An unhappy alternative is before you, Elizabeth. . . . Your mother will never see you again if you do not marry Mr. Collins, and I will never see you again if you do*" (Jane Austen). *Option* often stresses a power or liberty to choose that has been granted: *The committee gave us several options. Preference* indicates choice based on one's values, bias, or predilections: *our preference of wines. Selection* suggests a variety of things or persons to choose from: *a wide selection of movies. Election* emphasizes the use of judgment: *The university recommends the election of courses in composition.* See also Syns at **delicate.**

choir (kwīr) *n.* **1.** An organized company of singers, esp. one performing church music or singing in a church. **2.** The part of a church used by a choir. **3a.** A group of instruments of the same kind: *a string choir.* **b.** A division of some pipe organs, containing pipes suitable for accompanying a choir. **4.** An organized group: *a choir of dancers.* **5.** One of the orders of angels. ❖ *intr.v.* **choired, choir·ing, choirs** To sing in chorus. [ME *quer, quire* < OFr. *cuer* < Med.Lat. *chorus* < Lat., choral dance. See CHORUS.]

choir·boy (kwīr′boi′) *n.* A boy member of a choir.

choir·girl (kwīr′gûrl′) *n.* A girl member of a choir.

choir loft *n.* A gallery for a choir.

choir·mas·ter (kwīr′măs′tər) *n.* The director of a choir.

Choi·seul (shwä-zœl′) One of the Solomon Is. in the SW Pacific Ocean SE of Bougainville I.

choke (chōk) *v.* **choked, chok·ing, chokes** —*tr.* **1.** To interfere with the respiration of by compression or obstruction of the larynx or trachea. **2.** To check or slow the movement, growth, or action of: *The garden was choked with weeds.* **b.** To block up or obstruct by filling or clogging: *Mud choked the pipe.* **c.** To fill up; jam: *Traffic choked the highway.* **3.** *Sports* To reduce the air intake of (a carburetor), thus enriching the fuel mixture. **4.** *Sports* To grip (a bat, for example) nearer the hitting surface. —*intr.* **1.** To have difficulty in breathing, swallowing, or speaking. **2.** To become blocked up or obstructed. **3.** *Sports* To shorten one's grip on the handle, as of a bat. Often used with *up.* **4.** To fail to perform effectively because of nervous tension. ❖ *n.* **1.** The act or sound of choking. **2a.** Something that constricts or chokes. **b.** A narrow part, such as a chokebore. **3.** A device used in an internal-combustion engine to enrich the fuel mixture by reducing the flow of air to the carburetor. **4.** The fibrous inedible center of an artichoke head. —*phrasal verbs:* **choke back** To hold back; suppress. **choke off** To bring to an end as if by choking. **choke up** To be unable to speak because of emotion. [ME *choken,* short for *achoken* < OE *āceōcian* : *ā-*, intensive pref. + *cēoce,* jaw, cheek.]

choke·ber·ry (chōk′bĕr′ē) *n.* **1.** Any of various deciduous shrubs of the genus *Aronia* in the rose family, native to eastern North America and having tiny red to black applelike fruit. **2.** The fruit of any of these plants. [< its bitter fruit.]

choke·bore (chōk′bôr′, -bōr′) *n.* **1.** A shotgun bore that narrows toward the muzzle to prevent wide scattering of the shot. **2.** A gun with a narrowed bore near the muzzle.

choke chain *n.* See **choke collar.**

choke·cher·ry (chōk′chĕr′ē) *n.* **1.** A deciduous North American shrub or small tree (*Prunus virginiana*) in the rose family, having astringent, dark red to nearly black fruit. **2.** The fruit of this plant. [< its bitter fruit.]

choke coil *n. Electronics* A circuit element used to suppress or limit the flow of alternating current without affecting the flow of direct current.

choke collar *n.* A chain collar that tightens like a noose when the leash is pulled.

choke·damp (chōk′dămp′) *n.* See **blackdamp.** [< its causing suffocation in mines.]

choke·hold (chōk′hōld′) *n.* A restraining move in which one person seizes another around the neck in a tight grip.

cholla
chain-fruit cholla
Opuntia fulgida

choke·point or **choke point** (chōk′point′) *n.* **1.** A narrow passage through which shipping must pass. **2.** A point of congestion or obstruction.

chok·er (chō′kər) *n.* **1.** One that chokes or suffocates another. **2.** Something that fits closely around the neck or throat, as: **a.** A tight-fitting necklace. **b.** A high, tight collar. **c.** A narrow neckpiece of fur.

chok·ing (chō′kĭng) *adj.* **1.** Causing a choking or suffocating feeling. **2.** Having a strained or husky sound. —**chok′ing·ly** *adv.*

chok·y (chō′kē) *adj.* **-i·er, -i·est** **1.** Likely to cause choking. **2.** Tending to become choked.

cho·lan·gi·og·ra·phy (kō-lăn′jē-ŏg′rə-fē) *n.* X-ray examination of the bile ducts following administration of a radiopaque contrast medium. [CHOL(E)- + ANGIOGRAPHY.] —**cho·lan′gi·o·graph′ic** (-ə-grăf′ĭk) *adj.*

cho·late (kō′lāt′) *n.* A salt or ester of cholic acid. [CHOL(IC ACID) + -ATE².]

chole- or **chol-** *pref.* Bile: *cholesterol.* [< Gk. *kholē,* bile. See **ghel-** in App.]

cho·le·cal·cif·er·ol (kō′lĭ-kăl-sĭf′ə-rôl′, -rōl′, -rŏl′) *n.* See **vitamin D₃**.

cho·le·cyst (kō′lĭ-sĭst′) *n.* The gallbladder.

cho·le·cys·tec·to·my (kō′lĭ-sĭ-stĕk′tə-mē) *n., pl.* **-mies** Surgical removal of the gallbladder.

cho·le·cys·ti·tis (kō′lĭ-sĭ-stī′tĭs) *n.* Inflammation of the gallbladder.

cho·le·cys·to·ki·nin (kō′lĭ-sĭs′tə-kī′nĭn) *n.* A hormone produced principally by the small intestine in response to the presence of fats, causing contraction of the gallbladder, release of bile, and secretion of pancreatic digestive enzymes.

cho·le·li·thi·a·sis (kō′lə-lĭ-thī′ə-sĭs) *n.* The presence or formation of gallstones in the gallbladder or bile ducts.

chol·er (kŏl′ər, kō′lər) *n.* **1.** Anger; irritability. **2a.** One of the four humors of ancient and medieval physiology, thought to cause anger and bad temper when present in excess; yellow bile. **b.** *Obsolete* The quality or condition of being bilious. [ME *colre* < OFr. < Lat. *cholera,* cholera, jaundice < Gk. *kholera* < *kholē,* bile. See **ghel-** in App.]

chol·er·a (kŏl′ər-ə) *n.* **1.** An acute infectious disease of the small intestine, caused by the bacterium *Vibrio cholerae* and characterized by profuse watery diarrhea, vomiting, and severe dehydration. **2.** Any of various diseases of domesticated animals marked by severe gastroenteritis. [Lat., cholera, jaundice. See CHOLER.] —**chol′e·ra′ic** (-ə-rā′ĭk) *adj.* —**chol′e·roid′** (-ə-roid′) *adj.*

chol·er·ic (kŏl′ə-rĭk, kə-lĕr′ĭk) *adj.* **1.** Easily angered; bad-tempered. **2.** Showing or expressing anger. —**chol′er·i·cal·ly, chol′er·ic·ly** *adv.*

cho·le·sta·sis (kō′lĭ-stā′sĭs) *n.* Suppression of biliary flow. —**cho′le·stat′ic** (-stăt′ĭk) *adj.*

cho·les·ter·in (kə-lĕs′tər-ĭn) *n.* Cholesterol.

cho·les·ter·ol (kə-lĕs′tə-rôl′, -rōl′) *n.* A white crystalline substance, $C_{27}H_{45}OH$, in animal tissues and various foods, normally synthesized by the liver and a constituent of cell membranes and precursor to steroid hormones. [Earlier *cholester(in)* (CHOLE- + Gk. *stereos,* solid + -IN) + -OL¹.]

cho·le·styr·a·mine (kō′lĭ-stîr′ə-mēn′, kō-lĕs′tə-răm′ēn) *n.* A drug used to lower serum cholesterol levels and treat itching associated with jaundice through its ability to bind intestinal bile acids and promote their excretion. [CHOLE(STEROL) + STYR(ENE) + AMINE.]

cho·lic acid (kō′lĭk) *n.* An abundant crystalline bile acid, $C_{24}H_{40}O_5$, derived from cholesterol. [Gk. *kholikos,* bilious < *kholē,* bile. See CHOLE-.]

cho·line (kō′lēn′) *n.* A natural amine, $C_5H_{15}NO_2$, often classed in the vitamin B complex and a constituent of many other biologically important molecules, such as lecithin.

cho·li·ner·gic (kō′lə-nûr′jĭk) *adj.* **1.** Activated by or capable of liberating acetylcholine, esp. in the parasympathetic nervous system. **2.** Having physiological effects like those of acetylcholine. [(ACETYL)CHOLIN(E) + -ERGIC.]

cho·li·nes·ter·ase (kō′lə-nĕs′tə-rās′, -rāz′) *n.* An enzyme found chiefly at nerve terminals that catalyzes the hydrolysis of acetylcholine into acetic acid and choline. [CHOLIN(E) + ESTERASE.]

chol·la (choi′ə) *n.* Any of several spiny, shrubby, or treelike cacti of the genus *Opuntia,* having jointed stem segments. [Am.Sp. < obsolete Sp., upper part of the head, poss. < OFr. *cholle,* round lump, head, of Gmc. orig.]

Cho·lu·la (chə-loō′lə, chô-loō′lä) A town of E-central Mexico W of Puebla; site of an ancient Toltec center and a city sacred to the Aztecs. Pop. 26,748.

Cho·mo Lha·ri (chō′mō lär′ē) A peak, 7,318.8 m (23,996 ft), of the SE Himalaya Mts. on the Bhutan-China border.

chomp (chŏmp) *v.* **chomped, chomp·ing, chomps** —*tr.* To chew or bite on noisily. —*intr.* To chew or bite on something repeatedly: *chomping on a cigar.* ❖ *n.* The act or an instance of vigorous biting. [Variant of CHAMP¹.]

Chom·sky (chŏm′skē), **Noam** b. 1928. Amer. linguist and political theorist noted for his theory of generative grammar.

chon·dri·o·some (kŏn′drē-ə-sōm′) *n.* See **mitochondrion.**

chon·drite (kŏn′drīt′) *n.* A stone of meteoric origin characterized by chondrules. —**chon•drit•ic** (-drĭt′ĭk) *adj.*

chondro– or **chrondri–** or **chrondr–** *pref.* **1.** Cartilage: *chondrocranium.* **2.** Granule: *chondrite.* [< Gk. *khondros*, granule, cartilage. See **ghrendh-** in App.]

chon•dro•ma (kŏn-drō′mə) *n., pl.* **-mas** or **-ma•ta** (-mə-tə) A cartilaginous growth or tumor. —**chon•dro′ma•tous** (-mə-təs) *adj.*

chon•dro•ma•la•cia (kŏn′drō-mə-lā′shə) *n.* Abnormal softening or degeneration of cartilage of the joints, esp. of the knee. [CHONDRO- + Gk. *malakiā*, softness (< *malakos*, soft).]

chon•drule (kŏn′drōōl) *n.* A small round granule of extraterrestrial origin found embedded in some meteorites.

Chong•jin (chông′jĭn′, chœng′-) A city of NE North Korea on the Sea of Japan. Pop. 490,000.

Chong•qing (chông′chĭng′, chōōng′-) also **Chung•king** (chōōng′kĭng′, jōōng′gĭng′) A city of S-central China on the Yangtze R. (Chang Jiang). Pop. 3,122,704.

Chon•ju (chŏn′jōō′, chœn′-) A city of SW South Korea S of Seoul. Pop. 366,997.

choose (chōōz) *v.* **chose** (chōz), **cho•sen** (chō′zən), **choos•es** —*tr.* **1.** To select from a number of possible alternatives. **2a.** To prefer above others: *chooses the supermarket over the neighborhood grocery store.* **b.** To determine or decide: *chose to fly to Miami rather than drive.* —*intr.* To make a choice; make a selection. —*phrasal verb:* **choose up** To choose players and form sides or teams for a game. [ME *chesen* < OE *cēosan*. See **geus-** in App.] —**choos′er** *n.*

choos•y also **choos•ey** (chōō′zē) *adj.* **-i•er, -i•est** Very careful in choosing; highly selective. —**choos′i•ness** *n.*

Cho O•yu (chō′ ō-yōō′) A peak, 8,158.8 m (26,750 ft), of the central Himalaya Mts. on the Nepal-China border.

chop¹ (chŏp) *v.* **chopped, chop•ping, chops** —*tr.* **1a.** To cut by striking with a heavy sharp tool, such as an ax. **b.** To shape or form by chopping. **c.** To cut into small pieces. **d.** To curtail as if by chopping: *chop expenses.* **2.** *Sports* To hit or hit at with a short, swift downward stroke. —*intr.* **1.** To make heavy cutting strokes. **2.** *Archaic* To move roughly or suddenly. ❖ *n.* **1.** The act of chopping. **2a.** A swift, short, cutting blow or stroke. **b.** *Sports* A short downward stroke. **3.** A piece that has been chopped off, esp. a cut of meat, usu. taken from the rib, shoulder, or loin and containing a bone. **4a.** A short irregular motion of waves. **b.** An area of choppy water, as on an ocean. [ME *choppen*, prob. var. of *chappen*, to split. See **CHAP¹**.]

chop² (chŏp) *intr.v.* **chopped, chop•ping, chops** To change direction suddenly, as a ship in the wind. [Obsolete, to exchange < ME *choppen*, to barter, bargain, var. of *chapen* < OE *cēapian* < *cēap*, bargain, trade. See **CHEAP**.]

chop³ (chŏp) *n.* **1.** An official stamp or permit in the Far East. **2a.** A mark stamped on goods or coins to indicate their identity or quality. **b.** Quality; class: *first chop.* [Hindi *chāp*, seal.]

chop-chop (chŏp′chŏp′) *adv. Informal* Right away; quickly. [Pidgin E., redup. of *chop*, quick. See **CHOPSTICK**.]

chop•fall•en (chŏp′fô′lən) *adj.* Variant of **chapfallen.**

chop•house (chŏp′hous′) *n.* A restaurant that specializes in steaks and chops of meat.

Cho•pin (shō′păn′, shō-păn′), **Frédéric François** 1810–49. Polish-born French composer and pianist whose music was based on traditional Polish dance themes.

Cho•pin (shō′păn′), **Kate O'Flaherty** 1851–1904. Amer. writer whose works include *The Awakening* (1899).

cho•pine (chō-pēn′, chŏ-, chŏp′ĭn) *n.* A woman's high thick-soled shoe worn in the 16th and 17th centuries. [Obsolete Fr. *chapin* < OSpan. < *chapa*, covering < OFr. See **CHAPE**.]

chop•log•ic (chŏp′lŏj′ĭk) *n.* Complicated, often illogical or spurious argumentation. [< *to chop logic*, to bandy logic < obsolete *chop*, to bandy, exchange. See **CHOP²**.] —**chop′log′ic** *adj.*

chop•per (chŏp′ər) *n.* **1.** One that chops. **2.** *Archaeology* A crudely flaked core tool, esp. one of the early Paleolithic Period. **3.** A device that interrupts an electric current or a beam of radiation. **4.** *Informal* A helicopter. **5. choppers** *Slang* Teeth, esp. a set of false teeth. **6.** *Informal* A motorcycle.

chop•ping block (chŏp′ĭng) *n.* A wooden block on which food or wood is chopped.

chop•py¹ (chŏp′ē) *adj.* **-pi•er, -pi•est** Having many small waves: *choppy seas.* [< CHOP¹.] —**chop′pi•ly** *adv.* —**chop′pi•ness** *n.*

chop•py² (chŏp′ē) *adj.* **-pi•er, -pi•est** Abruptly shifting; variable. Used of the wind. [< CHOP².]

chops (chŏps) *pl.n.* **1.** The jaws. **2a.** The mouth. **b.** The lower cheeks or jowls. **c.** Muttonchops. **3.** *Slang* The technical skill with which a jazz or rock musician performs. —*idiom:* **bust (someone's) chops 1a.** To scold or insult someone. **b.** To disappoint or defeat someone. **2.** To hold a building contractor to the letter of an agreement. [Poss. akin to CHOP¹.]

chop shop *n. Slang* A place where stolen cars are disassembled for parts that are then sold.

chop•stick (chŏp′stĭk′) *n.* One of a pair of slender sticks made esp. of wood or ivory, held between the thumb and fingers and used as an eating utensil in Asia and in restaurants serving Asian food. [Pidgin E. *chop*, quick (prob. < Chin. (Cantonese) *kuài*) + STICK.]

chop su•ey (sōō′ē) *n.* A Chinese-American dish consisting of small pieces of meat or chicken cooked with bean sprouts and other vegetables and served with rice. [Chin. (Cantonese) *tsaápsui*, miscellaneous bits, equivalent to Chin. (Mandarin) *zá*, mixed + Chin. (Mandarin) *sui*, to break up, pieces.]

cho•ra•gus (kə-rā′gəs) *n., pl.* **-gi** (-jī′) **1.** One who undertook the expense of providing the chorus in ancient Greek drama. **2.** The leader of a group or movement. [Lat. *chorāgus* < Gk. *khorēgos, khorāgos : khoros*, chorus; see **gher-** in App. + *agein*, to lead; see **ag-** in App.] —**cho•rag′ic** (-răj′ĭk) *adj.*

cho•ral (kôr′əl, kōr′-) *adj.* **1.** Of or relating to a chorus or choir. **2.** Performed or written for performance by a chorus. [Med.Lat. *chorālis < chorus*, choral dance < Lat. See **CHORUS**.] —**cho′ral•ly** *adv.*

cho•rale also **cho•ral** (kə-rǎl′, -rǎl′) *n.* **1.** A Protestant hymn melody. **2.** A harmonized hymn, esp. one for organ. **3.** A chorus or choir. [Ger., short for *Choralgesang*, choral song, partial transl. of Med.Lat. *cantus chorālis*. See **CHORAL**.]

chorale prelude *n.* A composition chiefly in baroque style and based on the melody of a hymn or chorale.

choral speaking *n.* Recitation of poetry or prose by a chorus.

chord¹ (kôrd, kōrd) *n.* **1.** *Music* A combination of three or more pitches sounded simultaneously. **2.** Harmony, as of color. ❖ *v.* **chord•ed, chord•ing, chords** —*intr.* **1.** To be in accord; agree. **2.** *Music* To play chords on an instrument. —*tr.* **1.** *Music* To play chords on. **2.** To harmonize. [Alteration of ME *cord < accord*, agreement < OFr. *acorde < acorder*, to agree. See ACCORD.]

chord² (kôrd, kōrd) *n.* **1.** A line segment that joins two points on a curve. **2.** A straight line connecting the leading and trailing edges of an airfoil. **3.** *Anatomy* Variant of **cord** 5. **4.** An emotional feeling or response: *a sympathetic chord.* **5.** *Archaic* The string of a musical instrument. [Alteration of CORD.]

chord•al (kôr′dl) *adj.* **1.** Of or relating to the strings of an instrument. **2.** Relating to or consisting of a harmonic chord. **3.** Giving prominence to chordal rather than contrapuntal structure: *chordal music.*

chor•date (kôr′dāt′, -dĭt) *n.* Any of numerous animals in the phylum Chordata, having at some stage of development a dorsal nerve cord, a notochord, and gill slits. [< NLat. *Chordāta*, phylum name < Lat. *chorda*, cord. See CORD.] —**chor′date** *adj.*

chord organ *n. Music* An electronic or reed organ equipped with buttons for producing chords.

chore (chôr, chōr) *n.* **1.** A routine or minor duty or task. See Syns at **task. 2. chores** Daily or routine domestic tasks, esp. a farmer's routine morning and evening tasks. **3.** An unpleasant or burdensome task. [Variant of CHAR³.]

–chore *suff.* A plant distributed by a specified agency: *zoochore.* [< Gk. *khōrein*, to spread about < *khōros*, place, room. See **ghē-** in App.]

cho•re•a (kô-rē′ə, kō-, kə-) *n.* Any of various disorders of the nervous system marked by uncontrollable and irregular muscle movements, esp. of the arms, legs, and face. [NLat. *chorēa* (Sānctī Vītī), (St. Vitus') dance < Lat. *chorēa* < Gk. *khoreia*, choral dance < *khoros*. See CHORUS.]

cho•re•o•graph (kôr′ē-ə-grăf′, kōr′-) *v.* **-graphed, -graphing, -graphs** —*tr.* **1.** To create the choreography of: *choreograph a ballet.* **2.** To plan out or oversee the movement, development, or details of; orchestrate. —*intr.* To specialize in choreography. —**cho′re•og′ra•pher** (-ŏg′rə-fər) *n.*

cho•re•og•ra•phy (kôr′ē-ŏg′rə-fē, kōr′-) *n., pl.* **-phies 1a.** The art of creating and arranging dances or ballets. **b.** A work created by this art. **2.** Something likened to dance arrangements. [Fr. *chorégraphie* : Gk. *khoreia*, choral dance; see CHOREA + *-graphie*, writing (< Lat. *-graphia*, -graphy).] —**cho′re•o•graph′ic** (-ə-grăf′ĭk) *adj.* —**cho′re•o•graph′i•cal•ly** *adv.*

cho•ri•amb (kôr′ē-ămb′, -ăm′, kōr′-) *n.* **1.** A metrical foot consisting of a trochee followed by an iamb. **2.** A foot of verse used in lyric poetry having two unstressed syllables flanked by two rhythmic stresses marking the first and last syllables of the foot. [LLat. *choriambus* < Gk. *khoriambos : khoreios*, trochee (< *khoros*, chorus; see CHORUS) + *iambos*, iamb.] —**cho′ri•am′bic** (-ăm′bĭk) *adj.*

cho•ric (kôr′ĭk, kōr′-, kŏr′-) *adj.* Of or relating to a chorus. [LLat. *choricus* < Gk. *khorikos < khoros*, chorus. See **gher-¹** in App.]

cho•rine (kôr′ēn′, kōr′-) *n.* A chorus girl. [CHOR(US) + –INE¹.]

cho•ri•o•al•lan•to•is (kôr′ē-ō-là-lăn′tō-ĭs, kōr′-) *n.* The highly vascular fetal membrane that consists of the fused chorion and allantois. —**cho′ri•o•al′lan•to′ic** (-ō-ǎl′ən-tō′ĭk) *adj.*

cho•ri•on (kôr′ē-ŏn′, kōr′-) *n.* The outer membrane enclosing the embryo in reptiles, birds, and mammals. [Gk. *khorion.*] —**cho′ri•on′ic** (-ŏn′ĭk) *adj.*

chorionic villus sampling *n.* A prenatal test to detect birth defects that is performed at an early stage of pregnancy and involves retrieval and analysis of tissue from the chorionic villi.

cho•ri•pet•al•ous (kôr′ə-pĕt′l-əs, kōr′-) *adj.* Having separate petals. [Gk. *khōri, khōris*, apart; see **ghē-** in App. + PETALOUS.]

cho•ris•ter (kôr′ĭ-stər, kōr′-, kŏr′-) *n.* **1.** A singer in a choir. **2.** A leader of a choir. [ME *queristre* < AN *cueristre* < Med.Lat. *chorista < chorus*, chorus < Lat., choral dance. See CHORUS.]

cho•ri•zo (chə-rē′zō, -sō) *n., pl.* **-zos** A very spicy pork sausage

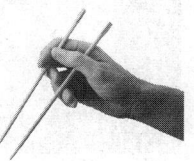
chopstick
pair of chopsticks

ă	pat	oi	boy
ā	pay	ou	out
âr	care	ŏŏ	took
ä	father	ōō	boot
ĕ	pet	ŭ	cut
ē	be	ûr	urge
ĭ	pit	th	thin
ī	pie	th	this
îr	pier	hw	which
ŏ	pot	zh	vision
ō	toe	ə	about,
ô	paw		item

Stress marks:
′ (primary);
′ (secondary), as in
lexicon (lĕk′sĭ-kŏn′)

that is seasoned esp. with garlic. [Sp.]

C horizon *n.* The third-deepest soil zone in ABC soil, unweathered and made up of the parent rock.

cho·rog·ra·phy (kə-rŏg′rə-fē) *n.* **1.** The technique of mapping a region or district. **2.** A description or map of a region. [Lat. *chōrographia* < Gk. *khōrographiā* : *khōros*, place; see **ghē-** in App. + *-graphiā*, -graphy.] —**cho′rog′ra·pher** *n.* —**cho′ro·graph′ic** (kôr′ə-grăf′ĭk, kōr′-), **cho′ro·graph′i·cal** *adj.* —**cho′ro·graph′i·cal·ly** *adv.*

cho·roid (kôr′oid′, kōr′-) *or* **cho·ri·oid** (kôr′ē-oid′, kōr′-) *n.* The dark-brown vascular coat of the eye between the sclera and the retina. ❖ *adj.* **1.** Resembling the chorion; membranous. **2.** Of or relating to the choroid. [< Gk. *khoroeidēs*, like an afterbirth, alteration of *khorioeidēs* : *khorion*, afterbirth; see CHORION + *-oeidēs*, -oid.]

chor·tle (chôr′tl) *n.* A snorting, joyful laugh or chuckle. ❖ *intr. & tr.v.* **-tled, -tling, -tles** To utter or express with a chortle. [Blend of CHUCKLE and SNORT.] —**chor′tler** *n.*

cho·rus (kôr′əs, kōr′-) *n., pl.* **-rus·es 1.** *Music* **a.** A composition in four or more parts written for a large number of singers. **b.** A refrain in which others, such as audience members, join a soloist in a song. **c.** A repeat of the opening statement of a popular song. **d.** A solo section based on the main melody of a popular song and played by a member of the group. **e.** A body of singers who perform choral compositions, usu. having more than one singer for each part. **f.** A body of vocalists and dancers who support the soloists and leading performers in operas, musical comedies, and revues. **2a.** A group of persons who speak or sing in unison a given part or composition in drama or poetry recitation. **b.** An actor in Elizabethan drama who recites the prologue and epilogue to a play and sometimes comments on the action. **3a.** A group of masked dancers who performed ceremonial songs at religious festivals in early Greek times. **b.** The group in a classical Greek drama whose songs and dances present an exposition of or, in later tradition, a disengaged commentary on the action. **c.** The portion of a classical Greek drama consisting of choric dance and song. **4.** A group or performer in a modern drama serving a purpose similar to the Greek chorus. **5.** The performers of a choral ode, esp. a Pindaric ode. **6a.** A speech, song, or other utterance made in concert by many people. **b.** A simultaneous utterance by a number of people: *a chorus of jeers.* **c.** The sounds so made. —**idiom: in chorus** All together; in unison. [Lat., choral dance < Gk. *khoros.* See **gher-** in App.] —**cho′rus** *v.*

chorus girl *n.* A female dancer in a theatrical chorus.

-chory *suff.* Plant dispersal by a specified agency: *zoochory.*

chose¹ (chōz) *v.* Past tense of **choose.**

chose² (shōz) *n. Law* An item of personal property; a chattel. [Fr. < Lat. *causa*, thing, case, reason.]

cho·sen (chō′zən) *v.* Past participle of **choose.** ❖ *adj.* **1.** Selected from or preferred above others: *the chosen few.* **2.** Having been selected by God; elect. ❖ *n.* (*used with a pl. verb*) The elect considered as a group. Often used with *the.*

Cho·sen (chō′sĕn′) *also* **Cho·sun** (-sŭn′) A name used for Korea since the second millennium B.C.

chott *also* **shott** (shŏt) *n.* **1.** The depression surrounding a salt marsh or lake, esp. in North Africa. **2.** The bed of a dried salt marsh. [Fr. < Ar. *šaṭṭ*, bank, coast < *šaṭṭa*, to exceed, deviate.]

Chou *or* **Chow** (jō) See **Zhou.**

chou·croute (shoō-kroōt′) *n.* An Alsatian dish of sauerkraut with wine, sausages, pork, and juniper berries. [Fr. *choucroute* (*garnie*), (garnished) sauerkraut, alteration (influenced by *chou*, cabbage) of Ger. dialectal *sûrkrût* : *sûr*, sour (< MHGer. *sūr* < OHGer.) + *krût*, cabbage, kraut (< MHGer. *krūt* < OHGer.).]

Chou En-lai (jō′ ĕn-lī′) See **Zhou Enlai.**

chough (chŭf) *n.* A crowlike Old World bird of the genus *Pyrrhocorax*, esp. *P. pyrrhocorax*, having black plumage and red legs. [ME.]

chow¹ (chou) *n.* Any of a breed of heavyset dog originating in China, having a long reddish-brown or black coat and a blue-black tongue. [Poss. < Chin. (Cantonese) *gǒu*, dog.]

chow² (chou) *Slang n.* Food; victuals. ❖ *intr.v.* **chowed, chowing, chows** To eat. [Poss. < Chin. (Cantonese) *tsaāp*, food, miscellany. See CHOP SUEY.]

chow chow *n.* See **chow¹.**

chow-chow (chou′chou′) *n.* **1.** A Chinese preserve of fruits, peels, and ginger. **2.** A relish consisting of chopped vegetables pickled in mustard. [Pidgin E., poss. redup. of Chin. (Cantonese) *tsaāp*, food, mixture. See CHOW².]

chow·der (chou′dər) *n.* **1.** A thick soup containing fish or shellfish, esp. clams, and vegetables in a milk or tomato base. **2.** A soup similar to this seafood dish. [Fr. *chaudière*, stew pot < OFr. < LLat. *caldāria.* See CAULDRON.]

chow·der·head (chou′dər-hĕd′) *n. Slang* A stupid person; a dolt. —**chow′der·head′ed** *adj.*

chow mein (chou′ mān′) *n.* A Chinese-American dish of stewed vegetables and meat served over fried noodles. [Chin. (Mandarin) *chǎo miàn* : *chǎo*, to stir-fry + *miàn*, noodles.]

Chr. *abbr.* **1.** Christ **2.** Christian **3.** *Bible* Chronicles

chres·ard (krĕs′ärd) *n.* Water present in the soil and available for plant absorption. [Gk. *khrēsis*, use (< *khrēsthai*, to use) + Gk. *ardein*, to water.]

Agatha Christie

Chrés·tien de Troyes *also* **Chré·tien de Troyes** (krā-tyăN′ də trwä′) fl. 1170. French trouvère who wrote the earliest surviving Arthurian romances.

chres·tom·a·thy (krĕ-stŏm′ə-thē) *n., pl.* **-thies 1.** A selection of literary passages, usu. by one author. **2.** An anthology used in studying a language. [Gk. *khrēstomatheia* : *khrēstos*, useful (< *khrēsthai*, to use) + *-matheia*, body of learning (< *manthanein*, *math-*, to learn).] —**chres′to·math′ic** (krĕs′tə-măth′ĭk) *adj.*

Chré·tien (krā-tyăN′), **Jean** b. 1934. Canadian prime minister (since 1993).

chrism (krĭz′əm) *n. Ecclesiastical* **1.** A consecrated mixture of oil and balsam for anointing in sacraments such as baptism and confirmation. **2.** A sacramental anointing. [ME *crisme*, chrism, chrisom < OE *crisma* < Lat. *chrīsma* < Gk. *khrīsma*, an anointing < *khrīein*, to anoint.] —**chris′mal** (krĭz′məl) *adj.*

chris·om (krĭz′əm) *n.* **1.** A white cloth or robe worn by an infant at baptism. **2.** *Archaic* An infant wearing a baptismal robe; a baby. [ME *crisom*, var. of *crisme.* See CHRISM.]

chrisom child *n. Archaic* An infant dead before one month.

Christ (krīst) *n.* **1.** The Messiah, as foretold by the Hebrew prophets. Often used with *the.* **2.** *Christianity* Jesus. [ME *Crist* < OE *Crīst* < Lat. *Chrīstus* < Gk. *Khrīstos* < *khrītos*, anointed, verbal adj. of *khrīein*, to anoint.] —**Christ′like′** *adj.* —**Christ′liness** *n.* —**Christ′ly** *adj.*

Christ·church (krīst′chûrch′) A city of E South I., New Zealand, near the Pacific coast. Pop. 293,700.

chris·ten (krĭs′ən) *tr.v.* **-tened, -ten·ing, -tens 1a.** To baptize into a Christian church. **b.** To give a name to at baptism. **2a.** To name. **b.** To name and dedicate ceremonially: *christen a ship.* **3.** To use for the first time. [ME *cristnen* < OE *cristnian* < *cristen*, Christian. See CHRISTIAN.]

Chris·ten·dom (krĭs′ən-dəm) *n.* **1.** Christians considered as a group. **2.** The Christian world. [ME *Cristendom* < OE *cristendōm* : *cristen*, Christian; see CHRISTIAN + *-dōm*, -dom.]

chris·ten·ing (krĭs′ə-nĭng) *n.* The Christian sacrament of baptizing and naming an infant.

Chris·tian (krĭs′chən) *adj.* **1.** Professing belief in Jesus as Christ or following the religion based on the life and teachings of Jesus. **2.** Relating to or derived from Jesus. **3.** Manifesting the qualities or spirit of Jesus. **4.** Relating to or characteristic of Christianity. **5.** Showing a loving concern for others; humane. ❖ *n.* **1.** One who professes belief in Jesus as Christ or follows the Christian religion. **2.** One who lives according to the teachings of Jesus. [ME *Cristen* < OE *cristen* < Lat. *Chrīstiānus* < *Chrīstus*, Christ. See CHRIST.] —**Chris′tian·ly** *adj. & adv.*

Christian, Charlie 1916–42. Amer. jazz guitarist and blues singer who was one of the first to amplify the guitar.

Christian X 1870–1947. King of Denmark (1912–47) noted for his passive resistance to the Nazi occupation of Denmark.

Christian Brother *n. Roman Catholic Church* A member of the order of Brothers of the Christian Schools that was founded in France in 1684 by Saint Jean Baptiste de la Salle (1651–1719) and is dedicated primarily to education.

Christian era *n.* The period beginning with the birth of Jesus.

chris·ti·an·i·a (krĭs′tē-ăn′ē-ə, -ä′nē-ə, krĭs′chē-) *n.* A christie. [Norw., after *Christiania* (Oslo), Norway.]

Chris·ti·a·ni·a (krĭs′tē-ăn′ē-ə, -ä′nē-ə, krĭs′chē-) See **Oslo.**

Chris·ti·an·i·ty (krĭs′chē-ăn′ĭ-tē, krĭs′tē-) *n.* **1.** The Christian religion. **2.** Christians as a group; Christendom. **3.** The state or fact of being a Christian. **4.** *pl.* **-ties** A particular form or sect of the Christian religion.

Chris·tian·ize (krĭs′chə-nīz′) *tr.v.* **-ized, -iz·ing, -iz·es** To convert (another) to Christianity; make Christian. —**Chris′tian·i·za′tion** (-chə-nī-zā′shən) *n.* —**Chris′tian·iz′er** *n.*

Christian name *n.* **1.** A name given at baptism. **2.** A name that precedes a person's family name.

Christian Science *n.* The church and religious system founded by Mary Baker Eddy. —**Christian Scientist** *n.*

chris·tie *or* **chris·ty** (krĭs′tē) *n., pl.* **-ties** A usu. high-speed ski turn used for changing direction or stopping, performed by shifting the weight forward and turning with the skis kept parallel. [Short for CHRISTIANIA.]

Chris·tie (krĭs′tē), Dame **Agatha Mary Clarissa** 1890–1976. British writer of more than 70 detective novels, including *The Murder of Roger Ackroyd* (1926).

Chris·ti·na (krĭ-stē′nə) 1626–89. Queen of Sweden (1632–54) who abdicated her throne, embraced Roman Catholicism, and spent much of the rest of her life in Rome.

Christ·mas (krĭs′məs) *n.* **1.** A Christian feast commemorating the birth of Jesus, usu. celebrated on December 25. **2.** Christmastide. [ME *Cristemas* < OE *Crīstes mæsse*, Christ's festival : *Crīst*, Christ; see CHRIST + *mæsse*, festival; see MASS.] —**Christ′mas·sy, Christ′mas·y** *adj.*

Christmas berry *n.* See **toyon.**

Christmas berry tree *n.* See **Brazilian pepper tree.**

Christmas cactus *n.* An epiphytic cactus (*Schlumbergera ×bridgesii*) of Brazilian ancestry, cultivated as a houseplant and having showy rose-purple flowers that bloom in winter.

Christmas card *n.* A greeting card sent at Christmas.

Christmas club *n.* A savings account, as in a bank, requiring periodic deposits to ensure money for shopping at Christmas.

Christmas disease *n.* A type of hemophilia that is caused by a deficiency of factor IX. [After Stephen *Christmas*, a 20th-cent. British boy who was first diagnosed with it.]

Christmas Eve *n.* The evening or day before Christmas.

Christmas fern *n.* A North American evergreen fern (*Polystichum acrostichoides*) having clusters of lance-shaped fronds.

Christmas Island 1. An Australian-administered island in the E Indian Ocean S of Java. **2.** See **Kiritimati.**

Christmas rose *n.* A European perennial evergreen herb (*Helleborus niger*) cultivated for its white or pinkish flowers.

Christ·mas·tide (krĭs′məs-tīd′) *n.* A Christian festival observed from Christmas Eve to the eve of Epiphany.

Christ·mas·time (krĭs′məs-tīm′) *n.* The season of Christmas.

Christmas tree *n.* **1.** An evergreen or artificial tree decorated, as with lights and ornaments, during the Christmas season. **2.** *Geology* A device consisting of pipes and valves that caps a producing natural gas or oil well and controls its flow.

Chris·to (krĭs′tō) Orig. Christo Vladimirov Javacheff. b. 1935. Bulgarian-born Amer. sculptor best known for wrapping large-scale objects in fabric.

Chris·to·gram (krĭs′tə-grăm′) *n.* See **Chi-Rho.**

Chris·tol·o·gy (krĭ-stŏl′ə-jē) *n., pl.* **-gies 1.** The theological study of Jesus. **2.** A doctrine or theory based on Jesus. —**Chris′to·log′i·cal** (krĭs′tə-lŏj′ĭ-kəl) *adj.*

Chris·tophe (krē-stôf′), **Henri** 1767–1820. King of Haiti (1811–20) who was instrumental in the liberation of Haiti from France (1804).

Chris·to·pher (krĭs′tə-fər), Saint. fl. 3rd cent. A.D. Christian martyr often depicted as a giant who carried travelers across a river.

Christ's thorn (krĭsts) also **Christ-thorn** (krīst′thôrn′) *n.* **1.** Either of two similar and related Old World spiny shrubs (*Ziziphus spina-christi* or *Paliurus spina-christi*) popularly believed to have been used for Jesus's crown of thorns. **2.** Any of several other plants, such as the crown-of-thorns.

chris·ty (krĭs′tē) *n.* Variant of **christie.**

chrom– *pref.* Variant of **chromo–.**

chro·ma (krō′mə) *n.* The aspect of color in the Munsell color system by which a sample appears to differ from a gray of the same lightness or brightness and that corresponds to saturation of the perceived color. [Gk. *khrōma*, color.]

chro·maf·fin (krō′mə-fĭn) *adj.* Readily stained with chromium salts. [Ger. : *Chrom*, chromium (< Fr. *chrome*; see CHROME) + Lat. *affinis*, related; see AFFINED.]

chro·mate (krō′māt′) *n.* A salt or ester of chromic acid.

chro·mat·ic (krō-măt′ĭk) *adj.* **1a.** Relating to colors or color. **b.** Relating to color perceived to have a saturation greater than zero. **2.** *Music* **a.** Of, relating to, or based on the chromatic scale. **b.** Relating to chords or harmonies based on nonharmonic tones. [Gk. *khrōmatikos < khrōma, khrōmat-*, color.] —**chro·mat′i·cal·ly** *adv.* —**chro·mat′i·cism** (-sĭz′əm) *n.*

chromatic aberration *n.* Color distortion in an image produced by a lens that cannot bring the various colors of light to focus at a single point.

chro·ma·tic·i·ty (krō′mə-tĭs′ĭ-tē) *n.* The aspect of color that includes consideration of its dominant wavelength and purity.

chro·mat·ics (krō-măt′ĭks) *n.* (*used with a sing. verb*) The scientific study of color. —**chro·ma·tist** (-ə-tĭst) *n.*

chromatic scale *n. Music* A scale consisting of 12 semitones.

chro·ma·tid (krō′mə-tĭd) *n.* Either of the two daughter strands of a duplicated chromosome that are joined by a single centromere and separate during cell division to become individual chromosomes.

chro·ma·tin (krō′mə-tĭn) *n.* A complex of nucleic acids and proteins, primarily histones, in the cell nucleus that stains readily with basic dyes and condenses to form chromosomes during cell division. —**chro′ma·tin′ic** *adj.*

chromato– or **chromat–** *pref.* **1.** Color: *chromatophore.* **2.** Chromatin: *chromatolysis.* [Gk. *khrōma, khrōmat-*, color.]

chro·mat·o·gram (krō-măt′ə-grăm′) *n.* The pattern of separated substances obtained by chromatography.

chro·mat·o·graph (krō-măt′ə-grăf′) *n.* An instrument that produces a chromatogram. ❖ *tr.v.* **-graphed, -graph·ing, -graphs** To separate and analyze by chromatography. —**chro·mat′o·graph′ic** *adj.* —**chro·mat′o·graph′i·cal·ly** *adv.*

chro·ma·tog·ra·phy (krō′mə-tŏg′rə-fē) *n.* Any of various techniques for the separation of complex mixtures that rely on the differential affinities of substances for a gas or liquid mobile medium and for a stationary adsorbing medium. —**chro′ma·tog′ra·pher** *n.*

chro·ma·tol·y·sis (krō′mə-tŏl′ĭ-sĭs) *n.* The dissolution or disintegration of chromophil material, such as chromatin, within a cell. —**chro·mat′o·lyt′ic** (-măt′ə-lĭt′ĭk) *adj.*

chro·mat·o·phil·ic (krō-măt′ə-fĭl′ĭk) *adj.* Chromophil.

chro·mat·o·phore (krō-măt′ə-fôr′, -fōr′) *n.* **1.** A pigment-containing or pigment-producing cell, esp. in certain lizards, that by expansion or contraction can change the color of the skin. **2.** A specialized pigment-bearing organelle in certain photosynthetic bacteria and cyanobacteria. —**chro·mat′o·phor′ic** (-fôr′ĭk, -fōr′-) *adj.*

chrome (krōm) *n.* **1a.** Chromium or a chromium alloy. **b.** Something plated with a chromium alloy. **2.** A pigment containing chromium. ❖ *tr.v.* **chromed, chrom·ing, chromes 1.** To plate with chromium. **2.** To tan or dye with a chromium compound. [Fr. < Gk. *khrōma*, color.]

–chrome *suff.* **1.** Colored: *polychrome.* **2.** Color; pigment: *urochrome.* [< Gk. *khrōma*, color.]

chrome alum *n.* A crystalline compound, CrK(SO₄)₂·12H₂O, used in tanning and in photography.

chrome green *n.* **1.** Any of a class of green pigments consisting of chrome yellow and iron blue in various proportions. **2.** A very dark yellowish green to moderate or strong green.

chrome red *n.* A light orange to red pigment consisting of basic lead chromate, PbCrO₄, with varying amounts of lead oxide, PbO.

chrome yellow *n.* Lead chromate, PbCrO₄, a yellow pigment often combined with lead sulfate, PbSO₄, for lighter hues.

chro·mic (krō′mĭk) *adj.* Of, relating to, or containing chromium, esp. with valence 3.

chromic acid *n.* **1.** A corrosive, oxidizing acid, H₂CrO₄, occurring only as salts or in solution. **2.** The anhydride of chromic acid, CrO₃, a crystalline material that reacts explosively with reducing agents and is used as an oxidizing agent.

chromic oxide *n.* A bright green crystalline powder, Cr₂O₃, used in metallurgy and as a paint pigment.

chro·mi·nance (krō′mə-nəns) *n.* The difference between one color and a reference color of the same brightness and chromaticity. [Blend of CHROMO– and LUMINANCE.]

chro·mite (krō′mīt′) *n.* A widely distributed, black to brownish-black chromium ore, FeCr₂O₄.

chro·mi·um (krō′mē-əm) *n. Symbol* **Cr** A lustrous hard metallic element, resistant to tarnish and corrosion and found primarily in chromite. It is used to harden steel alloys, in decorative platings, and as a pigment in glass. Atomic number 24; atomic weight 51.996; melting point 1,890°C; boiling point 2,482°C; specific gravity 7.18; valence 2, 3, 6. See table at **element.** [< Fr. *chrome.* See CHROME.]

chromo– or **chrom–** *pref.* **1.** Color: *chromoplast.* **2.** Chromium: *chromous.* [< Gk. *khrōma*, color.]

chro·mo·dy·nam·ics (krō′mō-dī-năm′ĭks) *n.* (*used with a sing. verb*) The theory of the strong interaction that postulates the exchange of gluons between color-carrying quarks.

chro·mo·gen (krō′mə-jən) *n.* **1.** *Chemistry* A substance capable of conversion into a pigment or dye. **2.** *Biology* A strongly pigmented or pigment-generating organelle, organ, or microorganism. —**chro′mo·gen′ic** (-jĕn′ĭk) *adj.*

chro·mo·lith·o·graph (krō′mə-lĭth′ə-grăf′) *n.* A colored print produced by chromolithography.

chro·mo·li·thog·ra·phy (krō′mə-lĭ-thŏg′rə-fē) *n.* The art or process of printing color pictures from a series of stone or zinc plates by lithography. —**chro′mo·li·thog′ra·pher** *n.* —**chro′mo·lith′o·graph′ic** (-lĭth′ə-grăf′ĭk) *adj.*

chro·mo·mere (krō′mə-mîr′) *n.* One of the serially aligned, beadlike granules of concentrated chromatin that constitutes a chromosome during the early phases of cell division. —**chro′mo·mer′ic** (-mĕr′ĭk, -mîr′-) *adj.*

chro·mo·ne·ma (krō′mə-nē′mə) *n., pl.* **-ma·ta** (-mə-tə) The spirally coiled central filament of a chromatid along which the chromomeres are aligned. [CHROMO(SOME) + Gk. *nēma*, thread; see ⑤ in App.] —**chro′mo·ne′mal** (-nē′məl), **chro′mo·ne·mat′al** (-nē-măt′l), **chro′mo·ne·mat′ic** (-nə-măt′ĭk), **chro′mo·ne′mic** (-nē′mĭk) *adj.*

chro·mo·phil (krō′mə-fĭl′) *adj.* or **chro·mo·phil·ic** (krō′mə-fĭl′ĭk) Readily stained with dyes. ❖ *n.* A chromophil cell or cell structure.

chro·mo·phore (krō′mə-fôr′, -fōr′) *n.* A chemical group capable of selective light absorption resulting in the coloration of certain organic compounds. —**chro′mo·phor′ic** (-fôr′ĭk, -fōr′-) *adj.*

chro·mo·plast (krō′mə-plăst′) *n.* A plastid that contains pigments other than chlorophyll, usu. yellow or orange carotenoids.

chro·mo·pro·tein (krō′mə-prō′tēn, -tē-ĭn) *n.* A conjugated protein, such as hemoglobin, that contains a pigmented prosthetic group, such as heme.

chro·mo·some (krō′mə-sōm′) *n.* **1.** A threadlike linear strand of DNA and associated proteins in the nucleus of eukaryotic cells that carries the genes and functions in the transmission of hereditary information. **2.** A circular strand of DNA in bacteria that contains the hereditary information necessary for cell life. —**chro′mo·so′mal** (-sō′məl), **chro′mo·so′mic** (-sō′mĭk) *adj.* —**chro′mo·so′mal·ly** *adv.*

chro·mo·sphere (krō′mə-sfîr′) *n.* **1.** An incandescent transparent layer of gas, primarily hydrogen, several thousand miles in depth, lying above and surrounding the photosphere of the sun. **2.** A gaseous layer similar to a chromosphere around a star. —**chro′mo·spher′ic** (-sfĭr′ĭk, -sfĕr′-) *adj.*

chro·mous (krō′məs) *adj.* Of, relating to, or containing chromium, esp. with valence 2.

Chron. *abbr. Bible* Chronicles

chro·nax·ie also **chro·nax·y** (krō′năk′sē, krŏn′ăk′-) *n., pl.* **-ies** The minimum time necessary to electrically stimulate a muscle or nerve fiber, using twice the minimum current needed to elicit a

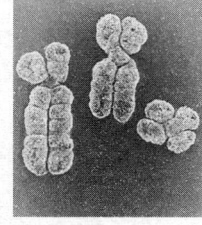

chromosome
scanning electron
micrograph of human
chromosomes

ă	pat	oi	boy
ā	pay	ou	out
âr	care	ōō	took
ä	father	ōō	boot
ĕ	pet	ŭ	cut
ē	be	ûr	urge
ĭ	pit	th	thin
ī	pie	th	this
îr	pier	hw	which
ŏ	pot	zh	vision
ō	toe	ə	about,
ô	paw		item

Stress marks:
′ (primary);
′ (secondary), as in
lexicon (lĕk′sĭ-kŏn′)

threshold response. [Fr. : Gk. *khronos*, time + Gk. *axiā*, value (< *axios*, worthy; see **ag-** in App.).]

chron•ic (krŏn′ĭk) *adj.* **1.** Of long duration; continuing: *chronic problems.* **2.** Lasting for a long period of time or marked by frequent recurrence: *chronic colitis.* **3.** Subject to a habit or pattern of behavior for a long time: *chronic drinker.* [Fr. *chronique* < Lat. *chronicus* < Gk. *khronikos*, of time < *khronos*, time.] —**chron′i•cal•ly** *adv.* —**chro•nic′i•ty** (krŏ-nĭs′ĭ-tē) *n.*

chronic fatigue immune dysfunction syndrome *n.* Chronic fatigue syndrome.

chronic fatigue syndrome *n.* A syndrome characterized primarily by chronic fatigue and a combination of flulike symptoms, such as swollen lymph glands, low-grade fever, and muscle pain or weakness.

chron•i•cle (krŏn′ĭ-kəl) *n.* **1.** An account of historical events presented in chronological order. **2.** A detailed narrative record or report. **3. Chronicles** (*used with a sing. verb*) See table at **Bible.** ❖ *tr.v.* **-cled, -cling, -cles** To record in or in the form of a historical record. [ME *cronicle* < AN, alteration of OFr. *cronique* < Lat. *chronica* < Gk. *khronika* (*biblia*), chronological (books), annals, neut. pl. of *khronikos*, of time. See CHRONIC.] —**chron′i•cler** (-klər) *n.*

chronic obstructive pulmonary disease *n.* A chronic lung disease in which there is persistent obstruction of the airways caused by emphysema or chronic bronchitis.

chrono- or **chron-** *pref.* Time: *chronometer.* [< Gk. *khronos*, time.]

chron•o•bi•ol•o•gy (krŏn′ō-bī-ŏl′ə-jē) *n.* The study of the effects of time and rhythmical phenomena on life processes.

chron•o•gram (krŏn′ə-grăm′, krō′nə-) *n.* **1.** The record produced by a chronograph. **2.** An inscribed phrase in which certain letters can be read as Roman numerals indicating a specific date. —**chron′o•gram•mat′ic** (-grə-măt′ĭk) *adj.* —**chron′o•gram•mat′i•cal•ly** *adv.*

chron•o•graph (krŏn′ə-grăf′, krō′nə-) *n.* An instrument that registers or graphically records time intervals. —**chron′o•graph′ic** *adj.* —**chron′o•graph′i•cal•ly** *adv.*

chron•o•log•i•cal (krŏn′ə-lŏj′ĭ-kəl, krō′nə-) also **chron•o•log•ic** (-lŏj′ĭk) *adj.* **1.** Arranged in order of time of occurrence. **2.** Relating to or in accordance with chronology. —**chron′o•log′i•cal•ly** *adv.*

chro•nol•o•gy (krə-nŏl′ə-jē) *n., pl.* **-gies 1.** The science that deals with the determination of dates and the sequence of events. **2.** The arrangement of events in time. **3.** A chronological list or table. —**chro•nol′o•gist, chro•nol′o•ger** *n.*

chro•nom•e•ter (krə-nŏm′ĭ-tər) *n.* An exceptionally precise timepiece. —**chron′o•met′ric** (krŏn′ə-mĕt′rĭk, krō′nə-), **chron′o•met′ri•cal** *adj.* —**chron′o•met′ri•cal•ly** *adv.*

chro•nom•e•try (krə-nŏm′ĭ-trē) *n.* The scientific measurement of time.

chron•o•scope (krŏn′ə-skōp′, krō′nə-) *n.* An optical instrument for the precise measurement of very small time intervals. —**chron′o•scop′ic** (-skŏp′ĭk) *adj.*

chrys•a•lid (krĭs′ə-lĭd) *n.* A chrysalis. ❖ *adj.* Relating to or resembling a chrysalis.

chrys•a•lis (krĭs′ə-lĭs) *n., pl.* **chrys•a•lis•es** or **chry•sal•i•des** (krĭ-săl′ĭ-dēz′) **1.** A pupa, esp. of a butterfly, enclosed in a firm case or cocoon. **2.** A protected stage of development. [Lat. *chrȳsallis* < Gk. *khrūsallis, khrūsallid-*, gold-colored pupa < *khrūsos*, gold. See CHRYSO-.]

chry•san•the•mum (krĭ-săn′thə-məm, -zăn′-) *n.* **1.** Any of numerous Eurasian plants of the genus *Chrysanthemum* in the composite family, many of which are cultivated for their showy flower heads. **2.** A flower head of one of these plants. [Lat. *chrȳsanthemum* < Gk. *khrūsanthemon*, gold flower : *khrūs-, khryso-* + *anthemon*, flower < *anthos*.]

chrys•el•e•phan•tine (krĭs′ĕl′ə-făn′tēn′, -tĭn′) *adj.* Made of gold and ivory. [Gk. *khrūselephantinos* : *khrūs-, chryso-* + *elephās, elephant-*, ivory; see ELEPHANT.]

chryso- or **chrys-** *pref.* Gold; golden: *chrysotherapy.* [Gk. *khrūs-, khrūso-* < *khrūsos*, gold, of Semitic orig.; akin to Heb. *ḥārūs.*]

chrys•o•ber•yl (krĭs′ə-bĕr′əl) *n.* A green to yellow vitreous mineral, BeAl₂O₄, used as a gemstone. [Lat. *chrȳsobēryllus* < Gk. *khrūsobērullos* : *khrūso-*, chryso- + *bērullos*, beryl; see BERYL.]

chrys•o•lite (krĭs′ə-līt′) *n.* See olivine. [ME *crisolite* < OFr. < Med.Lat. *crīsolitus* < Lat. *chrȳsolithus* < Gk. *khrūsolithos*, topaz : *khrūso-*, chryso- + *lithos*, stone.]

chrys•o•mel•id (krĭs′ə-mĕl′ĭd, -mē′lĭd) *n.* Any of various beetles of the family Chrysomelidae. [< NLat. *Chrȳsomēla*, type genus < Gk. *khrūsomēlon*, quince : *khrūso-*, chryso- + *mēlon*, apple.] —**chrys′o•mel′id** *adj.*

chrys•o•prase (krĭs′ə-prāz′) *n.* An apple-green chalcedony used as a gemstone. [ME *crisopase* < OFr. *crisopras* < Lat. *chrȳsoprasus* < Gk. *khrūsoprasos* : *khrūso-*, chryso- + *prason*, leek.]

Chry•sos•tom (krĭs′əs-təm, krĭ-sŏs′-), Saint **John** A.D. 347?–407. Antioch-born Greek prelate and patriarch of Constantinople (398–404).

chrys•o•ther•a•py (krĭs′ō-thĕr′ə-pē) *n.* The treatment of diseases, esp. rheumatoid arthritis, with gold compounds.

chrys•o•tile (krĭs′ə-tīl′) *n.* A fibrous mineral variety of serpentine forming part of commercial asbestos. [Ger. *Chrysotil* : Gk.

khrūso-, chryso- + Gk. *tilos*, something plucked (< *tillein*, to pluck).]

chthon•ic (thŏn′ĭk) also **chtho•ni•an** (thō′nē-ən) *adj. Greek Mythology* Of or relating to the underworld. [< Gk. *khthonios*, earthly < *khthōn*, earth. See dhghem- in App.]

Chu (chōō) A river of S Kazakhstan flowing c. 1,126 km (700 mi) E into Issyk-Kul.

Chuang Tzu (chwäng′ dzü′) c. 369–286 B.C. Chinese Taoist philosopher who advocated a skeptical approach to knowledge and a willing acceptance of change.

chub (chŭb) *n., pl.* **chub** or **chubs 1.** Any of various freshwater fishes of the family Cyprinidae related to the carps and minnows, esp. a Eurasian species, *Leuciscus cephalus.* **2.** Any of various North American fishes, such as a freshwater whitefish of the genus *Coregonus.* [ME *chubbe.*]

chub•by (chŭb′ē) *adj.* **-bi•er, -bi•est** Rounded and plump. See Syns at **fat.** [Prob. < CHUB (< the plumpness of the fish).] —**chub′bi•ly** *adv.* —**chub′bi•ness** *n.*

Chu•but (chə-bōōt′, chōō-) A river rising in SW Argentina and flowing c. 805 km (500 mi) E to the Atlantic Ocean.

chuck¹ (chŭk) *tr.v.* **chucked, chuck•ing, chucks 1.** To pat or squeeze fondly or playfully, esp. under the chin. **2a.** To throw or toss. **b.** *Informal* To throw out; discard. **c.** *Informal* To force out; eject: *chucking out the troublemakers.* **3.** *Informal* To give up; quit. ❖ *n.* **1.** An affectionate pat or squeeze under the chin. **2.** A throw, toss, or pitch. [Variant of *chock*, poss. < Fr. *choc*, knock, blow. See SHOCK¹.]

chuck² (chŭk) *n.* **1.** A cut of beef extending from the neck to the ribs and including the shoulder blade. **2a.** A clamp that holds a tool or the material being worked in a machine such as a lathe. **b.** A clamping device for holding a drill bit. **3.** *Informal* Food. [Dialectal *chuck*, lump, perh. var. of CHOCK.]

chuck³ (chŭk) *intr.v.* **chucked, chuck•ing, chucks** To make a clucking sound. ❖ *n.* A clucking sound. [ME *chukken*, of imit. orig.]

chuck•hole (chŭk′hōl′) *n.* See pothole 1. [Prob. < CHUCK¹.]

chuck•le (chŭk′əl) *intr.v.* **-led, -ling, -les 1.** To laugh quietly or to oneself. **2.** To cluck or chuck, as a hen. ❖ *n.* A quiet laugh. [Prob. freq. of CHUCK³.] —**chuck′ler** *n.* —**chuck′le•some** *adj.* —**chuck′ling•ly** (-lĭng-lē) *adv.*

chuck•le•head (chŭk′əl-hĕd′) *n. Informal* A stupid, gauche person. [Poss. < CHUCK².] —**chuck′le•head′ed** *adj.*

chuck wagon *n.* A wagon equipped with food and cooking utensils, as on a ranch or in a lumber camp.

chuck•wal•la (chŭk′wŏl′ə) *n.* A large herbaceous lizard (*Sauromalus obesus*) of the southwest United States and Mexico. [Am.Sp. *chacahuala* < Cahuilla *tcáxxwal.*]

chuck-will's-wid•ow (chŭk′wĭlz-wĭd′ō) *n.* A bird (*Caprimulgus carolinensis*) of the southern and central United States, resembling the whippoorwill. [Imit. of its call.]

chud•dar (chŭd′ər) *n.* **1.** A chador. **2.** A cotton shawl traditionally worn in India. [Urdu *chaddar*, cloth < Skt. *chattram*, screen, parasol < *chadati*, he covers, protects.]

chu•fa (chōō′fə) *n.* An Old World sedge (*Cyperus esculentus* var. *sativus*) having edible nutlike tubers. [< Sp. *chufar*, to make fun of, alteration of *chuflar*, to whistle, ridicule < VLat. *sufilāre*, alteration of Lat. *sībilāre, sīfilāre*, to hiss, whistle at.]

chuff¹ (chŭf) *n.* A rude, insensitive person; a boor. [ME *chuffe.*]

chuff² (chŭf) *intr.v.* **chuffed, chuff•ing, chuffs** To produce or move with chuffs. ❖ *n.* A noisy puffing or explosive sound. [Imit.]

chug¹ (chŭg) *n.* A dull explosive sound made repeatedly by a laboring engine. ❖ *intr.v.* **chugged, chug•ging, chugs 1.** To make dull explosive sounds. **2.** To move or travel while chugging. [Imit.] —**chug′ger** *n.*

chug² (chŭg) *tr. & intr.v.* **chugged, chug•ging, chugs** *Slang* To chugalug.

chug•a•lug (chŭg′ə-lŭg′) *Slang v.* **-lugged, -lug•ging, -lugs** —*tr.* To drink (a container of beer, for example) without pausing. —*intr.* To drink a beverage without pausing. [Imit.]

chu•kar (chə-kär′) *n.* A Eurasian partridge (*Alectoris chukar*) with grayish-brown plumage and red legs and bill. [Hindi *cakor* < Skt. *cakoraḥ.*]

Chuk•chi also **Chuk•chee** (chōōk′chē) *n., pl.* **Chukchi** or **-chis** also **Chukchee** or **-chees 1.** A member of a people of northeast Siberia. **2.** The language of the Chukchi. [Russ., pl. of *chukcha* < Chukchi *chawchaw.*]

Chukchi Peninsula A peninsula of extreme NE Russia across the Bering Strait from W AK and bordering on the **Chukchi Sea,** a section of the Arctic Ocean.

Chu Kiang (chōō′ kyäng′, jōō′ gyäng′) See **Zhu Jiang.**

chuk•ka (chŭk′ə) *n.* A short, ankle-length boot having two or three pairs of eyelets. [Alteration of CHUKKER.]

chuk•ker also **chuk•kar** (chŭk′ər) *n.* One of the periods of play, lasting 7½ minutes, in a polo match. [Hindi *cakkar*, circle, turn < Skt. *cakram.* See k**ʷel-** in App.]

Chu•la Vis•ta (chōō′lə vĭs′tə) A city of S CA S of San Diego. Pop. 173,556.

Chu•lym also **Chu•lim** (chə-lĭm′, chōō-) A river of S-central Russia flowing c. 1,730 km (1,075 mi) to the Ob R.

chum¹ (chŭm) *n.* An intimate friend or companion. ❖ *intr.v.*

chukar
Alectoris chukar

chummed, chum•ming, chums 1a. To be an intimate friend. **b.** To display good-natured friendliness. **2.** To share the same room, as in a dormitory. [Perh. short for *chamber fellow*, roommate.]

chum² (chŭm) *n.* Bait usu. consisting of oily fish ground up and scattered on the water. ❖ *v.* **chummed, chum•ming, chums** —*intr.* To fish with chum. —*tr.* To lure (fish) with chum. [?]

chum³ (chŭm) *n.* A chum salmon.

Chu•mash (chōō′măsh) *n., pl.* **Chumash** or **-mash•es** A member of a group of Hokan-speaking Native American peoples inhabiting the southern California coastal region around Santa Barbara.

chum•my (chŭm′ē) *adj.* **-mi•er, -mi•est** Intimate; friendly. —**chum′mi•ly** *adv.* —**chum′mi•ness** *n.*

chump¹ (chŭmp) *n.* A stupid or foolish person; a dolt. [Perh. blend of CHUNK and LUMP¹ or STUMP.]

chump² (chŭmp) *tr. & intr.v.* **chumped, chump•ing, chumps** To chew or make a chewing movement. [Variant of CHAMP¹.]

chump change *n. Slang* A small amount of money.

chum salmon *n.* A Pacific salmon (*Oncorhynchus keta*) with specks on its back. [Chinook Jargon *cam*, spotted, striped < Lower Chinook *c'ə́am*, *c'ə́am*-, variegated.]

Chung•king (chōōng′kĭng′, jōōng′gĭng′) See **Chongqing.**

chunk (chŭngk) *n.* **1.** A thick mass or piece. **2.** *Informal* A substantial amount. **3.** A strong stocky horse. ❖ *v.* **chunked, chunk•ing, chunks** —*tr.* To form into chunks. —*intr.* To make a dull clacking sound. [Perh. var. of CHUCK².]

chunk•y (chŭng′kē) *adj.* **-i•er, -i•est 1.** Short and thick; stocky. **2.** Containing small thick pieces: *chunky soup.* —**chunk′i•ly** *adv.* —**chunk′i•ness** *n.*

chun•nel (chŭn′əl) *n.* A railroad tunnel under the English Channel. [CH(ANNEL)¹ + (T)UNNEL.]

church (chûrch) *n.* **1.** A building for public, esp. Christian worship. **2.** often **Church a.** The company of all Christians regarded as a spiritual body. **b.** A specified Christian denomination. **c.** A congregation. **3.** Public divine worship in a church; a religious service. **4.** The clerical profession; clergy. **5.** Ecclesiastical power as distinguished from the secular. ❖ *tr.v.* **churched, church•ing, church•es** To conduct a church service for (a woman after childbirth). ❖ *adj.* Of or relating to the church; ecclesiastical. [ME *chirche* < OE *cirice*, ult. < Med.Gk. *kūrikon* < L.Gk. *kūriakon* (*dōma*), the Lord's (house), neut. of Gk. *kūriakos*, of the lord < *kūrios*, lord.]

Church, Frederick Edwin 1826–1900. Amer. painter who was a leader of the Hudson River School.

churched (chûrcht) *adj.* Belonging to or participating in a church. ❖ *n.* (*used with a pl. verb*) People who belong to or participate in a church considered as a group. Often used with *the.*

church father or **Church Father** *n.* Any of the authoritative early writers in the Christian church who formulated doctrines and codified religious observances.

church•go•er (chûrch′gō′ər) *n.* One who attends church. —**church′go′ing** *adj. & n.*

Chur•chill (chûr′chĭl′, chûrch′hĭl′), **Caryl** b. 1938. British playwright whose works include *Cloud 9* (1979).

Churchill, John 1st Duke of Marlborough. 1650–1722. English general and public figure during the reigns of James II, Anne, and George I.

Churchill, Mount A peak, 4,769.6 m (15,638 ft), in the Wrangell Mts. of S AK.

Churchill, Randolph Henry Spencer 1849–95. British politician who advocated social and constitutional reform.

Churchill, Winston 1871–1947. Amer. writer whose historical novels include *Richard Carvel* (1899).

Churchill, Sir Winston Leonard Spenser 1874–1965. British politician who served as prime minister (1940–45 and 1951–55) and won the 1953 Nobel Prize for literature. —**Chur•chill′i•an** (chûr-chĭl′ē-ən) *adj.*

Churchill Falls Formerly **Grand Falls.** A waterfall, 74.7 m (245 ft), of the Churchill R. in SW Labrador, Canada.

Churchill River 1. A river of E Canada flowing c. 965 km (600 mi) across Labrador to the Atlantic Ocean. **2.** A river rising in NW Saskatchewan, Canada, and flowing c. 1,609 km (1,000 mi) to Hudson Bay in N Manitoba.

church key *n.* A can or bottle opener usu. having a triangular head.

church•ly (chûrch′lē) *adj.* **1.** Of or relating to the church. **2.** Appropriate for a church. —**church′li•ness** *n.*

church•man (chûrch′mən) *n.* **1.** A man who is a cleric. **2.** A man who is a member of a church. —**church′man•ly** *adj.* —**church′man•ship** *n.*

Church of Christ, Scientist *n.* See **Christian Science.**

Church of England *n.* The episcopal and liturgical national church of England.

Church of Jesus Christ of Latter-day Saints *n.* See **Mormon Church.**

Church of Rome *n.* The Roman Catholic Church.

Church Slavonic *n.* See **Old Church Slavonic.**

church•war•den (chûrch′wôr′dn) *n.* **1.** A lay officer in the Anglican Church who handles the secular and legal affairs of the parish. **2.** One of two elected chief lay officers of the vestry in the Episcopal Church.

church•wom•an (chûrch′wŏŏm′ən) *n.* **1.** A woman who is a cleric. **2.** A woman who is a member of a church.

church•y (chûr′chē) *adj.* **-i•er, -i•est 1.** Conforming or adhering rigorously to the practices or creeds of a church. **2.** Of, suitable for, or suggesting a church.

church•yard (chûrch′yärd′) *n.* **1.** A yard next to a church, esp. a cemetery. **2.** The ground on which a church stands.

churl (chûrl) *n.* **1.** A rude, boorish person. **2.** A miserly person. **3a.** A ceorl. **b.** A medieval English peasant. [ME < OE *ceorl*, peasant.]

churl•ish (chûr′lĭsh) *adj.* **1.** Of, like, or befitting a churl; boorish or vulgar. **2.** Having a bad disposition; surly. **3.** Difficult to work with, such as soil; intractable. —**churl′ish•ly** *adv.* —**churl′ish•ness** *n.*

churn (chûrn) *n.* A vessel or device in which cream or milk is agitated to separate the oily globules from the caseous and serous parts, used to make butter. ❖ *v.* **churned, churn•ing, churns** —*tr.* **1a.** To agitate or stir (milk or cream) in order to make butter. **b.** To make by the agitation of milk or cream: *churn butter.* **2.** To shake or agitate vigorously: *wind churning up the fallen leaves.* —*intr.* **1.** To make butter by operating a churn. **2.** To move with or produce great agitation: *waves churning in the storm.* —*phrasal verb:* **churn out** To produce in an abundant or automatic manner. [ME *chirne* < OE *cyrn, cyrin.*] —**churn′er** *n.*

churr (chûr) *n.* The sharp whirring or trilling sound made by some insects and birds. [Imit.] —**churr** *v.*

chute (shōōt) *n.* **1.** An inclined trough, passage, or channel through or down which things may pass. **2.** A waterfall or rapid. **3.** A parachute. ❖ *v.* **chut•ed, chut•ing, chutes** —*tr.* To convey or deposit by a chute. —*intr.* To go or descend by a chute. [Fr., a fall, alteration (influenced by *chu*) of OFr. *cheoite* < fem. p. part. of *cheoir*, to fall < VLat. **cadēre* < Lat. *cadere.*]

chute-the-chute (shōōt′thə-shōōt′) *n.* Variant of **shoot-the-chute.**

chutist (shōō′tĭst) *n.* One who parachutes from an aircraft.

chut•ney (chŭt′nē) *n.* A pungent relish made of fruits, spices, and herbs. [Hindi *caṭnī* < *cāṭnā*, to taste.]

chutz•pah also **hutz•pah** (КНŎŌT′spə, hŏŏt′-) *n.* Utter nerve; effrontery. [Yiddish *khutspe* < Mishnaic Heb. *ḥuṣpāh < ḥaṣap*, to be insolent.]

Chuuk (chōōk) or **Truk** (trŭk, trŏŏk) An island group in the central Caroline Is.; part of the US Trust Territory of the Pacific Is.

Chu•vash (chōō-väsh′) *n., pl.* **Chuvash** or **-vash•es 1.** A member of a people located in the middle Volga River valley, chiefly in Chuvashia. **2.** The Turkic language spoken by the Chuvash. [Russ. < Chuvash *čăvaš.*]

Chu•va•shi•a (chōō-vä′shē-ə) An autonomous republic of W Russia in the Volga R. valley.

chyle (kīl) *n.* A milky fluid consisting of lymph and emulsified fat extracted from chyme by the lacteals during digestion and passed to the bloodstream through the thoracic duct. [Fr. < LLat. *chȳlus* < Gk. *khūlos*, juice. See **gheu-** in App.] —**chy′la′ceous** (kī-lā′shəs), **chy′lous** (kī′ləs) *adj.*

chy•lo•mi•cron (kī′lō-mī′krŏn′) *n.* One of the microscopic particles of emulsified fat found in the blood and lymph and formed during the digestion of fats. [CHYL(E) + Gk. *mikron*, small thing < neut. of *mīkros*, small.]

chyme (kīm) *n.* The thick semifluid mass of partly digested food that is passed from the stomach to the duodenum. [ME *chime*, humors, body fluids < OFr. < LLat. *chȳmus* < Gk. *khūmos*, juice. See **gheu-** in App.] —**chy′mous** (kī′məs) *adj.*

chy•mo•sin (kī′mə-sĭn) *n.* See **rennin.** [CHYM(E) + −OS(E)² + −IN.]

chy•mo•tryp•sin (kī′mə-trĭp′sĭn) *n.* A pancreatic digestive enzyme that catalyzes the hydrolysis of certain proteins in the small intestine into polypeptides and amino acids. [CHYM(E) + TRYPSIN.] —**chy′mo•tryp′tic** (-tĭk) *adj.*

Ci *abbr.* curie

CI *abbr.* **1.** certificate of insurance **2.** cost and insurance

CIA *abbr.* Central Intelligence Agency

ciao (chou) *interj.* Used to express greeting or farewell. [Ital. < dialectal *ciau*, alteration of Ital. *(sono vostro) schiavo*, (I am your) servant < Med.Lat. *sclavus*, slave, servant. See SLAVE.]

WORD HISTORY *Ciao* first appears in English in 1929 in Hemingway's *A Farewell to Arms*, which is set in northeast Italy during World War I. It is likely that this is where Hemingway learned the word, for *ciau* in Venetian dialect means "servant, slave," and as a casual greeting, "I am your servant." *Ciau* corresponds to standard Italian *schiavo*; both words come from Medieval Latin *sclavus*, "slave."

Cí•bo•la (sē′bə-lə) A vaguely defined historical region generally thought to be in present-day N NM; site of the fabled Seven Cities of Cíbola sought by Spanish explorers.

ci•bo•ri•um (sĭ-bôr′ē-əm, -bōr′-) *n., pl.* **-bo•ri•a** (-bôr′ē-ə, -bōr′-) **1.** A vaulted canopy permanently placed over an altar. **2.** A covered receptacle for holding the consecrated wafers of the Eucharist. [Med.Lat. *cibōrium* < Lat., a drinking cup < Gk. *kibōrion*, prob. of Egypt. orig.]

ci•ca•da (sĭ-kā′də, -kä′-) *n., pl.* **-das** or **-dae** (-dē′) Any of various insects of the family Cicadidae, having membranous wings

Sir Winston Churchill
portrait by Thomas Cantrell
Dugdale (1880–1952)

ă pat	oi boy
ā pay	ou out
âr care	ŏŏ took
ä father	ōō boot
ĕ be	ŭ cut
ē be	ûr urge
ĭ pit	th thin
ī pie	th this
îr pier	hw which
ŏ pot	zh vision
ō toe	ə about,
ô paw	item

Stress marks:
′ (primary);
′ (secondary), as in
lexicon (lĕk′sĭ-kŏn′)

and in the male a pair of resonating organs that produce a high-pitched droning sound. [ME < Lat. *cicāda*.]

ci·ca·la (sĭ-kä′lə) *n.* See **cicada**. [Ital. < Lat. *cicāda*.]

cic·a·trix (sĭk′ə-trĭks′, sĭ-kā′trĭks) *n., pl.* **cic·a·tri·ces** (sĭk′ə-trī′sēz, sĭ-kā′trĭ-sēz) A scar left by the formation of new connective tissue over a healing sore or wound. [ME *cicatrice* < Lat. *cicātrīx, cicātrīc-.*] —**cic′a·tri′cial** (sĭk′ə-trĭsh′əl), **ci·cat′ri·cose′** (-kōs′) *adj.*

cic·a·trize (sĭk′ə-trīz′) *tr. & intr.v.* **-trized, -triz·ing, -triz·es** To heal or become healed by the formation of scar tissue. [ME *cicatrizen* < OFr. *cicatriser* < Med.Lat. *cicātrizāre* < LLat. *cicātrīcārī,* to scar over < Lat. *cicātrīx; cicātrīc-,* cicatrix.] —**cic′a·tri·za′tion** (-trī-zā′shən) *n.*

Cic·e·ro (sĭs′ə-rō′), **Marcus Tullius** 106–43 B.C. Roman statesman, orator, and philosopher best known for his orations against Catiline. —**Cic′e·ro′ni·an** *adj.*

cic·e·ro·ne (sĭs′ə-rō′nē, chĭch′ə-, chē′chĕ-rō′nĕ) *n., pl.* **-nes** or **-ni** (nē) A guide for sightseers. [Ital. < Lat. *Cicerō, Cicerōn-,* Marcus Tullius Cicero.]

cich·lid (sĭk′lĭd) *n.* Any of various tropical and subtropical freshwater fishes of the family Cichlidae. [< NLat. *Cichla,* type genus < Gk. *kikhlē,* a kind of fish.] —**cich′lid** *adj.*

Cid (sĭd), **the** Orig. Rodrigo Díaz de Vivar. 1043?–99. Spanish national hero whose military exploits are recounted in several literary works.

CID *abbr.* Criminal Investigation Department

–cide *suff.* **1.** Killer: *bactericide.* **2.** Act of killing: *ecocide.* [ME < OFr. (< Lat. *-cīda,* killer), and < Lat. *-cīdium,* killing, both < *caedere,* to strike, kill.]

ci·der (sī′dər) *n.* The juice pressed from fruits, esp. apples, used as a beverage or to make other products, such as vinegar. [ME *sidre* < OFr. < LLat. *sīcera,* intoxicating drink < Gk. *sikera,* of Semitic orig.; akin to Heb. *šēkār,* intoxicating drink.]

ci-de·vant (sē′də-väN′) *adj.* Former. [Fr. : *ci,* here + *devant,* before.]

Cien·fue·gos (syĕn-fwā′gōs) A city of S-central Cuba on **Cienfuegos Bay,** an inlet of the Caribbean Sea. Pop. 129,665.

CIF *abbr.* cost, insurance, and freight

ci·gar (sĭ-gär′) *n.* A roll of tobacco leaves prepared for smoking. [Sp. *cigarro,* poss. < Maya *sik'ar* < *sik,* tobacco.]

ci·gar-box cedar (sĭ-gär′bŏks) *n.* See **Spanish cedar.**

cig·a·rette also **cig·a·ret** (sĭg′ə-rĕt′, sĭg′ə-rĕt′) *n.* **1.** A small roll of finely cut tobacco for smoking, enclosed in a wrapper of thin paper. **2.** A similar roll of another substance, such as marijuana. [Fr., dim. of *cigare,* cigar < Sp. *cigarro.* See CIGAR.]

cig·a·ril·lo (sĭg′ə-rĭl′ō) *n., pl.* **-los** A small narrow cigar. [Sp. *cigarrillo,* dim. of *cigarro,* cigar. See CIGAR.]

ci·gua·ter·a (sē′gwə-tĕr′ə) *n.* Poisoning caused by ingesting fish contaminated with ciguatoxin. [Am.Sp. < *ciguato,* one poisoned (with ciguatoxin) < *cigua, sigua,* snail, perh. < Arawakan orig.]

ci·gua·tox·in (sē′gwə-tŏk′sĭn) *n.* A potent neurotoxin that is secreted by dinoflagellates and can accumulate in certain marine fish. [CIGUA(TERA) + TOXIN.]

ci·lan·tro (sĭ-län′trō, -lăn′-) *n.* See **coriander.** [Sp., alteration of LLat. *coliandrum* < Lat. *coriandrum.* See CORIANDER.]

cil·i·ar·y (sĭl′ē-ĕr′ē) *adj.* **1.** Of or resembling cilia. **2.** Of or relating to the ciliary body and associated structures.

ciliary body *n.* A thickened portion of the vascular tunic of the eye located between the choroid and the iris.

cil·i·ate (sĭl′ē-ĭt, -āt′) *adj.* Ciliated. ❖ *n.* Any of various protozoans of the class Ciliata, characterized by numerous cilia. —**cil′i·ate·ly** *adv.* —**cil′i·a′tion** *n.*

cil·i·at·ed (sĭl′ē-ā′tĭd) *adj.* Having cilia.

cil·ice (sĭl′ĭs) *n.* A coarse cloth; haircloth. [Fr. < Lat. *cilicium,* a covering made of Cilician goat's hair < CILICIA.]

Ci·li·cia (sĭ-lĭsh′ə) An ancient region of SE Asia Minor on the Mediterranean Sea S of the Taurus Mts. —**Ci·li′cian** *adj. & n.*

Cilician Gates A pass in the Taurus Mts. of S Turkey.

cil·i·o·late (sĭl′ē-ə-lāt′) *adj.* Having minute cilia. [< NLat. *ciliolum,* dim. of *cilium,* cilium < Lat., eyelid. See CILIUM.]

cil·i·um (sĭl′ē-əm) *n., pl.* **-i·a** (-ē-ə) **1.** A microscopic hairlike process that extends from the surface of a cell or unicellular organism and acts in unison with other cilia to bring about the movement of the cell or of the surrounding medium. **2.** An eyelash. **3.** *Botany* One of the hairs along the edge of a structure, such as a leaf, usu. forming a fringe. [Lat., eyelid. See kel- in App.]

Ci·ma·bu·e (chē′mä-bōō′ĕ), **Giovanni** Orig. Cenni di Pepo. 1240?–1302? Italian painter considered the first master of the Florentine school.

Cim·ar·ron (sĭm′ə-rŏn′, -rōn′) A river rising in NE NM and flowing c. 1,123 km (698 mi) to the Arkansas R. in N OK.

ci·met·i·dine (sī-mĕt′ĭ-dēn′, -dĭn′) *n.* A drug, $C_{10}H_{16}N_6S$, that inhibits acid secretion in the stomach and is used to treat gastrointestinal disorders, such as peptic ulcers. [Alteration of CY(ANO–) + MET(HYL) + (GUAN)IDINE.]

ci·mex (sī′mĕks′) *n., pl.* **cim·i·ces** (sĭm′ĭ-sēz′) An insect of the genus Cimex, which includes bedbugs. [Lat. *cīmex.*]

Cim·me·ri·an (sĭ-mîr′ē-ən) *adj.* Very dark or gloomy. ❖ *n.* Greek Mythology One of a mythical people described by Homer

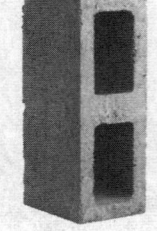

cinder block

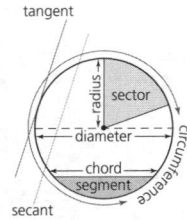

tangent

radius

sector

diameter

chord

segment

circumference

secant

circle

as inhabiting a land of perpetual darkness. [< Lat. *Cimmeriī,* the Cimmerians < Gk. *Kimmerioi.*]

CINC or **C in C** *abbr.* commander in chief

cinch (sĭnch) *n.* **1.** A girth for a pack or saddle. **2.** A firm grip. **3.** Something easy to accomplish. **4.** A sure thing; a certainty. ❖ *v.* **cinched, cinch·ing, cinch·es** —*tr.* **1.** To put a saddle girth on. **2.** To get a tight grip on. **3.** *Informal* To make certain; guarantee. —*intr.* To tighten a saddle girth. Often used with *up.* [Sp. *cincha,* fem. of *cincho,* belt < Lat. *cīnctus* < p. part. of *cingere,* to gird.]

cinch bug *n.* *Chiefly Southern & Midland US* Variant of **chinch bug.**

cin·cho·na (sĭng-kō′nə, sĭn-chō′-) *n.* **1.** Any of several trees and shrubs of the genus Cinchona, native chiefly to the Andes and cultivated for bark that yields quinine and quinidine, which are used to treat malaria. **2.** The dried bark of any of these plants. [NLat. *Cinchona,* genus name, reputedly after Francisca Henríquez de Ribera (1576–1639), Countess of *Chinchón.*] —**cin·chon′ic** (sĭng-kŏn′ĭk, sĭn-chŏn′-) *adj.*

cin·cho·nine (sĭng′kə-nēn′, sĭn′chə-) *n.* An alkaloid, $C_{19}H_{22}N_2O$, derived from the bark of various cinchona trees and used as an antimalarial agent. [CINCHON(A) + –INE².]

cin·cho·nism (sĭng′kə-nĭz′əm, sĭn′chə-) *n.* A pathological condition resulting from an overdose of cinchona bark or its derivatives and marked by headache and dizziness.

Cin·cin·na·ti (sĭn′sə-năt′ē, -năt′ə) A city of extreme SW OH on the Ohio R.; founded 1788. Pop. 331,285.

Cin·cin·na·tus (sĭn′sə-năt′əs, -nă′təs), **Lucius Quinctius** 519?–438 B.C. Roman statesman who according to tradition was twice called away from his farm to govern Rome (458 and 439).

Cin·co de Ma·yo (sēng′kō də mä′yō) *n.* May 5, observed by Mexican and Mexican-American communities in commemoration of the 1862 defeat of French troops at the Battle of Puebla. [Sp. : *cinco,* five + *de,* of + *Mayo,* May.]

cinc·ture (sĭngk′chər) *n.* **1.** The act of encircling or encompassing. **2a.** Something that encircles or surrounds. **b.** A belt or sash, esp. one worn with a vestment or habit. ❖ *tr.v.* **-tured, -tur·ing, -tures** To gird; encompass. [Lat. *cīnctūra* < *cīnctus,* p. part. of *cingere,* to gird.]

cin·der (sĭn′dər) *n.* **1a.** A burned substance, such as coal, that is not reduced to ashes but is incapable of further combustion. **b.** A partly charred substance that can burn further but without flame. **2.** cinders Ashes. **3.** cinders *Geology* See **scoria** 1. **4.** *Metallurgy* See **scoria** 2. **5.** Slag from a metal furnace. ❖ *tr.v.* **-dered, -der·ing, -ders** To burn or reduce to cinders. [Alteration (influenced by OFr. *cendre,* ashes) of ME *sinder* < OE, slag, dross.] —**cin′der·y** *adj.*

cinder block or **cin·der·block** (sĭn′dər-blŏk′) *n.* A usu. hollow building block made with concrete and coal cinders.

Cin·der·el·la (sĭn′də-rĕl′ə) *n.* One that achieves recognition or success after a period of obscurity and neglect. [After *Cinderella,* the fairy-tale character who escapes from drudgery.]

cin·e·aste also **cin·e·ast** (sĭn′ē-ăst, sĭn′ē-äst′) *n.* **1.** A film or movie enthusiast. **2.** A person involved in filmmaking. [Fr. *cinéaste* < *ciné,* cinema, short for *cinéma.* See CINEMA.]

cin·e·ma (sĭn′ə-mə) *n.* **1a.** A film or movie. **b.** A movie theater. **2a.** Films or movies considered as a group. **b.** The film or movie industry. **3.** The art or technique of making films or movies; filmmaking. [French *cinéma,* short for *cinématographe.* See CINEMATOGRAPH.] —**cin′e·mat′ic** (sĭn′ə-măt′ĭk) *adj.* —**cin′e·mat′i·cal·ly** *adv.*

cin·e·ma·theque (sĭn′ə-mə-tĕk′) *n.* A small movie theater showing classic or avant-garde films. [Fr. *cinémathèque* : *cinéma,* cinema; see CINEMA + (*biblio*)*thèque,* library (< Lat. *bibliotheca;* see BIBLIOTHECA).]

cin·e·mat·o·graph (sĭn′ə-măt′ə-grăf′) *n.* *Chiefly British* **1.** A movie camera or projector. **2.** A movie theater. [Fr. *cinématographe* : Gk. *kīnēma, kīnēmat-,* motion (< *kīnein,* to move; see kei-² in App.) + -*graphe,* -graph.]

cin·e·ma·tog·ra·pher (sĭn′ə-mə-tŏg′rə-fər) *n.* A movie photographer, esp. one who is in charge of shooting a movie.

cin·e·ma·tog·ra·phy (sĭn′ə-mə-tŏg′rə-fē) *n.* The art or technique of movie photography. —**cin′e·mat′o·graph′ic** (-măt′ə-grăf′ĭk) *adj.* —**cin′e·mat′o·graph′i·cal·ly** *adv.*

ci·né·ma vé·ri·té (sē′nä-mä′ vā′rē-tä′, sĭn′ə-mə vâr′ĭ-tā′) *n.* A style of documentary filmmaking that stresses unbiased realism. [Fr. *cinéma-vérité* : *cinéma,* cinema + *vérité,* truth.]

cin·e·ole also **cin·e·ol** (sĭn′ē-ōl′) *n.* See **eucalyptol.** [Alteration of NLat. *cinae oleum* : *cinae,* genitive of *cina,* wormseed + Lat. *oleum,* oil; see OLEO–.]

cin·e·phile (sĭn′ə-fīl′) *n.* A film or movie enthusiast. [Fr. *cinéphile* : *ciné,* cinema; see CINEASTE + *-phile,* -phile.]

cin·e·rar·i·a¹ (sĭn′ə-râr′ē-ə) *n.* Plural of **cinerarium.**

cin·e·rar·i·a² (sĭn′ə-râr′ē-ə) *n.* Any of several hybrid plants (*Senecio ×hybridus*) in the composite family, having showy flower heads and silvery foliage. [NLat. *Cinerāria,* genus name < fem. of Lat. *cinerārius,* of ashes (< the ash-colored down on its leaves). See CINERARIUM.]

cin·e·rar·i·um (sĭn′ə-râr′ē-əm) *n., pl.* **-i·a** (-ē-ə) A place for keeping the ashes of a cremated body. [Lat. *cinerārium* < neut. of *cinerārius,* of ashes < *cinis, ciner-,* ashes.] —**cin′er·ar′y** (sĭn′ə-rĕr′ē) *adj.*

ci·ne·re·ous (sĭ-nîr′ē-əs) *adj.* **1.** Consisting of or resembling ashes. **2.** Of a gray color tinged with black. [< Lat. *cinereus* < *cinis*, *ciner-*, ashes.]

cin·er·in (sĭn′ər-ĭn) *n.* Either of two compounds, $C_{20}H_{28}O_3$ or $C_{21}H_{28}O_5$, used in insecticides. [Lat. *cinis*, *ciner-*, ashes + *–IN*.]

cin·gu·lum (sĭng′gyə-ləm) *n., pl.* **-la** (-lə) *Biology* A girdlelike marking or structure, such as a band or ridge, on an animal. [Lat., girdle < *cingere*, to gird.] —**cin′gu·late** (-lĭt), **cin′gu·la·ted** (-lā′tĭd) *adj.*

cin·na·bar (sĭn′ə-bär′) *n.* **1.** A heavy reddish mercuric sulfide, HgS, that is the principal ore of mercury. **2.** Red mercuric sulfide used as a pigment. **3.** See **vermilion** 2. [ME *cinabare* < Lat. *cinnabaris* < Gk. *kinnabari.*] —**cin′na·bar′ine** (-bär′ĭn, -bə-rīn′) *adj.*

cinnamic acid *n.* A white crystalline acid, $C_6H_5CHCHCOOH$, found in cinnamon or made from balsams and used chiefly to manufacture perfume. [CINNAM(ON) + –IC.]

cin·na·mon (sĭn′ə-mən) *n.* **1a.** The dried inner bark of certain tropical Asian trees in the genus *Cinnamomum*, esp. *C. verum* and *C. loureirii*, often ground and used as a spice. **b.** A plant yielding this bark. **2.** A light reddish brown. ❖ *adj.* Of the color cinnamon. [ME *cinamome* < OFr. < Lat. *cinnamōmum* < Gk. *kinnamōmon*, prob. of Semitic orig.; akin to Heb. *qinnāmôn*.] —**cin·nam′ic** (sə-năm′ĭk) *adj.*

cinnamon bear *n.* A variety of the North American black bear (*Ursus americanus*) that has a reddish-brown coat.

cinnamon fern *n.* A New World fern (*Osmunda cinnamomea*) having narrow, spore-bearing cinnamon leaves first, which are later encircled by wider, sterile green leaves.

cinnamon stone *n.* See **essonite**.

cin·quain (sĭng′kān′, săng′-) *n.* A five-line stanza. [Fr. *cinq*, five (< OFr. *cinc*; see CINQUE) + (QUATR)AIN.]

cinque (sĭngk, săngk) *n. Games* The number five in cards or dice. [ME *cink* < OFr. *cinc* < Lat. *quīnque*, five. See **penk**[ʷ]**e** in App.]

cin·que·cen·tist (chĭng′kwĭ-chĕn′tĭst) *n.* An Italian, esp. a poet or an artist, of the 16th century.

cin·que·cen·to (chĭng′kwĭ-chĕn′tō) *n.* The 16th century, esp. in Italian art and literature. [Ital. < (*mil*) *cinquecento*, (one thousand) five hundred : *cinque*, five (< Lat. *quīnque*; see **penk**[ʷ]**e** in App.) + *cento*, hundred (< Lat. *centum*; see **dekm̥** in App.).]

cinque·foil (sĭngk′foil′, săngk′-) *n.* **1.** Any of several plants of the genus *Potentilla* in the rose family, having compound leaves that in some species bear five leaflets. **2.** *Architecture* A design having five sides composed of converging arcs, usu. used as a frame for glass or a panel. [ME *cinkfoil* : *cink*, five; see CINQUE + *foil*, leaf (transl. of OFr. *quintefeuille* < Lat. *quīnquefolium*, transl. of Gk. *pentaphullon*; see FOIL².]

Cinque Ports (sĭngk′) A group of seaports of SE England (orig. Hastings, Romney, Hythe, Dover, and Sandwich) that formed a maritime and defensive association in the 11th cent.

CIO *abbr.* **1.** chief information officer **2.** Congress of Industrial Organizations

ci·on (sī′ən) *n.* Variant of **scion** 2.

ciop·pi·no (chə-pē′nō) *n., pl.* **-nos** A stew made of several kinds of fish and shellfish, tomatoes, and white wine. [Ital., perh. var. of northwest Ital. *ciuppin*.]

Ci·pan·go (sĭ-păng′gō) Japan.

ci·pher also **cy·pher** (sī′fər) *n.* **1.** The mathematical symbol (0) denoting absence of quantity; zero. **2.** An Arabic numeral or figure; a number. **3.** One having no influence or value; a nonentity. **4a.** A cryptographic system in which units such as letters are arbitrarily transposed or substituted according to a predetermined code. **b.** The key to such a system. **c.** A message written or transmitted in such a system. **5.** A design combining or interweaving letters or initials; a monogram. ❖ *v.* **-phered, -pher·ing, -phers** —*intr.* To solve problems in arithmetic; calculate. —*tr.* **1.** To put in secret writing; encode. **2.** To solve by means of arithmetic. [ME *cifre* < OFr. < Med.Lat. *cifra* < Ar. *ṣifr* < *ṣafira*, to be empty (transl. of Skt. *śūnyam*, cipher, dot).]

ci·pher·text (sī′fər-tĕkst′) *n.* A text in encrypted form, as opposed to the plain text.

circ. *abbr.* **1.** circle **2.** circuit **3.** circulation **4.** circumference

cir·ca (sûr′kə) *prep.* In approximately; about. [Lat. *circā* < *circum*, around (prob. on the model of adverbs like *intrā*, within) < *circus*, circle. See CIRCLE.]

cir·ca·di·an (sər-kā′dē-ən, -kăd′ē-, sûr′kə-dī′ən, -dē′-) *adj. Biology* Relating to or exhibiting approx. 24-hour periodicity. [Lat. *circā*, around; see CIRCA + Lat. *diēs*, day; see **dyeu-** in App.] —**cir·ca′di·an·ly** *adv.*

circadian rhythm *n.* A daily rhythmic activity cycle, based on 24-hour intervals, that is exhibited by many organisms.

Cir·cas·sia (sər-kăsh′ə, -ē-ə) A historical region of SW Russia on the NE coast of the Black Sea N of the Caucasus Mts.

Cir·cas·sian (sər-kăsh′ən, -kăsh′ē-ən) *n.* **1.** A native or inhabitant of Circassia. **2.** The Caucasian language of the Circassians. —**Cir·cas′sian** *adj.*

Circassian walnut *n.* A type of English walnut, patterned with brown curves or black streaks.

Cir·ce (sûr′sē) *n. Greek Mythology* A goddess who turned Odysseus's men temporarily into swine but later gave them directions for their journey home. —**Cir′ce·an** (sûr′sē-ən, sər-sē′ən) *adj.*

cir·ci·nate (sûr′sə-nāt′) *adj.* **1.** Ring-shaped. **2.** *Botany* Rolled up in a coil with the tip in the center, as a fern frond. [Lat. *circinātus*, p. part. of *circināre*, to make circular < *circinus*, pair of compasses. See CIRCINUS.] —**cir′ci·nate′ly** *adv.*

Cir·ci·nus (sûr′sə-nəs) *n.* A constellation in the Southern Hemisphere near Musca and Triangulum Australe. [Lat. *circinus*, pair of compasses < *circus*, circle. See CIRCLE.]

cir·cle (sûr′kəl) *n.* **1.** A plane curve everywhere equidistant from a given fixed point, the center. **2.** A planar region bounded by a circle. **3.** Something, such as a ring, shaped like such a plane curve. **4.** A circular course, circuit, or orbit. **5.** A traffic circle. **6.** A curved section or tier of seats in a theater. **7.** A series or process that finishes at its starting point or repeats itself; a cycle. **8.** A group of people sharing an interest, activity, or achievement. **9.** A territorial or administrative division, esp. of a province, in some European countries. **10.** A sphere of influence or interest; domain. **11.** *Logic* A vicious circle. ❖ *v.* **-cled, -cling, -cles** —*tr.* **1.** To make or form a circle around; enclose. **2.** To move in a circle around. —*intr.* To move in a circle. —**idiom: circle the wagons** To take a defensive position. [ME *cercle* < OFr. < Lat. *circulus*, dim. of *circus*, circle < Gk. *kirkos, krikos*.] —**cir′cler** (-klər) *n.*

circle graph *n.* See **pie chart**.

cir·clet (sûr′klĭt) *n.* A small circle, esp. a circular ornament. [ME *cerclet* < OFr., dim. of *cercle*, circle. See CIRCLE.]

cir·cuit (sûr′kĭt) *n.* **1a.** A closed, usu. circular line that goes around an object or area. **b.** The region enclosed by such a line. **2a.** A path or route that returns to its starting point. **b.** The act of following such a path or route. **c.** A journey made on such a path or route. **3.** *Electronics* **a.** A closed path followed by an electric current. **b.** A configuration of electrically or electromagnetically connected components or devices. **4a.** A regular or accustomed course from place to place; a round: *the lecture circuit.* **b.** The area or district thus covered, esp. a territory under the jurisdiction of a judge in which periodic court sessions are held. **5a.** An association of theaters among which plays, acts, or films move for presentation. **b.** A group of nightclubs, show halls, or resorts at which entertainers appear in turn. **c.** An association of teams or clubs. **d.** A series of competitions held in different places. ❖ *intr. & tr.v.* **-cuit·ed, -cuit·ing, -cuits** To make a circuit or circuit of. [ME, circumference < OFr. < Lat. *circuitus*, a going around < p. part. of *circumīre*, to go around : *circum-*, circum- + *īre*, to go; see **ei-** in App.]

circuit board *n. Computer Science* An insulated board on which interconnected circuits and components such as microchips are mounted or etched.

circuit breaker *n.* An automatic switch that stops the flow of electric current in an overloaded electric circuit.

circuit court *n.* A state court that holds sessions at several different places within a judicial district.

cir·cu·i·tous (sər-kyōō′ĭ-təs) *adj.* Being or taking a roundabout, lengthy course. [Med.Lat. *circuitōsus* < Lat. *circuitus*, a going around. See CIRCUIT.] —**cir·cu′i·tous·ly** *adv.* —**cir·cu′i·ty, cir·cu′i·tous·ness** *n.*

circuit rider *n.* A cleric who travels from church to church.

cir·cuit·ry (sûr′kĭ-trē) *n., pl.* **-ries 1.** The design of or a detailed plan for an electric circuit. **2.** Electric circuits considered as a group.

cir·cu·lar (sûr′kyə-lər) *adj.* **1.** Of or relating to a circle. **2a.** Shaped like or nearly like a circle; round. **b.** Moving in or forming a circle. **3.** Circuitous; roundabout. **4.** Using a premise to prove a conclusion that in turn is used to prove the premise: *a circular argument.* **5.** Addressed or distributed to a large number of persons. ❖ *n.* A circular printed advertisement, directive, or notice. [ME *circuler* < AN < Lat. *circulāris* < *circulus*, circle. See CIRCLE.] —**cir′cu·lar′i·ty** (-lăr′ĭ-tē) *n.* —**cir′cu·lar·ly** *adv.*

circular function *n.* See **trigonometric function**.

cir·cu·lar·ize (sûr′kyə-lə-rīz′) *tr.v.* **-ized, -iz·ing, -iz·es 1.** To publicize with circulars. **2.** To canvass or poll using a questionnaire. —**cir′cu·lar·i·za′tion** (-lər-ĭ-zā′shən) *n.*

circular saw *n.* A power saw for cutting wood or metal consisting of a toothed disk rotated at high speed.

cir·cu·late (sûr′kyə-lāt′) *v.* **-lat·ed, -lat·ing, -lates** —*intr.* **1.** To move in or flow through a circle or circuit: *blood circulating through the body.* **2.** To move around, as from person to person or place to place. **3.** To move about or flow freely, as air. **5.** To spread widely among persons or places; disseminate. —*tr.* To cause to move about or be distributed. [< ME *circulat*, continuously distilled < Lat. *circulātus*, p. part. of *circulāre*, to make circular < *circulus*, circle. See CIRCLE.] —**cir′cu·la·tive** (-lā′tĭv) *adj.* —**cir′cu·la′tor** *n.*

cir·cu·lat·ing library (sûr′kyə-lā′tĭng) *n.* See **lending library**.

cir·cu·la·tion (sûr′kyə-lā′shən) *n.* **1.** Movement in a circle or circuit, esp. the movement of blood through the circulatory system. **2a.** Movement or passage through a system of vessels, as of water through pipes; flow. **b.** Free movement or passage. **3.** The passing of something, such as money, from place to place or person to person. **4a.** The condition of being passed about and widely known; distribution. **b.** Dissemination of printed material among readers. **c.** The number of copies of a publication sold or distributed.

cir·cu·la·to·ry (sûr′kyə-lə-tôr′ē, -tôr′ē) *adj.* **1.** Of or relating to

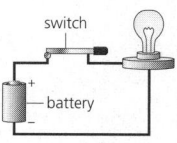

circuit
simple electrical circuit
system

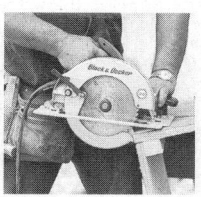

circular saw

circulation. **2.** Of or relating to the circulatory system.

circulatory system *n.* The system consisting of the heart and blood vessels that circulates blood throughout the body.

circum– *pref.* Around; about: *circumlunar.* [Lat. < *circum*, around, accusative of *circus*, circle. See CIRCLE.]

cir·cum·am·bi·ent (sûr′kəm-ăm′bē-ənt) *adj.* Encompassing on all sides; surrounding. —**cir′cum·am′bi·ence, cir′cum·am′bi·en·cy** *n.* —**cir′cum·am′bi·ent·ly** *adv.*

cir·cum·am·bu·late (sûr′kəm-ăm′byə-lāt′) *tr.v.* **-lat·ed, -lat·ing, -lates** To walk around (something), esp. as part of a ritual. —**cir′cum·am′bu·la′tion** *n.*

cir·cum·bo·re·al (sûr′kəm-bôr′ē-əl, -bōr′-) *adj.* Distributed or occurring chiefly throughout the boreal regions of North America and Eurasia. Used esp. of plants.

cir·cum·cise (sûr′kəm-sīz′) *tr.v.* **-cised, -cis·ing, -cis·es 1.** To remove the foreskin of (a male). **2.** To remove all or part of the clitoris, prepuce, or labia of (a female). [ME *circumcisen* < Lat. *circumcīdere, circumcīs-,* to cut around : *circum-, circum-* + *caedere,* to cut.] —**cir′cum·cis′er** *n.*

cir·cum·ci·sion (sûr′kəm-sĭzh′ən) *n.* **1.** The act of circumcising. **2.** A religious ceremony in which someone is circumcised. **3. Circumcision** A Christian feast celebrating the circumcision of Jesus, celebrated on January 1.

cir·cum·duc·tion (sûr′kəm-dŭk′shən) *n.* The circular movement of a limb such that the distal end of the limb delineates an arc. [Ult. < Lat. *circumdūcere,* to lead around : *circum-, circum-* + *dūcere,* to lead; see **deuk-** in App.]

cir·cum·fer·ence (sər-kŭm′fər-əns) *n.* **1.** The boundary line of a circle. **2a.** The boundary line of a figure, area, or object. **b.** The length of such a boundary. [ME < OFr. *circonference* < Lat. *circumferentia* < *circumferēns, circumferent-,* pr. part. of *circumferre,* to carry around : *circum-, circum-* + *ferre,* to carry; see **bher-**[1] in App.] —**cir′cum·fer·en′tial** (-fə-rĕn′shəl) *adj.*

cir·cum·flex (sûr′kəm-flĕks′) *n.* Any of several marks, esp. (ˆ), used over a vowel in certain languages or in phonetic keys to indicate quality of pronunciation. ❖ *adj.* **1.** Having this mark. **2.** Curving around: *a circumflex blood vessel.* [< Lat. *circumflexus,* bent around, circumflex, p. part. of *circumflectere,* to bend around : *circum-, circum-* + *flectere,* to bend.]

cir·cum·flu·ent (sər-kŭm′floo-ənt) also **cir·cum·flu·ous** (-əs) *adj.* Flowing around or surrounding.

cir·cum·fuse (sûr′kəm-fyooz′) *tr.v.* **-fused, -fus·ing, -fus·es 1.** To pour or diffuse around; spread. **2.** To surround, as with liquid; suffuse. [Lat. *circumfundere, circumfūs-* : *circum-, circum-* + *fundere,* to pour; see **gheu-** in App.] —**cir′cum·fu′sion** *n.*

cir·cum·ja·cent (sûr′kəm-jā′sənt) *adj.* Lying around; surrounding. [Lat. *circumiacēns, circumiacent-,* pr. part. of *circumiacēre,* to lie around : *circum-, circum-* + *iacēre,* to lie.]

cir·cum·lo·cu·tion (sûr′kəm-lō-kyoo′shən) *n.* **1.** The use of unnecessarily wordy and indirect language. **2.** Evasion in speech or writing. **3.** A roundabout expression. [Ult. < Lat. *circumlocūtiō, circumlocūtiōn-* < *circumlocūtus,* p. part. of *circumloquī* : *circum-, circum-* + *loquī,* to speak.] —**cir′cum·loc′u·to′ri·ly** (-lŏk′yə-tôr′ə-lē, -tōr′-) *adv.* —**cir′cum·loc′u·to′ry** (-tôr′ē, -tōr′ē) *adj.*

cir·cum·lu·nar (sûr′kəm-loo′nər) *adj.* Revolving about or surrounding the moon.

cir·cum·nav·i·gate (sûr′kəm-năv′ĭ-gāt′) *tr.v.* **-gat·ed, -gat·ing, -gates 1.** To proceed completely around: *circumnavigating the earth.* **2.** To go around; circumvent. —**cir′cum·nav′i·ga′tion** *n.* —**cir′cum·nav′i·ga′tor** *n.*

cir·cum·po·lar (sûr′kəm-pō′lər) *adj.* **1.** Located or found in one of the Polar Regions. **2.** *Astronomy* Being a star that from a given observer's latitude does not go below the horizon.

cir·cum·ro·tate (sûr′kəm-rō′tāt′) *intr.v.* **-tat·ed, -tat·ing, -tat·es** To turn like a wheel; revolve. —**cir′cum·ro·ta′tion** *n.* —**cir′cum·ro′ta·to′ry** (-tə-tôr′ē, -tōr′ē) *adj.*

cir·cum·scis·sile (sûr′kəm-sĭs′ĭl, -īl′) *adj. Botany* Splitting or opening along a circumference, with the top coming off as a lid: *a circumscissile seed capsule.* [CIRCUM- + Lat. *scissilis,* easily split, splitting; see SCISSILE.]

cir·cum·scribe (sûr′kəm-skrīb′) *tr.v.* **-scribed, -scrib·ing, -scribes 1.** To draw a line around; encircle. **2.** To limit narrowly; restrict. **3.** To determine the limits of; define. **4a.** To enclose (a polygon or polyhedron) within a configuration of lines or surfaces so that every vertex of the enclosed object is incident on the enclosing configuration. **b.** To erect (such a configuration) around a polygon or polyhedron. [ME *circumscriben* < Lat. *circumscrībere* : *circum-, circum-* + *scrībere,* to write; see **skrībh-** in App.] —**cir′cum·scrib′a·ble** *adj.*

cir·cum·scrip·tion (sûr′kəm-skrĭp′shən) *n.* **1.** The act of circumscribing or the state of being circumscribed. **2.** Something, such as a limit, that circumscribes. **3.** A circumscribed space or area. **4.** A circular inscription, as on a medallion. [Lat. *circumscrīptiō, circumscrīptiōn-* < *circumscrīptus,* p. part. of *circumscrībere,* to circumscribe. See CIRCUMSCRIBE.] —**cir′cum·scrip′tive** *adj.* —**cir′cum·scrip′tive·ly** *adv.*

cir·cum·so·lar (sûr′kəm-sō′lər) *adj.* Revolving around or surrounding the sun.

cir·cum·spect (sûr′kəm-spĕkt′) *adj.* Heedful of circumstances and potential consequences; prudent. [ME < Lat. *circumspectus,*

p. part. of *circumspicere,* to take heed : *circum-, circum-* + *specere,* to look; see **spek-** in App.] —**cir′cum·spect′ly** *adv.*

cir·cum·spec·tion (sûr′kəm-spĕk′shən) *n.* The state or quality of being circumspect. See Syns at **prudence.**

cir·cum·stance (sûr′kəm-stăns′) *n.* **1.** A condition or fact attending an event and having some bearing on it; a determining or modifying factor. **2.** A condition or fact that determines or must be considered in the determining of a course of action. **3.** The sum of determining factors beyond willful control. Often used in the plural. **4. circumstances** Financial status or means. **5.** Detail accompanying or surrounding an event, as in a narrative or series of events. **6.** Formal display; ceremony: *pomp and circumstance.* **7.** A particular incident or occurrence. See Syns at **occurrence.** ❖ *tr.v.* **-stanced, -stanc·ing, -stanc·es** To place in particular circumstances or conditions; situate. **—idioms: under no circumstances** In no case; never. **under (or in) the circumstances** Given these conditions; such being the case. [ME < OFr. *circonstance* < Lat. *circumstantia* < *circumstāns, circumstant-,* pr. part. of *circumstāre,* to stand around : *circum-, circum-* + *stāre,* to stand; see **stā-** in App.]

cir·cum·stan·tial (sûr′kəm-stăn′shəl) *adj.* **1.** Of, relating to, or dependent on circumstances. **2.** Of no primary significance; incidental. **3.** Complete and particular; full of detail: *a circumstantial report.* **4.** Full of ceremonial display. —**cir′cum·stan′tial·ly** *adv.*

circumstantial evidence *n.* Evidence bearing on various attendant circumstances from which the judge or jury might infer the occurrence of a fact in dispute.

cir·cum·stan·ti·al·i·ty (sûr′kəm-stăn′shē-ăl′ĭ-tē) *n., pl.* **-ties 1.** The quality of being fully or minutely detailed. **2.** A particular detail or circumstance.

cir·cum·stan·ti·ate (sûr′kəm-stăn′shē-āt′) *tr.v.* **-at·ed, -at·ing, -ates** To set forth or verify with circumstances; give detailed proof or description of.

cir·cum·ter·res·tri·al (sûr′kəm-tə-rĕs′trē-əl) *adj.* Revolving around or surrounding the earth.

cir·cum·val·late (sûr′kəm-văl′āt′) *tr.v.* **-lat·ed, -lat·ing, -lates** To surround with or as if with a rampart. ❖ *adj.* **1.** (*also* -ĭt) Surrounded with or as if with a rampart. **2.** *Anatomy* Surrounded by a ridge or wall-like structure. [Lat. *circumvallāre, circumvallāt-* : *circum-, circum-* + *vallum,* rampart with palisades (< *vallus,* post, stake).] —**cir′cum·val·la′tion** *n.*

cir·cum·vent (sûr′kəm-vĕnt′) *tr.v.* **-vent·ed, -vent·ing, -vents 1.** To surround (an enemy, for example); enclose or entrap. **2.** To go around; bypass: *a road that circumvents the city.* **3.** To avoid or get around by artful maneuvering. [ME *circumventen* < Lat. *circumvenīre, circumvent-* : *circum-, circum-* + *venīre,* to go, come; see **gʷā-** in App.] —**cir′cum·vent′er, cir′cum·ven′tor** *n.* —**cir′cum·ven′tion** *n.* —**cir′cum·ven′tive** *adj.*

cir·cum·vo·lu·tion (sər-kŭm′və-loo′shən, sûr′kəm-vō-) *n.* **1.** An act of turning, coiling, or folding about a center or axis. **2.** A single turn, coil, or fold; a convolution. [Ult. < Lat. *circumvolvere, circumvolāt-,* to roll around. See CIRCUMVOLVE.]

cir·cum·volve (sûr′kəm-vŏlv′) *intr. & tr.v.* **-volved, -volv·ing, -volves** To revolve or cause to revolve. [Lat. *circumvolvere* : *circum-, circum-* + *volvere,* to roll; see **wel-** in App.]

cir·cus (sûr′kəs) *n.* **1a.** A public entertainment consisting typically of a variety of performances by acrobats, clowns, and trained animals. **b.** A traveling company that performs such entertainments. **c.** A circular arena, surrounded by tiers of seats and often covered by a tent, for such shows. **2.** A roofless oval enclosure surrounded by tiers of seats, used in antiquity for public spectacles. **3.** *Chiefly British* An open circular place where several streets intersect. **4.** *Informal* Something suggestive of a circus. [ME, round arena < Lat., circus, circle. See CIRCLE.] —**cir′cus·y** *adj.*

ci·ré also **cire** (sĭ-rā′) *adj.* Having a highly glazed finish, usu. by the application of wax: *a ciré shirt.* ❖ *n.* A fabric or garment with such a finish. [Fr., p. part. of *cirer,* to wax < Lat. *cērāre.* See CE-RATED.]

cirque (sûrk) *n.* **1.** A steep bowl-shaped hollow occurring at the upper end of a mountain valley, esp. one forming the head of a glacier. **2.** A ring; a circle. [Fr. < Lat. *circus,* circle. See CIRCLE.]

cir·rate (sĭr′āt′) *adj. Biology* Having or resembling a cirrus or cirri. [Lat. *cirrātus,* curled < *cirrus,* curl of hair.]

cir·rho·sis (sĭ-rō′sĭs) *n.* A chronic disease of the liver marked by replacement of normal tissue with fibrous tissue, resulting from alcohol abuse, nutritional deprivation, or infection. **2.** Chronic interstitial inflammation of any tissue or organ. [NLat. : Gk. *kirros,* tawny (< the color of the diseased liver) + –OSIS.] —**cir·rhot′ic** (-rŏt′ĭk) *adj.*

cir·ri·ped (sĭr′ə-pĕd′) also **cir·ri·pede** (-pēd′) *n.* Any of various crustaceans of the subclass Cirripedia, which includes the barnacles and related organisms that attach themselves to objects or become parasitic in the adult stage. [< NLat. *Cirripedia,* order name : CIRR(US) + –PED.] —**cir′ri·ped′** *adj.*

cirro- or **cirri-** *pref.* Cirrus cloud: *cirrostratus.* [< CIRRUS.]

cir·ro·cu·mu·lus (sĭr′ō-kyoom′yə-ləs) *n.* A high-altitude cloud composed of a series of small, regularly arranged cloudlets in the form of ripples or grains.

cir·ro·strat·us (sĭr′ō-străt′əs, -strā′təs) *n.* A high-altitude, thin hazy cloud, usu. covering the sky and producing a halo effect.

cir•rus (sîr′əs) *n., pl.* **cir•ri** (sîr′ī′) **1.** A high-altitude cloud composed of narrow bands or patches of thin, generally white, fleecy parts. **2.** *Botany* **a.** A tendril or similar part. **b.** *Zoology* A slender flexible appendage, such as the fused cilia of certain protozoans. [Lat., curl of hair.]

CIS *abbr.* Commonwealth of Independent States

cis– *pref.* **1.** On this side: *cisatlantic.* **2.** A prefix used to denote a geometric isomer in which a pair of identical atoms or groups are located on the same side of a double bond or ring: *cis-2-butene.* [Lat. < *cis,* on this side of. See **ko-** in App.]

cis•al•pine (sĭs-ăl′pīn′) *adj.* Relating to, living on, or coming from the southern side of the Alps. [Lat. *Cisalpīnus* : *cis-*, cis- + *alpīnus,* alpine; see ALPINE.]

Cisalpine Gaul A section of ancient Gaul S and E of the Alps in present-day Italy.

cis•at•lan•tic (sĭs′ət-lăn′tĭk) *adj.* Situated on this side of the Atlantic Ocean.

CISC *abbr.* complex instruction set computer

Cis•cau•ca•sia (sĭs′kô-kā′zhə, -shə) A steppeland of SW Russia in the Caucasus N of the main range of the Caucasus Mts.

cis•co (sĭs′kō) *n., pl.* **-coes** or **-cos** Any of several North American freshwater fishes of the genus *Coregonus* or *Leucichthys,* related to the whitefish. [< Canadian Fr. *ciscoette* < Ojibwa *bemidewiskawed,* the (fish) with oily skin.]

Cis•kei (sĭs′kī) A former Black homeland of SE South Africa; reabsorbed into South Africa by the 1994 constitution. Cap. Zwelitsha. Pop. 645,000.

cis•lu•nar (sĭs-lo͞o′nər) *adj.* Situated between the earth and the moon.

cis•mon•tane (sĭs-mŏn′tān′) *adj.* Situated on this side of the mountains, esp. the Alps.

cis•pla•tin (sĭs-plă′tn) *n.* A platinum-containing chemotherapeutic drug, $Cl_2H_6N_2Pt$, used in the treatment of certain metastatic or advanced cancers. [CIS– + PLATIN(UM).]

cist[1] (sĭst) *n.* A wicker receptacle used in ancient Rome for carrying sacred utensils in a procession. [Lat. *cista* < Gk. *kistē.*]

cist[2] (sĭst, kĭst) also **kist** (kĭst) *n.* A stone-lined grave, often having a lid of stone or wood. [Welsh, chest < Lat. *cista,* basket. See CIST[1].]

Cis•ter•cian (sĭ-stûr′shən) *n.* A member of a contemplative monastic order founded by reformist Benedictines in France in 1098. [Fr. *Cistertien* < Med.Lat. *Cistercium,* Cîteaux, a village of E France, site of an abbey.] **—Cis•ter′cian** *adj.*

cis•tern (sĭs′tərn) *n.* **1.** A receptacle for holding water or other liquid, esp. a tank for catching and storing rainwater. **2.** *Anatomy* A cisterna. [ME *cisterne* < Lat. *cisterna* < *cista,* box < Gk. *kistē,* basket.] **—cis•tern′al** (sĭ-stûr′nəl) *adj.*

cis•ter•na (sĭ-stûr′nə) *n., pl.* **-nae** (-nē) **1.** A fluid-containing sac or cavity in the body of an organism. **2.** One of the saclike vesicles of the endoplasmic reticulum. [Lat., cistern. See CISTERN.] **—cis•ter′nal** *adj.*

cis•tron (sĭs′trŏn′) *n.* A section of DNA that contains the genetic code for a single polypeptide and functions as a hereditary unit. [< *cis-trans test,* a genetic test (CIS– + TRANS–) + –ON[1].] **—cis•tron′ic** *adj.*

cit. *abbr.* **1.** citation **2.** cited

cit•a•del (sĭt′ə-dəl, -dĕl′) *n.* **1.** A fortress in a commanding position in or near a city. **2.** A stronghold or fortified place; a bulwark. [Fr. *citadelle* < Ital. *cittadella,* dim. of *città,* city < Lat. *cīvitās.* See CITY.]

ci•ta•tion (sī-tā′shən) *n.* **1.** The act of citing. **2.** An authoritative source used for substantiation; a quotation. **3.** *Law* A reference to previous court decisions or authoritative writings. **4a.** An official commendation for meritorious action. **b.** A formal statement of the accomplishments of one being honored with an academic degree. **5.** An official summons, esp. one for appearance in court. **—ci•ta′tion•al** *adj.*

cite (sīt) *tr.v.* **cit•ed, cit•ing, cites 1.** To quote as an authority or example. **2.** To mention or bring forward as support, illustration, or proof. **3a.** To commend officially for meritorious action in military service. **b.** To honor formally. **4.** To summon before a court of law. [ME *citen,* to summon < OFr. *citer* < Lat. *citāre.* See **kei-**[2] in App.] **—cit′a•ble** *adj.* **—ci′ta•to′ry** (sī′tə-tôr′ē, -tōr′ē) *adj.*

cith•a•ra (sĭth′ər-ə, kĭth′-) also **kith•a•ra** (kĭth′-) *n. Music* An ancient instrument resembling the lyre. [Lat. < Gk. *kitharā.*]

cith•er (sĭth′ər, sĭth′-) *n.* A cittern. [Fr. *cithare, kitaire* < Lat. *cithara,* cithara. See CITHARA.]

cith•ern (sĭth′ərn, sĭth′-) *n.* Variant of **cittern.**

cit•ied (sĭt′ēd) *adj.* Having a city or cities.

cit•i•fied (sĭt′ĭ-fīd′) *adj.* Having or pretending to have the sophisticated style or manner associated with the city.

cit•i•fy (sĭt′ĭ-fī′) *tr.v.* **-fied, -fy•ing, -fies 1.** To cause to become urban. **2.** To impart the styles and manners of a city to. **—cit′i•fi•ca′tion** (-fĭ-kā′shən) *n.*

cit•i•zen (sĭt′ĭ-zən) *n.* **1.** A person owing loyalty to and entitled by birth or naturalization to the protection of a state or nation. **2.** A resident of a city or town, esp. one entitled to vote and enjoy other privileges there. **3.** A civilian. **4.** A native, inhabitant, or denizen of a particular place. [ME *citisein* < AN *citesein,* alteration (perh. influenced by *dainzain,* denizen) of OFr. *citeain* < *cite,* city. See CITY.] **—cit′i•zen•ly** *adj.*

cit•i•zen•ry (sĭt′ĭ-zən-rē) *n., pl.* **-ries** Citizens considered as a group.

cit•i•zen's arrest (sĭt′ĭ-zənz) *n.* An arrest made by a citizen, for whom legal authority arises from the fact of citizenship.

cit•i•zens band (sĭt′ĭ-zənz) *n.* A radio-frequency band officially allocated for private radio communications.

cit•i•zen•ship (sĭt′ĭ-zən-shĭp′) *n.* The status of a citizen with its attendant duties, rights, and privileges.

Ci•tlal•té•petl (sē′tläl-tā′pĕt-l) also **Mount O•ri•za•ba** (ôr′ĭ-zä′bə, ōr′-, ô′rē-sä′vä) An extinct volcanic peak, 5,702.6 m (18,697 ft), of S Mexico E of Mexico City.

cit•ral (sĭt′răl) *n.* A mobile pale-yellow liquid, $C_9H_{15}COH$, derived from lemon-grass oil and used in perfume and as a flavoring. [CITR(US) + –AL[3].]

cit•rate (sĭt′rāt′) *n.* A salt or ester of citric acid.

cit•ric (sĭt′rĭk) *adj.* Of or relating to citric acid.

citric acid *n.* A colorless translucent crystalline acid, $C_6H_8O_7$, principally derived by fermentation of carbohydrates or from lemon, lime, and pineapple juices and used in preparing citrates and in flavorings and metal polishes.

citric acid cycle *n.* See **Krebs cycle.**

cit•ri•cul•ture (sĭt′rĭ-kŭl′chər) *n.* The cultivation of citrus fruits. [CITR(US) + CULTURE.] **—cit′ri•cul′tur•ist** *n.*

ci•trine (sĭ-trēn′, sĭt′rēn′) *n.* **1.** A pale yellow variety of crystalline quartz resembling topaz. **2.** A light to moderate olive. [ME, reddish yellow < OFr. *citrin* < Med.Lat. *citrīnus* < Lat. *citrus,* citron tree.] **—ci•trine′** *adj.*

cit•ron (sĭt′rən) *n.* **1a.** A thorny evergreen shrub or small tree *(Citrus medica)* native to India with large lemonlike fruits that have a thick warty rind. **b.** The fruit of this plant, whose rind is often candied. **2.** A globose watermelon *(Citrullus lanatus* var. *citroides)* having white flesh that is candied or pickled. **3.** A grayish green yellow. [ME < OFr., alteration (influenced by *limon,* lemon) of Lat. *(mālum) citreum,* citron (fruit) < *citrus,* citron tree.] **—cit′ron** *adj.*

cit•ro•nel•la (sĭt′rə-nĕl′ə) *n.* **1.** A tropical Asian grass *(Cymbopogon nardus)* having lemon-scented leaves and an essential oil. **2.** The oil from this plant, used in perfumery, insect repellents, and commercial flavorings. [NLat. < Fr. *citronnelle,* lemon oil, dim. of *citron,* citron. See CITRON.]

cit•ro•nel•lal (sĭt′rə-nĕl′ăl′) *n.* An aromatic liquid, $C_{10}H_{18}O$, found in citronella and other essential oils and used in perfumes and flavorings. [CITRONELL(A) + –AL[3].]

cit•ro•nel•lol (sĭt′rə-nĕl′ôl, -ōl, -ŏl) *n.* A liquid, $C_{10}H_{20}O$, with a roselike odor, derived from any of several essential oils or synthesized and used in perfumery. [CITRONELL(A) + –OL[1].]

cit•rul•line (sĭt′rə-lēn′) *n.* An amino acid, $C_6H_{13}N_3O_3$ produced in the conversion of ornithine to arginine during urea formation in the liver. [NLat. *Citrullus,* watermelon genus (< Med.Lat. *citrullus,* watermelon < Ital. dialectal *citrulo* < LLat. *citrium* < Lat. *citrus,* citron) + –INE[2].]

cit•rus (sĭt′rəs) *n., pl.* **citrus** or **-rus•es 1.** Any of various evergreen shrubs or trees of the genus *Citrus,* such as the grapefruit, native to southern and southeast Asia and having unifoliolate compound leaves and juicy edible fruits. **2.** The fruit of any citrus. [Lat., citron tree.] **—cit′rus** *adj.* **—cit′rus•y** *adj.*

citrus canker *n.* A bacterial disease of citrus plants that causes defoliation and death.

Citrus Heights A city of N-central CA, a suburb of Sacramento. Pop. 85,071.

citrus red mite *n.* A large mite *(Panonychus citri)* that infests citrus plants and shrubs.

cit•tern (sĭt′ərn) also **cith•ern** (sĭth′ərn, sĭth′-) *n.* A 16th-century guitar with a flat pear-shaped body. [Perh. blend of Lat. *cithara,* cithara; see CITHARA, and obsolete E. *gittern* (< ME < OFr. *guiterne* < Lat. *cithara*).]

cit•y (sĭt′ē) *n., pl.* **-ies 1.** A center of population, commerce, and culture; a town of significant size and importance. **2a.** An incorporated municipality in the United States with definite boundaries and legal powers set forth in a charter granted by the state. **b.** A Canadian municipality of high rank, usu. determined by population. **c.** A large incorporated town in Great Britain, usu. the seat of a bishop, with its title conferred by the Crown. **3.** The inhabitants of a city. **4.** An ancient Greek city-state. [ME *cite* < OFr. < Lat. *cīvitās* < *cīvis,* citizen. See **kei-**[1] in App.]

city council *n.* The governing body of a city.

city editor *n.* **1.** A newspaper editor responsible for local news and reporters' assignments. **2.** *Chiefly British* A newspaper editor responsible for commercial and financial news.

city father *n.* A municipal official, such as a council member.

city hall *n.* **1.** The building housing municipal government offices. **2.** The municipal government, esp. its officials. **3.** *Slang* An entrenched and insensitive bureaucracy, esp. of a city.

city manager *n.* An administrator appointed by a city council to manage the affairs of the municipality.

cit•y•scape (sĭt′ē-skāp′) *n.* **1.** An artistic representation of a city. **2.** A city or section of a city regarded as a scene.

city slicker *n. Informal* A person with the sophistication and dress traditionally linked by rural people with the city.

cit•y-state (sĭt′ē-stāt′) *n.* A sovereign state consisting of an inde-

cirrus

cittern
detail from *The Concert,* by Pietro Paolini (1603–81)

ă	pat	oi	boy
ā	pay	ou	out
âr	care	o͝o	took
ä	father	o͞o	boot
ĕ	pet	ŭ	cut
ē	be	ûr	urge
ĭ	pit	th	thin
ī	pie	*th*	this
îr	pier	hw	which
ŏ	pot	zh	vision
ō	toe	ə	about,
ô	paw		item

Stress marks:
′ (primary);
′ (secondary), as in
lexicon (lĕk′sĭ-kŏn′)

pendent city and its surrounding territory.

cit·y·wide (sĭt′ē-wīd′) *adj.* Including or occurring in all parts of a city: *citywide busing; a citywide strike.*

Ci·u·dad Bo·lí·var (sē′ōō-däd′ bō-lē′vär, syōō-) A city of E-central Venezuela on the Orinoco R. SE of Caracas; formerly known as Angostura. Pop. 253,112.

Ciudad Gua·ya·na (gwä-yä′nə, gwä-yä′nä) A city of E Venezuela on the Orinoco R.; founded 1961. Pop. 523,578.

Ciudad Juá·rez also **Juárez** (wär′ĕz, hwä′rĕs) A city of N Mexico on the Rio Grande opposite El Paso TX. Pop. 544,496.

Ciudad Tru·jil·lo (trōō-hē′yō) See **Santo Domingo.**

civ·et (sĭv′ĭt) *n.* **1.** Any of various carnivorous catlike mammals of the family Viverridae of Africa and Asia, having anal scent glands that secrete a fluid with a musky odor. **2.** The thick yellowish fluid so secreted, used in perfumes. **3.** The fur of one of these mammals. [Fr. *civette* < OFr. < Catalan *civetta* < Med.Lat. *zibethus* < Ar. *zabād*, civet perfume.]

civ·ic (sĭv′ĭk) *adj.* Of, relating to, or belonging to a city, a citizen, or citizenship; municipal or civil. [Lat. *cīvicus* < *cīvis*, citizen. See **kei-¹** in App.] —**civ′i·cal·ly** *adv.*

civ·ics (sĭv′ĭks) *n.* (*used with a sing. verb*) The branch of political science that deals with civic affairs and the rights and duties of citizens.

civ·ies (sĭv′ēz) *pl.n. Slang* Variant of **civvies.**

civ·il (sĭv′əl) *adj.* **1.** Of, relating to, or befitting a citizen or citizens: *civil duties.* **2.** Of or relating to citizens and their interrelations with one another or with the state. **3.** Of ordinary citizens or ordinary community life as distinguished from the military or the ecclesiastical. **4.** Of or in accordance with organized society; civilized. **5.** Sufficiently observing or befitting accepted social usages; not rude. See Syns at **polite. 6.** Legally recognized as a division of time: *a civil year.* **7.** *Law* Relating to the rights of private individuals and legal proceedings concerning these rights, as distinguished from criminal, military, or international regulations or proceedings. [ME < Lat. *cīvīlis* < *cīvis*, citizen. See **kei-¹** in App.] —**civ′il·ly** *adv.*

civil death *n.* Total deprivation of civil rights, often resulting from conviction for treason or a felony.

civil defense *n.* Protective measures for civilian volunteers to take in the event of natural disaster or enemy attack.

civil disobedience *n.* Refusal to obey civil laws in order to induce governmental change, characterized by nonviolence.

civil engineer *n.* An engineer trained in the design and construction of public works and other large facilities. —**civil engineering** *n.*

civet
African civet
Civettictis civetta

ci·vil·ian (sĭ-vĭl′yən) *n.* **1.** A person following the pursuits of civil life, esp. one who is not an active member of the military or police. **2.** A specialist in Roman or civil law. ❖ *adj.* Of or relating to civilians or civil life. [ME, civil law judge < OFr. *civilien* < *civil*, civil < Lat. *cīvīlis.* See CIVIL.]

ci·vil·ian·ize (sĭ-vĭl′yə-nīz′) *tr.v.* **-ized, -iz·ing, -iz·es** To convert to civilian operation or control. —**ci·vil′ian·i·za′tion** (-ĭ-zā′shən) *n.*

ci·vil·i·ty (sĭ-vĭl′ĭ-tē) *n., pl.* **-ties 1.** Courteous behavior; politeness. **2.** A courteous act or utterance.

civ·i·li·za·tion (sĭv′ə-lĭ-zā′shən) *n.* **1.** An advanced state of development in human society, marked by progress in the arts and sciences, the extensive use of record-keeping, including writing, and complex political and social institutions. **2.** The type of culture and society developed by a particular nation or region or in a particular epoch. **3.** The act or process of civilizing or reaching a civilized state. **4.** Cultural or intellectual refinement; good taste. **5.** Modern society with its conveniences.

civ·i·lize (sĭv′ə-līz′) *tr.v.* **-lized, -liz·ing, -liz·es 1.** To raise from barbarism to civilization. **2.** To educate in matters of culture and refinement; polish. —**civ′i·liz′a·ble** *adj.* —**civ′i·liz′er** *n.*

civ·i·lized (sĭv′ə-līzd′) *adj.* **1.** Having a highly developed society and culture. **2.** Showing evidence of moral and intellectual advancement; humane, ethical, and reasonable. **3.** Marked by refined taste and manners; cultured; polished.

civil law *n.* **1.** The body of laws of a state or nation dealing with the rights of private citizens. **2.** The law of ancient Rome as embodied in the Justinian code, esp. that which applied to private citizens. **3.** A system of law having its origin in Roman law, as opposed to common law or canon law.

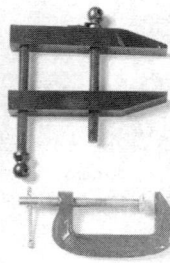

clamp
top: parallel clamp
bottom: C-clamp

civil libertarian *n.* One actively concerned with protecting those rights guaranteed to the individual by law or principle.

civil lib·er·ties (lĭb′ər-tēz) *pl.n.* Fundamental individual rights, such as freedom of speech and religion, protected by law against unwarranted governmental or other interference.

civil marriage *n.* A marriage ceremony by a civil official.

civil rights *pl.n.* The rights belonging to an individual by virtue of citizenship, esp. those guaranteed by the 13th and 14th Amendments to the US Constitution and by subsequent acts of Congress, including civil liberties and freedom from discrimination. ❖ *adj.* or **civ·il-rights** (sĭv′əl-rīts′) **1.** Of or relating to civil rights. **2.** Of or relating to a political movement, esp. during the 1950s and 1960s, devoted to securing equal treatment of minority groups. —**civil righter** *n.*

civil servant *n.* A person employed in the civil service.

civil service *n.* **1.** Those branches of public service that are not

legislative, judicial, or military and in which employment is usu. based on competitive examination. **2.** The entire body of persons employed by the civil branches of a government.

civil union *n.* A legal union of a same-sex couple, sanctioned by civil authority.

civil war *n.* **1.** A war between factions or regions of the same country. **2.** A state of hostility or conflict between elements within an organization. **3. Civil War** The war in the United States between the Union and the Confederacy from 1861 to 1865. **4. Civil War** The war in England between the Parliamentarians and the Royalists from 1642 to 1648.

civ·vies also **civ·ies** (sĭv′ēz) *pl.n. Slang* Civilian clothes.

CJ *abbr.* chief justice

ck. *abbr.* **1.** cask **2.** check

cl *abbr.* centiliter

Cl The symbol for the element **chlorine.**

cl. *abbr.* **1.** class **2.** classification **3.** clause **4.** clearance

c.l. *abbr.* **1.** carload **2.** civil law **3.** common law

clab·ber (klăb′ər) *n. Chiefly Southern, Midland, & Western US* Sour, curdled milk. ❖ *tr. & intr.v.* **-bered, -ber·ing, -bers** To curdle. [Short for BONNYCLABBER.]

clack (klăk) *v.* **clacked, clack·ing, clacks** —*intr.* **1.** To make an abrupt sharp sound. **2.** To chatter thoughtlessly or at length. **3.** To cackle or cluck, as a hen. —*tr.* To cause to make an abrupt sharp sound. ❖ *n.* **1.** A clacking sound. **2.** Something that makes a clacking sound. **3.** Thoughtless prolonged talk; chatter. [ME *clakken* < ON *klaka*, of imit. orig.] —**clack′er** *n.*

clack valve *n.* A hinged valve that permits fluids to flow in only one direction and clacks when the valve closes.

Clac·to·ni·an (klăk-tō′nē-ən) *adj.* Of or relating to a Lower Paleolithic tool culture of northwest Europe. [After Clacton, an urban district of SE England.]

clad¹ (klăd) *tr.v.* **clad, clad·ding, clads 1.** To sheathe or cover (a metal) with a metal. **2.** To cover with a protective or insulating layer of other material. [Back-formation < CLADDING.]

clad² (klăd) *v.* A past tense and a past participle of **clothe.**

clad·dagh (klä′də) *n.* A ring with a raised design of two hands clasping a crowned heart, usu. given as a token of love or friendship. [After *Claddagh*, a fishing village and suburb of Galway.]

clad·ding (klăd′ĭng) *n.* **1.** A metal coating bonded onto another metal under high pressure and temperature. **2.** The process of forming such a coating. **3.** A protective or insulating layer fixed to the outside of a building or another structure. [Earlier, clothing, poss. < CLAD².]

clade (klād) *n.* A group of organisms sharing homologous features derived from a common ancestor. [< Gk. *klados*, branch.]

cla·dist (klăd′ĭst, klā′dĭst) *n.* One who classifies organisms according to the principles of cladistics.

cla·dis·tics (klə-dĭs′tĭks) *n.* (*used with a sing. verb*) A system of organism classification based on phylogeny. —**cla·dis′tic, cla·dis′ti·cal** *adj.* —**cla·dis′ti·cal·ly** *adv.*

clad·oc·er·an (klə-dŏs′ər-ən) *n.* Any of various small, mostly freshwater crustaceans of the order Cladocera. [< NLat. *Cladocera*, order name : Gk. *klados*, branch + *keras*, horn; see **ker-¹** in App.] —**clad·oc′er·an** *adj.*

clad·ode (klăd′ōd′) *n.* See **cladophyll.** [NLat. *cladōdium* < L.Gk. *kladōdēs*, many-branched < Gk. *klados*, branch.] —**cla·do′di·al** (klə-dō′dē-əl) *adj.*

clad·o·gen·e·sis (klăd′ō-jĕn′ĭ-sĭs) *n.* The evolutionary change resulting when taxa branch off from common ancestral lineages. [Gk. *klados*, branch + –GENESIS.] —**clad′o·ge·net′ic** (-jə-nĕt′ĭk) *adj.* —**clad′o·ge·net′i·cal·ly** *adv.*

clad·o·gram (klăd′ə-grăm′, klā′də-) *n.* A branching treelike diagram showing the phylogenetic relationships of specific species of organisms and indicating points of evolutionary diversification. [Gk. *klados*, branch + –GRAM.]

clad·o·phyll (klăd′ə-fĭl′) *n.* A photosynthetic branch or portion of a stem that resembles and functions as a leaf, as in the asparagus. [Gk. *klados*, twig + –PHYLL.]

claim (klām) *tr.v.* **claimed, claim·ing, claims 1.** To demand, ask for, or take as one's own or one's right: *claim a reward.* See Syns at **demand. 2.** To take in a violent manner as if by right: *a hurricane claimed two lives.* **3.** To state to be true, esp. when open to question; maintain. **4.** To deserve or call for; require: *problems that claim attention.* ❖ *n.* **1.** A demand for something as rightful or due. **2.** A basis for demanding something; a title or right. **3.** Something claimed in a formal or legal manner, esp. a tract of public land staked out by a miner or homesteader. **4a.** A demand for payment in accordance with an insurance policy or other formal arrangement. **b.** The sum of money demanded. **5.** A statement of something as a fact; an assertion of truth. —*idiom:* **lay claim to** To assert one's right to or ownership of. [ME *claimen* < OFr. *clamer, claim-* < Lat. *clāmāre*, to call. See **kelə-** in App.] —**claim′a·ble** *adj.* —**claim′er** *n.*

claim·ant (klā′mənt) *n.* A party that makes a claim.

Clair (klâr), **René** Orig. René Chomette. 1898–1981. French filmmaker whose works include *Sous les Toits de Paris* (1929).

clair·au·di·ence (klâr-ô′dē-əns) *n.* The supposed power to hear things outside the range of normal perception. [CLAIR(VOYANCE) + AUDIENCE.] —**clair·au′di·ent** *adj. & n.*

clair de lune (klâr′ ə lōōn′) *n.* **1.** A pale grayish-blue glaze applied to various kinds of Chinese porcelain. **2.** The color of such a glaze. [Fr. : *clair*, light + *de*, of + *lune*, moon.]

claire-ob•scure (klâr′əb-skyo͝or′) *n.* See **chiaroscuro.** [Fr. *clair-obscur*, transl. of Ital. *chiaroscuro*.]

clair•voy•ance (klâr-voi′əns) *n.* **1.** The supposed power to see what cannot be perceived by the senses. **2.** Acute intuitive insight or perceptiveness.

clair•voy•ant (klâr-voi′ənt) *adj.* Of, relating to, or having clairvoyance. ❖ *n.* One possessing the supposed power of clairvoyance. [Fr. : *clair*, clear (< Lat. *clārus*; see **kelə-** in App.) + *voyant*, pr. part. of *voir*, to see (< Lat. *vidēre*; see **weid-** in App.).]

clam[1] (klăm) *n.* **1a.** Any of various usu. burrowing marine and freshwater bivalve mollusks of the class Pelecypoda, some of which are edible. **b.** The soft body of an edible clam. **2.** *Informal* A close-mouthed person. **3.** *Slang* A dollar. ❖ *intr.v.* **clammed, clam•ming, clams** To hunt clams. ***—phrasal verb:* clam up** *Informal* To refuse to talk. [< obsolete *clam-shell*, shell that clamps, clam < CLAM[2].] **—clam′mer** *n.*

clam[2] (klăm) *n.* A clamp or vise. [ME < OE *clam*, bond.]

cla•mant (klā′mənt, klăm′ənt) *adj.* **1.** Clamorous; loud. **2.** Demanding attention; pressing. [Lat. *clāmāns*, *clāmant-*, pr. part. of *clāmāre*, to cry out. See **kelə-** in App.] **—cla′mant•ly** *adv.*

clam•bake (klăm′bāk′) *n.* **1.** A seashore picnic where clams, fish, corn, and other foods are traditionally baked on heated stones covered with seaweed. **2.** *Informal* A gathering, esp. a noisy and lively one.

clam•ber (klăm′bər, klăm′ər) *intr.v.* **-bered, -ber•ing, -bers** To climb with difficulty, esp. on all fours; scramble. ❖ *n.* A difficult, awkward climb. [ME *clambren*, prob. freq. of *climben*, to climb. See CLIMB.] **—clam′ber•er** *n.*

clam•ber•ing (klăm′bər-ĭng, klăm′ər-) *adj.* Of or relating to a plant, often one without tendrils, that sprawls or climbs.

clam dig•gers or **clam•dig•gers** (klăm′dĭg′ərz) *pl.n.* Casual pants in a midcalf length.

clam-flat (klăm′flăt′) *n. New England* A level stretch of soft tidal mud where clams burrow.

clam•my (klăm′ē) *adj.* **-mi•er, -mi•est 1.** Disagreeably moist, sticky, and cold to the touch: *a clammy handshake.* **2.** Damp and unpleasant: *clammy weather.* **3.** Uneasy; apprehensive. [ME, sticky, prob. < *clam* (< OE, mud, clay) or < MLGer. *klam*, stickiness.] **—clam′mi•ly** *adv.* **—clam′mi•ness** *n.*

clam•or (klăm′ər) *n.* **1.** A loud outcry; a hubbub. **2.** A vehement expression of discontent or protest. **3.** A loud sustained noise. See Syns at **noise.** ❖ *v.* **-ored, -or•ing, -ors** *—intr.* **1.** To make a loud sustained noise or outcry. **2.** To make insistent demands or complaints. *—tr.* **1.** To exclaim insistently and noisily. **2.** To influence or force by clamoring. [ME *clamour* < OFr. < Lat. *clāmor*, shout < *clāmāre*, to cry out. See **kelə-** in App.] **—clam′or•er** *n.*

clam•or•ous (klăm′ər-əs) *adj.* **1.** Making or marked by outcry or sustained din. **2.** Insistently demanding attention; importunate. **—clam′or•ous•ly** *adv.*

clam•our (klăm′ər) *n. & v. Chiefly British* Variant of **clamor.**

clamp (klămp) *n.* **1.** Any of various devices used to join, grip, support, or compress mechanical or structural parts. **2.** Any of various tools with opposing sides or parts for bracing objects or holding them together. ❖ *tr.v.* **clamped, clamp•ing, clamps 1.** To fasten, grip, or support with or as if with a clamp. **2.** To establish by authority; impose. ***—phrasal verb:* clamp down** To become more strict or repressive; impose controls. [ME < MDu. *klampe*.]

clamp•down (klămp′doun′) *n.* An imposing of restrictions.

clamp•er (klăm′pər) *n.* One that clamps, esp. a spiked plate attached to the sole of a shoe to prevent slipping on ice.

clam•shell (klăm′shĕl′) *n.* **1.** The shell of a clam. **2.** Any of various devices with two hinged jaws, used to dredge or dig.

clam•worm (klăm′wûrm′) *n.* Any of various segmented burrowing marine worms of the genus *Nereis*, used as bait.

clan (klăn) *n.* **1.** A traditional social unit in the Scottish Highlands, consisting of families claiming a common ancestor and following the same hereditary chieftain. **2.** A tribal division tracing descent from a common ancestor. **3.** A large group of relatives, friends, or associates. [ME < Sc. Gael. *clann*, family < OIr. *cland*, offspring < Lat. *planta*, sprout.]

clan•des•tine (klăn-dĕs′tĭn) *adj.* Kept or done in secret, often to conceal an illicit or improper purpose. [Lat. *clandestīnus*, prob. blend of **clam-de*, secretly (< *clam*; see **kel-** in App.) and *intestīnus*, internal; see INTESTINE.] **—clan•des′tine•ly** *adv.* **—clan•des′tine•ness, clan′des•tin′i•ty** *n.*

clang (klăng) *n.* **1.** A loud, resonant, metallic sound. **2.** The strident call of a crane or goose. ❖ *intr. & tr.v.* **clanged, clang•ing, clangs** To make or cause a clang. [Prob. < Lat. *clangere*, to ring, clang.]

clang•er (klăng′ər) *n. Chiefly British* A blunder; a faux pas.

clan•gor (klăng′ər, klăng′gər) *n.* **1.** A clang or repeated clanging. **2.** A loud racket; a din. ❖ *intr.v.* **-gored, -gor•ing, -gors** To make a clangor. [Lat. < *clangere*, to clang.] **—clan′gor•ous** *adj.* **—clan′gor•ous•ly** *adv.*

clan•gour (klăng′ər, klăng′gər) *n. & v. Chiefly British* Variant of **clangor.**

clank (klăngk) *n.* A sharp, hard metallic sound that is not resonant. ❖ *intr.v.* **clanked, clank•ing, clanks** To make a clank. [Prob. imit.] **—clank′y** *adj.*

clan•nish (klăn′ĭsh) *adj.* **1.** Of, relating to, or characteristic of a clan. **2.** Inclined to cling together as a group and exclude outsiders. **—clan′nish•ly** *adv.* **—clan′nish•ness** *n.*

clans•man (klănz′mən) *n.* A man in a clan.

clans•wom•an (klănz′wo͝om′ən) *n.* A woman in a clan.

clap[1] (klăp) *v.* **clapped, clap•ping, claps** *—intr.* **1.** To strike the palms of the hands together with a sudden explosive sound. **2.** To come together suddenly with a sharp sound. *—tr.* **1.** To strike together with a sharp sound, as one hard surface on another. **2.** To strike (the hands) together with an abrupt loud sound, usu. repeatedly. **3.** To strike lightly but firmly with the open hand, as in greeting. **4.** To put or place quickly and firmly. **5.** To arrange hastily: *clapped together a plan.* ❖ *n.* **1.** The act or sound of clapping the hands. **2.** A sudden, loud, explosive sound. **3.** A sharp blow with the open hand; a slap. **4.** *Obsolete* A sudden stroke of fortune, esp. of bad luck. [ME *clappen* < OE *clæppan*, to throb, and < ON *klappa*, to clap, pat.]

clap[2] (klăp) *n. Vulgar Slang* Gonorrhea. [Prob. < obsolete Fr. *clapoir*, bubo < OFr. *clapier*, brothel < O Provençal, rabbit warren < *clap*, heap of stones, perh. of Celt. orig.]

clap•board (klăb′ərd, klăp′bôrd′, -bōrd′) *n.* A long narrow board with one edge thicker than the other, overlapped to cover the outer walls of frame structures. ❖ *tr.v.* **-board•ed, -board•ing, -boards** To cover with clapboards. [Partial transl. of Du. *klaphout* : *klappen*, to split, crack + MDu. *holt*, board.]

clap•per (klăp′ər) *n.* **1.** One who applauds. **2.** The tongue of a bell. **3.** *Slang* The tongue of a garrulous person. **4. clappers** Two flat wood pieces held in the fingers and struck rhythmically.

clapper rail *n.* A henlike North American bird *(Rallus longirostris)* of coastal marshes with brown plumage and a long bill.

clap skate *n.* A speed skate with the blade attached by a hinge at the heel, allowing greater efficiency by keeping the full length of the blade on the ice when the heel is raised.

clap•trap (klăp′trăp′) *n.* Pretentious, insincere, or empty language. [Obsolete *claptrap*, a theatrical trick to win applause : CLAP[1] + TRAP[1].]

claque (klăk) *n.* **1.** A group hired to applaud. **2.** A group of fawning admirers. [Fr. < *claquer*, to clap, of imit. orig.]

clar•ence (klăr′əns) *n.* A four-wheeled closed carriage with seats for four passengers. [After the Duke of *Clarence* (1765–1837), later William IV of England.]

Clar•en•don (klăr′ən-dən), 1st Earl of. See Edward **Hyde.**

Clare of As•si•si (klâr; ə-sē′zē, -sē, ə-sĭs′ē), Saint. 1194–1253. Italian religious leader who founded the Poor Clares with Saint Francis of Assisi.

clar•et (klăr′ĭt) *n.* **1a.** A dry red wine produced in the Bordeaux region of France. **b.** A similar wine made elsewhere. **2.** A dark or grayish purplish red to dark purplish pink. [ME, light-colored wine < OFr. *(vin) claret*, dim. of *clair*, clear < Lat. *clārus.* See CLEAR.]

clar•i•fy (klăr′ə-fī′) *v.* **-fied, -fy•ing, -fies** *—tr.* **1.** To make clear or easier to understand; elucidate. **2.** To clear of confusion or uncertainty. **3.** To make clear by removing impurities or solid matter, as by heating gently or filtering. *—intr.* To become clear. [ME *clarifien* < OFr. *clarifier* < LLat. *clārificāre* : Lat. *clārus*, clear; see CLEAR + Lat. *-ficāre*, -fy.] **—clar′i•fi•ca′tion** (-fĭ-kā′shən) *n.* **—clar′i•fi′er** *n.*

clar•i•net (klăr′ə-nĕt′) *n.* A woodwind instrument having a straight cylindrical tube with a flaring bell and a single-reed mouthpiece, played by means of finger holes and keys. [Fr. *clarinette*, fem. dim. of OFr. *clarin, clarion*, clarion; see CLARION, or of Provençal *clarin*, oboe (< O Provençal *clar*, clear < Lat. *clārus*; see CLEAR).] **—clar′i•net′ist, clar′i•net′tist** *n.*

clar•i•on (klăr′ē-ən) *adj.* Loud and clear. ❖ *n. Music* **1.** A medieval trumpet with a shrill clear tone. **2.** Its sound or a similar sound. [ME *clarioun*, a clarion < OFr. *clarion* < Med.Lat. *clāriō*, *clāriōn-* < Lat. *clārus*, clear. See CLEAR.]

clar•i•ty (klăr′ĭ-tē) *n.* **1.** Clearness of appearance. **2.** Clearness of thought or style; lucidity. [ME *clarite*, brightness < Lat. *clāritās*, clearness < *clārus*, clear. See CLEAR.]

Clark (klärk), **Charles Joseph** Known as "Joe." b. 1939. Canadian politician who served as prime minister (1979–80).

Clark, George Rogers 1752–1818. Amer. military leader who led raids on British troops and Native Americans in the Northwest Terr. during the Revolutionary War.

Clark, Kenneth Bancroft b. 1914. Panamanian-born Amer. psychologist who demonstrated the psychological effects of racial segregation and ghetto life.

Clark, Mark Wayne 1896–1984. Amer. general who was commander of United Nations forces in Korea (1952–53).

Clark, William 1770–1838. Amer. explorer who joined Meriwether Lewis in an expedition to the Pacific Ocean (1804–06).

Clarke (klärk), **Arthur Charles** b. 1917. British writer and scientist whose stories of space exploration include *2001: A Space Odyssey* (1968).

Clark Fork A river rising in SW MT and flowing c. 579 km (360 mi) to Pend Oreille Lake in the ID Panhandle.

clark•i•a (klär′kē-ə) *n.* Any of various annual, chiefly western North American plants of the genus *Clarkia.* [NLat. *Clarkia*, genus name, after William CLARK.]

clamshell

clarinet

ă	pat	oi	boy
ā	pay	ou	out
âr	care	o͝o	took
ä	father	o͞o	boot
ĕ	pet	ŭ	cut
ē	be	ûr	urge
ĭ	pit	th	thin
ī	pie	*th*	this
îr	pier	hw	which
ŏ	pot	zh	vision
ō	toe	ə	about, item
ô	paw		

Stress marks:
′ (primary);
′ (secondary), as in
lexicon (lĕk′sĭ-kŏn′)

Clarks·burg (klärks′bûrg′) A city of N WV SSE of Wheeling; an important Union supply base during the Civil War. Pop. 16,743.

Clarks·ville (klärks′vĭl′) A city of NW TN on the Cumberland and Red rivers NW of Nashville. Pop. 103,455.

clar·y (klâr′ē) *n., pl.* **-ies** A stout aromatic Mediterranean herb (*Salvia sclarea*) in the mint family, yielding an essential oil used as a flavoring and in perfumery. [ME *clare* < Med.Lat. *sclarea* and < OE *slaria.*]

clash (klăsh) *v.* **clashed, clash·ing, clash·es** —*intr.* **1.** To collide with a loud, harsh, usu. metallic noise: *cymbals clashing.* **2.** To come into conflict; be in opposition. **3.** To create an unpleasant visual impression when placed together. —*tr.* To strike together with a loud, harsh, metallic noise. ❖ *n.* **1.** A loud harsh noise, as of two metal objects in collision. **2.** A conflict, as between opposing ideas. **3.** An encounter between hostile forces; a battle or skirmish. [Imit.]

clasp (klăsp) *n.* **1.** A fastening, such as a hook, used to hold two or more objects or parts together. **2a.** An embrace or hug. **b.** A grip or grasp of the hand. **3.** A small metal bar or other device attached to a military decoration to indicate the action or service for which it was awarded or an additional award of the same medal. ❖ *tr.v.* **clasped, clasp·ing, clasps** **1.** To fasten with or as if with a clasp. **2.** To embrace tightly. **3.** To grip firmly in or with the hand; grasp. [ME *claspe,* prob. ult. < OE *clyppan,* to grasp, hold.]

clasp·er (klăs′pər) *n.* **1.** One that clasps. **2.** Any of the appendages of certain male insects and crustaceans that hold the female during copulation. **3.** A posterior extension on male elasmobranch pelvic fins, used in sperm transmission.

clasp·ing (klăs′pĭng) *adj. Botany* Being a leaf whose base partially or completely surrounds a stem.

clasp knife *n.* A pocketknife with a folding blade.

class (klăs) *n.* **1.** A set, group, or configuration containing members seen as having certain traits in common; a kind or category. **2.** A division based on quality, rank, or grade, as: **a.** A grade of mail: *sent third class.* **b.** A quality of accommodation on public transport: *tourist class.* **3a.** A social stratum whose members share certain economic, social, or cultural characteristics. **b.** Social rank or caste, esp. high rank. **c.** *Informal* Elegance of style, taste, and manner. **4a.** A group of students who are taught together because they have roughly the same level of academic development. **b.** A group of people who have the same year of academic graduation. **c.** A group of students who meet regularly to study the same subject. **d.** The period when such a group meets. **5.** *Biology* A taxonomic category ranking below a phylum or division and above an order. See table at **taxonomy. 6.** *Statistics* An interval in a frequency distribution. **7.** *Linguistics* A group of words belonging to the same grammatical category that share a particular set of inflections or other morphological properties. ❖ *tr.v.* **classed, class·ing, class·es** To arrange, group, or rate according to qualities or characteristics; assign to a class; classify. [Fr. *classe* < Lat. *classis,* class of citizens. See **kelə-** in App.]

class action *n.* A lawsuit brought on behalf of a large group with a common interest. —**class′-ac′tion** (klăs′ăk′shən) *adj.*

class-con·scious (klăs′kŏn′shəs) *adj.* **1.** Aware of belonging to a particular socioeconomic class. **2.** Supportive of class solidarity. —**class′-con′scious·ness** *n.*

clas·ses (klăs′ēz) *n.* Plural of **classis.**

clas·sic (klăs′ĭk) *adj.* **1a.** Belonging to the highest rank or class. **b.** Serving as the established model or standard. **c.** Having lasting significance or worth; enduring. **2a.** Adhering or conforming to established standards and principles. **b.** Of a well-known type; typical. **3.** Of or characteristic of the literature, art, and culture of ancient Greece and Rome; classical. **4a.** Formal, refined, and restrained in style. **b.** Simple and harmonious; elegant. **5.** Having historical or literary associations. ❖ *n.* **1.** An artist, author, or work considered to be of the highest rank or excellence. **2.** A work recognized as definitive in its field. **3a.** A literary work of ancient Greece or Rome. **b. classics** The languages and literature of ancient Greece and Rome. **c.** One that is of the highest rank or class. **4.** A typical or traditional example. **5.** *Informal* A superior or unusual example of its kind. **6.** A traditional event, esp. a major annual sporting event.

clas·si·cal (klăs′ĭ-kəl) *adj.* **1a.** Of or relating to the ancient Greeks and Romans, esp. their art, architecture, and literature. **b.** Conforming to the artistic and literary models of ancient Greece and Rome. **c.** Versed in the classics. **2.** Of or relating to the most artistically developed stage of a civilization. **3.** *Music* **a.** Of or relating to European music during the latter half of the 18th and the early 19th centuries. **b.** Of or relating to music in the educated European tradition, as opposed to popular or folk music. **4.** Of, relating to, or being a variety of a language that is epitomized by a prestigious body of literature. **5a.** Standard and authoritative rather than new or experimental. **b.** Well-known; classic. **6.** Of or relating to physics that can be described without the use of quantum mechanics or relativity. **7.** Relating to or consisting of studies in the humanities and general sciences. —**clas′si·cal′i·ty** (-kăl′ĭ-tē), **clas′si·cal·ness** *n.* —**clas′si·cal·ly** *adv.*

Classical Chinese *n.* The written form of Chinese from about the fifth century B.C. to the end of the Han dynasty in A.D. 220.

classical conditioning *n. Psychology* A process of behavior modification by which a subject comes to respond to a previously neutral stimulus repeatedly presented along with an unconditioned stimulus that elicits the desired response.

clas·si·cism (klăs′ĭ-sĭz′əm) also **clas·si·cal·ism** (-kə-lĭz′əm) *n.* **1.** Aesthetic attitudes and principles manifested in the art, architecture, and literature of ancient Greece and Rome and marked by emphasis on form, simplicity, proportion, and restraint. **2.** Adherence to such aesthetic values. **3.** Classical scholarship. **4.** A Greek or Latin expression.

clas·si·cist (klăs′ĭ-sĭst) *n.* **1.** One versed in the classics; a classical scholar. **2.** An adherent of classicism. **3.** An advocate of the study of ancient Greek and Latin.

clas·si·cize (klăs′ĭ-sīz′) *v.* **-cized, -ciz·ing, -ciz·es** —*tr.* To make classic or classical. —*intr.* To conform to classic style.

clas·si·fi·ca·tion (klăs′ə-fĭ-kā′shən) *n.* **1.** The act or result of classifying. **2.** A category or class. **3.** *Biology* The systematic grouping of organisms into categories on the basis of evolutionary or structural relationships between them; taxonomy. —**clas′si·fi·ca·to′ri·ly** (klăs′ə-fĭ-kə-tôr′ə-lē, -tōr′-, klə-sĭf′ĭ-) *adv.* —**clas′si·fi·ca·to′ry** (klăs′ə-fĭ-kə-tôr′ē, -tōr′ē, klə-sĭf′ĭ-klăs′ə-fĭ-kā′tə-rē) *adj.*

clas·si·fied (klăs′ə-fīd′) *adj.* **1.** Arranged in classes or categories. **2.** Available to authorized persons only, as for security.

classified advertisement *n.* A newspaper or magazine advertisement, usu. brief and in small type, printed with similar advertisements.

clas·si·fi·er (klăs′ə-fī′ər) *n.* A word or morpheme used in some languages in certain contexts, such as counting, that indicates the semantic class of an item.

clas·si·fy (klăs′ə-fī′) *tr.v.* **-fied, -fy·ing, -fies** **1.** To arrange or organize by class or category. **2.** To designate (a document, for example) as confidential or secret. —**clas′si·fi′a·ble** *adj.*

clas·sis (klăs′ĭs) *n., pl.* **-ses** (-ēz) **1.** A local governing body of pastors and elders in some Reformed churches. **2.** The district or churches under a classis. [Lat., class of citizens. See CLASS.]

class·ism (klăs′ĭz′əm) *n.* Bias based on social or economic class. —**class′ist** *adj. & n.*

class·less (klăs′lĭs) *adj.* **1.** Lacking social or economic class distinctions. **2.** Of no particular social or economic class.

class·mate (klăs′māt′) *n.* One in the same school class.

clas·son (klăs′ŏn) *n.* Either of two massless bosons, the photon and the graviton, that are quanta of the two classical fields, electromagnetic and gravitational. [CLASS(ICAL) + (BOS)ON.]

class·room (klăs′rōōm′, -rŏŏm′) *n.* A room or place esp. in a school in which classes are conducted.

class·y (klăs′ē) *adj.* **-i·er, -i·est** *Informal* Highly stylish; elegant. —**class′i·ness** *n.*

clast (klăst) *n.* A rock fragment or grain resulting from the mechanical weathering of larger rocks. [< Gk. *klastos,* broken < *klān,* to break.]

clas·tic (klăs′tĭk) *adj.* **1.** Separable into parts or having removable parts. **2.** *Geology* Made up of fragments of preexisting rock; fragmental. [< Gk. *klastos,* broken. See CLAST.] —**clas′tic** *n.*

clath·rate (klăth′rāt′) *adj.* **1.** *Biology* Having a latticelike structure or appearance. **2.** *Chemistry* Of or relating to inclusion complexes in which molecules of one substance are completely enclosed within the crystal structure of another. ❖ *n. Chemistry* A clathrate compound. [Lat. *clāthrātus,* p. part. of *clāthrāre,* to furnish with a lattice < *clāthrī, clātra,* lattice < Gk. *klēithra, klāithra,* pl. of *kleithron,* door bar < *kleiein,* to close.]

clat·ter (klăt′ər) *v.* **-tered, -ter·ing, -ters** —*intr.* **1.** To make a rattling sound. **2.** To move with a rattling sound. **3.** To talk rapidly and noisily; chatter. —*tr.* To cause to make a rattling sound. ❖ *n.* **1.** A rattling sound: *the clatter of dishes.* **2.** A loud disturbance; a racket. **3.** Noisy talk; chatter. [ME *clateren* < OE **clatrian.*] —**clat′ter·er** *n.*

Clau·del (klō-dĕl′), **Camille** 1864–1943. French sculptor best known for her bust models of Auguste Rodin (1888–92).

Claudel, Paul Louis Charles 1868–1955. French diplomat and writer whose works include poetry and plays.

clau·di·ca·tion (klô′dĭ-kā′shən) *n.* A halt or lameness in a person's walk. [Ult. < Lat. *claudicātiō, claudicātiōn-* < *claudicātus,* p. part. of *claudicāre,* to limp < *claudus,* lame.]

Clau·di·us I (klô′dē-əs) In full Tiberius Claudius Drusus Nero Germanicus. 10 B.C.–A.D. 54. Emperor of Rome (A.D. 41–54) who was poisoned by his wife, Agrippina, after her son Nero was named as heir.

Claudius II In full Marcus Aurelius Claudius Gothicus. A.D. 214–270. Emperor of Rome (268–270) who defeated the Goths in 269.

clause (klôz) *n.* **1.** *Grammar* A group of words containing a subject and a predicate and forming part of a compound or complex sentence. **2.** A distinct article, stipulation, or provision in a document. [ME < OFr. < Med.Lat. *clausa,* close of a rhetorical period < fem. of Lat. *clausus,* p. part. of *claudere,* to close.] —**claus′al** (klô′zəl) *adj.*

Clau·se·witz (klou′zə-vĭts), **Karl von** 1780–1831. Prussian army officer and military theorist who proposed the doctrines of total war and war as an instrument of policy.

Clau·si·us (klou′zē-ōōs), **Rudolf** 1822–88. German mathematician and physicist noted for his contributions to the laws of thermodynamics.

Claudius I
on a Roman silver coin

claus•tral (klô′strəl) *adj.* Variant of **cloistral.**
claus•tro•pho•bi•a (klô′strə-fō′bē-ə) *n.* An abnormal fear of being in narrow or enclosed spaces. [Lat. *claustrum,* enclosed place; see CLOISTER + -PHOBIA.] **—claus′tro•phobe′** *n.*
claus•tro•pho•bic (klô′strə-fō′bĭk) *adj.* **1a.** Relating to or suffering from claustrophobia. **b.** Uncomfortably closed or hemmed in. **2.** Tending to induce claustrophobia; uncomfortably confined or crowded. **—claus′tro•pho′bi•cal•ly** *adv.*
cla•vate (klā′vāt′) *adj. Biology* Having one end thickened; club-shaped. [< Lat. *clāva,* club.] **—cla′vate′ly** *adv.*
clave[1] (klāv) *v. Archaic* A past tense of **cleave**[1].
clave[2] (klāv) *v. Archaic* A past tense of **cleave**[2].
clave[3] *n.* **1.** One of a pair of cylindrical hardwood sticks beaten together as a percussion instrument. **2.** A syncopated two-bar musical pattern. [Am.Sp. < Sp., keystone < Lat. *clāvis,* key.]
cla•ver (klā′vər) *Scots intr.v.* **-vered, -ver•ing, -vers** To gossip or talk idly. ❖ *n.* Gossip; idle talk. [Perh. of Celt. orig.]
clav•i•chord (klăv′ĭ-kôrd′) *n.* An early keyboard instrument with a soft sound produced by small brass wedges striking horizontal strings. [ME *clavicord* < Med.Lat. *clāvichordium* : Lat. *clāvis,* key + Lat. *chorda,* string; see CORD.] **—clav′i•chord′ist** *n.*
clav•i•cle (klăv′ĭ-kəl) *n.* **1.** Either of two slender bones in humans that extend from the manubrium of the sternum to the acromion of the scapula. **2.** One of the bones of the pectoral girdle in many vertebrates. [NLat. *clāvīcula* < Lat., dim. of *clāvis,* key (< its shape).] **—cla•vic′u•lar** (klə-vĭk′yə-lər) *adj.* **—cla•vic′u•late′** (-lāt′) *adj.*
cla•vier (klə-vîr′, klā′vē-ər, klăv′ē-) *n. Music* **1.** A keyboard. **2.** A stringed keyboard instrument, as a clavichord. [Ger. *Klavier* < Fr. *clavier* < OFr., key-bearer < Lat. *clāvis,* key.]
claw (klô) *n.* **1.** A sharp, curved, horny structure on the toe of a mammal, reptile, or bird. **2a.** A chela or similar pincerlike structure on the end of a limb of a crustacean or other arthropod. **b.** A limb terminating in such a structure. **3.** Something that resembles a claw. **4.** *Botany* The narrow basal part of certain petals or sepals. ❖ *tr. & intr.v.* **clawed, claw•ing, claws** To scratch, dig, tear, or pull with or as if with claws. [ME *clawe* < OE *clawu.*] **—clawed** *adj.*
claw hammer *n.* **1.** A hammer having a head with one end forked for removing nails. **2.** *Informal* A tailcoat.
claw hatchet *n.* A hatchet having one end of the head forked.
clay (klā) *n.* **1a.** A fine-grained earthy material that is plastic when wet and hardens when heated, consisting primarily of hydrated silicates of aluminum and used for bricks, tiles, and pottery. **b.** A hardening or nonhardening similar material used for modeling. **2.** *Geology* A sedimentary material with grains less than 0.002 millimeter in diameter. **3.** Moist, sticky earth. **4.** The human body as opposed to the spirit. [ME *clei* < OE *clæg.*] **—clay′ey** (klā′ē), **clay′ish** *adj.*
Clay[1], **Cassius Marcellus** 1810–1903. Amer. abolitionist who was minister to Russia (1861–62 and 1863–69).
Clay[2], **Cassius Marcellus** See Muhammad **Ali.**
Clay, Henry Known as "the Great Compromiser." 1777–1852. Amer. politician who pushed the Missouri Compromise through the US House of Representatives (1820).
Clay, Lucius DuBignon 1897–1978. Amer. army officer who commanded US forces in Germany (1945–49).
clay mineral *n.* Any of various hydrous silicates that have a fine crystalline structure and are components of clay.
clay•more (klā′môr′, -mōr′) *n.* **1.** A claymore mine. **2.** A large double-edged broadsword formerly used by Scottish Highlanders. [Sc. Gael. *claidheamh mór,* large sword : *claidheamh,* sword (< OIr. *claideb*) + *mór,* great (< OIr.).]
claymore mine *n.* A ground-emplaced antipersonnel mine.
clay pigeon *n.* A clay disk target for skeet and trapshooting.
clean (klēn) *adj.* **clean•er, clean•est 1.** Free from dirt, stain, or impurities; unsoiled. **2a.** Free from foreign matter or pollution; unadulterated: *clean air.* **b.** Not infected. **3a.** Producing relatively little pollution: *a clean fuel.* **b.** Producing relatively little radioactive fallout or contamination. **4.** Having no imperfections or blemishes; regular or even: *a clean edge.* **5a.** Not ornate or intricate; spare. **b.** Sharply defined; clear-cut: *a clean outline against the sky.* **6.** Free from clumsiness; deft; adroit: *a clean throw.* **7.** Devoid of restrictions or encumbrances: *a clean bill of health.* **8.** Thorough; complete: *a clean getaway.* **9.** Having few alterations or corrections; legible. **10.** Blank. **11a.** Morally pure; virtuous. **b.** Having no marks of discredit or offense: *a clean record.* **12.** Fit for all readers or audiences; not ribald or obscene. **13.** Honest or fair: *a clean fight.* **14.** *Informal* **a.** Not carrying concealed weapons or drugs. **b.** Free from narcotics addiction or illegal drug use. **c.** Innocent of a suspected crime. ❖ *adv.* **cleaner, cleanest 1.** So as to be unsoiled: *washed clean.* **2.** In a fair manner: *plays clean.* **3.** In a clean or nonpolluting manner. **4.** *Informal* Entirely; wholly: *clean forgot.* ❖ *v.* **cleaned, clean•ing, cleans** *—tr.* **1.** To rid of dirt, rubbish, or impurities: *clean a room.* **2.** To get rid of (impurities or dirt, for example); remove: *cleaned off the stains.* **3.** To prepare (an animal) for cooking, as by removing the entrails or fat. **4.** To remove the contents from; empty. **5.** *Sports* To lift (a barbell) from the floor to the shoulders in one motion. *—intr.* To undergo or perform an act of cleaning. ***—phrasal verbs:*** **clean out 1.** To rid of dirt, rubbish, or impurities. **2.** To empty of contents or occupants. **3.** *Informal* To drive or force out. **4.** *Slang* To deprive completely of money or material wealth. **clean up 1.** To make clean or orderly. **2.** To make oneself clean, neat, or presentable. **3.** To dispose of; settle. **4.** *Slang* To make a large profit, often quickly. ***—idiom:*** **clean house** *Slang* To eliminate or discard what is undesirable. [ME *clene* < OE *clǣne.*] **—clean′a•ble** *adj.* **—clean′ness** *n.*

SYNONYMS *clean, antiseptic, cleanly, immaculate, spotless* These adjectives mean free from dirt: *clean clothing; antiseptic surgical instruments; a cleanly pet; an immaculate tablecloth; spotless gloves.*
ANTONYM *dirty*

clean and jerk *n.* A lift in weightlifting in which a weight is raised to shoulder height, held there briefly, and then pushed overhead in a rapid motion of the arms, typically accompanied by a spring or lunge from the legs.
clean-cut (klēn′kŭt′) *adj.* **1.** Clearly and sharply defined or outlined. **2.** Neat and trim in appearance.
clean•er (klē′nər) *n.* **1.** One whose work or business is cleaning. **2.** A machine or substance used in cleaning.
clean-hand•ed (klēn′hăn′dĭd) *adj.* Innocent; guiltless.
clean-limbed (klēn′lĭmd′) *adj.* Having well-formed limbs; well-proportioned.
clean•ly (klĕn′lē) *adj.* **-li•er, -li•est** Habitually and carefully neat and clean. See Syns at **clean.** ❖ *adv.* (klēn′lē) In a clean manner. **—clean′li•ness** (klĕn′lē-nĭs) *n.*
clean room *n.* A room that is maintained virtually free of contaminants, such as dust or bacteria, used in laboratory work and in electronic and aerospace production.
cleanse (klĕnz) *tr.v.* **cleansed, cleans•ing, cleans•es** To free from dirt, defilement, or guilt; purge or clean. [ME *clensen* < OE *clǣnsian* < *clǣne,* pure, clean.]
cleans•er (klĕn′zər) *n.* **1.** A detergent or other agent that removes dirt or grease. **2.** A lotion or cream to clean the face.
clean-shav•en (klēn′shā′vən) *adj.* **1.** Having the beard or hair shaved off. **2.** Having recently shaved.
Cle•an•thes (klē-ăn′thēz) 331?–232? B.C. Greek philosopher who succeeded Zeno as head of the Stoic school.
clean•up (klēn′ŭp′) *n.* **1.** A thorough cleaning or ordering. **2.** *Informal* The final, often routine tasks that complete a project. **3.** *Slang* A very large profit; a killing. **4.** *Baseball* The fourth position in the batting order. **—clean′up′** *adj.*
clear (klîr) *adj.* **clear•er, clear•est 1.** Free from clouds, mist, or haze: *a clear day.* **2.** Not obscured or darkened; bright: *a clear yellow.* **3.** Easily seen through; transparent. **4.** Free from flaw, blemish, or impurity: *a clear record.* **5.** Free from impediment, obstruction, or hindrance; open. **6.** Plain or evident to the mind; unmistakable. See Syns at **apparent. 7.** Easily perceptible to the eye or ear; distinct. **8.** Discerning or perceiving easily; keen. **9.** Free from doubt or confusion; certain. **10.** Free from qualification or limitation; absolute: *a clear winner.* **11.** Free from guilt; untroubled: *a clear conscience.* **12.** Having been freed from contact, proximity, or connection. **13.** Free from charges or deductions; net: *a clear profit.* **14.** Containing nothing. ❖ *adv.* **1.** Distinctly; clearly. **2.** Out of the way; completely away. **3.** *Informal* All the way; completely. ❖ *v.* **cleared, clear•ing, clears** *—tr.* **1.** To make light, clear, or bright. **2.** To rid of impurities, blemishes, muddiness, or foreign matter. **3.** To free from confusion, doubt, or ambiguity: *cleared up the question.* **4a.** To rid of objects or obstructions: *clear the table.* **b.** To make (a way or clearing) by removing obstructions. **c.** To remove (objects or obstructions). **5a.** To remove the occupants of: *clear the theater.* **b.** To remove (people). **6.** *Sports* To move or shoot (a ball or puck) away from the goal or out of the defensive zone. **7.** *Computer Science* **a.** To rid (a memory or buffer, for example) of instructions or data. **b.** To remove (instructions or data) from a memory. **8.** To free from a legal charge or imputation of guilt; acquit. **9.** To pass by, under, or over without contact. **10.** To settle (a debt). **11.** To gain (a given amount) as net profit or earnings. **12.** To pass (a bill of exchange, such as a check) through a clearing-house. **13a.** To secure the approval of. **b.** To authorize or approve. **14.** To free (a ship or cargo) from legal detention at a harbor by fulfilling customs and harbor requirements. **15.** To give clearance or authorization to. **16.** To free (the throat) of phlegm by making a rasping sound. *—intr.* **1.** To become clear. **2.** To go away; disappear: *The fog cleared.* **3a.** To exchange checks and bills or settle accounts through a clearing-house. **b.** To pass through the banking system and be debited and credited to the relevant accounts. **4.** To comply with customs and harbor requirements in discharging a cargo or in leaving or entering a port. ❖ *n.* A clear or open space. ***—phrasal verb:*** **clear out** *Informal* To leave a place, usu. quickly. ***—idioms:*** **clear the air** To dispel differences or emotional tensions. **in the clear 1.** Free from burdens or dangers. **2.** Not subject to suspicions or accusations of guilt. [ME *cler* < OFr. < Lat. *clārus,* clear, bright. See **kelə-** in App.] **—clear′a•ble** *adj.* **—clear′er** *n.* **—clear′ly** *adv.* **—clear′ness** *n.*
clear-air turbulence (klîr′âr′) *n.* Atmospheric turbulence that occurs under tranquil and cloudless conditions and subjects aircraft to strong updrafts and downdrafts.
clear•ance (klîr′əns) *n.* **1.** The act or process of clearing. **2.** A space cleared; a clearing. **3a.** The amount of space by which a

claw hammer

clean room

ă	pat	oi	boy
ā	pay	ou	out
âr	care	o͝o	took
ä	father	o͞o	boot
ĕ	pet	ŭ	cut
ē	be	ûr	urge
ĭ	pit	th	thin
ī	pie	*th*	this
îr	pier	hw	which
ŏ	pot	zh	vision
ō	toe	ə	about,
ô	paw		item

Stress marks:
′ (primary);
′ (secondary), as in
lexicon (lĕk′sĭ-kŏn′)

moving object clears something. **b.** The height or width of a passage. **4.** An intervening space or distance allowing free play, as between machine parts. **5.** Permission for a vehicle to proceed, as after an inspection. **6.** Official certification of blamelessness, trustworthiness, or suitability. **7.** A sale to dispose of old merchandise. **8.** The passage of checks and other bills of exchange through a clearing-house. **9.** *Physiology* **a.** The removal by the kidneys of a substance from blood plasma. **b.** Renal clearance.

clear-cut (klîr′kŭt′) *adj.* **1.** Distinctly and sharply defined or outlined. **2.** Not ambiguous; clear and obvious. See Syns at **apparent. 3.** Having been logged by clear-cutting. ❖ *v.* **-cut, -cut•ting, -cuts** —*tr.* To remove all of the trees in (a tract of timberland) at one time. —*intr.* To clear-cut an area. ❖ *n.* A clear-cut tract of timberland.

clear-eyed (klîr′īd′) *adj.* **1.** Having sharp, bright eyes; keen-sighted. **2.** Mentally acute or perceptive.

clear•head•ed (klîr′hĕd′ĭd) *adj.* Having a clear, orderly mind. —**clear′head′ed•ly** *adv.* —**clear′head′ed•ness** *n.*

clear•ing (klîr′ĭng) *n.* **1.** The act or process of making or becoming clear. **2.** A tract of land within an overgrown area from which trees and other obstructions have been removed. **3.** An open space. **4a.** The exchange among banks of checks, drafts, and notes and the settlement of consequent differences. **b. clearings** The total of daily claims at a clearing-house.

clear•ing-house or **clear•ing•house** (klîr′ĭng-hous′) *n.* An office where banks engage in clearing.

clear-sight•ed (klîr′sī′tĭd) *adj.* **1.** Having sharp, clear vision. **2.** Perceptive; discerning. —**clear′-sight′ed•ly** *adv.* —**clear′-sight′ed•ness** *n.*

clear•sto•ry (klîr′stôr′ē, -stōr′ē) *n.* Variant of **clerestory.**

Clear•wa•ter (klîr′wô′tər, -wŏt′ər) A city of W-central FL W of Tampa. Pop. 108,787.

Clearwater Mountains A range of N-central ID between the Salmon R. and the Bitterroot Range rising to c. 2,745 m (9,000 ft).

clear•weed (klîr′wēd′) *n.* Either of two eastern North American annual plants (*Pilea pumila* or *P. fontana*) having short drooping flower clusters and translucent stems and leaves.

clear•wing (klîr′wĭng′) *n.* Any of various wasplike moths of the family Sesiidae, with scaleless transparent wings.

cleat (klēt) *n.* **1.** A strip of wood or iron used to strengthen or support the surface to which it is attached. **2a.** A projecting piece of metal or hard rubber attached to the underside of a shoe to provide traction. **b. cleats** A pair of shoes with such projections on the soles. **3.** A piece of metal or wood having projecting arms or ends for winding or securing a line. **4.** A wedge-shaped piece of material that is fastened onto something to act as a support or prevent slippage. **5.** A spurlike device used to grip a tree or pole in climbing. ❖ *tr.v.* **cleat•ed, cleat•ing, cleats** To supply, support, secure, or strengthen with a cleat. [ME *clete* < OE **clēat,* lump, wedge.]

cleav•age (klē′vĭj) *n.* **1.** The act of splitting or cleaving. **2.** The state of being split or cleft; a fissure or division. **3.** *Mineralogy* The splitting or tendency to split of a crystallized substance along definite crystalline planes, yielding smooth surfaces. **4.** *Embryology* **a.** The series of mitotic cell divisions that produces a blastula from a fertilized ovum. **b.** Any single cell division in such a series. **5.** *Chemistry* The splitting of a complex molecule into simpler molecules. **6.** *Informal* The hollow between a woman's breasts.

cleave¹ (klēv) *v.* **cleft** (klĕft) or **cleaved** or **clove** (klōv), **cleft** or **cleaved** or **clo•ven** (klō′vən), **cleav•ing, cleaves** —*tr.* **1.** To split with or as if with a sharp instrument. See Syns at **tear¹. 2.** To make or accomplish by or as if by cutting. **3.** To pierce or penetrate. **4.** *Chemistry* To split (a complex molecule) into simpler molecules. —*intr.* **1.** *Mineralogy* To split or separate, esp. along a natural line of division. **2.** To make one's way; penetrate. [ME *cleven* < OE *clēofan.*] —**cleav′a•ble** *adj.*

cleave² (klēv) *intr.v.* **cleaved, cleav•ing, cleaves 1.** To adhere or stick fast. **2.** To be faithful. [ME *cleven* < OE *cleofian.*]

cleav•er (klē′vər) *n.* **1.** A heavy broad-bladed knife or hatchet used esp. by butchers. **2.** *Archaeology* A bifacial core tool flaked to produce a straight sharp edge at one end.

cleav•ers (klē′vərz) *pl.n.* (*used with a sing. or pl. verb*) See **bedstraw.** [ME *clivers,* prob. blend of *cliver,* burdock (< OE *clīfe*) and *clivres,* claws (< OE *clifras,* pl. of *clifer*).]

cleek (klēk) *n.* **1.** *Sports* **a.** A number one golf iron. **b.** A number four wood. **2.** *Scots* A large hook. [ME *cleike,* large hook < *cleken,* to grasp, var. of *clechen* < OE **clæcan;* prob. akin to *clyccan,* to clutch.]

clef (klĕf) *n. Music* A symbol indicating the pitch of one line of a staff, in relation to which the other pitches of the staff can be determined. [Fr., key < OFr. < Lat. *clāvis.*]

cleft (klĕft) *v.* Past tense and a past participle of **cleave¹.** ❖ *adj.* **1.** Divided; split. **2.** *Botany* Having indentations that extend about halfway to the center. ❖ *n.* **1.** A crack, crevice, or split. **2.** A split or indentation between two parts, as of the chin. [ME, p. part. of *cleven,* to split; see CLEAVE¹. N., ME, alteration (influenced by *cleft*) of *clift* < OE *geclyft.*]

cleft lip *n.* A congenital deformity characterized by a vertical cleft or pair of clefts in the upper lip, with or without involvement of the palate.

Samuel L. Clemens

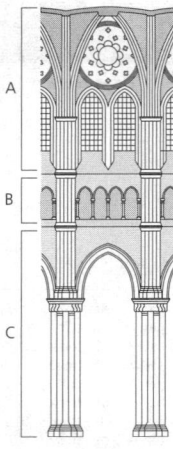

clerestory
High Gothic style cathedral nave wall
A. clerestory
B. triforium
C. arcade

cleft palate *n.* A congenital fissure in the roof of the mouth, resulting from incomplete fusion of the palate during embryonic development.

Cleis•the•nes¹ (klīs′thə-nēz′) or **Clis•the•nes** (klĭs′-) fl. 6th cent. B.C. Greek tyrant of Sicyon who led the Ionian population of the region in a revolt against the Dorians.

Cleis•the•nes² (klīs′thə-nēz′) or **Clis•the•nes** (klĭs′-) 570?–after 508 B.C. Athenian statesman who is generally regarded as the founder of Athenian democracy.

cleis•tog•a•mous (klī-stŏg′ə-məs) also **cleis•to•gam•ic** (klī′stə-găm′ĭk) *adj.* Of or relating to a flower that does not open and is self-pollinated in the bud. [Gk. *kleistos,* closed (< *kleiein,* to close) + –GAMOUS.] —**cleis•tog′a•mous•ly** *adv.* —**cleis•tog′a•my** (-mē) *n.*

cleis•to•the•ci•um (klī′stə-thē′sē-əm) *n., pl.* **-ci•a** (-sē-ə) A closed spherical ascocarp. [NLat. : Gk. *kleistos,* closed (< *kleiein,* to close) + Gk. *thēkion,* small case, dim. of *thēkē,* receptacle; see **dhē-** in App.]

clem•a•tis (klĕm′ə-tĭs, klĭ-măt′ĭs) *n.* Any of various mostly climbing plants of the genus *Clematis,* native chiefly to northern temperate regions and having showy flowers or fruit clusters. [Lat. *clēmatis,* a creeping plant < Gk. *klēmatis* < *klēma, klēmat-,* twig.]

Cle•men•ceau (klĕm′ən-sō′, klĕ-mäN-) **Georges** 1841–1929. French politician who served as premier (1906–09 and 1917–20) and played a key role in negotiating the Treaty of Versailles (1919).

clem•en•cy (klĕm′ən-sē) *n., pl.* **-cies 1.** A disposition to show mercy, esp. to an offender or enemy. See Syns at **mercy. 2.** A merciful, kind, or lenient act. **3.** Mildness, esp. of weather.

Clem•ens (klĕm′ənz), **Samuel Langhorne** Pen name **Mark Twain.** 1835–1910. Amer. author whose masterpieces of humor and sarcasm include *Tom Sawyer* (1876) and *The Adventures of Huckleberry Finn* (1884).

clem•ent (klĕm′ənt) *adj.* **1.** Inclined to be lenient or merciful. **2.** Mild: *clement weather.* [ME < Lat. *clēmēns, clēment-.*] —**clem′ent•ly** *adv.*

Clement I, Saint. Known as "Clement of Rome." Died c. A.D. 97. Pope (88–97) who was one of the Apostolic Fathers and the author of the First Epistle to the Corinthians (c. 96).

Clement V Orig. Bertrand de Got. 1264–1314. Pope (1305–14) befriended by Philip IV of France, who arranged his election.

Clement VII Orig. Giulio de' Medici. 1475?–1534. Pope (1523–34) who refused to grant the divorce of Henry VIII from Catherine of Aragon.

clem•en•tine (klĕm′ən-tīn′, -tēn′) *n.* A deep red-orange, often seedless mandarin orange. [Fr. *clémentine,* perhaps after Père *Clément* (fl. 1902), French missionary in Africa.]

Clement of Alexandria, Saint. A.D. 150?–220? Greek Christian theologian who combined Gnosticism with Platonism.

clench (klĕnch) *tr.v.* **clenched, clench•ing, clench•es 1.** To close tightly: *clench one's teeth.* **2.** To grasp or grip tightly. **3.** To clinch (a bolt, for example). **4.** *Nautical* To fasten with a clinch. ❖ *n.* **1.** A tight grip or grasp. **2.** Something, such as a mechanical device, that clenches or holds fast. **3.** *Nautical* See **clinch** 4. [ME *clenchen* < OE *beclencan.*]

cle•o•me (klē-ō′mē) *n.* Any of various often strong-smelling plants of the genus *Cleome,* native chiefly to warm regions. [NLat. *Cleome,* genus name.]

Cle•on (klē′ŏn) d. 422 B.C. Athenian politician who led the democratic faction after the death of Pericles (429).

Cle•o•pat•ra (klē′ə-pă′trə, -pä′trə, -pă′-) 69–30 B.C. Egyptian queen (51–49 and 48–30) who was defeated with Mark Antony by Octavian's forces at Actium (31).

clepe (klēp) *tr.v.* **cleped** (klĕpt, klēpt), **cleped** or **clept** (klĕpt) or **y•clept** (ĭ-klĕpt′) or **y•cleped** (ĭ-klĕpt′, ĭ-klĕpt′), **clep•ing, clepes** *Archaic* To call; name. [ME *clepen* < OE *cleopian,* to cry out.]

clep•sy•dra (klĕp′sĭ-drə) *n., pl.* **-dras** or **-drae** (-drē′) An ancient device that measured time by marking the regulated flow of water through a small opening. [Lat. < Gk. *klepsudrā : kleptein, kleps-,* to steal + *hudōr,* water; see **wed-** in App.]

clere•sto•ry also **clear•sto•ry** (klîr′stôr′ē, -stōr′ē) *n., pl.* **-ries 1.** The upper part of the nave, transepts, and choir of a church, containing windows. **2.** An upper portion of a wall containing windows. [ME *clerestorie* : perh. *cler,* giving light, clear; see CLEAR + *storie,* tier; see STORY².]

cler•gy (klûr′jē) *n., pl.* **-gies** The body of people ordained for religious service. See Usage Note at **collective noun.** [ME *clergie* < OFr. **clercīa* < LLat. *clēricus;* see CLERK) and < OFr. *clergié,* body of clerks (< VLat. **clercātus* < LLat. *clēricātus* < *clēricus,* clerk, cleric).]

cler•gy•man (klûr′jē-mən) *n.* A man who is a cleric.

cler•gy•wom•an (klûr′jē-wŏom′ən) *n.* A woman who is a cleric.

cler•ic (klĕr′ĭk) *n.* A member of the clergy. [LLat. *clēricus.* See CLERK.]

cler•i•cal (klĕr′ĭ-kəl) *adj.* **1.** Of or relating to office workers or work. **2.** Of, relating to, or typical of the clergy. **3.** Advocating clericalism. ❖ *n.* **1.** A cleric. **2. clericals** Garments worn by clerics. **3.** An advocate of clericalism. —**cler′i•cal•ly** *adv.*

clerical collar *n.* A stiff white collar fastened at the back of the neck, worn by certain members of the Christian clergy.

cler•i•cal•ism (klĕr′ĭ-kə-lĭz′əm) *n.* A policy of supporting the power and influence of the clergy in political or secular matters. —**cler′i•cal•ist** *n.*

cler•i•hew (klĕr′ə-hyo͞o′) *n.* A humorous verse, usu. consisting of two unmatched rhyming couplets, about a person whose name generally serves as one of the rhymes. [After Edmund *Clerihew* Bentley (1875–1956), British writer.]

cler•i•sy (klĕr′ĭ-sē) *n.* Educated people considered as a group; the literati. [Ger. *Klerisei*, clergy < Med.Lat. *clēricia* < LLat. *clēricus*, priest. See CLERK.]

clerk (klûrk; *British* klärk) *n.* **1.** A person who works in an office handling such things as records, correspondence, or files. **2a.** A person who keeps the records and performs the regular business of a court, legislative body, or municipal district. **b.** *Law* A law clerk, as for a judge. **3.** A person who works at a sales counter or service desk. **4.** A cleric. **5.** *Archaic* A scholar. ❖ *intr.v.* **clerked, clerk•ing, clerks** To work or serve as a clerk. [ME, clergyman, secretary < OE *clerc* and OFr. *clerc*, clergyman, both < LLat. *clēricus* < Gk. *klērikos*, belonging to the clergy < *klēros*, inheritance, lot.] —**clerk′dom** *n.* —**clerk′ship′** *n.*

clerk•ly (klûrk′lē) *adj.* **-li•er, -li•est 1.** Of, relating to, or typical of a clerk. **2.** *Archaic* Scholarly. —**clerk′li•ness** *n.*

Cleve•land (klēv′lənd) A city of NE OH on Lake Erie; laid out in 1796. Pop. 478,403.

Cleveland, (Stephen) Grover 1837–1908. The 22nd and 24th President of the US (1885–89 and 1893–97).

clev•er (klĕv′ər) *adj.* **-er•er, -er•est 1.** Mentally quick and original; bright. **2.** Nimble; dexterous. **3.** Exhibiting quick-wittedness: *a clever story.* **4.** *New England* Easily managed; docile. **5.** *New England* Affable but not esp. smart. **6.** *Chiefly Southern US* Good-natured; amiable. [ME *cliver*; akin to E Frisian *klifer, klüfer*, skillful.] —**clev′er•ly** *adv.* —**clev′er•ness** *n.*

SYNONYMS *clever, ingenious, shrewd* These adjectives refer to mental adroitness or to practical ingenuity and skill. *Clever* is the most comprehensive: *"Everybody's family doctor was remarkably clever, and was understood to have immeasurable skill in the management and training of the most skittish or vicious diseases"* (George Eliot). *Ingenious* implies originality and inventiveness: *"an ingenious solution to the storage problem"* (Linda Greider). *Shrewd* emphasizes mental astuteness and practical understanding: *a shrewd politician.*

Cleves (klēvz) See **Kleve.**

clev•is (klĕv′ĭs) *n.* A U-shaped metal fastening device with holes in each end for a pin or bolt. [< *clevi*, poss. of Scand. orig.; akin to ON *klofi*, cleft.]

clew¹ (klo͞o) *n.* **1.** A ball of yarn or thread. **2.** *Greek Mythology* The ball of thread Theseus used to escape the labyrinth. **3. clews** The cords used to suspend a hammock. **4.** also **clue** *Nautical* **a.** The lower aft corner of a fore-and-aft sail. **b.** One of the two lower corners of a square sail. ❖ *tr.v.* **clewed, clew•ing, clews 1.** To roll or coil into a ball. **2.** also **clue** *Nautical* To raise the lower corners of (a square sail) with ropes. Used with *up.* [ME *clewe* < OE *cliwen.*]

clew² (klo͞o) *n. & v. Chiefly British* Variant of **clue¹**.

Cli•burn (klī′bərn), **Van** b. 1934. Amer. pianist who was the first American to win the Tchaikovsky Prize (1958).

cli•ché also **cli•che** (klē-shā′) *n.* **1.** A trite or overused expression or idea. **2.** One whose behavior is predictable or superficial. [Fr., p. part. of *clicher*, to stereotype (imit. of sound of dropping a matrix into molten metal to make a stereotype plate).]

cli•chéd also **cli•ched** (klē-shād′) *adj.* Having become stale or commonplace through overuse; hackneyed.

Cli•chy (klē-shē′) A city of N-central France, a suburb of Paris. Pop. 46,895.

click (klĭk) *n.* **1.** A brief, sharp, nonresonant sound. **2.** A mechanical device that snaps into position. **3.** *Computer Science* An instance of pressing down and releasing a button on a pointing device, such as a mouse. **4.** *Linguistics* An implosive stop produced by raising the back of the tongue to make contact with the palate and simultaneously closing the lips or touching the teeth or alveolar ridge with the tip and sides of the tongue. ❖ *v.* **clicked, click•ing, clicks** —*intr.* **1.** To produce a click or series of clicks. **2.** *Computer Science* To press down and release a button on a pointing device. Often used with *on.* **3.** *Slang* **a.** To be a great success. **b.** To function well together; hit it off. **c.** To become clear; fall into place. —*tr.* **1.** To cause to click, as by striking together. **2.** *Computer Science* To press down and release (a button on a pointing device). [Imit.]

click beetle *n.* Any of various beetles of the family Elateridae, characterized by the ability to right themselves from an overturned position by flipping into the air with a clicking sound.

click•er (klĭk′ər) *n.* One that clicks, as: **a.** A remote control. **b.** A computer mouse. **c.** A mechanical counter.

click•stream (klĭk′strēm′) *n.* The sequence of links that are clicked on while browsing a website or series of websites.

click•wrap (klĭk′răp′) *adj.* Of or relating to a legal agreement, such as a software license, to which one indicates acceptance by clicking on a button or hyperlink. [CLICK + (SHRINK-)WRAP.]

cli•ent (klī′ənt) *n.* **1.** The party for which professional services are rendered, as by an attorney. **2.** A customer or patron. **3.** One who uses a social services agency. **4.** One dependent on the protection of another. **5.** A client state. **6.** *Computer Science* A computer or program that can download files or run applications from a file server. [ME < OFr. < Lat. *cliēns, client-*, dependent, follower. See **klei-** in App.] —**cli′ent•age** (-ən-tĭj) *n.* —**cli•en′tal** (klī-ĕn′tl, klī′ən-) *adj.*

cli•en•tele (klī′ən-tĕl′, klē′än-) *n.* **1.** The clients of a professional practice considered as a group. **2.** A body of customers or patrons: *a restaurant's clientele.* [Fr. *clientèle* < Lat. *clientēla*, clientship < *cliēns*, client. See CLIENT.]

client state *n.* A country that is dependent on the economic or military support of a larger, more powerful country.

cliff (klĭf) *n.* A high, steep, or overhanging face of rock. [ME *clif* < OE.] —**cliff′y** *adj.*

cliff brake *n.* Any of several ferns in the genus *Pellaea*, typically growing in dry rocky areas or on cliffs and having pinnately compound, often leathery leaves.

cliff dweller *n.* A member of certain Anasazi groups of the southwest United States who built dwellings on sheltered ledges in the sides of cliffs. —**cliff dwelling** *n.*

cliff•hang•er (klĭf′hăng′ər) *n.* **1.** A melodramatic serial in which each episode ends in suspense. **2.** A suspenseful situation at the end of a chapter, scene, or episode. **3.** A contest in which the outcome is uncertain until the end. —**cliff′hang′ing** *adj.*

cliff swallow *n.* A North American swallow *(Petrochelidon pyrrhonota)* that builds a bottle-shaped nest on the face of a cliff or bluff or under the eaves of a roof.

cli•mac•ter•ic (klī-măk′tər-ĭk, klī′măk-tĕr′ĭk) *n.* **1a.** A period of life characterized by physiological and psychological change that marks the end of a woman's reproductive capacity and terminates with the completion of menopause. **b.** A corresponding period in men marked by reduced sexual activity, although fertility is retained. **2.** A critical stage, period, or year. ❖ *adj.* **1.** Of or relating to a climacteric. **2.** Critical; crucial. [< Lat. *clīmactēricus*, of a dangerous period in life < Gk. *klīmaktērikos* < *klīmaktēr*, dangerous point, rung of a ladder < *klīmax*, ladder. See CLIMAX.]

cli•mac•tic (klī-măk′tĭk) also **cli•mac•ti•cal** (-tĭ-kəl) *adj.* Relating to or constituting a climax. —**cli•mac′ti•cal•ly** *adv.*

cli•mate (klī′mĭt) *n.* **1.** The characteristic meteorological conditions, including temperature, precipitation, and wind, of a particular region. **2.** A region of the earth having particular meteorological conditions. **3.** A prevailing condition or set of attitudes in human affairs. [ME *climat* < OFr. < LLat. *clima, climat-* < Gk. *klima*, surface of the earth, region. See **klei-** in App.]

cli•mat•ic (klī-măt′ĭk) *adj.* **1.** Of or relating to climate. **2.** *Ecology* Influenced or caused by the climate. —**cli•mat′i•cal•ly** *adv.*

cli•ma•tol•o•gy (klī′mə-tŏl′ə-jē) *n.* The meteorological study of climates and their phenomena. —**cli′ma•to•log′ic** (-mə-tl-ŏj′ĭk), **cli′ma•to•log′i•cal** (-ĭ-kəl) *adj.* —**cli′ma•to•log′i•cal•ly** *adv.* —**cli′ma•tol′o•gist** *n.*

cli•max (klī′măks′) *n.* **1.** The point of greatest intensity or force in an ascending series or progression; a culmination. **2a.** A series of statements or ideas in an ascending order of rhetorical force. **b.** The final point in such a series. **3a.** A moment of great or culminating intensity in a narrative or drama. **b.** The turning point in a plot or dramatic action. **4.** See **orgasm** 1. **5.** A stage in ecological development in which a community of organisms, esp. plants, is stable and capable of perpetuating itself. ❖ *tr. & intr.v.* **-maxed, -max•ing, -max•es** To bring to or reach a climax. [Lat. *clīmax*, rhetorical climax < Gk. *klīmax*, ladder. See **klei-** in App.]

climb (klīm) *v.* **climbed, climb•ing, climbs** —*tr.* **1.** To move upward on or mount, esp. with the hands and feet or the feet alone; ascend. **2.** To grow in an upward direction on or over. —*intr.* **1.** To move oneself upward, esp. with the hands and feet. **2.** To rise slowly, steadily, or effortfully; ascend. **3.** To move in a specified direction with the hands and feet. **4.** To slant or slope upward. **5.** To engage in mountain climbing. **6.** To grow in an upward direction, as some plants do, often with twining stems or tendrils. ❖ *n.* **1.** An act of climbing; an ascent. **2.** A place to be climbed. [ME *climben* < OE *climban.*] —**climb′a•ble** (klī′mə-bəl) *adj.*

climb•er (clī′mər) *n.* **1.** One that climbs, esp. a mountain climber. **2.** *Sports* A device used in mountain climbing. **3.** A climbing plant. **4.** One avidly seeking a higher social or professional position.

climb•ing fern (klī′mĭng) *n.* Any of various terrestrial ferns of the genus *Lygodium*, having a single pinnately compound leaf that climbs by twining.

climbing iron *n.* See **crampon** 2.

climbing perch *n.* A freshwater fish *(Anabas testudineus)* of tropical Asia having modified gills allowing it to breathe air and pectoral fins adapted for traveling on land.

clime (klīm) *n.* Climate: *warmer climes.* [ME, region of the earth < LLat. *clima* < Gk. *klima*. See CLIMATE.]

clin– *pref.* Variant of **clino–**.

–clinal *suff.* Sloping: *synclinal.* [< Gk. *klīnein*, to lean. See **klei-** in App.]

cli•nan•dri•um (klĭ-năn′drē-əm) *n., pl.* **-dri•a** (-drē-ə) *Botany* A hollow containing the anther in the upper part of the column of an orchid flower. [NLat. *clīnandrium* : Gk. *klīnē*, couch

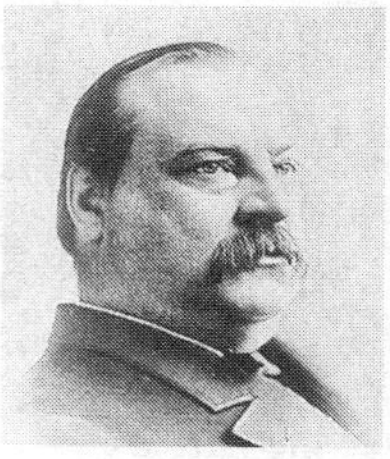

Grover Cleveland

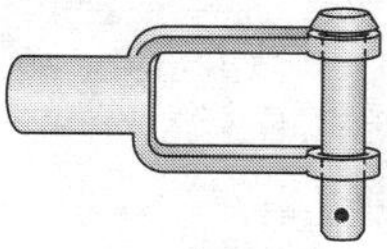

clevis

ă	pat	oi	boy
ā	pay	ou	out
âr	care	o͝o	took
ä	father	o͞o	boot
ĕ	pet	ŭ	cut
ē	be	ûr	urge
ĭ	pit	th	thin
ī	pie	*th*	this
îr	pier	hw	which
ŏ	pot	zh	vision
ō	toe	ə	about, item
ô	paw		

Stress marks:
′ (primary);
′ (secondary), as in
lexicon (lĕk′sĭ-kŏn′)

(< *klīnein*, to recline; see **klei-** in App.) + NLat. *-andrium*, stamen (< Gk. *anēr, andr-*, man; see –ANDRY).]

clinch (klĭnch) *v.* **clinched, clinch•ing, clinch•es** —*tr.* **1a.** To fix or secure (a nail, for example) by bending down or flattening the protruding pointed end. **b.** To fasten together thus. **2.** To settle definitely and conclusively. **3.** *Sports* To secure (a divisional championship, for instance) before the end of regular season play by having an insurmountable lead. **4.** *Nautical* To fasten with a clinch. —*intr.* **1.** To be held together securely. **2.** *Sports* To hold a boxing opponent with one or both arms to prevent or hinder punches. **3.** *Slang* To embrace amorously. ❖ *n.* **1.** Something, such as a clamp, that clinches. **2.** The clinched part of a nail, bolt, or rivet. **3.** *Sports* An act or instance of clinching in boxing. **4.** *Nautical* A half hitch in a rope with the end of the rope fastened back by seizing. **5.** *Slang* An amorous embrace. [Variant of CLENCH.]

clinch•er (klĭn′chər) *n.* **1.** One that clinches, as: **a.** A nail, screw, or bolt for clinching. **b.** A tool for clinching nails, screws, or bolts. **2.** *Informal* A decisive factor.

Clinch River A river rising in SW VA and flowing c. 483 km (300 mi) generally SW to the Tennessee R.

cline (klīn) *n.* A gradual change in a feature across the distributional range of a species or population, usu. correlated with an environmental or geographic transition. [< Gk. *klīnein*, to lean. See **klei-** in App.] —**clin′al** (klī′nəl) *adj.*

Cline, Virginia Patterson Known as "Patsy." 1932–63. Amer. singer whose country and western recordings include "I Fall to Pieces" (1960).

–cline *suff.* Slope: *anticline.* [Back-formation < –CLINAL.]

cling (klĭng) *intr.v.* **clung** (klŭng), **cling•ing, clings 1.** To hold fast or adhere to something, as by grasping or embracing. **2.** To remain close; resist separation. **3.** To remain emotionally attached; hold on. ❖ *n. Botany* A clingstone. [ME *clingen* < OE *clingan.*] —**cling′er** *n.* —**cling′y** *adj.*

cling•fish (klĭng′fĭsh′) *n., pl.* **clingfish** or **-fish•es** Any of various small marine fishes of the family Gobiesocidae, having a large sucking disk under the front part of the body by which they fasten themselves to rocks and seaweed.

Cling•mans Dome (klĭng′mənz) A mountain, 2,026.1 m (6,643 ft), in the Great Smoky Mts. on the TN-NC border.

cling•stone (klĭng′stōn′) *adj.* Of or relating to a fruit with flesh that adheres closely to the stone. ❖ *n.* A clingstone fruit.

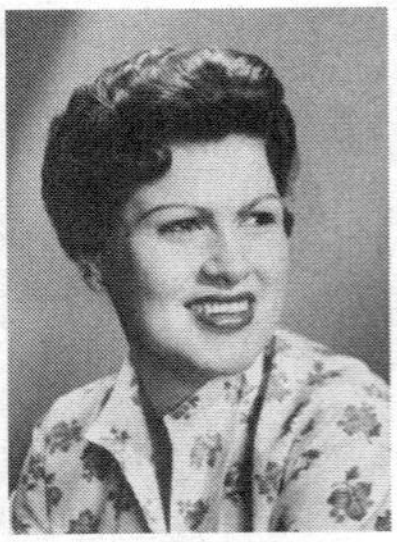

Patsy Cline

clin•ic (klĭn′ĭk) *n.* **1.** A facility devoted to the diagnosis and care of outpatients. **2.** A medical establishment run cooperatively by several specialists sharing the same facilities. **3.** A group session offering counsel or instruction in a particular field or activity. **4.** A training session with a patient for medical students. [Fr. *clinique* < Gk. *klīnikē (tekhnē)*, clinical (method), fem. of *klīnikos* < *klīnē*, couch. See **klei-** in App.]

–clinic *suff.* **1.** Sloping: *isoclinic.* **2.** Having a specified number of oblique axial intersections: *triclinic.*

clin•i•cal (klĭn′ĭ-kəl) *adj.* **1.** Of, relating to, or connected with a clinic. **2.** Involving or based on direct observation of the patient: *a clinical diagnosis.* **3.** Very objective and devoid of emotion; analytical. **4.** Suggestive of a medical clinic; austere and antiseptic: *a clinical style of decor.* —**clin′i•cal•ly** *adv.*

clinical thermometer *n.* A thermometer used to measure body temperature, esp. a small glass thermometer designed with a narrowing above the bulb so that the mercury column stays in position when the instrument is removed from the body.

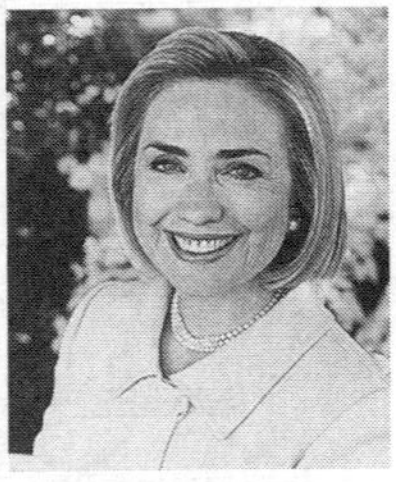

Hillary Rodham Clinton

cli•ni•cian (klĭ-nĭsh′ən) *n.* **1.** A health professional, such as a physician, nurse, or psychologist, who specializes in clinical practice. **2.** A health professional who practices at a clinic. [Fr. *clinicien* < *clinique*, clinic. See CLINIC.]

clink[1] (klĭngk) *intr. & tr.v.* **clinked, clink•ing, clinks** To make or cause to make a clink. ❖ *n.* A light sharp ringing sound. [ME *clinken*, prob. < MDu. *klinken*, of imit. orig.]

clink[2] (klĭngk) *n. Slang* A prison or a prison cell; a jail. [After *Clink*, a district of London famous for its prison.]

clink•er (klĭng′kər) *n.* **1.** The incombustible residue, fused into an irregular lump, that remains after coal combustion. **2.** A partially vitrified brick or a mass of bricks fused together. **3.** An extremely hard burned brick. **4.** Vitrified matter expelled by a volcano. **5.** *Slang* **a.** A sour note in a musical performance. **b.** A mistake; a blunder. **c.** Something of inferior quality; a conspicuous failure. **6.** *Chiefly British* Something admirable or first-rate. ❖ *intr.v.* **-ered, -er•ing, -ers** To form clinkers in burning. [Obsolete Du. *klinckaerd* < MDu. *klinken*, to clink. See CLINK[1].]

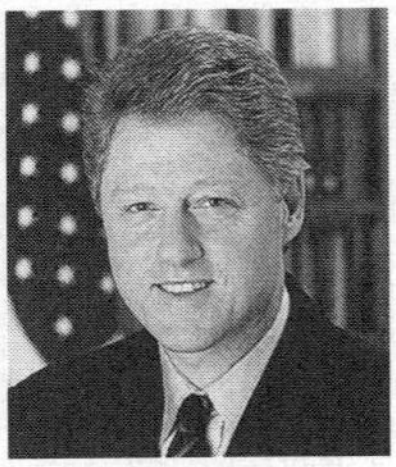

Bill Clinton

clink•er-built (klĭng′kər-bĭlt′) *adj.* Built with overlapping planks or boards. [< obsolete *clinker*, clinch-nail < ME *clinken*, prob. var. of *clenchen*, to clench < OE *beclencan*.]

clino– or **clin–** *pref.* Slope; slant: *clinometer.* [NLat. *clīno-* < Gk. *klīnein*, to slope. See **klei-** in App.]

cli•nom•e•ter (klī-nŏm′ĭ-tər) *n.* Any of various surveying instruments for measuring angles of elevation or incline. —**cli′no•met′ric** (-nə-mĕt′rĭk) *adj.* —**cli•nom′e•try** *n.*

clin•quant (klĭng′kənt, klăN-käN′) *adj.* Glittering with gold or tinsel. ❖ *n.* Imitation gold leaf; tinsel; glitter. [Fr., glistening, tinkling, pr. part. of obsolete *clinquer*, to clink, perh. < MDu. *klinken*. See CLINK[1].]

Clin•ton (klĭn′tən), **DeWitt** 1769–1828. Amer. politician who as governor of NY (1817–23 and 1825–28) was a principal supporter of the Erie Canal.

Clinton, George 1739–1812. Vice President of the US (1805–12).

Clinton, Sir **Henry** 1738–95. British general in the American Revolution who was commander in chief of British forces in North America (1778–81).

Clinton, Hillary Rodham b. 1947. Amer. attorney and First Lady of the US (1993–2001) who was elected to the US Senate in 2000.

Clinton, William Jefferson Known as "Bill." b. 1946. The 42nd President of the US (1993–2001) who signed the first balanced federal budget in 30 years and who was impeached (1999) on charges of perjury and obstruction of justice but was acquitted on both counts.

clin•to•ni•a (klĭn-tō′nē-ə) *n.* Any of various perennial herbs of the genus *Clintonia* in the lily family, native to North America and eastern Asia and having broad basal leaves, white, greenish-yellow, or purplish flowers, and blue or black berries. [NLat. *Clintonia*, genus name, after DeWitt CLINTON.]

Cli•o (klī′ō) *n. Greek Mythology* The Muse of history. [Lat. *Clīō* < Gk. *Kleiō* < *kleiein*, to tell. See **kleu-** in App.]

cli•o•met•rics (klī′ə-mĕt′rĭks) *n.* (*used with a sing. verb*) The study of history using economic models and advanced mathematical methods of data processing and analysis. —**cli′o•met′ric** *adj.* —**cli′o•me•tri′cian** (-mĭ-trĭsh′ən) *n.*

clip[1] (klĭp) *v.* **clipped, clip•ping, clips** —*tr.* **1.** To cut, cut off, or cut out with or as if with shears: *clip coupons.* **2.** To make shorter by cutting; trim. **3.** To cut off the edge of. **4.** To cut short; curtail. **5a.** To shorten (a word) by leaving out letters or syllables. **b.** To enunciate clearly and precisely. **6.** *Informal* To hit with a sharp blow. **7.** *Football* To block (an opponent) illegally from the rear. **8.** *Slang* To cheat, swindle, or rob. —*intr.* **1.** To cut something. **2.** *Informal* To move rapidly. ❖ *n.* **1.** The act of clipping. **2.** Something clipped off, esp.: **a.** The wool shorn at one shearing. **b.** A season's shearing. **3.** A short extract from a film or videotape. **4.** *Informal* A quick sharp blow. **5.** *Football* An illegal block from the rear. **6.** *Informal* A pace or rate. **7.** A single occasion; a time. **8.** **clips** A pair of shears or clippers. [ME *clippen* < ON *klippa*.]

clip[2] (klĭp) *n.* **1.** A device for gripping or holding things together; a clasp or fastener. **2.** A piece of jewelry that fastens with a clasp or clip; a brooch. **3.** A cartridge clip. ❖ *tr.v.* **clipped, clip•ping, clips 1.** To fasten with or as if with a clip; hold tightly. **2.** *Archaic* To embrace or encompass. [ME, hook < *clippen*, to clasp, embrace < OE *clyppan*.]

clip art *n.* Ready-made pieces of printed or digital graphic art that can be used to decorate an electronic document.

clip•board (klĭp′bôrd′, -bōrd′) *n.* **1.** A small writing board with a spring clip at the top for holding papers or a writing pad. **2.** *Computer Science* A file or an area in memory where cut or copied text and graphics can be stored before being moved.

clip joint *n. Slang* A restaurant, nightclub, or other business where customers are regularly overcharged.

clipped form (klĭpt) *n.* A word formed by dropping one or more syllables from a polysyllabic word, such as *prof.*

clip•per (klĭp′ər) *n.* **1.** One that cuts, shears, or clips. **2.** An instrument or tool for cutting, clipping, or shearing. Often used in the plural: *nail clippers.* **3.** *Nautical* A sharp-bowed sailing vessel of the mid-19th century that was built for great speed. **4.** One that moves very fast. **5.** *Electronics* See **limiter** 2.

clip•ping (klĭp′ĭng) *n.* **1.** Something cut off or out, esp. from a newspaper or magazine. **2.** See **clipped form.**

clip•sheet (klĭp′shēt′) *n.* A sheet of paper containing news items and other newspaper material, usu. printed on only one side for convenience in clipping and reprinting.

clique (klēk, klĭk) *n.* A small exclusive group of friends or associates. ❖ *intr.v.* **cliqued, cliqu•ing, cliques** *Informal* To form, associate in, or act as a clique. [Fr. < OFr., latch, or < obsolete Fr. *cliquer*, to click, clink, of imit. orig.] —**cliqu′ey, cliqu′y, cliqu′ish** *adj.* —**cliqu′ish•ly** *adv.* —**cliqu′ish•ness** *n.*

Clis•the•nes (klĭs′thə-nēz′) See **Cleisthenes.**

cli•tel•lum (klī-tĕl′əm) *n., pl.* **-tel•la** (-tĕl′ə) A glandular saddlelike epidermal region of certain annelid worms that secretes a fluid to form a cocoon for their eggs. [NLat. *clītellum*, sing. of Lat. *clītellae*, packsaddle. See **klei-** in App.]

clit•ic (klĭt′ĭk) *n.* An unstressed word, typically a function word, that is incapable of standing on its own and attaches in pronunciation to a stressed word, with which it forms a single accentual unit, as the definite article in French *l'arme*, "the arm." [Gk. *klitikos*, leaning < *klīnein*, to lean. See **klei-** in App.] —**clit′ic** *adj.* —**clit′i•cize** (-sīz′) *v.* —**clit′i•ci•za′tion** (-sĭ-zā′shən) *n.*

clit•o•ri•dec•to•my (klĭt′ər-ĭ-dĕk′tə-mē, klī′tər-) also **clit•o•rec•to•my** (klĭt′ə-rĕk′tə-mē, klī′tə-) *n., pl.* **-mies 1.** Surgical removal of the clitoris. **2.** See **female circumcision.** [Gk. *kleitoris, kleitorid-*, clitoris; see CLITORIS + –ECTOMY.]

clit•o•ris (klĭt′ər-ĭs, klĭ-tôr′ĭs, klī′tər-ĭs) *n.* A small elongated erectile organ at the anterior part of the vulva. [NLat. *clītoris* < Gk. *kleitoris.* See **klei-** in App.] —**clit′o•ral** (-ər-əl) *adj.*

Clive (klīv), **Robert.** Baron Clive of Plassey. 1725–74. British soldier who was instrumental in securing Great Britain's interests in India.

clo•a•ca (klō-ā′kə) *n., pl.* **-cae** (-sē′) **1.** A sewer or latrine. **2.** *Zoology* **a.** The common cavity into which the intestinal, genital, and urinary tracts open in vertebrates such as fish, reptiles, birds, and some primitive mammals. **b.** The posterior part of the intestinal tract in various invertebrates. [Lat. *cloāca*, sewer, canal.] **—clo•a′cal** (-kəl) *adj.*

cloak (klōk) *n.* **1.** A loose outer garment, such as a cape. **2.** Something that covers or conceals. ❖ *tr.v.* **cloaked, cloak•ing, cloaks** To cover or conceal with or as if with a cloak. See Syns at **hide**[1]. [ME *cloke* < ONFr. *cloque*, cloak, bell (< its shape) < Med.Lat. *clocca*. See CLOCK[1].]

cloak-and-dag•ger (klōk′ən-dăg′ər) *adj.* Marked by melodramatic intrigue and often by espionage.

cloak fern *n.* Any of various ferns in the genus *Notholaena*, native chiefly to the temperate and tropical Americas and having pinnately compound leaves.

cloak•room (klōk′ro͝om′, -ro͞om′) *n.* **1.** A room where coats and other articles may be left temporarily, as in a theater. **2.** A private lounge adjacent to a legislative chamber.

clob•ber (klŏb′ər) *tr.v.* **-bered, -ber•ing, -bers** *Slang* **1.** To strike violently and repeatedly; batter or maul. **2.** To defeat decisively. **3.** To criticize harshly. [?]

clo•chard (klō-shär′) *n., pl.* **-chards** (-shär′) A tramp; a vagrant. [Fr. < *clocher*, to limp < OFr. < VLat. **cloppicāre* < *cloppus*, lame person, alteration of Lat. *claudus*.]

cloche (klōsh) *n.* **1.** A close-fitting woman's hat with a bell-like shape. **2.** A usu. bell-shaped cover, used to protect plants from frost. [Fr. < OFr., bell < Med.Lat. *clocca*. See CLOCK[1].]

clock[1] (klŏk) *n.* **1.** An instrument other than a watch for measuring or indicating time, esp. a mechanical or electronic device. **2.** A time clock. **3.** A source of regularly occurring pulses used to measure the passage of time, as in a computer. **4.** Any of various devices that indicate measurement, such as a speedometer. **5.** A biological clock. **6.** *Botany* The downy flower head of a dandelion that has gone to seed. ❖ *v.* **clocked, clock•ing, clocks** *—tr.* **1.** To time, as with a stopwatch. **2.** To register or record with a mechanical device. *—intr.* To record working hours with a time clock: *clocks in at 8 A.M.* ***—idioms:* around (or round) the clock** Continuously. **clean (someone's) clock** *Slang* To beat or defeat decisively. [ME *clokke* < ONFr. *cloque*, bell, or < MDu. *clocke*, bell, clock, both < Med.Lat. *clocca*, of imit. orig.] **—clock′er** *n.*

clock[2] (klŏk) *n.* An embroidered or woven decoration on a stocking or sock. [Perh. < CLOCK[1], bell (obsolete).]

clock radio *n.* A radio having a built-in alarm clock that can be set to turn the radio on automatically.

clock•wise (klŏk′wīz′) *adv. & adj.* In the same direction as the rotating hands of a clock.

clock•work (klŏk′wûrk′) *n.* A mechanism of geared wheels driven by a wound spring, as in a mechanical clock. ***—idiom:* like clockwork** With machinelike regularity and precision.

clod (klŏd) *n.* **1.** A lump or chunk, esp. of earth or clay. **2.** Earth or soil. **3.** A dull, stupid person; a dolt. [ME, var. of *clot*, lump. See CLOT.] **—clod′dish** *adj.* **—clod′dish•ly** *adv.*

clod•hop•per (klŏd′hŏp′ər) *n.* **1.** A clumsy coarse person; a bumpkin. **2.** A big heavy shoe.

clo•fi•brate (klō-fī′brāt, -fĭb′rāt) *n.* A synthetic drug, $C_{12}H_{15}ClO_3$, used primarily to reduce abnormally elevated levels of plasma cholesterol and triglyceride. [*clofibr(ic acid)* (perh. C(H)LO(RO)– + FIBR(O)– + –IC) + –ATE[2].]

clog (klôg, klŏg) *n.* **1.** An obstruction or hindrance. **2.** A weight attached to the leg of an animal to hinder movement. **3.** A heavy, usu. wooden-soled shoe. ❖ *v.* **clogged, clog•ging, clogs** *—tr.* **1.** To obstruct movement on or in; block up. **2.** To hamper the function or activity of; impede. *—intr.* **1.** To become obstructed or choked up. **2.** To thicken or stick together; clot. **3.** To do a clog dance. [ME.]

clog dance *n.* A dance performed while wearing clogs and characterized by heavy stamping steps. **—clog dancer** *n.*

cloi•son•né (kloi′zə-nā′, klə-wä′zə-) *n.* **1.** Decorative enamelwork in which metal filaments are fused to the surface of an object to outline a design that is filled in with enamel paste. **2.** The art or process of producing such enamelware. [Fr., p. part. of *cloisonner*, to partition < OFr. *cloison*, partition < VLat. **clausiō*, *clausiōn-* < Lat. *clausus*, p. part. of *claudere*, to close, lock.] **—cloi•son•né′** *adj.*

clois•ter (kloi′stər) *n.* **1.** A covered walk with an open colonnade on one side, running along the walls of buildings that face a quadrangle. **2a.** A place, esp. a monastery or convent, devoted to religious seclusion. **b.** Life in a monastery or convent. **3.** A secluded, quiet place. ❖ *tr.v.* **-tered, -ter•ing, -ters 1.** To shut away from the world in or as if in a cloister; seclude. **2.** To furnish (a building) with a cloister. [ME *cloistre* < OFr., alteration of *clostre* < Lat. *claustrum*, enclosed place < *claudere*, to close.]

clois•tral (kloi′strəl) also **claus•tral** (klô′strəl) *adj.* **1.** Of, relating to, or like a cloister; secluded. **2.** Living in a cloister.

clomb (klōm) *v.* *Archaic* A past tense and a past participle of **climb.**

clomp (klŏmp) *intr.v.* **clomped, clomp•ing, clomps** To walk heavily and noisily. [Imit.]

clone (klōn) *n.* **1.** A cell, group of cells, or organism descended from and genetically identical to a single common ancestor. **2.** An organism descended asexually from a single ancestor, as a plant or polyp. **3.** A replica of a DNA sequence, such as a gene, produced by genetic engineering and transferred from one organism to another. **4.** One that copies or closely resembles another, as in appearance or function. ❖ *v.* **cloned, clon•ing, clones** *—tr.* **1.** To make multiple identical copies of (a DNA sequence). **2.** To create or propagate (an organism) from a clone cell: *clone a sheep.* **3.** To reproduce or propagate asexually: *clone a plant variety.* **4.** To produce a copy of; imitate closely. *—intr.* To grow as a clone. [Gk. *klōn*, twig.] **—clon′al** (klō′nəl) *adj.* **—clon′al•ly** *adv.* **—clon′er** *n.*

clo•nus (klō′nəs) *n., pl.* **-nus•es** An abnormality in neuromuscular activity characterized by rapidly alternating muscular contraction and relaxation. [NLat. < Gk. *klonos*, turmoil.] **—clo′nic** (klō′nĭk, klŏn′ĭk) *adj.* **—clo•nic′i•ty** (klō-nĭs′ĭ-tē, klŏ-), **clo′nism** (klō′nĭz′əm, klŏn′ĭz′əm) *n.*

clop (klŏp) *n.* A sharp hollow sound, as of a hoof on concrete. ❖ *intr.v.* **clopped, clop•ping, clops** To make or move with this sound. [Imit.]

clo•que also **clo•qué** (klō-kā′) *n.* A cotton, silk, or rayon fabric with a raised woven pattern and a puckered or quilted look. [Fr. *cloqué*, p. part. of *cloquer*, to become blistered < dialectal *cloque*, blister < Med.Lat. *clocca*, bell. See CLOCK[1].]

close (klōs) *adj.* **clos•er, clos•est 1.** Being near in space or time. **2.** Being near in relationship. **3.** Bound by mutual interests, loyalties, or affections; intimate: *close friends.* **4.** Having little or no space between elements or parts; tight and compact: *a close weave.* **5.** Being near the surface; short: *a close haircut.* **6.** Being on the brink of: *close to tears.* **7.** Decided by a narrow margin; almost even: *a close election.* **8.** Faithful to the original. **9.** Rigorous; thorough: *close attention.* **10.** Shut; closed. **11.** Shut in; enclosed. **12.** Confining or narrow; crowded: *close quarters.* **13.** Fitting tightly. **14.** Lacking fresh air; stuffy: *a close room.* **15.** Confined to specific persons or groups: *a close secret.* **16.** Strictly confined or guarded. **17.** Hidden from view; secluded. **18.** Secretive; reticent. **19.** Giving or spending with reluctance; stingy. **20.** Not easily acquired; scarce: *Money was close.* **21.** *Linguistics* Pronounced with the tongue near the palate, as the *ee* in *meet.* Used of vowels. **22.** Marked by more rather than less punctuation, esp. commas. ❖ *v.* (klōz) **closed, clos•ing, clos•es** *—tr.* **1.** To move (a door, for example) so that an opening or passage is covered or obstructed; shut. **2.** To bar access to. **3.** To fill or stop up: *closed the cracks.* **4.** To stop the operations of permanently or temporarily. **5.** To make unavailable for use: *closed the area for development.* **6.** To bring to an end; terminate: *close a letter.* **7.** To bring together all the elements or parts of: *closed ranks.* **8.** To join or unite; bring into contact: *close a circuit.* **9.** To draw or bind together the edges of: *close a wound.* **10.** To complete the final details or negotiations on: *close a deal.* **11.** *Archaic* To enclose on all sides. *—intr.* **1.** To become shut. **2.** To come to an end; finish. **3.** To reach an agreement; come to terms. **4.** To cease operation. **5.** To be priced or listed at a specified amount when trading ends: *Stocks closed higher today.* **6a.** To engage at close quarters. **b.** To draw near. **7.** To come together. **8.** *Baseball* To finish a game by protecting a lead. Used of relief pitchers. ❖ *n.* (klōz) **1.** The act of closing. **2.** A conclusion; a finish. **3.** *Music* The concluding part of a phrase or theme; a cadence. **4.** (klōs) An enclosed place, esp. land surrounding or beside a cathedral or other building. **5.** (klōs) *Chiefly British* A narrow way or alley. **6.** *Archaic* A fight at close quarters. ❖ *adv.* (klōs) **closer, closest** In a close position or manner; closely: *close together.* ***—phrasal verbs:* close in 1.** To seem to be gathering in on all sides. **2.** To advance on a target so as to block escape. **3.** To surround so as to make unusable. **close out 1.** To dispose of (a line of merchandise) at reduced prices. **2.** To terminate, as by selling. ***—idioms:* close to home** So as to affect one's feelings or interests. **close to the wind** At a close angle into the direction from which the wind blows. [ME *clos*, closed < OFr. < Lat. *clausus*, p. part. of *claudere*, to close.] **—close′ly** *adv.* **—close′ness** *n.* **—clos′ing** (klō′zĭng) *n.*

SYNONYMS *close, immediate, near, nearby, nigh, proximate* These adjectives mean not far from another in space, time, or relationship: *an airport close to town; her immediate family; his nearest relative; a nearby library; the nighest route; a proximate town.* **ANTONYM** *far*

close call (klōs) *n.* *Informal* A narrow escape.

close corporation (klōs) *n.* See **closed corporation.**

closed (klōzd) *adj.* **1.** Having boundaries; enclosed. **2.** Blocked or barred to passage or entry. **3.** Explicitly limited; restricted. **4.** Self-contained or self-sufficient. **5.** Barred to the public; conducted in secrecy. **6.** *Mathematics* **a.** Of or relating to a curve having no endpoints. **b.** Of or relating to a surface having no boundary curves. **c.** Of or relating to an interval containing both its endpoints. **d.** Characterized by or possessing the property by which an operation acting on an element in a set produces an element within the set. **7.** *Computer Science* Of or relating to a file that cannot be accessed. **8.** Allowing electricity to flow or pass: *a closed switch.* **9.** *Linguistics* Ending in a consonant. **10.** *Sports* Having the forward foot closer than the rear foot to the intended point of impact with the ball: *a closed batting stance.* **11.** *Physics* Of or relating to a model of the universe having sufficient matter to halt its expansion.

closed-cap•tioned (klōzd′kăp′shənd) *adj.* Broadcast with cap-

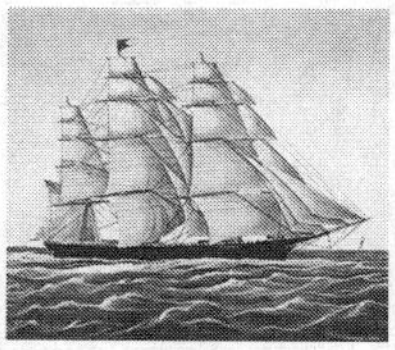

clipper
detail from *Clipper Ship 'Flying Cloud,'* an 1852 lithograph by Currier & Ives

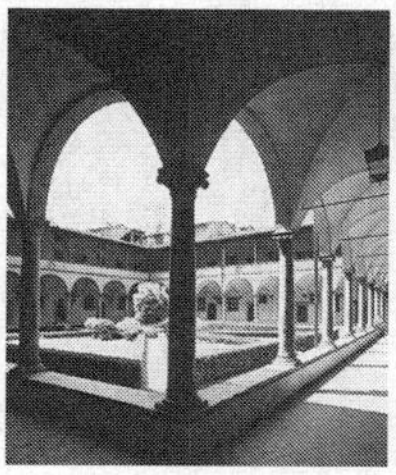

cloister
cloister at the church of San Lorenzo, Florence, Italy

ă	pat	oi	boy
ā	pay	ou	out
âr	care	o͝o	took
ä	father	o͞o	boot
ĕ	pet	ŭ	cut
ē	be	ûr	urge
ĭ	pit	th	thin
ī	pie	*th*	this
îr	pier	hw	which
ŏ	pot	zh	vision
ō	toe	ə	about, item
ô	paw		

Stress marks:
′ (primary);
′ (secondary), as in
lexicon (lĕk′sĭ-kŏn′)

tions seen only on a specially equipped receiver.

closed chain n. Chemistry See **ring**[1] 15.

closed circuit n. **1.** An electric circuit providing an uninterrupted, endless path for the flow of current. **2.** A television transmission circuit with a limited number of reception stations and no broadcast facilities. —**closed′-cir′cuit** (klōzd′sûr′kĭt) adj.

closed corporation n. A corporation in which the stock is held by relatively few persons and is not publicly traded.

closed couplet n. A rhymed couplet forming a complete thought or syntactic unit, for example, Should Humpty Dumpty chance to fall,/Who next will prance atop the wall?

closed-door (klōzd′dôr′, -dōr′) adj. Not open to the public.

closed-end (klōzd′ĕnd′) adj. Issuing a fixed number of shares that can be traded publicly but are not redeemable by the issuer: a closed-end investment company.

closed interval n. A set of numbers consisting of all the numbers between a pair of given numbers and including the endpoints.

close·down (klōz′doun′) n. A suspension or termination of operations: a plant closedown.

closed shop n. See **union shop**.

closed universe n. A model of the universe having sufficient matter and gravitational force to halt the expansion initiated by the big bang.

close-fist·ed (klōs′fĭs′tĭd) adj. Tightfisted; stingy.

close-grained (klōs′grānd′) adj. Dense or compact in structure or texture, as a wood composed of small-diameter cells.

close-hauled (klōs′hôld′) adv. & adj. Nautical With sails trimmed flat for sailing as close to the wind as possible.

close-knit (klōs′nĭt′) adj. Held tightly together, as socially.

close-mind·ed (klōs′mīn′dĭd, klōz′-) or **closed-mind·ed** (klōzd′-) adj. Intolerant of the beliefs and opinions of others; unreceptive to new ideas. —**close′-mind′ed·ness** n.

close-mouthed (klōs′mouthd′, -moutht′) adj. Tightlipped.

close-or·der drill (klōs′ôr′dər) n. A military drill in marching, maneuvering, and formal handling of arms in which the participants perform at close intervals.

close·out (klōz′out′) n. A sale in which all remaining stock is disposed of, usu. at greatly reduced prices.

clos·er (klō′zər) n. **1.** One that closes: the closer of the shop. **2.** Baseball A relief pitcher called upon to protect a lead late in a game.

close shave (klōs) n. Informal A narrow escape; a close call.

clos·et (klŏz′ĭt, klô′zĭt) n. **1.** A cabinet or enclosed recess for linens, household supplies, or clothing. **2.** A small private chamber, as for study or prayer. **3.** A water closet; a toilet. **4.** A state of secrecy or cautious privacy. ❖ tr.v. -et·ed, -et·ing, -ets To enclose or shut up in a private room, as for discussion. ❖ adj. **1.** Private; confidential: closet information. **2.** Being so or engaging only in private; secret. **3.** Based on theory and speculation rather than practice. [ME, private room < OFr., dim. of clos, enclosure < Lat. clausum < neut. of clausus, enclosed. See CLOSE.] —**clos′et·ful′** n.

closet drama n. A play to be read rather than performed.

clos·et·ed (klŏz′ĭ-tĭd, klô′zĭ-) adj. Being in a state of secrecy or cautious privacy.

close-up (klōs′ŭp′) n. **1.** A photograph, film, or television shot in which the subject is shown at a relatively large scale. **2.** An intimate view or description. —**close′-up′** adj.

clos·ing (klō′zĭng) n. **1.** The end or conclusion: the closing of a debate. **2.** A meeting for completing a transaction, esp. in transferring ownership of real estate.

closing transaction n. **1.** The last transaction for a security during a trading day. **2.** An option order that will eliminate or decrease the size of an existing option position.

clos·trid·i·um (klŏ-strĭd′ē-əm) n., pl. **-i·a** (-ē-ə) Any of various rod-shaped, spore-forming, chiefly anaerobic bacteria of the genus Clostridium. [NLat. Clostridium, genus name < Gk. klōstēr, klōstr-, spindle < klōthein, to spin.]

clo·sure (klō′zhər) n. **1.** The act of closing or the state of being closed: closure of an incision. **2.** Something that closes or shuts. **3.** A bringing to an end; a conclusion. **4.** See **cloture**. **5.** The property of being mathematically closed. ❖ tr.v. -sured, -sur·ing, -sures To cloture (a debate). [ME < OFr. < LLat. clausūra, fortress, lock < clausus, enclosed. See CLOSE.]

clot (klŏt) n. **1.** A thick, viscous, or coagulated mass or lump, as of blood. **2.** A clump, mass, or lump, as of clay. **3.** A compact group. ❖ v. **clot·ted, clot·ting, clots** —intr. To form into a clot or clots; coagulate. —tr. **1.** To cause to form into a clot or clots. **2.** To fill or cover with or as if with clots. [ME < OE clott, lump.]

cloth (klôth, klŏth) n., pl. **cloths** (klôths, klôthz, klôths, klŏthz) **1.** Fabric or material formed by weaving, knitting, pressing, or felting natural or synthetic fibers. **2.** A piece of fabric or material used for a specific purpose. **3.** Nautical **a.** Canvas. **b.** A sail. **4.** The characteristic attire of a profession, esp. that of the clergy. **5.** The clergy. —idiom: **in cloth** With a clothbound binding. [ME < OE clāth.]

cloth·bound (klôth′bound′, klŏth′-) n. Having a cover of thick paper boards covered with cloth. Used of a book.

clothe (klōth) tr.v. **clothed** or **clad** (klăd), **cloth·ing, clothes 1.** To put clothes on. **2.** To provide clothes for. **3.** To cover as with clothing. [ME clothen < OE clāthian < clāth, cloth.]

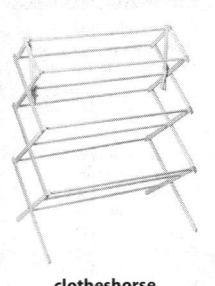

clotheshorse

clothes (klōz, klōthz) pl.n. **1.** Articles of dress; wearing apparel. **2.** Bedclothes. [ME < OE clāthas, pl. of clāth, cloth.]

clothes·horse (klōz′hôrs′, klōthz′-) n. **1.** A frame for drying or airing clothes. **2.** A person overconcerned with dress.

clothes·line (klōz′līn′, klōthz′-) n. A cord, rope, or wire on which clothes may be hung to dry or air.

clothes moth n. Any of various moths of the family Tineidae, whose larvae feed on wool, hair, fur, and feathers.

clothes·pin (klōz′pĭn′, klōthz′-) n. A clip of wood or plastic for fastening clothes to a clothesline.

clothes·press also **clothes press** (klōz′prĕs′, klōthz′-) n. A chest, closet, or wardrobe in which clothes are kept.

clothes tree n. An upright pole or stand with hooks or pegs on which to hang clothing.

cloth·ier (klōth′yər, klō′thē-ər) n. One that makes or sells clothing or cloth.

cloth·ing (klō′thĭng) n. **1.** Clothes considered as a group; wearing apparel. **2.** A covering.

Clo·tho (klō′thō) n. Greek Mythology One of the three Fates, the spinner of the thread of destiny. [Gk. Klōthō < klōthein, to spin.]

cloth yard n. The standard unit of cloth measurement, equal to 36 inches (0.914 meter).

clot·ted cream (klŏt′ĭd) n. A thick cream made primarily in England by heating milk until a layer of cream forms on its surface that is then cooled and skimmed off.

clo·ture (klō′chər) n. A parliamentary procedure by which debate is ended and an immediate vote is taken on the matter under discussion. ❖ tr.v. -tured, -tur·ing, -tures To apply cloture to (a parliamentary debate). [Fr. clôture < OFr. closture, prob. alteration of closure, closure. See CLOSURE.]

cloud (kloud) n. **1a.** A visible body of very fine water droplets or ice particles suspended in the atmosphere at altitudes ranging up to several miles above sea level. **b.** A mass, as of dust, suspended in the atmosphere or in outer space. **2.** A large moving body of things in the air or on the ground. **3.** Something that darkens or fills with gloom. **4.** A dark region or blemish, as on a polished stone. **5.** Something that obscures. **6.** Suspicion or a charge affecting a reputation. **7.** A collection of charged particles. ❖ v. **cloud·ed, cloud·ing, clouds** —tr. **1.** To cover with or as if with clouds. **2.** To make gloomy or troubled. **3.** To obscure. **4.** To cast aspersions on; sully. —intr. To become cloudy or overcast. —idiom: **in the clouds 1.** Imaginary; unreal; fanciful. **2.** Impractical. [ME, hill, cloud < OE clūd, rock, hill.] —**cloud′less** adj.

cloud·ber·ry (kloud′bĕr′ē) n. A creeping perennial herb (Rubus chamaemorus) in the rose family, native to northern regions and having white flowers and edible yellowish fruit.

cloud·burst (kloud′bûrst′) n. A sudden heavy rainstorm.

cloud chamber n. A gas-filled device in which the path of charged subatomic particles can be detected by the formation of chains of droplets on ions generated by their passage.

cloud·land (kloud′lănd′) n. A realm of imagination or fantasy.

cloud·let (kloud′lĭt) n. A small cloud or something like one.

cloud nine n. Informal A state of elation or great happiness.

cloud·y (kloud′ē) adj. **-i·er, -i·est 1.** Full of or covered with clouds; overcast. **2.** Of or like a cloud or clouds. **3.** Marked with indistinct masses or streaks: cloudy marble. **4.** Not transparent, as certain liquids. **5a.** Open to more than one interpretation. **b.** Not clearly perceived or perceptible. **6.** Troubled; gloomy. —**cloud′i·ly** adv. —**cloud′i·ness** n.

clout (klout) n. **1.** A blow, esp. with the fist. **2a.** Baseball A long powerful hit. **b.** Sports An archery target. **3.** Informal **a.** Influence; pull. **b.** Power; muscle. **4.** Chiefly Midland US A piece of cloth, esp. a baby's diaper. ❖ tr.v. **clout·ed, clout·ing, clouts** To hit, esp. with the fist. [ME, prob. < OE clūt, cloth patch.]

clove[1] (klōv) n. **1.** An evergreen tree (Syzygium aromaticum) native to the Moluccas and widely cultivated for its aromatic dried flower buds. **2.** A flower bud of this plant, used as a spice. Often used in the plural. [ME < OFr. clou (de girofle), nail (of the clove tree) < Lat. clāvus, nail.]

clove[2] (klōv) n. One of the small sections of a separable bulb, as that of garlic. [ME < OE clufu.]

clove[3] (klōv) v. **1.** A past tense of **cleave**[1]. **2.** Archaic A past participle of **cleave**[1].

clove[4] (klōv) v. Archaic A past tense of **cleave**[2].

clove hitch n. A knot used to secure a line to a spar, post, or other object, consisting of two half hitches made in opposite directions. [ME clove, split, p. part. of cleven, to split. See CLEAVE[1].]

clo·ven (klō′vən) v. A past participle of **cleave**[1]. ❖ adj. Split; divided.

cloven foot n. See **cloven hoof** 1. —**clo′ven-foot′ed** (klō′vən-fōōt′ĭd) adj.

cloven hoof n. **1.** A divided or cleft hoof, as in deer or cattle. **2.** Evil or Satan, often represented as a figure that has cleft hooves. —**clo′ven-hoofed′** (klō′vən-hōōft′, -hōōft′, -hōōvd′, -hōōvd′) adj.

clove oil n. An aromatic oil obtained from the buds, stems, or leaves of the clove tree. Used of a flavoring and perfumery.

clove pink n. See **carnation** 1.

clo·ver (klō′vər) n. **1.** Any of various herbs of the genus Trifolium in the pea family, having trifoliolate leaves and dense heads of small flowers. **2.** Any of several other plants in the pea family, such as sweet clover. **3.** Any of several nonleguminous plants, such as water clover. ***—idiom:* in clover** Living a carefree life. [ME < OE *clāfre.*]

clo•ver•leaf (klō′vər-lēf′) *n.* A highway interchange at which two highways have a series of entrance and exit ramps resembling the outline of a four-leaf clover and enabling vehicles to proceed in either direction on either highway. ❖ *adj.* Resembling or shaped like a leaf of the clover plant.

Clo•vis (klō′vĭs) *adj.* Of or relating to a culture widespread throughout North America from about 12,000 to 9,000 B.C., distinguished by sharp, fluted projectile points made of chalcedony or obsidian. [After *Clovis,* New Mexico.]

Clovis I A.D. 466?–511. King of the Franks (481–511) who unified Gaul as a single kingdom with Paris as its cap.

clown (kloun) *n.* **1a.** A buffoon or jester who entertains by jokes, antics, and tricks, as in a circus or play. **b.** One who jokes and plays tricks. **2.** A coarse, rude, vulgar person; a boor. **3.** A peasant; a rustic. ❖ *intr.v.* **clowned, clown•ing, clowns 1.** To behave like a buffoon or jester. **2.** To perform as a buffoon or jester. [Of Scand. orig. (akin to Icel. *klunni,* clumsy person) or of LGer. orig.] **—clown′ish** *adj.* **—clown′ish•ly** *adv.*

clown anemone *n.* See **anemone fish.**

clown fish *n.* See **anemone fish.**

cloy (kloi) *v.* **cloyed, cloy•ing, cloys** *—tr.* To cause distaste or disgust by supplying with too much of something originally pleasant, esp. something rich or sweet; surfeit. *—intr.* To be too filling, rich, or sweet. [Short for obsolete *accloy,* to clog < ME *acloien* < OFr. *encloer,* to drive a nail into < Med.Lat. *inclāvāre* : Lat. *in-,* in; see IN–[2] + Lat. *clāvāre,* to nail (< *clāvus,* nail).] **—cloy′ing•ly** *adv.* **—cloy′ing•ness** *n.*

clo•za•pine (klō′zə-pēn′, -pĭn) *n.* An antipsychotic drug used as a sedative and in the treatment of schizophrenia. [C(H)LO(RO)– + alteration of *(dia)zepine* (DIAZEP(AM) + –INE[2]).]

cloze (klōz) *adj.* Based on or being a test of reading comprehension that asks one to supply words systematically deleted from a text. [Alteration of CLOSURE.]

CLU *abbr.* chartered life underwriter

club (klŭb) *n.* **1.** A stout heavy stick, usu. thicker at one end, suitable for use as a weapon. **2.** *Sports* An implement used in some games to drive a ball, esp. a stick with a protruding head used in golf. **3.** *Games* **a.** A black figure shaped like a trefoil or clover leaf on certain playing cards. **b.** A playing card with this figure. **c. clubs** (*used with a sing. or pl. verb*) The suit of cards represented by this figure. **4.** A group of people organized for a common purpose, esp. a group that meets regularly: *a garden club.* **5.** The building, room, or other facility used for the meetings of an organized group. **6.** *Sports* An athletic team or organization. **7.** A nightclub. ❖ *v.* **clubbed, club•bing, clubs** *—tr.* **1.** To strike or beat with or as if with a club. **2.** To gather or combine (hair, for example) into a clublike mass. **3.** To contribute to a joint or common purpose. *—intr.* To join or combine for a common purpose; form a club. [ME < ON *klubba.*]

club•ba•ble also **club•a•ble** (klŭb′ə-bəl) *adj. Informal* Suited to membership in a social club; sociable.

clubbed (klŭbd) *adj.* Shaped like a club.

club•ber (klŭb′ər) *n.* **1.** One that wields a club. **2.** One who is active in a club.

club•by (klŭb′ē) *adj.* **-bi•er, -bi•est 1.** Typical of a club or club members. **2.** Friendly; sociable. **3.** Clannish; exclusive. **—club′bi•ness** *n.*

club car *n.* A railroad passenger car equipped with lounge chairs, tables, a buffet or bar, and other comforts.

club chair *n.* An easy chair with arms and a low back.

club•foot (klŭb′fo͝ot′) *n.* **1.** A congenital deformity of the foot, usu. marked by a curled shape or twisted position of the ankle, heel, and toes. **2.** A foot so deformed. **—club′foot′ed** *adj.*

club•house (klŭb′hous′) *n.* **1a.** A building occupied by a club. **b.** The main building of a country club. **2.** *Sports* The locker room of an athletic team.

club moss or **club-moss** (klŭb′môs′, -mŏs′) *n.* Any of various vascular plants of the genus *Lycopodium,* often resembling mosses and reproducing by spores. [< the club-shaped strobiles on some species of this plant.]

club root *n.* A disease of cabbage and related plants, caused by a fungus *(Plasmodiophora brassicae)* and characterized by knobby or club-shaped swellings on the roots and wilting, yellowing, and stunted growth of aboveground parts.

club sandwich *n.* A sandwich composed of two or three slices of bread with various meats, tomato, lettuce, and dressing.

club soda *n.* See **carbonated water.**

club steak *n.* See **Delmonico steak.**

cluck (klŭk) *n.* **1a.** The characteristic sound made by a hen when brooding or calling its chicks. **b.** A sound similar to this. **2.** *Informal* A stupid or foolish person. ❖ *v.* **clucked, cluck•ing, clucks** *—intr.* **1.** To utter a cluck. **2.** To make a cluck, as in coaxing a horse. *—tr.* **1.** To call by clucking. **2.** To express by clucking. [ME *clokken* < OE *cloccian.*]

clue[1] (klo͞o) *n.* Something that serves to guide or direct in the solution of a problem or mystery. ❖ *tr.v.* **clued, clue•ing** or **clu•ing, clues** To give (someone) guiding information. [Variant of CLEW[1] (< Theseus's use of a ball of thread as a guide through the Cretan labyrinth).]

clue[2] (klo͞o) *Nautical n.* Variant of **clew[1]** 4. ❖ *v.* Variant of **clew[1]** 2.

clue•less (klo͞o′lĭs) *adj.* Lacking understanding or knowledge.

Cluj-Na•po•ca (klo͞ozh′nä-pô′kä) A city of W-central Romania NW of Bucharest; founded in the 12th cent. Pop. 321,850.

Clum•ber spaniel also **clum•ber spaniel** (klŭm′bər) *n.* A dog of a breed developed in England, having short legs, a stocky body, and a silky, predominantly white coat. [After *Clumber Park,* an estate in Nottinghamshire, England.]

clump (klŭmp) *n.* **1.** A clustered mass; a lump: *clumps of soil.* **2.** A thick grouping, as of trees or bushes. **3.** A heavy dull sound; a thud. ❖ *v.* **clumped, clump•ing, clumps** *—intr.* **1.** To form clumps. **2.** To walk or move so as to make a clump. *—tr.* To gather into or form clumps of. [Prob. LGer. *klump* < MLGer. *klumpe,* cluster of trees.] **—clump′y** *adj.*

clum•sy (klŭm′zē) *adj.* **-si•er, -si•est 1.** Lacking physical coordination, skill, or grace; awkward. **2.** Awkwardly constructed; unwieldy. **3.** Gauche; inept. [< obsolete *clumse,* to be numb with cold < ME *clomsen,* of Scand. orig.] **—clum′si•ly** *adv.* **—clum′si•ness** *n.*

clung (klŭng) *v.* Past tense and past participle of **cling.**

clunk (klŭngk) *n.* **1.** A dull sound; a thump. **2.** A blow that produces a dull sound. **3.** *Informal* A stupid, dull person. ❖ *v.* **clunked, clunk•ing, clunks** *—intr.* **1.** To make or move with a clunk. **2.** To strike something so as to make a dull sound. *—tr.* To strike so as to make a dull sound. [Imit.]

clunk•er (clŭng′kər) *n. Informal* **1.** A decrepit machine, esp. an old car; a rattletrap. **2.** A failure; a flop.

clunk•y (klŭng′kē) *adj.* **-i•er, -i•est** Clumsy; awkward.

Clu•ny (klo͞o′nē, klo͞o-nē′, klü-) A town of E-central France NNW of Lyon; site of an abbey founded in 910. Pop. 4,724.

clu•pe•id (klo͞o′pē-ĭd) *n.* Any of various soft-finned fishes of the family Clupeidae, as herrings. [< NLat. *Clupeidae,* family name < Lat. *clupea,* a small fish.] **—clu′pe•id** *adj.*

clus•ter (klŭs′tər) *n.* **1.** A group of the same or similar elements gathered or occurring closely together; a bunch. **2.** *Linguistics* Two or more successive consonants in a word, as *cl* and *st* in the word *cluster.* **3.** A group of academic courses in a related area. ❖ *v.* **-tered, -ter•ing, -ters** *—intr.* To gather or grow into bunches. *—tr.* To cause to grow or form into bunches. [ME < OE *clyster.*]

cluster bean *n.* See **guar.**

cluster bomb *n.* A bomb or artillery shell that releases explosive fragments over a wide area.

clutch[1] (klŭch) *v.* **clutched, clutch•ing, clutch•es** *—tr.* **1.** To grasp and hold tightly. **2.** To seize; snatch. *—intr.* **1.** To attempt to grasp or seize. **2.** To engage or disengage a motor vehicle's clutch. ❖ *n.* **1.** A hand, claw, talon, or paw in the act of grasping. **2.** A tight grasp. **3.** Control or power. Often used in the plural. **4.** A device for gripping and holding. **5a.** Any of various devices for engaging and disengaging two working parts of a shaft or of a shaft and a driving mechanism. **b.** The apparatus, such as a lever or pedal, that activates one of these devices. **6.** A tense, critical situation. **7.** A clutch bag. ❖ *adj. Informal* **1.** Being or occurring in a tense or critical situation. **2.** Tending to be successful in tense or critical situations. [ME *clucchen* < OE *clyccan.*]

clutch[2] (klŭch) *n.* **1.** The complete set of eggs produced or incubated at one time. **2.** A brood of chickens. **3.** A group; a bunch. ❖ *tr.v.* **clutched, clutch•ing, clutch•es** To hatch (chicks). [Variant of dialectal *cletch* < ME *clekken,* to hatch < ON *klekja.*]

clutch bag *n.* A woman's purse that is strapless and carried in the hand.

clut•ter (klŭt′ər) *n.* **1.** A confused or disordered state or collection; a jumble. **2.** A confused noise; a clatter. ❖ *v.* **-tered, -ter•ing, -ters** *—tr.* **1.** To litter or pile in a disordered manner. **2.** To make disorderly by filling or covering with objects. *—intr.* **1.** To run or move with bustle and confusion. **2.** To make a clatter. [Prob. < ME *cloteren,* to clot < *clot,* lump < OE *clott.*]

Clyde (klīd) A river of SW Scotland flowing c. 171 km (106 mi) NW to the **Firth of Clyde,** an estuary of the North Channel.

Clydes•dale (klīdz′dāl′) *n.* A large powerful draft horse of a breed developed in the Clyde valley of Scotland.

clyp•e•us (klĭp′ē-əs) *n., pl.* **-e•i** (-ē-ī′) A shieldlike plate on the front of the head of an insect. [NLat. < Lat. *clipeus,* round shield.] **—clyp′e•al** (-ē-əl) *adj.*

clys•ter (klĭs′tər) *n.* An enema. [ME *clister,* ult. < Gk. *klustēr,* clyster pipe < *kluzein,* to wash out.]

Cly•tem•nes•tra also **Cly•taem•nes•tra** (klī′təm-nĕs′trə) *n. Greek Mythology* The wife of Agamemnon who with her lover Aegisthus murdered him and was later murdered by Orestes and Electra.

cm *abbr.* centimeter

Cm The symbol for the element **curium.**

CM *abbr.* **1.** center of mass **2.** common market **3.** court-martial

CMA *abbr.* certified medical assistant

Cmdr. *abbr.* commander

c'mon (kə-mŏn′, -môn′) *Informal* Contraction of *come on.*

CMOS *abbr.* complementary metal oxide semiconductor

CMSA *abbr.* Consolidated Metropolitan Statistical Area

CMSgt *abbr.* chief master sergeant

Clovis I
baptism of Clovis I in a detail from a 14th-century illuminated manuscript

Clydesdale

ă	pat	oi	boy
ā	pay	ou	out
âr	care	o͝o	took
ä	father	o͞o	boot
ĕ	pet	ŭ	cut
ē	be	ûr	urge
ĭ	pit	th	thin
ī	pie	*th*	this
îr	pier	hw	which
ŏ	pot	zh	vision
ō	toe	ə	about, item
ô	paw		

Stress marks:
′ (primary);
′ (secondary), as in
lexicon (lĕk′sĭ-kŏn′)

CMV *abbr.* cytomegalovirus

C/N *abbr.* credit note

cni·dar·i·an (nī-dâr′ē-ən) *n.* Any of various invertebrate animals of the phylum Cnidaria, characterized by a radially symmetrical body with a saclike internal cavity, and including the jellyfishes, hydras, sea anemones, and corals. ❖ *adj.* Of, relating to, or belonging to the phylum Cnidaria. [NLat. *Cnīdāria,* phylum name < Gk. *knīdē,* sea nettle.]

cni·do·blast (nī′də-blăst′) *n.* A cell in the epidermis of cnidarians in which a nematocyst is developed. [NLat. *cnida,* nematocyst (< Lat. *cnīdē,* nettle < Gk. *knīdē*) +‑BLAST.]

Cni·dus also **Cni·dos** (nī′dəs) An ancient Greek city of Asia Minor in present-day SW Turkey.

CNO *abbr.* chief of naval operations

Cnos·sos or **Cnos·sus** (nŏs′əs) See **Knossos.**

CNS *abbr.* central nervous system

Cnut (kə-nōōt′, -nyōōt′) See **Canute.**

Co¹ The symbol for the element **cobalt.**

Co² *abbr. Bible* Corinthians

CO *abbr.* **1.** cash order **2.** Colorado **3.** commanding officer **4.** conscientious objector

co. *abbr.* **1.** company **2.** county

c/o *abbr.* care of

co– *pref.* **1.** Together; joint; jointly; mutually: *coeducation.* **2a.** Partner or associate in an activity: *coauthor; cofounder.* **b.** Subordinate or assistant: *copilot.* **3.** To the same extent or degree: *coextensive.* **4.** Complement of an angle: *cotangent.* [ME < Lat., var. of *com‑,* com‑.]

CoA *abbr.* coenzyme A

co·ac·er·vate (kō-ăs′ər-vāt′, kō′ə-sûr′vĭt) *n.* A cluster of droplets separated out of a lyophilic colloid. ❖ *adj.* **1.** Of or relating to a cluster of droplets. **2.** *Biology* Growing in clusters. ❖ *tr.v.* **-vated, -vat·ing, -vates** To cause to form a coacervate. [< Lat. *coacervātus,* p. part. of *coacervāre,* to heap together : *co‑,* co‑ + *acervāre,* to heap (< *acervus,* a heap).] **—co·ac′er·vate** (-vāt′, -vĭt′) *adj.* **—co·ac′er·va′tion** *n.*

coach (kōch) *n.* **1a.** A motorbus. **b.** A railroad passenger car. **c.** A closed automobile, usu. with two doors. **d.** A large, closed, four-wheeled carriage with an exterior driver's seat; a stagecoach. **2.** An economical class of passenger accommodations on a commercial airplane or a train. **3.** *Sports* A person who trains or directs athletes or athletic teams. **4a.** A person who gives instruction, as in singing. **b.** A private tutor employed to prepare a student for an examination. ❖ *tr. & intr.v.* **coached, coach·ing, coach·es 1.** To train or tutor or to act as a trainer or tutor. **2.** To transport by or ride in a coach. [Fr. *coche* < obsolete Ger. *Kotsche* < Hung. *kocsi,* after *Kocs,* a town of NW Hungary (where such carriages were first made).] **—coach′a·ble** *adj.* **—coach′er** *n.*

coach dog *n.* See **Dalmatian.**

coach·man (kōch′mən) *n.* **1.** A man who drives a coach or carriage. **2.** An artificial fly used in angling.

co·ac·tion (kō-ăk′shən) *n.* **1.** An impelling or restraining force; a compulsion. **2.** Joint action. **3.** *Ecology* Any of the reciprocal actions or effects, such as symbiosis, that can occur in a community. [ME < Lat. *coaccioun* < *coāctiō, coāctiōn‑,* a collecting < *coāctus,* p. part. of *cōgere,* to collect, condense; see COAGULUM. Senses 2 and 3 : CO‑ + ACTION.] **—co·ac′tive** *adj.* **—co·ac′tive·ly** *adv.*

co·a·dapt·ed (kō′ə-dăp′tĭd) *adj.* **1.** Of or relating to genetic characteristics that have become established through mutually beneficial interaction between organisms in a community. **2.** Of or relating to interaction among genes at different loci that result in expression of these characteristics. **—co′ad·ap·ta′tion** (-ăd-ăp-tā′shən) *n.*

co·ad·ju·tant (kō-ăj′ə-tənt) *n.* A helper; an assistant.

co·ad·ju·tor (kō′ə-jōō′tər, kō-ăj′ə-tər) *n.* **1.** A coworker; an assistant. **2.** An assistant to a bishop. [ME *coadjutour,* assistant < Lat. *coadiūtor : co‑,* co‑ + *adiūtor,* assistant (< *adiūtāre,* to aid; see ADJUTANT).]

co·ad·u·nate (kō-ăj′ə-nĭt, -nāt′) *adj.* Closely joined; grown together; united. [LLat. *coadūnātus,* p. part. of *coadūnāre,* to combine : Lat. *co‑,* co‑ + Lat. *adūnāre,* to unite (*ad‑,* ad‑ + *ūnus,* one; see oi‑no‑ in App.).] **—co′ad·u·na′tion** (-nā′shən) *n.* **—co·ad′u·na′tive** *adj.*

co·ag·u·lant (kō-ăg′yə-lənt) *n.* An agent that causes a liquid or sol to coagulate. **—co·ag′u·lant** *adj.*

co·ag·u·lase (kō-ăg′yə-lās′, -lāz′) *n.* An enzyme, such as thrombin, that induces coagulation. [COAGUL(ATE) +‑ASE.]

co·ag·u·late (kō-ăg′yə-lāt′) *v.* **-lat·ed, -lat·ing, -lates** *—tr.* To cause transformation of (a liquid or sol, for example) into or as if into a soft, semisolid, or solid mass. *—intr.* To become coagulated. [ME *coagulaten* < Lat. *coāgulāre, coāgulāt‑ < coāgulum,* coagulator. See COAGULUM.] **—co·ag′u·la·bil′i·ty** *n.* **—co·ag′u·la·ble, co·ag′u·la′tive** (-lā′tĭv, -lə-tĭv) *adj.* **—co·ag′u·la′tion** *n.* **—co·ag′u·la′tor** *n.*

co·ag·u·lum (kō-ăg′yə-ləm) *n., pl.* **-la** (-lə) A coagulated mass, as of blood; a clot. [Lat. *coāgulum,* coagulator, rennet < *cōgere,* to condense : *co‑,* co‑ + *agere,* to drive; see **ag‑** in App.]

coal (kōl) *n.* **1a.** A natural, dark brown to black, graphitelike material used as a fuel, formed from fossilized plants and consisting of at least 50 percent carbon by weight. **b.** A piece of this sub-

Ty Cobb

cobblestone
cobblestone street on
Beacon Hill, Boston,
Massachusetts

stance. **2.** A glowing or charred piece of solid fuel. **3.** Charcoal. ❖ *v.* **coaled, coal·ing, coals** *—tr.* **1.** To burn (a combustible solid) to a charcoal residue. **2.** To provide with coal. *—intr.* To take on coal. [ME *col* < OE.]

co·a·lesce (kō′ə-lĕs′) *intr.v.* **-lesced, -lesc·ing, -lesc·es 1.** To grow together; fuse. **2.** To come together so as to form one whole; unite. [Lat. *coalēscere : co‑,* co‑ + *alēscere,* to grow, inchoative of *alere,* to nourish.] **—co′a·les′cence** *n.* **—co′a·les′cent** *adj.*

coal·fish (kōl′fĭsh′) *n.* Any of several black or dark-colored fishes, esp. the pollock or sablefish.

coal gas *n.* **1.** A gaseous mixture produced by the destructive distillation of bituminous coal and used as a commercial fuel. **2.** The gaseous mixture released by burning coal.

coal·i·fi·ca·tion (kō′lə-fĭ-kā′shən) *n.* Compression and hardening over long periods of time, by which coal is formed from plant materials.

co·a·li·tion (kō′ə-lĭsh′ən) *n.* **1.** An alliance, esp. a temporary one, of people, factions, parties, or nations. **2.** A combination into one body; a union. [Fr. < Med.Lat. *coalitiō, coalition‑* < Lat. *coalitus,* p. part. of *coalēscere,* to grow together. See COALESCE.] **—co′a·li′tion·ist** *n.*

coal measures *pl.n. Geology* **1.** **Coal Measures** A stratigraphic unit equivalent to the Pennsylvanian or Upper Carboniferous periods. **2.** Strata of the Carboniferous Period, usu. containing coal deposits.

coal oil *n.* See **kerosene.**

Coal·sack (kōl′săk′) *n.* **1.** A dark nebula that appears in the southern Milky Way. **2.** A similar dark nebula in the Northern Hemisphere near the constellation Cygnus.

coal tar *n.* A viscous black liquid containing numerous organic compounds that is obtained by the destructive distillation of coal and widely used, as in sealants or paints.

coam·ing (kō′mĭng) *n. Nautical* A raised rim or border around an opening designed to keep out water. [?]

co·an·chor or **co·an·chor** (kō-ăng′kər) *n.* Either of two news commentators coordinating a newscast. **—co·an′chor** *v.*

co·arc·tate (kō-ärk′tāt′) *adj. Zoology* **1.** Enclosed in an oval horny case. Used of an insect pupa. **2.** Constricted, narrowed, or compressed, as a segment of a blood vessel. [Lat. *coarctātus,* p. part. of *coarctāre,* to compress, alteration of *coartāre : co‑,* co‑ + *artāre,* to compress (< *artus,* tight, confined; see **ar‑** in App.).] **—co′arc·ta′tion** *n.*

coarse (kôrs, kōrs) *adj.* **coars·er, coars·est 1.** Of low, common, or inferior quality. **2a.** Lacking in delicacy or refinement. **b.** Vulgar or indecent. **3.** Consisting of large particles; not fine in texture. **4.** Rough, esp. to the touch: *a coarse tweed.* [ME *cars,* prob. < *course,* custom. See COURSE.] **—coarse′ly** *adv.* **—coars′en** *v.* **—coarse′ness** *n.*

coarse-grained (kôrs′grānd′, kōrs′-) *adj.* **1.** Having a rough, coarse texture. **2.** Not refined; indelicate and crude.

coast (kōst) *n.* **1a.** Land next to the sea; the seashore. **b.** **Coast** The Pacific coast of the United States. **2.** A hill or other slope down which one may coast. **3.** The act of sliding or coasting; slide. **4.** *Obsolete* The frontier or border of a country. ❖ *v.* **coast·ed, coast·ing, coasts** *—intr.* **1a.** To slide down an incline through the effect of gravity. **b.** To move effortlessly and smoothly. See Syns at **slide. 2.** To move without further use of propelling power. **3.** To act or move aimlessly or with little effort. **4.** *Nautical* To sail near or along a coast. *—tr. Nautical* To sail or move along the coast or border of. [ME *coste* < OFr. < Lat. *costa,* side.] **—coast′al** (kō′stəl) *adj.*

coast·er (kō′stər) *n.* **1.** One that coasts, as: **a.** One who acts in an aimless manner. **b.** A sled or toboggan. **c.** One who rides a sled or toboggan. **2.** *Nautical* A vessel engaged in coastal trade. **3.** A roller coaster. **4a.** A small mat or plate placed under a vessel to protect a tabletop or other surface beneath. **b.** A small tray, often on wheels, for passing something around a table. **5.** A resident of a coastal region.

coaster brake *n.* A brake and clutch on the rear wheel and drive mechanism of a bicycle operated through reverse pressure on the pedals.

coast guard also **Coast Guard** *n.* **1.** The branch of a nation's armed forces responsible for coastal defense, protection of life and property at sea, and enforcement of customs, immigration, and navigation laws. **2.** A coast guard member.

coast·guards·man (kōst′gärdz′mən) *n.* A member of a coast guard.

coast·land (kōst′lănd′) *n.* The land along a coast.

coast·line (kōst′līn′) *n.* The shape, outline, or boundary of a coast.

Coast Mountains A range of W British Columbia, Canada, and SE AK extending c. 1,609 km (1,000 mi) parallel to the Pacific coast and rising to 3,996.7 m (13,104 ft).

Coast Ranges A series of mountain ranges of extreme W North America extending from SE AK to Baja California along the coastline of the Pacific Ocean.

Coast Salish *n.* The Salish-speaking Native American peoples inhabiting the northwest Pacific coast from the Strait of Georgia to southwest Washington.

coast-to-coast (kōst′tə-kōst′) *adj.* Reaching, airing, or traveling from one coast to another.

cobra

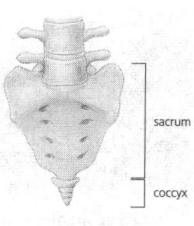

coccyx

coast·ward (kōst′wərd) *adv. & adj.* Toward or directed toward a coast. —**coast′wards** (-wərdz) *adv.*

coast·wise (kōst′wīz′) *adv. & adj.* Along, by way of, or following a coast.

coat (kōt) *n.* **1a.** A sleeved outer garment extending from the shoulders to the waist or below. **b.** A garment extending to just below the waist and usu. forming the top part of a suit. **2.** A natural outer covering; an integument. **3.** A layer of material covering something else; a coating. ❖ *tr.v.* **coat·ed, coat·ing, coats 1.** To provide or cover with a coat. **2.** To cover with a layer, as of paint. [ME *cote* < OFr., < Gmc. orig.] —**coat′ed** *adj.*

coat·dress (kōt′drĕs′) *n.* A dress that buttons up the front and is tailored somewhat like a coat.

co·a·ti (kō-ä′tē) *n., pl.* **coati** or **-tis** Any of four species of mammals of the genera *Nasua* or *Nasuella* of South and Central America and the southwest United States, related to the raccoon but having a longer snout and tail. [Sp. *coatí* and Port. *coati* < Tupi : *cua*, belt + *tim*, nose.]

co·a·ti·mun·di (kō-ä′tē-mŭn′dē) *n., pl.* **coatimundi** or **-dis** also **coatimondi** or **-dis** A coati. [Poss. Tupi *coati*; see COATI + *mundé*, animal trap.]

coat·ing (kō′tĭng) *n.* **1.** A layer of a substance spread over a surface for protection or decoration; a covering layer. **2.** Cloth for making coats.

coat of arms *n., pl.* **coats of arms** *Heraldry* **1.** A tabard or surcoat blazoned with bearings. **2a.** An arrangement of bearings, usu. depicted on and around a shield, that indicates ancestry and distinctions. **b.** A representation of bearings.

coat of mail *n., pl.* **coats of mail** An armored coat made of chain mail, interlinked rings, or overlapping metal plates; a hauberk.

coat·room (kōt′rōōm′, -rŏŏm′) *n.* See **cloakroom 1.**

coat·tail (kōt′tāl′) *n.* **1.** The loose back part of a coat that hangs below the waist. **2.** **coattails** The skirts of a formal or dress coat. —*idiom:* **on (someone's) coattails** As a result of the success of another.

coat tree *n.* See **clothes tree.**

co·au·thor or **co-au·thor** (kō-ô′thər) *n.* A collaborating or joint author. —**co·au′thor** *v.*

coax¹ (kōks) *v.* **coaxed, coax·ing, coax·es** —*tr.* **1.** To persuade or try to persuade by pleading or flattery; cajole. **2.** To obtain by persistent persuasion. **3.** To move to or adjust toward a desired end: *coaxed the girder into place.* **4.** *Obsolete* To caress; fondle. —*intr.* To use persuasion or inducement. [Obsolete *cokes*, to fool < *cokes*, fool.] —**coax′er** *n.*

co·ax² (kō′ăks, kō-ăks′) *n.* *Informal* A coaxial cable.

co·ax·i·al (kō-ăk′sē-əl) *adj.* Having or mounted on a common axis.

coaxial cable *n.* A cable consisting of a conducting metal tube enclosing and insulated from a central conducting core, used for transmitting high-frequency signals.

cob (kŏb) *n.* **1.** A corncob. **2.** A male swan. **3.** A thickset, stocky, short-legged horse. **4.** A small lump or mass, as of coal. **5.** A mixture of clay and straw used as a building material. [Prob. < obsolete *cob*, round object, head, testicle.]

co·bal·a·min (kō-băl′ə-mĭn) also **co·bal·a·mine** (-mēn′) *n.* See **vitamin B₁₂.** [COBAL(T) + (VIT)AMIN.]

co·balt (kō′bôlt′) *n.* *Symbol* **Co** A metallic element, used chiefly for magnetic alloys and high-temperature alloys and in the form of its salts for blue glass and ceramic pigments. Atomic number 27; atomic weight 58.9332; melting point 1,495°C; boiling point 2,900°C; specific gravity 8.9; valence 2, 3. See table at **element.** [Ger. *Kobalt* < MHGer. *kobolt*, var. of *kobold*, goblin (< silver miners' belief that cobalt had been placed by goblins who had stolen the silver).]

cobalt 60 *n.* A radioactive isotope of cobalt with mass number 60, used in radiotherapy, metallurgy, and materials testing.

cobalt blue *n.* **1.** A blue to green pigment consisting of a variable mixture of cobalt oxide and alumina. **2.** A moderate to deep vivid blue or greenish blue.

co·balt·ic (kō-bôl′tĭk) *adj.* Of or containing cobalt, esp. with valence 3.

co·balt·ite (kō′bôl-tīt′) also **co·balt·ine** (-tēn′) *n.* A rare mineral, cobalt sulfarsenide, CoAsS, that is a cobalt ore.

co·balt·ous (kō-bôl′təs) *adj.* Of or containing cobalt, esp. with valence 2.

Cobb (kŏb), **Tyrus Raymond ("Ty")** 1886–1961. Amer. baseball player and manager who was the first player elected to the National Baseball Hall of Fame (1936).

Cob·bett (kŏb′ĭt), **William** 1763?–1835. British journalist noted for his essays on the deterioration of rural life brought about by the Industrial Revolution.

cob·ble¹ (kŏb′əl) *n.* **1.** A cobblestone. **2.** *Geology* A rock fragment between 64 and 256 millimeters in diameter, esp. a naturally rounded one. **3.** **cobbles** See **cob coal.** ❖ *tr.v.* **-bled, -bling, -bles** To pave with cobblestones.

cob·ble² (kŏb′əl) *tr.v.* **-bled, -bling, -bles 1.** To make or mend (boots or shoes). **2.** To put together clumsily; bungle.

cob·bler¹ (kŏb′lər) *n.* **1.** One who mends or makes boots and shoes. **2.** *Archaic* One who is clumsy at work; a bungler. [ME *cobeler.*]

cob·bler² (kŏb′lər) *n.* **1.** A deep-dish fruit pie with a thick top crust. **2.** An iced drink made of wine or liqueur, sugar, and citrus fruit. [?]

cob·ble·stone (kŏb′əl-stōn′) *n.* A naturally rounded paving stone. [ME *cobelston* : obsolete *cobel*, prob. dim. of *cob*, round object; see COB + ME *ston*, stone, stone; see STONE.]

cob coal *n.* Coal in rounded lumps of various sizes.

Cob·den (kŏb′dən), **Richard** 1804–65. British politician who was a leading supporter of free trade.

co·bel·lig·er·ent (kō′bə-lĭj′ər-ənt) *n.* One, such as a nation, that assists another or others in waging war.

co·bi·a (kō′bē-ə) *n.* A large food and game fish (*Rachycentron canadum*) of tropical and subtropical seas. [Origin unknown.]

Co·blenz (kō′blĕnts′) See **Koblenz.**

cob·nut (kŏb′nŭt′) *n.* **1.** The large edible nut of a cultivated variety of hazel. **2.** The plant bearing this fruit.

CO·BOL or **Co·bol** (kō′bôl′) *n.* A programming language, used esp. for business applications, that is more like English than most other programming languages. [*Co(mmon) B(usiness-)O(riented) L(anguage)*.]

co·bra (kō′brə) *n.* **1.** Any of several venomous snakes, esp. of the genus *Naja*, that are native to Asia and Africa and capable of expanding the skin of the neck to form a flattened hood. **2.** Leather made from the skin of one of these snakes. [Short for Port. *cobra (de capello)*, snake (with a hood) < Lat. *colubra*, fem. of *coluber*.]

cob·web (kŏb′wĕb′) *n.* **1a.** The web spun by a spider to catch its prey. **b.** A single thread of a cobweb. **2.** Something resembling a cobweb. **3.** An intricate plot; a snare. **4.** **cobwebs** Confusion; disorder. ❖ *tr.v.* **-webbed, -web·bing, -webs** To cover with or as if with cobwebs. [ME *coppeweb*, spider (short for *attercoppe* < OE *ātorcoppe* : *ātor*, poison + *copp*, head) + *web*, web; see WEB.]

co·ca (kō′kə) *n.* **1.** Any of certain Andean evergreen shrubs or small trees of the genus *Erythroxylum*, esp. *E. coca*, whose leaves contain cocaine and other alkaloids. **2.** The dried leaves of such a plant, used for extraction of cocaine and other alkaloids. [Sp. < Quechua *kúka*.]

Coca, Imogene 1908–2001. Amer. comedian who costarred in comedy sketches with Sid Caesar on television.

co·caine (kō-kān′, kō′kān′) *n.* A colorless or white crystalline alkaloid, $C_{17}H_{21}NO_4$, extracted from coca leaves, sometimes used in medicine as a local anesthetic and widely used as an illicit drug for its euphoric and stimulating effects. [Fr. *cocaïne* < *coca*, coca < Sp. See COCA.]

co·cain·ism (kō-kā′nĭz′əm) *n.* The habitual or excessive use of cocaine.

co·cain·ize (kō-kā′nīz′) *tr.v.* **-ized, -iz·ing, -iz·es** To anesthetize (a body part) with cocaine.

co·car·cin·o·gen (kō′kär-sĭn′ə-jən, kō-kär′sĭn-ə-jĕn′) *n.* A substance or factor that will not promote cancer by itself but can potentiate cancer when acting with carcinogenic agents. —**co·car·cin·o·gen·ic** (-sə-nə-jĕn′ĭk) *adj.*

coc·cid (kŏk′sĭd) *n.* Any of various insects of the superfamily Coccoidea, such as the mealybugs. [< NLat. *Coccidae*, family name < *Coccus*, type genus < Gk. *kokkos*, grain.]

coc·cid·i·oi·do·my·co·sis (kŏk-sĭd′ē-oi′dō-mī-kō′sĭs) *n.* An infectious respiratory disease of humans and other animals caused by inhaling the fungus *Coccidioides immitis.* [NLat. *Coccidioides*, genus name (< *Coccidium*, former genus name; see COCCIDIUM + *-oīdēs* < Gk. *-oeidēs*, -oid) + MYCOSIS.]

coc·cid·i·o·sis (kŏk-sĭd′ē-ō′sĭs) *n.* A parasitic disease of many animals, including cattle and poultry, but rarely of humans, resulting from infestation of the alimentary canal by protozoans of the order Coccidia. [NLat. *Coccidia*, order name, pl. of *Coccidium*, former genus name; see COCCIDIUM + -OSIS.]

coc·cid·i·um (kŏk-sĭd′ē-əm) *n., pl.* **-i·a** (-ē-ə) Any of various parasitic protozoans belonging to the order Coccidia and responsible for coccidiosis. [NLat. *Coccidium*, former genus name : COCCUS + *-idium*, diminutive suff. (< Gk. *-idion*).]

coc·coid (kŏk′oid′) *adj.* Shaped like or resembling a coccus; spherical. ❖ *n.* A coccoid microorganism.

coc·co·lith (kŏk′ə-lĭth′) *n.* A microscopic calcite skeletal plate that protects certain marine phytoplankton and in a fossilized state forms chalk and limestone deposits. [COCC(US) (< its shape) + -LITH.]

coc·cus (kŏk′əs) *n., pl.* **coc·ci** (kŏk′sī, kŏk′ī) **1.** A bacterium having a spherical or spheroidal shape. **2.** *Botany* A division containing a single seed that splits apart from a many-lobed fruit. [NLat. < Gk. *kokkos*, grain.] —**coc′cal** (kŏk′əl) *adj.*

—coccus *suff.* A microorganism of spherical or spheroidal shape: *streptococcus.* [< COCCUS.]

coc·cyg·e·al (kŏk-sĭj′ē-əl) *adj.* Of or relating to the coccyx. [< NLat. *coccyx, coccyg-,* coccyx; see COCCYX.]

coc·cyx (kŏk′sĭks) *n., pl.* **coc·cy·ges** (kŏk-sī′jēz, kŏk′sĭ-jēz′) A small triangular bone at the spinal column base in humans and tailless apes, consisting of several fused rudimentary vertebrae. [NLat. *coccyx* < Gk. *kokkūx*, cuckoo, coccyx.]

Co·cha·bam·ba (kō′chə-bäm′bə, -chä-bäm′bä) A city of W-central Bolivia NNW of Sucre; founded 1574. Pop. 448,756.

Co·chin¹ (kō′chĭn) A city of SW India on the Malabar Coast of the Arabian Sea; colonized by the Portuguese in 1503. Pop. 513,249.

Co·chin² (kō′chĭn) n. See **Cochin China²**.

Cochin China¹ A region of S Indochina including the rich delta area of the Mekong R.

Cochin China² n. A large domestic fowl of a breed developed in Asia, having thickly feathered legs. [After Cochin China¹.]

coch·i·neal (kŏch′ə-nēl′, kŏch′ə-nēl′, kō′chə-, kō′chə-) n. **1.** A red dye made of the dried and pulverized bodies of female cochineal insects. **2.** A vivid red. [Fr. cochenille < Sp. cochinilla, cochineal insect, prob. < VLat. *coccinella < fem. dim. of Lat. coccinus, scarlet < Gk. kokkinos < kokkos, kermes berry.] —**coch′i·neal′** adj.

cochineal insect n. Any of several red scale insects of the family Dactylopiidae that feed on cacti and range from the southwest United States to Central America.

Co·chise (kō-chēs′, -chēz′) 1812?–74. Chiricahua Apache leader who directed Apache resistance to US troops in the Southwest (1861–72).

coch·le·a (kŏk′lē-ə, kō′klē-ə) n., pl. **-le·ae** (-lē-ē′, -lē-ī′) also **-le·as** A spiral-shaped cavity of the inner ear that contains nerve endings essential for hearing. [Lat., snail shell < Gk. kokhlias, snail < kokhlos, land snail.] —**coch′le·ar** adj.

cochlear implant n. A surgically implanted electronic device that allows people with severe hearing loss to recognize some sounds, esp. speech sounds, and that consists of a microphone and receiver, a processor that converts sound into electronic signals, and electrodes that transmit the signals to the auditory nerve.

cochlear nerve n. A division of the auditory nerve that conducts auditory stimuli to the brain.

coch·le·ate (kŏk′lē-ĭt, -āt′, kō′klē-) also **coch·le·at·ed** (-ā′tĭd) adj. Shaped like a snail shell; spirally twisted. [Lat. cochleātus < cochlea, snail shell. See COCHLEA.]

Coch·ran (kŏk′rən), **Jacqueline** 1910–80. Amer. aviator who held numerous national and international speed records.

cock¹ (kŏk) n. **1a.** An adult male chicken; a rooster. **b.** An adult male of various other birds. **2.** A weathervane shaped like a rooster; a weathercock. **3.** A leader or chief. **4.** A faucet or valve by which the flow of a liquid or gas can be regulated. **5a.** The hammer of a firearm. **b.** The position of the hammer of a firearm when cocked. **6.** A tilting or jaunty turn upward. **7.** Vulgar Slang The penis. **8.** Archaic The characteristic cry of a rooster early in the morning. ❖ v. **cocked, cock·ing, cocks** —tr. **1.** To set the hammer of (a firearm) in a position ready for firing. **2.** To set (a device, such as a camera shutter) in a position ready for use. **3.** To tilt or turn up or to one side, usu. in a jaunty or alert manner. **4.** To raise in preparation to throw or hit. —intr. **1.** To cock the hammer of a firearm. **2.** To turn or stick up. **3.** To strut; swagger. —**idioms: cock a snook** Chiefly British Slang To express scorn or derision by or as if by placing the thumb on the nose and wigling the fingers; thumb one's nose. **cock of the walk** An overbearing or domineering person. [ME cok < OE cocc, prob. < LLat. coccus < coco, a cackling, of imit. orig.]

cock² (kŏk) n. A cone-shaped pile of straw or hay. ❖ tr.v. **cocked, cock·ing, cocks** To arrange (straw or hay) into piles shaped like cones. [ME cok.]

cock·ade (kŏ-kād′) n. An ornament, such as a rosette, usu. worn on the hat as a badge. [Alteration of obsolete cockard < Fr. cocarde < OFr. coquarde, fem. of coquard, vain, cocky < coq, cock < LLat. coccus. See COCK¹.] —**cock·ad′ed** adj.

cock-a-hoop (kŏk′ə-hōōp′, -hŏŏp′) adj. **1.** Being in a state of boastful elation or exultation. **2.** Being askew. [< the phrase to set cock on hoop, to drink festively.] —**cock′-a-hoop′** adv.

Cock·aigne (kŏ-kān′) n. An imaginary land of easy and luxurious living. [ME cokaigne < OFr. < (pais de) cokaigne, (land of) plenty < MLGer. kōkenje, dim. of kōke, cake.]

cock-a-leek·ie also **cock·a·leek·ie** (kŏk′ə-lē′kē) n. A soup made with chicken broth and leeks. [Alteration of cockie (dim. of COCK¹) + leekie (dim. of LEEK).]

cock·a·lo·rum (kŏk′ə-lôr′əm, -lōr′-) n. **1.** A little man with an unduly high opinion of himself. **2.** Boastful talk; braggadocio. [Perh. alteration (influenced by Lat. -ōrum, genitive pl. ending) of obsolete Flem. kockeloeren, to crow, of imit. orig.]

cock·a·ma·mie also **cock·a·ma·my** (kŏk′ə-mā′mē) adj. Slang **1.** Trifling; nearly valueless. **2.** Ludicrous; nonsensical: a cockamamie reason. [Prob. alteration of DECALCOMANIA.]

cock-and-bull story (kŏk′ən-bōōl′) n. An absurd or highly improbable tale passed off as being true.

cock·a·tiel also **cock·a·teel** (kŏk′ə-tēl′) n. A small crested Australian parrot (Nymphicus hollandicus) having gray and yellow plumage. [Du. kaketielje, ult. < Malay kakatua, cockatoo. See COCKATOO.]

cock·a·too (kŏk′ə-tōō′) n., pl. **-toos** Any of various large parrots, esp. of the genus Kakatoe of Australia and adjacent areas, having a long erectile crest. [Du. kaketoe < Malay kakatua.]

cock·a·trice (kŏk′ə-trĭs, -trīs′) n. Mythology A serpent hatched from a cock's egg and having the power to kill by its glance. [ME cocatrice, basilisk < OFr. cocatris < Med.Lat. cocātrīx, cocātrīc-, poss. alteration of calcātrīx (transl. of Gk. ikhneumōn, tracker) < Lat. calcāre, to track < calx, calc-, heel.]

cock·boat (kŏk′bōt′) n. A small rowboat, esp. one used to ferry supplies from ship to shore. [ME cokboot : cok, cockboat (< AN

coque, prob. ult. < Lat. caudica < caudex, caudic-, tree trunk) + boot, boat < BOAT.]

cock·chaf·er (kŏk′chā′fər) n. Any of various European beetles of the family Scarabaeidae, esp. Melolontha melolontha, which is destructive to plants. [Poss. COCK¹ + CHAFER.]

Cock·croft (kŏk′krŏft, -krôft′), **Sir John Douglas** 1897–1967. British physicist who with Ernest Walton succeeded in splitting the atom (1931). They shared a 1951 Nobel Prize.

cock·crow (kŏk′krō′) n. The very beginning of the day; dawn.

cocked hat (kŏkt) n. A hat with the brim turned up in two or three places, esp. a three-cornered hat; a tricorn.

cock·er¹ (kŏk′ər) n. **1.** A cocker spaniel. **2a.** A person who keeps or trains gamecocks. **b.** A person who promotes or attends cockfights.

cock·er² (kŏk′ər) tr.v. **-ered, -er·ing, -ers** To pamper, spoil, or coddle. [ME cokeren.]

cock·er·el (kŏk′ər-əl) n. A young rooster. [ME cokerel, dim. of cok, cock. See COCK¹.]

cocker spaniel n. A dog of a breed originally developed in England, having long drooping ears and a variously colored silky coat. [< its original use in hunting woodcocks.]

cock·eye (kŏk′ī′) n. A squinting eye. [Prob. COCK¹ + EYE.]

cock·eyed (kŏk′īd′) adj. Informal **1.** Foolish; ridiculous; absurd. **2.** Askew; crooked. **3.** Intoxicated; drunk.

cock·fight (kŏk′fīt′) n. A fight between gamecocks, often fitted with metal gaffs. —**cock′fight′ing** adj. & n.

cock·horse (kŏk′hôrs′) n. **1.** Something used as a toy horse, such as the knee of an adult. **2.** A horse added to a team of horses to assist a wagon, as through high water. [?]

cock·le¹ (kŏk′əl) n. **1.** Any of various bivalve mollusks of the family Cardiidae, having rounded or heart-shaped shells with radiating ribs. **2.** The shell of a cockle. **3.** A wrinkle; a pucker. **4.** Nautical A cockleshell. ❖ intr. & tr.v. **-led, -ling, -les** To become or cause to become wrinkled or puckered. —**idiom: cockles of (one's) heart** One's innermost feelings. [ME cokel < OFr. coquille, shell < VLat. *cochillia < Lat. conchyllium < Gk. konkhulion, dim. of konkhē, mussel.]

cock·le² (kŏk′əl) n. Any of several weedy plants, esp. the corn cockle. [ME cokkel < OE coccel < Med.Lat. *cocculus, dim. of Lat. coccus, kermes berry < Gk. kokkos.]

cock·le·boat (kŏk′əl-bōt′) n. See cockboat.

cock·le·bur (kŏk′əl-bûr′) n. **1.** Any of several annual weeds of the genus Xanthium in the composite family, having fruits in a bur. **2.** A bur of this plant.

cock·le·shell (kŏk′əl-shĕl′) n. **1a.** The shell of a cockle. **b.** A shell like that of a cockle. **2.** Nautical A small light boat.

cock·loft (kŏk′lôft′, -lŏft′) n. A small loft, garret, or attic.

cock·ney or **Cock·ney** (kŏk′nē) n., pl. **-neys 1.** A native of the East End of London. **2.** The dialect or accent of the natives of the East End of London. [ME cokenei, cock's egg, pampered child, city dweller : coken, cock (poss. blend of cok; see COCK¹, and chiken, chicken; see CHICKEN) + ei, egg (< OE ǣg; see awi- in App.).] —**cock′ney** adj.

cock-of-the-rock (kŏk′əv-thə-rŏk′) n., pl. **cocks-of-the-rock** Either of two South American birds (Rupicola rupicola or R. peruviana) having a distinctive crest and bright orange or reddish plumage in the male. [< its habit of nesting on rocks.]

cock·pit (kŏk′pĭt′) n. **1a.** The space in the fuselage of a small airplane containing seats for the pilot, copilot, and sometimes passengers. **b.** The space set apart for the pilot and crew, as in a helicopter, large airliner, or transport aircraft. **2.** The driver's compartment in a racing car. **3.** An area for cockfights. **4.** A place where many battles have been fought. **5.** Nautical **a.** A compartment in an old warship below the water line, used as quarters and as a station for the wounded. **b.** An area in a small decked vessel, toward the stern and lower than the rest of the deck, from which the vessel is steered.

cock·roach (kŏk′rōch′) n. Any of numerous oval flat-bodied insects of the family Blattidae, including several species that are common household pests. [By folk ety. < obsolete cacarootch < Sp. cucaracha < cuca, caterpillar.]

cocks·comb (kŏks′kōm′) n. **1.** The comb of a rooster. **2.** The cap of a jester, decorated to resemble the comb of a rooster. **3.** An annual plant (Celosia cristata) cultivated for its fan-shaped or plumelike red or yellow flower clusters. **4.** Obsolete Variant of coxcomb 1.

cocks·foot (kŏks′fŏŏt′) n. Chiefly British Orchard grass.

cock·shy (kŏk′shī′) n., pl. **-shies** Chiefly British **1.** A mark aimed at in throwing contests. **2.** The throw in a throwing contest. [< a game in which sticks were shied at a cock.]

cock·spur hawthorn (kŏk′spûr′) n. A thorny North American tree (Crataegus crus-galli) having white flowers and small red fruit. [< the resemblance of its thorn to a cock's spur.]

cock·suck·er (kŏk′sŭk′ər) n. Vulgar Slang **1.** One who performs fellatio. **2.** A mean or despicable person.

cock·sure (kŏk′shŏŏr′) adj. **1.** Completely sure; certain. **2.** Too sure; overconfident. —**cock′sure′ly** adv. —**cock′sure′ness** n.

cock·tail (kŏk′tāl′) n. **1.** Any of various mixed alcoholic drinks consisting usu. of brandy, whiskey, vodka, or gin combined with fruit juices or other liquors and often served chilled. **2.** Medicine A mixture of drugs, usu. in solution, that is part of a treatment

cockatiel
Nymphicus hollandicus

cocker spaniel

cock-of-the-rock
Peruvian cock-of-the-rock
Rupicola peruviana

regimen. **3.** An appetizer, such as mixed fruit served with juice or seafood served with a sharp sauce: *shrimp cocktail.* ❖ *adj.* **1.** Of or relating to cocktails: *a cocktail party.* **2.** Suitable for wear on semiformal occasions. [?]

cocktail table *n.* See **coffee table.**

cock•y (kŏk′ē) *adj.* **-i•er, -i•est** Overly self-assertive or self-confident. —**cock′i•ly** *adv.* —**cock′i•ness** *n.*

Co•co (kō′kō) A river rising in N Nicaragua and flowing c. 483 km (300 mi) to the Caribbean Sea.

co•coa (kō′kō) *n.* **1a.** A powder made from cacao seeds after they have been fermented, roasted, shelled, ground, and freed of most of their fat. **b.** A beverage made by mixing this powder with sugar in hot water or milk. **2.** A moderate brown to reddish brown. [Alteration (influenced by *coco,* coconut palm; see COCONUT) of CACAO.] —**co′coa** *adj.*

cocoa bean *n.* See **cacao** 2.

cocoa butter *n.* A yellowish-white fatty solid obtained from cacao seeds and used in cosmetics, chocolate, and soap.

co•co•nut also **co•coa•nut** (kō′kə-nŭt′, -nət) *n.* **1.** The fruit of the coconut palm, consisting of a fibrous husk surrounding a large seed. **2.** The large, brown, hard-shelled seed of the coconut, containing white flesh surrounding a partially fluid-filled central cavity. **3.** The edible white flesh of the coconut. **4.** A coconut palm. [Port. *côco,* grinning skull, goblin, coconut (prob. < LLat. *coccum,* shell; see COCOON) + NUT.]

coconut milk *n.* **1.** A milky fluid extracted from the flesh of the coconut, used in foods or as a beverage. **2.** The watery fluid in the central cavity of the coconut, used chiefly as a beverage.

coconut oil *n.* An oil or semisolid fat obtained from the flesh of the coconut, used in foods, cosmetics, and soaps.

coconut palm *n.* A feather-leaved palm *(Cocos nucifera)* extensively cultivated in tropical regions for food, beverages, oil, thatching, fiber, utensils, and ornament.

co•coon (kə-ko͞on′) *n.* **1a.** A protective case of silk or similar fibrous material spun by the larvae of moths and other insects that serves as a covering for their pupal stage. **b.** A similar natural protective covering or structure, such as the egg case of a spider. **2.** A protective plastic coating that is placed over stored military or naval equipment. **3.** Something suggestive of a cocoon in appearance or purpose. ❖ *v.* **-cooned, -coon•ing, -coons** —*tr.* To envelop in or as if in a cocoon. —*intr.* To retreat as if into a cocoon. [Fr. *cocon* < Provençal *coucoun,* dim. of *coco,* shell < LLat. *coccum* < Lat., berry, oak gall < Gk. *kokkos,* seed, berry.]

coco plum or **co•co•plum** (kō′kō-plŭm′) *n.* An evergreen shrub or small tree *(Chrysobalanus icaco)* native to the American and African tropics and having plumlike fruit. [Alteration of Sp. *icaco* < Arawak *ikaku.*]

Co•cos Islands (kō′kōs) also **Kee•ling Islands** (kē′lĭng) An Australian-administered island group in the E Indian Ocean SW of Sumatra.

co•cotte (kô-kôt′) *n.* A woman prostitute. [Fr., chicken, prostitute < fem. dim. of *coq,* cock < OFr. See COCK[1].]

co•co•yam (kō′kō-yăm′) *n.* See **taro** 2. [COCO(A) + YAM.]

Coc•teau (kŏk-tō′, kôk-), **Jean** 1889–1963. French writer and filmmaker whose works include the novel *Les Enfants Terrible* (1929) and the film *Beauty and the Beast* (1945).

Co•cy•tus (kō-sī′təs, -sī′-) *n. Greek Mythology* One of the five rivers of Hades.

cod[1] (kŏd) *n., pl.* **cod** or **cods** Any of various marine fishes of the family Gadidae, esp. *Gadus morhua,* a food fish of northern Atlantic waters. [ME.]

cod[2] (kŏd) *n.* **1.** A husk or pod. **2.** *Archaic* The scrotum. **3.** *Obsolete* A bag. [ME < OE *codd.*]

Cod, Cape A hook-shaped peninsula of SE MA extending E and N into the Atlantic Ocean.

COD *abbr.* **1.** cash on delivery **2.** collect on delivery

co•da (kō′də) *n.* **1.** *Music* The concluding passage of a movement or composition. **2.** A conclusion or closing part of a statement. [Ital. < Lat. *cauda,* tail.]

cod•dle (kŏd′l) *tr.v.* **-dled, -dling, -dles 1.** To cook in water just below the boiling point. **2.** To treat indulgently; baby. [Poss. alteration of CAUDLE.] —**cod′dler** *n.*

code (kōd) *n.* **1.** A systematically arranged and comprehensive collection of laws. **2.** A systematic collection of regulations and rules of procedure or conduct: *a traffic code.* **3a.** A system of signals used to represent letters or numbers in transmitting messages. **b.** A system of symbols, letters, or words given certain arbitrary meanings, used for messages requiring secrecy or brevity. **4.** A system of symbols and rules used to represent instructions to a computer; a computer program. **5.** The genetic code. **6.** *Slang* A patient whose heart has stopped beating, as in cardiac arrest. ❖ *v.* **cod•ed, cod•ing, codes** —*tr.* **1.** To systematize and arrange (laws and regulations) into a code. **2.** To convert (a message, for example) into code. —*intr.* **1.** To specify the genetic code for an amino acid or a polypeptide. **2.** To write or revise a computer program. **3.** *Medicine* To go into cardiac arrest. [ME < OFr. < Lat. *cōdex,* book. See CODEX.]

code blue *n.* A medical emergency that involves signaling personnel to aid a person in cardiac arrest.

co•dec•li•na•tion (kō′dĕk-lə-nā′shən) *n. Astronomy* The complement of the declination.

co•de•fen•dant (kō′dĭ-fĕn′dənt) *n. Law* A joint defendant.

co•deine (kō′dēn′, -dē-ĭn) *n.* An alkaloid narcotic, $C_{18}H_{21}NO_3$, derived from opium or morphine and used as a cough suppressant, analgesic, and hypnotic. [Fr. *codéine* : Gk. *kōdeia,* poppy head (< *koos,* cavity) + *-ine,* alkaloid; see –INE[2].]

code name *n.* A name assigned to conceal the identity or existence of something or someone.

co•de•ter•mi•na•tion (kō′dĭ-tûr′mə-nā′shən) *n.* Cooperation, esp. between labor and management, in policymaking.

code word *n.* **1.** A secret word or phrase used as a code name or password. **2.** A euphemism.

co•dex (kō′dĕks′) *n., pl.* **co•di•ces** (kō′dĭ-sēz′, kŏd′ĭ-) A manuscript volume, esp. of a classic work or of the Scriptures. [Lat. *cōdex, cōdic-,* tree trunk, wooden tablet, book, var. of *caudex,* trunk.]

cod•fish (kŏd′fĭsh′) *n., pl.* **codfish** or **-fish•es** See **cod**[1].

codg•er (kŏj′ər) *n. Informal* A somewhat eccentric man, esp. an old one. [Perh. alteration of obsolete *cadger,* peddler. See CADGE.]

cod•i•cil (kŏd′ə-sĭl) *n.* A supplement or appendix, esp. to a will. [ME < OFr. *codicille* < Lat. *cōdicillus,* dim. of *cōdex, cōdic-,* codex. See CODEX.] —**cod′i•cil′la•ry** (kŏd′ə-sĭl′ə-rē) *adj.*

cod•i•fy (kŏd′ĭ-fī′, kō′də-) *tr.v.* **-fied, -fy•ing, -fies 1.** To reduce to a code: *codify laws.* **2.** To arrange or systematize. —**cod′i•fi•ca′tion** (-fĭ-kā′shən) *n.* —**cod′i•fi′er** *n.*

cod•ling[1] (kŏd′lĭng) also **cod•lin** (-lĭn) *n.* **1.** A greenish elongated English apple used for cooking. **2.** A small unripe apple. [Alteration of ME *querdlyng,* poss. < AN **querdelion,* lionheart : OFr. *cuer,* heart; see COURAGE + *de,* of (< Lat. *dē;* see DE–) + OFr. *lion,* lion; see LION.]

cod•ling[2] (kŏd′lĭng) *n., pl.* **codling** or **-lings** A young cod.

codling moth also **codlin moth** *n.* A grayish moth *(Carpocapsa pomonella)* whose larvae are destructive to various fruits.

cod-liv•er oil (kŏd′lĭv′ər) *n.* An oil obtained from the liver of cod and related fishes, used as a source of vitamins A and D.

co•dom•i•nance (kō-dŏm′ə-nəns) *n.* A condition in which both alleles are codominant.

co•dom•i•nant (kō-dŏm′ə-nənt) *adj.* **1.** *Genetics* Of or being two alleles of a gene pair in a heterozygote that are both fully expressed. **2a.** *Ecology* Being one of two or more of the most characteristic species in a biotic community. **b.** Influencing the presence and type of other species in the community. ❖ *n. Ecology* A codominant species in a biotic community.

co•don (kō′dŏn′) *n.* A sequence of three adjacent nucleotides constituting the genetic code that determines the insertion of a specific amino acid in a polypeptide chain during protein synthesis. [COD(E) + –ON[1].]

cod•piece (kŏd′pēs′) *n.* A pouch at the crotch of the tight-fitting breeches worn by men in the 15th and 16th centuries. [ME *codpece* : *cod,* bag, scrotum (< OE *codd,* bag) + *pece,* piece; see PIECE.]

cods•wal•lop (kŏdz′wŏl′əp) *n. Chiefly British Slang* Nonsense; rubbish. [?]

Co•dy (kō′dē), **William Frederick** Known as "Buffalo Bill." 1846–1917. Amer. frontier scout who after 1883 toured the US and Europe with his Wild West Show.

co•ed or **co-ed** (kō′ĕd′) *Informal n.* A woman who attends a coeducational college or university. ❖ *adj.* **1.** Coeducational. **2.** Open to both sexes. [Short for *coeducational.*]

co•ed•it (kō-ĕd′ĭt) *tr.v.* **-ed•it•ed, -ed•it•ing, -ed•its** To edit (a print publication or a film) jointly with another or others. —**co•ed′i•tor** *n.*

co•ed•u•ca•tion (kō-ĕj′ə-kā′shən) *n.* The system of education in which both sexes attend the same institution or classes. —**co•ed′u•ca′tion•al** *adj.* —**co•ed′u•ca′tion•al•ly** *adv.*

co•ef•fi•cient (kō′ə-fĭsh′ənt) *n.* **1.** A number or symbol multiplied with a variable or an unknown quantity in an algebraic term, as 4 in the term $4x$ or x in the term $x(a + b)$. **2.** A numerical measure of a physical or chemical property that is constant for a system under specified conditions.

–coel or **–coele** or **–cele** *suff.* Chamber; cavity: *blastocoel.* [NLat. *-coela* < Gk. *koilos,* hollow.]

coe•la•canth (sē′lə-kănth′) *n.* Any of various mostly extinct fishes of the order Coelacanthiformes. [NLat. *Coelacanthus,* former genus name : Gk. *koilos,* hollow; see –COEL + Gk. *akantha,* spine.] —**coe′la•can′thine′** (-kăn′thīn′, -thĭn), **coe′la•can′thous** (-thəs) *adj.*

coe•len•ter•ate (sĭ-lĕn′tə-rāt′, -tər-ĭt) *n.* See **cnidarian.** [< NLat. *Coelenterāta,* phylum name : *Coelenter(on),* coelenteron; see COELENTERON + Lat. *-āta,* neut. pl. of *-ātus,* -ate; see –ATE[1].] —**coe•len′ter•ate′, coe•len•ter′ic** (-tĕr′ĭk) *adj.*

coe•len•ter•on (sĭ-lĕn′tə-rŏn′, -tər-ən) *n., pl.* **-te•ra** (-tər-ə) The saclike cavity within the body of a coelenterate. [NLat. : Gk. *koilos,* hollow; see –COEL + ENTERON.]

coe•li•ac (sē′lē-ăk′) *adj.* Variant of **celiac.**

coe•lom also **ce•lom** or **coe•lome** (sē′ləm) *n.* The cavity within the body of all animals higher than the cnidarians and certain primitive worms, formed by the splitting of the embryonic mesoderm into two layers. [Ger. *Koelom* < Gk. *koilōma,* cavity < *koilos,* hollow.] —**coe•lom′ic** (sĭ-lŏm′ĭk, -lō′mĭk) *adj.*

coe•lo•mate (sē′lə-māt′) *adj.* Possessing a coelom: *a coelomate animal.* —**coe′lo•mate** *n.*

coeno– or **ceno–** *pref.* Common: *coenocyte.* [NLat. < Gk. *koino-*

coconut palm
Cocos nucifera

Buffalo Bill Cody

coelacanth
Latimeria chalumnae

ă	pat	oi	boy
ā	pay	ou	out
âr	care	o͝o	took
ä	father	o͞o	boot
ĕ	pet	ŭ	cut
ē	be	ûr	urge
ĭ	pit	th	thin
ī	pie	*th*	this
îr	pier	hw	which
ŏ	pot	zh	vision
ō	toe	ə	about, item
ô	paw		

Stress marks:
′ (primary);
′ (secondary), as in
lexicon (lĕk′sĭ-kŏn′)

< *koinos*. See **kom** in App.]

coen·o·bite (sĕn′ə-bīt′, sē′nə-) *n.* Variant of **cenobite**.

coe·no·cyte (sē′nə-sīt′) *n.* A multinucleate cytoplasmic mass enclosed by a single cell wall, as in slime molds and certain fungi and algae. —**coe′no·cyt′ic** (-sĭt′ĭk) *adj.*

coe·nu·rus (sĭ-noŏr′əs, -nyŏŏr′-) *n.*, *pl.* -**nu·ri** (-noŏr′ī′, -nyŏŏr′ī′) The parasitic larval stage of the tapeworm *Taenia multiceps*, consisting of a cyst in which the scolex develops and infecting the central nervous system of ruminants. [NLat. *coenūrus*, having a common tail (because the larva has many heads) : COEN(O)– + Gk. *ourā*, tail; see **ors–** in App.]

co·en·zyme (kō-ĕn′zīm′) *n.* A nonproteinaceous organic substance that usu. contains a vitamin or mineral and combines with the apoenzyme to form an active enzyme system. —**co′en·zy·mat′ic** (-zə-mă′tĭk) *adj.*

coenzyme A *n.* A coenzyme present in all living cells that functions as an acyl group carrier and is necessary for acetylation reactions.

coenzyme Q *n.* Ubiquinone.

co·e·qual (kō-ē′kwəl) *adj.* Equal with one another, as in rank or size. ❖ *n.* An equal. —**co′e·qual′i·ty** (-kwŏl′ĭ-tē) *n.* —**co·e′qual·ly** *adv.*

co·erce (kō-ûrs′) *tr.v.* -**erced**, -**erc·ing**, -**erc·es** **1.** To force to act or think in a certain way by use of pressure, threats, or intimidation; compel. **2.** To dominate, restrain, or control forcibly: *coerced the strikers into compliance.* **3.** To bring about by force or threat: *efforts to coerce agreement.* [Lat. *coercēre*, to control, restrain : *co-*, co- + *arcēre*, to enclose, confine.] —**co·erc′er** *n.* —**co·erc′i·ble** *adj.*

co·er·cion (kō-ûr′zhən, -shən) *n.* **1.** The act or practice of coercing. **2.** Power or ability to coerce. —**co·er′cion·ar′y** (-zhə-nĕr′ē, -shə-) *adj.*

co·er·cive (kō-ûr′sĭv) *adj.* Characterized by or inclined to coercion. —**co·er′cive·ly** *adv.* —**co·er′cive·ness** *n.*

co·er·civ·i·ty (kō′ər-sĭv′ĭ-tē) *n.* The intensity of the magnetic field needed to reduce the magnetization of a ferromagnetic material to zero.

co·es·sen·tial (kō′ĭ-sĕn′shəl) *adj.* Having the same essence or nature. —**co′es·sen′ti·al′i·ty** (-shē-ăl′ĭ-tē), **co′es·sen′tial·ness** *n.* —**co′es·sen′tial·ly** *adv.*

co·e·ta·ne·ous (kō′ĭ-tā′nē-əs) *adj.* Of equal age, duration, or period; coeval. [< LLat. *coaetāneus*, a contemporary : Lat. *co-*, co- + Lat. *aetās*, age; see **aiw-** in App.] —**co′e·ta′ne·ous·ly** *adv.* —**co′e·ta′ne·ous·ness** *n.*

co·e·ter·nal (kō′ĭ-tûr′nəl) *adj.* Equally or jointly eternal. —**co′e·ter′nal·ly** *adv.*

co·e·ter·ni·ty (kō′ĭ-tûr′nĭ-tē) *n.* Existence for eternity with another or others.

Coeur d'A·lene (kôr′ də-lān′, kôrd′l-ān′, kûrd′-) A city of N ID on **Coeur D'Alene Lake** in the Panhandle E of Spokane WA. Pop. 34,514.

co·e·val (kō-ē′vəl) *adj.* Originating or existing during the same period; lasting through the same era. [< LLat. *coaevus* : *co-*, co- + *aevum*, age; see **aiw-** in App.] —**co·e′val** *n.* —**co·e′val·ly** *adv.*

co·ev·o·lu·tion (kō′ĕv-ə-loō′shən, -ē-və-) *n.* The evolution of two or more interdependent species, each adapting to changes in the other. —**co′ev·o·lu′tion·ar·y** *adj.* —**co′e·volve′** (-ĭ-vŏlv′) *v.*

co·ex·ist (kō′ĭg-zĭst′) *intr.v.* -**ist·ed**, -**ist·ing**, -**ists** **1.** To exist together, at the same time or in the same place. **2.** To live in peace with another or others despite differences, esp. as a matter of policy. —**co′ex·is′tence** *n.* —**co′ex·is′tent** *adj.*

co·ex·tend (kō′ĭk-stĕnd′) *intr.* & *tr.v.* -**tend·ed**, -**tend·ing**, -**tends** To extend or cause to extend through the same space or duration. —**co′ex·ten′sion** *n.*

co·ex·ten·sive (kō′ĭk-stĕn′sĭv) *adj.* Having the same limits, boundaries, or scope. —**co′ex·ten′sive·ly** *adv.*

co·fac·tor (kō′făk′tər) *n.* **1.** A contributing factor. **2.** A substance, such as a metallic ion or coenzyme, that must be associated with an enzyme for the enzyme to function.

C. of C. *abbr.* chamber of commerce

C. of E. *abbr.* Church of England

cof·fee (kô′fē, kŏf′ē) *n.* **1a.** Any of various tropical African shrubs or trees of the genus *Coffea*, esp. *C. arabica*, cultivated for their seeds that are dried, roasted, and ground to prepare a stimulating aromatic drink. **b.** The beanlike seeds of this plant, enclosed within a pulpy fruit. **c.** The beverage prepared from coffee seeds. **2.** A moderate brown to dark brown or dark grayish brown. **3.** An informal social gathering at which coffee and other refreshments are served. [Alteration (influenced by Ital. *caffè*) of Ottoman Turk. *qahveh* < Ar. *qahwa*; akin to *qahiya*, to become weak.]

coffee break *n.* A short break from work during which coffee or other refreshments may be consumed.

cof·fee·cake (kô′fē-kāk′, kŏf′ē-) *n.* A cake or sweetened bread, often containing nuts or raisins.

cof·fee·house also **coffee house** (kô′fē-hous′, kŏf′ē-) *n.* A restaurant where coffee and other refreshments are served, esp. where people meet for conversation, games, or music.

coffee klatch or **coffee klatsch** also **kaf·fee·klatsch** (kôf′ē-klăch′, -kläch′, kô′fē-) *n.* A casual social gathering for coffee and

coffee
coffee beans and blossoms

coffer
detail of the ceiling at Union Station, Washington, DC

conversation. [Partial transl. of Ger. *Kaffeeklatsch* : *Kaffee*, coffee + *Klatsch*, gossip; see KLATSCH.]

cof·fee·mak·er also **coffee maker** (kô′fē-mā′kər, kŏf′ē-) *n.* An apparatus used to brew coffee.

coffee mill *n.* A device for grinding roasted coffee beans.

cof·fee·pot (kô′fē-pŏt′, kŏf′ē-) *n.* A pot for brewing or serving coffee.

coffee shop *n.* A small restaurant in which coffee and light meals are served.

coffee table *n.* A long low table, often placed before a sofa.

cof·fee-ta·ble book (kô′fē-tā′bəl, kŏf′ē-) *n.* An oversize book of elaborate design used for display, as on a coffee table.

cof·fer (kô′fər, kŏf′ər) *n.* **1.** A strongbox. **2a.** Financial resources; funds. Often used in the plural. **b.** A treasury. Often used in the plural. **3.** *Architecture* A decorative sunken panel in a ceiling, dome, soffit, or vault. **4.** The chamber formed by a canal lock. **5.** A cofferdam. **6.** A floating dock. ❖ *tr.v.* -**fered**, -**fer·ing**, -**fers** **1.** To put in a coffer. **2.** *Architecture* To supply (a ceiling, for example) with decorative sunken panels. [ME *cofre* < OFr., alteration of **cofne* < Lat. *cophinus*, basket. See COFFIN.]

cof·fer·dam (kô′fər-dăm′, kŏf′ər-) *n.* **1.** A temporary watertight enclosure that is pumped dry so that construction, as of piers, may be undertaken. **2.** A watertight chamber attached to the side of a ship to facilitate repairs below the water line.

cof·fin (kô′fĭn, kŏf′ĭn) *n.* **1.** An oblong box in which a corpse is buried. **2.** The horny part of a horse's hoof. ❖ *tr.v.* -**fined**, -**fin·ing**, -**fins** To place in or as if in a coffin. [ME *cofin*, basket < OFr. < Lat. *cophinus* < Gk. *kophinos*.]

coffin bone *n.* The bone enclosed inside a horse's hoof.

coffin nail *n. Slang* A cigarette.

cof·fle (kô′fəl, kŏf′əl) *n.* A group of animals, prisoners, or slaves chained together in a line. ❖ *tr.v.* -**fled**, -**fling**, -**fles** To fasten together in a coffle. [Ar. *qāfila*, caravan, fem. active part. of *qafala*, to close, return.]

co·found (kō-found′) *tr.v.* -**found·ed**, -**found·ing**, -**founds** To establish with another or others. —**co·found′er** *n.*

C. of S. *abbr.* chief of staff

co·func·tion (kō′fŭngk′shən) *n.* The trigonometric function of the complement of an angle: *The tangent is the cofunction of the cotangent.*

cog[1] (kŏg, kôg) *n.* **1.** One of a series of teeth, as on the rim of a wheel or gear, whose engagement transmits successive motive force to a corresponding wheel or gear. **2.** A cogwheel. **3.** A member of an organization who performs necessary but usu. minor or routine functions. [ME *cogge*, prob. of Scand. orig.; akin to Swed. *kugg, kugge*.]

cog[2] (kŏg, kôg) *v.* **cogged**, **cog·ging**, **cogs** —*tr.* To load or manipulate (dice) fraudulently. —*intr.* To cheat, esp. at dice. ❖ *n.* An instance of cheating; a swindle. [?]

cog[3] (kŏg, kôg) *n.* A tenon projecting from a wooden beam designed to fit into an opening in another beam to form a joint. ❖ *tr.v.* **cogged**, **cog·ging**, **cogs** To join with tenons. [Alteration (influenced by COG[1]) of *cock*, to join with tenons.]

cog. *abbr.* cognate

co·gen·er·a·tion (kō-jĕn′ə-rā′shən) *n.* A process in which an industrial facility uses its waste energy to produce heat or electricity.

co·gent (kō′jənt) *adj.* Appealing to the intellect or powers of reasoning; convincing. See Syns at **valid**. [Lat. *cōgēns, cōgent-*, pr. part. of *cōgere*, to force : *co-*, co- + *agere*, to drive; see **ag-** in App.] —**co′gen·cy** (-jən-sē) *n.* —**co′gent·ly** *adv.*

cog·i·ta·ble (kŏj′ĭ-tə-bəl) *adj.* Thinkable; conceivable.

cog·i·tate (kŏj′ĭ-tāt′) *intr.* & *tr.v.* -**tat·ed**, -**tat·ing**, -**tates** To take careful thought or think carefully about; ponder. [Lat. *cōgitāre, cōgitāt-* : *co-*, intensive pref.; see CO– + *agitāre*, to consider; see AGITATE.] —**cog′i·ta′tor** *n.*

cog·i·ta·tion (kŏj′ĭ-tā′shən) *n.* **1.** Thoughtful consideration; meditation. **2.** A serious thought.

cog·i·ta·tive (kŏj′ĭ-tā′tĭv) *adj.* **1.** Of or relating to cogitation. **2.** Inclined to or capable of cogitation. —**cog′i·ta′tive·ly** *adv.*

co·gnac (kōn′yăk′, kŏn′-, kôn′-) *n.* A brandy distilled from white wine and produced in the vicinity of Cognac.

Co·gnac (kōn′yăk′, kŏn′-, kô-nyăk′) A city of W France on the Charente R. NNE of Bordeaux; noted since the 18th cent. for its distilleries. Pop. 20,660.

cog·nate (kŏg′nāt′) *adj.* **1.** Related by blood; having a common ancestor. **2.** Related in origin, as certain words in genetically related languages descended from the same ancestral root. **3.** Related or analogous in nature, character, or function. ❖ *n.* **1.** One related by blood or origin with another, esp. a person sharing an ancestor. **2.** A word related to one in another language. [Lat. *cognātus* : *co-*, co- + *gnātus*, born, p. part. of *nāscī*, to be born; see **genə-** in App.] —**cog·na′tion** *n.*

cog·ni·tion (kŏg-nĭsh′ən) *n.* **1.** The mental process or faculty of knowing, including aspects such as awareness, perception, reasoning, and judgment. **2.** That which comes to be known, as through reasoning or intuition; knowledge. [ME *cognicioun* < Lat. *cognitiō, cognitiōn-* < *cognitus*, p. part. of *cognōscere*, to learn : *co-*, intensive pref.; see CO– + *gnōscere*, to know; see **gnō-** in App.] —**cog·ni′tion·al** *adj.*

cog·ni·tive (kŏg′nĭ-tĭv) *adj.* **1.** Of, characterized by, involving, or relating to cognition. **2.** Having a basis in or reducible to empirical factual knowledge. —**cog′ni·tive·ly** *adv.*

cognitive dissonance *n. Psychology* A condition of conflict or anxiety resulting from inconsistency between belief and action, such as opposing animal slaughter and eating meat.

cognitive science *n.* The study of the nature of various mental tasks and the processes that enable them to be performed.

cognitive therapy *n.* A form of psychotherapy using imagery, self-instruction, and related techniques to alter distorted attitudes and perceptions.

cog·ni·za·ble (kŏg′nĭ-zə-bəl, kŏg-nī′-) *adj.* **1.** Knowable or perceivable. **2.** *Law* That can be tried before a particular court. —**cog′ni·za·bly** *adv.*

cog·ni·zance (kŏg′nĭ-zəns) *n.* **1.** Conscious knowledge or recognition; awareness. **2.** The range of what one can know or understand. **3.** Observance; notice: *We will take cognizance of your objections.* **4.** *Heraldry* A crest or badge worn to distinguish the bearer. [ME *conissaunce* < OFr. *conoissance* < *connoistre*, to know < Lat. *cognōscere*, to learn. See COGNITION.]

cog·ni·zant (kŏg′nĭ-zənt) *adj.* Fully informed; conscious. See Syns at **aware.** [< COGNIZANCE.]

cog·no·men (kŏg-nō′mən) *n., pl.* **-no·mens** or **-nom·i·na** (-nŏm′ə-nə) **1a.** A family name; a surname. **b.** The third and usu. last name of a citizen of ancient Rome, as *Caesar* in *Gaius Julius Caesar.* **2.** A name, esp. a descriptive nickname or epithet. [Lat. *cognōmen* : *co-, con-, co-* (influenced by *cognōscere*, to know) + *nōmen*, name; see **nō-men-** in App.] —**cog·nom′i·nal** (-nŏm′ə-nəl) *adj.*

co·gno·scen·te (kŏn′yə-shĕn′tē, kŏg′nə-) *n., pl.* **-ti** (-tē) A person with superior knowledge or highly refined taste; a connoisseur. [Obsolete Ital. < Lat. *cognōscēns, cognōscent-*, pr. part. of *cognōscere*, to know. See COGNITION.]

co·gon (kō-gōn′) *n.* An Old World perennial grass (*Imperata cylindrica*), widespread as a weed in warm regions and used for thatching. [Sp. *cogón* < Tagalog *kugon*.]

cog railway *n.* A railway designed to operate on steep slopes and having a locomotive with a center cogwheel that engages with a cogged center rail to provide traction.

Cogs·well chair (kŏgz′wĕl′, -wəl) *n.* An upholstered easy chair, open under the armrests, with a sloping back and cabriole front legs. [Prob. < the name *Cogswell*.]

cog·wheel (kŏg′hwēl′, -wēl′, kŏg′-) *n.* **1.** A toothed wheel. **2.** One of a set of cogged wheels in a mechanism.

co·hab·it (kō-hăb′ĭt) *intr.v.* **-it·ed, -it·ing, -its 1.** To live together in a sexual relationship, esp. when not legally married. **2.** To coexist, as animals of different species. [LLat. *cohabitāre* : Lat. *co-, co-* + Lat. *habitāre*, to dwell; see INHABIT.] —**co·hab′i·tant, co·hab′it·er** *n.* —**co·hab′i·ta′tion** *n.* —**co·hab′i·ta′tion·al** *adj.*

Co·han (kō′hăn′), **George Michael** 1878–1942. Amer. singer, songwriter, and playwright whose songs include "I'm a Yankee Doodle Dandy."

co·heir (kō-âr′) *n.* A joint heir, as to an estate.

co·heir·ess (kō-âr′ĭs) *n.* A joint woman heir, as to an estate. See Usage Note at **-ess.**

co·here (kō-hîr′) *v.* **-hered, -her·ing, -heres** —*intr.* **1.** To stick or hold together in a mass that resists separation. **2.** To have internal elements or parts logically linked and aesthetically consistent: "*The movie as a whole failed to cohere*" (Robert Brustein). —*tr.* To cause to form a united, orderly, and aesthetically consistent whole. [Lat. *cohaerēre* : *co-, co-* + *haerēre*, to cling.]

co·her·ence (kō-hîr′əns, -hĕr′-) *n.* **1.** The quality or state of cohering, esp. a logical, orderly, and aesthetically consistent relationship of parts. **2.** *Physics* The property of being coherent.

co·her·en·cy (kō-hîr′ən-sē) *n., pl.* **-cies** Coherence.

co·her·ent (kō-hîr′ənt, -hĕr′-) *adj.* **1.** Sticking together; cohering. **2.** Marked by orderly, logical, and aesthetic consistency: *a coherent essay.* **3.** *Physics* Of, relating to, or having waves with a constant phase relationship that are capable of exhibiting interference. **4.** Of or relating to a system of units of measurement in which a small number of base units are defined from which all others are derived by multiplication or division only. —**co·her′ent·ly** *adv.*

co·he·sion (kō-hē′zhən) *n.* **1.** The act, process, or condition of cohering. **2.** *Physics* The intermolecular attraction by which the elements of a body are held together. **3.** *Botany* The congenital union of parts of the same kind. [< Lat. *cohaesus*, p. part. of *cohaerēre*, to cling together. See COHERE.] —**co·he′sive** (-sĭv, -zĭv) *adj.* —**co·he′sive·ly** *adv.* —**co·he′sive·ness** *n.*

co·he·sion·less (kō-hē′zhən-lĭs) *adj.* Composed of particles that do not cohere. Used of soil.

Cohn (kōn), **Ferdinand Julius** 1828–98. German botanist who is considered the founder of bacteriology.

co·ho (kō′hō) *n., pl.* **co·hos** or **coho** The coho salmon.

co·hort (kō′hôrt′) *n.* **1.** A group or band of people. **2.** A companion or associate. **3.** A generational group as defined in demographics, statistics, or market research. **4a.** One of the 10 divisions of a Roman legion, consisting of 300 to 600 men. **b.** A group of soldiers. [ME < OFr. *cohorte* < Lat. *cohors, cohort-*. See **gher-** in App.]

USAGE NOTE The use of *cohort* to refer to an individual rather than a group has gained currency in recent years and seems now to be the predominant usage. Seventy-one percent of the Usage Panel accepts the sentence *The cashiered dictator and his cohorts have all written their memoirs*, while only 43 percent accepts *The gangster walked into the room surrounded by his cohort.*

coho salmon *n.* A small silver edible fish (*Oncorhynchus kisutch*) native to North Pacific waters and introduced in the Great Lakes. [Alteration of *cohose* < Halkomelem (Salishan language of SW Brit. Columbia) *kʷʷaxʷʷɵθ*.]

co·hosh (kō′hŏsh′) *n.* Any of several North American plants, esp. blue cohosh, black cohosh, and baneberry. [< Eastern Abenaki *kkʷʷàhas.*]

co·host or **co-host** (kō′hōst′) *n.* A joint host, as of a social event. ❖ *tr.v.* **-host·ed, -host·ing, -hosts** To serve as a joint host of.

co·hous·ing (kō′hou′zĭng) *n.* A living arrangement combining private living quarters with common dining and activity areas in a community whose residents share in tasks such as childcare.

co·hune (kō-hōōn′) *n.* A feather-leaved Central American palm (*Orbignya cohune*) having hard-shelled fruits that yield a useful oil. [NLat., perh. < Am.Sp. < Mosquito *ókhún.*]

coif (koif) *n.* **1.** (*also* kwäf) A coiffure. **2.** A tight-fitting cap worn under a veil. **3.** A white skullcap once worn by English lawyers. **4.** A heavy skullcap of steel or leather, once worn under a helmet or mail hood. ❖ *tr.v.* **coifed, coif·ing, coifs 1.** (*also* kwäf) To arrange or dress (hair). **2.** To cover with or as if with a coif. [ME < OFr. *coife* < LLat. *cofea*, helmet, of Gmc. orig.]

coif·feur (kwä-fûr′) *n.* A man who is a hairdresser. [Fr. < *coiffer*, to coif < OFr. *coife*, coif. See COIF.]

coif·feuse (kwä-fyōōz′, -fœz′) *n.* A woman who is a hairdresser. [Fr., fem. of *coiffeur*, coiffeur. See COIFFEUR.]

coif·fure (kwä-fyōor′) *n.* A hairstyle. ❖ *tr.v.* **-fured, -fur·ing, -fures** To arrange or dress (hair). [Fr. < *coiffer*, to coif. See COIFFEUR.]

coign (koin, kwoin) *n. & v.* Variant of **quoin.**

coign of vantage (coin) *n.* An advantageous position.

coil¹ (koil) *n.* **1a.** A series of connected spirals or concentric rings formed by gathering or winding: *a coil of rope.* **b.** A single spiral or ring within such a series. **2.** A spiral pipe or series of spiral pipes, as in a radiator. **3.** *Electricity* **a.** A wound spiral of two or more turns of insulated wire, used to introduce inductance. **b.** Any of various devices that have such a spiral as the major component. **4.** A roll of postage stamps for use in a vending machine. ❖ *v.* **coiled, coil·ing, coils** —*tr.* **1.** To wind in concentric rings or spirals. **2.** To wind into a shape resembling a coil. —*intr.* **1.** To form concentric rings or spirals. **2.** To move in a spiral course: *black smoke coiling up into the sky.* [Prob. < obsolete Fr. *coillir*, to gather < Lat. *colligere*. See COLLECT¹.] —**coil′er** *n.*

coil² (koil) *n.* A disturbance; a fuss. [?]

Coim·ba·tore (koim′bə-tôr′, -tōr′) A city of S India SSW of Bangalore. Pop. 816,321.

coin (koin) *n.* **1.** A small piece of metal, usu. flat and circular, authorized by a government for use as money. **2.** Metal money considered as a whole. **3.** A flat circular object resembling metal money: *coins of pepperoni.* **4.** *Architecture* A corner or cornerstone. ❖ *tr.v.* **coined, coin·ing, coins 1.** To make (pieces of money) from metal; mint or strike: *coined silver dollars.* **2.** To make pieces of money from (metal): *coin gold.* **3.** To devise (a new word or phrase). ❖ *adj.* Requiring one or more pieces of metal money for operation: *a coin washing machine.* —**idiom: the other side of the coin** One of two differing or opposing views or sides. [ME < OFr., die for stamping coins, wedge < Lat. *cuneus*, wedge.] —**coin′a·ble** *adj.* —**coin′er** *n.*

coin·age (koi′nĭj) *n.* **1.** The right or process of making coins. **2a.** Metal currency. **b.** A system of metal currency. **3a.** A new word or phrase. **b.** The invention of new words.

co·in·cide (kō′ĭn-sīd′) *intr.v.* **-cid·ed, -cid·ing, -cides 1.** To occupy the same relative position or the same area in space. **2.** To happen at the same time or during the same period. **3.** To correspond exactly; be identical. **4.** To agree exactly, as in opinion; concur. [Med.Lat. *coincidere* : Lat. *co-, co-* + Lat. *incidere*, to occur; see INCIDENT.]

co·in·ci·dence (kō-ĭn′sĭ-dəns, -dĕns′) *n.* **1.** Occupation of the same relative position or area in space. **2.** A sequence of events that although accidental seems to have been planned.

co·in·ci·dent (kō-ĭn′sĭ-dənt) *adj.* **1.** Occupying the same area in space or happening at the same time. **2.** Being very similar to another, as in nature. **3.** Matching point for point; coinciding.

co·in·ci·den·tal (kō-ĭn′sĭ-dĕn′tl) *adj.* **1.** Occurring as or resulting from coincidence. **2.** Happening or existing at the same time. —**co·in′ci·den′tal·ly, co·in′ci·dent′ly** *adv.*

co·in·sur·ance (kō′ĭn-shōōr′əns) *n.* **1.** Insurance held by two or more insurers. **2.** A form of insurance in which one insures property for less than its value and is responsible for the difference.

co·in·sure (kō′ĭn-shōōr′) *tr.v.* **-sured, -sur·ing, -sures 1.** To insure jointly. **2.** To insure with coinsurance.

coir (koir) *n.* The fiber obtained from the husk of a coconut, used chiefly in making rope and matting. [Malayalam *kayar*, cord < *kayaru*, to be twisted.]

cog railway

å	pat	oi	boy
ā	pay	ou	out
âr	care	ŏŏ	took
ä	father	ōō	boot
ĕ	pet	ŭ	cut
ē	be	ûr	urge
ĭ	pit	th	thin
ī	pie	th	this
îr	pier	hw	which
ŏ	pot	zh	vision
ō	toe	ə	about,
ô	paw		item

Stress marks:
′ (primary);
′ (secondary), as in
lexicon (lĕk′sĭ-kŏn′)

co·i·tus (kō′ĭ-təs, kō-ē′-) *n.* Heterosexual union involving insertion of the penis into the vagina. [Lat. < p. part. of *coīre*, to copulate : *co-*, co- + *īre*, to go, come; see **ei-** in App.] —**co′i·tal** *adj.* —**co′i·tal·ly** *adv.*

coitus in·ter·rup·tus (ĭn′tə-rŭp′təs) *n.* Coitus deliberately interrupted by withdrawal of the penis prior to ejaculation. [NLat. : Lat. *coitus*, coitus + Lat. *interruptus*, p. part. of *interrumpere*, to interrupt.]

coke[1] (kōk) *n.* The solid residue of impure carbon obtained from coal and other carbonaceous materials by destructive distillation, used as a fuel and in making steel. ❖ *tr. & intr.v.* **coked, cok·ing, cokes** To convert or be converted into coke. [Perh. < ME *colk*, core.]

coke[2] (kōk) *Slang n.* Cocaine. ❖ *tr.v.* **coked, cok·ing, cokes** To affect or intoxicate with cocaine.

Coke (kōk) A trademark used for a soft drink. See Regional Note at **tonic.**

Coke (kook, kōk), Sir **Edward** 1552–1634. English jurist who as chief justice of the Court of Common Pleas (1606–16) ruled that the common law is supreme law.

col (kŏl) *n.* A pass between two mountain peaks or a gap in a ridge. [Fr. < OFr., neck < Lat. *collum.* See **kʷel-** in App.]

col. *abbr.* **1.** collect **2.** college **3.** colony **4.** column

Col. *abbr.* **1.** Colombia **2.** also **Col** or **COL** colonel **3.** Colorado **4.** *Bible* Colossians

col–[1] *pref.* Variant of **com–.**

col–[2] *pref.* Variant of **colo–.**

co·la[1] (kō′lə) *n.* A carbonated soft drink containing an extract of the cola nut and other flavorings.

co·la[2] (kō′lə) *n.* Plural of **colon**[1] 2.

co·la[3] (kō′lə) *n.* A plural of **colon**[2].

co·la[4] also **ko·la** (kō′lə) *n.* Either of two tropical African evergreen plants (*Cola acuminata* or *C. nitida*) having nutlike seeds yielding an extract that contains caffeine and theobromine and is used in carbonated beverages and pharmaceuticals. [Of W African orig.; akin to Temne *kɔla*, kola nut.]

COLA (kō′lə) *abbr.* cost-of-living adjustment

col·an·der (kŭl′ən-dər, kŏl′-) *n.* A bowl-shaped kitchen utensil with perforations for draining off liquids and rinsing food. [ME *colyndore*, prob. < a Romance source akin to O Provençal *colador*, strainer < VLat. **cōlātōr* < Lat. *cōlātus*, p. part. of *cōlāre*, to strain. See PERCOLATE.]

colander

Col·bert (kōl-bĕr′, kōl-), **Claudette** 1903–96. Amer. actress whose films include *It Happened One Night* (1934).

Colbert, Jean Baptiste 1619–83. French politician who served as an adviser to Louis XIV.

col·can·non (kŏl-kăn′ən) *n.* An Irish dish of mashed potatoes and cabbage. [Ir.Gael. *cál ceannan* : *cál*, cabbage (< OIr. < Lat. *caulis*) + *ceannan*, white-headed (*ceann*, head < OIr. *cenn* + *fionn*, white < OIr. *find*; see **weid-** in App.).]

Col·ches·ter (kōl′chĕs′tər, -chĭ-stər) A municipal borough of SE England near the North Sea; site of the first Roman colony in Britain. Pop. 149,087.

col·chi·cine (kŏl′chĭ-sēn′, kŏl′kĭ-) *n.* A poisonous alkaloid, $C_{22}H_{25}NO_6$, obtained from the autumn crocus and used in plant breeding to induce chromosome doubling and in medicine to treat gout. [COLCHIC(UM) + –INE[2].]

col·chi·cum (kŏl′chĭ-kəm, kŏl′kĭ-) *n.* **1.** Any of various bulbous plants of the genus *Colchicum*, such as the autumn crocus. **2.** The dried ripe seeds or corms of the autumn crocus, both of which yield colchicine. [Lat., poisonous plant < Gk. *kolkhikon*, meadow saffron, after *Kolkhos*, Colchis.]

Col·chis (kŏl′kĭs) An ancient region on the Black Sea S of the Caucasus Mts.

col·co·thar (kŏl′kə-thər, -thär′) *n.* A ferric oxide obtained as a residue after heating ferrous sulfate, used in glass polishing and as a pigment. [Med.Lat. < Sp. *colcótar* < Ar. *qulquṭār*, poss. < Gk. *khalkanthos*, copper sulfate : *khalkos*, copper + *anthos*, flower.]

cold (kōld) *adj.* **cold·er, cold·est 1a.** Having a low temperature. **b.** Having a temperature lower than normal body temperature. **c.** Feeling no warmth; uncomfortably chilled. **2a.** Marked by deficient heat: *a cold room.* **b.** Being at a temperature that is less than what is required: *cold oatmeal.* **c.** Chilled by refrigeration or ice: *cold beer.* **3.** Lacking emotion; objective: *cold logic.* **4.** Having no appeal to the senses or feelings: *a cold decor.* **5a.** Not affectionate or friendly; aloof: *a cold person.* **b.** Exhibiting or feeling no enthusiasm: *a cold audience.* **c.** Devoid of sexual desire; frigid. **6.** Being a tone or color that suggests little warmth. **7.** Having lost all freshness or vividness through passage of time: *a cold scent.* **8a.** Marked by or sustaining a loss of body heat: *cold hands.* **b.** Appearing to be dead; unconscious. **c.** Dead: *cold in his grave.* **9.** Marked by unqualified certainty or sure familiarity. **10.** So intense as to be almost uncontrollable: *cold fury.* **11.** Characterized by repeated failure, as in a sport. ❖ *adv.* **1.** To an unqualified degree; totally: *stone cold sober.* **2.** With complete finality: *We turned him down cold.* **3.** Without advance preparation or introduction: *took the exam cold and passed.* ❖ *n.* **1a.** Relative lack of warmth. **b.** The sensation resulting from lack of warmth; chill. **2.** A condition of low air temperature; cold weather. **3.** A viral infection characterized by inflammation of the mucous membranes lining the upper respiratory passages and usu. accompanied by fever, chills,

coughing, and sneezing. —*idiom:* **out in the cold** Lacking benefits given to others; neglected. [ME < OE *ceald.* See **gel-** in App.] —**cold′ly** *adv.* —**cold′ness** *n.*

SYNONYMS *cold, arctic, chilly, cool, frigid, frosty, gelid, glacial, icy* These adjectives mean having a low temperature: *cold air; an arctic climate; a chilly day; cool water; a frigid room; a frosty morning; gelid seas; glacial winds; icy hands.* **ANTONYM** *hot*

cold-blood·ed (kōld′blŭd′ĭd) *adj.* **1a.** Lacking feeling or emotion. **b.** Executed without emotion. **2.** Ectothermic. —**cold′-blood′ed·ly** *adv.* —**cold′-blood′ed·ness** *n.*

cold call *n.* A telephone call or visit made to someone who is not expecting contact, often in order to sell something. —**cold′-call′** (kōld′kôl′) *v.*

cold chisel *n.* A chisel made of hardened, tempered steel and used for cutting cold metal.

cold·cock (kōld′kŏk′) *tr.v.* **-cocked, -cock·ing, -cocks** *Slang* To knock (another) unconscious.

cold cream *n.* An emulsion for softening and cleaning skin.

cold cut *n.* A slice of cold cooked meat. Often used in the plural.

cold drink *n.* **1.** A drink served or taken cold. **2.** *Chiefly Southern US* See **soft drink.** See Regional Note at **tonic.**

cold duck *n.* A beverage made of sparkling Burgundy and champagne. [Transl. of Ger. *Kalte Ente,* a drink made from a mixture of wines.]

cold feet *pl.n. Slang* Fearfulness or timidity preventing the completion of a course of action.

cold frame *n.* A structure consisting of a wooden or concrete frame and a top of glass or clear plastic, used for protecting and acclimatizing seedlings and plants.

cold front *n.* The leading portion of a cold atmospheric air mass moving against and replacing a warm air mass.

Cold Harbor A locality in E VA ENE of Richmond; site of two Civil War battles (1862 and 1864).

cold-heart·ed (kōld′här′tĭd) *adj.* Devoid of sympathy or feeling. —**cold′-heart′ed·ly** *adv.* —**cold′-heart′ed·ness** *n.*

cold light *n.* **1.** Light producing little or no heat. **2.** Light emitted by a process other than incandescence.

cold pack *n.* **1.** A compress filled or moistened with a cold fluid and applied externally to swollen or injured body parts to relieve pain and swelling. **2.** A canning process in which uncooked food is packed in jars or cans, then sterilized by heat.

cold rubber *n.* A durable strong synthetic rubber polymerized at low temperatures.

cold·shoul·der (kōld′shōl′dər) *tr.v.* **-dered, -der·ing, -ders** *Informal* To slight or snub (someone).

cold shoulder *n. Informal* Deliberate coldness or disregard.

cold sore *n.* A small blister occurring on the lips and face and caused by herpes simplex.

cold storage *n.* **1.** Protective storage, as of foods or furs, in a refrigerated place. **2.** *Informal* A state of abeyance.

cold sweat *n.* A reaction to nervousness, pain, or shock, marked by perspiration, chill, and cold moist skin.

cold turkey *n. Slang* **1.** Immediate, complete withdrawal from something on which one has become dependent, such as an addictive drug. **2.** Blunt language or procedural method.

cold type *n.* Typesetting, such as photocomposition, done without the casting of metal.

cold war or **Cold War** *n.* A state of political tension and military rivalry between nations that stops short of full-scale war, esp. that which existed between the United States and Soviet Union following World War II. —**cold warrior** *n.*

cold water *n. Informal* Discouragement, deterrence, or deprecation, as of a silly proposal.

cold-wa·ter (kōld′wô′tər, -wŏt′ər) *adj.* Lacking modern plumbing or heating facilities: *a cold-water flat.*

cold wave *n.* An onset of unusually cold weather within a 24-hour period.

cold-weld (kōld′wĕld′) *tr.v.* **-weld·ed, -weld·ing, -welds** To weld under high pressure or vacuum without heat.

cold weld·ing *n.* The welding of two materials under high pressure or vacuum without the use of heat.

cole (kōl) *n.* See **kale** 1. [ME *col* < OE *cāl* < Lat. *caulis*, cabbage.]

Cole, Nat "King" 1919–65. Amer. singer and pianist who recorded such popular ballads as "Mona Lisa."

Cole, Thomas 1801–48. English-born Amer. painter and leader of the Hudson River School.

co·lec·to·my (kə-lĕk′tə-mē) *n., pl.* **-mies** Surgical removal of part or all of the colon.

Cole·man (kōl′mən), **Cy** b. 1929. Amer. composer and theatrical producer whose Broadway productions include *Sweet Charity* (1966).

Coleman, Ornette b. 1939. Amer. jazz saxophonist and composer known for his unrestrained improvisational style.

cole·man·ite (kōl′mə-nīt′) *n.* A natural hydrated calcium borate, $Ca_2B_6O_{11} \cdot 5H_2O$, a source of borax. [After William Tell *Coleman* (1824–93), American merchant in California.]

co·le·op·ter·an (kō′lē-ŏp′tər-ən, kŏl′ē-) also **co·le·op·ter·on** (-tə-rŏn′) *n.* Any of numerous insects of the order Coleoptera, having forewings modified to form protective covers for the hind wings and including the beetles and fireflies. ❖ *adj.* Of, relating to, or belonging to the order Coleoptera. [< NLat. *Coleoptera*, order name < Gk. *koleopteros*, sheath-winged : *koleon*, sheath; see **kel-** in App. + *pteron*, wing; see **pet-** in App.] **—co′le•op′ter•ous** (-tər-əs) *adj.*

co•le•op•tile (kō′lē-ŏp′tĭl, kŏl′ē-) *n.* A protective sheath enclosing the shoot tip and embryonic leaves of grasses. [< NLat. *coleoptilum* : Gk. *koleon*, sheath; see **kel-** in App. + Gk. *ptilon*, plume; see **pet-** in App.]

co•le•o•rhi•za (kō′lē-ə-rī′zə, kŏl′ē-) *n., pl.* **-zae** (-zē) A protective sheath enclosing the embryonic root of grasses. [NLat. : Gk. *koleon*, sheath; see **kel-** in App. + Gk. *rhiza*, root; see **wrād-** in App.]

Cole•ridge (kōl′rĭj, kō′lə-rĭj), **Samuel Taylor** 1772–1834. British poet and critic whose works include "The Rime of the Ancient Mariner" (1798).

cole•slaw also **cole slaw** (kōl′slô′) *n.* A salad of finely shredded raw cabbage dressed with mayonnaise or a vinaigrette. [Du. *koolsla* : *kool*, cabbage (< MDu. *cōle* < Lat. *caulis*) + *sla*, salad (short for *salade* < Fr. < OFr.; see SALAD).]

Col•et (kŏl′ət), **John** 1467?–1519. English scholar and theologian who founded Saint Paul's School in London (1509).

Co•lette (kō-lĕt′, kô-), **(Sidonie Gabrielle Claudine)** 1873–1954. French writer whose works include *Gigi* (1945).

co•le•us (kō′lē-əs) *n.* Any of various Old World herbs of the genus *Coleus* in the mint family, having multicolored leaves. [NLat. *Coleus*, genus name < Gk. *koleos*, sheath (< the way its filaments are joined). See **kel-** in App.]

cole•wort (kōl′wûrt′, -wôrt′) *n.* See **kale** 1.

coli– *pref.* Variant of **colo–.**

col•ic (kŏl′ĭk) *n.* Severe abdominal pain caused by spasm, obstruction, or distention of any of the hollow viscera, such as the intestines. ❖ *adj.* (*also* kō′lĭk) Of, relating to, or affecting the colon. [ME *colik*, affecting the colon, colic < OFr. *colique* < Lat. *cōlica (passiō)*, (suffering) of the colon, fem. of *cōlicus* < Gk. *kōlikos* < *kolon, kōlon*, colon.] **—col′ick•y** (kŏl′ĭ-kē) *adj.*

col•i•cin (kŏl′ĭ-sĭn, kō′lĭ-) *n.* Any of various antibacterial proteins produced by certain strains of the colon bacillus and lethal to related strains of bacteria. [COL(ON)² + –IC + –IN.]

col•ic•root (kŏl′ĭk-rōōt′, -rŏŏt′) *n.* **1.** Any of certain perennial herbs of the genus *Aletris* in the lily family, esp. *A. farinosa* of eastern North America, having racemes of white flowers and rootstocks formerly used to treat colic. **2.** Any of various other plants thought to relieve colic.

co•li•form (kō′lə-fôrm′, kŏl′ə-) *adj. Microbiology* Of or relating to the bacilli that commonly inhabit the intestines of humans and other vertebrates, esp. the colon bacillus. **—co′li•form′** *n.*

Co•li•gny or **Co•li•gni** (kô-lē-nyē′), **Gaspard de** 1519–72. French general and Huguenot leader who was one of the first victims of the Saint Bartholomew's Day Massacre (1572).

co•lin•e•ar (kō-lĭn′ē-ər) *adj.* **1.** Containing elements that correspond to one another and are arranged in the same linear sequence. **2.** Collinear. **—co•lin′e•ar′i•ty** (-ăr′ĭ-tē) *n.*

co•li•phage (kō′lə-fāj′) *n.* A bacteriophage that infects the bacterium *Escherichia coli.* [NLat. *(Escherichia) colī*, species name; see E. COLI + –PHAGE.]

col•i•se•um also **col•os•se•um** (kŏl′ĭ-sē′əm) *n.* A large amphitheater for public sports events, entertainment, or assemblies. [Med.Lat. *Colisēum*, an amphitheater in Rome, Italy, var. of Lat. *Colossēum* < neut. of *colossēus*, gigantic < *colossus*, huge statue. See COLOSSUS.]

co•lis•tin (kə-lĭs′tĭn, kō-) *n.* An antibiotic produced by the bacterium *Bacillus polymyxa* or *B. colistinus* that is effective against a wide range of gram-negative bacteria. [< NLat. *Colistīnus*, species name < COLI–.]

co•li•tis (kə-lī′tĭs) *n.* Inflammation of the colon.

coll. *abbr.* **1.** collateral **2.** collect **3.** college **4.** colloquial

coll– *pref.* Variant of **collo–.**

col•lab•o•rate (kə-lăb′ə-rāt′) *intr.v.* **-rat•ed, -rat•ing, -rates** **1.** To work together, esp. in an intellectual effort. **2.** To cooperate treasonably, as with an enemy. [LLat. *collabōrāre, collabōrāt-* : Lat. *com-*, com- + Lat. *labōrāre*, to work (< *labor*, toil).] **—col•lab′o•ra′tion** *n.* **—col•lab′o•ra′tive** *adj.* **—col•lab′o•ra′tor** *n.*

col•lab•o•ra•tion•ist (kə-lăb′ə-rā′shə-nĭst) *n.* One that collaborates with an enemy occupation force. **—col•lab′o•ra′tion•ism** *n.*

col•lage (kō-läzh′, kə-) *n.* **1a.** An artistic composition of materials and objects pasted over a surface. **b.** A work, such as a literary piece, composed of both borrowed and original material. **2.** The art of creating such compositions. **3.** An assemblage of diverse elements: *a collage of memories.* ❖ *v.* **-laged, -lag•ing, -lages** —*tr.* To paste (diverse materials) over a surface, thereby creating an artistic product. —*intr.* To create such an artistic product. [Fr. < *coller*, to glue < *colle*, glue < VLat. **colla* < Gk. *kolla*.] **—col•lag′ist** *n.*

col•la•gen (kŏl′ə-jən) *n.* The fibrous protein constituent of bone, tendon, and other connective tissue. [Gk. *kolla*, glue + –GEN.] **—col′la•gen′ic** (-jĕn′ĭk), **col•lag′e•nous** (kə-lăj′ə-nəs) *adj.*

col•lag•e•nase (kə-lăj′ə-nās′, -nāz′, kŏl′ə-jə-) *n.* Any of various enzymes that catalyze the hydrolysis of collagen and gelatin.

col•lapse (kə-lăps′) *v.* **-lapsed, -laps•ing, -laps•es** —*intr.* **1.** To fall down or inward suddenly; cave in. **2.** To break down suddenly in strength or health and cease to function. **3.** To fold compactly. —*tr.* To cause to fold, break down, or fall down or inward. ❖ *n.* **1.** The act of falling down or inward, as from loss of supports. **2.** An abrupt failure of function, strength, or health; a breakdown. **3.** An abrupt loss of perceived value or of effect. [Lat. *collābī, collāps-*, to fall together : *com-*, com- + *lābī*, to fall.] **—col•laps′i•bil′i•ty** *n.* **—col•laps′i•ble, col•laps′a•ble** *adj.*

col•lar (kŏl′ər) *n.* **1.** The part of a garment that encircles the neck. **2.** A necklace. **3a.** A restraining or identifying band put around the neck of an animal. **b.** The cushioned part of a harness that presses against the shoulders of a draft animal. **4.** *Biology* An encircling structure or bandlike marking, as around an animal's neck, suggestive of a collar. **5.** Any of various ringlike devices used to limit, guide, or secure a machine part. **6.** *Slang* An arrest, as of a criminal. ❖ *tr.v.* **-lared, -lar•ing, -lars** **1.** To furnish with a collar. **2.** *Slang* **a.** To seize or detain. **b.** To arrest (a criminal, for example). [ME *coler* < OFr. *colier* < Lat. *collāre* < *collum*, neck. See **kʷel-** in App.] **—col′lared** *adj.*

col•lar•bone (kŏl′ər-bōn′) *n.* See **clavicle** 1.

collar cell *n.* See **choanocyte.**

col•lard (kŏl′ərd) *n.* **1.** See **kale** 1. **2. collards** The leaves of kale, used as a vegetable. [Variant of COLEWORT.]

collared peccary *n.* A small wild hog *(Tayassu tajacu)* with a range from the southwest United States to northern Argentina, having a gray and black coat with a white band.

col•late (kə-lāt′, kŏl′āt′, kō′lāt′) *tr.v.* **-lat•ed, -lat•ing, -lates** **1.** To examine and compare carefully in order to note points of disagreement. **2.** To assemble in proper numerical or logical sequence. **3.** *Printing* **a.** To examine (gathered sheets) in order to arrange them in sequence before binding. **b.** To verify the order and completeness of (pages). **4.** *Ecclesiastical* To admit (a cleric) to a benefice. [< Lat. *collātus*, p. part. of *cōnferre*, to bring together : *com-*, com- + *lātus*, brought; see **telə-** in App.] **—col•la′tor** *n.*

col•lat•er•al (kə-lăt′ər-əl) *adj.* **1.** Situated or running side by side; parallel. **2.** Coinciding in tendency or effect; accompanying. **3.** Serving to support or corroborate. **4.** Of a secondary nature; subordinate. **5.** Of, relating to, or guaranteed by a security pledged against the performance of an obligation: *a collateral loan.* **6.** Having an ancestor in common but descended from a different line. ❖ *n.* **1.** Property acceptable as security for a loan or other obligation. **2.** A collateral relative. [ME < Med.Lat. *collāterālis* : Lat. *com-*, com- + Lat. *lātus, later-*, side.] **—col•lat′er•al•ly** *adv.*

col•lat•er•al•ize (kə-lăt′ər-ə-līz′) *tr.v.* **-ized, -iz•ing, -izes** **1.** To secure (a loan) through use of collateral. **2.** To pledge (property, for example) as collateral.

col•la•tion (kə-lā′shən, kŏ-, kō-) *n.* **1.** The act or process of collating. **2.** A light meal, esp. one permitted on fast days.

col•league (kŏl′ēg′) *n.* A fellow member of a profession, staff, or academic faculty; an associate. See Syns at **partner.** [Fr. *collègue* < Lat. *collēga* : *com-*, com- + *lēgāre*, to depute; see **leg-** in App.] **—col′league•ship′** *n.*

col•lect¹ (kə-lĕkt′) *v.* **-lect•ed, -lect•ing, -lects** —*tr.* **1.** To bring together in a group or mass; gather. **2.** To accumulate as a hobby or for study. **3.** To call for and obtain payment of: *collect taxes.* **4.** To recover control of: *collect one's emotions.* **5.** To call for (someone); pick up. —*intr.* **1.** To come together in a group or mass; gather. See Syns at **gather. 2.** To take in payments or donations. ❖ *adv. & adj.* With payment to be made by the receiver: *called collect.* [ME *collecten* < Lat. *colligere, collēct-* : *com-*, com- + *legere*, to gather; see **leg-** in App.]

col•lect² (kŏl′ĭkt, -ĕkt′) *n. Ecclesiastical* A brief prayer that is used in various Western liturgies before the epistle and varies with the day. [ME *collecte* < OFr. < Med.Lat. *collēcta*, short for *(ōrātiō ad) collēctam*, (prayer at the) gathering < Lat. *collēctus*, gathered, p. part. of *colligere*, to gather. See COLLECT¹.]

col•lec•ta•ne•a (kŏl′ĕk-tā′nē-ə) *pl.n.* A selection of passages from one or more authors; an anthology. [Lat. *collēctānea* < neut. pl. of *collēctāneus*, collected < *collēctus*. See COLLECT².]

col•lect•ed (kə-lĕk′tĭd) *adj.* **1.** Self-possessed; composed. **2.** Brought or culled from various sources: *collected poems.* **—col•lect′ed•ly** *adv.* **—col•lect′ed•ness** *n.*

col•lect•i•ble also **col•lect•a•ble** (kə-lĕk′tə-bəl) *n.* One of a group or class of objects sought by collectors. **—col•lect′i•ble** *adj.*

col•lec•tion (kə-lĕk′shən) *n.* **1.** The act or process of collecting. **2.** A group of objects or works to be seen or kept together. **3.** A line of products produced for one season, as clothes developed by a designer. **4.** An accumulation; a deposit. **5.** Money collected, as for charity.

col•lec•tive (kə-lĕk′tĭv) *adj.* **1.** Assembled or accumulated into a whole. **2.** Of, relating to, or made by a number of people acting as a group: *a collective decision.* ❖ *n.* **1.** An undertaking, such as a business operation, set up on the principles or system of collectivism. **2.** *Grammar* A collective noun. **—col•lec′tive•ly** *adv.* **—col•lec′tive•ness** *n.*

collective bargaining *n.* Negotiation between the representatives of organized workers and their employers to determine wages, hours, and working conditions.

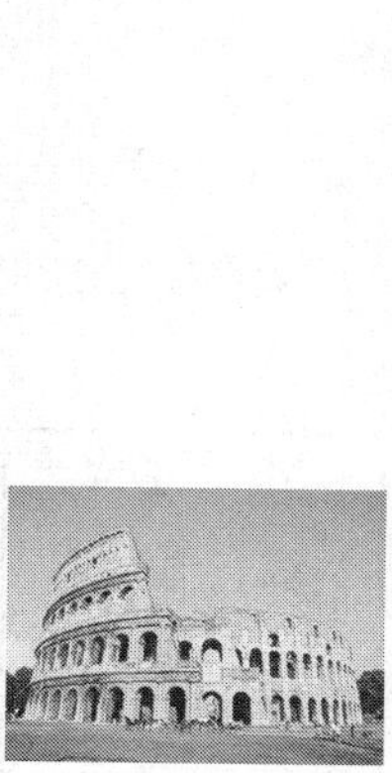

coliseum
the Colosseum, Rome, built 70–82 A.D.

ă	pat	oi	boy
ā	pay	ou	out
âr	care	ŏŏ	took
ä	father	ōō	boot
ĕ	pet	ŭ	cut
ē	be	ûr	urge
ĭ	pit	th	thin
ī	pie	*th*	this
îr	pier	hw	which
ŏ	pot	zh	vision
ō	toe	ə	about, item
ô	paw		

Stress marks:
′ (primary);
′ (secondary), as in
lexicon (lĕk′sĭ-kŏn′)

collective farm *n.* A farm or a group of farms managed and worked cooperatively by a group of laborers under state supervision, esp. in a communist country.

collective mark *n.* A trademark or service mark for a cooperative, association, or other collective organization.

collective memory *n.* **1.** The ability of a community to remember events. **2.** The collection of memories shared by a common culture.

collective noun *n.* A noun that denotes a collection of persons or things regarded as a unit.

USAGE NOTE In American usage, a collective noun takes a singular verb when it refers to the collection as a whole, as in *The family was united.* It takes a plural verb when it refers to the members of the group individually, as in *My family are always fighting each other.* A collective noun should not be treated as both singular and plural in the same construction; thus *The family is determined to press its* (not *their*) *claim.* Among the common collective nouns are *committee, clergy, company, enemy, group, family, flock, public,* and *team.* • In British usage, collective nouns are more often treated as plurals: *The government have not announced a new policy.* See Usage Notes at **government, group.**

collective unconscious *n.* In Jungian psychology, a part of the unconscious shared by a society, a people, or all humankind that preserves ancestral experience in symbolic form.

col•lec•tiv•ism (kə-lĕk′tə-vĭz′əm) *n.* The principles or system of ownership and control of the means of production and distribution by the people collectively, usu. under the supervision of a government. —**col•lec′tiv•ist** *n.* —**col•lec′tiv•is′tic** *adj.*

col•lec•tiv•i•ty (kŏl′ĕk-tĭv′ĭ-tē, kə-lĕk′-) *n.* **1.** The quality or condition of being collective. **2.** The people considered as a whole.

col•lec•tiv•ize (kə-lĕk′tə-vīz′) *tr.v.* **-ized, -iz•ing, -iz•es** To organize (an economy or enterprise) on the basis of collectivism. —**col•lec′tiv•i•za′tion** (-tə-vĭ-zā′shən) *n.*

col•lec•tor (kə-lĕk′tər) *n.* **1.** One that collects. **2.** A person employed to collect taxes or other payments. **3.** A person who collects, as stamps. **4.** An electrode collector. **5.** A solar collector. —**col•lec′tor•ship′** *n.*

col•leen (kŏ-lēn′, kŏl′ēn′) *n.* An Irish girl. [Ir.Gael. *cailín,* dim. of *caile,* girl < OIr.]

col•lege (kŏl′ĭj) *n.* **1a.** An institution of higher learning that grants the bachelor's degree in liberal arts or science or both. **b.** An undergraduate division or school of a university offering courses and granting degrees in a particular field. **c.** A school, sometimes a university, offering special instruction in professional or technical subjects. **d.** The students, faculty, and administration of such a school or institution. **e.** The building and buildings occupied by such a school or institution. **f.** *Chiefly British* A self-governing society of scholars for study or instruction, incorporated within a university. **g.** An institution in France for secondary education that is not supported by the state. **2a.** A body of persons having a common purpose or shared duties. **b.** An electoral college. **3.** A body of clerics living together on an endowment. [ME < OFr. < Lat. *collēgium.* See COLLEGIUM.]

College Board A service mark used for the administration of aptitude and achievement tests, used by some colleges and universities in admitting and placing students.

College of Cardinals *n. Roman Catholic Church* The body of cardinals that elect and assist the pope.

college try *n. Informal* A serious effort to do or achieve something.

col•le•gi•al (kə-lē′jē-əl, -jəl) *adj.* **1a.** Marked by or having power vested equally among colleagues. **b.** *Roman Catholic Church* Marked by the equal sharing of power among the bishops. **2.** Of, marked by, or similar to college life; collegiate. [ME < Lat. *collēgiālis,* of colleagues < *collēgium,* association. See COLLEGIUM.] —**col•le′gi•al•ly** *adv.*

col•le•gi•al•i•ty (kə-lē′jē-ăl′ĭ-tē) *n.* **1.** Collegial power. **2.** The doctrine that bishops share collegial power.

col•le•gian (kə-lē′jən, -jē-ən) *n.* A college student or recent college graduate.

col•le•giate (kə-lē′jĭt, -jē-ĭt) *adj.* **1.** Of, relating to, or held to resemble a college. **2.** Of, for, or typical of college students. **3.** Of or relating to a collegiate church.

collegiate church *n.* **1.** A Roman Catholic or Anglican church other than a cathedral, having a chapter of canons and a dean or provost. **2a.** A church in the United States associated with others under a common body of pastors. **b.** An association of such churches. **3.** A church in Scotland served by two or more ministers at the same time.

col•le•gi•um (kə-lē′jē-əm, -lĕg′ē-) *n., pl.* **-le•gi•a** (-lē′jē-ə, -lĕg′ē-ə) or **-le•gi•ums** **1.** An executive council or committee of equally empowered members, esp. one supervising an industry or commissariat in the Soviet Union. **2.** A group whose members pursue shared goals while working within a framework of mutual trust and respect. [Russ. *kollegiya* < Lat. *collēgium,* association < *collēga,* colleague. See COLLEAGUE.]

col•lem•bo•lan (kə-lĕm′bə-lən) *n.* See **springtail.** [COLL(O)- + Gk. *embolos,* peg, stopper; see EMBOLUS.]

col•len•chy•ma (kə-lĕng′kə-mə) *n.* A supportive tissue of

plants, consisting of elongated living cells with unevenly thickened walls. [COLL(O)- + –ENCHYMA.] —**col′len•chym′a•tous** (kŏl′ən-kĭm′ə-təs) *adj.*

col•len•chyme (kŏl′ən-kīm′) *n.* A gelatinous mesenchyme that constitutes a layer in the body wall of many cnidarians and ctenophores. [< COLLENCHYMA.]

col•let (kŏl′ĭt) *n.* **1.** A cone-shaped sleeve used for holding circular or rodlike pieces in a lathe or other machine. **2.** A metal collar used in watchmaking to join one end of a balance spring to the balance staff. **3.** A circular flange or rim into which a gem is set. [Fr., dim. of *col,* collar < Lat. *collum,* neck. See **k****wel-** in App.]

col•lide (kə-līd′) *intr.v.* **-lid•ed, -lid•ing, -lides** **1.** To come together with violent direct impact. **2.** To meet in opposition; conflict. [Lat. *collīdere* : *com-, com-* + *laedere,* to strike.]

col•lie (kŏl′ē) *n.* A dog of a breed originating in Scotland as a sheepdog, having a long narrow muzzle and either a long or short coat, depending on the variety. [Sc., perh. var. of *colly,* like *coal* < ME *col,* coal. See COAL.]

collie

col•lier (kŏl′yər) *n.* **1.** A coal miner. **2.** A coal ship. [ME *colier* < *col,* coal < OE.]

col•lier•y (kŏl′yə-rē) *n., pl.* **-ies** A coal mine together with its physical plant and outbuildings.

col•li•gate (kŏl′ĭ-gāt′) *tr.v.* **-gat•ed, -gat•ing, -gates** **1.** To tie or group together. **2.** *Logic* To bring (isolated facts) together by an explanation or hypothesis that applies to them all. [Lat. *colligāre, colligat-* : *com-, com-* + *ligāre,* to tie, bind.] —**col′li•ga′tion** *n.*

col•li•ga•tive (kŏl′ĭ-gā′tĭv) *adj.* Depending on the quantity of molecules but not on their chemical nature.

col•li•mate (kŏl′ə-māt′) *tr.v.* **-mat•ed, -mat•ing, -mates** **1.** To make parallel; line up. **2.** To adjust the line of sight of (an optical device). [NLat. *collīmāre, collīmāt-,* alteration of Lat. *collīneāre,* to aim : *com-, com-* + *līneāre,* to make straight (< *līnea,* line; see LINE[1]).] —**col′li•ma′tion** *n.*

col•li•ma•tor (kŏl′ə-mā′tər) *n.* A device capable of collimating radiation.

col•lin•e•ar (kə-lĭn′ē-ər, kō-) *adj.* **1.** Passing through or lying on the same straight line. **2.** Containing a common line; coaxial. —**col•lin′e•ar′i•ty** (- âr′ĭ-tē) *n.*

col•lins (kŏl′ənz) *n.* A tall iced drink made with liquor, such as gin, and lemon or lime juice. [Prob. < the name *Collins.*]

Collins[1], Michael 1890–1922. Irish nationalist and Sinn Fein leader who helped negotiate the establishment of the Irish Free State (1921).

Collins[2], Michael b. 1930. Italian-born Amer. astronaut who as a crew member of Apollo 11 piloted the spacecraft during its mission to the moon (1969).

Collins, (William) Wilkie 1824–89. British writer noted for his detective novels, including *The Woman in White* (1860).

col•lin•si•a (kə-lĭn′zē-ə) *n.* Any of various low-growing North American plants of the genus *Collinsia,* having whorled leaves and variously colored flowers. [NLat. *Collinsia,* genus name, after Zaccheus *Collins* (1764–1831), American botanist.]

col•li•sion (kə-lĭzh′ən) *n.* **1.** The act or process of colliding; a crash or conflict. **2.** *Physics* The close approach of two or more particles, such as atoms, resulting in an abrupt change of momentum or exchange of energy. [ME < LLat. *collīsiō, collīsiōn-* < Lat. *collīsus,* p. part. of *collīdere,* to collide. See COLLIDE.] —**col•li′sion•al** *adj.*

collision cross section *n.* See **cross section** 2.

collo– or **coll–** *pref.* **1.** Glue: *collenchyma.* **2.** Colloid: *collotype.* [NLat. < Gk. *kolla,* glue.]

col•lo•cate (kŏl′ə-kāt′) *tr.v.* **-cat•ed, -cat•ing, -cates** To place together, in proper order, or side by side. [Lat. *collocāre, collocāt-* : *com-, com-* + *locāre,* to place; see LOCATE.]

col•lo•ca•tion (kŏl′ō-kā′shən) *n.* **1.** The act of collocating or the state of being collocated. **2.** *Linguistics* An arrangement or juxtaposition of words or other elements, esp. those that commonly co-occur. —**col′lo•ca′tion•al** *adj.*

col•lo•di•on (kə-lō′dē-ən) *n.* A highly flammable, syrupy solution of pyroxylin, ether, and alcohol, used esp. as an adhesive to close small wounds and for making photographic plates. [Variant of *collodium* < NLat. *collōdium,* gluey substance < Gk. *kollōdēs,* glutinous, gluelike : *kolla,* glue + *-ōdēs,* adj. suff. (earlier, having the smell of < *ozein, ōd-,* to smell).]

col•logue (kə-lōg′) *intr.v.* **-logued, -logu•ing, -logues** **1.** To be on friendly or intimate terms with someone. **2a.** To consult or confer with someone. **b.** To chat. **3.** *Chiefly Upper Southern US* To conspire; intrigue. [Perh. alteration of *colleague,* to ally < OFr. *colleguer,* to collect. See COLLIGATE.]

col•loid (kŏl′oid′) *n.* **1.** *Chemistry* **a.** A system in which finely divided particles, which are approx. 10 to 10,000 angstroms in size, are dispersed in a continuous medium. **b.** The particulate matter so suspended. **2.** *Physiology* The gelatinous product of the thyroid gland, consisting mainly of thyroglobulin. **3.** *Pathology* Gelatinous material resulting from colloid degeneration in diseased tissue. ❖ *adj.* Of, relating to, containing, or having the nature of a colloid. —**col•loi′dal** (kə-loid′l, kō-) *adj.* —**col•loi′dal•ly** *adv.*

col•lop (kŏl′əp) *n.* **1.** A small portion or a slice of food, esp. of meat. **2.** A roll of fat flesh. [ME.]

col•lo•qui•al (kə-lō′kwē-əl) *adj.* **1.** Characteristic of or suited to

Colombia

the spoken language or to informal writing. **2.** Relating to conversation; conversational. [< COLLOQUY.] —**col•lo′qui•al** *n.* —**col•lo′qui•al•ly** *adv.* —**col•lo′qui•al•ness** *n.*

col•lo•qui•al•ism (kə-lō′kwē-ə-lĭz′əm) *n.* **1.** Colloquial style or quality. **2.** A colloquial expression.

col•lo•qui•um (kə-lō′kwē-əm) *n., pl.* **-qui•ums** or **-qui•a** (-kwē-ə) **1.** An informal meeting for the exchange of views. **2.** An academic seminar on a broad topic usu. led by a different lecturer at each meeting. [Lat., conversation < *colloquī,* to talk together : *com-,* com- + *loquī,* to speak.]

col•lo•quy (kŏl′ə-kwē) *n., pl.* **-quies 1.** A conversation, esp. a formal one. **2.** A written dialogue. [< Lat. *colloquium,* conversation. See COLLOQUIUM.] —**col′lo•quist** (-kwĭst) *n.*

col•lo•type (kŏl′ə-tīp′) *n.* **1.** A printing process employing a glass plate with a gelatin surface that carries the image to be reproduced. **2.** A print made by this process.

col•lude (kə-lōōd′) *intr.v.* **-lud•ed, -lud•ing, -ludes** To act together secretly to achieve a fraudulent, illegal, or deceitful purpose; conspire. [Lat. *collūdere* : *com-,* com- + *lūdere,* to play.] —**col•lud′er** *n.*

col•lu•sion (kə-lōō′zhən) *n.* A secret agreement between collusive parties. [ME < Lat. *collūsiō, collūsiōn-* < *collūsus,* p. part. of *collūdere,* to collude. See COLLUDE.]

col•lu•sive (kə-lōō′sĭv, -zĭv) *adj.* Acting in secret to achieve a fraudulent, illegal, or deceitful goal. —**col•lu′sive•ly** *adv.* —**col•lu′sive•ness** *n.*

col•lu•vi•um (kə-lōō′vē-əm) *n., pl.* **-vi•ums** or **-vi•a** (-vē-ə) A loose rock deposit accumulated through the action of gravity at the base of a cliff or slope. [Lat., a collection of washings, dregs < *colluere,* to wash thoroughly : *com-,* com- + *luere,* to wash; see **leu(ə)-** in App.] —**col•lu′vi•al** *adj.*

col•lyr•i•um (kə-lĭr′ē-əm) *n., pl.* **-i•ums** or **-i•a** (-ē-ə) A medicinal lotion applied to the eye; eyewash. [Lat. *collȳrium* < Gk. *kollū́rion,* eye salve, poultice, dim. of *kollū́rā,* roll of bread.]

col•ly•wob•bles (kŏl′ē-wŏb′əlz) *pl.n.* (*used with a sing.* or *pl. verb*) *Informal* Pain in the stomach or bowels. [Prob. alteration (influenced by COLIC and WOBBLE) of *cholera morbus,* gastroenteritis : Lat. *cholera,* jaundice; see CHOLER + Lat. *morbus,* disease; see MORBID.]

Colo. *abbr.* Colorado

colo– or **coli–** or **col–** *pref.* Colon: *colostomy.* [< COLON².]

col•o•bo•ma (kŏl′ə-bō′mə) *n., pl.* **-ma•ta** (-mə-tə) An anomaly of the eye, usu. a developmental defect, that often results in some loss of vision. [NLat. *colobōma* < Gk. *kolobōma,* part removed in mutilation < *koloboun,* to mutilate < *kolobos,* maimed.] —**col′o•bo′ma•tous** *adj.*

col•o•bus monkey (kŏl′ə-bəs, kə-lō′-) *n.* Any of various large African monkeys of the genus *Colobus,* having a long tail and vestigial thumbs. [NLat. *Colobus,* genus name < Gk. *kolobos,* maimed (< the appearance of its hands).]

col•o•cynth (kŏl′ə-sĭnth′) *n.* **1.** A tendril-bearing Old World vine (*Citrullus colocynthis*) with green-mottled fruit. **2.** The fruit of this plant, whose pulp is a laxative. [Lat. *colocynthis* < Gk. *kolokunthis* < *kolokunthē,* round gourd.]

co•log•a•rithm (kō-lôg′ə-rĭth′əm, -lŏg′ə-) *n.* The logarithm of the reciprocal of a number.

co•logne (kə-lōn′) *n.* A scented liquid made of alcohol and various fragrant oils. [Short for *cologne* (*water*), transl. of Fr. (*eau de*) *Cologne,* after COLOGNE.]

Co•logne (kə-lōn′) also **Köln** (kœln) A city of W Germany on the Rhine R. N of Bonn; a Roman settlement called Colonia Agrippina after A.D. 50. Pop. 962,517.

Co•lom•bi•a (kə-lŭm′bē-ə) A country of NW South America with coastlines on the Pacific Ocean and the Caribbean Sea; gained independence from Spain in 1819. Cap. Bogotá. Pop. 26,525,670. —**Co•lom′bi•an** *adj. & n.*

Co•lom•bo (kə-lŭm′bō) The cap. of Sri Lanka, in the W part on the Indian Ocean. Pop. 615,000.

co•lon¹ (kō′lən) *n., pl.* **-lons 1a.** A punctuation mark (:) used after a word introducing a quotation, explanation, series, or salutation. **b.** The sign (:) used between numbers in time expressions (2:30 A.M.) and ratios (1:2). **2.** *pl.* **co•la** (-lə) A section of a metrical period in quantitative verse, consisting of two to six feet and in Latin having one principal accent. [Lat. *cōlon,* part of a verse < Gk. *kôlon,* limb, metrical unit.]

co•lon² (kō′lən) *n., pl.* **-lons** or **-la** (-lə) The section of the large intestine from the cecum to the rectum. [ME < Lat. < Gk. *kolon,* large intestine.] —**co•lon′ic** *adj.*

co•lon³ (kō-lōn′) *n., pl.* **-lons** or **-lo•nes** (-lō′nās′) See table at **currency.** [Sp. *colón,* after Cristóbal Colón, Christopher Columbus.]

co•lon bacillus (kō′lən) *n.* A rod-shaped bacterium, esp. *Escherichia coli,* found in all vertebrate intestinal tracts, that is generally nonpathological but sometimes causes diarrhea and other dysenteric symptoms.

co•lo•nel (kûr′nəl) *n.* **1a.** A commissioned officer in the US Army, Air Force, or Marine Corps ranking above lieutenant colonel and below brigadier general. **b.** A person holding a similar rank in another military organization. **2.** An honorary civilian title awarded by some states of the United States. [Alteration of obsolete *coronel* < Fr. < OItal. *colonello* < dim. of *colonna,* column

of soldiers < Lat. *columna,* column.] —**co′lo•nel•cy, co′lo•nel•ship′** *n.*

Colonel Blimp *n. Chiefly British* A pompous, reactionary, ultranationalistic person. [After *Colonel Blimp,* a cartoon character created by Sir David Low (1891–1963), British cartoonist.]

co•lo•ni•al (kə-lō′nē-əl) *adj.* **1.** Of, relating to, possessing, or inhabiting a colony or colonies. **2.** often **Colonial.** Of or relating to the 13 British colonies that became the United States of America. **b.** Of or relating to the period of these colonies. **3.** often **Colonial.** Of, relating to, or being a style of architecture and furniture prevalent in the American colonies just before and during the Revolution. **4.** Living in, consisting of, or forming a colony. ❖ *n.* **1.** An inhabitant of a colony. **2.** A house designed in a colonial architectural style. —**co•lo′ni•al•ly** *adv.*

co•lo•ni•al•ism (kə-lō′nē-ə-lĭz′əm) *n.* A policy by which a nation maintains or extends its control over foreign dependencies. —**co•lo′ni•al•ist** *n.*

col•o•nist (kŏl′ə-nĭst) *n.* **1.** An original settler or founder of a colony. **2.** An inhabitant of a colony.

co•lon•i•tis (kō′lə-nī′tĭs) *n.* See **colitis.**

col•o•nize (kŏl′ə-nīz′) *v.* **-nized, -niz•ing, -niz•es** —*tr.* **1.** To form or establish a colony or colonies in. **2.** To migrate to and settle in; occupy as a colony. **3.** To resettle or confine (persons) in or as if in a colony. **4.** To subjugate (a population) to or as if to a colonial government. —*intr.* **1.** To form or establish a colony. **2.** To settle in a colony or colonies. —**col′o•ni•za′tion** (-nī-zā′shən) *n.* —**col′o•niz′er** *n.*

col•on•nade (kŏl′ə-nād′) *n. Architecture* A series of columns placed at regular intervals. [Fr., alteration of *colonnate* < Ital. *colonnato* < *colonna,* column < Lat. *columna.*] —**col′on•nad′ed** *adj.*

co•lon•o•scope (kō-lŏn′ə-skōp′, kə-) *n.* A long flexible endoscope, often equipped with a device for obtaining tissue samples, that is used for visual examination of the colon.

co•lon•os•co•py (kō′lə-nŏs′kə-pē) *n.* Examination of the colon by means of a colonoscope.

col•o•ny (kŏl′ə-nē) *n., pl.* **-nies 1a.** A group of emigrants or their descendants settled in a distant territory but subject to or closely associated with the parent country. **b.** A territory thus settled. **2.** A region controlled by a distant country; a dependency. **3a.** A group of people with the same interests or ethnic origin in a particular area. **b.** The area occupied by such a group. **4. Colonies** The British colonies that became the original 13 states of the United States. **5.** A group of people institutionalized in a relatively remote area. **6.** *Ecology* A group of the same kind of organisms living or growing together. **7.** *Microbiology* A visible growth of microorganisms, usu. in a solid or semisolid nutrient medium. [ME *colonie* < Lat. *colōnia* < *colōnus,* settler < *colere,* to cultivate. See **kʷel-** in App.]

colony stimulating factor *n.* A hormone produced in the cells lining the blood vessels that stimulates the bone marrow to synthesize white blood cells.

col•o•phon (kŏl′ə-fŏn′, -fən) *n.* **1.** An inscription, usu. at the end of a book, giving facts about its publication. **2.** A publisher's emblem or trademark, usu. on a title page. [LLat. *colophōn* < Gk. *kolophōn,* finishing touch.]

Col•o•phon (kŏl′ə-fŏn′) An ancient Greek city of Asia Minor NW of Ephesus.

col•or (kŭl′ər) *n.* **1.** That aspect of things that is caused by differing qualities of the light reflected or emitted by them, definable in terms of the observer or of the light, as: **a.** The appearance of objects or light sources as perceived by the individual and involving hue, lightness, and saturation for objects and hue, brightness, and saturation for light sources. **b.** The characteristics of light by which the individual is made aware of objects or light sources, described in terms of dominant wavelength, luminance, and purity. **2.** A substance, such as a dye or paint, that imparts a hue. **3a.** The general appearance of the skin; complexion. **b.** A ruddy complexion. **c.** A reddening of the face; a blush. **4.** The skin pigmentation of a person not categorized as white. **5. colors** A flag or banner, as of a country. **6. colors** The salute made during the ceremony of raising or lowering a flag. **7. colors** A distinguishing symbol, badge, ribbon, mark, or combination of colors. **8. colors** One's opinion or position: *Stick to your colors.* **9.** Character or nature. Often used in the plural. **10a.** Outward appearance, often deceptive: *a tale with the merest color of truth.* **b.** Appearance of authenticity: *testimony that lends color to an otherwise absurd notion.* **11a.** Variety of expression. **b.** Vivid, picturesque detail: *a story with a lot of color.* **12.** Traits of personality or behavior that attract interest. **13.** The use or effect of pigment in painting, as distinct from form. **14.** *Music* Quality of tone or timbre. **15.** *Law* Mere semblance of legal right. **16.** A particle or bit of gold found in auriferous gravel or sand. **17.** *Physics* A quantum characteristic of quarks that determines their role in the strong interaction. ❖ *v.* **-ored, -or•ing, -ors** —*tr.* **1.** To impart color to or change the color of. **2a.** To give a distinctive character or quality to; modify. **b.** To exert an influence on; affect: *The war colored the soldier's life.* **3a.** To misrepresent: *color the facts.* **b.** To gloss over; excuse. —*intr.* **1a.** To take on color. **b.** To change color. **2.** To become red in the face; blush. [ME *colour* < OFr. < Lat. *color.* See **kel-** in App.] —**col′or•er** *n.*

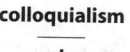

colonnade
the Jefferson Memorial,
Washington, DC

ă	pat	oi	boy
ā	pay	ou	out
âr	care	ŏŏ	took
ä	father	ōō	boot
ĕ	pet	ŭ	cut
ē	be	ûr	urge
ĭ	pit	th	thin
ī	pie	th	this
îr	pier	hw	which
ŏ	pot	zh	vision
ō	toe	ə	about,
ô	paw		item

Stress marks:
′ (primary);
′ (secondary), as in
lexicon (lĕk′sĭ-kŏn′)

col•or•a•ble (kŭl′ər-ə-bəl) *adj.* **1.** Meant to deceive; not genuine. **2.** Seemingly true or genuine; plausible. See Syns at **plausible.** —**col′or•a•bil′i•ty, col′or•a•ble•ness** *n.* —**col′or•a•bly** *adv.*

Col•o•ra•do (kŏl′ə-răd′ō, -rä′dō) A state of the W-central US; admitted as the 38th state in 1876. The region was added to the US through the Louisiana Purchase (1803) and a cession by Mexico (1848). Cap. Denver. Pop. 4,301,261. —**Col′o•ra′dan** *adj. & n.*

Colorado, Río A river of central Argentina rising in the Andes and flowing c. 853 km (530 mi) SE to the Atlantic Ocean.

Colorado blue spruce *n.* See **blue spruce.**

Colorado Desert A region of SE CA W of the Colorado R.

Colorado potato beetle *n.* A small striped beetle (*Leptinotarsa decemlineata*) that is a major agricultural pest.

Colorado River 1. A river of the SW US rising in the Rocky Mts. and flowing c. 2,333 km (1,450 mi) SW through the **Colorado Plateau** of W CO to the Gulf of California in NW Mexico. **2.** A river rising in NW TX and flowing c. 1,438 km (894 mi) SE to an inlet of the Gulf of Mexico.

Colorado Springs A city of central CO S of Denver; site of the US Air Force Academy (est. 1958). Pop. 360,890.

col•or•ant (kŭl′ər-ənt) *n.* Something, esp. a dye, pigment, ink, or paint, that colors or modifies the hue of something else. ❖ *adj.* Of or being a subtractive primary color.

col•or•a•tion (kŭl′ə-rā′shən) *n.* **1.** Arrangement of colors. **2.** The sum of the beliefs or principles of a person or group.

col•or•a•tu•ra (kŭl′ər-ə-toŏr′ə, -tyoŏr′ə) *n.* **1.** Florid ornamentation in vocal music, esp. trills and runs. **2.** A singer, esp. a soprano, specializing in coloratura. [Obsolete Ital. < LLat. *colōrātūra,* coloring < Lat. *colōrātus,* p. part. of *colōrāre,* to color < *color.* See COLOR.]

color bar *n.* See **color line.**

col•or•blind or **col•or-blind** (kŭl′ər-blīnd′) *adj.* **1.** Partially or totally unable to distinguish certain colors. **2a.** Not subject to racial prejudices. **b.** Not recognizing racial or class distinctions. —**col′or•blind′ness** *n.*

col•or•breed (kŭl′ər-brēd′) *tr.v.* **-bred** (-brĕd′), **-breed•ing,** **-breeds** To breed (plants or animals) selectively to produce new or desired colors.

col•or•cast (kŭl′ər-kăst′) *v.* **-cast** or **-cast•ed, -cast•ing, -casts** —*tr.* To broadcast (a television program) in color. [COLOR + (BROAD)CAST.] —**col′or•cast′** *n.*

col•or-code (kŭl′ər-kōd′) *tr.v.* **-cod•ed, -cod•ing, -codes** To color, as wires, according to a code for easy identification.

co•lo•rec•tal (kō′lə-rĕk′təl) *adj.* Relating to or involving both the colon and the rectum: *colorectal cancer.*

col•ored (kŭl′ərd) *adj.* **1.** Having color. **2.** often **Colored** *Offensive* **a.** Of or belonging to a racial group not regarded as white. **b.** Of mixed racial strains. **3.** Distorted or biased. ❖ *n.* also **Colored** *pl.* **colored** also **Coloreds** or **Coloreds** *Offensive* **1.** A person of a racial group not regarded as white. **2.** A person of mixed racial strains. See Usage Note at **black.**

col•or•fast (kŭl′ər-făst′) *adj.* Having color that will not run or fade with washing or wear. —**col′or•fast′ness** *n.*

color filter *n.* A photographic filter of colored glass that modifies light striking film by selectively absorbing colors.

col•or•ful (kŭl′ər-fəl) *adj.* **1.** Full of color; abounding in colors. **2.** Characterized by rich variety; vividly distinctive: *colorful language.* —**col′or•ful•ly** *adv.* —**col′or•ful•ness** *n.*

color guard *n.* A ceremonial escort for a flag.

col•or•if•ic (kŭl′ə-rĭf′ĭk) *adj.* Producing or imparting color.

col•or•im•e•ter (kŭl′ə-rĭm′ĭ-tər) *n.* **1.** Any of various instruments used to determine or specify colors, as by comparison with spectroscopic or visual standards. **2.** An instrument that measures the concentration of a known constituent of a solution by comparison with colors of standard solutions of that constituent. —**col′or•i•met′ric** (-ə-rə-mĕt′rĭk) *adj.* —**col′or•i•met′ri•cal•ly** *adv.* —**col′or•im′e•try** *n.*

Colorado potato beetle
Leptinotarsa decemlineata

color guard

Christopher Columbus

col•or•ing (kŭl′ər-ĭng) *n.* **1.** The art, manner, or process of applying color. **2.** A substance used to color something. **3.** Appearance with regard to color. **4.** Characteristic aspect, tone, or style. **5.** False or misleading appearance.

col•or•ist (kŭl′ər-ĭst) *n.* **1.** A painter skilled in achieving special effects with color. **2.** A hairdresser who specializes in dyeing hair. —**col′or•is′tic** *adj.*

col•or•ize (kŭl′ə-rīz′) *tr.v.* **-ized, -iz•ing, -iz•es** To impart color to (black-and-white film) by means of a computer-assisted process. —**col′or•i•za′tion** (-ər-ĭ-zā′shən) *n.* —**col′or•iz′er** *n.*

col•or•less (kŭl′ər-lĭs) *adj.* **1.** Lacking color. **2.** Weak in color; pallid. **3.** Lacking animation, variety, or distinction; dull. —**col′or•less•ly** *adv.* —**col′or•less•ness** *n.*

color line *n.* A barrier, created by custom, law, or economic differences, separating nonwhite persons from whites.

color wheel *n.* A circular diagram in which primary and usu. intermediate colors are arranged sequentially so that related colors are next to each other and complementary colors are opposite.

Co•los•sae (kə-lŏs′ē) An ancient city of central Asia Minor. —**Co•los′sian** (-lŏsh′ən) *adj. & n.*

co•los•sal (kə-lŏs′əl) *adj.* Of a size, extent, or degree that elicits awe or taxes belief; immense. [Fr. < Lat. *colossus,* colossus. See COLOSSUS.] —**co•los′sal•ly** *adv.*

Colossal order *n. Architecture* Any of the classical orders used in such a way that the columns extend from the ground through two or more stories of a building.

col•os•se•um (kŏl′ĭ-sē′əm) *n.* Variant of **coliseum.**

Co•los•sians (kə-lŏsh′ənz) *pl.n.* (used with a sing. verb) See table at **Bible.** [Lat. *Colossēnsēs,* inhabitants of Colossae < *Colossae,* Colossae < Gk. *Kolossai.*]

co•los•sus (kə-lŏs′əs) *n., pl.* **-los•si** (-lŏs′ī′) or **-los•sus•es 1.** A huge statue. **2.** Something likened to a huge statue, as in size or importance. [Lat. < Gk. *kolossos.*]

co•los•to•my (kə-lŏs′tə-mē) *n., pl.* **-mies 1.** Surgical construction of an artificial excretory opening from the colon. **2.** The opening created by such a surgical procedure.

co•los•trum (kə-lŏs′trəm) *n.* The thin yellowish fluid secreted by the mammary glands at the time of parturition that is rich in antibodies and minerals and precedes the production of true milk. [Lat.] —**co•los′tral** (-trəl) *adj.*

col•our (kŭl′ər) *n. & v. Chiefly British* Variant of **color.**

–colous *suff.* Having a specified kind of habitat: *rupicolous.* [< Lat. *-cola,* tiller, inhabitant. See kʷel- in App.]

col•pi•tis (kŏl-pī′tĭs) *n.* See **vaginitis.** [Gk. *kolpos,* vagina + –ITIS.]

col•por•tage (kŏl′pôr′tĭj, -pôr′-) *n.* A colporteur work.

col•por•teur (kŏl′pôr′tər, -pôr′-) *n.* A peddler of devotional literature. [Fr., alteration of OFr. *comporteur* < *comporter,* to conduct, peddle. See COMPORT.]

col•po•scope (kŏl′pə-skōp′) *n.* A magnifying and photographic device used as an aid in the diagnostic examination of the vaginal and cervical epithelia. [Gk. *kolpos,* vagina, womb + –SCOPE.] —**col′po•scop′ic** (-skōp′ĭk) *adj.*

col•pos•co•py (kŏl-pŏs′kə-pē) *n., pl.* **-pies** Examination of the vaginal and cervical epithelia by means of a colposcope. [Gk. *kolpos,* vagina, womb + –SCOPY.]

colt (kōlt) *n.* **1.** A young male horse. **2.** A youthful or inexperienced person; a novice. [ME < OE.]

Colt, Samuel 1814–62. Amer. firearms inventor and manufacturer who developed the first revolver.

colt•ish (kōl′tĭsh) *adj.* **1.** Relating to or suggestive of a colt. **2.** Lively and frisky. —**colt′ish•ly** *adv.* —**colt′ish•ness** *n.*

Col•trane (kōl′trān), **John William** 1926–67. Amer. jazz saxophonist and composer whose innovations broke through thematic and harmonic restrictions in jazz improvisation.

colts•foot (kōlts′foŏt′) *n., pl.* **-foots 1.** A perennial Eurasian herb (*Tussilago farfara*) in the composite family, having yellow flower heads and hoof-shaped leaves. **2.** The dried leaves or flower heads of this plant. **3.** See **galax.**

col•u•brid (kŏl′ə-brĭd, kŏl′yə-) *n.* Any of numerous, widely distributed, chiefly nonvenomous snakes of the family Colubridae, which includes the garter snakes. [< NLat. *Colubridae,* family name < Lat. *coluber, colubr-,* snake.] —**col′u•brid** *adj.*

col•u•brine (kŏl′ə-brīn′, kŏl′yə-) *adj.* **1.** Of, relating to, or resembling a snake. **2.** Colubrid.

co•lu•go (kə-loŏ′gō) *n., pl.* **-gos** See **flying lemur.** [Of Malayan orig.]

Co•lum•ba (kə-lŭm′bə) *n.* A constellation in the Southern Hemisphere near Caelum and Puppis. [Lat. *columba,* dove.]

Columba also **Col•um** (kŏl′əm), Saint. 521–597. Irish missionary who Christianized N Scotland.

col•um•bar•i•um (kŏl′əm-bâr′ē-əm) also **col•um•bar•y** (kŏl′əm-bĕr′ē) *n., pl.* **-i•a** (-ē-ə) also **-ies 1a.** A vault with niches for urns containing ashes of the dead. **b.** A niche in such a vault. **2a.** A dovecote. **b.** A pigeonhole in a dovecote. [Lat. *columbārium* < *columba,* dove.]

Co•lum•bi•a¹ (kə-lŭm′bē-ə) **1.** A community of N-central MD WSW of Baltimore. Pop. 88,254. **2.** A city of central MO NNW of Jefferson City; seat of the University of Missouri (est. 1839). Pop. 84,531. **3.** The cap. of SC, in the central part. Pop. 116,278.

Co·lum·bi·a² (kə-lŭm′bē-ə) *n.* The United States. [After Christopher COLUMBUS.]

Co·lum·bi·an (kə-lŭm′bē-ən) *adj.* **1.** Of or relating to the United States. **2.** Of or relating to Christopher Columbus.

Columbia River A river rising in SE British Columbia, Canada, and flowing c. 1,947 km (1,210 mi) S then W through the **Columbia Plateau** and along the WA-OR border to its outlet on the Pacific Ocean.

col·um·bine (kŏl′əm-bīn′) *n.* Any of various perennial herbs of the genus *Aquilegia*, native to north temperate regions and having showy flowers that have petals with long hollow spurs. [ME < Med.Lat. *columbīna* < fem. of Lat. *columbīnus*, dovelike (< the resemblance of the inverted flower to a cluster of doves) < *columba*, dove.]

co·lum·bite (kə-lŭm′bīt′) *n.* A black, red-brown, or colorless mineral, (Fe, Mn)(Nb, Ta)₂O₆, the principal ore of niobium. [COLUMB(IUM) + -ITE¹.]

co·lum·bi·um (kə-lŭm′bē-əm) *n.* Niobium. Not in scientific use. [After COLUMBIA².]

Co·lum·bus (kə-lŭm′bəs) **1.** The cap. of OH, in the central part; laid out in 1812. Pop. 711,470. **2.** A city of W GA on the Chattahoochee R. SSW of Atlanta; settled in 1828. Pop. 186,291.

Columbus, Christopher 1451–1506. Italian explorer in the service of Spain who attempted to reach Asia by sailing W from Europe, thereby discovering America (1492).

Columbus Day *n.* October 12, observed in the United States in commemoration of the discovery in 1492 of the New World by Christopher Columbus.

col·u·mel·la (kŏl′yə-mĕl′ə, kŏl′ə-) *n., pl.* **-mel·lae** (-mĕl′ē) Any small columnlike structure in various plants and animals, often forming the central axis of development for the organism or an anatomical structure. [Lat., dim. of *columna*, column. See COLUMN.] **—col′u·mel′lar** (-mĕl′ər) *adj.* **—col′u·mel′late′** (-mĕl′āt′) *adj.*

col·umn (kŏl′əm) *n.* **1.** *Architecture* A supporting pillar consisting of a base, a cylindrical shaft, and a capital. **2.** Something resembling an architectural pillar. **3a.** *Printing* One of two or more separated vertical sections of typed lines lying side by side on a page. **b.** A feature article that appears regularly in a publication. **4.** A formation, as of vehicles, in which all elements follow one behind the other. **5.** *Botany* A columnlike structure, as one formed by the union of a stamen and the style in an orchid flower. **6.** *Anatomy* Any of various tubular or pillarlike supporting structures in the body, usu. having a single tissue origin and function. [ME *columne* < Lat. *columna*.] **—col′umned** (kŏl′əmd) *adj.*

co·lum·nar (kə-lŭm′nər) *adj.* **1.** Having the shape of a column. **2.** Constructed with or having columns.

columnar epithelium *n.* Epithelium consisting of one or more cell layers, the most superficial of which is composed of elongated cylindrical cells projecting toward the surface.

co·lum·ne·a (kə-lŭm′nē-ə) *n.* Any of various bushy or trailing tropical American plants of the genus *Columnea*, having colorful tubular flowers. [NLat. *Columnea*, genus name, after Fabius Columna, Fabio Colonna (1567–1650?), Italian botanist.]

co·lum·ni·a·tion (kə-lŭm′nē-ā′shən) *n.* The use or arrangement of columns in a building.

col·um·nist (kŏl′əm-nĭst, -ə-mĭst) *n.* A writer of a column in a publication, such as a newspaper.

Col·ville (kŏl′vĭl′, kōl′-) A river rising in the Brooks Range of NW AK and flowing c. 603 km (375 mi) to the Arctic Ocean.

col·za (kŏl′zə, kōl′-) *n.* See rape². [Fr. < Du. *koolzaad* : *kool*, cabbage (< MDu. *cōle* < Lat. *caulis*) + *zaad*, seed (< MDu. *saet*; see sē- in App.).]

com. *abbr.* **1.** combustion **2.** comma **3.** commentary **4.** commerce **5.** commission **6.** committee **7.** commune

Com. *abbr.* **1.** commander **2.** commissioner **3.** commodore **4.** commonwealth **5.** communist

com- or **col-** or **con-** or **cor-** *pref.* Together; with; joint; jointly: *commingle*. [ME < Lat., together, intensive pref. < OLat. *com*. See kom in App.]

co·ma¹ (kō′mə) *n., pl.* **-mas** A state of deep unconsciousness, usu. due to injury, disease, or poison, in which one can neither sense nor respond to stimuli or internal needs. [Gk. *kōma*, deep sleep.]

co·ma² (kō′mə) *n., pl.* **-mae** (-mē) **1.** *Astronomy* The nebulous luminescent cloud containing the nucleus and constituting the major portion of the head of a comet. **2.** *Botany* A usu. terminal tuft or cluster, esp. a tuft of hairs on a seed. **3.** *Physics* A diffuse, comet-shaped image of a point source of light or radiation caused by aberration in the optical system. [Lat., hair < Gk. *komē*.] **—co′mal** *adj.*

Coma Ber·e·ni·ces (bĕr′ə-nī′sēz′) *n.* A constellation in the northern sky near Boötes and Leo. [NLat. *Coma Berenicēs* < *Coma* + Lat. *Berenicēs*, genitive of *Berenicē* < Gk. *Berenikēs*, genitive of *Berenikē* : *komē*, hair + Lat. *Berenicēs*, genitive of *Berenicē* (a queen of Egypt who promised her hair to Venus).]

Co·man·che (kə-măn′chē) *n., pl.* **Comanche** or **-ches** **1.** A member of a Native American people formerly ranging over the southern Great Plains from western Kansas to northern Texas and now located in Oklahoma. **2.** The Uto-Aztecan language of the Comanche. [Sp. < Ute *kimmanči*.] **—Co·man′che** *adj.*

co·mate¹ (kō′māt′) *adj.* Comose. [Lat. *comātus*, having long hair < *coma*, hair. See COMA².]

co·mate² (kō-māt′, kō′māt′) *n.* A mate; a companion.

co·ma·tose (kō′mə-tōs′, kŏm′ə-) *adj.* **1.** Of, relating to, or affected with coma; unconscious. **2.** Lethargic; torpid. [Gk. *kōma, kōmat-*, deep sleep + -OSE¹.] **—co′ma·tose′ly** *adv.*

co·mat·u·lid (kō-măch′ə-lĭd) also **co·mat·u·la** (-lə) *n., pl.* **-lids** also **-lae** (-lē) Any of various marine invertebrates of the class Crinoidea that are attached to a surface by a stalk when young but are free-swimming as adults. [< NLat. *Comatulidae*, former family name < LLat. *comātulus*, having neatly curled hair < Lat. *comātus*, having long hair. See COMATE¹.]

comb (kōm) *n.* **1a.** A thin toothed strip used to smooth, arrange, or fasten the hair. **b.** An implement, such as a wool card, that resembles a hair comb in shape or use. **c.** A currycomb. **2a.** The fleshy crest or ridge that grows on the crown of the head of certain birds and is most prominent in the male. **b.** Something resembling a fowl's comb. **3.** A honeycomb. ❖ *v.* **combed, comb·ing, combs** *—tr.* **1a.** To move a comb through (the hair) so as to arrange or groom. **b.** To move though or pass across with a raking action: *wind combing the wheatfields.* **2.** To card (wool or other fiber). **3.** To search thoroughly; look through: *combed the dresser drawers for a lost bracelet.* **4.** To remove with or as if with a comb: *combed the snarls out of his hair.* *—intr.* **1.** To roll and break. Used of waves. **2.** To make a thorough search: *combed through the documents.* [ME < OE. See gembh- in App.]

comb. *abbr.* **1.** combination **2.** combustion

com·bat (kəm-băt′, kŏm′băt′) *v.* **-bat·ed, -bat·ing, -bats** or **-bat·ted, -bat·ting, -bats** *—tr.* **1.** To oppose in battle; fight against. **2.** To oppose vigorously; struggle against. See Syns at **oppose.** *—intr.* To engage in fighting; contend or struggle. ❖ *n.* (kŏm′băt′) Fighting, esp. armed battle; strife. See Syns at **conflict.** [Fr. *combattre* < OFr. < LLat. *combattere* : Lat. *com-*, com- + *battere*, to beat.] **—com′bat′** *adj.*

com·bat·ant (kəm-băt′nt, kŏm′bə-tnt) *n.* One that takes part in armed strife. ❖ *adj.* Engaging in armed strife.

combat boot *n.* A boot that laces up the front and has a thick rubber outsole, worn esp. by infantry.

combat fatigue *n.* A condition of stress caused by usu. prolonged exposure to military combat.

com·bat·ive (kəm-băt′ĭv) *adj.* Eager or disposed to fight; belligerent. See Syns at **argumentative.** **—com·bat′ive·ly** *adv.* **—com·bat′ive·ness** *n.*

comb·er (kō′mər) *n.* **1.** One, such as a machine or a worker, that combs something, such as wool. **2.** A long wave that has peaked or broken into foam; a breaker.

com·bi·na·tion (kŏm′bə-nā′shən) *n.* **1.** The act of combining or the state of being combined. **2.** The result of combining. **3.** An alliance for a common purpose; an association. **4.** A sequence of numbers or letters used to open a combination lock. **5.** *Mathematics* One or more elements selected from a set without regard to the order of selection. **—com′bi·na′tion·al** *adj.*

combination lock *n.* A lock that will open only when its dial is turned through a combination.

com·bi·na·tive (kŏm′bə-nā′tĭv, kəm-bī′nə-tĭv) *adj.* **1.** Of, relating to, or resulting from combination. **2.** Tending, serving, or able to combine.

com·bi·na·to·ri·al (kŏm′bə-nə-tôr′ē-əl, -tōr′-, kəm-bī′nə-) *adj.* **1.** Relating to or involving combinations. **2.** Relating to the arrangement and counting of mathematical elements in sets.

com·bi·na·tor·ics (kŏm′bə-nə-tôr′ĭks, -tōr′-, kəm-bī′nə-) *n.* (*used with a sing. verb*) Combinatorial mathematics.

com·bi·na·to·ry (kŏm′bə-nə-tôr′ē, -tōr′ē, kəm-bī′nə-) *adj.* **1.** Combinative. **2.** Combinatorial.

com·bine (kəm-bīn′) *v.* **-bined, -bin·ing, -bines** *—tr.* **1.** To bring into a state of unity; merge. **2.** To join (two or more substances) to make a single substance; mix. **3.** To possess or exhibit in combination. **4.** (kŏm′bīn′) To harvest (a grain crop) using a combine. *—intr.* **1.** To become united; coalesce. **2.** To join forces for a common purpose. See Syns at **join.** **3.** *Chemistry* To form a compound. **4.** (kŏm′bīn′) To harvest a grain crop using a combine. ❖ *n.* (kŏm′bīn′) **1.** A power-operated harvesting machine that cuts, threshes, and cleans grain. **2.** An association for the furtherance of political or commercial interests. **3.** A combination. [ME *combinen* < OFr. *combiner* < LLat. *combīnāre* : Lat. *com-*, com- + *bīnī*, two by two; see dwo- in App.] **—com·bin′er** *n.*

comb·ings (kō′mĭngz) *pl.n.* Small loose pieces of material, such as hairs or wool, removed with a comb.

com·bin·ing form (kəm-bī′nĭng) *n.* A modified form of an independent word that occurs only in combination with words, affixes, or other combining forms to form compounds or derivatives, as *electro-* (from *electric*) in *electromagnet.*

comb jelly *n.* See ctenophore.

com·bo (kŏm′bō) *n., pl.* **-bos** **1.** *Music* A small jazz band. **2.** *Informal* The product or result of combining.

com·bust (kəm-bŭst′) *v.* **-bust·ed, -bust·ing, -busts** *—intr.* **1a.** To catch fire; burst into flame. **b.** To undergo combustion; burn. **2.** To become suddenly angry or agitated. *—tr.* **1.** To cause to burn; ignite. **2.** To cause to become angry or violent. [Back-formation < COMBUSTION.]

combine

capital

shaft

base

column
Ionic order column

com•bus•ti•ble (kəm-bŭs′tə-bəl) *adj.* **1.** Capable of igniting and burning. **2.** Easily aroused or excited. ❖ *n.* A combustible substance. —**com•bus′ti•bil′i•ty** *n.* —**com•bus′ti•bly** *adv.*

com•bus•tion (kəm-bŭs′chən) *n.* **1.** The process of burning. **2.** A chemical change, esp. oxidation, accompanied by the production of heat and light. **3.** Violent anger or agitation. [ME < LLat. *combustiō, combustiōn-* < Lat. *combustus*, p. part. of *combūrere*, to burn up, blend of *com-*, com-, and *ambūrere*, to burn around (*amb-, ambi-*, ambi- + *ūrere*, to burn).] —**com•bus′tive** (-tĭv) *adj.*

combustion chamber *n.* An enclosure in which combustion, esp. of a fuel or propellant, is initiated and controlled.

com•bus•tor (kəm-bŭs′tər) *n.* A combustion chamber and its igniters, injectors, and other related apparatus in a jet engine or gas turbine.

Comdr. *abbr.* commander

Comdt. *abbr.* commandant

come (kŭm) *intr.v.* **came** (kām), **come, com•ing, comes 1a.** To advance toward the speaker or toward a specified place; approach: *Come to me.* **b.** To advance in a specified manner: *The children came reluctantly.* **2a.** To make progress; advance. **b.** To fare: *How are things coming?* **3a.** To reach a particular point in a series or as a result of orderly progression. **b.** To arrive, as in due course: *Dawn comes at 5* A.M. *in June.* **4.** To move into view; appear: *The moon came over the horizon.* **5.** To occur in time; take place: *come rain or shine.* **6a.** To arrive at a particular result or end: *come to an understanding.* **b.** To arrive at or reach a particular state or condition: *Come to your senses!* **c.** To move or be brought to a particular position. **7.** To extend; reach: *water that came to my waist.* **8.** To have priority; rank. **9.** To happen as a result: *This comes of your carelessness.* **10.** To fall to one: *No good can come of this.* **11.** To occur in the mind. **12a.** To issue forth: *A cry came from the child.* **b.** To be derived; originate. **c.** To be descended: *They come from a good family.* **d.** To be within a given range or spectrum of reference or application. **13.** To be a native or resident: *He comes from Iowa.* **14.** To add up to a certain amount. **15a.** To become: *The knot came loose.* **b.** To turn out to be. **16.** To be available or obtainable: *shoes that come in all sizes.* **17.** *Vulgar Slang* To experience orgasm. ❖ *n. Vulgar Slang* Semen. ***—phrasal verbs:*** **come about 1.** To take place; happen. **2.** To turn around. **3.** *Nautical* To change tack. **come across 1.** To meet or find by chance. **2.** *Slang* **a.** To do what is wanted. **b.** To pay over money that is demanded. **3.** To give an impression. **come along 1.** To make advances to a goal; progress. **2.** To go with someone else who takes the lead: *I'll come along on the hike.* **3.** To show up; appear: *the first offer that comes along.* **come around (**or **round) 1.** To recover; revive: *fainted but soon came around.* **2.** To change one's opinion or position. **come at 1.** To obtain; get: *come at an education through study.* **2.** To rush at; attack. **come back 1.** To return to or regain past success after a period of misfortune. **2.** To retort; reply: *came back with a sharp riposte.* **3.** To recur to the memory. **come between** To cause to be in conflict or estrangement. **come by 1.** To gain possession of; acquire. **2.** To pay a visit. **come down 1.** To lose wealth or position. **2a.** To pass or be handed down by tradition. **b.** To be handed down from a higher authority. **3.** *Slang* To happen; occur: *What's coming down tonight?* **come in 1a.** To arrive: *Fall clothes will be coming in soon.* **b.** To become available for use: *New weather information just came in.* **c.** To start producing. Used of an oil well. **2.** To arrive among those who finish a contest or race: *came in fifth.* **3.** To perform or function in a particular way: *A food processor comes in handy.* **4.** To reply in a specified manner to a call or signal. **5.** To take on a specified role. **come into** To acquire, esp. as an inheritance. **come off 1.** To happen; occur: *The trip came off on schedule.* **2.** To acquit oneself. **3.** To turn out to be successful. **come on 1.** To convey a particular personal image. **2.** *Slang* To show sexual interest in someone. **3a.** To progress or advance in increments: *Darkness came on after seven.* **b.** To begin in small increments or by degrees: *Sleet came on after one o'clock.* **4.** To hurry up; move rapidly. Often used in the imperative: *Come on!* **5.** To stop an inappropriate behavior; abandon a position or an attitude; be obliging. Used chiefly in the imperative. **come out 1.** To become known: *The truth came out at the trial.* **2.** To be issued or brought out. **3.** To make a formal social debut. **4.** To end up; result. **5.** To declare oneself publicly. **6.** To reveal that one is a gay man, a lesbian, or a bisexual. **come over 1.** To change sides, as in a controversy. **2.** To pay a casual visit. **come through 1.** To do what is required or anticipated. **2a.** To become manifest. **b.** To be communicated in a specified manner. **come to** To recover consciousness: *The fainting victim came to.* **come up 1.** To manifest itself; arise: *The question never came up.* **2.** To rise above the horizon. **3.** To rise, as in status or rank. **4.** To draw near; approach. **come upon** To discover or meet by accident. ***—idioms:*** **come a cropper** To fail utterly. **come clean** To confess all. **come down on** To punish, oppose, or reprimand severely and often with force. **come down to 1.** To confront or deal with forthrightly. **2.** To amount to in essence. **come down with** To become sick with (an illness). **come in for** To receive; be subjected to. **come into (one's) own 1.** To get possession of what belongs to one. **2.** To obtain rightful recognition or prosperity. **come off it** *Slang* To stop acting or speaking foolishly or pretentiously. Often used in the imperative. **come out with 1.** To put into words; say. **2.** To reveal publicly. **come to blows** To begin a physical fight. **come to grief** To meet with disaster; fail. **come to grips with** To confront squarely and attempt to deal decisively with. **come to light (**or **hand)** To be clearly revealed or disclosed. **come to terms 1.** To confront squarely and come to understand fully and objectively. **2.** To reach mutual agreement. **come true** To happen as predicted. **come up against** To encounter, esp. a difficulty or major problem. **come up with** To bring forth or discover. [ME *comen* < OE *cuman.* See **gʷā-** in App.]

comet
Comet Hale-Bopp, February 1997

come•back (kŭm′băk′) *n.* **1a.** A return to formerly enjoyed status or prosperity. **b.** A return to popularity. **2.** The act of making up a deficit, as in a contest. **3.** A reply; a retort.

co•me•di•an (kə-mē′dē-ən) *n.* **1.** A professional entertainer who tells jokes or performs various other comic acts. **2.** An actor in comedy. **3.** A writer of comedy. **4.** A person who amuses or tries to amuse. [Fr. *comédien*, player, comedian < *comédie*, comedy < Med.Lat. *cōmēdia.* See COMEDY.]

co•me•dic (kə-mē′dĭk) *adj.* Of or relating to comedy. —**co•me′di•cal•ly** *adv.*

co•me•di•enne (kə-mē′dē-ĕn′) *n.* A woman professional entertainer who tells jokes or performs various other comic acts. [Fr. *comédienne*, fem. of *comédien*, comedian. See COMEDIAN.]

com•e•do (kŏm′ĭ-dō′) *n., pl.* **-dos** or **-do•nes** (-dō′nēz) See **blackhead** 1. [Lat. *comedō*, glutton (< a comparison of the wormlike shape of the waxy material that can be squeezed from a blackhead to a worm believed to feed on the body) < *comedere*, to eat up : *com-*, intensive pref.; see COM– + *edere*, to eat; see **ed-** in App.]

com•e•do•gen•ic (kŏm′ĭ-dō-jĕn′ĭk) *adj.* Tending to produce or aggravate acne. [COMEDO + –GENIC.]

come•down (kŭm′doun′) *n.* **1.** A decline to a lower status or level. **2a.** A feeling of disappointment or depression. **b.** A cause of disappointment or depression.

com•e•dy (kŏm′ĭ-dē) *n., pl.* **-dies 1a.** A dramatic work or film that is humorous or satirical and that usu. has a happy ending. **b.** The genre made up of such works. **2.** A literary work having humorous themes or characters. **3.** Popular entertainment composed of jokes, satire, or humorous performance. **4.** The art of composing or performing comedy. **5.** A humorous element of life or literature. **6.** A humorous occurrence. ***—idiom:*** **comedy of errors** A ludicrous event or sequence of events. [ME *comedie* < Med.Lat. *cōmēdia* < Lat. *cōmoedia* < Gk. *kōmōidia* < *kōmōidos*, comic actor : *kōmos*, revel + *aoidos*, singer (< *aeidein*, to sing).]

comedy of manners *n., pl.* **comedies of manners** A comedy satirizing the attitudes and behavior of a particular social group, often of fashionable society.

come-hith•er (kŭm-hĭth′ər) *adj.* Seductive; alluring.

come•ly (kŭm′lē) *adj.* **-li•er, -li•est 1.** Pleasing and wholesome in appearance; attractive. **2.** Suitable; seemly. [ME *comli*, alteration of *cumli* < OE *cȳmlic*, lovely, delicate < *cȳme*, beautiful.] —**come′li•ness** *n.*

Co•me•ni•us (kə-mē′nē-əs), **John Amos** 1592–1670. Moravian theologian who held that divine majesty is exalted and not threatened by science.

come-on (kŭm′ŏn′, -ôn′) *n.* **1.** Something offered to allure or attract; an inducement, esp. to buy. **2.** *Slang* A sexual or romantic approach or proposal.

com•er (kŭm′ər) *n.* **1.** One that arrives or comes. **2.** One showing promise of attaining success: *a political comer.*

co•mes•ti•ble (kə-mĕs′tə-bəl) *adj.* Fit to be eaten; edible. ❖ *n.* Something that can be eaten as food. [Fr. < OFr. < LLat. *comēstibilis* < Lat. *comēstus*, alteration of *comēsus*, p. part. of *comedere*, to eat up : *com-*, intensive pref.; see COM– + *edere*, to eat; see **ed-** in App.]

com•et (kŏm′ĭt) *n.* A celestial body having a head consisting of a solid nucleus surrounded by a nebulous coma up to 2.4 million kilometers (1.5 million miles) in diameter and a vapor tail arising only in that part of its orbit that is sufficiently close to the sun. [ME *comete* < OE *comēta* < LLat. < Lat. *comētēs* < Gk. *komētēs*, long-haired (star), comet < *komē*, hair.] —**com′et•ar′y** (-ĭ-tĕr′ē), **co•met′ic** (kə-mĕt′ĭk) *adj.*

come•up•pance (kŭm′ŭp′əns) *n.* A punishment or retribution that one deserves; one's just deserts.

com•fit (kŭm′fĭt, kŏm′-) *n.* A confection that consists of a piece of fruit, a seed, or a nut coated with sugar. [ME *confit* < OFr. < Lat. *cōnfectum*, thing prepared, neut. p. part. of *cōnficere*, to prepare : *com-*, com- + *facere*, to make; see **dhē-** in App.]

com•fort (kŭm′fərt) *tr.v.* **-fort•ed, -fort•ing, -forts 1.** To soothe in time of affliction or distress. **2.** To ease physically; relieve. ❖ *n.* **1.** A condition or feeling of pleasurable ease, well-being, and contentment. **2.** Solace in time of grief or fear. **3.** Help; assistance. **4.** One that brings or provides comfort. **5.** The capacity to give physical ease and well-being. **6.** *Chiefly Southern & Lower Northern US* A quilted bedcover; a comforter. [ME *comforten* < OFr. *conforter*, to strengthen < LLat. *cōnfortāre* : Lat. *com-*, com- + Lat. *fortis*, strong; see **bhergh-** in App.] —**com′fort•ing•ly** *adv.*

com•fort•a•ble (kŭm′fər-tə-bəl, kŭmf′tə-bəl, kŭmf′tər-) *adj.* **1.** Providing physical comfort. **2.** Free from stress or anxiety; at ease. **3.** Producing feelings of ease or security. **4.** Sufficient to

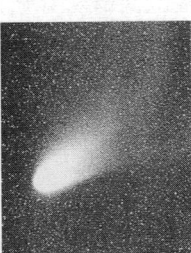

provide financial security: *comfortable earnings.* —**com′fort•a•ble•ness** *n.* —**com′fort•a•bly** *adv.*

com•fort•er (kŭm′fər-tər) *n.* **1.** One that comforts. **2.** **Comforter** *Christianity* The Holy Spirit. **3.** A quilted bedcover. **4.** A narrow, long, typically woolen neck scarf.

comfort station *n.* A public restroom or toilet.

comfort woman *n.* A woman forced to serve as a prostitute for Japanese servicemen during World War II. [Transl. of J. *ianfu* : *ian,* comfort + *fu,* woman.]

com•frey (kŭm′frē) *n., pl.* -**freys** Any of various hairy perennial Eurasian herbs of the genus *Symphytum,* esp. *S. officinale,* having flowers in coiled cymes and long used in herbal medicine. [ME *comferi* < OFr. *cumfirie* < VLat. *cōnferva* < *cōnfervēre,* to boil together : *com-,* com- + *fervēre,* to boil.]

com•fy (kŭm′fē) *adj.* -**fi•er, -fi•est** *Informal* Comfortable.

com•ic (kŏm′ĭk) *adj.* **1.** Characteristic of or having to do with comedy. **2.** Of or relating to comic strips. **3.** Amusing; humorous. ❖ *n.* **1a.** A comedian. **b.** A person whose behavior elicits laughter. **2a.** **comics** Comic strips. **b.** A comic book. **3.** A source of humor in art or life. [ME *comice* < Lat. *cōmicus* < Gk. *kōmikos* < *kōmos,* revel.]

com•i•cal (kŏm′ĭ-kəl) *adj.* **1.** Provoking mirth or amusement; funny. **2.** Of or relating to comedy. —**com′i•cal′i•ty** (-kăl′ĭ-tē), **com′i•cal•ness** *n.* —**com′i•cal•ly** *adv.*

comic book *n.* A book of comic strips or cartoons, often relating a narrative.

Co•mice (kō-mēs′, kə-) *n.* A cultivated variety of pear having blushed greenish-yellow skin and juicy flesh. [< Fr. *(Doyenne du) Comice,* (Dean of the) Show < *comice (agricole),* (agricultural) show < OFr., convention < Lat. *comitia.* See COMITIA.]

comic opera *n.* An opera or operetta with a humorous plot, mainly spoken dialogue, and usu. a happy ending.

com•ic-op•er•a (kŏm′ĭk-ŏp′ər-ə, -ŏp′rə) *adj.* Not to be taken seriously.

comic relief *n.* A humorous incident introduced into a serious literary work or drama in order to relieve dramatic tension or heighten emotional impact.

comic strip *n.* **1.** A usu. humorous narrative sequence of cartoon panels. **2.** A series or serialization of such narrative sequences.

Co•mines also **Com•mines** (kô-mēn′), **Philippe de** 1447?–1511. French historian noted for his *Mémoires* (1524).

com•ing (kŭm′ĭng) *adj.* **1.** Approaching; forthcoming; next. **2.** Showing promise of fame or success. ❖ *n.* Arrival; advent.

com•ing-out (kŭm′ĭng-out′) *n.* **1.** A social debut. **2.** A revelation or acknowledgment that one is a gay man, a lesbian, or a bisexual.

Com•in•tern (kŏm′ĭn-tûrn′) *n.* An association of Communist parties of the world, established in 1919 by Lenin and dissolved in 1943. [Russ. *komintern,* abbr. of *Kommunisticheskiĭ Internatsional,* Communist International.]

co•mi•ti•a (kə-mĭsh′ē-ə, -mĭsh′ə) *n., pl.* **comitia** A popular assembly in ancient Rome having legislative or electoral duties. [Lat. < pl. of *comitium,* assembly place : *com-,* com- + *itus,* p. part. of *īre,* to go; see **ei-** in App.] —**co•mi′tial** (-mĭsh′əl) *adj.*

com•i•ty (kŏm′ĭ-tē) *n., pl.* -**ties 1.** An atmosphere of social harmony. **2.** See **comity of nations 2. 3.** The principle by which the courts of one jurisdiction may accede or give effect to the laws or decisions of another. [Lat. *cōmitās* < *cōmis,* friendly.]

comity of nations *n.* **1.** Courteous recognition accorded by one nation to the laws and institutions of another. **2.** The nations observing international comity.

com•ix (kŏm′ĭks) *pl.n.* Comic books and comic strips, esp. of the alternative press. [Alteration of *comics,* pl. of COMIC.]

comm. *abbr.* **1.** commerce **2.** commission **3.** committee

Comm. *abbr.* **1.** commander **2.** commonwealth

com•ma (kŏm′ə) *n.* **1.** A punctuation mark (,) used to indicate a separation of ideas or elements within the structure of a sentence. **2.** A pause or separation; a caesura. **3.** Any of several butterflies of the genus *Polygonia,* having brownish wings with irregularly notched edges. [Lat. < Gk. *komma,* piece cut off, short clause < *koptein,* to cut.]

comma fault *n.* Improper use of a comma to join two independent clauses.

com•mand (kə-mănd′) *v.* -**mand•ed, -mand•ing, -mands** —*tr.* **1.** To direct with authority; give orders to. **2.** To have control or authority over; rule. **3.** To have at one's disposal. **4.** To deserve and receive as due; exact. **5a.** To exercise dominating, authoritative influence over. **b.** To dominate by physical position; overlook. —*intr.* **1.** To give orders. **2.** To exercise authority or control as or as if one is a commander. ❖ *n.* **1.** The act of commanding. **2.** An order given with authority. **3.** *Computer Science* A signal that initiates an operation defined by an instruction. **4a.** The authority to command. **b.** Possession and exercise of the authority to command. **5.** Ability to control or use; mastery. **6.** Dominance by location; extent of view. **7a.** The jurisdiction of a commander. **b.** A military unit, post, district, or region under the control of one officer. **c.** A unit of the US Air Force that is larger than an air force. ❖ *adj.* **1.** Of, relating to, or constituting a command. **2.** Done or performed in response to a command. [ME *commanden* < OFr. *comander* < LLat. *commandāre* : Lat. *com-,* intensive pref.; see COM– + Lat. *mandāre,* to entrust; see **man-²** in App.] —**com•mand′a•ble** *adj.*

com•man•dant (kŏm′ən-dănt′, -dänt′) *n.* The commanding officer of a military organization. [Fr. < pr. part. of *commander,* to command < OFr. *comander.* See COMMAND.]

command economy *n.* An economy that is planned and controlled by a central administration, as in the Soviet Union.

com•man•deer (kŏm′ən-dîr′) *tr.v.* -**deered, -deer•ing, -deers 1.** To force into military service. **2.** To seize for military use; confiscate. **3.** To take arbitrarily or by force. [Afr. *kommandeer* < Fr. *commander,* to command < OFr. *comander.* See COMMAND.]

com•mand•er (kə-măn′dər) *n.* **1.** A person who commands, esp. a commanding officer. **2a.** A commissioned officer in the US Navy or Coast Guard ranking above lieutenant commander and below captain. **b.** The chief commissioned officer of a military unit regardless of his or her rank. **3.** An officer in some knightly or fraternal orders.

commander in chief *n., pl.* **commanders in chief 1.** The supreme commander of all the armed forces of a nation. **2.** The officer commanding a major armed force.

com•mand•ing (kə-măn′dĭng) *adj.* **1.** Having command; controlling. **2.** Dominating: *a commanding view of the ocean.* —**com•mand′ing•ly** *adv.* —**com•mand′ing•ness** *n.*

commanding officer *n.* A military officer in charge of a unit, post, camp, base, or station.

com•mand•ment (kə-mănd′mənt) *n.* **1.** A command; an edict. **2.** *Bible* One of the Ten Commandments.

command module *n.* The portion of a spacecraft in which the astronauts live, communicate with a ground station, and operate controls during a flight.

com•man•do (kə-măn′dō) *n., pl.* -**dos** or -**does 1a.** A small fighting force specially trained for making quick, destructive raids against enemy-held areas. **b.** A member of such a force. **2a.** An organized force of Boer troops in South Africa. **b.** A raid made by such a force. [Afr. *kommando* < Du. *commando,* unit of troops < Sp. *comando* < *comandar,* to command < LLat. *commandāre.* See COMMAND.]

command post *n.* **1.** The field headquarters used by the commander of a military unit. **2.** A headquarters used by a team or organization.

comma splice *n.* See **comma fault.**

com•me•dia dell′ar•te (kə-mā′dē-ə dĕl-är′tĕ, -tĕ, -mĕd′ē-ə) *n.* A type of comedy developed in Italy in the 16th and 17th centuries and characterized by improvisation from a standard plot outline and the use of stock characters. [Ital. : *commedia,* comedy + *dell′arte,* of the guild, professional.]

comme il faut (kŭm′ ĕl fō′) *adj.* In accord with conventions or standards. [Fr. : *comme,* as + *il faut,* proper.]

com•mem•o•rate (kə-mĕm′ə-rāt′) *tr.v.* -**rat•ed, -rat•ing, -rates 1.** To honor the memory of with a ceremony. **2.** To serve as a memorial to. [Lat. *commemorāre, commemorāt-,* to remind : *com-,* com- + *memorāre* (< *memor,* mindful; see **(s)mer-** in App.).] —**com•mem′o•ra•tor** *n.* —**com•mem′o•ra•to′ry** (-ər-ə-tôr′ē, -tôr′ē) *adj.*

com•mem•o•ra•tion (kə-mĕm′ə-rā′shən) *n.* **1.** The act of commemorating someone or something. **2.** Something that commemorates.

com•mem•o•ra•tive (kə-mĕm′ər-ə-tĭv, -ə-rā′-) *adj.* Commemorating someone or something. ❖ *n.* Something commemorative.

com•mence (kə-mĕns′) *v.* -**menced, -menc•ing, -menc•es** —*tr.* To begin; start. —*intr.* To enter upon or have a beginning; start. [ME *commencen* < OFr. *comencier* < VLat. **cominitiāre* : Lat. *com-,* com- + LLat. *initiāre,* to begin (< Lat. *initium,* beginning; see **ei-** in App.).] —**com•menc′er** *n.*

com•mence•ment (kə-mĕns′mənt) *n.* **1.** A beginning; a start. **2a.** A ceremony at which academic degrees or diplomas are conferred. **b.** The day on which such a ceremony occurs.

com•mend (kə-mĕnd′) *tr.v.* -**mend•ed, -mend•ing, -mends 1.** To represent as worthy, qualified, or desirable; recommend. **2.** To express approval of; praise. See Syns at **praise. 3.** To commit to the care of another; entrust. [ME *commenden* < Lat. *commendāre : com-,* com- + *mandāre,* to entrust; see **man-²** in App.] —**com•mend′a•ble** *adj.* —**com•mend′a•ble•ness** *n.* —**com•mend′a•bly** *adv.*

com•men•da•tion (kŏm′ən-dā′shən) *n.* **1.** The act of commending. **2.** Something, as an award, that commends.

com•men•sal (kə-mĕn′səl) *adj.* Of, relating to, or characterized by commensalism. ❖ *n.* An organism participating in a commensal relationship. [ME, sharing a meal < Med.Lat. *commēnsālis* : Lat. *com-,* com- + Lat. *mēnsa,* table.] —**com•men′sal•ly** *adv.*

com•men•sal•ism (kə-mĕn′sə-lĭz′əm) *n.* A symbiotic relationship between two organisms of different species in which one derives some benefit while the other is unaffected.

com•men•su•ra•ble (kə-mĕn′sər-ə-bəl, -shər-) *adj.* **1.** Measurable by a common standard. **2.** Commensurate; proportionate. **3.** *Mathematics* Exactly divisible by the same unit an integral number of times. Used of two quantities. [LLat. *commēnsūrābilis* : Lat. *com-,* com- + *mēnsūrābilis,* measurable (< *mēnsūrāre,* to measure; see COMMENSURATE).] —**com•men′su•ra•bil′i•ty** *n.* —**com•men′su•ra•bly** *adv.*

com•men•su•rate (kə-mĕn′sər-ĭt, -shər-) *adj.* **1.** Of the same size, extent, or duration as another. **2.** Corresponding in size or

command module

ă	pat	oi	boy
ā	pay	ou	out
âr	care	ŏŏ	took
ä	father	ōō	boot
ĕ	pet	ŭ	cut
ē	be	ûr	urge
ĭ	pit	th	thin
ī	pie	th	this
îr	pier	hw	which
ŏ	pot	zh	vision
ō	toe	ə	about,
ô	paw		item

Stress marks:
′ (primary);
′ (secondary), as in
lexicon (lĕk′sĭ-kŏn′)

degree; proportionate. **3.** Measurable by a common standard; commensurable. [LLat. *commēnsūrātus* < Lat. *com-*, com- + *mēnsūrātus* < p. part. of *mēnsūrāre*, to measure (< Lat. *mēnsūra*, measure; see MEASURE).] —**com•men′su•rate•ly** *adv.* —**com•men′su•ra′tion** *n.*

com•ment (kŏm′ĕnt) *n.* **1a.** A written note intended as an explanation, illustration, or criticism of a passage in a book or other writing; an annotation. **b.** A series of annotations or explanations. **2a.** A statement of fact or opinion, esp. one that expresses a personal reaction or attitude. **b.** An implied conclusion or judgment. **3.** Talk; gossip. **4.** *Computer Science* A string of text in a program that does not function in the program itself but is used by the programmer to explain instructions. **5.** *Linguistics* The part of a sentence that provides new information about the topic. ❖ *v.* -ment•ed, -ment•ing, -ments —*intr.* **1.** To make a comment; remark. **2.** To serve as a judgmental commentary. —*tr.* To make comments on; annotate. [ME < LLat. *commentum*, interpretation < Lat., contrivance < neut. p. part. of *comminīscī*, to devise. See men-¹ in App.]

SYNONYMS *comment, observation, remark* These nouns denote an expression of fact, opinion, or explanation: *an unpleasant comment; an observation about the movie; an offensive remark.*

com•men•tar•y (kŏm′ən-tĕr′ē) *n., pl.* -ies **1.** A series of explanations or interpretations. **2.** An expository treatise or series of annotations; an exegesis. Often used in the plural. **3.** An apt explanation or illustration. **4.** A personal narrative; a memoir. Often used in the plural. —**com′men•tar′i•al** (-târ′ē-əl) *adj.*

com•men•tate (kŏm′ən-tāt′) *v.* -tat•ed, -tat•ing, -tates —*intr.* To serve as commentator. —*tr.* To make a running commentary on. [Back-formation < COMMENTATOR.]

com•men•ta•tor (kŏm′ən-tā′tər) *n.* **1.** A broadcaster or writer who reports and analyzes events in the news. **2.** One who writes or delivers a commentary or commentaries.

com•merce (kŏm′ərs) *n.* **1.** The buying and selling of goods, esp. on a large scale, as between cities or nations. See Syns at **business**. **2.** Intellectual exchange or social interaction. **3.** Sexual intercourse. [Fr. < OFr. < Lat. *commercium* : *com-*, com- + *merx, merc-*, merchandise.]

com•mer•cial (kə-mûr′shəl) *adj.* **1a.** Of or relating to commerce. **b.** Engaged in commerce. **c.** Involved in work that is intended for the mass market. **2.** Of, relating to, or being goods, often unrefined, produced and distributed in large quantities for use by industry. **3.** Having profit as a chief aim. **4.** Sponsored by an advertiser or supported by advertising. ❖ *n.* A paid advertisement on television or radio. —**com•mer′cial•ly** *adv.*

commercial bank *n.* A bank whose principal functions are to receive demand deposits and make short-term loans.

com•mer•cial•ism (kə-mûr′shə-lĭz′əm) *n.* **1.** The practices, methods, aims, and spirit of commerce or business. **2.** An attitude that emphasizes tangible profit or success. —**com•mer′cial•ist** *n.* —**com•mer′cial•is′tic** *adj.*

com•mer•cial•ize (kə-mûr′shə-līz′) *tr.v.* -ized, -iz•ing, -iz•es **1.** To apply business methods to for profit. **2a.** To do, exploit, or make chiefly for financial gain. **b.** To sacrifice the quality of for profit. —**com•mer′cial•i•za′tion** (-shə-lĭ-zā′shən) *n.*

commercial paper *n.* Short-term, unsecured, discounted, and negotiable notes sold by one company to another in order to satisfy immediate cash needs.

commercial traveler *n.* A traveling sales representative.

com•mie also **Com•mie** (kŏm′ē) *n. Informal* A Communist. [Short for COMMUNIST.]

com•mi•na•tion (kŏm′ə-nā′shən) *n.* A formal denunciation. [ME *comminacioun* < Lat. *comminātiō, comminātiōn-* < *comminātus*, p. part. of *comminārī*, to threaten : *com-*, com- + *minārī*, to threaten; see MENACE.] —**com•min′a•to′ry** (kə-mĭn′ə-tôr′ē, -tōr′ē, kŏm′ĭ-nə-) *adj.*

Com•mines (kô-mēn′), Philippe de See Philippe de **Comines**.

com•min•gle (kə-mĭng′gəl) *v.* -gled, -gling, -gles —*intr.* To become blended. —*tr.* To cause to blend together; mix.

com•mi•nute (kŏm′ə-nōōt′, -nyōōt′) *tr.v.* -nut•ed, -nut•ing, -nutes To reduce to powder; pulverize. [Lat. *comminuere, comminūt-* : *com-*, com- + *minuere*, to lessen.] —**com′mi•nu′tion** *n.*

com•mis•er•ate (kə-mĭz′ə-rāt′) *v.* -at•ed, -at•ing, -ates —*tr.* To feel or express sorrow or pity for; sympathize with. —*intr.* To feel or express sympathy. [Lat. *commiserārī, commiserāt-* : *com-*, com- + *miserārī*, to pity (< *miser*, wretched).] —**com•mis′er•a′tive** *adj.* —**com•mis′er•a′tive•ly** *adv.* —**com•mis′er•a′tor** *n.*

com•mis•er•a•tion (kə-mĭz′ə-rā′shən) *n.* The feeling or expression of pity or sorrow.

com•mis•sar (kŏm′ĭ-sär′) *n.* **1a.** An official of the Communist Party in charge of political indoctrination and the enforcement of party loyalty. **b.** The head of a commissariat in the Soviet Union until 1946. **2.** A person who tries to control public opinion. [Russ. *komissar* < Ger. *Kommissar*, deputy < Med.Lat. *commissārius*, agent. See COMMISSARY.]

com•mis•sar•i•at (kŏm′ĭ-sâr′ē-ĭt) *n.* **1.** A department of an army that provides supplies. **2.** A food supply. **3.** A major government department in the Soviet Union until 1946. [Fr. < Med.Lat. *commissārius*, agent. See COMMISSARY.]

com•mis•sar•y (kŏm′ĭ-sĕr′ē) *n., pl.* -ies **1a.** A supermarket for military personnel and their dependents, usu. located on a military installation. **b.** A store where food and equipment are sold, as in a mining camp. **2.** A lunchroom or cafeteria, esp. one in a film or television studio. **3.** A person to whom a special duty is given by a higher authority; a deputy. [ME *commissarie*, agent < Med.Lat. *commissārius* < Lat. *commissus*, entrusted. See COMMISSION.]

com•mis•sion (kə-mĭsh′ən) *n.* **1a.** The act of granting certain powers or the authority to carry out a particular task or duty. **b.** The authority so granted. **c.** The matter or task so authorized. **d.** A document conferring such authorization. **2a.** A group of people officially authorized to perform certain duties or functions. **b.** often **Commission** A ruling council within the Mafia. **3.** The act of committing or perpetrating. **4.** A fee or percentage allowed to a sales representative or an agent for services rendered. **5a.** An official document issued by a government, conferring on the recipient the rank of a commissioned officer in the armed forces. **b.** The rank and powers so conferred. ❖ *tr.v.* -sioned, -sion•ing, -sions **1.** To grant a commission to. **2.** To place an order for. **3.** To put (a ship) into active service. —*idioms:* **in commission 1.** In active service. Used of a ship. **2.** In use or in usable condition. **on commission** With a sales commission serving as full or partial recompense for the work done. **out of commission 1.** Not in active service. Used of a ship. **2.** Not in use or in working condition. [ME *commissioun* < Lat. *commissiō, commissiōn-* < *commissus*, p. part. of *committere*, to entrust. See COMMIT.] —**com•mis′sion•al** *adj.*

com•mis•sion•aire (kə-mĭsh′ə-nâr′) *n. Chiefly British* A uniformed attendant. [Fr. < Med.Lat. *commissiōnārius* < Lat. *commissiō, commissiōn-*, commission. See COMMISSION.]

com•mis•sioned officer (kə-mĭsh′ənd) *n.* An officer who holds a commission and ranks as a second lieutenant or above in the US Army, Air Force, or Marine Corps or as an ensign or above in the US Navy or Coast Guard.

com•mis•sion•er (kə-mĭsh′ə-nər) *n.* **1.** A member of a commission. **2.** A person authorized by a commission to perform certain duties. **3.** A governmental official in charge of a department. **4.** *Sports* An official selected by an athletic association or league to exercise administrative or regulatory powers over it. —**com•mis′sion•er•ship′** *n.*

commission merchant *n.* One that buys and sells goods for others on a commission basis.

commission plan *n.* Municipal government in which legislative and administrative functions and powers are vested in an elected commission rather than in a mayor and city council.

com•mis•sure (kŏm′ə-shoōr′) *n.* **1.** A line or place at which two things join. **2.** *Anatomy* **a.** A tract of nerve fibers passing from one side to the other of the spinal cord or brain. **b.** The point or surface where two parts, such as the eyelids, join or form a connection. [ME < Lat. *commissūra* < *commissus*, p. part. of *committere*, to join. See COMMIT.] —**com′mis•su′ral** *adj.*

com•mit (kə-mĭt′) *v.* -mit•ted, -mit•ting, -mits —*tr.* **1.** To do, perform, or perpetrate. **2.** To put in trust or charge; entrust. **3.** To place officially in confinement or custody. **4.** To consign for future use or reference or for preservation. **5.** To put into a place to be kept safe or to be disposed of. **6a.** To make known the views of (oneself) on an issue. **b.** To bind or obligate, as by a pledge. **7.** To refer (a legislative bill, for example) to a committee. —*intr.* To pledge or obligate one's own self. [ME *committen* < Lat. *committere* : *com-*, com- + *mittere*, to send.] —**com•mit′ta•ble** *adj.*

com•mit•ment (kə-mĭt′mənt) *n.* **1.** The act or an instance of committing, esp.: **a.** The act of referring a legislative bill to committee. **b.** Official consignment, as to a prison. **c.** A court order authorizing consignment to a prison. **2a.** A pledge to do. **b.** Something pledged, esp. an engagement by contract involving financial obligation. **3.** The state of being bound emotionally or intellectually to someone or something.

com•mit•tal (kə-mĭt′l) *n.* **1.** The act of entrusting. **2.** The act or an instance of committing to confinement. **3.** The act of pledging oneself to a particular view or position.

com•mit•tee (kə-mĭt′ē) *n.* **1.** A group of people officially delegated to perform a function. See Usage Note at **collective noun**. **2.** *Archaic* A person to whom a trust or charge is committed. [< ME *committe*, trustee < AN *comité*, p. part. of *cometre*, to commit < Lat. *committere*. See COMMIT.]

com•mit•tee•man (kə-mĭt′ē-mən, -măn′) *n.* **1.** A man who is a member of a committee. **2.** A man who is a party leader of a ward or precinct.

committee of the whole *n.* The whole membership of a legislative body sitting as a committee to consider a proposal.

com•mit•tee•wom•an (kə-mĭt′ē-wŏom′ən) *n.* **1.** A woman who is a member of a committee. **2.** A woman who is a party leader of a ward or precinct.

com•mix (kə-mĭks′, kō-) *v.* -mixed, -mix•ing, -mix•es —*intr.* To be or become mixed. —*tr.* To cause to mix. [< ME *commixt, mixed* < Lat. *commixtus*, p. part. of *commiscēre*, to mix : *com-*, com- + *miscēre*, to mix; see meik- in App.]

com•mix•ture (kə-mĭks′chər, kō-) *n.* **1.** The act or process of mixing. **2.** The result of mixing; a mixture.

com·mode (kə-mōd′) *n.* **1.** A low cabinet or chest of drawers, often elaborately decorated and usu. standing on legs or short feet. **2a.** A movable stand or cupboard containing a washbowl. **b.** A chair enclosing a chamber pot. **c.** A toilet. **3.** A woman's ornate headdress, fashionable around 1700. [Fr. < *commode*, convenient < Lat. *commodus*. See COMMODIOUS.]

com·mod·i·fy (kə-mŏd′ə-fī′) *tr.v.* **-fied, -fy·ing, -fies** To turn into or treat as a commodity; make commercial: "*Such music . . . commodifies the worst sorts of . . . stereotypes*" (Michiko Kakutani). [COMMODI(TY) + -FY.] **—com·mod′i·fi·a·ble** *adj.* **—com·mod′i·fi·ca′tion** (-fĭ-kā′shən) *n.*

com·mo·di·ous (kə-mō′dē-əs) *adj.* **1.** Spacious; roomy. **2.** *Archaic* Suitable; handy. [ME, convenient < Med.Lat. *commodiōsus* < Lat. *commodus* : *com-*, com- + *modus*, measure; see med- in App.] **—com·mo′di·ous·ly** *adv.* **—com·mo′di·ous·ness** *n.*

com·mod·i·ty (kə-mŏd′ĭ-tē) *n., pl.* **-ties 1.** Something useful that can be turned to commercial or other advantage. **2.** An article of trade or commerce, esp. an agricultural or mining product that can be transported. **3.** Advantage; benefit. **4.** *Obsolete* A quantity; lot. [ME *commodite* < OFr., convenience < Lat. *commoditās* < *commodus*, convenient. See COMMODIOUS.]

com·mo·dore (kŏm′ə-dôr′, -dōr′) *n.* **1a.** A former commissioned rank in the US Navy that is above captain and below rear admiral. **b.** One who holds this rank. **2a.** The senior captain of a naval squadron or merchant fleet. **b.** The presiding officer of a yacht club. [Obsolete *commandore*, prob. < Du. *komandeur*, commander < Fr. *commandeur* < OFr. < *comander*, to command. See COMMAND.]

Com·mo·dus (kŏm′ə-dəs), **Lucius Aelius Aurelius** A.D. 161–192. Emperor of Rome (180–192) who was murdered in a conspiracy led by his mistress.

com·mon (kŏm′ən) *adj.* **-er, -est 1a.** Belonging equally to or shared equally by two or more; joint: *common interests*. **b.** Of or relating to the community as a whole; public: *for the common good.* See Syns at **general.** See Usage Note at **mutual. 2.** Widespread; prevalent. **3a.** Occurring frequently or habitually; usual. **b.** Most widely known; ordinary: *the common housefly.* **4.** Having no special designation, status, or rank. **5a.** Not distinguished by superior or noteworthy characteristics; average. **b.** Of no special quality; standard. **c.** Of mediocre or inferior quality; second-rate. **6.** Unrefined or coarse in manner; vulgar. **7.** *Grammar* **a.** Either masculine or feminine in gender. **b.** Representing one or all of the members of a class; not designating a unique entity. ❖ *n.* **1. commons** The common people; commonalty. **2. commons** (*used with a sing. or pl. verb*) **a.** The political class composed of commoners. **b.** The parliamentary representatives of this class. **3. Commons** (*used with a sing. or pl. verb*) The House of Commons. **4.** A tract of land belonging to or used by a community as a whole. **5.** The legal right of a person to use the lands or waters of another, as for fishing. **6. commons** (*used with a sing. verb*) A building or hall for dining, typically at a university or college. **7.** Common stock. **8.** *Ecclesiastical* A service used for a particular class of festivals. **—idiom: in common** Equally with or by all. [ME *commune* < OFr. *commun* < Lat. *commūnis.*] **—com′mon·ly** *adv.* **—com′mon·ness** *n.*

com·mon·age (kŏm′ə-nĭj) *n.* **1.** The right to pasture animals on common land. **2.** The state of being held in common.

com·mon·al·i·ty (kŏm′ə-năl′ĭ-tē) *n., pl.* **-ties 1a.** The possession along with another or others of a certain attribute or set of attributes. **b.** A shared feature or attribute. **2.** See **commonalty** 1.

com·mon·al·ty (kŏm′ə-nəl-tē) *n., pl.* **-ties 1.** The common people as opposed to the upper classes. **2.** An incorporated body; a corporation. **3.** An entire group. [ME *communalte* < OFr. *comunalte* < Med.Lat. *commūnālitās* < LLat. *commūnālis*, of the community. See COMMUNAL.]

common bile duct *n.* The duct formed by the union of the cystic duct and the hepatic duct that carries bile from the liver and the gallbladder to the duodenum.

common carrier *n.* **1.** One that is in the business of transporting the public, goods, or messages for a fee. **2.** A company that provides telecommunications services to the public.

common cold *n.* See **cold** 3.

common denominator *n.* **1.** *Mathematics* A quantity into which all the denominators of a set of fractions may be divided without a remainder. **2.** A commonly shared theme or trait.

common divisor *n.* A quantity that is a factor of two or more quantities.

com·mon·er (kŏm′ə-nər) *n.* **1.** One of the common people. **2.** A person without noble rank or title.

Common Era *n.* The period coinciding with the Christian era.

common factor *n.* See **common divisor.**

common fraction *n.* A fraction with an integer as a numerator and an integer as a denominator.

common gender *n.* In Modern English, the gender of those nouns that apply to either sex, such as *spouse.*

common grackle *n.* A large grackle (*Quiscalus quiscula*) chiefly of eastern North America, existing in several variations, each having iridescent blackish-purple plumage and a long, wedge-shaped tail.

common ground *n.* A foundation for mutual understanding.

common law *n.* The system of laws originated and developed in England and based on court decisions, on the doctrines implicit in those decisions, and on customs and usages rather than on codified written laws. **—com′mon-law′** (kŏm′ən-lô′) *adj.*

common-law marriage *n.* A marriage existing by mutual agreement or the fact of cohabitation without a civil or religious ceremony.

common logarithm *n.* A logarithm to the base 10, esp. as distinguished from a natural logarithm.

common market *n.* An economic unit, typically formed of nations, intended to eliminate or markedly reduce trade barriers among its members.

Common Market See European Economic Community.

common measure *n.* A ballad stanza form in iambic meter, often rhyming in alternating pairs, that is typical of many church hymns.

common multiple *n.* A quantity into which each of two or more quantities may be divided with zero remainder.

common noun *n.* A noun, such as *book* or *dog*, that can be preceded by the definite article and represents one or all of the members of a class.

com·mon·place (kŏm′ən-plās′) *adj.* Having no remarkable features, characteristics, or traits; ordinary. ❖ *n.* **1a.** A trite or obvious remark; a platitude. **b.** Something that is ordinary or common. **2.** *Archaic* A passage marked for reference or entered in a commonplace book. [Transl. of Lat. *locus commūnis*, generally applicable literary passage, transl. of Gk. *koinos topos*.]

commonplace book *n.* A personal journal in which quotable passages, literary excerpts, and comments are written.

common pleas *pl.n.* (*used with a sing. verb*) In some states of the United States, a court of common pleas.

common room *n.* **1.** A faculty lounge in a college or university. **2.** A lounge for use by all members of a residential institution or community.

common salt *n.* **1.** See **salt** 1. **2.** Sodium chloride.

common school *n.* A public elementary school.

com·mon·sense (kŏm′ən-sĕns′) *adj.* Having or exhibiting native good judgment. **—com′mon·sen′si·ble, com′mon·sen′si·cal** *adj.*

common sense *n.* Sound judgment not based on specialized knowledge; native good judgment. [Transl. of Lat. *sēnsus commūnis*, common feelings of humanity.]

common stock *n.* Capital stock that is secondary to preferred stock in the distribution of dividends and often of assets.

common time *n.* A musical meter with four quarter notes to the measure.

common touch *n.* The ability to appeal to the interests and sensibilities of the ordinary person.

com·mon·weal (kŏm′ən-wēl′) *n.* **1.** The public good or welfare. **2.** *Archaic* A commonwealth or republic.

com·mon·wealth (kŏm′ən-wĕlth′) *n.* **1.** The people of a nation or state; the body politic. **2.** A nation or state governed by the people; a republic. **3. Commonwealth a.** Used to refer to Kentucky, Massachusetts, Pennsylvania, and Virginia. **b.** Used to refer to a self-governing autonomous political unit voluntarily associated with the United States, namely, Puerto Rico and the Northern Mariana Islands. **4.** The English state and government from the death of Charles I in 1649 to the restoration of the monarchy in 1660, including the Protectorate of 1653 to 1659. **5.** *Archaic* The public good.

Commonwealth of Independent States An association of self-governing states including most of the former Soviet republics; formed in 1991.

Commonwealth of Nations also **British Commonwealth** An association comprising the United Kingdom, its dependencies, and many former British colonies with a common allegiance to the British Crown; est. in 1931.

common wormwood *n.* See **absinthe** 1.

common year *n.* A calendar year having 365 days; a year without an intercalary period.

com·mo·tion (kə-mō′shən) *n.* **1.** A condition of turbulent motion. **2a.** An agitated disturbance; a hubbub. **b.** Civil disturbance or insurrection; disorder. [ME *commocioun* < OFr. *commotion* < Lat. *commōtiō, commōtiōn-* < *commōtus*, p. part. of *commovēre*, to disturb : *com-*, com- + *movēre*, to move.]

com·move (kə-mōōv′) *tr.v.* **-moved, -mov·ing, -moves 1.** To cause to move with force or violence; agitate. **2.** To rouse strong feelings; excite. [ME *commeven* < OFr. *commovoir, commeuv-* < Lat. *commovēre*. See COMMOTION.]

com·mu·nal (kə-myōō′nəl, kŏm′yə-) *adj.* **1.** Of or relating to a commune. **2.** Of or relating to a community. **3a.** Of, belonging to, or shared by the people of a community; public. **b.** Marked by collective ownership and control of goods and property. [Fr. < LLat. *commūnālis* < Lat. *commūnis*, common. See COMMON.] **—com′mu·nal′i·ty** (kŏm′yə-nălĭ-tē) *n.* **—com·mu′nal·ly** *adv.*

com·mu·nal·ism (kə-myōō′nə-lĭz′əm, kŏm′yə-nə-) *n.* **1.** Belief in or practice of communal ownership, as of goods and property. **2.** Strong devotion to the interests of one's own minority or ethnic group rather than those of society as a whole.

com·mu·nal·ist (kə-myōō′nə-lĭst) *n.* **1.** An advocate of communal living. **2.** One who is more interested in one's own minor-

commode

common grackle
Quiscalus quiscula

ă pat	oi boy
ā pay	ou out
âr care	ōō took
ä father	ōō boot
ĕ pet	ŭ cut
ē be	ûr urge
ĭ pit	th thin
ī pie	th this
îr pier	hw which
ŏ pot	zh vision
ō toe	ə about,
ô paw	item

Stress marks:
′ (primary);
′ (secondary), as in
lexicon (lĕk′sĭ-kŏn′)

ity or ethnic group than in society as a whole. **3.** One who is deeply concerned about the quality of community life. —**com·mu′nal·is′tic** *adj.*

com·mu·nal·ize (kə-myōō′nə-līz′, kŏm′yə-nə-) *tr.v.* **-ized, -iz·ing, -iz·es** To convert into communal property.

Com·mu·nard (kŏm′yə-närd′) *n.* **1.** A member or advocate of the Commune of Paris of 1871. **2. communard** One who lives in a commune. [Fr. < *commune,* commune. See COMMUNE².]

com·mune¹ (kə-myōōn′) *intr.v.* **-muned, -mun·ing, -munes** **1.** To be in a state of intimate, heightened sensitivity and receptivity, as with one's surroundings. **2.** To receive the Eucharist. [ME *communen,* to have common dealings with, converse < OFr. *communer,* to make common, share (< *common,* common; see COMMON) and perh. < OFr. *communier,* to share in the Communion (< LLat. *commūnicāre* < Lat., to communicate; see COMMUNICATE).]

com·mune² (kŏm′yōōn′, kə-myōōn′) *n.* **1a.** A relatively small, often rural community whose members share common interests, work, and income and often own property collectively. **b.** The people in such a community. **2.** The smallest local political division of various European countries. **3a.** A local community organized with a government for promoting local interests. **b.** A municipal corporation in the Middle Ages. **4.** often **Commune a.** The revolutionary group that controlled the government of Paris from 1789 to 1794. **b.** The insurrectionary, socialist government that controlled Paris from March 18 to May 28, 1871. [Fr., independent municipality < OFr. *comugne* < Med.Lat. *commūnia,* community < neut. of Lat. *commūnis,* common.]

com·mu·ni·ca·ble (kə-myōō′nĭ-kə-bəl) *adj.* **1.** Transmittable between persons or species; contagious. **2.** Readily communicated. **3.** Talkative. —**com·mu′ni·ca·bil′i·ty, com·mu′ni·ca·ble·ness** *n.* —**com·mu′ni·ca·bly** *adv.*

com·mu·ni·cant (kə-myōō′nĭ-kənt) *n.* **1.** A person who receives or is entitled to receive Communion. **2.** A person, esp. an informant, who communicates something. —**com·mu′ni·cant** *adj.*

com·mu·ni·cate (kə-myōō′nĭ-kāt′) *v.* **-cat·ed, -cat·ing, -cates** —*tr.* **1a.** To convey information about; make known; impart. **b.** To reveal clearly; manifest: *Her disapproval communicated itself in her frown.* **2.** To spread (a disease, for example) to others; transmit. —*intr.* **1.** To have an interchange, as of ideas. **2.** To express oneself in such a way that one is readily and clearly understood. **3.** *Ecclesiastical* To receive Communion. **4.** To be connected, one with another: *apartments that communicate.* [Lat. *commūnicāre, commūnicāt-* < *commūnis,* common.] —**com·mu′ni·ca′tor** *n.*

com·mu·ni·ca·tion (kə-myōō′nĭ-kā′shən) *n.* **1.** The act of communicating; transmission. **2a.** The exchange of thoughts, messages, or information. **b.** Interpersonal rapport. **3. communications** (*used with a sing. or pl. verb*) **a.** The art and technique of using words effectively in imparting one's ideas. **b.** The field of study concerned with the transmission of information by various means, such as print or broadcasting. **4.** Something communicated; a message. **5. communications** A means of communicating, esp.: **a.** A system, such as mail, telephone, or television, for sending and receiving messages. **b.** A network of routes for sending messages and transporting troops and supplies. **6. communications** The technology employed in transmitting messages. **7.** *Biology* The transmission of information from one organism to another, as by chemical signal or behavior. **8.** An opening or connecting passage, as between two structures. —**com·mu′ni·ca′tion·al** *adj.*

communication disorder *n.* Any of various disorders characterized by impaired language expression or comprehension, such as one arising from hearing loss or central nervous system damage.

com·mu·ni·ca·tions satellite (kə-myōō′nĭ-kā′shənz) *n.* An artificial satellite used to aid telecommunications.

com·mu·ni·ca·tive (kə-myōō′nĭ-kā′tĭv, -kə-tĭv) *adj.* **1.** Inclined to communicate readily; talkative. **2.** Of or relating to communication. —**com·mu′ni·ca′tive·ly** *adv.* —**com·mu′ni·ca′tive·ness** *n.*

com·mun·ion (kə-myōōn′yən) *n.* **1.** The act or an instance of sharing; sharing of thoughts. **2.** Religious or spiritual fellowship. **3.** A body of Christians with a common religious faith who practice the same rites; a denomination. **4. Communion a.** The sacrament of the Eucharist received by a congregation. **b.** The consecrated elements of the Eucharist. **c.** The part of the Mass or a liturgy in which the Eucharist is received. [ME *communion,* Christian fellowship, Eucharist < OFr. *communion* < LLat. *commūniō, commūniōn-* < Lat., mutual participation < *commūnis,* common. See COMMON.]

com·mu·ni·qué (kə-myōō′nĭ-kā′, -myōō′nĭ-kā′) *n.* An official announcement. [Fr., p. part. of *communiquer,* to announce < Lat. *commūnicāre,* to communicate. See COMMUNICATE.]

com·mu·nism (kŏm′yə-nĭz′əm) *n.* **1.** A theoretical economic system characterized by collective ownership of property and the organization of labor for the common advantage of all members. **2. Communism a.** A system of government in which the state controls the economy and a single party holds power, claiming to work toward a social order in which all goods are equally shared.

b. The Marxist-Leninist version of Communist doctrine that advocates the overthrow of capitalism by the revolution of the proletariat. [Fr. *communisme* < *commun,* common < OFr. < Lat. *commūnis.*]

Communism Peak also **Mount Communism** A mountain, 7,500 m (24,590 ft), in the Pamirs of NE Tajikistan.

Com·mu·nist (kŏm′yə-nĭst) *n.* **1a.** A member of a movement or political party that advocates Communism. **b.** A supporter of such a movement or party. **2.** A Communard. **3.** often **communist** A radical viewed as a subversive or revolutionary. ❖ *adj.* **1.** often **communist** Relating to, characteristic of, or held to resemble communism or Communists. **2. communist** Supporting, advocating, or serving to further communism.

com·mu·nis·tic (kŏm′yə-nĭs′tĭk) *adj.* Of, characteristic of, or inclined to communism. —**com′mu·nis′ti·cal·ly** *adv.*

com·mu·ni·tar·i·an (kə-myōō′nĭ-târ′ē-ən) *n.* A member or supporter of a small cooperative or a collectivist community.

com·mu·ni·ty (kə-myōō′nĭ-tē) *n., pl.* **-ties 1a.** A group of people living in the same locality and under the same government. **b.** The district or locality in which such a group lives. **2a.** A group of people having common interests. **b.** A group viewed as forming a distinct segment of society. **3a.** Similarity or identity. **b.** Sharing, participation, and fellowship. **4.** Society as a whole; the public. **5.** *Ecology* **a.** A group of plants and animals living and interacting with one another in a specific region under relatively similar environmental conditions. **b.** The region occupied by a community. [ME *communite,* citizenry < OFr. < Lat. *commūnitās,* fellowship < *commūnis,* common. See COMMON.]

community antenna television *n.* See **cable television.**

community center *n.* A meeting place used by members of a community for social, cultural, or recreational purposes.

community chest *n.* A fund financed by private contributions for aiding charitable organizations and welfare agencies.

community college *n.* A junior college without residential facilities that is often funded by the government.

community medicine *n.* Public health services for members of a given community or region.

community property *n.* Property owned jointly by spouses.

community service *n.* **1.** Service volunteered by individuals or an organization to benefit a community or its institutions. **2.** Similar work performed by law offenders to serve a sentence in lieu of or in addition to jail time.

com·mu·nize (kŏm′yə-nīz′) *tr.v.* **-nized, -niz·ing, -niz·es 1.** To subject to public ownership or control. **2.** To convert to Communist principles or control. —**com′mu·ni·za′tion** (-nĭ-zā′shən) *n.*

com·mut·a·ble (kə-myōō′tə-bəl) *adj.* **1.** That can be substituted, interchanged, or revoked: *a commutable prison sentence.* **2.** Accessible to commuters. —**com·mut′a·bil′i·ty** *n.*

com·mu·tate (kŏm′yə-tāt′) *tr.v.* **-tat·ed, -tat·ing, -tates** To reverse the direction of (an alternating electric current) each half-cycle to produce a unidirectional current. [Back-formation < COMMUTATOR.]

com·mu·ta·tion (kŏm′yə-tā′shən) *n.* **1.** A substitution, exchange, or interchange. **2a.** The substitution of one kind of payment for another. **b.** The payment substituted. **3.** The travel of a commuter. **4.** *Electricity* **a.** Conversion of alternating to unidirectional current. **b.** Reversal of current direction. **5.** *Law* Reduction of a penalty to a less severe one. [ME *commutacioun* < Lat. *commūtātiō, commūtātiōn-* < *commūtātus,* p. part. of *commūtāre,* to alter, exchange. See COMMUTE.]

commutation ticket *n.* A ticket issued at a reduced rate by a railroad or other transportation company for passage over a given route for a specified number of trips.

com·mu·ta·tive (kŏm′yə-tā′tĭv, kə-myōō′tə-tĭv) *adj.* **1.** Relating to, involving, or characterized by substitution, interchange, or exchange. **2.** Independent of order. Used of a logical or mathematical operation that combines objects or sets of objects two at a time. —**com·mu′ta·tiv′i·ty** (kə-myōō′tə-tĭv′ĭ-tē) *n.*

com·mu·ta·tor (kŏm′yə-tā′tər) *n.* A cylindrical arrangement of insulated metal bars connected to the coils of a direct-current electric motor or generator, providing a unidirectional current from the generator or a reversal of current into the coils of the motor.

com·mute (kə-myōōt′) *v.* **-mut·ed, -mut·ing, -mutes** —*intr.* **1.** To travel as a commuter. **2a.** To make substitution or exchange. **b.** To serve as a substitute. **3.** To pay in gross, usu. at a reduced rate, rather than in individual payments. **4.** *Mathematics & Logic* To satisfy or engage in a commutative operation. —*tr.* **1.** To substitute (one thing for another); exchange. **2.** To change (a penalty, debt, or payment) to a less severe one. ❖ *n.* An act or instance of commuting. [ME *commuten,* to transform < Lat. *commūtāre : com-, com- + mūtāre,* to change.]

com·mut·er (kə-myōō′tər) *n.* **1.** One that travels regularly from one place to another, as from suburb to city and back. **2.** An airplane or airline that carries passengers short distances and often serves small airports.

Co·mo (kō′mō) A resort city of N Italy near the Swiss border at the SW end of **Lake Como.** Pop. 95,183.

Com·o·rin (kŏm′ər-ĭn), **Cape** A cape at the southernmost point of India projecting into the Indian Ocean.

Com·o·ros (kŏm'ə-rōz') A country coextensive with the Comoro Islands in the Indian Ocean off SE Africa. The islands declared their independence from France in 1975, although Mayotte, the largest of the group, voted to retain its status as a French territory. Cap. Moroni. Pop. 630,000.

co·mose (kō'mōs') adj. Botany Having a coma; comate.

comp[1] (kŏmp) intr.v. **comped, comp·ing, comps** To play a jazz accompaniment. [Short for ACCOMPANY.]

comp[2] (kŏmp) n. Informal Something, such as a theater ticket or a book, given free of charge. [Short for COMPLIMENTARY.]

comp. abbr. **1.** comparative **2.** compensation **3.** compiled **4.** complete **5.** composer **6.** compound

com·pact[1] (kəm-păkt', kŏm-, kŏm'păkt') adj. **1.** Closely and firmly united or packed together; dense. **2.** Occupying little space compared with others of its type. **3.** Brief and to the point; concise. **4.** Marked by or having a short solid physique. ❖ v. (kəm-păkt') **-pact·ed, -pact·ing, -pacts** —tr. **1.** To press or join firmly together. **2a.** To make by pressing or joining together; compose. **b.** To consolidate; combine. —intr. To be capable of being pressed tightly together or to become so pressed: garbage that compacts easily. ❖ n. (kŏm'păkt') **1.** A small case containing a mirror, pressed powder, and a powder puff. **2.** An automobile that is bigger in size than a subcompact but smaller than an intermediate. [ME < Lat. compāctus, p. part. of compingere, to put together : com-, com- + pangere, to fasten.] —com·pact'ly adv. —com·pact'ness n.

com·pact[2] (kŏm'păkt') n. An agreement or a covenant. [Lat. compactum, neut. p. part. of compacīscī, to agree : com-, com- + pacīscī, to agree; see PACT.]

compact disk or **com·pact disc** (kŏm'păkt') n. A small optical disk on which data such as music, text, or graphic images is digitally encoded.

> **USAGE NOTE** Disk was originally spelled in English with a k in the mid-17th century. The c-spelling arose a half century later as a learned spelling derived from the word's Latin source, discus. Both forms were used interchangeably into the 1900s, with the British tending to use disc and Americans using disk. The spellings also began to be sorted out by function. In the late 1800s, for reasons that are not clear, people used disc to refer to phonograph recordings made on flat plates. The c-spelling became conventional for this sense, which is why we listen to disc jockeys and not disk jockeys. In the 1940s, however, American computer scientists chose the spelling disk to refer to flat storage devices. This became conventionalized in such compounds as hard disk and floppy disk. When the new storage technology of the compact disk arose in the 1970s, computer specialists preferred the familiar k-spelling, while people in the music industry referred to them as compact discs. Similarly, the computer industry created the optical disk, the format that the entertainment industry used to create the videodisc.

com·pac·tion (kəm-păk'shən) n. The process of compacting or the state of being compacted.

com·pac·tor or **com·pact·er** (kəm-păk'tər, kŏm'păk'-) n. An apparatus that compresses refuse into relatively small packs for handy disposal.

com·pa·dre (kəm-pä'drā) n. Chiefly Southwestern US A close friend or associate; a companion. [Sp., joint father, godfather, friend < Med.Lat. compater, joint priest, godfather : Lat. com-, com- + Lat. pater, father; see pəter- in App.]

com·pan·ion[1] (kəm-păn'yən) n. **1a.** A person who accompanies or associates with another; a comrade. **b.** A domestic partner. **2.** A person employed to assist, live with, or travel with another. **3.** One of a pair or set of things; a mate. ❖ tr.v. **-ioned, -ion·ing, -ions** To be a companion to; accompany. [ME compaignyon < OFr. compaignon < VLat. *compāniō, *compāniōn- : Lat. com-, com- + Lat. pānis, bread; see pā- in App.]

com·pan·ion[2] (kəm-păn'yən) n. Nautical A companionway.

com·pan·ion·a·ble (kəm-păn'yə-nə-bəl) adj. **1.** Having the qualities of a good companion; friendly. **2.** Suggestive of companionship. —com·pan'ion·a·ble·ness n. —com·pan'ion·a·bly adv.

com·pan·ion·ate (kəm-păn'yə-nĭt) adj. **1.** Having the qualities of a companion. **2.** Harmonious; suitable.

companionate marriage n. A marriage in which the partners agree to have no children, may divorce by mutual consent, and are not held responsible for the other's financial welfare.

com·pan·ion·ship (kəm-păn'yən-shĭp') n. The relationship of companions; fellowship.

com·pan·ion·way (kəm-păn'yən-wā') n. Nautical A staircase leading from a deck to the cabins or area below. [< companion, framed windows above a hatchway, companionway, prob. alteration of obsolete Du. kompanje < OFr. compagne, storeroom < OItal. (camera della) compagna, pantry < VLat. *compānia, things eaten with bread : Lat. com-, com- + Lat. pānis, bread; see COMPANION[1].]

com·pa·ny (kŭm'pə-nē) n., pl. **-nies 1.** A group of persons. **2a.** One's companions or associates. **b.** A guest or guests. **c.** The state of friendly companionship. **3a.** A business enterprise; a firm. **b.** A partner or partners not specifically named in a firm's title. **4.** A troupe of dramatic or musical performers. **5a.** A subdivision of a military regiment or battalion that constitutes the lowest administrative unit, made up of at least two platoons. **b.** A unit of firefighters. **6.** A ship's crew and officers. See Usage Note at collective noun. ❖ tr.v. **-nied, -ny·ing, -nies** To accompany or associate with. [ME compainie < OFr. compaignie < VLat. *compānia < *compāniō, companion. See COMPANION[1].]

com·pa·ny-grade officer (kŭm'pə-nē-grād') n. A commissioned officer having the rank of second lieutenant, first lieutenant, or captain in the US Army, Air Force, or Marine Corps.

company man n. A man whose primary allegiance is to his employer.

company woman n. A woman whose primary allegiance is to her employer.

com·pa·ra·ble (kŏm'pər-ə-bəl) adj. **1.** Admitting of comparison with another or others. **2.** Similar or equivalent. —com'pa·ra·bil'i·ty, com'pa·ra·ble·ness n. —com'pa·ra·bly adv.

comparable worth n. A theory holding that jobs held chiefly by women should pay the same as jobs held chiefly by men if the jobs are similar.

com·par·a·tist (kəm-păr'ə-tĭst) n. A person who employs the comparative method. [Fr. comparatiste < comparative, comparative < comparer, to compare. See COMPARE.]

com·par·a·tive (kəm-păr'ə-tĭv) adj. **1a.** Relating to, based on, or involving comparison. **b.** Of or relating to the scientific or historical comparison of different phenomena, institutions, or objects in an effort to understand their origins or relationships. **2.** Estimated by comparison; relative. **3.** Grammar Of, relating to, or being the intermediate degree of comparison of adjectives, as better or more wonderful, or adverbs, as more softly. ❖ n. Grammar **1.** The comparative degree. **2.** An adjective or adverb expressing the comparative degree. —com·par'a·tive·ly adv.

> **OUR LIVING LANGUAGE** Speakers of vernacular dialects often use double comparatives and superlatives such as more higher and most fastest. Although such constructions may seem redundant or even illogical, in reality both standard and nonstandard varieties of all languages are replete with such constructions. In English the redundant comparative dates back to the 1500s. The Modern English rule governing the distribution of –er/–est and more/most had not yet arisen, and such forms as eminenter, impudentest, and beautifullest occurred together with constructions like more near, most poor, and most foul. Double markings were commonly used to indicate special emphasis, and they do not appear to have been socially disfavored. In fact, even Shakespeare used double comparatives and superlatives, as in Mark Antony's statement "This was the most unkindest cut of all" from Julius Caesar. Nowadays, although double comparatives and superlatives are not considered standard usage, they are kept alive in vernacular dialects. See Note at might[2].

comparative method n. **1.** Comparison of languages with the goal of establishing their descent from a common ancestor. **2.** Comparison of phonemes, morphemes, words, or syntactic constructions in genetically related languages with the goal of reconstructing the sound system, grammar, or lexicon of the protolanguage.

com·pa·ra·tor (kŏm'pə-rā'tər, kəm-păr'ə-) n. Any of various instruments for comparing a measured property of an object, such as its shape, color, or brightness, with a standard.

com·pare (kəm-pâr') v. **-pared, -par·ing, -pares** —tr. **1.** To consider or describe as similar, equal, or analogous; liken. **2.** To examine in order to note the similarities or differences of. **3.** Grammar To form the positive, comparative, or superlative degree of (an adjective or adverb). —intr. **1.** To be worthy of comparison; bear comparison. **2.** To draw comparisons. ❖ n. Comparison. —idiom: compare notes To exchange ideas, views, or opinions. [ME comparen < OFr. comparer < Lat. comparāre < compār, equal : com-, com- + pār, equal; see perə- in App.] —com·par'er n.

> **USAGE NOTE** Compare usually takes the preposition to when it refers to the activity of describing the resemblances between unlike things: He compared her to a summer day. It takes with when it refers to the act of examining two like things in order to discern their similarities or differences: The police compared the forged signature with the original. When compare is used to mean "to liken (one) with another," with is traditionally considered the correct form: That little bauble is not to be compared with (not to) this enormous jewel. But to is frequently used in this context and is not incorrect.

com·par·i·son (kəm-păr'ĭ-sən) n. **1a.** The act of comparing or the process of being compared. **b.** A statement or estimate of similarities and differences. **2.** The quality of being similar or equivalent; likeness: no comparison between the two books. **3.** Grammar The modification or inflection of an adjective or adverb to denote the positive, comparative, and superlative degrees. [ME comparisoun < OFr. comparaison < Lat. comparātiō, comparātiōn- < comparātus, p. part. of comparāre, to compare. See COMPARE.]

com·part (kəm-pärt') tr.v. **-part·ed, -part·ing, -parts** To divide into parts. [Obsolete Fr. compartir < Ital. compartire < LLat. compartīrī, to share : Lat. com-, com- + partīrī, to divide

ă	pat	oi	boy
ā	pay	ou	out
âr	care	oŏ	took
ä	father	ōō	boot
ĕ	pet	ŭ	cut
ē	be	ûr	urge
ĭ	pit	th	thin
ī	pie	th	this
îr	pier	hw	which
ŏ	pot	zh	vision
ō	toe	ə	about,
ô	paw		item

Stress marks:
' (primary);
' (secondary), as in
lexicon (lĕk'sĭ-kŏn')

(< *pars*, *part*-, a part; see **perə-** in App.).]

com·part·ment (kəm-pärt′mənt) *n.* **1.** One of the parts or spaces into which an area is subdivided. **2.** A separate room, section, or chamber. ❖ *tr.v.* **-ment·ed, -ment·ing, -ments** To compartmentalize. —**com′part·ment′al** (kŏm′pärt-mĕn′tl) *adj.*

com·part·men·tal·ize (kŏm′pärt-mĕn′tl-īz′, kəm-pärt′-) *tr.v.* **-ized, -iz·ing, -iz·es** To separate into distinct parts, categories, or compartments. —**com′part·men′tal·i·za′tion** (-ĭ-zā′shən) *n.*

com·pass (kŭm′pəs, kŏm′-) *n.* **1a.** A device used to determine geographic direction, usu. consisting of a magnetic needle or needles free to pivot until aligned with the magnetic field of the earth. **b.** A device, such as a radio compass, used for determining geographic direction. **2.** A device for describing circles or circular arcs and for taking measurements, consisting of a pair of rigid, end-hinged legs, one of which is equipped with a marker that pivots around the other, sharp-pointed leg. **3a.** An enclosing line or boundary; a circumference. **b.** A restricted space or area. **c.** Range or scope, as of understanding. **4.** *Music* See **range** 2b. ❖ *tr.v.* **-passed, -pass·ing, -pass·es 1.** To make a circuit of; circle. **2.** To surround; encircle. **3.** To understand; comprehend. **4.** To succeed in carrying out. See Syns at **reach. 5.** To scheme; plot. ❖ *adj.* **1.** Forming a curved configuration. **2.** Semicircular. Used of bow windows. [ME *compas*, circle, compass < OFr. < *compasser*, to measure < VLat. *compassāre, to pace off : Lat. *com*-, com- + Lat. *passus*, step; see PACE¹.] —**com′pass·a·ble** *adj.*

compass card *n.* A freely pivoting circular disk carrying the magnetic needles of a compass and marked with the 32 points of the compass and the 360 degrees of the circle.

com·pas·sion (kəm-păsh′ən) *n.* Deep awareness of the suffering of another coupled with the wish to relieve it. [ME *compassioun* < LLat. *compassiō, compassiōn-* < *compassus*, p. part. of *compatī*, to sympathize : Lat. *com*-, com- + Lat. *patī*, to suffer.]

com·pas·sion·ate (kəm-păsh′ə-nĭt) *adj.* Feeling or showing compassion; sympathetic. See Syns at **humane.** ❖ *tr.v.* (-nāt′) **-at·ed, -at·ing, -ates** To pity. —**com·pas′sion·ate·ly** *adv.*

compass plant *n.* A perennial herb (*Silphium laciniatum*) in the composite family, native to the Midwest United States and having yellow flowers and basal pinnate leaves.

com·pat·i·ble (kəm-păt′ə-bəl) *adj.* **1.** Capable of existing or performing in harmonious, agreeable, or congenial combination. **2.** Capable of integration and operation in a system with no modification or conversion required. **3.** Capable of forming a chemically or biochemically stable system. **4.** Of or relating to a television system in which color broadcasts can be received in black and white by sets incapable of color reception. **5.** *Medicine* Capable of being grafted, transfused, or transplanted from one individual to another without rejection. ❖ *n.* A device that can be integrated into or used with another device or system of its type. [ME < Med.Lat. *compatibilis* < LLat. *compatī*, to sympathize. See COMPASSION.] —**com·pat′i·bil′i·ty, com·pat′i·ble·ness** *n.* —**com·pat′i·bly** *adv.*

com·pa·tri·ot (kəm-pā′trē-ət, -ŏt′) *n.* **1.** A person from one's own country. **2.** A colleague. [Fr. *compatriote* < LLat. *compatriōta* : Lat. *com*-, com- + LLat. *patriōta*, countryman; see PATRIOT.] —**com·pa′tri·ot′ic** (-ŏt′ĭk) *adj.*

com·peer (kŏm′pîr′, kəm-pîr′) *n.* **1.** A person of equal status or rank; a peer. **2.** A comrade, companion, or associate. [ME *comper* < OFr. < Lat. *compār*, equal. See COMPARE.]

com·pel (kəm-pĕl′) *tr.v.* **-pelled, -pel·ling, -pels 1.** To force, drive, or constrain. **2.** To necessitate or pressure by force; exact. **3.** To exert a strong irresistible force on; sway. [ME *compellen* < Lat. *compellere* : com-, com- + *pellere*, to drive; see pel-² in App.] —**com·pel′la·ble** *adj.* —**com·pel′ler** *n.*

com·pel·la·tion (kŏm′pə-lā′shən) *n.* **1.** The act of addressing or designating someone by name. **2.** A name; an appellation. [Lat. *compellātiō, compellātiōn-* < *compellātus*, p. part. of *compellāre*, to address. See pel-² in App.]

com·pel·ling (kəm-pĕl′ĭng) *adj.* **1.** Urgently requiring attention. **2.** Drivingly forceful: *compelling ambition.*

com·pend (kŏm′pĕnd′) *n.* A compendium.

com·pen·di·ous (kəm-pĕn′dē-əs) *adj.* Containing or stating briefly and concisely all the essentials. [ME < LLat. *compendiōsus* < Lat. *compendium*, a shortening. See COMPENDIUM.] —**com·pen′di·ous·ly** *adv.*

com·pen·di·um (kəm-pĕn′dē-əm) *n., pl.* **-di·ums** or **-di·a** (-dē-ə) **1.** A short, complete summary; an abstract. **2.** A list or collection of various items. [Lat., a shortening < *compendere*, to weigh together : com-, com- + *pendere*, to weigh.]

com·pen·sa·ble (kəm-pĕn′sə-bəl) *adj.* Being such as to entitle or warrant compensation: *compensable injuries.*

com·pen·sate (kŏm′pən-sāt′) *v.* **-sat·ed, -sat·ing, -sates** —*tr.* **1.** To offset; counterbalance. **2.** To make satisfactory payment or reparation to; recompense or reimburse. —*intr.* To serve as or provide a substitute or counterbalance. [Lat. *compēnsāre, compēnsāt*- : com-, com- + *pēnsāre*, to weigh, freq. of *pendere*.] —**com′pen·sa′tive** (kŏm′pən-sā′tĭv, kəm-pĕn′sə-tĭv) *adj.* —**com′pen·sa′tor** *n.* —**com·pen′sa·to·ry** (kəm-pĕn′sə-tôr′ē, -tōr′ē) *adj.*

com·pen·sa·tion (kŏm′pən-sā′shən) *n.* **1.** The act of compen-

sating or the state of being compensated. **2.** Something given or received as payment or reparation, as for a service or loss. **3.** *Biology* The increase in size or activity of one part of an organism or organ that makes up for the loss or dysfunction of another. **4.** *Psychology* Behavior that serves to offset a real or imagined deficiency. —**com′pen·sa′tion·al** *adj.*

compensatory time *n.* Time off given to an employee in place of overtime pay.

com·pere (kŏm′pâr′) *Chiefly British n.* The master of ceremonies, as of a variety show. [Fr. *compère* < OFr., godfather, companion < Med.Lat. *compater* : Lat. *com*-, com- + Lat. *pater*, father; see PATER.] —**com′pere′** *v.*

com·pete (kəm-pēt′) *intr.v.* **-pet·ed, -pet·ing, -petes** To strive against another or others to attain a goal. [LLat. *competere*, to strive together < Lat., to coincide, be suitable : com-, com- + *petere*, to seek; see pet- in App.]

com·pe·tence (kŏm′pĭ-təns) *n.* **1a.** The state or quality of being adequately or well qualified; ability. **b.** A specific range of skill, knowledge, or ability. **2.** *Law* The quality or condition of being legally qualified to perform an act. **3.** Sufficient means for a comfortable existence. **4.** *Microbiology* The ability of bacteria to be genetically transformable. **5.** *Medicine* The ability to respond immunologically to antigenic agents. **6.** *Linguistics* The knowledge that enables one to produce and comprehend a language.

com·pe·ten·cy (kŏm′pĭ-tən-sē) *n., pl.* **-cies** Competence.

com·pe·tent (kŏm′pĭ-tənt) *adj.* **1.** Properly or sufficiently qualified; capable. **2.** Adequate for the purpose. **3.** *Law* Legally qualified or fit to perform an act. [ME, adequate < OFr. < Lat. *competēns, competent*-, pr. part. of *competere*, to be suitable. See COMPETE.] —**com′pe·tent·ly** *adv.*

com·pe·ti·tion (kŏm′pĭ-tĭsh′ən) *n.* **1.** The act of competing, as for profit or a prize; rivalry. **2.** A test of skill or ability; a contest. **3.** Rivalry between two or more businesses. **4.** A competitor. **5.** *Ecology* The simultaneous demand by two or more organisms for limited environmental resources.

com·pet·i·tive (kəm-pĕt′ĭ-tĭv) *adj.* **1.** Of, involving, or determined by competition. **2.** Inclined to compete. —**com·pet′i·tive·ly** *adv.* —**com·pet′i·tive·ness** *n.*

com·pet·i·tor (kəm-pĕt′ĭ-tər) *n.* One that competes; a rival.

Com·piégne (kômp-yän′, kôN-pyěN′yə) A city of N France on the Oise R. NE of Paris. The armistice ending World War I was signed nearby on Nov. 11, 1918. Pop. 40,384.

com·pi·la·tion (kŏm′pə-lā′shən) *n.* **1.** The act of compiling. **2.** Something, such as a report, that is compiled.

com·pile (kəm-pīl′) *tr.v.* **-piled, -pil·ing, -piles 1.** To gather into a single book. **2.** To put together or compose from materials gathered from several sources. **3.** *Computer Science* To translate (a program) into machine language. [ME *compilen* < OFr. *compiler*, prob. < Lat. *compīlāre*, to plunder : com-, com- + *pīla*, heap (of stones); pillar.]

com·pil·er (kəm-pī′lər) *n.* **1.** One that compiles. **2.** *Computer Science* A program that translates another program into machine language.

com·pla·cence (kəm-plā′səns) *n.* **1.** Contented self-satisfaction. **2.** Total lack of concern.

com·pla·cen·cy (kəm-plā′sən-sē) *n.* **1.** A feeling of contentment or self-satisfaction, esp. when coupled with an unawareness of danger, trouble, or controversy. **2.** An instance of complacency.

com·pla·cent (kəm-plā′sənt) *adj.* **1.** Contented to a fault; self-satisfied and unconcerned. **2.** Eager to please; complaisant. [Lat. *complacēns, complacent*-, pr. part. of *complacēre*, to please : com-, com- + *placēre*, to please.] —**com·pla′cent·ly** *adv.*

com·plain (kəm-plān′) *intr.v.* **-plained, -plain·ing, -plains 1.** To express feelings of pain, dissatisfaction, or resentment. **2.** To make a formal accusation or bring a formal charge. [ME *compleinen* < OFr. *complaindre, complaign*- < VLat. *complangere : com-, com- + Lat. *plangere*, to lament; see plāk- in App.] —**com·plain′er** *n.*

com·plain·ant (kəm-plā′nənt) *n. Law* A party that makes a complaint or files a formal charge; a plaintiff.

com·plaint (kəm-plānt′) *n.* **1.** An expression of pain, dissatisfaction, or resentment. **2.** A cause or reason for complaining; a grievance. **3a.** A bodily disorder or disease; a malady or ailment. **b.** The symptom or distress about which a patient seeks medical assistance. **4.** *Law* **a.** A claim set forth by the plaintiff in a civil action. **b.** A formal charge, made under oath, of the commission of a crime or other such offense. [ME *compleinte* < OFr. *complainte* < fem. p. part. of *complaindre*, to complain. See COMPLAIN.]

com·plai·sance (kəm-plā′səns, -zəns) *n.* The inclination to comply willingly with the wishes of others; amiability.

com·plai·sant (kəm-plā′sənt, -zənt) *adj.* Exhibiting a desire or willingness to please; cheerfully obliging. [Fr. < OFr., pr. part. of *complaire*, to please < Lat. *complacēre*. See COMPLACENT.] —**com·plai′sant·ly** *adv.*

com·pleat (kəm-plēt′) *adj.* **1.** Of or characterized by a highly developed or wide-ranging skill or proficiency. **2.** Being an outstanding example of a kind; quintessential. [Variant of COMPLETE.]

com·plect (kəm-plĕkt′) *tr.v.* **-plect·ed, -plect·ing, -plects** To

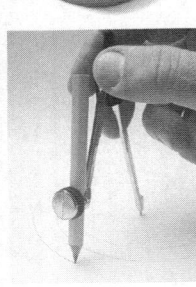

compass
top: directional compass
bottom: drawing a circle with a compass

join by weaving or twining together; interweave. [Lat. *complectī*, to entwine : *com-*, com- + *plectere*, to plait; see **plek-** in App.]

com·plect·ed (kəm-plĕk′tĭd) *adj. Informal* Marked by or having a particular facial complexion. Often used in combination: *ruddy-complected.* [Back-formation < COMPLECTION, var. of COMPLEXION.]

com·ple·ment (kŏm′plə-mənt) *n.* **1a.** Something that completes, makes up a whole, or brings to perfection. **b.** The quantity or number needed to make up a whole: *shelves with a full complement of books.* **c.** Either of two parts that complete the whole or mutually complete each other. **2.** An angle related to another so that the sum of their measures is 90°. **3.** *Grammar* A word or words used after a verb to complete a predicate construction. **4.** *Music* An interval that completes an octave when added to a given interval. **5.** The full crew of officers and enlisted personnel required to run a ship. **6.** *Immunology* A complex system of proteins found in normal blood serum that combines with antibodies to destroy pathogenic bacteria and other foreign cells. **7.** *Mathematics & Logic* For a universal set, the set of all elements in the set that are not in a specified subset. **8.** A complementary color. ❖ *tr.v.* (-mĕnt′) **-ment·ed, -ment·ing, -ments** To serve as a complement to. [ME < OFr. < Lat. *complēmentum* < *complēre*, to fill out. See COMPLETE.]

> **USAGE NOTE** *Complement* means "something that completes or brings to perfection": *The antique silver was a complement to the beautifully set table. Compliment* means "an expression or act of courtesy or praise": *They gave us a compliment on our beautifully set table.*

com·ple·men·tal (kŏm′plə-mĕn′tl) *adj.* Having to do with or being a complement. —**com′ple·men′tal·ly** *adv.*

com·ple·men·tar·i·ty (kŏm′plə-mĕn-tăr′ĭ-tē) *n.* The state or quality of being complementary.

com·ple·men·ta·ry (kŏm′plə-mĕn′tə-rē, -trē) *adj.* **1.** Forming or serving as a complement; completing. **2.** Supplying mutual needs or offsetting mutual lacks. **3.** *Biochemistry* Of or relating to the specific pairing of the purines and pyrimidines between strands of a DNA or an RNA molecule. —**com′ple·men′ta·ri·ly** (-tə-rə-lē, -trə-lē, -mĕn-târ′ə-lē) *adv.* —**com′ple·men′ta·ri·ness** *n.*

complementary angles *pl.n.* Two angles whose sum is 90°.

complementary color *n.* Either one of two colors whose mixture in the right proportions produces white (in the case of light) or gray (in the case of pigment).

complementary medicine *n.* A method of health care that combines the therapies and philosophies of conventional medicine with those of alternative medicines, such as acupuncture or herbal medicine.

complement fixation *n.* The binding of active serum complement to a specific antigen-antibody pair used in various diagnostic tests.

com·plete (kəm-plēt′) *adj.* **-plet·er, -plet·est** **1.** Having all necessary or normal parts, components, or steps; entire. **2.** *Botany* Having all principal parts, namely, the sepals, petals, stamens, and pistil or pistils. **3.** Having come to an end. **4.** Absolute; total. **5a.** Skilled; accomplished. **6.** Thorough; consummate. **6.** *Football* Caught by a receiver: *a complete pass.* ❖ *tr.v.* **-plet·ed, -plet·ing, -pletes** **1.** To bring to a finish or an end. **2.** To make whole, with all necessary elements or parts. **3.** *Football* To throw (a forward pass) so as to be caught by a receiver. [ME *complet* < Lat. *complētus*, p. part. of *complēre*, to fill out : *com-*, com- + *plēre*, to fill; see **pelə-¹** in App.] —**com·plete′ly** *adv.* —**com·plete′ness** *n.* —**com·ple′tive** *adj.*

> **USAGE NOTE** *Complete* is sometimes held to be an absolute term like *perfect* or *chief.* Nonetheless, it can be qualified. A majority of the Usage Panel accepts the example *His book is the most complete treatment of the subject.*

complete blood count *n.* The determination of the quantity of each type of blood cell in a given sample of blood.

complete metamorphosis *n.* The complete form of metamorphosis in which an insect passes through four separate stages of growth, as embryo, larva, pupa, and imago.

com·ple·tion (kəm-plē′shən) *n.* **1.** The act of completing or the state of being completed. **2.** *Football* A forward pass that is caught in bounds by a receiver.

com·plex (kəm-plĕks′, kŏm′plĕks′) *adj.* **1a.** Consisting of interconnected or interwoven parts; composite. **b.** Composed of two or more units: *a complex carbohydrate.* **2.** Involved or intricate; complicated. **3.** *Grammar* **a.** Consisting of at least one bound form. Used of a word. **b.** Consisting of an independent clause and at least one other independent or dependent clause. Used of a sentence. ❖ *n.* (kŏm′plĕks′) **1.** A whole composed of interconnected or interwoven parts. **2.** A group of related, often repressed ideas and impulses that compel habitual attitudes and behavior. **3.** An exaggerated or obsessive concern or fear. **4.** *Medicine* The combination of factors, symptoms, or signs of a disease or disorder that forms a syndrome. [Lat. *complexus*, p. part. of *complectī*, to entwine. See COMPLECT.] —**com·plex′ly** *adv.* —**com·plex′ness** *n.*

SYNONYMS *complex, complicated, intricate, involved, tangled, knotty* These adjectives mean having parts so interconnected as to make the whole perplexing. *Complex* implies a combination of many associated parts: *a complex set of musical variations. Complicated* stresses elaborate relationship of parts: *complicated politics that thwart a cohesive policy. Intricate* refers to a pattern of intertwining parts that is difficult to follow or analyze: *"No one could soar into a more intricate labyrinth of refined phraseology"* (Anthony Trollope). *Involved* stresses confusion arising from the commingling of parts and the consequent difficulty of separating them: *a plot line criticized as being too involved. Tangled* strongly suggests the random twisting of many parts: *"Oh, what a tangled web we weave,/When first we practice to deceive!"* (Sir Walter Scott). *Knotty* stresses intellectual complexity leading to difficulty of solution or comprehension: *a knotty problem.*

complex fraction *n.* A fraction in which the numerator or the denominator or both contain fractions.

com·plex·ion (kəm-plĕk′shən) *n.* **1.** The natural color, texture, and appearance of the skin, esp. of the face. **2.** General character, aspect, or appearance. **3.** A viewpoint, inclination, or attitude. **4.** The combination of the four humors of cold, heat, moistness, and dryness in specific proportions, thought in ancient and medieval physiology to control the temperament and the constitution of the body. [ME *complexioun*, physical constitution < OFr. *complexion* < LLat. *complexiō, complexiōn-*, balance of the humors < Lat., combination < *complexus*, p. part. of *complectī*, to entwine. See COMPLECT.] —**com·plex′ion·al** *adj.*

com·plex·ioned (kəm-plĕk′shənd) *adj.* Of or having a specified complexion. Often used in combination: *fair-complexioned.*

com·plex·i·ty (kəm-plĕk′sĭ-tē) *n., pl.* **-ties** **1.** The quality or condition of being complex. **2.** Something complex.

complexity theory *n.* The study of how order, structure, and pattern arise from extremely complicated, apparently chaotic systems.

complex number *n.* Any number of the form $a + bi$, where a and b are real numbers and i^2 equals −1.

complex plane *n.* A plane whose points have complex numbers as their coordinates.

com·pli·ance (kəm-plī′əns) *n.* **1.** The act of complying with a wish, request, or demand; acquiescence. **2.** A disposition or tendency to yield to the will of others. **3a.** Extension or displacement of a loaded structure per unit load. **b.** Flexibility.

com·pli·an·cy (kəm-plī′ən-sē) *n.* Compliance.

com·pli·ant (kəm-plī′ənt) *adj.* Disposed or willing to comply; submissive. —**com·pli′ant·ly** *adv.*

com·pli·ca·cy (kŏm′plĭk′ə-sē) *n., pl.* **-cies** **1.** The state of being complicated. **2.** A complication.

com·pli·cate (kŏm′plĭ-kāt′) *tr. & intr.v.* **-cat·ed, -cat·ing, -cates** **1.** To make or become complex or perplexing. **2.** To twist or become twisted together. ❖ *adj.* (-kĭt) **1.** Complex, intricate, and involved. **2.** *Biology* Folded longitudinally one or several times, as certain leaves. [Lat. *complicāre, complicāt-*, to fold together : *com-*, com- + *plicāre*, to fold; see **plek-** in App.]

com·pli·cat·ed (kŏm′plĭ-kā′tĭd) *adj.* **1.** Containing intricately combined or involved parts. **2.** See Syns at **complex.** —**com′pli·cat′ed·ly** *adv.* —**com′pli·cat′ed·ness** *n.*

com·pli·ca·tion (kŏm′plĭ-kā′shən) *n.* **1.** The act of complicating. **2.** A confused or intricate relationship of parts. **3.** A factor, condition, or element that complicates. **4.** *Medicine* A secondary disease, accident, or negative reaction occurring during an illness and usu. aggravating it.

com·plice (kŏm′plĭs) *n. Archaic* An associate; an accomplice. [ME < OFr. < LLat. *complex, complic-*, one closely connected with : Lat. *com-*, com- + Lat. *plicāre*, to fold; see **plek-** in App.]

com·plic·it (kəm-plĭs′ĭt) *adj.* Having complicity.

com·plic·i·ty (kəm-plĭs′ĭ-tē) *n., pl.* **-ties** Involvement as an accomplice in a questionable act or a crime.

com·pli·er (kəm-plī′ər) *n.* One that complies.

com·pli·ment (kŏm′plə-mənt) *n.* **1.** An expression of praise, admiration, or congratulation. **2.** A formal act of civility, courtesy, or respect. **3. compliments** Good wishes; regards. See Usage Note at **complement.** ❖ *tr.v.* **-ment·ed, -ment·ing, -ments** **1.** To pay a compliment to. **2.** To show fondness, regard, or respect for by giving a gift or performing a favor. [Fr. < Ital. *complimento* < Sp. *cumplimiento* < *cumplir*, to complete < Lat. *complēre*, to fill up : *com-*, com- + *plēre*, to fill; see **pelə-¹** in App.]

com·pli·men·ta·ry (kŏm′plə-mĕn′tə-rē, -trē) *adj.* **1.** Expressing, using, or resembling a compliment. **2.** Given free to repay a favor or as an act of courtesy. —**com′pli·men′ta·ri·ly** *adv.*

complimentary close (klōz) *n.* A polite termination of a letter just before the writer's signature, such as *Yours truly.*

com·pline or **Com·pline** (kŏm′plĭn, -plīn′) also **com·plin** or **Com·plin** (-plĭn) *n. Ecclesiastical* The last of the seven canonical hours recited or sung before retiring. [ME, alteration of *compli* < OFr. *complie* < Med.Lat. *(hōra) complēta*, final (hour) < Lat. *complētus*, p. part. of *complēre*, to complete. See COMPLETE.]

com·ply (kəm-plī′) *intr.v.* **-plied, -ply·ing, -plies** **1.** To act in accordance with another's command, request, rule, or wish. **2.** *Obsolete* To be courteous or obedient. [ME *complien*, to carry out, fulfill < OFr. *complir* < Lat. *complēre*. See COMPLETE.]

ă	pat	oi	boy
ā	pay	ou	out
âr	care	ŏŏ	took
ä	father	ōō	boot
ĕ	pet	ŭ	cut
ē	be	ûr	urge
ĭ	pit	th	thin
ī	pie	th	this
îr	pier	hw	which
ŏ	pot	zh	vision
ō	toe	ə	about,
ô	paw		item

Stress marks:
′ (primary);
′ (secondary); as in
lexicon (lĕk′sĭ-kŏn′)

com·po (kŏm′pō) n., pl. **-pos** Any of various combined substances, such as mortar or plaster, formed by mixing ingredients. [Short for COMPOSITION.]

com·po·nent (kəm-pō′nənt) n. **1.** A constituent element, as of a system. See Syns at **element. 2.** A part of a mechanical or electrical complex. **3.** *Mathematics* One of a set of two or more vectors having a sum equal to a given vector. **4.** Any of the minimum number of substances required to specify completely the composition of all phases of a chemical system. ❖ *adj.* Being or functioning as a constituent or an ingredient. [< Lat. *compōnēns, compōnent-*, pr. part. of *compōnere*, to put together : *com-, com-* + *pōnere*, to put; see **apo-** in App.] **—com′po·nen′tial** (kŏm′pə-nĕn′shəl) *adj.*

com·port (kəm-pôrt′, -pōrt′) v. **-port·ed, -port·ing, -ports** —*tr.* To conduct (oneself) in a particular manner. —*intr.* To agree, correspond, or harmonize. [ME *comporten* < OFr. *comporter*, to conduct < Lat. *comportāre*, to bring together : *com-, com-* + *portāre*, to carry; see **per-²** in App.]

com·port·ment (kəm-pôrt′mənt, -pōrt′-) n. Deportment.

com·pose (kəm-pōz′) v. **-posed, -pos·ing, -pos·es** —*tr.* **1.** To make up the constituent parts of; constitute or form. See Usage Note at **comprise. 2.** To make or create by putting together parts or elements. **3.** To create or produce (a literary or musical piece). **4.** To make (oneself) calm or tranquil. **5.** To settle or adjust; reconcile: *They managed to compose their differences.* **6.** To arrange aesthetically or artistically. **7.** *Printing* To arrange or set (type or matter to be printed). —*intr.* **1.** To create a literary or musical piece. **2.** *Printing* To set type. [ME *composen* < OFr. *composer*, alteration (influenced by *poser*, to put, place) of Lat. *compōnere*; see COMPONENT.]

com·posed (kəm-pōzd′) *adj.* Serenely self-possessed. **—com·pos′ed·ly** (-pō′zĭd-lē) *adv.* **—com·pos′ed·ness** n.

com·pos·er (kəm-pō′zər) n. One that composes, esp. music.

composing stick n. A small shallow tray, usu. metal and with an adjustable end, in which type is set by hand.

com·pos·ite (kəm-pŏz′ĭt) *adj.* **1.** Made up of distinct components; compound. **2.** *Mathematics* Having factors; factorable. **3.** *Botany* Of or relating to the Composite family. **4. Composite** *Architecture* Of or relating to the Composite order. ❖ n. **1.** A structure or entity made up of distinct components. See Syns at **mixture. 2.** A complex material in which two or more distinct, structurally complementary substances combine to produce structural or functional properties not present in any individual component. **3.** *Botany* A composite plant. **4.** *Mathematics* The application of one function to another. [Fr. < OFr. < Lat. *compositus*, p. part. of *compōnere*, to put together. See COMPONENT.] **—com·pos′ite·ly** *adv.* **—com·pos′ite·ness** n.

composite family n. The largest family of flowering plants, the Compositae (Asteraceae), characterized by many small flowers arranged in a head looking like a single flower and subtended by an involucre of bracts.

composite number n. An integer exactly divisible by at least one positive integer other than itself or 1.

Composite order
Composite order capital

Composite order n. *Architecture* A classical order formed by superimposing Ionic volutes on a Corinthian capital.

com·po·si·tion (kŏm′pə-zĭsh′ən) n. **1a.** The combining of distinct parts or elements to form a whole. **b.** The manner in which such parts are combined or related. **c.** General makeup: *the changing composition of the electorate.* **d.** The result or product of composing; a mixture or compound. **2.** Arrangement of artistic parts so as to form a unified whole. **3a.** The art or act of composing a musical or literary work. **b.** A work of music, literature, or art, or its structure or organization. **4.** A short essay, esp. one written as an academic exercise. **5.** *Law* A settlement whereby the creditors of a debtor about to enter bankruptcy agree to the discharge of their respective claims on receipt of a lesser amount than that actually owed. **6.** *Linguistics* The formation of compounds from separate words. **7.** *Printing* Typesetting. [ME *composicioun* < OFr. *composition* < Lat. *compositiō, compositiōn-* < *compositus*, p. part. of *compōnere*. See COMPONENT.] **—com′po·si′tion·al** *adj.* **—com′po·si′tion·al·ly** *adv.*

com·pos·i·tive (kəm-pŏz′ĭ-tĭv) *adj.* Synthetic; compounded.

com·pos·i·tor (kəm-pŏz′ĭ-tər) n. One that sets written material into type; a typesetter. [ME *compositur*, one who composes, settler of disputes < AN *compositour* < Lat., writer, compiler < *compōnere, composit-*, to put together. See COMPONENT.] **—com·pos′i·to′ri·al** (-tôr′ē-əl, -tōr′-) *adj.*

com·pos men·tis (kŏm′pəs mĕn′tĭs) *adj.* Of sound mind; sane. [Lat. : *compos*, having mastery of + *mentis*, genitive of *mēns*, mind.]

com·post (kŏm′pōst′) n. **1.** A mixture of decaying organic matter used to fertilize soil. **2.** A composition; a mixture. ❖ *tr.v.* **-post·ed, -post·ing, -posts 1.** To fertilize with a mixture of decaying organic matter. **2.** To convert (vegetable matter) to compost. [ME < OFr., mixture, compost < Lat. *compositum*, mixture < neut. p. part. of *compōnere*, to put together. See COMPONENT.]

com·post·ing toilet (kŏm′pō′stĭng) n. A toilet that uses little or no water, connected to a tank in which waste material is decomposed by aerobic bacteria.

com·po·sure (kəm-pō′zhər) n. A calm or tranquil state of

compound¹
left: pinnate compound leaf
right: palmate compound leaf

mind; self-possession. [< COMPOSE.]

com·pote (kŏm′pōt) n. **1.** Fruit stewed or cooked in syrup. **2.** A long-stemmed dish used for holding fruit, nuts, or candy. [Fr. < OFr. *composte*, mixture < Lat. *composita*, fem. p. part. of *compōnere*, to put together. See COMPONENT.]

com·pound¹ (kŏm-pound′, kəm-, kŏm′pound′) v. **-pound·ed, -pound·ing, -pounds** —*tr.* **1.** To combine so as to form a whole; mix. **2.** To produce or create by combining two or more ingredients or parts. **3.** To settle (a debt, for example) by agreeing on an amount less than the claim; adjust. **4.** To compute (interest) on the principal and accrued interest. **5.** To add to; increase. —*intr.* **1.** To form a compound. **2.** To come to terms; agree. ❖ *adj.* (kŏm′pound′, kŏm-pound′, kəm-) **1.** Consisting of two or more substances, ingredients, elements, or parts. **2.** *Botany* Composed of more than one part. ❖ n. (kŏm′pound′) **1.** A combination of two or more elements or parts. See Syns at **mixture. 2.** *Linguistics* A word that consists either of two or more elements that are independent words, such as *loudspeaker*, or of specially modified combining forms, such as Greek *philosophia*, from *philo-*, "loving," and *sophia*, "wisdom." **3.** *Chemistry* A substance consisting of atoms or ions of two or more different elements in definite proportions that cannot be separated by physical means. **4.** *Botany* **a.** A leaf whose blade is divided into two or more distinct leaflets. **b.** A pistil composed of two or more united carpels. [Alteration of ME *compounen* < OFr. *componre, compondre*, to put together < Lat. *compōnere*. See COMPONENT.] **—com·pound′a·ble** *adj.* **—com·pound′er** n.

com·pound² (kŏm′pound′) n. **1.** A building or buildings set off and enclosed by a barrier. **2.** An enclosed area used for prisoners of war. [Alteration of Malay *kampong*, village.]

com·pound-com·plex sentence (kŏm′pound-kŏm′plĕks) n. A sentence consisting of at least two coordinate independent clauses and one or more dependent clauses.

compound eye n. The eye of most insects and some crustaceans, which is composed of many light-sensitive elements, each forming a portion of an image.

compound fraction n. See complex fraction.

compound fracture n. A fracture in which broken bone fragments lacerate soft tissue and protrude through an open wound in the skin.

compound interest n. Interest computed on the accumulated unpaid interest as well as on the original principal.

compound lens n. See lens 2.

compound microscope n. A microscope consisting of an objective and an eyepiece at opposite ends of an adjustable tube.

compound number n. A quantity that is expressed in terms of two or more different units, such as 10 pounds 5 ounces or 3 feet 4 inches.

compound sentence n. A sentence of two or more coordinate independent clauses, often joined by a conjunction or conjunctions.

com·pra·dor also **com·pra·dore** (kŏm′prə-dôr′) n. **1.** A go-between; an intermediary. **2.** A native-born agent in China and certain other Asian countries formerly employed by a foreign business to help with commercial transactions. [Port. < LLat. *comparātor*, buyer < Lat. *comparāre*, to buy : *com-, com-* + *parāre*, to get.]

com·pre·hend (kŏm′prĭ-hĕnd′) *tr.v.* **-hend·ed, -hend·ing, -hends 1.** To take in the meaning, nature, or importance of; grasp. See Syns at **apprehend. 2.** To take in as a part; include. [ME *comprehenden* < Lat. *comprehendere* : *com-, com-* + *prehendere*, to grasp; see **ghend-** in App.] **—com′pre·hend′i·ble** *adj.* **—com′pre·hend′ing·ly** *adv.*

com·pre·hen·si·ble (kŏm′prĭ-hĕn′sə-bəl) *adj.* Readily comprehended or understood; intelligible. **—com′pre·hen′si·bil′i·ty** n. **—com′pre·hen′si·bly** *adv.*

com·pre·hen·sion (kŏm′prĭ-hĕn′shən) n. **1a.** The act or fact of grasping the meaning, nature, or importance of; understanding. **b.** The knowledge that is acquired in this way. **2.** Capacity to include. **3.** *Logic* The sum of meanings and corresponding implications inherent in a term. [ME *comprehensioun* < Lat. *comprehēnsiō, comprehēnsiōn-* < *comprehēnsus*, p. part. of *comprehendere*, to comprehend. See COMPREHEND.]

com·pre·hen·sive (kŏm′prĭ-hĕn′sĭv) *adj.* **1.** So large in scope or content as to include much: *a comprehensive history.* **2.** Marked by or showing extensive understanding. ❖ n. An examination covering the entire field of major study. Often used in the plural. [LLat. *comprehēnsīvus*, conceivable < Lat. *comprehēnsus*, p. part. of *comprehendere*, to comprehend. See COMPREHEND.] **—com′pre·hen′sive·ly** *adv.* **—com′pre·hen′sive·ness** n.

com·press (kəm-prĕs′) *tr.v.* **-pressed, -press·ing, -press·es 1.** To press together. **2.** To make more compact by or as if by pressing. **3.** *Computer Science* To transform (data) to minimize the space required for storage or transmission. ❖ n. (kŏm′prĕs′) **1.** *Medicine* A soft pad applied with pressure to a body part to control hemorrhage or supply heat, cold, moisture, or medication. **2.** A machine for compressing material. [ME *compressen* < OFr. *compresser* < LLat. *compressāre*, freq. of Lat. *comprimere* : *com-, com-* + *premere*, to press.]

com·pressed (kəm-prĕst′) *adj.* **1.** Pressed together or into less volume or space. **2.** *Biology* Flattened, esp. laterally or lengthwise, as certain leafstalks or the bodies of many fishes.

compressed air *n.* Air under greater than atmospheric pressure, esp. when used to power a mechanical device or provide a portable supply of oxygen.

com·press·i·ble (kəm-prĕs′ə-bəl) *adj.* That can be compressed. —**com·press′i·bil′i·ty, com·press′i·ble·ness** *n.*

com·pres·sion (kəm-prĕsh′ən) *n.* **1a.** The act or process of compressing. **b.** The state of being compressed. **2a.** The process by which the working substance in a heat engine is compressed. **b.** The engine cycle during which this process occurs. **3.** *Computer Science* The process by which data is compressed into a form that minimizes the space required to store or transmit it. —**com·pres′sion·al** *adj.*

compression ratio *n.* In an internal combustion engine, the ratio of the volume between the piston and cylinder head before and after a compression stroke.

compression wave *n.* A wave propagated by means of the compression of a fluid, as a sound wave.

com·pres·sive (kəm-prĕs′ĭv) *adj.* Serving to or able to compress. —**com·pres′sive·ly** *adv.*

com·pres·sor (kəm-prĕs′ər) *n.* One that compresses, esp. a machine used to compress gases.

com·prise (kəm-prīz′) *tr.v.* **-prised, -pris·ing, -pris·es 1.** To consist of; be composed of. **2.** To include; contain. **3.** *Usage Problem* To compose; constitute. [ME *comprisen* < OFr. *compris,* p. part. of *comprendre,* to include < Lat. *comprehendere, comprēndere.* See COMPREHEND.] —**com·pris′a·ble** *adj.*

USAGE NOTE In strict usage, the whole *comprises* the parts; the parts *compose* the whole: *The Union comprises 50 states. Fifty states compose the Union.* Despite this rule, *comprise* is increasingly used in place of *compose,* especially in the passive (*The Union is comprised of 50 states*), and our surveys show that opposition to this usage is abating. In the 1960s, 53 percent of the Usage Panel found this usage unacceptable, but in 1996, only 35 percent objected. See Usage Note at **include.**

com·pro·mise (kŏm′prə-mīz′) *n.* **1a.** A settlement of differences in which each side makes concessions. **b.** The result of such a settlement. **2.** Something that combines qualities or elements of different things. **3.** A concession to something detrimental or pejorative: *a moral compromise.* ❖ *v.* **-mised, -mis·ing, -mis·es** —*tr.* **1.** To settle by concessions. **2.** To expose or make liable to danger, suspicion, or disrepute. **3.** *Obsolete* To pledge mutually. —*intr.* To make a compromise. [ME *compromis* < OFr. < Lat. *comprōmissum,* mutual promise < neut. p. part. of *comprōmittere,* to promise mutually : *com-, com-* + *prōmittere,* to promise; see PROMISE.] —**com′pro·mis′er** *n.*

comp time *n. Informal* Compensatory time.

Comp·ton (kŏmp′tən) A city of S CA, a suburb between Los Angeles and Long Beach. Pop. 93,493.

Compton, Arthur Holly 1892–1962. Amer. physicist who shared a 1927 Nobel Prize.

comp·trol·ler (kən-trō′lər, kŏmp-trō′- kŏmp′trō′-) *n.* Variant of **controller** 2.

com·pul·sion (kəm-pŭl′shən) *n.* **1a.** The act of compelling. **b.** The state of being compelled. **2a.** An irresistible impulse to act, regardless of the rationality of the motivation. **b.** An act or acts performed in response to such an impulse. [ME < OFr. < LLat. *compulsiō, compulsiōn-* < Lat. *compulsus,* p. part. of *compellere,* to compel. See COMPEL.]

com·pul·sive (kəm-pŭl′sĭv) *adj.* **1.** Having the capacity to compel. **2.** *Psychology* Caused or conditioned by compulsion or obsession. ❖ *n.* A person with behavior patterns governed by a compulsion. —**com·pul′sive·ly** *adv.* —**com·pul′sive·ness, com′pul·siv′i·ty** (kŏm′pŭl-sĭv′ĭ-tē, kəm-) *n.*

com·pul·so·ry (kəm-pŭl′sə-rē) *adj.* **1.** Obligatory; required. **2.** Employing or exerting compulsion; coercive. —**com·pul′so·ri·ly** *adv.* —**com·pul′so·ri·ness** *n.*

com·punc·tion (kəm-pŭngk′shən) *n.* **1.** A strong uneasiness caused by a sense of guilt. **2.** A sting of conscience or a pang of doubt aroused by wrongdoing. [ME *compunccioun* < OFr. *componction* < LLat. *compūnctiō, compūnctiōn-,* sting of conscience, puncture < Lat. *compūnctus,* p. part. of *compungere,* to sting : *com-,* intensive pref.; see COM- + *pungere,* to prick.] —**com·punc′tious** (-shəs) *adj.* —**com·punc′tious·ly** *adv.*

com·pu·ta·tion (kŏm′pyoo-tā′shən) *n.* **1.** The act or process of computing. **b.** A method of computing. **2.** The result of computing. **3.** The act of operating a computer. —**com′pu·ta′tion·al** *adj.* —**com′pu·ta′tion·al·ly** *adv.*

com·pute (kəm-pyoot′) *v.* **-put·ed, -put·ing, -putes** —*tr.* **1.** To determine by mathematics, esp. by numerical methods. **2.** To determine by the use of a computer. —*intr.* **1.** To determine an amount or number. **2.** To use a computer. ❖ *n.* Computation. [Fr. *computer* < OFr., < Lat. *computāre : com-, com-* + *putāre,* to reckon. N., LLat. *computus* < Lat. *computāre,* to compute.] —**com·put′a·bil′i·ty** *n.* —**com·put′a·ble** *adj.*

com·put·er (kəm-pyoo′tər) *n.* **1.** A device that computes, esp. a programmable electronic machine that performs high-speed operations or assembles, stores, correlates, or otherwise processes information. **2.** One who computes.

computer age *n.* The current era as characterized by the devel-

opment, applications, and social consequences of computer technology.

computer graphics *n. (used with a sing. or pl. verb)* **1.** The set of technologies used to create art with computers. **2.** Art or designs created using such technologies.

com·put·er·ist (kəm-pyoo′tər-ĭst) *n.* One who uses a computer or is enthusiastic about computer technology.

com·put·er·ize (kəm-pyoo′tə-rīz′) *tr.v.* **-ized, -iz·ing, -iz·es 1.** To furnish with a computer or computer system. **2.** To enter, process, or store (information) in a computer or system of computers. —**com·put′er·iz′a·ble** *adj.* —**com·put′er·i·za′tion** (-tər-ĭ-zā′shən) *n.*

com·put·er·ized axial tomography (kəm-pyoo′tə-rīzd′) *n.* Tomography in which computer analysis of a series of cross-sectional scans made along a single axis of a body structure or tissue is used to construct a three-dimensional image of that structure.

computer literacy *n.* The ability to use a computer and its software to accomplish practical tasks. —**computer literate** *adj.*

computer science *n.* The study of computer technology, including hardware and software. —**computer scientist** *n.*

computer virus *n.* A computer program designed to corrupt a computer's memory or cause another program to malfunction, usu. by copying itself repeatedly.

Comr. *abbr.* commissioner

com·rade (kŏm′răd′, -rəd) *n.* **1.** A person who shares one's interests or activities; a friend or companion. **2.** often **Comrade** A fellow member of a group, esp. a fellow member of the Communist Party. [Fr. *camarade* < OFr., < roommate < OSpan. *camarada,* barracks company, roommate < *camara,* room < LLat. *camera.* See CHAMBER.] —**com′rade·ship′** *n.*

WORD HISTORY A comrade can be socially or politically close, a closeness found at the etymological heart of the word *comrade.* Spanish preserved the Latin word *camara,* with its Late Latin meaning "chamber, room," and formed the derivative *camarada,* with the sense "roommates, especially barrack mates." *Camarada* then came to have the general sense "companion." English *comrade,* first recorded in the 16th century, came from Spanish and French, French having borrowed from Spanish. The political sense of *comrade,* now associated with Communism, had its origin in the late-19th-century use of the word as a title by socialists and communists in order to avoid such forms of address as *mister.* This usage, which originated in France during the French Revolution, is first recorded in English in 1884.

com·rade·ry (kŏm′răd-rē, -rä-də-, -rəd-rē) *n.* Camaraderie; comradeship. [Alteration (influenced by COMRADE) of CAMARADERIE.]

Com·stock (kŏm′stŏk′, kŭm′-), **Anthony** 1844–1915. Amer. reformer notorious for his moral crusades against books and art that he considered obscene.

Com·stock·er·y (kŏm′stŏk′ə-rē, kŭm′-) *n.* Censorship of literature and other forms of expression because of perceived immorality or obscenity. [After Anthony COMSTOCK.]

Comstock Lode A rich vein of gold and silver discovered in 1859 at Virginia City in W NV.

Comte (kôNt), **(Isidore) Auguste (Marie François)** 1798–1857. French philosopher known as the founder of positivism and sociology. —**Com′ti·an** (kôN′tē-ən, kŏm′-) *adj.* —**Com′tism** (kŏm′tĭz′əm) *n.* —**Com′tist** (kŏm′tĭst) *n.*

con[1] (kŏn) *adv.* In opposition or disagreement; against. ❖ *n.* **1.** An argument or opinion against something. **2.** One who holds an opposing opinion or view. [Short for CONTRA.]

con[2] (kŏn) *tr.v.* **conned, con·ning, cons 1.** To study, peruse, or examine carefully. **2.** To learn or commit to memory. [ME *connen,* to know < OE *cunnan.* See **gnō-** in App.] —**con′ner** *n.*

con[3] or **conn** (kŏn) *Nautical tr.v.* **conned, con·ning, cons** or **conns** To direct the steering or course of (a vessel). ❖ *n.* **1.** The station or post of the person who steers a vessel. **2.** The act or process of steering a vessel. [< *cond* < ME *conduen* < OFr. *conduire* < Lat. *condūcere,* to lead together. See CONDUCE.]

con[4] (kŏn) *Slang tr.v.* **conned, con·ning, cons** To swindle (a victim) by first winning his or her confidence; dupe. ❖ *n.* A swindle. ❖ *adj.* Of, relating to, or involving a swindle or a fraud: *a con artist.* [Short for CONFIDENCE.]

con[5] (kŏn) *n. Slang* A convict.

con. *abbr.* **1.** concerto **2.** *Latin* conjunx (wife) **3.** consolidate **4. Con.** consul **5.** continued

con– *pref.* Variant of **com–.**

Con·a·kry (kŏn′ə-krē) The cap. of Guinea, in the SW part on the Atlantic Ocean. Pop. 600,000.

con a·mo·re (kŏn′ ə-môr′ē, -môr′-, kôn′ ä-mō′rä) *adv.* **1.** *Music* Lovingly; tenderly. **2.** With devotion or zeal. [Ital. : *con,* with + *amore,* love.]

Co·nant (kō′nənt), **James Bryant** 1893–1978. Amer. educator who was president of Harvard University (1933–53).

co·na·tion (kō-nā′shən) *n. Psychology* The aspect of mental processes or behavior directed toward action or change. [Lat. *cōnātiō, cōnātiōn-,* effort < *cōnātus,* p. part. of *cōnārī,* to try.] —**co·na′tion·al, co′na·tive** (kō′nə-tĭv, kŏn′ə-) *adj.*

con bri·o (kŏn brē′ō, kôn) *adv. Music* With great energy; vigorously. [Ital. : *con,* with + *brio,* vigor.]

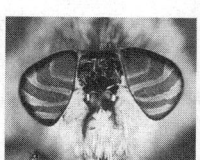

compound eye
close-up of the eyes of a horsefly

ă	pat	oi	boy
ā	pay	ou	out
âr	care	oo	took
ä	father	oo	boot
ĕ	pet	ŭ	cut
ē	be	ûr	urge
ĭ	pit	th	thin
ī	pie	th	this
îr	pier	hw	which
ŏ	pot	zh	vision
ō	toe	ə	about,
ô	paw		item

Stress marks:
′ (primary);
′ (secondary), as in
lexicon (lĕk′sĭ-kŏn′)

con·cat·e·nate (kŏn-kăt′n-āt′, kən-) *tr.v.* **-nat·ed, -nat·ing, -nates** **1.** To connect or link in a series or chain. **2.** *Computer Science* To arrange (strings of characters) into a chained list. ❖ *adj.* (-nĭt, -nāt′) Connected or linked in a series. [LLat. *concatēnāre, concatēnāt-* : *com-*, com- + *catēnāre,* to bind (< Lat. *catēna,* chain).] **—con·cat′e·na′tion** *n.*

con·cave (kŏn-kāv′, kŏn′kāv′) *adj.* Curved like the inner surface of a sphere. ❖ *n.* A concave surface, structure, or line. ❖ *tr.v.* **-caved, -cav·ing, -caves** To make concave. [ME < Lat. *concavus* : *com-*, com- + *cavus,* hollow.] **—con·cave′ly** *adv.* **—con·cave′ness** *n.*

con·cav·i·ty (kŏn-kăv′ĭ-tē) *n., pl.* **-ties** **1.** The state of being curved like the inner surface of a sphere. **2.** A surface or structure configured in such a curve.

con·ca·vo-con·cave (kŏn-kā′vō-kŏn-kāv′) *adj.* Concave on both surfaces; biconcave. Used of a lens.

con·ca·vo-con·vex (kŏn-kā′vō-kŏn-vĕks′) *adj.* **1.** Concave on one side and convex on the other. **2.** Having greater curvature on the concave side than on the convex side. Used of a lens.

con·ceal (kən-sēl′) *tr.v.* **-cealed, -ceal·ing, -ceals** To keep from being seen, found, or observed; hide. See Syns at **hide**[1]. [ME *concelen* < OFr. *conceler* < Lat. *concēlāre* : *com-*, com- + *cēlāre,* to hide; see **kel-** in App.] **—con·ceal′a·ble** *adj.* **—con·ceal′ment** *n.*

con·ceal·er (kən-sē′lər) *n.* **1.** One that conceals. **2.** A facial cosmetic used to cover blemished skin.

con·cede (kən-sēd′) *v.* **-ced·ed, -ced·ing, -cedes** —*tr.* **1.** To acknowledge, often reluctantly, as being true, just, or proper; admit. **2.** To yield or grant (a right, for example). —*intr.* To make a concession; yield. [Fr. *concéder* < Lat. *concēdere* : *com-*, com- + *cēdere,* to yield.] **—con·ced′ed·ly** (-sē′dĭd-lē) *adv.* **—con·ced′er** *n.*

con·ceit (kən-sēt′) *n.* **1.** A favorable and esp. unduly high opinion of one's own abilities or worth. **2.** An ingenious or witty turn of phrase or thought. **3a.** An elaborate or exaggerated metaphor or simile. **b.** A poem or passage consisting of such a metaphor or simile. **4a.** The result of intellectual activity; a thought or opinion. **b.** A fanciful thought or idea. **5a.** A fancy article; a knickknack. **b.** An extravagant, fanciful, and elaborate construction or structure. ❖ *tr.v.* **-ceit·ed, -ceit·ing, -ceits** *Chiefly British* To take a fancy to. **2.** *Obsolete* To understand; conceive. [ME, mind, conception < AN *conceite* < LLat. *conceptus.* See CONCEPT.]

con·ceit·ed (kən-sē′tĭd) *adj.* Holding or characterized by an unduly high opinion of oneself; vain. **—con·ceit′ed·ly** *adv.* **—con·ceit′ed·ness** *n.*

con·ceive (kən-sēv′) *v.* **-ceived, -ceiv·ing, -ceives** —*tr.* **1.** To become pregnant with (offspring). **2.** To form or develop in the mind; devise. **3.** To apprehend mentally; understand. **4.** To be of the opinion that; think. **5.** To begin or originate in a specific way: *a practice conceived in desperate times.* —*intr.* **1.** To form or hold an idea. **2.** To become pregnant. [ME *conceiven* < OFr. *concevoir, conceiv-* < Lat. *concipere* : *com-*, com- + *capere,* to take; see **kap-** in App.] **—con·ceiv′a·bil′i·ty, con·ceiv′a·ble·ness** *n.* **—con·ceiv′a·ble** *adj.* **—con·ceiv′a·bly** *adv.* **—con·ceiv′er** *n.*

con·cel·e·brate (kən-sĕl′ə-brāt′) *v.* **-brat·ed, -brat·ing, -brates** —*intr.* To take part in a concelebration of the Eucharist. —*tr.* To take part in (a Eucharist) as a joint celebrant. [Lat. *concelebrāre, concelebrāt-* : *com-*, com- + *celebrāre,* to celebrate; see CELEBRATE.] **—con·cel′e·brant** (-brənt) *n.*

con·cen·ter (kən-sĕn′tər, kŏn-) *tr. & intr.v.* **-tered, -ter·ing, -ters** To direct toward or come together at a common center. [Prob. Ital. *concentrare* or Fr. *concentrer,* both < Lat. *com-*, com- + Lat. *centrum,* center; see CENTER.]

con·cen·trate (kŏn′sən-trāt′) *v.* **-trat·ed, -trat·ing, -trates** —*tr.* **1a.** To direct or draw toward a common center; focus. **b.** To bring into one main body: *Authority was concentrated in the president.* **2.** To make (a solution or mixture) less dilute. —*intr.* **1a.** To converge toward or meet in a common center. **b.** To increase by degree; gather. **2.** To direct one's thoughts or attention: *concentrated on the task.* ❖ *n.* A product that has been concentrated, esp. a food that has been reduced in volume or bulk by the removal of liquid. [< CONCENTER.] **—con′cen·tra′tive** *adj.* **—con′cen·tra′tive·ly** *adv.* **—con′cen·tra′tor** *n.*

con·cen·tra·tion (kŏn′sən-trā′shən) *n.* **1a.** The act or process of concentrating, esp. the fixing of close, undivided attention. **b.** The condition of being concentrated. **2.** Something that has been concentrated. **3.** *Chemistry* The amount of a specified substance in a unit amount of another substance.

concentration camp *n.* A camp where civilians, enemy aliens, political prisoners, and sometimes prisoners of war are detained and confined, typically under harsh conditions.

con·cen·tric (kən-sĕn′trĭk) also **con·cen·tri·cal** (-trĭ-kəl) *adj.* Having a common center. [ME *concentrik* < Med.Lat. *concentricus* : Lat. *com-*, com- + Lat. *centrum,* center; see CENTER.] **—con·cen′tri·cal·ly** *adv.* **—con′cen·tric′i·ty** (kŏn′sĕn-trĭs′ĭ-tē) *n.*

Con·cep·ción (kən-sĕp′sē-ōn′, -sĕp′shən, kŏn′sĕp-syōn′) A city of W-central Chile near the Pacific coast SSW of Santiago; founded 1550. Pop. 306,464.

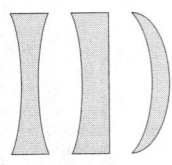

concave
left to right: biconcave, plano-concave, and concavo-convex lenses

con·cept (kŏn′sĕpt′) *n.* **1.** A general idea derived or inferred from specific instances or occurrences. **2.** Something formed in the mind; a thought or notion. See Syns at **idea**. **3.** A scheme; a plan: *a concept for a new mall.* [Lat. *conceptus* < Lat., p. part. of *concipere,* to conceive. See CONCEIVE.]

con·cep·ta·cle (kən-sĕp′tə-kəl) *n.* A hollow chamber containing reproductive structures that appears on the surface of receptacles in certain algae and fungi. [Lat. *conceptāculum,* receptacle < *conceptus,* p. part. of *concipere,* to conceive. See CONCEIVE.]

con·cep·tion (kən-sĕp′shən) *n.* **1a.** Formation of a viable zygote by the union of the sperm and the ovum; fertilization. **b.** The entity formed by the union of the sperm and the ovum; an embryo or zygote. **2a.** The ability to form or understand mental concepts and abstractions. **b.** Something conceived in the mind; a concept, plan, design, idea, or thought. See Syns at **idea**. **3.** *Archaic* A beginning; a start. [ME *concepcioun* < OFr. *conception* < Lat. *conceptiō, conceptiōn-* < *conceptus.* See CONCEPT.] **—con·cep′tion·al** *adj.* **—con·cep′tive** *adj.*

con·cep·tu·al (kən-sĕp′chōō-əl) *adj.* Of concepts or mental conception. [Med.Lat. *conceptuālis* < LLat. *conceptus,* a thought. See CONCEPT.] **—con·cep′tu·al·ly** *adv.*

conceptual art *n.* Art that is intended to convey an idea or concept and that may not involve the creation or appreciation of a traditional art object. **—conceptual artist** *n.*

con·cep·tu·al·ism (kən-sĕp′chōō-ə-lĭz′əm) *n.* *Philosophy* The doctrine that universals exist only within the mind and have no external or substantial reality. **—con·cep′tu·al·ist** *adj. & n.*

con·cep·tu·al·ize (kən-sĕp′chōō-ə-līz′) *v.* **-ized, -iz·ing, -iz·es** —*tr.* To form a concept or concepts of, esp. to interpret in a conceptual way. —*intr.* To form concepts. **—con·cep′tu·al·i·za′tion** (-ə-lī-zā′shən) *n.* **—con·cep′tu·al·iz′er** *n.*

con·cep·tus (kən-sĕp′təs) *n.* The product of conception at any point between fertilization and birth. [Lat., something conceived. See CONCEPT.]

con·cern (kən-sûrn′) *v.* **-cerned, -cern·ing, -cerns** —*tr.* **1.** To have to do with or relate to. **2.** To be of interest or importance to: *This problem concerns all of us.* **3.** To engage the attention of; involve: *concerned ourselves with the task.* **4.** To cause anxiety or uneasiness in. —*intr.* *Obsolete* To be of importance. ❖ *n.* **1.** A matter that relates to or affects one. **2.** Regard for or interest in someone or something. **3.** A troubled or anxious state of mind arising from solicitude or interest. See Syns at **anxiety**. **4.** A business establishment or enterprise; a firm. **5.** A contrivance; a gadget. [ME *concernen* < OFr. *concerner* < Med.Lat. *concernere* < LLat., to mingle together : Lat. *com-*, com- + Lat. *cernere,* to sift; see **krei-** in App.]

con·cerned (kən-sûrnd′) *adj.* **1.** Interested and involved. **2.** Anxious; troubled.

con·cern·ing (kən-sûr′nĭng) *prep.* In reference to. See Usage Note at **participle**.

con·cern·ment (kən-sûrn′mənt) *n.* **1.** A matter that is of concern. **2.** Reference, relation, or importance. **3.** Anxiety; worry.

con·cert (kŏn′sûrt′, -sərt) *n.* **1.** *Music* A performance given by one or more singers or instrumentalists or both. **2a.** Agreement in purpose, feeling, or action. **b.** Unity achieved by mutual communication of views, ideas, and opinions: *acted in concert.* **c.** Concerted action. ❖ *v.* (kən-sûrt′) **-cert·ed, -cert·ing, -certs** —*tr.* **1.** To plan or arrange by mutual agreement. **2.** To adjust; settle. —*intr.* To act together in harmony. [Fr. < Ital. *concerto* < OItal., agreement, harmony < *concertare,* to bring into agreement, poss. < VLat. **concertāre,* to settle by argument < Lat., to debate : *con-*, com- + *certāre,* to contend, freq. of *cernere,* to separate, decide by fighting; see **krei-** in App.]

con·cert·ed (kən-sûr′tĭd) *adj.* **1.** Planned or accomplished together; combined: *a concerted effort.* **2.** *Music* Arranged in parts for voices or instruments. **—con·cert′ed·ly** *adv.*

concert grand *n.* The largest grand piano, being roughly 2.7 meters (9 feet) in length and having the volume, tone, and timbre appropriate for use in concerts.

con·cer·ti·na (kŏn′sər-tē′nə) *n.* A small hexagonal accordion with bellows and with buttons for keys. [CONCERT + Ital. *-ina,* fem. dim. suff.]

concertina wire *n.* Barbed wire that is extended in a spiral for use as a barrier, as on a fence.

con·cer·ti·no (kŏn′chĕr-tē′nō) *n., pl.* **-nos** **1.** A short concerto. **2.** The solo group in a concerto grosso. [Ital., dim. of *concerto,* concert. See CONCERT.]

con·cer·tize (kŏn′sər-tīz′) *intr.v.* **-tized, -tiz·ing, -tiz·es** To give concerts or perform in concerts.

con·cert·mas·ter (kŏn′sərt-măs′tər) *n.* The first violinist in a symphony orchestra.

con·cert·mis·tress (kŏn′sərt-mĭs′trĭs) *n.* A woman first violinist in a symphony orchestra.

con·cer·to (kən-chĕr′tō) *n., pl.* **-tos** or **-ti** (-tē) A composition for an orchestra and one or more solo instruments, typically in three movements. [Ital., concert. See CONCERT.]

concerto gros·so (grō′sō) *n., pl.* **concerti gros·si** (grō′sē) A composition for a small group of instrumental soloists and an orchestra. [Ital. : *concerto,* concerto + *grosso,* large.]

concert pitch *n.* **1.** See **international pitch**. **2.** The state of being ready and tensely alert.

con·ces·sion (kən-sĕsh'ən) *n.* **1.** The act of conceding. **2a.** Something, such as a point claimed in argument, that is later conceded. **b.** An acknowledgment or admission. **3.** A grant of a tract of land, as by a government, in return for stipulated services or a promise that the land will be used for a specific purpose. **4a.** The privilege of maintaining a subsidiary business within certain premises. **b.** The space allotted for such a business. **c.** The business itself. [ME < Lat. *concessiō, concessiōn- < concessus,* p. part. of *concēdere,* to concede. See CONCEDE.] —**con·ces'sion·al** *adj.* —**con·ces'sion·ar'y** (-shə-nĕr'ē) *adj.*

con·ces·sion·aire (kən-sĕsh'ə-nâr') *n.* The holder or operator of a concession. [Fr. *concessionnaire < concession,* concession < Lat. *concessiō.* See CONCESSION.]

con·ces·sion·er (kən-sĕsh'ə-nər) *n.* A concessionaire.

con·ces·sive (kən-sĕs'ĭv) *adj.* **1.** Of the nature of or containing a concession. **2.** *Grammar* Expressing concession.

conch (kŏngk, kŏnch) *n., pl.* **conchs** (kŏngks) or **conch·es** (kŏn'chĭz) **1.** Any of various tropical marine gastropod mollusks, esp. of the genera *Strombus* and *Cassis,* having large, often brightly colored spiral shells and edible flesh. **2.** The shell of one of these gastropod mollusks, used as an ornament, in making cameos, or as a horn. **3.** *Anatomy* See **concha** 1. [ME *conche* < OFr. < Lat. *concha,* mussel < Gk. *konkhē.*]

con·cha (kŏng'kə) *n., pl.* **-chae** (-kē') **1.** *Anatomy* Any of various structures that resemble a shell in shape. **2.** *Architecture* The half dome over an apse. [LLat., semidome < Lat., mussel shell. See CONCH.] —**con'chal** (-kəl) *adj.*

con·chif·er·ous (kŏng-kĭf'ər-əs) *adj.* Having or forming a shell.

con·chi·o·lin (kŏng-kī'ə-lĭn, kŏn-) *n.* A protein substance that is the organic basis of mollusk shells. [CONCH + -OL¹ + -IN.]

concho– or **conchi–** or **conch–** *pref.* Shell: *conchology.* [Gk. *konkho– < konkhos,* shell.]

Con·cho·bar (kŏn-kŭv'ər, -kōō'hōōr, kŏn'ər) *n. Mythology* The king of Ulster who abducted Deirdre.

con·choi·dal (kŏng-koid'l) *adj.* Of, relating to, or being a surface characterized by smooth shell-like convexities and concavities. [< Gk. *konkhoeidēs,* musselike : *konkho-,* concho- + *-oeidēs,* -oid.] —**con·choi'dal·ly** *adv.*

con·chol·o·gy (kŏng-kŏl'ə-jē) *n.* The branch of zoology that deals with the study of mollusks and shells. —**con'cho·log'i·cal** (-lŏj'ĭ-kəl) *adj.* —**con·chol'o·gist** *n.*

con·cierge (kŏn-syârzh') *n.* **1.** A staff member of a hotel or apartment complex who assists guests or residents. **2.** A person, esp. in France, who lives in an apartment house, attends the entrance, and serves as a janitor. [Fr. < OFr. *cumcerges < VLat. *cōnservius,* alteration of Lat. *cōnservus,* fellow slave : *com-,* com- + *servus,* slave.]

con·cil·i·ar (kən-sĭl'ē-ər) *adj.* Of, relating to, or generated by a council. [< Lat. *concilium,* council. See COUNCIL.]

con·cil·i·ate (kən-sĭl'ē-āt') *v.* **-at·ed, -at·ing, -ates** —*tr.* **1.** To overcome the distrust or animosity of; appease. **2.** To regain or try to regain (friendship or goodwill) by pleasant behavior. **3.** To make or try to make compatible; reconcile. —*intr.* To gain or try to gain friendship or goodwill. See Syns at **pacify.** [Lat. *conciliāre, conciliāt- < concilium,* meeting. See **kelə-** in App.] —**con·cil'i·a·ble** (-ə-bəl) *adj.* —**con·cil'i·a'tion** *n.* —**con·cil'i·a'tor** *n.* —**con·cil'i·a·to'ry** (-ə-tôr'ē, -tōr'ē) *adj.*

con·cin·ni·ty (kən-sĭn'ĭ-tē) *n., pl.* **-ties** **1.** Harmony in the arrangement or interarrangement of parts with respect to a whole. **2.** Studied elegance and facility in style of expression. **3.** An instance of harmonious arrangement or studied elegance and facility. [< Lat. *concinnitās < concinnāre,* to put in order < *concinnus,* deftly joined.]

con·cise (kən-sīs') *adj.* Expressing much in few words; clear and succinct. [Lat. *concīsus,* p. part. of *concīdere,* to cut up : *com-,* com- + *caedere,* to cut.] —**con·cise'ly** *adv.* —**con·cise'ness** *n.*

con·ci·sion (kən-sĭzh'ən) *n.* **1.** The state or quality of being concise. **2.** *Archaic* A cutting apart or off.

con·clave (kŏn'klāv', kŏng'-) *n.* **1.** A secret or confidential meeting. **2.** *Roman Catholic Church* **a.** The private rooms in which the cardinals meet to elect a new pope. **b.** The meeting held to elect a new pope. **3.** A meeting of family members or associates. [ME, private chamber, conclave of cardinals < Lat. *conclāve,* lockable room : *com-,* com- + *clāvis,* key.]

con·clude (kən-klōōd') *v.* **-clud·ed, -clud·ing, -cludes** —*tr.* **1.** To bring to an end; close. **2.** To bring about (an agreement, for example). **3.** To reach a decision or form an opinion about. See Syns at **decide. 4.** To arrive at (a logical conclusion or end) by the process of reasoning; infer on the basis of convincing evidence. **5.** *Obsolete* To confine; enclose. —*intr.* **1.** To come to an end; close. **2.** To come to a decision or agreement. [ME *concluden* < Lat. *conclūdere : com-,* com- + *claudere,* to close.] —**con·clud'er** *n.*

con·clu·sion (kən-klōō'zhən) *n.* **1.** The close or last part; the end or finish. **2.** The result or outcome of an act or process. **3.** A judgment or decision reached after deliberation. **4.** A final arrangement or settlement, as of a treaty. **5.** *Law* The close of a plea or deed. **6a.** *Logic* The proposition that must follow from the major and minor premises in a syllogism. **b.** The proposition concluded from one or more premises; a deduction. [ME *conclusioun < OFr. conclusion <* Lat. *conclūsiō, conclūsiōn- < conclūsus,*

p. part. of *conclūdere,* to end. See CONCLUDE.]

con·clu·sive (kən-klōō'sĭv) *adj.* Serving to put an end to doubt, question, or uncertainty; decisive. —**con·clu'sive·ly** *adv.* —**con·clu'sive·ness** *n.*

con·clu·so·ry (kən-klōō'sə-rē) *adj.* **1.** Conclusive. **2.** *Law* Convincing but not so that contradiction is impossible.

con·coct (kən-kŏkt') *tr.v.* **-coct·ed, -coct·ing, -cocts 1.** To prepare by mixing ingredients. **2.** To devise, using skill and intelligence; contrive. [Lat. *concoquere, concoct-,* to boil together : *com-,* com- + *coquere,* to cook; see **pekʷ-** in App.] —**con·coct'er, con·coct'or** *n.* —**con·coc'tion** *n.*

con·com·i·tance (kən-kŏm'ĭ-təns) *n.* **1.** Occurrence or existence together or in connection with one another. **2.** A concomitant.

con·com·i·tant (kən-kŏm'ĭ-tənt) *adj.* Occurring or existing concurrently; attendant. ❖ *n.* One that is concomitant. [LLat. *concomitāns, concomitant-,* pr. part. of *concomitārī,* to accompany : Lat. *com-,* com- + Lat. *comitārī,* to accompany (< *comes, comit-,* companion; see **ei-** in App.).] —**con·com'i·tant·ly** *adv.*

con·cord (kŏn'kôrd', kŏng'-) *n.* **1.** Harmony or agreement of interests or feelings; accord. **2.** A treaty establishing peaceful relations. **3.** *Grammar* Agreement between words in person, number, gender, or case. **4.** *Music* A harmonious combination of simultaneously sounded tones. [ME *concorde < OFr.* < Lat. *concordia < concors, concord-,* agreeing : *com-,* com- + *cor, cord-,* heart; see **kerd-** in App.]

Con·cord (kŏng'kərd) **1.** The cap. of NH, in the S-central part on the Merrimack R. Pop. 40,687. **2.** A town of E MA on the **Concord River** WNW of Boston; site of an early battle of the Revolutionary War (Apr. 19, 1775). Pop. 16,993. **3.** A city of W-central CA NE of Oakland. Pop. 121,780.

con·cor·dance (kən-kôr'dns) *n.* **1.** Agreement; concord. **2.** An alphabetical index of all the words in a text or corpus of texts, showing every contextual occurrence of a word. **3.** *Genetics* The presence of a given trait in both members of a pair of twins.

con·cor·dant (kən-kôr'dnt) *adj.* Harmonious; agreeing. [ME *concordaunt < OFr. concordant <* Lat. *concordāns, concordant-,* pr. part. of *concordāre,* to agree < *concors, concord-,* agreeing. See CONCORD.] —**con·cor'dant·ly** *adv.*

con·cor·dat (kən-kôr'dăt') *n.* **1.** A formal agreement; a compact. **2.** *Roman Catholic Church* An agreement between the pope and a government for the regulation of church affairs. [Fr. < Med.Lat. *concordātum < neut. p. part. of Lat. *concordāre,* to agree < *concors, concord-,* agreeing. See CONCORD.]

Con·corde (kŏn'kôrd', kŏng'-) A trademark for a supersonic passenger aircraft used primarily for transatlantic travel.

Con·cord grape (kŏng'kərd) *n.* A cultivated variety of the fox grape having dark blue to purple-black skin, used for making jelly, juice, and wine. [After CONCORD, MA.]

con·course (kŏn'kôrs', -kōrs', kŏng'-) *n.* **1.** A large open space for the gathering or passage of crowds, as in an airport. **2.** A broad thoroughfare. **3.** A great crowd; a throng. **4.** The act of coming, moving, or flowing together. [ME *concours,* assembly < OFr. < Lat. *concursus < p. part. of concurrere,* to assemble : *com-,* com- + *currere,* to run.]

conch
queen conch
Strombus gigas

con·cres·cence (kən-krĕs'əns) *n.* **1.** *Biology* The growing together of related parts, tissues, or cells. **2.** The amassing of physical particles. [Lat. *concrēscentia < concrēscēns, concrēscent-,* pr. part. of *concrēscere,* to grow together. See CONCRETE.] —**con·cres'cent** *adj.*

con·crete (kŏn-krēt', kŏng-, kŏn'krēt', kŏng'-) *adj.* **1.** Of or relating to an actual, specific thing or instance; particular: *concrete evidence.* **2.** Existing in reality or in real experience; perceptible by the senses; real: *concrete objects.* **3.** Formed by the coalescence of separate particles or parts into one mass; solid. **4.** Made of concrete. ❖ *n.* (kŏn'krēt', kŏng'-, kŏn-krēt', kŏng-) **1.** A hard, strong construction material consisting of sand, conglomerate gravel, pebbles, broken stone, or slag in a mortar or cement matrix. **2.** A mass formed by the coalescence of particles. ❖ *v.* (kŏn'krēt', kŏng'-, kŏn-krēt', kŏng-) **-cret·ed, -cret·ing, -cretes** —*tr.* **1.** To build, treat, or cover with concrete. **2.** To form into a mass by coalescence or cohesion of particles or parts. —*intr.* To harden; solidify. [ME *concret < Lat. concrētus,* p. part. of *concrēscere,* to grow together, harden : *com-,* com- + *crēscere,* to grow; see **ker-²** in App.] —**con·crete'ly** *adv.* —**con·crete'ness** *n.*

concrete music *n. Musique concrète.*

concrete noun *n.* A noun, such as *flower* or *rain,* that denotes a material or tangible object or phenomenon.

concrete poetry *n.* Poetry that conveys meaning by graphic arrangement of letters, words, or symbols.

con·cre·tion (kən-krē'shən) *n.* **1a.** The act or process of concreting into a mass; coalescence. **b.** The state of having been concreted. **2.** A solid hard mass. **3.** *Geology* A rounded mass of mineral matter found in sedimentary rock. **4.** *Pathology* A solid mass, usu. inorganic, formed in a cavity or tissue of the body; a calculus. —**con·cre'tion·ar'y** (-shə-nĕr'ē) *adj.*

con·cret·ism (kŏn-krē'tĭz'əm, kŏng-) *n.* The practice of representing abstract concepts or qualities in concrete form, as in concrete poetry. —**con·cret'ist** *n.*

con·cre·tize (kŏn'krĭ-tīz', kŏng'-) *tr.v.* **-tized, -tiz·ing, -tiz·es** To make real or specific. —**con'cre·ti·za'tion** (-tĭ-zā'shən) *n.*

con·cu·bi·nage (kŏn-kyōō′bə-nĭj, kən-) *n.* **1.** *Law* Cohabitation without legal marriage. **2.** The state of being a concubine.

con·cu·bine (kŏng′kyə-bīn′, kŏn′-) *n.* **1.** A woman who cohabits with a man without being legally married to him. **2.** A secondary wife, often having few legal rights. [ME < OFr. < Lat. *concubīna* : *com-*, com- + *cubāre*, to lie down.]

con·cu·pis·cence (kŏn-kyōō′pĭ-səns) *n.* A strong desire, esp. sexual desire; lust. [ME < OFr. < LLat. *concupīscentia* < Lat. *concupīscēns*, *concupīscent-*, pr. part. of *concupīscere*, inchoative of *concupere*, to desire strongly : *com-*, com- + *cupere*, to desire.] **—con·cu′pis·cent** *adj.*

con·cur (kən-kûr′) *intr.v.* **-curred, -cur·ring, -curs 1.** To be of the same opinion; agree. See Syns at **assent. 2.** To act together; cooperate. **3.** To occur at the same time; coincide. **4.** *Obsolete* To converge. [ME *concurren* < Lat. *concurrere*, to meet : *com-*, com- + *currere*, to run.]

con·cur·rence (kən-kûr′əns, -kŭr′-) *n.* **1.** Agreement in opinion. **2.** Cooperation, as of agents, circumstances, or events. **3.** Simultaneous occurrence. **—con·cur′ren·cy** *n.*

con·cur·rent (kən-kûr′ənt, -kŭr′-) *adj.* **1.** Happening at the same time as something else. **2.** Operating or acting in conjunction with another. **3.** Meeting or tending to meet at the same point; convergent. **4.** Being in accordance; harmonious. **—con′cur′rent** *n.* **—con·cur′rent·ly** *adv.*

concurrent resolution *n.* A resolution adopted by both houses of a bicameral legislature that does not have the force of law and does not require the signature of the chief executive.

con·cuss (kən-kŭs′) *tr.v.* **-cussed, -cuss·ing, -cuss·es** To injure by concussion. [Lat. *concutere*, *concuss-*, to strike together : *com-*, com- + *quatere*, to strike.]

con·cus·sion (kən-kŭsh′ən) *n.* **1.** A violent jarring; a shock. **2.** An injury to an organ, esp. the brain, produced by a violent blow and followed by a temporary or prolonged loss of function. [ME *concussioun*, bruise, contusion < Lat. *concussiō*, *concussiōn-*, concussion < *concussus*, p. part. of *concutere*, to strike together. See CONCUSS.] **—con·cus′sive** (-kŭs′ĭv) *adj.* **—con·cus′sive·ly** *adv.*

cond. *abbr.* **1.** condition **2.** conditional **3.** conductor

Con·dé (kôn-dā′), Prince de. Title of Louis II de Bourbon. 1621–86. French general during the Thirty Years' War.

con·demn (kən-dĕm′) *tr.v.* **-demned, -demn·ing, -demns 1.** To express strong disapproval of. See Syns at **criticize. 2.** To pronounce judgment against; sentence. **3.** To judge or declare to be unfit for use or consumption, usu. by official order. **4.** To lend credence to or provide evidence for an adverse judgment against: *condemned by his actions.* **5.** *Law* To appropriate (property) for public use. [ME *condemnen* < OFr. *condemner* < Lat. *condemnāre* : *com-*, com- + *damnāre*, to sentence (< *damnum*, penalty).] **—con·dem′na·ble** (-dĕm′nə-bəl) *adj.* **—con·dem′na·to′ry** (-nə-tôr′ē, -tōr′ē) *adj.* **—con·demn′er, con·dem′nor** (-dĕm′ər, -dĕm-nôr′) *n.*

con·dem·na·tion (kŏn′dĕm-nā′shən) *n.* **1a.** The act of condemning. **b.** The state of being condemned. **2.** Severe reproof; strong censure. **3.** A reason or occasion for condemning.

con·den·sate (kŏn′dən-sāt′, -dĕn-, kən-dĕn′sāt′) *n.* A product of condensation.

con·den·sa·tion (kŏn′dĕn-sā′shən, -dən-) *n.* **1.** The act of condensing. **2.** The state of being condensed. **3.** A condensate. **4.** An abridgement or shortening, as of a written work. **5.** *Physics* **a.** The process by which a gas or vapor changes to a liquid. **b.** The liquid so formed. **6.** *Chemistry* A chemical reaction in which water or another simple substance is released by the combination of two or more molecules. **7.** *Psychology* The process by which a symbol or word is associated with the emotional content of a group of ideas, feelings, memories, or impulses. **—con′den·sa′tion·al** *adj.*

con·dense (kən-dĕns′) *v.* **-densed, -dens·ing, -dens·es** *—tr.* **1.** To reduce the volume or compass of. **2.** To make more concise; abridge or shorten. **3.** *Physics* **a.** To cause (a gas or vapor) to change to a liquid. **b.** To remove water from (milk, for example). *—intr.* **1.** To become more compact. **2.** To undergo condensation. [ME *condensen* < OFr. *condenser* < Lat. *condēnsāre* : *com-*, com- + *dēnsāre*, to thicken (< *dēnsus*, thick).] **—con·dens′a·bil′i·ty** *n.* **—con·dens′a·ble, con·dens′i·ble** *adj.*

con·densed matter physics (kən-dĕnst′) *n.* See **solid-state physics.**

condensed milk *n.* Cow's milk with sugar added, reduced by evaporation to a thick consistency.

con·dens·er (kən-dĕn′sər) *n.* **1.** One that condenses, esp. an apparatus used to condense vapor. **2.** See **capacitor. 3.** A mirror, lens, or combination of lenses used to gather light and direct it upon an object or through a projection lens.

con·de·scend (kŏn′dĭ-sĕnd′) *intr.v.* **-scend·ed, -scend·ing, -scends 1.** To descend to the level of one considered inferior. **2.** To deal with people in a patronizingly superior manner. [ME *condescenden* < OFr. *condescendre* < LLat. *condescendere* : Lat. *com-*, com- + *dēscendere*, to descend; see DESCEND.] **—con′de·scend′er** *n.*

con·de·scen·dence (kŏn′dĭ-sĕn′dəns) *n.* Condescension.

con·de·scend·ing (kŏn′dĭ-sĕn′dĭng) *adj.* Displaying a patronizingly superior attitude. **—con′de·scend′ing·ly** *adv.*

con·de·scen·sion (kŏn′dĭ-sĕn′shən) *n.* **1.** The act of conde-

scending. **2.** Condescending behavior or attitude. [LLat. *condēscēnsiō*, *condēscēnsiōn-* < *condēscēnsus*, p. part. of *condēscendere*, to condescend. See CONDESCEND.]

con·dign (kən-dīn′) *adj.* Deserved; adequate. [ME *condigne* < OFr. < Lat. *condignus* : *com-*, com- + *dignus*, worthy.] **—con·dign′ly** *adv.*

con·di·ment (kŏn′də-mənt) *n.* A substance, such as a relish, vinegar, or spice, used to flavor or complement food. [ME < OFr. < Lat. *condīmentum* < *condīre*, to season. See **dhē-** in App.] **—con′di·men′tal** (-mĕn′tl) *adj.*

con·di·tion (kən-dĭsh′ən) *n.* **1.** A mode or state of being. **2a.** A state of health. **b.** A state of readiness or physical fitness. **3.** A disease or physical ailment: *a heart condition.* **4.** Social position; rank. **5.** One that is indispensable to the appearance or occurrence of another; prerequisite. **6.** One that restricts or modifies another; a qualification. **7. conditions** Existing circumstances. **8.** *Grammar* The dependent clause of a conditional sentence; protasis. **9.** *Logic* A proposition on which another proposition depends; the antecedent of a conditional proposition. **10.** *Law* **a.** A provision making the effect of a legal instrument contingent on the occurrence of an uncertain future event. **b.** The event itself. **11.** An unsatisfactory grade given to a student, serving notice that deficiencies can be made up by the completion of additional work. **12.** *Obsolete* Disposition; temperament. ❖ *tr.v.* **-tioned, -tion·ing, -tions 1.** To make dependent on a condition or conditions. **2.** To stipulate as a condition. **3.** To render fit for work or use. **4.** To accustom (oneself or another) to; adapt. **5.** To air-condition. **6.** To give the grade of condition to. **7.** *Psychology* To cause an organism to respond in a specific manner to a conditioned stimulus in the absence of an unconditioned stimulus. **8.** To replace moisture or oils in (hair, for example) by use of a therapeutic product. [ME *condicioun* < OFr. *condicion* < LLat. *conditiō*, *conditiōn-*, alteration of Lat. *condiciō* < *condīcere*, to agree : *com-*, com- + *dīcere*, to talk; see **deik-** in App.]

con·di·tion·al (kən-dĭsh′ə-nəl) *adj.* **1.** Imposing, depending on, or containing a condition. **2.** *Grammar* Stating, containing, or implying a condition. **3.** *Psychology* Brought about by conditioning. ❖ *n. Grammar* A mood, tense, clause, word, or morpheme expressing a condition. **—con·di′tion·al′i·ty** (-dĭsh′ə-năl′ĭ-tē) *n.* **—con·di′tion·al·ly** *adv.*

conditional probability *n.* The probability that an event will occur, given that one or more other events have occurred.

con·di·tioned (kən-dĭsh′ənd) *adj.* **1.** Subject to or dependent on a condition or conditions. **2.** Physically fit. **3.** Prepared for a specific action or process. **4.** *Psychology* Exhibiting or trained to exhibit a conditioned response.

conditioned response *n. Psychology* A new or modified response elicited by a stimulus after conditioning.

conditioned stimulus *n. Psychology* A previously neutral stimulus that after repeated association with an unconditioned stimulus elicits the response effected by the unconditioned stimulus itself.

con·di·tion·er (kən-dĭsh′ə-nər) *n.* One that conditions, esp. an additive or application that improves a substance.

con·di·tion·ing (kən-dĭsh′ə-nĭng) *n. Psychology* A process of behavior modification by which a subject comes to associate a desired behavior with a previously unrelated stimulus.

con·do (kŏn′dō′) *n., pl.* **-dos** *Informal* A condominium.

con·dole (kən-dōl′) *intr.v.* **-doled, -dol·ing, -doles** To express sympathy or sorrow. [LLat. *condolēre*, to feel another's pain : Lat. *com-*, com- + Lat. *dolēre*, to grieve.] **—con·do′la·to′ry** (-dō′lə-tôr′ē, -tōr′ē) *adj.* **—con·dol′er** *n.*

con·do·lence (kən-dō′ləns) *n.* **1.** Sympathy with a person who has experienced pain, grief, or misfortune. **2.** An expression or declaration of such sympathy. **—con·do′lent** *adj.*

con·dom (kŏn′dəm, kŭn′-) *n.* **1.** A flexible sheath, usu. made of thin rubber or latex, designed to cover the penis during sexual intercourse for contraceptive purposes or as a means of preventing sexually transmitted diseases. **2.** A similar device, consisting of a loose-fitting polyurethane sheath closed at one end, that is inserted into the vagina before sexual intercourse. [?]

con·do·min·i·um (kŏn′də-mĭn′ē-əm) *n., pl.* **-min·i·ums** also **-min·i·a** (-mĭn′ē-ə) **1a.** A building or complex in which units of property, such as apartments, are owned by individuals and common parts of the property, such as the grounds, are owned jointly by the unit owners. **b.** A unit in such a complex. **2a.** Joint sovereignty, esp. joint rule of territory by two or more nations, or a plan to achieve it. **b.** A politically dependent territory. **—con′do·min′i·al** (-ē-əl) *adj.*

con·done (kən-dōn′) *tr.v.* **-doned, -don·ing, -dones** To overlook, forgive, or disregard (an offense) without protest or censure. See Syns at **forgive.** [Lat. *condōnāre* : *com-*, com- + *dōnāre*, to give (< *dōnum*, gift; see **dō-** in App.).] **—con′do·na′tion** *n.* **—con·don′er** *n.*

con·dor (kŏn′dôr′, -dər) *n.* **1.** Either of two New World vultures, *Vultur gryphus* of the Andes or *Gymnogyps californianus*, having a bare head and neck and dull black plumage containing variable amounts of white. **2.** A gold coin of some South American countries bearing the figure of a condor. [Sp. *cóndor* < Quechua *cuntur*.]

Con·dor·cet (kôn-dôr-sĕ′), Marquis de. Title of Marie Jean An-

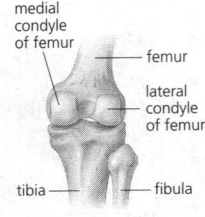

medial condyle of femur

femur

lateral condyle of femur

tibia

fibula

condyle
posterior view of a right knee joint

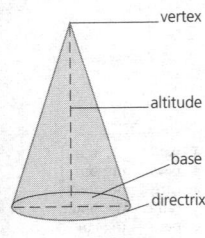

vertex

altitude

base

directrix

cone
right circular cone

toine Nicolas Caritat. 1743–94. French mathematician and philosopher known for his work on the theory of probability.

con•dot•tie•re (kŏn′də-tyâr′ē, -tyâr′ā) *n.*, *pl.* **-tie•ri** (-tyâr′ē) A leader of mercenary soldiers between the 14th and 16th centuries. [Ital. < *condotta*, troop of mercenaries < fem. p. part. of *condurre*, to conduct < Lat. *condūcere*, to lead together. See CONDUCE.]

con•duce (kən-do͞os′, -dyo͞os′) *intr.v.* **-duced, -duc•ing, -duc•es** To contribute or lead to a specific result. [Lat. *condūcere* : *com-*, com- + *dūcere*, to lead; see **deuk-** in App.] **—con•duc′er** *n.* **—con•duc′ing•ly** *adv.*

con•du•cive (kən-do͞o′sĭv, -dyo͞o′-) *adj.* Tending to cause or bring about; contributive. See Syns at **favorable. —con•du′cive•ness** *n.*

con•duct (kən-dŭkt′) *v.* **-duct•ed, -duct•ing, -ducts** *—tr.* **1.** To direct the course of; manage or control. **2.** To lead or guide. See Syns at **accompany. 3.** *Music* To lead (an orchestra, for example). **4.** To serve as a medium for conveying; transmit. **5.** To comport (oneself) in a specified way. *—intr.* **1.** To act as a conductor. **2.** To lead. ❖ *n.* (kŏn′dŭkt′) **1.** The way a person acts, esp. morally or ethically. See Syns at **behavior. 2.** The act of directing or controlling; management. **3.** *Obsolete* A guide; an escort. [ME *conducten* < Lat. *condūcere*, *conduct-*, to lead together. See CONDUCE.] **—con•duct′i•bil′i•ty** *n.* **—con•duct′i•ble** *adj.*

con•duc•tance (kən-dŭk′təns) *n. Symbol* **G** A measure of a material's ability to conduct electric charge; the reciprocal of the resistance.

con•duc•tim•e•try (kŏn′dŭk-tĭm′ĭ-trē) *n.* The scientific measurement of solution conductance. **—con•duc′to•met′ric** *adj.*

con•duc•tion (kən-dŭk′shən) *n.* The transmission or conveying of something through a medium or passage, esp. the transmission of electric charge or heat through a conducting medium without perceptible motion of the medium itself.

con•duc•tive (kən-dŭk′tĭv) *adj.* Exhibiting conductivity.

con•duc•tiv•i•ty (kŏn′dŭk-tĭv′ĭ-tē) *n.*, *pl.* **-ties 1.** The ability or power to conduct or transmit heat, electricity, or sound. **2.** The conductance of a material. **3.** *Physiology* The conductibility of a structure, esp. the ability of a nerve to transmit a wave of excitation.

con•duc•tor (kən-dŭk′tər) *n.* **1.** One who conducts, esp.: **a.** One who is in charge of a railroad train, bus, or streetcar. **b.** *Music* One who directs an orchestra or other such group. **2.** *Physics* A substance or medium that conducts heat, light, sound, or esp. an electric charge. **3.** A lightning rod, as on a house or barn. **—con′duc•to′ri•al** (kŏn′dŭk-tôr′ē-əl, -tōr′-) *adj.* **—con•duc′tor•ship′** *n.*

con•duit (kŏn′do͞o-ĭt, -dĭt) *n.* **1.** A pipe or channel for conveying fluids. **2.** A tube or duct for enclosing electric wires or cable. **3.** A means by which something is transmitted. **4.** *Archaic* A fountain. [ME < OFr. < Med.Lat. *conductus* < Lat., p. part. of *condūcere*, to lead together. See CONDUCE.]

con•du•pli•cate (kŏn-do͞o′plĭ-kĭt, -dyo͞o′-) *adj.* Folded together lengthwise, as certain petals in a bud. [Lat. *conduplicātus*, p. part. of *conduplicāre*, to double : *com-*, com- + *duplicāre*, to double (< *duplex*, *duplic-*, double; see **dwo-** in App.).] **—con′du•pli•ca′tion** (-kā′shən) *n.*

con•dyle (kŏn′dīl′, -dl) *n.* A rounded prominence at the end of a bone, most often for articulation with another bone. [Lat. *condylus*, knuckle < Gk. *kondulos*.] **—con′dy•lar** (-də-lər) *adj.* **—con′dy•loid′** (-dl-oid′) *adj.*

con•dy•lo•ma (kŏn′dl-ō′mə) *n.*, *pl.* **-mas** or **-ma•ta** (-mə-tə) A wartlike growth on the skin or mucous membrane, usu. in the area of the anus or external genitalia. [Gk. *kondulōma* < *kondulos*, knuckle.] **—con′dy•lo′ma•tous** (-mə-təs) *adj.*

cone (kōn) *n.* **1.** *Mathematics* **a.** The surface generated by a straight line, the generator, passing through a fixed point, the vertex, and moving along a fixed curve, the directrix. **b.** A right circular cone. **2a.** The solid formed by a cone, bound by its vertex and a plane section taken anywhere above or below the vertex. **b.** Something cone-shaped. **3.** *Botany* **a.** A unisexual reproductive structure of gymnospermous plants, typically consisting of a central axis around which there are scaly, overlapping, spirally arranged sporophylls that develop pollen-bearing sacs or naked ovules or seeds. **b.** A similar structure that produces spores on club mosses, horsetails, and spike mosses. **c.** Any reproductive structure resembling a cone. **4.** *Physiology* One of the photoreceptors in the retina of the eye that is responsible for daylight and color vision. **5.** Any of various gastropod mollusks of the family Conidae of tropical and subtropical seas, having a conical shell and a poisonous, sometimes fatal sting. ❖ *tr.v.* **coned, con•ing, cones** To shape (something) like a cone or a segment of one. [Fr. *cône* and ME *cone*, angle of a quadrant, both < Lat. *cōnus* < Gk. *kōnos*.]

cone•flow•er (kōn′flou′ər) *n.* Any of various North American plants of the genera *Rudbeckia*, *Ratibida*, and *Echinacea* in the composite family, having disk flowers on a cone-shaped central receptacle surrounded by colorful ray flowers.

cone•nose (kōn′nōz′) *n.* Any of various bloodsucking hemipterous insects of the family Reduviidae, esp. *Triatoma sanguisuga*, having sucking mouthparts and a painful toxic bite.

Con•es•to•ga (kŏn′ĭ-stō′gə) *n.*, *pl.* **Conestoga** or **-gas** See **Susquehannock** 1.

Conestoga wagon *n.* A heavy covered wagon with broad wheels, used esp. by American pioneers for westward travel. [After *Conestoga*, a village of SE Pennsylvania.]

co•ney[1] also **co•ny** (kō′nē, kŭn′ē) *n.*, *pl.* **-neys** also **-nies 1.** A rabbit, esp. the European rabbit *(Oryctolagus cuniculus)*. **2.** The fur of a rabbit. **3.** See **pika. 4.** See **hyrax. 5a.** A grouper *(Epinephelus fulvus)* of the tropical Atlantic Ocean having dark brown or sharply bicolored skin and a few blue and black spots. **b.** *Chiefly Florida Keys & West Indies* The red hind. **6.** *Archaic* A dupe; a simpleton. [ME *coni* < OFr. *conis*, pl. of *conil* < Lat. *cunīculus*; poss. akin to *cunnus*, *cunus*, female pudenda.]

co•ney[2] (kō′nē) *n. Informal* A Coney Island.

Co•ney Island[1] (kō′nē) A resort district of Brooklyn NY on the Atlantic Ocean, known for its amusement park.

Co•ney Island[2] (kō′nē) *n. Informal* A hot dog with condiments, esp. meat sauce and onions.

conf. *abbr.* **1.** *Latin* confer (compare) **2.** confidential

con•fab (kŏn′făb′) *Informal n.* A casual talk; confabulation. ❖ *intr.v.* (kən-făb′, kŏn′făb′) **-fabbed, -fab•bing, -fabs** To engage in casual talk.

con•fab•u•late (kən-făb′yə-lāt′) *intr.v.* **-lat•ed, -lat•ing, -lates 1.** To talk casually; chat. **2.** *Psychology* To fill in gaps in one's memory with fabrications that one believes to be facts. [Lat. *cōnfābulārī*, *cōnfābulāt-* : *com-*, com- + *fābulārī*, to talk (< *fābula*, conversation; see FABLE).] **—con•fab′u•la′tion** *n.* **—con•fab′u•la′tor** *n.* **—con•fab′u•la•to′ry** (-lə-tôr′ē, -tōr′ē) *adj.*

con•fect (kən-fĕkt′) *tr.v.* **-fect•ed, -fect•ing, -fects 1.** To make into a confection or preserve. **2.** To put together by combining materials. ❖ *n.* (kŏn′fĕkt′) A sweet confection. [ME *confecten*, to prepare < Lat. *cōnficere*, *cōnfect-* : *com-*, intensive pref.; see COM– + *facere*, to make; see **dhē-** in App.]

con•fec•tion (kən-fĕk′shən) *n.* **1.** The act or process of confecting or the result of it. **2.** A sweet preparation, such as candy. **3.** A sweetened medicinal compound; an electuary. **4.** A piece displaying splendid craft, skill, and work. ❖ *tr.v.* **-tioned, -tion•ing, -tions** To make into a confection.

con•fec•tion•ar•y (kən-fĕk′shə-nĕr′ē) *n.*, *pl.* **-ies 1.** A confectioner's shop. **2.** Sweet preparations; confections. **3.** *Obsolete* A confectioner. **—con•fec′tion•ar′y** *adj.*

con•fec•tion•er (kən-fĕk′shə-nər) *n.* One that makes or sells confections.

con•fec•tion•ers' sugar (kən-fĕk′shə-nərz) *n.* Finely pulverized sugar with cornstarch added.

con•fec•tion•er•y (kən-fĕk′shə-nĕr′ē) *n.*, *pl.* **-ies 1.** Candies and other confections considered as a group. **2.** The skill or occupation of a confectioner. **3.** A confectioner's shop.

confed. *abbr.* confederation

con•fed•er•a•cy (kən-fĕd′ər-ə-sē) *n.*, *pl.* **-cies 1a.** A union of persons, parties, or states; a league. **b.** The persons, parties, or states joined in such a union. **c. Confederacy** The Confederate States of America. **2.** A group of people united for unlawful practices; a conspiracy. [ME *confederacie* < AN < LLat. *cōnfoederātiō*, *cōnfoederātiōn-*, agreement < *cōnfoederātus*, p. part. of *cōnfoederāre*, to unite. See CONFEDERATE.]

con•fed•er•al (kən-fĕd′ər-əl, -fĕd′rəl) *adj.* **1.** Of confederation or a confederation. **2.** Of or involving the activities of two or more nations. **—con•fed′er•al•ist** *n.*

con•fed•er•ate (kən-fĕd′ər-ĭt) *n.* **1.** A member of a confederacy; an ally. **2.** One who assists in a plot; an accomplice. See Syns at **partner. 3. Confederate** A supporter of the Confederate States of America. ❖ *adj.* **1.** United in a confederacy; allied. **2. Confederate** Of or having to do with the American Confederacy. [< ME *confederat*, allied < LLat. *cōnfoederātus*, p. part. of *cōnfoederāre*, to unite : Lat. *com-*, com- + Lat. *foederāre*, to unite (< *foedus*, *foeder-*, league; see **bheidh-** in App.).] **—con•fed′er•ate′** (-ə-rāt′) *v.* **—con•fed′er•a′tive** *adj.*

Confederate States of America A republic composed of the 11 Southern states that seceded from the United States in 1860 and 1861; dissolved in 1865 after being defeated in the American Civil War.

con•fed•er•a•tion (kən-fĕd′ə-rā′shən) *n.* **1a.** The act of forming into or becoming part of a confederacy. **b.** The state of being confederated. **2.** A group of confederates, esp. of states or nations, united for a common purpose; a league. **3. Confederation** The federal union of the Canadian provinces and territories. **—con•fed′er•a′tion•ism** *n.* **—con•fed′er•a′tion•ist** *n.*

con•fer (kən-fûr′) *v.* **-ferred, -fer•ring, -fers** *—tr.* **1.** To bestow (an honor, for example). **2.** To invest with (a characteristic, for example). *—intr.* To meet in order to deliberate together or compare views; consult. [Lat. *cōnferre* : *com-*, com- + *ferre*, to bring; see **bher-**[1] in App.] **—con•fer′ment, con•fer′ral** *n.* **—con•fer′ra•ble** *adj.* **—con•fer′rer** *n.*

con•fer•ee also **con•fer•ree** (kŏn′fə-rē′) *n.* **1.** A participant in a conference. **2.** One upon whom something is conferred.

con•fer•ence (kŏn′fər-əns, -frəns) *n.* **1a.** A meeting for consultation or discussion. **b.** An exchange of views. **c.** A meeting of committees to settle differences between two legislative bodies. **2.** An assembly of clerical or of clerical and lay members from a particular district in Protestant churches. **3.** *Sports* An association of teams. **4.** The act of conferring, as of an academic degree. [Med.Lat. *cōnferentia* < Lat. *cōnferēns*, *cōnferent-*, pr. part. of *cōn-*

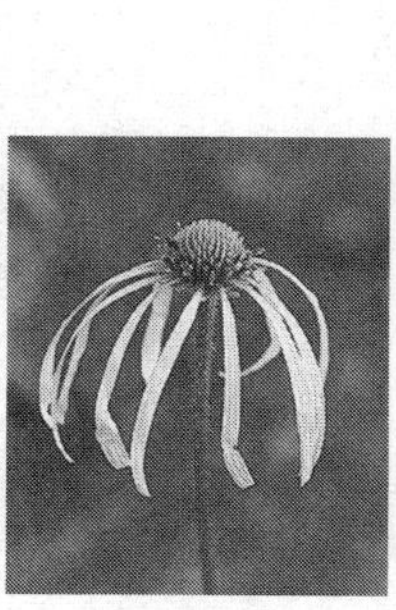

coneflower

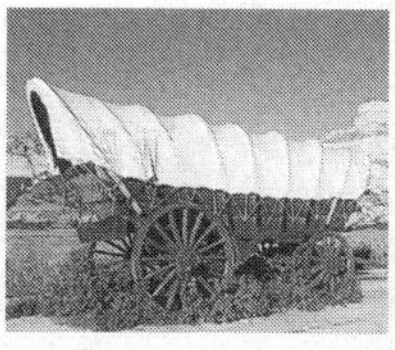

Conestoga wagon at the Oregon Trail Museum, Scotts Bluff National Monument, Nebraska

ă	pat	oi	boy
ā	pay	ou	out
âr	care	o͝o	took
ä	father	o͞o	boot
ĕ	pet	ŭ	cut
ē	be	ûr	urge
ĭ	pit	th	thin
ī	pie	*th*	this
îr	pier	hw	which
ŏ	pot	zh	vision
ō	toe	ə	about, item
ô	paw		

Stress marks:
′ (primary);
′ (secondary), as in
lexicon (lĕk′sĭ-kŏn′)

ferre, to bring together. See CONFER.] —con′fer•en′tial (-fə-rĕn′shəl) adj.

conference call n. A telephone call in which three or more people participate by means of a central switching unit.

con•fess (kən-fĕs′) v. **-fessed, -fess•ing, -fess•es** —tr. **1.** To disclose (something damaging or inconvenient to oneself); admit. **2.** To acknowledge belief or faith in. **3a.** To make known (one's sins), as to a priest. **b.** To hear the confession of (a penitent). —intr. **1.** To admit or acknowledge something damaging or inconvenient to oneself. **2a.** To disclose one's sins, as to a priest. **b.** To listen to a confession. [ME confessen < OFr. confesser < VLat. *cŏnfessāre < Lat. cŏnfitērī, cŏnfess- : com-, com- + fatērī, to admit; see bhā- in App.] —con•fess′a•ble adj. —con•fess′ed•ly (-ĭd-lē) adv.

con•fes•sion (kən-fĕsh′ən) n. **1.** The act or process of confessing. **2.** Something confessed, esp. disclosure of one's sins to a priest. **3.** A statement acknowledging guilt, made by one accused or charged with an offense. **4.** An avowal of belief in a particular faith; a creed. **5.** A church or group of worshipers adhering to a specific creed.

con•fes•sion•al (kən-fĕsh′ə-nəl) adj. Of, relating to, or resembling confession. ❖ n. A small enclosed stall in which a priest hears confessions.

con•fes•sor (kən-fĕs′ər) n. **1.** One who confesses. **2.** One who confesses faith in Christianity in the face of persecution but does not suffer martyrdom. **3a.** A priest who hears confession and gives absolution. **b.** A priest who is one's spiritual mentor.

con•fet•ti (kən-fĕt′ē) pl.n. (used with a sing. verb) Small pieces or streamers of colored paper that are scattered around during the course of festive occasions. [Ital., pl. of confetto, candy < Med.Lat. cŏnfectum < neut. of Lat. cŏnfectus, p. part. of cŏnficere, to prepare. See CONFECT.]

con•fi•dant (kŏn′fĭ-dănt′, -dänt′, kŏn′fĭ-dănt′, -dänt′) n. **1.** One to whom secrets or private matters are disclosed. **2.** A character in a drama or fiction, such as a friend, who is used to reveal the thoughts of a main character. [Fr. confident < Ital. confidente < Lat. cŏnfīdēns, cŏnfīdent-, pr. part. of cŏnfīdere, to rely on. See CONFIDE.]

con•fi•dante (kŏn′fĭ-dănt′, -dänt′, kŏn′fĭ-dănt′, -dänt′) n. **1.** A woman to whom secrets or private matters are disclosed. **2.** A woman character in a drama or fiction, such as a friend, who is used to reveal the thoughts of a main character. [Fr. confidente, fem. of confident, confidant. See CONFIDANT.]

con•fide (kən-fīd′) v. **-fid•ed, -fid•ing, -fides** —tr. **1.** To tell (something) in confidence; entrust. **2.** To put into another's care; entrust. —intr. To disclose private matters in confidence. [ME, to rely on < OFr. confider < Lat. cŏnfīdere : com-, intensive pref.; see COM- + fīdere, to trust; see bheidh- in App.] —con•fid′er n.

con•fi•dence (kŏn′fĭ-dəns) n. **1.** Trust or faith in a person or thing. **2.** A trusting relationship. **3a.** That which is confided; a secret. **b.** A feeling of assurance that a confidant will keep a secret. **4.** A feeling of assurance, esp. of self-assurance. **5.** The state or quality of being certain. ❖ adj. Of, relating to, or involving a swindle or fraud.

confidence game n. A swindle in which the victim is defrauded after his or her confidence has been won.

confidence interval n. A statistical range with a specified probability that a given parameter lies within the range.

confidence man n. A man who swindles his victims by using a confidence game.

con•fi•dent (kŏn′fĭ-dənt) adj. **1.** Marked by assurance, as of success. **2.** Marked by confidence in oneself; self-assured. **3.** Very bold; presumptuous. **4.** Obsolete Confiding; trustful. [Lat. cŏnfīdēns, cŏnfīdent-, pr. part. of cŏnfīdere, to rely on. See CONFIDE.] —con′fi•dent•ly adv.

con•fi•den•tial (kŏn′fĭ-dĕn′shəl) adj. **1.** Done or communicated in confidence; secret. **2.** Entrusted with the confidence of another. **3.** Indicating confidence or intimacy. **4.** Containing secret information, the unauthorized disclosure of which poses a threat to national security. —con′fi•den′ti•al′i•ty (-shē-ăl′ĭ-tē), con′fi•den′tial•ness n. —con′fi•den′tial•ly adv.

con•fid•ing (kən-fī′dĭng) adj. Having a tendency to confide; trusting. —con•fid′ing•ly adv. —con•fid′ing•ness n.

con•fig•u•ra•tion (kən-fĭg′yə-rā′shən) n. **1a.** Arrangement of parts or elements. **b.** The form, as of a figure, determined by the arrangement of its parts or elements. **2.** Psychology Gestalt. **3.** Chemistry The structural arrangement of atoms in a compound or molecule. **4.** Computer Science **a.** The way in which a system is set up or a network is connected. **b.** The set of components that make up a computer system. —con•fig′u•ra′tion•al•ly adv. —con•fig′u•ra′tive, con•fig′u•ra′tion•al adj.

con•fig•ure (kən-fĭg′yər) tr.v. **-ured, -ur•ing, -ures** To design, arrange, set up, or shape with a view to specific applications or uses. [Ult. < Lat. cŏnfigūrāre : com-, com- + figūrāre, to form (< figūra, shape; see dheigh- in App.].

con•fine (kən-fīn′) v. **-fined, -fin•ing, -fines** —tr. **1.** To keep within bounds; restrict. **2.** To shut up or keep in, esp. to imprison. **3.** To restrict in movement. —intr. Archaic To border. ❖ n. (kŏn′fīn′) **1. confines a.** The limits of a space or area; the borders. **b.** Restraining elements: the confines of politics. **c.** Purview; scope. **2a.** Archaic A restriction. **b.** Obsolete A prison. [Fr. confiner

< OFr. < confins, boundaries, ult. < Lat. cŏnfīne < neut. of cŏnfīnis, adjoining : com-, com- + fīnis, border.] —con•fin′a•ble, con•fine′a•ble adj. —con•fin′er n.

con•fine•ment (kən-fīn′mənt) n. **1.** The act of confining or the state of being confined. **2.** Lying-in.

con•firm (kən-fûrm′) tr.v. **-firmed, -firm•ing, -firms 1.** To support or establish the certainty or validity of; verify. **2.** To make firmer; strengthen. **3.** To make valid or binding by a formal or legal act; ratify. **4.** To administer the religious rite of confirmation to. [ME confirmen < OFr. confermer < Lat. cŏnfirmāre : com-, com- + firmāre, to strengthen (< firmus, strong).] —con•firm′a•bil′i•ty n. —con•firm′a•ble adj. —con•firm′a•to′ry (-fûr′mə-tôr′ē, -tōr′ē) adj. —con•firm′er n.

con•fir•ma•tion (kŏn′fər-mā′shən) n. **1a.** The act of confirming. **b.** Something that confirms; verification. **2a.** A Christian rite admitting a baptized person to full membership in a church. **b.** A Jewish ceremony marking completion of a young person's religious training.

con•firmed (kən-fûrmd′) adj. **1.** Being firmly settled in habit; inveterate. **2.** Having been ratified; verified. **3.** Having received the rite of confirmation. —con•firm′ed•ly (-fûr′mĭd-lē) adv.

con•fis•ca•ble (kən-fĭs′kə-bəl) adj. Subject to confiscation.

con•fis•cate (kŏn′fĭ-skāt′) tr.v. **-cat•ed, -cat•ing, -cates 1.** To seize (private property) for the public treasury. **2.** To seize by or as if by authority. ❖ adj. (kŏn′fĭ-skāt′, kən-fĭs′kāt) **1.** Seized by a government; appropriated. **2.** Having lost property through confiscation. [Lat. cŏnfiscāre, cŏnfiscāt- : com-, com- + fiscus, treasury.] —con′fis•ca′tion n. —con′fis•ca′tor n. —con•fis′ca•to′ry (kən-fĭs′kə-tôr′ē, -tōr′ē) adj.

con•fit (kōn-fē′, kôn-) n. **1.** Meat that has been salted, then cooked and preserved in its own fat. **2.** A condiment made by cooking seasoned fruit or vegetables to a jamlike consistency. [ME confyt < OFr. confit < Med.Lat. cŏnfectum < p. part. of cŏnficere, to prepare. See CONFECT.]

Con•fi•te•or (kən-fē′tē-ər, -ôr′) n. A prayer in which sins are confessed. [Lat. cŏnfiteor, I confess (its first word), first pers. sing. pr. t. of cŏnfitērī, to acknowledge. See CONFESS.]

con•fi•ture (kŏn′fĭ-chŏŏr′) n. A confection, preserve, or jam. [Fr. < OFr. < confit, confection. See COMFIT.]

con•fla•grant (kən-flā′grənt) adj. Burning intensely; blazing. [Lat. cŏnflagrāns, cŏnflagrant-, pr. part. of cŏnflagrāre, to burn up : com-, com- + flagrāre, to burn.]

con•fla•gra•tion (kŏn′flə-grā′shən) n. A large destructive fire. [Lat. cŏnflagrātiō, cŏnflagrātiōn- < cŏnflagrātus, p. part. of cŏnflagrāre, to burn up. See CONFLAGRANT.]

con•flate (kən-flāt′) tr.v. **-flat•ed, -flat•ing, -flates 1.** To bring together; meld or fuse. **2.** To combine (two variant texts, for example) into one whole. [Lat. cŏnflāre, cŏnflāt- : com-, com- + flāre, to blow.] —con•fla′tion n.

con•flict (kŏn′flĭkt′) n. **1.** A state of open, often prolonged fighting; a battle or war. **2.** A state of disharmony between incompatible or antithetical persons, ideas, or interests; a clash. **3.** Psychology A psychic struggle resulting from the opposition or simultaneous functioning of mutually exclusive impulses, desires, or tendencies. **4.** Opposition between characters or forces in a work of drama or fiction, esp. opposition affecting the plot. ❖ intr.v. (kən-flĭkt′) **-flict•ed, -flict•ing, -flicts 1.** To be in or come into opposition; differ. **2.** Archaic To engage in warfare. [ME < Lat. cŏnflīctus, collision < p. part. of cŏnflīgere, to strike together : com-, com- + flīgere, to strike.] —con•flic′tion n. —con•flic′tive adj. —con•flic′tu•al (kən-flĭk′chōō-əl) adj.

> **SYNONYMS** conflict, contest, combat, fight These nouns denote struggle between opposing forces for victory or supremacy. Conflict applies both to open fighting between hostile groups and to a struggle between antithetical forces: "The kind of victory MacArthur had in mind . . . victory by expanding the conflict to all of China—would have been the wrong kind of victory" (Harry S. Truman). Contest can refer either to friendly competition or to a hostile struggle to achieve an objective: a spelling contest; the gubernatorial contest. Combat commonly implies an encounter between two armed persons or groups: "Alexander had appeared to him, armed for combat" (Connop Thirlwall). Fight usually refers to a clash involving individual adversaries: A fight was scheduled between the boxing champion and the challenger.

con•flict•ed (kən-flĭk′tĭd) adj. Usage Problem Made uneasy by conflicting impulses.

> **USAGE NOTE** The adjective conflicted is most often associated with the jargon of pop psychology. Almost the entire Usage Panel (92 percent) rejects its use in the sentence Caught between loyalty to old employees and a recognition of the need to cut costs, many managers are conflicted about the reorganization plan.

conflict of interest n., pl. **conflicts of interest** A conflict between a person's private interests and public obligations.

con•flu•ence (kŏn′flōō-əns) n. **1a.** A flowing together of two or more streams. **b.** The point of juncture of such streams. **c.** The combined stream formed by this juncture. **2.** A gathering, flowing, or meeting together at one juncture or point.

con•flu•ent (kŏn′flōō-ənt) adj. **1.** Flowing together; blended into one. **2.** Pathology Merging or running together so as to form a mass, as sores in a rash. ❖ *n.* **1.** One of two or more confluent streams. **2.** A tributary. [ME < Lat. *cônfluêns, confluent-*, pr. part. of *cônfluere*, to flow together : *com-*, com- + *fluere*, to flow.]

con·flux (kŏn′flŭks′) *n.* A confluence. [< Lat. *cônflūxus*, p. part. of *cônfluere*, to flow together. See CONFLUENT.]

con·fo·cal (kŏn-fō′kəl) *adj.* Having the same focus or foci. Used of a lens.

con·form (kən-fôrm′) *v.* **-formed, -form·ing, -forms** —*intr.* **1.** To correspond in form or character; be similar. **2.** To act or be in accord or agreement; comply. **3.** To act in accordance with current customs or modes. See Syns at **adapt.** —*tr.* To bring into agreement or correspondence; make similar. [Ult. < Lat. *cônfôrmāre*, to shape after : *com-*, com- + *fôrmāre*, to shape (< *fôrma*, shape; see FORM).] —**con·form′er** *n.*

con·form·a·ble (kən-fôr′mə-bəl) *adj.* **1.** Corresponding; similar. **2.** Quick to comply; submissive. **3.** *Geology* Of, relating to, or being strata that are parallel to each other without interruption. —**con·form′a·bil′i·ty, con·form′a·ble·ness** *n.* —**con·form′a·bly** *adv.*

con·for·mal (kən-fôr′məl) *adj.* **1.** *Mathematics* Of, relating to, or being a mapping in which all angles between intersecting curves remain unchanged. **2.** Of or relating to a map projection in which small areas are rendered with true shape. [LLat. *cônfôr-mālis*, similar : Lat. *com-*, com- + Lat. *fôrma*, shape; see FORM.]

con·for·mance (kən-fôr′məns) *n.* Conformity.

con·for·ma·tion (kŏn′fər-mā′shən) *n.* **1.** The act of conforming or the state of being conformed. **2.** The structure or outline of an item or entity, determined by the arrangement of its parts. **3.** A symmetrical arrangement of the parts of a thing. **4.** A spatial arrangement of atoms in a molecule brought about by free rotation of the atoms about a single chemical bond. —**con′for·ma′tion·al** *adj.* —**con′for·ma′tion·al·ly** *adv.*

con·form·ist (kən-fôr′mĭst) *n.* A person who uncritically or habitually conforms to the customs, rules, or styles of a group. ❖ *adj.* Marked by conformity or convention. —**con·form′ism** *n.*

con·form·i·ty (kən-fôr′mĭ-tē) *n., pl.* **-ties 1.** Similarity in form or character; agreement. **2.** Action or behavior in correspondence with current customs, rules, or styles. **3.** The relationship between adjacent rock strata representing a continuous period of time.

con·found (kən-found′, kŏn-) *tr.v.* **-found·ed, -found·ing, -founds 1.** To cause to become confused or perplexed. **2.** To fail to distinguish; mix up. **3.** To make (something bad) worse. **4.** To cause to be ashamed; abash. **5.** To damn. **6a.** To frustrate. **b.** *Archaic* To bring to ruination. [ME *confounden* < AN *confundre* < Lat. *cônfundere*, to mix together, confuse : *com-*, com- + *fundere*, to pour; see **gheu-** in App.] —**con·found′er** *n.*

con·found·ed (kən-foun′dĭd, kŏn-) *adj.* **1.** Confused; befuddled. **2.** Used as an intensive: *a confounded fool.* —**con·found′ed·ly** *adv.* —**con·found′ed·ness** *n.*

con·fra·ter·ni·ty (kŏn′frə-tûr′nĭ-tē) *n., pl.* **-ties** An association of persons united in a common purpose or profession. [ME *confraternite* < OFr. < Med.Lat. *cônfrāternitās* < *cônfrāter*, colleague. See CONFRERE.]

con·frere (kŏn′frâr′) *n.* A fellow member of a fraternity or profession; a colleague. [ME < OFr. < Med.Lat. *cônfrāter* : Lat. *com-*, com- + *frāter*, brother; see **bhrāter-** in App.]

con·front (kən-frŭnt′) *v.* **-front·ed, -front·ing, -fronts** —*tr.* **1.** To come face to face with, esp. with defiance or hostility: *confronted her accuser in a court of law.* **2.** To bring face to face with: *was confronted with the truth.* **3.** To come up against; encounter: *confronted danger.* —*intr.* To engage in confrontation. [Fr. *confronter* < OFr., to adjoin < Med.Lat. *cônfrontāre* : Lat. *com-*, com- + Lat. *frôns, front-*, front.] —**con·fron·ta·tive** *adj.* —**con·front′er** *n.* —**con·front′ment** *n.*

con·fron·ta·tion (kŏn′frŭn-tā′shən) *n.* **1.** The act of confronting or the state of being confronted, esp. a meeting face to face. **2a.** A conflict involving armed forces: *a nuclear confrontation.* **b.** Discord or a clash of opinions and ideas: *ideological confrontation.* **3.** A focused comparison. —**con′fron·ta′tion·al** *adj.* —**con′fron·ta′tion·ist** *n.*

Con·fu·cius (kən-fyōō′shəs) Orig. Kong Fuzi. c. 551–479 B.C. Chinese philosopher whose *Analects* contain a collection of his sayings. —**Con·fu′cian** (-shən) *adj. & n.* —**Con·fu′cian·ism** *n.* —**Con·fu′cian·ist** *n.*

con·fuse (kən-fyōōz′) *v.* **-fused, -fus·ing, -fus·es** —*tr.* **1a.** To cause to be unable to think with clarity or act with intelligence or understanding. **b.** To cause to feel embarrassment. **2a.** To fail to differentiate from another: *confused flattery with admiration.* **b.** To make opaque; blur. **c.** To assemble without order or sense; jumble. **3.** *Archaic* To bring to ruination. —*intr.* To make something unclear or incomprehensible. [ME *confusen* < OFr. *confus,* perplexed < Lat. *cônfūsus,* p. part. of *cônfundere,* to mix together. See CONFOUND.] —**con·fus′a·ble** *adj.* —**con·fus′ing·ly** *adv.*

SYNONYMS confuse, addle, befuddle, discombobulate, fuddle, muddle, throw These verbs mean to cause to be unclear in mind or intent: *heavy traffic that confused the driver; problems that addle my brain; a question that befuddled even the professor; was discombobulated by the possibilities; a plot line that fuddled my comprehension; a student who was muddled by facts and figures; behavior that really threw me.*

con·fused (kən-fyōōzd′) *adj.* **1.** Being unable to think with clarity or act with understanding and intelligence. **2a.** Lacking logical order or sense. **b.** Chaotic; jumbled. —**con·fus′ed·ly** (-fyōō′zĭd-lē) *adv.* —**con·fus′ed·ness** *n.*

con·fu·sion (kən-fyōō′zhən) *n.* **1a.** The act of confusing or the state of being confused. **b.** An instance of being confused. **2.** *Psychology* Impaired orientation with respect to time, place, or person; a disturbed mental state. —**con·fu′sion·al** *adj.*

con·fu·ta·tion (kŏn′fyōō-tā′shən) *n.* **1.** The act of confuting. **2.** Something that confutes.

con·fute (kən-fyōōt′) *tr.v.* **-fut·ed, -fut·ing, -futes 1.** To prove to be wrong or in error; refute decisively. **2.** *Obsolete* To confound. [Lat. *cônfūtāre.*] —**con·fut′a·ble, con·fu′ta·tive** (kən-fyōō′tə-tĭv) *adj.* —**con·fut′er** *n.*

cong. *abbr. Pharmacology* congius (gallon)

Cong. *abbr.* **1.** Congregational **2.** Congress

con·ga (kŏng′gə) *n.* **1.** A dance in which the dancers form a long winding line. **2.** Music for this dance. **3.** A conga drum. ❖ *intr.v.* **-gaed, -ga·ing, -gas** To perform this dance. [Am.Sp. *(danza) Conga,* Conga (dance) < Sp. *Congo,* of the Congo < Kongo *-kongo,* Kongo language and people.]

conga drum *n.* A tall, usu. tapering single-headed drum typically played by beating with the hands.

con game *n. Slang* A confidence game.

con·gé (kŏn′zhā′, -jā′, kôn-zhā′) also **con·gee** (kŏn′jē) *n.* **1.** Formal or authoritative permission to depart. **2.** An abrupt dismissal. **3.** A leave-taking. **4.** A formal bow. **5.** *Architecture* A concave molding. [ME *conge* and Fr. *congé,* both < OFr. *congie* < Lat. *commeātus* < p. part. of *commeāre,* to come and go : *com-*, com- + *meāre,* to go.]

con·geal (kən-jēl′) *v.* **-gealed, -geal·ing, -geals** —*intr.* **1.** To solidify by or as if by freezing. **2.** To coagulate; jell. —*tr.* To cause to congeal. [ME *congelen* < OFr. *congeler* < Lat. *congelāre* : *com-*, com- + *gelāre,* to freeze; see **gel-** in App.] —**con·geal′a·ble** *adj.* —**con·geal′er** *n.* —**con·geal′ment** *n.*

con·gealed salad (kən-jēld′) *n. Chiefly Southern US* A molded salad made of flavored gelatin, chopped fruits or vegetables, and sometimes other ingredients.

con·ge·la·tion (kŏn′jə-lā′shən) *n.* The process of congealing or the state of being congealed.

con·ge·ner (kŏn′jə-nər) *n.* **1.** A member of the same kind, class, or group. **2.** An organism belonging to the same taxonomic genus as another organism. [< Lat., of the same race : *com-*, com- + *genus, gener-,* race; see **genə-** in App.] —**con′ge·ner′ic** (-nĕr′ĭk), **con·gen′er·ous** (kən-jĕn′ər-əs, kŏn-) *adj.*

con·gen·ial (kən-jēn′yəl) *adj.* **1.** Having the same tastes, habits, or temperament; sympathetic. **2.** Of a pleasant disposition; friendly: *a congenial host.* **3.** Suited to one's needs or nature; agreeable. [Prob. < CON- + Lat. *genius,* the personification of one's natural inclinations; see GENIUS.] —**con·ge′ni·al′i·ty** (-jē′nē-ăl′ĭ-tē), **con·gen′ial·ness** *n.* —**con·gen′ial·ly** *adv.*

con·gen·i·tal (kən-jĕn′ĭ-tl) *adj.* **1.** Existing at or before birth, as a defect or medical condition. **2.** Being or having an essential characteristic as if by nature; inherent or inveterate. [< Lat. *congenitus : com-*, com- + *genitus,* born, p. part. of *gignere,* to bear; see **genə-** in App.] —**con·gen′i·tal·ly** *adv.*

congenital anomaly *n.* See birth defect.

con·ger (kŏng′gər) *n.* Any of various large scaleless marine eels of the family Congridae, esp. *Conger oceanicus,* native to Atlantic waters. [ME *congre* < OFr., prob. < LLat. *congrus* < Lat. *conger* < Gk. *gongros.*]

con·ge·ries (kən-jîr′ēz′, kŏn′jə-rēz′) *n.* (used with a sing. verb) A collection; an aggregation. [Lat. *congeriēs* < *congerere,* to heap up. See CONGEST.]

con·gest (kən-jĕst′) *v.* **-gest·ed, -gest·ing, -gests** —*tr.* **1.** To overfill or overcrowd. **2.** *Pathology* To cause the accumulation of excessive blood or fluid in (a vessel or organ). —*intr.* To become congested. [Lat. *congerere, congest-,* to heap up, crowd together : *com-*, com- + *gerere,* to carry.] —**con·ges′tion** *n.* —**con·ges′tive** *adj.*

congestive heart failure *n.* A condition marked by weakness, edema, and shortness of breath that is caused by inadequate blood circulation in the peripheral tissues and the lungs.

con·gi·us (kŏn′jē-əs) *n., pl.* **-gi·i** (-jē-ī′) **1.** *Pharmacology* A gallon. **2.** An ancient Roman measure for liquids, equal to about seven eighths of a US gallon (3.3 liters). [ME, a liquid measure < Lat. < Gk. *konkhion,* dim. of *konkhē, konkhos,* shellful.]

con·glo·bate (kŏn-glō′bāt′, kŏng′glō-) *tr.v.* **-bat·ed, -bat·ing, -bates** To form into a globe or ball. [Lat. *conglobāre, conglobāt- : com-*, com- + *globus,* ball.] —**con·glo′bate** *adj.* —**con′glo·ba′tion** *n.*

con·globe (kən-glōb′) *tr.v.* **-globed, -glob·ing, -globes** To conglobate.

con·glom·er·ate (kən-glŏm′ə-rāt′) *intr. & tr.v.* **-at·ed, -at·ing, -ates** To form or cause to form into an adhering or rounded mass. ❖ *n.* (-ər-ĭt) **1.** A corporation made up of a number of different companies that operate in diversified fields. **2.** A collected heterogeneous mass; a cluster: *a conglomerate of colors.* **3.** *Geology* A rock consisting of pebbles and gravel embedded in cement. ❖ *adj.* (-ər-ĭt) **1.** Gathered into a mass; clustered. **2.** *Geology* Made

Confucius

up of loosely cemented heterogeneous material. [Lat. *conglomerāre, conglomerāt-* : *com-*, com- + *glomerāre*, to wind into a ball (< *glomus, glomer-*, ball).] —**con·glom′er·at′ic** (-ə-răt′ĭk), **con·glom′er·it′ic** (-ə-rĭt′ĭk) *adj.* —**con·glom′er·a′tor** *n.*

con·glom·er·a·tion (kən-glŏm′ə-rā′shən) *n.* **1a.** The act or process of conglomerating. **b.** The state of being conglomerated. **2.** An accumulation of miscellaneous things.

con·glu·ti·nate (kən-glo͞ot′n-āt′, kŏn-) *intr. & tr.v.* **-nat·ed, -nat·ing, -nates** To become or cause to become stuck or glued together. [ME *conglutinaten* < Lat. *conglūtināre, conglūtināt-* : *com-*, com- + *glūtināre*, to glue (< *glūten*, glue).] —**con·glu′ti·nate′** *adj.* —**con·glu′ti·na′tion** *n.*

Con·go (kŏng′gō) **1.** Officially **Republic of the Congo.** A country of W-central Africa with a coastline on the Atlantic Ocean; achieved independence from France in 1960. Cap. Brazzaville. Pop. 2,516,000. **2.** Officially **Democratic Republic of the Congo,** formerly **Za·ire** (zī′ĭr, zä-îr′) A country of central Africa astride the equator; a former Belgian colony, achieved independence in 1960. Cap. Kinshasa. Pop. 42,552,000.

Congo eel *n.* An eellike amphibian *(Amphiuma means)* of the southeast United States having two pairs of tiny nonfunctioning legs.

Congo Free State See **Congo** 2.

Con·go·lese (kŏng′gō-lēz′, -lēs′) *adj.* **1.** Of or relating to either the Republic of the Congo or the Democratic Republic of the Congo (formerly Zaire) or to their peoples or languages. **2.** Of or relating to the region surrounding the Congo River or its peoples or languages. [Fr. *congolais* < *Congo*, Congo (prob. on the model of *angolais*, Angolan).] —**Con′go·lese′** *n.*

Congo red *n.* A brownish-red powder, $C_{32}H_{22}N_6Na_2O_6S_2$, used as a dye, indicator, and biological stain.

Congo River Formerly also **Zaire River.** A river of central Africa flowing c. 4,666 km (2,900 mi) through the Democratic Republic of the Congo (formerly Zaire) to the Atlantic Ocean.

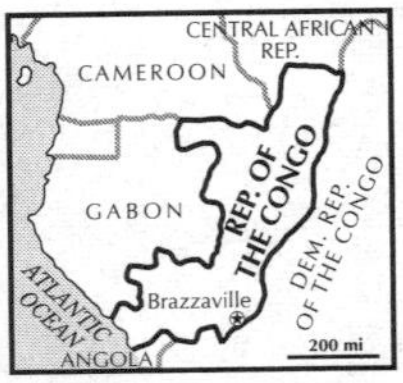

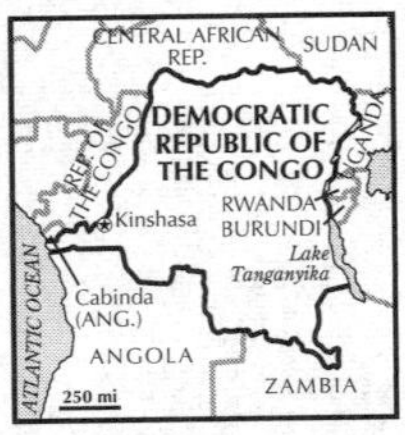

Congo
top: Republic of the Congo
bottom: Democratic Republic of the Congo

Congo snake *n.* See **Congo eel.**

con·gou (kŏng′gō, -go͞o) *n.* A grade of Chinese black tea. [Chin. (Amoy) *kong hu (te)*, elaborately prepared (tea), corresponding to Chin. (Mandarin) *gōngfu (chá)* < *gōngfu*, workmanship. See KUNG FU.]

con·grats (kən-grăts′) *Informal interj.* Congratulations. ❖ *pl.n.* Congratulations: *sent him my congrats.*

con·grat·u·late (kən-grăch′ə-lāt′, -grăj′-, kəng-) *tr.v.* **-lat·ed, -lat·ing, -lates** To express joy or acknowledgment, as for the achievement or good fortune of (another). [Lat. *congrātulārī, congrātulāt-* : *com-*, com- + *grātulārī*, to rejoice (< *grātus*, pleasing).] —**con·grat′u·la′tor** *n.* —**con·grat′u·la·to′ry** (-lə-tôr′ē, -tōr′ē) *adj.*

con·grat·u·la·tion (kən-grăch′ə-lā′shən, -grăj′-, kəng-) *n.* **1.** The act of expressing joy or acknowledgment, as for another's achievement or good fortune. **2.** An expression of such joy or acknowledgment. Often used in the plural. ❖ *interj.* Used to express such joy or acknowledgment.

con·gre·gant (kŏng′grĭ-gənt) *n.* One who congregates, esp. a member of a group of people gathered for religious worship.

con·gre·gate (kŏng′grĭ-gāt′) *tr. & intr.v.* **-gat·ed, -gat·ing, -gates** To bring or come together in a group, crowd, or assembly. ❖ *adj.* (-gĭt) **1.** Gathered; assembled. **2.** Involving a group. [ME *congregaten* < Lat. *congregāre, congregāt-* : *com-*, com- + *gregāre*, to assemble (< *grex, greg-*, herd).] —**con′gre·ga′tive** *adj.* —**con′gre·ga′tive·ness** *n.* —**con′gre·ga′tor** *n.*

con·gre·ga·tion (kŏng′grĭ-gā′shən) *n.* **1.** The act of assembling. **2.** A body of assembled people or things; a gathering. **3a.** A group of people gathered for religious worship. **b.** Those who regularly worship at a specific church or synagogue. **4.** *Roman Catholic Church* **a.** A religious institute in which only simple vows are taken. **b.** A division of the Curia.

con·gre·ga·tion·al (kŏng′grĭ-gā′shə-nəl) *adj.* **1.** Of or relating to a congregation. **2. Congregational** Of or relating to Congregationalism or Congregationalists.

con·gre·ga·tion·al·ism (kŏng′grĭ-gā′shə-nə-lĭz′əm) *n.* **1.** A church government in which each local congregation is self-governing. **2. Congregationalism** The system of government and religious beliefs of a Protestant denomination in which each member church is self-governing. —**con′gre·ga′tion·al·ist** *n.*

con·gress (kŏng′grĭs) *n.* **1.** A formal assembly of representatives to discuss problems. **2.** The national legislative body of a nation, esp. a republic. **3. Congress a.** The national legislative body of the United States, consisting of the Senate and the House of Representatives. **b.** The two-year session of this legislature between elections of the House of Representatives. **4a.** The act of coming together or meeting. **b.** A single meeting, as of a political party. **5.** Sexual intercourse. [ME *congresse*, body of attendants < Lat. *congressus*, meeting < p. part. of *congredī*, to meet : *com-*, com- + *gradī*, to go; see **ghredh-** in App.] —**con·gres′sion·al** (kən-grĕsh′ə-nəl, kəng-) *adj.* —**con·gres′sion·al·ly** *adv.*

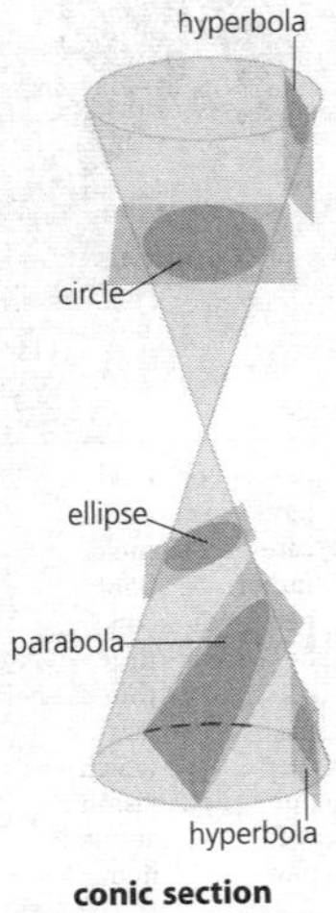

conic section
conic sections created by the intersection of various planes of right circular cones

Congress boot *n.* An ankle-high shoe with elastic material in the sides.

Congressional Medal of Honor *n.* The highest US military decoration, awarded in the name of Congress to members of the armed forces for gallantry and bravery beyond the call of duty.

con·gress·man (kŏng′grĭs-mən) *n.* A man who is a member of the US Congress, esp. of the House of Representatives.

con·gress·per·son (kŏng′grĭs-pûr′sən) *n.* A congressman or congresswoman.

con·gress·wom·an (kŏng′grĭs-wo͝om′ən) *n.* A woman who is a member of the US Congress, esp. of the House of Representatives.

Con·greve (kŏn′grēv′, kŏng′-), **William** 1670–1729. English playwright whose comedies include *The Way of the World* (1700).

con·gru·ence (kŏng′gro͞o-əns, kən-gro͞o′-) *n.* **1.** Agreement, harmony, conformity, or correspondence. **2.** *Mathematics* **a.** The state of being congruent. **b.** A statement that two quantities are congruent. —**con′gru·en·cy** *n.*

con·gru·ent (kŏng′gro͞o-ənt, kən-gro͞o′-) *adj.* **1.** Corresponding; congruous. **2.** *Mathematics* **a.** Coinciding exactly when superimposed. **b.** Of or relating to two numbers that have the same remainder when divided by a third number. [ME < Lat. *congruēns, congruent-*, pr. part. of *congruere*, to agree.] —**con′gru·ent·ly** *adv.*

con·gru·i·ty (kən-gro͞o′ĭ-tē, kŏn-) *n., pl.* **-ties 1.** The quality or fact of being congruous. **2.** The quality or fact of being congruent. **3.** A point of agreement.

con·gru·ous (kŏng′gro͞o-əs) *adj.* **1.** Corresponding in character or kind; appropriate or harmonious. **2.** *Mathematics* Congruent. [< Lat. *congruus* < *congruere*, to agree.] —**con′gru·ous·ly** *adv.* —**con′gru·ous·ness** *n.*

con·ic (kŏn′ĭk) *adj.* Conical. ❖ *n.* A conic section. [NLat. *cōnicus* < Gk. *kōnikos* < *kōnos*, cone.] —**co·nic′i·ty** (kə-nĭs′ĭ-tē) *n.*

con·i·cal (kŏn′ĭ-kəl) *adj.* Of, relating to, or shaped like a cone.

conic projection or **conical projection** *n.* A method of projecting maps of parts of the earth's spherical surface on a surrounding cone, which is then flattened to a plane surface having concentric circles as parallels of latitude and radiating lines from the apex as meridians.

conic section *n.* **1.** A plane curve generated from the intersection of a right circular cone and a plane, including the circle, ellipse, hyperbola, and parabola. **2.** A graph of the general quadratic equation in two variables.

co·nid·i·o·phore (kə-nĭd′ē-ə-fôr′, -fōr′) *n.* A specialized fungal hypha that produces conidia. [CONIDI(UM) + –PHORE.] —**co·nid′i·oph′or·ous** (kə-nĭd′ē-ŏf′ər-əs) *adj.*

co·nid·i·um (kə-nĭd′ē-əm) *n., pl.* **-i·a** (-ē-ə) An asexually produced fungal spore, formed on a conidiophore. [NLat. < Gk. *konis*, dust.] —**co·nid′i·al** (-əl) *adj.*

con·i·fer (kŏn′ə-fər, kō′nə-) *n.* Any of various mostly needle-leaved or scale-leaved, chiefly evergreen, cone-bearing gymnospermous trees or shrubs, such as pines, spruces, and firs. [< NLat. *Cōniferae*, family name < Lat., fem. pl. of *cōnifer*, cone-bearing : *cōnus*, cone (< Gk. *kōnos*) + *-fer*, -fer.] —**co·nif′er·ous** (kō-nĭf′ər-əs, kə-) *adj.*

co·ni·ine (kō′nē-ēn′) also **co·nin** (kō′nĭn) or **co·nine** (-nēn′) *n.* A poisonous colorless liquid alkaloid, $C_5H_{10}NC_3H_7$, found in the poison hemlock. [LLat. *cōnium*, conium; see CONIUM + –INE[2].]

co·ni·um (kō′nē-əm) *n.* The poison hemlock. [LLat. *cōnium* < Gk. *kōneion*, prob. < *kōna*, liquid pitch.]

conj. *abbr.* **1.** conjugation **2.** conjunction **3.** conjunctive

con·jec·tur·al (kən-jĕk′chər-əl) *adj.* **1.** Based on or involving conjecture. **2.** Tending to conjecture. —**con·jec′tur·al·ly** *adv.*

con·jec·ture (kən-jĕk′chər) *n.* **1.** Inference or judgment based on incomplete evidence; guesswork. **2.** A statement, opinion, or conclusion based on guesswork. ❖ *v.* **-tured, -tur·ing, -tures** —*tr.* To infer from inconclusive evidence; guess. —*intr.* To make a conjecture. [ME < OFr. < Lat. *coniectūra* < *coniectus*, p. part. of *conicere*, to infer : *com-*, com- + *iacere*, to throw.] —**con·jec′tur·a·ble** *adj.* —**con·jec′tur·a·bly** *adv.* —**con·jec′tur·er** *n.*

con·join (kən-join′) *tr. & intr.v.* **-joined, -join·ing, -joins** To join or become joined together; unite. [ME *conjoinen* < OFr. *conjoindre, conjoign-* < Lat. *coniungere* : *com-*, com- + *iungere*, to join; see **yeug-** in App.] —**con·join′er** *n.*

con·joint (kən-joint′) *adj.* **1.** Joined together; combined. **2.** Of, consisting of, or involving two or more combined or associated entities; joint. [ME < OFr., p. part. of *conjoindre*, to conjoin. See CONJOIN.] —**con·joint′ly** *adv.*

con·ju·gal (kŏn′jə-gəl) *adj.* Of or relating to marriage or the relationship of spouses. [Lat. *coniugālis* < *coniūnx, coniug-*, spouse < *coniungere*, to join in marriage. See CONJOIN.] —**con′ju·gal′i·ty** (-găl′ĭ-tē) *n.* —**con′ju·gal·ly** *adv.*

con·ju·gant (kŏn′jə-gənt) *n.* Either of a pair of organisms, cells, or gametes undergoing conjugation.

con·ju·gate (kŏn′jə-gāt′) *v.* **-gat·ed, -gat·ing, -gates** —*tr.* **1.** *Grammar* To inflect (a verb) in its forms for distinctions such as number, person, voice, mood, and tense. **2.** To join together. —*intr.* **1.** *Biology* To undergo conjugation. **2.** *Grammar* To be inflected. ❖ *adj.* (-gĭt, -gāt′) **1.** Joined together, esp. in a pair or pairs; coupled. **2.** *Mathematics & Physics* Inversely or oppositely related with respect to one of a group of otherwise identical properties. Used esp. of either or both of a pair of complex numbers differing only in the sign of the imaginary term. **3.** *Chemistry* Relating to an acid and a base that are related by the difference of a proton. **4.** *Linguistics* Derived from a common source, such as the words *foul* and *filth.* ❖ *n.* (-gĭt, -gāt′) *Mathematics & Physics* Any of a set of numbers that satisfy the same irreducible polynomial. [Lat. *coniugāre, coniugāt-,* to join together : *com-,* com- + *iugāre,* to join (< *iugum,* yoke; see **yeug-** in App.).] —**con′ju·gate′ly** *adv.* —**con′ju·ga′tive** *adj.* —**con′ju·ga′tor** *n.*

con·ju·gat·ed protein (kŏn′jə-gā′tĭd) *n.* A compound, such as hemoglobin, made up of a protein molecule and a nonprotein prosthetic group.

con·ju·ga·tion (kŏn′jə-gā′shən) *n.* **1a.** The act of conjugating. **b.** The state of being conjugated. **2.** *Grammar* **a.** The inflection of a particular verb. **b.** A presentation of the complete set of inflections of a verb. **c.** A class of verbs having similar inflected forms. **3.** *Biology* **a.** The temporary union of two bacterial cells during which one cell transfers part or all of its genome to the other. **b.** A process of sexual reproduction in which ciliate protozoans of the same species temporarily couple and exchange genetic material. **c.** A process of sexual reproduction in certain algae and fungi in which temporary or permanent fusion occurs, resulting in the union of the male and female gametes. —**con′ju·ga′tion·al** *adj.* —**con′ju·ga′tion·al·ly** *adv.*

con·junct (kən-jŭngkt′, kŏn′jŭngkt′) *adj.* **1.** Joined together; united. **2.** Acting in association; combined. **3.** *Music* Of or relating to successive tones of the scale, moving step by step. ❖ *n.* (kŏn′jŭngkt′) **1.** One that is in conjunction or association with another. **2.** *Logic* One of the components of a conjunction. [ME < Lat. *coniūnctus,* p. part. of *coniungere,* to join together. See CONJOIN.] —**con·junct′ly** *adv.*

con·junc·tion (kən-jŭngk′shən) *n.* **1a.** The act of joining. **b.** The state of being joined. **2.** A joint or simultaneous occurrence; concurrence. **3.** One resulting from or embodying a union; a combination. **4.** *Grammar* **a.** The part of speech that serves to connect words, phrases, clauses, or sentences. **b.** A word belonging to this part of speech, such as *and* or *because.* **5.** *Astronomy* The position of two celestial bodies on the celestial sphere when they have the same celestial longitude. **6.** *Logic* **a.** A compound proposition that has components joined by the word *and* or its symbol and is true only if all the components are true. **b.** The relationship between the components of a conjunction. [Ult. < Lat. *coniūnctiō, coniūnctiōn-,* a joining, conjunction, in grammatical sense transl. of Gk. *sundesmos,* binding together, conjunction.] —**con·junc′tion·al** *adj.*

con·junc·ti·va (kŏn′jŭngk-tī′və) *n., pl.* **-vas** or **-vae** (-vē) The mucous membrane that lines the inner surface of the eyelid and the exposed surface of the eyeball. [ME < Med.Lat. *(membrāna) coniūnctīva,* connective (membrane), fem. of LLat. *coniūnctīvus* < Lat. *coniūnctus,* p. part. of *coniungere,* to join together. See CONJOIN.] —**con′junc·ti′val** (-vəl) *adj.*

con·junc·tive (kən-jŭngk′tĭv) *adj.* **1.** Joining; connective. **2.** Joined together; combined. **3.** *Grammar* **a.** Of, relating to, or being a conjunction. **b.** Serving to connect elements of meaning and construction within sentences, as *and,* or between sentences, as *therefore.* ❖ *n. Grammar* A connective word, esp. a conjunction or conjunctive adverb. —**con·junc′tive·ly** *adv.*

conjunctive adverb *n.* A function word that connects two sentences and provides adverbial emphasis, as *therefore* in *This intersection is dangerous; therefore drive slowly.*

con·junc·ti·vi·tis (kən-jŭngk′tə-vī′tĭs) *n.* Inflammation of the conjunctiva, characterized by redness and often accompanied by a discharge.

con·junc·ture (kən-jŭngk′chər) *n.* **1.** A combination, as of events. **2.** A critical set of circumstances; a crisis.

con·jun·to (kŏn-hōōn′tō) *n., pl.* **-tos 1.** A dance band, esp. in Latin America. **2.** A style of popular dance music originating along the Texas-Mexico border, featuring accordion, drums, and 12-string bass guitar and traditionally based on polka, waltz, and bolero rhythms. [Sp. < Lat. *coniūnctus,* p. part. of *coniungere,* to join together. See CONJOIN.]

con·ju·ra·tion (kŏn′jə-rā′shən) *n.* **1.** The act or art of conjuring. **2.** A magic spell or incantation. **3.** A magic trick or magical effect. **4.** *Archaic* A solemn appeal; an entreaty.

con·jure (kŏn′jər, kən-jŏŏr′) *v.* **-jured, -jur·ing, -jures** —*tr.* **1a.** To summon (a devil or spirit) by magic or supernatural power. **b.** To influence or effect by or as if by magic: *conjure away my doubts.* **2a.** To call or bring to mind; evoke: *conjure up an image.* **b.** To imagine; picture. **3.** *Archaic* To call on or entreat solemnly, esp. by an oath. —*intr.* **1.** To perform magic tricks, esp. by sleight of hand. **2a.** To summon a devil by magic or supernatural power. **b.** To practice black magic. ❖ *n.* (kŏn′jər) *Chiefly Southern US* See **hoodoo** 1a. ❖ *adj.* (kŏn′jər) *Chiefly Southern US* Of or practicing folk magic: *a conjure woman.* [Ult. < LLat. *coniūrāre,* to pray by something holy < Lat., to swear together : *com-,* com- + *iūrāre,* to swear; see **yewes-** in App.]

con·jur·er also **con·jur·or** (kŏn′jər-ər, kŭn′-) *n.* **1.** One that performs magic tricks; a magician. **2.** A sorcerer or sorceress.

conk[1] (kŏngk) *Slang n.* **1a.** The head. **b.** A blow, esp. on the head. **2.** *Chiefly British* The human nose. ❖ *v.* **conked, conk·ing, conks** —*tr.* To hit, esp. on the head. —*intr.* **1.** To stop functioning; fail: *The engine conked out.* **2.** To fall asleep, esp. suddenly or heavily: *I conked out.* **3.** To pass out; faint. **4.** To die. [Orig. unknown. N., sense 1b, and v., prob. of imit. orig.]

conk[2] (kŏngk) *n.* A hard, shelflike, spore-bearing structure of certain wood-decaying fungi, found on stumps, logs, or trees. [Perh. alteration of CONCH.]

conk[3] (kŏngk) *n.* A hairstyle in which the hair is straightened, usu. by chemical means. ❖ *tr.v.* **conked, conk·ing, conks** To straighten (tightly curled hair) usu. by chemical means. [Perh. alteration of *congolene,* substance for straightening hair.]

con man *n. Slang* A confidence man.

conn (kŏn) *v. & n. Nautical* Variant of **con**[3].

Conn. *abbr.* Connecticut

Con·nacht (kŏn′ət, -əKHt) also **Con·naught** (-ôt′) A historical region of W-central Ireland.

con·nate (kŏn′āt′, kŏ-nāt′) *adj.* **1.** Existing at birth or from the beginning; inborn or inherent. **2.** Originating at the same time; related. **3.** Being in close accord or sympathy; congenial. **4.** *Biology* United to a structure of the same kind: *a connate leaf.* **5.** *Geology* Trapped in sediment or rock at the time of deposition: *connate water.* [LLat. *connātus,* p. part. of *connāscī,* to be born with : Lat. *com-,* com- + Lat. *nāscī,* to be born; see **genə-** in App.] —**con′nate′ly** *adv.* —**con′nate′ness** *n.*

con·nat·u·ral (kə-năch′ər-əl, kŏ-) *adj.* **1.** Innate; inborn. **2.** Related or similar in nature; cognate. [Med.Lat. *connātūrālis* : Lat. *com-,* com- + Lat. *nātūrālis,* by birth; see NATURAL.] —**con·nat′u·ral′i·ty** (-ə-răl′ĭ-tē) *n.* —**con·nat′u·ral·ly** *adv.* —**con·nat′u·ral·ness** *n.*

con·nect (kə-nĕkt′) *v.* **-nect·ed, -nect·ing, -nects** —*tr.* **1.** To join or fasten together. **2.** To associate or consider as related. See Syns at **join. 3.** To join to or by means of a communications circuit. **4.** To plug in (an electrical cord or device) to an outlet. —*intr.* **1.** To become joined or united. **2.** To be scheduled so as to provide continuing service, as between airplanes. **3.** To establish a rapport or relationship; relate: *The candidate failed to connect with the voters.* **4.** *Sports* To hit or play a ball successfully. [ME *connecten* < Lat. *cōnectere, connectere* : *cō-, com-,* com- + *nectere,* to bind.] —**con·nect′i·ble, con·nect′a·ble** *adj.* —**con·nec′tor, con·nect′er** *n.*

con·nect·ed (kə-nĕk′tĭd) *adj.* **1.** Joined or fastened together. **2.** *Mathematics* Having a continuous path between any two points. Used of a curve, set, or surface. **3.** Related by family. **4.** Logically or intelligibly ordered or presented; coherent. **5.** Associated with or related to influential or important people. —**con·nect′ed·ly** *adv.* —**con·nect′ed·ness** *n.*

Con·nect·i·cut (kə-nĕt′ĭ-kət) A state of the NE US; admitted as one of the original Thirteen Colonies in 1788. The Fundamental Orders, a constitution based on the consent of the governed, was adopted by the colony in 1639. Cap. Hartford. Pop. 3,405,565.

Connecticut River A river of the NE US flowing c. 655 km (407 mi) from N NH to its outlet on Long Island Sound.

con·nect·ing rod (kə-nĕk′tĭng) *n.* A rod that transmits motion or power from one moving part to another, esp. the rod connecting the crankshaft of a motor vehicle to a piston.

con·nec·tion (kə-nĕk′shən) *n.* **1a.** The act of connecting. **b.** The state of being connected. **2.** One that connects; a link. **3.** An association or relationship: *a connection between two crimes.* **4.** The logical or intelligible ordering of words or ideas; coherence. **5.** Reference or relation to something else; context. **6.** A usu. influential or important person with whom one is associated: *used my connections to land a job.* **7.** A conveyance or scheduled run providing continuing service between means of transportation. **8.** A physical link between two or more points in a telecommunications system. **9.** A means or channel of communication: *a bad phone connection.* —**con·nec′tion·al** *adj.*

con·nec·tive (kə-nĕk′tĭv) *adj.* Serving or tending to connect. ❖ *n.* **1.** One that connects. **2.** *Grammar* A word that connects words, phrases, clauses, and sentences. **3.** *Botany* The part of a stamen that connects the halves of an anther. —**con·nec′tive·ly** *adv.*

connective tissue *n.* Tissue arising chiefly from the embryonic mesoderm that is characterized by a highly vascular matrix and includes adipose tissue, cartilage, and bone.

con·nec·tiv·i·ty (kŏn′ĕk-tĭv′ĭ-tē) *n., pl.* **-ties 1.** The quality or condition of being connected or connective. **2.** The ability to make and maintain a connection between points in a telecommunications system.

Con·nel·ly (kŏn′ə-lē), **Marcus Cook ("Marc")** 1890–1980. Amer. playwright, producer, and director whose works include *The Green Pastures* (1930).

con·nex·ion (kə-nĕk′shən) *n. Chiefly British* Variant of **connection.**

con·ning tower (kŏn′ĭng) *n.* **1.** A raised, enclosed observation post in a submarine, often used as a means of entrance and exit. **2.** The armored pilothouse of a warship. [< CON[3].]

con·nip·tion (kə-nĭp′shən) *n. Informal* A fit of violent emotion, such as anger or panic. [Mock-Lat., perh. influenced by SNIP or SNAP.]

con·niv·ance also **con·niv·ence** (kə-nī′vəns) *n.* **1.** The act of conniving. **2.** *Law* Knowledge of and tacit consent to the commission of an illegal act by another.

con·nive (kə-nīv′) *intr.v.* **-nived, -niv·ing, -nives 1.** To cooperate secretly in an illegal or wrongful action; collude. **2.** To scheme; plot. **3.** To feign ignorance of or fail to act against a wrong, thus implying tacit consent: *conniving at the escape.* [Lat. *cōnīvēre, connīvēre,* to close the eyes.] —**con·niv′er** *n.* —**con·niv′er·y** *n.*

con·ni·vent (kə-nī′vənt) *adj. Biology* Converging and touching

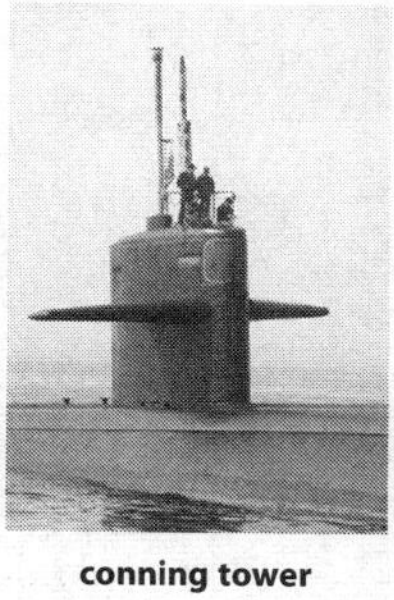

conning tower

ă	pat	oi	boy
ā	pay	ou	out
âr	care	ŏŏ	took
ä	father	ōō	boot
ĕ	pet	ŭ	cut
ē	be	ûr	urge
ĭ	pit	th	thin
ī	pie	*th*	this
îr	pier	hw	which
ŏ	pot	zh	vision
ō	toe	ə	about, item
ô	paw		

Stress marks:
′ (primary);
′ (secondary), as in
lexicon (lĕk′sĭ-kŏn′)

but not fused, as an insect's wings. [Lat. *connīvēns, connīvent-*, pr. part. of *cōnīvēre, connīvēre*, to be tightly closed.]

con·nois·seur (kŏn′ə-sûr′, -sōōr′) *n.* **1.** A person with expert knowledge or training, esp. in the fine arts. **2.** A person of informed and discriminating taste. [Obsolete Fr. < OFr. *connoisseur* < *connoistre*, to know < Lat. *cognōscere*, to learn, know. See COGNITION.] —**con′nois·seur′ship′** *n.*

Con·nol·ly (kŏn′ə-lē), **Maureen** Known as "Little Mo." 1934–69. Amer. tennis player who was the first to win the grand slam of US, British, French, and Australian women's championships (1953).

Con·nors (kŏn′ərz), **James Scott ("Jimmy")** b. 1952. Amer. tennis player who twice won both the US and Wimbledon men's singles titles (1974 and 1982) and also won the US title in 1976, 1978, and 1983.

con·no·ta·tion (kŏn′ə-tā′shən) *n.* **1.** The act or process of connoting. **2a.** An idea or meaning suggested by or associated with a word or thing. **b.** The set of associations implied by a word in addition to its literal meaning. **3.** *Logic* The set of attributes constituting the meaning of a term; intension. —**con′no·ta′tive** *adj.*

con·note (kə-nōt′) *tr.v.* **-not·ed, -not·ing, -notes** **1.** To suggest or imply in addition to literal meaning. See Usage Note at **denote**. **2.** To have as a related or attendant condition. [Med.Lat. *connotāre*, to mark along with : Lat. *com-*, com- + Lat. *notāre*, to mark (< *nota*, mark; see **gnō-** in App.).]

con·nu·bi·al (kə-nōō′bē-əl, -nyōō′-) *adj.* Relating to marriage or the married state; conjugal. [Lat. *cōnūbiālis* < *cōnūbium*, marriage : com-, com- + *nūbere*, to marry.] —**con·nu′bi·al·ism**, **con·nu′bi·al′i·ty** (-ăl′ĭ-tē) *n.*

co·no·dont (kō′nə-dŏnt′, kŏn′ə-) *n.* **1.** A member of an extinct group of primitive fishlike chordates, preserved primarily in the form of their conelike teeth. **2.** A fossil tooth of this chordate. [Gk. *kōnos*, cone + -ODONT.]

co·noid (kō′noid′) also **co·noi·dal** (kō-noid′l) *adj.* Shaped like a cone. —**co′noid** *n.*

con·quer (kŏng′kər) *v.* **-quered, -quer·ing, -quers** —*tr.* **1.** To defeat or subdue by force, esp. by force of arms. **2.** To gain or secure control of by or as if by force of arms: *conquering disease.* **3.** To overcome or surmount by physical, mental, or moral force: *conquered fear.* See Syns at **defeat.** —*intr.* To be victorious; win. [ME *conqueren* < OFr. *conquerre* < VLat. *conquaerere* < Lat. *conquīrere*, to procure : com-, com- + *quaerere*, to seek.] —**con′quer·a·ble** *adj.* —**con′quer·or, con′quer·er** *n.*

con·quest (kŏn′kwĕst′, kŏng′-) *n.* **1.** The act or process of conquering. **2.** Something acquired by conquering. **3.** One that has been captivated or overcome. [ME < OFr. < VLat. *conquaesīta*, fem. p. part. of *conquaerere*. See CONQUER.]

con·qui·an (kŏng′kē-ən) *n.* Variant of **cooncan.**

con·quis·ta·dor (kŏn-kwĭs′tə-dôr′, kŏng-kē′stə-) *n., pl.* **-dors** or **-dor·es** (-dôr′ās, -ēz) A conqueror, esp. one of the 16th-century Spanish soldiers who defeated the civilizations of the New World. [Sp. < *conquistar*, to conquer < VLat. *conquaesītāre*, freq. of Lat. *conquīrere*, to procure. See CONQUER.]

Con·rad (kŏn′răd′), **Joseph** 1857–1924. Polish-born British writer whose works include *Lord Jim* (1900).

cons. *abbr.* **1.** consigned **2.** consignment **3.** consolidated **4.** consonant **5.** constitution

Cons. *abbr.* **1.** constable **2.** consul

con·san·guin·e·ous (kŏn′săn-gwĭn′ē-əs, -săng-) also **con·san·guine** (kŏn-săng′gwĭn, kən-) *adj.* Of the same lineage or origin. [< Lat. *cōnsanguineus* : com-, com- + *sanguineus*, of blood; see SANGUINE.] —**con′san·guin′e·ous·ly** *adv.*

con·san·guin·i·ty (kŏn′săn-gwĭn′ĭ-tē, -săng-) *n., pl.* **-ties** **1.** Relationship by blood or by a common ancestor. **2.** A close affinity or connection.

con·science (kŏn′shəns) *n.* **1a.** The awareness of a moral or ethical aspect to one's conduct together with the urge to prefer right over wrong. **b.** A source of moral or ethical judgment or pronouncement. **c.** Conformity to one's own sense of right conduct. **2.** The part of the superego in psychoanalysis that judges the ethics of one's actions and thoughts and then transmits its judgments to the ego. **3.** *Obsolete* Consciousness. —*idiom:* **in (all good) conscience** In all truth or fairness. [ME < OFr. < Lat. *cōnscientia* < *cōnsciēns, cōnscient-*, pr. part. of *cōnscīre*, to be conscious of : com-, com- + *scīre*, to know.] —**con′science·less** *adj.*

conscience clause *n.* A clause in a law that relieves persons whose conscientious or religious scruples forbid compliance.

conscience money *n.* Money paid in compensation or atonement, as for a dishonest or morally objectionable act.

con·sci·en·tious (kŏn′shē-ĕn′shəs) *adj.* **1.** Guided by or in accordance with the dictates of conscience; principled. **2.** Thorough and assiduous: *conscientious work.* [Obsolete Fr. *conscientieux* < Med.Lat. *cōnscientiōsus* < Lat. *cōnscientia*, conscience. See CONSCIENCE.] —**con′sci·en′tious·ly** *adv.* —**con′sci·en′tious·ness** *n.*

conscientious objector *n.* One who on the basis of religion or principle refuses to bear arms or serve in the military.

con·scio·na·ble (kŏn′shə-nə-bəl) *adj.* **1.** Acceptable or permissible according to conscience; conscientious; principled. [Obsolete *conscions* (var. of CONSCIENCE) + -ABLE.]

con·scious (kŏn′shəs) *adj.* **1a.** Having an awareness of one's environment and one's own existence, sensations, and thoughts. See Syns at **aware. b.** Mentally perceptive or alert; awake. **2.** Capable of thought, will, or perception. **3.** Subjectively known or felt: *conscious remorse.* **4.** Intentionally conceived or done; deliberate: *a conscious insult.* **5.** Inwardly attentive or sensible; mindful: *conscious of being stared at.* **6.** Especially aware of or preoccupied with. Often used in combination: *a health-conscious diet.* ❖ *n.* In psychoanalysis, the component of waking awareness perceptible by a person at any given instant; consciousness. [< Lat. *cōnscius* : com-, com- + *scīre*, to know.] —**con′scious·ly** *adv.*

con·scious·ness (kŏn′shəs-nĭs) *n.* **1.** The state or condition of being conscious. **2.** A sense of identity, including the attitudes, beliefs, and sensitivities held by or considered characteristic of an individual or group. **3a.** Special awareness or sensitivity: *class consciousness.* **b.** Alertness to or concern for a particular issue or situation. **4.** In psychoanalysis.

con·scious·ness-rais·ing (kŏn′shəs-nĭs-rā′zĭng) *n.* The process of achieving greater awareness, as of one's own needs or of a political or social issue. —**con′scious·ness-rais′er** *n.*

con·script (kŏn′skrĭpt′) *n.* One compulsorily enrolled for service, esp. in the armed forces; a draftee. ❖ *adj.* Enrolled compulsorily; drafted. ❖ *tr.v.* (kən-skrĭpt′) **-script·ed, -script·ing, -scripts** To enroll compulsorily into service; draft. [Lat. *cōnscrīptus*, p. part. of *cōnscrībere*, to enroll : com-, com- + *scrībere*, to write; see **skribh-** in App.]

con·scrip·tion (kən-skrĭp′shən) *n.* **1.** Compulsory enrollment, esp. for the armed forces; draft. **2.** A monetary payment exacted by a government in wartime.

con·se·crate (kŏn′sĭ-krāt′) *tr.v.* **-crat·ed, -crat·ing, -crates** **1.** To declare or set apart as sacred. **2.** *Christianity* **a.** To produce the ritual transformation of (the elements of the Eucharist) into the body and blood of Jesus. **b.** To sanctify (bread and wine) for use in Communion. **c.** To initiate (a priest) into the order of bishops. **3.** To dedicate solemnly to a service or goal. **4.** To make venerable; hallow: *consecrated by time.* ❖ *adj.* Dedicated to a sacred purpose; sanctified. [ME *consecraten* < Lat. *cōnsecrāre, cōnsecrāt-* : com-, com- + *sacrāre*, to make sacred (< *sacer, sacr-*, sacred; see **sak-** in App.).] —**con′se·cra′tive** *adj.* —**con′se·cra′tor** *n.* —**con′se·cra·to′ry** (-krə-tôr′ē, -tōr′ē) *adj.*

con·se·cra·tion (kŏn′sĭ-krā′shən) *n.* **1.** The act, process, or ceremony of consecrating. **2.** The state of being consecrated.

con·se·cu·tion (kŏn′sĭ-kyōō′shən) *n.* **1.** A sequence or succession. **2.** *Logic* The relation of consequent to antecedent; deduction.

con·sec·u·tive (kən-sĕk′yə-tĭv) *adj.* **1.** Following one after another without interruption; successive. **2.** Marked by logical sequence. **3.** *Grammar* Expressing consequence or result. [Fr. *consécutif* < OFr. < Med.Lat. *cōnsecūtīvus* < *cōnsecūtus*, p. part. of Lat. *cōnsequī*, to follow closely. See CONSEQUENT.] —**con·sec′u·tive·ly** *adv.* —**con·sec′u·tive·ness** *n.*

con·sen·su·al (kən-sĕn′shōō-əl) *adj.* **1.** Of or expressing consensus: *a consensual decision.* **2a.** *Law* Existing or entered into by mutual consent without formalization by document or ceremony: *a consensual marriage.* **b.** Involving the willing participation of both or all parties, esp. in an illegal practice. **3.** *Physiology* **a.** Of or relating to a reflex of one body structure following stimulation of another. **b.** Of or relating to involuntary movement of a body part accompanying voluntary movement of another. —**con·sen′su·al·ly** *adv.*

con·sen·sus (kən-sĕn′səs) *n.* **1.** An opinion or position reached by a group as a whole. See Usage Note at **redundancy. 2.** General agreement. [Lat. *cōnsēnsus* < p. part. of *cōnsentīre*, to agree. See CONSENT.]

con·sent (kən-sĕnt′) *intr.v.* **-sent·ed, -sent·ing, -sents** **1.** To give assent, as to the proposal of another; agree. See Syns at **assent. 2.** *Archaic* To be of the same mind or opinion. ❖ *n.* **1.** Acceptance or approval of what is planned or done by another; acquiescence. **2.** Agreement as to opinion or a course of action: *chosen by common consent.* [ME *consenten* < OFr. *consentir* < Lat. *cōnsentīre* : com-, com- + *sentīre*, to feel.] —**con·sent′er** *n.*

con·sen·ta·ne·ous (kŏn′sĕn-tā′nē-əs) *adj.* **1.** Manifesting agreement; accordant. **2.** Unanimous. [< Lat. *cōnsentāneus* < *cōnsentīre*, to agree. See CONSENT.] —**con·sen′ta·ne′i·ty** (kən-sĕn′tə-nē′ĭ-tē), **con′sen·ta′ne·ous·ness** *n.* —**con′sen·ta′ne·ous·ly** *adv.*

consent decree *n.* A judicial decree expressing a voluntary agreement between parties to a suit, esp. an agreement by a defendant to cease activities alleged by the government to be illegal in return for an end to the charges.

con·se·quence (kŏn′sĭ-kwĕns′, -kwəns) *n.* **1.** Something that logically or naturally follows from an action or condition. See Syns at **effect. 2.** The relation of a result to its cause. **3.** A logical conclusion or inference. **4.** Significance; importance. —*idiom:* **in consequence** As a result; consequently.

con·se·quent (kŏn′sĭ-kwĕnt′, -kwənt) *adj.* **1a.** Following as a natural effect, result, or conclusion. **b.** Following as a logical conclusion. **2.** Logically correct or consistent. **3.** *Geology* Having a position or direction determined by the original form or slope of the earth's surface. ❖ *n.* **1.** *Logic* The conclusion, as of a syllogism or a conditional sentence. **2.** The second term of a ratio. [ME < OFr. < Lat. *cōnsequēns, cōnsequent-*, pr. part. of *cōnsequī*, to follow closely : com-, com- + *sequī*, to follow; see **sek**w-1 in App.]

con•se•quen•tial (kŏn′sĭ-kwĕn′shəl) *adj.* **1.** Following as an effect, result, or conclusion; consequent. **2.** Having important consequences; significant. **3a.** Important; influential. **b.** Pompous; self-important. —**con′se•quen′ti•al′i•ty** (-shē-ăl′ĭ-tē) *n.* —**con′se•quen′tial•ly** *adv.*

con•se•quent•ly (kŏn′sĭ-kwĕnt′lē, -kwənt-lē) *adv.* As a result; therefore.

con•ser•van•cy (kən-sûr′vən-sē) *n., pl.* **-cies 1.** Conservation, esp. of natural resources. **2a.** An organization dedicated to the conservation of wildlife and wildlife habitats in the United States. **b.** *Chiefly British* A commission supervising fisheries and navigation.

con•ser•va•tion (kŏn′sûr-vā′shən) *n.* **1.** The act or process of conserving. **2a.** Preservation or restoration from loss, damage, or neglect. **b.** The protection, preservation, management, or restoration of wildlife and natural resources such as forests and water. **3.** The maintenance of a physical quantity, such as mass, during a physical or chemical change. —**con′ser•va′tion•al** *adj.*

conservation biology *n.* The branch of biology that deals with the effects of humans on the environment and with the conservation of biological diversity.

con•ser•va•tion•ist (kŏn′sûr-vā′shə-nĭst) *n.* One practicing or advocating conservation, esp. of natural resources.

conservation of charge *n.* A principle stating that the total electric charge of an isolated system remains constant regardless of changes within the system.

conservation of energy *n.* A principle stating that the total energy of an isolated system remains constant regardless of changes within the system.

conservation of mass *n.* A principle in classical physics stating that the total mass of an isolated system is unchanged by interaction of its parts.

conservation of momentum *n.* A principle stating that the total linear momentum of an isolated system remains constant regardless of changes within the system.

con•ser•va•tism (kən-sûr′və-tĭz′əm) *n.* **1.** The inclination, esp. in politics, to maintain the existing or traditional order. **2.** A political philosophy or attitude emphasizing respect for traditional institutions, distrust of government activism, and opposition to sudden change. **3. Conservatism** The principles and policies of the Conservative Party or the Progressive Conservative Party. **4.** Caution; moderation.

con•ser•va•tive (kən-sûr′və-tĭv) *adj.* **1.** Favoring traditional views and values; tending to oppose change. **2.** Traditional or restrained in style: *a conservative suit.* **3.** Moderate; cautious. **4a.** Of or relating to the political philosophy of conservatism. **b.** Belonging to a conservative party, group, or movement. **5. Conservative** Of or belonging to the Conservative Party or the Progressive Conservative Party. **6. Conservative** Of or adhering to Conservative Judaism. **7.** Tending to conserve; preservative. ❖ *n.* **1.** One favoring traditional views and values. **2.** A supporter of political conservatism. **3. Conservative** A member or supporter of the Conservative Party or the Progressive Conservative Party. **4.** *Archaic* A preservative agent or principle. —**con•ser′va•tive•ly** *adv.* —**con•ser′va•tive•ness** *n.*

Conservative Judaism *n.* The branch of Judaism that allows for modifications in Jewish law when authorized by the Conservative rabbinate.

Conservative Party *n.* A major political party of the United Kingdom.

con•ser•va•tize (kən-sûr′və-tīz′) *tr.v.* **-tized, -tiz•ing, -tizes** To make conservative or more conservative. [CONSERVAT(IVE) + -IZE.]

con•ser•va•tor (kən-sûr′və-tər, kŏn′sər-vā′tər) *n.* **1.** A person in charge of maintaining or restoring valuable items, as in a museum. **2.** One that conserves or preserves from injury, violation, or infraction. **3.** *Law* One responsible for the person and property of an incompetent. —**con′ser•va•to′ri•al** (-tôr′ē-əl, -tōr′-) *adj.* —**con•ser′va•tor•ship′** *n.*

con•ser•va•to•ry (kən-sûr′və-tôr′ē, -tōr′ē) *n., pl.* **-ries 1.** A greenhouse, esp. one in which plants are arranged aesthetically for display. **2.** A school of music or dramatic art.

con•serve (kən-sûrv′) *v.* **-served, -serv•ing, -serves** —*tr.* **1a.** To protect from loss or harm; preserve. **b.** To use carefully or sparingly, avoiding waste. **2.** To keep (a quantity) constant through physical or chemical reactions or evolutionary changes. **3.** To preserve (fruits) with sugar. —*intr.* To economize. ❖ *n.* (kŏn′sûrv′) A jam made of fruits stewed in sugar. [ME *conserven* < OFr. *conserver* < Lat. *cōnservāre* : *com-*, com- + *servāre*, to preserve.] —**con•serv′a•ble** *adj.* —**con•serv′er** *n.*

con•sid•er (kən-sĭd′ər) *v.* **-ered, -er•ing, -ers** —*tr.* **1.** To think carefully about. **2.** To think or deem to be; regard as. See Usage Note at **as**1. **3.** To form an opinion about; judge: *considers waste to be criminal.* **4.** To take into account; bear in mind. **5.** To show consideration for: *considered the feelings of others.* **6.** To esteem; regard. **7.** To look at thoughtfully. —*intr.* To think carefully; reflect. [ME *consideren* < OFr. *considerer* < Lat. *cōnsīderāre* : *com-*, com- + *sīdus*, *sīder-*, star.] —**con•sid′er•er** *n.*

con•sid•er•a•ble (kən-sĭd′ər-ə-bəl) *adj.* **1.** Large in amount, extent, or degree. **2.** Worthy of consideration; significant. ❖ *n.*

Informal A considerable amount, extent, or degree. —**con•sid′er•a•bly** *adv.*

con•sid•er•ate (kən-sĭd′ər-ĭt) *adj.* **1.** Having or marked by regard for the needs or feelings of others. See Syns at **thoughtful**. **2.** Characterized by careful thought. —**con•sid′er•ate•ly** *adv.* —**con•sid′er•ate•ness** *n.*

con•sid•er•a•tion (kən-sĭd′ə-rā′shən) *n.* **1a.** Careful thought; deliberation. **b.** A result of considering; an opinion or judgment. **2.** A factor to be considered in forming a judgment or decision. **3.** A treatment or account. **4.** Thoughtful concern for others; solicitude. **5.** High regard; esteem. **6.** Payment given in exchange for a service rendered; recompense. **7.** *Law* Something promised, given, or done that has the effect of making an agreement a legally enforceable contract. —*idiom:* **in consideration of 1.** In view of; on account of. **2.** In return for.

con•sid•ered (kən-sĭd′ərd) *adj.* **1.** Reached after or done with careful thought; deliberate. **2.** Highly regarded; esteemed.

con•sid•er•ing (kən-sĭd′ər-ĭng) *prep.* In view of; taking into consideration. See Usage Note at **participle**. ❖ *adv. Informal* All things considered.

con•sign (kən-sīn′) *v.* **-signed, -sign•ing, -signs** —*tr.* **1.** To give over to the care of another; entrust. **2.** To turn over permanently to another's charge or to a lasting condition. **3.** To deliver (merchandise, for example) for custody or sale. **4.** To set apart, as for a special use or purpose; assign. —*intr. Obsolete* To submit; consent. [ME *consignen*, to certify by seal < OFr. *consigner* < Lat. *cōnsignāre* : *com-*, com- + *signāre*, to mark (< *signum*, mark; see **sek**w-1 in App.).] —**con•sign′a•ble** *adj.* —**con′sig•na′tion** (kŏn′sī-nā′shən, -sĭg-) *n.* —**con•sig′nor, con•sign′er** *n.*

con•sign•ee (kŏn′sī-nē′, kən-sī′nē′) *n.* The one to whom something, such as goods or merchandise, is consigned.

con•sign•ment (kən-sīn′mənt) *n.* **1.** The act of consigning. **2.** Something consigned. —*idiom:* **on consignment** With the provision that payment is expected only on completed sales and that unsold items may be returned.

con•sist (kən-sĭst′) *intr.v.* **-sist•ed, -sist•ing, -sists 1.** To be made up or composed. See Usage Note at **include**. **2.** To have a basis; reside or lie. **3.** To be compatible; accord. [Lat. *cōnsistere*, to stand still, to be composed of : *com-*, com- + *sistere*, to cause to stand; see **stā-** in App.]

con•sis•tence (kən-sĭs′təns) *n.* Consistency.

con•sis•ten•cy (kən-sĭs′tən-sē) *n., pl.* **-cies 1a.** Agreement or logical coherence among things or parts. **b.** Correspondence among related aspects; compatibility. **2.** Reliability or uniformity of successive results or events. **3.** Degree of density, firmness, or viscosity.

con•sis•tent (kən-sĭs′tənt) *adj.* **1.** In agreement; compatible. **2.** Being in agreement with itself; coherent and uniform. **3.** Reliable; steady. **4.** *Mathematics* Having at least one common solution, as of two or more equations. [Lat. *cōnsistēns, cōnsistent-*, pr. part. of *cōnsistere*, to stand still. See CONSIST.] —**con•sis′tent•ly** *adv.*

con•sis•to•ry (kən-sĭs′tə-rē) *n., pl.* **-ries 1a.** *Roman Catholic Church* An assembly of cardinals presided over by the pope for the solemn promulgation of papal acts. **b.** A governing body of a local congregation in certain Reformed churches. **c.** A regulatory court in Lutheran state churches. **d.** An Anglican diocesan court presided over by a bishop's chancellor or commissary. **2.** The meeting of a consistory. **3.** A council; a tribunal. [ME *consistorie* < OFr. < Lat. *cōnsistōrium*, place of assembly < *cōnsistere*, to stand together. See CONSIST.] —**con′sis•to′ri•al** (kŏn′sĭ-stôr′ē-əl, -stōr′-) *adj.*

con•so•ci•ate (kən-sō′shē-āt′) *tr. & intr.v.* **-at•ed, -at•ing, -ates** To bring or come into friendly or cooperative association. ❖ *adj.* (-ĭt) Associated; united. ❖ *n.* (-ĭt) An associate or partner. [Lat. *cōnsociāre, cōnsociāt-*, to associate : *com-*, com- + *sociāre*, to associate (< *socius*, companion; see **sek**w-1 in App.).]

con•so•ci•a•tion (kən-sō′shē-ā′shən) *n.* **1.** Friendly or cooperative association, as between groups. **2.** *Ecology* A subdivision of an association having one dominant species of plant. **3.** A political association in which various groups share power according to an agreed formula or mechanism. —**con•so′ci•a′tion•al** *adj.*

con•sol (kŏn′sŏl, kən-sŏl′) *n. Chiefly British* A government bond in Great Britain, originally issued in 1751, that pays perpetual interest and has no date of maturity. Often used in the plural. [Short for *Consolidated Annuity*.]

con•so•la•tion (kŏn′sə-lā′shən) *n.* **1a.** The act or an instance of consoling. **b.** The state of being consoled. **2.** One that consoles; a comfort: *Your kindness was a consolation.* **3.** *Sports* A competition or round of play for participants who have been eliminated before the final of a tournament.

consolation prize *n.* A prize given to a competitor who loses or does not win the first prize.

con•sole1 (kən-sōl′) *tr.v.* **-soled, -sol•ing, -soles** To allay the sorrow or grief of. [Fr. *consoler* < OFr. < Lat. *cōnsōlārī* : *com-*, com- + *sōlārī*, to comfort.] —**con•sol′a•ble** *adj.* —**con•so′la•to′ry** (-sŏl′ə-tôr′ē, -tōr′ē, -sōl′ə-) *adj.* —**con•sol′er** *n.* —**con•sol′ing•ly** *adv.*

con•sole2 (kŏn′sōl′) *n.* **1a.** A cabinet, as for a television set, designed to stand on the floor. **b.** A small freestanding storage cabinet. **2.** *Music* The desklike part of an organ that contains the keyboard, stops, and pedals. **3a.** A central control panel for a

console2

mechanical, electrical, or electronic system. **b.** An instrument panel. **4.** The portion of a computer or peripheral that houses the apparatus used to operate the machine manually. **5.** A small storage compartment mounted between bucket seats in an automobile. **6.** An often scroll-shaped bracket used for decoration or for supporting a projecting member. **7.** A console table. [Fr., perh. short for *consolider*, to strengthen < Lat. *consolidāre*. See CONSOLIDATE.]

con·sole table (kŏn′sōl′) *n.* **1.** A table supported by decorative consoles fixed to a wall. **2.** A small table, often with curved legs resembling consoles, set against a wall.

con·sol·i·date (kən-sŏl′ĭ-dāt′) *v.* **-dat·ed, -dat·ing, -dates** *—tr.* **1.** To unite into one system or whole; combine. **2.** To make strong or secure; strengthen. **3.** To make firm or coherent; form into a compact mass. *—intr.* **1.** To become solidified or united. **2.** To join in a merger or union. [Lat. *consolidāre, consolidāt-* : *com-, com-* + *solidāre*, to make firm (< *solidus*, firm; see **sol-** in App.).] **—con·sol′i·da′tor** *n.*

con·sol·i·dat·ed school (kən-sŏl′ĭ-dā′tĭd) *n.* A public school serving pupils from several adjacent districts.

con·sol·i·da·tion (kən-sŏl′ĭ-dā′shən) *n.* **1a.** The act or process of consolidating. **b.** The state of being consolidated. **2.** The merger of two or more commercial interests or corporations.

con·som·mé (kŏn′sə-mā′, kŏn′sə-mā′) *n.* A clear soup made of strained meat or vegetable stock, served hot or as a cold jelly. [Fr. < p. part. of *consommer*, to use up < Lat. *consummāre*, to finish. See CONSUMMATE.]

con·so·nance (kŏn′sə-nəns) *n.* **1.** Agreement; harmony; accord. **2a.** Close correspondence of sounds. **b.** The repetition of consonants or of a consonant pattern, esp. at the ends of words. **3.** *Music* A simultaneous combination of sounds not requiring resolution to another combination of sounds for finality of effect and conventionally regarded as pleasing.

con·so·nant (kŏn′sə-nənt) *adj.* **1.** Being in agreement or accord. **2.** Corresponding or alike in sound, as words. **3.** Harmonious in sound or tone. ❖ *n.* **1.** A speech sound produced by a partial or complete obstruction of the air stream by constriction of the speech organs, such as (p), (f), (r), (w), and (h). **2.** A letter or character representing such a speech sound. [ME < OFr. < Lat. *cōnsonāns, consonant-*, pr. part. of *cōnsonāre*, to agree : *com-, com-* + *sonāre*, to sound.] **—con′so·nant·ly** *adv.*

con·so·nan·tal (kŏn′sə-năn′tl) *adj.* **1.** Of, relating to, or having the nature of a consonant. **2.** Containing a consonant or consonants. **—con′so·nan′tal·ly** *adv.*

con·sort (kŏn′sôrt′) *n.* **1.** A husband or wife, esp. of a monarch. **2.** A companion or partner. **3.** A ship accompanying another in travel. **4.** Partnership; association. **5.** A group; a company. **6.** *Music* **a.** An instrumental ensemble. **b.** An ensemble using instruments of the same family. ❖ *v.* (kən-sôrt′) **-sort·ed, -sort·ing, -sorts** *—intr.* **1.** To keep company; associate. **2.** To be in accord or agreement. *—tr.* **1.** To unite in company; associate. **2.** *Obsolete* **a.** To escort; accompany. **b.** To espouse. [ME, colleague < OFr. < Lat. *cōnsors, cōnsort-* : *com-, com-* + *sors*, fate.]

con·sor·ti·um (kən-sôr′tē-əm, -shē-əm) *n., pl.* **-ti·a** (-tē-ə, -shē-ə) **1a.** An association or combination, as of businesses, in order to engage in a joint venture. **b.** A cooperative arrangement among groups or institutions. **2.** An association or society. **3.** *Law* A spouse's right to the company of, help of, affection of, and sexual relations with his or her mate. [Lat., fellowship < *cōnsors, cōnsort-*, partner. See CONSORT.] **—con·sor′ti·al** *adj.*

con·spe·cif·ic (kŏn′spĭ-sĭf′ĭk) *adj.* Of or belonging to the same species. **—con′spe·cif′ik** *n.*

con·spec·tus (kən-spĕk′təs) *n., pl.* **-tus·es 1.** A general survey of a subject. **2.** A synopsis. [Lat. < p. part. of *cōnspicere*, to observe. See CONSPICUOUS.]

con·spic·u·ous (kən-spĭk′yōō-əs) *adj.* **1.** Easy to notice; obvious. **2.** Attracting attention, as by being unusual; noticeable. [< Lat. *cōnspicuus* < *cōnspicere*, to observe : *com-, com-* + *specere*, to look; see **spek-** in App.] **—con′spic·u′i·ty** (kŏn′spĭ-kyōō′ĭ-tē), **con·spic′u·ous·ness** *n.* **—con·spic′u·ous·ly** *adv.*

conspicuous consumption *n.* The acquisition or display of expensive items to suggest that one is wealthy.

con·spir·a·cy (kən-spîr′ə-sē) *n., pl.* **-cies 1.** An agreement to perform together an illegal, wrongful, or subversive act. **2.** A group of conspirators. **3.** *Law* An agreement between two or more persons to commit a crime or accomplish a legal purpose through illegal action. **4.** A joining or acting together, as if by sinister design: *a devastating conspiracy of wind and tide.* [ME *conspiracie* < AN, prob. alteration of OFr. *conspiration* < Lat. *cōnspīrātiō, cōnspīrātiōn-* < *cōnspīrātus*, p. part. of *cōnspīrāre*, to conspire. See CONSPIRE.]

con·spir·a·tor (kən-spîr′ə-tər) *n.* One that engages in a conspiracy.

con·spir·a·to·ri·al (kən-spîr′ə-tôr′ē-əl, -tōr′-) *adj.* Of, relating to, or characteristic of conspirators or a conspiracy: *a conspiratorial act.* **—con·spir′a·to′ri·al·ly** *adv.*

con·spire (kən-spīr′) *v.* **-spired, -spir·ing, -spires** *—intr.* **1.** To plan together secretly to commit an illegal or wrongful act or accomplish a legal purpose illegally: *conspired to defraud unwitting investors.* **2.** To join or act together. *—tr.* To plan or plot secretly. [ME *conspiren* < OFr. < Lat. *cōnspīrāre* : *com-, com-* + *spīrāre*, to

John Constable
detail from a c. 1799
portrait by Richard Ramsay
Reinagle (1775–1862)

Constantine the Great
bronze bust

breathe.] **—con·spir′er** *n.* **—con·spir′ing·ly** *adv.*

con spi·ri·to (kŏn spîr′ĭ-tō′, kōn) *adv. Music* With spirit and vigor. [Ital. : *con*, with + *spirito*, spirit, soul.]

con·sta·ble (kŏn′stə-bəl, kŭn′-) *n.* **1.** A peace officer with less authority and smaller jurisdiction than a sheriff, empowered to serve writs and warrants and make arrests. **2.** A medieval officer of high rank, usu. serving as military commander in the absence of a monarch. **3.** The governor of a royal castle. **4.** *Chiefly British* A police officer. [ME < OFr. *conestable* < LLat. *comes stabulī*, officer of the stable : Lat. *comes*, officer, companion; see **ei-** in App. + Lat. *stabulī*, genitive of *stabulum*, stable; see **stā-** in App.] **—con′sta·ble·ship′** *n.*

Con·sta·ble (kŭn′stə-bəl, kŏn′-), **John** 1776–1837. British landscape painter whose works include *The Hay Wain* (1821).

con·stab·u·lar (kən-stăb′yə-lər) *adj.* Constabulary.

con·stab·u·lar·y (kən-stăb′yə-lĕr′ē) *n., pl.* **-ies 1.** The body of constables of a district or city. **2.** The district under a constable's jurisdiction. **3.** An armed police force organized like a military unit. ❖ *adj.* Of or relating to constables, constabularies, or their jurisdictions.

Con·stance (kŏn′stəns) See **Konstanz**.

Constance, Lake of or **Bo·den·see** (bōd′n-zā′) An Alpine lake bordering on S Germany, N Switzerland, and W Austria.

con·stan·cy (kŏn′stən-sē) *n.* **1.** Steadfastness; faithfulness. **2.** The condition or quality of being constant; changelessness.

con·stant (kŏn′stənt) *adj.* **1.** Continually occurring; persistent. **2.** Regularly recurring: *constant interruptions.* **3.** Unchanging in nature, value, or extent; invariable. See Syns at **continual. 4.** Steadfast in purpose, loyalty, or affection; faithful. See Syns at **faithful.** ❖ *n.* **1.** Something unchanging or invariable. **2a.** A quantity assumed to have a fixed value in a specified mathematical context. **b.** An experimental or theoretical condition, factor, or quantity that does not vary or is regarded as invariant in specified circumstances. [ME < OFr. < Lat. *cōnstāns, constant-*, pr. part. of *cōnstāre*, to stand firm : *com-, com-* + *stāre*, to stand; see **stā-** in App.] **—con′stant·ly** *adv.*

Con·stan·ţa (kən-stän′sə, kōn-stän′tsä) A city of SE Romania on the Black Sea E of Bucharest; founded in the 7th cent. B.C. Pop. 348,985.

con·stan·tan (kŏn′stən-tăn′) *n.* An alloy of 45 percent nickel and 55 percent copper, used chiefly in electrical instruments because of its constant resistance under varying temperatures. [< CONSTANT.]

Con·stant de Re·becque (kôN-stäN′ də rə-bĕk′), **Benjamin** 1767–1830. French writer and politician who was exiled in 1802 for denouncing Napoleon.

Con·stan·tine (kŏn′stən-tēn′, kôN-stäN-tēn′) A city of NE Algeria E of Algiers. Founded by Carthaginians and destroyed in A.D. 311, it was rebuilt by Constantine I and named in his honor. Pop. 344,454.

Con·stan·tine I¹ (kŏn′stən-tēn′, -tīn′) Known as "Constantine the Great." A.D. 285?–337. Emperor of Rome (306–337) who adopted the Christian faith.

Con·stan·tine I² (kŏn′stən-tēn, -tīn′) 1868–1923. King of Greece (1913–17) who opposed the Allies in World War I.

Constantine II b. 1940. King of Greece (1964–67) who went into exile after a coup d'état by army officers.

Con·stan·ti·no·ple (kŏn′stăn-tə-nō′pəl) See **Istanbul.**

constant velocity joint *n.* A universal joint used esp. in frontwheel drive cars that allows power to be transmitted from a transaxle to an axle or from an axle to a wheel even at sharp angles.

con·stel·late (kŏn′stə-lāt′) *intr. & tr.v.* **-lat·ed, -lat·ing, -lates** To form or cause to form a group or cluster.

con·stel·la·tion (kŏn′stə-lā′shən) *n.* **1.** *Astronomy* **a.** An arbitrary formation of stars perceived as a figure or design, esp. one of 88 recognized groups. **b.** An area of the celestial sphere occupied by one of the 88 recognized constellations. **2.** The configuration of planets at the time of one's birth, regarded by astrologers as determining one's character or fate. **3.** A gathering or assemblage, esp. of prominent persons or things. **4.** A set or configuration, as of related items, properties, ideas, or individuals. [Ult. < LLat. *cōnstēllātiō, cōnstēllātiōn-* : Lat. *com-, com-* + Lat. *stēlla*, star; see **ster-** in App.] **—con·stel′la·to·ry** (-stĕl′ə-tôr′ē, -tōr′ē) *adj.*

con·ster·nate (kŏn′stər-nāt′) *tr.v.* **-nat·ed, -nat·ing, -nates** To cause consternation in. [Lat. *cōnsternāre, cōnsternāt-* : *com-, com-* + *sternere*, to throw down.]

con·ster·na·tion (kŏn′stər-nā′shən) *n.* A state of paralyzing dismay. See Syns at **fear.**

con·sti·pate (kŏn′stə-pāt′) *tr.v.* **-pat·ed, -pat·ing, -pates 1.** To cause constipation in. **2.** To clog or make sluggish; obstruct. [Lat. *cōnstīpāre, cōnstīpāt-*, to crowd together : *com-, com-* + *stīpāre*, to cram.]

con·sti·pat·ed (kŏn′stə-pā′tĭd) *adj.* **1.** Affected with constipation. **2.** Stiff, stodgy, or recalcitrant.

con·sti·pa·tion (kŏn′stə-pā′shən) *n.* **1.** Difficult, incomplete, or infrequent evacuation of dry hardened feces from the bowels. **2.** Obstruction; stultification.

con·stit·u·en·cy (kən-stĭch′ōō-ən-sē) *n., pl.* **-cies 1a.** The body of voters of the residents of a district represented by an elected legislator or official. **b.** The district so represented. **2a.** A group of supporters or patrons. **b.** A group served by an organization or institution; a clientele.

con·stit·u·ent (kən-stĭch′ōō-ənt) *adj.* **1.** Serving as part of a whole; component: *a constituent element.* **2.** Empowered to elect or designate. **3.** Authorized to make or amend a constitution: *a constituent assembly.* ❖ *n.* **1.** A constituent part; a component. See Syns at **element. 2.** A resident of a district or member of a group represented by an elected official. **3.** One that authorizes another to act as a representative; a client. **4.** *Grammar* A functional unit of a grammatical construction, as a verb, noun phrase, or clause. [Lat. *cōnstituēns, cōnstituent-*, pr. part. of *cōnstituere*, to set up. See CONSTITUTE.] —**con·stit′u·ent·ly** *adv.*

constituent structure *n. Grammar* An analysis of the constituents of a construction, such as a sentence.

con·sti·tute (kŏn′stĭ-tōōt′, -tyōōt′) *tr.v.* **-tut·ed, -tut·ing, -tutes 1.** To be the elements or parts of; compose. **b.** To amount to; equal. **2a.** To set up or establish according to law or provision. **b.** To found (an institution, for example). **c.** To enact (a law or regulation). **3.** To appoint to an office, dignity, function, or task; designate. [ME *constituen* < Lat. *cōnstituere*, to set up : *com-*, com- + *statuere*, to set up; see **stā-** in App.] —**con′sti·tut′er, con′sti·tu′tor** *n.*

con·sti·tu·tion (kŏn′stĭ-tōō′shən, -tyōō′-) *n.* **1.** The act or process of composing, setting up, or establishing. **2a.** The composition or structure of something; makeup. **b.** The physical makeup of a person. **3a.** The system of fundamental laws and principles that prescribes the nature, functions, and limits of a government or another institution. **b.** The document recording such a system. **c. Constitution** The fundamental law of the US, framed in 1787, ratified in 1789, and variously amended since.

con·sti·tu·tion·al (kŏn′stĭ-tōō′shə-nəl, -tyōō′-) *adj.* **1.** Of or relating to a constitution: *a constitutional amendment.* **2.** Consistent with, sanctioned by, or permissible according to a constitution. **3.** Established by or operating under a constitution. **4.** Of or proceeding from the basic structure or nature of a person or thing; inherent. **5.** Of or relating to one's physical makeup. ❖ *n.* A walk taken regularly for one's health. —**con′sti·tu′tion·al·ly** *adv.*

con·sti·tu·tion·al·ism (kŏn′stĭ-tōō′shə-nə-lĭz′əm, -tyōō′-) *n.* **1.** Government in which power is distributed and limited by a system of laws that must be obeyed by the rulers. **2a.** A constitutional system of government. **b.** Advocacy of such a system. —**con′sti·tu′tion·al·ist** *n.*

con·sti·tu·tion·al·i·ty (kŏn′stĭ-tōō′shə-năl′ĭ-tē, -tyōō′-) *n.* Accordance with constitutional provisions or principles.

con·sti·tu·tion·al·ize (kŏn′stĭ-tōō′shə-nə-līz′, -tyōō′-) *tr.v.* **-ized, -iz·ing, -iz·es 1.** To provide with or make subject to a constitution. **2.** To incorporate into or sanction under a constitution. —**con′sti·tu′tion·al·i·za′tion** (-lĭ-zā′shən) *n.*

constitutional monarchy *n.* A monarchy in which the powers of the ruler are restricted to those granted under the constitution and laws of the nation.

con·sti·tu·tive (kŏn′stĭ-tōō′tĭv, -tyōō′-) *adj.* **1.** Making a thing what it is; essential. **2.** Having power to institute, establish, or enact. —**con′sti·tu′tive·ly** *adv.*

con·strain (kən-strān′) *tr.v.* **-strained, -strain·ing, -strains 1.** To compel by physical, moral, or circumstantial force; oblige: *felt constrained to object.* **2.** To keep within close bounds; confine. **3.** To inhibit or restrain; hold back. **4.** To produce in a forced or inhibited manner. [ME *constreinen* < OFr. *constraindre, constraign-* < Lat. *cōnstringere*, to restrain, compress : *com-*, com- + *stringere*, to bind, press together.] —**con·strain′a·ble** *adj.* —**con·strain′ed·ly** (-strā′nĭd-lē) *adv.* —**con·strain′er** *n.*

con·straint (kən-strānt′) *n.* **1.** The threat or use of force to prevent, restrict, or dictate the action or thought of others. **2.** The state of being restricted or confined within prescribed bounds. **3.** One that restricts, limits, or regulates; a check: *moral constraints.* **4.** Embarrassed reserve or reticence; awkwardness. [ME *constreinte* < OFr. < fem. p. part. of *constraindre*, to constrain. See CONSTRAIN.]

con·strict (kən-strĭkt′) *v.* **-strict·ed, -strict·ing, -stricts** —*tr.* **1.** To make smaller or narrower by binding or squeezing. **2.** To squeeze or compress. **3.** To restrict the scope or freedom of; cramp. —*intr.* To become constricted. [Lat. *cōnstringere, cōnstrict-*, to compress. See CONSTRAIN.] —**con·stric′tive** *adj.* —**con·stric′tive·ly** *adv.*

con·stric·tion (kən-strĭk′shən) *n.* **1a.** The act or process of constricting. **b.** The condition or result of being constricted. **c.** Something that constricts. **2.** A feeling of tightness or pressure. **3.** A constricted or narrow part.

con·stric·tor (kən-strĭk′tər) *n.* **1.** One that constricts, as a muscle that compresses a part of the body. **2.** Any of various snakes that tightly coil around and asphyxiate their prey.

con·stringe (kən-strĭnj′) *tr.v.* **-stringed, -string·ing, -string·es** To cause to contract; constrict. [Lat. *cōnstringere*. See CONSTRAIN.] —**con·strin′gen·cy** *n.* —**con·strin′gent** *adj.*

con·struct (kən-strŭkt′) *tr.v.* **-struct·ed, -struct·ing, -structs 1.** To form by assembling or combining parts; build. **2.** To create (a sentence, for example) by systematically arranging ideas or terms. **3.** *Mathematics* To draw (a geometric figure) that meets specific requirements. ❖ *n.* (kŏn′strŭkt′) **1.** Something formed

or constructed from parts. **2a.** A concept, model, or schematic idea. **b.** A concrete image or idea. [Lat. *cōnstruere, cōnstrūct-* : *com-*, com- + *struere*, to pile up.] —**con·struct′i·ble** *adj.* —**con·struc′tor, con·struct′er** *n.*

con·struc·tion (kən-strŭk′shən) *n.* **1a.** The act or process of constructing. **b.** The art, trade, or work of building. **2a.** A structure, such as a building. **b.** Something fashioned or devised systematically. **c.** An artistic composition using various materials; an assemblage or a collage. **3.** The way in which something is built or put together. **4.** The interpretation or explanation given to an expression or a statement. **5.** *Grammar* **a.** The arrangement of words in a meaningful phrase, clause, or sentence. **b.** A group of words so arranged. —**con·struc′tion·al** *adj.* —**con·struc′tion·al·ly** *adv.*

con·struc·tion·ist (kən-strŭk′shə-nĭst) *n.* A person who construes a legal text or document in a specified way.

construction paper *n.* A heavy paper produced in a variety of colors and used in artwork esp. for folded and cutout designs.

con·struc·tive (kən-strŭk′tĭv) *adj.* **1.** Serving to improve or advance; helpful. **2.** Of or relating to construction; structural. **3.** *Law* Based on an interpretation; not directly expressed. —**con·struc′tive·ly** *adv.* —**con·struc′tive·ness** *n.*

con·struc·tiv·ism (kən-strŭk′tə-vĭz′əm) *n.* A movement in modern art originating in Moscow in 1920 and characterized by the use of industrial materials to create nonrepresentational, often geometric objects. —**con·struc′tiv·ist** *n.*

con·strue (kən-strōō′) *v.* **-strued, -stru·ing, -strues** —*tr.* **1.** To adduce or explain the meaning of; interpret. **2.** *Grammar* **a.** To analyze the structure of (a clause or sentence). **b.** To use syntactically: *The noun fish can be construed as singular or plural.* **3.** To translate, esp. aloud. —*intr.* **1.** To analyze grammatical structure. **2.** To be subject to grammatical analysis. ❖ *n.* (kŏn′strōō′) An interpretation or translation. [ME *construen* < LLat. *cōnstruere* < Lat., to build. See CONSTRUCT.] —**con·stru′al** *n.*

con·sub·stan·tial (kŏn′səb-stăn′shəl) *adj.* Of the same substance, nature, or essence. [ME *consubstancial* < LLat. *cōnsubstantiālis* : Lat. com-, com- + LLat. *substantiālis*, substantial; see SUBSTANTIAL.]

con·sub·stan·ti·ate (kŏn′səb-stăn′shē-āt′) *tr. & intr.v.* **-at·ed, -at·ing, -ates** To unite or become united in one common substance, nature, or essence.

con·sub·stan·ti·a·tion (kŏn′səb-stăn′shē-ā′shən) *n.* The doctrine that the substance of the body and blood of Jesus coexists with the substance of the Eucharistic bread and wine.

con·sue·tude (kŏn′swĭ-tōōd′, -tyōōd′) *n.* Custom; usage. [ME < Lat. *cōnsuētūdō.* See CUSTOM.] —**con′sue·tu′di·nar′y** (-tōōd′n-ĕr′ē, -tyōōd′-) *adj.*

con·sul (kŏn′səl) *n.* **1.** An official appointed by a government to reside in a foreign country and represent that government's commercial interests and assist its citizens there. **2.** Either of the two chief magistrates of the Roman Republic, elected for a term of one year. **3.** Any of the three chief magistrates of the French Republic from 1799 to 1804. [ME, Roman consul < Lat. *cōnsul*; poss. akin to *cōnsulere*, to take counsel.] —**con′su·lar** (-sə-lər) *adj.* —**con′sul·ship′** *n.*

con·su·late (kŏn′sə-lĭt) *n.* **1.** The residence or official premises of a consul. **2.** The office, term of office, or jurisdiction of a consul. **3.** Government by consuls.

consulate general *n., pl.* **consulates general** The consulate occupied by a consul general.

consul general *n., pl.* **consuls general** A consul of the highest rank serving at a principal location and usu. responsible for other consular offices within a country.

con·sult (kən-sŭlt′) *v.* **-sult·ed, -sult·ing, -sults** —*tr.* **1a.** To seek advice or information of. **b.** To refer to: *consulted a directory.* **2.** To take into account; consider. —*intr.* **1.** To exchange views; confer. **2.** To work or serve as a consultant. ❖ *n.* (kən-sŭlt′, kŏn′sŭlt′) A consultation, esp. one involving physicians. [Fr. *consulter* < Lat. *cōnsultāre*, freq. of *cōnsulere*, to take counsel.] —**con·sult′er** *n.*

con·sul·tan·cy (kən-sŭl′tn-sē) *n., pl.* **-cies 1.** The act or an instance of consulting. **2.** A business or agency offering expert or professional advice in a field. **3.** A position as a consultant.

con·sul·tant (kən-sŭl′tənt) *n.* **1.** One who gives expert or professional advice. **2.** One who consults another. —**con·sul′tant·ship′** *n.*

con·sul·ta·tion (kŏn′səl-tā′shən) *n.* **1.** The act or process of consulting. **2a.** A conference at which advice is given or views are exchanged. **b.** A meeting between physicians to discuss the diagnosis or treatment of a case.

con·sul·ta·tive (kən-sŭl′tə-tĭv) also **con·sul·tive** (-sŭl′tĭv) or **con·sul·ta·to·ry** (-tôr′ē, -tōr′ē) *adj.* Of or relating to consultation; advisory.

con·sul·tor (kən-sŭl′tər) *n. Roman Catholic Church* **1.** A person, such as a priest, appointed to assist and advise a bishop. **2.** An adviser to a congregation of the Curia.

con·sum·a·ble (kən-sōō′mə-bəl) *adj.* **1.** That can be consumed: *consumable energy.* **2.** That may be depleted or worn out by use. ❖ *n.* A consumable good or service.

con·sume (kən-sōōm′) *v.* **-sumed, -sum·ing, -sumes** —*tr.* **1.** To take in as food; eat or drink up. **2a.** To expend; use up. **b.** To

ă	pat	oi	boy
ā	pay	ou	out
âr	care	ŏŏ	took
ä	father	ōō	boot
ĕ	pet	ŭ	cut
ē	be	ûr	urge
ĭ	pit	th	thin
ī	pie	th	this
îr	pier	hw	which
ŏ	pot	zh	vision
ō	toe	ə	about,
ô	paw		item

Stress marks:
′ (primary)
′ (secondary), as in
lexicon (lĕk′sĭ-kŏn′)

purchase (goods or services) for direct use or ownership. **3.** To waste; squander. **4.** To destroy totally: *flames that consumed the house.* **5.** To absorb; engross: *consumed with jealousy.* —*intr.* **1.** To be destroyed, expended, or wasted. **2.** To purchase economic goods and services. [ME *consumen* < Lat. *cōnsūmere* : *com-*, *com-* + *sūmere*, to take.]

con•sum•ed•ly (kən-soō′mĭd-lē) *adv.* Excessively.

con•sum•er (kən-soō′mər) *n.* **1.** One that consumes, esp. for direct use or ownership rather than for business. **2.** A heterotrophic organism that ingests other organisms or organic matter in a food chain. —**con•sum′er•ship** *n.*

consumer credit *n.* Credit granted to a consumer permitting use or ownership during a term of payment.

consumer goods *pl.n.* Goods, such as food and clothing, that satisfy human wants through their direct consumption or use.

con•sum•er•ism (kən-soō′mə-rĭz′əm) *n.* **1.** The movement to protect and inform consumers by requiring such practices as honest advertising. **2.** The theory that a progressively greater consumption of goods is economically beneficial. **3.** Attachment to materialistic values or possessions. —**con•sum′er•ist** *n.* —**con•sum′er•is′tic** *adj.*

consumer price index *n.* An index of prices used to measure the change in the cost of basic goods and services in comparison with a fixed base period.

con•sum•ing (kən-soō′mĭng) *adj.* Ardent or deeply felt: *a consuming passion.*

con•sum•mate (kŏn′sə-māt′) *tr.v.* **-mat•ed, -mat•ing, -mates** **1a.** To bring to completion or fruition; conclude: *consummate a business transaction.* **b.** To realize or achieve; fulfill. **2a.** To complete (a marriage) with the first act of sexual intercourse after the ceremony. **b.** To fulfill (a sexual desire or attraction) esp. by intercourse. —*adj.* (kən-sŭm′ĭt, kŏn′sə-mət) **1.** Complete or perfect in every respect: *consummate happiness.* See Syns at **perfect.** **2.** Supremely accomplished or skilled. **3.** Complete; utter: *a consummate bore.* [ME *consummaten* < Lat. *cōnsummāte*, *cōnsummāt-* : *com-*, *com-* + *summa*, sum; see SUM.] —**con•sum′mate•ly** (kən-sŭm′ĭt-lē) *adv.* —**con′sum•ma′tive, con•sum′ma•to′ry** (-sŭm′ə-tôr′ē, -tōr′ē) *adj.* —**con′sum•ma′tor** *n.*

con•sum•ma•tion (kŏn′sə-mā′shən) *n.* **1.** The act of consummating; a fulfillment. **2.** An ultimate goal or end.

con•sump•tion (kən-sŭmp′shən) *n.* **1a.** The act or process of consuming. **b.** The state of being consumed. **c.** An amount consumed. **2.** *Economics* The using up of goods and services by consumer purchasing or in the production of other goods. **3.** *Pathology* **a.** A progressive wasting of body tissue. **b.** Pulmonary tuberculosis. Not in scientific use. [ME *consumpcioun* < Lat. *cōnsūmptiō*, *cōnsūmptiōn-*, a consuming < *cōnsūmptus*, p. part. of *cōnsūmere*, to consume. See CONSUME.]

con•sump•tive (kən-sŭmp′tĭv) *adj.* **1.** Consuming or tending to consume. **2.** Of, relating to, or afflicted with consumption. ❖ *n.* A person afflicted with consumption. —**con•sump′tive•ly** *adv.*

cont. *abbr.* **1.** contents **2.** continent **3.** continued **4.** contraction

con•tact (kŏn′tăkt′) *n.* **1a.** A coming together or touching, as of objects or surfaces. **b.** The state or condition of touching or of immediate proximity. **2a.** Connection or interaction; communication: *in contact with the right people.* **b.** Visual observation. **c.** Association; relationship: *came into contact with new ideas.* **3.** A person who might be of use; a connection. **4a.** A connection between two conductors that permits a flow of current or heat. **b.** A part or device that makes or breaks such a connection. **5.** *Medicine* A person recently exposed to a contagious disease, usu. through close association with an infected individual. **6.** A contact lens. ❖ *v.* (kŏn′tăkt′, kən-tăkt′) **-tact•ed, -tact•ing, -tacts** —*tr.* **1.** To bring or put in contact. **2.** To get in touch with; communicate with. —*intr.* To be in or come into contact. ❖ *adj.* **1.** Of, sustaining, or making contact. **2.** Caused or transmitted by touching. [Lat. *contāctus* < p. part. of *contingere*, to touch : *com-*, *com-* + *tangere*, to touch; see **tag-** in App.] —**con•tac′tu•al** (kən-tăk′choō-əl) *adj.* —**con•tac′tu•al•ly** *adv.*

USAGE NOTE *Contact* has been widely used as a general verb meaning "to communicate with" for nearly a century. Despite its popularity, it has been decried by critics who object either to its supposedly vague meaning or to the fact that it was originally a noun that was converted into a verb. Yet the very broadness of the verb's meaning renders it particularly useful in an age of proliferating forms of communication, and turning nouns into verbs has been a standard feature of English for hundreds of years. Not surprisingly, resistance to the verb *contact* is abating: in 1969 only 34 percent of the Usage Panel accepted the use of *contact* as a verb, but in our most recent survey 65 percent of the Panel accepted the sentence *She immediately called an officer at the Naval Intelligence Service, who in turn contacted the FBI.* See Usage Note at **impact.**

---

contact dermatitis *n.* An acute or chronic skin inflammation resulting from contact with an irritating substance or allergen.

contact flight *n.* Aircraft navigation by visual observation of the horizon or of landmarks.

contact inhibition *n.* The cessation of cellular growth and division due to physical contact with other cells.

contact lens *n.* A thin plastic or glass lens that is fitted over the cornea of the eye to correct various vision defects.

con•tac•tor (kŏn′tăk′tər, kən-tăk′-) *n.* An electrical relay used to control the flow of power in a circuit.

contact print *n.* A print made by exposing a photosensitive surface in direct contact with a photographic negative.

contact sport *n.* A sport, such as hockey, that involves physical contact between players as part of normal play.

con•ta•gion (kən-tā′jən) *n.* **1a.** Disease transmission by direct or indirect contact. **b.** A disease so transmitted; a contagious disease. **c.** The causative agent, such as a virus, of a communicable disease. **2.** *Psychology* The propagation or spread of a behavior, attitude, or emotion among individuals. **3.** A harmful, corrupting influence. **4.** The tendency to spread, as of a doctrine. [ME *contagioun* < Lat. *contāgiō*, *contāgiōn-* < *contingere*, *contāct-*, to touch. See CONTACT.]

con•ta•gious (kən-tā′jəs) *adj.* **1.** Of or relating to contagion. **2.** Transmissible by direct or indirect contact; communicable. **3.** Capable of transmitting disease. **4.** Spreading or tending to spread from one to another; infectious. —**con•ta′gious•ly** *adv.* —**con•ta′gious•ness** *n.*

contagious abortion *n.* Brucellosis, esp. in cattle.

con•ta•gium (kən-tā′jəm) *n., pl.* **-gia** (-jə) The causative agent of a communicable disease; contagion. [Lat. *contāgium*, contagion, contamination < *contāgiō*. See CONTAGION.]

con•tain (kən-tān′) *tr.v.* **-tained, -tain•ing, -tains** **1a.** To have within; hold. **b.** To be capable of holding. **2.** To have as component parts; include or comprise. **3a.** To hold or keep within limits; restrain. **b.** To halt the spread or development of; check: *a method of containing disease.* **4.** To check the expansion or influence of (a hostile power or ideology) by containment. **5.** *Mathematics* To be exactly divisible by. [ME *conteinen* < OFr. *contenir* < Lat. *continēre* : *com-*, *com-* + *tenēre*, to hold; see **ten-** in App.] —**con•tain′a•ble** *adj.*

con•tain•er (kən-tā′nər) *n.* **1.** A receptacle in which material is held or carried. **2.** A large reusable receptacle accommodating smaller cartons or cases in a single shipment.

con•tain•er•board (kən-tā′nər-bôrd′, -bōrd′) *n.* A corrugated or solid cardboard used to make containers.

con•tain•er•ize (kən-tā′nə-rīz′) *tr.v.* **-ized, -iz•ing, -iz•es** To package (cargo) in large standardized containers for efficient shipping and handling. —**con•tain′er•i•za′tion** (-tə′nər-ĭ-zā′shən) *n.*

container ship *n.* A ship fitted for transporting containerized cargo.

con•tain•ment (kən-tān′mənt) *n.* **1.** The act or condition of containing. **2.** A policy of checking the expansion or influence of a hostile power or ideology. **3.** A structure or system designed to prevent the accidental release of radioactive materials from a reactor.

con•tam•i•nant (kən-tăm′ə-nənt) *n.* One that contaminates.

con•tam•i•nate (kən-tăm′ə-nāt′) *tr.v.* **-nated, -nat•ing, -nates** **1.** To make impure or unclean by contact or mixture. **2.** To expose to or permeate with radioactivity. ❖ *n.* (-nĭt) One that contaminates; a contaminant. [ME *contaminaten* < Lat. *contāminnāre*, *contāmināt-*. See **tag-** in App.] —**con•tam′i•na′tive** *adj.* —**con•tam′i•na′tor** *n.*

con•tam•i•na•tion (kən-tăm′ə-nā′shən) *n.* **1a.** The act or process of contaminating. **b.** The state of being contaminated. **2.** One that contaminates.

contd. *abbr.* continued

conte (kônt) *n., pl.* **contes** (kônt) **1.** A short story or novella. **2.** A medieval narrative tale. [Fr. < OFr. *conter*, to relate, recount. See COUNT[1].]

con•temn (kən-tĕm′) *tr.v.* **-temned, -temn•ing, -temns** To view with contempt; despise. See Syns at **despise.** [ME *contempnen*, to slight < Lat. *contemnere* : *com-*, *com-* + *temnere*, to despise.] —**con•temn′er** (-tĕm′ər, -tĕm′nər) *n.*

con•tem•plate (kŏn′təm-plāt′) *v.* **-plat•ed, -plat•ing, -plates** —*tr.* **1.** To consider carefully and at length; meditate on or ponder. **2.** To have in mind as an intention or possibility. **3.** To look at attentively and thoughtfully: *"It is interesting to contemplate an entangled bank, clothed with many plants"* (Charles Darwin). —*intr.* To ponder; meditate. [Lat. *contemplārī*, *contemplāt-* : *com-*, *com-* + *templum*, space for observing auguries.] —**con′tem•pla′tor** *n.*

con•tem•pla•tion (kŏn′təm-plā′shən) *n.* **1.** The act or state of contemplating. **2.** Thoughtful observation or study. **3.** Meditation on spiritual matters, esp. as a form of devotion. **4.** Intention or expectation: *contemplation of a career change.*

con•tem•pla•tive (kən-tĕm′plə-tĭv, kŏn′təm-plā′-) *adj.* Disposed to or characterized by contemplation. See Syns at **pensive.** ❖ *n.* **1.** A person given to contemplation. **2.** A member of a religious order emphasizing meditation. —**con•tem′pla•tive•ly** *adv.* —**con•tem′pla•tive•ness** *n.*

con•tem•po•ra•ne•ous (kən-tĕm′pə-rā′nē-əs) *adj.* Originating, existing, or happening during the same period of time. [Lat. *contemporāneus* : *com-*, *com-* + *tempus*, *tempor-*, time + *-āneus*, adj. suff.] —**con•tem′po•ra•ne′i•ty** (-pər-ə-nē′ĭ-tē, -nā′-), **con•tem′po•ra•ne•ous•ness** *n.* —**con•tem′po•ra•ne•ous•ly** *adv.*

con·tem·po·rar·y (kən-tĕm′pə-rĕr′ē) *adj.* **1.** Belonging to the same period of time: *a fact documented by two contemporary sources.* **2.** Of about the same age. **3.** Current; modern. ❖ *n., pl.* **-ies 1.** One of the same time or age. **2.** A person of the present age. [Med.Lat. *contemporārius* : Lat. *com-*, com- + Lat. *tempus, tempor-*, time + Lat. *-ārius*, -ary.] —**con′tem′po·rar′i·ly** (-tĕm′pə-râr′ə-lē) *adv.*

con·tem·po·rize (kən-tĕm′pə-rīz′) *v.* **-rized, -riz·ing, -riz·es** —*tr.* To modernize. —*intr.* To be contemporary. —**con·tem′po·ri·za′tion** (-tĕm′pər-ĭ-zā′shən) *n.*

con·tempt (kən-tĕmpt′) *n.* **1.** The feeling or attitude of regarding someone or something as inferior, base, or worthless; scorn. **2.** The state of being despised or dishonored; disgrace. **3.** Open disrespect or willful disobedience of the authority of a court of law or legislative body. [ME < Lat. *contemptus*, p. part. of *contemnere*, to despise. See CONTEMN.]

con·tempt·i·ble (kən-tĕmp′tə-bəl) *adj.* **1.** Deserving of contempt; despicable. **2.** *Obsolete* Contemptuous. —**con·tempt′i·bil′i·ty, con·tempt′i·ble·ness** *n.* —**con·tempt′i·bly** *adv.*

con·temp·tu·ous (kən-tĕmp′chōō-əs) *adj.* Manifesting or feeling contempt; scornful. —**con·temp′tu·ous·ly** *adv.* —**con·temp′tu·ous·ness** *n.*

con·tend (kən-tĕnd′) *v.* **-tend·ed, -tend·ing, -tends** —*intr.* **1.** To strive in opposition or against difficulties; struggle. **2.** To compete, as in a race; vie. **3.** To strive in controversy or debate; dispute. —*tr.* To maintain or assert. [ME *contenden* < Lat. *contendere* : *com-*, com- + *tendere*, to stretch, strive; see **ten-** in App.] —**con·tend′er** *n.*

con·tent[1] (kŏn′tĕnt′) *n.* **1.** Something contained, as in a receptacle. Often used in the plural. **2a.** Written material, such as information or documents, provided for publication. **b.** The individual items that together constitute a written work or document. Often used in the plural. **3a.** The substantive or meaningful part. **b.** The meaning or significance of a literary or artistic work. **4.** The proportion of a specified substance: *a high protein content.* [ME < Med.Lat. *contentum*, neut. p. part. of Lat. *continēre*, to contain. See CONTAIN.]

con·tent[2] (kən-tĕnt′) *adj.* **1.** Desiring no more than what one has; satisfied. **2.** Ready to accept or acquiesce; willing. ❖ *tr.v.* **-tent·ed, -tent·ing, -tents** To make content or satisfied. ❖ *n.* Contentment; satisfaction. [ME < OFr. < Lat. *contentus*, p. part. of *continēre*, to restrain. See CONTAIN.]

content analysis (kŏn′tĕnt′) *n.* A systematic analysis of the content of a communication including themes and symbols to determine its objective or meaning.

con·tent·ed (kən-tĕn′tĭd) *adj.* Satisfied with things as they are; content. —**con·tent′ed·ly** *adv.* —**con·tent′ed·ness** *n.*

con·ten·tion (kən-tĕn′shən) *n.* **1.** The act or an instance of striving in controversy or debate. **2.** A striving to win in competition; rivalry. **3.** An assertion put forward in argument. [Ult. < Lat. *contentiō, contentiōn-* < *contentus*, p. part. of *contendere*, to contend. See CONTEND.]

con·ten·tious (kən-tĕn′shəs) *adj.* **1.** Given to contention; quarrelsome. See Syns at **argumentative**. **2.** Involving or likely to cause contention; controversial. —**con·ten′tious·ly** *adv.* —**con·ten′tious·ness** *n.*

con·tent·ment (kən-tĕnt′mənt) *n.* **1.** The state of being contented; satisfaction. **2.** A source of satisfaction.

content word (kŏn′tĕnt′) *n.* A word, such as a noun or verb, having a statable lexical meaning rather than indicating a grammatical relationship.

con·ter·mi·nous (kən-tûr′mə-nəs) also **co·ter·mi·nous** (kō-) *adj.* **1.** Sharing a boundary; contiguous. **2.** Contained in the same boundaries; coextensive: *the conterminous states.* **3.** Sharing scope, range of meaning, or extent in time. [< Lat. *conterminus* : *com-*, com- + *terminus*, boundary.] —**con·ter′mi·nous·ly** *adv.* —**con·ter′mi·nous·ness** *n.*

contes (kônt) *n.* Plural of **conte.**

con·tes·sa (kən-tĕs′ə, kōn-tĕs′sä) *n.* An Italian countess. [Ital., fem. of *conte*, count < LLat. *comes, comit-*. See COUNT[2].]

con·test (kŏn′tĕst′) *n.* **1.** A struggle for superiority or victory between rivals. **2.** A competition, esp. one in which entrants perform separately and are rated by judges. See Syns at **conflict**. ❖ *v.* (kən-tĕst′, kŏn′tĕst′) **-test·ed, -test·ing, -tests** —*tr.* **1.** To compete or strive for. **2.** To call into question and take an active stand against; dispute or challenge. See Syns at **oppose**. —*intr.* To struggle or compete; contend. [Prob. < Fr. *conteste* < *contester*, to dispute < OFr., to call to witness < Lat. *contestārī* : *com-*, com- + *testis*, witness; see **trei-** in App.] —**con·test′a·ble** *adj.* —**con′tes·ta′tion** (kŏn′tĕ-stā′shən) *n.* —**con·test′er** *n.*

con·tes·tant (kən-tĕs′tənt, kŏn′tĕs′tənt) *n.* **1.** One taking part in a contest; a competitor. **2.** One that contests or disputes something, such as an election or a will.

con·text (kŏn′tĕkst′) *n.* **1.** The part of a text or statement that surrounds a particular word or passage and determines its mean-

ing. **2.** The circumstances in which an event occurs; a setting. [ME, composition < Lat. *contextus* < p. part. of *contexere*, to join together : *com-*, com- + *texere*, to weave.]

con·tex·tu·al (kən-tĕks′chōō-əl, kŏn-) *adj.* Of, involving, or depending on a context. —**con·tex′tu·al·ly** *adv.*

con·tex·tu·al·ize (kən-tĕks′chōō-ə-līz′) *tr.v.* **-ized, -iz·ing, -iz·es** To place (a word or idea, for example) in a particular context. —**con·tex′tu·al·i·za′tion** (-ə-lĭ-zā′shən) *n.*

con·tex·ture (kən-tĕks′chər, kŏn′tĕks′-) *n.* **1.** The act of weaving or assembling parts into a whole. **2.** An arrangement of interconnected parts; a structure. —**con·tex′tur·al** *adj.*

con·ti·gu·i·ty (kŏn′tĭ-gyōō′ĭ-tē) *n., pl.* **-ties 1.** The state of being contiguous. **2.** A continuous mass or series.

con·tig·u·ous (kən-tĭg′yōō-əs) *adj.* **1.** Sharing an edge or boundary; touching. **2.** Neighboring; adjacent. **3.** Connected in time or space without a break: *the 48 contiguous states.* [< Lat. *contiguus* < *contingere, contig-*, to touch. See CONTACT.] —**con·tig′u·ous·ly** *adv.* —**con·tig′u·ous·ness** *n.*

con·ti·nence (kŏn′tə-nəns) *n.* **1.** Self-restraint; moderation. **2.** Voluntary control over urinary and fecal discharge. **3.** Partial or complete abstention from sexual activity.

con·ti·nent[1] (kŏn′tə-nənt) *n.* **1.** One of the principal land masses of the earth. **2. Continent** The mainland of Europe. Used with *the.* [Lat. *(terra) continēns, continent-*, continuous (land), pr. part. of *continēre*, to hold together. See CONTAIN.]

con·ti·nent[2] (kŏn′tə-nənt) *adj.* Exercising continence. [ME < Lat. *continēns*, pr. part. of *continēre*, to restrain. See CONTAIN.] —**con·ti·nent·ly** *adv.*

con·ti·nen·tal (kŏn′tə-nĕn′tl) *adj.* **1.** Of, relating to, or characteristic of a continent. **2.** often **Continental** Of or relating to the mainland of Europe; European. **3. Continental** Of or relating to the American colonies during and immediately after the Revolutionary War. ❖ *n.* **1.** often **Continental a.** An inhabitant of a continent. **b.** An inhabitant of mainland Europe. **2.** A native of the continental United States living or working in Puerto Rico or the US Virgin Islands. **3. Continental** A soldier in the American army during the Revolutionary War. **4.** A piece of paper money issued by the Continental Congress during the Revolutionary War. —**con′ti·nen′tal·ly** *adv.*

continental breakfast *n.* A light breakfast consisting usu. of coffee or tea and a baked good.

Continental Celtic *n.* An extinct branch of the Celtic languages comprising Gaulish and Celtiberian, once spoken in continental Europe.

continental code *n.* See **international Morse code**.

continental divide *n.* An extensive stretch of high ground from each side of which the river systems of a continent flow in opposite directions.

Continental Divide A series of mountain ridges extending from AK to Mexico, mostly in the Rocky Mts.; often called the **Great Divide** in the US.

continental drift *n.* The movement, formation, or re-formation of continents described by the theory of plate tectonics.

continental shelf *n.* A submerged border of a continent that slopes gradually seaward and extends to a point of steeper descent to the ocean bottom.

continental shield *n.* See **shield** 6.

continental slope *n.* The descent from the continental shelf to the ocean bottom.

con·tin·gence (kən-tĭn′jəns) *n.* **1.** A joining or touching. **2.** Contingency.

con·tin·gen·cy (kən-tĭn′jən-sē) *n., pl.* **-cies 1a.** A possible but unlikely or unplanned event. **b.** A possibility that must be prepared for; a future emergency. **2.** The condition of dependence on chance; uncertainty. **3.** Something incidental to something else. —**con·tin′gen·cy** *adj.*

contingency fee *n.* A fee, as for an attorney, payable only in the event of a successful or satisfactory outcome.

contingency table *n.* A statistical table showing the observed frequencies of data elements classified in rows and columns according to two variables.

con·tin·gent (kən-tĭn′jənt) *adj.* **1.** Liable to occur but not certain; possible. **2.** Dependent on conditions or occurrences not yet established; conditional. **3.** Happening by chance or accident; fortuitous. **4.** *Logic* True only under certain conditions; not necessarily or universally true. ❖ *n.* **1.** An event or condition that is likely but not inevitable. **2.** A share or quota, as of troops, contributed to a general effort. **3.** A representative group forming part of an assemblage. [ME < Lat. *contingēns, contingent-*, pr. part. of *contingere*, to touch. See CONTACT.] —**con·tin′gent·ly** *adv.*

contingent worker *n.* A temporary or part-time worker, usu. working under contract for a fixed period.

con·tin·u·a (kən-tĭn′yōō-ə) *n.* A plural of **continuum**.

con·tin·u·al (kən-tĭn′yōō-əl) *adj.* **1.** Recurring regularly or frequently. **2.** Not interrupted; steady. —**con·tin′u·al·ly** *adv.*

SYNONYMS *continual, continuous, constant, ceaseless, incessant, perpetual, eternal, perennial, interminable* These adjectives mean occurring repeatedly over a long period of time. *Continual* is chiefly restricted to what is intermittent or repeated at intervals:

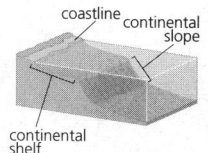

coastline · continental slope
continental shelf

continental shelf

the continual banging of the shutter in the wind. Continuous implies lack of interruption: a continuous line. Constant stresses steadiness or persistence and unvarying nature: constant chatter. Ceaseless and incessant pertain to uninterrupted activity: the ceaseless thunder of the surf; incessant questions. Perpetual emphasizes both steadiness and duration: a perpetual stream of visitors. Eternal refers to what is everlasting, especially to what is seemingly without temporal beginning or end: "That freedom can be retained only by the eternal vigilance which has always been its price" (Elmer Davis). Perennial describes existence that goes on year after year, often with the suggestion of self-renewal: perennial poverty. Interminable refers to what is or seems to be endless and is often applied to something prolonged and wearisome: an interminable argument.

con·tin·u·ance (kən-tĭn′yo͞o-əns) n. **1.** The act or fact of continuing. **2.** The time during which something exists or lasts; duration. **3.** A continuation or sequel. **4.** Law Postponement or adjournment to a future date.

USAGE NOTE Continuance is interchangeable with continuation in some of its senses. However, only continuance is used to refer to the duration of a state or condition, as in his continuance in office. Continuation applies especially to prolongation or resumption of action (a continuation of the meeting) or to physical extension (the continuation of the street).

con·tin·u·ant (kən-tĭn′yo͞o-ənt) n. A consonant, such as (s), (m), or (l), that can be prolonged without change while breath lasts.

con·tin·u·a·tion (kən-tĭn′yo͞o-ā′shən) n. **1a.** The act or fact of continuing. **b.** The state of being continued. **2.** An extension by which something is carried to a further point. **3.** A resumption after an interruption. See Usage Note at **continuance**.

con·tin·u·a·tive (kən-tĭn′yo͞o-ā′tĭv, -ə-tĭv) adj. Of, relating to, or serving to cause continuation. ❖ n. Something that expresses or causes continuation. —**con·tin′u·a′tive·ly** adv.

con·tin·u·a·tor (kən-tĭn′yo͞o-ā′tər) n. One that continues, esp. a person who carries on the work of another.

con·tin·ue (kən-tĭn′yo͞o) v. **-ued, -u·ing, -ues** —intr. **1.** To go on with a particular action or in a particular condition; persist. **2.** To exist over a prolonged period; last. **3.** To remain in the same state, capacity, or place. **4.** To go on after an interruption; resume. —tr. **1.** To carry forward; persist in. **2.** To carry further in time, space, or development; extend. **3.** To cause to remain or last; retain. **4.** To carry on after an interruption; resume. **5.** Law To postpone or adjourn. [ME continuen < OFr. continuer < Lat. continuāre < continuus, continuous < continēre, to hold together. See CONTAIN.] —**con·tin′u·a·ble** adj. —**con·tin′u·er** n.

con·tin·ued fraction (kən-tĭn′yo͞od) n. A fraction whose numerator is a whole number and whose denominator is a whole number plus a fraction that has a denominator consisting of a whole number plus a fraction, and so on.

con·tin·u·ing education (kən-tĭn′yo͞o-ĭng) n. **1.** An instructional program featuring recent advances in a particular area. **2.** Instructional courses esp. for adult part-time students.

con·ti·nu·i·ty (kŏn′tə-no͞o′ĭ-tē, -nyo͞o′-) n., pl. **-ties 1.** The state or quality of being continuous. **2.** An uninterrupted succession or flow; a coherent whole. **3a.** A detailed script or scenario consulted to avoid discrepancies from shot to shot in a film, allowing scenes to be shot out of order. **b.** Spoken matter serving to link parts of a radio or television program so that no break occurs.

con·tin·u·o (kən-tĭn′yo͞o-ō′) n., pl. **-os** An independent bass line, usu. realized on a keyboard instrument, in which numerals written underneath the notes indicate the kinds of harmony to be played. [Ital. < Lat. continuus, continuous. See CONTINUE.]

con·tin·u·ous (kən-tĭn′yo͞o-əs) adj. **1.** Uninterrupted in time, sequence, substance, or extent. See Syns at **continual**. **2.** Attached together in repeated units. **3.** Mathematics Of or relating to a line or curve that extends without a break or irregularity. —**con·tin′u·ous·ly** adv. —**con·tin′u·ous·ness** n.

continuous creation theory n. See **steady state theory**.

continuous spectrum n. A spectrum without lines or bands, esp. one of radiation distributed over an uninterrupted range of wavelengths.

continuous variation n. Variation within a population in which a graded series of intermediate phenotypes falls between the extremes.

continuous wave also **con·tin·u·ous-wave** (kən-tĭn′yo͞o-əs-wāv′) adj. Emitting or capable of emitting continuously; not pulsed: a continuous wave laser.

con·tin·u·um (kən-tĭn′yo͞o-əm) n., pl. **-tin·u·a** (-tĭn′yo͞o-ə) or **-tin·u·ums 1.** A continuous extent, succession, or whole, no part of which can be distinguished from neighboring parts except by arbitrary division. **2.** Mathematics **a.** A set having the same number of points as all the real numbers in an interval. **b.** The set of all real numbers. [Lat., neut. of continuus, continuous. See CONTINUE.]

con·tort (kən-tôrt′) v. **-tort·ed, -tort·ing, -torts** —tr. To twist, wrench, or bend severely out of shape. —intr. To become twisted into a strained form or expression. [Lat. contorquēre, contort-, to

twist : com-, com- + torquēre, to twist.] —**con·tor′tion** n. —**con·tor′tive** adj.

con·tort·ed (kən-tôr′tĭd) adj. **1.** Twisted or strained out of shape. **2.** Botany Twisted, bent, or partially rolled upon itself; convolute. —**con·tort′ed·ly** adv. —**con·tort′ed·ness** n.

con·tor·tion·ist (kən-tôr′shə-nĭst) n. One who contorts, esp. an acrobat. —**con·tor′tion·is′tic** adj.

con·tour (kŏn′to͞or′) n. **1a.** The outline of a figure, body, or mass. **b.** A line that represents such an outline. See Syns at **outline**. **2.** A surface, esp. of a curving form. Often used in the plural. **3.** A contour line. **4.** Linguistics The distinctive rising and falling patterns of pitch, tone, or stress. ❖ tr.v. **-toured, -tour·ing, -tours 1.** To make or shape the outline of; represent in contour. **2.** To build (a road, for example) to follow the contour of the land. ❖ adj. **1.** Following the contour lines of uneven terrain to limit erosion of topsoil. **2.** Shaped to fit the outline or form of something. [Fr., alteration of Ital. contorno < contornare, to draw in outline : Lat. com-, intensive pref.; see COM- + Lat. tornāre, to round off (< tornus, lathe < Gk. tornos; see terə-¹ in App.).]

contour feather n. Any of the outermost feathers of a bird, forming the visible body contour and plumage.

contour line n. A line on a map that joins points of equal elevation.

contour map n. A map showing elevations and surface configuration by means of contour lines.

contr. abbr. **1.** contraction **2.** contralto

con·tra (kŏn′trə) prep. In contrast or opposition to; against. ❖ adv. In opposition to something stated or expected; to the contrary. [Lat. contrā, against. See kom- in App.]

contra– pref. **1.** Against; opposite; contrasting: contraposition. **2.** Lower in pitch: contrabassoon. [ME < Lat. contrā- < contrā, against; see CONTRA. Sense 2, Ital. < Lat. contrā.]

con·tra·band (kŏn′trə-bănd′) n. **1.** Goods prohibited by law or treaty from being imported or exported. **2a.** Illegal traffic in contraband; smuggling. **b.** Smuggled goods. **3.** Goods that may be seized and confiscated by a belligerent if shipped to another belligerent by a neutral. **4.** During the Civil War, a slave who fled or was taken behind Union lines. ❖ adj. Prohibited from being imported or exported. [Ital. contrabbando : contra-, against (< Lat. contrā-; see CONTRA-) + bando, legal proclamation (< LLat. bannus, of Gmc. orig.; see bhā- in App.).] —**con′tra·band′age** n. —**con′tra·band′ist** n.

con·tra·bass (kŏn′trə-bās′) n. See **double bass**. ❖ adj. Pitched an octave below the normal bass range. [Obsolete Ital. contrabasso : Ital. contra-, against (< Lat. contrā-; see CONTRA-) + Ital. basso, bass (< Med.Lat. bassus, low).] —**con′tra·bass′ist** n.

con·tra·bas·soon (kŏn′trə-bə-so͞on′, -bă-) n. The largest and lowest pitched of the double-reed wind instruments, sounding an octave below the bassoon.

con·tra·cep·tion (kŏn′trə-sĕp′shən) n. Intentional prevention of conception or impregnation through the use of various devices, agents, drugs, sexual practices, or surgical procedures. [CONTRA- + (CON)CEPTION.]

con·tra·cep·tive (kŏn′trə-sĕp′tĭv) adj. Capable of preventing conception. ❖ n. A device, drug, or chemical agent that prevents conception.

con·tract (kŏn′trăkt) n. **1a.** An agreement between two or more parties, esp. one written and enforceable by law. **b.** The writing or document containing such an agreement. **2.** The branch of law dealing with formal agreements between parties. **3.** Marriage as a formal agreement; betrothal. **4.** Games **a.** The last and highest bid of a suit of one hand in bridge. **b.** The number of tricks thus bid. **5.** A paid assignment to murder someone. ❖ v. (kən-trăkt′, kŏn′trăkt′) **-tract·ed, -tract·ing, -tracts** —tr. **1.** To enter into by contract; establish or settle by formal agreement. **2.** To acquire or incur. **3a.** To reduce in size by drawing together; shrink. **b.** To pull together; wrinkle. **4.** Grammar To shorten (a word or words) by omitting or combining letters or sounds. —intr. **1.** To enter into an agreement. **2.** To become reduced in size by or as if by being drawn together. —**phrasal verb: contract out** To engage a person outside an organization by contract to undertake or produce (work). [ME < Lat. contractus, p. part. of contrahere, to draw together, make a contract : com-, com- + trahere, to draw.] —**con·tract′i·bil′i·ty, con·tract′i·ble·ness** n. —**con·tract′i·ble** adj.

contract bridge n. Auction bridge in which tricks in excess of the contract may not count toward game bonuses.

con·trac·tile (kən-trăk′təl, -tīl′) adj. Capable of contracting or causing contraction. —**con′trac·til′i·ty** (kŏn′trăk-tĭl′ĭ-tē) n.

contractile vacuole n. A membrane-bound organelle in certain protists that maintains osmotic equilibrium by pumping fluid cyclically from within the cell to the outside, alternately filling and contracting to release its contents on the cell surface.

con·trac·tion (kən-trăk′shən) n. **1.** The act of contracting or the state of being contracted. **2a.** A word or phrase formed by omitting or combining some sounds from a longer word or phrase. **b.** The formation of such a word. **3.** Physiology The shortening and thickening of functioning muscle or muscle fiber. **4.** A period of decreased business activity.

con·trac·tor (kŏn′trăk′tər, kən-trăk′-) n. **1.** One that agrees to provide materials or services at a specified price, esp. for construction work. **2.** Something, esp. a muscle, that contracts.

con·trac·tu·al (kən-trăk′chōō-əl) *adj.* Of, relating to, or having the nature of a contract. —**con·trac′tu·al·ly** *adv.*

con·trac·ture (kən-trăk′chər) *n.* **1.** An abnormal, often permanent shortening, as of scar tissue, that results in distortion or deformity, esp. of a body joint. **2.** Such a deformity.

con·tra·cy·cli·cal (kŏn′trə-sī′klĭ-kəl, -sĭk′lĭ-) *adj.* Acting counter to an economic cycle.

con·tra·dance or **con·tra·danse** (kŏn′trə-dăns′) *n.* Variants of **contredanse**.

con·tra·dict (kŏn′trə-dĭkt′) *v.* **-dict·ed, -dict·ing, -dicts** —*tr.* **1.** To assert or express the opposite of (a statement). **2.** To deny the statement of. **3.** To be contrary to; be inconsistent with. —*intr.* To utter a contradictory statement. [Lat. *contrādīcere, contrādict-,* to speak against : *contrā-,* contra- + *dīcere,* to speak; see **deik-** in App.] —**con′tra·dict′a·ble** *adj.* —**con′tra·dict′er, con′tra·dic′tor** *n.*

con·tra·dic·tion (kŏn′trə-dĭk′shən) *n.* **1a.** The act of contradicting. **b.** The state of being contradicted. **2.** A denial. **3.** Inconsistency; discrepancy. **4.** Something that contains contradictory elements.

con·tra·dic·to·ry (kŏn′trə-dĭk′tə-rē) *adj.* **1.** Involving, of the nature of, or being a contradiction. **2.** Given to contradicting. ❖ *n., pl.* **-ries** *Logic* Either of two propositions related in such a way that it is impossible for both to be true or both to be false. —**con′tra·dic′to·ri·ly** *adv.* —**con′tra·dic′to·ri·ness** *n.*

con·tra·dis·tinc·tion (kŏn′trə-dĭ-stĭngk′shən) *n.* Distinction by contrasting or opposing qualities. —**con′tra·dis·tinc′tive** *adj.* —**con′tra·dis·tinc′tive·ly** *adv.*

con·tra·dis·tin·guish (kŏn′trə-dĭ-stĭng′gwĭsh) *tr.v.* **-guished, -guish·ing, -guish·es** To distinguish by contrasting qualities.

con·tra·fac·tu·al (kŏn′trə-făk′chōō-əl) *n.* A linguistic construction expressing an idea that is presupposed to be false, as *I would go* in the sentence *I would go if I could.*

con·tra·ges·tive (kŏn′trə-jĕs′tĭv) *adj.* Capable of preventing gestation, either by preventing implantation or by causing the uterine lining to shed after implantation. ❖ *n.* A contragestive drug or agent. [CONTRA– + GEST(ATION) + –IVE.] —**con′tra·ges·ta′tion** (-jĕ-stā′shən) *n.*

con·trail (kŏn′trāl′) *n.* A visible trail of streaks of condensed water vapor or ice crystals sometimes forming in the wake of an aircraft. [*con*(*densation*) *trail.*]

con·tra·in·di·cate (kŏn′trə-ĭn′dĭ-kāt′) *tr.v.* **-cat·ed, -cat·ing, -cates** To indicate the inadvisability of (a medical drug, for example). —**con′tra·in′di·ca′tion** *n.* —**con′tra·in·dic′a·tive** (-ĭn-dĭk′ə-tĭv) *adj.*

con·tra·lat·er·al (kŏn′trə-lăt′ər-əl) *adj.* Taking place or originating in a corresponding part on an opposite side.

con·tral·to (kən-trăl′tō) *n., pl.* **-tos** *Music* **1.** The lowest female voice or voice part, intermediate in range between soprano and tenor. **2.** A woman with a contralto voice. [Ital. : *contra-,* below (< Lat. *contrā-,* contra-) + *alto,* alto; see **ALTO**.]

con·tra·po·si·tion (kŏn′trə-pə-zĭsh′ən) *n.* An opposite position; antithesis.

con·tra·pos·i·tive (kŏn′trə-pŏz′ĭ-tĭv) *n.* *Logic* A proposition derived by negating and permuting the terms of another, equivalent proposition.

con·trap·pos·to (kŏn′trə-pōs′tō) *n.* The position of a figure in painting or sculpture in which the hips and legs are turned in a different direction from that of the shoulders and head; the twisting of a figure on its own vertical axis. [Ital., p. part. of *trapporre,* to set opposite, contrast < Lat. *contrāpōnere* : *contrā-,* contra- + *pōnere,* to place; see **apo-** in App.]

con·trap·tion (kən-trăp′shən) *n.* A mechanical device; a gadget. [Perh. mock-Latinate blend of CONTRIVE and TRAP¹.]

con·tra·pun·tal (kŏn′trə-pŭn′tl) *adj.* *Music* Of, relating to, or incorporating counterpoint. [< obsolete Ital. *contrapunto,* counterpoint : Ital. *contra-,* against (< Lat. *contrā-;* see CONTRA–) + Ital. *punto,* point, note (< VLat. **punctum* < Lat. *pūnctum;* see PUNCTUAL).] —**con′tra·pun′tal·ly** *adv.*

con·tra·pun·tist (kŏn′trə-pŭn′tĭst) *n.* One who writes or composes counterpoint.

con·trar·i·an (kən-trâr′ē-ən) *n.* One who takes a contrary view or action, esp. an investor who makes decisions that contradict prevailing wisdom.

con·tra·ri·e·ty (kŏn′trə-rī′ĭ-tē) *n., pl.* **-ties** **1.** The quality or condition of being contrary. **2.** Something that is contrary.

con·tra·ri·ous (kən-trâr′ē-əs) *adj.* Perverse; inimical. —**con·trar′i·ous·ly** *adv.*

con·tra·ri·wise (kŏn′trĕr′ē-wīz′, kən-trâr′-) *adv.* **1.** From a contrasting point of view. **2.** In the opposite way or reverse order. **3.** In a perverse manner.

con·trar·y (kŏn′trĕr′ē) *adj.* **1.** Opposed, as in character or purpose. **2.** Opposite in direction or position. **3.** *Music* Moving in the opposite direction at a fixed interval. **4.** Adverse; unfavorable. **5.** (*also* kən-trâr′ē) Given to recalcitrant behavior; willful or perverse. ❖ *n., pl.* **-ies** **1.** Something that is opposite or contrary. **2.** Either of two opposing or contrary things. **3.** *Logic* A proposition related to another in such a way that if the latter is true, the former must be false, but if the latter is false, the former is not necessarily true. ❖ *adv.* In an opposite or contrary manner; counter.

—**idioms: by contraries** *Obsolete* In opposition to what is expected. **on the contrary** In opposition to what has been stated or what is expected. **to the contrary** To the opposite effect from what has been stated or what is expected. [ME *contrarie* < AN < Lat. *contrārius : contrā,* against; see **kom** in App. + *-ārius,* -ary.] —**con′trar′i·ly** (kŏn′trĕr′ə-lē, kən-trâr′-) *adv.* —**con′trar′i·ness** *n.*

con·trast (kən-trăst′, kŏn′trăst′) *v.* **-trast·ed, -trast·ing, -trasts** —*tr.* To set in opposition in order to show or emphasize differences. —*intr.* **1.** To show differences when compared: *a color that contrasted with the dark background.* **2.** *Linguistics* To evince a difference that can distinguish meaning, as (p) and (b) in English. ❖ *n.* (kŏn′trăst′) **1a.** The act of contrasting; a setting off of dissimilar entities or objects. **b.** The state of being contrasted: *red berries standing in contrast against the snow.* **2.** A difference between entities or objects compared. **3.** One thing that is strikingly dissimilar to another. **4.** The use of opposing elements, such as colors or lines, in proximity to produce an intensified effect in a work of art. **5.** The difference in brightness between the light and dark areas of a picture, such as a photograph or video image. [Fr. *contraster* < Ital. *contrastare* < Med.Lat. *contrāstāre* : Lat. *contrā-,* contra- + Lat. *stāre,* to stand; see **stā-** in App.] —**con·trast′a·ble** *adj.* —**con·trast′ing·ly** *adv.* —**con·tras·tive** *adj.*

USAGE NOTE The noun *contrast* may be followed by *between, with,* or *to: There is a sharp contrast between his earlier and later works. In contrast with* (or less frequently, *to*) *his early works, the later plays are less theatrical.* When *contrast* is used as a transitive verb, both *with* and *to* may follow, though *with* is more common.

contrast medium *n.* A substance, such as barium or air, used in radiography to increase the contrast of an image.

con·trast·y (kŏn′trăs′tē) *adj.* Having or producing sharp contrasts between light and dark areas in photography.

con·tra·vene (kŏn′trə-vēn′) *tr.v.* **-vened, -ven·ing, -venes** **1.** To act or be counter to; violate. **2.** To oppose in argument; gainsay. [Fr. *contrevenir* < Med.Lat. *contrāvenīre,* to transgress < LLat. *contrāvenīre,* to oppose < Lat. *contrā-,* contra- + *venīre,* to come; see **gʷā-** in App.] —**con′tra·ven′er** *n.*

con·tra·ven·tion (kŏn′trə-vĕn′shən) *n.* The act of contravening; a violation.

con·tre·danse also **con·tre·dance** or **con·tra·dance** or **con·tra·danse** (kŏn′trə-dăns′) *n.* **1.** A folk dance performed in two lines with the partners facing each other. **2.** The music for a contredanse. [Fr., alteration (influenced by *contre-,* opposite) of E. COUNTRY-DANCE.]

con·tre·temps (kŏn′trə-tän′, kôn′trə-tän′) *n., pl.* **contretemps** (-tänz′, -tänz′) An unforeseen event that disrupts the normal course of things; an inopportune occurrence. [Fr. : *contre-,* against (< Lat. *contrā-;* see CONTRA-) + *temps,* time (< Lat. *tempus*).]

con·trib·ute (kən-trĭb′yōōt) *v.* **-ut·ed, -ut·ing, -utes** —*tr.* **1.** To give or supply in common with others; give to a common fund or for a common purpose. **2.** To submit for publication. —*intr.* **1.** To make a contribution. **2.** To help bring about a result; act as a factor. **3.** To submit material for publication. [Lat. *contribuere, contribūt-,* to bring together : *com-,* com- + *tribuere,* to grant; see TRIBUTE.] —**con·trib′u·tive** *adj.* —**con·trib′u·tive·ly** *adv.* —**con·trib′u·tive·ness** *n.* —**con·trib′u·tor** *n.*

con·tri·bu·tion (kŏn′trĭ-byōō′shən) *n.* **1.** The act of contributing. **2.** Something contributed. **3.** A payment exacted for a special purpose; an impost or a levy. **4.** An article or other work submitted for publication.

con·trib·u·to·ry (kən-trĭb′yə-tôr′ē, -tōr′ē) *adj.* **1.** Of or relating to contribution. **2.** Helping to bring about a result. **3.** Subject to an impost or levy. ❖ *n., pl.* **-ries** One that contributes.

con·trite (kən-trīt′, kŏn′trīt′) *adj.* **1.** Feeling regret and sorrow for one's sins or offenses; penitent. **2.** Arising from or expressing contrition: *contrite words.* [ME *contrit* < Lat. *contrītus,* p. part. of *conterere,* to crush : *com-,* com- + *terere,* to grind; see **terə-¹** in App.] —**con·trite′ly** *adv.* —**con·trite′ness** *n.*

con·tri·tion (kən-trĭsh′ən) *n.* Sincere remorse for wrongdoing; repentance.

con·tri·vance (kən-trī′vəns) *n.* **1a.** The act of contriving. **b.** The state of being contrived. **2.** Something contrived, as a mechanical device or a clever plan.

con·trive (kən-trīv′) *v.* **-trived, -triv·ing, -trives** —*tr.* **1.** To plan with cleverness or ingenuity; devise. **2.** To invent or fabricate, esp. by improvisation. **3.** To plan with evil intent; scheme. **4.** To bring about, as by scheming; manage. —*intr.* To form plans or schemes. [ME *contreven* < OFr. *controver, contreuv-* < Med.Lat. *contropāre,* to compare : Lat. *com-,* com- + Lat. *tropus,* turn, manner, style (< Gk. *tropos*).] —**con·triv′er** *n.*

con·trived (kən-trīvd′) *adj.* Obviously planned or calculated; not spontaneous or natural; labored: *a novel with a contrived ending.* —**con·triv′ed·ly** (-trī′vĭd-lē, -trīvd′lē) *adv.*

con·trol (kən-trōl′) *tr.v.* **-trolled, -trol·ling, -trols** **1.** To exercise authoritative or dominating influence over; direct. **2.** To adjust to a requirement; regulate: *The valve controls the flow of water.* **3.** To hold in restraint; check: *controlled my temper.* **4.** To reduce or prevent the spread of: *control a fire.* **5a.** To verify or regulate (a

contrail

ă pat	oi boy
ā pay	ou out
âr care	ōō took
ä father	ōō boot
ĕ pet	ŭ cut
ē be	ûr urge
ĭ pit	th thin
ī pie	th this
îr pier	hw which
ŏ pot	zh vision
ō toe	ə about,
ô paw	item

Stress marks:
′ (primary);
′ (secondary), as in
lexicon (lĕk′sĭ-kŏn′)

scientific experiment) by conducting a parallel experiment or by comparing with another standard. **b.** To verify (an account, for example) by using a duplicate register for comparison. ❖ *n.* **1.** Authority or ability to manage or direct: *lost control of the skidding car.* **2a.** A controlling agent, device, or organization. **b.** An instrument or set of instruments used to operate, regulate, or guide a machine or vehicle. Often used in the plural. **3.** A straining device, measure, or limit; a curb: *price controls.* **4a.** A standard of comparison for checking or verifying the results of an experiment. **b.** An individual or group used as a standard of comparison in a control experiment. **5.** An intelligence agent who supervises or instructs another agent. **6.** A spirit presumed to speak or act through a medium. Often used in the plural. [ME *controllen* < AN *controreller* < Med.Lat. *contrārotulāre*, to check by duplicate register < *contrārotulus*, duplicate register : Lat. *contrā-*, contra- + Lat. *rotulus*, roll, dim. of *rota*, wheel.] —**con·trol′la·bil′i·ty** *n.* —**con·trol′la·ble** *adj.*

control experiment *n.* An experiment that isolates the effect of one variable on a system by holding constant all variables but the one under observation.

control freak *Slang n.* One who has an obsessive need to exert control over people and situations.

control key *n.* A key on a computer keyboard that is pressed in combination with another key to activate a command.

con·trolled substance (kən-trōld′) *n.* A drug or chemical substance whose possession and use are regulated under the Controlled Substances Act.

con·trol·ler (kən-trō′lər) *n.* **1.** One that controls: *a controller of events.* **2.** also **comp·trol·ler** (kən-trō′lər, kŏmp-trō′-, kŏmp′trō′-) An officer who audits accounts and supervises the financial affairs of a corporation or a governmental body. **3.** A regulating mechanism, as in a vehicle or electric device. —**con·trol′ler·ship′** *n.*

con·trol·ling interest (kən-trō′lĭng) *n.* Ownership of a sufficient number of shares of stock in a company to control company policy.

control tower *n.* A tower at an airfield from which air traffic is controlled by radio and observed physically and by radar.

con·tro·ver·sial (kŏn′trə-vûr′shəl, -sē-əl) *adj.* **1.** Of, producing, or marked by controversy. **2.** Fond of controversy; disputatious. —**con′tro·ver′sial·ist** *n.* —**con′tro·ver·si·al′i·ty** (-shē-ăl′ĭ-tē, -sē-) *n.* —**con′tro·ver′sial·ly** *adv.*

con·tro·ver·sy (kŏn′trə-vûr′sē) *n., pl.* **-sies** **1.** A dispute, esp. a public one, between sides holding opposing views. **2.** The act or practice of engaging in such disputes. [ME *controversie* < Lat. *contrōversia* < *contrōversus*, disputed : *contrā-*, contra- + *versus*, p. part. of *vertere*, to turn; see **wer-²** in App.]

con·tro·vert (kŏn′trə-vûrt′, kŏn′trə-vûrt′) *tr.v.* **-vert·ed, -vert·ing, -verts** To raise arguments against; voice opposition to. [Back-formation < CONTROVERSY.] —**con′tro·vert′i·ble** *adj.*

con·tu·ma·cious (kŏn′tə-mā′shəs, -tyə-) *adj.* Obstinately disobedient or rebellious; insubordinate. —**con′tu·ma′cious·ly** *adv.* —**con′tu·ma′cious·ness** *n.*

con·tu·ma·cy (kŏn′tŏō-mə-sē, -tyŏō-) *n., pl.* **-cies** Obstinate or contemptuous resistance to authority. [ME *contumacie* < Lat. *contumācia* < *contumāx, contumāc-*, insolent.]

con·tu·me·ly (kŏn′tŏō-mə-lē, -tyŏō-, -təm-lē) *n., pl.* **-lies** **1.** Rudeness or contempt arising from arrogance; insolence. **2.** An insolent or arrogant remark or act. [ME *contumelie* < OFr. < Lat. *contumēlia*; akin to *contumāx, contumāc-*, insolent.] —**con′tu·me′li·ous** (kŏn′tə-mē′lē-əs) *adj.* —**con′tu·me′li·ous·ly** *adv.*

con·tuse (kən-tŏōz′, -tyŏōz′) *tr.v.* **-tused, -tus·ing, -tus·es** To injure without breaking the skin; bruise. [ME *contusen* < Lat. *contundere, contūs-*, to beat : *com-*, com- + *tundere*, to beat.]

con·tu·sion (kən-tŏō′zhən, -tyŏō′-) *n.* An injury in which the skin is not broken; a bruise.

co·nun·drum (kə-nŭn′drəm) *n.* **1.** A riddle in which a fanciful question is answered by a pun. **2.** A paradoxical, insoluble, or difficult problem; a dilemma. [?]

con·ur·ba·tion (kŏn′ər-bā′shən) *n.* A predominantly urban region including adjacent towns and suburbs; a metropolitan area. [CON- + Lat. *urbs*, city + -ATION.]

con·va·lesce (kŏn′və-lĕs′) *intr.v.* **-lesced, -lesc·ing, -lesc·es** To return to health and strength after illness; recuperate. [Late ME *convalesshe* < Lat. *convalēscere* : *com-*, com- + *valēscere*, to grow strong, inchoative of *valēre*, to be strong.]

con·va·les·cence (kŏn′və-lĕs′əns) *n.* **1.** Gradual return to health and strength after illness. **2.** The period needed for returning to health after illness. —**con′va·les′cent** *adj. & n.*

con·vect (kən-vĕkt′) *v.* **-vect·ed, -vect·ing, -vects** —*tr.* To transfer (heat) by convection. —*intr.* To undergo convection. [Back-formation < CONVECTION.]

con·vec·tion (kən-vĕk′shən) *n.* **1.** The act or process of conveying; transmission. **2.** *Physics* **a.** Heat transfer in a gas or liquid by the circulation of currents from one region to another. **b.** Fluid motion caused by an external force such as gravity. **3.** *Meteorology* The transfer of heat or other atmospheric properties by massive vertical motion within the atmosphere, esp. by such motion directed upward. [LLat. *convectiō, convectiōn-* < *convectus*, p. part. of *convehere*, to carry together : Lat. *com-*, com- + Lat. *vehere*, to carry; see **wegh-** in App.] —**con·vec′tion·al** *adj.*

control tower

—**con·vec′tive** *adj.* —**con·vec′tive·ly** *adv.*

convection oven *n.* An oven having a fan that shortens cooking time by circulating hot air uniformly around the food.

con·vec·tor (kən-vĕk′tər) *n.* A partly enclosed, directly heated surface from which warm air circulates by convection.

con·vene (kən-vēn′) *v.* **-vened, -ven·ing, -venes** —*intr.* To come together usu. for an official or public purpose; assemble formally. —*tr.* **1.** To cause to convene; convoke. **2.** To summon to appear, as before a tribunal. [ME *convenen* < OFr. *convenir* < Lat. *convenīre* : *com-*, com- + *venīre*, to come; see **gʷā-** in App.] —**con·ven′a·ble** *adj.* —**con·ven′er, con·ven′or** *n.*

con·ven·ience (kən-vēn′yəns) *n.* **1.** The quality of being suitable to one's comfort, purposes, or needs. **2.** Personal comfort or advantage. **3.** Something that increases comfort or saves work. **4.** A suitable or agreeable time: *Reply at your earliest convenience.* **5.** *Chiefly British* A lavatory.

convenience food *n.* A prepackaged food that can be prepared quickly and easily.

convenience store *n.* A small retail store that is open long hours and that typically sells staple groceries and snacks.

con·ven·ien·cy (kən-vēn′yən-sē) *n., pl.* **-cies** *Archaic* Convenience.

con·ven·ient (kən-vēn′yənt) *adj.* **1.** Suited or favorable to one's comfort, purpose, or needs. **2a.** Easy to reach; accessible. **b.** Close at hand; near: *convenient to transportation.* **3.** *Obsolete* Fitting and proper; suitable. [ME < Lat. *conveniēns, convenient-*, pr. part. of *convenīre*, to be suitable, fit. See CONVENE.] —**con·ven′ient·ly** *adv.*

con·vent (kŏn′vənt, -vĕnt′) *n.* **1.** A community, esp. of nuns, bound by vows to a religious life under a superior. **2.** The building or buildings occupied by such a community. [ME *covent* < OFr. < Med.Lat. *conventus* < Lat., assembly < p. part. of *convenīre*, to assemble. See CONVENE.]

con·ven·ti·cle (kən-vĕn′tĭ-kəl) *n.* A religious meeting, esp. a secret or illegal one, such as those held by Dissenters in England and Scotland in the 16th and 17th centuries. [ME < Lat. *conventiculum*, meeting, dim. of *conventus*, assembly. See CONVENT.] —**con·ven′ti·cler** *n.*

con·ven·tion (kən-vĕn′shən) *n.* **1a.** A formal meeting of members, representatives, or delegates, as of a political party or profession. **b.** The body of persons attending such an assembly. **2.** An agreement between states, sides, or military forces. **3.** General agreement on or acceptance of certain practices or attitudes. **4.** A practice or procedure widely observed in a group; a custom. **5.** A widely used device or technique, as in literature or painting. [ME *convencioun* < Lat. *conventiō, conventiōn-*, meeting < *conventus*, p. part. of *convenīre*, to assemble. See CONVENE.]

con·ven·tion·al (kən-vĕn′shə-nəl) *adj.* **1.** Based on or in accordance with general agreement, use, or practice; customary. **2.** Conforming to established practice or accepted standards; traditional. **3a.** Devoted to or bound by conventions to the point of artificiality; ceremonious. **b.** Unimaginative; conformist. **4.** Represented, as in a work of art, in simplified or abstract form. **5.** Of, relating to, or resembling an assembly. **6.** Using means other than nuclear weapons or energy. —**con·ven′tion·al·ism** *n.* —**con·ven′tion·al·ist** *n.* —**con·ven′tion·al·ly** *adv.*

con·ven·tion·al·i·ty (kən-vĕn′shə-nǎl′ĭ-tē) *n., pl.* **-ties** **1.** The state, quality, or character of being conventional. **2.** A conventional act, idea, or practice. **3. conventionalities** The rules of conventional social behavior.

con·ven·tion·al·ize (kən-vĕn′shə-nə-līz′) *tr.v.* **-ized, -iz·ing, -iz·es** To make conventional. —**con·ven′tion·al·i·za′tion** (-lĭ-zā′shən) *n.*

con·ven·tion·eer (kən-vĕn′shə-nîr′) *n.* One who attends a convention.

con·ven·tu·al (kən-vĕn′chŏō-əl) *adj.* Of or relating to a convent. ❖ *n.* **1.** A member of a convent. **2. Conventual** A member of a branch of the Franciscan order that permits the accumulation and possession of common property. [ME < Med.Lat. *conventuālis* < *conventus*, convent. See CONVENT.]

con·verge (kən-vûrj′) *v.* **-verged, -verg·ing, -verg·es** —*intr.* **1a.** To tend toward or approach an intersecting point. **b.** To come together from different directions; meet. **2.** To tend toward or achieve union or a common conclusion or result. **3.** *Mathematics* To approach a limit. —*tr.* To cause to converge. [LLat. *convergere*, to incline together : Lat. *com-*, com- + Lat. *vergere*, to incline; see **wer-²** in App.]

con·ver·gence (kən-vûr′jəns) *n.* **1.** The act, condition, or fact of converging. **2.** *Mathematics* The property or manner of approaching a limit, such as a point, line, or value. **3.** The point of converging; a meeting place. **4.** *Physiology* The coordinated turning of the eyes inward to focus on an object at close range. **5.** *Biology* The adaptive evolution of superficially similar structures, such as bird wings, in unrelated species subjected to similar environments. —**con·ver′gen·cy** *n.* —**con·ver′gent** *adj.*

convergent evolution *n.* See **convergence** 5.

con·ver·sant (kən-vûr′sənt, kŏn′vər-) *adj.* **1.** Familiar, as by study or experience. **2.** Able to converse knowledgeably on a subject. [ME *conversaunt*, associated with < OFr. *conversant*, pr. part. of *converser*, to associate with < Lat. *conversārī*. See CONVERSE¹.] —**con·ver′sance, con·ver′san·cy** *n.* —**con·ver′sant·ly** *adv.*

con·ver·sa·tion (kŏn′vər-sā′shən) *n.* **1.** A spoken exchange of thoughts, opinions, and feelings; a talk. **2.** An informal discussion of a matter by representatives of governments, institutions, or organizations. —**con′ver·sa′tion·al** *adj.* —**con′ver·sa′tion·al·ly** *adv.*

con·ver·sa·tion·al·ist (kŏn′vər-sā′shə-nə-lĭst) also **con·ver·sa·tion·ist** (-shə-nĭst) *n.* One given to or skilled at conversation.

conversation piece *n.* **1.** An unusual object that arouses comment or interest. **2.** A genre painting, popular esp. in the 18th century, depicting a group of fashionable people.

con·ver·sa·zi·o·ne (kŏn′vər-sät′sē-ō′nĕ, kōn′vĕr-sä-tsyō′nĕ) *n., pl.* **-nes** or **-ni** (-nē) A meeting for conversation or discussion, esp. about art. [Ital. < Lat. *conversātiō, conversātiōn-*, dealings with persons < *conversātus*, p. part. of *conversārī*, to associate with. See CONVERSE[1].]

con·verse[1] (kən-vûrs′) *intr.v.* **-versed, -vers·ing, -vers·es** **1.** To engage in a spoken exchange of thoughts, ideas, or feelings; talk. **2.** *Archaic* To be familiar; associate. ❖ *n.* (kŏn′vûrs′) **1.** Spoken interchange of thoughts and feelings; conversation. **2.** *Obsolete* Social interaction. [ME *conversen*, to associate with < OFr. *converser* < Lat. *conversārī* : *com-*, com- + *versārī*, to occupy oneself; see **wer-[2]** in App.]

con·verse[2] (kən-vûrs′, kŏn′vûrs′) *adj.* Reversed, as in position, order, or action; contrary. ❖ *n.* (kŏn′vûrs′) **1.** Something that has been reversed; an opposite. **2.** *Logic* A proposition obtained by conversion. [Lat. *conversus*, p. part. of *convertere*, to turn around. See CONVERT.] —**con·verse′ly** *adv.*

con·ver·sion (kən-vûr′zhən, -shən) *n.* **1a.** The act of converting. **b.** The state of being converted. **2.** A change in which one adopts a new religion, faith, or belief. **3.** Something that is changed from one use, function, or purpose to another. **4.** *Law* **a.** The unlawful appropriation of another's property. **b.** The changing of real property to personal property or vice versa. **5.** The exchange of one type of security or currency for another. **6.** *Logic* The interchange of the subject and predicate of a proposition. **7.** *Football* A score made on a try for a point or points after a touchdown. **8.** *Psychology* A defense mechanism in which repressed ideas, conflicts, or impulses are manifested by bodily symptoms that have no physical cause. **9.** The expression of a quantity in alternative units, as of length or weight. [ME *conversioun*, religious conversion < OFr. *conversion* < Lat. *conversiō, conversiōn-*, a turning around < *conversus*, p. part. of *convertere*, to turn around. See CONVERT.] —**con·ver′sion·al, con·ver′sion·ar′y** (-zhə-nĕr′ē, -shə-) *adj.*

conversion disorder *n.* See **conversion reaction.**

conversion factor *n.* A numerical factor used to multiply or divide a quantity when converting from one system of units to another.

conversion reaction *n.* A condition characterized by the presence of physiologic symptoms having no discernible physical cause but for which there is evidence of a psychological conflict.

Con·ver·so (kən-vĕr′sō) *n., pl.* **-sos** A Spanish or Portuguese Jew who converted outwardly to Christianity in the late Middle Ages so as to avoid persecution or expulsion. [Sp., a convert < *converso* < Med.Lat. *conversus* < Lat., p. part. of *convertere*, to turn around, convert. See CONVERT.]

con·vert (kən-vûrt′) *v.* **-vert·ed, -vert·ing, -verts** —*tr.* **1.** To change (something) into another form, substance, state, or product; transform. **2.** To change (something) from one use, function, or purpose to another. **3.** To persuade or induce to adopt a particular religion, faith, or belief. **4.** To exchange for something of equal value. **5.** To exchange (a security, for example) by substituting an equivalent of another form. **6.** To express in alternative units. **7.** *Logic* To transform (a proposition) by conversion. **8.** *Law* **a.** To appropriate (another's property) without right to one's own use. **b.** To change (property) from real to personal or from joint to separate or vice versa. **9.** *Sports* **a.** To complete (a conversion or free throw, for example) successfully. **b.** To score (a spare) in bowling. —*intr.* **1.** To undergo a conversion: *converted to Islam.* **2.** To be converted: *a sofa that converts into a bed.* **3a.** *Football* To make a conversion. **b.** *Sports* To shoot and score a goal or basket after receiving a pass or gaining control of a rebound. ❖ *n.* (kŏn′vûrt′) One who has been converted, esp. from one religion or belief to another. [ME *converten* < OFr. *convertir* < Lat. *convertere*, to turn around : *com-*, com- + *vertere*, to turn; see **wer-[2]** in App.]

con·vert·ed rice (kən-vûr′tĭd) *n.* A white rice prepared from brown rice that has been soaked, steamed under pressure to force nutrients into the endosperm, and then dried and milled.

con·vert·er also **con·ver·tor** (kən-vûr′tər) *n.* **1.** A furnace in which pig iron is converted into steel by the Bessemer process. **2.** A machine that converts electric current from one kind to another. **3.** An electronic device that converts one frequency of a radio signal to another. **4.** A device that converts data from one code to another.

con·vert·i·ble (kən-vûr′tə-bəl) *adj.* **1.** That can be converted. **2.** Having a top that can be folded back or removed. **3.** Lawfully exchangeable for gold or another currency. ❖ *n.* **1.** Something that can be converted. **2.** A convertible automobile. **3.** A convertible security. —**con·vert′i·bil′i·ty** *n.* —**con·vert′i·bly** *adv.*

convertible security *n.* A security that at the holder's option

may be exchanged for another asset.

con·vert·i·plane also **con·vert·i·plane** (kən-vûr′tə-plān′) *n.* An airplane built to fly vertically as well as forward.

con·vex (kŏn′vĕks′, kən-vĕks′) *adj.* Having a surface or boundary that curves or bulges outward, as the exterior of a sphere. [Lat. *convexus*. See **wegh-** in App.] —**con′vex′ly** *adv.*

con·vex·i·ty (kən-vĕk′sĭ-tē) *n., pl.* **-ties** **1.** The state of being convex. **2.** A convex surface, body, part, or line.

con·vex·o-con·cave (kən-vĕk′sō-kən-kāv′) *adj.* **1.** Convex on one side and concave on the other. **2.** Having greater curvature on the convex side than on the concave side.

con·vex·o-con·vex (kən-vĕk′sō-kən-vĕks′) *adj.* Convex on both sides; biconvex. Used of a lens.

con·vey (kən-vā′) *tr.v.* **-veyed, -vey·ing, -veys** **1.** To take or carry from one place to another; transport. **2.** To serve as a medium of transmission for; transmit. **3.** To communicate or make known; impart. **4.** *Law* To transfer ownership of or title to. **5.** *Archaic* To steal. [ME *conveien* < OFr. *conveier* < Med.Lat. *conviāre*, to escort : Lat. *com-*, com- + *via*, way; see **wegh-** in App.] —**con·vey′a·ble** *adj.*

con·vey·ance (kən-vā′əns) *n.* **1.** The act of conveying. **2.** A means of conveying, esp. a vehicle for transportation. **3.** *Law* **a.** Transfer of title to property from one person to another. **b.** The document by which a property transfer is effected. —**con·vey′anc·er** *n.*

con·vey·anc·ing (kən-vā′ən-sĭng) *n.* The branch of legal practice dealing with the conveyance of property or real estate.

con·vey·or also **con·vey·er** (kən-vā′ər) *n.* One that conveys, esp. a mechanical apparatus that transports materials or items from one place to another.

conveyor belt *n.* A mechanical apparatus consisting of a continuous moving belt that transports materials.

con·vict (kən-vĭkt′) *v.* **-vict·ed, -vict·ing, -victs** —*tr.* **1.** *Law* To find or prove (someone) guilty of an offense or crime, esp. by the verdict of a court. **2.** To show or declare to be blameworthy; condemn: *His remarks convicted him of insensitivity.* **3.** To make aware of one's sinfulness or guilt. —*intr.* To return a verdict of guilty in a court. ❖ *n.* (kŏn′vĭkt′) *Law* **1.** A person found or declared guilty of an offense or crime. **2.** A person serving a sentence of imprisonment. ❖ *adj. Archaic* Found guilty; convicted. [ME *convicten* < Lat. *convincere, convict-.* See CONVINCE.]

con·vic·tion (kən-vĭk′shən) *n.* **1.** *Law* **a.** The judgment of a jury or judge that a person is guilty of a crime as charged. **b.** The state of being found or proved guilty. **2a.** The act or process of convincing. **b.** The state of being convinced. See Syns at **certainty. 3.** A fixed or strong belief. —**con·vic′tion·al** *adj.*

con·vic·tive (kən-vĭk′tĭv) *adj.* Having power or serving to convince or convict. —**con·vic′tive·ly** *adv.*

con·vince (kən-vĭns′) *tr.v.* **-vinced, -vinc·ing, -vinc·es** **1.** To bring by the use of argument or evidence to firm belief or a course of action. **2.** *Obsolete* To prove to be wrong or guilty. **3.** *Obsolete* To conquer; overpower. [Lat. *convincere*, to prove wrong : *com-*, com- + *vincere*, to conquer.] —**con·vince′ment** *n.* —**con·vinc′er** *n.* —**con·vinc′i·ble** *adj.*

con·vinc·ing (kən-vĭn′sĭng) *adj.* **1.** Serving to convince: *a convincing argument.* **2.** Believable; plausible. See Syns at **valid.** —**con·vinc′ing·ly** *adv.* —**con·vinc′ing·ness** *n.*

con·viv·i·al (kən-vĭv′ē-əl) *adj.* **1.** Fond of feasting, drinking, and good company; sociable. **2.** Merry; festive: *a convivial atmosphere.* [LLat. *convīviālis* < Lat. *convīvium*, banquet : *com-*, com- + *vīvere*, to live; see **gʷeiə-** in App.] —**con·viv′i·al′i·ty** (-ăl′ĭ-tē) *n.* —**con·viv′i·al·ly** *adv.*

con·vo·ca·tion (kŏn′və-kā′shən) *n.* **1a.** The act of convoking. **b.** A group of people convoked, esp. the members of a college or university community who are assembled for a ceremony. **2.** A clerical assembly of the Anglican Church similar to a synod but assembling only when called. **3.** An assembly of the clergy and representative laity of a section of a diocese of the Episcopal Church. —**con′vo·ca′tion·al** *adj.*

con·voke (kən-vōk′) *tr.v.* **-voked, -vok·ing, -vokes** To cause to assemble in a meeting; convene. [Fr. *convoquer* < OFr. < Lat. *convocāre* : *com-*, com- + *vocāre*, to call; see **wekʷ-** in App.] —**con·vok′er** *n.*

con·vo·lute (kŏn′və-lōōt′) *adj.* Rolled or coiled together in overlapping whorls, as certain leaves or shells. ❖ *intr. & tr.v.* **-lut·ed, -lut·ing, -lutes** To coil or fold or cause to coil or fold in overlapping whorls. [Lat. *convolūtus*, p. part. of *convolvere*, to convolve. See CONVOLVE.] —**con′vo·lute′ly** *adv.*

con·vo·lut·ed (kŏn′və-lōō′tĭd) *adj.* **1.** Having numerous overlapping coils or folds. **2.** Intricate; complicated.

con·vo·lu·tion (kŏn′və-lōō′shən) *n.* **1.** A form or part that is folded or coiled. **2.** One of the convex folds of the surface of the brain. —**con′vo·lu′tion·al** *adj.*

con·volve (kən-vŏlv′) *v.* **-volved, -volv·ing, -volves** —*tr.* To roll together; coil up. —*intr.* To form convolutions. [Lat. *convolvere* : *com-*, com- + *volvere*, to roll; see **wel-** in App.]

con·vol·vu·lus (kən-vŏl′vyə-ləs) *n., pl.* **-lus·es** or **-li** (-lī′) Any of various mostly trailing or twining plants of the widespread genus *Convolvulus*, having funnel-shaped flowers. [Lat., bindweed < *convolvere*, to intertwine. See CONVOLVE.]

con·voy (kŏn′voi′) *n.* **1.** The act of accompanying or escorting,

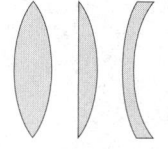

convex
left to right: biconvex, plano-convex, and convexo-concave lenses

esp. for protective purposes. **2.** An accompanying and protecting force, as of ships or troops. **3.** A group, as of ships or motor vehicles, traveling together with a protective escort or for safety or convenience. ❖ *tr.v.* (kŏn′voi′, kən-voi′) **-voyed, -voy•ing, -voys** To accompany, esp. for protection; escort. [< ME *convoyen*, to escort < OFr. *convoier*, var. of *conveier*, var. of *conveier*. See CONVEY.]

con•vul•sant (kən-vŭl′sənt) *adj.* Causing or producing convulsions. ❖ *n.* A convulsant agent, such as a drug.

con•vulse (kən-vŭls′) *v.* **-vulsed, -vuls•ing, -vuls•es** —*tr.* **1.** To shake or agitate violently. **2.** To affect with muscular convulsions. **3.** To cause to shake with laughter or strong emotion. —*intr.* To become affected by or as if by convulsions; shake. [Lat. *convellere, convuls-*, to pull violently : *com-, com-* + *vellere*, to pull.]

con•vul•sion (kən-vŭl′shən) *n.* **1.** An intense, paroxysmal, involuntary muscular contraction. **2.** An uncontrolled fit, as of laughter; a paroxysm. **3.** A violent disturbance.

con•vul•sive (kən-vŭl′sĭv) *adj.* **1.** Marked by or having the nature of convulsions. **2.** Having or producing convulsions. —**con•vul′sive•ly** *adv.* —**con•vul′sive•ness** *n.*

co•ny (kō′nē, kŭn′ē) *n.* Variant of **coney**[1].

coo (kōō) *v.* **cooed, coo•ing, coos** —*intr.* **1.** To utter the murmuring sound of a dove or pigeon or a sound resembling it. **2.** To talk fondly or amorously in murmurs. —*tr.* To express or utter with soft murmuring sounds. [Imit.] —**coo′er** *n.*

Cooch Be•har (kōōch′ bə-här′) A former princely state of NE India; came under British rule in 1772.

cook (kōōk) *v.* **cooked, cook•ing, cooks** —*tr.* **1.** To prepare (food) for eating by applying heat. **2.** To prepare or treat by heating. **3.** *Slang* To alter or falsify so as to make a more favorable impression; doctor. —*intr.* **1.** To prepare food for eating by applying heat. **2.** To undergo application of heat esp. for the purpose of later ingestion. **3.** *Slang* To happen or develop. **4.** *Slang* To proceed or perform very well. ❖ *n.* A person who prepares food for eating. —*phrasal verb:* **cook up** *Informal* To fabricate; concoct. [ME *coken* < *coke*, cook < OE *cōc* < VLat. **cōcus* < Lat. *cocus, coquus* < *coquere*, to cook. See **pek**ʷ- in App.]

Cook, James Known as "Captain Cook." 1728–79. British navigator and explorer who commanded three major voyages of discovery, charting many islands of the Pacific Ocean.

Cook, Mount also **A•o•rang•i** (ä′ō-räng′gē) A mountain, 3,766.4 m (12,349 ft), of New Zealand on South I. in the Southern Alps.

cook•book (kōōk′bŏōk′) *n.* A book containing recipes and other information about the preparation of food.

cook•er (kōōk′ər) *n.* **1.** One that cooks, esp. a utensil or an appliance for cooking. **2.** A person employed to operate cooking apparatuses in the commercial preparation of food and drink.

cook•er•y (kōōk′ə-rē) *n., pl.* **-ies 1.** The art or practice of preparing food. **2.** A place for cooking.

cook•ie also **cook•y** (kōōk′ē) *n., pl.* **-ies 1.** A small, usu. flat and crisp cake made from sweetened dough. **2.** *Slang* A person. **3.** *Computer Science* A collection of information stored on the local computer of a World Wide Web user, used chiefly by websites to identify previous users. [Du. *koekje*, dim. of *koek*, cake < MDu. *koeke*.]

cookie cutter *n.* A device for cutting flattened cookie dough into shapes before baking.

cook•ie-cut•ter (kōōk′ē-cŭt′ər) *adj.* Very similar or identical in appearance: *cookie-cutter houses.*

Cook Inlet An inlet of the Gulf of Alaska in S AK W of the Kenai Peninsula.

Cook Islands An island group of the S Pacific Ocean SE of Samoa; probably inhabited by Polynesians more than 1,500 years ago and first sighted by Capt. James Cook in 1773.

cook-off (kōōk′ôf′, -ŏf′) *n.* A cooking competition.

cook•out (kōōk′out′) *n.* A meal cooked and served outdoors.

cook•stove (kōōk′stōv′) *n.* A stove for cooking.

Cook Strait A narrow channel separating North I. and South I. in New Zealand.

cook•top (kōōk′tŏp′) *n.* A flat, usu. glass cooking surface making up the top of a stove or built into a countertop.

cook•ware (kōōk′wâr′) *n.* Cooking utensils.

cool (kōōl) *adj.* **cool•er, cool•est 1.** Neither warm nor very cold; moderately cold. See Syns at **cold. 2.** Giving or suggesting relief from heat: *a cool blouse.* **3.** Marked by calm self-control: *a cool negotiator.* **4.** Marked by indifference, disdain, or dislike; unfriendly or unresponsive: *a cool greeting.* **5.** Of, relating to, or characteristic of colors, such as blue and green, that produce the impression of coolness. **6.** *Slang* **a.** Excellent; first-rate: *a cool car.* **b.** Acceptable; satisfactory. **7.** *Slang* Entire; full: *worth a cool million.* ❖ *adv. Informal* In a casual manner; nonchalantly. ❖ *v.* **cooled, cool•ing, cools** —*tr.* **1.** To make less warm. **2.** To make less ardent, intense, or zealous. **3.** *Physics* To reduce the molecular or kinetic energy of (an object). —*intr.* **1.** To become less warm: *took a dip to cool off.* **2.** To become calmer. ❖ *n.* **1.** A cool place, part, or time. **2.** The state or quality of being cool. **3.** Composure; poise. —*idioms:* **cool it** *Slang* **1.** To calm down; relax. **2.** To stop doing something. **cool (one's) heels** *Informal* To wait or be kept waiting. [ME *cole* < OE *cōl.* See **gel-** in App.] —**cool′ish** *adj.* —**cool′ly** *adv.* —**cool′ness** *n.*

Captain Cook
1776 portrait by Nathaniel
Dance (1735–1811)

Calvin Coolidge

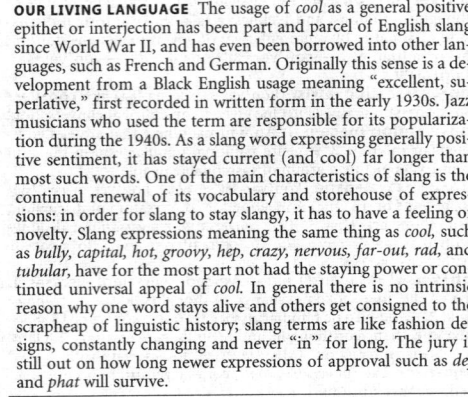

OUR LIVING LANGUAGE The usage of *cool* as a general positive epithet or interjection has been part and parcel of English slang since World War II, and has even been borrowed into other languages, such as French and German. Originally this sense is a development from a Black English usage meaning "excellent, superlative," first recorded in written form in the early 1930s. Jazz musicians who used the term are responsible for its popularization during the 1940s. As a slang word expressing generally positive sentiment, it has stayed current (and cool) far longer than most such words. One of the main characteristics of slang is the continual renewal of its vocabulary and storehouse of expressions: in order for slang to stay slangy, it has to have a feeling of novelty. Slang expressions meaning the same thing as *cool*, such as *bully, capital, hot, groovy, hep, crazy, nervous, far-out, rad,* and *tubular,* have for the most part not had the staying power or continued universal appeal of *cool.* In general there is no intrinsic reason why one word stays alive and others get consigned to the scrapheap of linguistic history; slang terms are like fashion designs, constantly changing and never "in" for long. The jury is still out on how long newer expressions of approval such as *def* and *phat* will survive.

cool•ant (kōō′lənt) *n.* An agent that produces cooling, esp. a fluid that draws off heat by circulating through an engine.

cool•down (kōōl′doun′) *n.* A period following strenuous physical activity in which stretching or milder exercise is performed to allow the body gradually to return to normal.

cool•er (kōō′lər) *n.* **1.** A device, container, or room that cools or keeps cool. **2.** A cold drink, often a mixture of white wine and juice. **3.** *Slang* A jail.

Coo•ley's anemia (kōō′lēz) *n.* A usu. fatal form of thalassemia in which normal hemoglobin is absent, characterized by severe anemia, enlargement of the heart, liver, and spleen, and skeletal deformation. [After Thomas Benton *Cooley* (1871–1945), American physician.]

cool-head•ed (kōōl′hĕd′ĭd) *adj.* Not easily excited or flustered.

Coo•lidge (kōō′lĭj), **Grace Goodhue** 1879–1957. First Lady of the US (1923–29).

Coolidge, (John) Calvin 1872–1933. The 30th President of the US (1923–29), whose business policies led to a stock market boom in the 1920s, followed by economic collapse.

coo•lie also **coo•ly** (kōō′lē) *n., pl.* **-lies** *Offensive* An unskilled Asian laborer. [Hindi *qulī*, laborer, perh. ult. < *Kulī*, a tribe in Gujarat.]

cool jazz *n.* A style of jazz that emerged by the early 1950s, marked by extensive legato passages and a reflective character. [On the model of *hot jazz*, bop.]

coon (kōōn) *n.* **1.** *Informal* A raccoon. **2.** *Offensive Slang* Used as a disparaging term for a Black person. [Short for RACCOON.]

coon•can (kōōn′kăn′) or **con•qui•an** (kŏng′kē-ən) *n.* A card game for two players that is an early version of rummy. [Alteration of Am.Sp. *conquián*, prob. < Sp. *con quién*, with whom? : *con*, with (< Lat. *cum*; see **kom** in App.) + *quien*, whom (< Lat. *quem*, accusative of *quis*, who; see **kʷo-** in App.).]

coon's age (kōōnz) *n. Slang* A long time.

coon•skin (kōōn′skĭn′) *n.* **1.** The pelt of a raccoon. **2.** An article, such as a hat, made from the pelts of raccoons.

coon•tie (kōōn′tē) *n.* Any of several evergreen species of the genus *Zamia*, native to southern Florida, Mexico, and the West Indies and having thickened underground stems that yield starch resembling arrowroot. [Florida Creek *kuntii*, arrowroot.]

coop (kōōp) *n.* **1.** An enclosure or cage, as for poultry or small animals. **2.** *Slang* **a.** An uncomfortably confined space. **b.** A prison. ❖ *tr.v.* **cooped, coop•ing, coops** To confine in or as if in a coop. Often used with *up.* —*idiom:* **fly** (or **blow**) **the coop** To make a getaway; escape. [ME *coupe*, poss. < MDu. *kūpe*, basket, tub < Gmc. **kūpōn*, poss. < Lat. *cūpa*, cask.]

co-op (kō′ŏp′, kō-ŏp′) *n.* A cooperative.

coop•er (kōō′pər) *n.* One that makes or repairs wooden barrels and tubs. [ME *couper* < *kūpe* < *kūpe*, basket, tub. See COOP.] —**coop′er** *v.* —**coop′er•age** *n.*

Cooper, Gary 1901–61. Amer. actor whose films include *High Noon* (1952).

Cooper, James Fenimore 1789–1851. Amer. writer whose frontier novels include *The Last of the Mohicans* (1826).

Cooper, Peter 1791–1883. Amer. manufacturer, inventor, and philanthropist who built the first locomotive in the US.

co•op•er•ate (kō-ŏp′ə-rāt′) *intr.v.* **-at•ed, -at•ing, -ates 1.** To work or act together toward a common end or purpose. **2.** To acquiesce willingly; be compliant. **3.** To form an association for common, usu. economic benefit. [LLat. *cooperārī, cooperāt-* : Lat. *co-, co-* + *operārī*, to work (< *opus, oper-*, work).] —**co•op′er•a′tor** *n.*

co•op•er•a•tion (kō-ŏp′ə-rā′shən) *n.* **1.** The act or practice of cooperating. **2.** The association of persons or businesses for common, usu. economic benefit. —**co•op′er•a′tion•ist** *n.*

co•op•er•a•tive (kō-ŏp′ər-ə-tĭv, -ə-rā′tĭv, -ŏp′rə-) *adj.* **1.** Done in cooperation with others. **2.** Marked by willingness to cooperate; compliant. **3.** Of, relating to, or formed as an enterprise or organization jointly owned or managed by those who use its facilities or services. ❖ *n.* A cooperative enterprise or organization. —co•op′er•a•tive•ly *adv.* —co•op′er•a•tive•ness *n.*

Coo•per's hawk (kōō′pərz, kŏŏp′ərz) *n.* A short-winged hawk (*Accipiter cooperii*) widespread throughout North America and having a dark back, a long tail, and a rusty-barred chest. [After William Cooper (1797–1864), American ornithologist.]

Coo•pers•town (kōō′pərz-toun′) A residential village of E-central NY WSW of Schenectady; site of the National Baseball Hall of Fame. Pop. 2,032.

co-opt (kō-ŏpt′, kō′ŏpt′) *tr.v.* **-opt•ed, -opt•ing, -opts** **1.** To elect as a fellow member of a group. **2.** To appoint summarily. **3.** To take or assume for one's own use; appropriate. **4.** To neutralize or win over through assimilation into an established group or culture. [Lat. *cooptāre* : *co-, co-* + *optāre,* to choose.] —co′-op•ta′tion (-ŏp′tā′tɪv) *adj.* —co-op′tion (-ŏp′shən) *n.* —co-op′tive *adj.*

co•or•di•nate (kō-ôr′dn-āt′, -ĭt) *n.* **1.** One that is equal in importance, rank, or degree. **2. coordinates** A set of articles designed to match or complement one other, as in style or color. **3.** *Mathematics* Any of a set of two or more numbers used to determine the position of a point, line, curve, or plane in a space of a given dimension with respect to a system of lines or other fixed reference. **4. coordinates** *Informal* Directions. ❖ *adj.* (-ĭt, -āt′) **1.** Of equal importance, rank, or degree. **2.** Of or involving coordination. **3.** Of or based on a system of coordinates. **4.** *Grammar* Having equal syntactic status. **5.** Of or relating to a university in which men and women are taught by the same faculty but in single-sex classes or on single-sex campuses. ❖ *v.* (-āt′) —*tr.* **-nat•ed, -nat•ing, -nates** **1.** To place in the same order, class, or rank. **2.** To harmonize in a common action or effort. **3.** *Grammar* To link (syntactically equivalent units) together. —*intr.* **1.** To be coordinate: *The generators coordinate so that one is always running.* **2.** To work together harmoniously. **3.** To form a pleasing combination; match: *shoes that coordinate with the dress.* [CO- + ORDINATE.] —co•or′di•nate•ly *adv.* —co•or′di•nate•ness (-ĭt-nĭs) *n.* —co•or′di•na′tive *adj.* —co•or′di•na′tor *n.*

coordinate bond *n.* A covalent chemical bond between two atoms that is produced when one atom shares a pair of electrons with another atom lacking such a pair.

co•or•di•nat•ed universal time (kō-ôr′dn-ā′tĭd) *n.* Universal time corrected by the addition or omission of leap seconds.

coordinate system *n.* A method of representing points in a space of given dimensions by coordinates.

co•or•di•nat•ing conjunction (kō-ôr′dn-ā′tĭng) *n.* A conjunction that connects two identically constructed or syntactically equal grammatical elements, such as *or* in *They don't know whether they're coming or going.*

co•or•di•na•tion (kō-ôr′dn-ā′shən) *n.* **1a.** The act of coordinating. **b.** The state of being coordinate; harmonious adjustment or interaction. **2.** *Physiology* Harmonious functioning of muscles or groups of muscles in the execution of movements. **3.** *Grammar* The linking of two syntactically equal units, as by a coordinate conjunction. [Fr. < Med.Lat. *coōrdinātiō, coōrdinātiōn-* : *co-, co-* + Lat. *ōrdinātiō,* arrangement (< *ōrdinātus,* p. part. of *ōrdināre,* to arrange in order < *ōrdō, ōrdin-,* order; see **ar-** in App.).]

coordination compound *n.* A chemical compound formed by joining independent molecules or ions usu. to a central metallic atom by coordinate bonds.

Coo•sa (kōō′sə) A river rising in NW GA and flowing c. 460 km (286 mi) through E AL to join the Tallapoosa R. and form the Alabama R.

coot (kōōt) *n.* **1.** Any of several dark-gray aquatic birds of the genus *Fulica,* native to North America and Europe and having lobed toes and a white bill. **2.** See **scoter. 3.** *Informal* An eccentric or crotchety person, esp. an eccentric old man. [ME *coote,* poss. < MDu. *coet.*]

coot•er (kōō′tər) *n. Lower Southern US* **1.** An edible freshwater turtle of the genus *Chrysemys.* **2.** Any of various turtles or tortoises. See Regional Note at **goober.** [Gullah, of Niger-Congo orig.; akin to Mandingo *kuta.*]

coo•tie (kōō′tē) *n. Slang* A body louse. [Prob. < Malay *kutu.*]

cop¹ (kŏp) *n. Informal* **1.** A police officer. **2.** One that regulates certain behaviors or actions. [Short for COPPER².]

cop² (kŏp) *Slang tr.v.* **copped, cop•ping, cops** **1.** To take unlawfully or without permission; steal. **2a.** To get hold of; gain or win: *copped a ticket to the game.* **b.** To take or catch: *copped a quick look.* —**phrasal verb: cop out** To avoid fulfilling a commitment or responsibility. —**idiom: cop a plea** To plead guilty to a lesser charge so as to avoid standing trial for a more serious charge. See CAPTURE. [Prob. var. of *cap,* to catch < OFr. *caper* < Lat. *capere.*]

cop³ (kŏp) *n.* **1.** A cone-shaped or cylindrical roll of yarn or thread wound on a spindle. **2.** *Chiefly British* A summit or crest, as of a hill. [ME, summit < OE.]

cop. *abbr.* copyright

Cop. *abbr.* Coptic

co•pa•cet•ic or **co•pa•set•ic** (kō′pə-sĕt′ĭk) *adj.* Very satisfactory or acceptable; fine. [?]

co•pai•ba (kō-pī′bə, -pā′-) *n.* A viscous oleoresin obtained from South American trees of the genus *Copaifera,* used in certain varnishes and as a fixative in some perfumes. [Sp. < Port. *copaíba* < Tupi *cupaiba.*]

co•pal (kō′pəl, -păl′) *n.* Any of several brittle resins of recent or fossil origin, obtained from various tropical trees and used in certain varnishes. [Sp. < Nahuatl *copalli,* resin.]

Co•pán (kō-pän′) A ruined Mayan city of W Honduras that flourished from c. 300 B.C. to A.D. 900.

co•par•ce•nar•y (kō-pär′sə-nĕr′ē) *n., pl.* **-ies** **1.** Joint inheritance or heirship of property. **2.** Joint ownership. —**co•par′ce•nar′y** *adj.*

co•par•ce•ner (kō-pär′sə-nər) *n.* One of two or more persons sharing an inheritance; a joint heir.

co•par•ent•ing (kō-pär′ən-tĭng, -păr′-) *n.* An arrangement in a divorce or separation by which parents share legal and physical custody of a child or children. —**co′par′ent** *n.*

co•part•ner (kō-pärt′nər, kō′pärt′-) *n.* A joint partner, as in a business enterprise; an associate. —**co•part′ner•ship′** *n.*

co•pay (kō′pā′) *n.* A copayment.

co•pay•ment (kō′pā′mənt) *n.* A fixed fee that subscribers to a medical plan must pay for their use of specific medical services covered by the plan.

cope¹ (kōp) *intr.v.* **coped, cop•ing, copes** **1.** To contend or strive, esp. on even terms or with success. **2.** To contend with difficulties and act to overcome them. [ME *copen, coupen,* to strike < OFr. *couper* < VLat. *colpāre* < LLat. *colpus,* blow. See COUP.] —**cop′er** *n.*

cope² (kōp) *n.* **1.** A long ecclesiastical vestment worn over an alb or surplice. **2.** A covering resembling a cloak or mantle. **3.** A coping. ❖ *tr.v.* **coped, cop•ing, copes** **1.** To cover or dress in a cope. **2.** To provide with coping: *cope a wall.* [ME *cope* < OE *-cāp* < Med.Lat. *cāpa,* cloak < LLat. *cappa.*]

Co•pen•ha•gen (kō′pən-hā′gən, -hä′-) The cap. of Denmark, in the E part on the E coast of Sjaelland. Pop. 619,288.

co•pe•pod (kō′pə-pŏd′) *n.* Any of numerous minute marine and freshwater crustaceans of the subclass Copepoda, having an elongated body and a forked tail. [< NLat. *Cōpēpoda,* order name : Gk. *kōpē,* oar; see **kap-** in App. + *-poda, -pod.*]

Co•per•ni•cus (kō-pûr′nə-kəs, kə-), **Nicolaus** 1473–1543. Polish astronomer who theorized that Earth and the other planets revolve around the sun. —**Co•per′ni•can** *adj. & n.*

cope•stone (kōp′stōn) *n.* A capstone. [COPE² + STONE.]

cop•i•er (kŏp′ē-ər) *n.* **1.** A machine that makes printed or graphic copies. **2.** One that transcribes or copies.

co•pi•lot (kō′pī′lət) *n.* The second or relief pilot of an aircraft.

cop•ing (kō′pĭng) *n.* The top layer or course of a masonry wall, usu. slanted to shed water; a cope. [< COPE².]

coping saw *n.* A light handsaw with a slender blade stretched across a U-shaped frame, used for cutting designs in wood.

co•pi•ous (kō′pē-əs) *adj.* **1.** Yielding or containing plenty; affording ample supply: *a copious harvest.* **2.** Large in quantity; abundant: *copious rainfall.* **3.** Abounding in matter, thoughts, or words; wordy. [ME < Lat. *cōpiōsus* < *cōpia,* abundance.] —**co′pi•ous•ly** *adv.* —**co′pi•ous•ness** *n.*

co•pla•nar (kō-plā′nər) *adj.* Lying or occurring in the same plane. —**co′pla•nar′i•ty** (kō′plə-năr′ĭ-tē) *n.*

Cop•land (kōp′lənd), **Aaron** 1900–90. Amer. composer whose works include the ballet *Appalachian Spring* (1944).

Cop•ley (kŏp′lē), **John Singleton** 1738–1815. Amer. painter whose works include portraits of Revolutionary leaders.

co•pol•y•mer (kō-pŏl′ə-mər) *n.* A polymer of two or more different monomers. —**co•pol′y•mer′ic** (-mĕr′ĭk) *adj.*

co•pol•y•mer•ize (kō-pŏl′ə-mə-rīz′, kō′pə-lĭm′ə-) *v.* **-ized, -iz•ing, -iz•es** —*tr.* To polymerize (different monomers) together. —*intr.* To react to form a copolymer. —**co•pol′y•mer•i•za′tion** (-mər-ĭ-zā′shən) *n.*

cop-out also **cop•out** (kŏp′out′) *n. Slang* **1.** A failure to fulfill a commitment or responsibility or to face a difficulty squarely. **2.** A person who fails to fulfill a commitment or responsibility. **3.** An excuse for inaction or evasion.

cop•per¹ (kŏp′ər) *n.* **1.** *Symbol* **Cu** A ductile malleable metallic element that is an excellent conductor of heat and electricity and is used for electrical wiring, water piping, and corrosion-resistant parts, either pure or in alloys such as brass and bronze. Atomic number 29; atomic weight 63.546; melting point 1,083°C; boiling point 2,595°C; specific gravity 8.96; valence 1, 2. See table at **element. 2.** A coin made of copper or a copper alloy. **3.** *Chiefly British* A large cooking pot made of copper or iron. **4.** Any of various small butterflies of the subfamily Lycaeninae, having copper-colored wings. **5.** A reddish brown. ❖ *tr.v.* **-pered, -per•ing, -pers** **1.** To coat or finish with a layer of copper. **2.** *Slang* To bet against, as in faro. [ME *coper* < OE < LLat. *cuprum* < Lat. *Cyprium (aes),* Cyprian (metal) < *Cyprius,* of Cyprus < Gk. *Kuprios* < *Kupros,* Cyprus.] —**cop′per•y** *adj.*

cop•per² (kŏp′ər) *n. Slang* A police officer. [< COP².]

Copper and Stone Age *n.* See **Chalcolithic.**

cop•per•as (kŏp′ər-əs) *n.* **ferrous sulfate.** [ME *coperose,* a metallic sulfate < OFr. < Med.Lat. *cuperōsa,* prob. short for **aqua cuprōsa,* copper water < LLat. *cuprum,* copper. See COPPER¹.]

cop•per•head (kŏp′ər-hĕd′) *n.* **1.** A venomous North American snake (*Agkistrodon contortrix*) with a reddish-brown body and darker crossbands. **2. Copperhead** A Northerner who sympathized with the South during the Civil War.

cop•per•leaf (kŏp′ər-lēf′) *n.* Any of various plants of the genus

cop³

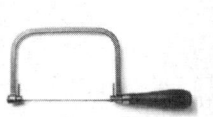

coping saw

ă	pat	oi	boy
ā	pay	ou	out
âr	care	ŏŏ	took
ä	father	ōō	boot
ĕ	pet	ŭ	cut
ē	be	ûr	urge
ĭ	pit	th	thin
ī	pie	th	this
îr	pier	hw	which
ŏ	pot	zh	vision
ō	toe	ə	about,
ô	paw		item

Stress marks:
′ (primary)
′ (secondary), as in
lexicon (lĕk′sĭ-kŏn′)

Acalypha, esp. *A. wilkesiana,* an ornamental shrub of the Pacific islands widely grown for its colorful leaves.

Cop·per·mine (kŏp′ər-mīn′) A river of N Northwest Terrs., Canada, flowing c. 845 km (525 mi) to the Arctic Ocean.

cop·per·plate (kŏp′ər-plāt′) *n.* **1.** A copper printing plate engraved or etched to form a recessed pattern of the matter to be printed. **2.** A copperplate print or engraving.

copper pyrites *n.* See chalcopyrite.

Copper River A river rising in the Wrangell Mts. of S AK and flowing c. 483 km (300 mi) to the Gulf of Alaska.

cop·per·smith (kŏp′ər-smĭth′) *n.* One who works or manufactures objects, esp. utensils, in copper.

copper sulfate *n.* A poisonous copper salt, $CuSO_4 \cdot 5H_2O$, used in agriculture, textile dyeing, and electroplating.

cop·per·ware (kŏp′ər-wâr′) *n.* Articles made of copper.

cop·pice (kŏp′ĭs) *n.* A thicket or grove of small trees or shrubs. [OFr. *copeiz.* See COPSE.]

co·pra (kō′prə, kŏp′rə) *n.* The dried flesh of the coconut from which coconut oil is extracted. [Port. < Malayalam *koppara.*]

copro– *pref.* Excrement; dung: *coprolite.* [< Gk. *kopros,* dung.]

co·proc·es·sor (kō′prŏs′ĕs-ər) *n.* A microprocessor that performs specialized functions that the central processing unit cannot perform or cannot perform as well and as quickly.

cop·ro·la·li·a (kŏp′rə-lā′lē-ə) *n.* Uncontrolled, often obsessive use of obscene or scatological language accompanying certain mental disorders. [COPRO– + Gk. *laliā,* babbling (< *lalein,* to talk).]

cop·ro·lite (kŏp′rə-līt′) *n.* Fossilized excrement. **—cop′ro·lit′ic** (-lĭt′ĭk) *adj.*

cop·rol·o·gy (kŏ-prŏl′ə-jē) *n.* Scatology.

cop·roph·a·gous (kŏ-prŏf′ə-gəs) *adj.* Feeding on excrement: *coprophagous beetles.* **—cop′roph′a·gy** (-ə-jē) *n.*

cop·ro·phil·i·a (kŏp′rə-fĭl′ē-ə) *n.* An abnormal, often obsessive interest in excrement. **—cop′ro·phil′i·ac′** (-ē-ăk′) *n.* **—cop′ro·phil′ic** *adj.*

cop·roph·i·lous (kŏ-prŏf′ə-ləs) *adj.* Living or growing on excrement, as certain fungi.

copse (kŏps) *n.* A thicket of small trees or shrubs. [ME *copys* < OFr. *copeiz,* thicket for cutting < *coper, couper,* to cut. See COPE¹.]

Copt (kŏpt) *n.* **1.** An Egyptian belonging to or descended from the people of ancient or pre-Islamic Egypt. **2.** A member of the Coptic Church. [Fr. *Copte* < NLat. *Coptus* < Ar. *Qubt,* Copts < Coptic *Gyptias* < Gk. *Aiguptios,* an Egyptian < *Aiguptos,* Egypt, of Egypt. orig.]

cop·ter (kŏp′tər) *n. Informal* A helicopter.

Cop·tic (kŏp′tĭk) *n.* The Afro-Asiatic language of the Copts. ❖ *adj.* Of or relating to the Copts, the Coptic Church, or the Coptic language.

Coptic Church *n.* The Christian church of Egypt, with dioceses elsewhere in Africa and the Near East, having a liturgy in Coptic and a Monophysite doctrine.

cop·u·la (kŏp′yə-lə) *n.* **1.** *Grammar* A verb, such as a form of *be* or *seem,* that identifies the predicate of a sentence with the subject. **2.** *Logic* The word or set of words that serves as a link between the subject and predicate of a proposition. [Lat. *cōpula,* link.] **—cop′u·lar** (-lər) *adj.*

cop·u·late (kŏp′yə-lāt′) *intr.v.* **-lat·ed, -lat·ing, -lates** To engage in coitus. ❖ *adj.* (-lĭt) Coupled; joined. [Lat. *cōpulāre, cōpulāt-,* to join together < *cōpula,* link.] **—cop′u·la′tion** *n.* **—cop′u·la·to′ry** (-lə-tôr′ē, -tōr′ē) *adj.*

cop·u·la·tive (kŏp′yə-lā′tĭv, -lə-tĭv) *adj.* **1.** *Grammar* **a.** Serving to connect coordinate words or clauses: *a copulative conjunction.* **b.** Serving as a copula: *a copulative verb.* **2.** Of or relating to copulation. ❖ *n. Grammar* A copulative word or group of words. **—cop′u·la·tive·ly** *adv.*

cop·y (kŏp′ē) *n., pl.* **-ies 1.** An imitation or reproduction of an original; a duplicate. **2.** One example of a printed text or picture: *an autographed copy of a novel.* **3.** Material, such as a manuscript, that is to be set in type. **4.** The words to be printed or spoken in an advertisement. **5.** Suitable source material for journalism: *Celebrities make good copy.* ❖ *v.* **-ied, -y·ing, -ies** *—tr.* **1.** To make a reproduction or copy of. **2.** To follow as a model or pattern; imitate. See Syns at **imitate.** *—intr.* **1.** To make a copy. **2.** To admit of being copied. [ME *copie* < OFr. < Med.Lat. *cōpia,* transcript < Lat., profusion.] **—cop′y·a·ble** *adj.*

cop·y·book (kŏp′ē-bŏŏk′) *n.* An exercise book containing models of penmanship. ❖ *adj.* Unoriginal; trite.

copy boy also **cop·y·boy** (kŏp′ē-boi′) *n.* A boy employed by a newspaper or broadcast news office to run errands.

cop·y·cat (kŏp′ē-kăt′) *Informal n.* One that closely imitates or mimics another. **—cop′y·cat′** *v. & adj.*

copy desk *n.* The desk in a news office where copy is edited and prepared for typesetting or broadcasting.

cop·y·ed·it or **cop·y-ed·it** (kŏp′ē-ĕd′ĭt) *tr.v.* **-it·ed, -it·ing, -its** To correct and prepare (a manuscript, for example) for typesetting and printing. **—cop′y·ed′i·tor** *n.*

copy girl also **cop·y·girl** (kŏp′ē-gûrl′) *n.* A girl employed by a newspaper or broadcast news office to run errands.

cop·y·hold·er (kŏp′ē-hōl′dər) *n.* **1.** An assistant who reads manuscript aloud to a proofreader. **2.** A device that holds copy in place, esp. for a typesetter.

coquina
Donax variabilis

corbel arch

cop·y·ist (kŏp′ē-ĭst) *n.* One who makes written copies.

cop·y·left (kŏp′ē-lĕft′) *n.* A form of licensing that encourages the distribution of software at no charge for noncommercial uses. [After COPYRIGHT.] **—cop′y·left′ed** (-lĕf′tĭd) *adj.*

copy protection *n.* A means of preventing the illegal or unauthorized copying of a software product, esp. a preventive routine that is incorporated into a copyrighted program. **—cop′y·pro·tect′ed** (-prə-tĕk′tĭd) *adj.*

cop·y·read·er (kŏp′ē-rē′dər) *n.* One who edits and corrects newspaper copy for publication.

cop·y·right (kŏp′ē-rīt′) *n.* The legal right to exclusive publication, production, sale, or distribution of a literary, musical, or artistic work. ❖ *adj.* **1.** Of or relating to a copyright: *a copyright agreement.* **2.** Protected by copyright. ❖ *tr.v.* **-right·ed, -right·ing, -rights** To secure a copyright for. **—cop′y·right′a·ble** *adj.* **—cop′y·right′er** *n.*

cop·y·writ·er (kŏp′ē-rī′tər) *n.* One who writes copy, esp. for advertising.

coq au vin (kōk′ ō văN′) *n.* A dish of chicken cooked in red wine. [Fr. : *coq,* chicken + *à,* with + *vin,* wine.]

co·quet (kō-kĕt′) *intr.v.* **-quet·ted, -quet·ting, -quets 1.** To engage in coquetry; flirt. **2.** To trifle; dally. [Fr. *coqueter < coquet,* flirtatious man, dim. of *coq,* cock < OFr. *coc* < LLat. *coccus.* See COCK¹.]

co·quet·ry (kō′kĭ-trē, kō-kĕt′rē) *n., pl.* **-ries** Dalliance; flirtation. [Fr. *coquetterie < coquette,* coquette. See COQUETTE.]

co·quette (kō-kĕt′) *n.* A woman who makes teasing sexual or romantic overtures; a flirt. [Fr., fem. of *coquet,* flirtatious man. See COQUET.] **—co·quet′tish** *adj.* **—co·quet′tish·ly** *adv.* **—co·quet′tish·ness** *n.*

co·quil·la nut (kō-kĕl′yə, -kē′yə) *n.* The thick-shelled seed of a Brazilian feather-leaved palm (*Attalea funifera*) used for carving or turning. [Port. *coquilho,* dim. of *côco,* coco. See COCONUT.]

co·quille (kō-kēl′) *n.* A scallop-shaped dish or a scallop shell in which various seafood dishes are browned and served. [Fr. < Lat. *conchȳlia,* pl. of *conchȳlium,* shellfish < Gk. *konkhulion,* dim. of *konkhos.*]

co·qui·na (kō-kē′nə) *n.* **1.** Any of various small marine clams of the genus *Donax* that have variously colored shells. **2.** A soft porous limestone, composed essentially of fragments of shells and coral, used as a building material. [Sp., cockle, prob. dim. of *concha,* shell < Lat., mussel. See CONCH.]

co·qui·to (kō-kē′tō) *n., pl.* **-tos** A feather-leaved palm (*Jubaea chilensis*) native to Chile and having a sugary sap used for making wine and a kind of honey. [Sp., dim. of *coco,* coco palm < Port. *côco,* dim. of COCONUT.]

Cor. *abbr. Bible* Corinthians

cor– *pref.* Variant of com–.

cor·a·cle (kôr′ə-kəl, kŏr′-) *n.* A small rounded boat made of waterproof material stretched on a wicker or wooden frame. [Welsh *corwgl* < MIr. *curach* < OIr.]

cor·a·coid (kôr′ə-koid′, kŏr′-) *n.* **1.** A bony process projecting from the scapula toward the sternum in mammals. **2.** A beak-shaped bone articulating with the scapula and sternum in most lower vertebrates, such as birds and reptiles. [NLat. *coracoīdēs* < Gk. *korakoeidēs,* ravenlike : *korax, korak-,* raven + *-oeidēs,* -oid.] **—cor′a·coid** *adj.*

cor·al (kôr′əl, kŏr′-) *n.* **1a.** A rocklike deposit consisting of the calcareous skeletons secreted by various anthozoans and often accumulating to form reefs or islands in warm seas. **b.** Any of numerous chiefly colonial marine polyps of the class Anthozoa that secrete such calcareous skeletons. **c.** The red-orange, pinkish, or white deposits secreted by corals of the genus *Corallium.* **d.** An object made of this material. **2.** A deep or strong pink to moderate red or reddish orange. **3.** The unfertilized eggs of a female lobster, which turn reddish when cooked. ❖ *adj.* Of the color coral. [ME < OFr. < Lat. *corallium* < Gk. *korallion.*]

cor·al-bells (kôr′əl-bĕlz′, kŏr′-) *pl.n.* (*used with a sing. or pl. verb*) A species of alumroot (*Heuchera sanguinea*) native to the southwest United States and Mexico and cultivated for its clusters of bell-shaped flowers.

cor·al·ber·ry (kôr′əl-bĕr′ē, kŏr′-) *n.* A North American deciduous shrub (*Symphoricarpos orbiculatus*) cultivated for its abundant clusters of coral-red, berrylike fruits.

coral fungus *n.* Any of numerous fungi, esp. of the family Clavariaceae, whose spore-bearing structures resemble coral.

cor·al·line (kôr′ə-lĭn, -līn′, kŏr′-) *adj.* **1.** Of, consisting of, or producing coral. **2.** Resembling coral, esp. in color. ❖ *n.* **1.** Any of various red algae of the family Corallinaceae whose fronds are covered with calcareous deposits. **2.** Any of various organisms that resemble coral. [Fr. *corallin* < LLat. *corallīnus* < Lat. *corallium,* coral. See CORAL.]

cor·al·loid (kôr′ə-loid′, kŏr′-) also **cor·al·loid·al** (-loid′l) *adj.* Resembling coral in appearance or form. [Lat. *corallium,* coral; see CORAL + –OID.]

coral pink *n.* A moderate to deep yellowish pink.

coral reef *n.* An erosion-resistant marine ridge or mound consisting chiefly of compacted coral.

cor·al·root (kôr′əl-rōōt′, -rŏŏt′, kŏr′-) *n.* Any of several saprophytic, chiefly New World orchids of the genus *Corallorhiza,* having leafless stems and small flowers.

Coral Sea An arm of the SW Pacific Ocean bounded by Vanuatu, NE Australia, and SE New Guinea.

coral snake *n.* Any of various venomous snakes of the genus *Micrurus*, native to tropical America and the southern United States and having red, yellow, and black bands.

Coral Springs A city of SE FL, a suburb of Fort Lauderdale. Pop. 117,549.

coral vine *n.* A climbing woody vine (*Antigonon leptopus*) native to Mexico and cultivated for its red to white flowers.

Co•ran•tijn (kôr′ən-tīn′, kôr′-) See **Courantyne.**

cor•ban (kôr′bən, -băn′) *n.* A sacrifice made to God by the ancient Hebrews at the Temple in Jerusalem. [ME < LLat. < Gk. *korbān* < Heb. *qurbān* < *qārab*, to approach.]

cor•beil also **cor•beille** (kôr′bəl, kôr-bā′) *n.* A sculptured basket of flowers or fruits used as an architectural element. [Fr. *corbeille* < LLat. *corbicula*, dim. of Lat. *corbis*, basket.]

cor•bel (kôr′bəl, -bĕl′) *n.* A bracket of stone, wood, or other building material, projecting from the face of a wall and generally used to support a cornice or an arch. ❖ *tr.v.* **-beled, -bel•ing, -bels** also **-belled, -bel•ling, -bels** To provide with or support by a corbel. [ME < OFr., dim. of *corp*, raven (being similar in shape to a raven's beak) < Lat. *corvus.*]

corbel arch *n.* An archlike structure in which the sides are formed by corbeling.

cor•bel•ing (kôr′bə-lĭng, -bĕl′-) *n.* An overlapping arrangement of bricks or stones in which each course extends farther out from the wall than the course below.

Cor•bett (kôr′bət), **James John** Known as "Gentleman Jim." 1866–1933. Amer. heavyweight boxing champion (1892–97).

cor•bie gable (kôr′bē) *n.* A gable finished with corbie-steps.

cor•bie-step also **cor•bie•step** (kôr′bē-stĕp′) *n.* One of a series of stepped masonry projections rising above roof level along the sides of a gable wall. [ME *corbie*, raven < OFr. *corbin* < Lat. *corvīnus*, ravenlike. See CORBINA.]

cor•bi•na (kôr-bē′nə) also **cor•vi•na** (-vē′nə) *n.* 1. A food and game fish (*Menticirrhus undulatus*) of North American Pacific waters. 2. Any of several related marine fishes of the family Sciaenidae. [Sp. *corbina, corvina* < fem. of *corvino*, ravenlike (< its color) < Lat. *corvīnus* < *corvus*, raven.]

Cor•co•va•do (kôr′kə-vä′dō, kôr′kô-vä′dŏŏ) A mountain, 704.6 m (2,310 ft) of SE Brazil overlooking Rio de Janeiro; site of an enormous concrete statue of Christ the Redeemer.

Cor•cy•ra (kôr-sī′rə) See **Corfu.**

cord (kôrd) *n.* 1. A slender rope usu. made of twisted strands or fibers. 2. An insulated flexible electric wire fitted with a plug or plugs. 3. A hangman's rope. 4. An influence, feeling, or force that binds or restrains; a bond or tie. 5. also **chord** (also kôrd) *Anatomy* A long ropelike structure, such as a nerve or tendon. 6a. A raised rib on the surface of cloth. b. A fabric or cloth with such ribs. 7. **cords** Trousers made of corduroy. 8. A unit of quantity for cut fuel wood, equal to a stack measuring 4 × 4 × 8 feet or 128 cubic feet (3.62 cubic meters). ❖ *tr.v.* **cord•ed, cord•ing, cords** 1. To fasten or bind with a cord. 2. To furnish with a cord. 3. To pile (wood) in cords. [ME < OFr. *corde* < Lat. *chorda* < Gk. *khordē.*] —**cord′er** *n.*

cord•age (kôr′dĭj) *n.* 1. Cords or ropes, esp. the ropes in the rigging of a ship. 2. The amount of wood in an area as measured in cords.

cor•date (kôr′dāt′) *adj.* Having a heart-shaped outline: *a cordate leaf.* [NLat. *cordātus* < Lat. *cor, cord-*, heart. See **kerd-** in App.] —**cor′date•ly** *adv.*

Cor•day (kôr-dā′, kôr′dā), **Charlotte** 1768–98. French Revolutionary heroine who was guillotined for the assassination of Jean Paul Marat in 1793.

cord•ed (kôr′dĭd) *adj.* 1. Tied or bound with cords. 2. Furnished with or made of cords. 3. Ribbed or twilled: *a corded bedspread.* 4. Stacked in cords: *corded firewood.*

cord grass *n.* Any of several perennial grasses of the genus *Spartina*, several of which form colonies in salt marshes.

cor•dial (kôr′jəl) *adj.* 1. Warm and sincere; friendly: *a cordial greeting.* 2. Strongly felt; fervent. 3. Serving to invigorate; stimulating. ❖ *n.* 1. A stimulant; a tonic. 2. A liqueur. [ME, of the heart < Med.Lat. *cordiālis* < Lat. *cor, cord-*, heart. See **kerd-** in App.] —**cor•dial′i•ty** (-jăl′ĭ-tē, -jē-ăl′-, -dē-ăl′-), **cor′dial•ness** *n.* —**cor′dial•ly** *adv.*

cor•di•er•ite (kôr′dē-ə-rīt′) *n.* A dichroic violet-blue to gray mineral silicate of magnesium, aluminum, and sometimes iron. [Fr., after Pierre L. *Cordier* (1777–1861), French geologist.]

cor•di•form (kôr′də-fôrm′) *adj.* Heart-shaped. [Lat. *cor, cord-*, heart; see **kerd-** in App. + -FORM.]

cor•dil•le•ra (kôr′dl-yâr′ə, kôr-dĭl′ər-ə) *n.* A chain of mountains, esp. the principal mountain system of a continent. [Sp. < OFr. *cordele*, dim. of *cuerda*, cord < Lat. *chorda*. See CORD.] —**cor′dil•le′ran** (-yâr′ən) *adj.*

Cor•dil•le•ra Cen•tral (kôr′dĭl-yĕr′ə sĕn-träl′, -dē-yĕ′rä) 1. The central of three ranges of the Andes in W Colombia. 2. A mountain range of central Dominican Republic. 3. A range of the Andes extending NW and SE in N-central Peru. 4. A range of S-central Puerto Rico.

Cordillera Mé•ri•da (mĕr′ĭ-də, mĕr′rē-dä) A mountain range of W Venezuela extending NE and SW.

Cordillera Oc•ci•den•tal (ŏk′sĭ-dĕn-täl′, ŏk′sē-) A range of the W Andes with branches in W Colombia and along the Pacific coast of Peru.

Cordillera O•rien•tal (ôr′ē-ĕn-täl′, ô′ryĕn-) A range of the E Andes with branches in central Bolivia, W Colombia, and SE Peru.

Cordillera Re•al (rā-äl′) A range of the Andes with branches in W Bolivia and central Ecuador.

Cor•dil•le•ras (kôr′dĭl-yâr′əz, -dē-yĕ′räs) The complex of mountain ranges in W North America, Central America, and South America, extending from AK to Cape Horn.

cord•ite (kôr′dīt′) *n.* A smokeless explosive powder consisting of nitrocellulose, nitroglycerin, and petrolatum that has been dissolved in acetone, dried, and extruded in cords.

cord•less (kôrd′lĭs) *adj.* Having no cord, usu. using batteries as a source of power: *a cordless telephone.* —**cord′less•ly** *adv.*

cor•do•ba (kôr′də-bə, -və) *n.* See table at **currency.** [Am.Sp. *córdoba*, after Francisco Fernández de *Córdoba* (1475?–1526?), Spanish explorer.]

Cór•do•ba (kôr′də-bə) 1. (*also* kôr′dō-vä) A city of N-central Argentina NW of Buenos Aires; founded 1573. Pop. 1,148,305. 2. (*also* kôr′thō-vä) A city of S Spain on the Guadalquivir R. ENE of Seville. Pop. 305,894. —**Cor′do•van** (-vən) *adj. & n.*

cor•don (kôr′dn) *n.* 1. A line of people, military posts, or ships stationed around an area to enclose or guard it. 2. A cord, braid, or ribbon worn as a fastening or ornament. 3. *Architecture* A stringcourse. 4. *Botany* A fruit tree pruned and trained to grow on a support as a ropelike stem. ❖ *tr.v.* **-doned, -don•ing, -dons** To form a cordon around (an area) so as to prevent movement in or out. [Fr. < OFr., dim. of *corde*, cord.]

cor•don bleu (kôr′dôn blœ′) *n., pl.* **cor•dons bleus** (kôr′dôn blœ′) A person highly distinguished in a field, esp. a master chef. [Fr. : *cordon*, ribbon + *bleu*, blue.]

cor•don sa•ni•taire (kôr-dôn′ să-nē-târ′) *n., pl.* **cor•dons sa•ni•taires** (kôr-dôn′ să-nē-târ′) 1. A barrier designed to prevent a disease from spreading. 2. A chain of states organized around a nation considered potentially hostile. [Fr., quarantine line : *cordon*, line + *sanitaire*, sanitary.]

cor•do•van (kôr′də-vən) *n.* A fine leather originally made of goatskin but now more frequently of split horsehide. [Sp. *cordován*, from *Córdova* (*Córdoba*), Spain.]

cor•du•roy (kôr′də-roi′) *n.* 1. A durable cut-pile fabric, usu. made of cotton, with vertical ribs. 2. **corduroys** Trousers made of corduroy. 3. A road made of logs laid down crosswise. ❖ *tr.v.* **-royed, -roy•ing, -roys** To build (a corduroy). [Prob. CORD + obsolete *duroy*, a coarse woolen fabric.] —**cor′du•roy′** *adj.*

cord•wood (kôrd′wŏŏd′) *n.* 1. Wood cut and piled in cords. 2. Wood sold by the cord.

core (kôr, kōr) *n.* 1. The hard or fibrous central part of certain fruits, containing the seeds. 2. The central or innermost part. 3. The basic or most important part; the essence. A set of subjects or courses that make up a required portion of a curriculum. 5. *Electricity* A soft iron rod in a coil or transformer that provides a path for and intensifies the magnetic field produced by the windings. 6a. *Computer Science* A memory, esp. one consisting of a series of tiny doughnut-shaped masses of magnetic material. b. One of the magnetic doughnut-shaped masses that make up such a memory. 7. The central portion of the earth below the mantle, beginning at a depth of about 2,900 kilometers (1,800 miles) and probably consisting of iron and nickel. 8. A mass of dry sand placed within a mold to provide openings or shape to a casting. 9. The part of a nuclear reactor where fission occurs. 10. A cylindrical sample of rock, ice, or other material obtained from the center of a mass by drilling or cutting. 11. The base to which veneer woods are glued. 12. *Archaeology* A stone from which one or more flakes have been removed, serving as a source for such flakes or as a tool itself. ❖ *tr.v.* **cored, cor•ing, cores** 1. To remove the core of: *core apples.* 2. To remove (a cylindrical sample) from something, such as a glacier. [ME.]

CORE *abbr.* Congress of Racial Equality

core dump *n.* A copy of the data stored in the core memory of a computer, usu. used for debugging purposes.

co•re•lig•ion•ist (kō′rĭ-lĭj′ə-nĭst) *n.* One having the same religion as another.

core memory *n.* See **core** 6a.

cor•e•op•sis (kôr′ē-ŏp′sĭs, kōr-) *n.* Any of various plants of the genus *Coreopsis* in the composite family, having showy radiate flower heads. [NLat. *Coreopsis*, genus name < Gk. *koris*, bedbug; see **sker-1** in App. + -OPSIS.]

co•re•pres•sor (kō′rĭ-prĕs′ər) *n.* A substance that combines with and activates a genetic repressor, thus preventing gene transcription and inhibiting protein synthesis.

cor•er (kôr′ər) *n.* A device for coring apples.

co•re•spon•dent (kō′rĭ-spŏn′dənt) *n.* A person charged with having committed adultery with the defendant in a divorce suit. —**co′re•spon′den•cy** *n.*

core tool *n.* *Archaeology* A stone tool consisting of a core that is flaked to produce a cutting edge or edges.

corf (kôrf) *n., pl.* **corves** (kôrvz) *Chiefly British* A truck, tub, or basket used in a mine. [ME, basket < MDu. *corf* or MLGer. *korf*, both prob. < Lat. *corbis.*]

corbie-step
City Hall in Frankfurt, Germany

ă	pat	oi	boy
ā	pay	ou	out
âr	care	ŏŏ	took
ä	father	ōō	boot
ĕ	pet	ŭ	cut
ē	be	ûr	urge
ĭ	pit	th	thin
ī	pie	th	this
îr	pier	hw	which
ŏ	pot	zh	vision
ō	toe	ə	about,
ô	paw		item

Stress marks:
′ (primary);
′ (secondary), as in
lexicon (lĕk′sĭ-kŏn′)

Cor•fu (kôr′fōō, -fyōō, kôr-fōō′) also **Kér•ki•ra** (kĕr′kē-rä′) Formerly **Cor•cy•ra** (kôr-sī′rə) An island of Greece in the Ionian Is. off the NW coast of the mainland; settled c. 700 B.C.

cor•gi (kôr′gē) n., pl. **-gis** A Welsh corgi. [Welsh : cor, dwarf + ci, dog; see **kwon-** in App.]

co•ri•a•ceous (kôr′ē-ā′shəs, kōr′-) adj. Of or like leather, esp. in texture. [< LLat. coriāceus < Lat. corium, leather. See **sker-**[1] in App.]

co•ri•an•der (kôr′ē-ăn′dər, kōr′-, kôr′ē-ăn′dər, kōr′-) n. **1a.** An aromatic annual Eurasian herb (Coriandrum sativum) in the parsley family, cultivated for its edible fruits, leafy shoots, and roots. **b.** The leaves of this herb, used as a flavoring and garnish. **2.** The seedlike fruit of this plant, used as a seasoning. [ME coriandre < OFr. < Lat. coriandrum < Gk. koriandron.]

Cor•inth (kôr′ĭnth, kŏr′-) also **Kó•rin•thos** (kô′rĭn-thôs′) A city of S Greece in the NE Peloponnesus on the Gulf of Corinth near the site of the ancient city of **Corinth**, a rich maritime power in the 7th and 6th cent. B.C. Pop. 22,658.

Corinth, Gulf of Formerly **Gulf of Le•pan•to** (lĭ-păn′tō, lĕ′pän-tô) An inlet of the Ionian Sea between the Peloponnesus and central Greece.

Corinth, Isthmus of A narrow isthmus connecting central Greece with the Peloponnesus and crossed by the **Corinth Canal** (constructed 1881–93).

Co•rin•thi•an (kə-rĭn′thē-ən) adj. **1.** Of or relating to ancient Corinth or its people or culture. **2.** Architecture Of or relating to the Corinthian order. **3.** Elegantly or elaborately ornate. **4.** Given to licentious and profligate luxury. ❖ n. **1.** A native or inhabitant of Corinth. **2.** A luxury-loving person; a bon vivant. **3.** A wealthy amateur sportsman, esp. an amateur yachtsman. **4.** **Corinthians** (used with a sing. verb) See table at **Bible**.

Corinthian order n. Architecture The most ornate of the three classical orders, marked by a slender fluted column having an ornate bell-shaped capital decorated with acanthus leaves.

Co•ri•o•lis force (kôr′ē-ō′lĭs, kōr′-) n. A pseudo-force used mathematically to describe motion, as of aircraft or cloud formations, relative to a uniformly rotating frame of reference such as Earth. [After Gaspard G. de Coriolis (1792–1843), French mathematician.]

co•ri•um (kôr′ē-əm, kōr′-) n., pl. **-ri•a** (-ē-ə) See **dermis**. [Lat., skin. See **sker-**[1] in App.]

cork (kôrk) n. **1.** The lightweight elastic outer bark of the cork oak, used esp. for bottle closures, insulation, and floats. **2a.** Something made of cork, esp. a bottle stopper. **b.** A bottle stopper made of other material, such as plastic. **3.** A small float used on a fishing line or net for buoyancy. **4.** Botany A nonliving water-resistant tissue formed on the outside of the cork cambium in many seed plants. ❖ tr.v. **corked, cork•ing, corks 1.** To stop or seal with a cork. **2.** To restrain or check; hold back: tried to cork my anger. **3.** To blacken with burnt cork. [ME < Du. kurk or LGer. korck, both < Sp. alcorque, cork-soled shoe, prob. < Ar. dialectal al-qūrq : al-, the + qūrq, cork (< Lat. quercus, oak; see **perk°u-** in App.).]

Cork A city of S Ireland near the head of **Cork Harbor**, an inlet of the Atlantic Ocean. Pop. 127,253.

cork•age (kôr′kĭj) n. A charge at a restaurant for serving a bottle of liquor that was not bought on the premises.

cork•board (kôrk′bôrd′, -bōrd′) n. A construction and insulating material made of compressed and baked granules of cork.

cork cambium n. A lateral ring of meristematic tissue found in woody seed plants, producing cork on the outside of the ring and parenchyma on the inside of the ring.

corked (kôrkt) adj. **1.** Sealed with or as if with a cork. **2.** Tainted in flavor by an unsound cork. **3.** Blackened by burnt cork.

cork•er (kôr′kər) n. **1.** One that corks bottles, for example. **2.** Slang A remarkable or astounding person or thing.

cork•ing (kôr′kĭng) Slang adj. Splendid; fine: a corking party. ❖ adv. Used as an intensive. [< CORKER.]

cork oak n. A Mediterranean evergreen oak tree (Quercus suber) having thick bark that yields commercial cork.

cork•screw (kôrk′skrōō′) n. A device for drawing corks from bottles, consisting of a pointed metal spiral attached to a handle. ❖ adj. Spiral in shape. ❖ intr. & tr.v. **-screwed, -screw•ing, -screws** To move or cause to move in a spiral or winding course.

cork•wood (kôrk′wōōd′) n. **1.** A deciduous shrub or small tree (Leitneria floridana) native to the southeast United States and having lightweight wood. **2.** See **balsa**.

cork•y (kôr′kē) adj. **-i•er, -i•est 1.** Of or resembling cork. **2.** Informal Lively; buoyant. —**cork′i•ness** n.

corm (kôrm) n. A food-storing underground stem, sometimes bearing papery scale leaves, as in the crocus. [NLat. cormus < Gk. kormos, a trimmed tree trunk. See **sker-**[1] in App.]

cor•mel (kôr′məl, kôr-mĕl′) n. A small young corm produced by a mature corm. [CORM + -el, dim. suff. (< Lat. -ellus).]

cor•mo•rant (kôr′mər-ənt, -mə-rănt′) n. **1.** Any of several large marine diving birds of the genus Phalacrocorax, having webbed feet, a hooked bill, and a distensible pouch. **2.** A greedy, rapacious person. ❖ adj. Greedy; rapacious. [ME cormoraunt < OFr. cormorant : corp, raven; see **CORBEL** + marenc, of the sea (< Lat. marīnus; see **MARINE**).]

corn[1] (kôrn) n. **1a.** Any of numerous cultivated forms of a usu.

Corinthian order
Corinthian order capital

cormorant
double-crested cormorant
Phalacrocorax auritus

tall annual cereal grass (Zea mays) bearing grains or kernels on large ears. **b.** The grains or kernels of this plant, used as food or fodder and yielding an edible oil or starch. **2.** An ear of this plant. **3.** Chiefly British Any of various cereal plants or grains, esp. wheat or oats. **4a.** A single grain of a cereal plant. **b.** A seed or fruit of various other plants, such as a peppercorn. **5.** Corn snow. **6.** Informal Corn whiskey. **7.** Slang Something considered trite, dated, melodramatic, or unduly sentimental. ❖ tr.v. **corned, corn•ing, corns 1.** To cause to form hard particles; granulate. **2a.** To season and preserve with granulated salt. **b.** To preserve (beef, for example) in brine. **3.** To feed (animals) with corn or grain. [ME, grain < OE. See **grə-no-** in App.]

corn[2] (kôrn) n. A horny thickening of the skin, usu. on or near a toe, resulting from pressure or friction. [ME corne < OFr., horn < Lat. cornū. See **ker-**[1] in App.]

corn•ball (kôrn′bôl′) Slang n. One who behaves in a mawkish or unsophisticated manner. ❖ adj. Mawkish or unsophisticated; corny: cornball humor. [< corn ball, a ball of popcorn and molasses.]

Corn Belt An agricultural region of the central US primarily in IA and IL but also including parts of IN, MN, SD, NE, KS, MO, and OH.

corn borer n. **1.** The larva of a European moth (Pyrausta nubilalis), now common in eastern North America, that feeds on and destroys corn and other plants. **2.** Any of various insect larvae similar to the corn borer that infest corn.

corn•braid (kôrn′brād′) tr.v. **-braid•ed, -braid•ing, -braids** To style (hair) in rows of braids; cornrow. —**corn′braid′** n.

corn bread or **corn•bread** (kôrn′brĕd′) n. Bread made from cornmeal.

corn cake or **corn•cake** (kôrn′kāk′) n. Chiefly Southern & Midland US See **johnnycake**. See Regional Note at **johnnycake**.

corn chip n. A thin crisp piece of food made from cornmeal.

corn•cob (kôrn′kŏb′) n. **1.** The hard cylindrical core on which the kernels of an ear of corn grow. **2.** A corncob pipe.

corncob pipe n. A pipe with a bowl made of a dried corncob.

corn cockle n. A weedy annual Mediterranean plant (Agrostemma githago) having reddish flowers and opposite leaves.

corn•crake (kôrn′krāk′) n. A common Eurasian bird (Crex crex) with brownish-yellow plumage, found in grain fields and meadows.

corn•crib (kôrn′krĭb′) n. A structure for storing and drying ears of corn.

corn•dodg•er (kôrn′dŏj′ər) n. **1.** Chiefly Southern US A small round cornmeal cake that is baked or fried. **2.** Chiefly Southern Atlantic US A dumpling of cornmeal that is boiled or steamed.

corn dog n. A frankfurter encased in corn bread batter before being baked or fried, usu. served on a stick.

cor•ne•a (kôr′nē-ə) n. The transparent convex anterior portion of the outer fibrous coat of the eyeball that covers the iris and the pupil. [Med.Lat. cornea (tēla), horny (tissue) < Lat. corneus < cornū, horn. See **ker-**[1] in App.] —**cor′ne•al** (-əl) adj.

corn earworm n. The large, destructive larva of a moth (Heliothis zea) that feeds on corn and many other plants.

Cor•neille (kôr-nā′), Pierre 1606–84. French playwright whose works include Le Cid (c. 1637) and Horace (1640).

cor•ne•i•tis (kôr′nē-ī′tĭs) n. Inflammation of the cornea.

cor•nel (kôr′nəl, -nĕl′) n. Any of various plants of the genus Cornus, which includes the bunchberry and dogwoods. [Short for Ger. Kornelbaum, cornel tree (< MHGer. kurnelboum < OHGer. kurnilboum), or < Fr. cornouille, both < Med.Lat. corniola < dim. of Lat. cornus.]

cor•nel•ian (kôr-nĕl′yən) n. Variant of **carnelian**.

cornelian cherry n. **1.** A deciduous Eurasian shrub or small tree (Cornus mas) having small yellow flowers and cherrylike fruits. **2.** The fruit of this plant. [< CORNEL.]

Cor•nell (kôr-nĕl′), Ezra 1807–74. Amer. businessman and philanthropist who cofounded Cornell University (1868).

cor•ne•ous (kôr′nē-əs) adj. Made of horn or a hornlike substance; horny. [< Lat. corneus < cornū, horn. See **ker-**[1] in App.]

cor•ner (kôr′nər) n. **1a.** The position at which two lines, surfaces, or edges meet and form an angle. **b.** The area enclosed or bounded by an angle formed in this manner: the corner of one's eye. **2.** The place where two roads or streets join or intersect. **3a.** Sports Any of the four angles of a boxing or wrestling ring where the ropes are joined. **b.** Baseball Either side of home plate, toward or away from the batter. **4.** A threatening or embarrassing position from which escape is difficult. **5.** A remote, secluded, or secret place: a beautiful corner of Paris. **6.** A part or piece made to fit on a corner, as in mounting or for protection. **7a.** A speculative monopoly of a stock or commodity created by purchasing all or most of the available supply in order to raise its price. **b.** Exclusive possession; monopoly. ❖ v. **-nered, -ner•ing, -ners** —tr. **1.** To furnish with corners. **2.** To place or drive into a corner. **3.** To form a corner in (a stock or commodity). —intr. **1.** To come together or be situated on or at a corner. **2.** To turn, as at a corner. ❖ adj. **1.** Located at a street corner. **2.** Designed for use in a corner. —**idiom: around the corner** About to happen; imminent. [ME < AN < OFr. corne, corner, horn < VLat. *corna < Lat. cornua, pl. of cornū, horn, point. See **ker-**[1] in App.]

cor•ner•back also **corner back** (kôr′nər-băk′) n. Football Either of two defensive halfbacks stationed a short distance behind the linebackers and relatively near the sidelines.

corner kick *n.* In soccer, a direct free kick from a corner of the field awarded to the attacking team when the ball has been driven out of bounds over the goal line by a defender.

cor•ner•stone also **corner stone** (kôr′nər-stōn′) *n.* **1a.** A stone at the corner of a building uniting two intersecting walls; a quoin. **b.** Such a stone, often inscribed, laid at a ceremony marking the origin of a building. **2.** An indispensable and fundamental basis: *the cornerstone of an argument.*

cor•ner•wise (kôr′nər-wīz′) also **cor•ner•ways** (-wāz′) *adv.* **1.** With a corner toward the front. **2.** So as to form a corner. **3.** From corner to corner; diagonally.

cor•net (kôr-nĕt′) *n.* **1.** *Music* A wind instrument of the trumpet class, having three valves operated by pistons. **2.** (*also* kôr′nĭt) A piece of paper twisted into a cone and used to hold small wares such as candy or nuts. **3.** (*also* kôr′nĭt) A headdress, often cone-shaped, worn by women in the 12th and 13th centuries. [ME < OFr., dim. of *corn,* horn < Lat. *cornū.* See **ker-**[1] in App.]

cor•net•ist also **cor•net•tist** (kôr-nĕt′ĭst) *n. Music* One who plays a cornet.

corn-fed (kôrn′fĕd′) *adj.* **1.** Fed on corn. **2.** *Slang* Healthy and strong but unsophisticated.

corn flakes *pl.n.* A crisp, flaky, commercially prepared cold cereal made from coarse cornmeal.

corn•flow•er (kôrn′flou′ər) *n.* An annual Eurasian plant (*Centaurea cyanus*) in the composite family, having blue, purple, pink, or white flowers.

corn•husk (kôrn′hŭsk′) *n.* The leafy husk of an ear of corn.

corn•husk•ing (kôrn′hŭs′kĭng) *n.* **1.** The husking of corn. **2.** A social gathering for husking corn. —**corn′husk′er** *n.*

cor•nice (kôr′nĭs) *n.* **1a.** A horizontal molded projection that crowns or completes a building or wall. **b.** The uppermost part of an entablature. **2.** The molding at the top of the walls of a room, between the walls and ceiling. **3.** An ornamental horizontal molding or frame used to conceal rods, picture hooks, or other devices. ❖ *tr.v.* **-niced, -nic•ing, -nic•es** To supply, decorate, or finish with or as if with a cornice. [Obsolete Fr. < Ital., poss. < Lat. *cornīx, cornīc-,* crow < its resemblance to a crow's beak (influenced by Gk. *korōnis,* curved line, flourish).]

cor•niche (kôr′nĭsh, kôr-nĕsh′) *n.* A road that winds along the side of a steep coast or cliff. [Short for Fr. *route en corniche* : *route,* road + *en,* on + *corniche,* rock ledge, cornice (< Ital. *cornice*; see CORNICE).]

cor•nic•u•late (kôr-nĭk′yə-lāt′, -lĭt) *adj.* Having horns or horn-like projections. [Lat. *corniculātus* < *corniculum,* dim. of *cornū,* horn. See **ker-**[1] in App.]

cor•ni•fi•ca•tion (kôr′nə-fĭ-kā′shən) *n.* The conversion of squamous epithelial cells into a horny material, such as hair, nails, or feathers. [Lat. *cornū,* horn; see **ker-**[1] in App. + –FICATION.]

Cor•nish (kôr′nĭsh) *adj.* Of or relating to Cornwall, its people, or the Cornish language. ❖ *n.* **1.** The Brittonic language of Cornwall, extinct since the late 18th century. **2.** Any of an English breed of domestic fowl often crossbred to produce roasters. [CORN(WALL) + –ISH.]

Cor•nish•man (kôr′nĭsh-mən) *n.* A man who is a native or inhabitant of Cornwall, England.

Cor•nish•wom•an (kôr′nĭsh-wōōm′ən) *n.* A woman who is a native or inhabitant of Cornwall, England.

Corn Law *n.* One of a series of British laws in force before 1846 that regulated the grain trade and restricted imports of grain.

corn lily *n.* Any of various bulbous herbs of the genus *Ixia,* native to southern Africa and widely cultivated as an ornamental for its showy colored flowers.

corn•meal also **corn meal** (kôrn′mēl′) *n.* Meal made from corn, used in a wide variety of foods.

corn oil *n.* A liquid obtained from the embryos of corn grains, used esp. as a cooking and salad oil and in margarines.

corn•pone or **corn pone** (kôrn′pōn′) *n. Chiefly Southern & Midland US* See johnnycake. See Regional Notes at johnnycake, **pone.** ❖ *adj. Informal* Folksy and homespun, as in manner.

corn poppy *n.* An annual Eurasian plant (*Papaver rhoeas*), having usu. scarlet flowers.

corn•row (kôrn′rō′) *tr.v.* **-rowed, -row•ing, -rows** To style (hair) by dividing into sections and braiding close to the scalp in rows. —**corn′row′** *n.*

corn salad *n.* Any of several plants of the genus *Valerianella,* esp. a Eurasian annual (*V. locusta* or *V. olitoria*), having small white to pale bluish flowers and edible young leaves.

corn silk *n.* The styles and stigmas that appear as a silky tuft or tassel at the tip of an ear of corn.

corn smut *n.* See cuitlacoche.

corn snow *n.* Snow that has melted and refrozen into a rough granular surface.

corn•stalk also **corn stalk** (kôrn′stôk′) *n.* The stalk or stem of a corn plant.

corn•starch (kôrn′stärch′) *n.* Starch prepared from corn grains, used industrially and as a thickener in cooking.

corn sugar *n.* Dextrose obtained from cornstarch.

corn syrup *n.* A syrup prepared from cornstarch, used in indus-

try and in numerous food products as a sweetener.

cor•nu (kôr′nōō, -nyōō) *n., pl.* **-nu•a** (-nōō-ə, -nyōō-ə) A part or structure, such as a bony protuberance, that resembles a horn. [Lat. *cornū,* horn. See **ker-**[1] in App.] —**cor′nu•al** (-əl) *adj.*

cor•nu•co•pi•a (kôr′nə-kō′pē-ə, -nyə-) *n.* **1.** A goat's horn overflowing with fruit, flowers, and grain, signifying prosperity. **2.** *Greek Mythology* The horn of the goat that suckled Zeus, which broke off and became filled with fruit. **3.** A cone-shaped ornament or receptacle. **4.** An overflowing store; an abundance. [LLat. *cornūcōpia* < Lat. *cornū cōpiae* : *cornū,* horn; see CORNU + *cōpiae,* genitive of *cōpia,* plenty.] —**cor′nu•co′pi•an** *adj.*

cor•nute (kôr-nōōt′, -nyōōt′) also **cor•nut•ed** (-nōō′tĭd, -nyōō′-) *adj.* **1.** Shaped like a horn. **2.** Having horns or horn-shaped processes. [Lat. *cornūtus* < *cornū,* horn. See CORNU.]

Corn•wall (kôrn′wôl′) A region of extreme SW England on a peninsula bounded by the Atlantic Ocean and English Channel.

Corn•wal•lis (kôrn-wŏl′ĭs, -wô′lĭs), **Charles.** 1st Marquis and 2nd Earl Cornwallis. 1738–1805. British military leader who surrendered at Yorktown (1781).

corn whiskey *n.* Whiskey distilled from corn.

corn•y (kôr′nē) *adj.* **-i•er, -i•est** Trite, dated, melodramatic, or mawkishly sentimental. [< CORN[1].] —**corn′i•ly** *adv.* —**corn′i•ness** *n.*

co•rol•la (kə-rŏl′ə, -rō′lə) *n.* The petals of a flower considered as a group or unit. [Lat. *corōlla,* small garland, dim. of *corōna,* garland. See CORONA.] —**co•rol′late** (-rōl′āt′) *adj.*

cor•ol•lar•y (kôr′ə-lĕr′ē, kŏr′-) *n., pl.* **-ies 1.** A proposition that follows with little or no proof required from one already proven. **2.** A deduction or an inference. **3.** A natural consequence or effect; a result. ❖ *adj.* Consequent; resultant. [ME *corolarie* < Lat. *corōllārium,* money paid for a garland, gratuity < *corōlla,* small garland. See COROLLA.]

Cor•o•man•del Coast (kôr′ə-măn′dl) A region of SE India bounded by the Bay of Bengal and the Eastern Ghats.

co•ro•na (kə-rō′nə) *n., pl.* **-nas** *or* **-nae** (-nē) **1.** *Astronomy* **a.** A faintly colored luminous ring appearing to surround a celestial body visible through a haze or thin cloud, caused by diffraction of light from suspended matter in the intervening medium. **b.** The luminous irregular envelope of highly ionized gas outside the chromosphere of the sun. **2.** *Architecture* The projecting top part of a cornice. **3.** A cigar with a long tapering body and blunt ends. **4.** *Anatomy* The crownlike upper portion of a body part or structure. **5.** *Botany* A crown-shaped, funnel-shaped, or trumpet-shaped outgrowth or appendage of the perianth of certain flowers, such as the daffodil. **6.** *Electricity* A faint glow enveloping the high-field electrode in a corona discharge. [Lat. *corōna.* See CROWN.]

Corona A city of S CA SW of Riverside. Pop. 124,966.

Corona Aus•tra•lis (ô-strā′lĭs) *n.* A constellation in the Southern Hemisphere near Telescopium and Sagittarius. [Lat. *Corōna austrālis* : *corōna,* crown + *austrālis,* southern.]

Corona Bo•re•al•is (bôr′ē-ăl′ĭs, bōr′ē-) *n.* A constellation in the Northern Hemisphere between Hercules and Boötes. [Lat. *Corōna boreālis* : *corōna,* crown + *boreālis,* northern.]

corona discharge *n.* An electrical discharge characterized by a corona and occurring when one of two electrodes in a gas has a shape causing the electric field at its surface to be significantly greater than that between the electrodes.

Co•ro•na•do (kôr′ə-nä′dō, kŏr′-, kō′rō-nä′thō), **Francisco Vásquez de** 1510–54. Spanish explorer who was the first European to explore the American Southwest.

co•ro•na•graph also **co•ro•no•graph** (kə-rō′nə-grăf′) *n.* A telescope equipped with a disk that blacks out most of the sun, used to photograph the sun's corona.

cor•o•nal (kôr′ə-nəl, kŏr′-, kə-rō′nəl) *n.* **1.** A garland, wreath, or circlet for the head. **2.** *Linguistics* A coronal consonant. ❖ *adj.* **1.** Of or relating to a corona, esp. of the head. **2.** Of, relating to, or having the direction of the coronal suture or of the plane dividing the body into front and back portions. **3.** *Linguistics* Articulated by raising the blade of the tongue, as (t) in *tip.*

coronal suture *n.* The suture extending across the skull between the two parietal bones and the frontal bone.

cor•o•nar•y (kôr′ə-nĕr′ē, kŏr′-) *adj.* **1.** Of, relating to, or being the coronary arteries or coronary veins. **2.** Of or relating to the heart. ❖ *n., pl.* **-ies** A coronary thrombosis or heart attack.

coronary artery *n.* Either of two arteries that originate in the aorta and supply blood to the muscular tissue of the heart.

coronary bypass surgery *n.* A surgical procedure performed to improve blood supply to the heart by removing a healthy blood vessel from another part of the body, such as the leg, and grafting it onto the heart to circumvent a blocked artery.

coronary care unit *n.* A hospital unit that is specially equipped to treat patients with serious heart conditions.

coronary occlusion *n.* The partial or complete obstruction of blood flow in a coronary artery, as by a thrombus.

coronary sinus *n.* A venous sinus that opens into the right atrium of the heart and serves to drain the coronary veins.

coronary thrombosis *n.* Obstruction of a coronary artery by a thrombus, often leading to destruction of heart muscle.

coronary vein *n.* Any one of the veins that drains blood from the muscular tissue of the heart into the coronary sinus.

corncrib
a row of corncribs

ă	pat	oi	boy
ā	pay	ou	out
âr	care	ōō	took
ä	father	ōō	boot
ĕ	pet	ŭ	cut
ē	be	ûr	urge
ĭ	pit	th	thin
ī	pie	*th*	this
îr	pier	hw	which
ŏ	pot	zh	vision
ō	toe	ə	about,
ô	paw		item

Stress marks:
′ (primary);
′ (secondary); as in
lexicon (lĕk′sĭ-kŏn′)

cor·o·na·tion (kôr′ə-nā′shən, kŏr′-) *n.* The act or ceremony of crowning a sovereign or the sovereign's consort. [ME *coronacioun* < Med.Lat. *corōnātiō, corōnātiōn-* < Lat. *corōnātus,* p. part. of *co-rōnāre,* to crown < *corōna,* crown. See CROWN.]

cor·o·ner (kôr′ə-nər, kŏr′-) *n.* A public officer who investigates by inquest any death thought to be of other than natural causes. [ME, officer of the crown < AN *corouner* < *coroune,* crown < Lat. *corōna.* See CROWN.] —**cor′o·ner·ship′** *n.*

cor·o·net (kôr′ə-nĕt′, kŏr′-) *n.* **1.** A small crown worn by nobles below the rank of sovereign. **2.** A chaplet or headband decorated with gold or jewels. **3.** The upper margin of a horse's hoof. [ME *coronette* < OFr., dim. of *corone,* crown < Lat. *corōna.* See CROWN.]

co·ro·no·graph (kə-rō′nə-grăf′) *n.* Variant of **coronagraph.**

Co·rot (kô-rō′, kə-), **Jean Baptiste Camille** 1796–1875. French painter noted for his sketches of Italian landscapes.

co·ro·tate (kō-rō′tāt′) *intr.v.* **-tat·ed, -tat·ing, -tates** To rotate in conjunction with another body. —**co′ro·ta′tion** *n.* —**co′ro·ta′tion·al** *adj.*

corp. *abbr.* corporation

cor·po·ra (kôr′pər-ə) *n.* Plural of **corpus.**

cor·po·ral[1] (kôr′pər-əl, kôr′prəl) *adj.* Of or relating to the body. See Syns at **bodily.** [ME < OFr. < Lat. *corporālis* < *corpus, corpor-,* body. See k^w**rep-** in App.] —**cor′po·ral′i·ty** (-pə-răl′ĭ-tē) *n.* —**cor′po·ral·ly** *adv.*

cor·po·ral[2] (kôr′pər-əl, kôr′prəl) *n.* A noncommissioned officer in the US Army ranking above private first class and below sergeant or in the US Marine Corps ranking above lance corporal and below sergeant. [Obsolete Fr., alteration of *caporal* < OItal. *caporale* < *capo,* head < Lat. *caput.* See kaput- in App.]

cor·po·ral[3] (kôr′pər-əl, kôr′prəl) *n. Ecclesiastical* A white linen cloth on which the consecrated elements are placed during the Eucharist. [ME < OFr. and < Med.Lat. *corporāle,* both < Lat. *corporālis,* of the body < *corpus, corpor-,* body. See k^w**rep-** in App.]

cor·po·rate (kôr′pər-ĭt, kôr′prĭt) *adj.* **1.** Formed into a corporation; incorporated. **2.** Of or relating to a corporation. **3.** United or combined into one body; collective. **4.** Of or relating to a corporative government or political system. [Lat. *corporātus,* p. part. of *corporāre,* to make into a body < *corpus, corpor-,* body. See k^w**rep-** in App.] —**cor′po·rate·ly** *adv.*

corporate welfare *n.* Financial aid, such as a subsidy or tax break, provided by a government to corporations or other businesses, esp. when viewed as wasteful or unjust.

cor·po·ra·tion (kôr′pə-rā′shən) *n.* **1.** A body that is granted a charter recognizing it as a separate legal entity having its own rights, privileges, and liabilities distinct from those of its members. **2.** Such a body created for purposes of government. **3.** A group of people combined into one body.

cor·po·ra·tist (kôr′pər-ə-tĭst′, kôr′prə-tĭst′) *adj.* Of or relating to a corporative state or system. —**cor′po·ra·tism** *n.*

cor·po·ra·tive (kôr′pər-ə-tĭv, -pə-rā′tĭv) *adj.* **1.** Of, relating to, or associated with a corporation. **2.** Of or relating to a government or political system in which the principal economic functions are organized as corporate entities.

cor·po·ra·tor (kôr′pə-rā′tər) *n.* A member of a corporation.

cor·po·re·al (kôr-pôr′ē-əl, -pōr′-) *adj.* **1.** Of, relating to, or characteristic of the body. See Syns at **bodily. 2.** Of a material nature; tangible. [< Lat. *corporeus < corpus, corpor-,* body. See k^w**rep-** in App.] —**cor′po′re·al′i·ty** (-ăl′ĭ-tē), **cor′po′re·al·ness** *n.* —**cor·po′re·al·ly** *adv.*

cor·po·re·i·ty (kôr′pə-rē′ĭ-tē, -rā′-) *n.* The state of being material or corporeal; physical existence.

cor·po·sant (kôr′pə-zănt) *n.* See **Saint Elmo's fire.** [Port. and obsolete Sp. *corpo santo,* both < Lat. *corpus sānctum,* holy body : *corpus,* body; see k^w**rep-** in App. + *sānctum,* neut. of *sānctus,* holy, p. part. of *sancīre,* to consecrate; see sak- in App.]

corps (kôr, kōr) *n., pl.* **corps** (kôrz, kōrz) **1a.** A separate specialized branch or department of the armed forces. **b.** A tactical unit of ground combat forces between a division and an army under a lieutenant general. **2.** A body of persons acting together or associated under common direction. [Fr. < OFr. < Lat. *corpus,* body. See k^w**rep-** in App.]

corps de bal·let (kôr′ də bă-lā′, kôr′) *n.* The dancers in a ballet company who perform as a group. [Fr. : *corps,* corps + *de,* of + *ballet,* ballet.]

corpse (kôrps) *n.* A dead body, esp. that of a human. [ME *corps* < Lat. *corpus.* See k^w**rep-** in App.]

corps·man (kôr′mən, kôr′-, kôrz′mən, kôrz′-) *n.* **1.** An enlisted person in the US Navy or Marines trained to give first aid and basic medical treatment. **2.** A member of a government-sponsored group designated as a corps.

cor·pu·lence (kôr′pyə-ləns) *n.* The condition of being excessively fat; obesity. [ME, corporality < Lat. *corpulentia,* corpulence < *corpulentus,* corpulent < *corpus,* body. See k^w**rep-** in App.]

cor·pu·lent (kôr′pyə-lənt) *adj.* Excessively fat. See Syns at **fat.** —**cor′pu·lent·ly** *adv.*

cor·pus (kôr′pəs) *n., pl.* **-po·ra** (-pər-ə) **1.** A large collection of writings of a specific kind or on a specific subject. **2.** A collection of writings or recorded remarks used for linguistic analysis. **3a.** The capital or principal amount, as of an estate or trust. **b.** The principal of a bond. **4.** *Anatomy* **a.** The main part of a body struc-

ture or organ. **b.** A distinct body mass or organ having a specific function. **5.** *Music* The overall length of a violin. [ME < Lat. See k^w**rep-** in App.]

corpus cal·lo·sum (kə-lō′səm) *n., pl.* **corpora cal·lo·sa** (kə-lō′sə) The arched bridge of nervous tissue that connects the two cerebral hemispheres, allowing communication between the right and left sides of the brain. [NLat. *corpus callōsum* : Lat. *corpus,* body + Lat. *callōsum,* neut. of *callōsus,* callous.]

Corpus Chris·ti[1] (krĭs′tē) A city of S TX on **Corpus Christi Bay,** an arm of the Gulf of Mexico. Pop. 277,454.

Corpus Chris·ti[2] (krĭs′tē) *n. Roman Catholic Church* A feast in honor of the Eucharist, traditionally observed on the first Thursday after Trinity Sunday. [ME < Med.Lat. *Corpus Chrīstī,* body of Christ : Lat. *corpus,* body + Lat. *Chrīstī,* genitive of *Chrīstus,* Christ.]

cor·pus·cle (kôr′pə-səl, -pŭs′əl) *n.* **1a.** An unattached body cell, such as a blood cell. **b.** A rounded globular mass of cells. **2.** A discrete particle, such as an electron. **3.** A minute globular particle. [Lat. *corpusculum,* dim. of *corpus,* body. See k^w**rep-** in App.] —**cor·pus′cu·lar** (kôr-pŭs′kyə-lər) *adj.*

corpus de·lic·ti (dĭ-lĭk′tī′) *n. Law* The material evidence in a homicide, such as the corpse, showing that a crime has been committed. **2.** A corpse. [NLat. *corpus dēlictī* : Lat. *corpus,* body + Lat. *dēlictī,* genitive of *dēlictum,* crime.]

corpus lu·te·um (lōō′tē-əm) *n., pl.* **corpora lu·te·a** (lōō′tē-ə) A yellow progesterone-secreting mass of cells that forms from an ovarian follicle after the release of a mature egg. [NLat. *corpus lūteum* : Lat. *corpus,* body + Lat. *lūteum,* neut. of *lūteus,* yellow.]

corpus stri·a·tum (strī-ā′təm) *n., pl.* **corpora stri·a·ta** (strī-ā′tə) Either of two gray and white, striated bodies of nerve fibers in the lower lateral wall of each cerebral hemisphere. [NLat. *corpus striātum* : Lat. *corpus,* body + Lat. *striātum,* neut. of *striātus,* striated.]

corr. *abbr.* **1.** correction **2.** correspondent

cor·rade (kə-rād′) *tr. & intr.v.* **-rad·ed, -rad·ing, -rades** To erode or be eroded by abrasion. [Lat. *corrādere,* to scrape together : *com-,* com- + *rādere,* to scrape.] —**cor·ra′sion** (-rā′zhən) *n.* —**cor·ra′sive** (-sĭv, -zĭv) *adj.*

cor·ral (kə-răl′) *n.* **1.** An enclosure for confining livestock. **2.** An enclosure formed by a circle of wagons for defense against attack during an encampment. ❖ *tr.v.* **-ralled, -ral·ling, -rals 1.** To drive into and hold in a corral. **2.** To arrange (wagons) in a corral. **3.** To take control or possession of. **4.** To gather; garner: *corralled support for the legislation.* [Sp. < VLat. **currāle,* enclosure for carts < Lat. *currus,* cart < *currere,* to run.]

cor·rect (kə-rĕkt′) *v.* **-rect·ed, -rect·ing, -rects** —*tr.* **1a.** To remove the errors from. **b.** To indicate the errors in. **2.** To punish for the purpose of improving or reforming. **3.** To remove, remedy, or counteract (a malfunction, for example). **4.** To adjust so as to meet a required standard or condition. —*intr.* **1.** To make corrections. **2.** To make adjustments; compensate. ❖ *adj.* **1.** Free from error or fault; true or accurate. **2.** Conforming to standards; proper. [ME *correcten* < Lat. *corrigere, corrēct-,* to correct : *com-,* com- + *regere,* to rule; see reg- in App.] —**cor·rect′a·ble, cor·rect′i·ble** *adj.* —**cor·rect′ly** *adv.* —**cor·rect′ness** *n.* —**cor·rec′tor** *n.*

SYNONYMS *correct, rectify, remedy, redress, reform, revise, amend* These verbs mean to make right what is wrong. *Correct* refers to eliminating faults, errors, or defects: *correct spelling mistakes. Rectify* stresses the idea of bringing something into conformity with a standard of what is right: *will rectify the omission. Remedy* involves removing or counteracting something considered a cause of harm or damage: *took courses to remedy his ignorance. Redress* refers to setting right something considered immoral or unethical and usually involves making reparation: *the wrong to be redressed. Reform* implies broad change that improves form or character: *"Let us reform our schools, and we shall find little reform needed in our prisons"* (John Ruskin). *Revise* suggests change that results from reconsideration: *revise a manuscript. Amend* implies improvement through alteration or correction: *"Whenever [the people] shall grow weary of the existing government, they can exercise their constitutional right of amending it"* (Abraham Lincoln).

cor·rec·tion (kə-rĕk′shən) *n.* **1.** The act or process of correcting. **2.** Something offered or substituted for a mistake or fault. **3a.** Punishment intended to rehabilitate or improve. **b. corrections** The treatment of offenders through a system of penal incarceration, rehabilitation, probation, and parole or the administrative system by which these are effectuated. **4.** An amount or quantity added or subtracted in order to correct. **5.** A decline in stock-market activity or prices following a period of increases. —**cor·rec′tion·al** *adj.*

cor·rec·ti·tude (kə-rĕk′tĭ-tōōd′, -tyōōd′) *n.* Appropriate manners and behavior; propriety.

cor·rec·tive (kə-rĕk′tĭv) *adj.* Tending or intended to correct: *corrective lenses.* ❖ *n.* An agent that corrects. —**cor·rec′tive·ly** *adv.*

Cor·reg·gio (kə-rĕj′ō, kō-rĕd′jō), **Antonio Allegri da** 1494–1534. Italian High Renaissance painter known for his use of chiaroscuro.

Cor·reg·i·dor (kə-rĕg′ĭ-dôr′, -dōr′, kôr-rĕ′hē-dôr′) An island of the N Philippines at the entrance to Manila Bay.

cor•re•late (kôr′ə-lāt′, kŏr′-) v. **-lat•ed, -lat•ing, -lates** —tr. **1.** To put or bring into causal, complementary, parallel, or reciprocal relation. **2.** To establish or demonstrate as having a correlation. —intr. To be related by a correlation. ❖ adj. (-lĭt, -lāt′) Related by a correlation, esp. having corresponding characteristics. ❖ n. (-lĭt, -lāt′) Either of two correlate entities; a correlative. [Back-formation < CORRELATION.] —**cor′re•la′tor** n.

cor•re•la•tion (kôr′ə-lā′shən, kŏr′-) n. **1.** A causal, complementary, parallel, or reciprocal relationship, esp. a structural, functional, or qualitative correspondence between two comparable entities. **2.** Statistics The simultaneous change in value of two numerically valued random variables: the negative correlation between age and normal vision. **3.** An act of correlating or the condition of being correlated. [Med.Lat. correlātiō, correlātiōn-: Lat. com-, com- + Lat. relātiō, relation, report (< relātus, p. part. of referre, to carry back; see RELATE).] —**cor′re•la′tion•al** adj.

correlation coefficient n. A measure of the interdependence of two random variables that ranges in value from −1 to +1, indicating perfect negative correlation at −1, absence of correlation at zero, and perfect positive correlation at +1.

cor•rel•a•tive (kə-rĕl′ə-tĭv) adj. **1.** Related; corresponding. **2.** Grammar Indicating a reciprocal or complementary relationship: a correlative conjunction. ❖ n. **1.** Either of two correlative entities; a correlate. **2.** Grammar A correlative word or expression. —**cor•rel′a•tive•ly** adv.

correlative conjunction n. Either of a pair of conjunctions, such as both . . . and, that connect two parts of a sentence and are not used adjacent to each other.

cor•re•spond (kôr′ĭ-spŏnd′, kŏr′-) intr.v. **-spond•ed, -spond•ing, -sponds 1.** To be in agreement, harmony, or conformity. **2.** To be similar or equivalent in character, quantity, origin, structure, or function: English navel corresponds to Greek omphalos. **3.** To communicate by letter, usu. over a period of time. [Fr. correspondre < Med.Lat. correspondēre : Lat. com-, com- + respondēre, to respond; see RESPOND.]

cor•re•spon•dence (kôr′ĭ-spŏn′dəns, kŏr′-) n. **1.** The act, fact, or state of agreeing or conforming. **2.** Similarity or analogy. **3a.** Communication by the exchange of letters. **b.** The letters written or received. —**cor′re•spon′den•cy** n.

correspondence course n. An educational course offered by a correspondence school.

correspondence principle n. The principle that predictions of quantum theory approach those of classical physics in the limit of large quantum numbers.

correspondence school n. A school that offers instruction by mail, sending lessons and examinations to a student.

cor•re•spon•dent (kôr′ĭ-spŏn′dənt, kŏr′-) n. **1.** One who communicates by means of letters. **2.** One employed by the print or broadcast media to supply news stories or articles. **3.** One that has regular business dealings with another, esp. at a distance. **4.** Something that corresponds; a correlative. ❖ adj. Corresponding. —**cor′re•spon′dent•ly** adv.

cor•re•spond•ing (kôr′ĭ-spŏn′dĭng, kŏr′-) adj. **1.** Having the same or nearly the same relationship. **2.** Accompanying another. **3a.** Having been assigned the responsibility of written communications. **b.** Participating at a distance from the rest of a group. —**cor′re•spond′ing•ly** adv.

cor•re•spon•sive (kôr′ĭ-spŏn′sĭv, kŏr′-) adj. Jointly responsive. —**cor′re•spon′sive•ly** adv.

cor•ri•da (kô-rē′də, -dä) n. A bullfight, esp. a program in which several bulls are engaged. [Sp. corrida (de toros), running (of the bulls), bullfight < p. part. of correr, to run < Lat. currere.]

cor•ri•dor (kôr′ĭ-dər, -dôr′, kŏr′-) n. **1.** A narrow hallway, passageway, or gallery, often with rooms or apartments opening onto it. **2a.** A tract of land forming a passageway, such as one that allows an inland country access to the sea through another country. **b.** A restricted tract of land for the passage of trains. **c.** Restricted airspace for the passage of aircraft. **d.** The restricted path followed by a spacecraft on a particular mission. **3.** A thickly populated strip of land connecting urban areas. —idiom: **corridors of power** A place in which powerful leaders work and rule. [Fr. < Ital. corridore < correre, to run < Lat. currere.]

cor•rie (kôr′ē, kŏr′ē) n. A round hollow in a hillside; a cirque. [Sc. Gael. coire, hollow, cauldron < OIr., cauldron.]

Cor•ri•en•tes (kôr′ē-ĕn′tĕs) A city of NE Argentina on the Paraná R.; founded 1588. Pop. 257,766.

Cor•ri•gan (kôr′ĭ-gən, kŏr′-), **Mairead** b. 1944. Irish peace activist who shared the 1976 Nobel Peace Prize.

cor•ri•gen•dum (kôr′ĭ-jĕn′dəm, kŏr′-) n., pl. **-da** (-də) **1.** An error to be corrected, esp. a printer's error. **2. corrigenda** A list of errors in a book along with their corrections. [Lat., neut. gerundive of corrigere, to correct. See CORRECT.]

cor•ri•gi•ble (kôr′ĭ-jə-bəl, kŏr′-) adj. Capable of being corrected, reformed, or improved. [ME < OFr. < Med.Lat. corrigibilis < Lat. corrigere, to correct. See CORRECT.] —**cor′ri•gi•bil′i•ty** n. —**cor′ri•gi•bly** adv.

cor•ri•val (kə-rī′vəl, kō-) n. A rival or opponent. [Fr. < Lat. corrīvālis : com-, com- + rīvālis, rival; see RIVAL.] —**cor•ri′val** adj. —**cor•ri′val•ry** (-rē) n.

cor•rob•o•rant (kə-rŏb′ər-ənt) adj. Archaic Producing or stim-

ulating physical vigor. Used of a medicine.

cor•rob•o•rate (kə-rŏb′ə-rāt′) tr.v. **-rat•ed, -rat•ing, -rates** To strengthen or support with other evidence; make more certain. [Lat. corrōborāre, corrōborāt- : com-, com- + rōborāre, to strengthen (< rōbur, rōbor-, strength; see reudh- in App.).] —**cor•rob′o•ra′tion** n. —**cor•rob′o•ra′tive** (-ə-rā′tĭv, -ər-ə-tĭv), **cor•rob′o•ra•to′ry** (-ər-ə-tôr′ē, -tōr′ē) adj. —**cor•rob′o•ra′tor** n.

cor•rob•o•ree (kə-rŏb′ə-rē) n. **1.** An Australian Aboriginal dance festival held at night. **2.** Australian **a.** A large, noisy celebration. **b.** A great tumult. [< Dharuk (Aboriginal language of SE Australia) garabari.]

cor•rode (kə-rōd′) v. **-rod•ed, -rod•ing, -rodes** —tr. **1.** To destroy a metal or alloy gradually, esp. by oxidation or chemical action. **2.** To impair steadily; deteriorate. —intr. To be eaten or worn away. [ME corroden < Lat. corrōdere, to gnaw away : com-, com- + rōdere, to gnaw.] —**cor•rod′i•ble, cor•ro′si•ble** (-rō′sə-bəl) adj.

cor•ro•sion (kə-rō′zhən) n. **1a.** The act or process of corroding. **b.** The condition produced by corroding. **2.** A substance, such as rust, formed by corroding. [ME corosioun, corrosion of tissue < OFr. corrosion < Med.Lat. corrōsiō, corrōsiōn-, the act of gnawing < Lat. corrōsus, p. part. of corrōdere, to gnaw away. See CORRODE.]

cor•ro•sive (kə-rō′sĭv, -zĭv) adj. **1.** Having the capability or tendency to cause corrosion. **2.** Gradually destructive; steadily harmful: corrosive anxiety. **3.** Spitefully sarcastic: corrosive wit. ❖ n. A substance having the capability to cause corrosion. —**cor•ro′sive•ly** adv. —**cor•ro′sive•ness** n.

corrosive sublimate n. See mercuric chloride.

cor•ru•gate (kôr′ə-gāt′, kŏr′-) tr. & intr.v. **-gat•ed, -gat•ing, -gates** To shape or become shaped into folds or parallel and alternating ridges and grooves. [Lat. corrūgāre, corrūgāt-, to wrinkle up : com-, com- + rūgāre, to wrinkle (< rūga, wrinkle).] —**cor′ru•gat′ed** (-gā′tĭd), **cor′ru•gate′** adj.

corrugated iron n. A structural sheet iron, usu. galvanized, shaped in parallel furrows and ridges for rigidity.

cor•ru•ga•tion (kôr′ə-gā′shən, kŏr′-) n. **1a.** The act or process of corrugating. **b.** The state of being corrugated. **2.** A groove or ridge on a corrugated surface.

cor•rupt (kə-rŭpt′) adj. **1.** Marked by immorality and perversion; depraved. **2.** Venal; dishonest: a corrupt mayor. **3.** Containing errors or alterations, as a text. **4.** Archaic Tainted; putrid. ❖ v. **-rupt•ed, -rupt•ing, -rupts** —tr. **1.** To destroy or subvert the honesty or integrity of. **2.** To ruin morally; pervert. **3.** To taint; contaminate. **4.** To cause to become rotten; spoil. **5.** To change the original form of (a text, for example). **6.** Computer Science To damage (data) in a file or on a disk. —intr. To become corrupt. [ME < Lat. corruptus, p. part. of corrumpere, to destroy : com-, com- + rumpere, to break; see reup- in App.] —**cor•rupt′er, cor•rup′tor** n. —**cor•rup′tive** adj. —**cor•rupt′ly** adv. —**cor•rupt′ness** n.

cor•rupt•i•ble (kə-rŭp′tə-bəl) adj. Capable of being corrupted: corruptible judges. —**cor•rupt′i•bil′i•ty, cor•rupt′i•ble•ness** n. —**cor•rupt′i•bly** adv.

cor•rup•tion (kə-rŭp′shən) n. **1a.** The act or process of corrupting. **b.** The state of being corrupt. **2.** Decay; rot. **3.** Archaic Something that corrupts.

cor•rup•tion•ist (kə-rŭp′shə-nĭst) n. One who defends or practices corruption, particularly in politics.

cor•sage (kôr-säzh′, -säj′) n. **1.** A small bouquet of flowers worn at the shoulder or waist or on the wrist. **2.** The bodice or waist of a dress. [ME, torso < OFr. < cors, body < Lat. corpus. See k\ʷrep- in App.]

cor•sair (kôr′sâr′) n. **1.** A pirate, esp. along the Barbary Coast. **2.** A swift pirate ship, often officially sanctioned. [Fr. corsaire < O Provençal corsari < OItal. corsaro < Med.Lat. cursārius < cursus, plunder < Lat., run, course. See COURSE.]

corse (kôrs) n. Archaic A corpse. [ME cors < OFr. < Lat. corpus. See k\ʷrep- in App.]

cor•se•let (kôr′slĭt) n. **1.** also **cors′let** Body armor, esp. a breastplate. **2.** also **cor•se•lette** (kôr′sə-lĕt′) An undergarment combining a light corset and a brassiere. [Fr., dim. of OFr. cors, body. See CORSET.]

cor•set (kôr′sĭt) n. **1.** A close-fitting undergarment, often reinforced by stays, worn to support and shape the waistline, hips, and breasts. **2.** A medieval outer garment, esp. a laced jacket or bodice. ❖ tr.v. **-set•ed, -set•ing, -sets** To enclose in or as if in a corset. [ME, bodice < OFr., dim. of cors, body < Lat. corpus. See k\ʷrep- in App.]

Cor•si•ca (kôr′sĭ-kə) An island of France in the Mediterranean Sea N of Sardinia; ceded to France by Genoa in 1768. —**Cor′si•can** adj. & n.

cor•tege also **cor•tège** (kôr-tĕzh′) n. **1.** A train of attendants, as of a distinguished person; a retinue. **2a.** A ceremonial procession. **b.** A funeral procession. [Fr. cortège < OItal. corteggio < corteggiare, to pay honor < corte, court < Lat. cohors, cohort-, throng. See gher- in App.]

Cor•tés (kôr-tĕz′, -tĕs′), **Hernando** or **Hernán** 1485–1547. Spanish conquistador who conquered Aztec Mexico.

cor•tex (kôr′tĕks′) n., pl. **-ti•ces** (-tĭ-sēz′) or **-tex•es 1.** Anatomy

corset
detail from a pastel by
Henri de Toulouse-Lautrec

Hernando Cortés

ă	pat	oi	boy
ā	pay	ou	out
âr	care	ŏŏ	took
ä	father	ōō	boot
ĕ	pet	ŭ	cut
ē	be	ûr	urge
ĭ	pit	th	thin
ī	pie	th	this
îr	pier	hw	which
ŏ	pot	zh	vision
ō	toe	ə	about,
ô	paw		item

Stress marks:
′ (primary);
′ (secondary), as in
lexicon (lĕk′sĭ-kŏn′)

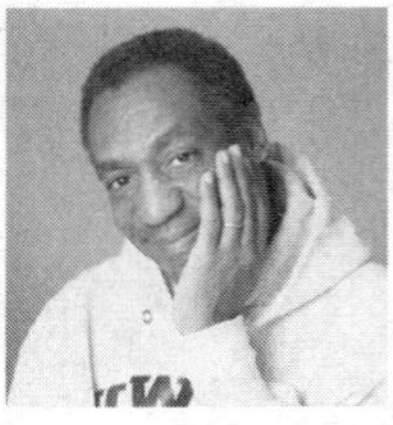

Bill Cosby

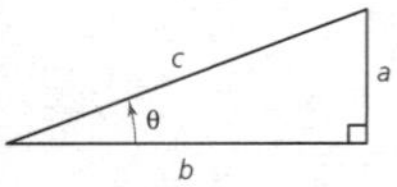

cosecant
$\csc \theta = \frac{c}{a}$

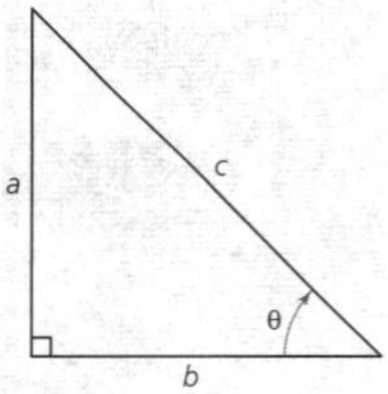

cosine
$\cos \theta = \frac{b}{c}$

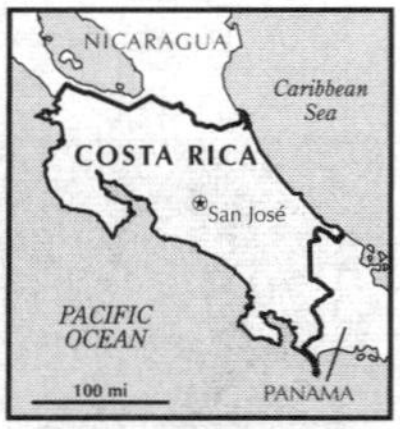

Costa Rica

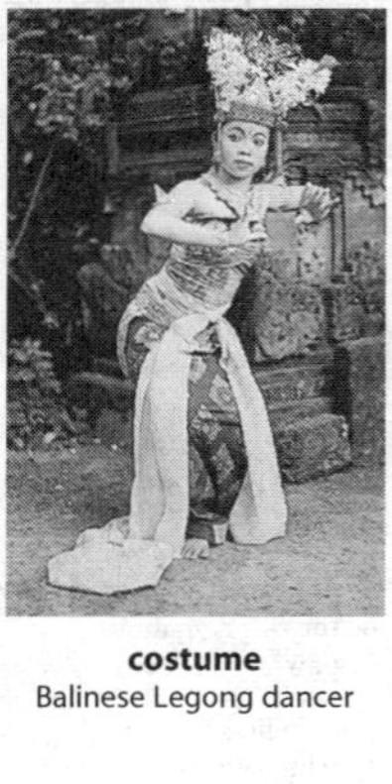

costume
Balinese Legong dancer

a. The outer layer of an internal organ or body structure, as of the kidney or adrenal gland. **b.** The outer layer of gray matter that covers the surface of the cerebral hemisphere. **2.** *Botany* The region of tissue in a root or stem between the epidermis and the vascular tissue. **3.** An external layer, such as bark or rind. [Lat., bark. See **sker-**[1] in App.]

cor•ti•cal (kôr′tĭ-kəl) *adj.* **1.** Of, relating to, derived from, or consisting of cortex. **2.** Of, relating to, associated with, or depending on the cerebral cortex. **—cor′ti•cal•ly** *adv.*

cortico– or **cortic–** *pref.* Cortex: *corticotropin.* [< Lat. *cortex, cortic-*, bark, rind. See CORTEX.]

cor•ti•coid (kôr′tĭ-koid′) *n.* A corticosteroid.

cor•ti•co•ste•roid (kôr′tĭ-kō-stîr′oid′,-stĕr′-) *n.* Any of the steroid hormones produced by the adrenal cortex or their synthetic equivalents, such as cortisol and aldosterone.

cor•ti•cos•ter•one (kôr′tĭ-kŏs′tə-rōn′) *n.* A corticosteroid, $C_{21}H_{30}O_4$, that functions in the metabolism of carbohydrates and proteins. [CORTICO– + STER(OL) + –ONE.]

cor•ti•co•tro•pin (kôr′tĭ-kō-trō′pən) also **cor•ti•co•tro•phin** (-trō′fĭn) *n.* See **ACTH.** [CORTICO– + –TROP(IC) + –IN.]

cor•tin (kôr′tn) *n.* An adrenal cortex extract that contains a mixture of hormones including cortisone. [CORT(EX) + –IN.]

cor•ti•sol (kôr′tĭ-sôl′, -zôl′, -sōl′, -zōl′) *n.* See **hydrocortisone** 1. [CORTIS(ONE) + –OL[1].]

cor•ti•sone (kôr′tĭ-sōn′, -zōn′) *n.* A naturally occurring corticosteroid, $C_{21}H_{28}O_5$, that functions primarily in carbohydrate metabolism and is used in the treatment of rheumatoid arthritis, adrenal insufficiency, certain allergies, and gout. [Shortening of CORTICOSTERONE.]

Cort•land (kôrt′lənd) *n.* A large, red-skinned cultivated variety of apple. [After *Cortland*, a county of central New York.]

Cor•to•na (kôr-tō′nə, -nä), **Pietro Berrettini da** 1596–1669. Italian painter and architect best known for the fresco *The Allegory of Divine Providence and Barberini Power* (1633–39).

co•run•dum (kə-rŭn′dəm) *n.* An extremely hard mineral, aluminum oxide, Al_2O_3, that occurs in gem varieties such as ruby and sapphire and in a common form used chiefly in abrasives. [Tamil *kuruntam.*]

co•rus•cant (kə-rŭs′kənt) *adj.* Giving forth flashes of light.

cor•us•cate (kôr′ə-skāt′, kŏr′-) *intr.v.* **-cat•ed, -cat•ing, -cates** **1.** To give forth flashes of light; sparkle and glitter: *coruscating diamonds.* **2.** To exhibit sparkling virtuosity. [Lat. *coruscāre, coruscāt-*, to flash.] **—cor′us•ca′tion** *n.*

Cor•val•lis (kôr-văl′ĭs) A city of W OR on the Willamette R. SSW of Salem. Pop. 49,322.

cor•vée (kôr-vā′, kôr′vā′) *n.* **1.** Labor exacted by a local authority for little or no pay or instead of taxes and used esp. in the maintenance of roads. **2.** A day of unpaid work required of a vassal by a feudal lord. [Fr. *corvée* and ME *corve*, both < OFr. *corovee* < Med.Lat. *(opera) corrogāta*, (work) requested, neut. pl. p. part. of Lat. *corrogāre*, to summon together : *com-*, com- + *rogāre*, to ask; see **reg-** in App.]

corves (kôrvz) *n.* Plural of **corf.**

cor•vette (kôr-vĕt′) *n.* **1.** A fast, lightly armed warship, smaller than a destroyer, often armed for antisubmarine operations. **2.** An obsolete sailing warship, smaller than a frigate, usu. armed with one tier of guns. [Fr., a kind of warship, prob. < MDu. *corf*, basket, small ship. See CORF.]

cor•vi•na (kôr-vē′nə) *n.* Variant of **corbina.**

cor•vine (kôr′vīn′, -vĭn) *adj.* Of, resembling, or characteristic of crows. [Lat. *corvīnus* < *corvus*, raven.]

Cor•vus (kôr′vəs) *n.* A constellation in the Southern Hemisphere near Crater and Virgo. [Lat. *corvus*, raven.]

Cor•y•bant (kôr′ə-bănt′, kŏr′-) *n., pl.* **-bants** or **-ban•tes** (-băn′tēz′) *Greek Mythology* A priest of Cybele whose rites were celebrated with ecstatic dances. **—Cor′y•ban′tic** *adj.*

co•ryd•a•lis (kə-rĭd′l-ĭs) *n.* Any of various herbs of the genus *Corydalis*, native chiefly to northern temperate regions and having finely divided leaves and spurred flowers. [NLat. *Corydalis*, genus name < Gk. *korudallis*, crested lark (< the shape of the flowers) < *korudos.* See **ker-**[1] in App.]

cor•ymb (kôr′ĭmb, -ĭm, kŏr′-) *n.* A usu. flat-topped flower cluster in which the flower stalks grow upward from various points of the main stem to approx. the same height. [Fr. *corymbe* < Lat. *corymbus*, flower bunch < Gk. *korumbos*, head. See **ker-**[1] in App.] **—cor′ym•bose′** (-ĭm-bōs′), **co•rym′bous** (kə-rĭm′bəs) *adj.*

co•ry•ne•bac•te•ri•um (kôr′ə-nē-băk-tîr′ē-əm, kə-rĭn′ə-) *n., pl.* **-te•ri•a** (-tîr′ē-ə) Any of various gram-positive, rod-shaped bacteria of the genus *Corynebacterium*, which includes many animal and plant pathogens. [NLat. *Corynēbacterium*, genus name : Gk. *korunē*, club; see **ker-**[1] in App. + BACTERIUM.]

co•ryn•e•form (kə-rĭn′ə-fôrm′) *adj.* Having the shape of a corynebacterium. [CORYNE(BACTERIUM) + –FORM.]

cor•y•phae•us (kôr′ə-fē′əs, kŏr′-) *n., pl.* **-phae•i** (-fē′ī′) **1.** The leader of a Greek chorus. **2.** A leader or spokesperson. [Lat., leader < Gk. *koruphaios* < *koruphē*, head. See **ker-**[1] in App.]

cor•y•phée (kôr′ə-fā′, kŏr′-) *n.* A ballet dancer ranking below a soloist and performing in small ensembles. [Fr. < Lat. *coryphaeus*, leader. See CORYPHAEUS.]

co•ry•za (kə-rī′zə) *n.* See **cold** 3. [LLat. *coryza* < Gk. *koruza*, catarrh.]

cos[1] (kôs, kŏs) *n.* See **romaine.** [After *Cos* (Kos).]

cos[2] *abbr.* cosine

Cos (kŏs, kôs) See **Kos.**

Cos•by (kôz′bē, kŏz′-), **William Henry, Jr.** Known as "Bill." b. 1937. Amer. comedian, actor, and producer who was the first African-American actor to star in a network television series, "I Spy" (1965–68).

co•se•cant (kō-sē′kănt′, -kənt) *n.* **1.** The reciprocal of the sine of an angle in a right triangle. **2.** The secant of the complement of a directed angle or arc.

co•seis•mal (kō-sīz′məl, -sīs′-) also **co•seis•mic** (-mĭk) *adj.* Relating to or being a line connecting the points on a map that indicate the places simultaneously affected by an earthquake shock. ❖ *n.* A coseismal line.

cosh[1] (kŏsh) *Chiefly British n.* A weighted weapon similar to a blackjack. [Perh. < Romany *kosh*, stick.] **—cosh** *v.*

cosh[2] *abbr.* hyperbolic cosine

co•sign (kō-sīn′) *tr.v.* **-signed, -sign•ing, -signs 1.** To sign (a document) jointly. **2.** To endorse (another's signature), as for a loan. **—co•sign′er** *n.*

co•sig•na•to•ry (kō-sĭg′nə-tôr′ē, -tōr′ē) *adj.* Signed jointly. ❖ *n., pl.* **-ries** One who cosigns.

co•sine (kō′sīn′) *n.* **1.** In a right triangle, the ratio of the length of the side adjacent to an acute angle to the length of the hypotenuse. **2.** The abscissa at the endpoint of an arc of a unit circle centered at the origin of a Cartesian coordinate system, the arc being of length *x* and subtending a positive or negative angle.

cos lettuce *n.* See **romaine.**

cos•met•ic (kŏz-mĕt′ĭk) *n.* **1.** A preparation that is designed to beautify the body by direct application. **2.** Something superficial that is used to cover a deficiency or defect. ❖ *adj.* **1.** Serving to beautify the body, esp. the face and hair. **2.** Serving to modify or improve the appearance of a physical feature, defect, or irregularity: *cosmetic surgery.* **3a.** Decorative rather than functional. **b.** Lacking depth or significance; superficial: *cosmetic changes.* [Fr. *cosmétique* < Gk. *kosmētikos*, skilled in arranging < *kosmētos*, well-ordered < *kosmein*, to arrange < *kosmos*, order.] **—cos•met′i•cal•ly** *adv.*

cos•me•ti•cian (kŏz′mĭ-tĭsh′ən) *n.* One whose occupation is manufacturing, selling, or applying cosmetics.

cos•met•i•cize (kŏz-mĕt′ĭ-sīz′) *tr.v.* **-cized, -ciz•ing, -ciz•es** To make superficially attractive or acceptable.

cos•me•tol•o•gy (kŏz′mĭ-tŏl′ə-jē) *n.* The study or art of cosmetics and their use. **—cos′me•tol′o•gist** *n.*

cos•mic (kŏz′mĭk) also **cos•mi•cal** (-mĭ-kəl) *adj.* **1.** Of or relating to the universe, esp. as distinct from Earth. **2.** Infinitely or inconceivably extended; vast. [Gk. *kosmikos* < *kosmos*, universe.] **—cos′mi•cal•ly** *adv.*

cosmic dust *n.* Clouds of fine solid particles of matter in interstellar space.

cosmic noise *n.* Radio-frequency radiation originating outside Earth's atmosphere, such as that originating from sunspots.

cosmic ray *n.* A stream of ionizing radiation of extraterrestrial origin, consisting chiefly of protons, alpha particles, and other atomic nuclei, that enters the atmosphere, collides with atomic nuclei, and produces secondary radiation.

cosmic string *n.* Any of numerous very long and thin alterations or topological defects in space hypothesized to have resulted from the big bang and to have made possible the conglomeration of mass into structures such as galaxies and the unequal distribution of mass in the universe.

cos•mid (kŏz′mĭd) *n. Genetics* A hybrid vector that has been spliced with plasmid DNA for cloning large genes or gene fragments. [Blend of *cos (sequence)*, sequence of DNA allowing the cosmid to form as a circle (short for *cohesive ends*) and PLASMID.]

cosmo– or **cosm–** *pref.* Universe; world: *cosmology.* [< Gk. *kosmos*, order, universe.]

cos•mo•chem•is•try (kŏz′mō-kĕm′ĭ-strē) *n.* The science of the chemical composition of the universe. **—cos′mo•chem′i•cal** (-ĭ-kəl) *adj.*

cos•mog•o•ny (kŏz-mŏg′ə-nē) *n., pl.* **-nies 1.** The astrophysical study of the origin and evolution of the universe. **2.** A specific theory or model of the origin and evolution of the universe. **—cos′mo•gon′ic** (-mə-gŏn′ĭk), **cos′mo•gon′i•cal** *adj.* **—cos′mo•gon′i•cal•ly** *adv.* **—cos•mog′o•nist** *n.*

cos•mog•ra•phy (kŏz-mŏg′rə-fē) *n., pl.* **-phies 1.** The study of the visible universe that includes geography and astronomy. **2.** A general description or depiction of the world or universe. **—cos•mog′ra•pher** *n.* **—cos′mo•graph′ic** (-mə-grăf′ĭk), **cos′mo•graph′i•cal** *adj.* **—cos′mo•graph′i•cal•ly** *adv.*

cos•mol•o•gy (kŏz-mŏl′ə-jē) *n., pl.* **-gies 1.** The study of the physical universe considered as a totality of phenomena in time and space. **2a.** The astrophysical study of the history, structure, and constituent dynamics of the universe. **b.** A specific theory or model of this structure and these dynamics. **—cos′mo•log′ic** (-mə-lŏj′ĭk), **cos′mo•log′i•cal** *adj.* **—cos′mo•log′i•cal•ly** *adv.* **—cos•mol′o•gist** *n.*

cos•mo•naut (kŏz′mə-nôt′) *n.* A Russian or Soviet astronaut. [Russ. *kosmonavt* : Gk. *kosmos*, universe + Gk. *nautēs*, sailor.]

cos•mop•o•lis (kŏz-mŏp′ə-lĭs) *n.* A large city inhabited by people from many different countries. [COSMO– + Gk. *polis*, city.]

cos·mo·pol·i·tan (kŏz′mə-pŏl′ĭ-tn) *adj.* **1.** Pertinent or common to the whole world. **2.** Having constituent elements from all over the world or from many different parts of the world. **3.** So sophisticated as to be at home in all parts of the world or conversant with many spheres of interest. **4.** *Ecology* Growing or occurring in many parts of the world; widely distributed. ❖ *n.* A cosmopolitan person or organism; a cosmopolite. —**cos′mo·pol′i·tan·ism** *n.*

cos·mop·o·lite (kŏz-mŏp′ə-līt′) *n.* **1.** A cosmopolitan person. **2.** *Ecology* An organism found in most parts of the world. **3.** See **painted lady.** [Gk. *kosmopolītēs : kosmos,* world + *polītēs* (< *polis,* city).] —**cos′mop′o·lit′ism** (-lī-tīz′əm, -lĭ-tīz′-) *n.*

cos·mos (kŏz′məs, -mŏs, -mōs′) *n.* **1.** The universe regarded as an orderly, harmonious whole. **2.** An ordered, harmonious whole. **3.** Harmony and order as distinct from chaos. **4.** *pl.* **-mos·es** or **cosmos** Any of various mostly Mexican herbs of the genus *Cosmos* in the composite family, having radiate flower heads. [ME < Gk. *kosmos,* order.]

co·spon·sor (kō-spŏn′sər) *tr.v.* **-sored, -sor·ing, -sors** To be a joint sponsor of. ❖ *n.* A joint sponsor. —**co·spon′sor·ship′** *n.*

Cos·sack (kŏs′ăk) *n.* A member of a people of southern European Russia and adjacent parts of Asia, noted as cavalry soldiers esp. during czarist times. [Russ. *kazak* and Ukrainian *kozak,* both < South Turkic *qazaq,* adventurer. See KAZAKH.] —**Cos′sack′** *adj.*

cos·set (kŏs′ĭt) *tr.v.* **-set·ed, -set·ing, -sets** To pamper. ❖ *n.* A pet, esp. a pet lamb. [Poss. < AN *coscet,* pet lamb < ME *cotsete,* cottage-dweller < OE *cotsǣta : cot,* cottage + *-sǣta, -sǣte,* inhabitant; see **sed-** in App.]

cost (kôst) *n.* **1.** An amount paid or required in payment for a purchase; a price. **2.** The expenditure of something, such as time, necessary for the attainment of a goal. **3. costs** *Law* The charges fixed for litigation, often payable by the losing party. ❖ *v.* **cost, cost·ing, costs** —*intr.* To require a specified payment, expenditure, effort, or loss. —*tr.* **1.** To have as a price. **2.** To cause to lose, suffer, or sacrifice. **3.** *past tense and past participle* **costed** To estimate or determine the cost of. [ME < OFr. < *coster,* to cost < Lat. *cōnstāre,* to be fixed, cost. See CONSTANT.]

cos·ta (kŏs′tə) *n., pl.* **-tae** (-tē) *Biology* A rib or a riblike part, such as the midrib of a leaf. [Lat.] —**cos′tal** *adj.*

Cos·ta Bra·va (kŏs′tə brä′və, kô′stä brä′vä) The Mediterranean coast of NE Spain from Barcelona to the French border.

cost accountant *n.* An accountant who keeps records of the costs of production and distribution. —**cost accounting** *n.*

Cos·ta del Sol (kŏs′tə dĕl sôl′, kô′stə, kô′-, kô′stä thĕl) The Mediterranean coast of S Spain NE of Gibraltar.

Cos·ta Me·sa (kŏs′tə mā′sə, kô′stə, kô′-) A city of S CA SSW of Santa Ana. Pop. 108,724.

co·star also **co-star** (kō′stär′) *n.* A starring actor given equal status with another or others in a play or film. —**co′star** *v.*

cos·tard (kŏs′tərd) *n.* **1.** An English variety of large cooking apple. **2.** *Archaic* The human head. [ME < ONFr., poss. < *coste,* rib < Lat. *costa.*]

Cos·ta Ri·ca (kŏs′tə rē′kə, kô′stə, kô′-) A country of Central America between Panama and Nicaragua; achieved independence from Spain in 1821. Cap. San José. Pop. 3,071,000. —**Cos′ta Ri′can** (rē′kən) *adj. & n.*

cos·tate (kŏs′tāt, kô′stāt′) *adj.* Having a costa or costae.

cost-ef·fec·tive (kôst′ĭ-fĕk′tĭv) *adj.* Economical in terms of the goods or services received for the money spent. —**cost′-ef·fec′tive·ly** *adv.* —**cost′-ef·fec′tive·ness** *n.*

Cos·tel·lo (kŏs-tĕl′ō), **John Aloysius** 1891–1976. Irish politician and prime minister (1948–51 and 1954–57) who took Ireland out of the Commonwealth of Nations (1949).

Costello, Lou 1908–59. Amer. comedian whose films with Bud Abbott include *Buck Privates* (1941).

cos·ter·mon·ger (kŏs′tər-mŭng′gər, -mŏng′-) *n. Chiefly British* One who sells goods from a cart, barrow, or stand in the streets. [Obsolete *costard-monger* : COSTARD + MONGER.]

cos·tive (kŏs′tĭv) *adj.* **1a.** Suffering from constipation. **b.** Causing constipation. **2.** Slow; sluggish. **3.** Stingy. [ME *costif* < OFr. *costeve,* p. part. of *costever,* to constipate < Lat. *cōnstīpāre.* See CONSTIPATE.] —**cos′tive·ly** *adv.* —**cos′tive·ness** *n.*

cost·ly (kôst′lē) *adj.* **-li·er, -li·est** **1.** Of high price or value; expensive. **2.** Entailing loss or sacrifice. —**cost′li·ness** *n.*

cost·mar·y (kôst′mâr′ē) *n., pl.* **-ies** A Eurasian perennial herb (*Chrysanthemum balsamita*) in the composite family, having aromatic foliage used for potpourri, tea, or flavoring. [ME *costmarie* : *cost,* costmary (< OE < Lat. *costum* < Gk. *kostos* < Skt. *kuṣṭhaḥ*) + *marie,* Mary, the mother of Jesus.]

cost of living *n.* **1.** The average cost of the basic necessities of life, such as food, shelter, and clothing. **2.** The cost of basic necessities as defined by an accepted standard. —**cost′-of-liv′ing** (kôst′ŭv-lĭv′ĭng) *adj.*

cost-of-living index *n.* See **consumer price index.**

cost-plus (kôst′plŭs′) *n.* The cost of production plus a fixed rate of profit. —**cost′-plus′** *adj.*

cost-push (kôst′pŏosh′) *n.* Inflation in which increased production costs, due to higher wages, tend to drive prices up.

cos·trel (kŏs′trəl) *n.* A flat pear-shaped drinking vessel with loops for attachment to the belt of the user. [ME < OFr. *costerel,* poss. < *costier,* at the side < *coste,* rib < Lat. *costa.*]

cos·tume (kŏs′tōōm′, -tyōōm′) *n.* **1.** A style of dress, including garments, accessories, and hairstyle, esp. as characteristic of a particular country, period, or people. **2.** An outfit or disguise worn on Mardi Gras, Halloween, or similar occasions. **3.** A set of clothes appropriate for a particular occasion or season. ❖ *tr.v.* (*also* kŏ-stōōm′, -styōōm′) **-tumed, -tum·ing, -tumes** **1.** To put a costume on; dress. **2.** To design or furnish costumes for. [Fr. < Ital., style, dress < Lat. *cōnsuētūdō,* custom. See CUSTOM.]

costume jewelry *n.* Jewelry made from inexpensive metals and imitation gems or semiprecious stones.

cos·tum·er (kŏs′tōō′mər, -tyōō′-, kŏ-stōō′mər, -styōō′-) also **cos·tum·i·er** (kŏ-stōō′mē-ər, -styōō′-, kôs′tōōm-yā′) *n.* One that makes or supplies costumes or costumes.

cos·tum·er·y (kŏ-stōō′mə-rē, -styōō′-) *n.* **1.** Articles of costume considered as a group. **2.** The art of costuming.

co·sy (kō′zē) *adj., v., & n.* Variant of **cozy.**

cot¹ (kŏt) *n.* **1.** A narrow bed, esp. one made of canvas on a collapsible frame. **2.** *Chiefly British* A crib. [Hindi *khāṭ* < Skt. *khaṭvā* < Tamil *kaṭṭu,* to bind, tie.]

cot² (kŏt) *n.* **1.** A small house. **2.** A protective covering or sheath. [ME < OE.]

cot³ *abbr.* cotangent

co·tan·gent (kō-tăn′jənt) *n.* **1.** The reciprocal of the tangent of an angle in a right triangle. **2.** The tangent of the complement of a directed angle or arc. —**co′tan·gen′tial** (-jĕn′shəl) *adj.*

cote¹ (kōt) *n.* A small shed or shelter for sheep or birds. [ME < OE.]

cote² (kōt) *tr.v.* **cot·ed, cot·ing, cotes** *Obsolete* To go around by the side of; skirt. [Prob. < Fr. *côtoyer,* to skirt < *côté,* side < OFr. *coste* < Lat. COSTREL.]

Côte d'A·zur (kōt′ də-zōōr′, dä-zür′) The Mediterranean coast of SE France.

Côte d'I·voire (dē-vwär′) also **Ivory Coast** A country of W Africa on the Gulf of Guinea; French colony until 1960. Cap. Yamoussoukro; Abidjan is the largest city and de facto administrative center. Pop. 7,920,000.

co·ten·ant (kō-tĕn′ənt) *n.* One of two or more tenants sharing property. —**co·ten′an·cy** *n.*

Co·ten·tin (kō-tän-tăn′) A peninsula of NW France extending into the English Channel E of the Channel Is.

co·ter·ie (kō′tə-rē, kō′tə-rē′) *n.* A small, often select group who associate with one another frequently. [Fr. < OFr., peasant association < *cotier,* cottager, ult. poss. of Gmc. orig.]

co·ter·mi·nous (kō-tûr′mə-nəs) *adj.* Variant of **conterminous.**

co·thur·nus (kō-thûr′nəs) *n., pl.* **-ni** (-nī′) **1.** A buskin worn by actors of classical tragedy. **2.** The ancient style of classical tragedy. [Lat. < Gk. *kothornos.*]

co·tid·al (kō-tīd′l) *adj.* **1.** Indicating coincidence of high tides or low tides. **2.** Of or relating to a line that passes through each location on a coastal map where tides occur at the same time of day.

co·til·lion also **co·til·lon** (kō-tĭl′yən, kə-) *n.* **1.** A formal ball, esp. one at which young women are presented to society. **2a.** A lively dance, originating in France in the 18th century, having intricate patterns and steps. **b.** A quadrille. **c.** Music for these dances. [Fr. *cotillon* < OFr., petticoat, dim. of *cote,* coat. See COAT.]

co·to·ne·as·ter (kə-tō′nē-ăs′tər) *n.* Any of various erect or creeping shrubs of the genus *Cotoneaster* in the rose family, native to Eurasia and having tiny red or black fruits. [NLat. *Cotoneaster,* genus name : Lat. *cotōneum,* quince; see QUINCE + Lat. *-aster,* partially resembling.]

Co·to·nou (kō′tn-ōō′) A city of S Benin on the Gulf of Guinea. Pop. 536,827.

Co·to·pax·i (kō′tə-păk′sē, -tō-päk′-) An active volcano, 5,900.8 m (19,347 ft), in the Andes of central Ecuador.

cot·quean (kŏt′kwēn′) *n. Archaic* **1.** A coarse or scolding woman. **2.** A man concerned with domestic matters traditionally regarded as suitable for women. [COT² + QUEAN.]

Cots·wold (kŏt′swōld′) *n.* A sheep of a breed distinguished by its long wool, originally developed in the Cotswold Hills.

Cotswold Hills A range of SW England extending c. 80 km (50 mi) NE from Bristol and rising to approx. 329 m (1,080 ft).

cot·ta (kŏt′ə) *n., pl.* **cot·tae** (kŏt′ē) or **cot·tas** A short surplice. [Med.Lat., of Gmc. orig.]

cot·tage (kŏt′ĭj) *n.* **1.** A small single-storied house, esp. in the country. **2.** A small vacation house. [ME *cotage* < AN < Med.Lat. *cotāgium,* of Gmc. orig.]

cottage cheese *n.* A soft white cheese made of strained and seasoned curds of skim milk.

cottage industry *n.* **1.** A usu. small-scale industry carried on at home by family members using their own equipment. **2.** A small, loosely organized industry.

cot·tag·er (kŏt′ĭ-jər) *n.* One who resides in a cottage.

cottage tulip *n.* A late-blooming type of garden tulip having long stems and egg-shaped, variously colored flowers.

cot·ter (kŏt′ər) *n.* **1.** A bolt, wedge, key, or pin inserted through a slot to hold parts together. **2.** A cotter pin. [?]

cotter pin *n.* A split cotter inserted through holes in two or more

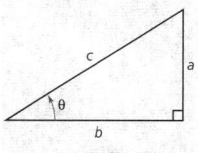

cotangent
$$\cot\theta = \frac{b}{a}$$

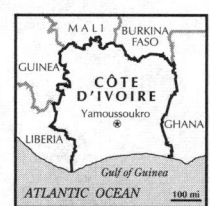

Côte d'Ivoire

pieces and bent at the ends to fasten the pieces together.

Cot•ti•an Alps (kŏt′ē-ən) A range of the Alps between NW Italy and SE France rising to 3,843.6 m (12,602 ft).

cot•ton (kŏt′n) *n.* **1a.** Any of various shrubby plants of the genus *Gossypium,* grown for the soft white downy fibers surrounding oil-rich seeds. **b.** The fiber of any of these plants, used in making textiles and other products. **c.** Thread or cloth manufactured from the fiber of these plants. **2.** The crop of these plants. **3.** Any of various soft downy substances produced by other plants. ❖ *intr.v.* **-toned, -ton•ing, -tons** *Informal* **1.** To take a liking; attempt to be friendly: *a dog that didn't cotton to strangers.* **2.** To come to understand. Often used with *to* or *onto.* [ME *cotoun* < OFr. *coton* < OItal. *cotone* < Ar. *quṭn, quṭun;* perh. akin to Akkadian *qaṭānu,* to become thin, fine (of textiles).]

Cotton, John 1584–1652. English-born Amer. cleric who fled religious persecution in England and settled in Boston, where he became a civil and religious leader.

Cotton Belt An agricultural region of the SE US, concentrated particularly in SC, GA, AL, and MS, where cotton became the predominant crop in the 19th cent.

cotton candy *n.* A light, very sweet candy of threaded sugar.

cotton gin *n.* A machine that separates the seeds, seed hulls, and other small objects from the fibers of cotton.

cotton grass *n.* Any of various perennial grasslike plants of the genus *Eriophorum,* bearing at maturity one or more conspicuous tufts of cottony bristles.

cot•ton•mouth (kŏt′n-mouth′) *n.* See **water moccasin** 1.

cot•ton-pick•ing (kŏt′n-pĭk′ĭng) *adj. Informal* Used as an intensive: *a cotton-picking fool.*

cot•ton•seed (kŏt′n-sēd′) *n.* The seed of the cotton plant.

cottonseed oil *n.* The usu. pale yellow oil obtained from cottonseed, used in manufacturing, industry, and cooking.

cotton stainer *n.* Any of various red and black bugs of the genus *Dysdercus* that pierce cotton bolls and stain the fibers.

cot•ton•tail (kŏt′n-tāl′) *n.* Any of several North American rabbits of the genus *Sylvilagus,* having grayish or brownish fur and a tail with a fluffy white underside.

cot•ton•weed (kŏt′n-wēd′) *n.* Any of various plants having cottony down, as some species of the genus *Froelichia.*

cot•ton•wood (kŏt′n-wŏŏd′) *n.* Any of several North American poplar trees, esp. *Populus deltoides,* having triangular leaves and a tuft of cottony hairs on the seeds.

cotton wool *n.* Cotton in its natural or raw state.

cot•ton•y (kŏt′n-ē) *adj.* **1.** Of or resembling cotton; fluffy. **2.** Covered with fibers resembling cotton; nappy.

co•tur•nix (kə-tûr′nĭks) *n.* A small stub-tailed Eurasian quail (*Coturnix coturnix*) having sandy streaked plumage and commonly used in laboratory research. [Lat. *coturnīx,* quail.]

Co•ty (kō-tē′, kô-), René 1882–1962. French politician and the last president (1953–59) of the Fourth Republic.

cot•y•le•don (kŏt′l-ēd′n) *n.* **1.** *Botany* A leaf of the embryo of a seed plant, which upon germination either remains in the seed or emerges, enlarges, and becomes green. **2.** *Anatomy* One of the lobules constituting the uterine side of the mammalian placenta, consisting mainly of a rounded mass of villi. [Lat. *cotylēdōn,* navelwort < Gk. *kotulēdōn* < *kotulē,* hollow object.] —**cot′y•le′don•ar′y** (-ēd′n-ĕr′ē), **cot′y•le′do•nous** (-ēd′n-əs) *adj.*

cot•y•lo•saur (kŏt′l-ə-sôr′) *n.* Any of an extinct order (Cotylosauria) of primitive reptiles of the Carboniferous and Permian periods that included the ancestors of all of the reptiles. [< NLat. *Cotylosauria,* order name : Gk. *kotulē,* hollow object, socket + Gk. *sauros,* lizard.]

couch (kouch) *n.* **1a.** A sofa. **b.** A sofa on which a patient lies while undergoing psychoanalysis or psychiatric treatment. **2a.** The frame or floor on which grain, usu. barley, is spread in malting. **b.** A layer of grain, usu. barley, spread to germinate. **3.** A priming coat of paint or varnish used in artistic painting. ❖ *v.* **couched, couch•ing, couch•es** —*tr.* **1.** To word in a certain manner; phrase. **2.** To cause (oneself) to lie down, as for rest. **3.** To embroider by laying thread flat on a surface and fastening it by stitches at regular intervals. **4.** To spread (grain) on a couch to germinate, as in malting. **5.** To lower (a spear, for example) to horizontal position, as for an attack. —*intr.* **1.** To lie down; recline, as for rest. **2.** To lie in ambush or concealment; lurk. **3.** To be in a heap or pile, as leaves for decomposition or fermentation. [ME *couche* < OFr. *culche, couche* < *couchier,* to lay down, lie down < Lat. *collocāre.* See COLLOCATE.] —**couch′er** *n.*

couch•ant (kou′chənt) *adj. Heraldry* Lying down with the head raised. [ME < OFr., pr. part. of *couchier,* to lie down. See COUCH.]

cou•chette (kōō-shĕt′) *n.* **1.** A compartment on a European passenger train equipped with four to six berths for sleeping. **2.** A sleeping berth in one of these compartments. [Fr., dim. of *couche,* bed < OFr. See COUCH.]

couch grass *n.* A Eurasian grass (*Agropyron repens*) that has whitish-yellow root stocks and has become a troublesome weed in the New World. [Alteration of QUITCH GRASS.]

couch potato *n. Slang* A person who spends much time sitting or lying down, usu. watching television.

cou•gar (kōō′gər) *n. Chiefly Western US* See **mountain lion.** [Fr. *couguar,* alteration of Port. *çuçuarana* < Tupi *suasuarana* : *suasú,* deer + *rana,* like (< its color).]

cotton

cottonwood
eastern cottonwood
Populus deltoides

cough (kôf, kŏf) *v.* **coughed, cough•ing, coughs** —*intr.* **1.** To expel air from the lungs suddenly and noisily, often to keep the respiratory passages free of irritating material. **2.** To make a noise similar to a cough. —*tr.* To expel by coughing. ❖ *n.* **1.** The act of coughing. **2.** An illness marked by frequent coughing. —*phrasal verb:* **cough up** *Slang* **1.** To hand over or relinquish (money or another possession), often reluctantly. **2.** To confess or disclose. [ME *coughen,* ult. of imit. orig.]

cough drop *n.* A small, often medicated and sweetened lozenge taken orally to ease coughing or soothe a sore throat.

cough syrup *n.* A sweetened medicated liquid taken orally to ease coughing.

could (kŏŏd) *aux.v.* Past tense of *can*[1]. **1.** Used to indicate ability or permission in the past: *I could run faster then. Only men could go to the club.* **2.** Used with hypothetical or conditional force: *If we could help, we would.* **3.** Used to indicate tentativeness or politeness: *I could be wrong. Could you come over here?*

could•est (kŏŏd′ĭst) or **couldst** (kŏŏdst) *aux.v. Archaic* A second person singular past tense of *can*[1].

could•n't (kŏŏd′nt) Contraction of *could not.*

cou•lee (kōō′lē) *n.* **1.** *Western US* A deep gulch or ravine with sloping sides, often dry in summer. **2.** *Louisiana & Southern Mississippi* **a.** A streambed, often dry. **b.** A small stream, bayou, or canal. **3.** *Upper Midwest* A valley with hills on either side. **4a.** A stream of molten lava. **b.** A sheet of solidified lava. [Canadian Fr. *coulée* < Fr., flow < *couler,* to flow < Lat. *cōlāre,* to filter < *cōlum,* sieve.]

cou•lis (kōō-lē′) *n.* A thick sauce made of puréed fruit or vegetables. [Fr., strained liquid < OFr. *couleis* < VLat. **cōlāticus* < Lat. *cōlātus,* p. part. of *cōlāre,* to strain. See COULEE.]

cou•lisse (kōō-lēs′) *n.* **1.** A grooved timber in which something slides. **2a.** A section of stage scenery placed in a wing of a theatre. **b.** The space between such pieces of scenery. **c.** A backstage area in a theater. [Fr. < OFr. *(porte) couleice,* sliding door. See PORT-CULLIS.]

cou•loir (kōōl-wär′) *n.* A deep mountainside gorge or gully, esp. in the Swiss Alps. [Fr. < *couler,* to slide. See COULEE.]

cou•lomb (kōō′lŏm′, -lôm′) *n.* The meter-kilogram-second unit of electrical charge equal to the quantity of charge transferred in one second by a steady current of one ampere. ❖ *adj.* also **cou•lom•bic** (kōō-lŏm′bĭk, -lôm′-) Of or relating to the Coulomb force. [After Charles Augustin de COULOMB.]

Cou•lomb (kōō′lŏm′, -lôm′, kōō-lŏm′, -lôn′), **Charles Augustin de** 1736–1806. French physicist who pioneered research in magnetism and electricity.

Coulomb force (kōō′lŏm′, -lôm′) *n.* An attractive or repulsive electrostatic force described by Coulomb's law.

Coulomb's law (kōō′lŏmz′, -lômz′) *n.* The fundamental law of electrostatics stating that the force between two charged particles is directly proportional to the product of their charges and inversely proportional to the square of the distance between them. [After Charles Augustin de COULOMB.]

cou•lom•e•ter (kōō-lŏm′ĭ-tər, kōō′lə-mē′tər) *n.* A device for determining the amount of a substance released during electrolysis. [COULO(MB) + -METER.]

cou•lom•e•try (kōō-lŏm′ĭ-trē) *n.* An analytical method for determining the amount of a substance released during electrolysis in which the number of coulombs used is measured. [COULO(MB) + -METRY.] —**cou′lo•met′ric** (-lə-mĕt′rĭk) *adj.* —**cou′lo•met′ri•cal•ly** *adv.*

coul•ter (kōl′tər) *n.* A blade or wheel attached to the beam of a plow that makes vertical cuts in the soil in advance of the plowshare. [ME *culter* < OE *culter* and < OFr. *coltre,* both < Lat. *culter,* knife, plowshare.]

Coulter pine *n.* A pine tree (*Pinus coulteri*) native to California and Baja California and having needles in bundles of three and sharp-scaled cones that are the heaviest of all pines. [After Thomas Coulter (1793–1843), Irish botanist.]

cou•ma•rin (kōō′mər-ĭn) *n.* A fragrant crystalline compound, $C_9H_6O_2$, extracted from several plants or produced synthetically and widely used in perfumes. [Fr. *coumarine* < *coumarou,* tonka bean tree < Sp. *coumarú* < Port. *cumaru* < Tupi *cumarú, comaru.*] —**cou′ma•ric** (-mər-ĭk) *adj.*

coun•cil (koun′səl) *n.* **1a.** An assembly of persons called together for consultation, deliberation, or discussion. **b.** A body of people elected or appointed to serve as administrators, legislators, or advisors. **c.** An assembly of church officials and theologians convened for regulating matters of doctrine and discipline. **2.** The discussion or deliberation that takes place in such an assembly or body. [ME *counceil* < OFr. *concile* < Lat. *concilium.* See kelə- in App.]

USAGE NOTE *Council* and *councilor* refer principally to a deliberative assembly, its work, and its membership. *Counsel* and *counselor* pertain chiefly to advice and guidance in general and to a person who provides it. *Consul* denotes an officer in the foreign service of a country.

Council Bluffs A city of SW IA on the Missouri R. opposite Omaha NE; settled in 1846. Pop. 58,268.

coun•cil•man (koun′səl-mən) *n.* A man who is a member of a council, esp. of the local governing body of a city or town.

council of ministers *n., pl.* **councils of ministers** A body of advisers to a head of state.

coun·cil·or (koun′sə-lər, -slər) *n.* A member of a council, as one convened to advise a governor. See Usage Note at **council.**

coun·cil·wom·an (koun′səl-wŏŏm′ən) *n.* A woman who is a member of a council, esp. of the local governing body of a city or town.

coun·sel (koun′səl) *n.* **1.** The act of exchanging opinions and ideas; consultation. **2.** Advice or guidance, esp. as solicited from a knowledgeable person. See Syns at **advice. 3.** A plan of action. **4.** Private, guarded thoughts or opinions. **5.** A lawyer or group of lawyers giving legal advice and esp. conducting a case in court. ❖ *v.* **-seled, -sel·ing, -sels** or **-selled, -sel·ling, -sels** —*tr.* **1.** To give counsel to; advise. **2.** To recommend. —*intr.* To give or take advice. See Usage Note at **council.** [ME *counseil* < OFr. *conseil* < Lat. *cōnsilium;* akin to *cōnsulere,* to take counsel, consult.]

coun·sel·or also **coun·sel·lor** (koun′sə-lər, -slər) *n.* **1.** A person who counsels. **2.** An attorney, esp. a trial lawyer. **3.** A person who supervises young people at a summer camp. See Usage Note at **council.** —**coun′se·lor·ship′** *n.*

coun·sel·or-at-law (koun′sə-lər-ət-lô′, -slər-) *n., pl.* **coun·sel·ors-at-law** An attorney; a counsel.

count¹ (kount) *v.* **count·ed, count·ing, counts** —*tr.* **1a.** To name or list (the units of a group or collection) one by one in order to determine a total; number. **b.** To recite numerals in ascending order up to and including. **c.** To include in a reckoning; take account of. **2.** *Informal* **a.** To include by or as if by counting. **b.** To exclude by or as if by counting. **3a.** To believe or consider to be; deem: *Count yourself lucky.* —*intr.* **1.** To recite or list numbers in order or enumerate items by units or groups. **2a.** To have importance: *You really count with me.* **b.** To have a specified proportion or value: *Each basket counts for two points.* **3.** *Music* To keep time by counting beats. ❖ *n.* **1.** The act of counting or calculating. **2a.** A number reached by counting. **b.** The totality of specific items in a particular sample. **3.** *Law* Any of the separate and distinct charges in an indictment. **4.** *Sports* The counting from one to ten seconds, during which time a boxer who has been knocked down must rise or be declared the loser. **5.** *Baseball* The number of balls and strikes that an umpire has called against a batter. —*phrasal verb:* **count on 1.** To rely on; depend on. **2.** To be confident of; anticipate: *counted on getting a raise.* —*idiom:* **count heads** (or **noses**) To make a count of members, attendees, or participants by or as if by noting bodily presence. [ME *counten* < OFr. *conter* < Lat. *computāre,* to calculate : *com-, com-* + *putāre,* to think.]

SYNONYMS *count, import, matter, signify, weigh* These verbs mean to be of significance or importance: *an opinion that counts; actions that import little; decisions that really matter; thoughts that signify much; considerations that weigh with her.*

count² (kount) *n.* **1.** A nobleman in some European countries. **2.** Used as a title for such a nobleman. [ME *counte* < OFr. *conte* < LLat. *comes, comit-,* occupant of any state office < Lat., companion. See **ei-** in App.]

count·a·ble (koun′tə-bəl) *adj.* **1.** That can be counted. **2.** *Mathematics* That can be put into a one-to-one correspondence with the positive integers. —**count′a·bil′i·ty** *n.* —**count′a·bly** *adv.*

count·down (kount′doun′) *n.* **1.** The counting backward aloud from an arbitrary starting number to indicate the time remaining before an event or operation. **2.** The checks and preparations carried out during this activity.

coun·te·nance (koun′tə-nəns) *n.* **1.** Appearance, esp. the expression of the face. **2.** The face or facial features. **3a.** A look or expression indicative of encouragement or of moral support. **b.** Support or approval. **4.** *Obsolete* Bearing; demeanor. ❖ *tr.v.* **-nanced, -nanc·ing, -nanc·es** To give sanction to; tolerate or approve. [ME *contenaunce* < OFr. < *contenir,* to behave. See CONTAIN.] —**coun′te·nanc·er** *n.*

coun·ter¹ (koun′tər) *adj.* Contrary; opposing. ❖ *n.* **1.** One that is an opposite. **2.** *Sports* A boxing blow given while receiving or parrying another. **3.** *Sports* A fencing parry in which one foil follows the other in a circular fashion. **4.** A stiff piece of leather around the heel of a shoe. **5.** The portion of a ship's stern extending from the water line to the extreme outward swell. **6.** *Printing* The depression between the raised lines of the face on a piece of type. ❖ *v.* **-tered, -ter·ing, -ters** —*tr.* **1.** To meet or return (a blow) by another blow. **2.** To move or act in opposition to; oppose. **3.** To offer in response. —*intr.* To move, act, or respond so as to be in opposition. ❖ *adv.* **1.** In a contrary manner or direction. **2.** To or toward an opposite or dissimilar course or outcome. [ME *countre* < OFr. *contre* < Lat. *contrā.* See COUNTER–.]

coun·ter² (koun′tər) *n.* **1.** A flat surface on which money is counted, business is transacted, or food is prepared or served. **2.** *Games* A piece, as of wood, used for keeping a count or a place. **3a.** An imitation coin; a token. **b.** A piece of money. —*idioms:* **over the counter 1.** Without being listed or available on an officially recognized stock exchange but in trade by direct negotiation between buyers and sellers. **2.** Without a doctor's prescription being legally required. **under the counter** In an illegal or surreptitious manner; illicitly. [ME *countour* < AN *counteour*

< Med.Lat. *computātōrium,* countinghouse < Lat. *computāre,* to calculate. See COUNT¹.]

count·er³ (koun′tər) *n.* One that counts, esp. an electronic or mechanical device that automatically counts occurrences or repetitions of phenomena or events.

counter– *pref.* **1.** Contrary; opposite; opposing: *counterclaim.* **2.** Corresponding; complementary: *counterfoil.* [ME *countre-* < OFr. *contre-* < Lat. *contrā.* See **kom** in App.]

coun·ter·act (koun′tər-ăkt′) *tr.v.* **-act·ed, -act·ing, -acts** To oppose and mitigate the effects of by contrary action; check. —**coun′ter·ac′tion** *n.* —**coun′ter·ac′tive** *adj.*

coun·ter·ar·gu·ment (koun′tər-är′gyə-mənt) *n.* **1.** An argument in opposition to another. **2.** Something that undermines an argument or deters someone from action.

coun·ter·at·tack (koun′tər-ə-tăk′) *n.* A return attack. ❖ *intr. & tr.v.* (koun′tər-ə-tăk′) **-tacked, -tack·ing, -tacks** To deliver a return attack or make a return attack against.

coun·ter·bal·ance (koun′tər-băl′əns, koun′tər-băl′əns) *n.* **1.** A force or influence equally counteracting another. **2.** A weight that acts to balance another; a counterpoise. ❖ *tr.v.* (koun′tər-băl′əns, koun′tər-băl′əns) **-anced, -anc·ing, -anc·es 1.** To act as a counteracting force, influence, or weight to; counterpoise. **2.** To oppose with an equal force; offset.

coun·ter·change (koun′tər-chānj′) *tr.v.* **-changed, -chang·ing, -chang·es 1.** To cause to change places; transpose. **2.** To make checkered; variegate.

coun·ter·charge (koun′tər-chärj′) *n.* A charge in opposition to another charge. ❖ *v.* (koun′tər-chärj′) **-charged, -charg·ing, -charg·es** —*tr.* To bring a charge against (one's accuser). —*intr.* To make a countercharge.

coun·ter·check (koun′tər-chĕk′) *n.* **1.** Something that serves to check, restrict, or limit something else. **2.** Something that verifies a previous check. ❖ *tr.v.* (koun′tər-chĕk′) **-checked, -check·ing, -checks 1.** To oppose or check by a counteraction. **2.** To check again in order to verify.

counter check *n.* A bank check for the use of customers making a withdrawal.

coun·ter·claim (koun′tər-klām′) *n.* An opposing claim, esp. in a legal action. ❖ *intr. & tr.v.* (koun′tər-klām′) **-claimed, -claim·ing, -claims** To plead a counterclaim or make a counterclaim against. —**coun′ter·claim′ant** (-klā′mənt) *n.*

coun·ter·clock·wise (koun′tər-klŏk′wīz′) *adv. & adj.* In a direction opposite to the rotating hands of a clock.

coun·ter·con·di·tion·ing (koun′tər-kən-dĭsh′ə-nĭng) *n.* *Psychology* Conditioning intended to replace a negative response to a stimulus with a positive response.

coun·ter·cul·ture (koun′tər-kŭl′chər) *n.* A culture with values or lifestyles in opposition to those of the established culture. —**coun′ter·cul′tur·al** *adj.* —**coun′ter·cul′tur·ist** *n.*

coun·ter·cur·rent (koun′tər-kûr′ənt, -kûr′-) *n.* A current that flows opposite to the flow of another current. —**coun′ter·cur′rent** *adj.* —**coun′ter·cur′rent·ly** *adv.*

coun·ter·cy·cli·cal (koun′tər-sĭk′lĭ-kəl, -sī′klĭ-) *adj.* Intended to limit extreme developments in a business cycle.

coun·ter·dem·on·stra·tion (koun′tər-dĕm′ən-strā′shən) *n.* A demonstration held in opposition to another demonstration. —**coun′ter·dem′on·stra′tor** *n.*

coun·ter·es·pi·o·nage (koun′tər-ĕs′pē-ə-näzh′, -nĭj) *n.* Espionage to detect and counteract enemy espionage.

coun·ter·ex·am·ple (koun′tər-ĭg-zăm′pəl) *n.* An example that refutes or disproves a hypothesis, proposition, or theorem.

coun·ter·fac·tu·al (koun′tər-făk′chōō-əl) *adj.* Running contrary to the facts. —**coun′ter·fac′tu·al** *adv.*

coun·ter·feit (koun′tər-fĭt′) *v.* **-feit·ed, -feit·ing, -feits** —*tr.* **1.** To make a copy of, usu. with the intent to defraud; forge. **2.** To make a pretense of; feign. —*intr.* **1.** To carry on a deception; dissemble. **2.** To make fraudulent copies of something valuable. ❖ *adj.* Made in imitation of what is genuine with the intent to defraud. **2.** Simulated; feigned. ❖ *n.* A fraudulent imitation or facsimile. [ME *countrefeten* < *contrefet,* made in imitation < OFr. *contrefait,* p. part. of *contrefaire,* to counterfeit : *contre-,* counter- + *faire,* to make (< Lat. *facere;* see **dhē-** in App.).] —**coun′ter·feit′er** *n.*

coun·ter·foil (koun′tər-foil′) *n.* The part of a check or other commercial paper retained by the issuer as a record.

coun·ter·force (koun′tər-fôrs′, -fōrs′) *n.* A contrary or opposing force.

coun·ter·glow (koun′tər-glō′) *n.* See **gegenschein.**

coun·ter·in·sur·gen·cy (koun′tər-ĭn-sûr′jən-sē) *n.* Political and military strategy or action intended to oppose and forcefully suppress insurgency. —**coun′ter·in·sur′gent** *n.*

coun·ter·in·tel·li·gence (koun′tər-ĭn-tĕl′ə-jəns) *n.* The branch of an intelligence service charged with keeping sensitive information from an enemy, preventing subversion and sabotage, and collecting political and military information.

coun·ter·in·tu·i·tive (koun′tər-ĭn-tōō′ĭ-tĭv, -tyōō′-) *adj.* Contrary to what intuition or common sense would indicate.

coun·ter·ir·ri·tant (koun′tər-ĭr′ĭ-tənt) *n.* An agent that induces local inflammation to relieve inflammation in underlying or adjacent tissues. ❖ *adj.* Of or producing the effect of such an agent. —**coun′ter·ir′ri·ta′tion** (-tā′shən) *n.*

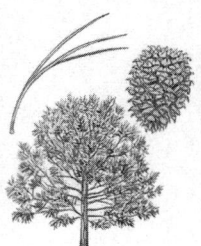

Coulter pine
Pinus coulteri

ă pat   oi boy
ā pay   ou out
âr care   ŏŏ took
ä father   ōō boot
ĕ pet   ŭ cut
ē be   ûr urge
ĭ pit   th thin
ī pie   th this
îr pier   hw which
ŏ pot   zh vision
ō toe   ə about,
ô paw   item

Stress marks:
′ (primary);
′ (secondary), as in
lexicon (lĕk′sĭ-kŏn′)

coun·ter·man (koun′tər-măn′, -mən) *n.* A man who tends a counter, as in a diner.

coun·ter·mand (koun′tər-mănd′, koun′tər-mănd′) *tr.v.* **-mand·ed, -mand·ing, -mands** **1.** To cancel or reverse (a previously issued command or order). **2.** To recall by a contrary order. ❖ *n.* (koun′tər-mănd′) **1.** An order or command reversing another one. **2.** Cancellation of an order or command. [ME *countremaunden* < OFr. *contremander* : *contre-*, counter- + *mander*, to command (< Lat. *mandāre*; see **man-²** in App.).]

coun·ter·march (koun′tər-märch′) *n.* **1.** A march back or in a reverse direction. **2.** A complete reversal of method or conduct. ❖ *intr. & tr.v.* **-marched, -march·ing, -march·es** To execute or cause to execute a countermarch.

coun·ter·mine (koun′tər-mīn′) *v.* **-mined, -min·ing, -mines** *—tr.* **1.** To frustrate or defeat by secret and opposite measures. **2.** To make or use a countermine against. *—intr.* To make or lay down countermines. ❖ *n.* (koun′tər-mīn′) **1.** A tunnel dug to intercept and destroy an enemy's mine. **2.** A plot to frustrate or defeat an attack.

coun·ter·move (koun′tər-mōōv′) *n.* A move made in opposition or retaliation to another. ❖ *intr.v.* (koun′tər-mōōv′) **-moved, -mov·ing, -moves** To make a move in retaliation or opposition. **—coun′ter·move′ment** *n.*

coun·ter·of·fen·sive (koun′tər-ə-fĕn′sĭv) *n.* A large-scale counterattack, intended to stop an enemy offensive.

coun·ter·of·fer (koun′tər-ô′fər, -ŏf′ər) *n.* An offer made in return by one who rejects an unsatisfactory offer.

coun·ter·pane (koun′tər-pān′) *n.* A cover for a bed; a bedspread. [Alteration of obsolete *counterpoint*, ult. < OFr. *coultepointe* < Med.Lat. *culcita pūncta*, stitched quilt : Lat. *culcita*, quilt, mattress; see QUILT + Lat. *pūncta*, fem. of *pūnctus*, stitched, pricked; see POINT.]

coun·ter·part (koun′tər-pärt′) *n.* **1a.** One that closely resembles another. **b.** One that has the same functions and characteristics as another; a corresponding person or thing. **2.** A copy or duplicate of a legal paper. **3a.** One of two parts that fit and complete each other. **b.** One that serves as a complement.

coun·ter·per·son (koun′tər-pûr′sən) *n.* A person who tends a counter, as in a diner.

coun·ter·plan (koun′tər-plăn′) *n.* **1.** A plan intended to counter or oppose another plan. **2.** An alternate plan.

coun·ter·plot (koun′tər-plŏt′) *n.* **1.** A plot or scheme intended to subvert another plot. **2.** See **subplot** 1. ❖ *v.* **-plot·ted, -plot·ting, -plots** *—intr.* To oppose or subvert one plot with another. *—tr.* To plot against; thwart with a counterplot.

coun·ter·point (koun′tər-point′) *n.* **1.** *Music* **a.** Melodic material that is added above or below an existing melody. **b.** The technique of combining two or more melodic lines in such a way that they establish a harmonic relationship while retaining their linear individuality. **c.** A composition or piece that incorporates or consists of contrapuntal writing. **2a.** A contrasting but parallel element, item, or theme. **b.** Use of contrasting elements in a work of art. ❖ *tr.v.* **-point·ed, -point·ing, -points** **1.** *Music* To write or arrange (music) in counterpoint. **2.** To set in contrast.

coun·ter·poise (koun′tər-poiz′) *n.* **1.** A counterbalancing weight. **2.** A force or influence that balances or equally counteracts another. **3.** The state of being in equilibrium. ❖ *tr.v.* **-poised, -pois·ing, -pois·es** **1.** To oppose with an equal weight; counterbalance. **2.** To act against with an equal force or power; offset. [Alteration (influenced by POISE¹) of ME *countrepeis* < OFr. *contrepeis* : *contre-*, counter- + *peis*, weight; see AVOIRDUPOIS.]

coun·ter·pose (koun′tər-pōz′) *tr.v.* **-posed, -pos·ing, -pos·es** To set in contrast, opposition, or balance.

coun·ter·pro·duc·tive (koun′tər-prə-dŭk′tĭv) *adj.* Tending to hinder rather than serve one's purpose. **—coun′ter·pro·duc′tive·ly** *adv.*

coun·ter·pro·pos·al (koun′tər-prə-pō′zəl) *n.* A proposal offered to nullify or substitute for a previous one.

coun·ter·punch (koun′tər-pŭnch′) *n.* A countering attack or blow, esp. one delivered by a boxer. **—coun′ter·punch′** *v.* **—coun′ter·punch′er** *n.*

coun·ter·ref·or·ma·tion (koun′tər-rĕf′ər-mā′shən) *n.* A reformation intended to counter the effects of a previous one.

Counter Reformation *n.* A reform movement within the Roman Catholic Church that arose in 16th-century Europe in response to the Protestant Reformation.

coun·ter·rev·o·lu·tion (koun′tər-rĕv′ə-lōō′shən) *n.* **1.** A revolution whose aim is the deposition and reversal of a political or social system set up by a previous revolution. **2.** A movement to oppose revolutionary tendencies and developments. **—coun′ter·rev′o·lu′tion·ar′y** (-shə-nĕr′ē) *adj. & n.* **—coun′ter·rev′o·lu′tion·ist** *n.*

coun·ter·shad·ing (koun′tər-shā′dĭng) *n.* Protective coloration in an animal or insect, marked by darker coloring of areas exposed to light and lighter coloring of shaded areas.

coun·ter·shaft (koun′tər-shăft′) *n.* An intermediate shaft between the powered and driven shafts in a belt drive.

coun·ter·sign (koun′tər-sīn′) *tr.v.* **-signed, -sign·ing, -signs** To sign (a previously signed document), as for authentication. ❖ *n.* **1.** A second or confirming signature. **2a.** A sign or signal to be

given to a sentry in order to pass; a password. **b.** A secret sign or signal given in answer to another.

coun·ter·sig·na·ture (koun′tər-sĭg′nə-chər) *n.* See **countersign** 1.

coun·ter·sink (koun′tər-sĭngk′) *n.* **1.** A hole with the top part enlarged so that the head of a screw or bolt will lie flush with or below the surface. **2.** A tool for making such a hole. ❖ *tr.v.* **-sunk** (-sŭngk′), **-sink·ing, -sinks** **1.** To make a countersink on or in. **2.** To drive (a screw or bolt) into a countersink.

coun·ter·spy (koun′tər-spī′) *n., pl.* **-spies** A spy working in opposition to enemy espionage.

coun·ter·stain (koun′tər-stān′) *n.* A stain used to color the components in a microscopic specimen that are not made visible by the principal stain. **—coun′ter·stain′** *v.*

coun·ter·sue (koun′tər-sōō′) *tr.v.* **-sued, -su·ing, -sues** To bring legal proceedings against (a plaintiff) in opposition to a suit against oneself. **—coun′ter·suit′** (-sōōt′) *n.*

coun·ter·ten·or (koun′tər-tĕn′ər) *n.* **1.** An adult male voice with a range above that of tenor. **2.** A singer having a voice within this range.

coun·ter·top (koun′tər-tŏp′) *n.* A level surface on a cabinet or display case, as in a kitchen or department store.

coun·ter·trans·fer·ence (koun′ər-trăns-fûr′əns, -trăns′fər-) *n.* A psychotherapist's own repressed feelings in reaction to the emotions, experiences, or problems of a person undergoing treatment.

coun·ter·vail (koun′tər-vāl′, koun′tər-vāl′) *v.* **-vailed, -vail·ing, -vails** *—tr.* **1.** To act against with equal force; counteract. **2.** To compensate for; offset. *—intr.* To act against an often detrimental influence or power. [ME *countrevaillen* < OFr. *contrevaloir, contrevail-* : *contre-*, counter- + *valoir*, to be worth (< Lat. *valēre*, to be strong).]

coun·ter·weigh (koun′tər-wā′) *intr. & tr.v.* **-weighed, -weigh·ing, -weighs** To counterbalance or cause to counterbalance.

coun·ter·weight (koun′tər-wāt′) *n.* **1.** A weight used as a counterbalance. **2.** A force or influence equally counteracting another. **—coun′ter·weight′ed** (-wā′tĭd) *adj.*

coun·ter·wom·an (koun′tər-wōōm′ən) *n.* A woman who tends a counter, as in a diner.

count·ess (koun′tĭs) *n.* **1.** A woman holding the title of count or earl. **2.** The wife or widow of a count or an earl. **3.** Used as a title for such a noblewoman. [ME *countes* < OFr. *contesse*, fem. of *conte*, count. See COUNT².]

count·ing·house also **count·ing house** (koun′tĭng-hous′) *n.* A building, room, or office in which a business firm carries on operations such as accounting and correspondence.

count·less (kount′lĭs) *adj.* Incapable of being counted; innumerable. See Syns at **incalculable.** **—count′less·ly** *adv.*

count noun *n.* A noun that refers to a single entity and that can form a plural or occur in a noun phrase construction with an indefinite article, with numerals, or with such terms as *many.*

count palatine *n., pl.* **counts palatine 1a.** Any of various noblemen originally exercising certain royal powers within their own domains, esp. a count of the Holy Roman Empire. **b.** A feudal lord having sovereign powers over his lands. **2.** The titled proprietor of a county palatine in England or Ireland.

coun·tri·fied also **coun·try·fied** (kŭn′trĭ-fīd′) *adj.* **1.** Resembling or having the characteristics of country life; rural. **2.** Lacking sophistication.

coun·try (kŭn′trē) *n., pl.* **-tries 1a.** A nation or state. **b.** The territory of a nation or state; land. **c.** The people of a nation or state; populace. **2.** The land of a person's birth or citizenship. **3.** A region, territory, or large tract of land distinguishable by features of topography, biology, or culture. **4.** An area or expanse outside cities and towns; a rural area. **5.** *Informal* Country music. ❖ *adj.* **1.** Of, relating to, or typical of the country. **2.** Of or relating to country music. [ME *countre* < OFr. *contree* < VLat. *(terra) contrāta*, (land) opposite, before < Lat. *contrā*, opposite. See **kom** in App.]

country and western *n.* See **country music.**

country club *n.* A suburban club for social and sports activities, usu. featuring a golf course.

country cousin *n.* A person with the unsophisticated or ingenuous manners associated with the country by city dwellers.

coun·try-dance (kŭn′trē-dăns′) *n.* A folk dance of English origin in which two lines of dancers face each other.

country gentleman *n.* A man who owns a country estate.

coun·try·man (kŭn′trē-mən) *n.* **1.** A person from one's own country; a compatriot. **2.** A native or an inhabitant of a particular country. **3.** A man who lives in the country.

country mile *n. Informal* A very great distance.

country music *n.* Popular music based on the folk style of the southern rural United States or on the music of cowboys in the American West.

coun·try·seat (kŭn′trē-sēt′) *n.* An estate or mansion in the country.

coun·try·side (kŭn′trē-sīd′) *n.* **1.** A rural region. **2.** The inhabitants of a rural region.

coun·try·wide (kŭn′trē-wīd′) *adv. & adj.* Throughout a whole country; nationwide: *a countrywide search.*

countersink
single-flute countersink bit

coun·try·wom·an (kŭn′trē-wŏŏm′ən) *n.* **1.** A woman from one's own country; a compatriot. **2.** A woman from a particular country. **3.** A woman who lives in the country.

coun·ty (koun′tē) *n., pl.* **-ties 1.** The largest administrative division of most states in the United States. **2a.** A territorial division exercising administrative, judicial, and political functions in Great Britain and Ireland. **b.** The territory under the jurisdiction of a count or earl. **3.** The people living in a county. [ME *counte,* territorial division < OFr. *conte,* the territory of a count < Med.Lat. *comitātus* < LLat., the office of count < Lat., retinue < *comes,* comit-, companion. See **ei-** in App.] —**coun′ty** *adj.*

county agent *n.* A government employee who serves as a consultant and adviser in a chiefly rural county on such matters as agriculture, education, and home economics.

county fair *n.* A fair usu. held every year in a county.

county palatine *n., pl.* **counties palatine** The domain of a count palatine in England or Ireland.

county seat *n.* A town or city that is the administrative center of its county.

county town *n. Chiefly British* A county seat.

coun·ty·wide (koun′tē-wīd′) *adv. & adj.* Throughout a whole county.

coup (kōō) *n., pl.* **coups** (kōōz) **1.** A brilliantly executed stratagem; a masterstroke. **2a.** A coup d'état. **b.** A sudden appropriation of leadership or power; a takeover. [Fr., stroke < OFr. *colp* < LLat. *colpus* < Lat. *colaphus* < Gk. *kolaphos.*]

coup de grâce (kōō′ də gräs′) *n., pl.* **coups de grâce** (kōō′) A deathblow delivered to end the misery of a mortally wounded victim. [Fr. : *coup,* stroke + *de,* of + *grâce,* mercy.]

coup de main (kōō′ də măn′) *n., pl.* **coups de main** (kōō′) A sudden action undertaken to surprise an enemy. [Fr. : *coup,* stroke, blow + *de,* of + *main,* hand.]

coup d'é·tat (kōō′ dā-tä′) *n., pl.* **coups d'état** (kōō′) or **coup d'é·tats** (dā-täz′) The sudden overthrow of a government by a usu. small group of persons in or previously in positions of authority. [Fr. : *coup,* blow, stroke + *de,* of + *état,* state.]

coup de thé·â·tre (kōō′ də tä-ä′trə) *n., pl.* **coups de théâtre** (kōō′) **1.** A sudden dramatic turn of events in a play. **2.** An unexpected and sensational event, esp. one that reverses or negates a situation. [Fr. : *coup,* stroke + *de,* of + *théâtre,* theater.]

coup d'oeil (kōō′ dœ′yə) *n., pl.* **coups d'oeil** (kōō′) A quick survey; a glance. [Fr. *coup d'œil : coup,* stroke + *de,* of + *œil,* eye.]

coupe[1] (kōōp) *n.* **1a.** A dessert of ice cream or fruit-flavored ice, garnished and served in a special dessert glass. **b.** The stemmed glass in which a coupe is served. **2.** A shallow bowl-shaped dessert dish. [Fr., cup < LLat. *cuppa.*]

coupe[2] (kōōp) *n.* Variant of **coupé** 2.

cou·pé (kōō-pā′) *n.* **1.** A closed four-wheel carriage with two seats inside and one outside. **2.** also **coupe** (kōōp) A closed two-door automobile. [Fr. < p. part. of *couper,* to cut < *coup,* blow. See COUP.]

Cou·pe·rin (kōō-pə-răn′, kōōp-răn′), **François** 1668–1733. French composer who was court organist to Louis XIV.

cou·ple (kŭp′əl) *n.* **1.** Two items of the same kind; a pair. **2.** Something that joins or connects two things together; a link. **3.** (*used with a sing. or pl. verb*) **a.** Two people united, as by marriage. **b.** Two people together. **4.** *Informal* A few; several: *a couple of days.* **5.** *Physics* A pair of forces of equal magnitude acting in parallel but opposite directions. ❖ *v.* **-pled, -pling, -ples** —*tr.* **1.** To link together; connect. **2a.** To join as spouses; marry. **b.** To join in sexual union. **3.** *Electricity* To link (two circuits or currents), as by magnetic induction. —*intr.* **1.** To form pairs; join. **2.** To unite sexually; copulate. **3.** To join chemically. ❖ *adj. Informal* Two or few. [ME < OFr. < Lat. *cōpula,* bond, pair.]

> **USAGE NOTE** When used to refer to two people who function socially as a unit, as in *a married couple,* the word *couple* may take either a singular or a plural verb, depending on whether the members are considered individually or collectively: *The couple were married last week. Only one couple was unaccounted for.* When a pronoun follows, *they* and *their* are more common than *it* and *its: The couple decided to spend their* (less commonly *its*) *vacation in Italy.* • Critics have sometimes maintained that *a couple of* is too inexact to be appropriate in formal writing. But the inexactitude of *a couple of* may usefully suggest that the writer is indifferent to the precise number of items involved. This usage should be considered unobjectionable on all levels of style. However, the omission of *of* in the phrase (as in *a couple books*) is considered incorrect by three-fourths of the Usage Panel.

cou·pler (kŭp′lər) *n.* **1.** One that couples, esp. a device for coupling two railroad cars. **2.** A device connecting two organ keyboards so that they may be played together.

cou·plet (kŭp′lĭt) *n.* **1.** A unit of verse consisting of two successive lines, usu. rhyming and having the same meter. **2.** Two similar things; a pair. [Fr. < OFr., dim. of *couple,* couple. See COUPLE.]

cou·pling (kŭp′lĭng) *n.* **1.** The act of linking together or forming couples. **2.** The act of uniting sexually. **3.** A device that links or connects. **4.** *Electronics* Transfer of energy from one circuit to another. **5.** The body part of a four-footed animal that connects the hindquarters to the forequarters.

cou·pon (kōō′pŏn′, kyōō′-) *n.* **1.** A negotiable certificate attached to a bond that represents a sum of interest due. **2a.** One of a set of detachable certificates that may be torn off and redeemed as needed. **b.** A detachable part, as of an advertisement, that entitles the bearer to certain benefits, such as a refund. **c.** A certificate accompanying a product that may be redeemed for a cash discount. **d.** A printed form to be used as an order blank or for requesting information or obtaining a discount. **3.** A detachable slip calling for periodic payments, as for merchandise bought on an installment plan. [Fr. < OFr. *colpon,* piece cut off < *colper,* to cut < *colp,* blow. See COUP.]

cour·age (kûr′ĭj, kŭr′-) *n.* The state or quality of mind or spirit that enables one to face danger, fear, or vicissitudes with self-possession and resolution; bravery. [ME *corage* < OFr. < VLat. **corāticum* < Lat. *cor,* heart. See **kerd-** in App.]

cou·ra·geous (kə-rā′jəs) *adj.* Having or characterized by courage; valiant. See Syns at **brave.** —**cou·ra′geous·ly** *adv.* —**cou·ra′geous·ness** *n.*

cou·rante (kōō-ränt′) *n.* **1.** A 17th-century French dance characterized by running and gliding steps to an accompaniment in triple time. **2.** *Music* The second movement of the classical baroque suite. [Fr. < fem. pr. part. of *courir,* to run < OFr. *courre* < Lat. *currere.*]

Cour·an·tyne also **Co·ran·tijn** (kôr′ən-tīn′, kôr′-) A river rising in SE Guyana and flowing c. 724 km (450 mi) to the Atlantic Ocean.

Cour·bet (kōōr-bā′, -bĕ′), **Gustave** 1819–77. French painter known for his realistic depiction of everyday scenes.

cour·gette (kōōr-zhĕt′) *n. Chiefly British* A zucchini. [Fr. dialectal, dim. of *courge,* gourd < OFr. *cohourde* < Lat. *cucurbita.*]

cou·ri·er (kōōr′ē-ər, kûr′-, kŭr′-) *n.* **1a.** A messenger, esp. one on official diplomatic business. **b.** A spy carrying secret information. **2a.** A personal attendant hired to make arrangements for a journey. **b.** An employee of a travel agency serving as a guide for tourists. [Fr. *courrier* < OFr. < OItal. *corriere* < *correre,* to run < Lat. *currere.*]

cour·lan (kōōr′lən) *n.* See **limpkin.** [Fr., perh. alteration of *courliri* < Galibi *kurliri.*]

Cour·land also **Kur·land** (kōōr′lənd) A historical region of S Latvia between the Baltic Sea and the Western Dvina R.

course (kôrs, kōrs) *n.* **1a.** Onward movement in a particular direction; progress. **b.** Movement in time; duration: *in the course of a year.* **2.** The direction of continuing movement. **3.** The route or path taken by something, such as a stream, that moves. See Syns at **way. 4.** A designated area of land or water on which a race is held or a sport played. **5.** A mode of action or behavior. **6.** A typical or natural manner of proceeding or developing; customary passage: *a fad that ran its course.* **7.** A systematic or orderly succession; a sequence. **8.** A continuous layer of building material, such as brick on a wall or roof of a building. **9a.** A complete body of prescribed studies constituting a curriculum. **b.** A unit of such a curriculum. **10.** A part of a meal served as a unit at one time. **11.** *Nautical* The lowest sail on a mast of a square-rigged ship. **12.** A point on the compass, esp. the one toward which a ship is sailing. ❖ *v.* **coursed, cours·ing, cours·es** —*tr.* **1.** To move swiftly through or over; traverse. **2a.** To hunt (game) with hounds. **b.** To set (hounds) to chase game. —*intr.* **1.** To proceed or move swiftly along a specified course. **2.** To hunt game with hounds. —**idioms: in due course** At the proper or right time. **of course 1.** In the natural or expected order of things; naturally. **2.** Without any doubt; certainly. [ME < OFr. *cours* < Lat. *cursus* < p. part. of *currere,* to run.]

cours·er[1] (kôr′sər, kōr′-) *n.* **1.** A dog trained for coursing. **2.** A huntsman.

cours·er[2] (kôr′sər, kōr′-) *n.* A swift horse; a charger.

cours·ing (kôr′sĭng, kōr′-) *n.* Hunting with dogs trained to chase game by sight instead of scent.

court (kôrt, kōrt) *n.* **1a.** An extent of open ground partially or completely enclosed by walls or buildings; a courtyard. **b.** A short street, esp. a wide alley walled by buildings on three sides. **c.** A large open section of a building, often with a glass roof or skylight. **d.** A large building standing in a courtyard. **2a.** The place of residence of a sovereign or dignitary. **b.** The retinue of a sovereign. **c.** A sovereign's governing body, including the council of ministers and state advisers. **d.** A formal meeting or reception presided over by a sovereign. **3.** *Law* **a.** A person or body of persons whose task is to hear and submit a decision on cases at law. **b.** The building, hall, or room in which such cases are heard and determined. **c.** The regular session of a judicial assembly. **d.** A similar authorized tribunal having military or ecclesiastical jurisdiction. **4.** *Sports* An open level area marked with appropriate lines, upon which a game is played. **5.** The body of directors of an organization, esp. of a corporation. **6.** A legislative assembly. ❖ *v.* **court·ed, court·ing, courts** —*tr.* **1a.** To attempt to gain; seek. **b.** To behave so as to invite or incur. **2.** To try to gain the love or affections of, esp. to seek to marry. **3.** To attempt to gain the favor of by attention or flattery. **4.** *Zoology* To behave so as to attract (a mate). —*intr.* **1.** To pursue a courtship; woo. **2.** *Zoology* To engage in courtship behavior. —*idiom:* **pay court to 1.** To flatter solicitously to obtain something or clear away antagonism. **2.** To seek someone's love; woo. [ME < OFr. *cort* < Lat. *cohors,*

coupler

Jacques Cousteau

covered bridge

cowboy boot
pair of cowboy boots

cohort-, courtyard, retinue. See **gher-** in App.]

Court, Margaret Smith b. 1942. Australian tennis player who won 26 major titles.

court bouillon (kōōr, kôr, kōr) n. A poaching liquid for fish, usu. including water, vinegar or wine, vegetables, and seasonings. [Fr. : *court*, short + *bouillon*, broth.]

cour•te•ous (kûr′tē-əs) adj. Characterized by gracious consideration toward others. See Syns at **polite**. [ME *corteis*, courtly < OFr. < *cort*, court. See COURT.] —**cour′te•ous•ly** adv. —**cour′te•ous•ness** n.

cour•te•san (kôr′tĭ-zən, kōr′-) n. A woman prostitute, esp. one whose clients are members of a royal court or men of high social standing. [Fr. *courtisane* < OFr. < OItal. *cortigiana*, fem. of *cortigiano*, courtier < *corte*, court < Lat. *cohors, cohort-*. See **gher-** in App.]

cour•te•sy (kûr′tĭ-sē) n., pl. **-sies 1a.** Polite behavior. **b.** A polite gesture or remark. **2a.** Consent or agreement in spite of fact; indulgence. **b.** Willingness or generosity in providing something needed. ❖ adj. **1.** Given or done as a polite gesture. **2.** Free of charge. [ME *courtesie* < OFr. < *corteis*, courtly. See COURTEOUS.]

courtesy title n. **1.** A title of no legal validity that is assumed or granted by custom. **2a.** In Great Britain, the title that the heir of a high-ranking peer customarily uses. **b.** In Great Britain, the prefixes *Lord* and *Lady* added to the given names of the younger children of dukes and marquises or *the Honourable* added to the children of viscounts and barons.

court•house (kôrt′hous′, kōrt′-) n. **1.** A building housing judicial courts. **2a.** A building housing the offices of a county government. **b.** A county seat.

court•i•er (kôr′tē-ər, -tyər, kōr′-) n. **1.** An attendant at a sovereign's court. **2.** One who seeks favor, esp. by insincere flattery or obsequious behavior. [ME *courteour* < AN < OFr. *cortoier*, to be at a royal court < *cort*, court. See COURT.]

court•ly (kôrt′lē, kōrt′-) adj. **-li•er, -li•est 1.** Suitable for a royal court; stately. **2.** Elegant; refined: *courtly manners.* **3.** Flattering in an insincere way; obsequious. ❖ adv. In a courtly manner; elegantly or politely. —**court′li•ness** n.

courtly love n. An idealized and often illicit form of love celebrated in the literature of the Middle Ages and the Renaissance in which a knight or courtier devotes himself to a noblewoman who is usu. married.

court-mar•tial (kôrt′mär′shəl, kōrt′-) n., pl. **courts-mar•tial** (kôrts′-, kōrts′-) **1.** A military or naval court of officers appointed by a commander to try persons for offenses under military law. **2.** A trial by such a military tribunal. ❖ tr.v. **-tialed, -tial•ing, -tials** also **-tialled, -tial•ling, -tials** To try by military tribunal. [< *martial court.*]

court of appeals (kôrt, kōrt) n., pl. **courts of appeals** A court to which appeals are made on points of law resulting from the judgment of a lower court.

court of chancery n., pl. **courts of chancery** A court with jurisdiction in equity.

court of claims n., pl. **courts of claims** A US federal court that determines claims brought by individuals against the government.

court of common pleas n., pl. **courts of common pleas 1.** A court in some states of the United States having general jurisdiction. **2.** A court in Great Britain that formerly heard civil cases between commoners.

court of domestic relations n., pl. **courts of domestic relations** A court having the judicial authority to investigate and decide on cases involving marital and esp. parental rights and obligations.

Court of Exchequer n. A former superior court in Great Britain dealing with matters of revenue.

court of inquiry n., pl. **courts of inquiry** A military court that inquires into and reports on questionable actions involving military personnel or property.

court of law n., pl. **courts of law** A court that hears cases and makes decisions based on statutes or the common law.

court of record n., pl. **courts of record** A court whose proceedings and decisions are retained on permanent record.

Court of Saint James's (jāmz′, jām′zĭz) n. The British royal court.

court order n. An order issued by a court that requires a person to do or refrain from doing something.

court plaster n. Cloth coated with an adhesive substance and used to cover cuts or scratches on the skin.

Cour•trai (kōōr-trā′, kōōr-) See **Kortrijk.**

court reporter n. A stenographer who makes a verbatim record and transcription of proceedings, as in a court.

court•room (kôrt′rōōm′, -rŏŏm′, kōrt′-) n. A room in which the proceedings of a court are held.

court•ship (kôrt′shĭp′, kōrt′-) n. **1.** The act, process, or period of courting. **2.** *Zoology* Specialized behavior in animals that leads to or initiates mating.

court•side (kôrt′sīd′, kōrt′-) n. The area immediately bordering the official court of play, as in tennis or basketball.

court tennis n. A form of tennis played in a large indoor court with a specially marked-out floor and high cement walls off which the ball may be played.

court•yard (kôrt′yärd′, kōrt′-) n. An open space surrounded by walls or buildings and adjoining or within a building.

cous•cous (kōōs′kōōs′) n. **1.** A pasta of North African origin made of crushed and steamed semolina. **2.** A North African dish consisting of pasta steamed with meat and vegetables. [Fr. < Ar. *kuskus < kaskasa*, to pulverize.]

cous•in (kŭz′ĭn) n. **1.** A child of one's aunt or uncle. **2.** A relative descended from a common ancestor by two or more steps in a diverging line. **3.** A relative by blood or marriage; a kinsman or kinswoman. **4.** A member of a kindred group or country: *our Canadian cousins.* **5.** Something similar in quality or character. **6.** Used as a form of address by a sovereign in addressing another sovereign or a high-ranking member of the nobility. [ME *cosin*, a relative < OFr. < Lat. *cōnsōbrīnus*, cousin : *com-*, com- + *sōbrīnus*, cousin on the mother's side; see **swesor-** in App.] —**cous′in•hood′** n. —**cous′in•ly** adj. —**cous′in•ship′** n.

cous•in-ger•man (kŭz′ĭn-jûr′mən) n., pl. **cous•ins-ger•man** (kŭz′ĭnz-) A child of one's aunt or uncle; a first cousin.

Cous•teau (kōō-stō′), Jacques Yves 1910–97. French explorer and film producer who developed underwater laboratories.

couth (kōōth) adj. Marked by or possessing a high degree of sophistication; refined. ❖ n. Refinement; sophistication. [Back-formation < UNCOUTH.]

cou•ture (kōō-tōōr′, -tür′) n. **1.** The business of designing, making, and selling high-fashion, usu. custom-made women's clothing. **2.** Dressmakers and fashion designers. **3.** The clothing created by designers. [Fr., sewing < OFr. *couture* < VLat. **cōnsūtūra* < Lat. *cōnsuere, cōnsūt-*, to sew together : *com-*, com- + *suere*, to sew; see **syū-** in App.]

cou•tu•rier (kōō-tōōr′ē-ər, -ē-ā′, -tür-yā′) n. **1.** An establishment engaged in couture. **2.** One who designs for or owns such an establishment. [Fr., dressmaker < OFr. *couturier < couture*, sewing. See COUTURE.]

cou•tu•rière (kōō-tōōr′ē-ər, -ē-âr′, -tür-yĕr′) n. A woman who designs for or owns an establishment engaged in couture. [Fr., dressmaker, seamstress < OFr. *couturiere*, fem. of *couturier*. See COUTURIER.]

cou•vade (kōō-väd′) n. A practice in certain cultures in which the husband of a woman in labor takes to his bed as though he were bearing the child. [Fr. < OFr. < *couver*, to incubate, hatch < Lat. *cubāre*, to lie down on.]

co•va•lence (kō-vā′ləns) n. The number of electron pairs an atom can share with other atoms. —**co•va′len•cy** n. —**co•va′lent** adj. —**co•va′lent•ly** adv.

covalent bond n. A chemical bond formed by the sharing of electrons, esp. pairs of electrons, between atoms.

co•var•i•ance (kō-vâr′ē-əns) n. A statistical measure of the variance of two random variables that are observed or measured in the same mean time period.

co•var•i•ant (kō-vâr′ē-ənt) adj. **1.** *Physics* Expressing or relating to the principle that physical laws have the same form regardless of the coordinate system in which they are expressed. **2.** *Statistics* Varying with another quantity in a manner that leaves a specified relationship unchanged.

cove¹ (kōv) n. **1.** A small sheltered bay in the shoreline of a sea, river, or lake. **2a.** A recess or small valley in the side of a mountain. **b.** A cave or cavern. **3.** A narrow gap or pass between hills or woods. **4.** *Architecture* **a.** A concave molding. **b.** A concave surface forming a junction between a ceiling and a wall. ❖ tr.v. **coved, cov•ing, coves** To make in an inward curving form. [ME, chamber, cave < OE *cofa*.]

cove² (kōv) n. *Chiefly British* A fellow; a man. [Prob. < Romany *kova*, man.]

co•vel•lite (kō-vĕl′īt′, kō′və-līt′) n. A lustrous indigo-blue mineral, CuS, a major copper ore. [After Nicolò *Covelli* (1790–1829), Italian mineralogist.]

cov•en (kŭv′ən, kō′vən) n. An assembly of 13 witches. [Perh. < ME *covent*, assembly, convent. See CONVENT.]

cov•e•nant (kŭv′ə-nənt) n. **1.** A binding agreement; a compact. **2.** *Law* **a.** A formal sealed agreement or contract. **b.** A suit to recover damages for violation of such a contract. **3.** In the Bible, God's promise to the human race. ❖ v. **-nant•ed, -nant•ing, -nants** —tr. To promise by or as if by a covenant. —intr. To enter into a covenant. [ME < OFr. < pr. part. of *convenir*, to agree. See CONVENE.] —**cov′e•nant′al** (-nǎn′tl) adj. —**cov′e•nant′al•ly** adv.

cov•e•nant•ee (kŭv′ə-nǎn-tē′, -nən-) n. The party to whom the promise in a covenant is made.

cov•e•nant•er (kŭv′ə-nǎn′tər) n. **1.** One who makes a covenant. **2. Covenanter** A Scottish Presbyterian who supported either the National Covenant of 1638 or the Solemn League and Covenant of 1643, intended to defend and extend Presbyterianism.

cov•e•nan•tor (kŭv′ə-nǎn′tər, -nən-, kŭv′ə-nǎn-tôr′) n. The party by whom the promise in a covenant is to be carried out.

Cov•ent Garden (kŭv′ənt, kŏv′-) An area in London long noted for its produce market (est. 1671) and its royal theater (built 1731–32). The market was moved in 1974.

Cov•en•try¹ (kŭv′ĭn-trē) A city of central England ESE of Birmingham; famous as the home of Lady Godiva in the 11th cent. Pop. 304,097.

Cov·en·try² (kŭv′ən-trē) *n.* A state of ostracism or exile. [After COVENTRY¹, England.]

cov·er (kŭv′ər) *v.* **-ered, -er·ing, -ers** —*tr.* **1.** To place something upon or over, so as to protect or conceal. **2.** To overlay or spread with something. **3a.** To put a cover or covering on. **b.** To wrap up; clothe. **4.** To invest (oneself) with a great deal of something. **5a.** To spread over the surface of. **b.** To extend over. **6a.** To copulate with (a female). Used esp. of horses. **b.** To sit on in order to hatch. **7.** To hide or screen from view or knowledge; conceal. **8a.** To protect or shield from harm, loss, or danger. **b.** To protect by insurance. **c.** To compensate or make up for. **9.** To be sufficient to defray, meet, or offset the cost or charge of. **10.** To make provision for; take into account. **11.** To deal with; treat of. **12.** To travel or pass over; traverse. **13a.** To have as one's territory or sphere of work. **b.** To be responsible for reporting the details of (an event or situation). **14.** To hold within the range and aim of a weapon, such as a firearm. **15.** To protect by occupying a strategic position. **16.** *Sports* **a.** To guard (an opponent playing offense). **b.** To defend (a position or area). **17.** To match (an opponent's stake) in a wager. **18.** To purchase (stock that one has shorted). **19.** *Games* To play a higher-ranking card than the one previously played). **20.** *Music* To record a cover of (a song). **21.** *Obsolete* To pardon or remit. —*intr.* **1.** To spread over a surface to protect or conceal something. **2.** To act as a substitute or replacement during someone's absence. **3.** To hide something in order to save someone from censure or punishment: *cover up for a colleague.* **4.** *Games* To play a higher card than the one previously played. ❖ *n.* **1.** Something that covers or is laid, placed, or spread over or upon something else, as: **a.** A lid or top. **b.** A binding or enclosure for a book or magazine. **c.** A covering, such as a sheet or blanket, used on a bed. **2a.** Something that provides shelter. **b.** Strategic protection given by armed units during hostile action. **3a.** Something, such as vegetation, covering the surface of the ground. **b.** Vegetation serving as protective concealment for wild animals. **4a.** Something, such as darkness, that screens, conceals, or disguises. **b.** A false background and identity, esp. for a spy. **5.** A table setting for one person. **6.** A cover charge. **7.** An envelope or wrapper for mail. **8.** Funds sufficient to meet an obligation or secure against loss. **9.** One who substitutes for another. **10.** *Music* A recording of a song that was previously recorded or made popular by another. —*idioms:* **cover (one's) tracks** To conceal traces so as to elude pursuers. **cover (the) ground 1.** To traverse a given distance with satisfying speed. **2.** To deal with or accomplish something in a certain manner. **take cover** To seek concealment or protection. **under cover 1.** In an enclosure for mailing. **2.** Being hidden or protected, as by darkness. [ME *coveren* < OFr. *covrir* < Lat. *cooperīre*, to cover completely : *co-*, intensive pref.; see CO– + *operīre*, to cover.] —**cov′er·a·ble** *adj.* —**cov′er·er** *n.* —**cov′er·less** *adj.*

cov·er·age (kŭv′ər-ĭj) *n.* **1.** The extent or degree to which something is observed, analyzed, and reported. **2a.** Inclusion in an insurance policy or protective plan. **b.** The extent of protection afforded by an insurance policy or plan. **3.** The amount of funds reserved to meet liabilities. **4.** The percentage of persons reached by a medium of communication, such as television.

cov·er·all (kŭv′ər-ôl′) *n.* A loose-fitting one-piece work garment worn to protect clothes. Often used in the plural.

cover boy *n.* An boy or man whose picture is featured on a magazine cover.

cover charge *n.* A fixed amount added to the bill at a nightclub or restaurant for entertainment or services.

cover crop *n.* A crop planted between periods of regular crop production to prevent soil erosion and provide humus or nitrogen.

Cov·er·dale (kŭv′ər-dāl′), **Miles** 1488–1568. English cleric who produced the first complete English Bible (1535).

cov·ered bridge (kŭv′ərd) *n.* A bridge whose roadway is protected by a roof and sides.

covered wagon *n.* A large wagon covered with an arched canvas top, used esp. by American pioneers for prairie travel.

cover girl *n.* An attractive woman whose picture is featured on a magazine cover.

cover glass *n.* **1.** A small thin piece of glass used to cover a specimen on a microscope slide. **2.** A protective sheet of glass for a transparency.

cov·er·ing (kŭv′ər-ĭng) *n.* Something that covers so as to protect or conceal.

cov·er·let (kŭv′ər-lĭt) also **cov·er·lid** (-lĭd) *n.* A bedspread. [ME *coverlite* < AN *coverlyth* : OFr. *covrir*, to cover; see COVER + OFr. *lit*, bed (< Lat. *lēctus*; see **legh-** in App.).]

cover letter *n.* A letter sent with other documents to explain more fully or provide information.

covers *abbr.* versed cosine

co·ver·sine (kō-vûr′sīn′) *n.* See **versed cosine**.

cover slip *n.* See **cover glass 1**.

cover story *n.* **1.** A story in a magazine concerning the cover illustration. **2.** A false story intended to deceive.

cov·ert (kŭv′ərt, kō′vərt, kō-vûrt′) *adj.* **1.** Not openly practiced, avowed, engaged in, accumulated, or shown. **2.** Covered or covered over; sheltered. **3.** *Law* Being married and therefore protected by one's husband. ❖ *n.* **1.** A covering or cover. **2a.** A cov-

ered place or shelter; a hiding place. **b.** Thick underbrush or woodland affording cover for game. **3.** *Zoology* One of the small feathers covering the bases of the longer feathers of a bird's wings or tail. **4.** A flock of coots. [ME < OFr. < p. part. of *covrir*, to cover. See COVER.] —**cov′ert·ly** *adv.* —**cov′ert·ness** *n.*

cov·er·ture (kŭv′ər-chər, -chŏŏr′) *n.* **1a.** A covering; a shelter. **b.** The state of being concealed; disguise. **2.** *Law* A married woman's status under common law. [ME < OFr. < *covert*, covered. See COVERT.]

cov·er-up or **cov·er·up** (kŭv′ər-ŭp′) *n.* **1.** An effort or strategy of concealment, esp. a planned effort to prevent scandal. **2.** A loose garment for wear over other clothing.

cov·et (kŭv′ĭt) *v.* **-et·ed, -et·ing, -ets** —*tr.* **1.** To feel blameworthy desire for (that which is another's). See Syns at **envy. 2.** To wish for longingly. See Syns at **desire.** —*intr.* To covet that which is another's. [ME *coveiten* < OFr. *coveitier* < *covitie*, desire < Lat. *cupiditās* < *cupidus*, desirous < *cupere*, to desire.] —**cov′et·a·ble** *adj.* —**cov′et·er** *n.* —**cov′et·ing·ly** *adv.*

cov·et·ous (kŭv′ĭ-təs) *adj.* **1.** Excessively and culpably desirous of the possessions of another. See Syns at **jealous. 2.** Marked by extreme desire to acquire or possess: *covetous of learning.* —**cov′et·ous·ly** *adv.* —**cov′et·ous·ness** *n.*

cov·ey (kŭv′ē) *n., pl.* **-eys 1.** A family or small flock of birds, esp. partridge or quail. **2.** A small group, as of persons. [ME < OFr. *covee*, brood < fem. p. part. of *cover*, to incubate < Lat. *cubāre*, to lie down.]

cov·ing (kō′vĭng) *n.* See **cove¹ 4**.

cow¹ (kou) *n.* **1.** The mature female of cattle of the genus *Bos.* **2.** The mature female of other large animals, such as whales, elephants, or moose. **3.** A domesticated bovine of either sex or any age. —*idiom:* **till the cows come home** *Informal* For a very long time; indefinitely. [ME *cou* < OE *cū*. See **g^wou-** in App.] —**cow′y** *adj.*

cow² (kou) *tr.v.* **cowed, cow·ing, cows** To frighten with threats or a show of force. [Prob. of Scand. orig.] —**cow′ed·ly** (-ĭd-lē) *adv.*

cow·ard (kou′ərd) *n.* One who shows cowardice. [ME < OFr. *couard* < *coue*, tail < Lat. *cauda*.] —**cow′ard** *adj.*

> **WORD HISTORY** A *coward* is one who "turns tail." The word comes from Old French *couart, coart,* "coward," and is related to Italian *codardo,* "coward." *Couart* is formed from *coe,* a northern French dialectal variant of *cue,* "tail" (from Latin *cōda*), to which the derogatory suffix *–ard* was added. This suffix appears in *bastard, laggard,* and *sluggard,* to name a few. A *coward* may also be one with his tail between his legs. In heraldry a *lion coward,* "cowardly lion," was depicted with his tail between his legs. So a *coward* may be one with his tail hidden between his legs or one who turns tail and runs like a rabbit, with his tail showing.

Coward, Sir Noel Pierce 1899–1973. British actor, playwright, and composer noted esp. for his witty comedies, such as *Private Lives* (1930).

cow·ard·ice (kou′ər-dĭs) *n.* Ignoble fear in the face of danger or pain. [ME *cowardise* < OFr. *couardise,* alteration of *couardie* < *couard,* coward. See COWARD.]

cow·ard·ly (kou′ərd-lē) *adj.* Exhibiting the characteristics of a coward. —**cow′ard·li·ness** *n.* —**cow′ard·ly** *adv.*

cow·bane (kou′bān′) *n.* **1.** A perennial North American herb (*Oxypolis rigidior*) having pinnately compound leaves and umbels of small white flowers. **2.** Any of several related plants, such as the water hemlock.

cow·bell (kou′bĕl′) *n.* A bell on a cow's collar.

cow·ber·ry (kou′bĕr′ē) *n.* **1.** A low creeping evergreen shrub (*Vaccinium vitis-idaea*) native to northern parts of North America and Eurasia. **2.** The edible red berry of this plant. [Approximate transl. of NLat. *Vaccīnium,* genus name < Lat. *vaccīnium,* bilberry (sense uncertain) < *vaccīnus,* of cows.]

cow·bird (kou′bûrd′) *n.* Any of various blackbirds of the genus *Molothrus,* esp. the common North American species *M. ater,* which lay their eggs in the nests of other birds.

cow·boy (kou′boi′) *n.* **1.** A hired man, esp. in the western United States, who tends cattle and performs many of his duties on horseback. See Regional Note at **vaquero. 2.** An adventurous hero. **3.** *Slang* A reckless person who ignores potential risks.

cowboy boot *n.* A high-arched boot with a high Cuban heel and usu. ornamental stitching.

cowboy hat *n.* A felt hat with a tall crown and wide brim.

cow·catch·er (kou′kăch′ər, -kĕch′-) *n.* The metal grille or frame projecting from the front of a locomotive and serving to clear the track of obstructions.

cow college *n. Informal* **1.** An agricultural college. **2.** A college or university considered to be provincial.

cow·er (kou′ər) *intr.v.* **-ered, -er·ing, -ers** To cringe in fear. [ME *couren,* of Scand. orig.]

cow·fish (kou′fĭsh′) *n., pl.* **cowfish** or **-fish·es 1.** Any of various aquatic mammals, esp. a whale of the genus *Mesoplodon,* having a pointed snout. **2.** Any of various marine fishes of the family Ostraciidae, esp. *Lactophrys quadricornis,* having hornlike spines over each eye.

cow·girl (kou′gûrl′) *n.* A hired woman, esp. in the western United States, who tends cattle and performs many of her duties

cowcatcher

on horseback. [COW(BOY) + GIRL.]

cow·hand (kou′hănd′) *n.* A cowboy or cowgirl.

cow·herd (kou′hûrd′) *n.* One who herds or tends cattle.

cow·hide (kou′hīd′) *n.* **1a.** The hide of a cow. **b.** The leather made from this hide. **2.** A heavy flexible whip, usu. made of braided leather. ✧ *tr.v.* **-hid·ed, -hid·ing, -hides** To beat with a heavy flexible whip.

cowl (koul) *n.* **1a.** The hood or hooded robe worn esp. by a monk. **b.** A draped neckline on a woman's garment. **2.** A hood-shaped covering used to increase the draft of a chimney. **3.** The top portion of the front part of an automobile body, supporting the windshield and dashboard. **4.** The cowling on an aircraft. ✧ *tr.v.* **cowled, cowl·ing, cowls** To cover with or as if with a cowl. [ME *coule* < OE *cugele* < LLat. *cuculla* < Lat. *cucullus,* hood.]

cowled (kould) *adj.* **1.** Wearing or supplied with a cowl; hooded. **2.** Having the shape of a hood.

Cow·ley (kou′lē), **Abraham** 1618–67. English metaphysical poet whose works include *Davideis* (1656).

cow·lick (kou′lĭk′) *n.* A tuft of hair on the head that grows in a different direction from the rest and will not lie flat.

cowl·ing (kou′lĭng) *n.* A removable metal covering for an engine, esp. an aircraft engine.

cow·man (kou′mən, -măn′) *n.* **1.** An owner of cattle or a cattle ranch. **2a.** See **cowboy** 1. **b.** A cowherd.

co·work·er or **co-work·er** (kō′wûr′kər) *n.* One that works with another; a fellow worker.

cow parsnip *n.* Any of several tall coarse herbs of the genus *Heracleum* in the parsley family, native chiefly to northern temperate regions and having compound umbels.

cow·pea (kou′pē′) *n.* **1.** An annual African plant (*Vigna unguiculata*) in the pea family, cultivated in warm regions for food, forage, and soil improvement. **2.** Its edible seed.

Cow·per (koo′pər, kou′-, koop′ər), **William** 1731–1800. British poet considered a precursor of romanticism.

Cow·per's gland (kou′pərz, koo′-) *n.* See **bulbourethral gland.** [After William *Cowper* (1666–1709), English surgeon.]

cow·pie (kou′pī′) *n. Informal* A rounded mass of cow excrement.

cow pilot *n.* See **sergeant major** 3.

cow·poke (kou′pōk′) *n.* See **cowboy** 1.

cow pony *n.* A small, agile horse used in herding cattle.

cow·pox (kou′pŏks′) *n.* A contagious skin disease of cattle, usu. characterized by pustules on the udder, that is caused by a virus and when transmitted to humans confers immunity to smallpox.

cow·punch·er (kou′pŭn′chər) *n.* See **cowboy** 1.

cow·rie or **cow·ry** (kou′rē) *n., pl.* **-ries** Any of various tropical marine gastropods of the family Cypraeidae, having glossy, often brightly marked shells, some of which are used as currency in the South Pacific and Africa. [Hindi *kaurī* < Skt. *kapardikā,* dim. of *kapardaḥ,* shell, of Dravidian orig.]

co·write or **co-write** (kō-rīt′) *tr.v.* **-wrote** (-rōt′), **-writ·ten** (-rĭt′n), **-writ·ing, -writes** To write jointly or in collaboration with another author. —**co′writ·er** *n.*

cow shark *n.* Any of several sharks of the family Hexanchidae of warm and temperate seas.

cow·shed (kou′shĕd′) *n.* A shed for housing cows.

cow·slip (kou′slĭp′) *n.* **1.** A Eurasian primrose (*Primula veris*) usu. having fragrant yellow flowers. **2.** See **marsh marigold.** **3.** The Virginia cowslip. [ME *cowslyppe* < OE *cūslyppe* : *cū,* cow; see gʷou- in App. + *slypa,* slime.]

cox (kŏks) *n.* A coxswain. —**cox** *v.*

COX-2 inhibitor (kŏks′too′) *n.* Any of a class of nonsteroidal anti-inflammatory drugs thought to have fewer side effects than traditional NSAIDs. [< *c*(*yclo*)*ox*(*ygenase*)*-2,* enzyme involved in the production of prostaglandins.]

cox·a (kŏk′sə) *n., pl.* **cox·ae** (kŏk′sē′) **1.** *Anatomy* The hip or hip joint. **2.** *Zoology* The segment of the leg of an insect or other arthropod that adjoins the body. [Lat., hip.] —**cox′al** *adj.*

cox·al·gi·a (kŏk-săl′jē-ə, -jə) *n.* Pain in or disease of the hip or hip joint. [COX(A) + –ALGIA.] —**cox·al′gic** (-jĭk) *adj.*

cox·comb (kŏks′kōm′) *n.* **1.** A conceited dandy; a fop. **2.** *Obsolete* A jester's cap; a cockscomb. [ME *cokkes comb,* crest of a cock : *cokkes,* genitive of *cok,* cock; see COCK[1] + *comb,* crest; see COMB.] —**cox·comb′i·cal** (-kōm′ĭ-kəl) *adj.*

cox·comb·ry (kŏk′skōm′rē, -skəm-) *n., pl.* **-ries** Behavior that is characteristic of a coxcomb; foppish conceit.

Cox·ey (kŏk′sē), **Jacob Sechler** 1854–1951. Amer. businessman and reformer who led a march on Washington DC to protest unemployment (1894).

cox·i·tis (kŏk-sī′tĭs) *n.* Inflammation of the hip joint.

cox·sack·ie·vi·rus also **Cox·sack·ie virus** (kook-să′kē-vī′rəs, kŏk-săk′ē-) *n.* Any of a group of enteroviruses associated with various diseases, such as meningitis, that chiefly affect children during the summer months. [After *Coxsackie,* a village of E-central New York.]

cox·swain (kŏk′sən, -swān′) *n.* **1.** A person who usu. steers a ship's boat and has charge of its crew. **2.** A person in a racing shell who usu. directs the rest of the crew. ✧ *intr. & tr.v.* **-swained, -swain·ing, -swains** To act as coxswain or serve as coxswain for. [ME *cokswayne : cok,* cockboat; see COCKBOAT + *swain,* servant; see SWAIN.]

coyote
Canis latrans

coy (koi) *adj.* **coy·er, coy·est** **1.** Tending to avoid people and social situations; reserved. **2.** Affectedly and usu. flirtatiously shy or modest. See Syns at **shy**[1]. **3.** Annoyingly unwilling to make a commitment. [ME < OFr. *quei, coi,* quiet, still < VLat. **quētus* < Lat. *quiētus,* p. part. of *quiēscere,* to rest.] —**coy′ly** *adv.* —**coy′ness** *n.*

coy·dog (kī′dôg′, -dŏg′) *n.* The hybrid offspring of a coyote and a feral dog. [COY(OTE) + DOG.]

coy·o·te (kī-ō′tē, kī′ōt′) *n.* **1.** A small wolflike carnivorous animal (*Canis latrans*) native to western North America. **2.** A person who smuggles illegal immigrants into the United States, esp. across the Mexican border. [Am.Sp. < Nahuatl *cóyotl.*]

coy·o·til·lo (koi′ə-tĭl′ō, -tē′yō, kī′ə-) *n., pl.* **-los** A poisonous shrub (*Karwinskia humboldtiana*) native to Texas and Mexico and having small greenish flowers and black fruits. [Am.Sp., dim. of *coyote,* coyote. See COYOTE.]

coy·pu (koi′poo) *n., pl.* **-pus** A large aquatic South American rodent (*Myocastor coypus*) having webbed feet and a long tail. [Am.Sp. *coipú* < Araucanian *kóypu.*]

coz (kŭz) *n. Informal* A cousin.

coz·en (kŭz′ən) *v.* **-ened, -en·ing, -ens** —*tr.* **1.** To mislead by means of a petty trick or fraud; deceive. **2.** To persuade or induce to do something by cajoling or wheedling. **3.** To obtain by deceit or persuasion. —*intr.* To act deceitfully. [Perh. < ME *cosin,* fraud, trickery.] —**coz′en·er** *n.*

coz·en·age (kŭz′ə-nĭj) *n.* **1.** The art or practice of cozening. **2.** An act or example of cozening.

Co·zu·mel (kō′zə-mĕl′, sōō-) An island off the coast of SE Mexico near Cancún.

co·zy also **co·sy** (kō′zē) *adj.* **-zi·er, -zi·est** also **-si·er, -si·est** **1.** Snug, comfortable, and warm. **2.** Marked by friendly intimacy. **3.** *Informal* Marked by close association for devious purposes. ✧ *intr.v.* **-zied, -zy·ing, -zies** also **-sied, -sy·ing, -sies** **1.** To make oneself snug and comfortable. **2.** *Informal* To try to get on friendly or intimate terms; ingratiate oneself. ✧ *n., pl.* **-zies** also **-sies** A padded or knitted covering placed esp. over a teapot to keep the tea hot. [Prob. of Scand. orig.] —**co′zi·ly** *adv.* —**co′zi·ness** *n.*

cp *abbr.* candlepower

cP *abbr.* centipoise

CP *abbr.* **1.** chemically pure **2.** command post **3.** Communist Party

cp. *abbr.* compare

CPA *abbr.* certified public accountant

cpd. *abbr.* compound

cpi *abbr. Printing* characters per inch

CPI *abbr.* consumer price index

CPL or **Cpl** also **Cpl.** *abbr.* corporal

cpm *abbr.* **1.** cost per thousand **2.** cycles per minute

CPO *abbr.* chief petty officer

CPR *abbr.* cardiopulmonary resuscitation

cps *abbr.* **1.** characters per second **2.** cycles per second

CPT *abbr.* captain

CPU *abbr.* central processing unit

CQ[1] (sē′kyōō′) *n.* Code letters used at the beginning of radio messages intended for all receivers. [?]

CQ[2] *abbr.* call to quarters

Cr The symbol for the element **chromium.**

CR *abbr.* **1.** conditioned reflex **2.** conditioned response **3.** Costa Rica

cr. *abbr.* **1.** credit **2.** Cr. creek **3.** crescendo **4.** crown

crab[1] (krăb) *n.* **1a.** Any of various predominantly marine crustaceans of the order Decapoda, characterized by a broad flattened cephalothorax covered by a hard carapace, short antennae, and five pairs of legs, of which the anterior pair are large and pincerlike. **b.** Any of various similar related crustaceans, such as the hermit crab. **c.** A horseshoe crab. **2a.** A crab louse. **b. crabs** *Slang* Infestation by crab lice. **3.** The maneuvering of an aircraft partially into a crosswind to compensate for drift. **4.** A machine for handling or hoisting heavy weights. **5. Crab** See **Cancer.** ✧ *v.* **crabbed, crab·bing, crabs** —*intr.* **1.** To hunt or catch crabs. **2.** To scurry sideways in the manner of a crab. **3.** To drift diagonally or sideways. **4.** To direct an aircraft into a crosswind. —*tr.* **1.** To direct (an aircraft) partly into a crosswind to eliminate drift. **2.** To cause to move or scurry sideways. —*idiom:* **catch a crab** To make a faulty stroke in rowing that causes the blade of the oar to strike the water on the recovery stroke. [ME *crabbe* < OE *crabba.* See gerbh- in App.] —**crab′ber** *n.*

crab[2] (krăb) *n.* **1.** A crab apple tree or its fruit. **2.** A quarrelsome, ill-tempered person. ✧ *v.* **crabbed, crab·bing, crabs** —*intr. Informal* To find fault; criticize someone or something. —*tr.* **1.** *Informal* To interfere with and ruin; spoil. **2.** *Informal* To find fault with; complain about. **3.** To make ill-tempered or sullen. [ME *crabbe,* poss. < *crab*[1] (shellfish). See CRAB[1].] —**crab′ber** *n.*

crab apple also **crab·ap·ple** (krăb′ăp′əl) *n.* **1.** Any of several deciduous trees of the genus *Malus,* native to North America and Eurasia. **2.** The small tart fruit of such a tree.

crab·bed (krăb′ĭd) *adj.* **1.** Irritable and perverse in disposition; ill-tempered. **2.** Difficult to understand; complicated. **3.** Difficult to read; cramped. [ME < *crabbe,* crab (influenced by CRAB[2]). See CRAB[1].] —**crab′bed·ly** *adv.* —**crab′bed·ness** *n.*

crab·by (krăb′ē) *adj.* **-bi·er, -bi·est** *Informal* Grouchy; ill-tempered. —**crab′bi•ly** *adv.* —**crab′bi•ness** *n.*

crab•grass or **crab grass** (krăb′grăs′) *n.* Any of certain grasses of the genus *Digitaria,* esp. *D. sanguinalis* or *D. ischaemum,* widely naturalized in North America.

crab louse *n.* A sucking louse (*Phthirus pubis*) that generally infests the pubic region and causes severe itching.

crab•meat (krăb′mēt′) *n.* The edible flesh of a crab.

crab′s eye (krăbz) *n.* See **rosary pea.**

crab•stick (krăb′stĭk′) *n.* **1.** A stick made of crab apple wood. **2.** A crabby, ill-tempered person.

crab•wise (krăb′wīz′) *adv.* **1.** Sideways. **2.** In a furtive or circumspect manner; indirectly.

crack (krăk) *v.* **cracked, crack•ing, cracks** —*intr.* **1.** To break or snap apart. **2.** To make a sharp snapping sound. **3.** To break without complete separation of parts; fissure: *The mirror cracked.* **4.** To change sharply in pitch or timbre, as from hoarseness or emotion. Used of the voice. **5.** To break down; fail: *The defendant's composure began to crack.* **6.** To have a mental or physical breakdown. **7.** To move or go rapidly. **8.** *Chemistry* To break into simpler molecules by means of heat. —*tr.* **1.** To cause to make a sharp snapping sound. **2.** To cause to break without complete separation of parts. **3a.** To break with a sharp snapping sound. See Syns at **break. b.** To crush (wheat, for example) into small pieces. **4.** To open to a slight extent: *crack a window.* **5.** To strike with a sudden sharp sound. **6.** *Informal* **a.** To break open or into: *crack a safe.* **b.** To open up for use or consumption: *crack a book.* **c.** To break through (an obstacle) in order to win acceptance or acknowledgment. **7.** To discover the solution to, esp. after considerable effort. **8.** To cause (the voice) to crack. **9.** *Informal* To tell (a joke), esp. on impulse or in an effective manner. **10.** To cause to have a mental or physical breakdown. **11.** To impair or destroy. **12.** To reduce (petroleum) to simpler compounds by cracking. ❖ *n.* **1.** A sharp snapping sound, such as the report of a firearm. **2a.** A partial split or break; a fissure. **b.** A slight narrow space. **3.** A sharp resounding blow. **4a.** A mental or physical impairment; a defect. **b.** A breaking, harshly dissonant vocal tone or sound, as in hoarseness. **5.** An attempt or try. **6.** A witty or sarcastic remark. **7.** A moment; an instant: *at the crack of dawn.* **8.** *Irish* Social amusement; fun. **9.** *Slang* Crack cocaine. ❖ *adj.* Excelling in skill or achievement; first-rate: *a crack shot.* —*phrasal verbs:* **crack down** To act more forcefully to regulate, repress, or restrain. **crack up** *Informal* **1.** To praise highly: *not the genius he was cracked up to be.* **2a.** To damage or wreck (a vehicle or vessel). **b.** To wreck a vehicle in an accident. **3.** To have a mental or physical breakdown. **4.** To experience or cause to experience a great deal of amusement. —*idiom:* **crack the whip** To behave in a domineering manner; demand hard work from those under one's control. [ME *craken* < OE *cracian.*]

crack baby *n.* An infant born to a mother who used crack cocaine during pregnancy.

crack•brain (krăk′brān′) *n.* A foolish or eccentric person. —**crack′brained′** *adj.*

crack cocaine *n.* Purified cocaine in pellet form that is smoked through a pipe and is highly addictive. [< its preparation by breaking cocaine crystals into pellets.]

crack•down (krăk′doun′) *n.* An act or example of forceful regulation, repression, or restraint: *a crackdown on crime.*

cracked (krăkt) *adj.* **1a.** Broken so that fissures appear on the surface: *a cracked mirror.* **b.** Broken into small or coarse pieces: *cracked corn.* **2.** Having a harsh or dissonant tone: *a cracked voice.* **3.** *Informal* Mentally deranged; crazy.

crack•er (krăk′ər) *n.* **1.** A thin crisp wafer or biscuit, usu. made of unsweetened dough. **2.** One that cracks, esp.: **a.** A firecracker. **b.** A small cardboard cylinder covered with decorative paper that holds candy or a party favor and pops open. **c.** The apparatus used in the cracking of petroleum. **d.** One who makes unauthorized use of a computer, esp. to tamper with data or programs. **3.** *Offensive* **a.** Used as a disparaging term for a poor white person of the rural, esp. southeast United States. **b.** Used as a disparaging term for a white person.

crack•er-bar•rel (krăk′ər-băr′əl) *adj.* Of or resembling the informal discussions carried on by persons at a country store: *cracker-barrel philosophy.*

crack•er•jack (krăk′ər-jăk′) also **crack•a•jack** (krăk′ə-) *adj. Slang* Of excellent quality or ability; fine. [Prob. < CRACK, first-rate + JACK.] —**crack′er•jack′** *n.*

crack•ers (krăk′ərz) *adj. Chiefly British Slang* Insane; mad. [Prob. < CRACKER, breakdown.]

crack•head (krăk′hĕd′) *n. Slang* A heavy user of crack cocaine.

crack•ing (krăk′ĭng) *n.* Thermal decomposition of a complex substance, esp. the breaking of petroleum molecules into shorter molecules to extract low-boiling fractions such as gasoline. ❖ *adj.* Excellent; great. ❖ *adv.* Used as an intensive: *a cracking good show.*

crack•le (krăk′əl) *v.* **-led, -ling, -les** —*intr.* **1.** To make a succession of slight sharp snapping noises. **2.** To show liveliness, energy, or intensity. **3.** To craze. —*tr.* **1.** To crush (paper, for example) with sharp snapping sounds. **2.** To craze (china, for example). ❖ *n.* **1.** The act or sound of crackling. **2a.** A network of fine cracks on the surface of glazed pottery, china, or glassware. **b.** Crackleware. [Frequentative of CRACK.]

crack•le•ware (krăk′əl-wâr′) *n.* Glazed pottery or glassware bearing a decorative surface network of fine cracks.

crack•ling (krăk′lĭng) *n.* **1.** A succession of slight sharp snapping noises. **2. cracklings** The crisp bits that remain after rendering fat from meat or frying or roasting the skin, esp. of a pig or a goose. [Sense 2, Du. *krakeling* < obsolete Du. *kraeckelingh* < MDu. *krākelinc* < *krāken,* to crack. See CRACKNEL.]

crack•ly (krăk′lē) *adj.* **-li•er, -li•est** Likely to crackle; crisp.

crack•nel (krăk′nəl) *n.* **1.** A hard crisp biscuit. **2. cracknels** Crisp bits of fried pork fat; cracklings. [ME *crakenele,* alteration of OFr. *craquelin* < MDu. *krākelinc,* small cake < *krāken,* to crack.]

crack•pot (krăk′pŏt′) *n.* An eccentric person, esp. one with bizarre ideas. ❖ *adj.* Foolish; harebrained. [CRACK(ED) + POT[1], skull (obsolete).]

crack•up or **crack-up** (krăk′ŭp′) *n. Informal* **1.** A crash, as one involving an airplane. **2.** A mental or physical breakdown.

Crac•ow (krăk′ou, krä′kou, -kōōf) See **Kraków.**

–cracy *suff.* Government; rule: *meritocracy.* [Fr. -*cratie* < OFr. < LLat. -*cratia* < Gk. -*kratiā* < *kratos,* strength, power.]

cra•dle (krād′l) *n.* **1.** A small low bed for an infant, often furnished with rockers. **2a.** The earliest period of life: *had an interest in music almost from the cradle.* **b.** A place of origin; a birthplace: *the cradle of civilization.* **3a.** A framework of wood or metal used to support something. **b.** A framework used to protect an injured limb. **4.** A low flat framework that rolls on casters, used by a mechanic working beneath an automobile. **5.** The part of a telephone that contains the connecting switch upon which the receiver and mouthpiece unit is supported. **6a.** A frame projecting above a scythe, used to catch grain as it is cut. **b.** A scythe equipped with such a frame. **7.** A boxlike device furnished with rockers, used for washing gold-bearing dirt. ❖ *v.* **-dled, -dling, -dles** —*tr.* **1a.** To place or retain in or as if in a cradle. **b.** To care for or nurture in infancy. **c.** To hold or support protectively: *cradled the cat in his arms.* **2.** To reap (grain) with a cradle. **3.** To place or support (a ship, for example) in a cradle. **4.** To wash (gold-bearing dirt) in a cradle. —*intr. Obsolete* To lie in or as if in a cradle. [ME *cradel* < OE.] —**cra′dler** *n.*

cradle cap *n.* A form of dermatitis that occurs in infants and is characterized by heavy yellow crusted lesions on the scalp.

cra•dle•song (krād′l-sông′, -sŏng′) *n.* A lullaby.

cra•dle-to-grave (krād′l-tə-grāv′) *adj.* Present or in effect throughout a person's lifetime: *cradle-to-grave health insurance.*

craft (krăft) *n.* **1.** Skill in doing or making something, as in the arts; proficiency. **2.** Skill in evasion or deception; guile. **3a.** An occupation or trade requiring manual dexterity or skilled artistry. **b.** The membership of such an occupation or trade; guild. **4.** *pl.* **craft** A boat, ship, or aircraft. ❖ *tr.v.* **craft•ed, craft•ing, crafts 1.** To make by hand. **2.** To make or construct (something) in a manner suggesting great care or ingenuity. [ME < OE *cræft.*] —**craft′er** *n.*

crafts•man (krăfts′mən) *n.* A man who practices a craft with great skill. —**crafts′man•like′** *adj.* —**crafts′man•ly** *adj.* —**crafts′man•ship′** *n.*

crafts•per•son (krăfts′pûr′sən) *n.* A craftsman or a craftswoman; an artisan.

crafts•wom•an (krăfts′wōōm′ən) *n.* A woman who practices a craft with great skill.

craft union *n.* A labor union limited in membership to workers engaged in the same craft.

craft•work (krăft′wûrk′) *n.* Work made or done by craftspeople. —**craft′work′er** *n.*

craft•y (krăf′tē) *adj.* **-i•er, -i•est 1.** Skilled in or marked by underhandedness, deviousness, or deception. **2.** *Chiefly British* Skillful; dexterous. [ME < OE *cræftig,* strong, skillful < *cræft,* skill.] —**craft′i•ly** *adv.* —**craft′i•ness** *n.*

crag (krăg) *n.* A steep rugged mass of rock projecting upward or outward. [ME < Welsh *craig* or Sc. Gael. *creagh.*] —**crag′ged** (krăg′ĭd) *adj.*

crag•gy (krăg′ē) *adj.* **-gi•er, -gi•est 1.** Having crags. **2.** Rugged and uneven. —**crag′gi•ly** *adv.* —**crag′gi•ness** *n.*

Craig (krăg), **Edward Gordon** 1872–1966. British theatrical producer, director, and designer known for his innovative productions and simplified stage designs.

Crai•gie (krā′gē), Sir **William Alexander** 1876–1957. British lexicographer and philologist who was joint editor of the *Oxford English Dictionary* (1901–33).

Cra•io•va (krä-yō′və, krä-yō′vä) A city of SW Romania W of Bucharest; on the site of a Roman settlement. Pop. 303,033.

crake (krāk) *n.* Any of several short-billed birds of the family Rallidae, such as the corncrake. [ME, crow, prob. < ON *krāka.*]

cram (krăm) *v.* **crammed, cram•ming, crams** —*tr.* **1.** To force, press, or squeeze into an insufficient space; stuff. **2.** To fill too tightly. **3a.** To gorge with food. **b.** To eat quickly and greedily. **4.** *Informal* To prepare (students) hastily for an impending examination. —*intr.* **1.** To gorge oneself with food. **2.** *Informal* To study hastily for an impending examination. ❖ *n.* **1.** A group that has been crammed together; a crush. **2.** *Informal* Hasty study for an impending examination. [ME *crammen* < OE *crammian.*] —**cram′mer** *n.*

cram•be (krăm′bē) *n.* Any of certain Old World annual plants of the genus *Crambe* in the mustard family, whose seeds yield a useful oil. [Lat. *crambē*, cabbage < Gk. *krambē*.]

cram·bo (krăm′bō) *n., pl.* **-boes** or **-bos** **1.** A word game in which a player or team must give a rhyme for a word or line presented by the opposing player or team. **2.** Doggerel. [Obsolete *crambe*, cabbage < Lat. *crambē (repetīta)*, (warmed-over) cabbage, said of pedestrian writing < Gk. *krambē*.]

cramp¹ (krămp) *n.* **1.** A sudden, involuntary, spasmodic muscular contraction causing severe pain, often resulting from strain or chill. **2.** A temporary partial paralysis of habitually or excessively used muscles. **3. cramps** Spasmodic contractions of the uterus, such as those occurring during menstruation or labor, usu. causing pain in the abdomen. ❖ *v.* **cramped, cramp·ing, cramps** —*tr.* To affect with or as if with a cramp. —*intr.* To suffer from or experience cramps. [ME *crampe* < OFr., of Gmc. orig.]

cramp² (krămp) *n.* **1.** An adjustable frame to hold pieces together; a clamp. **2.** A cramp iron. **3.** A compressing or restraining force, influence, or thing. **4.** A confined position or part. ❖ *tr.v.* **cramped, cramp·ing, cramps** **1.** To hold together with a cramp. **2a.** To shut in so closely as to restrict the physical freedom of. **b.** To confine; restrict. **3a.** To steer (the wheels of a vehicle) to make a turn. **b.** To jam (a wheel) by a short turn. ❖ *adj.* **1.** Restricted; narrowed. **2.** Difficult to read or decipher. —*idiom:* **cramp (one's) style** To restrict or prevent from free action or expression. [ME *crampe*, prob. < MDu., hook, cramp. Adj., prob. akin to Icel. *krappr*, constrained, tight, and OHGer. *cramf*, squeezed.]

cramped (krămpt) *adj.* **1.** Uncomfortably small or restricted: *cramped living quarters.* **2.** Small and difficult to read: *cramped handwriting.*

cramp·fish (krămp′fĭsh′) *n., pl.* **crampfish** or **-fish·es** See **electric ray.** [< CRAMP¹.]

cramp iron *n.* A bar, usu. of iron, with right-angle bends at both ends, used for holding together stones, timber, and other materials used in building.

cram·pon (krăm′pŏn′, -pən) *n.* **1.** A hinged pair of curved iron bars for raising heavy objects. Often used in the plural. **2.** A spiked iron or steel framework attached to the bottom of a shoe or boot to prevent slipping when walking or climbing on ice and snow. Often used in the plural. [ME < OFr., of Gmc. orig.]

Cra·nach (krä′näкн) *n.* **Lucas** Known as "the Elder." 1472–1553. German painter and engraver noted for his religious works.

cran·ber·ry (krăn′bĕr′ē) *n.* **1.** A mat-forming evergreen shrub (*Vaccinium macrocarpum*) of eastern North America. **2.** The tart red berries of this plant, used in sauces, jellies, relishes, and beverages. **3.** Any of several similar or related plants, esp. *V. oxycoccos.* [Partial transl. of LGer. *Kraanbere* : *Kraan*, crane (< MLGer. *kran*) + *bere*, berry.]

cranberry bush *n.* A North American shrub (*Viburnum trilobum*) having white flower clusters and scarlet fruit.

crane (krān) *n.* **1a.** Any of various large wading birds of the family Gruidae, having a long neck, long legs, and a long bill. **b.** A similar bird, such as a heron. **2.** A machine for hoisting and moving heavy objects by means of cables attached to a movable boom. **3.** Any of various devices with a swinging arm. ❖ *v.* **craned, cran·ing, cranes** —*tr.* **1.** To hoist or move with or as if with a crane. **2.** To strain and stretch (the neck, for example) in order to see better. —*intr.* **1.** To stretch one's neck toward something for a better view. **2.** To be irresolute; hesitate. [ME < OE *cran.*]

Crane, (Harold) Hart 1899–1932. Amer. poet whose works include *The Bridge* (1930).

Crane, Stephen 1871–1900. Amer. writer best known for *The Red Badge of Courage* (1895).

crane fly *n.* Any of numerous long-legged, slender-bodied flies of the family Tipulidae, resembling a large mosquito.

cranes·bill (krānz′bĭl′) *n.* See **geranium 1.**

cra·ni·a (krā′nē-ə) *n.* A plural of **cranium.**

cra·ni·al (krā′nē-əl) *adj.* Of or relating to the skull or cranium. [< CRANIUM.] —**cra′ni·al·ly** *adv.*

cranial index *n.* The ratio of the maximum breadth to the maximum length of the skull, multiplied by 100.

cranial nerve *n.* Any of several nerves that arise in pairs from the brain stem and reach the periphery through openings in the skull.

cra·ni·ate (krā′nē-ĭt, -āt′) *adj.* Having a skull or cranium. ❖ *n.* An animal or a human having a skull or cranium.

cra·ni·ec·to·my (krā′nē-ĕk′tə-mē) *n., pl.* **-mies** Surgical removal of a portion of the cranium.

cranio– or **crani–** *pref.* Cranium: *craniometer.* [< CRANIUM.]

cra·ni·o·cer·e·bral (krā′nē-ō-sĕr′ə-brəl, -sə-rē′brəl) *adj.* Of or relating to both the cranium and the cerebrum.

cra·ni·o·fa·cial (krā′nē-ō-fā′shəl) *adj.* Of or involving both the cranium and the face: *craniofacial surgery.*

cra·ni·ol·o·gy (krā′nē-ŏl′ə-jē) *n.* The scientific study of the skull, esp. in humans. —**cra′ni·o·log′i·cal** (-ə-lŏj′ĭ-kəl) *adj.* —**cra′ni·o·log′i·cal·ly** *adv.* —**cra′ni·ol′o·gist** *n.*

cra·ni·om·e·ter (krā′nē-ŏm′ĭ-tər) *n.* An instrument or device used to measure the skull. —**cra′ni·o·met′ric** (-ə-mĕt′rĭk), **cra′ni·o·met′ri·cal** *adj.*

cra·ni·om·e·try (krā′nē-ŏm′ĭ-trē) *n.* Measurement of the skull to determine its characteristics.

cra·ni·o·sa·cral (krā′nē-ō-sā′krəl, -săk′rəl) *adj.* **1.** Of or associated with both the cranium and the sacrum. **2.** Of or relating to the parasympathetic nervous system.

crampon
climber's boots equipped
with crampons

crappie
white crappie
Pomoxis annularis

cra·ni·ot·o·my (krā′nē-ŏt′ə-mē) *n., pl.* **-mies** **1.** Surgical incision into the skull. **2.** The breaking of the fetal skull to reduce it for removal when normal delivery is not possible.

cra·ni·um (krā′nē-əm) *n., pl.* **-ni·ums** or **-ni·a** (-nē-ə) **1.** The skull of a vertebrate. **2.** The portion of the skull enclosing the brain; the braincase. [ME *craneum* < Med.Lat. *crānium* < Gk. *krānion.* See **ker-¹** in App.]

crank¹ (krăngk) *n.* **1.** A device for transmitting rotary motion, consisting of a handle or arm attached at right angles to a shaft. **2.** A clever turn of speech; a verbal conceit: *quips and cranks.* **3.** A peculiar or eccentric idea or action. **4.** *Informal* **a.** A grouchy person. **b.** An eccentric person, esp. one who is unduly zealous. **5.** *Slang* Methamphetamine. ❖ *v.* **cranked, crank·ing, cranks** —*tr.* **1a.** To start or operate (an engine, for example) by turning a handle. **b.** To move or operate (a window, for example) by or as if by turning a handle. **2.** To make into the shape of a crank; bend. **3.** To provide with a handle that is used in turning. —*intr.* **1.** To turn a handle. **2.** To wind in a zigzagging course. ❖ *adj.* Of, being, or produced by an eccentric person. —*phrasal verbs:* **crank out** To produce, esp. mechanically and rapidly. **crank up 1.** To cause to start or get started. **2.** To cause to intensify: *cranks up the sound.* [ME < OE *cranc-*, as in *crancstæf*, weaving implement.]

crank² (krăngk) *adj. Nautical* Liable to capsize; unstable. [?]

crank·case (krăngk′kās′) *n.* The metal case enclosing the crankshaft and associated parts in a reciprocating engine.

crank·pin also **crank pin** (krăngk′pĭn′) *n.* A bar or cylinder on a crank that attaches to a connecting rod.

crank·shaft (krăngk′shăft′) *n.* A shaft that turns or is turned by a crank.

crank·y¹ (krăng′kē) *adj.* **-i·er, -i·est** **1.** Having a bad disposition; peevish. **2.** Having eccentric ways; odd. **3.** Full of bends and turns; crooked. **4.** Working unpredictably; erratic. **5.** Rickety; loose. —**crank′i·ly** *adv.* —**crank′i·ness** *n.*

crank·y² (krăng′kē) *adj.* **-i·er, -i·est** *Nautical* Liable to capsize.

Cran·mer (krăn′mər), **Thomas** 1489–1556. English prelate who as archbishop of Canterbury (1533–53) revised the *Book of Common Prayer* (1552). Under Mary I, a Roman Catholic, he was convicted of heresy and burned at the stake.

cran·nog (krăn′əg) *n.* An ancient Irish dwelling or fort built on an artificial island in a lake or marsh. [Ir.Gael. *crannóg*, wooden structure, pole < MIr. *crannóc* < OIr. < *crann*, tree.]

cran·ny (krăn′ē) *n., pl.* **-nies** A small opening, as in a wall or rock face; a crevice. [ME *crani*, perh. alteration of OFr. *cren, cran*, notch < *crener*, to notch.] —**cran′nied** *adj.*

Cran·ston (krăn′stən) A city of E-central RI S of Providence; settled in 1636. Pop. 79,269.

crap¹ (krăp) *Vulgar Slang* *n.* **1.** Excrement. **2.** An act of defecating. **3.** Worthless nonsense; rubbish. **4.** Cheap or shoddy material. **5.** Disorganized items; clutter. **6.** Insolent behavior or talk. ❖ *intr.v.* **crapped, crap·ping, craps** To defecate. ❖ *interj.* Used to express anger or displeasure. [ME *crappe*, chaff < OFr. *crappe* < Med.Lat. *crappa*, perh. of Gmc. orig.]

crap² (krăp) *n.* **1.** See **craps. 2.** A losing first throw in the game of craps. ❖ *v.* **crapped, crap·ping, craps** To make a losing throw in the game of craps. [Back-formation < CRAPS.]

crape (krāp) *n.* **1.** See **crepe 1. 2.** A black band worn in mourning. ❖ *tr.v.* **craped, crap·ing, crapes** To cover or drape with or as if with crepe. [Alteration of Fr. *crêpe.* See CREPE.]

crape·hang·er (krāp′hăng′gər) *n.* A morose, gloomy, or pessimistic person.

crape jasmine *n.* An evergreen shrub (*Tabernaemontana divaricata*) native to India and having fragrant white flowers.

crape myrtle also **crepe myrtle** *n.* A deciduous shrub (*Lagerstroemia indica*) native to China and having variously colored flowers with crinkled petals.

crap·per (krăp′ər) *n.* *Vulgar Slang* A toilet. [< CRAP¹.]

crap·pie (krŏp′ē) *n., pl.* **-pies** Either of two edible North American sunfishes, the black crappie (*Pomoxis nigromaculatus*) or the white crappie (*P. annularis*). [Canadian Fr. *crapet.*]

crap·py (krăp′ē) *adj.* **-pi·er, -pi·est** *Vulgar Slang* **1.** Inferior; worthless. **2.** Miserable; wretched. **3.** Mean; contemptible. [< CRAP¹.]

craps (krăps) *pl.n.* (*used with a sing. or pl. verb*) **1.** A gambling game played with two dice in which a first throw of 7 or 11 wins. **2.** A losing throw in this game. [Louisiana Fr., game of hazard < E. *crabs*, lowest throw in hazard < CRAB¹ or CRAP².]

crap·shoot (krăp′shoot′) *n. Slang* A risky enterprise.

crap·shoot·er (krăp′shoo′tər) *n.* One who plays craps.

crap·u·lence (krăp′yə-ləns) *n.* **1.** Sickness caused by excessive eating or drinking. **2.** Excessive indulgence; intemperance. [< CRAPULENT, sick from gluttony < LLat. *crāpulentus*, very drunk < Lat. *crāpula*, intoxication < Gk. *kraipalē*.] —**crap′u·lent** *adj.* —**crap′u·lous** *adj.*

crash¹ (krăsh) *v.* **crashed, crash·ing, crash·es** —*intr.* **1a.** To break violently or noisily; smash. **b.** To undergo sudden damage or destruction on impact: *Their car crashed into a guardrail.* **2.** To make a sudden loud noise: *breakers crashing against the rocks.* **3.** To move noisily or so as to cause damage: *went crashing through the woods.* **4.** To undergo a sudden severe downturn: *The stock market crashed.* **5.** *Computer Science* To stop functioning due to a crash. **6.** *Slang* To undergo a period esp. of depression after drug-taking. **7.** *Slang* **a.** To find temporary lodging or shelter. **b.** To go to sleep. —*tr.* **1.** To cause to crash. **2.** To dash to pieces; smash. **3.** *Informal* To join or enter (a party, for example) without invitation. ❖ *n.* **1.** A sudden loud noise, as of an object breaking. **2a.** A smashing to pieces. **b.** A collision, as between two automobiles. **3.** A sudden severe downturn: *a population crash.* **4.** *Computer Science* **a.** A sudden failure of a hard drive caused by damaging contact between the head and the storage surface, often resulting in the loss of data on the drive. **b.** A sudden failure of a program or operating system, usu. without serious consequences. **5.** *Slang* Mental depression after drug-taking. ❖ *adj. Informal* Of or characterized by an intensive effort to produce or accomplish: *a crash diet.* [ME *crasschen*; prob. akin to *crasen*, to shatter. See CRAZE.] —**crash′er** *n.*

crash[2] (krăsh) *n.* **1.** A coarse, light, unevenly woven fabric of cotton or linen, used for towels and curtains. **2.** Starched reinforced fabric used to strengthen the binding or the spine of a book. [< Russ. *krashenina*, colored linen < *krashenie*, coloring < *krasit′*, to color.]

Crash•aw (krăsh′ô), **Richard** 1613?–49. English metaphysical poet whose works include *Steps to the Temple* (1646).

crash dive *n.* A rapid dive made by a submarine, esp. in an emergency. —**crash′-dive′** (krăsh′dīv′) *v.*

crash helmet *n.* A padded helmet worn to protect the head.

crash•ing (krăsh′ĭng) *adj.* Total; absolute: *a crashing bore.*

crash-land (krăsh′lănd′) *v.* **-land•ed, -land•ing, -lands** —*tr.* To land (an aircraft or spacecraft) under emergency conditions, usu. with damage to the craft. —*intr.* To crash-land an aircraft or spacecraft. —**crash landing** *n.*

crash pad *n.* **1.** Padding inside vehicles for protecting occupants in the event of an accident or sudden stop. **2.** *Slang* A place affording free and usu. temporary lodging.

crash•wor•thy (krăsh′wûr′*th*ē) *adj.* Capable of withstanding the effects of a crash. —**crash′wor′thi•ness** *n.*

crass (krăs) *adj.* **crass•er, crass•est** So crude and unrefined as to be lacking in discrimination and sensibility. [Lat. *crassus*, dense.] —**crass′i•tude′** (-ĭ-to͞od′, -tyo͞od′), **crass′ness** *n.* —**crass′ly** *adv.*

Cras•sus (krăs′əs), **Marcus Licinius** 115?–53 B.C. Roman politician and general who joined Julius Caesar and Pompey in the first triumvirate to challenge the senate's power (60).

-crat *suff.* A participant in or supporter of a specified form of government: *technocrat.* [Fr. *-crate* < Gk. *-kratēs*, ruler < *kratos*, strength, power. See –CRACY.]

crate (krāt) *n.* **1.** A container, such as a slatted wooden case, used for storing or shipping. **2.** *Slang* An old rickety vehicle, esp. a decrepit automobile or aircraft. ❖ *tr.v.* **crat•ed, crat•ing, crates** To pack into a crate. [Lat. *crātis*, wickerwork.]

cra•ter (krā′tər) *n.* **1.** A bowl-shaped depression at the mouth of a volcano or geyser. **2a.** A bowl-shaped depression in a surface made by an explosion or the impact of a body, such as a meteoroid. **b.** A pit; a hollow. **3.** Variant of **krater. 4. Crater** A constellation in the Southern Hemisphere near Hydra and Corvus. ❖ *v.* **-tered, -ter•ing, -ters** —*tr.* To make craters in. —*intr.* **1.** To form a crater or craters. **2.** *Slang* **a.** To fall and crash violently from a great height. **b.** To fail utterly. [Lat. *crātēr* < Gk. *krātēr*, mixing vessel.]

Crater Lake A lake of SW OR in a volcanic crater of the Cascade Range.

cra•ton (krā′tŏn′) *n.* A large portion of a continental plate that has been relatively undisturbed since the Precambrian era and includes both shield and platform layers. [Ger. *Kraton* < Gk. *kratos*, power.] —**cra•ton′ic** (krə-tŏn′ĭk) *adj.*

cra•vat (krə-văt′) *n.* A scarf or band of fabric worn around the neck as a tie. [Fr. *cravate*, Croatian mercenary necktie < *Cravate*, a Croatian < Ger. dialectal *Krabate* < Serbo-Croatian *Hrvāt*.]

crave (krāv) *v.* **craved, crav•ing, craves** —*tr.* **1.** To have an intense desire for. See Syns at **desire. 2.** To need urgently; require. **3.** To beg earnestly for; implore. —*intr.* To have an eager or intense desire. [ME *craven* < OE *crafian*, to beg.] —**crav′er** *n.*

cra•ven (krā′vən) *adj.* Characterized by abject fear; cowardly. ❖ *n.* A coward. [ME *cravant*, perh. < OFr. *crevant*, pr. part. of *crever*, to burst < Lat. *crepāre*, to break.] —**cra′ven•ly** *adv.* —**cra′ven•ness** *n.*

crav•ing (krā′vĭng) *n.* A consuming desire; a yearning.

craw (krô) *n.* **1.** The crop of a bird or insect. **2.** The stomach of an animal. —***idiom:* stick in (one's) craw** To cause one to feel abiding discontent and resentment. [ME *crawe*.]

craw•dad (krô′dăd′) *n. Chiefly Southern & Western US* See **crayfish** 1. [CRAW(FISH) + DAD.]

craw•fish (krô′fĭsh′) *n. Chiefly Southern & Midland US* Variant of **crayfish.** ❖ *intr.v.* **-fished, -fish•ing, -fish•es** *Informal* To withdraw from an undertaking.

Craw•ford (krô′fərd), **Joan** 1908–77. Amer. actress noted for her performances in films such as *Mildred Pierce* (1945).

Crawford, Thomas 1814–57. Amer. sculptor whose works include *Armed Freedom* atop the US Capitol.

crawl[1] (krôl) *intr.v.* **crawled, crawl•ing, crawls 1.** To move slowly on the hands and knees or by dragging the body along the ground; creep. **2.** To advance slowly, feebly, laboriously, or with frequent stops. **3.** To proceed or act servilely. **4.** To be or feel as if swarming or covered with moving things. See Syns at **teem[1]. 5.** To swim the crawl. ❖ *n.* **1.** The action of crawling. **2.** An extremely slow pace. **3.** *Sports* A rapid swimming stroke consisting of alternating overarm strokes and a flutter kick. **4.** Words or figures that move across, up, or down a movie or television screen. [ME *craulen* < ON *krafla.* See **gerbh-** in App.] —**crawl′ing•ly** *adv.*

crawl[2] (krôl) *n.* A pen in shallow water, as for confining fish or turtles. [Afr. *kraal*, enclosure for animals. See KRAAL.]

crawl•er (krô′lər) *n.* **1.** One that crawls, esp. an early form of certain insect larvae. **2.** A vehicle, such as a bulldozer, that moves on continuous belts of metal plates.

crawl•space or **crawl space** (krôl′spās) *n.* A low or narrow space, such as one beneath the floor that gives workers access to plumbing or wiring equipment.

crawl•y (krô′lē) *adj.* **-i•er, -i•est** *Informal* **1.** Creepy. **2.** Feeling as if covered with moving things.

cray•fish (krā′fĭsh′) also **craw•fish** (krô′-) *n., pl.* **crayfish** or **-fish•es** also **crawfish** or **-fish•es 1.** Any of various freshwater crustaceans of the genera *Cambarus* and *Astacus*, resembling a lobster but considerably smaller. **2.** See **spiny lobster.** [By folk ety. < ME *crevise* < OFr. *crevice*, perh. < OHGer. *krebiz*, edible crustacean. See **gerbh-** in App.]

cray•on (krā′ŏn′, -ən) *n.* **1.** A stick of colored wax, charcoal, or chalk, used for drawing. **2.** A drawing made with one of these sticks. ❖ *tr.v.* **-oned, -on•ing, -ons** To draw, color, or decorate with a crayon. [Fr., dim. of *craie*, chalk < Lat. *crēta*.] —**cray′on•ist** (-ə-nĭst) *n.*

craze (krāz) *v.* **crazed, craz•ing, craz•es** —*tr.* **1.** To cause to become mentally deranged or obsessed. **2.** To produce a network of fine cracks in the surface or glaze of. —*intr.* **1.** To become crazed. **2.** To become covered with fine cracks. ❖ *n.* **1.** A short-lived popular fashion; a fad. **2.** A fine crack in a surface or glaze. [ME *crasen*, to shatter, of Scand. orig.]

cra•zy (krā′zē) *adj.* **-zi•er, -zi•est 1.** Affected with madness; insane. **2.** *Informal* Departing from proportion or moderation, esp.: **a.** Possessed by enthusiasm or excitement. **b.** Immoderately fond; infatuated. **c.** Intensely involved or preoccupied. **d.** Foolish or impractical; senseless. ❖ *n., pl.* **-zies** One who is or appears insane. —***idiom:* like crazy** *Informal* To an exceeding degree. —**cra′zi•ly** *adv.* —**cra′zi•ness** *n.*

crazy bone *n. Informal* The funny bone.

Crazy Horse Orig. Tashunca-Uitco. 1849?–77. Sioux leader who resisted the encroachment of whites in the Black Hills and joined Sitting Bull at the Battle of Little Bighorn (1876).

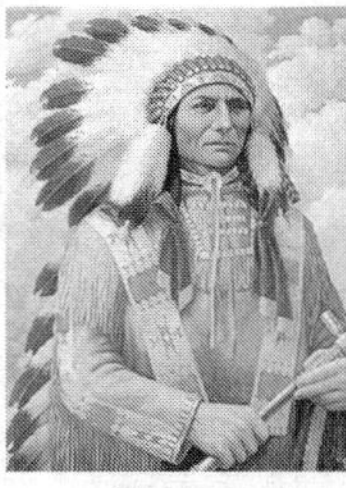

Crazy Horse
1940 painting by Robert Lindneux (1871–1970)

crazy quilt *n.* **1.** A patchwork quilt of pieces of cloth of various shapes, colors, and sizes, sewn together in an irregular pattern. **2.** A disorderly mixture; a hodgepodge.

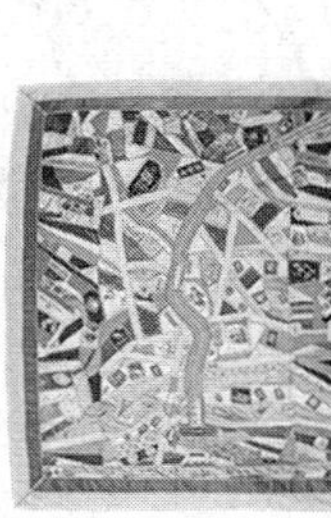

crazy quilt
c. 1885

cra•zy•weed (krā′zē-wēd′) *n.* See **locoweed.**

C-re•ac•tive protein (sē′rē-ăk′tĭv) *n.* A globulin that appears in the blood in certain acute inflammatory conditions, such as rheumatic fever. [*C-(polysaccharide) reactive.*]

creak (krēk) *intr.v.* **creaked, creak•ing, creaks 1.** To make a grating or squeaking sound. **2.** To move with a creaking sound. ❖ *n.* A grating or squeaking sound. [ME *creken*, to croak, complain, of imit. orig.] —**creak′ing•ly** *adv.*

creak•y (krē′kē) *adj.* **-i•er, -i•est 1.** Tending to creak. **2.** Shaky or infirm, as with age; decrepit. —**creak′i•ly** *adv.* —**creak′i•ness** *n.*

cream (krēm) *n.* **1a.** The yellowish fatty component of unhomogenized milk that tends to accumulate at the surface. **b.** Any of various substances resembling or containing cream: *hand cream.* **2.** A pale yellow to yellowish white. **3.** The choicest part: *the cream of the crop.* ❖ *v.* **creamed, cream•ing, creams** —*intr.* **1.** To form cream. **2.** To form foam or froth at the top. —*tr.* **1.** To remove the cream from; skim. **2.** To take or remove (the best part): *creamed off the best jobs for her cronies.* **3.** To beat into a creamy consistency. **4.** To prepare or cook in or with a cream sauce. **5.** To add cream to. **6.** *Slang* **a.** To defeat overwhelmingly. **b.** To damage severely; destroy. [ME *creme* < OFr. *craime* (< LLat. *crāmum*, of Celt. orig.) and < OFr. *cresme* (< Lat. *chrīsma*, an anointing < Gk. *khrīsma*, unguent < *khrīein*, to anoint).] —**cream** *adj.*

cream cheese *n.* A soft white cheese made of cream and milk.

cream•cups (krēm′kŭps′) *pl.n.* (*used with a sing. or pl. verb*) An annual plant (*Platystemon californicus*) native to the southwest United States and Mexico and cultivated for its cream-colored to yellowish flowers.

cream•er (krē′mər) *n.* **1.** A small jug or pitcher for cream. **2.** A machine or device for separating cream from milk. **3.** A refrigerator in which milk is placed to form cream. **4.** A substitute for cream: *a nondairy coffee creamer.*

cream•er•y (krē′mə-rē) *n., pl.* **-ies** An establishment where dairy products are prepared or sold.

cream of tartar *n.* See **potassium bitartrate.**

cream puff also **cream•puff** (krēm′pŭf′) *n.* **1.** A shell of light pastry filled with whipped cream, custard, or ice cream. **2.** *Slang* A weakling. **3.** *Slang* An old, esp. secondhand car in very good condition.

cream sauce *n.* A white sauce made by cooking together a mix-

ă	pat	oi	boy
ā	pay	ou	out
âr	care	o͝o	took
ä	father	o͞o	boot
ĕ	pet	ŭ	cut
ē	be	ûr	urge
ĭ	pit	th	thin
ī	pie	*th*	this
îr	pier	hw	which
ŏ	pot	zh	vision
ō	toe	ə	about, item
ô	paw		

Stress marks:
′ (primary);
′ (secondary), as in
lexicon (lĕk′sĭ-kŏn′)

ture of flour and butter with milk or cream.

cream soda *n.* A sweet carbonated drink with a vanilla flavor.

cream tea *n. Chiefly British* An afternoon refreshment consisting of scones, jam, and clotted cream served with tea.

cream·y (krē′mē) *adj.* **-i·er, -i·est** Rich in or resembling cream. **—cream′i·ly** *adv.* **—cream′i·ness** *n.*

crease (krēs) *n.* **1.** A line made by pressing, folding, or wrinkling. **2.** *Sports* **a.** An area marked off in front of the goal in hockey. **b.** One of the lines in cricket marking off the positions of the bowler and batter or the space between two of these lines. ❖ *v.* **creased, creas·ing, creas·es** —*tr.* **1.** To make a crease in. **2.** To graze or wound superficially with a bullet. —*intr.* To become wrinkled. [Alteration of *creaste*, perh. < ME *creste*, ridge. See CREST.] **—crease′less** *adj.* **—crease′proof′** *adj.* **—creas′er** *n.* **—creas′y** *adj.*

cre·ate (krē-āt′) *tr.v.* **-at·ed, -at·ing, -ates** **1.** To cause to exist; bring into being. See Syns at **found**[1]. **2.** To give rise to; produce: *created a stir.* **3.** To invest with an office or title; appoint. **4.** To produce through artistic or imaginative effort. ❖ *adj. Archaic* Created. [ME *createn* < Lat. *creāre*, *creāt-*. See **ker-**[2] in App.]

cre·a·tine (krē′ə-tēn′, -tĭn) also **cre·a·tin** (-tĭn) *n.* A nitrogenous organic acid, $C_4H_9N_3O_2$, that supplies energy for muscle contraction. [Fr. *créatine* : Gk. *kreas*, *kreat-*, flesh; see **kreuə-** in App. + -INE[2].]

creatine phosphate *n.* See **phosphocreatine.**

cre·at·i·nine (krē-ăt′n-ēn′, -ĭn) *n.* A creatine anhydride, $C_4H_7N_3O$, formed by the metabolism of creatine, that is found in muscle tissue and blood. [CREATIN(E) + -INE[2].]

cre·a·tion (krē-ā′shən) *n.* **1a.** The act of creating. **b.** The fact or state of having been created. **2.** The act of investing with a new office or title. **3a.** The world and all things in it. **b.** All creatures or a class of creatures. **4. Creation** The divine act by which, according to various religious and philosophical traditions, the world was brought into existence. **5.** An original product of human invention or artistic imagination. **—cre·a′tion·al** *adj.*

cre·a·tion·ism (krē-ā′shə-nĭz′əm) *n.* Belief in the literal interpretation of the account of the creation of the universe related in the Bible. **—cre·a′tion·ist** *adj. & n.*

creation science *n.* **1.** The effort to provide scientific evidence supporting the account of the creation of the universe related in the Bible. **2.** Creationism. **—creation scientist** *n.*

cre·a·tive (krē-ā′tĭv) *adj.* **1.** Having the ability or power to create. **2.** Productive; creating. **3.** Characterized by originality and expressiveness; imaginative. **—cre·a′tive·ly** *adv.* **—cre·a′tiv·i·ty** (-ĭ-tē), **cre·a′tive·ness** *n.*

cre·a·tor (krē-ā′tər) *n.* **1.** One that creates. **2. Creator** God.

crea·ture (krē′chər) *n.* **1.** Something created. **2a.** A living being, esp. an animal: *land creatures.* **b.** A human. **c.** An imaginary or fantastical being: *mythological creatures.* **3.** One dependent on or subservient to another; a tool. **—crea′tur·al** *adj.* **—crea′ture·li·ness** *n.* **—crea′ture·ly** *adj.*

creature comfort *n.* Something that contributes to physical comfort.

crèche (krĕsh) *n.* **1.** A representation of the Nativity, usu. with statues or figurines. **2.** A foundling hospital. **3.** *Chiefly British* A day nursery. [Fr. < OFr. *cresche*, crib, of Gmc. orig.]

Cré·cy (krĕs′ē, krā-sē′) or **Cré·cy-en-Pon·thieu** (-äN-pôN-tyœ′) A town of N France NW of Amiens; site of the first decisive battle of the Hundred Years' War (Aug. 26, 1346).

cre·dence (krēd′ns) *n.* **1.** Acceptance as true or valid; belief. **2.** Claim to acceptance; trustworthiness. **3.** Recommendation; credentials. **4.** A small table or shelf for the bread, wine, and vessels of the Eucharist when not in use at the altar. [ME < OFr. < Med.Lat. *crēdentia* < Lat. *crēdēns*, *crēdent-*, pr. part. of *crēdere*, to believe. See **kerd-** in App.]

cre·den·tial (krĭ-dĕn′shəl) *n.* **1.** That which entitles one to confidence, credit, or authority. **2. credentials** Evidence or testimonials concerning one's right to credit, confidence, or authority. ❖ *tr.v.* **-tialed, -tial·ing, -tials** To supply with credentials. [< Med.Lat. *crēdentiālis*, giving authority < *crēdentia*, trust. See CREDENCE.]

cre·den·za (krĭ-dĕn′zə) *n.* **1.** A buffet, sideboard, or bookcase, esp. one without legs. **2.** A piece of office furniture having a long flat top and usu. file drawers. [Ital. < Med.Lat. *crēdentia*, trust (poss. < the precautionary tasting of food placed on a sideboard before being served. See CREDENCE.]

cred·i·bil·i·ty (krĕd′ə-bĭl′ĭ-tē) *n.* **1.** The quality, capability, or power to elicit belief. **2.** A capacity for belief.

credibility gap *n.* **1.** Public skepticism about the truth of statements, esp. official claims and pronouncements. **2.** A discrepancy or disparity, esp. between words and actions.

cred·i·ble (krĕd′ə-bəl) *adj.* **1.** Capable of being believed; plausible. See Syns at **plausible.** **2.** Worthy of confidence; reliable. [ME < Lat. *crēdibilis* < *crēdere*, to believe. See **kerd-** in App.] **—cred′i·ble·ness** *n.* **—cred′i·bly** *adv.*

USAGE NOTE *Credible* is widely but incorrectly used where *credulous* would be appropriate. *Credulous* means "believing too readily," as in *He was credulous* (not *credible*) *enough to believe the claims.*

cred·it (krĕd′ĭt) *n.* **1.** Belief or confidence in the truth of some-

thing. **2.** A reputation for sound character or quality; standing. **3.** A source of honor or distinction. **4.** Recognition or approval for an act, ability, or quality. **5.** Influence based on the good opinion or confidence of others. **6.** An acknowledgment of work done. Often used in the plural. **7a.** Official certification or recognition of successful completion of a course of study. **b.** A unit of study so certified. **8.** Reputation for solvency and integrity entitling a person to be trusted in buying or borrowing. **9a.** An arrangement for deferred payment of a loan or purchase. **b.** The terms governing such an arrangement. **c.** The time allowed for deferred payment. **10.** *Accounting* **a.** The deduction of a payment made by a debtor from an amount due. **b.** The right-hand side of an account on which such amounts are entered. **c.** An entry or the sum of the entries on this side. **d.** The positive balance or amount remaining in a person's account. **e.** A credit line. ❖ *tr.v.* **-it·ed, -it·ing, -its** **1.** To believe in; trust. **2a.** To regard as having performed an action or being endowed with a quality. **b.** To ascribe to a person; attribute. **3.** *Accounting* **a.** To enter as a credit. **b.** To make a credit entry in: *credit an account.* **4.** To give or award an educational credit to. **5.** *Archaic* To bring honor or distinction to. [Fr. < OFr. < OItal. *credito* < Lat. *crēditum*, loan < neut. p. part. of *crēdere*, to entrust. See **kerd-** in App.]

cred·it·a·ble (krĕd′ĭ-tə-bəl) *adj.* **1.** Deserving of often limited praise or commendation. **2.** Worthy of belief. **3.** Deserving of commercial credit. **4.** That can be assigned. **—cred′it·a·bil′i·ty, cred′it·a·ble·ness** *n.* **—cred′it·a·bly** *adv.*

credit bureau *n.* An organization that provides credit information on prospective customers.

credit card *n.* A plastic card issued by a bank or business authorizing the holder to buy goods or services on credit.

credit hour *n.* A credit in a school or college, usu. representing one hour of class per week for one term.

credit line *n.* **1.** A line of copy acknowledging the source or origin of a news dispatch, published article, or other work. **2.** The maximum amount of credit given to a customer.

cred·i·tor (krĕd′ĭ-tər) *n.* One to whom money or its equivalent is owed.

credit rating *n.* An estimate of the amount of credit that can be extended to a company or person without undue risk.

credit union *n.* A cooperative organization that makes loans to its members at low interest rates.

cred·it·wor·thy (krĕd′ĭt-wûr′thē) *adj.* Having an acceptable credit rating. **—cred′it·wor′thi·ness** *n.*

cre·do (krē′dō, krā′-) *n., pl.* **-dos** **1.** A creed. **2. Credo a.** The Apostles' Creed or the Nicene Creed. **b.** The musical setting for the Nicene Creed, as in a choral Mass. [ME, the Apostles' Creed < Lat. *crēdō*, I believe (the first word of the Apostles' Creed or the Nicene Creed), first pers. sing. pr. t. of *crēdere*, to believe. See **kerd-** in App.]

cre·du·li·ty (krĭ-dōō′lĭ-tē, -dyōō′-) *n.* A disposition to believe too readily. [ME *credulite* < OFr. < Lat. *crēdulitās* < *crēdulus*, credulous. See CREDULOUS.]

cred·u·lous (krĕj′ə-ləs) *adj.* **1.** Disposed to believe too readily; gullible. **2.** Arising from or characterized by credulity. See Usage Note at **credible.** [< Lat. *crēdulus* < *crēdere*, to believe. See **kerd-** in App.] **—cred′u·lous·ly** *adv.* **—cred′u·lous·ness** *n.*

Cree (krē) *n., pl.* **Cree** or **Crees** **1.** A member of a Native American people inhabiting a large area from eastern Canada west to Alberta and the Great Slave Lake. **2.** The Algonquian language of the Cree. [Fr. *Cris*, shortening of *Cristineaux*, name of a 17th-cent. Cree band < Ojibwa (O Algonquin) *kiristino* < Cree.]

creed (krēd) *n.* **1.** A formal statement of religious belief; a confession of faith. **2.** A system of belief, principles, or opinions. [ME *crede* < OE *crēda* < Lat. *crēdō*, I believe. See CREDO.] **—creed′al, cre·dal** (krēd′l) *adj.*

creek (krēk, krĭk) *n.* **1.** A small stream, often a shallow or intermittent tributary to a river. **2.** A channel or stream running through a salt marsh. **3.** *Chiefly British* A small inlet in a shoreline, extending farther inland than a cove. —*idiom:* **up the creek (without a paddle)** *Informal* In a difficult or inextricable position. [ME *creke*, prob. < ON *kriki*, bend.]

Creek (krēk) *n., pl.* **Creek** or **Creeks** **1a.** A member of a Native American people formerly inhabiting eastern Alabama, southwest Georgia, and northwest Florida and now located in central Oklahoma and southern Alabama. **b.** The Muskogean language of the Creek. **2.** A member of a Native American confederacy made up of the Creek and various smaller southeast tribes. [< the picturesque creeks near which they lived.]

creel (krēl) *n.* **1.** A wicker basket, esp. one used by anglers for carrying fish. **2.** A frame for holding bobbins or spools in a spinning machine. [ME *crel* < OFr. *creille, latticework < Lat. *crātīcula*, gridiron, dim. of *crātis*, wickerwork.]

creep (krēp) *intr.v.* **crept** (krĕpt), **creep·ing, creeps** **1.** To move with the body close to the ground, as on hands and knees. **2a.** To move stealthily or cautiously. **b.** To move or proceed very slowly. **3.** *Botany* **a.** To grow or spread along a surface, rooting at intervals or clinging by means of suckers or tendrils. **b.** To grow horizontally under the ground, as the rhizomes of many plants. **4.** To slip out of place; shift gradually. **5.** To have a tingling sensation, made by or as if by things moving stealthily. ❖ *n.* **1.** The act of creeping; a creeping motion or progress. **2.** *Slang* An annoyingly

crenate
crenate leaf

unpleasant or repulsive person. **3.** A slow flow of metal when under high temperature or great pressure. **4.** A slow change in a characteristic of electronic equipment, such as a decrease in power with continued usage. **5.** *Geology* The slow movement of rock debris and soil down a weathered slope. **6. creeps** *Informal* A sensation of fear or repugnance, as if things were crawling on one's skin. [ME *crepen* < OE *crēopan.*]

creep·er (krē′pər) *n.* **1.** One that creeps. **2.** *Botany* A plant that spreads by means of stems that creep. **3.** See **cradle** 4. **4.** A grappling device for dragging bodies of water. **5.** A one-piece fitted garment for an infant. **6. creepers** A metal frame with a spike or spikes, attached to a shoe or boot to prevent slipping, esp. on ice.

creep·ing (krē′pĭng) *adj.* Developing gradually over time.

creeping Char·lie (chär′lē) *n.* See **moneywort.**

creeping eruption *n.* A human skin disease caused by hookworm or roundworm larvae beneath the skin and characterized by eruptions in the form of progressing reddish lines.

creeping Jen·nie also **creeping Jen·ny** (jĕn′ē) *n.* See **moneywort.**

creep·y (krē′pē) *adj.* **-i·er, -i·est** *Informal* **1.** Of or producing a sensation of uneasiness or fear, as of things crawling on one's skin. **2.** Annoyingly unpleasant; repulsive. **—creep′i·ness** *n.*

creese (krēs) *n.* Variant of **kris.**

cre·mains (krĭ-mānz′) *pl.n.* The ashes that remain after cremation of a corpse. [Blend of CREMATED and REMAINS.]

cre·mate (krē′māt, krĭ-māt′) *tr.v.* **-mat·ed, -mat·ing, -mates** To incinerate (a corpse). [Lat. *cremāre, cremāt-.*] **—cre·ma′tion** (krĭ-mā′shən) *n.* **—cre′ma′tor** *n.*

cre·ma·to·ri·um (krē′mə-tôr′ē-əm, -tōr′-) *n., pl.* **-to·ri·ums** or **-to·ri·a** (-tôr′ē-ə, -tōr′-) A furnace or establishment for the incineration of corpses.

cre·ma·to·ry (krē′mə-tôr′ē, -tōr′ē, krĕm′ə-) *n., pl.* **-ries** A crematorium. ❖ *adj.* Of or relating to cremation.

crème brû·lée (krĕm′ broō-lā′) *n.* A custard with a crust of caramelized sugar. [Fr., burnt cream : *crème,* cream + *brûlée,* burnt, fem. p. part. of *brûler,* to burn.]

crème car·a·mel (krĕm′ kăr′ə-mĕl′, krĕm′ kăr′ə-məl) *n.* A custard that is baked in a caramel coating and served chilled. [Fr. : *crème,* cream + *caramel,* caramel.]

crème de ca·cao (krĕm′ də kə-kou′, kə-kä′ō, krĕm′ də kō′kō′) *n.* A sweet white or brownish liqueur with a chocolate flavor. [Fr. : *crème,* cream + *de,* of + *cacao,* cacao.]

crème de la crème (krĕm′ də lä krĕm′) *n.* **1.** Something superlative. **2.** People of the highest social level. [Fr. : *crème,* cream + *de, of* + *la,* the + *crème,* cream.]

crème de menthe (krĕm′ də mänt′, mĕnth′, mĭnt′) *n.* A sweet green or white liqueur flavored with mint. [Fr. : *crème,* cream + *de,* of + *menthe,* mint.]

crème fraîche (krĕm′ frĕsh′) *n.* Slightly fermented and thickened cream. [Fr. : *crème,* cream + *fraîche,* fresh.]

cre·mi·ni or **cri·mi·ni** (krə-mē′nē) *n., pl.* **-nis** An edible, darkbrown mushroom (*Agaricus bisporus*) with a rounded cap. [Ital.]

cre·nate (krē′nāt′) also **cre·nat·ed** (-nā′tĭd) *adj.* Having a margin with low rounded or scalloped projections: *a crenate leaf.* [NLat. *crēnātus* < Late Med.Lat. *crēna,* notch < a reading of an uncertain Lat. word in a corrupt passage in Pliny the Elder (influenced by OFr. *cren*).] **—cre′nate′ly** *adv.*

cre·na·tion (krĭ-nā′shən) *n.* **1.** A rounded projection, as on the margin of a shell. **2.** The condition or state of being crenate. **3.** A process in which red blood cells in a hypertonic solution undergo shrinkage and acquire a notched or scalloped surface.

cren·a·ture (krĕn′ə-chər, krē′nə-) *n.* A rounded projection; a crenation.

cren·e·lat·ed also **cren·el·lat·ed** (krĕn′ə-lā′tĭd) *adj.* **1.** Having battlements. **2.** Indented; notched. [Prob. < Fr. *créneler,* to furnish with battlements < OFr. *crenel,* crenelation, dim. of *cren,* notch. See CRANNY.] **—cren′e·la′tion** *n.*

cren·shaw (krĕn′shô′) *n.* A variety of honeydew melon (*Cucumis melo* var. *inodorus*) having a greenish-yellow rind and sweet, usu. salmon-pink flesh. [?]

cren·u·late (krĕn′yə-lĭt, -lāt′) also **cren·u·lat·ed** (-lā′tĭd) *adj.* Having a margin with very small, low, rounded teeth: *a crenulate leaf.* [NLat. *crēnulātus* < *crēnula,* dim. of Med.Lat. *crēna,* notch.] **—cren′u·la′tion** *n.*

cre·o·dont (krē′ə-dŏnt′) *n.* Any of various extinct carnivorous mammals of the suborder Creodonta, of the Paleocene to the Pliocene. [< NLat. *Creodonta,* suborder name : Gk. *kreas,* flesh; see **kreuə-** in App. + Gk. *odous, odont-,* tooth.]

Cre·ole (krē′ōl′) *n.* **1.** A person of European descent born in the West Indies or Spanish America. **2a.** A person descended from or culturally related to the original French settlers of the southern United States, esp. Louisiana. **b.** The French dialect spoken by these people. **3.** A person descended from or culturally related to the Spanish and Portuguese settlers of the Gulf States. **4.** often **creole** A Black slave born in the Americas as opposed to one brought from Africa. **6. creole** A creolized language. **7.** Haitian Creole. ❖ *adj.* **1.** Of, relating to, or characteristic of the Creoles. **2. creole** Cooked with a spicy sauce containing tomatoes, onions, and peppers. [Fr. *créole* < Sp. *criollo,* person native to a locality < Port.

crioulo, dim. of *cria,* person raised in the house, esp. a servant < *criar,* to bring up < Lat. *creāre,* to beget. See **ker-²** in App.]

cre·o·lized language (krē′ə-līzd′) *n.* A language derived from a pidgin but more complex in grammar and vocabulary because it has become the native tongue of a community.

Cre·on (krē′ŏn′) *n. Greek Mythology* The brother of Jocasta and uncle of Antigone who became the king of Thebes after the fall of Oedipus.

cre·o·sol (krē′ə-sôl′, -sôl′, -sōl′) *n.* An aromatic liquid, $C_8H_{10}O_2$, a constituent of creosote. [CREOS(OTE) + -OL¹.]

cre·o·sote (krē′ə-sōt′) *n.* **1.** An oily liquid obtained by the destructive distillation of wood tar and formerly used as an expectorant. **2.** An oily liquid obtained from coal tar and used as a wood preservative and disinfectant. ❖ *tr.v.* **-sot·ed, -sot·ing, -sotes** To treat or paint with creosote. [Ger. *Kreosot* : Gk. *kreas,* flesh; see **kreuə-** in App. + Gk. *sōtēr,* preserver (< *sōzein,* to save).]

creosote bush *n.* Any of several resinous aromatic evergreen shrubs of the genus *Larrea,* esp. *L. tridentata,* a yellow-flowered plant of the southwest United States and Mexico.

crepe also **crêpe** (krāp) *n.* **1.** A light soft thin fabric of silk, cotton, or another fiber, with a crinkled surface. **2.** See **crape** 2. **3.** Crepe paper. **4.** Crepe rubber. **5.** (*also* krĕp) A thin small pancake, often stuffed and rolled up. [Fr. *crêpe* < OFr. *crespe,* curly < Lat. *crispus.*]

crêpe de Chine (krāp′ də shēn′) *n., pl.* **crêpes de Chine** (krāp′) also **crêpe de Chines** (shēn′) A silk crepe used for dresses and blouses. [Fr. : *crêpe,* crepe + *de,* of + *Chine,* China.]

crepe myrtle *n.* Variant of **crape myrtle.**

crepe paper *n.* Crinkled tissue paper, resembling the fabric crepe, used for decorations.

crepe rubber *n.* Rubber with a crinkled texture, used esp. for shoe soles.

crêpes su·zette (krāp′ soō-zĕt′, krĕp′) *n., pl.* **crêpes su·zettes** (-zĕt′) A dessert of crêpes warmed in an orange-butter sauce, often served with a flaming liqueur sauce. [Fr. : *crêpe,* pancake + *Suzette,* Suzy, allegedly after *Suzette* (for Suzanne) Reichenberg (1853–1924), French actress.]

crep·i·tate (krĕp′ĭ-tāt′) *intr.v.* **-tat·ed, -tat·ing, -tates** To make a crackling or popping sound; crackle. [Lat. *crepitāre, crepitāt-,* to crackle, freq. of *crepāre,* to creak.] **—crep′i·tant** (-tənt) *adj.* **—crep′i·ta′tion** *n.*

crept (krĕpt) *v.* Past tense and past participle of **creep.**

cre·pus·cu·lar (krĭ-pŭs′kyə-lər) *adj.* **1.** Of or like twilight; dim. **2.** *Zoology* Becoming active at twilight or before sunrise, as do bats and certain insects and birds.

cre·pus·cule (krĭ-pŭs′kyool) also **cre·pus·cle** (-pŭs′əl) *n.* Twilight. [ME < OFr. < Lat. *crepusculum* < *creper,* dark.]

cres·cen·do (krə-shĕn′dō) *n., pl.* **-dos** or **-di** (-dē) **1.** *Music* **a.** A gradual increase, esp. in the volume or intensity of sound in a passage. **b.** A passage played with a gradual increase in volume or intensity. **2a.** A steady increase in intensity or force. **b.** The climactic point or moment after such a progression. ❖ *adj.* Gradually increasing in volume, force, or intensity. ❖ *adv. Music* With a crescendo. ❖ *intr.v.* **-doed, -do·ing, -does** To build up to or reach a point of great intensity, force, or volume. [Ital., pr. part. of *crescere,* to increase < Lat. *crēscere.* See **ker-²** in App.]

cres·cent (krĕs′ənt) *n.* **1.** The figure of the moon as it appears in its first or last quarter, with concave and convex edges terminating in points. **2.** Something shaped like a crescent. ❖ *adj.* **1.** Crescent-shaped. **2.** Waxing, as the moon; increasing. [ME *cressaunt* < AN, var. of OFr. *creissant* < pr. part. of *creistre,* to grow < Lat. *crēscere.* See **ker-²** in App.] **—cres·cen′tic** (krə-sĕn′tĭk) *adj.*

cre·sol (krē′sôl′, -sôl′, -sōl′) *n.* Any of three isomeric phenols, $CH_3C_6H_4OH$, used in resins and as a disinfectant. [Alteration of CREOSOL.]

cress (krĕs) *n.* **1.** An Old World annual plant (*Lepidium sativum*) in the mustard family, cultivated for its edible seedlings and leaves. **2.** Any of several related plants, such as pennycress and watercress. [ME *cresse* < OE.]

cres·set (krĕs′ĭt) *n.* A metal cup, often suspended on a pole, containing burning oil or pitch and used as a torch. [ME < OFr., alteration of *croisuel,* probable < VLat. *croceolus,* small lamp.]

Cres·si·da (krĕs′ĭ-də) *n.* **1.** A Trojan woman in medieval romances who forsakes her lover Troilus for Diomedes. **2.** A satellite of Uranus.

crest (krĕst) *n.* **1a.** A usu. ornamental tuft, ridge, or similar projection on the head of a bird or other animal. **b.** An elevated, irregularly toothed ridge on the stigmas of certain flowers. **2a.** A ridge or appendage on a plant part, such as on a leaf. **2a.** A plume used as decoration on top of a helmet. **b.** A helmet. **3a.** *Heraldry* A device placed above the shield on a coat of arms. **b.** A representation of such a device. **4a.** The top, as of a wave. **b.** The highest or culminating point; the peak: *the crest of a flood.* **5.** The ridge on a roof. ❖ *v.* **crest·ed, crest·ing, crests** —*tr.* **1.** To decorate or furnish with a crest. **2.** To reach the crest of: *crested the ridge.* —*intr.* **1.** To form into a crest or crests: *waves cresting over the seawall.* **2.** To reach a crest: *The swollen river crested at midnight.* [ME *creste* < OFr. < Lat. *crista.* See **sker-²** in App.]

crest·ed (krĕs′tĭd) *adj.* Having a crest: *a crested black macaque.*

crested wheatgrass *n.* A Eurasian perennial grass (*Agropyron*

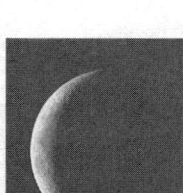

crescent

cristatum) cultivated for pasture and rangeland.

crest·fall·en (krĕst′fô′lən) *adj.* Dispirited and depressed; dejected. —**crest′fall′en·ly** *adv.* —**crest′fall′en·ness** *n.*

crest·ing (krĕs′tĭng) *n.* An ornamental ridge, as on top of a wall or roof.

Cres·tone Needle (krĕs′tōn) A peak, 4,330.1 m (14,197 ft), in the Sangre de Cristo Mts. of S-central CO.

Crestone Peak A mountain, 4,359.7 m (14,294 ft), in the Sangre de Cristo Mts. of S-central CO.

cre·syl (krĕ′sĭl) *n.* See **tolyl.** [CRESO(L) + -YL.]

cre·syl·ic (krĭ-sĭl′ĭk) *adj.* Of or relating to creosote or cresol. [CRES(OL) + -YL + -IC.]

cresylic acid *n.* **1.** Any of several acids derived from petroleum and coal tar that boil above 204°C, contain varying amounts of xylene and cresol, and are used in disinfectants, solvents, and electrical insulation. **2.** A mixture of the three isomers of cresol.

Cre·ta·ceous (krĭ-tā′shəs) *adj.* **1.** Of or belonging to the geologic time of the last period of the Mesozoic Era, characterized by the development of flowering plants and the disappearance of dinosaurs and many other forms of life. See table at **geologic time. 2. cretaceous** Of, containing, or resembling chalk. ❖ *n.* The Cretaceous Period or its deposits. [< Lat. *crētāceus,* chalky < *crēta,* chalk < *Crēta (terra),* Cretan (earth).] —**cre·ta′ceous·ly** *adv.*

Crete (krēt) An island of SE Greece in the E Mediterranean Sea. Its Minoan civilization reached the height of its wealth and power c. 1600 B.C. —**Cre′tan** *adj. & n.*

cre·tic (krē′tĭk) *n.* See **amphimacer.** [Lat. *Crēticus,* of Crete, Cretic foot < *Crēta,* Crete.]

cre·tin (krēt′n) *n.* **1.** A person afflicted with cretinism. **2.** *Offensive Slang* An idiot. [Fr. *crétin* < Fr. dialectal, mentally retarded person < VLat. **christiānus,* human being, poor fellow < Lat. *Chrīstiānus,* Christian. See CHRISTIAN.] —**cre′tin·oid** (-oid′) *adj.* —**cre′tin·ous** (-əs) *adj.*

cre·tin·ism (krēt′n-ĭz′əm) *n.* Congenital hypothyroidism.

cre·tonne (krĭ-tŏn′, krē′tŏn′) *n.* A heavy unglazed cotton, linen, or rayon fabric, colorfully printed and used for draperies and slipcovers. [After *Creton,* a village of NW France.]

Cre·ü·sa (krē-ōō′zə) *n. Greek Mythology* The wife of Aeneas who was lost while fleeing from Troy.

Creutz·feldt-Ja·kob disease (kroits′fĕlt-yä′kôp) *n.* A rare, usu. fatal disease of the brain that occurs most often in middle age and is caused by a slow virus. [After Hans G. *Creutzfeld* (1883–1964) and Alfons M. *Jakob* (1884–1931), German psychiatrists.]

cre·val·le (krĭ-văl′ē) *n.* Any of several fishes of the family Carangidae, such as the crevalle jack. [Alteration of CAVALLA.]

crevalle jack *n.* A food and game fish *(Caranx hippos)* of warm seas having a laterally compressed silvery body.

cre·vasse (krĭ-văs′) *n.* **1.** A deep fissure, as in a glacier; a chasm. **2.** A crack or breach in a dike or levee. ❖ *intr. & tr.v.* **-vassed, -vass·ing, -vass·es** To develop or cause to develop crevasses. [Fr. < OFr. *crevace,* crevice. See CREVICE.]

Crève·coeur (krĕv-kœr′), **Michel Guillaume Jean de** Pen name J. Hector Saint John. 1735–1813. French-born Amer. agriculturalist, writer, and diplomat whose works include *Letters from an American Farmer* (1782).

crev·ice (krĕv′ĭs) *n.* A narrow crack or opening; a fissure or cleft. [ME < OFr. *crevace,* prob. < VLat. **crepācia* < **crepa* < Lat. *crepāre,* to crack.] —**crev′iced** *adj.*

crew¹ (krōō) *n.* **1.** A group of people working together; a gang. **b.** A group of people gathered together temporarily; a crowd. **2a.** All personnel operating or serving aboard a ship. **b.** All of a ship's personnel except the officers. **c.** All personnel operating or serving aboard an aircraft in flight. **3.** *Sports* **a.** A team of rowers, as of a racing shell. **b.** The sport of rowing. ❖ *v.* **crewed, crew·ing, crews** —*intr.* To serve as a member of a crew. —*tr.* To serve as a crew member on (a ship, for example). [ME *creue,* military reinforcement < OFr., increase < fem. p. part. of *creistre,* to grow < Lat. *crēscere.* See ker-² in App.]

crew² (krōō) *v. Chiefly British* A past tense of **crow².**

crew·cut or **crew cut** (krōō′kŭt′) *n.* A closely cropped haircut. [So called because it was worn by rowers.]

crewed (krōōd) *adj.* Operated by an onboard crew.

crew·el (krōō′əl) *n.* Loosely twisted worsted yarn used for fancywork and embroidery. [ME *crule.*]

crew·el·work (krōō′əl-wûrk′) *n.* Needlework made with crewel.

crew neck *n.* **1.** A round close-fitting neckline. **2.** often **crew·neck** (krōō′nĕk′) A garment, esp. a sweater, with such a neckline. [< rowers' similar sweaters.]

crew sock *n.* A warm, usu. ribbed sock.

crib (krĭb) *n.* **1.** A bed with high sides for a young child or baby. **2a.** A small building, usu. with slatted sides, for storing corn. **b.** A rack or trough for fodder; a manger. **c.** A stall for cattle. **3.** A small crude cottage or room. **4.** *Slang* One's home. **5.** A framework to support or strengthen a mine or shaft. **6.** A wicker basket. **7a.** A petty theft. **b.** Plagiarism. **c.** See **pony** 4. **8.** *Games* A set of cards made up from discards by each player in cribbage, used by the dealer. ❖ *v.* **cribbed, crib·bing, cribs** —*tr.* **1.** To confine in or as if in a crib. **2.** To furnish with a crib. **3a.** To plagiarize (an idea or answer, for example). **b.** To steal. —*intr.* To plagiarize;

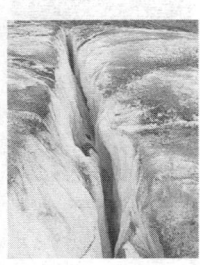

crevasse

cricket²

cheat. [ME, manger < OE *cribb.*] —**crib′ber** *n.*

crib·bage (krĭb′ĭj) *n.* A card game in which the score is kept by inserting pegs into holes arranged in rows on a small board. [< CRIB.]

crib death *n.* See **sudden infant death syndrome.**

crib·ri·form (krĭb′rə-fôrm′) *adj.* Perforated like a sieve. [Lat. *crībrum,* sieve; see krei- in App. + -FORM.]

cri·ce·tid (krī-sē′tĭd, -sĕt′ĭd) *n.* Any of various small rodents of the family Cricetidae, which includes muskrats and gerbils. [< NLat. *Cricetidae,* family name < *Cricetus,* hamster genus < Med.Lat. *cricetus,* hamster, perh. < O Czech *křeček,* dim. of *křeč,* of imit. orig.] —**cri·ce′tid** *adj.*

crick¹ (krĭk) *n.* A painful cramp or muscle spasm, as in the back or neck. ❖ *tr.v.* **cricked, crick·ing, cricks** To cause a crick in by turning or wrenching. [ME *crike.*]

crick² (krĭk) *n. Upper Northern & Western US* Variant of **creek.** See Regional Note at **run.**

Crick, Francis Henry Compton b. 1916. British biologist who with James D. Watson proposed a spiral model, the double helix, for the molecular structure of DNA. They shared a 1962 Nobel Prize.

crick·et¹ (krĭk′ĭt) *n.* Any of various insects of the family Gryllidae, having long antennae and legs adapted for leaping. [ME *criket* < OFr. *criquet* < *criquer,* to click, of imit. orig.]

crick·et² (krĭk′ĭt) *n.* **1.** A game played with bats, a ball, and wickets by 2 teams of 11 players each. **2.** Good sporting behavior and fair conduct: *It's not cricket to cheat.* ❖ *intr.v.* **-et·ed, -et·ing, -ets** To play the game of cricket. [Obsolete Fr. *criquet,* piece of wood < OFr., stick for a bowling game, perh. < MDu. *cricke,* walking stick.] —**crick′et·er, crick′et·eer′** (-ĭ-tîr′) *n.*

crick·et³ (krĭk′ĭt) *n.* A small wooden footstool. [?]

cri·coid (krī′koid′) *n.* A ring-shaped cartilage of the lower larynx that articulates with the thyroid cartilage and arytenoid cartilages. [NLat. *cricoīdēs* < Gk. *krikoeidēs,* ring-shaped : *krikos,* ring + *-oeidēs,* -oid.]

cri de coeur (krē′ də kœr′) *n., pl.* **cris de coeur** (krē′) An impassioned outcry, as of entreaty or protest. [Fr. *cri de cœur* : *cri,* cry + *de,* of + *cœur,* heart.]

cried (krīd) *v.* Past tense and past participle of **cry.**

cri·er (krī′ər) *n.* One that cries, esp.: **a.** An official who announces the orders of a court of law. **b.** A town crier. **c.** A hawker.

cries (krīz) *v.* Third person singular present tense of **cry.** ❖ *n.* Plural of **cry.**

crime (krīm) *n.* **1.** An act committed or omitted in violation of a law forbidding or commanding it and for which punishment is imposed upon conviction. **2.** Unlawful activity. **3.** A serious offense, esp. one in violation of morality. **4.** An unjust, senseless, or disgraceful act or condition: *It's a crime not to visit.* [ME < OFr. < Lat. *crīmen.* See krei- in App.]

Cri·me·a (krī-mē′ə, krĭ-) A region and peninsula of S Ukraine on the Black Sea; annexed by Russia in 1783 and the site of the Crimean War (1853–56). —**Cri·me′an** *adj.*

crim·i·nal (krĭm′ə-nəl) *adj.* **1.** Of, involving, or having the nature of crime. **2.** Relating to the administration of penal law. **3a.** Guilty of crime. **b.** Characteristic of a criminal. **4.** Shameful; disgraceful. ❖ *n.* One that has committed or been legally convicted of a crime. [ME < OFr. *criminel* < LLat. *crīminālis* < Lat. *crīmen, crīmin-,* accusation. See CRIME.] —**crim′i·nal·ly** *adv.*

criminal court *n.* A court empowered to hear and decide on cases involving offenses against criminal law.

crim·i·nal·ist (krĭm′ə-nə-lĭst) *n.* A specialist in the collection and examination of the physical evidence of crime. —**crim′i·nal·is′tics** *n.*

crim·i·nal·i·ty (krĭm′ə-năl′ĭ-tē) *n., pl.* **-ties 1.** The state, quality, or fact of being criminal. **2.** A criminal practice.

crim·i·nal·ize (krĭm′ə-nə-līz′) *tr.v.* **-ized, -iz·ing, -iz·es 1.** To impose a criminal penalty on or for; outlaw. **2.** To treat as a criminal. —**crim′i·nal·i·za′tion** (-lī-zā′shən) *n.*

criminal law *n.* Law that deals with crimes and their punishments.

crim·i·nate (krĭm′ə-nāt′) *tr.v.* **-nat·ed, -nat·ing, -nates** To incriminate. [Lat. *crīminārī, crīmināt-,* to accuse < *crīmen, crīmin-,* accusation. See CRIME.] —**crim′i·na′tion** *n.* —**crim′i·na′tive, crim′i·na·to′ry** (-nə-tôr′ē, -tōr′ē) *adj.* —**crim′i·na′tor** *n.*

cri·mi·ni (krə-mē′nē) *n.* Variant of **cremini.**

crim·i·no·gen·ic (krĭm′ə-nə-jĕn′ĭk) also **crim·o·gen·ic** (krī′mə-) *adj.* Producing or tending to produce crime.

crim·i·nol·o·gy (krĭm′ə-nŏl′ə-jē) *n.* The scientific study of criminal behavior and corrections. [Ital. *criminologia* < Lat. *crīmen, crīmin-,* accusation; see CRIME + Lat. *-logia,* -logy.] —**crim′i·no·log′i·cal** (-nə-lŏj′ĭ-kəl) *adj.* —**crim′i·no·log′i·cal·ly** *adv.* —**crim′i·nol′o·gist** *n.*

crimp¹ (krĭmp) *tr.v.* **crimped, crimp·ing, crimps 1.** To press or pinch into small regular folds or ridges. **2.** To bend or mold into shape. **3.** To cause (hair) to form tight curls or waves. **4.** To have a hampering or obstructive effect on. ❖ *n.* **1.** The act of crimping. **2.** Something made by or as if by crimping, as: **a.** Hair that has been tightly curled or waved. **b.** A series of curls, as of wool fibers. **c.** A crease or bend. **3.** An obstructing or hampering agent or force. [Du. or LGer. *krimpen* < MDu. or MLGer.] —**crimp′er** *n.*

crimp² (krĭmp) *n.* A person who tricks or coerces others into service as sailors or soldiers. ❖ *tr.v.* **crimped, crimp·ing, crimps** To procure (sailors or soldiers) by trickery or coercion. [?]

crimp·y (krĭm′pē) *adj.* **-i·er, -i·est** Full of crimps; wavy. —**crimp′i·ness** *n.*

crim·son (krĭm′zən) *n.* A deep to vivid purplish red to vivid red. ❖ *tr. & intr.v.* **-soned, -son·ing, -sons** To make or become deeply or vividly red. [ME *cremesin,* ult. < Ar. *qirmizī* < *qirmiz,* kermes insect. See KERMES.] —**crim′son** *adj.*

cringe (krĭnj) *intr.v.* **cringed, cring·ing, cring·es 1.** To shrink back, as in fear; cower. **2.** To behave in a servile way; fawn. ❖ *n.* An act or instance of cringing. [ME *crengen,* to bend haughtily, prob. ult. < OE *cringan,* to give way.]

crin·gle (krĭng′gəl) *n.* A small ring or grommet of rope or metal fastened to the edge of a sail. [LGer. *kringel,* dim. of *kring,* ring < MLGer.]

crin·kle (krĭng′kəl) *v.* **-kled, -kling, -kles** —*intr.* **1.** To form wrinkles or ripples. **2.** To make a soft crackling sound; rustle. —*tr.* To cause to crinkle. ❖ *n.* A wrinkle, ripple, or fold. [< ME *crinkled,* full of turnings.] —**crin′kly** *adj.*

crin·kle·root (krĭng′kəl-ro͞ot′, -ro͝ot′) *n.* A woodland plant (*Cardamine diphylla*) of eastern North America having fleshy rootstocks and trifoliolate leaves.

cri·noid (krī′noid′) *n.* Any of various echinoderms of the class Crinoidea, characterized by a cup-shaped body, feathery radiating arms, and either a stalk or clawlike base. [< NLat. *Crinoīdea,* class name : Gk. *krinon,* lily + Gk. *-oeidēs,* -oid.] —**cri′noid′** *adj.*

crin·o·line (krĭn′ə-lĭn) *n.* **1.** A coarse stiff fabric of cotton or horsehair used esp. to line and stiffen hats and garments. **2.** A petticoat made of this fabric. **3.** A hoop skirt. [Fr. < Ital. *crinolino : crino,* horsehair < Lat. *crīnis,* hair) + *lino,* flax (< Lat. *līnum).*] —**crin′o·line, crin′o·lined** (-lĭnd) *adj.*

cri·num (krī′nəm) *n.* Any of various bulbous plants of the genus *Crinum,* having strap-shaped leaves and showy flower umbels. [NLat. *Crinum,* genus name < Gk. *krinon,* lily.]

cri·ol·lo (krē-ō′lō, -yō) *n., pl.* **-los** (-lōz, -yōz) A Spanish American of European, usu. Spanish descent. ❖ *adj.* **1.** Of or relating to a criollo or criollos. **2.** Indigenous to or characteristic of a Spanish-American country. [Sp. See CREOLE.]

cripes (krīps) *interj.* Used to express annoyance, anger, or dismay. [Alteration of CHRIST.]

crip·ple (krĭp′əl) *n.* **1.** A person or animal that is partially disabled or unable to use a limb or limbs. **2.** A damaged or defective object or device. ❖ *tr.v.* **-pled, -pling, -ples 1.** To cause to lose the use of a limb or limbs. **2.** To disable, damage, or impair the functioning of. [ME *crepel* < OE *crypel.*] —**crip′pler** *n.*

cri·sis (krī′sĭs) *n., pl.* **-ses** (-sēz) **1a.** A crucial or decisive point or situation; a turning point. **b.** An unstable condition, as in political affairs, involving an impending abrupt or decisive change. **2.** A sudden change in the course of a disease or fever. **3.** An emotionally stressful event or a traumatic change in a person's life. **4.** A point in a story or drama when a conflict reaches its highest tension and must be resolved. [ME < Lat., judgment < Gk. *krisis* < *krīnein,* to separate, judge. See **krei-** in App.]

crisp (krĭsp) *adj.* **crisp·er, crisp·est 1.** Firm but easily broken or crumbled; brittle. **2.** Pleasingly firm and fresh. **3a.** Bracing; invigorating. **b.** Lively; sprightly. **4.** Conspicuously clean or new. **5.** Marked by clarity, conciseness, and briskness. **6.** Having small curls, waves, or ripples. ❖ *v.* **crisped, crisp·ing, crisps** —*tr.* To make or keep crisp. —*intr.* To become or remain crisp. ❖ *n.* **1.** Something crisp or easily crumbled. **2.** A dessert of fruit baked with a sweet crumbly topping. **3.** *Chiefly British* A potato chip. [ME, curly < OE < Lat. *crīspus.*] —**crisp′ly** *adv.* —**crisp′ness** *n.*

cris·pate (krĭs′pāt) also **cris·pat·ed** (-pā′tĭd) *adj.* Curled or ruffled, as the margins of certain leaves. [Lat. *crīspātus,* p. part. of *crīspāre,* to curl < *crīspus,* curly.]

cris·pa·tion (krĭs-pā′shən) *n.* **1a.** The act of crisping or curling. **b.** The state of being crisped or curled. **2.** A slight involuntary muscular contraction, often producing a crawling sensation of the skin.

crisped (krĭspt) *adj. Botany* Crispate.

crisp·er (krĭs′pər) *n.* One that crisps, esp. a compartment in a refrigerator used to keep vegetables fresh.

Cris·pin (krĭs′pĭn), Saint. 3rd cent. A.D. Roman shoemaker who with his brother Saint **Crispinian** sought to spread Christianity and was martyred.

crisp·y (krĭs′pē) *adj.* **-i·er, -i·est 1.** Firm but easily broken or crumbled; crisp. **2.** Having small curls, waves, or ripples. —**crisp′i·ness** *n.*

criss·cross (krĭs′krôs′, -krŏs′) *v.* **-crossed, -cross·ing, -cross·es** —*tr.* **1.** To mark with crossing lines. **2.** To move back and forth through or over. —*intr.* To move back and forth. ❖ *n.* **1.** A mark or pattern made of crossing lines. **2.** A state of being at conflicting or contrary purposes. ❖ *adj.* Crossing one another or marked by crossings. ❖ *adv.* In a manner or direction that crosses or is marked by crossings. [Alteration of ME *Cristcrosse,* mark of a cross, short for *Cristcross (me speed),* may Christ's cross (give me success).]

cris·sum (krĭs′əm) *n., pl.* **cris·sa** (krĭs′ə) The feathers or area under the tail of a bird surrounding the cloacal opening. [NLat.

< Lat. *crīssāre, crissāre,* to move the buttocks during intercourse.] —**cris′sal** (-əl) *adj.*

cris·ta (krĭs′tə) *n., pl.* **-tae** (-tē) **1.** *Anatomy* A crest or ridge. **2.** *Biology* One of the inward projections or folds of the inner membrane of a mitochondrion. [Lat.]

cris·tate (krĭs′tāt) also **cris·tat·ed** (-tā′tĭd) *adj.* Having or forming a crest or crista. [Lat. *cristātus < crista,* tuft.]

cri·te·ri·on (krī-tîr′ē-ən) *n., pl.* **-te·ri·a** (-tîr′ē-ə) or **-te·ri·ons** A standard, rule, or test on which a judgment or decision can be based. [Gk. *kritērion < kritēs,* judge < *krīnein,* to separate, judge. See **krei-** in App.] —**cri·te′ri·al** (-əl) *adj.*

USAGE NOTE Like the analogous etymological plurals *agenda* and *data,* criteria is widely used as a singular form. Unlike them, however, it is not yet acceptable in that use.

crit·ic (krĭt′ĭk) *n.* **1.** One who forms and expresses judgments of the merits, faults, value, or truth of a matter. **2.** One who analyzes, classifies, interprets, or evaluates literary or other artistic works. **3.** One who tends to make harsh or carping judgments. [Lat. *criticus* < Gk. *kritikos,* able to discern < *kritēs,* judge < *krīnein,* to separate, judge. See **krei-** in App.]

crit·i·cal (krĭt′ĭ-kəl) *adj.* **1.** Inclined to judge severely and find fault. **2.** Characterized by careful, exact evaluation and judgment. **3.** Of, relating to, or characteristic of critics or criticism. **4.** Forming or having the nature of a turning point. **5a.** Of or relating to a medical crisis. **b.** Being or relating to a grave physical condition. **6.** Indispensable; essential. **7.** Being in or verging on a state of crisis or emergency. **8.** Fraught with danger or risk. **9.** *Mathematics* Of or relating to a point at which a curve has a horizontal tangent line, as at a maximum or minimum. **10.** *Chemistry & Physics* Of or relating to the value of a measurement, such as temperature, at which an abrupt change in a quality, property, or state occurs. **11.** *Physics* Capable of sustaining a nuclear chain reaction. —**crit′i·cal·ly** *adv.* —**crit′i·cal·ness** *n.*

critical angle *n.* **1.** The smallest angle of incidence at which a light ray can be completely reflected from the boundary between two media. **2.** The angle of attack of an airfoil at which airflow abruptly changes, altering the lift and drag of an aircraft.

crit·i·cal·i·ty (krĭt′ĭ-kăl′ĭ-tē) *n., pl.* **-ties. 1.** The quality, state, or degree of being at the highest importance. **2.** *Physics* The point at which a nuclear reaction is self-sustaining.

critical mass *n.* **1.** The smallest mass of a fissionable material that will sustain a nuclear chain reaction. **2.** The amount of matter needed to generate sufficient gravitational force to halt the current expansion of the universe. **3.** An amount or level required for a specific result to occur.

critical point *n.* **1.** *Physics* The temperature and pressure at which the liquid and gaseous phases of a pure stable substance become identical. **2.** *Mathematics* A point at which a given function has derivative of zero or a derivative that is undefined.

critical state *n.* See **critical point** 1.

crit·ic·as·ter (krĭt′ĭ-kăs′tər) *n.* A petty or inferior critic. [CRITIC + Lat. *-aster,* pejorative suff.]

crit·i·cism (krĭt′ĭ-sĭz′əm) *n.* **1.** The act of criticizing, esp. adversely. **2.** A critical comment or judgment. **3a.** The practice of analyzing, classifying, interpreting, or evaluating literary or other artistic works. **b.** A critical article or essay; a critique. **c.** The investigation of the origin and history of literary documents; textual criticism.

crit·i·cize (krĭt′ĭ-sīz′) *v.* **-cized, -ciz·ing, -ciz·es** —*tr.* **1.** To find fault with. See Usage Note at **critique. 2.** To judge the merits and faults of; analyze and evaluate. —*intr.* To act as a critic. —**crit′i·ciz′a·ble** *adj.* —**crit′i·ciz′er** *n.*

SYNONYMS criticize, blame, reprehend, censure, condemn, denounce These verbs mean to express an unfavorable judgment. *Criticize* can mean merely to evaluate without necessarily finding fault; however, the word usually implies the expression of disapproval: *The review criticized the novel. Blame* emphasizes the finding of fault and the fixing of responsibility: *"People are always blaming their circumstances for what they are"* (George Bernard Shaw). *Reprehend* implies sharp disapproval: *"reprehends students who have protested apartheid"* (New York Times). *Censure* refers to open and strong expression of criticism; often it implies a formal reprimand: *"No man can justly censure or condemn another, because indeed no man truly knows another"* (Thomas Browne). *Condemn* denotes the pronouncement of harshly adverse judgment: *"The wrongs which we seek to condemn and punish have been so calculated, so malignant and so devastating that civilization cannot tolerate their being ignored"* (Robert H. Jackson). *Denounce* implies public proclamation of condemnation or repudiation: *The press denounced his policies.*

cri·tique (krĭ-tēk′) *n.* **1.** A critical review or commentary, esp. one dealing with works of art or literature. **2.** A critical discussion of a specified topic. **3.** The art of criticism. ❖ *tr.v.* **-tiqued, -tiqu·ing, -tiques** *Usage Problem* To review or discuss critically. [Fr. < Gk. *kritikē (tekhnē),* (art) of criticism, fem. of *kritikos,* critical. See CRITIC.]

USAGE NOTE *Critique* has been used as a verb meaning "to review or discuss critically" since the 18th century, but lately this

ă	pat	oi	boy
ā	pay	ou	out
âr	care	o͝o	took
ä	father	o͞o	boot
ĕ	pet	ŭ	cut
ē	be	ûr	urge
ĭ	pit	th	thin
ī	pie	*th*	this
îr	pier	hw	which
ŏ	pot	zh	vision
ō	toe	ə	about,
ô	paw		item

Stress marks:
′ (primary);
′ (secondary), as in
lexicon (lĕk′sĭ-kŏn′)

Croatia

usage has gained much wider currency, in part because the verb *criticize*, once neutral between praise and censure, is now mainly used in a negative sense. This use of *critique* is still regarded by many as pretentious jargon, although resistance appears to be weakening. In our 1997 ballot, 41 percent of the Usage Panel still rejected the sentence *As mock inquisitors grill him, top aides take notes and critique the answers with the President afterward.* In most contexts one can usually substitute *go over, review,* or *analyze.*

crit•ter (krĭt′ər) *n. Informal* **1.** A living creature. **2.** A domestic animal, esp. a cow, horse, or mule. **3.** A person. [Alteration of CREATURE.]

REGIONAL NOTE *Critter,* a pronunciation spelling of *creature,* actually reflects a pronunciation that would have been very familiar to Shakespeare: 16th- and 17th-century English had not yet begun to pronounce the *–ture* suffix with its modern (ch) sound. This archaic pronunciation still exists in American *critter.* The most common meaning of *critter* is "a living creature," whether wild or domestic. In old-fashioned speech *critter* and *beast* denoted a large domestic animal. The more restricted senses "a cow," "a horse," or "a mule" are still characteristic of the speech in specific US regions. The use of *critter* among younger speakers is almost always somewhat jocular or informal.

CRNA *abbr.* certified registered nurse anesthetist
croak (krōk) *n.* A low, hoarse sound, as that characteristic of frogs and crows. ❖ *v.* **croaked, croak•ing, croaks** —*tr.* **1.** To utter in a croak. **2.** *Slang* To kill. —*intr.* **1a.** To utter a croak. **b.** To speak with a low, hoarse voice. **2.** To mutter discontentedly; grumble. **3.** *Slang* To die. [< ME *croken,* to croak, prob. of imit. orig.] —**croak′i•ly** *adv.* —**croak′y** *adj.*
croak•er (krō′kər) *n.* **1a.** A croaking animal, esp. a frog. **b.** A person who grumbles or habitually predicts evil. **2.** Any of various fishes, chiefly of the family Sciaenidae, that make croaking or grunting sounds.
Croat (krō′ăt′, -ät′, krōt) *n.* **1a.** A native or inhabitant of Croatia. **b.** A person of Croatian descent. **2.** Serbo-Croatian as used in Croatia. [NLat. *Croata* < Serbo-Croatian *Hrvāt.*]
Cro•a•tia (krō-ā′shə, -shē-ə) A country of S Europe along the NE Adriatic coast; settled by Croats in the 7th cent. and later part of the Austro-Hungarian Empire and a constituent republic of Yugoslavia (after 1946). Croatia declared its independence in 1991. Cap. Zagreb. Pop. 4,396,397.
Cro•a•tian (krō-ā′shən) *n.* See **Croat.** ❖ *adj.* Of or relating to Croatia or its people, language, or culture.
croc (krŏk) *n. Informal* A crocodile.
Cro•ce (krō′chĕ), **Benedetto** 1866–1952. Italian philosopher noted for his *Philosophy of the Spirit* (1902–17).
cro•chet (krō-shā′) *v.* **-cheted** (-shād′), **-chet•ing** (-shā′ĭng), **-chets** (-shāz′) —*tr.* To make by looping thread with a hooked needle. —*intr.* To crochet a piece of needlework. ❖ *n.* Needlework made by crocheting. [< Fr. *crocheter* < OFr. *crochet,* hook, dim. of *croche,* fem. of *croc,* of Gmc. orig.] —**cro•chet′er** (-shā′ər) *n.*
cro•ci (krō′sī, -kī) *n.* A plural of **crocus.**
cro•cid•o•lite (krō-sĭd′l-īt′) *n.* A fibrous, lavender-blue or greenish mineral, a sodium iron silicate used as a commercial form of asbestos. [Gk. *krokis, krokid-,* nap on woolen cloth + -LITE.]
crock¹ (krŏk) *n.* **1a.** An earthenware vessel. **b.** A broken piece of earthenware. **2.** *Slang* Foolish talk; nonsense. [ME *crokke* < OE *crocc.* Sense 2, short for *crock of shit.*]
crock² (krŏk) *New England n.* Soot. ❖ *v.* **crocked, crock•ing, crocks** —*tr.* To soil with or as if with crock. —*intr.* To give off soot or color. [?]
crock³ (krŏk) *Chiefly British Slang n.* One that is worn-out, decrepit, or impaired; a wreck. ❖ *v.* **crocked, crock•ing, crocks** —*intr.* To become weak or disabled. Often used with *up.* —*tr.* To disable; wreck. Often used with *up.* [Earlier, old ewe that has ceased bearing; prob. akin to Norw. *krake,* sickly animal, and MDu. *kraecke,* broken-down horse.]
crocked (krŏkt) *adj. Slang* Intoxicated; drunk. [Poss. < CROCK³.]
crock•er•y (krŏk′ə-rē) *n.* Earthenware.
crock•et (krŏk′ĭt) *n. Architecture* A projecting ornament, usu. in the form of a cusp or curling leaf, placed along outer angles of pinnacles and gables. [ME *croket,* ornamental curl of hair, hook < ONFr. *croquet,* shepherd's crook, dim. of *croque,* var. of OFr. *croche.* See CROCHET.]
Crock•ett (krŏk′ĭt), **David ("Davy")** 1786–1836. Amer. frontiersman and politician who joined the Texas revolutionaries fighting against Mexico and died at the siege of the Alamo.
Crock-Pot (krŏk′pŏt′) A trademark used for an electric cooker that maintains a low temperature.
croc•o•dile (krŏk′ə-dīl′) *n.* **1.** Any of various large aquatic reptiles, chiefly of the genus *Crocodylus,* native to tropical and subtropical regions and having thick armorlike skin and long tapering jaws. **2.** A crocodilian reptile, such as an alligator, caiman, or gavial. **3.** Leather made from crocodile skin. [ME *cocodril* < OFr. < Lat. *cocodrillus,* var. of *crocodīlus* < Gk. *krokodīlos* : *krokē,* pebble + *drilos,* circumcised man, worm.]

crocodile bird *n.* A black and white African bird (*Pluvianus aegyptius*) that is related to the plover and feeds on insects that parasitize crocodiles.
Crocodile River See **Limpopo.**
crocodile tears *pl.n.* An insincere display of grief; false tears. [< the belief that crocodiles weep either to lure a victim or when eating one.]
croc•o•dil•i•an (krŏk′ə-dĭl′ē-ən, -dĭl′yən) *n.* Any of various reptiles of the order Crocodylia, which includes the alligators, crocodiles, caimans, and gavials. ❖ *adj.* **1.** Of, relating to, or resembling a crocodile. **2.** Belonging to the order Crocodylia.
croc•o•ite (krŏk′rō-īt′, krŏ′kō-) also **croc•oi•site** (krŏk′wə-zīt′) *n.* A rare lead chromate mineral, PbCrO₄, that forms brilliant orange crystals. [Alteration of Fr. *crocoise* < Gk. *krokoeis,* saffron-colored < *krokos,* saffron. See CROCUS.]
cro•cus (krō′kəs) *n., pl.* **-cus•es** or **-ci** (-sī, -kī) **1a.** Any of various perennial Eurasian herbs of the genus *Crocus,* having grasslike leaves and showy, variously colored flowers. **b.** Any of several other plants, such as the autumn crocus. **2.** A grayish to light reddish purple. **3.** A dark red powdered variety of iron oxide, Fe₂O₃, used as an abrasive for polishing. **4.** A coarse, loosely woven material like burlap. [ME *crocus* < OFr. < Lat. < Gk. *krokos*; perh. < a source akin to Ar. *kurkum,* saffron.]
Croe•sus¹ (krē′səs) d. c. 546 B.C. Last king of Lydia (560–546) whose kingdom fell to the Persians under Cyrus.
Croe•sus² (krē′səs) *n.* A very wealthy man. [After CROESUS¹.]
croft (krôft, krŏft) *n. Chiefly British* **1.** A small enclosed field or pasture near a house. **2.** A small farm, esp. a tenant farm. [ME < OE.]
croft•er (krôf′tər, krŏf′-) *n. Chiefly British* One who rents and cultivates a croft; a tenant farmer.
Crohn's disease (krōnz) *n.* An inflammatory bowel disease most commonly affecting the small intestine and characterized by abdominal pain, ulceration, and fibrous tissue buildup. [After Burrill Bernard Crohn (1884–1983), American physician.]
crois•sant (krwä-sän′, krə-sänt′) *n.* A rich crescent-shaped roll of leavened dough or puff pastry. [Fr. < OFr. *creissant, croissant,* crescent. See CRESCENT.]
Croix de Guerre (krwä′ də gâr′) *n., pl.* **Croix de Guerre** A French military decoration for bravery in combat. [Fr. : *croix,* cross + *de,* of, + *guerre,* war.]
Cro-Mag•non (krō-măg′nən, -măn′yən) *n.* An early form of modern human (*Homo sapiens*) inhabiting Europe in the late Paleolithic Period and characterized by a broad face and tall stature, known from skeletal remains found in the Cro-Magnon cave in southern France. —**Cro-Mag′non** *adj.*
crom•lech (krŏm′lĕk′) *n.* **1.** A prehistoric monument consisting of monoliths encircling a mound. **2.** A dolmen. [Welsh : *crom,* fem. of *crwm,* arched + *llech,* stone.]
Cromp•ton (krŏmp′tən), **Samuel** 1753–1827. British inventor of the spinning mule (1779).
Crom•well (krŏm′wĕl′, -wəl, krŭm′-), **Oliver** 1599–1658. English military, political, and religious figure who led the Parliamentary victory in the English Civil War (1642–49) and ruled as lord protector (1653–58). His son **Richard** (1626–1712) succeeded him briefly (1658–59) before the restoration of the monarchy. —**Crom•well′i•an** *adj.*
Cromwell, Thomas. Earl of Essex. 1485?–1540. English politician who proposed the legislation that established the monarch as head of the established church (1534).
crone (krōn) *n.* An ugly, withered old woman; a hag. [ME < ONFr. *carogne,* carrion, cantankerous woman < VLat. *carōnia,* carrion < Lat. *carō, carn-,* flesh. See **sker-¹** in App.]
Cron•kite (krŏn′kīt), **Walter** b. 1916. Amer. news broadcaster and editor who was the nightly news anchor (1962–81) for the Columbia Broadcasting System.
Cro•nus (krō′nəs) *n. Greek Mythology* A Titan who ruled the universe until dethroned by his son Zeus.
cro•ny (krō′nē) *n., pl.* **-nies** A longtime close friend or companion. [Poss. < Gk. *khronios,* long lasting < *khronos,* time.]
cro•ny•ism (krō′nē-ĭz′əm) *n.* Favoritism shown to old friends without regard for their qualifications.
crook¹ (krŏŏk) *n.* **1.** An implement or tool, such as a bishop's crosier with a bent or curved part. **2.** A part that is curved or bent like a hook. **3.** A curve or bend; a turn. **4.** *Informal* One who makes a living by dishonest methods. ❖ *v.* **crooked, crook•ing, crooks** —*tr.* To make a crook in; bend. —*intr.* To bend or curve. See Syns at **bend¹.** [ME *crok* < ON *krōkr.*]
crook² (krŏŏk) *adj. Australian* **1.** Out of order; faulty. **2.** Not well; ill. **3.** Of poor quality; inferior. **4.** Not honest; crooked. [< CROOKED < CROOK¹.]
crook•ed (krŏŏk′ĭd) *adj.* **1.** Having or marked by bends, curves, or angles. **2.** *Informal* Dishonest or unscrupulous; fraudulent. —**crook′ed•ly** *adv.* —**crook′ed•ness** *n.*
crook•er•y (krŏŏk′ə-rē) *n.* Dishonest practices, as in business.
Crookes (krŏŏks), Sir **William** 1832–1919. British chemist and physicist who discovered thallium (1861), invented the radiometer (1875), and studied cathode rays.
crook•neck (krŏŏk′nĕk′) *n.* Any of several edible varieties of summer squash having a narrow crooked or curved neck and a yellow rind and flesh.

crocus
saffron crocus
Crocus sativus

crop-dusting

cross
top: Maltese and St. Andrew's
center: patriarchal, Greek, and tau
bottom: Latin, Calvary, and Celtic

croon (kroon) v. **crooned, croon·ing, croons** —intr. **1.** To hum or sing softly. **2.** To sing popular songs in a soft, sentimental manner. **3.** Scots To roar or bellow. —tr. To sing softly or in a humming way. ❖ n. A crooning. [ME crounen < MDu. krōnen, to lament.] —croon'er n.

crop (krŏp) n. **1a.** Cultivated plants or agricultural produce, such as grain or fruit, considered as a group: Wheat is a common crop. **b.** The total yield of such produce in a particular season or place: a large crop of apples. **2.** A group, quantity, or supply appearing at one time: a crop of new ideas. **3.** A short haircut. **4.** An earmark on an animal. **5a.** A short whip used in horseback riding. **b.** The stock of a whip. **6.** Zoology **a.** A pouchlike enlargement of a bird's gullet in which food is partially digested or stored for regurgitation to nestlings. **b.** A similar enlargement in the digestive tract of annelids and insects. ❖ v. **cropped, crop·ping, crops** —tr. **1a.** To cut or bite off the tops or ends of. **b.** To cut (hair, for example) very short. **c.** To clip (an animal's ears, for example). **d.** To trim (a photograph or picture, for example). **2a.** To harvest. **b.** To cause to grow or yield a crop. —intr. **1.** To feed on growing grasses and herbage. **2.** To plant, grow, or yield a crop. —phrasal verb: **crop up** To appear unexpectedly or occasionally. [ME < OE cropp, ear of grain.]

crop-dust·er or **crop duster** (krŏp'dŭst'ər) n. **1.** A light airplane equipped for crop-dusting. **2.** A crop-duster pilot.

crop-dust·ing (krŏp'dŭs'tĭng) n. The process of spraying crops with powdered insecticides or fungicides from an airplane. —crop'-dust' v.

crop-eared (krŏp'îrd') adj. **1.** Having the ears cropped. **2.** Having the hair cut so short that the ears show.

crop·land (krŏp'lănd') n. Land that is fit or used for growing crops.

crop·per¹ (krŏp'ər) n. A sharecropper.

crop·per² (krŏp'ər) n. **1.** A heavy fall; a tumble. **2.** A disastrous failure; a fiasco. [Perh. < the phrase neck and crop, completely.]

crop rotation n. Successive planting of different crops on the same land to improve fertility and control insects and disease.

cro·quet (krō-kā') n. **1.** An outdoor game in which the players drive wooden balls through a series of wickets using long-handled mallets. **2.** The act of croqueting. ❖ tr.v. **-queted** (-kād'), **-quet·ing** (-kā'ĭng), **-quets** (-kāz') To drive away (an opponent's croquet ball) by hitting one's own ball when the two are in contact. [Fr. dialectal, hockey stick < ONFr., shepherd's crook.] See CROCKET.

cro·quette (krō-kĕt') n. A small cake of minced food, such as poultry, vegetables, or fish, usu. coated with bread crumbs and fried in deep fat. [Fr. < croquer, to crunch.]

Cros·by (krôz'bē), **Harry Lillis** Known as "Bing." 1904–77. Amer. singer and actor noted for his crooning voice.

cro·sier or **cro·zier** (krō'zhər) n. **1.** A staff with a crook or cross at the end, carried by or before an abbot, bishop, or archbishop as a symbol of office. **2.** Botany See fiddlehead. [ME croser < OFr. crossier, staff bearer < crosse, crosier, of Gmc. orig.]

cross (krôs, krŏs) n. **1a.** An upright post with a transverse piece near the top, on which condemned persons were executed in ancient times. **b.** often **Cross** The cross upon which Jesus was crucified. **c.** A crucifix. **d.** Any of various modifications of the cross design, such as a Maltese cross. **e.** A medal, emblem, or insignia in the form of a cross. **2. Cross** The Christian religion; Christianity. **3.** Christianity The sign of the cross. **4.** A trial, affliction, or frustration. See Syns at burden¹. **5.** A mark or pattern formed by the intersection of two lines, esp. such a mark (X) used as a signature. **6.** A pipe fitting with four branches in upright and transverse form, used as a junction for intersecting pipes. **7.** Biology **a.** A plant or animal produced by crossbreeding; a hybrid. **b.** The process of crossbreeding; hybridization. **8.** One that combines the qualities of two other things. **9.** Slang A contest whose outcome has been dishonestly prearranged. **10.** Sports A hook thrown over an opponent's punch in boxing. ❖ v. **crossed, cross·ing, cross·es** —tr. **1.** To go or extend across; pass from one side of to the other. **2.** To carry or conduct across something. **3.** To extend or pass through or over; intersect. **4a.** To delete or eliminate by or as if by drawing a line through: crossed it off my list. **b.** To make or put a line across: Cross your t's. **5.** To place crosswise one over the other. **6.** To make the sign of the cross upon or over as a sign of devotion: He crossed himself in passing. **7.** To combine the qualities of two things: The movie crosses horror with humor. **9a.** To interfere with; thwart or obstruct: Don't cross me. **b.** To betray or deceive; double-cross. Often used with up. **10.** Biology To crossbreed or cross-fertilize (plants or animals). —intr. **1.** To lie or pass across each other; intersect. **2a.** To move or extend from one side to another. **b.** To make a crossing: crossed into Germany. **3.** To move or be conveyed in opposite directions at the same time: Our letters crossed. **4.** Biology To crossbreed or cross-fertilize. ❖ adj. **1.** Lying or passing crosswise; intersecting: a cross street. **2.** Contrary or counter; opposing. **3.** Showing ill humor; annoyed. **4.** Involving interchange; reciprocal. **5.** Crossbred; hybrid. ❖ adv. Crosswise. **prep.** Across. —phrasal verb: **cross over 1.** To change from one condition or loyalty to another. **2.** Genetics To exchange genetic material. Used of homologous chromosomes. —idioms: **cross (someone's) palm** To pay, tip, or bribe. **cross swords** To quarrel or fight. [ME cros < OE, prob. < ON kross < OIr. cros < Lat. crux.] —cross'er n. —cross'ly adv. —cross'ness n.

cross·bar (krôs'bär', krŏs'-) n. A horizontal bar, line, or stripe.

cross·beam (krôs'bēm', krŏs'-) n. A horizontal or transverse beam, esp. a structural beam resting on two supports.

cross·bill (krôs'bĭl', krŏs'-) n. Any of various finches of the genus Loxia, having curved mandibles with narrow tips that cross when the bill is closed.

cross·bones (krôs'bōnz', krŏs'-) pl.n. A representation of two bones placed crosswise, usu. under a skull, symbolizing danger or death.

cross·bow (krôs'bō', krŏs'-) n. A weapon consisting of a bow fixed crosswise on a wooden stock, with grooves on the stock to direct the projectile. —cross'bow'man n.

cross·bred (krôs'brĕd, krŏs'-) adj. Produced by crossbreeding. —cross'bred' n.

cross·breed (krôs'brēd', krŏs'-) v. **-bred** (-brĕd'), **-breed·ing, -breeds** —tr. To produce (an organism) by the mating of individuals of different breeds, varieties, or species; interbreed. —intr. To mate so as to produce a hybrid; interbreed. ❖ n. An organism produced by crossbreeding.

cross·check (krôs'chĕk', krŏs'-) tr.v. **-checked, -check·ing, -checks 1.** To verify by comparing with parallel or supplementary data. **2.** Sports To check illegally in ice hockey by striking an opponent with one's hockey stick held in both hands and lifted off the ice. ❖ n. The act of crosschecking.

cross-coun·try (krôs'kŭn'trē, krŏs'-) adj. **1.** Moving or directed across open country rather than following tracks, roads, or runs. **2.** From one side of a country to the opposite side. ❖ n. A cross-country sport, esp. running or skiing. —cross'-coun'try adv.

cross-country skiing n. The sport of skiing over the countryside rather than on downhill runs.

cross-court (krôs'kôrt', -kōrt', krŏs'-) adv. & adj. To or toward the other side of a playing court, esp. a basketball or tennis court.

cross cousin n. A cousin who is the child of one's mother's brother or one's father's sister.

cross-cul·tur·al (krôs'kŭl'chər-əl, krŏs'-) adj. Comparing or dealing with two or more different cultures. —cross'-cul'tur·al·ly adv.

cross·cur·rent (krôs'kûr'ənt, -kŭr'-, krŏs'-) n. **1.** A current flowing across another current. **2.** A conflicting tendency, inclination, or movement.

cross·cut (krôs'kŭt', krŏs'-) v. **-cut, -cut·ting, -cuts** —tr. **1.** To cut or run across or through. **2.** To cut using a crosscut saw. **3.** To interweave (two separate, usu. concurrent scenes) in a film. —intr. To crosscut scenes in a film. ❖ adj. **1.** Constructed or used for cutting crosswise. **2.** Cut across or crosswise. ❖ n. **1.** A course or cut going crosswise. **2.** A path more direct than the main path; a shortcut. **3.** A level in a mine driven so that it intersects a vein of ore. **4.** A crosscut saw. **5.** An example of cinematic crosscutting.

crosscut saw n. A saw for cutting wood across the grain.

cross-country skiing

cross-dress (krôs'drĕs', krŏs'-) intr.v. **-dressed, -dress·ing, -dress·es** To dress in the clothing characteristic of the opposite sex. —cross'-dress'er n. —cross'-dress'ing n.

crosse (krôs, krŏs) n. The stick used in lacrosse. [Fr. < OFr., staff. See CROSIER.]

cross-ex·am·ine (krôs'ĭg-zăm'ĭn, krŏs'-) v. **-ined, -in·ing, -ines** —tr. **1.** To question (a person) closely, esp. with regard to answers or information given previously. **2.** Law To question (a witness already examined by the opposing side). —intr. To question a person closely. —cross'-ex·am'i·na'tion n. —cross'-ex·am'in·er n.

cross-eye (krôs'ī', krŏs'ī') n. **1.** Esotropia. **2.** An eye affected with esotropia. —cross'-eyed' adj.

cross-fer·til·i·za·tion (krôs'fûr'tl-ĭ-zā'shən, krŏs'-) n. **1.** Fertilization by the union of gametes from different individuals, sometimes of different varieties or species. **2.** Mutual exchange, as between dissimilar concepts, that produces something beneficial. —cross'-fer'tile adj.

cross-fer·til·ize (krôs'fûr'tl-īz', krŏs'-) intr. & tr.v. **-ized, -iz·ing, -iz·es** To undergo or cause to undergo cross-fertilization.

cross-file (krôs'fīl', krŏs'-) tr. & intr.v. **-filed, -fil·ing, -files** To register (someone) or be registered as a candidate in the primaries of more than one political party. —cross'-fil'er n.

cross-fire (krôs'fīr', krŏs'-) n. **1.** Lines of fire from two or more positions crossing each other at a single point. **2.** A confrontational situation in which opposing factions, forces, views, or opinions converge. **3.** Rapid, heated discussion.

Cross-Flo·ri·da Waterway (krôs'flôr'ĭ-də, -flōr'-, krŏs'-) See Lake Okeechobee.

cross-grained (krôs'grānd', krŏs'-) adj. **1.** Having an irregular, transverse, or diagonal grain, as opposed to a parallel grain. **2.** Troublesome to deal with; contrary.

cross hair or **cross·hair** (krôs'hâr', krŏs'-) n. Either of two fine strands of wire crossed in the focus of the eyepiece of an optical instrument and used as a calibration or sighting reference.

cross·hatch (krôs'hăch', krŏs'-) tr.v. **-hatched, -hatch·ing, -hatch·es** To mark or shade with two or more sets of intersecting parallel lines. ❖ n. **1.** A pattern made by such lines. **2.** The symbol (#).

cross·head (krôs'hĕd', krŏs'-) n. A beam that connects the pis-

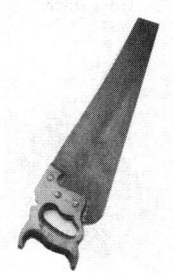

crosscut saw

ton rod to the connecting rod of a reciprocating engine.

cross·in·dex (krôs'ĭn'dĕks, krôs'-) *v.* **-dexed, -dex·ing, -dex·es** —*tr.* **1.** To index (a particular item) under more than one heading. **2.** To furnish (an index in a book, for example) with cross-references. —*intr.* To furnish cross-references. —**cross'in'dex** *n.*

cross·ing (krô'sĭng, krŏs'ĭng) *n.* **1.** The act or action of crossing. **2a.** A place at which roads, lines, or tracks intersect; an intersection. **b.** A place at which a river or highway, for example, may be crossed. **3.** The intersection of the nave and transept in a cruciform church.

crossing over or **cross·ing-o·ver** (krô'sĭng-ō'vər, krŏs'ĭng-) *n.* The exchange of genetic material between homologous chromosomes that occurs during meiosis and contributes to genetic variability.

cross-leg·ged (krôs'lĕg'ĭd, -lĕgd', krŏs'-) *adv. & adj.* **1.** With the legs or ankles crossed and the knees far apart. **2.** With one leg lying over and across the other leg.

cross-link (krôs'lĭngk', krŏs'-) *tr.v.* **-linked, -link·ing, -links** To join (adjacent chains of a polymer or protein) by creating covalent bonds. ❖ *n.* A chemical bond or link created by cross-linking.

cross matching *n.* The process of determining the compatibility of blood from a donor with that of a recipient before transfusion.

cross·mul·ti·ply (krôs'mŭl'tə-plī', krŏs'-) *intr.v.* **-plied, -ply·ing, -plies** To multiply the numerator of one of a pair of fractions by the denominator of the other. —**cross multiplication** *n.*

cros·sop·te·ryg·i·an (krŏ-sŏp'tə-rĭj'ē-ən) *n.* See **lobe-finned fish.** [< NLat. *Crossopterygiī*, group name : Gk. *krossoi*, fringe (< *krossōtos*, fringed < *krossai*, projecting stone blocks) + Gk. *pterugia*, fins, pl. dim. of *pterux, pterug-*, wing. See PTERYGOID.] —**cros'sop'te·ryg'i·an** *adj.*

cross·o·ver (krôs'ō'vər, krŏs'-) *n.* **1.** A place at which the means by which a crossing is made. **2.** A short connecting track by which a train can be transferred from one line to another. **3.** *Genetics* **a.** Crossing over. **b.** A characteristic resulting from crossing over. **4.** A registered member of one political party who votes in the primary of the other party. **5.** The adaptation of a musical style, as by blending elements of two or more styles or categories to gain wider appeal.

cross·patch (krôs'păch', krŏs'-) *n.* A peevish, irascible person; a grouch. [CROSS + *patch*, jester.]

cross·piece (krôs'pēs', krŏs'-) *n.* A transverse or horizontal piece, as of a structure or implement.

cross·pol·li·nate (krôs'pŏl'ə-nāt', krŏs'-) *tr.v.* **-nat·ed, -nat·ing, -nates 1.** To pollinate (a flower) by means of cross-pollination. **2.** To influence (another), esp. reciprocally.

cross·pol·li·na·tion (krôs'pŏl'ə-nā'shən, krŏs'-) *n.* The transfer of pollen from an anther of the flower of one plant to a stigma of the flower of another plant.

cross product *n.* See **vector product.**

cross·pur·pose (krôs'pûr'pəs, krŏs'-) *n.* A usu. unintentionally conflicting or contrary purpose. —*idiom:* **at cross-purposes** Misunderstanding each other's purposes.

cross·ques·tion (krôs'kwĕs'chən, krŏs'-) *tr.v.* **-tioned, -tion·ing, -tions** To question closely; cross-examine. ❖ *n.* A question asked during cross-examination.

cross·re·ac·tion (krôs'rē-ăk'shən, krŏs'-) *n.* The reaction between an antigen and an antibody that was generated against a different but similar antigen. —**cross'-re·act'** *v.* —**cross'-re·ac'tive** *adj.* —**cross'-re·ac·tiv'i·ty** *n.*

cross·re·fer (krôs'rĭ-fûr', krŏs'-) *v.* **-ferred, -fer·ring, -fers** —*tr.* To refer (a reader) from one part or passage to another. —*intr.* To make a cross-reference.

cross·ref·er·ence (krôs'rĕf'ər-əns, -rĕf'rəns, krŏs'-) *n.* A reference from one part of a book, index, catalog, or file to another part containing related information. ❖ *tr.v.* **-enced, -enc·ing, -enc·es** To provide with cross-references.

cross·re·sis·tance (krôs'rĭ-zĭs'təns, krŏs'-) *n.* Tolerance to a usu. toxic substance as a result of exposure to a similarly acting substance.

cross·road (krôs'rōd', krŏs'-) *n.* **1.** A road that intersects another road. **2. crossroads** (*used with a sing. or pl. verb*) **a.** A place where two or more roads meet. **b.** A small, usu. rural community at an intersection of two or more roads; *gas at a remote crossroads.* **c.** A place that is centrally located. **d.** A crucial point.

cross·ruff (krôs'rŭf', -rŭf', krŏs'-) *n.* A series of plays in games of the whist family in which partnership hands alternately trump suits led by one another. ❖ *v.* **-ruffed, -ruff·ing, -ruffs** —*intr.* To perform a crossruff or a series of crossruffs. —*tr.* To trump in alternating plays.

cross section also **cross-sec·tion** (krôs'sĕk'shən, krŏs'-) *n.* **1a.** A section formed by a plane cutting through an object, usu. at right angles to an axis. **b.** A piece so cut or a graphic representation of such a piece. **2.** *Physics* A measure of the probability that an encounter between particles will result in the occurrence of a particular atomic or nuclear reaction. **3.** *Statistics* A sample meant to be representative of a whole population. **4.** *Informal* A variety; a diversity. —**cross'-sec'tion·al** (krôs'sĕk'shə-nəl, krŏs'-) *adj.*

cross-stitch (krôs'stĭch', krŏs'-) *n.* **1.** A double stitch forming an

cross-stitch

crostino

croustade

X in sewing and embroidery. **2.** Needlework made with X-shaped stitches. —**cross'-stitch'** *v.*

cross·talk (krôs'tôk', krŏs'-) *n.* **1.** *Electronics* Undesired signals or sounds in a telephone or other communications device as a result of coupling between transmission circuits. **2.** Ancillary, incidental conversation.

cross·tie (krôs'tī', krŏs'-) *n.* A supporting transverse beam or rod, esp. a beam that connects the rails of a railroad.

cross·tol·er·ance (krôs'tŏl'ər-əns, krŏs'-) *n.* Resistance to the effects of a substance as a result of continued exposure to a different substance having a similar pharmacologic action.

cross·town or **cross-town** (krôs'toun', krŏs'-) *adv. & adj.* Running, extending, or going across a city or town.

cross-train (krôs'trān', krŏs'-) *v.* **-trained, -train·ing, -trains** —*intr.* **1.** To undergo or provide training in different tasks or skills. **2.** To train in different sports, mainly by alternating regimens, as in running, bicycling, and swimming. —*tr.* To train (another) in different tasks or skills.

cross-train·er (krôs'trā'nər, krŏs'-) *n.* **1.** A person who cross-trains, esp. in different sports. **2.** An athletic shoe designed for cross-training.

cross·tree (krôs'trē', krŏs'-) *n.* *Nautical* One of the two horizontal crosspieces at the upper ends of the lower masts in fore-and-aft-rigged vessels, serving to spread the shrouds.

cross vault *n.* A vault formed by the intersection of two or more barrel vaults.

cross vine *n.* See **bignonia.**

cross·walk (krôs'wôk', krŏs'-) *n.* A path marked off on a street to indicate where pedestrians should cross.

cross·way (krôs'wā', krŏs'-) *n.* A crossroad.

cross·wind (krôs'wĭnd', krŏs'-) *n.* A wind blowing at right angles to a given direction, as to an aircraft's line of flight.

cross·wise (krôs'wīz', krŏs'-) *adv.* also **cross·ways** (-wāz') So as to be or lie in a cross direction; across. ❖ *adj.* Crossing.

cross·word (krôs'wûrd', krŏs'-) *n.* A puzzle in which an arrangement of numbered squares is to be filled with words running both across and down in answer to clues that are correspondingly numbered.

cro·sti·no (krō-stē'nō) *n., pl.* **-ni** (-nē) **1.** A piece of thin crisp toast. **2.** An hors d'oeuvre made with a crostino and any of various toppings. [Ital., dim. of *crosta*, crust < Lat. *crūsta*.]

crotch (krŏch) *n.* **1.** The angle or region of the angle formed by the junction of two parts or members. **2a.** The area on a pair of pants, underpants, or shorts where the two leg panels are sewn together. **b.** A piece of material sewn into this area to join the legs. **3.** The fork of a pole or other support. [Poss. alteration of CRUTCH and partly < ME *croche*, crook, crosier (< OFr., hook, shepherd's crook, fem. of *croc*, hook; see CROCHET).] —**crotched** (krŏcht) *adj.*

crotch·et (krŏch'ĭt) *n.* **1.** An odd, whimsical, or stubborn notion. **2.** *Music* See **quarter note. 3.** *Obsolete* A small hook or hooklike structure. [ME *crochet*, hook < OFr. See CROCHET.]

crotch·et·y (krŏch'ĭ-tē) *adj.* Capriciously stubborn or eccentric; perverse. —**crotch'et·i·ness** *n.*

cro·ton (krōt'n) *n.* **1.** Any of various plants of the genus *Croton.* **2.** An Old World tropical evergreen shrub (*Codiaeum variegatum*) with glossy multicolored foliage. [NLat. *Croton,* genus name < Gk. *krotōn,* castor oil plant.]

Croton bug *n.* See **German cockroach.** [After the *Croton* River of SE New York.]

cro·ton·ic acid (krō-tŏn'ĭk) *n.* An organic acid, $C_4H_6O_2$, used in the preparation of pharmaceuticals and resins. [< NLat. *Croton,* plant genus. See CROTON.]

croton oil *n.* A brownish-yellow oil obtained from the seeds of a tropical Asian shrub or small tree (*Croton tiglium*) and formerly used as a cathartic.

crouch (krouch) *v.* **crouched, crouch·ing, crouch·es** —*intr.* **1a.** To stoop, esp. with bent knees. **b.** To press the body close to the ground with bent limbs. **2.** To bend servilely or timidly; cringe. —*tr.* To bend (the head, for example) low, as in fear. ❖ *n.* The act or posture of bending low or crouching. [ME *crouchen,* prob. < ONFr. **crouchir,* to bend, var. of OFr. *crochir* < *croche,* hook. See CROCHET.]

croup[1] (krōōp) *n.* A pathological condition of the larynx, esp. in infants and children, characterized by respiratory difficulty and a hoarse cough. [< dialectal *croup,* to croak.] —**croup'ous** (krōō'pəs), **croup'y** *adj.*

croup[2] (krōōp) *n.* The rump of a beast of burden, esp. a horse. [ME *croupe* < OFr., of Gmc. orig.]

crou·pi·er (krōō'pē-ər, -pē-ā') *n.* An attendant at a gaming table who collects and pays bets. [Fr., one behind another on a horse, croupier < *croupe,* rump < OFr. See CROUP[2].]

crouse (krōōs) *adj.* *Scots* Lively; vivacious. [ME *crous,* fierce, bold, perh. < MFlem. *cruus,* curly, bold.]

crous·tade (krōō-städ') *n.* A molded or hollowed bowllike crust, as of pastry, filled with another food. [Fr. < Provençal *crustado* < O Provençal < Lat. *crūstātus,* p. part. of *crūstāre,* to encrust < *crūsta,* crust. See CRUST.]

crou·ton (krōō'tŏn', krōō-tŏn') *n.* A small crisp piece of toasted or fried bread. [Fr. *croûton,* dim. of *croûte,* crust < OFr. *crouste* < Lat. *crūsta.*]

crow[1] (krō) *n.* **1.** Any of several large glossy black birds of the genus *Corvus,* having a characteristic raucous call, esp. *C. brachyrhynchos* of North America. **2.** A crowbar. **3. Crow** See **Corvus.** —*idiom:* **as the crow flies** In a straight line. [ME *croue* < OE *crāwe.* Sense 2 < the resemblance of its forked end to a crow's foot or beak.]

crow[2] (krō) *intr.v.* **crowed, crow·ing, crows 1.** To utter the shrill cry characteristic of a cock. **2.** To exult loudly, as over another's defeat; boast. **3.** To make a sound expressive of pleasure or well-being, characteristic of an infant. ❖ *n.* **1.** The shrill cry of a cock. **2.** A crowing sound. [ME *crouen* < OE *crāwan.*]

Crow *n., pl.* **Crow** or **Crows 1.** A member of a Native American people formerly inhabiting the northern Great Plains between the Platte and Yellowstone rivers and now in southeast Montana. **2.** The Siouan language of the Crow.

crow·bar (krō′bär′) *n.* A straight bar of iron or steel, with the working end shaped like a chisel and often slightly bent and forked, used as a lever. ❖ *tr.v.* **-barred, -bar·ring, -bars** To extract, remove, or insert forcibly. [CROW[1] + BAR[1].]

crow·ber·ry (krō′běr′ē) *n.* **1.** A low-growing evergreen shrub (*Empetrum nigrum*) native to cool regions of the Northern Hemisphere and having tiny leaves, small pinkish or purplish flowers, and black berrylike fruits. **2.** The fruit of this plant. [Prob. transl. of Ger. *Krähenbeere : Krähe,* crow + *Beere,* berry.]

crow blackbird *n.* See **grackle** 1.

crowd[1] (kroud) *n.* **1.** A large number of persons gathered together; a throng. **2.** The common people; the populace. **3.** A group of people united by a common characteristic, as age. **4.** A group of people attending a public function. **5.** A large number of things positioned or considered together. ❖ *v.* **crowd·ed, crowd·ing, crowds** —*intr.* **1.** To congregate in a restricted area; throng. **2.** To advance by pressing or shoving. —*tr.* **1.** To force by or as if by pressing or shoving. **2.** To draw or stand near to. **3.** To press, cram, or force tightly together. **4.** To fill or occupy to overflowing. **5.** *Informal* To put pressure on, as to pay a debt. —*idiom:* **crowd (on) sail** *Nautical* To spread a large amount of sail to increase speed. [< ME *crowden,* to crowd, press < OE *crūdan,* to hasten, press.] —**crowd′er** *n.*

crowd[2] (kroud, krŏŏd) *n.* **1.** An ancient Celtic stringed instrument that was bowed or plucked. **2.** *Chiefly British* A fiddle. [ME *croud* < M Welsh *crwth.*]

crow·foot (krō′fŏŏt′) *n.* **1.** *pl.* **-foots a.** Any of numerous plants of the genus *Ranunculus* that have palmately cleft or divided leaves, such as the buttercups. **b.** Any of several other plants having leaves or other parts somewhat resembling a bird's foot. **2.** *pl.* **-feet** (-fēt′) A caltrop used to delay the advance of mounted troops and infantry.

crown (kroun) *n.* **1.** An ornamental circlet or head covering, often made of precious metal set with jewels and worn as a symbol of sovereignty. **2.** often **Crown a.** The power, position, or empire of a monarch or of a state governed by constitutional monarchy. **b.** The monarch as head of state. **3.** A distinction or reward for achievement, esp. a title signifying championship in a sport. **4.** Something resembling a diadem in shape. **5a.** A coin stamped with a crown or crowned head. **b.** A silver coin formerly used in Great Britain and worth five shillings. **c.** Any one of several coins, such as the koruna, having a name that means "crown." **6a.** The top or highest part of the head. **b.** The head itself. **7.** The top or upper part of a hat. **8.** The highest point or summit. **9.** The highest, primary, or most valuable part, attribute, or state. **10.** *Dentistry* **a.** The part of a tooth that is covered by enamel and projects beyond the gum line. **b.** An artificial substitute for the natural crown of a tooth. **11.** *Nautical* The lowest part of an anchor, where the arms are joined to the shank. **12.** *Architecture* The highest portion of an arch. **13.** *Botany* **a.** The upper part of a tree, which includes the branches and leaves. **b.** The part of a plant where the stem and roots merge. **c.** The persistent, mostly underground base of a perennial herb. **d.** See **corona** 5. **14.** The crest of an animal, esp. of a bird. **15.** The portion of a cut gem above the girdle. ❖ *v.* **crowned, crown·ing, crowns** —*tr.* **1.** To put a crown or garland on the head of. **2.** To invest with regal power; enthrone. **3.** To confer honor, dignity, or reward upon. **4.** To surmount or be the highest part of. **5.** To form the crown, top, or chief ornament of. **6.** To bring to completion or successful conclusion; consummate. **7.** *Dentistry* To put a crown on (a tooth). **8.** To make (a piece in checkers that has reached the last row) into a king by placing another piece upon it. **9.** *Informal* To hit on the head. —*intr.* To reach a stage in labor when a large segment of the fetal scalp is visible at the vaginal opening. [ME *crowne* < AN *coroune* < Lat. *corōna,* wreath, garland, crown < Gk. *korōnē, korōna,* anything curved, kind of crown < *korōnos,* curved.]

crown canopy *n.* See **canopy** 5.

crown colony *n.* A British colony in which the government in London has some control of legislation, usu. administered by an appointed governor.

crown daisy *n.* See **garland chrysanthemum.**

crown glass *n.* **1.** A soda-lime optical glass that is exceptionally hard and clear, with low refraction and low dispersion. **2.** A form of window glass made by whirling a glass bubble to make a flat circular disk with a lump left in the center.

crown jewel *n.* **1a.** A precious stone that is part of a sovereign's

regalia. **b. crown jewels** The jewels used ceremonially by a sovereign. **2.** The most prized asset or possession in a group.

crown lens *n.* The crown-glass element in an achromatic lens.

crown-of-thorns (kroun′əv-thôrnz′) *n.* **1.** A trailing or climbing spiny shrub (*Euphorbia milii*) native to Madagascar and having showy flower clusters with usu. red petallike bracts. **2.** The Christ's thorn.

Crown Point A village of NE NY on the W shore of Lake Champlain; site of major battles during the French and Indian War and the American Revolution. Pop. 2,119.

crown prince *n.* The male heir apparent to a throne.

crown princess *n.* **1.** The female heir apparent or heir presumptive to a throne. **2.** The wife of a crown prince.

crown roast *n.* A roast consisting of the rib sections of two loins placed upright and fastened together in a circle.

crown saw *n.* A cylindrical saw with teeth on the bottom edge of the cylinder, used for cutting round holes.

crown vetch *n.* A perennial European herb (*Coronilla varia*) in the pea family, grown for forage and erosion control and having small flower clusters and pinnately compound leaves.

crow's-foot (krōz′fŏŏt′) *n., pl.* **-feet** (-fēt′) **1.** A wrinkle at the outer corner of the eye. Often used in the plural. **2.** A three-pointed embroidery stitch.

crow's-nest (krōz′něst′) *n.* **1.** A small lookout platform with a railing and windscreen, located near the top of a ship's mast or superstructure. **2.** A similar platform on shore.

croze (krōz) *n.* A groove inside the end of a barrel or cask into which the head is set. [Fr. *creux* < OFr. *crues,* groove < VLat. *crosus,* perh. of Celt. orig.]

cro·zier (krō′zhər) *n.* Variant of **crosier.**

CRP *abbr.* C-reactive protein

CRT *abbr.* cathode-ray tube

cru (krōō) *n., pl.* **crus 1.** A vineyard or wine-producing region in France. **2.** A grade or class of wine. [Fr. < p. part. of *croître,* to grow < OFr. *creistre.* See CRESCENT.]

cru·ces (krōō′sēz) *n.* A plural of **crux.**

cru·cial (krōō′shəl) *adj.* **1a.** Extremely significant or important. **b.** Vital to the resolution of a crisis; decisive. **2.** *Archaic* Having the form of a cross. [< NLat. (*īnstantia) crucis,* (*experīmentum) crucis,* crossroads (case), crossroads (experiment) < Lat. *crux, cruc-,* cross. Sense 2, Fr. < OFr. < Lat. *crux.*] —**cru′cial·ly** *adv.*

cru·ci·ate (krōō′shē-āt′) *adj.* **1.** Arranged in or forming a cross; cruciform. **2a.** Overlapping or crossing, as the wings of some insects when at rest. **b.** Shaped like a cross. [NLat. *cruciātus* < Lat. *crux, cruc-,* cross.] —**cru′ci·ate·ly** *adv.*

cru·ci·ble (krōō′sə-bəl) *n.* **1.** A vessel made of a refractory substance such as graphite or porcelain, used for melting and calcining materials at high temperatures. **2.** A severe test, as of belief. **3.** A situation or time characterized by powerful intellectual, social, or economic forces: *was raised in the crucible of the Depression.* [ME *crusible* < Med.Lat. *crūcibulum,* night-light, crucible, poss. < OFr. *croisuel,* cresset. See CRESSET.]

crucible steel *n.* See **drill steel.**

cru·ci·fer (krōō′sə-fər) *n.* **1.** One who bears a cross in a religious procession. **2.** *Botany* Any of various plants in the mustard family (Cruciferae or Brassicaceae), which includes the alyssum, cabbage, and many weeds. [LLat. : Lat. *crux, cruc-,* cross + Lat. *-fer, -fer.*] —**cru·cif′er·ous** (-sĭf′ər-əs) *adj.*

cru·ci·fix (krōō′sə-fĭks′) *n.* **1.** An image or figure of Jesus on the cross. **2.** A cross as a symbol of the Crucifixion. [ME < OFr. < LLat. *crucifixus* < Lat., p. part. of *crucifīgere,* crucify. See CRUCIFY.]

cru·ci·fix·ion (krōō′sə-fĭk′shən) *n.* **1a.** The act of crucifying; execution on a cross. **b. Crucifixion** The crucifying of Jesus on Calvary. **c.** A representation of Jesus on the cross. **2.** An extremely difficult, painful trial; torturous suffering.

cru·ci·form (krōō′sə-fôrm′) *adj.* Shaped like a cross; cruciate. [Lat. *crux, cruc-,* cross + -FORM.] —**cru′ci·form′** *n.* —**cru′ci·form′ly** *adv.*

cru·ci·fy (krōō′sə-fī′) *tr.v.* **-fied, -fy·ing, -fies 1.** To put (a person) to death by nailing or binding to a cross. **2.** To mortify or subdue (the flesh). **3.** To treat cruelly. **4.** To criticize harshly; pillory. [ME *crucifien* < OFr. *crucifier,* alteration of Lat. *crucifīgere : crux, cruc-,* cross + *fīgere,* to attach.] —**cru′ci·fi′er** *n.*

cru·ci·ver·bal·ist (krōō′sə-vûr′bə-lĭst) *n.* **1.** A constructor of crossword puzzles. **2.** An enthusiast of word games, esp. of crossword puzzles. [< Lat. *crux, cruc-,* cross + Lat. *verbum,* word (transl. of E. CROSSWORD).]

crud (krŭd) *n.* **1.** *Slang* **a.** A coating or incrustation of filth or refuse. **b.** Something loathsome, despicable, or worthless. **c.** One who is contemptible or disgusting. **2.** A disease or ailment, imaginary or real, esp. affecting the skin. [ME *crudde,* poss. < OE *crūden,* p. part. of *crūdan,* to press.]

crud·dy (krŭd′ē) *adj.* **-di·er, -di·est** *Slang* Worthless, loathsome, or disgusting. —**crud′di·ness** *n.*

crude (krōōd) *adj.* **crud·er, crud·est 1.** Being in an unrefined or natural state; raw. **2.** Lacking tact or taste; blunt or offensive. **3.** Characterized by uncultured simplicity; unsophisticated. **4.** Not carefully or skillfully made; rough: *a crude sketch.* **5.** Undisguised or unadorned; plain. **6.** *Statistics* In an unanalyzed form; not adjusted to allow for related circumstances or data. **7.** Displaying a

crowbar

crow's-nest

lack of knowledge or skill. **8.** *Archaic* Unripe or immature. ❖ *n.* A substance, esp. petroleum, in its unrefined state. [ME < Lat. *crūdus.* See **kreuə-** in App.] —**crude′ly** *adv.* —**cru′di•ty** (kro͞o′dĭ-tē), **crude′ness** *n.*

crude oil *n.* Unrefined petroleum.

cru•di•tés (kro͞o′dĭ-tā′) *pl.n.* Cut raw vegetables, such as carrot sticks, often served with a dip as an appetizer. [Fr., pl. of *crudité,* rawness < OFr. *crudite* < Lat. *crūditās,* indigestion, undigested food < *crūdus,* raw. See CRUDE.]

cru•el (kro͞o′əl) *adj.* **-el•er, -el•est** or **-el•ler, -el•lest 1.** Disposed to inflict pain or suffering. **2.** Causing suffering. [ME < OFr. < Lat. *crūdēlis.* See **kreuə-** in App.] —**cru′el•ly** *adv.*

SYNONYMS *cruel, fierce, ferocious, barbarous, inhuman, savage, vicious* These adjectives mean predisposed to inflict violence, pain, or hardship or to find satisfaction in the suffering of others: *a cruel tyrant; a fierce warrior; a ferocious attack dog; a barbarous crime; inhuman treatment of captured soldiers; a savage outburst of temper; a vicious kick.*

cru•el•ty (kro͞o′əl-tē) *n., pl.* **-ties 1.** The quality or condition of being cruel. **2.** Something that causes pain or suffering. **3.** *Law* The infliction of physical or mental distress, esp. when considered a determinant in granting a divorce.

cru•et (kro͞o′ĭt) *n.* **1.** A small glass bottle for holding a condiment, such as vinegar. **2.** *Ecclesiastical* A small vessel for holy water or for water or wine used in the consecration of the Eucharist. [ME < OFr., dim. of *crue,* flask, of Gmc. orig.]

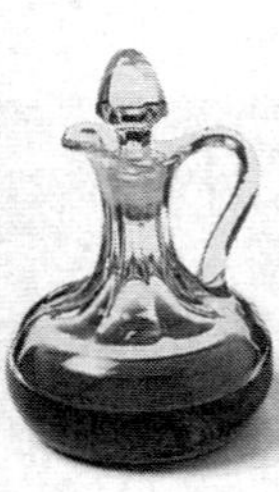

cruet

Cruik•shank (kro͝ok′shăngk′), **George** 1792–1878. British caricaturist and illustrator of works by Charles Dickens.

cruise (kro͞oz) *v.* **cruised, cruis•ing, cruis•es** —*intr.* **1a.** To sail or travel about, as for pleasure. **b.** To go or move along, esp. in an unhurried or unconcerned fashion. **2.** To travel at a constant speed or at a speed providing maximum operating efficiency for a sustained period. **3a.** *Informal* To move leisurely about an area in the hope of discovering something. **b.** *Slang* To look for a sexual partner, as in a public place. **4.** To inspect a wooded area to determine its lumber yield. —*tr.* **1.** To travel about or journey over. **2.** To inspect in order to determine lumber yield. ❖ *n.* The act or an instance of cruising, esp. a sea voyage for pleasure. [Du. *kruisen,* to cross < *kruis,* cross < MDu. *cruce* < Lat. *crux, cruc-,* cross.]

cruise control *n.* **1.** A system in a motor vehicle for maintaining a constant speed. **2.** Maintenance of a constant speed in such a vehicle.

cruise missile *n.* A guided missile that serves as a self-contained precision bomb.

cruis•er (kro͞o′zər) *n.* **1.** One of a class of fast warships of medium tonnage with a long cruising radius and less armor and firepower than a battleship. **2.** A cabin cruiser. **3.** See **squad car.**

cruis•er•weight (kro͞o′zər-wāt′) *n.* A professional boxer weighing more than 175 pounds and not more than 190 pounds (approx. 79.5–85.5 kilograms), heavier than a light heavyweight and lighter than a heavyweight. [Poss. after the *cruiser* warship, the second heaviest warship.]

crul•ler (krŭl′ər) *n.* **1.** *Chiefly Northeastern, Central Atlantic, & Upper Northern US* A small, usu. ring-shaped or twisted cake of sweet dough fried in deep fat. **2.** *Chiefly New England & Pennsylvania* An unraised doughnut, usu. twisted but also shaped into rings or oblongs. [< obsolete Du. *krulle-koken,* rolled-up cake < MDu. *crulle-koken* < *crulle,* curly.]

crumb (krŭm) *n.* **1.** A very small piece broken from a baked item, such as cake or bread. **2.** A small fragment, scrap, or portion: *eraser crumbs.* **3.** The soft inner portion of bread. **4.** *Slang* A contemptible, untrustworthy, or loathsome person. ❖ *v.* **crumbed, crumb•ing, crumbs** —*tr.* **1.** To break into very small pieces; crumble. **2.** To cover or prepare with very small pieces of bread. **3.** To brush (a table or cloth) clear of small scraps or fragments of food. —*intr.* To break apart in very small pieces. [ME *crome* < OE *cruma.*]

crum•ble (krŭm′bəl) *v.* **-bled, -bling, -bles** —*tr.* To break into small fragments or particles. —*intr.* **1.** To fall into small fragments or particles; disintegrate. **2.** To give way; collapse. [Alteration of ME *cremelen* < OE **crymelen,* freq. of *gecrymmian,* to break into crumbs < *cruma,* crumb.]

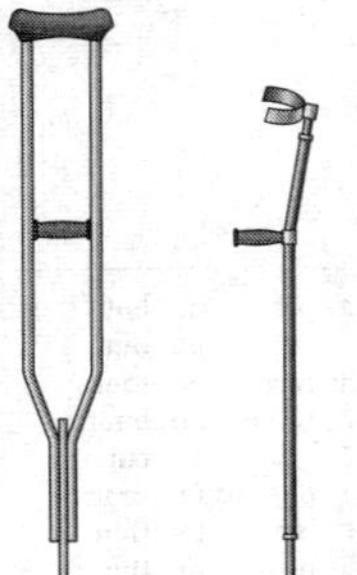

crutch
an axillary crutch (*left*) and a forearm crutch (*right*)

crum•bly (krŭm′blē) *adj.* **-bli•er, -bli•est** Easily crumbled; friable. —**crum′bli•ness** *n.*

crum•horn (krŭm′hôrn′) *n.* Variant of **krummhorn.**

crum•my also **crumb•y** (krŭm′ē) *adj.* **-mi•er, -mi•est** also **-i•er, -i•est** *Slang* **1.** Miserable or wretched. **2.** Shabby or cheap: *a crummy little rowboat.* [Prob. < CRUMB.]

crump (krŭmp) *v.* **crumped, crump•ing, crumps** —*tr.* **1.** To crush or crunch with the teeth. **2.** To strike heavily with a crunching sound. —*intr.* To make a crunching sound, esp. in walking over snow. ❖ *n.* **1a.** A crunching sound. **b.** The sound of an exploding shell. **2.** A heavy blow. [Imit.]

crum•pet (krŭm′pĭt) *n.* A small flat round of bread, baked on a griddle and usu. served toasted. [Poss. < ME *crompid (cake),* curled (cake), prob. p. part. of *crumpen,* to curl up, prob. < *crumb, crump,* crooked < OE.]

crum•ple (krŭm′pəl) *v.* **-pled, -pling, -ples** —*tr.* **1.** To crush together or press into wrinkles; rumple. **2.** To cause to collapse. —*intr.* **1.** To become wrinkled. **2.** To collapse. ❖ *n.* An irregular fold, crease, or wrinkle. [ME *crumplen,* prob. freq. of *crumpen,* to curl up. See CRUMPET.] —**crum′ply** *adj.*

crunch (krŭnch) *v.* **crunched, crunch•ing, crunch•es** —*tr.* **1.** To chew with a noisy crackling sound. **2.** To crush, grind, or tread noisily. **3.** *Slang* To perform operations on; manipulate or process (numerical or mathematical data). —*intr.* **1.** To chew noisily with a crackling sound. **2.** To move with a crushing sound. **3.** To produce or emit a crushing sound. ❖ *n.* **1.** The act or sound of crunching. **2a.** A decisive confrontation. **b.** A critical moment or situation. **3.** A sit-up having a small range of motion that reduces back strain. [Alteration of *craunch,* poss. of imit. orig.] —**crunch′a•ble** *adj.*

crunch•y (krŭn′chē) *adj.* **-i•er, -i•est** Making a crunching or cracking sound, as when chewed; crisp. —**crunch′i•ness** *n.*

crup•per (krŭp′ər) *n.* **1.** A leather strap looped under a horse's tail and attached to a harness or saddle to keep it from slipping forward. **2.** The rump of a horse; the croup. [ME *crouper* < OFr. *cropiere* < *croupe,* rump. See CROUP².]

cru•ral (kro͝or′əl) *adj.* Of or relating to the leg, shank, or thigh. [Lat. *crūrālis* < *crūs, crūr-,* leg.]

crus (kro͞os, krŭs) *n., pl.* **cru•ra** (kro͝or′ə) **1.** The section of the leg or hind limb between the knee and foot; shank. **2a.** A leglike part. **b.** A body part consisting of elongated masses or diverging bands that resemble legs or roots. [Lat. *crūs, crūr-,* leg.]

cru•sade (kro͞o-sād′) *n.* **1.** often **Crusade** Any of the military expeditions undertaken by European Christians in the 11th, 12th, and 13th centuries to recover the Holy Land from the Muslims. **2.** A holy war undertaken with papal sanction. **3.** A vigorous concerted movement for a cause or against an abuse. [Fr. *croisade* and Sp. *cruzada,* both ult. < Lat. *crux, cruc-,* cross.] —**cru•sade′** *v.* —**cru•sad′er** *n.*

cru•sa•do (kro͞o-sä′dō) also **cru•za•do** (-zä′-) *n., pl.* **-does** or **-dos** An old Portuguese coin of gold or silver having a cross pictured on the reverse. [Port. < p. part. of *cruzar,* to mark with a cross < *cruz,* cross < Lat. *crux, cruc-.*]

cruse (kro͞oz, kro͞os) *n.* A small earthenware container for holding liquids. [ME *crouse,* perh. < MDu. *cruyse,* pot.]

crush (krŭsh) *v.* **crushed, crush•ing, crush•es** —*tr.* **1.** To press between opposing bodies so as to break or injure. **2.** To break, pound, or grind (stone or ore, for example) into small fragments or powder. **3.** To put down; subdue. **4.** To overwhelm or oppress severely. **5.** To crumple or rumple. **6.** To hug, esp. with great force. **7.** To press upon, shove, or crowd. **8.** To extract or obtain by pressing or squeezing. **9.** *Archaic* To drink; quaff. —*intr.* **1.** To be or become crushed. **2.** To proceed or move by crowding or pressing. ❖ *n.* **1.** The act of crushing; extreme pressure. **2.** The state of being crushed. **3.** A great crowd. **4.** A substance prepared by or as if by crushing, esp. a fruit drink. **5.** *Informal* **a.** A usu. temporary infatuation. **b.** One who is the object of such an infatuation. **6.** A decisive or critical moment or situation. **7.** The process of stamping or crushing grapes for wine. [ME *crushen* < OFr. *croissir,* of Gmc. orig.] —**crush′a•ble** *adj.* —**crush′er** *n.* —**crush′proof′** (-pro͞of′) *adj.*

crushed (krŭsht) *adj.* Treated so as to have a permanently crinkled or rumpled appearance. Used of a fabric.

crust (krŭst) *n.* **1a.** The hard outer portion or surface area of bread. **b.** A piece of bread consisting mostly of the crust. **c.** A hard and dry piece of bread. **2.** A pastry shell, as of a pie. **3.** A hard crisp covering or surface: *snow with a firm crust.* **4.** A hard deposit formed on the interior of a wine bottle as the wine matures. **5.** *Geology* **a.** The exterior portion of the earth that lies above the Mohorovičić discontinuity. **b.** The outermost solid layer of a planet or moon. **6.** The hard outer covering of certain plants and animals. **7.** *Pathology* An outer layer formed by the drying of a bodily exudate such as blood; a scab. **8.** *Informal* Insolence; audacity; gall. ❖ *v.* **crust•ed, crust•ing, crusts** —*tr.* **1.** To cover with a crust. **2.** To form into a crust. —*intr.* **1.** To become covered with a crust. **2.** To harden into a crust. [ME *cruste* < OFr. *crouste* < Lat. *crūsta.*] —**crust′less** *adj.*

crus•ta•cean (krŭ-stā′shən) *n.* Any of various predominantly aquatic arthropods of the class Crustacea, including lobsters and crabs, characteristically having a segmented body, a chitinous exoskeleton, and paired jointed limbs. [< NLat. *Crūstācea,* class name, neut. pl. of *crustāceus,* hard-shelled < Lat. *crūsta,* shell.] —**crus•ta′cean** *n.*

crus•ta•ceous (krŭ-stā′shəs) *adj.* **1.** Having, resembling, or constituting a hard crust or shell. **2.** Crustacean. [Lat. *crūsta,* shell + -ACEOUS.]

crus•tose (krŭs′tōs′) *adj.* Of or relating to a lichen whose thallus is thin, crusty, and closely adherent to or embedded in the surface on which it grows. [Lat. *crūstōsus,* crusted < *crūsta,* crust.]

crust•y (krŭs′tē) *adj.* **-i•er, -i•est 1.** Having, resembling, or being a crust. **2.** Rough or surly in manner. —**crust′i•ly** *adv.* —**crust′i•ness** *n.*

crutch (krŭch) *n.* **1.** A staff or support used by the physically injured or disabled as an aid in walking, usu. designed to fit under the armpit and often used in pairs. **2.** A forked leg rest on a sidesaddle. **3.** A device used for assistance or support; a prop: *a mnemonic crutch.* **4.** The crotch of a person or an animal. **5.** A forked device or part. ❖ *tr.v.* **crutched, crutch•ing, crutch•es** To support on or as if on crutches; prop up. [ME *crucche* < OE *crycc*.]

Crut·zen (krŏŏt′sən, -sə), **Paul** b. 1933. Dutch meteorologist who shared a 1995 Nobel Prize in chemistry.

crux (krŭks, krŏŏks) *n.*, *pl.* **crux·es** or **cru·ces** (krŏŏ′sēz) **1.** The basic, central, or critical point or feature: *the crux of the matter.* **2.** A puzzling or apparently insoluble problem. **3. Crux** See **Southern Cross.** [Prob. short for Med.Lat. *crux (interpretum),* torment (of interpreters) < Lat. *crux,* cross.]

Cruz (krŏŏs), **Juana Inés de la** 1648?–95. Mexican nun and poet noted for her love lyrics, courtly tributes, satires, plays, and theological writings.

cru·za·do (krŏŏ-zä′dō) *n.* Variant of **crusado.**

Cru·zan (krŏŏ-zăn′) *n.* A native or inhabitant of St. Croix in the US Virgin Islands. [< Am.Sp. *Santa Cruz,* St. Croix.] —**Cru′zan** *adj.*

cru·zei·ro (krŏŏ-zâr′ō, -zâ′rŏŏ) *n.*, *pl.* **-ros** A monetary unit formerly used in Brazil. [Port. < *cruz,* cross (< the figure on the coin) < Lat. *crux.*]

crwth (krŏŏth) *n.* See **crowd**² 1. [Welsh < M Welsh.]

cry (krī) *v.* **cried** (krīd), **cry·ing, cries** (krīz) —*intr.* **1.** To sob or shed tears because of grief, sorrow, or pain; weep. **2.** To call loudly; shout. **3.** To utter a characteristic sound or call. Used of an animal. **4.** To demand or require immediate action or remedy: *cried out for change.* —*tr.* **1.** To utter loudly; call out. **2.** To proclaim or announce in public. **3.** To bring into a particular condition by weeping. **4.** *Archaic* To beg for; implore. ❖ *n.*, *pl.* **cries** (krīz) **1.** A loud utterance of an emotion, such as fear or despair. **2.** A loud exclamation; a shout or call. **3.** A fit of weeping. **4.** An urgent entreaty or appeal. **5.** A public or general demand or complaint. **6.** A common view or general report. **7.** An advertising of wares by calling out. **8.** A rallying call or appeal. **9.** A slogan, esp. a political one. **10.** The characteristic call or utterance of an animal. **11a.** The baying of hounds during the chase. **b.** A pack of hounds. **12.** *Obsolete* Clamor; outcry. **13.** *Obsolete* A public announcement; a proclamation. —*phrasal verbs:* **cry down** To belittle or disparage. **cry off** To break or withdraw from a promise, agreement, or undertaking. **cry up** To praise highly; extol. —*idioms:* **cry havoc** To sound an alarm; warn. **cry (one's) eyes (or heart) out** To weep inconsolably for a long time. **cry on (someone's) shoulder** To tell one's problems to gain sympathy. **cry over spilled milk** To regret in vain what cannot be undone or rectified. **cry wolf** To raise a false alarm. **in full cry** In hot pursuit, as hounds hunting. [ME *crien* < OFr. *crier* < VLat. **critāre* < Lat. *quirītāre,* to cry out, perh. < *Quirītēs,* Roman public officers to whom one would cry out in times of need.]

SYNONYMS *cry, weep, wail, keen, whimper, sob, blubber* These verbs mean to make inarticulate sounds of grief, unhappiness, or pain. *Cry* and *weep* both involve the shedding of tears; *cry* more strongly implies accompanying sound: "*She cried without trying to suppress any of the noisier manifestations of grief and confusion*" (J.D. Salinger). "*I weep for what I'm like when I'm alone*" (Theodore Roethke). *Wail* refers primarily to sustained, inarticulate mournful sound: "*The women . . . began to wail together*" (Joseph Conrad). *Keen* suggests wailing and lamentation for the dead: "*It is the wild Irish women keening over their dead*" (George A. Lawrence). *Whimper* refers to low, plaintive, broken or repressed cries: *The prisoner whimpered for clemency. Sob* is marked by convulsive breathing or gasping: "*sobbing and crying . . . as if her heart would break*" (Laurence Sterne). *Blubber* refers to noisy shedding of tears with broken or inarticulate speech: "*When he drew out what had been a fiddle, crushed to morsels in the greatcoat, he blubbered aloud*" (Emily Brontë).

cry·ba·by (krī′bā′bē) *n.*, *pl.* **-bies** A person who cries or complains frequently with little cause.

cry·ing (krī′ĭng) *adj.* **1.** Requiring action or attention. **2.** Abominable; reprehensible: *a crying shame.*

cryo– *pref.* Cold; freezing: *cryoscopy.* [< Gk. *kruos,* icy cold.]

cry·o·bank (krī′ə-băngk′) *n.* A cryogenic place of storage for semen or transplantable tissues.

cry·o·bi·ol·o·gy (krī′ō-bī-ŏl′ə-jē) *n.* The study of the effects of very low temperatures on living organisms. —**cry′o·bi′o·log′i·cal** (-bī′ə-lŏj′ĭ-kəl) *adj.* —**cry′o·bi·o·log′i·cal·ly** *adv.* —**cry′o·bi·ol′o·gist** *n.*

cry·o·gen (krī′ə-jən) *n.* A liquid, such as liquid nitrogen, that boils at a temperature below about 110°K (−160°C) and is used to obtain very low temperatures; a refrigerant.

cry·o·gen·ic (krī′ə-jĕn′ĭk) *adj.* **1.** Of or relating to low temperatures. **2.** Requiring or suitable to cryogenic storage. —**cry′o·gen′i·cal·ly** *adv.*

cry·o·gen·ics (krī′ə-jĕn′ĭks) *n.* (*used with a sing. or pl. verb*) The production of low temperatures or the study of low-temperature phenomena.

cry·og·e·ny (krī-ŏj′ə-nē) *n.* See **cryogenics.**

cry·o·lite (krī′ə-līt′) *n.* A vitreous natural fluoride of aluminum and sodium, Na₃AlF₆, used chiefly in the electrolytic recovery of aluminum.

cry·om·e·ter (krī-ŏm′ĭ-tər) *n.* A thermometer capable of measuring very low temperatures.

cry·on·ics (krī-ŏn′ĭks) *n.* (*used with a sing. verb*) The process of freezing and storing dead bodies under the assumption that they

may be reanimated. [CRY(O)– + *-onics,* as in BIONICS.] —**cry·on′ic** *adj.*

cry·o·phil·ic (krī′ə-fĭl′ĭk) also **cry·oph·i·lous** (krī-ŏf′ə-ləs) *adj.* Having an affinity for or thriving at low temperatures.

cry·o·probe (krī′ə-prōb′) *n.* A surgical instrument used to apply extreme cold to tissues during cryosurgery.

cry·o·scope (krī′ə-skōp′) *n.* An instrument used to measure the freezing point of a liquid.

cry·os·co·py (krī-ŏs′kə-pē) *n.* A technique for determining the molecular weight of a solute by dissolving a known quantity of it in a solvent and recording the amount by which the freezing point of the solvent drops. —**cry′o·scop′ic** (-ə-skŏp′ĭk) *adj.*

cry·o·stat (krī′ə-stăt′) *n.* An apparatus used to maintain constant low temperature. —**cry′o·stat′ic** *adj.*

cry·o·sur·ger·y (krī′ō-sûr′jə-rē) *n.* The selective exposure of tissues to extreme cold, often by applying a probe containing liquid nitrogen, to bring about the destruction or elimination of abnormal cells. —**cry′o·sur′geon** (-jən) *n.* —**cry′o·sur′gi·cal** (-jĭ-kəl) *adj.*

cry·o·ther·a·py (krī′ō-thĕr′ə-pē) *n.* The local or general use of low temperatures in medical therapy.

crypt (krĭpt) *n.* **1.** An underground vault or chamber, esp. one used as a burial place. **2.** *Anatomy* A small pit, recess, or glandular cavity in the body. [Lat. *crypta* < Gk. *kruptē* < fem. of *kruptos,* hidden < *kruptein,* to hide.]

crypt·a·nal·y·sis (krĭp′tə-năl′ĭ-sĭs) *n.* **1.** The analysis and deciphering of cryptographic writings or systems. **2.** also **crypt·an·a·lyt·ics** (krĭp′tăn-ə-lĭt′ĭks) (*used with a sing. verb*) The study of techniques for cryptanalysis. [CRYPT(OGRAM) + ANALYSIS.] —**crypt·an′a·lyst** (krĭp-tăn′ə-lĭst) *n.* —**crypt·an′a·lyt′ic** (-lĭt′ĭk) *adj.* —**crypt·an′a·lyze′** *v.*

cryp·tic (krĭp′tĭk) also **cryp·ti·cal** (-tĭ-kəl) *adj.* **1.** Having hidden meaning; mystifying. **2.** Secret or occult. **3.** Using code or cipher. **4.** *Biology* Tending to conceal or camouflage: *cryptic coloring.* [LLat. *crypticus* < Gk. *kruptikos* < *kruptos,* hidden < *kruptein,* to hide.] —**cryp′ti·cal·ly** *adv.* —**cryp′tic·ness** *n.*

cryp·to (krĭp′tō) *n.*, *pl.* **-tos** One who covertly supports a certain doctrine, group, or party. ❖ *adj.* **1.** Secret; covert. **2.** Of, relating to, or employing cryptography. [< CRYPTO–.]

crypto– or **crypt–** *pref.* Hidden; secret: *cryptoclastic.* [< Gk. *kruptos,* hidden < *kruptein,* to hide.]

cryp·to·clas·tic (krĭp′tō-klăs′tĭk) *adj.* Composed of microscopic rock fragments.

cryp·to·coc·co·sis (krĭp′tə-kŏ-kō′sĭs) *n.* A systemic infection caused by the fungus *Cryptococcus neoformans* that most often occurs in the central nervous system.

cryp·to·coc·cus (krĭp′tə-kŏk′əs) *n.* Any of various yeastlike fungi of the genus *Cryptococcus,* commonly occurring in the soil and including certain pathogenic species. —**cryp′to·coc′cal** *adj.*

cryp·to·crys·tal·line (krĭp′tō-krĭs′tə-lĭn, -lēn′) *adj.* Having a microscopic crystalline structure.

cryp·to·gam (krĭp′tə-găm′) *n. Botany* A member of a formerly recognized taxonomic group that included all seedless plants and plantlike organisms, such as mosses. [< NLat. *Cryptogamia,* former group name : CRYPTO– + Gk. *gamos,* wedding.] —**cryp′to·gam′ic, cryp·tog′a·mous** (-tŏg′ə-məs) *adj.*

cryp·to·gen·ic (krĭp′tə-jĕn′ĭk) also **cryp·tog·e·nous** (krĭp-tŏj′ə-nəs) *adj.* Of obscure or unknown origin.

cryp·to·gram (krĭp′tə-grăm′) *n.* **1.** A piece of writing in code or cipher. **2.** A figure or representation having a secret or occult significance. —**cryp′to·gram′mic** *adj.*

cryp·to·graph (krĭp′tə-grăf′) *n.* **1.** See **cryptogram** 1. **2.** A system of secret or cipher writing; a cipher. **3a.** A device for translating plain text into cipher. **b.** A device for deciphering codes and ciphers. ❖ *tr.v.* **-graphed, -graph·ing, -graphs** To write (a message, for example) in code or cipher.

cryp·tog·ra·pher (krĭp-tŏg′rə-fər) *n.* One who uses, studies, or develops cryptographic systems and writings.

cryp·tog·ra·phy (krĭp-tŏg′rə-fē) *n.* **1.** The process or skill of communicating in or deciphering secret writings or ciphers. **2.** Secret writing. —**cryp′to·graph′ic** (-tə-grăf′ĭk) *adj.* —**cryp′to·graph′i·cal·ly** *adv.*

cryp·to-Jew (krĭp′tō-jŏŏ′) *n.* A member of a Jewish community forced to convert to another religion and outwardly embracing it while secretly maintaining Jewish practices.

cryp·tol·o·gy (krĭp-tŏl′ə-jē) *n.* The study of cryptanalysis or cryptography. —**cryp′to·log′ic** (-tə-lŏj′ĭk), **cryp′to·log′i·cal** (-ĭ-kəl) *adj.* —**cryp·tol′o·gist** *n.*

cryp·to·me·ri·a (krĭp′tə-mîr′ē-ə) *n.* See **Japanese cedar.** [NLat. *Cryptomeria,* genus name : CRYPTO– + Gk. *meros,* part.]

crypt·or·chism (krĭp-tôr′kĭz′əm) also **crypt·or·chi·dism** (-kĭ-dĭz′əm) *n.* A developmental defect marked by the failure of the testes to descend into the scrotum. [< NLat. *cryptorchidismus* < Gk. *kruptorkhos,* having undescended testes : CRYPT(O)– + *orkhis,* orkhid-, testicle (< Gk. *orkhis*).] —**crypt′or′chid** *n.*

cryp·to·spo·rid·i·um (krĭp′tō-spə-rĭd′ē-əm) *n.* A protozoan of the genus *Cryptosporidium* that is an intestinal parasite in humans and other vertebrates and is capable of causing severe diarrhea. [NLat. *Cryptosporidium,* genus name : CRYPT(O)– + SPOR(O)– + Lat. *-idium,* diminutive suff. (< Gk. *-idion*).]

cryp·to·zo·ite (krĭp′tō-zō′īt′) *n.* A malarial parasite at the stage

ă pat	oi boy	
ā pay	ou out	
âr care	ŏŏ took	
ä father	ŏŏ boot	
ĕ pet	ŭ cut	
ē be	ûr urge	
ĭ pit	th thin	
ī pie	th this	
îr pier	hw which	
ŏ pot	zh vision	
ō toe	ə about,	
ô paw	item	

Stress marks:
′ (primary);
′ (secondary), as in
lexicon (lĕk′sĭ-kŏn′)

Cuba

of development in which it inhabits bodily tissue before invading the red blood cells. [CRYPTO– + ZO(O)– + –ITE¹.]

crys•tal (krĭs′təl) *n.* **1a.** A homogeneous solid formed by a repeating three-dimensional pattern of atoms, ions, or molecules and having fixed distances between constituent parts. **b.** The unit cell of such a pattern. **2.** A mineral, esp. a transparent form of quartz, having a crystalline structure, often characterized by external planar faces. **3a.** A natural or synthetic crystalline material having piezoelectric or semiconducting properties. **b.** An electronic device, such as a detector, using such a material. **4a.** A high-quality, clear, colorless glass. **b.** An object, esp. a vessel or ornament, made of such glass. **c.** Such objects considered as a group. **5.** A clear glass or plastic protective cover for the face of a watch or clock. **6.** *Slang* A stimulant drug, usu. methamphetamine, in its powdered form. ❖ *adj.* Clear or transparent. [ME *cristal* < OFr. < Lat. *crystallum* < Gk. *krustallos,* ice, crystal.]

crystal ball *n.* **1.** A globe of quartz crystal or glass in which images are supposedly visible to fortune tellers. **2.** A vehicle or technique for making predictions.

crystal detector *n.* A rectifying detector used esp. in early radio receivers and consisting of a semiconducting crystal in point contact with a fine metal wire.

crystal gazing *n.* **1.** Divination by gazing into a crystal ball. **2.** The making of determinations or predictions using questionable or unscientific means. —**crystal gazer** *n.*

crystal lattice *n.* A geometric arrangement of the points in space at which the atoms, molecules, or ions of a crystal occur.

crys•tal•lif•er•ous (krĭs′tə-lĭf′ər-əs) also **crys•tal•lig•er•ous** (-lĭj′-) *adj.* Producing or containing crystals.

crys•tal•line (krĭs′tə-lĭn, -lĭn′, -lēn′) *adj.* **1.** Being, relating to, or composed of crystal or crystals. **2.** Resembling crystal, as in transparency or structure. [ME *cristallin* < OFr. < Lat. *crystallinus* < Gk. *krustallinos* < *krustallos,* ice, crystal.] —**crys′tal•lin′i•ty** (-lĭn′ĭ-tē) *n.*

crystalline lens *n.* The lens of an eye.

crys•tal•lite (krĭs′tə-līt′) *n.* Any of numerous minute rudimentary crystalline bodies of unknown composition found in glassy igneous rocks. —**crys′tal•lit′ic** (-lĭt′ĭk) *adj.*

crys•tal•lize also **crys•tal•ize** (krĭs′tə-līz′) *v.* **-lized, -liz•ing, -liz•es** also **-ized, -iz•ing, -iz•es** —*tr.* **1.** To cause to form crystals or assume a crystalline structure. **2.** To give a definite and usu. permanent form to. **3.** To coat with crystals, as of sugar. —*intr.* **1.** To assume a crystalline form. **2.** To take on a definite and usu. permanent form. —**crys′tal•liz′a•ble** *adj.* —**crys′tal•li•za′tion** (-lĭ-zā′shən) *n.* —**crys′tal•liz′er** *n.*

crystallo– or **crystall–** *pref.* Crystal: *crystallize.* [< Gk. *krustallo–* < *krustallos,* crystal.]

crys•tal•log•ra•phy (krĭs′tə-lŏg′rə-fē) *n.* The science of crystal structure and phenomena. —**crys′tal•log′ra•pher** *n.* —**crys′tal•lo•graph′ic** (-lə-grăf′ĭk), **crys′tal•lo•graph′i•cal** *adj.* —**crys′tal•lo•graph′i•cal•ly** *adv.*

crys•tal•loid (krĭs′tə-loid′) *n.* **1.** *Chemistry* A substance that can be crystallized. **2.** *Botany* Any of various minute crystallike particles consisting of protein and found in certain plant cells, esp. oily seeds. —**crys′tal•loid′, crys′tal•loi′dal** (-loid′l) *adj.*

crystal pleat *n.* One of a series of very narrow pleats creased in the same direction.

crystal set *n.* An early radio receiver using a crystal detector.

crystal violet *n.* A dye derived from gentian violet that is used as a general biological stain and an acid-base indicator.

Cs The symbol for the element **cesium.**

CS *abbr.* **1.** capital stock **2.** chief of staff **3.** Christian Science **4.** civil service **5.** conditioned stimulus

CSA *abbr.* Confederate States of America

csc *abbr.* cosecant

csch *abbr.* hyperbolic cosecant

C-sec•tion (sē′sĕk′shən) *n.* A cesarean section.

CSF *abbr.* cerebrospinal fluid

CST *abbr.* Central Standard Time

c-store or **C-store** (sē′stôr′) *n.* A convenience store.

CT *abbr.* **1.** Central Time **2.** Connecticut

ct. *abbr.* **1.** cent **2.** certificate

Ct. *abbr.* **1.** Connecticut **2.** count (title) **3.** court

cten•oid (tĕn′oid′, tē′noid′) *adj. Biology* **1.** Comblike. **2.** Having marginal projections that resemble the teeth of a comb. [Gk. *ktenoeidēs : kteis, kten–,* comb + *-oeidēs,* -oid.]

cten•o•phore (tĕn′ə-fôr′, -fōr′) *n.* Any of various marine animals of the phylum Ctenophora, having transparent gelatinous bodies bearing eight rows of comblike cilia used for swimming. [< NLat. Ctenophora, phylum name : Gk. *kteis, kten–,* comb + NLat. *-phora* < neut. pl. of Gk. *-phoros,* -phore.] —**cte•noph′o•ran** (tĭ-nŏf′ər-ən) *adj.*

Ctes•i•phon (tĕs′ə-fŏn′, tē′sə-) An ancient city of central Iraq on the Tigris R. SE of Baghdad.

ctg. or **ctge.** *abbr.* cartage

ctn *abbr.* cotangent

ctr. *abbr.* center

ctrl *abbr.* control key

CTS *abbr.* carpal tunnel syndrome

CT scan (sē′tē′) *n.* See **CAT scan.**

CT scanner *n.* See **CAT scanner.**

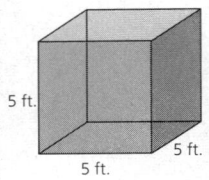

5 ft.

5 ft.

5 ft.

cube

To calculate the volume of a cube, multiply the length of an edge of the cube by itself twice. The volume of this cube is 125 cubic feet.

cubism
Violin and Guitar by Picasso

Cu The symbol for the element **copper**¹ **1.** [< LLat. *cuprum.* See COPPER¹.]

cu. *abbr.* cubic

cua•dril•la (kwä-drē′yə, -drēl′yə) *n., pl.* **-las** The group of assistants to the matador in a bullfight. [Sp., dim. of *cuadra,* square < Lat. *quadra.* See QUADRILLE¹.]

Cuan•do also **Kwan•do** (kwän′dō) A river rising in central Angola and flowing about 965 km (600 mi) generally SE and E to the Zambezi R.

Cuan•za also **Kwan•za** (kwän′zə) A river rising in central Angola and flowing c. 805 km (500 mi) to the Atlantic Ocean.

cuat•ro (kwä′trō) *n., pl.* **-ros** A small guitarlike instrument of Latin America, usu. having four or five pairs of strings. [Sp. < Lat. *quattuor,* four. See QUATRAIN.]

cub (kŭb) *n.* **1.** The young of certain carnivorous animals, such as the bear. **2.** A youth, esp. one who is inexperienced, awkward, or ill-mannered. **3.** A novice or learner, esp. in newspaper reporting. **4. Cub** A Cub Scout. [?]

Cu•ba (kyoō′bə) An island country in the Caribbean Sea S of FL; a Spanish colony until 1898. Cap. Havana. Pop. 10,960,000. —**Cu′ban** *adj. & n.*

cub•age (kyoō′bĭj) *n.* Cubic content, volume, or displacement.

cu•ba•nelle (kyoō′bə-nĕl′) *n.* A cultivar of the tropical pepper *Capsicum annuum* having long, sweet, pale green to red fruits used in cooking. [Ult. after CUBA.]

Cuban heel *n.* A broad heel of moderate height with a slightly tapered back and straight front, used in shoes and boots.

Cuban sandwich *n. Florida* See **submarine** 2. See Regional Note at **submarine.**

cu•ba•ture (kyoō′bə-choōr′, -chər) *n.* **1.** The determination of the volume of a solid. **2.** Cubage. [CUB(E) + (QUADR)ATURE.]

cub•by (kŭb′ē) *n., pl.* **-bies** A small room; a cubbyhole.

cub•by•hole (kŭb′ē-hōl′) *n.* **1.** A snug or cramped space or room. **2.** A small compartment. **3.** A category, esp. an overrestrictive one. [< *cub,* pen, hutch (perh. < Flem. *cubbe* < MFlem.) + HOLE.]

cube (kyoōb) *n.* **1.** *Mathematics* A regular solid having six congruent square faces. **2a.** Something having the general shape of a cube: *a cube of sugar.* **b.** A cubicle used for work or study. **3.** *Mathematics* The third power of a number or quantity. **4. cubes** *Slang* Cubic inches. Used esp. of an internal combustion engine. ❖ *tr.v.* **cubed, cub•ing, cubes 1.** *Mathematics* To raise (a quantity or number) to the third power. **2.** To determine the cubic contents of. **3.** To form or cut into cubes; dice. **4.** To tenderize (meat) by breaking the fibers with superficial cuts in a pattern of squares. [Lat. *cubus* < Gk. *kubos.* N., sense 2b, short for CUBICLE.] —**cub′er** *n.*

cu•bé also **cu•be** (kyoō-bā′, kyoō′bā′) *n.* Any of several tropical American woody plants of the genus *Lonchocarpus* in the pea family, whose roots are a source of rotenone. [Am.Sp.]

cu•beb (kyoō′bĕb′) *n.* **1.** A tropical southeast Asian shrubby vine *(Piper cubeba)* having spicy berrylike fruits and heart-shaped leaves. **2.** The dried unripe berrylike fruit of this plant, used in perfumery, pharmaceuticals, and flavorings. [ME *cubebe* < OFr. < Med.Lat. *cubeba* < Ar. dialectal *kubāba.*]

cube root *n.* A number whose cube is equal to a given number.

cube steak *n.* A thin slice of beef tenderized by cubing.

cu•bic (kyoō′bĭk) *adj.* **1a.** Having the shape of a cube. **b.** Shaped similar to a cube. **2a.** Having three dimensions. **b.** Having a volume equal to a cube whose edge is of a stated length. **3.** *Mathematics* Of the third power, order, or degree. **4.** Of or relating to a crystalline form that has three equal axes at right angles to each other; isometric. ❖ *n. Mathematics* A cubic expression, curve, or equation. —**cu′bic•ly** *adv.*

cu•bi•cal (kyoō′bĭ-kəl) *adj.* **1.** Cubic. **2.** Of or relating to volume. —**cu′bi•cal•ly** *adv.* —**cu′bi•cal•ness** *n.*

cu•bi•cle (kyoō′bĭ-kəl) *n.* A small compartment, as for work, sleep, or study. [ME < Lat. *cubiculum,* bed chamber < *cubāre,* to lie down.]

cubic measure *n.* A unit, such as a cubic foot, or a system of units used to measure volume or capacity.

cubic zirconia *n.* A synthetic gemstone, ZrO_2, used in jewelry as an artificial diamond.

cu•bi•form (kyoō′bə-fôrm′) *adj.* Having the shape of a cube.

cub•ism also **Cub•ism** (kyoō′bĭz′əm) *n.* A nonobjective school of painting and sculpture, marked by the use of abstract, often geometric structures usu. rendered as a set of discrete planes. —**cub′ist** *n.* —**cu•bis′tic** *adj.* —**cu•bis′ti•cal•ly** *adv.*

cu•bit (kyoō′bĭt) *n.* An ancient unit of linear measure, originally equal to the length of the forearm from the tip of the middle finger to the elbow, or about 17 to 22 inches (43 to 56 centimeters). [ME *cubite* < Lat. *cubitum,* cubit, elbow.]

cu•boid (kyoō′boid′) *adj.* Having the approximate shape of a cube. ❖ *n.* **1.** *Anatomy* A tarsal bone on the outer side of the foot in front of the calcaneus and behind the fourth and fifth metatarsal bones. **2.** *Mathematics* A rectangular parallelepiped. —**cu•boi′dal** (kyoō-boid′l) *adj.*

Cub Scout *n.* A member of the junior division of the Boy Scouts, for boys of ages eight through ten.

cu•chi•fri•to (koō′chǐ-frē′tō) *n., pl.* **-tos** A small deep-fried cube of pork. [Am.Sp. : *cuchí,* pig (alteration of Sp. *cochino,* dim.

of *coch*, interj. used to call pigs) + Sp. *frito*, p. part. of *freir*, to fry (< Lat. *frīgere*).

Cu·chul·ain (kŏŏ-kŭlʹĭn, -кнŭlʹ-) *n. Mythology* A hero of ancient Ulster who defended it against the rest of Ireland.

cuck·ing stool (kŭkʹĭng) *n.* An instrument of punishment, consisting of a chair in which the offender was tied and exposed to public derision or ducked in water. [ME *cukking stol* < *cukken*, to defecate, of Scand. orig.]

cuck·old (kŭkʹəld, kŏŏkʹ-) *n.* A man married to an unfaithful wife. ❖ *tr.v.* **-old·ed, -old·ing, -olds** To make a cuckold of. [ME *cokewald* < AN *cucuald < *cucu*, the cuckoo < VLat. *cuccūlus < Lat. *cucūlus*.]

cuck·old·ry (kŭkʹəl-drē, kŏŏkʹ-) *n.* **1.** The state of being a cuckold. **2.** The act of making someone a cuckold.

cuck·oo (kŏŏʹkŏŏ, kŏŏkʹŏŏ) *n., pl.* **-oos 1a.** A grayish European bird (*Cuculus canorus*) that has a characteristic two-note call and lays its eggs in the nests of birds of other species. **b.** Any of various related birds of the family Cuculidae, having grayish-brown plumage. **2.** The cuckoo's call or cry. **3.** *Slang* A foolish or crazy person. ❖ *tr.v.* **-ooed, -oo·ing, -oos** To repeat incessantly. ❖ *adj. Slang* Lacking in sense; foolish or crazy. [ME *cuccu*, of imit. orig.]

cuckoo clock *n.* A wall or shelf clock that announces intervals of time with a sound imitative of a cuckoo's call and often with the emergence of a mechanical bird from a small door.

cuck·oo·flow·er (kŏŏʹkŏŏ-flou′ər, kŏŏkʹŏŏ-) *n.* **1.** A perennial herb (*Cardamine pratensis*) in the mustard family, native to the northern temperate regions and having pink, purple, or white flowers. **2.** See **ragged robin.** [< the association of its time of blooming with the cuckoo's spring call.]

cuck·oo·pint (kŏŏʹkŏŏ-pīnt′, kŏŏkʹŏŏ-) *n.* A European plant (*Arum maculatum*) having arrow-shaped leaves and a yellow-green spathe. [< obsolete *cuckoopintle* < ME *cokkupintel* < *cokku, cuccu*, cuckoo; see CUCKOO + *pintel*, penis; see PINTLE.]

cuckoo spit *n.* A frothy mass of liquid secreted on plant stems as a protective covering by nymphs of the spittlebug.

cu·cul·late (kyŏŏ-kŭl-lāt′, kyŏŏʹkəl-lāt′) *adj. Botany* Having the shape of a cowl or hood; hooded. [Med.Lat. *cucullātus* < Lat. *cucullus*, hood.] —**cu′cul·late·ly** *adv.*

cu·cum·ber (kyŏŏʹkŭm′bər) *n.* **1a.** A tendril-bearing, climbing or sprawling annual plant (*Cucumis sativus*) having edible cylindrical fruit with a green rind and crisp white flesh. **b.** The edible fruit of this plant. **2.** Any of several related or similar plants, such as the bur cucumber. [ME *cucomer* < OFr. *coucombre* < Lat. *cucumis, cucumer-*.]

cucumber tree *n.* Any of certain magnolias, esp. *Magnolia acuminata*, a deciduous tree of eastern North America, having greenish-yellow flowers and a cucumber-shaped fruit.

cu·cur·bit (kyŏŏ-kûrʹbĭt) *n.* **1.** Any of various mostly climbing or trailing plants of the family Cucurbitaceae, which includes the squash, pumpkin, and cucumber. **2.** A gourd-shaped flask forming the body of an alembic, formerly used in distillation. [ME *cucurbite* < OFr. < Lat. *cucurbita*, gourd.]

Cú·cu·ta (kŏŏʹkə-tə, -kŏŏ-tä′) A city of NE Colombia near the Venezuelan border. Pop. 383,584.

cud (kŭd) *n.* **1.** Food regurgitated from the first stomach to the mouth of a ruminant and chewed again. **2.** Something held in the mouth and chewed. [ME < OE *cudu.*]

cud·bear (kŭdʹbâr′) *n.* A purplish-red dye derived from certain lichens. [After *Cuthbert* Gordon, 18th-cent. Scottish chemist.]

cud·dle (kŭdʹl) *v.* **-dled, -dling, -dles** —*tr.* To fondle in the arms; hug tenderly. —*intr.* To nestle; snuggle. ❖ *n.* The act of cuddling. [?] —**cud′dle·some, cud′dly** *adj.*

cud·dy[1] (kŭdʹē) *n., pl.* **-dies 1.** *Nautical* A small cabin or the galley on a ship. **2.** A small room, cupboard, or closet. [?]

cud·dy[2] (kŭdʹē) *n., pl.* **-dies** *Scots* **1.** A donkey. **2.** A fool; a dolt. [Perh. < *Cuddy*, nickname for *Cuthbert*.]

cudg·el (kŭjʹəl) *n.* A short heavy stick; a club. ❖ *tr.v.* **-eled, -el·ing, -els** or **-elled, -el·ling, -els** To beat or strike with or as if with a cudgel. [ME *cuggel* < OE *cycgel*.]

cud·weed (kŭdʹwēd′) *n.* **1.** Any of various woolly plants of the genus *Gnaphalium* in the composite family, having small whitish or yellowish flower heads. **2.** Any of several similar and related plants in the genus *Filago.*

cue[1] (kyŏŏ) *n.* **1.** *Games* A long tapered rod with a leather tip, used in billiards and pool. **2.** *Games* A long stick with a concave attachment at one end for shoving disks in shuffleboard. **3.** A queue of hair. **4.** A line of waiting people or vehicles; a queue. ❖ *v.* **cued, cu·ing, cues** —*tr.* **1.** *Games* To strike with a cue. **2.** To braid or twist (hair) into a queue. —*intr.* To form a line or queue. [Variant of QUEUE.]

cue[2] (kyŏŏ) *n.* **1.** A signal, such as a word, used to prompt another event in a performance, such as an actor's speech. **2a.** A reminder or prompting. **b.** A hint or suggestion. **3.** *Psychology* A stimulus that elicits or signals a type of behavior. **4.** *Archaic* One's assigned role or function. **5.** *Archaic* A mood; a disposition. ❖ *tr.v.* **cued, cu·ing, cues 1.** To give a cue to; signal or prompt. **2.** To insert into the sequence of a performance. **3.** To position (an audio or video recording) in readiness for playing: *cue up a record on the turntable.* —*phrasal verb:* **cue in** To give information or instructions to, as to a latecomer. [Perh. < *q, qu,* abbr. of Lat.

quandō, when, used for actors' copies of plays. See **kʷo-** in App.]

cue[3] (kyŏŏ) *n.* The letter *q.*

cue ball *n.* The white ball in billiards and pool.

Cuer·na·va·ca (kwĕr-nə-väʹkä, -nä-väʹkä) A city of S-central Mexico in the **Cuernavaca Valley** near Mexico City. Pop. 281,294.

cues·ta (kwĕsʹtə) *n.* A ridge with a gentle slope on one side and a cliff on the other. [Sp. < Lat. *costa*, side.]

cuff[1] (kŭf) *n.* **1a.** A fold used as trimming at the bottom of a sleeve. **b.** A band, often open with a button closure, at the bottom of a sleeve. **2.** The turned-up fold at the bottom of a trouser leg. **3.** The band at the top of a sock. **4.** The part of a glove over the wrist. **5.** A handcuff. **6.** *Medicine* An inflatable band used with a sphygmomanometer in measuring arterial blood pressure. ❖ *tr.v.* **cuffed, cuff·ing, cuffs 1.** To form a cuff on. **2.** To put handcuffs on. —*idioms:* **off the cuff** In an extemporaneous or informal manner. **on the cuff** On credit. [ME *cuffe*, mitten.]

cuff[2] (kŭf) *tr.v.* **cuffed, cuff·ing, cuffs** To strike with or as if with the open hand; slap. ❖ *n.* Such a blow or slap. [?]

cuff link *or* **cuff·link** (kŭfʹlĭngk′) *n.* A fastening for a shirt cuff, usu. of two buttons or buttonlike parts connected with a chain or shank that passes through two slits in the cuff.

Cu·fic (kŏŏʹfĭk, kyŏŏʹ-) *adj.* Variant of **Kufic.**

Cu·ia·bá (kŏŏ′yə-bäʹ) A city of W-central Brazil W of Brasília on the **Cuiabá River,** c. 483 km (300 mi). Pop. 401,303.

cui bo·no (kwē′ bōʹnō) *n.* Utility, advantage, or self-interest considered as the determinant of value or motivation. [< Lat., for whom (it is) of advantage : *cui*, to whose, dative of *quī* + *bonō*, dative of *bonum*, advantage.]

cui·rass (kwĭ-räsʹ) *n.* **1a.** A piece of armor for protecting the breast and back. **b.** The breastplate alone. **2.** A defense or protection. **3.** *Zoology* A protective covering of bony plates or scales. ❖ *tr.v.* **-rassed, -rass·ing, -rass·es** To protect with a cuirass. [ME *curas* < OFr. *curasse*, prob. alteration of O Provençal *coirassa* < LLat. *coriācea (vestis)*, leather (garment), fem. of *coriāceus* < Lat. *corium*, hide. See **sker-**[1] in App.]

cui·ras·sier (kwĭr′ə-sîr′) *n.* A horse soldier wearing a cuirass. [Fr. < *cuirasse*, cuirass < OFr. *curasse*. See CUIRASS.]

Cui·si·nart (kwē′zə-närt′, kwē′zə-närt′) A trademark used for a kind of food processor and its attachments.

cui·sine (kwĭ-zēnʹ) *n.* **1.** A characteristic manner or style of preparing food: *Spanish cuisine.* **2.** Food; fare. [Fr. < OFr. < VLat. **cocīna,* var. of Lat. *coquīna,* kitchen, cookery < *coquere,* to cook. See pekʷ- in App.]

cuisse (kwĭs) *also* **cuish** (kwĭsh) *n.* Plate armor worn to protect the front of the thigh. [ME *quisse*, prob. back-formation < *quisseues*, pl. of *quisseu*, cuisse < OFr. *quisseuz*, pl. of *quissel* < *quisse*, thigh < Lat. *coxa*, hip.]

cuit·la·co·che (kwēt′lä-kōʹchä) *also* **huit·la·co·che** (wēt′-) *n.* A bulbous black fungus (*Ustilago maydis*) that infects corn, producing kernels with a smoky-sweet flavor that are used in a variety of Mexican dishes. [Am.Sp. < Nahuatl *quitlacochtli : quitlatl, dung + cochtli*, asleep.]

cuke (kyŏŏk) *n. Informal* A cucumber.

Cul·bert·son (kŭlʹbərt-sən), **Ely** 1891–1955. Amer. contract bridge authority whose books include *The Contract Bridge Blue Book* (1930).

culch *or* **cultch** (kŭlch) *n.* **1.** A natural bed for oysters, consisting of gravel or crushed shells to which the oyster spawn may adhere. **2.** The spawn of the oyster. **3.** *also* **scultch** *or* **sculch** (skŭlch) *New England* Clean trash or rubbish, such as string, paper, and cloth. **4.** A person or thing not highly regarded. [Perh. ult. < OFr. *culche, couche*, couch. See COUCH.]

cul-de-sac (kŭlʹdĭ-săk′, kŏŏlʹ-) *n., pl.* **culs-de-sac** (kŭlz′-, kŏŏlz′-) *or* **cul-de-sacs** (kŭlʹ-) **1a.** A dead-end street. **b.** An impasse. **2.** *Anatomy* A saclike cavity or tube open only at one end. [Fr. : *cul*, bottom + *de*, of + *sac*, back.]

Cu·le·bra Cut (kŏŏ-lāʹbrə) See **Gaillard Cut.**

Culebra Peak A mountain, 4,284.3 m (14,047 ft), in the Sangre de Cristo Mts. of extreme S-central CO.

cu·let (kyŏŏʹlĭt, kŭlʹĭt) *n.* **1.** The small flat face at the bottom of a gem cut as a brilliant. **2.** Armor consisting of overlapping plates used to protect the buttocks. [Obsolete Fr., dim. of *cul*, rump < Lat. *cūlus.* See **(s)keu-** in App.]

cu·lex (kyŏŏʹlĕks) *n., pl.* **-li·ces** (-lĭ-sēz′) Any of various mosquitoes of the genus *Culex*, which includes the common house mosquito (*C. pipiens*). [Lat., gnat.]

Cu·lia·cán (kŏŏl′yə-känʹ) A city of W Mexico WNW of Durango on the **Culiacán River,** c. 282 km (175 mi); founded 1531. Pop. 304,826.

cu·li·nar·y (kyŏŏʹlə-nĕr′ē, kŭlʹə-) *adj.* Of or relating to a kitchen or to cookery. [Lat. *culīnārius* < *culīna*, kitchen. See pekʷ- in App.]

cull (kŭl) *tr.v.* **culled, cull·ing, culls 1.** To pick out from others; select. **2.** To gather; collect. **3.** To remove rejected members or parts from (a herd, for example). ❖ *n.* Something picked out from others, esp. one that is inferior. [ME *cullen* < OFr. *cuillir* < Lat. *colligere.* See **cull′er** *n.*]

Cul·len (kŭlʹən), **Countée** 1903–46. Amer. poet whose works include *Colors* (1926) and *Copper Sun* (1927).

cul·let (kŭlʹĭt) *n.* Scraps of broken or waste glass gathered for re-

cuckoopint
Arum maculatum

melting, esp. with new material. [Prob. alteration of *collet*, neck of glass left on the blowing iron < Fr., collar, dim. of *col*, neck < OFr. < Lat. *collum*. See k**w**el- in App.]

cul·lion (kŭl′yən) *n. Archaic* A contemptible fellow; a rascal. [ME *coilon*, testicle < OFr. *coillon* < Lat. *culleus*, bag.]

cul·lis (kŭl′ĭs) *n.* A gutter or groove in a roof. [ME *colis* < OFr. *coleis*, channel < *coler*, to pour < Lat. *cōlāre*, to filter < *cōlum*, sieve.]

Cul·lo·den Moor (kə-lŏd′n, -lŏd′n) A moor in N Scotland E of Inverness; site of the final defeat of the Highland Jacobites (1746).

cul·ly (kŭl′ē) *Archaic n., pl.* **-lies** A fool or dupe. ❖ *tr.v.* **-lied, -ly·ing, -lies** To fool; cheat. [Perh. < CULLION.]

culm[1] (kŭlm) *n.* The stem of a grass or similar plant. [Lat. *culmus*, stalk.]

culm[2] (kŭlm) *n.* **1.** Waste from anthracite coal mines, consisting of fine coal, coal dust, and dirt. **2a.** Carboniferous shale. **b.** Inferior anthracite coal. [ME *colme*, coal dust, perh. < OE *col*, coal.]

cul·mi·nant (kŭl′mə-nənt) *adj.* **1.** Being at the highest altitude. **2.** Reaching the highest point or degree; highest.

cul·mi·nate (kŭl′mə-nāt′) —*intr.* **-nat·ed, -nat·ing, -nates** **1a.** To reach the highest point or degree; climax. **b.** To come to completion; end. **2.** *Astronomy* To reach the highest point above an observer's horizon. Used of stars and other celestial bodies. —*tr.* To bring to the point of greatest intensity or to completion. [LLat. *culmināre, culmināt-* < Lat. *culmen, culmin-*, summit.] —**cul′mi·na′tion** *n.*

cu·lotte (kōō-lŏt′, kyōō-, kōō′lŏt′, kyōō′-) *n.* A woman's full trousers cut to resemble a skirt. Often used in the plural. [Fr., breeches, dim. of *cul*, rump < Lat. *cūlus*. See (s)keu- in App.]

cul·pa·ble (kŭl′pə-bəl) *adj.* Deserving of blame or censure as being wrong, evil, improper, or injurious. [ME *coupable* < OFr. < Lat. *culpābilis* < *culpāre*, to blame < *culpa*, fault.] —**cul′pa·bil′i·ty** *n.* —**cul′pa·bly** *adv.*

Cul·pep·er (kŭl′pĕp′ər), Lord **Thomas** 1635–89. English colonial administrator who governed Virginia (1677–83).

cul·prit (kŭl′prĭt) *n.* **1.** One charged with an offense or crime. **2.** One guilty of a fault or crime. [Prob. < *cul. prit*, abbr. for AN **culpable: prit d'averrer nostre bille*, guilty: (I am) ready to aver our indictment.]

culs-de-sac (kŭlz′dĭ-săk′, kōōlz′-) *n.* A plural of **cul-de-sac.**

cult (kŭlt) *n.* **1a.** A religion or religious sect generally considered to be extremist or false, with its followers often living communally under an authoritarian charismatic leader. **b.** The followers of such a religion or sect. **2.** A system or community of religious worship and ritual. **3.** The formal means of expressing religious reverence. **4.** A usu. nonscientific method claimed by its originator to cure a particular disease. **5a.** Obsessive, esp. faddish devotion to or veneration for a person, principle, or thing. **b.** The object of such devotion. **6.** An exclusive group of persons sharing an esoteric, usu. artistic or intellectual interest. [Lat. *cultus*, worship < p. part. of *colere*, to cultivate. See k**w**el- in App.] —**cul′tic, cult′ish** *adj.* —**cult′ism** *n.* —**cult′ist** *n.*

cultch (kŭlch) *n.* Variant of **culch.**

cul·ti (kŭl′tī) *n.* A plural of **cultus.**

cul·ti·gen (kŭl′tə-jən) *n.* An organism, esp. a cultivated plant, not known to have a wild or uncultivated counterpart. [CULTI(VATED) + -GEN.]

cul·ti·va·ble (kŭl′tə-və-bəl) *adj.* Capable of undergoing cultivation: *cultivable land.* —**cul′ti·va·bil′i·ty** *n.*

cul·ti·var (kŭl′tə-vär′, -vâr′) *n.* A race or variety of a plant that has been created or selected intentionally and maintained through cultivation. [*culti*(vated) *var*(iety).]

cul·ti·vate (kŭl′tə-vāt′) *tr.v.* **-vat·ed, -vat·ing, -vates** **1a.** To improve and prepare (land), as by plowing, for raising crops; till. **b.** To loosen or dig soil around (growing plants). **2.** To grow or tend (a plant or crop). **3.** To promote the growth of (a biological culture). **4.** To nurture; foster. See Syns at **nurture. 5.** To form and refine, as by education. **6.** To seek the acquaintance or goodwill of. [Med.Lat. *cultivāre, cultivāt-* < *cultīvus*, tilled < Lat. *cultus*, p. part. of *colere*, to till. See k**w**el- in App.] —**cul′ti·vat′a·ble** *adj.*

cul·ti·vat·ed (kŭl′tə-vā′tĭd) *adj.* **1.** Of, relating to, or produced in cultivation. **2.** Educated; polished; refined.

cul·ti·va·tion (kŭl′tə-vā′shən) *n.* **1a.** The act of cultivating. **b.** The state of being cultivated. **2.** Refinement; culture.

cul·ti·va·tor (kŭl′tə-vā′tər) *n.* **1.** One who cultivates. **2.** An implement or machine for loosening the soil and destroying weeds around growing plants.

cul·trate (kŭl′trāt′) also **cul·trat·ed** (-trā′tĭd) *adj.* Sharp-edged and pointed; knifelike: *cultrate leaves.* [Lat. *cultrātus* < *culter, cultr-*, knife.]

cul·tur·al (kŭl′chər-əl) *adj.* Of or relating to culture or cultivation. —**cul′tur·al·ly** *adv.*

cultural anthropology *n.* The scientific study of the development of human cultures based on ethnologic, ethnographic, linguistic, social, and psychological data and methods of analysis.

cul·ture (kŭl′chər) *n.* **1a.** The totality of socially transmitted behavior patterns, arts, beliefs, institutions, and all other products of human work and thought. **b.** These products considered as the expression of a particular period, class, community, or popula-

tion. **c.** These products considered with respect to a particular category, such as a field, subject, or mode of expression: *oral culture.* **d.** The predominating attitudes and behavior that characterize a group or organization: *corporate culture.* **2.** Intellectual and artistic activity and the works produced by it. **3a.** Development of the intellect through training or education. **b.** Enlightenment resulting from such training or education. **4.** A high degree of taste and refinement formed by aesthetic and intellectual training. **5.** Special training and development. **6.** The cultivation of soil; tillage. **7.** The breeding of animals or growing of plants, esp. to produce improved stock. **8.** *Biology* **a.** The culturing of microorganisms or other living matter. **b.** Such a growth or colony. ❖ *tr.v.* **-tured, -tur·ing, -tures** **1.** To cultivate. **2a.** To grow (microorganisms, for example) in a culture medium. **b.** To use (a substance) as a culture medium. [ME, cultivation < OFr. < Lat. *cultūra* < *cultus*, p. part. of *colere*. See CULTIVATE.]

cul·tured (kŭl′chərd) *adj.* **1.** Educated, polished, and refined. **2.** Produced under artificial and controlled conditions.

culture medium *n.* A liquid or gelatinous substance containing nutrients in which microorganisms or tissues are cultivated for scientific purposes.

culture shock *n.* A condition of confusion and anxiety affecting a person suddenly exposed to an alien culture or milieu.

cul·tus (kŭl′təs) *n., pl.* **-tus·es** or **-ti** (-tī) A cult, esp. a religious one. [Lat., veneration. See CULT.]

cul·ver (kŭl′vər) *n.* A dove or pigeon. [ME < OE *culufre* < VLat. *columbra < Lat. *columbula*, dim. of *columba*, dove.]

cul·ver·in (kŭl′vər-ĭn) *n.* **1.** An early, crudely made musket. **2.** A long heavy cannon used in the 16th and 17th centuries. [ME < OFr. *coulevrine* < *couleuvre*, snake < Lat. *colubra*, fem. of *coluber*.]

cul·vert (kŭl′vərt) *n.* **1.** A sewer or drain crossing under a road or embankment. **2a.** The part of a road or embankment over a culvert. **b.** The channel or conduit for a culvert. [?]

cum (kōōm, kŭm) *prep.* Together with; plus. Often used in combination: *our attic-cum-studio.* [Lat. See kom in App.]

cum. *abbr.* cumulative

Cu·mae (kyōō′mē) An ancient city and Greek colony of S-central Italy near present-day Naples; adopted Roman culture after the 2nd cent. B.C.

Cu·ma·ná (kōō′mä-nä′) A city of NE Venezuela on the Caribbean Sea E of Caracas; founded 1521. Pop. 232,228.

cum·ber (kŭm′bər) *tr.v.* **-bered, -ber·ing, -bers** **1.** To weigh down; burden: *cumbered with duties.* **2.** To hamper or hinder, as by being in the way. **3.** To litter; clutter up. **4.** *Archaic* To bother; distress. ❖ *n.* A hindrance; an encumbrance. [ME *cumbren*, to annoy < OFr. *combrer* < *combre*, hindrance < VLat. *comboros, of Celt. orig.] —**cum′ber·er** *n.*

Cum·ber·land Gap (kŭm′bər-lənd) A natural passage through the Cumberland Plateau near the junction of the KY, VA, and TN borders.

Cumberland Plateau or **Cumberland Mountains** The SW section of the Appalachian Mts., extending NE to SW from S WV through VA, KY, and TN into N AL.

Cumberland River A river rising in SE KY and flowing c. 1,105 km (687 mi) SW into N TN then NW to the Ohio R. in SW KY.

cum·ber·some (kŭm′bər-səm) *adj.* **1.** Difficult to handle because of weight or bulk. **2.** Troublesome or onerous. —**cum′ber·some·ly** *adv.*

cum·bi·a (kōōm′bē-ə) *n.* **1.** A Latin-American dance marked by short sliding steps. **2.** Music for this dance. [Am.Sp.]

Cum·bri·a (kŭm′brē-ə) A Celtic kingdom of NW England. The S part came under Anglo-Saxon control c. 944; the N portion passed to Scotland in 1018. —**Cum′bri·an** *adj. & n.*

cum·brous (kŭm′brəs) *adj.* Cumbersome. [ME < *cumbren*, to annoy. See CUMBER.] —**cum′brous·ly** *adv.* —**cum′brous·ness** *n.*

cum·in (kŭm′ĭn, kōō′mĭn, kyōō′-) *n.* **1a.** An annual Mediterranean herb (*Cuminum cyminum*) in the parsley family, having finely divided leaves and clusters of small white or pink flowers. **b.** The seedlike fruit of this plant used for seasoning. **2.** Black cumin. [ME < OFr. < Lat. *cumīnum* < Gk. *kumīnon*, prob. of Semitic orig.; akin to Akkadian *kamūnu, kammūnu.*]

cum lau·de (kōōm lou′də, lou′dĕ, kŭm lô′dĕ) *adv. & adj.* With honor. Used to express academic distinction: *graduated cum laude.* [Prob. Med.Lat. : Lat. *cum*, with + Lat. *laude*, ablative of *laus*, praise.]

cum·mer·bund (kŭm′ər-bŭnd′) *n.* A broad sash, esp. one worn as an article of formal dress, as with a dinner jacket. [Hindi *kamarband* < Pers. : *kamar*, waist + *band*, band; see BUND[1].]

Cum·mings (kŭm′ĭngz), **Edward Estlin** Usu. styled e.e. cummings. 1894–1962. Amer. writer best known for his lyrical and typographically inventive poetry.

cum·quat (kŭm′kwŏt′) *n.* Variant of **kumquat.**

cum·shaw (kŭm′shô′) *n.* A tip; a gratuity. [Pidgin E. < Chin. (Amoy) *gamsia*, an expression of thanks.]

cu·mu·late (kyōōm′yə-lāt′) *v.* **-lat·ed, -lat·ing, -lates** —*tr.* **1.** To gather in a heap; accumulate. **2.** To combine into one unit; merge. —*intr.* To become massed. ❖ *adj.* Having cumulated or been cumulated. [Lat. *cumulāre, cumulāt-* < *cumulus*, heap.] —**cu′mu·la′tion** *n.*

cummerbund

cu·mu·la·tive (kyōōm′yə-lā′tĭv, -yə-lə-tĭv) *adj.* **1.** Increasing or enlarging by successive addition. **2.** Acquired by or resulting from accumulation. **3.** Of or relating to interest or a dividend added to the next payment if not paid when due. **4.** *Law* **a.** Supporting the same point as earlier evidence. **b.** Imposed more severely upon a repeat offender. **c.** Following successively. **5.** *Statistics* **a.** Relating to the sum of the frequencies of experimentally determined values of a random variable that are less than or equal to a specified value. **b.** Relating to experimental error that increases in magnitude with each successive measurement. —**cu′mu·la′tive·ly** *adv.* —**cu′mu·la′tive·ness** *n.*

cumulative voting *n.* A system of voting in which each voter is given as many votes as there are positions to be filled and allowed to cast those votes for one candidate or distribute them in any way among the candidates.

cu·mu·li·form (kyōōm′yə-lə-fôrm′) *adj.* Having the shape of a cumulus.

cumulo– or **cumuli–** or **cumul–** *pref.* Cumulus: *cumulonimbus.* [< CUMULUS.]

cu·mu·lo·nim·bus (kyōōm′yə-lō-nĭm′bəs) *n., pl.* **-bus·es** or **-bi** (-bī) An extremely dense, vertically developed cumulus with a glaciated top extending to great heights, usu. producing heavy rains, thunderstorms, or hailstorms.

cu·mu·lous (kyōōm′yə-ləs) *adj.* Resembling a pile or mound.

cu·mu·lus (kyōōm′yə-ləs) *n., pl.* **-li** (-lī′) **1.** A dense, white, fluffy, flat-based, cloud with a multiple rounded top, usu. formed by the ascent of thermally unstable air masses. **2.** A pile, mound, or heap. [Lat., heap.]

Cu·na (kōō′nə) *n.* Variant of **Kuna.**

Cu·nax·a (kyōō-nǎk′sə) An ancient town of Babylonia NW of Babylon; site of a battle (401 B.C.) in which Artaxerxes II of Persia defeated his brother Cyrus the Younger.

cunc·ta·tion (kŭngk-tā′shən) *n.* Procrastination; delay. [Lat. *cūnctātiō,* *-tiōn- < cūnctātus,* p. part. of *cūnctārī,* to delay.] —**cunc′ta·tive** (kŭngk′tā′tĭv, -tə-tĭv), —**cunc′ta′tor** *n.*

cu·ne·al (kyōō′nē-əl) *adj.* Wedge-shaped. [NLat. *cuneālis* < Lat. *cuneus,* wedge.]

cu·ne·ate (kyōō′nē-ĭt, -āt′) *adj. Botany* Wedge-shaped. [Lat. *cuneātus,* p. part. of *cuneāre,* to make wedge-shaped < *cuneus,* wedge.] —**cu′ne·ate·ly** *adv.*

cu·ne·i·form (kyōō′nē-ə-fôrm′, kyōō-nē′-) *adj.* **1.** Wedge-shaped. **2a.** Being a character or characters formed by the arrangement of small wedge-shaped elements and used in ancient Sumerian, Akkadian, Assyrian, Babylonian, and Persian writing. **b.** Relating to, composed in, or using such characters. **3.** *Anatomy* Of, relating to, or being a wedge-shaped bone or cartilage. ❖ *n.* **1.** Writing typified by the use of cuneiform characters. **2.** *Anatomy* A wedge-shaped bone, esp. one in the tarsus of the foot. [Lat. *cuneus,* wedge + –FORM.]

Cu·ne·ne also **Ku·ne·ne** (kōō-nā′nə) A river rising in W-central Angola and flowing c. 1,207 km (750 mi) S and W to the Atlantic Ocean.

cun·ner (kŭn′ər) *n.* A small fish (*Tautogolabrus adspersus*) of North American Atlantic waters. [?]

cun·ni·lin·gus (kŭn′ə-lĭng′gəs) *n.* Oral stimulation of the clitoris or vulva. [NLat. < Lat., he who licks the vulva : *cunnus,* vulva; see **(s)keu–** in App. + *lingere,* to lick; see **leigh–** in App.] —**cun′ni·lin′gual** *adj.*

cun·ning (kŭn′ĭng) *adj.* **1.** Marked by or given to artful subtlety and deceptiveness. **2.** Executed with or exhibiting ingenuity. **3.** Delicately pleasing; pretty or cute. ❖ *n.* **1.** Skill in deception; guile. **2.** Skill or adeptness in execution or performance; dexterity. [ME, pr. part. of *connen,* to know < OE *cunnan.* See **gnō–** in App.] —**cun′ning·ly** *adv.* —**cun′ning·ness** *n.*

Cunningham (kŭn′ing-hăm′), **Merce** b. c. 1922. Amer. dancer and choreographer whose works include *Squaregame* (1976).

cunt (kŭnt) *n.* **1.** *Vulgar Slang* The female genitals. **2.** *Offensive Slang* **a.** Used as a disparaging term for a woman. **b.** Used as a disparaging term for a disagreeable person. [ME *cunte.*]

cup (kŭp) *n.* **1a.** A small open container, usu. with a flat bottom and a handle, used for drinking. **b.** Such a container and its contents. **2.** A unit of capacity or volume equal to 16 tablespoons or 8 fluid ounces (237 milliliters). **3.** The bowl of a drinking vessel. **4.** The chalice or the wine used in the Eucharist. **5.** A decorative cup-shaped vessel awarded as a prize or trophy. **6.** *Sports* A golf hole or the metal container inside a hole. **7.** Either of the two parts of a brassiere that fit over the breasts. **8.** An athletic supporter having a reinforcement of plastic or metal. **9.** A sweetened, flavored, usu. chilled beverage, esp. one made with wine. **10.** A dish served in a cup-shaped vessel. **11a.** A cuplike object. **b.** *Biology* A cuplike structure or organ. **12.** A lot or portion to be suffered or enjoyed. ❖ *tr.v.* **cupped, cup·ping, cups 1.** To place in or as in a cup. **2.** To shape like a cup. **3.** To subject to cupping. —**idioms: cup of tea 1.** Something that one excels in or enjoys. **2.** A matter to be reckoned or dealt with. **in (one's) cups** Intoxicated; drunk. [ME *cuppe* < OE < LLat. *cuppa,* drinking vessel, perh. var. of Lat. *cūpa,* tub, cask.]

cup·bear·er (kŭp′bâr′ər) *n.* One who fills and distributes cups of wine, as in a royal household.

cup·board (kŭb′ərd) *n.* A closet or cabinet, usu. with shelves for storing food, crockery, and utensils.

cup·cake (kŭp′kāk′) *n.* A small cake baked in a cup-shaped container.

cu·pel (kyōō′pəl, kyōō-pĕl′) *n.* **1.** A porous cup, often made of bone ash, used in assaying to separate precious metals from base elements. **2.** The bottom or receptacle in a silver-refining furnace. ❖ *tr.v.* **-peled, -pel·ing, -pels** or **-pelled, -pel·ling, -pels** To assay or separate from base metals in a cupel. [Fr. *coupelle* < OFr., dim. of *coupe,* cup < LLat. *cuppa,* drinking vessel.] —**cu′pel·ler, cu′pel·er** *n.*

cu·pel·la·tion (kyōō′pə-lā′shən) *n.* A refining process for nonoxidizing metals, such as gold, in which a metallic mixture is oxidized at high temperatures and base metals are separated by absorption into the walls of a cupel.

cup·ful (kŭp′fŏol′) *n., pl.* **-fuls 1.** The amount that a cup can hold. **2.** A measure of capacity equal to one cup.

cup fungus *n.* Any of various ascomycetous fungi, esp. of the family Pezizaceae, characterized by a spore-bearing structure that is often stalkless and cup-shaped or disk-shaped.

Cu·pid (kyōō′pĭd) *n.* **1.** *Roman Mythology* The god of love; the son of Venus. **2. cupid** A representation of Cupid as a naked cherubic boy usu. having wings and holding a bow and arrow, used as a symbol of love. [ME *Cupide* < OFr. < Lat. *cupīdō,* desire, Cupid < *cupere,* to desire.]

cu·pid·i·ty (kyōō-pĭd′ĭ-tē) *n.* Excessive desire, esp. for wealth; covetousness or avarice. [ME *cupidite* < OFr. < Lat. *cupiditās* < *cupidus,* desiring < *cupere,* to desire.]

Cupid's bow (kyōō′pĭdz bō′) *n., pl.* **Cupid's bows** An archery bow that curves inward at the center and usu. outward at the ends.

cu·po·la (kyōō′pə-lə) *n.* **1.** *Architecture* **a.** A domed roof or ceiling. **b.** A small domelike structure surmounting a roof. **2.** A cylindrical shaft type of blast furnace used for remelting metals before casting. **3.** A small rounded and domed structure on a tracked armored vehicle. [Ital. < LLat. *cūpula,* dim. of Lat. *cūpa,* tub.]

cup·pa (kŭp′ə) *n. Chiefly British* A cup of tea.

cup·ping (kŭp′ĭng) *n.* A treatment in which evacuated glass cups are applied to skin to draw blood to the surface.

cu·pre·ous (kōō′prē-əs, kyōō′-) *adj.* Of, resembling, or containing copper; coppery. [< LLat. *cupreus < cuprum,* copper. See COPPER[1].]

cu·pric (kōō′prĭk, kyōō′-) *adj.* Of or containing divalent copper.

cu·prif·er·ous (kōō-prĭf′ər-əs, kyōō-) *adj.* Containing copper.

cu·prite (kōō′prīt′, kyōō′-) *n.* A natural red secondary ore of copper, essentially Cu_2O, that forms as a result of weathering.

cupro– or **cupri–** or **cupr–** *pref.* Copper: *cupriferous.* [< LLat. *cuprum,* copper. See COPPER[1].]

cu·pro·nick·el (kōō′prō-nĭk′əl, kyōō′-) *n.* An alloy of copper that contains 10 to 30 percent nickel.

cu·prous (kōō′prəs, kyōō′-) *adj.* Of, relating to, or containing univalent copper.

cu·pu·late (kyōō′pyə-lāt′, -lĭt) also **cu·pu·lar** (-lər) *adj.* **1.** Resembling a small cup. **2.** Having or bearing a cupule.

cu·pule (kyōō′pyōōl) *n.* A small cup-shaped structure or organ, such as the cup at the base of an acorn. [LLat. *cūpula,* little cask, dim. of Lat. *cūpa,* tub.]

cur (kûr) *n.* **1.** A dog considered to be inferior or undesirable; a mongrel. **2.** A base or cowardly person. [ME *curre,* perh. of Scand. orig.]

cur·a·ble (kyōōr′ə-bəl) *adj.* Being such that curing or healing is possible: *curable diseases.* —**cur′a·bil′i·ty, cur′a·ble·ness** *n.* —**cur′a·bly** *adv.*

cu·ra·çao (kyōōr′ə-sō′, -sou′, kōōr′-) also **cu·ra·çoa** (-sō′ə) *n.* A liqueur flavored with the peel of the sour orange. [After CURAÇAO.]

Cu·ra·çao (kōōr′ə-sou′, kyōōr′-, kōōr′ə-sou′, kyōōr′-) An island of the Netherlands Antilles in the S Caribbean Sea off the NW coast of Venezuela; settled by the Spanish in 1527 and under Dutch control after 1634.

cu·ra·cy (kyōōr′ə-sē) *n., pl.* **-cies** The office, duties, or term of office of a curate. [CURA(TE)[1] + –CY.]

cu·ran·de·ra (kōō′rən-dâr′ə) *n.* A woman who practices folk medicine; an herb doctor. [Am.Sp., fem. of *curandero,* healer. See CURANDERO.]

cu·ran·de·ro (kōō′rən-dâr′ō) *n., pl.* **-ros** A man who practices folk medicine; an herb doctor. [Am.Sp. < Sp. *curar,* to cure < Lat. *cūrāre,* to cure, take care of. See CURATIVE.]

cu·ra·re also **cu·ra·ri** (kōō-rä′rē, kyōō-) *n.* **1.** A dark resinous extract obtained from several tropical American woody plants, esp. *Chondrodendron tomentosum* or certain species of *Strychnos,* used as an arrow poison by some Indian peoples of South America. **2.** *Medicine* A purified preparation or alkaloid obtained from *Chondrodendron tomentosum,* used to relax skeletal muscles. **3.** A plant yielding curare. [Port. or Sp. *curaré,* both of Cariban and Tupian orig.]

cu·ra·rize (kōō-rä′rīz′, kyōō-) *tr.v.* **-rized, -riz·ing, -riz·es 1.** To poison with curare. **2.** To treat with curare. —**cu·ra′ri·za′tion** (-rĭ-zā′shən) *n.*

cu·ras·sow (kōōr′ə-sō′, kyōōr′-) *n.* Any of several long-tailed crested South and Central American game birds of the family Cracidae. [Alteration of CURAÇAO.]

cu·rate[1] (kyōōr′ĭt) *n.* **1.** A cleric, esp. one in charge of a parish.

cupola

ă pat   oi boy
ā pay   ou out
âr care   ōō took
ä father ōō boot
ĕ pet   ŭ cut
ē be   ûr urge
ĭ pit   th thin
ī pie   *th* this
îr pier   hw which
ŏ pot   zh vision
ō toe   ə about,
ô paw   item

Stress marks:
′ (primary);
′ (secondary), as in
lexicon (lĕk′sĭ-kŏn′)

2. A cleric who assists a rector or vicar. [ME *curat* < Med.Lat. *cūrātus* < LLat. *cūra,* spiritual charge < Lat., care. See CURE.]

cu•rate² (kyŏŏr′āt′) *tr.v.* To act as curator of; organize and oversee. [Back-formation < CURATOR.]

cu•rate's egg (kyŏŏr′its) *n. Chiefly British* Something with both good and bad qualities. [< a story in *Punch* about a curate who, having been served a bad egg by his bishop, said that parts of it were excellent.]

cu•ra•tive (kyŏŏr′ə-tĭv) *adj.* **1.** Serving or tending to cure. **2.** Of or relating to the cure of disease. ❖ *n.* Something that cures; a remedy. [ME < OFr. *curatif* < Med.Lat. *cūrātīvus* < Lat. *cūrātus,* p. part. of *cūrāre,* to cure < *cūra,* care. See CURATIVE.] —**cu′ra•tive•ly** *adv.* —**cu′ra•tive•ness** *n.*

cu•ra•tor (kyŏŏ-rā′tər, kyŏŏr′ə-tər) *n.* One who manages or oversees, as the administrative director of a museum collection. [ME *curatour,* legal guardian < OFr. *curateur* < Lat. *cūrātor,* overseer < *cūrāre,* to take care of. See CURATIVE.] —**cu′ra•to′ri•al** (kyŏŏr′ə-tôr′ē-əl, -tōr′-) *adj.* —**cu•ra′tor•ship′** *n.*

curb (kûrb) *n.* **1.** A concrete border or row of joined stones forming part of a gutter along the edge of a street. **2.** An enclosing framework, such as that around a skylight. **3.** A raised margin along an edge used to confine or strengthen. **4.** Something that checks or restrains. **5.** A chain or strap that passes under a horse's lower jaw and helps restrain the horse. **6.** A market, originally on a street or sidewalk, for trading securities not listed on a stock exchange. ❖ *tr.v.* **curbed, curb•ing, curbs** **1.** To check, restrain, or control as if with a curb; rein in. **2.** To lead (a dog) off the sidewalk into the gutter so that it can defecate. **3.** To furnish with a curb. [Blend of ME, curved piece of wood (< OFr. *corbe,* curved object < *corbe,* curved < Lat. *curvus*) and ME *corbe,* horse strap (< *corben,* to bow down, halt < OFr. *corber,* to bow down < Lat. *curvāre* < *curvus,* curved, bent).]

curb•ing (kûr′bĭng) *n.* **1.** The material used to construct a curb. **2.** A row of curbstones; a curb.

curb roof *n.* A roof having two slopes on each side, as a gambrel roof or a mansard roof.

curb service *n.* Service or attendance, esp. from a restaurant, provided to customers remaining in their parked vehicles.

curb•side (kûrb′sīd′) *n.* **1.** The side of a pavement or street bordered by a curb. **2.** A sidewalk. —**curb′side′** *adj.*

curb•stone (kûrb′stōn′) *n.* A stone or row of stones that constitutes a curb. ❖ *adj.* Untrained or unsophisticated.

curb weight *n.* The weight of a fueled automobile with standard equipment but without cargo or passengers.

cur•cu•li•o (kər-kyōō′lē-ō′) *n., pl.* **-os** *snout beetle.* [NLat. *Curculiō,* type genus < Lat. *curculiō,* a kind of weevil.]

cur•cu•ma (kûr′kyə-mə) *n.* Any of various tropical Asian plants of the genus *Curcuma,* which includes turmeric. [NLat. *Curcuma,* genus name < Ar. *kurkum,* saffron.]

curd (kûrd) *n.* **1.** The part of milk that coagulates and is used to make cheese. **2.** A coagulated liquid that resembles milk curd. ❖ *intr. & tr.v.* **curd•ed, curd•ing, curds** To form or cause to form into curd. [ME, var. of *crud*; prob. akin to *crowden,* to press. See CROWD¹.] —**curd′y** *adj.*

curd cheese *n. Chiefly British* Cottage cheese.

cur•dle (kûr′dl) *v.* **-dled, -dling, -dles** —*intr.* **1a.** To change into curd. **b.** To become congealed as if by having changed into curd. **2.** To go bad or become spoiled. —*tr.* To cause to change into or as if into curd. [Frequentative of CURD.]

cure (kyŏŏr) *n.* **1.** Restoration of health; recovery from disease. **2.** A method or course of medical treatment used to restore health. **3.** An agent, that restores health; a remedy. **4.** Something that corrects or relieves a harmful or disturbing situation. **5.** *Ecclesiastical* Spiritual charge or care, as of a priest for a congregation. **6.** The office or duties of a curate. **7.** The act or process of preserving a product. ❖ *v.* **cured, cur•ing, cures** —*tr.* **1.** To restore to health. **2.** To effect a recovery from: *cure a cold.* **3.** To remove or remedy (something harmful or disturbing): *cure an evil.* **4.** To preserve (meat, for example), as by salting, smoking, or aging. **5.** To prepare, preserve, or finish (a substance) by a chemical or physical process. **6.** To vulcanize (rubber). —*intr.* **1.** To effect a cure or recovery. **2.** To be prepared, preserved, or finished by a chemical or physical process. [ME < OFr., medical treatment < Lat. *cūra* < Archaic Lat. *coisa-.*] —**cur′er** *n.*

SYNONYMS *cure, heal, remedy* These verbs mean to set right an undesirable or unhealthy condition: *cure an ailing economy; heal a wounded spirit; remedy a structural defect.*

cu•ré (kyŏŏ-rā′, kyŏŏr′ā′) *n.* A parish priest. [Fr. < OFr. < Med.Lat. *cūrātus.* See CURATE¹.]

cure-all (kyŏŏr′ôl′) *n.* A remedy that cures all diseases or evils.

cu•ret•tage (kyŏŏr′ĭ-täzh′) *n.* The removal of tissue or growths from a body cavity by scraping with a curette.

cu•rette also **cu•ret** (kyŏŏ-rĕt′) *n.* A surgical instrument shaped like a scoop or spoon, used to remove tissue or growths from a body cavity. [Fr. < OFr. < *curer,* to cure < Lat. *cūrāre,* to take care of < *cūra,* care. See CURE.]

cur•few (kûr′fyōō) *n.* **1.** A regulation requiring certain or all people to leave the streets or be home at a prescribed hour. **2a.** The time at which a curfew begins. **b.** The signal for a curfew. [ME

Marie Curie

curlew
long-billed curlew
Numenius americanus

curling

curfeu < OFr. *cuevrefeu* : *covrir,* to cover; see COVER + *feu,* fire (< Lat. *focus,* hearth).]

cu•ri•a (kŏŏr′ē-ə, kyŏŏr′-) *n., pl.* **cu•ri•ae** (kŏŏr′ē-ē′, kyŏŏr′-) **1a.** One of the ten subdivisions of a tribe in early Rome. **b.** The assembly place of such a subdivision. **2.** The Roman senate or any of the various buildings in which it met in republican Rome. **3.** The ensemble of central administrative and governmental services in imperial Rome. **4.** often **Curia** *Roman Catholic Church* The central administration governing the Church. **5a.** A medieval assembly or council. **b.** A medieval royal court of justice. [Lat. *cūria,* council, curia. See wī-ro- in App.] —**cu′ri•al** *adj.*

cu•rie (kyŏŏr′ē, kyŏŏ-rē′) *n.* A unit of radioactivity, equal to the amount of a radioactive isotope that decays at the rate of 3.7 ×10^10 disintegrations per second. [After Pierre CURIE.]

Cu•rie (kyŏŏr′ē, kyŏŏ-rē′, kū-) also **Cu•rie-Jo•li•ot** (-zhō-lyō′), **Irène** See Irène **Joliot-Curie.**

Curie, Marie 1867–1934. Polish-born French chemist who shared a 1903 Nobel Prize with her husband, **Pierre Curie** (1859–1906), and Henri Becquerel for research on radioactivity. In 1911 she won a second Nobel Prize for her discovery of radium and polonium.

Curie point *n.* A transition temperature marking a change in the magnetic or ferroelectric properties of a substance. [After Pierre CURIE.]

cu•ri•o (kyŏŏr′ē-ō′) *n., pl.* **-os** A curious or unusual object of art or piece of bric-a-brac. [Short for CURIOSITY.]

cu•ri•o•sa (kyŏŏr′ē-ō′sə, -zə) *pl.n.* Books or other writings dealing with unusual, esp. pornographic, topics. [NLat. *cūriōsa,* neut. pl. of Lat. *cūriōsus,* inquisitive. See CURIOUS.]

cu•ri•os•i•ty (kyŏŏr′ē-ŏs′ĭ-tē) *n., pl.* **-ties** **1.** A desire to know or learn. **2.** A desire to know about what does not concern one; nosiness. **3.** An object that arouses interest, as by being extraordinary. **4.** A strange or odd aspect. **5.** *Archaic* Fastidiousness. [ME *curiosite* < OFr. < Lat. *cūriōsitās* < *cūriōsus,* inquisitive. See CURIOUS.]

cu•ri•ous (kyŏŏr′ē-əs) *adj.* **1.** Eager to learn more. **2.** Unduly inquisitive; prying. **3.** Arousing interest because of novelty or strangeness. **4.** *Archaic* **a.** Accomplished with skill or ingenuity. **b.** Extremely careful; scrupulous. [ME < OFr. *curios* < Lat. *cūriōsus,* careful, inquisitive < *cūra,* care. See CURE.] —**cu′ri•ous•ly** *adv.* —**cu′ri•ous•ness** *n.*

SYNONYMS *curious, inquisitive, snoopy, nosy* These adjectives apply to persons who show a marked desire for information or knowledge. *Curious* most often implies an avid desire to know or learn: *a curious child. Inquisitive* frequently suggests excessive curiosity and the asking of many questions: "Remember, no revolvers. The police are, I believe, proverbially inquisitive" (Lord Dunsany). *Snoopy* suggests underhanded prying: *a snoopy hotel detective. Nosy* implies impertinent curiosity likened to that of an animal using its nose to examine or probe: *My nosy colleague went through my mail.* See also Syns at **strange.**

Cu•ri•ti•ba (kŏŏr′ĭ-tē′bə) A city of SE Brazil SW of São Paulo; founded 1654. Pop. 1,313,094.

cu•ri•um (kyŏŏr′ē-əm) *n.* *Symbol* **Cm** A metallic synthetic radioactive transuranic element. Atomic number 96; longest-lived isotope Cm 247; melting point (estimated) 1,350°C; valence 3. See table at **element.** [After Marie CURIE and Pierre CURIE.]

curl (kûrl) *v.* **curled, curl•ing, curls** —*tr.* **1.** To twist (the hair, for example) into ringlets or coils. **2.** To form into a coiled or spiral shape: *curled the ribbon.* **3.** To decorate with coiled or spiral shapes. **4.** To raise and turn under (the upper lip), as in snarling. —*intr.* **1.** To form ringlets or coils. **2.** To assume a spiral or curved shape. **3.** To move in a curve or spiral. **4.** *Sports* To engage in curling. ❖ *n.* **1.** Something with a spiral or coiled shape. **2.** A coil or ringlet of hair. **3.** A treatment in which the hair is curled. **4a.** The act of curling: *the curl of a meandering river.* **b.** The state of being curled. **5.** *Sports* A weightlifting exercise in which a barbell is raised to the chest or shoulder and lowered without moving the upper arms, shoulders, or back. **6.** Any of various plant diseases in which leaves roll up. —*phrasal verb:* **curl up** To assume a position with legs drawn up. [ME *curlen* < *crulle,* curly, perh. of MLGer. orig.]

Curl, Robert Floyd, Jr. b. 1933. Amer. chemist who shared a 1996 Nobel Prize for discovering fullerenes.

curl•er (kûr′lər) *n.* **1.** One that curls, as a device on which hair is wound for curling. **2.** *Sports* A player of curling.

cur•lew (kûrl′yōō, kûrl′lōō) *n.* Any of several brownish long-legged shore birds of the genus *Numenius,* having long, slender, downward-curving bills. [ME *curleu* < OFr. *courlieu,* perh. of imit. orig.]

Cur•ley (kûr′lē), **James Michael** 1874–1958. Amer. politician who was mayor of Boston four times between 1914 and 1950 and governor of MA (1935–37).

curl•i•cue also **curl•y•cue** (kûr′lĭ-kyōō′) *n.* A fancy twist or curl, such as a flourish made with a pen. [CURLY + CUE¹, tail, and poss. CUE³.] —**curl′i•cued** *adj.*

curl•ing (kûr′lĭng) *n.* A game originating in Scotland in which two four-person teams slide heavy oblate stones toward the center of a circle at either end of a length of ice.

curling iron *n.* A rod-shaped metal implement used when heated

CURRENCY TABLE: LISTED BY BASIC UNIT

Unit	Country	Unit	Country	Unit	Country	Unit	Country
afghani	Afghanistan		Saint Lucia	kip	Laos		Uruguay
			Saint Vincent and	koruna	Czech Republic	pound	Cyprus
baht	Thailand		the Grenadines		Slovakia		Egypt
balboa	Panama		Singapore	krona	Iceland		Ireland*
birr	Ethiopia		Solomon Islands		Sweden		Lebanon
bolivar	Venezuela		Taiwan	krone	Denmark		Syria
boliviano	Bolivia		Trinidad and Tobago		Norway		United Kingdom
			Tuvalu	kroon	Estonia	pula	Botswana
cedi	Ghana		United States	kuna	Croatia		
colon	Costa Rica		Zimbabwe	kwacha	Malawi	quetzal	Guatemala
	El Salvador	dong	Vietnam		Zambia		
cordoba	Nicaragua	drachma	Greece*	kwanza	Angola	rand	South Africa
		dram	Armenia	kyat	Myanmar	real	Brazil
dalasi	Gambia					rial	Iran
denar	Macedonia	escudo	Cape Verde	lari	Georgia		Oman
deutsche			Portugal*	lats	Latvia		Yemen
mark	Germany*			lek	Albania	riel	Cambodia
dinar	Algeria	forint	Hungary	lempira	Honduras	ringgit	Malaysia
	Bahrain	franc	Belgium*	leone	Sierra Leone	riyal	Qatar
	Iraq		Benin	leu	Moldova		Saudi Arabia
	Jordan		Burkina Faso		Romania	rubel	Belarus
	Kuwait		Burundi	lev	Bulgaria	ruble	Russia
	Libya		Cameroon	lilangeni	Swaziland	rufiyaa	Maldives
	Sudan		Central African	lira	Italy*	rupee	India
	Tunisia		Republic		Malta		Mauritius
	Yugoslavia		Chad		San Marino		Nepal
dirham	Morocco		Comoros		Turkey		Pakistan
	United Arab		Congo (Rep. of)		Vatican City		Seychelles
	Emirates		Congo (Dem. Rep. of)	litas	Lithuania		Sri Lanka
dobra	São Tomé and		Côte d'Ivoire	livre	Lebanon	rupiah	Indonesia
	Príncipe		Djibouti	loti	Lesotho		
dollar	Antigua and		Equatorial Guinea			schilling	Austria*
	Barbuda		France*	manat	Azerbaijan	sheqel	Israel
	Australia		Gabon		Turkmenistan	shilling	Kenya
	Bahamas		Guinea	marka	Bosnia and		Somalia
	Barbados		Guinea-Bissau		Herzegovina		Tanzania
	Belize		Liechtenstein	markka	Finland*		Uganda
	Brunei		Luxembourg*	metical	Mozambique	sol	Peru
	Canada		Madagascar			som	Kyrgyzstan
	Dominica		Mali	naira	Nigeria	somoni	Tajikistan
	Ecuador		Monaco	nakfa	Eritrea	sum	Uzbekistan
	Fiji		Niger	ngultrum	Bhutan		
	Grenada		Rwanda			taka	Bangladesh
	Guyana		Senegal	ouguiya	Mauritania	tala	Samoa
	Hong Kong		Switzerland			tenge	Kazakhstan
	Jamaica		Togo	pa'anga	Tonga	tolar	Slovenia
	Kiribati			pataca	Macao	tugrik	Mongolia
	Liberia	gourde	Haiti	peseta	Andorra		
	Marshall Islands	guarani	Paraguay		Spain*	vatu	Vanuatu
	Micronesia	guilder	Netherlands*	peso	Argentina		
	Namibia		Suriname		Chile	won	North Korea
	Nauru				Colombia		South Korea
	New Zealand	hryvnia	Ukraine		Cuba		
	Palau				Dominican Republic	yen	Japan
	Saint Kitts and Nevis	kina	Papua New Guinea		Mexico	yuan	China
					Philippines	zloty	Poland

* Banknotes denominated in euros begin circulating in 2002.

to curl the hair.

curl paper *n.* A piece of soft paper on which a lock of hair is rolled up for curling.

curl•y (kûr′lē) *adj.* **-i•er, -i•est 1.** Having curls. **2.** Tending to curl. **3.** Having a wavy grain. —**curl′i•ly** *adv.* —**curl′i•ness** *n.*

curly top *n.* A viral disease of many plants characterized by curled leaves and stunted growth.

cur•mudg•eon (kər-mŭj′ən) *n.* An ill-tempered person full of resentment and stubborn notions. [?] —**cur•mudg′eon•ly** *adj.* —**cur•mudg′eon•ry** *n.*

cur•rach also **cur•ragh** (kûr′əкн, kûr′ə) *n. Scots & Irish* A coracle. [ME *currok* < MIr. *curach.* See CORACLE.]

cur•rant (kûr′ənt, kŭr′-) *n.* **1.** Any of various deciduous shrubs of the genus *Ribes,* native chiefly to the Northern Hemisphere and having edible, variously colored berries. **2.** The fruits of any of these plants. **3.** A small seedless raisin of the Mediterranean region, used chiefly in baking. [ME *(raysons of) coraunte,* (raisins of) Corinth, currants < AN *(raisins de) Corauntz* < Lat. *Corinthus,* Corinth < Gk. *Korinthos.*]

cur•ren•cy (kûr′ən-sē, kŭr′-) *n., pl.* **-cies 1.** Money in any form when in actual use as a medium of exchange, esp. paper money. **2.** Transmission from person to person as a medium of exchange. **3.** General acceptance or use. **4.** The state of being current; up-to-dateness. [< ME *curraunt,* in circulation. See CURRENT.]

cur•rent (kûr′ənt, kŭr′-) *adj.* **1a.** Belonging to the present time. **b.** Being in progress now. **2.** Passing from one to another; circulating. **3.** Prevalent, esp. at the present time. **4.** Running; flowing. ❖ *n.* **1.** A steady, smooth onward movement. **2.** The part of a body of liquid or gas that has a continuous onward movement. **3.** A general tendency, movement, or course. **4.** *Symbol* **I** Electric-

ity **a.** A flow of electric charge. **b.** The amount of electric charge flowing past a specified circuit point per unit time. [ME *currant* < OFr. *corant,* pr. part. of *courre,* to run < Lat. *currere.*] —**cur′rent•ly** *adv.* —**cur′rent•ness** *n.*

current assets *pl.n.* Cash or assets convertible into cash at short notice.

current density *n. Physics* **1.** *Symbol* **j, J** The ratio of the magnitude of current flowing in a conductor to the cross-sectional area perpendicular to it, expressed as a vector whose direction is the same as that of the current. **2.** The number of subatomic particles per unit time crossing a unit area in a designated plane perpendicular to the direction of particle movement.

cur•ri•cle (kûr′ĭ-kəl) *n.* A light, open two-wheeled carriage, drawn by two horses abreast. [< Lat. *curriculum,* course, racing chariot < *currere,* to run. See CURRENT.]

cur•ric•u•lum (kə-rĭk′yə-ləm) *n., pl.* **-la** (-lə) or **-lums 1.** All the courses of study offered by an educational institution. **2.** A group of related courses, often in a special field of study. [Lat., course < *currere,* to run. See CURRENT.] —**cur•ric′u•lar** (-lər) *adj.*

curriculum vi•tae (vī′tē, vē′tī, wē′tī′) *n., pl.* **curricula vitae** A summary of one's education, professional history, and job qualifications. [Lat. *curriculum vītae,* the race of life : *curriculum,* course + *vītae,* genitive of *vīta,* life.]

cur•ri•er (kûr′ē-ər, kŭr′-) *n.* One that prepares tanned hides for use. [ME *curreiour* < OFr. < Lat. *coriārius* < *corium,* leather. See sker-¹ in App.]

Currier, Nathaniel 1813–88. Amer. lithographer who with his partner James Merritt Ives produced more than 7,000 prints.

cur•ri•er•y (kûr′ē-ə-rē, kŭr′-) *n., pl.* **-ies** The trade, work, or shop of a currier.

currant
garden red currant
Ribes sativum

ă	pat	oi	boy
ā	pay	ou	out
âr	care	ŏŏ	took
ä	father	ōō	boot
ĕ	pet	ŭ	cut
ē	be	ûr	urge
ĭ	pit	th	thin
ī	pie	th	this
îr	pier	hw	which
ŏ	pot	zh	vision
ō	toe	ə	about,
ô	paw		item

Stress marks:
′ (primary);
′ (secondary); as in
lexicon (lĕk′sĭ-kŏn′)

currycomb

cur·rish (kûr′ĭsh) *adj.* Snarling and bad-tempered. —**cur′rish·ly** *adv.*

cur·ry[1] (kûr′ē, kŭr′ē) *tr.v.* **-ried, -ry·ing, -ries** **1.** To groom (a horse) with a currycomb. **2.** To prepare (tanned hides) for use, as by soaking. —*idiom:* **curry favor** To seek or gain favor by fawning. [ME *curreien* < AN *curreier*, to arrange, curry < VLat. **corrēdāre* : Lat. *com-*, com- + VLat. **rēdāre*, to make ready (of Gmc. orig.). *Curry favor*, by folk ety. < ME *currayen favel* < OFr. *correier fauvel*, to curry a fallow-colored horse, be hypocritical (< the fallow horse as a medieval symbol of deceit).]

cur·ry[2] also **cur·rie** (kûr′ē, kŭr′ē) *n.*, *pl.* **-ries** **1.** Curry powder. **2.** A heavily spiced sauce or relish made with curry powder. **3.** A dish seasoned with curry powder. ❖ *tr.v.* **-ried, -ry·ing, -ries** To season (food) with curry. [Tamil *kaṟi.*]

cur·ry·comb (kûr′ē-kōm′, kŭr′-) *n.* A comb with plastic or rubber teeth, used for grooming horses. ❖ *tr.v.* **-combed, -comb·ing, -combs** To groom with a currycomb.

curry leaf *n.* The fragrant leaf of the curry-leaf tree (*Murraya koenigii*), a plant native to India, used as a seasoning in cooking.

curry powder *n.* A pungent seasoning prepared from cumin, coriander, turmeric, and other spices.

curse (kûrs) *n.* **1a.** An appeal or prayer for evil or misfortune to befall someone or something. **b.** The evil or misfortune that comes in or as if in response to such an appeal. **2.** One that is accursed. **3.** A source or cause of evil; a scourge. **4.** A profane word or phrase; a swearword. **5.** *Ecclesiastical* A censure, ban, or anathema. **6.** *Slang* Menstruation. Used with *the.* ❖ *v.* **cursed** or **curst** (kûrst), **curs·ing, curs·es** —*tr.* **1.** To invoke evil or misfortune upon; damn. **2.** To swear at. **3.** To bring evil upon; afflict. **4.** *Ecclesiastical* To put under a ban or an anathema; excommunicate. —*intr.* To utter curses; swear. [ME < OE *curs.*] —**curs′er** *n.*

curs·ed (kûr′sĭd, kûrst) also **curst** (kûrst) *adj.* So wicked and detestable as to deserve to be cursed. —**curs′ed·ly** *adv.* —**curs′ed·ness** *n.*

cur·sive (kûr′sĭv) *adj.* Having the successive letters joined together: *cursive writing.* ❖ *n.* **1.** A cursive character or letter. **2.** A manuscript written in cursive characters. **3.** *Printing* A type style that imitates handwriting. [Fr. (*écriture*) *cursive*, cursive (handwriting) < Med.Lat. (*scripta*) *cursīva* < Lat. *cursus*, p. part. of *currere*, to run.] —**cur′sive·ly** *adv.* —**cur′sive·ness** *n.*

cur·sor (kûr′sər) *n. Computer Science* A movable indicator on a display, marking the position at which a character can be entered, corrected, or deleted. [ME, runner < Lat. < *cursus*, p. part. of *currere*, to run.]

cur·so·ri·al (kûr-sôr′ē-əl, -sōr′-) *adj.* Adapted to or specialized for running. [< LLat. *cursōrius*, of running. See CURSORY.]

cur·so·ry (kûr′sə-rē) *adj.* Performed with haste and scant attention to detail. [LLat. *cursōrius*, of running < Lat. *cursor*, runner. See CURSOR.] —**cur′so·ri·ly** *adv.* —**cur′so·ri·ness** *n.*

curt (kûrt) *adj.* **curt·er, curt·est** **1.** Rudely brief or abrupt, as in speech or manner. **2.** Using few words; terse. **3.** Having been shortened. [ME, short, brief < AN < Lat. *curtus.* See SKER-[1] in App.] —**curt′ly** *adv.* —**curt′ness** *n.*

cur·tail (kər-tāl′) *tr.v.* **-tailed, -tail·ing, -tails** To cut short or reduce. [ME *curtailen*, to restrict, prob. blend of OFr. *courtauld*, docked; see CURTAL, and ME *taillen*, to cut (< OFr. *tailler*; see TAILOR).] —**cur·tail′er** *n.* —**cur·tail′ment** *n.*

cur·tain (kûr′tn) *n.* **1.** Material that hangs over an opening as a decoration, shade, or screen. **2.** Something that functions as or resembles a screen, cover, or barrier: *a curtain of mist.* **3a.** The movable screen or drape that separates a stage from an auditorium or serves as a backdrop. **b.** The rising or opening of a theater curtain at the beginning of a performance or act. **c.** The time at which a theatrical performance begins or is scheduled to begin. **d.** The fall or closing of a theater curtain at the end of a performance or act. **4.** The part of a rampart or parapet connecting two bastions or gates. **5.** *Architecture* A curtain wall. **6. curtains** *Slang* **a.** The end. **b.** Absolute ruin. **c.** Death. ❖ *tr.v.* **-tained, -tain·ing, -tains** **1.** To provide (something) with or as if with a curtain. **2.** To shut off (something) with or as if with a curtain. [ME *cortine* < OFr. < LLat. *cōrtīna* < Lat. *cōrs, cōrt-*, var. of *cohors*, court. See COURT.]

curtain call *n.* The appearance of performers or a performer at the end of a performance to receive applause.

curtain raiser *n.* **1.** A short play or skit presented before the principal production. **2.** A preliminary event.

curtain wall *n.* **1.** An outer or enclosing wall, esp. one connecting two towers or turrets. **2.** A nonbearing outer wall, often of glass and steel, serving esp. as cladding.

cur·tal (kûr′tl) *n.* **1.** An animal with a docked tail. **2.** Something cut short or docked. ❖ *adj. Obsolete* Cut short or docked. [Obsolete Fr. *courtault* < OFr. < *court*, short < Lat. *curtus.* See SKER-[1] in App.]

curtal ax *n. Archaic* A cutlass. [By folk ety. < earlier *coutelace, curtelace*, cutlass < OFr. *coutelas.* See CUTLASS.]

cur·tate (kûr′tāt′) *adj.* Having been shortened; abbreviated. [Lat. *curtātus*, p. part. of *curtāre*, to shorten < *curtus*, cut short. See CURT.]

cur·te·sy (kûr′tĭ-sē) *n.*, *pl.* **-sies** The life tenure that by common law is held by a man over the property of his deceased wife if children with rights of inheritance were born during the marriage. [ME *courtesie, curtesie.* See COURTESY.]

cur·ti·lage (kûr′tl-ĭj) *n. Law* The enclosed area immediately surrounding a house or dwelling. [ME < OFr. *courtillage* < *courtil*, dim. of *cort*, court. See COURT.]

Cur·tis (kûr′tĭs), **Benjamin Robbins** 1809–74. Amer. jurist; associate justice of the US Supreme Court (1851–57).

Cur·tiss (kûr′tĭs), **Glenn Hammond** 1878–1930. Amer. aviation pioneer who developed the first seaplane (1911).

curt·sy or **curt·sey** (kûrt′sē) *n.*, *pl.* **-sies** or **-seys** A gesture of respect or reverence made chiefly by women by bending the knees with one foot forward and lowering the body. ❖ *intr.v.* **-sied, -sy·ing, -sies** or **-seyed, -sey·ing, -seys** To make a curtsy. [Variant of COURTESY.]

cu·rule (kyoŏr′oōl′) *adj.* Privileged to sit in a curule chair; of superior rank. [Lat. *curūlis*, of a curule chair < *currus*, chariot < *currere*, to run.]

curule chair *n.* A seat with heavy curved legs and no back, reserved for the use of the highest officials in ancient Rome.

cur·va·ceous (kûr-vā′shəs) *adj.* Having the curves of a full or voluptuous figure. —**cur·va′ceous·ness** *n.*

cur·va·ture (kûr′və-choŏr′, -chər) *n.* **1.** The act of curving or the state of being curved. **2.** *Mathematics* **a.** The ratio of the change in the angle of a tangent that moves over a given arc to the length of the arc. **b.** The reciprocal of the radius of a circle. **3.** *Medicine* A curving or bending, esp. an abnormal one: *curvature of the spine.* [ME < Lat. *curvātūra* < *curvātus*, p. part. of *curvāre*, to bend < *curvus*, curved.]

curve (kûrv) *n.* **1a.** A line that bends in a smooth continuous fashion. **b.** A surface that bends in a smooth continuous fashion. **c.** Something characterized by such a line or surface, esp. a contour of the human body. **2.** A relatively smooth bend in a road or other course. **3a.** A line representing data on a graph. **b.** A trend derived from or as if from such a graph. **4.** A method of grading students based on relative performance. **5.** *Mathematics* **a.** The graph of a function on a coordinate plane. **b.** The intersection of two surfaces in three dimensions. **c.** The graph of the solutions to any equation of two variables. **6.** *Baseball* A curve ball. **7.** *Slang* Something that is unexpected or designed to trick or deceive. ❖ *v.* **curved, curv·ing, curves** —*intr.* To move in or take the shape of a curve. —*tr.* **1.** To cause to curve. See Syns at BEND[1]. **2.** *Baseball* To pitch a curve ball to. **3.** To grade (students, for example) on a curve. [< ME, curved < Lat. *curvus.*] —**curv′ed·ness** *n.* —**curv′y** *adj.*

curve ball or **curve·ball** (kûrv′bôl′) *n. Baseball* **1.** A pitched ball that veers or breaks to the left when thrown with the right hand and to the right when thrown with the left hand. **2.** Something that is unexpected or designed to trick or deceive.

cur·vet (kûr-vĕt′) *n.* A light leap by a horse, in which both hind legs leave the ground just before the forelegs are set down. ❖ *v.* **-vet·ted, -vet·ting, -vets** or **-vet·ed, -vet·ing, -vets** —*intr.* **1.** To leap in a curvet. **2.** To prance; frolic. —*tr.* To cause to leap in a curvet. [Ital. *corvetta* < OItal. < OFr. *courbette* < *courber*, to curve < Lat. *curvāre* < *curvus*, curved.]

cur·vi·lin·e·ar (kûr′və-lĭn′ē-ər) also **cur·vi·lin·e·al** (-əl) *adj.* Formed, bounded, or characterized by curved lines. [Lat. *curvus*, curved; see CURVE + LINEAR.] —**cur′vi·lin′e·ar′i·ty** (-ē-ăr′ĭ-tē) *n.* —**cur′vi·lin′e·ar·ly** *adv.*

Cus·co (koōs′kō) See CUZCO.

cu·sec (kyoō′sĕk′) *n.* A volumetric unit for measuring the flow of liquids, equal to one cubic foot per second.

Cush[1] (kŭsh, koŏsh) In the Bible, the eldest son of Ham.

Cush[2] also **Kush** (kŭsh, koŏsh) **1.** An ancient region of NE Africa where the biblical descendants of Cush settled. It is often identified with Ethiopia. **2.** An ancient kingdom of Nubia in N Sudan that flourished from the 11th cent. B.C. to the 4th cent. A.D. —**Cush′ite** *adj. & n.*

cu·shaw (kə-shô′, koō-shô′) *n.* Any of several kinds of winter squash (*Cucurbita mixta*) having a curved neck. [?]

Cush·ing (koŏsh′ĭng), **Harvey Williams** 1869–1939. Amer. neurologist noted for his study of the brain and the pituitary gland.

Cush·ing's disease (koŏsh′ĭngz) *n.* The form of Cushing's syndrome involving the pituitary gland.

Cushing's syndrome *n.* A syndrome caused by an increased production of ACTH or by excessive intake of glucocorticoids, characterized by obesity and weakening of the muscles. [After Harvey Williams CUSHING.]

cush·ion (koŏsh′ən) *n.* **1.** A pad or pillow with a soft filling, used for resting, reclining, or kneeling. **2.** Something resilient used as a rest, support, or shock absorber. **3.** A padlike body part. **4.** *Games* The rim bordering the playing surface of a billiard table. **5.** A pillow used in lacemaking. **6.** Something that mitigates or relieves an adverse effect. ❖ *tr.v.* **-ioned, -ion·ing, -ions** **1.** To provide with a cushion. **2.** To place or seat on a cushion. **3.** To cover or hide (something) with or as if with a cushion. **4.** To protect as if with cushions. **5.** To mitigate the effects of. [ME *cushin* < OFr. *coussin* < VLat. **coxīnum* < Lat. *coxa*, hip.] —**cush′ion·y** *adj.*

Cush·it·ic (koō-shĭt′ĭk) *n.* A branch of the Afro-Asiatic language family spoken in Somalia, Ethiopia, Eritrea, and northern Kenya and including Beja, Oromo, and Somali. —**Cush·it′ic** *adj.*

cush·y (koŏsh′ē) *adj.* **-i·er, -i·est** *Informal* Making few demands; comfortable: *a cushy job.* [?] —**cush′i•ly** *adv.* —**cush′i•ness** *n.*

cusk (kŭsk) *n., pl.* **cusk** or **cusks 1.** A food fish *(Brosme brosme)* of North Atlantic coastal waters that is related to the cod. **2.** See **burbot.** [Prob. alteration of *tusk,* a kind of codfish, perh. < Norw. dialectal, var. of Norw. *torsk, tosk* < ON *thorskr.* See **ters-** in App.]

cusp (kŭsp) *n.* **1.** A point or pointed end. **2.** *Anatomy* **a.** A pointed or rounded projection on the chewing surface of a tooth. **b.** A triangular fold or flap of a heart valve. **3.** *Mathematics* A point at which a curve crosses itself and at which the two tangents to the curve coincide. **4.** *Architecture* The point of intersection of two ornamental arcs or curves. **5.** *Astronomy* Either point of a crescent moon. **6.** A transitional point or time, as between two astrological signs. [Lat. *cuspis,* point.]

cus•pate (kŭs′pāt′) also **cus•pat•ed** (-pā′tĭd) *adj.* **1.** Having a cusp. **2.** Shaped like a cusp.

cus•pid (kŭs′pĭd) *n.* See **canine** 2. [< Lat. *cuspis, cuspid-,* point.]

cus•pi•date (kŭs′pĭ-dāt′) also **cus•pi•dat•ed** (-dā′tĭd) *adj.* **1.** Having a cusp. **2.** *Biology* Terminating in or tipped with a sharp firm point. [Lat. *cuspidātus,* p. part. of *cuspidāre,* to make pointed < *cuspis, cuspid-,* point.]

cus•pi•da•tion (kŭs′pĭ-dā′shən) *n. Architecture* Decoration with cusps.

cus•pi•dor (kŭs′pĭ-dôr′, -dōr′) *n.* A spittoon. [Port. < *cuspir,* to spit < Lat. *cōnspuere,* to spit upon : *com-,* com- + *spuere,* to spit.]

cuss (kŭs) *Informal intr. & tr.v.* **cussed, cuss•ing, cuss•es** To curse or curse at. ❖ *n.* **1.** A curse. **2.** An odd or perverse person or creature. [Alteration of CURSE.]

cuss•ed (kŭs′ĭd) *adj. Informal* **1.** Perverse; stubborn. **2.** Cursed. —**cuss′ed•ly** *adv.* —**cuss′ed•ness** *n.*

cus•tard (kŭs′tərd) *n.* A dish consisting of milk, eggs, flavoring, and sometimes sugar, boiled or baked until set. [ME *crustade, custard,* a pie with a crust, prob. < O Provençal *croustado.* See CROUSTADE.] —**cus′tard•y** *adj.*

custard apple *n.* **1.** Any of several tropical American trees of the genus *Annona,* esp. *A. reticulata,* having large, nearly heart-shaped edible fruits. **2.** The fruit of any of these trees.

Cus•ter (kŭs′tər), **George Armstrong** 1839–76. Amer. soldier who was killed and his troops annihilated by Sioux and Cheyenne warriors at Little Bighorn.

cus•to•di•al (kŭ-stō′dē-əl) *adj.* **1.** Of or relating to the work of guarding or maintaining. **2a.** Having custody, esp. of a child. **b.** Of or relating to child custody. **3.** Marked by care and supervision rather than efforts to cure.

cus•to•di•an (kŭ-stō′dē-ən) *n.* **1.** One in charge of something; a caretaker. **2.** A janitor. —**cus•to′di•an•ship′** *n.*

cus•to•dy (kŭs′tə-dē) *n., pl.* **-dies 1.** The act or right of guarding, esp. such a right granted by a court. **2.** Care, supervision, and control exerted by one in charge. See Syns at **care. 3.** The state of being detained or held under guard, esp. by the police: *took the suspect into custody.* [ME *custodie* < Lat. *custōdia* < *custōs, custōd-,* guard. See **sed-** in App.]

cus•tom (kŭs′təm) *n.* **1.** A practice followed by people of a particular group or region. **2.** A habitual practice of a person. See Syns at **habit. 3.** *Law* A common tradition or usage so long established that it has the force or validity of law. **4a.** Habitual patronage. **b.** Habitual customers; patrons. **5. customs a.** Duties or taxes imposed on imported and, less commonly, exported goods. **b.** (*used with a sing. verb*) The governmental agency authorized to collect these duties. **c.** (*used with a sing. verb*) The procedure for inspecting goods and baggage entering a country. **6.** Tribute, service, or rent paid by a feudal tenant to a lord. ❖ *adj.* **1.** Made to order. **2.** Specializing in the making or selling of made-to-order goods: *a custom tailor.* [ME *custume* < OFr. *costume* < Lat. *cōnsuētūdō, cōnsuētūdin-* < *cōnsuētus,* p. part. of *cōnsuēscere,* to accustom : *com-,* com- + *suēscere,* to become accustomed; see **s(w)e-** in App.]

cus•tom•a•ble (kŭs′tə-mə-bəl) *adj.* Subject to tariffs.

cus•tom•ar•y (kŭs′tə-mĕr′ē) *adj.* **1.** Commonly practiced, used, or encountered; usual. See Syns at **usual. 2.** Based on custom or tradition rather than written law or contract. —**cus′tom•ar′i•ly** (-mâr′ə-lē) *adv.* —**cus′tom•ar′i•ness** *n.*

cus•tom-built (kŭs′təm-bĭlt′) *adj.* Built according to the specifications of the buyer.

cus•tom•er (kŭs′tə-mər) *n.* **1.** One that buys goods or services. **2.** *Informal* An individual with whom one must deal.

cus•tom•house (kŭs′təm-hous′) also **cus•toms•house** (-təmz-) *n.* A governmental building or office where customs are collected and ships are cleared for entering or leaving the country.

cus•tom•ize (kŭs′tə-mīz′) *tr.v.* **-ized, -iz•ing, -iz•es** To make or alter to individual or personal specifications. —**cus′tom•i•za′tion** (-ĭ-zā′shən) *n.* —**cus′tom•iz′er** *n.*

cus•tom-made (kŭs′təm-mād′) *adj.* Made according to the specifications of an individual purchaser.

customs union *n.* An international association organized to eliminate customs restrictions between member nations and establish a uniform tariff policy toward nonmember nations.

cut (kŭt) *v.* **cut, cut•ting, cuts** —*tr.* **1.** To penetrate with a sharp edge; strike a narrow opening in. **2.** To separate into parts with or as if with a sharp-edged instrument; sever: *cut cloth with scissors.* **3.** To sever the edges or ends of; shorten: *cut one's hair.* **4.** To mow, reap, or harvest: *cut grain.* **5.** To fell by sawing; hew. **6.** To have (a new tooth) grow through the gums. **7.** To form or shape by severing or incising. **8a.** To form by penetrating, probing, or digging: *cut a trench.* **b.** To exhibit the appearance or give the impression of: *cuts a fine figure.* **9.** To separate from a main body; detach: *cut a limb from the tree.* **10.** To discharge from a group or number: *had to cut six players from the team.* **11.** To pass through or across; cross: *a sailboat cutting the water.* **12.** *Games* To divide (a deck of cards) into two parts. **13.** To reduce the size, extent, or duration of; curtail or shorten: *cut a budget.* **14a.** To remove or delete: *cut a line from the script.* **b.** *Computer Science* To remove (a segment) from a document or graphics file for storage in a buffer. **15.** To lessen the strength of; dilute: *cut whiskey with water.* **16.** To dissolve by breaking down the fat of: *Soap cuts grease.* **17.** To injure the feelings of; hurt keenly. **18.** To refuse to speak to or recognize; snub: *cut me dead at the party.* **19.** To fail to attend purposely: *cut a class.* **20.** *Informal* To cease; stop: *cut an engine.* **21.** *Sports* To strike (a ball) so that it spins in a reverse direction. **22a.** To perform: *cut a caper.* **b.** To make out and issue: *cut a check.* **23.** *Slang* To be able to manage; handle successfully: *couldn't cut the long hours anymore.* **24.** To stop filming (a movie scene). **25a.** To record a performance on (a phonograph record or other medium). **b.** To make a recording of. **26.** To edit (film or recording tape). —*intr.* **1.** To make an incision or separation: *Cut along the dotted line.* **2.** To allow incision or severing: *Butter cuts easily.* **3.** To function as a sharp-edged instrument. **4.** To injure someone's feelings: *a remark that cut.* **5.** To grow through the gums. Used of teeth. **6.** To change direction abruptly: *Cut to the left.* **7.** To go directly and often hastily: *cut across a field.* **8.** *Games* To cut a deck of cards. **9.** To make an abrupt change of image or sound, as in filming. ❖ *n.* **1.** The act of cutting. **2.** The result of cutting, esp. an opening or wound made by a sharp edge. **3.** A part that has been cut from a main body: *a cut of cloth.* **4.** A passage made by digging or probing. **5.** The elimination or removal of a part. **6.** A reduction: *a cut in salary.* **7.** *Sports* The remainder of contestants in a competition, esp. in golf, after some have been eliminated. **8.** The style in which a garment is cut. **9.** *Informal* A portion of profits or earnings; a share. **10.** A wounding remark; an insult. **11.** An unexcused absence, as from school. **12.** A step in a scale of value or quality; degree: *a cut above the average.* **13.** *Printing* **a.** An engraved block or plate. **b.** A print made from such a block. **14.** *Sports* A stroke that causes a ball to spin in a reverse direction. **15.** *Baseball* A swing of a bat. **16.** *Games* The act of cutting a deck of cards. **17.** One of the objects used in drawing lots. **18.** An abrupt change of image or sound, as between shots in a film. **19.** A transition from one scene to another in a film, video, or television program. **20.** A movie at a given stage in its editing. **21.** A single selection of music from a recording. ***—phrasal verbs:* cut back 1.** To shorten by cutting; prune. **2.** To reduce or decrease. **cut down 1.** To kill or strike down. **2.** To alter by removing extra or additional fittings. **3.** To reduce the amount taken or used. **cut in 1.** To move into a line of people or things out of turn. **2.** To interrupt. **3.** To interrupt a dancing couple in order to dance with one of them. **4.** To connect or become connected into an electrical circuit. **5.** To mix in with or as if with cutting motions. **6.** To include, esp. among those profiting. **cut off 1.** To separate from others; isolate. **2.** To stop suddenly; discontinue. **3.** To shut off; bar. **4.** To interrupt the course or passage of. **5.** To interrupt or break the line of communication of. **6.** To disinherit. **cut out 1.** To remove by or as if by cutting. **2.** To form or shape by or as if by cutting. **3.** To take the place of; supplant. **4.** To suit or fit by nature. **5.** To assign beforehand or by necessity; predetermine. **6.** To deprive. **7.** To stop; cease. **8.** *Informal* To depart hastily. **9.** *Chiefly Southern US* To turn off (a light or television set). **cut up** *Informal* **1.** To behave in a playful, comic, or boisterous way; clown. **2.** To criticize severely. ***—idioms:* cut corners** To do something in the easiest or most inexpensive way. **cut down to size** To deflate the self-importance of. **cut loose** To speak or act without restraint. **cut no ice** To make no effect or impression. **cut (one's) losses** To withdraw from a losing situation. **cut (one's) teeth on** To learn or do as a beginner. **cut short** To stop before the end; abbreviate. **cut the mustard** To perform up to expectations or to a required standard. **cut to the chase** To get to the matter at hand. [ME *cutten.*] —**cut′ta•ble** *adj.*

cut-and-dried (kŭt′n-drīd′) also **cut-and-dry** (-drī′) *adj.* **1.** Prepared and arranged in advance; settled. **2.** Ordinary.

cut-and-paste (kŭt′ənd-pāst′) *adj.* Pieced together from several sources.

cu•ta•ne•ous (kyo͞o-tā′nē-əs) *adj.* Of, relating to, or affecting the skin. [< NLat. *cutāneus,* ult. < Lat. *cutis,* skin. See **(s)keu-** in App.] —**cu•ta′ne•ous•ly** *adv.*

cut•a•way (kŭt′ə-wā′) *n.* **1.** A man's formal daytime coat, with front edges sloping diagonally from the waist and forming tails at the back. **2.** A brief shot that interrupts the main action of a film, often to depict related matter or supposedly concurrent action. **3.** A model or diagram of an object with part of the outer layer removed so as to reveal the interior.

cut•back (kŭt′băk′) *n.* **1.** A decrease; a curtailment. **2.** A sharp

George Armstrong Custer

ă	pat	oi	boy
ā	pay	ou	out
âr	care	o͝o	took
ä	father	o͞o	boot
ĕ	pet	ŭ	cut
ē	be	ûr	urge
ĭ	pit	th	thin
ī	pie	*th*	this
îr	pier	hw	which
ŏ	pot	zh	vision
ō	toe	ə	about, item
ô	paw		

Stress marks:
′ (primary);
′ (secondary), as in
lexicon (lĕk′sĭ-kŏn′)

reversal of direction, as of a ball carrier in football.

cutch (kŭch) *n.* See **catechu** 1. [Malay *kachu,* of Dravidian orig.]

cute (kyo͞ot) *adj.* **cut•er, cut•est 1.** Delightfully pretty or dainty. **2.** Obviously contrived to charm; precious. **3.** Shrewd; clever. [Short for ACUTE.] —**cute′ly** *adv.* —**cute′ness** *n.*

WORD HISTORY *Cute* was originally a shortened form of *acute* in the sense "keenly perceptive or discerning, shrewd." In this sense *cute* is first recorded in a dictionary published in 1731. Probably *cute* came to be used as a term of approbation for things demonstrating acuteness, and so it went on to develop its own sense of "pretty, fetching."

cute•sy (kyo͞ot′sē) *adj.* **-si•er, -si•est** *Informal* Deliberately or affectedly cute; precious. —**cute′si•ness** *n.*

cut flower *n.* Any of various showy flowers used in fresh arrangements.

cut glass *n.* Glassware shaped or decorated by cutting instruments or abrasive wheels. —**cut′-glass′** (kŭt′glăs′) *adj.*

cut•grass also **cut grass** (kŭt′grăs′) *n.* **1.** Any of several grasses of the genus *Leersia,* having leaves with very rough margins. **2.** Any of several other grasses with rough margins.

cu•ti•cle (kyo͞o′tĭ-kəl) *n.* **1.** The outermost layer of the skin of vertebrates; epidermis. **2.** The strip of hardened skin at the base and sides of a fingernail or toenail. **3.** Dead or hardened epidermis. **4.** *Zoology* The noncellular, hardened or membranous protective covering of many invertebrates. **5.** *Botany* The layer of cutin covering the epidermis of the aerial parts of plants. [Lat. *cutīcula,* dim. of *cutis,* skin. See **(s)keu-** in App.] —**cu•tic′u•lar** (-tĭk′yə-lər) *adj.*

cut•ie also **cut•ey** (kyo͞o′tē) *n., pl.* **-ies** also **-eys** *Informal* A cute person.

cu•tin (kyo͞ot′n) *n.* A waxlike water-repellent material present in the walls of some plant cells and forming the cuticle. [Lat. *cutis,* skin; see **(s)keu-** in App. + -IN.]

cu•tin•ize (kyo͞ot′n-īz′) *v.* **-ized, -iz•ing, -iz•es** —*tr.* To coat or impregnate with cutin. —*intr.* To become coated or impregnated with cutin. —**cu′tin•i•za′tion** (-ĭ-zā′shən) *n.*

cu•tis (kyo͞o′tĭs) *n., pl.* **-tes** (-tēz) or **-tis•es** (-tĭs-ĭz) [Lat., skin. See **(s)keu-** in App.]

cut•lass also **cut•las** (kŭt′ləs) *n.* **1.** A short heavy sword with a curved single-edged blade, once used as a weapon by sailors. **2.** *Caribbean* A machete. [Fr. *coutelas* < OFr. *coutelasse,* prob. augmentative of *coutel,* knife < Lat. *cultellus,* dim. of *culter,* knife.]

cutlass fish *n.* Any of several marine fishes of the genus *Trichiurus,* having a long ribbonlike body and a pointed tail.

cut•ler (kŭt′lər) *n.* One who makes, repairs, or sells knives or other cutting instruments. [ME *cuteler* < OFr. *coutelier* < *coutel,* knife. See CUTLASS.]

cut•ler•y (kŭt′lə-rē) *n.* **1.** Cutting instruments and tools. **2.** Utensils such as knives, forks, and spoons used as tableware. **3.** The occupation of a cutler. [M English *cutellerie* < OFr. *coutelerie* < *coutel,* knife. See CUTLASS.]

cut•let (kŭt′lĭt) *n.* **1.** A thin slice of meat, usu. veal or lamb, cut from the leg or ribs. **2.** A patty of chopped meat or fish, usu. coated with bread crumbs and fried; a fish croquette. [Fr. *côtelette* < OFr. *costelette,* dim. of *coste,* rib < Lat. *costa.*]

cut•off also **cut-off** (kŭt′ôf′, -ŏf′) *n.* **1.** A designated limit or point of termination. **2.** A shortcut or bypass. **3.** A new channel cut by a river across the neck of an oxbow. **4.** The act or an instance of cutting off. **5.** *Baseball* The interception by an infielder of a throw to home plate from the outfield. **6.** A device that cuts off a flow of fluid. **7.** *Music* A conductor's signal for a stop or break. **8. cutoffs** Pants made into shorts by cutting off part of the legs. ❖ *adj.* Being a limit or point of termination.

cut•out (kŭt′out′) *n.* **1.** Something cut out or intended to be cut out from something else. **2.** *Electricity* A device that interrupts, bypasses, or disconnects a circuit or circuit element.

cut•o•ver (kŭt′ō′vər) *adj.* Cleared of trees, esp. those that bear valuable lumber.

cut•purse (kŭt′pûrs′) *n.* A pickpocket.

cut-rate (kŭt′rāt′) *adj.* Sold or on sale at a reduced price.

Cut•tack (kŭt′ək) A city of E India SW of Calcutta; long noted for its gold and silver filigree work. Pop. 403,418.

cut•ter (kŭt′ər) *n.* **1.** One that cuts, esp. in tailoring. **2.** A device or machine that cuts. **3.** *Nautical* **a.** A single-masted sailing vessel with two or more headsails and a mast set somewhat farther aft than that of a sloop. **b.** A ship's boat used for transporting stores or passengers. **4.** A small, lightly armed boat used by the Coast Guard. **5.** A small sleigh, usu. seating one person and drawn by a single horse.

cut•throat (kŭt′thrōt′) *n.* **1.** A murderer, esp. one who cuts throats. **2.** An unprincipled, ruthless person. ❖ *adj.* **1.** Cruel; murderous. **2.** Relentless or merciless in competition. **3.** *Sports & Games* Being a form of a game in which each of three or more players acts and scores individually.

cutthroat trout *n.* A large trout (*Salmo clarkii*) found in western North American waters similar to the rainbow trout, but with red or orange markings on the lower jaw.

cut time *n. Music* Duple meter in which the half note is the unit of time.

cut•ting (kŭt′ĭng) *adj.* **1.** Capable of or designed for incising,

shearing, or severing. **2.** Sharply penetrating; piercing. **3.** Injuring or capable of injuring the feelings of others. ❖ *n.* **1.** A part cut off from a main body. **2.** A part removed from a plant to propagate a new plant. **3.** An excavation made through high ground in a construction project. **4.** The editing of film or recording tape. **5.** *Chiefly British* A clipping, as from a newspaper. —**cut′ting•ly** *adv.*

cutting edge *n.* **1.** An effective quality or element. **2.** The position of greatest advancement or importance; the forefront.

cutting horse *n.* A saddle horse trained to separate individual animals from a cattle herd.

cut•tle•bone (kŭt′l-bōn′) *n.* The calcareous internal shell of a cuttlefish, used as a dietary supplement for cage birds or ground into powder for use as a polishing agent. [ME *cotilbone* : *codel, cutil,* cuttlefish; see CUTTLEFISH + *bone,* bone; see BONE.]

cut•tle•fish (kŭt′l-fĭsh′) *n., pl.* **cuttlefish** or **-fish•es** Any of various squidlike cephalopod marine mollusks of the genus *Sepia,* having a calcareous internal shell. [ME *codel, cutil,* cuttlefish (< OE *cudele*) + FISH.]

cut•up (kŭt′ŭp′) *n. Informal* A mischievous person.

cut•wa•ter (kŭt′wô′tər, -wŏt′ər) *n.* **1.** The forward part of a ship's prow. **2.** The wedge-shaped end of a bridge pier, designed to divide the current and break up ice floes.

cut•work (kŭt′wûrk′) *n.* Openwork embroidery in which the ground fabric is cut away from the design.

cut•worm (kŭt′wûrm′) *n.* The larva of various moths of the family Noctuidae that feed on and destroy many plants.

cu•vette (kyo͞o′vĕt′) *n.* A small, transparent, often tubular laboratory vessel. [Fr., dim. of *cuve,* tub < Lat. *cūpa.*]

Cu•vier (kyo͞o′vē-ā′, ko͞ov-yā′, kü-vyā′), Baron **Georges Léopold Chrétien Frédéric Dagobert** 1769–1832. French naturalist considered the founder of comparative anatomy.

Cuy•a•ho•ga Falls (kī′ə-hō′gə, kə-hō′-, -hô′-, -hä′-) A city of NE OH, a suburb of Akron on the **Cuyahoga River,** c. 129 km (80 mi). Pop. 49,374.

Cuz•co (ko͞oz′kō, ko͞os′-) also **Cus•co** (ko͞os′-) A city of S Peru in the Andes ESE of Lima; built on the site of an ancient Incan city supposedly founded in the 12th cent. Pop. 302,700.

CV *abbr.* **1.** Cape Verde **2.** cardiovascular **3.** curriculum vitae

cv. *abbr.* cultivar

CVA *abbr.* cerebrovascular accident

CV joint (sē′vē′) *n.* See **constant velocity joint.**

CVS *abbr.* chorionic villus sampling

cvt. *abbr.* convertible

CW *abbr.* **1.** chemical warfare **2.** continuous wave

cw. *abbr.* clockwise

cwm (ko͞om) *n.* See **cirque** 1. [Welsh, valley.]

CWO *abbr.* **1.** cash with order **2.** chief warrant officer

cwt. *abbr.* hundredweight

CY *abbr.* calendar year

-cy *suff.* **1.** State; condition; quality: *bankruptcy.* **2.** Rank; office: *baronetcy.* [ME *-cie* < OFr. *-cie, -tie* < Lat. *-cia, -tia* and Gk. *-kiā, -keia, -tiā, -teia.*]

cy•an (sī′ăn′, -ən) *n.* A greenish blue, one of the subtractive primary colors. [Gk. *kuanos,* dark blue.]

cyan- *pref.* Variant of **cyano-.**

cy•an•am•ide also **cy•an•am•id** (sī-ăn′ə-mīd) *n.* **1.** A caustic acidic crystalline compound, NHCNH, prepared by treating calcium cyanamide with sulfuric acid. **2.** Calcium cyanamide.

cy•a•nate (sī′ə-nāt′, -nət) *n.* A salt or ester of cyanic acid.

cy•an•ic (sī-ăn′ĭk) *adj.* **1.** Relating to or containing cyanogen. **2.** Of a blue or bluish hue.

cyanic acid *n.* A poisonous, unstable, highly volatile organic acid, HOCN, used to prepare cyanates.

cy•a•nide (sī′ə-nīd′) *n.* also **cy•a•nid** (-nĭd) Any of various salts or esters of hydrogen cyanide containing a CN group, esp. the extremely poisonous compounds potassium cyanide and sodium cyanide. ❖ *tr.v.* **-nid•ed, -nid•ing, -nides 1.** To treat (a metal surface) with cyanide to produce a hard surface. **2.** To treat (an ore) with cyanide to extract gold or silver.

cyanide process *n.* A process of extracting gold or silver from ores by treating them with a solution of sodium cyanide or calcium cyanide.

cy•a•nine (sī′ə-nēn′, -nĭn) *n.* Any of various blue dyes, used to sensitize photographic emulsions to a greater range of light.

cy•a•nite (sī′ə-nīt′) *n.* Variant of **kyanite.**

cyano- or **cyan-** *pref.* **1.** Blue: *cyanotype.* **2a.** Cyanogen: *cyanic.* **b.** Cyanide: *cyanogenesis.* [Gk. *kuano-* < *kuanos,* dark blue.]

cy•a•no•ac•ry•late (sī′ə-nō-ăk′rə-lāt′, sī-ăn′ō-) *n.* A strongly adhesive substance that is used in industry and medicine.

cy•a•no•bac•te•ri•um (sī′ə-nō-băk-tîr′ē-əm, sī-ăn′ō-) *n., pl.* **-te•ri•a** (-tîr′ē-ə) A photosynthetic bacterium of the class Coccogoneae or Hormogoneae, generally blue-green in color.

cy•a•no•co•bal•a•min (sī′ə-nō′kō-băl′ə-mĭn, sī-ăn′ō-) *n.* See **vitamin B₁₂.**

cy•an•o•gen (sī-ăn′ə-jən) *n.* **1.** A colorless, flammable, pungent, highly poisonous gas, C_2N_2, used as a rocket propellant, insecticide, and chemical weapon. **2.** A univalent radical, CN.

cy•a•no•hy•drin (sī′ə-nō-hī′drĭn, sī-ăn′ō-) *n.* Any of several compounds that contain both the CN and OH radicals. [CYANO- + HYDR(O)- + -IN.]

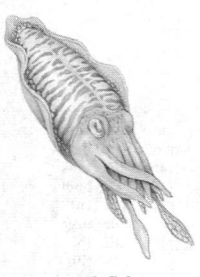

cutter
US Coast Guard patrol boat

cuttlefish
common cuttlefish
Sepia officinalis

cy•a•no•sis (sī′ə-nō′sĭs) *n.* A bluish discoloration of the skin and mucous membranes resulting from inadequate oxygenation of the blood. —**cy′a•not′ic** (-nŏt′ĭk) *adj.*

cy•an•o•type (sī-ăn′ə-tīp′) *n.* See **blueprint** 1a.

Cyb•e•le (sĭb′ə-lē) *n. Greek Mythology* A goddess of nature and fertility in Asia Minor and Greece.

cyber– *pref.* **1.** Computer: *cyberpunk.* **2.** Computer network: *cyberspace.* See Usage Note at **virtual.** [< CYBERNETICS.]

cy•ber•ca•fe (sī′bər-kă-fā′, -kə-) *n.* **1.** A cafe from which customers can access the Internet. **2.** A chatroom.

cy•ber•cast (sī′bər-kăst′) *n.* A news or entertainment program transmitted over the Internet. [CYBER– + (NEWS)CAST.]

cy•ber•cul•ture (sī′bər-kŭl′chər) *n.* The culture arising from the use of computer networks, as for communication, entertainment, work, and business.

cy•ber•nate (sī′bər-nāt′) *tr.v.* **-nat•ed, -nat•ing, -nates** To control (an industrial process) by computer. [CYBERN(ETICS) + –ATE[1].] —**cy′ber•na′tion** *n.*

cy•ber•net•ics (sī′bər-nĕt′ĭks) *n.* (*used with a sing. verb*) The theoretical study of communication and control processes in biological, mechanical, and electronic systems, esp. the comparison of these processes in biological and artificial systems. [< Gk. *kubernētēs*, governor < *kubernān*, to govern.] —**cy′ber•net′ic** *adj.* —**cy′ber•net′i•cal•ly** *adv.* —**cy′ber•net′i•cist, cy′ber•ne•ti′cian** (-nĭ-tĭsh′ən) *n.*

cy•ber•punk (sī′bər-pŭngk′) *n.* Fast-paced science fiction involving futuristic computer-based societies. [CYBER(NETICS) + PUNK.] —**cy′ber•punk′** *adj.*

cy•ber•sex (sī′bər-sĕks′) *n.* Sexual activity or arousal through communication by computer.

cy•ber•space (sī′bər-spās′) *n.* The electronic medium of computer networks, in which online communication takes place.

cy•borg (sī′bôrg′) *n.* A human who has certain physiological processes aided or controlled by mechanical or electronic devices. [*cyb(ernetic) org(anism).*]

cy•cad (sī′kăd′, -kəd) *n.* Any of various palmlike gymnospermous cone-bearing evergreen plants of the division Cycadophyta, native to warm regions and having large, pinnately compound leaves. [NLat. *Cycas, Cycad-*, genus name < Gk. *kukas*, erroneous reading of *koïkas*, accusative pl. of *koïx*, a kind of palm tree, perh. of Egypt. orig.]

cycl– *pref.* Variant of **cyclo–.**

Cyc•la•des (sĭk′lə-dēz′) also **Ki•klá•dhes** (kē-klä′*th*ēs) A group of islands of SE Greece in the S Aegean Sea. The name was used in ancient times for the islands surrounding Delos.

cy•cla•mate (sī′klə-māt′, sĭk′lə-) *n.* A salt of cyclamic acid formerly used as an artificial sweetener, esp. sodium cyclamate or calcium cyclamate. [CYCLAM(IC ACID) + –ATE[2].]

cy•cla•men (sī′klə-mən, sĭk′lə-) *n.* Any of various plants of the genus *Cyclamen*, having decorative leaves and showy flowers with reflexed petals. [NLat. *Cyclamen*, genus name < Lat. *cyclamīnos* < Gk. *kuklamīnos*, prob. < *kuklos*, circle, wheel (perh. < its bulbous roots). See CYCLE.]

cyc•la•mic acid (sĭk′lə-mĭk′, sī′klə-) *n.* A crystalline acid, $C_6H_{13}NO_3S$, used to produce cyclamates. [CYCLO– + AM(IDE) + –IC.]

cy•clase (sī′klās′, -klāz′) *n.* An enzyme that acts as a catalyst in the cyclization of a compound. [CYCL(IC) + –ASE.]

cy•cle (sī′kəl) *n.* **1.** An interval of time during which a characteristic, often regularly repeated event or sequence of events occurs. **2a.** A single complete execution of a periodically repeated phenomenon: *A year constitutes a cycle of the seasons.* **b.** A periodically repeated sequence of events: *the cycle of birth, growth, and death.* **3.** The orbit of a celestial body. **4.** A long period of time; an age. **5a.** The aggregate of traditional poems or stories organized around a central theme or hero: *the Arthurian cycle.* **b.** A series of poems or songs on the same theme: *Schubert's song cycles.* **6.** A bicycle, motorcycle, or similar vehicle. **7.** *Botany* A circular or whorled arrangement of flower parts. ❖ *v.* **-cled, -cling, -cles** —*intr.* **1.** To occur in or pass through a cycle. **2.** To move in or as if in a cycle. **3.** To ride a bicycle, motorcycle, or similar vehicle. —*tr.* To use in or put through a cycle. [ME < LLat. *cyclus* < Gk. *kuklos*, circle. See **kʷel-** in App.] —**cy′cler** *n.*

cy•clic (sī′klĭk, sĭk′lĭk) or **cy•cli•cal** (sī′klĭ-kəl, sĭk′lĭ-kəl) *adj.* **1a.** Of, relating to, or characterized by cycles. **b.** Recurring or moving in cycles. **2.** *Chemistry* Of or relating to compounds having atoms arranged in a ring or closed-chain structure. **3.** *Botany* **a.** Having parts arranged in a whorl. **b.** Forming a whorl. —**cy′cli•cal′i•ty** (sĭk′lə-kăl′ĭ-tē, sī′klə-) *n.* —**cy′cli•cal•ly** *adv.*

cyclic AMP *n.* A cyclic nucleotide of adenosine that acts to regulate various metabolic processes and mediate hormone activity at the cellular level.

cyclic GMP *n.* A cyclic nucleotide of guanosine that acts to regulate various metabolic processes and mediate hormone activity at the cellular level, possibly as an antagonist to cyclic AMP.

cy•clin (sī′klĭn) *n.* A class of proteins that fluctuate in concentration at specific points during the cell cycle and that regulate the cycle by binding to a kinase.

cy•cling (sī′klĭng) *n.* The act, sport, or technique of riding or racing on a bicycle, motorcycle, or similar vehicle. ❖ *adj.* Relating to or used in cycling.

cy•clist (sī′klĭst) *n.* One who rides or races a bicycle, motorcycle, or similar vehicle.

cy•cli•za•tion (sī′klĭ-zā′shən, sĭk′lĭ-) *n.* The formation of one or more rings in a hydrocarbon.

cyclo– or **cycl–** *pref.* **1.** Circle; cycle: *cyclorama.* **2.** A cyclic compound: *cyclohexane.* [Gk. *kuklo-* < *kuklos*, circle. See **kʷel-** in App.]

cy•clo•al•kane (sī′klō-ăl′kān) *n.* An alicyclic hydrocarbon with a saturated ring.

cy•clo•hex•ane (sī′klō-hĕk′sān′) *n.* An extremely flammable, colorless mobile liquid, C_6H_{12}, obtained from petroleum and benzene and used in the manufacture of nylon and as a solvent.

cy•clo•hex•i•mide (sī′klō-hĕk′sə-mīd′, -mĭd) *n.* A colorless crystalline compound, $C_{15}H_{23}NO_4$, used as a fungicide.

cy•cloid (sī′kloid′) *adj.* **1.** Resembling a circle. **2.** *Zoology* **a.** Thin, rounded, and smooth-edged; disklike. Used of fish scales. **b.** Having or composed of such scales. **3.** *Psychology* Afflicted with or relating to cyclothymia. ❖ *n.* **1.** *Mathematics* The curve traced by a point on the circumference of a circle that rolls on a straight line. **2.** *Zoology* A fish having cycloid scales. [Fr. *cycloïde* < Gk. *kukloeidēs*, circular : *kuklos*, circle; see **kʷel-**[1] in App. + *-oeidēs*, -oid.] —**cy•cloi′dal** (-kloid′l) *adj.*

cy•clom•e•ter (sī-klŏm′ĭ-tər) *n.* **1.** An instrument that records the revolutions of a wheel to indicate distance traveled. **2.** An instrument that measures circular arcs. —**cy′clo•met′ric** (-klə-mĕt′rĭk) *adj.* —**cy•clom′e•try** *n.*

cy•clone (sī′klōn′) *n.* **1.** *Meteorology* An atmospheric system characterized by the rapid inward circulation of air masses about a low-pressure center, circulating counterclockwise in the Northern Hemisphere and clockwise in the Southern Hemisphere. **2.** A violent rotating windstorm. **3.** Any of various devices using centrifugal action to separate materials. [< Gk. *kuklōn*, pr. part. of *kukloun*, to rotate < *kuklos*, circle. See **kʷel-** in App.] —**cy•clon′ic** (-klŏn′ĭk), **cy•clon′i•cal** *adj.*

cyclone cellar *n.* An underground shelter in or adjacent to a house, used for protection from severe windstorms.

cy•clo•par•af•fin (sī′klō-păr′ə-fĭn) *n.* See **cycloalkane.**

cy•clo•pe•an (sī′klə-pē′ən, sī-klō′pē-) *adj.* **1.** often **Cyclopean** Relating to or suggestive of a Cyclops. **2.** Of or constituting a primitive style of masonry characterized by the use of massive stones of irregular shape and size.

cy•clo•pe•di•a also **cy•clo•pae•di•a** (sī′klə-pē′dē-ə) *n.* An encyclopedia. [Short for ENCYCLOPEDIA.] —**cy′clo•pe′dic** (-dĭk) *adj.* —**cy′clo•pe′dist** (-dĭst) *n.*

cy•clo•phos•pha•mide (sī′klə-fŏs′fə-mīd′) *n.* An immunosuppressive antineoplastic drug, $C_7H_{15}Cl_2N_2P$, used to treat Hodgkin's disease, lymphoma, and certain leukemias.

cy•clo•ple•gia (sī′klə-plē′jə) *n.* Paralysis of the ciliary muscles of the eye, resulting in the loss of visual accommodation.

cy•clo•pro•pane (sī′klə-prō′pān′) *n.* A highly flammable, explosive, colorless gas, C_3H_6, sometimes used as an anesthetic.

Cy•clops (sī′klŏps) *n., pl.* **Cy•clo•pes** (sī-klō′pēz) *Greek Mythology* **1.** Any of the three one-eyed Titans who forged thunderbolts for Zeus. **2.** Any of a race of one-eyed giants, reputedly descended from these Titans, inhabiting Sicily. [Lat. < Gk. *Kuklōps* : *kuklos*, circle; see CYCLE + *ōps*, eye; see MYOPIA.]

cy•clo•ram•a (sī′klə-răm′ə, -rä′mə) *n.* **1.** A large composite picture placed on the walls of a cylindrical room so as to appear in natural perspective to a spectator standing in the center of the room. **2.** A large curtain or wall, usu. concave, at the rear of a stage. [CYCL(O)– + (PAN)ORAMA.]

cy•clo•sis (sī-klō′sĭs) *n., pl.* **-ses** (-sēz) The streaming rotary motion of protoplasm within a cell. [NLat. < Gk. *kuklōsis*, a surrounding < *kukloun*, to surround < *kuklos*, circle. See **kʷel-** in App.]

cy•clo•spor•ine (sī′klə-spôr′ēn, -ĭn, -spōr′-) also **cy•clo•spor•in** (-ĭn) *n.* An immunosuppressive drug obtained from certain soil fungi, used mainly to prevent the rejection of transplanted organs.

cy•clo•stome (sī′klə-stōm′) *n.* Any of various primitive eellike vertebrates of the class Agnatha, lacking jaws and true teeth and having a circular, sucking mouth. [< NLat. *Cyclostomī* and *Cyclostomata*, class names : CYCLO– + Gk. *stoma, stomat-*, mouth.] —**cy•clos′to•mate′** (sī-klŏs′tə-māt′, -mĭt), **cy′clo•stom′a•tous** (sī′klə-stŏm′ə-təs, -stō′mə-) *adj.*

cy•clo•thy•mi•a (sī′klə-thī′mē-ə) *n.* A mild affective disorder characterized by alternating periods of elation and depression. —**cy′clo•thy′mic** (-mĭk) *adj. & n.*

cy•clo•tron (sī′klə-trŏn′) *n.* A circular particle accelerator in which charged subatomic particles generated at a central source are accelerated spirally outward in a plane perpendicular to a fixed magnetic field by an alternating electric field.

cy•der (sī′dər) *n. Chiefly British* Variant of **cider.**

cyg•net (sĭg′nĭt) *n.* A young swan. [ME *cignet* < AN, dim. of OFr. *cygne*, swan < Lat. *cygnus* < Gk. *kuknos.*]

Cyg•nus (sĭg′nəs) *n.* A constellation in the Northern Hemisphere near Lacerta and Lyra. [Lat. *cygnus*, swan. See CYGNET.]

cyl•in•der (sĭl′ən-dər) *n.* **1.** *Mathematics* **a.** The surface generated by a straight line intersecting and moving along a closed plane curve, the directrix, while remaining parallel to a fixed straight line that is not on or parallel to the plane of the directrix.

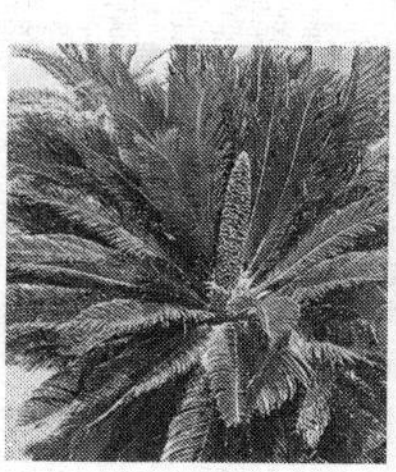

cycad
sago palm
Cycas revoluta

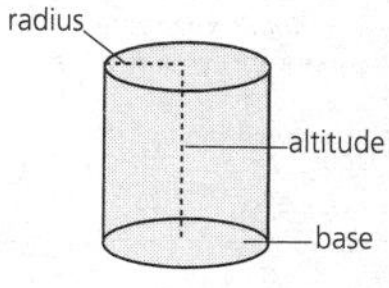

cylinder
To calculate the volume of a right circular cylinder, multiply the area of the base by the altitude.

ă	pat	oi	boy
ā	pay	ou	out
âr	care	o͝o	took
ä	father	o͞o	boot
ĕ	pet	ŭ	cut
ē	be	ûr	urge
ĭ	pit	th	thin
ī	pie	*th*	this
îr	pier	hw	which
ŏ	pot	zh	vision
ō	toe	ə	about, item
ô	paw		

Stress marks:
′ (primary);
′ (secondary), as in
lexicon (lĕk′sĭ-kŏn′)

b. The portion of such a surface bounded by two parallel planes and the regions of the planes bounded by the surface. **c.** A solid bounded by two parallel planes and such a surface, esp. such a surface having a circle as its directrix. **2.** A cylindrical container or object. **3.** *Engineering* **a.** The chamber in which a piston of a reciprocating engine moves. **b.** The chamber of a pump from which fluid is expelled by a piston. **4.** The rotating chamber of a revolver that holds the cartridges. **5.** Any of several rotating parts in a printing press, esp. one that carries the paper. **6.** *Archaeology* A cylindrical stone or clay object with an engraved design or inscription. [Lat. *cylindrus* < Gk. *kulindros* < *kulindein*, to roll.]

cylinder head *n.* The closed, often detachable end of a cylinder in an internal-combustion engine.

cy·lin·dri·cal (sə-lĭn′drĭ-kəl) also **cy·lin·dric** (-drĭk) *adj.* **1.** Of or having the shape of a cylinder, esp. of a circular one. **2.** *Mathematics* Of or relating to the coordinate system formed by two polar coordinates in a plane and a rectangular coordinate measured from the plane. —**cy·lin·dri·cal·i·ty** (-kăl′ĭ-tē) *n.* —**cy·lin′dri·cal·ly** *adv.*

cyl·in·droid (sĭl′ən-droid′) *n.* A cylindrical surface or solid, all of whose sections perpendicular to the elements are elliptical. ❖ *adj.* Resembling a cylinder.

cy·ma (sī′mə) *n.* A molding having a partly concave and partly convex curve in profile, used esp. in classical architecture. [NLat. *cȳma* < Gk. *kūma*, wave, cyma < *kuein*, to swell.]

cy·ma·tium (sī-mā′shəm, -shē-əm) *n., pl.* **-tia** (-shə, -shē-ə) **1.** See **cyma. 2.** The topmost molding of a classical cornice. [Lat. *cȳmatium* < Gk. *kūmation*, dim. of *kūma*, cyma. See CYMA.]

cym·bal (sĭm′bəl) *n.* A percussion instrument consisting of a concave brass plate that makes a loud clashing tone when hit with a drumstick or when used in pairs. [ME < OE and < OFr. *cymbale*, both < Lat. *cymbalum* < Gk. *kumbalon* < *kumbē*, bowl.] —**cym′bal·eer** (sĭm′bə-lîr′), **cym′bal·er, cym′bal·ist** *n.*

cym·bid·i·um (sĭm-bĭd′ē-əm) *n.* Any of various epiphytic orchids of the genus *Cymbidium*, native to tropical Asia and Australia and having elongate clusters of showy blooms. [NLat. *Cymbidium*, genus name < Lat. *cymba*, boat < Gk. *kumbē*.]

cyme (sīm) *n.* A usu. flat-topped or convex flower cluster in which the main axis and each branch end in a flower. [Lat. *cȳma*, young cabbage sprout < Gk. *kūma*, anything swollen, sprout. See CYMA.] —**cy·mif′er·ous** (sī-mĭf′ər-əs) *adj.*

cy·mene (sī′mēn′) *n.* Any of three isomeric liquid hydrocarbons, C₁₀H₁₄, obtained chiefly from the essential oils of cumin and thyme and used to manufacture synthetic resins. [Fr. *cymène* < Gk. *kuminon*, cumin. See CUMIN.]

cym·ling (sĭm′lĭng) also **cym·lin** (-lĭn) *n.* See **pattypan squash.** [Alteration of SIMNEL.]

cy·mo·gene (sī′mə-jēn′) *n.* A flammable gaseous fraction of petroleum, consisting chiefly of butane. [CYM(ENE) + *-gene* (var. of *-GEN*).]

cy·moid (sī′moid′) *adj.* **1.** *Architecture* Resembling a cyma. **2.** *Botany* Resembling a cyme.

cy·mo·phane (sī′mə-fān′) *n.* An opalescent variety of chrysoberyl having a shimmering luster. [Fr. : Gk. *kūma*, wave, cyma; see CYMA + Gk. *-phanēs*, appearing; see *-PHANE*.]

cy·mose (sī′mōs′) also **cy·mous** (-məs) *adj.* **1.** Relating to or resembling a cyme; determinate. **2.** Bearing a cyme or cymes. [CYM(E) + *-OSE¹*.] —**cy′mose·ly** *adv.*

Cym·ric (kĭm′rĭk, sĭm′-) *adj.* Of or relating to the Cymry. ❖ *n.* See **Welsh** 2.

Cym·ry (kĭm′rē, sĭm′-) *n.* (*used with a pl. verb*) **1.** The Brythonic Celts of Wales, Cornwall, and Brittany. **2.** The Welsh. [Welsh, pl. of *Cymro*, the Welsh people, Wales. See **merg-** in App.]

Cyn·e·wulf (kĭn′ə-wŏŏlf′) or **Cyn·wulf** (kĭn′wŏŏlf′) fl. c. 900. Anglo-Saxon poet whose works include *Juliana.*

cyn·ic (sĭn′ĭk) *n.* **1.** A person who believes all people are motivated by selfishness. **2.** A person whose outlook is scornfully and often habitually negative. **3.** *Cynic* A member of a sect of ancient Greek philosophers who believed virtue to be the only good and self-control to be the only means of achieving virtue. ❖ *adj.* **1.** Cynical. **2.** *Cynic* Of or relating to the Cynics or their beliefs. [Lat. *cynicus*, Cynic philosopher < Gk. *kunikos* < *kuōn, kun-*, dog. See **kwon-** in App.]

cyn·i·cal (sĭn′ĭ-kəl) *adj.* **1.** Believing or showing the belief that people are motivated chiefly by base or selfish concerns. **2.** Selfishly or callously calculating. **3.** Negative or pessimistic, as from world-weariness. **4.** Expressing jaded or scornful skepticism or negativity. —**cyn′i·cal·ly** *adv.* —**cyn′i·cal·ness** *n.*

cyn·i·cism (sĭn′ĭ-sĭz′əm) *n.* **1.** A cynical attitude or quality. **2.** A cynical comment or act. **3.** *Cynicism* The beliefs of the Cynics.

cy·no·sure (sī′nə-shŏŏr′, sĭn′ə-) *n.* **1.** An object that serves as a focal point of attention and admiration. **2.** Something that serves to guide. [Fr., Ursa Minor (which contains the guiding star Polaris) < Lat. *cynosura* < Gk. *kunosoura*, dog's tail, Ursa Minor : *kunos*, genitive of *kuōn*, dog; see **kwon-** in App. + *ourā*, tail; see **ors-** in App.] —**cy′no·sur′al** *adj.*

cy·pher (sī′fər) *n. & v.* Variant of **cipher.**

cy pres (sē′ prā′) *n.* The legal doctrine that allows a court freedom in interpreting the terms of a will or gift if carrying out the terms literally would be impracticable or illegal and as long as the general intent of the testator or donor is observed. [ME < AN :

cy, so, as (< Lat. *sīc*, so; see SIC¹) + *pres*, near (< LLat. *pressē*, close to < Lat. *pressus*, p. part. of *premere*, to press closely; see PRESS¹).]

cy·press (sī′prĭs) *n.* **1a.** Any of various Eurasian and North American evergreen trees or shrubs of the genus *Cupressus*, having scalelike leaves and globose woody cones. **b.** Any of several similar or related coniferous trees. **c.** The wood of any of these trees. **2.** Cypress branches used as a symbol of mourning. [ME *cipres* < OFr. *cypressus*, prob. blend of Lat. *cupressus* and *cyparissus* < Gk. *kuparissos*.]

cypress vine *n.* An annual twining tropical American vine (*Ipomoea quamoclit*) having pinnately cut leaves and showy, usu. scarlet flowers.

Cyp·ri·an (sĭp′rē-ən) *adj.* **1.** Of or relating to Cyprus; Cypriot. **2a.** Of or relating to the ancient worship of Aphrodite on Cyprus. **b.** Licentious; wanton. ❖ *n.* **1.** See **Cypriot** 1. **2.** also **cyprian a.** A wanton person. **b.** A prostitute.

Cyprian, Saint. d. A.D. 258. Christian prelate and martyr in North Africa.

cyp·ri·nid (sĭp′rə-nĭd) *n.* Any of the freshwater fishes of the family Cyprinidae, which includes the minnows, carps, and shiners. [< NLat. *Cyprīnidae*, family name < *Cyprīnus*, type genus < Lat. *cyprīnus*, carp < Gk. *kuprīnos.*] —**cyp′ri·nid** *adj.*

cy·prin·o·dont (sĭ-prĭn′ə-dŏnt′, -prī′nə-) *n.* Any of various small soft-finned fishes of the family Cyprinodontidae, which includes the killifishes and topminnows. [Lat. *cyprīnus*, carp (< Gk. *kuprīnos*) + *-ODONT*.] —**cy·prin′o·dont** *adj.*

cyp·ri·noid (sĭp′rə-noid′, sĭ-prī′-) *adj.* Of, relating to, or resembling a carp or other cyprinid fish. ❖ *n.* A cyprinoid fish. [< NLat. *Cyprīnoīdea*, suborder name : *Cyprīnus*, type genus; see CYPRINID + *-oīdea*, neut. pl. of *-oīdēs*, -oid.]

Cyp·ri·ot (sĭp′rē-ət, -ŏt′) also **Cyp·ri·ote** (-ōt′, -ət) *n.* **1.** A native or inhabitant of Cyprus. **2.** The ancient or modern Greek dialect of Cyprus. ❖ *adj.* **1.** Of or relating to Cyprus or its people or culture. **2.** Of or relating to Cypriot Greek. [Fr. *cypriote* < Gk. *Kupriōtēs* < *Kupros*, Cyprus.]

cyp·ri·pe·di·um (sĭp′rĭ-pē′dē-əm) *n.* Any of various orchids of the genus *Cypripedium*, such as the lady's slipper. [NLat. *Cypripedium*, genus name : LLat. *Cypris*, Venus (< Gk. *Kupris*, Aphrodite < *Kupros*, Cyprus, legendary birthplace of Aphrodite) + NLat. *-pedium* (alteration of Gk. *pedilon*, sandal; see **ped-** in App.).]

Cy·prus (sī′prəs) An island country in the E Mediterranean Sea S of Turkey; site of an ancient Neolithic culture and settled by Phoenicians c. 800 B.C. It achieved independence from Great Britain in 1960. Cap. Nicosia. Pop. 734,000.

cyp·se·la (sĭp′sə-lə) *n., pl.* **-lae** (-lē′) An achene fruit derived from an inferior ovary, characteristic of plants in the composite family. [NLat. < Gk. *kupselē*, hollow vessel.]

Cy·ra·no de Ber·ge·rac (sîr′ə-nō də bûr′zhə-răk′, bĕr′-), **Savinien de** 1619–55. French satirist and duelist whose works include the drama *The Pedant Imitated* (1654).

Cyr·e·na·ic (sîr′ə-nā′ĭk, sī′rə-) *adj.* **1.** Of or relating to Cyrenaica or Cyrene. **2.** Of or advocating the doctrines of Aristippus of Cyrene, who argued that pleasure is the only good in life. —**Cyr′e·na′ic** *n.*

Cyr·e·na·i·ca (sîr′ə-nā′ĭ-kə, sī′rə-) An ancient region of NE Libya bordering on the Mediterranean Sea; colonized by Greeks in the 7th cent. B.C.

Cy·re·ne (sī-rē′nē) An ancient Greek city of Cyrenaica; founded c. 630 B.C. and noted as an intellectual center.

Cyr·il (sîr′əl), Saint. 827–869. Christian missionary and theologian who with his brother Saint Methodius (826–885) worked in Moravia, translating the Scriptures into Old Church Slavonic.

Cy·ril·lic (sə-rĭl′ĭk) *adj.* Of or being any of the alphabets based on Glagolitic and used for certain Slavic languages, such as Russian. [Invention incorrectly attributed to St. CYRIL.]

Cy·rus (sī′rəs) Known as "the Younger." 424?–401 B.C. Persian prince who led a mammoth force of Greeks against his brother Artaxerxes II. The retreat that followed his defeat and death are described in Xenophon's *Anabasis.*

Cyrus II Known as "Cyrus the Great." 600?–529? B.C. King of Persia (550–529) and founder of the Persian Empire.

cyst (sĭst) *n.* **1.** *Pathology* An abnormal membranous sac containing a gaseous, liquid, or semisolid substance. **2.** *Anatomy* A sac or vesicle in the body. **3.** *Biology* A small capsulelike sac that encloses certain organisms in their dormant or larval stage. **4.** *Botany* A thick-walled resting spore, as in certain algae or fungi. [NLat. *cystis* < Gk. *kustis*, bladder.]

cyst– *pref.* Variant of **cysto–.**

cys·tec·to·my (sĭ-stĕk′tə-mē) *n., pl.* **-mies 1.** Surgical removal of a cyst. **2a.** Surgical removal of the gallbladder. **b.** Surgical removal of all or part of the urinary bladder.

cys·te·ine (sĭs′tə-ēn′, -ĭn, -tē-) *n.* An amino acid, C₃H₇O₂NS, derived from cystine and found in most proteins. [Alteration of CYSTINE.]

cys·tic (sĭs′tĭk) *adj.* **1.** Of, relating to, or having the characteristic of a cyst. **2.** Having or containing cysts or a cyst. **3.** Enclosed in a cyst. **4.** *Anatomy* Of, relating to, or involving the gallbladder or urinary bladder.

cystic duct *n.* The duct that conveys bile from the gallbladder to the common bile duct.

cyma
top: cyma recta
bottom: cyma reversa

cypress
Monterey cypress
Cupressus macrocarpa

cys·ti·cer·coid (sĭs'tĭ-sûr'koid) *n.* The larval stage of certain tapeworms, resembling a cysticercus but having the scolex completely filling the enclosing cyst. [CYSTICERC(US) + –OID.]

cys·ti·cer·co·sis (sĭs'tĭ-sər-kō'sĭs) *n.* The condition of being infested with cysticerci. [CYSTICERC(US) + –OSIS.]

cys·ti·cer·cus (sĭs'tĭ-sûr'kəs) *n., pl.* **-ci** (-sī') The larval stage of many tapeworms, consisting of a single invaginated scolex enclosed in a fluid-filled cyst. [NLat. : Gk. *kustis*, cyst; see CYST + Gk. *kerkos*, tail.]

cystic fibrosis *n.* A hereditary disease of the exocrine glands, affecting mainly the pancreas, respiratory system, and sweat glands and characterized by the production of abnormally viscous mucus, usu. resulting in chronic respiratory infections and impaired pancreatic function.

cys·tine (sĭs'tēn') *n.* A white crystalline amino acid, $C_6H_{12}N_2O_4S_2$, found in many proteins, esp. keratin. [< its discovery in bladder stones.]

cys·ti·tis (sĭ-stī'tĭs) *n.* Inflammation of the urinary bladder.

cysto– or **cyst–** *pref.* Bladder; cyst; sac: *cystocele.* [< NLat. *cystis*, bladder < Gk. *kustis.*]

cys·to·cele (sĭs'tə-sēl') *n.* Herniation of the urinary bladder through the wall of the vagina.

cys·toid (sĭs'toid') *adj.* Formed like or resembling a cyst. ❖ *n.* A cystoid structure.

cys·to·lith (sĭs'tə-lĭth') *n.* **1.** *Botany* A mineral concretion, usu. of calcium carbonate, occurring in the epidermal cells of certain plants, such as figs. **2.** See **urinary calculus**.

cys·to·scope (sĭs'tə-skōp') *n.* A tubular instrument used to examine the interior of the urinary bladder and ureter. —**cys'to·scop'ic** (-skŏp'ĭk) *adj.* —**cys·tos'co·py** (sĭ-stŏs'kə-pē) *n.*

cys·tos·to·my (sĭ-stŏs'tə-mē) *n., pl.* **-mies** The surgical formation of an opening into the urinary bladder.

–cyte *suff.* Cell: *leukocyte.* [NLat. *-cyta* < Gk. *kutos*, hollow vessel. See **(s)keu-** in App.]

Cy·the·ra (sĭ-thîr'ə, sĭth'ər-ə) also **Kí·thi·ra** (kē'thē-rä') An island of S Greece in the Mediterranean Sea S of the Peloponnesus; chief center for the worship of Aphrodite.

Cyth·e·re·a (sĭth'ə-rē'ə) *n. Greek Mythology* See **Aphrodite**.

cy·ti·dine (sī'tĭ-dēn') *n.* A nucleoside, $C_9H_{13}N_3O_5$, composed of cytosine and ribose. [CYT(O)– + –ID(E) + –INE.]

cyto– or **cyt–** *pref.* Cell: *cytoplasm.* [< Gk. *kutos*, hollow vessel. See **(s)keu-** in App.]

cy·to·chem·is·try (sī'tō-kĕm'ĭ-strē) *n.* The branch of biochemistry that studies the chemical composition and activity of cells. —**cy'to·chem'i·cal** (-kĕm'ĭ-kəl) *adj.*

cy·to·chrome (sī'tə-krōm') *n.* Any of a class of iron-containing proteins important in cell respiration as catalysts of oxidation-reduction reactions.

cy·to·gen·e·sis (sī'tō-jĕn'ĭ-sĭs) *n.* The formation, development, and variation of cells.

cy·to·ge·net·ics (sī'tō-jə-nĕt'ĭks) *n.* (*used with a sing. verb*) The branch of biology that deals with heredity and the cellular components associated with heredity. —**cy'to·ge·net'ic**, **cy'to·ge·net'i·cal** *adj.* —**cy'to·ge·net'i·cal·ly** *adv.* —**cy'to·ge·net'i·cist** (-sĭst) *n.*

cy·tog·e·ny (sī-tŏj'ə-nē) *n.* See **cytogenesis**.

cy·to·kine (sī'tə-kīn') *n.* Any of several proteins, such as the interleukins and lymphokines, that act as intercellular mediators in an immune response. [CYTO– + Gk. *kīnein*, to move; see KININ.]

cy·to·ki·ne·sis (sī'tō-kə-nē'sĭs, -kī-) *n.* The division of the cytoplasm of a cell following the division of the nucleus. —**cy'to·ki·net'ic** (-nĕt'ĭk) *adj.*

cy·to·ki·nin (sī'tə-kī'nĭn) *n.* Any of a class of plant hormones that promote cell division and growth and delay the senescence of leaves.

cy·tol·o·gy (sī-tŏl'ə-jē) *n.* The branch of biology that deals with cell formation, structure, and function. —**cy'to·log'ic** (-tə-lŏj'ĭk), **cy'to·log'i·cal** *adj.* —**cy·tol'o·gist** *n.*

cy·tol·y·sin (sī-tŏl'ĭ-sĭn) *n.* A substance, such as an antibody, capable of dissolving or destroying cells. [CYTOLYS(IS) + –IN.]

cy·tol·y·sis (sī-tŏl'ĭ-sĭs) *n.* The dissolution or destruction of a cell. —**cy'to·lyt'ic** (sī'tə-lĭt'ĭk) *adj.*

cy·to·me·gal·ic (sī'tō-mĭ-găl'ĭk) *adj.* Of, relating to, or characterized by greatly enlarged cells.

cy·to·meg·a·lo·vi·rus (sī'tō-mĕg'ə-lō-vī'rəs) *n.* Any of a group of herpes viruses that attack and enlarge epithelial cells.

cy·to·mem·brane (sī'tə-mĕm'brān) *n.* See **cell membrane**.

cy·to·path·ic (sī'tə-păth'ĭk) *adj.* Of or relating to degeneration or disease of cells.

cy·to·path·o·gen·ic (sī'tə-păth'ə-jĕn'ĭk) *adj.* Of, relating to, or producing pathological changes in cells. —**cy'to·path'o·ge·nic'i·ty** (-jə-nĭs'ĭ-tē) *n.*

cy·to·phil·ic (sī'tə-fĭl'ĭk) *adj.* Having an affinity for cells.

cy·to·pho·tom·e·ter (sī'tō-fō-tŏm'ĭ-tər) *n.* An instrument used to identify and locate the chemical compounds within a cell by measuring the intensity of light passing through stained sections of the cytoplasm. —**cy'to·pho'to·met'ric** (-tə-mĕt'rĭk) *adj.* —**cy'to·pho·tom'e·try** *n.*

cy·to·plasm (sī'tə-plăz'əm) *n.* The protoplasm outside the nucleus of a cell. —**cy'to·plas'mic** (-plăz'mĭk) *adj.* —**cy'to·plas'mi·cal·ly** *adv.*

cy·to·plast (sī'tə-plăst') *n.* The intact cytoplasm of a single cell. —**cy'to·plas'tic** (-plăs'tĭk) *adj.*

cy·to·sine (sī'tə-sēn') *n.* A pyrimidine base, $C_4H_5N_3O$, that is the constituent of DNA and RNA involved in base-pairing with guanine. [CYT(O)– + (RIB)OS(E) + –INE².]

cy·to·skel·e·ton (sī'tə-skĕl'ĭ-tn) *n.* The internal framework of a cell, composed largely of actin filaments and microtubules.

cy·to·sol (sī'tə-sôl', -sŏl') *n.* The fluid component of cytoplasm, excluding organelles and the insoluble, usu. suspended cytoplasmic components. [CYTO– + SOL(UTION).]

cy·to·sta·sis (sī'tō-stā'sĭs, -stăs'ĭs) *n.* Arrest of cellular growth and multiplication.

cy·to·stat·ic (sī'tə-stăt'ĭk) *adj.* Inhibiting or suppressing cellular growth and multiplication. ❖ *n.* A cytostatic agent. —**cy'to·stat'i·cal·ly** *adv.*

cy·to·tax·on·o·my (sī'tō-tăk-sŏn'ə-mē) *n.* The classification of organisms based on cellular structure and function, esp. on the structure and number of chromosomes. —**cy'to·tax·o·nom'ic** (-tăk'sə-nŏm'ĭk) *adj.* —**cy'to·tax·on'o·mist** *n.*

cy·to·tech·nol·o·gist (sī'tə-tĕk-nŏl'ə-jĭst) *n.* A technician trained in medical examination and identification of cellular abnormalities. —**cy'to·tech·nol'o·gy** *n.*

cy·to·tox·ic (sī'tə-tŏk'sĭk) *adj.* Of, relating to, or producing a toxic effect on cells. —**cy'to·tox·ic'i·ty** (-tŏk-sĭs'ĭ-tē) *n.*

cytotoxic T cell *n.* See **killer cell**.

cy·to·tox·in (sī'tə-tŏk'sĭn) *n.* A substance having a specific toxic effect on certain cells.

CZ *abbr.* Canal Zone

czar (zär, tsär) *n.* **1.** also **tsar** or **tzar** (zär, tsär) A male monarch or emperor, esp. one of the emperors who ruled Russia before the revolution of 1917. **2.** A person having great power; an autocrat. **3.** *Informal* An appointed official having special powers to regulate or supervise an activity. [Russ. *tsar'* < ORuss. *tsĭsarĭ*, emperor, king < O Church Slavonic *tsĕsarĭ* < Goth. *kaisar* < Gk. < Lat. *Caesar*, emperor. See CAESAR.] —**czar'dom** *n.*

USAGE NOTE The word *czar* can also be spelled *tsar. Czar* is the most common form in American usage and virtually the only one employed in the extended senses "any tyrant" or, informally, "one in authority." But *tsar* more accurately transliterates the Russian and appears more often in scholarly writing with reference to one of the Russian emperors.

czar·das (chär'däsh') *n.* **1.** An intricate Hungarian dance characterized by variations in tempo. **2.** Music for this dance. [Hung. *csárdás* < *csárda*, wayside tavern < Serbo-Croatian *čardāk*, watchtower < Turk. *çardak*, hut, trellis < Pers. *chār ṭāq* < *chahār ṭāq*, four-cornered vault : *chahār*, four (< OIran. *cathwārō*; see **k^wetwer-** in App.) + *ṭāq*, vault (< Ar., arch).]

czar·e·vitch (zär'ə-vĭch', tsär'-) *n.* The eldest son of a Russian czar. [Russ. *tsarevich* : *tsar'*, czar; see CZAR + *-evich*, masc. patronymic suff.]

cza·rev·na (zä-rĕv'nə, tsä-) *n.* **1.** The daughter of a Russian czar. **2.** The wife of a czarevitch. [Russ. *tsarevna* : *tsar'*, czar; see CZAR + *-evna*, fem. patronymic suff.]

cza·ri·na (zä-rē'nə, tsä-) *n.* The wife of a Russian czar. [Alteration (perh. influenced by Lat. *rēgīna*, queen) of Russ. *tsaritsa*; see CZARITZA.]

czar·ism (zär'ĭz'əm, tsär'-) *n.* The system of government in Russia under the czars. —**czar'ist** *adj. & n.*

cza·rit·za (zä-rĭt'sə, tsä-rēt'-) *n.* An empress of Russia. [Russ. *tsaritsa* : *tsar'*, czar; see CZAR + *-itsa*, fem. suff.]

Czech (chĕk) *n.* **1a.** A native or inhabitant of the Czech Republic. **b.** A native or inhabitant of Bohemia. **c.** A person of Czech descent. **2.** The Slavic language of the Czechs. [Pol. < Czech *Čech.*] —**Czech** *adj.*

Czech·o·slo·va·ki·a (chĕk'ə-slō-vä'kē-ə, -slō-) A former country of central Europe; formed in 1918 and divided in 1993 into the Czech Republic and Slovakia. —**Czech'o·slo'vak, Czech'o·slo·va'ki·an** *adj. & n.*

Czech Republic A country of central Europe; part of Czechoslovakia from 1918–93. Cap. Prague. Pop. 10,333,000.

Czer·ny (chĕr'nē), **Karl** 1791–1857. Austrian pianist and composer whose works include *School of the Left Hand.*

Czę·sto·cho·wa (chĕn'stə-kō'və, chĕn'stô-hô'vä) A city of S Poland N of Katowice. Pop. 258,266.

Cyprus

Czech Republic

ă	pat	oi	boy
ā	pay	ou	out
âr	care	oŏ	took
ä	father	ōō	boot
ĕ	pet	ŭ	cut
ē	be	ûr	urge
ĭ	pit	th	thin
ī	pie	*th*	this
îr	pier	hw	which
ŏ	pot	zh	vision
ō	toe	ə	about,
ô	paw		item

Stress marks:
' (primary);
' (secondary); as in
lexicon (lĕk'sĭ-kŏn')

Dd

d¹ or **D** (dē) *n., pl.* **d's** or **D's** also **ds** or **Ds 1.** The fourth letter of the modern English alphabet. **2.** Any of the speech sounds represented by the letter *d.* **3.** The fourth in a series. **4.** Something shaped like the letter D. **5. D** The lowest passing grade given to a student in a school or college. **6.** *Music* **a.** The second tone in the scale of C major or the fourth tone in the relative minor scale. **b.** A key or scale in which D is the tonic.

d² *abbr.* **1.** deuteron **2.** diameter **3.** differential **4.** down quark

D¹ **1.** The symbol for the isotope deuterium. **2.** also **d** The symbol for the Roman numeral 500.

D² *abbr.* **1.** dative **2.** day **3.** Democrat **4.** down

d. *abbr.* **1.** date **2.** daughter **3.** died **4.** dose **5.** *Chiefly British* penny (¹⁄₁₂ of a shilling)

D. *abbr.* **1.** diopter **2.** Don (title) **3.** duchess **4.** duke

'd 1. Contraction of *had.* **2.** Contraction of *would.* **3.** Contraction of *did.*

DA¹ (dē′ā′) *n. Slang* A ducktail. [Abbreviation of *duck's ass.*]

DA² *abbr.* **1.** delayed action **2.** deposit account **3.** district attorney **4.** Doctor of Arts **5.** don't answer

Da. *abbr.* Danish

dab¹ (dăb) *v.* **dabbed, dab·bing, dabs** —*tr.* **1.** To apply with short poking strokes: *dabbed paint on the spot.* **2.** To cover lightly with or as if with a moist substance. **3.** To strike or hit lightly. —*intr.* To tap gently; pat. ❖ *n.* **1.** A small amount: *a dab of jelly.* **2.** A quick light pat. [ME *dabben,* to strike.]

dab² (dăb) *n.* Any of various flatfishes, chiefly of the genera *Limanda* and *Hippoglossoides.* [ME *dabbe.*]

dab³ (dăb) *n. Chiefly British* A dab hand. [?]

dab·ber (dăb′ər) *n.* A cushioned pad used by printers and engravers to apply ink.

dab·ble (dăb′əl) *v.* **-bled, -bling, -bles** —*tr.* To splash or spatter with or as if with a liquid. —*intr.* **1.** To splash liquid gently and playfully. **2.** To undertake something without serious intent. **3.** To bob forward and under in shallow water to feed off the bottom. [Poss. < Du. *dabbelen,* freq. of *dabben,* to strike, tap.]

dab·bler (dăb′lər) *n.* One who engages in an activity superficially or without serious intent.

dab·bling duck (dăb′lĭng) *n.* Any of various ducks, chiefly of the genus *Anas,* including the mallards and teals, that feed by dabbling in shallow water.

dab·chick (dăb′chĭk′) *n.* Any of various small grebes of the genus *Podiceps.* [Alteration of *dobchick* : ME *doppe,* diving bird (< OE *-doppa*) + CHICK.]

dab hand *n.* A person skilled in a particular activity.

da ca·po (dä kä′pō) *adv. Music* From the beginning. [Ital. : *da,* from + *capo,* head.]

Dac·ca (dăk′ə, dä′kə) See **Dhaka.**

dace (dās) *n., pl.* **dace** or **dac·es** Any of various small freshwater fishes of the family Cyprinidae, which also includes carps and minnows. [ME *dace, darce* < OFr. *dars* < LLat. *darsus,* poss. of Celt. orig.]

da·cha (dä′chə) *n.* A Russian country house or villa. [Russ., gift, land, country house. See **dō-** in App.]

Da·chau (dä′kou′, -ᴋʜou′) A city of SE Germany NNW of Munich; site of a Nazi concentration camp. Pop. 33,141.

dachs·hund (däks′hŏŏnt′, däk′sənt, däk′sənd) *n.* A small dog of a breed developed in Germany, having a long body, a usu. short-haired dark coat, and very short legs. [Ger. : *Dachs,* badger (< MHGer. *dahs* < OHGer.) + *Hund,* dog (< MHGer. *hunt* < OHGer.; see **kwon-** in App.).]

dachshund

Da·ci·a (dā′shē-ə, -shə) An ancient region and Roman province corresponding roughly to present-day Romania; abandoned to the Goths after A.D. 270. —**Da′ci·an** *adj. & n.*

da·cite (dā′sīt′) *n.* A light gray, fine-grained extrusive rock composed chiefly of sodic plagioclase and free quartz. [After DACIA.]

da·coit (də-koit′) *n.* A member of a robber band or gang in India or Myanmar (Burma). [Hindi *ḍakait.*]

da·coit·y (də-koi′tē) *n.* Robbery by a band or gang of dacoits. [Hindi *ḍakaitī* < *ḍakait,* dacoit.]

dac·quoise (dä-kwŏz′) *n.* A cake made of layers of nut meringue with cream fillings between the layers. [Fr. < fem. of *dacquois,* of Dax, a town of SW France.]

Da·cron (dā′krŏn′, dăk′rŏn′) A trademark used for a synthetic polyester fabric or the fiber from which it is made.

dac·tyl (dăk′təl) *n.* **1.** A metrical foot consisting of one accented syllable followed by two unaccented or of one long syllable followed by two short, as in *flattery.* **2.** A finger, toe, or similar part or structure; a digit. [ME *dactil* < Lat. *dactylus* < Gk. *daktulos,* finger, dactyl.] —**dac·tyl′ic** (-tĭl′ĭk) *adj. & n.*

dactylo– or **dactyl–** *pref.* Finger; toe; digit: *dactylogram.* [< Gk. *daktulos,* finger.]

dac·tyl·o·gram (dăk-tĭl′ə-grăm′) *n.* A fingerprint.

dac·ty·log·ra·phy (dăk′tə-lŏg′rə-fē) *n.* The study of fingerprints as a method of identification. —**dac′ty·lo·graph′ic** (-lō-grăf′ĭk) *adj.*

dac·ty·lol·o·gy (dăk′tə-lŏl′ə-jē) *n.* The use of the fingers to communicate, as in the manual alphabet.

dad (dăd) *n. Informal* A father. [Of baby-talk orig.]

Da·da or **da·da** (dä′dä) *n.* A European artistic and literary movement (1916–23) that flouted conventional values by producing works marked by nonsense and travesty. [Fr. *dada,* hobbyhorse, Dada, of baby-talk orig.] —**Da′da·ism** *n.* —**Da′da·ist** *adj. & n.* —**Da′da·is′tic** *adj.*

dad·dy (dăd′ē) *n., pl.* **-dies** *Informal* A father.

daddy long·legs (lông′lĕgz′, lŏng′-) *n., pl.* **daddy longlegs 1.** Any of various arachnids of the order Phalangida, with a small rounded body and long slender legs. **2.** See **crane fly.**

daddy track *n.* A career path determined by work arrangements offering fathers certain benefits, such as flexible schedules, but usu. providing fewer opportunities for advancement.

dad·gum (dăd′gŭm′) *adj. Chiefly Southern US* Used as an intensive to express mild annoyance. See Regional Note at **damned.** [Alteration of GODDAMN.]

da·do (dā′dō) *n., pl.* **-does 1.** *Architecture* The section of a pedestal between base and surbase. **2.** The lower portion of the wall of a room, decorated differently from the upper section. **3a.** A rectangular groove cut into a board so that a like piece may be fitted into it. **b.** The board so cut. ❖ *tr.v.* **-doed, -do·ing, -does 1.** To furnish with a dado. **2.** To cut a dado in. [Ital. < Lat. *datum,* neut. p. part. of *dare,* to give. See **dō-** in App.]

dae·dal (dēd′l) *adj.* **1.** Intricate in design or function. **2.** Finely or skillfully made or employed; artistic. [Lat. *daedalus* < Gk. *daidalos.*]

Dae·da·lus (dēd′l-əs) *n. Greek Mythology* A legendary artist and inventor, builder of the Labyrinth. —**Dae·da′li·an, Dae·da′le·an** (dĭ-dā′lē-ən, -dāl′yən) *adj.*

dae·mon (dē′mən) *n.* **1.** *Chiefly British* Variant of **demon. 2.** Variant of **daimon. 3.** *Computer Science* A program or process that is open but remains inactive until invoked.

dae·mon·ic (dĭ-mŏn′ĭk) *adj.* Variant of **demonic.**

daf·fo·dil (dăf′ə-dĭl) *n.* **1a.** Any of various bulbous plants of the genus *Narcissus,* esp. *N. pseudonarcissus,* having usu. yellow flowers with a trumpet-shaped central crown. **b.** The flower of this plant. **2.** A brilliant to vivid yellow. [Alteration of ME *affodil* < Lat. *asphodelus,* asphodel. See ASPHODEL.]

daf·fy (dăf′ē) *adj.* **-fi·er, -fi·est** *Informal* **1.** Silly; foolish. **2.** Crazy. [< obsolete *daff,* fool < ME *daffe;* prob. akin to *dafte,* foolish. See DAFT.] —**daf′fi·ly** *adv.* —**daf′fi·ness** *n.*

daft (dăft) *adj.* **daft·er, daft·est 1.** Mad; crazy. **2.** Foolish; stupid. **3.** *Scots* Frolicsome. [ME *dafte,* foolish < OE *gedæfte,* meek.] —**daft′ly** *adv.* —**daft′ness** *n.*

dag¹ (dăg) *n.* **1.** A lock of matted or dung-coated wool. **2.** A hanging end or shred. [ME *dagge,* shred.]

dag² *abbr.* decagram

Da·gan (dä′gän′) *n. Mythology* The Babylonian god of the earth.

Da·ges·tan (dä′gĭ-stän′, däg′ĭ-stän′) An autonomous republic of SW Russia on the Caspian Sea; settled in the 1st millennium B.C.

dag·ger (dăg′ər) *n.* **1.** A short pointed weapon with sharp edges. **2.** Something that agonizes, torments, or wounds. **3.** *Printing* **a.** See **obelisk** 2. **b.** A double dagger. —*idiom:* **look daggers at** To glare at angrily or hatefully. [ME *daggere,* alteration of OFr. *dague,* ult. perh. < VLat. **dāca (ēnsis),* Dacian (knife) < fem. of Lat. *Dācus.*]

da·go also **Da·go** (dā′gō) *n., pl.* **-gos** or **-goes** *Offensive Slang* Used as a disparaging term for an Italian, Spaniard, or Portuguese. [Alteration of Sp. *Diego,* a given name < Lat. *Iacōbus,* Jacob.]

Da·gon (dā′gŏn′) *n. Mythology* The chief god of the ancient Philistines, represented as half-man and half-fish.

Da·guerre (də-gâr′, dä-gĕr′), **Louis Jacques Mandé** 1789–1851. French artist who invented the daguerreotype process.

da·guerre·o·type (də-gâr′ə-tīp′) *n.* **1.** An early photographic process with the image made on a light-sensitive silver-coated metallic plate. **2.** A photograph made by this process. ❖ *tr.v.* **-typed, -typ·ing, -types** To make a daguerreotype of. [Fr., after Louis Jacques Mandé DAGUERRE.] —**da·guerre′o·typ′er** *n.* —**da·guerre′o·typ′y** *n.*

Dalai Lama

dag·wood also **Dag·wood** (dăg′wŏod′) *n.* A multilayered sandwich. [After *Dagwood* Bumstead in the comic strip *Blondie*.]

dah (dä) *n.* A dash in radio and telegraph code. [Imit.]

dahl (däl) *n.* **1.** See **pigeon pea**. **2.** or **dal** An East Indian stew made with lentils, onions, and various spices. [Hindi *dāl*, dahl seed < Skt. *dalaḥ, dalam,* piece split off < *dalati,* he splits.]

Dahl, Roald 1916–90. British writer best known for his children's books, including *James and the Giant Peach* (1961).

dahl·ia (dăl′yə, däl′-, dāl′-) *n.* Any of several plants of the genus *Dahlia,* native to Mexico and Central America and having tuberous roots and showy rayed flower heads. [NLat. *Dahlia,* genus name, after Anders *Dahl* (1751–87), Swedish botanist.]

Da·ho·mey (də-hō′mē, dä-ô-mā′) See **Benin** 2. —**Da·ho′me·an** (də-hō′mē-ən), **Da·ho′man** (-mən) *adj. & n.*

da·hoon (də-hōōn′) *n.* A small tree (*Ilex cassine*) of the southeast United States having red or orange to yellow fruit and leathery dark green leaves. [?]

dai·kon (dī′kŏn′, -kən) *n.* A white radish (*Raphanus sativus* var. *longipinnatus*) of Japan having a long edible root. [J. : *dai,* big (< M Chin. *daj, thaj*) + *kon,* root (< M Chin. *kən*).]

dai·ly (dā′lē) *adj.* **1.** Of or occurring during the day. **2.** Happening or done every day. **3.** Computed or assessed for each day: *a daily record.* **4.** Everyday: *clothes for daily use.* ❖ *adv.* **1.** Every day. **2.** Once a day. ❖ *n., pl.* **-lies 1.** A newspaper published every day or every weekday. **2. dailies** The first, unedited print of all the alternative shots or takes of a motion picture, usu. viewed after a day's shooting; the rushes. [ME *dayly* < OE *dæglīc* < *dæg,* day.] —**dai′li·ness, daily·ness** *n.*

daily double *n.* A bet won by choosing both winners of two specified races on one day, as in horseracing.

daily dozen *n.* **1.** A set of exercises that one does every day. **2.** A set of routine tasks.

dai·mi·o or **dai·my·o** (dī′mē-ō′, dīm′yō′) *n., pl.* **daimio** or **-mi·os** also **daimyo** or **-my·os** A feudal lord of Japan. [J. *daimyō* : *dai,* great; see DAIKON + *myō,* name (< M Chin. *mjiajng*).]

dai·mon (dī′mōn′) also **de·mon** or **dae·mon** (dē′mən) *n. Greek Mythology* **1.** An inferior deity, such as a deified hero. **2.** An attendant spirit; a genius. [Gk. *daimōn.* See **dā-** in App.]

dain·ty (dān′tē) *adj.* **-ti·er, -ti·est 1.** Delicately beautiful or charming; exquisite. **2.** Delicious or choice. See Syns at **delicate**. **3.** Of refined taste; discriminating. **4.** Overfastidious; squeamish. ❖ *n., pl.* **-ties** Something delicious; a delicacy. [ME *deinte,* excellence, excellent < OFr. *deintie* < Lat. *dignitās < dignus,* worthy.] —**dain′ti·ly** *adv.* —**dain′ti·ness** *n.*

daiq·ui·ri (dăk′ə-rē, dī′kə-) *n., pl.* **-ris** A cocktail of rum, lime or lemon juice, and sugar. [After *Daiquiri,* a village of eastern Cuba.]

Dai·ren (dī′rĕn′) See **Dalian**.

dair·y (dâr′ē) *n., pl.* **-ies 1.** A commercial establishment for processing or selling milk and milk products. **2.** A place where milk and cream are stored and processed. **3.** A dairy farm. **4.** The dairy business; dairying. ❖ *adj.* **1.** Of, for, or relating to milk or milk products. **2.** Of or relating to dairying. **3.** *Judaism* Containing or intended for use with dairy products exclusively, in accordance with kashrut. [ME *daierie* : *daie,* dairymaid (< OE *dǣge,* bread kneader; see **dheigh-** in App.) + AN *-erie,* place (< OFr.; see -ERY).]

dairy cattle *pl.n.* Cows raised for milk rather than meat.

dairy farm *n.* A farm for producing milk and milk products.

dair·y·ing (dâr′ē-ĭng) *n.* The business of operating a dairy.

dair·y·maid (dâr′ē-mād′) *n.* A woman or girl who works in a dairy.

dair·y·man (dâr′ē-mən) *n.* **1.** A man who owns or manages a dairy. **2.** A man who works in a dairy.

dair·y·wom·an (dâr′ē-wŏom′ən) *n.* **1.** A woman who owns or manages a dairy. **2.** A woman who works in a dairy.

da·is (dā′ĭs, dī′-) *n.* A raised platform for speakers or guests. [ME *deis* < AN, platform < LLat. *discus,* table < Lat. *discus,* quoit. See DISK.]

dai·shi·ki (dī-shē′kē) *n.* Variant of **dashiki**.

dai·sy (dā′zē) *n., pl.* **-sies 1.** Any of several plants of the composite family, esp. a Eurasian plant (*Chrysanthemum leucanthemum*) having flower heads with a yellow center and white rays. **2.** A European plant (*Bellis perennis*) having flower heads with pink or white rays. **3.** *Slang* One deemed excellent. [ME *daisie* < OE *dæges ēage,* genitive of *dæg,* day + *ēage,* eye; see **okʷ-** in App.]

daisy chain *n.* **1.** A garland or chain made of linked daisies. **2.** A series of connected events, activities, or experiences.

daisy wheel *n.* A printing device used in some electric typewriters and printers, consisting of printing characters fixed at the ends of spokes on a wheel.

Da·kar (də-kär′, dăk′är′) The cap. of Senegal, in the W part on the Atlantic Ocean; former cap. of French West Africa (1904–59). Pop. 1,641,358.

Da·ko·ta (də-kō′tə) *n., pl.* **Dakota** or **-tas 1.** A member of any of the Sioux peoples, esp. any of the peoples of the Santee branch. **2.** The Siouan language of the Dakota. —**Da·ko′tan** *adj. & n.*

Da·ko·tas (də-kō′təz) The Dakota Terr. or (after 1889) the states of ND and SD.

Dakota Territory A territory of the N-central US organized in 1861 and divided into the states of ND and SD in 1889.

dal¹ (däl) *n.* Variant of **dahl** 2.

dal² *abbr.* decaliter

Da·la·dier (də-lä′dē-ā′, dä-lä-dyä′), **Édouard** 1884–1970. French public official who signed the Munich Pact with Adolf Hitler in Sep. 1938.

Da·lai Lama (dä′lī) *n.* The traditional governmental ruler and highest priest of the dominant sect of Buddhism in Tibet and Mongolia. [Tibetan : Mongolian *dalai,* ocean + Tibetan *bla-ma,* monk (< his being known as the ocean of compassion).]

da·la·si (dä-lä′sē) *n., pl.* **dalasi** See table at **currency**. [Mandingo, poss. ult. < E. *dollars,* pl. of DOLLAR.]

dale (dāl) *n.* A valley. [ME < OE *dæl.*]

Dale, Sir Henry Hallett 1875–1968. British physiologist who shared a 1936 Nobel Prize.

Dale, Sir Thomas d. 1619. English-born colonial administrator noted for his strict rule of Virginia (1611–16).

da·leth (dä′lĭd, -lĕt, -lĕth) *n.* The fourth letter of the Hebrew alphabet. [Heb. *dālet* < Phoenician *dalt,* door, fourth letter of the Phoenician alphabet.]

Da·ley (dā′lē), **Richard Joseph** 1902–76. Amer. politician who was mayor of Chicago (1955–76).

Dal·hou·sie (dăl-hōō′zē, -hou′-), **10th Earl and 1st Marquis of**. Title of James Andrew Broun Ramsay. 1812–60. British colonial administrator who served as governor-general in India (1847–56).

Da·lí (dä′lē, dä-lē′), **Salvador** 1904–89. Spanish surrealist artist whose works include *The Persistence of Memory* (1931). —**Da′li·esque′** (-ĕsk′) *adj.*

Salvador Dalí

Da·li·an (dä′lyän′) also **Ta·lien** (tä′lyĕn′) Formerly **Dai·ren** (dī′rĕn′) A city of NE China on the Bo Hai; opened to foreign commerce in 1901. Pop. 1,723,302.

Dal·las (dăl′əs) A city of NE TX on the Trinity R. E of Fort Worth; founded by French settlers in 1841. Pop. 1,188,580.

dalles (dălz) *pl.n.* The rapids of a river between the precipices of a gorge or narrow valley. [Fr., pl. of *dalle,* gutter < OFr. < ON *dæla.*]

Dalles, The (dălz) A city of N OR on the Columbia R. E of Portland. Pop. 19,587.

dal·li·ance (dăl′ē-əns) *n.* **1.** Frivolous spending of time; dawdling. **2.** Playful flirtation.

Dal·lis grass (dăl′ĭs) *n.* A tall South American perennial grass (*Paspalum dilatatum*) grown for pasturage in the southern United States. [Prob. alteration of DALLAS.]

Dall sheep (dôl) or **Dall's sheep** (dôlz) *n.* A wild sheep (*Ovis dalli*) of the mountains of northwest North America having curved yellowish horns. [After William Healey *Dall* (1845–1927), American naturalist.]

Dall sheep
Ovis dalli

dal·ly (dăl′ē) *v.* **-lied, -ly·ing, -lies** —*intr.* **1.** To play amorously; flirt. **2.** To trifle; toy. **3.** To waste time; dawdle. —*tr.* To waste (time). [ME *dalien* < OFr. *dalier.*] —**dal′li·er** *n.* —**dal′ly·ing·ly** *adv.*

Dal·ma·ti·a (dăl-mā′shə) A historical region of SE Europe on the Adriatic Sea; divided between Serbia and Croatia in the 10th cent. and held by numerous powers after the 15th cent.

Dal·ma·tian (dăl-mā′shən) *n.* **1.** A native or inhabitant of Dalmatia. **2.** also **dalmatian** A dog of a breed believed to have originated in Dalmatia, having a short, smooth white coat covered with dark spots. ❖ *adj.* Of or relating to Dalmatia or its inhabitants or culture.

dal·mat·ic (dăl-măt′ĭk) *n.* **1.** A wide-sleeved garment worn over the alb by a deacon or bishop at Mass. **2.** A wide-sleeved garment worn by an English monarch at coronation. [ME *dalmatik* < OFr. *dalmatique* < Med.Lat. *dalmatica (vestis),* Dalmatian (garment) < Lat. *dalmaticus,* Dalmatian.]

dalmatian

dal se·gno (däl sān′yō) *adv. Music* From the place marked by the sign ❀ to a designated point. Used as a direction to repeat a passage. [Ital. : *da,* from + *il,* the + *segno,* sign.]

dal·ton (dôl′tən) *n.* See **atomic mass unit**. [After John DALTON.]

Dalton, John 1766–1844. British chemist who formulated the atomic theory and studied colorblindness.

Dalton, Robert 1867–92. Amer. outlaw noted for his exploits as a horse thief, train robber, and leader of the Dalton gang.

dal·ton·ism also **Dal·ton·ism** (dôl′tə-nĭz′əm) *n.* An inherited defect in perception of red and green. [After John DALTON.] —**dal′to′ni·an** (-tō′nē-ən), **dal·ton′ic** (-tŏn′ĭk) *adj.*

dam¹ (dăm) *n.* **1a.** A barrier built across a waterway to control the flow or raise the level of water. **b.** A body of water controlled by such a barrier. **2.** A barrier against the passage of liquid or loose material, as a rubber sheet used in dentistry to isolate a tooth. **3.** An obstruction; a hindrance. ❖ *tr.v.* **dammed, dam·ming, dams 1.** To hold back by a dam. **2.** To close up; obstruct. [ME.]

dam² (dăm) *n.* **1.** A female parent. Used of a four-legged animal. **2.** *Archaic* A mother. [ME *dam, dame,* lady, mother. See DAME.]

dam³ *abbr.* decameter

dam·age (dăm′ĭj) *n.* **1.** Harm or injury to property or a person, resulting in loss of value or the impairment of usefulness. **2. damages** *Law* Money ordered to be paid as compensation for injury or loss. **3.** *Informal* Cost; price. ❖ *v.* **-aged, -ag·ing, -ag·es** —*tr.* To cause damage to: *Some insects damage plants.* —*intr.* To suffer or be susceptible to damage. [ME < OFr. : *dam,* loss (< Lat. *damnum*) + *-age,* -age.] —**dam′age·a·bil′i·ty** *n.* —**dam′age·**

ă	pat	oi	boy
ā	pay	ou	out
âr	care	ŏŏ	took
ä	father	ōō	boot
ĕ	pet	ŭ	cut
ē	be	ûr	urge
ĭ	pit	th	thin
ī	pie	th	this
îr	pier	hw	which
ŏ	pot	zh	vision
ō	toe	ə	about,
ô	paw		item

Stress marks: ′ (primary); ′ (secondary), as in **lexicon** (lĕk′sĭ-kŏn′)

a•ble adj. —dam′ag•ing•ly adv.

damage control n. An effort to minimize damage or loss.

Da•man (də-măn′) A former Portuguese colony of NW India on the E shore of the Gulf of Khambhat; annexed by India in 1961.

Da•man•hur (däm′ən-hŏŏr′, dä′män-hŏŏr′) A city of NE Egypt on the Nile delta NW of Cairo. Pop. 222,000.

dam•ar (dăm′ər) n. Variant of **dammar**.

dam•a•scene (dăm′ə-sēn′, dăm′ə-sēn′) tr.v. -scened, -scen•ing, -scenes To decorate (metal) with wavy patterns of inlay or etching. ❖ n. Metalwork that is damascened. ❖ adj. 1. Of or relating to damascening. 2. Of or relating to damask. [Fr. damasquiner < damasquin, of Damascus < Lat. Damascēnus < Gk. Damaskēnos < Damaskos, Damascus.]

Da•mas•cus (də-măs′kəs) Cap. of Syria, in the SW part; inhabited since prehistoric times. Pop. 1,549,000. —**Dam′a•scene′** (dăm′ə-sēn′) adj. & n.

Damascus steel n. An early form of steel having wavy markings, developed in Near Eastern countries and used chiefly in sword blades.

dam•ask (dăm′əsk) n. 1. A rich patterned fabric of cotton, linen, silk, or wool. 2. A fine twilled table linen. 3. Damascus steel. 4. The wavy pattern on Damascus steel. ❖ tr.v. -asked, -ask•ing, -asks 1. To damascene. 2. To decorate or weave with rich patterns. [ME, Damascus, damask < Lat. Damascus < Gk. Damaskos.] —**dam′ask** adj.

damask rose n. A rose (Rosa damascena) native to Asia that has fragrant red or pink flowers and is used as a source of attar. [< ME Damask, Damascus. See DAMASK.]

damask steel n. Damascus steel.

dame (dām) n. 1. Used formerly as a courtesy title for a woman in authority or a mistress of a household. 2a. A married woman; a matron. b. An elderly woman. 3. Slang A woman. 4. Chiefly British a. A woman holding a nonhereditary title conferred by a sovereign. b. The wife or widow of a knight. c. Used as the title for such a woman. [ME < OFr. < Lat. domina, fem. of dominus, lord, master. See dem- in App.]

dame's rocket (dāmz) n., pl. **dame's rockets** A European plant (Hesperis matronalis) having clusters of fragrant flowers.

Da•mien de Veus•ter (dā′mē-ən də myăN′ də vœ-stēr′), **Joseph** Known as "Father Damien." 1840–89. Belgian Roman Catholic missionary who ministered to the leper colony on Molokai (1873–89).

dam•mar or **dam•ar** also **dam•mer** (dăm′ər) n. Any of various hard resins obtained from trees of the genera Shorea, Balanocarpus, and Hopea, native to southeast Asia and used in varnishes and lacquers. [Malay damar, resin.]

dam•mit (dăm′ĭt) interj. Used to express anger, irritation, or disappointment. [Alteration of damn it.]

damn (dăm) v. **damned**, **damn•ing**, **damns** —tr. 1. To pronounce an adverse judgment upon. 2. To cause the failure of; ruin. 3. To condemn as harmful, illegal, or immoral. 4. To condemn to everlasting punishment. 5. To swear at. —intr. To swear; curse. ❖ interj. Used to express anger, irritation, contempt, or disappointment. ❖ n. 1. The saying of "damn" as a curse. 2. Informal The least bit; a jot. ❖ adv. & adj. Damned. —**idiom: damn it** Used to express anger, annoyance, or disappointment: We must finish, damn it. [ME dampnen < OFr. dampner < Lat. damnāre, to condemn, inflict loss upon < damnum, loss.] —**damn′ing•ly** adv.

dam•na•ble (dăm′nə-bəl) adj. Deserving condemnation; odious. —**dam′na•ble•ness** n. —**dam′na•bly** adv.

dam•na•tion (dăm-nā′shən) n. 1. The act of damning or the condition of being damned. 2a. Condemnation to everlasting punishment. b. Everlasting punishment. 3. Ruin caused by adverse criticism. ❖ interj. Used to express anger or annoyance. See Regional Note at tarnation.

dam•na•to•ry (dăm′nə-tôr′ē, -tōr′ē) adj. Threatening with or expressing condemnation; damning.

damned (dămd) adj. **damned•er** (dăm′dər), **damned•est** (dăm′dĭst) 1. Condemned, esp. to eternal punishment. 2. Informal Detestable. 3. Used as an intensive. ❖ adv. **damneder**, **damnedest** Used as an intensive. ❖ n. Souls doomed to eternal punishment.

REGIONAL NOTE There are many regional variants, mostly euphemisms, for damned, both as an oath and as a mild intensive. Southern exclamations and intensives tend to begin with dad–, a euphemism for "god"; hence dadblamed, dadblasted, dadburn, and dadgum. Another such euphemism is the better known doggone, probably originally Southern but now widespread. Like dadgum, doggone is used as a mild intensive: "The best doggone deals in Alabama" (billboard in Montgomery). A common Southern and South Midland variant of damned is durn, also euphemistic and relatively mild.

damned•est (dăm′dĭst) adj. Superlative of **damned**. ❖ n. All that is possible; the utmost: did my damnedest.

Dam•o•cles (dăm′ə-klēz′) fl. 4th cent. B.C. Greek courtier to Dionysius the Elder who according to legend was forced to sit under a sword suspended by a single hair to demonstrate the precariousness of a king's fortunes.

Da•mon (dā′mən) n. A legendary Greek who pledged his life so

his condemned friend Pythias could arrange his affairs.

dam•o•sel also **dam•oi•selle** or **dam•o•zel** (dăm′ə-zĕl′) n. Archaic A young woman; a damsel. [ME damoisele < OFr. damoiselle, damsel. See DAMSEL.]

damp (dămp) adj. **damp•er**, **damp•est** 1. Slightly wet. See Syns at **wet**. 2. Archaic Dejected. ❖ n. 1. Moisture in the air; humidity. 2. Foul or poisonous gas in the air in coal mines. 3. Lowness of spirits; depression. 4. A restraint or check; a discouragement. ❖ tr.v. **damped**, **damp•ing**, **damps** 1. To make damp or moist; moisten. 2. To extinguish (a fire, for example) by cutting off air. 3. To restrain or check; discourage. 4. Music To slow or stop the vibrations of (the strings of a keyboard instrument) with a damper. 5. Physics To decrease the amplitude of (an oscillating system). —**phrasal verb: damp off** Botany To be affected by damping off. [ME, poison gas, perh. < MDu., vapor.] —**damp′ish** adj. —**damp′ly** adv. —**damp′ness** n.

damp•en (dăm′pən) v. -ened, -en•ing, -ens —tr. 1. To make damp. 2. To deaden, restrain, or depress. 3. To soundproof. —intr. To become damp. —**damp′en•er** n.

damp•er (dăm′pər) n. 1. One that deadens or restrains. 2. An adjustable plate, as in a furnace flue, for controlling the draft. 3. Music a. A device in keyboard instruments for deadening the vibrations of the strings. b. A mute for various brass instruments. 4. A device that eliminates or diminishes vibrations or oscillations.

damp•ing (dăm′pĭng) n. The capacity built into a mechanical or electrical device to prevent excessive correction and the resulting instability or oscillatory conditions.

damping off n. A disease of seedlings that is caused by fungi and results in wilting and death.

dam•sel (dăm′zəl) n. A young woman or girl; a maiden. [ME damisele < OFr. dameisele, damoiselle < VLat. *dominicella, dim. of domina, lady. See DAME.]

dam•sel•fish (dăm′zəl-fĭsh′) n., pl. **damselfish** or **-fish•es** Any of various small, usu. brightly colored tropical marine fishes of the family Pomacentridae.

dam•sel•fly (dăm′zəl-flī′) n. Any of various often brightly colored predatory insects having a long slender body and elongated wings that fold together when the insect is at rest.

dam•son (dăm′zən, -sən) n. 1a. A Eurasian plum tree (Prunus insititia) having edible fruit. 2. The oval, bluish-black plum of this tree. [ME damson, damacene < Lat. (prūnum) Damascēnum, (plum) of Damascus, neut. of Damascēnus. See DAMASCENE.]

dan also **Dan** (dän, dän) n. 1a. Any of 12 levels of proficiency at the grade of black belt in martial arts such as judo and karate. b. One at such a level. 2. An expert or expert level in shogi and other such games. [J. < M Chin. dan.]

Dan¹ (dän) In the Bible, a son of Jacob and the forebear of one of the tribes of Israel.

Dan² (dän) n. Archaic Used formerly as a title of honor for respected men, such as clerics and poets. [ME < OFr. < Med.Lat. Domnus < Lat. dominus, master, lord. See dem- in App.]

Dan. abbr. 1. Bible Daniel 2. Danish

Da•na (dā′nə), **Richard Henry** 1815–82. Amer. lawyer and writer best known for his Two Years Before the Mast (1840).

Dan•a•e also **Dan•a•ë** (dăn′ə-ē′) n. Greek Mythology The daughter of Eurydice and Acrisius and mother of Perseus who was imprisoned by her father in a bronze chamber.

Da•na•i•des or **Da•na•ï•des** (də-nā′ĭ-dēz′) pl.n. Greek Mythology The daughters of Danaus who at their father's command murdered their bridegrooms and were condemned in Hades to pour water eternally into a leaky vessel.

Dan•a•kil (dăn′ə-kĭl′, də-nä′kēl) A desert region of NE Ethiopia, S Eritrea and N Djibouti bordering on the Red Sea.

Da Nang or **Da•nang** (də-năng′, dä′näng′) Formerly **Tou•rane** (tōō-rän′) A city of central Vietnam on the South China Sea; site of a US military base during the Vietnam War. Pop. 382,674.

Dan•a•us also **Dan•a•üs** (dăn′ē-əs) n. Greek Mythology A king of Argos and father of the Danaides.

dance (dăns) v. **danced**, **danc•ing**, **danc•es** —intr. 1. To move rhythmically, usu. to music, using prescribed or improvised steps and gestures. 2a. To leap or skip about excitedly. b. To appear to flash or twinkle. c. Informal To appear to skip about; vacillate. 3. To bob up and down. —tr. 1. To perform (a dance). 2. To cause to dance. 3. To bring to a particular condition by dancing. ❖ n. 1. A series of motions and steps, usu. performed to music. 2. The art of dancing. 3. A party of people for dancing; a ball. 4. One round or turn of dancing: May I have this dance? 5. A musical or rhythmical piece composed or played for dancing. 6. The act or an instance of dancing. [ME daunce < OFr. danser, perh. < Gmc. orig.] —**dance′a•ble** adj. —**danc′er** n.

dan•cer•cise (dăn′sər-sīz′) n. Energetic dancing done for the purpose of aerobic exercise. [Blend of DANCE and EXERCISE.]

D & C abbr. dilation and curettage

dan•de•li•on (dăn′dl-ī′ən) n. 1. A Eurasian plant (Taraxacum officinale) of the composite family, having yellow flower heads and deeply notched leaves. 2. Any of several related plants. 3. A brilliant to vivid yellow. [ME dent-de-lioun < OFr. dentdelion < Med.Lat. dēns leōnis, lion's tooth : Lat. dēns, dent-, tooth; see dent- in App. + Lat. leōnis, genitive of leō, lion; see LION.]

dan•der¹ (dăn′dər) n. Informal Temper or anger: What got their

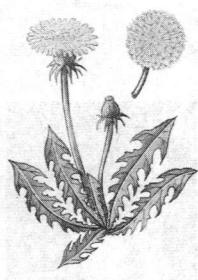

damascene

dandelion
common dandelion
Taraxacum officinale

Dante Alighieri
detail of Dante Declaiming the Divine Comedy, c. 1465, by Domenico di Michelino (1417–91)

dander up? [Perh. alteration of *dunder*, fermented cane juice used in rum-making, fermentation, poss. alteration of Sp. *redundar*, to overflow < Lat. *redundāre*. See REDUNDANT.]

dan·der² (dăn′dər) *n.* Scurf from the coat or feathers of animals, often of an allergenic nature. [Alteration of DANDRUFF.]

Dan·die Din·mont (dăn′dē dĭn′mŏnt′) *n.* A small terrier having a rough grayish or brownish coat and drooping ears. [After *Dandie Dinmont*, the owner of two such dogs in *Guy Mannering*, a novel by Sir Walter Scott.]

dan·di·fy (dăn′də-fī′) *tr.v.* **-fied, -fy·ing, -fies** To dress as or cause to resemble a dandy. —**dan′di·fi·ca′tion** (-fĭ-kā′shən) *n.*

dan·dle (dăn′dl) *tr.v.* **-dled, -dling, -dles** **1.** To move (a small child) up and down on the knees or in the arms in a playful way. **2.** To pamper or pet. [?] —**dan′dler** *n.*

Dan·dong (dăn′dŏong′) also **Tan·tung** (tän′tŏong′) or **An·tung** (än′tŏong′) A city of NE China on the Yalu R. opposite North Korea. Pop. 660,518.

dan·druff (dăn′drəf) *n.* A scaly scurf formed on the scalp, sometimes caused by seborrhea. [*dand*-, of unknown orig. + dialectal *hurf*, scurf (< OE *hrufa*, crust, scab).] —**dan′druff·y** *adj.*

dan·dy (dăn′dē) *n., pl.* **-dies** **1.** A man who affects extreme elegance in clothes and manners; a fop. **2.** Something very agreeable. ❖ *adj.* **-di·er, -di·est** **1.** Suggestive of a dandy; foppish. **2.** Fine; good. [Perh. short for *jack-a-dandy*, fop.] —**dan′di·ly** *adv.* —**dan′dy·ish** *adj.* —**dan′dy·ism** *n.*

Dane (dān) *n.* **1.** A native or inhabitant of Denmark. **2.** A person of Danish ancestry. [ME *Dan* < ON *Danr*.]

Dane·geld (dān′gĕld′) also **Dane·gelt** (-gĕlt′) *n.* A tax levied in England from the 10th to the 12th century to finance protection against Danish invasion. [ME : *Dane*, genitive pl. of *Dan*, Dane; see DANE + *geld*, tribute (< OE *geld, gield*, payment).]

Dane·law also **Dane·lagh** (dān′lô′) *n.* **1.** The body of law established by the Danish invaders in northeast England in the ninth and tenth centuries. **2.** The sections of England under this law. [ME *Denelage* < OE *Dena lagu* : *Dena*, genitive of *Dene*, the Danes + *lagu*, law; see LAW.]

dang (dăng) *interj., adv., adj., v., & n.* Damn. [Alteration of DAMN.]

dan·ger (dān′jər) *n.* **1.** Exposure or vulnerability to harm or risk. **2.** A source or an instance of risk or peril. **3.** *Obsolete* Power, esp. power to harm. [ME *daunger*, power, peril < OFr. *dangier* < VLat. *dominiārium*, power < Lat. *dominium*, sovereignty < *dominus*, lord, master. See dem- in App.]

dan·ger·ous (dān′jər-əs) *adj.* **1.** Involving or filled with danger; perilous. **2.** Being able or likely to do harm. —**dan′ger·ous·ly** *adv.* —**dan′ger·ous·ness** *n.*

dan·gle (dăng′gəl) *v.* **-gled, -gling, -gles** —*intr.* **1.** To hang loosely and swing to and fro. **2.** To be a hanger-on. —*tr.* **1.** To cause to hang loosely or swing. **2.** To cause (one's hopes) to hang uncertainly. ❖ *n.* **1.** The act or an instance of dangling. **2.** Something dangled. [Perh. < Dan. *dangle* or Swed. *dangla*.] —**dan′gler** *n.* —**dan′gly** *adj.*

dan·gle·ber·ry (dăng′gəl-bĕr′ē) *n.* A deciduous shrub (*Gaylussacia frondosa*) of the eastern United States having dark blue fruits. [Prob. alteration of *tangleberry*.]

dan·gling (dăng′glĭng) *adj.* Of or being a modifier, esp. a participle or participial phrase, that grammatically modifies the subject of its sentence but semantically modifies another element of the sentence or an unstated referent, as *approaching Dallas* in the sentence *Approaching Dallas, the skyline came into view.*

Dan·iel¹ (dăn′yəl) **1.** In the Bible, a Hebrew prophet of the 6th cent. B.C. [Heb. *Dānî′ēl, Dānîyēl*, God is my judge : *dān*, judge + -*î*, my + *'ēl*, God.]

Dan·iel² (dăn′yəl) *n.* See table at Bible. [After DANIEL¹.]

da·ni·o (dā′nē-ō′) *n., pl.* **-os** Any of various small, often brightly colored freshwater fishes of the genera *Danio* and *Brachydanio*, popular as aquarium fish. [NLat. *Danio*, genus name.]

Dan·ish (dā′nĭsh) *adj.* Of or relating to Denmark, the Danes, their language, or their culture. ❖ *n.* **1.** The North Germanic language of the Danes. **2.** *pl.* **Danish** or **-ish·es** A Danish pastry. [ME, alteration (influenced by ON *Danr*, Dane) of *Denish* < OE *Denisc* < *Dene*, the Danes.]

Danish pastry *n.* A sweet pastry made with raised dough.

Dan·ite (dăn′īt′) *Bible n.* A descendant of Dan. ❖ *adj.* Of or relating to the Hebrew tribe descended from Dan.

dank (dăngk) *adj.* **dank·er, dank·est** Disagreeably damp or humid. See Syns at wet. [ME, prob. of Scand. orig.] —**dank′ly** *adv.* —**dank′ness** *n.*

D'An·nun·zio (dän-nŏon′tsyō), **Gabriele** 1863–1938. Italian writer who supported Benito Mussolini's fascist regime.

Da·no-Nor·we·gian (dā′nō-nôr-wē′jən) *n.* An official literary form of Norwegian based on written Danish.

dan·seur (dän-sœr′) *n., pl.* **-seurs** (-sœr′) A man who dances. [Fr. < OFr. < *danser*, to dance. See DANCE.]

dan·seuse (dän-sœz′) *n., pl.* **-seuses** (-sœz′) A woman who dances. [Fr., fem. of *danseur*, danseur. See DANSEUR.]

Dan·te A·li·ghie·ri (dän′tā ä′lē-gyě′rē) 1265–1321. Italian poet renowned for *The Divine Comedy* (completed 1321). —**Dan′te·an** *adj. & n.* —**Dan·tesque** (dän-těsk′) *adj.*

Dan·ton (dän-tôn′), **Georges Jacques** 1759–94. French Revolutionary leader who was guillotined for his opposition to the

excesses of the Reign of Terror.

Dan·ube (dăn′yōob) A river of S-central Europe rising in SW Germany and flowing c. 2,848 km (1,770 mi) SE to the Black Sea. —**Dan·u′bi·an** *adj.*

Dan·zig (dän′sĭg, dăn′tsĭk) See **Gdańsk.**

Danzig Free City A former state (1919–39) on the Gulf of Gdańsk surrounding and including the city of Gdańsk.

dap (dăp) *intr.v.* **dapped, dap·ping, daps** **1.** To fish by letting a baited hook fall onto the water. **2.** To dip quickly into water, as a bird does. **3.** To skip or bounce, esp. over water. [Prob. alteration of DAB¹.]

daph·ne (dăf′nē) *n.* Any of several Eurasian shrubs of the genus *Daphne*, often cultivated for their glossy evergreen foliage and small bell-shaped flowers. [Lat. *daphnē*, laurel < Gk.]

Daphne *n.* *Greek Mythology* A nymph who metamorphosed into a laurel tree as a means of escaping from Apollo.

daph·ni·a (dăf′nē-ə) *n., pl.* **daphnia** Any of various water fleas of the genus *Daphnia*, some species of which are used as food for aquarium fish. [NLat. *Daphnia*, genus name < Gk. *Daphnē*, Daphne.]

Daph·nis (dăf′nĭs) *n.* *Greek Mythology* A Sicilian shepherd famed as a musician and the inventor of pastoral poetry.

Da Pon·te (də pŏn′tē, dä pŏn′tĕ), **Lorenzo** 1749–1838. Italian-born Amer. educator who wrote the libretto for Mozart's *Marriage of Figaro* (1786).

dap·per (dăp′ər) *adj.* **1a.** Neatly dressed; trim. **b.** Very stylish in dress. **2.** Lively and alert. [ME *daper*, elegant, prob. < MDu. *dapper*, quick, strong.] —**dap′per·ly** *adv.* —**dap′per·ness** *n.*

dap·ple (dăp′əl) *n.* **1a.** Mottled or spotted marking, as on a horse's coat. **b.** An individual spot. **2.** An animal with a dappled skin or coat. ❖ *tr.v.* **-pled, -pling, -ples** To mark or mottle with spots. —**dap′ple** *adj.*

dap·pled (dăp′əld) *adj.* Spotted; mottled. [ME, prob. < ON *depill*, spot, splash, dim. of *dapi*, pool.]

dap·ple-gray (dăp′əl-grā′) *adj.* Gray with a mottled pattern of darker gray. ❖ *n.* A horse having a coat of mottled gray. [ME *dappel-grai*, prob. alteration (influenced by DAPPLED) of **appel-grai*, apple-gray < ON *apalgrār* : **apall*, apple + *grār*, gray.]

dap·sone (dăp′sōn′, -zōn′) *n.* An antibacterial drug, $C_{12}H_{12}N_2O_2S$, used to treat leprosy and some forms of dermatitis. [D(I)—¹ + A(MINO)– + (DI)P(HENYL) + S(ULF)ONE.]

DAR *abbr.* Daughters of the American Revolution

Dar·by and Joan (där′bē; jōn) *n.* An elderly, happily married couple who are seldom seen apart. [Probably after *Darby and Joan*, a couple in an 18th-cent. English ballad.]

Dard (därd) also **Dar·dic** (där′dĭk) *n.* A group of Indic languages spoken in the upper Indus River valley.

Dar·dan (där′dn) or **Dar·da·ni·an** (där-dā′nē-ən) *n.* *Archaic* A Trojan. [After *Dardanus*, the mythical founder of Troy.] —**Dar′dan** *adj.*

Dar·da·nelles (där′dn-ĕlz′) Formerly **Hel·les·pont** (hĕl′ĭ-spŏnt′) A strait connecting the Aegean Sea with the Sea of Marmara; scene of the exploits of Hero and Leander.

Dar·da·nus (där′dn-əs) *n.* *Greek Mythology* The founder of Troy.

dare (dâr) *v.* **dared, dar·ing, dares** —*tr.* **1.** To have the courage for. **2.** To challenge (someone) to do something requiring boldness. **3.** To confront boldly; defy. —*intr.* To be bold enough to do or try something: *Dive if you dare.* —*aux.* To be courageous or bold enough to: *I dare not say.* ❖ *n.* An act of daring; a challenge. [ME *daren* < OE *dearr*, first and third pers. sing. pr. t. of *durran*, to venture, dare. See dhers- in App.] —**dar′er** *n.*

Dare, Virginia 1587–87? The first child of English parents born in America; disappeared with other members of the Lost Colony of Roanoke I.

DARE *abbr. Dictionary of American Regional English*

dare·dev·il (dâr′dĕv′əl) *n.* One who is recklessly bold. —**dare′dev′il** *adj.* —**dare′dev′il·ry, dare′dev′il·try** (-trē) *n.*

dare·say (dâr′sā′) *tr.v.* To think very likely or almost certain; suppose. Used in the first person sing. present tense. ❖ *intr.v.* To suppose; conjecture. Used in the first person sing. present tense.

Dar es Sa·laam (där′ ĕs sə-läm′) The de facto cap. of Tanzania, in the E part on an arm of the Indian Ocean; founded 1862. Pop. 1,096,000.

Dar·fur (där-fŏor′) A region and former sultanate of W Sudan; occupied since prehistoric times.

Da·ri·én (dâr′ē-ĕn′, där-yĕn′) A region of E Panama on the **Gulf of Darién**, a wide bay of the Caribbean between E Panama and NW Colombia. Vasco Núñez de Balboa led an expedition across the **Isthmus of Darién** (now the Isthmus of Panama) and became the first European to view the Pacific Ocean from the New World.

dar·ing (dâr′ĭng) *adj.* Willing to take risks; bold and venturesome. ❖ *n.* Audacious bravery; boldness. —**dar′ing·ly** *adv.* —**dar′ing·ness** *n.*

Da·rí·o (dä-rē′ō), **Rubén** 1867–1916. Nicaraguan poet whose works include *Cantos de Vida y Esperanza* (1905).

Da·ri·us I (də-rī′əs) Known as "Darius the Great." 550?–486 B.C. King of Persia (521–486) who expanded the empire, organized a highly efficient administrative system, and invaded Greece.

Dar·jee·ling¹ (där-jē′lĭng) A town of NE India in the Himalaya

dapple-gray

Darius I
bas-relief from the royal palace at Persepolis

ă	pat	oi	boy
ā	pay	ou	out
âr	care	ŏŏ	took
ä	father	ōō	boot
ĕ	pet	ŭ	cut
ē	be	ûr	urge
ĭ	pit	th	thin
ī	pie	th	this
îr	pier	hw	which
ŏ	pot	zh	vision
ō	toe	ə	about,
ô	paw		item

Stress marks:
′ (primary);
′ (secondary), as in
lexicon (lĕk′sĭ-kŏn′)

Mts. at an altitude of 2,287.5 m (7,500 ft). Pop. 73,000.

Dar·jee·ling² (där-jē′lĭng) *n.* A fine variety of black tea grown esp. in the northern part of India.

dark (därk) *adj.* **dark·er, dark·est** **1a.** Lacking or having very little light: *a dark corner.* **b.** Lacking brightness: *a dark day.* **2.** Reflecting only a small fraction of incident light. **3.** Of a shade tending toward black in comparison with other shades. Used of a color. **4.** Having a swarthy complexion. **5.** Served without milk or cream: *dark coffee.* **6.** Gloomy; dismal. **7.** Sullen or threatening: *a dark scowl.* **8.** Difficult to understand; obscure. **9.** Concealed or secret; mysterious. **10.** Lacking enlightenment or culture: *a dark age in history.* **11.** Exhibiting or stemming from evil characteristics; sinister. **12.** Being or characterized by morbid or grimly satiric humor. **13.** Having richness or depth: *a dark vocal tone.* **14.** Not giving performances; closed. **15.** *Linguistics* Pronounced with the back of the tongue raised toward the velum. Used of the sound (l) in words like *full.* ❖ *n.* **1.** Absence of light. **2.** A place having little or no light. **3.** Night; nightfall: *home before dark.* **4.** A deep hue or color. —*idiom:* **in the dark 1.** In a state of ignorance; uninformed. **2.** In secret. [ME *derk* < OE *deorc.*] —**dark′ish** *adj.* —**dark′ly** *adv.* —**dark′ness** *n.*

SYNONYMS *dark, dim, murky, dusky, obscure* These adjectives indicate the absence of light or clarity. *Dark,* the most widely applicable, can refer to insufficiency of illumination for seeing (*a dark evening,*) deepness of shade or color (*dark brown*), absence of cheer (*a dark, somber mood*), or lack of rectitude (*a dark past*). *Dim* suggests lack of clarity of outline: *"life and the memory of it cramped,/dim, on a piece of Bristol board"* (Elizabeth Bishop). It can also apply to a source of light to indicate insufficiency: *"storied Windows richly dight,/Casting a dim religious light"* (John Milton). *Murky* implies darkness, often extreme, such as that produced by smoke or fog: *"The path was altogether indiscernible in the murky darkness which surrounded them"* (Sir Walter Scott). *Dusky* suggests the dimness that is characteristic of diminishing light, as at twilight: *"The dusky night rides down the sky,/And ushers in the morn"* (Henry Fielding). Also, it refers to deepness of shade of a color: *"A dusky blush rose to her cheek"* (Edith Wharton). *Obscure* usually means unclear to the mind or senses but it can refer to physical darkness: *the obscure rooms of a shuttered mansion.*

dark adaptation *n.* The adjustments of the eye, including increased activity of rods in the retina, that make vision possible in relative darkness. —**dark′-a·dapt′** (därk′ə-dăpt′) *v.* —**dark′-a·dapt′ed** (därk′ə-dăp′tĭd) *adj.*

Dark Age *n.* **1.** An era of ignorance, superstition, or social chaos or repression. Often used in the plural. **2. Dark Ages a.** The period in Europe from the fall of Rome in the fifth century A.D. to about the year 1000. **b.** The entire Middle Ages, esp. when viewed as a troubled period marked by the loss of classical learning. No longer in use by historians.

dark comedy *n.* **1.** A comedy having gloomy or disturbing elements, esp. one in which a character suffers an irreparable loss. **2.** A comedy having morbid or grimly satiric humor.

dark·en (där′kən) *v.* **-ened, -en·ing, -ens** —*tr.* **1a.** To make dark or darker. **b.** To give a darker hue to. **2.** To fill with sadness. **3.** To render vague or uncertain. **4.** To tarnish or stain. —*intr.* To become dark or gloomy. —**dark′en·er** *n.*

dark-field microscope (därk′fēld′) *n.* A microscope in which an object is illuminated only from the sides so that it appears bright against a dark background.

dark horse *n.* **1.** One who achieves unexpected political success, typically as a nominee at a party's convention. **2.** A little-known, unexpectedly successful entrant.

dark lantern *n.* A lantern whose light can be blocked, as by a sliding panel.

dar·kle (där′kəl) *v.* **-kled, -kling, -kles** —*intr.* **1.** To appear darkly or indistinctly. **2a.** To grow dark. **b.** To become gloomy. —*tr.* To make dark or indistinct.

dark·ling (där′klĭng) *adv.* In the dark. ❖ *adj.* **1.** Occurring in the dark. **2.** Dark; dim. ❖ *n.* The dark.

darkling beetle *n.* A beetle of the family Tenebrionidae, having a brown or black body and feeding on decaying vegetation, living plants, or stored grain.

dark matter *n.* Physical objects or particles that emit little or no detectable radiation and are postulated to exist because of unexplained gravitational forces observed on other astronomical objects.

dark·room (därk′rōōm′, -rŏŏm′) *n.* A room in which photographic materials are processed, either in complete darkness or with a safelight.

dark·some (därk′səm) *adj.* Dark and somber.

dark star *n.* A star normally obscure or too faint for visual observation, esp. the component of an eclipsing binary star detectable by spectral analysis or in the eclipse of the bright component.

dark·y also **dark·ie** (där′kē) *n., pl.* **-ies** *Offensive* Used as a disparaging term for a Black person.

Dar·lan (där-län′), **Jean Louis Xavier François** 1881–1942. French admiral who helped persuade French territories in N and W Africa to side with the Allies after 1942.

dar·ling (där′lĭng) *n.* **1.** A dearly beloved person. **2.** One that is

Clarence Darrow

greatly liked or preferred; a favorite. ❖ *adj.* **1.** Dearly beloved. **2.** Regarded with special favor; favorite. **3.** *Informal* Charming or amusing: *a darling hat.* [ME *dereling* < OE *dēorling : dēore,* dear + *-ling,* dim. suff.]

Darling Range An upland region of SW Australia extending along the Pacific coast N and S of Perth.

Darling River A river rising in SE Australia and flowing c. 2,739 km (1,702 mi) to the Murray R.

Darm·stadt (därm′stät, -shtät′) A city of SW Germany SE of Frankfurt; chartered 1330. Pop. 139,754.

darn¹ (därn) *v.* **darned, darn·ing, darns** —*tr.* To mend (a garment, for example) by weaving thread or yarn across a gap or hole. —*intr.* To repair a hole, as in a garment, by weaving thread or yarn across it. ❖ *n.* A hole so repaired. [Fr. dialectal *darner,* perh. < Norman Fr. *darne,* piece < Breton *darn.*]

darn² (därn) *interj., adv., adj., v., & n.* Damn. [Alteration of DAMN.]

dar·na·tion (där-nā′shən) *n. & interj.* Damnation. See Regional Note at **tarnation.**

darned (därnd) *adj.* Damned.

darned·est or **darnd·est** (därn′dĭst) *n.* The most possible.

dar·nel (där′nəl) *n.* Any of several Eurasian grasses of the genus *Lolium,* esp. *L. temulentum* or *L. perenne.* [ME.]

darn·er (där′nər) *n.* **1.** One that darns. **2.** *Northeastern, Upper Northern, & Western US* See **dragonfly.** See Regional Note at **dragonfly.** [< its resemblance to a *darner,* darning needle.]

darn·ing needle (där′nĭng) *n.* **1.** A long large-eyed needle used in darning. **2.** *Northeastern, Upper Northern, & Western US* See **dragonfly.** See Regional Note at **dragonfly.**

Darn·ley (därn′lē), Lord. Title of Henry Stewart or Stuart. 1545–67. Scottish nobleman and second husband (1565–67) of Mary Queen of Scots.

Dar·row (där′ō), **Clarence Seward** 1857–1938. Amer. lawyer known for his staunch opposition to capital punishment and for his defense in the Scopes evolution trial (1925).

dart (därt) *n.* **1a.** A slender, pointed missile, often having tail fins, thrown by hand, shot from a blowgun, or expelled by an exploding bomb. **b.** An object like a dart in shape, use, or effect. **2.** The stinger of an insect. **3. darts** (*used with a sing. or pl. verb*) *Games* A game in which darts are thrown at a target. **4.** A sudden, rapid movement. **5.** A tapered tuck sewn to adjust the fit of a garment. ❖ *v.* **dart·ed, dart·ing, darts** —*intr.* To move suddenly and rapidly. —*tr.* **1.** To thrust or throw suddenly and rapidly. **2.** To cause to move swiftly and abruptly. [ME < OFr., of Gmc. orig.]

dart·board (därt′bôrd′, -bōrd′) *n.* A circular board, often of cork, used as the target in a game of darts.

dart·er (där′tər) *n.* **1.** One that moves suddenly and rapidly. **2.** See **anhinga.** **3.** Any of various small, often brilliantly colored eastern North American freshwater fishes of the family Percidae, closely related to the perches.

Dart·moor (därt′mŏŏr′, -môr′, -mōr′) An upland region of SW England noted for its bare granite tors.

Dar·von (där′vŏn) A trademark used for a preparation of propoxyphene.

Dar·win (där′wĭn), **Charles Robert** 1809–82. British naturalist who developed a theory of evolution based on natural selection in works such as *On the Origin of Species* (1859). —**Dar·win′i·an** *adj. & n.*

Darwin, Erasmus 1731–1802. British physician, scientist, reformer, and poet who wrote *Zoonomia* (1794–96).

Dar·win·ism (där′wĭ-nĭz′əm) *n.* A theory of biological evolution developed by Charles Darwin and others, stating that all species of organisms arise and develop through the natural selection of inherited variations that increase the individual's ability to survive and reproduce. —**Dar′win·ist** *n.* —**Dar′win·is′tic** *adj.*

dash¹ (dăsh) *v.* **dashed, dash·ing, dash·es** —*tr.* **1.** To break or smash by striking violently. **2.** To hurl, knock, or thrust with sudden violence. **3.** To splash; bespatter. **4a.** To write hastily. Often used with *off: dash off a letter.* **b.** To drink hastily. Often used with *down.* **5a.** To add an enlivening or altering element to. **b.** To affect by adding an element to. **6a.** To destroy or wreck. **b.** To confound; abash. —*intr.* **1.** To strike violently; smash. **2.** To move with haste; rush. ❖ *n.* **1.** A swift, violent blow or stroke. **2a.** A splash. **b.** A small amount of an added ingredient. **3.** A quick stroke, as with a pencil or brush. **4.** A sudden movement; a rush. **5.** *Sports* A short footrace run at top speed. **6.** A spirited quality; verve. **7.** A punctuation mark (—) used in writing. **8.** In Morse code, the long sound or signal used with the dot and silent intervals to represent letters or numbers. **9.** A dashboard. [ME *dashen,* prob. of Scand. orig.; akin to Dan. *daske,* to beat.]

dash² (dăsh) *tr.v.* **dashed, dash·ing, dash·es** To damn. [Alteration of DAMN.]

dash·board (dăsh′bôrd′, -bōrd′) *n.* A panel under the windshield of a vehicle, containing indicator dials, compartments, and sometimes controls.

da·sheen (dă-shēn′) *n.* *Caribbean* **1.** A variety of taro having large yellowish tubers. **2.** The tuber of this plant. [?]

dash·er (dăsh′ər) *n.* One that dashes, esp. the plunger of an ice-cream freezer.

da·shi (dä′shē) *n.* A clear soup stock, usu. with a fish or vegetable base. [J., broth.]

da·shi·ki (də-shē′kē) also **dai·shi·ki** (dī-) *n., pl.* **-kis** A loose, brightly colored African garment. [Yoruba *dànṣíkí* < Hausa *dán cíkí.*]

dash·ing (dăsh′ĭng) *adj.* **1.** Audacious and gallant; spirited. **2.** Marked by showy elegance; splendid. —**dash′ing·ly** *adv.*

Dasht-e-Ka·vir (dăsht′ē-kə-vîr′, dăsht′ē-kä-vîr′) A salt desert of N-central Iran SE of the Elburz Mts.

Dasht-e-Lut (dăsht′ē-loot′) A sand and stone desert of E Iran extending S from the Dasht-e-Kavir.

das·sie (dăs′ē) *n.* See **hyrax.** [Afr., dim. of *das*, badger < MDu.]

das·tard (dăs′tərd) *n.* A sneaking, malicious coward. [ME, prob. alteration of ON *dæstr*, exhausted < p. part. of *dæsa*, to languish, decay.]

das·tard·ly (dăs′tərd-lē) *adj.* Cowardly and malicious; base. —**das′tard·li·ness** *n.*

das·y·ure (dăs′ē-yŏŏr′) *n.* Any of various often carnivorous marsupials of the family Dasyuridae of Australia, Tasmania, and adjacent islands. [NLat. *Dasyurus*, genus name : Gk. *dasus*, hairy + *oura*, tail; see **ors-** in App.]

DAT *abbr.* digital audiotape

dat. *abbr.* dative

da·ta (dä′tə, dăt′ə, dä′tə) *pl.n. (used with a sing. or pl. verb)* **1.** Factual information, esp. information organized for analysis. **2.** Numerical or other information represented in a form suitable for computer processing. **3.** Values derived from scientific experiments. **4.** Plural of **datum** 1. [Lat., pl. of *datum*. See DATUM.]

USAGE NOTE Although the word *data* comes from the plural of Latin *datum*, "something given," in English *data* is not always treated as a plural noun. Sometimes scientists think of *data* as plural, as in *These data do not support the conclusions.* But more often scientists and researchers think of data as a singular mass entity like information, and most people now follow this in general usage. Sixty percent of the Usage Panel accepts the use of *data* with a singular verb and pronoun in the sentence *Once the data is in, we can begin to analyze it.* A still larger number, 77 percent, accepts the sentence *We have very little data on the efficacy of such programs,* where the quantifier *very little,* which is not used with similar plural nouns such as *facts* and *results,* implies that *data* here is indeed singular.

data bank or **da·ta·bank** (dä′tə-băngk′, dăt′ə-) *n.* **1.** See **database. 2.** An organization chiefly concerned with building, maintaining, and using a database.

da·ta·base (dä′tə-bās′, dăt′ə-) *Computer Science n.* also **data base** A collection of data arranged for ease of retrieval. ❖ *tr.v.* **-based, -bas·ing, -bas·es** To put (data) into a database.

data carrier *n.* A medium, such as magnetic tape, that records or communicates data.

data highway *n.* **1.** A network of computer networks, other devices, and switching systems used for the transfer of digitized information. **2.** The integrated circuitry of a computer chip.

data processing *n.* **1.** Conversion of data into a form that can be processed by computer. **2.** The storing or processing of data by a computer. —**da·ta-pro′cess·ing** (dä′tə-prŏs′ĕs′ĭng, -prŏ′sĕs′-, dăt′ə-) *adj.*

data processor *n.* **1.** A device, such as a calculator or computer, that performs operations on data. **2.** A person who processes data.

data set *n.* **1.** An electronic device that provides an interface in the transmission of data to a remote station. **2.** A collection of related data records on a computer-readable medium, such as a disk.

date[1] (dāt) *n.* **1a.** Time stated in terms of the day, month, and year. **b.** A statement of calendar time, as on a document. **2.** A specified day of a month. **3.** A particular point or period of time at which something happened or is expected to happen. **4.** The time during which something lasts; duration. **5.** The time or historical period to which something belongs. **6.** An appointment: *a lunch date with a client.* See Syns at **engagement. 7a.** An engagement to go out socially with another person, often out of romantic interest. **b.** A person's companion on such an outing. **8.** An engagement for a performance. ❖ *v.* **dat·ed, dat·ing, dates** —*tr.* **1.** To mark or supply with a date. **2.** To determine the date of. **3.** To betray the age of: *Pictures of old cars date the book.* **4.** To go on a date with. —*intr.* **1.** To have origin in a particular time in the past: *This statue dates from 500 B.C.* **2.** To become old-fashioned. **3.** To go on dates. —*idiom:* **to date** Until now: *To date, six people have accepted the invitation.* [ME < OFr. < Med.Lat. *data,* < Lat. *data (Romae),* issued (at Rome) (on a certain day), fem. p. part. of *dare,* to give. See **dō-** in App.] —**dat′a·ble,** **date′a·ble** *adj.* —**dat′er** *n.*

date[2] (dāt) *n.* **1.** The edible fruit of the date palm, containing a thin hard seed. **2.** A date palm. [ME < OFr. < O Provençal *datil* < Lat. *dactylus* < Gk. *daktulos,* finger, date (< its shape).]

date·book (dāt′bŏŏk′) *n.* A notebook or calendar for listing information such as appointments or events.

dat·ed (dā′tĭd) *adj.* **1.** Displaying a date. **2.** Old-fashioned; out-of-date. —**dat′ed·ly** *adv.* —**dat′ed·ness** *n.*

date·less (dāt′lĭs) *adj.* **1.** Having no date. **2.** So ancient that no date can be determined. **3.** Having no limits in time.

date·line (dāt′līn′) *n.* A phrase at the head of a newspaper or magazine article giving the date and place of origin. —**date′-line′** *v.*

date line *n.* The International Date Line.

date palm *n.* A palm tree *(Phoenix dactylifera)* of western Asia and northern Africa having featherlike leaves and bearing clusters of dates.

date rape *n.* Rape perpetrated by the victim's social escort. —**date′-rape′** *adj.*

da·tive (dā′tĭv) *adj.* Of, relating to, or being the grammatical case that marks the recipient of action, the indirect object of the verb, or the object of certain prepositions. ❖ *n.* **1.** The dative case. **2.** A word or form in the dative case. [ME *datif* < Lat. *(cāsus) datīvus,* (case) of giving (transl. of Gk. *dotikē ptōsis*) < *datus,* p. part. of *dare,* to give. See **dō-** in App.] —**da′tive·ly** *adv.*

Da·tong (dä′tŏŏng′) also **Ta·tung** (tä′tŏŏng′) A city of NE China W of Beijing. Pop. 1,277,310.

dATP (dē′ā′tē′pē′) *n.* One of the two purine nucleotides that are used to synthesize DNA. [D(EOXY)– + ATP.]

da·tum (dā′təm, dăt′əm, dä′təm) *n.* **1.** *pl.* **-ta** (-tə) A fact or proposition used to draw a conclusion or make a decision. See Usage Note at **data. 2.** *pl.* **-tums** A point, line, or surface used as a reference, as in surveying. [Lat., something given < neut. p. part. of *dare,* to give. See **dō-** in App.]

da·tu·ra (də-tŏŏr′ə, -tyŏŏr′ə) *n.* Any of several plants of the genus *Datura,* having large trumpet-shaped flowers, prickly fruits, and leaves and seeds that yield narcotic alkaloids. [NLat. *Datura,* genus name < Hindi *dhatūrā,* datura < Skt. *dhattūraḥ.*]

daub (dôb) *v.* **daubed, daub·ing, daubs** —*tr.* **1.** To cover or smear with a soft adhesive substance, such as plaster or grease. **2.** To apply paint to (a surface) with crude strokes. **3.** To apply with quick or crude strokes: *daubed paint on the paper.* —*intr.* **1.** To paint with crude strokes. **2.** To daub a sticky material. ❖ *n.* **1.** The act or a stroke of daubing. **2.** A soft adhesive coating material, such as plaster or grease. **3.** Matter daubed on; a smear. **4.** A crude painting or picture. [ME *dauben* < OFr. *dauber* < Lat. *dēalbāre,* to whitewash : *dē-,* intensive pref.; see DE- + *albus,* white; see **albho-** in App.] —**daub′er** *n.* —**daub′er·y** (dô′bə-rē) *n.*

Dau·bi·gny (dō-bē-nyē′), **Charles François** 1817–78. French painter known for his sensitive portrayal of light.

Dau·det (dō-dā′), **Alphonse** 1840–97. French writer whose naturalistic stories include *Lettres de mon Moulin* (1869).

daugh·ter (dô′tər) *n.* **1.** One's female child. **2.** A female descendant. **3.** A woman considered as if in a relationship of child to parent. **4.** One personified or regarded as a female descendant. **5.** *Physics* The immediate product of the radioactive decay of an element. ❖ *adj.* **1.** Possessing the characteristics or relationship of a daughter. **2.** *Biology* Of or relating to a cell, organelle, or other structure produced by division or replication. **3.** *Physics* Produced by or resulting from the decay of a radioactive element. [ME *doughter* < OE *dohtor.* See **dhugəter-** in App.] —**daugh′ter·ly** *adj.*

daugh·ter-in-law (dô′tər-ĭn-lô′) *n., pl.* **daugh·ters-in-law** (dô′tərz-) The wife of one's son.

Dau·mier (dō-myā′), **Honoré** 1808–79. French artist best known for his bitterly satirical lithographs.

daunt (dônt, dänt) *tr.v.* **daunt·ed, daunt·ing, daunts** To abate the courage of; discourage. [ME *daunten* < OFr. *danter* < Lat. *domitāre,* freq. of *domāre,* to tame.] —**daunt′er** *n.* —**daunt′ing·ly** *adv.*

daunt·less (dônt′lĭs, dänt′-) *adj.* Incapable of being intimidated or discouraged; fearless. —**daunt′less·ly** *adv.* —**daunt′less·ness** *n.*

dau·phin (dô′fĭn) *n.* **1.** The eldest son of the king of France from 1349 to 1830. **2.** Used as a title for such a nobleman. [ME < OFr., title of the lords of Dauphiné < *Dalphin, Dalfin,* a surname < *dalfin,* dolphin (< the device on the family's coat of arms). See DOLPHIN.]

dau·phine (dô-fēn′) *n.* The wife of a dauphin. [Fr., fem. of *dauphin.* See DAUPHIN.]

Dau·phi·né (dō-fē-nā′) A historical region and former province of SE France bordering on Italy.

DAV *abbr.* Disabled American Veterans

Da·vao (dä′vou′) A city of SE Mindanao, Philippines, on **Davao Gulf,** an inlet of the Pacific. Pop. 960,910.

da·ven (dä′vən) *intr.v.* **-vened, -ven·ing, -vens** To recite Jewish liturgical prayers. [Yiddish *davnen.*]

dav·en·port (dăv′ən-pôrt′, -pôrt′) *n.* **1.** A large sofa, often convertible into a bed. **2.** A small desk. [< obsolete *davenport,* a small writing desk, prob. < manufacturer's name.]

Davenport A city of E IA on the Mississippi R. opposite Rock Island IL. Pop. 98,359.

Da·vid (dā′vĭd) d. c. 962 B.C. The second king of Judah and Israel; reputed author of many of the Psalms. [Heb. *dāwīd,* beloved, kinsman (sense uncertain).]

David, Saint. c. 520–601. Patron saint of Wales, whose shrine was a pilgrimage site during the Middle Ages.

David I 1082?–1153. King of Scotland (1124–53) who transformed his realm into a feudalistic society.

Da·vid (dä′vət), **Gerard** 1460?–1523. Dutch painter of religious subjects; one of the most important Flemish primitives.

Da·vid (dä-vēd′), **Jacques Louis** 1748–1825. French painter whose works include *The Death of Marat* (1793).

date palm
Phoenix dactylifera

ă	pat	oi	boy
ā	pay	ou	out
âr	care	ŏŏ	took
ä	father	ōō	boot
ĕ	pet	ŭ	cut
ē	be	ûr	urge
ĭ	pit	th	thin
ī	pie	th	this
îr	pier	hw	which
ŏ	pot	zh	vision
ō	toe	ə	about,
ô	paw		item

Stress marks:
′ (primary);
′ (secondary); as in
lexicon (lĕk′sĭ-kŏn′)

Da·vid·son (dā′vĭd-sən), **Jo(seph)** 1883–1952. Amer. sculptor known for his portrait busts.

Da·vies (dā′vēz), **Arthur Bowen** 1862–1928. Amer. painter and organizer of the revolutionary Armory Show in 1913.

Dá·vi·la y Pa·di·lla (dä′vē-lä ē pä-dē′yä), **Agustín** 1562–1604. Mexican prelate who wrote a noted study of the Spanish colonial era.

da Vin·ci (də vĭn′chē, dä), **Leonardo** See **Leonardo da Vinci.**

Da·vis (dā′vĭs), **Benjamin Oliver** 1877–1970. Amer. cavalry officer who was the first African-American general in the US Army (1940–48). His son **Benjamin Oliver Davis, Jr.** (b. 1912), was the first African-American general in the US Air Force (1954–70).

Davis, Bette 1908–89. Amer. actress whose films include *Dangerous* (1935) and *Jezebel* (1938).

Davis, Jefferson 1808–89. Amer. soldier and president of the Confederacy (1861–65); indicted for treason (1866) but never prosecuted.

Davis, Miles Dewey, Jr. 1926–91. Amer. jazz musician acclaimed for his warm, often muted trumpet style.

Davis, Richard Harding 1864–1916. Amer. writer known as the leading war correspondent of his day.

Davis, Stuart 1894–1964. Amer. artist who often incorporated jazz tempos into his canvases.

Davis Strait A strait of the N Atlantic between SE Baffin I. and SW Greenland.

dav·it (dăv′ĭt, dā′vĭt) *n.* Any of various small cranes that project over the side of a ship and are used for hoisting. [ME *daviot* < Norman Fr. *daviot,* dim. of *Davi,* David.]

Da·vy (dā′vē), **Sir Humphry** 1778–1829. British chemist who was a pioneer of electrochemistry.

Davy Jones (jōnz′) *n.* The bottom of the sea, as personified in songs and stories. [?]

Davy Jones's locker (jōn′zĭz, jōnz) *n.* The bottom of the sea, esp. as the grave of all who perish at sea.

daw (dô) *n.* A jackdaw. [ME *dawe.*]

daw·dle (dôd′l) *v.* **-dled, -dling, -dles** *—intr.* **1.** To take more time than necessary. **2.** To move aimlessly or lackadaisically. *—tr.* To waste (time) by idling. [Perh. alteration of dialectal *daddle,* to diddle.] —**daw′dler** *n.* —**daw′dling·ly** *adv.*

Dawes (dôz), **Charles Gates** 1865–1951. Vice President of the US (1925–29) who shared the 1925 Nobel Peace Prize.

Dawes, William 1745–99. Amer. patriot who rode with Paul Revere on Apr. 18, 1775, to warn of the British advance on Lexington and Concord.

dawn (dôn) *n.* **1.** The time at which daylight first begins. **2.** A first appearance; a beginning: *the dawn of history.* See Syns at **beginning.** ✦ *intr.v.* **dawned, dawn·ing, dawns** **1.** To begin to become daylight. **2.** To begin to appear or develop; emerge. **3.** To begin to be perceived. [< ME *daunen,* to dawn, prob. ult. < OE *dagung* < *dagian,* to dawn.]

dawn redwood *n.* A cone-bearing Chinese tree (*Metasequoia glyptostroboides*) related to the redwood.

Daw·son (dô′sən) A town of W Yukon Terr., Canada, at the confluence of the Yukon and Klondike rivers; a boom town during the Klondike gold rush of the late 1890s. Pop. 1,287.

Dawson Creek A city of NE British Columbia, Canada; S terminus of the Alaska Highway. Pop. 11,125.

day (dā) *n.* **1.** The period of light between dawn and nightfall; the interval from sunrise to sunset. **2a.** The 24-hour period during which earth completes one rotation on its axis. **b.** The period during which a celestial body makes a similar rotation. **3.** One of the numbered 24-hour periods into which a week, month, or year is divided. **4.** The portion of a 24-hour period that is devoted to work, school, or business: *an eight-hour day.* **5.** A 24-hour period or a portion of it reserved for a certain activity: *a day of rest.* **6a.** A period, as of vigor or success, in one's lifetime. **b.** A period of opportunity or prominence. **7.** A period of time in history; an era. **8. days** Period of life or activity: *Your days are numbered.* ✦ *adj.* **1.** Of or relating to the day. **2.** Working during the day. **3.** Occurring after nightfall: *a day hike.* —**idioms: day after day** For many days; continuously. **day in, day out** Every day without fail; continuously. [ME *dai, day* < OE *dæg.*]

Day, Clarence Shepard, Jr. 1874–1935. Amer. writer best known for his autobiographical *Life with Father* (1935).

Day, Dorothy 1897–1980. Amer. journalist and reformer who cofounded the *Catholic Worker* in 1933.

Day or **Daye** (dā), **Stephen** 1594?–1668. English-born colonist who printed the *Bay Psalm Book* in 1640.

Day·ak (dä′yăk′) or **Dy·ak** (dī′-) *n., pl.* **Dayak** or **-aks** also **Dyak** or **-aks** **1.** A member of any of various Indonesian peoples inhabiting Borneo. **2.** The language of the Dayak. [Dayak *Daya, Dayaq,* upcountry person, Dayak.]

Da·yan (dä-yän′), **Moshe** 1915–81. Israeli military leader who directed the 1956 Sinai campaign and 1967 Six-Day War.

day bed or **day·bed** (dā′bĕd′) *n.* A couch or sofa that is convertible into a bed.

day·book (dā′bŏŏk′) *n.* **1.** A book in which daily transactions are recorded. **2.** A diary.

day·break (dā′brāk′) *n.* The beginning of day; dawn.

day camp *n.* A children's camp providing recreation and meals during the day but no overnight facilities.

Jefferson Davis
detail from an 1849
watercolor on ivory by
George Lethbridge
Saunders (1807–63)

Miles Davis

davit
row of lifeboats suspended
from davits

day·care or **day care** (dā′kâr′) *n.* Provision of daytime training, supervision, and recreation for children, the disabled, or the elderly.

day·dream (dā′drēm′) *n.* A dreamlike musing while awake, esp. of the fulfillment of wishes. ✦ *intr.v.* **-dreamed** or **-dreamt** (-drĕmt′), **-dream·ing, -dreams** To have dreamlike musings while awake. —**day′dream′er** *n.*

day·flow·er (dā′flou′ər) *n.* Any of various plants of the genus *Commelina,* having blue or purplish flowers that wilt quickly.

day·fly (dā′flī′) *n.* See **mayfly.**

Day-Glo (dā′glō′) A trademark used for fluorescent coloring agents and materials.

day job *n.* One's primary job, usu. at daytime and enabling one to pursue a secondary activity from which one would eventually like to draw an income.

day labor *n.* Labor paid by the day. —**day laborer** *n.*

day letter *n.* A telegram sent during the day.

Day Lewis, Cecil 1904–72. Irish-born poet and critic who became poet laureate in 1968.

day·light (dā′līt′) *n.* **1.** The light of day; sunlight. **2a.** Daybreak. **b.** Daytime. **3.** Exposure to public notice. **4.** Understanding of what had been obscure. **5.** *Sports* An opening, as between defenders. **6. daylights** *Slang* One's wits.

day·light-sav·ing time (dā′līt-sā′vĭng) or **day·light-sav·ings time** (-vĭngz) *n.* Time during which clocks are set one hour or more ahead of standard time to provide more daylight at the end of the working day during late spring, summer, and early fall.

day lily or **day·lil·y** (dā′lĭl′ē) *n.* Any of several perennial Eurasian herbs of the genus *Hemerocallis* in the lily family, having lily-like flowers.

day·long (dā′lông′, -lŏng′) *adj.* Lasting through the whole day. ✦ *adv.* Through the day (all).

day nursery *n.* A facility for the supervision of preschool children, esp. during the hours that their parents are at work.

Day of Atonement *n.* See **Yom Kippur.** [Transl. of Heb. *yôm kippûr.*]

Day of Judgment *n.* See **Judgment Day** 1.

Day of the Dead *n.* November 1 and November 2 collectively, celebrated concurrently with All Saints' Day and All Souls' Day in Mexico and parts of Central America in commemoration of the dead. [Transl. of Sp. *Día de los Muertos.*]

day one *n.* *Informal* The very beginning; the first day.

day room *n.* A recreation room, as in a barracks.

days (dāz) *adv.* During the daytime on every day or most days: *works days in the store.*

day school *n.* **1.** A private school for pupils living at home. **2.** A school that holds classes during the day.

day·side (dā′sīd′) *n.* **1.** Office personnel who work days. **2.** The side of a planet facing the sun. —**day′side′** *adj.*

days of grace *pl.n.* Extra days allowed for payment of a note or bill after it has come due. [Transl. of Lat. *diēs grātiae* : *diēs,* pl. of *diēs,* day + *grātiae,* genitive of *grātia,* grace.]

day·star (dā′stär′) *n.* **1.** The morning star. **2.** The sun.

day student *n.* A student at a school who does not reside in the facilities provided by the institution.

day·time (dā′tīm′) *n.* The time between sunrise and sunset. ✦ *adj.* Occurring in or appropriate for use during the day.

day-to-day (dā′tə-dā′) *adj.* **1.** Occurring on a routine or daily basis. **2.** Subsisting one day at a time.

Day·ton (dāt′n) A city of SW OH NNE of Cincinnati; home of Orville and Wilbur Wright. Pop. 166,179.

Day·to·na Beach (dā-tō′nə) A city of NE FL on the Atlantic coast NNE of Orlando; site of automobile speed trials and races since the early 1900s. Pop. 64,112.

day trade *n.* A trade of a security that is opened and closed on the same day.

day trader *n.* A speculator who buys and sells securities on the basis of small short-term price movements. —**day trading** *n.*

day-trip·per (dā′trĭp′ər) *n.* One who takes a trip during the day without an overnight stop.

daze (dāz) *tr.v.* **dazed, daz·ing, daz·es** **1.** To stun, as with a heavy blow or shock; stupefy. **2.** To dazzle, as with strong light. ✦ *n.* A stunned or bewildered condition. [ME *dasen,* of Scand. orig.; akin to ON *dasask,* to become weary.]

daz·zle (dăz′əl) *v.* **-zled, -zling, -zles** *—tr.* **1.** To dim the vision of, esp. by intense light. **2.** To amaze or bewilder with spectacular display: *a skater who dazzled the audience.* *—intr.* **1.** To become blinded. **2.** To inspire admiration or wonder. ✦ *n.* The act of dazzling or the state of being dazzled. [Frequentative of DAZE.] —**daz′zler** *n.* —**daz′zling·ly** *adv.*

dB *abbr.* decibel

Db The symbol for the element **dubnium.**

DBA *abbr.* **1.** Doctor of Business Administration **2.** doing business as

DBE *abbr.* Dame Commander of the British Empire

dbh *abbr.* diameter at breast height

D.Bib. *abbr.* Douay Bible

DC *abbr.* **1.** da capo **2.** direct current **3.** District of Columbia **4.** Doctor of Chiropractic

DCL *abbr.* **1.** Doctor of Canon Law **2.** Doctor of Civil Law

DCM *abbr.* Distinguished Conduct Medal

dCTP (dē′sē′tē′pē′) *n.* One of the two pyrimidine nucleotides that are used to synthesize DNA. [D(EOXY)– + C(YTIDINE) + T(RI)P(HOSPHATE).]

DD *abbr.* **1.** demand draft **2.** dishonorable discharge **3.** *Latin* Divinitatis Doctor (Doctor of Divinity)

dd. *abbr.* delivered

D-day (dē′dā′) *n.* **1.** The unnamed day on which an operation or offensive is to be launched. **2.** The day on which the Allied forces invaded France during World War II (June 6, 1944). [*D* (abbr. of DAY).]

DDC or **ddC** (dē′dē-sē′) *n.* A nucleoside analogue that inhibits the replication of retroviruses such as HIV. [*d(i)d(eoxy)c(ytidine)*.]

DDI or **ddI** (dē′dē-ī′) *n.* A nucleoside analogue antiviral drug that inhibits replication of retroviruses such as HIV. [*d(i)d(eoxy)-i(nosine)*. See DIDANOSINE.]

DDS *abbr.* **1.** Doctor of Dental Science **2.** Doctor of Dental Surgery

DDT (dē′dē-tē′) *n.* A colorless contact insecticide, $C_{14}H_9Cl_5$, banned in the United States for most uses since 1972. [D(ICHLORO)D(IPHENYL)T(RICHLOROETHANE).]

DE *abbr.* Delaware

de– *pref.* **1.** Do or make the opposite of; reverse: *decriminalize*. **2.** Remove or remove from: *delouse*. **3.** Out of: *deplane*. **4.** Reduce; degrade: *declass*. **5.** Derived from: *deverbative*. [ME *de-* < OFr. *de-* (< Lat. *dē-*, from, off, apart, away, down, out, completely < *dē*; see **de-** in App.) or < OFr. *des-*, out, off, apart, away, completely (< Lat. *dis-*, dis-, and *dē-*).]

de·ac·ces·sion (dē′ăk-sĕsh′ən) *v.* **-sioned, -sion·ing, -sions** —*tr.* To remove and sell (a work of art) from a museum collection, esp. to purchase other works of art. —*intr.* To deaccession a work of art. —**de′ac·ces′sion** *n.*

dea·con (dē′kən) *n.* **1.** A cleric ranking below a priest in the Anglican, Eastern Orthodox, and Roman Catholic churches. **2.** A Protestant layperson who assists the minister. **3.** Used as a title prefixed to the surname of such a person: *Deacon Brown.* [ME *deken* < OE *dīacon* < LLat. *diāconus* < Gk. *diākonos*, attendant, minister.]

dea·con·ess (dē′kə-nĭs) *n.* **1.** A Protestant woman who assists the minister. **2.** Used as a title prefixed to the surname of such a woman: *Deaconess Brown.*

dea·con·ry (dē′kən-rē) *n., pl.* **-ries 1.** The office or position of a deacon. **2.** Deacons considered as a group.

de·ac·ti·vate (dē-ăk′tə-vāt′) *tr.v.* **-vat·ed, -vat·ing, -vates 1.** To render inactive or ineffective. **2.** To inhibit, block, or disrupt the action of (a biological agent). **3.** To remove from active military status. —**de·ac′ti·va′tion** *n.* —**de·ac′ti·va′tor** *n.*

dead (dĕd) *adj.* **dead·er, dead·est 1.** Having lost life; no longer alive. **2.** Marked for death; doomed. **3a.** Having the physical appearance of death: *a dead pallor.* **b.** Lacking feeling or sensitivity; unresponsive. **c.** Weary and worn-out; exhausted. **4a.** Not having the capacity to live; inanimate or inert. **b.** Not having the capacity to produce or sustain life; barren: *dead soil.* **5a.** No longer in existence, use, or operation. **b.** No longer having significance or relevance. **c.** Physically inactive; dormant: *a dead volcano.* **6a.** Not commercially productive; idle: *dead capital.* **b.** Not circulating or running; stagnant: *dead air.* **7a.** Devoid of activity; quiet: *a dead town.* **b.** Lacking animation or excitement; dull. **8.** Having no resonance. Used of sounds. **9.** Having grown cold; extinguished: *dead coals.* **10.** Lacking elasticity or bounce. **11.** Out of operation because of a fault or breakdown. **12a.** Sudden; abrupt: *a dead stop.* **b.** Complete; utter: *dead silence.* **c.** Exact; unerring: *the dead center of a target.* **13.** *Sports* Out of play. Used of a ball. **14a.** Lacking connection to electric current. **b.** Drained of electric charge; discharged: *a dead battery.* ❖ *n.* **1.** One who has died: *respect for the dead.* **2.** The period of greatest intensity: *the dead of winter.* ❖ *adv.* **1.** Absolutely; altogether. **2.** Directly; exactly. **3.** Suddenly. —*idioms:* **dead and buried** No longer relevant. **dead in the water** Unable to function or move. **dead to rights** In the very act of making an error or committing a crime. [ME *ded* < OE *dēad.* See **dheu-²** in App.] —**dead′ness** *n.*

dead air *n.* An unintended interruption in a broadcast during which there is no sound.

dead·beat¹ (dĕd′bēt′) *Informal n.* **1.** One who does not pay debts. **2.** A lazy person; a loafer. —**dead′beat′** *adj.*

dead·beat² (dĕd′bēt′) *adj.* Having an indicator that stops without oscillation.

dead bolt also **dead·bolt** (dĕd′bōlt′) *n.* A bolt on a lock that is moved by turning the key or knob without activation of a spring.

dead center *n.* The point at the end of each stroke of a moving crank and connecting rod at which the two lie in the same straight line and the turning force applied by the connecting rod is zero.

dead duck *n. Slang* One doomed to failure or to death.

dead·en (dĕd′n) *v.* **-ened, -en·ing, -ens** —*tr.* **1.** To render less intense or vigorous: *deaden the pain.* **2.** To make soundproof. **3.** To make less colorful or brilliant. —*intr.* **1.** To become dead. **2.** To lose vigor, brilliance, or liveliness. —**dead′en·er** *n.*

dead end *n.* **1.** An end of a passage, such as a street, that affords no exit. **2.** A point beyond which no movement or progress can be made; an impasse.

dead-end (dĕd′ĕnd′) *adj.* **1.** Having no exit. **2.** Permitting no advancement: *a dead-end job.* **3.** *Informal* Tough and rowdy: *a dead-*

end gang. ❖ *intr.v.* **-end·ed, -end·ing, -ends** To terminate with no exit or possibility of advancement.

dead·en·ing (dĕd′n-ĭng) *n.* Material used for soundproofing.

dead·eye (dĕd′ī′) *n.* **1.** *Nautical* A flat disk with a grooved perimeter, pierced by holes through which the lanyards are passed to fasten the shrouds. **2.** *Slang* An expert shooter.

dead·fall (dĕd′fôl′) *n.* **1.** A trap for large animals in which a heavy weight falls on the prey. **2.** A mass of fallen timber and brush.

dead hand *n.* **1.** The ever-present, oppressive influence of past events. **2.** Mortmain. [ME *dede hond,* transl. of OFr. *mortemain* or Med.Lat. *manus mortua,* mortmain.]

dead·head (dĕd′hĕd′) *Informal n.* **1.** A person who uses a free ticket for admittance or entertainment. **2.** A vehicle carrying no passengers or freight. **3.** A sluggish or dull-witted person. **4.** A partially submerged log or trunk. ❖ *tr.v.* **-head·ed, -head·ing, -heads 1.** To pilot or drive (a vehicle) carrying no passengers or freight. **2.** To pull (dead or dying blossoms) off a flower. ❖ *adv.* Without passengers or freight.

dead heat *n.* **1.** *Sports* A race in which two or more contestants compete evenly or finish at the same time. **2.** A political campaign or other contest that is so close that it is impossible to predict the winner.

dead language *n.* A language, such as Latin, that is no longer learned as a native language by a speech community.

dead letter *n.* **1.** An unclaimed or undelivered letter that after a time is destroyed or returned to the sender by the postal service. **2.** A law, directive, or factor formally in effect but no longer valid or enforced.

dead lift *n.* A lift in weightlifting in which the weight is lifted from the floor to the level of the hips and then lowered by controlled effort to the floor.

dead·light (dĕd′līt′) *n.* **1.** *Nautical* **a.** A strong shutter fastened over a porthole in stormy weather. **b.** A thick window in a ship's side or deck. **2.** A skylight that cannot be opened.

dead·line (dĕd′līn′) *n.* **1.** A time limit, as for payment of a debt. **2.** A line in a prison that prisoners can cross only at the risk of being shot. ❖ *tr.v.* **-lined, -lin·ing, -lines** To govern by setting a time limit.

dead load *n.* See **dead weight** 3.

dead·lock (dĕd′lŏk′) *n.* **1.** A standstill resulting from the opposition of two unrelenting forces. **2.** *Sports* A tied score. ❖ *tr. & intr.v.* **-locked, -lock·ing, -locks** To bring or come to a deadlock.

dead·ly (dĕd′lē) *adj.* **-li·er, -li·est 1.** Causing or tending to cause death. **2.** Suggestive of death. **3.** Wanting to kill; implacable. **4a.** Destructive in effect: *a deadly critique.* **b.** Tending to take away vitality, effectiveness, or force. **5.** Absolute; utter: *deadly concentration.* **6.** Extreme or terrible. **7.** Extremely accurate; unerring. **8.** Dull, tedious, and boring. ❖ *adv.* **1.** So as to suggest death. **2.** To an extreme. —**dead′li·ness** *n.*

deadly nightshade *n.* **1.** See **belladonna** 1. **2.** See **bittersweet** nightshade.

deadly sin *n.* One of the seven sins—anger, covetousness, envy, gluttony, lust, pride, and sloth—that are regarded as fatal to one's soul.

dead-man's float (dĕd′mănz′) *n.* A floating position in which a person lies face down and extends the arms forward.

dead march *n.* A slow, solemn funeral march.

dead meat *n. Slang* **1.** A corpse or carcass. **2.** One that is doomed, as to ruin or death.

dead nettle *n.* Any of several weedy plants of the genus *Lamium,* having clusters of small, usu. purplish flowers.

dead-on (dĕd′ôn′, -ŏn′) *adj. Informal* Precisely accurate and to the point.

dead·pan (dĕd′păn′) *n.* **1.** An expressionless face. **2.** A person, esp. a performer, who has or assumes a blank expression. ❖ *adj.* Impassively matter-of-fact, as in style or expression: *deadpan delivery of the joke.* ❖ *adv.* With a deadpan face. ❖ *tr. & intr.v.* **-panned, -pan·ning, -pans** To express or express oneself in a deadpan way.

dead point *n.* See **dead center**.

dead reckoning *n.* **1.** A method of estimating the position of an aircraft or a ship without astronomical observations, as by applying to a known position the course and distance traveled since. **2.** Prediction based on inference; guesswork. [Poss. alteration of *ded.,* abbr. of *deduced* < *deduce,* to trace from the beginning. See DEDUCE.]

Dead Sea A salt lake, c. 397 m (1,300 ft) below sea level, between Israel and Jordan; the lowest point on the earth.

Dead Sea Scrolls *pl.n.* The papyrus scrolls and scroll fragments discovered by the Dead Sea, mostly dating from the last two centuries B.C., containing passages from the Hebrew Scriptures, apocryphal biblical books, and sectarian writings.

dead weight *n.* **1.** The unrelieved weight of a heavy motionless mass. **2.** An oppressive burden or difficulty. **3.** The fixed weight of a structure or piece of equipment, such as a bridge on its supports.

dead·wood (dĕd′wŏŏd′) *n.* **1.** Dead branches or wood on a tree. **2.** One that is burdensome or superfluous. **3.** *Nautical* The vertical planking between the keel of a vessel and the sternpost.

deaf (dĕf) *adj.* **deaf·er, deaf·est 1.** Partially or completely lack-

deadeye

ă pat	oi boy
ā pay	ou out
âr care	ŏŏ took
ä father	ōō boot
ĕ pet	ŭ cut
ē be	ûr urge
ĭ pit	th thin
ī pie	th this
îr pier	hw which
ŏ pot	zh vision
ō toe	ə about,
ô paw	item

Stress marks:
′ (primary)
′ (secondary), as in
lexicon (lĕk′sĭ-kŏn′)

ing in the sense of hearing. **2. Deaf** Of or relating to the Deaf or their culture. ❖ *n.* **1.** Deaf people considered as a group. Used with *the.* **2. Deaf** The community of deaf people who use American Sign Language as a primary means of communication. Used with *the.* [ME *def, deef* < OE *dēaf.*] —**deaf′ly** *adv.* —**deaf′ness** *n.*

USAGE NOTE Some writers have lately introduced a distinction between the lowercase noun *deaf,* which is used to refer simply to people with extensive hearing disorders, and the capitalized noun *Deaf,* which refers to the community that uses American Sign Language as a primary means of communication.

deaf·en (dĕf′ən) *v.* **-ened, -en·ing, -ens** —*tr.* **1.** To make deaf, esp. momentarily by a loud noise. **2.** To make soundproof. —*intr.* To cause deafness. —**deaf′en·ing·ly** *adv.*

deaf-mute also **deaf mute** (dĕf′myōot′) *Often Offensive n.* A person who can neither hear nor speak. ❖ *adj.* (dĕf-myōot′) Unable to speak or hear.

deal¹ (dēl) *v.* **dealt** (dĕlt), **deal·ing, -ens** —*tr.* **1.** To give out as a share or portion; apportion. **2.** To distribute among several recipients. See Syns at **distribute. 3.** *Slang* To sell: *deal cocaine.* **4.** To administer; deliver: *dealt him a blow.* **5.** *Games* **a.** To distribute (playing cards) among players. **b.** To give (a specific card) to a player while so distributing. —*intr.* **1.** To be occupied or concerned: *The book deals with the Middle Ages.* **2.** To behave in a specified way toward another or others; have transactions: *She deals honestly with me.* **3.** To take action with respect to someone or something: *dealing with complaints.* See Syns at **treat. 4.** *Informal* To cope: *can't deal with stress.* **5a.** To do business; trade: *dealing in diamonds.* **b.** *Slang* To buy and sell drugs, esp. illegally. **6.** *Games* To distribute playing cards. ❖ *n.* **1.** The act or a round of apportioning or distributing. **2.** *Games* **a.** Distribution of playing cards. **b.** The cards so distributed; a hand. **c.** The right or turn of a player to distribute the cards. **3.** An indefinite quantity or degree. **4.** An agreement often arranged secretly, as in politics. **5a.** A business transaction. **b.** An agreement, esp. one that is mutually beneficial. **6.** *Informal* A sale favorable esp. to the buyer; a bargain. **7.** *Informal* Treatment received: *a raw deal.* [ME *delen* < OE *dǣlan,* to divide, share.]

deal² (dēl) *n.* **1.** A fir or pine board cut to standard dimensions. **2.** Fir or pine wood. [ME *dele* < MDu. and MLGer. *dele,* plank.]

de·a·late (dē-ā′lāt′) or **de·a·lat·ed** (-lā′tĭd) *adj.* Having lost the wings. Used of insects that shed their wings after a mating flight. ❖ *n.* A dealate insect. —**de′a·la′tion** *n.*

deal·er (dē′lər) *n.* **1.** One engaged in buying and selling: *a drug dealer.* **2.** *Games* The one who distributes cards.

deal·er·ship (dē′lər-shĭp′) *n.* A franchise to sell specified items in a certain area.

deal·fish (dēl′fĭsh′) *n., pl.* **dealfish** or **-fish·es** An Atlantic ribbonfish (*Trachipterus arcticus*) having a compressed, tapering silvery body. [< DEAL².]

deal·ing (dē′lĭng) *n.* **1. dealings** Transactions or relations with others, usu. in business. **2.** Method or manner of conduct in relation to others; treatment: *honest dealing.*

de·am·i·nate (dē-ăm′ə-nāt′) *tr.v.* **-nat·ed, -nat·ing, -nates** To remove an amino group, NH₂, from (an organic compound). —**de·am′i·na′tion** *n.*

de·am·i·nize (dē-ăm′ə-nīz′) *tr.v.* **-nized, -niz·ing, -niz·es** To deaminate. —**de·am′i·ni·za′tion** (-nī-zā′shən) *n.*

dean (dēn) *n.* **1a.** An administrative officer in charge of a college, faculty, or division in a university. **b.** An officer of a college or high school who counsels students and supervises the enforcement of rules. **2.** *Ecclesiastical* The head of the chapter of canons governing a cathedral or collegiate church. **3.** *Roman Catholic Church* A priest appointed to oversee a group of parishes within a diocese. **4.** The senior member of a body or group. [ME *deen* < OFr. *deien* < LLat. *decānus,* chief of ten < *decem,* ten, or < Gk. *dekānos,* chief of ten (< *deka,* ten). See **dekm** in App.] —**dean′ship′** *n.*

Dean, James Byron 1931–55. Amer. actor whose films include *East of Eden* and *Rebel Without a Cause* (both 1955).

dean·er·y (dē′nə-rē) *n., pl.* **-ies** The office, jurisdiction, or official residence of an ecclesiastical dean.

dean's list (dēnz) *n., pl.* **deans' lists** A list of students, esp. in a college, who have attained high academic rank.

dear¹ (dîr) *adj.* **dear·er, dear·est 1a.** Loved and cherished: *my dearest friend.* **b.** Greatly valued; precious: *lost everything dear to them.* **2.** Highly esteemed or regarded. Used in direct address, esp. in salutations. **3a.** High-priced; expensive. **b.** Charging high prices. **4.** Earnest; ardent. **5.** Heartfelt: *my dearest wish.* **6.** *Obsolete* Noble; worthy. ❖ *n.* **1.** One that is greatly loved. **2.** An endearing, lovable, or kind person. ❖ *adv.* **1.** With fondness; affectionately. **2.** At a high cost: *sold their wares dear.* ❖ *interj.* Used as a polite exclamation, chiefly of surprise or distress. [ME *dere* < OE *dēore.*] —**dear′ly** *adv.* —**dear′ness** *n.*

dear² (dîr) *adj.* Severe; grievous. [ME *dere* < OE *dēor.*]

Dear·born (dîr′bôrn′, -bərn) A city of SE MI W of Detroit. Pop. 97,775.

Dear John *n.* A letter, as to a serviceman, requesting a divorce or ending a personal relationship.

dearth (dûrth) *n.* **1.** A scarce supply; a lack. **2.** Shortage of food;

famine. [ME *derthe* < OE **dēorthu,* costliness < *dēore,* costly. See DEAR¹.]

death (dĕth) *n.* **1.** The act of dying; termination of life. **2.** The state of being dead. **3.** The cause of dying. **4.** A manner of dying: *a heroine's death.* **5.** often **Death** A personification of the destroyer of life, usu. represented as a skeleton holding a scythe. **6a.** Bloodshed; murder. **b.** Execution. **7.** *Law* Civil death. **8.** The termination or extinction of something. —*idioms:* **at death's door** Near to death; gravely ill or injured. **be the death of** To distress or irritate to an intolerable degree. **put to death** To execute. **to death** To an intolerable degree; extremely. [ME *deeth* < OE *dēath.* See **dheu-²** in App.]

death·bed (dĕth′bĕd′) *n.* **1.** The bed on which a person dies. **2.** The last hours before death.

death benefit *n.* Insurance money payable to a deceased person's stipulated beneficiary.

death·blow (dĕth′blō′) *n.* **1.** A stroke or blow that causes death. **2.** A destructive event or occurrence.

death camas also **death camass** *n.* Any of several plants of the genus *Zigadenus* of western North America that have clusters of greenish flowers and are poisonous to livestock.

death camp *n.* A concentration camp in which those held captive are likely to die or be killed.

death cap *n.* A poisonous, usu. white mushroom (*Amanita phalloides*) having a prominent cup-shaped base.

death cup *n.* See **death cap.**

death duty *n. Chiefly British* A tax on inherited property; an inheritance tax.

death house *n.* See **death row.**

death instinct *n.* **1.** A primitive impulse for destruction, decay, and death, postulated by Sigmund Freud as coexisting with and opposing the life instinct. **2.** Death wish.

death·less (dĕth′lĭs) *adj.* Not subject to termination or death; immortal. —**death′less·ly** *adv.* —**death′less·ness** *n.*

death·ly (dĕth′lē) *adj.* **1.** Of, resembling, or characteristic of death: *a deathly silence.* **2.** Causing death; fatal. ❖ *adv.* **1.** In the manner of death. **2.** Extremely; very: *deathly cold.*

death mask *n.* A cast of a person's face taken after death.

death penalty *n.* A sentence of punishment by execution.

death rate *n.* The ratio of total deaths to total population in a specified community or area over a specified period of time.

death rattle *n.* A gurgling or rattling sound sometimes made in the throat of a dying person, caused by breath passing through mucus.

death row (rō) *n.* The part of a prison for housing inmates who have received the death penalty.

death's-head (dĕths′hĕd′) *n.* The human skull as a symbol of mortality or death.

deaths·man (dĕths′mən) *n. Archaic* An executioner.

death squad *n.* A clandestine military or paramilitary group employed to carry out political assassinations.

death tax *n.* **1.** See **inheritance tax. 2.** See **estate tax.**

death·trap (dĕth′trăp′) *n.* **1.** An unsafe building or other structure. **2.** A perilous circumstance or situation.

Death Valley An arid desert basin of E CA and W NV.

death warrant *n.* **1.** *Law* An official order authorizing a person's execution. **2.** Something that destroys hope or expectation; a deathblow.

death·watch (dĕth′wŏch′) *n.* **1.** A vigil kept beside a dying or dead person. **2.** One who guards a condemned person before execution. **3.** A deathwatch beetle.

deathwatch beetle *n.* Any of several wood-burrowing beetles of the family Anobiidae, esp. *Xestobium rufovillosum,* whose head makes a clicking sound that was superstitiously regarded as a portent of death.

death wish *n.* **1.** *Psychiatry* A desire for self-destruction, often accompanied by feelings of depression, hopelessness, and self-reproach. **2.** The desire for the death of another person toward whom one has unconscious hostility.

Deau·ville (dō′vĭl, dō-vēl′) A resort city of NW France on the English Channel. Pop. 4,682.

deb (dĕb) *n. Informal* A debutante.

de·ba·cle (dĭ-bä′kəl, -băk′əl, dĕb′ə-kəl) *n.* **1.** A sudden collapse, downfall, or defeat; a rout. **2.** A total, often ludicrous failure. **3.** The breaking up of ice in a river. **4.** A violent flood. [Fr. *débâcle* < *débâcler,* to unbar < OFr. *desbacler: des-,* de- + *bacler,* to bar, ult. < Lat. *baculum,* rod.]

De Ba·key (də bā′kē), **Michael Ellis** b. 1908. Amer. surgeon who implanted the first totally artificial heart in a human (1966).

de·bar (dē-bär′) *tr.v.* **-barred, -bar·ring, -bars 1.** To exclude or shut out; bar. **2.** To forbid, hinder, or prevent. [ME *debarren* < OFr. *desbarer,* to unbar : *des-,* de- + *barer,* to bar (< *barre,* bar; see BAR¹).] —**de·bar′ment** *n.*

de·bark (dĭ-bärk′) *v.* **-barked, -bark·ing, -barks** —*tr.* To unload, as from a ship or an airplane. —*intr.* To disembark. [Fr. *débarquer : dé-,* from (< OFr. *de-*; see DE-) + *barque,* ship (< OFr.; see BARK³).] —**de′bar·ka′tion** (dē′bär-kā′shən) *n.*

de·base (dĭ-bās′) *tr.v.* **-based, -bas·ing, -bas·es** To lower in character, quality, or value; degrade. See Syns at **degrade.** [DE- + BASE².] —**de·base′ment** *n.* —**de·bas′er** *n.*

de·bat·a·ble (dĭ-bā′tə-bəl) *adj.* **1.** That can be argued or discussed. **2.** Open to dispute. **—de•bat′a•bly** *adv.*

de•bate (dĭ-bāt′) *v.* **-bat•ed, -bat•ing, -bates** *—intr.* **1.** To consider something; deliberate. **2.** To engage in argument by discussing opposing points. **3.** To engage in a formal discussion or argument. **4.** *Obsolete* To fight or quarrel. *—tr.* **1.** To deliberate on; consider. **2.** To dispute or argue about. **3.** To discuss or argue (a question, for example) formally. **4.** *Obsolete* To fight or argue for or over. ❖ *n.* **1.** A discussion involving opposing points; an argument. **2.** Deliberation; consideration: *passed the motion with little debate.* **3.** A formal contest of argumentation in which two opposing teams defend and attack a given proposition. **4.** *Obsolete* Conflict; strife. [ME *debaten* < OFr. *debatre* : *de-*, de- + *battre*, to beat; see BATTER[1].] **—de•bate′ment** *n.* **—de•bat′er** *n.*

de•bauch (dĭ-bôch′) *v.* **-bauched, -bauch•ing, -bauch•es** *—tr.* **1a.** To corrupt morally. **b.** To lead away from excellence or virtue. **2.** To reduce the value or quality of; debase. **3.** *Archaic* To cause to forsake allegiance. *—intr.* To indulge in dissipation. ❖ *n.* **1.** The act or a period of debauchery. **2.** An orgy. [Fr. *débaucher* < OFr. *desbauchier*, to lead astray, rough-hew timber : *des-*, de- + *bauch*, beam, of Gmc. orig.] **—de•bauch′ed•ly** (-bô′chĭd-lē) *adv.* **—de•bauch′er** *n.*

de•bauch•ee (dĭ-bô′chē′, dĕb′ə-shē′, -shā′) *n.* A person who habitually indulges in debauchery or dissipation; a libertine.

de•bauch•er•y (dĭ-bô′chə-rē) *n., pl.* **-ies** **1a.** Extreme indulgence in sensual pleasures; dissipation. **b. debaucheries** Orgies. **2.** *Archaic* Seduction from morality, allegiance, or duty.

de•ben•ture (dĭ-bĕn′chər) *n.* **1.** A certificate or voucher acknowledging a debt. **2.** An unsecured bond issued by a corporation or governmental agency and backed only by the credit standing of the issuer. **3.** A customhouse certificate providing for the payment of a drawback. [ME *debentur* < Lat. *dēbentur*, they are due, third pers. pl. pr. passive of *dēbēre*, to owe. See **ghabh-** in App.]

de•bil•i•tate (dĭ-bĭl′ĭ-tāt′) *tr.v.* **-tat•ed, -tat•ing, -tates** To sap the strength or energy of; enervate. [Lat. *dēbilitāre*, *dēbilitāt-* < *dēbilis*, weak. See **bel-** in App.] **—de•bil′i•ta′tion** *n.* **—de•bil′i•ta′tive** *adj.*

de•bil•i•tat•ed (dĭ-bĭl′ĭ-tā′tĭd) *adj.* Showing impairment of energy or strength; enfeebled.

de•bil•i•ty (dĭ-bĭl′ĭ-tē) *n., pl.* **-ties** The state of being weak or feeble; infirmity. [ME *debilite* < OFr. < Lat. *dēbilitās* < *dēbilis*, weak. See **bel-** in App.]

deb•it (dĕb′ĭt) *n.* **1a.** An item of debt as recorded in an account. **b.** An entry of a sum in the debit or left-hand side of an account. **c.** The sum of such entries. **d.** The left-hand side of an account where bookkeeping entries are made. **2.** A drawback; a detriment. ❖ *tr.v.* **-it•ed, -it•ing, -its** **1.** To enter (a sum) on the left-hand side of an account. **2.** To charge with a debit. [ME *debite* < Lat. *dēbitum*, debt. See DEBT.]

debit card *n.* A bankcard used to make an electronic withdrawal from funds on deposit in a bank, as in purchasing goods or obtaining cash advances.

deb•o•nair also **deb•o•naire** (dĕb′ə-nâr′) *adj.* **1.** Suave; urbane. **2.** Affable; genial. **3.** Carefree and gay; jaunty. [ME *debonaire*, gracious, kindly < OFr. < *de bon aire*, of good lineage or disposition : *de*, of (< Lat. *dē*; see DE–) + *bon, bonne*, good (< Lat. *bonus*; see **deu-**[2] in App.) + *aire*, nest, family; see AERIE.] **—deb′o•nair′ly** *adv.* **—deb′o•nair′ness** *n.*

de•bone (dē-bōn′) *tr.v.* **-boned, -bon•ing, -bones** To remove the bones from: *debone a chicken breast.*

Deb•o•rah (dĕb′ər-ə, dĕb′rə) In the Bible, a judge who aided the Israelites in their victory over the Canaanites. [Heb. *dəbôrâ*, bee.]

de•bouch (dĭ-bouch′, -bo͞osh′) *v.* **-bouched, -bouch•ing, -bouch•es** *—intr.* **1.** To march from a narrow or confined area into the open. **2.** To emerge; issue. *—tr.* To cause to emerge or issue. [Fr. *déboucher* : *dé-*, out of (< OFr. *des-*; see DE–) + *bouche*, mouth (< Lat. *bucca*).]

de•bouch•ment (dĭ-bouch′mənt, -bo͞osh′-) *n.* **1.** The act or an instance of marching from a narrow confined area into the open. **2.** A debouchure.

de•bou•chure (dĭ-bo͞o′sho͝or′) *n.* An opening or mouth, as of a river or stream.

De•bre•cen (dĕb′rĭt-sĕn′, -rĕ-tsĕn′) A city of E Hungary near the Romanian border E of Budapest. Pop. 217,497.

de•bride•ment (dā′brēd-mäN′, dĭ-brēd′mənt) *n.* Surgical removal of dead or contaminated tissue and foreign matter from a wound. [Fr. *débridement* < *débrider*, to unbridle, debride (< the likening of constricting bands of tissue to bridles) < OFr. *desbrider* : *des-*, de- + *bride*, bridle (prob. < MHGer. *brīdel*, rein).] **—de•bride′** *v.*

de•brief (dē-brēf′) *tr.v.* **-briefed, -brief•ing, -briefs** **1.** To question to obtain knowledge or intelligence gathered esp. on a military mission. **2.** To instruct not to reveal classified information after leaving employment.

de•bris also **dé•bris** (də-brē′, dā-, dā′brē′) *n.* **1a.** The scattered remains of something broken or destroyed; rubble or wreckage. **b.** Carelessly discarded refuse; litter. **2.** *Geology* An accumulation of relatively large rock fragments: *glacial debris.* [Fr. *débris* < OFr. *debrisier*, to break to pieces : *de-*, intensive pref.; see DE– + *brisier*, to break (< VLat. *_brīsāre_, to press grapes, prob. of Celt. orig.).]

Debs (dĕbz), **Eugene Victor** 1855–1926. Amer. labor organizer and socialist leader who ran unsuccessfully for President five times between 1900 and 1920.

debt (dĕt) *n.* **1.** Something owed, such as money, goods, or services. **2a.** An obligation or liability to pay or render something to someone else. **b.** The condition of owing. **3.** An offense requiring forgiveness or reparation; a trespass. [ME *dette* < OFr. < VLat. *_dēbita_, pl. of Lat. *dēbitum*, debt, neut. p. part. of *dēbēre*, to owe. See **ghabh-** in App.] **—debt′less** *adj.*

debt•or (dĕt′ər) *n.* **1.** One that owes something to another. **2.** One who is guilty of a trespass or sin. [ME *dettour* < OFr. *dettor* < Lat. *dēbitor* < *dēbitus*, p. part. of *dēbēre*, to owe. See DEBT.]

de•bug (dē-bŭg′) *tr.v.* **-bugged, -bug•ging, -bugs** **1.** To remove a hidden electronic device, such as a microphone, from. **2.** To search for and correct malfunctioning elements or errors in: *debug a computer program.* **3.** To remove insects from, as with a pesticide. **—de•bug′ger** *n.*

de•bunk (dē-bŭngk′) *tr.v.* **-bunked, -bunk•ing, -bunks** To expose or ridicule the falseness or exaggerated claims of: *debunk a supposed miracle drug.* **—de•bunk′er** *n.*

De•bus•sy (də-byo͞o′sē, dĕb′yo͞o-sē′, də-bü-sē′), **Claude Achille** 1862–1918. French composer considered the first exponent of musical impressionism.

de•but also **dé•but** (dā-byo͞o′, də-, dā′byo͞o′) *n.* **1.** A first public appearance, as of a performer. **2.** The formal presentation of a young woman to society. **3.** The beginning of a course of action. ❖ *tr. & intr.v.* **-buted** (-byo͞od′), **-but•ing** (-byo͞o′ĭng), **-buts** (-byo͞oz′) *Usage Problem* To present in or make a debut. [Fr. *début* < *débuter*, to give the first stroke in a game, begin : *dé-*, from, away (< OFr. *de-*; see DE–) + *but*, goal, target (< OFr. *butte*; see BUTT[3]).]

USAGE NOTE *Debut* is widely used as a verb, both intransitively (*Her new series will debut next March on network television*) and transitively (*The network will debut her new series next March*). These usages are well established in connection with entertainment and the performing arts but are not entirely acceptable when used of other sorts of introductions, as of products or publications.

deb•u•tante (dĕb′yo͞o-tänt′, dā′byo͞o-) *n.* A young woman making a formal debut into society. [Fr. *débutante*, fem. pr. part. of *débuter*, to begin. See DEBUT.]

De•bye (də-bī′), **Peter Joseph Wilhelm** 1884–1966. Dutch-born Amer. physicist who won a 1936 Nobel Prize.

dec. *abbr.* **1.** deceased **2.** declension **3.** declination **4.** decorated **5.** decrescendo

Dec. *abbr.* December

deca– or **dec–** also **deka–** or **dek–** *pref.* Ten: *decane.* [Gk. *deka-* < *deka*, ten. See **dekm̥** in App.]

dec•ade (dĕk′ād′, dĕ-kād′) *n.* **1.** A period of ten years. **2.** A group or series of ten. [ME, a group of ten < OFr. < LLat. *decas*, *decad-* < Gk. *dekas* < *deka*, ten. See **dekm̥** in App.]

dec•a•dence (dĕk′ə-dəns, dĭ-kād′ns) *n.* **1.** A process, condition, or period of deterioration or decline, as in morals or art; decay. **2.** often **Decadence** A literary movement esp. of late 19th-century France and England characterized by refined aestheticism, artifice, and the quest for new sensations. [Fr. *décadence* < OFr. *decadence* < Med.Lat. *dēcadentia*, a decaying, declining < VLat. *_dēcadere_, to decay. See DECAY.]

dec•a•den•cy (dĕk′ə-dən-sē, dĭ-kād′n-) *n.* Decadence.

dec•a•dent (dĕk′ə-dənt, dĭ-kād′nt) *adj.* **1.** Being in a state of decline or decay. **2.** Marked by or providing unrestrained gratification; self-indulgent. **3.** often **Decadent** Of or relating to literary Decadence. ❖ *n.* **1.** A person in a condition or process of mental or moral decay. **2.** often **Decadent** A member of the Decadence movement. [Fr. *décadent*, back-formation < *décadence*, decadence. See DECADENCE.] **—dec′a•dent•ly** *adv.*

de•caf (dē′kăf′) *n. Informal* Decaffeinated coffee. **—de′caf′** *adj.*

de•caf•fein•at•ed (dē-kăf′ə-nā′tĭd, -kăf′ē-ə-) *adj.* Having the caffeine removed: *decaffeinated coffee.* **—de•caf′fein•ate′** *v.* **—de•caf′fein•a′tion** *n.*

dec•a•gon (dĕk′ə-gŏn′) *n.* A polygon with ten angles and ten sides. [Med.Lat. *decagōnum* < Gk. *dekagōnon* < neut. of *dekagōnos*, having ten angles : *deka*, ten; see **dekm̥** in App. + *-gōnos*, angled; see –GON.] **—de•cag′o•nal** (dĭ-kăg′ə-nəl) *adj.* **—de•cag′o•nal•ly** *adv.*

dec•a•he•dron (dĕk′ə-hē′drən) *n., pl.* **-drons** or **-dra** (-drə) A polyhedron with ten faces. **—dec′a•he′dral** *adj.*

de•cal (dē′kăl′, dĭ-kăl′) *n.* **1.** A picture or design transferred by decalcomania. **2.** A decorative sticker. [Short for DECALCOMANIA.]

de•cal•ci•fy (dē-kăl′sə-fī′) *v.* **-fied, -fy•ing, -fies** *—tr.* To remove calcium or calcium compounds from (bones or teeth, for example). *—intr.* To lose calcium or calcium compounds. **—de•cal′ci•fi•ca′tion** (-fĭ-kā′shən) *n.* **—de•cal′ci•fi′er** *n.*

de•cal•co•ma•ni•a (dē-kăl′kə-mā′nē-ə, -mān′yə) *n.* **1.** The process of transferring pictures or designs printed on specially prepared paper to materials such as glass or metal. **2.** A decal. [Fr. *décalcomanie* : < *décalquer*, to transfer a tracing (*de-*, from < Lat. *dē-*; see DE– + *calquer*, to trace; see CALQUE) + *manie*, craze, from its popularity in the 19th cent. (< Lat. *mania*, madness; see MANIA).]

de•ca•les•cence (dē′kə-lĕs′əns) *n.* A sudden slowing in the rate

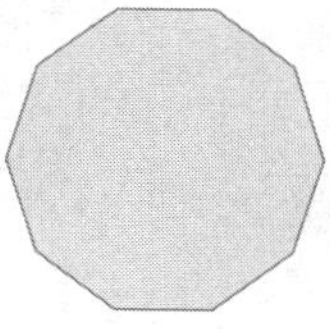

decagon

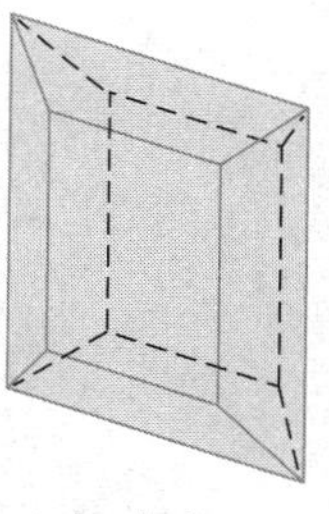

decahedron

ă pat	oi boy
ā pay	ou out
âr care	o͝o took
ä father	o͞o boot
ĕ pet	ŭ cut
ē be	ûr urge
ĭ pit	th thin
ī pie	*th* this
îr pier	hw which
ŏ pot	zh vision
ō toe	ə about, item
ô paw	

Stress marks:
′ (primary);
′ (secondary), as in
lexicon (lĕk′sĭ-kŏn′)

of temperature increase in a metal being heated, caused by endothermic structural changes. [< DE– + Lat. *calēscere*, to become warm, inchoative of *calēre*, to be warm.] —**de′ca·les′cent** *adj.*

Dec·a·logue or **Dec·a·log** (dĕk′ə-lôg′, -lŏg′) *n. Bible* The Ten Commandments. [ME *decalog* < LLat. *decalogus* < Gk. *dekalogos* : *deka*, ten; see **dekm̥** in App. + *logos*, word, pronouncement; see **leg-** in App.]

de·camp (dĭ-kămp′) *intr.v.* -**camped, -camp·ing, -camps** 1. To depart secretly or suddenly. 2. To depart from a camp. [Fr. *décamper* < OFr. *descamper*, to strike camp : *des-*, de– + *camp*, camp; see CAMP[1].] —**de·camp′ment** *n.*

dec·ane (dĕk′ān′) *n.* Any of various liquid isomers, $C_{10}H_{22}$, of the methane series.

dec·a·no·ic acid (dĕk′ə-nō′ĭk) *n.* See **capric acid.**

de·cant (dĭ-kănt′) *tr.v.* -**cant·ed, -cant·ing, -cants** 1. To pour off (wine, for example) without disturbing the sediment. 2. To pour (a liquid) from one container into another. [Med.Lat. *dēcanthāre* : Lat. *dē-*, de– + Lat. *canthus*, rim of a vessel (of Celt. orig.).] —**de·can·ta·tion** (dē′kăn-tā′shən) *n.*

de·cant·er (dĭ-kănt′ər) *n.* A vessel for decanting, esp. a decorative bottle used for serving wine.

de·cap·i·tate (dĭ-kăp′ĭ-tāt′) *tr.v.* -**tat·ed, -tat·ing, -tates** To cut off the head of; behead. [LLat. *dēcapitāre, dēcapitāt-* : Lat. *dē-*, de– + Lat. *caput, capit-*, head; see **kaput-** in App.] —**de·cap′i·ta′tion** *n.* —**de·cap′i·ta′tor** *n.*

dec·a·pod (dĕk′ə-pŏd′) *n.* 1. A crustacean of the order Decapoda, such as a crab or shrimp, typically having ten legs, each joined to a segment of the thorax. 2. A cephalopod mollusk, such as a squid, having ten armlike tentacles. [< NLat. *Decapoda*, order name : DECA– + *-poda*, -pod.] —**dec′a·pod, de·cap′o·dal** (dĭ-kăp′ə-dəl), **de·cap′o·dan** (-dən), **de·cap′o·dous** (-dəs) *adj.*

De·cap·o·lis (dĭ-kăp′ə-lĭs) A confederacy in NE Palestine of ten Roman-controlled cities settled by Greeks.

de·car·bon·ate (dē-kär′bə-nāt′) *tr.v.* -**at·ed, -at·ing, -ates** To remove carbon dioxide or carbonic acid from. —**de·car′bon·a′tion** *n.*

de·car·bon·ize (dē-kär′bə-nīz′) *tr.v.* -**ized, -iz·ing, -iz·es** To remove carbon from; decarburize. —**de·car′bon·i·za′tion** (-bə-nĭ-zā′shən) *n.* —**de·car′bon·iz′er** *n.*

de·car·box·yl·a·tion (dē′kär-bŏk′sə-lā′shən) *n.* Removal of a carboxyl group from a chemical compound, usu. with hydrogen replacing it.

de·car·bu·rize (dē-kär′bə-rīz′, -byə-) *tr.v.* -**rized, -riz·ing, -riz·es** To decarbonize. —**de·car′bu·ri·za′tion** (-rĭ-zā′shən) *n.*

dec·are (dĕk′âr′, -är′) *n.* A metric unit of area equal to 10 ares.

dec·a·syl·la·ble (dĕk′ə-sĭl′ə-bəl) *n.* A line of verse having ten syllables. —**dec′a·syl·lab′ic** (-sə-lăb′ĭk) *adj.*

de·cath·lete (dĭ-kăth′lēt) *n.* An athlete who participates in a decathlon.

de·cath·lon (dĭ-kăth′lən, -lŏn′) *n.* A track-and-field event usu. for men that includes the 100-meter, 400-meter, and 1,500-meter runs; the 110-meter high hurdle; the discus and javelin throws; the shot put; the pole vault; the high jump; and the long jump. [DECA– + (PENTA)THLON.]

De·ca·tur (dĭ-kā′tər) A city of central IL E of Springfield. Pop. 81,860.

Decatur, Stephen 1779–1820. Amer. naval officer active in the Tripolitan War and the War of 1812.

de·cay (dĭ-kā′) *v.* -**cayed, -cay·ing, -cays** —*intr.* 1. *Biology* To break down into component parts; rot. 2. *Physics* To disintegrate or diminish by radioactive decay. 3. *Electronics* To decrease gradually in magnitude. Used of voltage or current. 4. *Aerospace* To decrease in orbit. 5. To fall into ruin. 6. *Pathology* To decline in health or vigor; waste away. 7. To decline from a state of normality, excellence, or prosperity; deteriorate. —*tr.* To cause to decay. ❖ *n.* **1a.** The destruction or decomposition of organic matter as a result of bacterial or fungal action; rot. **b.** Rotted matter. 2. *Physics* Radioactive decay. 3. *Aerospace* The decrease in orbital altitude of an artificial satellite. 4. A gradual deterioration to an inferior state: *urban decay.* 5. A falling into ruin. [ME *decayen* < OFr. *decair* < VLat. **dēcadere* : Lat. *dē-*, de– + Lat. *cadere*, to fall.] —**de·cay′er** *n.*

Dec·can (dĕk′ən) A plateau of S-central India. The name is also used for the entire Indian peninsula S of the Narmada R.

decd. *abbr.* deceased

de·cease (dĭ-sēs′) *intr.v.* -**ceased, -ceas·ing, -ceas·es** To die. ❖ *n.* The act of dying; death. [ME *decesen* < *deces*, death < OFr. < Lat. *dēcessus*, departure, death < p. part. of *dēcēdere*, to depart, die : *dē-*, de– + *cēdere*, to go.]

de·ceased (dĭ-sēst′) *adj.* No longer living; dead. ❖ *n.* A dead person.

de·ce·dent (dĭ-sēd′nt) *n. Law* A dead person. [Lat. *dēcēdēns, dēcēdent-*, pr. part. of *dēcēdere*, to depart, die. See DECEASE.]

de·ceit (dĭ-sēt′) *n.* 1. The act or practice of deceiving; deception. 2. A stratagem; a trick. 3. The quality of being deceitful; falseness. [ME *deceite* < OFr. < p. part. of *deceveir*, to deceive. See DECEIVE.]

de·ceit·ful (dĭ-sēt′fəl) *adj.* 1. Given to cheating or deceiving. 2. Deliberately misleading; deceptive. —**de·ceit′ful·ly** *adv.* —**de·ceit′ful·ness** *n.*

de·ceive (dĭ-sēv′) *v.* -**ceived, -ceiv·ing, -ceives** —*tr.* 1. To cause to believe what is not true; mislead. 2. *Archaic* To catch by

guile; ensnare. —*intr.* 1. To practice deceit. 2. To give a false impression: *appearances can deceive.* [ME *deceiven* < OFr. *deceveir* < VLat. **dēcipēre* < Lat. *dēcipere*, to ensnare, deceive : *dē-*, de– + *capere*, to seize; see **kap-** in App.] —**de·ceiv′a·ble** *adj.* —**de·ceiv′er** *n.* —**de·ceiv′ing·ly** *adv.*

SYNONYMS *deceive, betray, mislead, beguile, delude, dupe* These verbs mean to lead another into error, danger, or a disadvantageous position, often by underhand means. *Deceive* involves the deliberate misrepresentation of the truth: *"We are inclined to believe those whom we do not know, because they have never deceived us"* (Samuel Johnson). *Betray* implies treachery: *"When you betray somebody else, you also betray yourself"* (Isaac Bashevis Singer). *Mislead* means to lead in the wrong direction or into error of thought or action: *"My manhood, long misled by wandering fires,/Followed false lights"* (John Dryden). *Beguile* suggests deceiving or misleading by means of charm or allure: *They beguiled unwary investors.* To *delude* is to mislead the mind or judgment: *The government deluded the public about radiation.* *Dupe* implies playing upon another's susceptibilities or naiveté: *Gullible shoppers are easily duped.*

de·cel·er·ate (dē-sĕl′ə-rāt′) *v.* -**at·ed, -at·ing, -ates** —*tr.* 1. To decrease the velocity of. 2. To slow down the rate of advancement of: *decelerated the arms buildup.* —*intr.* To decrease in velocity. [DE– + (AC)CELERATE.] —**de·cel′er·a′tion** *n.* —**de·cel′er·a′tor** *n.*

De·cem·ber (dĭ-sĕm′bər) *n.* The 12th month of the year in the Gregorian calendar. See table at **calendar.** [ME *decembre* < OFr. < Lat. *December*, the tenth month of the Roman year, prob. < **decemmembris* < *decem-mēnsris* : *decem*, ten; see **dekm̥** in App. + *mēnsis*, month; see MENSES.]

De·cem·brist (dĭ-sĕm′brĭst) *n.* A participant in the attempt to overthrow Czar Nicholas I of Russia in December 1825.

de·cem·vir (dĭ-sĕm′vər) *n., pl.* -**virs** or -**vi·ri** (-və-rī′) 1. One of a body of ten Roman magistrates, esp. a member of one of two bodies appointed in 451 and 450 B.C. to draw up a code of laws. 2. One of an authoritative body of ten. [ME < Lat., sing. of *decemvirī*, commission of ten men : *decem*, ten; see **dekm̥** in App. + *virī*, pl. of *vir*, man; see **wī-ro-** in App.] —**de·cem′vi·ral** *adj.* —**de·cem′vi·rate** (-vər-ĭt, -və-rāt′) *n.*

de·cen·cy (dē′sən-sē) *n., pl.* -**cies** 1. The state or quality of being decent; propriety. 2. Conformity to prevailing standards of propriety or modesty. 3. **decencies a.** Social or moral proprieties. **b.** The necessities for an acceptable standard of living.

de·cen·na·ry (dĭ-sĕn′ə-rē) *adj.* Of or relating to a ten-year period. ❖ *n., pl.* -**ries** A period of ten years; a decade. [< Lat. *decennis*, lasting for ten years. See DECENNIUM.]

de·cen·ni·al (dĭ-sĕn′ē-əl) *adj.* 1. Relating to or lasting for ten years. 2. Occurring every ten years. ❖ *n.* A tenth anniversary. [< Lat. *decennium*, a period of ten years. See DECENNIUM.] —**de·cen′ni·al·ly** *adv.*

de·cen·ni·um (dĭ-sĕn′ē-əm) *n., pl.* -**cen·ni·ums** or -**cen·ni·a** (-sĕn′ē-ə) A period of ten years. [Lat. < *decennis*, lasting for ten years : *decem*, ten; see **dekm̥** in App. + *annus*, year.]

de·cent (dē′sənt) *adj.* 1. Characterized by conformity to standards of propriety or morality. 2. Free from indelicacy; modest. 3. Fairly good; adequate: *a decent salary.* **4a.** Morally upright; respectable. **b.** Kind or obliging: *decent of them to help you.* 5. *Informal* Properly or modestly dressed. [Lat. *decēns, decent-*, pr. part. of *decēre*, to be fitting.] —**de′cent·ly** *adv.* —**de′cent·ness** *n.*

de·cen·tral·ize (dē-sĕn′trə-līz′) *v.* -**ized, -iz·ing, -iz·es** —*tr.* 1. To distribute the administrative functions or powers of (a central authority) among local authorities. 2. To cause to withdraw or disperse from a center of concentration. —*intr.* To undergo decentralization. —**de·cen′tral·i·za′tion** (-trə-lĭ-zā′shən) *n.* —**de·cen′tral·i·za′tion·ist** *adj. & n.*

de·cep·tion (dĭ-sĕp′shən) *n.* 1. The use of deceit. 2. The fact or state of being deceived. 3. A ruse; a trick. [ME *decepcioun* < OFr. *deception* < LLat. *dēceptiō, dēceptiōn-* < Lat. *dēceptus*, p. part. of *dēcipere*, to deceive. See DECEIVE.]

de·cep·tive (dĭ-sĕp′tĭv) *adj.* Deceiving or tending to deceive. —**de·cep′tive·ly** *adv.* —**de·cep′tive·ness** *n.*

de·cer·e·brate (dē-sĕr′ə-brāt′) *tr.v.* -**brat·ed, -brat·ing, -brates** To eliminate cerebral brain function in (an animal), as by removing the cerebrum in an experiment. ❖ *adj.* (*also* -brĭt) 1. Deprived of cerebral function, as by surgery. 2. Resulting from or as if from decerebration. 3. Lacking intelligence or reason. ❖ *n.* (*also* -brĭt) A decerebrate animal or person. —**de·cer′e·bra′tion** *n.*

de·cer·ti·fy (dē-sûr′tə-fī′) *tr.v.* -**fied, -fy·ing, -fies** To revoke the certification of: *voted to decertify the union.* —**de·cer′ti·fi·ca′tion** (dē-sûr′tə-fĭ-kā′shən, dē′sər-) *n.*

deci– *pref.* One tenth (10^{-1}): *decigram.* [Fr. *déci-* < Lat. *decimus*, tenth < *decem*, ten. See **dekm̥** in App.]

dec·i·bel (dĕs′ə-bəl, -bĕl′) *n.* A unit used to express relative difference in power or intensity, usu. between two acoustic or electric signals, equal to ten times the common logarithm of the ratio of the two levels. [DECI– + BEL.]

de·cide (dĭ-sīd′) *v.* -**cid·ed, -cid·ing, -cides** —*tr.* **1a.** To settle conclusively all contention or uncertainty about: *decide a case.* **b.**

To come to a decision about: *decide what to do.* **2.** To influence or determine the outcome of. **3.** To cause to make or reach a decision. —*intr.* **1.** To pronounce a judgment; announce a verdict. **2.** To make up one's mind. [ME *deciden* < OFr. *decider* < Lat. *dēcīdere,* to cut off, decide : *dē-,* de- + *caedere,* to cut.] **—de•cid′a•bil′i•ty** *n.* **—de•cid′a•ble** *adj.* **—de•cid′er** *n.*

SYNONYMS decide, determine, settle, rule, conclude, resolve These verbs mean to come to a decision. *Decide* is the least specific: "*If two laws conflict with each other, the courts must decide on the operation of each*" (John Marshall). *Determine* often involves somewhat narrower issues: *A jury will determine the verdict. Settle* stresses finality of decision: "*The lama waved a hand to show that the matter was finally settled in his mind*" (Rudyard Kipling). *Rule* implies that the decision is handed down by someone in authority: *The committee ruled that changes should be implemented. Conclude* suggests that a decision, opinion, or judgment has been arrived at after careful consideration: *She concluded that the criticism was unjust. Resolve* stresses the exercise of choice in making a firm decision: *I resolved to diet.*

de•cid•ed (dĭ-sī′dĭd) *adj.* **1.** Without doubt or question; definite: *a decided success.* **2.** Free from hesitation or vacillation; resolute. **—de•cid′ed•ly** *adv.* **—de•cid′ed•ness** *n.*

de•cid•u•a (dĭ-sĭj′ōō-ə) *n., pl.* **-u•as** or **-u•ae** (-ōō-ē′) A mucous membrane lining the uterus, modified during pregnancy and shed at parturition or during menstruation. [NLat. (*membrāna*) *dēcidua,* (membrane) that falls off < fem. of Lat. *dēciduus,* falling off. See DECIDUOUS.] **—de•cid′u•al** *adj.*

de•cid•u•ate (dĭ-sĭj′ōō-ĭt) *adj.* **1.** Characterized by or having a decidua. **2.** Characterized by shedding.

de•cid•u•ous (dĭ-sĭj′ōō-əs) *adj.* **1.** Falling off or shed at a specific season or stage of growth: *deciduous antlers.* **2.** Shedding or losing foliage at the end of the growing season: *deciduous trees.* **3.** Not lasting; ephemeral. [< Lat. *dēciduus* < *dēcidere,* to fall off : *dē-,* de- + *cadere,* to fall.] **—de•cid′u•ous•ly** *adv.* **—de•cid′u•ous•ness** *n.*

dec•i•gram (dĕs′ĭ-grăm′) *n.* A metric unit of mass or weight equal to one-tenth (10^{-1}) of a gram.

dec•ile (dĭs′īl′, -əl) *n. Statistics* **1.** Any one of the numbers or values dividing the distribution of the individuals in a series into ten groups of equal frequency. **2.** Any one of the ten groups. [DEC(I)- + -ILE².]

de•cil•lion (dĭ-sĭl′yən) *n.* **1.** The cardinal number equal to 10^{33}. **2.** *Chiefly British* The cardinal number equal to 10^{60}. [Lat. *decem,* ten; see DECI- + (M)ILLION.] **—de•cil′lion** *adj.*

de•cil•lionth (dĭ-sĭl′yənth) *n.* **1.** The ordinal number matching the number decillion in a series. **2.** One of a decillion equal parts. **—de•cil′lionth** *adv. & adj.*

dec•i•mal (dĕs′ə-məl) *n.* **1.** A linear array of digits that represents a real number, every decimal place indicating a multiple of a negative power of 10. For example, the decimal 0.12 = $^{12}/_{100}$. **2.** A number written using the base 10. ❖ *adj.* **1.** Expressed or expressible as a decimal. **2a.** Based on 10. **b.** Numbered or ordered by groups of 10. [Med.Lat. *decimālis,* of tenths or tithes < Lat. *decima,* a tenth part or tithe < *decem,* ten. See dekm̥ in App.] **—dec′i•mal•ly** *adv.*

dec•i•mal•ize (dĕs′ə-mə-līz′) *tr.v.* **-ized, -iz•ing, -iz•es** To change to a decimal system. **—dec′i•mal•i•za′tion** (-mə-lĭ-zā′shən) *n.*

decimal place *n.* The position of a digit to the right of a decimal point.

decimal point *n.* A dot written in a decimal number, as in 8.375, to indicate the place where values change from positive to negative powers of 10.

decimal system *n.* **1.** A number system based on units of 10. **2.** A system of measurement in which all derived units are multiples of 10 of the fundamental unit.

dec•i•mate (dĕs′ə-māt′) *tr.v.* **-mat•ed, -mat•ing, -mates** **1.** To destroy or kill a large part of (a group). **2.** *Usage Problem* **a.** To inflict great destruction or damage on. **b.** To reduce markedly in amount: *He decimated his trust fund.* **3.** To select by lot and kill one in every ten of. [Lat. *decimāre, decimāt-,* to punish every tenth person < *decimus,* tenth < *decem,* ten. See dekm̥ in App.] **—dec′i•ma′tion** *n.*

USAGE NOTE *Decimate* originally referred to the killing of every tenth person, a punishment used in the Roman army for mutinous legions. Today this meaning is commonly extended to include the killing of any large proportion of a group. Sixty-six percent of the Usage Panel accepts this extension in the sentence *The Jewish population of Germany was decimated by the war,* even though it is common knowledge that the number of Jews killed was much greater than a tenth of the original population. *Decimate* is also used to refer to large-scale destruction other than killing, as in *The supply of fresh produce was decimated by the accident at Chernobyl,* but this usage is acceptable to only 26 percent of the Panel.

dec•i•me•ter (dĕs′ə-mē′tər) *n.* A metric unit of length equal to one-tenth (10^{-1}) of a meter.

de•ci•pher (dĭ-sī′fər) *tr.v.* **-phered, -pher•ing, -phers** **1.** To read or interpret (ambiguous, obscure, or illegible matter). See

Syns at **solve. 2.** To convert from a code or cipher to plain text; decode. **—de•ci′pher•a•ble** *adj.* **—de•ci′pher•er** *n.* **—de•ci′pher•ment** *n.*

de•ci•sion (dĭ-sĭzh′ən) *n.* **1.** The passing of judgment on an issue under consideration. **2.** The act of reaching a conclusion or making up one's mind. **3.** A conclusion or judgment reached or pronounced; a verdict. **4.** Firmness of character or action; determination. **5.** *Sports* A victory won on points, as in boxing when no knockout has occurred. **6.** *Baseball* A win or loss accorded to a pitcher. [ME *decisioun* < OFr. *decision* < Lat. *dēcīsiō, dēcīsiōn-,* curtailment, settlement < *dēcīsus,* p. part. of *dēcīdere,* to cut off, decide. See DECIDE.] **—de•ci′sion•al** *adj.*

de•ci•sive (dĭ-sī′sĭv) *adj.* **1.** Having the power to decide; conclusive. **2.** Characterized by decision and firmness; resolute. **3.** Beyond doubt; unmistakable: *a decisive defeat.* **—de•ci′sive•ly** *adv.* **—de•ci′sive•ness** *n.*

deck¹ (dĕk) *n.* **1.** A platform extending from one side of a ship to the other. **2a.** A platform or surface likened to a ship's deck. **b.** A roofless, floored structure, typically with a railing, that adjoins a house. **c.** The roadway of a bridge or an elevated freeway. **3.** A pack of playing cards. **4.** A tape deck. **5.** *Slang* A packet of narcotics. ❖ *tr.v.* **decked, deck•ing, decks** **1.** To furnish with or as if with a deck. **2.** *Slang* To knock down, as with a punch. **—idioms: clear the deck** *Informal* To prepare for action. **hit the deck** *Slang* **1.** To get out of bed. **2.** To fall or drop to a prone position. **3.** To prepare for action. **on deck 1.** On hand; present. **2.** *Sports* Waiting to take one's turn. [ME *dekke* < MDu. *dec,* roof, covering. See (s)teg- in App.]

deck² (dĕk) *tr.v.* **decked, deck•ing, decks** **1.** To clothe with finery; adorn. Often used with *out.* **2.** To decorate. [Du. *dekken,* to cover < MDu. *decken.* See (s)teg- in App.]

deck chair *n.* A folding chair usu. with arms and a leg rest.

deck•er (dĕk′ər) *n.* Something having a deck or an indicated number of levels. Often used in combination: *double-decker buses.*

deck hand *n.* A member of a ship's crew who performs manual labor.

deck•house (dĕk′hous′) *n.* A short, houselike structure on the upper deck of a ship.

deck•le (dĕk′əl) *n.* **1.** A frame used in making paper by hand to form paper pulp into sheets of a desired size. **2.** A deckle edge. [Ger. *Deckel* < *Decke,* cover < *decken,* to cover < MHGer. < OHGer. *decchen.* See (s)teg- in App.]

deckle edge *n.* The rough edge of handmade paper formed in a deckle. **—deck′le-edged′** (dĕk′əl-ĕjd′) *adj.*

deck tennis *n.* A game in which a small ring is tossed back and forth over a net.

de•claim (dĭ-klām′) *v.* **-claimed, -claim•ing, -claims** —*intr.* **1.** To deliver a formal recitation, esp. as an exercise in rhetoric or elocution. **2.** To speak loudly and vehemently; inveigh. —*tr.* To utter or recite with rhetorical effect. [ME *declamen* < Lat. *dēclāmāre : dē-,* intensive pref.; see DE- + *clāmāre,* to cry out; see kelə- in App.] **—de•claim′er** *n.*

dec•la•ma•tion (dĕk′lə-mā′shən) *n.* **1.** A recitation delivered as an exercise in rhetoric or elocution. **2a.** Vehement oratory. **b.** A speech marked by strong feeling; a tirade. [ME *declamacioun* < Lat. *dēclāmātiō, dēclāmātiōn-* < *dēclāmātus,* p. part. of *dēclāmāre,* to declaim. See DECLAIM.]

de•clam•a•to•ry (dĭ-klăm′ə-tôr′ē, -tōr′ē) *adj.* **1.** Characteristic of a declamation. **2.** Pompously rhetorical; bombastic.

de•clar•ant (dĭ-klâr′ənt) *n.* One who makes a declaration, as an alien who has signed a declaration of intent to become a US citizen.

dec•la•ra•tion (dĕk′lə-rā′shən) *n.* **1.** An explicit formal announcement, either oral or written. **2.** The act or process of declaring. **3.** A statement of taxable goods or of properties subject to duty. **4.** *Games* A bid, esp. the final bid of a hand in certain card games.

de•clar•a•tive (dĭ-klâr′ə-tĭv, -klăr′-) *adj.* **1.** Serving to declare or state. **2.** *Grammar* Of, relating to, or being an element or construction used to make a statement. ❖ *n. Grammar* A sentence or expression that makes a statement. **—de•clar′a•tive•ly** *adv.*

de•clar•a•to•ry (dĭ-klâr′ə-tôr′ē, -tōr′ē) *adj.* Declarative.

de•clare (dĭ-klâr′) *v.* **-clared, -clar•ing, -clares** —*tr.* **1.** To make known formally or officially. **2.** To state emphatically or authoritatively; affirm. **3.** To reveal or make manifest; show. **4.** To make a full statement of (dutiable goods, for example). —*intr.* **1.** To make a declaration. **2.** To proclaim one's support, choice, opinion, or resolution. **3.** To choose the order in which cards are to be played from the dummy as well as from one's own hand in games such as bridge. [ME *declaren* < OFr. *declarer* < Lat. *dēclārāre : dē-,* intensive pref.; see DE- + *clārāre,* to make clear (< *clārus,* clear; see kelə- in App.).] **—de•clar′a•ble** *adj.* **—de•clar′er** *n.*

de•class (dē-klăs′) *tr.v.* **-classed, -class•ing, -class•es** To lower in class or status.

dé•clas•sé (dā′klä-sā′) *adj.* **1.** Lowered in class, rank, or social position. **2.** Lacking high station or birth; of inferior social status. [Fr., p. part. of *déclasser,* to lower in class : *dé-,* down (< Lat. *dē-;* see DE-) + *classe,* class; see CLASS.]

de•clas•si•fy (dē-klăs′ə-fī′) *tr.v.* **-fied, -fy•ing, -fies** To remove security classification from (a document). **—de•clas′si•fi′a•ble**

ă pat   oi boy
ā pay   ou out
âr care   ōō took
ä father ōō boot
ĕ pet   ŭ cut
ē be   ûr urge
ĭ pit   th thin
ī pie   th this
îr pier   hw which
ō toe   ə about,
ŏ pot   zh vision
ô paw   item

Stress marks:
′ (primary);
′ (secondary); as in
lexicon (lĕk′sĭ-kŏn′)

adj. —**de·clas'si·fi·ca'tion** (-fĭ-kā'shən) *n.*

de·claw (dē-klô') *tr.v.* **-clawed, -claw·ing, -claws** To remove the claws from: *declaw a cat.*

de·clen·sion (dĭ-klĕn'shən) *n.* **1.** *Linguistics* **a.** In certain languages, the inflection of nouns, pronouns, and adjectives in categories such as case, number, and gender. **b.** A class of words of one language with the same or a similar system of inflections. **2.** A descending slope; a descent. **3.** A decline or decrease; deterioration. **4.** A deviation, as from a standard or practice. [ME *declension* < OFr. *declinaison* < Lat. *dēclīnātiō, dēclīnātiōn-*, grammatical declension, declination. See DECLINATION.] —**de·clen'sion·al** *adj.*

dec·li·na·tion (dĕk'lə-nā'shən) *n.* **1.** A sloping or bending downward. **2.** A falling off, esp. from prosperity or vigor. **3.** A deviation, as from a specific direction or standard. **4.** A refusal to accept. **5.** Magnetic declination. **6.** *Astronomy* The angular distance to a point on a celestial object, measured north or south from the celestial equator. [ME *declinacioun* < OFr. *declination* < Lat. *dēclīnātiō, dēclīnātiōn-* < *dēclīnātus*, p. part. of *dēclīnāre*, to turn away. See DECLINE.] —**dec'li·na'tion·al** *adj.*

de·cline (dĭ-klīn') *v.* **-clined, -clin·ing, -clines** —*intr.* **1.** To express polite refusal. **2a.** To slope downward; descend. **b.** To bend downward; droop. **3.** To degrade or lower oneself; condescend. **4.** To deteriorate gradually; fail. **5a.** To sink, as the setting sun. **b.** To draw to a gradual close; wane. —*tr.* **1.** To refuse politely. **2.** To cause to slope or bend downward. **3.** *Grammar* To inflect (a noun, a pronoun, or an adjective) for number and case. ❖ *n.* **1.** The process or result of declining. **2.** A downward movement. **3.** The period when something approaches an end. **4.** A downward slope; a declivity. **5.** A disease that gradually weakens or wastes the body. [ME *declinen* < OFr. *decliner* < Lat. *dēclīnāre*, to turn away, bend downward, change the form of a word : *dē-*, de- + *-clīnāre*, to lean, bend; see **klei-** in App.] —**de·clin'a·ble** *adj.* —**de·clin'er** *n.*
Syns at **refuse¹**.

de·cliv·i·tous (dĭ-klĭv'ĭ-təs) *adj.* Moderately steep.

de·cliv·i·ty (dĭ-klĭv'ĭ-tē) *n., pl.* **-ties** A downward slope. [Lat. *dēclīvitās* < *dēclīvis*, sloping down : *dē-*, de- + *clīvus*, slope; see **klei-** in App.]

dec·o (dĕk'ō) *n.* Art deco.

de·coct (dĭ-kŏkt') *tr.v.* **-coct·ed, -coct·ing, -cocts 1.** To extract the flavor of by boiling. **2.** To make concentrated; boil down. [ME *decocten*, to boil < Lat. *dēcoquere, dēcoct-*, to boil down or away : *dē-*, de- + *coquere*, to boil, to cook; see **pekʷ-** in App.] —**de·coc'tion** *n.*

de·code (dē-kōd') *tr.v.* **-cod·ed, -cod·ing, -codes 1.** To convert from code into plain text. **2.** To convert from a scrambled electronic signal into an interpretable one. **3.** To extract the underlying meaning from: *decode a literary text.*

de·cod·er (dē-kōd'dər) *n.* **1.** One that decodes. **2.** A device that decodes a scrambled electronic signal to make it interpretable.

de·col·late¹ (dĭ-kŏl'āt') *tr.v.* **-lat·ed, -lat·ing, -lates** To behead. [Lat. *dēcollāre, dēcollāt-* : *dē-*, de- + *collum*, neck; see **kʷel-** in App.] —**de'col·la'tion** *n.*

de·col·late² (dĕk'ə-lāt', dē-kō'-) *tr.v.* **-lat·ed, -lat·ing, -lates** To separate the copies of (a computer printout, for example). —**de'col·la'tor** *n.*

dé·colle·tage (dā'kŏl-täzh') *n.* **1.** A low neckline on a woman's garment. **2.** A dress with a low neckline in front. [Fr. < *décolleté*, having a low neckline. See DÉCOLLETÉ.]

dé·colle·té (dā'kôl-tā') *adj.* **1.** Cut low at the neckline: *a décolleté dress.* **2.** Wearing a garment that is low-cut or strapless. [Fr., p. part. of *décolleter*, to lower a neckline, uncover the neck : *dé-*, off (< Lat. *dē-*; see DE-) + *collet*, collar (< OFr., dim. of *col*, neck, collar < Lat. *collum*, neck; see **kʷel-** in App.).]

de·col·o·nize (dē-kŏl'ə-nīz') *tr.v.* **-nized, -niz·ing, -niz·es** To free (a colony) from dependent status. —**de·col'o·ni·za'tion** (-nĭ-zā'shən) *n.*

de·col·or·ant (dē-kŭl'ər-ənt) *n.* A bleaching agent.

de·col·or·ize (dē-kŭl'ə-rīz') *tr.v.* **-ized, -iz·ing, -iz·es** To remove the color from. —**de·col'or·i·za'tion** (-kŭl'ər-ĭ-zā'shən) *n.* —**de·col'or·iz'er** *n.*

de·com·mis·sion (dē'kə-mĭsh'ən) *tr.v.* **-sioned, -sion·ing, -sions** To withdraw (a ship, for example) from active service.

de·com·pen·sa·tion (dē·kŏm-pən-sā'shən) *n.* **1.** Failure of the heart to maintain adequate blood circulation. **2.** The inability to maintain defense mechanisms in response to stress, resulting in psychological disturbance. —**de·com'pen·sate'** *v.*

de·com·pose (dē'kəm-pōz') *v.* **-posed, -pos·ing, -pos·es** —*tr.* **1.** To separate into components or basic elements. **2.** To cause to rot. —*intr.* **1.** To become broken down into components; disintegrate. **2.** To decay; putrefy. —**de'com·pos'a·bil'i·ty** *n.* —**de'com·pos'a·ble** *adj.*

de·com·pos·er (dē'kəm-pō'zər) *n.* An organism, often a bacterium or fungus, that feeds on and breaks down dead plant or animal matter.

de·com·po·si·tion (dē-kŏm'pə-zĭsh'ən) *n.* **1.** The act or result of decomposing; disintegration. **2a.** *Chemistry* Separation into constituents by chemical reaction. **b.** *Biology* Breakdown or decay of organic materials. —**de·com'po·si'tion·al** *adj.*

de·com·pound¹ (dē-kŏm'pound', dē'kəm-pound') *adj.* **1.** Compounded or consisting of things or parts that are already compound. **2.** *Botany* Having or consisting of compound divisions; bipinnate: *a decompound leaf.*

de·com·pound² (dē'kəm-pound') *tr.v.* **-pound·ed, -pound·ing, -pounds** To decompose.

de·com·press (dē'kəm-prĕs') *v.* **-pressed, -press·ing, -press·es** —*tr.* **1.** To relieve of pressure or compression. **2.** To bring (a person exposed to conditions of increased pressure) gradually back to normal atmospheric pressure. —*intr.* **1.** To adjust to normal atmospheric conditions after being exposed to increased pressure. **2.** *Informal* To relax.

de·com·pres·sion (dē'kəm-prĕsh'ən) *n.* **1.** The act or process of decompressing. **2.** A surgical procedure used to relieve pressure on an organ or part, such as the abdomen.

decompression chamber *n.* A compartment in which atmospheric pressure can be gradually raised or lowered, used esp. in readjusting divers to normal atmospheric pressure.

decompression sickness *n.* A disorder, seen esp. in deep-sea divers, caused by the formation of nitrogen bubbles in the blood following a rapid drop in pressure and marked by severe pains in the joints and chest, skin irritation, cramps, and paralysis.

de·con·di·tion (dē'kən-dĭsh'ən) *v.* **-tioned, -tion·ing, -tions** —*tr.* **1.** *Psychology* To cause (a conditioned response, such as a phobia) to become extinct. **2.** To cause to decline from a condition of physical fitness. —*intr.* To lose physical fitness.

de·con·gest (dē'kən-jĕst') *tr.v.* **-gest·ed, -gest·ing, -gests** To relieve the congestion of (sinuses, for example). —**de'con·ges'tion** (-jĕs'chən) *n.* —**de'con·ges'tive** *adj.*

de·con·ges·tant (dē'kən-jĕs'tənt) *n.* A medication or treatment that breaks up congestion, as of the sinuses, by reducing swelling. ❖ *adj.* Capable of relieving congestion.

de·con·struct (dē'kən-strŭkt') *tr.v.* **-struct·ed, -struct·ing, -structs 1.** To break down into components; dismantle. **2.** To write about or analyze (a literary text, for example), following the tenets of deconstruction.

de·con·struc·tion (dē'kən-strŭk'shən) *n.* A philosophical movement and theory of literary criticism that asserts that words can only refer to other words and tries to demonstrate how statements about any text subvert their own meanings. —**de'con·struc'tion·ism** *n.* —**de'con·struc'tion·ist** *n.* & *adj.*

de·con·tam·i·nate (dē'kən-tăm'ə-nāt') *tr.v.* **-nat·ed, -nat·ing, -nates 1.** To eliminate contamination in. **2.** To make safe by eliminating harmful substances, such as noxious chemicals or radioactive material. —**de'con·tam'i·nant** (-nənt) *n.* —**de'con·tam'i·na'tion** *n.* —**de'con·tam'i·na'tor** *n.*

de·con·trol (dē'kən-trōl') *tr.v.* **-trolled, -trol·ling, -trols** To stop control of, esp. by the government. —**de'con·trol'** *n.*

dé·cor or **de·cor** (dā'kôr', dā-kôr') *n.* **1a.** Decoration. **b.** A decorative style or scheme, as of a room. **2.** A stage setting; scenery. [Fr. < *décorer*, to decorate < Lat. *decorāre*, to beautify. See DECORATE.]

dec·o·rate (dĕk'ə-rāt') *tr.v.* **-rat·ed, -rat·ing, -rates 1.** To furnish or adorn with something ornamental; embellish. **2.** To confer a medal or other honor on. [< ME *decorat*, made beautiful < Lat. *decorātus*, p. part. of *decorāre*, to beautify < *decus, decor-*, honor, ornament.]

dec·o·ra·tion (dĕk'ə-rā'shən) *n.* **1.** The act, process, or art of decorating. **2.** Something used to decorate. **3.** An emblem of honor, such as a medal or badge.

Decoration Day *n.* See **Memorial Day**.

dec·o·ra·tive (dĕk'ər-ə-tĭv, -ə-rā'-) *adj.* Serving to decorate or embellish; ornamental. —**dec'o·ra·tive·ly** *adv.* —**dec'o·ra·tive·ness** *n.*

dec·o·ra·tor (dĕk'ə-rā'tər) *n.* One that decorates, esp. an interior decorator.

dec·o·rous (dĕk'ər-əs, dĭ-kôr'əs, -kōr'-) *adj.* Characterized by or exhibiting decorum; proper: *decorous behavior.* [< Lat. *decōrus*, becoming, handsome < *decor*, seemliness, beauty.] —**dec'o·rous·ly** *adv.* —**dec'o·rous·ness** *n.*

de·cor·ti·cate (dē-kôr'tĭ-kāt') *tr.v.* **-cat·ed, -cat·ing, -cates 1.** To remove the bark, husk, or outer layer from; peel. **2.** To remove the surface layer, membrane, or fibrous cover of. [Lat. *dēcorticāre, dēcorticāt-* : *dē-*, de- + *cortex, cortic-*, bark, rind; see **sker-¹** in App.] —**de·cor'ti·ca'tion** *n.* —**de·cor'ti·ca'tor** *n.*

de·co·rum (dĭ-kôr'əm, -kōr'-) *n.* **1.** Appropriateness of behavior or conduct; propriety. **2. decorums** The conventions of polite behavior. **3.** The appropriateness of an element of an artistic or literary work, such as style or tone, to other elements, such as subject matter and character. [Lat. *decōrum* < *decōrus*, becoming, handsome. See DECOROUS.]

de·cou·page also **dé·cou·page** (dā'kōō-päzh') *n.* **1.** The technique of decorating a surface with cutouts, as of paper. **2.** A creation produced by this technique. [Fr. *découpage* < *découper*, to cut up or out < OFr. *descolper* : *des-*, de- + *colper*, to cut (< *colp*, stroke; see COUP).]

de·cou·ple (dē-kŭp'əl) *tr.v.* **-pled, -pling, -ples 1.** *Electronics* To reduce or eliminate the coupling of (one circuit or one part to another). **2.** To separate or detach. —**de·cou'pler** *n.*

de·coy (dē'koi', dĭ-koi') *n.* **1a.** A living or artificial bird or other animal used to entice game into a trap or within shooting range. **b.** An enclosed place into which wildfowl are lured for capture. **2.** A means used to mislead or lead into danger. ❖ *tr.v.* (dĭ-koi')

décolletage
detail from a portrait by
Anthony Vandyke

decoy
carved wood duck

-coyed, -coy•ing, -coys To lure or entrap by or as if by a decoy. [Poss. < Du. *de kooi*, the cage : *de*, the (< MDu.; see **to-** in App.) + *kooi*, cage (< MDu. *côie* < Lat. *cavea*).] **—de•coy′er** *n.*

de•crease (dĭ-krēs′) *intr. & tr.v.* **-creased, -creas•ing, -creas•es** To grow or cause to grow gradually less or smaller, as in number, amount, or intensity. ❖ *n.* (dē′krēs′) **1.** The act or process of decreasing. **2.** The amount by which something decreases. [ME *decresen* < OFr. *decreistre, decreiss-* < Lat. *dēcrēscere* : *dē-*, de- + *crēscere*, to grow; see **ker-**² in App.] **—de•creas′ing•ly** *adv.*

SYNONYMS *decrease, lessen, reduce, dwindle, abate, diminish, subside* These verbs mean to become or cause to become smaller or less. *Decrease* and *lessen* refer to steady or gradual diminution: *Lack of success decreases confidence. His appetite lessens as his illness progresses. Reduce* emphasizes bringing down in size, degree, or intensity: *The workers reduced their wage demands. Dwindle* suggests decreasing bit by bit to a vanishing point: *Their savings dwindled away. Abate* stresses a decrease in amount or intensity and suggests a reduction of excess: *Toward evening the fire began to abate. Diminish* implies taking away or removal: *The warden's authority diminished after the revolt. Subside* implies a falling away to a more normal level: *Our wild enthusiasm did not subside.*

de•cree (dĭ-krē′) *n.* **1.** An authoritative order having the force of law. **2.** *Law* The judgment of a court of equity, admiralty, probate, or divorce. ❖ *v.* **-creed, -cree•ing, -crees** —*tr.* To ordain, establish, or decide by decree. See Syns at **dictate.** —*intr.* To issue a decree. [ME *decre* < OFr. *decret* < Lat. *dēcrētum*, principle, decision < neut. p. part. of *dēcernere*, to decide : *dē-*, de- + *cernere*, to sift; see **krei-** in App.] **—de•cree′a•ble** *adj.* **—de•cre′er** *n.*

dec•re•ment (dĕk′rə-mənt) *n.* **1.** The act or process of decreasing or becoming gradually less. **2.** The amount that is lost by gradual diminution or waste. **3.** *Mathematics* The amount by which a variable is decreased; a negative increment. [Lat. *dēcrēmentum* < *dēcrēscere, dēcrē-*, to decrease. See DECREASE.] **—dec′re•ment′al** (-mĕn′tl) *adj.*

de•crep•it (dĭ-krĕp′ĭt) *adj.* Weakened, worn out, impaired, or broken down by old age, illness, or hard use. [ME < OFr. < Lat. *dēcrepitus*, worn out : *dē-*, de- + *crepitus*, p. part. of *crepāre*, to burst.] **—de•crep′it•ly** *adv.*

de•crep•i•tate (dĭ-krĕp′ĭ-tāt′) *v.* **-tat•ed, -tat•ing, -tates** —*tr.* To roast or calcine (crystals or salts) until they emit a crackling sound or until crackling stops. —*intr.* To make a crackling sound when roasted. [NLat. *dēcrepitāre, dēcrepitāt-* : Lat. *dē-*, de- + Lat. *crepitāre*, to crackle, freq. of *crepāre*, to burst, crack.] **—de•crep′i•ta′tion** *n.*

de•crep•i•tude (dĭ-krĕp′ĭ-to͞od′, -tyo͞od′) *n.* The quality or condition of being weakened, worn out, impaired, or broken down by old age, illness, or hard use.

de•cre•scen•do (dā′krə-shĕn′dō, dē′-) *Music adv. & adj.* With gradually diminishing force or loudness. ❖ *n., pl.* **-dos 1.** A gradual decrease in force or loudness. **2.** A decrescendo passage. [Ital., gerund of *decrescere*, to decrease < Lat. *dēcrēscere*. See DECREASE.]

de•cres•cent (dĭ-krĕs′ənt) *adj.* Becoming gradually less; waning. [Lat. *dēcrēscēns, dēcrēscent-*, pr. part. of *dēcrēscere*, to decrease. See DECREASE.]

de•cre•tal (dĭ-krēt′l) *n. Roman Catholic Church* A decree, esp. a papal letter giving a decision on a point of canon law. [ME < OFr. *decretale* < LLat. *dēcrētālis*, fixed by decree < Lat. *dēcrētum*, principle, decision. See DECREE.]

de•cre•tive (dĭ-krē′tĭv) *adj.* Decretory.

dec•re•to•ry (dĕk′rĭ-tôr′ē, -tōr′ē, dĭ-krē′tə-rē) *adj.* Of, relating to, or having the force of a decree.

de•crim•i•nal•ize (dē-krĭm′ə-nə-līz′) *tr.v.* **-ized, -iz•ing, -iz•es** To reduce or abolish criminal penalties for. **—de•crim′i•nal•i•za′tion** (-nə-lĭ-zā′shən) *n.*

de•cry (dĭ-krī′) *tr.v.* **-cried, -cry•ing, -cries 1.** To condemn openly. **2.** To depreciate (currency, for example) by official proclamation or by rumor. [Fr. *décrier* < OFr. *descrier* : *des-*, de- + *crier*, to cry; see CRY.] **—de•cri′er** *n.*

de•crypt (dē-krĭpt′) *tr.v.* **-crypt•ed, -crypt•ing, -crypts 1.** To decipher. **2.** To decode. ❖ *n.* (dē′krĭpt′) A deciphered or decoded message. [DE- + *-crypt* (< CRYPTOGRAM).] **—de•cryp′tion** *n.*

de•cu•bi•tus ulcer (dĭ-kyo͞o′bĭ-təs) *n.* See **bedsore.** [Med.Lat. *dēcubitus*, lying down, being bedridden < p. part. of Lat. *dēcumbere*, to lie down. See DECUMBENT.]

de•cum•bent (dĭ-kŭm′bənt) *adj.* **1.** Lying down; reclining. **2.** *Botany* Lying or growing on the ground but with erect or rising tips. [Lat. *dēcumbēns, dēcumbent-*, pr. part. of *dēcumbere*, to lie down : *dē-*, de- + *-cumbere*, to lie down.] **—de•cum′bence** (-bəns), **de•cum′ben•cy** (-bən-sē) *n.*

dec•u•ple (dĕk′yə-pəl) *adj.* **1.** Consisting of ten parts or members. **2.** Ten times as much in size, strength, number, or amount. ❖ *n.* A number ten times larger than another. ❖ *intr. & tr.v.* **-pled, -pling, -ples** To multiply or be multiplied by ten. [ME < OFr. < LLat. *decuplus* : Lat. *decem*, ten; see **dekm̥** in App. + Lat. *-plus*, -fold.]

de•cu•ri•on (dĭ-kyo͝or′ē-ən) *n.* **1.** An officer in command of ten men in the army of ancient Rome. **2.** A member of a municipal senate in ancient Rome. [Lat. *decuriō* < *decuria*, group of ten men, administrative body of ten families < **decu-viria* : *decem*, ten; see **dekm̥** in App. + *vir*, man; see **wī-ro-** in App.]

de•cur•rent (dĭ-kûr′ənt, -kŭr′-) *adj. Botany* Having the leaf base extending down the stem below the insertion. [ME < Lat. *dēcurrēns, dēcurrent-*, pr. part. of *dēcurrere*, to run down : *dē-*, de- + *currere*, to run.] **—de•cur′rent•ly** *adv.*

de•cus•sate (dĭ-kŭs′āt′, dĕk′ə-sāt′) *tr. & intr.v.* **-sat•ed, -sat•ing, -sates** To cross or become crossed so as to form an X; intersect. ❖ *adj.* **1.** Intersected or crossed in the form of an X. **2.** *Botany* Arranged on a stem in opposite pairs at right angles to those above or below. [Lat. *decussāre, decussāt-* < *decussis*, the number ten, intersection of two lines (< the Romans' use of X for the numeral 10), a ten as coin : *decem*, ten; see **dekm̥** in App. + *assis*, as (coin).] **—de•cus′sate′ly** *adv.*

dec•us•sa•tion (dĕk′ə-sā′shən, dē′kə-) *n.* **1.** A crossing in the shape of an X. **2.** *Anatomy* An X-shaped crossing, esp. of nerves or bands of nerve fibers, connecting corresponding parts on opposite sides of the brain or spinal cord.

DEd *abbr.* Doctor of Education

de•dans (də-däN′) *n., pl.* **dedans** (-däN′, -däNz′) **1.** A screened gallery for spectators at the service end of a court tennis court. **2.** The spectators at a court tennis match. [Fr. < *dedans*, inside < OFr. *dedenz* : *de*, of, from (< Lat. *dē*; see DE–) + *denz*, within (< LLat. *deintus*, from within : Lat. *dē*, from; see DE– + Lat. *intus*, within; see **en** in App.).]

ded•i•cate (dĕd′ĭ-kāt′) *tr.v.* **-cat•ed, -cat•ing, -cates 1.** To set apart for a deity or for religious purposes; consecrate. **2.** To set apart for a special use: *dedicated their money to scientific research.* **3.** To commit (oneself) to a particular course of thought or action. **4.** To address or inscribe (a literary work, for example) to another as a mark of respect or affection. **5a.** To open (a building, for example) to public use. **b.** To show to the public for the first time: *dedicate a monument.* [ME *dedicaten* < Lat. *dēdicāre, dēdicāt-* : *dē-*, de- + *dicāre*, to proclaim; see **deik-** in App.] **—ded′i•ca′tor** *n.*

ded•i•cat•ed (dĕd′ĭ-kā′tĭd) *adj.* **1.** Wholly committed to a particular course of thought or action; devoted. **2.** Designed for a particular use or function. **—ded′i•cat′ed•ly** (-kā′tĭd-lē) *adv.*

ded•i•ca•tion (dĕd′ĭ-kā′shən) *n.* **1.** The act of dedicating or the state of being dedicated. **2.** A note prefixed to a literary or other artistic work dedicating it to someone. **3.** A rite or ceremony of dedicating. **4.** Selfless devotion. **—ded′i•ca′tive, ded′i•ca•to′ry** (-kə-tôr′ē, -tōr′ē) *adj.*

de•dif•fer•en•ti•a•tion (dē′dĭf-ə-rĕn′shē-ā′shən) *n. Biology* Regression of a specialized cell or tissue to a simpler, more embryonic unspecialized form. **—de′dif•fer•en′ti•ate′** *v.*

de•duce (dĭ-do͞os′, -dyo͞os′) *tr.v.* **-duced, -duc•ing, -duc•es 1.** To reach (a conclusion) by reasoning. **2.** To infer from a general principle; reason deductively. **3.** To trace the origin or derivation of. [ME *deducen* < Lat. *dēdūcere*, to lead away or down : *dē-*, de- + *dūcere*, to lead; see **deuk-** in App.] **—de•duc′i•ble** *adj.*

de•duct (dĭ-dŭkt′) *v.* **-duct•ed, -duct•ing, -ducts** —*tr.* **1.** To take away (a quantity) from another; subtract. **2.** To derive by deduction; deduce. —*intr.* To take away a desirable part. [ME *deducten* < Lat. *dēdūcere, dēduct-*, to lead away. See DEDUCE.]

de•duct•i•ble (dĭ-dŭk′tə-bəl) *adj.* That can be deducted, esp. with respect to income taxes: *deductible expenses.* ❖ *n.* **1.** Something, such as an expense, that can be deducted, as for income tax purposes. **2.** A clause in an insurance policy that exempts the insurer from paying a specified amount in the event of a claim. **—de•duct′i•bil′i•ty** *n.*

de•duc•tion (dĭ-dŭk′shən) *n.* **1.** The act of deducting; subtraction. **2.** An amount that is or may be deducted: *tax deductions.* **3.** *Logic* **a.** The process of reasoning in which a conclusion follows necessarily from the premises; reasoning from the general to the specific. **b.** A conclusion reached by deduction.

de•duc•tive (dĭ-dŭk′tĭv) *adj.* **1.** Of or based on deduction. **2.** Involving deduction in reasoning. **—de•duc′tive•ly** *adv.*

dee (dē) *n.* The letter *d.*

Dee 1. A river rising in the Cairngorm Mts. of E Scotland and flowing c. 145 km (90 mi) to the North Sea. **2.** A river of N Wales and W England flowing c. 113 km (70 mi) partially along the Welsh-English border to the Irish Sea.

deed (dēd) *n.* **1.** Something that is carried out; an act or action. **2.** A praiseworthy act; a feat or exploit. **3.** Action or performance in general. **4.** *Law* A document sealed as an instrument of bond, contract, or conveyance, esp. relating to property. ❖ *tr.v.* **deed•ed, deed•ing, deeds** To transfer by means of a legal deed. [ME *dede* < OE *dǣd.* See **dhē-** in App.]

dee•jay (dē′jā′) *n. Informal* A disc jockey. [Pronunciation of DJ[1].]

deem (dēm) *v.* **deemed, deem•ing, deems** —*tr.* **1.** To have as an opinion; judge. **2.** To regard as; consider: *deemed the results unsatisfactory.* See Usage Note at **as**[1]. —*intr.* To have an opinion; think. [ME *demen* < OE *dēman.* See **dhē-** in App.]

de-em•pha•size (dē-ĕm′fə-sīz′) *tr.v.* **-sized, -siz•ing, -siz•es** To decrease the emphasis on; minimize the importance of. **—de-em′pha•sis** (-sĭs) *n.*

deep (dēp) *adj.* **deep•er, deep•est 1a.** Extending far downward below a surface: *a deep hole in the road.* **b.** Extending far inward from an outer surface: *a deep cut.* **c.** Extending far backward from front to rear: *a deep closet.* **d.** Extending far from side to side from a center: *a deep yard.* **e.** Far distant down or in: *deep in*

ă	pat	oi	boy
ā	pay	ou	out
âr	care	o͝o	took
ä	father	o͞o	boot
ĕ	pet	ŭ	cut
ē	be	ûr	urge
ĭ	pit	th	thin
ī	pie	*th*	this
îr	pier	hw	which
ŏ	pot	zh	vision
ō	toe	ə	about, item
ô	paw		

Stress marks:
′ (primary);
′ (secondary), as in
lexicon (lĕk′sĭ-kŏn′)

the woods. **f.** Coming from or penetrating to a depth: *a deep sigh.* **g.** *Sports* Located or taking place near the outer boundaries of the area of play: *deep left field.* **2.** Extending a specific distance in a given direction: *snow four feet deep.* **3.** Far distant in time or space: *deep in the past.* **4a.** Difficult to penetrate or understand; recondite. **b.** Of a mysterious or obscure nature: *a deep secret.* **c.** Very learned or intellectual; wise. **5a.** Of a grave or extreme nature: *deep trouble.* **b.** Very absorbed or involved: *deep in thought.* **6.** Rich and intense in shade. Used of a color. **7.** Low in pitch; resonant. **8.** Covered or surrounded to a designated degree. Often used in combination: *waist-deep in snow.* **9.** Large in quantity or size; big. **10.** *Sports* Having a sufficient number of capable reserve players: *That team is not very deep.* ❖ *adv.* **1.** To a great depth; deeply: *dig deep.* **2.** Well along in time; late. **3.** *Sports* Close to the outer boundaries of the area of play. ❖ *n.* **1a.** A deep place in land or in a body of water. **b.** A vast, immeasurable extent. **2.** The extent of encompassing time or space; firmament. **3.** The most intense or extreme part: *the deep of night.* **4.** The ocean. **5.** *Nautical* A distance estimated in fathoms between successive marks on a sounding line. —**idiom: in deep water** In difficulty. [ME *dep* < OE *dēop.* See **dheub-** in App.] —**deep′ly** *adv.* —**deep′ness** *n.*
deep-dish (dēp′dĭsh′) *adj.* Made or used in a deep baking dish.
deep ecology *n.* A form of environmentalism that advocates radical measures to protect the natural environment regardless of their effect on the welfare of people. —**deep ecologist** *n.*
deep•en (dē′pən) *tr. & intr.v.* **-ened, -en•ing, -ens** To make or become deep or deeper.
deep freeze *n.* A condition of being held in temporary suspension or inactivity.
deep-freeze (dēp′frēz′) *tr.v.* **-froze** (-frōz′), **-fro•zen** (-frō′zən), **-freez•ing, -freez•es** **1.** To quick-freeze. **2.** To store in a frozen condition. **3.** To suspend or defer indefinitely.
deep freezer *n.* A freezer for the quick-freezing and long-term storage of food.
deep-fry (dēp′frī′) *tr.v.* **-fried, -fry•ing, -fries** To fry by immersing in a deep utensil of fat or oil.
deep fryer *n.* An appliance used for deep-frying food.
deep pocket *n.* A source of substantial wealth or financial support. Often used in the plural.
Deep River A river rising in N-central NC and flowing c. 201 km (125 mi) to the Cape Fear R.
deep-root•ed (dēp′rōo′tĭd, -rōot′ĭd) *adj.* Firmly implanted.
deep-sea (dēp′sē′) *adj.* Of, relating to, or taking place in the deeper parts of the sea: *deep-sea exploration.*
deep-seat•ed (dēp′sē′tĭd) *adj.* **1.** Being far below the surface. **2.** Deeply rooted; ingrained: *deep-seated differences.*
deep-set (dēp′sĕt′) *adj.* **1.** Deeply set or placed: *deep-set eyes.* **2.** Deep-seated: *deep-set hatred.*
deep six *n. Slang* **1.** Burial at sea. **2.** Disposal or rejection of something. [American slang, a grave, referring to the conventional depth of a grave (six feet).]
deep-six (dēp′sĭks′) *tr.v.* **-sixed, -six•ing, -six•es** *Slang* **1.** To toss overboard. **2.** To toss out; get rid of.
Deep South A region of the SE US, usu. comprising AL, GA, LA, MS, and SC.
deep space *n.* The regions beyond the gravitational influence of Earth.
deep structure *n.* In generative grammar, an abstract underlying structure from which the actual form of a sentence is derived.
deer (dîr) *n., pl.* **deer** Any of various hoofed ruminant mammals of the family Cervidae, having deciduous antlers borne chiefly by the males. [ME *der,* beast < OE *dēor.*]
deer fly or **deer•fly** (dîr′flī′) *n.* Any of various blood-sucking flies of the genus *Chrysops,* having spotted or banded wings.
deer grass *n.* See **meadow beauty.**
deer•hound (dîr′hound′) *n.* A dog of a breed developed in Scotland for hunting deer, related to the greyhound but larger and having a wiry coat.
deer mouse *n.* A North American mouse *(Peromyscus maniculatus)* having white feet and underparts and a long tail.
deer•skin (dîr′skĭn′) *n.* **1.** Leather made from the hide of a deer. **2.** A garment made from deerskin.
deer•stalk•er (dîr′stô′kər) *n.* A tight-fitting hat with visors in the front and back, originally worn by hunters.
deer tick *n.* Any of several ticks of the genus *Ixodes* that are parasitic on deer and other animals and transmit the infectious agents of febrile diseases, such as Lyme disease.
de-es•ca•late or **de•es•ca•late** (dē-ĕs′kə-lāt′) *v.* **-lat•ed, -lat•ing, -lates** —*tr.* To decrease the size, scope, or intensity of (a war, for example). —*intr.* To decrease in size, scope, or intensity. —**de-es′ca•la′tion** *n.* —**de-es′ca•la•tor′y** (-lə-tôr′ē, -tōr′ē) *adj.*
deet (dēt) *n.* A colorless oily liquid, $C_{12}H_{17}NO$, that has a mild odor and is used as an insect repellent. [< *d.t.,* abbr. of DIETHYL TOLUAMIDE.]
def (dĕf) *adj.* **def•fer, def•fest** *Slang* Excellent; first-rate. [Short for DEFINITE.]
def. *abbr.* **1.** defendant **2.** defense **3.** definite **4.** definition
de•face (dĭ-fās′) *tr.v.* **-faced, -fac•ing, -fac•es** **1.** To mar or spoil the appearance or surface of; disfigure. **2.** To impair the usefulness or value of. **3.** *Obsolete* To obliterate; destroy. [ME *de-*

deer mouse
Peromyscus maniculatus

deer tick
adult female deer tick
Ixodes scapularis

facen < OFr. *desfacier* : *des-, de-* + *face,* face; see FACE.] —**de•face′a•ble** *adj.* —**de•face′ment** *n.* —**de•fac′er** *n.*
de fac•to (dĭ făk′tō, dā) *adv.* In reality or fact; actually. ❖ *adj.* Exercising power or functioning without being legally or officially established: *a de facto government.* [Lat. *dē factō* : *dē,* from, according to + *factō,* ablative of *factum,* fact.]
de•fal•cate (dĭ-făl′kāt′, -fôl′-, dĕf′əl-) *intr.v.* **-cat•ed, -cat•ing, -cates** To misuse funds; embezzle. [Med.Lat. *dēfalcāre, dēfalcāt-,* to mow, deduct : Lat. *dē-, de-* + Lat. *falx, falc-,* sickle.] —**de′fal•ca′tion** (dē′făl-kā′shən, -fôl-, dĕf′əl-) *n.* —**de•fal′ca•tor** *n.*
def•a•ma•tion (dĕf′ə-mā′shən) *n.* The act of defaming; calumny. —**de•fam′a•to′ry** (dĭ-făm′ə-tôr′ē, -tōr′ē) *adj.*
de•fame (dĭ-fām′) *tr.v.* **-famed, -fam•ing, -fames** **1.** To damage the reputation or character of by slander or libel. **2.** *Archaic* To disgrace. [ME *defamen* < OFr. *defamer* < Med.Lat. *dēfāmāre,* alteration of Lat. *diffāmāre,* to spread news of, slander : *dis-,* abroad, apart; see DIS- + *fāma,* rumor, reputation; see **bhā-** in App.] —**de•fam′er** *n.*
de•fang (dē-făng′) *tr.v.* **-fanged, -fang•ing, -fangs** **1.** To remove the fangs of (a snake, for example). **2.** To undermine the power of; make ineffectual: *defanged the opposition.*
de•fat (dē-făt′) *tr.v.* **-fat•ted, -fat•ting, -fats** To remove fat from: *had to defat the chicken stock.*
de•fault (dĭ-fôlt′) *n.* **1.** Failure to perform a task or fulfill an obligation, esp. failure to meet a financial obligation. **2.** *Law* Failure to make a required court appearance. **3.** The failure of one or more competitors or teams to participate in a contest. **4.** *Computer Science* A particular setting or value for a variable that is assigned automatically by an operating system and remains in effect unless overridden by the operator. ❖ *v.* **-fault•ed, -fault•ing, -faults** —*intr.* **1a.** To fail to do what is required. **b.** To fail to pay money when it is due. **2.** *Law* **a.** To fail to appear in court when summoned. **b.** To lose a case by not appearing. **3.** To default a scheduled contest. —*tr.* **1.** To fail to perform or pay. **2.** *Law* To lose (a case) by failing to appear in court. **3.** To fail to take part in or complete (a contest, for example). —**idiom: in default of** Through the failure, absence, or lack of. [ME *defaute* < OFr. < p. part. of *defaillir,* to fail, grow weak : *de-,* intensive pref.; see DE- + *faillir;* see FAIL.] —**de•fault′er** *n.*
de•fea•sance (dĭ-fē′zəns) *n.* **1.** A rendering void; an annulment. **2a.** The voiding of a contract or deed. **b.** A clause within a contract or deed providing for annulment. [ME *defesaunce* < AN < OFr. *defesance* < *defesant,* pr. part. of *desfaire,* to destroy. See DEFEAT.]
de•fea•si•ble (dĭ-fē′zə-bəl) *adj.* Capable of being annulled or invalidated. —**de•fea′si•bil′i•ty, de•fea′si•ble•ness** *n.*
de•feat (dĭ-fēt′) *tr.v.* **-feat•ed, -feat•ing, -feats** **1.** To win victory over; beat. **2.** To prevent the success of; thwart. ❖ *n.* **1.** The act of defeating or state of being defeated. **2.** Failure to win. **3.** A coming to naught; frustration. [ME *defeten* < *defet,* disfigured < OFr. *desfait,* p. part. of *desfaire,* to destroy < Med.Lat. *disfacere,* to destroy, undo : Lat. *dis-,* dis- + Lat. *facere,* to do; see **dhē-** in App.] —**de•feat′er** *n.*

SYNONYMS *defeat, conquer, vanquish, beat, rout, subdue, subjugate, overcome* These verbs mean to triumph over an adversary. *Defeat* is the most general: *"Whether we defeat the enemy in one battle, or by degrees, the consequences will be the same"* (Thomas Paine). *Conquer* suggests decisive and often wide-scale victory: *"The Franks . . . having conquered the Gauls, established the kingdom which has taken its name from them"* (Alexander Hamilton). *Vanquish* emphasizes total mastery: *Napoleon's forces were vanquished at Waterloo. Beat* is similar to *defeat,* though less formal and more emphatic: *"To win battles . . . you beat the soul . . . of the enemy man"* (George S. Patton). *Rout* implies complete victory followed by the disorderly flight of the defeated force: *The enemy was routed in the first battle. Subdue* suggests mastery and control achieved by overpowering: *"It cost [the Romans] two great wars, and three great battles, to subdue that little kingdom [Macedonia]"* (Adam Smith). *Subjugate* more strongly implies reducing an opponent to submission: *"The last foreigner to subjugate England was a Norman duke in the Middle Ages named William"* (Stanley Meisler). To *overcome* is to prevail over, often by persevering: *overcome an enemy; overcome a disability.*

de•feat•ism (dĭ-fē′tĭz′əm) *n.* Acceptance of or resignation to the prospect of defeat. —**de•feat′ist** *adj. & n.*
def•e•cate (dĕf′ĭ-kāt′) *v.* **-cat•ed, -cat•ing, -cates** —*intr.* To void feces. —*tr.* **1.** To remove (impurities, as in a solution). **2.** To void (feces) from the bowels. [Lat. *dēfaecāre,* to clean the dregs from : *dē-, de-* + *faex, faec-,* dregs.] —**def′e•ca′tion** *n.* —**def′e•ca′tor** *n.*
de•fect (dē′fĕkt′, dĭ-fĕkt′) *n.* **1.** The lack of something necessary or desirable for completion or perfection. **2.** An imperfection that causes inadequacy or failure; a shortcoming. ❖ *intr.v.* (dĭ-fĕkt′) **-fect•ed, -fect•ing, -fects** **1.** To disown allegiance to one's country and take up residence in another. **2.** To abandon a position or association, often to join an opposing group. [ME < Lat. *dēfectus,* failure, want < p. part. of *dēficere,* to desert, be wanting : *dē-, de-* + *facere,* to do; see **dhē-** in App.] —**de•fec′tion** *n.* —**de•fec′tor** *n.*
de•fec•tive (dĭ-fĕk′tĭv) *adj.* **1a.** Having a defect; faulty. **b.**

Marked by subnormal structure, function, intelligence, or behavior. **2.** *Grammar* Lacking one or more of the inflected forms normal for a particular kind of word, as the verb *may*. ❖ *n. Offensive* One who is physically or mentally deficient. **—de·fec′tive·ly** *adv.* **—de·fec′tive·ness** *n.*

de·fence (dĭ-fĕns′) *n. & v. Chiefly British* Variant of **defense.**

de·fend (dĭ-fĕnd′) *v.* **-fend·ed, -fend·ing, -fends** *—tr.* **1.** To make or keep safe from danger, attack, or harm. **2.** *Sports* **a.** To attempt to prevent the opposition from scoring while playing in or near (a goal, for example). **b.** To be responsible for guarding (an opposing player). **c.** To compete against a challenger in an attempt to retain (a championship). **3.** To support or maintain, as by argument or action; justify. **4.** *Law* **a.** To represent (a defendant) in a civil or criminal action. **b.** To attempt to disprove or invalidate (an action or claim). *—intr.* **1.** To make a defense. **2.** *Sports* To play defense. [ME *defenden* < OFr. *defendre* < Lat. *dēfendere,* to ward off. See **gʷhen-** in App.] **—de·fend′a·ble** *adj.* **—de·fend′er** *n.*

SYNONYMS defend, protect, guard, preserve, shield, safeguard These verbs mean to make or keep safe from danger, attack, or harm. *Defend* implies repelling an attack: *defending her territory. Protect* often suggests providing a barrier to discomfort, injury, or attack: *bought a dog to protect the children. Guard* suggests keeping watch: *guarded the house against intruders.* To *preserve* is to take measures to maintain something in safety: *ecologists working to preserve our resources. Shield* suggests protecting with a piece of defensive armor: *His lawyers tried to shield him from reporters. Safeguard* stresses protection against potential danger: *The Bill of Rights safeguards our individual liberties.*

de·fen·dant (dĭ-fĕn′dənt, -dănt′) *n. Law* The party against which an action is brought.

de·fen·es·tra·tion (dē-fĕn′ĭ-strā′shən) *n.* An act of throwing someone or something out of a window. [< DE– + Lat. *fenestra,* window.] **—de·fen′es·trate′** *v.*

de·fense (dĭ-fĕns′) *n.* **1.** The act of defending against attack, danger, or injury. **2.** A means or method of defending or protecting. **3.** An argument in support or justification of something. **4.** *Law* **a.** The action of the defendant in opposition to complaints against him or her. **b.** The defendant and his or her legal counsel. **5.** The science or art of defending oneself; self-defense. **6.** (*often* dē′fĕns′) *Sports* **a.** The means or tactics used in trying to stop the opposition from scoring. **b.** The team or those players on the team attempting to stop the opposition from scoring. **c.** The act or an instance of defending a championship against a challenger. **7.** The military, governmental, and industrial complex, esp. as it manages weaponry production. ❖ *tr.v.* **-fensed, -fens·ing, -fens·es** *Sports* To attempt to stop (the opposition) from scoring. [ME < OFr. < Lat. *dēfēnsa* < fem. p. part. of *dēfendere,* to ward off. See DEFEND.] **—de·fense′less** *adj.* **—de·fense′less·ly** *adv.* **—de·fense′less·ness** *n.*

de·fense·man (dĭ-fĕns′mən, -măn′) *n.* A team member, as in hockey, who plays a defensive zone or position.

defense mechanism *n.* **1.** *Biology* A physiological reaction of an organism used in self-protection, as against infection. **2.** *Psychology* Any of various usu. unconscious mental processes that protect the ego from shame, anxiety, or other unacceptable feelings or thoughts.

de·fen·si·ble (dĭ-fĕn′sə-bəl) *adj.* Capable of being defended, protected, or justified: *defensible arguments.* **—de·fen′si·bil′i·ty, de·fen′si·ble·ness** *n.* **—de·fen′si·bly** *adv.*

de·fen·sive (dĭ-fĕn′sĭv) *adj.* **1.** Intended or appropriate for defending; protective. **2a.** Intended to withstand or deter aggression or attack. **b.** Of or relating to the effort to prevent an opponent from gaining points in a game or athletic contest. **c.** Performed so as to avoid risk, danger, or legal liability: *defensive medicine.* **3.** *Psychology* Constantly protecting oneself from criticism or other real or perceived threats to the ego. ❖ *n.* **1.** A means of defense. **2.** An attitude or position of defense. **—idiom: on the defensive** Prepared to withstand or counter aggression or attack. **—de·fen′sive·ly** *adv.* **—de·fen′sive·ness** *n.*

de·fer¹ (dĭ-fûr′) *v.* **-ferred, -fer·ring, -fers** *—tr.* **1.** To put off; postpone. **2.** To postpone the induction of (one eligible for the military draft). *—intr.* To procrastinate. [ME *differen,* to postpone, alter. See DIFFER.] **—de·fer′ra·ble** *adj.* **—de·fer′rer** *n.*

de·fer² (dĭ-fûr′) *v.* **-ferred, -fer·ring, -fers** *—intr.* To submit to the opinion or wishes of another through respect or recognition of authority. See Syns at **yield.** *—tr.* To commit or entrust to another. [ME *deferen* < OFr. *deferer* < Lat. *dēferre,* to carry away, refer to : *dē-,* de– + *ferre,* to carry; see **bher-¹** in App.] **—de·fer′rer** *n.*

def·er·ence (dĕf′ər-əns, dĕf′rəns) *n.* **1.** Submission or courteous yielding to the opinion or wishes of another. **2.** Courteous respect.

def·er·ent¹ (dĕf′ər-ənt, dĕf′rənt) *adj.* Showing deference; deferential.

def·er·ent² (dĕf′ər-ənt, dĕf′rənt) *adj.* **1.** *Anatomy* Carrying down or away. Used of a duct or vessel. **2.** Serving or adapted to carry or transport. [ME *deferent* < Lat. *dēferēns, dēferent-,* pr. part. of *dēferre,* to carry away. See DEFER².]

def·er·en·tial (dĕf′ə-rĕn′shəl) *adj.* Marked by or exhibiting

---

deference. **—def′er·en′tial·ly** *adv.*

de·fer·ment (dĭ-fûr′mənt) *n.* **1.** The act or an instance of delaying or putting off. **2.** Officially sanctioned postponement of compulsory military service.

de·fer·ral (dĭ-fûr′əl) *n.* Deferment.

de·ferred (dĭ-fûrd′) *adj.* **1.** Postponed or delayed: *deferred gratification.* **2.** Withheld until a future date.

de·fer·ves·cence (dē′fər-vĕs′əns) *n.* The abatement of a fever. [< Lat. *dēfervēscēns, dēfervēscent-,* pr. part. of *dēfervēscere,* to stop boiling, cool off : *dē-,* de– + *fervēscere,* to grow hot, inchoative of *fervēre,* to be hot, boil.] **—de′fer·ves′cent** *adj.*

de·fi·ance (dĭ-fī′əns) *n.* **1.** The act or an example of defying; bold resistance to an opposing force or authority. **2.** Intentionally contemptuous behavior or attitude; readiness to contend or resist. **—idiom: in defiance of** In spite of; contrary to. [ME *defiaunce* < OFr. *desfiance* < *desfier,* to defy. See DEFY.]

de·fi·ant (dĭ-fī′ənt) *adj.* Marked by defiance; boldly resisting. **—de·fi′ant·ly** *adv.*

de·fib·ril·late (dē-fĭb′rə-lāt′, -fī′brə-) *tr.v.* **-lat·ed, -lat·ing, -lates** To stop the fibrillation of (a heart) and restore normal contractions through the use of drugs or an electric shock. **—de·fib′ril·la′tion** *n.*

de·fib·ril·la·tor (dē-fĭb′rə-lā′tər, -fī′brə-) *n.* A device used to defibrillate the heart by applying an electric shock.

de·fi·cien·cy (dĭ-fĭsh′ən-sē) *n., pl.* **-cies 1.** The quality or condition of being deficient; incompleteness or inadequacy. **2.** A lack or shortage, esp. of something essential to health.

deficiency disease *n.* A disease, such as rickets or scurvy, that is caused by a dietary deficiency of specific nutrients, esp. a vitamin or mineral.

de·fi·cient (dĭ-fĭsh′ənt) *adj.* **1.** Lacking an essential quality or element. **2.** Inadequate in amount or degree; insufficient. [Lat. *dēficiēns, dēficient-,* pr. part. of *dēficere,* to fail, be wanting. See DEFECT.] **—de·fi′cient·ly** *adv.*

def·i·cit (dĕf′ĭ-sĭt) *n.* **1a.** Inadequacy or insufficiency. **b.** A deficiency or impairment in mental or physical functioning. **c.** An unfavorable condition or position; a disadvantage. **2a.** The amount by which a sum of money falls short of the required or expected amount; a shortage. **b.** A business loss. [Fr. *déficit* < Lat. *déficit,* it is lacking, third pers. sing. pr. t. of *dēficere,* to fail, be lacking. See DEFECT.]

deficit spending *n.* The spending of public funds obtained by borrowing rather than by taxation.

de·fi·er (dĭ-fī′ər) *n.* One that defies: *a defier of tradition.*

def·i·lade (dĕf′ə-lād′, -läd′) *tr.v.* **-lad·ed, -lad·ing, -lades** To arrange (fortifications) in such a way as to give protection from enfilading and other fire. ❖ *n.* **1.** The act or procedure of defilading. **2.** A fortified position offering protection from enfilading and other fire. [DE– + (EN)FILADE.]

de·file¹ (dĭ-fīl′) *tr.v.* **-filed, -fil·ing, -files 1.** To make filthy or dirty; pollute. **2.** To debase the pureness or excellence of; corrupt. **3.** To profane or sully (a reputation, for example). **4.** To make unclean or unfit for ceremonial use; desecrate. **5.** To violate the chastity of. [ME *defilen,* alteration (influenced by *filen* < OE *fȳlan;* see **pū-** in App.) of *defoulen,* to trample on, abuse, pollute < OFr. *defouler,* to trample, full cloth : *de-,* de– + *fouler,* to trample, beat down; see FULL².] **—de·file′ment** *n.* **—de·fil′er** *n.* **—de·fil′ing·ly** *adv.*

de·file² (dĭ-fīl′) *intr.v.* **-filed, -fil·ing, -files** To march in single file or in files or columns. ❖ *n.* **1.** A narrow gorge or pass that restricts lateral movement, as of troops. **2.** A march in a line. [Fr. *défiler* : *dé-,* away, off (< OFr. *de-;* see DE–) + *file,* line, file (< OFr. *filer,* to spin thread, march in line; see FILE¹). N. < Fr. *défilé* < p. part. of *défiler.*]

de·fine (dĭ-fīn′) *v.* **-fined, -fin·ing, -fines** *—tr.* **1a.** To state the precise meaning of (a word, for example). **b.** To describe the nature or basic qualities of; explain: *a study that defines people according to their incomes.* **2a.** To delineate the outline or form of. **b.** To specify distinctly: *define the software's new features.* **3.** To give form or meaning to; characterize: *"For him, a life is defined by action"* (Jay Parini). *—intr.* To make or write a definition. [ME *definen, diffinen* < OFr. *definir, diffiner* < Lat. *dēfīnīre,* to limit, determine : *dē-,* intensive pref. + *fīnis,* boundary, limit.] **—de·fin′a·bil′i·ty** *n.* **—de·fin′a·ble** *adj.* **—de·fin′a·bly** *adv.* **—de·fine′ment** *n.* **—de·fin′er** *n.*

de·fin·i·en·dum (dĭ-fĭn′ē-ĕn′dəm) *n., pl.* **-da** (-də) A word or expression that is being defined. [Lat. *dēfīniendum,* neut. gerundive of *dēfīnīre,* to define. See DEFINE.]

de·fin·i·ens (dĭ-fĭn′ē-ĕnz′) *n., pl.* **-en·ti·a** (-ĕn′shē-ə, -shə) The word or words serving to define another word or expression, as in a dictionary entry. [Lat. *dēfīniēns,* pr. part. of *dēfīnīre,* to define.]

def·i·nite (dĕf′ə-nĭt) *adj.* **1.** Having distinct limits: *definite restrictions on smoking.* **2.** Indisputable; certain: *a definite victory.* **3.** Clearly defined; explicitly precise. **4.** *Grammar* Limiting or particularizing. **5.** *Botany* **a.** Of a specified number not exceeding 20, as certain floral organs, esp. stamens. **b.** Cymose; determinate. [ME *diffinite,* defined < Lat. *dēfīnītus,* p. part. of *dēfīnīre,* to define. See DEFINE.] **—def′i·nite·ly** *adv.* **—def′i·nite·ness** *n.*

USAGE NOTE *Definite* and *definitive* both apply to what is pre-

---

ă pat   oi boy
ā pay   ou out
âr care   oŏ took
ä father   oō boot
ĕ pet   ŭ cut
ē be   ûr urge
ĭ pie   th thin
ĭ pie   th this
îr pier   hw which
ŏ pot   zh vision
ō toe   ə about,
ô paw   item

Stress marks:
′ (primary);
′ (secondary), as in
lexicon (lĕk′sĭ-kŏn′)

cisely defined or explicitly set forth. But *definitive* generally refers specifically to a judgment or description that serves as a standard or reference point for others, as in *the definitive decision of the court* (which sets forth a final resolution of a judicial matter).

definite article *n.* A member of the class of determiners that restricts or particularizes a noun, as *the* in English.

definite integral *n.* An integral that is calculated between two specified limits, usu. expressed as $\int_a^b f(x)dx$, whose value is the area bounded by the curve $f(x)$, the limits a and b, and the x-axis.

def·i·ni·tion (dĕf′ə-nĭsh′ən) *n.* **1a.** A statement conveying fundamental character. **b.** A statement of the meaning of a word, phrase, or term. **2.** The act or process of stating a precise meaning or significance; formulation of a meaning. **3a.** The act of making clear and distinct. **b.** The state of being closely outlined or determined. **4a.** The clarity of detail in an optically produced image, such as a photograph, effected by a combination of resolution and contrast. **b.** The degree of clarity with which a televised image or broadcast signal is received. [ME *diffinicioun* < OFr. *definition* < Lat. *dēfīnītiō-, dēfīnītiōn-* < *dēfīnītus*, p. part. of *dēfīnīre*, to define. See DEFINE.] —**def′i·ni′tion·al** *adj.*

de·fin·i·tive (dĭ-fĭn′ĭ-tĭv) *adj.* **1.** Precisely defined or explicit. **2.** Supplying or being a final settlement or decision; conclusive. **3.** Authoritative and complete: *a definitive biography.* See Usage Note at **definite. 4.** *Biology* Fully formed or developed, as an organ or structure. ❖ *n. Grammar* A word that defines or limits, such as the definite article. —**de·fin′i·tive·ly** *adv.* —**de·fin′i·tive·ness** *n.*

definitive host *n.* An organism in or on which a parasite develops to an adult or sexually mature stage.

def·in·i·tude (dĭ-fĭn′ĭ-tōōd′, -tyōōd′) *n.* The quality of being definite or exact; precision.

def·la·grate (dĕf′lə-grāt′) *intr. & tr.v.* **-grat·ed, -grat·ing, -grates** To burn or cause to burn with great heat and intense light. [Lat. *dēflagrāre, dēflagrāt-* : *dē-*, intensive pref.; see DE- + *flagrāre*, to blaze.] —**def′la·gra′tion** *n.*

de·flate (dĭ-flāt′) *v.* **-flat·ed, -flat·ing, -flates** —*tr.* **1a.** To release contained air or gas from. **b.** To collapse by releasing contained air or gas. **2.** To reduce the size or importance of. **3.** *Economics* **a.** To reduce the amount or availability of (currency or credit), effecting a decline in prices. **b.** To produce deflation in (an economy). —*intr.* To be or become deflated. [DE- + (IN)FLATE.] —**de·fla′tor** *n.*

de·fla·tion (dĭ-flā′shən) *n.* **1.** The act of deflating or the condition of being deflated. **2.** A persistent decrease in the level of consumer prices or a persistent increase in the purchasing power of money because of a reduction in available currency and credit. **3.** The erosion and transport of loose particles, as sand in a desert, by wind. —**de·fla′tion·ar′y** (-shə-nĕr′ē) *adj.* —**de·fla′tion·ist** *n.*

de·flect (dĭ-flĕkt′) *intr. & tr.v.* **-flect·ed, -flect·ing, -flects** To turn aside or cause to turn aside; bend or deviate. [Lat. *dēflectere* : *dē-*, de- + *flectere*, to bend.] —**de·flect′a·ble** *adj.* —**de·flec′tive** *adj.* —**de·flec′tor** *n.*

de·flec·tion (dĭ-flĕk′shən) *n.* **1.** The act of deflecting or the condition of being deflected. **2.** Deviation or a specified amount of deviation. **3.** The deviation of an indicator of a measuring instrument from zero or from its normal position.

de·flexed (dĭ-flĕkst′, dē′flĕkst′) *adj. Botany* Bent or turned downward at a sharp angle: *deflexed petals.* [< Lat. *dēflexus*, p. part. of *dēflectere*, to bend. See DEFLECT.]

de·flex·ion (dĭ-flĕk′shən) *n. Chiefly British* Variant of **deflection.**

def·lo·ra·tion (dĕf′lə-rā′shən) *n.* **1.** The act of deflowering. **2.** Rupture of the hymen, typically in sexual intercourse. [ME *defloracioun* < LLat. *dēflōrātiō, dēflōrātiōn-* < *dēflōrātus*, p. part. of *dēflōrāre*, to deflower. See DEFLOWER.]

de·flow·er (dē-flou′ər) *tr.v.* **-ered, -er·ing, -ers 1.** To take away the virginity of (a woman). **2.** To destroy the innocence, integrity, or beauty of; ravage. [ME *deflouren* < OFr. *defflourer* < LLat. *dēflōrāre* : Lat. *dē-*, de- + Lat. *flōs, flōr-*, flower; see *bhel-* in App.] —**de·flow′er·er** *n.*

de·fo·cus (dē-fō′kəs) *tr.v.* **-cused, -cus·ing, -cus·es** or **-cussed, -cus·sing, -cus·ses** To cause (a beam or a lens) to deviate from accurate focus. ❖ *n.* The act or result of defocusing a lens.

De·foe (dĭ-fō′), **Daniel** 1660–1731. British writer whose works include *Robinson Crusoe* (1719).

de·fog (dē-fôg′, -fŏg′) *tr.v.* **-fogged, -fog·ging, -fogs** To remove condensed water vapor from. —**de·fog′ger** *n.*

de·fo·li·ant (dē-fō′lē-ənt) *n.* A chemical sprayed or dusted on plants to cause the leaves to fall off.

de·fo·li·ate (dē-fō′lē-āt′) *v.* **-at·ed, -at·ing, -ates** —*tr.* **1.** To deprive of foliage. **2.** To cause the leaves to fall off of, esp. by the use of chemicals. —*intr.* To lose foliage. [LLat. *dēfoliāre, dēfoliāt-* : Lat. *dē-*, de- + Lat. *folium*, leaf; see *bhel-* in App.] —**de·fo′li·ate** (-ĭt) *adj.* —**de·fo′li·a′tion** *n.* —**de·fo′li·a′tor** *n.*

de·force (dē-fôrs′, -fōrs′) *tr.v.* **-forced, -forc·ing, -forc·es** *Law* To withhold (something) by force from the rightful owner. [ME *deforcen* < AN *deforcer* < OFr. *desforcier* : *des-*, de- + *forcier*, to

Charles de Gaulle

force (< VLat. **fortiāre* < Lat. *fortis*, strong; see *bhergh-* in App.] —**de·force′ment** *n.*

de·for·est (dē-fôr′ĭst, -fŏr′-) *tr.v.* **-est·ed, -est·ing, -ests** To cut down and clear away the trees or forests from. —**de·for′es·ta′tion** (-ĭ-stā′shən) *n.* —**de·for′est·er** *n.*

De For·est (dĭ fôr′ĭst, fŏr′-), **Lee** 1873–1961. Amer. electrical engineer and originator of radio news broadcasts (1916).

de·form (dĭ-fôrm′) *v.* **-formed, -form·ing, -forms** —*tr.* **1.** To spoil the natural form of; misshape. **2.** To spoil the beauty or appearance of; disfigure. **3.** *Physics* To alter the shape of by pressure or stress. **4.** *Geology* To change the original state of (a rock mass), esp. by folding. —*intr.* To become deformed. [ME *deformen* < OFr. *deformer* < Lat. *dēfōrmāre* : *dē-*, de- + *fōrma*, form; see BHEL[1].] —**de·form′a·bil′i·ty** *n.* —**de·form′a·ble** *adj.*

de·for·ma·tion (dē′fôr-mā′shən, dĕf′ər-) *n.* **1a.** The act or process of deforming. **b.** The condition of being deformed. **2.** An alteration of form for the worse. **3.** *Physics* **a.** An alteration of shape, as by pressure or stress. **b.** The resultant shape. —**de·for·ma′tion·al** *adj.*

de·formed (dĭ-fôrmd′) *adj.* Distorted in form; misshapen.

de·for·mi·ty (dĭ-fôr′mĭ-tē) *n., pl.* **-ties 1.** The state of being deformed. **2.** A bodily malformation, distortion, or disfigurement. **3.** One that is deformed. **4.** Gross ugliness or distortion.

de·frag (dĭ-frăg′) *tr.v.* **-fragged, -frag·ging, -frags** *Informal* To defragment. —**de·frag′ger** *n.*

de·frag·ment (dĭ-frăg′mənt) *tr.v.* **-ment·ed, -ment·ing, -ments** To reorganize (a computer file) to eliminate fragmentation. —**de·frag′men·ta′tion** (-mən-tā′shən, -mĕn-) *n.* —**de·frag′ment·er** *n.*

de·fraud (dĭ-frôd′) *tr.v.* **-fraud·ed, -fraud·ing, -frauds** To take something from by fraud; swindle. [ME *defrauden* < OFr. *defrauder* < Lat. *dēfraudāre* : *dē-*, de- + *fraudāre*, to cheat (< *fraus, fraud-*, fraud).] —**de′fraud·a′tion** (dē′frô-dā′shən) *n.* —**de·fraud′er** *n.*

de·fray (dĭ-frā′) *tr.v.* **-frayed, -fray·ing, -frays** To undertake the payment of (costs or expenses); pay. [Fr. *défrayer* < OFr. *desfrayer* : *des-*, de- + **frai*, expense (< Lat. *frāctum* < neut. p. part. of *frangere*, to break; see *bhreg-* in App.).] —**de·fray′al** *n.*

de·frock (dĭ-frŏk′) *tr.v.* **-frocked, -frock·ing, -frocks 1.** To strip of priestly privileges and functions. **2.** To deprive of the right to practice a profession. **3.** To deprive of an honorary position.

de·frost (dē-frôst′, -frŏst′) *v.* **-frost·ed, -frost·ing, -frosts** —*tr.* **1.** To remove ice or frost from. **2.** To cause to thaw. —*intr.* **1.** To become free of ice or frost. **2.** To become thawed.

de·frost·er (dē-frô′stər, -frŏs′tər) *n.* **1.** A device to remove or prevent frost. **2.** A device that thaws frozen goods.

deft (dĕft) *adj.* **deft·er, deft·est** Quick and skillful; adroit. See Syns at **dexterous.** [ME, gentle, humble, var. of *dafte*, foolish. See DAFT.] —**deft′ly** *adv.* —**deft′ness** *n.*

de·fu·el (dē-fyōō′əl) *tr.v.* **-eled, -el·ing, -els** also **-elled, -el·ling, -els** To remove the fuel from: *defuel a rocket.*

de·funct (dĭ-fŭngkt′) *adj.* Having ceased to exist or live. [Lat. *dēfūnctus*, p. part. of *dēfūngī*, to finish : *dē-*, de- + *fungī*, to perform.] —**de·func′tive** *adj.* —**de·funct′ness** *n.*

de·fund (dē-fŭnd′) *tr.v.* **-fund·ed, -fund·ing, -funds** To stop the flow of funds to: *defund a federal program.*

de·fuse (dē-fyōōz′) *tr.v.* **-fused, -fus·ing, -fus·es 1.** To remove the fuse from (an explosive device). **2.** To make less dangerous, tense, or hostile.

de·fy (dĭ-fī′) *tr.v.* **-fied, -fy·ing, -fies 1a.** To oppose or resist with boldness and assurance. **b.** To refuse to submit to or cooperate with. **2.** To be unaffected by; resist or withstand. **3.** To challenge or dare (someone) to do something. [ME *defien* < OFr. *desfier* < VLat. **disfīdāre* : Lat. *dis-*, dis- + Lat. *fīdus*, faithful; see *bheidh-* in App.]

deg. *abbr.* degree

dé·ga·gé (dā′gä-zhā′) *adj.* Free and relaxed in manner; casual. [Fr., p. part. of *dégager*, to disengage < OFr. *desgagier* : *des-*, de- + *gage*, pledge (of Gmc. orig.).]

De·ga·na·wi·dah (də-gä′nə-wē′də) fl. 1550–1600. Huron leader, legendary founder with Hiawatha of the Iroquois confederacy.

De·gas (də-gä′), **(Hilaire Germain) Edgar** 1834–1917. French painter and sculptor noted for his studies of ballet dancers.

de Gaulle (də gōl′, gôl′), **Charles André Joseph Marie** 1890–1970. French general and politician who was the first president (1959–69) of the Fifth Republic.

de·gauss (dē-gous′) *tr.v.* **-gaussed, -gauss·ing, -gauss·es 1.** To neutralize the magnetic field of (a ship, for example). **2.** To erase information from (a magnetic disk or other storage device). [DE- + GAUSS.] —**de·gauss′er** *n.*

de·gen·er·a·cy (dĭ-jĕn′ər-ə-sē) *n., pl.* **-cies 1.** The process of degenerating. **2.** The state of being degenerate. **3.** Corrupt, vulgar, vicious behavior, esp. sexual. **4.** *Genetics* The presence in a genetic code of multiple codons for the same amino acid.

de·gen·er·ate (dĭ-jĕn′ər-ĭt) *adj.* **1.** Having declined, as in function or nature, from a former or original state. **2.** Having fallen to an inferior or undesirable state, esp. mentally or morally. **3.** *Physics* Relating to two or more quantum states that share the same quantum numbers: *degenerate energy levels.* **4.** *Physics*

Characterized by great density and consisting of atoms stripped of electrons: *degenerate matter.* **5.** *Medicine* Characterized by degeneration, as of tissue. **6.** *Biology* Having lost one or more highly developed functions, characteristics, or structures through evolution. **7.** *Genetics* **a.** Coding for the same amino acid as another codon. **b.** Having more than one codon that may code for the same amino acid. ❖ *n.* **1.** A depraved, corrupt, or vicious person. **2.** A person lacking or having progressively lost normative biological or psychological characteristics. ❖ *intr.v.* (-ə-rāt′) **-at·ed, -at·ing, -ates 1.** To fall below a normal or desirable state, esp. functionally or morally; deteriorate. **2.** To decline in quality. **3.** To undergo degeneration. [Lat. *dēgenerātus*, p. part. of *dēgenerāre,* to depart from one's own kind, deteriorate : *dē-,* de- + *genus, gener-,* race; see **genə-** in App.] —**de·gen′er·ate·ly** *adv.* —**de·gen′er·ate·ness** *n.*

de·gen·er·a·tion (dĭ-jĕn′ə-rā′shən) *n.* **1.** The process of degenerating. **2.** The state of being degenerate. **3.** *Medicine* Gradual deterioration of specific tissues, cells, or organs with corresponding impairment or loss of function. **4.** *Biology* The evolutionary decline or loss of a function, characteristic, or structure in an organism or species. **5.** *Electronics* Loss of or gain in power in an amplifier caused by unintentional negative feedback.

de·gen·er·a·tive (dĭ-jĕn′ər-ə-tĭv) *adj.* Of, relating to, causing, or characterized by degeneration: *a degenerative disease.*

degenerative joint disease *n.* See **osteoarthritis.**

de·gla·ci·a·tion (dē-glā′shē-ā′shən, -sē-) *n.* The uncovering of glaciated land because of melting or sublimation of the glacier.

de·glam·or·ize (dē-glăm′ə-rīz′) *tr.v.* **-ized, -iz·ing, -iz·es** To make less glamorous.

de·glaze (dē-glāz′) *tr.v.* **-glazed, -glaz·ing, -glaz·es 1.** To remove glaze from (pottery, for example). **2.** To dissolve what remains of a sauté or roast in (a pan or pot) by heating with liquid.

de·glu·ti·nate (dē-glōōt′n-āt′) *tr.v.* **-nat·ed, -nat·ing, -nates** To extract the gluten from (wheat flour, for example). [Lat. *dēglūtināre, dēglūtināt- : dē-,* de- + *glūten, glutin-,* glue.] —**de·glu′ti·na′tion** *n.*

de·glu·ti·tion (dē′glōō-tĭsh′ən) *n.* The act or process of swallowing. [Fr. *déglutition* < *déglutir,* to swallow < Lat. *dēglūtīre : dē-,* de- + *glūtīre,* to gulp.] —**de·glu′ti·to·ry** (-tĭ-tôr′ē, -tōr′ē) *adj.*

de·grad·a·ble (dĭ-grā′də-bəl) *adj.* That can be chemically degraded: *degradable paper products.* —**de·grad′a·bil′i·ty** *n.*

deg·ra·da·tion (dĕg′rə-dā′shən) *n.* **1.** The act or process of degrading. **2.** The state of being degraded; degeneration. **3.** A decline to a lower condition, quality, or level. **4.** *Geology* A general lowering of the earth's surface by erosion or weathering. **5.** *Chemistry* Decomposition of a compound by stages, exhibiting well-defined intermediate products. —**deg′ra·da′tive** *adj.*

de·grade (dĭ-grād′) *v.* **-grad·ed, -grad·ing, -grades** —*tr.* **1.** To reduce in grade, rank, or status; demote. **2.** To lower in dignity; dishonor or disgrace. **3.** To lower in moral or intellectual character; debase. **4.** To reduce in worth or value: *degrade a currency.* **5.** To impair in physical structure or function. **6.** *Geology* To lower or wear by erosion or weathering. **7.** To cause (an organic compound) to undergo degradation. —*intr.* **1.** To fall below a normal state; deteriorate. **2.** To undergo degradation; decompose. [ME *degraden* < OFr. *degrader* < LLat. *dēgradāre* : Lat. *dē-,* de- + Lat. *gradus,* step; see **ghredh-** in App.] —**de·grad′er** *n.*

SYNONYMS *degrade, abase, debase, demean, humble, humiliate* These verbs mean to deprive of self-esteem or self-worth. *Degrade* implies reduction to a state of shame or disgrace: *"If I pitied you for crying . . . you should spurn such pity. . . . Rise, and don't degrade yourself into an abject reptile!"* (Emily Brontë). *Abase* refers principally to loss of rank or prestige: *"He would . . . abase himself like a worm before the injured damsel"* (Louisa May Alcott). *Debase* implies reduction in quality or value: *"debasing the moral currency"* (George Eliot). *Demean* suggests lowering in social position: *"It puts him where he can make the advances without demeaning himself"* (William Dean Howells). *Humble* refers to lowering in rank or to reducing in pride: *Loss humbled him.* To *humiliate* is to subject to loss of self-respect or dignity: *a humiliating defeat.*

de·grad·ed (dĭ-grā′dĭd) *adj.* **1.** Reduced in rank, dignity, or esteem. **2.** Having been corrupted or depraved. **3.** Having been reduced in quality or value. —**de·grad′ed·ly** *adv.* —**de·grad′ed·ness** *n.*

de·grad·ing (dĭ-grā′dĭng) *adj.* Tending or intended to degrade. —**de·grad′ing·ly** *adv.*

de·gran·u·la·tion (dē-grăn′yə-lā′shən) *n.* The process of losing granules.

de·grease (dē-grēs′, -grēz′) *tr.v.* **-greased, -greas·ing, -greas·es** To remove grease from. —**de·greas′er** *n.*

de·gree (dĭ-grē′) *n.* **1.** One of a series of steps in a process, course, or progression; a stage. **2.** A step in a direct hereditary line of descent or ascent. **3.** Relative social or official rank, dignity, or position. **4.** Relative intensity or amount, as of a quality or attribute: *degree of accuracy.* **5.** The extent or measure of a state of being, an action, or a relation. **6.** A unit division of a temperature scale. **7.** *Mathematics* A planar unit of angular measure equal in magnitude to ⅟₃₆₀ of a complete revolution. **8.** A unit of latitude or longitude, equal to ⅟₃₆₀ of a great circle. **9.** *Mathematics* **a.** The

greatest sum of the exponents of the variables in a term of a polynomial or polynomial equation. **b.** The exponent of the derivative of highest order in a differential equation in standard form. **10a.** An academic title given by a college or university to a student who has completed a course of study. **b.** A similar title conferred as an honorary distinction. **11.** *Law* A division or classification of a specific crime according to its seriousness: *second-degree murder.* **12.** A classification of the severity of an injury, esp. a burn: *a third-degree burn.* **13.** *Grammar* One of the forms used in the comparison of adjectives and adverbs. **14.** *Music* **a.** One of the seven notes of a diatonic scale. **b.** A space or line of the staff. —*idioms:* **by degrees** Little by little; gradually. **to a degree** To a small extent; in a limited way. [ME *degre* < OFr. < VLat. **dēgradus* : Lat. *dē-,* de- + Lat. *gradus,* step; see **ghredh-** in App.]

de·greed (dĭ-grēd′) *adj.* Having or requiring an academic degree.

de·gree-day (dĭ-grē′dā′) *n.* A unit of measurement equal to a difference of one degree between the mean outdoor temperature on a certain day and a reference temperature.

degree of freedom *n., pl.* **degrees of freedom 1.** *Statistics* Any of the unrestricted independent random variables that constitute a statistic. **2.** *Physics* **a.** Any of the minimum number of coordinates required to specify completely the motion of a mechanical system. **b.** Any of the independent thermodynamic variables, such as pressure, required to specify a system with a given number of phases and components.

de·gres·sion (dĭ-grĕsh′ən, dē-) *n.* A descent by stages or steps. [ME < Med.Lat. *dēgressiō, dēgressiōn-,* descent < Lat. *dēgressus,* p. part. of *dēgredī,* to step down : *dē-,* de- + *gradī,* to step; see **ghredh-** in App.] —**de·gres′sive** *adj.*

de·gust (dĭ-gŭst′, dē-) *tr.v.* **-gust·ed, -gust·ing, -gusts** To taste with relish; savor. [Lat. *dēgustāre : dē-,* de- + *gustāre,* to taste; see **geus-** in App.] —**de·gus′ta′tion** (dē′gŭ-stā′shən) *n.*

de·hisce (dĭ-hĭs′) *intr.v.* **-hisced, -hisc·ing, -hisc·es 1.** *Botany* To open at definite places, discharging seeds or other contents. **2.** *Medicine* To rupture or break open. [Lat. *dehīscere : dē-,* de- + *hīscere,* to split, inchoative of *hiāre,* to be open.]

de·his·cence (dĭ-hĭs′əns) *n.* **1.** *Botany* An opening at definite places at maturity to release or expose the contents, such as seeds from a fruit. **2.** *Medicine* A splitting open or a rupture, as of a surgical wound. —**de·his′cent** *adj.*

de·horn (dē-hôrn′) *tr.v.* **-horned, -horn·ing, -horns 1.** To remove the horns from. **2.** To prevent growth in the horns of (cattle, for example), as by cauterization.

Deh·ra Dun (dā′rə dōōn′) A city of N India NNE of Delhi. Pop. 270,159.

de·hu·man·ize (dē-hyōō′mə-nīz′) *tr.v.* **-ized, -iz·ing, -iz·es 1.** To deprive of human qualities such as compassion. **2.** To render mechanical and routine. —**de·hu′man·i·za′tion** (-mə-nĭ-zā′shən) *n.*

de·hu·mid·i·fy (dē′hyōō-mĭd′ə-fī′) *tr.v.* **-fied, -fy·ing, -fies** To remove atmospheric moisture from. —**de′hu·mid′i·fi·ca′tion** (-fĭ-kā′shən) *n.* —**de′hu·mid′i·fi′er** *n.*

de·hy·dra·tase (dē-hī′drə-tās′, -tāz′) *n.* An enzyme that catalyzes the removal of oxygen and hydrogen from organic compounds in the form of water.

de·hy·drate (dē-hī′drāt′) *v.* **-drat·ed, -drat·ing, -drates** —*tr.* **1.** To remove water from; make anhydrous. **2.** To preserve by removing water from (vegetables, for example). **3.** To deplete the bodily fluids of: *The hot weather dehydrated the runners.* —*intr.* To lose water or bodily fluids.

de·hy·dra·tion (dē′hī-drā′shən) *n.* **1.** The process of removing water from a substance or compound. **2.** Excessive loss of water from the body, organ, or body part.

de·hy·dra·tor (dē-hī′drā′tər) *n.* **1.** A substance that removes water. **2.** An appliance or an engineered system for removing water from substances such as absorbents or food.

de·hy·dro·chlor·in·ase (dē-hī′drə-klôr′ə-nās′, -nāz′, -klōr′-) *n.* An enzyme that catalyzes the removal of hydrogen and chlorine from a chlorinated hydrocarbon.

de·hy·dro·chlor·in·ate (dē-hī′drə-klôr′ə-nāt′, -klōr′-) *tr.v.* **-at·ed, -at·ing, -ates** To remove hydrogen and chlorine or hydrogen chloride from (a compound). —**de·hy′dro·chlo′ri·na′tion** *n.*

de·hy·dro·gen·ase (dē′hī-drŏj′ə-nās′, -nāz′, dē-hī′drə-jə-) *n.* An enzyme that catalyzes the removal of hydrogen from a substrate and the transfer of hydrogen to an acceptor in an oxidation-reduction reaction.

de·hy·dro·gen·ate (dē′hī-drŏj′ə-nāt′, dē-hī′drə-jə-) *tr.v.* **-at·ed, -at·ing, -ates** To remove hydrogen from. —**de·hy′dro·gen·a′tion** *n.*

de·hy·dro·gen·ize (dē′hī-drŏj′ə-nīz′, dē-hī′drə-jə-) *tr.v.* **-ized, -iz·ing, -iz·es** To dehydrogenate. —**de·hy′dro·gen·i·za′tion** (-ə-nĭ-zā′shən) *n.*

de·hyp·no·tize (dē-hĭp′nə-tīz′) *tr.v.* **-tized, -tiz·ing, -tiz·es** To arouse from a hypnotic state.

de·ice (dē-īs′) *tr.v.* **-iced, -ic·ing, -ic·es** To make or keep free of ice; melt ice from: *deiced the plane's wings.*

de·ic·er (dē-ī′sər) *n.* **1.** A device that is used on an aircraft to keep or remove ice from the wings and propeller. **2.** A compound

ă	pat	oi	boy
ā	pay	ou	out
âr	care	ŏŏ	took
ä	father	ŏŏ	boot
ĕ	pet	ŭ	cut
ē	be	ûr	urge
ĭ	pit	th	thin
ī	pie	th	this
îr	pier	hw	which
ŏ	pot	zh	vision
ō	toe	ə	about,
ô	paw		item

Stress marks:
′ (primary);
′ (secondary), as in
lexicon (lĕk′sĭ-kŏn′)

that is used to prevent the formation of ice.

deic·tic (dīk′tĭk) *adj.* **1.** *Logic* Directly proving by argument. **2.** *Linguistics* Of or relating to a word whose referent is determined from the context. In *I want him to come here now*, the deictic words are *I*, *here*, *him*, and *now*. [Gk. *deiktikos < deiktos*, able to show directly < *deiknunai*, to show. See **deik-** in App.] —**deic′ti·cal·ly** *adv.*

de·if·ic (dē-ĭf′ĭk, dā-) *adj.* **1.** Making or tending to make divine. **2.** Of or characterized by divine or godlike nature. [LLat. *deificus* : Lat. *deus*, god; see **dyeu-** in App. + Lat. *-ficus*, *-fic.*]

de·i·fi·ca·tion (dē′ə-fĭ-kā′shən, dā′-) *n.* **1a.** The act or process of deifying. **b.** The condition of being deified. **2.** One that embodies the qualities of a god.

de·i·fy (dē′ə-fī′, dā′-) *tr.v.* **-fied, -fy·ing, -fies** **1.** To make a god of; raise to the condition of a god. **2.** To worship or revere as a god: *deify a leader.* **3.** To idealize; exalt: *deifying success.* [ME *deifien < OFr. deifier < LLat. deificāre < deificus*, deific. See DEIFIC.] —**de′i·fi′er** *n.*

deign (dān) *v.* **deigned, deign·ing, deigns** —*intr.* To think it appropriate to one's dignity; condescend. —*tr.* To condescend to give; vouchsafe. [ME *deinen < OFr. deignier*, to regard as worthy < Lat. *dignārī < dignus*, worthy.]

deil (dēl) *n. Scots* **1.** The devil; Satan. **2.** A mischievous person; an imp. [Sc. < ME *dele*, var. of *devel*. See DEVIL.]

Dei·mos (dē′mōs, dā′-, dī′mōs) *n.* A satellite of Mars. [Gk., one of the sons of Ares < *deimos*, fear, terror.]

de·in·dus·tri·al·ize (dē′ĭn-dŭs′trē-ə-līz′) *v.* **-ized, -iz·ing, -iz·es** —*tr.* To cause (a nation or area) to lose or be deprived of industrial capability or strength. —*intr.* To undergo or suffer loss of industrial infrastructure and potential. —**de′in·dus′tri·al·i·za′tion** (-ə-lĭ-zā′shən) *n.*

de·in·sti·tu·tion·al·ize (dē-ĭn′stĭ-tōō′shə-nə-līz′, -tyōō′-) *tr.v.* **-ized, -iz·ing, -iz·es** **1.** To remove the institutional status of. **2.** To release (a mental health patient, for example) from an institution for placement and care in the community. —**de·in′sti·tu′tion·al·i·za′tion** (-lĭ-zā′shən) *n.*

de·i·on·ize (dē-ī′ə-nīz′) *tr.v.* **-ized, -iz·ing, -iz·es** To remove ions from (a solution) using an ion-exchange process. —**de·i′on·i·za′tion** (-nĭ-zā′shən) *n.* —**de·i′on·iz′er** *n.*

Deir·dre (dîr′drə, -drē) *n.* A legendary princess of Ulster who killed herself after King Conchobar murdered her lover.

de·ism (dē′ĭz′əm, dā′-) *n.* The belief, based on reason, in a God who created the universe and has since assumed no control over life, exerted no influence on nature, and given no supernatural revelation. [Fr. *déisme < Lat. deus*, god. See **dyeu-** in App.] —**de′ist** *n.* —**de·is′tic, de·is′ti·cal·ly** *adv.*

de·i·ty (dē′ĭ-tē, dā′-) *n., pl.* **-ties** **1.** A god or goddess. **2a.** The essential nature or condition of being a god; divinity. **b. Deity** God. Used with *the.* [ME *deite < OFr. < LLat. deitās*, divine nature < Lat. *deus*, god. See **dyeu-** in App.]

deix·is (dīk′sĭs) *n.* The function of a deictic word in specifying its referent in a given context. [Gk., display, demonstrative reference < *deiknunai*, to show. See **deik-** in App.]

dé·jà vu (dā′zhä vōō′) *n.* **1.** *Psychology* The illusion of having already experienced something actually being experienced for the first time. **2a.** An impression of having seen or experienced something before. **b.** Dull familiarity; monotony. [Fr. : *déjà*, already + *vu*, seen.]

de·ject (dĭ-jĕkt′) *tr.v.* **-ject·ed, -ject·ing, -jects** To lower the spirits of; dishearten. [ME *dejecten < Lat. dēicere, dēiect-*, to cast down : *dē-, de-* + *iacere*, to throw.]

de·ject·ed (dĭ-jĕk′tĭd) *adj.* Being in low spirits; depressed. —**de·ject′ed·ly** *adv.* —**de·ject′ed·ness** *n.*

de·jec·tion (dĭ-jĕk′shən) *n.* **1.** The state of being dejected; low spirits. **2.** Evacuation of the intestinal tract; defecation.

de ju·re (dē jŏŏr′ē, dā yŏŏr′ā) *adv. & adj.* According to law; by right. [Lat. *dē iūre* : *dē*, from + *iūre*, ablative of *iūs*, law.]

deka- or **dek-** *pref.* Variants of **deca-**.

deke (dēk) *tr.v.* **deked, dek·ing, dekes** To deceive (an opponent) by a fake. ❖ *n.* A fake, intended to deceive an opponent. [Short for DECOY.]

de Klerk (də klûrk′, klĕrk′), **F(rederik) W(illem)** b. 1936. South African president (1989–94) who shared the 1993 Nobel Peace Prize.

de Koo·ning (dĭ kōō′nĭng), **Willem** 1904–97. Dutch-born Amer. painter and leader of the abstract expressionist school. His wife, **Elaine Fried de Kooning** (1920–89), also a painter, was noted for her portraits.

Del. *abbr.* Delaware

De·la·croix (də-lä-krwä′), **(Ferdinand Victor) Eugène** 1798–1863. French romantic painter known for his vast, dramatic canvases, such as *Liberty Leading the People* (1830).

Del·a·go·a Bay (dĕl′ə-gō′ə) An inlet of the Indian Ocean in S Mozambique; explored by the Portuguese after 1544.

de la Mare (də la mâr′, dĕl′ə-mâr′), **Walter John** 1873–1956. British writer whose works include *Early One Morning* (1935) and *O Lovely England* (1953).

de·lam·i·nate (dē-lăm′ə-nāt′) *intr.v.* **-nat·ed, -nat·ing, -nates** To split into thin layers.

de·lam·i·na·tion (dē-lăm′ə-nā′shən) *n.* **1.** The act of splitting or separating a laminate into layers. **2.** *Embryology* The splitting

delft
bud vase

of the blastoderm into two cell layers to form a gastrula.

De·la·ney (də-lā′nē), **Shelagh** b. 1930. British playwright best known for *A Taste of Honey* (1958).

De·lan·y (də-lā′nē), **Martin Robinson** 1812–85. Amer. physician who cofounded and edited the *North Star* (1847–49).

Del·a·ware[1] (dĕl′ə-wâr′) *n., pl.* **Delaware** or **-wares** **1.** A member of a group of closely related Native American peoples formerly inhabiting the Delaware and Hudson river valleys and the area between and now living in Oklahoma, Kansas, Wisconsin, and Ontario. **2.** One or both of the Algonquian languages of the Delaware. [After the DELAWARE RIVER.] —**Del·a·war′e·an** *adj.*

Del·a·ware[2] (dĕl′ə-wâr′) A state of the E US on the Atlantic Ocean; admitted as the first of the original Thirteen Colonies in 1787. The region was settled by the Dutch in 1631 and by Swedes in 1638. Cap. Dover. Pop. 783,600.

Del·a·ware[3] (dĕl′ə-wâr′) *n.* A variety of grape having sweet, light red fruit. [After DELAWARE[2].]

Delaware Bay An estuary of the Delaware R. emptying into the Atlantic Ocean between E DE and S NJ.

Delaware River A river rising in SE NY and flowing c. 451 km (280 mi) to N DE, where it enters Delaware Bay.

De La Warr (dĕl′ə wâr′, wər), Baron. Title of Thomas West. 1577–1618. English-born Amer. colonial administrator chosen as the first governor of the Virginia Company colony.

de·lay (dĭ-lā′) *v.* **-layed, -lay·ing, -lays** —*tr.* **1.** To postpone until a later time; defer. **2.** To cause to be later or slower than expected or desired: *Traffic delayed us.* —*intr.* To act or move slowly; put off an action or a decision. ❖ *n.* **1.** The act of delaying; postponement. **2.** The condition of being delayed; detainment. **3.** The period of time during which one is delayed. **4.** The interval of time between two events. [ME *delaien < AN delaier < OFr. deslaier : des-, de-* + *laier*, to leave, of Gmc. orig.] —**de·lay′er** *n.*

Del·brück (dĕl′brŏŏk′, -brük′), **Max** 1906–81. German-born Amer. biologist who shared a 1969 Nobel Prize.

de·le (dē′lē) *n.* A sign indicating that something is to be removed from printed or written matter. ❖ *tr.v.* **-led, -le·ing, -les** **1.** To remove, esp. from printed or written matter; delete. **2.** To mark with a sign indicating deletion. [Lat. *dēlē*, second pers. sing. imper. of *dēlēre*, to delete.]

de·lec·ta·ble (dĭ-lĕk′tə-bəl) *adj.* **1.** Greatly pleasing; delightful. **2.** Greatly pleasing to the taste; delicious. ❖ *n.* Something delectable. [ME < OFr. < Lat. *dēlectābilis < dēlectāre*, to please. See DELIGHT.] —**de·lec′ta·bil′i·ty, de·lec′ta·ble·ness** *n.* —**de·lec′ta·bly** *adv.*

de·lec·ta·tion (dē′lĕk-tā′shən) *n.* **1.** Delight. **2.** Enjoyment; pleasure. [ME *delectacioun < OFr. < Lat. dēlectātiō, dēlectātiōn- < dēlectus*, p. part. of *dēlectāre*, to please. See DELIGHT.]

De·led·da (dĕ-lĕd′dä), **Grazia** 1875–1936. Italian writer who won the 1926 Nobel Prize for literature.

del·e·ga·cy (dĕl′ĭ-gə-sē) *n., pl.* **-cies** **1.** The act of delegating or state of being delegated. **2.** The authority, office, or position of a delegate. **3.** A body of delegates; a delegation.

de·le·gal·ize (dē-lē′gə-līz′) *tr.v.* **-ized, -iz·ing, -iz·es** To make illegal. —**de·le′gal·i·za′tion** (-gə-lĭ-zā′shən) *n.*

del·e·gate (dĕl′ĭ-gāt′, -gĭt) *n.* **1.** A person authorized to act as another's representative; a deputy or agent. **2.** A representative to a conference or convention. **3.** A member of a House of Delegates, the lower house of the Maryland, Virginia, or West Virginia legislature. **4.** A representative of a US territory in the House of Representatives who is entitled to speak but not vote. ❖ *tr.v.* (-gāt′) **-gat·ed, -gat·ing, -gates** **1.** To authorize and send (another person) as one's representative. **2.** To commit or entrust (a task or power) to another. **3.** *Law* To appoint (one's debtor) as a debtor to one's creditor in place of oneself. [ME *delegat < Med.Lat. dēlēgātus < p. part. of dēlēgāre*, to dispatch : Lat. *dē-, de-* + *lēgāre*, to send; see **leg-** in App.] —**del′e·ga′tor** *n.*

del·e·ga·tion (dĕl′ĭ-gā′shən) *n.* **1a.** The act of delegating. **b.** The condition of being delegated. **2.** A person or group of persons officially elected or appointed as representatives.

de·le·git·i·mize (dē′lə-jĭt′ə-mīz′) *tr.v.* **-mized, -miz·ing, -miz·es** To revoke the legal or legitimate status of. —**de·le·git′i·mi·za′tion** (-mĭ-zā′shən) *n.*

de Les·seps (də lĕs′əps, lĕ-sĕps′), Vicomte **Ferdinand Marie** See Ferdinand Marie de **Lesseps.**

de·lete (dĭ-lēt′) *tr.v.* **-let·ed, -let·ing, -letes** To remove by striking out or canceling. See Syns at **erase.** [Lat. *dēlēre, dēlēt-*, to wipe out.]

del·e·te·ri·ous (dĕl′ĭ-tîr′ē-əs) *adj.* Having a harmful effect; injurious. [< Gk. *dēlētērios < dēlētēr*, destroyer < *dēleisthai*, to harm.] —**del′e·te′ri·ous·ly** *adv.* —**del′e·te′ri·ous·ness** *n.*

de·le·tion (dĭ-lē′shən) *n.* **1.** The act of deleting; removal by striking out. **2.** Material that has been removed from a written text. **3.** *Genetics* The loss, as through mutation, of one or more nucleotides from a chromosome.

delft (dĕlft) *n.* **1.** A style of glazed earthenware, usu. blue and white, originally made in Delft, Netherlands. **2.** Such pottery. [After DELFT, where it was first made.]

Delft A city of SW Netherlands SE of The Hague; noted for its pottery since the 16th cent. Pop. 86,733.

Del·hi (dĕl′ē) A city of N-central India on the Yamuna R. The new section of Delhi is the cap. of India. Pop. 7,206,704.

del•i (dĕl′ē) *n., pl.* **-is** *Informal* A delicatessen.

de•lib•er•ate (dĭ-lĭb′ər-ĭt) *adj.* **1.** Done with or marked by full consciousness of the nature and effects; intentional: *a deliberate insult.* **2.** Arising from or marked by careful consideration: *a deliberate decision.* See Syns at **voluntary. 3.** Unhurried in action, movement, or manner, as if trying to avoid error. ❖ *v.* (-ə-rāt′) **-at•ed, -at•ing, -ates** —*intr.* **1.** To think carefully and often slowly, as about a choice to be made. **2.** To consult with another or others in a process of reaching a decision. —*tr.* To consider (a matter) carefully and often slowly, as by weighing alternatives. [Lat. *dēlīberātus,* p. part. of *dēlīberāre,* to consider, weigh : *dē-,* de- + *lībrāre,* to balance (< *lībra,* a balance, scales).] —**de•lib′er•ate•ly** *adv.* —**de•lib′er•ate•ness** *n.*

de•lib•er•a•tion (dĭ-lĭb′ə-rā′shən) *n.* **1.** The act or process of deliberating. **2. deliberations** Discussion and consideration of all sides of an issue. **3.** Thoughtfulness in decision or action. **4.** Leisureliness in motion or manner.

de•lib•er•a•tive (dĭ-lĭb′ə-rā′tĭv, -ər-ə-tĭv) *adj.* **1.** Assembled or organized for deliberation or debate. **2.** Characterized by or for use in deliberation or debate. —**de•lib′er•a′tive•ly** *adv.* —**de•lib′er•a′tive•ness** *n.*

De•libes (də-lēb′), **(Clément Philibert) Léo** 1836–91. French composer whose melodic works include *Coppélia* (1870).

del•i•ca•cy (dĕl′ĭ-kə-sē) *n., pl.* **-cies 1.** The quality of being delicate. **2.** Something pleasing and appealing, esp. a choice food. **3.** Fineness of appearance, construction, or execution; elegance. **4.** Frailty of bodily constitution or health. **5.** Sensitivity of perception, discrimination, or taste; refinement. **6a.** Sensitivity to the feelings of others; tact. **b.** Sensitivity to what is proper; propriety. **c.** Undue sensitivity to or concern with what may be considered offensive or improper; squeamishness. **7.** The need for tact in treatment or handling: *a topic of some delicacy.* **8.** Sensitivity to very small changes; precision. [ME *delicacie* < *delicat,* delicate. See DELICATE.]

del•i•cate (dĕl′ĭ-kĭt) *adj.* **1.** Pleasing to the senses, esp. in a subtle way: *a delicate violin passage.* **2.** Exquisitely fine or dainty. **3.** Frail in constitution or health. **4.** Easily broken or damaged. **5.** Marked by sensitivity of discrimination: *a critic's delicate ear.* **6a.** Considerate of the feelings of others. **b.** Concerned with propriety. **c.** Squeamish or fastidious. **7.** Requiring tactful treatment. **8.** Fine or soft in touch or skill. **9.** Measuring, indicating, or responding to very small changes; precise. **10.** Very subtle in difference or distinction. [ME *delicat* and Fr. *délicat,* both < Lat. *dēlicātus,* pleasing; akin to Lat. *dēlicia,* pleasure. See DELICIOUS.] —**del′i•cate•ly** *adv.* —**del′i•cate•ness** *n.*

SYNONYMS *delicate, choice, dainty, elegant, exquisite, fine* These adjectives mean appealing to refined taste: *a delicate flavor; choice exotic flowers; a dainty dish; elegant handwriting; an exquisite wine; the finest embroidery.* See also Syns at **fragile.**

del•i•ca•tes•sen (dĕl′ĭ-kə-tĕs′ən) *n.* **1.** A shop that sells foods ready for serving. **2.** Ready-to-serve foods such as cheeses and salads. [Ger. *Delikatessen* < pl. of *Delikatesse,* delicacy < Fr. *délicatesse* < Ital. *delicatezza* < *delicato,* delicate, dainty < Lat. *dēlicātus,* pleasing. See DELICATE.]

de•li•cious (dĭ-lĭsh′əs) *adj.* **1.** Highly pleasing or agreeable to the senses, esp. of taste or smell. **2.** Very pleasant; delightful: *a delicious revenge.* [ME < AN < LLat. *dēliciōsus,* pleasing < Lat. *dēlicia,* pleasure : *dē-,* intensive pref.; see DE– + *lacere,* to entice.] —**de•li′cious•ly** *adv.* —**de•li′cious•ness** *n.*

Delicious *n.* A variety of sweet apple whose flesh is often streaked with yellow and red.

de•lict (dĭ-lĭkt′) *n.* A legal offense; a misdemeanor. [Lat. *dēlictum* < neut. p. part. of *dēlinquere,* to offend. See DELINQUENT.]

de•light (dĭ-līt′) *n.* **1.** Great pleasure; joy. **2.** Something giving great pleasure or enjoyment. ❖ *v.* **-light•ed, -light•ing, -lights** —*intr.* **1.** To take great pleasure or joy: *delights in dogs.* **2.** To give great pleasure or joy: *a vista that delights.* —*tr.* To please greatly. [ME *delit* < OFr., a pleasure < *delitier,* to please, charm < Lat. *dēlectāre* : *dē-,* de- + *lactāre,* freq. of *lacere,* to entice.]

de•light•ed (dĭ-lī′tĭd) *adj.* **1.** Filled with delight. **2.** *Obsolete* Delightful. —**de•light′ed•ly** *adv.* —**de•light′ed•ness** *n.*

de•light•ful (dĭ-līt′fəl) *adj.* Greatly pleasing. —**de•light′ful•ly** *adv.* —**de•light′ful•ness** *n.*

de•light•some (dĭ-līt′səm) *adj.* Delightful. —**de•light′some•ly** *adv.* —**de•light′some•ness** *n.*

De•li•lah (də-lī′lə) In the Bible, a lover of Samson who betrayed him to the Philistines.

de•lim•it (dĭ-lĭm′ĭt) also **de•lim•i•tate** (-ĭ-tāt′) *tr.v.* **-it•ed, -it•ing, -its** also **-tat•ed, -tat•ing, -tates** To establish the limits or boundaries of; demarcate. [Fr. *délimiter* < Lat. *dēlīmitāre* : *dē-,* de- + *līmitāre,* to limit (< *līmes, līmit-,* boundary line).] —**de•lim′i•ta′tion** *n.* —**de•lim′i•ta′tive** *adj.*

de•lim•it•er (dĭ-lĭm′ĭ-tər) *n. Computer Science* A character or sequence of characters marking the beginning or end of a unit of data.

de•lin•e•ate (dĭ-lĭn′ē-āt′) *tr.v.* **-at•ed, -at•ing, -ates 1.** To draw or trace the outline of; sketch out. **2.** To represent pictorially; depict. **3.** To depict in words or gestures; describe. [Lat. *dēlīneāre, dēlīneāt-* : *dē-,* de- + *līnea,* line, thread; see LINE[1].] —**de•lin′e•a′tion** *n.* —**de•lin′e•a′tive** *adj.* —**de•lin′e•a′tor** *n.*

de•lin•quen•cy (dĭ-lĭng′kwən-sē, -lĭn′-) *n., pl.* **-cies 1.** Juvenile delinquency. **2.** Failure to do what law or duty requires. **3.** An offense or a misdemeanor; a misdeed. **4.** A debt or other financial obligation on which payment is overdue. ❖ *adj.* Of or relating to juvenile delinquency.

de•lin•quent (dĭ-lĭng′kwənt, -lĭn′-) *adj.* **1.** Failing to do what law or duty requires. **2.** Overdue in payment. ❖ *n.* **1.** A juvenile delinquent. **2.** A person who neglects or fails to do what law or duty requires. [Lat. *dēlinquēns, dēlinquent-,* pr. part. of *dēlinquere,* to offend : *dē-,* de- + *linquere,* to leave, abandon; see **leikʷ-** in App.] —**de•lin′quent•ly** *adv.*

del•i•quesce (dĕl′ĭ-kwĕs′) *intr.v.* **-quesced, -quesc•ing, -quesc•es 1a.** To melt away. **b.** To disappear as if by melting. **2.** *Chemistry* To dissolve and become liquid by absorbing moisture from the air. **3.** *Botany* **a.** To branch out into numerous subdivisions that lack a main axis. **b.** To become fluid or soft on maturing, as certain fungi. [Lat. *dēliquēscere* : *dē-,* de- + *liquēscere,* to melt, inchoative of *liquēre,* to be liquid.] —**del′i•ques′cence** *n.* —**del′i•ques′cent** *adj.*

de•lir•i•ous (dĭ-lîr′ē-əs) *adj.* **1.** Of, suffering from, or characteristic of delirium. **2.** Marked by uncontrolled excitement or emotion; ecstatic. —**de•lir′i•ous•ly** *adv.* —**de•lir′i•ous•ness** *n.*

de•lir•i•um (dĭ-lîr′ē-əm) *n., pl.* **-i•ums** or **-i•a** (-ē-ə) **1.** A temporary state of mental confusion and fluctuating consciousness, characterized by anxiety, disorientation, hallucinations, and incoherent speech. **2.** A state of uncontrolled excitement or emotion. [Lat. *dēlīrium* < *dēlīrāre,* to be deranged : *dē-,* de- + *līra,* furrow.] —**de•lir′i•ant** *adj.*

delirium tre•mens (trē′mənz) *n.* An acute, sometimes fatal episode of delirium usu. caused either by withdrawal from alcohol following habitual excessive drinking or by an episode of heavy alcohol consumption. [NLat. *dēlīrium tremēns* : Lat. *dēlīrium,* delirium + Lat. *tremēns,* trembling.]

de•list (dē-lĭst′) *tr.v.* **-list•ed, -list•ing, -lists** To remove from a list, esp. from a list of securities that may be traded on a stock exchange.

De•lius (dē′lē-əs, dēl′yəs), **Frederick** 1862–1934. British composer of romantic, impressionistic works.

de•liv•er (dĭ-lĭv′ər) *v.* **-ered, -er•ing, -ers** —*tr.* **1.** To bring or transport to the proper place or recipient; distribute. **2.** To surrender (someone or something) to another; hand over. **3.** To secure (something promised or desired), as for a candidate or political party. **4.** To throw or hurl. **5.** To strike (a blow). **6.** To express in words; declare or utter. **7a.** To give birth to. **b.** To assist (a woman) in giving birth. **c.** To assist or aid in the birth of. **8.** To give forth or produce. **9.** To set free, as from misery, peril, or evil. —*intr.* **1.** To produce or achieve what is desired or expected; make good. **2.** To give birth. ***—idiom:*** **deliver (oneself) of** To pronounce; utter. [ME *deliveren* < OFr. *delivrer* < LLat. *dēlīberāre* : Lat. *dē-,* de- + *līberāre,* to free (< *līber,* free; see **leudh-** in App.).] —**de•liv′er•a•bil′i•ty** *n.* —**de•liv′er•a•ble** *adj.* —**de•liv′er•er** *n.*

de•liv•er•ance (dĭ-lĭv′ər-əns, -lĭv′rəns) *n.* **1.** The act of delivering or the condition of being delivered. **2.** Rescue from bondage or danger. **3.** A publicly expressed opinion or judgment, such as the verdict of a jury.

de•liv•er•y (dĭ-lĭv′ə-rē, -lĭv′rē) *n., pl.* **-ies 1a.** The act of conveying or delivering. **b.** Something delivered, as a shipment. **2a.** The act of transferring to another. **b.** *Law* A formal act of transferring ownership of property to another. **3.** The act of giving up; surrender. **4.** The act or manner of throwing or discharging. **5.** The act of giving birth; parturition. **6a.** Utterance or enunciation. **b.** The act or manner of speaking or singing. **7.** The act of releasing or rescuing.

delivery room *n.* **1.** A room or area in a hospital that is equipped for delivering babies. **2.** A room or an area set aside for making or receiving deliveries.

dell (dĕl) *n.* A small wooded valley. [ME *del* < OE *dell.*]

del•la Rob•bia (dĕl′ə rō′bē-ə, dĕl′lä rōb′byä), **Luca** 1400?–82. Italian sculptor noted for his terra-cotta works.

dells (dĕlz) *pl.n.* The rapids of a river. [Alteration of DALLES.]

Del•mar•va Peninsula (dĕl-mär′və) A peninsula of the E US separating Chesapeake Bay from Delaware Bay and the Atlantic Ocean and including DE and parts of E MD and VA.

Del•mon•i•co (dĕl-mŏn′ĭ-kō′), **Lorenzo** 1813–81. Swiss-born Amer. restaurateur who popularized European cuisine in New York City.

Delmonico steak *n.* A small, often boned steak from the front section of the short loin of beef. [After Lorenzo DELMONICO.]

de•lo•cal•ize (dē-lō′kə-līz′) *tr.v.* **-ized, -iz•ing, -iz•es 1.** To remove from a native or usual locality. **2.** To broaden the range or scope of. —**de•lo′cal•i•za′tion** (-kə-lĭ-zā′shən) *n.*

De•lorme or **de l'Orme** (də-lôrm′), **Philibert** 1515?–70. French architect who built the Tuileries in Paris.

De•los (dē′lŏs′, dĕl′ŏs) An island of SE Greece in the Cyclades Is. of the S Aegean; traditionally sacred to Apollo.

de•louse (dē-lous′) *tr.v.* **-loused, -lous•ing, -lous•es** To rid (a person or an animal) of lice by physical or chemical means.

Del•phi (dĕl′fī′) An ancient town of central Greece near Mt. Parnassus; seat of a famous oracle of Apollo.

ă	pat	oi	boy
ā	pay	ou	out
âr	care	o͝o	took
ä	father	o͞o	boot
ĕ	pet	ŭ	cut
ē	be	ûr	urge
ĭ	pit	th	thin
ī	pie	*th*	this
îr	pier	hw	which
ŏ	pot	zh	vision
ō	toe	ə	about,
ô	paw		item

Stress marks:
′ (primary);
′ (secondary), as in
lexicon (lĕk′sĭ-kŏn′)

Del·phic (dĕl′fĭk) also **Del·phi·an** (-fē-ən) *adj.* **1.** *Greek Mythology* Of or relating to Delphi or to the oracle of Apollo at Delphi. **2.** Obscurely prophetic; oracular. —**Del′phi·cal·ly** *adv.*

del·phin·i·um (dĕl-fĭn′ē-əm) *n.* A plant of the genus *Delphinium,* esp. any of several tall cultivated varieties with palmate leaves and long racemes of spurred flowers. [NLat. *Delphinium,* genus name < Gk. *delphinion,* larkspur, prob. dim. of *delphīs, delphīn-,* dolphin (< the shape of the nectary). See DOLPHIN.]

Del·phi·nus (dĕl-fī′nəs) *n.* A constellation in the Northern Hemisphere near Pegasus and Aquila. [Lat. *delphīnus,* dolphin. See DOLPHIN.]

del·ta (dĕl′tə) *n.* **1.** The fourth letter of the Greek alphabet. **2.** An object shaped like a triangle. **3a.** A usu. triangular alluvial deposit at the mouth of a river. **b.** A similar deposit at the mouth of a tidal inlet, caused by tidal currents. **4.** *Mathematics* A finite increment in a variable. [ME < Lat. < Gk. < Phoenician **dalt,* door, fourth letter of the Phoenician alphabet.] —**del·ta′ic** (-tā′ĭk), **del′tic** (-tĭk) *adj.*

delta ray *n.* An electron ejected from matter by ionizing radiation.

delta wave *n.* A brain wave with a frequency of one to three hertz that is associated with deep sleep in normal adults.

delta wing *n.* An aircraft with swept-back wings that give it the appearance of an isosceles triangle.

del·ti·ol·o·gy (dĕl′tē-ŏl′ə-jē) *n.* The collection and study of postcards. [< Gk. *deltion,* dim. of *deltos,* letter.]

del·toid (dĕl′toid′) *n.* A thick triangular muscle covering the shoulder joint, used to raise the arm from the side. ❖ *adj.* **1.** Triangular. **2.** Of or relating to the deltoid. [NLat. *deltoīdēs* < Gk. *deltoeidēs,* triangular : *delta,* delta; see DELTA + *-oeidēs,* -oid.]

de·lude (dĭ-lōōd′) *tr.v.* **-lud·ed, -lud·ing, -ludes** **1.** To deceive the mind or judgment of: *deluding consumers.* See Syns at **deceive. 2.** *Obsolete* To elude or evade. **3.** *Obsolete* To frustrate the hopes or plans of. [ME *deluden* < Lat. *dēlūdere : dē-,* de- + *lūdere,* to play.] —**de·lud′er** *n.* —**de·lud′ing·ly** *adv.*

del·uge (dĕl′yōōj, -yōōzh, dā′lōōj, -lōōzh, dĭ-lōōj′, -lōōzh′) *n.* **1a.** A great flood. **b.** A heavy downpour. **2.** Something that overwhelms as if by a great flood: *a deluge of mail.* **3. Deluge** In the Bible, the great flood that occurred in the time of Noah. ❖ *tr.v.* **-uged, -ug·ing, -ug·es** **1.** To overrun with water; inundate. **2.** To overwhelm with a large number or amount; swamp. [< ME, flood < OFr. < Lat. *dīluvium* < *dīluere,* to wash away : *dis-,* apart; see DIS- + *-luere,* to wash; see **leu(ə)-** in App.]

de·lu·sion (dĭ-lōō′zhən) *n.* **1a.** The act or process of deluding. **b.** The state of being deluded. **2.** A false belief or opinion. **3.** *Psychology* A false belief held strongly held in spite of invalidating evidence, esp. as a symptom of mental illness. [ME *delusioun* < Lat. *dēlūsiō, dēlūsiōn-* < *dēlūsus,* p. part. of *dēlūdere,* to delude. See DELUDE.] —**de·lu′sion·al** *adj.*

de·lu·sive (dĭ-lōō′sĭv) *adj.* **1.** Tending to delude. **2.** Having the nature of a delusion; false. —**de·lu′sive·ly** *adv.* —**de·lu′sive·ness** *n.*

de·lu·so·ry (dĭ-lōō′sə-rē, -zə-) *adj.* Tending to deceive.

de·luxe also **de luxe** (dĭ-lŭks′, -lōōks′) *adj.* Particularly elegant and luxurious; sumptuous. ❖ *adv.* In an elegant and luxurious manner; sumptuously. [Fr. *de luxe,* of luxury : *de,* of + *luxe,* luxury.]

delve (dĕlv) *v.* **delved, delv·ing, delves** —*intr.* **1.** To search deeply and laboriously: *delved into archives.* **2.** To dig the ground, as with a spade. —*tr. Archaic* To dig (ground) with a spade. [ME *delven,* to dig < OE *delfan.*] —**delv′er** *n.*

dem. *abbr.* **1.** demonstrative **2.** demurrage

Dem. *abbr.* **1.** Democrat **2.** Democratic

de·mag·net·ize (dē-măg′nĭ-tīz′) *tr.v.* **-ized, -iz·ing, -iz·es** **1.** To remove magnetic properties from. **2.** To erase (a magnetic storage device). —**de·mag′net·i·za′tion** (-nĭ-tĭ-zā′shən) *n.* —**de·mag′net·iz′er** *n.*

dem·a·gog·ic (dĕm′ə-gŏj′ĭk, -gŏg′-, -gō′jĭk) also **dem·a·gog·i·cal** (-gŏj′ĭ-kəl, -gŏg′-, -gō′jĭ-kəl) *adj.* Of or relating to a demagogue. —**dem′a·gog′i·cal·ly** *adv.*

dem·a·gog·ism (dĕm′ə-gô′gĭz-əm, -gŏg′ĭz-) *n.* Demagoguery.

dem·a·gogue (dĕm′ə-gôg′, -gŏg′) *n.* **1.** A leader who obtains power by means of impassioned appeals to emotions and prejudices. **2.** A leader of the common people in ancient times. [Gk. *dēmagōgos,* popular leader : *dēmos,* people; see **dā-** in App. + *agōgos,* leading (< *agein,* to lead; see **ag-** in App.).]

dem·a·gogu·er·y (dĕm′ə-gô′gə-rē, -gŏg′ə-) *n.* The practices or rhetoric of a demagogue.

dem·a·gog·y (dĕm′ə-gŏj′ē, -gô′jē, -gŏg′ē, -gō′jē) *n.* The character or practices of a demagogue; demagoguery.

de·mand (dĭ-mănd′) *v.* **-mand·ed, -mand·ing, -mands** —*tr.* **1.** To ask for urgently or peremptorily. **2.** To claim as just or due: *demand payment.* **3.** To ask to be informed of. **4.** To require as useful, just, proper, or necessary; call for. **5.** *Law* To claim formally; lay legal claim to. —*intr.* To make a demand. ❖ *n.* **1.** The act of demanding. **2.** Something demanded. **3.** An urgent requirement or need. **4.** The state of being sought after: *in demand as a speaker.* **5.** *Economics* **a.** The desire to possess a commodity or make use of a service, combined with the ability to purchase it. **b.** The amount of a commodity or service that people are ready to buy for a given price: *supply and demand.* **6.** *Computer Science*

A coding technique in which a command to read or write is initiated as the need for a new block of data occurs, thus eliminating the need to store data. **7.** *Law* A formal claim. **8.** *Archaic* An emphatic question or inquiry. —*idiom:* **on demand 1.** When presented for payment. **2.** When needed or asked for. [ME *demanden* < OFr. *demander,* to charge with doing, and < Med.Lat. *dēmandāre,* to demand, both < Lat., to entrust : *dē-,* de- + *mandāre,* to entrust; see **man-2** in App.] —**de·mand′a·ble** *adj.* —**de·mand′er** *n.*

de·man·dant (dĭ-măn′dənt) *n. Archaic* A plaintiff.

demand deposit *n.* A bank deposit that can be withdrawn without advance notice.

de·mand·ing (dĭ-măn′dĭng) *adj.* Requiring much effort or attention. —**de·mand′ing·ly** *adv.*

demand loan *n.* See **call loan.**

demand note *n.* A bill or draft payable on demand.

de·mand-pull (dĭ-mănd′pŏŏl′) *n.* Increased demand for a limited supply of goods and services, tending to cause consumer prices to increase. —**de·mand′-pull′** *adj.*

de·man·toid (dĭ-măn′toid′) *n.* A transparent green variety of garnet used as a gem. [Ger. < *archaic Demant,* diamond < MHGer. *diemant* < OFr. *diamant.* See DIAMOND.]

de·mar·cate (dĭ-mär′kāt′, dē′mär-kāt′) *tr.v.* **-cat·ed, -cat·ing, -cates** **1.** To set the boundaries of; delimit. **2.** To separate clearly as if by boundaries; distinguish: *demarcate categories.* [Back-formation < DEMARCATION.] —**de·mar′ca′tor** *n.*

de·mar·ca·tion also **de·mar·ka·tion** (dē′mär-kā′shən) *n.* **1.** The setting or marking of boundaries or limits. **2.** A separation; a distinction. [Sp. *demarcación* < *demarcar,* to mark boundaries : *de-,* off (< Lat. *dis-*) + *marcar,* to mark (< Ital. *marcare* < OItal., of Gmc. orig.; see **merg-** in App.).]

dé·marche (dā-märsh′) *n.* **1.** A course of action; a maneuver. **2.** A diplomatic representation or protest. **3.** A statement or protest addressed by citizens to public authorities. [Fr. < OFr. *demarche,* gait < *demarchier,* to march : *de-,* de- + *marchier,* to march; see MARCH[1].]

de·ma·te·ri·al·ize (dē′mə-tîr′ē-ə-līz′) *tr. & intr.v.* **-ized, -iz·ing, -iz·es** To deprive of or lose apparent physical substance; make or become immaterial. —**de′ma·te′ri·al·i·za′tion** (-ə-lĭ-zā′shən) *n.*

deme (dēm) *n.* **1.** One of the townships of ancient Attica. **2.** *Ecology* A local, usu. stable population of interbreeding organisms of the same kind. [Gk. *dēmos,* people. See **dā-** in App.]

de·mean1 (dĭ-mēn′) *tr.v.* **-meaned, -mean·ing, -means** To conduct or behave (oneself) in a particular manner. [ME *demeinen,* to govern < OFr. *demener : de-,* de- + *mener,* to conduct (< Lat. *mināre,* to drive (animals) < *minārī,* to threaten < *minae,* threats).]

de·mean2 (dĭ-mēn′) *tr.v.* **-meaned, -mean·ing, -means** **1.** To debase, as in dignity. **2.** To humble (oneself). See Syns at **degrade.** [DE- + MEAN[2].] —**de·mean′ing·ly** *adv.*

de·mean·or (dĭ-mē′nər) *n.* The way in which a person behaves; deportment.

de·ment (dĭ-mĕnt′) *tr.v.* **-ment·ed, -ment·ing, -ments** **1.** To make insane. **2.** To cause to lose intellectual capacity. [LLat. *dēmentāre* < Lat. *dēmēns, dēment-,* senseless : *dē-,* de- + *mēns,* mind; see **men-1** in App.]

de·ment·ed (dĭ-mĕn′tĭd) *adj.* **1.** Mentally ill; insane. **2.** Suffering from dementia. —**de·ment′ed·ly** *adv.* —**de·ment′ed·ness** *n.*

de·men·tia (dĭ-mĕn′shə) *n.* **1.** Deterioration of intellectual faculties resulting from an organic disease or disorder of the brain and sometimes accompanied by emotional disturbance. **2.** Madness; insanity. [Lat. *dēmentia,* madness < *dēmēns, dēment-,* senseless. See DEMENT.] —**de·men′tial** *adj.*

de·mer·it (dĭ-mĕr′ĭt) *n.* **1a.** A quality or characteristic deserving of blame or censure; a fault. **b.** Absence of merit. **2.** A mark made against one's record for a fault or for misconduct. [ME *demerite,* offense < OFr. *desmerite* < Lat. *dēmeritum* < neut. p. part. of *dēmerēre,* to deserve : *dē-,* de- + *merēre,* to earn.] —**de·mer′i·to′ri·ous** (-tôr′ē-əs, -tōr′-) *adj.* —**de·mer′i·to′ri·ous·ly** *adv.*

Dem·er·ol (dĕm′ə-rôl′, -rŏl′, -rōl′) A trademark used for a preparation of meperidine.

de·mer·sal (dĭ-mûr′səl) *adj.* Dwelling at or near, sinking to, or deposited near the bottom of a body of water. [< Lat. *dēmersus,* p. part. of *dēmergere,* to sink : *dē-,* de- + *mergere,* to sink.]

de·mesne (dĭ-mān′, -mēn′) *n.* **1.** Manorial land retained for the private use of a feudal lord. **2.** The grounds belonging to a mansion or country house. **3.** An extensive piece of landed property; an estate. **4.** A district; a territory. **5.** A realm; a domain. [Anglo-Fr., respelling of ME *demeine* (influenced by Fr. legal phrase *mesne* (lord), middle lord, lord holding a manor of a superior lord) < AN < OFr. *demaine.* See DOMAIN.]

De·me·ter (dĭ-mē′tər) *n. Greek Mythology* The goddess of the harvest, daughter of Rhea and Cronus and mother of Persephone. [Gk. *Dēmētēr.* See **māter-** in App.]

demi– *pref.* **1.** Half: *demirelief.* **2.** To some degree; part; partly:

delta wing
NASA aircraft F-16XL

demijohn

demigod. [ME *demi,* a half of a measure or unit < OFr. < Med.Lat. *dīmedius* < Lat. *dīmidius,* divided in half : *dis-,* dis- + *medius,* half; see MEDIUM.]

dem·i·god (dĕm′ē-gŏd′) *n.* **1.** *Mythology* **a.** A male being, often the offspring of a deity and a mortal, who has some divine powers. **b.** An inferior deity; a minor god. **c.** A deified man. **2.** A person who is highly honored or revered.

dem·i·god·dess (dĕm′ē-gŏd′ĭs) *n.* **1.** A female being, often the offspring of a deity and a mortal, who has some divine powers. **2.** A deified woman.

dem·i·john (dĕm′ē-jŏn′) *n.* A large narrow-necked bottle made of glass or earthenware, usu. encased in wickerwork. [Prob. alteration of Fr. *dame-Jeanne* : *dame,* lady; see DAME + *Jeanne,* personal name.]

de·mil·i·ta·rize (dē-mĭl′ĭ-tə-rīz′) *tr.v.* **-rized, -riz·ing, -riz·es** To remove or forbid military troops in (an area). —**de·mil′i·ta·ri·za′tion** (-tər-ĭ-zā′shən) *n.*

De Mille (də mĭl′), **Agnes George** 1905–93. Amer. choreographer whose works include innovative dances for musicals such as *Oklahoma!* (1943) and *Carousel* (1945).

De Mille, Cecil Blount 1881–1959. Amer. filmmaker known for his spectacular epic productions, including *The Ten Commandments* (1923 and 1956).

dem·i·mon·daine (dĕm′ē-mŏn-dān′, -mŏn′dān′) *n.* A woman belonging to the demimonde. [Fr. < *demi-monde,* demimonde. See DEMIMONDE.]

dem·i·monde (dĕm′ē-mŏnd′) *n.* **1a.** A class of women financially supported by lovers or protectors. **b.** Women prostitutes considered as a group. **2.** A group whose respectability is dubious or whose success is marginal. [Fr. *demi-monde* : *demi-,* demi- + *monde,* world (< Lat. *mundus*).]

de·min·er·al·i·za·tion (dē-mĭn′ər-ə-lĭ-zā′shən) *n.* **1.** The act or process of removing minerals or mineral salts from a liquid. **2.** The loss, deprivation, or removal of minerals or mineral salts from the body, esp. through disease.

de·min·er·al·ize (dē-mĭn′ər-ə-līz′) *tr.v.* **-ized, -iz·ing, -iz·es** To remove minerals or mineral salts from (a liquid). —**de·min′er·al·i′zer** *n.*

dem·i·re·lief (dĕm′ē-rĭ-lēf′) *n.* See half relief.

dem·i·rep (dĕm′ē-rĕp′) *n.* A person of doubtful reputation or respectability. [DEMI- + REP(UTATION).]

de·mise (dĭ-mīz′) *n.* **1a.** Death. **b.** The end of existence or activity; termination: *the demise of the streetcar.* **2.** *Law* Transfer of an estate by lease or will. **3.** The transfer of a ruler's authority by death or abdication. ❖ *v.* **-mised, -mis·ing, -mis·es** —*tr.* **1.** *Law* To transfer (an estate) by lease or will. **2.** To transfer (sovereignty) by abdication or will. —*intr.* **1.** *Law* To be transferred by will or descent. **2.** To die. [ME, transfer of property < OFr. *dimis,* p. part. of *demettre,* to release. See DEMIT.] —**de·mis′a·ble** *adj.*

dem·i·sem·i·qua·ver (dĕm′ē-sĕm′ē-kwā′vər) *n.* Chiefly British A thirty-second note.

de·mis·sion (dĭ-mĭsh′ən) *n.* Relinquishment of an office or function. [Ult. < Lat. *dīmissiō, dīmissiōn-,* dismissal < *dīmissus,* p. part. of *dīmittere.* See DEMIT.]

de·mit (dĭ-mĭt′) *v.* **-mit·ted, -mit·ting, -mits** —*tr.* **1.** To relinquish (an office or function). **2.** *Archaic* To dismiss. —*intr.* To give up an office or position; resign. [ME *dimitten,* to release < OFr. *demettre* < Lat. *dīmittere* : *dis-,* away; see DIS- + *mittere,* to send.]

dem·i·tasse (dĕm′ē-tăs′, -täs′) *n.* **1.** A small cup of strong black coffee or espresso. **2.** The small cup used to serve this drink. [Fr. *demi-tasse* : *demi-,* demi- + *tasse,* cup (< OFr. < Ar. *ṭašt,* basin < Pers. *tašt*).]

dem·i·urge (dĕm′ē-ûrj′) *n.* **1.** A powerful creative force or personality. **2.** A public magistrate in some ancient Greek states. **3. Demiurge** A deity in Gnosticism, Manichaeism, and other religions who creates the material world and is often viewed as the originator of evil. **4. Demiurge** A Platonic deity who orders or fashions the material world out of chaos. [LLat. *dēmiurgus,* artisan : *dēmiourgos,* artisan : *dēmios,* public (< *dēmos,* people; see dā- in App.) + *ergos,* worker (< *ergon,* work; see werg- in App.).] —**dem′i·ur′geous** (-ûr′jəs), **dem′i·ur′gic** (-jĭk), **dem′i·ur′gi·cal** (-jĭ-kəl) *adj.* —**dem′i·ur′gi·cal·ly** *adv.*

dem·i·world (dĕm′ē-wûrld′) *n.* See demimonde 2.

dem·o¹ (dĕm′ō) *n., pl.* **-os** *Informal* **1a.** A demonstration, as of a product. **b.** A brief recording illustrating the abilities of a musician or other performer. **2.** A product used for demonstration and often sold later at a discount. —**dem′o** *v.*

dem·o² (dĕm′ō) *n. Informal* Demolition.

de·mob (dē-mŏb′) Chiefly British *tr.v.* **-mobbed, -mob·bing, -mobs** To demobilize (armed forces).

de·mo·bil·ize (dē-mō′bə-līz′) *tr.v.* **-ized, -iz·ing, -iz·es** **1.** To discharge from military service or use. **2.** To disband (troops). —**de·mo′bi·li·za′tion** (-bə-lĭ-zā′shən) *n.*

de·moc·ra·cy (dĭ-mŏk′rə-sē) *n., pl.* **-cies** **1.** Government by the people, exercised either directly or through elected representatives. **2.** A society with such a government. **3.** The common people, considered as the primary source of political power. **4.** Majority rule. **5.** The principles of social equality and individual rights. [Fr. *démocratie* < LLat. *dēmocratia* < Gk. *dēmokratiā* :

dēmos, people; see dā- in App. + *-kratiā,* -cracy.]

dem·o·crat (dĕm′ə-krăt′) *n.* **1.** An advocate of democracy. **2. Democrat** A Democratic Party member. [Fr. *démocrate,* back-formation < *démocratie,* democracy. See DEMOCRACY.]

Democrat, Mount A peak, 4,315.1 m (14,148 ft), of central CO in the Park Range of the Rocky Mts.

dem·o·crat·ic (dĕm′ə-krăt′ĭk) *adj.* **1.** Of, characterized by, or advocating democracy: *democratic government.* **2.** Of or for the people in general; popular. **3.** Believing in or practicing social equality. **4. Democratic** Of, relating to, or characteristic of the Democratic Party. —**dem′o·crat′i·cal·ly** *adv.*

Democratic Party *n.* One of the two major US political parties, owing its origin to a split in the Democratic-Republican Party under Andrew Jackson in 1828.

Dem·o·crat·ic-Re·pub·li·can Party (dĕm′ə-krăt′ĭk-rĭ-pŭb′lĭ-kən) *n.* A US political party founded by Thomas Jefferson in 1792 in opposition to the Federalist Party.

de·moc·ra·tize (dĭ-mŏk′rə-tīz′) *tr.v.* **-tized, -tiz·ing, -tiz·es** To make democratic. —**de·moc·ra·ti·za′tion** (-tĭ-zā′shən) *n.*

De·moc·ri·tus (dĭ-mŏk′rĭ-təs) 460?–370? B.C. Greek philosopher who believed that pleasure, along with self-control, is the goal of human life.

dé·mo·dé (dā′mō-dā′) *adj.* No longer in fashion; outmoded. [Fr., p. part. of *démoder,* to outmode : *dé-,* out (< OFr. *de-*; see DE-) + *mode,* fashion; see MODE.]

de·mod·u·late (dē-mŏj′ə-lāt′, -mŏd′yə-) *tr.v.* **-lat·ed, -lat·ing, -lates** To extract (information) from a modulated carrier wave. —**de·mod′u·la′tor** *n.*

de·mod·u·la·tion (dē-mŏj′ə-lā′shən) *n.* The conversion of a modulated carrier wave into a current equivalent to the original signal.

De·mo·gor·gon (dē′mə-gôr′gən, dē′mə-gôr′-) *n. Mythology* A terrifying ancient deity or demon of the underworld. [LLat. *dēmogorgōn.*]

dem·o·graph·ic (dĕm′ə-grăf′ĭk, dē′mə-) *adj.* also **dem·o·graph·i·cal** (-ĭ-kəl) Of or relating to demography. ❖ *n.* A portion of a population, esp. considered as consumers. —**dem′o·graph′i·cal·ly** *adv.*

dem·o·graph·ics (dĕm′ə-grăf′ĭks, dē′mə-) *n. (used with a pl. verb)* The characteristics of human populations and population segments, esp. when used to identify consumer markets.

de·mog·ra·phy (dĭ-mŏg′rə-fē) *n.* The study of the characteristics of human populations. [Fr. *démographie* : Gk. *dēmos,* people; see dā- in App. + Fr. *-graphie,* writing (< Gk. *-graphiā,* -graphy).] —**de·mog′ra·pher** *n.*

dem·oi·selle (dĕm′wə-zĕl′) *n.* **1.** A young woman. **2.** A demoiselle crane. **3.** See damselfly. **4.** See damselfish. [Fr., damsel < OFr. *dameisele.* See DAMSEL.]

demoiselle crane *n.* A small crane (*Anthropoides virgo*) of Asia, northern Africa, and Europe having gray and black plumage and white plumes at the side of the head.

de·mol·ish (dĭ-mŏl′ĭsh) *tr.v.* **-ished, -ish·ing, -ish·es** **1.** To tear down completely; raze. **2.** To do away with completely; put an end to. **3.** To damage (someone's reputation, for example) severely. [Fr. *démolir, démoliss-* < Lat. *dēmōlīrī* : *dē-,* de- + *mōlīrī,* to build (< *mōlēs,* mass).] See Syns at **ruin.**

dem·o·li·tion (dĕm′ə-lĭsh′ən, dē′mə-) *n.* **1.** The act or process of wrecking or destroying, esp. by explosives. **2. demolitions** Explosives, esp. when designed or used as weapons. [Fr. *démolition* < Lat. *dēmōlītiō, dēmōlītiōn-* < *dēmōlīrī,* to demolish. See DEMOLISH.] —**dem′o·li′tion·ist** *n.*

demolition derby *n.* A contest in which drivers crash old cars into each other until only one is left running.

de·mon (dē′mən) *n.* **1.** An evil supernatural being; a devil. **2.** A persistently tormenting person, force, or passion. **3.** One who is extremely zealous, skillful, or diligent. **4.** Variant of **daimon.** [ME < LLat. *daemōn* < Lat., spirit < Gk. *daimōn,* divine power. See dā- in App.]

demon. *abbr.* demonstrative

de·mon·e·tize (dē-mŏn′ĭ-tīz′, -mŭn′-) *tr.v.* **-tized, -tiz·ing, -tiz·es** **1.** To divest (a coin, for example) of monetary value. **2.** To stop using (a metal) as a monetary standard. [Fr. *démonétiser* : *dé-,* away from (< OFr. *de-*; see DE-) + Lat. *monēta,* coin; see MONEY.] —**de·mon·e·ti·za′tion** (-tĭ-zā′shən) *n.*

de·mo·ni·ac (dĭ-mō′nē-ăk′) also **de·mo·ni·a·cal** (dē′mə-nī′ə-kəl) *adj.* **1.** Possessed, produced, or influenced by a demon. **2.** Of, resembling, or suggestive of a devil; fiendish. ❖ *n.* One who is or seems to be possessed by a demon. [ME *demoniak* < LLat. *daemoniacus* < *daimoniakos* < *daimonios* < *daimōn,* divine power. See DEMON.] —**de·mo·ni·a·cal·ly** *adv.*

de·mon·ic also **dae·mon·ic** (dĭ-mŏn′ĭk) *adj.* **1.** Befitting a demon; fiendish. **2.** Motivated by a spiritual force or genius; inspired. —**de·mon′i·cal·ly** *adv.*

de·mon·ize (dē′mə-nīz′) *tr.v.* **-ized, -iz·ing, -iz·es** **1.** To turn into or as if into a demon. **2.** To possess by or as if by a demon. **3.** To represent as evil or diabolic: *demonized the enemy.* —**de′mon·i·za′tion** (-mə-nĭ-zā′shən) *n.*

de·mon·ol·a·try (dē′mə-nŏl′ə-trē) *n.* Worship of demons.

de·mon·ol·o·gy (dē′mə-nŏl′ə-jē) *n.* **1.** The study of demons. **2.** Belief in or worship of demons. **3.** A list or catalog of one's enemies. —**de′mon·o·log′ic** (-ə-lŏj′ĭk), **de′mon·o·log′i·cal**

Cecil B. De Mille

demoiselle crane
Anthropoides virgo

ă pat	oi boy
ā pay	ou out
âr care	oŏ took
ä father	oō boot
ĕ pet	ŭ cut
ē be	ûr urge
ĭ pit	th thin
ī pie	th this
îr pier	hw which
ŏ pot	zh vision
ō toe	ə about,
ô paw	item

Stress marks:
′ (primary);
′ (secondary), as in
lexicon (lĕk′sĭ-kŏn′)

(-ĭ-kəl) *adj.* —**de'mon·ol'o·gist** *n.*

de·mon·stra·ble (dĭ-mŏn'strə-bəl) *adj.* **1.** Capable of being demonstrated or proved. **2.** Obvious; apparent. —**de·mon'stra·bil'i·ty, de·mon'stra·ble·ness** *n.* —**de·mon'stra·bly** *adv.*

dem·on·strate (dĕm'ən-strāt') *v.* **-strat·ed, -strat·ing, -strates** —*tr.* **1.** To show clearly and deliberately; manifest. **2.** To show to be true by reasoning or adducing evidence; prove. **3.** To present by experiments, examples, or practical application; explain and illustrate. **4.** To show the use of (an article) to a prospective buyer. —*intr.* **1.** To give a demonstration. **2.** To participate in a public display of opinion, as by marching. [Lat. *dēmōnstrāre, dēmōnstrāt-* : *dē-*, completely; see DE- + *mōnstrāre*, to show (< *mōnstrum*, divine portent < *monēre*, to warn; see **men-¹** in App.).]

dem·on·stra·tion (dĕm'ən-strā'shən) *n.* **1.** The act of showing or making clear. **2.** Conclusive evidence; proof. **3.** An illustration or explanation by exemplification or practical application. **4.** A manifestation, as of one's feelings. **5.** A public display of group opinion.

de·mon·stra·tive (dĭ-mŏn'strə-tĭv) *adj.* **1.** Serving to manifest or prove. **2.** Involving or characterized by demonstration. **3.** Given to or marked by the open expression of emotion. **4.** *Grammar* Specifying or singling out the person or thing referred to. ❖ *n. Grammar* A demonstrative pronoun or adjective. —**de·mon'stra·tive·ly** *adv.* —**de·mon'stra·tive·ness** *n.*

dem·on·stra·tor (dĕm'ən-strā'tər) *n.* **1.** One that demonstrates, as at a rally. **2.** An article used in a demonstration.

de·mor·al·ize (dĭ-môr'ə-līz', -mŏr'-) *tr.v.* **-ized, -iz·ing, -iz·es 1.** To undermine the confidence or morale of: *an inconsistent policy that demoralized the staff.* **2.** To disorder; confuse. **3.** To debase the morals of; corrupt. —**de·mor'al·i·za'tion** (-ə-lĭ-zā'shən) *n.*

De Mor·gan (dĭ môr'gən), **Augustus** 1806–71. British mathematician who with George Boole laid the foundation for modern symbolic logic.

de·mos (dē'mŏs') *n.* **1.** The common people; the populace. **2.** The common people of an ancient Greek state. [Gk. *dēmos*, district, people. See **dā-** in App.]

De·mos·the·nes (dĭ-mŏs'thə-nēz') 384–322 B.C. Greek orator whose reputation is based mainly on his *Philippics.*

de·mote (dĭ-mōt') *tr.v.* **-mot·ed, -mot·ing, -motes** To reduce in grade, rank, or status. [DE- + (PRO)MOTE.] —**de·mo'tion** *n.*

de·mot·ic (dĭ-mŏt'ĭk) *adj.* **1.** Of or relating to the common people; popular. **2.** Of, relating to, or written in the simplified form of ancient Egyptian hieratic writing. **3. Demotic** Of or relating to a form of modern Greek based on colloquial use. ❖ *n.* **Demotic** Demotic Greek. [Gk. *dēmotikos* < *dēmotēs*, a commoner < *dēmos*, people. See **dā-** in App.]

de·mount (dē-mount') *tr.v.* **-mount·ed, -mount·ing, -mounts** To remove (a motor, for example) from a position on a mounting or other support. —**de·mount'a·ble** *adj.*

Demp·sey (dĕmp'sē), **William Harrison ("Jack")** 1895–1983. Amer. prizefighter who won the world heavyweight title in 1919.

de·mul·cent (dĭ-mŭl'sənt) *adj.* Serving to soothe or soften. ❖ *n.* A usu. mucilaginous or oily substance used esp. to soothe pain in mucuous membranes. [Lat. *dēmulcēns, dēmulcent-*, pr. part. of *dēmulcēre*, to soften : *dē-*, de- + *mulcēre*, to stroke.]

de·mur (dĭ-mûr') *intr.v.* **-murred, -mur·ring, -murs 1.** To voice opposition; object. See Syns at **object. 2.** *Law* To enter a demurrer. **3.** To delay. ❖ *n.* **1.** The act of demurring. **2.** An objection. **3.** A delay. [ME *demuren*, to delay < AN *demurer* < Lat. *dēmorārī* : *dē-*, de- + *morārī*, to delay (< *mora*, delay).] —**de·mur'ra·ble** *adj.*

de·mure (dĭ-myoor') *adj.* **-mur·er, -mur·est 1.** Modest and reserved in manner or behavior. **2.** Affectedly shy, modest, or reserved. See Syns at **shy¹.** [ME, prob. < AN (influenced by OFr. *mur, meur*, mature, serious), p. part. of *demurer*, to delay, wait. See DEMUR.] —**de·mure'ly** *adv.* —**de·mure'ness** *n.*

de·mur·rage (dĭ-mûr'ĭj, -mŭr'-) *n.* **1.** Detention of a ship or other cargo conveyance during loading or unloading beyond the scheduled time of departure. **2.** Compensation paid for such detention.

de·mur·ral (dĭ-mûr'əl, -mŭr'-) *n.* The act of demurring, esp. a mild, polite, or considered expression of opposition.

de·mur·rer (dĭ-mûr'ər, -mŭr'-) *n.* **1.** One that demurs; an objector. **2.** An objection. **3.** *Law* A method of objecting that admits the facts of the opponent's argument but denies that they sustain the pleading based upon them.

de·my (dĭ-mī') *n., pl.* **-mies** Any of several standard sizes of paper, esp. paper measuring 16 by 21 inches. [Alteration of DEMI-.]

de·my·e·lin·ate (dē-mī'ə-lə-nāt') *tr.v.* **-at·ed, -at·ing, -ates** To destroy or remove the myelin sheath of (a nerve fiber), as through disease. —**de·my'e·lin·a'tion** *n.*

de·mys·ti·fy (dē-mĭs'tə-fī') *tr.v.* **-fied, -fy·ing, -fies** To make less mysterious; clarify. —**de·mys'ti·fi·ca'tion** (-fĭ-kā'shən) *n.* —**de·mys'ti·fi'er** *n.*

de·my·thol·o·gize (dē'mĭ-thŏl'ə-jīz') *tr.v.* **-gized, -giz·ing, -giz·es 1.** To rid of mythological elements in order to discover the underlying meaning. **2.** To remove the mysterious or mythical aspects from. —**de'my·thol·o·gi·za'tion** (-jĭ-zā'shən) *n.*

dendrite

—**de'my·thol'o·giz'er** *n.*

den (dĕn) *n.* **1.** The shelter or retreat of a wild animal; a lair. **2.** A cave or hollow used as a refuge or hiding place. **3.** A hidden or squalid dwelling place: *a den of thieves.* **4.** A secluded room for study or relaxation. **5.** A unit of about eight to ten Cub Scouts. ❖ *intr.v.* **denned, den·ning, dens** To inhabit or hide in a den. [ME < OE *denn.*]

Den. *abbr.* Denmark

De·na·li (də-nä'lē) See Mount **McKinley.**

den·ar (dĕn'är') *n., pl.* **den·a·ri** (dĕn'är-ē) See table at **currency.** [Macedonian < O Church Slavonic *dinarii* < L.Gk. *dēnarion* < Lat. *dēnārius.* See DENARY.]

de·nar·i·us (dĭ-nâr'ē-əs) *n., pl.* **-i·i** (-ē-ī') **1.** An ancient Roman silver coin. **2.** An ancient Roman gold coin valued at 25 silver denarii. [ME < Lat. *dēnārius.* See DENARY.]

den·a·ry (dĕn'ə-rē) *adj.* **1.** Tenfold. **2.** Divided or counted by tens; decimal. [Lat. *dēnārius* < *dēnī*, by tens. See **dekm** in App.]

de·na·tion·al·ize (dē-năsh'ə-nə-līz') *tr.v.* **-ized, -iz·ing, -iz·es 1.** To deprive of national rights or characteristics. **2.** To transfer (an industry, for example) from governmental to private ownership. —**de·na'tion·al·i·za'tion** (-lĭ-zā'shən) *n.*

de·nat·u·ral·ize (dē-năch'ər-ə-līz') *tr.v.* **-ized, -iz·ing, -iz·es 1.** To make unnatural. **2.** To deprive of the rights of citizenship. —**de·nat'u·ral·i·za'tion** (-ər-ə-lĭ-zā'shən) *n.*

de·na·ture (dē-nā'chər) *tr.v.* **-tured, -tur·ing, -tures 1.** To change the nature or natural qualities of. **2.** To render unfit to eat or drink without destroying other uses, esp. to add methanol to (ethyl alcohol). **3.** *Biochemistry* **a.** To alter (a protein) structurally, as with heat, so that its original properties, esp. its biological activity, are diminished or eliminated. **b.** To cause (double-stranded DNA) to separate into individual strands. **4.** *Physics* To add nonfissionable matter to (fissionable material) so as to prevent use in an atomic weapon. —**de·na'tur·ant** *n.* —**de·na'tur·a'tion** *n.*

den·dri·form (dĕn'drə-fôrm') *adj.* Shaped like or having the form of a tree.

den·dri·mer (dĕn'drə-mər) *n.* A polymer in which the atoms are arranged in branches along a central backbone of carbon atoms. [DENDR(O)- + alteration of (POL)YMER.]

den·drite (dĕn'drīt') *n.* **1a.** A mineral crystallizing in another mineral in the form of a branching or treelike mark. **b.** A rock or mineral bearing such a mark or marks. **2.** A branched protoplasmic extension of a nerve cell that conducts impulses from adjacent cells inward toward the cell body.

den·drit·ic (dĕn-drĭt'ĭk) also **den·drit·i·cal** (-ĭ-kəl) *adj.* **1.** Of, relating to, or resembling a dendrite. **2.** Of or relating to a dendritic cell. **3.** Dendriform. —**den·drit'i·cal·ly** *adv.*

dendritic cell *n.* An antigen-presenting immune cell that functions to initiate the immune response by activating lymphocytes and stimulating the secretion of cytokines.

dendro– or **dendri–** or **dendr–** *pref.* Tree; treelike: *dendrochronology.* [< Gk. *dendron*, tree. See **deru-** in App.]

den·dro·chro·nol·o·gy (dĕn'drō-krə-nŏl'ə-jē) *n.* The study of climate changes and past events by comparing the successive annual growth rings of trees or old timber. —**den'dro·chron'o·log'i·cal** (-krŏn'ə-lŏj'ĭ-kəl) *adj.* —**den'dro·chron'o·log'i·cal·ly** *adv.* —**den'dro·chro·nol'o·gist** *n.*

den·droid (dĕn'droid') also **den·droi·dal** (dĕn-droid'l) *adj.* Shaped like a tree.

den·drol·o·gy (dĕn-drŏl'ə-jē) *n.* The botanical study of trees and other woody plants. —**den'dro·log'ic** (-drə-lŏj'ĭk), **den'dro·log'i·cal** *adj.* —**den·drol'o·gist** *n.*

den·dron (dĕn'drŏn') *n.* See **dendrite** 2. [Gk., tree. See **deru-** in App.]

dene (dēn) *n. Chiefly British* A sandy tract or dune by the seashore. [Poss. E Frisian *düne*, a sand dune; akin to DUNE.]

De·ne also **Dé·né** (dä'nē, dä-nā') *n. (used with a pl. verb)* The Athabaskan-speaking peoples of northwest Canada and inland Alaska considered as a group.

De·neb (dĕn'ĕb') *n.* The brightest star in the constellation Cygnus. [Ar. *danab*, tail.]

De·neb·o·la (də-nĕb'ə-lə) *n.* A star in the constellation Leo. [< shortening of Ar. *danab al-'asad*, tail of the lion : *danab*, tail + *al-*, the + *'asad*, lion.]

den·e·ga·tion (dĕn'ĭ-gā'shən) *n.* A denial. [Ult. < Lat. *dēnegāre, dēnegāt-*, to deny. See DENY.]

de·ner·vate (dē-nûr'vāt') *tr.v.* **-vat·ed, -vat·ing, -vates** To deprive (an organ or body part) of a nerve supply, as by surgery or with drugs. —**de·ner·va'tion** *n.*

den·gue (dĕng'gē, -gā) *n.* An acute, infectious tropical disease caused by an arbovirus transmitted by mosquitoes and marked by high fever, rash, headache, and severe muscle and joint pain. [Am.Sp., alteration (influenced by *dengue*, affectation) of Swahili *-dinga.*]

Deng Xiao·ping (dŭng' shou'pĭng', shyou'-) also **Teng Hsiao-ping** (tŭng' shyou'pĭng', dŭng') 1904–97. Chinese Communist leader who officially retired as head of state in Nov. 1989.

de·ni·a·ble (dĭ-nī'ə-bəl) *adj.* **1.** Possible to contradict or declare untrue. **2.** Being such that plausible disavowal is possible. —**de·ni'a·bil'i·ty** *n.* —**de·ni'a·bly** *adv.*

de·ni·al (dĭ-nī'əl) *n.* **1.** A refusal to comply with or satisfy a request. **2a.** A refusal to grant the truth of a statement or allegation; a contradiction. **b.** *Law* The opposing by a defendant of an allegation of the plaintiff. **3a.** A refusal to accept or believe something, such as a belief. **b.** *Psychology* An unconscious defense mechanism marked by refusal to acknowledge painful realities, thoughts, or feelings. **4.** The act of disowning or disavowing; repudiation. **5.** Self-denial.

de•ni•er¹ (dĭ-nī′ər) *n.* One that denies.

den•ier² (dən-yä′) *n.* **1.** (*also* dĕn′yər) A unit of fineness for rayon, nylon, and silk, based on a standard mass per length of 1 gram per 9,000 meters of yarn. **2.** (*also* də-nîr′) **a.** A small coin of varying composition and value current in western Europe from the eighth century until the French Revolution. **b.** *Archaic* A small trifling sum. [ME *denere*, a coin < OFr. *dener* < Lat. *dēnārius*. See DENARIUS.]

den•i•grate (dĕn′ĭ-grāt′) *tr.v.* **-grat•ed, -grat•ing, -grates** **1.** To attack the character or reputation of; speak ill of; defame. **2.** To disparage; belittle. [Lat. *dēnigrāre, dēnigrāt-*, to blacken, defame : *dē-, de-* + *niger, nigr-*, black; see nek^w-t- in App.] —**den′i•gra′tion** *n.* —**den′i•gra′tor** *n.*

den•im (dĕn′ĭm) *n.* **1a.** A coarse twilled cloth, usu. cotton, used for jeans, overalls, and work uniforms. **b. denims** Trousers or another garment made of this cloth. **2.** A similar but finer fabric used in draperies and upholstery. [Fr. (*serge*) *de Nîmes*, (serge) of Nîmes.]

De•nis or **De•nys** (dĕn′ĭs, də-nē′), Saint. 3rd cent. A.D. First bishop of Paris and patron saint of France.

de•ni•tri•fy (dē-nī′trə-fī′) *tr.v.* **-fied, -fy•ing, -fies** **1.** To remove nitrogen or nitrogen groups from (a compound). **2.** To reduce (nitrates or nitrites) to nitrogen-containing gases. —**de•ni′tri•fi•ca′tion** (-fĭ-kā′shən) *n.*

den•i•zen (dĕn′ĭ-zən) *n.* **1.** An inhabitant; a resident. **2.** One that frequents a particular place. **3.** *Ecology* An animal or a plant naturalized in a region. **4.** *Chiefly British* A foreigner who is granted rights of residence and sometimes of citizenship. ✦ *tr.v.* **-zened, -zen•ing, -zens** *Chiefly British* To make a denizen of. [ME *denisein* < AN *denzein* < *deinz*, within < LLat. *deintus*, from within. See DEDANS.] —**den′i•zen•a′tion** *n.*

Den•mark (dĕn′märk′) A country of N Europe on Jutland and adjacent islands; united with Sweden until 1523 and with Norway until 1814. Cap. Copenhagen. Pop. 5,205,000.

Denmark Strait A channel between Greenland and Iceland connecting the Arctic Ocean with the N Atlantic Ocean.

den mother A woman who supervises a den of Cub Scouts.

de•nom•i•nate (dĭ-nŏm′ə-nāt′) *tr.v.* **-nat•ed, -nat•ing, -nates** **1.** To issue or express in terms of a given monetary unit. **2.** To give a name to; designate. ✦ *adj.* (-ə-nĭt) Of or relating to a quantity as a multiple of a unit: *12 in 12 pounds is denominate.* [Lat. *dēnōmināre, dēnōmināt-* : *dē-, de-* + *nōmināre*, to name (< *nōmen, nōmin-*, name; see nō-men- in App.).] —**de•nom′i•na•ble** (-nə-bəl) *adj.*

de•nom•i•na•tion (dĭ-nŏm′ə-nā′shən) *n.* **1.** A large group of religious congregations united under a common faith and name and administratively organized. **2.** One of a series of kinds, values, or sizes, as of currency or weights. **3.** A name or designation, esp. for a class or group. —**de•nom′i•na′tion•al** *adj.* —**de•nom′i•na′tion•al•ly** *adv.*

de•nom•i•na•tion•al•ism (dĭ-nŏm′ə-nā′shə-nə-lĭz′əm) *n.* **1.** The tendency to divide into religious denominations. **2.** Support of such division. **3.** Strict denominational adherence; sectarianism. —**de•nom′i•na′tion•al•ist** *adj. & n.*

de•nom•i•na•tive (dĭ-nŏm′ə-nā′tĭv, -nə-tĭv) *adj.* **1.** Giving or constituting a name; naming. **2.** Formed from a noun or adjective. ✦ *n.* A word, esp. a verb, that derives from a noun or adjective.

de•nom•i•na•tor (dĭ-nŏm′ə-nā′tər) *n.* **1.** *Mathematics* The expression written below the line in a common fraction that indicates the number of parts into which one whole is divided. **2.** A common trait or characteristic. **3.** An average level or standard.

de•no•ta•tion (dē′nō-tā′shən) *n.* **1.** The act of denoting; indication. **2.** Something, such as a sign, that denotes. **3.** Something signified or referred to; a particular meaning of a symbol. **4.** The most specific or direct meaning of a word, in contrast to its figurative or associated meanings.

de•no•ta•tive (dĭ-nō′tə-tĭv, dē′nō-tā′-) *adj.* **1.** Denoting or naming; designative. **2.** Specific; direct. —**de•no′ta•tive•ly** *adv.*

de•note (dĭ-nōt′) *tr.v.* **-not•ed, -not•ing, -notes** **1.** To mark; indicate. **2.** To serve as a symbol or name for the meaning of; signify. **3.** To signify directly; refer to specifically. [Fr. *dénoter* < Lat. *dēnotāre* : *dē-, de-* + *notāre*, to mark; see CONNOTE.] —**de•not′a•ble** *adj.* —**de•no′tive** *adj.*

> **USAGE NOTE** In speaking of words or expressions *denote* describes the relation between the expression and the thing it conventionally names, whereas *connote* describes the relation between the word and the images or associations it evokes. Thus the word *river* denotes a moving body of water and may connote such things as the relentlessness of time and the changing nature of life.

de•noue•ment also **dé•noue•ment** (dā′nōō-män′) *n.* **1a.** The final resolution of a dramatic or narrative plot. **b.** The events fol-

lowing the climax of a drama or novel in which such a resolution takes place. **2.** The outcome of a sequence of events; the end result. [Fr. *dénouement* < OFr. *desnouement*, an untying < *desnouer*, to undo : *des-, de-* + *nouer*, to tie (< Lat. *nōdāre* < *nōdus*, knot).]

de•nounce (dĭ-nouns′) *tr.v.* **-nounced, -nounc•ing, -nounc•es** **1.** To condemn openly as being evil or reprehensible. See Syns at **criticize. 2.** To accuse formally. **3.** To give formal announcement of the ending of (a treaty). [ME *denouncen*, to proclaim < AN *denuncier* and Med.Lat. *dēnūntiāre*, both < Lat. : *dē, de-* + *nūntiāre*, to announce (< *nūntius*, messenger).] —**de•nounce′ment** *n.* —**de•nounc′er** *n.*

de no•vo (dĭ nō′vō, dā) *adv. & adj.* Over again, anew. [Lat. *dē novō.*]

dense (dĕns) *adj.* **dens•er, dens•est** **1a.** Having a high concentration of parts or mass per unit. **b.** Crowded closely together; compact. **2.** Hard to penetrate; thick: *a dense jungle.* **3a.** Permitting little light to pass through, because of compactness of matter: *a dense fog.* **b.** Opaque, with good contrast between light and dark. Used of a photographic negative. **4.** Difficult to understand because of complexity or obscurity. **5.** Slow to apprehend; thickheaded. [ME < Lat. *dēnsus.*] —**dense′ly** *adv.* —**dense′ness** *n.*

den•sim•e•ter (dĕn-sĭm′ĭ-tər) *n.* An instrument used to measure density or specific gravity. [Lat. *dēnsus*, dense + -METER.] —**den′si•met′ric** (-sə-mĕt′rĭk) *adj.*

den•si•tom•e•ter (dĕn′sĭ-tŏm′ĭ-tər) *n.* **1.** An apparatus for measuring the optical density of a material. **2.** See **densimeter.** [DENSIT(Y) + -METER.] —**den′si•tom′e•try** (-ĭ-trē) *n.*

den•si•ty (dĕn′sĭ-tē) *n., pl.* **-ties** **1.** The quality or condition of being dense. **2a.** The quantity of something per unit measure, esp. per unit length, area, or volume. **b.** The mass per unit volume of a substance under specified conditions of pressure and temperature. **3.** *Computer Science* The number of units of useful information contained within a linear dimension. **4.** The number of beings or objects per unit of area. **5.** The degree of optical opacity of a medium or material, as of a photographic negative. **6.** Thickness of consistency; impenetrability. **7.** Complexity of structure or content. **8.** Stupidity; dullness.

dent¹ (dĕnt) *n.* **1.** A depression in a surface made by pressure or a blow. **2.** *Informal* A significant, usu. diminishing effect. **3.** *Informal* Meaningful progress; headway. ✦ *v.* **dent•ed, dent•ing, dents** —*tr.* To make a dent in. —*intr.* To become dented. [ME *dent*, var. of *dint*, blow < OE *dynt.*]

dent² (dĕnt) *n.* See **tooth** 3. [Fr. See DENTIST.]

dent- *pref.* Variant of **denti-.**

den•tal (dĕn′tl) *adj.* **1.** Of, relating to, or for the teeth. **2.** Of, relating to, or intended for dentistry. **3.** *Linguistics* Articulated with the tip of the tongue near or against the upper front teeth, as English *t* and *d.* ✦ *n. Linguistics* A dental consonant. [NLat. *dentālis* < Lat. *dēns, dent-*, tooth. See **dent-** in App.]

dental caries *n.* The formation of cavities in the teeth by the action of bacteria; tooth decay.

dental floss *n.* A waxed or unwaxed thread used to remove food particles and plaque from between the teeth and under the gums.

dental hygienist *n.* A person trained and licensed to provide preventive dental services, usu. in conjunction with a dentist.

dental implant *n.* A tooth, usu. artificial, anchored in the gums or jawbone to replace a missing tooth.

den•ta•li•um (dĕn-tā′lē-əm) *n., pl.* **-li•a** (-lē-ə) or **-li•ums** Any of various tooth shells of the genus *Dentalium.* [NLat. *Dentālium*, genus name < *dentālis*, toothy. See DENTAL.]

dental plate *n.* See **denture** 1.

dental technician *n.* One who makes dental devices, such as bridges, to the specifications of a dentist.

den•tate (dĕn′tāt′) *adj.* Edged with toothlike projections; toothed: *dentate leaves.* [Lat. *dentātus* < *dēns, dent-*, tooth. See **dent-** in App.] —**den′tate′ly** *adv.*

den•ta•tion (dĕn-tā′shən) *n.* **1.** The condition of being dentate. **2.** A toothlike part or projection.

dent corn *n.* A tall-growing variety of corn (*Zea mays* var. *indentata*) having yellow or white kernels indented at the tip.

denti- or **dent-** *pref.* **1.** Tooth: *dentoid.* **2.** Dental: *dentilabial.* [< Lat. *dēns, dent-*, tooth. See **dent-** in App.]

den•ti•cle (dĕn′tĭ-kəl) *n.* A small tooth or toothlike projection. [ME < Lat. *denticulus*, dim. of *dēns, dent-*, tooth. See **dent-** in App.] —**den•tic′u•lar** (-tĭk′yə-lər) *adj.*

den•tic•u•late (dĕn-tĭk′yə-lĭt) also **den•tic•u•lat•ed** (-lā′tĭd) *adj.* **1.** Finely toothed or notched; minutely dentate. **2.** *Architecture* Having dentils. [Lat. *denticulātus < denticulus*, denticle. See DENTICLE.] —**den•tic′u•late•ly** *adv.* —**den•tic′u•la′tion** *n.*

den•ti•form (dĕn′tə-fôrm′) *adj.* Shaped like a tooth.

den•ti•frice (dĕn′tə-frĭs′) *n.* A substance, such as a paste or powder, for cleaning the teeth. [Fr. < OFr. < Lat. *dentifricium* : *denti-*, denti- + *fricāre*, to rub.]

den•tig•er•ous (dĕn-tĭj′ər-əs) *adj.* Having or furnished with teeth. [DENTI- + Lat. *gerere*, to bear.]

den•til (dĕn′tĭl) *n.* One of a series of small rectangular blocks projecting like teeth from a molding or beneath a cornice. [Obsolete Fr. *dentille* < OFr., dim. of *dent*, tooth. See DENTIST.]

den•tin (dĕn′tĭn) or **den•tine** (-tēn′) *n.* The main calcareous part of a tooth beneath the enamel, surrounding the pulp chamber and root canals. —**den′tin•al** (dĕn′tə-nəl, dĕn-tē′-) *adj.*

Denmark

dentate
dentate leaf

den·tist (dĕn′tĭst) *n.* A person who is trained and licensed to practice dentistry. [Fr. *dentiste* < *dent*, tooth < OFr. < Lat. *dēns, dent-*. See **dent-** in App.]

den·tist·ry (dĕn′tĭ-strē) *n.* The medical science concerned with diseases of the teeth, gums, and related oral structures, including the restoration of defective teeth.

den·ti·tion (dĕn-tĭsh′ən) *n.* **1.** The type, number, and arrangement of teeth. **2.** The process of growing new teeth; teething. [Lat. *dentītiō, dentītiōn-* < *dentītus,* p. part. of *dentīre,* to teethe < *dēns, dent-,* tooth. See DENTIST.]

den·toid (dĕn′toid′) *adj.* Tooth-shaped; toothlike.

den·tu·lous (dĕn′chə-ləs) *adj.* Possessing teeth; toothed. [Back-formation < EDENTULOUS, toothless.]

den·ture (dĕn′chər) *n.* **1.** A partial or complete set of artificial teeth for either jaw. **2.** A complete set of removable artificial teeth for both jaws. Often used in the plural. [Fr. < OFr. < *dent,* tooth. See DENTIST.]

de·nu·cle·ar·ize (dē-nōō′klē-ə-rīz′, -nyōō′-) *v.* **-ized, -iz·ing, -iz·es** —*tr.* To remove or ban nuclear weapons from. —*intr.* To reduce or eliminate a store of nuclear weapons. —**de·nu′cle·ar·i·za′tion** (-ər-ĭ-zā′shən) *n.*

de·nu·date (dĭ-nōō′dāt′, -nyōō′-) *tr.v.* **-dat·ed, -dat·ing, -dates** To divest of covering. ❖ *adj.* Bare; denuded. [Lat. *dēnūdāre, dēnūdāt-.* See DENUDE.]

de·nude (dĭ-nōōd′, -nyōōd′) *tr.v.* **-nud·ed, -nud·ing, -nudes** **1.** To divest of covering; make bare. **2.** *Geology* To expose (rock strata) by erosion. [Lat. *dēnūdāre : dē-, de- + nūdāre,* to make bare (< *nūdus,* nude).] —**de′nu·da′tion** (dē′nōō-dā′shən, -nyōō-, dĕn′yōō-) *n.*

de·nu·mer·a·ble (dĭ-nōō′mər-ə-bəl, -nyōō′-) *adj.* Countable. [< *denumerate,* to count < LLat. *dēnumerāre, dēnumerāt-,* alteration of Lat. *dīnumerāre : dī-, dis-, dis- + numerāre,* to number; see NUMERATE.] —**de·nu′mer·a·bil′i·ty** *n.* —**de·nu′mer·a·bly** *adv.*

de·nun·ci·a·tion (dĭ-nŭn′sē-ā′shən, -shē-) *n.* **1.** The act or an instance of denouncing, esp. publically. **2.** The act of accusing another of a crime before a public prosecutor. [ME *denunciacioun* < Lat. *dēnūntiātiō, dēnūntiātiōn-* < *dēnūntiātus,* p. part. of *dēnūntiāre,* to announce. See DENOUNCE.] —**de·nun′ci·a·tive** (-ā′tĭv, -ə-tĭv) *adj.* —**de·nun′ci·a·to·ry** (-ə-tôr′ē, -tōr′ē) *adj.*

Den·ver (dĕn′vər) The cap. of CO, in the N-central part on the South Platte R.; settled in 1858. Pop. 554,636.

Denver boot *n.* A device locked to the wheel of a vehicle to keep it from being driven, used esp. to force settlement of traffic violations.

de·ny (dĭ-nī′) *tr.v.* **-nied, -ny·ing, -nies** **1.** To declare untrue; contradict. **2.** To refuse to believe; reject. **3.** To refuse to recognize or acknowledge; disavow. **4a.** To decline to grant or allow; refuse. **b.** To give a refusal to; turn down or away. **c.** To restrain (oneself) esp. from indulgence in pleasures. [ME *denien* < OFr. *denier* < Lat. *dēnegāre : dē-, de- + negāre,* to say no; see **ne** in App.]

De·nys (dĕn′ĭs, də-nē′), Saint. See Saint **Denis**.

de·o·dar (dē′ə-där′) or **de·o·dar·a** (-där′ə) *n.* A tall cedar (*Cedrus deodara*) that has drooping branches and is an important timber tree in India. [Hindi *deodār* < Skt. *devadāru : deva-,* divine; see **dyeu-** in App. + *dāru,* wood; see **deru-** in App.]

de·o·dor·ant (dē-ō′dər-ənt) *n.* A substance used to mask or suppress unwanted odors. ❖ *adj.* Capable of masking or neutralizing odors.

de·o·dor·ize (dē-ō′də-rīz′) *tr.v.* **-ized, -iz·ing, -iz·es** **1.** To mask or neutralize the odor of. **2.** To make more acceptable, as by elimination or suppression of an offensive aspect. —**de·o′dor·i·za′tion** (-dər-ĭ-zā′shən) *n.* —**de·o′dor·iz′er** *n.*

de·on·tic (dē-ŏn′tĭk) *adj.* Of, relating to, or concerning duties or obligations. [Gk. *deon, deont-,* obligation, necessity. See DEON-TOLOGY.]

de·on·tol·o·gy (dē′ŏn-tŏl′ə-jē) *n.* Ethical theory concerned with duties and rights. [Gk. *deon, deont-,* obligation, necessity (< neut. pr. part. of *dein,* to need, lack; see **deu-¹** in App.) + –LOGY.] —**de·on′to·log′i·cal** (-tə-lŏj′ĭ-kəl) *adj.* —**de·on′tol′o·gist** *n.*

de·ox·i·dize (dē-ŏk′sĭ-dīz′) *tr.v.* **-dized, -diz·ing, -diz·es** To remove oxygen from (a compound); reduce. —**de·ox′i·di·za′tion** (-dĭ-zā′shən) *n.* —**de·ox′i·diz′er** *n.*

deoxy– *pref.* Being a molecule containing less oxygen than another to which it is closely related: *deoxycorticosterone.*

de·ox·y·cor·ti·cos·ter·one (dē-ŏk′sē-kôr′tĭ-kŏs′tə-rōn′) *n.* A steroid hormone, $C_{21}H_{30}O_3$, that is secreted by the adrenal cortex and is a precursor of corticosterone.

de·ox·y·gen·ate (dē-ŏk′sə-jə-nāt′) *tr.v.* **-at·ed, -at·ing, -ates** To remove dissolved oxygen from (a liquid, such as water). —**de·ox′y·gen·a′tion** *n.*

de·ox·y·ri·bo·nu·cle·ase (dē-ŏk′sē-rī′bō-nōō′klē-ās′, -āz′, -nyōō′-) *n.* DNase.

de·ox·y·ri·bo·nu·cle·ic acid (dē-ŏk′sē-rī′bō-nōō-klē′ĭk, -klā′-, -nyōō-) *n.* DNA.

de·ox·y·ri·bo·nu·cle·o·tide (dē-ŏk′sē-rī′bō-nōō′klē-ə-tīd′, -nyōō′-) *n.* A nucleotide containing deoxyribose.

de·ox·y·ri·bose (dē-ŏk′sē-rī′bōs′) *n.* A sugar, $C_5H_{10}O_4$, that is a constituent of DNA.

Denver boot

deodar
Cedrus deodara cv. 'Aurea'

dep. *abbr.* **1.** department **2.** departure **3.** dependency **4.** deponent **5.** deposed **6.** deposit **7.** depot **8.** deputy

de·part (dĭ-pärt′) *v.* **-part·ed, -part·ing, -parts** —*intr.* **1.** To go away; leave. **2.** To die. **3.** To vary, as from a regular course; deviate. See Syns at **swerve.** —*tr.* To go away from; leave. [ME *departen* < OFr. *departir,* to split, divide : *de-, de- + partir,* to divide (< Lat. *partīre < pars, part-,* part; see PART).]

de·part·ed (dĭ-pär′tĭd) *adj.* **1.** Bygone; past. **2.** Dead. ❖ *n.* A dead person, esp. one who has died recently.

de·part·ment (dĭ-pärt′mənt) *n.* **1.** A distinct, usu. specialized division of a large organization, esp.: **a.** A principal administrative division of a government. **b.** A specialized division of a business: *the personnel department.* **c.** A division of a school or college dealing with a particular subject: *the physics department.* **2. Department** One of the principal executive divisions of the US government, headed by a cabinet officer. **3.** A section of a department store selling a particular line of merchandise. **4.** An administrative district in France. **5.** A unit of a warship's crew, organized by function. **6.** An area of particular knowledge or responsibility; a specialty. [Fr. *département* < OFr., separation < *departir,* to divide. See DEPART.] —**de′part·men′tal** (dē′pärt-mĕn′tl) *adj.* —**de′part·men′tal·ly** *adv.*

de·part·men·tal·ize (dē′pärt-mĕn′tl-īz′) *tr.v.* **-ized, -iz·ing, -iz·es** To organize into departments. —**de′part·men′tal·i·za′tion** (-ĭ-zā′shən) *n.*

department store *n.* A large retail store offering a variety of merchandise and services in separate departments.

de·par·ture (dĭ-pär′chər) *n.* **1.** The act of leaving. **2.** A starting out, as on a trip or a course of action. **3.** A divergence or deviation, as from an established rule or procedure.

de·pau·per·ate (də-pô′pər-ĭt) *adj.* **1.** Arrested in growth or development; stunted. **2.** Severely diminished; impoverished. —**de·pau′pe·ra′tion** (-pə-rā′shən) *n.*

de·pend (dĭ-pĕnd′) *intr.v.* **-pend·ed, -pend·ing, -pends** **1.** To rely, esp. for support or maintenance. **2.** To place trust or confidence. **3.** To be determined, conditioned, or contingent. **4.** To have a dependence or addiction. **5.** To be pending or undecided, as in a court. **6.** To hang down. [ME *dependen,* to hang down < OFr. *dependre* < Lat. *dēpendēre : dē-, de- + pendēre,* to hang.]

> **USAGE NOTE** In writing or formal speech, *depend,* indicating condition or contingency, is always followed by *on* or *upon,* as in *It depends on who is in charge.*

de·pend·a·ble (dĭ-pĕn′də-bəl) *adj.* Trustworthy. —**de·pend′a·bil′i·ty, de·pend′a·ble·ness** *n.* —**de·pend′a·bly** *adv.*

de·pen·dence also **de·pen·dance** (dĭ-pĕn′dəns) *n.* **1.** The state of being dependent, as for support. **2a.** Subordination to someone or something needed or greatly desired. **b.** Trust; reliance. **3.** The state of being determined, influenced, or controlled by something else. **4.** A compulsive or chronic need; an addiction: *an alcohol dependence.*

de·pen·den·cy also **de·pen·dan·cy** (dĭ-pĕn′dən-sē) *n., pl.* **-cies** **1.** Dependence. **2.** Something dependent or subordinate. **3.** A territory under the jurisdiction of a state of which it does not form an integral part.

de·pen·dent (dĭ-pĕn′dənt) *adj.* **1.** also **de·pen·dant** (dĭ-pĕn′dənt) Contingent on another. **2.** Subordinate. **3.** Relying on or requiring the aid of another for support. **4.** Hanging down. ❖ *n.* One who relies on another esp. for financial support. —**de·pen′dent·ly** *adv.*

dependent clause *n.* A clause that cannot stand alone as a full sentence and functions as a noun, adjective, or adverb within a sentence.

dependent variable *n.* **1.** *Mathematics* A variable whose value is determined by the value assumed by an independent variable. **2.** *Statistics* The observed variable in an experiment whose changes are determined by one or more independent variables.

de·per·son·al·ize (dē-pûr′sə-nə-līz′) *tr.v.* **-ized, -iz·ing, -iz·es** **1.** To deprive of individual character or a sense of personal identity. **2.** To render impersonal. —**de·per′son·al·i·za′tion** (-lĭ-zā′shən) *n.*

de·pict (dĭ-pĭkt′) *tr.v.* **-pict·ed, -pict·ing, -picts** **1.** To represent in a picture or sculpture. **2.** To represent in words; describe. [ME *depicten* < Lat. *dēpingere, dēpict- : dē-, de- + pingere,* to picture.] —**de·pic′tion** *n.*

de·pig·men·ta·tion (dē-pĭg′mən-tā′shən, -mĕn-) *n.* Loss or removal of normal pigmentation.

dep·i·late (dĕp′ə-lāt′) *tr.v.* **-lat·ed, -lat·ing, -lates** To remove hair from (the body). [Lat. *dēpilāre, dēpilāt- : dē-, de- + pilāre,* to deprive of hair (< *pilus,* hair).] —**dep′i·la′tion** *n.* —**dep′i·la′tor** *n.*

de·pil·a·to·ry (dĭ-pĭl′ə-tôr′ē, -tōr′ē) *adj.* Having the capability to remove hair. ❖ *n., pl.* **-ries** A preparation that is used to remove unwanted hair from the body.

de·plane (dē-plān′) *intr.v.* **-planed, -plan·ing, -planes** To disembark from an airplane.

de·plete (dĭ-plēt′) *tr.v.* **-plet·ed, -plet·ing, -pletes** To decrease the fullness of; use up or empty out. [Lat. *dēplēre, dēplēt-,* to empty : *dē-, de- + plēre,* to fill; see **pelə-¹** in App.] —**de·plet′a·ble** *adj.*

SYNONYMS *deplete, drain, exhaust, impoverish, enervate* These verbs mean to weaken severely by removing something essential. *Deplete* refers to using up gradually and only hints at harmful consequences: *Our food supply was soon depleted. Drain* suggests gradual drawing off and implies more harm: *War drains a nation's economy. Exhaust* stresses reduction to a point of no further usefulness: *"The resources of civilization are not yet exhausted"* (William Ewart Gladstone). *Impoverish* refers to severe reduction of essential resources or qualities: *"His death . . . impoverished the public stock of harmless pleasure"* (Samuel Johnson). *Enervate* refers to weakening or destruction of vitality or strength: *Idleness enervates the will to succeed.*

de•ple•tion (dĭ-plē′shən) *n.* **1.** The act or process of depleting. **2.** The state of being depleted; exhaustion. **3.** The use or consumption of a resource faster than it is replenished.

de•plor•a•ble (dĭ-plôr′ə-bəl, -plōr′-) *adj.* **1.** Worthy of severe condemnation or reproach. **2.** Lamentable; woeful. **3.** Wretched; bad. **—de•plor′a•ble•ness, de•plor′a•bil′i•ty** *n.* **—de•plor′a•bly** *adv.*

de•plore (dĭ-plôr′, -plōr′) *tr.v.* **-plored, -plor•ing, -plores 1.** To feel or express strong disapproval of; condemn. **2.** To express sorrow or grief over. **3.** To regret; bemoan. [Fr. *déplorer*, lament, regret < Lat. *dēplōrāre* : *dē-*, de- + *plōrāre*, to wail.]

de•ploy (dĭ-ploi′) *v.* **-ployed, -ploy•ing, -ploys** *—tr.* **1a.** To position (troops) in readiness for combat. **b.** To bring (forces or material) into action. **c.** To base (a weapons system) in the field. **2.** To distribute (persons or forces) systematically or strategically. **3.** To put into use or action. *—intr.* To be or become deployed. [Fr. *déployer* < OFr. *despleier* < Lat. *displicāre*, to scatter : *dis-*, dis- + *plicāre*, to fold; see **plek-** in App.] **—de•ploy′a•bil′i•ty** *n.* **—de•ploy′a•ble** *adj.* **—de•ploy′er** *n.* **—de•ploy′ment** *n.*

de•plume (dē-plo͞om′) *tr.v.* **-plumed, -plum•ing, -plumes** To pluck the feathers from. **—de′plu•ma′tion** *n.*

de•po•lar•ize (dē-pō′lə-rīz′) *tr.v.* **-ized, -iz•ing, -iz•es 1.** To eliminate or counteract the polarization of. **2.** To demagnetize. **—de•po′lar•i•za′tion** (-lər-ĭ-zā′shən) *n.*

de•po•lit•i•cize (dē′pə-lĭt′ĭ-sīz′) *tr.v.* **-cized, -ciz•ing, -ciz•es** To remove the political aspect from. **—de′po•lit′i•ci•za′tion** (-sĭ-zā′shən) *n.*

de•pone (dĭ-pōn′) *v.* **-poned, -pon•ing, -pones** *—tr.* To testify or declare under oath. *—intr.* To give testimony. [ME *deponen* < Med.Lat. *dēpōnere* < Lat., to put down : *dē-*, de- + *pōnere*, to put; see **apo-** in App.]

de•po•nent (dĭ-pō′nənt) *adj. Grammar* Being a verb of active meaning but passive or middle form, as certain Latin and Greek verbs. ❖ *n.* **1.** *Grammar* A deponent verb. **2.** *Law* One who testifies under oath, esp. in writing. [ME < LLat. *(verbum) dēpōnēns, dēpōnent-*, deponent (verb), pr. part. of Lat. *dēpōnere*, to put down. See DEPONE.]

de•pop•u•late (dē-pŏp′yə-lāt′) *tr.v.* **-lat•ed, -lat•ing, -lates** To reduce sharply the population of, as by disease, war, or forcible relocation. [Lat. *dēpopulārī, dēpopulāt-*, to lay waste : *dē-*, de- + *populārī*, to ravage (< *populus*, people, throng).] **—de•pop′u•la′tion** *n.* **—de•pop′u•la′tor** *n.*

de•port (dĭ-pôrt′, -pōrt′) *tr.v.* **-port•ed, -port•ing, -ports 1.** To expel from a country. See Syns at **banish. 2.** To behave or conduct (oneself) in a given manner; comport. [Fr. *déporter*, to banish < Lat. *dēportāre*, to carry away : *dē-*, de- + *portāre*, to carry; see **per-**[2] in App. Sense 2, ME < OFr. *deporter*, to behave < Lat. *dēportāre*.]

de•port•a•ble (dĭ-pôr′tə-bəl, -pōr′-) *adj.* **1.** Subject to deportation: *a deportable alien.* **2.** Punishable by deportation.

de•por•ta•tion (dē′pôr-tā′shən, -pōr-) *n.* **1.** The act or an instance of deporting. **2.** Expulsion of an undesirable alien from a country.

de•port•ee (dē′pôr-tē′, -pōr-) *n.* A deported person.

de•port•ment (dĭ-pôrt′mənt, -pōrt′-) *n.* A manner of personal conduct; behavior. See Syns at **behavior.**

de•pos•al (dĭ-pō′zəl) *n.* The act or an instance of deposing from office.

de•pose (dĭ-pōz′) *v.* **-posed, -pos•ing, -pos•es** *—tr.* **1a.** To remove from office or power. **b.** To dethrone. **2.** *Law* **a.** To state or affirm in a deposition or by affidavit. **b.** To take a deposition from. **3.** To put or lay down; deposit. *—intr. Law* To give a deposition; testify. [ME *deposen* < OFr. *deposer*, alteration (influenced by *poser*, to put) of Lat. *dēpōnere*, to put down; see DEPONE.] **—de•pos′a•ble** *adj.*

de•pos•it (dĭ-pŏz′ĭt) *v.* **-it•ed, -it•ing, -its** *—tr.* **1.** To put or set down; place. **2.** To lay down or leave behind by a natural process. **3a.** To give over or entrust for safekeeping. **b.** To put (money) in a bank or financial account. **4.** To give as partial payment or security. *—intr.* To become deposited; settle. ❖ *n.* **1.** Something that is entrusted for safekeeping. **2.** The condition of being deposited. **3.** A partial or initial payment of a cost or debt. **4.** A sum of money given as security for an item acquired for temporary use. **5.** A depository. **6.** Something deposited, esp. by a natural process, as: **a.** *Geology* A concentration of mineral matter or sediment in a layer, vein, or pocket. **b.** *Physiology* An accumulation of organic or inorganic material in a body tissue, structure, or fluid. **c.** A sediment or precipitate that has settled out of a solution. **7.** A coating or crust left on a surface, as by evaporation. [Lat. *dēpōnere, dēposit-*. See DEPONE.] **—de•pos′i•tor** *n.*

de•pos•i•tar•y (dĭ-pŏz′ĭ-tĕr′ē) *n., pl.* **-ies 1.** One entrusted with something for preservation or safekeeping. **2.** A depository.

dep•o•si•tion (dĕp′ə-zĭsh′ən) *n.* **1.** The act of deposing, as from high office. **2.** The act of depositing, esp. the laying down of matter by a natural process. **3.** Something deposited; a deposit. **4.** *Law* Testimony under oath, esp. a statement by a witness that is written down or recorded for use in court. **5. Deposition** The removal of Jesus from the cross. **—dep′o•si′tion•al** *adj.*

de•pos•i•to•ry (dĭ-pŏz′ĭ-tôr′ē, -tōr′ē) *n., pl.* **-ries 1.** A place where something is deposited, as for storage or safekeeping; a repository. **2.** A trustee; a depositary.

de•pot (dē′pō, dĕp′ō) *n.* **1.** A railroad or bus station. **2.** A warehouse or storehouse. **3a.** A storage installation for military equipment and supplies. **b.** A station for assembling military recruits and forwarding them to active units. [Fr. *dépôt* < OFr. *depost* < Lat. *dēpositum*, something deposited < neut. p. part. of *dēpōnere*, to put down, deposit. See DEPOSIT.]

de•prave (dĭ-prāv′) *tr.v.* **-praved, -prav•ing, -praves** To debase, esp. morally. [ME *depraven*, to corrupt < OFr. *depraver* < Lat. *dēprāvāre* : *dē-*, de- + *prāvus*, crooked.] **—dep′ra•va′tion** (dĕp′rə-vā′shən) *n.* **—de•prav′er** *n.*

de•praved (dĭ-prāvd′) *adj.* Morally corrupt; perverted. **—de•prav′ed•ly** (-prā′vĭd-lē, -prāvd′lē) *adv.*

de•prav•i•ty (dĭ-prăv′ĭ-tē) *n., pl.* **-ties 1.** Moral corruption or degradation. **2.** A depraved act or condition.

dep•re•cate (dĕp′rĭ-kāt′) *tr.v.* **-cat•ed, -cat•ing, -cates 1.** To express disapproval of; deplore: *deprecated the terrible working conditions.* **2.** To belittle; depreciate. [Lat. *dēprecārī, dēprecāt-*, to ward off by prayer : *dē-*, de- + *precārī*, to pray; see **prek-** in App.] **—dep′re•ca′tion** *n.* **—dep′re•ca′tor** *n.*

USAGE NOTE The first and fully accepted meaning of *deprecate* is "to express disapproval of." But the word is now used, almost to the exclusion of *depreciate*, in the sense "to belittle or mildly disparage," as in *He deprecated his own contribution.* In an earlier survey this newer sense was approved by a majority of the Usage Panel.

dep•re•ca•to•ry (dĕp′rĭ-kə-tôr′ē, -tōr′ē) also **dep•re•ca•tive** (-kā′tĭv) *adj.* **1.** Expressing disapproval or criticism. **2.** Mildly disparaging or uncomplimentary, esp. of oneself. **—dep′re•ca•to′ri•ly** *adv.*

de•pre•cia•ble (dĭ-prē′shə-bəl) *adj.* That can be depreciated in value: *depreciable assets.*

de•pre•ci•ate (dĭ-prē′shē-āt′) *v.* **-at•ed, -at•ing, -ates** *—tr.* **1.** To lessen the price or value of. **2.** To think or speak of as being of little worth; belittle. See Usage Note at **deprecate.** *—intr.* To diminish in price or value. [Med.Lat. *dēpreciāre, dēpreciāt-*, alteration of Lat. *dēpretiāre* : *dē-*, de- + *pretium*, price.] **—de•pre′ci•a′tor** *n.*

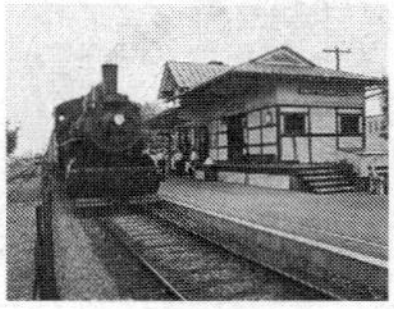

depot
the Strasburg Railroad in Pennsylvania

de•pre•ci•a•tion (dĭ-prē′shē-ā′shən) *n.* **1.** A loss in value, as because of wear. **2.** *Accounting* An allowance made for a loss in value of property. **3.** Reduction in the purchasing value of money. **4.** An instance of disparaging or belittlement.

de•pre•cia•to•ry (dĭ-prē′shə-tôr′ē, -tōr′ē) also **de•pre•cia•tive** (-shə-tĭv, -shē-ā′tĭv) *adj.* **1.** Diminishing in value. **2.** Disparaging; belittling.

dep•re•date (dĕp′rĭ-dāt′) *v.* **-dat•ed, -dat•ing, -dates** *—tr.* To ransack; plunder. *—intr.* To engage in plundering. [LLat. *dēpraedārī, dēpraedāt-* : Lat. *dē-*, de- + Lat. *praedārī*, to plunder (< *praeda*, booty; see **ghend-** in App.).] **—dep′re•da′tor** *n.* **—de•pred′a•to′ry** (dĭ-prĕd′ə-tôr′ē, -tōr′ē, dĕp′rĭ-də-) *adj.*

dep•re•da•tion (dĕp′rĭ-dā′shən) *n.* **1.** A predatory attack; a raid. **2.** Damage or loss; ravage: *the depredations of time.*

de•press (dĭ-prĕs′) *tr.v.* **-pressed, -press•ing, -press•es 1.** To lower in spirits; deject. **2a.** To cause to drop or sink; lower. **b.** To press down: *depress the typewriter key.* **3.** To lessen the activity or force of; weaken. **4.** To lower prices in (a financial market). [ME *depressen*, to push down < OFr. *depresser* < Lat. *dēprimere, dēpress-* : *dē-*, de- + *premere*, to press.] **—de•press′i•ble** *adj.*

de•pres•sant (dĭ-prĕs′ənt) *adj.* Tending to lower the rate of vital physiological activities. ❖ *n.* A depressant agent, esp. a drug.

de•pressed (dĭ-prĕst′) *adj.* **1.** Low in spirits; dejected. **2.** Suffering from psychological depression. **3.** Sunk below the surrounding region. **4.** Lower in amount, degree, or position. **5a.** Sluggish in growth or activity. **b.** Suffering from social and economic hardship: *a depressed region.*

de•press•ing (dĭ-prĕs′ĭng) *adj.* **1.** Causing esp. emotional depression. **2.** Dismal; dreary. **—de•press′ing•ly** *adv.*

de•pres•sion (dĭ-prĕsh′ən) *n.* **1a.** The act of depressing. **b.** The condition of being depressed. **2.** An area that is sunk below its surroundings; a hollow. **3.** The condition of feeling sad or despondent. **4.** *Psychology* A psychiatric disorder characterized by an inability to concentrate, insomnia, loss of appetite, and feelings of extreme sadness, dejection, and hopelessness. **5a.** A reduction in activity or force. **b.** A reduction in physiological vigor or activity. **c.** A lowering in amount, degree, or position. **6a.** *Economics* A period of drastic decline in an economy, characterized by decreasing business activity, falling prices, and unemployment. **b. Depression** The worldwide economic depression from

ă	**pat**	oi	**boy**
ā	**pay**	ou	**out**
âr	**care**	o͝o	**took**
ä	**father**	o͞o	**boot**
ĕ	**pet**	ŭ	**cut**
ē	**be**	ûr	**urge**
ĭ	**pit**	th	**thin**
ī	**pie**	*th*	**this**
îr	**pier**	hw	**which**
ŏ	**pot**	zh	**vision**
ō	**toe**	ə	**about, item**
ô	**paw**		

Stress marks:
′ (primary);
′ (secondary), as in
lexicon (lĕk′sĭ-kŏn′)

the late 1920s through the 1930s. **7.** *Meteorology* A region of low barometric pressure. **8.** The angular distance below the horizontal plane through the point of observation.

de·pres·sive (dĭ-prĕs′ĭv) *adj.* **1.** Tending to depress or lower. **2.** Depressing; gloomy. **3.** Of or relating to psychological depression. ❖ *n.* A person suffering from psychological depression. —**de·pres′sive·ly** *adv.* —**de·pres′sive·ness** *n.*

de·pres·sor (dĭ-prĕs′ər) *n.* **1.** Something that depresses or is used to depress: *a tongue depressor.* **2.** A muscle that draws down a part of the body.

de·pres·sur·ize (dē-prĕsh′ə-rīz′) *tr.v.* **-ized, -iz·ing, -iz·es** To reduce the air or gas pressure within (a chamber, for example). —**de·pres′sur·i·za′tion** (-prĕsh′ər-ĭ-zā′shən) *n.*

de·priv·al (dĭ-prī′vəl) *n.* Deprivation.

dep·ri·va·tion (dĕp′rə-vā′shən) *n.* **1a.** The act or an instance of depriving; loss. **b.** The condition of being deprived; privation. **2.** A removal of rank or office.

de·prive (dĭ-prīv′) *tr.v.* **-prived, -priv·ing, -prives 1.** To take something away from: *deprived me of the inheritance.* **2.** To keep from possessing or enjoying; deny. **3.** To remove from office. [ME *depriven* < OFr. *depriver* < Med.Lat. *dēprīvāre* : Lat. *dē-*, de- + Lat. *prīvāre*, to rob (< *prīvus*, alone, without; see **per**[1] in App.).] —**de·priv′a·ble** *adj.*

de·prived (dĭ-prīvd′) *adj.* **1.** Marked by deprivation, esp. of economic or social necessities. **2.** Lacking in advantage, opportunity, or experience.

de·pro·gram (dē-prō′grăm′, -grəm) *tr.v.* **-grammed, -gram·ming, -grams** or **-gramed, -gram·ing, -grams** To counteract or try to counteract the effect of an indoctrination, esp. of a religion or cult. —**de·pro′gram′mer** *n.*

dept. *abbr.* **1.** department **2.** deputy

depth (dĕpth) *n.* **1.** The condition or quality of being deep. **2a.** The extent, measurement, or dimension downward, backward, or inward. **b.** The measurement or sense of distance from an observation point, such as linear perspective in painting. **3.** A deep part or place. Often used in the plural. **4a.** The most profound or intense part or stage. **b.** Intensity; force: *the depth of their feelings.* **5.** The severest or worst part. **6.** A low point, level, or degree. **7.** Intellectual complexity or penetration; profundity. **8.** The range of one's understanding or competence. **9.** Strength held in reserve, esp. a supply of capable replacements. **10.** The degree of richness or intensity: *depth of color.* **11.** Lowness in pitch. **12.** Complete detail; thoroughness. [ME *depthe* < *dep*, deep. See DEEP.]

depth charge *n.* A charge designed for detonation at a preset depth under water, used esp. against submarines.

depth perception *n.* The ability to perceive spatial relationships, esp. distances between objects, in three dimensions.

depth psychology *n.* **1.** Psychology of the unconscious mind. **2.** Psychoanalysis.

depth sounder *n.* An ultrasonic instrument used to measure the depth of water under a ship.

dep·u·rate (dĕp′yə-rāt′) *tr. & intr.v.* **-rat·ed, -rat·ing, -rates** To cleanse or purify or become cleansed or purified. [Med.Lat. *dēpūrāre, dēpūrāt-* : Lat. *dē-*, de- + *pūrus*, pure.] —**dep′u·ra′tion** *n.* —**dep′u·ra′tor** *n.*

dep·u·ta·tion (dĕp′yə-tā′shən) *n.* **1.** A person or group appointed to represent another or others; a delegation. **2a.** The act of deputing. **b.** The state of being deputed.

de·pute (dĭ-pyōōt′) *tr.v.* **-put·ed, -put·ing, -putes 1.** To appoint or authorize as an agent or representative. **2.** To assign (authority or duties) to another; delegate. [ME *deputen* < OFr. *deputer* < LLat. *dēputāre*, to allot < Lat., to consider : *dē-*, de- + *putāre*, to ponder.]

dep·u·tize (dĕp′yə-tīz′) *tr. & intr.v.* **-tized, -tiz·ing, -tiz·es** To appoint or serve as a deputy. —**dep′u·ti·za′tion** (-tĭ-zā′shən) *n.*

dep·u·ty (dĕp′yə-tē) *n., pl.* **-ties 1.** A person appointed or empowered to act for another. **2.** An assistant exercising full authority in the absence of a superior and equal authority in emergencies. **3.** A representative in a legislative body in certain countries. [ME *depute* < OFr. < p. part. of *deputer*, to depute. See DEPUTE.]

De Quin·cey (dĭ kwĭn′sē, -zē), Thomas 1785–1859. British writer noted for *Confessions of an English Opium Eater* (1821).

der. *abbr.* **1.** derivation **2.** derivative

de·rac·i·nate (dĭ-răs′ə-nāt′) *tr.v.* **-nat·ed, -nat·ing, -nates 1.** To pull out by the roots; uproot. **2.** To displace from one's native or accustomed environment. [< Fr. *déraciner* < OFr. *desraciner* : *des-*, de- + *racine*, root (< LLat. *rādīcīna* < Lat. *rādīx, rādīc-*; see **wrād-** in App.).] —**de·rac′i·na′tion** *n.*

de·rail (dē-rāl′) *intr. & tr.v.* **-railed, -rail·ing, -rails 1.** To run or cause to run off the rails. **2.** To come or bring to a sudden halt. [Fr. *dérailler* : *dé-*, off (< OFr. *de-*; see DE–) + *rail*, rail (< E. RAIL[1]).] —**de·rail′ment** *n.*

de·rail·leur (dĭ-rā′lər) *n.* A device for shifting gears on a bicycle by moving the chain between sprocket wheels of different sizes. [Fr. *dérailleur* < *dérailler*, to derail. See DERAIL.]

De·rain (də-răN′), André 1880–1954. French painter and sculptor who was a founder of fauvism.

de·range (dĭ-rānj′) *tr.v.* **-ranged, -rang·ing, -rang·es 1.** To disturb the order or arrangement of. **2.** To upset the normal condition or functioning of. **3.** To disturb mentally; make insane.

derby

derrick
over an oil well

dervish
Istanbul, Turkey

[Fr. *déranger* < OFr. *desrengier* : *des-*, de- + *reng*, line (of Gmc. orig.).] —**de·range′ment** *n.*

der·by (dûr′bē) *n., pl.* **-bies 1.** *Sports* Any of various annual horseraces, esp. for three-year-olds. **2.** *Sports* A formal race usu. having an open field of contestants: *a motorcycle derby.* **3.** A stiff felt hat with a round crown and a narrow, curved brim. [After Edward Stanley, 12th Earl of *Derby* (1752–1834), founder of the English Derby.]

Der·by (där′bē) A city of central England W of Nottingham; settled by the Romans. Pop. 228,648.

de·reg·u·late (dē-rĕg′yə-lāt′) *tr.v.* **-lat·ed, -lat·ing, -lates** To free from regulation, esp. government regulation: *deregulate the airline industry.* —**de·reg′u·la′tion** *n.* —**de·reg′u·la′tor** *n.* —**de·reg′u·la·to′ry** (-lə-tôr′ē, -tōr′ē) *adj.*

der·e·lict (dĕr′ə-lĭkt′) *adj.* **1.** Deserted by an owner or keeper; abandoned. **2.** Run-down; dilapidated. **3.** Neglectful of duty or obligation; remiss. ❖ *n.* **1.** Abandoned property, esp. a ship abandoned at sea. **2.** A homeless or jobless person; a vagrant. [Lat. *dērelictus*, p. part. of *dērelinquere*, to abandon : *dē-*, de- + *relinquere*, to leave behind; see RELINQUISH.]

der·e·lic·tion (dĕr′ə-lĭk′shən) *n.* **1.** Willful neglect, as of duty or principle. **2a.** The act of abandoning; abandonment. **b.** A state of abandonment or neglect.

de·ride (dĭ-rīd′) *tr.v.* **-rid·ed, -rid·ing, -rides** To speak of or treat with contemptuous mirth. See Syns at ridicule. [Lat. *dērīdēre* : *dē-*, de- + *rīdēre*, to laugh at.] —**de·rid′er** *n.*

de ri·gueur (də rē-gœr′) *adj.* Required by the current fashion or custom. [Fr. : *de*, of + *rigueur*, rigor, strictness.]

de·ri·sion (dĭ-rĭzh′ən) *n.* **1a.** Contemptuous or jeering laughter; ridicule. **b.** A state of being derided. **2.** An object of ridicule; a laughingstock. [ME *derisioun* < AN < LLat. *dērīsiō, dērīsiōn-* < Lat. *dērīsus*, p. part. of *dērīdēre*, to deride. See DERIDE.]

de·ri·sive (dĭ-rī′sĭv, -zĭv, -rīs′ĭv, -rīz′-) *adj.* Mocking; jeering. —**de·ri′sive·ly** *adv.* —**de·ri′sive·ness** *n.*

de·ri·so·ry (dĭ-rī′sə-rē, -zə-) *adj.* **1.** Expressing derision; derisive. **2.** Laughable; ridiculous.

deriv. *abbr.* **1.** derivation **2.** derivative

der·i·vate (dĕr′ə-vāt′) *adj.* Derivative.

der·i·va·tion (dĕr′ə-vā′shən) *n.* **1.** The act or process of deriving. **2.** The state or fact of being derived; originating. **3.** Something derived; a derivative. **4.** The form or source from which something is derived; an origin. **5.** The historical origin and development of a word; an etymology. **6.** *Linguistics* **a.** The process by which words are formed from existing words or bases by adding affixes, as *singer* from *sing*, by changing the shape of the word or base, as *song* from *sing*, or by adding an affix and changing the pronunciation of the word or base, as *electricity* from *electric*. **b.** A linguistic description of word formation. **c.** A formal representation or description of the series of ordered rules and operations that generate a surface structure from a deep structure. **7.** *Logic & Mathematics* A process indicating through a sequence of statements that a result necessarily follows from the initial assumptions. —**der′i·va′tion·al** *adj.*

de·riv·a·tive (dĭ-rĭv′ə-tĭv) *adj.* **1.** Resulting from or employing derivation. **2.** Copied or adapted from others. ❖ *n.* **1.** Something derived. **2.** *Linguistics* A word formed from another by derivation. **3.** *Mathematics* **a.** The limiting value of the ratio of the change in a function to the corresponding change in its independent variable. **b.** The instantaneous rate of change of a function with respect to its variable. **c.** The slope of the tangent line to the graph of a function at a given point. **4.** *Chemistry* A compound derived or obtained from another and containing essential elements of the parent substance. **5.** *Business* An investment that derives its value from another more fundamental investment, as a commitment to buy a bond for a certain sum on a certain date. —**de·riv′a·tive·ly** *adv.* —**de·riv′a·tive·ness** *n.*

de·rive (dĭ-rīv′) *v.* **-rived, -riv·ing, -rives** —*tr.* **1.** To obtain or receive from a source. **2.** To arrive at by reasoning; deduce or infer. **3.** To trace the origin or development of (a word). **4.** *Linguistics* To generate (a surface structure) from a deep structure. **5.** *Chemistry* To produce or obtain (a compound) from another substance by chemical reaction. —*intr.* To issue from a source; originate. See Syns at stem[1]. [ME *deriven*, to be derived from < OFr. *deriver* < Lat. *dērīvāre*, to derive, draw off : *dē-*, de- + *rīvus*, stream.] —**de·riv′a·ble** *adj.* —**de·riv′er** *n.*

–derm *suff.* Skin; covering: *blastoderm.* [< Gk. *derma*, skin (poss. influenced by Fr. *-derme*).]

der·ma[1] (dûr′mə) *n.* See dermis. [Gk., skin.]

der·ma[2] (dûr′mə) *n.* Beef casing stuffed with a seasoned mixture of matzo meal or flour, onion, and suet. [Poss. Yiddish *gederem*, intestines < MHGer. *darm*, intestine < OHGer. See **tera-**[1] in App.]

derma– or **derm–** or **dermo–** *pref.* Skin: *dermal.* [< Gk. *derma*, skin.]

–derma *suff.* Skin; skin disease: *scleroderma.* [NLat. < Gk. *derma*, skin.]

der·ma·bra·sion (dûr′mə-brā′zhən) *n.* A surgical procedure to remove skin imperfections, such as scars, by abrading the surface of the skin with fine sandpaper or wire brushes.

der·mal (dûr′məl) also **der·mic** (-mĭk) *adj.* Of or relating to the skin or dermis.

der•map•ter•an (dər-măp′tər-ən) *n.* Any of various insects of the order Dermaptera, having an elongated body with pincerlike appendages at the posterior end. [< NLat. *Dermaptera*, order name : DERMA– + Gk. *ptera*, pl. of *pteron*, wing; see –PTER.] —**der•map′ter•an** *adj.*

der•ma•ti•tis (dûr′mə-tī′tĭs) *n.* Inflammation of the skin.

dermato– or **dermat–** *pref.* Skin: *dermatophyte.* [Gk. *derma, dermat-*, skin.]

der•mat•o•gen (dûr-măt′ə-jən) *n.* See **protoderm.**

der•ma•toid (dûr′mə-toid′) also **der•moid** (-moid′) *adj.* Resembling skin; skinlike.

der•ma•tol•o•gy (dûr′mə-tŏl′ə-jē) *n.* The branch of medicine that is concerned with the physiology and pathology of the skin. —**der′ma•to•log′i•cal** (-tə-lŏj′ĭ-kəl), **der′ma•to•log′ic** *adj.* —**der′ma•tol′o•gist** *n.*

der•ma•tome (dûr′mə-tōm′) *n.* **1.** *Anatomy* An area of skin innervated by sensory fibers from a single spinal nerve. **2.** *Medicine* An instrument used in cutting thin slices of the skin, as for skin grafts. **3.** *Embryology* The part of a mesodermal somite from which the dermis develops. [DERMA– + –TOME.]

der•mat•o•phyte (dûr-măt′ə-fīt′, dûr′mə-tə-) *n.* Any of various fungi that can cause parasitic skin infections. —**der•mat′o•phyt′ic** (-fĭt′ĭk) *adj.*

der•ma•to•phy•to•sis (dûr′mə-tō′fī-tō′sĭs) *n.* A fungal infection of the skin, esp. athlete's foot.

der•ma•to•plas•ty (dûr′mə-tō-plăs′tē) *n.* The use of skin grafts in plastic surgery to correct defects or replace skin.

der•ma•to•sis (dûr′mə-tō′sĭs) *n., pl.* **-ses** (-sēz) A skin disease, esp. one without inflammation.

–dermatous *suff.* Having a specified kind of skin: *sclerodermatous.* [Gk. *derma, dermat-*, skin + –OUS.]

der•mic (dûr′mĭk) *adj.* Variant of **dermal.**

der•mis (dûr′mĭs) *n.* The sensitive connective tissue layer of the skin located below the epidermis, containing nerve endings, sweat and sebaceous glands, and blood and lymph vessels. [NLat., back-formation < LLat. *epidermis*, epidermis. See EPIDERMIS.]

dermo– *pref.* Variant of **derma–.**

der•moid (dûr′moid′) *adj.* Variant of **dermatoid.**

der•nier cri (dĕr′nyā krē′) *n.* The latest thing; the newest fashion. [Fr. : *dernier*, last, latest + *cri*, cry.]

der•o•gate (dĕr′ə-gāt′) *v.* **-gat•ed, -gat•ing, -gates** —*intr.* **1.** To take away; detract. **2.** To deviate from a standard or expectation; go astray. —*tr.* To disparage; belittle. [ME *derogaten* < Lat. *dērogāre, dērogāt-* : *dē-*, de- + *rogāre*, to ask; see **reg-** in App.] —**der′o•ga′tion** *n.*

de•rog•a•tive (dĭ-rŏg′ə-tĭv, dĕr′ə-gā′-) *adj.* **1.** Tending to derogate; detractive. **2.** Disparaging; derogatory. —**de•rog′a•tive•ly** *adv.*

de•rog•a•to•ry (dĭ-rŏg′ə-tôr′ē, -tōr′ē) *adj.* **1.** Disparaging; belittling. **2.** Tending to detract or diminish. —**de•rog′a•to′ri•ly** *adv.* —**de•rog′a•to′ri•ness** *n.*

der•rick (dĕr′ĭk) *n.* **1.** A machine for hoisting and moving heavy objects, consisting of a movable boom equipped with cables and pulleys and connected to the base of an upright stationary beam. **2.** A tall framework over a drilled hole, esp. an oil well, used to support boring equipment. [Obsolete *derick*, hangman, gallows, after *Derick*, 16th-cent. English hangman.]

Der•ri•da (dĕr′ĭ-dä′, dĕ′rē-), **Jacques** b. 1930. Algerian-born French philosopher who developed the theory of deconstruction.

der•ri•ère also **der•ri•ere** (dĕr′ē-âr′) *n.* The buttocks; the rear. [Fr., behind < OFr. *deriere*, in back of < VLat. **dē retrō* : Lat. *dē*, from, of; see DE– + Lat. *retrō*, back; see RETRO–.]

der•ring-do (dĕr′ĭng-do͞o′) *n.* Daring or reckless action. [Misinterpretation of earlier *derrynge do*, misprint of Late ME *dorryng do*, daring to do < ME *durring don* : *durring*, pr. part. of *durren*, to dare (< OE *durran*; see DARE) + *don*, to do; see DO[1].]

der•rin•ger (dĕr′ĭn-jər) *n.* A short-barreled pistol that has a large bore and is small enough to be carried in a pocket. [After Henry *Deringer* (1786–1868), American gunsmith.]

der•ris (dĕr′ĭs) *n.* Any of various usu. woody vines of the genus *Derris* of tropical Asia, whose roots yield the insecticide rotenone. [NLat. *Derris*, genus name < Gk., covering.]

Der•ry (dĕr′ē) also **Lon•don•der•ry** (lŭn′dən-dĕr′ē, lŭn′dən-dĕr′ē) A borough of NW Northern Ireland NW of Belfast; built on the site of an abbey founded in 546. Pop. 68,000.

der•vish (dûr′vĭsh) *n.* **1.** A member of any of various Muslim mystical or ascetic orders, many of which are known for acts of ecstatic devotion. **2.** One that possesses abundant, often frenzied energy. [Turk. *derviş*, mendicant < Pers. *darvēsh.*]

DES (dē′ē-ĕs′) *n.* Diethylstilbestrol.

de•sa•cral•ize (dē-sā′krə-līz′, -săk′rə-) *tr.v.* **-ized, -iz•ing, -iz•es** To divest of sacred or religious significance.

de•sal•i•nate (dē-săl′ə-nāt′) *tr.v.* **-nat•ed, -nat•ing, -nates** To desalinize. —**de•sal′i•na′tion** *n.* —**de•sal′i•na′tor** *n.*

de•sal•i•nize (dē-săl′ə-nīz′) *tr.v.* **-nized, -niz•ing, -niz•es** To remove salts and other chemicals from (seawater or soil, for example). —**de•sal′i•ni•za′tion** (-nĭ-zā′shən) *n.*

de•salt (dē-sôlt′) *tr.v.* **-salt•ed, -salt•ing, -salts** To desalinize.

De•sargues (dā-zärg′), **Gérard** 1591–1661. French army officer regarded as one of the founders of modern geometry.

des•cant (dĕs′kănt′) *n.* **1.** also **dis•cant** (dĭs′-) *Music* **a.** An ornamental melody or counterpoint sung or played above a theme. **b.** The highest part sung in part music. **2.** A discussion or discourse on a theme. ❖ *intr.v.* (dĕs′kănt′, dĕ-skănt′) **-cant•ed, -cant•ing, -cants 1.** To comment at length; discourse. **2.** also **dis•cant** (dĭs′kănt′, dĭ-skănt′) *Music* **a.** To sing or play a descant. **b.** To sing melodiously. [ME *descant* < AN *descaunt* < Med.Lat. *discantus*, a refrain : Lat. *dis-*, dis- + Lat. *cantus*, song < p. part. of *canere*, to sing; see **kan-** in App.] —**des′cant′er** *n.*

Des•cartes (dā-kärt′), **René** 1596–1650. French mathematician and philosopher who founded analytic geometry and is known for his rationalistic premise "I think, therefore I am."

de•scend (dĭ-sĕnd′) *v.* **-scend•ed, -scend•ing, -scends** —*intr.* **1.** To move from a higher to a lower place; come or go down. **2.** To slope, extend, or incline downward. **3a.** To come from an ancestor or ancestry. **b.** To come down from a source; derive. **c.** To pass by inheritance. **4.** To lower oneself; stoop. **5.** To proceed or progress downward, as in rank. **6.** To arrive or attack in a sudden or an overwhelming manner. —*tr.* **1a.** To move from a higher to a lower part of; go down. **b.** To get down from. **2.** To extend or proceed downward along. [ME *descenden* < OFr. *descendre* < Lat. *dēscendere* : *dē-*, de- + *scandere*, to climb.] —**de•scend′i•ble, de•scend′a•ble** *adj.*

de•scen•dant (dĭ-sĕn′dənt) *n.* **1.** A person, an animal, or a plant whose descent can be traced to a particular individual or group. **2.** Something derived from a prototype or earlier form. **3.** In astrology, the point of the ecliptic or the sign of the zodiac that sets in the west at the time of a person's birth or other event.

de•scen•dent also **de•scen•dant** (dĭ-sĕn′dənt) *adj.* **1.** Moving downward; descending. **2.** Proceeding by descent from an ancestor.

de•scend•er (dĭ-sĕn′dər) *n.* **1.** One that descends. **2.** *Printing* **a.** The part of the lowercase letters, such as *q*, that extends below the other lowercase letters. **b.** A letter with such a part.

de•scent (dĭ-sĕnt′) *n.* **1.** The act or an instance of descending. **2.** A way down. **3.** A downward incline or passage. **4a.** Hereditary derivation; lineage. **b.** One generation of a specific lineage. **5a.** The fact or process of coming down or being derived from a source. **b.** Development in form or structure during transmission from an original source. **6.** *Law* Transference of property by inheritance. **7.** A lowering or decline, as in level. **8.** A sudden visit or attack; an onslaught. [ME < OFr. < *descendre*, to descend. See DESCEND.]

Des•chutes (dā-sho͞ot′, də-sho͞ots′) A river rising in the Cascade Range of W-central OR and flowing c. 402 km (250 mi) to the Columbia R. near The Dalles.

de•scram•ble (dē-skrăm′bəl) *tr.v.* **-bled, -bling, -bles** To unscramble (a coded message or signal, for example).

de•scribe (dĭ-skrīb′) *tr.v.* **-scribed, -scrib•ing, -scribes 1.** To give an account of in speech or writing. **2.** To convey an idea or impression of; characterize. **3.** To represent pictorially; depict. **4.** To trace the form or outline of: *describe a circle with a compass.* [ME *describen* < Lat. *dēscrībere*, to write down : *dē-*, de- + *scrībere*, to write; see **skrībh-** in App.] —**de•scrib′a•ble** *adj.* —**de•scrib′er** *n.*

de•scrip•tion (dĭ-skrĭp′shən) *n.* **1.** The act, process, or technique of describing. **2.** A statement or an account describing something. **3.** A pictorial representation. **4.** A kind. [ME *descripcioun* < AN < Lat. *dēscrīptiō, dēscrīptiōn-* < *dēscrīptus*, p. part. of *dēscrībere*, to write down. See DESCRIBE.]

de•scrip•tive (dĭ-skrĭp′tĭv) *adj.* **1.** Involving or characterized by description; serving to describe. **2.** Concerned with classification or description: *a descriptive science.* **3.** *Grammar* **a.** Expressing an attribute of the modified noun, as *green* in *green grass.* Used of an adjective or adjectival clause. **b.** Nonrestrictive. **4.** Of or relating to the study of a language with emphasis on constructing a grammar without regard to historical development, comparison with other languages, or advocated norms for proper usage. —**de•scrip′tive•ly** *adv.* —**de•scrip′tive•ness** *n.*

descriptive clause *n.* A nonrestrictive clause.

de•scrip•tor (dĭ-skrĭp′tər) *n.* *Computer Science* Information used to identify an item in a data storage and retrieval system. [LLat. *dēscrīptor*, describer < Lat. *dēscrībere, dēscrīpt-*, to describe. See DESCRIBE.]

de•scry (dĭ-skrī′) *tr.v.* **-scried, -scry•ing, -scries 1.** To catch sight of (something difficult to discern). See Syns at **see**[1]. **2.** To discover by careful observation or scrutiny; detect. [ME *descrien* < OFr. *descrier*, to call, cry out. See DECRY.] —**de•scri′er** *n.*

Des•de•mo•na (dĕz′də-mō′nə) *n.* A satellite of Uranus. [After *Desdemona*, wife of Othello in *Othello* by William Shakespeare.]

des•e•crate (dĕs′ĭ-krāt′) *tr.v.* **-crat•ed, -crat•ing, -crates** To violate the sacredness of; profane. [DE– + (CON)SECRATE.] —**des′e•crat′er, des′e•cra′tor** *n.* —**des′e•cra′tion** *n.*

de•seg•re•gate (dē-sĕg′rĭ-gāt′) *v.* **-gat•ed, -gat•ing, -gates** —*tr.* **1.** To abolish or eliminate segregation in. **2.** To open (a school or workplace, for example) to members of all races or ethnic groups, esp. by force of law. —*intr.* To become open to members of all races or ethnic groups. —**de•seg′re•ga′tion** *n.* —**de•seg′re•ga′tion•ist** *n.*

de•sen•si•tize (dē-sĕn′sĭ-tīz′) *tr.v.* **-tized, -tiz•ing, -tiz•es 1.** To render insensitive or less sensitive. **2.** *Immunology* To make (an individual) nonreactive or insensitive to an antigen. **3.** To

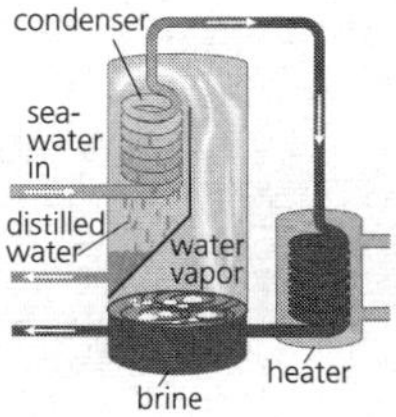

desalinize
flash-distillation process to desalinize seawater

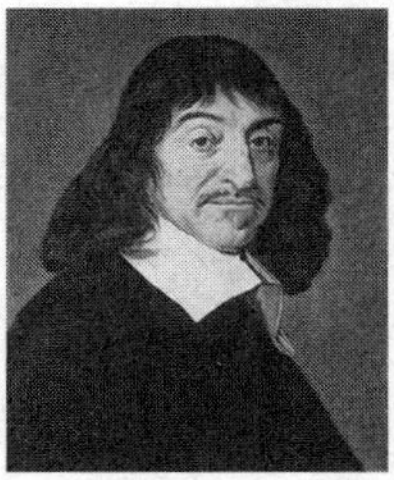

Descartes
after a painting by Frans Hals

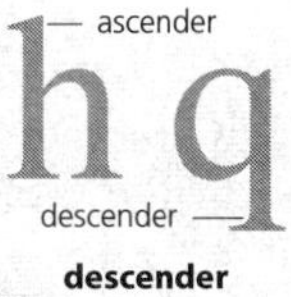

descender

ă pat	oi boy
ā pay	ou out
âr care	o͝o took
ä father	o͞o boot
ĕ pet	ŭ cut
ē be	ûr urge
ĭ pit	th thin
ī pie	*th* this
îr pier	hw which
ŏ pot	zh vision
ō toe	ə about, item
ô paw	

Stress marks:
′ (primary);
′ (secondary), as in **lexicon** (lĕk′sĭ-kŏn′)

make emotionally insensitive or unresponsive, as by long exposure or repeated shocks. **4.** To make (a photographic film or substance) less sensitive to light. **—de·sen′si·ti·za′tion** (-tī-zā′shən) *n.* **—de·sen′si·tiz′er** *n.*

Des·er·et (dĕz′ə-rēt′) An area in the SW US proposed by the Mormons in 1849 as an independent state or a US state.

des·ert[1] (dĕz′ərt) *n.* **1.** A barren or desolate area, esp.: **a.** A dry, often sandy region of little rainfall, extreme temperatures, and sparse vegetation. **b.** A region of permanent cold that is largely or entirely devoid of life. **2.** An empty or forsaken place; a wasteland. **3.** *Archaic* A wild, uncultivated, and uninhabited region. ❖ *adj.* **1.** Of, relating to, characteristic of, or inhabiting a desert: *desert fauna.* **2.** Barren and uninhabited; desolate. [ME < OFr. < LLat. *dēsertum* < neut. p. part. of *dēserere,* to desert. See DESERT[3].]

de·sert[2] (dĭ-zûrt′) *n.* **1.** Something that is deserved or merited, esp. a punishment. Often used in the plural. **2.** The state or fact of deserving reward or punishment. [ME < OFr. *deserte* < fem. p. part. of *deservir,* to deserve. See DESERVE.]

WORD HISTORY When Shakespeare says in Sonnet 72, "Unless you would devise some virtuous lie,/To do more for me than mine own desert," he is using the word *desert* in the sense of "worthiness; deserving," a word that is most familiar in the phrase *just deserts.* This word goes back to the Latin word *dēservīre,* "to devote to the service of," which in Vulgar Latin came to mean "to merit by service." *Dēservīre* is made up of *dē-,* meaning "thoroughly," and *servīre,* "to serve." Knowing this, we can distinguish this *desert* from *desert,* "a wasteland," and *desert,* "to abandon," both of which go back to Latin *dēserere,* "to forsake, leave uninhabited," which is made up of *dē-,* expressing the notion of undoing, and the verb *serere,* "to link together."

de·sert[3] (dĭ-zûrt′) *v.* **-sert·ed, -sert·ing, -serts** *—tr.* **1.** To leave empty or alone; abandon. **2.** To withdraw from, esp. in spite of a responsibility or duty; forsake. **3.** To abandon (a military post, for example) in violation of orders or an oath. *—intr.* To forsake one's duty or post, esp. to be absent without leave from the armed forces with no intention of returning. [Fr. *déserter* < LLat. *dēsertāre,* freq. of Lat. *dēserere,* to abandon : *dē-,* de- + *serere,* to join.] **—de·sert′er** *n.*

de·sert·i·fi·ca·tion (dĭ-zûr′tə-fĭ-kā′shən) *n.* The transformation of arable or habitable land to desert.

de·ser·tion (dĭ-zûr′shən) *n.* **1a.** The act or an instance of deserting. **b.** The state of being deserted. **2.** *Law* Willful abandonment of one's spouse or children or both without their consent and with the intention of forsaking all legal obligations to them.

de·serve (dĭ-zûrv′) *v.* **-served, -serv·ing, -serves** *—tr.* To be worthy of; merit. See Syns at **earn**[1]. *—intr.* To be worthy or deserving. [ME *deserven* < OFr. *deservir* < Lat. *dēservīre,* to serve zealously : *dē-,* intensive pref.; see DE- + *servīre,* to serve; see SERVE.]

de·served (dĭ-zûrvd′) *adj.* Merited or earned. **—de·serv′ed·ly** (-zûr′vĭd-lē) *adv.* **—de·serv′ed·ness** *n.*

de·serv·ing (dĭ-zûr′vĭng) *adj.* Worthy, as of reward, praise, or aid. ❖ *n.* Merit; worthiness. **—de·serv′ing·ly** *adv.*

de Se·ver·sky (də sə-vĕr′skē), **Alexander Procofieff** 1894–1974. Russian-born Amer. aeronautical engineer who invented various airplane devices, including a bombsight.

de·sex (dē-sĕks′) *tr.v.* **-sexed, -sex·ing, -sex·es** To remove part or all of the reproductive organs; neuter.

de·sex·u·al·ize (dē-sĕk′shoo-ə-līz′) *tr.v.* **-ized, -iz·ing, -iz·es** **1.** To take away the sexual quality of. **2.** To desex. **—de·sex′u·al·i·za′tion** (-ə-lĭ-zā′shən) *n.*

des·ha·bille (dĕs′ə-bēl′, -bĕl′) *n.* Variant of **dishabille.**

De Si·ca (də sē′kə), **Vittorio** 1901–74. Italian filmmaker whose works include *The Bicycle Thief* (1948).

des·ic·cant (dĕs′ĭ-kənt) *n.* A substance, such as calcium oxide or silica gel, that has a high affinity for water and is used as a drying agent. [< Lat. *dēsiccāns, dēsiccant-,* pr. part. of *dēsiccāre,* to desiccate. See DESICCATE.] **—des′ic·cant** *adj.*

des·ic·cate (dĕs′ĭ-kāt′) *v.* **-cat·ed, -cat·ing, -cates** *—tr.* **1.** To dry out thoroughly. **2.** To preserve (foods) by removing the moisture. **3.** To make dry, dull, or lifeless. *—intr.* To become dry; dry out. ❖ *adj.* (*also* -kĭt) Lacking spirit or animation; arid. [Lat. *dēsiccāre, dēsiccāt-* : *dē-,* de- + *siccāre,* to dry up (< *siccus,* dry).] **—des′ic·ca′tion** *n.* **—des′ic·ca′tive** *adj.* **—des′ic·ca′tor** *n.*

de·sid·er·ate (dĭ-sĭd′ə-rāt′) *tr.v.* **-at·ed, -at·ing, -ates** To wish to have or see happen. [Lat. *dēsīderāre, dēsīderāt-,* to desire. See DESIRE.] **—de·sid′er·a′tion** *n.*

de·sid·er·a·tive (dĭ-sĭd′ər-ə-tĭv, -ə-rā′-, zĭd′-) *adj.* **1.** Of, relating to, or expressing desire. **2.** *Grammar* Being a clause, a sentence, or in some languages an inflected verb form that expresses desire.

de·sid·er·a·tum (dĭ-sĭd′ə-rä′təm, -rä′-) *n., pl.* **-ta** (-tə) Something considered necessary or highly desirable. [Lat. *dēsīderātum* < neut. p. part. of *dēsīderāre,* to desire. See DESIRE.]

de·sign (dĭ-zīn′) *v.* **-signed, -sign·ing, -signs** *—tr.* **1a.** To conceive or fashion in the mind; invent. **b.** To formulate a plan for; devise. **2.** To plan out in systematic, usu. graphic form. **3.** To create or contrive for a particular purpose or effect. **4.** To have as a goal or purpose; intend. **5.** To create or execute in an artistic or

desert[1]

highly skilled manner. *—intr.* **1.** To make or execute plans. **2.** To have a goal or purpose in mind. **3.** To create designs. ❖ *n.* **1a.** A drawing or sketch. **b.** A graphic representation, esp. a detailed plan for construction or manufacture. **2.** The purposeful or inventive arrangement of parts or details. **3.** The art or practice of designing or making designs. **4.** Something designed, esp. a decorative or an artistic work. **5.** An ornamental pattern. **6.** A basic scheme or pattern that affects and controls function or development. **7.** A plan; a project. See Syns at **plan. 8a.** A reasoned purpose; an intent. **b.** Deliberate intention. **9.** A secretive plot or scheme. Often used in the plural. [ME *designen* < Lat. *dēsignāre,* to designate. See DESIGNATE.] **—de·sign′a·ble** *adj.*

des·ig·nate (dĕz′ĭg-nāt′) *tr.v.* **-nat·ed, -nat·ing, -nates** **1.** To indicate or specify; point out. **2.** To give a name or title to; characterize. **3.** To select and set aside for a duty, an office, or a purpose. See Syns at **allocate.** ❖ *adj.* (-nĭt) Appointed but not yet installed in office. [Lat. *dēsignāre, dēsignāt-* : *dē-,* de- + *signāre,* to mark (< *signum,* sign; see **sek**ʷ-[1] in App.).] **—des′ig·na′tive, des′ig·na·to′ry** (-nə-tôr′ē, -tōr′ē) *adj.* **—des′ig·na′tor** *n.*

des·ig·nat·ed driver (dĕz′ĭg-nā′tĭd) *n.* One who agrees to remain sober, as at a party, in order to be able to drive others home safely.

designated hitter *n. Baseball* A player designated at the start of a game to bat instead of the pitcher.

des·ig·na·tion (dĕz′ĭg-nā′shən) *n.* **1.** The act of designating; a marking or pointing out. **2.** Nomination or appointment. **3.** A distinguishing name or title.

des·ig·nee (dĕz′ĭg-nē′) *n.* A person who has been designated.

de·sign·er (dĭ-zī′nər) *n.* One that produces designs. ❖ *adj.* **1.** Bearing the name, signature, or identifying pattern of a specific designer. **2.** Conceived or created by a designer.

designer drug *n.* A drug with properties and effects similar to a known drug but slightly altered, esp. in order to evade legal restrictions.

designer gene *n.* A gene modified or created by genetic engineering.

de·sign·ing (dĭ-zī′nĭng) *adj.* **1.** Conniving; crafty. **2.** Showing or exercising forethought. **—de·sign′ing·ly** *adv.*

des·i·nence (dĕs′ə-nəns) *n.* A grammatical ending; an inflection. [Fr. *désinence* < Med.Lat. *dēsinentia* < Lat. *dēsinēns, dēsinent-,* pr. part. of *dēsinere,* to come to an end : *dē-,* off; see DE- + *sinere,* to leave.] **—des′i·nen′tial** (-nĕn′shəl) *adj.*

de·sir·a·ble (dĭ-zīr′ə-bəl) *adj.* **1.** Worth having or seeking, as by being useful, advantageous, or pleasing. **2.** Worth doing or achieving; advisable. **3.** Arousing desire, esp. sexual desire. ❖ *n.* A desirable person or thing. **—de·sir′a·bil′i·ty, de·sir′a·ble·ness** *n.* **—de·sir′a·bly** *adv.*

de·sire (dĭ-zīr′) *tr.v.* **-sired, -sir·ing, -sires** **1.** To wish or long for; want. **2.** To express a wish for; request. ❖ *n.* **1.** A wish or longing. **2.** A request or petition. **3.** The object of longing. **4.** Sexual appetite; passion. [ME *desiren* < OFr. *desirer* < Lat. *dēsīderāre* : *dē-,* de- + *sīdus, sīder-,* star.] **—de·sir′er** *n.*

SYNONYMS *desire, covet, crave, want, wish* These verbs mean to have a strong longing for: *desire peace; coveted the new convertible; craving fame and fortune; wanted a drink of water; got all she wished.*

de·sir·ous (dĭ-zīr′əs) *adj.* Having or expressing desire; desiring. **—de·sir′ous·ly** *adv.* **—de·sir′ous·ness** *n.*

de·sist (dĭ-sĭst′, -zĭst′) *intr.v.* **-sist·ed, -sist·ing, -sists** To cease doing something; forbear. See Syns at **stop.** [ME *desisten* < OFr. *desister* < Lat. *dēsistere* : *dē-,* de- + *sistere,* to bring to a standstill; see **stā-** in App.]

desk (dĕsk) *n.* **1.** A piece of furniture typically having a flat or sloping top for writing and often drawers or compartments. **2.** A table, counter, or booth at which specified functions are performed. **3.** A department of a large organization in charge of a specified operation. **4.** A lectern. **5.** A music stand in an orchestra. [ME *deske* < Med.Lat. *desca,* table < OItal. *desco* < Lat. *discus,* quoit. See DISK.]

desk·man (dĕsk′măn′, -mən) *n.* A man who works at a desk, esp. a newspaper writer.

desk·top (dĕsk′tŏp′) *n.* **1.** The top of a desk. **2.** *Computer Science* The background image of a display screen, on which windows, icons, and other graphical items appear. **—desk′top** *adj.*

desktop publishing *n.* The design and production of publications using personal computers with graphics capability.

des·man (dĕs′mən) *n., pl.* **-mans** Either of two aquatic insectivorous molelike mammals, *Desmana moschata* of eastern Europe and western Asia or *Galemys pyrenaicus* of southwest Europe, having a long snout and a flattened scaly tail. [Short for Swed. *desmanråtta,* muskrat : *desman,* musk (< MLGer. *desem* < Med.Lat. *bisamum,* of Semitic orig.; akin to Heb. *bōśem, bāśām,* balsam) + *råtta,* rat.]

des·mid (dĕs′mĭd) *n.* Any of various green unicellular freshwater algae of the family Desmidiaceae, often forming colonies. [< NLat. *Desmidiáceae,* family name < *Desmidium,* type genus < Gk. *desmos,* bond < *dein,* to bind.]

Des Moines (dĭ moin′) The cap. of IA, in the S-central part on the Des Moines R. Pop. 198,682.

Des Moines River A river rising in SW MN and flowing c. 861

km (535 mi) across IA to the Mississippi R.

Des•na (də-snä′, dyə-) A river rising in W Russia and flowing c. 885 km (550 mi) to the Dnieper R. in the Ukraine.

des•o•late (dĕs′ə-lĭt, dĕz′-) *adj.* **1a.** Devoid of inhabitants; deserted. **b.** Barren; lifeless. **2.** Rendered unfit for habitation or use. **3.** Dreary; dismal. **4.** Bereft of friends or hope; sad and forlorn. ❖ *tr.v.* (-lāt′) **-lat•ed, -lat•ing, -lates** **1.** To rid or deprive of inhabitants. **2.** To lay waste; devastate. **3.** To forsake; abandon. **4.** To make lonely, forlorn, or wretched. [ME *desolat* < Lat. *dēsōlātus*, p. part. of *dēsōlāre*, to abandon : *dē-*, de- + *sōlus*, alone; see **s(w)e-** in App.] **—des′o•late•ly** *adv.* **—des′o•late•ness** *n.* **—des′o•lat′er, des′o•la′tor** *n.*

des•o•la•tion (dĕs′ə-lā′shən, dĕz′-) *n.* **1.** The act or an instance of desolating. **2.** The state of being desolate. **3.** Devastation; ruin. **4a.** The state of being abandoned or forsaken; loneliness. **b.** Wretchedness; misery.

de•sorb (dē-sôrb′, -zôrb′) *tr.v.* **-sorbed, -sorb•ing, -sorbs** To remove (an absorbed or adsorbed substance) from. [DE- + (AB)SORB or (AD)SORB.] **—de•sorp′tion** (-sôrp′shən, -zôrp′-) *n.*

de So•to (dĭ sō′tō, dĕ), **Hernando** or **Fernando** 1496?–1542. Spanish explorer who explored much of S North America, crossing the Mississippi R. in 1541.

de•spair (dĭ-spâr′) *intr.v.* **-spaired, -spair•ing, -spairs** **1.** To lose all hope. **2.** To be overcome by a sense of futility or defeat. ❖ *n.* **1.** Complete loss of hope. **2.** One despaired of or causing despair. [ME *despeiren* < OFr. *desperer* < Lat. *dēspērāre* : *dē-*, de- + *spērāre*, to hope.]

de•spair•ing (dĭ-spâr′ĭng) *adj.* Characterized by or resulting from despair; hopeless. **—de•spair′ing•ly** *adv.*

des•patch (dĭ-spăch′) *v. & n.* Variant of dispatch.

des•per•a•do (dĕs′pə-rä′dō, -rā′-) *n., pl.* **-does** or **-dos** A bold or desperate outlaw, esp. of the American frontier. [Prob. < Sp. *desperado, desesperado*, desperate person < p. part. of *desesperar*, to despair < Lat. *dēspērāre*. See DESPAIR.]

des•per•ate (dĕs′pər-ĭt) *adj.* **1.** Having lost all hope; despairing. **2.** Marked by, arising from, or showing despair. **3.** Reckless or violent because of despair. **4.** Undertaken out of extreme urgency or as a last resort. **5.** Nearly hopeless; critical. **6.** Suffering or driven by great need or distress. **7.** Extremely intense. [ME *desperat* < Lat. *dēspērātus*, p. part. of *dēspērāre*, to despair. See DESPAIR.] **—des′per•ate•ly** *adv.* **—des′per•ate•ness** *n.*

des•per•a•tion (dĕs′pə-rā′shən) *n.* **1.** The condition of being desperate. **2.** Recklessness arising from despair.

de•spic•a•ble (dĭ-spĭk′ə-bəl, dĕs′pĭ-kə-) *adj.* Deserving of contempt or scorn; vile. [LLat. *dēspicābilis* < Lat. *dēspicārī*, to despise. See **spek-** in App.] **—de•spic′a•ble•ness** *n.* **—de•spic′a•bly** *adv.*

De•spi•na (də-spē′nə) *n.* A satellite of Neptune. [< Gk. *Despoina*, the Mistress, Arcadian goddess who was the daughter of Poseidon < Despoina, queen, lady, mistress, fem. of *despotēs*, master. See **dem-** in App.]

de•spise (dĭ-spīz′) *tr.v.* **-spised, -spis•ing, -spis•es** **1.** To regard with contempt or scorn. **2.** To dislike intensely; loathe. **3.** To regard as unworthy of one's interest or concern: *despised any thought of their own safety.* [ME *despisen* < OFr. *despire, despis-* < Lat. *dēspicere* : *dē-*, de- + *specere*, to look; see **spek-** in App.] **—de•spis′al** (-spī′zəl) *n.* **—de•spis′er** *n.*

SYNONYMS *despise, contemn, disdain, scorn, scout* These verbs mean to regard with utter contempt: *despises incompetence; contemned the dictator's actions; disdained my suggestion; scorns sentimentality; scouted simplistic explanations.* **ANTONYM** esteem

de•spite (dĭ-spīt′) *prep.* In spite of; notwithstanding. ❖ *n.* **1.** Contemptuous defiance or disregard. **2.** Spite; malice. [Short for *in despite of* < ME *despit*, spite < OFr. < Lat. *dēspectus* < p. part. of *dēspicere*, to despise. See DESPISE.]

de•spite•ful (dĭ-spīt′fəl) *adj.* Full of malice; spiteful. **—de•spite′ful•ly** *adv.* **—de•spite′ful•ness** *n.*

de•spit•e•ous (dĭ-spĭt′ē-əs) *adj. Archaic* Despiteful. **—de•spit′e•ous•ly** *adv.*

de•spoil (dĭ-spoil′) *tr.v.* **-spoiled, -spoil•ing, -spoils** **1.** To sack; plunder. **2.** To deprive of something valuable by force; rob. [ME *despoilen* < OFr. *despoillier* < Lat. *dēspoliāre* : *dē-*, de- + *spoliāre*, to plunder (< *spolium*, booty).] **—de•spoil′er** *n.* **—de•spoil′ment** *n.*

de•spo•li•a•tion (dĭ-spō′lē-ā′shən) *n.* The act of despoiling or the condition of being despoiled. [LLat. *dēspoliātiō, dēspoliātiōn-* < Lat. *dēspoliātus*, p. part. of *dēspoliāre*, to despoil. See DESPOIL.]

de•spond (dĭ-spŏnd′) *intr.v.* **-spond•ed, -spond•ing, -sponds** To become disheartened or discouraged. ❖ *n.* Despondency. [Lat. *dēspondēre*, to give up : *dē-*, de- + *spondēre*, to promise; see **spend-** in App.] **—de•spond′ing•ly** *adv.*

de•spon•dence (dĭ-spŏn′dəns) *n.* Despondency.

de•spon•den•cy (dĭ-spŏn′dən-sē) *n.* Depression of spirits from loss of hope, confidence, or courage; dejection.

de•spon•dent (dĭ-spŏn′dənt) *adj.* Feeling or expressing despondency; dejected. **—de•spon′dent•ly** *adv.*

des•pot (dĕs′pət) *n.* **1.** A ruler with absolute power. **2.** A person who wields power oppressively; a tyrant. **3a.** A Byzantine emperor or prince. **b.** An Eastern Orthodox bishop or patriarch. [Fr. *despote* < Med.Lat. *despota* < Gk. *despotēs*, master. See **dem-** in

App.] **—des•pot′ic** (dĭ-spŏt′ĭk) *adj.* **—des•pot′i•cal•ly** *adv.*

des•pot•ism (dĕs′pə-tĭz′əm) *n.* **1.** Rule by or as if by a despot; absolute power or authority. **2.** The actions of a despot; tyranny. **3a.** A government or political system in which the ruler exercises absolute power. **b.** A state so ruled.

Des•prez (dā-prā′), **Josquin** See Josquin Desprez.

des•qua•mate (dĕs′kwə-māt′) *intr.v.* **-mat•ed, -mat•ing, -mates** To shed, peel, or come off in scales. Used of skin. [Lat. *dēsquāmāre, dēsquāmāt-* : *dē-*, de- + *squāma*, scale.] **—des′qua•ma′tion** *n.*

Des•sa•lines (dĕ-sä-lēn′), **Jean Jacques** 1758?–1806. African-born emperor of Haiti (1804–06) who defeated the French (1803) to gain the island's independence.

des•sert (dĭ-zûrt′) *n.* **1.** A usu. sweet course or dish served at the end of a meal. **2.** *Chiefly British* Fresh fruit, nuts, or sweetmeats served after the sweet course of a dinner. [Fr. < OFr. *desservir*, to clear the table : *des-*, de- + *servir*, to serve; see SERVE.]

des•sert•spoon (dĭ-zûrt′spoon′) *n.* A spoon intermediate between a tablespoon and a teaspoon, used for dessert.

dessert wine *n.* Any of various sweet wines, such as port or Sauternes, served with or after dessert.

de•sta•bi•lize (dē-stā′bə-līz′) *tr.v.* **-lized, -liz•ing, -liz•es** **1.** To upset the stability or smooth functioning of. **2.** To undermine the power of (a government or leader) by subversive or terrorist acts. **—de•sta′bi•li•za′tion** (-lĭ-zā′shən) *n.*

de•stain (dē-stān′) *tr.v.* **-stained, -stain•ing, -stains** To remove stain from (a specimen) to aid in microscopic study.

de•ster•i•lize (dē-stĕr′ə-līz′) *tr.v.* **-lized, -liz•ing, -liz•es** To release (gold) from an inactive status and return it to use as a backing for credit and new currency.

de Stijl (də stīl′, stäl′) *n.* A school of art originating in the Netherlands in 1917 and characterized by the use of rectangular shapes and primary colors. [Du. : *de*, the + *stijl*, style.]

des•ti•na•tion (dĕs′tə-nā′shən) *n.* **1.** The place to which one is going or directed. **2.** The ultimate purpose for which something is created or intended. **3.** *Archaic* An act of appointing or setting aside for a specific purpose.

des•tine (dĕs′tĭn) *tr.v.* **-tined, -tin•ing, -tines** **1.** To determine beforehand; preordain. **2.** To assign for a specific end, use, or purpose. **3.** To direct toward a given destination: *a flight destined for Tokyo.* [ME *destinen* < OFr. *destiner* < Lat. *dēstināre*, to determine. See **stā-** in App.]

des•ti•ny (dĕs′tə-nē) *n., pl.* **-nies** **1.** The fate to which a particular person or thing is destined; one's lot. **2.** A predetermined course of events considered as something beyond human control. **3.** The power or agency thought to predetermine events; fate. [ME *destine* < OFr. *destinee* < fem. p. part. of *destiner*, to destine < Lat. *dēstināre*, to determine. See **stā-** in App.]

des•ti•tute (dĕs′tĭ-tōōt′, -tyōōt′) *adj.* **1.** Utterly lacking; devoid. **2.** Lacking resources or the means of subsistence; completely impoverished. See Syns at **poor.** [ME < Lat. *dēstitūtus*, p. part. of *dēstituere*, to abandon : *dē-*, de- + *statuere*, to set; see **stā-** in App.] **—des′ti•tute′ness** *n.*

des•ti•tu•tion (dĕs′tĭ-tōō′shən, -tyōō′-) *n.* **1.** Extreme want of resources or the means of subsistence; complete poverty. **2.** A deprivation or lack; a deficiency.

des•tri•er (dĕs′trē-ər, dĭ-strîr′) *n. Archaic* A war horse. [ME *destrer* < AN < VLat. **dextrārius*, right-hand < Lat. *dexter*, right. See **deks-** in App.]

de•stroy (dĭ-stroi′) *v.* **-stroyed, -stroy•ing, -stroys** —*tr.* **1.** To ruin completely; spoil. **2.** To tear down or break up; demolish. See Syns at **ruin.** **3.** To do away with; put an end to. **4.** To kill. **5.** To subdue or defeat completely; crush. **6.** To render useless or ineffective: *destroyed her testimony.* —*intr.* To be destructive; cause destruction. [ME *destroien* < OFr. *destruire* < VLat. **dēstrūgere*, back-formation < Lat. *dēstrūctus*, p. part. of *dēstruere* : *dē-*, de- + *struere*, to pile up.]

de•stroy•er (dĭ-stroi′ər) *n.* **1.** One that destroys. **2.** A small, fast, highly maneuverable warship armed with guns, torpedoes, depth charges, and guided missiles.

destroyer escort *n.* A warship, usu. smaller than a destroyer, used in antisubmarine action.

de•stroy•ing angel (dĭ-stroi′ĭng) *n.* Any of several poisonous mushrooms of the genus *Amanita.*

de•struct (dĭ-strŭkt′, dē′strŭkt′) *n.* The intentional, usu. remote-controlled destruction of a rocket or missile after launching. ❖ *v.* **-struct•ed, -struct•ing, -structs** —*tr.* To destroy intentionally (a rocket or missile) after launch. —*intr.* To self-destruct. [Back-formation < DESTRUCTION.]

de•struc•ti•ble (dĭ-strŭk′tə-bəl) *adj.* Breakable or easily destroyed. **—de•struc′ti•bil′i•ty, de•struc′ti•ble•ness** *n.*

de•struc•tion (dĭ-strŭk′shən) *n.* **1a.** The act of destroying. **b.** The condition of having been destroyed. **2.** The cause or means of destroying. [ME < OFr. < Lat. *dēstrūctiō, dēstrūctiōn-* < *dēstrūctus*, p. part. of *dēstruere*, to destroy. See DESTROY.]

de•struc•tion•ist (dĭ-strŭk′shə-nĭst) *n.* One who believes in or advocates destruction, esp. of existing social institutions.

de•struc•tive (dĭ-strŭk′tĭv) *adj.* **1.** Causing or wreaking destruction; ruinous. **2.** Designed or tending to disprove or discredit: *destructive criticism.* **—de•struc′tive•ly** *adv.* **—de•struc′tive•ness, de′struc•tiv′i•ty** (dē′strŭk-tĭv′ĭ-tē) *n.*

destructive distillation *n.* The decomposition of organic sub-

ă pat
ā pay
âr care
ä father
ĕ pet
ē be
ĭ pit
ī pie
îr pier
ŏ pot
ō toe
ô paw

oi boy
ou out
ŏŏ took
ōō boot
ŭ cut
ûr urge
th thin
th this
hw which
zh vision
ə about,
item

Stress marks:
′ (primary);
′ (secondary), as in
lexicon (lĕk′sĭ-kŏn′)

stances such as wood or coal by heat in the absence of air to produce products such as coke or charcoal.

de•struc•tor (dǐ-strŭk′tər) *n.* **1.** An incinerator for refuse. **2.** An explosive device for effecting a destruct.

des•ue•tude (dĕs′wǐ-tōōd′, -tyōōd′) *n.* A state of disuse or inactivity. [Fr. *désuétude* < Lat. *dēsuētūdō* < *dēsuētus*, p. part. of *dēsuēscere*, to put out of use : *dē-*, de- + *suēscere*, to become accustomed; see **s(w)e-** in App.]

de•sul•fur•ize (dē-sŭl′fə-rīz′) *tr.v.* **-ized, -iz•ing, -iz•es** To eliminate sulfur from (petroleum, for example). **—de•sul′fur•i•za′tion** (-fər-ĭ-zā′shən) *n.*

des•ul•to•ry (dĕs′əl-tôr′ē, -tōr′ē, dĕz′-) *adj.* **1.** Moving or jumping from one thing to another; disconnected: *a desultory speech.* **2.** Occurring haphazardly; random. See Syns at **chance.** [Lat. *dēsultōrius,* leaping < *dēsultor,* a leaper < *dēsultus,* p. part. of *dēsilīre,* to leap down : *dē-,* de- + *salīre,* to jump.] **—des′ul•to′ri•ly** *adv.* **—des′ul•to′ri•ness** *n.*

de•tach (dǐ-tăch′) *t.v.* **-tached, -tach•ing, -tach•es 1.** To separate or unfasten; disconnect. **2.** To remove from association or union with something: *detached herself from the group.* **3.** To send (troops, for example) on a special mission. [Fr. *détacher* < OFr. *destachier* : *des-,* de- + *attachier,* to attach; see ATTACH.] **—de•tach′a•bil′i•ty** *n.* **—de•tach′a•ble** *adj.* **—de•tach′a•bly** *adv.*

de•tached (dǐ-tăcht′) *adj.* **1.** Separated; disconnected. **2.** Standing apart from others; separate. **3.** Marked by an absence of emotional involvement; aloof or impartial. **—de•tach′ed•ly** (-tăch′ĭd-lē, -tăcht′lē) *adv.* **—de•tach′ed•ness** *n.*

de•tach•ment (dǐ-tăch′mənt) *n.* **1.** The act or process of disconnecting or detaching; separation. **2.** The state of being separate or detached. **3.** Indifference to or remoteness from the concerns of others; aloofness. **4.** Absence of prejudice or bias; disinterest. **5a.** The dispatch of a military unit from a larger body for a special duty or mission. **b.** The unit so dispatched. **c.** A permanent unit, usu. smaller than a platoon, organized for special duties.

de•tail (dǐ-tāl′, dē′tāl′) *n.* **1.** An individual part or item; a particular. See Syns at **item. 2.** Particulars considered individually and in relation to a whole. **3.** A minor or inconsequential item or aspect; a minutia. **4.** A minute or thorough treatment or account. **5a.** A discrete part or portion of a work, such as a painting or building, esp. when considered in isolation. **b.** A representation of such a part or portion: *a detail of a Rembrandt portrait.* **6a.** A small elaborated element of a work of art, craft, or design. **b.** Such elements considered together. **c.** The rendering of artistic detail. **7a.** The selection of one or more troops for a particular duty, usu. a fatigue duty. **b.** The personnel so selected. **c.** The duty assigned. ❖ *tr.v.* (dǐ-tāl′) **-tailed, -tail•ing, -tails 1.** To report or relate minutely or in particulars. **2.** To name or state explicitly. **3.** To provide with artistic or decorative detail. **4.** To clean (a car interior, for example) meticulously. **5.** To select and dispatch for a particular duty. **—idiom: in detail** With attention to particulars; thoroughly or meticulously. [Fr. *détail* < OFr. *detail,* a piece cut off < *detaillir,* to cut up : *de-,* de- + *tailler, taillier,* to cut; see TAILOR.] **—de•tail′er** *n.*

de•tailed (dǐ-tāld′, dē′tāld′) *adj.* Characterized by abundant use of detail or thoroughness of treatment: *a detailed report.*

detail man *n.* A representative of a manufacturer of drugs or medical supplies who calls on doctors, pharmacists, and other professional distributors to promote new drugs and supplies.

de•tain (dǐ-tān′) *tr.v.* **-tained, -tain•ing, -tains 1.** To keep from proceeding; delay or retard. **2.** To keep in custody or temporary confinement. **3.** *Obsolete* To retain or withhold (payment or property, for example). [ME *deteinen* < OFr. *detenir* < VLat. **detēnīre* < Lat. *dētinēre* : *dē-,* de- + *tenēre,* to hold; see **ten-** in App.] **—de•tain′ment** *n.*

de•tain•ee (dē′tā-nē′, dǐ-tā′-) *n.* A person held in custody or confinement: *a political detainee.*

de•tain•er (dǐ-tā′nər) *n.* **1.** A withholding from the rightful owner of property that has lawfully come into the possession of the current holder. **2.** The detention of a person, esp. in custody. **3.** A writ authorizing the further detention of a person in custody, pending further action.

de•tect (dǐ-tĕkt′) *tr.v.* **-tect•ed, -tect•ing, -tects 1.** To discover or ascertain the existence, presence, or fact of. **2.** To discern (something hidden or subtle): *detect a note of sarcasm in his voice.* **3.** *Electronics* To demodulate. [ME *detecten* < Lat. *dētegere, dētēct-,* to uncover : *dē-,* de- + *tegere,* to cover; see **(s)teg-** in App.] **—de•tect′a•ble, de•tect′i•ble** *adj.* **—de•tect′er** *n.*

de•tec•tion (dǐ-tĕk′shən) *n.* **1.** The act or process of detecting; discovery. **2.** See **demodulation.**

de•tec•tive (dǐ-tĕk′tǐv) *n.* A person, usu. a member of a police force, who investigates crimes and obtains evidence or information. ❖ *adj.* **1.** Of or relating to detectives or their work: *detective novels.* **2.** Suited for or used in detection.

de•tec•tor (dǐ-tĕk′tər) *n.* One that detects, esp. a device that automatically identifies and records or registers a stimulus, such as a change in pressure, an electric signal, or radiation.

de•tent (dǐ-tĕnt′) *n.* A catch or lever that locks the movement of one part of a mechanism. [Fr. *détente,* a loosening < OFr. *destente* < fem. p. part. of *destendre,* to release : *des-,* de- + *tendre,* to stretch (< Lat. *tendere;* see **ten-** in App.).]

dé•tente (dā-tänt′, -täNt′) *n.* **1.** A relaxing or easing, as of ten-

sion between rivals. **2.** A policy toward a rival nation or bloc characterized by increased diplomatic, commercial, and cultural contact and a desire to reduce tensions. [Fr. See DETENT.] **—dé•tent′ist** *n.*

de•ten•tion (dǐ-tĕn′shən) *n.* **1a.** The act of detaining. **b.** The state or a period of being detained, esp. a period of temporary custody before trial. **c.** Punishment requiring a student to stay after regular school hours. **2.** A forced or punitive delay. [ME *detencioun,* withholding < AN < Lat. *dētentiō, dētentiōn- < dētentus,* p. part. of *dētinēre,* to detain. See DETAIN.]

detention home *n.* A place where juvenile offenders are held in custody, esp. temporarily while awaiting court action.

de•ter (dǐ-tûr′) *v.* **-terred, -ter•ring, -ters** *—tr.* To prevent or discourage from acting, as by means of fear or doubt. *—intr.* To prevent or discourage the occurrence of an action, as by means of fear or doubt. [Lat. *dēterrēre : dē-,* de- + *terrēre,* to frighten.] **—de•ter′ment** *n.* **—de•ter′ra•ble** *adj.* **—de•ter′rer** *n.*

de•terge (dǐ-tûrj′) *tr.v.* **-terged, -terg•ing, -terg•es** To wash or wipe off (a wound, for example); cleanse. [Fr. *déterger* < Lat. *dētergēre : dē-,* de- + *tergēre,* to wipe.]

de•ter•gence (dǐ-tûr′jəns) *n.* Detergency.

de•ter•gen•cy (dǐ-tûr′jən-sē) *n.* The power or quality of cleansing.

de•ter•gent (dǐ-tûr′jənt) *n.* A synthetic cleansing substance that acts similarly to soap. ❖ *adj.* Having cleansing power.

de•te•ri•o•rate (dǐ-tîr′ē-ə-rāt′) *v.* **-rat•ed, -rat•ing, -rates** *—tr.* To diminish or impair in quality, character, or value. *—intr.* **1.** To grow worse; degenerate: *The weather deteriorated overnight.* **2.** To weaken or disintegrate; decay. [LLat. *dēteriōrāre, dēteriōrāt-* < Lat. *dēterior,* worse.] **—de•te′ri•o•ra′tion** *n.* **—de•te′ri•o•ra′tive** *adj.*

de•ter•mi•na•ble (dǐ-tûr′mə-nə-bəl) *adj.* **1.** Capable of being determined, limited, or fixed. **2.** *Law* Capable of being settled or decided: *matters determinable by common law.* **—de•ter′min•a•ble•ness** *n.* **—de•ter′min•a•bly** *adv.*

de•ter•mi•na•cy (dǐ-tûr′mə-nə-sē) *n.* **1.** The quality or condition of being determinate. **2.** The condition of being determined or characterized.

de•ter•mi•nant (dǐ-tûr′mə-nənt) *adj.* Determinative. ❖ *n.* **1.** An influencing or determining element or factor. **2.** *Mathematics* The value that is computed from a square matrix of numbers by a rule of combining products of the matrix entries and that characterizes the solvability of simultaneous linear equations. **3.** *Immunology* An epitope.

de•ter•mi•nate (dǐ-tûr′mə-nǐt) *adj.* **1.** Precisely limited or defined; definite: *a determinate distance.* **2.** Conclusively settled; final. **3.** Firm in purpose; resolute. **4.** *Botany* Terminating in a flower; cymose. [ME < Lat. *dēterminātus,* p. part. of *dētermināre,* to determine. See DETERMINE.] **—de•ter′mi•nate•ly** *adv.* **—de•ter′mi•nate•ness** *n.*

de•ter•mi•nat•er (dǐ-tûr′mə-nā′tər) *n.* A determiner.

de•ter•mi•na•tion (dǐ-tûr′mə-nā′shən) *n.* **1a.** The act of making or arriving at a decision. **b.** The decision reached. **2a.** Firmness of purpose; resolve. **b.** A fixed intention or resolution. **3a.** The settling of a question or case by an authoritative decision or pronouncement, esp. by a judicial body. **b.** The decision or pronouncement made. **4a.** The ascertaining or fixing of the quantity, quality, position, or character of something. **b.** The result of such ascertaining. **5.** A fixed movement or tendency toward an object or end. **6.** *Logic* **a.** The defining of a concept through its constituent elements. **b.** The qualification of a concept or proposition to render it more definite or specific.

de•ter•mi•na•tive (dǐ-tûr′mə-nā′tǐv, -nə-) *adj.* Tending, able, or serving to determine. ❖ *n.* A determining factor. **—de•ter′mi•na′tive•ly** *adv.* **—de•ter′mi•na′tive•ness** *n.*

de•ter•mine (dǐ-tûr′mǐn) *v.* **-mined, -min•ing, -mines** *—tr.* **1a.** To decide or settle (a dispute, for example) conclusively and authoritatively. **b.** To end or decide, as by judicial action. **2.** To establish or ascertain definitely, as after investigation or calculation. See Syns at **discover. 3.** To cause (someone) to come to a conclusion or resolution. **4.** To be the cause of; regulate. **5.** To give direction to: *The committee determines departmental policy.* **6.** To limit in scope or extent. **7.** *Mathematics* To fix or define the position, form, or configuration of. **8.** *Logic* To explain or limit by adding differences. **9.** *Law* To put an end to; terminate. *—intr.* **1.** To reach a decision; resolve. See Syns at **decide. 2.** *Law* To come to an end. [ME *determinen* < OFr. *determiner* < Lat. *dētermināre,* to limit : *dē-,* de- + *terminus,* boundary.]

de•ter•mined (dǐ-tûr′mǐnd) *adj.* **1.** Marked by or showing determination; resolute. **2.** Decided or resolved. **—de•ter′mined•ly** *adv.* **—de•ter′mined•ness** *n.*

de•ter•min•er (dǐ-tûr′mə-nər) *n.* **1.** One that determines. **2.** *Grammar* A word belonging to a group of noun modifiers, which includes articles, demonstratives, possessive adjectives, and words such as *any, both,* or *whose,* and in English occurring first in a noun phrase or after another determiner.

de•ter•min•ism (dǐ-tûr′mə-nǐz′əm) *n.* The philosophical doctrine that every state of affairs, including every human event, act, and decision, is the inevitable consequence of antecedent states of affairs. **—de•ter′min•ist** *n.* **—de•ter′min•is′tic** *adj.* **—de•ter′min•is′ti•cal•ly** *adv.*

detector
archaeologist using a
metal detector

de·ter·rence (dĭ-tûr′əns, -tŭr′-) *n.* **1.** The act or a means of deterring. **2.** Measures taken by a state or an alliance of states to prevent hostile action by another state.

de·ter·rent (dĭ-tûr′ənt, -tŭr′-) *adj.* Tending to deter: *deterrent weapons.* ❖ *n.* **1.** Something that deters. **2.** A retaliatory means of discouraging enemy attack: *a nuclear deterrent.*

de·ter·sive (dĭ-tûr′sĭv, -zĭv) *adj.* Detergent. [Fr. *détersif* < Lat. *dētersus*, p. part. of *dētergēre*, to deterge. See DETERGE.] —**de·ter′sive** *n.*

de·test (dĭ-tĕst′) *tr.v.* **-test·ed, -test·ing, -tests** To dislike intensely; abhor: *detests hairy spiders.* [Fr. *détester* < Lat. *dētestārī*, to curse : *dē-*, de- + *testārī*, to invoke (< *testis*, witness; see **trei-** in App.).] —**de·test′er** *n.*

de·test·a·ble (dĭ-tĕs′tə-bəl) *adj.* Inspiring or deserving abhorrence or scorn. —**de·test′a·bil′i·ty, de·test′a·ble·ness** *n.* —**de·test′a·bly** *adv.*

de·tes·ta·tion (dē′tĕ-stā′shən) *n.* **1.** Strong dislike or hatred; abhorrence. **2.** One that is detested.

de·thatch (dē-thăch′) *v.* **-thatched, -thatch·ing, -thatch·es** —*tr.* To remove (dead grass) from a lawn, usu. to aerate the soil. —*intr.* To dethatch grass. —**de·thatch′er** *n.*

de·throne (dē-thrōn′) *tr.v.* **-throned, -thron·ing, -thrones 1.** To remove from the throne; depose. **2.** To remove from a prominent or powerful position. —**de·throne′ment** *n.*

det·i·nue (dĕt′n-ōō′, -yōō′) *n. Law* **1a.** An action to recover possession or the value of property wrongfully detained. **b.** The writ authorizing such action. **2.** The act of unlawfully detaining personal property. [ME *detenue* < OFr., detention < fem. p. part. of *detenir*, to detain. See DETAIN.]

det·o·nate (dĕt′n-āt′) *intr. & tr.v.* **-nat·ed, -nat·ing, -nates** To explode or cause to explode: *detonated the bomb.* [Lat. *dētonāre*, *dētonāt-*, to thunder down : *dē-*, de- + *tonāre*, to thunder; see **(s)tenə-** in App.] —**det′o·nat′a·ble** *adj.*

det·o·na·tion (dĕt′n-ā′shən) *n.* **1.** The act of exploding. **2.** An explosion.

det·o·na·tor (dĕt′n-ā′tər) *n.* **1.** A device, such as a percussion cap, used to set off an explosive charge. **2.** An explosive.

de·tour (dē′tŏŏr′, dĭ-tŏŏr′) *n.* **1.** A roundabout way or course, esp. a road used temporarily instead of a main route. **2.** A deviation from a direct course of action. ❖ *intr. & tr.v.* **-toured, -tour·ing, -tours** To go or cause to go by a roundabout way. [Fr. *détour* < OFr. *destor* < *destorner*, to turn away : *des-*, de- + *torner*, to turn; see TURN.]

de·tox (dē-tŏks′) *Informal tr.v.* **-toxed, -tox·ing, -tox·es** To subject to detoxification. ❖ *n.* (dē′tŏks′) A part of a hospital or clinic in which patients are detoxified.

de·tox·i·cate (dē-tŏk′sĭ-kāt′) *tr.v.* **-cat·ed, -cat·ing, -cates** To detoxify.

de·tox·i·fi·ca·tion (dē-tŏk′sə-fĭ-kā′shən) *n.* **1.** The process of detoxifying. **2.** The state or condition of being detoxified. **3.** *Physiology* The metabolic process by which the toxic qualities of a poison or toxin are reduced by the body. **4.** A medically supervised treatment program for alcohol or drug addiction to purge the body of intoxicating or addictive substances.

de·tox·i·fy (dē-tŏk′sə-fī′) *tr.v.* **-fied, -fy·ing, -fies 1.** To counteract or destroy the toxic properties of. **2.** To remove the effects of poison from. **3.** To treat (a person) for alcohol or drug dependence by detoxification. [DE- + TOXI(C) + -FY.]

de·tract (dĭ-trăkt′) *v.* **-tract·ed, -tract·ing, -tracts** —*tr.* **1.** To draw or take away; divert: *They could detract little from so solid an argument.* **2.** *Archaic* To speak ill of; belittle. —*intr.* To reduce the value, importance, or quality of something. Often used with *from.* [ME *detracten* < Lat. *dētrahere, dētract-*, to remove : *dē-*, de- + *trahere*, to pull.] —**de·trac′tive** *adj.* —**de·trac′tive·ly** *adv.* —**de·trac′tor** *n.*

de·trac·tion (dĭ-trăk′shən) *n.* **1.** The act of detracting or taking away. **2.** A derogatory or damaging comment on a person's character or reputation; disparagement.

de·train (dē-trān′) *intr. & tr.v.* **-trained, -train·ing, -trains** To leave or cause to leave a train. —**de·train′ment** *n.*

de·trib·al·ize (dē-trī′bə-līz′) *tr.v.* **-ized, -iz·ing, -iz·es** To cause to lose tribal membership and customs. —**de·trib′al·i·za′tion** (-trī′bə-lĭ-zā′shən) *n.*

det·ri·ment (dĕt′rə-mənt) *n.* **1.** Damage, harm, or loss. See Syns at **disadvantage. 2.** Something that causes damage, harm, or loss: *Smoking is a detriment to good health.* [ME < OFr. < Lat. *dētrīmentum < dētrītus*, p. part. of *dēterere*, to lessen, wear down : *dē-*, de- + *terere*, to rub; see **terə-¹** in App.]

det·ri·men·tal (dĕt′rə-mĕn′tl) *adj.* Causing damage or harm; injurious. —**det′ri·men′tal·ly** *adv.*

de·tri·tion (dĭ-trĭsh′ən) *n.* The act of wearing away by friction. [Med.Lat. *dētrītiō, dētrītiōn-* < Lat. *dētrītus*, p. part. of *dēterere*, to lessen, rub away. See DETRIMENT.]

de·tri·tus (dĭ-trī′təs) *n., pl.* **detritus 1.** Loose fragments or grains that have been worn away from rock. **2.** Disintegrated material; debris. [Fr. < Lat. *dētrītus* < p. part. of *dēterere*, to lessen, wear away. See DETRIMENT.] —**de·tri′tal** (-trīt′l) *adj.*

De·troit (dĭ-troit′) A city of SE MI opposite Windsor, Ontario, on the **Detroit River**; founded by French settlers in 1701. Pop. 951,270.

de trop (də trō′) *adj.* Too much or too many; excessive or super-

fluous. [Fr. : *de*, in, of + *trop*, excess.]

de·tu·mes·cence (dē′tŏŏ-mĕs′əns, -tyŏŏ-) *n.* Reduction or lessening of a swelling, esp. of a swollen organ. [< Lat. *dētumēscere*, to subside : *dē-*, de- + *tumēscere*, to swell, inchoative of *tumēre*.] —**de′tu·mes′cent** *adj.*

Deu·ca·li·on (dōō-kā′lē-ən, dyōō-) *n. Greek Mythology* A son of Prometheus who with his wife, Pyrrha, built an ark and floated in it to survive the deluge sent by Zeus.

deuce¹ (dōōs, dyōōs) *n.* **1a.** A playing card having two spots or the side of a die bearing two pips. **b.** A cast of dice totaling two. **2.** A tied score in tennis in which each player or side has 40 points and one player or side must win 2 successive points to win the game. [ME *deus* < OFr., two < Lat. *duōs*, masc. accusative of *duo*. See **dwo-** in App.]

deuce² (dōōs, dyōōs) *Informal n.* **1.** The devil. **2.** An outstanding example, esp. of something bad. **3.** Used as an intensive: *What the deuce were they thinking of?* [Prob. < LGer. *duus*, a throw of two in dice games, bad luck, ult. < Lat. *duo*, two. See DEUCE¹.]

deuc·ed (dōō′sĭd, dyōō′-) *adj. Informal* Darned; confounded. [< DEUCE².]

de·us ex ma·chi·na (dā′əs ĕks mä′kə-nə, -nä′, măk′ə-nə) *n.* **1.** In Greek and Roman drama, a god lowered by stage machinery to resolve a plot. **2.** An unexpected, artificial, or improbable character, device, or event introduced in a work of fiction or drama to resolve a situation. [NLat. *deus ex māchinā* : Lat. *deus*, god + Lat. *ex*, from + Lat. *māchinā*, ablative of *māchina*, machine (transl. of Gk. *theos apo mēkhanēs*).]

Deut. *abbr. Bible* Deuteronomy

deu·ter·ag·o·nist (dōō′tə-răg′ə-nĭst, dyōō-) *n.* The character second in importance to the protagonist in classical Greek drama. [Gk. *deuteragōnistēs*, an actor of second-class parts : *deuteros*, second + *agōnistēs*, actor; see PROTAGONIST.]

deu·ter·a·no·pi·a (dōō′tər-ə-nō′pē-ə, dyōō-) *n.* A form of colorblindness characterized by insensitivity to green. [DEUTER(O)- + Gk. *anōpia*, blindness (*an-*, not; see **A-¹** + *-ōpia*, -opia), so called because green is considered the second of the primary colors.] —**deu′ter·a·nope** (-nōp′) *n.* —**deu′ter·a·nop′ic** (-nŏp′ĭk, -nō′pĭk) *adj.*

deu·ter·ate (dōō′tə-rāt′, dyōō-) *tr.v.* **-at·ed, -at·ing, -ates** To introduce deuterium into (a chemical compound). [DEUTER(IUM) + -ATE¹.] —**deu′ter·a′tion** *n.*

deu·te·ri·um (dōō-tîr′ē-əm, dyōō-) *n.* **Symbol D** An isotope of hydrogen with one proton and one neutron in the nucleus having an atomic weight of 2.014. [DEUTER(O)- + -IUM.]

deuterium oxide *n.* An isotopic form of water with composition D_2O, used as a moderator in nuclear reactors.

deutero- or **deuter-** *pref.* Second; secondary: *deuterocanonical.* [Gk. *deuteros*, second, secondary.]

deu·ter·o·ca·non·i·cal (dōō′tə-rō′kə-nŏn′ĭ-kəl, dyōō-) *adj. Bible* Of, relating to, or being a second canon, esp. that consisting of sections of the Bible not included in the original Roman Catholic canon but accepted by theologians in 1548 at the Council of Trent.

deu·ter·og·a·my (dōō′tə-rŏg′ə-mē, dyōō-) *n.* See **digamy.**

deu·ter·on (dōō′tə-rŏn′, dyōō-) *n.* The nucleus of a deuterium atom, consisting of a bound proton and neutron. [DEUTER(IUM) + -ON¹.]

Deu·ter·on·o·my (dōō′tə-rŏn′ə-mē, dyōō-) *n.* See table at **Bible.** [LLat. *deuteronomium* < Gk. *deuteronomion*, a second law (< *(to) deuteronomion (touto)*, Septuagint, mistranslation of Heb. *mišnê hattôrâ hazzō't*, a copy of this law) : *deuteros*, second + *nomos*, law; see **nem-** in App.] —**Deu′ter·o·nom′ic** (-tər-ə-nŏm′ĭk) *adj.*

deuto- or **deut-** *pref.* Second; secondary: *deutoplasm.* [Alteration of DEUTERO-.]

deu·to·plasm (dōō′tə-plăz′əm, dyōō′-) *n.* The nutritive substances or yolk in the cytoplasm of an ovum or other cell. —**deu′to·plas′mic** *adj.*

deut·sche mark also **deut·sche·mark** (doi′chə-märk′) *n.* See table at **currency.** [Ger. : *deutsch*, Ger. + *Mark*, mark.]

deut·zi·a (dōōt′sē-ə, dyōōt′-) *n.* Any of various shrubs of the genus *Deutzia*, cultivated for their white or pinkish flowers. [After Jan van der *Deutz*, 18th-cent. Dutch patron of botany.]

dev. *abbr.* deviation

De Va·le·ra (dĕv′ə-lĕr′ə, -lîr′ə), **Eamon** 1882–1975. Amer.-born Irish political leader and first president of the Republic of Ireland (1959–73).

de·val·ue (dē-văl′yōō) also **de·val·u·ate** (-văl′yōō-āt′) *v.* **-ued, -u·ing, -ues** also **-at·ed, -at·ing, -ates** —*tr.* **1.** To lessen or cancel the value of. **2.** To lower the exchange value of (a currency) by lowering its gold equivalency. —*intr.* To devalue a currency. —**de·val′u·a′tion** *n.*

De·va·na·ga·ri (dā′və-näd′gə-rē) *n.* The alphabet in which Sanskrit and many modern Indian languages are written. [Skt. *devanāgarī*, royal city writing (< its supposedly having been invented in Pataliputra, a royal city in India) : *deva-*, divine, royal; see **dyeu-** in App. + *nāgarī*, fem. of *nāgara*, of a city (< *nagaram*, city, prob. of Dravidian orig.).]

dev·as·tate (dĕv′ə-stāt′) *tr.v.* **-tat·ed, -tat·ing, -tates 1.** To lay waste; destroy. **2.** To overwhelm; confound; stun. [Lat. *dēvāstāre, dēvāstāt-* : *dē-*, de- + *vāstāre*, to lay waste (< *vāstus*, empty,

Eamon De Valera

ă	pat	oi	boy
ā	pay	ou	out
âr	care	ŏŏ	took
ä	father	ōō	boot
ĕ	pet	ŭ	cut
ē	be	ûr	urge
ĭ	pit	th	thin
ī	pie	*th*	this
îr	pier	hw	which
ŏ	pot	zh	vision
ō	toe	ə	about,
ô	paw		item

Stress marks:
′ (primary);
′ (secondary), as in
lexicon (lĕk′sĭ-kŏn′)

desolate).] —dev′as·tat′ing·ly adv. —dev′as·ta′tion n. —dev′as·ta′tor n.

de·vel·op (dĭ-vĕl′əp) v. -oped, -op·ing, -ops —tr. **1.** To bring from latency to or toward fulfillment. **2a.** To expand or enlarge. **b.** To aid in the growth of; strengthen. **c.** To improve the quality of; refine: *developing my piano technique.* **3.** To cause to become more complex; elaborate. **b.** *Music* To elaborate (a theme) with rhythmic and harmonic variations. **4a.** To bring into being gradually: *develop a new industry.* **b.** To set forth or clarify by degrees. **5a.** To come to have gradually; acquire: *develop a taste for opera.* **b.** To become affected with; contract; *developed a rash.* **6.** To cause gradually to acquire a specific role, function, or form, as: **a.** To influence the behavior of. **b.** To cause (a tract of land) to serve a particular purpose. **c.** To make available and effective to fulfill a particular end. **d.** To convert or transform: *developed the play into a movie.* **7.** *Games* To move (a chess piece) to or toward a more strategic position. **8a.** To process (a photosensitive material), esp. with chemicals, in order to render a recorded image visible. **b.** To render (an image) visible by this means. —*intr.* **1a.** To grow by degrees into a more advanced, evolved, or mature state. See Syns at **mature. b.** To increase or expand. **2.** To come gradually into existence or activity. **3.** To come gradually to light; be disclosed. [Fr. *développer* < OFr. *desveloper* : *des-*, dis- + *voloper*, to wrap (poss. of Celt. orig.).] —de·vel′op·a·ble adj.

de·vel·oped (dĭ-vĕl′əpt) adj. Advanced in industrial capability, technological sophistication, and economic productivity.

de·vel·op·er (dĭ-vĕl′ə-pər) n. **1.** One that develops: *a developer of hidden talent.* **2.** A person who develops real estate, esp. for residential or commercial use. **3.** A chemical used to render visible the image recorded on a photosensitive surface.

de·vel·op·ing (dĭ-vĕl′ə-pĭng) adj. Having a relatively low level of industrial capability, technological sophistication, and economic productivity.

de·vel·op·ment (dĭ-vĕl′əp-mənt) n. **1.** The act of developing. **2.** The state of being developed. **3.** A significant event, occurrence, or change. **4.** A group of dwellings built by the same contractor. **5.** Determination of the best techniques for applying a new device or process to production of goods or services. **6.** *Music* **a.** Elaboration of a theme with rhythmic and harmonic variations. **b.** The central section of a movement in sonata form, in which the theme is elaborated and explored. —de·vel′op·men′tal (-mĕn′tl) adj. —de·vel′op·men′tal·ly adv.

SYNONYMS *development, evolution, progress* These nouns mean a progression from a simpler or lower to a more advanced, mature, or complex form or stage: *the development of an idea into reality; the evolution of a plant from a seed; attempts made to foster social progress.*

developmental disability n. A mental or physical disability arising before adulthood and usu. lasting throughout life.

de·ver·bal n. See deverbative.

de·ver·ba·tive (dē-vûr′bə-tĭv) adj. **1.** Formed from a verb, such as the noun *worker* derived from the verb *work.* **2.** Used in derivation from a verb, such as the suffix *-er* in *teacher.* ❖ n. A deverbative word or element.

Dev·er·eux (dĕv′ə-rōō′), Robert. 2nd Earl of Essex. 1566–1601. English noble and favorite of Elizabeth I.

de·vest (dĭ-vĕst′) tr.v. -vest·ed, -vest·ing, -vests **1.** *Law* To take away (a right or possession, for example). **2.** *Archaic* **a.** To remove the clothing or covering of. **b.** To deprive of a title, right, or item of property. [Obsolete Fr. *desvestir*, to undress < Med.Lat. *disvestīre* : Lat. *dis-*, dis- + Lat. *vestis*, garment; see wes-2 in App.]

De·vi (dā′vē) n. *Hinduism* A mother goddess having various manifestations and roles, esp. that of consort to Shiva. [Skt. *devī*, fem. of *devah*, god. See dyeu- in App.]

de·vi·ant (dē′vē-ənt) adj. Differing from a norm or from the accepted standards of a society. ❖ n. One that differs from a norm, esp. a person whose behavior is deviant. [ME *deviaunt* < LLat. *dēviāns, dēviant-*, pr. part. of *dēviāre*, to deviate. See DEVIATE.] —de′vi·ance, de′vi·an·cy n.

de·vi·ate (dē′vē-āt′) v. -at·ed, -at·ing, -ates —intr. **1.** To turn aside from a course or way. **2.** To depart, as from a norm or purpose; stray. See Syns at **swerve.** —tr. To cause to turn aside or differ. ❖ n. (-ĭt) A deviant. [LLat. *dēviāre, dēviāt-* : Lat. *dē-*, de- + Lat. *via*, road; see wegh- in App.] —de′vi·a′tor n. —de′vi·a·to′ry (-ə-tôr′ē, -tōr′ē) adj.

de·vi·a·tion (dē′vē-ā′shən) n. **1.** The act of deviating or turning aside. **2.** An abnormality; a departure. **3.** Deviant behavior or attitudes. **4.** Divergence from an accepted political policy or party line. **5.** Deflection of a compass needle caused by local magnetic influence. **6.** *Statistics* The difference, esp. the absolute difference, between one number in a set and the mean of the set. —de′vi·a′tion·ism n. —de′vi·a′tion·ist adj. & n.

de·vice (dĭ-vīs′) n. **1.** A contrivance or an invention serving a particular purpose. **2a.** A technique or means. **b.** A plan or scheme, esp. a malign one. **3.** A literary contrivance, such as parallelism or personification, used to achieve a particular effect. **4.** A decorative design or pattern, as one used in embroidery. **5.** A graphic symbol or motto, esp. in heraldry. **6.** *Archaic* The act, state, or power of devising. —*idiom:* leave to (one's) own devices To allow to do as one pleases. [ME < OFr. *devis*, division,

Devi
seventh-century
Cambodian sandstone
sculpture

wish, and OFr. *devise*, design, both < Lat. *dīvīsus, dīvīsa*, p. part. of *dīvidere*, to divide. See DIVIDE.]

dev·il (dĕv′əl) n. **1.** often **Devil** In many religions, the major personified spirit of evil, ruler of Hell, and foe of God. Used with *the.* **2.** A subordinate evil spirit; a demon. **3.** A wicked or malevolent person. **4.** A person: *the poor devil.* **5.** An energetic, mischievous, daring, or clever person. **6.** *Printing* A printer's devil. **7.** A device or machine, esp. one having teeth or spikes and used for tearing. **8.** An outstanding example, esp. of something difficult or bad. **9.** A severe reprimand or expression of anger. **10.** *Informal* Used as an intensive: *Who the devil do you think you are?* ❖ tr.v. -iled, -il·ing, -ils or -illed, -il·ling, -ils **1.** To season (food) heavily. **2.** To annoy, torment, or harass. **3.** To tear up (cloth or rags) in a toothed machine. —**idioms: between the devil and the deep blue sea** Between two equally unacceptable choices. **give the devil his due** To give credit to a disagreeable or malevolent person. **go to the devil 1.** To be unsuccessful; fail. **2.** To become depraved. **3.** Used in the imperative to express anger or impatience. [ME *devel* < OE *dēofol* < Lat. *diabolus* < L.Gk. *diabolos* < Gk., slanderer < *diaballein*, to slander : *dia-*, dia- + *ballein*, to hurl; see gʷelə- in App.]

dev·il·fish (dĕv′əl-fĭsh′) n., pl. devilfish or -fish·es **1.** See manta 2. **2.** See octopus 1. **3.** See gray whale.

dev·il·ish (dĕv′ə-lĭsh) adj. **1.** Of, resembling, or characteristic of a devil, as: **a.** Malicious; evil. **b.** Mischievous, teasing, or annoying. **2.** Excessive; extreme: *devilish heat.* ❖ adv. Extremely; very. —dev′il·ish·ly adv. —dev′il·ish·ness n.

dev·il·kin (dĕv′əl-kĭn) n. A little devil; an imp.

dev·il-may-care (dĕv′əl-mā-kâr′) adj. **1.** Heedless of caution; reckless. **2.** Jovial and rakish in manner.

dev·il·ment (dĕv′əl-mənt) n. Devilish behavior; mischief.

dev·il's advocate (dĕv′əlz) n. **1.** One who argues against a cause or position simply for the sake of argument or to determine the validity of the cause or position. **2.** *Roman Catholic Church* An official appointed to present arguments against a proposed canonization or beatification. [Transl. of Med.Lat. *advocātus diabolī*, one arguing for the devil's plea against canonizing a saint.]

devil's bit n. See blazing star 1.

devil's darning needle n. *Northeastern, Upper Northern, & Western US* See dragonfly. See Regional Note at dragonfly. **2.** See damselfly.

devil's food cake n. A rich chocolate cake.

Dev·il's Island (dĕv′īlz) An island in the Caribbean off French Guiana; a French penal colony after the 1850s.

devil's paintbrush n. See orange hawkweed.

devil's walking stick n. See Hercules' club 1.

dev·il·try (dĕv′əl-trē) or dev·il·ry (-əl-rē) n., pl. -tries or -ries **1.** Reckless mischief. **2.** Extreme cruelty; wickedness. **3.** Evil magic; witchcraft. **4.** An act of mischief, cruelty, or witchcraft. [< DEVIL (influenced by such words as GALLANTRY).]

dev·il·wood (dĕv′əl-wŏŏd′) n. A tree (*Osmanthus americanus*) of the southeast United States having fragrant greenish flowers, hard wood, and whitish bark.

De Vin·ne (də vĭn′ē), Theodore Low 1828–1914. Amer. printer who wrote *The Practice of Typography* (1900–04).

de·vi·ous (dē′vē-əs) adj. **1.** Not straightforward; shifty. **2.** Departing from the correct or accepted way; erring. **3.** Deviating from the straight or direct course; roundabout. **4.** Away from a main road or course; distant or removed. [< Lat. *dēvius*, out-of-the-way : *dē-*, de- + *via*, road; see wegh- in App.] —de′vi·ous·ly adv. —de′vi·ous·ness n.

de·vise (dĭ-vīz′) tr.v. -vised, -vis·ing, -vis·es **1.** To form, plan, or arrange in the mind; design or contrive. **2.** *Law* To transmit or give (real property) by will. **3.** *Archaic* To suppose; imagine. ❖ n. *Law* **1a.** The act of transmitting or giving real property by will. **b.** The property or lands so transmitted or given. A will or clause in a will transmitting or giving real property. [ME *devisen* < OFr. *deviser* < VLat. *dēvīsāre* < Lat. *dīvīsāre*, freq. of *dīvidere*, to divide. See DIVIDE.] —de·vis′a·ble adj. —de·vis′er n.

de·vi·see (dĭ-vī′zē′, dĕv′ĭ-zē′) n. *Law* One to whom a devise is made.

de·vi·sor (dĭ-vī′zər, dĕv′ĭ-zôr′) n. *Law* One that makes a devise.

de·vi·tal·ize (dē-vīt′l-īz′) tr.v. -ized, -iz·ing, -iz·es To diminish or destroy the strength or vitality of. —de·vit′al·i·za′tion (-ĭ-zā′shən) n.

de·vit·ri·fy (dē-vĭt′rə-fī′) tr.v. -fied, -fy·ing, -fies To cause (a glassy material) to become crystalline and brittle. —de·vit′ri·fi′a·ble adj. —de·vit′ri·fi·ca′tion (-fĭ-kā′shən) n.

de·vo·cal·ize (dē-vō′kə-līz′) tr.v. -ized, -iz·ing, -iz·es To devoice. —de·vo′cal·i·za′tion (-kə-lĭ-zā′shən) n.

de·voice (dē-vois′) tr.v. -voiced, -voic·ing, -voic·es To pronounce (a normally voiced sound) without vibration of the vocal chords so as to make it wholly or partly voiceless.

de·void (dĭ-void′) adj. Completely lacking. [ME, p. part. of *devoiden*, to remove, eliminate < OFr. *desvoidier* : *des-*, de- + *voidier*, to empty (< *voide*, empty; see VOID).]

de·voir (dəv-wär′, dĕv′wär′) n. **1.** An act or expression of respect or courtesy; civility. Often used in the plural. **2.** Duty or responsibility. [ME, duty < OFr. < *devoir*, to owe < Lat. *dēbēre*. See ghabh- in App.]

de·vol·a·til·ize (dē-vŏl′ə-tl-īz′) tr.v. -ized, -iz·ing, -iz·es To remove volatile material from: *devolatilize coal.* —**de•vol′a•til•i•za′tion** *n.*

dev•o•lu•tion (dĕv′ə-lōō′shən, dē′və-) *n.* **1.** A passing down or descent through successive stages of time or a process. **2.** Transference, as of rights or qualities, to a successor. **3.** Delegation of duties to a subordinate or substitute. **4.** A transfer of powers from a central government to local units. **5.** *Biology* Degeneration. [LLat. *dēvolūtiō, dēvolūtiōn-* < Lat. *dēvolūtus,* p. part. of *dēvolvere,* to roll down, fall to. See DEVOLVE.] —**dev′o•lu′tion•ar′y** (-shə-nĕr′ē) *adj.* —**dev′o•lu′tion•ist** *n.*

de•volve (dĭ-vŏlv′) *v.* **-volved, -volv•ing, -volves** —*tr.* **1.** To pass on or delegate to another. **2.** *Archaic* To cause to roll onward or downward. —*intr.* **1.** To be passed on or transferred to another. **2.** To degenerate or deteriorate gradually: *The meeting devolved into a shouting match.* **3.** *Archaic* To roll onward or downward. [ME *devolven,* to transfer < OFr. *devolver,* to confer, ascribe < Lat. *dēvolvere,* to roll down, fall to : *dē-, de-* + *volvere,* to roll; see **wel-** in App.] —**de•volve′ment** *n.*

Dev•on[1] (dĕv′ən) A region of SW England on the English Channel; part of Wessex after the 8th cent.

Dev•on[2] (dĕv′ən) *n.* Any of a breed of reddish cattle raised primarily for beef. [After DEVON[1], where the breed was orig. developed.]

De•vo•ni•an (dĭ-vō′nē-ən) *adj.* Of or belonging to the geologic time of the fourth period of the Paleozoic Era, characterized by the appearance of forests and amphibians. See table at **geologic time.** ❖ *n.* The Devonian Period or its deposits. [After *Devon,* a county of SW England.]

Devon Island An island of N Nunavut, Canada, between Baffin and Ellesmere islands.

Dev•on•shire cream (dĕv′ən-shîr′, -shər) *n.* See **clotted cream.** [After *Devonshire,* or Devon, a county of SW England.]

de•vote (dĭ-vōt′) *tr.v.* **-vot•ed, -vot•ing, -votes 1.** To give or apply (one's time, attention, or self) to an activity, cause, or person. **2.** To set apart for a purpose or use. **3.** To set apart by or as if by a vow or solemn act; consecrate: *a temple devoted to Apollo.* [Lat. *dēvovēre, dēvōt-,* to vow : *dē-, de-* + *vovēre,* to vow.] —**de•vote′ment** *n.*

de•vot•ed (dĭ-vō′tĭd) *adj.* **1.** Feeling or displaying strong affection or attachment; ardent. **2.** Having been consecrated; dedicated. —**de•vot′ed•ly** *adv.* —**de•vot′ed•ness** *n.*

dev•o•tee (dĕv′ə-tē′, -tā′) *n.* **1.** One who is ardently devoted to something; an enthusiast or advocate: *a devotee of sports.* **2.** An ardent or fanatical adherent of a religion.

de•vo•tion (dĭ-vō′shən) *n.* **1.** Ardent, often selfless affection and dedication, as to a person or principle. See Syns at **love. 2.** Religious ardor or zeal; piety. **3a.** An act of religious observance or prayer. Often used in the plural. **b. devotions** Prayers or religious texts. **4.** The act of devoting or the state of being devoted.

de•vo•tion•al (dĭ-vō′shə-nəl) *adj.* Of, relating to, expressive of, or used in devotion, esp. of a religious nature. ❖ *n.* A short religious service. —**de•vo′tion•al•ly** *adv.*

de•vour (dĭ-vour′) *tr.v.* **-voured, -vour•ing, -vours 1.** To eat up greedily. **2.** To destroy, consume, or waste: *Flames devoured the house.* **3.** To take in eagerly: *devour a novel.* **4.** To prey upon voraciously: *devoured by jealousy.* [ME *devouren* < OFr. *devourer* < Lat. *dēvorāre* : *dē-, de-* + *vorāre,* to swallow.] —**de•vour′er** *n.* —**de•vour′ing•ly** *adv.*

de•vout (dĭ-vout′) *adj.* **-er, -est 1.** Devoted to religion or religious obligations. **2.** Displaying reverence or piety. **3.** Sincere; earnest: *devout wishes for their success.* [ME < OFr. < Lat. *dēvōtus,* p. part. of *dēvovēre,* to vow. See DEVOTE.] —**de•vout′ly** *adv.* —**de•vout′ness** *n.*

De Vries (də vrēs′), **Hugo** 1848–1935. Dutch botanist who studied evolution by observing mutations.

dew (dōō, dyōō) *n.* **1.** Water droplets condensed from the air, usu. onto cool surfaces. **2.** Something moist, fresh, pure, or renewing. **3.** Moisture, as in the form of tears, that appears in small drops. ❖ *tr.v.* **dewed, dew•ing, dews** To wet with or as if with dew. [ME *deu* < OE *dēaw.*]

de•wan (dĭ-wän′) *n.* Any of various government officials in India. [Hindi *dīvān* < Pers., account book.]

Dew•ar (dōō′ər, dyōō′-), **Sir James** 1842–1923. Scottish-born chemist who invented cordite (1889) with Sir Frederick Abel.

Dewar flask *n.* A container used esp. to store liquefied gases, having a double wall with a vacuum between the walls and silvered surfaces facing the vacuum. [After Sir James DEWAR.]

de•wa•ter (dē-wô′tər, -wŏt′ər) *tr.v.* **-tered, -ter•ing, -ters** To remove water from (a waste product, for example).

dew•ber•ry (dōō′bĕr′ē, dyōō′-) *n.* **1.** Any of several trailing forms of the blackberry, such as *Rubus hispidus* of North America. **2.** The fruit of any of these plants.

dew•claw (dōō′klô′, dyōō′-) *n.* A digit or claw not reaching the ground and found on the feet of certain mammals. [Perh. DEW + CLAW.] —**dew′clawed′** *adj.*

dew•drop (dōō′drŏp′, dyōō′-) *n.* A drop of dew.

Dew•ey (dōō′ē, dyōō′ē), **George** 1837–1917. Amer. naval officer active in the Spanish-American War.

Dewey, John 1859–1952. Amer. philosopher and educator who was a leading exponent of philosophical pragmatism.

Dewey, Melvil 1851–1931. Amer. librarian and founder of the

decimal system of classification (1876).

Dewey, Thomas Edmund 1902–71. Amer. politician who was the Republican nominee for President in 1944 and 1948.

Dewey decimal classification *n.* A system used in libraries for organizing publications into subject categories corresponding to three-digit numerals, with further specification expressed by numerals following a decimal point. [After Melvil DEWEY.]

dew•fall (dōō′fôl′, dyōō′-) *n.* **1.** The formation of dew. **2.** The time of evening when dew begins to form.

dew•lap (dōō′lăp′, dyōō′-) *n.* **1.** A fold of loose skin hanging from the neck of certain animals. **2.** A pendulous part similar to this, such as the wattle of a bird. **3.** A fold of loose skin hanging from a person's throat. [ME *dewlappe* : *dew,* of unknown meaning (akin to Dan. and Norw. *dog-* in Dan. *doglæb* and Norw. *doglæp,* dewlap) + *lappe,* fold; see LAP[2].]

DEW line (dōō, dyōō) *n.* A line of radar stations near the 70th parallel across North America, maintained by the United States and Canada to give advance warning of enemy aircraft and missiles. [*D(istant) E(arly) W(arning).*]

de•worm (dē-wûrm′) *tr.v.* **-wormed, -worm•ing, -worms** To cure (an animal) of worms; worm. —**de•worm′er** *n.*

dew point *n.* The temperature at which air becomes saturated and produces dew.

dew-worm also **dew worm** (dōō′wûrm′, dyōō′-) *n.* An earthworm found on or near the surface of the ground and used as fishing bait.

dew•y (dōō′ē, dyōō′ē) *adj.* **-i•er, -i•est 1.** Moist with or as if with dew: *dewy grass.* **2.** Accompanied by dew: *a dewy morning.* **3.** Suggestive of the freshness or purity of dew, as in innocence. —**dew′i•ly** *adv.* —**dew′i•ness** *n.*

dew•y-eyed (dōō′ē-īd′, dyōō′-) *adj.* Innocent; naive.

dex•a•meth•a•sone (dĕk′sə-mĕth′ə-sōn′, -zōn′) *n.* A synthetic glucocorticoid used primarily in the treatment of inflammatory disorders. [*dexa-* (blend of DECA– and HEXA–) + METH(YL) + prob. alteration of (CORT)ISONE.]

Dex•e•drine (dĕk′sĭ-drĭn, -drēn′) A trademark used for dextroamphetamine.

dex•ie (dĕk′sē) *n. Slang* A pill or tablet containing dextroamphetamine.

dex•ter (dĕk′stər) *adj.* **1.** Of or located on the right side. **2.** *Heraldry* Situated on or being the side of a shield on the wearer's right. **3.** *Obsolete* Auspicious; favorable. [Lat. See **deks-** in App.]

dex•ter•i•ty (dĕk-stĕr′ĭ-tē) *n.* **1.** Skill and grace in physical movement, esp. in the use of the hands; adroitness. **2.** Mental skill or adroitness; cleverness. [Fr. *dextérité* < Lat. *dexteritās* < *dexter,* skillful. See DEXTER.]

dex•ter•ous (dĕk′stər-əs, -strəs) also **dex•trous** (-strəs) *adj.* **1.** Skillful in the use of the hands. **2.** Having mental skill or adroitness. **3.** Done with dexterity. [< Lat. *dexter,* skillful. See DEXTER.] —**dex′ter•ous•ly** *adv.* —**dex′ter•ous•ness** *n.*

dex•tral (dĕk′strəl) *adj.* **1.** Of, relating to, or located on the right side; right. **2.** Right-handed. **3.** *Zoology* Of or relating to a gastropod shell that coils clockwise and has its aperture to the right when facing the observer with the apex upward. —**dex•tral′i•ty** (dĕk-străl′ĭ-tē) *n.* —**dex′tral•ly** *adv.*

dex•tran (dĕk′străn′, -strən) *n.* Any of a group of long-chain polymers of glucose with various molecular weights that are used as plasma volume expanders. [DEXTR(OSE) + –AN[2].]

dex•trin (dĕk′strĭn) also **dex•trine** (dĕk′strĭn, -strēn′) *n.* Any of various soluble polysaccharides obtained from starch by the application of heat or acids used mainly as adhesives and thickening agents.

dex•tro (dĕk′strō) *adj.* Dextrorotatory.

dex•tro- or **dextr-** *pref.* **1.** On or to the right; right: *dextrorotation.* **2.** Dextrorotatory: *dextrose.* [Lat. < *dexter,* on the right side. See **deks-** in App.]

dex•tro•am•phet•a•mine (dĕk′strō-ăm-fĕt′ə-mēn′, -mĭn) *n.* A white crystalline compound, $C_9H_{13}N$, the dextrorotatory isomer of amphetamine, used in the form of its phosphate or sulfate salt as a stimulant.

dex•tro•glu•cose (dĕk′strə-glōō′kōs′) *n.* See **dextrose.**

dex•tro•ro•ta•tion (dĕk′strə-rō-tā′shən) *n.* A turning to the right. Used esp. of the plane of polarization of light.

dex•tro•ro•ta•to•ry (dĕk′strə-rō′tə-tôr′ē, -tōr′ē) also **dex•tro•ro•ta•ry** (-rō′tə-rē) *adj.* Of or relating to an optically active chemical that rotates the plane of polarized light to the right or clockwise.

dex•trorse (dĕk′strôrs′) *adj. Botany* Growing upward in a spiral that turns from left to right. [Lat. *dextrōrsus* < *dextrōversus,* turning toward the right : *dexter,* right; see DEXTRO- + *versus,* p. part. of *vertere,* to turn; see **wer-**[2] in App.] —**dex′trorse•ly** *adv.*

dewlap

dex•trose (dĕk′strōs′) *n.* The dextrorotatory form of glucose, $C_6H_{12}O_6 \cdot H_2O$, found naturally in animal and plant tissue and derived synthetically from starch. [DEXTR(OGLUC)OSE.]

dex•trous (dĕk′strəs) *adj.* Variant of **dexterous.**

dey (dā) *n.* **1.** Used formerly as the title of the governor of Algiers before the French conquest in 1830. **2.** Used formerly as the title for rulers of the states of Tunis and Tripoli. [Fr. < Turk. *dayı,* maternal uncle.]

Dezh•nev (dĕzh′nəf, dĕzh′nē-ôf′, dĭzh-nyôf′), **Cape** also **East Cape** A cape of extreme NE Russia on the Bering Strait opposite AK.

DFA *abbr.* Doctor of Fine Arts

DFC *abbr.* Distinguished Flying Cross

dg *abbr.* decigram

dGTP (dē′jē′tē′pē′) *n.* One of the two purine nucleotides that are used to synthesize DNA. [D(EOXY) + G(UANOSINE) + T(RI)P(HOSPHATE).]

DH *abbr.* **1.** designated hitter **2.** Doctor of Humanities

Dha•ka or **Dac•ca** (dăk′ə, dä′kə) The cap. of Bangladesh, in the E-central part; under British rule 1765–1947. Pop. 3,397,187.

dhar•ma (där′mə, dûr′-) *n.* **1.** *Hinduism & Buddhism* **a.** The principle or law that orders the universe. **b.** Individual conduct in conformity with this principle. **2.** *Hinduism* Individual obligation with respect to caste, social custom, and law. **3.** *Buddhism* The body of teachings expounded by the Buddha. [Skt. *dharmaḥ,* statute, law.] —**dhar′mic** *adj.*

dhar•na (där′nə, dûr′-) also **dhur•na** (dûr′nə) *n.* A fast conducted at the door of an offender, esp. a debtor, in India as a means of obtaining compliance with a demand for justice. [Hindi *dharnā* < Prakrit *dharaṇa* < Skt. *dharaṇam,* act of support, stay.]

Dha•ruk (där′ŏŏk) *n., pl.* **Dharuk** or **-ruks 1.** A member of an Aboriginal people of southeast Australia, now culturally assimilated into the Australian population. **2.** Their extinct Pama-Nyungan language.

Dhau•la•gi•ri (dou′lə-gîr′ē) A peak, 8,177.1 m (26,810 ft) in the Himalaya Mts. of W-central Nepal.

DHEA (dē′āch′ē′ā′) *n.* An androgenic steroid hormone secreted by the adrenal cortex or prepared synthetically for sale as a nutritional supplement. [*d(e)h(ydro)e(pi)a(ndrosterone)*.]

Dhe•gi•ha (dā′jē-hä′) *n., pl.* **Dhegiha** or **-has 1.** A branch of the Siouan linguistic family comprising the Omaha, Ponca, Osage, Kansa, and Quapaw languages. **2.** A member of any of the peoples speaking Dhegiha.

DHL *abbr.* **1.** Doctor of Hebrew Letters **2.** Doctor of Hebrew Literature

dhole (dōl) *n.* A wild Asian dog (*Cuon alpinus*) usu. hunting with a pack. [Perh. < Kannada *tōḷa,* wolf.]

dho•ti (dō′tē) also **dhoo•tie** (dōō′-) *n., pl.* **-tis** also **-ties 1.** A loincloth worn by Hindu men in India. **2.** The cotton fabric used for such loincloths. [Hindi *dhotī* < *dhautta, *dhotta,* cloth, prob. < p. part. of *dhauvati,* he washes < Skt. *dhūnoti, dhau-,* he shakes.]

dhow (dou) *n.* A usu. one- or two-masted, lateen-rigged ship used along the coasts of the Indian Ocean. [Perh. of E African orig.]

Dhu'l-Hij•jah (dōōl-hĭj′ä) *n.* The 12th month of the year in the Islamic calendar. See table at **calendar.** [Ar. *ḏū-l-ḥijja : ḏū,* the one of + *al-,* the + *ḥijja,* pilgrimage (< *ḥajja,* to make a pilgrimage).]

Dhu'l-Qa'•dah (dōōl-kä′dä) *n.* The 11th month of the year in the Islamic calendar. See table at **calendar.** [Ar. *ḏū-l-qa'da : ḏū,* the one of + *al-,* the + *qa'da,* sitting (< *qa'ada,* to sit).]

dhur•rie (dûr′ē) *n.* A flat-woven cotton rug made in India. [Hindi *darī* < M Indic *darita,* split cane, mat < var. of Skt. *dalita-,* p. part. of *dalati,* he splits.]

Di The symbol for didymium 1.

di-[1] *pref.* **1.** Two; twice; double: *dichromatic.* **2.** Containing two atoms, radicals, or groups: *dichloride.* [Gk. See **dwo-** in App.]

di-[2] *pref.* Variant of **dia-.**

dia- or **di-** *pref.* **1.** Through: *diachronic.* **2.** Across: *diatropism.* [Gk. < *dia,* through.]

di•a•base (dī′ə-bās′) *n.* A dark gray to black, fine-textured igneous rock composed mainly of feldspar and pyroxene and used for monuments and as crushed stone. [Fr., partly < Gk. *diabasis,* a crossing over (< *diabainein,* to pass through or over; see DIABETES) and partly < *diabase* (dia-, two, alteration of *di-* < Gk. *di-;* see DI-[1] + *base,* basis < OFr.; see BASE[1].)]

di•a•be•tes (dī′ə-bē′tĭs, -tēz) *n.* Any of several metabolic disorders marked by excessive discharge of urine and persistent thirst, esp. one of the two types of diabetes mellitus. [ME *diabete* < Med.Lat. *diabētēs* < Lat. < Gk., siphon, diabetes < *diabainein,* to cross over, straddle : *dia-,* dia- + *bainein,* to go; see gʷā- in App.]

diabetes in•sip•i•dus (ĭn-sĭp′ĭ-dəs) *n.* A chronic metabolic disorder characterized by intense thirst and excessive urination, caused by a deficiency of the pituitary hormone vasopressin. [NLat. *diabētēs īnsipidus : diabētēs,* diabetes + Lat. *īnsipidus,* insipid.]

diabetes mel•li•tus (mə-lī′təs, mĕl′ĭ-) *n.* **1.** A severe chronic form of diabetes that typically appears in childhood or adolescence, is caused by insufficient production of insulin, and is characterized by increased sugar in the blood and urine, excessive

thirst, frequent urination, and wasting. **2.** A mild form of diabetes that typically appears first in adulthood, is exacerbated by obesity, and is treated with changes in diet and an exercise regimen. [NLat. *diabētēs mellitus : Lat. diabētēs,* diabetes + Lat. *mellī-tus,* honey-sweet.]

di•a•bet•ic (dī′ə-bĕt′ĭk) *adj.* **1.** Of, relating to, or having diabetes: *a diabetic coma.* **2.** Intended for use by a person with diabetes. ❖ *n.* A person who has diabetes.

di•a•ble•rie (dē-ä′blə-rē, -äb′lə-) *n.* **1.** Sorcery; witchcraft. **2.** Representation of devils or demons, as in paintings or fiction. **3.** Devilish conduct; deviltry. [Fr. < OFr. < *diable,* devil < Lat. *diabolus.* See DEVIL.]

di•a•bol•i•cal (dī′ə-bŏl′ĭ-kəl) also **di•a•bol•ic** (-ĭk) *adj.* **1.** Of, concerning, or characteristic of the devil; satanic. **2.** Wicked, fiendish, or cruel. [< ME *deabolik* < OFr. *diabolique* < LLat. *diabolicus* < Lat. *diabolus,* devil. See DEVIL.] —**di′a•bol′i•cal•ly** *adv.* —**di′a•bol′i•cal•ness** *n.*

di•ab•o•lism (dī-ăb′ə-lĭz′əm) *n.* **1.** Dealings with or worship of the devil or demons; sorcery. **2.** Devilish conduct or character. —**di•ab′o•list** *n.*

di•ab•o•lize (dī-ăb′ə-līz′) *tr.v.* **-lized, -liz•ing, -liz•es 1.** To cause to be diabolical. **2.** To represent as diabolical.

di•a•ce•tyl•mor•phine (dī′ə-sĕt′l-môr′fēn′, dī-ăs′ĭ-tl-) *n.* See **heroin.** [DI-[1] + ACETYL + MORPHINE.]

di•a•chron•ic (dī′ə-krŏn′ĭk) *adj.* Of or concerned with phenomena as they change through time. [< DIA- + Gk. *khronos,* time.] —**di′a•chron′i•cal•ly** *adv.*

di•ach•ro•ny (dī-ăk′rə-nē) *n.* **1.** Diachronic arrangement or analysis. **2.** Change occurring over time. [DIACHRON(IC) + -Y[2].]

di•ac•o•nal (dī-ăk′ə-nəl) *adj.* Of or concerning a deacon or the diaconate. [LLat. *diāconālis* < *diāconus,* deacon. See DEACON.]

di•ac•o•nate (dī-ăk′ə-nĭt, -nāt′) *n.* **1.** The rank, office, or tenure of a deacon. **2.** Deacons considered as a group. [LLat. *diāco-nātus* < *diāconus,* deacon. See DEACON.]

di•a•crit•ic (dī′ə-krĭt′ĭk) *adj.* **1.** Diacritical. **2.** *Medicine* Diagnostic or distinctive. ❖ *n.* A mark, such as the cedilla of *façade* or the acute accent of *resumé,* added to a letter to indicate a special phonetic value or distinguish words that are otherwise graphically identical. [Gk. *diakritikos,* distinguishing < *diakritos,* distinguished < *diakrīnein,* to distinguish : *dia-,* apart; see DIA- + *krei-,* to separate; see **krei-[1]** in App.]

di•a•crit•i•cal (dī′ə-krĭt′ĭ-kəl) *adj.* **1.** Marking a distinction; distinguishing. **2.** Able to discriminate or distinguish. **3.** Serving as a diacritic. —**di′a•crit′i•cal•ly** *adv.*

Dí•a de la Ra•za (dē′ä dĕ lä rä′sä) *n.* October 12, celebrated as a holiday in Spain, Latin America, and Hispanic regions and territories of the United States to commemorate the arrival of Christopher Columbus in the New World in 1492. [Am.Sp., day of the people.]

Día de los Muer•tos (lōs mwĕr′tōs) *n.* See **Day of the Dead.** [Sp. : *día,* day + *de,* of + *los,* the + *muertos,* pl. of *muerto,* dead.]

di•a•del•phous (dī′ə-dĕl′fəs) *adj.* Having the filaments of a flower united into two groups: *diadelphous stamens.* [DI-[1] + Gk. *adelphos,* brother; see **sem-[1]** in App.]

di•a•dem (dī′ə-dĕm′, -dəm) *n.* **1.** A crown worn as a sign of royalty. **2.** Royal power or dignity. ❖ *tr.v.* **-demed, -dem•ing, -dems** To adorn with or as if with a diadem. [ME *diademe* < OFr. < Lat. *diadēma* < Gk., band < *diadein,* to bind around : *dia-,* dia- + *dein,* to bind.]

di•aer•e•sis (dī-ĕr′ĭ-sĭs) *n.* Variant of **dieresis.**

di•a•gen•e•sis (dī′ə-jĕn′ĭ-sĭs) *n.* The process of chemical and physical change in deposited sediment during its conversion to rock. —**di′a•ge•net′ic** (-jə-nĕt′ĭk) *adj.*

di•a•ge•ot•ro•pism (dī′ə-jē-ŏt′rə-pĭz′əm) *n. Botany* The tendency of growing parts, such as roots, to become oriented at right angles to the direction of gravitational force. —**di′a•ge′o•trop′ic** (-ə-trŏp′ĭk, -trŏp′pĭk) *adj.*

Dia•ghi•lev (dē-ä′gə-lĕf′, dyä′gĭ-lĭf), **Sergei Pavlovich** 1872–1929. Russian ballet impresario who founded (1909) the Ballets Russes company in Paris.

di•ag•nose (dī′əg-nōs′, -nōz′) *v.* **-nosed, -nos•ing, -nos•es** —*tr.* **1.** To distinguish or identify (a disease, for example) by diagnosis. **2.** To identify a disease or condition in (a person). **3.** To analyze the nature or cause of. —*intr.* To make a diagnosis. [Back-formation < DIAGNOSIS.] —**di′ag•nos′a•ble** *adj.*

di•ag•no•sis (dī′əg-nō′sĭs) *n., pl.* **-ses** (-sēz) **1.** *Medicine* **a.** The act or process of determining the nature and cause of a disease or injury through examination of a patient. **b.** The opinion derived from such an examination. **2a.** A critical analysis of the nature of something. **b.** The conclusion reached by such analysis. **3.** *Biology* A brief description of an organism, as for taxonomic classification. [Gk. *diagnōsis,* discernment < *diagignōskein,* to distinguish : *dia-,* apart; see DIA- + *gignōskein, gnō-,* to come to know, discern; see gnō- in App.]

di•ag•nos•tic (dī′əg-nŏs′tĭk) *adj.* **1.** Of, relating to, or used in a diagnosis. **2.** Serving to identify a particular disease; characteristic. ❖ *n.* **1.** The art or practice of medical diagnosis. Often used in the plural with a sing. verb. **2.** A symptom or a distinguishing feature serving as evidence in a diagnosis. **3.** An instrument or a technique used in medical diagnosis. [Gk. *diagnōstikos,* able to distinguish < *diagnōstos,* distinguished < *diagignōskein,* to distin-

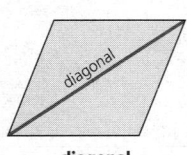

diagonal

guish. See DIAGNOSIS.] **—di′ag•nos′ti•cal•ly** *adv.*

di•ag•nos•ti•cian (dī′əg-nŏ-stĭsh′ən) *n.* A person who diagnoses, esp. a physician specializing in medical diagnostics.

di•ag•o•nal (dī-ăg′ə-nəl) *adj.* **1.** *Mathematics* **a.** Joining two nonadjacent vertices of a polygon. **b.** Joining two vertices of a polyhedron not in the same face. **2.** Having a slanted or oblique direction. **3.** Having oblique lines or markings. **4.** Relating to or being the front left and back right feet or the front right and back left feet of a quadruped. ❖ *n.* **1.** *Mathematics* A diagonal line or plane. **2.** Something, such as a row or part, that is arranged obliquely. **3.** A fabric woven with diagonal lines. **4.** A virgule. [Lat. *diagōnālis* < Gk. *diagōnios*, from angle to angle : *dia-*, dia- + *gōniā*, angle, corner; see **genu-** in App.] **—di•ag′o•nal•ly** *adv.*

di•a•gram (dī′ə-grăm′) *n.* **1.** A plan, drawing, or outline designed to demonstrate or explain how something works or clarify the relationship between the parts of a whole. **2.** *Mathematics* A graphic representation of an algebraic or geometric relationship. **3.** A chart or graph. ❖ *tr.v.* **-grammed, -gram•ming, -grams** or **-gramed, -gram•ing, -grams** To indicate or represent by or as if by a diagram. [Lat. *diagramma*, figure < Gk., a figure worked out by lines, plan < *diagraphein*, to mark out, delineate : *dia-*, dia- + *graphein*, to write; see **gerbh-** in App.] **—di′a•gram′ma•ble** *adj.* **—di′a•gram•mat′ic** (-grə-măt′ĭk), **di′a•gram•mat′i•cal** *adj.* **—di′a•gram•mat′i•cal•ly** *adv.*

di•a•ki•ne•sis (dī′ə-kə-nē′sĭs, -kī-) *n., pl.* **-ses** (-sēz) The final stage of prophase in meiosis, marked by shortening and thickening of paired chromosomes, formation of spindle fibers, disappearance of the nucleolus, and degeneration of the nuclear membrane. **—di′a•ki•net′ic** (-nĕt′ĭk) *adj.*

di•al (dī′əl) *n.* **1.** A graduated surface or face on which a measurement, such as speed, is indicated by a moving needle or pointer. **2a.** The face of a clock. **b.** A sundial. **3a.** The panel or face on a radio or television receiver on which the frequencies or channels are indicated. **b.** A movable control knob or other device used to change these frequencies or channels. **4.** A rotatable disk on a telephone with numbers and letters, used to signal the number to which a call is made. ❖ *v.* **-aled, -al•ing, -als** or **-alled, -al•ling, -als** *—tr.* **1.** To measure with or as if with a dial. **2.** To point to, indicate, or register by means of a dial. **3.** To control by means of a dial. **4a.** To signal (a number) in making a telephone call. **b.** To call (a party) on a telephone. *—intr.* **1.** To use a dial, as on a telephone. **2.** To use a telephone. [ME, sundial, clock < OFr. *dyal* < Med.Lat. *diāle* < neut. of *diālis*, daily < Lat. *diēs*, day. See **dyeu-** in App.] **—di′al•er** *n.*

di•a•lect (dī′ə-lĕkt′) *n.* **1.** A variety of a language distinct from the standard variety in pronunciation, grammar, or vocabulary. **2.** The language peculiar to the members of a group, esp. in an occupation; jargon. **3.** The manner or style of expressing oneself in language or the arts. **4.** A language considered as part of a larger family of languages or a linguistic branch. Not in scientific use. [Fr. *dialecte* < OFr. < Lat. *dialectus*, form of speech < Gk. *dialektos*, speech < *dialegesthai*, to discourse, use a dialect : *dia-*, between, over; see DIA– + *legesthai*, middle voice of *legein*, to speak; see **leg-** in App.] **—di′a•lec′tal** *adj.* **—di′a•lec′tal•ly** *adv.*

dialect atlas *n.* See **linguistic atlas.**

dialect geography *n.* See **linguistic geography.**

di•a•lec•tic (dī′ə-lĕk′tĭk) *n.* **1.** The art or practice of arriving at the truth by using conversation involving question and answer. **2a.** The process esp. associated with Hegel of arriving at the truth by consideration of a thesis, development of an antithesis in reaction to this, and combination of the thesis and antithesis into a coherent synthesis. **b.** Hegel's critical method for the investigation of this process. **3a.** The Marxian process of change through the conflict of opposing forces. Often used in the plural with a sing. or pl. verb. **b.** The Marxian critique of this process. **4. dialectics** (*used with a sing. verb*) A method of argument that weighs contradictory facts or ideas with a view to their resolution. **5.** The contradiction between two conflicting forces viewed as the determining factor in their interaction. [ME *dialetik* < OFr. *dialetique* < Lat. *dialectica*, logic < Gk. *dialektikē (tekhnē)*, (art of) debate, fem. of *dialektikos* < *dialektos*, speech, conversation. See DIALECT.] **—di′a•lec′ti•cal, di′a•lec′tic** *adj.* **—di′a•lec′ti•cal•ly** *adv.*

dialectical materialism *n.* The Marxian interpretation of reality that views matter as the sole subject of change and all change as the product of a constant conflict between the contradictions inherent in all events, ideas, and movements.

di•a•lec•ti•cian (dī′ə-lĕk-tĭsh′ən) *n.* **1.** One who specializes in the study of dialects. **2.** One who is skilled in dialectic.

di•a•lec•tol•o•gy (dī′ə-lĕk-tŏl′ə-jē) *n.* The study of dialects. **—di′a•lec′to•log′i•cal** (-tə-lŏj′ĭ-kəl) *adj.* **—di′a•lec′to•log′i•cal•ly** *adv.* **—di′a•lec•tol′o•gist** *n.*

di•a•log (dī′ə-lôg′, -lŏg′) *n. & v.* Variant of **dialog.**

dialog box *n.* A window that appears on a computer screen, presenting information or requesting input.

di•a•log•ic (dī′ə-lŏj′ĭk) also **di•a•log•i•cal** (-ĭ-kəl) *adj.* Of, relating to, or written in dialogue. **—di′a•log′i•cal•ly** *adv.*

di•al•o•gist (dī-ăl′ə-jĭst, dī′ə-lô′gĭst, -lŏg′ĭst) *n.* **1.** A writer of dialogue. **2.** One who speaks in a dialogue. **—di′a•lo•gis′tic** (dī′ə-lə-jĭs′tĭk), **di′a•lo•gis′ti•cal** *adj.*

di•a•logue or **di•a•log** (dī′ə-lôg′, -lŏg′) *n.* **1.** A conversation between two or more people. **2a.** Conversation between characters in a drama or narrative. **b.** The lines or passages in a script that are intended to be spoken. **3.** A literary work written in the form of a conversation: *the dialogues of Plato.* **4.** *Music* A composition or passage for two or more parts, suggestive of conversational interplay. **5.** An exchange of ideas or opinions. ❖ *v.* **-logued, -logu•ing, -logues** or **-loged, -log•ing, -logs** *—tr.* To express as or in a dialogue. *—intr.* **1.** To converse in a dialogue. **2.** To engage in an informal exchange of views. [ME *dialog* < OFr. *dialogue* < Lat. *dialogus* < Gk. *dialogos*, conversation < *dialegesthai*, to discuss. See DIALECT.] **—di′a•log′uer** *n.*

dial tone *n.* A low steady tone in a telephone receiver indicating that a number may be dialed.

di•al-up (dī′əl-ŭp′, dīl′-) *adj.* Of or relating to a network connection, as to the Internet, which requires that a telephone number be dialed.

di•al•y•sis (dī-ăl′ĭ-sĭs) *n., pl.* **-ses** (-sēz′) **1.** The separation of smaller molecules from larger molecules or of dissolved substances from colloidal particles in a solution by selective diffusion through a semipermeable membrane. **2.** Hemodialysis. [Gk. *dialusis*, separating, dissolution < *dialūein*, to break up, dissolve : *dia-*, apart; see DIA– + *lūein*, to loosen; see **leu-** in App.] **—di′a•lyt′ic** (-ə-lĭt′ĭk) *adj.* **—di′a•lyt′i•cal•ly** *adv.*

di•a•lyze (dī′ə-līz′) *tr. & intr.v.* **-lyzed, -lyz•ing, -lyz•es** To subject to or undergo dialysis. [Back-formation < DIALYSIS.] **—di′a•lyz′a•bil′i•ty** *n.* **—di′a•lyz′a•ble** *adj.*

di•a•lyz•er (dī′ə-lī′zər) *n.* A machine equipped with a semipermeable membrane and used for performing dialysis.

diam. *abbr.* diameter

di•a•mag•net (dī′ə-măg′nĭt) *n.* A diamagnetic substance.

di•a•mag•net•ic (dī′ə-măg-nĕt′ĭk) *adj.* Of or relating to a substance that is repelled by a magnet. **—di′a•mag′ne•tism** (-nĭ-tĭz′əm) *n.*

di•a•man•te or **di•a•man•té** (dē′ə-män-tā′) *n.* **1.** A small glittering ornament, such as a sequin, applied to fabric. **2.** Fabric covered with many of these ornaments. [Fr. *diamanté*, decorated with diamonds < *diamant*, diamond. See DIAMOND.]

di•am•e•ter (dī-ăm′ĭ-tər) *n.* **1.** *Mathematics* **a.** A straight line segment passing through the center of a figure, esp. of a circle or sphere, and terminating at the periphery. **b.** The length of such a segment. **2.** Thickness or width. **3.** A unit of magnification equal to the number of times an object's linear dimensions are increased by the magnifying apparatus. [ME *diametre* < OFr. < Lat. *diametrus* < Gk. *diametros (grammē)*, diagonal (line) : *dia-*, dia- + *metron*, measure; see **mē-**^{1} in App.] **—di•am′e•tral** (-trəl) *adj.*

di•a•met•ri•cal (dī′ə-mĕt′rĭ-kəl) also **di•a•met•ric** (-rĭk) *adj.* **1.** Of, relating to, or along a diameter. **2.** Exactly opposite; contrary. **—di′a•met′ri•cal•ly** *adv.*

di•am•ine (dī-ăm′ēn′, -ĭn, dī′ə-mēn′, -mĭn) *n.* Any of various chemical compounds containing two amino groups.

di•a•mond (dī′ə-mənd, dī′mənd) *n.* **1.** An extremely hard crystalline form of carbon that is usu. colorless and is used as a gemstone and in abrasives, cutting tools, and other applications. **2.** A figure with four equal sides forming two inner obtuse angles and two inner acute angles; a rhombus or lozenge. **3.** *Games* **a.** A red lozenge-shaped figure on certain playing cards. **b.** A playing card with this figure. **c. diamonds** (*used with a sing. or pl. verb*) The suit of cards represented by this figure. **4.** *Baseball* **a.** An infield. **b.** The whole playing field. ❖ *tr.v.* **-mond•ed, -mond•ing, -monds** To adorn with or as if with diamonds. ***—idiom:* diamond in the rough** One having exceptionally good qualities but lacking refinement. [ME *diamaunt* < OFr. *diamant* < Med.Lat. *diamās, diamant-*, alteration of Lat. *adamās.* See ADAMANT.]

di•a•mond•back moth (dī′ə-mənd-băk′, dī′mənd-) *n.* One of several small moths of the family Plutellidae, having front wings that reveal diamond-shaped spots when folded.

diamondback rattlesnake *n.* Either of two large venomous rattlesnakes *(Crotalus adamanteus* or *C. atrox)* that are found in the southern and western United States and in Mexico and have diamond-shaped markings on the back.

diamondback terrapin *n.* One of several edible turtles of the genus *Malaclemys* of the southern Atlantic and Gulf coasts of the United States, having a carapace with diamond-shaped markings.

Diamond Head A promontory, 232.1 m (761 ft), on the SE coast of Oahu HI.

di•a•mond•if•er•ous (dī′ə-mən-dĭf′ər-əs, dī′mən-) *adj.* Bearing or yielding diamonds.

Di•an•a (dī-ăn′ə) *n. Roman Mythology* The virgin goddess of hunting and childbirth, traditionally associated with the moon. [ME < Lat. *Diāna.* See **dyeu-** in App.]

Diana, Princess of Wales. Title of Lady Diana Frances Spencer. 1961–97. Consort (1981–96) of Charles, Prince of Wales, heir to the British throne.

di•an•drous (dī-ăn′drəs) *adj. Botany* Having two stamens.

Di•ane de Poi•tiers (dē-ăn′ də pwä-tyā′) Duchesse de Valentinois. 1499–1566. French lover of Henry II.

di•an•thus (dī-ăn′thəs) *n.* A plant of the genus *Dianthus,* which includes carnations and pinks. [NLat. *Dianthus*, genus name, prob. alteration (influenced by DI–^{1}), of Gk. *diosanthos*, carnation : *Dios*, genitive of *Zeus*, Zeus; see **dyeu-** in App. + *anthos*, flower.]

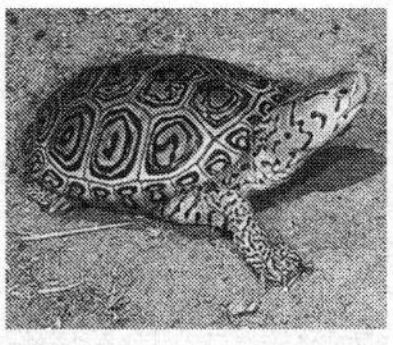

diamondback terrapin
Northern diamondback terrapin
Malaclemys terrapin terrapin

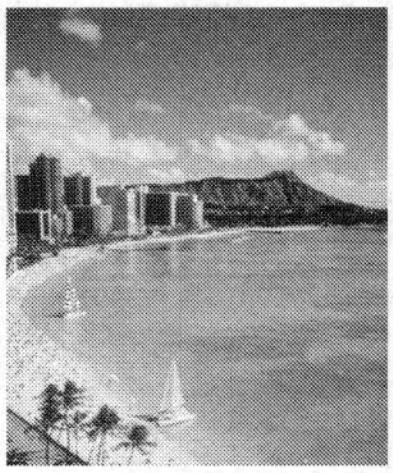

Diamond Head
Waikiki Beach with Diamond Head in the distance

ă	pat	oi	boy
ā	pay	ou	out
âr	care	ŏŏ	took
ä	father	ōō	boot
ĕ	pet	ŭ	cut
ē	be	ûr	urge
ĭ	pit	th	thin
ī	pie	*th*	this
îr	pier	hw	which
ŏ	pot	zh	vision
ō	toe	ə	about, item
ô	paw		

Stress marks:
′ (primary);
′ (secondary), as in
lexicon (lĕk′sĭ-kŏn′)

di·a·pa'son (dī'ə-pā'zən, -sən) *n.* **1.** A rich outpouring of harmonious sound. **2.** The entire range of an instrument or voice. **3.** Either of the two principal stops on a pipe organ that form the tonal basis for the entire scale of the instrument. **4.** The interval and the consonance of an octave. **5.** A standard indication of pitch. **6.** A tuning fork. [ME *diapasoun* < Lat. *diapāsōn*, the whole octave < Gk. *dia pāsōn* (*khordōn*), through all (the notes) : *dia*, through; see DIA– + *pāsōn*, fem. genitive pl. of *pās*, every.]

di·a·pause (dī'ə-pôz') *n. Zoology* A period of suspended development and diminished physiological activity, as in certain insects. [Gk. *diapausis*, pause < *diapauein*, to pause : *dia-*, between; see DIA– + *pauein*, to stop.]

di·a·pe·de·sis (dī'ə-pī-dē'sĭs) *n., pl.* **-ses** (-sēz) The movement of blood cells, esp. white blood cells, through capillary walls into body tissue. [Gk. *diapēdēsis*, transudation < *diapēdān*, to ooze through : *dia-*, dia– + *pēdān*, to leap, throb; see **ped-** in App.] —**di'a·pe·det'ic** (-dĕt'ĭk) *adj.*

di·a·per (dī'ə-pər, dī'pər) *n.* **1a.** A folded piece of absorbent material, such as cloth, that is placed between a baby's legs and fastened at the waist to contain excretions. **b.** A similar piece of material, worn by incontinent adults. **2a.** A white cotton or linen fabric patterned with small diamond-shaped figures. **b.** A piece of such cloth. **c.** Such a pattern. ❖ *tr.v.* **-pered, -per·ing, -pers** **1.** To put a diaper on. **2.** To weave or decorate in a diamond-shaped pattern. [ME, a patterned fabric < OFr. *diapre, diaspre* < Med.Lat. *diasprum*, a white silken material < Med.Gk. *diaspros*, pure white < Gk. *dia-*, intensive pref.; see DIA– + L.Gk. *aspros*, white (prob. < Lat. *asper*, rough).]

di·aph·a·nous (dī-ăf'ə-nəs) *adj.* **1.** Of such fine texture as to be transparent or translucent. **2.** Characterized by delicacy of form. See Syns at **airy**. **3.** Vague or insubstantial. [< Med.Lat. *diaphanus*, transparent < Gk. *diaphanēs* < *diaphainein*, to be transparent : *dia-*, dia– + *phainein, phan-*, to show.] —**di'a·pha·ne'i·ty** (dī'ə-fə-nē'ĭ-tē), **di·aph'a·nous·ness** *n.* —**di·aph'a·nous·ly** *adv.*

di·a·pho·re·sis (dī'ə-fə-rē'sĭs, dī-ăf'ə-) *n.* Perspiration, esp. when copious and medically induced. [LLat. *diaphorēsis* < Gk. < *diaphorein*, to disperse : *dia-*, dia– + *phorein*, to convey, freq. of *pherein*, to carry; see **bher-**¹ in App.]

di·a·pho·ret·ic (dī'ə-fə-rĕt'ĭk, dī-ăf'ə-) *adj.* Producing or increasing perspiration. ❖ *n.* A diaphoretic medicine or other agent. [DIAPHOR(ESIS) + –ETIC.]

di·a·phragm (dī'ə-frăm') *n.* **1.** *Anatomy* A muscular membranous partition separating the abdominal and thoracic cavities and functioning in respiration. **2.** A membranous part that divides or separates. **3.** A thin disk, as in a telephone receiver, that vibrates in response to sound waves to produce electric signals or vibrates in response to electric signals to produce sound waves. **4.** A contraceptive device consisting of a thin flexible disk, usu. made of rubber, that covers the uterine cervix to prevent the entry of sperm during sexual intercourse. **5.** A disk having a fixed or variable opening used to restrict the amount of light traversing a lens or optical system. [ME *diafragma* < LLat. *diaphragma*, midriff < Gk., partition < *diaphrassein*, to barricade : *dia-*, intensive pref.; see DIA– + *phrassein, phrag-*, to enclose.] —**di'a·phrag·mat'ic** (-frăg-măt'ĭk) *adj.* —**di'a·phrag·mat'i·cal·ly** *adv.*

di·aph·y·sis (dī-ăf'ĭ-sĭs) *n., pl.* **-ses** (-sēz') The shaft of a long bone. [Gk. *diaphusis*, spinous process of the tibia < *diaphuesthai*, to grow between : *dia-*, dia– + *phuesthai*, to grow, middle voice of *phuein*; see **bheuə-** in App.] —**di'a·phys'i·al** (dī'ə-fĭz'ē-əl), **di·aph'y·se'al** (-ăf'ĭ-sē'əl) *adj.*

di·a·pir (dī'ə-pîr') *n.* An anticlinal fold in which a mobile core, such as gypsum, has pierced through the more brittle overlying rock. [Fr. < Gk. *diapeirein*, to push through : *dia-*, dia– + *peirein*, to pierce; see **per-**² in App.] —**di'a·pir'ic** *adj.*

di·a·poph·y·sis (dī'ə-pŏf'ĭ-sĭs) *n., pl.* **-ses** (-sēz') *Anatomy* The superior or articular surface of the transverse process of a vertebra. [DI(A)– + APOPHYSIS.] —**di·ap'o·phys'i·al** (-ăp'ə-fĭz'ē-əl) *adj.*

di·ap·sid (dī-ăp'sĭd) *n.* Any of various reptiles having a skull with two pairs of temporal openings and including snakes and dinosaurs. [NLat. *Diapsida*, former subclass name : DI–¹ + Gk. *hapsis, hapsid-*, loop, arch; see APSIS.] —**di·ap'sid** *adj.*

di·ar·chy also **dy·ar·chy** (dī'är'kē) *n., pl.* **-chies** Government by two joint rulers.

di·a·rist (dī'ə-rĭst) *n.* A person who keeps a diary.

di·ar·rhe·a also **di·ar·rhoe·a** (dī'ə-rē'ə) *n.* Excessive and frequent evacuation of watery feces, usu. indicating gastrointestinal disorder. [ME *diaria* < Med.Lat. < LLat. *diarrhoea* < Gk. *diarroia* < *diarrein*, to flow through : *dia-*, dia– + *rhein*, to flow, run; see **sreu-** in App.] —**di'ar·rhe'al, di·ar·rhe'ic** (-ĭk), **di'ar·rhet'ic** (-rĕt'ĭk) *adj.*

di·ar·thro·sis (dī'är-thrō'sĭs) *n., pl.* **-ses** (-sēz) Any of several types of bone articulation permitting free motion in a joint, as that of the shoulder or hip. [Gk. *diarthrōsis < diarthroun*, to articulate : *dia-*, between; see DIA– + *arthroun*, to fasten by a joint (< *arthron*, joint; see **ar-** in App.).] —**di'ar·thro'di·al** (-dē-əl) *adj.*

di·a·ry (dī'ə-rē) *n., pl.* **-ries 1.** A daily record, esp. a personal record of events, experiences, and observations; a journal. **2.** A book for use in keeping a diary. [Lat. *diārium*, daily allowance, daily

diatom
photomicrograph of a
variety of diatoms

dibble

journal < *diēs*, day. See **dyeu-** in App.]

Di·as (dē'əs, -ash), **Bartolomeu** 1450?–1500. Portuguese navigator; the first to round the Cape of Good Hope (1488).

di·as·po·ra (dī-ăs'pər-ə) *n.* **1.** The dispersion of Jews outside Israel from the sixth century B.C., when they were exiled to Babylonia, until the present time. **2.** often **diaspora** The body of Jews or Jewish communities outside Palestine or modern Israel. **3. diaspora a.** A dispersion of a people from their homeland. **b.** The community formed by such a people. **4. diaspora** A dispersion of an originally homogeneous entity, such as a language or culture. [Gk. *diasporā*, dispersion < *diaspeirein*, to spread about : *dia-*, apart; see DIA– + *speirein*, to sow, scatter.] —**di·as'po·ric** *adj.*

di·a·spore (dī'ə-spôr', -spōr') *n.* **1.** A pearly hydrous aluminum oxide, AlO(OH), found in bauxite and corundum and used as a refractory and abrasive. **2.** *Botany* See **disseminule**. [< Gk. *diasporā*, dispersion, scattering. See DIASPORA.]

di·a·stase (dī'ə-stās', -stāz') *n.* An amylase or a mixture of amylases, found in milk, that converts starch to dextrin and maltose. [Fr. < Gk. *diastasis*, separation < *diistanai, diasta-*, to separate : *dia-*, apart; see DIA– + *histanai*, to cause to stand; see **stā-** in App.] —**di·a·sta'sic** (-stā'sĭk, -zĭk) *adj.*

di·a·ste·ma (dī'ə-stē'mə) *n., pl.* **-ma·ta** (-mə-tə) A gap or space between two teeth. [LLat. *diastēma*, interval < Gk. < *diistanai, diastē-*, to separate. See DIASTASE.] —**di'a·ste·mat'ic** (-stə-măt'ĭk) *adj.*

di·as·to·le (dī-ăs'tə-lē) *n.* **1.** *Physiology* The normal rhythmically occurring relaxation and dilatation of the heart chambers, during which they fill with blood. **2.** The lengthening of a short syllable in Greek and Latin verse. [Gk. *diastolē*, dilation < *diastellein*, to expand : *dia-*, apart; see DIA– + *stellein*, to place; see **stel-** in App.] —**di'as·tol'ic** (dī'ə-stŏl'ĭk) *adj.*

di·as·tro·phism (dī-ăs'trə-fĭz'əm) *n.* The process of deformation by which the major features of the earth's crust are formed. [< Gk. *diastrophē*, distortion < *diastrephein*, to distort : *dia-*, apart; see DIA– + *strephein*, to twist.] —**di'a·stroph'ic** (dī'ə-strŏf'ĭk, -strō'fĭk) *adj.*

di·a·tes·sa·ron (dī'ə-tĕs'ər-ən) *n.* The four Gospels combined into a single narrative. [ME, interval of a fourth < Lat. *diatessarōn*, made of four (ingredients) < Gk. *dia tessarōn*, out of four : *dia-*, according to; see DIA– + *tessarōn*, genitive of *tessares*, four; see **kʷetwer-** in App.]

di·a·ther·my (dī'ə-thûr'mē) *n.* The therapeutic generation of local heat in body tissues by high-frequency electromagnetic currents. —**di'a·ther'mic** (-mĭk) *adj.*

di·ath·e·sis (dī-ăth'ĭ-sĭs) *n., pl.* **-ses** (-sēz') **1.** A hereditary predisposition of the body to a disease, allergy, or other disorder. **2.** *Grammar* See **voice**. **3.** [Gk., disposition, condition < *diatithenai, diathe-*, to dispose : *dia-*, dia– + *tithenai*, to place, set; see **dhē-** in App.] —**di'a·thet'ic** (dī'ə-thĕt'ĭk) *adj.*

di·a·tom (dī'ə-tŏm') *n.* Any of various microscopic one-celled or colonial algae of the class Bacillariophyceae, having cell walls of silica consisting of two interlocking symmetrical valves. [NLat. *diatoma* < Gk. *diatomos*, cut in half < *diatemnein*, to cut in half : *dia-*, dia– + *temnein*, to cut.]

di·a·to·ma·ceous (dī'ə-tə-mā'shəs, dī-ăt'ə-) *adj.* Consisting of diatoms or their skeletons.

diatomaceous earth *n.* A light-colored porous rock composed of the shells of diatoms.

di·a·tom·ic (dī'ə-tŏm'ĭk) *adj.* Made up of two atoms.

di·at·o·mite (dī-ăt'ə-mīt') *n.* Powdered diatomaceous earth used as a filler, a filtering agent, and an absorbent.

di·a·ton·ic (dī'ə-tŏn'ĭk) *adj. Music* Of or using only the seven tones of a standard scale without chromatic alterations. [LLat. *diatonicus* < Gk. *diatonikos* : *dia-*, dia– + *tonos*, tone; see TONE.] —**di'a·ton'i·cal·ly** *adv.* —**di'a·ton'i·cism** (-ĭ-sĭz'əm) *n.*

di·a·tribe (dī'ə-trīb') *n.* A bitter, abusive denunciation. [Lat. *diatriba*, learned discourse < Gk. *diatribē*, pastime, lecture < *diatribein*, to consume, wear away : *dia-*, intensive pref.; see DIA– + *tribein*, to rub; see **terə-**¹ in App.]

di·at·ro·pism (dī-ăt'rə-pĭz'əm) *n.* The tendency of certain plants or their parts to arrange themselves at right angles to a stimulus. —**di'a·trop'ic** (dī'ə-trŏp'ĭk, -trō'pĭk) *adj.*

Dí·az (dē'äs, -äz), **(José de la Cruz) Porfirio** 1830–1915. Mexican soldier and politician who served as president (1877–80 and 1884–1911).

Dí·az del Cas·til·lo (dē'äth thĕl kä-stēl'yō), **Bernal** 1492?–1581. Spanish soldier and historian noted for his eyewitness account of the conquest of Mexico (1519–21).

di·az·e·pam (dī-ăz'ə-păm') *n.* A tranquilizer, $C_{16}H_{13}ClN_2O$, used in the treatment of anxiety and as a sedative, muscle relaxant, and anticonvulsant. [DIAZ(O) + EP(OXIDE) + AM(MONIA).]

di·a·zine (dī'ə-zēn', dī-ăz'ĭn) *n.* A heterocyclic compound with four carbon atoms and two nitrogen atoms, esp. any of three isomers of $C_4H_4N_2$. [DIAZ(O) + –INE².]

di·az·i·non (dī-ăz'ə-nŏn') *n.* A liquid, $C_{12}H_{21}N_3O_3PS$, used as an insecticide. [DIAZIN(E) + –ON³.]

di·az·o (dī-ăz'ō) *adj.* Relating to or containing a pair of bonded nitrogen atoms.

di·a·zo·ni·um (dī'ə-zō'nē-əm) *n.* Any of various compounds containing the cation N_2 attached to an organic group, esp. an aromatic hydrocarbon. [DIAZ(O) + (AMM)ONIUM.]

di•ba•sic (dī-bā′sĭk) *adj.* **1.** Containing two replaceable hydrogen atoms. **2.** Of or relating to salts or acids forming salts with two atoms of a univalent metal.

dib•ber (dĭb′ər) *n.* A dibble. [Alteration of DIBBLE.]

dib•ble (dĭb′əl) *n.* A pointed gardening implement used to make holes in soil. ❖ *tr.v.* **-bled, -bling, -bles 1.** To make holes in (soil) with a dibble. **2.** To plant by means of a dibble. [ME *dibbel.*] **—dib′bler** *n.*

di•bro•mide (dī-brō′mīd′, -mĭd) *n.* A chemical compound containing two bromine atoms.

dibs (dĭbz) *pl.n. Slang* **1.** A claim; rights: *I have dibs on that piece of pie.* **2.** Money, esp. in small amounts. [Short for *dibstones,* counters used in a game, prob. < obsolete *dib,* to tap.]

di•car•box•yl•ic (dī-kär′bŏk-sĭl′ĭk) *adj.* Containing two carboxyl groups per molecule.

di•cast (dī′kăst′, dĭk′ăst′) *n.* One of 6,000 citizens chosen yearly in ancient Athens to sit in the law courts and act as judge and juror. [Gk. *dikastēs,* judge < *dikazein,* to judge < *dikē,* right, custom. See **deik-** in App.] **—di•cas′tic** *adj.*

dice (dīs) *n.* **1.** Plural of **die**[2] 3. **2.** *pl.* **dice** also **dices** A small cube, as of food. ❖ *v.* **diced, dic•ing, dic•es** *—intr.* To play or gamble with dice. *—tr.* **1.** To win or lose (money) by gambling with dice. **2.** To cut (food) into small cubes. **3.** To decorate with dicelike figures. [Pl. of DIE[2].]

di•cen•tra (dī-sĕn′trə) *n.* A plant of the genus *Dicentra,* which includes the bleeding heart. [NLat. *Dicentra,* genus name : DI–[1] + Greek *kentron,* point (< *kentein,* to prick).]

di•ceph•a•lous (dī-sĕf′ə-ləs) *adj.* Having two heads.

dic•er (dī′sər) *n.* A device used for dicing food.

dic•ey (dī′sē) *adj.* **-i•er, -i•est** Involving or fraught with danger or risk. [< DICE.]

di•cha•si•um (dī-kā′zē-əm, -zhē-əm, -zhəm) *n., pl.* **-si•a** (-zē-ə, -zhē-ə, -zhə) A cyme having two lateral flowers or branches originating from opposite points beneath a terminal flower. [NLat. < Gk. *dikhasis,* division < *dikhazein,* to divide in two < *dikha,* in two. See **dwo-** in App.] **—di•cha′si•al** (-zē-əl, -zhē-əl, -zhəl) *adj.* **—di•cha′si•al•ly** *adv.*

di•chlo•ride (dī-klôr′īd′, -klōr′-) *n.* A chemical compound containing two chlorine atoms.

di•chlo•ro•di•phen•yl•tri•chlo•ro•eth•ane (dī-klôr′ō-dī-fĕn′əl-trī-klôr′ō-ĕth′ān′, -klōr′-, -fē′nəl-, dī-klōr′-) *n.* DDT.

dicho– or **dich–** *pref.* In two; into two parts: *dichogamous.* [Gk. *dikho-* < *dikha,* in two. See **dwo-** in App.]

di•chog•a•mous (dī-kŏg′ə-məs) *adj.* Having pistils and stamens that mature at different times, thus promoting cross-pollination. **—di•chog′a•my** (-mē) *n.*

di•chon•dra (dī-kŏn′drə) *n.* A small creeping herb *(Dichondra micrantha)* cultivated as a substitute for lawn grass. [NLat., genus name : DI–[1] + Gk. *khondros,* granule; see CHONDRO–.]

di•chot•o•mize (dī-kŏt′ə-mīz′) *v.* **-mized, -miz•ing, -miz•es** *—tr.* To separate into two parts or classifications. *—intr.* To be or become divided into parts or branches; fork. **—di•chot′o•mist** (-mĭst) *n.* **—di•chot′o•mi•za′tion** (-mĭ-zā′shən) *n.*

di•chot•o•mous (dī-kŏt′ə-məs) *adj.* **1.** Divided or dividing into two parts or classifications. **2.** Marked by dichotomy. **—di•chot′o•mous•ly** *adv.* **—di•chot′o•mous•ness** *n.*

di•chot•o•my (dī-kŏt′ə-mē) *n., pl.* **-mies 1.** Division into two usu. contradictory parts or opinions. **2.** *Astronomy* The phase of the moon, Mercury, or Venus when half of the disk is illuminated. **3.** *Botany* Branching characterized by successive forking into two approximately equal divisions. [Gk. *dikhotomiā* < *dikhotomos,* divided in two : *dikho-,* dicho- + *temnein,* to cut.]

di•chro•ic (dī-krō′ĭk) *adj.* **1.** Manifesting dichroism. **2.** *Pathology* Dichromatic. [< Gk. *dikhroos,* bicolored : *di-,* two; see DI–[1] + *khrōs,* color, skin.]

di•chro•ism (dī′krō-ĭz′əm) *n. Chemistry* **1.** The property possessed by some solutions of showing different colors at different concentrations. **2.** The property possessed by some crystals of exhibiting two different colors when viewed along different axes.

di•chro•ite (dī-krō′īt′) *n.* See **cordierite.** [DICHRO(IC) + –ITE[1].]

di•chro•mate (dī-krō′māt′, dī′krō-) *n.* A compound containing the divalent negative ion, Cr_2O_7, usu. having a characteristic orange-red color.

di•chro•mat•ic (dī′krō-măt′ĭk) *adj.* **1.** Possessing or exhibiting two colors. **2.** *Zoology* Having two distinct color phases not associated with season, sex, or age, as certain species of birds. **3.** *Pathology* Of or relating to dichromatism.

di•chro•ma•tism (dī-krō′mə-tĭz′əm) also **di•chro•mism** (-mĭz′əm) *n.* **1.** The quality or condition of being dichromatic. **2.** *Pathology* A form of colorblindness in which only two of the three fundamental colors can be distinguished because of a lack of one of the cone pigments.

di•chro•mic (dī-krō′mĭk) *adj.* **1.** *Pathology* Dichromatic. **2.** *Chemistry* Containing two chromium atoms per molecule.

dichromic acid *n.* An acid, $H_2Cr_2O_7$, known only in solution.

dick[1] (dĭk) *n. Slang* A detective. [Shortening and alteration of DETECTIVE.]

dick[2] (dĭk) *Slang n.* **1.** *Chiefly British* A fellow; a guy. **2.** *Vulgar* A penis. **3.** A mean or contemptible person, esp. a man. [< *Dick,* nickname for *Richard.*]

Dick, George Frederick 1881–1967. Amer. medical researcher who teamed with his wife, **Gladys Henry Dick** (1881–1963), to isolate the germ that causes scarlet fever.

dick•cis•sel (dĭk-sĭs′əl, dĭk′sĭs′-) *n.* A sparrowlike bird *(Spiza americana)* native to southern Ontario and the central United States, the male of which has a yellow breast marked with a small black bib on the throat. [Imit. of its song.]

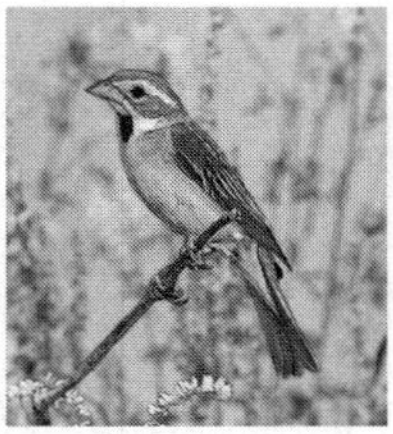

dickcissel
Spiza americana

dick•ens (dĭk′ənz) *n. Informal* **1.** A severe reprimand or expression of anger: *gave me the dickens for being late.* **2.** Used as an intensive: *What in the dickens is that?* [Alteration of DEVIL (influenced by the name DICKENS).]

Dickens, Charles John Huffam Pen name "Boz." 1812–70. British writer known for his tales of Victorian life, including *David Copperfield* (1849–50). **—Dick•en′si•an** (dĭ-kĕn′zē-ən) *adj.*

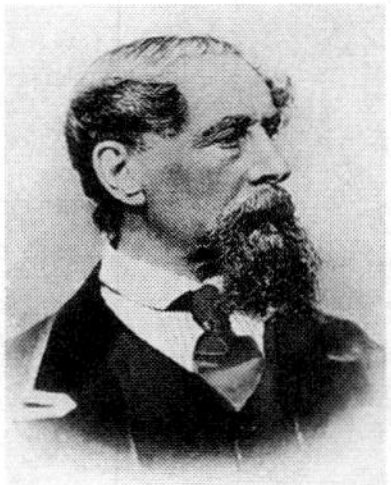

Charles Dickens

dick•er (dĭk′ər) *intr.v.* **-ered, -er•ing, -ers** To bargain; barter. ❖ *n.* The act or process of bargaining. [Prob. < *dicker,* a quantity of ten, ten hides < ME *diker,* perh. < OE **dicor* < Lat. *decuria,* set of ten < *decem,* ten. See **dekm̥** in App.]

dick•ey also **dick•ie** or **dick•y** (dĭk′ē) *n., pl.* **-eys** also **-ies 1a.** A woman's blouse front worn under a suit jacket or low-necked garment. **b.** A detachable shirt front or collar. **c.** A child's bib or pinafore. **2.** A donkey. **3.** A small bird. **4a.** The driver's seat on a carriage. **b.** A rear seat for servants on a carriage. [< dim. of *Dick,* nickname for *Richard.*]

Dick•in•son (dĭk′ĭn-sən), **Emily Elizabeth** 1830–86. Amer. poet who wrote more than a thousand verses.

Dickinson, John 1732–1808. Amer. Revolutionary politician who wrote *Letters from a Farmer in Pennsylvania* (1767–68).

Dick test *n.* A skin test used to determine immunity or susceptibility to scarlet fever. [After George Frederick DICK and Gladys Henry DICK.]

dick•y[1] (dĭk′ē) *n.* Variant of **dickey.**

dick•y[2] (dĭk′ē) *adj. Informal* Impaired; faulty; weak. [?]

di•cli•nous (dī-klī′nəs) *adj.* Having stamens and pistils in separate flowers: *a diclinous plant.* [DI–[1] + Gk. *klīnē,* bed, couch; see **klei-** in App. + –OUS.] **—di′cli′ny** (dī′klī′nē) *n.*

di•cot•y•le•don (dī′kŏt′l-ēd′n) also **di•cot** (dī′kŏt′) *n.* A flowering plant with two embryonic seed leaves or cotyledons that usu. appear at germination. **—di′cot′y•le′don•ous** (-l-ēd′n-əs) *adj.*

di•cro•tism (dī′krə-tĭz′əm) *n.* A condition in which the pulse is felt as two beats per single heartbeat. [< Gk. *dikrotos,* double-beating : *di-,* two; see DI–[1] + *krotos,* rattling noise.] **—di•crot′ic** (-krŏt′ĭk) *adj.*

Dic•ta•phone (dĭk′tə-fōn′) A trademark used for an apparatus that records and reproduces dictation for transcription.

dic•tate (dĭk′tāt′, dĭk-tāt′) *v.* **-tat•ed, -tat•ing, -tates** *—tr.* **1.** To say or read aloud to be recorded or written by another. **2a.** To prescribe with authority; impose. **b.** To control or command. *—intr.* **1.** To dictate material. **2.** To issue orders or commands. ❖ *n.* (dĭk′tāt′) **1.** A directive; a command. **2.** A guiding principle. [Lat. *dictāre, dictāt-,* freq. of *dīcere,* to say. See **deik-** in App.]

SYNONYMS *dictate, decree, impose, ordain, prescribe* These verbs mean to set forth expressly and authoritatively: *victors dictating the terms of surrender; martial law decreed by the governor; impose obedience; a separation ordained by fate; taxes prescribed by law.*

dic•ta•tion (dĭk-tā′shən) *n.* **1a.** The act or process of dictating material to another for transcription. **b.** The material so dictated. **2.** An authoritative command or order.

dic•ta•tor (dĭk′tā′tər, dĭk-tā′-) *n.* **1a.** An absolute ruler. **b.** A tyrant; a despot. **2.** An ancient Roman magistrate appointed temporarily to deal with an immediate crisis or emergency. **3.** One who dictates: *the dictator of the letter.*

dic•ta•to•ri•al (dĭk′tə-tôr′ē-əl, -tōr′-) *adj.* **1.** Tending to dictate; domineering. **2.** Of, relating to, or characteristic of a dictator or dictatorship; autocratic. **—dic′ta•to′ri•al•ly** *adv.*

dic•ta•tor•ship (dĭk-tā′tər-shĭp′, dĭk′tā′-) *n.* **1.** The office or tenure of a dictator. **2.** A state or government under dictatorial rule. **3.** Absolute or despotic control or power.

dic•tion (dĭk′shən) *n.* **1.** Choice and use of words in speech or writing. **2.** Distinctness of pronunciation in speech or singing. [ME *diccion,* a saying, word < OFr. < Lat. *dictiō, dictiōn-,* rhetorical delivery < *dictus,* p. part. of *dīcere,* to say. See **deik-** in App.] **—dic′tion•al** *adj.* **—dic′tion•al•ly** *adv.*

dic•tion•ar•y (dĭk′shə-nĕr′ē) *n., pl.* **-ies 1.** A reference book containing an alphabetical list of words, with information given for each word, usu. including meaning, pronunciation, and etymology. **2.** A book listing the words of a language with translations into another language. **3.** A book listing words or other linguistic items in a particular category or subject with information about them: *a medical dictionary.* **4.** *Computer Science* A list of words stored in machine-readable form for reference, as by spell-ing-checking software. [Med.Lat. *dictiōnārium* < Lat. *dictiō, dictiōn-,* diction. See DICTION.]

dic•tum (dĭk′təm) *n., pl.* **-ta** (-tə) or **-tums 1.** An authoritative, often formal pronouncement. **2.** *Law* See **obiter dictum** 1. [Lat. < neut. p. part. of *dīcere,* to say. See **deik-** in App.]

dic•ty•o•some (dĭk′tē-ə-sōm′) *n.* The Golgi apparatus in plant cells. [Gk. *diktuon,* net (< *dikein,* to throw; see **deik-** in App.) + –SOME[3].]

ă	pat	oi	boy
ā	pay	ou	out
âr	care	o͝o	took
ä	father	o͞o	boot
ĕ	pet	ŭ	cut
ē	be	ûr	urge
ĭ	pit	th	thin
ī	pie	*th*	this
îr	pier	hw	which
ŏ	pot	zh	vision
ō	toe	ə	about, item
ô	paw		

Stress marks:
′ (primary);
′ (secondary), as in
lexicon (lĕk′sĭ-kŏn′)

did (dĭd) *v.* Past tense of **do**[1].

di·dact (dī′dăkt′) *n.* A didactic person. [Back-formation < DIDACTIC.]

di·dac·tic (dī-dăk′tĭk) also **di·dac·ti·cal** (-tĭ-kəl) *adj.* **1.** Intended to instruct. **2.** Morally instructive. **3.** Inclined to teach or moralize excessively. [Gk. *didaktikos*, skillful in teaching < *didaktos*, taught < *didaskein*, *didak-*, to teach, educate.] —**di·dac′ti·cal·ly** *adv.* —**di·dac′ti·cism** (-tĭ-sĭz′əm) *n.*

di·dac·tics (dī-dăk′tĭks) *n.* (*used with a sing. or pl. verb*) Instruction; teaching; pedagogy.

di·dan·o·sine (dī-dăn′ə-sēn′, -sĭn) *n.* See DDI. [Shortening and alteration of *dideoxyinosine* : DI-[1] + DEOXY- + *inosine*, a nucleoside (Gk. *īs*, *īn-*, sinew + −OS(E)[2] + −INE[2]).]

di·dap·per (dī′dăp′ər) *n.* A small grebe, such as the dabchick. [ME *didopper*, alteration of *divedap* < OE *dūfedoppa*, pelican : *dūfan*, to dive + *-doppa*, a kind of bird.]

did·dle[1] (dĭd′l) *tr.v.* **-dled, -dling, -dles** *Slang* To cheat; swindle. [Perh. akin to OE *dydrian*, to deceive, or < var. of dialectal *doodle*, fool, simpleton (akin to LGer. *dudeldopp*).] —**did′dler** *n.*

did·dle[2] (dĭd′l) *v.* **-dled, -dling, -dles** —*tr.* **1.** To jerk up and down or back and forth. **2.** *Vulgar Slang* **a.** To have intercourse with (a woman). **b.** To practice masturbation upon. —*intr.* **1.** To shake rapidly; jiggle. **2.** *Slang* To play; fiddle. **3.** *Slang* To waste time: *diddled around all morning.* [Prob. alteration of dialectal *didder*, to quiver, tremble < ME *dideren*, var. of *daderen*, *doderen*. See DODDER[1].]

did·dly (dĭd′lē) *n.* *Slang* A small or worthless amount. [Short for *diddlyshit*. See DIDDLY-SQUAT.]

did·dly-squat (dĭd′lē-skwŏt′) *n.* *Slang* Diddly. [Alteration of *diddlyshit* (influenced by *doodly-squat*) : *diddly* (prob. < DIDDLE[2]) + SHIT, added as an intensive.]

Di·de·rot (dē′də-rō′, dē-drō′), **Denis** 1713–84. French philosopher and writer whose supreme accomplishment was his work on the *Encyclopédie* (1751–72).

didj·er·i·doo or **didg·er·i·doo** (dĭj′ə-rē-dōō′, dĭj′ə-rē-dōō′) *n., pl.* **-doos** A musical instrument of the Aboriginal peoples of Australia, consisting of a long hollow branch or stick that makes a deep drone when blown into. [Imit. of its sound.]

did·n't (dĭd′nt) Contraction of *did not.*

di·do (dī′dō) *n., pl.* **-dos** or **-does** A mischievous prank or antic; a caper. [?]

Dido *n.* *Roman Mythology* The founder and queen of Carthage, who fell in love with Aeneas and killed herself when he abandoned her.

Did·rik·son (dĭd′rĭk-sən), **Mildred Ella** See Mildred Ella Didrikson Zaharias.

didst (dĭdst) *v.* *Archaic* Second person singular past tense of **do**[1].

di·dym·i·um (dī-dĭm′ē-əm) *n.* **1.** *Symbol* **Di** A metallic mixture, once considered an element, composed of neodymium and praseodymium. **2.** A mixture of rare-earth elements and oxides used chiefly in manufacturing and coloring various forms of glass. [< Gk. *didumos*, twin, double. See dwo- in App.]

did·y·mous (dĭd′ə-məs) *adj.* Arranged or occurring in pairs; twin. [< Gk. *didumos*, twin. See dwo- in App.]

di·dyn·a·mous (dī-dĭn′ə-məs) *adj.* Having four stamens in two pairs of unequal length. [< NLat. *Didynamia*, former class name : DI-[1] + Gk. *dunamis*, power; see DYNAMIC.]

die[1] (dī) *intr.v.* **died, dy·ing** (dī′ĭng), **dies** **1.** To cease living; become dead; expire. **2.** To cease existing, esp. by degrees; fade. **3.** To experience an agony or suffering suggestive of that of death. **4.** *Informal* To desire something greatly. **5a.** To cease operation; stop. **b.** To be destroyed, as in combat. —*phrasal verbs:* **die back** *Botany* To be affected by dieback. **die down** To lose strength; subside. **die off** To undergo a sudden sharp decline in population. **die out** To cease living completely; become extinct. —*idiom:* **die hard** To take a long time in passing out of existence. [ME *dien*, prob. < ON *deyja*. See dheu-[2] in App.]

die[2] (dī) *n., pl.* **dies** or **dice** (dīs) **1.** *pl.* **dies** A device used for cutting out, forming, or stamping material, esp.: **a.** An engraved metal piece used for impressing a design onto a softer metal, as in coining money. **b.** One of several component pieces that are fitted into a diestock to cut threads on screws or bolts. **c.** A part on a machine that punches shaped holes in, cuts, or forms sheet metal, cardboard, or other stock. **d.** A metal block containing small conical holes through which plastic, metal, or other ductile material is extruded or drawn. **2.** *pl.* **dies** *Architecture* The dado of a pedestal, esp. when cube-shaped. **3.** *pl.* **dice a.** A small cube marked on each side with from one to six dots, usu. used in pairs in gambling and in various other games. **b.** **dice** (*used with a sing. verb*) A game of chance using dice. ❖ *tr.v.* **died, die·ing, dies** To cut, form, or stamp with or as if with a die. —*idioms:* **load the dice 1.** To make an outcome highly probable; predetermine a result. **2.** To put another at a distinct disadvantage, as through prior maneuver. **the die is cast** The decision has been made and is irrevocable. [ME *de*, gaming die < OFr. < Lat. *datum*, given < neut. p. part. of *dare*, to give. See dō- in App.]

die·back (dī′băk′) *n.* The gradual dying of plant shoots, starting at the tips, caused by disease or climate.

di·e·cious (dī-ē′shəs) *adj.* Variant of dioecious.

Die·fen·ba·ker (dē′fən-bā′kər), **John George** 1895–1979. Canadian politician who served as prime minister (1957–63).

dief·fen·bach·i·a (dē′fən-bä′kē-ə, -băk′ē-ə) *n.* Any of several plants of the genus *Dieffenbachia* native to tropical America and having jointed stems and variegated leaves. [NLat., genus name, after Ernst *Dieffenbach* (1811–55), German naturalist.]

die-hard also **die·hard** (dī′härd′) *adj.* Stubbornly resisting change or clinging to a seemingly hopeless or dated cause. ❖ *n.* A diehard person. —**die′-hard′ism** *n.*

diel·drin (dēl′drĭn) *n.* A chlorinated hydrocarbon, $C_{12}H_8Cl_6O$, used as an insecticide and in mothproofing. [< *Diel(s-Al)d(e)r* (*reaction*), chemical reaction by which it is obtained < aldrin, after Otto Paul Hermann DIELS and Kurt ALDER.]

di·e·lec·tric (dī′ĭ-lĕk′trĭk) *n.* A nonconductor of electricity, esp. a substance with electrical conductivity of less than a millionth (10^{-6}) of a siemens. [DI(A)- + ELECTRIC.] —**di·e·lec′tric** *adj.* —**di·e·lec′tri·cal·ly** *adv.*

dielectric constant *n.* *Physics* See **permittivity.**

dielectric heating *n.* The heating of electrically nonconducting materials by a rapidly varying electromagnetic field.

Diels (dēlz, dēls), **Otto Paul Hermann** 1876–1954. German chemist who shared a 1950 Nobel Prize.

Di·em (dē-ĕm′, dyĕm), **Ngo Dinh** 1901–63. Vietnamese politician who was president of South Vietnam (1954–63).

Dien Bien Phu (dyĕn′ byĕn′ fōō′) A town of NW Vietnam near the Laos border; site of a French military base that fell to Vietminh troops on May 7, 1954, after a 56-day siege.

di·en·ceph·a·lon (dī′ĕn-sĕf′ə-lŏn′, -lən) *n.* The posterior part of the forebrain that connects the midbrain with the cerebral hemispheres, encloses the third ventricle, and contains the thalamus and hypothalamus. [DI(A)- + ENCEPHALON.] —**di·en·ce·phal′ic** (-sə-făl′ĭk) *adj.*

die-off (dī′ôf′, -ŏf′) *n.* The elimination of a species, population, or community of plants or animals as a result of natural causes.

Di·eppe (dē-ĕp′, dyĕp) A city of NE France on the English Channel N of Rouen; site of a disastrous Allied commando raid (Aug. 19, 1942). Pop. 35,957.

di·er·e·sis or **di·aer·e·sis** (dī-ĕr′ĭ-sĭs) *n., pl.* **-ses** (-sēz′) **1.** *Linguistics* **a.** A mark (̈) placed over the second of two adjacent vowels to indicate that they are to be pronounced as separate sounds rather than a diphthong, as in *naïve*. **b.** A mark (̈) placed over a vowel, such as the final vowel in *Brontë*, to indicate that the vowel is not silent. **2.** *Poetry* A break or pause in a line of verse when the end of a word and the end of a metrical foot coincide. [LLat. *diaeresis* < Gk. *diairesis* < *diairein*, to divide : *dia-*, apart; see DIA- + *hairein*, to take.]

die·sel (dē′zəl, -səl) *n.* **1.** A diesel engine. **2.** A vehicle powered by a diesel engine. **3.** Fuel designed to power a diesel engine.

Die·sel (dē′zəl), **Rudolf** 1858–1913. German engineer who devised and patented (1892) an internal-combustion engine.

diesel engine (dē′zəl, -səl) *n.* An internal-combustion engine that uses the heat of highly compressed air to ignite a spray of fuel introduced after the compression stroke starts. [After Rudolf DIESEL.]

die·sink·er (dī′sĭng′kər) *n.* One that makes or engraves metal dies for stamping or shaping. —**die′sink′ing** *n.*

Di·es I·rae (dē′ās ĭr′ā′) *n.* A medieval Latin hymn describing Judgment Day, used in some masses for the dead. [Med.Lat. *Diēs irae*, day of wrath (the first words of the hymn) : Lat. *diēs*, day + Lat. *īrae*, genitive of *īra*, wrath.]

di·e·sis (dī′ĭ-sĭs) *n., pl.* **-ses** (-sēz′) See **double dagger.** [Med. Lat., semitone (shown by a double dagger) < Lat., quarter tone < Gk., letting through < *diēnai*, to send through : *dia-*, dia- + *hīenai*, *he-*, to send.]

die·stock (dī′stŏk′) *n.* An apparatus for holding the dies that cut threads on screws, bolts, pipes, or rods.

di·es·trus (dī-ĕs′trəs) also **di·es·trum** (-trəm) *n.* The sexually inactive period of the estrous cycle. [DI(A)- + ESTRUS.] —**di·es′trous** *adj.*

di·et[1] (dī′ĭt) *n.* **1.** The usual food and drink of a person or animal. **2.** A regulated selection of foods, esp. as medically prescribed or for cosmetic weight loss. **3.** Something used, enjoyed, or provided regularly: *a diet of detective novels.* ❖ *adj.* **1.** Of or relating to foods ingested as part of a specially regulated diet. **2.** Having few or no calories: *diet soft drinks.* ❖ *v.* **-et·ed, -et·ing, -ets** —*intr.* To eat and drink according to a regulated system, esp. so as to lose weight or control a medical condition. —*tr.* To regulate or prescribe food and drink for. [ME *diete* < OFr. < Lat. *diaeta*, way of living, diet < Gk. *diaita*, back-formation < *diaitasthai*, to live one's life, middle voice of *diaitān*, to treat.] —**di′et·er** *n.*

di·et[2] (dī′ĭt) *n.* **1.** A national or local legislative assembly in certain countries, such as Japan. **2.** A formal general assembly of the princes or estates of the Holy Roman Empire. [ME *diete*, day's journey, day for meeting, assembly < Med.Lat. *diēta*, alteration (influenced by Lat. *diēs*, day) of Lat. *diaeta*, daily routine; see DIET[1].]

di·e·tar·y (dī′ĭ-tĕr′ē) *adj.* Of or relating to diet. ❖ *n., pl.* **-ies 1.** A system or regimen of dieting. **2.** A regulated daily food allowance. —**di′e·tar′i·ly** (-târ′ə-lē) *adv.*

dietary law *n.* *Judaism* The body of regulations prescribing the kinds and combinations of food that may be eaten.

di·e·tet·ic (dī′ĭ-tĕt′ĭk) *adj.* **1.** Of or relating to diet or its regulation. **2.** Specially prepared or processed for restrictive diets. [LLat. *diaetēticus* < Gk. *diaitētikos* < *diaita*, diet. See DIET[1].] **—di′e•tet′i•cal•ly** *adv.*

di•e•tet•ics (dī′ĭ-tĕt′ĭks) *n.* (*used with a sing. verb*) The study of nutrition as it relates to health.

di•eth•yl•car•bam•a•zine citrate (dī-ĕth′əl-kär-băm′ə-zēn′) *n.* An anthelmintic agent, $C_{16}H_{29}O_8N_3$, used esp. in the treatment of ascariasis and filariasis. [DI–[1] + ETHYL + CARBAM(IC ACID) + (PIPER)AZINE.]

di•eth•yl ether (dī-ĕth′əl) *n.* See **ether** 2.

di•eth•yl•stil•bes•trol (dī-ĕth′əl-stĭl-bĕs′trôl′, -trŏl′, -trōl′) *n.* A synthetic compound, $C_{18}H_{20}O_2$, with estrogenic properties that is used in the treatment of prostate cancer and that was once used to prevent miscarriage but later found to be associated with disorders of the reproductive organs in the children of women for whom it was prescribed.

diethyl tol•u•am•ide (tŏl′yo͞o-ăm′īd′, -ĭd) *n.* Deet. [DI–[1] + ETHYL + TOLU(ENE) + AMIDE.]

di•e•ti•tian or **di•e•ti•cian** (dī′ĭ-tĭsh′ən) *n.* A person specializing in dietetics. [DIET[1] + *-itian* (alteration of –ICIAN).]

Die•trich (dē′trĭk, -trĭKH), **Marlene** 1901–92. German-born Amer. actress and singer whose films include *The Blue Angel* (1930) and *Destry Rides Again* (1939).

diff (dĭf) *n. Informal* Difference: "*[His] flaw . . . starts with a fleshy calculation, an instinct to blunt disagreement and split the diff*" (Peggy Noonan).

dif•fer (dĭf′ər) *intr.v.* **-fered, -fer•ing, -fers 1.** To be dissimilar or unlike in nature, quality, amount, or form. **2.** To be of a different opinion; disagree. **3.** *Obsolete* To quarrel; dispute. [ME *differen* < OFr. *differer* < Lat. *differre*, to differ, delay : *dis-*, apart; see DIS– + *ferre*, to carry; see **bher-**[1] in App.]

dif•fer•ence (dĭf′ər-əns, dĭf′rəns) *n.* **1.** The quality or condition of being unlike or dissimilar. **2a.** An instance of disparity or unlikeness. **b.** A degree or amount by which things differ. **c.** A specific point distinguishing one thing from another. **3.** A noticeable change or effect. **4a.** A disagreement or controversy. **b.** A cause of a disagreement or controversy. **5.** Discrimination in taste or choice; distinction. **6.** *Mathematics* **a.** The amount by which one quantity is greater or less than another. **b.** The amount that remains after one quantity is subtracted from another. **7.** *Archaic* A distinct mark or peculiarity. ❖ *tr.v.* **-enced, -enc•ing, -enc•es** To distinguish.

SYNONYMS *difference, dissimilarity, unlikeness, divergence, variation, distinction, discrepancy* These nouns refer to a lack of correspondence or agreement. *Difference* is the most general: *differences in color and size; a difference of opinion. Dissimilarity* is difference between things otherwise alike or comparable: *a dissimilarity between the twins' personalities. Unlikeness* usually implies greater and more obvious difference: *an unlikeness among their teaching styles. Divergence* suggests an increasing difference: *points of divergence between British and American English. Variation* occurs between things of the same class or species; often it refers to modification of something original, prescribed, or typical: *variations in temperature; a variation in shape. Distinction* often means a difference in detail, determinable only by close inspection: *the distinction between "good" and "excellent." A discrepancy* is a difference between things that should correspond or match: *a discrepancy between words and actions.*

dif•fer•ent (dĭf′ər-ənt, dĭf′rənt) *adj.* **1.** Unlike in form, quality, amount, or nature; dissimilar. **2.** Distinct or separate: *That's a different issue.* **3.** Various or assorted: *interviewed different people.* **4.** Differing from all others; unusual. ❖ *adv.* In a different way or manner; otherwise. [ME < OFr. < Lat. *differēns*, *different-*, pr. part. of *differre*, to differ. See DIFFER.] **—dif′fer•ent•ly** *adv.* **—dif′fer•ent•ness** *n.*

USAGE NOTE *Different from* and *different than* are both common in British and American English. Critics since the 18th century have singled out *different than* as incorrect, though it is well attested in the works of reputable writers. Where the comparison is drawn directly between two persons or things, *from* is usually the safer choice: *My book is different from* (not *than*) *yours.* But *different than* is more acceptably used, particularly in American usage, where the object of comparison is expressed by a full clause: *The campus is different than it was 20 years ago* (or *The campus is different from how it was 20 years ago*). • The construction *different to* is chiefly British.

dif•fer•en•ti•a (dĭf′ə-rĕn′shē-ə, -shə) *n., pl.* **-ti•ae** (-shē-ē′) An attribute that distinguishes one entity from another, esp. one species from others of the same genus. [Lat., difference < *differēns*, *different-*, pr. part. of *differre*, to differ. See DIFFER.]

dif•fer•en•tia•ble (dĭf′ə-rĕn′shə-bəl, -shē-ə-) *adj.* **1.** That can be differentiated: *differentiable species.* **2.** *Mathematics* Possessing a derivative. **—dif′fer•en′tia•bil′i•ty** *n.*

dif•fer•en•tial (dĭf′ə-rĕn′shəl) *adj.* **1.** Of, relating to, or showing a difference. **2.** Being or making a difference; distinctive. **3.** Dependent on or using a specific difference or distinction. **4.** *Mathematics* Of or relating to differentiation. **5.** Involving differences in speed or direction of motion. ❖ *n.* **1.** *Mathematics* **a.** An infinitesimal increment in a variable. **b.** The product of the derivative of a function of one variable and the increment of the independent variable. **2.** Differential gear. **3.** A difference between comparable things, as in price. **—dif′fer•en′tial•ly** *adv.*

differential calculus *n.* **1.** The mathematics of the variation of a function with respect to changes in independent variables. **2.** The study of slopes of curves, accelerations, maxima, and minima by means of derivatives and differentials.

differential coefficient *n.* See **derivative** 3.

differential equation *n.* An equation that expresses a relationship between functions and their derivatives.

differential gear *n.* An arrangement of gears in an epicyclic train permitting the rotation of two shafts at different speeds, used on the rear axle of automotive vehicles to allow different rates of wheel rotation on curves.

differential windlass *n.* A hoisting device that has two drums of different sizes on the same axis and a line wound on the larger and unwound from the smaller drum for extra lifting power.

dif•fer•en•ti•ate (dĭf′ə-rĕn′shē-āt′) *v.* **-at•ed, -at•ing, -ates** *—tr.* **1.** To constitute the distinction between. **2.** To perceive or show the difference in or between; discriminate. **3.** To make different by alteration or modification. **4.** *Mathematics* To calculate the derivative or differential of (a function). *—intr.* **1.** To become distinct or specialized. **2.** To make distinctions; discriminate. **3.** *Biology* To undergo differentiation.

dif•fer•en•ti•a•tion (dĭf′ə-rĕn′shē-ā′shən) *n.* **1a.** The act or process of differentiating. **b.** The state of becoming differentiated. **2.** *Mathematics* The process of computing a derivative. **3.** *Biology* The process by which cells or tissues undergo a change toward a more specialized form or function, esp. during embryonic development.

dif•fi•cult (dĭf′ĭ-kŭlt′, -kəlt) *adj.* **1.** Hard to do or accomplish; demanding considerable effort or skill; arduous. **2.** Hard to endure; trying. **3.** Hard to comprehend or solve. **4.** Hard to please, satisfy, or manage. **5.** Hard to persuade or convince; stubborn. [ME, back-formation < *difficulte*, difficulty. See DIFFICULTY.] **—dif′fi•cult′ly** *adv.*

dif•fi•cul•ty (dĭf′ĭ-kŭl′tē, -kəl-) *n., pl.* **-ties 1.** The condition or quality of being difficult. **2.** Something not easily done, comprehended, or solved. **3.** A troublesome or embarrassing state of affairs, esp. of financial affairs. Often used in the plural. **4.** A laborious effort; a struggle; trouble. **5.** A disagreement or dispute. **6.** Reluctance or an objection; unwillingness. [ME *difficulte* < OFr. *dificulte* < Lat. *difficultās* < *difficilis*, difficult : *dis-*, dis- + *facilis*, easy; see **dhē-** in App.]

SYNONYMS *difficulty, hardship, rigor, vicissitude* These nouns denote something that requires great effort to overcome: *grappling with financial difficulties; a life of hardship; undergoing the rigors of prison; withstood the vicissitudes of an army career.*

dif•fi•dence (dĭf′ĭ-dəns, -dĕns′) *n.* The quality or state of being diffident; timidity or shyness.

dif•fi•dent (dĭf′ĭ-dənt, -dĕnt′) *adj.* **1.** Lacking or marked by a lack of self-confidence; shy and timid. See Syns at **shy**[1]. **2.** Reserved in manner. [ME < Lat. *diffīdēns*, *diffīdent-*, pr. part. of *diffīdere*, to mistrust : *dis-*, dis- + *fīdere*, to trust; see **bheidh-** in App.] **—dif′fi•dent•ly** *adv.*

dif•fract (dĭ-frăkt′) *intr. & tr.v.* **-fract•ed, -fract•ing, -fracts** To undergo or cause to undergo diffraction. [Back-formation < DIFFRACTION.] **—dif•frac′tive** *adj.* **—dif•frac′tive•ly** *adv.* **—dif•frac′tive•ness** *n.*

dif•frac•tion (dĭ-frăk′shən) *n.* Change in the directions and intensities of a group of waves after passing by an obstacle or through an aperture whose size is approx. the same as the wavelength of the waves. [NLat. *diffrāctiō*, *diffrāctiōn-* < Lat. *diffrāctus*, p. part. of *diffringere* : *dis-*, apart; see DIS– + *frangere*, to break; see **bhreg-** in App.]

diffraction grating *n.* A usu. glass or polished metal surface having a large number of very fine parallel grooves or slits in order to diffract light.

dif•fuse (dĭ-fyo͞oz′) *v.* **-fused, -fus•ing, -fus•es** *—tr.* **1.** To pour out and cause to spread freely. **2.** To spread about or scatter; disseminate. **3.** To make less brilliant; soften. *—intr.* **1.** To become widely dispersed; spread out. **2.** *Physics* To undergo diffusion. ❖ *adj.* (dĭ-fyo͞os′) **1.** Widely spread or scattered; not concentrated. **2.** Verbose or unclear: *diffuse writing.* [< ME, dispersed < AN *diffus* < Lat. *diffūsus*, p. part. of *diffundere*, to spread : *dis-*, out, apart; see DIS– + *fundere*, to pour; see **gheu-** in App.] **—dif•fuse′ly** (-fyo͞os′lē) *adv.* **—dif•fuse′ness** (-fyo͞os′nĭs) *n.*

dif•fus•er (dĭ-fyo͞o′zər) *n.* **1.** One that diffuses, as: **a.** A light fixture that spreads light evenly. **b.** A medium that scatters light, used in photography to soften shadows. **c.** A device placed in front of a loudspeaker diaphragm to diffuse the sound waves. **2.** A flow passage in a wind tunnel that decelerates a stream of gas or liquid from a high to a low velocity.

dif•fus•i•ble (dĭ-fyo͞o′zə-bəl) *adj.* Capable of diffusing or of undergoing diffusion: *diffusible dyes.* **—dif•fus′i•bly** *adv.*

dif•fu•sion (dĭ-fyo͞o′zhən) *n.* **1.** The process of diffusing or the condition of being diffused. **2.** Needless profusion of words; prolixity. **3.** *Physics* **a.** The scattering of incident light by reflection from a rough surface. **b.** The transmission of light through a translucent material. **c.** The spontaneous intermingling of the

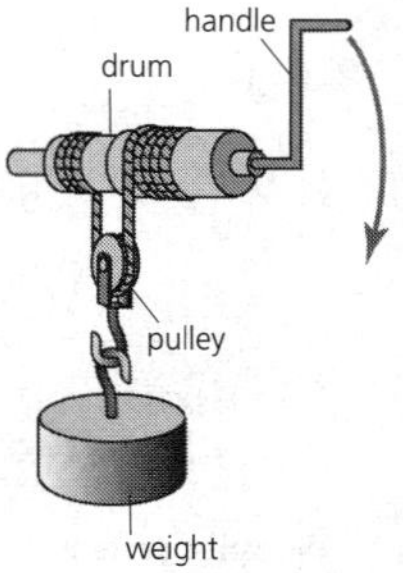

differential windlass
A differential windlass requires minimum effort to lift considerable weight.

ă pat	oi boy
ā pay	ou out
âr care	o͝o took
ä father	o͞o boot
ĕ pet	ŭ cut
ē be	ûr urge
ĭ pit	th thin
ī pie	*th* this
îr pier	hw which
ŏ pot	zh vision
ō toe	ə about, item
ô paw	

Stress marks:
′ (primary);
′ (secondary), as in
lexicon (lĕk′sĭ-kŏn′)

particles of two or more substances as a result of random thermal motion. **—dif•fu′sion•al** *adj.*

dif•fu•sive (dĭ-fyo͞o′sĭv, -zĭv) *adj.* Characterized by diffusion. **—dif•fu′sive•ly** *adv.* **—dif•fu′sive•ness** *n.*

dig (dĭg) *v.* **dug** (dŭg), **dig•ging, digs** *—tr.* **1.** To break up, turn over, or remove (earth, for example), as with a shovel. **2.** To make or form by removing earth or other material: *dug my way out of the snow.* **3.** To obtain by digging: *dig coal.* **4.** To learn or discover by careful research or investigation: *dug out the real facts.* **5.** To force down and into something; thrust. **6.** To poke or prod. **7.** *Sports* To strike or redirect (a ball) just before it hits the ground, as in tennis. **8.** *Slang* **a.** To understand fully: *Do you dig me?* **b.** To like, enjoy, or appreciate. **c.** To take notice of. *—intr.* **1.** To loosen, turn over, or remove earth or other material. **2.** To make one's way by or as if by pushing aside or removing material. **3.** *Slang* To have understanding. ❖ *n.* **1.** A poke or thrust. **2.** A sarcastic, taunting remark; a gibe. **3.** An archaeological excavation. **4.** *Sports* An act or an instance of digging a ball. **5. digs** *Chiefly British* Lodgings. ***—phrasal verb:* dig in 1.** To dig trenches for protection. **2.** To hold on stubbornly, as to a position; entrench oneself. **3a.** To begin to work intensively. **b.** To begin to eat heartily. [ME *diggen*; perh. akin to OFr. *digue*, dike, trench. V., tr., sense 8 and intr., sense 3, perh. influenced by Wolof *degg*, to hear, find out, understand, or Ir.Gael. *tuigim*, I understand.]

di•gam•ma (dī-găm′ə) *n.* A letter occurring in certain early forms of Greek and transliterated in English as *w.* [Lat. < Gk. : *di-*, two; see DI–[1] + *gamma*, gamma (because its shape resembles two gammas); see GAMMA.]

dig•a•my (dĭg′ə-mē) *n.* Remarriage after the death or divorce of one's first husband or wife. **—dig′a•mous** (-məs) *adj.*

di•gas•tric (dī-găs′trĭk) *Anatomy adj.* Having two fleshy ends connected by a thinner tendinous portion. Used of certain muscles. ❖ *n.* A muscle of the lower jaw that elevates the hyoid bone and assists in lowering the jaw.

dig•er•a•ti (dĭj′ə-rä′tē) *pl.n.* People who are knowledgeable about digital technologies such as computer programming and design. [DIG(ITAL) + (LIT)ERATI.]

di•gest (dī-jĕst′, dĭ-) *v.* **-gest•ed, -gest•ing, -gests** *—tr.* **1.** *Physiology* To convert (food) into simpler chemical compounds that can be absorbed and assimilated by the body, as by chemical and muscular action in the alimentary canal. **2.** To absorb or assimilate mentally. **3a.** To organize into a systematic arrangement, usu. by summarizing or classifying. **b.** To condense or abridge (a written work). **4.** To endure or bear patiently. **5.** *Chemistry* To soften or disintegrate by means of chemical action, heat, or moisture. *—intr.* **1.** *Physiology* **a.** To become assimilated into the body. **b.** To assimilate food substances. **2.** *Chemistry* To undergo exposure to heat, liquids, or chemical agents. ❖ *n.* (dī′jĕst′) **1.** A collection of previously published material, such as articles, usu. edited or condensed. **2.** *Law* A systematic arrangement of statutes or court decisions. **3.** A periodical containing literary abridgments or other condensed works. **4. Digest** See **pandect** 3. [ME *digesten* < Lat. *dīgerere, dīgest-*, to separate, arrange : *dī-, dis-*, apart; see DIS– + *gerere*, to carry.]

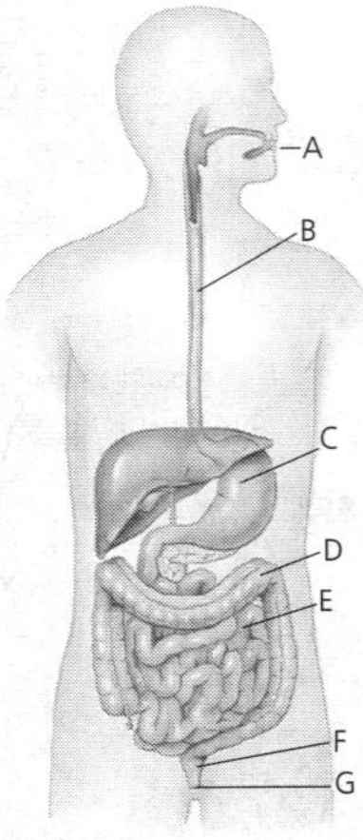

digestive system
A. mouth
B. esophagus
C. stomach
D. large intestine
E. small intestine
F. rectum
G. anus

di•gest•er (dī-jĕs′tər, dĭ-) *n.* **1.** One that makes a digest. **2.** *Chemistry* A vessel in which substances are softened or decomposed, usu. for further processing.

di•gest•i•ble (dī-jĕs′tə-bəl, dĭ-) *adj.* Easy to digest. **—di•gest′i•bil′i•ty, di•gest′i•ble•ness** *n.* **—di•gest′i•bly** *adv.*

di•ges•tion (dī-jĕs′chən, dĭ-) *n.* **1.** *Physiology* **a.** The process by which food is converted into substances that can be absorbed and assimilated by the body. **b.** The result of this process. **c.** The ability to digest food. **2.** The process of decomposing organic matter in sewage by bacteria. **3.** Assimilation of ideas or information; understanding.

di•ges•tive (dī-jĕs′tĭv, dĭ-) *adj.* **1.** Relating to or aiding digestion. **2.** Serving to digest food. ❖ *n.* A substance that aids digestion. **—di•ges′tive•ly** *adv.* **—di•ges′tive•ness** *n.*

digestive gland *n.* A gland, such as the pancreas, that secretes into the alimentary canal substances necessary for digestion.

digestive system *n.* The alimentary canal and digestive glands regarded as an integrated system responsible for the ingestion, digestion, and absorption of food.

digestive tract *n.* See **alimentary canal.**

dig•ger (dĭg′ər) *n.* **1a.** One that digs. **b.** A tool or machine used for digging or excavating. **2.** often **Digger** *Informal* A soldier from New Zealand or Australia, esp. in World War I. **3.** also **Digger** *Offensive* A member of any of various Native American peoples of the Great Basin. Used esp. in the 19th century. [Sense 3 < their use of digging sticks as foraging tools.]

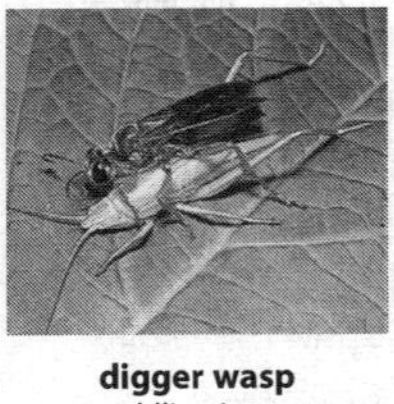

digger wasp
straddling its prey

digger wasp *n.* Any of various wasps of the family Sphecidae that burrow into the ground to build their nests and store prey.

dig•gings (dĭg′ĭngz) *pl.n.* **1.** An excavation site, as for mining ore. **2.** Excavated materials. **3.** *Chiefly British* Rooms; lodgings.

dight (dīt) *tr.v.* **dight** or **dight•ed, dight•ing, dights** *Archaic* To dress; adorn. [ME *dighten* < OE *dihtan*, to arrange < Lat. *dictāre*, to dictate. See DICTATE.]

dig•it (dĭj′ĭt) *n.* **1a.** A human finger or toe. **b.** A corresponding part in other vertebrates. **2.** A unit of length derived from the breadth of a finger and equal to about ¾ of an inch (2.0 centimeters). **3a.** One of the ten Arabic number symbols, 0 through 9. **b.** Such a symbol used in a system of numeration. [ME < Lat. *digitus*, finger, toe. See **deik-** in App.]

dig•i•tal (dĭj′ĭ-tl) *adj.* **1.** Of, relating to, or resembling a digit, esp. a finger. **2.** Operated or done with the fingers. **3.** Having digits. **4.** Expressed in numerical form, esp. for use by a computer. **5.** *Computer Science* Of or relating to a device that can read, write, or store information represented in numerical form. See Usage Note at **virtual. 6.** Using or giving a reading in digits: *a digital clock.* ❖ *n.* A key played with the finger, as on a piano. **—dig′i•tal•ly** *adv.*

digital computer *n.* A computer that performs calculations and logical operations with quantities represented as digits, usu. in the binary number system.

dig•i•tal•in (dĭj′ĭ-tăl′ĭn) *n.* **1.** A white crystalline glycoside, $C_{36}H_{56}O_{14}$, obtained from the seeds of the common foxglove. **2.** One of several mixtures of digitalis glycosides extracted from common foxglove leaves or seeds. [DIGITAL(IS) + –IN.]

dig•i•tal•is (dĭj′ĭ-tăl′ĭs) *n.* **1.** A plant of the genus *Digitalis*, which includes the foxgloves. **2.** A drug prepared from the seeds and dried leaves of this plant, used in medicine as a cardiac stimulant. [Lat. *digitālis*, of a finger (< the finger-shaped corollas of foxglove) < *digitus*, finger. See DIGIT.]

dig•i•tal•ize (dĭj′ĭ-tl-īz′) *tr.v.* **-ized, -iz•ing, -iz•es 1.** To administer digitalis in a dosage sufficient to achieve the maximum therapeutic effect without producing toxic symptoms. **2.** To digitize. **—dig′i•tal•i•za′tion** (-ĭ-zā′shən) *n.*

digital photography *n.* A method of photography in which an image is digitally encoded and stored for later reproduction.

digital recording *n.* **1.** A method of recording in which portions of sound waves are converted into numbers and stored for later reproduction. **2.** A record, tape, or disk that is recorded using this process.

digital satellite system *n.* A system in which a satellite dish receives, decodes, and passes a digital signal to a television, radio receiver, or computer.

dig•i•tate (dĭj′ĭ-tāt′) also **dig•i•tat•ed** (-tā′tĭd) *adj.* **1.** Having digits or fingerlike projections. **2.** *Botany* Having parts arising from a common point; palmate. **—dig′i•tate′ly** *adv.*

dig•i•ta•tion (dĭj′ĭ-tā′shən) *n.* **1.** Division into fingerlike parts. **2.** A fingerlike part or process.

dig•i•ti•grade (dĭj′ĭ-tĭ-grād′) *adj.* Relating to an animal, such as a horse or dog, whose weight is borne on the toes. [Fr. : Lat. *digitus*, toe; see DIGIT + Lat. *gradus*, step; see GRADE.]

dig•i•tize (dĭj′ĭ-tīz′) *tr.v.* **-tized, -tiz•ing, -tiz•es** To put (data, for example) into digital form. **—dig′i•ti•za′tion** (-tĭ-zā′shən) *n.* **—dig′i•tiz′er** *n.*

dig•i•tox•in (dĭj′ĭ-tŏk′sĭn) *n.* A highly active glycoside, $C_{41}H_{64}O_{13}$, derived from digitalis and prescribed in the treatment of certain cardiac conditions. [DIGI(TALIS) + TOXIN.]

di•glos•si•a (dī-glô′sē-ə, -glŏs′ē-ə) *n.* The use of two markedly different varieties of a language in different social situations, such as a formal variety at work and an informal variety at home. [< Gk. *diglōssos*, speaking two languages : *di-*, two; see DI–[1] + *glōssa*, language.] **—di•glos′sic** *adj.*

di•glyc•er•ide (dī-glĭs′ə-rīd′) *n.* An ester of two fatty acids and glycerol.

dig•ni•fied (dĭg′nə-fīd′) *adj.* Having or expressing dignity. **—dig′ni•fied′ly** (-fīd′lē, -fī′ĭd-lē) *adv.*

dig•ni•fy (dĭg′nə-fī′) *tr.v.* **-fied, -fy•ing, -fies 1.** To confer dignity or honor on; give distinction to: *dignified him with a title.* **2.** To raise the status of (something unworthy or lowly); make honorable. [ME *dignifien* < OFr. *dignifier* < LLat. *dignificāre* : Lat. *dignus*, worthy + Lat. *-ficāre*, -fy.]

dig•ni•tar•y (dĭg′nĭ-tĕr′ē) *n., pl.* **-ies** A person of high rank or position.

dig•ni•ty (dĭg′nĭ-tē) *n., pl.* **-ties 1.** The quality or state of deserving esteem or respect. **2.** Inherent nobility and worth. **3a.** Poise and self-respect. **b.** Stateliness and formality in manner and appearance. **4.** The respect and honor associated with an important position. **5.** A high office or rank. **6. dignities** The ceremonial symbols and observances attached to high office. **7.** *Archaic* A dignitary. [ME *dignite* < OFr. < Lat. *dignitās* < *dignus*, worthy.]

dig•ox•in (dĭj-ŏk′sĭn) *n.* A cardiac glycoside, $C_{41}H_{64}O_{14}$, obtained from the leaves of a foxglove, *Digitalis lanata*, with pharmacological effects similar to digitalis. [DIG(ITALIS) + (T)OXIN.]

di•graph (dī′grăf′) *n.* **1.** A pair of letters representing a single speech sound, such as the *ph* in *pheasant.* **2.** A single character consisting of two letters run together and representing a single sound, such as Old English *æ.* **—di•graph′ic** (dī-grăf′ĭk) *adj.*

di•gress (dī-grĕs′, dĭ-) *intr.v.* **-gressed, -gress•ing, -gress•es** To turn aside, esp. from the main subject in writing or speaking; stray. See Syns at **swerve.** [Lat. *dīgredī, dīgress-* : *dī-, dis-*, apart; see DIS– + *gradī*, to go; see **ghredh-** in App.]

di•gres•sion (dī-grĕsh′ən, dĭ-) *n.* **1.** The act of digressing. **2.** An instance of digressing, esp. a written or spoken passage with no bearing on the main topic. **—di•gres′sion•al** *adj.*

di•gres•sive (dī-grĕs′ĭv, dĭ-) *adj.* Marked by digressions; rambling. **—di•gres′sive•ly** *adv.* **—di•gres′sive•ness** *n.*

di•he•dral (dī-hē′drəl) *adj. Mathematics* **1.** Formed by or having two plane faces; two-sided. **2.** Relating to, having, or forming a dihedral angle. ❖ *n.* **1.** *Mathematics* A dihedral angle. **2.** *Aeronau-*

tics The upward or downward inclination of an aircraft wing from true horizontal.

dihedral angle *n.* **1.** *Mathematics* The angle formed by two intersecting planes. **2.** *Aeronautics* The dihedral of an aircraft wing.

di·hy·brid (dī-hī′brĭd) *n. Genetics* The hybrid of parents that differ at only two gene loci, for which each parent is homozygous with different alleles.

di·hy·dric (dī-hī′drĭk) *adj.* Containing two hydroxyl radicals.

di·hy·drox·y·phen·yl·al·a·nine (dī′hī-drŏk′sē-fĕn′əl-ăl′ə-nēn′, -fē′nəl-) *n.* Dopa.

Di·jon (dē-zhôn′) A city of E France N of Lyon; noted for its foodstuffs. Pop. 146,723.

dik-dik (dĭk′dĭk′) *n.* Any of several small African antelopes of the genus *Madoqua.* [Of E African orig., perh. imit. of its cry.]

dike¹ also **dyke** (dīk) *n.* **1a.** An embankment of earth and rock built to prevent floods. **b.** *Chiefly British* A low wall, often of sod, dividing or enclosing lands. **2.** A barrier blocking a passage, esp. for protection. **3.** A raised causeway. **4.** A ditch; a channel. **5.** *Geology* A long mass of igneous rock that cuts across the structure of adjacent rock. ❖ *tr.v.* **diked, dik·ing, dikes** also **dyked, dyk·ing, dykes** **1.** To protect, enclose, or provide with a dike. **2.** To drain with dikes or ditches. [ME < OE *dīc,* trench, and < ON *dīki,* ditch.] —**dik′er** *n.*

dike² (dīk) *n. Offensive Slang* Variant of **dyke².**

dik·tat (dĭk-tät′) *n.* **1.** A harsh, unilaterally imposed settlement with a defeated party. **2.** An authoritative or dogmatic statement or decree. [Ger. < Lat. *dictātum* < neut. p. part. of *dictāre,* to dictate. See DICTATE.]

Di·lan·tin (dī-lăn′tĭn) A trademark used for phenytoin.

di·lap·i·date (dī-lăp′ĭ-dāt′) *tr. & intr.v.* **-dat·ed, -dat·ing, -dates** **1.** To bring or fall into a state of partial ruin, decay, or disrepair. **2.** *Archaic* To squander; waste. [Lat. *dīlapidāre, dīlapidāt-,* to demolish, destroy : *dī-, dis-,* apart; see DIS- + *lapidāre,* to throw stones (< *lapis, lapid-,* stone).] —**di·lap′i·da′tion** *n.*

di·lap·i·dat·ed (dī-lăp′ĭ-dā′tĭd) *adj.* Having fallen into a state of disrepair or deterioration; broken-down and shabby.

di·la·tan·cy (dī-lāt′n-sē, dĭ-) *n., pl.* **-cies** **1.** The increase in volume of a granular substance when its shape is changed, caused by greater distance between its component particles. **2.** The phenomenon whereby a viscous substance solidifies under pressure.

di·la·tant (dī-lāt′nt, dĭ-) *adj.* **1.** Tending to dilate; dilating. **2.** Exhibiting dilatancy. ❖ *n.* A dilator.

di·la·ta·tion (dĭl′ə-tā′shən, dī′lə-) *n.* **1a.** The act or process of expanding; dilation. **b.** The condition of being expanded or stretched. **c.** A dilated formation or part. **2.** *Medicine* The condition of being abnormally enlarged or dilated, as of an organ or tubular structure. **3.** Lengthy explanation or elaboration of a subject in writing or speech. —**dil′a·ta′tion·al** *adj.*

dil·a·ta·tor (dĭl′ə-tā′tər, dī′lə-) *n.* A dilator.

di·late (dī-lāt′, dī′lāt′) *v.* **-lat·ed, -lat·ing, -lates** —*tr.* To make wider or larger. —*intr.* **1.** To become wider or larger. **2.** To speak or write at great length; expatiate. [ME *dilaten* < OFr. *dilater* < Lat. *dīlātāre,* to enlarge : *dī-, dis-,* apart; see DIS- + *lātus,* wide.] —**di·lat′a·bil′i·ty** *n.* —**di·lat′a·ble** *adj.* —**di·lat′a·bly** *adv.* —**di·la′tive** *adj.*

di·lat·ed (dī-lā′tĭd, dī′lā′-) *adj.* **1.** Having been widened; expanded. **2.** Distended. —**di·lat′ed·ness** *n.*

di·la·tion (dī-lā′shən, dĭ-) *n.* **1.** The act of expanding or the state of being expanded. **2.** *Medicine* See **dilatation** 2.

dilation and curettage *n.* A surgical procedure in which the cervix is expanded with a dilator and the uterine lining scraped with a curette, performed to diagnose and treat certain uterine conditions.

dil·a·tom·e·ter (dĭl′ə-tŏm′ĭ-tər, dī′lə-) *n.* An instrument used to measure thermal expansion and dilation in solids and liquids. [DILATE + –METER.] —**dil′a·to·met′ric** (-tə-mĕt′rĭk) *adj.* —**dil′a·tom′e·try** *n.*

di·la·tor (dī-lā′tər, dī′lā′-, dī-lā′-) *n.* **1.** A muscle that dilates a body part, such as a blood vessel. **2.** An instrument that dilates a body part, such as a cavity, canal, or orifice.

dil·a·to·ry (dĭl′ə-tôr′ē, -tōr′ē) *adj.* **1.** Intended to delay. **2.** Tending to postpone or delay. [ME *dilatorie* < Lat. *dīlātōrius* < *dīlātor,* delayer < *dīlātus,* p. part. of *differre,* to delay : *dī-, dis-,* apart; see DIS- + *lātus,* carried; see **tel·a**- in App.] —**dil′a·to′ri·ly** *adv.* —**dil′a·to′ri·ness** *n.*

dil·do also **dil·doe** (dĭl′dō) *n., pl.* **-dos** also **-does** An object having the shape and often the appearance of an erect penis, used in sexual stimulation. [?]

di·lem·ma (dĭ-lĕm′ə) *n.* **1.** A situation that requires a choice between equally unfavorable or mutually exclusive options. **2.** *Usage Problem* A problem that seems to defy a satisfactory solution. **3.** *Logic* An argument that presents two or more alternatives, each of which has the same consequence. [LLat. < Gk. *dilēmma,* ambiguous proposition : *di-,* two; see DI-¹ + *lēmma,* proposition; see LEMMA¹.] —**dil′em·mat′ic** (dĭl′ə-măt′ĭk) *adj.*

spread use of the term meaning simply "problem" or "predicament" and involving no issue of choice, 58 percent of the Usage Panel in our 1999 survey rejected the sentence *Historically, race has been the great dilemma of democracy.*

dil·et·tante (dĭl′ĭ-tänt′, dĭl′ĭ-tänt′e, -tănt′, -tănt′ē) *n., pl.* **-tantes** also **-tan·ti** (-tän′tē, -tăn′-) **1.** A dabbler in an art or a field of knowledge. **2.** A lover of the fine arts; a connoisseur. ❖ *adj.* Superficial; amateurish. [Ital., lover of the arts < pr. part. of *dilettare,* to delight < Lat. *delectāre.* See DELIGHT.] —**dil′et·tan′tish** *adj.* —**dil′et·tan′tism** *n.*

dil·i·gence¹ (dĭl′ə-jəns) *n.* **1.** Earnest, persistent application to an undertaking; assiduity. **2.** Attentive care; heedfulness.

dil·i·gence² (dĭl′ə-jəns, dē′lē-zhäns′) *n.* A large stagecoach. [Fr. < *carrosse de) diligence,* speed (coach) < OFr., dispatch < Lat. *dīligentia* < *dīligēns, dīligent-,* diligent. See DILIGENT.]

dil·i·gent (dĭl′ə-jənt) *adj.* Marked by persevering, painstaking effort. [ME < OFr. < Lat. *dīligēns, dīligent-,* pr. part. of *dīligere,* to esteem, love : *dī-, dis-,* apart; see DIS- + *legere,* to choose; see **leg-** in App.] —**dil′i·gent·ly** *adv.*

dill (dĭl) *n.* **1.** An aromatic herb (*Anethum graveolens*) native to Eurasia and having finely dissected leaves and small yellow flowers clustered in umbels. **2.** The leaves or seeds of this plant, used as a seasoning. [ME *dile* < OE.]

dill pickle *n.* A pickled cucumber flavored with dill.

dil·ly (dĭl′ē) *n., pl.* **-lies** *Slang* One that is remarkable or extraordinary, as in size or quality: *had a dilly of a fight.* [Obsolete *dilly,* delightful, shortening and alteration of DELIGHTFUL.]

dil·ly-dal·ly (dĭl′ē-dăl′ē) *intr.v.* **-lied, -lying, -lies** To waste time, esp. in indecision; dawdle or vacillate. [Reduplication of DALLY.] —**dil′ly-dal′li·er** *n.*

dil·u·ent (dĭl′yōō-ənt) *adj.* Serving to dilute. ❖ *n. Chemistry* An inert substance used to dilute. [Lat. *dīluēns, dīluent-,* pr. part. of *dīluere,* to dilute. See DILUTE.]

di·lute (dī-lōōt′, dĭ-) *tr.v.* **-lut·ed, -lut·ing, -lutes** **1.** To make thinner or less concentrated by adding a liquid. **2.** To lessen the force, strength, purity, or brilliance of, esp. by admixture. **3.** To decrease the value of (shares of stock) by increasing the total number of shares. ❖ *adj.* Weakened; diluted. [Lat. *dīluere, dīlūt-* : *dī-, dis-,* apart, away; see DIS- + *-luere,* to wash (< *lavere;* see **leu(ə)-** in App.).] —**di·lut′er, di·lut′or** *n.* —**di·lu′tive** *adj.*

di·lu·tion (dī-lōō′shən, dĭ-) *n.* **1a.** The process of making weaker or less concentrated. **b.** A dilute or weakened condition. **2.** A diluted substance. **3.** A decrease in the equity position of a share of stock because of the issuance of additional shares.

di·lu·vi·al (dī-lōō′vē-əl) also **di·lu·vi·an** (-ən) *adj.* Of, relating to, or produced by a flood. [LLat. *dīluviālis* < Lat. *dīluvium,* flood < *dīluere,* to wash away. See DILUTE.]

dim (dĭm) *adj.* **dim·mer, dim·mest** **1a.** Lacking in brightness: *a dim room.* **b.** Emitting only a small amount of light; faint: *a dim lightbulb.* **2.** Lacking luster; dull and subdued. **3a.** Faintly outlined; indistinct. **b.** Obscure to the mind or the senses: *a dim recollection.* See Syns at **dark. 4.** Lacking sharpness or clarity of understanding or perception. **5.** Lacking keenness or vigor. **6.** Negative, unfavorable, or disapproving. **7.** *Slang* Dimwitted. ❖ *tr. & intr.v.* **dimmed, dim·ming, dims** To make or become dim. ❖ *n.* **1a.** A parking light on a motor vehicle. **b.** A low beam. **2.** *Archaic* Dusk. [ME < OE.] —**dim′ly** *adv.* —**dim′ness** *n.*

dim. *abbr.* **1.** dimension **2.** diminished **3.** diminuendo **4.** diminutive

Di·Mag·gio (də-mä′zhē-ō, -măj′ē-ō), **Joseph Paul** Known as "Jolting Joe." 1914–99. Amer. baseball player considered the best all-around player ever at center field.

dime (dīm) *n.* **1.** A coin of the United States or Canada worth ten cents. **2.** *Slang* A dime bag. —*idioms:* **a dime a dozen** Overabundant; commonplace. **on a dime** At a precise point; within a narrowly defined area: *a sports car that stops on a dime.* [ME, tenth part < OFr. *disme* < Lat. *decima (pars),* tenth (part) < *decem,* ten. See **dekm** in App.]

di·men·hy·dri·nate (dī′mĕn-hī′drə-nāt′) *n.* An antihistamine, $C_{24}H_{28}ClN_5O_3$, used to treat motion sickness and allergies. [DIME(THYL) + (AMI)N(E) + *hydrinate* (hydr(am)in(e) + –ATE²).]

dime novel *n.* A melodramatic novel of romance or adventure, usu. in paperback. [After the *Dime Book Series,* published by Erastus Flavel Beadle (1821–94).] —**dime novelist** *n.*

di·men·sion (dī-mĕn′shən, dĭ-) *n.* **1.** A measure of spatial extent, esp. width, height, or length. **2.** Extent or magnitude; scope. Often used in the plural. **3.** Aspect; element. **4.** *Mathematics* **a.** The least number of independent coordinates required to specify uniquely the points in a space. **b.** The range of such a coordinate. **5.** *Physics* A physical property, such as mass, length, time, or a combination thereof, regarded as a fundamental measure or as one of a set of fundamental measures of a physical quantity. ❖ *tr.v.* **-sioned, -sion·ing, -sions** **1.** To cut or shape to specified dimensions. **2.** To mark with specified dimensions. [ME *dimensioun* < Lat. *dīmēnsiō, dīmēnsiōn-,* extent < *dīmēnsus,* p. part. of *dīmētīrī,* to measure out : *dī-, dis-, dis-* + *mētīrī,* to measure; see **mē-¹** in App.] —**di·men′sion·al** *adj.* —**di·men′sion·al′i·ty** (-shə-năl′ĭ-tē) *n.* —**di·men′sion·al·ly** *adv.* —**di·men′sion·less** *adj.*

di·mer (dī′mər) *n.* **1.** A molecule consisting of two identical sim-

Joe DiMaggio
photographed in 1939

pler molecules. **2.** A chemical compound consisting of dimers. [DI-[1] + (POLY)MER.] —**di•mer′ic** (dī-mĕr′ĭk) *adj.*

di•mer•cap•rol (dī′mər-kăp′rôl, -rōl, -rŏl) *n.* An oily viscous liquid, $C_3H_8OS_2$, used as an antidote for poisoning caused by lewisite, organic arsenic compounds, and heavy metals including lead. [DI-[1] + MERCAP(TAN) + (P)R(OPANE) + -OL(E).]

dim•er•ous (dīm′ər-əs) *adj.* **1.** Consisting of two parts or segments, as the tarsus in certain insects. **2.** *Botany* Having flower parts in sets of two. —**dim′er•ism** *n.*

dime store *n.* See **five-and-ten.**

dim•e•ter (dĭm′ĭ-tər) *n.* **1.** A line of verse consisting of two metrical feet. **2.** A line of verse consisting of two measures of two feet each. [LLat. *dimeter, dimetrus,* having two verses < Gk. *dimetros : di-,* two; see DI-[1] + *metron,* meter; see METER[1].]

di•meth•yl (dī-mĕth′əl) *n.* An organic compound, esp. ethane, containing two methyl groups.

di•meth•yl•ni•tros•a•mine (dī-mĕth′əl-nī-trō′sə-mēn′, -nī′-trō-săm′īn) *n.* A carcinogenic nitrosamine, $C_2H_6N_2O$, that occurs in tobacco smoke and certain foods.

di•meth•yl•sulf•ox•ide (dī-mĕth′əl-sŭl-fŏk′sīd′) *n.* DMSO.

dimin. *abbr.* **1.** diminuendo **2.** diminutive

di•min•ish (dĭ-mĭn′ĭsh) *v.* **-ished, -ish•ing, -ish•es** —*tr.* **1a.** To make smaller or less or to appear so. **b.** To detract from the authority, reputation, or prestige of. **2.** To cause to taper. **3.** *Music* To reduce (a perfect or minor interval) by a semitone. —*intr.* **1.** To become smaller or less. See Syns at **decrease. 2.** To taper. [ME *diminishen,* blend of *diminuen,* to lessen (< OFr. *diminuer* < Lat. *diminuere,* var. of *dēminuere* < *dē-,* de- + *minuere,* to lessen) and *minishen,* to reduce (< OFr. *minuiser* < VLat. **minūtiāre* < Lat. *minūtia,* smallness < *minūtus,* small < p. part. of *minuere,* to lessen).] —**di•min′ish•a•ble** *adj.* —**di•min′ish•ment** *n.*

di•min•ished capacity (dĭ-mĭn′ĭsht) *n.* Lack of ability to comprehend the nature of a crime one has committed or to restrain oneself from committing a crime.

di•min•ish•ing returns (dĭ-mĭn′ĭ-shĭng) *pl.n.* A yield rate that after a certain point fails to increase proportionately to additional outlays of capital or investments of time and labor.

di•min•u•en•do (dĭ-mĭn′yōō-ĕn′dō) *n., adv., & adj. Music* Decrescendo. [Ital., pr. part. of *diminuire,* to diminish < Lat. *dīminuere.* See DIMINISH.]

dim•i•nu•tion (dĭm′ə-nōō′shən, -nyōō′-) *n.* **1a.** The act or process of diminishing. **b.** The resulting reduction; decrease. **2.** *Music* Statement of a theme in notes of lesser duration, usu. one-half, of the original. [ME *diminucioun* < OFr. *diminution* < Lat. *dīminūtiō, dēminūtiō- < dīminūtus,* p. part. of *dīminuere.* See DIMINISH.] —**dim′i•nu′tion•al** *adj.*

di•min•u•tive (dĭ-mĭn′yə-tĭv) *adj.* **1.** Extremely small in size; tiny. See Syns at **small. 2.** *Grammar* Of or being a suffix that indicates smallness, youth, familiarity, affection, or contempt, as *-kin* in *lambkin.* ❖ *n.* **1.** *Grammar* A diminutive suffix, word, or name. **2.** A very small person or thing. [ME *diminutif* < OFr. < Lat. *dīminūtīvus,* var. of *dēminūtīvus < dēminūtus,* p. part. of *dēminuere,* to lessen. See DIMINISH.] —**di•min′u•tive•ly** *adv.* —**di•min′u•tive•ness** *n.*

dim•i•ty (dĭm′ĭ-tē) *n., pl.* **-ties** A sheer crisp cotton fabric with raised woven stripes or checks. [ME *demyt* < Med.Lat. *dimitum* < Gk. *dimiton* < neut. of *dimitos,* double-threaded : *di-,* two; see DI-[1] + *mitos,* thread.]

DIMM *abbr. Computer Science* dual in-line memory module

dim•mer (dĭm′ər) *n.* **1.** A rheostat or other device used to vary the intensity of an electric light. **2a.** A parking light on a motor vehicle. **b.** A low beam.

di•mor•phic (dī-môr′fĭk) also **di•mor•phous** (-fəs) *adj.* Existing or occurring in two distinct forms; exhibiting dimorphism.

di•mor•phism (dī-môr′fĭz′əm) *n.* **1.** *Biology* The existence, within a species of animals, of two distinct forms that differ in one or more characteristics, as in the coloration of male and female birds. **2.** *Botany* The occurrence of two distinct forms of the same plants in one plant or in two plants of the same species, as in the juvenile and adult leaves of ivy. **3.** *Chemistry & Physics* Dimorphic crystallization.

dim-out (dĭm′out′) *n.* **1.** Restricted use of lights at night, as to make a city less visible from the air in wartime. **2.** The semidarkness resulting from restricted use of lights at night.

dim•ple (dĭm′pəl) *n.* **1.** A small natural indentation in the flesh on a part of the human body, as in the cheek. **2.** A slight depression or indentation in a surface. ❖ *v.* **-pled, -pling, -ples** —*intr.* To form dimples by smiling. —*tr.* To produce dimples in. [ME *dimpel.*] —**dim′ply** *adj.*

dim sum (dĭm′ sōōm′, sŭm′) *n.* A traditional Chinese meal in which small portions of a variety of foods, including dumplings, are served in succession. [Chin. (Cantonese) *tímsàm,* light refreshments, equivalent to Chin. (Mandarin) *diǎn,* spot, drop + *xīn,* heart.]

dim•wit (dĭm′wĭt′) *n. Slang* A stupid person. —**dim′wit′ted** *adj.* —**dim′wit′ted•ly** *adv.* —**dim′wit′ted•ness** *n.*

din (dĭn) *n.* A jumble of loud, usu. discordant sounds. See Syns at **noise.** ❖ *v.* **dinned, din•ning, dins** —*tr.* **1.** To stun with deafening noise. **2.** To instill by wearying repetition. —*intr.* To make a loud noise. [ME *dine* < OE *dyne.*]

dimorphism
male (*top*) and female
(*bottom*) black widow
spiders

dingo
Canis dingo

di•nar (dĭ-när′, dē′när′) *n.* **1.** See table at **currency. 2.** Any of several units of gold and silver currency formerly used in the Middle East. [Ar. *dīnār* < L.Gk. *dēnarion* < Lat. *dēnārius.* See DENARIUS.]

Di•nar•ic Alps (dĭ-när′ĭk) A range of the Balkan Peninsula extending c. 644 km (400 mi) along the E coast of the Adriatic Sea.

dine (dīn) *v.* **dined, din•ing, dines** —*intr.* **1.** To have dinner. —*tr.* To give dinner to; entertain at dinner. [ME *dinen* < OFr. *diner, disner* < VLat. **disiūnāre < *disiêiūnāre :* Lat. *dis-,* dis- + Lat. *iēiūnium,* fast.]

Di•né (dĭ′nĕ′) *n.* **1.** (*used with a pl. verb*) The Navajo people. **2.** The Navajo language. [Navajo, the people.]

din•er (dī′nər) *n.* **1.** One that dines. **2.** See **dining car. 3.** A small, usu. inexpensive restaurant with a long counter and booths housed in a building resembling a dining car.

Di•ne•sen (dē′nə-sən, dĭn′ĭ-), Isak Pen name of Baroness Karen Blixen. 1885–1962. Danish writer who is best known for her memoir *Out of Africa* (1937).

di•nette (dī-nĕt′) *n.* **1.** A nook or alcove located in or near a kitchen and used for informal meals. **2.** The table and chairs used to furnish such an area. [DINE + -ETTE.]

ding¹ (dĭng) *v.* **dinged, ding•ing, dings** —*intr.* **1.** To ring; clang. **2.** To speak persistently and repetitiously. —*tr.* **1.** To cause to clang. **2.** To instill with constant repetition. ❖ *n.* A ringing sound. [Partly imit. and partly alteration of DIN.]

ding² (dĭng) *Informal n.* A small dent or nick, as in a car. ❖ *tr.v.* **dinged, ding•ing, dings** **1.** To dent; nick. **2.** To hit; strike. [< *ding,* to strike, beat on (< ME *dingen;* akin to ON *dengja*) and < DING¹.]

ding-a-ling (dĭng′ə-lĭng) *n. Slang* A scatterbrained or eccentric person.

ding•bat (dĭng′băt′) *n.* **1.** *Slang* A stupid or silly person. **2.** An object, such as a brick, used as a missile. **3.** *Slang* An unspecified gadget or other small article. **4.** *Printing* A typographical ornament or symbol. [DING¹ + BAT² (as in *bats in the belfry*).]

ding-dong (dĭng′dông′, -dŏng′) *n.* **1.** The peal of a bell. **2.** *Slang* An empty-headed person; a fool. ❖ *intr.v.* **-donged, -dong•ing, -dongs** To ring; jingle. ❖ *adj.* Characterized by a hammering exchange, as of blows. [Imit.]

dinge (dĭnj) *n.* Grime or squalor; dinginess. [Back-formation < DINGY.]

din•ghy (dĭng′ē) *n., pl.* **-ghies 1.** A small open boat carried as a tender, lifeboat, or pleasure craft on a larger boat. **2.** A small rowboat. **3.** An inflatable rubber life raft. [Hindi *ḍiṅgī,* var. of *ḍeṅgī, ḍeṅgā,* float, raft.]

din•gle (dĭng′gəl) *n.* A small wooded valley; a dell. [ME, dell, hollow.]

Ding Ling (dĭng′ lĭng′) 1904–86. Chinese writer whose novels, stories, and plays explore the role of women in Communist China.

din•go (dĭng′gō) *n., pl.* **-goes** A wild dog (*Canis dingo*) of Australia having a reddish-brown or yellowish-brown coat. [Dharuk (Aboriginal language of SE Australia) *ḍiṅgu.*]

din•gus (dĭng′əs) *n. Slang* An article whose name is unknown or forgotten. [Du. *dinges, whatchamacallit* < Ger. *Dings* < MHGer. *dinges,* genitive of *dinc,* thing < OHGer. *ding, thing,* assembly, case, thing.]

din•gy (dĭn′jē) *adj.* **-gi•er, -gi•est 1.** Darkened with smoke or grime; dirty or discolored. **2.** Shabby, drab, or squalid. [Poss. < ME *dinge, dung,* var. of *dung.* See DUNG.] —**din′gi•ly** *adv.* —**din′gi•ness** *n.*

din•ing car (dī′nĭng) *n.* A railroad car in which meals are served.

dining room *n.* A room in which meals are eaten.

di•ni•tro•ben•zene (dī-nī′trō-bĕn′zēn′, -bĕn-zēn′) *n.* Any of three isomeric compounds, $C_6H_4(NO_2)_2$, made from a mixture of nitric acid, sulfuric acid, and heated benzene and used in celluloid manufacture, in dyes, and in organic synthesis.

dink (dĭngk) *n.* A drop shot. [< *dink,* sound of a weakly hit or dropped ball.]

DINK or **dink** (dĭngk) *n.* A member of a two-career couple with no children. [D(*ual*) I(*ncome*) N(*o*) K(*ids*).]

Din•ka (dĭng′kə) *n., pl.* **Dinka** or **-kas 1.** A member of a traditionally pastoral people of the Nile valley in southern Sudan. **2.** Their Nilotic language. [Prob. ult. < Dinka *jieng,* person.]

din•key also **din•ky** (dĭng′kē) *n., pl.* **-keys** also **-kies** A small locomotive used in a railroad yard, as for shunting. [< DINKY.]

din•kum (dĭng′kəm) *Australian adj.* Genuine; real. ❖ *adv.* Honestly; truly. [< E. dialectal and Australian, *work.*]

din•ky (dĭng′kē) *adj.* **-ki•er, -ki•est** *Informal* **1.** Of small size or consequence; insignificant. **2.** Of poor quality; shabby. [Prob. < Sc. *dink,* neat, trim.]

din•ner (dĭn′ər) *n.* **1a.** The chief meal of the day, eaten in the evening or at midday. **b.** A banquet or formal meal in honor of a person or an event. **c.** The food prepared for either of these meals. **2.** A full-course meal served at a fixed price. [ME *diner,* morning meal < OFr. *disner, diner,* to dine, morning meal. See DINE.]

WORD HISTORY In Middle English *dinner* meant "breakfast," as did the Old French word *disner,* or *diner,* which was the source of our word. The Old French word came from the Vulgar Latin word *disiūnāre, meaning "to break one's fast; that is, to eat one's first meal," a notion also contained in our word *breakfast*. The Vulgar Latin word was derived from an earlier word, *disiēiūnāre*, the Latin elements of which are *dis-*, denoting reversal, and *iēiūnium*, "fast." Middle English *diner* not only meant "breakfast" but, echoing usage of the Old French word *diner*, more commonly meant "the first big meal of the day, usually eaten between 9 A.M. and noon." Customs change, however, and over the years we have let the chief meal become the last meal of the day.

dinner jacket *n.* See **tuxedo** 1.
dinner theater *n.* A restaurant that presents a play during or after dinner.
din·ner·ware (dĭn'ər-wâr') *n.* **1.** The tableware used in serving a meal. **2.** A set of dishes.
di·no·flag·el·late (dī'nō-flăj'ə-lĭt, -lāt', -flə-jĕl'ĭt) *n.* Any of numerous minute, chiefly marine protozoans of the order Dinoflagellata, having two flagella and a cellulose covering and forming a chief constituent of plankton. [< NLat. *Dīnoflagellāta*, class name < Gk. *dīnos*, whirling (< *dīnein*, to whirl) + Lat. *flagellum*, flagellum; see FLAGELLUM.]
di·no·saur (dī'nə-sôr') *n.* **1.** Any of various extinct, often gigantic, chiefly terrestrial reptiles of the orders Saurischia and Ornithischia that lived in the Mesozoic Era. **2.** A relic of the past. **3.** One hopelessly outmoded or unwieldy. [NLat. *Dīnosauria*, group name < *Dīnosaurus*, former genus name : Gk. *deinos*, monstrous + Gk. *sauros*, lizard.] —**di'no·sau'ri·an** (-sôr'ē-ən) *adj. & n.* —**di'no·sau'ric** *adj.*
di·no·there (dī'nə-thîr') *n.* Any of various extinct elephantlike mammals of the genus *Dinotherium* that existed during the Miocene, Pliocene, and Pleistocene epochs. [< NLat. *Dīnothērium*, genus name : Gk. *deinos*, monstrous + Gk. *thērion*, wild beast; see TREACLE.]
dint (dĭnt) *n.* **1.** Force or effort; power: *by dint of hard work.* **2.** A dent. ❖ *tr.v.* **dint·ed, dint·ing, dints 1.** To put a dent in. **2.** To impress or drive in forcibly. [ME. See DENT[1].]
di·nu·cle·o·tide (dī-nōō'klē-ə-tīd', -nyōō'-) *n.* A molecule that consists of a combination of two nucleotides.
Din·wid·die (dĭn-wĭd'ē, dĭn'wĭd-ē), Robert 1693–1770. Scottish-born British colonial administrator who was lieutenant governor of Virginia (1751–58).
di·oc·e·san (dī-ŏs'ĭ-sən) *adj.* Of or relating to a diocese. ❖ *n.* The bishop of a diocese.
di·o·cese (dī'ə-sĭs, -sēs', -sēz') *n.* The district under the jurisdiction of a bishop. [ME *diocise* < OFr. < LLat. *diocēsis* < Lat. *dioecēsis*, jurisdiction < Gk. *dioikēsis*, administration < *dioikein*, to keep house, administer : *dia-*, intensive pref.; see DIA- + *oikein*, to inhabit (< *oikos*, house; see **weik-** in App.).]
Di·o·cle·tian (dī'ə-klē'shən) A.D. 245?–313? Emperor of Rome (284–305) who divided the empire into east and west (286) and led the last persecution of the Christians (303).
di·ode (dī'ōd') *n.* **1.** An electronic device that restricts current flow chiefly to one direction. **2.** An electron tube having a cathode and an anode. **3.** A two-terminal semiconductor device used chiefly as a rectifier.
diode laser *n.* See **semiconductor laser.**
di·oe·cious also **di·e·cious** (dī-ē'shəs) *adj. Botany* Having the male and female reproductive organs on separate individuals of the same species. [< NLat. *Dioecia*, former class name : DI-[1] + Gk. *oikiā*, a dwelling; see **weik-** in App.] —**di·oe'cious·ly** *adv.* —**di·oe'cism** (-sĭz'əm) *n.*
Di·og·e·nes (dī-ŏj'ə-nēz') d. *c.* 320 B.C. Greek philosopher who founded the Cynic school of philosophy.
Di·o·mede Islands (dī'ə-mēd') Two rocky islands in the Bering Strait between AK and Siberia. **Little Diomede** belongs to the US; **Big Diomede**, to Russia.
Di·o·me·des (dī'ə-mēd'dēz) *n. Greek Mythology* One of the Greek heroes of the Trojan War.
Di·o·ne (dī-ō'nē) *n.* **1.** *Greek Mythology* The mother of Aphrodite by Zeus. **2.** A satellite of Saturn. [Gk. *Diōnē* < *Zeus*, *Di-*, Zeus; see **dyeu-** in App.]
Di·o·nys·i·a (dī'ə-nĭz'ē-ə, -nĭzh'ē-ə, -nĭs'ē-ə) *pl.n.* Ancient Greek festivals held chiefly at Athens in honor of Dionysus, esp. fall festivals related to the development of Greek drama. [Lat. *Dionȳsia* < Gk. *Dionūsia (hiera)*, (festivities) of Dionysus, neut. pl. of *Dionūsios*. See DIONYSIAN.]
Di·o·nys·i·ac (dī'ə-nĭs'ē-ăk') *adj.* **1a.** *Greek Mythology* Of or relating to Dionysus. **b.** Of or relating to the Dionysia. **2.** often **dionysiac** Ecstatic or wild; Dionysian. [Lat. *Dionȳsiacus* < Gk. *Dionūsiakos* < *Dionūsios* < *Dionūsos*, Dionysus.]
Di·o·nys·i·an (dī'ə-nĭsh'ən, -nĭzh'ən, -nĭs'ē-ən) *adj.* **1.** *Greek Mythology* **a.** Of or relating to Dionysus. **b.** Of or devoted to the worship of Dionysus. **2.** often **dionysian** Of an ecstatic, orgiastic, or irrational nature; frenzied or undisciplined. **3.** often **dionysian** In the philosophy of Nietzsche, of or displaying creative-intuitive power as opposed to critical-rational power. [< Lat. *Dionȳsius* < Gk. *Dionūsios* < *Dionūsos*, Dionysus.]
Di·o·nys·i·us (dī'ə-nĭsh'ē-əs, -nĭsh'əs, -nī'sē-əs) Known as "the Elder." 430?–367 B.C. Tyrant of Syracuse (405–367) noted for his campaigns against the Carthaginians in Sicily. His son **Dionysius** (395?–343?), "the Younger," succeeded him as tyrant in

367 and was exiled in 343 for his despotic rule.
Dionysius Ex·ig·u·us (ĕg-zĭg'yōō-əs, ĕk-sĭg'-) A.D. 500?–560? Scythian monk and scholar who introduced the method of reckoning the Christian era from the birth of Jesus.
Dionysius of Halicarnassus 1st cent. B.C. Greek historian who wrote a 20-volume history of Rome, of which 10 books are extant.
Di·o·ny·sus (dī'ə-nī'səs, -nē'-) *n. Greek & Roman Mythology* The god of wine and of an orgiastic religion celebrating the power and fertility of nature. [Lat. *Dionȳsus* < Gk. *Dionūsos.*]
Di·o·phan·tine analysis (dī'ə-făn'tīn', -tĭn) *n.* A collection of methods for determining integral solutions of certain algebraic equations. [After *Diophantus*, 3rd-cent. A.D. Greek mathematician.]
Diophantine equation *n.* An algebraic equation with two or more variables whose coefficients are integers, studied to determine all integral solutions. [After *Diophantus*, 3rd-cent. A.D. Greek mathematician.]
di·op·side (dī-ŏp'sīd') *n.* A light green monoclinic pyroxene mineral, $CaMgSi_2O_6$, used as a gemstone and refractory. [Fr. : *di-*, two (< Gk.; see DI-[1]) + Gk. *-opsis*, appearance.]
di·op·ter (dī-ŏp'tər) *n.* A unit of measurement of the refractive power of lenses equal to the reciprocal of the focal length measured in meters. [Obsolete *diopter*, an instrument for measuring angles < Lat. *dioptra* < Gk. *dioptrā* : *dia-*, dia- + *optos*, visible; see **okʷ-** in App.] —**di·op'tral** (-trəl) *adj.*
di·op·tom·e·ter (dī'ŏp-tŏm'ĭ-tər) *n.* An instrument used for measuring ocular refraction. [DI(A)– + OPT(IC) + –METER.] —**di'op·tom'e·try** *n.*
di·op·tric (dī-ŏp'trĭk) also **di·op·tri·cal** (-trĭ-kəl) *adj.* **1.** Of or relating to dioptrics. **2.** Relating to optical refraction; refractive. [Gk. *dioptrikos* < *dioptrā*, an optical instrument. See DIOPTER.]
di·op·trics (dī-ŏp'trĭks) *n.* (used with a sing. verb) The study of the refraction of light.
Di·or (dē-ôr'), Christian 1905–57. French fashion designer best known for his New Look of 1947.
di·o·ram·a (dī'ə-răm'ə, -rä'mə) *n.* **1.** A three-dimensional scene in which figures, stuffed wildlife, or other objects are arranged naturalistically against a painted background. **2.** A scene reproduced on cloth transparencies with lights shining through the cloths to produce changes in effect, intended for viewing at a distance through an aperture. [Fr., blend of *dia-*, through (< Gk.; see DIA–) and *panorama*, panorama (< E. PANORAMA).] —**di'o·ram'ic** (-răm'ĭk) *adj.*
di·o·rite (dī'ə-rīt') *n.* Any of various dark granite-textured crystalline rocks rich in plagioclase. [Fr. < Gk. *diorizein*, to distinguish : *dia-*, apart, between; see DIA– + *horizein*, to divide, limit; see HORIZON.] —**di'o·rit'ic** (-rĭt'ĭk) *adj.*
Di·os·cu·ri (dī-ŏs'kyə-rī', dī'ə-skyōōr'ī) *pl.n. Greek Mythology* Castor and Pollux, the twin sons of Leda, who were transformed by Zeus into the constellation Gemini. [Gk. *Dioskouroi* : *Dios*, genitive of *Zeus*, Zeus; see **dyeu-** in App. + *kouroi*, pl. of *kouros*, boy; see **ker-[2]** in App.]
di·ox·ane (dī-ŏk'sān') *n.* A flammable, potentially explosive liquid, $C_4H_8O_2$, that is used as a solvent for fats, greases, and resins. [DI-[1] + OX(O)– + –ANE.]
di·ox·ide (dī-ŏk'sīd') *n.* A compound with two oxygen atoms per molecule.
di·ox·in (dī-ŏk'sĭn) *n.* Any of several carcinogenic or teratogenic heterocyclic hydrocarbons that occur as impurities in petroleum-derived herbicides. [DI-[1] + OX(O)– + –IN.]
dip (dĭp) *v.* **dipped, dip·ping, dips** —*tr.* **1.** To plunge briefly into a liquid, as in order to wet, coat, or saturate. **2.** To color or dye by immersing. **3.** To immerse (an animal) in a disinfectant solution. **4.** To form (a candle) by repeatedly immersing a wick in melted wax or tallow. **5.** To galvanize or plate (metal) by immersion. **6.** To scoop up by plunging the hand or a receptacle below the surface, as of a liquid; ladle: *dip water out of a bucket.* **7.** To lower and raise (a flag) in salute. **8.** To lower or drop (something) suddenly. —*intr.* **1.** To plunge into water or other liquid and come out quickly. **2.** To plunge the hand or a receptacle into liquid or a container, esp. so as to take something up or out. **3.** To withdraw a small amount from a fund: *We dipped into our savings.* **4.** To drop down or sink out of sight suddenly. **5.** To drop suddenly before climbing. Used of an aircraft. **6.** To slope downward; decline: *The road dipped.* **7.** To decline slightly and usu. temporarily. **8.** *Geology* To lie at an angle to the horizontal plane, as a rock stratum or vein. **9a.** To read here and there at random; browse. **b.** To investigate a subject superficially; dabble. ❖ *n.* **1.** A brief plunge or immersion, esp. a quick swim. **2.** A liquid into which something is dipped, as for dyeing or disinfecting. **3.** A savory creamy mixture into which food may be dipped. **4.** An amount taken up by dipping. **5.** A container for dipping. **6.** A candle made by repeated dipping in tallow or wax. **7.** A downward slope; a decline. **8.** A sharp downward course; a drop. **9.** *Geology* The downward inclination of a rock stratum or vein in reference to the plane of the horizon. **10.** Magnetic dip. **11.** A hollow or depression. **12.** *Slang* A pickpocket. **13.** *Slang* A foolish or stupid person. [ME *dippen* < OE *dyppan*. See **dheub-** in App. Sense 13, back-formation < DIPPY.]
di·pep·ti·dase (dī-pĕp'tĭ-dās', -dāz') *n.* An enzyme that hy

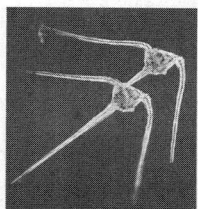
dinoflagellate
Ceratium sp.

diorama

ă	pat	oi	boy
ā	pay	ou	out
âr	care	ŏŏ	took
ä	father	ōō	boot
ĕ	pet	ŭ	cut
ē	be	ûr	urge
ĭ	pit	th	thin
ī	pie	*th*	this
îr	pier	hw	which
ŏ	pot	zh	vision
ō	toe	ə	about,
ô	paw		item

Stress marks:
' (primary);
' (secondary), as in
lexicon (lĕk'sĭ-kŏn')

drolyzes dipeptides into their constituent amino acids.

di·pep·tide (dī-pĕp′tīd′) *n.* A peptide that is composed of two amino acid molecules linked by a peptide bond.

di·pet·al·ous (dī-pĕt′l-əs) *adj.* Having two petals.

di·phase (dī′fāz′) also **di·pha·sic** (dī-fā′zĭk) *adj.* Having two phases.

di·phen·yl (dī-fĕn′əl, -fē′nəl) *n.* See **biphenyl.**

di·phen·yl·a·mine (dī-fĕn′əl-ə-mēn′, -ăm′ĭn, -fē′nəl-) *n.* A crystalline compound, $(C_6H_5)_2NH$, used as a stabilizer for plastics and in the manufacture of dyes and explosives.

di·phen·yl·hy·dan·to·in (dī-fĕn′əl-hī-dăn′tō-ĭn, -fē′nəl-) *n.* See **phenytoin.** [DIPHENYL + *hydantoin* (HYD(ROGEN) + (ALL)ANTO(IS) + −IN).]

di·phos·gene (dī-fŏz′jĕn′) *n.* A liquid, $ClCO_2CCl_3$, used in organic synthesis, yielding a poison gas used in World War I.

di·phos·phate (dī-fŏs′fāt′) *n.* An ester of phosphoric acid containing two phosphate groups.

di·phos·pho·gly·cer·ic acid (dī-fŏs′fō-glĭ-sĕr′ĭk) *n.* A diphosphate of glyceric acid that is an important intermediate in various metabolic processes, such as photosynthesis.

diph·the·ri·a (dĭf-thîr′ē-ə, dĭp-) *n.* An acute infectious disease caused by the bacillus *Corynebacterium diphtheriae,* characterized by the production of a systemic toxin and the formation of a false membrane in the throat and causing difficulty in breathing, high fever, and weakness. [NLat. *diphthēria* < Fr. *diphthérie* < Gk. *diphtherā,* piece of hide, leather. See LETTER.] —**diph′the·rit′ic** (-thə-rĭt′ĭk) *adj.* —**diph·ther′ic** (-thĕr′ĭk), **diph·ther′i·al** *adj.*

diph·thong (dĭf′thŏng′, -thŏng′, dĭp′-) *n.* A complex speech sound or glide that begins with one vowel and gradually changes to another vowel within the same syllable, as (oi) in *boil.* [ME *diptonge* < OFr. *diptongue* < LLat. *diphthongus* < Gk. *diphthongos : di-,* two; see DI−[1] + *phthongos,* sound.] —**diph·thon′gal** *adj.*

diph·thong·ize (dĭf′thŏng-īz′, -thŏng′-, dĭp′-) *tr. & intr.v.* **-ized, -iz·ing, -iz·es** To pronounce as or become a diphthong. —**diph′thong·i·za′tion** (-ĭ-zā′shən) *n.*

di·phy·let·ic (dī′fī-lĕt′ĭk) *adj.* Descended from two ancestral lines or individuals.

di·phyl·lous (dī-fĭl′əs) *adj. Botany* Having two leaves.

di·phy·o·dont (dī-fī′ə-dŏnt′) *adj.* Having two successive sets of teeth, deciduous and permanent. [< Gk. *diphuēs,* double (*di-,* two; see DI−[1]) + *phuein,* to grow; see **bheuə-** in App.]

di·ple·gia (dī-plē′jə, -jē-ə) *n.* Paralysis of corresponding parts on both sides of the body.

di·plex (dī′plĕks′) *adj.* Capable of simultaneous transmission or reception of two messages in the same radio channel. [DI−[1] + (DU)PLEX.]

di·plex·er (dī′plĕk-sər) *n.* A coupling device that permits two radio transmitters to share the same antenna.

diplo- or **dipl-** *pref.* **1.** Double: *diplococcus.* **2.** Having double the basic number of chromosomes; diploid: *diplont.* [< Gk. < *diploos,* double. See **dwo-** in App.]

dip·lo·blas·tic (dĭp′lō-blăs′tĭk) *adj.* Derived from the ectoderm and the endoderm. Used of lower invertebrates.

dip·lo·coc·cus (dĭp′lō-kŏk′əs) *n., pl.* **-coc·ci** (-kŏk′sī′, -kŏk′ī′) Any of various paired spherical bacteria, including those of the genus *Diplococcus,* some of which are pathogenic. —**dip′lo·coc′cal** (-kŏk′əl), **dip′lo·coc′cic** (-kŏk′sĭk, -kŏk′ĭk) *adj.*

di·plod·o·cus (dĭ-plŏd′ə-kəs, dī-) *n.* A very large herbivorous dinosaur of the genus *Diplodocus* that existed during the Jurassic Period. [NLat. *Diplodocus,* genus name : Gk. *diplo-,* diplo- + Gk. *dokos,* beam.]

dip·lo·e (dĭp′lō-ē′) *n.* The spongy, porous bony tissue between the hard outer and inner bone layers of the cranium. [Gk. *diploē,* a fold, doubling < fem. of *diploos,* twofold. See **dwo-** in App.] —**dip·lo′ic** (-lō-ĭk) *adj.*

dip·loid (dĭp′loid′) *adj.* **1.** Double or twofold. **2.** *Genetics* Having a pair of each type of chromosome, so that the basic chromosome number is doubled. ❖ *n. Genetics* An organism having diploid cells. [Gk. *diploos,* double; see **dwo-** in App. + −OID.] —**dip′loi·dy** (-loi′dē) *n.*

di·plo·ma (dĭ-plō′mə) *n.* **1.** A document issued by an educational institution to testify that the recipient has earned a degree or successfully completed a particular course of study. **2.** A certificate conferring a privilege or honor. **3.** An official document or charter. [Lat. *diplōma,* letter of introduction < Gk., document, folded paper < *diploos,* double. See **dwo-** in App.]

di·plo·ma·cy (dĭ-plō′mə-sē) *n.* **1.** The art or practice of conducting international relations, as in negotiating alliances. **2.** Tact and skill in dealing with people.

diploma mill *n. Informal* An unaccredited institution of higher education that grants degrees without ensuring that students are properly qualified.

dip·lo·mat (dĭp′lə-măt′) *n.* **1.** One appointed to represent a government in its relations with other governments. **2.** One who uses skill and tact in dealing with others. [Fr. *diplomate,* back-formation < *diplomatique,* diplomatic. See DIPLOMATIC.]

dip·lo·mate (dĭp′lə-māt′) *n.* One granted a diploma, esp. a physician certified as a specialist by a board of examiners.

dip·lo·mat·ic (dĭp′lə-măt′ĭk) *adj.* **1.** Of, relating to, or involving diplomacy or diplomats. **2.** Using or marked by tact and sensitivity in dealing with others. **3a.** Of or relating to diplomatics.

b. Being an exact copy of the original. [Fr. *diplomatique* < NLat. *diplōmaticus* < Lat. *diplōma, diplōmat-,* letter of introduction. See DIPLOMA.] —**dip′lo·mat′i·cal·ly** *adv.*

diplomatic corps *n.* The body of diplomatic personnel in residence at a nation's capital.

diplomatic immunity *n.* The exemption from taxation and ordinary processes of law afforded to diplomatic personnel in a foreign country.

dip·lo·mat·ics (dĭp′lə-măt′ĭks) *n.* (*used with a sing. verb*) The branch of paleography that deals with the study of ancient official documents and determines their age and authenticity.

di·plo·ma·tist (dĭ-plō′mə-tĭst) *n.* A diplomat.

dip·lont (dĭp′lŏnt′) *n.* An organism having somatic cells with the diploid number of chromosomes. —**dip·lont′ic** (-lŏn′tĭk) *adj.*

dip·lo·pi·a (dĭ-plō′pē-ə) *n.* See **double vision.** —**di·plo′pic** (-plō′pĭk, dĭ-plŏp′ĭk) *adj.*

dip·lo·pod (dĭp′lə-pŏd′) *n.* See **millipede.** —**dip·lop′o·dous** (-lŏp′ə-dəs) *adj.*

dip·lo·sis (dĭ-plō′sĭs) *n.* The formation during fertilization of the diploid number of chromosomes by the fusion of the nuclei of two haploid gametes. [NLat. *diplōsis* < Gk., a doubling < *diploun,* to double < *diploos,* double. See DIPLO−.]

dip·no·an (dĭp′nō-ən) *n.* Any of various fishes of the group Dipnoi, marked by modified lungs that enable them to breathe atmospheric air. [< NLat. *Dipnoī,* order name < Gk. *dipnooi,* pl. of *dipnoos,* having two apertures for breathing : *di-,* two; see DI−[1] + *pnoē,* breath (< *pnein,* to breathe).] —**dip′no·an** *adj.*

dip·o·dy (dĭp′ə-dē) *n., pl.* **-dies** A prosodic unit consisting of two feet. [LLat. *dipodia* < Gk. *dipodiā* < *dipous,* two-footed : *di-,* two; see DI−[1] + *pous, pod-,* foot; see −POD.]

di·pole (dī′pōl′) *n.* **1.** *Physics* A pair of equal and opposite electric charges or magnetic poles, separated by a small distance. **2.** *Chemistry* A molecule having two such charges or poles. **3.** *Electronics* An antenna, usu. fed from the center, consisting of two equal horizontal rods. —**di·po′lar** *adj.*

dipole moment *n.* **1.** The product of either charge in an electric dipole with the distance separating them. **2.** Magnetic moment.

dip·per (dĭp′ər) *n.* **1.** One that dips, esp. a container for taking up water. **2.** One of several small birds of the genus *Cinclus* that dive into swift streams and feed along the bottom. **3. Dipper a.** The Big Dipper. **b.** The Little Dipper.

dip·py (dĭp′ē) *adj.* **-pi·er, -pi·est** *Slang* Foolish. [?]

di·pro·pel·lant (dī′prə-pĕl′ənt) *n.* See **bipropellant.**

di·prot·ic (dī-prŏt′ĭk) *adj.* Having two hydrogen ions to donate to bases in an acid-base reaction. [DI−[1] + PROT(ON) + −IC.]

dip·shit (dĭp′shĭt′) *Vulgar Slang n.* A foolish or contemptible person. ❖ *adj.* Foolish or contemptible.

dip·so·ma·ni·a (dĭp′sə-mā′nē-ə, -mān′yə) *n.* An insatiable craving for alcoholic beverages. [Gk. *dipsa,* thirst + −MANIA.] —**dip′so·ma′ni·ac** (-ăk′) *adj. & n.* —**dip′so·ma·ni′a·cal** (-mə-nī′ə-kəl) *adj.*

dip·stick (dĭp′stĭk′) *n.* **1.** A graduated rod for measuring the depth or amount of liquid in a container. **2.** *Slang* A foolish or contemptible person.

dip·ter·al (dĭp′tər-əl) *adj.* **1.** *Architecture* Having a double row of columns on all sides. **2.** *Biology* Dipterous. [< Gk. *dipteros,* temple with a double peristyle : *di-,* di- + *pteron,* feather, wing; see **pet-** in App.]

dip·ter·an (dĭp′tər-ən) also **dip·ter·on** (-tə-rŏn′) *n.* A dipterous insect. —**dip′ter·an** *adj.*

dip·ter·ous (dĭp′tər-əs) *adj.* **1.** Of, relating to, or belonging to the Diptera, a large order of insects that includes the true flies and mosquitoes and is characterized by a single pair of membranous wings and a pair of club-shaped balancing organs. **2.** Having two wings, as certain insects, or winglike appendages, as certain fruits and seeds. [< NLat. *Diptera,* order name < Gk. *dipteros,* having two wings : *di-,* two; see DI−[1] + *pteron,* wing; see −PTER.]

dip·tych (dĭp′tĭk) *n.* **1.** A work consisting of two painted or carved panels that are hinged together. **2.** An ancient writing tablet having two leaves hinged together. **3.** A list of names of Christians for whom special prayers are made during the liturgy in many churches. [LLat. *diptycha* < Gk. *diptukha* < neut. pl. of *diptukhos,* folded double : *di-,* two; see DI−[1] + *ptukhē,* fold (< *ptussein, ptukh-,* to fold).]

di·pyr·id·a·mole (dī-pĭr′ĭ-də-mōl′, -pə-rĭd′ə-) *n.* A drug, $C_{24}H_{40}N_8O_4$, that acts as a coronary vasodilator. [DI−[1] + PYRID(INE) + −AM(INE) + −OLE.]

di·quat (dī′kwăt′) *n.* A strong crystalline herbicide, $C_{12}H_{12}Br_2N_2$, used to control water weeds. [DI−[1] + QUAT(ERNARY).]

dir. *abbr.* director

Di·rac (dĭ-răk′), **Paul Adrien Maurice** 1902–84. British mathematician and physicist who shared a 1933 Nobel Prize.

Dirac sea *n.* In quantum mechanics, the negative energy electron state that constitutes a vacuum. [After Paul Adrien Maurice DIRAC.]

dire (dīr) *adj.* **dir·er, dir·est 1.** Warning of or having dreadful consequences; calamitous: *a dire economic forecast; dire threats.* **2.** Urgent; desperate: *dire poverty.* [Lat. *dīrus,* fearsome, terrible.] —**dire′ly** *adv.* —**dire′ness** *n.*

di·rect (dĭ-rĕkt′, dī-) *v.* **-rect·ed, -rect·ing, -rects** —*tr.* **1.** To manage or conduct the affairs of; regulate. **2.** To have or take

dipteral

director's chair

charge of; control. **3.** To give authoritative instructions to: *directed them to answer.* **4.** To cause to move toward a goal; aim. **5.** To show or indicate the way for. **6.** To cause to move in or follow a straight course. **7.** To indicate the intended recipient on (a letter, for example). **8.** To address or adapt (remarks, for example) to a specific person, audience, or purpose. **9a.** To give guidance and instruction to (musicians, for example) in the performance of a work. **b.** To supervise the performance of. *—intr.* **1.** To give commands or directions. **2.** To conduct a performance or rehearsal. ❖ *adj.* **1.** Proceeding without interruption in a straight course or line; not deviating or swerving. **2.** Straightforward and candid; frank. **3.** Having no intervening persons, conditions, or agencies; immediate. **4.** Effected by action of the voters rather than through elected representatives or delegates. **5.** Being of unbroken descent; lineal: *a direct descendant.* **6.** Consisting of the exact words of the writer or speaker. **7.** Lacking compromising or mitigating elements; absolute. **8.** *Mathematics* Varying in the same manner as another quantity, esp. increasing if another quantity increases or decreasing if it decreases. **9.** *Astronomy* Moving west to east in the same direction as the sun's movement against the stars. Used of a planet. **10.** *Sports* Being a free kick in soccer by which a goal can be scored without the ball being touched by a second player. ❖ *adv.* Straight; directly. [ME *directen* < Lat. *dīrigere, dīrēct-*, to give direction to : *dī-, dis-*, apart; see DIS– + *regere*, to guide; see **reg-** in App.]

direct action *n.* The strategic use of immediately effective acts, such as strikes or sabotage, to achieve a political or social end.

direct current *n.* An electric current flowing in one direction only.

di•rect•ed (dĭ-rĕk′tĭd) *adj. Mathematics* Having an indicated positive sense: *directed angle; directed distance.*

di•rec•tion (dĭ-rĕk′shən, dī-) *n.* **1.** The act or function of directing. **2.** Management, supervision, or guidance of an action or operation. **3.** The art or action of musical or theatrical directing. **4.** *Music* A word or phrase in a score indicating how a passage is to be played or sung. **5.** An instruction or series of instructions for doing or finding something. Often used in the plural. **6.** An authoritative indication; an order or command. **7a.** The distance-independent relationship between two points in space that specifies the angular position of either with respect to the other; the relationship by which the alignment or orientation of any position with respect to any other position is established. **b.** A position to which motion or another position is referred. **c.** A line leading to a place or point. **d.** The line or course along which a person or thing moves. **8.** The statement in degrees of the angle measured between due north and a given line or course on a compass. **9.** A course or area of development; a tendency toward a particular end or goal: *charting a new direction for the company.* [ME, arrangement < Lat. *dīrēctiō, dīrēctiōn-* < *dīrēctus*, p. part. of *dīrigere*, to direct. See DIRECT.] **—di•rec′tion•less** *adj.*

di•rec•tion•al (dĭ-rĕk′shə-nəl, dī-) *adj.* **1.** Of or indicating direction. **2.** *Electronics* Capable of receiving or sending signals in one direction only. **3.** Relating to guidance in effort, behavior, or thought. **4.** Serving to point the future direction, as of fashion. ❖ *n.* A directional signal. **—di•rec′tion•al′i•ty** (-shə-năl′ĭ-tē) *n.*

directional antenna *n.* An antenna that receives or sends signals most effectively in a particular direction.

directional signal *n.* One of two lights on the front and rear of an automotive vehicle that indicate the direction of a turn.

direction finder *n.* A device for determining the source of a transmitted signal, consisting mainly of a radio receiver and a coiled rotating antenna.

di•rec•tive (dĭ-rĕk′tĭv, dī-) *n.* An order or instruction, esp. one from a central authority. ❖ *adj.* Serving to direct.

di•rect•ly (dĭ-rĕkt′lē, dī-) *adv.* **1.** In a direct line or manner; straight. **2.** Without anyone or anything intervening. **3.** Exactly or totally. **4.** At once; instantly. **5.** Candidly; frankly. **6.** *Chiefly Southern US* In a little while; shortly. ❖ *conj. Chiefly British* As soon as.

direct mail *n.* Advertisements or other printed matter mailed directly to prospective customers or contributors. **—di•rect′-mail′** (dĭ-rĕkt′māl′, dī-) *adj.* **—direct mailer** *n.*

direct object *n.* A word or phrase in a sentence referring to the one receiving the action of a transitive verb. For example, in *mail the letter, letter* is the direct object.

di•rec•tor (dĭ-rĕk′tər, dī-) *n.* **1.** One that supervises, controls, or manages. **2.** A member of a group of persons chosen to govern the affairs of an institution or corporation. **3.** A person who supervises the creative aspects of a dramatic production or film and instructs the actors and crew. **4.** The conductor of an orchestra or chorus. **—di•rec′tor•ship′** *n.*

di•rec•tor•ate (dĭ-rĕk′tər-ĭt, dī-) *n.* **1.** The office or position of a director. **2.** A board of directors, as of a corporation. **3.** The entire staff of a bureau or department.

di•rec•to•ri•al (dĭ-rĕk′tôr′ē-əl, -tōr′-, dī-) *adj.* **1.** Of or relating to a director or directorate. **2.** Serving to direct; directive. **—di•rec′to′ri•al•ly** *adv.*

di•rec•tor's chair (dĭ-rĕk′tərz, dī-) *n.* A folding armchair with a usu. canvas back and seat.

director's cut *n.* The version of a film in which the editing is executed or approved by the director, usu. including footage not in the standard release.

di•rec•to•ry (dĭ-rĕk′tə-rē, dī-) *n., pl.* **-ries 1.** A book containing an alphabetical or classified listing of names, addresses, and other data. **2.** *Computer Science* **a.** A listing of the files contained in a storage device, such as a magnetic disk. **b.** A description of the various characteristics of a file, such as the layout of the fields in it. **3.** A book of rules or directions. **4.** A group or body of directors. ❖ *adj.* Serving to direct.

direct primary *n.* A primary in which a party's candidates for public office are nominated by direct vote of the people.

di•rec•trix (dĭ-rĕk′trĭks, dī-) *n., pl.* **di•rec•trix•es** or **di•rec•tri•ces** (dĭ′rĕk-trī′sēz) **1.** *Mathematics* A fixed curve traversed by a generatrix in generating a conic section or a cylinder. **2.** The median line in the trajectory of fire of an artillery piece.

direct tax *n.* A tax levied directly on the taxpayer.

dire•ful (dīr′fəl) *adj.* **1.** Inspiring dread; terrible. **2.** Foreshadowing evil or disaster; ominous. **—dire′ful•ly** *adv.*

dire wolf *n.* A large wolflike mammal *(Canis dirus)* that inhabited North America during the Pleistocene Epoch.

dirge (dûrj) *n.* **1.** *Music* **a.** A funeral hymn or lament. **b.** A slow, mournful musical composition. **2.** A mournful or elegiac poem or other literary work. [ME, an antiphon at Matins in the Office for the Dead < Med.Lat. *dīrige Domine*, direct, Lord, sing. imper. of *dīrigere*, to direct. See DIRECT.] **—dirge′ful** *adj.*

dir•ham (də-răm′) *n.* See table at **currency.** [Ar. < Gk. *drakhmē*, drachma.]

dir•i•gi•ble (dĭr′ə-jə-bəl, də-rĭj′ə-bəl) *n.* See **airship.** [Lat. *dīrigere*, to direct; see DIRECT + –IBLE.]

dirk (dûrk) *n.* A dagger. ❖ *tr.v.* **dirked, dirk•ing, dirks** To stab with a dirk. [Sc. *durk.*]

dirn•dl (dûrn′dl) *n.* **1.** A full-skirted dress with a tight bodice and low neck, that is sleeveless or has short full sleeves. **2.** A full skirt with a gathered waistband. [Ger., short for *Dirndlkleid* : Ger. dialectal *Dirndl*, dim. of *Dirne*, girl (< OHGer. *diorna*) + *Kleid*, dress.]

dirt (dûrt) *n.* **1.** Earth or soil. **2a.** A filthy or soiling substance, such as mud. **b.** Excrement. **3.** A squalid or filthy condition. **4.** One that is mean or vile. **5a.** Obscene language or subject matter. **b.** Malicious or scandalous gossip. **c.** Information that embarrasses or accuses. **6.** Unethical behavior; corruption. **7.** Material, such as gravel, from which metal is extracted in mining. [ME, var. of *drit*, excrement, filth, mud < ON.]

dirt•bag (dûrt′băg′) *n. Slang* A filthy or vile person.

dirt bike *n.* **1.** A lightweight motorcycle designed for use on rough surfaces, such as dirt roads or trails. **2.** See **mountain bike.**

dirt-cheap (dûrt′chēp′) *adv. & adj.* Very cheap.

dirt dauber *n. Chiefly Southern US* See **mud dauber.** See Regional Note at **mud dauber.**

dirt farmer *n. Informal* A farmer who does all the work on his or her property. **—dirt farming** *n.*

dirt-poor (dûrt′po͝or′) *adj.* Lacking most of life's necessities.

dirt•y (dûr′tē) *adj.* **-i•er, -i•est 1a.** Soiled, as with dirt; unclean. **b.** Spreading dirt; polluting. **c.** Apt to soil with dirt or grime. **d.** Contaminated with infectious microorganisms. **2.** Squalid or filthy; run-down. **3a.** Obscene or indecent. **b.** Malicious or scandalous: *a dirty lie.* **4a.** Unethical or sordid: *dirty politics.* **b.** Not sportsmanlike: *a dirty fighter.* **c.** Acquired by illicit or improper means: *dirty money.* **d.** *Slang* Possessing or using illegal drugs. **5a.** Unpleasant or distasteful; thankless. **b.** Very unfortunate or regrettable: *a dirty shame.* **6.** Expressing disapproval or hostility: *a dirty look.* **7.** Not bright and clear in color; somewhat drab. Often used in combination: *dirty-blonde hair.* **8.** Producing a great amount of long-lived radioactive fallout. Used of nuclear weapons. **9.** Stormy; rough: *dirty weather.* ❖ *v.* **-ied, -y•ing, -ies** *—tr.* **1.** To make soiled. **2.** To stain or tarnish with dishonor. *—intr.* To become soiled. **—dirt′i•ly** *adv.* **—dirt′i•ness** *n.*

dirty laundry *n. Informal* Personal affairs that could cause embarrassment or distress if made public.

dirty old man *n. Informal* A middle-aged or elderly man with lewd or lecherous inclinations.

dirty pool *n. Slang* Unjust or dishonest conduct. [< POOL[2].]

dirty rice *n. Southern Louisiana* A dish of white rice cooked with chicken livers and gizzards, onions, peppers, and seasonings.

dirty tricks *pl.n. Informal* **1.** Covert intelligence operations that disrupt the economy or the political situation in another country. **2.** Unethical behavior, esp. acts that destroy the credibility of an opponent. **3.** Commercial espionage. **—dirty trickster** *n.*

dirty word *n.* **1.** An obscene or vulgar word. **2.** A word, expression, or concept viewed as odious or intolerable.

dis or **diss** (dĭs) *tr.v.* **dissed, diss•ing, diss•es** *Informal* To show disrespect to, often by insult or criticism. [African American Vernacular E., short for DISRESPECT.]

Dis (dĭs) *n. Roman Mythology* **1.** The god of the underworld; Pluto. **2.** The underworld. [Lat. *Dīs* < var. of *dīves*, wealthy (since the underworld was viewed as the source of wealth from the ground). See **dyeu-** in App.]

dis– *pref.* **1.** Not: *dissimilar.* **2a.** Absence of: *disinterest.* **b.** Opposite of: *disfavor.* **3.** Undo; do the opposite of: *disarrange.* **4a.** Deprive of: *disfranchise.* **b.** Remove: *disbud.* **5.** Free from: *disintoxicate.* **6.** Used as an intensive: *disannul.* [ME < OFr. *des-*

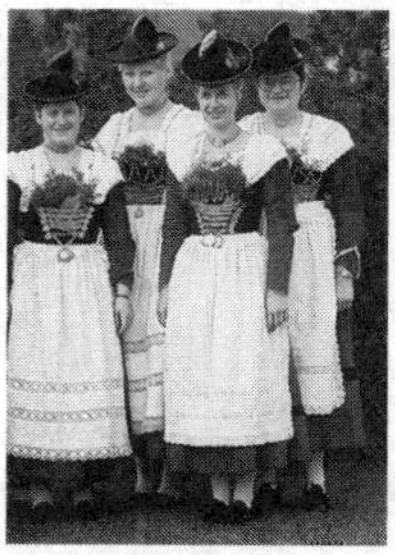

dirndl
German folk costumes

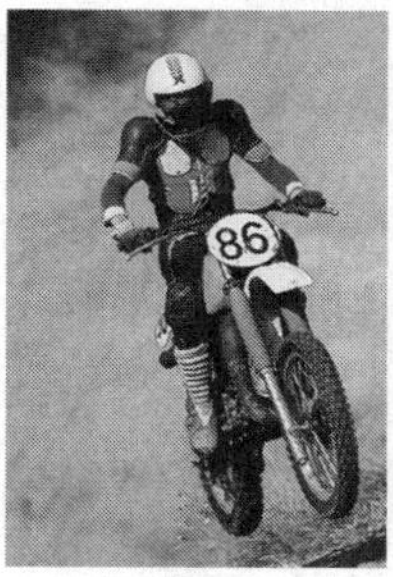

dirt bike

ă	pat	oi	boy
ā	pay	ou	out
âr	care	o͝o	took
ä	father	o͞o	boot
ĕ	pet	ŭ	cut
ē	be	ûr	urge
ĭ	pit	th	thin
ī	pie	*th*	this
îr	pier	hw	which
ŏ	pot	zh	vision
ō	toe	ə	about, item
ô	paw		

Stress marks:
′ (primary);
′ (secondary), as in
lexicon (lĕk′sĭ-kŏn′)

< Lat. *dis-* < *dis*, apart, asunder.]

dis•a•bil•i•ty (dĭs′ə-bĭl′ĭ-tē) *n., pl.* **-ties 1a.** The condition of being disabled; incapacity. **b.** The period of such a condition. **2.** A disadvantage or deficiency, esp. a physical or mental impairment that impedes access or performance. **3.** Something that hinders or incapacitates. **4.** A legal incapacity or disqualification.

dis•a•ble (dĭs-ā′bəl) *tr.v.* **-bled, -bling, -bles 1.** To deprive of capability or effectiveness, esp. to impair the physical abilities of. **2.** *Law* To render legally disqualified. —**dis•a′ble•ment** *n.*

dis•a•bled (dĭs-ā′bəld) *adj.* **1.** Inoperative: *a disabled vehicle.* **2.** Impaired, as in physical functioning: *a disabled veteran.* ❖ *n.* (*used with a pl. verb*) Physically impaired people considered as a group. See Usage Note at **handicapped.**

dis•a•buse (dĭs′ə-byōoz′) *tr.v.* **-bused, -bus•ing, -bus•es** To free from a falsehood or misconception. [Fr. *désabuser* : *dés-*, dis- + *abuser*, to delude (< OFr., to misuse; see ABUSE).]

di•sac•cha•ri•dase (dī-săk′ər-ĭ-dās′, -dāz′) *n.* An enzyme, such as invertase or lactase, that catalyzes the hydrolysis of disaccharides to monosaccharides.

di•sac•cha•ride (dī-săk′ə-rīd′) *n.* Any of a class of sugars, including lactose and sucrose, composed of two monosaccharides.

dis•ac•cord (dĭs′ə-kôrd′) *n.* Lack of harmony; disagreement. ❖ *intr.v.* **-cord•ed, -cord•ing, -cords** To disagree. [< ME *disaccorden*, to disagree < OFr. *desacorder* : *des-*, dis- + *acorder*, to agree; see ACCORD.]

dis•ac•cus•tom (dĭs′ə-kŭs′təm) *tr.v.* **-tomed, -tom•ing, -toms** To render (a person) unaccustomed to something to which the person had been accustomed. [ME *disacustome* < OFr. *desacostumer* : *des-*, dis- + *acostumer*, to accustom; see ACCUSTOM.]

dis•ad•van•tage (dĭs′əd-văn′tĭj) *n.* **1.** An unfavorable condition. **2.** Something that places one in an unfavorable condition. **3.** Damage or loss, esp. to reputation or finances; detriment. ❖ *tr.v.* **-taged, -tag•ing, -tag•es** To put at a disadvantage; hinder or harm. [ME *disavauntage* < OFr. *desavantage* : *des-*, dis- + *avantage*, advantage; see ADVANTAGE.]

> **SYNONYMS** *disadvantage, detriment, drawback, handicap* These nouns denote a condition, circumstance, or characteristic unfavorable to success: *Poor health is a disadvantage to athletes. To its detriment, the museum has no parking lot. Every job has its drawbacks. Illiteracy is a serious handicap in life.*

dis•ad•van•taged (dĭs′əd-văn′tĭjd) *adj.* **1.** Deprived of some necessities or advantages of life, such as adequate housing or medical care. **2.** Being at a disadvantage, esp. with respect to competitive or opposing elements or forces. ❖ *n.* (*used with a pl. verb*) Deprived people considered as a group.

dis•ad•van•ta•geous (dĭs-ăd′văn-tā′jəs, dĭs′ăd-vən-) *adj.* Detrimental; unfavorable. —**dis′ad•van′ta•geous•ly** *adv.*

dis•af•fect (dĭs′ə-fĕkt′) *tr.v.* **-fect•ed, -fect•ing, -fects** To cause to lose affection or loyalty. —**dis′af•fec′tion** *n.*

dis•af•fect•ed (dĭs′ə-fĕk′tĭd) *adj.* Resentful and rebellious, esp. against authority. —**dis′af•fect′ed•ly** *adv.*

dis•af•fil•i•ate (dĭs′ə-fĭl′ē-āt′) *v.* **-at•ed, -at•ing, -ates** —*tr.* To remove from association. —*intr.* To end an affiliation. —**dis′af•fil′i•a′tion** *n.*

dis•af•firm (dĭs′ə-fûrm′) *tr.v.* **-firmed, -firm•ing, -firms** To deny or contradict. —**dis′af•fir′mance** (dĭs′ə-fûr′məns), **dis•af′fir•ma′tion** (dĭs-ăf′ər-mā′shən) *n.*

dis•ag•gre•gate (dĭs-ăg′rĭ-gāt′) *v.* **-gat•ed, -gat•ing, -gates** —*tr.* To divide into parts. —*intr.* To break up or apart. —**dis•ag′gre•ga′tion** *n.* —**dis•ag′gre•ga′tive** *adj.*

dis•a•gree (dĭs′ə-grē′) *intr.v.* **-greed, -gree•ing, -grees 1.** To fail to correspond. **2a.** To have a differing opinion. **b.** To dispute or quarrel. **3.** To cause adverse effects. [ME *disagreen* < OFr. *desagreer* : *des-*, dis- + *agreer*, to agree; see AGREE.]

dis•a•gree•a•ble (dĭs′ə-grē′ə-bəl) *adj.* **1.** Not to one's liking; unpleasant or offensive. **2.** Having a quarrelsome, bad-tempered manner. —**dis′a•gree′a•ble•ness** *n.* —**dis′a•gree′a•bly** *adv.*

dis•a•gree•ment (dĭs′ə-grē′mənt) *n.* **1.** A failure or refusal to agree. **2.** A disparity; an inconsistency. **3a.** A conflict or difference of opinion. **b.** A quarrel.

dis•al•low (dĭs′ə-lou′) *tr.v.* **-lowed, -low•ing, -lows 1.** To refuse to allow. **2.** To reject as invalid, untrue, or improper: *disallow an unsigned will as evidence.* [ME *disallowen* < OFr. *desalouer*, to reprimand : *des-*, dis- + *alouer*, to approve; see ALLOW.] —**dis′al•low′a•ble** *adj.* —**dis′al•low′ance** *n.*

dis•am•big•u•ate (dĭs′ăm-bĭg′yōo-āt′) *tr.v.* **-at•ed, -at•ing, -ates** To establish a single grammatical or semantic interpretation for. —**dis′am•big′u•a′tion** *n.*

dis•an•nul (dĭs′ə-nŭl′) *tr.v.* **-nulled, -null•ing, -nuls** To annul or cancel. —**dis′an•nul′ment** *n.*

dis•ap•pear (dĭs′ə-pîr′) *v.* **-peared, -pear•ing, -pears** —*intr.* **1.** To pass out of sight or existence: *The ship disappeared over the horizon.* **2.** To cease to exist. —*tr.* To cause (someone) to disappear, esp. by kidnapping or murder. —**dis′ap•pear′ance** *n.*

> **SYNONYMS** *disappear, evanesce, evaporate, fade, vanish* These verbs mean to pass out of sight or existence: *a skyscraper disappearing in the fog; time seeming to evanesce; courage evaporating under pressure; memories fading away; hope slowly vanishing.*

dis•ap•point (dĭs′ə-point′) *v.* **-point•ed, -point•ing, -points**

—*tr.* **1.** To fail to satisfy the hope, desire, or expectation of. **2.** To frustrate or thwart. —*intr.* To cause disappointment. [ME *disappointen* < OFr. *desapointier*, to remove from office : *des-*, dis- + *apointer, apointier*, to appoint; see APPOINT.]

dis•ap•point•ed (dĭs′ə-poin′tĭd) *adj.* Thwarted in hope, desire, or expectation. —**dis′ap•point′ed•ly** *adv.*

dis•ap•point•ing (dĭs′ə-poin′tĭng) *adj.* Not up to expectations or hopes. —**dis′ap•point′ing•ly** *adv.*

dis•ap•point•ment (dĭs′ə-point′mənt) *n.* **1a.** The act of disappointing. **b.** The condition or feeling of being disappointed. **2.** One that disappoints.

dis•ap•pro•ba•tion (dĭs-ăp′rə-bā′shən) *n.* Moral disapproval; condemnation.

dis•ap•prov•al (dĭs′ə-prōo′vəl) *n.* The act of disapproving; condemnation or censure.

dis•ap•prove (dĭs′ə-prōov′) *v.* **-proved, -prov•ing, -proves** —*tr.* **1.** To have an unfavorable opinion of; condemn. **2.** To refuse to approve; reject. —*intr.* To have an unfavorable opinion. —**dis′ap•prov′er** *n.* —**dis′ap•prov′ing•ly** *adv.*

dis•arm (dĭs-ärm′) *v.* **-armed, -arm•ing, -arms** —*tr.* **1.** To divest of weapons. **b.** To deprive of the means of attack or defense; render harmless. **2a.** To overcome or allay the suspicion, hostility, or antagonism of. **b.** To win the confidence of. —*intr.* **1.** To lay down arms. **2.** To reduce or abolish armed forces. [ME *disarmen* < OFr. *desarmer* : *des-*, dis- + *armer*, to arm (< Lat. *armāre* < *arma*, weapons; see **ar-** in App.).] —**dis•arm′er** *n.*

dis•ar•ma•ment (dĭs-är′mə-mənt) *n.* **1.** The act of laying down arms, esp. the reduction or abolition of a nation's military forces and armaments. **2.** The condition of being disarmed.

dis•arm•ing (dĭs-är′mĭng) *adj.* Tending to allay suspicion or hostility; winning favor. —**dis•arm′ing•ly** *adv.*

dis•ar•range (dĭs′ə-rānj′) *tr.v.* **-ranged, -rang•ing, -rang•es** To upset the proper order of. —**dis′ar•range′ment** *n.*

dis•ar•ray (dĭs′ə-rā′) *n.* **1.** A state of disorder; confusion. **2.** Disorderly dress. ❖ *tr.v.* **-rayed, -ray•ing, -rays 1.** To throw into confusion; upset. **2.** To undress.

dis•ar•tic•u•late (dĭs′är-tĭk′yə-lāt′) *v.* **-lat•ed, -lat•ing, -lates** —*tr.* To separate at the joints. —*intr.* To become disjointed. —**dis′ar•tic′u•la′tion** *n.* —**dis′ar•tic′u•la′tor** *n.*

dis•as•sem•ble (dĭs′ə-sĕm′bəl) *v.* **-bled, -bling, -bles** —*tr.* To take apart. —*intr.* **1.** To come apart. **2.** To break up in random fashion. —**dis′as•sem′bly** *n.*

dis•as•so•ci•ate (dĭs′ə-sō′shē-āt′, -sē-) *tr.v.* **-at•ed, -at•ing, -ates** To remove from association; dissociate. —**dis′as•so′ci•a′tion** *n.*

dis•as•ter (dĭ-zăs′tər, -săs′-) *n.* **1a.** An occurrence causing widespread destruction and distress; a catastrophe. **b.** A grave misfortune. **2.** *Informal* A total failure. **3.** *Obsolete* An evil influence of a star or planet. [Fr. *désastre* < Ital. *disastro* : *dis-*, pejorative pref. (< Lat. *dis-*; see DIS-) + *astro*, star (< Lat. *astrum* < Gk. *astron*; see **ster-** in App.).]

disaster area *n.* An area that officially qualifies for emergency governmental aid as a result of a catastrophe.

dis•as•trous (dĭ-zăs′trəs, -săs′-) *adj.* **1.** Accompanied by or causing distress or disaster; calamitous. **2.** Extremely bad; terrible. —**dis•as′trous•ly** *adv.* —**dis•as′trous•ness** *n.*

dis•a•vow (dĭs′ə-vou′) *tr.v.* **-vowed, -vow•ing, -vows** To disclaim knowledge of, responsibility for, or association with. [ME *disavowen* < OFr. *desavouer* : *des-*, dis- + *avouer*, to avow; see AVOW.] —**dis′a•vow′a•ble** *adj.* —**dis′a•vow′al** *n.*

dis•band (dĭs-bănd′) *v.* **-band•ed, -band•ing, -bands** —*tr.* To dissolve the organization of (a corporation, for example). —*intr.* **1.** To cease to function as an organization. **2.** To separate and move in different directions; disperse. [Obsolete Fr. *desbander*, to separate someone from a troop : *des-*, dis- + OFr. *band*, troop; see BAND².] —**dis•band′ment** *n.*

dis•bar (dĭs-bär′) *tr.v.* **-barred, -bar•ring, -bars** To expel (an attorney) from the practice of law by official action or procedure. —**dis•bar′ment** *n.*

dis•be•lief (dĭs′bĭ-lēf′) *n.* Refusal or reluctance to believe.

dis•be•lieve (dĭs′bĭ-lēv′) *v.* **-lieved, -liev•ing, -lieves** —*tr.* To refuse to believe in; reject. —*intr.* To withhold or reject belief. —**dis′be•liev′er** *n.* —**dis′be•liev′ing•ly** *adv.*

dis•branch (dĭs-brănch′) *tr.v.* **-branched, -branch•ing, -branch•es 1.** To cut or break a branch from (a tree). **2.** To remove (a limb or branch) from a tree.

dis•bud (dĭs-bŭd′) *tr.v.* **-bud•ded, -bud•ding, -buds 1.** To remove buds from (a plant) to promote better blooms or control its shape. **2a.** To prevent the growth of developing horns on (livestock). **b.** To remove such horns from (livestock).

dis•bur•den (dĭs-bûr′dn) *v.* **-dened, -den•ing, -dens** —*tr.* **1a.** To relieve (a pack animal, for example) of a burden. **b.** To free of a burden or trouble. **2.** To unload. —*intr.* To unload a burden. —**dis•bur′den•ment** *n.*

dis•bur•sal (dĭs-bûr′səl) *n.* Disbursement.

dis•burse (dĭs-bûrs′) *tr.v.* **-bursed, -burs•ing, -burs•es** To pay out; expend. See Syns at **spend.** [Obsolete Fr. *desbourser* < OFr. *desborser* : *des-*, dis- + *borse*, purse (< LLat. *bursa*; see BURSA).] —**dis•burs′a•ble** *adj.* —**dis•burs′er** *n.*

dis•burse•ment (dĭs-bûrs′mənt) *n.* **1.** The act or process of disbursing. **2.** Money paid out; expenditure.

disc (dĭsk) *n. & v.* Variant of **disk.**

disc. *abbr.* discount

disc– *pref.* Variant of **disco–.**

dis•calced (dĭs-kălst′) *adj.* Barefoot or wearing sandals. Used of certain religious orders. [< Lat. *discalceātus* : *dis-,* dis- + *calceātus,* shod (< *calceus,* shoe < *calx, calc-,* heel).]

dis•cant (dĭs′kănt′) *n.* Variant of **descant** 1. ❖ *v.* (dĭs′kănt′, dĭ-skănt′) Variant of **descant** 2.

dis•card (dĭs-kärd′) *v.* **-card•ed, -card•ing, -cards** —*tr.* **1.** To throw away; reject. **2a.** To throw out (a playing card) from a hand. **b.** To play (a card other than a trump) from a suit different from that of the card led. —*intr.* To discard a playing card. ❖ *n.* (dĭs′kärd′) **1a.** The act of discarding in a card game. **b.** A discarded playing card. **2.** One that is discarded. —**dis•card′a•ble** *adj.* —**dis•card′er** *n.*

dis•car•nate (dĭs-kär′nĭt, -nāt′) *adj.* Having no material body or form. [DIS– + (IN)CARNATE.] —**dis•car′nate** *n.*

disc brake also **disk brake** *n.* A brake in which the friction is caused by a set of pads that press against a rotating disk.

dis•cern (dĭ-sûrn′, -zûrn′) *v.* **-cerned, -cern•ing, -cerns** —*tr.* **1.** To perceive with the eyes or intellect; detect. **2.** To recognize or comprehend mentally. **3.** To perceive or recognize as distinct; distinguish. See Syns at **see**[1]. —*intr.* To perceive differences: *discern between right and wrong.* [ME *discernen* < OFr. *discerner* < Lat. *discernere,* to separate : *dis-,* apart; see DIS– + *cernere,* to perceive; see **krei-** in App.] —**dis•cern′er** *n.*

dis•cern•i•ble (dĭ-sûr′nə-bəl, -zûr′-) *adj.* Perceptible, as by vision or the intellect. See Syns at **perceptible.** —**dis•cern′i•bly** *adv.*

dis•cern•ing (dĭ-sûr′nĭng, -zûr′-) *adj.* Exhibiting keen insight and good judgment; perceptive. —**dis•cern′ing•ly** *adv.*

dis•cern•ment (dĭ-sûrn′mənt, -zûrn′-) *n.* **1.** The act or process of exhibiting keen insight and good judgment. **2.** Keenness of insight and judgment.

dis•charge (dĭs-chärj′) *v.* **-charged, -charg•ing, -charg•es** —*tr.* **1a.** To relieve of a burden or contents; unload. **b.** To unload or empty (contents). **2a.** To release, as from confinement or duty. **b.** To let go; empty out: *a train discharging commuters.* **c.** To pour forth; emit. **d.** To shoot. **3.** To remove from office or employment. **4.** To perform the obligations or demands of (an office, duty, or task). **5.** To comply with the terms of (a promise, for example). **6.** *Law* **a.** To acquit completely. **b.** To set aside; annul. **7.** To remove (color) from cloth, as by chemical bleaching. **8.** To cause the release of stored energy or electric charge from (a battery, for example). **9.** *Architecture* **a.** To apportion (weight) evenly, as over a door. **b.** To relieve (a part) of excess weight by distribution of pressure. **10.** To clear the record of the loan of (a returned library book). —*intr.* **1.** To get rid of a burden or weight. **2a.** To go off; fire: *The musket discharged loudly.* **b.** To pour forth, emit, or release contents. **c.** To become blurred, as a dye; run. **3.** To undergo the release of stored energy or electric charge. ❖ *n.* (dĭs′chärj′, dĭs-chärj′) **1.** The act of removing a load or burden. **2.** The act of shooting or firing a projectile or weapon. **3a.** A flowing out or pouring forth; emission; secretion. **b.** The amount or rate of emission or ejection. **c.** Something discharged, released, emitted, or excreted. **4.** The act or an instance of removing an obligation, burden, or responsibility. **5a.** Fulfillment of the terms of something, such as a debt. **b.** Performance, as of an office. **6a.** Dismissal or release from employment, service, care, or confinement. **b.** An official document certifying such release, esp. from military service. **7.** *Law* An annulment or acquittal; dismissal, as of a court order. **8.** *Electricity* **a.** Release of stored energy in a capacitor. **b.** Conversion of chemical energy to electric energy in a storage battery. **c.** A flow of electricity in a dielectric, esp. in a rarefied gas. **d.** Elimination of net electric charge from a charged body. [ME *dischargen* < OFr. *deschargier* < LLat. *discarricāre* : Lat. *dis-,* dis- + LLat. *carricāre,* to load; see CHARGE.] —**dis•charge′a•ble** *adj.* —**dis•charg•ee′** *n.* —**dis•charg′er** *n.*

discharge lamp *n.* A lamp that generates light by means of an internal electrical discharge between electrodes in a gas.

discharge tube *n.* A closed insulating vessel containing a gas at low pressure through which an electric current flows when sufficient voltage is applied to its electrodes.

disc harrow *n.* Variant of **disk harrow.**

disci– *pref.* Variant of **disco–.**

dis•ci•form (dĭs′ə-fôrm′, dĭs′kə-) *adj.* Flat and rounded in shape; discoid: *disciform fungi.*

dis•ci•ple (dĭ-sī′pəl) *n.* **1a.** One who assists in spreading the teachings of another. **b.** An active adherent, as of a movement. **2.** often **Disciple** One of the original followers of Jesus. **3. Disciple** A member of the Disciples of Christ. [ME < OE *discipul* and < OFr. *desciple,* both < Lat. *discipulus,* pupil < *discere,* to learn.] —**dis•ci′ple•ship′** *n.*

Dis•ci•ples of Christ (dĭ-sī′pəlz) *pl.n.* (*used with a sing. or pl. verb*) A Christian denomination founded in 1809 that accepts the Bible as the only rule of Christian faith and practice.

dis•ci•plin•a•ble (dĭs′ə-plĭn′ə-bəl, dĭs′ə-plīn′-) *adj.* **1.** Deserving of or subject to discipline. **2.** Easily taught.

dis•ci•pli•nar•i•an (dĭs′ə-plə-nâr′ē-ən) *n.* One that enforces or believes in strict discipline. ❖ *adj.* Disciplinary.

dis•ci•pli•nar•y (dĭs′ə-plə-nĕr′ē) *adj.* **1.** Of, relating to, or used for discipline: *disciplinary measures.* **2.** Of or relating to a specific field of academic study. —**dis′ci•pli•nar′i•ly** (-nâr′ə-lē) *adv.* —**dis′ci•pli•nar′i•ty** (-nâr′ĭ-tē, -nâr′-) *n.*

dis•ci•pline (dĭs′ə-plĭn) *n.* **1.** Training expected to produce a specific character or pattern of behavior, esp. training that produces moral or mental improvement. **2.** Controlled behavior resulting from disciplinary training; self-control. **3a.** Control obtained by enforcing compliance or order. **b.** A systematic method to obtain obedience. **c.** Order based on submission to authority. **4.** Punishment to correct or train. **5.** A set of rules or methods, as those regulating the practice of a church or monastic order. **6.** A branch of knowledge or teaching. ❖ *tr.v.* **-plined, -plin•ing, -plines** **1.** To train by instruction and practice, esp. to teach self-control to. **2.** To teach to accept authority. **3.** To punish to gain control or enforce obedience. **4.** To impose order on. [ME < OFr. *descepline* < Lat. *disciplīna* < *discipulus,* pupil. See DISCIPLE.] —**dis′ci•pli•nal** (-plə-nəl) *adj.* —**dis′ci•plin′er** *n.*

dis•ci•plined (dĭs′ə-plĭnd) *adj.* Possessing or indicative of discipline.

disc jockey also **disk jockey** *n.* An announcer who presents popular recorded music, esp. on the radio; a DJ.

dis•claim (dĭs-klām′) *v.* **-claimed, -claim•ing, -claims** —*tr.* **1.** To deny or renounce claim to or connection with; disown. **2.** To deny the validity of; repudiate. **3.** *Law* To renounce one's right or claim to. —*intr.* *Law* To renounce a right or claim. [ME *disclaimen* < AN *desclaimer* : *des-,* dis- + *claimer,* to claim (< Lat. *clāmāre,* to cry out; see CLAIM).]

dis•claim•er (dĭs-klā′mər) *n.* **1.** A repudiation or denial of responsibility or connection. **2.** *Law* A renunciation of one's right or claim. [ME, denial of a feudal claim < AN *desclaimer,* to disclaim, denial of a feudal claim. See DISCLAIM.]

dis•cla•ma•tion (dĭs′klə-mā′shən) *n.* The act or an instance of disavowing; renunciation. [Med.Lat. *disclāmātiō, disclāmātiōn-,* to disclaim < *disclāmātus,* p. part. of *disclāmāre,* to disclaim, prob. < AN *desclaimer, disclamer.* See DISCLAIM.]

dis•cli•max (dĭs-klī′măks′) *n. Ecology* A climax community disturbed by various influences, esp. by humans and domestic animals.

dis•close (dĭ-sklōz′) *tr.v.* **-closed, -clos•ing, -clos•es** **1.** To expose to view, as by removing a cover. **2.** To make known (something secret). [ME *disclosen* < OFr. *desclore, desclos-* : *des-,* dis- + *clore,* to close (< Lat. *claudere*).] —**dis•clos′a•ble** *adj.* —**dis•clos′er** *n.*

dis•clos•ing agent (dĭ-sklō′zĭng) *n.* A dye used in dentistry to reveal the presence of dental plaque.

dis•clo•sure (dĭ-sklō′zhər) *n.* **1.** The act or process of revealing or uncovering. **2.** Something uncovered; a revelation.

dis•co (dĭs′kō) *n., pl.* **-cos** **1.** A discotheque. **2a.** *Music* Popular dance music, esp. of the late 1970s, characterized by strong repetitive bass rhythms. **b.** A style of dancing usu. done to disco music. [Short for DISCOTHEQUE.] —**dis′co** *adj. & v.*

disco– or **disc–** also **disci–** *pref.* **1.** Disk: *discoid.* **2.** Phonograph record: *discophile.* [Lat. < Gk. *disko-* < *diskos,* disk. See DISK.]

dis•cog•ra•phy (dĭ-skŏg′rə-fē) *n., pl.* **-phies** **1.** The study and cataloging of phonograph records. **2.** A comprehensive list of the recordings made by a performer or of a composer's works. —**dis•cog′ra•pher** *n.* —**dis′co•graph′i•cal** (dĭs′kə-grăf′ĭ-kəl), **dis′co•graph′ic** (-grăf′ĭk) *adj.*

dis•coid (dĭs′koid′) also **dis•coi•dal** (dĭ-skoid′l) *adj.* **1.** Disk-shaped. **2.** Relating to or having a disk. **3.** *Botany* Having disk flowers only. Used of a composite flower head. —**dis′coid′** *n.*

dis•col•or (dĭs-kŭl′ər) *v.* **-ored, -or•ing, -ors** —*tr.* To alter or spoil the color of; stain. —*intr.* To become altered or spoiled in color. [ME *discolouren* < OFr. *discolerer* : *des-,* dis- + *colourer,* to color (< Lat. *colōrāre* < *color,* color; see COLOR).]

dis•col•or•a•tion (dĭs-kŭl′ə-rā′shən) *n.* **1a.** The act of discoloring. **b.** The condition of being discolored. **2.** A discolored spot, smudge, or area; a stain.

dis•com•bob•u•late (dĭs′kəm-bŏb′yə-lāt′) *tr.v.* **-lat•ed, -lat•ing, -lates** To throw into confusion. See Syns at **confuse.** [Perh. mock-Latin alteration of DISCOMPOSE.] —**dis′com•bob′u•la′tion** *n.*

dis•com•fit (dĭs-kŭm′fĭt) *tr.v.* **-fit•ed, -fit•ing, -fits** **1.** To make uneasy or perplexed; disconcert. **2.** To thwart the plans of; frustrate. **3.** *Archaic* To defeat in battle. ❖ *n.* Discomfiture. [ME *discomfiten* < OFr. *desconfit,* p. part. of *desconfire, descumfire,* to defeat : *des-,* dis- + *confire,* to make (< Lat. *cōnficere,* to prepare; see COMFIT).]

USAGE NOTE *Discomfit* originally meant "to defeat, frustrate," and its newer meaning "to embarrass, disconcert," probably arose in part through confusion with *discomfort.* But the newer sense is now the most common and should be considered standard.

dis•com•fi•ture (dĭs-kŭm′fĭ-chŏŏr′, -chər) *n.* **1.** Frustration or disappointment. **2.** Lack of ease; perplexity and embarrassment. **3.** *Archaic* Defeat.

dis•com•fort (dĭs-kŭm′fərt) *n.* **1.** Mental or bodily distress. **2.** Something that disturbs one's comfort; an annoyance. ❖ *tr.v.* **-fort•ed, -fort•ing, -forts** To make uncomfortable; distress. See Usage Note at **discomfit.** [ME < OFr. *desconfort < desconforter,* to discourage : *des-*, *dis-* + *conforter*, to strengthen; see COMFORT.] —**dis·com′fort·a·ble** (-kŭm′fər-tə-bəl, -kŭmf′tə-bəl) *adj.* —**dis·com′fort·ing·ly** *adv.*

dis·com·mend (dĭs′kə-mĕnd′) *tr.v.* -**mend·ed**, -**mend·ing**, -**mends** 1. To show or voice disapproval of. 2. To cause to come into disfavor or ill regard. —**dis′com·mend′a·ble** *adj.*

dis·com·mode (dĭs′kə-mōd′) *tr.v.* -**mod·ed**, -**mod·ing**, -**modes** To put to inconvenience; trouble. [DIS- + *commode*, to suit (< Lat. *commodāre* < *commodus*, convenient; see COMMODIOUS).]

dis·com·pose (dĭs′kəm-pōz′) *tr.v.* -**posed**, -**pos·ing**, -**pos·es** 1. To disturb the composure or calm of; perturb. 2. To disorder. —**dis′com·pos′ed·ly** (-pō′zĭd-lē) *adv.* —**dis′com·pos′ing·ly** *adv.* —**dis′com·po′sure** (-pō′zhər) *n.*

dis·con·cert (dĭs′kən-sûrt′) *tr.v.* -**cert·ed**, -**cert·ing**, -**certs** 1. To upset the self-possession of; ruffle. 2. To frustrate (plans, for example) by throwing into disorder; disarrange. [Obsolete Fr. *disconcerter* < OFr. *desconcerter* : *des-*, *dis-* + *concerter*, to bring into agreement (< OItal. *concertare*; see CONCERT).] —**dis′con·cert′ing·ly** *adv.*

dis·con·form·i·ty (dĭs′kən-fôr′mĭ-tē) *n.*, *pl.* -**ties** 1. *Geology* A type of unconformity in which the rock layers are parallel. 2. Refusal or failure to conform; nonconformity.

dis·con·nect (dĭs′kə-nĕkt′) *v.* -**nect·ed**, -**nect·ing**, -**nects** —*tr.* 1. To interrupt the connection of or between: *disconnected the hose.* 2. *Electricity* To shut off the current in (an appliance) by removing its connection to a power source. —*intr.* To interrupt a connection. ❖ *n.* (dĭs′kə-nĕkt′) A lack of connection; a disparity. —**dis′con·nec′tion** *n.*

dis·con·nect·ed (dĭs′kə-nĕk′tĭd) *adj.* 1. Not connected; separate. 2. Marked by unrelated parts; incoherent. —**dis′con·nect′ed·ly** *adv.* —**dis′con·nect′ed·ness** *n.*

dis·con·so·late (dĭs-kŏn′sə-lĭt) *adj.* 1. Seeming beyond consolation; extremely dejected. 2. Cheerless; gloomy. [ME < Med.Lat. *disconsōlātus* : Lat. *dis-*, *dis-* + *cōnsōlātus*, p. part. of *cōnsōlārī*, to console; see CONSOLE[1].] —**dis·con′so·late·ly** *adv.* —**dis·con′so·late·ness**, **dis·con′so·la′tion** (-kŏn′sə-lā′shən) *n.*

dis·con·tent (dĭs′kən-tĕnt′) *n.* 1a. Absence of contentment; dissatisfaction. b. A restless longing for better circumstances. 2. One who is discontented. ❖ *adj.* Discontented. ❖ *tr.v.* -**tent·ed**, -**tent·ing**, -**tents** To make discontented. —**dis′con·tent′ment** *n.*

dis·con·tent·ed (dĭs′kən-tĕn′tĭd) *adj.* Restlessly unhappy. —**dis′con·tent′ed·ly** *adv.* —**dis′con·tent′ed·ness** *n.*

dis·con·tin·u·ance (dĭs′kən-tĭn′yōō-əns) *n.* The act or an instance of discontinuing or the condition of being discontinued; cessation.

dis·con·tin·u·a·tion (dĭs′kən-tĭn′yōō-ā′shən) *n.* A cessation; a discontinuance.

dis·con·tin·ue (dĭs′kən-tĭn′yōō) *v.* -**ued**, -**u·ing**, -**ues** —*tr.* 1. To stop doing or providing (something): *discontinued the ferry service.* 2. To cease making or manufacturing. —*intr.* To come to an end. See Syns at **stop**. [ME *discontinuen* < OFr. *descontinuer* < Med.Lat. *discontinuāre* : Lat. *dis-*, *dis-* + Lat. *continuāre*, to continue; see CONTINUE.]

dis·con·ti·nu·i·ty (dĭs-kŏn′tə-nōō′ĭ-tē, -nyōō′-) *n.*, *pl.* -**ties** 1. Lack of continuity, logical sequence, or cohesion. 2. A break or gap. 3. *Geology* A surface at which seismic wave velocities change. 4. *Mathematics* a. A point at which a function is defined but is not continuous. b. A point at which a function is undefined.

dis·con·tin·u·ous (dĭs′kən-tĭn′yōō-əs) *adj.* 1a. Marked by interruptions; intermittent. b. Consisting of distinct or unconnected elements. c. Being without sequential order or coherent form. 2. *Mathematics* Possessing one or more discontinuities. —**dis′con·tin′u·ous·ly** *adv.* —**dis′con·tin′u·ous·ness** *n.*

dis·co·phile (dĭs′kə-fīl′) *n.* A collector of or specialist in phonograph records.

dis·cord (dĭs′kôrd′) *n.* 1a. Lack of agreement. b. Tension or strife resulting from a lack of agreement; dissension. 2. A confused or harsh sound or mingling of sounds. 3. *Music* An inharmonious combination of simultaneously sounded tones; a dissonance. ❖ *intr.v.* (dĭ-skôrd′, dĭs′kôrd′) -**cord·ed**, -**cord·ing**, -**cords** To fail to agree or harmonize; clash. [ME < OFr. *descorde* < Lat. *discordia* < *discors*, disagreeing : *dis-*, apart; see DIS- + *cor*, *cord-*, heart; see **kerd-** in App.]

dis·cor·dance (dĭ-skôr′dns) *n.* 1. The state or an instance of disagreement; discord. 2. *Genetics* The presence of a given genetic trait in only one member of a pair of identical twins.

dis·cor·dant (dĭ-skôr′dnt) *adj.* 1. Not being in accord; conflicting. 2. Disagreeable in sound; harsh or dissonant. —**dis·cor′dan·cy** *n.* —**dis·cor′dant·ly** *adv.*

Dis·cor·di·a (dĭ-skôr′dē-ə) *n. Roman Mythology* The goddess of strife. [Lat. < *discordia*, discord. See DISCORD.]

dis·co·theque also **dis·co·thèque** (dĭs′kə-tĕk′, dĭs′kə-tĕk′) *n.* A nightclub that features dance music, often showy decor, and elaborate lighting. [Fr. < Ital. *discoteca*, record library : *disco*, disk, record (< Lat. *discus*, quoit; see DISCUS) + *biblioteca*, library (< Lat. *bibliothēca*; see BIBLIOTHECA).]

dis·count (dĭs′kount′, dĭs-kount′) *v.* -**count·ed**, -**count·ing**, -**counts** —*tr.* 1. To subtract from a cost or price. 2a. To purchase or sell (a commercial paper) at a reduction equal to the amount of interest that will accumulate before it matures. b. To lend money on (a commercial paper not immediately payable) after deducting the interest. 3a. To sell at a reduced price. b. To reduce in quantity or value. 4a. To leave out of account as untrustworthy; disregard. b. To underestimate the significance of; minimize. c. To regard with doubt. 5. To anticipate and make allowance for; reckon with in advance. —*intr.* To lend money after deduction of interest. ❖ *n.* (dĭs′kount′) 1. A reduction from the full or standard amount of a price or debt. 2. The discount rate on a commercial paper. 3. The act or an instance of discounting a commercial paper. [Alteration (influenced by DIS- and COUNT[1]) of Fr. *décompter* < OFr. *desconter* : *des-*, away; see DIS- + *conter*, to count; see COUNT[1].] —**dis′count′a·ble** *adj.*

dis·coun·te·nance (dĭs-koun′tə-nəns) *tr.v.* -**nanced**, -**nanc·ing**, -**nanc·es** 1. To view or treat with disfavor. 2. To put out of countenance; disconcert. ❖ *n.* Disfavor.

dis·count·er (dĭs-koun′tər) *n.* One that discounts, as a person who runs a discount business.

discount rate *n.* 1. The interest deducted in advance on a commercial paper. 2. The interest rate charged by a central bank on loans to its member banks.

dis·cour·age (dĭ-skûr′ĭj, -skûr′-) *tr.v.* -**aged**, -**ag·ing**, -**ag·es** 1. To deprive of confidence, hope, or spirit. 2. To hamper by discouraging; deter. 3. To try to prevent by expressing disapproval or raising objections. [ME *discoragen* < OFr. *descoragier* : *des-*, *dis-* + *corage*, courage; see COURAGE.] —**dis·cour′age·a·ble** *adj.* —**dis·cour′ag·er** *n.* —**dis·cour′ag·ing·ly** *adv.*

dis·cour·age·ment (dĭ-skûr′ĭj-mənt, -skûr′-) *n.* 1a. The act of discouraging. b. The condition of being discouraged. 2. Something that discourages.

dis·course (dĭs′kôrs′, -kōrs′) *n.* 1. Verbal expression in speech or writing. 2. Conversation. 3. A formal written or spoken discussion of a subject. 4. *Archaic* The process or power of reasoning. ❖ *v.* (dĭ-skôrs′, -skōrs′) -**coursed**, -**cours·ing**, -**cours·es** —*intr.* 1. To speak or write formally and at length. 2. To engage in conversation or discussion; converse. —*tr.* *Archaic* To narrate or discuss. [ME *discours*, process of reasoning < Med.Lat. *discursus* < Lat., a running about < p. part. of *discurrere*, to run about : *dis-*, apart; see DIS- + *currere*, to run.] —**dis′cours′er** *n.*

dis·cour·te·ous (dĭs-kûr′tē-əs) *adj.* Exhibiting no courtesy. —**dis·cour′te·ous·ly** *adv.* —**dis·cour′te·ous·ness** *n.*

dis·cour·te·sy (dĭs-kûr′tĭ-sē) *n.*, *pl.* -**sies** 1. Lack of courtesy; rudeness. 2. A rude act or statement.

dis·cov·er (dĭ-skŭv′ər) *tr.v.* -**ered**, -**er·ing**, -**ers** 1. To notice or learn: *discovered that the painting was missing.* 2. To be the first, or the first of one's group or kind, to find, learn of, or observe. b. To learn about for the first time in one's experience: *discovered a new restaurant.* 3. To learn something about: *discovered the painting to be a fake.* 4. To identify (a person) as a potentially prominent performer. 5. *Archaic* To reveal or expose. [ME *discoveren*, to reveal < OFr. *descovrir* < LLat. *discooperīre* : Lat. *dis-* + *cooperīre*, to cover; see COVER.] —**dis·cov′er·a·ble** *adj.* —**dis·cov′er·er** *n.*

SYNONYMS *discover, ascertain, determine, learn* These verbs mean to gain knowledge or awareness of something not known before: *discovered a distant star; ascertaining the facts; tried to determine his origins; learned my name.*

dis·cov·er·y (dĭ-skŭv′ə-rē) *n.*, *pl.* -**ies** 1. The act or an instance of discovering. 2. Something discovered. 3. *Law* The compulsory disclosure of pertinent facts or documents to the opposing party in a civil action, usu. before a trial begins.

dis·cred·it (dĭs-krĕd′ĭt) *tr.v.* -**it·ed**, -**it·ing**, -**its** 1. To damage in reputation; disgrace. 2. To cause to be doubted or distrusted. 3. To refuse to believe. ❖ *n.* 1. Damage to one's reputation. 2. Lack of trust or belief; doubt. 3. Something damaging to one's reputation or stature.

dis·cred·it·a·ble (dĭs-krĕd′ĭ-tə-bəl) *adj.* Harmful to one's reputation; blameworthy. —**dis·cred′it·a·bly** *adv.*

dis·creet (dĭ-skrēt′) *adj.* 1. Showing prudence and self-restraint; circumspect. 2. Free from ostentation; modest. [ME < OFr. *discret* < Med.Lat. *discrētus* < Lat., p. part. of *discernere*, separate, to discern. See DISCERN.] —**dis·creet′ly** *adv.* —**dis·creet′ness** *n.*

dis·crep·ance (dĭ-skrĕp′əns) *n.* Discrepancy.

dis·crep·an·cy (dĭ-skrĕp′ən-sē) *n.*, *pl.* -**cies** 1. Divergence or disagreement, as between facts or claims; difference. 2. An instance of discrepancy. See Syns at **difference**.

dis·crep·ant (dĭ-skrĕp′ənt) *adj.* Marked by discrepancy; disagreeing. [ME *discrepaunt* < Lat. *discrepāns*, *discrepant-*, pr. part. of *discrepāre*, to disagree : *dis-*, apart; see DIS- + *crepāre*, to rattle.] —**dis·crep′ant·ly** *adv.*

dis·crete (dĭ-skrēt′) *adj.* 1. Constituting a separate thing. 2. Consisting of unconnected distinct parts. 3. *Mathematics* Defined for a finite or countable set of values; not continuous. [ME < OFr. < Lat. *discrētus*, p. part. of *discernere*, to separate. See DISCREET.] —**dis·crete′ly** *adv.* —**dis·crete′ness** *n.*

discrete variable *n.* A variable that assumes only values in a discrete set, such as the integers.

dis·cre·tion (dĭ-skrĕsh′ən) *n.* 1. The quality of being discreet; circumspection. See Syns at **prudence**. 2. The ability or power to decide responsibly. 3. The freedom to act or judge on one's own.

—**dis·cre′tion·al** *adj.* —**dis·cre′tion·al·ly** *adv.*

dis·cre·tion·ar·y (dĭ-skrĕsh′ə-nĕr′ē) *adj.* **1.** Left to or regulated by one's own discretion or judgment. **2.** Available for use as needed or desired: *a discretionary fund.* —**dis·cre′tion·ar·i·ly** (-när′ə-lē) *adv.*

discretionary account *n.* A stock or commodity account in which an agent is free to trade without first consulting.

dis·cret·i·za·tion (dĭ-skrē′tĭ-zā′shən) *n.* The act of making mathematically discrete.

dis·crim·i·na·bil·i·ty (dĭ-skrĭm′ə-nə-bĭl′ĭ-tē) *n.* **1.** The quality of being discriminable. **2.** The capacity or power to discriminate.

dis·crim·i·na·ble (dĭs-krĭm′ə-nə-bəl) *adj.* That can be discriminated; distinguishable. —**dis·crim′i·na·bly** *adv.*

dis·crim·i·nant (dĭ-skrĭm′ə-nənt) *n.* An expression used to distinguish or separate other expressions in a quantity or equation.

discriminant function *n. Statistics* A function of a set of variables used to classify an object or event.

dis·crim·i·nate (dĭ-skrĭm′ə-nāt′) *v.* **-nat·ed, -nat·ing, -nates** —*intr.* **1a.** To make a clear distinction; distinguish. **b.** To make sensible decisions; judge wisely. **2.** To distinguish by class or category without regard to individual merit; show preference or prejudice. —*tr.* **1.** To perceive the distinguishing features of; recognize as distinct. **2.** To distinguish by noting differences; differentiate. [Lat. *discrīmināre, discrīmināt-* < *discrīmen, discrīmin-,* distinction. See **krei-** in App.] —**dis·crim′i·nate** (-nĭt) *adj.* —**dis·crim′i·nate·ly** *adv.*

dis·crim·i·nat·ing (dĭ-skrĭm′ə-nā′tĭng) *adj.* **1a.** Able to recognize or draw fine distinctions; perceptive. **b.** Showing careful judgment or fine taste. **2.** Separating into distinct parts; analytical. **3.** Serving to distinguish; distinctive. **4.** Showing bias; discriminatory. —**dis·crim′i·nat′ing·ly** *adv.*

dis·crim·i·na·tion (dĭ-skrĭm′ə-nā′shən) *n.* **1.** The act of discriminating. **2.** The ability or power to see or make fine distinctions; discernment. **3.** Treatment or consideration based on class or category rather than individual merit; partiality or prejudice. —**dis·crim′i·na′tion·al** *adj.*

dis·crim·i·na·tive (dĭ-skrĭm′ə-nā′tĭv, -nə-tĭv) *adj.* **1.** Drawing distinctions. **2.** Showing prejudice. —**dis·crim′i·na′tive·ly** *adv.*

dis·crim·i·na·tor (dĭ-skrĭm′ə-nā′tər) *n.* **1.** One that discriminates. **2.** *Electronics* A device that converts a property of an input signal, such as frequency or phase, into an amplitude variation.

dis·crim·i·na·to·ry (dĭ-skrĭm′ə-nə-tôr′ē, -tōr′ē) *adj.* **1.** Marked by or showing prejudice; biased. **2.** Making distinctions. —**dis·crim′i·na·to′ri·ly** *adv.*

dis·cur·sive (dĭ-skûr′sĭv) *adj.* **1.** Covering a wide field of subjects; rambling. **2.** Proceeding to a conclusion through reason. [Med.Lat. *discursīvus* < Lat. *discursus,* running about. See **DISCOURSE.**] —**dis·cur′sive·ly** *adv.* —**dis·cur′sive·ness** *n.*

dis·cus (dĭs′kəs) *n., pl.* **-cus·es 1.** *Sports* **a.** A disk, typically wooden or plastic with a metal rim, thrown for distance in athletic competitions. **b.** A track-and-field event in which a discus is thrown. **2.** A small, brilliantly colored South American freshwater fish (*Symphysodon discus*) having a disk-shaped body. **3.** Something resembling a flat circular plate; a disk. **4.** *Botany* See **disk 5.** [Lat. See **DISK.**]

dis·cuss (dĭ-skŭs′) *tr.v.* **-cussed, -cuss·ing, -cuss·es 1.** To speak with another or others about. **2.** To consider (a subject) in speech or writing. [ME *discussen* < AN *discusser* < Lat. *discussus,* p. part. of *discutere,* to break up : *dis-,* apart; see **DIS-** + *quatere,* to shake.] —**dis·cuss′a·ble, dis·cuss′i·ble** *adj.* —**dis·cuss′er** *n.*

dis·cus·sant (dĭ-skŭs′ənt) *n.* A participant in a formal discussion.

dis·cus·sion (dĭ-skŭsh′ən) *n.* **1.** Consideration of a subject by a group; an earnest conversation. **2.** A formal discourse on a topic; an exposition.

dis·dain (dĭs-dān′) *tr.v.* **-dained, -dain·ing, -dains 1.** To regard or treat with haughty contempt; despise. See Syns at **despise. 2.** To consider or reject as beneath oneself. ❖ *n.* A feeling or show of contempt and aloofness; scorn. [ME *disdeinen* < OFr. *desdeignier* < VLat. **disdignāre* < Lat. *dēdignārī : dē-,* de- + *dignārī,* to deem worthy (< *dignus,* worthy; see **dek-** in App.).]

dis·dain·ful (dĭs-dān′fəl) *adj.* Showing disdain. See Syns at **proud.** —**dis·dain′ful·ly** *adv.* —**dis·dain′ful·ness** *n.*

dis·ease (dĭ-zēz′) *n.* **1.** A pathological condition in an organism resulting from infection or genetic defect, for example, and characterized by identifiable symptoms. **2.** A condition or tendency, as of society, regarded as abnormal and harmful. **3.** *Obsolete* Lack of ease; trouble. [ME *disese* < OFr. : *des-,* dis- + *aise,* ease; see **EASE.**] —**dis·eased′** *adj.*

dis·em·bark (dĭs′ĕm-bärk′) *v.* **-barked, -bark·ing, -barks** —*intr.* **1.** To go ashore from a ship. **2.** To leave a vehicle or aircraft. —*tr.* To take ashore from a ship. [Prob. obsolete Fr. *desembarquer* < Fr. : *des-,* dis- + *embarquer,* to embark; see **EMBARK.**] —**dis·em′bar·ka′tion** *n.*

dis·em·bar·rass (dĭs′ĕm-băr′əs) *tr.v.* **-rassed, -rass·ing, -rass·es** To free from something bothersome or encumbering; relieve. —**dis·em′bar′rass·ment** *n.*

dis·em·bod·y (dĭs′ĕm-bŏd′ē) *tr.v.* **-ied, -y·ing, -ies 1.** To free (the soul or spirit) from the body. **2.** To divest of material existence or substance. —**dis·em·bod′i·ment** *n.*

dis·em·bogue (dĭs′ĕm-bōg′) *v.* **-bogued, -bogu·ing, -bogues** —*intr.* To flow out or empty, as water from a channel. —*tr.* To discharge or pour forth (water, for example). [< Sp. *desemboque,* mouth of a river < *desembocar,* to flow out : *des-,* reversal (< Lat. *dis-;* see **DIS-**) + *embocar,* to put into the mouth (*en-,* in < Lat. *in-;* see **IN-²** + *boca,* mouth < Lat. *bucca,* cheek).] —**dis·em·bogue′ment** *n.*

dis·em·bow·el (dĭs′ĕm-bou′əl) *tr.v.* **-eled, -el·ing, -els** or **-elled, -el·ling, -els 1.** To remove the entrails from. **2.** To deprive of meaning or substance. —**dis·em·bow′el·ment** *n.*

dis·em·ploy (dĭs′ĕm-ploi′) *tr.v.* **-ployed, -ploy·ing, -ploys** To deprive of employment. —**dis·em·ploy′ment** *n.*

dis·em·pow·er (dĭs′ĕm-pou′ər) *tr.v.* **-ered, -er·ing, -ers** To deprive of power or influence. —**dis·em·pow′er·ment** *n.*

dis·en·a·ble (dĭs′ĕ-nā′bəl) *tr.v.* **-bled, -bling, -bles** To make unable or incapable; prevent.

dis·en·chant (dĭs′ĕn-chănt′) *tr.v.* **-chant·ed, -chant·ing, -chants** To free from illusion or false belief; undeceive. [Obsolete Fr. *desenchanter* < OFr., to break a spell : *des-,* dis- + *enchanter,* to enchant; see **ENCHANT.**] —**dis·en·chant′er** *n.* —**dis·en·chant′ing·ly** *adv.* —**dis·en·chant′ment** *n.*

dis·en·cum·ber (dĭs′ĕn-kŭm′bər) *tr.v.* **-bered, -ber·ing, -bers** To relieve of burdens or hardships. [Obsolete Fr. *desencombrer* < OFr. : *des-,* dis- + *encombrer,* to encumber; see **ENCUMBER.**] —**dis·en·cum′ber·ment** *n.*

dis·en·fran·chise (dĭs′ĕn-frăn′chīz′) *tr.v.* **-chised, -chis·ing, -chis·es** To disfranchise. —**dis·en·fran′chise′ment** (-chīz′mənt, -chĭz-) *n.*

dis·en·gage (dĭs′ĕn-gāj′) *v.* **-gaged, -gag·ing, -gag·es** —*tr.* **1.** To release from something that holds fast, connects, or entangles. **2.** To release (oneself) from an engagement or obligation. —*intr.* To free or detach oneself; withdraw. —**dis·en·gage′ment** *n.*

dis·en·tail (dĭs′ĕn-tāl′) *tr.v.* **-tailed, -tail·ing, -tails** *Law* To release (an estate) from entail. —**dis·en·tail′ment** *n.*

dis·en·tan·gle (dĭs′ĕn-tăng′gəl) *v.* **-gled, -gling, -gles** —*tr.* **1.** To extricate from entanglement; free. **2.** To clear up (a plot, for example); unravel. —*intr.* To become free of entanglement. —**dis·en·tan′gle·ment** *n.*

dis·en·thrall (dĭs′ĕn-thrôl′) *tr.v.* **-thralled, -thrall·ing, -thralls** To free from a controlling force or influence.

dis·e·quil·i·brate (dĭs′ĭ-kwĭl′ə-brāt′) *tr.v.* **-brat·ed, -brat·ing, -brates** To upset the equilibrium of (the economy, for example); unbalance. —**dis·e·quil′i·bra′tion** *n.*

dis·e·qui·lib·ri·um (dĭs′ē-ē′kwə-lĭb′rē-əm, -ĕk′wə-) *n.* Loss or lack of stability or equilibrium.

dis·es·tab·lish (dĭs′ĭ-stăb′lĭsh) *tr.v.* **-lished, -lish·ing, -lish·es 1.** To alter the status of (something established by authority or general acceptance). **2.** To deprive (a church) of official governmental support. —**dis·es·tab′lish·ment** *n.*

dis·es·tab·lish·men·tar·i·an or **Dis·es·tab·lish·men·tar·i·an** (dĭs′ĭ-stăb′lĭsh-mən-târ′ē-ən) *n.* An opponent of an established order, esp. one who opposes state support of an established church. —**dis·es·tab′lish·men·tar′i·an** *adj.* —**dis·es·tab′lish·men·tar′i·an·ism** *n.*

dis·es·teem (dĭs′ĭ-stēm′) *tr.v.* **-teemed, -teem·ing, -teems** To hold in disfavor. ❖ *n.* Lack of esteem; disfavor.

di·seur (dē-zûr′, -zœr′) *n.* A man who is a skilled and usu. professional performer of monologues. [Fr. < OFr. < *dire, dis-,* to say < Lat. *dīcere.* See **DICTION.**]

di·seuse (dē-zœz′, də-) *n.* A woman who is a skilled and usu. professional performer of monologues. [Fr., fem. of *diseur.* See **DISEUR.**]

dis·fa·vor (dĭs-fā′vər) *n.* **1.** Unfavorable opinion or regard; disapproval. **2.** The condition of being so regarded. ❖ *tr.v.* **-vored, -vor·ing, -vors** To view or treat with disfavor.

dis·fea·ture (dĭs-fē′chər) *tr.v.* **-tured, -tur·ing, -tures** To disfigure: *disfeatured by a scar.* —**dis·fea′ture·ment** *n.*

dis·fig·ure (dĭs-fĭg′yər) *tr.v.* **-ured, -ur·ing, -ures** To spoil the appearance or shape of; deform. [ME *disfiguren* < OFr. *desfigurer : des-,* dis- + *figure,* figure (< Lat. *figūra,* shape; see **dheigh-** in App.).] —**dis·fig′u·ra′tion, dis·fig′ure·ment** *n.* —**dis·fig′ur·er** *n.*

dis·fran·chise (dĭs-frăn′chīz′) *tr.v.* **-chised, -chis·ing, -chis·es 1.** To deprive of a privilege, immunity, or right of citizenship, esp. the right to vote; disenfranchise. **2.** To deprive (a corporation, for example) of a privilege or franchise. —**dis·fran′chise′ment** (-chīz′mənt, -chĭz-) *n.* —**dis·fran′chis·er** *n.*

dis·frock (dĭs-frŏk′) *tr.v.* **-frocked, -frock·ing, -frocks** To defrock.

dis·func·tion (dĭs-fŭngk′shən) *n.* Variant of **dysfunction.**

dis·gorge (dĭs-gôrj′) *v.* **-gorged, -gorg·ing, -gorg·es** —*tr.* **1.** To vomit from the throat or stomach. **2.** To discharge violently; spew. **3.** To surrender (stolen money, for example) unwillingly. —*intr.* To discharge or pour forth contents. [ME *disgorgen* < OFr. *desgorger : des-,* dis- + *gorger,* to pack (< *gorge,* throat; see **GORGE.**] —**dis·gorge′ment** *n.*

dis·grace (dĭs-grās′) *n.* **1.** Loss of honor or reputation; shame. **2.** The condition of being strongly and generally disapproved of. **3.** One that brings disfavor or discredit. ❖ *tr.v.* **-graced, -grac·ing, -grac·es 1.** To bring shame or dishonor on. **2.** To deprive of

discus

favor or good repute; treat with disfavor. [Fr. *disgrâce* < Ital. *disgrazia* : *dis-*, not (< Lat.; see DIS–) + *grazia*, favor (< Lat. *grātia* < *grātus*, pleasing).] —**dis•grac′er** *n.*

dis•grace•ful (dĭs-grās′fəl) *adj.* Bringing or warranting disgrace. —**dis•grace′ful•ly** *adv.* —**dis•grace′ful•ness** *n.*

dis•grun•tle (dĭs-grŭn′tl) *tr.v.* **-tled, -tling, -tles** To discontent. [DIS- + *gruntle*, to grumble (< ME *gruntelen*, freq. of *grunten*, to grunt; see GRUNT).] —**dis•grun′tle•ment** *n.*

dis•guise (dĭs-gīz′) *tr.v.* **-guised, -guis•ing, -guis•es 1a.** To modify the manner or appearance of to prevent recognition. **b.** To furnish with a disguise. **2.** To conceal or obscure by dissemblance; misrepresent. ❖ *n.* **1a.** The act or an instance of disguising. **b.** The condition of being disguised. **2.** Clothes or accessories concealing one's identity. **3a.** Appearance that misrepresents the character of something. **b.** A pretense or misrepresentation. [ME *disguisen* < OFr. *desguiser* : *des-*, dis- + *guise*, manner; see GUISE.] —**dis•guis′ed•ly** (-gī′zĭd-lē) *adv.* —**dis•guise′ment** *n.* —**dis•guis′er** *n.*

dis•gust (dĭs-gŭst′) *tr.v.* **-gust•ed, -gust•ing, -gusts 1.** To excite nausea or loathing in; sicken. **2.** To offend the taste or moral sense of; repel. ❖ *n.* Profound repugnance excited by something offensive. [Late OFr. *desgouster*, to lose one's appetite : *des-*, dis- + *gouster*, to eat, taste (< Lat. *gustāre*; see **geus-** in App.).]

SYNONYMS *disgust, nauseate, repel, revolt, sicken* These verbs mean to offend the senses or feelings of: *a stench that disgusted us; hypocrisy that nauseated me; repelled by arrogance; brutality that revolts my sensibilities; a fetid odor that sickened the workers.*

dis•gust•ed (dĭs-gŭs′tĭd) *adj.* Filled with disgust or irritated impatience. —**dis•gust′ed•ly** *adv.*

dis•gust•ful (dĭs-gŭst′fəl) *adj.* **1.** Causing disgust; repugnant. **2.** Full of or marked by disgust. —**dis•gust′ful•ly** *adv.*

dis•gust•ing (dĭs-gŭs′tĭng) *adj.* Arousing disgust; repugnant. —**dis•gust′ing•ly** *adv.*

dish (dĭsh) *n.* **1a.** An open, usu. shallow concave container for holding, cooking, or serving food. **b. dishes** The containers and often the utensils used when eating. **c.** A shallow concave container. **2.** The amount a dish can hold. **3a.** The food contained in a dish. **b.** A particular variety or preparation of food: *a Japanese dish.* **4a.** A depression similar to that in a food dish. **b.** The degree of concavity in such a depression. **5.** *Electronics* A dish antenna. **6.** *Slang* A good-looking person, esp. a woman. **7.** *Informal* Idle talk; gossip. ❖ *v.* **dished, dish•ing, dish•es** *—tr.* **1.** To serve (food) in or as if in a dish. **2.** To present: *dished up the entertainment.* **3.** To hollow out; make concave. **4.** *Informal* To gossip about. **5.** *Chiefly British Slang* To ruin, foil, or defeat. *—intr. Informal* To talk idly, esp. to gossip. —*phrasal verb:* **dish out** To give out; dispense freely. —*idiom:* **dish it out** *Slang* To deal out criticism or abuse. [ME < OE *disc* < Lat. *discus.* See DISK.]

dis•ha•bille (dĭs′ə-bēl′, -bē′) also **des•ha•bille** (dĕs′-) *n.* **1.** The state of being partially or very casually dressed. **2.** Casual or lounging attire. **3.** An intentionally careless manner. [Fr. *déshabillé* < p. part. of *déshabiller*, to undress : *des-*, dis- + *habiller*, to clothe; see HABILIMENT.]

dish antenna

dish antenna *n.* A transmitter or receiver of electromagnetic energy, esp. microwaves or radiowaves, consisting of a concave parabolic reflector.

dis•har•mo•ni•ous (dĭs′här-mō′nē-əs) *adj.* Lacking in harmony. —**dis′har•mo′ni•ous•ly** *adv.*

dis•har•mo•nize (dĭs-här′mə-nīz′) *tr.v.* **-nized, -niz•ing, -niz•es** To make disharmonious.

dis•har•mo•ny (dĭs-här′mə-nē) *n.* Lack of harmony; discord.

dish•cloth (dĭsh′klôth′, -klŏth′) *n.* A cloth for washing dishes.

dishcloth gourd *n.* See **loofa 2.**

dis•heart•en (dĭs-här′tn) *tr.v.* **-ened, -en•ing, -ens** To shake or destroy the courage or resolution of; dispirit. —**dis•heart′en•ing•ly** *adv.* —**dis•heart′en•ment** *n.*

dished (dĭsht) *adj.* **1.** Concave. **2.** Slanting toward one another at the bottom. Used of a pair of wheels.

di•shev•el (dĭ-shĕv′əl) *tr.v.* **-eled, -el•ing, -els** or **-elled, -el•ling, -els 1a.** To let fall (hair or clothing) in disarray. **b.** To disarrange the hair or clothing of. **2.** To throw into disorder. [Back-formation < DISHEVELED.] —**di•shev′el•ment** *n.*

di•shev•eled or **di•shev•elled** (dĭ-shĕv′əld) *adj.* **1.** Being in loose disarray; unkempt, as hair. **2.** Marked by disorder; untidy. [ME *discheveled* < OFr. *deschevele*, p. part. of *descheveler*, to disarrange the hair : *des-*, apart; see DIS- + *chevel*, hair (< Lat. *capillus*).]

dis•hon•est (dĭs-ŏn′ĭst) *adj.* **1.** Disposed to lie, cheat, defraud, or deceive. **2.** Resulting from or marked by a lack of honesty. [ME *dishoneste*, dishonorable < OFr. *deshoneste*, prob. < Med.Lat. *dishonestus* : Lat. *dis-*, dis- + Lat. *honestus*, honorable; see HONEST.] —**dis•hon′est•ly** *adv.*

dis•hon•es•ty (dĭs-ŏn′ĭ-stē) *n., pl.* **-ties 1.** Lack of honesty or integrity; improbity. **2.** A dishonest act or statement.

dis•hon•or (dĭs-ŏn′ər) *n.* **1.** Loss of honor or reputation. **2.** The condition of having lost honor or good repute. **3.** A cause of loss of honor: *was a dishonor to the club.* **4.** Failure to pay or refusal to accept a commercial obligation. ❖ *tr.v.* **-ored, -or•ing, -ors 1.** To bring disgrace upon. **2.** To treat in a disrespectful manner. **3.** To fail or refuse to accept or pay (a bill, for example). [ME *dis-*

honour < OFr. *deshonor* : *des-*, dis- + *honor*, honor; see HONOR.] —**dis•hon′or•er** *n.*

dis•hon•or•a•ble (dĭs-ŏn′ər-ə-bəl) *adj.* **1.** Marked by or causing dishonor or discredit. **2.** Lacking integrity; unprincipled. —**dis•hon′or•a•ble•ness** *n.* —**dis•hon′or•a•bly** *adv.*

dishonorable discharge *n.* Discharge from the armed forces for a grave offense, such as cowardice or murder.

dish•pan (dĭsh′păn′) *n.* A flat-bottomed basin for washing dishes.

dish•rag (dĭsh′răg′) *n.* A dishcloth.

dish•tow•el (dĭsh′tou′əl) *n.* A towel for drying dishes.

dish•wash•er (dĭsh′wŏsh′ər, -wô′shər) *n.* **1.** A person who washes dishes. **2.** A machine for washing dishes.

dish•wa•ter (dĭsh′wô′tər, -wŏt′ər) *n.* Water in which dishes are washed.

dish•y (dĭsh′ē) *adj.* **-i•er, -i•est 1.** *Informal* Gossipy; sensational. **2.** *Chiefly British Slang* Good-looking; attractive.

dis•il•lu•sion (dĭs′ĭ-lōō′zhən) *tr.v.* **-sioned, -sion•ing, -sions** To free or deprive of illusion. ❖ *n.* **1.** The act of disenchanting. **2.** The condition or fact of being disenchanted. —**dis•il•lu′sion•ment** *n.* —**dis•il•lu′sive** (-sĭv, -zĭv) *adj.*

dis•in•cen•tive (dĭs′ĭn-sĕn′tĭv) *n.* Something that prevents or discourages action; a deterrent.

dis•in•cli•na•tion (dĭs-ĭn′klə-nā′shən) *n.* A lack of inclination; a mild aversion or reluctance.

dis•in•cline (dĭs′ĭn-klīn′) *v.* **-clined, -clin•ing, -clines** *—tr.* To make reluctant or averse. *—intr.* To be unwilling.

dis•in•clined (dĭs′ĭn-klīnd′) *adj.* Unwilling or reluctant.

dis•in•fect (dĭs′ĭn-fĕkt′) *tr.v.* **-fect•ed, -fect•ing, -fects** To cleanse so as to destroy or prevent the growth of disease-carrying microorganisms. —**dis′in•fec′tion** *n.*

dis•in•fec•tant (dĭs′ĭn-fĕk′tənt) *n.* An agent, such as heat or a chemical, that destroys, neutralizes, or inhibits the growth of disease-carrying microorganisms. ❖ *adj.* Serving to disinfect.

dis•in•fest (dĭs′ĭn-fĕst′) *tr.v.* **-fest•ed, -fest•ing, -fests** To rid of vermin. —**dis•in•fes•ta•tion** (-fĕ-stā′shən) *n.*

dis•in•fes•tant (dĭs′ĭn-fĕs′tənt) *n.* An agent that eradicates an infestation, as of vermin.

dis•in•fla•tion (dĭs′ĭn-flā′shən) *n.* Downward movement of inflated prices to a more normal level. —**dis′in•fla′tion•ar′y** (-shə-nĕr′ē) *adj.*

dis•in•form (dĭs′ĭn-fôrm′) *tr.v.* **-formed, -form•ing, -forms** To give disinformation to. [Back-formation < DISINFORMATION.] —**dis•in•form′er**, **dis′in•form′ant** *n.*

dis•in•for•ma•tion (dĭs-ĭn′fər-mā′shən) *n.* **1.** Deliberately misleading information announced or leaked by a government to influence another nation. **2.** Dissemination of disinformation. [Poss. transl. of Russ. *dezinformatsiya.*]

dis•in•gen•u•ous (dĭs′ĭn-jĕn′yōō-əs) *adj.* Not straightforward or candid; insincere. —**dis′in•gen′u•ous•ly** *adv.* —**dis′in•gen′u•ous•ness** *n.*

dis•in•her•it (dĭs′ĭn-hĕr′ĭt) *tr.v.* **-it•ed, -it•ing, -its 1.** To exclude from inheritance. **2.** To deprive of a right or privilege. —**dis′in•her′i•tance** *n.*

dis•in•hi•bi•tion (dĭs′ĭn-hə-bĭsh′ən, -ĭn-ə-, dĭs-ĭn′-) *n.* **1.** A loss of inhibition, as through the influence of drugs or alcohol, resulting in unrestrained behavior. **2.** Removal of an inhibitory substance or stimulus.

dis•in•te•grate (dĭs-ĭn′tĭ-grāt′) *v.* **-grat•ed, -grat•ing, -grates** *—intr.* **1.** To become reduced to components, fragments, or particles. **2.** To lose cohesion or unity: *a family that disintegrated.* **3.** *Physics & Chemistry* To decay or undergo a transformation from a more massive to a less massive nucleus by the emission of particles or radiation. *—tr.* To cause to disintegrate. —**dis•in′te•gra′tion** *n.* —**dis•in′te•gra′tive** *adj.* —**dis•in′te•gra′tor** *n.*

dis•in•ter (dĭs′ĭn-tûr′) *tr.v.* **-terred, -ter•ring, -ters 1.** To dig up or remove from a grave or tomb; exhume. **2.** To bring to public notice; disclose. —**dis′in•ter′ment** *n.*

dis•in•ter•est (dĭs-ĭn′tər-ĭst, -ĭn′trĭst) *n.* **1.** Freedom from selfish bias or self-interest; impartiality. **2.** Lack of interest; indifference. ❖ *tr.v.* **-est•ed, -est•ing, -ests** To divest of interest.

dis•in•ter•est•ed (dĭs-ĭn′trĭ-stĭd, -ĭn′tə-rĕs′tĭd) *adj.* **1.** Free of bias and self-interest; impartial. **2a.** Not interested; indifferent. **b.** Having lost interest. —**dis•in′ter•est•ed•ly** *adv.* —**dis•in′ter•est•ed•ness** *n.*

USAGE NOTE Many maintain that the word *disinterested* can legitimately be used only in its sense of "having no stake in an outcome or issue," as in *Since the judge stands to profit from the sale of the company, she cannot be considered a disinterested party in the dispute.* The Usage Panel favors this position, rejecting the use of *disinterested* to mean "uninterested." In a 1988 survey, 89 percent rejected the sentence *His unwillingness to give five minutes of his time proves that he is disinterested* [uninterested] *in finding a solution to the problem,* a proportion that is not significantly different from the 93 percent who disapproved of it in a 1980 survey.

dis•in•tox•i•cate (dĭs′ĭn-tŏk′sĭ-kāt′) *tr.v.* **-cat•ed, -cat•ing, -cates** To free from the effects of intoxication or from dependence on intoxicating agents. —**dis′in•tox′i•ca′tion** *n.*

dis•in•vest•ment (dĭs′ĭn-vĕst′mənt) *n.* Withdrawal of capital

dis•join (dĭs-join′) v. **-joined, -join•ing, -joins** —tr. To undo the joining of; separate. —intr. To become separated. [ME disjoinen < OFr. desjoindre < Lat. disiungere : dis-, dis- + iungere, to join; see JOIN.]

dis•joint (dĭs-joint′) v. **-joint•ed, -joint•ing, -joints** —tr. **1.** To put out of joint; dislocate. **2.** To take apart at the joints. **3.** To destroy the coherence or connections of. **4.** To separate; disjoin. —intr. **1.** To come apart at the joints. **2.** To become dislocated. ❖ adj. Mathematics Having no elements in common. Used of sets. [ME disjointen, to destroy, ult. < OFr. desjoint, p. part. of desjoindre, to disjoin. See DISJOIN.]

dis•joint•ed (dĭs-join′tĭd) adj. **1.** Separated at the joints. **2.** Out of joint; dislocated. **3.** Lacking order or coherence. —dis•joint′ed•ly adv. —dis•joint′ed•ness n.

dis•junct (dĭs-jŭngkt′) adj. **1.** Characterized by separation. **2.** Music Relating to progression by intervals larger than major seconds. [ME disjuncte < Lat. disiūnctus, p. part. of disiungere, to disjoin. See DISJOIN.]

dis•junc•tion (dĭs-jŭngk′shən) n. **1.** The act of disjoining or the condition of being disjoined. **2.** Logic **a.** A proposition that presents two or more alternative terms, with the assertion that only one is true. **b.** A proposition that presents two or more alternative terms, with the assertion that at least one is true. **3.** Genetics The separation of homologous chromosomes during meiosis.

dis•junc•tive (dĭs-jŭngk′tĭv) adj. **1.** Serving to separate or divide. **2.** Grammar Serving to establish a relationship of contrast or opposition, as the conjunction but in rich but unhappy. **3.** Logic **a.** Of a proposition that presents two or more alternative terms. **b.** Of a syllogism that contains a disjunction as one premise. ❖ n. Grammar A disjunctive conjunction. —dis•junc′tive•ly adv.

dis•junc•ture (dĭs-jŭngk′chər) n. Disjunction; separation.

disk also **disc** (dĭsk) n. **1.** A thin, flat, circular object or plate. **2.** Something resembling such an object. **3a.** The disk used in a disc brake. **b.** A disk used on a disk harrow. **4.** A round flattened structure in an animal, such as an intervertebral disk. **5.** Botany The flower head of composite plants, such as the daisy. **6.** Computer Science **a.** A magnetic disk, such as a floppy disk or hard disk. **b.** An optical disk, esp. a compact disk. See Usage Note at **compact disk**. **7.** A phonograph record. **8.** A circular grid in a phototypesetting machine. ❖ tr.v. **disked, disk•ing, disks** also **disced, disc•ing, discs** To work (soil) with a disk harrow. [Lat. discus, quoit < Gk. diskos < dikein, to throw. See **deik-** in App.]

disk brake n. Variant of **disc brake**.

disk drive n. Computer Science A device that reads data stored on a magnetic or optical disk and writes data onto the disk for storage.

disk•ette (dĭ-skĕt′) n. See **floppy disk**.

disk flower n. Any of the tiny tubular flowers in the center of the flower head of certain composite plants, such as the daisy.

disk harrow or **disc harrow** n. A harrow equipped with a series of sharp metal disks set on edge or at an angle on one or more axles.

disk jockey n. Variant of **disc jockey**.

disk wheel n. A spokeless wheel in which a disk joins the hub to the rim.

dis•like (dĭs-līk′) tr.v. **-liked, -lik•ing, -likes** To regard with distaste or aversion. ❖ n. An attitude or a feeling of distaste or aversion. —dis•lik′a•ble, dis•like′a•ble adj.

dis•lo•cate (dĭs′lō-kāt′, dĭs-lō′kāt′) tr.v. **-cat•ed, -cat•ing, -cates** **1.** To put out of usual or proper position or relationship. **2.** To displace (a body part), esp. to displace a bone from its normal position. **3.** To throw into confusion; disrupt. [Med.Lat. dislocāre, dislocāt- : dis-, dis- + Lat. locāre, to place (< locus, place).]

dis•lo•ca•tion (dĭs′lō-kā′shən) n. **1.** The act or process of dislocating or the state of having been dislocated. **2.** Displacement of a body part, esp. the temporary displacement of a bone from its normal position. **3.** Chemistry An imperfection in a crystal structure resulting from an absence of an atom or atoms in one or more layers. **4.** Geology See **displacement** 5.

dis•lodge (dĭs-lŏj′) v. **-lodged, -lodg•ing, -lodg•es** —tr. To remove or force out from a position or dwelling previously occupied. —intr. To move or go from a dwelling or former position. [ME disloggen < OFr. deslogier : des-, dis- + logier, to lodge (< loge, shed, of Gmc. orig.).] —dis•lodge′ment, dis•lodg′ment n.

dis•loy•al (dĭs-loi′əl) adj. Lacking loyalty. [Late ME < OFr. desloial : des-, dis- + loial, loyal; see LOYAL.] —dis•loy′al•ly adv.

dis•loy•al•ty (dĭs-loi′əl-tē) n., pl. **-ties 1.** The quality of being disloyal; faithlessness. **2.** A disloyal act.

dis•mal (dĭz′məl) adj. **1.** Causing gloom or depression; dreary: dismal weather. **2.** Characterized by ineptitude, dullness, or a lack of merit. **3.** Obsolete Dreadful; disastrous. ❖ n. Chiefly South Atlantic US See **pocosin**. [ME, unlucky days < AN, unlucky days < Med.Lat. diēs malī : Lat. diēs, pl. of diēs, day; see **dyeu-** in App. + Lat. malī, pl. of malus, evil; see **mel-** in App.] —dis′mal•ly adv. —dis′mal•ness n.

Dismal Swamp A swampy region of SE VA and NE NC.

dis•man•tle (dĭs-măn′tl) tr.v. **-tled, -tling, -tles 1a.** To take apart; disassemble. **b.** To put an end to in a gradual systematic way. **2.** To strip of furnishings or equipment. **3.** To strip of covering or clothing. [Obsolete Fr. desmanteler, to raze fortifications

round a town < OFr. : des-, dis- + (em)manteler, to cover with a coat, shelter (ult. < mantel, cloak; see MANTLE).] —dis•man′tle•ment n.

dis•mast (dĭs-măst′) tr.v. **-mast•ed, -mast•ing, -masts** Nautical To remove or break off the mast of.

dis•may (dĭs-mā′) tr.v. **-mayed, -may•ing, -mays 1.** To destroy the courage or resolution of by exciting dread or apprehension. **2.** To cause to lose enthusiasm; disillusion. **3.** To upset or alarm. ❖ n. A sudden or complete loss of courage in the face of trouble or danger. [ME dismaien < AN *desmaiier : prob. de-, intensive pref.; see DE- + OFr. esmaier, to frighten (< VLat. *exmagāre, to deprive of power : Lat. ex-, ex- + Gmc. *magan, to be able to).] —dis•may′ing•ly adv.

dis•mem•ber (dĭs-mĕm′bər) tr.v. **-bered, -ber•ing, -bers 1.** To cut, tear, or pull off the limbs of. **2.** To divide into pieces. [ME dismembren < OFr. desmembrer < VLat. *dismembrāre : dis-, dis- + Lat. membrum, limb; see MEMBER.] —dis•mem′ber•ment n.

dis•miss (dĭs-mĭs′) tr.v. **-missed, -miss•ing, -miss•es 1.** To end the employment or service of; discharge. **2.** To direct or allow to leave. **3a.** To stop considering; rid one's mind of; dispel. **b.** To refuse to accept or recognize; reject. **4.** Law To put (a claim or action) out of court without further hearing. [ME dismissen < Med.Lat. dismittere, dismiss-, var. of Lat. dīmittere : dī-, dis-, apart; see DIS- + mittere, to send.] —dis•miss′i•ble adj. —dis•mis′sion (-mĭsh′ən) n.

dis•miss•al (dĭs-mĭs′əl) n. **1a.** The act of dismissing. **b.** The condition of being dismissed. **2.** An order or notice of discharge.

dis•mis•sive (dĭs-mĭs′ĭv) adj. **1.** Serving to dismiss. **2.** Showing indifference or disregard: a dismissive shrug.

dis•mount (dĭs-mount′) v. **-mount•ed, -mount•ing, -mounts** —intr. To get off or down, as from a horse. —tr. **1.** To remove from a support, setting, or mounting. **2.** To unseat or throw off, as from a horse. **3.** To disassemble (a mechanism, for example). ❖ n. (dĭs′mount′) The act or manner of dismounting, esp. from a horse. [Prob. alteration of obsolete Fr. desmonter, to unseat : des-, dis- + monter, to mount; see MOUNT¹.] —dis•mount′a•ble adj.

Dis•ney (dĭz′nē), **Walter Elias ("Walt")** 1901–66. Amer. animator and motion picture executive whose full-length animated features include Snow White (1938).

dis•o•be•di•ence (dĭs′ə-bē′dē-əns) n. Refusal or failure to obey. —dis′o•be′di•ent adj. —dis′o•be′di•ent•ly adv.

dis•o•bey (dĭs′ə-bā′) v. **-beyed, -bey•ing, -beys** —intr. To refuse or fail to follow an order or rule. —tr. To refuse or fail to obey (an order, for example). [ME disobeien < OFr. desobeir < VLat. *disobedīre : Lat. dis-, dis- + Lat. oboedīre, to obey; see OBEY.] —dis′o•bey′er n.

dis•o•blige (dĭs′ə-blīj′) tr.v. **-bliged, -blig•ing, -blig•es 1.** To refuse or neglect to act in accord with the wishes of. **2.** To inconvenience. **3.** To give offense to; affront. —dis′o•blig′ing•ly adv.

dis•or•der (dĭs-ôr′dər) n. **1.** A lack of order or regular arrangement; confusion. **2.** A breach of civic order; a public disturbance. **3.** An ailment that affects the mind or body. ❖ tr.v. **-dered, -der•ing, -ders 1.** To throw into confusion or disarray. **2.** To disturb the normal physical or mental health of; derange.

dis•or•dered (dĭs-ôr′dərd) adj. **1.** Being in a condition of confusion or disarray. **2.** Physically or mentally ill. —dis•or′dered•ly adv. —dis•or′dered•ness n.

dis•or•der•ly (dĭs-ôr′dər-lē) adj. **1.** Lacking regular or logical order or arrangement. **2.** Undisciplined. **3.** Law Disturbing the public peace or decorum. —dis•or′der•li•ness n.

disorderly conduct n. Law An offense involving disturbance of the public peace and decency.

dis•or•gan•ize (dĭs-ôr′gə-nīz′) tr.v. **-ized, -iz•ing, -iz•es** To destroy the organization, systematic arrangement, or unity of. —dis•or′gan•i•za′tion (-gə-nĭ-zā′shən) n.

dis•o•ri•ent (dĭs-ôr′ē-ĕnt′, -ŏr′-) tr.v. **-ent•ed, -ent•ing, -ents** To cause (a person, for example) to experience disorientation.

dis•o•ri•en•ta•tion (dĭs-ôr′ē-ĕn-tā′shən) n. **1.** Loss of one's sense of direction, position, or relationship with one's surroundings. **2.** Mental confusion or impaired awareness, esp. regarding place, time, or personal identity.

dis•own (dĭs-ōn′) tr.v. **-owned, -own•ing, -owns** To refuse to acknowledge or accept as one's own; repudiate.

dis•par•age (dĭ-spăr′ĭj) tr.v. **-aged, -ag•ing, -ag•es 1.** To speak of in a slighting or disrespectful way; belittle. **2.** To reduce in esteem or rank. [ME disparagen < OFr. desparager : des-, dis- + parage, high birth (< per, peer; see PEER².)] —dis•par′age•ment n. —dis•par′ag•er n. —dis•par′ag•ing•ly adv.

dis•pa•rate (dĭs′pər-ĭt, dĭ-spăr′ĭt) adj. **1.** Fundamentally distinct or different; entirely dissimilar. **2.** Containing dissimilar or opposing elements: a disparate group of people. [Lat. disparātus, p. part. of disparāre, to separate : dis-, apart; see DIS- + parāre, to prepare.] —dis′pa•rate•ly adv. —dis′pa•rate•ness n.

dis•par•i•ty (dĭ-spăr′ĭ-tē) n., pl. **-ties 1.** The condition or fact of being unequal, as in age; difference. **2.** Unlikeness; incongruity. [Fr. disparité < OFr. desparite < LLat. disparitās : Lat. dis-, dis- + LLat. paritās, equality; see PARITY¹.]

dis•pas•sion (dĭs-păsh′ən) n. Freedom from passion, bias, or emotion; objectivity.

disk harrow

Walt Disney

dis·pas·sion·ate (dĭs-păsh′ə-nĭt) *adj.* Devoid of or unaffected by passion, emotion, or bias. See Syns at **fair**¹. —**dis·pas′sion·ate·ly** *adv.* —**dis·pas′sion·ate·ness** *n.*

dis·patch also **des·patch** (dĭ-spăch′) *tr.v.* **-patched, -patch·ing, -patch·es 1.** To relegate to a specific destination or send on specific business. **2a.** To complete, transact, or dispose of promptly. **b.** To eat up (food); finish off (a dish or meal). **3.** To put to death summarily. ❖ *n.* **1.** The act of sending off, as to a specific destination. **2.** Dismissal or rejection of something regarded as unimportant or unworthy of consideration. **3.** The act of putting to death. **4.** Speed in performance or movement. See Syns at **haste**. **5.** (*also* dĭs′păch′) A written message, esp. an official communication, sent with speed. **6.** (*also* dĭs′păch′) A news item sent to a news organization, as by a correspondent. [Sp. *despachar* or Ital. *dispacciare*, both prob. ult. < O Provençal *empachar*, to impede < VLat. *impāctāre*, freq. of Lat. *impingere*, to dash against. See IMPINGE.] —**dis·patch′er** *n.*

dis·pel (dĭ-spĕl′) *tr.v.* **-pelled, -pel·ling, -pels 1.** To rid one's mind of: *managed to dispel my doubts.* **2.** To drive away or off by or as if by scattering. [ME *dispellen* < Lat. *dispellere* : *dis-*, apart; see DIS- + *pellere*, to drive; see **pel-**² in App.]

dis·pens·a·ble (dĭ-spĕn′sə-bəl) *adj.* **1.** Not essential; unimportant. **2.** Capable of being dispensed, administered, or distributed. **3.** Subject to dispensation, as a vow or church law. —**dis·pens′a·bil′i·ty** *n.*

dis·pen·sa·ry (dĭ-spĕn′sə-rē) *n., pl.* **-ries 1.** An office in a hospital, school, or other institution from which medical supplies, preparations, and treatments are dispensed. **2.** A public institution that dispenses medicines or medical aid.

dis·pen·sa·tion (dĭs′pən-sā′shən, -pĕn-) *n.* **1a.** The act of dispensing. **b.** Something dispensed. **c.** A specific arrangement or system by which something is dispensed. **2.** An exemption or release from an obligation or rule, granted by or as if by an authority. **3a.** An exemption from a church law or a vow granted by an ecclesiastical authority. **b.** The document containing this exemption. **4.** *Theology* **a.** The divine ordering of worldly affairs. **b.** A religious system considered to have been divinely revealed or appointed. [Med.Lat. *dispēnsātiō, dispēnsātiō* < Lat., distribution, management < *dispēnsātus*, p. part. of *dispēnsāre*, to distribute. See DISPENSE.] —**dis·pen·sa′tion·al** *adj.*

dis·pen·sa·to·ry (dĭ-spĕn′sə-tôr′ē, -tōr′ē) *n., pl.* **-ries** A book in which the contents, preparation, and uses of medicines are described; a pharmacopoeia.

dis·pense (dĭ-spĕns′) *v.* **-pensed, -pens·ing, -pens·es** —*tr.* **1.** To deal out in parts or portions; distribute. See Syns at **distribute**. **2.** To prepare and give out (medicines). **3.** To administer (laws, for example). **4.** To exempt or release, as from a duty or religious obligation. —*intr.* To grant a dispensation or exemption. —*phrasal verb:* **dispense with 1.** To manage without; forgo: *Let's dispense with the formalities.* **2.** To get rid of; do away with. [ME *dispensen* < OFr. *dispenser* < Lat. *dispēnsāre*, to distribute, freq. of *dispendere*, to weigh out : *dis-*, out; see DIS- + *pendere*, to weigh.]

dis·pens·er (dĭ-spĕn′sər) *n.* One that dispenses or gives out, esp. a machine or container that allows the contents to be removed and used in convenient or prescribed amounts.

dis·peo·ple (dĭs-pē′pəl) *tr.v.* **-pled, -pling, -ples** To depopulate.

dis·per·sal (dĭ-spûr′səl) *n.* The act or process of dispersing or the condition of being dispersed; distribution.

dis·per·sant (dĭ-spûr′sənt) *n. Chemistry* A liquid or gas added to a mixture to promote dispersion or to maintain dispersed particles in suspension.

dis·perse (dĭ-spûrs′) *v.* **-persed, -pers·ing, -pers·es** —*tr.* **1a.** To drive off or scatter in different directions: *The police dispersed the crowd.* **b.** To strew or distribute widely. **2.** To cause to vanish or disappear. **3.** To disseminate (knowledge, for example). **4.** To separate (light) into spectral rays. **5.** To distribute (particles) evenly throughout a medium. —*intr.* **1.** To separate and move in different directions; scatter. **2.** To vanish; dissipate. [ME *dispersen* < OFr. *disperser* < Lat. *dispergere, dispers-*, to disperse : *dis-*, apart; see DIS- + *spargere*, to scatter.] —**dis·persed′·ly** (-spûr′sĭd-lē) *adv.* —**dis·pers′er** *n.* —**dis·pers′i·ble** *adj.*

disperse phase *n.* The particles or droplets in a disperse system that are dispersed throughout a medium.

disperse system *n. Chemistry* A system, such as a colloid, consisting of a disperse phase in a dispersion medium.

dis·per·sion (dĭ-spûr′zhən, -shən) *n.* **1a.** The act or process of dispersing. **b.** The state of being dispersed. **2. Dispersion** The Diaspora of the Jews. **3.** *Statistics* The degree of scatter of data, usu. about an average value, such as the median. **4.** *Physics* **a.** Separation of a complex wave into its component parts according to a given characteristic, such as wavelength. **b.** Separation of visible light into colors by refraction or diffraction. **5.** *Chemistry* See **disperse system**.

dispersion medium *n.* The continuous medium, such as a gas, liquid, or solid, in which a disperse phase is distributed.

dis·per·sive (dĭ-spûr′sĭv, -zĭv) *adj.* **1.** Tending to become dispersed. **2.** Tending to produce dispersion. —**dis·per′sive·ly** *adv.* —**dis·per′sive·ness** *n.*

dis·pir·it (dĭ-spîr′ĭt) *tr.v.* **-it·ed, -it·ing, -its** To lower in or de-

prive of spirit; dishearten. [DI(S)- + SPIRIT.]

dis·pir·it·ed (dĭ-spîr′ĭ-tĭd) *adj.* Marked by low spirits; dejected. —**dis·pir′it·ed·ly** *adv.*

dis·place (dĭs-plās′) *tr.v.* **-placed, -plac·ing, -plac·es 1.** To move from the usual place or position, esp. to force to leave a homeland. **2.** To take the place of; supplant. **3.** To discharge from an office or position. —**dis·place′a·ble** *adj.* —**dis·plac′er** *n.*

dis·placed person (dĭs-plāst′) *n.* One who has been driven from one's homeland by war or internal upheaval.

dis·place·ment (dĭs-plās′mənt) *n.* **1a.** The act of displacing. **b.** The condition of having been displaced. **2.** *Chemistry* A reaction in which an atom, radical, or molecule replaces another in a compound. **3.** *Physics* **a.** A vector or the magnitude of a vector from the initial position to a subsequent position assumed by a body. **b.** The weight or volume of a fluid displaced by a floating body. **4.** The volume displaced by a single stroke of a piston in an engine or pump. **5.** *Geology* **a.** The relative movement between the two sides of a fault. **b.** The distance between the two sides of a fault. **6.** *Psychology* A defense mechanism in which emotion, affect, or desire shifts from the original object to a more acceptable or immediate substitute.

displacement ton *n.* A unit for measuring the displacement of a ship afloat, equivalent to one long ton or about one cubic meter of salt water.

dis·play (dĭ-splā′) *v.* **-played, -play·ing, -plays** —*tr.* **1a.** To present or hold up to view. **b.** *Computer Science* To provide (information or graphics) on a screen. **2.** To give evidence of; manifest. **3.** To exhibit ostentatiously; show off. **4.** To be endowed with an identifiable form or character. **5.** To express, as by gestures or bodily posture: *a smirk that displayed contempt.* **6.** To spread out; unfurl. —*intr.* *Zoology* To engage in courtship behavior. ❖ *n.* **1a.** The act of displaying. **b.** A public exhibition. **c.** Objects or merchandise set out for viewing by the public. **2.** A demonstration or manifestation. **3a.** *Biology* A specialized pattern of visually communicative behavior such as the presentation of colors or plumage as part of courtship. **b.** An instance of such behavior. **4.** Ostentatious exhibition. **5.** An advertisement or headline designed to catch the eye. **6a.** *Computer Science* A device that gives information in a visual form, as on a screen. **b.** A visual representation of information. [ME *displayen* < AN *despleier* < Med.Lat. *displicāre*, to unfold < Lat., to scatter : *dis-*, apart; see DIS- + *plicāre*, to fold; see **plek-** in App.]

dis·please (dĭs-plēz′) *v.* **-pleased, -pleas·ing, -pleas·es** —*tr.* To cause annoyance or vexation to. —*intr.* To cause annoyance or displeasure. [ME *displesen* < OFr. *desplaire, desplais-* < VLat. *displacēre* < Lat. *displicēre* : Lat. *dis-*, dis- + Lat. *placēre*, to please; see PLEASE.] —**dis·pleas′ing·ly** *adv.*

dis·pleas·ure (dĭs-plĕzh′ər) *n.* **1.** The condition or fact of being displeased; dissatisfaction. **2.** Discomfort, uneasiness, or pain. **3.** *Archaic* An injurious offense. [ME *displesure* < OFr. *desplaisir* : *des-*, dis- + *plaisir*, pleasure; see PLEASURE.]

dis·plode (dĭ-splōd′) *tr. & intr.v.* **-plod·ed, -plod·ing, -plodes** *Archaic* To explode. [Lat. *displōdere* : *dis-*, dis- + *plaudere*, to clap, beat.]

dis·port (dĭ-spôrt′, -spōrt′) *v.* **-port·ed, -port·ing, -ports** —*intr.* To amuse oneself in a light frolicsome manner. —*tr.* **1.** To amuse (oneself) in a light frolicsome manner. **2.** To display. ❖ *n.* Frolicsome diversion. [ME *disporten* < OFr. *desporter*, to divert : *des-*, apart; see DIS- + *porter*, to carry (< Lat. *portāre*; see PORT⁵).]

dis·pos·a·ble (dĭ-spō′zə-bəl) *adj.* **1.** Designed to be disposed of after use: *disposable razors.* **2a.** Remaining to a person after taxes have been deducted: *disposable income.* **b.** Free for use; available. ❖ *n.* An article, such as a paper diaper, that can be disposed of after one use. —**dis·pos′a·bil′i·ty** *n.*

dis·pos·al (dĭ-spō′zəl) *n.* **1.** A particular order, distribution, or placement. **2.** A particular method of attending to or settling matters. **3.** Transference by gift or sale. **4.** The act or process of getting rid of something. **5.** An electric device installed below a sink that grinds garbage so it can be flushed away. **6.** The liberty or power to dispose of: *funds at our disposal.*

dis·pose (dĭ-spōz′) *v.* **-posed, -pos·ing, -pos·es** —*tr.* **1.** To place or set in a particular order; arrange. **2.** To put (business affairs, for example) into correct, definitive, or conclusive form. **3.** To put into a willing or receptive frame of mind; incline. See Syns at **incline**. —*intr.* To settle or decide a matter. ❖ *n. Obsolete* **1.** Disposal. **2.** Disposition; demeanor. —*phrasal verb:* **dispose of 1.** To attend to; settle: *disposed of the problem quickly.* **2.** To transfer or part with. **3.** To get rid of; throw out. **4.** To kill or destroy. [ME *disposen* < OFr. *disposer*, alteration (influenced by *poser*, to put, place) of Lat. *dispōnere*, to arrange : *dis-*, apart; see DIS- + *pōnere*, to put; see **apo-** in App.] —**dis·pos′er** *n.*

dis·po·si·tion (dĭs′pə-zĭsh′ən) *n.* **1.** One's usual mood; temperament. **2a.** A habitual inclination; a tendency. **b.** A physical property or tendency. **3.** Arrangement, positioning, or distribution. **4.** A final settlement. **5.** An act of disposing; a bestowal or transfer to another. **6a.** The power or liberty to control, direct, or dispose. **b.** Management; control. [ME *disposicioun* < OFr. *disposition* < Lat. *dispositiō, disposition-* < *dispositus*, p. part. of *dispōnere*, to dispose. See DISPOSE.]

dis·pos·i·tive (dĭs-pŏz′ĭ-tĭv) *adj.* Relating to or affecting a disposition or settlement, esp. of a legal case or will.

dis·pos·sess (dĭs′pə-zĕs′) *tr.v.* **-sessed, -sess·ing, -sess·es** To deprive (another) of the possession or occupancy of something. **—dis′pos·ses′sion** (-zĕsh′ən) *n.* **—dis′pos·ses′sor** *n.* **—dis′·pos′ses′so·ry** (-zĕs′ə-rē) *adj.*

dis·pos·sessed (dĭs′pə-zĕst′) *adj.* **1.** Deprived of possession. **2.** Spiritually impoverished or alienated. **—dis′pos·sessed′** *n.*

dis·praise (dĭs-prāz′) *tr.v.* **-praised, -prais·ing, -prais·es** To express disapproval of; censure. ❖ *n.* Disapproval; censure. [ME *dispreisen* < OFr. *despreiser,* var. of *despriser* < LLat. *dēpretiāre.* See DEPRECIATE.] **—dis′prais′er** *n.* **—dis′prais′ing·ly** *adv.*

dis·prize (dĭs-prīz′) *tr.v.* **-prized, -priz·ing, -priz·es** *Archaic* To disdain or undervalue; scorn. [ME *disprisen* < OFr. *desprisier.* See DISPRAISE.]

dis·proof (dĭs-pro͞of′) *n.* **1.** The act of refuting or disproving. **2.** Evidence that refutes or disproves.

dis·pro·por·tion (dĭs′prə-pôr′shən, -pôr′-) *n.* **1.** Absence of proportion, symmetry, or proper relation. **2.** An instance of a disproportionate relation. ❖ *tr.v.* **-tioned, -tion·ing, -tions** To make disproportionate.

dis·pro·por·tion·al (dĭs′prə-pôr′shə-nəl, -pôr′-) *adj.* Disproportionate. **—dis′pro·por′tion·al·ly** *adv.*

dis·pro·por·tion·ate (dĭs′prə-pôr′shə-nĭt, -pôr′-) *adj.* Out of proportion, as in size, shape, or amount. **—dis′pro·por′tion·ate·ly** *adv.* **—dis′pro·por′tion·ate·ness** *n.*

dis·prove (dĭs-pro͞ov′) *tr.v.* **-proved, -prov·ing, -proves** To prove to be false, invalid, or in error; refute. [ME *disproven* < OFr. *desprover* : *des-,* dis- + *prover,* to prove; see PROVE.] **—dis·prov′a·ble** *adj.* **—dis·prov′al** *n.*

dis·put·a·ble (dĭ-spyo͞o′tə-bəl, dĭs′pyə-) *adj.* Open to dispute; debatable. **—dis·put′a·bil′i·ty** *n.* **—dis·put′a·bly** *adv.*

dis·pu·tant (dĭ-spyo͞ot′nt, dĭs′pyə-tənt) *adj.* Engaged in dispute or argument. ❖ *n.* One engaged in a dispute.

dis·pu·ta·tion (dĭs′pyə-tā′shən) *n.* **1.** The act of disputing; debate. **2.** An academic exercise consisting of a formal debate or an oral defense of a thesis.

dis·pu·ta·tious (dĭs′pyə-tā′shəs) *adj.* Inclined to dispute. See Syns at **argumentative. —dis′pu·ta′tious·ly** *adv.* **—dis′pu·ta′tious·ness** *n.*

dis·pute (dĭ-spyo͞ot′) *v.* **-put·ed, -put·ing, -putes** —*tr.* **1.** To argue about; debate. **2.** To question the truth or validity of; doubt. **3.** To strive to win (a prize, for example); contest for. **4.** To strive against; resist. —*intr.* **1.** To engage in discussion or argument; debate. **2.** To quarrel angrily. ❖ *n.* **1.** A verbal controversy; a debate. **2.** An angry altercation; a quarrel. [ME *disputen* < OFr. *desputer* < Lat. *disputāre,* to examine : *dis-,* apart; see DIS- + *putāre,* to reckon.] **—dis·put′er** *n.*

dis·qual·i·fi·ca·tion (dĭs-kwŏl′ə-fĭ-kā′shən) *n.* **1.** The act of disqualifying or the condition of having been disqualified. **2.** Something that disqualifies.

dis·qual·i·fy (dĭs-kwŏl′ə-fī′) *tr.v.* **-fied, -fy·ing, -fies 1a.** To render unqualified or unfit. **b.** To declare unqualified or ineligible. **2.** To deprive of legal rights, powers, or privileges.

dis·qui·et (dĭs-kwī′ĭt) *tr.v.* **-et·ed, -et·ing, -ets** To deprive of peace or rest; trouble. ❖ *n.* Absence of peace or rest; anxiety. *adj. Archaic* Uneasy; restless. **—dis·qui′et·ing·ly** *adv.* **—dis·qui′et·ly** *adv.* **—dis·qui′et·ness** *n.*

dis·qui·e·tude (dĭs-kwī′ĭ-to͞od′, -tyo͞od′) *n.* Worried unease.

dis·qui·si·tion (dĭs′kwĭ-zĭsh′ən) *n.* A formal discourse on a subject, often in writing. [Lat. *disquīsītiō, disquīsītiōn-,* investigation < *disquīsītus,* p. part. of *disquīrere,* to investigate : *dis-* + *quaerere,* to search for.]

Dis·rae·li (dĭz-rā′lē), **Benjamin. 1st** Earl of Beaconsfield. 1804–81. British politician and novelist who served as prime minister (1868 and 1874–80).

dis·rate (dĭs-rāt′) *tr.v.* **-rat·ed, -rat·ing, -rates** To reduce in rank or rating; demote.

dis·re·gard (dĭs′rĭ-gärd′) *tr.v.* **-gard·ed, -gard·ing, -gards 1.** To pay no attention or heed to. **2.** To treat without proper respect or attentiveness. ❖ *n.* Lack of thoughtful attention or regard. **—dis′re·gard′er** *n.* **—dis′re·gard′ful** *adj.*

dis·rel·ish (dĭs-rĕl′ĭsh) *tr.v.* **-ished, -ish·ing, -ish·es** To have distaste for; dislike. ❖ *n.* Distaste; aversion.

dis·re·mem·ber (dĭs′rĭ-mĕm′bər) *v.* **-bered, -ber·ing, -bers** *Informal* —*tr.* To fail to remember. —*intr.* To forget.

dis·re·pair (dĭs′rĭ-pâr′) *n.* The condition of needing repair.

dis·rep·u·ta·ble (dĭs-rĕp′yə-tə-bəl) *adj.* Lacking respectability, as in character or appearance. **—dis·rep′u·ta·bil′i·ty, dis·rep′u·ta·ble·ness** *n.* **—dis·rep′u·ta·bly** *adv.*

dis·re·pute (dĭs′rĭ-pyo͞ot′) *n.* Damage to or loss of reputation.

dis·re·spect (dĭs′rĭ-spĕkt′) *n.* Lack of respect, esteem, or courteous regard. ❖ *tr.v.* **-spect·ed, -spect·ing, -spects** To show a lack of respect for: *disrespected her elders.*

dis·re·spect·a·ble (dĭs′rĭ-spĕk′tə-bəl) *adj.* Unworthy of respect. **—dis′re·spect′a·bil′i·ty** *n.*

dis·re·spect·ful (dĭs′rĭ-spĕkt′fəl) *adj.* Having or exhibiting a lack of respect; rude and discourteous. **—dis′re·spect′ful·ly** *adv.* **—dis′re·spect′ful·ness** *n.*

dis·robe (dĭs-rōb′) *v.* **-robed, -rob·ing, -robes** —*tr.* To remove the clothing or covering from. —*intr.* To undress oneself. **—dis·rob′er** *n.*

dis·rupt (dĭs-rŭpt′) *tr.v.* **-rupt·ed, -rupt·ing, -rupts 1.** To

throw into confusion or disorder. **2.** To interrupt or impede the progress, movement, or procedure of. **3.** To break or burst; rupture. [Lat. *disrumpere, disrupt-,* to break apart : *dis-,* dis- + *rumpere,* to break; see reup- in App.] **—dis·rupt′er, dis·rupt′or** *n.* **—dis·rup′tion** *n.*

dis·rup·tive (dĭs-rŭp′tĭv) *adj.* Relating to, causing, or produced by disruption. **—dis·rup′tive·ly** *adv.*

diss (dĭs) *v.* Variant of **dis.**

diss. *abbr.* dissertation

dis·sat·is·fac·tion (dĭs-săt′ĭs-făk′shən) *n.* **1.** The condition or feeling of being displeased or unsatisfied; discontent. **2.** A cause of discontent.

dis·sat·is·fac·to·ry (dĭs-săt′ĭs-făk′tə-rē) *adj.* Unsatisfactory.

dis·sat·is·fied (dĭs-săt′ĭs-fīd′) *adj.* Feeling or exhibiting a lack of satisfaction. **—dis·sat′is·fied′ly** *adv.*

dis·sat·is·fy (dĭs-săt′ĭs-fī′) *tr.v.* **-fied, -fy·ing, -fies** To fail to satisfy; disappoint.

dissd. *abbr.* dissolved

dis·seat (dĭs-sēt′) *tr.v.* **-seat·ed, -seat·ing, -seats** *Archaic* To unseat.

dis·sect (dĭ-sĕkt′, dī-, dī′sĕkt′) *tr.v.* **-sect·ed, -sect·ing, -sects 1.** To cut apart or separate (tissue), esp. for anatomical study. **2.** To examine, analyze, or criticize in minute detail. See Syns at **analyze.** [Lat. *dissecāre, dissect-,* to cut apart : *dis-,* dis- + *secāre,* to cut up; see sek- in App.] **—dis·sec′ti·ble** *adj.* **—dis·sec′tor** *n.*

dis·sect·ed (dĭ-sĕk′tĭd, dī-) *adj.* **1.** *Botany* Divided into many deep, narrow segments: *dissected leaves.* **2.** *Geology* Cut by irregular valleys and hills.

dis·sec·tion (dĭ-sĕk′shən, dī-) *n.* **1.** The act or an instance of dissecting. **2.** Something that has been dissected, such as a tissue specimen under study. **3.** A detailed examination or analysis.

dis·seize also **dis·seise** (dĭs-sēz′) *tr.v.* **-seized, -seiz·ing, -seiz·es** also **-seised, -seis·ing, -seis·es** To dispossess unlawfully of real property; oust. [ME *disseisen* < AN *disseisir,* var. of OFr. *dessaisir* : *des-,* dis- + *saisir,* to seize; see SEIZE.]

dis·sei·zin also **dis·sei·sin** (dĭs-sē′zĭn) *n.* Wrongful dispossession of one in the possession of real property. [ME *disseisine* < AN, var. of OFr. *dessaisine* : *des-,* dis- + *seisine,* seisin; see SEISIN.]

dis·sem·ble (dĭ-sĕm′bəl) *v.* **-bled, -bling, -bles** —*tr.* **1.** To disguise or conceal behind a false appearance; feign. **2.** To make a false show of; feign. —*intr.* To dissemble one's real nature, motives, or feelings. [ME *dissemblen* < OFr. *dessembler,* to be different : *des-,* dis- + *sembler,* to appear, seem; see SEMBLABLE.] **—dis·sem′blance** *n.* **—dis·sem′bler** *n.* **—dis·sem′bling·ly** *adv.*

dis·sem·i·nate (dĭ-sĕm′ə-nāt′) *v.* **-nat·ed, -nat·ing, -nates** —*tr.* **1.** To scatter widely, as in sowing seed. **2.** To spread abroad; promulgate: *disseminate information.* —*intr.* To become diffused; spread. [Lat. *dissēmināre, dissēmināt-* : *dis-,* dis- + *sēmināre,* to sow (< *sēmen, sēmin-,* seed; see sē- in App.).] **—dis·sem′i·na′tion** *n.* **—dis·sem′i·na′tor** *n.*

dis·sem·i·nat·ed (dĭ-sĕm′ə-nā′tĭd) *adj.* Spread over a large area of a body, tissue, or organ.

dis·sem·i·nule (dĭ-sĕm′ə-nyo͞ol′) *n.* A reproductive plant part, such as a seed, fruit, or spore, that is modified for dispersal. [DISSEMIN(ATE) + -ULE.]

dis·sen·sion (dĭ-sĕn′shən) *n.* Difference of opinion. [ME *dissencioun* < OFr. *dissension* < Lat. *dissēnsiō, dissēnsiōn-* < *dissēnsus,* p. part. of *dissentīre,* to dissent. See DISSENT.]

dis·sent (dĭ-sĕnt′) *intr.v.* **-sent·ed, -sent·ing, -sents 1.** To differ in opinion or feeling; disagree. **2.** To withhold assent or approval. ❖ *n.* **1.** Difference of opinion or feeling; disagreement. **2.** The refusal to conform to the authority or doctrine of an established church; nonconformity. **3.** *Law* A justice's refusal to concur with the opinion of a majority, as on a higher court. [ME *dissenten* < Lat. *dissentīre* : *dis-,* dis- + *sentīre,* to feel.] **—dis·sent′ing·ly** *adv.*

dis·sent·er (dĭ-sĕn′tər) *n.* **1.** One who dissents. **2.** often **Dissenter** One who refuses to accept the doctrines of an established church, esp. the Church of England.

dis·sen·tient (dĭ-sĕn′shənt) *adj.* Dissenting, esp. from the sentiment or policies of a majority. ❖ *n.* A dissenter. **—dis·sen′tience** *n.*

dis·sent·ing opinion *n.* See **dissent 3.**

dis·sep·i·ment (dĭ-sĕp′ə-mənt) *n.* *Botany* A partition dividing an organ into chambers. [Lat. *dissaepīmentum,* partition < *dissaepīre,* to divide : *dis-* + *saepīre,* hedge off (< *saepēs,* hedge).] **—dis·sep′i·men′tal** (-mĕn′tl) *adj.*

dis·ser·tate (dĭs′ər-tāt′) also **dis·sert** (dĭ-sûrt′) *intr.v.* **-tat·ed, -tat·ing, -tates** also **-sert·ed, -sert·ing, -serts** To discourse formally. [Lat. *dissertāre, dissertāt-,* freq. of *disserere,* to discuss : *dis-,* dis- + *serere,* to connect.] **—dis′ser·ta′tor** *n.*

dis·ser·ta·tion (dĭs′ər-tā′shən) *n.* A lengthy formal treatise, esp. one written by a candidate for the doctoral degree at a university; a thesis.

dis·serve (dĭs-sûrv′) *tr.v.* **-served, -serv·ing, -serves** To treat badly; harm.

dis·ser·vice (dĭs-sûr′vĭs) *n.* A harmful action; an injury.

dis·sev·er (dĭ-sĕv′ər) *v.* **-ered, -er·ing, -ers** —*tr.* **1.** To separate; sever. **2.** To divide into parts; break up. —*intr.* To become separated or disunited. [ME *disseveren* < OFr. *dessevrer* < LLat. *dissē-*

Benjamin Disraeli
1881 portrait by Sir John
Everett Millais

parāre : Lat. *dis-*, dis- + Lat. *sēparāre*; see SEPARATE.] **—dis•sev′er•ance, dis•sev′er•ment** *n.*

dis•si•dence (dĭs′ĭ-dəns) *n.* Disagreement, as of opinion or belief; dissent.

dis•si•dent (dĭs′ĭ-dənt) *adj.* Disagreeing, as in opinion or belief. ❖ *n.* One who disagrees; a dissenter. [Lat. *dissidēns, dissident-*, pr. part. of *dissidēre*, to disagree : *dis-*, apart; see DIS– + *sedēre*, to sit; see **sed-** in App.]

dis•sim•i•lar (dĭ-sĭm′ə-lər) *adj.* Unlike; different. **—dis•sim′i•lar•ly** *adv.*

dis•sim•i•lar•i•ty (dĭ-sĭm′ə-lăr′ĭ-tē) *n., pl.* **-ties 1.** The quality of being distinct or unlike; difference. **2.** A point of distinction or difference. See Syns at **difference.**

dis•sim•i•late (dĭ-sĭm′ə-lāt′) *v.* **-lat•ed, -lat•ing, -lates** *—tr.* **1.** To make unlike or dissimilar. **2.** *Linguistics* To cause to undergo dissimilation. *—intr.* **1.** To become unlike or dissimilar. **2.** *Linguistics* To undergo dissimilation. [DIS– + (AS)SIMILATE.]

dis•sim•i•la•tion (dĭ-sĭm′ə-lā′shən) *n.* **1.** The act or process of making or becoming dissimilar. **2.** *Linguistics* The process by which one of two similar or identical sounds in a word becomes less like the other, such as the *l* in English *marble* (from French *marbre*).

dis•si•mil•i•tude (dĭs′ə-mĭl′ĭ-to͞od′, -tyo͞od′) *n.* Lack of resemblance; dissimilarity. [ME < Lat. *dissimilitūdō* < *dissimilis*, different : *dis-*, dis- + *similis*, like; see SIMILAR.]

dis•sim•u•late (dĭ-sĭm′yə-lāt′) *v.* **-lat•ed, -lat•ing, -lates** *—tr.* To disguise (one's intentions, for example) under a feigned appearance. *—intr.* To conceal one's feelings or intentions. [ME *dissimulaten* < Lat. *dissimulāre, dissimulāt-* : *dis-*, dis- + *simulāre*, to simulate; see SIMULATE.] **—dis•sim′u•la′tion** *n.* **—dis•sim′u•la′tive** *adj.* **—dis•sim′u•la′tor** *n.*

dis•si•pate (dĭs′ə-pāt′) *v.* **-pat•ed, -pat•ing, -pates** *—tr.* **1.** To drive away; disperse. **2.** To attenuate to or almost to the point of disappearing. **3a.** To spend or expend intemperately or wastefully; squander. **b.** To use up, esp. recklessly; exhaust: *dissipated their energy.* **4.** To cause to lose (energy, such as heat) irreversibly. *—intr.* **1.** To vanish by dispersion. **2.** To indulge in the intemperate pursuit of pleasure. [ME *dissipaten* < Lat. *dissipāre, dissipāt-*.] **—dis′si•pat′er, dis′si•pa′tor** *n.* **—dis′si•pa′tive** *adj.*

dis•si•pat•ed (dĭs′ə-pā′tĭd) *adj.* **1.** Intemperate in the pursuit of pleasure; dissolute. **2.** Wasted or squandered. **3.** Irreversibly lost. Used of energy. **—dis′si•pat′ed•ly** *adv.*

dis•si•pa•tion (dĭs′ə-pā′shən) *n.* **1.** The act of dissipating or the condition of having been dissipated. **2.** Wasteful expenditure or consumption. **3.** Dissolute indulgence in sensual pleasure; intemperance. **4.** An amusement; a diversion.

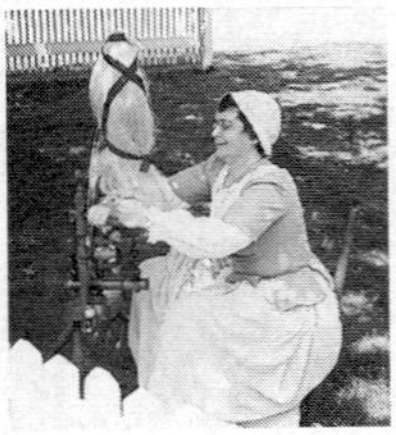

distaff

dis•so•cia•ble (dĭ-sō′shə-bəl, -shē-ə-bəl) *adj.* That can be dissociated; separable. **—dis•so′cia•bil′i•ty, dis•so′cia•ble•ness** *n.* **—dis•so′cia•bly** *adv.*

dis•so•ci•ate (dĭ-sō′shē-āt′, -sē-) *v.* **-at•ed, -at•ing, -ates** *—tr.* **1.** To remove from association; separate. **2.** *Chemistry* To cause to undergo dissociation. *—intr.* **1.** To cease associating; part. **2.** *Biology* To mutate or change morphologically, often reversibly. **3.** *Chemistry* To undergo dissociation. [Lat. *dissociāre, dissociāt-* : *dis-*, dis- + *sociāre*, to unite (< *socius*, companion; see **sek^{w}-[1]** in App.).] **—dis•so′ci•a′tive** *adj.*

dis•so•ci•a•tion (dĭ-sō′sē-ā′shən, -shē-) *n.* **1.** The act of dissociating or the condition of having been dissociated. **2.** *Chemistry* **a.** The process by which the action of a solvent or a change in physical condition, as in temperature, causes a molecule to split into simpler groups of atoms or ions. **b.** The separation of an electrolyte into ions of opposite charge. **3.** *Psychology* A defense mechanism in which anxiety-provoking thoughts, emotions, or physical sensations are separated from the rest of the psyche.

dis•sol•u•ble (dĭ-sŏl′yə-bəl) *adj.* That can be dissolved. [Lat. *dissolūbilis* < *dissolūtus*, p. part. of *dissolvere*, to dissolve. See DISSOLVE.] **—dis′sol•u•bil′i•ty, dis•sol′u•ble•ness** *n.*

dis•so•lute (dĭs′ə-lo͞ot′) *adj.* Lacking moral restraint; indulging in sensual pleasures or vices. [ME < Lat. *dissolūtus*, p. part. of *dissolvere*, to dissolve. See DISSOLVE.] **—dis′so•lute′ly** *adv.* **—dis′so•lute′ness** *n.*

dis•so•lu•tion (dĭs′ə-lo͞o′shən) *n.* **1.** Decomposition into fragments or parts; disintegration. **2.** Indulgence in sensual pleasures; debauchery. **3.** Termination or extinction by disintegration or dispersion. **4.** Extinction of life; death. **5.** Annulment or termination of a formal or legal bond, or contract. **6.** Formal dismissal of an assembly or legislature. **7.** Reduction to a liquid form; liquefaction. **—dis′so•lu′tive** *adj.*

dis•solve (dĭ-zŏlv′) *v.* **-solved, -solv•ing, -solves** *—tr.* **1.** To cause to pass into solution. **2.** To reduce (solid matter) to liquid form; melt. **3.** To cause to disappear or vanish; dispel. **4.** To break into component parts; disintegrate. **5.** To bring to an end by or as if by breaking up; terminate. **6.** To dismiss (a legislative body, for example). **7.** To cause to break down emotionally or psychologically; upset. **8.** To cause to lose definition; blur; confuse. **9.** *Law* To annul; abrogate. *—intr.* **1.** To pass into solution. **2.** To become liquid; melt. **3.** To break up or disperse. **4.** To become disintegrated; disappear. **5.** To be overcome emotionally or psychologically. **6.** To lose clarity or definition; fade away. **7.** To shift shots in a film or videotape by having one shot fade out while the next simultaneously grows clearer. ❖ *n.* A transition in a film or videotape made by fading out one shot while the next one grows clearer. [ME *dissolven* < Lat. *dissolvere* : *dis-*, dis- + *solvere*, to release; see **leu-** in App.] **—dis•solv′a•ble** *adj.* **—dis•solv′er** *n.*

dis•sol•vent (dĭ-zŏl′vənt) *adj.* Capable of dissolving a substance; solvent. ❖ *n.* A solvent.

dis•so•nance (dĭs′ə-nəns) *n.* **1.** A harsh disagreeable combination of sounds; discord. **2.** Lack of agreement, consistency, or harmony; conflict. **3.** *Music* A combination of tones considered to suggest unrelieved tension and require resolution.

dis•so•nan•cy (dĭs′ə-nən-sē) *n., pl.* **-cies** Dissonance.

dis•so•nant (dĭs′ə-nənt) *adj.* **1.** Harsh and inharmonious in sound; discordant. **2.** Being at variance; disagreeing. **3.** *Music* Constituting or producing a dissonance. [ME *dissonaunt* < OFr. *dissonant* < Lat. *dissonāns, dissonant-*, pr. part. of *dissonāre*, to be dissonant : *dis-*, apart; see DIS– + *sonāre*, to sound.] **—dis′so•nant•ly** *adv.*

dis•suade (dĭ-swād′) *tr.v.* **-suad•ed, -suad•ing, -suades** To deter (a person) from a course of action or a purpose by persuasion or exhortation. [Lat. *dissuādēre* : *dis-*, dis- + *suādēre*, to advise; see **swād-** in App.] **—dis•suad′er** *n.*

dis•sua•sion (dĭ-swā′zhən) *n.* The act or an instance of dissuading. [Ult. < Lat. *dissuāsiō, dissuāsiōn-* < *dissuāsus*, p. part. of *dissuādēre*, to dissuade. See DISSUADE.] **—dis•sua′sive** *adj.* **—dis•sua′sive•ly** *adv.* **—dis•sua′sive•ness** *n.*

dis•syl•la•ble (dĭ′sĭl′ə-bəl, dĭ-sĭl′-, dī-) *n.* Variant of **disyllable.**

dis•sym•me•try (dĭs-sĭm′ĭ-trē) *n., pl.* **-tries** Lack of symmetry. **—dis′sym•met′ric** (dĭs′sĭ-mĕt′rĭk), **dis′sym•met′ri•cal** (-rĭ-kəl) *adj.* **—dis′sym•met′ri•cal•ly** *adv.*

dist. *abbr.* **1.** distance **2.** district

dis•taff (dĭs′tăf′) *n.* **1a.** A staff that holds the unspun flax, wool, or tow from which thread is drawn in spinning by hand. **b.** An attachment for a spinning wheel that serves this purpose. **2.** Work and concerns traditionally considered important to women. **3.** Women considered as a group. [ME *distaf* < OE *distæf* : *dis-*, bunch of flax + *stæf*, staff.]

distaff side *n.* The female line or maternal branch of a family.

dis•tal (dĭs′təl) *adj.* **1.** Anatomically located far from a point of reference. **2.** Situated farthest from the middle and front of the jaw, as a tooth. [DIST(ANT) + –AL[1].] **—dis′tal•ly** *adv.*

dis•tance (dĭs′təns) *n.* **1.** The extent of space between two objects or places; an intervening space. **2.** The fact or condition of being apart in space; remoteness. **3.** *Mathematics* The length or numerical value of a straight line or curve. **4a.** The extent of space between points on a measured course. **b.** The length of a race, esp. of a horserace. **5a.** A point or an area that is far away. **b.** A depiction of such a point or area. **6.** A stretch of space without designation of limit; an expanse. **7.** The extent of time between two events; an intervening period. **8.** A point removed in time. **9.** The full period or length of a contest or game. **10.** An amount of progress. **11.** Difference or disagreement. **12.** Emotional separateness or reserve. ❖ *tr.v.* **-tanced, -tanc•ing, -tanc•es 1.** To place or keep at or as if at a distance. **2.** To cause to appear at a distance. **3.** To leave far behind; outrun.

distance learning *n.* Education in which students take academic courses by accessing information and communicating with the instructor asynchronously over a computer network.

dis•tant (dĭs′tənt) *adj.* **1a.** Separate or apart in space. **b.** Far removed; remote. **2.** Coming from or going to a distance: *a distant sound.* **3.** Far removed or apart in time: *the distant past.* **4.** Far apart in relationship: *a distant cousin.* **5.** Minimally similar: *a distant likeness.* **6.** Far removed mentally. **7.** Aloof or chilly. [ME *distaunt* < OFr. < Lat. *distāns, distant-*, pr. part. of *distāre*, to be remote : *dī-, dis-*, apart; see DIS– + *stāre*, to stand; see **stā-** in App.] **—dis′tant•ly** *adv.*

dis•taste (dĭs-tāst′) *n.* Dislike or aversion. ❖ *tr.v.* **-tast•ed, -tast•ing, -tastes** *Archaic* **1.** To feel repugnance for; dislike. **2.** To offend; displease.

dis•taste•ful (dĭs-tāst′fəl) *adj.* **1a.** Unpleasant; disagreeable. **b.** Objectionable; offensive. **2.** Expressing aversion or dislike. **—dis•taste′ful•ly** *adv.* **—dis•taste′ful•ness** *n.*

Dist. Atty. *abbr.* district attorney

dis•tel•fink (dĭs′tl-fĭngk) *n.* A traditional Pennsylvania Dutch folk art motif of a bird or birds symbolizing good luck and happiness. [< Ger., goldfinch < MHGer. *distelvinke* < OHGer. *distilvinko* : *distil*, thistle + *vinko*, finch.]

dis•tem•per[1] (dĭs-tĕm′pər) *n.* **1a.** An infectious viral disease occurring in dogs, characterized by catarrh, vomiting, fever, lethargy, partial paralysis, and sometimes death. **b.** A similar viral disease of cats characterized by fever, vomiting, diarrhea leading to dehydration, and sometimes death. **c.** Any of various similar mammalian diseases. **2.** An illness or disease; an ailment. **3.** Ill humor; testiness. **4.** Disorder or disturbance, esp. of a social or political nature. ❖ *tr.v.* **-pered, -per•ing, -pers 1.** To put out of order. **2.** *Archaic* To unsettle; derange. [< ME *distemperen*, to upset the balance of the humors < OFr. *destemprer*, to disturb < LLat. *distemperāre* : Lat. *dis-*, dis- + Lat. *temperāre*, to mix properly.]

dis•tem•per[2] (dĭs-tĕm′pər) *n.* **1a.** A process of painting in which pigments are mixed with water and a glue-size or casein binder, used esp. for flat wall decoration. **b.** The paint used in this process. **2.** A painting made by this process. ❖ *tr.v.* **-pered, -per•**

ing, -pers 1. To mix (powdered pigments or colors) with water and size. **2.** To paint (a work) in distemper. [ME *distemperen,* to dilute. See DISTEMPER[1].]

dis•tend (dĭ-stĕnd′) *v.* **-tend•ed, -tend•ing, -tends** *—intr.* To swell out or expand from or as if from internal pressure. *—tr.* **1.** To cause to distend; dilate. **2.** To extend. [ME *distenden* < Lat. *distendere* : *dis-,* dis- + *tendere,* to stretch; see **ten-** in App.]

dis•ten•si•ble (dĭ-stĕn′sə-bəl) *adj.* That can be distended: *a fish with a distensible stomach.* **—dis•ten′si•bil′i•ty** *n.*

dis•ten•tion also **dis•ten•sion** (dĭ-stĕn′shən) *n.* The act of distending or the state of being distended. [ME *distensioun* < OFr. < Lat. *distēnsiō, distēnsiōn-,* alteration of *distentiō* < *distentus,* p. part. of *distendere,* to distend. See DISTEND.]

dis•tich (dĭs′tĭk) *n., pl.* **-tichs 1.** A unit of verse consisting of two lines, esp. as used in Greek and Latin elegiac poetry. **2.** A rhyming couplet. [Lat. *distichon* < Gk. *distikhon* < neut. of *distikhos,* having two rows or verses : *di-,* two; see DI–[1] + *stikhos,* line of verse; see **steigh-** in App.]

dis•ti•chous (dĭs′tĭ-kəs) *adj. Botany* Arranged in two vertical rows on opposite sides of an axis: *distichous leaves.* [< Lat. *distichus,* having two rows < Gk. *distikhos.* See DISTICH.] **—dis′ti•chous•ly** *adv.*

dis•till also **dis•til** (dĭ-stĭl′) *v.* **-tilled, -till•ing, -tills** also **-tilled, -til•ling, -tils** *—tr.* **1.** To subject (a substance) to distillation. **2.** To separate (a distillate) by distillation. **3.** To increase the concentration of, separate, or purify by or as if by distillation. **4.** To separate or extract the essential elements of. **5.** To exude or give off (matter) in drops or small quantities. *—intr.* **1.** To undergo or be produced by distillation. **2.** To fall or exude in drops or small quantities. [ME *distillen* < OFr. *distiller* < Lat. *distillāre,* var. of *dēstillāre,* to trickle : *dē-,* de- + *stillāre,* to drip (< *stilla,* drop).] **—dis•till′a•ble** *adj.*

dis•til•late (dĭs′tə-lāt′, -lĭt, dĭ-stĭl′ĭt) *n.* **1.** A liquid condensed from vapor in distillation. **2.** A purified form; an essence.

dis•til•la•tion (dĭs′tə-lā′shən) *n.* **1.** The evaporation and subsequent collection of a liquid by condensation as a means of purification. **2.** The extraction of the volatile components of a mixture by the condensation and collection of the vapors that are produced as the mixture is heated. **3.** A distillate.

dis•till•er (dĭ-stĭl′ər) *n.* **1.** One that distills, as a condenser. **2.** One that makes alcoholic liquors by the process of distillation.

dis•till•er•y (dĭ-stĭl′ə-rē) *n., pl.* **-ies** An establishment for distilling, esp. for distilling alcoholic liquors.

dis•tinct (dĭ-stĭngkt′) *adj.* **1.** Readily distinguishable from all others; discrete. **2.** Easily perceived by the senses or intellect; clear. See Syns at **apparent. 3.** Clearly defined; unquestionable: *at a distinct disadvantage.* **4.** Very likely; probable. **5.** Notable: *a distinct honor.* [ME, p. part. of *distincten,* to discern < OFr. *destincter* < Lat. *dīstīnctus,* p. part. of *dīstinguere,* to distinguish. See DISTINGUISH.] **—dis•tinct′ly** *adv.* **—dis•tinct′ness** *n.*

dis•tinc•tion (dĭ-stĭngk′shən) *n.* **1.** The act of distinguishing; differentiation. **2.** The condition or fact of being dissimilar or distinct; difference. See Syns at **difference. 3.** A distinguishing factor, attribute, or characteristic. **4a.** Excellence or eminence, as of performance, character, or reputation. **b.** A special feature or quality conferring superiority. **5.** Recognition of achievement or superiority; honor.

dis•tinc•tive (dĭ-stĭngk′tĭv) *adj.* **1.** Serving to identify; distinguishing. **2.** Characteristic or typical. **3.** *Linguistics* Phonemically relevant and capable of conveying a difference in meaning, as nasalization in the initial sound of *mat* versus *bat.* **—dis•tinc′tive•ly** *adv.* **—dis•tinc′tive•ness** *n.*

dis•tin•gué (dēs′tăng-gā′, dĭs′-, dĭ-stăng′gā) *adj.* Distinguished in appearance, manner, or bearing. [Fr., p. part. of *distinguer,* to distinguish < OFr. See DISTINGUISH.]

dis•tin•guish (dĭ-stĭng′gwĭsh) *v.* **-guished, -guish•ing, -guish•es** *—tr.* **1.** To perceive as being different or distinct. **2.** To perceive distinctly; discern. **3.** To make noticeable or different; set apart. **4.** To cause (oneself) to be eminent or recognized. *—intr.* To perceive or indicate differences; discriminate: *distinguish between right and wrong.* [Alteration of obsolete *distingue* < ME *distinguen* < OFr. *distinguer* < Lat. *dīstinguere,* to separate.] **—dis•tin′guish•a•ble** *adj.* **—dis•tin′guish•a•bly** *adv.*

dis•tin•guished (dĭ-stĭng′gwĭsht) *adj.* **1.** Characterized by excellence or distinction; eminent. **2.** Dignified in conduct or appearance.

Distinguished Conduct Medal *n.* A British military decoration for distinguished conduct in the field.

Distinguished Flying Cross *n.* **1.** A US military decoration awarded for heroism or extraordinary achievement in aerial combat. **2.** A British military decoration awarded to officers of the Royal Air Force for extraordinary achievement.

Distinguished Service Cross *n.* **1.** A US Army decoration awarded for exceptional heroism in combat. **2.** A British military decoration awarded to officers of the Royal Navy for gallantry in action.

Distinguished Service Medal *n.* **1.** A US military decoration awarded for distinguished performance in a duty of great responsibility. **2.** A British military decoration awarded to noncommissioned officers and members of the Royal Navy and Royal Marines for distinguished conduct in war.

Distinguished Service Order *n.* A British military decoration for gallantry in action.

dis•tort (dĭ-stôrt′) *tr.v.* **-tort•ed, -tort•ing, -torts 1.** To twist out of a proper or natural relation of parts; misshape. **2.** To give a false or misleading account of; misrepresent. **3.** To cause to work in a twisted or disorderly manner; pervert. [Lat. *distorquēre, distort-* : *dis-,* apart; see DIS– + *torquēre,* to twist.] **—dis•tort′er** *n.* **—dis•tor′tive** (-stôr′tĭv) *adj.*

dis•tor•tion (dĭ-stôr′shən) *n.* **1a.** The act or an instance of distorting. **b.** The condition of being distorted. **2.** A statement that twists fact; a misrepresentation. **3.** A change in the shape of an image resulting from imperfections in an optical system, such as a lens. **4.** *Electronics* **a.** An undesired change in the waveform of a signal. **b.** A consequence of such a change, esp. a lack of fidelity in reception or reproduction. **5.** *Psychology* The modification of unconscious impulses into forms acceptable by conscious or dreaming perception. **—dis•tor′tion•al, dis•tor′tion•ar′y** *adj.*

dis•tract (dĭ-străkt′) *tr.v.* **-tract•ed, -tract•ing, -tracts 1.** To cause to turn away from the original focus of attention or interest; divert. **2.** To pull in conflicting emotional directions; unsettle. [ME *distracten* < Lat. *distrahere, distract-,* to pull away : *dis-,* apart; see DIS– + *trahere,* to draw.] **—dis•tract′ing•ly** *adv.* **—dis•trac′tive** *adj.*

dis•tract•ed (dĭ-străk′tĭd) *adj.* **1.** Having the attention diverted. **2.** Suffering conflicting emotions; distraught. **—dis•tract′ed•ly** *adv.*

dis•tract•er also **dis•trac•tor** (dĭ-străk′tər) *n.* One of the incorrect answers presented as a choice in a multiple-choice test.

dis•trac•tion (dĭ-străk′shən) *n.* **1.** The act of distracting or the condition of being distracted. **2.** Something, esp. an amusement, that distracts. **3.** Extreme mental or emotional disturbance; obsession: *loved the puppy to distraction.*

dis•train (dĭ-strān′) *v.* **-trained, -train•ing, -trains** *Law —tr.* **1.** To seize and hold (property) to compel payment or reparation. **2.** To seize the property of (a person) in order to compel payment of debts. *—intr.* To levy a distress. [ME *distreinen* < OFr. *destreindre, destreign-* < Med.Lat. *dīstringere, dīstrinct-* < Lat., to hinder : *dī-, dis-,* apart; see DIS– + *stringere,* to draw tight.] **—dis•train′a•ble** *adj.* **—dis•train′ment** *n.* **—dis•trai′nor, dis•train′er** *n.*

dis•train•ee (dĭs′trā-nē′) *n. Law* One that has been distrained.

dis•traint (dĭ-strānt′) *n. Law* The act or process of distraining; distress. [< DISTRAIN (on the model of such pairs as *constrain, constraint*).]

dis•trait (dĭ-strā′) *adj.* Inattentive or preoccupied, esp. because of anxiety. [ME < OFr., p. part. of *distraire,* to distract < Lat. *distrahere.* See DISTRACT.]

dis•traught (dĭ-strôt′) *adj.* **1.** Deeply agitated, as from emotional conflict. **2.** Mad; insane. [ME, alteration of *distract,* p. part. of *distracten,* to distract. See DISTRACT.]

dis•tress (dĭ-strĕs′) *tr.v.* **-tressed, -tress•ing, -tress•es 1.** To cause strain, anxiety, or suffering to. See Syns at **trouble. 2.** To mar or otherwise treat (a fabric, for example) to give the appearance of an antique or of heavy use. **3.** *Archaic* To constrain or overcome by harassment. ❖ *n.* **1.** Anxiety or mental suffering. **2a.** Severe strain resulting from exhaustion or an accident. **b.** Acute physical discomfort. **c.** Physical deterioration caused by hard use over time. **3.** The condition of being in need of immediate help: *a motorist in distress.* [ME *distressen* < OFr. *destresser* < *destresse,* constraint < VLat. **dīstrictia* < Lat. *dīstrictus,* p. part. of *dīstringere,* to hinder. See DISTRAIN.] **—dis•tress′ing•ly** *adv.*

dis•tressed (dĭ-strĕst′) *adj.* **1.** Suffering distress. **2.** Damaged or previously used. **3.** Having been foreclosed and offered for sale, usu. below market value. **4.** Intentionally marred or faded to convey an antique or used look.

dis•tress•ful (dĭ-strĕs′fəl) *adj.* Causing or experiencing distress. **—dis•tress′ful•ly** *adv.* **—dis•tress′ful•ness** *n.*

distress signal *n.* An international signal used by a distressed ship or aircraft to request help.

dis•trib•u•tar•y (dĭ-strĭb′yə-tĕr′ē) *n., pl.* **-ies** A branch of a river that flows away from the main stream.

dis•trib•ute (dĭ-strĭb′yo͞ot) *v.* **-ut•ed, -ut•ing, -utes** *—tr.* **1.** To divide and dispense in portions. **2a.** To supply (goods) to retailers. **b.** To deliver or pass out. **3a.** To spread or diffuse over an area; scatter. **b.** To apportion so as to be evenly spread throughout a given area. **4.** To separate into categories; classify. **5.** *Logic* To use (a term) so as to include all individuals or entities of a given class. *—intr. Mathematics* To be distributive. [ME *distributen* < Lat. *distribuere, distribūt-* : *dis-,* apart; see DIS– + *tribuere,* to give; see TRIBUTE.]

SYNONYMS *distribute, divide, dispense, dole, deal, ration* These verbs mean to give out in portions or shares. *Distribute* is the least specific: *The government distributed land to settlers. Divide* implies giving out portions, often equal, on the basis of a plan or purpose: *The estate will be divided among the heirs. Dispense* stresses the careful determination of portions, often according to measurement or weight: *dispensed the medication. Dole,* often followed by *out,* implies careful, usually sparing measurement of portions: *The professor doled out praise to the best students. Deal* implies orderly equitable distribution, often piece by piece: *dealt five cards to each player. Ration* refers to equitable division in lim-

ă	pat	oi	boy
ā	pay	ou	out
âr	care	o͝o	took
ä	father	o͞o	boot
ĕ	pet	ŭ	cut
ē	be	ûr	urge
ĭ	pit	th	thin
ī	pie	*th*	this
îr	pier	hw	which
ŏ	pot	zh	vision
ō	toe	ə	about, item
ô	paw		

Stress marks:
′ (primary);
′ (secondary), as in
lexicon (lĕk′sĭ-kŏn′)

ited portions of scarce, often necessary items: *rationing fuel during the war.*

dis•tri•bu•tion (dĭs′trə-byo͞o′shən) *n.* **1.** The act of distributing or the condition of being distributed; apportionment. **2.** Something distributed; an allotment. **3.** The act of dispersing or the condition of being dispersed; diffusion. **4a.** The geographic occurrence or range of an organism. **b.** The geographic occurrence or range of a custom, usage, or other feature. **5.** Division into categories; classification. **6.** The process of marketing and supplying goods, esp. to retailers. **7.** A spatial or temporal array of objects or events. **8.** *Law* The division of an estate or property among rightful heirs. **9.** *Statistics* A set of numbers and their frequency of occurrence collected from measurements over a statistical population. **10.** *Mathematics* A generalized function used in the study of partial differential equations. **—dis′tri•bu′tion•al** *adj.*

dis•trib•u•tive (dĭ-strĭb′yə-tĭv) *adj.* **1a.** Of, relating to, or involving distribution. **b.** Serving to distribute. **2.** *Mathematics* Of or relating to a rule that the same product results in multiplication when performed on a set of numbers as when performed on members of the set individually. If $a \times (b + c) = a \times b + a \times c$, then × is distributive over +. **3.** *Grammar* Referring to each individual or entity of a group separately rather than collectively, as *every* in the sentence *Every employee attended the meeting.* ❖ *n.* A distributive word or term. **—dis•trib′u•tive•ly** *adv.* **—dis•trib′u•tive•ness** *n.*

dis•trib•u•tor (dĭ-strĭb′yə-tər) *n.* **1.** One that distributes, esp. a device that applies electric current in proper sequence to the spark plugs of an engine. **2.** One that markets or sells merchandise, esp. a wholesaler. **—dis•trib′u•tor•ship′** *n.*

dis•trict (dĭs′trĭkt) *n.* **1.** A division of an area, as for administrative purposes. **2.** A region or locality marked by a distinguishing feature: *the lake district.* ❖ *tr.v.* **-trict•ed, -trict•ing, -tricts** To mark off or divide into districts. [Fr. < OFr. < Med.Lat. *dīstrictus* < Lat., p. part. of *dīstringere,* to hinder. See DISTRAIN.] **—dis′trict•wide′** *adv. & adj.*

district attorney *n.* The prosecuting officer of a judicial district.

district court *n.* **1.** A US federal trial court serving a judicial district. **2.** A state court of general jurisdiction in some states.

District of Columbia A federal district of the E US, on the Potomac R. between VA and MD; coextensive with the city of Washington.

dis•trust (dĭs-trŭst′) *n.* Lack of trust or confidence. ❖ *tr.v.* **-trust•ed, -trust•ing, -trusts** To have no confidence in.

dis•trust•ful (dĭs-trŭst′fəl) *adj.* Feeling or showing doubt. **—dis•trust′ful•ly** *adv.* **—dis•trust′ful•ness** *n.*

dis•turb (dĭ-stûrb′) *tr.v.* **-turbed, -turb•ing, -turbs 1.** To break up or destroy the tranquillity or settled state of. **2.** To trouble emotionally or mentally; upset. **3a.** To interfere with; interrupt. **b.** To intrude on; inconvenience. **4.** To put out of order; disarrange. [ME *distourben* < OFr. *destourber* < Lat. *disturbāre* : Lat. *dis-,* dis- + Lat. *turbāre,* to agitate (< *turba,* confusion, prob. < Gk. *turbē*).] **—dis•turb′er** *n.* **—dis•turb′ing•ly** *adv.*

dis•tur•bance (dĭ-stûr′bəns) *n.* **1a.** The act of disturbing. **b.** The condition of being disturbed. **2.** Something that disturbs, as a commotion. **3.** Mental or emotional unbalance or disorder. **4.** A variation in normal wind conditions. **5.** *Geology* Folding or faulting that affects a relatively large area.

dis•turbed (dĭ-stûrbd′) *adj.* Showing signs or symptoms of mental or emotional illness.

di•sul•fide (dī-sŭl′fīd′) *n.* A chemical compound containing two sulfur atoms combined with other elements or radicals.

dis•un•ion (dĭs-yo͞on′yən) *n.* **1.** The state of being disunited; separation. **2.** Lack of unity; discord.

dis•un•ion•ist (dĭs-yo͞on′yə-nĭst) *n.* An advocate of disunion, esp. a secessionist during the US Civil War.

dis•u•nite (dĭs′yo͞o-nīt′) *tr. & intr.v.* **-nit•ed, -nit•ing, -nites** To separate or become separate.

dis•u•ni•ty (dĭs-yo͞o′nĭ-tē) *n., pl.* **-ties** Lack of unity.

dis•use (dĭs-yo͞os′) *n.* The state of not being used or of being no longer in use.

dis•u•til•i•ty (dĭs′yo͞o-tĭl′ĭ-tē) *n.* The state or fact of being useless or counterproductive.

dis•val•ue (dĭs-văl′yo͞o) *tr.v.* **-ued, -u•ing, -ues 1.** To regard as of little or no value. **2.** *Archaic* To disparage. ❖ *n.* **1.** A negative value of something. **2.** *Obsolete* Disesteem.

di•syl•la•ble also **dis•syl•la•ble** (dī′sĭl′ə-bəl, dī-sĭl′-, dĭ-) *n.* A word with two syllables. **—di′syl•lab′ic** (dī′sĭ-lăb′ĭk, dĭs′sĭ-) *adj.*

dit (dĭt) *n.* The dot in radio and telegraph code. [Imit.]

ditch (dĭch) *n.* A long narrow trench or furrow dug in the ground, as for irrigation. ❖ *v.* **ditched, ditch•ing, ditch•es** *—tr.* **1.** To dig or make a ditch in. **2.** To surround with a ditch. **3a.** To drive (a vehicle) into a ditch. **b.** To derail (a train). **4.** *Slang* **a.** To get rid of; discard. **b.** To get away from (a person). **c.** *Slang* To discontinue use of or association with. **d.** To skip (class or school). **5.** To crash-land (an aircraft) on water. *—intr.* **1.** To dig a ditch. **2.** To crash-land in water. [ME *dich* < OE *dīc.*]

dith•er (dĭth′ər) *n.* A state of indecisive agitation. ❖ *intr.v.* **-ered, -er•ing, -ers** To be nervously irresolute in acting or doing. [Alteration of *didder* < ME *dideren,* to tremble. See DIDDLE².]

dith•y•ramb (dĭth′ĭ-răm′, -rămb′) *n.* **1.** A frenzied impassioned choric hymn and dance of ancient Greece in honor of Dionysus. **2.** An irregular poetic expression suggestive of the ancient Greek dithyramb. **3.** A wildly enthusiastic speech or piece of writing. [Lat. *dīthyrambus* < Gk. *dīthurambos.*] **—dith′y•ramb′ic** *adj.*

di•tran•si•tive (dī-trăn′sĭ-tĭv, -zĭ-) *adj.* Of or relating to a verb that takes or can take two objects, as *find* in *She found him a job.* ❖ *n.* A ditransitive verb. **—di•tran′si•tiv′i•ty** *n.*

dit•sy also **dit•zy** (dĭt′sē) *adj.* **-si•er, -si•est** also **-zi•er, -zi•est** *Slang* Eccentric or scatterbrained. [Perh. blend of DOTTY + DIZZY.]

dit•ta•ny (dĭt′n-ē) *n., pl.* **-nies 1.** An aromatic woolly plant *(Origanum dictamnus)* native to Crete and formerly believed to have magical powers. **2.** See **gas plant.** [ME *ditaine* < OFr. *ditan* < Lat. *dictamnus* < Gk. *diktamnon,* perhaps after Mount *Diktē* (Dhíkti), a peak in eastern Crete.]

dit•to (dĭt′ō) *n., pl.* **-tos 1.** The same as stated above or before. **2.** A duplicate; a copy. **3.** A pair of small marks (") used to indicate that the word, phrase, or figure given above is to be repeated. ❖ *adv.* As before. ❖ *tr.v.* **-toed, -to•ing, -tos** To duplicate (a document, for example). [Ital. dialectal, p. part. of Ital. *dire,* to say < Lat. *dīcere.* See **deik-** in App.]

dit•ty (dĭt′ē) *n., pl.* **-ties** A simple song. [ME *dite,* a literary composition < OFr. *dite* < Lat. *dictātum,* thing dictated < neut. p. part. of *dictāre,* to dictate. See DICTATE.]

ditty bag *n.* A bag used by armed forces personnel to carry small items such as sewing implements. [?]

Di•u (dē′o͞o) An island of W India NW of Mumbai (Bombay); annexed by India (1962).

di•u•re•sis (dī′ə-rē′sĭs) *n.* Excessive discharge of urine. [NLat. < LLat. *diūrēticus,* diuretic. See DIURETIC.]

di•u•ret•ic (dī′ə-rĕt′ĭk) *adj.* Tending to increase the discharge of urine. ❖ *n.* A diuretic substance or drug. [ME *diuretik* < OFr. *diuretique* < LLat. *diūrēticus* < Gk. *diourētikos* < *diourein,* to pass urine : *dia-,* dia- + *ourein,* to urinate.] **—di′u•ret′ic•al•ly** *adv.*

di•ur•nal (dī-ûr′nəl) *adj.* **1.** Relating to or occurring in a 24-hour period; daily. **2.** Occurring or active during the daytime rather than at night: *diurnal animals.* **3.** *Botany* Opening during daylight hours and closing at night. ❖ *n.* **1.** A book containing all the offices for the daily canonical hours of prayer except matins. **2.** *Archaic* **a.** A diary or journal. **b.** A daily newspaper. [ME < LLat. *diurnālis* < Lat. *diurnus* < *diēs,* day. See **dyeu-** in App.] **—di•ur′nal•ly** *adv.*

div. *abbr.* **1.** divergence **2.** divided **3.** dividend **4.** division **5.** divorced

di•va (dē′və) *n., pl.* **-vas** or **-ve** (-vā) **1.** An operatic prima donna. **2.** A very successful singer of nonoperatic music. [Ital. < Lat. *dīva,* goddess, fem. of *dīvus,* god. See **dyeu-** in App.]

di•va•gate (dī′və-gāt′, dĭv′ə-) *intr.v.* **-gat•ed, -gat•ing, -gates 1.** To wander or drift about. **2.** To ramble; digress. [LLat. *dīvagārī, dīvagāt-* : Lat. *dī-, dis-,* apart; see DIS– + Lat. *vagārī,* to wander (< *vagus,* wandering).] **—di′va•ga′tion** *n.*

di•va•lent (dī-vā′lənt) *adj.* Having a valence of 2.

di•van (dĭ-văn′, -văn′) *n.* **1.** A long backless sofa, esp. one set with pillows against a wall. **2.** (*also* dī-văn′) A census taken under the early Islamic caliphs. **3.** (*also* dī-văn′) A government department or office in Muslim countries. **4.** (*also* dī-văn′) A book of poems or prose, esp. one written in Arabic or Persian by a single author. [Fr. < Turk. < Pers. *dīvān,* place of assembly, roster, prob. < OPers. **dipivahanam,* document house : *dipī-,* writing, document (< Akkadian *ṭuppu,* tablet, letter < Sumerian *dub*) + *vahanam,* house; see **wes-**¹ in App.]

di•var•i•cate (dī-văr′ĭ-kāt′, dĭ-) *intr.v.* **-cat•ed, -cat•ing, -cates** To diverge at a wide angle; spread apart. ❖ *adj.* (dī-văr′ə-kĭt, -kāt′, dĭ-) **1.** *Biology* Branching or spreading widely from a point or axis, as branches; diverging. **2.** Relating to a separation of two bones normally adjacent or attached but not located in a joint; distatic. [Lat. *dīvāricāre, dīvāricāt-* : *dī, dis-,* dis- + *vāricāre,* to straddle (< *vārus,* bent).] **—di•var′i•cate′ly** *adv.*

di•var•i•ca•tion (dī-văr′ĭ-kā′shən, dĭ-) *n.* **1.** The act of divaricating. **2.** The point at which branching occurs. **3.** A divergence of opinion.

dive¹ (dīv) *v.* **dived** or **dove** (dōv), **dived, div•ing, dives** *—intr.* **1a.** To plunge, esp. headfirst, into water. **b.** To execute a dive in athletic competition. **c.** To participate in the sport of competitive diving. **2a.** To go toward the bottom of a body of water; submerge. **b.** To engage in the activity of scuba diving. **c.** To submerge under power. Used of a submarine. **3a.** To fall head down through the air. **b.** To descend nose down at an acceleration usu. exceeding that of free fall. Used of an airplane. **c.** To engage in the sport of skydiving. **4.** To drop sharply and rapidly; plummet. **5a.** To rush headlong and vanish into. **b.** To plunge one's hand into. **6.** To lunge. **7.** To plunge into an activity or enterprise. *—tr.* To cause (an aircraft, for example) to dive. ❖ *n.* **1a.** A plunge into water, esp. headfirst and in a way established for athletic competition. **b.** The act or an instance of submerging, as of a submarine or a skin diver. **c.** A nearly vertical descent at an accelerated speed through the air. **d.** A quick, pronounced drop. **2.** *Slang* A disreputable or rundown bar or nightclub. **3.** *Sports* **a.** A knockout feigned by a prizefighter. **b.** An exaggerated fall, esp. by a hockey player, intended to draw a penalty against an opponent. **4.** A lunge or a headlong jump. [ME *diven* < OE *dȳfan,* to dip, and < *dūfan,* to sink. See **dheub-** in App.]

di•ve (dē′vā) *n.* A plural of **diva**.

dive-bomb (dīv′bŏm′) *tr.v.* **-bombed, -bomb•ing, -bombs** To bomb from an airplane at the end of a steep dive toward the target. **—dive′-bomb′er** *n.*

dive brake *n.* A flap that can be extended on an aircraft to increase drag and reduce the speed of descent.

div•er (dī′vər) *n.* **1.** One that dives. **2.** One that works under water, esp. one equipped with breathing apparatus. **3.** Any of several diving water birds, esp. the loon.

di•verge (dĭ-vûrj′, dī-) *v.* **-verged, -verg•ing, -verg•es** *—intr.* **1.** To go or extend in different directions from a common point; branch out. **2.** To differ, as in opinion or manner. **3.** To depart from a set course or norm; deviate. See Syns at **swerve. 4.** *Mathematics* To fail to approach a limit. *—tr.* To cause (light rays, for example) to diverge; deflect. [Lat. *dīvergere* : Lat. *dī, dis-*, apart; see DIS– + Lat. *vergere*, to bend; see **wer-²** in App.]

di•ver•gence (dĭ-vûr′jəns, dī-) *n.* **1a.** The act of diverging. **b.** The state of being divergent. **c.** The degree by which things diverge. **2.** *Physiology* A turning of the eyes outward from a common point. **3.** Departure from a norm; deviation. **4.** Difference, as of opinion. See Syns at **difference. 5.** *Biology* The evolutionary tendency or process by which related life forms evolve into different forms when living under different conditions. **6.** *Mathematics* Failure to approach a limit. **7.** A meteorological condition characterized by the expansion in volume of a mass of air over a region.

di•ver•gen•cy (dĭ-vûr′jən-sē) *n., pl.* **-cies 1.** The state of being divergent. **2.** A divergence or deviation.

di•ver•gent (dĭ-vûr′jənt, dī-) *adj.* **1.** Drawing apart from a common point; diverging. **2.** Departing from convention. **3.** Differing from another. **4.** *Mathematics* Failing to approach a limit; not convergent. **—di•ver′gent•ly** *adv.*

di•vers (dī′vərz) *adj.* Various; several; sundry. [ME. See DIVERSE.]

di•verse (dĭ-vûrs′, dī-, dī′vûrs′) *adj.* **1.** Differing from one another. **2.** Made up of distinct characteristics, qualities, or elements: *a diverse history.* [ME *divers* < OFr. *divers* < Lat. *dīversus*, p. part. of *dīvertere*, to divert. See DIVERT.] **—di•verse′ly** *adv.* **—di•verse′ness** *n.*

di•ver•si•form (dĭ-vûr′sə-fôrm′, dī-) *adj.* Having different forms; variform.

di•ver•si•fy (dĭ-vûr′sə-fī′, dī-) *v.* **-fied, -fy•ing, -fies** *—tr.* **1a.** To give variety to; vary. **b.** To extend (business activities) into disparate fields. **2.** To distribute (investments) among different companies or securities. *—intr.* To diversify activities or investments. [ME *diversifien* < OFr. *diversifier* < Med.Lat. *dīversificāre* : Lat. *dīversus*; see DIVERSE + Lat. *-ficāre*, -fy.] **—di•ver′si•fi•ca′tion** (-fĭ-kā′shən) *n.*

di•ver•sion (dĭ-vûr′zhən, -shən, dī-) *n.* **1.** The act or an instance of diverting or turning aside; deviation. **2.** Something that distracts the mind and relaxes or entertains. **3.** A maneuver that draws the attention of an opponent away from a planned point of action, as in a battle. [LLat. *dīversiō, dīversiōn-*, act of turning aside < Lat. *dīversus*, p. part. of *dīvertere*, to divert. See DIVERT.] **—di•ver′sion•ar′y** *adj.*

di•ver•sion•ist (dĭ-vûr′zhə-nĭst, -shə-, dī-) *n.* One engaged in diversionary, disruptive, or subversive activities.

di•ver•si•ty (dĭ-vûr′sĭ-tē, dī-) *n., pl.* **-ties 1a.** The fact or quality of being diverse; difference. **b.** A point or respect in which things differ. **2.** Variety or multiformity.

di•vert (dĭ-vûrt′, dī-) *v.* **-vert•ed, -vert•ing, -verts** *—tr.* **1.** To turn aside from a course or direction. **2.** To distract. **3.** To entertain by distracting from worrisome thoughts or cares; amuse. *—intr.* To turn aside. [ME *diverten* < OFr. *divertir* < Lat. *dīvertere* : *dī-, dis-*, aside; see DIS– + *vertere*, to turn; see **wer-²** in App.] **—di•vert′er** *n.* **—di•vert′ing•ly** *adv.*

di•ver•tic•u•li•tis (dī′vûr-tĭk′yə-lī′tĭs) *n.* Inflammation of a diverticulum or of diverticula in the intestinal tract, causing fecal stagnation and pain.

di•ver•tic•u•lo•sis (dī′vûr-tĭk′yə-lō′sĭs) *n.* A condition characterized by numerous diverticula in the colon.

di•ver•tic•u•lum (dī′vûr-tĭk′yə-ləm) *n., pl.* **-la** (-lə) A pouch or sac branching out from a hollow organ or structure, such as the intestine. [NLat. < Lat. *dēverticulum*, by-path < *dēvertere*, to turn aside : *dē-*, de- + *vertere*, to turn; see DIVERT.] **—di′ver•tic′u•lar** *adj.*

di•ver•ti•men•to (dĭ-vĕr′tə-mĕn′tō) *n., pl.* **-tos** or **-ti** (-tē) A chiefly 18th-century form of instrumental chamber music having several short movements. [Ital. < *divertire*, to divert < OFr. *divertir*. See DIVERT.]

di•ver•tisse•ment (də-vûr′tĭs-mənt, dē-vĕr-tēs-mäN′) *n.* **1.** A short performance, typically a ballet, that is presented as an interlude in an opera or play. **2.** *Music* See **divertimento. 3.** A diversion; an amusement. [Fr. < *divertir*, to divert < OFr. See DIVERT.]

Di•ves (dī′vēz′) *n.* A man of great wealth. [ME < Lat. *dīves*, wealthy. See **dyeu-** in App.]

di•vest (dĭ-vĕst′, dī-) *tr.v.* **-vest•ed, -vest•ing, -vests 1.** To strip, as of clothes. **2a.** To deprive, as of rights or property; dispossess. **b.** To free of; rid. **3.** To sell off or otherwise dispose of (a subsidiary company or an investment). **4.** *Law* To devest. [Alteration (influenced by Med.Lat. *dīvestīre*, to undress) of DEVEST.] **—di•vest′ment** *n.*

di•ves•ti•ture (dĭ-vĕs′tĭ-chər, -cho͝or′, dī-) *n.* **1.** An act of divesting. **2.** The sale, liquidation, or spinoff of a corporate division or subsidiary. [< Med.Lat. *dīvestītus*, p. part. of *dīvestīre*, to undress, var. of *disvestīre* : Lat. *dis-*, dis- + Lat. *vestīre*, to dress; see VESTMENT.]

di•vide (dĭ-vīd′) *v.* **-vid•ed, -vid•ing, -vides** *—tr.* **1a.** To separate into parts, sections, groups, or branches. See Syns at **separate. b.** To sector into units of measurement; graduate. **c.** To separate and group according to kind; classify: *divided the plants by genus.* **2a.** To separate into opposing factions; disunite. **b.** To cause (members of a parliament) to vote by separating into groups, as pro and con. **3.** To separate from something else; cut off. **4.** To apportion among a number. See Syns at **distribute. 5.** *Mathematics* **a.** To subject (a number) to the process of division: *divided 20 by 4.* **b.** To be a divisor of: *3 divides 9.* **c.** To use (a number) as a divisor: *divided 5 into 35.* *—intr.* **1a.** To become separated into parts. **b.** To branch out, as a river. **c.** To form into factions; take sides. **d.** To vote by dividing. **2.** *Mathematics* To perform the operation of division. **3.** *Biology* To undergo cell division. ❖ *n.* **1.** A dividing point or line. **2.** A ridge of land; a watershed. [ME *dividen* < Lat. *dīvidere* : *dī-, dis-*, dis- + *-videre*, to separate.] **—di•vid′a•ble** *adj.*

di•vid•ed (dĭ-vī′dĭd) *adj.* **1.** Separated into parts or pieces. **2.** Being in a state of disagreement or disunity. **3.** Moved by conflicting interests, emotions, or activities: *divided loyalties.* **4.** Separated by distance. **5.** Having the lanes for opposing traffic separated. **6.** *Botany* Having indentations extending to the midrib or base and forming distinct lobes. **—di•vid′ed•ly** *adv.*

div•i•dend (dĭv′ĭ-dĕnd′) *n.* **1.** *Mathematics* A quantity to be divided. **2a.** A share of profits received by a stockholder or by a policyholder in a mutual insurance society. **b.** A payment pro rata to a creditor of a person adjudged bankrupt. **3a.** A share of a surplus; a bonus. **b.** An unexpected gain, benefit, or advantage. [Alteration of ME *divident* < Lat. *dīvidēns, dīvident-*, pr. part. of *dīvidere*, to divide. See DIVIDE.]

di•vid•er (dĭ-vī′dər) *n.* **1a.** One that divides, esp. a screen or other partition. **b.** *Chiefly British* A highway median strip. **2.** A device resembling a compass, used for dividing lines and transferring measurements.

div•i-div•i (dĭv′ē-dĭv′ē) *n., pl.* **-is 1.** A small tree *(Caesalpinia coriaria)* of the West Indies and South America having compound leaves and long pods. **2.** Tannin extracted from its pods. [Sp. *dividivi*, prob. of Cariban or Arawakan orig.]

div•i•na•tion (dĭv′ə-nā′shən) *n.* **1.** The art or act of foretelling future events or revealing occult knowledge by means of augury or an alleged supernatural agency. **2.** An inspired guess or presentiment. **3.** Something that has been divined. **—di•vin′a•to′ry** (dĭ-vĭn′ə-tôr′ē, -tōr′ē) *adj.*

di•vine (dĭ-vīn′) *adj.* **-vin•er, -vin•est 1a.** Having the nature of or being a deity. **b.** Of, relating to, emanating from, or being the expression of a deity. **c.** Being in the service or worship of a deity; sacred. **2.** Superhuman; godlike. **3a.** Supremely good or beautiful; magnificent: *a divine performance.* **b.** Extremely pleasant; delightful. **4.** Heavenly; perfect. ❖ *n.* **1.** A cleric. **2.** A theologian. ❖ *v.* **-vined, -vin•ing, -vines** *—tr.* **1.** To foretell through or as if through the art of divination. **2a.** To know by inspiration, intuition, or reflection. **b.** To guess. **3.** To locate (underground water or minerals) with a divining rod; douse. *—intr.* **1.** To practice divination. **2.** To guess. [ME < OFr. *devine* < Lat. *dīvīnus*, divine, foreseeing < *dīvus*, god. See **deiw-** in App. V., ME *divinen* < OFr. *deviner* < Lat. *dīvīnāre* < *dīvīnus* < *dīvus*. See **dyeu-** in App.] **—di•vine′ly** *adv.* **—di•vine′ness** *n.* **—di•vin′er** *n.*

Divine Liturgy *n.* The Eastern Orthodox Eucharistic rite.

Divine Office *n.* The office of the breviary.

divine right *n.* The doctrine that monarchs derive their right to rule directly from God and are accountable only to God.

div•ing bell (dī′vĭng) *n.* A large vessel for underwater work, open on the bottom and supplied with air under pressure.

diving board *n.* A flexible board projecting over water from which a dive may be executed.

diving suit *n.* A heavy waterproof garment with a detachable air-fed helmet, used for underwater work.

di•vin•ing rod (dĭ-vī′nĭng) *n.* A forked branch or stick that is believed to indicate subterranean water or minerals by bending downward when held over a source.

di•vin•i•ty (dĭ-vĭn′ĭ-tē) *n., pl.* **-ties 1.** The state or quality of being divine. **2a. Divinity** The godhead; God. Used with *the.* **b.** A deity, such as a god or goddess. **3.** Godlike character. **4.** Theology. **5.** A soft white candy, usu. containing nuts.

di•vis•i•ble (dĭ-vĭz′ə-bəl) *adj.* Capable of being divided, esp. with no remainder. **—di•vis′i•bil′i•ty, di•vis′i•ble•ness** *n.* **—di•vis′i•bly** *adv.*

di•vi•sion (dĭ-vĭzh′ən) *n.* **1a.** The act or process of dividing. **b.** The state of having been divided. **2.** *Mathematics* The operation of determining how many times one quantity is contained in another; the inverse of multiplication. **3.** The proportional distribution of a quantity or entity. **4.** Something, such as a partition, that serves to divide. **5.** One of the parts, sections, or groups into which something is divided. **6a.** An administrative or functional unit of government or corporate activity. **b.** A territorial section marked off for political or governmental purposes. **7a.** A self-

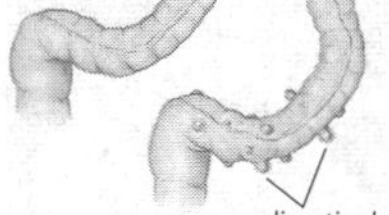

diverticulosis
left: healthy section of intestine
right: diseased section of intestine

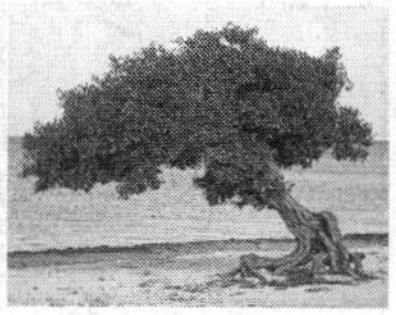

divi-divi
Caesalpinia coriaria

ă	pat	oi	boy
ā	pay	ou	out
âr	care	o͝o	took
ä	father	o͞o	boot
ĕ	pet	ŭ	cut
ē	be	ûr	urge
ĭ	pit	*th*	thin
ī	pie	*th*	this
îr	pier	hw	which
ŏ	pot	zh	vision
ō	toe	ə	about, item
ô	paw		

Stress marks:
′ (primary);
′ (secondary), as in
lexicon (lĕk′sĭ-kŏn′)

contained administrative and tactical military unit that is smaller than a corps. **b.** A group of several ships of similar type forming a tactical unit in the US Navy. **c.** A unit of the US Air Force larger than a wing and smaller than an air force. **8.** *Botany* The highest taxonomic category corresponding approximately to a phylum in zoological classification. See table at **taxonomy. 9.** A category created for purposes of competition, as in boxing. **10a.** Variance of opinion; disagreement. **b.** A splitting into factions; disunion. **11.** The separation of members of a parliament according to their stand on an issue put to vote. **12.** *Biology* Cell division. **13.** A type of propagation in which plants grow from parts of a parent plant such as bulbs, suckers, or rhizomes. [ME *divisioun* < OFr. *division* < Lat. *dīvīsiō, dīvīsiōn-* < *dīvīsus,* p. part. of *dīvidere,* to divide. See DIVIDE.] —**di·vi′sion·al** *adj.*

di·vi·sion·ism (də-vĭzh′ə-nĭz′əm) *n.* A branch of neoimpressionism in which colors are divided into their components and arranged so that the eye organizes the shape.

division sign *n.* **1.** The symbol (÷) placed between two quantities written on a single line to indicate the division of the first by the second. **2.** The symbol (/) placed between two quantities written horizontally, as in ⅔, or the symbol (—) placed between two quantities written vertically, as in ⅔, to indicate a fraction.

di·vi·sive (dĭ-vī′sĭv) *adj.* Creating dissension or discord. —**di·vi′sive·ly** *adv.* —**di·vi′sive·ness** *n.*

di·vi·sor (dĭ-vī′zər) *n.* The quantity by which another quantity, the dividend, is to be divided.

di·vorce (dĭ-vôrs′, -vōrs′) *n.* **1.** The legal dissolution of a marriage. **2.** A complete or radical severance of closely connected things. ❖ *v.* **-vorced, -vorc·ing, -vorc·es** —*tr.* **1.** To dissolve the marriage between. **2.** To end marriage with (one's spouse) by divorce. **3.** To cut off or separate. See Syns at **separate.** —*intr.* To obtain a divorce. [ME < OFr. < Lat. *dīvortium* < *dīvortere,* to divert, var. of *dīvertere.* See DIVERT.]

di·vor·cé (dĭ-vôr-sā′, -sē′, -vōr-, -vôr′sā′, -sē′, -vōr′-) *n.* A divorced man. [Fr., masc. p. part. of *divorcer,* to divorce < OFr. < *divorce.* See DIVORCE.]

di·vor·cée (dĭ-vôr-sā′, -sē′, -vōr-, -vôr′sā′, -sē′, -vōr′-) *n.* A divorced woman. [Fr., fem. p. part. of *divorcer,* to divorce < OFr. < *divorce.* See DIVORCE.]

di·vorce·ment (dĭ-vôrs′mənt, -vōrs′-) *n.* Complete separation.

div·ot (dĭv′ət) *n.* **1.** A piece of turf torn up, esp. by a golf club in striking a ball. **2.** *Scots* A thin square of turf or sod used for roofing. [Sc., a turf.]

di·vulge (dĭ-vŭlj′) *tr.v.* **-vulged, -vulg·ing, -vulg·es** To make known (something private or secret). [ME *divulgen* < OFr. *divulguer* < Lat. *dīvulgāre,* to publish : *dī-, dis-,* among; see DIS- + *vulgāre,* to spread among the multitude (< *vulgus,* common people).] —**di·vul′gence** *n.* —**di·vulg′er** *n.*

div·vy (dĭv′ē) *Slang tr.v.* **-vied, -vy·ing, -vies** To divide. Often used with *up: divvied up the loot.* ❖ *n., pl.* **-vies** A share or portion. [Shortening and alteration of DIVIDEND.]

Dix (dĭks), **Dorothea Lynde** 1802–87. Amer. educator who worked to improve treatment of the mentally ill.

Dix·ie¹ (dĭk′sē) A region of the S and E US, usu. comprising the states that joined the Confederacy during the Civil War. The term was popularized in the song "Dixie's Land" (1859) by Daniel D. Emmett (1815–1904).

Dix·ie² (dĭk′sē) *n.* Any one of several songs of this name, popular as Confederate war songs. —*idiom:* **whistle Dixie** *Slang* To engage in unrealistically rosy fantasizing.

Dix·ie·crat (dĭk′sē-krăt′) *n.* A member of a dissenting group of Democrats in the South who formed the States' Rights Party in 1948. [DIXIE¹ + (DEMO)CRAT.] —**Dix′ie·crat′ic** *adj.*

Dix·ie·land (dĭk′sē-lănd′) *n.* A style of instrumental jazz associated with New Orleans and characterized by a relatively fast two-beat rhythm and by group and solo improvisations.

Dix·on (dĭk′sən), **Willie** 1915–92. Amer. musician and songwriter who was a major figure on the Chicago blues scene.

DIY *abbr.* do-it-yourself

Di·yar·ba·kir (dĭ-yär′bə-kîr′, dē-yär′bŭk-ər) A city of SE Turkey on the Tigris R.; captured by the Ottoman Turks in 1515. Pop. 448,300.

di·zen (dī′zən, dĭz′ən) *tr.v.* **-zened, -zen·ing, -zens** *Archaic* To deck out in fine clothes and ornaments; bedizen. [Poss. MDu. *disen,* to prepare a distaff with flax for spinning < MLGer. *dise, disene,* bunch of flax.] —**di′zen·ment** *n.*

di·zy·got·ic (dī′zī-gŏt′ĭk) or **di·zy·gous** (dī-zī′gəs) *adj.* Derived from two separately fertilized eggs. Used esp. of fraternal twins.

diz·zy (dĭz′ē) *adj.* **-zi·er, -zi·est 1.** Having a whirling sensation and a tendency to fall. **2.** Bewildered or confused. **3a.** Producing or tending to produce giddiness: *a dizzy height.* **b.** Caused by giddiness; reeling. **4.** Characterized by impulsive haste; very rapid. **5.** *Slang* Scatterbrained or silly. ❖ *tr.v.* **-zied, -zy·ing, -zies 1.** To make dizzy. **2.** To confuse or bewilder. [ME *dusie, disi* < OE *dysig,* foolish.] —**diz′zi·ly** *adv.* —**diz′zi·ness** *n.* —**diz′zy·ing·ly** *adv.*

DJ¹ (dē′jā′) *n.* A disc jockey. ❖ *v.* **DJ′ed, DJ′ing, DJ′s** —*tr.* To act as a disc jockey at (a social gathering or radio station). —*intr.* To act as a disc jockey.

DJ² *abbr.* **1.** district judge **2.** *Latin* Doctor Juris (Doctor of Law)

Dja·kar·ta (jə-kär′tə) See **Jakarta.**

djel·la·ba or **djel·la·bah** also **jel·la·ba** (jə-lä′bə) or **ga·la·bi·a** (-bē-ə) *n.* A long, loose, hooded garment with full sleeves, worn esp. in Muslim countries. [Fr. < Ar. *jallābīya* < *jallāb,* attractive < *jalaba,* to bring, fetch.]

Dji·bou·ti (jĭ-boō′tē) **1.** Formerly **A·fars and Is·sas** (ə-färz′; ĭ′səs) A country of E Africa on the Gulf of Aden; gained independence from France in 1977. **2.** The capital of Djibouti, in the SE part on an inlet of the Gulf of Aden; founded by the French in 1888. Pop. 300,000.

Dji·las (jĭl′äs), **Milovan** 1911–95. Montenegrin writer and politician who was dismissed in 1954 for criticizing the Communist regime.

djin·ni or **djin·ny** (jĭn′ē, jĭ-nē′) *n.* Variant of **jinni.**

dk. *abbr.* **1.** dark **2.** deck **3.** dock

dl *abbr.* deciliter

D layer *n.* The lowest layer of the ionosphere, existing only during the day.

DLit or **DLitt** *abbr. Latin* Doctor Litterarum (Doctor of Letters; Doctor of Literature)

DLS *abbr.* Doctor of Library Science

dm *abbr.* decimeter

DM *abbr.* **1.** data management **2.** deutsche mark

DMA *abbr.* Doctor of Musical Arts

DMD *abbr. Latin* Dentariae Medicinae Doctor (Doctor of Dental Medicine)

DML *abbr.* Doctor of Modern Languages

DMSO (dē′ĕm-ĕs-ō′) *n.* A colorless hygroscopic liquid, $(CH_3)_2SO$, used as an industrial solvent and as a penetrant to convey medications into the tissues. [D(I)M(ETHYL)S(ULF)O(XIDE).]

DMV *abbr.* Department of Motor Vehicles

Dn *abbr. Bible* Daniel

DNA (dē′ĕn-ā′) *n.* A nucleic acid that carries the genetic information in the cell and is capable of self-replication and synthesis of RNA, consisting of two long chains of nucleotides twisted into a double helix and joined by hydrogen bonds, the sequence of nucleotides determining individual hereditary characteristics. [D(EOXYRIBO)N(UCLEIC) A(CID).]

DNA fingerprint *n.* An individual's unique sequence of DNA base pairs, determined by exposing a DNA sample to molecular probes. —**DNA fingerprinting** *n.*

DNA polymerase *n.* An enzyme that functions in the replication and repair of DNA by using single-stranded DNA as a template.

DNase also **DNAse** (dē-ĕn′ās) or **DNAase** (dē′ĕn-ā′ās) *n.* An enzyme that catalyzes the hydrolysis of DNA.

DNA virus *n.* A virus having a genome composed of DNA.

Dnie·per (nē′pər, dnyē′-) A river rising in W-central Russia near Smolensk and flowing c. 2,285 km (1,420 mi) S through Belarus and Ukraine to the Black Sea.

Dnies·ter (nē′stər, dnyē′-) A river rising in W Ukraine and flowing c. 1,368 km (850 mi) generally SE to the Black Sea near Odessa.

Dni·pro·pe·trovs'k (nē′prō-pə-trôfsk′, dnyē′-) or **Dne·pro·pe·trovsk** (nĕp′rō-, dnyĭ′prō-) A city of E-central Ukraine on the Dnieper R. SSW of Kharkov; founded 1787. Pop. 1,153,000.

DNR *abbr.* **1.** Department of Natural Resources **2.** do not resuscitate

do¹ (doō) *v.* **did** (dĭd), **done** (dŭn), **do·ing, does** (dŭz) —*tr.* **1a.** To perform or execute: *doing your assigned task.* **b.** To fulfill the requirements of: *did my duty.* **c.** To carry out; commit: *a crime done on purpose.* **2a.** To produce, esp. by creative effort. **b.** To play the part or role of in a creative production. **c.** To mimic. **3a.** To bring about; effect: *Crying won't do any good.* **b.** To render; give: *Do honor to your family.* **4.** To put forth; exert: *Do your best.* **5a.** To take care of or put in order: *did the bedrooms.* **b.** To prepare for further use esp. by washing: *did the dishes.* **6a.** To set or style (the hair). **b.** To apply cosmetics to. **7.** To have as an occupation or profession. **8.** To work out by studying: *doing a homework assignment.* **9.** Used as a substitute for an antecedent verb or verb phrase: *I know it, and she does too.* **10.** *Informal* **a.** To travel (a specified distance): *do a mile a minute.* **b.** To make a tour of; visit. **11a.** To be sufficient for; serve: *This room will do us nicely.* **b.** *Informal* To serve (a prison term). **12.** *Slang* To cheat; swindle. **13.** *Slang* To take (drugs) illegally. **14.** *Slang* To kill; murder. **15.** *Vulgar Slang* To have sex with; bring to orgasm. —*intr.* **1.** To behave or conduct oneself; act: *Do as I say.* **2a.** To get along; fare. **b.** To carry on; manage: *We can do without you.* **c.** To make good use of something out of need: *I could do with a hot bath.* **3a.** To serve a purpose. **b.** To be proper or fitting. **4.** To take place; happen. **5.** Used as a substitute for an antecedent verb: *worked as hard as we did.* **6.** Used after another verb for emphasis: *Run quickly, do!* —*aux.* **1.** Used with the infinitive without *to* in questions, negative statements, and inverted phrases: *Do you understand? I did not sleep well. Little did we know!* **2.** Used as a means of emphasis: *I do want to be sure.* ❖ *n., pl.* **dos** or **do's 1.** A statement of what should be done. **2.** *Informal* An entertainment; a party. **3.** A commotion. **4.** *Chiefly British Slang* A swindle; a cheat. **5.** *Slang* Excrement. **6.** *Archaic* Duty; deed. —*phrasal verbs:* **do by** To behave with respect to; deal with. **do for** To care or provide for; take care of. **do in** *Slang* **1.** To tire completely; exhaust. **2.** To kill. **3.** To ruin utterly. **do up 1.** To adorn or dress lavishly. **2.** To wrap and tie (a package). **3.** To fasten: *do up the buttons.* **do without** To

Dorothea Dix
c. 1849 daguerreotype

Djibouti

DNA

manage despite the absence of. ***—idioms:* do a disappearing act** *Informal* To vanish. **do away with 1.** To make an end of; eliminate. **2.** To destroy; kill. **do (one) proud** To act or perform in a way that gives cause for pride. **do (one's) bit** To contribute toward an overall effort. **do (one's) business** *Slang* To defecate. Used esp. of a pet. **do (one's) own thing** *Slang* To do what one does or likes best. **do or die** To exert supreme effort. [ME *don* < OE *dōn*. See **dhē-** in App.]

do² (dō) *n. Music* The first tone of the diatonic scale in solfeggio. [Ital., more singable replacement of *ut*. See GAMUT.]

do³ (do͞o) *n., pl.* **dos** *Slang* A hairdo.

DO *abbr.* **1.** Doctor of Optometry **2.** Doctor of Osteopathy

DOA *abbr.* dead on arrival

do•a•ble (do͞o′ə-bəl) *adj.* Possible to do.

DOB *abbr.* date of birth

dob•bin (dŏb′ĭn) *n.* A horse, esp. a working farm horse. [< *Dobbin*, alteration of *Robin*, nickname for *Robert*.]

dob•by (dŏb′ē) *n., pl.* **-bies 1.** A part in a loom that controls the harnesses to permit the weaving of small geometric figures. **2a.** Such a woven figure. **b.** A fabric with dobbies. [Perh. < *Dobbie*, dim. of *Dob*, alteration of *Rob*, nickname for *Robert*.]

Do•ber•man pin•scher (dō′bər-mən pĭn′shər) *n.* A medium-sized to large dog of a breed originating in Germany, having short hair and a smooth, usu. dark coat. [Ger. *Dobermann* (after Ludwig *Dobermann*, 19th-cent. German dog breeder) + Ger. *Pinscher*, terrier (prob. < E. PINCH < the cropping of its ears and tail).]

do•bra (dō′brə) *n.* See table at **currency.** [Port., ult. < Lat. *duplus*, double. See DUPLE.]

Do•bro (dō′brō) A trademark used for stringed musical instruments, esp. guitars and banjos.

dob•son (dŏb′sən) *n.* See **hellgrammite.** [Prob. < the name *Dobson*.]

dob•son•fly (dŏb′sən-flī′) *n.* An insect *(Corydalus cornutus)* having four large many-veined wings and in the male long pincerlike mandibles.

doc (dŏk) *n. Informal* A physician, dentist, or veterinarian. [Short for DOCTOR.]

DOC *abbr.* Department of Commerce

do•cent (dō′sənt, dō-sĕnt′) *n.* **1.** A teacher or lecturer at a university who is not a regular faculty member. **2.** A lecturer or tour guide in a museum or cathedral. [Ger. *Dozent* < Lat. *docēns, docent-*, pr. part. of *docēre*, to teach.]

Do•ce•tism (dō-sē′tĭz′əm, dō′sə-tĭz′əm) *n.* An opinion esp. associated with the Gnostics that Jesus had no human body and only appeared to have died on the cross. [Prob. < L.Gk. *Dokētai*, espousers of Docetism < Gk. *dokein*, to seem.] **—Do•ce′tist** *n.*

doc•ile (dŏs′əl, -īl′) *adj.* **1.** Ready and willing to be taught; teachable. **2.** Yielding to supervision or direction; tractable. [Lat. *docilis* < *docēre*, to teach.] **—doc′ile•ly** *adv.* **—do•cil′i•ty** (dŏ-sĭl′ĭ-tē, dō-) *n.*

dock¹ (dŏk) *n.* **1.** The area of water between two piers or alongside a pier that receives a ship for loading, unloading, or repairs. **2.** A pier; a wharf. **3.** A group of piers on a commercial waterfront that serve as a landing area for ships or boats. Often used in the plural. **4.** A platform at which trucks or trains load or unload cargo. ❖ *v.* **docked, dock•ing, docks** *—tr.* **1.** To maneuver (a vessel or vehicle) into or next to a dock. **2.** To couple (two or more spacecraft, for example) in space. *—intr.* To move or come into a dock. [Du. *dok* < MDu. *doc* < *dūken*, to go under water, dive.]

dock² (dŏk) *n.* **1.** The solid or fleshy part of an animal's tail. **2.** The tail of an animal after it has been bobbed or clipped. ❖ *tr.v.* **docked, dock•ing, docks 1.** To clip short or cut off (an animal's tail, for example). **2.** To deprive of a benefit or a part of one's wages, esp. as a punishment. **3.** To withhold or deduct a part from (one's salary or wages). [ME *dok*.]

dock³ (dŏk) *n.* An enclosed place where the defendant stands or sits in a court of law. ***—idiom:* in the dock** On trial or under intense scrutiny. [Obsolete Flem. *docke*, cage.]

dock⁴ (dŏk) *n.* See **sorrel¹** 1. [ME < OE *docce*.]

dock•age (dŏk′ĭj) *n.* **1.** A charge for docking privileges. **2.** Facilities for docking vessels. **3.** The docking of ships.

dock•er¹ (dŏk′ər) *n.* A dockhand.

dock•er² (dŏk′ər) *n.* One that docks something, such as an animal's tail.

dock•et (dŏk′ĭt) *n.* **1.** *Law* **a.** A calendar of the cases awaiting action in a court. **b.** A brief entry of the court proceedings in a legal case. **c.** The book containing such entries. **2.** A summary or other brief statement of the contents of a document; an abstract. **3.** A list of things to be done. **4.** A label or ticket on a package listing the contents or directions for assembling or operating. ❖ *tr.v.* **-et•ed, -et•ing, -ets 1.** *Law* To enter in a court calendar or a record of court proceedings. **2.** To provide with a brief identifying statement. **3.** To label or ticket (a parcel). [ME *doggett*, summary, digest.]

dock•hand (dŏk′hănd′) *n.* A longshoreman.

dock•mack•ie (dŏk′măk′ē) *n.* A shrub *(Viburnum acerifolium)* of eastern North America having clusters of white flowers. [Prob. < American Du., perh. of Mahican orig.]

dock•side (dŏk′sīd′) *n.* The area adjacent to a boating dock.

dock•work•er (dŏk′wûr′kər) *n.* A dockhand.

dock•yard (dŏk′yärd′) *n.* **1.** An area, often bordering a body of water, with facilities for dry-docking ships. **2.** *Chiefly British* A navy yard.

doc•tor (dŏk′tər) *n.* **1.** A person, esp. a physician, dentist, or veterinarian, trained in the healing arts and licensed to practice. **2a.** A person who has earned the highest academic degree awarded by a college or university in a specified discipline. **b.** A person awarded an honorary degree by a college or university. **3.** Used as a title and form of address for a person holding the degree of doctor. **4.** *Roman Catholic Church* An eminent theologian. **5.** A practitioner of folk medicine or folk magic. **6.** A rig or device contrived for a special use, as in an emergency. ❖ *v.* **-tored, -tor•ing, -tors** *—tr.* **1.** *Informal* To give medical treatment to. **2.** To repair, esp. in a makeshift manner; rig. **3a.** To falsify or change in such a way as to make favorable to oneself. **b.** To add ingredients to improve or conceal the taste, appearance, or quality of. **c.** To alter or modify for a specific end. *—intr. Informal* To practice medicine. [ME, an expert, authority < OFr. *docteur* < Lat. *doctor*, teacher < *docēre*, to teach.] **—doc′tor•al** *adj.* **—doc′tor•ly** *adj.*

doc•tor•ate (dŏk′tər-ĭt) *n.* The degree or status of a doctor as conferred by a university.

doc•tri•naire (dŏk′trə-nâr′) *n.* A doctrinaire person. ❖ *adj.* Of or characteristic of a person inflexibly attached to a practice or theory without regard to its practicality. [Fr. < *doctrine*, doctrine < OFr. See DOCTRINE.] **—doc′tri•nair′ism** *n.* **—doc′tri•nar′i•an** *n.*

doc•tri•nal (dŏk′trə-nəl, dŏk-trī′nəl) *adj.* Characterized by, belonging to, or concerning doctrine. **—doc′tri•nal•ly** *adv.*

doc•trine (dŏk′trĭn) *n.* **1.** A principle or system presented for acceptance or belief, as by a religious or philosophic group; dogma. **2.** A rule or principle of law, esp. established by precedent. **3.** A statement of government policy, esp. in foreign affairs and military strategy. **4.** *Archaic* Something taught; a teaching. [ME < OFr. < Lat. *doctrīna* < *doctor*, teacher. See DOCTOR.]

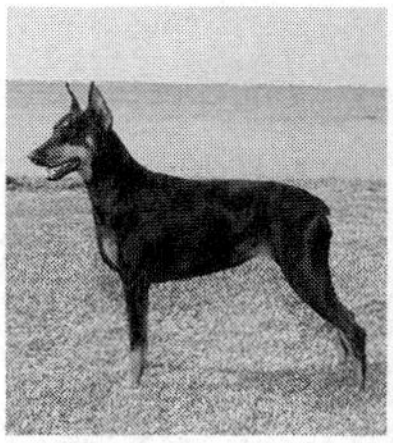

Doberman pinscher

doc•u•ment (dŏk′yə-mənt) *n.* **1a.** A written or printed paper that bears the original, official, or legal form of something and can furnish evidence or information. **b.** Something, such as a recording or photograph, that can furnish evidence or information. **c.** A writing that contains information. **d.** *Computer Science* A piece of work created with an application, as with a word processor. **e.** *Computer Science* A computer file that is not an executable file and contains data for use by applications. **2.** Something, esp. a material substance such as a coin bearing a symbol or mark, that serves as evidence. ❖ *tr.v.* (-mĕnt′) **-ment•ed, -ment•ing, -ments 1.** To furnish with a document or documents. **2.** To support (a claim, for example) with evidence or information. **3.** To support (statements in a book, for example) with written references or citations; annotate. [ME, precept < OFr. < Lat. *documentum*, example, proof < *docēre*, to teach.] **—doc′u•ment′a•ble** *adj.* **—doc′u•ment′al** (-mĕn′tl) *adj.* **—doc′u•ment′er** *n.*

doc•u•ment•al•ist (dŏk′yə-mĕn′tl-ĭst′) *n.* A specialist in documentation.

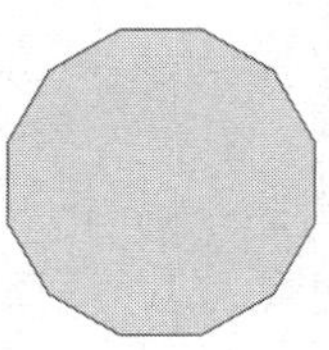

dodecagon

doc•u•men•tar•i•an (-mĕn-târ′ē-ən, -mən-) also **doc•u•men•ta•rist** (dŏk′yə-mĕn′tər-ĭst) *n.* One that makes documentaries or a documentary.

doc•u•men•ta•ry (dŏk′yə-mĕn′tə-rē) *adj.* **1.** Consisting of, concerning, or based on documents. **2.** Presenting facts objectively without editorializing or inserting fictional matter. ❖ *n., pl.* **-ries** A work, such as a film, presenting its subject matter factually, often with news films, interviews, and narration.

doc•u•men•ta•tion (dŏk′yə-mĕn-tā′shən) *n.* **1a.** The act or an instance of supplying documents, references, or records. **b.** The documents or references supplied. **2.** The collation, synopsizing, and coding of printed material for reference. **3.** *Computer Science* The organized collection of material that describes a computer program, operating system, or hardware device.

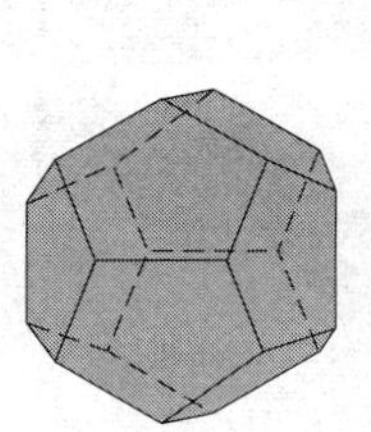

dodecahedron

DOD *abbr.* Department of Defense

dod•der¹ (dŏd′ər) *intr.v.* **-dered, -der•ing, -ders 1.** To shake or tremble, as from age; totter. **2.** To progress feebly and unsteadily. [Alteration of ME *daderen*, perh. < LGer.] **—dod′der•er** *n.*

dod•der² (dŏd′ər) *n.* Any of various leafless annual parasitic herbs of the genus *Cuscuta*, having slender twining stems and small whitish flowers. [ME *doder*, poss. < MDu., yolk of an egg.]

dod•dered (dŏd′ərd) *adj.* **1.** *Botany* Lacking the top branches because of age or decay. **2.** Infirm; feeble. [Prob. alteration of *dodded*, p. part. of dialectal *dod*, to lop off < ME *dodden*, perh. < *dodde*, a measure of grain.]

dod•der•ing (dŏd′ər-ĭng) *adj.* Infirm, feeble, and often senile.

do•dec•a•gon (dō-dĕk′ə-gŏn′) *n.* A polygon with 12 sides. [Gk. *dōdekagōnon* : *dōdeka*, twelve (*duo*, two; see **dwo-** in App. + *deka*, ten; see **dekm̥** in App.) + *-gōnon*, -gon.] **—do′de•cag′o•nal** (dō′dĕ-kăg′ə-nəl) *adj.*

do•dec•a•he•dron (dō′dĕk-ə-hē′drən) *n., pl.* **-drons** or **-dra** (-drə) A polyhedron with 12 faces. [Gk. *dōdekaedron* : *dōdeka*, twelve; see DODECAGON + *-edron*, -hedron.] **—do′dec•a•he′dral** *adj.*

Do•dec•a•nese (dō-dĕk′ə-nēz′, -nēs′) An island group of SE Greece in the Aegean Sea between Turkey and Crete; held by Turkey from 1522 until 1912.

do•dec•a•phon•ic (dō′dĕk-ə-fŏn′ĭk) *adj.* Relating to, composed in, or consisting of twelve-tone music. [Gk. *dōdeka*, twelve;

ă	pat	oi	boy
ā	pay	ou	out
âr	care	o͝o	took
ä	father	o͞o	boot
ĕ	pet	ŭ	cut
ē	be	ûr	urge
ĭ	pit	th	thin
ī	pie	*th*	this
îr	pier	hw	which
ŏ	pot	zh	vision
ō	toe	ə	about, item
ô	paw		

Stress marks:
′ (primary);
′ (secondary), as in
lexicon (lĕk′sĭ-kŏn′)

see DODECAGON + PHON(O)–, tone, pitch + –IC.] **—do•dec′a•** **phon•ist** (dō-dĕk′ə-fə-nĭst, dō′də-kăf′ə-) *n.* **—do•dec′a•** **phon′y** (dō-dĕk′ə-fō′nē, dō′də-kăf′ə-), **do•dec′a•phon•ism** *n.*

dodge (dŏj) *v.* **dodged, dodg•ing, dodg•es** *—tr.* **1.** To avoid (a blow, for example) by moving or shifting quickly aside. **2.** To evade (an obligation, for example) by cunning or deceit. **3.** To blunt or reduce the intensity of (a section of a photograph) by shading during the printing process. *—intr.* **1.** To move aside or in a given direction by shifting or twisting suddenly. **2.** To practice trickery or cunning; prevaricate. ❖ *n.* **1.** The act of dodging. **2.** An ingenious expedient intended to evade or trick. [?]

Dodge, Mary Elizabeth Mapes 1831–1905. Amer. writer best known for *Hans Brinker, or the Silver Skates* (1865).

dodge ball *n.* A game in which players on one team try to eliminate players on another by hitting them with an inflated ball.

Dodge City A city of SW KS on the Arkansas R. W of Wichita; laid out on the Santa Fe Trail in 1872. Pop. 25,176.

dodg•er (dŏj′ər) *n.* **1.** One that dodges or evades. **2.** A shifty, dishonest person; a trickster. **3.** A small printed handbill. **4.** *Chiefly Southern Atlantic US* See **corndodger** 2.

Dodg•son (dŏj′sən), **Charles Lutwidge** Pen name Lewis Carroll. 1832–98. British mathematician and writer renowned for the classics *Alice's Adventures in Wonderland* (1865) and *Through the Looking-Glass* (1872).

dodg•y (dŏj′ē) *adj.* **-i•er, -i•est** *Chiefly British* **1.** Evasive; shifty. **2.** Unsound, unstable, and unreliable. **3.** So risky as to require very deft handling.

do•do (dō′dō) *n., pl.* **-does** or **-dos 1.** A large clumsy flightless bird (*Raphus cucullatus*) formerly of the island of Mauritius in the Indian Ocean and extinct since the late 17th century. **2.** *Informal* One who is out-of-date, as in dress or ideas. **3.** *Informal* A stupid person; an idiot. [Port. *dodó*, alteration of obsolete Du. *dodors* : Du. *dot*, tuft of feathers + obsolete Du. *ors*, tail (< MDu. *ærs*; see **ors-** in App.).]

Do•do•ma (dō′də-mä, -dō-) A city of Tanzania, in the central part; designated to become the cap. by 2005. Pop. 203,833.

doe (dō) *n., pl.* **doe** or **does 1.** The female of a deer or related animal. **2.** The female of various mammals, such as the hare, goat, or kangaroo. [ME *do* < OE *dā*.]

DOE *abbr.* Department of Energy

Doe•nitz also **Dö•nitz** (dœ′nĭts), **Karl** 1891–1980. German officer who was chief naval commander during World War II.

do•er (dōō′ər) *n.* **1.** One who does something. **2.** A particularly active, energetic person: *a real doer in party politics.*

does (dŭz) *v.* Third person singular present tense of **do**[1].

doe•skin (dō′skĭn′) *n.* **1a.** The skin of a doe, deer, or goat. **b.** Leather made from this skin, used esp. for gloves. **2.** A fine woolen fabric. **3.** A densely napped finish for certain woolen fabrics.

does•n't (dŭz′ənt) Contraction of *does not.*

do•est (dōō′ĭst) *v. Archaic* A second person singular present tense of **do**[1].

do•eth (dōō′əth) *v. Archaic* A third person singular present tense of **do**[1].

doff (dôf, dŏf) *tr.v.* **doffed, doff•ing, doffs 1.** To take off; remove. **2.** To tip or remove (one's hat) in salutation. **3.** To put aside; discard. [ME *doffen* < *don off*, to do off : *don*, to do; see DO[1] + *off*, off; see OFF.]

dog (dôg, dŏg) *n.* **1.** A domesticated canid (*Canis familiaris*) related to foxes and wolves and raised in many breeds. **2.** Any of various members of the family Canidae, such as the dingo. **3.** A male animal of the family Canidae, esp. of the fox or a domesticated breed. **4.** Any of various other animals, such as the prairie dog. **5.** *Informal* **a.** A person: *you lucky dog!* **b.** A contemptible person: *You stole my watch, you dog.* **6.** *Slang* **a.** An unattractive or uninteresting person. **b.** Something of inferior or low quality. **c.** An investment that produces a low return or a loss. **7. dogs** *Slang* The feet. **8.** See **andiron.** **9.** *Slang* A hot dog; a wiener. **10.** Any of various hooked or U-shaped metallic devices used for gripping or holding heavy objects. **11.** *Astronomy* A sun dog. ❖ *adv.* Totally; completely. Often used in combination: *dog-tired.* ❖ *tr.v.* **dogged, dog•ging, dogs 1.** To track or trail persistently. **2.** To hold or fasten with a dog. *—idioms:* **dog it** *Slang* To fail to expend the effort to accomplish something. **go to the dogs** To go to ruin; degenerate. **put on the dog** *Informal* To make an ostentatious display. [ME *dogge* < OE *docga*.]

dog-and-po•ny show (dôg′ən-pō′nē, dŏg′-) *n. Slang* An elaborate presentation orchestrated to gain approval, as for a policy. [< the razzle-dazzle of animal acts at circuses.]

dog•bane (dôg′bān′, dŏg′-) *n.* Any of several plants of the genus *Apocynum*, having milky juice and bell-shaped flowers.

dog•ber•ry (dôg′bĕr′ē, dŏg′-) *n.* **1.** A wild gooseberry (*Ribes cynosbati*) of eastern North America bearing large prickly berries. **2.** A wild mountain ash (*Pyrus decora*) of eastern North America. **3.** The fruit of either of these plants.

dog biscuit *n.* A hard cracker for dogs.

dog•cart (dôg′kärt′, dŏg′-) *n.* **1.** A vehicle for two persons seated back to back and drawn by one horse. **2.** A cart pulled by dogs.

dog•catch•er (dôg′kăch′ər, dŏg′-) *n.* A dog officer.

dog collar *n.* **1.** A collar for a dog. **2.** *Informal* A clerical collar. **3.**

dogsled

dogtooth

A tight-fitting necklace; a choker.

dog days *pl.n.* **1.** The sultry period of summer between early July and early September. **2.** A period of stagnation. [Transl. of LLat. *diēs canīculārēs*, Dog Star days (so called because the Dog Star (Sirius) rises and sets with the sun during this time) : Lat. *diēs*, pl. of *diēs*, day + LLat. *canīculārēs*, pl. of *canīculāris*, of the Dog Star.]

doge (dōj) *n.* The elected chief magistrate of the former republics of Venice and Genoa. [Ital. dialectal < Lat. *dux, duc-*, leader < *dūcere*, to lead. See **deuk-** in App.]

dog-ear (dôg′îr′, dŏg′-) *n.* A turned-down corner of a page in a book. ❖ *tr.v.* **-eared, -ear•ing, -ears 1.** To turn down the corner of (a page of a book). **2.** To make worn or shabby from overuse. **—dog′-eared′** *adj.*

dog-eat-dog (dôg′ĕt-dôg′, dŏg′ĕt-dŏg′) *adj.* Ruthlessly acquisitive or competitive: *a dog-eat-dog society.*

dog•face (dôg′fās′, dŏg′-) *n. Slang* A US Army foot soldier, esp. in World War II.

dog fennel *n.* **1.** A strong-smelling European weed (*Anthemis cotula*) naturalized in North America. **2.** A weedy plant (*Eupatorium capillifolium*) of the southeast United States having pinnately divided leaves and long clusters of greenish flowers.

dog•fight (dôg′fīt′, dŏg′-) *n.* **1a.** A violent fight between or as if between dogs. **b.** An illegal organized fight between dogs. **2.** An aerial battle between fighter planes. **—dog′fight′er** *n.*

dog•fish (dôg′fĭsh′, dŏg′-) *n., pl.* **dogfish** or **-fish•es 1.** Any of various small sharks, chiefly of the family Squalidae, of Atlantic and Pacific coastal waters. **2.** See **bowfin.**

dog•ged (dô′gĭd, dŏg′ĭd) *adj.* Stubbornly persevering; tenacious. See Syns at **obstinate. —dog′ged•ly** *adv.* **—dog′ged•ness** *n.*

Dog•ger Bank (dô′gər, dŏg′ər) An extensive sandbank of the central North Sea between England and Denmark.

dog•ger•el (dô′gər-əl, dŏg′ər-) also **dog•grel** (dŏg′rəl, dŏg′-) *n.* Clumsy verse, often having an irregular form and monotonous rhymes. [< ME, poor, worthless < *dogge*, dog. See DOG.] **—dog′ger•el** *adj.*

dog•gish (dô′gĭsh, dŏg′ĭsh) *adj.* **1.** Relating to or suggestive of a dog. **2.** Surly; gruff. **3.** *Informal* Showily stylish. **—dog′gish•ly** *adv.* **—dog′gish•ness** *n.*

dog•go (dô′gō, dŏg′ō) *adv. Informal* In concealment. [Prob. < DOG.]

dog•gone (dôg′gôn′, -gŏn′, dŏg′-) *Informal tr. & intr.v.* **-goned, -gon•ing, -gones** To damn. ❖ *interj. & n.* Damn. ❖ *adv. & adj.* also **dog•goned** Damned. See Regional Note at **damned.** [Alteration of Sc. *dagone* < *dag on (it)*, alteration of GODDAMN.]

dog•gy or **dog•gie** (dô′gē, dŏg′ē) *n., pl.* **-gies** A dog, esp. a small one. ❖ *adj.* **-gi•er, -gi•est** Of or suggestive of a dog; doggish.

doggy bag or **doggie bag** *n.* A bag for leftover food that a customer of a restaurant may take home after a meal.

dog•hanged (dôg′hăngd, dŏg′-) *adj. Chiefly Southern US* Hangdog. See Regional Note at **everywhere.**

dog•house (dôg′hous′, dŏg′-) *n.* A small shelter for a dog. **—idiom: in the doghouse** *Slang* In great disfavor or trouble.

do•gie also **do•gy** (dō′gē) *n., pl.* **-gies** *Western US* A stray or motherless calf. [?]

dog iron *n. Chiefly Southern & South Midland US* See **andiron.** See Regional Note at **andiron.** [(FIRE)DOG + (AND)IRON.]

dog•leg (dôg′lĕg′, dŏg′-) *n.* **1a.** Something that has a sharp bend, esp. a road or route that bends abruptly. **b.** A sharp bend or turn. **2.** *Sports* A golf hole in which the fairway is abruptly angled. ❖ *intr.v.* **-legged, -leg•ging, -legs** To make a sharp bend or turn. **—dog′leg′ged** (-lĕg′ĭd, -lĕgd′) *adj.*

dog•ma (dôg′mə, dŏg′-) *n., pl.* **-mas** or **-ma•ta** (-mə-tə) **1.** A doctrine or a system relating to matters such as morality and faith, set forth authoritatively by a church. **2.** An authoritative principle, belief, or statement of ideas or opinion, esp. one considered to be absolutely true. **3.** A principle or belief or a group of them. [Lat. < Gk., opinion, belief < *dokein*, to seem, think.]

dog•mat•ic (dôg-măt′ĭk, dŏg′-) *adj.* **1.** Relating to, characteristic of, or resulting from dogma. **2.** Characterized by an authoritative, arrogant assertion of unproved or unprovable principles. [LLat. *dogmaticus* < Gk. *dogmatikos* < *dogma, dogmat-*, belief. See DOGMA.] **—dog•mat′i•cal•ly** *adv.*

dog•mat•ics (dôg-măt′ĭks, dŏg′-) *n.* (used with a sing. verb) The study of religious dogmas, esp. of a Christian church.

dog•ma•tism (dôg′mə-tĭz′əm, dŏg′-) *n.* Arrogant, stubborn assertion of opinion or belief.

dog•ma•tist (dôg′mə-tĭst, dŏg′-) *n.* **1.** An arrogantly assertive person. **2.** One who expresses or sets forth dogma.

dog•ma•tize (dôg′mə-tīz′, dŏg′-) *v.* **-tized, -tiz•ing, -tiz•es** *—intr.* To express oneself dogmatically. *—tr.* To proclaim as dogma. **—dog′ma•ti•za′tion** (-tĭ-zā′shən) *n.*

dog officer *n.* One appointed or elected to impound stray dogs.

do-good•er (dōō′gŏŏd′ər) *n.* A naive idealist who supports philanthropic or humanitarian causes or reforms. **—do′-good′** *adj.* **—do′-good′ing** *adj. & n.* **—do′-good′ism** *n.*

dog paddle *n.* A prone swimming stroke in which the arms and legs remain submerged and each limb moves in alternation.

Dog•rib (dôg′rĭb′, dŏg′-) *n., pl.* **Dogrib** or **-ribs 1.** A member of a Native American people inhabiting an area between the Great Bear and Great Slave lakes in the Northwest Territories of Canada. **2.** The Athabaskan language of this people. [Transl. of Cree *atimospikay.*]

dog rose *n.* A prickly wild rose *(Rosa canina)* native to Europe and having fragrant pink or white flowers. [Transl. of Med.Lat. *rosa canīna* : Lat. *rosa,* rose + Lat. *canīna,* fem. of *canīnus,* of a dog.]

dogs·bod·y (dôgz′bŏd′ē, dŏgz′-) *n., pl.* **-ies** *Chiefly British Slang* One who does menial work; a drudge. [Brit. slang, naval rations (obsolete), midshipman.]

dog's chance (dôgz, dŏgz) *n. Slang* A very slim chance.

dog·sled or **dog sled** (dôg′slĕd′, dŏg′-) *n.* A sled pulled by one or more dogs. **—dog′sled′** *v.* **—dog′sled′der** *n.* **—dog′sled′-ding** *n.*

dog's life *n. Slang* A miserably unhappy existence.

dog's mercury *n.* A creeping ill-smelling Old World weed *(Mercurialis perennis)* having small greenish flowers.

Dog Star *n.* **1.** See **Sirius. 2.** See **Procyon.** [The brightest star in the constellation Canis Major, the Big Dog.]

dog tag *n.* **1.** A metal identification disk attached to a dog's collar. **2.** A metal identification tag worn on a chain around the neck by members of the armed forces.

dog-tired (dôg′tīrd′, dŏg′-) *adj.* Extremely tired.

dog·tooth (dôg′tooth′, dŏg′-) *n.* **1.** A canine tooth; an eyetooth. **2.** *Architecture* A medieval ornament consisting of four leaflike projections radiating from a raised center.

dogtooth violet *n.* Any of several plants of the genus *Erythronium,* having leaves with reddish blotches and lilylike flowers on leafless stems.

dog·trot (dôg′trŏt′, dŏg′-) *n.* **1.** A steady trot like that of a dog. **2.** *Chiefly Southern US* A roofed passage between two parts of a structure. **—dog′trot′** *v.*

dog·watch (dôg′wŏch′, dŏg′-) *n.* **1.** *Nautical* Either of two periods of watch duty, from 4 to 6 P.M. or 6 to 8 P.M. **2.** A late night shift. [Prob. < *dog-sleep,* a light or interrupted sleep.]

dog·wood (dôg′wood′, dŏg′-) *n.* **1.** A tree *(Cornus florida)* of eastern North America having small greenish flowers surrounded by four large showy white or pink bracts that resemble petals. **2.** Any of several trees or shrubs of the genus *Cornus.*

do·gy (dō′gē) *n. Western US* Variant of **dogie.**

Do·ha (dō′hə, -hä) The cap. of Qatar, on the Persian Gulf. Pop. 217,294.

DOI *abbr.* Department of the Interior

doi·ly (doi′lē) *n., pl.* **-lies 1.** A small ornamental mat, usu. of lace or linen. **2.** A small table napkin. [After *Doily* or *Doyly,* 18th-cent. London draper.]

do·ing (doo′ing) *n.* **1.** Performance of an act. **2.** **doings a.** Daily activities. **b.** Social events and activities.

do-it-your·self (doo′ĭt-yər-sĕlf′) *adj.* Of, relating to, or designed to be done by an amateur. **—do′-it-your·self′er** *n.*

DOJ *abbr.* Department of Justice

do·jo (dō′jō) *n., pl.* **-jos** A school for training in Japanese arts of self-defense, such as judo and karate. [J. *dōjō : dō,* art; see AIKIDO + *jō,* place (< M Chin. *driang, trhiang).*]

DOL *abbr.* Department of Labor

dol. *abbr.* dolce

do·lab·ri·form (dō-lăb′rə-fôrm′) also **do·lab·rate** (-rāt′) *adj. Biology* Having the shape of the head of an ax. [Lat. *dolābra,* pickax (< *dolāre,* to hew) + -FORM.]

Dol·by (dōl′bē) A trademark used for an electronic device that eliminates noise from recorded sound and audio signals.

dol·ce (dōl′chā) *adv. & adj. Music* In a gentle and sweet manner. [< Ital., sweet < Lat. *dulcis.*]

dolce vi·ta (vē′tə, -tä) *n.* A luxurious self-indulgent way of life. [Ital. : *dolce,* sweet + *vita,* life.]

dol·drums (dōl′drəmz′, dôl′-, dŏl′-) *pl.n. (used with a sing. or pl. verb)* **1.** A period of stagnation or slump. **b.** A period of depression or unhappy listlessness. **2a.** A region of the ocean near the equator, characterized by calms, light winds, or squalls. **b.** The weather conditions of these regions. [Prob. < obsolete *doldrum,* dullard, alteration (influenced by TANTRUM) of ME *dold,* p. part. of *dullen,* to dull < *dul,* dull. See DULL.]

dole[1] (dōl) *n.* **1.** Charitable dispensation of goods, esp. money, food, or clothing. **2.** A share of money, food, or clothing charitably given. **3.** *Chiefly British* The distribution of government relief payments to the unemployed; welfare. **4.** *Archaic* One's fate. ❖ *tr.v.* **doled, dol·ing, doles 1.** To dispense as charity. **2.** To give out in small portions. See Syns at **distribute. —idiom:** on the dole Receiving regular relief payments. [ME *dol,* part, share < OE *dāl.*]

dole[2] (dōl) *n. Archaic* Sorrow; grief; dolor. [ME *dol* < OFr. *dol, deul* < Lat. *dolus* < Lat. *dolēre,* to feel pain, grieve.]

dole·ful (dōl′fəl) *adj.* **1.** Filled with or expressing grief; mournful. See Syns at **sad. 2.** Causing grief: *a doleful loss.* **—dole′ful·ly** *adv.* **—dole′ful·ness** *n.*

dol·er·ite (dŏl′ə-rīt′) *n. Chiefly British* A dark fine-grained igneous rock; diabase. [Fr. *dolérite* < Gk. *doleros,* deceitful (< its easily being mistaken for diorite < *dolos,* trick).] **—dol′er·it′ic** (-rĭt′ĭk) *adj.*

dol·i·cho·ce·phal·ic (dŏl′ĭ-kō-sə-făl′ĭk) also **dol·i·cho·ceph·a·lous** (-sĕf′ə-ləs) *adj.* Having a relatively long head with a cephalic index below 76. [Gk. *dolikhos,* long; see **del-** in App.

+ -CEPHALIC.] **—dol′i·cho·ceph′a·lism** (-sĕf′ə-lĭz′əm), **dol′i·cho·ceph′a·ly** (-sĕf′ə-lē) *n.*

dol·i·cho·cra·ni·al (dŏl′ə-kō-krā′nē-əl) also **dol·i·cho·cra·nic** (-nĭk) *adj.* Having a relatively long skull with a cranial index of 74.9 or less. [Gk. *dolikhos,* long; see **del-** in App. + CRANIAL.] **—dol′i·cho·cra′ny** *n.*

do·lit·tle (doo′lĭt′l) *n. Informal* A lazy person.

doll (dŏl) *n.* **1.** A child's usu. small toy having the likeness of a human. **2.** A pretty child. **3.** *Slang* **a.** An attractive person. **b.** A woman. **c.** A sweetheart or darling. **d.** A helpful or obliging person. **—phrasal verb: doll up** *Slang* **1.** To dress oneself smartly and often ostentatiously, esp. for a special occasion. **2.** To embellish to make much more attractive. [< *Doll,* nickname for *Dorothy.*]

dol·lar (dŏl′ər) *n.* **1.** See table at **currency. 2.** A coin or note worth one dollar. [LGer. *daler,* taler < Ger. *Taler,* short for *Joachimstaler,* after *Joachimstal* (Jáchymov), a town of northwest Czech Republic where similar coins were first minted.]

dollar cost averaging *n.* Periodic investment of a fixed dollar amount, as in a stock, on the belief that the average value of the investment will rise over time.

dollar diplomacy *n.* **1.** A policy aimed at furthering US interests abroad by encouraging the investment of capital in foreign countries. **2.** A policy intended to safeguard a nation's foreign investments.

dol·lar·fish (dŏl′ər-fĭsh′) *n., pl.* **dollarfish** or **-fish·es** See **moonfish** 1.

dol·lar·i·za·tion (dŏl′ər-ĭ-zā′shən) *n.* The replacement of a country's system of currency with US dollars.

dollar sign *n.* The symbol ($), used mainly to indicate a dollar amount.

Doll·fuss (dŏl′foos), **Engelbert** 1892–1934. Austrian politician who as chancellor (1932–34) established an authoritarian one-party state.

doll·house (dŏl′hous′) *n.* **1.** A small model house used as a children's toy or to display miniature dolls and furniture. **2.** A house so small that it is likened to a toy house.

dol·lop (dŏl′əp) *n.* **1.** A large lump or portion of a solid matter. **2.** A small quantity or splash of a liquid. **3.** A modicum; a bit. [Earlier, tuft, clump; perh. akin to Norw. *dolp,* lump.]

dol·ly (dŏl′ē) *n., pl.* **-lies 1.** *Informal* A child's doll. **2a.** A low mobile platform that rolls on casters, used for transporting heavy loads. **b.** Such a platform used for work underneath a motor vehicle. **3.** A wheeled apparatus used to transport a movie or television camera about a set. **4.** A small locomotive, as for use on a construction site. **5.** A tool used to hold one end of a rivet while the other end is hammered to form a head. **6.** A small piece of wood or metal placed on the head of a pile to prevent damage while it is being driven.

Dolly Var·den (vär′dn) *n.* A colorfully spotted trout *(Salvelinus malma)* of northwest North America and eastern Asia. [After *Dolly Varden,* a character known for her colorful costume in the novel *Barnaby Rudge* by Charles Dickens.]

dol·ma (dōl′mə, -mä) *n., pl.* **dol·mas** or **dol·ma·des** (dōl-mä′dĕs) A dish consisting of a fruit or vegetable, esp. a grape leaf, cooked with a filling of ground meat, rice, and herbs. [Turk., filling.]

dol·man (dōl′mən) *n., pl.* **-mans** A woman's garment having capelike arm pieces. [Fr. < Ger. < Hung. *dolmany* < Turk. *dōlāmān,* robe < *dolamak,* to wind.]

dolman sleeve *n.* A full sleeve that is very wide at the armhole and narrow at the wrist.

dol·men (dōl′mən, dôl′-) *n.* See **portal tomb.** [Fr. < Breton *taolvean : *taol,* alteration of *tol,* key + *men,* stone; see MENHIR.]

dol·o·mite (dō′lə-mīt′, dŏl′ə-) *n.* **1.** A mineral, CaMg(CO$_3$)$_2$, used in fertilizer and in construction. **2.** A magnesia-rich sedimentary rock resembling limestone. [Fr., after Déodat de Dolomieu (1750–1801), French geologist.] **—dol′o·mit′ic** (-mĭt′ĭk) *adj.* **—dol′o·mit′i·za′tion** (-mĭt′ĭ-zā′shən) *n.* **—dol′o·mit·ize′** (-mī-tīz′) *v.*

Dolomite Alps A range of the E Alps in NE Italy rising to 3,344.3 m (10,965 ft).

do·lor (dō′lər) *n.* Sorrow; grief. [ME *dolour* < OFr. < Lat. *dolor,* pain < *dolēre,* to suffer, feel pain.]

do·lo·ro·so (dō′lə-rō′sō) *adv. & adj. Music* In a mournful or plaintive manner. [Ital. < Lat. *dolōrōsus,* dolorous. See DOLOROUS.]

do·lor·ous (dō′lər-əs, dŏl′ər-) *adj.* Marked by or exhibiting sorrow, grief, or pain. [ME < OFr. *doloros* < LLat. *dolōrōsus* < *dolor,* dolor. See DOLOR.] **—do′lor·ous·ly** *adv.* **—do′lor·ous·ness** *n.*

dol·phin (dŏl′fĭn, dôl′-) *n., pl.* **dolphin** or **-phins 1.** Any of various cetaceans of the family Delphinidae, related to whales but usu. smaller and having a beaklike snout. **2a.** A large marine food and game fish *(Coryphaena hippurus)* having a long continuous dorsal fin and an iridescent blue back with yellow sides. **b.** A similar fish *(C. equisetis)* of smaller size, having silvery or pale yellow sides. [ME < OFr. *daulfin,* blend of *daufin* and O Provençal *dalfin,* both < Med.Lat. *dalfinus* < Lat. *delphīnus* < Gk. *delphīs, delphīn-* < *delphus,* womb (< its shape).]

dol·phin·fish (dŏl′fĭn-fĭsh′, dôl′-) *n., pl.* **dolphinfish** or **-fish·es** See **dolphin** 2a, 2b.

dogwood
Cornus florida

dolphin
Atlantic spotted dolphin
Stenella frontalis

ă	pat	oi	boy
ā	pay	ou	out
âr	care	oo	took
ä	father	oo	boot
ĕ	pet	ŭ	cut
ē	be	ûr	urge
ĭ	pit	th	thin
ī	pie	th	this
îr	pier	hw	which
ŏ	pot	zh	vision
ō	toe	ə	about,
ô	paw		item

Stress marks: ′ (primary); ′ (secondary), as in **lexicon** (lĕk′sĭ-kŏn′)

dolphin kick *n.* A swimming kick used mainly in butterfly in which the legs are extended straight back and moved up and down in unison.

dolphin striker *n.* A small vertical spar under the bowsprit of a sailboat that extends and helps support the martingale.

dolt (dōlt) *n.* A stupid person. [ME *dulte* < p. part. of *dullen*, to dull < *dul*, dull. See DULL.] —**dolt'ish** *adj.* —**dolt'ish•ly** *adv.* —**dolt'ish•ness** *n.*

Dom (dŏm) *n.* **1.** (*also* dōōN) Used formerly as a title for men of the Portuguese and Brazilian royalty, aristocracy, and hierarchy, preceding the given name. **2.** *Roman Catholic Church* Used as a title before the names of Benedictine and Carthusian monks in orders. [Port. < Lat. *dominus*, lord, master. See **dem-** in App.]

Dom. *abbr.* **1.** Dominica **2.** Dominican **3.** dominion

-dom *suff.* **1.** State; condition: *stardom.* **2a.** Domain; position; rank: *dukedom.* **b.** Those that collectively have a specified position, office, or character: *officialdom.* [ME < OE *-dōm.* See **dhē-** in App.]

do•main (dō-mān') *n.* **1.** A territory over which rule or control is exercised. **2.** A sphere of activity, concern, or function; a field. **3.** *Physics* A region in a ferromagnetic material in which the direction of spontaneous magnetization is uniform and different from that in neighboring regions. **4.** *Law* Public domain. **5.** *Mathematics* **a.** The set of all possible values of an independent variable of a function. **b.** An open connected set that contains at least one point. **6.** *Biology* Any of three primary divisions of living systems, consisting of the eukaryotes, bacteria, and archaea, that are considered to rank above a kingdom in taxonomic systems based on similarities of DNA sequences. **7.** *Computer Science* A group of networked computers that share a common communications address. [Fr. *domaine*, blend of OFr. *demaine* < LLat. *dominicum*) and Lat. *dominium*, property, both < *dominus*, lord. See **dem-** in App.]

domain name *n.* A series of alphanumeric strings separated by periods, such as *www.hmco.com,* that is an address of a computer network connection and that identifies the owner of the address.

dome (dōm) *n.* **1.** A vaulted roof having a circular, polygonal, or elliptical base and a generally hemispherical or semispherical shape. **2.** A domelike structure, object, or natural formation. **3.** *Slang* The human head. **4.** *Chemistry* A form of crystal with two similarly inclined faces that meet at an edge parallel to the horizontal axis. **5.** *Archaic* A large stately building. ❖ *v.* **domed, dom•ing, domes** —*tr.* **1.** To cover with or as if with a dome. **2.** To shape like a dome. —*intr.* To rise or swell into the shape of a dome. [< Fr. *dôme,* dome, cathedral < Ital. *duomo,* cathedral < Lat. *domus,* house; see **dem-** in App.) and < Fr. *dôme,* roof (< Provençal *doma* < Gk. *dōma,* house; see **dem-** in App.).]

Domes•day Book (dōōmz'dā', dōmz'-) *also* **Dooms•day Book** (dōōmz'-) *n.* The written census and survey of English landowners made by order of William the Conqueror in 1085–86. [< ME *domesday,* doomsday. See DOOMSDAY.]

do•mes•tic (də-mĕs'tĭk) *adj.* **1.** Of or relating to the family or household: *domestic chores.* **2.** Fond of home life and household affairs. **3.** Tame or domesticated. Used of animals. **4.** Of or relating to a country's internal affairs. **5.** Produced in or indigenous to a particular country: *domestic wine.* ❖ *n.* **1.** A household servant. **2a.** Cotton cloth. **b.** Household linens. Often used in the plural. **3.** A product or substance of domestic origin. [ME < OFr. *domestique* < Lat. *domesticus* < *domus,* house. See **dem-** in App.] —**do•mes'ti•cal•ly** *adv.*

do•mes•ti•cate (də-mĕs'tĭ-kāt') *tr.v.* **-cat•ed, -cat•ing, -cates** **1.** To make comfortable at home; make domestic. **2.** To adopt or fit for domestic use or life. **3a.** To train or adapt (an animal or plant) to live with and be of use to humans. **b.** To introduce and accustom (an animal or plant) into another region; naturalize. **4.** To bring down to an ordinary person's level. **5.** A plant or animal adapted to live among humans. —**do•mes'ti•ca'tion** *n.*

do•mes•tic•i•ty (dō'mĕ-stĭs'ĭ-tē) *n., pl.* **-ties** **1.** The quality or condition of being domestic. **2.** Home life or devotion to it. **3.** **domesticities** Household affairs.

do•mes•ti•cize (də-mĕs'tĭ-sīz') *tr.v.* **-cized, -ciz•ing, -ciz•es** To domesticate.

domestic partner *n.* A person, other than a spouse, with whom one cohabits.

domestic prelate *n.* *Roman Catholic Church* A priest who is an honorary member of the papal household.

domestic relations court *n.* In certain US states, a court with jurisdiction over family disputes, esp. involving the welfare of children.

domestic science *n.* Home economics.

domestic violence *n.* Violence toward or physical abuse of one's spouse or domestic partner.

do•mi•cal (dō'mĭ-kəl, dŏm'ĭ-) *adj.* Shaped like or having a dome. [DOM(E) + (CON)ICAL.] —**do'mi•cal•ly** *adv.*

dom•i•cile (dŏm'ĭ-sīl', -səl, dō'mĭ-) *n.* **1.** A residence; a home. **2.** One's legal residence. ❖ *v.* **-ciled, -cil•ing, -ciles** —*tr.* **1.** To establish (one) in a residence. **2.** To provide with often temporary lodging. —*intr.* To dwell. [ME *domicilie* < OFr. *domicile* < Lat. *domicilium* < *domus,* house. See **dem-** in App.] —**dom'i•cil'i•ar'y** (-sĭl'ē-ĕr'ē) *adj.*

dom•i•nance (dŏm'ə-nəns) *n.* The condition or fact of being

dominant: *a company's dominance in the marketplace.*

dom•i•nant (dŏm'ə-nənt) *adj.* **1.** Exercising the most influence or control. **2.** Most prominent, as in position; ascendant. **3.** *Genetics* Of, relating to, or being an allele that produces the same phenotypic effect whether inherited with a homozygous or heterozygous allele. **4.** *Ecology* Of, relating to, or being a species that is most characteristic of an ecological community, usu. determining the presence, abundance, and type of other species. **5.** *Music* Relating to or based on the dominant. ❖ *n.* **1.** *Genetics* A dominant allele or trait. **2.** *Ecology* A dominant species. **3.** *Music* The fifth tone of a diatonic scale. [ME *dominaunt* < OFr. < Lat. *domināns, dominant-,* pr. part. of *dominārī,* to dominate. See DOMINATE.] —**dom'i•nant•ly** *adv.*

dom•i•nate (dŏm'ə-nāt') *v.* **-nat•ed, -nat•ing, -nates** —*tr.* **1.** To control or govern by superior authority or power. **2.** To exert a supreme, guiding influence on or over. **3.** To enjoy a commanding or controlling position in: *dominating the market.* **4.** To overlook from a height. —*intr.* **1.** To have or exert strong authority or mastery. **2.** To be situated in or occupy a position more elevated or decidedly superior to others. [Lat. *dominārī, domināt-,* to rule < *dominus,* lord. See **dem-** in App.] —**dom'i•na'tive** *adj.* —**dom'i•na'tor** *n.*

dom•i•na•tion (dŏm'ə-nā'shən) *n.* **1a.** Control or power over another or others. **b.** The exercise of such control or power. **2.** **dominations** *Christianity* The fourth of the nine orders of angels.

dom•i•na•trix (dŏm'ə-nā'trĭks) *n., pl.* **-na•trix•es** or **-na•tri•ces** (-nā'trĭ-sēz', -nə-trī'sēz) **1.** A woman who is the dominating partner in a sadomasochistic relationship. **2.** A woman regarded as overbearing.

dom•i•neer (dŏm'ə-nîr') *v.* **-neered, -neer•ing, -neers** —*tr.* To rule or control arbitrarily or arrogantly; tyrannize. —*intr.* To rule or control in such a way. [Du. *domineren* < Fr. *dominer* < Lat. *dominārī,* to dominate. See DOMINATE.]

dom•i•neer•ing (dŏm'ə-nîr'ĭng) *adj.* Tending to domineer; overbearing. —**dom'i•neer'ing•ly** *adv.*

Dom•i•nic (dŏm'ə-nĭk), Saint. 1170?–1221. Spanish-born priest who founded the Dominican order (1216).

Dom•i•ni•ca (dŏm'ə-nē'kə, də-mĭn'ĭ-kə) An island country of the E Caribbean between Guadeloupe and Martinique; gained its independence from Great Britain in 1978. Cap. Roseau. Pop. 71,000. —**Dom'i•ni'can** *adj. & n.*

do•min•i•cal (də-mĭn'ĭ-kəl) *adj.* *Ecclesiastical* **1.** Of or associated with Jesus as the Lord. **2.** Relating to Sunday as the Lord's day. [LLat. *dominicālis* < Lat. *dominicus,* of a lord < *dominus,* lord. See **dem-** in App.]

Do•min•i•can[1] (də-mĭn'ĭ-kən) *adj.* Of or relating to the Dominican Republic or its people or culture. ❖ *n.* **1.** A native or inhabitant of the Dominican Republic. **2.** A person of Dominican ancestry.

Do•min•i•can[2] (də-mĭn'ĭ-kən) *n.* *Roman Catholic Church* A member of an order of preaching friars established in 1216 by Saint Dominic. —**Do•min'i•can** *adj.*

Dominican Republic A country of the West Indies on the E part of Hispaniola; became independent from Haiti in 1844. Cap. Santo Domingo. Pop. 7,760,000.

dom•i•nie (dŏm'ə-nē', dō'mə-) *n.* *Scots* **1.** A cleric. **2.** A schoolmaster. [Obsolete *domine,* clergyman < Lat., vocative of *dominus,* lord. See **dem-** in App.]

do•min•ion (də-mĭn'yən) *n.* **1.** Control or the exercise of control; sovereignty. **2.** A territory or sphere of influence or control; a realm. **3.** often **Dominion** One of the self-governing nations in the British Commonwealth. **4.** **dominions** *Christianity* See **domination** 2. [ME *dominioun* < OFr. *dominion* < Med.Lat. *dominiō, dominiōn-* < Lat. *dominium,* property < *dominus,* lord. See **dem-** in App.]

Dominion Day *n.* July 1, observed in Canada in commemoration of the formation of the Dominion in 1867.

Dom•i•nique (dŏm'ə-nēk', dŏm'ə-nĭk) *also* **Dom•i•nick** (dŏm'ə-nĭk) *n.* One of a breed of American domestic fowl having gray barred plumage, yellow legs, and a rose-colored comb. [After DOMINICA.]

dom•i•no[1] (dŏm'ə-nō') *n., pl.* **-noes** or **-nos** *Games* **1.** A small rectangular block, the face of which is divided into halves, each half being blank or marked by dots. **2.** **dominoes** (*used with a sing. or pl. verb*) A game played with these small blocks. [Fr., prob. < *domino,* mask, perh. because of the resemblance between the eyeholes and the spots on some of the tiles. See DOMINO[2].]

dom•i•no[2] (dŏm'ə-nō') *n., pl.* **-noes** or **-nos** **1a.** A costume consisting of a hooded robe worn with an eye mask at a masquerade. **b.** The mask so worn. **2.** One wearing this costume. [Fr., prob. < Lat. *(benedīcāmus) dominō,* (let us praise) the Lord, dative of *dominus,* lord. See **dem-** in App.]

Domino, Fats b. 1928. Amer. singer whose songs of the early 1950s include *Blue Monday.*

domino effect *n.* A cumulative effect produced when one event sets off a chain of similar events. [Because a row of dominoes stood on end will fall in succession if the first one is knocked over.]

domino theory *n.* A theory that one event will set off a train of similar events.

dome
dome of the Cathedral of Santa Maria del Fiore, Florence, Italy, 1420–36, by Filippo Brunelleschi

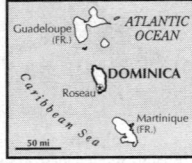

Dominica

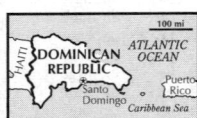

Dominican Republic

Do·mi·tian (də-mĭsh′ən) Originally Titus Flavius Domitianus A.D. 51–96. Emperor of Rome (81–96) who completed the conquest of Britain.

don¹ (dŏn) *n.* **1. Don** (*also* dōn) Used as a courtesy title before the name of a man in a Spanish-speaking area. **2.** *Chiefly British* **a.** A head, tutor, or fellow at a college of Oxford or Cambridge. **b.** A college or university professor. **3.** The leader of an organized-crime family. **4.** *Archaic* An important personage. [Sp. dialectal and Ital., both < Lat. *dominus*, lord. See DOM- in App.]

don² (dŏn) *tr.v.* **donned, don·ning, dons 1.** To put on (clothing). **2.** To assume or take on: *donned the air of the injured party.* [ME, contraction of *do on*, to put on. See DO¹.]

Do·ña (dō′nyä) *n.* Used as a courtesy title before the name of a woman in a Spanish-speaking area. [Sp. < Lat. *domina*, fem. of *dominus*, lord. See DON¹.]

do·nate (dō′nāt′, dō-nāt′) *tr.v.* **-nat·ed, -nat·ing, -nates 1.** To present as a gift, as to a fund or cause; contribute. **2.** *Medicine* To provide (an organ, for example) for implantation or transplant. **3.** *Chemistry* To provide (an electron or atom, for example) for combination with an acceptor. [Back-formation < DONATION.] —**do′na·tor** *n.*

Don·a·tel·lo (dŏn′ə-tĕl′ō, dō′nä-tĕl′lō) 1386?–1466. Italian sculptor renowned for his lifelike figures, such as the bronze *David*.

do·na·tion (dō-nā′shən) *n.* **1.** The act of giving to a fund or cause. **2.** Something that is donated. [ME *donacioun*, gift, benefice < OFr. < Lat. *dōnātiō, dōnātiōn-* < *dōnātus*, p. part. of *dōnāre*, to give < *dōnum*, gift. See dō- in App.]

Don·a·tist (dō′nə-tĭst, dŏn′ə-) *n.* A member of a rigoristic, schismatic Christian sect that arose in North Africa in the fourth century A.D. [Med.Lat. *Donatista*, after *Donatus*, 4th-cent. A.D. ecclesiastic.] —**Don′a·tism** *n.*

don·a·tive (dō′nə-tĭv, dŏn′ə-) *n.* A special donation; a gift. ❖ *adj.* Characterized by, constituting, or subject to donation. [Lat. *dōnātīvum* < neut. of *dōnātīvus*, of a donation < *dōnātus*, p. part. of *dōnāre*, to give. See DONATION.]

Don·cas·ter (dŏng′kə-stər) A borough of N-central England NE of Sheffield. Pop. 292,729.

done (dŭn) *v.* Past participle of do¹. ❖ *adj.* **1.** Carried out or accomplished; finished. **2.** Cooked adequately. **3.** Socially acceptable. **4.** *Informal* Worn out; exhausted. —*idioms:* **done for** *Informal* Doomed to death or destruction. **done in** Worn out; exhausted. —**done′ness** *n.*

do·nee (dō-nē′) *n.* The recipient of a gift. [DON(OR) + -EE¹.]

Do·nets (də-nĕts′, dŭ-nyĕts′) A river rising in W Russia and flowing c. 1,046 km (650 mi) through E Ukraine to join the Don R.

Donets Basin *also* **Don·bas** (dŏn′bäs) A major industrial region of E Ukraine and SW Russia N of the Sea of Azov and W of the Donets R.; developed after the 1870s.

Do·nets′k (də-nĕtsk′, dŭ-nyĕts′) A city of E Ukraine ESE of Kiev; founded c. 1870. Pop. 1,121,400.

dong¹ (dông, dŏng) *n., pl.* **dong** See table at **currency**. [Vietnamese *dông* < Chin. (Mandarin) *tóng*, copper coin.]

dong² (dông, dŏng) *n. Vulgar Slang* A penis. [?]

don·gle (dŏng′gəl, dông′-) *n.* A hardware device that serves as copy protection for certain software by rendering the software inoperable when the device is not plugged into a printer port. [Prob. arbitrary coinage.]

dong quai (dŏong kwä, kwī) *n.* A perennial aromatic herb (*Angelica sinensis*) native to China and Japan, yielding a root that is used esp. to treat menstrual disorders. [Chin. (Mandarin) *dāng guī* : *dāng*, should, ought + *guī*, return (< the belief that it causes blood to return where it should).]

Dö·nitz (dœ′nĭts), **Karl** See **Karl Doenitz**.

Don·i·zet·ti (dŏn′ĭ-zĕt′ē, dō′nē-dzĕt′tē), **Gaetano** 1797–1848. Italian composer whose operas include *Lucia di Lammermoor* (1835).

don·jon (dŏn′jən, dŭn′-) *n.* The fortified main tower of a castle; a keep. [Variant of DUNGEON.]

Don Juan (wŏn′, hwŏn′, jōō′ən) *n.* **1.** A libertine; a profligate. **2.** A man who obsessively seduces women. [After *Don Juan*, legendary 14th-cent. Spanish nobleman.]

don·key (dŏng′kē, dŏng′-, dông′-) *n., pl.* **-keys 1.** The domesticated ass (*Equus asinus*). **2.** *Slang* An obstinate or stupid person. [Perh. < the name *Duncan* or, of imit. orig.]

donkey engine *n.* **1.** A small auxiliary steam engine used for hoisting or pumping, esp. on a ship. **2.** A small locomotive.

don·key·work (dŏng′kē-wûrk′, dŭng′-, dông′-) *n. Slang* Hard physical labor.

Don·na (dŏn′ə, dōn′nä) *n.* Used as a courtesy title before the name of a woman in an Italian-speaking area. [Ital. < Lat. *domina*. See DOÑA.]

Donne (dŭn), **John** 1572–1631. English cleric and metaphysical poet whose works include *Divine Poems* (1607).

don·née (dô-nā′) *n.* A set of literary or artistic principles or assumptions on which a creative work is based. [Fr. < fem. p. part. of *donner*, to give < OFr. < Lat. *dōnāre*. See DONATE.]

Don·ner Pass (dŏn′ər) A pass, 2,162.1 m (7,089 ft), in the Sierra Nevada of E CA near Lake Tahoe; named after the Donner Party, trapped here in Oct. 1846.

---

don·nish (dŏn′ĭsh) *adj.* Of, relating to, or held to be characteristic of a university don; bookish or pedantic.

don·ny·brook (dŏn′ē-brook′) *n.* An uproar; a free-for-all. [After *Donnybrook* fair, held in Donnybrook, a suburb of Dublin, Ireland, and noted for its brawls.]

do·nor (dō′nər) *n.* **1.** One that contributes something to a cause or fund. **2.** *Medicine* One from whom blood, tissue, or an organ is taken for transfusion, implantation, or transplant. **3.** *Chemistry* An atom, molecule, or ion that provides a component to an acceptor, esp. an atom that provides two electrons to form a molecular bond. **4.** *Electronics* An element introduced into a semiconductor with a negative valence greater than that of the pure semiconductor. [ME < AN *donour* < Lat. *dōnātor* < *dōnāre* to give. See DONATION.]

Do·no·so (dō-nō′sō), **José** 1924–96. Chilean writer whose novels include *The Obscene Bird of Night* (1970).

do-noth·ing (dōō′nŭth′ĭng) *Informal adj.* Offering no initiative for change, esp. in politics. ❖ *n.* An idle or lazy person. —**do′noth′ing·ism** *n.*

Don Qui·xo·te (kē-hō′tē, kwĭk′sət) *n.* An impractical idealist bent on righting incorrigible wrongs. [After *Don Quixote*, hero of a satiric romance by Miguel de Cervantes.]

Don River A river of W Russia flowing c. 1,963 km (1,220 mi) to the Sea of Azov.

don't (dōnt) **1.** Contraction of *do not.* **2.** *Nonstandard* Contraction of *does not.* ❖ *n.* A statement of what should not be done: *a list of dos and don'ts.*

do·nut (dō′nŭt′, -nət) *n.* Variant of **doughnut**.

doo·bie (dōō′bē) *n. Slang* A marijuana cigarette. [?]

doo·dad (dōō′dăd′) *n. Informal* An unnamed or nameless gadget or trinket.

doo·dle (dōōd′l) *v.* **-dled, -dling, -dles** —*intr.* **1.** To scribble aimlessly, esp. when preoccupied. **2.** To kill time. —*tr.* To draw (figures) while preoccupied. ❖ *n.* A figure, design, or scribble drawn or written absent-mindedly. [E. dialectal, to fritter away time, perh. < *doodle*, fool. See DOODLEBUG.] —**doo′dler** *n.*

doo·dle·bug (dōōd′l-bŭg′) *n. Chiefly Southern US* **1.** See **ant lion**. **2.** See **pill bug**. **3.** See **sow bug**. **4.** A divining rod. [Perh. dialectal *doodle*, fool, simpleton; see DIDDLE¹ + BUG.]

doo-doo (dōō′dōō′) *n. Slang* Fecal matter or something likened to it. [Baby-talk doubling of DO¹.]

doo·fus (dōō′fəs) *n., pl.* **-fus·es** *Slang* An incompetent, foolish, or stupid person. [Perh. blend of *doof*, fool (< Sc.) and *goofus*, fool (< GOOF).]

doo·hick·ey (dōō′hĭk′ē) *n., pl.* **-eys** *Informal* An unnamed gadget or trinket. [Perh. DOO(DAD) + HICKEY.]

Doo·lit·tle (dōō′lĭt′l), **Hilda** Pen name H.D. 1886–1961. Amer. poet known for works such as *Sea Garden* (1916).

doom (dōōm) *n.* **1.** Inevitable destruction or ruin. **2.** Fate, esp. a tragic or ruinous one. **3.** A decision or judgment, esp. an official condemnation to a severe penalty. **4.** Judgment Day. **5.** A statute or ordinance, esp. in Anglo-Saxon England. ❖ *tr.v.* **doomed, doom·ing, dooms 1.** To condemn to ruination or death. **2.** To destine to an unhappy end. [ME *dom* < OE *dōm*, judgment. See dhē- in App.]

doom palm *n.* A palm (*Hyphaene thebaica*) native to the Nile Valley and having fruits the size of an orange with a distinctive aroma and taste. [Prob. < Ar. dialectal *dōm*, var. of Ar. *dawm*.]

dooms·ay·er (dōōm′sā′ər) *n.* One who predicts calamity at every opportunity.

dooms·day (dōōmz′dā′) *n.* Judgment Day. [ME *domesday* < OE *dōmes dæg* : *dōmes*, genitive of *dōm*, judgment; see DOOM + *dæg*, day.]

Doomsday Book *n.* Variant of **Domesday Book**.

door (dôr, dōr) *n.* **1a.** A movable structure used to close off an entrance, typically consisting of a panel that swings on hinges or that slides or rotates. **b.** A similar part on a piece of furniture or a vehicle. **2.** A doorway. **3.** The room or building to which a door belongs. **4.** A means of approach or access. —*idioms:* **at (one's) door** Within one's sphere of accountability. **close** (or **shut**) **the door on** To refuse to allow for the possibility of. **leave the door open** To allow for the possibility of: *Leave the door open for changes.* **show (someone) the door** *Informal* **1.** To eject (someone) from the premises. **2.** To terminate the employment of; fire. [ME *dor* < OE *duru, dor*. See dhwer- in App.] —**door′less** *adj.*

door·bell (dôr′bĕl′, dōr′-) *n.* A bell, chime, or buzzer outside a door that is rung to announce the presence of a visitor.

do-or-die (dōō′ər-dī′) *adj.* Requiring supreme effort to avoid the consequences of failure: *a do-or-die situation.*

door·jamb (dôr′jăm′, dōr′-) *n.* Either of the two vertical pieces framing a doorway and supporting the lintel.

door·keep·er (dôr′kē′pər, dōr′-) *n.* One who is employed to guard an entrance or gateway.

door·knob (dôr′nŏb′, dōr′-) *n.* A knob-shaped handle for opening and closing a door.

door·man (dôr′măn′, -mən, dōr′-) *n.* A man employed to attend the entrance of a building.

door·mat (dôr′măt′, dōr′-) *n.* **1.** A mat placed before a doorway for wiping the shoes. **2.** *Slang* One who submits meekly to domination or mistreatment by others.

Donatello

donkey
Equus asinus

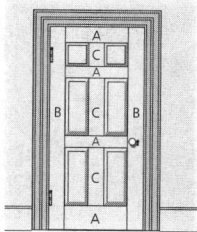

door
A. rails
B. stiles
C. muntins

---

door·nail (dôr′nāl′, dōr′-) *n.* A large-headed nail. **—idiom:** **dead as a doornail** Undoubtedly dead.

Door Peninsula A peninsula of E WI between Green Bay and Lake Michigan.

door·post (dôr′pōst′, dōr′-) *n.* See **doorjamb.**

door prize *n.* A prize awarded by lottery to the holder of a ticket purchased at or before a function.

door·sill (dôr′sĭl′, dōr′-) *n.* The threshold of a doorway.

door·step (dôr′stĕp′, dōr′-) *n.* A step leading to a door.

door·stop (dôr′stŏp′, dōr′-) *n.* **1.** A wedge inserted under a door to hold it open. **2.** A weight or spring that prevents a door from slamming. **3.** A rubber-tipped projection on a wall to protect it from the impact of an opening door.

door-to-door (dôr′tə-dôr′, dōr′tə-dōr′) *adj.* **1.** Going to or making appeals at residences, as when selling or canvassing. **2.** Delivered directly from a store or business to a residence. **—door′-to-door′** *adv.*

door·way (dôr′wā′, dōr′-) *n.* The entranceway to a room, building, or passage.

door·wom·an (dôr′wŏŏm′ən, dōr′-) *n.* A woman employed to attend the entrance of a building.

door·yard (dôr′yärd′, dōr′-) *n.* The yard in front of the door of a house.

doo-wop or **doo·wop** (dōō′wŏp′) *n.* A style of rhythm and blues of the 1950s, characterized by words and nonsense syllables sung in harmony by small groups against a stylized rhythmic melody. [Imit. of the vocals in such music.] **—doo′-wop′** *adj.*

doo·zy or **doo·zie** (dōō′zē) *n., pl.* **-zies** *Slang* Something extraordinary or bizarre. [Poss. blend of DAISY and Duesenberg, a luxury car of the late 1920s and 1930s.]

do·pa (dō′pə) *n.* An amino acid, $C_9H_{11}NO_4$, formed in the liver from tyrosine and converted to dopamine in the brain. [*d*(*ihydr*)*o*(*xy*)*p*(*henyl*)*a*(*lanine*).]

do·pa·mine (dō′pə-mēn′) *n.* A monoamine neurotransmitter formed in the brain by the decarboxylation of dopa and essential to the normal functioning of the central nervous system. [DOP(A) + AMINE.]

do·pa·mi·ner·gic (dō′pə-mə-nûr′jĭk) *adj.* Of, relating to, or activated by dopamine or related substances. [DOPAMIN(E) + –ERGIC.]

dop·ant (dō′pənt) *n.* An impurity added to a pure semiconductor material to alter its conductive properties for use in transistors and diodes. [DOP(E) + –ANT.]

dope (dōp) *n.* **1.** *Informal* **a.** A narcotic, esp. an addictive one. **b.** Narcotics considered as a group. **c.** An illicit drug, esp. marijuana. **2.** A narcotic preparation used to stimulate a racehorse. **3.** *Informal* A stupid person; a dolt. **4.** *Informal* Factual information, esp. of a private nature. **5.** *Chemistry* An absorbent or adsorbent material used in manufacturing, such as nitroglycerin used in dynamite. **6.** A lacquer formerly used to protect, waterproof, and tauten the cloth surfaces of airplane wings. **7.** *Chiefly Southern US* See **cola** [1]. **8.** *Lower Northern US* Syrup or sweet sauce poured on ice cream. ❖ *v.* **doped, dop·ing, dopes** *—tr.* **1.** *Informal* **a.** To administer a narcotic to. **b.** To add a narcotic to. **c.** To administer a performance-enhancing substance to (an athlete). **2.** *Informal* To figure out (a puzzle, for example). **3.** *Informal* To make a rough plan of: *doped out a plan.* **4.** *Electronics* To treat (a semiconductor) with a dopant. *—intr. Informal* To take narcotics or a performance-enhancing substance. [Du. *doop*, sauce < *dopen*, to dip.] **—dop′er** *n.*

REGIONAL NOTE Before it came to refer to narcotics, *dope* was borrowed into English from the Dutch word *doop*, "sauce." Throughout the 19th century it meant "gravy." In the North Midland United States, particularly Ohio, *dope* is still heard as the term for an ice-cream topping, such as syrup. In the South, particularly in South Carolina, *dope* means "a cola-flavored soft drink." The term might be related to the Northern usage as a reference to the syrup base of a cola drink. However, folk wisdom has it that *dope* recalls the minute amounts of cocaine in the original Atlanta recipe for Coca-Cola, which was named after this exotic ingredient.

dope sheet *n. Slang* A scratch sheet.

dope·ster (dōp′stər) *n.* One who analyzes and forecasts future events, as in sports or politics.

dop·ey also **dop·y** (dō′pē) *adj.* **dop·i·er, dop·i·est** *Slang* **1.** Dazed or lethargic, as if drugged. **2.** Stupid; doltish: *a dopey kid.* **3.** Silly; foolish: *a dopey answer.*

dop·ing (dō′pĭng) *n.* The use of a drug, such as a steroid, or a blood product, such as erythropoietin, to improve athletic performance.

dop·pel·gäng·er or **dop·pel·gang·er** (dŏp′əl-găng′ər, -gĕng′-) *n.* A ghostly double of a living person, esp. one that haunts its living counterpart. [Ger., a double : *doppel*, double (< Fr. *double*; see DOUBLE) + *Gänger*, goer (< *Gang*, a going < MHGer. *ganc* < OHGer.).]

Dop·pler (dŏp′lər) *adj.* Of, relating to, or using the Doppler effect or Doppler radar.

Doppler effect *n. Physics* A change in the observed frequency of a wave, as of sound or light, when the source and observer are in motion relative to each other, the frequency increasing as the source and observer approach each other and decreasing as they move apart. [After Christian Johann *Doppler* (1803–53), Austrian physicist and mathematician.]

Doppler radar *n.* Radar that uses the Doppler effect to measure velocity.

Doppler shift *n.* See **Doppler effect.**

Dor. *abbr.* Doric

do·ra·do (də-rä′dō) *n.* **1.** See **dolphin** 2a. **2. Dorado** A constellation of the Southern Hemisphere near Reticulum and Pictor. [Sp., dolphin (fish) < LLat. *deaurātus*, p. part. of *deaurāre*, to gild. See DORY[2].]

dor·bee·tle (dôr′bēt′l) *n.* A European dung beetle (*Geotrupes stercorarius*) that flies with a droning sound. [Obsolete *dor*, a buzzing bee or beetle (< ME *dorre* < OE *dora*) + BEETLE[1].]

Dor·dogne (dôr-dôn′, -dōn′yə) A river rising in the Auvergne Mts. of S-central France and flowing c. 483 km (300 mi) SW to join the Garonne R. N of Bordeaux.

Dor·drecht (dôr′drĕkt′, -drĕkнт′) also **Dort** (dôrt) A city of SW Netherlands on the Meuse R. SE of Rotterdam; founded in the 11th cent. Pop. 113,041.

Do·ré (dô-rā′), **(Paul) Gustave** 1832–83. French artist best known for his imaginative drawings and lithographs.

Do·ri·an (dôr′ē-ən, dōr′-) *n.* One of a Hellenic people that invaded Greece around 1100 B.C. [Lat. *Dōriānus* < *Dōrius* < Gk. *Dōrios* < *Dōris*, Doris.] **—Do′ri·an** *adj.*

Dor·ic (dôr′ĭk, dŏr′-) *n.* A dialect of ancient Greek spoken in the Peloponnesus, Crete, certain Aegean Islands, Sicily, and Italy. ❖ *adj.* **1.** Of, relating to, or being Doric. **2.** In the style of or being the Doric order. [Lat. *Dōricus* < Gk. *Dōrikos* < *Dōris*, Doris.]

Doric order *n.* The oldest and simplest of the three orders of classical Greek architecture, characterized by heavy columns with plain, saucer-shaped capitals and no base.

Dor·is (dôr′ĭs, dŏr′-, dōr′-) An ancient region of central Greece; traditional homeland of the Dorians.

dork (dôrk) *n.* **1.** *Slang* A stupid, inept, or foolish person. **2.** *Vulgar Slang* The penis. [Perh. < *dork*, var. of DIRK.] **—dork′i·ness** *n.* **—dork′y** *adj.*

Dor·king (dôr′kĭng) *n.* A heavy-bodied domestic fowl having five toes on each foot and raised chiefly for food. [After *Dorking*, an urban district of southern England.]

dorm (dôrm) *n. Informal* A dormitory.

dor·mant (dôr′mənt) *adj.* **1.** Lying asleep or as if asleep; inactive. **2.** Latent but capable of being activated. **3.** Temporarily quiescent. See Syns at **inactive.** **4.** In a condition of biological rest or inactivity. [ME < OFr. < pr. part. of *dormir*, to sleep < Lat. *dormīre*.] **—dor′man·cy** *n.*

dor·mer (dôr′mər) *n.* **1.** A window set vertically into a small gable projecting from a sloping roof. **2.** The gable holding such a window. [Obsolete Fr. *dormeor*, sleeping room < *dormir*, to sleep. See DORMANT.]

dor·mie also **dor·my** (dôr′mē) *adj.* Ahead of an opponent in a golf match by as many holes as remain to be played. [?]

dor·min (dôr′mĭn) *n.* Abscisic acid. [DORM(ANCY) + –IN.]

dor·mi·to·ry (dôr′mĭ-tôr′ē, -tōr′ē) *n., pl.* **-ries 1.** A room providing sleeping quarters for a number of persons. **2.** A building for housing a number of persons, as at a school or resort. [ME *dormitorie* < Lat. *dormītōrium* < *dormītōrius*, of sleep < *dormītus*, p. part. of *dormīre*, to sleep.]

dor·mouse (dôr′mous′) *n.* Any of various squirrellike Old World rodents of the family Gliridae. [ME, prob. alteration (influenced by *mous*, mouse) of AN *dormeus*, inclined to sleep, hibernating < OFr. *dormir*, to sleep. See DORMANT.]

dor·nick[1] (dôr′nĭk) *n.* A coarse damask. [ME, after *Doornik* (Tournai), a city of southwest Belgium.]

dor·nick[2] (dôr′nĭk) *n. Lower Northern US* A stone small enough to throw from a field being cleared. [Prob. < Ir.Gael. *dornóg*, a small round stone.]

do·ron·i·cum (də-rŏn′ĭ-kəm) *n.* A plant of the genus *Doronicum*, which includes the leopard's bane. [NLat. < Ar. *darawnaj* < Pers. *darūnak*.]

dorp (dôrp) *n. South African* A small town. [Afr. < MDu.]

dor·sa (dôr′sə) *n.* Plural of **dorsum.**

dor·sad (dôr′săd′) *adv.* In the direction of the back; dorsally.

dor·sal (dôr′səl) *adj.* **1.** *Anatomy* Of, toward, on, in, or near the back or upper surface of an organ, part, or organism. **2.** *Botany* Of or on the outer surface, underside, or back of an organ. [ME < Med.Lat. *dorsālis* < Lat. *dorsuālis* < *dorsum*, back.] **—dor′sal·ly** *adv.*

dorsal fin *n.* The main fin located on the back of fishes and certain marine mammals.

dorsal root *n.* The more posterior of the two nerve fiber bundles of a spinal nerve that carries sensory information to the central nervous system.

Dor·set[1] (dôr′sĭt) *n.* A Native American culture flourishing in northern Greenland and the eastern Canadian Arctic south to Newfoundland from about 800 B.C. to A.D. 1000. [After Cape Dorset, Baffin Island, site of excavations.]

Dor·set[2] (dôr′sĭt) A region of SW England on the English Channel; part of the Anglo-Saxon kingdom of Wessex.

Dorset Horn *n.* A domestic sheep of a breed having large horns and medium-length, fine-textured wool. [After DORSET[2].]

Doric order
Doric order capital

dormer

Dor•sey (dôr′sē), **Tommy** 1905–56. Amer. band leader who with his brother **Jimmy** (1904–57) established swing bands popular in the 1930s and 1940s.

dor•si•ven•tral (dôr′sĭ-vĕn′trəl) or **dor•so•ven•tral** (-sō-) *adj.* **1.** *Botany* Flattened having distinct upper and lower surfaces, as most leaves do. **2.** *Biology* Extending from a dorsal to a ventral surface. —**dor′si•ven′tral•ly** *adv.*

dorso– or **dorsi–** or **dors–** *pref.* **1.** Back: *dorsad.* **2.** Dorsal: *dorsoventral.* [< Lat. *dorsum,* back.]

dor•so•lat•er•al (dôr′sō-lăt′ər-əl) *adj.* Of or involving both the back and the side. —**dor′so•lat′er•al•ly** *adv.*

dor•sum (dôr′səm) *n., pl.* **-sa** (-sə) *Anatomy* **1.** The back. **2.** The upper outer surface, as of an organ or part. [Lat., back.]

Dort (dôrt) See **Dordrecht.**

Dort•mund (dôrt′mənd, -mŏŏnt′) A city of W-central Germany NNE of Cologne; first mentioned c. 885. Pop. 601,966.

do•ry[1] (dôr′ē, dōr′ē) *n., pl.* **-ries** A small narrow flatbottom boat with high sides and a sharp prow. [?]

do•ry[2] (dôr′ē, dōr′ē) *n., pl.* **-ries 1.** John Dory. **2.** See **walleye** 1. [ME *dorre* < OFr. *doree* < fem. p. part. of *dorer,* to gild < LLat. *deaurāre* : Lat. *dē-,* de- + Lat. *aurum,* gold.]

DOS (dŏs, dôs) *n. Computer Science* An operating system that resides on a disk. [*d(isk) o(perating) s(ystem)*.]

dos•age (dō′sĭj) *n.* **1a.** Administration of a therapeutic agent in prescribed amounts. **b.** Determination of that amount. **c.** The amount so administered. **2.** Addition of an ingredient to a substance in a specific amount, esp. to wine.

dose (dōs) *n.* **1a.** A specified quantity of a therapeutic agent prescribed to be taken at one time or at stated intervals. **b.** The amount of radiation administered as therapy to a given site. **2.** An ingredient added, esp. to wine, to impart flavor or strength. **3.** An amount, esp. of something unpleasant, to which one is subjected. **4.** *Slang* A venereal infection. ❖ *tr.v.* **dosed, dos•ing, dos•es 1.** To give (someone) a dose, as of medicine. **2.** To give or prescribe (medicine) in specified amounts. [Fr. < LLat. *dosis* < Gk., something given < *didonai,* to give. See **dō-** in App.] —**dos′er** *n.*

do-si-do (dō′sē-dō′) *n., pl.* **-dos 1.** A movement in square dancing in which two dancers approach each other and circle back to back, then return to their original positions. **2.** The call given to signal such a movement. [Alteration of Fr. *dos à dos,* back to back : *dos,* back (< OFr.; see DOSSIER) + *à,* to (< OFr. < Lat. *ad,* to, at.)]

do•sim•e•ter (dō-sĭm′ĭ-tər) *n.* An instrument that measures the amount of radiation absorbed in a given period.

do•sim•e•try (dō-sĭm′ĭ-trē) *n.* The accurate measurement of doses, esp. of radiation. —**do•sim′et′ric** (-sə-mĕt′rĭk) *adj.*

Dos Pas•sos (dŏs păs′ōs), **John Roderigo** 1896–1970. Amer. writer best known for the trilogy *U.S.A.* (1930–36).

doss (dŏs) *Chiefly British Slang n.* **1.** Sleep; rest. **2.** A crude or makeshift bed. ❖ *intr.v.* **dossed, doss•ing, doss•es** To go to bed, esp. in a crude or makeshift bed; sleep. [Perh. alteration of *dorse,* back < Lat. *dorsum.*]

dos•sal also **dos•sel** (dŏs′əl) *n.* An ornamental hanging of rich fabric, as behind an altar. [Med.Lat. *dossāle* < neut. of *dossālis,* dorsal < LLat. *dorsālis.* See DORSAL.]

dos•si•er (dŏs′ē-ā′, dô′sē-ā′) *n.* A collection of papers giving detailed information about a person or subject. [Fr. < OFr., papers labeled on the back < *dos,* back < Lat. *dorsum.*]

dost (dŭst) *v. Archaic* A second person singular present tense of **do**[1].

Dos•to•yev•sky or **Dos•to•ev•ski** (dŏs′tə-yĕf′skē, -toi-, dŭs-), **Feodor Mikhailovich** 1821–81. Russian writer whose works include *Crime and Punishment* (1866) and *The Brothers Karamazov* (1879–80). —**Dos′to•yev′ski•an** *adj.*

dot[1] (dŏt) *n.* **1a.** A tiny round mark made by or as if by a pointed instrument; a spot. **b.** Such a mark used in orthography, as above an *i.* **c.** The basic unit of resolution for images produced by a printing device. **2.** A tiny amount. **3.** In Morse and similar codes, the short sound or signal used in combination with the dash and silent intervals to represent letters, numbers, or punctuation. **4.** *Mathematics* **a.** A decimal point. **b.** A symbol (·) indicating multiplication. **5.** *Music* A mark after a note indicating an increase in time value by half. **6.** *Computer Science* A period, as used as in URLs and e-mail addresses, to separate strings of words. ❖ *v.* **dot•ted, dot•ting, dots** —*tr.* **1.** To mark with a dot. **2.** To form or make with dots. **3.** To cover with or as if with dots. —*intr.* To make a dot. —*idiom:* **on** (or **at**) **the dot** Punctual or punctually. [ME **dot* < OE *dott,* head of a boil.] —**dot′ter** *n.*

dot[2] (dŏt) *n.* A woman's marriage portion; a dowry. [Fr. < Lat. *dōs, dōt-,* dowry. See **dō-** in App.]

DOT *abbr.* Department of Transportation

dot•age (dō′tĭj) *n.* A deterioration of mental faculties associated with aging. [ME < *doten,* to dote.]

dot•ard (dō′tərd) *n.* A person who is in his or her dotage. [ME < *doten,* to dote.]

dot-com (dŏt′kŏm′) *adj.* **1.** Of or relating to business conducted on the Internet. **2.** Of or relating to a company whose products or services deal with or are sold on the Internet. ❖ *n.* A dot-com company. [Pronunciation of *.com,* commercial organization (in Internet addresses).]

dot-com•mer (dŏt′kŏm′ər) *n.* One who works, esp. in a professional or managerial capacity, for an Internet business.

dote (dōt) *intr.v.* **dot•ed, dot•ing, dotes** To show excessive love or fondness. [ME *doten.*]

doth (dŭth) *v. Archaic* A third person singular present tense of **do**[1].

dot matrix *n.* A dense grid of dots or pins used to form alphanumeric characters or designs.

dot product *n.* See **scalar product.** [< the use of a dot to indicate the function, as in *x · y.*]

dot•ted swiss (dŏt′ĭd) *n.* A sheer, crisp cotton fabric with dots.

dot•tle (dŏt′l) *n.* The plug of tobacco ash left in the bowl of a pipe after it has been smoked. [< DOT[1], lump (obsolete).]

dot•ty (dŏt′ē) *adj.* **-ti•er, -ti•est 1a.** Mentally unbalanced; crazy. **b.** Amusingly eccentric or unconventional. **c.** Ridiculous or absurd. **2.** Having a feeble or unsteady gait; shaky. **3.** Obsessively infatuated or enamored. [Prob. alteration of Sc. *dottle,* silly < ME *doten,* to dote.] —**dot′ti•ly** *adv.* —**dot′ti•ness** *n.*

Dou•ai (dōō-ā′) Formerly **Dou•ay** (dōō-ā′) A town of N France NE of Amiens; site of a Roman Catholic college for English priests founded by Philip II of Spain. Pop. 42,576.

Dou•a•la also **Du•a•la** (dōō-ä′lä) A city of SW Cameroon on the Bight of Biafra. Pop. 1,029,731.

Dou•ay Bible (dōō′ā, dōō-ā′) *n.* The first English translation of the Vulgate Bible authorized by the Roman Catholic Church, published 1582–1610. [After DOUAI.]

dou•ble (dŭb′əl) *adj.* **1.** Twice as much in size, strength, number, or amount. **2.** Composed of two like parts: *double doors.* **3.** Composed of two unlike parts; dual: *a double meaning.* **4.** Accommodating or designed for two: *a double bed.* **5.** Characterized by duplicity; deceitful. **6.** *Botany* Having many more than the usual number of petals, usu. in a crowded or an overlapping arrangement. ❖ *n.* **1.** Something increased twofold. **2.** One that closely resembles another; a duplicate. **3a.** An actor's understudy. **b.** An actor who takes the place of another actor in scenes requiring special skills or preparations. **4.** An apparition; a wraith. **5a.** A sharp turn in a direction of movement; a reversal. **b.** A sharp, often devious change in position or argument; a shift. **6. doubles** *Sports* A form of a game having two players on each side. **7.** *Baseball* See **two-base hit. 8.** *Games* A bid doubling one's opponent's bid in bridge, indicating the ability to take tricks and increasing the penalties and bonuses in scoring. ❖ *v.* **-bled, -bling, -bles** —*tr.* **1.** To make twice as great. **2.** To be twice as much as. **3.** To fold in two. **4.** To clench (one's fist). **5.** To duplicate; repeat. **6.** *Games* To challenge (an opponent's bid) with a double in bridge. **7.** *Music* To duplicate (another part or voice) an octave higher or lower or in unison. **8.** *Nautical* To sail around. —*intr.* **1.** To be increased twofold. **2.** To turn sharply or all the way around; reverse one's course: *doubled back.* **3.** To serve in an additional capacity. **4.** To replace an actor in the actor's absence or in a certain scene. **5.** *Baseball* To hit a two-base hit. **6.** *Games* To announce a double in bridge. ❖ *adv.* **1.** To twice the amount or extent; doubly. **2.** Two together; in pairs. **3.** In two: *bent double.* —*phrasal verb:* **double up 1.** To bend suddenly, as in pain. **2.** To share accommodations meant for one. —*idiom:* **on** (or **at**) **the double 1.** Immediately. **2.** In double time. [ME < OFr. < Lat. *duplus.* See **dwo-** in App.] —**dou′ble•ness** *n.*

double agent *n.* A person pretending to spy for one government while actually spying for another.

double bar *n. Music* A double vertical or heavy black line through a staff marking the end of a main section of a composition.

dou•ble-bar•reled (dŭb′əl-băr′əld) *adj.* **1.** Having two barrels mounted side by side. **2.** Serving two purposes; twofold.

double bass (bās) *n.* The largest bowed stringed instrument in the modern orchestra, also used in jazz, having a deep range that goes as low as three octaves below middle C. [DOUBLE, tuned an octave lower than (because a string that is twice the length of another gives a pitch an octave lower) + BASS[2].]

double bassoon *n.* See **contrabassoon.**

double bind *n.* **1.** A psychological impasse created by contradictory demands. **2.** A situation in which one must choose between equally unsatisfactory alternatives.

double blind *n.* A testing procedure, designed to eliminate bias, in which the identity of those receiving a test treatment is concealed from both administrators and subjects until the study ends. —**dou′ble-blind′** (dŭb′əl-blīnd′) *adj.*

double boiler *n.* A cooking utensil consisting of two nested pans, designed to allow slow, even cooking or heating of food in the upper pan by the action of water boiling in the lower.

double bond *n.* A covalent bond in which two electron pairs are shared between two atoms.

dou•ble-book (dŭb′əl-bŏŏk′) *tr.v.* **-booked, -book•ing, -books 1.** To overbook (an airline flight, for example). **2.** To make two reservations for (a hotel room, for example) in order to be certain of obtaining one.

dou•ble-breast•ed (dŭb′əl-brĕs′tĭd) *adj.* **1.** Fastened by lapping one front edge of a garment over the other and usu. having a double row of buttons with a single row of buttonholes. Used esp. of a coat or jacket. **2.** Having a double-breasted coat.

double check *n.* A careful reinspection or reexamination to assure accuracy or proper condition; verification. —**dou′ble-**

double bass

check′ (dŭb′əl-chĕk′) *v.*

double chin *n.* A fold of fatty flesh beneath the chin.

dou•ble-click (dŭb′əl-klĭk′) *v.* **-clicked, -click•ing, -clicks** —*tr.* To press down and release a button on (a pointing device) twice in rapid succession in order to activate a command or function represented graphically on a display screen. —*intr.* To double-click a pointing device.

dou•ble-cross (dŭb′əl-krôs′, -krŏs′) *tr.v.* **-crossed, -cross•ing, -cross•es** To betray by violating a prior agreement. ❖ *n.* **1.** often **double cross** An act of betrayal. **2. double cross** *Genetics* A cross in which each parent is the product of a single cross. —**dou′ble-cross′er** *n.*

double dagger *n.* A reference mark (‡) used in printing and writing.

double date *n.* A date in which two couples participate. —**dou′ble-date′** (dŭb′əl-dāt′) *v.*

Dou•ble•day (dŭb′əl-dā′), **Abner** 1819–93. Amer. army officer traditionally considered the inventor of baseball.

dou•ble-deal•ing (dŭb′əl-dē′lĭng) *adj.* Duplicitous or deceitful; treacherous. ❖ *n.* Duplicity or deceit; treachery. —**dou′ble-deal′er** *n.*

dou•ble-deck•er (dŭb′əl-dĕk′ər) *n.* Something, such as a structure or sandwich, that has two decks, floors, or layers.

double decomposition *n.* A chemical reaction between two compounds in which the first and second parts of one reactant are united, respectively, with the second and first parts of the other.

dou•ble-dig•it (dŭb′əl-dĭj′ĭt) *adj.* Being between 10 and 99 percent.

double dipping *n.* The practice of drawing two incomes from the government, usu. by holding a government job and receiving a pension. —**double dipper** *n.*

double dribble *n. Basketball* An illegal dribble in which a player uses both hands simultaneously to dribble the ball or begins to dribble the ball a second time after a complete stop.

double dutch also **double Dutch** (dŭch) *n.* A jump rope game in which two ropes are swung crisscross by two turners.

dou•ble-edged (dŭb′əl-ĕjd′) *adj.* **1.** Having two cutting edges: *a double-edged blade.* **2a.** Effective or capable of being interpreted in two ways. **b.** Having a dual purpose.

dou•ble-en•ten•dre (dŭb′əl-än-tän′drə, dōō-blän-tän′drə) *n.* **1.** A word or phrase having a double meaning, esp. when the second meaning is risqué. **2.** The use of such a word or phrase; ambiguity. [Obsolete Fr. : *double,* double + *entendre,* meaning, interpretation.]

double entry *n.* A method of bookkeeping in which a transaction is entered as a debit to one account and a credit to another, so that the totals of debits and credits are equal.

dou•ble-faced (dŭb′əl-fāst′) *adj.* **1.** Having two faces or aspects. **2.** Usable on both sides. **3.** Duplicitous; hypocritical.

double fault *n.* Two successive service faults in tennis, resulting in the loss of a point. —**dou′ble-fault′** (dŭb′əl-fôlt′) *v.*

double feature *n.* A movie program consisting of two full-length films.

double fertilization *n.* The union in flowering plants of one sperm nucleus with an egg, forming a diploid zygote, and another with two polar nuclei, forming an endosperm.

double genitive *n.* A phrasal construction in English in which possession is indicated by the word *of* followed by the possessive form of a noun or pronoun, as in *a relative of mine* or *a friend of Pat's.* See Usage Note at **of.**

dou•ble-head•er also **dou•ble-head•er** (dŭb′əl-hĕd′ər) *n.* **1.** *Sports* Two events held in succession on the same program, esp. in baseball. **2.** A train pulled by two locomotives.

double helix *n.* The coiled structure of double-stranded DNA in which strands linked by hydrogen bonds form a spiral configuration.

double indemnity *n.* A clause in an insurance policy that provides for payment of double the face value of the contract in case of accidental death.

double jeopardy *n.* The act of putting one already tried or convicted through a second trial for the same offense.

dou•ble-joint•ed (dŭb′əl-join′tĭd) *adj.* Having unusually flexible joints, esp. of the limbs or fingers.

double knit also **dou•ble-knit** (dŭb′əl-nĭt′) *n.* A jerseylike knit fabric of two interlocked sides. —**dou′ble-knit′** *adj.*

double negative *n.* A construction that employs two negatives, esp. to express a single negation.

double-decker

Douglas fir
Pseudotsuga menziesii

Frederick Douglass

USAGE NOTE Double negatives are acceptably used when they combine to form an affirmative: *He cannot just do nothing* (that is, "he must do something"). An affirmative meaning is also assigned when *not* is used together with an adjective or adverb that begins with a negative prefix such as *in-* or *un-,* conveying a weaker affirmative than does the positive adjective or adverb by itself; for example, *a not infrequent visitor* may visit less frequently than *a frequent visitor.* • A double (or more accurately, multiple) negative is considered unacceptable when it is used to convey or reinforce a negative meaning, as in *He didn't say nothing* (meaning "he didn't say anything"). Such constructions were once wholly acceptable in English. But in the 18th century the view was advanced that "two Negatives in English destroy one another, or are equivalent to an Affirmative"; and today this view is generally accepted. • The restriction on multiple negatives extends to the combination of negatives with adverbs such as *hardly* and *scarcely;* therefore it is regarded as incorrect to say *I couldn't hardly do it.* • Multiple negatives continue to be widely used in a number of nonstandard varieties of English and are often used by speakers of all backgrounds when they want to strike a colloquial or popular note, as in *You ain't seen nothing yet!* But constructions like these are usually considered marks of ignorance or illiteracy when they appear in formal speech or in writing. See Usage Notes at **hardly, scarcely.**

dou•ble-park (dŭb′əl-pärk′) *tr. & intr.v.* **-parked, -park•ing, -parks** To park alongside another vehicle already parked parallel to the curb. —**dou′ble-park′er** *n.*

double play *n. Baseball* A play in which two players are put out.

double pneumonia *n.* Pneumonia affecting both lungs.

dou•ble-quick (dŭb′əl-kwĭk′) *adj.* Very quick; rapid. ❖ *n.* A marching cadence; double time. ❖ *intr. & tr.v.* **-quicked, -quick•ing, -quicks** To double-time.

dou•bler (dŭb′lər) *n.* A device that doubles the frequency or voltage of an input signal.

double reed *n.* **1.** A pair of joined reeds that vibrate together to produce sound in certain wind instruments. **2.** An instrument using a double reed. —**dou′ble-reed′** *adj.*

double refraction *n.* See **birefringence.**

double salt *n.* A salt that ionizes in solution as if it were two salts but forms a single substance upon crystallization.

dou•ble-space (dŭb′əl-spās′) *intr. & tr.v.* **-spaced, -spac•ing, -spac•es** To type or format so that there is a full space between lines.

dou•ble•speak (dŭb′əl-spēk′) *n.* See **double talk** 2.

double standard *n.* A set of principles permitting greater opportunity or liberty to one than to another, esp. the granting of greater sexual freedom to men than to women.

double star *n.* See **binary star.**

dou•blet (dŭb′lĭt) *n.* **1.** A close-fitting jacket worn by European men between the 15th and 17th centuries. **2a.** A pair of similar or identical things. **b.** A member of such a pair. **c.** *Physics* A multiplet with two members. **3.** *Linguistics* One of two words derived from the same historical source by different routes of transmission. **4. doublets** *Games* A throw of two dice such that the same face of each lands on top. [ME < OFr., dim. of *double,* double. See DOUBLE.]

double take *n.* A delayed reaction to an unusual remark or circumstance, often used as a comic device.

double talk *n.* **1.** Meaningless speech that consists of nonsense syllables mixed with intelligible words; gibberish. **2.** Deliberately ambiguous or evasive language.

dou•ble-team (dŭb′əl-tēm′) *tr.v.* **-teamed, -team•ing, -teams** *Sports* To guard or cover (an offensive player) with two defensive players simultaneously.

dou•ble-think (dŭb′əl-thĭngk′) *n.* Thought marked by the acceptance of gross contradictions and falsehoods, esp. when used as a technique of self-indoctrination.

double time *n.* **1.** A marching pace of 180 three-foot steps per minute. **2.** A rate of pay that is twice the regular rate. —**dou′ble-time′** (dŭb′əl-tīm′) *v.*

dou•ble•ton (dŭb′əl-tən) *n.* A pair of cards that are the only ones of their suit in a hand dealt to a player. [DOUBLE + (SINGLE)TON.]

dou•ble-tongue (dŭb′əl-tŭng′) *intr.v.* **-tongued, -tongu•ing, -tongues** To play a rapidly repeated series of notes on a wind instrument by placing the tongue alternately between the positions for *t* and *k.*

dou•ble•tree (dŭb′əl-trē′) *n.* A crossbar on a wagon or carriage to which two whiffletrees are attached for harnessing two animals abreast.

dou•ble-u (dŭb′əl-yōō′) *n.* The letter *w.*

double vision *n.* A disorder of vision in which a single object appears double.

dou•bloon (dŭ-blōōn′) *n.* A gold coin formerly used in Spain and Spanish America. [Sp. *doblón,* augmentative of *dobla,* Sp. coin < Lat. *dupla,* fem. of *duplus,* double. See **dwo-** in App.]

dou•bly (dŭb′lē) *adv.* **1.** To a double degree; twice: *doubly protected; made doubly certain.* **2.** In a twofold manner.

Doubs (dōō) A river rising in the Jura Mts. of E France and flowing c. 434 km (270 mi) to the Saône R.

doubt (dout) *v.* **doubt•ed, doubt•ing, doubts** —*tr.* **1.** To be undecided or skeptical about. **2.** To tend to disbelieve; distrust. **3.** To regard as unlikely. **4.** *Archaic* To suspect; fear. —*intr.* To be undecided or skeptical. ❖ *n.* **1.** A lack of certainty that often leads to irresolution. See Syns at **uncertainty. 2.** A lack of trust. **3.** A point about which one is uncertain or skeptical. **4.** The condition of being unsettled or unresolved. —*idioms:* **beyond** (or **without**) **doubt** Without question; certainly; definitely. **no doubt 1.** Certainly. **2.** Probably. [ME *douten* < OFr. *douter* < Lat. *dubitāre,* to waver. See **dwo-** in App.] —**doubt′er** *n.*

USAGE NOTE *Doubt* and *doubtful* may be followed by clauses introduced by *that, whether,* or *if. Whether* normally introduces an indirect question and is therefore the traditional choice when the subject is in a state of genuine uncertainty about alternative possibilities: *I doubt whether he meant what he said. It was doubtful whether she would recover from her wounds. If* may also be used as a substitute for *whether* but is more informal in tone. By contrast, *that* is the choice when one uses *doubt* as an understated way of expressing disbelief: *I doubt that we have seen the last of* that *problem,* meaning "I think we haven't seen the last of that problem." *That* is also the usual choice when the truth of the clause following *doubt* is assumed, as in negative sentences and questions. Thus *I never doubted for a minute that I would be rescued* implies "I was certain that I would be rescued." By the same token, *Do you doubt that you will be paid?* seems to pose a rhetorical question ("Surely you believe that you will be paid"), whereas using *whether* in the same question may express a genuine request for information. • In informal speech the clause following *doubt* is sometimes introduced with *but: I don't doubt but* (or *but what) he will come.* Although modern critics sometimes object to its use in formal writing, reputable precedent exists for this construction, as in Richard Steele's remark *"I do not doubt but England is at present as polite a Nation as any in the World."*

doubt•ful (dout′fəl) *adj.* **1.** Subject to or causing doubt: *a doubtful claim; doubtful prospects.* **2.** Experiencing or showing doubt. **3.** Of uncertain outcome; undecided. **4.** Raising doubts as to legitimacy, honesty, or respectability; suspicious: *the candidate's doubtful past.* **—doubt′ful•ly** *adv.* **—doubt′ful•ness** *n.*

doubt•ing Thomas (dou′tĭng) *n.* One who is habitually doubtful. [After Saint THOMAS, who doubted Jesus's resurrection until he had proof of it.]

doubt•less (dout′lĭs) *adv.* **1.** Certainly. **2.** Presumably; probably. ❖ *adj.* Certain; assured. **—doubt′less•ly** *adv.*

dou•ceur (do͞o-sûr′, -sœr′) *n.* Money given as a tip, gratuity, or bribe. [Fr. < LLat. *dulcor,* sweetness < Lat. *dulcis,* sweet.]

douche (do͞osh) *n.* **1a.** A stream of water often containing medicinal or cleansing agents and applied to a body part or cavity. **b.** A stream of air applied similarly. **2.** The application of a douche. **3.** An instrument for applying a douche. ❖ *v.* **douched, douch•ing, douch•es** *—tr.* To cleanse or treat by means of a douche. *—intr.* To apply a douche to oneself. [Fr., shower < Ital. *doccia,* conduit, back-formation < *doccione,* pipe < Lat. *ductiō, ductiōn-,* act of leading < *ductus,* p. part. of *dūcere,* to lead. See **deuk-** in App.]

dough (dō) *n.* **1a.** A soft thick mixture of dry ingredients, such as flour, and liquid that is kneaded, shaped, and baked, esp. as bread or pastry. **b.** A pasty mass similar to this mixture. **2.** *Slang* Money. [ME *dogh* < OE *dāg.* See **dheigh-** in App.]

dough•boy (dō′boi′) *n.* **1.** A piece of bread dough rolled thin and fried in deep fat. **2.** An American World War I infantryman. [Sense 2, perh. < the large buttons on American uniforms of the 1860s, said to resemble doughboys (sense 1).]

dough•face (dō′fās) *n.* A Northerner who sided with the South in the US Civil War, esp. a proslavery member of Congress.

dough•nut also **do•nut** (dō′nŭt′, -nət) *n.* **1.** A small ring-shaped cake made of rich light dough fried in deep fat. **2.** Something whose form is reminiscent of a doughnut. **3.** A fast, tight 360° turn made in a motor vehicle or motorized boat.

dough•ty (dou′tē) *adj.* **-ti•er, -ti•est** Marked by stouthearted courage. [ME < OE *dohtig.*] **—dough′ti•ly** *adv.* **—dough′ti•ness** *n.*

dough•y (dō′ē) *adj.* **-i•er, -i•est** Having the consistency or appearance of dough. **—dough′i•ness** *n.*

Doug•las (dŭg′ləs), **Stephen Arnold** 1813–61. Amer. politician who served as US representative (1843–47) and senator (1847–61) from IL; engaged Abraham Lincoln in a famous series of debates (1858).

Douglas, William Orville 1898–1980. Amer. jurist; associate justice of the US Supreme Court (1939–75).

Douglas fir *n.* A tall evergreen timber tree *(Pseudotsuga menziesii* formerly *P. taxifolia)* of northwest North America having short needles and egg-shaped cones. [After David *Douglas* (1798–1834), Scottish botanist.]

Doug•las-Home (dŭg′ləs-hyo͞om′), Sir **Alexander Frederick** 1903–95. British prime minister (1963–64).

Doug•lass (dŭg′ləs), **Frederick** 1817–95. Amer. abolitionist and journalist who escaped from slavery (1838) and wrote *Narrative of the Life of Frederick Douglass* (1845).

Dou•kho•bor (do͞o′kə-bôr′) *n.* Variant of **Dukhobor.**

dou•la (do͞o′lə) *n.* A woman who assists another woman during labor and after childbirth. [Mod.Gk. *doula* < Gk. dialectal *doulā,* servant-woman, slave.]

doum (do͞om) *n.* See **doom palm.** [Fr., prob. < Ar. dialectal *dōm.* See DOOM PALM.]

dour (do͝or, dour) *adj.* **dour•er, dour•est 1.** Marked by sternness or harshness; forbidding. **2.** Silently ill-humored; gloomy. **3.** Sternly obstinate; unyielding. [ME, poss. < MIr. *dúr,* prob. < Lat. *dūrus,* hard. See **deru-** in App.] **—dour′ly** *adv.* **—dour′ness** *n.*

USAGE NOTE The word *dour,* which is etymologically related to *duress* and *endure,* traditionally rhymes with *tour.* The variant pronunciation that rhymes with *sour* is, however, widely used and must be considered acceptable. In a recent survey, 65 percent of the Usage Panel preferred the traditional pronunciation, and 33 percent preferred the variant.

dou•ra or **dou•rah** (do͝or′ə) *n.* Variants of **durra.**

dou•rine (do͞o-rēn′) *n.* A contagious venereal disease of mules, horses, and asses, caused by the protozoan parasite *Trypanosoma equiperdum.* [French < Ar. *darina,* mangy (said of a female camel), fem. of *darin,* dirty < *darina,* to be dirty.]

Dou•ro (dôr′o͞o, dō′ro͞o) also **Due•ro** (dwĕr′ō) A river rising in N-central Spain and flowing c. 772 km (480 mi) along the Spanish-Portuguese border to the Atlantic Ocean.

douse[1] also **dowse** (dous) *v.* **doused, dous•ing, dous•es** also **dowsed, dows•ing, dows•es** *—tr.* **1.** To plunge into liquid; immerse. **2.** To wet thoroughly; drench. **3.** To put out (a light or fire); extinguish. *—intr.* To become thoroughly wet. ❖ *n.* A thorough drenching. [< obsolete *douse,* to strike.] **—dous′er** *n.*

douse[2] (douz) *v.* Variant of **dowse[1].**

dove[1] (dŭv) *n.* **1.** Any of various birds of the family Columbidae, having a small head and a characteristic cooing call. **2.** A gentle innocent person. **3.** A person who advocates peace, conciliation, or negotiation. **4. Dove** See **Columba.** [ME *douve* < OE **dūfe.*] **—dov′ish** *adj.* **—dov′ish•ness** *n.*

dove[2] (dōv) *v.* See Regional Note at **wake[1].**

dove•cote (dŭv′kōt′, -kŏt′) also **dove•cot** (-kŏt′) *n.* A compartmental structure, often raised on a pole, for housing domesticated pigeons.

dove•kie also **dove•key** (dŭv′kē) *n.* A small black-and-white sea bird *(Alle alle)* of the Arctic and northern Atlantic oceans having a short bill and a stout body. [Dim. of DOVE[1].]

Do•ver (dō′vər) **1.** A municipal borough of SE England on the Strait of Dover opposite Calais, France; a strategic port since medieval times. Pop. 33,700. **2.** The cap. of DE in the central part; founded 1683. Pop. 32,135.

Dover, Strait of A narrow channel at the E end of the English Channel between SE England and N France.

dove•tail (dŭv′tāl′) *n.* **1.** A fan-shaped tenon that forms a tight interlocking joint when fitted into a corresponding mortise. **2.** A joint formed by interlocking one or more such tenons and mortises. ❖ *v.* **-tailed, -tail•ing, -tails** *—tr.* **1.** To cut into or join by means of dovetails. **2.** To connect or combine precisely or harmoniously. *—intr.* **1.** To be joined together by means of dovetails. **2.** To combine or interlock into a unified whole.

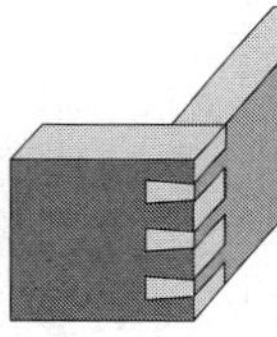
dovetail

dow•a•ger (dou′ə-jər) *n.* **1.** A widow who holds a title or property derived from her deceased husband. **2.** An elderly woman of high social station. [Obsolete Fr. *douagière* < *douage,* dower < *douer,* to endow < Lat. *dōtāre* < *dōs, dōt-,* dowry. See **dō-** in App.]

dow•a•ger's hump (dou′ə-jərz) *n.* An abnormal curvature of the spine that is primarily manifested as a rounded hump in the upper back and typically affects older women.

dow•dy (dou′dē) *adj.* **-di•er, -di•est 1.** Lacking stylishness or neatness; shabby. **2.** Old-fashioned; antiquated. ❖ *n., pl.* **-dies** A dowdy person; a frump. [< ME *doude,* immoral, unattractive, or shabbily dressed woman.] **—dow′di•ly** *adv.* **—dow′di•ness** *n.* **—dow′dy•ish** *adj.*

dow•el (dou′əl) *n.* **1.** A usu. round pin that fits tightly into a corresponding hole to fasten or align two adjacent pieces. **2.** A piece of wood driven into a wall to act as an anchor for nails. ❖ *tr.v.* **-eled, -el•ing, -els** also **-elled, -el•ling, -els 1.** To fasten or align with dowels. **2.** To equip with dowels. [ME *doule,* part of a wheel, perh. < MLGer. *dovel,* plug, or < OFr. *doele,* barrel stave (dim. of *douve* < LLat. *doga,* vessel < Gk. *dokhē,* receptacle < *dekhesthai,* to take).]

dow•er (dou′ər) *n.* **1.** The part or interest of a deceased man's real estate allotted by law to his widow for her lifetime. **2.** See **dowry** 1. **3.** A natural endowment or gift; a dowry. ❖ *tr.v.* **-ered, -er•ing, -ers** To give a dower to; endow. [ME *douere* < OFr. *douaire* < Med.Lat. *dōtārium, dōārium* < Lat. *dōs, dōt-,* dowry. See **dō-** in App.]

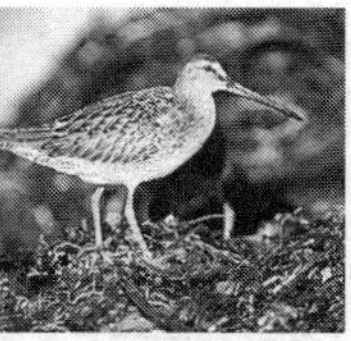
dowitcher
long-billed dowitcher
Limnodromus scolopaceus

dow•itch•er (dou′ĭ-chər) *n.* Either of two shore birds *(Limnodromus griseus* or *L. scolopaceus)* of northern regions having brownish plumage and a long straight bill. [Perh. < Mohawk *tawistawis,* snipe.]

Dow Jones Averages (dou) A trademark used for three indexes of the relative price of selected industrial, transportation, and utility stocks based on a formula developed and periodically revised by Dow Jones & Company, Inc.

down[1] (doun) *adv.* **1a.** From a higher to a lower place or position. **b.** Toward, to, or on the ground, floor, or bottom: *tripped and fell down.* **2.** In or into a sitting, kneeling, or reclining position. **3.** Toward or in the south; southward. **4a.** Away from a place considered central or a center of activity, such as a city or town. **b.** Away from the present place. **5.** To a specific location or source: *tracking a rumor down.* **6.** Toward or at a low or lower point on a scale. **7a.** To or in a quiescent or subdued state: *calmed down.* **b.** In or into an inactive or inoperative state. **8.** To or at a lower intensity. **9.** To or into a lower or inferior condition, as of subjection, defeat, or disgrace. **10.** To an extreme degree; heavily: *worn down.* **11.** Seriously or vigorously: *get down to work.* **12.** From earlier times or people. **13.** To a reduced or concentrated form. **14.** In writing; on paper: *wrote it down.* **15.** In partial payment at

ă pat	oi boy
ā pay	ou out
âr care	o͝o took
ä father	o͞o boot
ĕ pet	ŭ cut
ē be	ûr urge
ĭ pit	th thin
ī pie	*th* this
îr pier	hw which
ŏ pot	zh vision
ō toe	ə about, item
ô paw	

Stress marks:
′ (primary);
′ (secondary), as in
lexicon (lĕk′sĭ-kŏn′)

the time of purchase. **16.** Into or toward a secure position: *nailed down the boards.* ❖ *adj.* **1a.** Moving or directed downward. **b.** Low or lower: *prices were down.* **c.** Reduced; diminished. **2.** Afflicted; sick: *down with a cold.* **3.** Malfunctioning or not operating, esp. temporarily. **4.** Low in spirits; depressed. **5a.** *Sports & Games* Trailing an opponent: *down 20 points.* **b.** *Football* Not in play. **c.** *Football* Having had one's forward progress in carrying the ball stopped, esp. by being tackled. **d.** *Baseball* Retired; out. **6.** Completed; done: *three down, two to go.* **7.** Learned or known perfectly: *had algebra down.* **8.** *Slang* Knowledgeable; aware. Used with *with.* ❖ *prep.* **1.** In a descending direction along, upon, into, or through. **2.** Along the course of: *walking down the street.* **3.** In or at. ❖ *n.* **1.** A downward movement; descent. **2.** *Football* Any of a series of four plays during which a team must advance at least ten yards to keep the ball. ❖ *v.* **downed, down·ing, downs** —*tr.* **1.** To bring, put, strike, or throw down. **2.** To swallow hastily; gulp. **3.** *Football* **a.** To put (the ball) out of play by touching it to the ground. **b.** To stop the advancement of the ball by (a ball carrier), as by tackling. —*intr.* To go or come down; descend. —**idioms: down on** *Informal* Hostile or negative toward; ill-disposed to. **down on (one's) luck** Afflicted by misfortune. [ME *doun* < OE *-dūne* (as in *ofdūne,* downwards) < *dūne,* dative of *dūn,* hill. See **dheuə-** in App.]

down² (doun) *n.* **1.** Fine, soft, fluffy feathers forming the first plumage of a young bird and underlying the contour feathers in certain adult birds. **2.** *Botany* A covering of soft short hairs, as on some leaves or fruit. **3.** A soft, silky, or feathery substance. [ME *doun* < ON *dūnn.*]

down³ (doun) *n.* **1.** An expanse of rolling, grassy, treeless upland used for grazing. Often used in the plural. **2.** *often* **Down** Any of several breeds of sheep having short wool, originally bred in the Downs of southern England. [ME *doune* < OE *dūn,* hill. See **dheuə-** in App.]

down-and-dirt·y (doun′ənd-dûr′tē) *adj. Informal* **1.** Intently and fiercely competitive, often unscrupulously so. **2.** Bawdy; lewd.

down-and-out or **down and out** (doun′ənd-out′, -ən-) *adj.* **1.** Lacking funds, resources, or prospects; destitute. **2.** Incapacitated; prostrate. —**down′-and-out′,** **down′-and-out′er** *n.*

down-at-heel (doun′ət-hēl′) or **down-at-the-heel** (-ət-thə-) *adj.* **1.** Worn out from long use or neglect; dilapidated. **2.** Shabbily dressed because of poverty; seedy.

down·beat (doun′bēt′) *n.* **1.** *Music* **a.** The downward stroke made by a conductor to indicate the first beat of a measure. **b.** The first beat of a measure. **2.** *Informal* A period of stagnation or inactivity. ❖ *adj.* Cheerless; pessimistic.

down-bow or **down·bow** (doun′bō′) *n.* A stroke made by drawing a bow from handle to tip across the strings of a violin or other bowed instrument.

down·burst (doun′bûrst′) *n.* An extremely powerful downward air current from a cumulonimbus cloud, typically associated with thunderstorm activity.

down·cast (doun′kăst′) *adj.* **1.** Directed downward. **2.** Low in spirits; depressed.

down·court (doun-kôrt′, -kōrt′) *adv. & adj. Sports* To, into, or in the far end of the court, esp. in basketball.

down·draft (doun′drăft′) *n.* **1.** A strong downward current of air. **2.** A downward trend; downturn.

Down East also **down East** New England, esp. Maine. —**Down Easter** *n.* —**Down Eastern** *adj.*

down·er (dou′nər) *n. Slang* **1.** A depressant or sedative drug. **2.** One that depresses, such as an experience or person.

Dow·ney (dou′nē) A city of S CA, a suburb of Los Angeles. Pop. 107,323.

down·fall (doun′fôl′) *n.* **1a.** A sudden loss of wealth, rank, reputation, or happiness; ruin. **b.** A cause of sudden ruin. **2.** A fall of rain or snow, esp. a heavy or unexpected one.

down·fall·en (doun′fô′lən) *adj.* Fallen, as from high position; ruined.

down·field (doun′fēld′) *adv. & adj. Sports* To, into, or in the defensive team's end of the field.

down·grade (doun′grād′) *n.* **1.** A descending slope, as in a road. **2.** A turn or trend downward. **3.** A decline, as in fortune. ❖ *tr.v.* **-grad·ed, -grad·ing, -grades** **1.** To lower the status or salary of. **2.** To minimize the importance, value, or reputation of.

down·haul (doun′hôl′) *n. Nautical* A rope or set of ropes for hauling down or securing a sail or spar.

downspout

down·heart·ed (doun′här′tĭd) *adj.* Low in spirits; depressed. —**down′heart′ed·ly** *adv.* —**down′heart′ed·ness** *n.*

down·hill (doun′hĭl′) *adv.* **1.** Down the slope of a hill. **2.** Toward a lower or worse condition. ❖ *adj.* **1.** Sloping downward; descending. **2.** *Sports* Of, relating to, or constituting skiing down a slope. ❖ *n.* **1.** A downhill skiing race. **2.** A downward gradient; a descending slope.

down-home (doun′hōm′) *adj.* Of, relating to, or reminiscent of a simple, wholesome, unpretentious lifestyle, esp. that associated with the rural southern United States.

Dow·ning (dou′nĭng), **Andrew Jackson** 1815–52. Amer. landscape architect who designed the grounds of the US Capitol.

Downing Street¹ A thoroughfare in London, England, off Whitehall. No. 10 Downing Street is the official residence of the first lord of the Treasury, who is usu. the prime minister of Great Britain.

Downing Street² *n.* The British government.

down·link (doun′lĭngk′) *n.* A transmission path by which radio or other signals are sent to the earth from an aircraft or communications satellite.

down·load (doun′lōd′) *tr.v.* **-load·ed, -load·ing, -loads** **1.** To unload. **2.** *Computer Science* To transfer (data or programs) from a server or host computer to one's own computer or device.

down·mar·ket also **down·mar·ket** (doun′mär′kĭt) *adj.* Appealing to or designed for low-income consumers; downscale.

down payment *n.* A partial payment made at the time of purchase with the balance to be paid later.

down·play (doun′plā′) *tr.v.* **-played, -play·ing, -plays** To minimize the significance of; play down.

down·pour (doun′pôr′, -pōr′) *n.* A heavy fall of rain.

down quark *n.* A quark, with a charge of −⅓ and a mass about 20 times that of the electron, that is a component of protons and neutrons.

down·range (doun′rānj′) *adv. & adj.* Away from the launch site and along the flight line of a missile test range.

down·rig·ger (doun′rĭg′ər) *n. Nautical* A trolling rig that consists of a weighted cable attached below the boat to a fishing line, used to troll live bait at or near the float.

down·right (doun′rīt′) *adj.* **1.** Thoroughgoing; unequivocal. **2.** Forthright; candid. ❖ *adv.* Thoroughly; absolutely.

down·riv·er (doun′rĭv′ər) *adv. & adj.* Toward or near the mouth of a river; in the direction of the current.

Downs (dounz) Two roughly parallel ranges of chalk hills in SE England: the **North Downs** extending c. 161 km (100 mi) from W to E; the **South Downs,** c. 105 km (65 mi).

down·scale (doun′skāl′) *adj.* Of, for, or relating to low-income consumers. ❖ *tr. & intr.v.* **-scaled, -scal·ing, -scales** To reduce in scale; scale down.

down·shift (doun′shĭft′) *intr.v.* **-shift·ed, -shift·ing, -shifts** **1.** To shift a motor vehicle into a lower gear. **2.** To reduce the speed, rate, or intensity of something. **3.** To simplify or reduce one's commitments, esp. in work hours. —**down′shift′** *n.*

down·side (doun′sīd′) *n.* **1.** The lower side or portion. **2.** A disadvantageous aspect. **3.** A downward tendency.

down·size (doun′sīz′) *v.* **-sized, -siz·ing, -siz·es** —*tr.* **1.** To reduce in number or size: *a company that downsized its work force.* **2.** To dismiss or lay off from work. **3.** To make in a smaller size: *a car that was downsized for its new model.* —*intr.* To become smaller in size by reductions in personnel.

OUR LIVING LANGUAGE Nothing fails so miserably as a failed euphemism—though there have been plenty of successes. The English language, especially business jargon, is littered with words that now seem ordinary but were once regarded as euphemisms. Consider the terms *senior* for old person, *custodian* for janitor, and *rest room* for toilet (itself a euphemism). These words arise from a natural tendency to ease the pain or embarrassment associated with things such as death or bodily functions, or from a conscious desire to recast something unpleasant in a more dignified light. *Downsize* is a recent example of a euphemism that found broad acceptance in the language and is not particularly thought of as a deceptive attempt to smooth over the pain of large-scale firings. But the search for less harmful terms goes on and on. The attempt to find even more positive-sounding ways to say "downsize" has led business executives and people working in human resources and public relations (both euphemists themselves) to float a number of alternatives. Companies were being "reengineered" and even "right-sized"; laid-off workers had to be "separated" or "unassigned" for being "nonessential"; their jobs were said to be "no longer going forward." Most of these terms were met with scorn, being regarded as cynical attempts to sugarcoat an inherently distressing phenomenon, and as failed euphemisms they accomplished the exact opposite of what they were designed to. Why one euphemism should be accepted while another is not remains something of a mystery, but the selection of such terms indicates one way in which social attitudes have a powerful effect on language change.

down·slide (doun′slīd′) *n.* A downward course; a decline.

down·spout (doun′spout′) *n.* A vertical pipe for carrying rainwater down from a roof gutter.

down·stage (doun′stāj′) *adv.* Toward, at, or on the front part of a stage. —**down′stage′** *adj. & n.*

down·stairs (doun′stârz′) *adv.* **1.** Down the stairs. **2.** To or on a lower floor. ❖ *n.* (*used with a sing. verb*) The lower or main floor. ❖ *adj.* **downstairs** (doun′stârz′) also **down·stair** (-stâr′) Located on a lower or main floor.

down·state (doun′stāt′) *n.* The southerly section of a state in the United States. ❖ *adv. & adj.* To, from, or in the southerly section of a state. —**down′stat′er** *n.*

down·stream (doun′strēm′) *adv. & adj.* In the direction of a stream's current.

down·swing (doun′swĭng′) *n.* **1.** A swing downward, as of a golf club. **2.** A decline, as of a business.

Down syndrome or **Down's syndrome** *n.* A congenital disorder, caused by the presence of an extra 21st chromosome, in which the affected person has mild to moderate mental retardation, short stature, and a flattened facial profile. [After John Langdon Haydon *Down* (1828–96), British physician.]

down•tick (doun′tĭk′) *n.* **1.** A decrease, esp. a small or incremental one. **2.** A transaction in a stock market security below the price of the previous transaction.

down•time (doun′tīm′) *n.* The period of time when something is not in operation, esp. as the result of a malfunction.

down-to-earth (doun′tōō-ûrth′, -tə-) *adj.* **1.** Realistic; sensible. **2a.** Unpretentious or unaffected. **b.** Simple in style; unornate.

down•town (doun′toun′) *n.* The lower part or the business center of a city or town. ❖ *adv.* (doun′toun′) To, toward, or in the downtown area. ❖ *adj.* (doun′toun′) Of, relating to, or located downtown.

down•trend (doun′trĕnd′) *n.* A downward trend; a downturn. —**down′trend′** *v.*

down•trod•den (doun′trŏd′n) *adj.* Oppressed; tyrannized.

down•turn (doun′tûrn′) *n.* A tendency downward, esp. in business or economic activity.

down under *adv. Informal* To or in Australia or New Zealand. ❖ *n. also* **Down Under** Australia and often New Zealand.

down•ward (doun′wərd) *adv. or* **down•wards** (-wərdz) **1.** In, to, or toward a lower place, level, or position. **2.** From a prior source or earlier time: *passed downward through the ages.* ❖ *adj.* Directed toward a lower place or position. —**down′ward•ly** *adv.*

down•wash (doun′wŏsh′, -wôsh′) *n.* The downward deflection of air from a moving object, such as an airplane wing.

down•wind (doun′wĭnd′) *adv.* In the direction in which the wind blows. —**down′wind′** *adj.*

down•y (dou′nē) *adj.* **-i•er, -i•est** **1.** Made of or covered with down. **2a.** Resembling down. **b.** Quietly soothing; soft.

downy brome *n.* A Eurasian grass (*Bromus tectorum*), now widespread in grasslands of the western United States.

downy mildew *n.* A disease of plants caused by fungi of the order Peronosporales and characterized by gray, velvety patches of spores on the lower surfaces of leaves.

downy woodpecker *n.* A North American woodpecker (*Picoides pubescens*) having a solid white back and a small bill.

dow•ry (dou′rē) *n., pl.* **-ries** **1.** Money or property brought by a bride to her husband at marriage. **2.** A sum of money required of a postulant at a convent. **3.** A natural endowment or gift; a talent. **4.** *Archaic* See **dower** 1. [ME *douerie* < AN *douarie* < Med.Lat. *dōtārium, dōārium*, dower. See DOWER.]

dowse¹ *also* **douse** (douz) *intr.v.* **dowsed, dows•ing, dows•es** *also* **doused, dous•ing, dous•es** To use a divining rod to search for underground water or minerals. [?]

dowse² (dous) *v. & n.* Variant of **douse¹**.

dows•er (dou′zər) *n.* **1.** A person who uses a divining rod to search for underground water or minerals. **2.** A divining rod.

dox•ol•o•gy (dŏk-sŏl′ə-jē) *n., pl.* **-gies** An expression of praise to God, esp. a short hymn sung as part of a Christian worship service. [Med.Lat. *doxologia* < Gk. *doxologiā*, praise : *doxa*, glory, honor (< *dokein*, to seem) + *logos*, saying; see –LOGY.] —**dox′o•log′i•cal** (dŏk′sə-lŏj′ĭ-kəl) *adj.* —**dox′o•log′i•cal•ly** *adv.*

dox•y (dŏk′sē) *n., pl.* **-ies** *Slang* **1.** A female lover; a mistress. **2.** A sexually promiscuous woman. [Perh. < obsolete Du. *docke*, doll.]

doy•en (doi-ĕn′, doi′ən, dwä-yăn′) *n.* A man who is the eldest or senior member of a group. [Prob. Fr. < OFr. *doien* < LLat. *decānus*, chief of ten. See DEAN.]

doy•enne (doi-ĕn′, dwä-yĕn′) *n.* A woman who is the eldest or senior member of a group. [Fr., fem. of *doyen*, senior member. See DOYEN.]

Doyle (doil), Sir **Arthur Conan** 1859–1930. British writer known chiefly for his stories featuring Sherlock Holmes.

D'Oy•ly Carte (doi′lē kärt′), **Richard** See Richard D'Oyly **Carte.**

doz. *abbr.* dozen

doze (dōz) *v.* **dozed, doz•ing, doz•es** —*intr.* To sleep lightly and intermittently. —*tr.* To spend (time) dozing or as if dozing. ❖ *n.* A short light sleep. —*phrasal verb:* **doze off** To fall into a doze. [Prob. of Scand. orig.] —**doz′er** *n.*

doz•en (dŭz′ən) *n., pl.* **dozen** A set of 12. **2. dozens** An indefinite large number. ❖ *adj.* Twelve. [ME *dozeine* < OFr. *dozaine* < *dozze*, twelve, ult. < Lat. *duodecim* : *duo*, two; see **dwo-** in App. + *decem*, ten; see **dekm̥** in App.] —**doz′enth** (-ənth) *adj.*

do•zy (dō′zē) *adj.* **-zi•er, -zi•est** Half asleep; drowsy. —**doz′i•ly** *adv.* —**do′zi•ness** *n.*

DP *abbr.* **1.** data processing **2.** dew point **3.** displaced person **4.** double play

D particle *n.* Either of two subatomic particles in the meson family, one neutral and one positively charged, having masses 3,649 and 3,658 times that of the electron.

DPh *or* **DPhil** *abbr.* Doctor of Philosophy

dpi *abbr.* dots per inch

dpt. *abbr.* **1.** department **2.** deponent

DPT vaccine (dē′pē-tē′) *n.* Variant of **DTP vaccine.**

dr. *abbr.* **1.** debtor **2.** drachma **3.** dram

Dr. *abbr.* **1.** doctor **2.** drive

drab¹ (drăb) *adj.* **drab•ber, drab•best** **1a.** Of a dull grayish to yellowish brown color. **b.** Of a light olive brown or khaki color. **2.** Faded and dull in appearance. **3.** Dull or commonplace in charac-

ter; dreary. ❖ *n.* **1.** A dull grayish to yellowish or light olive brown. **2.** Cloth of this color or of an unbleached natural color. [Alteration of obsolete Fr. *drap*, cloth < OFr. See DRAPE.] —**drab′ly** *adv.* —**drab′ness** *n.*

drab² (drăb) *n.* **1.** A slattern. **2.** A woman prostitute. ❖ *intr.v.* **drabbed, drab•bing, drabs** To consort with prostitutes. [Poss. of Celt. orig. (akin to Sc. Gael. *dràbag* and Ir.Gael. *drabóg*, slattern) or < Du. *drab*, dregs.]

drab³ (drăb) *n.* A negligible amount: *finished the work in dribs and drabs.* [Prob. alteration of DRIB.]

drab•ble (drăb′əl) *tr. & intr.v.* **-bled, -bling, -bles** To make or become wet and soiled by dragging; draggle. [ME *drabelen*.]

dra•cae•na (drə-sē′nə) *n.* Any of several tropical plants of the genera *Dracaena* and *Cordyline*, having decorative foliage. [LLat., female dragon < Gk. *drakaina*, fem. of *drakōn*, serpent. See DRAGON.]

drachm (drăm) *n.* **1.** A dram. **2.** A drachma.

drach•ma (drăk′mə) *n., pl.* **-mas** *or* **-mae** (-mē) **1.** See table at **currency. 2.** An ancient Greek silver coin. **3.** One of several modern units of weight, esp. the dram. [Lat. < Gk. *drakhmē* < *drassesthai, drakh-*, to grasp.]

Dra•co¹ (drā′kō) 7th cent. B.C. Athenian politician whose legal code (c. 621) was noted for its severity. —**Dra•co′ni•an** *adj.*

Dra•co² (drā′kō) *n.* A constellation in the polar region of the Northern Hemisphere near Cepheus and Ursa Major. [Lat. *dracō*, dragon. See DRAGON.]

dra•co•ni•an (drā-kō′nē-ən, drə-) *adj.* Exceedingly harsh; very severe: *draconian budget cuts.* [After DRACO¹.]

dra•con•ic¹ (drā-kŏn′ĭk) *adj.* Of or suggestive of a dragon. [< Lat. *dracō, dracōn-*, dragon. See DRAGON.]

dra•con•ic² (drā-kŏn′ĭk, drə-) *adj.* Draconian. —**dra•con′i•cal•ly** *adv.*

draft (drăft) *n.* **1.** A current of air in an enclosed area. **2.** A device that regulates the flow or circulation of air. **3a.** The act of pulling loads; traction. **b.** Something that is pulled or drawn; a load. **c.** A team of animals used to pull loads. **4.** *Nautical* The depth of a vessel's keel below the water line, esp. when loaded. **5.** A heavy demand on resources. **6.** A written order directing the payment of money from an account or fund. **7a.** A gulp, swallow, or inhalation. **b.** The amount taken in by a single act of drinking or inhaling. **c.** A measured portion; a dose. **8a.** The drawing of a liquid, as from a keg. **b.** An amount drawn. **9a.** The process or method of selecting one or more individuals from a group, as for a duty. **b.** Compulsory enrollment in the armed forces; conscription. **c.** A body of people selected or conscripted. **10.** *Sports* A system in which the exclusive rights to new players are distributed among professional teams. **11a.** The act of drawing in a fishnet. **b.** The quantity of fish caught. **12a.** A preliminary version of a plan, document, or picture. **b.** A representation of something to be constructed. **13.** A narrow line chiseled on a stone to guide a stonecutter in leveling its surface. **14.** A slight taper given a die to facilitate the removal of a casting. **15.** An allowance made for loss in weight of merchandise. ❖ *v.* **draft•ed, draft•ing, drafts** —*tr.* **1.** To select from a group for some usu. compulsory service. **2.** To select (a player) in a sports draft. **3.** To draw up a preliminary version of or plan for. **4.** To create by thinking and writing; compose. —*intr.* To move, ride, or drive close behind a fast-moving object to take advantage of the slipstream. ❖ *adj.* **1.** Suited for or used for drawing heavy loads. **2.** Drawn from a cask or tap. —*idiom:* **on draft** Drawn from a large container, such as a keg. [ME *draught*, act of drawing < OE *dreaht*; akin to *dragan*, to draw.]

draft board *n.* A local board of civilians in charge of the selection of persons for compulsory military service.

draft•ee (drăf-tē′) *n.* One who is drafted, esp. for military service.

draft•er (drăf′tər) *n.* One that drafts, esp. a person who drafts plans or designs or composes a document.

draft•ing (drăf′tĭng) *n.* The systematic representation and dimensional specification of mechanical and architectural structures.

drafts•man (drăfts′mən) *n.* **1.** A man who draws plans or designs, as of structures to be built. **2.** A man who draws, esp. an artist. —**drafts′man•ship′** *n.*

drafts•per•son (drăfts′pûr′sən) *n.* A drafter.

drafts•wom•an (drăfts′wŏŏm′ən) *n.* **1.** A woman who draws plans or designs, as of structures to be built. **2.** A woman who draws, esp. an artist.

draft•y (drăf′tē) *adj.* **-i•er, -i•est** Having or exposed to drafts of air. —**draft′i•ly** *adv.* —**draft′i•ness** *n.*

drag (drăg) *v.* **dragged, drag•ging, drags** —*tr.* **1.** To pull along with difficulty or effort; haul. See Syns at **pull. 2.** To cause to trail along a surface, esp. the ground. **3.** *Computer Science* **a.** To move (a pointing device) while pressing down on one of its buttons. **b.** To move (an item) on a screen using a pointing device. **4.** To move or bring by force or with great effort. **5a.** To search or sweep the bottom of (a body of water), as with a dragnet. **b.** To bring up or catch by such means. **6.** To prolong tediously: *dragged the story out.* **7.** *Baseball* To hit (a bunt) while taking the first steps toward first base. **8.** To break up, rake, or smooth out (land or dirt), esp. by pulling a drag or heavy mesh. —*intr.* **1.** To trail

downy woodpecker
Picoides pubescens

dowser

ă	pat	oi	boy
ā	pay	ou	out
âr	care	ŏŏ	took
ä	father	ōō	boot
ĕ	pet	ŭ	cut
ē	be	ûr	urge
ĭ	pit	th	thin
ī	pie	*th*	this
îr	pier	hw	which
ŏ	pot	zh	vision
ō	toe	ə	about,
ô	paw		item

Stress marks:
′ (primary);
′ (secondary), as in
lexicon (lĕk′sĭ-kŏn′)

along the ground. **2.** To move slowly or with effort. **3.** To lag behind. **4.** To pass or proceed slowly, tediously, or laboriously. **5.** *Computer Science* To move a pointing device while pressing down on one of its buttons. **6.** To search or dredge the bottom of a body of water. **7.** To take part in or as if in a drag race. **8.** To draw on a cigarette, pipe, or cigar. ❖ *n.* **1.** The act of dragging. **2.** Something, such as a harrow, that is dragged along the ground. **3.** A device, such as a grappling hook, that is used for dragging under water. **4.** A heavy sledge or cart for hauling loads. **5.** A large four-horse coach with seats inside and on top. **6.** Something, such as a sea anchor, that retards motion. **7.** One that impedes or slows progress; a drawback or burden. **8.** The degree of resistance involved in dragging or hauling. **9.** The retarding force exerted on a moving body by a fluid medium such as air. **10.** A slow laborious motion or movement. **11a.** The scent or trail of an animal. **b.** Something that provides an artificial scent. **12.** *Slang* One that is obnoxiously tiresome. **13.** A puff on a cigarette, pipe, or cigar. **14.** *Slang* A street or road. **15.** The clothing characteristic of one sex when worn by a member of the opposite sex. —*idiom:* **drag (one's) feet (or heels)** To act or work with intentional slowness; delay. [ME *draggen* < ON *draga* or var. of ME *drawen*; see DRAW.]

drag bunt *n. Baseball* A bunt executed while taking the first steps toward first base.

dra·gée (drä-zhāʹ) *n.* **1.** A small, often medicated candy. **2.** A tiny hard candy used to decorate baked goods. [Fr. < OFr. *dragie*. See DREDGE².]

drag·ger (drăgʹər) *n.* One that drags, esp. a boat equipped to tow fishing gear, such as a trawl net, along the bottom of the sea.

drag·gle (drăgʹəl) *v.* **-gled, -gling, -gles** —*tr.* To make wet and dirty by dragging on the ground. —*intr.* **1.** To become wet and muddy by being dragged. **2.** To follow slowly; straggle. [Prob. freq. of DRAG.]

drag·gy (drăgʹē) *adj.* **-gi·er, -gi·est 1.** Dull and listless. **2.** *Slang* Very tiresome.

drag·line (drăgʹlīnʹ) *n.* **1.** A line used for dragging. **2.** A kind of dredging machine.

drag link *n.* A link for transmitting rotary motion between cranks on two parallel but slightly offset shafts.

drag·net (drăgʹnĕtʹ) *n.* **1.** A system of coordinated procedures to catch wanted persons such as criminals. **2a.** A net for trawling; a trawl. **b.** A net for catching small game.

drag·o·man (drăgʹə-mən) *n., pl.* **-mans** or **-men** An interpreter or guide in countries where Arabic, Turkish, or Persian is spoken. [ME *dragman*, ult. < Akkadian *targumannu*, interpreter, perh. < *ragāmu*, to speak, call.]

drag·on (drăgʹən) *n.* **1.** A mythical monster traditionally represented as a gigantic reptile with a lion's claws, a serpent's tail, wings, and a scaly skin. **2a.** A fiercely vigilant or intractable person. **b.** Something very formidable or dangerous. **3.** Any of various lizards, such as the Komodo dragon. **4. Dragon** See **Draco²**. **5.** *Archaic* A large snake or serpent. [ME < OFr. < Lat. *dracō, dracōn-*, large serpent < Gk. *drakōn*, perh. < *derkesthai*, to look.]

drag·on·et (drăgʹə-nĭt) *n.* Any of various small, often brightly colored marine fishes of the family Callionymidae, having a slender body and a flattened head. [ME, young dragon < OFr., dim. of *dragon*, dragon. See DRAGON.]

drag·on·fly (drăgʹən-flīʹ) *n.* Any of various insects of the order Odonata or suborder Anisoptera, having a long slender body and two pairs of net-veined wings.

REGIONAL NOTE Regional terms for the dragonfly abound. The greatest variety of terms are in the South, where the most widespread term is *snake doctor* (from a folk belief that dragonflies take care of snakes). The Midland equivalent is *snake feeder.* Speakers from the Lower South and the Mississippi Valley are more likely to refer to the same insect as a *mosquito fly, mosquito hawk,* or, in the South Atlantic states, a *skeeter hawk.* The imagery outside the South often alludes to the insect's shape: speakers in the West, Upper North, and New England call it a *darner, darning needle,* or, less commonly, a *devil's darning needle,* and those in the Upper North also refer to it just as a *needle;* those in coastal New Jersey call it a *spindle;* and those in the San Francisco Bay area, an *ear sewer,* that is, a creature that sews up your ears.

dragon
detail from the Nine-Dragon Wall in Beihai Park, Beijing, China

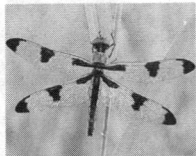

dragonfly

drag·on·head (drăgʹən-hĕdʹ) *n.* Any of several plants of the genera *Dracocephalum* and *Physostegia*, having terminal spikes of rose-pink or purplish flowers.

drag·on·root (drăgʹən-rōōtʹ, -rŏŏtʹ) *n.* See **green dragon.**

drag·on's blood (drăgʹənz) *n.* **1.** A red, resinous substance obtained from the fruit of a climbing palm (*Daemonorops draco*) of tropical Asia. **2.** Any of several resins similar to this substance.

dragon's mouth *n.* See **swamp pink.**

dragon tree *n.* A tree (*Dracaena draco*) of the Canary Islands having a thick trunk, sword-shaped leaves, and orange fruit.

dra·goon (drə-gōōnʹ, dră-) *n.* A member of a European military unit trained and armed to fight mounted or on foot. ❖ *tr.v.* **-gooned, -goon·ing, -goons 1.** To subjugate or persecute by the imposition of troops. **2.** To compel by violent measures or threats; coerce. [Fr. *dragon*, carbine, dragoon < OFr., dragon. See DRAGON.]

drag queen *n. Slang* A man, esp. a performer, who dresses as a woman.

drag race *n.* A race between two cars to determine which can accelerate faster from a standstill. [< DRAG, an automobile (slang).] —**drag racer** *n.* —**drag racing** *n.*

drag·ster (drăgʹstər) *n.* **1.** An automobile specially built or modified for drag racing. **2.** One who races a dragster.

drag strip *n.* A short straight course or track for drag racing.

drain (drān) *v.* **drained, drain·ing, drains** —*tr.* **1.** To draw off (a liquid) by a gradual process: *drained water from the sink.* **2a.** To cause liquid to go out from; empty: *drained the bathtub.* **b.** To draw off the surface water of. **3.** To drink all the contents of. **4a.** To deplete gradually, esp. to the point of complete exhaustion. See Syns at **deplete. b.** To fatigue or spend emotionally or physically. —*intr.* **1.** To flow off or out. **2.** To become empty by the drawing off of liquid. **3.** To discharge surface or excess water. **4.** To become gradually depleted; dwindle. ❖ *n.* **1.** A pipe or channel by which liquid is drawn off. **2.** *Medicine* A device, such as a tube, inserted into the opening of a wound or body cavity to facilitate discharge of fluid or purulent material. **3.** The act or process of draining. **4a.** A gradual outflow or loss; consumption or depletion. **b.** Something that causes a gradual loss. —*idiom:* **down the drain** To or into the condition of being wasted or lost. [ME *dreinen*, to strain, drain < OE *drēahnian*.] —**drainʹa·ble** *adj.* —**drainʹer** *n.*

drain·age (drāʹnĭj) *n.* **1.** The action or a method of draining. **2.** A system of drains. **3.** Something drained off. **4.** *Medicine* The removal of fluid or purulent material from a wound or body cavity.

drainage basin *n.* An area drained by a river system.

drain·pipe (drānʹpīpʹ) *n.* A pipe for carrying off water or sewage.

Draize test (drāz) *n.* A test to determine the degree to which a substance such as a cosmetic or pharmaceutical irritates human tissues, in which a small amount of the substance is applied directly in the eye of a rabbit, and the rabbit is then monitored. [After John Henry *Draize* (1900–92), American pharmacologist.]

drake¹ (drāk) *n.* A male duck. [ME.]

drake² (drāk) *n.* A mayfly used as fishing bait. [ME, dragon < OE *draca* < West Gmc. **drako* < Lat. *dracō*. See DRAGON.]

Drake, Sir Francis 1540?–96. English explorer who was the first Englishman to circumnavigate the world (1577–80).

Dra·kens·burg Mountains (dräʹkənz-bûrgʹ) A range of E South Africa, Lesotho, and Swaziland rising to 3,164.6 m (11,425 ft).

Drake Passage A strait between Cape Horn and the South Shetland Islands that connects the S Atlantic and Pacific oceans.

dram¹ (drăm) *n.* **1a.** A unit of weight in the US Customary System equal to ¹⁄₁₆ of an ounce or 27.34 grains (1.77 grams). See table at **measurement. b.** A unit of apothecary weight equal to ⅛ of an ounce or 60 grains (3.89 grams). **2a.** A small draft: *took a dram of brandy.* **b.** A small amount; a bit. [ME *dragme*, a drachma, a unit of weight < OFr. < LLat. *dragma* < Lat. *drachma*. See DRACHMA.]

dram² *n., pl.* **dram** See table at **currency.** [Armenian, ult. < Gk. *drakhmē*. See DRACHMA.]

DRAM (dēʹrămʹ) *n. Computer Science* A memory chip that stores information as electrical charges in capacitors. [D(YNAMIC) RAM.]

dra·ma (dräʹmə, drămʹə) *n.* **1a.** A prose or verse composition, esp. one telling a serious story, that is intended for representation by actors impersonating the characters and performing the dialogue and action. **b.** A serious narrative work or program for television, radio, or the cinema. **2.** Theatrical plays of a particular kind or period: *Elizabethan drama.* **3.** The art or practice of writing or producing dramatic works. **4.** A situation or succession of events in real life having the dramatic progression or emotional effect characteristic of a play. **5.** The quality or condition of being dramatic. [LLat. *drāma, drāmat-* < Gk. < *drān*, to do, perform.]

Dram·a·mine (drămʹə-mēnʹ) A trademark used for dimenhydrinate.

dra·mat·ic (drə-mătʹĭk) *adj.* **1.** Of or relating to drama or the theater. **2.** Marked by or expressive of the action or emotion associated with drama or the theatre. **3.** Arresting or forceful in appearance or effect. **4.** *Music* Having a powerful, expressive singing voice. [LLat. *drāmaticus* < Gk. *drāmatikos* < *drāma, drāmat-*, drama. See DRAMA.] —**dra·matʹi·cal·ly** *adv.*

dramatic irony *n.* The dramatic effect achieved by a speech that shows an incongruity of which the characters in the play remain unaware.

dramatic monologue *n.* A literary, usu. verse composition revealing a speaker's character in a monologue addressed to the reader or to a presumed listener.

dra·mat·ics (drə-mătʹĭks) *n.* (*used with a sing. or pl. verb*) **1.** The art or practice of acting and stagecraft. **2.** Dramatic or stagy behavior: *Cut the dramatics.*

dram·a·tis per·so·nae (drămʹə-tĭs pər-sōʹnē, drăʹmə-tĭs pər-sōʹnīʹ) *pl.n.* **1.** The characters in a play or story. **2.** A list of the characters in a play or story. [Lat. *drāmatis*, genitive of *drāma*, drama + *persōnae*, pl. of *persōna*, character.]

dram·a·tist (drămʹə-tĭst, drăʹmə-) *n.* One who writes plays.

dram·a·ti·za·tion (drămʹə-tĭ-zāʹshən, drăʹmə-) *n.* **1.** The act or art of dramatizing, as of a literary work. **2.** A work adapted for dramatic presentation.

dram•a•tize (drăm′ə-tīz′, drä′mə-) *v.* **-tized, -tiz•ing, -tiz•es** —*tr.* **1.** To adapt (a literary work) for performance. **2.** To present or view in a dramatic or melodramatic way. —*intr.* **1.** To be adaptable to dramatic form. **2.** To self-dramatize.

dram•a•turge (drăm′ə-tûrj′, drä′mə-) *n.* A writer or adapter of plays; a playwright. [Fr. < Gk. *drāmatourgos* : *drāma, drāmat-*, drama; see DRAMA + *ergon*, work; see **werg-** in App.]

dram•a•tur•gy (drăm′ə-tûr′jē, drä′mə-) *n.* The art of the theater, esp. the writing of plays. —**dram′a•tur′gic, dram′a•tur′gi•cal** *adj.*

drank (drăngk) *v.* Past tense of **drink.**

dr. ap. *abbr.* apothecaries' dram

drape (drāp) *v.* **draped, drap•ing, drapes** —*tr.* **1.** To cover, dress, or hang with or as if with cloth in loose folds. **2.** To arrange or let fall in loose folds. **3.** To hang or rest limply: *draped my legs over the chair.* —*intr.* To fall or hang in loose folds. ❖ *n.* **1.** A drapery; a curtain. **2.** The way in which cloth falls or hangs. [ME *drapen*, to weave < OFr. *draper* < *drap*, cloth < LLat. *drappus.*]

drap•er (drā′pər) *n. Chiefly British* A dealer in cloth or clothing and dry goods. [ME, weaver or seller of cloth < OFr. *drapier* < *drap*, cloth. See DRAPE.]

Draper, Henry 1837–82. Amer. astronomer who was the first to photograph a stellar spectrum (1872).

drap•er•y (drā′pə-rē) *n., pl.* **-ies 1.** Cloth or clothing gracefully arranged in loose folds. **2.** A piece or pieces of heavy fabric hanging straight in loose folds, used as a curtain. **3.** Cloth; fabric. **4.** *Chiefly British* The business of a draper.

dras•tic (drăs′tĭk) *adj.* **1.** Severe or radical in nature; extreme. **2.** Taking violent or rapid effect. [Gk. *drastikos*, active < *drastos*, to be done < *drān*, to do.] —**dras′ti•cal•ly** *adv.*

drat (drăt) *interj.* Used to express annoyance. [Short for *God rot.*]

drat•ted (drăt′ĭd) *adj.* Damned; confounded.

draught (drăft) *n., v., & adj. Chiefly British* Variant of **draft.**

draughts (drăfts, dräfts) *n.* (*used with a sing. or pl. verb*) *Chiefly British* The game of checkers. [ME *draughtes*, pl. of *draught*, act of pulling, move at chess. See DRAFT.]

Dra•va or **Dra•ve** (drä′və) also **Drau** (drou) A river rising in the Carnic Alps of S Austria and flowing c. 724 km (450 mi) through NE Slovenia and N Croatia to the Danube R.

dr. avdp. *abbr.* avoirdupois dram

Dra•vid•i•an (drə-vĭd′ē-ən) *n.* **1.** A large family of languages spoken esp. in southern India and northern Sri Lanka that includes Tamil, Telugu, Malayalam, and Kannada. **2.** A member of any Dravidian-speaking people, esp. the pre-Indo-European ones of southern India. [< Sanksrit *drāviḍaḥ*, a Dravidian.] —**Dra•vid′i•an, Dra•vid′ic** (-vĭd′ĭk) *adj.*

draw (drô) *v.* **drew** (dro͞o), **drawn** (drôn), **draw•ing, draws** —*tr.* **1a.** To cause to move after or toward one by applying continuous force; drag. See Syns at **pull. b.** To cause to move in a given direction or to a given position, as by leading: *drew the children with him.* **c.** To move or pull so as to cover or uncover something: *draw the curtains.* **2.** To cause to flow forth: *drew blood.* **3.** To suck or take in (air, for example); inhale. **4.** To require (a specified depth of water) for floating. **5.** To take or pull out: *drew out a wallet.* **6.** To extract or take for one's own use: *drew strength from faith.* **7.** To eviscerate; disembowel. **8a.** To cause to come by attracting; attract. **b.** To select or take in from a given group, type, or region. **9.** To bring to a certain condition or action; lead. **10.** To bring about deliberately; provoke: *drew enemy fire.* **11.** To evoke as a response; elicit. **12.** To earn; gain: *drew interest.* **13a.** To withdraw (money). **b.** To use (a check, for example) when paying. **c.** To receive on a regular basis or at a specified time: *draw a pension.* **14.** To take or receive by chance: *draw lots.* **15.** *Games* **a.** To take (cards) from a dealer or central stack. **b.** To force (a card) to be played. **16.** To end or leave (a contest) tied or undecided. **17.** To hit or strike (a ball) so as to give it backspin. **18.** To pull back the string of (a bow). **19.** To distort the shape of. **20.** To stretch taut. **21a.** To flatten, stretch, or mold (metal) by hammering or die stamping. **b.** To shape or elongate (a wire, for example) by pulling through dies. **22a.** To inscribe (a line or lines) with a pencil or other marking implement. **b.** To make a likeness of on a surface, using mostly lines; depict with lines. **c.** To portray in writing or speech; depict with words. **23.** To formulate or devise from evidence or data at hand: *drew a comparison.* **24.** To compose or write out in legal format. —*intr.* **1.** To proceed or move steadily. **2.** To attract customers or spectators. **3.** To pour forth liquid. **4.** To cause suppuration. **5.** To take in a draft of air. **6.** To steep in or as if in the manner of tea. **7.** To pull out a weapon for use. **8.** To use or call upon part of a fund or supply. **9.** To contract or tighten. **10.** To conclude a contest without either side winning; tie. **11.** To make a likeness with lines on a surface; sketch. ❖ *n.* **1a.** An act of drawing. **b.** The result of drawing. **2.** Something drawn, esp. a lot, card, or cards drawn at random. **3.** *Sports & Games* A matchup or opponent in a tournament in which the matchups are made at random. **4.** An inhalation, esp. through a pipe or other smoking implement. **5.** One that attracts interest, customers, or spectators. **6.** The movable part of a drawbridge. **7.** A special advantage; an edge. **8.** A contest ending without either side winning. **9.** A small natural depression that water drains into; a shallow gully. **10.** *Football* A play in which the quarterback drops back as if to pass and then hands off to a running back. **11.** *Sports* A face-off. —***phrasal verbs:*** **draw away** To move ahead of competitors. **draw back** To retreat. **draw down** To deplete by consuming or spending. **draw on** To approach. **draw out 1.** To prolong; protract. **2.** To induce to speak freely. **draw up 1.** To compose or write in a set form; write out. **2.** To bring (troops, for example) into order. **3.** To bring or come to a halt. **4.** To bring (oneself) into an erect posture, often as an expression of dignity or indignation. **5.** *Chiefly Southern US* To shrink when washed. Used of clothes. —***idioms:*** **draw a blank** To fail to find or remember something. **draw and quarter 1.** To execute (a prisoner) by tying each limb to a horse and driving the horses in different directions. **2.** To disembowel and dismember after hanging. **draw straws** To decide by a lottery with straws of unequal lengths. [ME *drauen* < OE *dragan.*]

draw•back (drô′băk′) *n.* **1.** A disadvantage or inconvenience. See Syns at **disadvantage. 2.** A refund or remittance.

draw•bar (drô′bär′) *n.* **1.** A bar across the rear of a tractor for hitching machinery. **2.** A railroad coupler.

draw•bridge (drô′brĭj′) *n.* A bridge that can be raised or drawn aside either to prevent access or to permit passage.

draw•down (drô′doun′) *n.* **1.** The act, process, or result of depleting: *the drawdown of oil supplies.* **2.** A lowering of the water level in a reservoir or other body of water.

draw•ee (drô′ē′) *n.* The party on which an order for the payment of money is drawn.

draw•er (drô′ər) *n.* **1.** One that draws, esp. one that draws an order for the payment of money. **2.** (*also* drôr) A boxlike compartment in furniture that can be pulled out and pushed in. **3. drawers** (drôrz) Underpants.

draw•ing (drô′ĭng) *n.* **1.** The act or an instance of drawing. **2a.** The art of representing objects or forms on a surface chiefly by means of lines. **b.** A work produced by this art.

drawing card *n.* An attraction drawing large audiences.

drawing pin *n. Chiefly British* A thumbtack.

drawing room *n.* **1.** A large room in which guests are entertained. **2.** A ceremonial reception. **3.** A large private room on a railroad sleeping car. [Short for earlier *withdrawing room.*]

draw•knife (drô′nīf′) *n.* A knife with a handle at each end of the blade, used with a drawing motion to shave a surface.

drawbridge

drawl (drôl) *v.* **drawled, drawl•ing, drawls** —*intr.* To speak with lengthened or drawn-out vowels. —*tr.* To utter with lengthened or drawn-out vowels. ❖ *n.* The speech or manner of speaking of one who drawls. [Prob. < LGer. *drauelen*, to loiter, delay.] —**drawl′er** *n.*

drawn (drôn) *v.* Past participle of **draw.** ❖ *adj.* Haggard, as from fatigue or ill health.

drawn butter *n.* Melted or clarified butter, often seasoned and used as a sauce. [*drawn*, p. part. of DRAW, to bring to a proper consistency (obsolete).]

draw poker *n.* Poker in which each player is dealt five cards and may replace some after the first round of betting.

draw•shave (drô′shāv′) *n.* See **drawknife.**

draw•string (drô′strĭng′) *n.* A cord or ribbon run through a hem or casing and pulled to tighten or close an opening.

drawknife

draw•tube (drô′to͞ob′, -tyo͞ob′) *n.* A tube that slides within another tube, as in a small hand telescope.

dray (drā) *n.* A low heavy cart without sides, used for haulage. ❖ *tr.v.* **drayed, dray•ing, drays** To haul by means of a dray. [ME *draie*, sledge, cart < OE *dragan*, to draw.]

dray•age (drā′ĭj) *n.* **1.** Transport by dray. **2.** A charge for transport by dray.

dray•man (drā′mən) *n.* A driver of a dray.

Dray•ton (drāt′n), **Michael** 1563–1631. English poet whose works include *Idea, The Shepherd's Garland* (1593).

dread (drĕd) *v.* **dread•ed, dread•ing, dreads** —*tr.* **1.** To be in terror of. **2.** To anticipate with alarm, distaste, or reluctance. **3.** *Archaic* To hold in awe or reverence. —*intr.* To be very afraid. ❖ *n.* **1.** Profound fear; terror. **2.** Fearful or distasteful anticipation. See Syns at **fear. 3.** An object of fear, awe, or reverence. **4.** *Archaic* Awe; reverence. ❖ *adj.* **1.** Causing terror or fear. **2.** Inspiring awe. [ME *dreden*, short for *adreden* < OE *adrǣdan* < *ondrǣdan*, to advise against, fear : *ond-, and-*, against; see UN–[2] + *rǣdan*, to advise.]

dread•ful (drĕd′fəl) *adj.* **1.** Inspiring dread; terrible. **2.** Extremely unpleasant; distasteful or shocking: *dreadful heat.* —**dread′ful•ly** *adv.* —**dread′ful•ness** *n.*

dread•locks (drĕd′lŏks′) *pl.n.* **1.** A natural hairstyle in which the hair is twisted into long matted or ropelike locks. **2.** A similar hairstyle consisting of long thin braids radiating from the scalp. —**dread′locked′** *adj.*

dread•nought (drĕd′nôt′) *n.* A heavily armed battleship.

dreads (drĕdz) *pl.n. Informal* Dreadlocks.

dream (drēm) *n.* **1.** A series of images, ideas, emotions, and sensations occurring involuntarily in the mind during certain stages of sleep. **2.** A daydream; a reverie. **3.** A state of abstraction; a trance. **4.** A wild fancy or hope. **5.** A condition or achievement that is longed for; an aspiration. **6.** One exceptionally gratifying, excellent, or beautiful. ❖ *v.* **dreamed** or **dreamt** (drĕmt), **dream•ing, dreams** —*intr.* **1.** To experience a dream in sleep. **2.** To daydream. **3.** To have a deep aspiration: *dreaming of peace.* **4.** To regard something as feasible or practical: *wouldn't dream of*

ă	pat	oi	boy
ā	pay	ou	out
âr	care	o͝o	took
ä	father	o͞o	boot
ĕ	pet	ŭ	cut
ē	be	ûr	urge
ĭ	pit	th	thin
ī	pie	*th*	this
îr	pier	hw	which
ŏ	pot	zh	vision
ō	toe	ə	about, item
ô	paw		

Stress marks:
′ (primary);
′ (secondary), as in
lexicon (lĕk′sĭ-kŏn′)

going. —*tr.* **1.** To experience a dream of while asleep. **2.** To conceive of; imagine. **3.** To pass (time) idly or in reverie. ***—phrasal verb:* dream up** To invent; concoct. [ME *drem* < OE *drēam,* joy, music; akin to O Saxon *drōm,* mirth, dream.]

dream•er (drē′mər) *n.* **1.** One that dreams. **2a.** A visionary. **b.** An idealist. **3.** A habitually impractical person.

dream•land (drēm′lănd′) *n.* **1.** An ideal or imaginary land. **2.** A state of sleep.

dream•scape (drēm′skāp′) *n.* A dreamlike scene or picture having surreal qualities. [DREAM + (LAND)SCAPE.]

dream vision *n.* A narrative poem, esp. in medieval literature, in which the main character falls asleep and experiences events having allegorical, didactic, or moral significance.

dream•y (drē′mē) *adj.* **-i•er, -i•est 1.** Resembling a dream; ethereal or vague. **2.** Given to daydreams or reverie. **3.** Soothing and serene. **4.** *Informal* Inspiring delight; wonderful. **—dream′i•ly** *adv.* **—dream′i•ness** *n.*

drear (drîr) *adj.* Dreary.

drea•ry (drîr′ē) *adj.* **-ri•er, -ri•est 1.** Dismal; bleak. **2.** Boring; dull: *dreary tasks.* [ME *dreri,* bloody, frightened, sad < OE *drēorig,* bloody, sad < *drēor,* gore.] **—drea′ri•ly** *adv.* **—drea′ri•ness** *n.*

dreck (drĕk) *n. Slang* Trash, esp. inferior merchandise. [Ger., dirt, trash, and Yiddish *drek,* excrement, both < MHGer. *drec* < OHGer. See **sker-**[2] in App.] **—dreck′y** *adj.*

dredge[1] (drĕj) *n.* **1.** Any of various machines equipped with scooping or suction devices and used to deepen harbors and waterways and in underwater mining. **2.** *Nautical* A boat or barge equipped with a dredge. **3.** An implement consisting of a net on a frame, used for gathering shellfish. ❖ *v.* **dredged, dredg•ing, dredg•es** —*tr.* **1.** To clean, deepen, or widen with a dredge. **2.** To bring up with a dredge: *dredged up the silt.* **3.** To come up with; unearth: *dredged up bitter memories.* —*intr.* To use a dredge. [ME *dreg-,* in *dreg-boat,* boat for dredging; akin to OE *dragan,* to draw.]

dredge[2] (drĕj) *tr.v.* **dredged, dredg•ing, dredg•es** To coat (food) by sprinkling with a powder, such as sugar. [< obsolete *dredge,* a sweetmeat < ME *dragge* < OFr. *dragie,* alteration of Lat. *tragēmata,* confectionary < Gk., pl. of *tragēma,* sweetmeat. See **terə-**[1] in App.]

dredg•er[1] (drĕj′ər) *n.* **1.** A dredging machine. **2.** *Nautical* A barge or boat equipped with a dredge.

dredg•er[2] (drĕj′ər) *n.* A container with a perforated lid used for coating food with a powder, such as flour or sugar.

D region *n.* See **D layer.**

dreg (drĕg) *n.* **1.** The sediment in a liquid; lees. Often used in the plural. **2.** The basest or least desirable portion. Often used in the plural. **3.** A small amount; a residue. [ME *dreg* < ON *dregg.*]

drei•del also **drei•dl** (drād′l) *n.* A spinning top commemorating the rededication of the Temple in Jerusalem and used in Hanukkah games. [Yiddish *dreydl* < *dreyen,* to turn < MHGer. *dræjen* < OHGer. *drāen.*]

Drei•ser (drī′sər, -zər), **Theodore Herman Albert** 1871–1945. Amer. writer and editor whose novels include *Sister Carrie* (1900) and *An American Tragedy* (1925).

drench (drĕnch) *tr.v.* **drenched, drench•ing, drench•es 1.** To wet through and through; soak. **2.** To administer a drench to (an animal). **3.** To provide with something in great abundance; surfeit. ❖ *n.* **1.** The act of wetting or becoming wet through and through. **2.** A large dose of liquid medicine, esp. one administered to an animal by pouring down the throat. [ME *drenchen,* to drown < OE *drencan,* to give to drink, drown. See **dhreg-** in App.] **—drench′er** *n.*

Dres•den (drĕz′dən) A city of E-central Germany ESE of Leipzig; long noted for its china industry. Pop. 479,273.

Dresden china *n.* Meissen porcelain. [After DRESDEN.]

dress (drĕs) *v.* **dressed, dress•ing, dress•es** —*tr.* **1a.** To put clothes on; clothe. **b.** To furnish with clothing. **2.** To decorate or adorn. **3.** To arrange a display in: *dress a store window.* **4.** To arrange (troops) in ranks; align. **5.** To apply medication, bandages, or other therapeutic materials to (a wound). **6.** To arrange and groom (the hair), as by styling, combing, or washing. **7.** To groom (an animal); curry. **8.** To cultivate (land or plants). **9.** To clean (fish or fowl) for cooking or sale. **10a.** To trim and finish the surface of (wood, for example). **b.** To tan or prepare (a hide) in leather-making. —*intr.* **1.** To put on clothes. **2.** To wear clothes of a certain kind or style. **3.** To wear formal clothes. **4.** To get into proper alignment with others. ❖ *n.* **1.** Clothing; apparel. **2.** A style of clothing. **3.** A one-piece outer garment for women or girls. **4.** Outer covering or appearance; guise. ❖ *adj.* **1.** Suitable for formal occasions. **2.** Requiring formal clothes. ***—phrasal verbs:* dress down 1.** To scold; reprimand. **2.** To wear informal clothes, befitting an occasion or location. **dress up** To wear formal or fancy clothes. ***—idiom:* dress ship** *Nautical* To display the ensign, signal flags, and bunting on a ship. [ME *dressen,* to arrange, put on clothing < OFr. *drecier,* to arrange < VLat. **dīrēctiāre* < Lat. *dīrēctus,* p. part. of *dīrigere,* to direct. See DIRECT.]

WORD HISTORY A dress is such a common article of modern attire that it is difficult to imagine that the word *dress* has not always referred to this garment. The earliest noun sense of *dress,* recorded in a work written before 1450, was "speech, talk." This *dress* comes from the verb *dress,* which goes back through Old French *drecier,* "to arrange," and the assumed Vulgar Latin **dīrēctiāre* to Latin *dīrēctus,* a form of the verb *dīrigere,* "to direct." In accordance with its etymology, the verb *dress* has meant and still means "to place," "to arrange," and "to put in order." The sense "to clothe" is related to the notion of putting in order, specifically in regard to clothing. This verb sense then gave rise to the noun sense "personal attire" as well as to the specific garment sense. The earliest noun sense, "speech," comes from a verb sense having to do with addressing or directing words to other people.

dres•sage (drə-säzh′, drĕ-) *n.* The guiding of a horse through a series of complex maneuvers by slight movements of the rider's hands, legs, and weight. [Fr., preparation, training, dressage < *dresser,* to set up, arrange, train < OFr. *drecier,* to set up, arrange. See DRESS.]

dress circle *n.* A section of seats in a theater or opera house, usu. the first tier above the orchestra.

dress code *n.* A set of rules, as in a school, indicating the approved manner of dress.

dress•er[1] (drĕs′ər) *n.* **1.** One that dresses: *a careful dresser.* **2.** A wardrobe assistant, as for an actor.

dress•er[2] (drĕs′ər) *n.* **1.** A low chest of drawers often supporting a mirror and typically used for holding clothes and personal items. **2.** A cupboard or set of shelves for dishes or kitchen utensils. [ME *dressour,* table for preparing food < OFr. *dreceur* < *drecier,* to set up, arrange. See DRESS.]

dress•ing (drĕs′ĭng) *n.* **1.** A therapeutic or protective material applied to a wound. **2.** A sauce for certain dishes, such as salads. **3.** A stuffing, as for fish. **4.** Fertilizing material for soil.

dressing gown *n.* A robe worn for lounging or before dressing.

dressing room *n.* A room, as in a theater, for changing costumes or clothes and applying makeup.

dressing table *n.* A low table with a mirror at which one sits while applying makeup.

dress•mak•er (drĕs′mā′kər) *n.* One that makes women's clothing, esp. dresses. **—dress′mak′ing** *n.*

dress rehearsal *n.* A full uninterrupted rehearsal of a play with costumes and stage properties.

dress•y (drĕs′ē) *adj.* **-i•er, -i•est 1.** Showy or elegant in dress or appearance. **2.** Smart; stylish. **—dress′i•ness** *n.*

drew (dro͞o) *v.* Past tense of **draw.**

Drew Family of Amer. actors, including **John** (1827–62), his wife, **Louisa** (1820–97), and their son **John** (1853–1927).

Drew, Daniel 1797–1879. Amer. financier who as a director of the Erie Railroad manipulated stock prices.

Drey•fus (drī′fəs, drā-), **Alfred** 1859–1935. French army officer who was convicted of treason (1894) but later acquitted when the evidence against him was shown to have been forged by anti-Semites.

drib (drĭb) *n.* A negligible amount. [Perh. < DRIBLET.]

drib•ble (drĭb′əl) *v.* **-bled, -bling, -bles** —*intr.* **1.** To flow or fall in drops or an unsteady stream; trickle. **2.** To let saliva drip from the mouth; drool. **3.** *Sports* **a.** To dribble a ball or puck. **b.** To advance by dribbling. —*tr.* **1.** To let flow or fall in drops or an unsteady stream. **2.** *Sports* **a.** To move (a ball or puck) by repeated light bounces or kicks, as in basketball or soccer. **b.** To hit (a baseball, for example) so that it bounces slowly. ❖ *n.* **1.** A weak, unsteady stream; a trickle. **2.** A small quantity; a bit. **3.** *Sports* The act of dribbling a ball. [Frequentative of obsolete *drib,* alteration of DRIP.] **—drib′bler** *n.*

drib•let (drĭb′lĭt) *n.* **1.** A tiny falling drop of liquid. **2.** A small amount or portion. [< obsolete *drib,* to fall in drops, alteration of DRIP.]

dried (drīd) *v.* Past tense and past participle of **dry.**

dri•er[1] also **dry•er** (drī′ər) *n.* **1.** One that dries. **2.** A substance added to paint, varnish, or ink to speed drying.

dri•er[2] (drī′ər) *adj.* A comparative of **dry.**

dries (drīz) *v.* Third person singular present tense of **dry.**

dri•est (drī′ĭst) *adj.* A superlative of **dry.**

drift (drĭft) *v.* **drift•ed, drift•ing, drifts** —*intr.* **1.** To be carried along by currents of air or water. **2.** To proceed or move unhurriedly and smoothly. **3.** To move leisurely or sporadically from place to place, esp. without purpose or regular employment. **4a.** To wander from a set course or point of attention; stray. **b.** To vary from or oscillate randomly about a fixed setting, position, or mode of operation. **5.** To be piled up in banks or heaps by the force of a current. —*tr.* **1.** To cause to be carried in a current. **2.** To pile up in banks or heaps. **3.** *Western US* To drive (livestock) slowly or far afield, esp. for grazing. ❖ *n.* **1.** The act or condition of drifting. **2.** Something moving along in a current of air or water. **3.** A bank or pile, as of sand or snow, heaped up by currents of air or water. **4.** *Geology* Rock debris transported and deposited by or from ice, esp. by or from a glacier. **5a.** A general trend or tendency, as of opinion. **b.** General meaning or purport; tenor: *caught my drift.* **6a.** A gradual change in position. **b.** A gradual deviation from an original course, model, method, or intention. **c.** Variation or random oscillation about a fixed setting, position, or mode of behavior. **7.** A gradual change in the output of a circuit or amplifier. **8.** The rate of flow of a water current. **9a.** A tool for ramming or driving something down. **b.** A tapered

dredge[1]
top: dredging a harbor
bottom: harvesting oysters in Chesapeake Bay, Maryland

dreidel

steel pin for enlarging and aligning holes. **10a.** A horizontal or nearly horizontal passageway in a mine running through or parallel to a vein. **b.** A secondary mine passageway between two main shafts or tunnels. **11.** A drove or herd, esp. of swine. [< ME, drove, herd, act of driving; akin to ON *drift*, snowdrift.] **—drift′y** *adj.*

drift•age (drĭf′tĭj) *n.* Matter borne or deposited by air or water.

drift•er (drĭf′tər) *n.* One that drifts, esp. a person who moves aimlessly from place to place or from job to job.

drift net *n.* A large fishing net buoyed up by floats that is carried along with the current or tide.

drift•wood (drĭft′wo͝od′) *n.* Wood floating in or washed up by a body of water.

drill[1] (drĭl) *n.* **1a.** An implement with cutting edges or a pointed end for boring holes in hard materials, usu. by a rotating abrasion or repeated blows; a bit. **b.** The hand-operated or hand-powered holder for this implement. **c.** A harsh loud noise made by or as if by a powered tool of this kind. **2a.** Disciplined repetitious exercise as a means of teaching and perfecting a skill or procedure. **b.** A task or exercise of this kind. **3.** The training of soldiers in marching and the manual of arms. **4.** Any of various marine gastropod mollusks, chiefly of the genus *Urosalpinx*, that bore holes into the shells of bivalve mollusks. ❖ *v.* **drilled, drill•ing, drills** —*tr.* **1a.** To make a hole in (a hard material) with a drill. **b.** To make (a hole) with or as if with a drill. **2.** To strike or hit sharply. **3a.** To instruct thoroughly by repetition in a skill or procedure. **b.** To infuse knowledge of or skill in by repetitious instruction. **4.** To train (soldiers) in marching and the manual of arms. —*intr.* **1.** To make a hole with or as if with a drill. **2.** To perform a training exercise. [Obsolete Du. *dril* < *drillen*, to bore < MDu. *drillen*. See **terə-**[1] in App.] **—drill′er** *n.*

drill[2] (drĭl) *n.* **1.** A shallow trench or furrow in which seeds are planted. **2.** A row of planted seeds. **3.** A machine or implement for planting seeds in holes or furrows. ❖ *tr.v.* **drilled, drill•ing, drills 1.** To sow (seeds) in rows. **2.** To plant (a field) in drills. [Perh. < *drill*, rill < ME *drille*, sip.]

drill[3] (drĭl) *n.* Durable cotton or linen twill of varying weights, generally used for work clothes. [Short for *drilling*, alteration of Ger. *Drillich* < MHGer. *drilich*, threefold, fabric woven with three threads < OHGer. *drilīh*, alteration of Lat. *trilīx*, triple-twilled. See TRELLIS.]

drill[4] (drĭl) *n.* A baboon *(Papio leucophaeus)* of western Africa. [Poss. of West African orig.]

drill instructor *n.* A noncommissioned officer who instructs recruits in military drill and discipline.

drill•mas•ter (drĭl′măs′tər) *n.* **1.** A drill instructor. **2.** An instructor given to extremely rigorous training.

drill press *n.* A powered vertical drilling machine in which the drill is pressed to the work automatically or by a hand lever.

drill steel *n.* A high-grade steel used in tools and dies that is made by fusing low-carbon steel with charcoal or cast iron.

drill•stock (drĭl′stŏk′) *n.* The part of a drilling tool or machine that holds the shank of a drill or bit.

Drin (drēn) A river of Albania flowing c. 282 km (175 mi) to the Adriatic Sea.

Dri•na (drē′nə, -nä) A river rising in E Bosnia and Herzegovina flowing c. 459 km (285 mi) to the Sava R.

drink (drĭngk) *v.* **drank** (drăngk), **drunk** (drŭngk), **drink•ing, drinks** —*tr.* **1.** To take into the mouth and swallow (a liquid). **2.** To swallow the liquid contents of (a vessel). **3.** To take in or soak up; absorb. **4.** To take in eagerly through the senses or intellect: *drank in its beauty.* **5a.** To give or make (a toast). **b.** To toast (a person or an occasion, for example). **6.** To bring to a specific state by drinking alcoholic liquors: *drank our sorrows away.* —*intr.* **1.** To swallow liquid: *drank noisily.* **2.** To imbibe alcoholic liquors: *drink socially.* **3.** To salute a person or an occasion with a toast: *drank to you.* ❖ *n.* **1.** A liquid for drinking; a beverage. **2.** An amount of liquid swallowed. **3.** An alcoholic beverage. **4.** Excessive or habitual indulgence in alcoholic liquor. **5.** *Chiefly Southern US* See **soft drink.** See Regional Note at **tonic. 6.** *Slang* A body of water; the sea. [ME *drinken* < OE *drincan*. See **dhreg-** in App.]

drink•a•ble (drĭng′kə-bəl) *adj.* Suitable or fit for drinking; potable. ❖ *n.* A beverage. **—drink′a•bil′i•ty** *n.*

drink•er (drĭng′kər) *n.* **1.** One that drinks. **2.** One who drinks alcoholic liquors, esp. habitually or excessively.

drink•ing fountain (drĭng′kĭng) *n.* A device with a nozzle that when activated provides a stream of drinking water.

drip (drĭp) *v.* **dripped, drip•ping, drips** —*intr.* **1.** To fall in drops. **2.** To shed drops: *The umbrella dripped all over the floor.* **3.** To ooze or be saturated with or as if with liquid. —*tr.* To let fall in or as if in drops. ❖ *n.* **1.** The process of forming and falling in drops. **2a.** Liquid or moisture that falls in drops. **b.** A slight intermittent flow or leak. **3.** The sound made by liquid falling in drops. **4.** A projection on a cornice or sill from which rainwater can drip, protecting the wall below. **5.** *Slang* A tiresome or annoying person. [ME *drippen*.]

drip-dry (drĭp′drī′) *adj.* Made of a fabric that will not wrinkle when hung dripping wet for drying. ❖ *intr.v.* **-dried, -dry•ing, -dries** To dry with no wrinkles when hung dripping wet.

drip•less (drĭp′lĭs) *adj.* Made or designed to prevent dripping.

drip pan *n.* **1.** A pan for catching liquid waste. **2.** See **dripping pan.**

drip•ping (drĭp′ĭng) *n.* **1.** The act or sound of something falling in drops. **2.** The fat and juices exuded from roasting meat, often used in making gravy. Often used in the plural.

dripping pan *n.* A pan for catching the drippings from roasting meat.

drip•py (drĭp′ē) *adj.* **-pi•er, -pi•est 1.** Characterized by dripping; drizzly. **2.** *Slang* **a.** Tiresome or annoying. **b.** Mawkishly sentimental. **—drip′pi•ly** *adv.* **—drip′pi•ness** *n.*

drip•stone (drĭp′stōn′) *n.* **1.** A protective drip made of stone, as on a cornice over a door. **2.** Calcium carbonate in the form of stalactites or stalagmites.

drive (drīv) *v.* **drove** (drōv), **driv•en** (drĭv′ən), **driv•ing, drives** —*tr.* **1.** To push, propel, or press onward forcibly; urge forward. **2.** To repulse or put to flight by force or influence. **3.** To guide, control, or direct (a vehicle). **4a.** To convey or transport in a vehicle. **b.** To traverse in a vehicle. **5a.** To supply the motive force or power to and cause to function. **b.** To cause or sustain, as if by supplying force or power: *an economy driven by exports.* **6.** To compel or force to work, often excessively. **7.** To force into or from a particular act or state: *drove me crazy.* **8.** To force to go through or penetrate. **9.** To create or produce by penetrating forcibly: *drove a hole in the tire.* **10.** To carry through vigorously to a conclusion: *drive a hard bargain.* **11a.** *Sports* To throw, strike, or cast (a ball, for example) hard or rapidly. **b.** *Baseball* To cause (a run) to be scored by batting. **12a.** To chase (game) into the open or into traps or nets. **b.** To search (an area) for game in such a manner. —*intr.* **1.** To move along or advance quickly as if pushed by an impelling force. **2.** To rush, dash, or advance violently against an obstruction. **3.** To operate a vehicle, such as a car. **4.** To go or be transported in a vehicle. **5a.** *Sports* To hit, throw, or impel a ball or other missile forcibly. **b.** *Basketball* To move directly to the basket with the ball. **6.** To make an effort to reach or achieve an objective; aim. ❖ *n.* **1.** The act of driving. **2.** A trip or journey in a vehicle. **3.** A road for automobiles and other vehicles. **4a.** The means or apparatus for transmitting motion or power to a machine or from one machine part to another. **b.** The position or operating condition of such a mechanism: *put the car in drive.* **c.** The means by which automotive power is applied to a roadway: *four-wheel drive.* **5.** *Computer Science* A device that reads data from and often writes data onto a storage medium, such as a floppy disk. **6.** A strong organized effort to accomplish a purpose. **7.** Energy, push, or aggressiveness. **8.** *Psychology* A strong motivating tendency or instinct related to self-preservation, reproduction, or aggression that prompts activity toward a particular end. **9.** A massive sustained military offensive. **10a.** *Sports* The act of hitting, knocking, or thrusting a ball very swiftly. **b.** *Sports* The stroke or thrust by which a ball is driven. **c.** *Basketball* The act of driving. **11a.** A rounding up and driving of cattle to new pastures or to market. **b.** A gathering and driving of logs down a river. **c.** The cattle or logs thus driven. ***—phrasal verb:* drive at** To mean to do or say. [ME *driven* < OE *drīfan*.] **—driv′a•bil′i•ty** *n.* **—driv′a•ble** *adj.*

drill press

drive bay *n.* A space in a computer where a drive can be installed.

drive-by (drīv′bī′) *adj.* Performed from a moving vehicle: *a drive-by murder.* ❖ *n.* An act, such as a shooting, performed from a moving vehicle.

drive-in (drīv′ĭn′) *n.* An establishment designed to permit customers to remain in their motor vehicles while being accommodated. **—drive′-in′** *adj.*

drive-through

driv•el (drĭv′əl) *v.* **-eled, -el•ing, -els** or **-elled, -el•ling, -els** —*intr.* **1.** To slobber; drool. **2.** To flow like spittle or saliva. **3.** To talk stupidly or childishly. —*tr.* **1.** To allow to flow from the mouth. **2.** To say (something) stupidly. ❖ *n.* **1.** Saliva flowing from the mouth. **2.** Stupid or senseless talk. [ME *drevelen* < OE *dreflian*.] **—driv′el•er** *n.*

drive•line (drīv′līn′) *n.* See **drive train.**

driv•en (drĭv′ən) *v.* Past participle of **drive.** ❖ *adj.* **1.** Piled up or carried along by a current: *driven snow.* **2.** Motivated by or having a compulsive quality or need: *a driven person.* **3.** Caused, sustained, or stimulated: *an export-driven economy.* **4.** Powered, operated, or controlled: *a piston-driven airplane.*

driv•er (drī′vər) *n.* **1.** One that drives, as the operator of a motor vehicle. **2.** A tool, such as a hammer, used to impart forceful pressure. **3.** A machine part that transmits motion or power to another part. **4.** A piece of software that enables a computer to communicate with a peripheral. **5.** *Sports* A golf club with a wide head and a long shaft, used for long shots from the tee. **6.** *Nautical* A jib-headed spanker.

driver ant *n.* See **army ant.**

driv•er's seat (drī′vərz) *n.* A position of control or authority.

drive shaft also **drive•shaft** (drīv′shăft′) *n.* A rotating shaft that transmits mechanical power from a motor or an engine to a point or region of application.

drive-through or **drive-thru** (drīv′thro͞o′) *adj.* **1.** Relating to or conducting exchanges with clients who drive up to a window: *drive-thru banking.* **2.** Performed or provided quickly and routinely. ❖ *n.* A drive-through establishment, esp. a restaurant.

drive train *n.* The components of an automotive vehicle that connect the transmission with the driving axles.

ă pat	oi boy
ā pay	ou out
âr care	o͝o took
ä father	o͞o boot
ĕ pet	ŭ cut
ē be	ûr urge
ĭ pit	th thin
ī pie	*th* this
îr pier	hw which
ŏ pot	zh vision
ō toe	ə about, item
ô paw	

Stress marks:
′ (primary);
′ (secondary), as in
lexicon (lĕk′sĭ-kŏn′)

drive-up (drīv'ŭp') *adj.* Designed to serve customers in their motor vehicles. —**drive'-up'** *n.*

drive·way (drīv'wā') *n.* A private road that connects a house, garage, or other building with the street.

driv·ing (drī'vĭng) *adj.* **1.** Transmitting power or motion. **2.** Violent, intense, or forceful: *a driving rain.* **3.** Energetic or active: *a driving personality.* —**driv'ing·ly** *adv.*

driz·zle (drĭz'əl) *v.* **-zled, -zling, -zles** —*intr.* To rain gently in fine mistlike drops. —*tr.* **1.** To let fall in fine drops or particles. **2.** To moisten with fine drops. ❖ *n.* A fine, gentle, misty rain. [Perh. < ME *drisning,* fall of dew < OE *-drysnian* (in *gedrysnian,* to pass away, vanish).] —**driz'zly** *adj.*

Dro·ghe·da (drô'ĭ-də, drô'hĭ-) A municipal borough of E Ireland on the Boyne R.; overrun by Oliver Cromwell (1649). Pop. 23,247.

drogue (drōg) *n.* **1.** *Nautical* See **sea anchor. 2.** A drogue parachute. **3.** A funnel-shaped device towed behind an aircraft as a target. **4.** A funnel-shaped device at the end of the hose of a tanker aircraft, used as a receptacle for the probe of a receiving aircraft. [Perh. alteration of DRAG (influenced by obsolete *drogue,* drug).]

drogue parachute *n.* **1.** A parachute used to stabilize or decelerate a fast-moving object, esp. a small parachute used to slow down a reentering spacecraft. **2.** A small parachute used to pull a main parachute from its storage pack.

droit (droit, drwä) *n.* **1.** A legal right. **2.** Something to which one has legal right. [ME, a fee allowed by law < OFr., right < LLat. *dīrēctum* < neut. of Lat. *dīrēctus,* straight. See DIRECT.]

droit du seign·eur (drwä dü sĕn-yœr') *n.* The supposed right of a feudal lord to have sexual relations with a vassal's bride on her wedding night. [Fr. : *droit,* right + *du,* of the + *seigneur,* lord of a manor.]

droll (drōl) *adj.* **droll·er, droll·est** Amusingly odd or whimsically comical. ❖ *n. Archaic* A buffoon. [Fr. *drôle,* buffoon, droll < OFr. *drolle,* bon vivant, poss. < MDu. *drol,* goblin.] —**droll'ness** *n.* —**drol'ly** *adv.*

droll·er·y (drō'lə-rē) *n., pl.* **-ies 1.** A comical or whimsical quality. **2.** A comical or whimsical way of acting or talking. **3a.** The act of joking. **b.** Something comical or whimsical.

–drome *suff.* **1.** Racecourse: *hippodrome.* **2.** Field; arena: *airdrome.* **3.** Running: *palindrome.* [Lat. *-dromus* < Gk. *dromos,* racecourse.]

drom·e·dar·y (drŏm'ĭ-dĕr'ē, drŭm'-) *n., pl.* **-ies** The one-humped domesticated camel (*Camelus dromedarius*) of northern Africa and western Asia. [ME *dromedarie* < OFr. *dromedaire* < LLat. *dromedārius* < Lat. *dromas, dromad-* < Gk., running.]

drom·ond (drŏm'ənd, drŭm'-) *n. Nautical* A large medieval sailing galley. [ME < AN *dromund* < LLat. *dromō, dromōn-,* kind of ship < L.Gk. *dromōn* < Gk. *dromos,* race.]

–dromous *suff.* Running; moving: *catadromous.* [< NLat. *-dromus* < Gk. *-dromos* < *dromos,* act of running.]

drone¹ (drōn) *n.* **1.** A male bee, esp. a honeybee, that has no sting, performs no work, and has the sole function of mating with the queen bee. **2.** An idle person who lives off others. **3.** A person who does tedious or menial work; a drudge. **4.** A pilotless, remote-controlled aircraft. [ME < OE *drān.*]

drone² (drōn) *v.* **droned, dron·ing, drones** —*intr.* **1.** To make a continuous low dull humming sound. **2.** To speak in a monotonous tone. **3.** To pass or act in a monotonous way. —*tr.* To utter in a monotonous low tone. ❖ *n.* **1.** A continuous low humming or buzzing sound. **2.** *Music* **a.** Any of the pipes of a bagpipe that lack finger holes and produce a single tone. **b.** A long sustained tone. **c.** Any of various instruments that produce only a constant pitch. [< DRONE¹ (< the bee's humming sound).]

drool (drōōl) *v.* **drooled, drool·ing, drools** —*intr.* **1.** To let saliva run from the mouth; drivel. **2.** *Informal* To show extravagant appreciation or desire. **3.** *Informal* To talk nonsense. —*tr.* To let run from the mouth. ❖ *n.* **1.** Saliva. **2.** *Informal* Senseless talk; drivel. [Perh. alteration of DRIVEL.]

droop (drōōp) *v.* **drooped, droop·ing, droops** —*intr.* **1.** To bend or hang downward. **2.** To bend or sag gradually. **3.** To sag in dejection or exhaustion. —*tr.* To let bend or hang down. ❖ *n.* The act or condition of drooping. [ME *droupen* < ON *drūpa.*] —**droop'i·ly** *adv.* —**droop'ing·ly** *adv.*

drop (drŏp) *n.* **1.** The smallest quantity of liquid heavy enough to fall in a spherical mass. See table at **measurement. 2.** A small quantity of a substance. **3.** *drops* Liquid medicine administered in drops. **4.** A trace or hint: *not a drop of pity.* **5a.** Something shaped or hanging like a drop. **b.** A small globular piece of hard candy. **6.** The act of falling; descent. **7.** A swift decline or decrease, as in quality, quantity, or intensity. **8a.** The vertical distance from a higher to a lower level. **b.** The distance through which something falls or drops. **9.** A sheer incline, such as the face of a cliff. **10a.** A descent by parachute. **b.** Personnel and equipment landed by means of parachute. **11.** Something that is arranged to fall or be lowered. **12.** A drop curtain. **13.** A slot through which something is deposited in a receptacle. **14.** A central place or establishment where something, such as mail, is brought and subsequently distributed. **15a.** A predetermined location for the deposit and subsequent removal of secret communications or illicit goods. **b.** The act of depositing such communi-

drogue parachute

cations or materials. **16.** *Electronics* A connection made available for an input or output unit on a transmission line. ❖ *v.* **dropped, drop·ping, drops** —*intr.* **1.** To fall in drops. **2.** To fall from a higher to a lower place or position. **3.** To become less, as in number, intensity, or volume. **4.** To descend from one level to another. **5.** To fall or sink into a state of exhaustion or death. **6.** To pass or slip into a specified state or condition. —*tr.* **1.** To let fall by releasing hold of. **2.** To let fall in drops. **3.** To cause to become less; reduce. **4.** To cause to fall, as by hitting or shooting. **5.** To give birth to. Used of animals. **6.** To say or offer casually: *drop a hint.* **7.** To write at one's leisure: *drop me a note.* **8.** To cease consideration or treatment of. **9.** To terminate an association or a relationship with. **10.** To leave unfinished. **11.** To leave out (a letter, for example) in speaking or writing. **12.** To leave or set down at a particular place; unload. **13.** To spend (money), esp. lavishly or rashly. **14.** To parachute. **15.** To lower the level of (the voice). **16.** To lose (a game or contest, for example). **17.** *Slang* To take, as a drug, by mouth. —*phrasal verbs:* **drop back** *Football* To back away from the line of scrimmage. **drop behind** To fall behind; fail to keep up. **drop by** To stop in for a short visit. **drop off 1.** To fall asleep. **2.** To decrease. **drop out 1.** To withdraw from participation, as in a school. **2.** To withdraw from established society, esp. because of disillusion with conventional values. —*idiom:* **get** (or **have**) **the drop on** To achieve a distinct advantage over. [ME *droppe* < OE *dropa.*]

drop cloth *n.* A sheet, as of cloth or plastic, for protection against spills or dripping, used esp. by painters.

drop curtain *n.* **1.** An unframed curtain that is lowered to a stage from the flies, often serving as background scenery. **2.** A theater curtain that is lowered or raised vertically rather than drawn to the side.

drop·forge (drŏp'fôrj', -fōrj') *tr.v.* **-forged, -forg·ing, -forg·es** To forge or stamp (a metal) between dies by the force of a falling weight such as a drop hammer.

drop hammer *n.* A machine consisting of an anvil aligned with a hammer that is dropped to forge or stamp molten metal.

drop-in (drŏp'ĭn') *n.* **1.** One who casually drops in, as to visit or obtain an appointment. **2.** An informal social event. ❖ *adj.* Provided for short-term use.

drop kick *n. Football* A kick made by dropping the ball to the ground and kicking it just as it starts to rebound. —**drop'-kick'** (drŏp'kĭk') *v.*

drop leaf *n.* A hinged wing on a table that can be folded down when not in use.

drop·let (drŏp'lĭt) *n.* A tiny drop.

droplet infection *n.* An infection transmitted by droplets of moisture expelled from the upper respiratory tract, as through coughing.

drop·light (drŏp'lĭt') *n.* A hanging lamp that can be lowered and raised on its cord.

drop-off (drŏp'ôf', -ŏf') *n.* **1.** A steep or abrupt downward slope. **2.** A noticeable decrease: *a drop-off in attendance.* **3.** A designated place where people or things can be left.

drop·out (drŏp'out') *n.* **1a.** One who quits school. **b.** One who has withdrawn from a given social group. **2.** *Computer Science* **a.** A segment of magnetic tape lacking expected information. **b.** The failure to read a bit of stored information.

drop pass *n.* A pass, as in hockey, in which the passer advances beyond the puck or ball, leaving it for a trailing teammate.

dropped egg (drŏpt) *n. New England* A poached egg.

drop·per (drŏp'ər) *n.* One that drops, esp. a small tube with a suction bulb at one end for drawing in a liquid and releasing it in drops.

drop·ping (drŏp'ĭng) *n.* **1.** Something dropped. **2. droppings** The excrement of animals.

drop shot *n.* A shot in various racquet games in which a ball or shuttlecock drops quickly after crossing the net or hitting the wall.

drop·sy (drŏp'sē) *n.* Edema. Not in scientific use. [ME *dropesie,* short for *hydropesie,* ult. < Gk. *hudrōpiāsis* < *hudrōps,* dropsy, a dropsical person : *hudro-,* water; see HYDRO- + *ōps,* face; see **ok^w-** in App.] —**drop'si·cal** (-sĭ-kəl) *adj.* —**drop'si·cal·ly** *adv.*

drop·wort (drŏp'wôrt', -wûrt') *n.* A Eurasian plant (*Filipendula vulgaris*) having finely divided leaflets and small white flowers.

dros·er·a (drŏs'ər-ə) *n.* See **sundew.** [Gk., fem. of *droseros,* dewy < *drosos,* dew.]

drosh·ky (drŏsh'kē) also **dros·ky** (drŏs'-) *n., pl.* **-kies** also **-kys** An open four-wheeled horse-drawn carriage formerly used in Russia and Poland. [Russ. *drozhki,* dim. of *drogi,* wagon, pl. of *droga,* shaft of a wagon.]

dro·soph·i·la (drō-sŏf'ə-lə, drə-) *n.* Any of various small fruit flies of the genus *Drosophila,* esp. *D. melanogaster,* used in genetic research. [NLat. *Drosophila,* genus name : Gk. *drosos,* dew + NLat. *-phila,* fem. of *-philus, -phile.*]

dross (drŏs, drôs) *n.* **1.** Waste or impure matter. **2.** The scum that forms on the surface of molten metal as a result of oxidation. **3.** Worthless, commonplace, or trivial matter. [ME *dros* < OE *drōs,* dregs.] —**dross'y** *adj.*

drought (drout) also **drouth** (drouth) *n.* **1.** A long period of abnormally low rainfall. **2.** A prolonged dearth or shortage. [ME < OE *drūgoth;* akin to *dryge,* dry.] —**drought'y** *adj.*

drought

drove¹ (drōv) *v.* Past tense of **drive.**

drove² (drōv) *n.* **1.** A flock or herd being driven in a body. **2a.** A large mass of people moving or acting as a body. **b.** A large body of like things. **3a.** A stonemason's broad-edged chisel used for rough hewing. **b.** A stone surface dressed with such a chisel. [ME < OE *drāf* < *drīfan*, to drive.]

drov·er (drō′vər) *n.* One that drives cattle or sheep.

drown (droun) *v.* **drowned, drown·ing, drowns** —*tr.* **1.** To kill by submerging and suffocating in water or another liquid. **2.** To drench thoroughly or cover with or as if with a liquid. **3.** To deaden one's awareness of; blot out. **4.** To muffle or mask (a sound) by a louder sound. —*intr.* To die by suffocating in water or another liquid. [ME *drounen*, prob. of Scand. orig. See **dhreg-** in App.]

drowse (drouz) *v.* **drowsed, drows·ing, drows·es** —*intr.* To be half-asleep. —*tr.* **1.** To make drowsy. **2.** To pass (time) by drowsing. ❖ *n.* The condition of being sleepy. [Perh. ult. < OE *drūsian*, to sink, be sluggish.]

drows·y (drou′zē) *adj.* **-i·er, -i·est** **1.** Dull with sleepiness; sluggish. **2.** Produced or marked by sleepiness. **3.** Inducing sleepiness. —**drows′i·ly** *adv.* —**drows′i·ness** *n.*

dr. t. *abbr.* troy dram

drub (drŭb) *v.* **drubbed, drub·bing, drubs** —*tr.* **1.** To thrash with a stick. **2.** To instill forcefully: *drubbed the lesson into my head.* **3a.** To defeat soundly. **b.** To berate harshly. **4.** To stamp (the feet). —*intr.* **1.** To beat the ground; stamp. **2.** To pound; throb. ❖ *n.* A blow with a heavy instrument. [Perh. Ar. dialectal *drab* < *daraba*, to hit.] —**drub′ber** *n.*

drub·bing (drŭb′ĭng) *n.* **1.** A severe thrashing. **2.** A total defeat.

drudge¹ (drŭj) *n.* A person who performs drudgery. ❖ *intr.v.* **drudged, drudg·ing, drudg·es** To perform drudgery. [< ME *druggen*, to labor; akin to OE *drēogan*, to work, suffer.] —**drudg′er** *n.* —**drudg′ing·ly** *adv.*

drudge² (drŭj) *n. & v. Chesapeake Bay* Variant of **dredge**¹.

drudg·er·y (drŭj′ə-rē) *n., pl.* **-ies** Tedious, menial, or unpleasant work.

drudge·work (drŭj′wûrk′) *n.* Drudgery.

drug (drŭg) *n.* **1a.** A substance used in the diagnosis, treatment, or prevention of a disease or as a component of a medication. **b.** Such a substance as recognized or defined by the US Food, Drug, and Cosmetic Act. **2.** A chemical substance, such as a narcotic, that affects the central nervous system, causing changes in behavior and often addiction. **3.** *Obsolete* A chemical or dye. ❖ *tr.v.* **drugged, drug·ging, drugs** **1.** To administer a drug to. **2.** To poison or mix (food or drink) with a drug. **3.** To stupefy or dull with or as if with a drug. [ME *drogge* < OFr. *drogue*, drug, perh. < MDu. *droge* (vate), dry (cases), pl. of *drog*, dry.]

drug·get (drŭg′ĭt) *n.* **1a.** A heavy felted fabric of wool or wool and cotton, used as a floor covering. **b.** A coarse rug of this fabric, made in India. **2.** A fabric woven wholly or partly of wool, formerly used for clothing. [Fr. *droguet*, prob. < *drogue*, drug, worthless object. See DRUG.]

drug·gie also **drug·gy** (drŭg′ē) *n., pl.* **-gies** *Slang* One that takes or is addicted to drugs.

drug·gist (drŭg′ĭst) *n.* **1.** A pharmacist. **2.** One who sells drugs.

drug·gy¹ (drŭg′ē) *Slang adj.* **-gi·er, -gi·est** Of or relating to drugs or drug use.

drug·gy² (drŭg′ē) *n.* Variant of **druggie.**

drug holiday *n.* A brief period during which a drug that is typically taken daily is not taken or is replaced with another, usu. to minimize side effects.

drug·store also **drug store** (drŭg′stôr′, -stōr′) *n.* A store where prescriptions are filled and drugs and other items are sold; a pharmacy.

dru·id also **Dru·id** (drōō′ĭd) *n.* A member of an order of priests in ancient Gaul and Britain who appear in Welsh and Irish legend as prophets and sorcerers. [< Lat. *druidēs*, druids, of Celt. orig. See **deru-** in App.] —**dru·id′ic** (drōō-ĭd′ĭk), **dru·id′i·cal** (-ĭ-kəl) *adj.* —**dru·id′i·cal·ly** *adv.* —**dru′id·ism** *n.*

drum (drŭm) *n.* **1a.** A percussion instrument consisting of a hollow cylinder or hemisphere with a membrane stretched tightly over one or both ends, played by beating with the hands or sticks. **b.** A sound produced by this instrument. **2.** Something resembling a drum in shape or structure, esp. a barrellike metal container or a metal cylinder wound with cable, wire, or heavy rope. **3.** *Architecture* **a.** A circular or polygonal wall supporting a dome or cupola. **b.** Any of the cylindrical stone blocks stacked to form the shaft of a column. **4.** Any of various marine and freshwater fishes of the family Sciaenidae that make a drumming sound. **5.** *Anatomy* The eardrum. ❖ *v.* **drummed, drum·ming, drums** —*intr.* **1.** To play a drum or drums. **2.** To thump or tap rhythmically or continually. **3.** To produce a booming reverberating sound by beating the wings, as certain birds do. —*tr.* **1.** To perform (a piece or tune) on or as if on a drum. **2.** To summon by or as if by beating a drum. **3.** To make known or force upon (a person) by constant repetition. **4.** To expel or dismiss in disgrace. Often used with *out: was drummed out of the army.* —*phrasal verb:* **drum up** **1.** To bring about by continuous, persistent effort. **2.** To devise or invent: *drummed up an alibi.* [ME *drom*, prob. alteration of MDu. *tromme*, prob. of imit. orig.]

drum·beat (drŭm′bēt′) *n.* **1.** The sound produced by beating a

drum. **2.** Vehement, persistent advocacy of a cause.

drum·beat·er (drŭm′bē′tər) *n.* One that supports a cause, esp. vehemently. —**drum′beat′ing** *n.*

drum brake *n.* A brake in which the friction is caused by a set of pads that press against the inner surface of a rotating drum.

drum·fire (drŭm′fīr′) *n.* **1.** Heavy continuous gunfire. **2.** Something likened to continuous gunfire.

drum·head (drŭm′hĕd′) *n.* **1.** *Music* The material stretched over one or both ends of a drum. **2.** *Nautical* The circular top part of a capstan, used to hold bars for turning.

drum·lin (drŭm′lĭn) *n.* An elongated hill or ridge of glacial drift. [< *drum* < Ir.Gael. *druim*, back, ridge < OIr.]

drum machine *n.* A programmable electronic device having a sequencer that can arrange and alter digitally stored drum sounds.

drum major *n.* A man who leads a marching band or drum corps, often twirling a baton.

drum majorette *n.* A woman who leads a marching band or drum corps, often twirling a baton.

drum·mer (drŭm′ər) *n.* One who plays a drum.

drum printer *n.* A line printer in which a revolving cylinder acts as the printing element.

drum·roll (drŭm′rōl′) *n.* **1.** A rapid succession of short sounds produced by beating a drum. **2.** Emphatic support for a cause.

drum·stick (drŭm′stĭk′) *n.* **1.** *Music* A stick for beating a drum. **2.** The lower part of the leg of a cooked fowl.

drunk (drŭngk) *v.* Past participle of **drink.** ❖ *adj.* **1a.** Intoxicated with alcoholic liquor to the point of impairment of physical and mental faculties. **b.** Caused or influenced by intoxication. **2.** Overcome by strong feeling or emotion: *drunk with power.* ❖ *n.* **1.** A drunkard. **2.** A bout of drinking.

USAGE NOTE As an adjective the form *drunk* is used after a verb while the form *drunken* is now used only in front of a noun: *He was drunk last night. A drunken man sat at the table beside us.* Using *drunk* in front of a noun is generally unacceptable in formal style. But the phrases *drunk driver* and *drunk driving* are supported not only by common usage but also, in many jurisdictions, by a legal distinction between *drunk driver* (a driver whose alcohol level exceeds the legal limit) and *drunken driver* (a driver who is inebriated).

drunk·ard (drŭng′kərd) *n.* One who is habitually drunk.

drunk·en (drŭng′kən) *adj.* **1.** Delirious with or as if with strong drink; intoxicated. **2.** Habitually drunk. **3.** Of, involving, or occurring during intoxication. See Usage Note at **drunk.** **4.** Cooked with wine or another alcoholic beverage: *drunken mushrooms.* —**drunk′en·ly** *adv.* —**drunk′en·ness** *n.*

dru·pa·ceous (drōō-pā′shəs) *adj.* **1.** Resembling, relating to, or consisting of a drupe. **2.** Producing drupes.

drupe (drōōp) *n.* A fleshy fruit, such as a peach, usu. having a single hard stone that encloses a seed. [Lat. *drūpa, druppa,* overripe olive < Gk. *druppā*, olive, poss. alteration of *drupepēs*, ripened on the tree : *drūs, dru-*, tree; see **deru-** in App. + *peptein, pep-*, to ripen; see **pekʷ-** in App.]

drupe·let (drōōp′lĭt) *n.* A small drupe, such as one of the many subdivisions of a raspberry or blackberry.

druse (drōōz) *n.* A crust of tiny crystals lining a rock cavity, usu. composed of the same minerals that occur in the rock. [Ger., weathered ore, prob. < MHGer. *druos*, gland, tumor < OHGer.]

druth·ers (drŭth′ərz) *pl.n. Informal* A choice or preference. [Alteration of the phrase *'d rather* < *would rather*.]

Druze also **Druse** (drōōz) *n.* A member of a Syrian people following a religion marked by monotheism and a belief in al-Hakim (985–1021), an Ismaili caliph, as the embodiment of God. [Ar. *Durūz,* pl. of *durzī,* a Druse, after Ismail al-*Darazi* (died c. 1019), Muslim religious leader.]

dry (drī) *adj.* **dri·er** (drī′ər), **dri·est** (drī′ĭst) or **dry·er, dry·est** **1.** Free from liquid or moisture: *dry clothes.* **2.** Having or characterized by little or no rain. **3.** Marked by the absence of natural or normal moisture. **4.** Not under water. **5.** Having all the water or liquid drained away, evaporated, or exhausted: *a dry river.* **6.** No longer yielding liquid, esp. milk. **7.** Lacking a mucous or watery discharge: *a dry cough.* **8.** Not shedding tears. **9.** Needing or desiring drink; thirsty. **10.** No longer wet: *The paint is dry.* **11.** Of or relating to solid rather than liquid substances or commodities: *dry weight.* **12.** Not sweet as a result of the decomposition of sugar during fermentation. Used of wines. **13.** Having a large proportion of strong liquor to other ingredients: *a dry martini.* **14.** Eaten or served without butter, gravy, or other garnish. **15.** Having no adornment or coloration; plain. **16.** Devoid of bias or personal concern. **17a.** Lacking tenderness, warmth, or involvement; severe. **b.** Matter-of-fact or indifferent in manner. **18.** Wearisome; dull. **19.** Humorous or sarcastic in a shrewd, impersonal way: *dry wit.* **20.** Prohibiting or opposed to the sale or consumption of alcoholic beverages: *a dry law.* **21.** Unproductive of the expected results. **22.** Constructed without mortar or cement: *dry masonry.* ❖ *v.* **dried** (drīd), **dry·ing, dries** (drīz) —*tr.* **1.** To remove the moisture from; make dry. **2.** To preserve (food, for example) by extracting the moisture. —*intr.* To become dry. ❖ *n., pl.* **drys** *Informal* A prohibitionist. —*phrasal verbs:* **dry out** *Informal* To undergo a cure for alcoholism. **dry up** **1.** To make or become unproductive, esp. to do so gradually. **2.** *Infor-*

mal To stop talking. [ME *drie* < OE *drӯge*.] —**dry′ly, dri′ly** *adv.* —**dry′ness** *n.*

dry•ad (drī′əd, -ăd′) *n. Greek Mythology* A divinity presiding over forests and trees; a wood nymph. [ME *Driad* < Lat. *Dryas, Dryad-* < Gk. *Druas* < *drūs*, tree. See **deru-** in App.] —**dry′ad′ic** (-ăd′ĭk) *adj.*

dry•as•dust or **dry-as-dust** (drī′əz-dŭst′) *n.* A dull pedant. [After Dr. Jonas *Dryasdust*, a fictitious character to whom Sir Walter Scott dedicated some of his novels.]

dry cell *n.* A voltage-generating cell having an electrolyte in the form of moist paste. [Because its contents cannot spill.]

dry-clean (drī′klēn′) *tr.v.* **-cleaned, -clean•ing, -cleans** To clean (clothing or fabrics) with chemical solvents that have little or no water. —**dry cleaner** *n.* —**dry cleaning** *n.*

Dry•den (drīd′n), **John** 1631–1700. English writer whose works include critical essays, dramas, and poems.

dry dock *n.* A large dock in the form of a basin from which the water can be emptied, used for building or repairing a ship below its water line.

dry-dock (drī′dŏk′) *tr. & intr.v.* **-docked, -dock•ing, -docks** To place in or go into a dry dock.

dry•er (drī′ər) *n.* **1.** An appliance that removes moisture by heating or another process: *a hair dryer.* **2.** Variant of **drier**[1].

dry farming *n.* A type of farming practiced in arid areas without irrigation by planting drought-resistant crops and mulching or tilling to protect the soil moisture from evaporation. —**dry farm** *n.* —**dry′-farm′** (drī′färm′) *v.* —**dry farmer** *n.*

dry fly *n.* An artificial fly used in fishing that floats on the surface of the water when cast.

dry gangrene *n.* Gangrene that develops as a result of arterial obstruction and is characterized by mummification of the dead tissue and absence of bacterial decomposition.

dry goods *pl.n.* Textiles, clothing, and related articles of trade.

dry ice *n.* Solid carbon dioxide that sublimates at −78.5°C (−110°F) and is used as a coolant. [Orig. a trademark.]

dry•ing oil (drī′ĭng) *n.* An organic oil used as a binder in paints and varnishes.

dry kiln *n.* An oven for drying and seasoning cut lumber.

dry measure *n.* A system of units for measuring dry commodities such as grains, fruits, and vegetables.

dry mop *n.* See **dust mop**.

dry nurse *n.* A nurse employed to care for but not breast-feed an infant. —**dry′-nurse′** (drī′nûrs′) *v.*

dry•o•pith•e•cine (drī′ō-pĭth′ĭ-sēn′) *n.* An extinct ape of the genus *Dryopithecus*, known from Old World Miocene and Pliocene fossils and considered an ancestor of the anthropoid apes and humans. [< NLat. *Dryopithēcus*, genus name : Gk. *drūs*, oak; see **deru-** in App. + Gk. *pithēkos*, ape.] —**dry′o•pith′e•cine′** *adj.*

dry point *n.* **1.** A technique of intaglio engraving in which a hard steel needle is used to incise lines in a metal plate, with the rough burr at the sides of the incised lines often retained. **2.** An engraving or print made using this technique.

dry rot *n.* **1.** A fungal disease that causes timber to become brittle and crumble into powder. **2.** A plant disease in which the plant tissue remains dry while bulbs, fruits, or woody tissues decay.

dry run *n.* **1.** A trial exercise; a rehearsal. **2.** A test exercise in combat skills without the use of live ammunition.

dry-salt•er (drī′sôl′tər) *n. Chiefly British* A dealer in chemical products and dyes. —**dry′salt′er•y** *n.*

dry socket *n.* A painful inflamed condition at the site of extraction of a tooth that occurs when a blood clot fails to form properly or is dislodged.

Dry Tor•tu•gas (tôr-tōō′gəz) An island group of S FL W of Key West; named *Tortugas* ("turtles") by Ponce de León in 1513.

dry wall or **dry•wall** (drī′wôl′) *n.* **1a.** Plasterboard. **b.** A wall or ceiling constructed of a prefabricated material, such as plasterboard or paneling. **2.** A wall constructed from rocks that are not cemented together.

dry wash *n.* Cleaned but not ironed laundry.

dry well also **dry•well** (drī′wĕl′) *n.* A subterranean chamber near a building, with stones or gravel inside, used to collect rainwater from the roof to prevent soil erosion.

DS *abbr.* dal segno

DSC *abbr.* Distinguished Service Cross

DSM *abbr.* Distinguished Service Medal

DSO *abbr.* Distinguished Service Order

D-s particle (dē′ĕs′) *n.* A positively charged meson having a mass 3,852 times that of the electron.

DSS *abbr.* **1.** Department of Social Services **2.** digital satellite system

DST *abbr.* daylight-saving time

DT *abbr.* Doctor of Theology

DTD (dē′tē-dē′) *n.* A set of rules for marking up a document in SGML. [D(ocument) T(ype) D(efinition).]

DTP vaccine (dē′tē-pē′) or **DPT vaccine** (dē′pē-tē′) *n.* A vaccine administered to immunize children against diphtheria, tetanus, and pertussis.

DTs or **DT's** (dē′tēz′) *n.* (*used with a sing. or pl. verb*) Delirium tremens.

dTTP (dē′tē-tē′pē′) *n.* One of the two pyrimidine nucleotides that

---

are used to synthesize DNA. [D(EOXY)- + T(HYMIDINE) + T(RI)-P(HOSPHATE).]

Du. *abbr.* **1.** duke **2.** Dutch

du•ad (dōō′ăd′, dyōō′-) *n.* A unit of two objects; a pair. [Gk. *duas, duad-*, two < *duo*. See **dwo-** in App.]

du•al (dōō′əl, dyōō′-) *adj.* **1.** Composed of two usu. like or complementary parts; double. **2.** Having a double character or purpose. **3.** *Grammar* Of, relating to, or being a number category that indicates two persons or things. ❖ *n. Grammar* **1.** The dual number. **2.** An inflected form of a noun, adjective, pronoun, or verb used with two items or people. [Lat. *duālis* < *duo*, two. See **dwo-** in App.] —**du′al•ly** *adv.*

Du•a•la (dōō-ä′lä) See **Douala**.

du•al•ism (dōō′ə-lĭz′əm, dyōō′-) *n.* **1.** The state of being double; duality. **2.** *Philosophy* The view that the world consists of or is explicable as two basic entities, such as mind and matter. **3.** *Psychology* The view that the mind and body function separately, without interchange. **4.** *Theology* **a.** The view that the world is ruled by the antagonistic forces of good and evil. **b.** The view that humans have two basic natures, the physical and the spiritual. —**du′al•ist** *n.* —**du′al•is′tic** *adj.* —**du′al•is′ti•cal•ly** *adv.*

du•al•i•ty (dōō-ăl′ĭ-tē, dyōō-) *n.* The quality or character of being twofold; dichotomy.

du•al-pur•pose (dōō′əl-pûr′pəs, dyōō′-) *adj.* Designed for or serving two purposes.

dub[1] (dŭb) *tr.v.* **dubbed, dub•bing, dubs** **1.** To tap lightly on the shoulder to confer knighthood. **2.** To honor with a new title or description. **3.** To give a name to facetiously or playfully; nickname. **4.** To strike, cut, or rub (timber, for example) so as to make even or smooth. **5.** To dress (a fowl). **6.** To execute (a golf stroke, for example) poorly. ❖ *n.* An awkward person or player; a bungler. [ME *dubben* < OE *dubbian*, perh. < OFr. *aduber*.]

dub[2] (dŭb) *v.* **dubbed, dub•bing, dubs** —*tr.* **1.** To thrust at; poke. **2.** To beat (a drum). —*intr.* **1.** To make a thrust. **2.** To beat on a drum. ❖ *n.* **1.** The act of dubbing. **2.** A drumbeat. [Perh. < LGer. *dubben*, to hit, strike.]

dub[3] (dŭb) *tr.v.* **dubbed, dub•bing, dubs** **1a.** To transfer (recorded material) onto a new recording medium. **b.** To copy (a record or tape). **2.** To insert a new soundtrack, esp. a synchronized translation of the original dialogue, into (a film). **3.** To add (sound) into a film or tape. ❖ *n.* **1.** The new sounds added by dubbing. **2.** A dubbed copy of a tape or record. [Short for DOU-BLE.] —**dub′ber** *n.*

dub[4] (dŭb) *n. Scots* A puddle or small pool. [?]

Du Bar•ry (dōō bär′ē, dyōō′), **Comtesse**. Marie Jeanne Bécu. Title of "Madame Du Barry." 1743–93. French courtier and influential lover of Louis XV.

Du•bawnt (dōō-bônt′) A river, c. 933 km (580 mi), of SE Northwest Terrs., Canada, flowing through **Dubawnt Lake** and into SW Nunavut.

Du•bayy or **Du•bai** (dōō-bī′) A city and sheikdom of E United Arab Emirates on the Persian Gulf. Pop. 265,702.

dub•bin (dŭb′ĭn) also **dub•bing** (-ĭng) *n.* An application of tallow and oil for dressing leather. [< dub[1].]

Dub•ček (dōōb′chĕk, dōōp′-), **Alexander** 1921–92. Czechoslovakian politician who became head of a democratically elected parliament in 1990.

du Bel•lay (dōō bə-lā′, dü bĕ-lā′), **Joachim** See Joachim du **Bellay**.

du•bi•e•ty (dōō-bī′ĭ-tē, dyōō-) *n., pl.* **-ties** **1.** A feeling of doubt that often results in wavering. See Syns at **uncertainty**. **2.** A matter of doubt. [LLat. *dubietās* < Lat. *dubius*, doubtful. See DUBIOUS.]

Du•bin•sky (dōō-bĭn′skē), **David** 1892–1982. Russian-born Amer. labor leader who was president of the International Ladies' Garment Workers Union (1932–66).

du•bi•ous (dōō′bē-əs, dyōō′-) *adj.* **1.** Fraught with uncertainty or doubt; undecided. **2.** Arousing doubt; doubtful. **3.** Of questionable character. [< Lat. *dubius*. See **dwo-** in App.] —**du′bi•ous•ly** *adv.* —**du′bi•ous•ness** *n.*

du•bi•ta•ble (dōō′bĭ-tə-bəl, dyōō′-) *adj.* Subject to doubt or question; uncertain. [Lat. *dubitābilis* < *dubitāre*, to doubt. See DOUBT.] —**du′bi•ta•bly** *adv.*

Dub•lin (dŭb′lĭn) The cap. of Ireland, in the E-central part on the Irish Sea; scene of the Easter Rebellion of Apr. 24, 1916. Pop. 533,929. —**Dub′lin•er** *n.*

dub•ni•um (dōōb′nē-əm) *n. Symbol* **Db** An artificially produced radioactive element with atomic number 105 whose most long-lived isotopes have mass numbers of 258, 261, 262, and 263 with half-lives of 4.2, 1.8. 34, and 30 seconds, respectively. See table at **element**. [After *Dubna*, Russia, location of the United Institute of Nuclear Research.]

Du Bois (dōō bois′), **W(illiam) E(dward) B(urghardt)** 1868–1963. Amer. civil rights leader who cofounded the NAACP.

Du•bon•net (dōō′bə-nā′, dyōō′-) A trademark used for apéritif wines.

Du•bos (dōō-bôs′, -bō′, dü-), **René Jules** 1901–82. French-born Amer. bacteriologist noted for his research on natural antibiotics.

Du•brov•nik (dōō′brôv-nĭk′) Formerly **Ra•gu•sa** (rə-gōō′zə, rä-gōō′zä) A city of extreme S Croatia on the Adriatic Sea; medieval center of Serbo-Croatian culture and literature. Pop. 55,638.

dry dock
Jacksonville Shipyards,
Jacksonville, Florida

dry wall
constructing a dry wall

W.E.B. Du Bois
detail from an undated
portrait by Laura Wheeler
Waring (1887–1948)

Du·buf·fet (dōō-bə-fāʹ, dü-bü-fēʹ), **Jean** 1901–85. French artist known for his *art brut*, or "raw art."

Du·buque (də-byōōkʹ) A city of E IA on the Mississippi R. opposite the IL-WI border; settled in 1833. Pop. 57,686.

du·cal (dōōʹkəl, dyōōʹ-) *adj.* Of or relating to a duke or duchy. [ME < OFr. < LLat. *ducālis* < Lat. *dux, duc-,* leader. See DUKE.] —**duʹcal·ly** *adv.*

duc·at (dŭkʹət) *n.* **1.** Any of various gold coins formerly used in certain European countries. **2.** *Slang* **a.** A piece of money. **b.** An admission ticket. [ME < OFr. < OItal. *ducato* < Med.Lat. *ducātus,* duchy. See DUCHY.]

du·ce (dōōʹchā) *n.* A leader or commander; a chief. [Ital. < Lat. *dux, duc-.* See DUKE.]

Du·champ (dōō-shänʹ, dü) **Marcel** 1887–1968. French-born artist known for *Nude Descending a Staircase* (1912).

Du·chenne's muscular dystrophy (dōō-shĕnʹ) *n.* The most common form of muscular dystrophy, affecting almost exclusively males, beginning in early childhood and usu. causing death before adulthood. [After Guillaume B.A. *Duchenne* (1806–75), French physician.]

duch·ess (dŭchʹĭs) *n.* **1.** A noblewoman of the highest rank, esp. in British peerage. **2.** A woman holding title to a duchy in her own right. **3.** The wife or widow of a duke. **4.** Used as the title for such a noblewoman. [ME *duchesse* < OFr. < Med.Lat. *ducissa* < Lat. *dux, duc-,* leader. See DUKE.]

duch·y (dŭchʹē) *n., pl.* **-ies** The territory ruled by a duke or duchess; a dukedom. [ME < OFr. *duche* < Med.Lat. *ducātus* < Lat. *dux, duc-,* leader. See DUKE.]

duck¹ (dŭk) *n.* **1.** Any of various wild or domesticated swimming birds of the family Anatidae, characteristically having a broad flat bill, short legs, and webbed feet. **2.** A female duck. **3.** The flesh of a duck used as food. **4.** *Slang* A person, esp. one thought of as peculiar. **5.** *Chiefly British* A dear. Often used in the plural with a singular verb. [ME *doke* < OE *dūce,* poss. < **dūcan,* to dive. See DUCK².]

duck² (dŭk) *v.* **ducked, duck·ing, ducks** —*tr.* **1.** To lower quickly, esp. so as to avoid something: *ducked his head.* **2.** To evade; dodge: *duck responsibility.* **3.** To push suddenly under water. **4.** *Games* To deliberately play a card that is lower than (an opponent's card). —*intr.* **1.** To lower the head or body. **2.** To move swiftly, esp. so as to escape being seen. **3.** To submerge the head or body briefly in water. **4.** To evade a responsibility or obligation. Often used with *out.* **5.** *Games* To lose a trick by deliberately playing lower than one's opponent. ❖ *n.* **1.** A quick lowering of the head or body. **2.** A plunge into water. [ME *douken,* to dive, poss. < OE **dūcan;* akin to MLGer. and MDu. *dūken.*] —**duckʹer** *n.*

duck³ (dŭk) *n.* **1.** A durable, closely woven heavy cotton or linen fabric. **2. ducks** Clothing made of duck, esp. white trousers. [Du. *doek,* cloth < MDu. *doec.*]

duck⁴ (dŭk) *n.* **1.** An amphibious military truck used during World War II. **2.** An amphibious truck used in emergencies, as to evacuate flood victims. [Alteration (influenced by DUCK¹) of *DUKW,* its code designation.]

duck·bill (dŭkʹbĭl') *n.* **1.** See platypus. **2.** See hadrosaur.

duck-billed dinosaur (dŭkʹbĭld') *n.* See hadrosaur.

duck-billed platypus *n.* See platypus.

duck·board (dŭkʹbôrd', -bōrd') *n.* A board or boardwalk laid across wet or muddy ground or flooring.

duck hawk *n.* See peregrine falcon.

duck·ing stool (dŭkʹĭng) *n.* A device formerly used in Europe and New England for punishment, consisting of a chair in which an offender was tied and ducked into water.

duck·ling (dŭkʹlĭng) *n.* A young duck.

duck·pin (dŭkʹpĭn') *n.* **1.** A bowling pin that is shorter and squatter than a tenpin. **2. duckpins** (*used with a sing. verb*) A bowling game played with such pins and a small ball.

ducks and drakes (drāks) *n.* The game of skipping flat stones along the surface of water. —*idiom:* **make ducks and drakes of** (or **play ducks and drakes with**) To squander; waste.

duck soup *n. Slang* An easily accomplished task.

duck·tail (dŭkʹtāl') *n.* A hairstyle in which the hair is swept back at the sides to meet in an upturned point in back.

duck·weed (dŭkʹwēd') *n.* Any of various small, free-floating, stemless aquatic flowering plants of the genus *Lemna.*

duck·y (dŭkʹē) *adj.* **-i·er, -i·est** *Slang* Excellent; fine.

Du·com·mun (dü-kô-mônʹ), **Élie** 1833–1906. Swiss journalist who shared the 1902 Nobel Peace Prize.

duct (dŭkt) *n.* **1.** An often enclosed passage or channel for conveying a substance, esp. a liquid or gas. **2.** *Anatomy* A tubular body canal or passage, esp. one carrying a glandular secretion: *a tear duct.* **3.** A tube or pipe for enclosing electrical cables or wires. ❖ *tr.v.* **duct·ed, duct·ing, ducts** **1.** To channel through a duct: *duct the moist air away.* **2.** To supply with ducts. [Lat. *ductus,* act of leading < p. part. of *dūcere,* to lead. See deuk- in App.] —**ductʹal** *adj.* —**ductʹless** *adj.*

duc·tile (dŭkʹtəl, -tīl') *adj.* **1.** Easily drawn into wire or hammered thin: *ductile metals.* **2.** Easily molded or shaped. **3.** Capable of being readily persuaded or influenced. [ME *ductil* < OFr. < Lat. *ductilis* < *ductus,* p. part. of *dūcere,* to lead. See deuk- in App.] —**duc·tilʹi·ty** (-tĭlʹĭ-tē), **duc·tiʹli·bilʹi·ty** (-lə-bĭlʹĭ-tē) *n.*

duct·ing (dŭkʹtĭng) *n.* **1.** A duct or system of ducts. **2.** Material for making ducts.

duct·less gland (dŭktʹlĭs) *n.* See endocrine gland.

duct tape *n.* A waterproof, usu. silver adhesive cloth tape designed esp. for sealing ducts.

duc·tule (dŭkʹtōol') *n.* A small duct.

duct·work (dŭktʹwûrk') *n.* A group or system of ducts.

dud (dŭd) *n.* **1.** A bomb, shell, or explosive round that fails to detonate. **2.** *Informal* One that is disappointingly ineffective or unsuccessful. **3. duds** *Informal* **a.** Clothing. **b.** Personal belongings. [ME *dudde,* a cloak.]

dude (dōōd, dyōōd) *n.* **1.** *Informal* An Easterner or city person who vacations on a ranch in the West. **2.** *Informal* A man who is very fancy or sharp in dress and demeanor. **3.** *Slang* **a.** A man; a fellow. **b. dudes** Persons of either sex. ❖ *tr.v.* **dud·ed, dud·ing, dudes** *Slang* To dress elaborately or flamboyantly. [?]

du·deen (dōō-dēnʹ) *n.* A short-stemmed clay pipe. [Ir.Gael. *dúidín,* dim. of *dúd,* stump, pipe.]

dude ranch *n.* A resort patterned after a Western ranch, with outdoor activities such as horseback riding.

dudg·eon¹ (dŭjʹən) *n.* A sullen, angry, or indignant humor. [?]

dudg·eon² (dŭjʹən) *n.* **1.** *Obsolete* A wood used to make knife handles. **2.** *Archaic* **a.** A dagger with a hilt of this wood. **b.** The hilt of a dagger. [ME *dogeon,* poss. < AN.]

Dud·ley (dŭdʹlē) A borough of W-central England WNW of Birmingham. Pop. 311,478.

Dudley, Robert. 1st Earl of Leicester. 1532?–88. English courtier, politician, and favorite of Elizabeth I.

Dudley, Thomas 1576–1653. English colonial administrator who served as governor of Massachusetts Bay Colony (1634, 1640, 1645, and 1650).

due (dōō, dyōō) *adj.* **1.** Payable immediately or on demand. **2.** Owed as a debt; owing. **3.** In accord with right, convention, or courtesy; appropriate. **4.** Meeting special requirements; sufficient: *due cause.* **5a.** Expected or scheduled, esp. appointed to arrive. **b.** Expected to give birth. **6a.** Anticipated; looked for. **b.** Expecting or ready for something as part of a normal course or sequence. **7.** Capable of being attributed. ❖ *n.* **1.** Something owed or deserved: *received your due.* **2. dues** A charge or fee for membership, as in a club. ❖ *adv.* **1.** Straight; directly: *Go due west.* **2.** *Archaic* Duly. [ME < OFr. *deu,* p. part. of *devoir,* to owe < Lat. *dēbēre,* to owe. See ghabh- in App.]

due bill *n.* A written acknowledgment of indebtedness to a given party but not payable to order or transferable by endorsement.

du·el (dōōʹəl, dyōōʹ-) *n.* **1.** A prearranged formal combat between two persons, usu. over a point of honor. **2.** A struggle for domination between two contending persons, groups, or ideas. ❖ *v.* **-eled, -el·ing, -els** or **-elled, -el·ling, -els** —*tr.* **1.** To engage (another) in or as if in formal combat. **2.** To oppose actively and forcefully. —*intr.* To engage in or as if in formal combat. [ME *duelle* < Med.Lat. < Lat., war, archaic var. of *bellum.*] —**du·elʹer, du·elʹist** *n.*

du·en·de (dōō-ĕnʹdā') *n.* The ability to attract others by personal magnetism and charm. [Sp. dialectal, poss. < OSpan., owner, proprietor < *duen de (casa),* lord of (a house) : *duen,* lord (< Lat. *dominus;* see dem- in App.) + *de,* of (< Lat. *dē;* see DE–).]

due process *n.* A set course for judicial or other government activities designed to protect the individual's legal rights.

Due·ro (dwĕrʹō) See Douro.

du·et (dōō-ĕtʹ, dyōō-) *n.* **1.** *Music* **a.** A composition for two voices or two instruments. **b.** The two performers of a duet. **2.** A pair. [Ital. *duetto,* dim. of *duo* < Lat., two. See dwo- in App.]

due to *prep.* Because of.

Du·fay (dōō-fāʹ, dü-), **Guillaume** 1400?–74. Flemish composer particularly known for his Mass compositions.

duff¹ (dŭf) *n.* A stiff flour pudding boiled in a cloth bag or steamed. [Dialectal variation of DOUGH.]

duff² (dŭf) *n.* **1.** Decaying leaves and branches covering a forest floor. **2.** Fine coal; slack. [?]

duff³ (dŭf) *n. Slang* The buttocks. [?]

duf·fel or **duf·fle** (dŭfʹəl) *n.* **1.** A blanket fabric made of low-grade woolen cloth with a nap on both sides. **2.** Clothing and other personal gear carried by a camper. [Du., after *Duffel,* a town of northern Belgium.]

duff·er (dŭfʹər) *n.* **1.** *Informal* **a.** An incompetent or dull-witted person. **b.** A casual or mediocre player of a sport, esp. golf. **2.** *Slang* A peddler of cheap merchandise. **3.** *Slang* Something worthless or useless. [?]

duffle bag or **duffel bag** *n.* A large cylindrical cloth bag of canvas or duck for carrying personal belongings.

duffle coat or **duffel coat** *n.* A warm, usu. hooded coat made of duffel or a similar material and fastened with toggles.

Du·fy (dōō-fēʹ, dü-), **Raoul** 1877–1953. French painter noted for his brightly colored scenes of racing and the seaside.

dug¹ (dŭg) *n.* An udder, breast, or teat of a female animal. [?]

dug² (dŭg) *v.* Past tense and past participle of **dig.**

du·gong (dōōʹgông', -gŏng') *n.* A herbivorous marine mammal (*Dugong dugon*) of the Indian Ocean having flipperlike forelimbs and a deeply notched tail fin. [NLat. *Dugong,* genus name, poss. < Malay *duyong.*]

dugong
Dugong dugon

dug•out (dŭg′out′) *n.* **1.** A boat or canoe made of a hollowed-out log. **2.** A pit dug into the ground or on a hillside and used as a shelter. **3.** *Baseball* Either of two shelters at the side of a field where the players stay while not on the field.

duh (dŭ) *interj.* Used to express disdain for something deemed stupid or obvious. [Imit. of an utterance attributed to slow-witted people.]

DUI *abbr.* driving under the influence (of drugs or alcohol)

dui•ker (dī′kər) *n.* Any of various small African antelopes of the genera *Cephalophus* or *Sylvicapra*. [Afr. < Du. *duiken*, to dive < MDu. *dūken*.]

Duis•burg (dōos′bûrg′, dooz′-, düs′bŏŏrk′) A city of W-central Germany at the confluence of the Rhine and Ruhr rivers. Pop. 536,797.

du jour (də zhŏŏr, doo) *adj.* **1.** Prepared for a given day: *soup du jour.* **2.** Most recent; current: *the trend du jour.* [Fr. : *du*, of the + *jour*, day.]

duke (dook, dyook) *n.* **1.** A nobleman of the highest rank, esp. in British peerage. **2.** A sovereign prince who rules an independent duchy in some European countries. **3.** Used as the title for such a nobleman. **4.** *Slang* A fist. Often used in the plural: *Put up your dukes!* **5.** *Botany* A type of cherry intermediate between a sweet and a sour cherry. ❖ *intr.v.* **duked, duk•ing, dukes** To fight, esp. with fists. [ME < OFr. *duc* < Lat. *dux, duc-,* leader < *dūcere,* to lead. See **deuk-** in App.]

duke•dom (dook′dəm, dyook′-) *n.* **1.** A duchy. **2.** The office, rank, or title of a duke.

Du•kho•bor also **Dou•kho•bor** (doo′kə-bôr′) *n.* A member of a Russian Christian movement founded in the 18th century and marked by rejection of ecclesiastical and state authority. [Russ. *Dukhobor*: *dukh,* spirit, Holy Ghost + *-bor,* fighter (< *borot′sya,* to fight).]

Dul•bec•co (dŭl-bĕk′ō), **Renato** b. 1914. Italian-born Amer. virologist who shared a 1975 Nobel Prize.

dul•cet (dŭl′sĭt) *adj.* **1a.** Pleasing to the ear; melodious. **b.** Having a soothing agreeable quality. **2.** *Archaic* Sweet to the taste. [Alteration of ME *doucet* < OFr., dim. of *douce,* fem. of *doux,* sweet < Lat. *dulcis.*] —**dul′cet•ly** *adv.*

dul•ci•fy (dŭl′sə-fī′) *tr.v.* **-fied, -fy•ing, -fies 1.** To make agreeable or gentle; mollify. **2.** To sweeten. [LLat. *dulcificāre,* to sweeten : Lat. *dulcis,* sweet + *-ficāre,* -fy.] —**dul′ci•fi•ca′tion** (-fĭ-kā′shən) *n.*

dul•ci•mer (dŭl′sə-mər) *n.* **1.** A narrow, often hourglass-shaped stringed instrument having three or four strings and a fretted fingerboard, typically held flat across the knees while sitting and played by plucking or strumming. **2.** The hammered dulcimer. [Alteration (influenced by Lat. *dulcis,* sweet) of ME *doucemere* < OFr. *doulcemer, doulcemele,* prob. < Lat. *dulce melos,* sweet song : *dulce,* neut. of *dulcis,* sweet + *melos,* song (< Gk.).]

duiker
zebra duiker
Cephalophus zebra

dull (dŭl) *adj.* **dull•er, dull•est 1.** Intellectually weak or obtuse; stupid. **2.** Lacking responsiveness or alertness; insensitive. **3.** Dispirited; depressed. **4.** Not brisk or rapid; sluggish. **5.** Not having a sharp edge or point; blunt. **6.** Not intensely or keenly felt. **7.** Arousing no interest or curiosity; boring. **8.** Not bright or vivid. Used of a color. **9.** Cloudy or overcast. **10.** Not clear or resonant: *a dull thud.* ❖ *tr. & intr.v.* **dulled, dull•ing, dulls** To make or become dull. [ME *dul;* akin to OE *dol.*] —**dull′ish** *adj.* —**dull′ness, dul′ness** *n.* —**dul′ly** *adv.*

dull•ard (dŭl′ərd) *n.* One regarded as mentally dull; a dolt.

Dul•les (dŭl′ĭs), **John Foster** 1888–1959. Amer. diplomat who served as US secretary of state (1953–59).

dulls•ville (dŭlz′vĭl) *n. Slang* A dull place, thing, or condition.

dulse (dŭls) *n.* An edible red alga (*Palmaria palmata*) that grows on rocky shores on both sides of the northern Atlantic Ocean. [Sc. Gael. *duileasg* < OIr. *duilesc.*]

Du•luth (də-looth′) A city of NE MN on Lake Superior opposite Superior WI; settled in the 1850s. Pop. 86,918.

du•ly (doo′lē, dyoo′-) *adv.* **1.** In a proper manner. **2.** At the expected time. [ME *duely* < *due,* due. See **DUE.**]

du•ma (doo′mə) *n.* A Russian national parliament during czarist times. [Russ., of Gmc. orig. See **dhē-** in App.]

dump truck

Du•mas (doo-mä′, dyoo′-, dü-), **Alexandre** Known as "Dumas *père.*" 1802–70. French writer of historical romances, such as *The Count of Monte Cristo* and *The Three Musketeers* (both 1844). His son **Alexandre** (1824–95), known as "Dumas *fils,*" was a dramatist whose works include *La Dame aux Camélias* (1852).

du Mau•ri•er (doo môr′ē-ā′, dyoo, dü mô-ryā′), Dame **Daphne** 1907–89. British writer best known for *Rebecca* (1938).

du Maurier, George Louis Palmella Busson 1834–96. British illustrator and writer noted for his caricatures in *Punch* and his novel *Trilby* (1894).

dumb (dŭm) *adj.* **dumb•er, dumb•est 1a.** Lacking the power of speech. Used of animals and inanimate objects. **b.** *Often Offensive* Incapable of using speech; mute. Used of humans. **2.** Temporarily speechless, as with shock or fear: *dumb with disbelief.* **3.** Unwilling to speak; taciturn. **4.** Not expressed or articulated in sounds or words. **5.** Conspicuously unintelligent; stupid. **6.** Unintentional; haphazard: *dumb luck.* **7.** *Computer Science* Incapable of processing data independently of a host computer: *a dumb terminal.* ❖ *tr.v.* **dumbed, dumb•ing, dumbs** To make silent or dumb. —*phrasal verb:* **dumb down** *Slang* To rewrite for a less

dung beetle

educated or less sophisticated audience. [ME < OE.] —**dumb′ly** *adv.* —**dumb′ness** *n.*

dumb•bell (dŭm′bĕl′) *n.* **1.** A weight consisting of a short bar with a metal ball or disk at each end that is lifted for muscular exercise. **2.** *Slang* A stupid person; a dolt. [< an apparatus like that used to ring a church bell but without the bell.]

dumb cane *n.* See **dieffenbachia.** [So called because its leaves contain a substance that swells the throat when eaten.]

dumb•found also **dum•found** (dŭm′found′) *tr.v.* **-found•ed, -found•ing, -founds** To fill with astonishment and perplexity; confound. [DUMB + (CON)FOUND.]

dum•bo (dŭm′bō) *n., pl.* **-bos** *Slang* A stupid person.

dumb plant *n.* See **dieffenbachia.** [See DUMB CANE.]

dumb show *n.* **1.** A part of a play, esp. in medieval and Renaissance drama, enacted silently. **2.** Communication or acting by expressive gestures; pantomime.

dumb•struck (dŭm′strŭk′) *adj.* So shocked or astonished as to be rendered speechless.

dumb•wait•er (dŭm′wā′tər) *n.* **1.** A small elevator used to convey food or other goods from one floor of a building to another. **2.** A portable serving stand or table.

dum•dum (dŭm′dŭm′) *n.* A hollow-point small-arms bullet designed to expand upon impact, inflicting a gaping wound. [After *Dum Dum,* a town of northeast India.]

dum•ka (doom′kə) *n.* A song, esp. a Slavic folksong, that has alternating happy and sad passages. [Slovak, Ukrainian folksong < Ukrainian, dim. of *duma,* thought, memory, narrative poem, of Gmc. orig. See **dhē-** in App.]

dumm•kopf (doom′kôf′, -kôpf′, dŭm′-) *n.* A stupid person. [Ger. : *dumm,* dumb (< MHGer. *tump, tumb* < OHGer. *tumb* < Kopf,* head (< MHGer., cup, cranium < OHGer., cup < LLat. *cuppa.*)]

dum•my (dŭm′ē) *n., pl.* **-mies 1.** An imitation of a real or original object, intended as a practical substitute. **2a.** A mannequin for displaying clothes. **b.** A figure manipulated by a ventriloquist. **c.** A stuffed or pasteboard figure used as a target. **d.** *Football* A heavy stuffed cylindrical bag used for blocking and tackling practice. **3.** A stupid person; a dolt. **4.** A silent or taciturn person. **5.** A person or an agency secretly in the service of another. **6.** *Printing* **a.** One of a set of model pages with text and illustrations pasted into place to direct the printer. **b.** A set of bound blank pages used as a model to show the size and general appearance of a book being published. **7.** *Games* **a.** The partner in bridge whose exposed hand is played by the declarer. **b.** The hand thus exposed. **8.** *Computer Science* A character or other piece of information entered into a computer only to meet prescribed conditions, such as word length, and not affecting operations. ❖ *adj.* **1.** Simulating or replacing something but lacking its function. **2.** Serving as a front or cover for another: *a dummy corporation.* **3.** *Computer Science* Entered or provided only to meet prescribed conditions: *a dummy variable.* ❖ *tr.v.* **-mied, -my•ing, -mies** *Printing* To make a model of (a publication or page). —*phrasal verb:* **dummy up** *Slang* To keep silence; clam up. [< DUMB.]

dump (dŭmp) *v.* **dumped, dump•ing, dumps** —*tr.* **1.** To release or throw down in a large mass. **2a.** To empty (material) out of a container or vehicle. **b.** To empty out (a container or vehicle), as by overturning or tilting. **3a.** To get rid of; discard. **b.** *Informal* To discard or reject unceremoniously. **4.** To place (goods or stock, for example) on the market in large quantities and at a low price. **5.** *Computer Science* To transfer (data stored internally in a computer) from one place to another without processing. **6.** *Slang* To knock down; beat. —*intr.* **1.** To fall or drop abruptly. **2.** To discharge cargo or contents; unload. **3.** *Slang* To criticize another severely. ❖ *n.* **1.** A place where refuse is dumped. **2.** A storage place for goods or supplies; a depot. **3.** An unordered accumulation; a pile. **4.** *Computer Science* An instance or the result of dumping stored data. **5.** *Slang* A poorly maintained or disreputable place. **6.** *Vulgar Slang* An act of defecating. Often used with *take.* [ME *dumpen,* to fall suddenly, drop, of Scand. orig.] —**dump′er** *n.*

dump•ling (dŭmp′lĭng) *n.* **1.** A piece of dough, sometimes filled, that is cooked in liquid such as water or soup. **2.** Sweetened dough wrapped around fruit, baked and served as a dessert. **3.** *Informal* A short chubby creature. [Earlier *dumplin,* perh. < *dump,* lump.]

dumps (dŭmps) *pl.n.* A gloomy, melancholy state of mind; depression. Often used with *the.* [Prob. < Du. *domp,* haze < MDu. *damp,* vapor.]

dump•site (dŭmp′sīt′) *n.* The location of a dump, esp. a garbage dump.

Dump•ster (dŭmp′stər) A trademark used for containers designed for receiving, transporting, and dumping waste materials.

dump truck *n.* A heavy-duty truck having a bed that tilts backward to dump loose material.

dump•y¹ (dŭm′pē) *adj.* **-i•er, -i•est** Short and stout. [Prob. < *dump,* lump.] —**dump′i•ly** *adv.* —**dump′i•ness** *n.*

dump•y² (dŭm′pē) *adj.* **-i•er, -i•est** Resembling a dump, as in shabbiness; disreputable.

dumpy level *n.* A surveyor's instrument having a short telescope fixed rigidly to a horizontally rotating table.

dun¹ (dŭn) *tr.v.* **dunned, dun•ning, duns** To importune (a debtor) for payment. ❖ *n.* **1.** One that duns. **2.** An importunate demand for payment. [?]

dun[2] (dŭn) *n.* **1.** An almost neutral brownish gray to dull grayish brown. **2.** A fishing fly having this color. **3.** A horse of this color. [ME < OE *dunn,* perh. of Celt. orig.]

Du•nant (do͞o-näN′, dü-), **Jean Henri** 1828–1910. Swiss philanthropist who founded the International Red Cross (1864) and shared the 1901 Nobel Peace Prize.

Dun•bar (dŭn′bär), **Paul Laurence** 1872–1906. Amer. writer noted for his poetry, as in *Lyrics of Lowly Life* (1896).

Dun•bar (dŭn-bär′), **William** 1460?–1520? Scottish poet whose works include *The Thrissill and the Rois* (1503).

Dun•can (dŭng′kən), **Isadora** 1878–1927. Amer. dancer whose simple costumes and free movement greatly influenced modern dance.

dunce (dŭns) *n.* A stupid person; a dolt. [After John DUNS SCOTUS, whose writings were ridiculed in the 16th cent.]

dunce cap also **dunce's cap** (dŭn′sĭz) *n.* A cone-shaped paper cap, formerly placed on the head of a slow or lazy pupil.

Dun•dee (dŭn-dē′) A burgh of E-central Scotland on the N bank of the Firth of Tay; a stronghold of the Covenanters in the Scottish Reformation. Pop. 170,120.

dun•der•head (dŭn′dər-hĕd′) *n.* A dunce. [Perh. Du. *donder,* thunder (< MDu. *doner;* see **(s)tenə-** in App.) + HEAD.]

dun•drear•ies (dŭn-drîr′ēz) *pl.n.* Long sideburns worn with a clean-shaven chin. [After Lord *Dundreary,* a character in the play *Our American Cousin* by Tom Taylor (1817–80).]

dune (do͞on, dyo͞on) *n.* A hill or ridge of wind-blown sand. [Fr. < OFr. < MDu. *dūne.* See **dheuə-** in App.]

dune buggy *n.* A recreational vehicle having oversize tires designed for use on sand dunes or beaches.

dung (dŭng) *n.* **1a.** Animal excrement. **b.** Manure. **2.** Something foul or abhorrent. ❖ *tr.v.* **dunged, dung•ing, dungs** To fertilize (land) with manure. [ME < OE.] **—dung′y** *adj.*

dun•ga•ree (dŭng′gə-rē′) *n.* **1.** A sturdy, often blue denim fabric. **2. dungarees** Pants or overalls made of this. [Hindi *duṁgrī.*]

dung beetle *n.* Any of various beetles of the family Scarabaeidae that form balls of dung on which they feed and in which they lay their eggs.

Dun•ge•ness crab (dŭn′jə-nĕs′, -nĭs) *n.* An edible crab *(Cancer magister)* common along the Pacific coast from Alaska to northern California. [After *Dungeness,* a town of northwest Washington.]

dun•geon (dŭn′jən) *n.* **1.** A dark, often underground chamber or cell used to confine prisoners. **2.** A donjon. [ME *donjon,* castle keep, dungeon < OFr., keep, prob. < Med.Lat. *domniō, domniōn-,* the lord's tower < Lat. *dominus,* master. See **dem-** in App.]

dung•hill (dŭng′hĭl′) *n.* **1.** A heap of animal excrement. **2.** A foul degraded condition or place.

du•nite (do͞o′nīt′, dŭn′īt′) *n.* A dense igneous rock that consists mainly of olivine and is a source of magnesium. [After Mount *Dun* in northern South Island, New Zealand.] **—du•nit′ic** (do͞o-nĭt′ĭk, də-) *adj.*

dunk (dŭngk) *v.* **dunked, dunk•ing, dunks** *—tr.* **1.** To plunge into liquid; immerse. **2.** To dip (food) into a liquid before eating it. **3.** *Basketball* To slam (a ball) through the basket from above. *—intr.* **1.** To submerge oneself briefly in water. **2.** *Basketball* To make a dunk shot. ❖ *n.* **1.** The act or an instance of dunking. **2.** *Basketball* A dunk shot. [Penn. Dutch *dunke* < MHGer. *dunken* < OHGer. *dunkōn.*] **—dunk′er** *n.*

Dunk•er (dŭng′kər) also **Dun•kard** (-kərd) *n.* A member of the German Baptist Brethren, a group opposed to military service and the taking of legal oaths. [Penn. Dutch < *dunke,* to dunk (< baptism by immersion). See DUNK.]

Dun•kirk (dŭn′kûrk′) or **Dun•kerque** (dœN-kĕrk′) A city of N France on the North Sea. In World War II more than 330,000 Allied troops were evacuated from its beaches in the face of enemy fire (May–Jun. 1940). Pop. 73,120.

dunk shot *n. Basketball* A shot made by jumping and slamming the ball down through the basket.

dun•lin (dŭn′lĭn) *n.* A rust-brown and white sandpiper *(Calidris alpina)* native to northern regions of North America, Europe, and Asia. [DUN[2] + –LIN(G)[1].]

Dun•more (dŭn-môr′, -mōr′), 4th Earl of. Title of John Murray. 1732–1809. British colonial governor of Virginia (1771–76) who opposed the independence of the colonies.

dun•nage (dŭn′ĭj) *n.* **1.** Loose packing material used to protect a ship's cargo from damage during transport. **2.** Personal baggage. [ME *dennage* < MDu. *denne,* flooring of a ship.]

Duns Sco•tus (dŭnz skō′təs), **John** Known as "the Subtle Doctor." 1265?–1308. Scottish Franciscan monk and theologian who wrote *On the First Principal.*

Dun•stan (dŭn′stən), Saint. 924–988. English prelate who as archbishop of Canterbury (959–978) attempted to integrate the Danes and the English as a nation.

du•o (do͞o′ō, dyo͞o′ō) *n., pl.* **-os 1.** *Music* A duet, esp. two performers singing or playing together. **2.** Two people or two things in close association. [Ital. < Lat., two. See **dwo-** in App.]

duo– *pref.* Two: *duopoly.* [Lat. < *duo,* two. See **dwo-** in App.]

du•o•de•cil•lion (do͞o′ō-dĭ-sĭl′yən, dyo͞o′-) *n.* **1.** The cardinal number equal to 10^{39}. **2.** *Chiefly British* The cardinal number equal to 10^{72}. [Lat. *duodecim,* twelve; see DUODECIMAL + (M)ILLION.] **—du′o•de•cil′lion** *adj.* **—du′o•de•cil′lionth** *adj., adv. & n.*

du•o•dec•i•mal (do͞o′ə-dĕs′ə-məl, dyo͞o′-) *adj.* **1.** Of, relating to, or based on the number 12. **2.** Of or relating to twelfths. ❖ *n.* A twelfth. [< Lat. *duodecimus,* twelfth < *duodecim,* twelve : *duo,* two; see **dwo-** in App. + *decem,* ten; see **dek̂m** in App.]

du•o•dec•i•mo (do͞o′ə-dĕs′ə-mō′, dyo͞o′-) *n., pl.* **-mos 1.** The size (5 by 7¾ inches) of book pages formed by folding single sheets from a printing press into 12 leaves each. **2.** A book composed of pages of this size. [Lat. *(in) duodecimō,* (in) a twelfth, ablative of *duodecimus,* twelfth. See DUODECIMAL.]

du•o•de•num (do͞o′ə-dē′nəm, dyo͞o′-, do͞o-ŏd′n-əm, dyo͞o-) *n., pl.* **du•o•de•na** (do͞o′ə-dē′nə, dyo͞o′-, do͞o-ŏd′n-ə, dyo͞o-) or **du•o•de•nums** The beginning portion of the small intestine, starting at the lower end of the stomach and extending to the jejunum. [ME < Med.Lat., short for *intestīnum duodēnum digitōrum,* intestine of twelve finger-widths (in length) < Lat. *duodēnum,* genitive pl. of *duodēnī,* twelve each < *duodecim,* twelve. See DUODECIMAL.] **—du′o•de′nal** (do͞o′ə-dē′nəl, dyo͞o′-, do͞o-ŏd′n-əl, dyo͞o-) *adj.*

du•o•logue (do͞o′ə-lôg′, -lŏg′, dyo͞o′-) *n.* A dialogue or conversation between two persons. [DUO + (MONO)LOGUE.]

duo•mo (dwō′mō) *n., pl.* **-mos** A cathedral, esp. one in Italy. [Ital. See DOME.]

du•op•o•ly (do͞o-ŏp′ə-lē, dyo͞o-) *n.* An economic or political condition in which power is concentrated in two persons or groups. [DUO– + (MONO)POLY.]

dupe (do͞op, dyo͞op) *n.* **1.** An easily deceived person. **2.** A person who functions as the tool of another person or power. ❖ *tr.v.* **duped, dup•ing, dupes** To deceive (an unwary person). See Syns at **deceive.** [Fr. < OFr., prob. alteration of *huppe,* hoopoe (< the bird's stupid appearance). See HOOPOE.] **—dup′a•bil′i•ty** *n.* **—dup′a•ble** *adj.* **—dup′er** *n.*

dup•er•y (do͞o′pə-rē, dyo͞o′-) *n., pl.* **-ies** The act of duping or the condition of having been duped.

du•ple (do͞o′pəl, dyo͞o′-) *adj.* **1.** Consisting of two; double. **2.** *Music* Consisting of two or a multiple of two beats to the measure. [Lat. *duplus.* See **dwo-** in App.]

du•plex (do͞o′plĕks′, dyo͞o′-) *adj.* **1.** Twofold; double. **2.** Having two apartments, divisions, or floors. **3.** Relating to or being a single assembly of machinery having two identical units capable of operating simultaneously or independently. **4.** *Electronics* Of or relating to a communications mode that provides simultaneous transmission and reception in both directions. ❖ *n.* **1.** A house divided into two living units or residences. **2.** Something that is duplex. [Lat. See **dwo-** in App.] **—du•plex′i•ty** (-plĕk′sĭ-tē) *n.*

duplex apartment *n.* An apartment having rooms on two adjoining floors connected by an inner staircase.

du•pli•cate (do͞o′plĭ-kĭt, dyo͞o′-) *adj.* **1.** Identically copied from an original. **2.** Existing or growing in two corresponding parts; double. **3.** Of or being a manner of play in cards in which several different partnerships or teams play the same deals and compare scores at the end. ❖ *n.* **1.** An identical copy; a facsimile. **2.** One that corresponds exactly to another, esp. an original. **3.** A duplicate card game. ❖ *v.* (-kāt′) **-cat•ed, -cat•ing, -cates** *—tr.* **1.** To make an exact copy of. **2.** To make twofold; double. **3.** To make or perform again; repeat. *—intr.* To become duplicate. [ME < Lat. *duplicātus,* p. part. of *duplicāre,* to double < *duplex, duplic-,* twofold. See **dwo-** in App.] **—du′pli•ca•ble, du′pli•cat′a•ble** (-kā′tə-bəl) *adj.* **—du′pli•cate•ly** *adv.* **—du′pli•ca′tive** *adj.* **—du′pli•ca•to′ry** (-kĭ-tôr′ē, -tōr′ē) *adj.*

du•pli•ca•tion (do͞o′plĭ-kā′shən, dyo͞o′-) *n.* **1a.** The act or procedure of duplicating. **b.** The condition of being duplicated. **2.** A duplicate; a replica. **3.** *Genetics* **a.** The occurrence of a repeated section of genetic material in a chromosome. **b.** The formation of such a duplication.

du•pli•ca•tor (do͞o′plĭ-kā′tər, dyo͞o′-) *n.* A machine, such as a mimeograph, that reproduces printed or written material.

du•plic•i•tous (do͞o-plĭs′ĭ-təs, dyo͞o-) *adj.* Given to or marked by deliberate deceptiveness in behavior or speech. **—du•plic′i•tous•ly** *adv.* **—du•plic′i•tous•ness** *n.*

du•plic•i•ty (do͞o-plĭs′ĭ-tē, dyo͞o-) *n., pl.* **-ties 1a.** Deliberate deceptiveness in behavior or speech. **b.** An instance of duplicity; double-dealing. **2.** The quality or state of being twofold or double. [ME *duplicite* < OFr. < LLat. *duplicitās,* doubleness < Lat. *duplex, duplic-,* twofold. See **dwo-** in App.]

Du Pont de Ne•mours (do͞o pŏnt′ də nə-mo͝or′, dü pôN′), **Pierre Samuel** 1739–1817. French-born economist and politician who helped negotiate the Louisiana Purchase (1803). His son **Éleuthère Irénée** (1771–1834) is best known for founding a gunpowder works (1802) in Delaware.

du Pré (do͞o prā′, dyo͞o), **Jacqueline** 1945–87. British cellist noted for her performance of Elgar's *Concerto.*

Du•que de Ca•xi•as (do͞o′kē də kə-shē′əs, do͞o′kĭ dĭ kä-shē′äs) A city of SE Brazil, a suburb of Rio de Janeiro. Pop. 665,343.

du•ra•ble (do͝or′ə-bəl, dyo͝or′-) *adj.* **1.** Capable of withstanding wear and tear or decay. **2.** Able to perform or compete over a long period, as by avoiding injuries. **3.** Lasting; stable: *a durable friendship.* **4.** *Economics* Not depleted or consumed by use. ❖ *n. Economics* A durable manufactured product, such as an automobile.

Dungeness crab
Cancer magister

dunk shot

duomo
Santa Maria dell'Assunta, Siena, Italy

ă	pat	oi	boy
ā	pay	ou	out
âr	care	o͝o	took
ä	father	o͞o	boot
ĕ	pet	ŭ	cut
ē	be	ûr	urge
ĭ	pit	th	thin
ī	pie	*th*	this
îr	pier	hw	which
ŏ	pot	zh	vision
ō	toe	ə	about, item
ô	paw		

Stress marks:
′ (primary);
′ (secondary), as in
lexicon (lĕk′sĭ-kŏn′)

[ME < OFr. < Lat. *dūrābilis* < *dūrāre*, to last.] —**du′ra·bil′i·ty,** **du′ra·ble·ness** n. —**du′ra·bly** adv.

durable press n. See **permanent press.**

du·ral (dŏŏr′əl, dyŏŏr′-) adj. Of or relating to the dura mater.

du·ra ma·ter (dŏŏr′ə mā′tər, mă′-, dyŏŏr′ə) n. The outermost tough fibrous membrane covering the brain and the spinal cord and lining the inner surface of the skull. [ME < Med.Lat. *dūra māter* (cerebrī), hard mother (of the brain), dura mater (transl. of Ar. *'umm ad-dimāğ aṣ-ṣāfigah*, the dense mother of the brain, matrix of the brain) : Lat. *dūra*, fem. of *dūrus*, hard; see DURAMEN + Lat. *māter*, mother; see MATER.]

du·ra·men (dŏŏ-rā′mən, dyŏŏ-) n. See **heartwood.** [Lat. *dūrāmen*, hard growth of a vine < *dūrāre*, to harden < *dūrus*, hard. See deru- in App.]

du·rance (dŏŏr′əns, dyŏŏr′-) n. Confinement or restraint by force; imprisonment. [ME *duraunce*, duration < OFr. *durance* < *durer*, to last < Lat. *dūrāre*.]

Du·rand (də-rănd′), **Asher Brown** 1796–1886. Amer. artist known for his paintings of the Hudson R. valley.

Du·ran·go (də-răng′gō, dŏŏ-räng′-) A city of N-central Mexico NNW of Guadalajara; founded c. 1560. Pop. 257,915.

Du·rant (də-rănt′), **William James** Known as "Will." 1885–1981. Amer. historian who with his wife **Ariel** (1898–1981) wrote *The Story of Civilization* (11 volumes, 1935–75).

Du·ran·te (də-răn′tē), **Jimmy** 1893–1980. Amer. comedian remembered for his work on television and in films and Broadway shows, including *Red, Hot, and Blue* (1936).

du·ra·tion (dŏŏ-rā′shən, dyŏŏ-) n. **1.** Continuance or persistence in time. **2.** A period of existence or persistence. [ME *duracioun* < OFr. *duration* < Med.Lat. *dūrātiō, dūrātiōn-* < Lat. *dūrātus*, p. part. of *dūrāre*, to last.]

Dur·ban (dûr′bən) A city of E South Africa on **Durban Bay,** an inlet of the Indian Ocean; settled in 1824. Pop. 715,669.

dur·bar (dûr′bär′) n. **1.** A state reception formerly given by Indian princes for a British sovereign or one given for an Indian prince by his subjects. **2.** The court of an Indian prince. [Urdu *darbār*, audience hall, court < Pers. : *dar*, indoors (< MPers., door < OPers. *duvara*-); see dhwer- in App. + *bār*, audience hall (< East Iran. *dwāra*-, courtyard; see dhwer- in App.)]

Dü·rer (dŏŏr′ər, dyŏŏr′-, dü′rər), **Albrecht** 1471–1528. German painter and engraver who incorporated the classicism of the Italian Renaissance into N European art.

du·ress (dŏŏ-rĕs′, dyŏŏ-) n. **1.** Constraint by threat; coercion. **2.** *Law* **a.** Illegal coercion. **b.** Forcible confinement. [ME *duresse,* harshness, compulsion < OFr. *durece,* hardness < Lat. *dūritia* < *dūrus*, hard. See deru- in App.]

Dur·ga·pur (dŏŏr′gə-pŏŏr′, -gä-) A city of NE India NW of Calcutta. Pop. 425,836.

Dur·ham¹ (dûr′əm) A city of N-central NC E of Greensboro; settled c. 1750. Pop. 187,035.

Dur·ham² (dûr′əm) n. See **shorthorn.** [After *Durham,* a county of northern England.]

du·ri·an (dŏŏr′ē-ən, -än′, dyŏŏr′-) n. **1.** A southeast Asian tree (*Durio zibethinus*). **2.** The edible fruit of this plant, having a hard prickly rind and soft pulp. [Malay < *duri,* thorn.]

dur·ing (dŏŏr′ĭng, dyŏŏr′-) prep. **1.** Throughout the course or duration of. **2.** At some time in. [ME < pr. part. of *duren,* to last < OFr. *durer* < Lat. *dūrāre*.]

Durk·heim (dûrk′hīm, dür-kĕm′), **Émile** 1858–1917. French social scientist and a founder of sociology.

dur·mast (dûr′măst′) n. A European oak (*Quercus petraea*) with tough elastic wood. [Perh. alteration of *dun mast* : DUN² + MAST².]

durn (dûrn) *Chiefly Southern US interj., adv., adj., & v.* Variant of **darn².** See Regional Note at **damned.**

du·roc also **Du·roc** (dŏŏr′ŏk′, dyŏŏr′-) n. A large red hog of a breed developed in the 19th century in the United States. [After *Duroc,* a horse of the breed's developer.]

Du·ro·cher (də-rō′chər, -shər), **Leo Ernest** 1906–91. Amer. baseball player and manager remembered for his pithy sayings, such as "Nice guys finish last."

Du·roc-Jer·sey (dŏŏr′ŏk-jûr′zē, dyŏŏr′-) n. See **duroc.**

dur·ra also **dou·ra** or **dou·rah** (dŏŏr′ə) n. An Asian and northern African cereal plant (*Sorghum bicolor*). [Ar. *dura,* grain.]

Dur·rell (dûr′əl), **Lawrence George** 1912–90. British writer best known for *The Alexandria Quartet* (1957–60).

Dür·ren·matt (dŏŏr′ən-mät′, dyŏŏr′-, dür′-), **Friedrich** b. 1921. Swiss writer known for his absurdist novels and plays, such as *The Visit* (1956).

durst (dûrst) v. *Archaic* A past tense and a past participle of **dare.**

du·rum (dŏŏr′əm, dyŏŏr′-, dûr′-) n. A hardy wheat (*Triticum turgidum,* formerly *T. durum*) used chiefly in making pasta. [< Lat. *dūrum,* neut. of *dūrus,* hard. See deru- in App.]

Du·se (dŏŏ′zĕ), **Eleonora** 1859?–1924. Italian actress who was highly acclaimed for her roles in the plays of Gabriele D'Annunzio and Henrik Ibsen.

Du·shan·be (dŏŏ-shäm′bə, -shäm′-, -shän′-) The cap. of Tajikistan, in the W part of the republic. Pop. 602,000.

dusk (dŭsk) n. The darker stage of twilight, esp. in the evening. ❖ adj. Tending to darkness; dusky. ❖ intr. & tr.v. **dusked, dusk·ing, dusks** To become or make dark or dusky. [< ME, dark, alteration of OE *dox.*]

dusk·y (dŭs′kē) adj. **-i·er, -i·est 1.** Characterized by little or inadequate light; shadowy. **2.** Rather dark in color. See Syns at **dark.** —**dusk′i·ly** adv. —**dusk′i·ness** n.

dusky grouse n. See **blue grouse.**

Düs·sel·dorf (dŏŏs′əl-dôrf′, dŭs′-) A city of W-central Germany on the Rhine R. NNW of Cologne; chartered 1288. Pop. 514,936.

dust (dŭst) n. **1.** Fine dry particles of matter. **2.** A cloud of fine dry particles. **3.** Particles of matter regarded as the result of disintegration. **4a.** Earth, esp. when regarded as the substance of the grave. **b.** The surface of the ground. **5.** A debased or despised condition. **6.** Something of no worth. **7.** *Chiefly British* Rubbish readied for disposal. **8.** Confusion; agitation; commotion. ❖ v. **dust·ed, dust·ing, dusts** —tr. **1.** To remove dust from by wiping, brushing, or beating. **2.** To sprinkle with a powdery substance. **3.** To apply or strew in fine particles. —intr. **1.** To clean by removing dust. **2.** To cover itself with dust. Used of a bird. —**phrasal verb: dust off** To restore to use. [ME < OE *dūst.*]

dust·bin (dŭst′bĭn′) n. *Chiefly British* A trash can.

dust bowl n. A region left arid by drought and dust storms. [After the *Dust Bowl,* region in the S-central US that was stricken with drought in the 1930s.]

dust bunny n. *Informal* A mass of fine, dry particles, esp. of hair and skin;, that is formed by static electricity.

dust cover n. **1.** A removable or hinged plastic cover used to protect a piece of equipment. **2.** See **dust jacket.**

dust devil n. A small whirlwind, usu. of short duration, that swirls dust, debris, and sand to great heights.

dust·er (dŭs′tər) n. **1.** One that dusts, esp.: **a.** A cloth or brush used to remove dust. **b.** A device for sifting or scattering a powdered substance. **2.** A smock worn to protect one's clothing from dust. **3.** A woman's loose dress-length housecoat.

dust·ing (dŭs′tĭng) n. **1.** A light sprinkling: *a dusting of new snow.* **2.** *Slang* A beating or defeat.

dusting powder n. A fine powder used on the skin.

dust jacket n. **1.** A removable paper cover used to protect a book. **2.** A cardboard sleeve for a phonograph record.

dust mite n. Either of two mites, *Dermatophagoides pteronyssinus* or *D. farinae,* that feed on shed skin cells and produce excrement that is a common household allergen.

dust mop n. A mop used dry to remove dust from floors.

dust·pan (dŭst′păn′) n. A short-handled pan or scoop into which dust is swept.

dust ruffle n. A gathered or pleated strip of cloth reaching from the bottom of a mattress or box spring to the floor.

dust storm n. A severe windstorm that sweeps clouds of dust across an extensive area, esp. in an arid region.

dust·up (dŭst′ŭp′) n. *Slang* A row; a dispute.

dust·y (dŭs′tē) adj. **-i·er, -i·est 1.** Covered or filled with dust. **2.** Consisting of or resembling dust; powdery. **3.** Tinged with gray. **4.** Timeworn; stale. —**dust′i·ly** adv. —**dust′i·ness** n.

dusty miller n. Any of various plants of the genera *Artemisia, Centaurea, Chrysanthemum, Lychnis,* and *Senecio,* having leaves and stems covered with dustlike down.

Dutch (dŭch) adj. **1a.** Of or relating to the Netherlands or its people or culture. **b.** Of or relating to the Dutch language. **2.** *Archaic* **a.** German. **b.** Of or relating to any of the Germanic peoples or languages. **3.** Of or relating to the Pennsylvania Dutch. ❖ n. **1a.** (used with a pl. verb) The people of the Netherlands. **b.** *Archaic* A Germanic people. **c.** The Pennsylvania Dutch. **2a.** The official West Germanic language of the Netherlands and one of the official languages of Belgium. **b.** See **Pennsylvania Dutch** 2. **3.** *Slang* Anger or temper. —**idioms: go Dutch** To pay one's own expenses on a date or outing. **in Dutch** In disfavor or trouble. [ME *Duch,* German, Dutch < MDu. *Dūtsch.* See teutā- in App.]

Dutch auction n. An auction in which an item is initially offered at a high price that is lowered until a bid is made and the item sold.

Dutch cheese n. *Chiefly Northern US* See **cottage cheese.**

Dutch clover n. See **white clover.**

Dutch courage n. *Informal* Courage from drinking liquor.

Dutch door n. A door divided in two horizontally so that either part can be left open or closed.

Dutch East Indies See **Indonesia.**

Dutch elm disease n. A disease of elm trees caused by the fungus *Ceratocystis ulmi,* characterized by brown streaks in the wood and resulting in eventual death. [< its having been discovered in the Netherlands.]

Dutch Guiana See **Suriname.**

Dutch hoe n. See **scuffle².**

Dutch·man (dŭch′mən) n. **1a.** A man who is a native or inhabitant of the Netherlands. **b.** A man of Dutch ancestry. **2a.** *Archaic* A member of any of the Germanic peoples of central or northern Europe. **b.** *Northern & Western US* A person of German ancestry. **3. dutchman** Something used to conceal faulty construction.

Dutch·man's breeches (dŭch′mənz) pl.n. (used with a sing. or pl. verb) *Chiefly Northern US* A woodland plant (*Dicentra cucullaria*) of eastern North America having yellowish flowers with two spurs.

Dutchman's pipe n. See **pipe vine.**

Dutch metal n. An alloy of 80 percent copper and 20 percent zinc

Albrecht Dürer
detail from a self-portrait, 1500

dust storm
near Tsavo, Kenya

Dutch door

Dutchman's breeches
Dicentra cucullaria

used to make jewelry and as an imitation of gold leaf.
Dutch oven *n.* **1.** A large heavy pot or kettle, usu. of cast iron and with a tight lid, used for slow cooking. **2.** A metal utensil open on one side and equipped with shelves, placed before an open fire for baking or roasting food. **3.** A wall oven in which food is baked by means of preheated brick walls.
Dutch treat *n.* An outing in which all pay for themselves.
Dutch uncle *n.* A stern, candid critic or adviser.
Dutch West Indies See **Netherlands Antilles.**
Dutch•wom•an (dŭch′wo͝om′ən) *n.* **1.** A woman who is a native or inhabitant of the Netherlands. **2.** A woman of Dutch ancestry.
du•te•ous (do͞o′tē-əs, dyo͞o′-) *adj.* Obedient or dutiful. [< DUTY.] **—du′te•ous•ly** *adv.*
du•ti•a•ble (do͞o′tē-ə-bəl, dyo͞o′-) *adj.* Subject to import tax.
du•ti•ful (do͞o′tĭ-fəl, dyo͞o′-) *adj.* **1.** Careful to fulfill obligations. **2.** Expressing or filled with a sense of obligation. **—du′ti•ful•ly** *adv.* **—du′ti•ful•ness** *n.*
du•ty (do͞o′tē, dyo͞o′-) *n., pl.* **-ties 1.** An act or a course of action required by custom, law, or religion. **2a.** Moral obligation. **b.** The compulsion felt to meet such obligation. **3.** A service, function, or task assigned to one, esp. in the armed forces. **4.** Function or work; service. See Syns at **function. 5.** A government tax, esp. on imports. **6a.** The work performed by a machine under specified conditions. **b.** A measure of efficiency expressed as the amount of work done per unit of energy used. **7.** The total volume of water required to irrigate an area in order to cultivate a crop until harvest. ***—idioms:*** **duty bound** Obliged. **off duty** Not engaged in or responsible for assigned work. **on duty** Engaged in or responsible for assigned work. [ME *duete* < AN < *due*, var. of OFr. *deu*, due. See DUE.]
du•ty-free (do͞o′tē-frē′, dyo͞o′-) *adj.* **1.** Exempt from customs duties: *duty-free merchandise.* **2.** Of, relating to, or being a region or establishment in which imported goods are exempt from customs duties: *a duty-free shop.* **—du′ty-free′** *adv.*
du•um•vir (do͞o-ŭm′vər, dyo͞o-) *n.* A member of a duumvirate. [Lat. : *duum*, genitive pl. of *duo*, two; see **dwo-** in App. + *vir*, man; see **wī-ro-** in App.]
du•um•vi•rate (do͞o-ŭm′vər-ĭt, dyo͞o-) *n.* **1.** Any of various two-man executive boards in the Roman Republic. **2.** A regime or partnership of two persons.
Du•va•lier (do͞o′väl-yā′, dü-), **François** Known as "Papa Doc." 1907–71. Haitian dictator who was elected president in 1957 and declared himself president for life in 1964. His son **Jean-Claude** (b. 1951), "Baby Doc," succeeded him in 1971 but fled the country in 1986 after widespread civil unrest.
du•vet (do͞o-vā′, dyo͞o-) *n.* A quilt, usu. with a washable cover, used in place of a bedspread and top sheet. [Fr., down < OFr., alteration of *dumet*, dim. of *dum* < ON *dūnn.*]
du•ve•tyn also **du•ve•tyne** (do͞o′və-tēn′, dyo͞o′-, do͞o′və-tēn′, dyo͞o′-) *n.* A soft short-napped fabric with a twill weave, made of wool, cotton, rayon, or silk. [Fr. *duvetine* < *duvet*, down. See DUVET.]
du Vi•gneaud (do͞o vēn′yō, dyo͞o), **Vincent** 1901–78. Amer. biochemist who won a 1955 Nobel Prize.
Du•wa•mish (də-wä′mĭsh) also **Dwa•mish** (dwä′mĭsh) *n., pl.* **Duwamish** or **-mish•es** also **Dwamish** or **-mish•es 1.** A member of a Native American people of the eastern shore of Puget Sound near Seattle, Washington. **2.** Their Coast Salish language.
D.V. *abbr.* **1.** *Latin* Deo volente (God willing) **2.** Douay Version
DVD (dē′vē-dē′) *n.* A high-density compact disk, esp. one that holds high-resolution audio-visual material. [*d(igital) v(ideo) d(isk)* and *d(igital) v(ersatile) d(isk).*]
Dvi•na (dvē-nä′) **1.** also **Northern Dvina** A river, c. 748 km (465 mi), of W Russia flowing N and NE into **Dvina Bay,** an arm of the White Sea. **2.** also **Western Dvina** A river rising in W-central Russia and flowing c. 1,022 km (635 mi) generally W through Belarus and Latvia to the Gulf of Riga.
DVM *abbr.* Doctor of Veterinary Medicine
Dvo•rak (dvôr′ăk) *adj.* Of, relating to, or being a configuration of typewriter or computer keyboard keys arranged to increase the speed and ease of typing, the home row of keys being for the characters A, O, E, U, I, D, H, T, N, and S. [After August *Dvorak* (1894–1975), American educator.]
Dvoř•ák (dvôr′zhäk, -zhăk), **Anton** or **Antonín** 1841–1904. Czechoslovakian composer best known for his final symphony, *From the New World* (1893).
DVR *abbr.* digital video recorder
DW *abbr.* **1.** dead weight **2.** distilled water
D/W *abbr. Law* dock warrant
dwarf (dwôrf) *n., pl.* **dwarfs** or **dwarves** (dwôrvz) **1a.** An abnormally small person, often having limbs and features atypically proportioned or formed. **b.** An atypically small animal or plant. **2.** A small creature resembling a human, appearing in legends and fairy tales. **3.** A dwarf star. ❖ *v.* **dwarfed, dwarf•ing, dwarfs** *—tr.* **1.** To check the natural growth or development of; stunt. **2.** To cause to appear small by comparison. *—intr.* To become stunted or grow smaller. [ME *dwerf* < OE *dweorh.*] **—dwarf′ish** *adj.* **—dwarf′ish•ness** *n.*
dwarf cornel *n.* A herbaceous plant *(Cornus canadensis)* of northern North America having creeping rhizomes, scarlet fruit, and greenish flowers surrounded by four white bracts.
dwarf huckleberry *n.* See **dangleberry.**
dwarf•ism (dwôr′fĭz′əm) *n.* A pathological condition of arrested growth having various causes.
dwarf shoot *n.* A lateral branch that is much smaller than the main one, as in the cedar, larch, and ginkgo.
dwarf star *n.* A star, such as the sun, having relatively low mass, small size, and average or below average luminosity.
dweeb (dwēb) *n. Slang* A person regarded as socially inept or foolish, often on account of being overly studious. [?]
dwell (dwĕl) *intr.v.* **dwelt** (dwĕlt) or **dwelled, dwell•ing, dwells 1.** To live as a resident; reside. **2.** To be in a given place or condition. **3a.** To fasten one's attention. See Syns at **brood. b.** To speak or write at length. [ME *dwellen* < OE *dwellan*, to mislead, delay, dwell.] **—dwell′er** *n.*
dwell•ing (dwĕl′ĭng) *n.* A place to live in; an abode.
DWI *abbr.* driving while intoxicated
Dwight (dwīt), **Timothy** 1752–1817. Amer. cleric and educator who was a leading supporter of Federalism.
dwin•dle (dwĭn′dl) *v.* **-dled, -dling, -dles** *—intr.* To become gradually less until little remains. *—tr.* To cause to dwindle. See Syns at **decrease.** [Frequentative of ME *dwinen*, to waste away < OE *dwīnan*, to shrink. See **dheu-**[2] in App.]
dwt. *abbr.* pennyweight
Dy The symbol for the element **dysprosium.**
dy. *abbr.* **1.** delivery **2.** duty
dy•ad (dī′ăd′, -əd) *n.* **1.** Two individuals or units regarded as a pair. **2.** *Biology* One pair of homologous chromosomes due to division of a tetrad during meiosis. **3.** *Chemistry* A divalent atom or radical. **4.** *Mathematics* A function that draws a correspondence from any vector **u** to the vector (**v**•**u**)**w** and is denoted **vw**, where **v** and **w** are a fixed pair of vectors and **v**•**u** is the scalar product of **v** and **u.** ❖ *adj.* Made up of two units. [< Gk. *duas, duad-* < *duo*, two. See **dwo-** in App.]
dy•ad•ic (dī-ăd′ĭk) *adj.* **1.** Twofold. **2.** Of or relating to a dyad. ❖ *n. Mathematics* The sum of a finite number of dyads.
Dy•ak (dī′ăk′) *n.* Variant of **Dayak.**
dy•ar•chy (dī′är′kē) *n.* Variant of **diarchy.**
dyb•buk (dĭb′o͝ok, dē-bo͝ok′) *n., pl.* **dyb•buks** or **dyb•buk•im** (dĭ-bo͝ok′ĭm, dē′bo͞o-kēm′) In Jewish folklore, the wandering soul of a dead person that enters the body of a living person and controls his or her behavior. [Yiddish *dibek* < Heb. *dibbūq*, prob. < *dābaq*, to cling.]
dye (dī) *n.* **1.** A substance used to color materials. **2.** A color imparted by dyeing. ❖ *v.* **dyed, dye•ing, dyes** *—tr.* To color (a material), esp. by soaking in a solution. *—intr.* To take on or impart color. ***—idiom:*** **of the deepest dye** Of the most extreme sort. [ME *deie* < OE *dēag, dēah.*] **—dy′er** *n.*
dyed-in-the-wool (dīd′ĭn-*th*ə-wo͝ol′) *adj.* **1.** Thoroughgoing; out-and-out. **2.** Dyed before being woven into cloth.
Dy•er (dī′ər), **Mary** d. 1660. English-born Amer. Quaker martyr who was twice banished from Boston because of her beliefs and hanged after returning to the city a second time.
dy•er's broom (dī′ərz) *n.* See **dyer's greenweed.**
dyer's greenweed *n.* A small Eurasian shrub *(Genista tinctoria)* having yellow flower clusters that yield a dye.
dyer's rocket *n.* A European plant *(Reseda luteola)* having long spikes of small flowers that yield a yellow dye.
dy•er's-weed (dī′ərz-wēd′) *n.* Any of various plants yielding coloring matter used as dye.
dye•stuff (dī′stŭf′) *n.* See **dye** 1.
dye•wood (dī′wo͝od′) *n.* A wood used as a dyestuff.
dy•ing (dī′ĭng) *v.* Present participle of **die**[1]. ❖ *adj.* **1.** About to die. **2.** Drawing to an end; declining: *the dying hours of the empire.* **3.** Done or uttered just before death.
dyke[1] (dīk) *n. & v.* Variant of **dike**[1].
dyke[2] (dīk) also **dike** *n. Offensive Slang* Used as a disparaging term for a lesbian. [?] **—dyke′y** *adj.*
Dy•lan (dĭl′ən), **Bob** Orig. Robert Zimmerman. b. 1941. Amer. musician and composer who drew on blues, country and western, and folk music to create distinctive protest music in the 1960s.
dyn *abbr.* dyne
dy•nam•ic (dī-năm′ĭk) *adj.* also **dy•nam•i•cal** (-ĭ-kəl) **1a.** Of or relating to energy or to objects in motion. **b.** Of or relating to the study of dynamics. **2.** Characterized by continuous change, activity, or progress. **3.** Marked by intensity and vigor; forceful. **4.** Of or relating to variation of intensity, as in musical sound. ❖ *n.* **1.** An interactive system or process, esp. one involving competing or conflicting forces. **2.** A force. [Fr. *dynamique*, ult. < Gk. *dunamikos*, powerful < *dunamis*, power < *dunasthai*, to be able. See **deu-**[2] in App.] **—dy•nam′i•cal•ly** *adv.*
dynamical system *n. Mathematics* A space and its transformations, such as the solar system and its transformations over time in accordance with celestial mechanics.
dynamic RAM *n.* See **DRAM.**
dy•nam•ics (dī-năm′ĭks) *n.* **1a.** (*used with a sing. verb*) The branch of mechanics concerned with the effects of forces on the motion of a body or system of bodies, esp. of forces that do not originate within the system itself. **b.** (*used with a pl. verb*) The forces and motions that characterize a system. **2.** (*used with a pl. verb*) The social, intellectual, or moral forces that produce activity and change in a given sphere. **3.** (*used with a pl. verb*) Variation

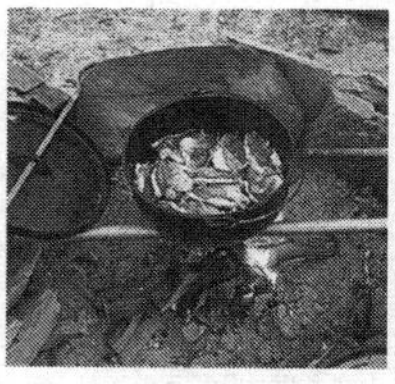

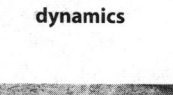

Dutch oven

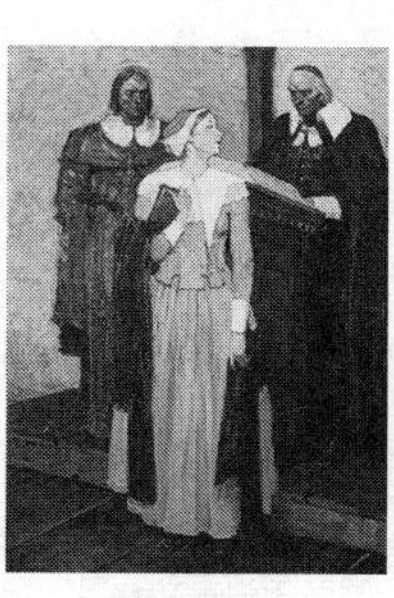

Mary Dyer
detail from a painting by
Edwin Austin Abbey
(1852–1911)

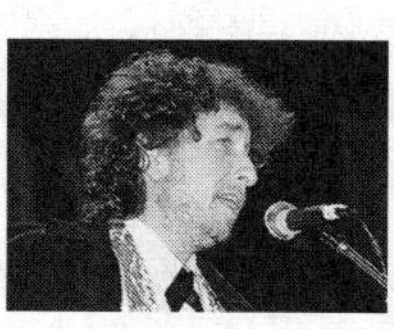

Bob Dylan

ă	pat	oi	boy
ā	pay	ou	out
âr	care	o͝o	took
ä	father	o͞o	boot
ĕ	pet	ŭ	cut
ē	be	ûr	urge
ĭ	pit	th	thin
ī	pie	*th*	this
îr	pier	hw	which
ŏ	pot	zh	vision
ō	toe	ə	about,
ô	paw		item

Stress marks:
′ (primary);
′ (secondary), as in
lexicon (lĕk′sĭ-kŏn′)

in force or intensity, esp. in musical sound. **4.** (*used with a sing. verb*) Psychodynamics.

dy·na·mism (dī′nə-mĭz′əm) *n.* **1.** Any of various theories or philosophical systems that explain the universe in terms of force or energy. **2.** A process or mechanism responsible for the development or motion of a system. **3.** Continuous change, activity, or progress; vigor. [Fr. *dynamisme* < Gk. *dunamis*, power. See DYNAMIC.] —**dy′na·mist** *n.* —**dy′na·mis′tic** *adj.*

dy·na·mite (dī′nə-mīt′) *n.* **1.** Any of a class of powerful explosives composed of nitroglycerin or ammonium nitrate dispersed in an absorbent medium with a combustible dope and an antacid, used in blasting and mining. **2.** *Slang* **a.** Something exceptionally exciting or wonderful. **b.** Something exceptionally dangerous. ❖ *tr.v.* -**mit·ed**, -**mit·ing**, -**mites** **1.** To blow up, shatter, or otherwise destroy with or as if with dynamite. **2.** To charge with dynamite. ❖ *adj. Slang* Outstanding; superb: *a dynamite performance.* [Swed. *dynamit* < Gk. *dunamis*, power. See DYNAMIC.] —**dy′na·mit′er** *n.*

dy·na·mo (dī′nə-mō′) *n., pl.* -**mos** **1.** A generator, esp. one for producing direct current. **2.** An extremely energetic and forceful person. [Short for *dynamoelectric machine.*]

dy·na·mo·e·lec·tric (dī′nə-mō′ĭ-lĕk′trĭk) also **dy·na·mo·e·lec·tri·cal** (-trĭ-kəl) *adj.* Of or relating to the conversion of mechanical energy to electrical energy or vice versa. [Gk. *dunamis*, power; see DYNAMIC + ELECTRIC.]

dy·na·mom·e·ter (dī′nə-mŏm′ĭ-tər) *n.* Any of several instruments used to measure mechanical power. [Fr. *dynamomètre* < Gk. *dunamis*, power; see DYNAMIC + -*mètre*, -meter.] —**dy′na·mo·met′ric** (-mō-mĕt′rĭk), **dy′na·mo·met′ri·cal** (-rĭ-kəl) *adj.* —**dy′na·mom′e·try** *n.*

dy·na·mo·tor (dī′nə-mō′tər) *n.* A rotating electric machine with two armatures, used to convert alternating current to direct current. [Gk. *dunamis*, power; see DYNAMIC + MOTOR.]

dy·nast (dī′năst′, -nəst) *n.* A ruler, esp. a hereditary one. [Lat. *dynastēs* < Gk. *dunastēs*, lord < *dunasthai*, to be able. See deu-² in App.]

dy·nas·ty (dī′nə-stē) *n., pl.* -**ties** **1.** A succession of rulers from the same family or line. **2.** A family or group that maintains power for several generations. [ME *dynastie* < OFr. < Lat. *dynastīa*, lordship < Gk. *dunasteia* < *dunastēs*, lord. See DYNAST.] —**dy·nas′tic** (dī-năs′tĭk) *adj.* —**dy·nas′ti·cal·ly** *adv.*

dy·na·tron (dī′nə-trŏn′) *n.* A tetrode with grid and plate potentials so arranged that plate current decreases when plate potential increases. [Gk. *dunamis*, power; see DYNAMIC + -TRON.]

dyne (dīn) *n.* A centimeter-gram-second unit of force, equal to the force required to impart an acceleration of one centimeter per second per second to a mass of one gram. [< Gk. *dunamis*, power. See DYNAMIC.]

dy·node (dī′nōd′) *n.* An electrode used in certain electron tubes to provide secondary emission. [Gk. *dunamis*, power; see DYNAMIC + -ODE.]

dys- *pref.* **1.** Abnormal: *dysplasia.* **2a.** Impaired: *dysgraphia.* **b.** Difficult: *dysphonia.* **3.** Bad: *dyslogistic.* [Lat. *dys-*, bad < Gk. *dus-*.]

dys·ar·thri·a (dĭs-är′thrē-ə) *n.* Difficulty in articulating words, caused by impairment of the muscles used in speech. [DYS- + Gk. *arthron*, joint, (vocal) articulation.]

dys·cal·cu·li·a (dĭs′kăl-kyōō′lē-ə) *n.* Impairment of the ability to solve mathematical problems, usu. resulting from brain dysfunction. [DYS- + CALCUL(ATE) + -IA¹.]

dys·cra·sia (dĭs-krā′zhə, -zhē-ə) *n.* An abnormal bodily condition, esp. of the blood. [Med.Lat., bad mixture, disease < Gk. *duskrāsiā* : *dus-*, dys- + *krāsis*, mixing.]

dys·en·ter·y (dĭs′ən-tĕr′ē) *n.* An inflammatory disorder of the lower intestinal tract, usu. caused by a bacterial, parasitic, or protozoan infection and resulting in pain, fever, and severe diarrhea, often accompanied by the passage of blood and mucus. [ME *dissenterie* < OFr. < Lat. *dysenteria* < Gk. *dusenteriā* : *dus-*, dys- + *enteron*, intestine; see en in App.] —**dys′en·ter′ic** *adj.*

dys·func·tion also **dis·func·tion** (dĭs-fŭngk′shən) *n.* Abnormal or impaired functioning, esp. of a body system or social group. —**dys·func′tion·al** *adj.*

dys·gen·e·sis (dĭs-jĕn′ĭ-sĭs) *n.* Defective or abnormal development of an organ, esp. of the gonads.

dys·gen·ic (dĭs-jĕn′ĭk) *adj.* Relating to or causing the deterioration of hereditary qualities in offspring.

dys·gen·ics (dĭs-jĕn′ĭks) *n.* (*used with a sing. verb*) The biological study of the factors producing degeneration in offspring, esp. of a particular race or species.

dys·graph·i·a (dĭs-grăf′ē-ə) *n.* Impairment of the ability to write, usu. caused by brain dysfunction or disease. [NLat. : DYS- + Gk. -*graphiā*, -graphy.] —**dys·graph′ic** *adj.*

dys·ki·ne·sia (dĭs′kə-nē′zhə, -kī-) *n.* An impairment in the ability to control movements, characterized by spasmodic or re-

petitive motions or lack of coordination.

dys·lex·i·a (dĭs-lĕk′sē-ə) *n.* A learning disorder marked by impairment of the ability to recognize and comprehend written words. [NLat. : DYS- + Gk. *lexis*, speech (< *legein*, to speak; see leg- in App.).]

dys·lex·ic (dĭs-lĕk′sĭk) or **dys·lec·tic** (-tĭk) *n.* A person who is affected by dyslexia. ❖ *adj.* Of or relating to dyslexia.

dys·lo·gis·tic (dĭs′lə-jĭs′tĭk) *adj.* Conveying censure. [DYS- + (EU)LOGISTIC.] —**dys′lo·gis′ti·cal·ly** *adv.*

dys·men·or·rhe·a also **dys·men·or·rhoe·a** (dĭs-mĕn′ə-rē′ə) *n.* Painful menstruation. [NLat. : DYS- + Gk. *mēn*, month; see mē-¹ in App. + -RRHEA.] —**dys·men′or·rhe′al** (-rē′əl), **dys·men′or·rhe′ic** (-rē′ĭk) *adj.*

dys·pep·si·a (dĭs-pĕp′shə, -sē-ə) *n.* Disturbed digestion; indigestion. [Lat. < Gk. *duspepsiā* : *dus-*, dys- + -*pepsiā*, digestion; see pekʷ- in App.]

dys·pep·tic (dĭs-pĕp′tĭk) *adj.* **1.** Relating to or having dyspepsia. **2.** Of or displaying a morose disposition. ❖ *n.* A person who is affected by dyspepsia. —**dys·pep′ti·cal·ly** *adv.*

dys·pha·gia (dĭs-fā′jə, -jē-ə) *n.* Difficulty in swallowing. —**dys·phag′ic** (-făj′ĭk) *adj.*

dys·pha·sia (dĭs-fā′zhə, -zhē-ə) *n.* Impairment of speech and verbal comprehension, esp. when associated with brain injury. —**dys·pha′sic** (-zĭk) *adj. & n.*

dys·pho·ni·a (dĭs-fō′nē-ə) *n.* Difficulty in speaking, usu. evidenced by hoarseness. [NLat. : DYS- + Gk. -*phōniā*, -phony.] —**dys·phon′ic** (-fŏn′ĭk) *adj.*

dys·pho·ri·a (dĭs-fôr′ē-ə, -fōr′-) *n.* An emotional state characterized by anxiety, depression, or unease. [NLat. < Gk. *dusphoriā*, distress < *dusphoros*, hard to bear : *dus-*, dys- + -*phoros*, -phorous.] —**dys·phor′ic** (-fôr′ĭk, -fōr′-) *adj.*

dys·pla·sia (dĭs-plā′zhə, -zhē-ə) *n.* Abnormal development or growth of tissues, organs, or cells. —**dys·plas′tic** (-plăs′tĭk) *adj.*

dysp·ne·a (dĭsp-nē′ə) *n.* Difficulty in breathing, often associated with lung or heart disease and resulting in shortness of breath. [Lat. *dyspnoea* < Gk. *duspnoia* : *dus-*, dys- + *pnoiā*, -pnoia, breathing.] —**dysp·ne′ic** (-nē′ĭk) *adj.*

dys·pro·si·um (dĭs-prō′zē-əm, -zhē-əm) *n. Symbol* **Dy** A soft, silvery rare-earth element used in nuclear research. Atomic number 66; atomic weight 162.50; melting point 1,407°C; boiling point 2,600°C; specific gravity 8.536; valence 3. See table at **element.** [NLat. < Gk. *dusprositos*, difficult to approach (< its rarity in nature) : *dus-*, dys- + *prositos*, approachable (< *prosienai*, to approach : *pros-*, toward + *ienai*, i-, to go; see ei- in App.).]

dys·rhyth·mi·a (dĭs-rĭth′mē-ə) *n.* An abnormality in an otherwise normal rhythmic pattern, as of brain waves. [NLat. : DYS- + Lat. *rhythmus*, rhythm; see RHYTHM.]

dys·tel·e·ol·o·gy (dĭs-tĕl′ē-ŏl′ə-jē, -tē′lē-) *n.* **1.** The doctrine of purposelessness in nature. **2.** Purposelessness in natural structures, as manifested by the existence of vestigial or nonfunctional organs or parts. —**dys·tel′e·o·log′i·cal** (-ə-lŏj′ĭ-kəl) *adj.* —**dys·tel′e·ol′o·gist** *n.*

dys·thy·mi·a (dĭs-thī′mē-ə) *n.* A mood disorder characterized by mild depression. [NLat. *dysthȳmia* < Gk. *dusthūmiā*, despondency : *dus-*, dys- + -*thūmiā*, -thymia.] —**dys·thy′mic** *adj.*

dys·to·ni·a (dĭs-tō′nē-ə) *n.* Abnormal muscle tone, usu. involving prolonged involuntary muscle contraction. —**dys·ton′ic** (-tŏn′ĭk) *adj.*

dys·to·pi·a (dĭs-tō′pē-ə) *n.* **1.** An imaginary place or state in which the condition of life is extremely bad, as from deprivation, oppression, or terror. **2.** A work describing such a place or state. [DYS- + (U)TOPIA.]

dys·to·pi·an (dĭs-tō′pē-ən) *adj.* **1.** Of or relating to a dystopia. **2.** Dire; grim.

dys·troph·ic (dĭ-strŏf′ĭk, -strōf′fĭk) *adj.* **1.** *Medicine* Of, relating to, or afflicted with dystrophy. **2.** *Ecology* Having brownish acidic waters, a high concentration of humic matter, and a small plant population. Used of a lake or pond. —**dys·tro·phi·ca′tion** (dĭs′trə-fĭ-kā′shən) *n.*

dys·tro·phy (dĭs′trə-fē) also **dys·tro·phi·a** (dĭ-strō′fē-ə) *n.* **1.** A degenerative disorder caused by inadequate or defective nutrition. **2.** Any of several disorders, esp. muscular dystrophy, in which the muscles weaken and atrophy. **3.** *Ecology* The condition of being dystrophic.

dys·u·ri·a (dĭs-yŏōr′ē-ə) *n.* Painful or difficult urination. [ME *dissure, dissuria* < OFr. *dissure* < Med.Lat. *dissuria* < LLat. *dysūria* < Gk. *dusouriā* : *dus-*, dys- + -*ouriā*, -uria.] —**dys·u′ric** (-yŏōr′ĭk) *adj.*

dz. *abbr.* dozen

Dzer·zhinsk (dər-zhĭnsk′, dzĭr-) A city of W-central Russia on the Oka R. W of Kazan. Pop. 286,479.

Dzham·bul (jäm-bōōl′) See **Zhambyl.**

Dzun·gar·i·a (dzōōng-gâr′ē-ə, zōōng-) A vast historical region of NW China; a Mongol kingdom from the 11th to the 14th cent. and conquered by the Chinese in the 1750s.

Ee

e¹ or **E** (ē) *n.*, *pl.* **e's** or **E's** also **es** or **Es** **1.** The fifth letter of the modern English alphabet. **2.** Any of the speech sounds represented by the letter *e*. **3.** The fifth in a series. **4.** Something shaped like the letter E. **5. E** A grade that indicates failing status. **6.** *Music* **a.** The third tone in the scale of C major or the fifth tone in the relative minor scale. **b.** A key or scale in which E is the tonic. **7. e** *Mathematics* The base of the natural system of logarithms, having a numerical value of approx. 2.71828.

e² *abbr.* electron

E *abbr.* **1a.** east **b.** eastern **2.** energy **3.** *Baseball* error **4.** excellent

E. *abbr.* **1.** earl **2.** English

e– also **E–** *pref.* Computer or computer network: *e-cash; e-zine.* See Usage Note at **virtual.** [< E-MAIL.]

E•a (ā′ä) *n. Mythology* The Babylonian god of primordial waters. [Akkadian < O Akkadian **hayy-*, living.]

each (ēch) *adj.* Being one of two or more considered individually; every: *Each person voted.* ❖ *pron.* Every one of a group considered individually; each one. ❖ *adv.* For or to each one; apiece. [ME *ech* < OE *ǣlc.*]

USAGE NOTE The traditional rule holds that when the subject of a sentence begins with *each*, it is grammatically singular, and the verb and following pronouns must be singular as well: *Each of the suites has its own bath.* When *each* follows a plural subject, however, the verb and subsequent pronouns remain in the plural: *The suites each have their own baths.* See Usage Notes at **every, he¹.**

---

each other *pron.* Each the other. Used to indicate that a relationship or action is reciprocal: *The boys like each other.*

ea•ger¹ (ē′gər) *adj.* **-ger•er, -ger•est 1.** Having or showing keen interest, intense desire, or impatient expectancy. See Usage Note at **anxious. 2.** *Obsolete* Tart; sharp; cutting. [ME *eger*, sour, sharp, impetuous < AN *egre* < Lat. *ācer.* See **ak-** in App.] **—ea′ger•ly** *adv.* **—ea′ger•ness** *n.*

ea•ger² (ē′gər, ā′gər) *n.* Variant of **eagre.**

eager beaver *n. Informal* One who is exceptionally industrious or zealous. **—ea′ger-bea′ver** (ē′gər-bē′vər) *adj.*

ea•gle (ē′gəl) *n.* **1.** Any of various large birds of prey of the family Accipitridae, having a hooked bill, keen vision, and long broad wings. **2.** A representation of an eagle used as an emblem or insignia. **3.** A gold coin formerly used in the United States, stamped with an eagle on the reverse side and worth ten dollars. **4.** A golf score of two strokes under par on a hole. ❖ *v.* **-gled, -gling, -gles** *—tr.* To shoot (a hole in golf) in two strokes under par. *—intr.* To score an eagle in golf. [ME *egle* < AN < O Provençal *aigla* < Lat. *aquila.*]

eagle eye *adj.* **1.** Keen eyesight. **2.** The ability or tendency to pay attention to detail. **—ea•gle-eyed** (ē′gəl-īd′) *adj.*

eagle ray *n.* Any of numerous rays of the family Myliobatidae, having massive jaws and winglike pectoral fins.

Eagle Scout *n.* One holding the highest rank in the Boy Scouts.

ea•glet (ē′glĭt) *n.* A young eagle.

ea•gre also **ea•ger** (ē′gər, ā′gər) *n.* See **bore³.** [?]

Ea•kins (ā′kĭnz), **Thomas** 1844–1916. Amer. painter whose works include *Max Schmitt in a Single Scull* (1871).

eal•dor•man (ôl′dər-mən) *n.* The chief magistrate of a district in Anglo-Saxon England. [OE. See ALDERMAN.]

Eames (ēmz), **Charles** 1907–78. Amer. designer noted for his chairs made of aluminum tubing and molded plywood.

Eames chair A trademark for a functional chair with seat and back shaped to the contours of the human body.

ear¹ (îr) *n.* **1.** *Anatomy* **a.** The vertebrate organ of hearing, which maintains equilibrium as well as senses sound. **b.** The part of this organ that is externally visible. **2.** An invertebrate organ analogous to the mammalian ear. **3.** The sense of hearing. **4.** Sensitivity or receptiveness to sound, esp.: **a.** Sharpness or refinement of hearing: *a good ear for harmony.* **b.** The ability to play a passage of music solely from hearing it: *plays the piano by ear.* **c.** Responsiveness to the sounds or forms of spoken language. **5.** Sympathetic or favorable attention. **6.** Something resembling the external ear in position or shape, esp.: **a.** A flexible tuft of feathers located above the eyes of certain birds that functions only in visual communication. **b.** A projecting handle, as on a vase. **7.** A small box in the upper corner of the page in a newspaper or periodical that contains a printed notice. **8. ears** *Informal* Headphones. **—idioms: all ears** *Informal* Acutely attentive. **coming out of (one's) ears** In more than adequate amounts; overabundant. **give (or lend) an ear** To pay close attention; listen attentively. **have (or keep) an ear to the ground** To be on the watch

for new trends or information. **in one ear and out the other** Without any influence or effect; unheeded. **on its** (or **someone's) ear** In a state of amazement, excitement, or uproar. **play it by ear** *Informal* To act according to the circumstances; improvise. [ME *ere* < OE *ēare.* See **ous-** in App.]

ear² (îr) *n.* The seed-bearing spike of a cereal plant, such as corn. ❖ *intr.v.* **eared, ear•ing, ears** To form or grow ears. [ME *ere* < OE *ēar.* See **ak-** in App.]

ear•ache (îr′āk′) *n.* Pain in the ear; otalgia.

ear canal *n.* The narrow tubelike passage through which sound enters the ear.

ear•drop (îr′drŏp′) *n.* **1.** An earring, esp. one with a pendant. **2. eardrops** Liquid medicine administered into the ear.

ear•drum (îr′drŭm′) *n.* The thin oval-shaped membrane that separates the middle ear from the external ear.

eared (îrd) *adj.* **1.** Having ears or earlike projections. **2.** Having a specified kind or number of ears.

eared seal *n.* Any of various seals of the family Otariidae, which includes the fur seals, characterized by external ears, oarlike front flippers, and hind flippers for walking on land.

ear•flap (îr′flăp′) *n.* A flap on a cap that may be turned down to cover the ears.

ear•ful (îr′fʊl′) *n.* **1.** An abundant or excessive amount of something heard. **2.** Gossip, esp. of an intimate or scandalous nature. **3.** A scolding or reprimand.

Ear•hart (âr′härt′), **Amelia** 1897?–1937. Amer. aviator who was the first woman to fly solo across the Atlantic Ocean (1932). She crashed and disappeared in the Pacific Ocean while attempting to fly around the world.

ear•ing (îr′ĭng) *n. Nautical* A short line attaching an upper corner of a sail to the yard. [Perh. < EAR¹.]

earl (ûrl) *n.* **1.** A British nobleman next in rank above a viscount and below a marquis. **2.** Used as a title for such a nobleman. [ME *erl*, nobleman of high rank < OE *eorl.*]

ear•lap (îr′lăp′) *n.* See **earflap.**

earl•dom (ûrl′dəm) *n.* The rank, title, or territory of an earl.

ear•less seal (îr′lĭs) *n.* Any of various seals of the family Phocidae, marked by short fore flippers, reduced hind flippers for swimming, and the absence of external ears.

ear•lobe also **ear lobe** (îr′lōb′) *n.* The soft, fleshy, pendulous lower part of the external ear.

ear•lock (îr′lŏk′) *n.* A lock of curled hair that hangs in front of the ear.

ear•ly (ûr′lē) *adj.* **-li•er, -li•est 1.** Of or occurring near the beginning of a given series, period of time, or course of events. **2a.** Of or belonging to a previous or remote period of time. **b.** Of or belonging to an initial stage of development. **3.** Occurring, developing, or appearing before the expected or usual time. **4.** Maturing or developing relatively soon. **5.** Occurring in the near future. ❖ *adv.* **-lier, -liest 1a.** Near the beginning of a given series, period of time, or course of events. **b.** At or near the beginning of the morning. **2.** At or during a remote or initial period. **3.** Before the expected or usual time. **4.** Soon in relation to others of its kind. **—idiom: early on** At an early stage or point. [ME *erli* < OE *ǣrlīce* : *ǣr*, before + *-līce*, adv. suff.; see –LY².] **—ear′li•ness** *n.*

Early, Jubal Anderson 1816–94. Amer. Confederate general whose forces threatened Washington DC (1864) but were ultimately defeated by Union troops.

early bird *n. Informal* **1.** A person who arises early in the morning. **2.** One that arrives or takes place early or before others. [< the expression "*The early bird catches the worm.*"] **—ear′ly-bird′** (ûr′lē-bûrd′) *adj.*

early music *n.* Western music from the start of the Middle Ages to about 1750, including the medieval, Renaissance, and Baroque periods.

ear•mark (îr′märk′) *n.* **1.** An identifying feature or characteristic. **2.** An identifying mark on the ear of a domestic animal. ❖ *tr.v.* **-marked, -mark•ing, -marks 1.** To reserve or set aside for a particular purpose. See Syns at **allocate. 2.** To mark in an identifying or distinctive way. **3.** To mark the ear of (a domestic animal) for identification.

ear•muff (îr′mŭf′) *n.* Either of a pair of ear coverings often attached to a headband and worn to protect the ears.

earn (ûrn) *tr.v.* **earned, earn•ing, earns 1.** To gain esp. for the performance of service, labor, or work. **2.** To acquire or deserve as a result of effort or action. **3.** To yield as return or profit. **—idiom: earn (one's) spurs** (or **stripes**) To gain a position through hard work, often in the face of difficulties. [ME *ernen* < OE *earnian.*] **—earn′er** *n.*

eagle ray
spotted eagle ray
Aetobatus narinari

Eames chair

Amelia Earhart

SYNONYMS **earn, deserve, merit, rate, win** These verbs mean to gain as a result of one's behavior or effort: *earns a large salary; deserves congratulations; a plan that merits consideration; an event that rates attention; a candidate who won wide support.*

earn² (ûrn) *intr.v.* **earned, earn·ing, earns** Obsolete To yearn. [ME *ernen,* var. of *yernen.* See YEARN.]

earned run (ûrnd) *n.* Baseball A run scored without the aid of an error, used in computing earned run averages.

earned run average *n.* Baseball A measure of a pitcher's performance obtained by dividing the total of earned runs by the total of innings pitched and multiplying by nine.

ear·nest¹ (ûr′nĭst) *adj.* **1.** Marked by or showing deep sincerity or seriousness: *an earnest gesture of goodwill.* **2.** Of an important or weighty nature; grave. See Syns at **serious.** —*idiom:* **in earnest 1.** With a purposeful or sincere intent: *study in earnest.* **2.** Serious; determined. [ME *ernest* < OE *eornoste.* See **er-** in App.] —**ear′nest·ly** *adv.* —**ear′nest·ness** *n.*

ear·nest² (ûr′nĭst) *n.* **1.** Money paid in advance as part payment to bind a contract or bargain. **2.** A token of something to come; a promise or assurance. [ME *ernest,* var. of *ernes,* alteration of OFr. *erres,* pl. of *erre,* pledge < Lat. *arra,* alteration of *arrabō* < Gk. *arrabōn,* earnest-money < Canaanite *ʾirrabōn,* surety < *ʾārab,* to pledge.]

earn·ings (ûr′nĭngz) *pl.n.* **1.** Salary or wages. **2a.** Business profits. **b.** Gains from investments.

Earp (ûrp), **Wyatt** 1848–1929. Amer. law officer involved in the gunfight at the O.K. Corral in Tombstone AZ (1881).

ear·phone (îr′fōn′) *n.* A device that converts electric signals to audible sound and fits over or in the ear.

ear·piece (îr′pēs′) *n.* **1.** A part, as of a hearing aid, that fits in or is held next to the ear. **2.** See **earphone. 3.** Either of the two parts of an eyeglasses frame that fit on the ear.

ear·plug (îr′plŭg′) *n.* **1.** An object made of a soft pliable material and fitted into the ear canal to block the entry of water or sound. **2.** An earphone, esp. one that fits into the ear.

ear·ring (îr′rĭng, îr′ĭng) *n.* An ornament worn on or pendent from the ear, esp. the earlobe.

ear rot *n.* Any of various fungus diseases of corn characterized by decay and molding of the ears.

ear sew·er (sō′ər) *n.* Northern California See **dragonfly.** See Regional Note at **dragonfly.**

ear shell *n.* **1.** See **abalone. 2.** The shell of the abalone.

ear·shot (îr′shŏt′) *n.* The range within which sound can be heard by the unaided ear; hearing distance.

ear·split·ting (îr′splĭt′ĭng) *adj.* Loud and shrill enough to hurt the ears.

earth (ûrth) *n.* **1a.** The land surface of the world. **b.** The softer friable part of land; soil, esp. productive soil. **2.** often **Earth** The third planet from the sun. See table at **planet. 3.** The realm of mortal existence; the temporal world. **4.** The human inhabitants of the world. **5a.** Worldly affairs and pursuits. **b.** Everyday life; reality. **6.** The substance of the human body; clay. **7.** The lair of a burrowing animal. **8.** *Chiefly British* The ground of an electrical circuit. **9.** *Chemistry* Any of several metallic oxides, such as alumina, that are difficult to reduce. ❖ *v.* **earthed, earth·ing, earths** —*tr.* **1.** To cover or heap (plants) with soil for protection. **2.** To chase (an animal) into an underground hiding place. —*intr.* To burrow or hide in the ground. Used of a hunted animal. —*idiom:* **on earth** Among all the possibilities: *Why on earth did you go?* [ME *erthe* < OE *eorthe.*]

Earth

earth·born (ûrth′bôrn′) *adj.* **1.** Springing from or born on the earth. **2.** Human; mortal: *earthborn existence.*

earth·bound also **earth-bound** (ûrth′bound′) *adj.* **1.** Fastened in or to the soil. **2.** Confined or restricted to the earth or to earthly concerns. **b.** Unimaginative; ordinary.

earth·en (ûr′thən, -thən) *adj.* Made of earth or clay: *an earthen fortification; an earthen pot.* **2.** Earthly; worldly.

earth·en·ware (ûr′thən-wâr′, -thən-) *n.* Pottery made from a porous clay that is fired at relatively low temperatures.

earth·light (ûrth′līt′) *n.* See **earthshine.**

earth·ling (ûrth′lĭng) *n.* **1.** One, esp. a human, that inhabits the planet Earth. **2.** A person devoted to the world.

earth·ly (ûrth′lē) *adj.* **1.** Of, relating to, or characteristic of this earth. **2a.** Terrestrial; not heavenly or divine. **b.** Worldly: *earthly delights.* **3.** Conceivable; possible: *no earthly reason for agreeing.* —**earth′li·ness** *n.*

earth·man (ûrth′măn′) *n.* A human inhabitant of the planet Earth; an earthling.

earth mother *n.* **1.** A goddess or female spirit representing the earth as the giver of life. **2.** A woman combining maternal and sensual qualities.

earth·mov·er (ûrth′moo′vər) *n.* A machine, such as a backhoe, used for digging or pushing earth. —**earth′mov′ing** *adj.*

earth·nut (ûrth′nŭt′) *n.* **1a.** A Eurasian and northern African plant (*Conopodium denudatum*) having tuberous roots that are edible when roasted. **b.** The tuber of this plant. **2.** Any of various other similar plants, such as the peanut.

earth·quake (ûrth′kwāk′) *n.* A sudden movement of the earth's crust caused by the release of stress accumulated along geologic faults or by volcanic activity.

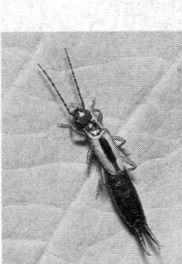

earwig
European earwig
Forficula auricularia

earth·rise (ûrth′rīz′) *n.* The rising of the earth above the horizon as seen from the moon.

earth science *n.* Any of several sciences concerned with the origin, structure, and physical phenomena of the earth.

earth·shak·ing (ûrth′shā′kĭng) *adj.* Very important.

earth·shat·ter·ing (ûrth′shăt′ər-ĭng) *adj.* Earthshaking.

earth·shine (ûrth′shīn′) *n.* The sunlight reflected from the earth's surface that illuminates part of the moon.

earth smoke *n.* See **fumitory.**

earth station *n.* An on-ground terminal linked to a spacecraft or satellite by an antenna and associated electronic equipment for transmitting or receiving messages, tracking, or control.

earth tone *n.* Any of various rich warm colors with tones of brown.

earth·ward (ûrth′wərd) *adv. & adj.* To or toward the earth. —**earth′wards** *adv.*

earth·work (ûrth′wûrk′) *n.* **1.** An earthen embankment, esp. one used as a fortification. **2.** *Engineering* Excavation and embankment of earth. **3.** A work of art made by altering an area of land or a natural geographic feature.

earth·worm (ûrth′wûrm′) *n.* Any of various terrestrial annelid worms of the class Oligochaeta, esp. those of the family Lumbricidae, that help aerate and enrich soil.

earth·y (ûr′thē) *adj.* **-i·er, -i·est 1.** Of, relating to, consisting of, or resembling earth: *an earthy smell.* **2.** Relating to or characteristic of this world; worldly. **3.** Crude or off-color; indecent. **4.** Hearty or uninhibited; natural: *an earthy enjoyment of life.* **5.** Unadorned and simple in style. —**earth′i·ly** *adv.* —**earth′i·ness** *n.*

ear trumpet *n.* A horn-shaped device formerly used to direct sound into the ear of a hearing-impaired person.

ear tuft *n.* See **ear¹** 6a.

ear·wax (îr′wăks′) *n.* The yellowish waxlike secretion of certain glands lining the canal of the external ear.

ear·wig (îr′wĭg′) *n.* Any of various elongate insects of the order Dermaptera, having a pair of pincerlike appendages protruding from the rear of the abdomen. ❖ *tr.v.* **-wigged, -wig·ging, -wigs** To attempt to influence by persistent confidential argument or talk. [ME *erwig* < OE *ēarwicga* : *ēare,* ear; see EAR¹ + *wicga,* insect; see **wegh-** in App.]

ear·wit·ness (îr′wĭt′nĭs) *n.* A person who has heard someone or something and can bear witness to the fact. [EAR¹ + (EYE)WITNESS.]

ear·worm (îr′wûrm′) *n.* See **corn earworm.**

ease (ēz) *n.* **1.** The condition of being comfortable or relieved. **2a.** Freedom from pain, worry, or agitation. **b.** Freedom from constraint or embarrassment; naturalness. **3a.** Freedom from difficulty or effort. **b.** Readiness or dexterity in performance; facility. **4.** Freedom from financial difficulty; affluence: *a life of ease.* **5.** A state of rest, relaxation, or leisure. ❖ *v.* **eased, eas·ing, eas·es** —*tr.* **1.** To free from pain, worry, or agitation. **2a.** To lessen the discomfort or pain of. **b.** To alleviate; assuage: *a drug to ease the pain.* **3.** To give respite from: *eased the burden on her staff.* **4.** To slacken the strain, pressure, or tension of; loosen. **5.** To reduce the difficulty or trouble of: *eased the requirements.* **6.** To move or maneuver slowly and carefully. —*intr.* **1.** To lessen, as in discomfort, pressure, or stress. **2.** To move or proceed with little effort. —*idiom:* **at ease 1.** In a relaxed position, esp. standing silently at rest with the right foot stationary. **2.** Used as a command for troops to assume a relaxed position. [ME *ese* < OFr. *aise,* elbowroom, physical comfort < VLat. *asium.*]

ease·ful (ēz′fəl) *adj.* Affording or characterized by comfort and peace; restful. —**ease′ful·ly** *adv.* —**ease′ful·ness** *n.*

ea·sel (ē′zəl) *n.* An upright frame for displaying or supporting something, such as an artist's canvas. [Du. *ezel,* ass, easel < MDu. *esel* < Lat. *asellus,* dim. of *asinus.*]

ease·ment (ēz′mənt) *n.* **1.** The act of easing or the condition of being eased. **2.** Something that affords ease or comfort. **3.** *Law* A right, such as a right of way, afforded a person to make limited use of another's real property.

eas·i·ly (ē′zə-lē) *adv.* **1.** In an easy manner; with ease. **2.** Without question; certainly. **3.** In all likelihood; well.

east (ēst) *n.* **1a.** The cardinal point on the compass 90° clockwise from due north and directly opposite west. **b.** The direction of the earth's axial rotation. **2.** An area or a region lying in the east. **3.** often **East a.** The eastern part of the earth, esp. eastern Asia. **b.** The eastern part of a region or country. **4.** often **East a.** The region of the United States east of the Allegheny Mountains and north of the Mason-Dixon Line. **b.** The former Communist bloc of countries in Asia and Eastern Europe. ❖ *adj.* **1.** To, toward, of, facing, or in the east. **2.** Originating in or coming from the east: *a cool east wind.* ❖ *adv.* In, from, or toward the east. [ME *est* < OE *ēast.* See **aus-** in App.]

East Africa A region of E Africa including S Somalia, Kenya, and Tanzania.

East Anglia A region and Anglo-Saxon kingdom of E England; settled by Angles in the late 5th cent. A.D. and controlled by the Danes from 886 to 917.

East Asia A region of Asia coextensive with the Far East. —**East Asian** *adj. & n.*

East Berlin See **Berlin.**

east·bound (ēst′bound′) *adj.* Going toward the east.

East•bourne (ēst′bôrn′, -bōrn′) A borough of SE England on the English Channel SSE of London. Pop. 77,300.

east by north n. The direction or compass point halfway between due east and east-northeast, or 78°45′ east of due north. ❖ *adv. & adj.* Toward or from east by north.

east by south n. The direction or compass point halfway between due east and east-southeast, or 101°15′ east of due north. ❖ *adv. & adj.* Toward or from east by south.

East Cape See Cape **Dezhnev**.

East China Sea An arm of the W Pacific bounded by China, South Korea, Taiwan, and the Ryukyu and Kyushu islands.

East Coast A region of the E US along the Atlantic coastline, esp. the urban corridor from Boston to Washington DC.

East End A section of E London N of the Thames R.; long a densely populated working-class and immigrant area centered around the docks and warehouses.

Eas•ter (ē′stər) n. **1.** A Christian feast commemorating the Resurrection of Jesus, traditionally observed on the first Sunday following the full moon that occurs on or next after the vernal equinox. **2.** Eastertide. [ME *ester* < OE *ēastre*. See **aus-** in App.]

Easter egg n. A dyed or decorated egg associated with Easter.

Easter Island Locally **Ra•pa Nu•i** (rä′pə nōō′ē) An island of Chile in the S Pacific Ocean W of the mainland; famous for its colossal heads carved from volcanic rock.

Easter lily n. Any of various lilies, esp. *Lilium longiflorum* var. *eximium*, having large white trumpet-shaped flowers that are displayed during the Easter season.

east•er•ly (ē′stər-lē) adj. **1.** Situated toward the east. **2.** Coming or being from the east: *easterly winds.* ❖ *n., pl.* **-lies** A storm or wind coming from the east. —**east′er•ly** adv.

Easter Monday n. The Monday following Easter, observed as a holiday in some countries and in North Carolina.

east•ern (ē′stərn) adj. **1.** Situated in, toward, or facing the east. **2.** Coming from the east: *eastern breezes.* **3.** Native to or growing in the east. **4.** often **Eastern** Of, relating to, or characteristic of eastern regions or the East. **5. Eastern a.** Of or relating to the Eastern Church. **b.** Of or relating to the Eastern Orthodox Church. [ME *estern* < OE *ēasterne*. See **aus-** in App.] —**east′ern•ness′** n.

Eastern Church n. **1.** The church of the Byzantine Empire. **2.** The Eastern Orthodox Church. **3.** often **Eastern church** A Uniat church.

Eastern Empire The Byzantine Empire.

east•ern•er also **East•ern•er** (ē′stər-nər) n. A native or inhabitant of the east, esp. the eastern United States.

Eastern Europe The countries of E Europe, esp. those allied with the USSR in the Warsaw Pact (1955–91).

Eastern Ghats See **Ghats**.

Eastern Hemisphere The half of the earth comprising Europe, Africa, Asia, and Australia.

east•ern•most (ē′stərn-mōst′) adj. Farthest east.

Eastern Orthodox Church n. The body of modern churches, including the Greek and Russian Orthodox, that is derived from the church of the Byzantine Empire, adheres to the Byzantine rite, and acknowledges the honorary primacy of the patriarch of Constantinople.

Eastern Shore A region of MD and VA E of Chesapeake Bay.

Eastern Shoshone n. See **Shoshone** 1c.

Eastern Standard Time n. Standard time in the fifth time zone west of Greenwich, England, reckoned at 75° west and used, for example, in the eastern part of North America.

Eas•ter•tide (ē′stər-tīd′) n. The Easter season.

East Frisian Islands See **Frisian Islands**.

East Germanic n. The subdivision of the Germanic languages that includes Gothic.

East Germany Officially **German Democratic Republic**. A former country of N Europe on the Baltic Sea; formed in 1949 from the zone occupied by Soviet troops after World War II and reunified with West Germany in Oct. 1990. —**East German** adj. & n.

East In•dies (ĭn′dēz) Indonesia. The term is sometimes used to refer to all of Southeast Asia. —**East Indian** adj. & n.

east•ing (ē′stĭng) n. **1.** The difference in longitude between two positions as a result of movement to the east. **2.** Progress toward the east.

East•main (ēst′mān′) A river rising in central Quebec, Canada, and flowing c. 821 km (510 mi) E to James Bay.

East•man (ēst′mən), **George** 1854–1932. Amer. industrialist who invented a dry-plate process of photographic film development, flexible film, and a process for color photography.

east-north•east (ēst′nôrth′ēst′) n. The direction or compass point halfway between due east and northeast, or 67°30′ east of due north. ❖ *adj.* To, toward, of, facing, or in the east-northeast. ❖ *adv.* In, from, or toward the east-northeast.

East Pakistan A former region of S Asia on the Bay of Bengal; held by Pakistan from 1947 to 1971, when it achieved independence as Bangladesh.

East Prussia A historical region and former province of Prussia on the Baltic Sea; separated from Germany by the Polish Corridor from 1919 to 1939 and divided between Poland and the USSR in 1945.

East River A narrow tidal strait connecting Upper New York Bay with Long Island Sound and separating the boroughs of Manhattan and the Bronx from Brooklyn and Queens.

East Saint Louis A city of SW IL on the Mississippi R. opposite St. Louis MO. Pop. 31,542.

East Siberian Sea An arm of the Arctic Ocean from Wrangel I. to the New Siberian Is.

East Slavic n. A subdivision of the Slavic languages that includes Belarusian, Russian, and Ukrainian.

east-south•east (ēst′south′ēst′) n. The direction or compass point halfway between due east and southeast, or 112°30′ east of due north. ❖ *adj.* To, toward, of, facing, or in the east-southeast. ❖ *adv.* In, from, or toward the east-southeast.

East Timor See **Timor**.

east•ward (ēst′wərd) adv. & adj. Toward, to, or in the east. ❖ n. An eastward direction, point, or region. —**east′ward•ly** adv. & adj. —**east′wards** adv.

eas•y (ē′zē) adj. **-i•er, -i•est 1.** Capable of being accomplished or acquired with ease; posing no difficulty. **2.** Requiring or exhibiting little effort or endeavor; undemanding. **3.** Free from worry, anxiety, trouble, or pain. **4a.** Affording comfort or relief; soothing: *soft light that was easy on the eyes.* **b.** Prosperous; well-off. **5.** Causing little hardship or distress. **6.** Socially at ease. **7a.** Relaxed in attitude; easygoing. **b.** Not strict or severe; lenient. **8.** Readily exploited, imposed on, or tricked. **9a.** Not hurried or forced; moderate: *an easy pace.* **b.** Light; gentle. **10.** Not steep or abrupt; gradual. **11.** *Economics* **a.** Less in demand and therefore readily obtainable. **b.** Plentiful and therefore at low interest rates. **12.** Promiscuous; loose. ❖ *adv.* **1.** Without haste or agitation. **2.** With little effort; easily. **3.** In a restrained or moderate manner. **4.** Without much hardship or cost. —*idiom:* **easy as pie** *Informal* Capable of being accomplished or done with no difficulty. [ME *esi* < OFr. *aaisie*, p. part. of *aaisier*, to put at ease : *a-*, to (< Lat. *ad-*, ad- + *aise*, ease; see EASE).] —**eas′i•ness** n.

SYNONYMS *easy, simple, effortless* These adjectives mean requiring little effort or posing little if any difficulty. *Easy* applies to tasks that require little effort: *clear handwriting that is easy to read. Simple* implies lack of complexity that facilitates understanding or performance: *spoke in plain, simple terms. Effortless* refers to performance in which the application of great strength or skill makes the execution seem easy: *wrote effortless prose.*

easy chair n. A large, comfortable, well-upholstered chair.

eas•y•go•ing also **eas•y-go•ing** (ē′zē-gō′ĭng) adj. **1a.** Living without undue worry or concern; calm. **b.** Lax or negligent; careless. **c.** Relaxed in attitude or standards. **2.** Not rigorous; demanding, or stressful. **3.** Leisurely; unhurried.

easy street n. *Informal* A condition of financial security.

eat (ēt) v. **ate** (āt), **eat•en** (ēt′n), **eat•ing, eats** —*tr.* **1a.** To take into the body by the mouth for digestion or absorption. **b.** To take in and absorb as food: *a plant that eats insects.* **c.** To include habitually or by preference in one's diet. **2.** To consume, ravage, or destroy by or as if by ingesting. **3.** To erode or corrode: *Waves ate away the beach.* **4.** To produce by or as if by eating. **5.** *Slang* To absorb the cost or expense of. **6.** *Informal* To bother or annoy. **7.** *Vulgar Slang* To perform cunnilingus on. Often used with *out.* —*intr.* **1a.** To consume food. **b.** To have or take a meal. **2.** To exercise a consuming or eroding effect. **3.** To cause persistent annoyance or distress. —*phrasal verb:* **eat up** *Slang* **1.** To receive or enjoy enthusiastically or avidly. **2.** To believe without question. —*idioms:* **eat crow** To be forced to accept a humiliating defeat. **eat (one's) heart out 1.** To feel bitter anguish or grief. **2.** To be consumed by jealousy. **eat (one's) words** To retract something that one has said. **eat out of (someone's) hand** To be manipulated or dominated by another. **eat (someone) alive** *Slang* To overwhelm or defeat thoroughly. [ME *eten* < OE *etan*. See **ed-** in App.] —**eat′er** n.

eat•a•ble (ē′tə-bəl) adj. Fit to be eaten; edible: *an eatable meal.* ❖ n. **1.** Something fit to be eaten. **2. eatables** Food.

eat•er•y (ē′tə-rē) n., pl. **-ies** *Informal* A restaurant.

eat•ing (ē′tĭng) adj. **1.** Suitable for being eaten, esp. without cooking. **2.** Used in the ingestion of food, as at the table.

eating disorder n. Any of various psychological disorders, such as anorexia nervosa or bulimia, that involve insufficient or excessive food intake.

eats (ēts) pl.n. *Slang* Food, esp. snacks.

Eau Claire (ō klâr′) A city of W-central WI. Pop. 61,704.

eau de co•logne (ō′ də kə-lōn′) n., pl. **eaux de cologne** (ō′, ōz′) See **cologne**. [Fr. *eau de Cologne*. See COLOGNE.]

eau de vie (ō′ də vē′) n., pl. **eaux de vie** (ō′, ōz′) Colorless brandy distilled from fermented fruit juice. [Fr. *eau-de-vie* : *eau*, water + *de*, of + *vie*, life.]

eaves (ēvz) pl.n. The projecting overhang at the lower edge of a roof. [ME *eves* < OE *efes.* See **upo** in App.]

eaves•drop (ēvz′drŏp′) intr.v. **-dropped, -drop•ping, -drops** To listen secretly to the private conversation of others. [Prob. back-formation < *eavesdropper*, one who eavesdrops < ME *evesdropper* < *evesdrop*, place where water falls from the eaves < OE *yfesdrype.* See **upo** in App.] —**eaves′drop′per** n.

eaves spout n. *Northern US* See **gutter** 2.

eaves trough n. *Northern & Western US* See **gutter** 2.

E•ban (ē′bən), **Abba** b. 1915. South African-born Israeli politi-

Easter Island

ă	pat	oi	boy
ā	pay	ou	out
âr	care	ŏŏ	took
ä	father	ōō	boot
ĕ	pet	ŭ	cut
ē	be	ûr	urge
ĭ	pit	th	thin
ī	pie	*th*	this
îr	pier	hw	which
ŏ	pot	zh	vision
ō	toe	ə	about,
ô	paw		item

Stress marks:
′ (primary);
′ (secondary), as in
lexicon (lĕk′sĭ-kŏn′)

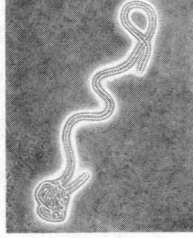
Ebola virus
transmission electron
micrograph of a single
Ebola virus strand

echidna
Tachyglossus aculeatus

echinacea

manner. **2.** A repetition or an imitation. **3.** A remnant or vestige. **4.** One who imitates another, as in opinions or dress. **5.** A sympathetic response. **6.** A consequence or repercussion. **7.** Repetition of certain sounds or syllables in poetry, as in echo verse. **8.** *Music* Soft repetition of a note or phrase. **9.** *Electronics* A reflected wave received by a radio or radar. ❖ *v.* **-oed, -o•ing, -oes** —*tr.* **1.** To repeat (a sound) by the reflection of sound waves from a surface. **2.** To repeat or imitate. —*intr.* **1.** To be repeated by or as if by an echo. **2.** To resound with or as if with an echo; reverberate. [ME < OFr. < Lat. *ēchō* < Gk. *ēkhō*.] **—ech′o•er** *n.* **—ech′o•ey** *adj.*

Echo *n. Greek Mythology* A nymph who pined away out of love for Narcissus until nothing but her voice remained.

ech•o•car•di•o•gram (ĕk′ō-kär′dē-ə-grăm′) *n.* A visual record produced by an echocardiograph.

ech•o•car•di•o•graph (ĕk′ō-kär′dē-ə-grăf′) *n.* An instrument that employs the differential transmission and reflection of ultrasonic waves to image structural and functional abnormalities of the heart. **—ech′o•car′di•o•graph′ic** *adj.* **—ech′o•car′di•og′ra•phy** (-ŏg′rə-fē) *n.*

echo chamber *n.* A room or enclosure with acoustically reflective walls that produce echoes or similar sound effects.

ech•o•en•ceph•a•lo•gram (ĕk′ō-ĕn-sĕf′ə-lə-grăm′, -ə-lō-) *n.* A visual record produced by an echoencephalograph.

ech•o•en•ceph•a•lo•graph (ĕk′ō-ĕn-sĕf′ə-lə-grăf′, -ə-lō-) *n.* An instrument that uses the differential transmission and reflection of ultrasonic waves to create a detailed visual image of the brain. **—ech′o•en•ceph′a•lo•graph′ic** *adj.* **—ech′o•en•ceph′a•log′ra•phy** (-lŏg′rə-fē) *n.*

ech•o•gram (ĕk′ō-grăm′) *n.* See **sonogram.**

e•chog•ra•phy (ĕ-kŏg′rə-fē) *n.* See **ultrasonography.**

e•cho•ic (ĕ-kō′ĭk) *adj.* **1.** Of or resembling an echo. **2.** Imitative of natural sounds; onomatopoeic: *an echoic word.*

ech•o•la•li•a (ĕk′ō-lā′lē-ə) *n.* **1.** *Medicine* The immediate and involuntary repetition of words or phrases just spoken by others. **2.** An infant's repetition of the sounds made by others. [ECHO + Gk. *laliā*, talk (< *lalos*, talkative).]

ech•o•lo•ca•tion (ĕk′ō-lō-kā′shən) *n.* **1.** A sensory system in certain animals, such as bats and dolphins, in which usu. high-pitched sounds are emitted and their echoes interpreted to determine the direction and distance of objects. **2.** *Electronics* A process for determining the location of objects by emitting sound waves and analyzing the waves reflected back to the sender by the object. **—ech′o•lo•cate′** *v.*

echo sounder *n.* A device for measuring depth of water by sending pressure waves down from the surface and recording the time until the echo returns from the bottom.

ech•o•vi•rus (ĕk′ō-vī′rəs) *n., pl.* **-rus•es** Any of a number of retroviruses of the family Picornaviridae, inhabiting the gastrointestinal tract and associated with various diseases. [*e(nteric) c(ytopathogenic) h(uman) o(rphan) virus.*]

echt (ĕkt) *adj.* Real; genuine. ❖ *adv.* Really; genuinely. [Ger. < MHGer. *echte*; akin to OHGer. *ēohaft*, customary.]

Eck (ĕk), **Johann** 1486–1543. German Roman Catholic theologian and opponent of the reforms of Martin Luther.

Eck•hart also **Eck•art** or **Eck•ardt** (ĕk′härt′, -ärt′), **Johannes** Known as "Meister Eckhart." 1260?–1327? German theologian regarded as the founder of mysticism in Germany.

é•clair (ā-klâr′, ā′klâr′) *n.* An oblong pastry filled with custard or whipped cream and usu. iced with chocolate. [Fr. < OFr. *esclair*, lightning < *esclairier*, to light up < VLat. **exclāriāre* < Lat. *exclārāre* : *ex-*, intensive pref.; see EX– + *clārus*, clear; see **kelə-** in App.]

e•clamp•si•a (ĭ-klămp′sē-ə) *n.* Coma and convulsions during or immediately after pregnancy, accompanied by edema, hypertension, and proteinuria. [NLat. < Gk. *eklampsis*, a shining forth, sudden development < *eklampein*, to shine forth : *ek-*, out; see ECTO– + *lampein*, to shine.] **—e•clamp′tic** (-tĭk) *adj.*

é•clat (ā-klä′, ā′klä′) *n.* **1.** Great brilliance, as of performance or achievement. **2.** Conspicuous success. **3.** Great acclamation or applause. **4.** *Archaic* Notoriety; scandal. [Fr., brilliance < OFr. *esclat*, splinter < *esclater*, to burst out, splinter, prob. of Gmc. orig.]

e•clec•tic (ĭ-klĕk′tĭk) *adj.* **1.** Selecting or employing individual elements from a variety of sources. **2.** Made up of or combining elements from a variety of sources. ❖ *n.* One that follows an eclectic method. [Gk. *eklektikos*, selective < *eklektos*, selected < *eklegein*, to select : *ek-*, out; see ECTO– + *legein*, to gather; see **leg-** in App.] **—e•clec′ti•cal•ly** *adv.*

e•clec•ti•cism (ĭ-klĕk′tə-sĭz′əm) *n.* An eclectic system.

e•clipse (ĭ-klĭps′) *n.* **1a.** The partial or complete obscuring of one celestial body by another. **b.** The period of time during which an eclipse occurs. **2.** A temporary or permanent dimming or cutting off of light. **3a.** A fall into obscurity or disuse; a decline. **b.** A disgraceful or humiliating end; a downfall: *the eclipse of the governor's career.* ❖ *tr.v.* **e•clipsed, e•clips•ing, e•clips•es 1a.** To cause an eclipse of. **b.** To obscure; darken. **2a.** To obscure or diminish in importance, fame, or reputation. **b.** To surpass; outshine. [ME < OFr. < Lat. *eclīpsis* < Gk. *ekleipsis* < *ekleipein*, to fail to appear, suffer an eclipse : *ek-*, out; see ECTO– + *leipein*, to leave; see **leikʷ-** in App.]

e•clip•tic (ĭ-klĭp′tĭk) *n.* **1.** The intersection plane of the earth's orbit with the celestial sphere, along which the sun appears to move as viewed from the earth. **2.** A great circle inscribed on a terrestrial globe inclined at an approx. angle of 23°27′ to the equator and representing the apparent path of the sun during a year. [ME *ecliptik* < Med.Lat. *(līnea) eclīptica*, ecliptic (line) < Lat. *eclīpticus*, of an eclipse < Gk. *ekleiptikos* < *ekleipein*, to fail to appear. See ECLIPSE.]

ec•lo•gite (ĕk′lə-jīt′) *n.* A coarse-grained greenish rock consisting primarily of garnet and sodic pyroxene. [Fr. *éclogite* < Gk. *eklogē*, selection (because the minerals it contains are not usu. found together). See ECLOGUE.]

ec•logue (ĕk′lôg′, -lŏg′) *n.* A pastoral poem, usu. in the form of a dialogue between shepherds. [ME *eclog* < Lat. *ecloga* < Gk. *eklogē*, selection < *eklegein*, to select. See ECLECTIC.]

e•clo•sion (ĭ-klō′zhən) *n.* The emergence of an adult insect from a pupal case or an insect larva from an egg. [Fr. *éclosion* < *éclore*, to open < OFr. < VLat. **exclaudere*, to shut out : Lat. *ex-*, ex- + Lat. *claudere*, to shut.]

ECM *abbr.* **1.** European Common Market **2.** electronic countermeasures (to jam or confuse transmissions)

E•co (ĕ′kō), **Umberto** b. 1932. Italian writer best known for his novels, including *The Name of the Rose* (1981).

eco– *pref.* Ecology; ecological: *ecosystem.* [< ECOLOGY.]

e•co•cide (ē′kō-sīd′, ĕk′ō-) *n.* Heedless or deliberate destruction of the natural environment, as by pollutants.

E. co•li (ē kō′lī) *n.* A bacillus *(Escherichia coli)* normally found in the human gastrointestinal tract and existing as numerous strains, some of which are capable of causing severe illness. [NLat. *E(scherichia) colī* : Theodor *Escherich* (1857–1911), German physician + Lat. *colī*, genitive of *colon*, colon; see COLON².]

e•col•o•gy (ĭ-kŏl′ə-jē) *n., pl.* **-gies 1a.** The science of the relationships between organisms and their environments. **b.** The relationship between organisms and their environment. **2.** The branch of sociology that studies the relationships between human groups and their physical and social environments. **3.** The study of the detrimental effects of modern civilization on the environment. [Ger. *Ökologie* : Gk. *oikos*, house; see **weik-** in App. + Ger. *-logie*, -logy (< Gk. *-logiā*).] **—ec′o•log′i•cal** (ĕk′ə-lŏj′ĭ-kəl, ē′kə-), **ec′o•log′ic** (-ĭk) *adj.* **—ec′o•log′i•cal•ly** *adv.* **—e•col′o•gist** *n.*

e•co•man•age•ment (ē′kō-măn′ĭj-mənt, ĕk′ō-) *n.* Any of various strategies to minimize the adverse effects of human activities on the environment.

e-com•merce (ē′kŏm′ərs) *n.* Commerce that is transacted electronically, as over the Internet.

e•con•o•met•rics (ĭ-kŏn′ə-mĕt′rĭks) *n.* *(used with a sing. verb)* Application of mathematical and statistical techniques to economics in the study of problems, theories, and models and in data analysis. **—e•con′o•met′ric** *adj.* **—e•con′o•met′ri•cal•ly** *adv.* **—e•con′o•me•tri′cian** (-mĭ-trĭsh′ən), **e•con′o•met′rist** *n.*

ec•o•nom•ic (ĕk′ə-nŏm′ĭk, ē′kə-) *adj.* **1a.** Of or relating to the production, development, and management of material wealth, as of a country or household. **b.** Of or relating to an economy. **2.** Of or relating to the science of economics. **3.** Of or relating to the practical necessities of life; material. **4a.** Financially rewarding; economical. **b.** Efficient; economical.

ec•o•nom•i•cal (ĕk′ə-nŏm′ĭ-kəl, ē′kə-) *adj.* **1.** Prudent and thrifty in management. See Syns at **sparing. 2.** Intended to save money, as by efficient operation; economic. **—ec′o•nom′i•cal•ly** *adv.*

economic rent *n.* See **rent**¹ 3.

ec•o•nom•ics (ĕk′ə-nŏm′ĭks, ē′kə-) *n.* **1.** *(used with a sing. verb)* The social science that deals with the production, distribution, and consumption of goods and services and with the theory and management of economies or economic systems. **2.** *(used with a sing. or pl. verb)* Economic matters, esp. relevant financial considerations.

e•con•o•mist (ĭ-kŏn′ə-mĭst) *n.* **1.** A specialist in economics. **2.** *Archaic* An economical person.

e•con•o•mize (ĭ-kŏn′ə-mīz′) *v.* **-mized, -miz•ing, -miz•es** —*intr.* **1.** To practice economy, as by reducing expenditures. **2.** To make economical use of something. —*tr.* To use or manage with thrift. **—e•con′o•miz′er** *n.*

e•con•o•my (ĭ-kŏn′ə-mē) *n., pl.* **-mies 1a.** Careful, thrifty management of resources, such as money, materials, or labor. **b.** An example or result of such management; a saving. **2a.** The system or range of economic activity in a country, region, or community. **b.** A specific type of economic system. **3.** An orderly functional arrangement of parts; an organized system. **4.** Efficient, sparing, or conservative use. **5.** The least expensive class of accommodations, esp. on an airplane. **6.** *Theology* The method of God's government of and activity within the world. ❖ *adj.* Economical or inexpensive to buy or use. [ME *yconomye*, management of a household < Lat. *oeconomia* < Gk. *oikonomiā* < *oikonomos*, one who manages a household : *oikos*, house; see **weik-** in App. + *nemein*, to allot, manage; see **nem-** in App.]

economy of scale *n., pl.* **economies of scale** The decrease in unit cost of a product or service resulting from large-scale operations, as in mass production.

e•co•spe•cies (ē′kō-spē′shēz, -sēz, ĕk′ō-) *n., pl.* **ecospecies** A taxonomic species considered in terms of its ecological characteristics and usu. including several interbreeding ecotypes.

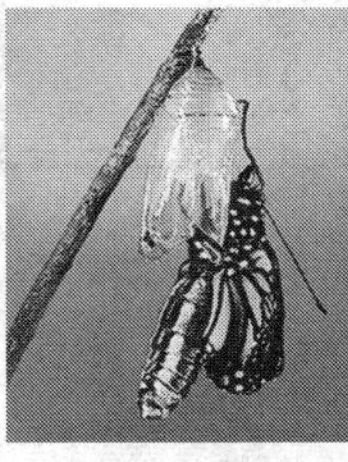

eclosion
monarch butterfly emerging from cocoon

ă	pat	oi	boy
ā	pay	ou	out
âr	care	o͝o	took
ä	father	o͞o	boot
ĕ	pet	ŭ	cut
ē	be	ûr	urge
ĭ	pit	th	thin
ī	pie	*th*	this
îr	pier	hw	which
ŏ	pot	zh	vision
ō	toe	ə	about, item
ô	paw		

Stress marks:
′ (primary);
′ (secondary), as in
lexicon (lĕk′sĭ-kŏn′)

e·co·sphere (ē′kō-sfîr′, ĕk′ō-) *n.* The regions of the universe, esp. on the earth, that are capable of supporting life.

e·co·sys·tem (ē′kō-sĭs′təm, ĕk′ō-) *n.* A biological community together with its environment, functioning as a unit.

e·co·ter·ror·ism (ē′kō-tĕr′ə-rĭz′əm, ĕk′ō-) *n.* Terrorism or sabotage committed in the name of environmental causes. —**e′co·ter′ror·ist** *adj. & n.*

e·co·tour·ism (ē′kō-tŏŏr′ĭz′əm, ĕk′ō-) *n.* Tourism involving travel to areas of ecological interest. —**e′co·tour′ist** *adj. & n.*

e·co·type (ē′kə-tīp′, ĕk′ə-) *n.* The smallest taxonomic subdivision of an ecospecies, consisting of populations adapted to particular environmental conditions. —**e′co·typ′ic** (-tĭp′ĭk) *adj.*

ec·ru (ĕk′rōō, ā′krōō) *n.* A grayish to pale yellow or light grayish-yellowish brown. [Fr. *écru*, raw, unbleached < OFr. *escru* : *es-*, intensive pref. (< Lat. *ex-*; see EX–) + *cru*, raw (< Lat. *crūdus*; see *kreuə-* in App.]

ec·sta·sy (ĕk′stə-sē) *n., pl.* **-sies 1.** Intense joy or delight. **2.** A state of emotion so intense that one is carried beyond rational thought and self-control: *an ecstasy of rage.* **3.** The trance, frenzy, or rapture associated with mystic or prophetic exaltation. **4.** *Slang* MDMA. [ME *extasie* < OFr. < LLat. *extasis*, terror < Gk. *ekstasis*, astonishment, distraction < *existanai*, to displace, derange : *ek-*, *ex-*, out of; see EXO– + *histanai*, to place; see *stā-* in App.]

ec·stat·ic (ĕk-stăt′ĭk) *adj.* **1.** Marked by or expressing ecstasy. **2.** Being in a state of ecstasy; enraptured. [Fr. *extatique* < Gk. *ekstatikos* < *ekstasis*, distraction. See ECSTASY.] —**ec·stat′i·cal·ly** *adv.*

ECT *abbr.* electroconvulsive therapy

ecto– *pref.* Outer; external: *ectoparasite.* [L.Gk. *ekto-* < Gk. *ektos*, outside < *ek*, *ek-*, out. See *eghs* in App.]

ec·to·derm (ĕk′tə-dûrm′) *n.* **1.** The outermost of the three primary germ layers of an embryo, from which the epidermis, nervous tissue, and, in vertebrates, sense organs develop. **2.** The outer layer of a diploblastic animal, such as a jellyfish. —**ec′to·der′mal, ec′to·der′mic** *adj.*

ec·tog·e·nous (ĕk-tŏj′ə-nəs) also **ec·to·gen·ic** (ĕk′tə-jĕn′ĭk) *adj. Biology* Able to live and develop outside a host.

ec·to·morph (ĕk′tə-môrf′) *n.* An individual having a lean, slightly muscular body build in which tissues derived from the embryonic ectoderm predominate. [ECTO(DERM) + –MORPH.] —**ec′to·mor′phic** *adj.*

–ectomy *suff.* Surgical removal: *tonsillectomy.* [NLat. *-ectomia* : Gk. *ek-*, out; see ECTO– + *-tomiā*, *-tomy.*]

ec·to·par·a·site (ĕk′tə-păr′ə-sīt′) *n.* A parasite, such as a flea, that lives on the exterior of another organism. —**ec′to·par′a·sit′ic** (-sĭt′ĭk) *adj.* —**ec′to·par′a·sit·ism** *n.*

ec·to·pi·a (ĕk-tō′pē-ə) *n.* An abnormal location or position of an organ or body part, occurring congenitally or as the result of injury. [NLat. < Gk. *ektopos*, away from a place : *ek-*, away from, out of; see *topos*, place.] —**ec·top′ic** (-tŏp′ĭk) *adj.*

ectopic pregnancy *n.* Implantation and subsequent development of a fertilized ovum outside the uterus.

ec·to·plasm (ĕk′tə-plăz′əm) *n.* **1.** *Biology* The outer portion of the cytoplasm of a cell, sometimes distinguishable as a somewhat rigid gelled layer beneath the cell membrane. **2a.** The visible substance believed to emanate from the body of a spiritualistic medium during communication with the dead. **b.** An immaterial or ethereal substance, esp. the transparent corporeal presence of a spirit or ghost. —**ec′to·plas′mic** *adj.*

ec·to·therm (ĕk′tə-thûrm′) *n.* An organism that regulates its body temperature largely by exchanging heat with its surroundings; a poikilotherm.

ec·to·ther·mic (ĕk′tə-thûr′mĭk) also **ec·to·ther·mal** (ĕk′tə-thûr′məl) or **ec·to·ther·mous** (-məs) *adj.* Of or relating to an ectotherm; cold-blooded.

é·cu (ā-kyōō′) *n., pl.* **é·cus** (ā-kyōō′) Any of various old French coins, esp. a silver five-franc piece. [Fr. < OFr. *escu* < Lat. *scūtum*, shield.]

Ec·ua·dor (ĕk′wə-dôr′) A country of NW South America on the Pacific Ocean; liberated from Spain in 1822 but remained part of Colombia until 1830. Cap. Quito. Pop. 11,221,000. —**Ec′ua·dor′i·an** *adj. & n.*

ec·u·men·i·cal (ĕk′yə-mĕn′ĭ-kəl) also **ec·u·men·ic** (-mĕn′ĭk) *adj.* **1.** Of worldwide scope; universal. **2a.** Of or relating to the worldwide Christian church. **b.** Concerned with establishing or promoting unity among churches or religions. [< LLat. *oecūmenicus* < Gk. *oikoumenikos* < *oikoumenē* (*gē*), inhabited (world), fem. pr. passive part. of *oikein*, to inhabit < *oikos*, house. See *weik-* in App.] —**ec′u·men′i·cal** *n.* —**ec′u·men′i·cal·ism** *n.* —**ec′u·men′i·cal·ly** *adv.*

ecumenical patriarch *n.* The patriarch of Constantinople, the highest ecclesiastical official of the Eastern Orthodox Church.

ec·u·men·i·cism (ĕk′yə-mĕn′ĭ-sĭz′əm) *n.* Ecumenism. —**ec′u·men′i·cist** *n.*

ec·u·me·nism (ĕk′yə-mə-nĭz′əm, ĭ-kyōō′-) *n.* **1.** A movement promoting unity among Christian churches or denominations. **2.** A movement promoting unity among religions through cooperation and understanding. —**ec′u·men′ist** *n.*

ec·ze·ma (ĕk′sə-mə, ĕg′zə-, ĭg-zē′-) *n.* A noncontagious inflammation of the skin, characterized chiefly by redness, itching, and the outbreak of lesions. [NLat. < Gk. *ekzema* < *ekzein*, to boil over : *ek-*, out; see ECTO– + *zein*, to boil.] —**ec·zem′a·tous** (ĕg-

zĕm′ə-təs, -zē′mə-təs, ĭg-) *adj.*

ed (ĕd) *n. Informal* Education: *driver's ed.*

ED *abbr.* **1.** effective dose **2.** erectile dysfunction

ed. *abbr.* **1.** edition **2.** editor

–ed¹ *suff.* Used to form the past tense of regular verbs: *tasted.* [ME *-ede* < OE *-ade*, *-ede*, *-ode.*]

–ed² *suff.* Used to form the past participle of regular verbs: *absorbed.* [ME < OE *-ad*, *-ed*, *-od.*]

–ed³ *suff.* Having; characterized by; resembling: *blackhearted.* [ME *-ede*, *-de* < OE *-ad*, *-od.*]

e·da·cious (ĭ-dā′shəs) *adj.* Characterized by voracity; devouring. [< Lat. *edāx*, *edāc-* < *edere*, to eat. See *ed-* in App.] —**e·dac′i·ty** (ĭ-dăs′ĭ-tē) *n.*

E·dam (ē′dəm, ē′dăm′) *n.* A mild yellow Dutch cheese, usu. covered with red wax. [After *Edam*, a town in the western Netherlands.]

e·daph·ic (ĭ-dăf′ĭk) *adj.* **1.** Of or relating to soil, esp. as it affects living organisms. **2.** Influenced by the soil rather than by the climate. [< Gk. *edaphos*, ground, soil. See *sed-* in App.]

Ed·da (ĕd′ə) *n.* **1.** A collection of Old Norse poems, called the Elder or Poetic Edda, assembled in the early 13th century. **2.** A manual of Icelandic poetry, called the Younger or Prose Edda, written by Snorri Sturluson (1179–1241). [ON.] —**Ed′dic** *adj.*

Ed·ding·ton (ĕd′ĭng-tən), Sir **Arthur Stanley** 1882–1944. British mathematician, astronomer, and physicist who was an early exponent of the theory of relativity.

ed·do (ĕd′ō) *n., pl.* **-does 1.** A variety of taro having small purplish tubers. **2.** The tuber of this plant. [Of Niger-Congo orig.; akin to Fante *edwo*, yam.]

ed·dy (ĕd′ē) *n., pl.* **-dies 1.** A current, as of water or air, moving contrary to the main current, esp. in a circular motion. **2.** A drift or tendency counter to or separate from a main current, as of history. ❖ *v.* **-died, -dy·ing, -dies** *—intr.* To move in or as if in an eddy. *—tr.* To cause to eddy. [ME *ydy*, prob. of Scand. orig.; akin to ON *idha.*]

Eddy, Mary (Morse) Baker 1821–1910. Amer. religious leader who founded Christian Science (1879).

Ed·dy·stone Rocks (ĕd′ĭ-stən) A rocky islet of SW England in the English Channel S of Plymouth.

E·de (ā′dā, ā-dā′) A city of W Nigeria NE of Ibadan; a former center of Yoruba culture. Pop. 216,400.

e·del·weiss (ā′dəl-vīs′, -wīs′) *n.* An alpine plant (*Leontopodium alpinum*) native to Europe and having leaves covered with whitish down and small flower heads surrounded by whitish bracts. [Ger., edel, noble (< MHGer. *edele* < OHGer. *edili*) + *weiss*, white (< MHGer. *wīz* < OHGer. *wīz*, *hwīz*).]

e·de·ma also **oe·de·ma** (ĭ-dē′mə) *n., pl.* **-mas** or **-ma·ta** (-mə-tə) **1.** *Pathology* An excessive accumulation of serous fluid in tissue spaces or a body cavity. **2.** *Botany* Extended swelling in plant organs caused primarily by an excessive accumulation of water. [ME *ydema* < Gk. *oidēma*, a swelling < *oidein*, to swell.] —**e·dem′a·tous** (ĭ-dĕm′ə-təs) *adj.*

E·den (ēd′n) *n.* **1.** *Bible* The garden of God and the first home of Adam and Eve. **2.** A delightful place; a paradise. **3.** A state of innocence or ultimate happiness. [ME < LLat. < Gk. *Ēden* < Heb. *'ēden*, delight, Eden.] —**E·den′ic** (ē-dĕn′ĭk) *adj.*

Eden, Sir (Robert) Anthony. 1st Earl of Avon. 1897–1977. British politician who served as prime minister (1955–57).

e·den·tate (ē-dĕn′tāt′) *adj.* **1.** Lacking teeth. **2.** Of or belonging to the order Edentata, which includes mammals having few or no teeth, such as anteaters and sloths. [Lat. *ēdentātus*, p. part. of *ēdentāre*, to knock out the teeth : *ē-*, *ex-*, ex- + *dēns*, *dent-*, tooth; see *dent-* in App.] —**e·den′tate** *n.*

e·den·tu·lous (ē-dĕn′chə-ləs) *adj.* Toothless. [< Lat. *ēdentulus* : *ē-*, *ex-*, ex- + *dēns*, *dent-*, tooth; see *dent-* in App.]

E·der (ā′dər) A river rising in central Germany and flowing c. 177 km (110 mi) E to the Fulda R.

E·der·le (ā′dər-lē), **Gertrude Caroline** b. 1906. Amer. swimmer; the first woman to swim the English Channel (1926).

E·des·sa (ĭ-dĕs′ə) An ancient city of Mesopotamia on the site of Urfa in SE Turkey; captured by Crusaders in 1097.

edge (ĕj) *n.* **1a.** A thin sharpened side, as of the blade of a cutting instrument. **b.** The degree of sharpness of a cutting blade. **c.** A penetrating, incisive quality. **d.** A slight sharpness or harshness. **2.** Keenness, as of desire; zest. **3a.** The line of intersection of two surfaces. **b.** A rim or brink. **c.** The point at which something is likely to begin: *on the edge of war.* **4a.** The area or part away from the middle; an extremity. **b.** A dividing line; a border. See Syns at **border. 5.** A margin of superiority; an advantage. **6.** A provocative or discomforting quality, as from audacity. ❖ *v.* **edged, edg·ing, edg·es** *—tr.* **1a.** To give an edge to (a blade); sharpen. **b.** To tilt (a ski or both skis) in such a way that an edge or both edges bite into the snow. **2a.** To put a border or edge on. **b.** To act as or be an edge of. **3.** To advance or push slightly or gradually. **4.** To trim or shape the edge of. *—intr.* To move gradually or hesitantly. *—phrasal verb:* **edge out** To surpass or beat by a small margin. *—idioms:* **on edge** Highly tense or nervous; irritable. **on the edge 1.** In a precarious position. **2.** In a state of keen excitement, as from risk. [ME *egge* < OE *ecg.* See *ak-* in App.]

edge city *n.* A sizeable commercial center offering a mixture of employment, shopping, and entertainment and serving a primar-

Ecuador

Mary Baker Eddy

edelweiss
Leontopodium alpinum

ily suburban area. [After *Edge City: Life on the New Frontier*, title of a 1991 book by Amer. writer Joel Garreau.]

edg•er (ĕj′ər) *n.* One that edges.

edge tool *n.* A tool, such as a chisel, that has a cutting edge.

edge•wise (ĕj′wīz′) also **edge•ways** (-wāz′) *adv.* **1.** With the edge foremost. **2.** On, by, with, or toward the edge.

Edge•worth (ĕj′wûrth′), **Maria** 1767–1849. British writer noted for her realistic novels, such as *Castle Rackrent* (1800).

edg•ing (ĕj′ĭng) *n.* Something that forms or serves as an edge or border.

edg•y (ĕj′ē) *adj.* **-i•er, -i•est 1.** Nervous or irritable. **2.** Having a sharp or biting edge. **3.** Daring, provocative, or trend-setting. **—edg′i•ly** *adv.* **—edg′i•ness** *n.*

edh also **eth** (ĕth) *n.* **1.** A letter (ð) appearing in Old English, Old Saxon, Old Norse, and modern Icelandic to represent an interdental fricative. **2.** The symbol (ð) in the International Phonetic Alphabet for the voiced interdental fricative, as in *either.* [Icel.]

E•di•a•ca•ran (ē′dē-ă′kə-rən) *adj.* Of or relating to a soft-bodied marine organism of the Precambrian Era, thought to be the earliest multicellular form of life. [After the *Ediacara* Hills in S Australia, where the first such fossils were found.]

ed•i•ble (ĕd′ə-bəl) *adj.* Fit to be eaten. ❖ *n.* Something edible; food. [LLat. *edibilis* < Lat. *edere*, to eat. See **ed-** in App.] **—ed′i•bil′i•ty, ed′i•ble•ness** *n.*

e•dict (ē′dĭkt′) *n.* **1.** A decree or proclamation issued by an authority and having the force of law. **2.** A formal pronouncement or command. [Lat. *ēdictum* < neut. p. part. of *ēdīcere*, to declare : *ē-, ex-,* ex- + *dīcere*, to speak; see **deik-** in App.]

ed•i•fi•ca•tion (ĕd′ə-fĭ-kā′shən) *n.* Intellectual, moral, or spiritual improvement; enlightenment.

ed•i•fice (ĕd′ə-fĭs) *n.* **1.** A building, esp. one of imposing appearance or size. **2.** An elaborate conceptual structure. [ME < OFr. < Lat. *aedificium* < *aedificāre*, to build : *aedis*, a building + *-ficāre*, -fy.]

ed•i•fy (ĕd′ə-fī′) *tr.v.* **-fied, -fy•ing, -fies** To instruct esp. so as to encourage intellectual, moral, or spiritual improvement. [ME *edifien* < OFr. *edifier* < LLat. *aedificāre*, to instruct spiritually < Lat., to build. See EDIFICE.] **—ed′i•fi′er** *n.*

Ed•in•burgh (ĕd′n-bûr′ə, -bûr′ə, -brə) The cap. of Scotland, in the E part on the Firth of Forth. Pop. 441,620.

E•dir•ne (e-dîr′nĕ) Formerly **A•dri•a•no•ple** (ā′drē-ə-nō′pəl) A city of NW Turkey NW of Istanbul; founded c. A.D. 125 by the Roman emperor Hadrian. Pop. 71,914.

Ed•i•son (ĕd′ĭ-sən) A community of central NJ NE of New Brunswick. Pop. 97,687.

Edison, Thomas Alva 1847–1931. Amer. inventor who patented more than a thousand inventions, among them the phonograph (1878) and an incandescent lamp (1879).

ed•it (ĕd′ĭt) *tr.v.* **-it•ed, -it•ing, -its 1a.** To prepare (written material) for publication or presentation, as by correcting, revising, or adapting. **b.** To prepare an edition of. **c.** To modify or adapt so as to make suitable or acceptable. **2.** To supervise the publication of (a magazine, for example). **3.** To assemble the components of (a soundtrack, for example), as by cutting and splicing. **4.** To eliminate; delete: *edited the best scene out.* ❖ *n.* An act or instance of editing. [Partly back-formation < EDITOR and partly < Fr. *éditer* (< Lat. *ēditus*, p. part. of *ēdere* : *ē-, ex-,* ex- + *dare*, to give; see **dō-** in App.).]

e•di•tion (ĭ-dĭsh′ən) *n.* **1a.** The entire number of copies of a publication issued at one time or from a single set of type. **b.** A single copy from this group. **c.** The form in which a publication is issued: *a paperback edition.* **d.** A version of an earlier publication having substantial changes or additions. **2.** All the copies of a specified issue of a newspaper. **3.** A broadcast of a radio or television news program. **4a.** The entire number of like or identical items issued or produced as a set. **b.** Any of the various or successive forms in which something is offered or presented. **5.** One that closely resembles an original; a version. [ME *edicion*, version < Lat. *ēditiō, ēditiōn-*, publication, production < *ēditus*, p. part. of *ēdere*, to publish, produce. See EDIT.]

ed•i•tor (ĕd′ĭ-tər) *n.* **1.** One who edits, esp. as an occupation. **2.** One who writes editorials. **3.** A device for editing film, consisting basically of a splicer and viewer. **4.** *Computer Science* A program used to edit text or data files. [LLat. *ēditor*, publisher < Lat. *ēditus*, p. part. of *ēdere*, to publish. See EDIT.]

ed•i•to•ri•al (ĕd′ĭ-tôr′ē-əl, -tōr′-) *n.* **1.** An article in a publication expressing the opinion of its editors or publishers. **2.** A commentary on television or radio expressing the opinion of the station or network. ❖ *adj.* **1.** Of or relating to an editor or editing. **2.** Of or resembling an editorial, esp. in expressing an opinion. **—ed′i•to′ri•al•ly** *adv.*

ed•i•to•ri•al•ist (ĕd′ĭ-tôr′ē-ə-lĭst, -tōr′-) *n.* One who writes or presents editorials.

ed•i•to•ri•al•ize (ĕd′ĭ-tôr′ē-ə-līz′, -tōr′-) *intr.v.* **-ized, -iz•ing, -iz•es 1.** To express an opinion in or as if in an editorial. **2.** To present an opinion as an objective report. **—ed′i•to′ri•al•i•za′tion** (-ə-lĭ-zā′shən) *n.*

editor in chief *n., pl.* **editors in chief** The editor having final responsibility for the operations and policies of a publication.

ed•i•tor•ship (ĕd′ĭ-tər-shĭp′) *n.* The position, functions, or guidance of an editor.

EdM *abbr. Latin* Educationis Magister (Master of Education)

Ed•mond (ĕd′mənd) A city of central OK N of Oklahoma City. Pop. 68,315.

Ed•mon•ton (ĕd′mən-tən) The cap. of Alberta, Canada, in the central part N of Calgary; founded 1795 as a fort and trading post of the Hudson's Bay Company. Pop. 616,306.

Ed•mund II (ĕd′mənd) Known as "Edmund Ironside." 993?–1016. King of the English (1016) who partitioned the kingdom in a settlement with Canute.

E•do (ĕd′ō) See Tokyo.

E•dom (ē′dəm) An ancient country of Palestine between the Dead Sea and the Gulf of Aqaba. According to the Bible, the original inhabitants were descendants of Esau.

E•dom•ite (ē′də-mīt′) *n.* A member of a Semitic people inhabiting Edom in ancient times. **—E′dom•it′ish** *adj.*

EDP *abbr.* electronic data processing

EDT *abbr.* Eastern Daylight Time

EDTA (ē′dē-tē-ā′) *n.* A crystalline acid, $C_{10}H_{16}N_2O_8$, that is a strong chelating agent and whose sodium salt is used as an antidote for metal poisoning and as an anticoagulant. [e(thylene)d(iamine)t(etraacetic) a(cid).]

ed•u•ca•ble (ĕj′ə-kə-bəl) *adj.* Capable of being educated or taught: *educable youngsters.* **—ed′u•ca•bil′i•ty** *n.*

ed•u•cate (ĕj′ə-kāt′) *v.* **-cat•ed, -cat•ing, -cates** *—tr.* **1.** To develop the innate capacities of, esp. by schooling or instruction. See Syns at **teach. 2.** To provide with knowledge or training in a particular area or for a particular purpose. **3a.** To provide with information; inform. **b.** To bring to an understanding or acceptance. **4.** To stimulate or develop the mental or moral growth of. **5.** To develop or refine (one's taste or appreciation, for example). *—intr.* To teach or instruct a person or group. [ME *educaten* < Lat. *ēducāre, ēducātus.* See **deuk-** in App.]

ed•u•cat•ed (ĕj′ə-kā′tĭd) *adj.* **1.** Having an education, esp. one above the average. **2a.** Showing evidence of schooling, training, or experience. **b.** Having or exhibiting cultivation; cultured. **3.** Based on experience or factual knowledge.

ed•u•ca•tion (ĕj′ə-kā′shən) *n.* **1.** The act or process of educating or being educated. **2.** The knowledge or skill obtained or developed by a learning process. **3.** A program of instruction of a specified kind or level: *driver education.* **4.** The field of study concerned with the pedagogy of teaching and learning. **5.** An instructive or enlightening experience.

ed•u•ca•tion•al (ĕj′ə-kā′shə-nəl) *adj.* **1.** Of or relating to education. **2.** Serving to educate; instructive. **—ed′u•ca′tion•al•ly** *adv.*

educational quotient *n.* A measure of the effectiveness of an educational system, based on factors such as student to teacher ratio and standardized test scores.

educational television *n.* **1.** See **public television. 2.** An often closed-circuit video system that provides education.

ed•u•ca•tion•ist (ĕj′ə-kā′shə-nĭst) also **ed•u•ca•tion•al•ist** (-shə-nə-lĭst) *n.* A specialist in the theory of education.

ed•u•ca•tive (ĕj′ə-kā′tĭv) *adj.* Educational.

ed•u•ca•tor (ĕj′ə-kā′tər) *n.* **1.** One trained in teaching; a teacher. **2a.** A specialist in the theory and practice of education. **b.** An administrator of a school or an educational institution.

e•duce (ĭ-dōōs′, ĭ-dyōōs′) *tr.v.* **e•duced, e•duc•ing, e•duc•es 1.** To draw or bring out; elicit. **2.** To assume or work out from given facts; deduce. [ME *educen*, to direct the flow of < Lat. *ēdūcere* : *ē-, ex-,* ex- + *dūcere*, to lead; see **deuk-** in App.] **—e•duc′i•ble** *adj.* **—e•duc′tion** (ĭ-dŭk′shən) *n.*

ed•u•tain•ment (ĕj′ōō-tān′mənt, ĕj′ə-) *n.* **1.** The act of learning through a medium that both educates and entertains. **2.** Any of various media, such as computer software, that educate and entertain. [EDU(CATION) : (ENTER)TAINMENT.]

Ed•ward[1] (ĕd′wərd) Known as "the Confessor." 1003?–66. King of the English (1042–66) whose reign was marked by political conflict between Norman and English groups.

Ed•ward[2] (ĕd′wərd) Prince of Wales. Known as "the Black Prince." 1330–76. English soldier during the Hundred Years' War who fought at Crécy (1346) and Poitiers (1356).

Edward I 1239–1307. King of England (1272–1307) whose Model Parliament of 1295 is sometimes considered England's first full parliament.

Edward II 1284–1327. King of England (1307–27) who was defeated at Bannockburn by the Scots (1314).

Edward III 1312–77. King of England (1327–77) who reigned during the beginning of the Hundred Years' War.

Edward IV 1442–83. King of England (1461–70 and 1471–83) who was crowned after the Yorkist victory in the Wars of the Roses, dethroned in 1470, and recrowned in 1471.

Edward V 1470–83. King of England (1483) who was crowned at the age of 13 on the death of his father, Edward IV, and was immediately confined in the Tower of London, where he and his younger brother were murdered.

Edward VI 1537–53. King of England and Ireland (1547–53) who was the son of Henry VIII and Jane Seymour.

Edward VII 1841–1910. King of Great Britain and Ireland (1901–10) who was known for his elegant, sporting style. **—Ed•ward′i•an** (ĕd-wôr′dē-ən, -wär′-) *adj. & n.*

Edward VIII Later known as Duke of Windsor. 1894–1972. King

Gertrude Ederle

Thomas Edison
1926 portrait by Ellis M.
Silvette (1876–1933)

ă	pat	oi	boy
ā	pay	ou	out
âr	care	ōō	took
ä	father	ōō	boot
ĕ	pet	ŭ	cut
ē	be	ûr	urge
ĭ	pit	th	thin
ī	pie	*th*	this
îr	pier	hw	which
ŏ	pot	zh	vision
ō	toe	ə	about,
ô	paw		item

Stress marks:
′ (primary);
′ (secondary), as in
lexicon (lĕk′sĭ-kŏn′)

of Great Britain and Ireland (1936) who abdicated in order to marry (1937) Wallis Warfield Simpson, an Amer. divorcée.

Edward, Lake A lake in the Great Rift Valley of central Africa on the Uganda-Congo (formerly Zaire) border.

Ed·wards (ĕd′wərdz), **Jonathan** 1703–58. Amer. theologian whose works stimulated the Great Awakening, a period of renewed American interest in religion.

Ed·win (ĕd′wĭn) 585?–633. King of Northumbria (617–633) who was converted to Christianity (627).

EE *abbr.* 1. electrical engineer 2. electrical engineering

–ee[1] *suff.* **1a.** One that receives or benefits from a specified action: *addressee*. **b.** One that possesses a specified thing: *mortgagee*. **2.** One that performs a specified action: *absentee*. [ME < OFr. *-e, -ee*, p.part. suff. < Lat. *-ātus*. See ATE[1].]

USAGE NOTE The suffix *–ee* was first used in English to refer to indirect objects and then direct objects of transitive verbs, as in *donee* or *draftee*. Beginning around the mid-19th century, primarily in American English, it was often extended to denote the agent or subject of an intransitive verb; for example, *standee*. Although the pattern is very common, in general such words retain an informal character as jocular nonce words. Formations like *attendee* where the suffix denotes the agent of a transitive verb, are rarer.

–ee[2] *suff.* **1a.** One resembling: *goatee*. **b.** A particular, esp. a diminutive kind of: *bootee*. **2.** One connected with: *bargee*. [Variant of –Y[1].]

EEC *abbr.* European Economic Community

EEG *abbr.* **1.** electroencephalogram **2.** electroencephalograph

eel (ēl) *n., pl.* **eel** or **eels** **1.** Any of various long, snakelike, scaleless marine or freshwater fishes of the order Anguilliformes or Apodes that characteristically migrate from fresh to salt water to spawn. **2.** Any of several similar fishes, such as the lamprey. [ME *ele* < OE *ǣl*.]

eel·grass (ēl′grăs′) *n.* Any of several submersed aquatic plants of the genus *Vallisneria*.

eel·pout (ēl′pout′) *n., pl.* **eelpout** or **-pouts** **1.** Any of various bottom-dwelling marine fishes of the family Zoarcidae, having an elongated body and a large head. **2.** See **burbot**.

eel·worm (ēl′wûrm′) *n.* Any of various often parasitic nematode worms, such as the vinegar eel.

e'en[1] (ēn) *n.* Evening.

e'en[2] (ēn) *adv.* Even.

EEOC *abbr.* Equal Employment Opportunity Commission

–eer *suff.* One associated with, concerned with, or engaged in: *balladeer*. [Fr. *-ier* < OFr. < Lat. *-ārius, -ary*.]

e'er (âr) *adv.* Ever.

ee·rie or **ee·ry** (îr′ē) *adj.* **-ri·er, -ri·est** **1a.** Inspiring inexplicable fear, dread, or uneasiness. **b.** Suggestive of the supernatural; mysterious. **2.** *Scots* Frightened or intimidated by superstition. [ME *eri*, fearful < OE *earg*, cowardly.] —**ee′ri·ly** *adv.* —**ee′ri·ness** *n.*

ef (ĕf) *n.* The letter *f*.

egg-and-dart

ef·face (ĭ-fās′) *tr.v.* **-faced, -fac·ing, -fac·es** **1.** To rub or wipe out. See Syns at **erase**. **2.** To make indistinct as if by rubbing. **3.** To conduct (oneself) inconspicuously. [ME *effacen* < Fr. *effacer* < OFr. *esfacier* : *es-*, out (< Lat. *ex-, ex-*) + *face*, face; see FACE.] —**ef·face′a·ble** *adj.* —**ef·face′ment** *n.* —**ef·fac′er** *n.*

ef·fect (ĭ-fĕkt′) *n.* **1.** Something brought about by a cause or agent; a result. **2.** The power to produce an outcome or achieve a result; influence. **3.** A scientific law, hypothesis, or phenomenon. **4.** Advantage; avail. **5.** The condition of being in full force or execution. **6a.** Something that produces a specific impression or supports a general design or intention. **b.** A particular impression. **c.** Production of a desired impression. **7.** The basic or general meaning; import. **8. effects** Movable belongings; goods. ❖ *tr.v.* **-fect·ed, -fect·ing, -fects** **1.** To bring into existence. **2.** To produce as a result. **3.** To bring about. See Usage Note at **affect**[1]. —**idiom: in effect** In essence; to all purposes. [ME < OFr. < Lat. *effectus* < p. part. of *efficere*, to accomplish : *ex-, ex-* + *facere*, to make; see **dhē-** in App.] —**ef·fect′er** *n.* —**ef·fect′i·ble** *adj.*

SYNONYMS *effect, consequence, result, outcome, upshot* These nouns denote an occurrence, situation, or condition that is caused by an antecedent. An *effect* is produced by the action of an agent or cause and follows it in time: *"Every cause produces more than one effect"* (Herbert Spencer). A *consequence* has a less sharply definable relationship to its cause: *reported on the consequences of urban crime*. A *result* is viewed as the end product of the operation of the cause: *analyzed the experiment's results*. An *outcome* implies finality and may suggest the operation of a cause over a relatively long period: *an unlikely outcome for the story*. An *upshot* is a decisive result, often climactic: *"The upshot of the matter . . . was that she showed both of them the door"* (Robert Louis Stevenson).

eggplant
Solanum melongena var.
esculenta

ef·fec·tive (ĭ-fĕk′tĭv) *adj.* **1a.** Having an intended or expected effect. **b.** Producing a strong impression or response; striking. **2.** Operative; in effect. **3.** Existing in fact; actual: *a decline in the effective demand.* **4.** Prepared for use or action, esp. in warfare. ❖ *n.* A soldier or a piece of military equipment that is ready for combat. —**ef·fec′tive·ness, ef′fec·tiv′i·ty** *n.*

ef·fec·tive·ly (ĭ-fĕk′tĭv-lē) *adv.* **1.** In an effective way. **2.** For all practical purposes; in effect.

ef·fec·tor (ĭ-fĕk′tər) *n.* **1.** A muscle, gland, or organ capable of responding to a stimulus, esp. a nerve impulse. **2.** A nerve ending that carries impulses to an effector. **3.** *Biochemistry* A molecule that when bound to an allosteric site of an enzyme causes either a decrease or an increase in the activity of the enzyme. **4.** *Computer Science* A device used to produce a desired change in an object in response to input.

ef·fec·tu·al (ĭ-fĕk′chōō-əl) *adj.* Producing or sufficient to produce a desired effect; fully adequate. [ME *effectuel* < OFr. < LLat. *effectuālis* < Lat. *effectus*, result, effect. See EFFECT.] —**ef·fec′tu·al′i·ty** (-ăl′ĭ-tē), **ef·fec′tu·al·ness** *n.* —**ef·fec′tu·al·ly** *adv.*

ef·fec·tu·ate (ĭ-fĕk′chōō-āt′) *tr.v.* **-at·ed, -at·ing, -ates** To bring about; effect. [Med.Lat. *effectuāre, effectuāt-* < Lat. *effectus*, an effect. See EFFECT.] —**ef·fec′tu·a′tion** *n.*

ef·fem·i·na·cy (ĭ-fĕm′ə-nə-sē) *n.* The quality or condition of being effeminate.

ef·fem·i·nate (ĭ-fĕm′ə-nĭt) *adj.* **1.** Having qualities or characteristics more often associated with women than men. **2.** Marked by weakness and excessive refinement. [ME *effeminat* < Lat. *effēminātus*, p. part. of *effēmināre*, to make feminine : *ex-, ex-* + *fēmina*, woman.] —**ef·fem′i·nate** *n.* —**ef·fem′i·nate·ly** *adv.*

ef·fen·di (ĭ-fĕn′dē) *n., pl.* **-dis** Used as a title of respect for men in Turkey. [Turk. *efendi* < Med.Gk. *aphentēs*, master, alteration of Gk. *authentēs*.]

ef·fer·ent (ĕf′ər-ənt) *adj.* **1.** Directed away from a central organ or section. **2.** Carrying impulses from the central nervous system to an effector. ❖ *n.* An efferent organ or body part, such as a blood vessel. [< Lat. *efferēns, efferent-*, pr. part. of *efferre*, to carry off : *ex-, ex-* + *ferre*, to carry; see **bher-**[1] in App.] —**ef′fer·ent·ly** *adv.*

ef·fer·vesce (ĕf′ər-vĕs′) *intr.v.* **-vesced, -vesc·ing, -vesc·es** **1.** To emit small bubbles of gas, as a carbonated or fermenting liquid. **2.** To escape from a liquid as bubbles; bubble up. **3.** To show high spirits or animation. [Lat. *effervescere* : *ex-*, up, out; see EX– + *fervēscere*, to start boiling, inchoative of *fervēre*, to boil.] —**ef′fer·ves′cence, ef′fer·ves′cen·cy** *n.* —**ef′fer·ves′cent** *adj.* —**ef′fer·ves′cent·ly** *adv.*

ef·fete (ĭ-fēt′) *adj.* **1.** Depleted of vitality, force, or effectiveness; exhausted. **2.** Marked by self-indulgence, triviality, or decadence: *an effete intellectual.* **3.** Overrefined; effeminate. **4.** No longer productive; infertile. [Lat. *effētus*, worn out, exhausted : *ex-, ex-* + *fētus*, bearing young, pregnant.] —**ef·fete′ly** *adv.*

ef·fi·ca·cious (ĕf′ĭ-kā′shəs) *adj.* Producing or capable of producing a desired effect. [< Lat. *efficāx, efficāc-* < *efficere*, to effect. See EFFECT.] —**ef′fi·ca′cious·ly** *adv.*

ef·fi·ca·cy (ĕf′ĭ-kə-sē) *n.* Power or capacity to produce a desired effect; effectiveness. [Lat. *efficācia* < *efficāx, efficāc-*, efficacious. See EFFICACIOUS.]

ef·fi·cien·cy (ĭ-fĭsh′ən-sē) *n., pl.* **-cies** **1a.** The quality or property of being efficient. **b.** The degree to which this quality is exercised. **2a.** The ratio of the effective or useful output to the total input in any system. **b.** The ratio of the energy delivered by a machine to the energy supplied for its operation. **3.** An efficiency apartment.

efficiency apartment *n.* A small, usu. furnished apartment with a private bathroom and kitchenette.

ef·fi·cient (ĭ-fĭsh′ənt) *adj.* **1a.** Acting or producing effectively with a minimum of waste, expense, or unnecessary effort: *an efficient worker.* **b.** Exhibiting a high ratio of output to input. **2.** Acting directly to produce an effect: *an efficient cause.* [ME < OFr. < Lat. *efficiēns, efficient-*, pr. part. of *efficere*, to effect. See EFFECT.] —**ef·fi′cient·ly** *adv.*

ef·fi·gy (ĕf′ə-jē) *n., pl.* **-gies** **1.** A crude figure or dummy representing a hated person or group. **2.** A likeness or image, esp. of a person. —**idiom: in effigy** Symbolically, esp. in the form of an effigy. [Fr. *effigie* < Lat. *effigiēs*, likeness < *effingere*, to portray : *ex-, ex-* + *fingere*, to shape; see **dheigh-** in App.]

ef·flo·resce (ĕf′lə-rĕs′) *intr.v.* **-resced, -resc·ing, -resc·es** **1.** To blossom; bloom. **2.** *Chemistry* **a.** To become a powder by losing water of crystallization, as when a hydrated crystal is exposed to air. **b.** To become covered with a powdery deposit. [Lat. *efflōrēscere* : *ex-, ex-* + *flōrēscere*, inchoative of *flōrēre*, to blossom (< *flōs, flōr-*, flower; see **bhel-** in App.).]

ef·flo·res·cence (ĕf′lə-rĕs′əns) *n.* **1.** *Botany* A state or time of flowering; anthesis. **2a.** A gradual process of unfolding or developing. **b.** The highest point; the culmination. **3.** *Chemistry* **a.** The deposit that results from the process of efflorescing. **b.** The process of efflorescing. **c.** A growth of salt crystals on a surface caused by evaporation of salt-laden water. **4.** *Pathology* Redness, a rash, or an eruption on the skin. —**ef′flo·res′cent** *adj.*

ef·flu·ence (ĕf′lōō-əns) *n.* **1.** The act or an instance of flowing out. **2.** Something that flows out or forth; an emanation.

ef·flu·ent (ĕf′lōō-ənt) *adj.* Flowing out or forth. ❖ *n.* Something that flows out or forth, esp.: **a.** A stream flowing out of a body of water. **b.** An outflow from a sewer or sewage system. **c.** A discharge of liquid waste, as from a factory or nuclear plant. [ME < Lat. *effluēns, effluent-*, pr. part. of *effluere*, to flow out : *ex-, ex-* + *fluere*, to flow.]

ef·flu·vi·um (ĭ-flōō′vē-əm) *n., pl.* **-vi·a** (-vē-ə) or **-vi·ums** **1.** A usu. invisible emanation or exhalation. **2a.** A byproduct or residue; waste. **b.** The fumes given off by waste or decaying matter. **3.** An impalpable emanation; an aura. [Lat. < *effluere*, to flow out. See EFFLUENT.] **—ef•flu′vi•al** *adj.*

ef•flux (ĕf′lŭks′) *n.* **1.** A flowing outward. **2.** Something that flows out or forth; an effluence. **3.** A passing or an expiration, as of time. [< Lat. *efflūxus*, p. part. of *effluere*, to flow out. See EFFLUENT.] **—ef•flux′ion** (ĭ-flŭk′shən) *n.*

ef•fort (ĕf′ərt) *n.* **1.** The use of physical or mental energy to do something. **2.** A difficult exertion of the strength or will. **3.** A usu. earnest attempt. **4.** Something done or produced through exertion; an achievement. **5.** *Physics* Force applied against inertia. [ME < OFr. *esfort* < *esforcier*, to force, exert < Med.Lat. *exfortiāre* : Lat. *ex-*, ex- + Lat. *fortis*, strong; see **bhergh-** in App.] **—ef′fort•ful** *adj.* **—ef′fort•ful•ly** *adv.*

ef•fort•less (ĕf′ərt-lĭs) *adj.* Calling for, requiring, or showing little or no effort. See Syns at **easy.** **—ef′fort•less•ly** *adv.* **—ef′fort•less•ness** *n.*

ef•front•er•y (ĭ-frŭn′tə-rē) *n., pl.* **-ies** Brazen boldness; presumptuousness. [Fr. *effronterie* < *effronté*, shameless < OFr. *esfronte* < VLat. **effrontātus*, alteration of LLat. *effrōns, effront-* : *ex-*, ex- + *frōns, front-*, front, forehead.]

ef•ful•gence (ĭ-fo͝ol′jəns, ĭ-fŭl′-) *n.* A brilliant radiance.

ef•ful•gent (ĭ-fo͝ol′jənt, ĭ-fŭl′-) *adj.* Shining brilliantly; resplendent. See Syns at **bright.** [Lat. *effulgēns, effulgent-*, pr. part. of *effulgēre*, to shine out : *ex-*, ex- + *fulgēre*, to shine.]

ef•fuse (ĭ-fyo͞os′) *adj. Botany* Spreading out loosely. ❖ *v.* (ĭ-fyo͞oz′) **-fused, -fus•ing, -fus•es** *—tr.* **1.** To pour out (a liquid). **2.** To radiate; diffuse. *—intr.* **1.** To spread or flow out. **2.** To ooze forth; exude. [Lat. *effūsus*, p. part. of *effundere*, to pour out : *ex-*, ex- + *fundere*, to pour; see **gheu-** in App.]

ef•fu•sion (ĭ-fyo͞o′zhən) *n.* **1a.** The act or an instance of effusing. **b.** Liquid or other matter poured forth. **2.** An unrestrained outpouring of feeling, as in speech or writing. **3.** *Pathology* **a.** The seeping of serous, purulent, or bloody fluid into a body cavity or tissue. **b.** The effused fluid.

ef•fu•sive (ĭ-fyo͞o′sĭv) *adj.* **1.** Unrestrained or excessive in emotional expression; gushy. **2.** Profuse; overflowing: *effusive praise.* **—ef•fu′sive•ly** *adv.* **—ef•fu′sive•ness** *n.*

Ef•ik (ĕf′ĭk) *n., pl.* **Efik** or **-iks 1.** A member of a people inhabiting southern Nigeria. **2.** The Niger-Congo language of the Efik people, closely related to Ibibio. **—Ef′ik** *adj.*

eft (ĕft) *n.* An immature newt. [ME *evete* < OE *efeta.*]

EFTA *abbr.* European Free Trade Association

EFTS *abbr.* electronic funds transfer system

eft•soons (ĕft-so͞onz′) *adv. Archaic* **1.** Soon afterward; presently. **2.** Once again. [< ME *eftsone* < OE *eftsōna* : *eft*, again; see **apo-** in App. + *sōna*, soon.]

e.g. *abbr. Latin* exempli gratia (for example)

e•gad (ĭ-găd′) or **e•gads** (ĭ-gădz′) *interj.* Used as a mild exclamation. [Alteration of *oh God.*]

Eg•a•di Islands (ĕg′ə-dē) also **Ae•ga•de•an Isles** (ē-gā′dē-ən) or **Ae•ga•tes** (-tēz) An island group of SW Italy in the Mediterranean Sea W of Sicily.

e•gal•i•tar•i•an (ĭ-găl′ĭ-târ′ē-ən) *adj.* Affirming, promoting, or characterized by belief in equal political, economic, and social rights for all people. [< Fr. *égalitaire* < *égalité*, equality < Lat. *aequālitās* < *aequālis*, equal. See EQUAL.] **—e•gal′i•tar′i•an** *n.* **—e•gal′i•tar′i•an•ism** *n.*

Eg•bert (ĕg′bərt) d. 839. West Saxon king (802–839) who became the first overlord of all the English peoples (829).

E•ge•ri•a (ĭ-jîr′ē-ə) *n.* A woman adviser or counselor. [After *Egeria*, Roman adviser to Numa Pompilius, a legendary king.]

e•gest (ē-jĕst′) *tr.v.* **e•gest•ed, e•gest•ing, e•gests** To discharge or excrete from the body. [Lat. *ēgerere, ēgest-*, to carry out : *ē-, ex-*, ex- + *gerere*, to carry.] **—e•ges′tion** *n.* **—e•ges′tive** *adj.*

e•ges•ta (ē-jĕs′tə) *pl.n.* Egested matter. [Lat., neut. pl. of *ēgestus*, p. part. of *ēgerere*, to carry out. See EGEST.]

egg[1] (ĕg) *n.* **1a.** A female gamete; an ovum. **b.** The round or oval reproductive body of various animals, consisting usu. of an embryo surrounded by nutrient material and a protective covering. **c.** A bird egg, esp. that of a hen, used as food. **2.** Something that is egg-shaped. **3.** *Slang* A person: *a good egg.* ❖ *tr.v.* **egged, egg•ing, eggs 1.** To cover with beaten egg, as in cooking. **2.** *Slang* To throw eggs at. ***—idioms:* put** (or **have**) **all (one's) eggs in one basket** *Informal* To risk everything on one venture. **egg on (one's) face** *Informal* Embarrassment; humiliation. [ME *egge*, bird's egg < ON *egg.* See **awi-** in App.] **—egg′y** *adj.*

egg[2] (ĕg) *tr.v.* **egged, egg•ing, eggs** To encourage or incite to action. Used with *on: egged on the mischief makers.* [ME *eggen* < ON *eggja.* See **ak-** in App.]

egg-and-dart (ĕg′ən-därt′) *n.* A decorative molding consisting of a series of egg-shaped figures alternating with dart-shaped, anchor-shaped, or tongue-shaped figures.

egg•beat•er (ĕg′bē′tər) *n.* A hand-held kitchen utensil with rotating blades for beating, whipping, or mixing.

egg case *n.* An ootheca.

egg cell *n.* See **egg**[1] 1a.

egg cream *n.* A drink made of milk, syrup, and soda water.

egg•cup (ĕg′kŭp′) *n.* A cup for holding a usu. soft-boiled egg.

eg•ger also **eg•gar** (ĕg′ər) *n.* Any of various moths of the family Lasiocampidae, whose larvae often construct tentlike webs among the branches of trees.

egg•fruit (ĕg′fro͞ot′) *n.* See **canistel.**

egg•head (ĕg′hĕd′) *n. Informal* An intellectual; a highbrow.

egg•head•ed (ĕg′hĕd′ĭd) *adj. Informal* Befitting or having the qualities of an intellectual. **—egg′head′ed•ness** *n.*

egg•nog (ĕg′nŏg′) *n.* A drink consisting of milk or cream, sugar, and eggs beaten together and often mixed with an alcoholic liquor such as rum or brandy. [EGG[1] + *nog*, ale.]

egg•plant (ĕg′plănt′) *n.* **1a.** An Indian plant *(Solanum melongena* var. *esculenta)* cultivated for its edible, ovoid, usu. purple-skinned fruit. **b.** The fruit of this plant. **2.** A blackish purple.

egg roll *n.* A usu. deep-fried cylindrical casing of thin egg dough around minced vegetables and often seafood or meat.

eggs Benedict (ĕgz) *pl.n. (used with a sing. or pl. verb)* A dish consisting of toasted halves of English muffin topped with broiled ham, poached eggs, and hollandaise sauce. [Prob. < the name *Benedict.*]

egg•shell (ĕg′shĕl′) *n.* **1.** The thin brittle exterior covering of the egg of a bird or reptile. **2.** A pale yellow to yellowish white.

egg timer *n.* A small hourglass running three to five minutes, used for timing the boiling of eggs.

egg tooth *n.* A toothlike projection from the beak of embryonic birds or the upper jaw of embryonic reptiles, used to cut the egg membrane and shell upon hatching.

e•gis (ē′jĭs) *n.* Variant of **aegis.**

eg•lan•tine (ĕg′lən-tīn′, -tēn′) *n.* See **sweetbrier.** [ME *eglentin* < OFr. *eglantine*, dim. of *aiglent* < VLat. **aculentum* < neut. of **aculentus*, spiny < Lat. *aculeus*, spine < *acus*, needle. See **ak-** in App.]

e•go (ē′gō, ĕg′ō) *n., pl.* **e•gos 1.** The self, esp. as distinct from the world and other selves. **2.** In psychoanalysis, the part of the psyche that is conscious, most directly controls thought and behavior, and is most aware of external reality. **3a.** An exaggerated sense of self-importance. **b.** Appropriate pride in oneself. [NLat. < Lat., I. See **eg** in App. Sense 2, transl. of Ger. *Ich*, a special use of *ich*, I, as a psychoanalytic term.]

e•go•cen•tric (ē′gō-sĕn′trĭk, ĕg′ō-) *adj.* **1.** Holding the view that the ego is the center, object, and norm of all experience. **2a.** Confined in attitude or interest to one's own needs or affairs. **b.** Caring only about oneself; selfish. **3.** *Philosophy* **a.** Viewed or perceived from one's own mind as a center. **b.** Taking one's own self as the starting point in a philosophical system. **—e′go•cen′tric** *n.* **—e′go•cen′tric•al•ly** *adv.* **—e′go•cen•tric′i•ty** (-trĭs′ĭ-tē), **e′go•cen′trism** *n.*

ego ideal *n.* In psychoanalysis, the part of one's ego containing an idealized self based on people one wishes to emulate.

e•go•ism (ē′gō-ĭz′əm, ĕg′ō-) *n.* **1a.** The ethical doctrine that morality is based on self-interest. **b.** The ethical belief that self-interest justly and properly motivates all conduct. **2.** Excessive preoccupation with one's own well-being and interests, usu. accompanied by conceit. **3.** Egotism; conceit.

e•go•ist (ē′gō-ĭst, ĕg′ō-) *n.* **1.** One devoted to one's own interests and advancement; an egocentric person. **2.** An egotist. **3.** An adherent of egoism. **—e′go•is′tic, e′go•is′ti•cal** *adj.* **—e′go•is′ti•cal•ly** *adv.*

e•go•ma•ni•a (ē′gō-mā′nē-ə, -mān′yə, ĕg′ō-) *n.* Obsessive egoism. **—e′go•ma′ni•ac′** (-nē-ăk′) *n.* **—e′go•ma•ni′a•cal** (-mə-nī′ə-kəl) *adj.* **—e′go•ma•ni′a•cal•ly** *adv.*

e•go•tism (ē′gə-tĭz′əm, ĕg′ə-) *n.* **1.** The tendency to speak or write of oneself excessively and boastfully. **2.** An inflated sense of one's own importance; conceit. [EGO + *-tism*, as in NEPOTISM.]

e•go•tist (ē′gə-tĭst, ĕg′ə-) *n.* **1.** A conceited, boastful person. **2.** A selfish, self-centered person. **—e′go•tis′tic, e′go•tis′ti•cal** *adj.* **—e′go•tis′ti•cal•ly** *adv.*

ego trip *n. Slang* An act or experience that gratifies the ego.

e•go-trip (ē′gō-trĭp′, ĕg′ō-) *intr.v.* **-tripped, -trip•ping, -trips** *Slang* To act egotistically. **—e′go-trip′per** *n.*

e•gre•gious (ĭ-grē′jəs, -jē-əs) *adj.* Conspicuously bad or offensive. [< Lat. *ēgregius*, outstanding : *ē-, ex-*, ex- + *grex, greg-*, herd.] **—e•gre′gious•ly** *adv.* **—e•gre′gious•ness** *n.*

e•gress (ē′grĕs′) *n.* **1.** The act of coming or going out; emergence. **2.** The right to leave or go out. **3.** A path or opening for going out; an exit. **4.** *Astronomy* The emergence of a celestial body from eclipse or occultation. ❖ *intr.v.* **e•gressed, e•gress•ing, e•gress•es** To go out; emerge. [Lat. *ēgressus* < p. part. of *ēgredī*, to go out : *ē-, ex-*, ex- + *gradī*, to go; see **ghredh-** in App.]

e•gres•sion (ĭ-grĕsh′ən) *n.* The act or process of emerging; egress.

e•gret (ē′grĭt, ĕg′rĭt) *n.* Any of several usu. white herons of the genera *Bubulcus, Casmerodius, Egretta*, and related genera, characteristically having long showy drooping plumes during the breeding season. [ME < OFr. *aigrette* < O Provençal *aigreta* < *aigron*, heron, of Gmc. orig.]

E•gypt (ē′jĭpt) Formerly (1958–61) **United Arab Republic.** A country of NE Africa on the Mediterranean Sea. A flourishing ancient kingdom and one of the earliest known civilizations, it became an independent state in 1922. Cap. Cairo. Pop. 48,503,000.

E•gyp•tian (ĭ-jĭp′shən) *n.* **1.** A native or inhabitant of Egypt. **2.** The extinct Afro-Asiatic language of the ancient Egyptians. ❖

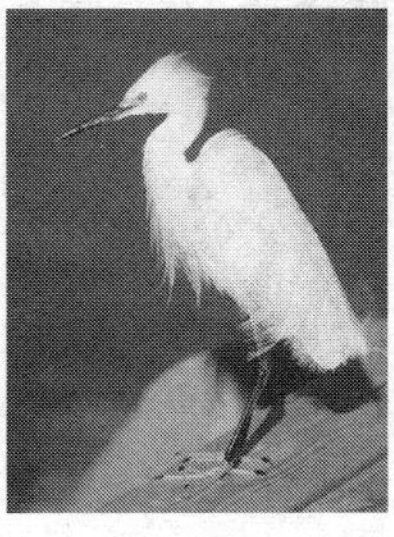

egret
snowy egret
Egretta thula

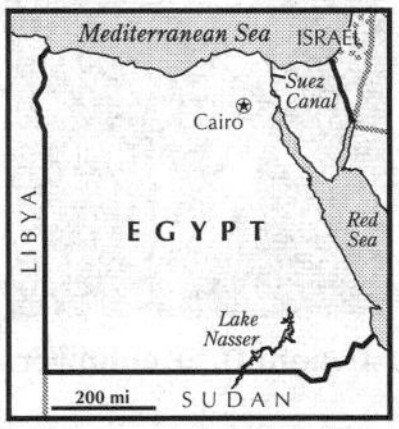

Egypt

ă	pat	oi	boy
ā	pay	ou	out
âr	care	o͝o	took
ä	father	o͞o	boot
ĕ	pet	ŭ	cut
ē	be	ûr	urge
ĭ	pit	th	thin
ī	pie	*th*	this
îr	pier	hw	which
ŏ	pot	zh	vision
ō	toe	ə	about,
ô	paw		item

Stress marks:
′ (primary);
′ (secondary), as in
lexicon (lĕk′sĭ-kŏn′)

adj. 1. Of or relating to Egypt or its people or culture. **2.** Of the language of the ancient Egyptians.

Egyptian clover *n.* See **berseem**.

Egyptian cotton *n.* A fine long-staple cotton grown chiefly in northern Africa.

E•gyp•tol•o•gy (ē′jĭp-tŏl′ə-jē) *n.* The study of the culture and artifacts of the ancient Egyptian civilization. —**E•gyp′to•log′i•cal** (ĭ-jĭp′tə-lŏj′ĭ-kəl) *adj.* —**E•gyp′tol•o•gist** *n.*

eh (ā, ĕ) *interj.* **1.** Used in asking a question or in seeking repetition or confirmation of a statement. **2.** Used to ascertain or reinforce a listener's interest or agreement.

EHF *abbr.* extremely high frequency

EHP *abbr.* **1.** effective horsepower **2.** electric horsepower

Eh•ren•burg (ĕr′ən-bŏŏrg′, ĕr′yĭn-bŏŏrk′), **Ilya Grigorievich** 1891–1967. Russian writer whose novels include *The Storm* (1948) and *The Thaw* (1954).

Ehr•lich (âr′lĭκн), **Paul** 1854–1915. German bacteriologist who shared a 1908 Nobel Prize.

EHV *abbr.* extra-high voltage

EHz *abbr.* exahertz

Eich•mann (īk′mən, īκн′-, īκн-män′), **Adolf** 1906–62. German Nazi official who was head of the Gestapo's Jewish section (1939–45). Captured by the Israeli secret service (1960), he was tried and executed in Israel.

ei•co•sa•pen•ta•e•no•ic acid (ī′kō-sə-pĕn′tə-ĭ-nō′ĭk) *n.* An omega-3 fatty acid found in fish oils. [Gk. *eikosa*, twenty, from its twenty carbon atoms (< *eikosi*; see **wīkṃtī** in App.) + *-pentaen(e)*, having five double bonds (PENTA- + -ENE) + -OIC.]

ei•der (ī′dər) *n.* Any of several large sea ducks, esp. of the genus *Somateria* of northern regions, having soft, commercially valuable down and predominantly black and white plumage in the male. [Back-formation < EIDERDOWN.]

ei•der•down also **eider down** (ī′dər-doun′) *n.* **1.** The down of the eider duck. **2.** A quilt stuffed with eiderdown. **3.** A warm, napped fabric. [Swed. *ejderdun* < Icel. *ædhar-dún* : *ædhar*, genitive of *ædhr*, eider (< ON *ædhr*) + *dún*, down (< ON *dūnn*).]

eider duck *n.* The eider.

ei•det•ic (ī-dĕt′ĭk) *adj.* Of, relating to, or marked by detailed and vivid recall of visual images. [Ger. *eidetisch* < Gk. *eidos*, form. See **weid-** in App.] —**ei•det′i•cal•ly** *adv.*

ei•do•lon (ī-dō′lən) *n., pl.* **-lons** or **-la** (-lə) **1.** A phantom; an apparition. **2.** An image of an ideal. [Gk. *eidōlon* < *eidos*, form. See **weid-** in App.]

Eid al-Fitr (ĭd əl-fĭt′ər) *n.* Variant of **'Id al-Fitr**.

Eif•fel (ī′fəl, ĭ-fĕl′), **Alexandre Gustave** 1832–1923. French engineer who designed the Eiffel Tower, 300 m (984 ft) high, for the Paris Exhibition of 1889.

eight (āt) *n.* **1.** The cardinal number equal to 7 + 1. **2.** The eighth in a set or sequence. **3.** Something having eight parts, units, or members. [ME *eighte* < OE *eahta*. See **oktō(u)** in App.] —**eight** *adj. & pron.*

eight ball *n. Games* A black pool ball that bears the number eight. —*idiom:* **behind the eight ball** *Slang* In an unfavorable or uncomfortable position.

eight•een (ā-tēn′) *n.* **1.** The cardinal number equal to 17 + 1. **2.** The 18th in a set or sequence. [ME *eightetene* < OE *eahtatēne*. See **oktō(u)** in App.] —**eight′een′** *adj. & pron.*

eight•een•mo (ā-tēn′mō) *n., pl.* **-mos** See **octodecimo**. [< *18mo*, abbr. of OCTODECIMO.]

eight•eenth (ā-tēnth′) *n.* **1.** The ordinal number matching the number 18 in a series. **2.** One of 18 equal parts. —**eight′eenth′** *adv. & adj.*

eight•een-wheel•er (ā′tēn-hwē′lər, -wē′-) *n. Informal* A combination of a tractor and a semitrailer.

eighth (ātth, āth) *n.* **1.** The ordinal number matching the number eight in a series. **2.** One of eight equal parts. [ME *eighthe* < OE *eahtotha* < *eahta*, eight. See **oktō(u)** in App.] —**eighth** *adv. & adj.*

eighth note *n. Music* A note having one-eighth the time value of a whole note.

eight•i•eth (ā′tē-ĭth) *n.* **1.** The ordinal number matching the number 80 in a series. **2.** One of 80 equal parts. —**eight′i•eth** *adv. & adj.*

eight•pen•ny nail (āt′pĕn′ē) *n.* A nail 2½ inches (6.4 centimeters) long. [< the former price per hundred.]

eight•vo (āt′vō′) *n., pl.* **-vos** See **octavo**. [< *8vo*, abbr. of OCTAVO.]

eight•y (ā′tē) *n., pl.* **-ies 1.** The cardinal number equal to 8 × 10. **2. eighties a.** A decade or the numbers from 80 to 89. **b.** often **Eighties** The decade from 80 to 89 in a century. [ME *eighti* < OE *eahtatig*. See **oktō(u)** in App.] —**eight′y** *adj. & pron.*

eight•y-eight (ā′tē-āt′) *n.* **1.** A high-velocity gun with a caliber of 88 millimeters, used by German troops during World War II. **2.** An artillery shell, esp. one fired by this gun. **3.** *Slang* A piano. [Sense 3 < the number of its keys.]

eight•y-six or **86** (ā′tē-sĭks′) *tr.v.* **eight•y-sixed, eight•y-six•ing, eight•y-six•es** or **86•ed, 86•ing, 86•es** *Slang* **1.** To refuse to serve (an unwelcome customer) at a bar or restaurant. **2a.** To throw out; eject. **b.** To throw away; discard. [Perhaps after Chumley's bar and restaurant at *86* Bedford Street in Greenwich Village, New York City.]

–ein *suff.* A chemical compound related to a specified compound with a similar name ending in *–in* or *–ine*: *phthalein.* [Alteration of –IN.]

Eind•ho•ven (īnt′hō′vən) A city of S Netherlands SE of Rotterdam; chartered 1232. Pop. 195,632.

ein•korn (īn′kôrn′) *n.* A one-seeded wheat (*Triticum monococcum*) grown in arid regions. [Ger. < MHGer. < OHGer. : *ein*, one; see **oi-no-** in App. + *korn*, grain; see **grə-no-** in App.]

Ein•stein (īn′stīn′), **Albert** 1879–1955. German-born Amer. theoretical physicist whose theories of relativity revolutionized modern thought. He won a 1921 Nobel Prize.

Albert Einstein
photographed c. 1932

ein•stei•ni•um (īn-stī′nē-əm) *n. Symbol* **Es** A radioactive transuranic element synthesized by neutron irradiation of plutonium or other elements. Its longest-lived isotope is Es 254 with a half-life of 276 days. Atomic number 99; melting point 860°C. See table at **element**. [After Albert EINSTEIN.]

Eir•e (âr′ə, ī′rə, âr′ē, ī′rē) See **Ireland**[2].

Ei•sen•how•er (ī′zən-hou′ər), **Dwight David** Known as "Ike." 1890–1969. Amer. general and the 34th President of the US (1953–61). As supreme commander of the Allies (1943–45) he launched the invasion of Normandy (Jun. 6, 1944) and oversaw the defeat of Germany (1945).

Eisenhower, Mamie Geneva Doud 1896–1979. First Lady of the US (1953–61).

Ei•sen•staedt (ī′zən-stät′), **Alfred** 1898–1995. German-born Amer. photographer who pioneered photojournalism.

Ei•sen•stein (ī′zən-stīn′), **Sergei Mikhailovich** 1898–1948. Soviet filmmaker whose influential works include *Potemkin* (1925).

Dwight D. Eisenhower

eis•tedd•fod (ā-stĕth′vŏd, ī-stĕth′-) *n., pl.* **-fods** or **eis•tedd•fod•au** (ā′stĕth-vŏd′ī, ī′stĕth-) An annual competitive festival of Welsh poets and musicians. [Welsh : *eistedd*, sitting; see **sed-** in App. + *bod*, to be; see **bheuə-** in App.]

ei•ther (ē′thər, ī′thər) *pron.* The one or the other: *Either will be fine.* ❖ *conj.* Used before the first of two or more coordinates or clauses linked by *or*: *Either we go or we stay.* ❖ *adj.* **1.** Any one of two; one or the other: *Wear either coat.* **2.** One and the other; each: *rings on either hand.* ❖ *adv.* Likewise; also. Used as an intensive following negative statements: *If you don't order a dessert, I won't either.* [ME < OE *æther, æghwæther.* See **kʷo-** in App.]

USAGE NOTE The traditional rule holds that *either* as a pronoun or an adjective should be used only to refer to one of two items and that *any* is required when more than two items are involved: *Any* (not *either*) *of the three candidates would be good.* But reputable writers have often violated this rule. • In *either . . . or* constructions the two conjunctions should be followed by parallel elements. The following is regarded as correct: *You may have either the ring or the bracelet.* The following is incorrect: *You may either have the ring or the bracelet.* • When used as a pronoun, *either* is singular and takes a singular verb: *The two left-wing parties disagree with each other more than either does with the right.* When followed by *of* and a plural noun, *either* is often used with a plural verb: *Either of the parties have enough support to form a government.* But this usage is widely regarded as incorrect; in an earlier survey it was rejected by 92 percent of the Usage Panel. • When all the elements in an *either . . . or* construction (or a *neither . . . nor* construction) used as the subject of a sentence are singular, the verb is singular; when the elements are plural, the verb is plural. When the construction mixes singular and plural elements, it has sometimes been suggested that the verb should agree with whichever noun phrase is closest to it; thus one would write *Either Eve or the Kays have been invited,* but *Either the Kays or Eve has been invited.* This pattern is accepted by 54 percent of the Usage Panel. Others have maintained that such sentences should be rewritten. See Usage Notes at **every, neither, or**[1].

ei•ther-or (ē′thər-ôr′, ī′thər-) *n.* A strictly limited choice or division between two options. —**ei′ther-or′** *adj.*

e•jac•u•late (ĭ-jăk′yə-lāt′) *v.* **-lat•ed, -lat•ing, -lates** —*tr.* **1.** To eject or discharge abruptly, esp. to discharge (semen) in orgasm. **2.** To utter suddenly and passionately; exclaim. —*intr.* To eject semen. ❖ *n.* (ĭ-jăk′yə-lĭt) The semen ejaculated in orgasm. [Lat. *ēiaculārī, ēiaculāt-* : *ē-, ex-, ex- + iaculārī,* to throw (< *iaculum,* dart).] —**e•jac′u•la′tor** *n.*

e•jac•u•la•tion (ĭ-jăk′yə-lā′shən) *n.* **1a.** The act of ejaculating. **b.** An abrupt discharge of fluid, esp. of seminal fluid. **2.** A sudden short exclamation, esp. a brief pious utterance or prayer. —**e•jac′u•la•to′ry** (-yə-lə-tôr′ē, -tôr′ē) *adj.*

e•ject (ĭ-jĕkt′) *v.* **e•ject•ed, e•ject•ing, e•jects** —*tr.* **1.** To throw out forcefully; expel. **2a.** To compel to leave. **b.** To evict. —*intr.* To make an emergency exit from an aircraft by deployment of an ejection seat or capsule. [ME *ejecten* < Lat. *ēicere, ēiect-* : *ē-, ex-, ex- + iacere,* to throw.] —**e•ject′a•ble** *adj.* —**e•jec′tive** *adj.*

SYNONYMS *eject, expel, evict, oust* These verbs mean to put out by force. To *eject* is to throw or cast out from within: *The fire ejected yellow flames into the night sky.* *Expel* means to drive out or away and implies permanent removal: *expelled the student for cheating.* *Evict* most commonly refers to the expulsion of persons from property by legal process: *evicted the noisy tenants.* *Oust* is applied chiefly to the removal of a person from a position lawfully or otherwise: *ousting the prime minister.*

Mamie Eisenhower
in her inaugural gown,
1959; painting by Thomas
Edgar Stephens
(1886–1966)

e•jec•ta (ĭ-jĕk′tə) *pl.n.* Ejected matter, as that from an erupting volcano. [NLat. *ēiecta* < neut. pl. of Lat. *ēiectus*, p. part. of *ēicere*, to throw out. See EJECT.]

e•jec•tion (ĭ-jĕk′shən) *n.* **1.** The act of ejecting or the condition of being ejected. **2.** Ejected matter.

ejection seat *n.* A seat designed to eject the occupant clear of an aircraft during an in-flight emergency.

e•ject•ment (ĭ-jĕkt′mənt) *n.* **1.** The act or an instance of ejecting; dispossession. **2.** *Law* An action to regain possession of real estate held by another.

e•jec•tor (ĭ-jĕk′tər) *n.* **1.** One that ejects, as a device in a gun that ejects the empty shell after each firing. **2.** A pump using a jet of water, air, or steam to withdraw a fluid from a space.

eke¹ (ēk) *tr.v.* **eked, ek•ing, ekes 1.** To supplement with great effort. Used with *out.* **2.** To get with great effort or strain. Used with *out.* **3.** To make (a supply) last by practicing strict economy. Used with *out.* [ME *eken*, to increase < OE *ēcan*.]

eke² (ēk) *adv. Archaic* Also. [ME < OE *ēac, ēc.*]

EKG *abbr.* **1.** electrocardiogram **2.** electrocardiograph

e•kis•tics (ĭ-kĭs′tĭks) *n.* (*used with a sing. verb*) The science of human settlements, including city or community design. [Mod.Gk. *oikistikē* < fem. of Gk. *oikistikos*, of settlements < *oikistēs*, colonizer, founder < *oikizein*, to settle < *oikos*, house. See ECONOMY.] **—e•kis′tic, e•kis′ti•cal** *adj.* **—ek′is•ti′cian** (ĕk′ĭ-stĭsh′ən) *n.*

el¹ also **ell** (ĕl) *n.* The letter *l.*

el² (ĕl) *n. Informal* An elevated railway.

el. *abbr.* elevation

e•lab•o•rate (ĭ-lăb′ər-ĭt) *adj.* **1.** Planned or executed with painstaking attention to details. **2.** Intricate and rich in detail. ❖ *v.* (ĭ-lăb′ə-rāt′) **-rat•ed, -rat•ing, -rates** *—tr.* **1.** To work out with care and detail; develop thoroughly. **2.** To produce by effort; create. *—intr.* **1.** To become elaborate. **2.** To express at greater length or in greater detail: *I elaborated on my proposal.* [Lat. *ēlabōrātus*, p. part. of *ēlabōrāre*, to work out : *ē-*, *ex-*, intensive pref.; see EX– + *labōrāre*, to work (< *labor*, work).] **—e•lab′o•rate•ly** *adv.* **—e•lab′o•ra′tion** *n.* **—e•lab′o•ra′tor** *n.*

El•a•gab•a•lus (ĕl′ə-găb′ə-ləs) See **Heliogabalus.**

E•laine (ĭ-lān′) *n.* **1.** In Arthurian legend, a woman who died of unrequited love of Lancelot. **2.** In Arthurian legend, the mother of Galahad by Lancelot.

El Al•a•mein (ĕl ăl′ə-mān′, ä′lə-) A town of N Egypt on the Mediterranean Sea; site of a decisive Allied victory in World War II (Nov. 1942).

E•lam (ē′ləm) also **Su•si•a•na** (so͞o′zē-ă′nə, -ăn′ə) An ancient country of SW Asia; est. E of the Tigris R. before 3000 B.C. and known for its warlike people, traditionally thought to be descended from Noah's son Shem.

E•la•mite (ē′lə-mīt′) *n.* **1.** A native or inhabitant of Elam. **2.** The language of the ancient Elamites.

é•lan (ā-läN′, ā-län′) *n.* **1.** Enthusiastic vigor and liveliness. **2.** Distinctive style or flair. [Fr. < OFr. *eslan*, rush < *eslancer*, to hurl : *es-*, out (< Lat. *ex-*; see EX–) + *lancer*, to throw (< LLat. *lanceāre*, to throw a lance < Lat. *lancea*, lance).]

e•land (ē′lənd) *n., pl.* **eland** also **e•lands** Either of two large African antelopes *(Taurotragus oryx* or *T. derbianus)* having a light brown or grayish coat and spirally twisted horns. [Afr. < Du., elk < obsolete Ger. *Elend*, of Balt. orig.; akin to Lith. *elnias*, deer.]

élan vi•tal (vē-tăl′) *n.* The vital force hypothesized by Henri Bergson as a source of efficient causation and evolution in nature. [Fr. : *élan*, ardor + *vital*, vital.]

el•a•pid (ĕl′ə-pĭd) *n.* Any of several venomous snakes of the family Elapidae, which includes the cobras, mambas, and coral snakes. [< NLat. *Elapidae*, family name < L.Gk. *elaps*, *elap-*, fish, var. of Gk. *ellops*.] **—el′a•pid** *adj.*

e•lapse (ĭ-lăps′) *intr.v.* **e•lapsed, e•laps•ing, e•laps•es** To slip by; pass. ❖ *n.* Passage; lapse. [Lat. *ēlābī*, *ēlāps-* : *ē-*, *ex-*, ex- + *lābī*, to slip.]

E•la•ra (ē′lər-ə) *n.* A moon of Jupiter. [Gk., mother by Zeus of the giant Tityus.]

e•las•mo•branch (ĭ-lăz′mə-brăngk′) *n.* Any of numerous fishes of the class Chondrichthyes, characterized by a cartilaginous skeleton and placoid scales and including the sharks, rays, and skates. [< NLat. *Elasmobranchiī*, former subclass name : Gk. *elasmos*, metal beaten out (< *elaunein*, *elas-*, to beat) + Lat. *branchia*, gill; see BRANCHIA.] **—e•las′mo•branch′** *adj.*

e•las•tase (ĭ-lăs′tās, -tāz) *n.* An enzyme found esp. in pancreatic juice that catalyzes the hydrolysis of elastin.

e•las•tic (ĭ-lăs′tĭk) *adj.* **1a.** Easily resuming original shape after being stretched or expanded; flexible. **b.** Springy; rebounding. **2.** *Physics* Returning to or capable of returning to an initial form or state after deformation. **3.** Quick to recover: *an elastic spirit.* **4.** Capable of adapting to change or a variety of circumstances. ❖ *n.* **1a.** A flexible stretchable fabric made with interwoven strands of rubber or an imitative synthetic fiber. **b.** An object made of this fabric. **2.** A rubber band. [NLat. *elasticus* < L.Gk. *elastos*, beaten, ductile, var. of Gk. *elatos* < *elaunein*, to beat out.] **—e•las′ti•cal•ly** *adv.*

elastic collision *n. Physics* A collision of particles in which the total kinetic energy of the particles is conserved.

elastic fiber *n.* A thick yellow connective-tissue fiber composed principally of elastin and characterized by great elasticity.

e•las•tic•i•ty (ĭ-lă-stĭs′ĭ-tē, ē′lă-) *n.* **1.** The condition or property of being elastic; flexibility. **2.** *Physics* **a.** The property of being elastic. **b.** The degree of elasticity.

e•las•ti•cized (ĭ-lăs′tĭ-sīzd′) *adj.* Made with strands or inserts of elastic.

elastic tissue *n.* A type of connective tissue consisting mainly of elastic fibers.

e•las•tin (ĭ-lăs′tĭn) *n.* A protein that is the principal structural component of elastic fibers. [ELAST(IC) + –IN.]

e•las•to•mer (ĭ-lăs′tə-mər) *n.* Any of various polymers having the elastic properties of natural rubber. [ELAST(IC) + (POLY)MER.] **—e•las′to•mer′ic** (-mĕr′ĭk) *adj.*

e•late (ĭ-lāt′) *tr.v.* **e•lat•ed, e•lat•ing, e•lates** To make proud or joyful: *My success elated my family.* ❖ *adj.* Elated. [< Lat. *ēlātus*, p. part. of *efferre*, to bring out, exalt : *ē-*, *ex-*, ex- + *lātus*, brought; see **telə-** in App.] **—e•la′tion** *n.*

e•lat•ed (ĭ-lā′tĭd) *adj.* Exultantly proud and joyful. **—e•lat′ed•ly** *adv.* **—e•lat′ed•ness** *n.*

el•a•ter (ĕl′ə-tər) *n.* **1.** An elaterid beetle. **2.** *Botany* A tiny elongated structure that forces the dispersal of spores. [Gk. *elatēr*, driver < *elaunein*, to drive.]

e•lat•er•id (ĭ-lăt′ər-ĭd) *n.* Any of numerous beetles of the family Elateridae, which includes the click beetles. [< NLat. *Elatēridae*, family name < Gk. *elatēr*, driver. See ELATER.] **—e•lat′er•id** *adj.*

e•lat•er•ite (ĭ-lăt′ə-rīt′) *n.* A brown-to-black, soft, elastic hydrocarbon resin. [ELATER, elasticity (obsolete) + –ITE¹.]

E layer *n.* A region of the ionosphere, extending from about 90 to 150 kilometers (55 to 95 miles) above earth that strongly reflects radio waves in the range from one to three megahertz.

El•ba (ĕl′bə) An island of Italy in the Tyrrhenian Sea between Corsica and the mainland; site of Napoleon Bonaparte's first exile (May 1814–Feb. 1815).

El•be (ĕl′bə, ĕlb) A river of the Czech Republic and Germany flowing c. 1,167 km (725 mi) to the North Sea.

El•bert (ĕl′bərt), **Mount** A peak, 4,402.1 m (14,433 ft), in the Sawatch Range of central CO.

el•bow (ĕl′bō′) *n.* **1a.** The joint or bend of the arm between the forearm and the upper arm. **b.** The bony outer projection of this joint. **2.** A joint, as of a bird, corresponding to the human elbow. **3.** Something having a bend or angle similar to an elbow, esp.: **a.** A length of pipe with a sharp bend in it. **b.** A sharp bend in a river or road. ❖ *v.* **-bowed, -bow•ing, -bows** *—tr.* **1.** To push, jostle, or shove with the elbow. **2.** To open up (a means of passage, for example) by or as if by use of the elbow. *—intr.* **1.** To make one's way by pushing with the elbow. **2.** To turn at an angle; bend. ***—idioms:*** **at (one's) elbow** Close at hand; nearby. **out at the elbows 1.** Poorly dressed. **2.** Lacking money. [ME *elbowe* < OE *elnboga* < Gmc. **elino-bugōn-*, bend in the forearm, elbow.]

elbow grease *n. Informal* Strenuous physical effort.

el•bow•room (ĕl′bō-ro͞om′, -ro͝om′) *n.* **1.** Room to move around or work freely. **2.** Ample scope.

El•brus (ĕl-bro͞os′), **Mount** A peak, 5,645.6 m (18,510 ft), in the Caucasus Mts. of SW Russia.

El•burz Mountains (ĕl-bo͝orz′) A range of N Iran rising to 5,774.9 m (18,934 ft).

El Cap•i•tan (ĕl′ kăp′ĭ-tăn′) A peak, 2,308.5 m (7,569 ft), in the Sierra Nevada of central CA.

El•che (ĕl′chĕ) A city of SE Spain SW of Alicante; held by the Moors from the 8th to the 13th cent. Pop. 188,062.

El Cid (sĭd′) See El **Cid.**

eld•er¹ (ĕl′dər) *adj.* **1.** Greater than another in age or seniority. **2.** Superior to another or others, as in rank. ❖ *n.* **1.** An older person. **2.** An older, influential member of a family, tribe, or community. **3.** One of the governing officers of a church, often having pastoral or teaching functions. [ME *eldre* < OE *eldra.*] **—el′der•ship′** *n.*

USAGE NOTE In comparisons between two persons, *elder* means "older" but not necessarily "old": *My elder sister is sixteen; my younger, ten.* (*Eldest* is used when three or more persons are compared: *He is the eldest of six brothers.*) In other contexts *elder* denotes relatively advanced age along with respect for a person's achievement, as in *an elder statesman.* If age alone is to be expressed, one should use *older* or *elderly* rather than *elder: a survey of older Americans; an elderly waiter.*

el•der² (ĕl′dər) *n.* Any of various shrubs or small trees of the genus *Sambucus,* having clusters of small white flowers and red or purplish-black berrylike fruit. [ME *eldre* < OE *ellærn.*]

el•der•ber•ry (ĕl′dər-bĕr′ē) *n.* **1.** The small edible purplish-black fruit of the common American elder *(Sambucus canadensis).* **2.** A shrub or tree that bears elderberries.

eld•er•care (ĕl′dər-kâr′) *n.* Social and medical programs and facilities intended for the care of the aged.

eld•er•ly (ĕl′dər-lē) *adj.* **1.** Being past middle age and approaching old age; rather old. See Usage Note at **old. 2.** Of, relating to, or characteristic of older persons or life in later years. ❖ *n.* **1.** *pl.* **-lies** An elderly person. **2.** Older people considered as a group. **—el′der•li•ness** *n.*

elder statesman *n.* An older man who is prominent or experienced in a particular field.

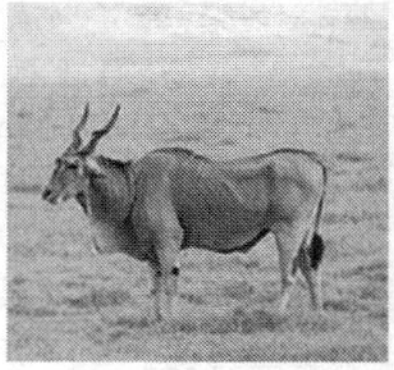

eland
common eland
Taurotragus oryx

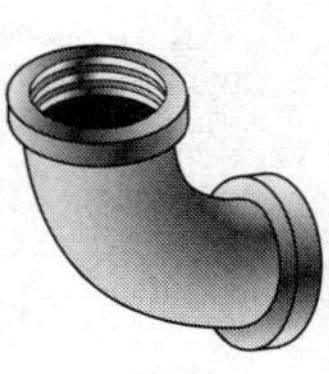

elbow
90° angle elbow with female threads at both ends

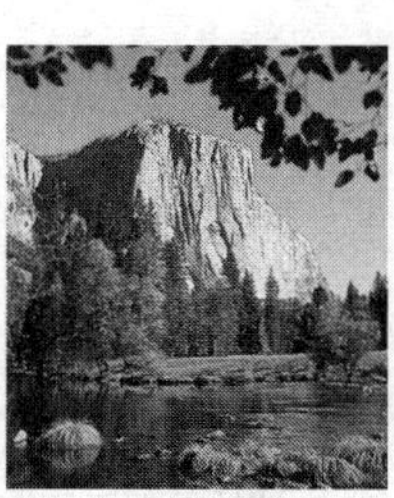

El Capitan

ă	pat	oi	boy
ā	pay	ou	out
âr	care	o͝o	took
ä	father	o͞o	boot
ĕ	pet	ŭ	cut
ē	be	ûr	urge
ĭ	pit	th	thin
ī	pie	*th*	this
îr	pier	hw	which
ŏ	pot	zh	vision
ō	toe	ə	about, item
ô	paw		

Stress marks:
′ (primary);
′ (secondary), as in
lexicon (lĕk′sĭ-kŏn′)

elder stateswoman *n.* An older woman who is prominent or experienced in a particular field.

eld·est (ĕl′dĭst) *adj.* Greatest in age or seniority. See Usage Note at **elder**[1]. [ME < OE *eldesta*.]

El Di·en·te Peak (dē-ĕn′tē) A mountain, 4,318.5 m (14,159 ft) high, in the Rocky Mts. of SW CO.

El Do·ra·do[1] (də-rä′dō, -rä′-) A legendary city or historical region of the New World, often thought to be in South America; fabled for its great wealth.

El Do·ra·do[2] (də-rä′dō, -rä′-) *n.* A place of fabulous wealth or inordinately great opportunity. [After EL DORADO[1].]

el·dritch (ĕl′drĭch) *adj.* Strange or unearthly; eerie. [Perh. ME *elriche* : OE *el-*, strange, other; see **al-** in App. + OE *rīce*, realm; see **reg-** in App.]

E·le·a (ē′lē-ə) also **Ve·li·a** (vē′lē-ə) An ancient Greek colony of S Italy; center of the Eleatic school of philosophy.

El·ea·nor of Aquitaine (ĕl′ə-nər, -nôr′) 1122?–1204. Queen of France (1137–52) and England (1152–1204). Her marriage to Louis VII of France was annulled in 1152, and she then married Henry II of England.

El·e·at·ic (ĕl′ē-ăt′ĭk) *adj.* Of or characteristic of the philosophical tradition founded by Zeno of Elea and by Parmenides, holding that there is one indivisible and unchanging reality. [Lat. *Eleāticus* < Gk. *Eleātikos*, from Elea.] —**El′e·a′tic** *n.* —**El′e·at′i·cism** (-ĭ-sĭz′əm) *n.*

el·e·cam·pane (ĕl′ĭ-kăm-pān′) *n.* A tall plant (*Inula helenium*) native to central Asia and having rayed yellow flower heads. [ME *elecampana* : OE *elene* (ult. < Gk. *helenion* < *Helenē*, Helen; see HELEN) + Med.Lat. *campāna*, of the field (< Lat. *campānea*, fem. of *campāneus* < *campus*, field).]

e·lect (ĭ-lĕkt′) *v.* **e·lect·ed, e·lect·ing, e·lects** —*tr.* **1.** To select by vote for an office or for membership. **2.** To pick out; select. **3.** To decide, esp. by preference. **4.** To select by divine will for salvation. —*intr.* To make a choice or selection. ❖ *adj.* **1.** Chosen deliberately; singled out. **2a.** Elected but not yet installed. Often used in combination: *the governor-elect.* **b.** Chosen for marriage. Often used in combination: *the bride-elect.* **3.** Selected by divine will for salvation. ❖ *n.* **1.** One that is chosen or selected. **2.** One selected by divine will for salvation. **3.** (*used with a pl. verb*) An exclusive group of people. [ME *electen* < Lat. *ēligere, ēlēct-*, to select : *ē-, ex-, ex-* + *legere*, to choose; see **leg-** in App.] —**e·lect′a·bil′i·ty** *n.* —**e·lect′a·ble** *adj.*

e·lec·tion (ĭ-lĕk′shən) *n.* **1a.** The act or power of electing. **b.** The fact of being elected. **2.** The right or ability to make a choice. See Syns at **choice**. **3.** Predestined salvation, esp. as conceived by Calvinists.

Election Day *n.* A day set by law for the election of public officials.

e·lec·tion·eer (ĭ-lĕk′shə-nîr′) *intr.v.* **-eered, -eer·ing, -eers** To work actively for a candidate or political party. —**e·lec′tion·eer′er** *n.*

e·lec·tive (ĭ-lĕk′tĭv) *adj.* **1.** Of or relating to a selection by vote. **2.** Filled or obtained by election. **3.** Having the power or authority to elect; electoral. **4.** Permitting or involving a choice; optional: *elective surgery.* ❖ *n.* An optional academic course or subject. —**e·lec′tive·ly** *adv.* —**e·lec′tive·ness** *n.*

e·lec·tor (ĭ-lĕk′tər) *n.* **1.** A qualified voter in an election. **2.** A member of the Electoral College. **3.** One of the German princes of the Holy Roman Empire entitled to elect the emperor.

e·lec·tor·al (ĭ-lĕk′tər-əl) *adj.* **1.** Of, relating to, or composed of electors. **2.** Relating to election. —**e·lec′tor·al·ly** *adv.*

Electoral College *n.* An electoral body chosen to elect the US President and Vice President.

e·lec·tor·ate (ĭ-lĕk′tər-ĭt) *n.* **1.** A body of qualified voters. **2.** The dignity or territory of an elector of the Holy Roman Empire.

electr– *pref.* Variant of **electro–**.

E·lec·tra (ĭ-lĕk′trə) *n. Greek Mythology* A daughter of Clytemnestra and Agamemnon who with her brother Orestes avenged their father's death by killing their mother and her lover Aegisthus.

Electra complex *n.* In psychoanalysis, a daughter's unconscious libidinal desire for her father.

e·lec·tret (ĭ-lĕk′trĭt) *n.* A solid dielectric that exhibits persistent dielectric polarization. [ELECTR(ICITY) + (MAGN)ET.]

e·lec·tric (ĭ-lĕk′trĭk) *adj.* **1.** also **e·lec·tri·cal** (-trĭ-kəl) Of, relating to, producing, or operated by electricity. **2a.** Of or related to sound created or altered by an electrical device. **b.** Amplified by an electronic device: *an electric guitar.* **3a.** Emotionally exciting; thrilling. **b.** Exceptionally tense; highly charged with emotion. ❖ *n.* An electrically powered machine or vehicle. [NLat. *ēlectricus*, deriving from amber, as by rubbing < Lat. *ēlectrum*, amber < Gk. *ēlektron*.] —**e·lec′tri·cal·ly** *adv.*

electrical engineering *n.* The branch of engineering that deals with the technology of electricity, esp. the design and application of circuitry and equipment for power generation and distribution, machine control, and communications. —**electrical engineer** *n.*

electrical storm *n.* A thunderstorm.

electric arc *n.* A luminous discharge that is formed when a current jumps a gap in a circuit or between two electrodes.

electric chair *n.* **1.** A chair used in the electrocution of a prisoner sentenced to death by law. **2.** Execution by means of electrocu-

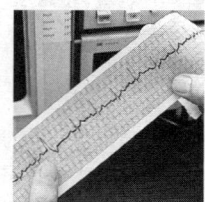

electrocardiogram

tion. **3.** The sentence of death by electrocution.

electric eel *n.* A long eellike freshwater fish (*Electrophorus electricus*) of northern South America having organs capable of producing a powerful electric discharge.

electric eye *n.* See **photoelectric cell**.

electric field *n.* A region of space characterized by the existence of a force generated by electric charge.

e·lec·tri·cian (ĭ-lĕk-trĭsh′ən, ē′lĕk-) *n.* One whose occupation is the installation, maintenance, repair, or operation of electric equipment and circuitry.

e·lec·tric·i·ty (ĭ-lĕk-trĭs′ĭ-tē, ē′lĕk-) *n.* **1a.** The physical phenomena arising from the behavior of electrons and protons caused by attraction of particles with opposite charges and repulsion of particles with the same charge. **b.** The physical science of such phenomena. **2.** Electric current as a source of power. **3.** Intense, contagious emotional excitement.

electric ray *n.* Any of various tropical or subtropical marine fishes of the family Torpedinidae, capable of producing an electric discharge that is used to stun or kill prey.

e·lec·tri·fy (ĭ-lĕk′trə-fī′) *tr.v.* **-fied, -fy·ing, -fies 1.** To produce electric charge on or in (a conductor). **2a.** To wire or equip (a building, for example) for the use of electric power. **b.** To provide with electric power. **c.** *Music* To amplify (music) by electronic means. **3.** To thrill, startle greatly, or shock. —**e·lec′tri·fi′a·ble** *adj.* —**e·lec′tri·fi·ca′tion** (-fĭ-kā′shən) *n.* —**e·lec′tri·fi′er** *n.* —**e·lec′tri·fy′ing·ly** *adv.*

electro– or **electr–** *pref.* **1a.** Electricity: *electromagnet.* **b.** Electric; electrically: *electrocute.* **2.** Electrolysis: *electrodeposit.* **3.** Electron: *electronegative.* [NLat. *ēlectro–* < Lat. *ēlectrum*, amber. See ELECTRIC.]

e·lec·tro·a·cous·tics (ĭ-lĕk′trō-ə-kōō′stĭks) *n.* (*used with a sing. verb*) The science that deals with the interaction or interconversion of electric and acoustic phenomena. —**e·lec′tro·a·cous′tic** *adj.*

e·lec·tro·car·di·o·gram (ĭ-lĕk′trō-kär′dē-ə-grăm′) *n.* The curve traced by an electrocardiograph.

e·lec·tro·car·di·o·graph (ĭ-lĕk′trō-kär′dē-ə-grăf′) *n.* An instrument used in the detection and diagnosis of heart abnormalities that generates a record of the electrical currents associated with heart muscle activity. —**e·lec′tro·car′di·o·graph′ic** (-grăf′ĭk) *adj.* —**e·lec′tro·car′di·o·graph′i·cal·ly** *adv.* —**e·lec′tro·car′di·og′ra·phy** (-kär′dē-ŏg′rə-fē) *n.*

e·lec·tro·chem·i·cal cell (ĭ-lĕk′trō-kĕm′ĭ-kəl) *n.* See **cell** 6a.

e·lec·tro·chem·is·try (ĭ-lĕk′trō-kĕm′ĭ-strē) *n.* The science of the interaction or interconversion of electric and chemical phenomena. —**e·lec′tro·chem′i·cal·ly** *adv.* —**e·lec′tro·chem′ist** *n.*

e·lec·tro·chro·mic (ĭ-lĕk′trō-krō′mĭk) *adj.* Of or relating to a substance that changes color when subjected to charged electrodes, as in the liquid crystal display of many calculators. [ELECTRO– + CHROM(O)– + –IC.]

e·lec·tro·con·vul·sive therapy (ĭ-lĕk′trō-kən-vŭl′sĭv) *n.* Administration of electric current to the brain through electrodes on the head to induce seizure activity, used esp. to treat severe depression.

e·lec·tro·cute (ĭ-lĕk′trə-kyōōt′) *tr.v.* **-cut·ed, -cut·ing, -cutes 1.** To kill with electricity. **2.** To execute (a condemned prisoner) by means of electricity. [ELECTRO– + (EXE)CUTE.] —**e·lec′tro·cu′tion** (-kyōō′shən) *n.*

e·lec·trode (ĭ-lĕk′trōd′) *n.* **1.** A solid electric conductor through which an electric current enters or leaves an electrolytic cell or other medium. **2.** A collector or emitter of electric charge or of electric-charge carriers, as in a semiconducting device.

electrode collector *n.* An electrode in an electron tube that collects electrons that have finished carrying current.

e·lec·tro·de·pos·it (ĭ-lĕk′trō-dĭ-pŏz′ĭt) *tr.v.* **-it·ed, -it·ing, -its** To deposit (a dissolved or suspended substance) on an electrode by electrolysis. ❖ *n.* The substance so deposited. —**e·lec′tro·dep′o·si′tion** (-dĕp′ə-zĭsh′ən, -dē′pə-) *n.*

e·lec·tro·di·al·y·sis (ĭ-lĕk′trō-dī-ăl′ĭ-sĭs) *n., pl.* **-ses** (-sēz′) Dialysis at a rate increased by the application of an electric potential across the dialysis membrane.

e·lec·tro·dy·nam·ics (ĭ-lĕk′trō-dī-năm′ĭks) *n.* (*used with a sing. verb*) The study of moving electric charges and their interaction with magnetic and electric fields. —**e·lec′tro·dy·nam′ic** *adj.*

e·lec·tro·dy·na·mom·e·ter (ĭ-lĕk′trō-dī′nə-mŏm′ĭ-tər) *n.* An instrument that measures current by indicating the level of magnetic attraction or repulsion between a fixed and a movable coil, one of which carries the unknown current.

e·lec·tro·en·ceph·a·lo·gram (ĭ-lĕk′trō-ĕn-sĕf′ə-lə-grăm′) *n.* A graphic record of the electrical activity of the brain as recorded by an electroencephalograph.

e·lec·tro·en·ceph·a·lo·graph (ĭ-lĕk′trō-ĕn-sĕf′ə-lə-grăf′) *n.* An instrument that generates a record of the electrical activity of the brain. —**e·lec′tro·en·ceph′a·lo·graph′ic** *adj.* —**e·lec′tro·en·ceph′a·log′ra·phy** (-lŏg′rə-fē) *n.*

e·lec·tro·form (ĭ-lĕk′trə-fôrm′) *tr.v.* **-formed, -form·ing, -forms** To produce or reproduce (an object) by electrodeposition on a mold.

e·lec·tro·gas·dy·nam·ics (ĭ-lĕk′trə-găs′dī-năm′ĭks) *n.* (*used* with a sing. verb) Generation of electrical energy from the kinetic energy contained in a high-pressure, ionized, moving combustion gas. —e•lec′tro•gas′dy•nam′ic adj.

e•lec•tro•gen•e•sis (ĭ-lĕk′trə-jĕn′ĭ-sĭs) n. Production of electrical impulses in living organisms or tissues. —e•lec′tro•gen′ic adj.

e•lec•tro•graph (ĭ-lĕk′trə-grăf′) n. 1. An electrically produced graph or tracing. 2. Equipment used to produce such a graph or tracing in facsimile transmission.

e•lec•tro•hy•drau•lic (ĭ-lĕk′trō-hī-drô′lĭk) adj. Of, relating to, or involving a combination of electric and hydraulic mechanisms. —e•lec′tro•hy•drau′li•cal•ly adv.

e•lec•tro•jet (ĭ-lĕk′trō-jĕt′) n. An electric current that moves in an ionized layer above the equator in the earth's upper atmosphere. [ELECTRO– + JET (STREAM).]

e•lec•tro•kin•et•ics (ĭ-lĕk′trō-kə-nĕt′ĭks, -kī-) n. (used with a sing. verb) The electrodynamics of heating effects and current distribution in electric networks.

e•lec•trol•o•gist (ĭ-lĕk-trŏl′ə-jĭst, ē′lĕk-) n. One who removes body hair by means of an electric current.

e•lec•tro•lu•mi•nes•cence (ĭ-lĕk′trō-loo′mə-nĕs′əns) n. 1. Direct conversion of electric energy to light by a solid phosphor subjected to an alternating electric field. 2. Emission of light that is caused by electric discharge in a gas. —e•lec′tro•lu′mi•nes′cent adj.

e•lec•trol•y•sis (ĭ-lĕk-trŏl′ĭ-sĭs, ē′lĕk-) n. 1. Chemical decomposition, produced in an electrolyte by an electric current. 2. Destruction of living tissue, esp. of hair roots, by means of an electric current applied with a needle-shaped electrode.

e•lec•tro•lyte (ĭ-lĕk′trə-līt′) n. 1. A chemical compound that ionizes when dissolved or molten to produce an electrically conductive medium. 2. Physiology Any of various ions required by cells to regulate the electric charge and flow of water molecules across the cell membrane.

e•lec•tro•lyt•ic (ĭ-lĕk′trə-lĭt′ĭk) adj. 1a. Of or relating to electrolysis. b. Produced by electrolysis. 2. Of or relating to electrolytes. —e•lec′tro•lyt′i•cal•ly adv.

e•lec•tro•lyze (ĭ-lĕk′trə-līz′) tr.v. -lyzed, -lyz•ing, -lyz•es To cause to decompose by electrolysis.

e•lec•tro•mag•net (ĭ-lĕk′trō-măg′nĭt) n. A magnet consisting essentially of a coil of insulated wire around a soft iron core, magnetized only when current flows through the wire.

e•lec•tro•mag•net•ic (ĭ-lĕk′trō-măg-nĕt′ĭk) adj. Of or exhibiting electromagnetism. —e•lec′tro•mag•net′i•cal•ly adv.

electromagnetic field n. The field associated with electric charge in motion, having both electric and magnetic components.

electromagnetic pulse n. 1. The pulse of intense electromagnetic radiation generated by a nuclear explosion. 2. The pulse of electromagnetic radiation emitted by the transmission of certain devices as citizen band radios and cellular phones.

electromagnetic spectrum n. The entire range of radiation extending in frequency from approx. 10²³ hertz to 0 hertz or, in wavelengths, from 10⁻¹³ centimeter to infinity.

electromagnetic unit n. Any of various systems of units for electricity and magnetism in which the permeability of free space is taken as unity and the abampere is the fundamental unit of current.

electromagnetic wave n. A wave propagated as a periodic disturbance of the electromagnetic field when an electric charge oscillates or accelerates.

e•lec•tro•mag•net•ism (ĭ-lĕk′trō-măg′nĭ-tĭz′əm) n. 1. Magnetism produced by electric charge in motion. 2. The physics of electricity and magnetism.

e•lec•tro•me•chan•i•cal (ĭ-lĕk′trō-mə-kăn′ĭ-kəl) adj. Relating to a mechanical device or system that is actuated or controlled by electricity.

e•lec•tro•met•al•lur•gy (ĭ-lĕk′trō-mĕt′l-ûr′jē) n. The use of electric and electrolytic processes to purify metals or reduce metallic compounds to metals. —e•lec′tro•met′al•lur′gi•cal adj.

e•lec•trom•e•ter (ĭ-lĕk-trŏm′ĭ-tər, ē′lĕk-) n. An instrument for measuring voltage.

e•lec•tro•mo•tive (ĭ-lĕk′trō-mō′tĭv) adj. Of, relating to, or producing electric current.

electromotive force n. The energy per unit charge that is converted from chemical, mechanical, or other forms of energy into electrical energy in a battery or dynamo.

e•lec•tro•my•o•gram (ĭ-lĕk′trō-mī′ō-grăm′) n. A graphic record of the electrical activity of a muscle as recorded by an electromyograph.

e•lec•tro•my•o•graph (ĭ-lĕk′trō-mī′ə-grăf′) n. An instrument that produces an audio or visual record of the electrical activity of a skeletal muscle. —e•lec′tro•my′o•graph′ic adj. —e•lec′tro•my•og′ra•phy (-mī-ŏg′rə-fē) n.

e•lec•tron (ĭ-lĕk′trŏn′) n. A stable subatomic particle in the lepton family having a rest mass of 9.1066 × 10⁻²⁸ grams and a unit negative electric charge of approx. 1.602 × 10⁻¹⁹ coulombs. [ELECTR(IC) + –ON¹.]

e•lec•tro•neg•a•tive (ĭ-lĕk′trō-nĕg′ə-tĭv) adj. 1. Having a negative electric charge. 2. Tending to attract electrons to form a chemical bond. 3. Capable of acting as a negative electrode.

electron gun n. The electrode, esp. in a cathode-ray tube, that produces a beam of accelerated electrons.

electron hole n. See hole 9.

e•lec•tron•ic (ĭ-lĕk-trŏn′ĭk, ē′lĕk-) adj. 1. Of or relating to electrons. 2. Of, relating to, or involving the controlled conduction of electrons or other charge carriers, esp. in a vacuum, gas, or semiconducting material. 3. Of, relating to, or produced by means of electronics: electronic books. 4. Of or relating to music produced or altered by electronic means, as by a synthesizer. 5. Of, implemented on, or controlled by a computer or computer network. —e•lec′tron′i•cal•ly adv.

electronic mail n. E-mail.

e•lec•tron•ics (ĭ-lĕk-trŏn′ĭks, ē′lĕk-) n. 1. (used with a sing. verb) The science and technology of electronic phenomena. 2. (used with a pl. verb) Electronic devices and systems.

electron lens n. Any of various devices that use an electric or magnetic field to focus a beam of electrons.

electron microscope n. Any of a class of microscopes that use electrons rather than visible light to produce images with linear magnification approaching or exceeding a million (10⁶).

electron multiplier n. A vacuum tube in which current amplification occurs through repeated collisions of secondary electrons with a series of anodes.

electron neutrino n. A stable elementary particle in the lepton family having a mass of zero, or very close to zero, and no charge.

electron optics n. (used with a sing. verb) The science of the control of electron motion by electron lenses in systems or under conditions analogous to those involving or affecting visible light.

electron pair n. Two electrons functioning or regarded as functioning in concert, esp. two electrons that form a nonpolar covalent bond between atoms.

electron transport n. The successive passage of electrons from one cytochrome or flavoprotein to another by a series of oxidation-reduction reactions during the aerobic production of ATP.

electron tube n. A sealed enclosure, either highly evacuated or containing a controlled quantity of gas, in which electrons can be made sufficiently mobile to act as the principal carriers of current between at least one pair of electrodes.

electron volt n. A unit of energy equal to the energy acquired by an electron falling through a potential difference of one volt, approx. 1.602 ×10⁻¹⁹ joules.

e•lec•tro•phile (ĭ-lĕk′trə-fīl′) n. A chemical compound or group attracted to electrons and tending to accept them.

e•lec•tro•pho•re•sis (ĭ-lĕk′trō-fə-rē′sĭs) n. 1. The migration of charged colloidal particles or molecules through a solution in an electric field. 2. A method of analyzing substances based on the rate of movement of each component in a colloidal suspension while in an electric field. —e•lec′tro•pho•ret′ic (-rĕt′ĭk) adj.

e•lec•tro•pho•ret•o•gram (ĭ-lĕk′trō-fə-rĕt′ə-grăm′) n. A record of the results of an electrophoresis.

e•lec•troph•o•rus (ĭ-lĕk-trŏf′ər-əs, ē′lĕk-) n., pl. -o•ri (-ə-rī′, -ə-rē′) An apparatus for generating static electricity, consisting of a hard rubber disk and a metal plate. [NLat. : ELECTRO– + Gk. -phoros, -phorous.]

e•lec•tro•phys•i•ol•o•gy (ĭ-lĕk′trō-fĭz′ē-ŏl′ə-jē) n. 1. The branch of physiology that studies the relationship between electric phenomena and bodily processes. 2. The electric activity associated with a bodily part or function. —e•lec′tro•phys′i•o•log′ic (-ə-lŏj′ĭk), e•lec′tro•phys′i•o•log′i•cal (-ĭ-kəl) adj. —e•lec′tro•phys′i•o•log′i•cal•ly adv. —e•lec′tro•phys′i•ol′o•gist n.

e•lec•tro•plate (ĭ-lĕk′trə-plāt′) tr.v. -plat•ed, -plat•ing, -plates To coat with a thin layer of metal by electrodeposition.

e•lec•tro•pos•i•tive (ĭ-lĕk′trō-pŏz′ĭ-tĭv) adj. 1. Having a positive electric charge. 2. Capable of acting as a positive electrode. 3. Tending to release electrons to form a chemical bond.

e•lec•tro•re•cep•tor (ĭ-lĕk′trō-rĭ-sĕp′tər) n. Any of a series of sensory organs in certain fish that detect electric fields.

e•lec•tro•rhe•ol•o•gy (ĭ-lĕk′trō-rē-ŏl′ə-jē) n. The study of the changes in flow properties that occur in certain fluids exposed to electric fields. —e•lec′tro•rhe′o•log′i•cal (-ə-lŏj′ĭ-kəl) adj.

e•lec•tro•scope (ĭ-lĕk′trə-skōp′) n. An instrument used to detect the presence, sign, and in some configurations the magnitude of an electric charge by the mutual attraction or repulsion of metal foils or pith balls. —e•lec′tro•scop′ic (-skŏp′ĭk) adj.

e•lec•tro•shock (ĭ-lĕk′trō-shŏk′) or electroshock therapy n. See electroconvulsive therapy.

e•lec•tro•stat•ic (ĭ-lĕk′trō-stăt′ĭk) adj. 1a. Of or relating to electric charges at rest. b. Produced or caused by such charges. 2. Of or relating to electrostatics. —e•lec′tro•stat′i•cal•ly adv.

electrostatic generator n. Any of various devices, such as the Van de Graaff generator, that generate high voltages by accumulating large quantities of electric charge.

electrostatic precipitation n. The removal of very fine particles suspended in a gas by electrostatic charging and subsequent precipitation onto a collector in a strong electric field.

electrostatic printing n. A process for printing or copying in which electrostatic charges are used to form the image in powder or ink on the surface to be printed.

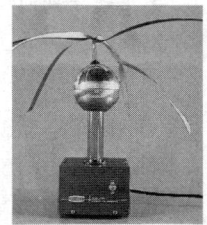

electrostatic generator
The ribbons and dome of this Van de Graaff generator become negatively charged and are repelled from each other.

e•lec•tro•stat•ics (ĭ-lĕk′trō-stăt′ĭks) *n.* *(used with a sing. verb)* The physics of electrostatic phenomena.

electrostatic unit *n.* Any unit of electricity or magnetism in the centimeter-gram-second system based on the forces of interaction between electric charges.

e•lec•tro•sur•ger•y (ĭ-lĕk′trō-sûr′jə-rē) *n.* The surgical use of high-frequency electric current. **—e•lec′tro•sur′gi•cal** (-jĭ-kəl) *adj.*

e•lec•tro•ther•a•peu•tics (ĭ-lĕk′trō-thĕr′ə-pyo͞o′tĭks) *n.* *(used with a sing. verb)* See **electrotherapy.**

e•lec•tro•ther•a•py (ĭ-lĕk′trō-thĕr′ə-pē) *n., pl.* **-pies** Medical therapy using electric currents.

e•lec•tro•ther•mal (ĭ-lĕk′trō-thûr′məl) *adj.* **1.** Of, relating to, or involving both electricity and heat. **2.** Of or relating to the production of heat by electricity.

e•lec•trot•o•nus (ĭ-lĕk′trŏt′n-əs, ē′lĕk-) *n.* Alteration in nerve or muscle excitability and conductivity while a constant electric current passes through. **—e•lec′tro•ton′ic** (-trə-tŏn′ĭk) *adj.*

e•lec•tro•type (ĭ-lĕk′trə-tīp′) *n.* **1.** A metal plate used in letterpress printing, made by electroplating a lead or plastic mold of the page to be printed. **2.** The process of making an electrotype. **—e•lec′tro•type′** *v.* **—e•lec′tro•typ′er** *n.* **—e•lec′tro•typ′ic** (-trō-tĭp′ĭk) *adj.*

e•lec•tro•va•lence (ĭ-lĕk′trō-vā′ləns) *n.* **1.** Valence characterized by the transfer of electrons from atoms of one element to atoms of another during the formation of an ionic bond between the atoms. **2.** The number of electric charges lost or gained by an atom in such a transfer. **—e•lec′tro•va′lent** *adj.*

e•lec•tro•va•len•cy (ĭ-lĕk′trō-vā′lən-sē) *n.* Electrovalence.

electrovalent bond *n.* See **ionic bond.**

e•lec•tro•weak (ĭ-lĕk′trō-wēk′) *adj.* Of or relating to the combination of the electromagnetic and weak nuclear forces in a unified theory.

e•lec•trum (ĭ-lĕk′trəm) *n.* An alloy of silver and gold. [ME < Lat. *ēlectrum*, amber < Gk. *ēlektron.*]

e•lec•tu•ar•y (ĭ-lĕk′cho͞o-ĕr′ē) *n., pl.* **-ies** A drug mixed with sugar and water or honey into a pasty mass suitable for oral administration. [ME *electuarie* < LLat. *ēlēctuārium*, prob. alteration of Gk. *ekleikton* < *ekleikhein*, to lick up : *ek-*, out; see **eghs** in App. + *leikhein*, to lick; see **leigh-** in App.]

el•ee•mos•y•nar•y (ĕl′ə-mŏs′ə-nĕr′ē, ĕl′ē-ə-) *adj.* **1.** Of, relating to, or dependent on charity. **2.** Contributed as an act of charity; gratuitous. [Med.Lat. *eleēmosynārius* < LLat. *eleēmosyna*, alms. See ALMS.]

el•e•gance (ĕl′ĭ-gəns) *n.* **1a.** Refinement, grace, and beauty in movement, appearance, or manners. **b.** Tasteful opulence in form, decoration, or presentation. **2a.** Restraint and grace of style. **b.** Scientific precision. **3.** Something elegant.

el•e•gan•cy (ĕl′ĭ-gən-sē) *n., pl.* **-cies** Elegance.

el•e•gant (ĕl′ĭ-gənt) *adj.* Characterized by or exhibiting refined, tasteful beauty of manner, form, or style. See Syns at **delicate.** [ME < OFr. < Lat. *ēlegāns*, *ēlegant-*, ult. < *ēligere*, to select. See ELECT.] **—el′e•gant•ly** *adv.*

el•e•gi•ac (ĕl′ə-jī′ək, ĭ-lē′jē-ăk′) *adj.* **1.** Of, relating to, or involving elegy or mourning or expressing sorrow for that which is irrecoverably past. **2.** Of or composed in elegiac couplets. [LLat. *elegīacus* < Gk. *elegeiakos* < *elegeia*, elegy. See ELEGY.] **—el′e•gi′ac** *n.* **—el′e•gi′a•cal** *adj.* **—el′e•gi′a•cal•ly** *adv.*

elegiac couplet *n.* A unit of verse in Greek and Roman prosody consisting of a line of dactylic hexameter followed by a line of dactylic pentameter.

elegiac stanza *n.* A four-line stanza in iambic pentameter rhyming on alternate lines.

el•e•gist (ĕl′ə-jĭst) *n.* The composer of an elegy.

el•e•gize (ĕl′ə-jīz′) *v.* **-gized, -giz•ing, -giz•es** *—intr.* To compose an elegy. *—tr.* To compose an elegy upon or for.

el•e•gy (ĕl′ə-jē) *n., pl.* **-gies 1.** A poem composed in elegiac couplets. **2a.** A poem or song composed esp. as a lament for a deceased person. **b.** Something resembling such a poem or song. **3.** *Music* A composition that is melancholy or pensive in tone. [Fr. *élégie* < Lat. *elegīa* < Gk. *elegeia*, pl. of *elegeion*, elegiac distich < *elegos*, song, mournful song.]

el•e•ment (ĕl′ə-mənt) *n.* **1.** A fundamental, essential, or irreducible constituent of a composite entity. **2. elements** The basic assumptions or principles of a subject. **3.** *Mathematics* **a.** A member of a set. **b.** A point, line, or plane. **c.** A part of a geometric configuration, such as an angle in a triangle. **d.** The generatrix of a geometric figure. **e.** Any of the terms in the rectangular array of terms that constitute a matrix or determinant. **4.** *Chemistry & Physics* A substance composed of atoms having an identical number of protons in each nucleus. See table on pages 454-455. **5.** One of four substances, earth, air, fire, or water, formerly regarded as a fundamental constituent of the universe. **6.** *Electricity* The resistance wire in an electrical appliance such as a heater or oven. **7. elements** The forces that constitute the weather, esp. severe or inclement weather. **8.** An environment naturally suited to or associated with an individual. **9.** A distinct group within a larger community. **10.** A part of a military force, esp.: **a.** A ground unit in an air force comparable to a platoon. **b.** A unit of an air force equal to two or three aircraft. **11. elements** The bread and wine of the Eucharist. [ME < OFr. < Lat. *elementum*, perh. ult. < *l m n*, first three letters of the second half of the Canaanite alphabet, recited by ancient scribes when learning it.]

SYNONYMS *element, component, constituent, factor, ingredient* These nouns denote one of the individual parts of which a composite entity is made up: *the grammatical elements of a sentence; jealousy, a component of his character; melody and harmony, two of the constituents of a musical composition; ambition as a key factor in her success; humor, an effective ingredient of a speech.*

element 110 *n.* An artificially produced radioactive element with atomic number 110 whose isotope has a mass number of 269 and a half-life of 10 milliseconds.

element 111 *n.* An artificially produced radioactive element with atomic number 111 whose isotope has a mass number of 272 and a half-life of 1.5 milliseconds.

element 112 *n.* An artificially produced radioactive element with atomic number 112 whose isotope has a mass number of 277 and a half-life of 280 milliseconds.

el•e•men•tal (ĕl′ə-mĕn′tl) *adj.* **1.** Of, relating to, or being an element. **2a.** Fundamental or essential; basic. **b.** Of or relating to fundamentals; elementary. **c.** Constituting an integral part; inborn. **3.** Of such character as to resemble a force of nature in power or effect. **—el′e•men′tal** *n.* **—el′e•men′tal•ly** *adv.*

el•e•men•ta•ry (ĕl′ə-mĕn′tə-rē, -trē) *adj.* **1.** Of, relating to, or constituting the basic, essential, or fundamental part. **2.** Relating to or involving the basic or simplest aspects of a subject. **3.** Relating to an elementary school or elementary education. **—el′e•men•ta′ri•ly** (-tĕr′ə-lē) *adv.* **—el′e•men′ta•ri•ness** *n.*

elementary particle *n.* Any of the subatomic particles that compose matter and energy, esp. one hypothesized or regarded as an irreducible constituent of matter.

elementary school *n.* **1.** A school for the first four to eight years of a child's formal education, often including kindergarten. **2.** The first four to eight years of formal education.

el•e•mi (ĕl′ə-mē) *n., pl.* **-mis** Any of various oily resins derived from certain tropical trees, esp. *Canarium luzonicum*, and used in making varnishes and inks. [Prob. ult. < Ar. *al-lāmī* : *al-*, the + *lāmī*, a resin.]

el•e•phant (ĕl′ə-fənt) *n.* **1.** Either of two very large herbivorous mammals, *Elephas maximus* of south-central Asia or *Loxodonta africana* of Africa, having thick skin, a long prehensile trunk, and long curved ivory tusks. **2.** Any of various extinct or living animals related to either of these two animals. [ME *elefaunt* < OFr. *olifant* < VLat. **olifantus* < Lat. *elephantus* < Gk. *elephās*, *elephant-*.]

elephant folio *n.* A book or publication of the largest size, often about 60 centimeters (2 feet) in height.

el•e•phan•ti•a•sis (ĕl′ə-fən-tī′ə-sĭs) *n.* Chronic, often extreme enlargement and hardening of cutaneous and subcutaneous tissue, esp. of the legs and external genitals, usu. caused by infestation of the lymph glands and vessels with a filarial worm. [Lat. *elephantiāsis* < Gk. : *elephās*, *elephant-*, elephant + *-iāsis*, -iasis.]

el•e•phan•tine (ĕl′ə-făn′tēn′, -tīn′, ĕl′ə-fən-) *adj.* **1.** Of or relating to an elephant. **2.** Enormous in size or strength. **3.** Ponderously clumsy.

elephant seal *n.* Either of two large seals, *Mirounga angustirostris* mainly of Pacific coastal waters of California or *M. leonina* of coastal waters of the Southern Hemisphere, the males of which have an inflatable trunklike proboscis.

el•e•phant's foot (ĕl′ə-fənts) *n., pl.* **elephant's foots 1.** An African species of yam *(Dioscorea elephantipes)* with clusters of tubers that grow above the ground. **2.** Any of several plants of the genus *Elephantopus* in the composite family, having purplish flowers grouped in discoid flower heads.

Eleusinian mysteries *pl.n.* The ancient religious rites celebrated at Eleusis in honor of Demeter. [< Lat. *Eleusīnius*, of Eleusis < Gk. *Eleusīnios* < *Eleusis*, *Eleusīn-*, Eleusis.]

E•leu•sis (ĭ-lo͞o′sĭs) An ancient city of E Greece near Athens. **—El′eu•sin′i•an** (ĕl′yo͞o-sĭn′ē-ən) *adj. & n.*

elev. *abbr.* elevation

el•e•vate (ĕl′ə-vāt′) *tr.v.* **-vat•ed, -vat•ing, -vates 1.** To move (something) to a higher place or position from a lower one; lift. **2.** To increase the amplitude, intensity, or volume of. **3.** To promote to a higher rank. **4.** To raise to a higher moral, cultural, or intellectual level. **5.** To lift the spirits of; elate. See Syns at **lift.** [ME *elevaten* < Lat. *ēlevāre*, *ēlevāt-* : *ē-*, *ex-*, up; see EX– + *levāre*, to raise.]

el•e•vat•ed (ĕl′ə-vā′tĭd) *adj.* **1a.** Raised esp. above the ground. **b.** Increased in amount or degree. **2a.** Morally or intellectually superior. **b.** Formal; lofty. **3.** Elated in feeling or mood; high-spirited. ❖ *n.* An elevated railway.

elevated railway *n.* A railway that operates on a raised structure in order to permit passage beneath it.

el•e•va•tion (ĕl′ə-vā′shən) *n.* **1a.** The act or an instance of elevating. **b.** The condition of being elevated. **2.** An elevated place or position. **3.** The height to which something is elevated above a point of reference. **4.** Loftiness of thought or feeling. **5.** A scale drawing of the side, front, or rear of a structure. **6.** The height of a thing above a reference level; altitude. **7a.** The ability to achieve height in a jump. **b.** The degree of height reached by such a jump.

el•e•va•tor (ĕl′ə-vā′tər) *n.* **1a.** A platform or an enclosure raised

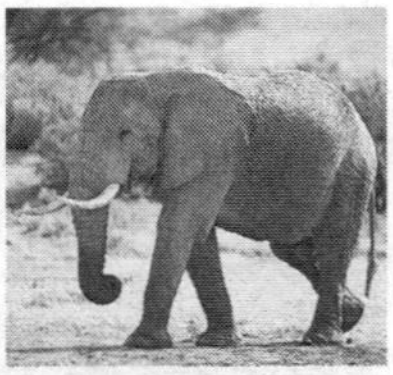
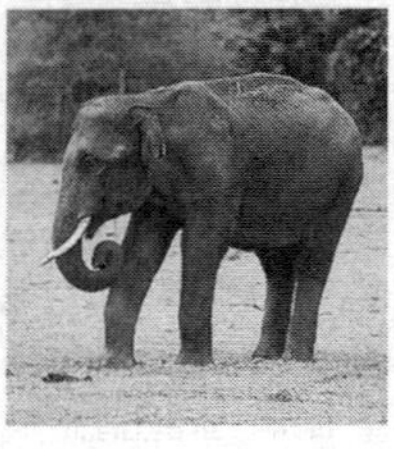

elephant
top: African elephant
Loxodonta africana
bottom: Indian elephant
Elephas maximus

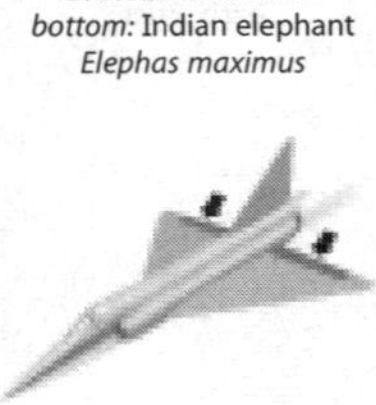

elevon
delta wing aircraft

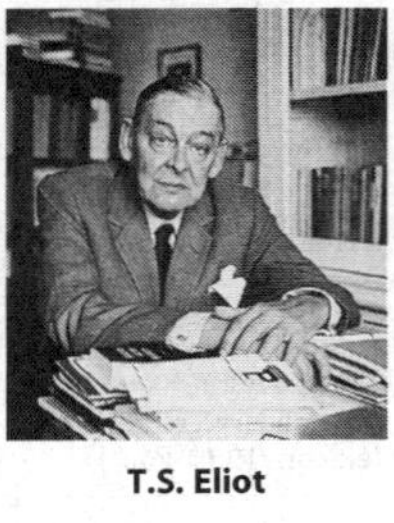

T.S. Eliot

and lowered in a vertical shaft to transport people or freight. **b.** The enclosure or platform with its operating equipment, motor, cables, and accessories. **2.** A movable control surface, usu. attached to the horizontal stabilizer of an aircraft, that is used to produce motion up or down. **3.** A mechanism, often with buckets or scoops attached to a conveyor, used for hoisting materials. **4.** A granary equipped with devices for hoisting and discharging grain.

e•lev•en (ĭ-lĕv′ən) *n.* **1.** The cardinal number equal to 10 + 1. **2.** The 11th in a set or sequence. **3.** Something with 11 parts or members, esp. a football team. [ME *elleven* < OE *endleofan.* See **oi-no-** in App.] **—e•lev′en** *adj. & pron.*

e•lev•ens•es (ĭ-lĕv′ən-zəs) *pl.n. Chiefly British* Tea or coffee taken at midmorning and often accompanied by a snack.

e•lev•enth (ĭ-lĕv′ənth) *n.* **1.** The ordinal number matching the number 11 in a series. **2.** One of 11 equal parts. **—e•lev′enth** *adv. & adj.*

eleventh hour *n.* The latest possible time.

el•e•von (ĕl′ə-vŏn′) *n.* A control surface on an airplane that combines the functions of an elevator and an aileron.

elf (ĕlf) *n., pl.* **elves** (ĕlvz) **1.** A small, often mischievous creature considered to have magical powers. **2a.** A lively mischievous child. **b.** A usu. sprightly or mischievous or sometimes spiteful person. [ME < OE *ælf.* See **albho-** in App.]

ELF *abbr.* extremely low frequency

El Fer•rol (fə-rōl′, fĕ-) also **El Ferrol del Cau•dil•lo** (dĕl′ kou-dē′ō, *-thē′ō*) A city of NW Spain on the Atlantic Ocean; an important naval station since the 18th cent. Pop. 90,410.

elf•in (ĕl′fĭn) *adj.* **1a.** Relating to or suggestive of an elf. **b.** Made, done, or produced by an elf. **2.** Small and sprightly or mischievous. **3.** Having a magical quality or charm; fairylike. [Prob. < ME *elvene,* pl. of *elve,* elf < OE *-elfen* (as in *wuduelfen,* dryad). See **albho-** in App.]

elf•ish (ĕl′fĭsh) also **elv•ish** (ĕl′vĭsh) *adj.* **1.** Of or relating to elves. **2.** Prankish; mischievous. **—elf′ish•ly** *adv.* **—elf′ish•ness** *n.*

elf•lock (ĕlf′lŏk′) *n.* A lock of hair tangled as if by elves. Often used in the plural.

El•gar (ĕl′gär′, -gər), Sir **Edward** 1857–1934. British composer whose works include *Enigma Variations* (1896).

El•gin (ĕl′jĭn) A city of NE IL on the Fox R. WNW of Chicago. Pop. 94,487.

El Grec•o (grĕk′ō) See El **Greco.**

el•hi (ĕl′hī′) *adj. Informal* Of, relating to, involving, or designed for use in grades 1 to 12.

E•li (ē′lī) In the Bible, a judge of Israel who was the teacher of Samuel.

e•lic•it (ĭ-lĭs′ĭt) *tr.v.* **-it•ed, -it•ing, -its 1a.** To bring or draw out (something latent); educe. **b.** To arrive at (a truth, for example) by logic. **2.** To call forth, draw out, or provoke (a reaction, for example). [Lat. *ēlicere, ēlicit-* : *ē-, ex-,* ex- + *lacere,* to entice.] **—e•lic′i•ta′tion** *n.* **—e•lic′i•tor** *n.*

e•lide (ĭ-līd′) *tr.v.* **e•lid•ed, e•lid•ing, e•lides 1a.** To omit or slur over (a syllable, for example) in pronunciation. **b.** To strike out (something written). **2a.** To eliminate or leave out of consideration. **b.** To cut short; abridge. [Lat. *ēlīdere,* to strike out : *ē-, ex-,* ex- + *laedere,* to strike.]

el•i•gi•ble (ĕl′ĭ-jə-bəl) *adj.* **1.** Qualified or entitled to be chosen. **2.** Desirable and worthy of choice, esp. for marriage. **3.** *Football* Allowed under the rules to catch a forward pass. ❖ *n.* A person who is eligible. [ME < OFr. < LLat. *ēligibilis* < Lat. *ēligere,* to select. See ELECT.] **—el′i•gi•bil′i•ty** *n.* **—el′i•gi•bly** *adv.*

E•li•jah (ĭ-lī′jə) 9th cent. B.C. A Hebrew prophet who according to the Bible was carried skyward in a chariot of fire.

e•lim•i•nate (ĭ-lĭm′ə-nāt′) *tr.v.* **-nat•ed, -nat•ing, -nates 1.** To get rid of; remove. **2a.** To leave out or omit from consideration; reject. **b.** To remove from consideration by defeating, as in a contest. **3.** *Mathematics* To remove (an unknown quantity) by combining equations. **4.** *Physiology* To excrete (bodily wastes). [Lat. *ēlīmināre, ēlīmināt-,* to banish : *ē-, ex-,* ex- + *līmen, līmin-,* threshold.] **—e•lim′i•na′tion** *n.* **—e•lim′i•na′tive, e•lim′i•na•to′ry** (-nə-tôr′ē, -tōr′ē) *adj.* **—e•lim′i•na′tor** *n.*

El•i•ot (ĕl′ē-ət), **Charles William** 1834–1926. Amer. educator who was president of Harvard University (1869–1909).

Eliot, George Pen name of Mary Ann Evans. 1819–80. British writer whose novels include *Middlemarch* (1871–72).

Eliot, John 1604–90. English missionary who contributed to *The Bay Psalm Book* (1640), the first book printed in New England.

Eliot, T(homas) S(tearns) 1888–1965. Amer.-born British poet and critic whose works include "The Love Song of J. Alfred Prufrock" (1915) and *The Waste Land* (1922). He won the 1948 Nobel Prize for literature.

E•lis (ē′lĭs) A region and city of ancient Greece in the W Peloponnesus; site of the original Olympic Games.

ELISA (ĭ-lī′zə, -sə) *n.* A sensitive immunoassay that uses an enzyme linked to an antibody or antigen as a marker for the detection of a specific protein, esp. an antigen or antibody. [*e(nzyme)-l(inked) i(mmunoad)s(orbent) a(ssay).*]

E•lis•a•beth•ville (ĭ-lĭz′ə-bəth-vĭl′) See **Lubumbashi.**

E•li•sha (ĭ-lī′shə) 9th cent. B.C. A Hebrew prophet who was chosen by Elijah to be his successor.

e•li•sion (ĭ-lĭzh′ən) *n.* **1a.** Omission of a final or initial sound in pronunciation. **b.** Omission of an unstressed vowel or syllable, as in scanning a verse. **2.** The act or an instance of omitting something. [Lat. *ēlīsiō, ēlīsiōn-* < *ēlīsus,* p. part. of *ēlīdere,* to strike out. See ELIDE.]

e•lite or **é•lite** (ĭ-lēt′, ā-lēt′) *n., pl.* **elite** or **e•lites 1a.** A group or class of persons or a member of such a group or class, enjoying superior intellectual, social, or economic status. **b.** The best or most skilled members of a group. **2.** A size of type on a typewriter, equal to 12 characters per linear inch. [Fr. *élite* < OFr. *eslite* < fem. p. part. of *eslire,* to choose < Lat. *ēligere.* See ELECT.] **—e•lite′** *adj.*

e•lit•ism or **é•lit•ism** (ĭ-lē′tĭz′əm, ā-lē′-) *n.* **1.** The belief that certain persons or members of certain groups deserve favored treatment by virtue of their perceived superiority. **2a.** The sense of entitlement enjoyed by such a group. **b.** Control, rule, or domination by such a group. **—e•lit′ist** *adj. & n.*

e•lix•ir (ĭ-lĭk′sər) *n.* **1.** A sweetened aromatic solution of alcohol and water, serving as a vehicle for medicine. **2a.** See **philosophers' stone. b.** A substance believed to maintain life indefinitely. **c.** A substance or medicine believed to have the power to cure all ills. **3.** An underlying principle. [ME, a substance of transmutative properties < OFr. *elissir* < Med.Lat. *elixir* < Ar. *al-'iksīr* : *al-,* the + *'iksīr,* elixir (prob. < Gk. *xērion,* desiccative powder < *xēros,* dry).]

E•liz•a•beth[1] (ĭ-lĭz′ə-bəth) The mother of John the Baptist and a kinswoman of Mary.

Elizabeth[2] 1843–1916. Queen of Romania (1881–1916) and poet who wrote as Carmen Sylva.

Elizabeth[3] b. 1900. Queen of Great Britain and Northern Ireland (1936–52) as the wife of George VI.

Elizabeth[4] A city of NE NJ S of Newark; settled in 1664. Pop. 120,568.

Elizabeth I 1533–1603. Queen of England and Ireland (1558–1603) who reestablished Protestantism in England. Her reign was marked by the execution of Mary Queen of Scots (1587) and the defeat of the Spanish Armada (1588). **—E•liz′a•be′than** (ĭ-lĭz′ə-bē′thən, -bĕth′ən) *adj. & n.*

Elizabeth II b. 1926. Queen of Great Britain and Northern Ireland (since 1952).

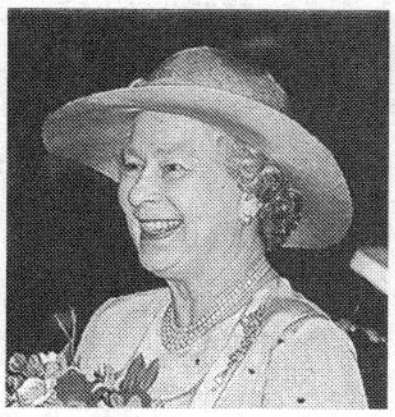

Elizabeth II

Elizabethan sonnet *n.* See **Shakespearean sonnet.**

Elizabeth Pe•trov•na (pə-trôv′nə) 1709–62. Empress of Russia (1741–62) during the War of the Austrian Succession (1740–48) and the Seven Years' War (1756–63).

elk (ĕlk) *n., pl.* **elk** or **elks 1.** See **wapiti. 2.** The moose. **3.** A light pliant leather of horsehide or calfskin, tanned and finished to resemble elk hide. [ME, prob. alteration of OE *eolh.*]

elk•hound (ĕlk′hound′) *n.* The Norwegian elkhound.

Elk Mountains A range of the Rocky Mts. in W-central CO rising to 4,350.8 m (14,265 ft).

ell[1] (ĕl) *n.* **1.** A wing of a building at right angles to the main structure. **2.** A right-angled bend in a pipe or conduit; an elbow. [< its L shape or short for ELBOW.]

ell[2] (ĕl) *n.* An English linear measure equal to 45 inches (114 centimeters). [ME < OE *eln,* the length from the elbow to the middle finger's tip, ell.]

ell[3] (ĕl) *n.* Variant of **el**[1].

el•lag•ic acid (ĭ-lăj′ĭk) *n.* A yellow crystalline compound, $C_{14}H_6O_8$, that is obtained from tannins and used as a hemostatic. [Fr. *ellagique* < *ellag,* backward spelling of *galle,* plant gall < Lat. *galla.*]

Elles•mere Island (ĕlz′mîr′) An island of N Nunavut, Canada, in the Arctic Ocean near Greenland.

El•lice Islands (ĕl′ĭs) See **Tuvalu.**

El•ling•ton (ĕl′ĭng-tən), **Edward Kennedy** Known as "Duke." 1899–1974. Amer. composer, pianist, and bandleader whose compositions include "Mood Indigo" (1930).

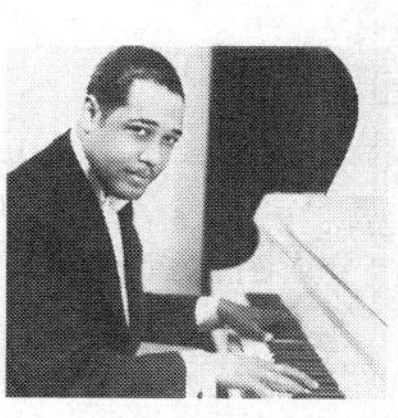

Duke Ellington

el•lipse (ĭ-lĭps′) *n.* **1.** A plane curve, esp.: **a.** A conic section whose plane is not parallel to the axis, base, or generatrix of the intersected cone. **b.** The locus of points for which the sum of the distances from each point to two fixed points is equal. **2.** Ellipsis. [Fr. < Lat. *ellīpsis* < Gk. *elleipsis,* a falling short, ellipse < *elleipein,* to fall short (< the relationship between the line joining the vertices of a conic and the line through the focus and parallel to the directrix of a conic) : *en-,* in; see EN–[2] + *leipein,* to leave; see **leik**[w]- in App.]

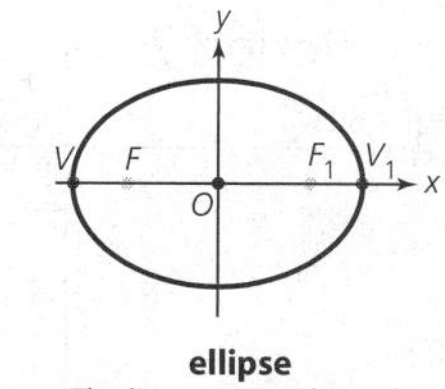

ellipse
The line running through the foci (F and F_1) of an ellipse is the major axis. The vertices (V and V_1) mark where the major axis intersects the ellipse.

el•lip•sis (ĭ-lĭp′sĭs) *n., pl.* **-ses** (-sēz) **1a.** The omission of a word or phrase necessary for a complete syntactical construction but not necessary for understanding. **b.** An example of such omission. **2.** A mark or series of marks (. . . or • • • , for example) used in writing or printing to indicate an omission. [Lat. *ellīpsis* < Gk. *elleipsis* < *elleipein,* to fall short. See ELLIPSE.]

el•lip•soid (ĭ-lĭp′soid′) *n.* A geometric surface, all of whose plane sections are either ellipses or circles. **—el•lip′soid′, el•lip′soi′dal** (-soid′l) *adj.*

el•lip•tic (ĭ-lĭp′tĭk) or **el•lip•ti•cal** (-tĭ-kəl) *adj.* **1.** Of, relating to, or having the shape of an ellipse. **2.** Containing or characterized by ellipsis. **3a.** Of or relating to extreme economy of oral or written expression. **b.** Marked by deliberate obscurity of style or expression. [NLat. *ellīpticus* < Gk. *elleiptikos,* defective < *elleipsis,* a falling short, ellipsis < *elleipein,* to fall short. See ELLIPSIS.] **—el•lip′ti•cal•ly** *adv.*

ă	pat	oi	boy
ā	pay	ou	out
âr	care	o͝o	took
ä	father	o͞o	boot
ĕ	pet	ŭ	cut
ē	be	ûr	urge
ĭ	pit	th	thin
ī	pie	*th*	this
îr	pier	hw	which
ŏ	pot	zh	vision
ō	toe	ə	about, item
ô	paw		

Stress marks:
′ (primary);
′ (secondary), as in
lexicon (lĕk′sĭ-kŏn′)

PERIODIC TABLE OF THE ELEMENTS

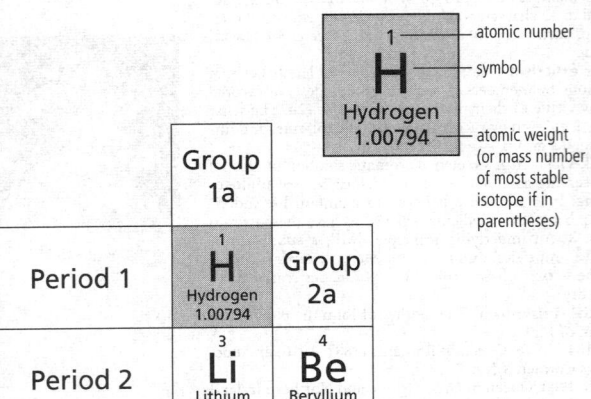

atomic number — 1
symbol — H
Hydrogen
atomic weight — 1.00794
(or mass number of most stable isotope if in parentheses)

The periodic table arranges the chemical elements in two ways. The first is by **atomic number**, starting with hydrogen (atomic number = 1) in the upper left-hand corner and continuing in ascending order from left to right. The second is by the number of electrons in the outermost **shell**. Elements having the same number of electrons in the outermost shell are placed in the same column. Since the number of electrons in the outermost shell in large part determines the chemical nature of an element, elements in the same column have similar chemical properties.

This arrangement of the elements was devised by **Dmitri Mendeleev** in 1869, before many of the elements now known were discovered. To maintain the overall logic of the table, Mendeleev allowed space for undiscovered elements whose existence he predicted. This space has since been partly filled in, most recently by the addition of elements 104–112. Elements 110–112 have been isolated experimentally but not yet officially named.

The **lanthanide** series (elements 57–71) and the **actinide** series (elements 89–103) are composed of elements with Group 3b chemical properties. They are placed below the main body of the table to make it easier to read.

	Group 1a	Group 2a	Group 3b	Group 4b	Group 5b	Group 6b	Group 7b	Group 8	Group 8
Period 1	1 **H** Hydrogen 1.00794								
Period 2	3 **Li** Lithium 6.941	4 **Be** Beryllium 9.0122							
Period 3	11 **Na** Sodium 22.9898	12 **Mg** Magnesium 24.305							
Period 4	19 **K** Potassium 39.098	20 **Ca** Calcium 40.08	21 **Sc** Scandium 44.956	22 **Ti** Titanium 47.87	23 **V** Vanadium 50.942	24 **Cr** Chromium 51.996	25 **Mn** Manganese 54.9380	26 **Fe** Iron 55.845	27 **Co** Cobalt 58.9332
Period 5	37 **Rb** Rubidium 85.47	38 **Sr** Strontium 87.62	39 **Y** Yttrium 88.906	40 **Zr** Zirconium 91.22	41 **Nb** Niobium 92.906	42 **Mo** Molybdenum 95.94	43 **Tc** Technetium (98)	44 **Ru** Ruthenium 101.07	45 **Rh** Rhodium 102.905
Period 6	55 **Cs** Cesium 132.905	56 **Ba** Barium 137.33	57–71* Lanthanides	72 **Hf** Hafnium 178.49	73 **Ta** Tantalum 180.948	74 **W** Tungsten 183.84	75 **Re** Rhenium 186.2	76 **Os** Osmium 190.2	77 **Ir** Iridium 192.2
Period 7	87 **Fr** Francium (223)	88 **Ra** Radium (226)	89–103** Actinides	104 **Rf** Rutherfordium (261)	105 **Db** Dubnium (262)	106 **Sg** Seaborgium (266)	107 **Bh** Bohrium (264)	108 **Hs** Hassium (265)	109 **Mt** Meitnerium (268)

*LANTHANIDES	57 **La** Lanthanum 138.91	58 **Ce** Cerium 140.12	59 **Pr** Praseodymium 140.908	60 **Nd** Neodymium 144.24	61 **Pm** Promethium (145)	62 **Sm** Samarium 150.36	63 **Eu** Europium 151.96
**ACTINIDES	89 **Ac** Actinium (227)	90 **Th** Thorium 232.038	91 **Pa** Protactinium 231.036	92 **U** Uranium 238.03	93 **Np** Neptunium (237)	94 **Pu** Plutonium (244)	95 **Am** Americium (243)

ALPHABETICAL TABLE OF THE ELEMENTS

Element	Symbol	Atomic Number	Element	Symbol	Atomic Number	Element	Symbol	Atomic Number	Element	Symbol	Atomic Number
Actinium	Ac	89	Cadmium	Cd	48	Element 110	–	110	Helium	He	2
Aluminum	Al	13	Calcium	Ca	20	Element 111	–	111	Holmium	Ho	67
Americium	Am	95	Californium	Cf	98	Element 112	–	112	Hydrogen	H	1
Antimony	Sb	51	Carbon	C	6	Erbium	Er	68	Indium	In	49
Argon	Ar	18	Cerium	Ce	58	Europium	Eu	63	Iodine	I	53
Arsenic	As	33	Cesium	Cs	55	Fermium	Fm	100	Iridium	Ir	77
Astatine	At	85	Chlorine	Cl	17	Fluorine	F	9	Iron	Fe	26
Barium	Ba	56	Chromium	Cr	24	Francium	Fr	87	Krypton	Kr	36
Berkelium	Bk	97	Cobalt	Co	27	Gadolinium	Gd	64	Lanthanum	La	57
Beryllium	Be	4	Copper	Cu	29	Gallium	Ga	31	Lawrencium	Lr	103
Bismuth	Bi	83	Curium	Cm	96	Germanium	Ge	32	Lead	Pb	82
Bohrium	Bh	107	Dubnium	Db	105	Gold	Au	79	Lithium	Li	3
Boron	B	5	Dysprosium	Dy	66	Hafnium	Hf	72	Lutetium	Lu	71
Bromine	Br	35	Einsteinium	Es	99	Hassium	Hs	108	Magnesium	Mg	12

Metals	Nonmetals	Noble gases

								Group 0
			Group 3a	Group 4a	Group 5a	Group 6a	Group 7a	2 **He** Helium 4.0026
			5 **B** Boron 10.811	6 **C** Carbon 12.011	7 **N** Nitrogen 14.0067	8 **O** Oxygen 15.9994	9 **F** Fluorine 18.9984	10 **Ne** Neon 20.183
Group 8	Group 1b	Group 2b	13 **Al** Aluminum 26.9815	14 **Si** Silicon 28.086	15 **P** Phosphorus 30.9738	16 **S** Sulfur 32.066	17 **Cl** Chlorine 35.453	18 **Ar** Argon 39.948
28 **Ni** Nickel 58.69	29 **Cu** Copper 63.546	30 **Zn** Zinc 65.39	31 **Ga** Gallium 69.72	32 **Ge** Germanium 72.61	33 **As** Arsenic 74.9216	34 **Se** Selenium 78.96	35 **Br** Bromine 79.904	36 **Kr** Krypton 83.80
46 **Pd** Palladium 106.4	47 **Ag** Silver 107.868	48 **Cd** Cadmium 112.41	49 **In** Indium 114.82	50 **Sn** Tin 118.71	51 **Sb** Antimony 121.76	52 **Te** Tellurium 127.60	53 **I** Iodine 126.9045	54 **Xe** Xenon 131.29
78 **Pt** Platinum 195.08	79 **Au** Gold 196.967	80 **Hg** Mercury 200.59	81 **Tl** Thallium 204.38	82 **Pb** Lead 207.2	83 **Bi** Bismuth 208.98	84 **Po** Polonium (210)	85 **At** Astatine (210)	86 **Rn** Radon (222)
110† (269)	111† (272)	112† (277)						

† Until official names are given to new elements, names based on a Latin translation of the atomic number are used; e.g. *ununbium* (Latin *unus* '1' + *unus* '1' + *bi-* '2') for element 112.

64 **Gd** Gadolinium 157.25	65 **Tb** Terbium 158.925	66 **Dy** Dysprosium 162.50	67 **Ho** Holmium 164.930	68 **Er** Erbium 167.26	69 **Tm** Thulium 168.934	70 **Yb** Ytterbium 173.04	71 **Lu** Lutetium 174.97
96 **Cm** Curium (247)	97 **Bk** Berkelium (247)	98 **Cf** Californium (251)	99 **Es** Einsteinium (252)	100 **Fm** Fermium (257)	101 **Md** Mendelevium (258)	102 **No** Nobelium (259)	103 **Lr** Lawrencium (262)

Element	Symbol	Atomic Number	Element	Symbol	Atomic Number	Element	Symbol	Atomic Number	Element	Symbol	Atomic Number
Manganese	Mn	25	Palladium	Pd	46	Ruthenium	Ru	44	Terbium	Tb	65
Meitnerium	Mt	109	Phosphorus	P	15	Rutherfordium	Rf	104	Thallium	Tl	81
Mendelevium	Md	101	Platinum	Pt	78	Samarium	Sm	62	Thorium	Th	90
Mercury	Hg	80	Plutonium	Pu	94	Scandium	Sc	21	Thulium	Tm	69
Molybdenum	Mo	42	Polonium	Po	84	Seaborgium	Sg	106	Tin	Sn	50
Neodymium	Nd	60	Potassium	K	19	Selenium	Se	34	Titanium	Ti	22
Neon	Ne	10	Praseodymium	Pr	59	Silicon	Si	14	Tungsten	W	74
Neptunium	Np	93	Promethium	Pm	61	Silver	Ag	47	Uranium	U	92
Nickel	Ni	28	Protactinium	Pa	91	Sodium	Na	11	Vanadium	V	23
Niobium	Nb	41	Radium	Ra	88	Strontium	Sr	38	Xenon	Xe	54
Nitrogen	N	7	Radon	Rn	86	Sulfur	S	16	Ytterbium	Yb	70
Nobelium	No	102	Rhenium	Re	75	Tantalum	Ta	73	Yttrium	Y	39
Osmium	Os	76	Rhodium	Rh	45	Technetium	Tc	43	Zinc	Zn	30
Oxygen	O	8	Rubidium	Rb	37	Tellurium	Te	52	Zirconium	Zr	40

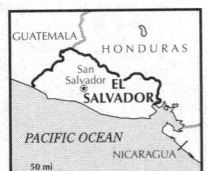

El Salvador

el·lip·tic·i·ty (ĭ-lĭp′tĭs′ĭ-tē) *n.* **1.** Deviation from perfect circular or spherical form toward elliptic or ellipsoidal form. **2.** The degree of this deviation.

El·lis (ĕl′ĭs), **(Henry) Havelock** 1859–1939. British psychologist and writer known for his pioneering works on sexuality.

Ellis Island An island of Upper New York Bay SW of Manhattan; chief immigration station of the US (1892–1943).

El·li·son (ĕl′ĭ-sən), **Ralph Waldo** 1914–94. Amer. writer whose works include *Invisible Man* (1952).

Ells·worth (ĕlz′wûrth′), **Lincoln** 1880–1951. Amer. explorer who took part in several polar expeditions.

Ellsworth, Oliver 1745–1807. Amer. jurist; chief justice of the US Supreme Court (1796–1800).

Ellsworth Land A high plateau of W Antarctica S of the Antarctic Peninsula that includes the **Ellsworth Mountains**, rising to 5,142.3 m (16,860 ft).

elm (ĕlm) *n.* Any of various deciduous trees of the genus *Ulmus*, characteristically having arching or curving branches and serrate leaves with asymmetrical bases. [ME < OE.]

El·man (ĕl′mən), **Mischa** 1891–1967. Russian-born Amer. violinist regarded as one of the foremost violinists of his time.

El Man·su·ra (măn-soŏr′ə) A city of N Egypt on a branch of the Nile R. Pop. 371,000.

elm bark beetle *n.* Either of two bark beetles (*Scolytus multistriatus* or *Hylurgopinus rufipes*) that transmit the fungus causing Dutch elm disease.

El Mis·ti (mē′stē) A dormant volcano, 5,825.8 m (19,101 ft), in the Cordillera Occidental of S Peru.

El Mon·te (mŏn′tē) A city of S CA E of Los Angeles. Pop. 115,965.

El Ni·ño (nēn′yō) *n. Oceanography* A warming of the ocean surface off the western coast of South America, occurring every 4 to 12 years when cold water does not rise toward the surface, creating unusual weather patterns in various parts of the world. [Am.Sp. < Sp., the Christ child (the onset of the warming being at Christmastide) : *el*, the (< Lat. *ille*; see **al-** in App.) + *niño*, child (< OSpan. *ninno* < VLat. *ninnus*).]

El O·beid (ō-bād′) also **Al U·bay·yid** (äl′ oŏ-bā′ĭd, äl′) A city of central Sudan SW of Khartoum; founded in the 1820s. Pop. 228,096.

el·o·cu·tion (ĕl′ə-kyoŏ′shən) *n.* **1.** The art of public speaking. **2.** A style or manner of speaking, esp. in public. [ME *elocucion* < Lat. *ēlocūtiō, ēlocūtiōn-* < *ēlocūtus*, p. part. of *ēloquī*, to speak out : *ē-, ex-, ex-* + *loquī*, to speak.] —**el′o·cu′tion·ar′y** (-shə-nĕr′ē) *adj.* —**el′o·cu′tion·ist** *n.*

e·lo·de·a (ĭ-lō′dē-ə) *n.* Any of various small submersed herbs of the genus *Elodea*, having grasslike leaves. [NLat. *Elōdea*, genus name < Gk. *helōdēs*, marshy < *helos*, marsh.]

El·o·him (ĕl′ō-hēm′, -hĭm′, ə-lō′hĭm) *n.* A name for God in the Hebrew Scriptures. [Heb. *ĕlōhîm* < *ĕlōah*, god.]

El·o·hist (ĕl′ō-hĭst′, ə-lō′-) *n.* The putative author of the earliest sources of the Pentateuch in which God is called Elohim. —**El′o·his′tic** *adj.*

e·loign (ĭ-loin′) *tr.v.* **e·loigned, e·loign·ing, e·loigns** *Archaic* **1.** To remove or carry away to a distance, esp. so as to conceal. **2.** To take (oneself) to a distance. [ME *elongen* < OFr. *esloigner* < LLat. *ēlongāre* : Lat. *ē-, ex-, ex-* + Lat. *longus*, long, distant; see **del-** in App.]

e·lon·gate (ĭ-lông′gāt′, ĭ-lŏng′-) *tr. & intr.v.* **-gat·ed, -gat·ing, -gates** To make or grow longer. ❖ *adj.* or **elongated 1.** Made longer; extended. **2.** Having more length than width; slender. [LLat. *ēlongāre, ēlongāt-*. See **ELOIGN.**]

e·lon·ga·tion (ĭ-lông′gā′shən, ĭ-lŏng′-, ē′lông-, ē′lŏng-) *n.* **1.** The act of elongating or the condition of being elongated. **2.** Something that elongates; an extension. **3.** The angular distance between two celestial bodies as seen from Earth.

e·lope (ĭ-lōp′) *intr.v.* **e·loped, e·lop·ing, e·lopes 1.** To run away with a lover, esp. with the intention of getting married. **2.** To run away; abscond. [Perh. AN *aloper*, to run away < one's husband with a lover < MDu. *ontlopen*, to run away : *ont-*, away from, along; see **ant-** in App. + *lopen*, to run.] —**e·lope′ment** *n.* —**e·lop′er** *n.*

el·o·quence (ĕl′ə-kwəns) *n.* **1a.** Persuasive powerful discourse. **b.** The skill or power of using such discourse. **2.** The quality of persuasive powerful expression.

el·o·quent (ĕl′ə-kwənt) *adj.* **1.** Characterized by eloquence. **2.** Vividly or movingly expressive. See Syns at **expressive.** [ME < OFr. < Lat. *ēloquēns, ēloquent-*, pr. part. of *ēloquī*, to speak out. See **ELOCUTION.**] —**el′o·quent·ly** *adv.* —**el′o·quent·ness** *n.*

El Pas·o (păs′ō) A city of extreme W TX on the Rio Grande opposite Ciudad Juárez, Mexico. Pop. 563,662.

El Sal·va·dor (săl′və-dôr′, säl′vä-dôr′) A country of Central America on the Pacific; achieved independence from Spain in 1821. Cap. San Salvador. Pop. 4,949,000. —**El Sal′va·dor′i·an** (săl′və-dôr′ē-ən, -dôr′-) *adj. & n.*

else (ĕls) *adj.* **1.** Other; different: *Ask somebody else.* **2.** Additional; more: *anything else.* ❖ *adv.* **1.** In a different or additional time, place, or manner: *Where else did he go?* **2.** If not; otherwise: *Be careful, or else you will fall.* —**idiom: or else** Regardless of any extenuating circumstances: *Be there or else!* [ME *elles* < OE. See **al-** in App.]

else·where (ĕls′hwâr′, -wâr′) *adv.* In or to a different or another place: *has property at the shore and elsewhere.*

El·si·nore (ĕl′sə-nôr′, -nōr′) See **Helsingør.**

el·u·ate (ĕl′yoŏ-ĭt, -āt′) *n.* The solution of solvent and dissolved matter resulting from elution. [Lat. *ēluere*, to wash out; see **ELUTE** + -ATE¹.]

e·lu·ci·date (ĭ-loŏ′sĭ-dāt′) *v.* **-dat·ed, -dat·ing, -dates** —*tr.* To make clear or plain, esp. by explanation. —*intr.* To give an explanation that clarifies. [LLat. *ēlūcidāre, ēlūcidāt-*: Lat. *ē-, ex-*, intensive pref.; see **EX-** + Lat. *lūcidus*, bright (< *lūcēre*, to shine; see **leuk-** in App.).] —**e·lu′ci·da′tion** *n.* —**e·lu′ci·da′tive** *adj.* —**e·lu′ci·da′tor** *n.*

e·lu·cu·brate (ĭ-loŏ′kyoŏ-brāt′) *tr.v.* **-brat·ed, -brat·ing, -brates** To produce (a written work) by working long and diligently. [Back-formation < ELUCUBRATION.]

e·lu·cu·bra·tion (ĭ-loŏ′kyoŏ-brā′shən) *n.* **1.** The act or process of elucubrating. **2.** A written work produced by elucubrating. [Lat. *ēlūcubrāre, ēlūcubrāt-*, to work at night by lamplight over : *ē-, ex-, ex-* + *lūcubrāre*, to work at night by lamplight; see **LUCU-BRATE.**]

e·lude (ĭ-loŏd′) *tr.v.* **e·lud·ed, e·lud·ing, e·ludes 1.** To evade or escape from, as by daring, cleverness, or skill. **2.** To escape the understanding or grasp of. [Lat. *ēlūdere* : *ē-, ex-, ex-* + *lūdere*, to play (< *lūdus*, play).]

el·u·ent also **el·u·ant** (ĕl′yoŏ-ənt) *n.* A substance used as a solvent in extracting one material from another. [Lat. *ēluēns, ēluent-*, pr. part. of *ēluere*, to wash out. See **ELUTE.**]

E·lul (ĕl′oŏl, ĕ-loŏl′) *n.* The 12th month of the year in the Jewish calendar. See table at **calendar.** [Heb. *ĕlûl* < Akkadian *elûlu*, a month name (August/September), prob. < *elēlu*, to become pure, become holy.]

e·lu·sion (ĭ-loŏ′zhən) *n.* The act or an instance of eluding or escaping; evasion. [Med.Lat. *ēlūsiō, ēlūsiōn-*, mockery, contempt < Lat. *ēlūsus*, p. part. of *ēlūdere*, to escape, mock. See **ELUDE.**]

e·lu·sive (ĭ-loŏ′sĭv, -zĭv) *adj.* **1.** Tending to elude capture, perception, comprehension, or memory. **2.** Difficult to define or describe. [< Lat. *ēlūsus*, p. part. of *ēlūdere*, to elude. See **ELUDE.**] —**e·lu′sive·ly** *adv.* —**e·lu′sive·ness** *n.*

e·lute (ĭ-loŏt′) *tr.v.* **e·lut·ed, e·lut·ing, e·lutes** To extract (one material) from another, usu. by means of a solvent. [< Lat. *ēluere, ēlūt-*, to wash out : *ē-, ex-, ex-* + *-luere*, to wash; see **leu(ə)-** in App.] —**e·lu′tion** *n.*

e·lu·tri·ate (ĭ-loŏ′trē-āt′) *tr.v.* **-at·ed, -at·ing, -ates 1.** To purify, separate, or remove (ore, for example) by washing, decanting, and settling. **2.** To wash away the lighter or finer particles of (soil, for example). [Lat. *elutriāre, elutriāt-* (< **elutrium*, vat, bath < Gk. **elutrion*, dim. of *elutron*, tank; see ELYTRON) or *ēlūtriāre* (< **ēlūtor*, one who washes < *ēluere*, to wash out; see **ELUTE.**)] —**e·lu′tri·a′tion** *n.*

e·lu·vi·ate (ĭ-loŏ′vē-āt′) *intr.v.* **-at·ed, -at·ing, -ates** To undergo eluviation.

e·lu·vi·a·tion (ĭ-loŏ′vē-ā′shən) *n.* The lateral or downward movement of dissolved or suspended material in soil when rainfall exceeds evaporation. [ELUVI(UM) + -ATION.]

e·lu·vi·um (ĭ-loŏ′vē-əm) *n.* Residual deposits of soil, dust, and rock particles produced by the wind. [NLat. *ēluvium* < Lat. *ēluere*, to wash out. See **ELUTE.**] —**e·lu′vi·al** (-əl) *adj.*

el·ver (ĕl′vər) *n.* See **glass eel.** [Alteration of *eelfare*, a brood of young eels : EEL + FARE, journey (obsolete).]

elves (ĕlvz) *n.* Plural of **elf.**

elv·ish (ĕl′vĭsh) *adj.* Variant of **elfish.**

E·ly (ē′lē), **Isle of** A region of E-central England with extensive drained fens. The city of **Ely** (pop. 10,268) is noted for its cathedral, dating from the 11th cent.

E·ly·sian (ĭ-lĭzh′ən) *adj.* **1.** *Greek Mythology* Of or relating to Elysium. **2.** Blissful; delightful.

Elysian Fields *pl.n. Greek Mythology* The abode of the blessed dead.

E·ly·si·um (ĭ-lĭz′ē-əm, ĭ-lĭzh′-) *n.* **1.** *Greek Mythology* The Elysian Fields. **2.** A place or condition of ideal happiness. [Lat. *Ēlysium* < Gk. *Ēlusion (pedion)*, Elysian (fields).]

El·y·tis (ĕl′ē-tēs′), **Odysseus** 1911–96. Greek poet who won the 1979 Nobel Prize for literature.

el·y·tron (ĕl′ĭ-trŏn′) *n., pl.* **-tra** (-trə) Either of the leathery or chitinous forewings of a beetle or a related insect, serving to encase the thin hind wings used in flight. [NLat. < Gk. *elutron*, sheath. See **wel-** in App.] —**el′y·troid′** (-troid′) *adj.*

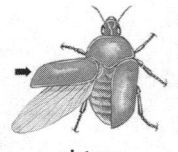

elytron

em (ĕm) *n.* **1.** The letter *m.* **2.** *Printing* **a.** The width of a square piece of type, used as a unit of measure for matter set in that size of type. **b.** Such a measure for 12-point type; a pica.

EM *abbr.* **1.** electromagnetic **2.** Engineer of Mines **3.** enlisted man

em-¹ *pref.* Variant of **en-¹.**

em-² *pref.* Variant of **en-².**

'em (əm) *pron. Informal* Contraction of *them.* [< ME *hem* < OE *him, heom*, dative and accusative pl. of *hē*, he. See **HE¹.**]

e·ma·ci·ate (ĭ-mā′shē-āt′) *tr. & intr.v.* **-at·ed, -at·ing, -ates** To make or become extremely thin, as by starvation. [Lat. *ēmaciāre, ēmaciāt-* : *ē-, ex-*, intensive pref.; see **EX-** + *maciāre*, to make thin.] —**e·ma′ci·a′tion** *n.*

e-mail or **e·mail** or **E-mail** (ē′māl′) *n.* **1.** A system for sending and receiving messages electronically over a computer network.

2. A message or messages sent or received by such a system. —*tr.* **-mailed, -mail•ing, -mails** To send (a message) by such a system. [E(LECTRONIC) MAIL.]

em•a•lan•ge•ni (ĕm′ə-läng-gĕn′ē) *n.* Plural of **lilangeni.**

em•a•nate (ĕm′ə-nāt′) *intr. & tr.v.* **-nat•ed, -nat•ing, -nates** To come or send forth, as from a source. See Syns at **stem**[1]. [Lat. *ēmānāre, ēmānāt-*, to flow out : *ē-, ex-*, ex- + *mānāre*, to flow.] —**em′a•na′tive** *adj.*

em•a•na•tion (ĕm′ə-nā′shən) *n.* **1.** The act or an instance of emanating. **2a.** Something that issues from a source; an emission. **b.** *Chemistry* An isotope of radon. Not in scientific use. —**em′a•na′tion•al** *adj.*

e•man•ci•pate (ĭ-măn′sə-pāt′) *tr.v.* **-pat•ed, -pat•ing, -pates 1.** To free from bondage, oppression, or restraint; liberate. **2.** *Law* To release (a child) from the control of parents or a guardian. [Lat. *ēmancipāre, ēmancipāt-* : *ē-, ex-*, ex- + *mancipāre*, to sell, transfer (< *manceps, mancip-*, purchaser; see **man-**[2] in App.).] —**e•man′ci•pa′tion** *n.* —**e•man′ci•pa′tive, e•man′ci•pa•to′ry** (-pə-tôr′ē, -tōr′ē) *adj.* —**e•man′ci•pa′tor** *n.*

e•mar•gi•nate (ĭ-mär′jə-nĭt, -nāt′) *adj. Botany* Having a shallow notch at the tip. [Lat. *ēmarginātus*, p. part. of *ēmargināre*, to take the edge away : *ē-, ex-*, ex- + *margō, margin-*, margin; see **merg-** in App.] —**e•mar′gi•na′tion** (-nā′shən) *n.*

e•mas•cu•late (ĭ-măs′kyə-lāt′) *tr.v.* **-lat•ed, -lat•ing, -lates 1.** To castrate. **2.** To deprive of virility, strength, or vigor; weaken. ❖ *adj.* (-lĭt) Deprived of virility, strength, or vigor. [Lat. *ēmasculāre, ēmasculāt-* : *ē-, ex-*, ex- + *masculus*, male, dim. of *mās*, male, man.] —**e•mas′cu•la′tion** *n.* —**e•mas′cu•la′tive, e•mas′cu•la•to′ry** (-lə-tôr′ē, -tōr′ē) *adj.* —**e•mas′cu•la′tor** *n.*

em•balm (ĕm-bäm′) *tr.v.* **-balmed, -balm•ing, -balms 1.** To treat (a corpse) with preservatives to prevent decay. **2.** To protect from change or oblivion; preserve. **3.** To impart fragrance to; perfume. [ME *embaumen* < OFr. *embasmer* : *en-*, in; see EN–[1] + *basme*, balm; see BALM.] —**em•balm′er** *n.* —**em•balm′ment** *n.*

em•bank (ĕm-băngk′) *tr.v.* **-banked, -bank•ing, -banks** To confine, support, or protect with an embankment.

em•bank•ment (ĕm-băngk′mənt) *n.* **1.** The act of embanking. **2.** A mound of earth or stone built to hold back water or support a roadway.

em•bar•ca•de•ro (ĕm-bär′kə-dâr′ō) *n., pl.* **-ros** *California* A pier, wharf, or landing place, esp. on a river or inland waterway. [Sp. < *embarcar*, to embark < OSpan. < Med.Lat. *imbarcāre*. See EMBARK.]

em•bar•go (ĕm-bär′gō) *n., pl.* **-goes 1.** A government order prohibiting the movement of merchant ships into or out of its ports. **2.** A prohibition by a government on certain or all trade with a foreign nation. **3.** A prohibition; a ban. ❖ *tr.v.* **-goed, -go•ing, -goes** To impose an embargo on. [Sp. < *embargar*, to impede < VLat. **imbarricāre*, to barricade : Lat. *in-*, in; see EN–[1] + VLat. **barricāre*, to barricade (< **barrīca*, barrel, barrier < **barra*, bar, barrier).]

em•bark (ĕm-bärk′) *v.* **-barked, -bark•ing, -barks** —*tr.* **1.** To cause to board a vessel or aircraft. **2.** To enlist (a person or persons) or invest (capital) in an enterprise. —*intr.* **1.** To go aboard a vessel or aircraft. **2.** To set out on a venture; commence. [Fr. *embarquer* < Late OFr., prob. < Med.Lat. *imbarcāre* : Lat. *in-*, in + *barca*, boat.] —**em′bar•ka′tion, em•bark′ment** *n.*

em•bar•rass (ĕm-băr′əs) *tr.v.* **-rassed, -rass•ing, -rass•es 1.** To cause to feel self-conscious or ill at ease; disconcert. **2.** To involve in or hamper with financial difficulties. **3.** To hinder with obstacles or difficulties; impede. **4.** To complicate. [Fr. *embarrasser*, to encumber, hamper < Sp. *embarazar* < Ital. *imbarazzare* < *imbarazzo*, obstacle, obstruction < *imbarrare*, to block, bar : *in-*, in (< Lat.; see EN–[1]) + *barra*, bar (< VLat. **barra*).] —**em•bar′rassed•ly** *adv.* —**em•bar′rass•ing•ly** *adv.*

em•bar•rass•ment (ĕm-băr′əs-mənt) *n.* **1.** The act or an instance of embarrassing. **2.** The state of being embarrassed. **3.** A source of embarrassment. **4.** An overabundance.

em•bas•sage (ĕm′bə-sĭj) *n. Archaic* An embassy. [ME *ambassage*, office or function of an ambassador, poss. var. of *ambassade* < OFr. *ambassade, ambaxade*, ult. < Med.Lat. *ambactiāta* < *ambactia*. See AMBASSADOR.]

em•bas•sy (ĕm′bə-sē) *n., pl.* **-sies 1.** A building containing the offices of an ambassador and staff. **2.** The position, function, or assignment of an ambassador. **3.** A mission to a foreign government headed by an ambassador. **4.** A staff of diplomatic representatives headed by an ambassador. [Variant of *ambassy*, office or function of an ambassador < obsolete Fr. *ambassée* < Med.Lat. *ambactiāta*. See EMBASSAGE.]

em•bat•tle (ĕm-băt′l) *tr.v.* **-tled, -tling, -tles 1.** To prepare for battle; array. **2.** To furnish with battlements for defense. [ME *embataillen* < OFr. *embataillier* : *en-*, in; see EN–[1] + *bataillier*, to battle (< *bataille*, battle; see BATTLE).]

em•bat•tled (ĕm-băt′ld) *adj.* **1.** Prepared or fortified for battle or engaged in battle. **2.** Beset, as with criticism.

em•bat•tle•ment (ĕm-băt′l-mənt) *n.* See **battlement.**

em•bay (ĕm-bā′) *tr.v.* **-bayed, -bay•ing, -bays** To put, shelter, or detain in or as if in a bay.

em•bay•ment (ĕm-bā′mənt) *n.* **1.** A bay or baylike shape. **2.** The formation of a bay.

em•bed (ĕm-bĕd′) also **im•bed** (ĭm-) *v.* **-bed•ded, -bed•ding, -beds** —*tr.* **1.** To fix firmly in a surrounding mass: *embed a post in concrete.* **2.** To enclose snugly or firmly. **3.** To cause to be an integral part of a surrounding whole. —*intr.* To become embedded. —**em•bed′ment** *n.*

em•bel•lish (ĕm-bĕl′ĭsh) *tr.v.* **-lished, -lish•ing, -lish•es 1.** To make beautiful, as by ornamentation. **2.** To add ornamental or fictitious details to (a story, for example). [ME *embelishen* < OFr. *embellir, embelliss-* : *en-*, causative pref.; see EN–[1] + *bel*, beautiful (< Lat. *bellus*; see **deu-**[2] in App.).] —**em•bel′lish•er** *n.*

em•bel•lish•ment (ĕm-bĕl′ĭsh-mənt) *n.* **1.** The act of embellishing or the state of being embellished. **2.** Something that embellishes. **3.** *Music* A note that embellishes a melody.

em•ber (ĕm′bər) *n.* **1.** A small glowing piece of coal or wood, as in a dying fire. **2. embers** The smoldering coal or ash of a dying fire. [ME *embre* < OE *ǣmerge*.]

Ember Day *n.* A day for prayer and fasting in some Christian churches, observed on the Wednesday, Friday, and Saturday after the first Sunday of Lent, after Whitsunday, after September 14, and after December 13. [ME *ymber daye* < OE *ymbrendæg* : *ymbryne*, recurrence, course of time (*ymbe*, around; see **ambhi** in App. + *ryne*, a running) + *dæg*, day.]

em•bez•zle (ĕm-bĕz′əl) *tr.v.* **-zled, -zling, -zles** To take (money, for example) for one's own use in violation of a trust. [ME *embesilen* < AN *enbesiler* : OFr. *en-*, intensive pref.; see EN–[1] + OFr. *besillier*, to ravage.] —**em•bez′zle•ment** *n.* —**em•bez′zler** *n.*

em•bit•ter (ĕm-bĭt′ər) *tr.v.* **-tered, -ter•ing, -ters 1.** To make bitter in flavor. **2.** To arouse bitter feelings in: *was embittered by years of unrewarded labor.* —**em•bit′ter•ment** *n.*

em•blaze[1] (ĕm-blāz′) *tr.v.* **-blazed, -blaz•ing, -blaz•es 1.** To set on fire. **2.** To cause to glow; light up.

em•blaze[2] (ĕm-blāz′) *tr.v.* **-blazed, -blaz•ing, -blaz•es** *Archaic* **1.** To emblazon. **2.** To decorate lavishly.

em•bla•zon (ĕm-blā′zən) *tr.v.* **-zoned, -zon•ing, -zons 1a.** To adorn (a surface) richly with prominent markings. **b.** To inscribe (a prominent marking) on a surface: *emblazon an X on a flag.* **2.** To make resplendent with brilliant colors. **3.** To make illustrious; celebrate. —**em•bla′zon•er** *n.* —**em•bla′zon•ment** *n.*

em•bla•zon•ry (ĕm-blā′zən-rē) *n., pl.* **-ries 1.** The act or art of emblazoning. **2.** Colorful or prominent decoration.

em•blem (ĕm′bləm) *n.* **1.** An object or representation that functions as a symbol. **2.** A distinctive badge, design, or device. **3.** An allegorical picture usu. inscribed with a verse or motto presenting a moral lesson. [ME, pictorial fable < Lat. *emblēma, emblēmat-*, raised ornament < Gk., embossed design < *emballein*, to insert, set in : *en-*, in; see EN–[2] + *ballein*, to throw; see **g**^{w}**elə-** in App.]

em•blem•at•ic (ĕm′blə-măt′ĭk) or **em•blem•at•i•cal** (-ĭ-kəl) *adj.* Of, relating to, or serving as an emblem; symbolic. —**em′blem•at′i•cal•ly** *adv.*

em•blem•a•tize (ĕm-blĕm′ə-tīz′) also **em•blem•ize** (ĕm′blə-mīz′) *tr.v.* **-tized, -tiz•ing, -tiz•es** also **-ized, -iz•ing, -iz•es** To represent with or as if with an emblem; symbolize.

em•ble•ments (ĕm′blə-mənts) *pl.n.* The crops or products of the land legally belonging to a tenant. [< ME *emblaiment* < OFr. *emblaement* < *emblaer*, to sow with grain < Med.Lat. *imblādāre* : Lat. *in-*, in; see EN–[1] + Med.Lat. *blādum, blādium*, grain (of Gmc. orig.; see **bhel-** in App.).]

em•bod•y (ĕm-bŏd′ē) *tr.v.* **-bod•ied, -bod•y•ing, -bod•ies 1.** To give a bodily form to; incarnate. **2.** To represent in bodily or material form. **3.** To make part of a system or whole; incorporate. —**em•bod′i•ment** *n.*

em•bold•en (ĕm-bōl′dən) *tr.v.* **-ened, -en•ing, -ens** To foster boldness or courage in; encourage.

em•bo•lec•to•my (ĕm′bə-lĕk′tə-mē) *n., pl.* **-mies** Surgical removal of an embolus. [EMBOL(US) + –ECTOMY.]

em•bol•ic (ĕm-bŏl′ĭk) *adj.* **1.** *Pathology* Of, relating to, or caused by an embolus or an embolism. **2.** *Embryology* Of or relating to emboly.

em•bo•lism (ĕm′bə-lĭz′əm) *n.* **1.** Obstruction or occlusion of a blood vessel by an embolus. **2.** An embolus. [ME *embolisme*, insertion < LLat. *embolismus* < Gk. *embolismos* < *emballein*, to insert. See EMBLEM.] —**em′bo•lis′mic** *adj.*

em•bo•lus (ĕm′bə-ləs) *n., pl.* **-li** (-lī′) A mass, such as a blood clot, that travels through the bloodstream and lodges so as to obstruct or occlude a blood vessel. [Lat., piston of a pump < Gk. *embolos*, stopper, plug < *emballein*, to insert. See EMBLEM.]

em•bo•ly (ĕm′bə-lē) *n., pl.* **-lies** The formation of a gastrula from a blastula by invagination. [Gk. *embolē*, insertion < *emballein*, to insert. See EMBLEM.]

em•bon•point (äN′bôN-pwăN′) *n.* The condition of being plump; stoutness. [Fr. < *en bon point*, in good condition : *en*, in (< Lat. *in*; see IN–[2]) + *bon*, good (< OFr.; see BOON[2]) + *point*, condition; see POINT.]

em•bos•om (ĕm-bo͝oz′əm, -bo͞o′zəm) *tr.v.* **-omed, -om•ing, -oms 1.** To enclose protectively; envelop. **2.** *Archaic* To clasp to or hold in the bosom.

em•boss (ĕm-bôs′, -bŏs′) *tr.v.* **-bossed, -boss•ing, -boss•es 1.** To mold or carve in relief: *emboss a design on a coin.* **2.** To decorate with or as if with a raised design: *emboss leather.* **3.** To adorn; decorate. [ME *embosen* < OFr. *embocer* : *en-*, in; see EN–[1] + *boce*, knob.] —**em•boss′er** *n.*

em•boss•ment (ĕm-bôs′mənt, -bŏs′-) *n.* **1.** The act or process

emarginate
emarginate leaf

emblem
universal recycling emblem

ă	**pat**	oi	**boy**
ā	**pay**	ou	**out**
âr	**care**	o͝o	**took**
ä	**father**	o͞o	**boot**
ĕ	**pet**	ŭ	**cut**
ē	**be**	ûr	**urge**
ĭ	**pit**	th	**thin**
ī	**pie**	*th*	**this**
îr	**pier**	hw	**which**
ŏ	**pot**	zh	**vision**
ō	**toe**	ə	**about, item**
ô	**paw**		

Stress marks:
′ (primary);
′ (secondary), as in
lexicon (lĕk′sĭ-kŏn′)

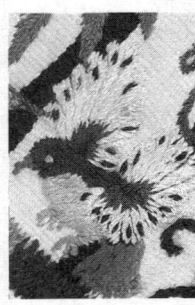

embroidery
detail of an embroidered
blouse

Ralph Waldo Emerson
c. 1875 photograph by
Frederick Gutekunst
(1831–1917)

empennage

of embossing or the condition of being embossed. **2.** Embossed ornamentation. **3.** The distance between the nondeformed part of a document surface and a specified point on a printed character in optical character recognition.

em·bou·chure (äm′boō-shŏōr′) *n.* **1.** The mouth of a river. **2.** *Music* **a.** The mouthpiece of a woodwind or brass instrument. **b.** The manner in which the lips and tongue are applied to such a mouthpiece. [Fr. < *emboucher*, to put or go into the mouth < OFr. : *en-*, in; see EN-¹ + *bouche*, mouth (< Lat. *bucca*, cheek).]

em·bowed (ĕm-bōd′) *adj.* **1.** Bent or curved like a bow. **2.** *Architecture* Having an arch or arches.

em·bow·el (ĕm-bou′əl) *tr.v.* **-eled, -el·ing, -els** or **-elled, -el·ling, -els 1.** To disembowel. **2.** *Obsolete* To enclose. [Obsolete Fr. *emboueler*, alteration of OFr. *esbouler* : *es-*, out (< Lat. *ex-*; see EX–) + *boeler* (< *boel, bouele*, entrails; see BOWEL). Sense 2, EN–¹ + BOWEL.]

em·bow·er (ĕm-bou′ər) *tr.v.* **-ered, -er·ing, -ers** To enclose in or as if in a bower.

em·brace (ĕm-brās′) *v.* **-braced, -brac·ing, -brac·es** —*tr.* **1.** To clasp or hold close with the arms, usu. as an expression of affection. **2a.** To surround; enclose. **b.** To twine around. **3.** To include as part of something broader. **4.** To take up willingly or eagerly. **5.** To avail oneself of. —*intr.* To join in an embrace. ❖ *n.* **1.** An act of embracing; a hug. **2.** An enclosure or encirclement. **3.** Eager acceptance. [ME *embracen* < OFr. *embracer* : *en-*, in; see EN–¹ + *brace*, the two arms; see BRACE.] —**em·brace′a·ble** *adj.* —**em·brace′ment** *n.* —**em·brac′er** *n.*

em·branch·ment (ĕm-brănch′mənt) *n.* **1.** A branching out, as of a mountain range or river. **2.** A branch or ramification.

em·bran·gle (ĕm-brăng′gəl) *tr.v.* **-gled, -gling, -gles** To entangle; embroil. [EN–¹ + dialectal *brangle*, to shake, waver, confuse (var. of *branle* < Fr. *branler* < OFr. *brandeler*, perh. < *brand*, sword; see BRANDISH).] —**em·bran′gle·ment** *n.*

em·bra·sure (ĕm-brā′zhər) *n.* **1.** An opening in a thick wall for a door or window, esp. one with sides angled so that the opening is larger on the inside than on the outside. **2.** A flared opening for a gun in a wall or parapet. [Fr. < *embraser*, to widen an opening.] —**em·bra′sured** *adj.*

em·brit·tle (ĕm-brĭt′l) *tr. & intr.v.* **-tled, -tling, -tles** To make or become brittle. —**em·brit′tle·ment** *n.*

em·bro·cate (ĕm′brə-kāt′) *tr.v.* **-cat·ed, -cat·ing, -cates** To moisten and rub (a part of the body) with a liniment or lotion. [Med.Lat. *embrocāre, embrocāt-* < LLat. *embrocha*, lotion < Gk. *embrokhē < embrekhein*, to foment : *en-*, in; see EN–² + *brekhein*, to wet.]

em·bro·ca·tion (ĕm′brə-kā′shən) *n.* **1.** The act or process of moistening and rubbing a part of the body with a liniment or lotion. **2.** A liniment or lotion.

em·broi·der (ĕm-broi′dər) *v.* **-dered, -der·ing, -ders** —*tr.* **1.** To ornament with needlework. **2.** To make by means of needlework: *embroider a design.* **3.** To add embellishments to: *embroider the truth.* —*intr.* **1.** To make needlework. **2.** To add embellishments. [ME *embrouderen,* partly < *embrouder* (< *brouden, broiden,* braided, embroidered < OE *brogden,* p. part. of *bregdan,* to weave; see BRAID) and partly < OFr. *embroder* (*en-,* intensive pref.; see EN–¹ + *broder, brosder,* to embroider, of Gmc. orig.).] —**em·broi′der·er** *n.*

em·broi·der·y (ĕm-broi′də-rē) *n., pl.* **-ies 1.** The act or art of embroidering. **2.** Ornamentation of fabric with needlework. **3.** A piece of embroidered fabric. **4.** Embellishment with fanciful details.

em·broil (ĕm-broil′) *tr.v.* **-broiled, -broil·ing, -broils 1.** To involve in argument, contention, or hostile actions. **2.** To throw into confusion or disorder; entangle. [Fr. *embrouiller* : *en-,* intensive pref.; see EN–¹ + *brouiller,* to confuse (< OFr.; see BROIL²).] —**em·broil′ment** *n.*

em·brown (ĕm-broun′) *tr.v.* **-browned, -brown·ing, -browns 1.** To make brown or dusky. **2.** To darken.

em·brue (ĕm-broō′) *v.* Variant of **imbrue.**

em·bry·o (ĕm′brē-ō′) *n., pl.* **-os 1a.** An organism in its early stages of development, esp. before it has reached a recognizable form. **b.** An organism at any time before full development, birth, or hatching. **2a.** The fertilized egg of a vertebrate animal following cleavage. **b.** In humans, the product of conception from implantation through the eighth week of development. **3.** *Botany* The rudimentary plant contained within a seed or an archegonium. **4.** A rudimentary or beginning stage. [Med.Lat. *embryō* < Gk. *embruon* : *en-,* in; see EN–² + *bruein,* to be full to bursting.]

em·bry·o·gen·e·sis (ĕm′brē-ō-jĕn′ĭ-sĭs) also **em·bry·og·e·ny** (-ŏj′ə-nē) *n.* The development and growth of an embryo. —**em′bry·o·gen′ic** (-jĕn′ĭk), **em′bry·o·ge·net′ic** (-ō-jə-nĕt′ĭk) *adj.*

em·bry·ol·o·gy (ĕm′brē-ŏl′ə-jē) *n.* **1.** The branch of biology that deals with the formation, early growth, and development of living organism. **2.** The embryonic structure or development of a particular organism. —**em′bry·o·log′ic** (-ə-lŏj′ĭk), **em′bry·o·log′i·cal** *adj.* —**em′bry·o·log′i·cal·ly** *adv.* —**em′bry·ol′o·gist** *n.*

em·bry·on·ic (ĕm′brē-ŏn′ĭk) also **em·bry·on·al** (ĕm′brē-ə-nəl) *adj.* **1.** Of, relating to, or being an embryo. **2.** also **em·bry·ot·ic** (-ŏt′ĭk) Rudimentary; incipient: *an embryonic nation.*

[< Med.Lat. *embryō, embryōn-,* embryo. See EMBRYO.] —**em′bry·on′ic·al·ly** *adv.*

embryonic disk *n.* **1.** A platelike mass of cells in the blastocyst from which a mammalian embryo develops. **2.** See **germinal disk.**

embryonic membrane *n.* Any of the membranous structures closely associated with or surrounding a vertebrate embryo, including the amnion, chorion, allantois, and yolk sac.

embryonic shield *n.* See **embryonic disk** 1.

embryo sac *n.* The female gametophyte of a seed plant, within which the embryo develops.

embryo transfer *n.* The transfer of a fertilized egg, such as one fertilized in vitro, to a recipient uterus.

em·cee (ĕm′sē′) *n.* A master of ceremonies. [Pronunciation of MC¹.] —**em′cee′** *v.*

em·dash or **em dash** (ĕm′dăsh′) *n.* A symbol (—) used in writing and printing to indicate a break in thought or sentence structure, to introduce an emphatic or explanatory phrase, or to separate two clauses. [< its being the width of an *m* in printing.]

–eme *suff.* A distinctive unit of linguistic structure: *semanteme.* [Fr. *-ème < phonème,* phoneme. See PHONEME.]

e·mend (ĭ-mĕnd′) *tr.v.* **e·mend·ed, e·mend·ing, e·mends** To improve by critical editing. [ME *emenden* < Lat. *ēmendāre* : *ē-, ex-,* ex- + *mendum,* defect, fault.] —**e·mend′er** *n.*

e·men·date (ē′mĕn-dāt′, ĭ-mĕn′-) *tr.v.* **-dat·ed, -dat·ing, -dates** To make textual corrections in. [Lat. *ēmendāre, ēmendāt-,* to emend. See EMEND.] —**e′men·da′tor** (-dā′tər) *n.* —**e·men′da·to·ry** (ĭ-mĕn′də-tôr′ē, -tōr′ē) *adj.*

e·men·da·tion (ē′mĕn-dā′shən, ĕ′mĕn-) *n.* **1.** The act of emending. **2.** An alteration intended to improve.

em·er·ald (ĕm′ər-əld, ĕm′rəld) *n.* **1.** A brilliant green to grass-green transparent variety of beryl, used as a gemstone. **2.** A strong yellowish green. ❖ *adj.* Of a strong yellowish green. [ME *emeraude* < OFr. < Med.Lat. *esmeralda, esmeraldus* < Lat. *smaragdus* < Gk. *smaragdos.*]

e·merge (ĭ-mûrj′) *intr.v.* **e·merged, e·merg·ing, e·merg·es 1.** To rise from or as if from a surrounding fluid. **2.** To come forth from obscurity: *new leaders who may emerge.* **3.** To become evident. **4.** To come into existence. [Lat. *ēmergere* : *ē-, ex-,* ex- + *mergere,* to immerse.]

e·mer·gence (ĭ-mûr′jəns) *n.* **1.** The act or process of emerging. **2.** A superficial outgrowth of plant tissue.

e·mer·gen·cy (ĭ-mûr′jən-sē) *n., pl.* **-cies 1.** A serious situation or occurrence that happens unexpectedly and demands immediate action. **2.** A condition of urgent need for action or assistance. ❖ *adj.* For use during emergencies.

emergency brake *n.* An additional brake system in a vehicle, commonly used as a parking brake.

emergency room *n.* The section of a health care facility for providing rapid treatment for victims of sudden illness or trauma.

e·mer·gent (ĭ-mûr′jənt) *adj.* **1a.** Coming into view, existence, or notice. **b.** Emerging: *emergent nations.* **2.** Rising above a surrounding medium, esp. a fluid. **3a.** Arising or occurring unexpectedly. **b.** Demanding prompt action; urgent. **4.** Occurring as a consequence. ❖ *n.* One that is coming into view or existence.

e·merg·ing (ĭ-mûr′jĭng) *adj.* Newly formed or just coming into prominence; emergent: *emerging markets.*

e·mer·i·ta (ĭ-mĕr′ĭ-tə) *adj.* Retired but retaining an honorary title corresponding to that held immediately before retirement. Used of a woman. ❖ *n., pl.* **-tae** (-tē′) or **-tas** A woman who holds emerita status. [Lat. *ēmerita,* fem. of *ēmeritus.* See EMERITUS.]

e·mer·i·tus (ĭ-mĕr′ĭ-təs) *adj.* Retired but retaining an honorary title corresponding to that held immediately before retirement. ❖ *n., pl.* **-ti** (-tī′) One who holds emeritus status. [Lat. *ēmeritus,* p. part. of *ēmerērī,* to earn by service : *ē-, ex-,* from; see EX– + *merērī,* to deserve, earn.]

e·mersed (ĭ-mûrst′) *adj. Botany* Rising above the surface of water: *emersed plants.* [< Lat. *ēmersus.* See EMERSION.]

e·mer·sion (ĭ-mûr′zhən, -shən) *n.* The act of emerging; emergence. [< Lat. *ēmersus,* p. part. of *ēmergere,* to emerge. See EMERGE.]

Em·er·son (ĕm′ər-sən), **Ralph Waldo** 1803–82. Amer. writer and philosopher whose works include *Nature* (1836). —**Em′er·so′ni·an** (-sō′nē-ən) *adj.*

em·er·y (ĕm′ə-rē, ĕm′rē) *n.* A fine-grained impure corundum used for grinding and polishing. [ME < OFr. *emeri, emeril* < LLat. *smericulum* < Gk. *smiris.*]

emery board *n.* A nail file consisting of a strip of cardboard coated with powdered emery.

em·e·sis (ĕm′ĭ-sĭs) *n., pl.* **-ses** (-sēz′) The act of vomiting. [Gk. < *emein,* to vomit. See **wemə-** in App.]

e·met·ic (ĭ-mĕt′ĭk) *adj.* Causing vomiting. ❖ *n.* An agent that causes vomiting. [Lat. *emeticus* < Gk. *emetikos < emetos,* vomiting < *emein,* to vomit. See **wemə-** in App.] —**e·met′i·cal·ly** *adv.*

em·e·tine (ĕm′ĭ-tēn′) *n.* A bitter-tasting crystalline alkaloid, $C_{29}H_{40}N_2O_4$, derived from ipecac root and used in the treatment of amebiasis and as an emetic. [Fr. *émétine < émétique,* emetic < Lat. *emeticus.* See EMETIC.]

EMF *abbr.* electromotive force

EMG *abbr.* electromyogram

–emia or **–hemia** also **–aemia** or **–haemia** *suff.* Blood: *leukemia.* [NLat. < Gk. *-aimiā* < *haima*, blood.]

em•i•grant (ĕm′ĭ-grənt) *n.* One that emigrates. ❖ *adj.* Of or relating to emigrants or the act of emigrating.

em•i•grate (ĕm′ĭ-grāt′) *intr.v.* **-grat•ed, -grat•ing, -grates** To leave one country or region to settle in another. See Usage Note at **migrate.** [Lat. *ēmigrāre, ēmigrāt-* : *ē-, ex-*, ex- + *migrāre*, to move.] —**em′i•gra′tion** (ĕm′ĭ-grā′shən) *n.*

é•mi•gré (ĕm′ĭ-grā′) *n.* One who has left a native country, esp. for political reasons. [Fr. < p. part. of *émigrer*, to emigrate < Lat. *ēmigrāre*. See EMIGRATE.]

E•mi•lia-Ro•ma•gna (ĕ-mēl′yə-rō-mä′nyä) A region of N Italy bordering on the Adriatic Sea.

em•i•nence (ĕm′ə-nəns) *n.* **1.** A position of great distinction or superiority: *rose to eminence as a surgeon.* **2.** A rise of ground; a hill. **3a.** A person of high station or great achievements. **b.** also **Eminence** *Roman Catholic Church* Used with *His* or *Your* as a title and form of address for a cardinal. **4.** *Anatomy* A projecting part, esp. from a bone.

ém•i•nence grise (ā-mē-näns grēz′) *n., pl.* **ém•i•nence grises** (ā-mē-näns grēz′) A powerful adviser or decision-maker who operates secretly or unofficially. [Fr., the power behind the throne : *éminence*, power + *grise*, fem. of *gris*, gray, shadowy.]

em•i•nen•cy (ĕm′ə-nən-sē) *n., pl.* **-cies** Eminence.

em•i•nent (ĕm′ə-nənt) *adj.* **1.** Towering or standing out above others; prominent. **2.** Of high rank, station, or quality; noteworthy. **3.** Outstanding, as in character or performance; distinguished. See Syns at **noted.** [ME < Lat. *ēminēns, ēminent-*, pr. part. of *ēminēre*, to stand out : *ē-, ex-*, ex- + *-minēre*, to jut out.] —**em′i•nent•ly** *adv.*

eminent domain *n.* The right of a government to appropriate private property for public use, usu. with compensation to the owner.

e•mir (ĭ-mîr′, ā-mîr′) also **a•mir** (ə-mîr′, ā-mîr′) *n.* A prince, chieftain, or governor, esp. in the Middle East. [Fr. *émir* < Ar. *'amīr*, commander, prince < *'amara*, to command.]

e•mir•ate (ĭ-mîr′ĭt, -āt′) *n.* **1.** The office of an emir. **2.** The nation or territory ruled by an emir.

em•is•sar•y (ĕm′ĭ-sĕr′ē) *n., pl.* **-ies** An agent sent on a mission to represent or advance the interests of another.

e•mis•sion (ĭ-mĭsh′ən) *n.* **1.** The act or an instance of emitting. **2.** Something emitted. **3.** A substance discharged into the air, esp. a pollutant. [Lat. *ēmissiō, ēmissiōn-*, a sending out < *ēmissus*, p. part. of *ēmittere*, to send out. See EMIT.]

emission spectrum *n.* The characteristic spectrum of radiation directly emitted by a substance subjected to a specific excitation.

e•mis•sive (ĭ-mĭs′ĭv) *adj.* Having the power or tendency to emit matter or energy; emitting.

em•is•siv•i•ty (ĕm′ĭ-sĭv′ĭ-tē) *n.* The ratio of the radiation emitted by a surface to the radiation emitted by a blackbody at the same temperature.

e•mit (ĭ-mĭt′) *tr.v.* **e•mit•ted, e•mit•ting, e•mits 1.** To give or send out (matter or energy). **2a.** To give out as sound; utter. **b.** To voice; express. **3.** To issue with authority, esp. to put (currency) into circulation. [Lat. *ēmittere*, to send out : *ē-, ex-*, ex- + *mittere*, to send.] —**e•mit′ter** *n.*

em•men•a•gogue (ĭ-mĕn′ə-gôg′, -gŏg′) *n.* A drug or agent that induces or hastens menstrual flow. [Gk. *emmēna*, the menses (< neut. pl. of *emmēnos*, monthly : *en-*, in; see EN–[2] + *mēn*, month; see **mē-**[1] in App.) + –AGOGUE.]

em•mer (ĕm′ər) *n.* A Eurasian wheat *(Triticum dicoccum)* first cultivated by the Babylonians. [Ger. < MHGer. *amer, emeri* < OHGer. *amaro.*]

em•met (ĕm′ĭt) *n. Archaic* An ant. [ME *emete* < OE *ǣmete.*]

em•me•tro•pi•a (ĕm′ĭ-trō′pē-ə) *n.* The condition of the normal eye when parallel rays are focused exactly on the retina and vision is perfect. [Gk. *emmetros*, well-proportioned, fitting (*en*, in; see EN–[2] + *metron*, measure; see METER[2]) + –OPIA.] —**em′me•trop′ic** (-trŏp′ĭk, -trō′pĭk) *adj.*

Em•my (ĕm′ē) A trademark for an award for excellence in the creation and production of television programming.

e•mol•lient (ĭ-mŏl′yənt) *adj.* **1.** Softening and soothing, esp. to the skin. **2.** Making less harsh or abrasive; mollifying. ❖ *n.* **1.** An agent that softens or soothes the skin. **2.** An agent that assuages or mollifies. [Lat. *ēmolliēns, ēmollient-*, pr. part. of *ēmollīre*, to soften : *ē-, ex-*, intensive pref.; see EX– + *mollīre*, to soften (< *mollis*, soft).]

e•mol•u•ment (ĭ-mŏl′yə-mənt) *n.* Payment for an office or employment; compensation. [ME < Lat. *ēmolumentum*, gain, orig. a miller's fee for grinding grain < *ēmolere*, to grind out : *ē-, ex-*, ex- + *molere*, to grind; see **melə-** in App.]

e•mote (ĭ-mōt′) *intr.v.* **e•mot•ed, e•mot•ing, e•motes** To express emotion, esp. in an excessive or theatrical manner. [Back-formation < EMOTION.] —**e•mot′er** *n.*

e•mo•ti•con (ĭ-mō′tĭ-kŏn′) *n.* A sideways facial glyph used in e-mail to indicate an emotion or attitude, as [:-)] to indicate intended humor. [EMOT(ION) + ICON.]

e•mo•tion (ĭ-mō′shən) *n.* **1.** A mental state arising spontaneously rather than through conscious effort; a feeling. **2.** A state of mental agitation or disturbance: *a quavering voice that betrayed emotion.* See Syns at **feeling. 3.** The part of the consciousness that involves feeling; sensibility. [Fr. *émotion* < OFr. < *esmovoir*, to excite < VLat. **exmovēre* : Lat. *ex-*, ex- + Lat. *movēre*, to move.]

e•mo•tion•al (ĭ-mō′shə-nəl) *adj.* **1.** Of or relating to emotion. **2.** Readily affected with or stirred by emotion. **3.** Arousing or intended to arouse the emotions: *an emotional appeal.* **4.** Marked by or exhibiting emotion. —**e•mo′tion•al′i•ty** (-shə-năl′ĭ-tē) *n.* —**e•mo′tion•al•ly** *adv.*

emotional intelligence *n.* Intelligence regarding the emotions, esp. in the ability to monitor one's own or others' emotions.

e•mo•tion•al•ism (ĭ-mō′shə-nə-lĭz′əm) *n.* **1.** An inclination to rely on or place too much value on emotion. **2.** Undue display of emotion.

e•mo•tion•al•ist (ĭ-mō′shə-nə-lĭst) *n.* **1.** One whose conduct, thought, or rhetoric is governed by emotion rather than reason. **2.** A very emotional person. —**e•mo′tion•al•is′tic** *adj.*

e•mo•tion•al•ize (ĭ-mō′shə-nə-līz′) *tr.v.* **-ized, -iz•ing, -iz•es** To impart an emotional quality to.

e•mo•tive (ĭ-mō′tĭv) *adj.* **1.** Of or relating to emotion. **2.** Characterized by, expressing, or exciting emotion: *an emotive trial lawyer.* —**e•mo′tive•ly** *adv.* —**e•mo′tive•ness, e′mo•tiv′i•ty** (ē′mō-tĭv′ĭ-tē) *n.*

EMP *abbr.* electromagnetic pulse

em•pa•na•da (ĕm′pə-nä′də) *n.* A Spanish or Latin-American turnover with a flaky crust and a spicy or sweet filling. [Sp. < fem. p. part. of *empanar*, to coat with breadcrumbs : *en-*, in (< Lat. *in-*; see EN–[1]) + *pan*, bread; see PANADA.]

em•pan•el (ĕm-păn′əl) *v.* Variant of **impanel.**

em•pa•thet•ic (ĕm′pə-thĕt′ĭk) *adj.* Empathic. —**em′pa•thet′i•cal•ly** *adv.*

em•path•ic (ĕm-păth′ĭk) *adj.* Of, relating to, or characterized by empathy.

em•pa•thize (ĕm′pə-thīz′) *intr.v.* **-thized, -thiz•ing, -thiz•es** To feel or experience empathy. —**em′pa•thiz′er** *n.*

em•pa•thy (ĕm′pə-thē) *n.* **1.** Identification with and understanding of another's situation, feelings, and motives. **2.** The attribution of one's feelings to an object. [EN–[2] + –PATHY.]

Em•ped•o•cles (ĕm-pĕd′ə-klēz′) 5th cent. B.C. Greek philosopher who believed that all matter is made of earth, air, fire and water, and that all change is caused by attraction and repulsion.

em•pen•nage (ĕm′pə-nĭj) *n.* The tail of an airplane. [Fr. < *empenner*, to feather an arrow : *en-*, in; see EN–[1] + *penne*, feather (< Lat. *penna*; see **pet-** in App.).]

em•per•or (ĕm′pər-ər) *n.* **1.** The male ruler of an empire. **2a.** The emperor butterfly. **b.** The emperor moth. [ME *emperour* < OFr. *empereor* < Lat. *imperātor* < *imperāre*, to command : *in-*, in; see EN–[1] + *parāre*, to prepare.] —**em′per•or•ship′** *n.*

emperor butterfly *n.* Any of several butterflies of the family Nymphalidae, having orange wings with dark markings.

emperor moth *n.* Any of several moths of the family Saturnidae, esp. *Saturnia pavonia* of Eurasia, having distinctively patterned wings.

emperor penguin *n.* A large penguin *(Aptenodytes forsteri)* of Antarctic regions having yellow-orange patches on the neck.

em•per•y (ĕm′pə-rē) *n., pl.* **-ies** Absolute dominion or jurisdiction; sovereignty. [ME *emperie* < OFr. < Lat. *imperium.* See EMPIRE.]

em•pha•sis (ĕm′fə-sĭs) *n., pl.* **-ses** (-sēz′) **1.** Special forcefulness of expression that gives importance to something singled out; stress. **2.** Special attention or effort directed toward something. **3.** Prominence given to a syllable, word, or words, as by raising the voice or printing in italic type. [Lat. < Gk. < *emphainein*, to exhibit, display : *en-*, in; see EN–[2] + *phainein*, to show.]

SYNONYMS *emphasis, accent, stress* These nouns mean special weight placed on something considered important: *an education with an emphasis on science; will study music with an accent on jazz; laid heavy stress on law and order.*

em•pha•size (ĕm′fə-sīz′) *tr.v.* **-sized, -siz•ing, -siz•es** To give emphasis to; stress. [< EMPHASIS.]

em•phat•ic (ĕm-făt′ĭk) *adj.* **1.** Expressed or performed with emphasis: *an emphatic "no."* **2.** Forceful and definite in expression or action. **3.** Standing out in a striking way. [Med.Lat. *emphaticus* < Gk. *emphatikos* < *emphainein*, to exhibit, display. See EMPHASIS.] —**em•phat′i•cal•ly** *adv.*

em•phy•se•ma (ĕm′fĭ-sē′mə, -zē′-) *n.* **1.** A pathological condition of the lungs marked by an abnormal increase in the size of the air spaces, resulting in labored breathing and an increased susceptibility to infection. **2.** An abnormal distention of body tissues caused by retention of air. [Gk. *emphusēma*, inflation < *emphūsān*, to blow in : *en-*, in; see EN–[2] + *phūsān*, to blow (< *phūsa*, bellows, bladder).] —**em′phy•sem′a•tous** (-sĕm′ə-təs, -sē′mə-, -zĕm′ə-, -zē′mə-) *adj.* —**em′phy•se′mic** *adj. & n.*

em•pire (ĕm′pīr′) *n.* **1a.** A political unit comprising a number of territories or nations and ruled by a single supreme authority. **b.** The territory included in such a unit. **2.** An extensive enterprise under a unified authority: *a publishing empire.* **3.** Imperial or imperialistic sovereignty or domination. [ME < OFr. < Lat. *imperium* < *imperāre*, to command. See EMPEROR.]

Em•pire (ŏm-pîr′, ĕm′pīr′) *adj.* Of or relating to a neoclassic style, as in furniture, prevalent in France during the first part of the 19th century. [After the First *Empire* of France (1804–15).]

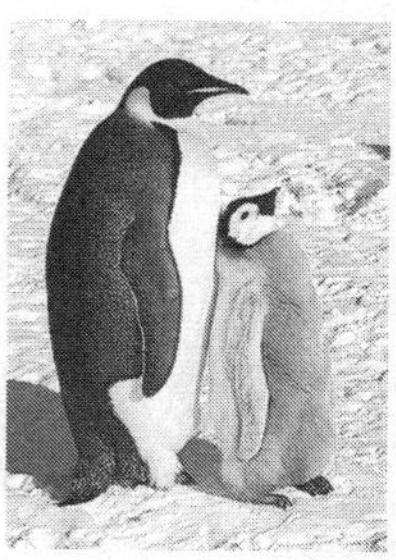

emperor penguin
Aptenodytes forsteri
adult with chick

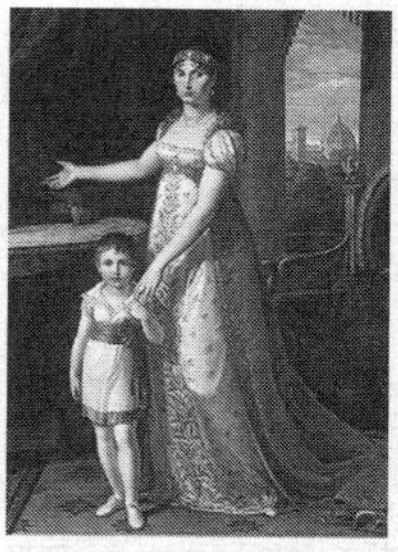

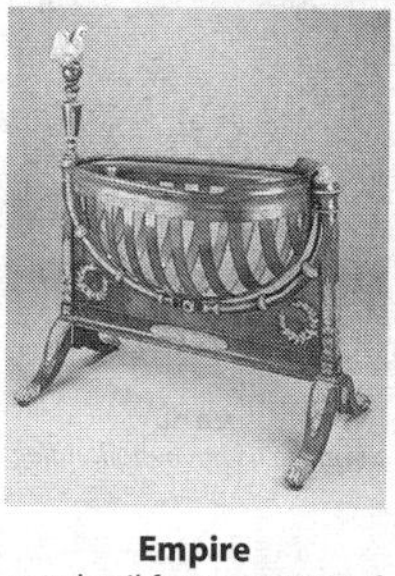

Empire
top: detail from a portrait of Elisa Bonaparte and her daughter Napoleone-Elisa by Pietro Benvenuti (1769–1844)
bottom: mahogany slatted cradle-on-stand

ă	pat	oi	boy
ā	pay	ou	out
âr	care	ŏŏ	took
ä	father	ōō	boot
ĕ	pet	ŭ	cut
ē	be	ûr	urge
ĭ	pit	th	thin
ī	pie	*th*	this
îr	pier	hw	which
ŏ	pot	zh	vision
ō	toe	ə	about, item
ô	paw		

Stress marks:
′ (primary);
′ (secondary), as in
lexicon (lĕk′sĭ-kŏn′)

em·pir·ic (ĕm-pîr′ĭk) *n.* **1.** One who is guided by practical experience rather than precepts or theory. **2.** An unqualified or dishonest practitioner; a charlatan. ❖ *adj.* Empirical. [Lat. *empīricus* < Gk. *empeirikos*, experienced < *empeiros*, skilled : *en-*, in; see EN–[2] + *peirān*, to try (< *peira*, try, attempt).]

em·pir·i·cal (ĕm-pîr′ĭ-kəl) *adj.* **1a.** Relying on or derived from observation or experiment. **b.** Verifiable or provable by means of observation or experiment. **2.** Guided by practical experience and not theory, esp. in medicine. —**em·pir′i·cal·ly** *adv.*

empirical formula *n.* A chemical formula that indicates the relative proportions of the elements in a molecule rather than the actual number of atoms of the elements.

em·pir·i·cism (ĕm-pîr′ĭ-sĭz′əm) *n.* **1.** The view that experience, esp. of the senses, is the only source of knowledge. **2a.** Employment of empirical methods, as in science. **b.** An empirical conclusion. **3.** The practice of medicine that disregards theory and relies solely on practical experience. —**em·pir′i·cist** *n.*

em·place (ĕm-plās′) *tr.v.* **-placed, -plac·ing, -plac·es** To put into place or position: *emplace a fortification on the hilltop.*

em·place·ment (ĕm-plās′mənt) *n.* **1.** A prepared position, such as a mounting or silo, for a military weapon. **2.** The act of putting into a certain position; placement. **3.** Position; location. [Fr. < obsolete *emplacer*, to put in position : *en-*, in; see EN–[1] + OFr. *place*, open space; see PLACE.]

em·plane (ĕm-plān′) *v.* Variant of enplane.

em·ploy (ĕm-ploi′) *tr.v.* **-ployed, -ploy·ing, -ploys 1a.** To engage the services of; put to work. **b.** To provide with gainful work: *factories that employ thousands.* **2.** To put to use or service. **3.** To devote (time, for example) to an activity or purpose. ❖ *n.* **1.** The state of being employed. **2.** *Archaic* Occupation. [ME *emploien* < OFr. *emploier* < Lat. *implicāre*, to involve : *in-*, in; see EN–[1] + *plicāre*, to fold; see **plek-** in App.] —**em·ploy′a·bil′i·ty** *n.* —**em·ploy′a·ble** *adj.* —**em·ploy′er** *n.*

em·ploy·ee also **em·ploy·e** (ĕm-ploi′ē, -ĭm-, ĕm′ploi-ē′) *n.* A person who works for another in return for compensation.

em·ploy·ment (ĕm-ploi′mənt) *n.* **1a.** The act of employing. **b.** The state of being employed. **2.** The work in which one is engaged; occupation. **3.** An activity to which one devotes time. **4.** The percentage or number of people gainfully employed.

employment agency *n.* An agency that finds jobs for people seeking them and finds people to fill particular jobs.

em·poi·son (ĕm-poi′zən) *tr.v.* **-soned, -son·ing, -sons 1.** To fill with venom; embitter. **2.** *Archaic* To poison.

em·po·ri·um (ĕm-pôr′ē-əm, -pōr′-) *n., pl.* **-po·ri·ums** or **-po·ri·a** (-pôr′ē-ə, -pōr′-) **1.** A place where various goods are bought and sold; a marketplace. **2.** A large retail store or place of business. [Lat. < Gk. *emporos*, traveler, merchant : *en-*, in; see EN–[2] + *poros*, journey; see **per-**[2] in App.]

em·pow·er (ĕm-pou′ər) *tr.v.* **-ered, -er·ing, -ers 1.** To invest with power, esp. legal power or official authority. **2.** To equip or supply with an ability; enable. —**em·pow′er·ment** *n.*

em·press (ĕm′prĭs) *n.* **1.** The woman ruler of an empire. **2.** The wife or widow of an emperor. [ME *emperesse* < OFr., fem. of *empereor*, emperor. See EMPEROR.]

em·presse·ment (äN′prĕs-mäN′) *n.* Effusive cordiality. [Fr. < (s′)*empresser*, to be eager : *en-*, in; see EN–[1] + *presser*, to press (< OFr.; see PRESS[1]).]

em·prise (ĕm-prīz′) *n.* **1.** A chivalrous or adventurous undertaking. **2.** Chivalrous daring or prowess. [ME < OFr. < fem. p. part. of *emprendre*, to undertake < VLat. *imprēndere* : Lat. *in-*, in; see EN–[1] + Lat. *prehendere, prēndere*, to take, grasp; see **ghend-** in App.]

emp·ty (ĕmp′tē) *adj.* **-ti·er, -ti·est 1a.** Holding or containing nothing. **b.** *Mathematics* Having no elements or members; null. **2.** Having no occupants or inhabitants; vacant. **3.** Lacking force or power: *an empty threat.* **4.** Lacking purpose or substance; meaningless. **5.** Not put to use; idle. **6.** Needing nourishment; hungry. **7.** Devoid; destitute. ❖ *v.* **-tied, -ty·ing, -ties** —*tr.* **1.** To remove the contents of. **2.** To transfer or pour off completely. **3.** To unburden; relieve. —*intr.* **1.** To become empty. **2.** To discharge its contents. ❖ *n., pl.* **-ties** *Informal* An empty container. [ME < OE *ǣmtig*, vacant, unoccupied < *ǣmetta*, leisure. See **med-** in App.] —**emp′ti·ly** *adv.* —**emp′ti·ness** *n.*

emp·ty-hand·ed (ĕmp′tē-hăn′dĭd) *adj.* **1.** Bearing nothing. **2.** Having received or gained nothing.

emp·ty-head·ed (ĕmp′tē-hĕd′ĭd) *adj.* Lacking sense or discretion; scatterbrained.

empty nest syndrome *n.* A feeling of depression experienced by some parents after their children have grown and left home.

Empty Quarter See Rub al Khali.

em·pur·ple (ĕm-pûr′pəl) *tr. & intr.v.* **-pled, -pling, -ples** To make or become purple.

em·py·e·ma (ĕm′pī-ē′mə) *n., pl.* **-ma·ta** (-mə-tə) The presence of pus in a body cavity, esp. the pleural cavity. [Med.Lat. *empyēma* < Gk. *empuēma* < *empuein*, to suppurate. See **pŭ-** in App.] —**em′py·e′mic** *adj.*

em·py·re·al (ĕm′pī-rē′əl, ĕm-pîr′ē-əl) *adj.* **1.** Empyrean. **2.** Of the sky; celestial. **3.** Elevated; sublime. [ME *emperiall* < Med.Lat. *empyreus* < LLat. *empyrius*, fiery < Gk. *empurios* : *en-*, in; see EN–[2] + *pūr*, fire; see **paəwr̥** in App.]

em·py·re·an (ĕm′pī-rē′ən, ĕm-pîr′ē-ən) *n.* **1a.** The highest reaches of heaven, believed by the ancients to be a realm of pure fire or light. **b.** The abode of God and the angels; paradise. **2.** The sky. [< Med.Lat. *empyreum* < *empyreus*, empyreal. See EMPYREAL.] —**em′py·re′an** *adj.*

Ems (ĕmz, ĕms) A river of NW Germany flowing c. 335 km (208 mi) to the North Sea at the Netherlands border.

EMS *abbr.* **1.** electrical muscle stimulation **2.** Emergency Medical Service **3.** European Monetary System

EMT *abbr.* emergency medical technician

e·mu (ē′myōō) *n.* A large flightless Australian bird (*Dromiceius novaehollandiae*) related to and resembling the ostrich and the cassowary. [Port. *ema*, rhea.]

EMU *abbr.* **1.** also **emu** electromagnetic unit **2.** European Monetary Union

em·u·late (ĕm′yə-lāt′) *tr.v.* **-lat·ed, -lat·ing, -lates 1.** To strive to equal or excel, esp. through imitation. **2.** To compete with successfully; approach or attain equality with. **3.** *Computer Science* To imitate the function of (another system), as by modifications to hardware or software. ❖ *adj.* (-lĭt) *Obsolete* Ambitious; emulous. [Lat. *aemulārī, aemulāt-* < *aemulus*, emulous. See EMULOUS.] —**em′u·la′tive** *adj.* —**em′u·la′tive·ly** *adv.* —**em′u·la′tor** *n.*

em·u·la·tion (ĕm′yə-lā′shən) *n.* **1.** Effort or ambition to equal or surpass another. **2.** Imitation of another. **3.** *Computer Science* The process or technique of emulating. **4.** *Obsolete* Jealous rivalry.

em·u·lous (ĕm′yə-ləs) *adj.* **1.** Eager or ambitious to equal or surpass another. **2.** Characterized or prompted by a spirit of rivalry. **3.** *Obsolete* Covetous of power or honor; envious. [< Lat. *aemulus*. See **aim-** in App.] —**em′u·lous·ly** *adv.*

e·mul·si·ble (ĭ-mŭl′sə-bəl) *adj.* That can be emulsified.

e·mul·si·fy (ĭ-mŭl′sə-fī′) *tr.v.* **-fied, -fy·ing, -fies** To make into an emulsion. [EMULSI(ON) + –FY.] —**e·mul′si·fi·ca′tion** (-fĭ-kā′shən) *n.* —**e·mul′si·fi′er** *n.*

e·mul·sion (ĭ-mŭl′shən) *n.* **1.** A suspension of small globules of one liquid in a second liquid with which the first will not mix: *an emulsion of oil in vinegar.* **2.** A photosensitive coating, usu. of silver halide grains in a thin gelatin layer, on photographic film, paper, or glass. [NLat. *ēmulsiō, ēmulsiōn-* < Lat. *ēmulsus*, p. part. of *ēmulgēre*, to milk out : *ē-, ex-, ex-* + *mulgēre*, to milk; see **melg-** in App.] —**e·mul′sive** *adj.*

e·munc·to·ry (ĭ-mŭngk′tə-rē) *adj.* Serving to carry waste out of the body; excretory. ❖ *n., pl.* **-ries** An emunctory organ. [ME *emunctorie* < Med.Lat. *ēmunctōrius* < Lat. *ēmunctus*, p. part. of *ēmungere*, to blow one's nose : *ē-, ex-*, intensive pref.; see EX– + *mungere*, to blow one's nose.]

en (ĕn) *n.* **1.** The letter *n.* **2.** *Printing* A space equal to half the width of an em.

en–[1] or **em–** or **in–** *pref.* **1a.** To put into or onto: *encapsulate.* **b.** To go into or onto: *enplane.* **2.** To cover or provide with: *enrobe.* **3.** To cause to be: *endear.* **4.** Thoroughly. Used often as an intensive: *entangle.* [ME < OFr. < Lat. *in-*, in. See **en** in App.]

en–[2] or **em–** *pref.* In; into; within: *enzootic.* [ME < Lat. < Gk. See **en** in App.]

–en[1] *suff.* **1a.** To cause to be: *cheapen.* **b.** To become: *redden.* **2a.** To cause to have: *hearten.* **b.** To come to have: *lengthen.* [ME *-enen, -nen* < OE *-nian.*]

–en[2] *suff.* Made of; resembling: *earthen.* [ME < OE.]

en·a·ble (ĕ-nā′bəl) *tr.v.* **-bled, -bling, -bles 1a.** To supply with the means, knowledge, or opportunity; make able. **b.** To make feasible or possible. **2.** To give legal power, capacity, or sanction to. **3.** To make operational; activate. —**en·a′bler** *n.*

en·act (ĕn-ăkt′) *tr.v.* **-act·ed, -act·ing, -acts 1.** To make into law: *Congress enacted a tax reform bill.* **2.** To act (something) out, as on a stage. —**en·act′a·ble** *adj.* —**en·ac′tor** *n.*

en·act·ment (ĕn-ăkt′mənt) *n.* **1a.** The act of enacting. **b.** The state of being enacted. **2.** Something that has been enacted.

e·nam·el (ĭ-năm′əl) *n.* **1.** A vitreous, usu. opaque protective or decorative coating baked on metal, glass, or ceramic ware. **2.** An object having such a coating, as in a piece of cloisonné. **3.** A coating that dries to a hard glossy finish. **4.** A paint that dries to a hard glossy finish. **5.** *Anatomy* The hard calcareous substance covering a tooth. ❖ *tr.v.* **-eled, -el·ing, -els** or **-elled, -el·ling, -els 1.** To coat, inlay, or decorate with enamel. **2.** To give a glossy or brilliant surface to. **3.** To adorn with a brightly colored surface. [< ME *enamelen*, to put on enamel < AN *enamailler* : *en-*, on (< OFr.; see EN–[1]) + *amail*, enamel (< OFr. *esmail*, of Gmc. orig.).] —**e·nam′el·er, e·nam′el·ist** *n.*

e·nam·el·ware (ĭ-năm′əl-wâr′) *n.* Articles coated or decorated with enamel.

en·am·or (ĭ-năm′ər) *tr.v.* **-ored, -or·ing, -ors** To inspire with love; captivate. [ME *enamouren* < OFr. *enamourer* : *en-*, causative pref.; see EN–[1] + *amour*, love; see AMOUR.]

en·am·our (ĭ-năm′ər) *v. Chiefly British* Variant of enamor.

en·an·ti·o·mer (ĭ-năn′tē-ə-mər) *n.* See enantiomorph. [Gk. *enantios*, opposite; see **ant-** in App. + –MER(E).] —**en·an′ti·o·mer′ic** (-mĕr′ĭk) *adj.*

en·an·ti·o·morph (ĭ-năn′tē-ə-môrf′) *n.* Either of a pair of crystals, molecules, or compounds that are mirror images of each other but are not identical. [Gk. *enantios*, opposite; see **ant-** in App. + –MORPH.] —**en·an′ti·o·mor′phic, en·an′ti·o·mor′phous** *adj.* —**en·an′ti·o·mor′phism** *n.*

emu
Dromiceius novaehollandiae

enamel
gold, enamel, and ivory
brooch, c. 1900

en·ar·thro·sis (ĕn'är-thrō'sĭs) *n.,* *pl.* **-ses** (-sēz) *Anatomy* See **ball-and-socket joint** 1. [Gk. *enarthrōsis < enarthros,* jointed : *en-,* in; see EN–² + *arthron,* joint.]

e·nate (ī-nāt', ē'nāt') *adj.* **1.** Growing outward. **2.** also **e·nat·ic** (ī-năt'ĭk) Related on the mother's side. ❖ *n.* A relative on one's mother's side. [Lat. *ēnātus,* p. part. of *ēnāscī,* to issue forth : *ē-, ex-,* ex- + *nāscī,* to be born; see **genə-** in App.]

e·na·tion (ē-nā'shən) *n. Botany* An outgrowth on the surface of an organ.

en bloc (äN blôk', ĕn blôk') *adv.* As a unit; all together. [Fr. : *en,* in + *bloc,* lump, bloc.]

en bro·chette (äN' brô-shĕt') *adv.* On a skewer: *lamb en brochette.* [Fr. : *en,* on + *brochette,* stick, skewer.]

enc. *abbr.* **1.** enclosed **2.** enclosure

en·cage (ĕn-kāj') *tr.v.* **-caged, -cag·ing, -cag·es** To confine in or as if in a cage.

en·camp (ĕn-kămp') *v.* **-camped, -camp·ing, -camps** —*intr.* To set up camp or live in a camp. —*tr.* To provide quarters for in a camp.

en·camp·ment (ĕn-kămp'mənt) *n.* **1a.** The act of encamping. **b.** The state of being encamped. **2.** A camp; quarters.

en·cap·su·late (ĕn-kăp'sə-lāt') *v.* **-lat·ed, -lat·ing, -lates** —*tr.* **1.** To encase in or as if in a capsule. **2.** To express in a brief summary: *encapsulated the news.* —*intr.* To become encapsulated. —**en·cap'su·la'tion** *n.* —**en·cap'su·la'tor** *n.*

en·cap·su·lat·ed (ĕn-kăp'sə-lā'tĭd) *adj.* Enclosed by a protective coating or membrane: *an encapsulated bacterium.*

en·cap·sule (ĕn-kăp'səl, -sōōl) *tr.v.* **-suled, -sul·ing, -sules** To encapsulate.

en·case (ĕn-kās') *tr.v.* **-cased, -cas·ing, -cas·es** To enclose in or as if in a case. —**en·case'ment** *n.*

en·caus·tic (ĕn-kô'stĭk) *n.* **1.** A paint consisting of pigment mixed with beeswax and fixed with heat after application. **2.** The art of painting with this substance. **3.** A painting produced with this substance. [Lat. *encausticus < Gk. enkaustikos < enkaiein, enkau-,* to paint in encaustic : *en-,* in; see EN–² + *kaiein,* to burn.]

–ence *suff.* **1.** State or condition: *dependence.* **2.** Action: *emergence.* [ME < Lat. *-entia* (< *-ēns,* -ent), and < OFr. *-ance,* -ance.]

en·ceinte¹ (ĕn-sānt', än-sänt') *adj.* Carrying an unborn child; pregnant. [Fr. < OFr., ult. < Lat. *inciēns,* pregnant.]

en·ceinte² (ĕn-sänt', än-sänt', äN-säNt') *n.* **1.** An encircling fortification around a fort, castle, or town. **2.** A structure or an area protected by an encircling fortification. [Fr. < LLat. *incīncta* < fem. p. part. of *incingere,* to surround closely : Lat. *in-,* in; see IN–¹ + *cingere,* to gird.]

En·cel·a·dus (ĕn-sĕl'ə-dəs) *n.* **1.** *Greek Mythology* A giant who was defeated in battle and buried under Mount Etna by Athena. **2.** A satellite of Saturn. [Lat. < Gk. *Enkelados.*]

en·ce·phal·ic (ĕn'sə-făl'ĭk) *adj.* **1.** Of or relating to the brain. **2.** Located within the cranial cavity.

en·ceph·a·li·tis (ĕn-sĕf'ə-lī'tĭs) *n.* Inflammation of the brain. —**en·ceph'a·lit'ic** (-lĭt'ĭk) *adj.*

encephalo– or **encephal–** *pref.* Brain: *encephalitis.* [NLat. < Gk. (*muelos*) *enkephalos,* (marrow) in the head : *en-,* in; see EN–² + *kephalē,* head; see **ghebh-el-** in App.]

en·ceph·a·lo·gram (ĕn-sĕf'ə-lə-grăm', -ə-lō-) *n.* **1.** An x-ray picture of the brain taken by encephalography. **2.** See **electroencephalogram.**

en·ceph·a·lo·graph (ĕn-sĕf'ə-lə-grăf', -ə-lō-) *n.* **1.** See **encephalogram** 1. **2.** See **electroencephalograph.**

en·ceph·a·log·ra·phy (ĕn-sĕf'ə-lŏg'rə-fē) *n., pl.* **-phies** Radiographic examination of the brain in which some of the cerebrospinal fluid is replaced with air or another gas that acts as a contrasting medium. —**en·ceph'a·lo·graph'ic** (-ə-lə-grăf'ĭk, -ə-lō-) *adj.* —**en·ceph'a·lo·graph'i·cal·ly** *adv.*

en·ceph·a·lo·my·e·li·tis (ĕn-sĕf'ə-lō-mī'ə-lī'tĭs) *n.* Inflammation of the brain and spinal cord.

en·ceph·a·lon (ĕn-sĕf'ə-lŏn') *n., pl.* **-la** (-lə) The brain of a vertebrate. [Gk. *enkephalon,* neut. of *enkephalos,* in the head. See ENCEPHALO–.] —**en·ceph'a·lous** *adj.*

en·ceph·a·lop·a·thy (ĕn-sĕf'ə-lŏp'ə-thē) *n., pl.* **-thies** Any of various diseases of the brain. —**en·ceph'a·lo·path'ic** (-lə-păth'ĭk) *adj.*

en·chain (ĕn-chān') *tr.v.* **-chained, -chain·ing, -chains** To bind with or as if with chains. —**en·chain'ment** *n.*

en·chant (ĕn-chănt') *tr.v.* **-chant·ed, -chant·ing, -chants** **1.** To cast a spell over; bewitch. **2.** To attract and delight; entrance. See Syns at **charm.** [ME *enchanten* < OFr. *enchanter* < Lat. *incantāre,* to cast a spell : *in-,* against; see EN–¹ + *cantāre,* to sing, freq. of *canere;* see **kan-** in App.]

en·chant·er (ĕn-chăn'tər) *n.* **1.** One that delights or fascinates. **2.** A sorcerer or magician.

en·chant·ing (ĕn-chăn'tĭng) *adj.* Having the power to enchant; charming: *enchanting music.* —**en·chant'ing·ly** *adv.*

en·chant·ment (ĕn-chănt'mənt) *n.* **1a.** The act of enchanting. **b.** The state of being enchanted. **2.** Something that enchants.

en·chant·ress (ĕn-chăn'trĭs) *n.* **1.** A woman of great charm or fascination. **2.** A woman who practices magic; a sorceress.

en·chase (ĕn-chās') *tr.v.* **-chased, -chas·ing, -chas·es** **1.** To set (a gem, for example). **2.** To set with or as if with gems: *enchase a brooch.* **3.** To decorate or ornament by inlaying or engraving.

[ME, to engrave < OFr. *enchasser,* to set gems : *en-,* in; see EN–¹ + *chasse,* case (< Lat. *capsa,* box).]

en·chi·la·da (ĕn'chə-lä'də) *n.* A dish consisting of a tortilla rolled and stuffed, as with meat, and baked in a chili sauce. [Am.Sp. : *en-,* in (< Lat. *in-;* see EN–¹) + *chile,* chili pepper; see CHILI + *-ada,* fem. adj. suff.]

en·chi·rid·i·on (ĕn'kī-rĭd'ē-ən) *n., pl.* **-i·ons** or **-i·a** (-ē-ə) A handbook; a manual. [LLat. *enchiridion* < Gk. *enkheiridion : en-,* in; see EN–² + *kheir,* hand; see **ghes-** in App. + *-idion,* diminutive suff.]

–enchyma *suff.* Cellular tissue: *chlorenchyma.* [< PARENCHYMA.]

en·ci·na (ĕn-sē'nə) *n.* See **live oak.** [Sp., holm oak < LLat. *īlicīna* < Lat. *īlex, īlic-.*]

en·ci·pher (ĕn-sī'fər) *tr.v.* **-phered, -pher·ing, -phers** To put (a message, for example) into cipher. —**en·ci'pher·er** *n.* —**en·ci'pher·ment** *n.*

en·cir·cle (ĕn-sûr'kəl) *tr.v.* **-cled, -cling, -cles** **1.** To form a circle around; surround. **2.** To move or go around completely; make a circuit of. —**en·cir'cle·ment** *n.*

encl. *abbr.* **1.** enclosed **2.** enclosure

en·clasp (ĕn-klăsp') *tr.v.* **-clasped, -clasp·ing, -clasps** To hold in a clasp; embrace.

en·clave (ĕn'klāv', ŏn'-) *n.* **1.** A country or part of a country lying wholly within the boundaries of another. **2.** A distinctly bounded area enclosed within a larger unit: *ethnic enclaves in a city.* [Fr. < OFr. *enclaver,* to enclose < VLat. **inclāvāre* : Lat. *in-,* in; see EN–¹ + Lat. *clāvis,* key.]

en·clit·ic (ĕn-klĭt'ĭk) *n.* **1.** A clitic that is attached to the end of another word, for example, the *–n't* of *don't.* **2.** A clitic. ❖ *adj.* Forming an enclitic. [LLat. *encliticus* < Gk. *enklitikos < enklīnein,* to lean on : *en-,* on, in; see EN–² + *klīnein,* to lean; see **klei-** in App.] —**en'clis·is** (-klĭs-ĭs) *n.*

en·close (ĕn-klōz') also **in·close** (ĭn-) *tr.v.* **-closed, -clos·ing, -clos·es** **1.** To surround on all sides; close in. **2.** To fence in. **3.** To contain, esp. so as to envelop or shelter. **4.** To insert into the same envelope or package. [ME *enclosen* < OFr. *enclos,* p. part. of *enclore* < Lat. *inclūdere.* See INCLUDE.]

en·clo·sure (ĕn-klō'zhər) *n.* **1a.** The act of enclosing. **b.** The state of being enclosed. **2.** Something enclosed: *a letter with a supplemental enclosure.* **3.** Something that encloses.

en·code (ĕn-kōd') *tr.v.* **-cod·ed, -cod·ing, -codes** **1.** To put into code. **2.** *Computer Science* To format (electronic data) according to a standard format. **3.** *Genetics* To specify the genetic code for (a protein molecule, for example). —**en·cod'er** *n.*

en·co·mi·ast (ĕn-kō'mē-ăst', -əst) *n.* One who delivers or writes an encomium; a eulogist. [Gk. *enkōmiastēs < enkōmiazein,* to praise < *enkōmion,* encomium. See ENCOMIUM.] —**en·co'mi·as'tic** (-ăs'tĭk), **en·co'mi·as'ti·cal** (-tĭ-kəl) *adj.*

en·co·mi·um (ĕn-kō'mē-əm) *n., pl.* **-mi·ums** or **-mi·a** (-mē-ə) **1.** Warm, glowing praise. **2.** A formal expression of praise; a tribute. [Lat. *encōmium* < Gk. *enkōmion (epos),* (speech) praising a victor, neut. of *enkōmios,* of the victory procession : *en-,* in; see EN–² + *kōmos,* celebration.]

en·com·pass (ĕn-kŭm'pəs) *tr.v.* **-passed, -pass·ing, -pass·es** **1.** To form a circle or ring around; surround. **2.** To enclose; envelop. **3.** To constitute or include. **4.** To accomplish; achieve. —**en·com'pass·ment** *n.*

en·core (ŏn'kôr', -kōr') *n.* **1.** A demand by an audience for an additional performance, usu. expressed by applause. **2.** An additional performance in response to the demand of an audience. ❖ *tr.v.* **-cored, -cor·ing, -cores** To demand an encore of. ❖ *interj.* Used to demand an additional performance. [Fr., still, yet, again, prob. < VLat. **hinc ad hōram,* from that to this hour : Lat. *hinc,* from here (< *hic,* this) + Lat. *ad,* to + Lat. *hōram,* accusative of *hōra,* hour; see HOUR.]

en·coun·ter (ĕn-koun'tər) *n.* **1.** A meeting, esp. one that is unexpected or brief. **2.** A hostile or adversarial confrontation or meeting. ❖ *v.* **-tered, -ter·ing, -ters** —*tr.* **1.** To meet, esp. unexpectedly. **2.** To confront in battle or contention. **3.** To come up against: *encounter obstacles.* —*intr.* To meet, esp. unexpectedly. [ME *encountre* < OFr. < *encontrer,* to meet < LLat. *incontrāre* : Lat. *in-,* in; see EN–¹ + Lat. *contrā,* against; see **kom** in App.]

encounter group *n.* A psychotherapy group designed to enhance sensitivity and self-awareness.

en·cour·age (ĕn-kûr'ĭj, -kûr'-) *tr.v.* **-aged, -ag·ing, -ag·es** **1.** To inspire with hope, courage, or confidence. **2.** To give support to; foster. **3.** To stimulate; spur. [ME *encouragen* < OFr. *encoragier : en-,* causative pref.; see EN–¹ + *corage,* courage; see COURAGE.] —**en·cour'ag·er** *n.*

en·cour·age·ment (ĕn-kûr'ĭj-mənt, -kûr'-) *n.* **1.** The act of encouraging. **2.** The state of being encouraged. **3.** One that encourages.

en·cour·ag·ing (ĕn-kûr'ə-jĭng, -kûr'-) *adj.* Giving courage, confidence, or hope. —**en·cour'ag·ing·ly** *adv.*

en·croach (ĕn-krōch') *intr.v.* **-croached, -croach·ing, -croach·es** **1.** To take another's possessions or rights gradually or stealthily. **2.** To advance beyond proper or former limits. [ME *encrochen,* to seize illegally < OFr. *encrochier,* to seize : *en-,* in; see EN–¹ + *croc,* hook (of Gmc. orig.).] —**en·croach'er** *n.*

en·croach·ment (ĕn-krōch'mənt) *n.* **1.** The act or an instance of encroaching. **2.** *Football* A violation of the rules in which a player enters the neutral zone and makes contact with an opponent prior to the snap of the ball.

en·crust (ĕn-krŭst′) also **in·crust** (ĭn-) tr.v. **-crust·ed, -crust·ing, -crusts 1.** To cover or coat with or as if with a crust. **2.** To decorate by inlaying or overlaying with a contrasting material. [Poss. < Fr. *incruster* < Lat. *incrūstāre* : *in-*, on; see EN–[1] + *crūsta*, crust.]

en·crus·ta·tion (ĕn′krŭs-tā′shən) n. Variant of **incrustation.**

en·crypt (ĕn-krĭpt′) tr.v. **-crypt·ed, -crypt·ing, -crypts 1.** To put into code or cipher. **2.** *Computer Science* To alter (a file, for example) using a secret code so as to be unintelligible to unauthorized parties. [EN–[1] + (DE)CRYPT.] —**en·cryp′tion** n.

en·cum·ber (ĕn-kŭm′bər) tr.v. **-bered, -ber·ing, -bers 1.** To put a heavy load on; burden. **2.** To hinder or impede the action or performance of. **3.** To burden with legal or financial obligations. [ME *encombren* < OFr. *encombrer*, to block up : *en-*, in; see EN–[1] + *combre*, hindrance (< Gaulish *comboros).]

en·cum·brance (ĕn-kŭm′brəns) n. **1.** One that encumbers; a burden or impediment. **2.** *Law* A lien or claim on property.

en·cum·branc·er (ĕn-kŭm′brən-sər) n. *Law* One that holds an encumbrance.

-ency suff. Condition or quality: *complacency.* [ME, var. of *-ence, -ence.*]

en·cyc·li·cal (ĕn-sĭk′lĭ-kəl) adj. Intended for general or wide circulation. ❖ n. *Roman Catholic Church* A papal letter addressed to the bishops of the Church or the hierarchy of a particular country. [< Med.Lat. *encyclicus*, circular < Gk. *enkuklios* : *en-*, in; see EN–[2] + *kuklos*, circle; see **kʷel-**[1] in App.]

en·cy·clo·pe·di·a (ĕn-sī′klə-pē′dē-ə) n. A reference work containing articles on a wide range of subjects or on numerous aspects of a field, usu. arranged alphabetically. [Med.Lat. *encyclopaedia*, general education course < alteration of Gk. *enkuklios paideia*, general education : *enkuklios*, circular, general; see ENCYCLICAL + *paideia*, education (< *pais, paid-*, child).]

en·cy·clo·pe·dic (ĕn-sī′klə-pē′dĭk) adj. **1.** Of, relating to, or characteristic of an encyclopedia. **2.** Embracing many subjects; comprehensive. —**en·cy′clo·pe′di·cal·ly** adv.

en·cy·clo·pe·dism (ĕn-sī′klə-pē′dĭz′əm) n. Encyclopedic learning.

en·cy·clo·pe·dist (ĕn-sī′klə-pē′dĭst) n. **1.** A person who writes for or compiles an encyclopedia. **2. Encyclopedist** One of the writers of the French *Encyclopédie* (1751–72), including its editors, Diderot and d'Alembert.

en·cyst (ĕn-sĭst′) v. **-cyst·ed, -cyst·ing, -cysts** —tr. To enclose in a cyst. —intr. To take the form of or become enclosed in a cyst. —**en·cyst′ment, en′cys·ta′tion** n.

end (ĕnd) n. **1.** Either extremity of something that has length: *the end of the pier.* **2.** The outside or extreme edge or physical limit; a boundary. **3.** The point in time when an action, event, or phenomenon ceases or is completed; the conclusion. **4.** A result; an outcome. **5.** Something toward which one strives; a goal. See Syns at **intention. 6.** The termination of life or existence; death. **7.** The ultimate extent; the very limit. **8.** *Slang* The very best; the ultimate. **9.** A remainder; a remnant. **10a.** A share of a responsibility or obligation. **b.** A particular area of responsibility. **11.** *Football* **a.** Either of the players in the outermost position on the line of scrimmage. **b.** The position played by such a player. ❖ v. **ended, end·ing, ends** —tr. **1.** To bring to a conclusion. **2.** To form the last or concluding part of. **3.** To destroy. —intr. **1.** To come to a finish; cease. **2.** To arrive at a place, situation, or condition as a result of a course of action. Often used with *up.* **3.** To die. —**idioms: in the end** Eventually; ultimately. **no end** A great deal. **on end 1.** Having one end down; upright. **2.** Without stopping: *drove for hours on end.* [ME *ende* < OE. See **ant-**[1] in App.]

end– pref. Variant of **endo–.**

en·da·moe·ba (ĕn′də-mē′bə) n. Variant of **entamoeba.**

en·dan·ger (ĕn-dān′jər) tr.v. **-gered, -ger·ing, -gers 1.** To expose to harm or danger; imperil. **2.** To threaten with extinction. —**en·dan′ger·ment** n.

SYNONYMS *endanger, hazard, imperil, jeopardize, risk* These verbs mean to subject to danger, loss, or destruction: *driving that endangers lives; hazarded his health by smoking; a forest imperiled by fire; strikes that jeopardize profits; risked her life's savings.*

---

en·dan·gered species (ĕn-dān′jərd) n. A species present in such small numbers that it is at risk of extinction.

end·arch (ĕnd′ärk′) adj. Of or relating to a xylem whose early development is from the center outward. [END(O)– + Gk. *arkhē*, beginning (< *arkhein*, to begin, rule).]

end·ar·te·rec·to·my (ĕn′där-tə-rĕk′tə-mē) n., pl. **-mies** Surgical excision of the inner lining of an artery that is clogged with plaque. [NLat. *endartērium*, inner lining of an artery (ENDO– + Lat. *artēria*, artery; see ARTERY) +-ECTOMY.]

end·ar·te·ri·tis (ĕn′där-tə-rī′tĭs) n. Inflammation of the inner lining of an artery. [NLat. *endartērium*, inner lining of an artery; see ENDARTERECTOMY + -ITIS.]

en·dash or **en dash** (ĕn′dăsh′) n. A symbol (–) used in writing or printing to connect continuing or inclusive numbers or to connect elements of a compound adjective when either of the elements is an open compound. [< its being the width of an *n* in printing.]

end·brain (ĕnd′brān′) n. See **telencephalon.**

en·dear (ĕn-dîr′) tr.v. **-deared, -dear·ing, -dears** To make beloved or sympathetic.

en·dear·ing (ĕn-dîr′ĭng) adj. Inspiring affection or warm sympathy: *an endearing smile.* —**en·dear′ing·ly** adv.

en·dear·ment (ĕn-dîr′mənt) n. **1.** The act of endearing. **2.** An expression of affection, such as a caress.

en·deav·or (ĕn-dĕv′ər) n. **1.** A conscientious or concerted effort toward an end; an earnest attempt. **2.** Purposeful or industrious activity. ❖ v. **-ored, -or·ing, -ors** —tr. To attempt (fulfillment of a responsibility, for example) by employment or expenditure of effort. —intr. To work with a set or specified goal or purpose. [ME *endeveren* < *endeveren*, to make an effort < *(putten) in dever*, (to put oneself) in duty : *in*, in; see IN[1] + *dever*, duty (< OFr. *deveir, devoir*; see DEVOIR).] —**en·deav′or·er** n.

en·deav·our (ĕn-dĕv′ər) n. & v. *Chiefly British* Variant of **endeavor.**

En·de·cott also **En·di·cott** (ĕn′dĭ-kət, -kŏt′), **John** 1588?–1665. English-born Amer. colonial administrator who was a founder and governor of the Massachusetts Bay Colony.

en·dem·ic (ĕn-dĕm′ĭk) adj. **1.** Prevalent in or peculiar to a particular locality, region, or people. **2.** *Ecology* Native to or confined to a certain region. ❖ n. *Ecology* An endemic plant or animal. [< Gk. *endēmos*, native, endemic : *en-*, in; see EN–[2] + *dēmos*, people; see **dā-** in App.] —**en·dem′i·cal·ly** adv. —**en·dem′ism** n.

En·der·by Land (ĕn′dər-bē) A region of Antarctica between Queen Maud Land and Wilkes Land; claimed by Australia.

end·er·gon·ic (ĕn′dər-gŏn′ĭk) adj. Requiring energy. [END(O)– + Gk. *ergon*, work; see **werg-** in App. +-IC.]

en·der·mic (ĕn-dûr′mĭk) adj. Acting medicinally by absorption through the skin. —**en·der′mi·cal·ly** adv.

En·ders (ĕn′dərz), **John Franklin** 1897–1985. Amer. bacteriologist who shared a 1954 Nobel Prize.

end·game also **end game** (ĕnd′gām′) n. **1.** *Games* The final stage of a chess game after most of the pieces have been removed from the board. **2.** The final stage of an extended process or course of events.

end·ing (ĕn′dĭng) n. **1.** A conclusion or termination. **2.** A concluding part; a finale. **3.** *Grammar* The final morpheme added to a word base to make an inflectional form.

en·dive (ĕn′dīv′, ŏn′dēv′) n. **1a.** An Indian plant (*Cichorium endivia*) cultivated for its leaves used in salads. **b.** Escarole. **2.** A variety of the common chicory (*Cichorium intybus*) cultivated to produce narrow, pointed, blanched leaves used in salads. [ME < OFr. *endive* < Med.Gk. *entubia*, pl. dim. of Gk. *entubon*, perh. < Egypt. *tybi*, January (because the plant grows in this month).]

end leaf n. See **endpaper.**

end·less (ĕnd′lĭs) adj. **1.** Being or seeming to be without an end or limit; boundless. **2.** Formed with the ends joined; continuous. —**end′less·ly** adv. —**end′less·ness** n.

end line n. *Sports* A line perpendicular to the sidelines that marks an end boundary of a playing field or court.

end·long (ĕnd′lông′, -lŏng′) adv. *Archaic* Lengthwise.

end man n. The person at the end of a line or row.

end·most (ĕnd′mōst′) adj. Being at or closest to the end; last.

end·note (ĕnd′nōt′) n. A note placed at the end of an article, chapter, or book that comments on or cites a reference for a designated part of the text.

endo– pref. Inside; within: *endometrium.* [Gk. < *endon*, within. See **en** in App.]

en·do·bi·ot·ic (ĕn′də-bī-ŏt′ĭk) adj. Living as a parasite or symbiont within the tissues of a host.

en·do·car·di·tis (ĕn′dō-kär-dī′tĭs) n. Inflammation of the endocardium. [ENDOCARD(IUM) + -ITIS.] —**en′do·car·dit′ic** (-dĭt′ĭk) adj.

en·do·car·di·um (ĕn′dō-kär′dē-əm) n., pl. **-di·a** (-dē-ə) The thin serous membrane, composed of endothelial tissue, that lines the interior of the heart. [NLat. : ENDO– + Gk. *kardiā*, heart; see **kerd-** in App.] —**en′do·car′di·al** adj.

en·do·carp (ĕn′dō-kärp′) n. The hard inner layer of the pericarp of many fruits, as a peach pit. —**en′do·car′pal** adj.

en·do·cra·ni·um (ĕn′dō-krā′nē-əm) n., pl. **-ni·a** (-nē-ə) **1.** The outermost layer of the dura mater. **2.** The inner surface of the skull.

en·do·crine (ĕn′də-krĭn, -krēn′, -krīn′) adj. **1.** Secreting internally. **2.** Of or relating to endocrine glands or the hormones secreted by them. ❖ n. **1.** The secretion of an endocrine gland; a hormone. **2.** An endocrine gland. [Fr. : Gk. *endo-*, endo- + Gk. *krīnein*, to separate; see **krei-** in App.]

endocrine gland n. Any of various glands, such as the thyroid, adrenal, or pituitary, producing hormonal secretions that pass directly into the bloodstream.

en·do·cri·nol·o·gy (ĕn′dō-krə-nŏl′ə-jē) n. The study of the glands and hormones of the body and their related disorders. —**en′do·cri′no·log′ic** (-krĭn′ə-lŏj′ĭk), **en′do·crin′o·log′i·cal** adj. —**en′do·cri·nol′o·gist** n.

en·do·cy·to·sis (ĕn′dō-sī-tō′sĭs) n. A process of cellular ingestion by which the plasma membrane folds inward to bring substances into the cell. —**en′do·cyt′ic** (-sĭt′ĭk), **en′do·cy·tot′ic** (-sī-tŏt′ĭk) adj. —**en′do·cy·tose′** (-tōs′) v.

---

endive
top: Belgian
bottom: curly

en·do·derm (ĕn′də-dûrm′) also **en·to·derm** (ĕn′tə-) *n.* The innermost of the three primary germ layers of an animal embryo, developing into the gastrointestinal tract, the lungs, and associated structures. —**en′do·der′mal** *adj.*

en·do·der·mis (ĕn′də-dûr′mĭs) *n.* The innermost layer of the cortex that forms a sheath around the vascular tissue of roots and some stems. [ENDO– + (EPI)DERMIS.]

en·do·don·tia (ĕn′dō-dŏn′shə, -shē-ə) *n.* Endodontics.

en·do·don·tics (ĕn′dō-dŏn′tĭks) *n.* (*used with a sing. verb*) The branch of dentistry that deals with diseases of the tooth root, dental pulp, and surrounding tissue. [ENDO– + (ORTHO)DONTICS.] —**en′do·don′tic** *adj.* —**en′do·don′tist** *n.*

en·do·en·zyme (ĕn′dō-ĕn′zīm′) *n.* An enzyme that acts on or is retained within the cell producing it.

en·do·er·gic (ĕn′dō-ûr′jĭk) *adj. Chemistry* Endothermic. [ENDO– + Gk. *ergon,* work; see **werg–** in App. + –IC.]

en·dog·a·my (ĕn-dŏg′ə-mē) *n.* **1.** *Anthropology* Marriage within a particular group in accordance with custom or law. **2.** *Botany* Fertilization resulting from pollination among flowers of the same plant. **3.** *Biology* Reproduction by the fusion of gametes of similar ancestry. —**en·dog′a·mous** *adj.*

en·dog·e·nous (ĕn-dŏj′ə-nəs) *adj.* **1.** Produced or growing from within. **2.** Originating or produced within an organism, tissue, or cell: *endogenous secretions.* —**en·dog′e·nous·ly** *adv.* —**en·dog′e·ny** *n.*

en·do·lymph (ĕn′də-lĭmf′) *n.* The fluid in the labyrinth of the inner ear. —**en′do·lym·phat′ic** (-lĭm-făt′ĭk) *adj.*

en·do·me·tri·o·sis (ĕn′dō-mē′trē-ō′sĭs) *n.* A condition, usu. resulting in pain and dysmenorrhea, characterized by the abnormal occurrence of endometrial tissue outside the uterus.

en·do·me·tri·um (ĕn′dō-mē′trē-əm) *n., pl.* **-tri·a** (-trē-ə) The membrane that lines the uterus. [NLat. *endometrium :* ENDO– + Gk. *mētrā,* uterus; see METRO–.] —**en′do·me′tri·al** *adj.*

en·do·mi·to·sis (ĕn′dō-mī-tō′sĭs) *n.* A process by which chromosomes replicate without the division of the cell nucleus. —**en′do·mi·tot′ic** (-tŏt′ĭk) *adj.*

en·do·morph (ĕn′də-môrf′) *n.* **1.** A mineral enclosed within another mineral, such as tourmaline in quartz. **2.** An individual characterized by prominence of the abdomen and other soft body parts developed from the embryonic endodermal layer. [ENDO(DERM) + –MORPH.]

en·do·mor·phic (ĕn′də-môr′fĭk) *adj.* **1.** Of or relating to an endomorph. **2.** Created through endomorphism.

en·do·mor·phism (ĕn′də-môr′fĭz′əm) *n.* **1.** A change within an intrusive igneous rock caused by the assimilation of portions of the surrounding rock. **2.** A homomorphism that maps a mathematical system into itself.

en·do·nu·cle·ase (ĕn′dō-nōō′klē-ās′, -āz′, -nyōō′-) *n.* Any of a group of enzymes that catalyze the hydrolysis of bonds between nucleic acids in the interior of a DNA or an RNA molecule.

en·do·par·a·site (ĕn′dō-păr′ə-sīt′) *n.* A parasite, such as a tapeworm, that lives within another organism. —**en′do·par·a·sit′ic** (-sĭt′ĭk) *adj.* —**en′do·par′a·sit·ism** (-sī-tĭz′əm) *n.*

en·do·pep·ti·dase (ĕn′dō-pĕp′tĭ-dās′, -dāz′) *n.* Any of a large group of enzymes that catalyze the hydrolysis of peptide bonds in the interior of a polypeptide chain or protein molecule.

en·do·phyte (ĕn′də-fīt′) *n.* A plant, such as a fungus, growing within another plant. —**en′do·phyt′ic** (-dō-fĭt′ĭk) *adj.*

en·do·plasm (ĕn′də-plăz′əm) *n.* A central, less viscous portion of the cytoplasm that is distinguishable in certain cells, esp. motile cells. —**en′do·plas′mic** *adj.*

endoplasmic reticulum *n.* A membrane network within the cytoplasm of cells involved in the synthesis, modification, and transport of cellular materials.

end organ *n.* The encapsulated termination of a sensory nerve.

en·dor·phin (ĕn-dôr′fĭn) *n.* Any of a group of peptide hormones that are found mainly in the brain and reduce the sensation of pain. [ENDO(GENOUS) + (MO)RPHIN(E).]

en·dorse (ĕn-dôrs′) also **in·dorse** (ĭn-) *tr.v.* **-dorsed, -dors·ing, -dors·es** **1.** To write one's signature on the back of (a check, for example) as evidence of the legal transfer of its ownership, esp. in return for the cash or credit indicated on its face. **2.** To place (one's signature), as on a contract, to indicate approval of its contents or terms. **3.** To acknowledge (receipt of payment) by signing a bill or other instrument. **4.** To give approval of or support to, esp. publicly; sanction: *endorse a political candidate.* See Syns at **approve.** [ME *endosen* < AN *endosser* < Med.Lat. *indorsāre :* Lat. *in-,* upon, in; see EN–[1] + Lat. *dorsum,* back.] —**en·dors′a·ble** *adj.* —**en·dors′er, en·dor′sor** *n.*

en·dor·see (ĕn′dôr-sē′) *n.* One to whom ownership of a negotiable document is transferred by endorsement.

en·dorse·ment (ĕn-dôrs′mənt) *n.* **1.** The act of endorsing. **2.** Something, such as a signature, that endorses or validates. **3.** Approbation; sanction. **4.** An amendment to a contract, such as an insurance policy, by which the original terms are changed.

en·do·scope (ĕn′də-skōp′) *n.* An instrument for viewing the interior of a body canal or a hollow organ such as the colon. —**en′do·scop′ic** (-skŏp′ĭk) *adj.* —**en′do·scop′i·cal·ly** *adv.* —**en·dos′co·py** (ĕn-dŏs′kə-pē) *n.*

en·do·skel·e·ton (ĕn′dō-skĕl′ĭ-tn) *n.* An internal supporting skeleton, derived from the mesoderm, characteristic of verte-

brates and certain invertebrates. —**en′do·skel′e·tal** (-ĭ-tl) *adj.*

en·dos·mo·sis (ĕn′dŏz-mō′sĭs, -dŏs-) *n.* The inward flow of a fluid through a permeable membrane toward a fluid of greater concentration. —**en′dos·mot′ic** (-mŏt′ĭk) *adj.* —**en′dos·mot′i·cal·ly** *adv.*

en·do·sperm (ĕn′də-spûrm′) *n.* The nutritive tissue within seeds of flowering plants, surrounding the embryo.

en·do·spore (ĕn′də-spôr′, -spōr′) *n.* **1.** A small asexual spore, as that formed by some bacteria. **2.** The inner layer of the wall of a spore.

en·do·stat·in (ĕn′dō-stăt′n) *n.* A potent, naturally occurring antiangiogenic protein that inhibits the formation of the blood vessels that feed tumors. [ENDO(THELIAL) + –STAT + –IN.]

en·dos·te·um (ĕn-dŏs′tē-əm) *n., pl.* **-te·a** (-tē-ə) The thin layer of cells lining the medullary cavity of a bone. [NLat. : END(O)– + Gk. *osteon,* bone; see **ost–** in App.]

en·do·the·ci·um (ĕn′dō-thē′sē-əm, -shē-əm) *n., pl.* **-ci·a** (-sē-ə, -shē-ə) The inner tissue of an anther or a moss capsule. [NLat. *endothēcium :* ENDO– + Gk. *thēkion,* dim. of *thēkē,* chest, receptacle; see **dhē–** in App.]

en·do·the·li·o·ma (ĕn′dō-thē′lē-ō′mə) *n., pl.* **-ma·ta** (-mə-tə) or **-mas** Any of various neoplasms derived from endothelium.

en·do·the·li·um (ĕn′dō-thē′lē-əm) *n., pl.* **-li·a** (-lē-ə) A layer of epithelial cells that lines serous cavities, lymph vessels, and blood vessels. [NLat. *endothēlium :* ENDO– + Gk. *thēlē,* nipple.] —**en′do·the′li·al, en′do·the′li·oid′** *adj.*

en·do·therm (ĕn′də-thûrm′) *n.* An organism that generates heat to maintain its body temperature, typically above the temperature of its surroundings; a homeotherm.

en·do·ther·mic (ĕn′dō-thûr′mĭk) also **en·do·ther·mal** (-məl) *adj.* **1.** *Chemistry* Characterized by or causing the absorption of heat; endoergic. **2.** *Biology* Of or relating to an endotherm; warm-blooded. —**en′do·ther′my** *n.*

en·do·tox·in (ĕn′dō-tŏk′sən) *n.* A toxin produced by certain bacteria and released upon destruction of the bacterial cell. —**en′do·tox′ic** *adj.*

en·do·tra·che·al (ĕn′də-trā′kē-əl) *adj.* Within or passing through the trachea: *an endotracheal tube.*

en·dow (ĕn-dou′) *tr.v.* **-dowed, -dow·ing, -dows** **1.** To provide with property or income. **2a.** To equip or supply with a talent or quality. **b.** To imagine as having a usu. favorable trait: *endowed the dog with human intelligence.* **3.** *Obsolete* To provide with a dower. [ME *endowen* < AN *endouer :* OFr. *en-,* intensive pref.; see EN–[1] + OFr. *douer,* to give a dowry to (< Lat. *dōtāre* < *dōs, dōt-,* dowry; see **dō–** in App.).]

en·dow·ment (ĕn-dou′mənt) *n.* **1.** The act of endowing. **2.** Funds or property donated to an institution, individual, or group. **3.** A natural gift, ability, or quality.

end·pa·per also **end paper** (ĕnd′pā′pər) *n.* Either of two folded sheets of heavy paper having one half pasted to the inside front or back cover of a book and the other half pasted to the base of the first or last page.

end plate *n.* The area of synaptic contact between a motor nerve and a muscle fiber.

end·play (ĕnd′plā′) *n.* A play in bridge that forces an opponent to lead and results in the opponents' losing one or more tricks that they would have had they not been leading. ❖ *tr.v.* **-played, -play·ing, -plays** To force (a bridge opponent) to lead disadvantageously.

end·point or **end point** (ĕnd′point′) *n.* **1.** Either of two points marking the end of a line segment. **2.** *Chemistry* The point in a titration at which no more titrant should be added. **3.** A tip or point of termination.

end product *n.* The result of a completed series of processes or changes.

end run *n.* **1.** *Football* A play in which the ball carrier tries to run around one end of the defensive line. **2.** *Informal* A maneuver in which impediments are bypassed, often by deceit or trickery.

end-run (ĕnd′rŭn′) *tr.v.* **-ran** (-răn′), **-run·ning, -runs** *Informal* To bypass (an impediment) often by deceit or trickery.

end-stopped (ĕnd′stŏpt′) *adj.* Ending in a syntactic and rhythmic pause. Used of a line of verse or a couplet.

end table *n.* A small table, usu. placed at either end of a couch or beside a chair.

en·due (ĕn-dōō′, -dyōō′) also **in·due** (ĭn-) *tr.v.* **-dued, -du·ing, -dues** **1.** To provide with a quality or trait; endow. **2.** To put on (a piece of clothing). [ME *enduen* < OFr. *enduire,* to lead in, induct < Lat. *indūcere;* see INDUCE. Sense 2, ME *induen,* to clothe < Lat. *induere,* to put on.]

en·dur·a·ble (ĕn-dōōr′ə-bəl, -dyōōr′-) *adj.* Possible to be endured; tolerable or bearable. —**en·dur′a·bly** *adv.*

en·dur·ance (ĕn-dōōr′əns, -dyōōr′-) *n.* **1.** The act, quality, or power of withstanding hardship or stress. **2.** The state or fact of persevering. **3.** Continuing existence; duration.

en·dure (ĕn-dōōr′, -dyōōr′) *v.* **-dured, -dur·ing, -dures** —*tr.* **1.** To carry on through, despite hardships; undergo. **2.** To bear with tolerance. See Syns at **bear**[1]. —*intr.* **1.** To continue in existence; last: *endured for centuries.* **2.** To suffer patiently without yielding. [ME *enduren* < OFr. *endurer* < Lat. *indūrāre,* to make hard : *in-,* against, into; see EN–[1] + *dūrus,* hard; see **deru–** in App.]

en·dur·ing (ĕn-dōōr′ĭng, -dyōōr′-) *adj.* **1.** Lasting; continuing;

ă	pat	oi	boy
ā	pay	ou	out
âr	care	ŏŏ	took
ä	father	ōō	boot
ĕ	pet	ŭ	cut
ē	be	ûr	urge
ĭ	pit	th	thin
ī	pie	*th*	this
îr	pier	hw	which
ŏ	pot	zh	vision
ō	toe	ə	about,
ô	paw		item

Stress marks:
′ (primary);
′ (secondary), as in
lexicon (lĕk′sĭ-kŏn′)

durable: *a novel of enduring interest.* **2.** Long-suffering; patient. —**en·dur′ing·ly** *adv.* —**en·dur′ing·ness** *n.*

en·dur·o (ĕn-dŏŏr′ō, -dyŏŏr′ō) *n., pl.* **-os** A race, as of motorcycles, that tests endurance.

end user also **end-us·er** (ĕnd′yŏŏ′zər) *n.* The final consumer of a product, esp. the one for whom the product is designed.

end·wise (ĕnd′wīz′) also **end·ways** (-wāz′) *adv.* **1.** On end; upright. **2.** With the end foremost. **3.** Lengthwise. **4.** End to end.

En·dym·i·on (ĕn-dĭm′ē-ən) *n. Greek Mythology* A handsome young man who was loved by Selene and whose youth was preserved by eternal sleep.

end zone *n. Football* The area at either end of the playing field between the goal line and the end line.

ENE *abbr.* east-northeast

-ene *suff.* An unsaturated organic compound, esp. one containing a double bond between carbon atoms: *ethylene.* [< Gk. *-ēnē,* fem. adj. suff.]

en·e·ma (ĕn′ə-mə) *n.* **1.** The injection of liquid into the rectum through the anus for therapeutic or diagnostic purposes, such as stimulating evacuation of the bowels. **2.** The fluid so injected. [LLat. < Gk. < *enienai,* to send in, inject : *en-,* in; see EN-² + *hīenai, he-,* to send.]

en·e·my (ĕn′ə-mē) *n., pl.* **-mies 1.** One who feels hatred toward, intends injury to, or opposes another; a foe. **2a.** A hostile power or force, such as a nation. **b.** A member or unit of such a force. **3.** A group of foes or hostile forces. See Usage Note at **collective noun. 4.** Something destructive or injurious in its effects. ❖ *adj.* Of, relating to, or being a hostile power or force. [ME *enemi* < OFr. < Lat. *inimicus* : *in-,* not; see IN-¹ + *amīcus,* friend.]

SYNONYMS *enemy, foe, opponent* These nouns denote one who is hostile to or opposes the purposes or interests of another: *betrayed by enemies; a foe of fascism; a political opponent.*

en·er·get·ic (ĕn′ər-jĕt′ĭk) *adj.* **1.** Possessing, exerting, or displaying energy. **2.** Of or relating to energy. [Gk. *energētikos* < *energein,* to be active < *energos,* active. See ENERGY.] —**en′er·get′i·cal·ly** *adv.*

en·er·get·ics (ĕn′ər-jĕt′ĭks) *n.* (*used with a sing. verb*) **1.** The study of the flow and transformation of energy. **2.** The flow and transformation of energy within a particular system.

en·er·gize (ĕn′ər-jīz′) *v.* **-gized, -giz·ing, -giz·es** —*tr.* **1.** To give energy to; activate or invigorate. **2.** To supply with an electric current. —*intr.* To release or put out energy. —**en′er·giz′er** *n.*

en·er·gy (ĕn′ər-jē) *n., pl.* **-gies 1.** The capacity for work or vigorous activity; vigor; power. See Syns at **strength. 2a.** Exertion of vigor or power. **b.** Vitality and intensity of expression. **3a.** Usable heat or power. **b.** A source of usable power, such as petroleum or coal. **4.** *Physics* The capacity of a physical system to do work. [Fr. *énergie* < LLat. *energīa* < Gk. *energeia* < *energos,* active : *en-,* in, at; see EN-² + *ergon,* work; see **werg-** in App.]

energy audit *n.* An evaluation of energy consumption, as in a home or business, to determine how energy can be conserved.

energy density *n.* The energy per unit volume of a region of space.

energy efficiency ratio *n.* A measure of the efficiency of a heating or cooling unit, equal to the unit's output in BTUs per hour divided by its consumption of energy in watts.

energy level *n.* **1.** The energy characteristic of a stationary state of a physical system, esp. a quantum mechanical system. **2.** The stationary state of a quantum mechanical system.

energy state *n.* See **energy level.**

en·er·vate (ĕn′ər-vāt′) *tr.v.* **-vat·ed, -vat·ing, -vates 1.** To weaken or destroy the strength or vitality of. See Syns at **deplete. 2.** *Medicine* To remove a nerve or part of a nerve. ❖ *adj.* (ĭ-nûr′vĭt) Deprived of strength; debilitated. [Lat. *ēnervāre, ēnervāt-* : *ē-, ex-,* ex- + *nervus,* sinew.] —**en′er·va′tion** *n.* —**en′er·va′tive** *adj.* —**en′er·va′tor** *n.*

USAGE NOTE Sometimes people mistakenly use *enervate* to mean "to invigorate" or "to excite" by assuming that it is a close cousin of *energize.* In fact, *enervate* means essentially the opposite. It comes from Latin *nervus,* "sinew," and thus means "to cause to become 'out of muscle'," that is, "to weaken or deplete of strength." It has no historical connection with *energize.*

E·nes·co (ə-nĕs′kō, ĕ-nĕs′-), **Georges** 1881–1955. Romanian-born violinist and composer whose works include the opera *Oedipus* (1936).

En·e·we·tak or **En·i·we·tok** (ĕn′ə-wē′tŏk′, ə-nē′wĭ-) An atoll in the Ralik Chain of the Marshall Is. in the W-central Pacific; site of US atomic tests (1948–54).

en·face (ĕn-fās′) *tr.v.* **-faced, -fac·ing, -fac·es** To write on the face of (a check, for example). —**en·face′ment** *n.*

en·fant ter·ri·ble (äN-fäN′ tĕ-rē′blə) *n.* **en·fants ter·ri·bles** (äN-fäN′ tĕ-rē′blə) One whose startlingly unconventional behavior, work, or thought embarrasses or disturbs others. [Fr. : *enfant,* child + *terrible,* frightful.]

en·fee·ble (ĕn-fē′bəl) *tr.v.* **-bled, -bling, -bles** To make feeble; weaken. —**en·fee′ble·ment** *n.* —**en·fee′bler** *n.*

en·feoff (ĕn-fĕf′, -fēf′) *tr.v.* **-feoffed, -feoff·ing, -feoffs** To invest with a feudal estate or fee. [ME *enfeffen* < AN *enfeoffer* : OFr. *en-,* causative pref.; see EN-¹ + OFr. *fief,* fief; see FEE.]

en·fet·ter (ĕn-fĕt′ər, ĭn-) *tr.v.* **-tered, -ter·ing, -ters** To bind in fetters; enchain.

En·field rifle (ĕn′fēld′) *n.* Any of several rifles formerly used by British and American troops, esp. the .30 or .303 caliber bolt-action breechloading model. [After *Enfield,* a borough of London, England.]

en·fi·lade (ĕn′fə-lād′, -läd′) *n.* **1.** Gunfire directed along the length of a target, such as a column of troops. **2.** A target vulnerable to sweeping gunfire. **3.** *Architecture* A linear arrangement of a series of interior doorways, as to a suite of rooms, so as to provide a vista when the doors are open. ❖ *tr.v.* **-lad·ed, -lad·ing, -lades** To rake with gunfire. [Fr., series, string, row < *enfiler,* to string together, run through < OFr. : *en-,* in, on; see EN-¹ + *fil,* thread (< Lat. *fīlum).*]

en·fleu·rage (ŏN′flə-räzh′, -räj′) *n.* A process in making perfume in which odorless fats or oils absorb the fragrance of fresh flowers. [Fr. < *enfleurer,* to saturate with the perfume of flowers : *en-,* causative pref.; see EN-¹ + *fleur,* flower (< OFr. *flour* < Lat. *flōs, flōr-;* see **bhel-³** in App.).]

en·fold (ĕn-fōld′) *tr.v.* **-fold·ed, -fold·ing, -folds 1.** To cover with or as if with folds; envelop. **2.** To hold within limits; enclose. **3.** To embrace. —**en·fold′er** *n.*

en·force (ĕn-fôrs′, -fōrs′) *tr.v.* **-forced, -forc·ing, -forc·es 1.** To compel observance of or obedience to. **2.** To impose (a kind of behavior); compel. **3.** To give force to; reinforce. [ME *enforcen* < OFr. *enforcier,* to exert force, compel, and < *enforcir,* to strengthen : *en-,* causative pref.; see EN-¹ + *force,* strength; see FORCE.] —**en·force′a·bil′i·ty** *n.* —**en·force′a·ble** *adj.* —**en·force′ment** *n.* —**en·forc′er** *n.*

en·fran·chise (ĕn-frăn′chīz′) *tr.v.* **-chised, -chis·ing, -chis·es 1.** To bestow a franchise on. **2.** To endow with the rights of citizenship, esp. the right to vote. **3.** To free, as from bondage. [ME *enfraunchisen* < OFr. *enfranchir, enfranchiss-,* to set free : *en-,* intensive pref.; see EN-¹ + *franchir* (< *franc,* free; see FRANK¹).] —**en·fran′chise′ment** *n.*

Eng. *abbr.* **1.** England **2.** English

En·ga·dine (ĕng′gə-dēn′) A valley of the Inn R. in E Switzerland, divided into the Upper Engadine in the SW and the Lower Engadine in the NE.

en·gage (ĕn-gāj′) *v.* **-gaged, -gag·ing, -gag·es** —*tr.* **1.** To obtain the services of; employ. **2.** To arrange for the use of; reserve. **3.** To pledge or promise, esp. to marry. **4.** To attract and hold the attention of; engross. **5.** To win over or attract. **6.** To draw into; involve. **7.** To require the use of; occupy. **8.** To enter or bring into conflict with. **9.** To interlock or cause to interlock; mesh: *engage the clutch.* **10.** To give or take as security. —*intr.* **1.** To involve oneself or become occupied; participate. **2.** To assume an obligation; agree. **3.** To enter into conflict or battle. **4.** To become meshed or interlocked. [ME *engagen,* to pledge something as security for repayment of debt < OFr. *engagier* : *en-,* in; see EN-¹ + *gage,* pledge, of Gmc. orig.] —**en·gag′er** *n.*

en·ga·gé (ŏN′gä-zhā′) *adj.* Actively committed, as to a political cause. [Fr., p. part. of *engager,* to engage < OFr. *engagier,* to pledge. See ENGAGE.]

en·gaged (ĕn-gājd′) *adj.* **1.** Employed, occupied, or busy. **2.** Committed, as to a cause. **3.** Pledged to marry; betrothed. **4.** Involved in conflict or battle. **5.** Being in gear; meshed. **6.** Partly embedded in or attached to another part.

en·gage·ment (ĕn-gāj′mənt) *n.* **1.** The act of engaging or the state of being engaged. **2.** Betrothal. **3.** Something that serves to engage; a pledge. **4.** A promise or agreement to be at a particular place at a particular time. **5a.** Employment, esp. for a specified time. **b.** A specified period of employment. **6.** A hostile encounter; a battle. **7.** The condition of being in gear.

SYNONYMS *engagement, appointment, assignation, date, rendezvous, tryst* These nouns denote a commitment to appear at a certain time and place: *a business engagement; a dental appointment; a secret assignation; a date to play tennis; a rendezvous of agents at the border; a lovers' tryst.*

en·gag·ing (ĕn-gā′jĭng) *adj.* Charming; attractive: *an engaging smile.* —**en·gag′ing·ly** *adv.*

en garde (äN gärd′) *interj.* Used to warn a fencer to assume the position preparatory to a match. [Fr. : *en,* on + *garde,* guard.]

en·gar·land (ĕn-gär′lənd) *tr.v.* **-land·ed, -land·ing, -lands** To encircle or deck with or as if with a garland.

En·gels (ĕng′əls, -əls), **Friedrich** 1820–95. German socialist theorist who collaborated with Karl Marx on *The Communist Manifesto* (1848).

en·gen·der (ĕn-jĕn′dər) *v.* **-dered, -der·ing, -ders** —*tr.* **1.** To bring into existence; give rise to. **2.** To procreate; propagate. —*intr.* To come into existence; originate. [ME *engendren* < OFr. *engendrer* < Lat. *ingenerāre* : *in-,* in; see EN-¹ + *generāre,* to produce; see GENERATE.] —**en·gen′der·er** *n.*

en·gine (ĕn′jĭn) *n.* **1a.** A machine that converts energy into mechanical force or motion. **b.** Such a machine distinguished from an electric, spring-driven, or hydraulic motor by use of a fuel. **2a.** A mechanical appliance, instrument, or tool. **b.** An agent, instrument, or means of accomplishment. **3.** A locomotive. **4.** A fire engine. **5.** A search engine. ❖ *tr.v.* **-gined, -gin·ing, -gines** To equip with an engine or engines. [ME *engin,* skill, machine

< OFr., innate ability < Lat. *ingenium*. See **genə-** in App.]

engine block *n.* The cast metal block containing the cylinders of an internal-combustion engine.

en·gi·neer (ĕn′jə-nîr′) *n.* **1.** One who is trained or professionally engaged in a branch of engineering. **2.** One who operates an engine. **3.** One who skillfully or shrewdly manages an enterprise. ❖ *tr.v.* **-neered, -neer·ing, -neers 1.** To plan, construct, or manage as an engineer. **2.** To alter or produce by methods of genetic engineering. **3.** To plan, manage, and put through by skillful acts or contrivance; maneuver. [ME *enginour* < OFr. *engigneor* < Med.Lat. *ingeniātor*, contriver < *ingeniāre*, to contrive < Lat. *ingenium*, ability. See ENGINE.]

en·gi·neer·ing (ĕn′jə-nîr′ĭng) *n.* **1a.** The application of science to practical ends such as the design, manufacture, and operation of structures, machines, and systems. **b.** The profession of or the work performed by an engineer. **2.** Skillful maneuvering or direction: *social engineering.*

en·gird (ĕn-gûrd′) *tr.v.* **-girt** (-gûrt′), **-gird·ing, -girds** *Archaic* To encircle.

en·gir·dle (ĕn-gûr′dl) *tr.v.* **-dled, -dling, -dles** To encircle or surround with or as if with a girdle.

en·gla·cial (ĕn-glā′shəl) *adj.* Located or occurring within a glacier.

Eng·land (ĭng′glənd) A division of the United Kingdom, the S part of the island of Great Britain. Acts of union joined England with Wales (1536) and Scotland (1707) to create the political entity of Great Britain and with Ireland (1801) to form the United Kingdom. Cap. London. Pop. 46,220,955.

Eng·lish (ĭng′glĭsh) *adj.* **1.** Of, relating to, or characteristic of England or its people or culture. **2.** Of or relating to the English language. ❖ *n.* **1.** The people of England. **2a.** The West Germanic language of England, the United States, and other countries that are or have been under English influence. **b.** The English language of a particular time, region, person, or group of persons: *American English.* **3.** A translation into or an equivalent in the English language. **4.** A course or class in the study of English language, literature, or composition. **5.** also **english a.** The spin given to a propelled ball by striking it on one side or releasing it with a sharp twist. ❖ *tr.v.* **-lished, -lish·ing, -lish·es 1.** To translate into English. **2.** To adapt into English; Anglicize. [ME < OE *Englisc* < *Engle*, the Angles.] —**Eng′lish·ness** *n.*

English bulldog *n.* A shorthaired stocky dog; a bulldog.

English Channel An arm of the Atlantic Ocean between W France and S England opening into the North Sea.

English daisy *n.* See **daisy** 2.

English foxhound *n.* Any of a breed of medium-sized hunting dog originating in England and having straight legs and a smooth black and white or tan and white coat.

English horn *n.* A double-reed woodwind instrument similar to but larger than the oboe and pitched lower by a fifth. [Transl. of Fr. *cor anglais*, perh. alteration of *cor anglé*, bent horn (< the curved crook to which the mouthpiece is attached) : *cor*, horn + *anglé*, bent.]

Eng·lish·man (ĭng′glĭsh-mən) *n.* **1.** A man who is a native or inhabitant of England. **2.** A man of English descent.

English muffin *n.* A flat round muffin made from yeast dough, baked on a griddle and usu. split and toasted.

English plantain *n.* See **ribgrass.**

English saddle *n.* A light hornless saddle with a steel cantle and pommel, a padded seat, and full side flaps.

English setter *n.* Any of a breed of medium-sized dog developed in England and having a long silky white coat usu. with black or brownish markings.

English sheepdog *n.* An Old English sheepdog.

English sonnet *n.* See **Shakespearean sonnet.**

English sparrow *n.* See **house sparrow.**

English springer spaniel *n.* Any of a breed of medium-sized hunting dog originating in England and having a silky liver and white or black and white coat.

English walnut *n.* **1.** A Eurasian tree (*Juglans regia*) cultivated in southern Europe and California for its valuable wood and its large edible nuts. **2.** The nut of this tree.

Eng·lish·wom·an (ĭng′glĭsh-wŏŏm′ən) *n.* **1.** A woman who is a native or inhabitant of England. **2.** A woman of English descent.

en·glut (ĕn-glŭt′) *tr.v.* **-glut·ted, -glut·ting, -gluts** To gulp down; swallow greedily. [AN *englutir* < LLat. *inglūtīre* : Lat. *in-*, intensive pref.; see IN-² + Lat. *gluttīre*, to swallow.]

en·gorge (ĕn-gôrj′) *v.* **-gorged, -gorg·ing, -gorg·es** —*tr.* **1.** To devour greedily. **2.** To gorge; glut. **3.** To fill to excess, as with blood or other fluid. —*intr.* To feed ravenously. [Fr. *engorger* < OFr. *engorgier* : *en-*, in; see EN-¹ + *gorge*, throat; see GORGE.] —**en·gorge′ment** *n.*

en·graft (ĕn-grăft′) *tr.v.* **-graft·ed, -graft·ing, -grafts 1.** To graft (a scion) onto or into another plant. **2.** To plant firmly; establish. —**en·graft′ment** *n.*

en·grailed (ĕn-grāld′) *adj.* **1.** *Heraldry* Indented along the edge with small curves. **2.** Having an edge or a margin formed by a series of raised dots. [ME *engreled* < OFr. *engresle*, p. part. of *engresler*, to engrail : *en-*, causative pref.; see EN-¹ + *gresle*, slender, tapered (< Lat. *gracilis*).]

en·grain (ĕn-grān′) *tr.v.* **-grained, -grain·ing, -grains** To ingrain. [ME *engreinen*, to dye with cochineal or kermes < OFr. *engrainer* : *en-*, causative pref.; see EN-¹ + *graine*, grain; see GRAIN.]

en·gram (ĕn′grăm′) *n.* A physical alteration thought to occur in living neural tissue in response to stimuli, posited as an explanation for memory. [Ger. *Engramm* : EN-² + Gk. *-gramma*, -gram.]

en·grave (ĕn-grāv′) *tr.v.* **-graved, -grav·ing, -graves 1.** To carve, cut, or etch into a material. **2.** To carve, cut, or etch a design or letters into. **3a.** To carve, cut, or etch into a block or surface used for printing. **b.** To print from a block or plate made by such a process. **4.** To impress deeply as if by carving or etching. —**en·grav′er** *n.*

en·grav·ing (ĕn-grā′vĭng) *n.* **1.** The art or technique of one that engraves. **2.** A design or text engraved on a surface. **3.** An engraved surface for printing. **4.** A print made from an engraved plate or block.

en·gross (ĕn-grōs′) *tr.v.* **-grossed, -gross·ing, -gross·es 1.** To occupy exclusively; absorb. **2.** To acquire most or all of (a commodity); monopolize (a market). **3a.** To write or transcribe in a large clear hand. **b.** To write or print the final draft of (an official document). [ME *engrossen*, to collect in large quantity, monopolize < OFr. *engrossier* < *en gros*, in large quantity : *en*, in (< Lat. *in*; see IN-²) + *gros*, large; see GROSS.] —**en·gross′er** *n.* —**en·gross′ment** *n.*

en·gross·ing (ĕn-grō′sĭng) *adj.* Occupying one's complete attention; wholly absorbing. —**en·gross′ing·ly** *adv.*

en·gulf (ĕn-gŭlf′) *tr.v.* **-gulfed, -gulf·ing, -gulfs** To swallow up or overwhelm by or as if by overflowing and enclosing. —**en·gulf′ment** *n.*

en·hance (ĕn-hăns′) *tr.v.* **-hanced, -hanc·ing, -hanc·es 1.** To make greater, as in value, beauty, or effectiveness; augment: *The flower garden enhanced the grounds.* **2.** To provide with improved, advanced, or sophisticated features. [ME *enhauncen* < AN *enhauncer*, var. of OFr. *enhaucier* < VLat. **inaltiāre* < LLat. *inaltāre* : Lat. *in-*, causative pref.; see EN-¹ + Lat. *altus*, high.] —**en·hance′ment** *n.* —**en·hanc′er** *n.* —**en·hanc′ive** *adj.*

en·har·mon·ic (ĕn′här-mŏn′ĭk) *adj. Music* Of or relating to tones that are identical in pitch but are written according to the key in which they occur, as C sharp and D flat, for example. [LLat. *enharmonicus* < Gk. *enarmonios* : *en-*, in; see EN-² + *harmoniā*, harmony; see HARMONY.] —**en·har·mon′i·cal·ly** *adv.*

e·nig·ma (ĭ-nĭg′mə) *n.* **1.** One that is puzzling or inexplicable. **2.** A perplexing speech or text; a riddle. [Lat. *aenigma* < Gk. *ainigma* < *ainissesthai*, *ainig-*, to speak in riddles < *ainos*, fable.]

en·ig·mat·ic (ĕn′ĭg-măt′ĭk) or **en·ig·mat·i·cal** (-ĭ-kəl) *adj.* Resembling an enigma; puzzling. [Gk. *ainigmatikos* < *ainigma*, *ainigmat-*, riddle. See ENIGMA.] —**en·ig·mat′i·cal·ly** *adv.*

en·isle (ĕn-īl′) *tr.v.* **-isled, -isl·ing, -isles 1.** To make into an island. **2.** To set apart from others; isolate.

En·i·we·tok (ĕn′ə-wē′tŏk′, ə-nē′wĭ-) See **Enewetak.**

en·jamb·ment or **en·jambe·ment** (ĕn-jăm′mənt, -jämb′) *n.* The continuation of a syntactic unit from one line or couplet of a poem to the next with no pause. [Fr. *enjambement* < OFr. *enjamber*, to straddle : *en-*, causative pref.; see EN-¹ + *jambe*, leg; see JAMB.]

en·join (ĕn-join′) *tr.v.* **-joined, -join·ing, -joins 1.** To direct or impose with authority and emphasis. **2.** To prohibit or forbid. See Syns at **forbid.** [ME *enjoinen* < OFr. *enjoindre* < Lat. *iniungere* : *in-*, causative pref.; see EN-¹ + *iungere*, to join; see **yeug-** in App.] —**en·join′er** *n.* —**en·join′ment** *n.*

en·join·der (ĕn-join′dər) *n.* An authoritative request or injunction. [< ENJOIN (modeled on REJOINDER).]

en·joy (ĕn-joi′) *v.* **-joyed, -joy·ing, -joys** —*tr.* **1.** To receive pleasure or satisfaction from. **2.** To have the use or benefit of. —*intr.* To have a pleasurable or satisfactory time. [ME *enjoien* < OFr. *enjoir* : *en-*, intensive pref.; see EN-¹ + *joir*, to rejoice (< Lat. *gaudēre*).] —**en·joy′a·ble** *adj.* —**en·joy′a·bly** *adv.* —**en·joy′er** *n.*

en·joy·ment (ĕn-joi′mənt) *n.* **1.** The act or state of enjoying. **2.** Use or possession of something beneficial or pleasurable. **3.** Something that gives pleasure. **4.** *Law* The exercise of a right.

en·keph·a·lin (ĕn-kĕf′ə-lĭn) *n.* Either of two polypeptides having opiate qualities that are produced in the brain. [Gk. *enkephalos*, in the head (*en-*, in; see EN-² + *kephalē*, head; see **ghebh-el-** in App.) + -IN.]

En·ki (ĕn′kē) *n. Mythology* The Mesopotamian god of waters and primeval establisher of law and order. [Sumerian *en-ki-k*, lord of the earth : *en*, lord + *ki*, earth + *-k*, genitive suff.]

en·kin·dle (ĕn-kĭn′dl) *v.* **-dled, -dling, -dles** —*tr.* **1.** To set afire; light. **2.** To incite; arouse. **3.** To make luminous and glowing. —*intr.* To catch fire. —**en·kin′dler** *n.*

en·lace (ĕn-lās′) also **in·lace** (ĭn-) *tr.v.* **-laced, -lac·ing, -lac·es 1.** To wrap or wind about with or as if with a lace or laces; encircle. **2.** To interlace; entwine. —**en·lace′ment** *n.*

en·large (ĕn-lärj′) *v.* **-larged, -larg·ing, -larg·es** —*tr.* **1.** To make larger; add to. **2.** To give greater scope to; expand. See Syns at **increase.** —*intr.* **1.** To become larger; grow. **2.** To speak or write at greater length or in greater detail; elaborate. [ME *enlargen* < OFr. *enlargier* : *en-*, causative pref.; see EN-¹ + *large*, large; see LARGE.] —**en·larg′er** *n.*

en·large·ment (ĕn-lärj′mənt) *n.* **1.** An act of enlarging or the state of being enlarged. **2.** Something that enlarges; an addition. **3.** Something that has been enlarged.

en·light·en (ĕn-līt′n) *tr.v.* **-ened, -en·ing, -ens** **1.** To give spiritual or intellectual insight to. **2.** To give information to; inform or instruct. **—en·light′en·er** *n.*

en·light·en·ment (ĕn-līt′n-mənt) *n.* **1a.** The act or a means of enlightening. **b.** The state of being enlightened. **2. Enlightenment** A philosophical movement of the 18th century that emphasized the use of reason to examine accepted doctrines and traditions and brought about many humanitarian reforms. Used with *the.* **3.** *Buddhism & Hinduism* A state in which the individual transcends desire and suffering and attains Nirvana.

En·lil (ĕn′lĭl) *n. Mythology* The chief Mesopotamian tutelary deity. [Sumerian, folk-etymological alteration (influenced by *en,* lord, and *lil,* wind) of *illil, ellil* < Semitic *ʾilil,* god of gods (sense uncertain).]

en·list (ĕn-lĭst′) *v.* **-list·ed, -list·ing, -lists** —*tr.* **1.** To engage (persons or a person) for service in the armed forces. **2.** To engage the support of. —*intr.* **1.** To enter the armed forces. **2.** To participate actively in a cause. **—en·list′ment** *n.*

en·list·ed (ĕn-lĭs′tĭd) *adj.* Of, relating to, or being a member of a military rank below a commissioned officer or warrant officer.

en·list·ee (ĕn-lĭs′tē′) *n.* A person who enlists or is enlisted for service in the armed forces.

en·liv·en (ĕn-lī′vən) *tr.v.* **-ened, -en·ing, -ens** To make lively; animate. **—en·liv′en·er** *n.* **—en·liv′en·ment** *n.*

en masse (ŏn măs′) *adv.* In one group or body; all together: *marched en masse to the capitol.* [Fr. : *en,* in + *masse,* mass.]

en·mesh (ĕn-mĕsh′) also **im·mesh** (ĭm-) *tr.v.* **-meshed, -mesh·ing, -mesh·es** To entangle, involve, or catch in or as if in a mesh. See Syns at **catch.** **—en·mesh′ment** *n.*

en·mi·ty (ĕn′mĭ-tē) *n., pl.* **-ties** Deep-seated, often mutual hatred. [ME *enemite* < OFr. *enemistie* < VLat. *inimīcitās* < Lat. *inimīcus,* enemy. See ENEMY.]

en·ne·ad (ĕn′ē-ăd′) *n.* A group or set of nine. [Gk. *enneas, ennead-* < *ennea,* nine. See **newn** in App.]

En·ni·us (ĕn′ē-əs), **Quintus** 239–169 B.C. Roman poet whose works survive only in fragments.

en·no·ble (ĕn-nō′bəl) *tr.v.* **-bled, -bling, -bles** **1.** To make noble; dignify. **2.** To confer nobility upon. [ME *ennoblen* < OFr. *ennoblir* : *en-,* causative pref.; see EN-[1] + *noble,* noble; see NOBLE.] **—en·no′ble·ment** *n.* **—en·no′bler** *n.*

en·nui (ŏn-wē′, ŏn′wē) *n.* Listlessness and dissatisfaction resulting from lack of interest; boredom. [Fr. < OFr. *enui* < *ennuyer,* to annoy, bore. See ANNOY.]

WORD HISTORY No one likes being bored, and this aversion lies at the root of our word *ennui.* The Latin phrase *mihi in odiō est* (literally translated as "to me in a condition of dislike or hatred is"), meaning "I hate or dislike," gave rise to the Vulgar Latin verb *ʾinodiāre,* "to make odious," the source of Modern French *ennuyer,* "to annoy, bore." This was borrowed into English by around 1275 as *anoien,* our *annoy.* From the Old French verb a noun meaning "worry, boredom" was derived, which became *ennui* in modern French. This noun, with the sense "boredom," was borrowed into English in the 18th century, perhaps filling a need in polite, cultivated society.

e·no·ki (ē-nōk′ē) *n., pl.* **-kis** Enokidake.

e·no·ki·da·ke (ĭ-nō′kē-dä′kē) *n.* A widely cultivated mushroom (*Flammulina velutipes*) native to North America and eastern Asia. [J. : *enoki,* Chin. nettle tree + *take,* bamboo, mushroom.]

e·nol (ē′nôl′, ē′nōl′) *n.* An organic compound containing a hydroxyl group attached to a doubly bonded carbon atom. [< —EN(E) + -OL[1].] **—e·nol′ic** (ē-nōl′ĭk) *adj.*

e·no·lase (ē′nə-lās′, -lāz′) *n.* An enzyme present in muscle tissue that acts in carbohydrate metabolism.

e·nol·o·gy also **oe·nol·o·gy** (ē-nōl′ə-jē) *n.* The study of wine and the making of wine. [Gk. *oinos,* wine + -LOGY.] **—e′no·log′i·cal** (ē′nə-lōj′ĭ-kəl) *adj.* **—e·nol′o·gist** *n.*

e·no·phile (ē′nə-fīl′) *n.* Variant of **oenophile.**

e·nor·mi·ty (ĭ-nôr′mĭ-tē) *n., pl.* **-ties** **1.** The quality of passing all moral bounds; excessive wickedness or outrageousness. **2.** A monstrous offense or evil; an outrage. **3.** *Usage Problem* Great size; immensity. [Fr. *énormité* < OFr. < Lat. *ēnormitās* < *ēnormis,* unusual, enormous. See ENORMOUS.]

USAGE NOTE *Enormity* is frequently used to refer simply to the property of being great in size or extent. But many would prefer that *enormousness* or *immensity* be used for this sense and that *enormity* be reserved for a property that evokes a negative moral judgment, as in *We only later became aware of the enormity of his crimes.* A majority of Usage Panelists approve of this distinction. Fifty-nine percent reject the use of *enormity* in the sentence *At that point the engineers sat down to design an entirely new viaduct, apparently undaunted by the enormity of their task.*

e·nor·mous (ĭ-nôr′məs) *adj.* **1.** Very great in size, extent, number, or degree. **2.** *Archaic* Very wicked; heinous. [< Lat. *ēnormis,* unusual, huge : *ē-, ex-, ex-* + *norma,* norm; see gnō- in App. Sense 2 < ME *enormious* < Lat. *ēnormis.*] **—e·nor′mous·ly** *adv.* **—e·nor′mous·ness** *n.*

ensign

e·nough (ĭ-nŭf′) *adj.* Sufficient to satisfy a need or a desire; adequate. ❖ *pron.* An adequate number or quantity. ❖ *adv.* **1.** To a satisfactory amount or degree; sufficiently: *cooked enough.* **2.** Very; fully; quite: *glad enough to leave.* **3.** Tolerably; rather: *sang well enough.* ❖ *interj.* Used to express impatience or exasperation. [ME *enogh* < OE *genōg.*]

e·nounce (ĭ-nouns′) *tr.v.* **e·nounced, e·nounc·ing, e·nounc·es** **1.** To declare formally; state. **2.** To pronounce clearly; enunciate. [< Fr. *énoncer* < Lat. *ēnūntiāre,* to speak out. See ENUNCIATE.] **—e·nounce′ment** *n.*

e·now (ĭ-nou′) *adj. & adv. Archaic* Enough. [ME, var. of *enogh.* See ENOUGH.]

en pas·sant (äN′ pä-säN′) *adv.* **1.** In passing; by the way; incidentally. **2.** Used in reference to a move in chess in which a pawn that has just completed an initial advance to its fourth rank is captured by an opponent pawn as if it had only moved to its third rank. [Fr. : *en,* in + *passant,* passing.]

en·phy·tot·ic (ĕn′fī-tŏt′ĭk) *adj.* Of or relating to a plant disease that causes a relatively constant amount of damage each year. [EN-[2] + -PHYT(E) + -OTIC.] **—en′phy·tot′ic** *n.*

en·plane (ĕn-plān′) also **em·plane** (ĕm-) *intr.v.* **-planed, -plan·ing, -planes** To board an airplane.

en prise (äN prēz′, äN) *adj.* Exposed to possible capture. Used of a chess piece. [Fr. : *en,* in + *prise,* grip, grasp.]

en·quire (ĕn-kwīr′) *v.* Variant of **inquire.**

en·quir·y (ĕn-kwīr′ē, ĕn′kwə-rē) *n., pl.* **-ies** Variant of **inquiry.**

en·rage (ĕn-rāj′) *tr.v.* **-raged, -rag·ing, -rag·es** To put into a rage; infuriate. [ME *enragen* < OFr. *enrager* : *en-,* causative pref.; see EN-[1] + *rage,* rage; see RAGE.] **—en·rage′ment** *n.*

en rap·port (äN′ rə-pôr′, -pōr′, rä-) *adj.* Being in agreement; harmonious. [Fr. : *en,* in + *rapport,* agreement.]

en·rapt (ĕn-răpt′) *adj.* Filled with delight; enraptured.

en·rap·ture (ĕn-răp′chər) *tr.v.* **-tured, -tur·ing, -tures** To fill with rapture or delight. **—en·rap′ture·ment** *n.*

en·rich (ĕn-rĭch′) *tr.v.* **-riched, -rich·ing, -rich·es** **1.** To make rich or richer. **2.** To make fuller, more meaningful, or more rewarding. **3.** To add fertilizer to. **4.** To add nutrients to. **5.** To add to the beauty or character of; adorn. **6.** *Physics* To increase the amount of one or more radioactive isotopes in (a material, esp. a nuclear fuel). [ME *enrichen* < OFr. *enrichier* : *en-,* causative pref.; see EN-[1] + *riche,* rich; see RICH.] **—en·rich′er** *n.*

en·rich·ment (ĕn-rĭch′mənt) *n.* **1.** The act of enriching or the state of being enriched. **2.** Something that enriches.

en·robe (ĕn-rōb′) *tr.v.* **-robed, -rob·ing, -robes** To dress in or as if in a robe.

en·roll also **en·rol** (ĕn-rōl′) *v.* **-rolled, -roll·ing, -rolls** also **-rols** —*tr.* **1.** To enter or register in a roll, list, or record. **2.** To roll or wrap up. **3.** To write or print a final copy of; engross. —*intr.* To place one's name on a roll or register. [ME *enrollen* < OFr. *enroller* : *en-,* in; see EN-[1] + *rolle,* roll (< Lat. *rotula,* little wheel; see ROLL).] **—en·roll·ee′** *n.*

en·roll·ment also **en·rol·ment** (ĕn-rōl′mənt) *n.* **1a.** The act or process of enrolling. **b.** The state of being enrolled. **2.** The number enrolled. **3.** A record or an entry.

en·root (ĕn-rōōt′, -rōōt′) *tr.v.* **-root·ed, -root·ing, -roots** To establish firmly by or as if by roots; implant.

en route (ŏn rōōt′, ĕn) *adv. & adj.* On or along the way. [Fr. : *en,* on + *route,* route.]

ENS or **Ens.** *abbr.* ensign

en·san·guine (ĕn-săng′gwĭn) *tr.v.* **-guined, -guin·ing, -guines** To cover or stain with or as if with blood.

En·sche·de (ĕn′skə-dā′, -sKHə-) A city of E Netherlands near the German border. Pop. 147,486.

en·sconce (ĕn-skŏns′) *tr.v.* **-sconced, -sconc·ing, -sconc·es** **1.** To settle (oneself) securely or comfortably. **2.** To place or conceal in a secure place. [EN-[1] + SCONCE[1].]

en·sem·ble (ŏn-sŏm′bəl) *n.* **1.** A unit or group of parts that contribute to a single effect, esp.: **a.** A coordinated outfit or costume. **b.** A coordinated set of furniture. **c.** A group of musicians, singers, dancers, or actors who perform together. **2.** *Music* **a.** A work for two or more vocalists or instrumentalists. **b.** The performance of such a work. [Fr. < OFr., together < LLat. *īnsimul,* at the same time : *in-,* intensive pref.; see IN-[2] + *simul,* at the same time; see sem-[1] in App.]

En·se·na·da (ĕn′sə-nä′də) A city of NW Mexico on the Pacific Ocean. Pop. 120,483.

en·sheathe (ĕn-shēth′) *tr.v.* **-sheathed, -sheath·ing, -sheathes** To cover or enclose with or as with a sheathe.

en·shrine (ĕn-shrīn′) also **in·shrine** (ĭn-) *tr.v.* **-shrined, -shrin·ing, -shrines** **1.** To enclose in or as if in a shrine. **2.** To cherish as sacred. **—en·shrine′ment** *n.*

en·shroud (ĕn-shroud′) *tr.v.* **-shroud·ed, -shroud·ing, -shrouds** To cover with or as if with a shroud.

en·si·form (ĕn′sə-fôrm′) *adj.* Shaped like a sword, as the leaf of an iris. [Lat. *ēnsis,* sword + -FORM.]

en·sign (ĕn′sən, -sīn′) *n.* **1.** A national flag displayed on ships and aircraft, often with the insignia of an armed forces unit. **2.** A standard or banner, as of a military unit. **3.** *Archaic* A standard-bearer. **4.** (ĕn′sən) A commissioned officer in the US Navy or Coast Guard, ranking below lieutenant junior grade. **5a.** A badge of office or power; an emblem. **b.** A sign; a token. [ME *ensigne*

< OFr. *enseigne* < Lat. *īnsignia*, insignia. See INSIGNIA.]

en•si•lage (ĕn′sə-lĭj) *n.* **1.** The process of storing and fermenting green fodder in a silo. **2.** Fodder preserved in a silo; silage. ❖ *tr.v.* **-laged, -lag•ing, -lag•es** To ensile. [Fr. < *ensiler*, to ensile. See ENSILE.]

en•sile (ĕn-sīl′) *tr.v.* **-siled, -sil•ing, -siles** To store (fodder) in a silo for preservation. [Fr. *ensiler* < Sp. *ensilar* : *en-*, in (< Lat. *in-*); see EN–[1] + *silo*, silo.]

en•slave (ĕn-slāv′) *tr.v.* **-slaved, -slav•ing, -slaves** To make into a slave. **—en•slave′ment** *n.* **—en•slav′er** *n.*

en•snare (ĕn-snâr′) also **in•snare** (ĭn-) *tr.v.* **-snared, -snar•ing, -snares** To take or catch in or as if in a snare. See Syns at **catch.** **—en•snare′ment** *n.* **—en•snar′er** *n.*

en•snarl (ĕn-snärl′) *tr.v.* **-snarled, -snarl•ing, -snarls** To entangle in or as if in a snarl.

En•sor (ĕn′sôr), **James** 1860–1949. Belgian painter whose works include *Entry of Christ into Brussels* (1888).

en•soul (ĕn-sōl′) also **in•soul** (ĭn-) *tr.v.* **-souled, -soul•ing, -souls 1.** To endow with a soul. **2.** To place, receive, or cherish in the soul.

en•sphere (ĕn-sfîr′) also **in•sphere** (ĭn-) *tr.v.* **-sphered, -spher•ing, -spheres** To enclose in or as if in a sphere.

en•sta•tite (ĕn′stə-tīt′) *n.* A variety of orthorhombic pyroxene having a magnesium silicate base, mainly $MgSiO_3$, usu. found embedded in igneous rocks and meteorites. [Gk. *enstatēs*, adversary (because of its refractory quality) : *en-*, in, at, near; see EN–[2] + *-statēs*, one that stands; see **stā-** in App. + –ITE[1].]

en•sue (ĕn-so͞o′) *intr.v.* **-sued, -su•ing, -sues 1.** To follow as a result. See Syns at **follow. 2.** To take place subsequently. [ME *ensuen* < OFr. *ensuivre, ensu-* < VLat. **īnsequere* < Lat. *īnsequī*, to follow closely : *in-*, intensive pref.; see EN–[1] + *sequī*, to follow; see **sekʷ-**[1] in App.]

en suite (äɴ swĕt′) *adv. & adj.* In or as part of a series or set. [Fr. : *en*, in + *suite*, a following, sequence.]

en•sure (ĕn-sho͝or′) *tr.v.* **-sured, -sur•ing, -sures** To make sure or certain; insure. See Usage Note at **assure.** [ME *ensuren* < AN *enseurer* : OFr. *en-*, causative pref.; see EN–[1] + OFr. *seur*, secure, var. of *sur*; see SURE.]

ENT *abbr. Medicine* ear, nose, and throat

ent– *pref.* Variant of **ento–.**

–ent *suff.* **1a.** Performing, promoting, or causing a specified action: *absorbent.* **b.** Being in a specified state or condition: *bivalent.* **2.** One that performs, promotes, or causes a specified action: *referent.* [ME < OFr. < Lat. *-ēns, -ent-*, pr. part. suff.]

en•tab•la•ture (ĕn-tăb′lə-cho͝or′) *n.* The upper section of a classical building, resting on the columns and constituting the architrave, frieze, and cornice. [Obsolete Fr. < Ital. *intavolatura* < *intavolare*, to put on a table : *in-*, in, on (< Lat.; see EN–[1]) + *tavola*, table (< Lat. *tabula*, board).]

en•tail (ĕn-tāl′, ĭn-) *tr.v.* **-tailed, -tail•ing, -tails 1.** To have, impose, or require as a necessary accompaniment or consequence. **2.** To limit the inheritance of (property) to a specified succession of heirs. **3.** To bestow or impose on a person or a specified succession of heirs. ❖ *n.* **1a.** The act of entailing, esp. property. **b.** The state of being entailed. **2.** An entailed estate. **3.** A predetermined order of succession, as to an estate or an office. **4.** Something transmitted as if by unalterable inheritance. [ME *entaillen*, to limit inheritance to specific heirs : *en-*, intensive pref.; see EN–[1] + *taille*, tail; see TAIL[2].] **—en•tail′ment** *n.*

en•ta•moe•ba (ĕn′tə-mē′bə) also **en•da•moe•ba** (ĕn′də-) *n., pl.* **-bas** or **-bae** (-bē) Any of several parasitic amoebas of the genus *Entamoeba*, esp. *E. histolytica*, which causes amoebic dysentery. [NLat. *Entamoeba*, genus name : ENT(O)– + AMOEBA.]

en•tan•gle (ĕn-tăng′gəl) *tr.v.* **-gled, -gling, -gles 1.** To twist together or entwine into a confusing mass; snarl. **2.** To complicate; confuse. **3.** To involve in or as if in a tangle. See Syns at **catch.** **—en•tan′gle•ment** *n.* **—en•tan′gler** *n.*

en•ta•sis (ĕn′tə-sĭs) *n., pl.* **-ses** (-sēz′) A slight convexity, as in the shaft of a column, to compensate for the illusion of concavity resulting from straight sides. [Lat. < Gk., tension < *enteinein*, to stretch tight : *en-*, intensive pref.; see EN–[2] + *teinein*, to stretch; see **ten-** in App.]

En•teb•be (ĕn-tĕb′ə, -tĕb′ē) A town of S Uganda on Lake Victoria; cap. of Uganda (1894–1962). Pop. 41,638.

en•tel•e•chy (ĕn-tĕl′ĭ-kē) *n., pl.* **-chies 1.** In the philosophy of Aristotle, the condition of a thing whose essence is fully realized; actuality. **2.** In some philosophical systems, a vital force that directs an organism toward self-fulfillment. [LLat. *entelechīa* < Gk. *entelekheia* : *entelēs*, complete (*en-*, in; see EN–[2] + *telos*, completion; see **kʷel-** in App.) + *ekhein*, to have; see **segh-** in App.]

en•tente (ŏn-tŏnt′) *n.* **1.** An agreement between two or more governments or powers for cooperative action or policy. **2.** The parties to such an agreement. [Fr. < OFr., intent < fem. p. part. of *entendre*, to understand, intend. See INTEND.]

en•ter (ĕn′tər) *v.* **-tered, -ter•ing, -ters** *—tr.* **1.** To come or go into. **2.** To penetrate; pierce. **3.** To introduce; insert. **4a.** To become a participant, member, or part of; join. **b.** To gain admission to (a school, for example). **5.** To cause to become a participant, member, or part of; enroll. **6.** To embark on; begin. **7.** To make a beginning in; take up: *entered medicine.* **8.** To write or put in. **9.** To place formally on record; submit. **10.** To go to or occupy in order to claim possession of (land). **11.** To report (a ship or cargo) to customs. *—intr.* **1.** To come or go in; make an entry. **2.** To effect penetration. **3.** To become a member or participant. ***—phrasal verbs:* enter into 1.** To participate in; take an active role or interest in. **2.** To become party to (a contract). **3.** To become a component of; form a part of. **4.** To consider; investigate. **enter on** (or **upon**) **1.** To set out on; begin. **2.** To begin considering; take up. **3.** To take possession of. [ME *entren* < OFr. *entrer* < Lat. *intrāre* < *intrā*, inside. See **en** in App.] **—en′ter•a•ble** *adj.*

en•ter•ic (ĕn-tĕr′ĭk) also **en•ter•al** (ĕn′tər-əl) *adj.* Of, relating to, or being within the intestine.

enteric fever *n.* See **typhoid fever.**

en•ter•i•tis (ĕn′tə-rī′tĭs) *n.* Inflammation of the intestinal tract, esp. of the small intestine.

entero– or **enter–** *pref.* Intestine: *enteritis.* [NLat. < Gk. *enteron*, intestine. See **en** in App.]

en•ter•o•bac•te•ri•um (ĕn′tə-rō-băk-tîr′ē-əm) *n., pl.* **-te•ri•a** (-tîr′ē-ə) Any of various gram-negative rod-shaped bacteria of the family Enterobacteriaceae that includes some pathogens of plants and animals, such as the colon bacillus and salmonella.

en•ter•o•bi•a•sis (ĕn′tə-rō-bī′ə-sĭs) *n.* Infestation of the intestine with pinworms. [NLat. *Enterobius*, pinworm genus (ENTERO– + Gk. *bios*, life; see BIO–) + –IASIS.]

en•ter•o•coele (ĕn′tə-rō-sēl′) *n.* The coelom formed from a pocketlike outgrowth of the wall of the archenteron, esp. in echinoderms and chordates.

en•ter•o•gas•trone (ĕn′tə-rō-găs′trōn′) *n.* A hormone released by the upper intestinal mucosa that inhibits gastric motility and secretion. [ENTERO– + GASTR(O)– + (HORM)ONE.]

en•ter•o•hep•a•ti•tis (ĕn′tə-rō-hĕp′ə-tī′tĭs) *n.* See **blackhead** 2.

en•ter•o•ki•nase (ĕn′tə-rō-kī′nās′, -nāz′, -kĭn′ās′, -āz′) *n.* An enzyme secreted by the upper intestinal mucosa that catalyzes the conversion of trypsinogen to trypsin.

en•ter•on (ĕn′tə-rŏn′) *n.* The alimentary canal; the intestines. [Gk. See **en** in App.]

en•ter•o•tox•in (ĕn′tə-rō-tŏk′sĭn) *n.* A toxin produced by bacteria that is specific for intestinal cells and causes the vomiting and diarrhea associated with food poisoning.

en•ter•o•vi•rus (ĕn′tə-rō-vī′rəs) *n., pl.* **-rus•es** Any of a subgroup of picornaviruses, including polioviruses, that infect the gastrointestinal tract and often spread to other areas of the body, esp. the nervous system. **—en′ter•o•vi′ral** *adj.*

en•ter•prise (ĕn′tər-prīz′) *n.* **1.** An undertaking, esp. one of some scope, complication, and risk. **2.** A business organization. **3.** Industrious systematic activity, esp. when directed toward profit. **4.** Willingness to undertake new ventures; initiative. [ME < OFr. *entreprise* < p. part. of *entreprendre*, to undertake : *entre-*, between (< Lat. *inter-*; see INTER–) + *prendre*, to take (< Lat. *prehendere, prēndere*; see **ghend-** in App.).] **—en′ter•pris′er** *n.*

en•ter•pris•ing (ĕn′tər-prī′zĭng) *adj.* Showing initiative and enterprise. **—en′ter•pris′ing•ly** *adv.*

en•ter•tain (ĕn′tər-tān′) *v.* **-tained, -tain•ing, -tains** *—tr.* **1.** To hold the attention of with something amusing or diverting. **2.** To extend hospitality toward. **3a.** To consider; contemplate. **b.** To hold in mind; harbor. **4.** *Archaic* To continue with; maintain. **5.** *Obsolete* To employ; hire. **6.** To give admittance to; receive. *—intr.* **1.** To show hospitality to guests. **2.** To provide entertainment. [ME *entertinen*, to maintain < OFr. *entretenir* < Med.Lat. *intertenēre* : Lat. *inter*, among; see INTER– + Lat. *tenēre*, to hold; see **ten-** in App.] **—en′ter•tain′er** *n.*

en•ter•tain•ing (ĕn′tər-tā′nĭng) *adj.* Agreeably diverting; amusing. **—en′ter•tain′ing•ly** *adv.*

en•ter•tain•ment (ĕn′tər-tān′mənt) *n.* **1.** The act of entertaining. **2.** The art or field of entertaining. **3.** Something that amuses, pleases, or diverts, esp. a performance or show. **4.** The pleasure afforded by being entertained; amusement. **5.** *Archaic* Maintenance; support. **6.** *Obsolete* Employment.

en•thal•py (ĕn′thăl′pē, ĕn-thăl′-) *n., pl.* **-pies** *Symbol* **H** A thermodynamic function of a system, equal to its internal energy plus the product of its volume and pressure. [< Gk. *enthalpein*, to heat in (*en-*, in; see EN–[2] + *thalpein*, to heat) + –Y[2].]

en•thrall (ĕn-thrôl′) *tr.v.* **-thralled, -thrall•ing, -thralls 1.** To hold spellbound; captivate. **2.** To enslave. [ME, to put in bondage : *en-*, causative pref.; see EN–[1] + *thrall*, slave; see THRALL.] **—en•thrall′ing•ly** *adv.* **—en•thrall′ment** *n.*

en•throne (ĕn-thrōn′) *tr.v.* **-throned, -thron•ing, -thrones 1a.** To seat on a throne. **b.** To invest with sovereign power or with the authority of high office. **2.** To raise to a lofty position; exalt. **—en•throne′ment** *n.*

en•thuse (ĕn-tho͞oz′) *v.* **-thused, -thus•ing, -thus•es** *—tr.* To make enthusiastic. *—intr.* To show or express enthusiasm.

en•thu•si•asm (ĕn-tho͞o′zē-ăz′əm) *n.* **1.** Great excitement for or interest in a subject or cause. **2.** A source or cause of great excitement or interest. **3.** *Archaic* **a.** Ecstasy arising from supposed possession by a god. **b.** Religious fanaticism. [LLat. *enthūsiasmus* < Gk. *enthousiasmos* < *enthousiazein*, to be inspired by a god < *entheos*, possessed : *en-*, in; see EN–[2] + *theos*, god; see **dhēs-** in App.]

en•thu•si•ast (ĕn-tho͞o′zē-ăst′) *n.* **1.** One who is filled with enthusiasm; one who is ardently absorbed in an interest or pursuit.

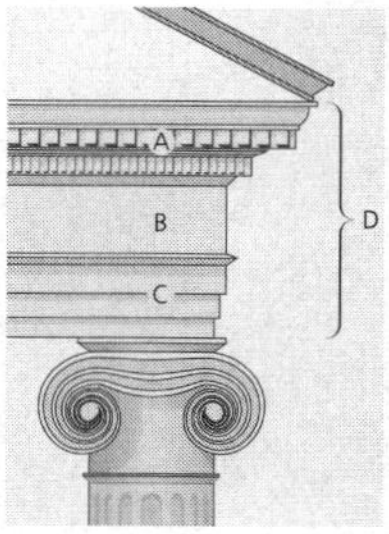

entablature
an Ionic order entablature
A. cornice
B. frieze
C. architrave
D. entablature

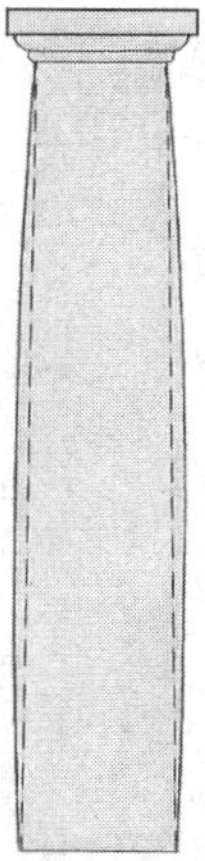

entasis

ă	pat	oi	boy
ā	pay	ou	out
âr	care	o͝o	took
ä	father	o͞o	boot
ĕ	pet	ŭ	cut
ē	be	ûr	urge
ĭ	pit	th	thin
ī	pie	*th*	this
îr	pier	hw	which
ŏ	pot	zh	vision
ō	toe	ə	about, item
ô	paw		

Stress marks:
′ (primary);
′ (secondary), as in
lexicon (lĕk′sĭ-kŏn′)

2. A zealot; a fanatic. [Gk. *enthousiastēs*, possessed person < *enthousiazein*, to be inspired. See ENTHUSIASM.]

en·thu·si·as·tic (ĕn-thōō′zē-ăs′tĭk) *adj.* Having or demonstrating enthusiasm. —**en·thu′si·as′ti·cal·ly** *adv.*

en·thy·meme (ĕn′thə-mēm′) *n. Logic* A syllogism in which one of the premises or the conclusion is not stated explicitly. [Lat. *enthȳmēma* < Gk. *enthūmēma*, a rhetorical argument < *enthūmeisthai*, to consider : *en-*, in; see EN-² + *thūmos*, mind.]

en·tice (ĕn-tīs′) *tr.v.* **-ticed, -tic·ing, -tic·es** To attract by arousing hope or desire; lure. [ME *enticen* < OFr. *enticier*, to instigate, poss. < VLat. **intitiāre*, to set afire : Lat. *in-*, in; see EN-¹ + Lat. *titiō*, firebrand.] —**en·tice′ment** *n.* —**en·tic′er** *n.*

en·tire (ĕn-tīr′) *adj.* **1.** Having no part excluded or left out; whole. See Syns at **whole. 2.** With no reservations or limitations; complete. **3.** All in one piece; intact. **4.** Of one piece; continuous. **5.** Not castrated. **6.** *Botany* Not having an indented margin: *an entire leaf.* **7.** Unmixed or unalloyed; pure or homogenous. ❖ *n.* **1.** The whole; the entirety. **2.** An uncastrated horse; a stallion. [ME < OFr. *entier* < Lat. *integrum*, neut. of *integer*. See **tag-** in App.] —**en·tire′ness** *n.*

en·tire·ly (ĕn-tīr′lē) *adv.* **1.** Wholly; completely: *entirely satisfied.* **2.** Solely or exclusively: *He was entirely to blame.*

en·tire·ty (ĕn-tī′rĭ-tē, -tīr′tē) *n., pl.* **-ties 1.** The state of being entire or complete. **2.** The entire amount or extent; the whole.

en·ti·tle (ĕn-tīt′l) *tr.v.* **-tled, -tling, -tles 1.** To give a name or title to. **2.** To furnish with a right or claim to something. [ME *entitlen* < OFr. *entiteler* < Med.Lat. *intitulāre* : Lat. *in-*, provide with; see EN-¹ + Lat. *titulus*, title.]

en·ti·tle·ment (ĕn-tīt′l-mənt) *n.* **1.** The act or process of entitling. **2.** The state of being entitled. **3.** A government program that guarantees and provides benefits to a particular group.

en·ti·ty (ĕn′tĭ-tē) *n., pl.* **-ties 1.** Something that exists as a discrete unit. **2.** The fact of existence; being. **3.** The existence of something considered apart from its properties. [Med.Lat. *entitās* < Lat. *ēns, ent-*, pr. part. of *esse*, to be. See **es-** in App.]

ento- or **ent-** *pref.* Inside; within: *entoblast.* [NLat. < Gk. *entos*, within. See **en** in App.]

en·to·blast (ĕn′tə-blăst′) *n.* Any of the blastomeres of an embryo from which the endoderm develops.

en·to·derm (ĕn′tə-dûrm′) *n.* Variant of **endoderm.**

en·toil (ĕn-toil′) *tr.v.* **-toiled, -toil·ing, -toils** *Archaic* To ensnare; entrap.

en·tomb (ĕn-tōōm′) *tr.v.* **-tombed, -tomb·ing, -tombs 1.** To place in or as if in a tomb or grave. **2.** To serve as a tomb for. —**en·tomb′ment** *n.*

entomo- *pref.* Insect: *entomology.* [Fr. < Gk. *entomon* < neut. of *entomos*, cut (< its segmented body) < *entemnein*, to cut up : *en-*, in; see EN-² + *temnein*, to cut.]

en·to·mol·o·gy (ĕn′tə-mŏl′ə-jē) *n.* The scientific study of insects. —**en′to·mo·log′ic** (-mə-lŏj′ĭk), **en′to·mo·log′i·cal** (-ĭ-kəl) *adj.* —**en′to·mo·log′i·cal·ly** *adv.* —**en′to·mol′o·gist** *n.*

en·to·moph·a·gous (ĕn′tə-mŏf′ə-gəs) *adj.* Feeding on insects; insectivorous.

en·to·moph·i·lous (ĕn′tə-mŏf′ə-ləs) *adj.* Pollinated by insects. —**en·to·moph′i·ly** *n.*

en·tou·rage (ŏn′tōō-räzh′) *n.* **1.** A group of attendants or associates; a retinue. **2.** One's environment or surroundings. [Fr. < *entourer*, to surround < OFr. *entour*, surroundings : *en-*, in; see EN-¹ + *tour*, circuit; see TOUR.]

en·tr'acte (ŏn′trăkt′, äN-träkt′) *n.* **1a.** The interval between two acts of a theatrical performance. **b.** Another performance, as of music or dance, provided between two acts of a theatrical performance. **2.** An interval likened to the one occurring between two acts of a drama. [Fr. : *entre*, between (< Lat. *inter*; see INTER–) + *acte*, act (< OFr.; see ACT).]

en·trails (ĕn′trālz′, -trəlz) *pl.n.* **1.** The internal organs, esp. the intestines. **2.** Internal parts. [< ME *entraille* < OFr. < Med.Lat. *intrālia*, alteration of Lat. *interānea* < neut. pl. of *interāneus*, internal < *inter*, within. See **en** in App.]

en·train¹ (ĕn-trān′) *tr.v.* **-trained, -train·ing, -trains 1.** To pull or draw along after itself. **2.** *Chemistry* To carry (suspended particles, for example) along in a current. [Fr. *entrainer* < OFr. : *en-*, in; see EN-¹ + *trainer*, to drag; see TRAIN.] —**en·train′er** *n.* —**en·train′ment** *n.*

en·train² (ĕn-trān′) *v.* **-trained, -train·ing, -trains** *—intr.* To go aboard a train. *—tr.* To put aboard a train.

en·trance¹ (ĕn′trəns) *n.* **1.** The act or an instance of entering. **2.** A means or point by which to enter. **3.** Permission or power to enter; admission. **4.** The point, as in a musical score, at which a performer begins. **5.** The first entry of an actor into a scene. **6.** The immersed part of a ship's hull forward of the middle body. [ME *entraunce*, right to enter < OFr. < *entrer*, to enter. See ENTER.]

en·trance² (ĕn-trăns′) *tr.v.* **-tranced, -tranc·ing, -tranc·es 1.** To put into a trance. **2.** To fill with delight, wonder, or enchantment. See Syns at **charm.** —**en·trance′ment** *n.* —**en·tranc′ing·ly** *adv.*

en·trance·way (ĕn′trəns-wā′) *n.* An entryway.

en·trant (ĕn′trənt) *n.* One that enters, esp. a competition. [Fr. < pr. part. of *entrer*, to enter < OFr. See ENTER.]

en·trap (ĕn-trăp′) *tr.v.* **-trapped, -trap·ping, -traps 1.** To catch in or as if in a trap. **2a.** To lure into danger, difficulty, or a compromising situation. See Syns at **catch. b.** To lure into performing an illegal act. [Fr. *entraper* < OFr. : *en-*, in; see EN-¹ + *trape*, trap (of Gmc. orig.).] —**en·trap′ment** *n.*

en·treat (ĕn-trēt′) *also* **en·treat** (ĭn-) *v.* **-treat·ed, -treat·ing, -treats** *—tr.* **1.** To make an earnest request of. **2.** To ask for earnestly; petition for. **3.** *Archaic* To deal with; treat. *—intr.* To make an earnest request or petition; plead. [ME *entreten* < AN *entreter* : *en-*, causative pref.; see EN-¹ + *treter*, to treat; see TREAT.] —**en·treat′ing·ly** *adv.* —**en·treat′ment** *n.*

en·treat·y (ĕn-trē′tē) *n., pl.* **-ies** An earnest request or petition; a plea.

en·tre·chat (ŏn′trə-shä′) *n.* A jump in ballet during which the dancer crosses the legs a number of times, alternately back and forth. [Fr. < earlier *entrechas*, alteration of Ital. *(capriola) intrecciata*, intricate (caper), fem. p. part. of *intrecciare*, to intertwine : *in-*, in (< Lat.; see IN–²) + *treccia*, tress; see TRESS.]

en·tre·côte (äN′trə-kōt′) *n.* A cut of steak taken from between the ribs. [Fr. : *entre*, between (< Lat. *inter*; see INTER–) + *côte*, rib (< Lat. *costa*; see COSTA).]

en·trée or **en·tree** (ŏn′trā, ŏn-trā′) *n.* **1a.** The main dish of a meal. **b.** A dish served in formal dining immediately before the main course or between two principal courses. **2a.** The act of entering. **b.** The power, permission, or liberty to enter; admittance. [Fr. < OFr. See ENTRY.]

en·tre·mets (ŏn′trə-mā′, -mĕ′) *n., pl.* **-mets** (-māz′, -mĕ′) A side dish served in addition to the principal course. [ME *entremetes* < OFr. *entremes, entremets* : *entre*, between (< Lat. *inter*; see INTER–) + *mes, mets*, dish; see MESS.]

en·trench (ĕn-trĕnch′) *also* **in·trench** (ĭn-) *v.* **-trenched, -trench·ing, -trench·es** *—tr.* **1.** To provide with a trench, esp. for fortifying or defending. **2.** To fix firmly or securely. *—intr.* **1.** To dig or occupy a trench. **2.** To encroach, infringe, or trespass. —**en·trench′ment** *n.*

en·tre·pôt (ŏn′trə-pō′) *n.* **1.** A place where goods are stored and from which they are distributed. **2.** A trading or market center. [Fr. < *entreposer*, to store : *entre*, in, among (< Lat. *inter-*; see INTER–) + *poser*, to place (< OFr.; see POSE².)]

en·tre·pre·neur (ŏn′trə-prə-nûr′, -nŏŏr′) *n.* A person who organizes, operates, and assumes the risk for a business venture. [Fr. < OFr. < *entreprendre*, to undertake. See ENTERPRISE.] —**en′tre·pre·neur′i·al** *adj.* —**en′tre·pre·neur′i·al·ism, en′tre·pre·neur′ism, en′tre·pre·neur′ship′** *n.*

en·tre·sol (ĕn′tər-sŏl′, ĕn′trə-, ŏn-trə-sôl′) *n.* The floor just above the ground floor of a building; a mezzanine. [Fr. : *entre-*, between (< Lat. *inter-*; see INTER–) + *sol*, floor (< Lat. *solum*).]

en·tro·py (ĕn′trə-pē) *n., pl.* **-pies 1.** *Symbol* S For a closed thermodynamic system, a measure of the thermal energy unavailable to do work. **2.** A measure of the disorder or randomness in a closed system. **3.** A measure of the loss of information in a transmitted message. **4.** The tendency for all matter and energy in the universe toward a state of inert uniformity. **5.** Inevitable and steady deterioration of a system or society. [Ger. *Entropie* < Gk. *en-*, in; see EN-² + Gk. *tropē*, transformation.] —**en·tro′pic** (ĕn-trō′pĭk, -trŏp′ĭk) *adj.* —**en·tro′pi·cal·ly** *adv.*

en·trust (ĕn-trŭst′) *also* **in·trust** (ĭn-) *tr.v.* **-trust·ed, -trust·ing, -trusts 1.** To give over (something) to another for care, protection, or performance. **2.** To give as a trust to (someone).

en·try (ĕn′trē) *n., pl.* **-tries 1a.** The act or an instance of entering. **b.** The privilege or right of entering. **2.** A means or place by which to enter. **3a.** The inclusion or insertion of an item, as in a record. **b.** An item entered in this way. **4a.** An entry word, as in a dictionary; a headword. **b.** A headword along with its text. **5.** One in a competition. [ME *entre* < OFr. *entree* < fem. p. part. of *entrer*, to enter. See ENTER.]

en·try·way (ĕn′trē-wā′) *n.* A passage by which to enter.

entry word *n.* See **headword 1.**

en·twine (ĕn-twīn′) *v.* **-twined, -twin·ing, -twines** *—tr.* To twine around or together. *—intr.* To twine or twist together. —**en·twine′ment** *n.*

en·twist (ĕn-twĭst′) *tr.v.* **-twist·ed, -twist·ing, -twists** To twist together; entwine.

e·nu·cle·ate (ĭ-nōō′klē-āt′, ĭ-nyōō′-) *tr.v.* **-at·ed, -at·ing, -ates 1.** *Medicine* To remove (a tumor, for example) whole from an enveloping cover or sac. **2.** *Biology* To remove the nucleus of. **3.** *Archaic* To explain; elucidate. ❖ *adj.* (-ĭt, -āt′) *Biology* Lacking a nucleus. [Lat. *ēnucleāre, ēnucleāt-*, to take out the kernel : *ē-, ex-*, ex- + *nucleus*, kernel; see NUCLEUS.] —**e·nu′cle·a′tion** *n.* —**e·nu′cle·a′tor** *n.*

e·nu·mer·a·ble (ĭ-nōō′mər-ə-bəl, ĭ-nyōō′-) *adj.* Capable of being put into one-to-one correspondence with the positive integers; denumerable.

e·nu·mer·ate (ĭ-nōō′mə-rāt′, -nyōō′-) *tr.v.* **-at·ed, -at·ing, -ates 1.** To count off or name one by one; list. **2.** To determine the number of; count. [Lat. *ēnumerāre, ēnumerāt-*, to count out : *ē-, ex-*, ex- + *numerus*, number; see **nem-** in App.] —**e·nu′mer·a′tion** *n.* —**e·nu′mer·a′tive** (-mə-rā′tĭv, -mər-ə-) *adj.* —**e·nu′mer·a′tor** *n.*

e·nun·ci·ate (ĭ-nŭn′sē-āt′) *v.* **-at·ed, -at·ing, -ates** *—tr.* **1.** To pronounce; articulate. **2.** To state or set forth precisely or systematically. **3.** To announce; proclaim. —*intr.* To pronounce words; speak aloud. [Lat. *ēnūntiāre, ēnūntiāt-* : *ē-, ex-,* ex- + *nūntiāre,* to announce (< *nūntius,* messenger).] —**e•nun′ci•a•ble** (-ə-bəl) *adj.* —**e•nun′ci•a′tion** *n.* —**e•nun′ci•a•tive** (-sē-ā′tĭv, -sē-ə-tĭv) *adj.* —**e•nun′ci•a′tive•ly** *adv.* —**e•nun′ci•a′tor** *n.*

en•ure (ĭn-yŏor′) *v.* Variant of **inure.**

en•u•re•sis (ĕn′yə-rē′sĭs) *n.* The involuntary discharge of urine. [NLat. < Gk. *enourein,* to urinate in : *en-,* in; see **EN-²** + *ourein,* to urinate.] —**en′u•ret′ic** (-rĕt′ĭk) *adj.*

en•vel•op (ĕn-vĕl′əp) *tr.v.* **-oped, -op•ing, -ops 1.** To enclose or encase completely with or as if with a covering. **2.** To attack (an enemy's flank). [ME *envolupen,* to be involved in < OFr. *envoluper, envoloper* : *en-,* in; see **EN-¹** + *voloper,* to wrap up.] —**en•vel′op•er** *n.* —**en•vel′op•ment** *n.*

en•ve•lope (ĕn′və-lōp′, ŏn′-) *n.* **1.** A flat paper container, esp. for a letter. **2.** Something that envelops; a wrapping. **3.** *Biology* An enclosing structure or cover, such as a membrane or the outer coat of a virus. **4.** The bag containing the gas in a balloon or airship. **5.** The set of limitations within which a technological system, esp. an aircraft, can perform safely and effectively. **6.** The coma of a comet. **7.** *Mathematics* A curve or surface that is tangent to every one of a family of curves or surfaces. [Fr. *enveloppe* < *envelopper,* to envelop < OFr. *envoloper.* See ENVELOP.]

en•ven•om (ĕn-vĕn′əm) *tr.v.* **-omed, -om•ing, -oms 1.** To make poisonous or noxious. **2.** To embitter. [ME *envenimen,* to poison < OFr. *envenimer* : *en-,* cover with; see **EN-¹** + *venim,* venom; see VENOM.]

en•vi•a•ble (ĕn′vē-ə-bəl) *adj.* So desirable as to arouse envy. —**en′vi•a•bly** *adv.*

en•vi•ous (ĕn′vē-əs) *adj.* **1.** Feeling, expressing, or characterized by envy. See Syns at **jealous. 2.** *Archaic* Eager to emulate; emulous. —**en′vi•ous•ly** *adv.* —**en′vi•ous•ness** *n.*

en•vi•ron (ĕn-vī′rən, -vī′ərn) *tr.v.* **-roned, -ron•ing, -rons** To encircle; surround. [ME *environen* < OFr. *environner* < *environ,* round about : *en-,* in; see **EN-¹** + *viron,* circle (< *virer,* to turn; see VEER¹).]

en•vi•ron•ment (ĕn-vī′rən-mənt, -vī′ərn-) *n.* **1.** The conditions that surround one; surroundings. **2.** The totality of circumstances around an organism or group of organisms, esp.: **a.** The combination of external conditions that affect organisms. **b.** The social and cultural conditions affecting an individual or community.

en•vi•ron•men•tal (ĕn-vī′rən-mĕn′tl, -vī′ərn-) *adj.* **1.** Of or relating to the environment. **2.** Relating to or concerned with the ecological impact of altering the environment. **3.** *Medicine* Of or relating to potentially harmful factors originating in the environment. —**en•vi′ron•men′tal•ly** *adv.*

en•vi•ron•men•tal•ism (ĕn-vī′rən-mĕn′tl-ĭz′əm, -vī′ərn-) *n.* **1.** Advocacy for or work toward protecting the natural environment. **2.** The theory that environment rather than heredity is the primary influence on intellectual growth and cultural development. —**en•vi′ron•men′tal•ist** *n.*

environmental medicine *n.* The study of the effects of environmental exposure to synthetic chemicals on the immune system.

en•vi•rons (ĕn-vī′rənz, -vī′ərnz) *pl.n.* **1.** A surrounding area, esp. of a city. **2.** Surroundings; environment. [Fr. < OFr., pl. of *environ,* circuit < *environ,* round about. See ENVIRON.]

en•vis•age (ĕn-vĭz′ĭj) *tr.v.* **-aged, -ag•ing, -ag•es 1.** To conceive an image of, esp. as a future possibility. **2.** To consider or regard in a certain way. [Fr. *envisager* : OFr. *en-,* in; see **EN-¹** + OFr. *visage,* face; see VISAGE.]

en•vi•sion (ĕn-vĭzh′ən) *tr.v.* **-sioned, -sion•ing, -sions** To picture in the mind; imagine.

en•voy¹ (ĕn′voi′, ŏn′-) *n.* **1.** A representative of a government sent on a diplomatic mission. **2.** A minister plenipotentiary assigned to a foreign embassy, ranking below the ambassador. **3.** A messenger; an agent. [Fr. *envoyé,* messenger < p. part. of *envoyer,* to send < OFr. *envoier* < LLat. *inviāre,* to be on the way : Lat. *in-,* in, on; see **EN-¹** + Lat. *via,* way; see **wegh-** in App.]

en•voy² also **en•voi** (ĕn′voi′, ŏn′-) *n.* **1.** A short closing stanza in certain verse forms, such as the ballade or sestina. **2.** The concluding portion of a prose work or a play. [ME *envoie* < OFr. < *envoier,* to send. See ENVOY¹.]

en•vy (ĕn′vē) *n., pl.* **-vies 1a.** A feeling of discontent and resentment aroused by desire for the possessions or qualities of another. **b.** The object of such feeling. **2.** *Obsolete* Malevolence. ❖ *tr.v.* **-vied, -vy•ing, -vies 1.** To feel envy toward. **2.** To regard with envy. [ME *envie* < OFr. < Lat. *invidia* < *invidus,* envious < *invidēre,* to envy : *in-,* in, on; see **EN-¹** + *vidēre,* to see; see **weid-** in App.] —**en′vi•er** *n.*

SYNONYMS *envy, begrudge, covet* These verbs mean to feel resentful or painful desire for another's advantages or possessions. *Envy,* the most general, combines discontent, resentment, and desire: *"When I peruse . . . the victories of mighty generals, I do not envy the generals"* (Walt Whitman). *Begrudge* stresses ill will and reluctance to acknowledge another's right or claim: *begrudged him success. Covet* stresses a secret or culpable longing for something to which one has no right: *"We hate no people and covet no people's lands"* (Wendell L. Willkie).

---

en•wind (ĕn-wīnd′) *tr.v.* **-wound** (-wound′), **-wind•ing,**

-winds To wind around or about.

en•womb (ĕn-wŏom′) *tr.v.* **-wombed, -womb•ing, -wombs** To enclose in or as if in a womb.

en•wrap (ĕn-răp′) *tr.v.* **-wrapped, -wrap•ping, -wraps 1a.** To wrap up; enclose. **b.** To envelop. **2.** To absorb completely; engross.

en•wreathe (ĕn-rēth′) *tr.v.* **-wreathed, -wreath•ing, -wreathes** To surround with or as if with a wreath.

en•zo•ot•ic (ĕn′zō-ŏt′ĭk) *adj.* Affecting or peculiar to animals of a specific geographic area. Used of a disease. ❖ *n.* An enzootic disease. [**EN-²** + ZO(O)- + -OTIC.]

en•zyme (ĕn′zīm) *n.* Any of numerous proteins or conjugated proteins produced by living organisms and functioning as biochemical catalysts. [Ger. *Enzym* < Med.Gk. *enzūmos,* leavened : Gk. *en-,* in; see **EN-²** + Gk. *zūmē,* leaven, yeast.] —**en′zy•mat′ic** (-zə-măt′ĭk), **en•zy′mic** (-zī′mĭk, -zĭm′ĭk) *adj.* —**en′zy•mat′i•cal•ly, en•zy′mi•cal•ly** *adv.*

en•zy•mol•o•gy (ĕn′zə-mŏl′ə-jē) *n.* The branch of science that deals with enzymes. —**en′zy•mol′o•gist** *n.*

EO *abbr.* executive order

e.o. *abbr. Latin* ex officio (by virtue of office)

eo- *pref.* Most primitive; earliest: *eohippus.* [< Gk. *ēōs,* dawn. See **aus-** in App.]

E•o•cene (ē′ə-sēn′) *adj.* Of or belonging to the geologic time of the second epoch of the Tertiary Period, characterized by the rise of mammals. See table at **geologic time.** ❖ *n.* The Eocene Epoch or its deposits.

EOE *abbr.* equal opportunity employer

e•o•hip•pus (ē′ō-hĭp′əs) *n.* Hyracotherium. [NLat. : EO- + Gk. *hippos,* horse; see **ekwo-** in App.]

e•o•li•an also **ae•o•li•an** (ē-ō′lē-ən, ē-ōl′yən) *adj.* Relating to, caused by, or carried by the wind. [< AEOLUS.]

e•o•lith (ē′ə-lĭth′) *n.* A crude stone artifact, such as a flake.

E•o•lith•ic (ē′ə-lĭth′ĭk) *adj.* Of or relating to the postulated earliest period of human culture preceding the Lower Paleolithic. Not in scientific use.

E•o•lus (ē-ō′ləs), **Mount** A peak, 4,295.3 m (14,083 ft), in the San Juan Mts. of SW CO.

EOM *abbr.* end of month

e•on also **ae•on** (ē′ŏn′, ē′ən) *n.* **1.** An indefinitely long period of time; an age. **2.** The longest division of geologic time, containing two or more eras. [LLat. *aeōn* < Gk. *aiōn.* See **aiw-** in App.]

e•o•ni•an also **ae•o•ni•an** (ē-ō′nē-ən) *adj.* Of, relating to, or constituting an eon.

E•os (ē′ŏs′) *n. Greek Mythology* The goddess of the dawn. [Gk. *Ēōs* < *ēōs,* dawn. See **aus-** in App.]

e•o•sin (ē′ə-sən) *n.* **1.** A red crystalline powder, $C_{20}H_8O_5Br_4$, used in textile dyeing and ink manufacturing. **2.** The red sodium or potassium salt of this powder, used in biology to stain cells. [Gk. *ēōs,* dawn (< its color); see **aus-** in App. + -IN.]

e•o•sin•o•phil (ē′ə-sĭn′ə-fĭl′) also **e•o•sin•o•phile** (-fīl′) *n.* **1.** A type of white blood cell containing cytoplasmic granules easily stained by eosin or other acid dyes. **2.** A microorganism, cell, or histological element easily stained by eosin or other acid dyes. —**e′o•sin′o•phil′, e′o•sin′o•phil′ic, e′o•si•noph′i•lous** (ē′ə-sī-nŏf′ə-ləs) *adj.*

e•o•sin•o•phil•i•a (ē′ə-sĭn′ə-fĭl′ē-ə) *n.* An increase in the number of eosinophils in the blood.

-eous *suff.* Having the nature of; resembling: *gaseous.* [ME < OFr. *-eux, -eus* (< Lat. *-ōsus*) and < Lat. *-eus.*]

Ep *abbr. Bible* Ephesians

EP *abbr.* **1.** European plan **2.** extended play

ep- *pref.* Variant of **epi-.**

EPA *abbr.* **1.** eicosapentaenoic acid **2.** Environmental Protection Agency

e•pact (ē′păkt′) *n.* The period of time necessary to bring the solar calendar into harmony with the lunar calendar. [Fr. *épacte* < LLat. *epacta* < Gk. *epaktē* (*hēmera*), intercalary (day), fem. of *epaktos,* brought in, inserted < *epagein,* to bring in, introduce : *ep-, epi-,* epi- + *agein,* to lead; see **ag-** in App.]

ep•arch (ĕp′ärk′) *n. Eastern Orthodox Church* A bishop or metropolitan. [Med.Gk. *eparkhos* < Gk., governor, ruler < *eparkhein,* to rule over : *ep-, epi-,* epi- + *arkhein,* to rule.]

ep•ar•chy (ĕp′är′kē) *n., pl.* **-chies** A diocese of an Eastern Orthodox Church. [Gk. *eparkhiā,* provincial government < *eparkhein,* to rule over : *ep-, epi-,* epi- + *arkhein,* to rule.]

ep•au•let also **ep•au•lette** (ĕp′ə-lĕt′, ĕp′ə-lĕt′) *n.* A shoulder ornament, esp. a fringed strap worn on military uniforms. [Fr. *épaulette,* dim. of *épaule,* shoulder < OFr. *espaule* < LLat. *spatula,* shoulder blade. See ESPALIER.]

ep•a•zo•te (ĕp′ə-zō′tē) *n.* **1.** See wormseed 1. **2.** The pungent leaves of the wormseed plant, used as a seasoning in Mexican cooking. [Am.Sp. < Nahuatl *epazotl* : *epatl,* skunk + *tzotl,* filth (< its smell).]

é•pée also **e•pee** (ā-pā′, ĕp′ā) *n.* **1.** A fencing sword with a bowl-shaped guard and a long narrow fluted blade with no cutting edge and a blunted point. **2.** The art or sport of fencing with an épée. [Fr. < OFr. *espee* < Lat. *spatha,* broad double-edged sword. See SPATHE.] —**é•pée′ist** *n.*

ep•ei•rog•e•ny (ĕp′ī-rŏj′ə-nē) *n., pl.* **-nies** Uplift or depression of the earth's crust, affecting large land areas or ocean bottom.

epaulet

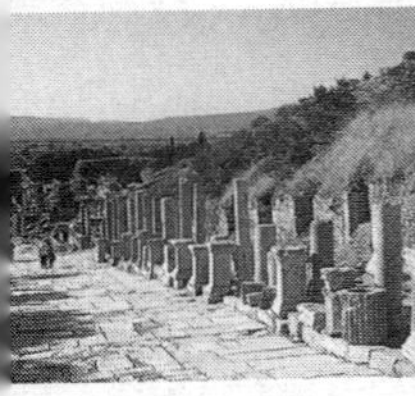

Ephesus
the Curetes Way

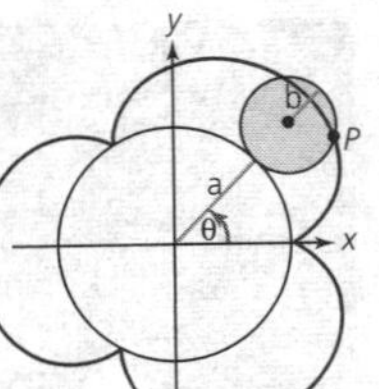

epicycloid
The parametric equations of a three-cusped epicycloid are:

$$x = (a + b)\cos\theta - b\cos\frac{a+b}{b}\theta,$$

$$y = (a + b)\sin\theta - b\sin\frac{a+b}{b}\theta.$$

[Gk. *ēpeiros*, continent + –GENY.] **—e•pei′ro•gen′ic** (ĭ-pī′rō-jĕn′ĭk) *adj.* **—e•pei′ro•gen′i•cal•ly** *adv.*

e•pen•the•sis (ĭ-pĕn′thĭ-sĭs) *n., pl.* **-ses** (-sēz′) The insertion of a sound in the middle of a word. [LLat. < Gk. < *epentithenai*, to insert : *ep-*, *epi-*, epi- + *en-*, in; see EN–² + *tithenai*, to place; see **dhē-** in App.] **—ep′en•thet′ic** (ĕp′ĭn-thĕt′ĭk) *adj.*

e•pergne (ĭ-pûrn′, ā-pârn′) *n.* A large table centerpiece consisting of a frame with extended arms or branches supporting holders, as for flowers. [Perh. alteration of Fr. *épargne*, a saving < *épargner*, to save < OFr. *espargnier*, of Gmc. orig.]

ep•ex•e•ge•sis (ĕp-ĕk′sə-jē′sĭs) *n.* Additional explanation or explanatory material. [Gk. *epexēgēsis* < *epexēgeisthai*, to explain in detail : *ep-*, *epi-*, epi- + *exēgeisthai*, to explain; see EXEGESIS.] **—ep•ex′e•get′ic** (-jĕt′ĭk), **ep•ex′e•get′i•cal** *adj.*

Eph. *abbr. Bible* Ephesians

e•phah also **e•pha** (ē′fə, ĕf′ä) *n.* An ancient Hebrew unit of dry measure, equal to a tenth of a homer or about one bushel (35 liters). [Heb. *'êpâ*, prob. < Egypt. *'pt.*]

e•phebe (ĕf′ēb′, ĭ-fēb′) also **e•phe•bus** (ĭ-fē′bəs) *n., pl.* **e•phebes** also **e•phe•bi** (ĭ-fē′bī) A youth between 18 and 20 in ancient Greece. [Lat. *ephēbus* < Gk. *ephēbos* : *ep-*, *epi-*, epi- + *hēbē*, early manhood.] **—e•phe′bic** *adj.*

e•phed•ra (ĭ-fĕd′rə, ĕf′ĭ-drə) *n.* **1.** Any of various plants of the genus *Ephedra*, some of which are used as a source of ephedrine. **2.** A stimulant derived from a plant of this genus. [Lat. *ephedra*, horsetail < Gk. *ephedrā* < fem. of *ephedros*, sitting upon : *ep-*, *epi-*, epi- + *hedrā*, seat; see **sed-** in App.]

e•phed•rine (ĭ-fĕd′rĭn, ĕf′ĭ-drēn′) *n.* An odorless powdered or crystalline alkaloid, $C_{10}H_{15}NO$, used to treat allergies and asthma. [Lat. *ephedra*, horsetail; see EPHEDRA + –INE².]

e•phem•er•al (ĭ-fĕm′ər-əl) *adj.* **1.** Lasting for a markedly brief time. **2.** Living or lasting only for a day. ❖ *n.* A markedly short-lived thing. [< Gk. *ephēmeros* : *ep-*, *epi-*, epi- + *hēmerā*, day.] **—e•phem′er•al′i•ty** *n.* **—e•phem′er•al•ly** *adv.*

e•phem•er•id (ĭ-fĕm′ər-ĭd) *n.* An insect of the order Ephemeroptera; a mayfly. [< NLat. *Ephēmeridae*, former order name < Gk. *ephēmeron*, mayfly. See EPHEMERON.]

e•phem•er•is (ĭ-fĕm′ər-ĭs) *n., pl.* **eph•e•mer•i•des** (ĕf′ə-mĕr′ə-dēz′) A table giving the coordinates of a celestial body at a number of specific times during a given period. [LLat. *ephēmeris* < Gk., diary < *ephēmeros*, daily. See EPHEMERAL.]

ephemeris time *n.* A system for the measurement of time based on the orbital positions of the earth, moon, and planets.

e•phem•er•on (ĭ-fĕm′ə-rŏn′) *n., pl.* **-er•a** (-ər-ə) or **-er•ons 1.** A short-lived thing. **2. ephemera** Printed matter of passing interest. [Gk. *ephēmeron*, mayfly < neut. of *ephēmeros*, daily, short-lived. See EPHEMERAL.]

E•phe•sian (ĭ-fē′zhən) *n.* **1.** A native or inhabitant of Ephesus. **2. Ephesians** (*used with a sing. verb*) See table at **Bible.** [< Lat. *Ephesiī*, inhabitants of Ephesus < Gk. *Ephesioi* < *Ephesos*, Ephesus.] **—E•phe′sian** *adj.*

Eph•e•sus (ĕf′ĭ-səs) An ancient city of Greek Asia Minor in W Turkey. Its temple, dedicated to Artemis, or in Roman times Diana, was one of the Seven Wonders of the World.

eph•od (ĕf′ŏd′, ē′fŏd′) *n.* An upper garment of the ancient Hebrew high priest. [ME < LLat. < Heb. *'ēpôd.*]

eph•or (ĕf′ôr′, -ər) *n., pl.* **-ors** or **-o•ri** (-ə-rī′) One of a body of five elected magistrates exercising supervisory power over the kings of Sparta. [Lat. *ephorus* < Gk. *ephoros* < *ephorān*, to oversee : *ep-*, *epi-*, epi- + *horān*, to see.] **—eph′or•ate′** (-ə-rāt′, -ə-rĭt) *n.*

epi- or **ep-** *pref.* **1.** On; upon: *epiphyte.* **2.** Over; above: *epicenter.* **3.** Around: *epicarp.* **4.** Close to; near: *epicalyx.* **5.** Besides: *epiphenomenon.* **6.** After: *epilogue.* [Gk. < *epi*, upon. See **epi** in App.]

ep•i•blast (ĕp′ə-blăst′) *n.* The outer layer of a blastula that gives rise to the ectoderm after gastrulation. **—ep′i•blas′tic** *adj.*

e•pib•o•ly (ĭ-pĭb′ə-lē) *n.* The growth of a rapidly dividing group of cells around a more slowly dividing group of cells, as in the formation of a gastrula. [Gk. *epibolē*, a laying on < *epiballein*, to throw on : *epi-*, epi- + *ballein*, to throw; see **gʷelə-** in App.] **—ep′i•bol′ic** (ĕp′ə-bŏl′ĭk) *adj.*

ep•ic (ĕp′ĭk) *n.* **1.** An extended narrative poem in elevated or dignified language, celebrating the feats of a legendary or traditional hero. **2.** A literary or dramatic composition resembling an epic. **3.** A series of events considered appropriate to an epic. ❖ *adj.* **1.** Of, constituting, or suggestive of a literary epic. **2.** Surpassing the usual or ordinary, esp. in scope or size. **3.** Heroic and impressive in quality. [< Lat. *epicus* < Gk. *epikos* < *epos*, word, song. See **wekʷ-** in App.] **—ep′i•cal•ly** *adv.*

ep•i•ca•lyx (ĕp′ĭ-kā′lĭks, -kăl′ĭks) *n., pl.* **-ca•lyx•es** or **-ca•ly•ces** (-kā′lĭ-sēz′, -kăl′ĭ-) A series of bracts subtending and resembling a calyx, as in the carnation.

ep•i•can•thic fold (ĕp′ĭ-kăn′thĭk) *n.* A fold of skin of the upper eyelid that partially covers the inner corner of the eye.

ep•i•can•thus (ĕp′ĭ-kăn′thəs) *n., pl.* **-thi** (-thī, -thē) See **epicanthic fold.** [NLat. : EPI– + CANTHUS.]

ep•i•car•di•um (ĕp′ĭ-kär′dē-əm) *n., pl.* **-di•a** (-dē-ə) The inner layer of the pericardium that is in actual contact with the surface of the heart. [NLat. : EPI– + Gk. *kardiā*, heart; see **kerd-** in App.] **—ep′i•car′di•al** *adj.*

ep•i•carp (ĕp′ĭ-kärp′) *n.* See **exocarp.**

ep•i•cene (ĕp′ĭ-sēn′) *adj.* **1.** Belonging to or resembling both the male and the female. **2.** Effeminate; unmanly. **3.** Sexless; neuter. **4.** *Linguistics* Having a single noun form for both the male and the female. ❖ *n.* **1.** One that is epicene. **2.** *Linguistics* An epicene word. [ME, having one noun form for either gender < Lat. *epicoenus* < Gk. *epikoinos*, in common : *epi-*, epi- + *koinos*, common; see **kom** in App.] **—ep′i•cen′ism** *n.*

ep•i•cen•ter (ĕp′ĭ-sĕn′tər) *n.* **1.** The point of the earth's surface directly above the focus of an earthquake. **2.** A focal point: *at the epicenter of the crisis.* **—ep′i•cen′tral** *adj.*

ep•i•chlo•ro•hy•drin (ĕp′ĭ-klôr′ə-hī′drĭn, -klōr′-) *n.* A colorless liquid, C_3H_5OCl, used as a solvent in making resins.

ep•i•con•dyle (ĕp′ĭ-kŏn′dīl, -dl) *n.* A rounded projection at the end of a bone, located on or above a condyle and usu. serving as a place of attachment for ligaments and tendons.

ep•i•cot•yl (ĕp′ĭ-kŏt′l) *n.* The stem of a seedling or embryo located between the cotyledons and the first true leaves.

ep•i•crit•ic (ĕp′ĭ-krĭt′ĭk) *adj.* Of or relating to sensory nerve fibers that enable the perception of slight differences in the intensity of stimuli, esp. touch or temperature. [Gk. *epikritikos*, decisive < *epikritēs*, decider < *epikrīnein*, to decide : *epi-*, epi- + *krīnein*, to judge; see **krei-** in App.]

epic simile *n.* An extended simile elaborated in great detail.

Ep•ic•te•tus (ĕp′ĭk-tē′təs) A.D. 55?–135? Phrygian-born Stoic philosopher who believed that one should act in life as one would at a banquet, by taking a polite portion of all that is offered.

ep•i•cure (ĕp′ĭ-kyo͝or′) *n.* **1.** A person with refined taste, esp. in food and wine. **2.** A person devoted to sensuous pleasure and luxurious living. See Usage Note at **gourmet.** [ME, an Epicurean < Med.Lat. *epicūrus* < Lat. *Epicūrus*, Epicurus < Gk. *Epikouros.*]

ep•i•cu•re•an (ĕp′ĭ-kyo͝o-rē′ən, -kyo͝or′ē-) *adj.* **1.** Devoted to the pursuit of pleasure, esp. to the enjoyment of good food and comfort. **2.** Suited to an epicure's tastes. **3. Epicurean** Of or relating to Epicurus or Epicureanism. ❖ *n.* **1.** A devotee of epicurean living; an epicure. **2. Epicurean** A follower of Epicurus. [ME *Epicurien* < *Epicure.* See EPICURE.]

Ep•i•cu•re•an•ism (ĕp′ĭ-kyo͝o-rē′ə-nĭz′əm, -kyo͝or′ē-) *n.* **1.** The philosophy of Epicurus that considered happiness or the avoidance of pain to be the highest good. **2.** also **epicureanism** Devotion to a life of pleasure and luxury.

ep•i•cur•ism (ĕp′ĭ-kyo͝o-rĭz′əm, ĕp′ĭ-kyo͝or′ĭz-əm) *n.* The beliefs, tastes, or lifestyle of an epicure.

Ep•i•cu•rus (ĕp′ĭ-kyo͝or′əs) 341?–270 B.C. Greek philosopher who founded the school of Epicureanism in c. 306.

ep•i•cu•ti•cle (ĕp′ĭ-kyo͞o′tĭ-kəl) *n.* The outermost layer of cuticle of an arthropod exoskeleton, composed mostly of wax.

ep•i•cy•cle (ĕp′ĭ-sī′kəl) *n.* **1.** In Ptolemaic cosmology, a small circle, the center of which moves on the circumference of a larger circle at whose center is the earth and the circumference of which describes the orbit of a planet. **2.** *Mathematics* A circle whose circumference rolls along the circumference of a fixed circle. [ME *epicicle* < LLat. *epicyclus* < Gk. *epikuklos* : *epi-*, epi- + *kuklos*, circle; see **kʷel-**¹ in App.] **—ep′i•cy′clic** (-sī′klĭk, -sĭk′lĭk) *adj.*

epicyclic train *n.* A system of gears in which at least one rotating gear revolves about another.

ep•i•cy•cloid (ĕp′ĭ-sī′kloid′) *n.* *Mathematics* The curve described by a point on the circumference of an epicycle. **—ep′i•cy•cloid′al** (-kloid′l) *adj.*

Ep•i•dau•rus (ĕp′ĭ-dôr′əs) An ancient city of Greece on the NE coast of the Peloponnesus.

ep•i•dem•ic (ĕp′ĭ-dĕm′ĭk) also **ep•i•dem•i•cal** (-ĭ-kəl) *adj.* **1.** Spreading rapidly and extensively by infection and affecting many individuals at the same time. **2.** Widely prevalent. ❖ *n.* **1.** An outbreak of an epidemic disease. **2.** A rapid spread, growth, or development. [Fr. *épidémique*, ult. < Gk. *epidēmiā*, prevalence of an epidemic disease < *epidēmos*, prevalent : *epi-*, epi- + *dēmos*, people; see **dā-** in App.] **—ep′i•dem′i•cal•ly** *adv.*

ep•i•de•mi•ol•o•gy (ĕp′ĭ-dē′mē-ŏl′ə-jē, -dĕm′ē-) *n.* The branch of medicine that deals with the causes, distribution, and control of disease in populations. [Med.Lat. *epidēmia*, an epidemic; see EPIDEMIC + –LOGY.] **—ep′i•de′mi•o•log′ic** (-ə-lŏj′ĭk), **ep′i•de′mi•o•log′i•cal** (-ĭ-kəl) *adj.* **—ep′i•de′mi•o•log′i•cal•ly** *adv.* **—ep′i•de′mi•ol′o•gist** *n.*

ep•i•der•mis (ĕp′ĭ-dûr′mĭs) *n.* **1.** The outer protective nonvascular layer of the skin of vertebrates, covering the dermis. **2.** An integument or outer layer of various invertebrates. **3.** The outermost layer of cells covering the leaves and young parts of a plant. [LLat. < Gk. : *epi-*, epi- + *derma*, skin.] **—ep′i•der′mal** (-məl), **ep′i•der′mic** *adj.*

ep•i•der•moid (ĕp′ĭ-dûr′moid′) *adj.* Composed of or resembling epidermal tissue: *epidermoid carcinoma.*

ep•i•di•a•scope (ĕp′ĭ-dī′ə-skōp′) *n.* A machine for projecting the images of opaque objects or transparencies on a screen. [EPI– + DIA– + –SCOPE.]

ep•i•did•y•mis (ĕp′ĭ-dĭd′ə-mĭs) *n., pl.* **-mi•des** (-mĭ-dēz′) A long narrow convoluted tube that lies on the posterior aspect of each testicle, connecting it to the vas deferens. [Gk. *epididumis* : *epi-*, epi- + *didumoi*, twins, testicles < pl. of *didumos*, double; see **dwo-** in App.] **—ep′i•did′y•mal** *adj.*

ep•i•dote (ĕp′ĭ-dōt′) *n.* A lustrous yellow, green, or black mineral, $Ca_2(Al, Fe)_3(SiO_4)_3OH$, found in metamorphic rock. [Fr. *épi-*

dote < Gk. *epididonai*, to increase (< the shape of its crystalline structure) : *epi-*, epi- + *didonai*, to give; see **dō-** in App.] —**ep'i·dot'ic** (-dŏt'ĭk) *adj.*

ep·i·du·ral (ĕp'ĭ-dŏŏr'əl, -dyŏŏr'-) *adj.* Located on or over the dura mater. ❖ *n.* An injection into the epidural space of the spine, as an anesthetic to control pain during childbirth.

ep·i·gas·tri·um (ĕp'ĭ-găs'trē-əm) *n., pl.* **-tri·a** (-trē-ə) The upper middle region of the abdomen. [NLat. < Gk. *epigastrion* < neut. of *epigastrios*, over the belly : *epi-*, epi- + *gastēr*, *gastr-*, stomach.] —**ep'i·gas'tric** (-trĭk) *adj.*

ep·i·ge·al (ĕp'ə-jē'əl) also **ep·i·ge·an** (-ən) or **ep·i·ge·ous** (-əs) *adj.* 1. *Biology* Living or occurring on or near the surface of the ground. 2. *Botany* Of or relating to the emergence of cotyledons above the surface of the ground after germination. [< Gk. *epigeios*, on the earth : *epi-*, epi- + *gē*, earth.]

ep·i·gene (ĕp'ə-jēn') *adj.* Formed, originating, or occurring on or just below the surface of the earth. [Fr. *épigène* < Gk. *epigenēs*, growing after : *epi-*, epi- + *-genēs*, -born; see **genə-** in App.]

ep·i·gen·e·sis (ĕp'ə-jĕn'ĭ-sĭs) *n.* 1. *Biology* The theory that an individual is developed by successive differentiation of an unstructured egg rather than by a simple enlarging of a preformed entity. 2. *Geology* Change in the mineral content of a rock because of outside influences. —**ep'i·ge·net'ic** (-jə-nĕt'ĭk) *adj.*

e·pig·e·nous (ĭ-pĭj'ə-nəs) *adj. Botany* Developing or growing on an upper surface, as fungi on leaves.

ep·i·glot·tis (ĕp'ĭ-glŏt'ĭs) *n., pl.* **-glot·tis·es** or **-glot·ti·des** (-glŏt'ĭ-dēz') The thin cartilaginous structure that folds over the glottis to keep food and liquid from the trachea. [Gk. *epiglōttis* : *epi-*, epi- + *glōttis*, glottis; see GLOTTIS.] —**ep'i·glot'tic** (-glŏt'ĭk) *adj.*

ep·i·gone (ĕp'ĭ-gōn') *n.* A second-rate imitator or follower, esp. of an artist or a philosopher. [Fr. *épigone*, sing. of *épigones* < Gk. *Epigonoi*, sons of the seven heroes against Thebes < pl. of *epigonos*, born after : *epi-*, epi- + *gonos*, child, seed; see **genə-** in App.] —**ep'i·gon'ic** (-gŏn'ĭk) *adj.* —**e·pig'o·nism** (ĭ-pĭg'ə-nĭz'əm) *n.*

ep·i·gram (ĕp'ĭ-grăm') *n.* 1. A short witty poem expressing a single thought or observation. 2. A concise, clever, often paradoxical statement. 3. Epigrammatic discourse or expression. [ME < OFr. *epigramme* < Lat. *epigramma* < Gk. < *epigraphein*, to mark the surface, inscribe : *epi-*, epi- + *graphein*, to write; see **gerbh-** in App.]

ep·i·gram·mat·ic (ĕp'ĭ-grə-măt'ĭk) also **ep·i·gram·mat·i·cal** (-ĭ-kəl) *adj.* 1. Of or having the nature of an epigram. 2. Containing or given to the use of epigrams. [Lat. *epigrammaticus* < Gk. *epigramma*, *epigrammat-*, epigram. See EPIGRAM.] —**ep'i·gram·mat'i·cal·ly** *adv.*

ep·i·gram·ma·tism (ĕp'ĭ-grăm'ə-tĭz'əm) *n.* Literary style marked by the use of epigrams. —**ep'i·gram'ma·tist** *n.*

ep·i·gram·ma·tize (ĕp'ĭ-grăm'ə-tīz') *v.* **-tized, -tiz·ing, -tiz·es** —*tr.* To express in an epigram. —*intr.* To create an epigram.

ep·i·graph (ĕp'ĭ-grăf') *n.* 1. An inscription, as on a statue. 2. A motto or quotation, as at the beginning of a literary composition, setting forth a theme. [Gk. *epigraphē* < *epigraphein*, to write on. See EPIGRAM.] —**ep'i·graph'ic, ep'i·graph'i·cal** *adj.* —**ep'i·graph'i·cal·ly** *adv.*

e·pig·ra·phy (ĭ-pĭg'rə-fē) *n.* 1. Inscriptions considered as a group. 2a. The study of inscriptions. b. Decipherment, esp. of ancient inscriptions. —**e·pig'ra·pher, e·pig'ra·phist** *n.*

e·pig·y·nous (ĭ-pĭj'ə-nəs) *adj.* Having floral parts attached to or near the summit of the ovary. —**e·pig'y·ny** (-nē) *n.*

ep·i·lep·sy (ĕp'ə-lĕp'sē) *n., pl.* **-sies** Any of various neurological disorders characterized by sudden recurring attacks of motor, sensory, or psychic malfunction with or without loss of consciousness or convulsive seizures. [Fr. *épilepsie* < Lat. *epilepsia* < Gk. *epilēpsis* < *epilambanein*, to lay hold of : *epi-*, epi- + *lambanein*, *lēp-*, to seize.]

ep·i·lep·tic (ĕp'ə-lĕp'tĭk) *adj.* 1. Affected with epilepsy. 2. Of, relating to, or associated with epilepsy. ❖ *n.* One who has epilepsy. [Fr. *épileptique* < LLat. *epilēpticus* < Gk. *epilēptikos* < *epilēpsis*, epilepsy. See EPILEPSY.]

ep·i·lep·to·gen·ic (ĕp'ə-lĕp'tə-jĕn'ĭk) *adj.* Having the capacity to induce epilepsy.

ep·i·lep·toid (ĕp'ə-lĕp'toid') *adj.* Resembling epilepsy. [EPILEPT(IC) + -OID.]

ep·i·logue also **ep·i·log** (ĕp'ə-lôg', -lŏg') *n.* 1a. A short poem or speech spoken directly to the audience at the end of a play. b. The performer who delivers an epilogue. 2. A short section at the end of a literary or dramatic work, often discussing the future of its characters. [ME *epiloge* < OFr. *epilogue* < Lat. *epilogus* < Gk. *epilogos*, conclusion of a speech : *epi-*, epi- + *logos*, word, speech; see **leg-** in App.]

Epimetheus *n.* 1. *Greek Mythology* A Titan, husband of Pandora, who together with his brother Prometheus took part in the creation of the human race. 2. A satellite of Saturn. [Gk. *Epimētheus* < *epimētheus*, afterthought (because after bestowing a special quality on each animal he had none left to give to humans), modeled on *Promētheus*, Prometheus (folk-etymologized by the Greeks as *promētheus*, forethought).]

ep·i·mys·i·um (ĕp'ə-mĭz'ē-əm, -mĭzh'ē-) *n., pl.* **-mys·i·a** (-mĭz'ē-ə, -mĭzh'-) The external sheath of connective tissue surrounding a muscle. [NLat. *epimȳsium* : EPI- + Gk. *mūs*, muscle; see **mūs-** in App.]

ep·i·nas·ty (ĕp'ə-năs'tē) *n., pl.* **-ties** A downward bending of leaves or other plant parts, resulting from excessive growth of the upper side. [EPI- + -NASTY.] —**ep'i·nas'tic** (-tĭk) *adj.*

ep·i·neph·rine also **ep·i·neph·rin** (ĕp'ə-nĕf'rĭn) *n.* 1. A hormone secreted by the adrenal medulla in response to physical or mental stress, as from fear, initiating many bodily responses, including an increase in heart rate and blood pressure. 2. A crystalline compound, $C_9H_{13}NO_3$, isolated from the adrenal glands of certain mammals or synthesized and used in medicine as a heart stimulant, vasoconstrictor, and bronchial relaxant. [EPI- + NEPHR(O)- + -INE².]

ep·i·neu·ri·um (ĕp'ə-nŏŏr'ē-əm, -nyŏŏr'-) *n., pl.* **-neu·ri·a** (-nŏŏr'ē-ə, -nyŏŏr'-) The thick sheath of connective tissue surrounding a nerve trunk. [NLat. : EPI- + Gk. *neuron*, nerve, tendon; see NEURON.] —**ep'i·neu'ri·al** *adj.*

ep·i·pe·lag·ic (ĕp'ə-pə-lăj'ĭk) *adj.* Of or relating to the part of the ocean into which enough sunlight enters for photosynthesis to take place.

e·pi·pet·al·ous (ĕp'ə-pĕt'l-əs) *adj.* Borne on or attached to the petals or corolla, as the stamens of the petunia.

e·piph·a·ny (ĭ-pĭf'ə-nē) *n., pl.* **-nies** 1. **Epiphany** A Christian feast celebrating the manifestation of the divine nature of Jesus to the Gentiles as represented by the Magi, traditionally observed on January 6. 2. A revelatory manifestation of a divine being. 3a. A sudden manifestation of the essence or meaning of something. b. A comprehension or perception of reality by means of a sudden intuitive realization. [ME *epiphanie* < OFr. < LLat. *epiphania*, manifestation < Gk. *epiphaneia* < *epiphainesthai*, to appear : *epi-*, forth; see EPI- + *phainein*, *phan-*, to show.] —**ep'i·phan'ic** (ĕp'ə-făn'ĭk) *adj.*

ep·i·phe·nom·e·nal·ism (ĕp'ə-fĭ-nŏm'ə-nə-lĭz'əm) *n. Philosophy* The doctrine holding that mental activities are simply epiphenomena of the neural processes of the brain.

ep·i·phe·nom·e·non (ĕp'ə-fĭ-nŏm'ə-nŏn') *n., pl.* **-na** (-nə) 1. A secondary phenomenon that results from and accompanies another. 2. *Pathology* An additional though not necessarily connected condition or symptom in the course of a disease. —**ep'i·phe·nom'e·nal** *adj.*

e·piph·y·sis (ĭ-pĭf'ĭ-sĭs) *n., pl.* **-ses** (-sēz') 1. The end of a long bone that is originally separated from the main shaft by cartilage and later unites to the main shaft through ossification. 2. See **pineal gland.** [Gk. *epiphusis*, an excrescence : *epi-*, epi- + *phusis*, growth; see **bheuə-** in App.] —**ep'i·phys'i·al** (ĕp'ə-fĭz'ē-əl), **ep'i·phys'e·al** *adj.*

ep·i·phyte (ĕp'ə-fīt') *n.* A plant that depends on another plant for mechanical support but not for nutrients. —**ep'i·phyt'ic** (-fĭt'ĭk), **ep'i·phyt'i·cal** *adj.*

ep·i·phy·tot·ic (ĕp'ə-fī-tŏt'ĭk) *adj.* Of, relating to, or characterized by a sudden or abnormally destructive, often widespread outbreak of a plant disease. —**ep'i·phy·tot'ic** *n.*

E·pi·rus (ĭ-pī'rəs) An ancient country on the Ionian Sea in present-day NW Greece and S Albania.

Epis. *abbr.* 1. Episcopal 2. Episcopalian 3. or **Epist.** Epistle

e·pis·co·pa·cy (ĭ-pĭs'kə-pə-sē) *n., pl.* **-cies** 1. See **episcopate** 3. 2. A system of church government in which bishops are the chief clerics. [< EPISCOPATE.]

e·pis·co·pal (ĭ-pĭs'kə-pəl) *adj.* 1. Of or relating to a bishop. 2. Of or relating to church government by bishops. 3. **Episcopal** Of or relating to the Episcopal Church. [ME < LLat. *episcopālis* < *episcopus*, bishop. See BISHOP.] —**e·pis'co·pal·ly** *adv.*

Episcopal Church *n.* The church in the United States that is in communion with the see of Canterbury.

E·pis·co·pa·lian (ĭ-pĭs'kə-pāl'ē-ən, -pāl'yən) *adj.* 1. Of, relating to, or belonging to the Episcopal Church. 2. **episcopalian** Of or advocating church government by bishops. —**E·pis'co·pa'lian** *n.*

e·pis·co·pate (ĭ-pĭs'kə-pĭt, -pāt') *n.* 1. The position, term, or office of a bishop. 2. The area of jurisdiction of a bishop; a diocese. 3. Bishops considered as a group. [LLat. *episcopātus* < *episcopus*, bishop. See BISHOP.]

e·pis·i·ot·o·my (ĭ-pĭz'ē-ŏt'ə-mē, ĭ-pē'zē-) *n., pl.* **-mies** Surgical incision of the perineum during childbirth to facilitate delivery. [Gk. *epision*, pubic region + -TOMY.]

ep·i·sode (ĕp'ĭ-sōd') *n.* 1a. An incident or event that is part of a progression or a larger sequence. b. One of a series of related events in the course of a continuous account. See Syns at **occurrence.** 2. A portion of a narrative that relates an event or a series of connected events and forms a coherent story in itself; an incident. 3a. A separate part of a serialized work, such as a novel. b. A separate program that is part of a television or radio series. 4. A section of a classic Greek tragedy that occurs between two choric songs. 5. *Music* A passage between statements of a main subject or theme, as in a fugue. [Fr. *épisode* < Gk. *epeisodion*, parenthetic narrative < neut. of *epeisodios*, coming in besides : *epi-*, epi- + *eisodios*, entering (*eis*, into; see **en** in App. + *hodos*, way, journey).]

ep·i·sod·ic (ĕp'ĭ-sŏd'ĭk) also **ep·i·sod·i·cal** (-ĭ-kəl) *adj.* 1. Relating to or resembling an episode. 2. Composed of a series of episodes: *an episodic novel.* 3. Limited to the duration of an episode; temporary. —**ep'i·sod'i·cal·ly** *adv.*

ă	pat	oi	boy
ā	pay	ou	out
âr	care	ŏŏ	took
ä	father	ōō	boot
ĕ	pet	ŭ	cut
ē	be	ûr	urge
ĭ	pit	th	thin
ī	pie	th	this
îr	pier	hw	which
ŏ	pot	zh	vision
ō	toe	ə	about,
ô	paw		item

Stress marks:
' (primary);
' (secondary), as in
lexicon (lĕk'sĭ-kŏn')

ep•i•some (ĕp'ĭ-sōm') *n.* A genetic particle of certain cells, esp. bacteria, that can exist either autonomously in the cytoplasm or as part of a chromosome. —**ep'i•so'mal** *adj.*

e•pis•ta•sis (ĭ-pĭs'tə-sĭs) *n., pl.* **-ses** (-sēz') **1.** An interaction between nonallelic genes, esp. an interaction in which one gene suppresses the expression of another. **2.** A film on the surface of a urine specimen. **3.** The suppression of a bodily discharge or secretion. [Gk., stoppage < *epistanai,* to stop : *ep-, epi-,* epi- + *histanai,* to place; see **stā-** in App.] —**ep'i•stat'ic** (ĕp'ĭ-stăt'ĭk) *adj.*

ep•i•stax•is (ĕp'ĭ-stăk'sĭs) *n., pl.* **-stax•es** (-stăk'sēz') A nosebleed. [Gk. < *epistazein, epistag-,* to bleed from the nose : *epi-,* epi- + *stazein,* to drip.]

ep•i•ste•mic (ĕp'ĭ-stē'mĭk) *adj.* Of, relating to, or involving knowledge; cognitive. [< Gk. *epistēmē,* knowledge. See EPISTEMOLOGY.] —**ep'i•ste'mi•cal•ly** *adv.*

e•pis•te•mol•o•gy (ĭ-pĭs'tə-mŏl'ə-jē) *n.* The branch of philosophy that studies the nature of knowledge, its presuppositions and foundations, and its extent and validity. [Gk. *epistēmē,* knowledge (< *epistasthai,* to understand : *epi-,* epi- + *histasthai,* middle voice of *histanai, stē-,* to place, determine; see **stā-** in App.) + −LOGY.] —**e•pis'te•mo•log'i•cal** (-mə-lŏj'ĭ-kəl) *adj.* —**e•pis'te•mo•log'i•cal•ly** *adv.* —**e•pis'te•mol'o•gist** *n.*

e•pis•tle (ĭ-pĭs'əl) *n.* **1.** A letter, esp. a formal one. **2.** A literary composition in the form of a letter. **3.** *Epistle Bible* **a.** One of the letters included as a book in the New Testament. **b.** An excerpt from one of these letters, read as part of a religious service. [ME *epistel* < OFr. *epistle* < Lat. *epistola* < Gk. *epistolē* < *epistellein,* to send a message to : *epi-,* epi- + *stellein,* to send; see **stel-** in App.]

e•pis•tler (ĭ-pĭs'lər) *n.* One who writes an epistle.

epistle side also **Epistle Side** *n.* **1.** In the traditional orientation of some Christian churches, the south side of a chancel or sanctuary when the altar or Eucharistic table faces east. **2.** In some Christian churches, the side of a chancel or sanctuary on the congregation's right.

e•pis•to•lar•y (ĭ-pĭs'tə-lĕr'ē) *adj.* **1.** Of or associated with letters or the writing of letters. **2.** Being in the form of a letter or letters. **3.** Carried on by or composed of letters. [< Lat. *epistolāris* < *epistola,* epistle. See EPISTLE.]

ep•i•style (ĕp'ĭ-stīl') *n.* See **architrave** 1. [Lat. *epistȳlium* < Gk. *epistȳlion* : *epi-,* epi- + *stūlos,* pillar; see **stā-** in App.]

ep•i•taph (ĕp'ĭ-tăf') *n.* **1.** An inscription on a tombstone in memory of the one buried there. **2.** A brief literary piece commemorating a deceased person. [ME < OFr. *epitaphe* < Lat. *epitaphium* < Gk. neut. of *epitaphios,* funerary : *epi-,* epi- + *taphos,* tomb.] —**ep'i•taph'ic** *adj.*

e•pit•a•sis (ĭ-pĭt'ə-sĭs) *n., pl.* **-ses** (-sēz') The middle part of a play that develops the action leading to the catastrophe. [Gk., stretching, intensity < *epiteinein,* to stretch, intensify : *epi-,* epi- + *teinein, ta-,* to stretch; see **ten-** in App.]

ep•i•tax•y (ĕp'ĭ-tăk'sē) *n., pl.* **-ies** The growth of the crystals of one mineral on the crystal face of another mineral, such that the crystalline substrates of both minerals have the same structural orientation.

ep•i•tha•la•mi•um (ĕp'ə-thə-lā'mē-əm) or **ep•i•tha•la•mi•on** (-ən) *n., pl.* **-mi•ums** or **-mi•a** (-mē-ə) A lyric ode in honor of a bride and bridegroom. [Lat. < Gk. *epithalamion* < neut. of *epithalamios,* of a wedding : *epi-,* epi- + *thalamos,* bridal chamber.]

ep•i•the•li•al•ize (ĕp'ə-thē'lē-ə-līz') or **ep•i•the•lize** (-thē'līz) *v.* **-ized, -iz•ing, -iz•es** or **-lized, -liz•ing, -liz•es** —*tr.* To cover (a wound, for example) with epithelial tissue. —*intr.* To become covered with epithelial tissue. —**ep'i•the'li•al•i•za'tion, ep'i•the'li•al•i•za'tion** (-ə-lĭ-zā'shən) *n.*

ep•i•the•li•o•ma (ĕp'ə-thē'lē-ō'mə) *n., pl.* **-ma•ta** (-mə-tə) or **-mas** A benign or malignant tumor derived from epithelium. —**ep'i•the'li•om'a•tous** (-ŏm'ə-təs) *adj.*

ep•i•the•li•um (ĕp'ə-thē'lē-əm) *n., pl.* **-li•ums** or **-li•a** (-lē-ə) Membranous tissue composed of one or more compact layers of cells that covers most internal and external surfaces of the body and its organs. [NLat. *epithēlium* : EPI- + Gk. *thēlē,* nipple.] —**ep'i•the'li•al, ep'i•the'li•oid** *adj.*

ep•i•thet (ĕp'ə-thĕt') *n.* **1a.** A term used to characterize a person or thing, such as *rosy-fingered* in *rosy-fingered dawn.* **b.** A term used as a descriptive substitute for a person's name or title, such as *The Great Emancipator* for Abraham Lincoln. **2.** An abusive or contemptuous word or phrase. **3.** *Biology* A word in the scientific name of an animal or plant following the genus name and denoting a species, variety, or other division of the genus, as *sativa* in *Lactuca sativa.* [Lat. *epitheton* < Gk., neut. of *epithetos,* added, attributed < *epitithenai,* to add to : *epi-,* epi- + *tithenai, the-,* to place; see **dhē-** in App.] —**ep'i•thet'ic, ep'i•thet'i•cal** *adj.*

USAGE NOTE Strictly speaking, an epithet need not be derogatory, but the term is commonly used as a simple synonym for "term of abuse" or "slur," as in the sentence *There is no place for racial epithets in a police officer's vocabulary.* This usage is accepted by 80 percent of the Usage Panel.

e•pit•o•me (ĭ-pĭt'ə-mē) *n.* **1.** A representative or example of a class or type. **2.** A brief summary; an abstract. [Lat. *epitomē,* a summary < Gk., an abridgment < *epitemnein,* to cut short : *epi-,* epi- + *temnein,* to cut.]

e•pit•o•mize (ĭ-pĭt'ə-mīz') *tr.v.* **-mized, -miz•ing, -miz•es 1.** To make an epitome of. **2.** To be a typical example of.

ep•i•tope (ĕp'ĭ-tōp') *n.* The portion of an immunogenic molecule with which an antibody or lymphocyte reacts. [EPI- + Gk. *topos,* place, spot.]

ep•i•zo•ic (ĕp'ĭ-zō'ĭk) *adj.* Living or growing on the external surface of an animal. —**ep'i•zo'ism** *n.*

ep•i•zo•on (ĕp'ĭ-zō'ŏn, -ən) *n., pl.* **-zo•a** (-zō'ə) An epizoic organism.

ep•i•zo•ot•ic (ĕp'ĭ-zō-ŏt'ĭk) *adj.* Affecting a large number of animals at the same time within a particular region or geographic area. Used of a disease. ❖ *n.* An epizootic disease.

ep•och (ĕp'ək, ē'pŏk') *n.* **1a.** A particular period of history, esp. one considered noteworthy. **b.** A notable event marking the beginning of an epoch. **2.** *Geology* A subdivision of a period. **3.** *Astronomy* An instant in time that is arbitrarily selected as a point of reference. [Med.Lat. *epocha,* measure of time < Gk. *epokhē,* a point in time. See **segh-** in App.]

ep•och•al (ĕp'ə-kəl, -ōk'əl) *adj.* **1.** Of, relating to, or characteristic of an epoch. **2a.** Highly significant or important; momentous. **b.** Without parallel: *epochal stupidity.*

ep•ode (ĕp'ōd') *n.* **1.** A lyric poem characterized by couplets of a long line followed by a shorter one. **2.** The third division of a Pindaric ode, differing in form from the strophe and antistrophe. **3.** The part of a choral ode in classical Greek drama following the strophe and antistrophe. [Lat. *epōdos,* a type of lyric poem < Gk. *epōidos,* sung after < *epaeidein, epaidein,* to sing after : *epi-,* epi- + *aeidein,* to sing.]

ep•o•nym (ĕp'ə-nĭm') *n.* **1.** A person whose name is or is thought to be the source of the name of something, such as a city. **2.** *Medicine* A name of a drug, structure, or disease based on or derived from the name of a person. [Fr. *éponyme* < Gk. *epōnumos,* named after : *epi-,* epi- + *onoma, onuma,* name; see **nō-men-** in App.] —**ep'o•nym'ic** *adj.*

e•pon•y•mous (ĭ-pŏn'ə-məs) *adj.* Of, relating to, or constituting an eponym. [< Gk. *epōnumos.* See EPONYM.]

e•pon•y•my (ĭ-pŏn'ə-mē) *n.* Derivation of a name of a place or thing from that of a person.

ep•o•pee (ĕp'ə-pē') *n.* **1.** Epic poetry, esp. as a literary genre. **2.** An epic poem. [Fr. *épopée* < Gk. *epopoiiā : epos,* song, word; see **wekʷ-** in App. + *poiein,* to make.]

ep•os (ĕp'ŏs') *n.* **1.** A number of poems, not formally united, that treat an epic theme. **2.** An epic. [Lat. < Gk. See **wekʷ-** in App.]

ep•ox•ide (ĕ-pŏk'sīd, ĭ-pŏk'-) *n.* **1.** A ring-shaped chemical structure consisting of an oxygen atom bonded to two other atoms, usu. of carbon, that are already bonded to each other. **2.** A compound containing such a structure.

ep•ox•y (ĭ-pŏk'sē) *n., pl.* **-ies 1.** Any of various usu. thermosetting resins capable of forming tight cross-linked polymer structures characterized by toughness, strong adhesion, and low shrinkage, used esp. in surface coatings and adhesives. **2.** See **epoxide.** ❖ *tr.v.* **-ied, -y•ing, -ies** To fasten together with epoxy. [EP(I)- + OXY(GEN).]

Ep•ping Forest (ĕp'ĭng) A former royal hunting preserve of SE England NE of London, now a public park.

EPROM (ē'prŏm') *n. Computer Science* A programmable read-only memory erasable by exposure to ultraviolet light and reprogrammable. [*e(rasable) p(rogrammable) r(ead-)o(nly) m(emory).*]

ep•si•lon (ĕp'sə-lŏn', -lən) *n.* The fifth letter of the Greek alphabet. [Gk. *e psilon,* simple *e : e, e* + *psilon,* neut. of *psilos,* simple.]

Ep•som salts (ĕp'səm) *pl.n.* (*used with a sing. verb*) Hydrated magnesium sulfate, $MgSO_4 \cdot 7H_2O$, used as a cathartic and as an agent to reduce inflammation. [After *Epsom,* former name of Epsom and Ewell, England.]

Ep•stein (ĕp'stīn'), Sir **Jacob** 1880–1959. Amer.-born British sculptor who is particularly noted for his busts.

Ep•stein-Barr virus (ĕp'stīn-bär') *n.* A herpes virus that causes infectious mononucleosis and is also associated with various types of human cancers. [After Michael A. *Epstein* and Y.M. *Barr,* 20th-cent. British virologists.]

EQ¹ (ē'kyōō') *n.* Emotional intelligence. [*e(motional) q(uotient).*]

EQ² *abbr.* educational quotient

eq. *abbr.* **1.** equal **2.** equation **3.** equivalent

eq•ua•ble (ĕk'wə-bəl, ē'kwə-) *adj.* **1a.** Unvarying; steady. **b.** Free from extremes. **2.** Not easily disturbed; serene. [Lat. *aequābilis* < *aequāre,* to make even < *aequus,* even.] —**eq'ua•bil'i•ty, eq'ua•ble•ness** *n.* —**eq'ua•bly** *adv.*

e•qual (ē'kwəl) *adj.* **1.** Having the same quantity, measure, or value as another. **2.** *Mathematics* Being the same or identical to in value. **3a.** Having the same privileges, status, or rights. **b.** Being the same for all members of a group. **4a.** Having the requisite qualities for a task or situation. **b.** Adequate in extent, amount, or degree. **5.** Impartial; just. **6.** Tranquil; equable. **7.** Showing or having no variance in proportion, structure, or appearance. ❖ *n.* One that is equal to another. ❖ *tr.v.* **e•qualed, e•qual•ing, e•quals** or **e•qualled, e•qual•ling, e•quals 1.** To be equal to, esp. in value. **2.** To do, make, or produce something equal to. [ME < Lat. *aequālis* < *aequus,* even, level.] —**e'qual•ly** *adv.*

e•qual•i•tar•i•an (ĭ-kwŏl'ĭ-târ'ē-ən) *adj.* Egalitarian. —**e•qual'i•tar'i•an•ism** *n.*

e•qual•i•ty (ĭ-kwŏl′ĭ-tē) *n., pl.* **-ties 1.** The state or quality of being equal. **2.** *Mathematics* A statement, usu. an equation, that one thing equals another. [ME *equalite* < OFr. < Lat. *aequālitās* < *aequālis*, equal. See EQUAL.]

e•qual•ize (ē′kwə-līz′) *v.* **-ized, -iz•ing, -iz•es** —*tr.* **1.** To make equal: *equalized responsibilities.* **2.** To make uniform. —*intr.* To constitute or induce equality, equilibrium, or balance. —**e′qual•i•za′tion** (ē′kwə-lĭ-zā′shən) *n.*

e•qual•iz•er (ē′kwə-lī′zər) *n.* **1.** One that equalizes, as: **a.** A device for equalizing pressure or strain. **b.** A tone control system designed to compensate for frequency distortion in audio systems. **2.** *Slang* A deadly weapon, such as a firearm.

equal opportunity *n.* Absence of discrimination, as in the workplace, based on race, color, age, gender, national origin, religion, or mental or physical disability.

equal sign *n.* The symbol (=) used to indicate logical or mathematical equality.

e•qua•nim•i•ty (ē′kwə-nĭm′ĭ-tē, ĕk′wə-) *n.* The quality of being calm and even-tempered; composure. [Lat. *aequanimitās* < *aequanimus*, even-tempered, impartial : *aequus*, even + *animus*, mind; see **anə-** in App.]

e•quate (ĭ-kwāt′) *v.* **e•quat•ed, e•quat•ing, e•quates** —*tr.* **1.** To make equal or equivalent. **2.** To reduce to a standard or average; equalize. **3.** To consider, treat, or depict as equal or equivalent. —*intr.* To be or seem to be equal; correspond. [ME *equaten* < Lat. *aequāre, aequāt-* < *aequus*, even, equal.]

e•qua•tion (ĭ-kwā′zhən, -shən) *n.* **1.** The act or process of equating or of being equated. **2.** The state of being equal. **3.** *Mathematics* A statement asserting the equality of two expressions, usu. written as a linear array of symbols that are separated into left and right sides and joined by an equal sign. **4.** *Chemistry* A representation of a chemical reaction, usu. written as a linear array in which the symbols and quantities of the reactants are separated from those of the products by an equal sign, an arrow, or a set of opposing arrows. **5.** A complex of variable elements or factors. —**e•qua′tion•al** *adj.* —**e•qua′tion•al•ly** *adv.*

e•qua•tor (ĭ-kwā′tər) *n.* **1a.** The imaginary great circle around the earth's surface, equidistant from the poles and perpendicular to the earth's axis of rotation, dividing the earth into the Northern Hemisphere and the Southern Hemisphere. **b.** A similar great circle drawn on the surface of a celestial body at right angles to the axis of rotation. **2.** The celestial equator. **3.** A circle that divides a sphere or other surface into congruent parts. [ME < Med.Lat. *aequātor (diēī et noctis)*, equalizer (of day and night) < Lat. *aequāre*, to equalize. See EQUATE.]

e•qua•to•ri•al (ē′kwə-tôr′ē-əl, -tōr′-, ĕk′wə-) *adj.* **1a.** Of, relating to, or resembling the earth's equator. **b.** Relating to conditions that exist at the earth's equator. **2.** Having or constituting a telescope mounting with two perpendicular axes, one of which is parallel to the earth's rotational axis. —**e′qua•to′ri•al•ly** *adv.*

Equatorial Guinea A country of W-central Africa including islands in the Gulf of Guinea; gained independence from Spain in 1968. Cap. Malabo. Pop. 389,000.

equatorial plate *n.* The plane located midway between the poles of a dividing cell during the metaphase stage of mitosis or meiosis.

eq•uer•ry (ĕk′wə-rē) *n., pl.* **-ries 1.** A personal attendant to the British royal household. **2.** An officer who supervises the horses belonging to a royal or noble household. [Fr. *écurie*, stable < OFr. *escurie* < *escuier*, squire. See SQUIRE.]

e•ques•tri•an (ĭ-kwĕs′trē-ən) *adj.* **1.** Of or relating to horseback riding or horseback riders. **2.** Depicted or represented on horseback. ❖ *n.* One who rides or performs on horseback. [< Lat. *equester, equestr-* < *eques*, horseman < *equus*, horse. See **ekwo-** in App.] —**e•ques′tri•an•ism, e•ques′tri•an•ship** *n.*

e•ques•tri•enne (ĭ-kwĕs′trē-ĕn′) *n.* A woman who rides or performs on horseback. [EQUESTR(IAN) + *-ienne*, fem. suff. (< Fr., fem. of *-ien*, -ian).]

equi– *pref.* Equal; equally: *equiangular.* [ME < Lat. *aequi-* < *aequus*, equal.]

e•qui•an•gu•lar (ē′kwē-ăng′gyə-lər, ĕk′wē-) *adj.* Having all angles equal.

e•qui•dis•tant (ē′kwĭ-dĭs′tənt, ĕk′wĭ-) *adj.* Equally distant. —**e′qui•dis′tance** (-təns) *n.* —**e′qui•dis′tant•ly** *adv.*

e•qui•lat•er•al (ē′kwə-lăt′ər-əl, ĕk′wə-) *adj.* Having all sides or faces equal. ❖ *n.* **1.** A side exactly equal to others. **2.** An equilateral geometric figure. —**e′qui•lat′er•al•ly** *adv.*

e•quil•i•brate (ĭ-kwĭl′ə-brāt′) *v.* **-brat•ed, -brat•ing, -brates** —*intr.* To be in or bring about equilibrium. —*tr.* To maintain in or bring into equilibrium. —**e•quil′i•bra′tion** *n.* —**e•quil′i•bra•to′ry** (-brə-tôr′ē, -tōr′ē) *adj.*

e•quil•i•bra•tor (ĭ-kwĭl′ə-brā′tər) *n.* A device that brings about and helps maintain equilibrium.

e•quil•i•brist (ĭ-kwĭl′ə-brĭst) *n.* A person who performs feats of balance. [Fr. *équilibriste* < *équilibre*, equilibrium < Lat. *aequilībrium*. See EQUILIBRIUM.] —**e•quil′i•bris′tic** *adj.*

e•qui•lib•ri•um (ē′kwə-lĭb′rē-əm, ĕk′wə-) *n., pl.* **-ri•ums** or **-ri•a** (-rē-ə) **1.** A condition in which all acting influences are canceled by others, resulting in a stable, balanced, or unchanging system. **2.** Mental or emotional balance; poise. **3.** *Physics* The state of a body or physical system at rest or in unaccelerated motion in which the resultant of all forces acting on it is zero and the sum of all torques about any axis is zero. **4.** *Chemistry* The state of a chemical reaction in which its forward and reverse reactions occur at equal rates so that the concentration of the reactants and products does not change with time. [Lat. *aequilībrium* : *aequi-*, equi- + *lībra*, balance.]

e•qui•mo•lar (ē′kwə-mō′lər, ĕk′wə-) *adj. Chemistry* Having an equal number of moles.

e•quine (ē′kwīn′, ĕk′wīn′) *adj.* **1.** Of, relating to, or characteristic of a horse. **2.** Of or belonging to the family Equidae, which includes horses and zebras. [Lat. *equīnus* < *equus*, horse. See **ekwo-** in App.] —**e′quine′** *n.*

equine infectious anemia *n.* A viral disease in horses marked by progressive anemia, a staggering gait, and fever.

e•qui•noc•tial (ē′kwə-nŏk′shəl, ĕk′wə-) *adj.* **1.** Relating to an equinox. **2.** Relating to the celestial equator. ❖ *n.* **1.** A violent wind and rain storm at or near the time of the equinox. **2.** See **celestial equator.** [ME *equinoxial* < OFr. < Lat. *aequinoctiālis* < *aequinoctium*, equinox. See EQUINOX.]

equinoctial circle *n.* See **celestial equator.**

e•qui•nox (ē′kwə-nŏks′, ĕk′wə-) *n.* **1.** Either of two points on the celestial sphere at which the ecliptic intersects the celestial equator. **2.** Either of the two times during a year when the sun crosses the celestial equator and when day and night are of approximately equal length. [ME < OFr. *equinoxe* < Med.Lat. *aequinoxium* < Lat. *aequinoctium* : *aequi-*, equi- + *nox, noct-*, night; see **nekʷ-t-** in App.]

e•quip (ĭ-kwĭp′) *tr.v.* **e•quipped, e•quip•ping, e•quips 1a.** To supply with necessities such as provisions. **b.** To furnish with the qualities necessary for performance. **2.** To dress up. [Fr. *équiper* < OFr. *esquiper*, of Gmc. orig.]

eq•ui•page (ĕk′wə-pĭj) *n.* **1.** Equipment or furnishings. **2a.** A horse-drawn carriage with attendants. **b.** The carriage itself. **3.** *Archaic* A retinue, as of a royal personage. **4.** *Archaic* A collection of small articles for personal or household use. [Fr. *équipage* < *équiper*, to equip. See EQUIP.]

e•quip•ment (ĭ-kwĭp′mənt) *n.* **1.** The act of equipping or the state of being equipped. **2.** Something with which a person, an organization, or a thing is equipped. **3.** The rolling stock esp. of a transportation system. **4.** The qualities or traits that make up the mental and emotional resources of an individual.

e•qui•poise (ē′kwə-poiz′, ĕk′wə-) *n.* **1.** Equality in distribution, as of weight or emotional forces; equilibrium. **2.** A counterpoise; a counterbalance.

e•qui•pol•lent (ē′kwə-pŏl′ənt, ĕk′wə-) *adj.* **1.** Equal in force, power, effectiveness, or significance. **2.** *Logic* Validly derived from each other; deducible. **3.** Equivalent. ❖ *n.* An equivalent. [ME < OFr. < Lat. *aequipollēns, aequipollent-* : *aequi-*, equi- + *pollēns*, pr. part. of *pollēre*, to be powerful.] —**e′qui•pol′lence** *n.*

e•qui•pon•der•ance (ē′kwə-pŏn′dər-əns, ĕk′wə-) *n.* Equality of weight; equipoise. [< *equiponderant*, having equal weight < Med.Lat. *aequiponderāns, aequiponderant-*, pr. part. of *aequiponderāre*, to weigh the same. See EQUIPONDERATE.] —**e′qui•pon′der•ant** *adj.*

e•qui•pon•der•ate (ē′kwə-pŏn′də-rāt′, ĕk′wə-) *tr.v.* **-at•ed, -at•ing, -ates 1.** To counterbalance. **2.** To give equal balance or weight to. [Med.Lat. *aequiponderāre, aequiponderāt-* : Lat. *aequi-*, equi- + Lat. *ponderāre*, to weigh.]

e•qui•po•ten•tial (ē′kwə-pə-tĕn′shəl, ĕk′wə-) *adj.* **1.** Having equal potential. **2.** *Physics* Having the same electric potential at every point.

e•qui•prob•a•ble (ē′kwə-prŏb′ə-bəl, ĕk′wə-) *adj.* Having equal mathematical or logical probability.

eq•ui•se•tum (ĕk′wə-sē′təm) *n., pl.* **-tums** or **-ta** (-tə) See **horsetail.** [Lat. *equisaetum*, horsetail : *equus*, horse; see **ekwo-** in App. + *saeta*, bristle, stiff hair.]

eq•ui•ta•ble (ĕk′wĭ-tə-bəl) *adj.* Marked by or having equity; just and impartial. See Syns at **fair**¹. [Fr. *équitable* < OFr. < *equite*, equity. See EQUITY.] —**eq′ui•ta•bly** *adv.*

eq•ui•tant (ĕk′wĭ-tənt) *adj.* Overlapping at the base to form a flat fanlike arrangement in two ranks, as the leaves of some irises. [Lat. *equitāns, equitant-*, pr. part. of *equitāre*, to ride horseback < *eques, equit-*, horseman < *equus*, horse. See **ekwo-** in App.]

eq•ui•ta•tion (ĕk′wĭ-tā′shən) *n.* The art and practice of riding a horse. [Lat. *equitātiō, equitātiōn-* < *equitāre*, to ride horseback. See EQUITANT.]

eq•ui•ty (ĕk′wĭ-tē) *n., pl.* **-ties 1.** The state, quality, or ideal of being just, impartial, and fair. **2.** Something that is just, impartial, and fair. **3.** *Law* **a.** Justice applied in circumstances covered by law yet influenced by principles of ethics and fairness. **b.** A system of jurisprudence supplementing and serving to modify the rigor of common law. **c.** An equitable right or claim. **d.** Equity of redemption. **4.** The residual value of a business or property beyond any mortgage thereon and liability therein. **5a.** The market value of securities less any debt incurred. **b.** Common stock and preferred stock. **6.** Funds provided to a business by the sale of stock. [ME *equite* < OFr. < Lat. *aequitās* < *aequus*, even, fair.]

equity of redemption *n.* The right of one who has mortgaged property to redeem that property upon payment of the sum due within a reasonable time after the due date.

e•quiv•a•lence (ĭ-kwĭv′ə-ləns) *n.* **1.** The state or condition of

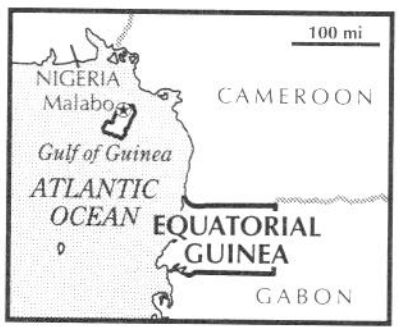

Equatorial Guinea

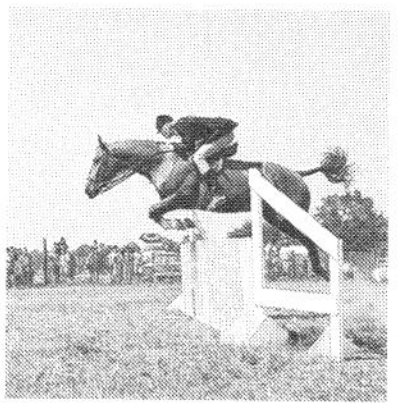

equestrian

ă	pat	oi	boy
ā	pay	ou	out
âr	care	o͝o	took
ä	father	o͞o	boot
ĕ	pet	ŭ	cut
ē	be	ûr	urge
ĭ	pit	th	thin
ī	pie	*th*	this
îr	pier	hw	which
ŏ	pot	zh	vision
ō	toe	ə	about,
ô	paw		item

Stress marks:
′ (primary);
′ (secondary), as in
lexicon (lĕk′sĭ-kŏn′)

being equivalent; equality. **2.** An equivalence relation.

e·quiv·a·lence relation *n.* A reflexive, symmetric, and transitive relationship between elements of a set, such as congruence for the set of all triangles in a plane.

e·quiv·a·len·cy (ĭ-kwĭv′ə-lən-sē) *n., pl.* **-cies** Equivalence.

e·quiv·a·lent (ĭ-kwĭv′ə-lənt) *adj.* **1a.** Equal, as in value, force, or meaning. **b.** Having similar or identical effects. **2.** Being essentially equal, all things considered. **3.** *Mathematics* **a.** Capable of being put into a one-to-one relationship. Used of two sets. **b.** Having similar, corresponding, or congruent parts. **4.** *Chemistry* Having the same ability to combine. ❖ *n.* **1.** Something that is essentially equal to another. **2.** *Chemistry* Equivalent weight. [ME < LLat. *aequivalēns, aequivalent-,* pr. part. of *aequivalēre,* to have equal force : Lat. *aequi-,* equi- + Lat. *valēre,* to be strong.] —e·quiv′a·lent·ly *adv.*

equivalent weight *n.* The weight of a substance that will combine with or replace one mole of hydrogen or one-half mole of oxygen, equal to the atomic weight divided by the valence.

e·quiv·o·cal (ĭ-kwĭv′ə-kəl) *adj.* **1.** Open to two or more interpretations and often intended to mislead; ambiguous. **2.** Of uncertain significance. **3.** Of a doubtful or uncertain nature. [< LLat. *aequivocus* : Lat. *aequi-,* equi- + Lat. *vocāre,* to call; see **wekʷ-** in App.] —e·quiv′o·cal′i·ty (-kăl′ĭ-tē), e·quiv′o·cal·ness *n.* —e·quiv′o·cal·ly *adv.*

e·quiv·o·cate (ĭ-kwĭv′ə-kāt′) *intr.v.* **-cat·ed, -cat·ing, -cates** **1.** To use equivocal language intentionally. **2.** To avoid making an explicit statement. [ME *equivocaten* < Med.Lat. *aequivocāre, aequivocāt-* < LLat. *aequivocus,* equivocal. See EQUIVOCAL.] —e·quiv′o·ca′tor *n.*

e·quiv·o·ca·tion (ĭ-kwĭv′ə-kā′shən) *n.* **1.** The use of equivocal language. **2.** An equivocal statement or expression.

eq·ui·voque also **eq·ui·voke** (ĕk′wə-vōk′, ē′kwə-) *n.* **1.** An equivocal word, phrase, or expression. **2.** A pun. **3.** A double meaning. [Fr. *équivoque* < LLat. *aequivocus,* ambiguous. See EQUIVOCAL.]

er (ûr) *interj.* Used to express hesitation or uncertainty.

Er The symbol for the element **erbium.**

ER *abbr.* emergency room

-er¹ *suff.* **1a.** One that performs a specified action: *swimmer.* **b.** One that undergoes or is capable of undergoing a specified action: *broiler.* **c.** One that has: *ten-pounder.* **d.** One associated or involved with: *banker.* **2a.** Native or resident of: *New Yorker.* **b.** One that is: *foreigner.* [ME, partly < OE *-ere* (< Gmc. *-ārjaz* < Lat. *-ārius,* -ary), partly < Anglo-Fr. *-er* (< OFr. *-ier* < Lat. *-ārius*) and partly < OFr. *-ere, -eor;* see OR¹.]

-er² *suff.* Used to form the comparative degree of adjectives and adverbs: *darker; faster.* [ME < OE *-re, -ra.*]

e·ra (îr′ə, ĕr′ə) *n.* **1.** A period of time as reckoned from a specific point in history. **2a.** A period of time characterized by particular circumstances, events, or personages. **b.** A point that marks the beginning of such a period of time. **3.** The longest division of geologic time, made up of one or more periods. [LLat. *aera* < Lat., counters, pl. of *aes, aer-,* bronze coin.]

ERA *abbr.* **1.** earned run average **2.** Equal Rights Amendment

e·rad·i·cate (ĭ-răd′ĭ-kāt′) *tr.v.* **-cat·ed, -cat·ing, -cates** **1.** To tear up by the roots. **2.** To get rid of as if by tearing up by the roots: *eradicating poverty.* [ME *eradicaten* < Lat. *ērādīcāre, ērādīcāt-* : *ē-, ex-,* ex- + *rādīx, rādīc-,* root; see **wrād-** in App.] —e·rad′i·ca·ble (-kə-bəl) *adj.* —e·rad′i·ca′tion *n.* —e·rad′i·ca′tive *adj.* —e·rad′i·ca′tor *n.*

e·rase (ĭ-rās′) *tr.v.* **e·rased, e·ras·ing, e·ras·es** **1a.** To remove (something written, for example) by rubbing, wiping, or scraping. **b.** To remove (recorded material) from a magnetic tape or other storage medium. **c.** To remove recorded material from (a magnetic tape, for example). **2.** To remove all traces of. **3.** To remove or destroy as if by wiping out. [Lat. *ērādere, ērās-,* to scratch out : *ē-, ex-,* ex- + *rādere,* to scrape.] —e·ras′a·bil′i·ty *n.* —e·ras′a·ble *adj.*

SYNONYMS erase, expunge, efface, delete, cancel These verbs mean to remove or invalidate something, especially something stored, recorded, or written down. To *erase* is to wipe or rub out, literally or figuratively: *erased the marks from the margin; erased the thought from her mind. Expunge* and *efface* imply thorough removal: *expunged their names from the list; tried to efface prejudice from his thinking.* To *delete* is to remove matter from a manuscript or data from a computer application: *deleted expletives from the transcript. Cancel* refers to invalidating by or as if by drawing lines through something written: *cancelled the stamp.*

e·ras·er (ĭ-rā′sər) *n.* An implement, such as a piece of rubber, used for erasing.

E·ras·mus (ĭ-răz′məs), **Desiderius** 1466?–1536. Dutch Renaissance scholar and Roman Catholic theologian whose works include *The Praise of Folly* (1509).

E·ras·tus (ĭ-răs′təs), **Thomas** 1524–83. Swiss Protestant theologian who opposed Calvinism.

e·ra·sure (ĭ-rā′shər) *n.* **1.** The act or an instance of erasing. **2.** The state of being erased.

Er·a·to (ĕr′ə-tō′) *n. Greek Mythology* The Muse of lyric poetry and mime. [Gk. *Eratō* < *erasthai,* to love.]

E·ra·tos·the·nes (ĕr′ə-tŏs′thə-nēz′) 3rd cent. B.C. Greek as-

tronomer and geographer who devised a map of the world and estimated the circumference of the earth.

er·bi·um (ûr′bē-əm) *n. Symbol* **Er** A soft rare-earth element, used in metallurgy and nuclear research. Atomic number 68; atomic weight 167.26; melting point 1,497°C; boiling point 2,900°C; specific gravity 9.051; valence 3. See table at **element.** [After *Ytterby,* a town in Sweden.]

ere (âr) *prep.* Previous to; before. ❖ *conj.* Rather than; before. [ME *er* < OE *ǣr.*]

Er·e·bus (ĕr′ə-bəs) *n. Greek Mythology* The region of the underworld through which the dead pass before reaching Hades.

e·rect (ĭ-rĕkt′) *adj.* **1.** Being in an upright position. **2.** Vertical, as a straight line or plane. **3.** Being in a stiff, rigid physiological condition. **4.** *Archaic* Wide-awake; alert. ❖ *tr.v.* **e·rect·ed, e·rect·ing, e·rects** **1.** To construct by assembling. **2.** To raise to a rigid or upright condition. **3.** To fix in an upright position. **4.** To set up; establish. **5.** *Mathematics* To construct (a perpendicular, for example) from or on a given base. [ME < Lat. *ērēctus,* p. part. of *ērigere,* to set up : *ē-, ex-,* ex- + *regere,* to guide; see **reg-** in App.] —e·rect′a·ble *adj.* —e·rect′ly *adv.* —e·rect′ness *n.*

e·rec·tile (ĭ-rĕk′təl, -tīl′) *adj.* **1.** Capable of being raised to an upright position. **2.** *Anatomy* Of or relating to tissue that is capable of filling with blood and becoming rigid. —e·rec·til′i·ty (-tĭl′ĭ-tē) *n.*

erectile dysfunction *n.* The inability to achieve penile erection or to maintain an erection until ejaculation.

e·rec·tion (ĭ-rĕk′shən) *n.* **1.** The act of erecting. **2.** Something erected; a construction. **3.** *Physiology* **a.** The firm and enlarged condition of a body part or organ when the erectile tissue surrounding it becomes filled with blood, esp. of the penis or clitoris. **b.** The process of filling with blood.

e·rec·tor (ĭ-rĕk′tər) *n.* **1.** One that erects. **2.** A muscle that causes or maintains the erection of a body part.

E region *n.* See **E layer.**

ere·long (âr-lông′, -lŏng′) *adv.* Before long; soon.

er·e·mite (ĕr′ə-mīt′) *n.* A recluse or hermit, esp. a religious recluse. [ME < LLat. *erēmīta.* See HERMIT.] —er′e·mit′ic (-mĭt′ĭk), er′e·mit′i·cal *adj.*

er·e·mur·us (ĕr′ə-myŏŏr′əs) *n.* Any of several Asiatic plants of the genus *Eremurus* in the lily family, having a tall cluster of bell-shaped flowers. [NLat. *Erēmūrus,* genus name : Gk. *erēmos,* solitary + Gk. *ourā,* tail; see **ors-** in App.]

ere·now (âr-nou′) *adv.* Before now; heretofore.

E·resh·ki·gal (ā-rĕsh′kē′găl, ĕr′ĕsh-kĭg′əl) *n. Mythology* The Mesopotamian goddess of the underworld. [Sumerian *ereš-ki-gal* : *ereš,* lady + *ki,* earth + *gal,* great.]

er·e·thism (ĕr′ə-thĭz′əm) *n.* Abnormal irritability or sensitivity of an organ or a body part to stimulation. [Fr. *éréthisme* < Gk. *erethisma,* a provocation < *erethizein,* to irritate.] —er′e·this′mic (-mĭk) *adj.*

E·re·van (yĕ′rĭ-vän′) See **Yerevan.**

ere·while (âr-hwīl′, -wīl′) also **ere·whiles** (-hwīlz′, -wīlz′) *adv. Archaic* Some time ago; heretofore.

Er·furt (ĕr′fərt, -fŏŏrt′) A city of central Germany SW of Leipzig; a member of the Hanseatic League. Pop. 200,799.

erg (ûrg) *n.* The centimeter-gram-second unit of energy or work equal to the work done by a force of one dyne acting over a distance of one centimeter. [< Gk. *ergon,* work. See **werg-** in App.]

er·ga·tive (ûr′gə-tĭv) *adj.* **1.** Of or relating to a language, such as Georgian, in which the subject of an intransitive verb and the object of a transitive verb are expressed by one grammatical case, and the subject of a transitive verb is expressed by another. **2.** Of or relating to the grammatical case of the subject of a transitive verb in such a language. ❖ *n.* **1.** The ergative case. **2.** A word or form in the ergative case. [< Gk. *ergatēs,* worker < *ergon,* work. See **werg-** in App.] —er′ga·tiv′i·ty *n.*

-ergic *suff.* Activated or produced by: *cholinergic.* [Gk. *ergon,* work; see **werg-** in App. + –IC.]

er·go (ûr′gō, âr′-) *conj.* Consequently; therefore. ❖ *adv.* Consequently; hence. [Lat. *ergō.* See **reg-** in App.]

er·go·graph (ûr′gə-grăf′) *n.* A device for measuring the work capacity of a muscle or muscle group during contraction. [Gk. *ergon,* work; see **werg-** in App. + –GRAPH.] —er′go·graph′ic *adj.*

er·gom·e·ter (ûr-gŏm′ĭ-tər) *n.* An instrument for measuring the amount of work done by a muscle or group of muscles. [Gk. *ergon,* work; see **werg-** in App. + –METER.] —er′go·met′ric (ûr′gə-mĕt′rĭk) *adj.*

er·go·nom·ics (ûr′gə-nŏm′ĭks) *n.* **1.** (*used with a sing. verb*) The applied science of equipment design intended to maximize productivity by reducing operator fatigue and discomfort. **2.** (*used with a pl. verb*) Design factors based on ergonomics. [Gk. *ergon,* work; see **werg-** in App. + (ECO)NOMICS.] —er′go·nom′ic, er′go·no·met′ric (-nə-mĕt′rĭk) *adj.* —er′go·nom′i·cal·ly *adv.*

er·gos·ter·ol (ûr-gŏs′tə-rôl′, -rŏl′) *n.* A crystalline sterol, $C_{28}H_{43}OH$, synthesized by yeast from sugars or derived from ergot and converted to vitamin D_2 when exposed to ultraviolet radiation. [ERGO(T) + STEROL.]

er·got (ûr′gət, -gŏt′) *n.* **1.** A fungus (*Claviceps purpurea*) that infects cereal plants and forms compact black masses of branching filaments that replace many of the grains of the host plant. **2.** The disease caused by such a fungus. **3.** The dried sclerotia of ergot, usu. obtained from rye seed and used as a source of several alkaloids and as the basic source of lysergic acid. [Fr. < OFr. *argot,* cock's spur (< its shape).] **—er•got′ic** *adj.*

er•got•a•mine (ûr-gŏt′ə-mēn′, -mĭn) *n.* A crystalline alkaloid, $C_{33}H_{35}N_5O_5$, derived from ergot that induces vasoconstriction and is used esp. in treating migraine.

er•got•ism (ûr′gə-tĭz′əm) *n.* Poisoning caused by consuming ergot-infected grain or grain products or from excessive use of drugs containing ergot.

Er•gun He (ĕr′gŏŏn′ hĕ′, ĕr′gwän′ hŭ′) See **Argun River.**

Er•ic•son also **Er•ics•son** (ĕr′ĭk-sən), **Leif** fl. c. 1000. Norwegian navigator who according to Norse sagas discovered Vinland.

Er•ics•son (ĕr′ĭk-sən), **John** 1803–89. Amer. engineer who built the first ironclad warship, the *Monitor* (1862).

Er•ic the Red (ĕr′ĭk) fl. 10th cent. Norwegian navigator who explored and named Greenland. (c. 985).

E•rid•a•nus (ĭ-rĭd′n-əs) *n.* A constellation in the Southern Hemisphere near Fornax and Cetus. [Gk. *Ēridanos,* mythical river associated with the myth of Phaeton.]

E•rie¹ (îr′ē) *n., pl.* **Erie** or **E•ries 1.** A member of a Native American people formerly inhabiting the southern shore of Lake Erie in northern Ohio, northwest Pennsylvania, and western New York. **2.** The Iroquoian language of the Erie.

E•rie² (îr′ē) A city of NW PA on Lake Erie SW of Buffalo, NY; laid out in 1795. Pop. 103,717.

Erie, Lake One of the Great Lakes, bounded by S Ontario, W NY, NW PA, N OH, and SE MI and linked with the Hudson R. by the New York State Barge Canal.

Erie Canal An artificial waterway extending c. 579 km (360 mi) across central NY from Albany to Buffalo; constructed from 1817 to 1825.

E•rig•e•na (ĭ-rĭj′ə-nə, -rē′jə-) or **Er•iu•ge•na** (ĕr-yōō′jə-), **John Scotus** 810?–877? Irish-born theologian and philosopher who sought to reconcile Neo-Platonism and Christian belief.

Er•ik•son (ĕr′ĭk-sən), **Erik Homburger** 1902–94. German-born Amer. psychoanalyst who proposed that people acquire mature psychosexual traits by overcoming personal crises.

Er•in (ĕr′ĭn) Ireland.

E•rin•y•es (ĭ-rĭn′ē-ēz′) *pl.n. Greek Mythology* The Furies.

E•ris (îr′ĭs, ĕr′-) *n. Greek Mythology* The goddess of discord.

ERISA *abbr.* Employee Retirement Income Security Act

e•ris•tic (ĭ-rĭs′tĭk) also **e•ris•ti•cal** (-tĭ-kəl) *adj.* Given to or characterized by disputatious, often specious argument. ❖ *n.* **1.** One given to or expert in dispute or argument. **2.** The art or practice of disputation and polemics. [Gk. *eristikos* < *erizein,* to wrangle, quarrel < *eris, erid-,* strife.]

Er•i•tre•a (ĕr′ĭ-trē′ə) A country N of Ethiopia bordering on the Red Sea. It was part of Ethiopia from 1952 to 1993. Pop. 3,437,000 **—Er′i•tre′an** *adj. & n.*

E•ri•van (yĕ′rĭ-vän′) See **Yerevan.**

Er•len•mey•er flask (ûr′lən-mī′ər, âr′-) *n.* A conical laboratory flask with a narrow neck and flat, broad bottom. [After Richard August Carl Emil *Erlenmeyer* (1825–1909), German chemist.]

er•mine (ûr′mĭn) *n.* **1.** A weasel (*Mustela erminea*) of northern regions having a black-tipped tail and dark brown fur that in winter changes to white. **2.** The commercially valuable white fur of this animal. [ME *ermin* < OFr. *ermine,* poss. of Gmc. orig., or < Med.Lat. *(mūs) Armenius,* Armenian (mouse).]

erne also **ern** (ûrn) *n.* Any of several sea eagles, esp. *Haliaeetus albicilla,* of Europe. [ME *ern* < OE *earn.*]

Ernst (ĕrnst), **Max** 1891–1976. German-born artist and a founder of Dada and surrealism.

e•rode (ĭ-rōd′) *v.* **e•rod•ed, e•rod•ing, e•rodes** *—tr.* **1.** To wear (something) away by abrasion. **2.** To eat into; corrode. **3.** To make or form by wearing away. **4.** To cause to diminish, deteriorate, or disappear as if by eating into or wearing away. *—intr.* To become worn or eaten away. [Lat. *ērōdere,* to gnaw off, eat away : *ē-, ex-,* ex- + *rōdere,* to gnaw.] **—e•rod′i•bil′i•ty** *n.* **—e•rod′i•ble** *adj.*

e•rog•e•nous (ĭ-rŏj′ə-nəs) *adj.* **1.** Responsive or sensitive to sexual stimulation: *erogenous zones.* **2.** Arousing sexual desire. [Gk. *erōs,* sexual love + –GENOUS.]

Er•os (ĕr′ŏs′, îr′-) *n.* **1.** *Greek Mythology* The god of love, son of Aphrodite. **2.** often **eros** Creative, often sexual yearning, love, or desire. **3a.** Sexual drive; libido. **b.** The sum of all instincts for self-preservation. [Lat. *Erōs* < Gk. < *erōs,* sexual love.]

e•rose (ĭ-rōs′) *adj.* Irregularly notched, toothed, or indented: *erose leaves.* [< Lat. *ērōsus,* p. part. of *ērōdere,* to gnaw off. See ERODE.] **—e•rose′ly** *adv.*

e•ro•sion (ĭ-rō′zhən) *n.* **1.** The process of eroding or the condition of being eroded: *erosion of the beach.* **2.** The group of natural processes, including weathering, corrosion, and abrasion, by which material is eroded. [Lat. *ērōsiō, ērōsiōn-,* an eating away < *ērōsus,* eaten away. See ERODE.] **—e•ro′sion•al** *adj.* **—e•ro′sion•al•ly** *adv.*

e•ro•sive (ĭ-rō′sĭv) *adj.* Causing erosion. **—e•ro′sive•ness, e•ro′siv′i•ty** *n.*

e•rot•ic (ĭ-rŏt′ĭk) *adj.* **1.** Of or concerning sexual love and desire;

amatory. **2.** Tending to arouse sexual desire. **3.** Dominated by sexual love or desire. [Gk. *erōtikos* < *erōs, erōt-,* sexual love.] **—e•rot′ic n.** **—e•rot′i•cal•ly** *adv.*

e•rot•i•ca (ĭ-rŏt′ĭ-kə) *pl.n.* (*used with a sing. or pl. verb*) Literature or art intended to arouse sexual desire. [Gk. *erōtika* < neut. pl. of *erōtikos,* erotic. See EROTIC.]

e•rot•i•cism (ĭ-rŏt′ĭ-sĭz′əm) *n.* **1.** An erotic quality or theme. **2.** Sexual excitement. **3.** Abnormally persistent sexual excitement. **—e•rot′i•cist** *n.*

e•rot•i•cize (ĭ-rŏt′ĭ-sīz′) *tr.v.* **-cized, -ciz•ing, -ciz•es** To make erotic. **—e•rot′i•ci•za′tion** (-sĭ-zā′shən) *n.*

er•o•tism (ĕr′ə-tĭz′əm) *n.* Eroticism.

er•o•tize (ĕr′ə-tīz′) *tr.v.* **-tized, -tiz•ing, -tiz•es** To imbue with erotic feeling or import.

e•ro•to•ma•ni•a (ĭ-rō′tə-mā′nē-ə, ĭ-rŏt′ə-) *n. Psychology* **1.** Excessive sexual desire. **2.** A delusional, romantic preoccupation with a stranger, esp. a public figure. [Gk. *erōtomania: erōs, erōt-,* sexual love + *-mania,* -mania.] **—e•ro′to•ma′ni•ac′** (-ăk′) *adj.*

err (ûr, ĕr) *intr.v.* **erred, err•ing, errs 1.** To make an error or a mistake. **2.** To violate accepted moral standards; sin. **3.** *Archaic* To stray. [ME *erren* < OFr. *errer* < Lat. *errāre,* to wander.]

er•ran•cy (ĕr′ən-sē) *n., pl.* **-cies** The state of erring or an instance of it.

er•rand (ĕr′ənd) *n.* **1a.** A short trip taken to perform a specified task, usu. for another. **b.** The purpose or object of such a trip. **2.** *Archaic* **a.** A mission; an embassy. **b.** An oral message that has been entrusted to one. [ME *erand* < OE *ærend.*]

er•rant (ĕr′ənt) *adj.* **1.** Roving, esp. in search of adventure: *knights errant.* **2.** Straying from the proper course or standards. **3a.** Wandering outside established limits. **b.** Aimless or irregular in motion. [ME *erraunt* < AN, partly < OFr. *errer,* to travel about (< VLat. **iterāre* < Lat. *iter,* journey; see **ei-** in App.) and partly < OFr. *errer,* to err; see ERR.] **—er′rant** *n.* **—er′rant•ly** *adv.*

er•rant•ry (ĕr′ən-trē) *n.* The condition of traveling or roving about, esp. in search of adventure.

er•rat•ic (ĭ-răt′ĭk) *adj.* **1.** Having no fixed or regular course; wandering. **2.** Lacking consistency, regularity, or uniformity. **3.** Deviating from the customary course in conduct or opinion; eccentric. [ME *erratik* < OFr. *erratique* < Lat. *errāticus* < *errāre,* to wander.] **—er•rat′i•cal•ly** *adv.* **—er•rat′i•cism** (-sĭz′əm) *n.*

er•ra•tum (ĭ-rä′təm, ĭ-rā′-) *n., pl.* **-ta** (-tə) An error in printing or writing, esp. one in a correction list bound into a book. [Lat. *errātum* < neut. p. part. of *errāre,* to stray.]

er•rhine (ĕr′īn′) *adj.* Promoting or inducing nasal discharge. ❖ *n.* An errhine medication. [NLat. *errhīnum,* an errhine medicine < Gk. *errīnon : en-,* in; see EN-² + *rhīs, rhīn-,* nose.]

Er Rif (ĕr rĭf′) A hilly region along the coast of N Morocco.

er•ro•ne•ous (ĭ-rō′nē-əs) *adj.* Containing or derived from error; mistaken. [ME < Lat. *errōneus* < *errō, errōn-,* a vagabond < *errāre,* to err, wander.] **—er•ro′ne•ous•ly** *adv.* **—er•ro′ne•ous•ness** *n.*

er•ror (ĕr′ər) *n.* **1.** An act, assertion, or belief that unintentionally deviates from what is correct, right, or true. **2.** The condition of having incorrect or false knowledge. **3.** The act or an instance of deviating from an accepted code of behavior. **4.** A mistake. **5.** *Mathematics* The difference between a computed or measured value and a true or theoretically correct value. **6.** *Baseball* A defensive fielding or throwing misplay when a play normally should have resulted in an out or prevented an advance by a base runner. [ME *errour* < OFr. < Lat. *error* < *errāre,* to err.] **—er′ror•less** *adj.*

er•satz (ĕr′zäts′, ĕr-zäts′) *adj.* Being an imitation or a substitute, usu. inferior; artificial: *ersatz coffee.* See Syns at **artificial.** [Ger., replacement < *ersetzen,* to replace < *ersetzen : ir-,* out; see **ud-** in App. + *sezzan,* to set; see **sed-** in App.] **—er′satz′** *n.*

Erse (ûrs) *n.* **1.** See **Irish Gaelic. 2.** See **Scottish Gaelic.** [ME *Ersch,* Irish < OE *Iras,* the Irish. See IRISH.]

erst (ûrst) *adv. Archaic* Erstwhile. [ME *erest* < OE *ǣrest.*]

erst•while (ûrst′hwīl′, -wīl′) *adv.* In the past; at a former time; formerly. ❖ *adj.* Former.

ERT *abbr.* estrogen replacement therapy

Er•té (ĕr-tā′) Romain de Tertoff. 1892–1990. Russian-born French designer and illustrator.

e•ru•cic acid (ĭ-rōō′sĭk) *n.* A fatty acid, $C_{22}H_{42}O_2$, in rapeseed, wallflower seed, and mustard seed. [< NLat. *Ērūca,* cabbage genus < Lat. *ērūca,* rocket, cabbage.]

e•ruct (ĭ-rŭkt′) *tr. & intr.v.* **e•ruct•ed, e•ruct•ing, e•ructs** To belch. [Lat. *ēructāre : ē-, ex-,* ex- + *ructāre,* to belch.] **—e•ruc•ta′tion** (ĭ-rŭk-tā′shən) *n.*

er•u•dite (ĕr′yə-dīt′, ĕr′ə-) *adj.* Characterized by erudition. See Syns at **learned.** [ME *erudit* < Lat. *ērudītus,* p. part. of *ērudīre,* to instruct : *ē-, ex-,* ex- + *rudis,* untaught; see RUDE.] **—er′u•dite′ly** *adv.*

er•u•di•tion (ĕr′yə-dĭsh′ən, ĕr′ə-) *n.* Deep wide learning.

e•rum•pent (ĭ-rŭm′pənt) *adj.* Bursting through or as if through a surface or covering. [Lat. *ērumpēns, ērumpent-,* pr. part. of

Eritrea

erosion
exposed eucalyptus tree roots

ă	pat	oi	boy
ā	pay	ou	out
âr	care	ŏŏ	took
ä	father	ōō	boot
ĕ	pet	ŭ	cut
ē	be	ûr	urge
ĭ	pit	th	thin
ī	pie	th	this
îr	pier	hw	which
ŏ	pot	zh	vision
ō	toe	ə	about,
ô	paw		item

Stress marks:
′ (primary);
′ (secondary), as in
lexicon (lĕk′sĭ-kŏn′)

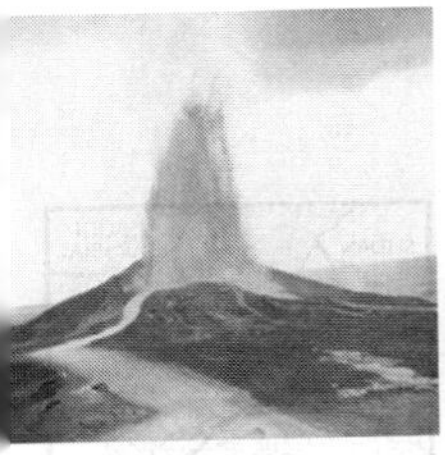

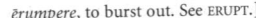

eruption
eruption of Kilauea volcano near Pu'u O'o, Hawaii Volcanoes National Park

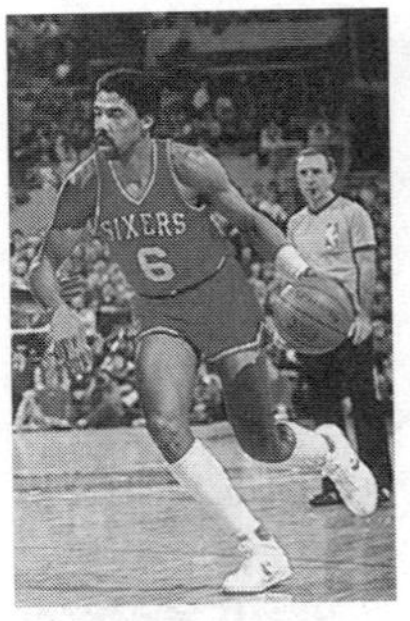

Julius Erving

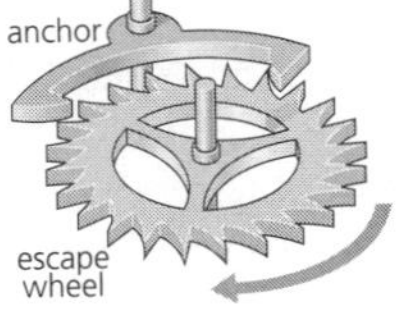

escapement

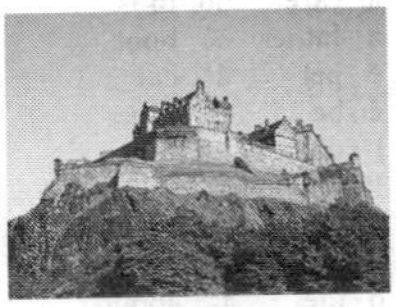

escarpment
Edinburgh Castle, Scotland

ērumpere, to burst out. See ERUPT.]

e•rupt (ĭ-rŭpt′) *v.* **e•rupt•ed, e•rupt•ing, e•rupts** —*intr.* **1.** To emerge violently from restraint or limits; explode. **2.** To become violently active. **3.** To force out or release something with violence or suddenness. **4a.** To break through the gums in developing. Used of teeth. **b.** To appear on the skin. Used of a rash or blemish. —*tr.* To force out violently. [Lat. *ērumpere, ērupt-* : *ē-, ex-,* ex- + *rumpere,* to break; see **reup-** in App.] —**e•rup′tive** *adj.* —**e•rup′tive•ly** *adv.*

e•rup•tion (ĭ-rŭp′shən) *n.* **1a.** The act or process of erupting. **b.** An instance of erupting. **2.** A sudden, often violent outburst. **3a.** An appearance of a rash or blemish on the skin. **b.** Such a rash or blemish. **4.** The emergence of a tooth through the gums.

Er•ving (ûr′vĭng), **Julius Winfield** Known as "Dr. J." b. 1950. Amer. professional basketball player for the Philadelphia 76ers (1976–87).

–ery or **–ry** *suff.* **1.** A place for: *bakery.* **2.** A collection or class: *finery.* **3.** A state or condition: *slavery.* **4.** Act; practice: *bribery.* **5.** Characteristics or qualities of: *snobbery.* [ME *-erie* < OFr. : *-er,* agent suff. (partly < *-ier;* see –ER[1], and partly < *-ere, -eor;* see –OR[1]) + *-ie,* n. suff.; see –Y[2].]

Er•y•man•thos or **Er•y•man•thus** (ĕr′ə-măn′thəs, -thŏs, ĕ-rē′män-thôs′) A mountain range of S Greece in the NW Peloponnesus rising to c. 2,225 m (7,295 ft) at **Mount Erymanthos.** —**Er′y•man′thi•an** *adj.*

e•ryn•go (ĭ-rĭng′gō) *n., pl.* **-goes** Any of several plants of the genus *Eryngium,* having spiny leaves and dense clusters of small bluish flowers. [Alteration of Lat. *ēryngion,* sea holly < Gk. *ērungion,* dim. of *ērungos.*]

er•y•sip•e•las (ĕr′ĭ-sĭp′ə-ləs, ĭr′-) *n.* An acute disease of the skin and subcutaneous tissue caused by a species of hemolytic streptococcus and marked by localized inflammation and fever. [ME *erisipila* < Lat. *erysipelas* < Gk. *erusipelas* : *erusi-,* red; see **reudh-** in App. + *-pelas,* skin; see **pel-**[1] in App.] —**er′y•si•pel′a•tous** (-sĭ-pĕl′ə-təs) *adj.*

er•y•the•ma (ĕr′ə-thē′mə) *n.* Redness of the skin caused by dilatation and congestion of the capillaries, often a sign of inflammation or infection. [Gk. *eruthēma* < *eruthainein,* to redden, be red < *eruthros,* red. See **reudh-** in App.] —**er′y•them′a•tous** (-thĕm′ə-təs, -thē′mə-), **er′y•the•mat′ic** (-măt′ĭk), **er′y•the′mic** *adj.*

er•y•thor•bic acid (ĕr′ə-thôr′bĭk) *n.* An optical isomer of ascorbic acid used as an antioxidant. [ERYTH(RO)– + (ASC)ORBIC ACID.]

er•y•thrism (ĕr′ə-thrĭz′əm) *n.* Unusual red pigmentation, as of hair or plumage. —**er′y•thris′mal** (-thrĭz′məl) *adj.*

er•y•thrite (ĕr′ə-thrīt′) *n.* A reddish secondary cobalt mineral, $CO_3(AsO_4)_2{\cdot}8H_2O$, found in veins bearing cobalt and arsenic and used in coloring glass.

erythro– or **erythr–** *pref.* **1.** Red: *erythrocyte.* **2.** Erythrocyte: *erythropoiesis.* [< Gk. *eruthros,* red. See **reudh-** in App.]

e•ryth•ro•blast (ĭ-rĭth′rə-blăst′) *n.* Any of the nucleated cells normally found only in bone marrow that develop into erythrocytes. —**e•ryth′ro•blas′tic** *adj.*

e•ryth•ro•blas•to•sis (ĭ-rĭth′rō-blă-stō′sĭs) *n., pl.* **-ses** (-sēz) The abnormal presence of erythroblasts in the blood. [NLat. *erythroblastōsis fētālis* : *erythroblastōsis,* erythroblastosis + *fētālis,* fetal.]

erythroblastosis fe•ta•lis (fē-tā′lĭs) *n.* A severe hemolytic disease of a fetus or newborn infant caused by the production of maternal antibodies against the fetal red blood cells, usu. involving Rh incompatibility between the mother and fetus. [NLat. *erythroblastōsis fētālis,* fetal erythroblastosis : *erythroblastōsis,* erythroblastosis + *fētālis,* fetal.]

e•ryth•ro•cyte (ĭ-rĭth′rə-sīt′) *n.* See **red blood cell.** —**e•ryth′ro•cyt′ic** (-sĭt′ĭk) *adj.*

e•ryth•ro•cy•tom•e•ter (ĭ-rĭth′rə-sī-tŏm′ĭ-tər) *n.* A device for counting the number of red blood cells in a blood sample.

e•ryth•ro•my•cin (ĭ-rĭth′rə-mī′sĭn) *n.* An antibiotic, $C_{37}H_{67}NO_{13}$, obtained from a strain of the actinomycete *Streptomyces erythreus* and used to treat a variety of infections.

e•ryth•ro•poi•e•sis (ĭ-rĭth′rō-poi-ē′sĭs) *n.* The formation or production of red blood cells. —**e•ryth′ro•poi•et′ic** (-ĕt′ĭk) *adj.*

e•ryth•ro•poi•e•tin (ĭ-rĭth′rō-poi-ē′tĭn) *n.* A glycoprotein hormone that stimulates the production of red blood cells by stem cells in the bone marrow in response to decreased blood oxygen levels. [ERYTHROPOIET(IC) + –IN.]

Erz•ge•bir•ge (ĕrts′gə-bîr′gə) A mountain range extending c. 153 km (95 mi) along the border of Germany and the Czech Republic; rising to 1,244.4 m (4,080 ft).

Es The symbol for the element **einsteinium.**

–es[1] *suff.* Variant of **–s**[1].

–es[2] *suff.* Variant of **–s**[2].

E•sau (ē′sô) The eldest son of Isaac and Rebecca who sold his birthright to his twin, Jacob, for a mess of pottage.

es•ca•drille (ĕs′kə-drĭl′, -drē′) *n.* A unit of a European air command, typically containing ten or more aircraft. [Fr. < Sp. *escuadrilla,* dim. of *escuadra,* squadron < *escuadrar,* to square off < VLat. **exquadrāre.* See SQUARE.]

es•ca•lade (ĕs′kə-lād′, -läd′) *n.* The act of scaling a fortified wall or rampart. [Fr. < Ital. *scalata,* ult. < Lat. *scālae,* ladder.] —**es′ca•lade′** *v.* —**es′ca•lad′er** *n.*

es•ca•late (ĕs′kə-lāt′) *v.* **-lat•ed, -lat•ing, -lates** —*tr.* To increase, enlarge, or intensify. —*intr.* To increase in intensity or extent. [Back-formation < ESCALATOR.] —**es′ca•la′tion** *n.* —**es′ca•la•to′ry** (-lə-tôr′ē, -tōr′ē) *adj.*

es•ca•la•tor (ĕs′kə-lā′tər) *n.* **1.** A moving stairway consisting of steps attached to a continuously circulating belt. **2.** An escalator clause. [Orig. a trademark.]

escalator clause *n.* A provision in a contract stipulating an increase or a decrease, as in wages, benefits, or prices, under certain conditions, such as changes in the cost of living.

es•cal•lop (ĭ-skŏl′əp, ĭ-skăl′-) *n. & v.* Variant of **scallop.** [ME *escalop* < OFr. *escalope.* See SCALLOP.]

es•ca•pade (ĕs′kə-pād′) *n.* An adventurous unconventional act or undertaking. [Fr., a trick, an escape < OFr., ult. < VLat. **excappāre,* to escape. See ESCAPE.]

es•cape (ĭ-skāp′) *v.* **-caped, -cap•ing, -capes** —*intr.* **1.** To break loose from confinement; get free. **2.** To issue from confinement or an enclosure; leak or seep out. **3.** To avoid a serious or unwanted outcome. **4.** *Botany* To become established in the wild. Used of a cultivated species. **5.** To interrupt a command, exit a program, or change levels within a program by pressing the escape key. —*tr.* **1.** To succeed in avoiding. **2.** To break loose from; get free of. **3.** To elude the memory or comprehension of. **4.** To issue involuntarily from. ❖ *n.* **1.** The act or an instance of escaping. **2.** A means of escaping. **3.** A means of temporarily avoiding worry, care, or unpleasantness. **4.** A gradual effusion from an enclosure; a leakage. **5.** *Botany* A plant that has escaped. **6.** *Computer Science* A key on a keyboard pressed to interrupt a command, exit a program, or change levels within a program. [ME *escapen* < ONFr. *escaper* < VLat. **excappāre,* to get out of one's cape, get away : Lat. *ex-,* ex- + Med.Lat. *cappa,* cloak.] —**es•cap′a•ble** *adj.* —**es•cap′er** *n.*

escape clause *n.* A clause in a contract that specifies the conditions under which the promisor is relieved of liability for failure to meet the terms of the contract.

es•cap•ee (ĭ-skā′pē′, ĕs′kā-) *n.* One that has escaped, esp. an escaped prisoner. See Usage Note at **–ee**[1].

es•cape•ment (ĭ-skāp′mənt) *n.* **1.** A mechanism consisting in general of an escape wheel and an anchor, used esp. in timepieces to control movement of the wheel and provide periodic energy impulses to a pendulum or balance. **2.** A mechanism, as in a typewriter, that controls the lateral movement of the carriage. **3a.** An escape. **b.** A means or way of escape.

escape velocity *n.* The minimum velocity that a body must attain to escape a gravitational field completely.

escape wheel *n.* The rotating notched wheel periodically engaged and disengaged by the anchor in an escapement.

es•cap•ism (ĭ-skā′pĭz′əm) *n.* The tendency to escape from daily reality or routine by indulging in daydreaming, fantasy, or entertainment. —**es•cap′ist** *adj.* —**es•cap′ist** *n.*

es•cap•ol•o•gy (ĕs′kā-pŏl′ə-jē) *n.* The art, skill, or practice of escaping. —**es′cap•ol′o•gist** *n.*

es•car•got (ĕs′kär-gō′) *n., pl.* **-gots** (-gō′) An edible snail, esp. one prepared as an appetizer or entrée. [Fr. < OFr. *escargol* < O Provençal *escaragol,* prob. ult. < Lat. *scarabaeus,* beetle. See SCARAB.]

es•ca•role (ĕs′kə-rōl′) *n.* A variety of endive *(Cichorium endivia)* having leaves with irregular frilled edges and often used in salads. [Fr. < OFr. *scariole* < LLat. *ēscāriola,* chicory < Lat. *ēscārius,* of food < *ēsca,* food < *edere, ēs-,* to eat. See **ed-** in App.]

es•carp (ĭ-skärp′) *n.* **1.** A steep slope or cliff; an escarpment. **2.** The inner wall of a ditch or trench dug around a fortification. ❖ *tr.v.* **-carped, -carp•ing, -carps 1.** To cause to form a steep slope. **2.** To furnish with an escarp. [Fr. *escarpe* < Ital. *scarpa.* See SCARP.]

es•carp•ment (ĭ-skärp′mənt) *n.* **1.** A steep slope or long cliff caused by erosion or faulting separating two level areas of differing heights. **2.** A steep slope before a fortification.

–escence *suff.* State; process. Used to form nouns from adjectives in *-escent* or verbs in *-esce: fluorescence.* [Fr. < OFr. < Lat. *-ēscentia* < *-ēscēns, -ēscent-,* -escent.]

–escent *suff.* **1.** Beginning to be; becoming: *juvenescent.* **2.** Characterized by; resembling: *opalescent.* [Fr. < OFr. < Lat. *-ēscēns, -ēscent-,* pr. part. suff. of inchoative verbs in *-ēscere.*]

esch•a•lot (ĕsh′ə-lŏt′) *n.* See **shallot.** [Obsolete Fr. *eschalotte.* See SHALLOT.]

es•char (ĕs′kär′) *n.* A dry scab or slough formed on the skin as a result of a burn or by the action of a corrosive or caustic substance. [ME *escare* < OFr. See SCAR[1].]

es•cha•rot•ic (ĕs′kə-rŏt′ĭk) *adj.* Producing an eschar. ❖ *n.* A caustic or corrosive substance or drug.

es•cha•tol•o•gy (ĕs′kə-tŏl′ə-jē) *n.* **1.** The branch of theology dealing with the end of the world or of humanity. **2.** A belief or doctrine concerning the last things, such as death, the destiny of humanity, the Second Coming, or the Last Judgment. [Gk. *eskhatos,* last; see **eghs** in App. + –LOGY.] —**es•chat′o•log′i•cal** (ĭ-skăt′l-ŏj′ĭ-kəl, ĕs′kə-tə-lŏj′-) *adj.* —**es•chat′o•log′i•cal•ly** *adv.* —**es′cha•tol′o•gist** *n.*

es•cheat (ĭs-chēt′) *n.* **1.** Reversion of land held under feudal ten-

ure to the manor in the absence of legal heirs or claimants. **2.** *Law* **a.** Reversion of property to the state in the absence of legal heirs or claimants. **b.** Property that has reverted to the state when no legal heirs or claimants exist. ❖ *intr. & tr.v.* **-cheat·ed, -cheat·ing, -cheats** *Law* To revert or cause to revert by escheat. [ME *eschete* < OFr. (< *escheoir*, to fall out) and < Med.Lat. *escheta*, both < VLat. *excadēre*, to fall out : Lat. *ex-*, ex- + Lat. *cadere*, to fall.] —**es·cheat′a·ble** *adj.*

es·cheat·age (ĭs-chē′tĭj) *n. Law* The right of the state to acquire property by escheat.

es·chew (ĕs-chōō′) *tr.v.* **-chewed, -chew·ing, -chews** To avoid; shun. [ME *eschewen* < OFr. *eschivir*, of Gmc. orig.; akin to SHY[1].] —**es·chew′al** (-əl) *n.*

Es·cof·fier (ĕs-kô-fyā′), **Auguste** 1846–1935. French chef whose cookery books include *Le Guide Culinaire* (1903).

es·co·lar (ĕs′kə-lär′) *n., pl.* **escolar** or **-lars** Any of several slender fishes of the family Gempylidae, esp. *Lepidocybium flavobrunneum*, of warm marine waters. [Sp., student (< the spectaclelike rings around its eyes) < LLat. *scholāris*, of a school. See SCHOLAR.]

Es·con·di·do (ĕs′kən-dē′dō) A city of S CA N of San Diego. Pop. 133,559.

Es·co·ri·al (ĕs-skôr′ē-əl, -skôr′-, ĕs′kō-rē-äl′) A monastery and palace of central Spain near Madrid (built 1563–84).

es·cort (ĕs′kôrt′) *n.* **1a.** One or more persons accompanying another to guide, protect, or show honor. **b.** A man who is the companion of a woman, esp. on a social occasion. **c.** A person, often a prostitute, who is hired to spend time with another as a companion. **2a.** One or more vehicles accompanying another vehicle to guide, protect, or honor its passengers. **b.** One or more warships or planes used to defend or protect other craft from attack. **3.** The state of being escorted. ❖ *tr.v.* (ĭ-skôrt′, ĕ-skôrt′, ĕs′kôrt′) **-cort·ed, -cort·ing, -corts** To accompany as an escort. See Syns at **accompany.** [Fr. *escorte* < Ital. *scorta* < *scorgere*, to guide < VLat. *excorrigere* : Lat. *ex-*, ex- + Lat. *corrigere*, to set right; see CORRECT.]

es·cri·toire (ĕs′krĭ-twär′) *n.* **1.** A writing table; a desk. **2.** A desk with a top section for books. [Obsolete Fr. < OFr. *escriptoire*, study < Med.Lat. *scrīptōrium*. See SCRIPTORIUM.]

es·crow (ĕs′krō, ĕ-skrō′) *n.* Money, property, a deed, or a bond put into the custody of a third party for delivery to a grantee only after the fulfillment of the conditions specified. ❖ *tr.v.* **-crowed, -crow·ing, -crows** To place in escrow. —*idiom:* **in escrow** In trust as an escrow. [AN *escrowe*, var. of OFr. *escroe*, scroll. See SCROLL.]

es·cu·do (ĭ-skōō′dō) *n., pl.* **-dos** See table at **currency.** [Port. and Sp., shield, escudo < Lat. *scūtum*, shield.]

es·cu·lent (ĕs′kyə-lənt) *adj.* Suitable for eating; edible. [Lat. *ēsculentus* < *ēsca*, food < *edere*, ĕs-, to eat. See ed- in App.] —**es′cu·lent** *n.*

es·cutch·eon (ĭ-skŭch′ən) *n.* **1.** *Heraldry* A shield or shield-shaped emblem bearing a coat of arms. **2.** An ornamental or protective plate, as for a keyhole. **3.** The plate on the stern of a ship inscribed with the ship's name. —*idiom:* **a blot on (one's) escutcheon** Dishonor to one's reputation. [ME *escochon* < AN *escuchon* < VLat. *scūtiō, scūtiōn-* < Lat. *scūtum*, shield.] —**es·cutch′eoned** *adj.*

Esd. or **Esdr.** *abbr.* Esdras

Es·dra·e·lon (ĕs′drā-ē′lŏn, -drə-, ĕz′-), **Plain of** A fertile plain of N Israel extending from the coastal lowlands near Mt. Carmel to the Jordan R. valley.

Es·dras (ĕz′drəs) *n. Bible* One of four books of the Vulgate, the first two of which correspond to Ezra and Nehemiah and the second two of which are sometimes included as an appendix to the New Testament as 1 and 2 Esdras.

ESE *abbr.* east-southeast

-ese *suff.* **1.** Of, relating to, characteristic of, or originating in a specified place: *Vietnamese.* **2.** Native or inhabitant of: *Taiwanese.* **3a.** Language or dialect of: *Chinese.* **b.** Literary style or diction of: *journalese.* [ME < Ital. < Lat. *-ēnsis*, originating in.]

es·er·ine (ĕs′ə-rēn′) *n.* See **physostigmine.** [Efik *esere*, Calabar bean + -INE[2].]

Es·fa·han (ĕs′fə-hän′) or **Is·fa·han** (ĭs′-) A city of central Iran S of Tehran; cap. of Persia from 1598 to 1722. Pop. 1,220,595.

e-signature (ē′sĭg′nə-chər) *n.* An electronic sound, symbol, or process attached to or associated with a contract or other record and used as the legal equivalent of a written signature.

Esk. *abbr.* Eskimo

es·ker (ĕs′kər) *n.* A long narrow ridge of coarse gravel deposited by a stream flowing in or under a decaying glacial ice sheet. [Ir. Gael. *eiscir* < OIr. *escir.*]

Es·ki·mo (ĕs′kə-mō′) *n., pl.* **Eskimo** or **-mos 1.** A member of a group of peoples inhabiting the Arctic coastal regions of North America and parts of Greenland and northeast Siberia. See Usage Note at **Native American. 2.** Any of the languages of the Eskimo peoples. [Fr. *Esquimaux*, Esquimau < Sp. *esquimao, esquimal* < Montagnais *ayashkimew*, Micmac.] —**Es′ki·mo′an** *adj.*

USAGE NOTE *Eskimo* has come under attack for its supposed offensiveness, and many Americans today either avoid this term or feel uneasy using it. *Inuit* is now the preferred term when refer-

ring to the Inuit-speaking peoples of Arctic Canada and Greenland. In Alaska and Arctic Siberia, where Inuit is not spoken, the comparable terms are *Inupiaq* and *Yupik*, neither of which has gained as much popularity as *Inuit*. While it makes sense to use these terms when speaking of the appropriate linguistic group, none of them can be used of the Eskimoan peoples as a whole; the only inclusive term remains *Eskimo.* • The claim that *Eskimo* is offensive is based primarily on a popular but disputed etymology tracing its origin to an Abenaki word meaning "eaters of raw meat." Many linguists now speculate that the term may actually derive from a Montagnais word referring to the manner of lacing a snowshoe.

Es·ki·mo-A·leut (ĕs′kə-mō′ə-lōōt′, -āl′ē-ōōt′) *n.* The language family containing the Eskimoan and Aleut languages.

Eskimo dog *n.* A large dog of a breed used in Arctic regions for pulling sleds and having a thick coat and a plumed tail.

Es·ki·şe·hir (ĕs′kĭ-shə-hîr′) A city of W-central Turkey W of Ankara. Pop. 451,000.

ESL *abbr.* English as a second language

ESOP (ē′sŏp) *n.* A plan under which the employees of a company or corporation acquire its capital stock. [E(mployee) S(tock) O(wnership) P(lan).]

e·soph·a·gus also **oe·soph·a·gus** (ĭ-sŏf′ə-gəs) *n., pl.* **-gi** (-jī′, -gī′) The muscular tube for the passage of food from the pharynx to the stomach; the gullet. [ME *isophagus* < Med.Lat. *ēsophagus* < Gk. *oisophagos*, arbitrary medical coinage perh. < *ois-*, fut. t. stem of *pherein*, to carry + *-phagos*, food (unattested sense) (< *phagein*, to eat; see **bhag-** in App.).] —**e·soph′a·ge′al** (-jē′əl) *adj.*

es·o·ter·ic (ĕs′ə-tĕr′ĭk) *adj.* **1a.** Meant for or understood by only a specific group. See Syns at **mysterious. b.** Of or relating to what is known by a restricted number of people. **2a.** Confined to a small group. **b.** Not publicly disclosed; confidential. [Gk. *esōterikos* < *esōterō*, comp. of *esō*, within. See **en** in App.] —**es′o·ter′i·cal·ly** *adv.*

es·o·ter·i·ca (ĕs′ə-tĕr′ĭ-kə) *pl.n.* (used with a sing. or pl. verb) Esoteric matters or items. [Gk. *esōterika* < neut. pl. of *esōterikos*, esoteric. See ESOTERIC.]

es·o·ter·i·cism (ĕs′ə-tĕr′ĭ-sĭz′əm) *n.* **1.** Esoteric teachings or practices. **2.** The quality or condition of being esoteric.

es·o·tro·pi·a (ĕs′ə-trō′pē-ə) *n.* A form of strabismus in which one or both of the eyes deviate inward. [NLat. *esōtropia* : Gk. *esō*, within; see **en** in App. + Gk. *tropē*, a turning; see –TROPIC.] —**es′o·trop′ic** (-trŏp′ĭk, -trō′pĭk) *adj.*

ESP (ē′ĕs-pē′) *n.* Communication or perception by means other than the physical senses. [e(xtra)s(ensory) p(erception).]

esp. *abbr.* especially

es·pa·drille (ĕs′pə-drĭl′) *n.* A shoe usu. having a fabric upper and a flexible sole, as of rope. [Fr. < Provençal *espardilho*, dim. of *espart*, esparto < Lat. *spartum*. See ESPARTO.]

es·pal·ier (ĭ-spăl′yər, -yā′) *n.* **1.** A tree or shrub trained to grow flat against a wall, often in a symmetrical pattern. **2.** A trellis or other framework on which an espalier is grown. ❖ *tr.v.* **-iered, -ier·ing, -iers 1.** To train as or on an espalier. **2.** To provide with an espalier. [Fr. < Ital. *spalliera*, shoulder support < *spalla*, shoulder < LLat. *spatula*, shoulder blade < Lat. See SPATULA.]

es·par·to (ĭ-spär′tō) *n., pl.* **-tos** A tough wiry grass (*Stipa tenacissima*) of northern Africa, used in making paper and cordage. [Sp. < Lat. *spartum* < Gk. *sparton*, rope.]

es·pe·cial (ĭ-spĕsh′əl) *adj.* **1.** Of special importance or significance; exceptional. **2.** Relating to or directed toward a particular person, group, or purpose. **3.** Peculiar to the individual; characteristic. [ME < OFr. < Lat. *speciālis*, of a kind < *speciēs*, species. See **spek-** in App.]

es·pe·cial·ly (ĭ-spĕsh′ə-lē, ĭ-spĕsh′-) *adv.* To an extent or degree deserving of special emphasis; particularly.

es·per·ance (ĕs′pər-əns) *n. Obsolete* Hope. [ME *esperaunce* < OFr. < VLat. *spērantia* < Lat. *spērāns, spērant-*, pr. part. of *spērāre*, to hope.]

Es·pe·ran·to (ĕs′pə-rän′tō, -răn′-) *n.* An artificial international language with vocabulary based on words common to many European languages and regularized inflections. [After Dr. *Esperanto*, "one who hopes," pseudonym of its inventor, Ludwik Lejzer Zamenhof (1859–1917), Polish philologist.] —**Es′pe·ran′tist** *adj. & n.*

es·pi·al (ĭ-spī′əl) *n.* **1.** The act of watching or observing. **2.** A taking notice of something; a discovery. **3.** The fact of being seen or noticed. [ME *espiaille* < OFr. < *espier*, to watch. See ESPY.]

es·pi·o·nage (ĕs′pē-ə-näzh′, -nĭj) *n.* The act or practice of spying or of using spies to obtain secret information. [Fr. *espionnage* < *espionner*, to spy < OFr. *espion*, spy < OItal. *spione*, of Gmc. orig. See **spek-** in App.]

Es·pí·ri·tu San·to (ĕ-spîr′ĭ-tōō sän′tō) An island of Vanuatu in the S Pacific Ocean.

es·pla·nade (ĕs′plə-näd′, -nād′) *n.* A flat open stretch of pavement or grass, esp. one designed as a promenade along a shore. [Fr. < Ital. *spianata* < *spianare*, to level < Lat. *explānāre*, to make plain. See EXPLAIN.]

Es·poo (ĕs′pō, -pô) A town of S Finland, a suburb of Helsinki. Pop. 180,851.

Escorial

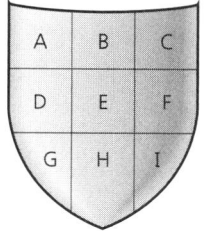

escutcheon
the areas of a shield
A. dexter chief
B. center chief
C. sinister chief
D. dexter flank
E. fess point
F. sinister flank
G. dexter base
H. center base
I. sinister base

espadrille
pair of espadrilles

ă	pat	oi	boy
ā	pay	ou	out
âr	care	ŏŏ	took
ä	father	ōō	boot
ĕ	pet	ŭ	cut
ē	be	ûr	urge
ĭ	pit	th	thin
ī	pie	th	this
îr	pier	hw	which
ŏ	pot	zh	vision
ō	toe	ə	about,
ô	paw		item

Stress marks:
′ (primary);
′ (secondary), as in
lexicon (lĕk′sĭ-kŏn′)

es·pous·al (ĭ-spou′zəl, -səl) *n.* **1a.** A betrothal. **b.** A wedding ceremony. **2.** Adoption of an idea or a cause. [ME *espousaille* < sing. of OFr. *espousailles*, betrothal < Lat. *spōnsālia* < neut. pl. of *spōnsālis*, of a betrothal < *spōnsus*, spouse. See SPOUSE.]

es·pouse (ĭ-spouz′) *tr.v.* **-poused, -pous·ing, -pous·es 1a.** To take in marriage; marry. **b.** To give (a woman) in marriage. **2.** To give one's loyalty or support to (a cause, for example); adopt. [ME *espousen* < OFr. *espouser* < Lat. *spōnsāre*, freq. of *spondēre*, to betroth. See **spend-** in App.] —**es·pous′er** *n.*

es·pres·so (ĭ-sprĕs′ō, ĕ-sprĕs′ō) also **ex·pres·so** (ĭk-sprĕs′ō, ĕk-) *n., pl.* **-sos** A strong coffee brewed by forcing steam under pressure through darkly roasted powdered coffee beans. [Ital. (*caffè*) *espresso*, espresso (coffee), p. part. of *esprimere*, to press out < Lat. *exprimere* : *ex-*, ex- + *premere*, to press.]

es·prit (ĕ-sprē′) *n.* **1.** Liveliness of mind or spirit. **2.** Esprit de corps. [Fr. < Lat. *spīritus*, spirit. See SPIRIT.]

esprit de corps (də kôr′) *n.* A common spirit of comradeship, enthusiasm, and devotion to a cause among the members of a group. [Fr. : *esprit*, spirit + *de*, of + *corps*, group.]

es·py (ĭ-spī′) *tr.v.* **-pied, -py·ing, -pies** To catch sight of (something distant, partially hidden, or obscure); glimpse. See Syns at **see**[1]. [ME *espien* < OFr. *espier*, to watch, of Gmc. orig. See **spek-** in App.]

Esq. *abbr.* esquire (title)

-esque *suff.* In the manner of; resembling: *Lincolnesque.* [Fr. < Ital. *-esco* < VLat. *-iscus*, of Gmc. orig.]

Es·qui·line (ĕs′kwə-līn′, -lĭn) One of the seven hills of ancient Rome; site of Nero's Golden House and Trajan's Thermae, or hot baths. —**Es′qui·line′** *adj.*

Es·qui·mau (ĕs′kə-mō′) *n., pl.* **Esquimau** or **-maux** (-mōz′) An Eskimo. [Fr., sing. of *Esquimaux*, Eskimo. See ESKIMO.]

es·quire (ĕs′kwīr, ĭ-skwīr′) *n.* **1.** A man or boy of the English gentry ranking directly below a knight. **2.** Used as an honorific usu. in its abbreviated form, esp. after the name of an attorney or a consular officer: *John Doe, Esq.* **3.** In medieval times, a candidate for knighthood who served a knight as an attendant and a shield bearer. **4.** *Archaic* An English country gentleman; a squire. [ME *esquier* < OFr. *escuier* < LLat. *scūtārius*, shield bearer < Lat. *scūtum*, shield.]

ess (ĕs) *n.* The letter *s*.

-ess *suff.* Female: *lioness.* [ME *-esse* < OFr. < LLat. *-issa* < Gk.]

es·say (ĕs′ā′, ĕ-sā′) *n.* **1.** (ĕs′ā′) **a.** A short literary composition on a single subject, usu. presenting the personal view of the author. **b.** Something resembling such a composition. **2.** A testing or trial of the value or nature of a thing: *an essay of my capabilities.* **3.** An initial attempt or endeavor, esp. a tentative attempt. ❖ *tr.v.* (ĕ-sā′, ĕs′ā′) **-sayed, -say·ing, -says 1.** To make an attempt at; try. **2.** To subject to a test. [Fr. *essai*, trial, attempt < OFr. < *essayer*, to attempt < VLat. *exagiāre*, to weigh out < LLat. *exagium*, a weighing : Lat. *ex-*, ex- + Lat. *agere*, to drive; see **ag-** in App. V., ME *assaien* < OFr. *assaer, assaier*, var. of *essayer*.] —**es·say′er** *n.*

es·say·ist (ĕs′ā-ĭst) *n.* A writer of essays.

es·say·is·tic (ĕs′ā-ĭs′tĭk) *adj.* **1.** Of or relating to an essay or a writer of essays. **2.** Resembling an essay in nature or quality.

Es·sen (ĕs′ən) A city of W-central Germany N of Cologne; founded in the 9th cent. Pop. 622,380.

es·sence (ĕs′əns) *n.* **1.** The intrinsic or indispensable properties that characterize or identify something. **2.** The most important ingredient; the crucial element. **3.** The inherent unchanging nature of a thing or class of things. **4a.** An extract that has the fundamental properties of a substance in concentrated form. **b.** Such an extract in a solution of alcohol. **c.** A perfume or scent. **5.** One that has or shows an abundance of a quality as if highly concentrated. **6.** Something that exists, esp. a spiritual or incorporeal entity. —*idioms:* **in essence** By nature; essentially. **of the essence** Of the greatest importance; crucial. [ME *essencia* and Fr. *essence,* both < Lat. *essentia* < *essēns, *essent-,* presumed pr. part. of *esse,* to be (created to translate Gk. *ousiā > ousa,* fem. pr. part. of *einai,* to be). See **es-** in App.]

Es·sene (ĕs′ēn′, ĭ-sēn′) *n.* A member of an ascetic Jewish sect that existed in ancient Palestine from the second century B.C. to the second century A.D. —**Es·se′ni·an** (ĕ-sē′nē-ən), **Es·sen′ic** (ĭ-sĕn′ĭk) *adj.* —**Es·se′nism** *n.*

es·sen·tial (ĭ-sĕn′shəl) *adj.* **1.** Constituting or being part of the essence of something; inherent. **2.** Basic or indispensable; necessary. See Syns at **indispensable. 3.** *Medicine* Of, relating to, or being a dysfunction or a disease of an unknown cause. **4.** *Biochemistry* Being a substance that is required for normal functioning but cannot be synthesized by the body and therefore must be included in the diet. ❖ *n.* **1.** Something fundamental. **2.** Something necessary or indispensable. —**es·sen′ti·al′i·ty** (-shē-ăl′ĭ-tē), *n.* —**es·sen′tial·ness** *n.* —**es·sen′tial·ly** *adv.*

es·sen·tial·ism (ĭ-sĕn′shə-lĭz′əm) *n.* The metaphysical theory that the essential properties of an object can be distinguished from those that are accidental to it.

es·sen·tial·ize (ĭ-sĕn′shə-līz′) *tr.v.* **-ized, -iz·ing, -izes** To express or extract the essential form of.

essential oil *n.* A volatile oil, usu. having the odor or flavor of the plant it is from, used in perfumes and flavorings.

Es·se·qui·bo (ĕs′ĭ-kwē′bō) A river rising on the Brazilian border of S Guyana and flowing c. 965 km (600 mi) generally N to the Atlantic Ocean.

Es·sex (ĕs′ĭks) A historical region and Anglo-Saxon kingdom of SE England.

Essex, 2nd Earl of. See Robert **Devereux.**

es·so·nite (ĕs′ə-nīt′) also **hes·so·nite** (hĕs′-) *n.* A brown or yellowish-brown variety of garnet. [Fr. < Gk. *hēssōn,* inferior, comp. of *ēka, hēka,* slightly.]

EST *abbr.* Eastern Standard Time

est. *abbr.* **1.** established **2.** estate **3.** estimate

Est. *abbr.* **1.** *Bible* Esther **2a.** Estonia **b.** Estonian

-est[1] *suff.* Used to form the superlative degree of adjectives and adverbs: *greatest; earliest.* [ME < OE *-est, -ast, -ost.*]

-est[2] or **-st** *suff.* Used to form the archaic second person singular of English verbs: *comest.* [ME < OE *-est, -ast.*]

es·tab·lish (ĭ-stăb′lĭsh) *tr.v.* **-lished, -lish·ing, -lish·es 1a.** To set up; found. See Syns at **found**[1]. **b.** To bring about; generate. **2a.** To place in a secure position or condition; install. **b.** To make firm or secure. **3.** To cause to be recognized and accepted. **4.** To introduce and put (a law, for example) into force. **5.** To prove the validity or truth of (a claim). **6.** To make a state institution of (a church). [ME *establishen* < OFr. *establir, establiss-* < Lat. *stabilīre* < *stabilis,* firm. See **stā-** in App.] —**es·tab′lish·er** *n.*

es·tab·lished church (ĭ-stăb′lĭsht) *n.* A church that a government recognizes and supports as a national institution.

es·tab·lish·ment (ĭ-stăb′lĭsh-mənt) *n.* **1a.** The act of establishing. **b.** The condition or fact of being established. **2.** Something established, as: **a.** An arranged order or system, esp. a legal code. **b.** A permanent civil, political, or military organization. **c.** An established church. **d.** A place of residence or business with its possessions and staff. **e.** A public or private institution, such as a hospital or school. **3.** often **Establishment** An established social order, as: **a.** A group of influential, powerful people in a government or society. **b.** A controlling group in a given field of activity.

es·tab·lish·men·tar·i·an (ĭ-stăb′lĭsh-mən-târ′ē-ən) *adj.* Of, relating to, or supporting a political or social establishment. —**es·tab′lish·men·tar′i·an** *n.* —**es·tab′lish·men·tar′i·an·ism** *n.*

es·ta·mi·net (ĕ-stä′mē-nā′) *n.* A small café. [Fr., prob. < Walloon *èstaminê, staminê,* cowshed, little café, prob. < *stamen,* post to which a cow is tied at the feeding trough, prob. of Gmc. orig. See **stā-** in App.]

es·tan·cia (ĕ-stän′syä) *n.* A large estate or cattle ranch in Spanish America. [Sp., room, enclosure, country estate < VLat. *stantia,* something standing < Lat. *stāns, stant-,* pr. part. of *stāre,* to stand. See **stā-** in App.]

es·tate (ĭ-stāt′) *n.* **1.** A landed property, usu. large in size. **2.** All of one's possessions, esp. the property and debts left at death. **3.** *Law* The nature and extent of an owner's rights to land or other property. **4.** *Chiefly British* A housing development. **5.** The situation or circumstances of one's life. **6.** Social position or rank, esp. of high order. **7.** A major social class, such as the clergy, the nobility, or the commons, formerly possessing distinct political rights. **8.** *Archaic* Display of wealth or power; pomp. [ME *estat,* condition < OFr. See STATE.]

Es·tates-Gen·er·al (ĭ-stāts′jĕn′ər-əl) *pl.n.* See **States-General** 2. [Transl. of Fr. *états généraux.*]

estate tax *n.* A tax imposed on the right to transfer property by inheritance and assessed on the net value of a decedent's estate before distribution to the heirs.

Es·te (ĕs′tā) Italian noble family that prospered from the late 10th to the early 19th cent. and exerted great influence on Renaissance literature.

es·teem (ĭ-stēm′) *tr.v.* **-teemed, -teem·ing, -teems 1.** To regard with respect; prize. See Syns at **appreciate. 2.** To regard as; consider. ❖ *n.* **1.** Favorable regard. **2.** *Archaic* Judgment; opinion. [ME *estemen,* to appraise < OFr. *estimer* < Lat. *aestimāre.*]

es·ter (ĕs′tər) *n.* Any of a class of organic compounds corresponding to the inorganic salts and formed from an organic acid and an alcohol. [Ger., shortening of *Essigäther* : *Essig,* vinegar (< MHGer. *ezzich* < OHGer. *ezzīh* < Lat. *acētum;* see **ak-** in App.) + *Äther,* ether (< Lat. *aethēr;* see ETHER).]

es·ter·ase (ĕs′tə-rās′, -rāz′) *n.* Any of various enzymes that catalyze the hydrolysis of an ester.

Es·ter·há·zy (ĕs′tər-hä′zē) Hungarian princely family of politicians, military officers, and art patrons.

es·ter·i·fi·ca·tion (ĕ-stĕr′ə-fĭ-kā′shən) *n.* A chemical reaction resulting in the formation of at least one ester product.

es·ter·i·fy (ĕ-stĕr′ə-fī′) *intr. & tr.v.* **-fied, -fy·ing, -fies** To change or cause to change to an ester.

Es·ther[1] (ĕs′tər) In the Bible, the Jewish queen of Persia who saved her people from massacre. [Heb. *estēr* < Pers. *sitareh*, star; see **ster-** in App., or Akkadian *Ištar*, Ishtar.]

Es·ther[2] (ĕs′tər) *n.* See table at **Bible.** [After ESTHER[1].]

es·the·sia (ĕs-thē′zhə) *n.* Variant of **aesthesia.**

es·the·si·om·e·ter (ĕs-thē′zē-ŏm′ĭ-tər) *n.* An instrument used to measure tactile sensitivity. [ESTHESI(A) + −METER.]

es·thete (ĕs′thēt) *n.* Variant of **aesthete.**

es·thet·ic (ĕs-thĕt′ĭk) *adj. & n.* Variant of **aesthetic.**

es·the·ti·cian (ĕs′thĭ-tĭsh′ən) *n.* Variant of **aesthetician.**

es·thet·i·cism (ĕs-thĕt′ĭ-sĭz′əm) *n.* Variant of **aestheticism.**

es·thet·ics (ĕs-thĕt′ĭks) *n.* Variant of **aesthetics.**

es·ti·ma·ble (ĕs′tə-mə-bəl) *adj.* **1.** Possible to estimate. **2.** Deserving of esteem; admirable: *an estimable book.* —**es′ti·ma·ble·ness** *n.* —**es′ti·ma·bly** *adv.*

es·ti·mate (ĕs′tə-māt′) *tr.v.* **-mat·ed, -mat·ing, -mates 1.** To calculate approximately (the amount, extent, magnitude, position, or value of something). **2.** To form an opinion about; evaluate. ❖ *n.* (-mĭt) **1.** The act of evaluating or appraising. **2.** A rough calculation, as of size. **3.** A statement of the approximate cost of work to be done. **4.** A judgment based on one's impressions; an opinion. [Lat. *aestimāre, aestimāt-.*] —**es′ti·ma′tive** *adj.* —**es′ti·ma′tor** *n.*

SYNONYMS estimate, appraise, assess, assay, evaluate, rate These verbs mean to form a judgment of worth or significance. *Estimate* usually implies a subjective and somewhat inexact judgment: *difficult to estimate results in advance.* *Appraise* stresses expert judgment: *appraised works of art.* *Assess* implies authoritative judgment in setting a monetary value on something as a basis for taxation: *assessing real estate.* *Assay* refers to careful examination, especially to chemical analysis of an ore: *will assay the ingot.* In extended senses *appraise, assess,* and *assay* can refer to any critical analysis. *Evaluate* implies considered judgment in ascertaining value: *evaluating a student's thesis.* *Rate* involves determining the rank or grade of someone or something in relation to others: *rated the restaurant higher than any other in the city.*

es·ti·ma·tion (ĕs′tə-mā′shən) *n.* **1a.** The act or an instance of estimating. **b.** The amount, extent, position, size, or value reached in an estimate. **2.** An opinion or judgment. **3.** Favorable regard; esteem.

es·ti·val also **aes·ti·val** (ĕs′tə-vəl) *adj.* Of, relating to, or appearing in summer. [ME < OFr. < Lat. *aestīvālis < aestīvus < aestās,* summer.]

es·ti·vate also **aes·ti·vate** (ĕs′tə-vāt′) *intr.v.* **-vat·ed, -vat·ing, -vates 1.** To spend the summer, as at a special place. **2.** *Zoology* To pass the summer in a dormant or torpid state. [Lat. *aestīvāre, aestīvāt- < aestīvus,* estival. See ESTIVAL.]

es·ti·va·tion also **aes·ti·va·tion** (ĕs′tə-vā′shən) *n.* **1.** The act of spending or passing the summer. **2.** *Zoology* A state of dormancy or torpor during the summer. **3.** *Botany* The arrangement of flower parts in the bud.

Es·to·ni·a (ĕ-stō′nē-ə) A country of NE Europe on the Baltic Sea. Settled before the 1st cent. A.D., it declared its independence in 1917 but was incorp. into the USSR as a constituent republic in 1940. It gained full independence in 1991. Cap. Tallinn. Pop. 1,499,000.

Es·to·ni·an (ĕ-stō′nē-ən) *adj.* Of or relating to Estonia or its people, language, or culture. ❖ *n.* **1a.** A native or inhabitant of Estonia. **b.** A person of Estonian descent. **2.** The Finno-Ugric language of Estonia.

es·top (ĕ-stŏp′) *tr.v.* **-topped, -top·ping, -tops 1.** To impede or prohibit by estoppel. **2.** *Archaic* To stop up. [ME *estoppen* < AN *estopper* < VLat. **stuppāre,* to stop up. See STOP.] —**es·top′page** (ĕ-stŏp′ĭj) *n.*

es·top·pel (ĕ-stŏp′əl) *n. Law* A bar preventing one from contradicting what one has previously stated as the truth. [Obsolete Fr. *estouppail* < OFr. *estouper,* to stop up < VLat. **stuppāre.* See STOP.]

es·tra·di·ol (ĕs′trə-dī′ôl′, -ōl′, -ŏl′) *n.* An estrogenic hormone, $C_{18}H_{24}O_2$, produced by the ovaries and used in treating estrogen deficiency. [*estra-,* estrogen hormone (ESTRUS) + DI−[1] + −OL[1].]

es·trange (ĭ-strānj′) *tr.v.* **-tranged, -trang·ing, -trang·es 1.** To make hostile, unsympathetic, or indifferent; alienate. **2.** To remove from an accustomed place or set of associations. [ME *estraungen* < OFr. *estrangier* < Lat. *extrāneāre,* to treat as a stranger, disown < *extrāneus,* foreign. See STRANGE.] —**es·trange′ment** *n.* —**es·trang′er** *n.*

es·tray (ĭ-strā′) *Archaic n.* A stray. ❖ *intr.v.* **-trayed, -tray·ing, -trays** To stray. [ME *astrai* < AN *estray < estraier,* to stray < OFr. See STRAY.]

Es·tre·ma·du·ra (ĕs′trə-mə-dōōr′ə, ĕs′trä-mä-thōō′rä) **1.** A historical region and former province of W Portugal surrounding Lisbon. **2.** A historical region of W-central Spain bordering

on Portugal; reconquered from the Moors in the 12th and 13th cent. —**Es′tre·ma·du′ran** *adj. & n.*

es·tri·ol (ĕs′trī-ôl′, -ōl′, -ŏl′, ē-strī′ôl′-) *n.* An estrogenic hormone, $C_{18}H_{24}O_3$, found in the urine during pregnancy. [ES(TRUS) + TRI− + −OL[1].]

es·tro·gen also **oes·tro·gen** (ĕs′trə-jən) *n.* Any of several steroid hormones produced chiefly by the ovaries and responsible for promoting estrus and the development and maintenance of female secondary sex characteristics. —**es′tro·gen′ic** (-jĕn′ĭk) *adj.* —**es′tro·gen′i·cal·ly** *adv.*

estrogen replacement therapy *n.* The administration of estrogen to relieve menopausal symptoms and to protect against osteoporosis and heart disease.

es·trone (ĕs′trōn′) *n.* An estrogenic hormone, $C_{18}H_{22}O_2$, used in the treatment of estrogen deficiency.

es·trous (ĕs′trəs) *adj.* Of, relating to, or being in estrus.

estrous cycle *n.* The recurrent set of physiological and behavioral changes that take place from one period of estrus to another.

es·trus also **oes·trus** (ĕs′trəs) *n.* The periodic state of sexual excitement in most female mammals, excluding humans, preceding ovulation and during which the female is most receptive to mating; heat. [NLat. < Lat. *oestrus,* frenzy, gadfly < Gk. *oistros.* See **eis−** in App.]

es·tu·a·rine (ĕs′chōō-ə-rīn′, -rēn′) *adj.* Of, relating to, or found in an estuary.

es·tu·ar·y (ĕs′chōō-ĕr′ē) *n., pl.* **-ies 1.** The part of the wide lower course of a river where its current is met by the tides. **2.** An arm of the sea that meets the mouth of a river. [Lat. *aestuārium < aestus,* tide, surge, heat.] —**es·tu·ar′i·al** (-âr′ē-əl) *adj.*

esu *abbr.* electrostatic unit

e·su·ri·ent (ĭ-sōōr′ē-ənt, ĭ-zŏor′-) *adj.* Hungry; greedy. [Lat. *ēsuriēns, ēsurient-,* pr. part. of *ēsurīre,* desiderative of *edere,* to eat. See **ed−** in App.] —**e·su′ri·ence** (-əns), **e·su′ri·en·cy** (-ən-sē) *n.* —**e·su′ri·ent·ly** *adv.*

ET *abbr.* **1.** eastern time **2.** elapsed time **3.** extraterrestrial

−et *suff.* **1.** Small: *falconet.* **2.** Something worn on: *labret.* [ME < OFr. < VLat. **-ittum.*]

e·ta (ā′tə, ē′tə) *n.* The seventh letter of the Greek alphabet. [Gk. *ēta,* of Phoenician orig.; akin to Heb. *ḥêt,* heth.]

ETA *abbr.* estimated time of arrival

e·ta-c particle (ā′tə-sē′, ē′tə-) *n.* A neutral meson having a mass 5,832 times that of the electron and a mean lifetime of approx. 3.1×10^{-22} seconds.

é·ta·gère also **e·ta·gere** (ā′tä-zhâr′) *n.* A piece of furniture with open shelves for small ornaments. [Fr. < OFr. *estagiere,* scaffold < *estage,* floor. See STAGE.]

e-tail·er (ē′tā′lər) *n.* One that sells goods or commodities to consumers electronically, as over the Internet. [E− + (RE)TAILER.]

et al. *abbr.* Latin *et alii* (and others)

et·a·mine (ĕt′ə-mēn′) *n.* A soft, light, loosely woven cotton or worsted. [Fr. < OFr. *estamine* < Lat. *stāminea* < fem. of *stāmineus,* made of threads < *stāmen,* thread. See **stā−** in App.]

eta particle *n.* A neutral meson having a mass 1,071 times that of an electron.

et cet·er·a (ĕt sĕt′ər-ə, sĕt′rə) And other things of the same class; and so forth. ❖ *n.* **et·cet·er·a** (ĕt′sĕt′-) **1.** A number of persons or things. **2.** etceteras Additional odds and ends; extras. [Lat. : *et,* and + *cētera,* the rest, neut. pl. of *cēterus*; see **ko−** in App.]

etch (ĕch) *v.* **etched, etch·ing, etch·es** —*tr.* **1a.** To cut into the surface of (glass, for example) by the action of acid. **b.** To make or create by this method. **2.** To impress, delineate, or imprint clearly. —*intr.* To engage in etching. [Du. *etsen* < Ger. *ätzen* < MHGer. *etzen* < OHGer. *ezzen,* to eat. See **ed−** in App.] —**etch′er** *n.*

etch·ing (ĕch′ĭng) *n.* **1.** The art of preparing etched plates for printing designs and pictures. **2.** A design etched on a plate. **3.** An impression made from an etched plate.

ETD *abbr.* estimated time of departure

E·te·o·cles (ĭ-tē′ə-klēz′) *n. Greek Mythology* A son of Oedipus and Jocasta who agreed to reign in Thebes in alternating years with his brother, Polynices, but refused to resign after the first year.

e·ter·nal (ĭ-tûr′nəl) *adj.* **1.** Having no beginning or end; existing outside time. See Syns at **infinite. 2.** Continuing without interruption; perpetual. See Syns at **continual. 3.** Forever true or changeless. **4.** Seemingly endless; interminable. **5.** Of or relating to spiritual communion with God, esp. in the afterlife. ❖ *n.* **1.** Something timeless, uninterrupted, or endless. **2. Eternal** God. [ME < OFr. < LLat. *aeternālis* < Lat. *aeternus.* See **aiw−** in App.] —**e·ter·nal·i·ty** (ē′tər-năl′ĭ-tē), **e·ter′nal·ness** *n.* —**e·ter′nal·ly** *adv.*

e·ter·nal·ize (ĭ-tûr′nə-līz′) *tr.v.* **-ized, -iz·ing, -iz·es** To eternize.

e·terne (ĭ-tûrn′) *adj. Archaic* Eternal. [ME < OFr. < Lat. *aeternus.* See ETERNAL.]

e·ter·ni·ty (ĭ-tûr′nĭ-tē) *n., pl.* **-ties 1.** Time without beginning or end; infinite time. **2.** The state or quality of being eternal. **3a.** The timeless state following death. **b.** The afterlife; immortality. **4.** A very long or seemingly endless time: *waited for an eternity.*

Estonia

[ME *eternite* < OFr. < Lat. *aeternitās* < *aeternus*, eternal. See ETERNAL.]

e·ter·nize (ĭ-tûr′nīz′) *tr.v.* **-nized, -niz·ing, -niz·es 1a.** To make eternal. **b.** To protract for an indefinite period. **2.** To make perpetually famous. [Fr. *éterniser* < OFr. *eterne*, eternal. See ETERNE.] —**e·ter′ni·za′tion** (-nĭ-zā′shən) *n.*

e·te·sian (ĭ-tē′zhən) *adj.* Occurring annually. Used of the northerly summer winds of the Mediterranean. [< Lat. *etēsius* < Gk. *etēsios* < *etos*, year. See **wet-**[2] in App.] —**e·te′sian** *n.*

eth (ĕth) *n.* Variant of **edh**.

-eth[1] or **-th** *suff.* Used to form the archaic third person singular present indicative of verbs: *leadeth.* [ME < OE *-eth, -ath.*]

-eth[2] *suff.* Variant of **-th**[3].

eth·ane (ĕth′ān′) *n.* A colorless odorless gaseous alkane, C_2H_6, that occurs as a constituent of natural gas and is used as a fuel and a refrigerant. [ETH(YL) + -ANE.]

eth·a·nol (ĕth′ə-nôl′, -nōl, -nŏl′) *n.* See **alcohol** 1. [ETHAN(E) + -OL[1].]

eth·a·nol·a·mine (ĕth′ə-nŏl′ə-mēn′, -nō′lə-) *n.* A colorless liquid, $NH_2(CH_2)_2ON$, used in the purification of petroleum, in dry cleaning, and in paints and pharmaceuticals.

Eth·el·bert (ĕth′əl-bûrt′) 552?-616. Anglo-Saxon king who ruled Britain S of the Humber and codified English law (604).

Eth·el·red II also **Aeth·el·red II** (ĕth′əl-rĕd′) Called "Ethelred the Unready." 968?-1016. King of the English (978-1016) whose kingdom was ultimately conquered by the Danes.

eth·ene (ĕth′ēn′) *n.* See **ethylene**. [ETH(YL) + -ENE.]

e·ther (ē′thər) *n.* **1.** Any of a class of organic compounds in which two hydrocarbon groups are linked by an oxygen atom. **2.** A volatile, highly flammable liquid, $C_2H_5OC_2H_5$, that is derived from the distillation of ethyl alcohol with sulfuric acid, used as a reagent and solvent and formerly as an anesthetic. **3.** The regions of space beyond the earth's atmosphere; the heavens. **4.** The element once believed to fill all space above the sphere of the moon and compose the stars and planets. **5.** *Physics* An all-pervading, infinitely elastic, massless medium formerly postulated as the medium of propagation of electromagnetic waves. [ME, upper air < Lat. *aethēr* < Gk. *aithēr*.] —**e·ther′ic** (ĭ-thĕr′ĭk, ĭ-thîr′-) *adj.*

e·the·re·al (ĭ-thîr′ē-əl) *adj.* **1.** Light and insubstantial; intangible. See Syns at **airy**. **2.** Highly refined; delicate. **3a.** Of the celestial spheres; heavenly. **b.** Not of this world; spiritual. **4.** *Chemistry* Of or relating to ether. [< Lat. *aetherius* < Gk. *aitherios* < *aithēr*, upper air.] —**e·the′re·al′i·ty** (-ăl′ĭ-tē), **e·the′re·al·ness** *n.* —**e·the′re·al·ly** *adv.*

e·the·re·al·ize (ĭ-thîr′ē-ə-līz′) *tr. & intr.v.* **-ized, -iz·ing, -iz·es** To make or become ethereal. —**e·the′re·al·i·za′tion** (-ə-lĭ-zā′shən) *n.*

Eth·er·ege (ĕth′ər-ĭj, ĕth′rĭj) Sir **George** 1635?-92? English playwright known for *She Would if She Could* (1668).

e·ther·i·fy (ĭ-thĕr′ə-fī′) *tr.v.* **-fied, -fy·ing, -fies** To convert (an alcohol) into an ether. —**e·ther′i·fi·ca′tion** (-fĭ-kā′shən) *n.*

e·ther·ize (ē′thə-rīz′) *tr.v.* **-ized, -iz·ing, -iz·es 1.** To subject to the fumes of ether; anesthetize. **2.** To etherify. —**e′ther·i·za′tion** (ē′thər-ĭ-zā′shən) *n.* —**e′ther·iz′er** *n.*

E·ther·net (ē′thər-nĕt′) A trademark for a LAN protocol.

eth·ic (ĕth′ĭk) *n.* **1a.** A set of principles of right conduct. **b.** A theory or a system of moral values. **2. ethics** (*used with a sing. verb*) The study of the general nature of morals and of specific moral choices; moral philosophy. **3. ethics** (*used with a sing. or pl. verb*) The rules or standards governing the conduct of a person or the members of a profession: *medical ethics.* [ME *ethik* < OFr. *ethique* (< LLat. *ēthica* < Gk. *ēthika*, ethics) and < Lat. *ēthicē* (< Gk. *ēthikē*), both < Gk. *ēthikos*, ethical < *ēthos*, character. See **s(w)e-** in App.]

eth·i·cal (ĕth′ĭ-kəl) *adj.* **1.** Of, relating to, or dealing with ethics. **2.** Being in accordance with the accepted principles that govern the conduct of a profession. See Syns at **moral**. **3.** Of or relating to a drug dispensed solely on the prescription of a physician. ❖ *n.* An ethical drug. —**eth′i·cal·ly** *adv.* —**eth′i·cal·ness, eth′i·cal′i·ty** (-kăl′ĭ-tē) *n.*

eth·i·cist (ĕth′ĭ-sĭst) also **e·thi·cian** (ĕ-thĭsh′ən) *n.* A specialist in ethics.

E·thi·o·pi·a (ē′thē-ō′pē-ə) Formerly **Ab·ys·sin·i·a** (ăb′ĭ-sĭn′ē-ə) A country of NE Africa. An ancient kingdom converted to Christianity in the 4th cent. A.D., it became independent in 1896. Cap. Addis Ababa. Pop. 32,775,000.

E·thi·o·pi·an (ē′thē-ō′pē-ən) *adj.* **1.** Of or relating to Ethiopia or its peoples or cultures. **2.** Of or relating to the zoogeographic region that includes Africa and most of Arabia. ❖ *n.* A native or inhabitant of Ethiopia.

Ethiopian Jew *n.* A member of a people living since ancient times in central Ethiopia and practicing a form of Judaism. Most Ethiopian Jews are now resettled in Israel. —**Ethiopian Jewry** *n.*

E·thi·op·ic (ē′thē-ŏp′ĭk, -ō′pĭk) *n.* Ge'ez. ❖ *adj.* **1.** Of or relating to Ge'ez. **2.** Ethiopian.

eth·moid (ĕth′moid′) also **eth·moi·dal** (ĕth-moid′l) *adj.* Of, relating to, or being a light spongy bone forming part of the walls and septum of the superior nasal cavity and containing numerous perforations for the passage of the olfactory nerve fibers. ❖ *n.* The ethmoid bone. [Fr. *ethmoïde* < Gk. *ēthmoeidēs*, sievelike :

Ethiopia

ēthmos, strainer (< *ēthein*, to sift) + *-oeidēs*, -oid.]

eth·narch (ĕth′närk′) *n.* The ruler of a province or a people. [Gk. *ethnarchēs* : *ethnos*, nation; see ETHNIC + *-archēs*, -arch.] —**eth′nar′chy** *n.*

eth·nic (ĕth′nĭk) *adj.* **1a.** Of or relating to a sizable group of people sharing a common and distinctive racial, national, religious, linguistic, or cultural heritage. **b.** Being a member of a particular ethnic group, esp. belonging to a national group by heritage but residing outside its national boundaries: *ethnic Chinese living in Indonesia.* **c.** Of, relating to, or distinctive of members of such a group. **2.** Relating to a people not Christian or Jewish. ❖ *n.* A member of a particular ethnic group, esp. one with the language or customs of the group. [ME, heathen < LLat. *ethnicus* < Gk. *ethnikos* < *ethnos*, people. See **s(w)e-** in App.]

eth·ni·cal (ĕth′nĭ-kəl) *adj.* **1.** Ethnic. **2.** Of or relating to ethnology. —**eth′ni·cal·ly** *adv.*

ethnic cleansing *n.* The systematic elimination of an ethnic group or groups from a region or society, as by forced emigration or genocide.

eth·nic·i·ty (ĕth-nĭs′ĭ-tē) *n.* **1.** Ethnic character, background, or affiliation. **2.** An ethnic minority.

ethno- *pref.* Race; people: *ethnology.* [Gk. < *ethnos*, people. See **s(w)e-** in App.]

eth·no·cen·trism (ĕth′nō-sĕn′trĭz′əm) *n.* **1.** Belief in the superiority of one's own ethnic group. **2.** Overriding concern with race. —**eth′no·cen′tric** (-trĭk) *adj.* —**eth′no·cen′tri·cal·ly** *adv.* —**eth′no·cen·tric′i·ty** (-sĕn-trĭs′ĭ-tē) *n.*

eth·nog·ra·phy (ĕth-nŏg′rə-fē) *n.* The branch of anthropology that deals with the scientific description of specific human cultures. —**eth·nog′ra·pher** *n.* —**eth′no·graph′ic** (ĕth′nə-grăf′ĭk), **eth′no·graph′i·cal** *adj.* —**eth′no·graph′i·cal·ly** *adv.*

eth·no·his·to·ry (ĕth′nō-hĭs′tə-rē) *n.* The study of esp. native or non-Western peoples from a combined historical and anthropological viewpoint. —**eth′no·his·to′ri·an** (-hī-stôr′ē-ən, -stôr′-, stôr′-) *n.* —**eth′no·his·to′ric** (-hī-stôr′ĭk, -stôr′-), **eth′no·his·to′ri·cal** *adj.*

eth·nol·o·gy (ĕth-nŏl′ə-jē) *n.* **1.** The science that analyzes and compares human cultures; cultural anthropology. **2.** The branch of anthropology that deals with the origin, distribution, and characteristics of human racial groups. —**eth′no·log′ic** (ĕth′nə-lŏj′ĭk), **eth′no·log′i·cal** *adj.* —**eth′no·log′i·cal·ly** *adv.* —**eth·nol′o·gist** *n.*

eth·no·mu·si·col·o·gy (ĕth′nō-myoo′zĭ-kŏl′ə-jē) *n.* **1.** The scientific study of music, esp. traditional or non-Western music, as an aspect of culture. **2.** The comparative study of music of different cultures. —**eth′no·mu′si·co·log′i·cal** (-kə-lŏj′ĭ-kəl) *adj.* —**eth′no·mu′si·col′o·gist** *n.*

eth·no·nym (ĕth′nō-nĭm′) *n.* The name of a people or ethnic group. —**eth′no·nym′ic** *adj.*

e·tho·gram (ē′thə-grăm′) *n.* A pictorial catalog of the behavioral patterns of an organism or a species.

e·thol·o·gy (ĭ-thŏl′ə-jē, ē-thŏl′-) *n.* **1.** The scientific study of animal behavior, esp. in nature. **2.** The study of human ethos and its formation. [Fr. *éthologie* < Lat. *ēthologia*, art of depicting character < Gk. *ēthologia* : *ēthos*, character; see ETHOS + *logos*, speech, expression; see -LOGY.] —**eth′o·log′i·cal** (ĕth′ə-lŏj′ĭ-kəl) *adj.* —**e·thol′o·gist** *n.*

e·thos (ē′thŏs′) *n.* The disposition, character, or fundamental values peculiar to a specific person, people, culture, or movement. [Gk. *ēthos*, character. See **s(w)e-** in App.]

eth·ox·yl (ĭ-thŏk′səl) also **eth·ox·y** (ĭ-thŏk′sē) *n.* The univalent radical C_2H_5O. [ETH(YL) + OX(O)- + -YL.]

eth·yl (ĕth′əl) *n.* A univalent organic radical, C_2H_5. [ETH(ER) + -YL.] —**eth·yl′ic** (ĕ-thĭl′ĭk) *adj.*

ethyl acetate *n.* A colorless volatile flammable liquid, $CH_3COOC_2H_5$, used in perfumes, flavorings, lacquers, pharmaceuticals, and rayon and as a general solvent.

ethyl alcohol *n.* See **alcohol** 1.

eth·yl·a·mine (ĕth′ə-lə-mēn′, -lăm′ən) *n.* A colorless volatile liquid, $C_2H_5NH_2$, used in petroleum refining and detergents and in organic synthesis.

eth·yl·ate (ĕth′ə-lāt′) *tr.v.* **-at·ed, -at·ing, -ates** To introduce the ethyl group into (a compound). —**eth′yl·a′tion** *n.*

ethyl chloride *n.* A chemical compound, C_2H_5Cl, a gas at ordinary temperatures and a colorless volatile flammable liquid when compressed, used as a solvent and refrigerant.

eth·yl·ene (ĕth′ə-lēn′) *n.* A colorless flammable gas, C_2H_4, used as a source of organic compounds, in welding metals, to color citrus fruits, and as an anesthetic. —**eth′yl·e′nic** (-ə-lē′nĭk, -lĕn′ĭk) *adj.*

ethylene glycol *n.* A colorless syrupy alcohol, $HOCH_2CH_2OH$, used as an antifreeze.

ethyl ether *n.* See **ether** 2.

eth·yne (ĕth′īn′) *n.* See **acetylene**.

-etic *suff.* Used to form adjectives usu. from nouns ending in *-esis*, as in *aphaeretic* from *aphaeresis*. [Lat. *-eticus* < Gk. *-etikos* < *-etos*, verbal adj. suff.]

e-tick·et (ē′tĭk′ĭt) *n.* A reservation, as for a seat on an airplane, for which confirmation is granted electronically in lieu of a printed ticket.

e·ti·o·late (ē′tē-ə-lāt′) v. -lat·ed, -lat·ing, -lates —tr. **1.** Botany To cause (a plant) to develop without chlorophyll by preventing exposure to sunlight. **2a.** To cause to appear pale and sickly. **b.** To make weak by stunting the growth or development of. —intr. Botany To become blanched or whitened, as when grown without sunlight. [Fr. étioler < Norman Fr. étieuler, to grow into haulm < éteule, stalk < OFr. esteule < VLat. *stupula < Lat. stipula.] —e′ti·o·la′tion n.

e·ti·ol·o·gy also **ae·ti·ol·o·gy** (ē′tē-ŏl′ə-jē) n., pl. -gies **1a.** The study of causes or origins. **b.** The branch of medicine that deals with the causes or origins of disease. **2a.** Assignment of a cause, origin, or reason for something. **b.** The cause or origin of a disease or disorder as determined by medical diagnosis. [LLat. aetiologia < Gk. aitiologiā : aitiā, cause + -logiā, -logy.] —e′ti·o·log′ic (-ə-lŏj′ĭk), e′ti·o·log′i·cal adj. —e′ti·o·log′i·cal·ly adv. —e′ti·ol′o·gist n.

et·i·quette (ĕt′ĭ-kĕt′, -kĭt) n. The practices and forms prescribed by social convention or by authority. [Fr. < OFr. estiquet, label. See TICKET.]

Et·na also **Aet·na** (ĕt′nə), **Mount** An active volcano, 3,325.1 m (10,902 ft), of E Sicily; first known eruption 475 B.C.

E·ton (ĕt′n) An urban district of SE-central England on the Thames R. opposite Windsor; site of the largest of England's public schools (founded 1440). Pop. 3,523.

Eton collar n. A broad white collar worn over the lapels of a jacket. [After Eton College, England.]

Eton jacket n. A waist-length black jacket that has wide lapels and is cut square at the hips. [After Eton College, England.]

é·touf·fée (ā′tōō-fā′) n., pl. -fées (-fā′) A spicy Cajun stew of vegetables and seafood, esp. crayfish. [Louisiana Fr. < Fr. (à l')étouffée, stewed, alteration of étuvée, fem. p. part. of étuver, to stew < Fr. estuver. See STEW.]

E·tru·ri·a (ĭ-trōōr′ē-ə) An ancient country of W-central Italy in Tuscany and parts of Umbria; center of the Etruscan civilization until the 3rd cent. B.C. —**E·tru′ri·an** adj. & n.

E·trus·can (ĭ-trŭs′kən) adj. Of or relating to ancient Etruria or its people, language, or culture. ❖ n. **1.** A native or inhabitant of ancient Etruria. **2.** The extinct language of the Etruscans, of unknown linguistic affiliation.

et seq. abbr. Latin et sequens (and the following one or ones)

-ette suff. **1.** Small; diminutive: kitchenette. **2.** Female: usherette. **3.** An imitation or inferior kind of cloth: leatherette. [ME < OFr., fem. of -et, -et.]

e·tude (ā′tōōd′, -tōōd′) n. Music **1.** A piece composed for the development of a specific point of technique. **2.** A composition featuring a point of technique but performed because of its artistic merit. [Fr. étude < OFr. estudie, study. See STUDY.]

é·tui (ā-twē′) n., pl. é·tuis (ā-twēz′) A small, usu. ornamental case for holding articles such as needles. [Fr. < OFr. estui, prison < estuier, to guard < VLat. *estudiāre, to treat carefully < Lat. studium, study. See STUDY.]

et ux. abbr. Latin et uxor (and wife)

ETV abbr. educational television

et·y·mo·log·i·cal (ĕt′ə-mə-lŏj′ĭ-kəl) also **et·y·mo·log·ic** (-lŏj′ĭk) adj. Of or relating to etymology or based on the principles of etymology. —et′y·mo·log′i·cal·ly adv.

et·y·mol·o·gist (ĕt′ə-mŏl′ə-jĭst) n. A specialist in etymology.

et·y·mol·o·gize (ĕt′ə-mŏl′ə-jīz′) v. -gized, -giz·ing, -giz·es —tr. To trace and state the etymology of. —intr. To give or suggest the etymology of a word.

et·y·mol·o·gy (ĕt′ə-mŏl′ə-jē) n., pl. -gies **1.** The origin and historical development of a linguistic form as shown by determining its basic elements, earliest known use, and changes in form and meaning, tracing its transmission from one language to another, identifying its cognates in other languages, and reconstructing its ancestral form where possible. **2.** The branch of linguistics that deals with etymologies. [ME etimologie < OFr. ethimologie < Med.Lat. ethimologia < Lat. etymologia < Gk. etumologiā : etumon, true sense of a word; see ETYMON + -logiā, -logy.]

et·y·mon (ĕt′ə-mŏn′) n., pl. -mons or -ma (-mə) **1.** An earlier form of a word in the same language or in an ancestor language. **2.** A word or morpheme from which compounds and derivatives are formed. **3.** A foreign word from which a particular loan word is derived. [Lat. < Gk. etumon, true sense of a word < neut. of etumos, true.]

Eu The symbol for the element europium.

EU abbr. European Union

eu– pref. **1.** Good; well; true: euplastic. **2.** A derivative of a specified substance: eucaine. [ME < Lat. < Gk.]

Eu·boe·a (yōō-bē′ə) also **Ev·voia** (ĕv′yä) An island of central Greece in the Aegean Sea E of the mainland.

eu·caine (yōō-kān′) n. A crystalline substance, $C_{15}H_{21}NO_2$, used as a local anesthetic in veterinary medicine.

eu·ca·lyp·tol (yōō′kə-lĭp′tôl′, -tōl′, -tŏl′) also **eu·ca·lyp·tole** (-tōl′) n. A colorless oily liquid, $C_{10}H_{18}O$, derived from eucalyptus and used in pharmaceuticals and flavoring.

eu·ca·lyp·tus (yōō′kə-lĭp′təs) n., pl. -tus·es or -ti (-tī) Any of numerous trees of the genus Eucalyptus, native to Australia and having wood valued as timber and aromatic leaves that yield an oil used medicinally. [NLat. Eucalyptus, genus name : Gk. eu-, eu-

+ Gk. kaluptos, covered (< kaluptein, to cover; see **kel-** in App.).]

eu·car·y·ote (yōō-kâr′ē-ōt′, -ē-ət) n. Variant of **eukaryote.**

Eu·cha·rist (yōō′kər-ĭst) n. **1.** A sacrament and the central act of worship in many Christian churches, in which bread and wine are consecrated and consumed in remembrance of Jesus's death; Communion. **2.** The consecrated elements of this rite; Communion. [ME eukarist < OFr. eucariste < LLat. eucharistia < Gk. eukharistiā < eukharistos, grateful, thankful : eu-, eu- + kharizesthai, to show favor (< kharis, grace).] —**Eu′cha·ris′tic, Eu′cha·ris′ti·cal** adj.

eu·chre (yōō′kər) n. **1.** A card game played usu. with the highest 32 cards, in which each player is dealt 5 cards and the player making the trump is required to take at least 3 tricks to win. **2.** The act of euchring an opponent. ❖ tr.v. -chred, -chring, -chres **1.** To prevent (an opponent) from taking 3 tricks in euchre. **2.** To deceive by sly or underhand means; cheat: euchred us out of our savings. [?]

eu·chro·ma·tin (yōō-krō′mə-tĭn′) n. Chromosomal material that is genetically active and stains lightly with basic dyes. —**eu′chro·mat′ic** (yōō′krō-măt′ĭk) adj.

Eu·clid (yōō′klĭd) 3rd cent. B.C. Greek mathematician who applied the deductive principles of logic to geometry. —**Eu·clid′e·an, Eu·clid′i·an** adj.

eu·dae·mon also **eu·dai·mon** or **eu·de·mon** (yōō-dē′mən) n. A good or benevolent spirit.

eu·dae·mon·ism also **eu·dai·mon·ism** or **eu·de·mon·ism** (yōō-dē′mə-nĭz′əm) n. A system of ethics that evaluates actions in terms of their capacity to produce happiness. —**eu·dae′mo·nist** n. —**eu·dae′mon·is′tic, eu·dae′mon·is′ti·cal** adj.

Eu·gene (yōō-jēn′) A city of W OR on the Willamette R. S of Salem. Pop. 137,893.

eu·gen·ic (yōō-jĕn′ĭk) adj. **1.** Of or relating to eugenics. **2.** Relating or adapted to the production of good or improved offspring. —**eu·gen′i·cal·ly** adv.

eu·gen·i·cist (yōō-jĕn′ĭ-sĭst) also **eu·gen·ist** (yōō′jə-nĭst) n. An advocate of or a specialist in eugenics.

eu·gen·ics (yōō-jĕn′ĭks) n. (used with a sing. verb) The study of hereditary improvement of the human race by controlled selective breeding.

Eu·gé·nie (yōō-jē′nē, œ-zhä-nē′) 1826–1920. Empress of France (1853–71) as the wife of Napoleon III who acted as regent during the emperor's absences.

eu·ge·nol (yōō′jə-nôl′, -nōl′, -nŏl′) n. A colorless aromatic liquid, $C_{10}H_{12}O_2$, made from clove oil and used as a dental analgesic and in perfumery. [NLat. Eugenia, genus of the clove plant (after Eugene, Prince of Savoy (1663–1736), Austrian general) + -OL(E).]

eu·gle·na (yōō-glē′nə) n. Any of various single-celled freshwater organisms of the genus Euglena, marked by the presence of chlorophyll, a reddish eyespot, and one anterior flagellum. [NLat. : Gk. eu-, eu- + Gk. glēnē, eyeball.]

eu·he·mer·ism (yōō-hē′mə-rĭz′əm, -hĕm′ə-) n. A theory attributing the origin of the gods to the deification of historical heroes. [After Euhemerus, 4th-cent. B.C. Greek philosopher.] —**eu·he′mer·ist** n. —**eu·he′mer·is′tic** adj. —**eu·he′mer·is′ti·cal·ly** adv. —**eu·he′mer·ize** v.

eu·kar·y·ote also **eu·car·y·ote** (yōō-kăr′ē-ōt, -ē-ət) n. An organism whose cells contain a distinct membrane-bound nucleus. [EU- + Gk. karuōtos, having nuts (< karuon, nut).] —**eu·kar′y·ot′ic** (-ŏt′ĭk) adj.

eu·la·chon (yōō′lə-kŏn′) n., pl. eulachon or -chons See candlefish. [Chinook Jargon ulákân.]

Eu·ler (oi′lər), **Leonhard** 1707–83. Swiss mathematician who introduced much of the basic notation in mathematics.

eu·lo·gize (yōō′lə-jīz′) tr.v. -gized, -giz·ing, -giz·es To praise highly in speech or writing, esp. in a formal eulogy. —**eu′lo·gist** (-jĭst), **eu′lo·giz′er** n. —**eu′lo·gis′tic** (-jĭs′tĭk) adj.

eu·lo·gy (yōō′lə-jē) n., pl. -gies **1.** A laudatory speech or piece of writing, esp. for someone who has died. **2.** High praise or commendation. [ME euloge < Med.Lat. eulogium < Gk. eulogiā, praise : eu-, eu- + logos, speech; see -LOGY.] —**eu′lo·gis′tic** (-jĭs′tĭk) adj. —**eu′lo·gis′ti·cal·ly** adv.

Eu·men·i·des (yōō-mĕn′ĭ-dēz′) pl.n. Greek Mythology The Furies. [Gk. eumenides (theai), gracious (goddesses), euphemism for the Furies < eumenē, good-spirited : eu-, eu- + menos, spirit, disposition; see men-¹ in App.]

eu·nuch (yōō′nək) n. **1.** A castrated man employed as a harem attendant or as a functionary in certain Asian courts. **2.** A man or boy whose testes are nonfunctioning or have been removed. **3.** Informal An ineffectual or powerless man. [ME eunuk < Lat. eunūchus < Gk. eunoukhos : eunē, bed + -okhos, keeping (< ekhein, to keep; see segh- in App.).] —**eu′nuch·ism** n.

WORD HISTORY The word eunuch does not derive, as one might think, from the operation that produced a eunuch but rather from one of his functions. Eunuch goes back to the Greek word eunoukhos, "a castrated person employed to take charge of the women of a harem and act as chamberlain." The Greek word is derived from eunē, "bed," and ekhein, "to keep." A eunuch, of course, was ideally suited to guard the bedchamber of women.

eu·on·y·mus (yōō-ŏn′ə-məs) n. Any of various plants of the

Etruscan
bronze statuette of a female
warrior, sixth–fourth
century B.C.

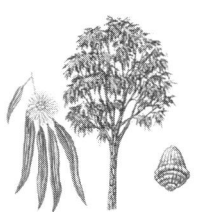

eucalyptus
blue gum eucalyptus
Eucalyptus globulus

ă	pat	oi	boy
ā	pay	ou	out
âr	care	ōō	took
ä	father	ōō	boot
ĕ	pet	ŭ	cut
ē	be	ûr	urge
ĭ	pit	th	thin
ī	pie	th	this
îr	pier	hw	which
ŏ	pot	zh	vision
ō	toe	ə	about,
ô	paw		item

Stress marks:
′ (primary);
′ (secondary); as in
lexicon (lĕk′sĭ-kŏn′)

genus *Euonymus*, having decorative foliage or fruits. [Lat. *euōnymus*, a tree of Lesbos < Gk. *euōnumos*, of good name : *eu-*, eu- + *onuma*, name; see **nǒ-men-** in App.]

eu·pat·rid (yōō-păt′rĭd, yōō′pə-trĭd) *n.*, *pl.* **-ri·dae** (-rĭ-dē′) or **-rids** A member of the hereditary aristocracy of ancient Athens. [Gk. *eupatridēs* : *eu-*, eu- + *patēr*, *patr-*, father; see **pəter-** in App. + *-idēs*, patronymic suff.] —**eu·pat′rid** *adj.*

eu·pep·si·a (yōō-pĕp′sē-ə, -shə) *n.* Good digestion. [Gk. < *eupeptos*, eupeptic. See EUPEPTIC.]

eu·pep·tic (yōō-pĕp′tĭk) *adj.* **1a.** Relating to or having good digestion. **b.** Conducive to digestion. **2.** Cheerful; happy. [< Gk. *eupeptos* : *eu-*, eu- + *peptein*, to digest; see **pekʷ-** in App.] —**eu·pep′ti·cal·ly** *adv.*

eu·phe·mism (yōō′fə-mĭz′əm) *n.* The act or an example of substituting a mild, indirect, or vague term for a harsh, blunt, or offensive one. [Gk. *euphēmismos* < *euphēmizein*, to use auspicious words < *euphēmiā*, use of auspicious words : *eu-*, eu- + *phēmē*, speech; see **bhā-** in App.] —**eu′phe·mist** *n.* —**eu′phe·mis′tic** (-mĭs′tĭk) *adj.* —**eu′phe·mis′ti·cal·ly** *adv.*

eu·phe·mize (yōō′fə-mīz′) *v.* **-mized, -miz·ing, -miz·es** —*tr.* To speak of or refer to by means of a euphemism. —*intr.* To use euphemisms. —**eu′phe·miz′er** *n.*

eu·phen·ics (yōō-fĕn′ĭks) *n.* (*used with a sing. verb*) The study or practice of phenotypic improvement of humans after birth. [Blend of EUGENICS and PHENOTYPE.] —**eu·phen′ic** *adj.*

eu·pho·ni·ous (yōō-fō′nē-əs) *adj.* Pleasing or agreeable to the ear. —**eu·pho′ni·ous·ly** *adv.* —**eu·pho′ni·ous·ness** *n.*

eu·pho·ni·um (yōō-fō′nē-əm) *n.* A brass wind instrument similar to the tuba but having a somewhat higher pitch and a mellower sound. [< Gk. *euphōnos*, sweet-voiced. See EUPHONY.]

eu·pho·ny (yōō′fə-nē) *n.*, *pl.* **-nies** Agreeable sound, esp. in the phonetic quality of words. [Fr. *euphonie* < LLat. *euphōnia* < Gk. *euphōniā*, sweet-voiced : *eu-*, eu- + *phōnē*, sound; see **bhā-** in App.] —**eu·phon′ic** (yōō-fŏn′ĭk) *adj.* —**eu·phon′i·cal·ly** *adv.* —**eu′pho·nize** *v.*

eu·phor·bi·a (yōō-fôr′bē-ə) *n.* A plant of the genus *Euphorbia*, which includes the spurges. [ME *euforbia* < Lat. *euphorbea*, after *Euphorbus*, 1st-cent. A.D. Greek physician.]

eu·pho·ri·a (yōō-fôr′ē-ə, -fōr′-) *n.* A feeling of great happiness or well-being. [NLat. < Gk. < *euphoros*, healthy : *eu-*, eu- + *pherein*, to bear; see **bher-1** in App.] —**eu·phor′ic** (-fôr′ĭk, -fōr′-) *adj.* —**eu·phor′i·cal·ly** *adv.*

eu·pho·ri·ant (yōō-fôr′ē-ənt, -fōr′-) *n.* A drug that tends to produce euphoria. —**eu·pho′ri·ant** *adj.*

eu·phot·ic (yōō-fōt′ĭk) *adj.* Of, relating to, or being the uppermost layer of a body of water that receives sufficient light for photosynthesis and the growth of green plants.

Eu·phra·tes (yōō-frā′tēz) A river of SW Asia flowing c. 2,735 km (1,700 mi) from central Turkey through Syria and into Iraq, where it joins the Tigris R.

Eu·phros·y·ne (yōō-frŏs′ə-nē) *n.* Greek Mythology One of the three Graces.

eu·phu·ism (yōō′fyoo-ĭz′əm) *n.* **1.** A literary style of the late 16th and early 17th centuries, characterized by elaborate alliteration, antitheses, and similes. **2.** Affected elegance of language. [After *Euphues*, a character created by John Lyly < Gk. *euphuēs*, shapely : *eu-*, eu- + *phuein*, to grow, bring forth; see **bheuə-** in App.] —**eu′phu·ist** *n.* —**eu′phu·is′tic, eu′phu·is′ti·cal** *adj.* —**eu′phu·is′ti·cal·ly** *adv.*

eu·plas·tic (yōō-plăs′tĭk) *adj.* Readily transformed into tissue, as in the healing of a wound.

eu·ploid (yōō′ploid′) *adj.* Having a chromosome number that is an exact multiple of the haploid number. ❖ *n.* A euploid cell or organism. —**eu′ploi′dy** *n.*

eup·ne·a (yōōp-nē′ə) *n.* Normal breathing. [NLat. < Gk. *eupnoia* < *eupnoos*, breathing well : *eu-*, eu- + *pnein*, to breathe.] —**eup·ne′ic** *adj.*

Eur. *abbr.* **1.** Europe **2.** European

Eur·a·sia (yōō-rā′zhə) The land mass comprising the continents of Europe and Asia.

Eur·a·sian (yōō-rā′zhən) *adj.* **1.** Of or relating to Eurasia. **2.** Of mixed European and Asian descent. ❖ *n.* **1.** A native or inhabitant of Eurasia. **2.** A person of mixed European and Asian descent. See Usage Note at **Amerasian.**

EURATOM *abbr.* European Atomic Energy Community

eu·re·ka (yōō-rē′kə) *interj.* Used to express triumph upon finding or discovering something. [Gk. *heurēka*, I have found (it) (supposedly exclaimed by Archimedes upon discovering how to measure the volume of an irregular solid), first pers. sing. perfect of *heuriskein*, to find.]

eu·rhyth·mics (yōō-rĭth′mĭks) *n.* Variant of **eurythmics.**

eu·rhyth·my (yōō-rĭth′mē) *n.* Variant of **eurythmy.**

Eu·rip·i·des (yōō-rĭp′ĭ-dēz′) 480?–406 B.C. Greek dramatist whose surviving works include *Medea* and *The Trojan Women.* —**Eu·rip′i·de′an** *adj.*

eu·ri·pus (yōō-rī′pəs) *n.*, *pl.* **-pi** (-pī′) A sea channel characterized by turbulent and unpredictable currents. [Lat. *eurīpus* < Gk. *eurīpos* : *eu-*, eu- + *rhīpē*, rush (< *rhīptein*, to throw).]

eu·ro or **Eu·ro** (yōōr′ō) *n.*, *pl.* **-ros** or **-ro's** The basic unit of currency among members of the European Monetary Union. [After EUROPE.]

Euro– *pref.* Europe; European: *Eurocrat.*

Eu·ro-A·mer·i·can (yōōr′ō-ə-mĕr′ĭ-kən) *n.* A US citizen or resident of European descent. ❖ *adj.* **1.** Of or relating to Euro-Americans. **2.** Of or relating to Europe and America.

Eu·ro·cen·tric (yōōr′ō-sĕn′trĭk) also **Eu·ro·po·cen·tric** (yōōr-ō′pə-) *adj.* Centered or focused on Europe and the Europeans, esp. in relation to historical or cultural influence. —**Eu′ro·cen′trism** *n.*

Eu·ro·crat (yōōr′ə-krăt′) *n.* An administrative official at the headquarters of the European Union. —**Eu′ro·crat′ic** *adj.*

Eu·ro·cur·ren·cy (yōōr′ō-kûr′ən-sē, -kûr′-) *n.*, *pl.* **-cies** Funds deposited in a bank when those funds are denominated in a currency differing from the bank's domestic currency.

Eu·ro·dol·lar (yōōr′ō-dŏl′ər) *n.* A US dollar on deposit with a bank abroad, esp. in Europe.

Eu·ro·pa (yōō-rō′pə) *n.* **1.** Greek Mythology A Phoenician princess abducted to Crete by Zeus in the form of a bull and the mother of Minos, Rhadamanthus, and Sarpedon. **2.** A satellite of Jupiter. [Lat. *Eurōpa* < Gk. *Eurōpē*.]

Eu·rope (yōōr′əp) The sixth-largest continent, extending W from the Dardanelles, Black Sea, and Ural Mts. It is technically a vast peninsula of the Eurasian landmass.

Eu·ro·pe·an (yōōr′ə-pē′ən) *n.* **1.** A native or inhabitant of Europe. **2.** A person of European descent. ❖ *adj.* Of or relating to Europe or its peoples, languages, or cultures.

European Community An economic and political organization of European Economic Community members, formed in 1967.

European corn borer *n.* See **corn borer** 1.

European Economic Community An economic organization est. in 1958 to promote trade and cooperation among the countries of Belgium, Luxembourg, the Netherlands, France, Italy, and West Germany. The United Kingdom, Ireland, and Denmark joined in 1973, Greece in 1981, Spain and Portugal in 1986, and Austria, Finland, and Sweden in 1995.

Eu·ro·pe·an·ize (yōōr′ə-pē′ə-nīz′) *tr.v.* **-ized, -iz·ing, -iz·es** To make European. —**Eu′ro·pe·an·i·za′tion** (-ə-nī-zā′shən) *n.*

European Monetary Union An agreement by participating European Union member countries that includes protocols for the pooling of currency reserves and the introduction of a common currency.

European plan *n.* A hotel plan in which the rates include only the charges for a room and not for meals.

European Union An economic and political union established in 1993 by members of the European Community.

eu·ro·pi·um (yōō-rō′pē-əm) *n. Symbol* **Eu** A rare-earth element occurring in monazite and bastnaesite and used as a neutron absorber in nuclear research. Atomic number 63; atomic weight 151.96; melting point 826°C; boiling point 1,439°C; specific gravity 5.259; valence 2, 3. See table at **element.** [After EUROPE.]

Eu·ro·po·cen·tric (yōōr-ō′pə-sĕn′trĭk) *adj.* Variant of **Euro-centric.**

Eu·rus (yōōr′əs) *n.* Greek Mythology The god of the east or southeast wind.

eury– *pref.* Wide; broad: *eurythermal.* [< Gk. *eurus*, wide.]

eu·ry·bath·ic (yōōr′ə-băth′ĭk) *adj.* Capable of living in a wide range of water depths. Used of an aquatic organism. —**eu′ry·bath′** *n.*

Eu·ryd·i·ce (yōō-rĭd′ĭ-sē) *n.* Greek Mythology The wife of Orpheus, whom he failed to rescue from the underworld when he looked back at her and so violated the command of Hades.

eu·ry·ha·line (yōōr′ə-hā′lĭn′, -hăl′ĭn′) *adj.* Capable of tolerating a wide range of salt water concentrations. Used of an aquatic organism.

eu·ryp·ter·id (yōō-rĭp′tər-ĭd) *n.* Any of various large segmented aquatic arthropods of the order Eurypterida that existed from the Ordovician Period to the Permian Period. [< NLat. *Eurypterida*, order name < *Eurypterus*, genus name : EURY– + Gk. *pteron*, wing; see –PTER-.]

eu·ry·ther·mal (yōōr′ə-thûr′məl) also **eu·ry·ther·mic** (-mĭk) or **eu·ry·ther·mous** (-məs) *adj.* Adaptable to a wide range of temperatures. Used of an organism. —**eu′ry·therm′** *n.*

eu·ryth·mics also **eu·rhyth·mics** (yōō-rĭth′mĭks) *n.* (*used with a sing. verb*) The art of interpreting music by rhythmical free-style bodily movement. —**eu·ryth′mic** *adj.*

eu·ryth·my also **eu·rhyth·my** (yōō-rĭth′mē) *n.* **1.** Harmony of proportion in architecture. **2.** A system of rhythmical bodily movements performed to a recitation of verse or prose. [Lat. *eurythmia* < Gk. *euruthmiā* < *euruthmos*, rhythmic, well-proportioned : *eu-*, eu- + *rhuthmos*, proportion; see RHYTHM.]

eu·ry·top·ic (yōōr′ĭ-tŏp′ĭk) *adj.* Able to adapt to a wide range of environmental conditions; widely distributed. Used of a plant or an animal. [EURY– + Gk. *topos*, place + –IC.] —**eu′ry·to·pic′i·ty** (-tō-pĭs′ĭ-tē) *n.*

Eu·se·bi·us of Cae·sa·re·a (yōō-sē′bē-əs; sē′zə-rē′ə, sĕs′ə-, sĕz′ə-) A.D. 260?–340? Palestinian theologian who wrote a history of the Christian church until the year 324.

eu·sta·chian tube or **Eu·sta·chian tube** (yōō-stā′shən, -shē-ən, -kē-ən) *n. Anatomy* A slender tube that connects the tympanic cavity with the nasal part of the pharynx and serves to equalize air pressure on either side of the eardrum. [After Bartolommeo EUSTACHIO.]

Euripides
marble bust

Eu·sta·chi·o (ĕ′ōō-stä′kyō), **Bartolommeo** 1520–74. Italian anatomist noted for his descriptions of the human ear and heart.

eu·sta·sy (yōō′stə-sē) n., pl. **-sies** A uniform worldwide change in sea level. [< *eustatic*, of eustasy < Ger. *eustatisch* : EU– + STAT(O)– + *-isch*, adj. suff.] —**eu·stat′ic** (-stăt′ĭk) adj.

eu·stele (yōō′stēl, yōō-stē′lē) n. Botany The central cylinder in which the primary vascular tissue is arranged around a pith.

eu·tec·tic (yōō-tĕk′tĭk) adj. **1.** Of, relating to, or formed at the lowest possible temperature of solidification for any mixture of specified constituents. **2.** Exhibiting the constitution or properties of such a solid. ❖ n. **1.** A eutectic mixture, solution, or alloy. **2.** The eutectic temperature. [< Gk. *eutēktos*, easily melted : *eu-*, eu- + *tēktos*, melted (< *tēkein*, to melt).]

eu·tec·toid (yōō-tĕk′toid′) adj. Of or relating to a eutectic mixture or alloy. ❖ n. A eutectic mixture or alloy.

Eu·ter·pe (yōō-tûr′pē) n. Greek Mythology The Muse of lyric poetry and music.

eu·tha·na·sia (yōō′thə-nā′zhə, -zhē-ə) n. The act or practice of ending the life of an individual suffering from a terminal illness or an incurable condition. [Gk. *euthanasiā*, a good death : *eu-*, eu- + *thanatos*, death.]

eu·than·ize (yōō′thə-nīz′) also **eu·than·a·tize** (yōō-thăn′ə-tīz′) tr.v. **-ized, -iz·ing, -iz·es** also **-a·tized, -a·tiz·ing, -a·tiz·es** To subject to euthanasia. [EUTHAN(ASIA) + –IZE.]

eu·then·ics (yōō-thĕn′ĭks) n. (used with a sing. verb) The study of the improvement of human functioning and well-being by improvement of living conditions. [< Gk. *euthenein*, to flourish.] —**eu·then′ist** n.

eu·the·ri·an (yōō-thîr′ē-ən) adj. Of or belonging to the infraclass Eutheria, including the placental mammals. [< NLat. *Euthēria*, infraclass name : Gk. *eu-*, eu- + Gk. *thēria*, pl. of *thērion*, wild animal; see TREACLE.] —**eu·ther′i·an** n.

eu·troph·ic (yōō-trŏf′ĭk, -trō′fĭk) adj. Having waters rich in mineral and organic nutrients, causing plant life, esp. algae, to proliferate, thereby reducing the dissolved oxygen content and often killing off other organisms. [< Gk. *eutrophos*, well-nourished : *eu-*, eu- + *trephein*, to nourish.] —**eu·troph′i·ca′tion** n. —**eu′tro·phy** (yōō′trə-fē) n.

eV abbr. electron volt

EVA abbr. extravehicular activity

e·vac·u·ant (ĭ-văk′yōō-ənt) adj. Causing evacuation, esp. of the bowels; purgative. ❖ n. A purgative.

e·vac·u·ate (ĭ-văk′yōō-āt′) v. **-at·ed, -at·ing, -ates** —tr. **1a.** To empty or remove the contents of. **b.** To create a vacuum in. **2.** To discharge waste matter from (the bowel, for example). **3a.** To relinquish military possession or occupation of (a town, for example). **b.** To withdraw or send away (troops or inhabitants) from a threatened area. **4.** To withdraw or depart from; vacate. —intr. **1.** To evacuate a place or area, esp. as a protective measure. **2.** To excrete waste matter from the body. [ME *evacuaten* < Lat. *ēvacuāre, ēvacuāt-*, to empty out : *ē-, ex-*, ex- + *vacuus*, empty (< *vacāre*, to be empty).] —**e·vac′u·a·tive** adj. —**e·vac′u·a′tor** n.

e·vac·u·a·tion (ĭ-văk′yōō-ā′shən) n. **1.** The act of evacuating or the condition of being evacuated. **2.** Physiology **a.** Discharge of waste materials from the excretory passages of the body, esp. from the bowels. **b.** The material so discharged.

e·vac·u·ee (ĭ-văk′yōō-ē′) n. A person evacuated from a dangerous area.

e·vade (ĭ-vād′) v. **e·vad·ed, e·vad·ing, e·vades** —tr. **1.** To escape or avoid by cleverness or deceit: *evade arrest.* **2a.** To avoid fulfilling, answering, or performing: *evade responsibility.* **b.** To fail to make payment of (taxes). **3.** To avoid giving a direct answer to. **4.** To baffle or elude. —intr. **1.** To practice evasion. **2.** To use cleverness or deceit in avoiding or escaping. [Fr. *évader* < Lat. *ēvādere* : *ē-, ex-*, ex- + *vādere*, to go.] —**e·vad′a·ble, e·vad′i·ble** adj. —**e·vad′er** n.

e·vag·i·nate (ĭ-văj′ə-nāt′) tr.v. **-nat·ed, -nat·ing, -nates** To cause (a body part) to turn inside out by eversion of an inner surface. [Lat. *ēvāgināre, ēvāgināt-*, to unsheath : *ē-, ex-*, ex- + *vāgīna*, sheath.] —**e·vag′i·na′tion** n.

e·val·u·ate (ĭ-văl′yōō-āt′) tr.v. **-at·ed, -at·ing, -ates** **1.** To ascertain or fix the value or worth of. **2.** To examine and judge carefully; appraise. See Syns at **estimate. 3.** Mathematics To calculate the numerical value of; express numerically. [Ult. < Fr. *évaluation* < OFr. < *evaluer*, to evaluate : *e-*, out (< Lat. *ē-, ex-*; see EX–) + *value*, value; see VALUE.] —**e·val′u·a·tive** adj. —**e·val′u·a′tor** n.

ev·a·nesce (ĕv′ə-nĕs′) intr.v. **-nesced, -nesc·ing, -nesc·es** To dissipate or disappear like vapor. See Syns at **disappear.** [Lat. *ēvānēscere*, to vanish : *ē-, ex-*, ex- + *vānēscere*, to disappear (< *vānus*, empty).] —**ev′a·nes′cence** n.

ev·a·nes·cent (ĕv′ə-nĕs′ənt) adj. Vanishing or likely to vanish like vapor. —**ev′a·nes′cent·ly** adv.

e·van·gel (ĭ-văn′jəl) n. **1.** The Christian gospel. **2.** An evangelist. [ME *evaungel* < LLat. *ēvangelium* < Gk. *euangelion*, good news < *euangelos*, bringing good news : *eu-*, eu- + *angelos*, messenger.]

e·van·gel·i·cal (ē′văn-jĕl′ĭ-kəl, ĕv′ən-) also **e·van·gel·ic** (-jĕl′ĭk) adj. **1.** Of, relating to, or in accordance with the Christian gospel, esp. one of the four gospel books of the New Testament. **2.** Evangelical Of, relating to, or being a Protestant church that

founds its teaching on the gospel. **3.** Evangelical Of, relating to, or being a Christian church believing in the authority of the Bible, in salvation through regeneration, and in a transformed personal life. **4.** Of or relating to the group in the Church of England that stresses personal conversion and salvation by faith. **5.** Marked by ardent or crusading enthusiasm. ❖ n. Evangelical A member of an evangelical church or party. —**e·van′gel·i·cal·ly** adv.

e·van·gel·i·cal·ism (ē′văn-jĕl′ĭ-kə-lĭz′əm, ĕv′ən-) n. **1.** often Evangelicalism Evangelical beliefs or doctrines. **2.** Adherence to a church or party professing evangelicalism.

e·van·gel·ism (ĭ-văn′jə-lĭz′əm) n. **1.** Zealous preaching and dissemination of the gospel, as through missionary work. **2.** Militant zeal for a cause. —**e·van′gel·is′tic** (-jə-lĭs′tĭk) adj. —**e·van′gel·is′ti·cal·ly** adv.

e·van·gel·ist (ĭ-văn′jə-lĭst) n. **1.** often Evangelist Any one of the authors of the four New Testament gospel books. **2.** One who practices evangelism.

e·van·gel·ize (ĭ-văn′jə-līz′) v. **-ized, -iz·ing, -iz·es** —tr. **1.** To preach the gospel to. **2.** To convert to Christianity. —intr. To preach the gospel. —**e·van′gel·i·za′tion** (-jə-lĭ-zā′shən) n. —**e·van′gel·iz′er** n.

Ev·ans (ĕv′ənz), Sir **Arthur John** 1851–1941. British archaeologist who unearthed remnants of the Bronze Age Minoan civilization in Crete.

Evans, Herbert McLean 1882–1971. Amer. anatomist who discovered vitamin E (1922).

Evans, Mount A peak, 4,350.5 m (14,264 ft), of N-central CO in the Front Range of the Rocky Mts.

Evans, Walker 1903–75. Amer. photographer noted for his images of the rural South during the 1930s.

Evans, William John ("Bill") 1929–64. Amer. jazz pianist known for his lyrical style.

Ev·ans·ton (ĕv′ən-stən) A city of NE IL on Lake Michigan N of Chicago. Pop. 74,239.

Ev·ans·ville (ĕv′ənz-vĭl′) A city of extreme SW IN on the Ohio R. and the KY border. Pop. 121,582.

e·vap·o·ra·ble (ĭ-văp′ər-ə-bəl) adj. That can evaporate or undergo evaporation. —**e·vap′o·ra·bil′i·ty** n.

e·vap·o·rate (ĭ-văp′ə-rāt′) v. **-rat·ed, -rat·ing, -rates** —tr. **1a.** To convert or change into a vapor. **b.** To draw off in the form of vapor. **2.** To draw moisture from, as by heating, leaving only the dry solid portion. **3.** To deposit (a metal) on a substrate by vacuum sublimation. —intr. **1a.** To change into vapor. **b.** To pass off in or as vapor. **2.** To produce vapor. **3.** To disappear; vanish. See Syns at **disappear.** [ME *evaporaten* < Lat. *ēvapōrāre, ēvapōrāt-* : *ē-, ex-*, ex- + *vapor*, steam.] —**e·vap′o·ra′tion** n. —**e·vap′o·ra′tive** adj. —**e·vap′o·ra′tive·ly** adv. —**e·vap′o·ra′tiv′i·ty** (-ərə-tĭv′ĭ-tē) n. —**e·vap′o·ra′tor** n.

e·vap·o·rat·ed milk (ĭ-văp′ə-rā′tĭd) n. Concentrated milk made by evaporating some of the water from whole milk.

e·vap·o·rite (ĭ-văp′ə-rīt′) n. A sedimentary deposit that results from the evaporation of seawater. [EVAPOR(ATION) + –ITE[1].] —**e·vap′o·rit′ic** (-rĭt′ĭk) adj.

e·va·sion (ĭ-vā′zhən) n. **1.** The act or an instance of evading. **2.** A means of evading; a subterfuge. [ME *evasioun* < OFr. *evasion* < LLat. *ēvāsiō, ēvāsiōn-* < Lat. *ēvāsus*, p. part. of *ēvādere*, to evade. See EVADE.]

e·va·sive (ĭ-vā′sĭv) adj. **1.** Inclined or intended to evade. **2.** Intentionally vague or ambiguous; equivocal: *an evasive statement.* —**e·va′sive·ly** adv. —**e·va′sive·ness** n.

eve (ēv) n. **1.** The evening or day preceding a special day. **2.** The period immediately preceding a certain event: *the eve of war.* **3.** Evening. [ME, var. of *even.* See EVEN[2].]

Eve In the Bible, the first woman and the wife of Adam. [LLat. *Ēva, Hēva* < Heb. *ḥawwâ*, living, life < *ḥāyâ*, to live.]

e·vec·tion (ĭ-vĕk′shən) n. Solar perturbation of the lunar orbit. [Lat. *ēvectiō, ēvection-*, a going up < *ēvectus*, p. part. of *ēvehere*, to raise up : *ē-, ex-*, up from; see EX– + *vehere*, to carry; see **wegh-** in App.] —**e·vec′tion·al** adj.

e·ven[1] (ē′vən) adj. **1a.** Having a horizontal surface; flat. **b.** Having no irregularities, roughness, or indentations; smooth. **c.** Being in the same plane or line; parallel. **2a.** Having no variations or fluctuations; uniform. **b.** Of uniform distribution. **c.** Placid; calm. **3a.** Equal or identical in degree, extent, or amount. **b.** Equally matched or balanced. **c.** Just; fair. **d.** Having nothing due on either side; square. **e.** Having exacted full revenge. **4.** Having equal probability; as likely as not. **5.** Sports **a.** Having an equal score. **b.** Being equal for each opponent. Used of a score. **6.** Mathematics **a.** Exactly divisible by 2. **b.** Characterized or indicated by a number exactly divisible by 2. **7a.** Having an even number in a sequence. **b.** Having an even number of members. **8.** Having an exact amount, extent, or number; precise. ❖ adv. **1a.** To a greater degree or extent. Used as an intensive with comparative adjectives and adverbs: *looked sick and felt even worse.* **b.** Indeed; moreover. Used as an intensive: *Even I know better.* **c.** Used as an intensive to indicate something that is unexpected: *declined even to consider the idea.* **2.** At the same time; already; just. **3.** To a degree that extends; fully: *loyal even unto death.* **4.** Exactly; precisely. ❖ tr. & intr.v. **e·vened, e·ven·ing, e·vens** To make or become even. —**idiom: on an even keel** In a stable or unim-

ă	pat	oi	boy
ā	pay	ou	out
âr	care	ŏŏ	took
ä	father	ōō	boot
ĕ	pet	ŭ	cut
ē	be	ûr	urge
ĭ	pit	th	thin
ī	pie	th	this
îr	pier	hw	which
ŏ	pot	zh	vision
ō	toe	ə	about,
ô	paw		item

Stress marks:
′ (primary);
′ (secondary), as in
lexicon (lĕk′sĭ-kŏn′)

Mount Everest

Chris Evert
with her 1981 Wimbledon trophy

paired state. [ME < OE *efen*.] —**e′ven•er** *n.* —**e′ven•ly** *adv.* —**e′ven•ness** *n.*

e•ven² (ē′vən) *n. Archaic* Evening. [ME < OE *æfen*.]

e•ven•fall (ē′vən-fôl′) *n.* The beginning of evening; twilight.

eve•ning (ēv′nĭng) *n.* **1.** The period of decreasing daylight between afternoon and night. **2.** The period between sunset or the evening meal and bedtime. **3.** A later period or time. **4.** *Chiefly Southern US* The time from noon to twilight. [ME < OE *æfnung* < *æfnian*, to become evening < *æfen*, evening.]

evening clothes *pl.n.* See **evening dress** 1.

evening dress *n.* **1.** Clothing worn for evening social events. **2.** See **evening gown**.

evening gown *n.* A woman's formal dress.

Evening Prayer (prâr) *n.* See **evensong** 1.

evening primrose *n.* Any of various North American plants of the genus *Oenothera*, characteristically having four-petaled yellow flowers that open in the evening.

evening star *n.* A planet, esp. Venus or Mercury, that is prominent in the west shortly after sunset.

E•ven•ki (ĭ-wĕng′kē, ĭ-vĕng′-) also **E•wen•ki** (ĭ-wĕng′kē) *n., pl.* **Evenki** or **-kis** also **Ewenki** or **-kis 1.** A member of a people inhabiting a large area of eastern Siberia and northern Nei Monggol (Inner Mongolia). **2.** The Tungusic language of the Evenki. [Russ., Evenki people < Evenki *śwənkī*.]

e•ven-pin•nate (ē′vən-pĭn′āt) *adj.* Of or relating to a compound leaf not terminating in a leaflet.

e•ven•song (ē′vən-sông′, -sŏng′) *n.* **1.** A daily evening service in the Anglican Church. **2.** A song sung in the evening. **3.** *Archaic* Evening.

e•ven-ste•ven (ē′vən-stē′vən) *adj. Informal* **1.** Having nothing due or owed on either side: *an even-steven transaction.* **2.** Having an equal score, as in a game or contest.

e•vent (ĭ-vĕnt′) *n.* **1a.** Something that takes place; an occurrence. **b.** A significant occurrence or happening. See Syns at **occurrence. c.** A social gathering or activity. **2.** The final result; the outcome. **3.** *Sports* A contest or an item in a sports program. **4.** *Physics* A point in space-time. —*idioms:* **at all events** In any case. **in any event** In any case. **in the event** If it should happen; in case. [Lat. *ēventus* < p. part. of *ēvenīre*, to happen : ē-, ex-, ex- + *venīre*, to come; see gⁱⁱā- in App.]

e•ven-tem•pered (ē′vən-tĕm′pərd) *adj.* Easygoing; calm.

e•vent•ful (ĭ-vĕnt′fəl) *adj.* **1.** Full of events. **2.** Important; momentous. —**e•vent′ful•ly** *adv.* —**e•vent′ful•ness** *n.*

event horizon *n.* The region, usu. described as spherical, marking the outer boundary of a black hole.

e•ven•tide (ē′vən-tīd′) *n. Archaic* Evening. [ME < OE *æfentīd : æfen*, evening + *tīd*, time; see dā- in App.]

e•ven•tu•al (ĭ-vĕn′chōō-əl) *adj.* **1.** Occurring at some future time; ultimate: *his eventual failure.* **2.** *Archaic* Dependent on circumstance; contingent. [Fr. *éventuel* < Lat. *ēventus*, outcome. See EVENT.]

e•ven•tu•al•i•ty (ĭ-vĕn′chōō-ăl′ĭ-tē) *n., pl.* **-ties** Something that may occur; a possibility.

e•ven•tu•al•ly (ĭ-vĕn′chōō-ə-lē) *adv.* At an unspecified future time.

e•ven•tu•ate (ĭ-vĕn′chōō-āt′) *intr.v.* **-at•ed, -at•ing, -ates** To result ultimately.

ev•er (ĕv′ər) *adv.* **1.** At all times; always: *ever hoping to strike it rich.* **2a.** At any time. **b.** In any way; at all: *How did they ever manage?* **3.** To a great extent or degree. Used for emphasis often with *so: He was ever so sorry.* —*idioms:* **ever and again anon** Now and then; occasionally. **for ever and a day** Always; forever. [ME < OE *æfre*. See aiw- in App.]

ev•er•bloom•ing (ĕv′ər-blōō′mĭng) *adj.* Blooming throughout the growing season.

Ev•er•est (ĕv′ər-ĭst, ĕv′rĭst), **Mount** A mountain, 8,850 m (29,035 ft), of the central Himalaya Mts. on the border of Xizang (Tibet) and Nepal; first scaled in 1953.

ev•er•glade (ĕv′ər-glād′) *n.* A tract of marshland, usu. under water and with patches of tall grass. [After the EVERGLADES.]

Ev•er•glades (ĕv′ər-glādz′) A subtropical swamp area of S FL including **Everglades National Park.**

ev•er•green (ĕv′ər-grēn′) *adj.* **1.** Having foliage that persists and remains green through the year. **2.** Perennially fresh or interesting; enduring. ❖ *n.* **1.** An evergreen tree, shrub, or plant. **2.** **evergreens** Twigs or branches of evergreen plants used as decoration.

ev•er•last•ing (ĕv′ər-lăs′tĭng) *adj.* **1.** Lasting forever; eternal. **2a.** Continuing indefinitely or for a long period of time. **b.** Persisting too long; tedious. ❖ *n.* **1. Everlasting** God. **2.** Eternal duration; eternity. **3.** Any of various plants that retain form and color long after they are dry. —**ev′er•last′ing•ly** *adv.* —**ev′er•last′ing•ness** *n.*

ev•er•more (ĕv′ər-môr′, -mōr′) *adv.* **1.** Forever; always. **2.** In a future time.

Ev•ers (ĕv′ərz), **Medgar Wiley** 1925–63. Amer. civil rights worker in MS who was killed by a sniper. His work was continued by his brother **Charles** (b. 1923).

e•ver•sion (ĭ-vûr′zhən, -shən) *n.* **1a.** The act of turning inside out. **b.** The condition of being turned inside out. **2.** The condition of being turned outward. [ME *eversioun* < OFr. *eversion* < Lat. *ēversiō, ēversiōn-* < *ēversus*, p. part. of *ēvertere*, to overturn. See EVERT.] —**e•ver′si•ble** (-sə-bəl) *adj.*

e•vert (ĭ-vûrt′) *tr.v.* **e•vert•ed, e•vert•ing, e•verts** To turn inside out or outward. [Back-formation < ME *everted*, turned upside down < Lat. *ēvertere*, to overturn : ē-, ex-, ex- + *vertere*, to turn; see wer-² in App.]

Ev•ert (ĕv′ərt), **Christine Marie** Known as "Chris." b. 1954. Amer. tennis player who won women's singles titles at the US Open (1975–78, 1980, and 1982) and Wimbledon (1974, 1976, and 1981).

ev•er•where (ĕv′ər-hwâr′, -wâr′) *adv. Chiefly Southern US* **1.** Everywhere. **2.** Wherever.

REGIONAL NOTE Inversion—the reversal of the two halves of a compound word—is a common process in the dialects of the southern Appalachians and the Ozarks. The commonly occurring *everwhere* (especially common in Texas) is an example of inversion when it means "wherever." Other examples of Southern inversion cited by Craig M. Carver in *American Regional Dialects* are *peckerwood, hoppergrass, doll-baby, doghanged* (meaning "hangdog"), *tie-tongued,* and *right-out* ("outright").

ev•er•which (ĕv′ər-hwĭch′, -wĭch′) *pron. Chiefly Southern US* Whichever. See Regional Note at **everwhere.**

eve•ry (ĕv′rē) *adj.* **1a.** Constituting each and all members of a group without exception. **b.** Being all possible: *every chance of winning.* **2.** Being each of a specified succession of objects or intervals: *every two hours.* **3.** The highest degree or expression of: *had every hope of succeeding.* —*idioms:* **every bit** *Informal* In all ways; equally. **every now and then again** From time to time; occasionally. **every once in a while** From time to time; occasionally. **every other** Each alternate: *every other week.* **every so often** At intervals; occasionally. **every which way** *Informal* **1.** In every direction. **2.** In complete disorder. [ME *everi, everich* < OE *æfre ælc : æfre*, ever; see aiw- in App. + *ælc*, each.]

USAGE NOTE *Every* is representative of a large class of English words and expressions that are singular in form but felt to be plural in sense. The class includes, for example, noun phrases introduced by *every, any,* and certain uses of *some.* These expressions invariably take a singular verb; we say *Every car has* (not *have*) *been tested.* But if a sentence contains a pronoun referring back to a noun phrase introduced by *every,* people often use a plural pronoun, especially in speech: *Every car must have their* (rather than *its) brakes tested.* The use of plural pronouns in such cases is still widely regarded as incorrect in writing. • When a phrase introduced by *every* or *any* refers to a group containing both men and women, there can be uncertainty over what the gender of the singular pronoun should be. This matter is discussed in the Usage Notes at **he** and **they.** See Usage Notes at **any, either, he¹, neither, none.**

eve•ry•bod•y (ĕv′rē-bŏd′ē, -bŭd′ē) *pron.* Every person; everyone.

eve•ry•day (ĕv′rē-dā′) *adj.* **1.** Appropriate for ordinary days or routine occasions: *everyday wear.* **2.** Commonplace; ordinary: *everyday worries.* ❖ *n.* The ordinary or routine day or occasion. —**eve′ry•day′ness** *n.*

Eve•ry•man or **eve•ry•man** (ĕv′rē-măn′) *n.* **1.** An ordinary person, representative of humanity and usu. perceived as male. **2.** An ordinary man, representative of all men.

eve•ry•one (ĕv′rē-wŭn′) *pron.* Every person; everybody. See Usage Notes at **every, he¹.**

eve•ry•place (ĕv′rē-plās′) *adv. Informal* Everywhere.

eve•ry•thing (ĕv′rē-thĭng′) *pron.* **1a.** All things or all of a group of things. **b.** All relevant matters: *told me everything.* **2.** The most important fact or consideration.

eve•ry•where (ĕv′rē-hwâr′, -wâr′) *adv.* In any or every place; in all places.

Eve•ry•wom•an or **eve•ry•wom•an** (ĕv′rē-wōōm′ən) *n.* An ordinary woman, representative of all women.

evg. *abbr.* evening

e•vict (ĭ-vĭkt′) *tr.v.* **e•vict•ed, e•vict•ing, e•victs 1.** To put out (a tenant, for example) by legal process; expel. **2.** To force out; eject. See Syns at **eject. 3.** *Law* To recover (property, for example) by a superior claim or legal process. [ME *evicten* < Lat. *ēvincere, ēvict-*, to vanquish : ē-, ex-, intensive pref.; see EX- + *vincere*, to defeat.] —**e•vict•ee′** (ĭ-vĭk-tē′, ĭ-vĭk′tē) *n.* —**e•vic′tion** *n.* —**e•vic′tor** *n.*

ev•i•dence (ĕv′ĭ-dəns) *n.* **1.** A thing or things helpful in forming a conclusion or judgment: *evidence of a burglary.* **2.** Something indicative; an outward sign: *evidence of grief.* **3.** *Law* The documentary or oral statements and the material objects admissible as testimony in a court of law. ❖ *tr.v.* **-denced, -denc•ing, -denc•es 1.** To indicate clearly; exemplify or prove. **2.** To support by testimony; attest. —*idiom:* **in evidence 1.** Plainly visible; to be seen. **2.** *Law* As legal evidence. [ME < OFr. < LLat. *ēvidentia* < Lat. *ēvidēns, ēvident-*, obvious. See EVIDENT.]

ev•i•dent (ĕv′ĭ-dənt) *adj.* Easily seen or understood; obvious. See Syns at **apparent.** [ME < OFr. < Lat. *ēvidēns, ēvident- : ē-, ex-*, ex- + *vidēns*, pr. part. of *vidēre*, to see; see weid- in App.]

ev·i·den·tial (ĕv′ĭ-dĕn′shəl) *adj. Law* Of, providing, or constituting evidence. —**ev′i·den′tial·ly** *adv.*

ev·i·den·tia·ry (ĕv′ĭ-dĕn′shə-rē, -shē-ĕr′ē) *adj. Law* **1.** Of evidence; evidential. **2.** For the presentation or determination of evidence: *an evidentiary hearing.*

ev·i·dent·ly (ĕv′ĭ-dənt-lē, ĕv′ĭ-dĕnt′lē) *adv.* **1.** Obviously; clearly. **2.** According to the evidence available.

e·vil (ē′vəl) *adj.* **e·vil·er, e·vil·est** **1.** Morally bad or wrong; wicked. **2.** Causing ruin, injury, or pain; harmful. **3.** Characterized by or indicating future misfortune; ominous. **4.** Bad or blameworthy by report; infamous. **5.** Marked by anger or spite; malicious. ❖ *n.* **1.** The quality of being morally bad or wrong; wickedness. **2.** That which causes harm, misfortune, or destruction. **3.** An evil force, power, or personification. **4.** Something that is a cause or source of suffering, injury, or destruction. ❖ *adv. Archaic* In an evil manner. [ME < OE *yfel.*] —**e′vil·ly** *adv.* —**e′vil·ness** *n.*

e·vil·do·er (ē′vəl-dōō′ər) *n.* One that performs evil acts. —**e′vil·do′ing** *n.*

evil eye *n.* **1.** A look or stare believed to harm others. **2.** The presumed power to harm others by magic or supernatural means.

e·vil-mind·ed (ē′vəl-mīn′dĭd) *adj.* Having evil thoughts, opinions, or intentions. —**e′vil-mind′ed·ly** *adv.* —**e′vil-mind′ed·ness** *n.*

e·vince (ĭ-vĭns′) *tr.v.* **e·vinced, e·vinc·ing, e·vinc·es** To show or demonstrate clearly; manifest. [Lat. *ēvincere,* to prevail, prove. See EVICT.] —**e·vinc′i·ble** *adj.*

e·vis·cer·ate (ĭ-vĭs′ə-rāt′) *v.* **-at·ed, -at·ing, -ates** —*tr.* **1.** To remove the entrails of; disembowel. **2.** To take away a vital or essential part of. **3.** *Medicine* **a.** To remove the contents of (an organ). **b.** To remove an organ, such as an eye, from (a patient). —*intr. Medicine* To protrude through a wound or surgical incision. [Lat. *ēviscerāre, ēviscerāt-* : *ē-, ex-,* ex- + *viscera,* internal organs; see VISCERA.] —**e·vis′cer·a′tion** *n.*

ev·i·ta·ble (ĕv′ĭ-tə-bəl) *adj.* Avoidable. [Lat. *ēvītābilis < ēvītāre,* to shun : *ex-, ex-* + *vītāre,* to avoid.]

ev·o·ca·tion (ĕv′ə-kā′shən, ē′və-) *n.* **1.** The act of evoking. **2.** Creation anew through memory or imagination. —**ev′o·ca′tor** *n.*

e·voc·a·tive (ĭ-vŏk′ə-tĭv) *adj.* Tending or having the power to evoke. —**e·voc′a·tive·ly** *adv.* —**e·voc′a·tive·ness** *n.*

e·voke (ĭ-vōk′) *tr.v.* **e·voked, e·vok·ing, e·vokes** **1.** To summon or call forth. **2.** To call to mind by naming, citing, or suggesting. **3.** To re-create, esp. through imagination. [Lat. *ēvocāre* : *ē-, ex-,* ex- + *vocāre,* to call; see wek-* in App.] —**ev′o·ca·ble** (ĕv′ə-kə-bəl, ĭ-vō′kə-) *adj.*

ev·o·lute (ĕv′ə-lōōt′, ē′və-) *n. Mathematics* The locus of the centers of curvature of a given curve. [< Lat. *ēvolūtus,* p. part. of *ēvolvere,* to unroll. See EVOLVE.]

ev·o·lu·tion (ĕv′ə-lōō′shən, ē′və-) *n.* **1.** A gradual process in which something changes into a different and usu. more complex or better form. See Syns at **development. 2a.** The process of developing. **b.** Gradual development. **3.** *Biology* **a.** Change in the genetic composition of a population over time through natural selection, resulting in the development of new species. **b.** The historical development of a related group of organisms; phylogeny. **4.** A movement that is part of a set of ordered movements. **5.** *Mathematics* The extraction of a root of a quantity. [Lat. *ēvolūtiō, ēvolūtiōn-* < *ēvolūtus,* p. part. of *ēvolvere,* to unroll. See EVOLVE.] —**ev′o·lu′tion·al, ev′o·lu′tion·ar′y** (-shə-nĕr′ē) *adj.* —**ev′o·lu′tion·ar′i·ly** *adv.*

ev·o·lu·tion·ism (ĕv′ə-lōō′shə-nĭz′əm, ē′və-) *n.* **1.** A theory of biological evolution, esp. that of Darwin. **2.** Advocacy of or belief in biological evolution. —**ev′o·lu′tion·ist** *n.*

e·volve (ĭ-vŏlv′) *v.* **e·volved, e·volv·ing, e·volves** —*tr.* **1a.** To develop or achieve gradually: *evolve a style of one's own.* **b.** To work (something) out; devise. **2.** *Biology* To develop (a characteristic) by evolutionary processes. **3.** To give off; emit. —*intr.* **1.** To undergo gradual change; develop. **2.** *Biology* To develop or arise through evolutionary processes. [Lat. *ēvolvere,* to unroll : *ē-, ex-,* + *volvere,* to roll; see wel- in App.] —**e·volv′a·ble** *adj.* —**e·volve′ment** *n.*

e·vul·sion (ĭ-vŭl′shən) *n.* A forcible extraction. [Lat. *ēvolsiō, ēvulsiō < ēvulsus,* p. part. of *ēvellere,* to pull out : *ē-, ex-,* ex- + *vellere,* to pull.]

Ev·voia (ĕv′yä) See **Euboea.**

ev·zone (ĕv′zōn′) *n.* An infantryman of a special corps of the Greek army. [Mod.Gk. *euzōnos* < Gk., well-girded, dressed for exercise : *eu-,* well; see EU– + *zōnē,* girdle.]

EW *abbr.* enlisted woman

ewe (yōō) *n.* A female sheep, esp. when full grown. [ME < OE *ēwe, ēowu.* See owi- in App.]

E·we (ā′wā′, ā′wē) *n., pl.* **Ewe** or **E·wes** **1.** A member of a people inhabiting southeast Ghana, southern Togo, and southern Benin. **2.** The Gbe language of the Ewe people.

Ew·ell (yōō′əl), **Richard Stoddert** 1817–72. Amer. Confederate general in the US Civil War.

ewe-neck (yōō′nĕk′) *n.* A defect in a horse or dog in which the neck is thin and has a concave arch. —**ewe′-necked′** *adj.*

E·wen·ki (ĭ-wĕng′kē) *n.* Variant of **Evenki.**

ew·er (yōō′ər) *n.* A pitcher, esp. a decorative one with a base, an oval body, and a flaring spout. [ME *euer* < AN < VLat. **aquāria* < Lat. *aquārius,* of water < *aqua,* water. See akʷ-ā- in App.]

ex¹ (ĕks) *prep.* **1.** Not including; without: *a stock price ex dividend.* **2.** *Business* Free of any transport or handling charges incurred before removal from a given location. **3.** From, but not having graduated with, the class of: *Lat.* See **eghs** in App.]

ex² (ĕks) *n.* The letter *x.* ❖ *tr.v.* **exed, ex·ing, ex·es** To delete or cross out: *exed each item off.*

ex³ (ĕks) *n. Slang* A former spouse or partner. [< EX–.]

Ex *abbr. Bible* Exodus

ex. *abbr.* **1.** examination **2.** example **3a.** except **b.** exception **4.** exchange **5.** executive **6.** express **7.** extra

ex– *pref.* **1.** Outside; out of; away from: *exodontia.* **2.** Not; without: *excaudate.* **3.** Former: *ex-president.* [ME < OFr. < Lat. and Gk.; see **eghs** in App.]

exa– *pref.* One quintillion (10¹⁸): *exahertz.* [Alteration of HEXA– (< its representing the sixth power of a thousand).]

ex·ac·er·bate (ĭg-zăs′ər-bāt′) *tr.v.* **-bat·ed, -bat·ing, -bates** To increase the severity, violence, or bitterness of; aggravate. [Lat. *exacerbāre, exacerbāt-* : *ex-,* intensive pref.; see EX– + *acerbāre,* to make harsh (< *acerbus,* harsh; see ak- in App.).] —**ex·ac′er·ba′tion** *n.*

ex·act (ĭg-zăkt′) *adj.* **1.** Strictly and completely in accord with fact; not deviating from truth or reality. **2.** Marked by accurate measurements or inferences with small margins of error. **3.** Marked by strict adherence to standards or rules. ❖ *tr.v.* **-act·ed, -act·ing, -acts** **1.** To force the payment or yielding of; extort. **2.** To demand and obtain by or as if by force or authority. See Syns at **demand.** [Lat. *exāctus,* p. part. of *exigere,* to weigh out, demand : *ex-, ex-* + *agere,* to weigh; see ag- in App.] —**ex·act′a·ble** *adj.* —**ex·act′ness** *n.* —**ex·ac′tor, ex·act′er** *n.*

ex·act·a (ĭg-zăk′tə) *n.* A method of betting in which the bettor must correctly pick those finishing in the first and second places in that sequence. [Short for Am.Sp. *quiniela exacta,* exact quiniela (a game of chance) < Sp. *exacta,* fem. of *exacto* < Lat. *exāctus.* See EXACT.]

ex·act·ing (ĭg-zăk′tĭng) *adj.* **1.** Making severe demands; rigorous: *an exacting instructor.* **2.** Requiring great care, effort, or attention. —**ex·act′ing·ly** *adv.* —**ex·act′ing·ness** *n.*

ex·ac·tion (ĭg-zăk′shən) *n.* **1a.** The act of exacting. **b.** Excessive demand; extortion. **2.** Something exacted.

ex·ac·ti·tude (ĭg-zăk′tĭ-tōōd′, -tyōōd′) *n.* The state or quality of being exact.

ex·act·ly (ĭg-zăkt′lē) *adv.* **1.** In an exact manner; accurately. **2.** In all respects; just. **3.** As you say.

ex·ag·ger·ate (ĭg-zăj′ə-rāt′) *v.* **-at·ed, -at·ing, -ates** —*tr.* **1.** To represent as greater than is actually the case; overstate. **2.** To enlarge or increase to an abnormal degree. —*intr.* To make overstatements. [Lat. *exaggerāre, exaggerāt-,* to heap up, magnify : *ex-,* intensive pref.; see EX– + *aggerāre,* to pile up (< *agger,* pile < *aggerere,* to bring to : *ad-,* ad- + *gerere,* to bring).] —**ex·ag′ger·at′ed·ly** *adv.* —**ex·ag′ger·a′tion** *n.* —**ex·ag′ger·a′tive, ex·ag′ger·a·to′ry** (-ə-tôr′ē, -tōr′ē) *adj.* —**ex·ag′ger·a′tor** *n.*

SYNONYMS *exaggerate, inflate, magnify, overstate* These verbs mean to represent something as being larger or greater than it actually is: *exaggerated the size of the fish; inflated his own importance; magnifying her part in their success; overstated their income.* ANTONYM *minimize*

ex·a·hertz (ĕk′sə-hûrts′) *n.* One quintillion (10¹⁸) hertz.

ex·alt (ĭg-zôlt′) *tr.v.* **-alt·ed, -alt·ing, -alts** **1.** To raise in rank, character, or status; elevate. **2.** To glorify, praise, or honor. **3.** To increase the effect or intensity of; heighten. **4.** *Obsolete* To fill with sublime emotion; elate. [ME *exalten* < Lat. *exaltāre* : *ex-,* up, away; see EX– + *altus,* high.] —**ex·alt′er** *n.*

ex·al·ta·tion (ĕg′zôl-tā′shən) *n.* **1.** The act of exalting or the condition of being exalted. **2.** A state or feeling of intense, often excessive exhilaration or well-being.

ex·alt·ed (ĭg-zôl′tĭd) *adj.* **1.** Elevated in rank, character, or status. **2.** Lofty; sublime; noble. **3.** Exaggerated; inflated. —**ex·alt′ed·ly** *adv.* —**ex·alt′ed·ness** *n.*

ex·am (ĭg-zăm′) *n.* An examination; a test.

ex·a·men (ĭg-zā′mən) *n.* An examination; an investigation. [Lat. *exāmen,* a weighing out. See EXAMINE.]

ex·am·i·nant (ĭg-zăm′ə-nənt) *n.* **1.** One who examines. **2.** One who is examined; an examinee.

ex·am·i·na·tion (ĭg-zăm′ə-nā′shən) *n.* **1.** The act of examining or the state of being examined. **2.** A set of questions or exercises testing knowledge or skill. **3.** A formal interrogation: *examination of the witness.* —**ex·am′i·na′tion·al** *adj.*

ex·am·ine (ĭg-zăm′ĭn) *tr.v.* **-ined, -in·ing, -ines** **1a.** To observe carefully or critically; inspect. **b.** To study or analyze. **2.** To test or check the condition or health of. **3.** To determine the qualifications, aptitude, or skills of by means of questions or exercises. **4.** To question formally, as to elicit information; interrogate. See Syns at **ask.** [ME *examinen* < OFr. *examiner* < Lat. *exāmināre* < *exāmen,* a weighing out < *exigere,* to weigh out. See EXACT.] —**ex·am′in·a·ble** *adj.* —**ex·am′in·er** *n.*

ex·am·in·ee (ĭg-zăm′ə-nē′) *n.* One that is examined.

ex·am·ple (ĭg-zăm′pəl) *n.* **1.** One that is representative of a

ewer
glazed earthenware ewer
from the Tang Dynasty

group as a whole. **2.** One serving as a pattern of a specific kind. **3.** A similar case that constitutes a model or precedent. **4a.** A punishment given as a warning or deterrent. **b.** One that has been given such a punishment. **5.** A problem or exercise used to illustrate a principle or method. —*idiom:* **for example** As an illustrative instance. [ME < OFr. *example, essaumple* < Lat. *exemplum* < *eximere,* to take out : *ex-,* ex- + *emere,* to take.]

ex·an·the·ma (ĕg′zăn-thē′mə) *also* **ex·an·them** (ĭg-zăn′thəm) *n., pl.* **-them·a·ta** (-thĕm′ə-tə) *or* **-the·mas** *also* **-thems 1.** A skin eruption accompanying certain infectious diseases. **2.** A disease, such as measles or scarlet fever, accompanied by a skin eruption. [LLat. *exanthēma* < Gk., eruption < *exanthein,* to burst forth : *ex-,* ex- + *anthein,* to blossom (< *anthos,* flower).] —**ex·an′the·mat′ic** (ĭg-zăn′thə-măt′ĭk), **ex′an·them′a·tous** (ĕg′zăn-thĕm′ə-təs) *adj.*

ex·ap·ta·tion (ĕg′zăp-tā′shən) *n. Biology* The utilization of a structure or feature for a function other than that for which it was developed through natural selection. [EX- + (AD)APTATION.] —**ex·ap′ted** *adj.* —**ex·ap′tive** *adj.*

ex·arch¹ (ĕk′särk) *n.* **1.** A bishop in the Eastern Orthodox Church ranking immediately below a patriarch. **2.** The ruler of a province in the Byzantine Empire. [LLat. *exarchus,* an overseer < Gk. *exarkhos* < *exarkhein,* to lead : *ex-,* ex- + *arkhein,* to rule.] —**ex·arch′al** *adj.* —**ex′ar′chate** (ĕk′sär′kāt), **ex′ar′chy** (-kē) *n.*

ex·arch² (ĕk′särk) *adj. Botany* Of or relating to a xylem whose early development is away from the center and toward the periphery. [EX(O)– + Gk. *arkhē,* beginning (< *arkhein,* to rule, begin).] —**ex′arch** *n.*

ex·as·per·ate (ĭg-zăs′pə-rāt′) *tr.v.* **-at·ed, -at·ing, -ates 1.** To make very angry or impatient; annoy greatly. **2.** To increase the gravity or intensity of. [Lat. *exasperāre, exasperāt-* : *ex-,* intensive pref.; see EX– + *asperāre,* to make rough (< *asper,* rough).] —**ex·as′per·at′ed·ly** *adv.* —**ex·as′per·at′er** *n.*

ex·as·per·a·tion (ĭg-zăs′pə-rā′shən) *n.* **1.** The act or an instance of exasperating. **2.** The state of being exasperated.

Exc. *abbr.* Excellency

Ex·cal·i·bur (ĕk-skăl′ə-bər) *n.* In Arthurian legend, the sword belonging to King Arthur. [ME, alteration (perh. influenced by Lat. *chalybs,* steel) of Med.Lat. *Caliburnus* < M Welsh *Caletuwlch* or MIr. *Caladbolg,* a legendary sword.]

ex ca·the·dra (ĕks′ kə-thē′drə) *adv. & adj.* With the authority derived from one's office or position. [Lat. *ex cathedrā* : *ex,* from + *cathedrā,* ablative of *cathedra,* chair.]

ex·cau·date (ĕk-skô′dāt′) *adj.* Without a tail; tailless.

ex·ca·vate (ĕk′skə-vāt′) *v.* **-vat·ed, -vat·ing, -vates** —*tr.* **1.** To make a hole in; hollow out. **2.** To form by hollowing out. **3.** To remove by digging or scooping out. **4.** To expose or uncover by or as if by digging. —*intr.* To engage in excavation. [Lat. *excavāre, excavāt-,* to hollow out : *ex-,* ex- + *cavāre,* to hollow (< *cavus,* hollow).]

ex·ca·va·tion (ĕk′skə-vā′shən) *n.* **1.** The act or process of excavating. **2.** A hole formed by excavating.

ex·ca·va·tor (ĕk′skə-vā′tər) *n.* One that excavates, esp. a backhoe.

ex·ceed (ĭk-sēd′) *tr.v.* **-ceed·ed, -ceed·ing, -ceeds 1.** To extend beyond or outside of: *The river exceeded its banks.* **2.** To be greater than; surpass: *The results exceeded his hopes.* **3.** To go beyond the limits of: *I exceeded my allowance.* [ME *exceden* < OFr. *exceder* < Lat. *excēdere* : *ex-,* ex- + *cēdere,* to go.]

ex·ceed·ing (ĭk-sē′dĭng) *adj.* Extreme; extraordinary: *exceeding darkness.* ❖ *adv. Archaic* Exceedingly.

ex·ceed·ing·ly (ĭk-sē′dĭng-lē) *adv.* To an advanced or unusual degree; extremely.

ex·cel (ĭk-sĕl′) *v.* **-celled, -cel·ling, -cels** —*tr.* To do or be better than; surpass. —*intr.* To show superiority; surpass others. [ME *excellen* < Lat. *excellere.*]

ex·cel·lence (ĕk′sə-ləns) *n.* **1.** The state, quality, or condition of excelling; superiority. **2.** Something in which one excels. **3.** **Excellence** Excellency.

Ex·cel·len·cy (ĕk′sə-lən-sē) *n., pl.* **-cies** Used with *His, Her,* or *Your* as a title and form of address for certain high officials.

ex·cel·lent (ĕk′sə-lənt) *adj.* **1.** Of the highest or finest quality; exceptionally good of its kind. **2.** *Archaic* Superior. [ME < OFr. < Lat. *excellēns, excellent-,* pr. part. of *excellere,* to excel. See EXCEL.] —**ex′cel·lent·ly** *adv.*

ex·cel·si·or (ĭk-sĕl′sē-ər) *n.* Slender curved wood shavings used esp. for packing. [Orig. a trademark.]

ex·cept (ĭk-sĕpt′) *prep.* With the exclusion of; other than; but. ❖ *conj.* **1.** If it were not for the fact that; only: *I would buy the suit, except that it costs too much.* **2.** Otherwise than: *They didn't open their mouths except to complain.* **3.** Unless. ❖ *v.* **-cept·ed, -cept·ing, -cepts** —*tr.* To leave out; exclude. —*intr.* To object. —*idiom:* **except for** Were it not for. [ME < Lat. *exceptus,* p. part. of *excipere,* to exclude : *ex-,* ex- + *capere,* to take; see **kap-** in App.]

ex·cept·ing (ĭk-sĕp′tĭng) *prep.* With the exception of. ❖ *conj.* Except.

ex·cep·tion (ĭk-sĕp′shən) *n.* **1.** The act of excepting or the condition of being excepted; exclusion. **2.** One that is excepted, esp. a case that does not conform to a rule or generalization. **3.** An objection or a criticism. **4.** *Law* A formal objection taken in the course of an action or a proceeding.

ex·cep·tion·a·ble (ĭk-sĕp′shə-nə-bəl) *adj.* Open or liable to objection or debate; objectionable or debatable. —**ex·cep′tion·a·bil′i·ty** *n.* —**ex·cep′tion·a·bly** *adv.*

ex·cep·tion·al (ĭk-sĕp′shə-nəl) *adj.* **1.** Being an exception; uncommon. **2.** Well above average; extraordinary. See Usage Note at **exceptionable. 3.** Deviating widely from a norm, as of physical or mental ability. —**ex·cep′tion·al′i·ty, ex·cep′tion·al·ness** *n.* —**ex·cep′tion·al·ly** (-shə-nəl′ī-tē) *adv.*

ex·cep·tive (ĭk-sĕp′tĭv) *adj.* **1.** Of, being, or containing an exception. **2.** *Archaic* Captious; faultfinding.

ex·cerpt (ĕk′sûrpt′) *n.* A passage or segment taken from a longer work, such as a literary composition. ❖ *tr.v.* (ĭk-sûrpt′) **-cerpt·ed, -cerpt·ing, -cerpts 1.** To select or use (an excerpt). **2.** To select or use material from (a longer work). [< ME, excerpted < Lat. *excerptus,* p. part. of *excerpere,* to pick out : *ex-,* ex- + *carpere,* to pluck; see **kerp-** in App.]

ex·cess (ĭk-sĕs′, ĕk′sĕs′) *n.* **1.** The state of exceeding what is normal or sufficient: *rains that filled the reservoir to excess.* **2.** An amount or quantity beyond what is normal or sufficient; a surplus. **3.** The amount or degree by which one quantity exceeds another: *the excess of sales over costs.* **4.** Intemperance; overindulgence. **5.** A behavior or an action that exceeds proper or lawful bounds. ❖ *adj.* Being more than is usual, required, or permitted. See Syns at **superfluous.** ❖ *tr.v.* **-cessed, -cess·ing, -cess·es** To eliminate the job or position of. —*idiom:* **in excess of** Greater than; more than. [ME < OFr. < Lat. *excessus,* p. part. of *excēdere,* to exceed. See EXCEED.]

ex·ces·sive (ĭk-sĕs′ĭv) *adj.* Exceeding a normal, usual, reasonable, or proper limit. —**ex·ces′sive·ly** *adv.* —**ex·ces′sive·ness** *n.*

SYNONYMS *excessive, exorbitant, extravagant, immoderate, inordinate* These adjectives mean exceeding a normal, usual, reasonable, or proper limit. *Excessive* describes a quantity, amount, or degree that is more than what is justifiable, tolerable, or desirable: *excessive drinking. Exorbitant* usually refers to a quantity or degree that far exceeds what is customary or fair: *an exorbitant fee. Extravagant* sometimes specifies lavish or unwise expenditure (*extravagant gifts*); often it implies unbridled divergence from the bounds of reason or sound judgment (*extravagant claims*). *Immoderate* denotes lack of due moderation: *immoderate enthusiasm. Inordinate* implies an overstepping of bounds imposed by authority or dictated by good sense: *inordinate demands.*

exch. *abbr.* **1.** exchange **2.** *also* **Exch.** exchequer

ex·change (ĭks-chānj′) *v.* **-changed, -chang·ing, -chang·es** —*tr.* **1.** To give in return for something received; trade. **2.** To give and receive reciprocally; interchange. **3.** To give up for a substitute. **4.** To turn in for replacement. —*intr.* **1.** To give something in return for something received; make an exchange. **2.** To be received in exchange: *The British pound once exchanged for $2.80.* ❖ *n.* **1.** The act or an instance of exchanging. **2.** One that is exchanged. **3.** A place where things are exchanged, esp. a center where securities or commodities are bought and sold. **4.** A telephone exchange. **5a.** A system of payments using instruments, such as negotiable drafts, instead of money. **b.** The fee or percentage charged for participating in such a system of payment. **6.** A bill of exchange. **7.** A rate of exchange. **8.** The amount of difference in the actual value of two or more currencies or between values of the same currency at two or more places. **9.** A dialogue: *a heated exchange.* ❖ *adj.* Of or relating to a reciprocal arrangement between a local and a foreign institution or group: *an exchange student.* [ME *eschaungen* < AN *eschaungier* < VLat. **excambiāre* : Lat. *ex-,* ex- + LLat. *cambīre,* to exchange, barter; see CHANGE.] —**ex·change′a·ble** *adj.*

exchange rate *n.* A rate of exchange.

ex·cheq·uer (ĕks′chĕk′ər, ĭks-chĕk′ər) *n.* **1. Exchequer** The British governmental department charged with the collection and management of the national revenue. **2. Exchequer** In Great Britain, the Court of Exchequer. **3.** A treasury, as of a nation or an organization. **4.** Financial resources; funds. [Alteration of ME *escheker* < OFr. *eschequier,* counting table, chessboard < *eschec,* check. See CHECK.]

ex·ci·mer (ĕk′sə-mər) *n.* A diatomic molecule existing in an energy level above the ground state. [EXC(ITED) + (D)IMER.]

ex·cip·i·ent (ĭk-sĭp′ē-ənt) *n.* An inert substance used as a diluent or vehicle for a drug. [Lat. *excipiēns, excipient-,* pr. part. of *excipere,* to take out, exclude. See EXCEPT.]

ex·cise¹ (ĕk′sīz′) *n.* **1.** An internal tax imposed on the production, sale, or consumption of a commodity or the use of a service within a country. **2.** A licensing charge or a fee levied for certain privileges. ❖ *tr.v.* **-cised, -cis•ing, -cis•es** To levy an excise on. [MDu. *excijs*, alteration of *accijs*, tax, prob. < OFr. *acceis*, partly < VLat. **accēnsum* (Lat. *ad-*, ad- + Lat. *cēnsus*, tax; see CENSUS) and partly < OFr. *assise*, legislative ordinance; see ASSIZE.] **—ex•cis′a•ble** *adj.*

ex•cise² (ĭk-sīz′) *tr.v.* **-cised, -cis•ing, -cis•es** To remove by or as if by cutting. [Lat. *excīdere, excīs-* : *ex-*, ex- + *caedere*, to cut.] **—ex•ci′sion** (-sĭzh′ən) *n.*

ex•cit•a•ble (ĭk-sī′tə-bəl) *adj.* **1.** Easily excited. **2.** Capable of responding to stimuli. **—ex•cit′a•bil′i•ty, ex•cit′a•ble•ness** *n.* **—ex•cit′a•bly** *adv.*

ex•ci•tant (ĭk-sī′tnt) *adj.* Tending to excite; stimulating. ❖ *n.* An agent or stimulus that excites; a stimulant.

ex•ci•ta•tion (ĕk′sī-tā′shən) *n.* **1.** The act or process of exciting or an instance of it. **2.** The state or condition of being excited. **3.** *Physiology* The activity produced in an organ, tissue, or part, such as a nerve cell, as a result of stimulation.

ex•ci•ta•tive (ĭk-sī′tə-tĭv) or **ex•ci•ta•to•ry** (-sī′tə-tôr′ē, -tōr′ē) *adj.* Causing or tending to cause excitation.

ex•cite (ĭk-sīt′) *tr.v.* **-cit•ed, -cit•ing, -cites 1.** To stir to activity. **2.** To call forth (a reaction, for example); elicit. **3.** To arouse strong feeling in: *excited the crowd.* **4.** *Physiology* To produce increased activity or response in (an organ, tissue, or part). **5.** *Physics* **a.** To increase the energy of. **b.** To raise (an atom, for example) to a higher energy level. [ME *exciten* < Lat. *excitāre*, freq. of *exciēre* : *ex-*, ex- + *ciēre*, to set in motion; see **kei-²** in App.]

ex•cit•ed (ĭk-sī′tĭd) *adj.* **1.** Being in a state of excitement; emotionally aroused; stirred. **2.** *Physics* Being at an energy level higher than the ground state. **—ex•cit′ed•ly** *adv.*

ex•cite•ment (ĭk-sīt′mənt) *n.* **1a.** The act or an instance of exciting. **b.** The condition of being excited. **2.** Something that excites.

ex•cit•er (ĭk-sī′tər) *n.* **1.** One that excites: *an exciter of animosity.* **2.** An auxiliary generator used to provide field current for a larger generator or alternator. **3.** *Electronics* An oscillator for generating the carrier frequency of a transmitter.

ex•cit•ing (ĭk-sī′tĭng) *adj.* Creating or producing excitement: *an exciting story.* **—ex•cit′ing•ly** *adv.*

ex•ci•ton (ĕk′sī-tŏn′, -sī-) *n.* An electrically neutral excited state of an insulator or semiconductor, often regarded as a bound state of an electron and a hole. [EXCIT(ATION) + -ON¹.]

ex•ci•ton•ics (ĕk′sī-tŏn′ĭks, -sī-) *n.* (used with a sing. verb) The study of excitons and their behavior in semiconductors and dielectrics.

ex•ci•tor (ĭk-sī′tər) *n.* A nerve whose stimulation induces an increase in activity of the part it supplies.

excl. *abbr.* **1.** exclamation **2.** excluding **3.** exclusive

ex•claim (ĭk-sklām′) *v.* **-claimed, -claim•ing, -claims** *—intr.* To cry out suddenly or vehemently, as from surprise. *—tr.* To express or utter (something) suddenly or vehemently. [Fr. *exclamer* < Lat. *exclāmāre* : *ex-*, ex- + *clāmāre*, to call; see **kelə-** in App.] **—ex•claim′er** *n.*

ex•cla•ma•tion (ĕk′sklə-mā′shən) *n.* **1.** An abrupt forceful utterance. **2.** An outcry, as of protest. **3.** *Grammar* An interjection.

exclamation mark *n.* See exclamation point.

exclamation point *n.* A punctuation mark (!) used after an exclamation.

ex•clam•a•tory (ĭk-sklăm′ə-tôr′ē, -tōr′ē) *adj.* Constituting, containing, relating to, or using exclamation.

ex•clave (ĕk′sklāv′) *n.* A part of a country that is isolated from the main part and surrounded by foreign territory. [EX– + (EN)CLAVE.]

ex•clo•sure (ĕk-sklō′zhər) *n.* **1.** An area of land enclosed by a barrier to protect vegetation, esp. from grazing animals. **2.** The practice of fencing off an area to protect vegetation. [EX– : (EN)CLOSURE.]

ex•clude (ĭk-sklood′) *tr.v.* **-clud•ed, -clud•ing, -cludes 1.** To prevent from entering; keep out; bar. **2.** To prevent from being included, considered, or accepted; reject. **3.** To put out; expel. [ME *excluden* < Lat. *exclūdere* : *ex-*, ex- + *claudere*, to shut.] **—ex•clud′a•bil′i•ty** *n.* **—ex•clud′a•ble, ex•clud′i•ble** *adj. & n.* **—ex•clud′er** *n.*

ex•clu•sion (ĭk-skloo′zhən) *n.* **1.** The act or practice of excluding. **2.** The condition or fact of being excluded. [ME *exclusioun* < Lat. *exclūsiō, exclūsiōn-* < *exclūsus*, p. part. of *exclūdere*, to shut. See EXCLUDE.] **—ex•clu′sion•ar′y** (-zhə-nĕr′ē) *adj.*

exclusionary rule *n.* A rule that forbids the use of illegally obtained evidence in a criminal trial.

ex•clu•sion•ist (ĭk-skloo′zhə-nĭst) *n.* One that advocates the exclusion of another or others, as from exercising a right. **—ex•clu′sion•ism** *n.* **—ex•clu′sion•ist, ex•clu′sion•is′tic** *adj.*

exclusion principle *n.* The principle that two particles of a given type, such as electrons, cannot simultaneously occupy a particular quantum state.

ex•clu•sive (ĭk-skloo′sĭv) *adj.* **1.** Excluding or tending to exclude. **2.** Not allowing something else; incompatible. **3.** Not divided or shared with others. **4.** Not accompanied by others; single or sole. **5.** Complete; undivided. **6.** Excluding some or most, as

from membership. **7.** Not including the specified extremes or limits but only the area between them: *20–25, exclusive; that is, 21, 22, 23 and 24.* **8.** Catering to a wealthy clientele; expensive. **9.** *Linguistics* Of, relating to, or being a first person plural pronoun that excludes the addressee. ❖ *n.* **1.** A news item initially released to only one publication or broadcaster. **2.** An exclusive right or privilege. **—ex•clu′sive•ly** *adv.* **—ex•clu′sive•ness, ex′clu•siv′i•ty** (ĕk′skloo-sĭv′ĭ-tē) *n.*

exclusive of *prep.* Not including or considering.

exclusive OR *n.* See XOR.

ex•cog•i•tate (ĭk-skŏj′ĭ-tāt′) *tr.v.* **-tat•ed, -tat•ing, -tates** To consider or think (something) out carefully and thoroughly. [Lat. *excōgitāre, excōgitāt-*, to find out by thinking : *ex-*, ex- + *cōgitāre*, to think; see COGITATE.] **—ex•cog′i•ta′tion** *n.* **—ex•cog′i•ta′tive** *adj.*

ex•com•mu•ni•ca•ble (ĕks′kə-myoo′nĭ-kə-bəl) *adj.* Meriting, liable to, or punishable by excommunication.

ex•com•mu•ni•cate (ĕks′kə-myoo′nĭ-kāt′) *tr.v.* **-cat•ed, -cat•ing, -cates 1.** To deprive of the right of church membership by ecclesiastical authority. **2.** To exclude by or as if by decree from membership or participation in a group. ❖ *n.* (-kĭt) A person who has been excommunicated. ❖ *adj.* (-kĭt, -kāt′) Having been excommunicated. [ME *excommunicaten* < LLat. *excommūnicāre, excommūnicāt-* : Lat. *ex-*, ex- + Lat. *commūnicāre*, to share (< *commūnis*, common).] **—ex′com•mu′ni•ca′tive** (-kā′tĭv, -kə-), **ex′com•mu′ni•ca•to•ry** (-kə-tôr′ē, -tōr′ē) *adj.* **—ex′com•mu′ni•ca′tor** *n.*

ex•com•mu•ni•ca•tion (ĕks′kə-myoo′nĭ-kā′shən) *n.* **1.** The act of excommunicating. **2.** The state of being excommunicated. **3.** An excommunicative ecclesiastical censure.

ex•co•ri•ate (ĭk-skôr′ē-āt′, -skōr′-) *tr.v.* **-at•ed, -at•ing, -ates 1.** To tear or wear off the skin of; abrade. **2.** To censure strongly; denounce. [ME *excoriaten* < Lat. *excoriāre, excoriāt-* : *ex-*, ex- + *corium*, skin; see **sker-¹** in App.] **—ex•co′ri•a′tion** *n.* **—ex•co′ri•a′tor** *n.*

ex•cre•ment (ĕk′skrə-mənt) *n.* Waste material, esp. fecal matter, expelled after digestion. [Lat. *excrēmentum* < *excernere, excrē-*, to excrete. See EXCRETE.] **—ex′cre•men′tal, ex′cre•men′ti′tious** (-mĕn-tĭsh′əs) *adj.*

ex•cres•cence (ĭk-skrĕs′əns) *n.* **1.** An outgrowth or enlargement, esp. an abnormal one, such as a wart. **2.** A usu. unwanted or unnecessary accretion. [ME < Lat. *excrēscentia* < neut. pl. of *excrēscēns, excrēscent-*, pr. part. of *excrēscere*, to grow out : *ex-*, ex- + *crēscere*, to grow; see **ker-²** in App.]

ex•cres•cen•cy (ĭk-skrĕs′ən-sē) *n., pl.* **-cies 1.** The state or condition of being excrescent. **2.** An excrescence.

ex•cres•cent (ĭk-skrĕs′ənt) *adj.* **1.** Growing out abnormally, excessively, or superfluously. **2.** *Linguistics* Of or relating to epenthesis; epenthetic. **—ex•cres′cent•ly** *adv.*

ex•cre•ta (ĭk-skrē′tə) *pl.n.* Waste matter, such as sweat, urine, or feces, discharged from the body. [Lat. *excrēta* < neut. pl. p. part. of *excernere*, to excrete. See EXCRETE.] **—ex•cre′tal** *adj.*

ex•crete (ĭk-skrēt′) *tr.v.* **-cret•ed, -cret•ing, -cretes** To separate and discharge (waste) from blood, tissues, or organs. [Lat. *excernere, excrēt-* : *ex-*, ex- + *cernere*, to separate; see **krei-** in App.]

ex•cre•tion (ĭk-skrē′shən) *n.* **1.** The act or process of excreting. **2.** The excreted matter.

ex•cre•to•ry (ĕk′skrĭ-tôr′ē, -tōr′ē) *adj.* Of, relating to, or used in excretion: *excretory organs.*

ex•cru•ci•ate (ĭk-skroo′shē-āt′) *tr.v.* **-at•ed, -at•ing, -ates 1.** To inflict severe pain on; torture. **2.** To inflict great mental distress on. [Lat. *excruciāre, excruciāt-* : *ex-*, intensive pref.; see EX– + *cruciāre*, to crucify, torture (< *crux, cruc-*, cross; see CROSS).] **—ex•cru′ci•a′tion** *n.*

ex•cru•ci•at•ing (ĭk-skroo′shē-ā′tĭng) *adj.* **1.** Intensely painful; agonizing. **2.** Very intense or extreme. **—ex•cru′ci•at′ing•ly** *adv.*

ex•cul•pate (ĕk′skəl-pāt′, ĭk-skŭl′-) *tr.v.* **-pat•ed, -pat•ing, -pates** To clear of guilt or blame. [Med.Lat. *exculpāre, exculpāt-* : Lat. *ex-*, ex- + Lat. *culpa*, guilt.] **—ex•cul′pa•ble** (ĭk-skŭl′pə-bəl) *adj.* **—ex′cul•pa′tion** *n.*

ex•cul•pa•to•ry (ĭk-skŭl′pə-tôr′ē, -tōr′ē) *adj.* Acting or tending to exculpate.

ex•cur•rent (ĭk-skûr′ənt, -skûr′-) *adj.* **1a.** Running or flowing outwardly. **b.** Marked by an outward flow of current. **2.** *Botany* **a.** Having a single undivided trunk with lateral branches. **b.** Extending beyond the apex of a leaf. [Lat. *excurrēns, excurrent-*, part. of *excurrere*, to run out. See EXCURSION.]

ex•cur•sion (ĭk-skûr′zhən) *n.* **1.** A usu. short journey made for pleasure; an outing. **2.** A roundtrip on a passenger vehicle at a special low fare. **3.** A group taking a short pleasure trip together. **4.** A diversion or deviation from a main topic; a digression. **5.** *Physics* **a.** A movement from and back to a mean position or axis in an oscillating or alternating motion. **b.** The distance traversed in such a movement. [Lat. *excursiō, excursiōn-* < *excursus*, p. part. of *excurrere*, to run out : *ex-*, ex- + *currere*, to run; see EXCURSION.]

ex•cur•sive (ĭk-skûr′sĭv) *adj.* Of, given to, or characterized by digression. **—ex•cur′sive•ly** *adv.* **—ex•cur′sive•ness** *n.*

ex•cur•sus (ĭk-skûr′səs) *n., pl.* **-sus•es 1.** A lengthy appended exposition of a topic or point. **2.** A digression. [Lat. < p. part. of *excurrere*, to run out. See EXCURSION.]

excurrent
red spruce tree

ă	pat	oi	boy
ā	pay	ou	out
âr	care	oo	took
ä	father	oo	boot
ĕ	pet	ŭ	cut
ē	be	ûr	urge
ĭ	pit	th	thin
ī	pie	th	this
îr	pier	hw	which
ŏ	pot	zh	vision
ō	toe	ə	about,
ô	paw		item

Stress marks:
′ (primary);
′ (secondary), as in
lexicon (lĕk′sĭ-kŏn′)

ex·cus·a·to·ry (ĭk-skyōō′zə-tôr′ē, -tōr′ē) *adj.* Tending or serving to excuse.

ex·cuse (ĭk-skyōōz′) *tr.v.* **-cused, -cus·ing, -cus·es 1a.** To explain (a fault or offense) in the hope of being forgiven or understood. **b.** To apologize for (oneself) for an act that could cause offense. **2a.** To grant pardon to; forgive. **b.** To make allowance for; overlook. See Syns at **forgive. 3.** To serve as justification for. **4.** To free, as from an obligation or duty; exempt. **5.** To give permission to leave; release. ❖ *n.* (ĭk-skyōōs′) **1.** An explanation offered to justify or obtain forgiveness. **2.** A reason or grounds for excusing. **3.** The act of excusing. **4.** A note explaining an absence. **5.** *Informal* An inferior example. **—idiom: excuse me 1.** Used to acknowledge and ask forgiveness for an action that could cause offense. **2.** Used to request that a statement be repeated. [ME *excusen* < OFr. *excuser* < Lat. *excūsāre : ex-, ex-* + *causa,* accusation; see CAUSE.] **—ex·cus′a·ble** *adj.* **—ex·cus′a·ble·ness** *n.* **—ex·cus′a·bly** *adv.* **—ex·cus′er** *n.*

ex·ec (ĭg-zĕk′) *n. Informal* **1.** An executive. **2.** The executive officer of a unit of the armed forces.

exec. *abbr.* executor

ex·e·cra·ble (ĕk′sĭ-krə-bəl) *adj.* **1.** Deserving of execration; hateful. **2.** Extremely inferior; very bad. [ME < Lat. *execrābilis* < *execrārī,* to execrate. See EXECRATE.] **—ex′e·cra·ble·ness** *n.* **—ex′e·cra·bly** *adv.*

ex·e·crate (ĕk′sĭ-krāt′) *tr.v.* **-crat·ed, -crat·ing, -crates 1.** To declare to be hateful or abhorrent; denounce. **2.** To feel loathing for; abhor. **3.** *Archaic* To invoke a curse on. [Lat. *execrārī, execrāt-: ex-, ex-* + *sacrāre,* to consecrate (< *sacer,* sacred; see sak- in App.).] **—ex′e·cra′tive, ex′e·cra·to′ry** (-krə-tôr′ē, -tōr′ē) *adj.* **—ex′e·cra′tor** *n.*

ex·e·cra·tion (ĕk′sĭ-krā′shən) *n.* **1.** The act of cursing. **2.** A curse. **3.** Something that is cursed or loathed.

ex·ec·u·tant (ĭg-zĕk′yə-tənt) *n.* One who performs or carries out, esp. a skilled performer.

ex·e·cute (ĕk′sĭ-kyōōt′) *tr.v.* **-cut·ed, -cut·ing, -cutes 1.** To put into effect; carry out. **2.** To perform; do. **3.** To create (a work of art, for example) in accordance with a prescribed design. **4.** To make valid, as by signing. **5.** To perform or carry out what is required by: *executed the terms of a will.* **6.** To put to death, esp. by carrying out a lawful sentence. **7.** *Computer Science* To run (a program or an instruction). [ME *executen* < OFr. *executer* < Med.Lat. *execūtāre* < Lat. *execūtor,* executor < *execūtus,* p. part. of *exequī, exsequī,* to pursue, carry out : *ex-, ex-* + *sequī,* to follow; see sekʷ-¹ in App.] **—ex′e·cut′a·ble** *adj.* **—ex′e·cut′er** *n.*

ex·e·cu·tion (ĕk′sĭ-kyōō′shən) *n.* **1a.** The act of executing something. **b.** The state of being executed. **2.** The manner, style, or result of performance. **3.** The act or an instance of putting to death or being put to death as a lawful penalty. **4.** *Law* **a.** The carrying into effect of a court judgment. **b.** A writ empowering an officer to enforce a judgment. **c.** Validation of a legal document by the performance of all necessary formalities. **5.** *Archaic* Effective, punitive, or destructive action.

ex·e·cu·tion·er (ĕk′sĭ-kyōō′shə-nər) *n.* One who executes, esp. one who puts a condemned person to death.

ex·ec·u·tive (ĭg-zĕk′yə-tĭv) *n.* **1.** A person or group having administrative or managerial authority in an organization. **2.** The chief officer of a government, state, or political division. **3.** The executive branch of government. **4.** *Computer Science* A set of coded instructions designed to process and control other coded instructions. ❖ *adj.* **1.** Of, relating to, capable of, or suited for carrying out or executing. **2.** Having, characterized by, or relating to administrative or managerial authority: *executive skills.* **3.** Of or relating to the branch of government charged with the execution of a country's laws and the administration of its functions. [ME, to be carried out < OFr. *exécutif* < *executer,* to carry out. See EXECUTE.]

executive agreement *n.* An agreement made between the executive branch of the US government and a foreign government without ratification by the Senate.

executive council *n.* **1.** A council that advises or assists a political executive. **2.** A council having the highest executive authority.

executive officer *n.* **1a.** The officer second in command of a military unit smaller than a division. **b.** The officer second in command of a naval unit. **2.** A person with executive power in an organization.

executive order *n.* See **regulation** 3.

executive privilege *n.* The principle that members of the executive branch of government cannot legally be forced to disclose confidential communications when such disclosure would adversely affect executive operations or procedures.

executive secretary *n.* A secretary having administrative duties and responsibilities.

executive session *n.* A session, as of a committee, often closed to the public, in which executive business is transacted.

ex·ec·u·tor (ĭg-zĕk′yə-tər, ĕk′sĭ-kyōō′tər) *n.* **1.** One who carries out or performs something. **2.** *Law* One appointed by a testator to execute the testator's will. **—ex·ec′u·to′ri·al** (-tôr′ē-əl, -tōr′-) *adj.* **—ex·ec′u·tor·ship′** *n.*

ex·ec·u·to·ry (ĭg-zĕk′yə-tôr′ē, -tōr′ē) *adj.* **1.** Of or relating to execution or administration; executive. **2.** In effect; operative. **3.** *Law* Intended to go into effect or having the potential of becom-

ing effective at a future time; contingent.

ex·ec·u·trix (ĭg-zĕk′yə-trĭks′) *n., pl.* **-trix·es** or **-tri·ces** (-trī′sēz′) *Law* A woman who is appointed by a testator to execute the testator's will.

ex·e·dra (ĕk′sĭ-drə, ĭk-sē′-) *n.* **1.** A usu. curved outdoor bench with a high back. **2.** An often semicircular portico with seats that was used in ancient Greece and Rome as a place for discussions. [Lat. < Gk. *exedrā : ex-, ex-* + *hedrā,* seat; see sed- in App.]

ex·e·ge·sis (ĕk′sə-jē′sĭs) *n., pl.* **-ses** (-sēz) Critical interpretation or explanation, esp. textual. [Gk. *exēgēsis < exēgeisthai,* to interpret : *ex-, ex-* + *hēgeisthai,* to lead.]

ex·e·gete (ĕk′sə-jēt′) also **ex·e·ge·tist** (ĕk′sə-jĕt′ĭst) *n.* A person skilled in exegesis. [Gk. *exēgētēs < exēgeisthai,* to interpret.] See EXEGESIS.

ex·e·get·ic (ĕk′sə-jĕt′ĭk) also **ex·e·get·i·cal** (-ĭ-kəl) *adj.* Of or relating to exegesis. **—ex′e·get′i·cal·ly** *adv.*

ex·em·plar (ĭg-zĕm′plär′, -plər) *n.* **1.** One that is worthy of imitation; a model. **2.** One that is typical or representative; an example. **3.** An ideal that serves as a pattern; an archetype. **4.** A copy, as of a book. [ME *exemplere* < LLat. *exemplārium* < Lat. *exemplum,* example. See EXAMPLE.]

ex·em·pla·ry (ĭg-zĕm′plə-rē) *adj.* **1.** Worthy of imitation; commendable: *exemplary behavior.* **2.** Serving as a model. **3.** Serving as an illustration; typical. **4.** Serving as a warning; admonitory. [< Lat. *exemplāris, exemplāre,* an exemplar. See EXEMPLAR.] **—ex′em·plar′i·ly** (ĕg′zəm-plâr′ə-lē) *adv.* **—ex·em′pla·ri·ness, ex′em·plar′i·ty** (ĕg′zəm-plăr′ĭ-tē) *n.*

ex·em·pli·fi·ca·tion (ĭg-zĕm′plə-fĭ-kā′shən) *n.* **1.** The act of exemplifying. **2.** One that exemplifies; an example.

ex·em·pli·fy (ĭg-zĕm′plə-fī′) *tr.v.* **-fied, -fy·ing, -fies 1.** To illustrate by example. **2.** To serve as an example of. [ME *exemplifien* < OFr. *exemplifier* < Med.Lat. *exemplificāre* < Lat. *exemplum,* example; see EXAMPLE + Lat. *-ficāre,* -fy.] **—ex·em′pli·fi′a·ble** *adj.* **—ex·em′pli·fi′er** *n.*

ex·em·pli gra·ti·a (ĭg-zĕm′plē grä′shē-ə, ĕk-sĕm′plē grä′tē-ä′) *adv.* For example. [Lat. *exemplī grātiā,* for the sake of example : *exemplī,* genitive of *exemplum,* example + *grātiā,* ablative of *grātia,* grace, sake.]

ex·em·plum (ĭg-zĕm′pləm) *n., pl.* **-pla** (-plə) **1.** An example. **2.** A brief story used to make a point in an argument or illustrate a moral truth. [Lat. See EXAMPLE.]

ex·empt (ĭg-zĕmpt′) *tr.v.* **-empt·ed, -empt·ing, -empts 1.** To make exempt. **2.** *Obsolete* To set apart; isolate. ❖ *adj.* **1.** Freed from an obligation, duty, or liability to which others are subject. **2.** *Obsolete* Set apart; isolated. ❖ *n.* One who is exempt. [ME *exempten* < OFr. *exempter* < *exempt,* exempt < Lat. *exemptus,* p. part. of *eximere,* to take out. See EXAMPLE.] **—ex·empt′i·ble** *adj.*

ex·emp·tion (ĭg-zĕmp′shən) *n.* **1.** The act or an instance of exempting. **2.** The state of being exempt; immunity. **3.** One that is exempted, esp. an amount of income that is exempted from taxation.

ex·en·ter·ate (ĭg-zĕn′tə-rāt′) *tr.v.* **-at·ed, -at·ing, -ates 1.** To disembowel; eviscerate. **2.** *Medicine* To remove the contents of (an organ). [Lat. *exenterāre, exenterāt-,* to disembowel : *ex-, ex-* + Gk. *enteron,* entrails; see en in App.] **—ex·en′ter·a′tion** *n.*

ex·er·cise (ĕk′sər-sīz′) *n.* **1.** An act of employing or putting into play; use. **2.** The discharge of a duty, function, or office. **3.** Activity that requires physical or mental exertion, esp. when performed to develop or maintain fitness. **4.** A task, problem, or other effort performed to develop or maintain fitness or increase skill. **5.** An activity having a specified aspect: *an exercise in futility.* **6. exercises** A program that includes speeches, presentations, and other ceremonial activities performed before an audience. ❖ *v.* **-cised, -cis·ing, -cis·es** *—tr.* **1.** To put into play or operation; employ. **2.** To bring to bear; exert. **3a.** To subject to practice or exertion in order to train, strengthen, or develop. **b.** To put through exercises. See Syns at **practice. 4a.** To carry out the functions of; execute. **b.** To execute the terms of (a stock option, for example). **5a.** To absorb the attentions of, esp. by worry or anxiety. **b.** To stir to anger or alarm; upset. *—intr.* To take exercise. [ME < OFr. *exercice* < Lat. *exercitium < exercitus,* p. part. of *exercēre,* to exercise : *ex-, ex-* + *arcēre,* to restrain.] **—ex′er·cis′a·ble** *adj.*

exercise bicycle *n.* A fitness device having a seat, handlebars, and pedals with adjustable resistance, used to simulate pedaling a bicycle.

exercise book *n.* A booklet for students, usu. containing problems or exercises and space for answers or practice.

ex·er·cis·er (ĕk′sər-sī′zər) *n.* **1.** One that exercises: *an exerciser of racehorses.* **2.** A device for exercising the body.

ex·er·ci·ta·tion (ĭg-zûr′sĭ-tā′shən) *n.* The act or an instance of exercising. [ME *exercitacioun* < Lat. *exercitātiō, exercitātiōn- < exercitāre,* freq. of *exercēre,* to exercise. See EXERCISE.]

ex·er·gon·ic (ĕk′sər-gŏn′ĭk) *adj.* Releasing energy. [EX(O)– + Gk. *ergon,* work; see werg- in App. + –IC.]

ex·er·gue (ĕk′sûrg′, ĕg′zûrg′) *n.* A space on the reverse of a coin or medal, usu. below the central design and often giving the date and place of engraving. [Fr. : Gk. *ex-, ex-* + Gk. *ergon,* work; see werg- in App.]

ex·ert (ĭg-zûrt′) *tr.v.* **-ert·ed, -ert·ing, -erts 1.** To put to use or effect; put forth. **2.** To bring to bear; exercise. **3.** To put (oneself)

exercise bicycle

to strenuous effort. [Lat. *exserere, exsert-*, to put forth, stretch out : *ex-, ex-* + *serere*, to join.]

ex•er•tion (ĭg-zûr′shən) *n.* The act or an instance of exerting, esp. a strenuous effort.

Ex•e•ter (ĕk′sĭ-tər) A borough of SW England NE of Plymouth; strategically important since Roman times. Pop. 105,087.

ex•e•unt (ĕk′sē-ənt, -ŏont′) Used as a stage direction to indicate that two or more performers leave the stage. [Lat., third pers. pl. pr. t. of *exīre*, to go out. See EXIT.]

ex•fo•li•ate (ĕks-fō′lē-āt′) *v.* **-at•ed, -at•ing, -ates** —*tr.* **1.** To remove (a layer of bark, for example) in flakes or scales; peel. **2.** To cast off in scales, flakes, or splinters. —*intr.* To come off or separate into flakes, scales, or layers. [Lat. *exfoliāre, exfoliāt-*, to strip of leaves : *ex-, ex-* + *folium*, leaf; see **bhel-** in App.] —**ex•fo′li•a′tion** *n.* —**ex•fo′li•a′tive** *adj.* —**ex•fo′li•a′tor** *n.*

ex•ha•lant also **ex•ha•lent** (ĕks-hā′lənt, ĕk-sā′-) *adj.* Functioning in exhalation. ❖ *n.* An organ, such as the siphon of a clam, that is used for exhalation.

ex•ha•la•tion (ĕks′hə-lā′shən, ĕk′sə-) *n.* **1.** The act or an instance of exhaling. **2.** Something, such as air, that is exhaled.

ex•hale (ĕks-hāl′, ĕk-sāl′) *v.* **-haled, -hal•ing, -hales** —*intr.* **1a.** To breathe out. **b.** To emit air or vapor. **2.** To be given off or emitted. —*tr.* **1.** To blow (something) out or breathe (something) out. **2.** To give off; emit. [ME *exalen* < Lat. *exhālāre* : *ex-, ex-* + *hālāre*, to breathe.]

ex•haust (ĭg-zôst′) *v.* **-haust•ed, -haust•ing, -hausts** —*tr.* **1.** To wear out completely. **2.** To drain of resources or properties; deplete. See Syns at **deplete**. **3.** To use up completely. **4.** To treat completely; cover thoroughly: *exhaust a topic*. **5.** To draw out the contents of; drain. **6.** To let out or draw off. —*intr.* To escape or pass out. ❖ *n.* **1a.** The escape or release of vaporous waste material, as from an engine. **b.** The fumes or gases so released. **2.** A duct or pipe through which waste material is emitted. **3.** An apparatus for drawing out noxious air or waste material by means of a partial vacuum. [Lat. *exhaurīre, exhaust-* : *ex-, ex-* + *haurīre*, to draw.] —**ex•haust′ed•ly** *adv.* —**ex•haust′er** *n.* —**ex•haust′i•bil′i•ty** *n.* —**ex•haust′i•ble** *adj.* —**ex•haust′ing•ly** *adv.*

ex•haus•tion (ĭg-zôs′chən) *n.* **1.** The act or an instance of exhausting. **2.** The state of being exhausted; extreme fatigue.

ex•haus•tive (ĭg-zô′stĭv) *adj.* **1.** Treating all parts or aspects without omission; thorough. **2.** Tending to exhaust. —**ex•haus′tive•ly** *adv.* —**ex•haus′tive•ness** *n.* —**ex′haus•tiv′i•ty** *n.*

ex•haust•less (ĭg-zôst′lĭs) *adj.* Never exhausted; inexhaustible. —**ex•haust′less•ly** *adv.* —**ex•haust′less•ness** *n.*

exhaust pipe *n.* See **tailpipe**.

ex•hib•it (ĭg-zĭb′ĭt, ĕg-) *v.* **-it•ed, -it•ing, -its** —*tr.* **1.** To show outwardly; display: *exhibited pleasure by smiling.* **2a.** To present for others to see. **b.** To present in a public exhibition or contest. **3.** To give evidence or an instance of; demonstrate. **4.** *Law* **a.** To submit (evidence or documents) in a court. **b.** To present or introduce officially. —*intr.* To put something on public display. ❖ *n.* **1.** The act or an instance of exhibiting. **2.** Something exhibited. **3.** A public showing; an exhibition. **4.** *Law* Something, such as a document, formally introduced as evidence in court. [ME *exhibiten* < Lat. *exhibēre, exhibit-* : *ex-, ex-* + *habēre*, to hold; see **ghabh-** in App.] —**ex•hib′i•tor, ex•hib′it•er** *n.* —**ex•hib′i•to′ry** (-ĭ-tôr′ē, -tōr′ē) *adj.*

ex•hi•bi•tion (ĕk′sə-bĭsh′ən) *n.* **1.** The act or an instance of exhibiting. **2.** Something exhibited; an exhibit. **3.** A large-scale public showing, as of art. **4.** *Chiefly British* A grant given to a scholar by a school or university.

ex•hi•bi•tion•ism (ĕk′sə-bĭsh′ə-nĭz′əm) *n.* **1.** The act or practice of deliberately behaving so as to attract attention. **2.** A psychosexual disorder marked by the compulsive exposure of the genitals in public. —**ex′hi•bi′tion•ist** *n.* —**ex′hi•bi′tion•is′tic** *adj.*

ex•hib•i•tive (ĭg-zĭb′ĭ-tĭv) *adj.* Tending to exhibit: *behavior exhibitive of certain instincts.* —**ex•hib′i•tive•ly** *adv.*

ex•hil•a•rant (ĭg-zĭl′ər-ənt) *adj.* Serving to exhilarate; exhilarating. ❖ *n.* Something that exhilarates or stimulates.

ex•hil•a•rate (ĭg-zĭl′ə-rāt′) *tr.v.* **-rat•ed, -rat•ing, -rates 1.** To cause to feel happily refreshed and energetic; elate. **2.** To invigorate; stimulate. [Lat. *exhilarāre, exhilarāt-* : *ex-*, intensive pref.; see EX-+ *hilarāre*, to make cheerful (< *hilaris, hilarus*, cheerful < Gk. *hilaros*).] —**ex•hil′a•ra′ting** *adj.* —**ex•hil′a•rat′ing•ly** *adv.* —**ex•hil′a•ra′tion** *n.* —**ex•hil′a•ra′tive** *adj.* —**ex•hil′a•ra′tor** *n.*

ex•hort (ĭg-zôrt′) *v.* **-hort•ed, -hort•ing, -horts** —*tr.* To urge by strong, often stirring argument, admonition, advice, or appeal: *exhorted the troops to hold the line.* —*intr.* To make urgent appeal. [ME *exhorten* < Lat. *exhortārī* : *ex-*, intensive pref.; see EX-+ *hortārī*, to encourage.] —**ex•hort′er** *n.*

ex•hor•ta•tion (ĕg′zôr-tā′shən, ĕk′sôr-) *n.* **1.** The act or an instance of exhorting. **2.** A speech or discourse that exhorts.

ex•hor•ta•tive (ĭg-zôr′tə-tĭv) *adj.* also **ex•hor•ta•to•ry** (-tôr′ē, -tōr′ē) *adj.* Acting or intended to exhort.

ex•hume (ĭg-zōōm′, -zyōōm′, ĭk-syōōm′, ĕks-hyōōm′) *tr.v.* **-humed, -hum•ing, -humes 1.** To remove from a grave; disinter. **2.** To bring to light, esp. after a period of obscurity. [Fr. *exhumer* < Med.Lat. *exhumāre* : Lat. *ex-, ex-* + Lat. *humus*, ground; see **dhghem-** in App.] —**ex′hu•ma′tion** (ĕg′zyōō-mā′shən,

---

ĕks′hyōō-) *n.* —**ex•hum′er** *n.*

ex hy•poth•e•si (ĕks′ hī-pŏth′ĭ-sī′) *adv.* By hypothesis. [NLat. *ex hypothesī* : Lat. *ex*, out of, by + Lat. *hypothesī*, ablative of *hypothesis*, hypothesis.]

ex•i•gence (ĕk′sə-jəns) *n.* Exigency.

ex•i•gen•cy (ĕk′sə-jən-sē, ĭg-zĭj′ən-) *n., pl.* **-cies 1.** The state or quality of requiring much effort or immediate action. **2.** A pressing or urgent situation. **3.** A requirement or need. Often used in the plural.

ex•i•gent (ĕk′sə-jənt) *adj.* **1.** Requiring immediate action or remedy. See Syns at **urgent**. **2.** Requiring much effort or expense; demanding. [Lat. *exigēns, exigent-*, pr. part. of *exigere*, to demand. See EXACT.] —**ex′i•gent•ly** *adv.*

ex•i•gu•i•ty (ĕk′sĭ-gyōō′ĭ-tē) *n.* The quality or condition of being scanty or meager.

ex•ig•u•ous (ĭg-zĭg′yōō-əs, ĭk-sĭg′-) *adj.* Quite scanty; meager. [< Lat. *exiguus* < *exigere*, to measure out, demand. See EXACT.] —**ex•ig′u•ous•ly** *adv.* —**ex•ig′u•ous•ness** *n.*

ex•ile (ĕg′zīl′, ĕk′sīl′) *n.* **1a.** Enforced removal from one's native country. **b.** Self-imposed absence from one's country. **2.** The condition or a period of living away from one's native country. **3.** One who lives in exile, whether forced or voluntary. ❖ *tr.v.* **-iled, -il•ing, -iles** To send into exile; banish. See Syns at **banish**. [ME *exil* < OFr. < Lat. *exilium* < *exul, exsul*, exiled person, wanderer.] —**ex•il′ic** (ĭg-zĭl′ĭk, ĭk-sĭl′-) *adj.*

ex•ine (ĕk′sēn′, -sīn′) *n.* The outer layer of the wall of a spore or pollen grain. [EX(O)– + Gk. *īs, īn-*, tendon.]

ex•ist (ĭg-zĭst′) *intr.v.* **-ist•ed, -ist•ing, -ists 1.** To have actual being; be real. **2.** To have life; live. **3.** To live at a minimal level; subsist. **4.** To continue to be; persist. **5.** To be present under certain circumstances or in a specified place; occur. [Lat. *existere, exsistere*, to come forth, be manifest : *ex-, ex-* + *sistere*, to stand; see **stā-** in App.]

ex•is•tence (ĭg-zĭs′təns) *n.* **1.** The fact or state of existing; being. **2.** The fact or state of continued being; life. **3a.** All that exists. **b.** A thing that exists; an entity. **4.** A mode or manner of existing. **5.** Specific presence; occurrence.

ex•is•tent (ĭg-zĭs′tənt) *adj.* **1.** Having life or being; existing. **2.** Occurring or present at the moment; current. ❖ *n.* One that exists.

ex•is•ten•tial (ĕg′zĭ-stĕn′shəl, ĕk′sĭ-) *adj.* **1.** Of or relating to existence. **2.** Based on experience; empirical. **3.** Of or as conceived by existentialism. **4.** *Linguistics* Relating to a construction or part of a construction that indicates existence, as the words *there is* in the sentence *There is a cat on the mat.* ❖ *n. Linguistics* An existential word or construction. —**ex′is•ten′tial•ly** *adv.*

ex•is•ten•tial•ism (ĕg′zĭ-stĕn′shə-lĭz′əm, ĕk′sĭ-) *n.* A philosophy that emphasizes the uniqueness and isolation of the individual in a hostile or indifferent universe, regards existence as unexplainable, and stresses free choice and responsibility for one's actions. —**ex′is•ten′tial•ist** *adj. & n.*

ex•it (ĕg′zĭt, ĕk′sĭt) *n.* **1.** The act of going away or out. **2.** A passage or way out. **3.** The departure of a performer from the stage. **4.** Death. ❖ *v.* **-it•ed, -it•ing, -its** —*intr.* To make one's exit; depart. —*tr.* To go out of; leave. **2.** *Computer Science* To terminate the execution of (an application). [< Lat., third pers. sing. pr. t. of *exīre*, to go out : *ex-, ex-* + *īre*, to go; see **ei-** in App. N., sense 2 < Lat. *exitus* < p. part. of *exīre*.]

exit poll *n.* A poll taken of a sample of voters as they leave a polling place, used esp. to predict the outcome of an election.

ex li•bris (ĕks lī′brĭs, lē′-) *n., pl.* **ex libris** See **bookplate**. [Lat. *ex librīs*, from the books : *ex*, from + *librīs*, ablative pl. of *liber*, book.]

ex ni•hi•lo (ĕks nē′ə-lō′, nĭ′-, nī′-) *adv. & adj.* Out of nothing. [Lat. *ex nihilō* : *ex*, out of + *nihilō*, ablative of *nihil*, nothing.]

exo– *pref.* Outside; external: *exoskeleton.* [< Gk. *exō*, outside < *ex*, out of. See **eghs** in App.]

ex•o•bi•ol•o•gy (ĕk′sō-bī-ŏl′ə-jē) *n.* The branch of biology that deals with the search for extraterrestrial life and the effects of extraterrestrial surroundings on living organisms. —**ex′o•bi′o•log′i•cal** (-ə-lŏj′ĭ-kəl) *adj.*

ex•o•carp (ĕk′sō-kärp′) *n. Botany* The outermost layer of the fruit wall.

ex•o•crine (ĕk′sə-krĭn, -krēn, -krīn′) *adj.* **1.** Secreting externally, directly or through a duct: *exocrine cells.* **2.** Of, relating to, or produced by an exocrine gland. [EXO- + Gk. *krīnein*, to separate; see **krei-** in App.]

exocrine gland *n.* An externally secreting gland, such as a salivary gland or sweat gland.

ex•o•cy•clic (ĕk′sō-sī′klĭk, -sĭk′lĭk) *adj.* External to a chemical ring structure: *an exocyclic double bond.*

ex•o•cy•to•sis (ĕk′sō-sī-tō′sĭs) *n., pl.* **-ses** (-sēz′) A process of cellular secretion or excretion in which substances contained in vesicles are discharged from the cell by fusion of the vesicular membrane with the outer cell membrane. —**ex′o•cy•tose′** (-tōs′) *v.* —**ex′o•cy•tot′ic** (-tŏt′ĭk) *adj.*

Exod. *abbr. Bible* Exodus

ex•o•don•tia (ĕk′sō-dŏn′shə, -shē-ə) *n.* Exodontics.

ex•o•don•tics (ĕk′sə-dŏn′tĭks) *n. (used with a sing. verb)* The dental specialty that deals with extraction of teeth. —**ex′o•don′tist** *n.*

ă	pat	oi	boy
ā	pay	ou	out
âr	care	ŏŏ	took
ä	father	ōō	boot
ĕ	pet	ŭ	cut
ē	be	ûr	urge
ĭ	pit	th	thin
ī	pie	th	this
îr	pier	hw	which
ŏ	pot	zh	vision
ō	toe	ə	about,
ô	paw		item

Stress marks:
′ (primary);
′ (secondary), as in
lexicon (lĕk′sĭ-kŏn′)

ex•o•dus (ĕk′sə-dəs) n. 1. A departure of a large number of people. 2. **Exodus a.** The departure of the Israelites from Egypt. **b.** See table at **Bible.** [LLat. < Gk. exodos : ex-, out; see EXO– + hodos, way, journey.]

ex•o•en•zyme (ĕk′sō-ĕn′zīm′) n. An enzyme that functions outside the cell from which it originates.

ex•o•er•gic (ĕk′sō-ûr′jĭk) adj. Exothermic. [EXO– + Gk. ergon, work; see **werg-** in App. + –IC.]

ex of•fi•ci•o (ĕks′ ə-fĭsh′ē-ō′) adv. & adj. By virtue of office or position. [Lat. ex officiō.]

ex•og•a•my (ĕk-sŏg′ə-mē) n. 1. The custom of marrying outside a social unit, such as a tribe. 2. Biology The fusion of two gametes that are not closely related. —**ex′o•gam′ic** (ĕk′sə-găm′ĭk), **ex•og′a•mous** (ĕk-sŏg′ə-məs) adj.

ex•og•e•nous (ĕk-sŏj′ə-nəs) adj. 1. Biology Derived or developed from outside the body; originating externally. 2. Botany Characterized by the addition of layers of woody tissue. 3. Medicine Having a cause external to the body. Used of diseases. [Fr. exogène : Gk. exō-, exo- + Fr. -gène, -gen.] —**ex•og′e•nous•ly** adv.

ex•on (ĕk′sŏn) n. A nucleotide sequence of DNA that codes information for protein synthesis for transcription to messenger RNA. [ex(pressed) + –ON[1].] —**ex•on′ic** adj.

ex•on•er•ate (ĭg-zŏn′ə-rāt′) tr.v. -at•ed, -at•ing, -ates 1. To free from blame. 2. To free from a responsibility, obligation, or task. [ME exoneraten < Lat. exonerāre, exonerāt-, to free from a burden : ex-, ex- + onus, oner-, burden.] —**ex•on′er•a′tion** n. —**ex•on′er•a′tive** adj.

ex•o•nu•cle•ase (ĕk′sō-nōō′klē-ās′, -āz′, -nyōō′-) n. Any of a group of enzymes that catalyze the hydrolysis of single nucleotides from the end of a DNA or RNA chain.

ex•o•nym (ĕk′sō-nĭm) n. A name by which one people or social group refers to another and by which the group so named does not refer to itself.

ex•o•pep•ti•dase (ĕk′sō-pĕp′tĭ-dās′, -dāz′) n. Any of a group of enzymes that catalyze the hydrolysis of single amino acids from the end of a polypeptide chain.

ex•oph•thal•mic goiter (ĕk′sŏf-thăl′mĭk) n. See **Graves′ disease.**

ex•oph•thal•mos also **ex•oph•thal•mus** (ĕk′sŏf-thăl′məs) n. Abnormal protrusion of the eyeball. [< Gk. exophthalmos, with prominent eyes : ex-, outside; see EXO– + ophthalmos, eye; see **okʷ-** in App.] —**ex′oph•thal′mic** adj.

ex•or•bi•tance (ĭg-zôr′bĭ-təns) n. 1. Excessiveness, as of price. 2. Behavior or an action exceeding what is right or proper.

ex•or•bi•tant (ĭg-zôr′bĭ-tənt) adj. Exceeding all bounds, as of custom or fairness. See Syns at **excessive.** [ME, aberrant, flagrant < OFr., excessive, extreme < LLat. exorbitāns, exorbitant-, pr. part. of exorbitāre, to deviate : Lat. ex-, ex- + Lat. orbita, path, track; see ORBIT.] —**ex•or′bi•tant•ly** adv.

ex•or•cise (ĕk′sôr-sīz′, -sər-) tr.v. -cised, -cis•ing, -cis•es 1. To expel (an evil spirit) by or as if by incantation, command, or prayer. 2. To free from evil spirits or malign influences. [ME exorcisen < LLat. exorcizāre < Gk. exorkizein : ex-, out of; see EXO– + horkizein, to make one swear (< horkos, oath).] —**ex′or•cis′er** n.

ex•or•cism (ĕk′sôr-sĭz′əm, -sər-) n. 1. The act, practice, or ceremony of exorcising. 2. A formula used in exorcising. —**ex′or•cist** n.

ex•or•di•um (ĭg-zôr′dē-əm, ĭk-sôr′-) n., pl. -di•ums or -di•a (-dē-ə) A beginning or introductory part, esp. of a speech or treatise. [Lat. < exōrdīrī, to begin : ex-, intensive pref.; see EX– + ōrdīrī, to begin.] —**ex•or′di•al** adj.

ex•o•skel•e•ton (ĕk′sō-skĕl′ĭ-tn) n. A hard outer structure, such as the shell of a crustacean, that provides protection or support for an organism. —**ex′o•skel′e•tal** (-ĭ-tl) adj.

ex•os•mo•sis (ĕk′sŏz-mō′sĭs, -sŏs-) n. The passage of a fluid through a semipermeable membrane toward a solution of lower concentration, esp. the passage of water through a cell membrane into the surrounding medium. [EX(O)– + OSMOSIS.] —**ex′os•mot′ic** (-mŏt′ĭk) adj.

ex•o•sphere (ĕk′sō-sfîr′) n. 1. The outermost region of a planet's atmosphere. 2. The outermost region of the earth's atmosphere, lying above the ionosphere and extending far into space. —**ex′o•spher′ic** (-sfîr′ĭk, -sfĕr′-) adj.

ex•o•spore (ĕk′sō-spôr′, -spōr′) n. The outermost layer of a spore in some algae and fungi.

ex•o•spor•i•um (ĕk′sō-spôr′ē-əm, -spōr′-) n., pl. -i•a (-ē-ə) See **exine.** [NLat. : EXO– + Gk. sporā, spore.]

ex•os•to•sis (ĕk′sŏ-stō′sĭs) n., pl. -ses (-sēz) A bony growth on the surface of a bone or tooth. [Gk. exostōsis : ex-, out of; see EXO– + osteon, bone; see **ost-** in App. + -ōsis, -osis.]

ex•o•ter•ic (ĕk′sə-tĕr′ĭk) adj. 1. Not confined to an inner circle of disciples or initiates. 2. Comprehensible to or suited to the public; popular. 3. Of or relating to the outside; external. [Lat. exōtericus, external < Gk. exōterikos < exōterō, comp. of exō, outside. See EXO–.] —**ex′o•ter′i•cal•ly** adv.

ex•o•ther•mic (ĕk′sō-thûr′mĭk) also **ex•o•ther•mal** (-məl) adj. Releasing heat. —**ex′o•ther′mi•cal•ly** adv.

ex•ot•ic (ĭg-zŏt′ĭk) adj. 1. From another part of the world. 2. Intriguingly unusual or different. See Syns at **fantastic.** 3. Of or involving striptease. ❖ n. 1. One that is exotic. 2. A striptease performer. [Lat. exōticus < Gk. exōtikos < exō, outside < ex, out. See eghs in App.] —**ex•ot′i•cal•ly** adv. —**ex•ot′i•cism** (-ĭ-sĭz′əm), **ex•ot′ic•ness** n.

ex•ot•i•ca (ĭg-zŏt′ĭ-kə) pl.n. Things that are curiously unusual or excitingly strange. [Lat. exōtica < neut. pl. of exōticus, exotic. See EXOTIC.]

ex•o•tox•in (ĕk′sō-tŏk′sĭn) n. A poisonous substance secreted by a microorganism and released externally.

ex•o•tro•pi•a (ĕk′sō-trō′pē-ə) n. A form of strabismus in which one or both of the eyes deviate outward. [NLat. : EXO– + Gk. tropē, a turning; see –TROPIC.] —**ex′o•trop′ic** (-trŏp′ĭk, -trō′pĭk) adj.

exp abbr. 1. exponent 2. exponential

exp. abbr. 1. expenses 2. experiment 3. expiration 4. export 5. express

ex•pand (ĭk-spănd′) v. -pand•ed, -pand•ing, -pands —tr. 1. To increase the size, volume, quantity, or scope of; enlarge. See Syns at **increase.** 2. To express at length or in detail. 3. To open (something) up or out. 4. Mathematics To write (a quantity) as a sum of terms in an extended form. —intr. 1. To become greater in size, volume, quantity, or scope. 2. To speak or write at length or in detail. 3. To open up or out; unfold. 4. To feel expansive. [ME expanden, to spread out < Lat. expandere : ex-, ex- + pandere, to spread.] —**ex•pand′a•ble** adj. —**ex•pand′er** n.

ex•pand•ing universe theory (ĭk-spăn′dĭng) n. 1. The cosmological theory holding that the universe is expanding, based on the interpretation of the red shift as indicating that all galaxies are moving away from one another. 2. The cosmogonical theory holding that all matter and energy in the universe originated from the big bang.

ex•panse (ĭk-spăns′) n. 1. A wide and open extent, as of surface, land, or sky. 2a. Expansion. **b.** The distance or amount of expansion. [Lat. expānsum < neut. p. part. of expandere, to spread out. See EXPAND.]

ex•pan•si•ble (ĭk-spăn′sə-bəl) adj. That can expand or be expanded: an expansible antenna. —**ex•pan′si•bil′i•ty** n.

ex•pan•sile (ĭk-spăn′səl, -sīl′) adj. Of, relating to, or capable of expansion.

ex•pan•sion (ĭk-spăn′shən) n. 1a. The act or process of expanding. **b.** The state of being expanded. 2a. An expanded part. **b.** A product of expanding: The book is an expansion of a PhD thesis. 3. The extent or amount by which something has expanded. 4. Mathematics **a.** A quantity written in an extended form. **b.** The process of obtaining this form. 5. An expanse. 6. A period of increased economic or business activity.

ex•pan•sion•ar•y (ĭk-spăn′shə-nĕr′ē) adj. Tending toward or causing expansion or expansionism.

expansion board n. See **expansion card.**

expansion bolt n. A bolt having an attachment that expands as the bolt is driven into a surface.

expansion card n. A circuit board that can be installed to enhance a computer's capabilities.

ex•pan•sion•ism (ĭk-spăn′shə-nĭz′əm) n. A nation's practice or policy of territorial or economic expansion. —**ex•pan′sion•ist** adj. & n.

ex•pan•sive (ĭk-spăn′sĭv) adj. 1. Capable of expanding or tending to expand. 2. Broad in size or extent; comprehensive. 3. Open and communicative; talkative or effusive. 4. Grand in scale. —**ex•pan′sive•ly** adv. —**ex•pan′sive•ness, ex′pan•siv′i•ty** (ĕk′spăn-sĭv′ĭ-tē) n.

ex par•te (ĕks pär′tē) adv. & adj. 1. Law From or on one side only, with the other side absent or unrepresented. 2. From a one-sided or strongly biased point of view. [Lat.]

ex•pa•ti•ate (ĭk-spā′shē-āt′) intr.v. -at•ed, -at•ing, -ates 1. To speak or write at length. 2. To wander freely. [Lat. expatiārī, expatiāt- : ex-, ex- + spatiārī, to spread (< spatium, space).] —**ex•pa′ti•a′tion** n.

ex•pa•tri•ate (ĕk-spā′trē-āt′) v. -at•ed, -at•ing, -ates —tr. 1. To send into exile. See Syns at **banish.** 2. To remove (oneself) from residence in one's native land. —intr. 1. To give up residence in one's homeland. 2. To renounce allegiance to one's homeland. ❖ n. (-ĭt, -āt′) 1. One who has taken up residence in a foreign country. 2. One who has renounced one's native land. ❖ adj. (-ĭt, -āt′) Residing in a foreign country; expatriated. [Med.Lat. expatriāre, expatriāt- : Lat. ex-, ex- + Lat. patria, native land (< patrius, paternal < pater, father; see **pəter-** in App.).] —**ex•pa′tri•a′tion** n.

ex•pect (ĭk-spĕkt′) v. -pect•ed, -pect•ing, -pects —tr. 1a. To look forward to the probable occurrence or appearance of. **b.** To consider likely or certain. 2. To consider reasonable or due. 3. To consider obligatory; require. 4. Informal To presume; suppose. —intr. 1. To look forward to the birth of one's child. Used in progressive tenses: She is expecting in May. 2. To be pregnant. Used in progressive tenses. [Lat. expectāre : ex-, ex- + spectāre, to look at, freq. of specere; see **spek-** in App.] —**ex•pect′a•ble** adj. —**ex•pect′a•bly, ex•pect′ed•ly** adv.

ex•pec•tance (ĭk-spĕk′təns) n. Expectancy.

ex•pec•tan•cy (ĭk-spĕk′tən-sē) n., pl. -cies 1. The act or state of expecting; expectation. 2. The state of being expected. 3. Something expected. 4. An expected amount calculated on the basis of actuarial data: a life expectancy of 70 years.

ex·pec·tant (ĭk-spĕk′tənt) *adj.* **1.** Having or marked by expectation. **2.** Pregnant. —**ex·pec′tant·ly** *adv.*

ex·pec·ta·tion (ĕk′spĕk-tā′shən) *n.* **1a.** The act of expecting. **b.** Eager anticipation. **2.** The state of being expected. **3a.** Something expected. **b. expectations** Prospects, esp. of success or gain. **4.** *Statistics* The expected value of a random variable. **b.** The mean of a random variable. —**ex′pec·ta′tion·al** *adj.*

ex·pec·ta·tive (ĭk-spĕk′tə-tĭv) *adj.* Of, relating to, or characterized by expectation.

ex·pect·ed value (ĭk-spĕk′tĭd) *n.* **1.** The sum of all possible values for a random variable, each value multiplied by its probability. **2.** The integral of the probability density function over a continuous random variable over its range of values.

ex·pec·to·rant (ĭk-spĕk′tər-ənt) *adj.* Promoting or facilitating the secretion or expulsion of matter from the respiratory tract. ❖ *n.* An expectorant medicine.

ex·pec·to·rate (ĭk-spĕk′tə-rāt′) *v.* **-rat·ed, -rat·ing, -rates** *—tr.* **1.** To eject from the mouth; spit. **2.** To cough up and eject by spitting. *—intr.* **1.** To spit. **2.** To clear out the chest and lungs by expectorating. [Lat. *expectorāre, expectorāt-*, to drive from the chest : *ex-*, ex- + *pectus, pector-*, chest.] —**ex·pec′to·ra′tion** *n.*

ex·pe·di·ence (ĭk-spē′dē-əns) *n.* Expediency.

ex·pe·di·en·cy (ĭk-spē′dē-ən-sē) *n., pl.* **-cies** **1.** Appropriateness to the purpose at hand; fitness. **2.** Adherence to self-serving means. **3.** A means; an expedient. **4.** *Obsolete* Speed.

ex·pe·di·ent (ĭk-spē′dē-ənt) *adj.* **1.** Appropriate to a purpose. **2a.** Serving to promote one's interest. **b.** Based on or marked by a concern for self-interest rather than principle; self-interested. **3.** *Obsolete* Speedy; expeditious. ❖ *n.* **1.** Something that is a means to an end. **2.** Something contrived or used to meet an urgent need. [ME < Lat. *expediēns, expedient-*, pr. part. of *expedīre*, to make ready. See EXPEDITE.] —**ex·pe′di·ent·ly** *adv.*

ex·pe·di·en·tial (ĭk-spē′dē-ĕn′shəl) *adj.* Of or relating to what is expedient. —**ex·pe′di·en′tial·ly** *adv.*

ex·pe·dite (ĕk′spĭ-dīt′) *tr.v.* **-dit·ed, -dit·ing, -dites** **1.** To speed up the progress of; accelerate. **2.** To perform quickly and efficiently. **3.** To issue officially; dispatch. [Lat. *expedīre, expedīt-*, to free from entanglements, make ready. See **ped-** in App.] —**ex′pe·dit′er, ex′pe·di′tor** *n.*

ex·pe·di·tion (ĕk′spĭ-dĭsh′ən) *n.* **1a.** A journey undertaken by a group of people with a definite objective. **b.** The group undertaking such a journey. **2.** Speed in performance; promptness. See Syns at **haste.** [ME *expedicioun*, military campaign < OFr. *expedition* < Lat. *expedītiō, expedītiōn-* < *expedītus*, p. part. of *expedīre*, to make ready. See EXPEDITE.]

ex·pe·di·tion·ar·y (ĕk′spĭ-dĭsh′ə-nĕr′ē) *adj.* **1.** Relating to or constituting an expedition. **2.** Sent on or designed for military operations abroad.

ex·pe·di·tious (ĕk′spĭ-dĭsh′əs) *adj.* Acting or done with speed and efficiency. See Syns at **fast**[1]. —**ex′pe·di′tious·ly** *adv.* —**ex′pe·di′tious·ness** *n.*

ex·pel (ĭk-spĕl′) *tr.v.* **-pelled, -pel·ling, -pels** **1.** To force or drive out. **2.** To discharge from or as if from a receptacle. **3.** To force to leave; deprive of membership. See Syns at **eject.** [ME *expellen* < Lat. *expellere* : *ex-*, ex- + *pellere*, to drive; see **pel-**[2] in App.] —**ex·pel′la·ble** *adj.* —**ex·pel′ler** *n.*

ex·pel·lant also **ex·pel·lent** (ĭk-spĕl′ənt) *adj.* Expelling or tending to expel.

ex·pel·lee (ĭk′spĕl-lē′) *n.* One who is expelled.

ex·pend (ĭk-spĕnd′) *tr.v.* **-pend·ed, -pend·ing, -pends** **1.** To lay out; spend. See Syns at **spend.** **2.** To use up; consume. [ME *expenden* < Lat. *expendere*, to pay out : *ex-*, ex- + *pendere*, to weigh.]

ex·pend·a·ble (ĭk-spĕn′də-bəl) *adj.* **1.** Subject to use or consumption: *an expendable source.* **2.** Not worth salvaging or reusing. **3.** Not strictly necessary; dispensable: *an expendable budget item.* **4.** Open to sacrifice in the interests of gaining an objective, esp. a military one. —**ex·pend′a·ble** *n.*

ex·pen·di·ture (ĭk-spĕn′də-chər) *n.* **1.** The act or process of expending; outlay. **2a.** An amount expended. **b.** An expense. [Med. Lat. *expenditus*, p. part. of *expendere*, to expend; see EXPEND + -URE.]

ex·pense (ĭk-spĕns′) *n.* **1a.** Something spent to attain a goal or accomplish a purpose. **b.** A loss for the sake of something gained; a sacrifice. **2.** An expenditure of money; a cost. **3. expenses** Charges incurred by an employee in the performance of work. **b.** *Informal* Money allotted for payment of such charges. **4.** Something requiring the expenditure of money. **5.** *Archaic* The act of expending. ❖ *tr.v.* **-pensed, -pens·ing, -pens·es** **1.** To charge with expenses. **2.** To write off as an expense. *—idiom:* **at (one's) expense** To one's detriment or chagrin. [ME < AN < Lat. *(pecūnia) expēnsa*, (money) paid out, fem. p. part. of *expendere*, to pay out. See EXPEND.]

expense account *n.* An account of expenses for repayment to an employee.

ex·pen·sive (ĭk-spĕn′sĭv) *adj.* **1.** Requiring a large expenditure; costly. **2.** Marked by high prices: *expensive stores.* —**ex·pen′sive·ly** *adv.* —**ex·pen′sive·ness** *n.*

ex·pe·ri·ence (ĭk-spîr′ē-əns) *n.* **1.** The apprehension of an object, thought, or emotion through the senses or mind. **2a.** Active participation in events or activities, leading to the accumulation

of knowledge or skill. **b.** The knowledge or skill so derived. **3a.** An event or a series of events participated in or lived through. **b.** The totality of such events in the past of an individual or group. ❖ *tr.v.* **-enced, -enc·ing, -enc·es** To participate in personally; undergo. [ME < OFr. < Lat. *experientia* < *experiēns, experient-*, pr. part. of *experīrī*, to try.] —**ex·pe′ri·enc·er** *n.*

ex·pe·ri·enced (ĭk-spîr′ē-ənst) *adj.* **1.** Having had experience in an activity or in life in general. **2.** Skilled or knowledgeable as the result of active participation or practice.

ex·pe·ri·en·tial (ĭk-spîr′ē-ĕn′shəl) *adj.* Relating to or derived from experience. —**ex·pe′ri·en′tial·ly** *adv.*

ex·per·i·ment (ĭk-spĕr′ə-mənt) *n.* **1a.** A test under controlled conditions that is made to demonstrate a known truth, examine the validity of a hypothesis, or determine the efficacy of something previously untried. **b.** The process of conducting such a test; experimentation. **2.** An innovative act or procedure. **3.** The result of experimentation. ❖ *intr.v.* (-mĕnt′) **-ment·ed, -ment·ing, -ments** **1.** To conduct an experiment. **2.** To try something new, esp. in order to gain experience. [ME < OFr. < Lat. *experīmentum* < *experīrī*, to try.] —**ex·per′i·ment′er** *n.*

ex·per·i·men·tal (ĭk-spĕr′ə-mĕn′tl) *adj.* **1a.** Relating to or based on experiment. **b.** Given to experimenting. **2.** Of the nature of an experiment; being or undergoing a test. **3.** Based on experience; empirical. —**ex·per′i·men′tal·ly** *adv.*

ex·per·i·men·tal·ism (ĭk-spĕr′ə-mĕn′tl-ĭz′əm) *n.* Use of empirical or experimental methods in determining the validity of ideas. —**ex·per′i·men′tal·ist** *n.*

ex·per·i·men·ta·tion (ĭk-spĕr′ə-mĕn-tā′shən) *n.* The act, process, or practice of experimenting.

experiment station *n.* An establishment in which scientific experiments are conducted in a specific field, such as agriculture, and practical uses are developed.

ex·pert (ĕk′spûrt′) *n.* **1.** A person with a high degree of skill in or knowledge of a certain subject. **2a.** The highest grade that can be achieved in marksmanship. **b.** One who has achieved this grade. ❖ *adj.* (ĕk′spûrt, ĭk-spûrt′) Having, involving, or demonstrating great skill, dexterity, or knowledge as the result of experience or training. See Syns at **proficient.** [ME < OFr., experienced < Lat. *expertus*, p. part. of *experīrī*, to try.] —**ex′pert′ly** *adv.* —**ex′pert′ness** *n.*

ex·per·tise (ĕk′spûr-tēz′) *n.* **1.** Expert advice or opinion. **2.** Skill or knowledge in a particular area. [Fr. < *expert*, experienced. See EXPERT.]

expert system *n.* A computer program that uses available information, heuristics, and inference to suggest solutions to problems in a particular discipline.

ex·pi·ate (ĕk′spē-āt′) *v.* **-at·ed, -at·ing, -ates** *—tr.* To make amends or reparation for; atone: *expiate one's sins by acts of penance.* *—intr.* To make amends; atone. [Lat. *expiāre, expiāt-* : *ex-*, intensive pref.; see EX– + *piāre*, to atone (< *pius*, devout).] —**ex′pi·a·ble** (-ə-bəl), **ex′pi·a·to·ry** (-ə-tôr′ē, -tōr′ē) *adj.* —**ex′pi·a′tion** *n.* —**ex′pi·a′tor** *n.*

ex·pi·ra·tion (ĕk′spə-rā′shən) *n.* **1.** The act of ending; termination. **2.** The act of exhalation. **3.** *Archaic* Death.

expiration date *n.* **1.** The date on which something, such as a warranty, is no longer valid or in effect. **2.** The date past which a product must be sold or removed from availability because it is no longer expected to be fresh or effective.

ex·pi·ra·to·ry (ĭk-spîr′ə-tôr′ē, -tōr′ē) *adj.* Of, relating to, or involving the expiration of air from the lungs.

ex·pire (ĭk-spîr′) *v.* **-pired, -pir·ing, -pires** *—intr.* **1.** To come to an end; terminate. **2.** To breathe one's last breath; die. **3.** To exhale; breathe out. *—tr.* **1.** To breathe (something) out. **2.** *Archaic* To give (something) off. [ME *expiren* < OFr. *expirer* < Lat. *exspīrāre* : *ex-*, ex- + *spīrāre*, to breathe.]

ex·pi·ry (ĭk-spîr′ē) *n., pl.* **-ries** **1.** An expiration, esp. of a contract or an agreement. **2.** Death.

ex·plain (ĭk-splān′) *v.* **-plained, -plain·ing, -plains** *—tr.* **1.** To make plain or comprehensible. **2.** To define; expound. **3a.** To offer reasons for or a cause of; justify: *explain an error.* **b.** To offer reasons for the actions, beliefs, or remarks of (oneself). *—intr.* To make something plain or comprehensible. *—phrasal verb:* **explain away** **1.** To dismiss or get rid of by explaining. **2.** To minimize by explanation. [ME *explanen* < Lat. *explānāre* : *ex-*, intensive pref.; see EX– + *plānus*, clear; see **pelə-**[2] in App.] —**ex·plain′a·ble** *adj.*

ex·pla·na·tion (ĕk′splə-nā′shən) *n.* **1.** The act or process of explaining. **2.** Something that explains. **3.** A mutual clarification of misunderstandings; a reconciliation.

ex·plan·a·tive (ĭk-splăn′ə-tĭv) *adj.* Explanatory. —**ex·plan′a·tive·ly** *adv.*

ex·plan·a·to·ry (ĭk-splăn′ə-tôr′ē, -tōr′ē) *adj.* Serving or intended to explain. —**ex·plan′a·to′ri·ly** *adv.*

ex·plant (ĕk-splănt′) *tr.v.* **-plant·ed, -plant·ing, -plants** To remove (living tissue) from the natural site of growth and place in a medium for culture. ❖ *n.* (ĕks′plănt′) Explanted tissue. [EX– + (IM)PLANT.] —**ex′plan·ta′tion** *n.*

ex·ple·tive (ĕk′splĭ-tĭv) *n.* **1.** An exclamation or oath, esp. one that is profane, vulgar, or obscene. **2a.** A word or phrase that does not contribute any meaning but is added only to fill out a sentence or a metrical line. **b.** *Linguistics* A word or grammatical ele-

ă	pat	oi	boy
ā	pay	ou	out
âr	care	ŏŏ	took
ä	father	ōō	boot
ĕ	pet	ŭ	cut
ē	be	ûr	urge
ĭ	pit	th	thin
ī	pie	*th*	this
îr	pier	hw	which
ŏ	pot	zh	vision
ō	toe	ə	about,
ô	paw		item

Stress marks:
′ (primary);
′ (secondary), as in
lexicon (lĕk′sĭ-kŏn′)

ment that fills a syntactic position but has no meaning, such as the word *it* in *It's raining.* ❖ *adj.* Added or inserted in order to fill out something, such as a sentence. [< LLat. *explētīvus*, serving to fill out < Lat. *explētus*, p. part. of *explēre*, to fill out : *ex-*, *ex-* + *plēre*, to fill; see **pelə-**[1] in App.]

ex·ple·to·ry (ĕk′splĭ-tôr′ē, -tōr′ē) *adj.* Expletive.

ex·pli·ca·ble (ĭk-splĭk′ə-bəl, ĕk′splĭ-kə-) *adj.* Possible to explain: *explicable phenomena.* —**ex·plic′a·bly** *adv.*

ex·pli·cate (ĕk′splĭ-kāt′) *tr.v.* **-cat·ed, -cat·ing, -cates** To make clear the meaning of; explain. [Lat. *explicāre, explicāt-*, to unfold, explain : *ex-*, *ex-* + *plicāre*, to fold; see **plek-** in App.] —**ex′pli·ca′tion** *n.* —**ex′pli·ca′tor** *n.*

ex·pli·ca·tion de texte (ĕk-splē-kä-syôn′ də tĕkst′) *n., pl.* **ex·pli·ca·tions de texte** (-syôn) A method of literary criticism in which aspects of a written work are analyzed in order to understand its structure and meanings. [Fr., explanation of (a) text.]

ex·pli·ca·tive (ĕk′splĭ-kā′tĭv, ĭk-splĭk′ə-tĭv) *adj.* Serving to explain. —**ex′pli·ca′tive·ly** *adv.*

ex·plic·it (ĭk-splĭs′ĭt) *adj.* **1a.** Fully and clearly expressed. **b.** Fully and clearly defined or formulated. **2.** Forthright and unreserved in expression. **3a.** Readily observable. **b.** Depicting nudity or sexual activity in graphic detail. [Lat. *explicitus*, p. part. of *explicāre*, to unfold. See EXPLICATE.] —**ex·plic′it·ly** *adv.* —**ex·plic′it·ness** *n.*

explicit function *n.* A function, such as $y = 4x + 3$, whose value may be computed from the independent variable.

ex·plode (ĭk-splōd′) *v.* **-plod·ed, -plod·ing, -plodes** —*intr.* **1.** To release mechanical, chemical, or nuclear energy by the sudden production of gases in a confined space. **2.** To burst violently as a result of internal pressure. **3.** To shatter with a loud noise. **4.** To make an emotional outburst: *exploded in rage.* **5.** To increase suddenly, sharply, and without control: *The population of deer exploded.* **6.** To change state or appearance suddenly. —*tr.* **1.** To cause to release energy or burst violently and noisily. **2.** To show to be false or unreliable. [Lat. *explōdere*, to drive out by clapping : *ex-*, *ex-* + *plaudere*, to clap.] —**ex·plod′er** *n.*

ex·plod·ed view (ĕk-splō′dĭd) *n.* An illustration or diagram of a construction that shows its parts separately but in positions that indicate their proper relationships to the whole.

ex·ploit (ĕk′sploit′, ĭk-sploit′) *n.* An act or deed, esp. a brilliant or heroic one. ❖ *tr.v.* (ĕk-sploit′, ĕk′sploit′) **-ploit·ed, -ploit·ing, -ploits** **1.** To employ to the greatest possible advantage. **2.** To make use of selfishly or unethically. See Syns at **manipulate. 3.** To advertise; promote. [ME < OFr. *esploit* < Lat. *explicitum*, neut. p. part. of *explicāre*, to unfold. See EXPLICATE.] —**ex·ploit′a·bil′i·ty** *n.* —**ex·ploit′a·ble** *adj.* —**ex·ploit′a·tive, ex·ploit′ive** *adj.* —**ex·ploit′a·tive·ly, ex·ploit′ive·ly** *adv.* —**ex·ploit′er** *n.*

ex·ploi·ta·tion (ĕk′sploi-tā′shən) *n.* **1.** The act of employing to the greatest possible advantage. **2.** Utilization of another selfishly. **3.** An advertising or a publicity program.

ex·plo·ra·tion (ĕk′splə-rā′shən) *n.* The act or an instance of exploring. —**ex·plor′a·to′ry** (ĭk-splôr′ə-tôr′ē, -splōr′ə-tōr′ē) *adj.*

ex·plore (ĭk-splôr′, -splōr′) *v.* **-plored, -plor·ing, -plores** —*tr.* **1.** To investigate systematically; examine. **2.** To search into or travel in for the purpose of discovery. **3.** *Medicine* To examine for diagnostic purposes. —*intr.* To make a careful examination or search. [Lat. *explōrāre* : *ex-*, *ex-* + perh. *plōrāre*, to cry out, as to rouse game.]

ex·plor·er (ĭk-splôr′ər, -splōr′-) *n.* **1.** One that explores, esp. one that explores a geographic area. **2.** An implement or a tool used for exploring; a probe. **3.** **Explorer** A person aged 14 to 21 who is a participant in the exploring program of the Boy Scouts of America.

ex·plo·sion (ĭk-splō′zhən) *n.* **1a.** A release of mechanical, chemical, or nuclear energy in a sudden and often violent manner with the generation of high temperature and usu. with the release of gases. **b.** A violent bursting as a result of internal pressure. **c.** The loud sharp sound made as a result of either of these actions. **2.** A sudden, often vehement outburst: *an explosion of rage.* **3.** A sudden great increase. **4.** *Linguistics* See **plosion.** [Lat. *explōsiō, explōsiōn-*, a driving off < *explōsus*, p. part. of *explōdere*, to drive out by clapping. See EXPLODE.]

ex·plo·sive (ĭk-splō′sĭv) *adj.* **1.** Relating to or having the nature of an explosion. **2.** Tending to explode. ❖ *n.* **1.** A substance, esp. a prepared chemical, that explodes or causes explosion. **2.** *Linguistics* A plosive. —**ex·plo′sive·ly** *adv.* —**ex·plo′sive·ness** *n.*

ex·po (ĕk′spō) *n., pl.* **-pos** *Informal* An exposition.

ex·po·nent (ĭk-spō′nənt, ĕk′spō′nənt) *n.* **1.** One that expounds or interprets. **2.** One that represents or advocates. **3.** *Mathematics* A number or symbol, as 3 in $(x + y)^3$, denoting the power to which another number or expression is to be raised. ❖ *adj.* Expository; explanatory. [Lat. *expōnēns, expōnent-*, pr. part. of *expōnere*, to expound. See EXPOUND.]

ex·po·nen·tial (ĕk′spə-nĕn′shəl) *adj.* **1.** Of or relating to an exponent. **2.** *Mathematics* **a.** Containing, involving, or expressed as an exponent. **b.** Expressed in terms of a designated power of *e*, the base of natural logarithms. —**ex′po·nen′tial·ly** *adv.*

ex·po·nen·ti·a·tion (ĕk′spə-nĕn′shē-ā′shən) *n. Mathematics* The act of raising a quantity to a power.

ex·port (ĭk-spôrt′, -spōrt′, ĕk′spôrt′, -spōrt′) *v.* **-port·ed,**

-port·ing, -ports —*tr.* **1.** To send or transport (as a commodity) abroad, esp. for trade. **2.** To cause the spread of (an idea, for example) in another part of the world; transmit. **3.** *Computer Science* To send (data) from one program to another. —*intr.* To export merchandise, esp. for trade. ❖ *n.* (ĕk′spôrt′, -spōrt′) Exportation. [ME *exsport* < Lat. *exportāre* : *ex-*, *ex-* + *portāre*, to carry; see **per-**[2] in App.] —**ex·port′a·bil′i·ty** *n.* —**ex·port′a·ble** *adj.* —**ex·port′er** *n.*

ex·por·ta·tion (ĕk′spôr-tā′shən, -spōr-) *n.* **1.** The act of exporting. **2.** Something exported; an export.

ex·pose (ĭk-spōz′) *tr.v.* **-posed, -pos·ing, -pos·es 1a.** To subject or allow to be subjected to an action, influence, or condition. **b.** To subject (a photographic film, for example) to the action of light. **c.** To deprive of shelter or protection; lay open to danger or harm. **2.** To make visible. **3a.** To make known (something discreditable). **b.** To reveal the guilt or wrongdoing of. **4.** To engage in indecent exposure of (oneself). [ME *exposen* < OFr. *exposer*, alteration (influenced by *poser*, to put, place) of Lat. *expōnere*, to set forth; see EXPOUND.] —**ex·pos′er** *n.*

ex·po·sé (ĕk′spō-zā′) *n.* **1.** An exposure or a revelation of something discreditable. **2.** A formal exposition of facts. [Fr., p. part. of *exposer*, to expose < OFr. See EXPOSE.]

ex·po·si·tion (ĕk′spə-zĭsh′ən) *n.* **1.** The systematic explanation of a subject. **2a.** A discourse that conveys information about or explains a subject. **b.** The art or technique of composing such discourses. **3.** *Music* **a.** The first part of a composition in sonata form that introduces the themes. **b.** The opening section of a fugue. **4.** The part of a play that provides the background information needed to understand the characters and the action. **5.** An act or example of exposing. **6.** A public exhibition, as of industrial developments. [ME *exposicioun* < OFr. *exposition* < Lat. *expositiō, expositiōn-* < *expositus*, p. part. of *expōnere*, to expound. See EXPOUND.] —**ex·pos′i·tive** (ĭk-spŏz′ĭ-tĭv), **ex·pos′i·to·ry** (-tôr′ē, -tōr′ē) *adj.* —**ex·pos′i·tor** *n.*

ex post fac·to (ĕks′ pōst făk′tō) *adj.* Formulated, enacted, or operating retroactively. Used esp. of a law. [Lat. *ex postfactō* : *ex*, from + *postfactō*, ablative of *postfactum*, that which is done afterward.]

ex·pos·tu·late (ĭk-spŏs′chə-lāt′) *intr.v.* **-lat·ed, -lat·ing, -lates** To reason earnestly with someone in an effort to dissuade or correct; remonstrate. See Syns at **object.** [Lat. *expostulāre, expostulāt-* : *ex-*, intensive pref.; see EX– + *postulāre*, to demand; see **prek-** in App.] —**ex·pos′tu·la′tion** *n.* —**ex·pos′tu·la′tor** *n.* —**ex·pos′tu·la·to′ry** (-lə-tôr′ē, -tōr′ē), **ex·pos′tu·la′tive** *adj.*

ex·po·sure (ĭk-spō′zhər) *n.* **1.** The act or an instance of exposing, as: **a.** An act of subjecting or an instance of being subjected to an action or influence. **b.** Appearance in public or in the mass media. **c.** Revelation, esp. of crime or guilt. **d.** The act of presenting a body part, esp. the genitals, to view. **2.** The condition of being exposed, esp. to severe weather or other forces of nature. **3.** A position in relation to climatic or weather conditions or points of the compass. **4a.** The act of exposing sensitized photographic film or plate. **b.** A photographic plate or a piece of film so exposed. **c.** The amount of radiant energy needed to expose a photographic film.

exposure meter *n.* A photoelectric instrument that measures the light intensity in a given area and in photographic use indicates the correct settings for an optimum exposure.

ex·pound (ĭk-spound′) *v.* **-pound·ed, -pound·ing, -pounds** —*tr.* **1.** To give a detailed statement of; set forth. **2.** To explain in detail; elucidate. —*intr.* To make a detailed statement: *expounded on a favorite topic.* [ME *expounden* < AN *espoundre* < Lat. *expōnere* : *ex-*, *ex-* + *pōnere*, to place; see **apo-** in App.] —**ex·pound′er** *n.*

ex·press (ĭk-sprĕs′) *tr.v.* **-pressed, -press·ing, -press·es 1.** To set forth in words; state. **2.** To manifest or communicate, as by a gesture; show. See Syns at **vent**[1]. **3.** To make known the feelings or opinions of (oneself), as by statement or art. **4.** To convey or suggest a representation of; depict. **5.** To represent by a sign or a symbol; symbolize. **6.** To squeeze or press out, as juice from an orange. **7.** To send by special messenger or rapid transport. **8.** *Genetics* **a.** To cause (itself) to produce an effect or a phenotype. Used of a gene. **b.** To manifest the effects of (a gene). **c.** To manifest (a genetic trait). ❖ *adj.* **1.** Definitely and explicitly stated. **2.** Particular; specific. **3a.** Sent out with or moving at high speed. **b.** Direct, rapid, and usu. nonstop: *an express bus.* **c.** Of, relating to, or appropriate for rapid travel: *express lanes.* ❖ *adv.* By express delivery or transport. ❖ *n.* **1a.** A rapid, efficient system for the delivery of goods and mail. **b.** Goods and mail conveyed by such a system. **2.** A means of transport, such as a train, that travels rapidly and makes few or no stops before its destination. **3.** *Chiefly British* **a.** A special messenger. **b.** A message delivered by special courier. [ME *expressen* < OFr. *expresser* < Med.Lat. *expressāre*, freq. of Lat. *exprimere* : *ex-*, *ex-* + *premere*, to press.] —**ex·press′er** *n.* —**ex·press′i·ble** *adj.*

ex·pres·sion (ĭk-sprĕsh′ən) *n.* **1.** The act of expressing, conveying, or representing in words, art, music, or movement; a manifestation. **2.** Something that expresses or communicates. **3.** *Mathematics* A symbol or combination of symbols that represents a quantity or a relationship between quantities. **4.** The manner in which one expresses oneself, esp. in speaking, depicting, or performing. **5.** A particular word or phrase. **6.** The outward manifestation of a mood or a disposition. **7.** A facial aspect or a look that conveys a special feeling. **8.** The act of pressing or squeezing out. **9.** *Genetics* The act or process of expressing a gene.

ex•pres•sion•ism (ĭk-sprĕsh′ə-nĭz′əm) *n.* A movement in the arts during the early part of the 20th century that emphasized subjective expression of the artist's inner experiences. —**ex•pres′sion•ist** *n.* —**ex•pres′sion•is′tic** *adj.* —**ex•pres′sion•is′ti•cal•ly** *adv.*

ex•pres•sion•less (ĭk-sprĕsh′ən-lĭs) *adj.* Lacking expression.

ex•pres•sive (ĭk-sprĕs′ĭv) *adj.* **1.** Of, relating to, or characterized by expression. **2.** Serving to express or indicate. **3.** Full of expression; significant: *an expressive glance.* —**ex•pres′sive•ly** *adv.* —**ex•pres′sive•ness** *n.*

SYNONYMS *expressive, eloquent, meaningful, significant* These adjectives mean effectively conveying a feeling, idea, or mood: *an expressive gesture; an eloquent speech; a meaningful look; a significant smile.*

ex•pres•siv•i•ty (ĕk′sprĕ-sĭv′ĭ-tē) *n., pl.* **-ties 1.** The quality of being expressive. **2.** *Genetics* The degree to which an expressed gene produces its effects in an organism.

ex•press•ly (ĭk-sprĕs′lē) *adv.* **1.** In an express or a definite manner; explicitly. **2.** Especially; particularly.

ex•pres•so (ĭk-sprĕs′ō, ĕk-) *n.* Variant of **espresso.**

ex•press•way (ĭk-sprĕs′wā′) *n.* A major divided highway designed for high-speed travel, having few or no intersections.

ex•pro•pri•ate (ĕk-sprō′prē-āt′) *tr.v.* **-at•ed, -at•ing, -ates 1.** To deprive of possession. **2.** To transfer (another's property) to oneself. [Med.Lat. *expropriāre, expropriāt-* : Lat. *ex-*, ex- + Lat. *propriāre*, to appropriate (< *proprius*, one's own; see PROPER).] —**ex•pro′pri•a′tion** *n.* —**ex•pro′pri•a′tor** *n.* —**ex•pro′pri•a•to′ry** (-ə-tôr′ē, -tōr′ē) *adj.*

ex•pul•sion (ĭk-spŭl′shən) *n.* The act of expelling or the state of being expelled. [ME *expulsioun* < OFr. *expulsion* < Lat. *expulsiō, expulsiōn-* < *expulsus*, p. part. of *expellere*, to expel. See EXPEL.]

ex•punc•tion (ĭk-spŭngk′shən, -spŭng′shən) *n.* The act of expunging or the condition of being expunged. [LLat. *expūnctiō, expūnctiōn-*, execution < Lat. *expūnctus*, p. part. of *expungere*, to strike out. See EXPUNGE.]

ex•punge (ĭk-spŭnj′) *tr.v.* **-punged, -pung•ing, -pung•es 1.** To erase or strike out. **2.** To eliminate completely; annihilate. See Syns at **erase.** [Lat. *expungere* : *ex-*, ex- + *pungere*, to prick.] —**ex•pung′er** *n.*

ex•pur•gate (ĕk′spər-gāt′) *tr.v.* **-gat•ed, -gat•ing, -gates** To remove erroneous, vulgar, obscene, or otherwise objectionable material from (a book, for example) before publication. [Lat. *expūrgāre, expūrgāt-*, to purify : *ex-*, intensive pref.; see EX– + *pūrgāre*, to cleanse.] —**ex′pur•ga′tion** *n.* —**ex′pur•ga′tor** *n.*

ex•pur•ga•to•ry (ĭk-spûr′gə-tôr′ē, -tōr′ē) also **ex•pur•ga•to•ri•al** (-tôr′ē-əl, -tōr′-) *adj.* Of or relating to expurgation or an expurgator.

expwy or **expy** *abbr.* expressway

ex•qui•site (ĕk′skwĭ-zĭt, ĭk-skwĭz′ĭt) *adj.* **1.** Marked by intricate and beautiful design or execution. **2.** Of such beauty or delicacy as to arouse intense delight. See Syns at **delicate. 3.** Excellent; flawless. **4.** Acutely perceptive or discriminating. **5.** Intense; keen. **6.** *Obsolete* Ingeniously devised or thought out. ❖ *n.* One excessively fastidious in dress, manners, or taste. [ME *exquisit*, carefully chosen < Lat. *exquīsītus*, p. part. of *exquīrere*, to search out : *ex-*, ex- + *quaerere*, to seek.] —**ex′qui•site•ly** *adv.* —**ex′qui•site•ness** *n.*

exr. *abbr.* executor

exrx. *abbr.* executrix

ex•san•gui•nate (ĕks-săng′gwə-nāt′) *tr. & intr.v.* **-nat•ed, -nat•ing, -nates** To drain or be drained of blood. [< Lat. *exsanguinātus*, drained of blood : *ex-*, ex- + *sanguis, sanguin-*, blood.] —**ex•san′gui•na′tion** *n.*

ex•san•guine (ĕks-săng′gwĭn) *adj.* Lacking blood; anemic. [Lat. *exsanguis, exsanguin-* : *ex-*, ex- + *sanguis*, blood.]

ex•scind (ĭk-sĭnd′) *tr.v.* **-scind•ed, -scind•ing, -scinds** To cut out; excise. [Lat. *exscindere* : *ex-*, ex- + *scindere*, to cut.]

ex•sert (ĭk-sûrt′) *tr.v.* **-sert•ed, -sert•ing, -serts** To thrust (something) out or forth; cause to protrude. ❖ *adj.* also **ex•sert•ed** (-sûr′tĭd) Thrust outward or protruding. [Lat. *exserere, exsert-*. See EXERT.] —**ex•ser′tion** *n.*

ex•sic•cate (ĕk′sĭ-kāt′) *intr. & tr.v.* **-cat•ed, -cat•ing, -cates** To dry up or cause to dry up. [Ult. < Lat. *exsiccāre, exsiccāt-* : *ex-*, ex- + *siccāre*, to dry (< *siccus*, dry).] —**ex′sic•ca′tion** *n.* —**ex′sic•ca′tive** *adj.* —**ex′sic•ca′tor** *n.*

ex•stip•u•late (ĕks-stĭp′yə-lĭt) *adj.* Lacking stipules.

ext. *abbr.* **1.** extension **2.** external **3.** extinct **4.** extra **5.** extract

ex•tant (ĕk′stənt, ĕk-stănt′) *adj.* **1.** Still in existence; not destroyed, lost, or extinct. **2.** *Archaic* Standing out; projecting. [Lat. *exstāns, exstant-*, pr. part. of *exstāre*, to stand out : *ex-*, ex- + *stāre*, to stand; see **stā-** in App.]

ex•tem•po•ral (ĭk-stĕm′pər-əl) *adj.* *Archaic* Extemporaneous. [Lat. *extemporālis* < *ex tempore*. See EXTEMPORE.]

ex•tem•po•ra•ne•ous (ĭk-stĕm′pə-rā′nē-əs) *adj.* **1.** Carried out or performed with little or no preparation; impromptu. **2.** Prepared in advance but delivered without notes or text. **3.** Skilled at or given to unrehearsed speech or performance. **4.** Provided, made, or adapted as an expedient; makeshift. [< LLat. *extemporāneus* < Lat. *ex tempore*. See EXTEMPORE.] —**ex•tem′po•ra•ne′i•ty** (-pər-ə-nē′ĭ-tē), **ex•tem′po•ra′ne•ous•ness** *n.* —**ex•tem′po•ra′ne•ous•ly** *adv.*

ex•tem•po•rar•y (ĭk-stĕm′pə-rĕr′ē) *adj.* Spoken, done, or composed with little or no preparation or forethought. [< EXTEMPORE.] —**ex•tem′po•rar′i•ly** (-râr′ə-lē) *adv.*

ex•tem•po•re (ĭk-stĕm′pə-rē) *adj.* Extemporary. ❖ *adv.* In an extemporaneous manner. [Lat. *ex tempore* : *ex*, of; see EX– + *tempore*, ablative of *tempus*, time.]

ex•tem•po•rize (ĭk-stĕm′pə-rīz′) *v.* **-rized, -riz•ing, -riz•es** —*tr.* To do or perform (something) without prior preparation or practice. —*intr.* To perform an act or utter something in an impromptu manner; improvise. [< EXTEMPORE.] —**ex•tem′po•ri•za′tion** (-pər-ĭ-zā′shən) *n.* —**ex•tem′po•riz′er** *n.*

ex•tend (ĭk-stĕnd′) *v.* **-tend•ed, -tend•ing, -tends** —*tr.* **1.** To open or straighten (something) out; unbend. **2.** To stretch or spread (something) out to greater or fullest length. **3a.** To exert (oneself) vigorously or to full capacity. **b.** To cause to move at full gallop. Used of a horse. **4a.** To increase in quantity or bulk by adding a cheaper substance. **b.** To adulterate. **5a.** To enlarge the area, scope, or range of. **b.** To expand the influence of. **c.** To make more comprehensive or inclusive. See Syns at **increase. 6a.** To offer: *extend one's greetings.* **b.** To make available; provide. **7a.** To cause (something) to be or last longer. **b.** To prolong the time allowed for payment of. **8.** *Chiefly British* **a.** To appraise or assess; value. **b.** To seize or make a levy on for the purpose of settling a debt. —*intr.* To be or become long, large, or comprehensive. [ME *extenden* < OFr. *extendre* < Lat. *extendere* : *ex-*, ex- + *tendere*, to stretch; see **ten-** in App.] —**ex•tend′i•bil′i•ty** *n.* —**ex•tend′a•ble, ex•tend′i•ble** *adj.*

ex•tend•ed (ĭk-stĕn′dĭd) *adj.* **1.** Stretched or pulled out: *an extended telescope.* **2.** Continued for a long period of time; protracted. **3.** Enlarged or broad in meaning, scope, or influence. —**ex•tend′ed•ly** *adv.*

extended family *n.* A family group that consists of parents, children, and other relatives, often in close proximity.

ex•tend•er (ĭk-stĕn′dər) *n.* A substance added to another substance to modify, dilute, or adulterate it.

ex•ten•si•ble (ĭk-stĕn′sə-bəl) *adj.* **1.** Capable of being extended or protruded. **2.** *Computer Science* Of or relating to a programming language or a system that can be modified by changing or adding features. —**ex•ten′si•bil′i•ty** *n.*

ex•ten•sile (ĭk-stĕn′sĭl) *adj.* Extensible.

ex•ten•sion (ĭk-stĕn′shən) *n.* **1.** The act of extending or the condition of being extended. **2.** The amount, degree, or range to which something extends or can extend. **3a.** The act of straightening or extending a limb. **b.** The position assumed by an extended limb. **4.** *Medicine* The application of traction to a fractured or dislocated limb to restore the normal position. **5a.** An addition that increases the area, influence, operation, or contents of something. **b.** An additional telephone connected to a main line. **6a.** An allowance of extra time, esp. for the repayment of a debt. **b.** The period of this extra time. **7.** The property of an object by which it occupies space. **8.** A program in a university, college, or school for students unable to attend at the usual time or in the usual place. **9.** *Logic* The class of objects designated by a specific term or concept; denotation. **10.** *Mathematics* A set that includes a given and similar set as a subset. **11.** *Computer Science* A set of characters that follow a filename and a period, used to identify the kind of file. [ME *extensioun* < OFr. *extension* < Lat. *extēnsiō, extēnsiōn-* < *extēnsus*, p. part. of *extendere*, to extend. See EXTEND.] —**ex•ten′sion•al** *adj.*

extension cord *n.* An insulated electric wire fitted with a plug and one or more outlets, allowing one to plug in devices with cords not long enough to reach a wall outlet.

ex•ten•si•ty (ĭk-stĕn′sĭ-tē) *n., pl.* **-ties 1a.** The quality of having extension or being extensive. **b.** A specific degree or range of extension. **2.** The attribute of sensation that enables one to perceive space or size.

ex•ten•sive (ĭk-stĕn′sĭv) *adj.* **1.** Large in extent, range, or amount. **2.** Of or relating to the cultivation of vast areas of land with a minimum of labor or expense. —**ex•ten′sive•ly** *adv.* —**ex•ten′sive•ness** *n.*

ex•ten•som•e•ter (ĕk′stĕn-sŏm′ĭ-tər) *n.* An instrument used to measure minute deformations in a test specimen of a material. [EXTENS(ION) + –METER.]

ex•ten•sor (ĭk-stĕn′sər) *n.* A muscle that extends or straightens a limb or body part. [NLat. *extēnsor* < Lat. *extēnsus*, p. part. of *extendere*, to stretch out. See EXTEND.]

ex•tent (ĭk-stĕnt′) *n.* **1a.** The range, magnitude, or distance over which a thing extends. **b.** The degree to which a thing extends. **2.** An extensive space or area. **3.** *Archaic* An assessment or valuation, esp. for taxation. [ME *extente*, assessment on land < AN < fem. p. part. of *extendre*, to extend < Lat. *extendere*. See EXTEND.]

ex•ten•u•ate (ĭk-stĕn′yo͞o-āt′) *tr.v.* **-at•ed, -at•ing, -ates 1.** To lessen or attempt to lessen the magnitude or seriousness of, esp. by providing partial excuses. **2.** *Archaic* **a.** To make thin or emaciated. **b.** To reduce the strength of. **3.** *Obsolete* To belittle; dispar-

expressionism
Street Scene by Ernst Ludwig Kirchner

ă	pat	oi	boy
ā	pay	ou	out
âr	care	o͝o	took
ä	father	o͞o	boot
ĕ	pet	ŭ	cut
ē	be	ûr	urge
ĭ	pit	th	thin
ī	pie	*th*	this
îr	pier	hw	which
ŏ	pot	zh	vision
ō	toe	ə	about, item
ô	paw		

Stress marks:
′ (primary);
′ (secondary), as in
lexicon (lĕk′sĭ-kŏn′)

age. [Lat. *extenuāre, extenuāt-* : *ex-*, ex- + *tenuāre,* to make thin (< *tenuis,* thin; see **ten-** in App.).] —**ex•ten′u•a′tive** *adj. & n.* —**ex•ten′u•a′tor** *n.* —**ex•ten′u•a•to′ry** (-ə-tôr′ē, -tōr′ē) *adj.*

ex•ten•u•a•tion (ĭk-stĕn′yōō-ā′shən) *n.* **1.** The act of extenuating or the condition of being extenuated; partial justification. **2.** A partial excuse.

ex•te•ri•or (ĭk-stîr′ē-ər) *adj.* **1.** Outer; external. **2.** Originating or acting from the outside. **3.** Suitable for use outside: *an exterior paint.* ❖ *n.* **1.** A part or a surface that is outside. **2.** An external or outward appearance. **3.** A representation in visual art of the outdoors. [Lat., comp. of *exter,* outward. See **eghs** in App.] —**ex•te′ri•or•ly** *adv.*

exterior angle *n.* **1.** The angle between any side of a polygon and an extended adjacent side. **2.** Any of the four angles that do not include a region of the space between two lines intersected by a transversal.

ex•te•ri•or•i•ty (ĭk-stîr′ē-ôr′ĭ-tē, -ōr′-) *n.* Outwardness; externality.

ex•te•ri•or•ize (ĭk-stîr′ē-ə-rīz′) *tr.v.* **-ized, -iz•ing, -iz•es 1.** To turn outward; externalize. **2.** *Medicine* To expose (an interior body part) in surgery.

ex•ter•mi•nate (ĭk-stûr′mə-nāt′) *tr.v.* **-nat•ed, -nat•ing, -nates** To get rid of by destroying completely; extirpate. [Lat. *extermināre, extermināt-,* to drive out : *ex-*, ex- + *termināre,* to mark boundaries (< *terminus,* boundary marker).] —**ex•ter′mi•na′tion** *n.* —**ex•ter′mi•na′tive, ex•ter′mi•na•to′ry** (-nə-tôr′ē, -tōr′ē) *adj.*

ex•ter•mi•na•tor (ĭk-stûr′mə-nā′tər) *n.* One that exterminates, esp. one whose occupation is the killing of vermin.

ex•tern or **ex•terne** (ĕk′stûrn′) *n.* A person associated with but not officially residing in an institution, esp. a nonresident physician on a hospital staff. [Lat. *externus,* external. See **EXTERNAL.**] —**ex′tern•ship′** *n.*

ex•ter•nal (ĭk-stûr′nəl) *adj.* **1.** Relating to, existing on, or connected with the outside or an outer part; exterior. **2.** Suitable for application to the outside. **3.** Existing independently of the mind. **4.** Acting or coming from the outside: *external pressures.* **5.** Of or relating chiefly to outward appearance; superficial. **6.** Of or relating to foreign affairs or foreign countries. ❖ *n.* **1.** An exterior part or surface. **2. externals a.** Outer circumstances. **b.** Outward appearances. [ME < Lat. *externus,* outward < *exter.* See **eghs** in App.] —**ex•ter′nal•ly** *adv.*

external auditory canal *n.* See **ear canal.**

ex•ter•nal-com•bus•tion engine (ĭk-stûr′nəl-kəm-bŭs′chən) *n.* An engine, such as a steam engine, in which the fuel is burned outside the engine cylinder.

external ear *n.* The outer portion of the ear including the auricle and the passage leading to the eardrum.

ex•ter•nal•ism (ĭk-stûr′nə-lĭz′əm) *n.* Excessive concern with outer circumstances or appearances. —**ex•ter′nal•ist** *n.*

ex•ter•nal•i•ty (ĕk′stər-năl′ĭ-tē) *n., pl.* **-ties 1.** The state or quality of being external or externalized. **2.** Something that is external.

ex•ter•nal•ize (ĭk-stûr′nə-līz′) *tr.v.* **-ized, -iz•ing, -iz•es 1a.** To make external. **b.** To manifest externally. **2.** To attribute to outside causes. **3.** To project or attribute (inner conflicts or feelings) to external circumstances or causes. —**ex•ter′nal•i•za′tion** (-lĭ-zā′shən) *n.*

external respiration *n.* The exchange of oxygen and carbon dioxide between the environment and respiratory organs.

ex•ter•o•cep•tor (ĕk′stə-rō-sĕp′tər) *n.* A sense organ, such as the ear, that receives and responds to stimuli originating from outside the body. [Lat. *exter,* outside; see **EXTERIOR** + (RE)CEPTOR.] —**ex′ter•o•cep′tive** *adj.*

ex•ter•ri•to•ri•al (ĕks′tĕr-ĭ-tôr′ē-əl, -tōr′-) *adj.* Extraterritorial. —**ex′ter•ri•to•ri•al′i•ty** (-ăl′ĭ-tē) *n.* —**ex′ter•ri•to′ri•al•ly** *adv.*

ex•tinct (ĭk-stĭngkt′) *adj.* **1.** No longer existing or living. **2.** No longer burning or active. **3.** No longer in use. **4.** *Law* Lacking a claimant; void. [ME < Lat. *exstīnctus,* p. part. of *exstinguere,* to extinguish. See **EXTINGUISH.**]

ex•tinc•tion (ĭk-stĭngk′shən) *n.* **1a.** The act of extinguishing. **b.** The condition of being extinguished. **2.** The fact of being extinct or the process of becoming extinct. **3.** *Psychology* A reduction or a loss in the strength or rate of a conditioned response when the unconditioned stimulus or reinforcement is withheld.

ex•tinc•tive (ĭk-stĭngk′tĭv) *adj.* Tending to extinguish or make extinct.

ex•tin•guish (ĭk-stĭng′gwĭsh) *tr.v.* **-guished, -guish•ing, -guish•es 1.** To put out (a fire, for example); quench. **2.** To put an end to (hopes, for example); destroy. **3.** To obscure; eclipse. **4.** *Law* **a.** To settle or discharge (a debt). **b.** To nullify. **5.** *Psychology* To bring about the extinction of (a conditioned response). [Lat. *exstinguere* : *ex-*, intensive pref.; see **EX–** + *stinguere,* to quench.] —**ex•tin′guish•a•ble** *adj.* —**ex•tin′guish•ment** *n.*

ex•tin•guish•er (ĭk-stĭng′gwĭ-shər) *n.* One that extinguishes, esp.: **a.** Any of various portable mechanical devices for spraying a fire with chemicals. **b.** A small metal cone or cup on a long handle, used to snuff out candles; a snuffer.

ex•tir•pate (ĕk′stər-pāt′) *tr.v.* **-pat•ed, -pat•ing, -pates 1.** To pull up by the roots. **2.** To destroy totally; exterminate. **3.** To re-

move by surgery. [Lat. *exstirpāre, exstirpāt-* : *ex-*, ex- + *stirps,* root.] —**ex′tir•pa′tion** *n.* —**ex′tir•pa′tive** *adj.* —**ex′tir•pa′tor** *n.*

ex•tol also **ex•toll** (ĭk-stōl′) *tr.v.* **-tolled, -tol•ling, -tols** also **-tolled, -toll•ing, -tolls** To praise highly; exalt. See Syns at **praise.** [ME *extollen* < Lat. *extollere,* to lift up, praise : *ex-*, up from; see **EX–** + *tollere,* to lift; see **telə–** in App.] —**ex•tol′ler** *n.* —**ex•tol′ment** *n.*

ex•tort (ĭk-stôrt′) *tr.v.* **-tort•ed, -tort•ing, -torts** To obtain from another by coercion or intimidation. [Lat. *extorquēre, extort-,* to wrench out, extort : *ex-*, ex- + *torquēre,* to twist.] —**ex•tort′er** *n.* —**ex•tort′ive** *adj.*

ex•tor•tion (ĭk-stôr′shən) *n.* **1.** The act or an instance of extorting. **2.** Illegal use of one's official position or powers to obtain property, funds, or patronage. **3.** An excessive or exorbitant charge. **4.** Something extorted. —**ex•tor′tion•ar′y** (-shə-nĕr′ē) *adj.* —**ex•tor′tion•ist, ex•tor′tion•er** *n.*

ex•tor•tion•ate (ĭk-stôr′shə-nĭt) *adj.* **1.** Marked by extortion. **2.** Exorbitant; immoderate. —**ex•tor′tion•ate•ly** *adv.*

ex•tra (ĕk′strə) *adj.* **1.** More than or beyond what is usual, normal, expected, or necessary. See Syns at **superfluous. 2.** Better than ordinary; superior. **3.** Subject to an additional charge. ❖ *n.* **1.** Something more than is usual or necessary. **2.** Something for which an additional charge is made. **3.** A special edition of a newspaper. **4a.** An additional or alternate worker. **b.** A performer hired to play a minor part, as in a crowd scene in a film. **5.** Something of exceptional quality. ❖ *adv.* To an exceptional extent or degree; unusually. [Prob. short for **EXTRAORDINARY.**]

extra– or **extro–** *pref.* Outside; beyond: *extraterritorial.* [Lat. *extrā-* < *extrā.* See **eghs** in App.]

ex•tra-base hit (ĕk′strə-bās′) *n. Baseball* A double, a triple, or a home run.

ex•tra•cel•lu•lar (ĕk′strə-sĕl′yə-lər) *adj.* Located or occurring outside a cell or cells. —**ex′tra•cel′lu•lar•ly** *adv.*

ex•tra•cor•po•re•al (ĕk′strə-kôr-pôr′ē-əl, -pōr′-) *adj.* Situated or occurring outside the body. —**ex′tra•cor•po′re•al•ly** *adv.*

ex•tract (ĭk-străkt′) *tr.v.* **-tract•ed, -tract•ing, -tracts 1.** To draw or pull out, often with great force or effort. **2.** To obtain despite resistance. **3.** To obtain from a substance by chemical or mechanical action, as by pressure, distillation, or evaporation. **4.** To remove for separate consideration or publication; excerpt. **5a.** To derive or obtain (information, for example) from a source. **b.** To deduce (a principle or doctrine); construe (a meaning). **c.** To derive (pleasure or comfort) from an experience. **6.** *Mathematics* To determine or calculate (the root of a number). ❖ *n.* (ĕk′străkt′) Something extracted, esp.: **a.** A passage from a literary work; an excerpt. **b.** A concentrated preparation of the essential constituents of a food, flavoring, or other substance. [ME *extracten* < Lat. *extrahere, extract-* : *ex-* + *trahere,* to draw.] —**ex•tract′a•ble, ex•tract′i•ble** *adj.* —**ex•trac′tor** *n.*

ex•trac•tion (ĭk-străk′shən) *n.* **1.** The act of extracting or the condition of being extracted. **2.** Something obtained by extracting; an extract. **3.** Origin; lineage.

ex•trac•tive (ĭk-străk′tĭv) *adj.* **1.** Used in or obtained by extraction. **2.** Possible to extract. ❖ *n.* **1.** Something that may be extracted. **2.** The insoluble portion of an extract. —**ex•trac′tive•ly** *adv.*

ex•tra•cur•ric•u•lar (ĕk′strə-kə-rĭk′yə-lər) *adj.* **1.** Being outside the regular curriculum of a school or college. **2.** Being outside one's usual duties. **3.** *Informal* Extramarital.

ex•tra•dit•a•ble (ĕk′strə-dī′tə-bəl) *adj.* **1.** Subject to extradition: *extraditable fugitives.* **2.** Making liable to extradition.

ex•tra•dite (ĕk′strə-dīt′) *v.* **-dit•ed, -dit•ing, -dites** —*tr.* **1.** To give up or deliver (a fugitive, for example) to the legal jurisdiction of another government or authority. **2.** To obtain the extradition of. See Syns at **banish.** —*intr.* To perform or engage in the process of extradition.

ex•tra•di•tion (ĕk′strə-dĭsh′ən) *n.* Legal surrender of a fugitive to the jurisdiction of another state, country, or government for trial. [Fr. : Lat. *ex-*, ex- + Lat. *trāditiō, trāditiōn-,* a handing over; see **TRADITION.**]

ex•tra•dos (ĕk′strə-dŏs′, -dōs′) *n., pl.* **-dos** (-dōz′) or **-dos•es** (-dŏs′ĭz) *Architecture* The upper or exterior curve of an arch. [Fr. : Lat. *extrā,* outside; see **EXTRA–** + Fr. *dos,* back (< Lat. *dorsum).*]

ex•tra•ga•lac•tic (ĕk′strə-gə-lăk′tĭk) *adj.* Located or originating beyond the Milky Way.

ex•tra-high voltage (ĕk′strə-hī′) *n.* A voltage higher than 345 kilovolts.

ex•tra•ju•di•cial (ĕk′strə-jōō-dĭsh′əl) *adj.* **1.** Outside the authority of a court. **2.** Outside the usual judicial proceedings. —**ex′tra•ju•di′cial•ly** *adv.*

ex•tra•le•gal (ĕk′strə-lē′gəl) *adj.* Not permitted or governed by law. —**ex′tra•le′gal•ly** *adv.*

ex•tra•mar•i•tal (ĕk′strə-măr′ĭ-tl) *adj.* Being in violation of marriage vows; adulterous: *an extramarital affair.*

ex•tra•mun•dane (ĕk′strə-mŭn-dān′, -mŭn′dān′) *adj.* Occurring or existing outside the physical world or universe.

ex•tra•mu•ral (ĕk′strə-myŏor′əl) *adj.* Occurring or situated outside the walls or boundaries, as of a community.

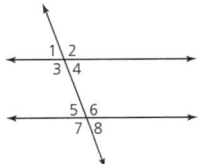

exterior angle
Angles 1, 2, 7, and 8 are exterior angles.

extinguisher
fire extinguisher

ex·tra·ne·ous (ĭk-strā′nē-əs) *adj.* **1.** Not constituting a vital element or part. **2.** Inessential or unrelated to the topic or matter at hand; irrelevant. **3.** Coming from the outside. [< Lat. *extrāneus* < *extrā*, outside. See EXTRA–.] —**ex·tra′ne·ous·ly** *adv.* —**ex·tra′ne·ous·ness** *n.*

ex·tra·net (ĕk′strə-nĕt′) *n.* An extension of an institution's intranet that provides outsiders with limited access.

ex·tra·nu·cle·ar (ĕk′strə-nōō′klē-ər, -nyōō′-) *adj.* **1.** Located or occurring outside the nucleus of a cell. **2.** Existing or acting outside the nucleus of an atom.

ex·tra·oc·u·lar muscle (ĕk′strə-ŏk′yə-lər) *n.* Any of the six small muscles that control movement of the eyeball within the socket.

ex·tra·or·di·naire (ĕk′strə-ôr′dn-âr′) *adj.* Extraordinary: *a jazz singer extraordinaire.* [Fr. < OFr. < Lat. *extraōrdinārius.* See EXTRAORDINARY.]

ex·traor·di·nar·y (ĭk-strôr′dn-ĕr′ē, ĕk′strə-ôr′-) *adj.* **1.** Beyond what is ordinary or usual. **2.** Highly exceptional; remarkable. **3.** Employed or used for a special service, function, or occasion. [ME *extraordinarie* < Lat. *extraōrdinārius* : *extrā*, outside; see EXTRA– + *ōrdō*, *ōrdin-*, order.] —**ex·traor′di·nar′i·ly** (-dn-âr′ə-lē) *adv.*

ex·trap·o·late (ĭk-străp′ə-lāt′) *v.* **-lat·ed, -lat·ing, -lates** —*tr.* **1.** To infer or estimate by extending or projecting known information. **2.** *Mathematics* To estimate (a value of a variable outside a known range) from values within a known range. —*intr.* To engage in the process of extrapolating. [EXTRA– + (INTER)POLATE.] —**ex·trap′o·la′tion** *n.* —**ex·trap′o·la′tive** *adj.* —**ex·trap′o·la′tor** *n.*

ex·tra·py·ram·i·dal (ĕk′strə-pĭ-răm′ĭ-dl) *adj.* Relating to or involving neural pathways situated outside or independent of the pyramidal tracts.

ex·tra·sen·so·ry (ĕk′strə-sĕn′sə-rē) *adj.* Being outside the normal range or bounds of the senses.

extrasensory perception *n.* ESP.

ex·tra·sys·to·le (ĕk′strə-sĭs′tə-lē) *n.* A premature contraction of the heart, causing momentary arrhythmia.

ex·tra·ter·res·tri·al (ĕk′strə-tə-rĕs′trē-əl) *adj.* Originating, located, or occurring outside Earth or its atmosphere: *intelligent extraterrestrial being or life.* ❖ *n.* An extraterrestrial being or life form.

ex·tra·ter·ri·to·ri·al (ĕk′strə-tĕr′ĭ-tôr′ē-əl, -tōr′-) *adj.* **1.** Located outside territorial boundaries. **2.** Of or relating to persons exempt from the legal jurisdiction of the country in which they reside. —**ex′tra·ter′ri·to′ri·al·ly** *adv.*

ex·tra·ter·ri·to·ri·al·i·ty (ĕk′strə-tĕr′ĭ-tôr′ē-ăl′ĭ-tē, -tōr′-) *n.* Exemption from local legal jurisdiction, such as that granted to foreign diplomats.

ex·tra·u·ter·ine (ĕk′strə-yōō′tər-ĭn, -tə-rīn′) *adj.* Located or occurring outside the uterus.

ex·trav·a·gance (ĭk-străv′ə-gəns) *n.* **1.** The quality of being extravagant. **2.** Immoderate expense or display. **3.** Something extravagant.

ex·trav·a·gan·cy (ĭk-străv′ə-gən-sē) *n., pl.* **-cies 1.** Extravagance. **2.** Something extravagant.

ex·trav·a·gant (ĭk-străv′ə-gənt) *adj.* **1.** Given to lavish or imprudent expenditure. **2.** Exceeding reasonable bounds: *extravagant demands.* See Syns at **excessive. 3.** Extremely abundant; profuse. **4.** Unreasonably high; exorbitant. **5.** *Archaic* Straying beyond limits or bounds; wandering. [ME, unusual, rambling < OFr. < Med.Lat. *extrāvagāns, extrāvagant-*, pr. part. of *extrāvagārī*, to wander : Lat. *extrā*, outside; see EXTRA– + Lat. *vagārī*, to wander.] —**ex·trav′a·gant·ly** *adv.*

ex·trav·a·gan·za (ĭk-străv′ə-găn′zə) *n.* **1.** An elaborate spectacular entertainment or display. **2.** *Music* A composition marked by freedom and diversity of form, often with burlesque elements and satirical or parodic intent. [Ital. *estravaganza,* extravagance < *estravagare* < Med.Lat. *extrāvagāns, extrāvagant-*, pr. part. of *extrāvagārī*, to wander. See EXTRAVAGANT.]

ex·trav·a·gate (ĭk-străv′ə-gāt′) *intr.v.* **-gat·ed, -gat·ing, -gates** *Archaic* To exceed reasonable limits or bounds. [Med.Lat. *extrāvagārī, extrāvagāt-*, to wander. See EXTRAVAGANT.]

ex·trav·a·sate (ĭk-străv′ə-sāt′) *v.* **-sat·ed, -sat·ing, -sates** —*tr.* **1.** *Pathology* To force the flow of (blood or lymph) from a vessel out into surrounding tissue. **2.** *Geology* To cause (molten lava) to pour forth from a volcanic vent. —*intr.* **1.** *Pathology* To exude from a vessel into surrounding tissue. **2.** *Geology* To erupt. [EXTRA– + VAS(O)– + –ATE¹.] —**ex·trav′a·sa′tion** *n.*

ex·tra·vas·cu·lar (ĕk′strə-văs′kyə-lər) *adj.* **1.** Located or occurring outside a blood or lymph vessel. **2.** Lacking vessels; nonvascular.

ex·tra·ve·hic·u·lar activity (ĕk′strə-vē-hĭk′yə-lər) *n.* Activity or maneuvers performed by an astronaut outside a spacecraft in space.

ex·tra·ver·sion (ĕk′strə-vûr′zhən) *n.* Variant of **extroversion.**

ex·tra·vert (ĕk′strə-vûrt′) *n.* Variant of **extrovert.** [EXTRA– + Lat. *vertere*, to turn; see **wer-²** in App.]

ex·tra·vert·ed (ĕk′strə-vûr′tĭd) *adj.* Variant of **extroverted.**

ex·treme (ĭk-strēm′) *adj.* **1.** Most remote in any direction; outermost or farthest. **2.** Being in or attaining the greatest or highest degree; very intense. **3.** Extending far beyond the norm; excessive. **4.** Of the greatest severity; drastic. **5.** *Biology* **a.** Characterized by

severe, usu. oxygen-poor environmental conditions. **b.** Having an affinity for such conditions: *an extreme microorganism.* **6.** *Sports* **a.** Very dangerous or difficult: *extreme rafting.* **b.** Participating in a very dangerous or difficult sport: *an extreme skier.* **7.** *Archaic* Final; last. ❖ *n.* **1.** The greatest or utmost degree or point. **2.** Either of the two things situated at opposite ends of a range. **3.** An extreme condition. **4.** A drastic expedient: *resorted to extremes.* **5.** *Mathematics* **a.** The first or last term of a ratio or a series. **b.** A maximum or minimum value of a function. **6.** *Logic* The major or minor term of a syllogism. [ME < OFr. < Lat. *extrēmus.* See **eghs** in App.] —**ex·treme′ly** *adv.* —**ex·treme′ness** *n.*

extremely high frequency *n.* A radio-frequency band with a range of 30,000 to 300,000 megahertz.

extremely low frequency *n.* A radio frequency below 300 hertz.

extreme unction *n. Roman Catholic Church* The Anointing of the Sick. No longer in Ecclesiastical use.

ex·trem·ist (ĭk-strē′mĭst) *n.* One who advocates or resorts to measures beyond the norm, esp. in politics. —**ex·trem′ist** *adj.*

ex·trem·i·ty (ĭk-strĕm′ĭ-tē) *n., pl.* **-ties 1.** The outermost or farthest point or portion. **2.** The greatest or utmost degree. **3a.** Grave danger, necessity, or distress. **b.** A moment at which death or ruin is imminent. **4.** An extreme or severe measure. **5a.** A bodily limb or appendage. **b.** A hand or foot.

ex·tri·cate (ĕk′strĭ-kāt′) *tr.v.* **-cat·ed, -cat·ing, -cates 1.** To release from an entanglement or difficulty; disengage. **2.** *Archaic* To distinguish from something related. [Lat. *extrīcāre, extrīcāt-* : *ex-*, ex- + *trīcae*, hindrances, perplexities.] —**ex′tri·ca·ble** (-kə-bəl) *adj.* —**ex′tri·ca′tion** *n.*

ex·trin·sic (ĭk-strĭn′sĭk, -zĭk) *adj.* **1.** Not forming an essential or inherent part of a thing; extraneous. **2.** Originating from the outside; external. [Lat. *extrīnsecus,* from outside : *exter*, outside; see EXTERIOR + *-im*, adv. suff. + *secus*, alongside; see **sekʷ-¹** in App.] —**ex·trin′si·cal·ly** *adv.*

extrinsic factor *n.* See vitamin B₁₂.

extro– *pref.* Variant of **extra–.**

ex·trorse (ĕk′strôrs′) *adj. Botany* Facing outward; turned away from the axis: *extrorse anthers.* [LLat. *extrōrsus,* turned outward (modeled on Lat. *intrōrsum,* turned inward) : Lat. *extrā*, outside; see EXTRA– + Lat. *versus*, p. part. of *vertere*, to turn; see **wer-²** in App.]

ex·tro·ver·sion also **ex·tra·ver·sion** (ĕk′strə-vûr′zhən) *n.* **1.** Interest in or behavior directed toward others or one's environment rather than oneself. **2.** A turning inside out, as of an organ. —**ex′tro·ver′sive·ly** *adv.* —**ex′tro·ver′sive·ly** *adv.*

ex·tro·vert also **ex·tra·vert** (ĕk′strə-vûrt′) *n.* An extroverted person. [Alteration (influenced by INTROVERT) of EXTRAVERT.]

ex·tro·vert·ed also **ex·tra·vert·ed** (ĕk′strə-vûr′tĭd) *adj.* Marked by extroversion; gregarious or outgoing.

ex·trude (ĭk-strōōd′) *v.* **-trud·ed, -trud·ing, -trudes** —*tr.* **1.** To push or thrust out. **2.** To shape (a plastic, for instance) by forcing it through a die. —*intr.* To protrude or project. [Lat. *extrūdere* : *ex-*, ex- + *trūdere*, to thrust.]

ex·tru·sion (ĭk-strōō′zhən) *n.* **1.** The act or process of pushing or thrusting out. **2.** The act or process of shaping by forcing through a die. **3.** An object or material produced by extruding. [Med.Lat. *extrūsiō, extrūsiōn-* < Lat. *extrūsus,* p. part. of *extrūdere,* to thrust out. See EXTRUDE.]

ex·tru·sive (ĭk-strōō′sĭv, -zĭv) *adj.* **1.** Tending to push or thrust out. **2.** Tending to protrude or project. **3.** Derived from magma poured out or ejected at the earth's surface. Used of igneous rocks.

ex·u·ber·ance (ĭg-zōō′bər-əns) *n.* **1.** The quality or condition of being exuberant. **2.** An exuberant act or expression.

ex·u·ber·ant (ĭg-zōō′bər-ənt) *adj.* **1.** Full of unrestrained enthusiasm or joy. **2.** Lavish; extravagant. **3.** Extreme in degree, size, or extent. **4.** Growing, producing, or produced abundantly; plentiful. [ME, overabundant < OFr. < Lat. *exūberāns, exūberant-*, pr. part. of *exūberāre,* to exuberate. See EXUBERATE.] —**ex·u′ber·ant·ly** *adv.*

ex·u·ber·ate (ĭg-zōō′bə-rāt′) *intr.v.* **-at·ed, -at·ing, -ates 1.** To be exuberant. **2.** *Archaic* To abound; overflow. [ME *exuberaten,* to make fruitful < Lat. *exūberāre, exūberāt-* : *ex-*, intensive pref.; see EX– + *ūberāre,* to be fruitful (< *ūber*, fertile).]

ex·u·date (ĕks′yōō-dāt′) *n.* A substance that has oozed forth. [Lat. *exsūdātum,* neut. p. part. of *exsūdāre,* to exude. See EXUDE.]

ex·u·da·tion (ĕks′yōō-dā′shən) *n.* **1.** The act or an instance of oozing forth. **2.** An exudate.

ex·ude (ĭg-zōōd′, ĭk-sōōd′) *v.* **-ud·ed, -ud·ing, -udes** —*intr.* To ooze forth. —*tr.* **1.** To discharge or emit (a liquid or gas, for example) gradually. **2.** To exhibit in abundance. [Lat. *exsūdāre* : *ex-*, ex- + *sūdāre,* to sweat; see **sweid-** in App.]

ex·ult (ĭg-zŭlt′) *intr.v.* **-ult·ed, -ult·ing, -ults 1.** To rejoice greatly; be jubilant or triumphant. **2.** *Obsolete* To leap upward, esp. for joy. [Lat. *exsultāre* : *ex-*, ex- + *saltāre,* to dance, freq. of *salīre,* to leap.] —**ex·ul′tance, ex·ul′tan·cy** *n.*

ex·ul·tant (ĭg-zŭl′tənt) *adj.* Marked by great joy or jubilation; triumphant. —**ex·ul′tant·ly** *adv.*

ex·ul·ta·tion (ĕk′səl-tā′shən, ĕg′zəl-) *n.* The act or condition of rejoicing greatly.

extravehicular activity

ă pat	oi boy
ā pay	ou out
âr care	ōō took
ä father	ōō boot
ĕ pet	ŭ cut
ē be	ûr urge
ĭ pit	th thin
ī pie	th this
îr pier	hw which
ŏ pot	zh vision
ō toe	ə about,
ô paw	item

Stress marks:
′ (primary);
′ (secondary), as in
lexicon (lĕk′sĭ-kŏn′)

eyeblack

ex·urb (ĕk′sûrb′) *n.* A region lying beyond the suburbs of a city, esp. one inhabited principally by wealthy people. [EX– + (SUB)URB.] —**ex·ur′ban** *adj.* —**ex·ur′ban·ite**′ *n.*

ex·ur·bi·a (ĕk-sûr′bē-ə, ĕg-zûr′-) *n.* An exurban area.

ex·u·vi·ae (ĭg-zōō′vē-ē′) *pl.n.* The cast-off skins or coverings of various organisms. [Lat. < *exuere,* to take off.] —**ex·u′vi·al** (-vē-əl) *adj.*

ex·u·vi·ate (ĭg-zōō′vē-āt′) *v.* **-at·ed, -at·ing, -ates** —*tr.* To shed or cast off (a covering). —*intr.* To shed or cast off exuviae; molt. [EXUVI(AE) + –ATE¹.] —**ex·u′vi·a′tion** *n.*

-ey *suff.* Variant of **-y¹.**

ey·as (ī′əs) *n.* A nestling hawk or falcon, esp. one to be trained for falconry. [ME *eias* < *an eias,* alteration of **a nias,* an eyas < OFr. *niais* < Lat. *nīdus,* nest. See **sed-** in App.]

Eyck (īk), **Jan van** 1390?–1441. Flemish painter known esp. for his portraits and altarpieces.

eye (ī) *n.* **1.** An organ of vision or of light sensitivity. **2a.** Either of a pair of hollow structures located in bony sockets of the skull, each having a lens that focuses light on a retina; the vertebrate organ of vision. **b.** The external visible portion of this organ together with associated structures, such as the eyelids and eyebrows. **c.** The pigmented iris of this organ. **3.** The faculty of seeing; vision. **4.** The ability to make intellectual or aesthetic judgments. **5a.** A way of regarding something; a point of view. **b.** Attention. **6.** Something suggestive of the vertebrate organ of vision, esp.: **a.** An opening in a needle. **b.** A camera aperture. **c.** A loop, as of metal, rope, or thread. **d.** A circular marking on a peacock's feather. **e.** *Chiefly Southern US* The round flat cover over the hole on a wood-burning stove. **7.** A photosensitive device, such as a photoelectric cell. **8.** *Botany* **a.** A bud on a twig or tuber: *the eye of a potato.* **b.** The often differently colored center of the corolla of some flowers. **9a.** *Meteorology* The circular area of relative calm at the center of a hurricane. **b.** The center or focal point of attention or action. **10.** *Informal* A detective, esp. a private detective. **11.** A choice center cut of meat. ❖ *tr.v.* **eyed, eye·ing** or **ey·ing** (ī′ĭng), **eyes 1.** To look at. **2.** To watch closely. **3.** To supply with an eye or hole. —*idioms:* **all eyes** Fully attentive. **an eye for an eye** Punishment in which an offender suffers what the victim has suffered. **clap** (or **lay** or **set**) **(one's) eye on** To look at. **eye to eye** In agreement. **have eyes for** To be interested in. **have (one's) eye on 1.** To look at, esp. attentively or continuously. **2.** To have as one's objective. **in the eye of the wind** *Nautical* Directly into the wind. **in the public eye 1.** Frequently seen in public or in the media. **2.** Widely publicized; well-known. **my eye** *Slang* In no way; not at all. Used interjectionally. **with an eye to** With a view to. [ME < OE *ēge, ēage.* See **ok**ʷ- in App.]

eye·ball (ī′bôl′) *n.* **1.** The globe-shaped portion of the eye surrounded by the socket and covered externally by the eyelids. **2.** The eye itself. ❖ *tr.v.* **-balled, -ball·ing, -balls** *Informal* **1.** To look over carefully; scrutinize. **2.** To measure or estimate roughly by sight.

eye·ball-to-eye·ball (ī′bôl′tə-ī′bôl′) *adv. & adj. Informal* Face-to-face.

eye bank *n.* A place at which corneas obtained from human bodies immediately after death are stored and preserved for subsequent transplantation to patients with corneal defects.

eye bath *n.* See **eyecup.**

eye·black (ī′blăk′) *n.* Any of various dark pigments applied under the eyes esp. by athletes to reduce sun glare.

eye·blink (ī′blĭngk′) *n.* An extremely short period of time; an instant.

eye·bolt (ī′bōlt′) *n.* A bolt having a looped head designed to receive a hook or rope.

eye·bright (ī′brīt′) *n.* Any of several plants of the genus *Euphrasia,* having opposite toothed leaves and flowers in spikes.

eye·brow (ī′brou′) *n.* **1.** The bony ridge extending over the eye. **2.** The arch of short hairs covering this ridge.

eyebrow pencil *n.* A cosmetic pencil used for extending or darkening the eyebrows.

eye candy *n. Informal* One that is visually attractive or pleasing to look at, esp. in a superficial way.

eye-catch·ing (ī′kăch′ĭng) *adj.* Visually attractive. —**eye′-catch′er** *n.*

eye chart *n.* A chart of letters and figures of various sizes, used to test visual acuity.

eye contact *n.* Direct visual contact with another's eyes.

eye·cup (ī′kŭp′) *n.* A small cup with a rim contoured to fit the socket of the eye, used for applying a liquid medicine or wash to the eye.

eyed (īd) *adj.* Having eyes of a specified number or kind. Often used in combination: *brown-eyed.*

eye dialect *n.* The use of nonstandard spellings, such as *enuff* for *enough,* to represent uneducated, colloquial, dialectal, or nonstandard speech.

eyed·ness (īd′nĭs) *n.* A preference for use of one eye rather than the other.

eyespot
buckeye butterfly

eyestalk
close-up of a hermit crab

eye chart

eye·drop·per (ī′drŏp′ər) *n.* A dropper for administering liquid medicines, esp. one for dispensing them into the eye.

eye·ful (ī′fŏŏl′) *n.* **1.** A complete view. **2.** One that is pleasing to the sight. **3.** Sufficient observation to discover more than one had expected or enough to be satisfied. **4.** An amount of material blown or directed into the eye.

eye·glass (ī′glăs′) *n.* **1a. eyeglasses** Glasses for the eyes. **b.** A single lens in a pair of glasses; a monocle. **2.** See **eyepiece. 3.** See **eyecup.**

eye·hole (ī′hōl′) *n.* **1.** The socket of an eye. **2.** See **peephole.**

eye·hook (ī′hŏŏk′) *n.* A hook attached to a ring at the end of a rope or chain.

eye·lash (ī′lăsh′) *n.* **1.** Any of the short hairs fringing the edge of the eyelid. **2.** A row of hairs fringing the eyelid.

eye·let (ī′lĭt′) *n.* **1a.** A small hole or perforation, used for fastening with a cord or hook. **b.** A metal ring designed to reinforce such a hole; a grommet. **2.** A small hole edged with embroidered stitches as part of a design. **3.** A peephole. **4.** A small eye. [Alteration (influenced by EYE) of ME *oilet* < OFr. *oillet,* dim. of *oil,* eye < Lat. *oculus.* See **ok**ʷ- in App.]

eye·lid also **eye-lid** (ī′lĭd′) *n.* Either of two folds of skin and muscle that can be closed over the exposed portion of the eyeball.

eye·lift (ī′lĭft′) *n.* Cosmetic surgery of the tissue around the eye to reduce or eliminate folds, wrinkles, and sags.

eye·lin·er (ī′lī′nər) *n.* Makeup used to outline the eyes.

eye opener *n. Informal* **1.** A startling or shocking revelation. **2.** A drink of liquor taken to stimulate, esp. upon awakening.

eye·piece (ī′pēs′) *n.* The lens or lens group closest to the eye in an optical instrument; an ocular.

eye-pop·ping (ī′pŏp′ĭng) *adj. Informal* Eliciting wonder or astonishment. —**eye′-pop′per** *n.*

eye rhyme *n.* A rhyme consisting of words, such as *lint* and *pint,* with similar spellings but different sounds.

eye·shade (ī′shād′) *n.* A visor fastened about the head and used for protection against glare.

eye shadow *n.* A cosmetic available in various colors or tints and applied esp. to the eyelids to enhance the eyes.

eye·shine (ī′shīn′) *n.* The glow reflected from the eyes of some animals when struck by light in dark surroundings.

eye·shot (ī′shŏt′) *n.* The range of vision; sight.

eye·sight (ī′sīt′) *n.* **1.** The faculty of sight; vision. **2.** Range of vision; view.

eyes-on·ly (īz′ōn′lē) *adj.* Of or relating to privileged information: *an eyes-only memo.* [< the phrase *for your eyes only.*]

eye·sore (ī′sôr′, ī′sōr′) *n.* Something, such as a distressed building, that is unpleasant or offensive to view.

eye·spot (ī′spŏt′) *n.* **1.** A light-sensitive patch of pigment in certain algae and unicellular organisms. **2.** A simple visual organ of certain invertebrates composed of light-sensitive pigmented cells covering a sensory ending. **3.** A rounded eyelike marking, as on the tail of a peacock. **4.** *Botany* Either of two fungal diseases that affect grasses and are characterized by oval lesions.

eye·stalk (ī′stôk′) *n.* A movable stalklike structure in certain crustaceans, such as crabs, that bears an eye at the tip.

eye·strain (ī′strān′) *n.* Pain and fatigue of the eyes, often accompanied by headache, caused by prolonged use of the eyes, uncorrected visual defects, or an imbalance of the eye muscles.

eye·tooth (ī′tōōth′) *n.* A canine tooth of the upper jaw.

eye·wash (ī′wŏsh′, ī′wôsh′) *n.* **1.** A medicated or nonmedicated solution applied as a cleanser for the eyes. **2.** *Informal* Actions or remarks intended to hide the facts.

eye·wear (ī′wâr′) *n.* **1.** Eyeglasses, goggles, or other objects worn over the eyes. **2.** Fashionable eyeglasses.

eye·wink (ī′wĭngk′) *n.* **1.** A wink of the eye. **2.** An instant. **3.** *Obsolete* A glance.

eye·wit·ness (ī′wĭt′nĭs) *n.* A person who has seen someone or something and can bear witness to the fact.

eyre (âr) *n.* A circuit court held by itinerant royal justices in medieval England. [ME < AN *eire* < Lat. *iter,* journey. See **ei-** in App.]

Eyre (âr), **Lake** A shallow salt lake of S-central Australia.

Eyre Peninsula A peninsula of S Australia between Spencer Gulf and the Great Australian Bight.

ey·rie or **ey·ry** (âr′ē, îr′ē) *n.* Variants of **aerie.**

Ezek. or **Ezk** *abbr. Bible* Ezekiel

Ez·e·ki·as (ĕz′ĭ-kī′əs) See **Hezekiah.**

E·ze·ki·el¹ (ĭ-zē′kē-əl) A Hebrew prophet of the 6th cent. B.C. who called for the Jews exiled in Babylon to return to godliness and faith. [Heb. *yəḥezqē'l,* God has strengthened : *yəḥezaq,* he has strengthened (reduced form of *yəḥazzēq < ḥizzēq,* to strengthen) + *'ēl,* God.]

E·ze·ki·el² (ĭ-zē′kē-əl) *n.* See table at **Bible.** [After EZEKIEL¹.]

e-zine (ē′zēn′) *n.* A magazine that is published electronically, esp. on the Internet.

Ezr *abbr. Bible* Ezra

Ez·ra¹ (ĕz′rə) A Hebrew high priest of the 5th cent. B.C. who led many Jews back to Jerusalem after their Babylonian exile. [Heb. *'ezrā,* a nickname, perh. for *'azrī'ēl,* God is my help.]

Ez·ra² (ĕz′rə) *n.* See table at **Bible.** [After EZRA¹.]

Ff

f¹ or **F** (ĕf) *n., pl.* **f's** or **F's** also **fs** or **Fs** **1.** The sixth letter of the modern English alphabet. **2.** Any of the speech sounds represented by the letter *f*. **3.** The sixth in a series. **4.** Something shaped like the letter F. **5.** F A grade that indicates failing status. **6.** *Music* **a.** The fourth tone in the scale of C major or the sixth tone in the relative minor scale. **b.** A key or scale in which F is the tonic.

f² *abbr.* **1.** *Grammar* feminine **2.** *focal length* **3.** forte **4.** function

F¹ The symbol for the element **fluorine.**

F² *abbr.* **1.** Fahrenheit **2.** fail **3.** farad **4.** female **5.** *Genetics* filial generation **6.** foul **7.** franc **8.** Friday

f. *abbr.* **1.** farthing **2.** *Metallurgy* fine **3.** also **F.** folio **4.** following

F. *abbr.* French

f/ *abbr.* f-stop

fa (fä) *n. Music* The fourth tone of the diatonic scale in solfeggio. [ME < Med.Lat. See GAMUT.]

FAA *abbr.* Federal Aviation Administration

fab¹ (făb) *n. Informal* Fabrication: *a shed of metal fab.*

fab² (făb) *adj. Slang* Fabulous; wonderful.

Fa•ber•gé (făb′ər-zhā′), **Peter Carl** 1846–1920. Russian goldsmith and jeweler whose works include jeweled and enameled Easter eggs for European royalty.

Fa•bi•an (fā′bē-ən) *adj.* **1a.** Of or relating to the caution and avoidance of direct confrontation typical of Quintus Fabius Maximus. **b.** Cautious or dilatory, as in taking action. **2.** Of, relating to, or being a member of the Fabian Society, which was committed to gradual means for spreading socialist principles. [Lat. *Fabiānus*, after Quintus FABIUS MAXIMUS VERRUCOSUS.] **—Fa′bi•an** *n.* **—Fa′bi•an•ism** *n.* **—Fa′bi•an•ist** *n.*

Fa•bi•us Max•i•mus Ver•ru•co•sus (fā′bē-əs măk′sə-məs věr-yōō-kō′səs, -ōō-), **Quintus** d. 203 B.C. Roman general who defeated Hannibal (209) through delaying tactics.

fa•ble (fā′bəl) *n.* **1.** A usu. short narrative making an edifying or cautionary point and often employing animal characters that act like humans. **2.** A story about legendary persons and exploits. **3.** A falsehood; a lie. ❖ *v.* **-bled, -bling, -bles** *—tr.* To recount as if true. *—intr. Archaic* To compose fables. [ME < OFr. < Lat. *fābula* < *fārī,* to speak. See **bhā-** in App.] **—fa′bler** *n.*

fa•bled (fā′bəld) *adj.* **1.** Made known or famous by fables; legendary. **2.** Existing only in fables; fictitious.

fab•li•au (făb′lē-ō′) *n., pl.* **-li•aux** (-lē-ō′, -ōz′) A medieval tale in verse characterized by comic ribald treatment of themes drawn from life. [Fr. < ONFr. < OFr. *fablel,* dim. of *fable,* fable. See FABLE.]

fab•ric (făb′rĭk) *n.* **1a.** A cloth produced esp. by knitting, weaving, or felting fibers. **b.** The texture or quality of such cloth. **2.** A complex underlying structure. **3a.** A method or style of construction. **b.** A structural material, such as masonry. **c.** A physical structure; a building. [ME *fabryke,* something constructed < OFr. *fabrique* < Lat. *fabrica,* craft, workshop < *faber, fabr-,* workman, artificer.]

fab•ric•a•ble (făb′rĭ-kə-bəl) *adj.* Capable of being shaped or formed: *a fabricable alloy.* **—fab′ric•a•bil′i•ty** *n.*

fab•ri•cate (făb′rĭ-kāt′) *tr.v.* **-cat•ed, -cat•ing, -cates** **1.** To make; create. **2.** To construct by combining or assembling diverse, typically standardized parts. **3.** To concoct in order to deceive: *fabricated an excuse.* [ME *fabricaten* < Lat. *fabricārī, fabricāt-,* to make < *fabrica,* craft. See FABRIC.] **—fab′ri•ca′tion** *n.* **—fab′ri•ca′tor** *n.*

fab•u•late (făb′yə-lāt′) *intr.v.* **-lat•ed, -lat•ing, -lates** To compose fables or stories, esp. employing fantasy. [Lat. *fābulārī, fābulāt-,* < *fābula,* tale, talk. See FABLE.] **—fab′u•la′tion** *n.* **—fab′u•la′tor** *n.*

fab•u•list (făb′yə-lĭst) *n.* **1.** A composer of fables. **2.** A teller of tales; a liar. [Fr. *fabuliste* < Lat. *fābula,* fable. See FABLE.]

fab•u•lous (făb′yə-ləs) *adj.* **1.** Barely credible; astonishing. **2.** Extremely pleasing or successful: *a fabulous vacation.* **3a.** Of the nature of a fable or myth; legendary. **b.** Told of or celebrated in fables or legends. [ME, mythical < OFr. *fabuleux* < Lat. *fābulōsus* < *fābula,* fable. See FABLE.] **—fab′u•lous•ly** *adv.* **—fab′u•lous•ness** *n.*

fac. *abbr.* **1.** facsimile **2.** faculty

fa•çade also **fa•cade** (fə-säd′) *n.* **1.** The face of a building, esp. the principal face. **2.** An artificial or deceptive front. [Fr. < Ital. *facciata* < *faccia,* face < VLat. **facia* < Lat. *faciēs.* See **dhē-** in App.]

face (fās) *n.* **1a.** The front of the head from the top of the forehead to the base of the chin and from ear to ear. **b.** A person. **2.** A person's countenance. **3.** A contorted facial expression; a grimace. **4.** Facial cosmetics: *put one's face on.* **5.** Outward appearance.

6a. Value or standing in the eyes of others; prestige: *lose face.* **b.** Self-assurance; confidence. **7.** Effrontery; impudence. **8.** The most significant or prominent surface of an object, esp.: **a.** The surface presented to view; the front. **b.** A façade. **c.** Outer surface: *the face of the earth.* **d.** A marked side: *the face of a clock.* **e.** The right side, as of fabric. **f.** An exposed, often precipitous surface of rock. **9.** A planar surface of a geometric solid. **10.** Any of the surfaces of a rock or crystal. **11.** The end, as of a mine or tunnel, at which work is advancing. **12.** The appearance and geologic surface features of an area of land; topography. **13.** *Printing* **a.** A typeface or range of typefaces. **b.** The raised printing surface of a piece of type. ❖ *v.* **faced, fac•ing, fac•es** *—tr.* **1.** To occupy a position with the face toward: *faced the audience.* **2.** To front on: *The window faced the south.* **3a.** To confront with complete awareness: *has to face the facts.* **b.** To overcome by confronting boldly or bravely. **c.** To confront with impudence. **4a.** To be certain to encounter; have in store: *faced a long ordeal.* **b.** To bring or to be brought face to face with. **5.** To cause (troops) to change direction by giving a command. **6.** *Games* To turn (a playing card) so that the face is up. **7.** To furnish with a surface or cover of a different material. **8.** To line or trim the edge of, esp. with contrasting material. **9.** To treat the surface of so as to smooth. *—intr.* **1.** To be turned or placed with the front toward a specified direction. **2.** To turn the face in a specified direction. **—phrasal verbs: face down** To attain mastery over or overcome by confronting in a determined manner. **face off** *Sports* To start play in ice hockey, lacrosse, and other games by releasing the puck or ball between two opposing players. **face up** To confront, an unpleasant situation, for example, with resolution. **—idioms: face the music** To accept the unpleasant consequences, esp. of one's own actions. **in the face (or teeth) of** In opposition to or defiance of. **on the face of it** From appearances alone; apparently. **show (one's) face** To make an appearance. **to (one's) face** In the view or hearing of. [ME < OFr. < VLat. **facia* < Lat. *faciēs.* See **dhē-** in App.] **—face′a•ble** *adj.*

face angle *n.* The angle formed between two edges of a polyhedral angle.

face card *n.* A king, queen, or jack of a deck of cards.

face•cloth also **face cloth** (fās′klôth′, -klŏth′) *n.* See **washcloth.**

face-down also **face down** (fās′doun′) *adv.* In a position so that the face is down: *floating face-down in the water.*

face-hard•en (fās′här′dn) *tr.v.* **-hard•ened, -hard•en•ing, -hard•ens** To harden the surface of (a metal).

face•less (fās′lĭs) *adj.* **1.** Having no face. **2.** Without character or identity; anonymous. **—face′less•ness** *n.*

face•lift also **face•lift** (fās′lĭft′) *n.* **1.** Plastic surgery to remove wrinkles or other visible signs of aging for cosmetic purposes. **2.** A restyling or modernization, as of a building. **—face′-lift′** *v.*

face•mask (fās′măsk′) *n.* A protective or disguising cover for the face, often enveloping the entire head.

facemask
ice hockey facemask

face-off (fās′ôf′, -ŏf′) *n.* **1.** A method of starting play in ice hockey, lacrosse, and other games in which an official drops the puck or ball between two opposing players who contend for its control. **2.** A confrontation.

face•plate (fās′plāt′) *n.* **1.** A disk attached to the mandrel of a lathe to hold the work to be turned. **2.** The glass front of a cathode-ray tube upon which the image is displayed. **3.** A protective plate covering the human face, as of a welder.

faceplate

fac•er (fā′sər) *n.* **1.** One that faces, esp. a device used in smoothing or dressing a surface. **2.** An unexpected stunning blow or defeat.

face-sav•er (fās′sā′vər) *n.* Something that prevents loss of dignity or self-esteem. **—face′-sav′ing** *adj. & n.*

fac•et (fās′ĭt) *n.* **1.** One of the flat polished surfaces cut on a gemstone or occurring naturally on a crystal. **2.** *Anatomy* A small smooth flat surface, as on a bone or tooth. **3.** *Biology* One of the lenslike visual units of a compound eye, as of an insect. **4.** One of numerous aspects, as of a subject; a phase. [Fr. *facette* < OFr., dim. of *face,* face. See FACE.] **—fac′et•ed, fac′et•ted** *adj.*

fa•cete (fə-sēt′) *adj. Archaic* Witty; facetious. [Lat. *facētus.*]

fa•ce•ti•ae (fə-sē′shē-ē′) *pl.n.* Witty or humorous writings and sayings. [Lat. *facētiae,* pl. of *facētia,* jest. See FACETIOUS.]

face time *n.* Time spent interacting in the presence of or in the same location as another or others: *put in face time at the office.*

fa•ce•tious (fə-sē′shəs) *adj.* Playfully jocular; humorous. [Fr. *facétieux* < *facétie,* jest < Lat. *facētia* < *facētus,* witty.] **—fa•ce′tious•ly** *adv.* **—fa•ce′tious•ness** *n.*

face-to-face (fās′tə-fās′) *adj.* Being in the presence of another; facing: *had a face-to-face discussion to negotiate the contract.* ❖

ă	pat	oi boy
ā	pay	ou out
âr	care	ōō took
ä	father	ōō boot
ĕ	pet	ŭ cut
ē	be	ûr urge
ĭ	pit	th thin
ī	pie	th this
îr	pier	hw which
ŏ	pot	zh vision
ō	toe	ə about,
ô	paw	item

Stress marks:
′ (primary);
′ (secondary); as in
lexicon (lĕk′sĭ-kŏn′)

adv. also **face to face** In person; directly.

face-up also **face up** (fās′ŭp′) *adv.* In a position so that the face is up.

face value *n.* **1.** The value printed or written on the face, as of a bill or bond. **2.** Apparent significance or value.

fa·cial (fā′shəl) *adj.* Of or concerning the face: *facial hair.* ❖ *n.* A treatment for the face, usu. consisting of a massage and the application of cosmetic creams. **—fa′cial·ly** *adv.*

facial index *n.* The ratio of facial length to facial width multiplied by 100.

facial nerve *n.* Either of the seventh pair of cranial nerves that control facial muscles and relay sensation from the taste buds of the front part of the tongue.

–facient *suff.* **1.** Causing; bringing about: *somnifacient.* **2.** Something that causes or brings about: *abortifacient.* [< Lat. *faciēns, facient-,* pr. part. of *facere,* to do. See **dhē-** in App.]

fa·ci·es (fā′shē-ēz′, -shēz) *n., pl.* **facies 1.** *Biology* The general aspect or outward appearance, as of a given growth of flora. **2.** *Medicine* The appearance or expression of the face, esp. when typical of a disorder or disease. **3.** *Geology* A rock or stratified body distinguished from others by its appearance or composition. [Lat. *faciēs.* See **dhē-** in App.]

fac·ile (fās′əl) *adj.* **1.** Done or achieved with little effort or difficulty; easy. **2.** Working, acting, or speaking with effortless ease and fluency. **3.** Arrived at without due care, effort, or examination; superficial. **4.** Readily manifested, together with an aura of insincerity and lack of depth: *a facile slogan.* **5.** *Archaic* Pleasingly mild, as in disposition or manner. [ME < OFr. < Lat. *facilis.* See **dhē-** in App.] **—fac′ile·ly** *adv.* **—fac′ile·ness** *n.*

fa·cil·i·tate (fə-sĭl′ĭ-tāt′) *tr.v.* **-tat·ed, -tat·ing, -tates** To make easy or easier. [< Fr. *faciliter* < OFr. < Ital. *facilitare* < *facile,* facile < Lat. *facilis.* See FACILE.] **—fa·cil′i·ta′tive** (-tā′tĭv) *adj.* **—fa·cil′i·ta′tor** *n.*

fa·cil·i·ta·tion (fə-sĭl′ĭ-tā′shən) *n.* **1a.** The act of making easy or easier. **b.** The state of being made easy or easier. **2.** *Physiology* The lowering of the threshold for propagation of an action potential of a neuron.

fa·cil·i·ty (fə-sĭl′ĭ-tē) *n., pl.* **-ties 1.** Ease in moving, acting, or doing; aptitude. **2.** Readiness to be persuaded; pliability. **3.** Something that facilitates an action or process. Often used in the plural. **4.** Something created to serve a particular function: *health care facilities.* **5. facilities** *Informal* A restroom.

fac·ing (fā′sĭng) *n.* **1.** A piece of material sewn to the edge of a garment, such as a dress or coat, as lining or decoration. **2.** An outer layer or coating applied to a surface for protection or decoration.

fac·sim·i·le (făk-sĭm′ə-lē) *n.* **1.** An exact copy or reproduction, as of a document. **2.** See **fax.** ❖ *adj.* **1.** Of or used to produce exact reproductions, as of documents. **2.** Exactly reproduced; duplicate. [Lat. *fac simile,* make similar : *fac,* sing. imper. of *facere,* to make; see **dhē-** in App. + *simile,* neut. of *similis,* similar; see SIMILAR.]

fact (făkt) *n.* **1.** Knowledge or information based on real occurrences. **2a.** Something demonstrated to exist or known to have existed. **b.** A real occurrence; an event: *the facts of the accident.* **c.** Something believed to be true or real: *mistaken facts.* **3.** A thing that has been done, esp. a crime: *an accessory before the fact.* **4.** *Law* The aspect of a case at law comprising events determined by evidence. **—idiom: in (point of) fact** In reality or in truth; actually. [Lat. *factum,* deed < neut. p. part. of *facere,* to do. See **dhē-** in App.]

USAGE NOTE Expressions like *true facts* and *real facts* may occasion qualms among critics who hold that facts cannot be other than true or real, but these phrases are often useful for emphasis. *The true facts of the case* implies something different from *the facts of the case,* which can refer to all the particulars surrounding the case, not just to what actually happened to bring the case about.

fact-find·ing (făkt′fīn′dĭng) *n.* Discovery or determination of facts or accurate information. ❖ *adj.* Of, relating to, or used in the discovery or determination of facts. **—fact′-find′er** *n.*

fac·tic·i·ty (făk-tĭs′ĭ-tē) *n.* The quality or condition of being a fact: *historical facticity.*

fac·tion¹ (făk′shən) *n.* **1.** A group of persons forming a cohesive, usu. contentious minority within a larger group. **2.** Conflict within an organization or nation; internal dissension. [Fr. < Lat. *factiō, factiōn-* < *factus,* p. part. of *facere,* to do. See **dhē-** in App.] **—fac′tion·al** *adj.* **—fac′tion·al·ism** *n.* **—fac′tion·al·ly** *adv.*

fac·tion² (făk′shən) *n.* A form of fiction incorporating real people or events as essential elements. [Blend of FACT and FICTION.]

–faction *suff.* Production; making: *petrifaction.* [ME *-faccioun* < OFr. *-faction* < Lat. *-factiō, -factiōn-* < *factus,* p. part. of *facere,* to make. See **dhē-** in App.]

fac·tion·al·ize (făk′shə-nə-līz′) *tr.v.* **-ized, -iz·ing, -iz·es** To split (a group, for example) into disputatious factions.

fac·tious (făk′shəs) *adj.* **1.** Of, relating to, produced by, or characterized by internal dissension. **2.** Given to or promoting internal dissension. **—fac′tious·ly** *adv.* **—fac′tious·ness** *n.*

fac·ti·tious (făk-tĭsh′əs) *adj.* **1.** Produced artificially rather than by a natural process. **2.** Lacking authenticity or genuineness;

sham. [< Lat. *factīcius* < *factus,* p. part. of *facere,* to make. See **dhē-** in App.] **—fac·ti′tious·ly** *adv.* **—fac·ti′tious·ness** *n.*

fac·ti·tive (făk′tĭ-tĭv) *adj.* Of or constituting a transitive verb that renders to a thing a certain character or status and that in English can take an objective complement modifying its direct object, such as *make* in *That makes me angry.* [NLat. *factitīvus* < Lat. *factitāre,* to do, practice, freq. of *facere,* to do. See **dhē-** in App.] **—fac′ti·tive·ly** *adv.*

fact of life *n., pl.* **facts of life 1.** Something unavoidable that must be faced or dealt with. **2. facts of life** The basic physiological functions involved in sex and reproduction.

fac·toid (făk′toid) *n.* **1.** A piece of inaccurate or false information that is accepted as true because of repetition in the media. **2.** A brief, somewhat interesting fact. **—fac·toi′dal** *adj.*

fac·tor (făk′tər) *n.* **1.** One that actively contributes to an accomplishment, result, or process. See Syns at **element. 2a.** One who acts for someone else; an agent. **b.** A person or firm that accepts accounts receivable as security for short-term loans. **3.** *Mathematics* One of two or more quantities that divides a given quantity without a remainder. For example, 2 and 3 are factors of 6. **4.** A quantity by which a stated quantity is multiplied or divided, so as to indicate an increase or decrease in a measurement. **5.** A gene. No longer in technical usage. **6.** *Physiology* A substance that functions in a specific biochemical reaction or bodily process, such as blood coagulation. ❖ *tr.v.* **-tored, -tor·ing, -tors** To determine or indicate explicitly the factors of. **—phrasal verb: factor in** To figure in. [ME *factour,* perpetrator, agent < OFr. *facteur* < Lat. *factor,* maker < *facere,* to make. See **dhē-** in App.] **—fac′tor·a·ble** *adj.* **—fac′tor·ship′** *n.*

factor VIII *n.* See **antihemophilic factor.**

factor IX *n.* A protein substance in blood plasma that participates in and is essential for the blood-clotting process.

fac·tor·age (făk′tər-ĭj) *n.* **1.** The business of a factor. **2.** The commission or fee paid to a factor.

fac·to·ri·al (făk-tôr′ē-əl, -tōr′-) *n.* The product of all the positive integers from 1 to a given number. For example, 4 factorial, usu. written 4!, is equal to 24 ($1 \times 2 \times 3 \times 4 = 24$). ❖ *adj.* Of or relating to a factor or factorial.

fac·tor·ize (făk′tə-rīz′) *tr.v.* **-ized, -iz·ing, -iz·es** *Mathematics* To factor. **—fac′tor·i·za′tion** (-tər-ĭ-zā′shən) *n.*

fac·to·ry (făk′tə-rē) *n., pl.* **-ries 1a.** A building or group of buildings in which goods are manufactured; a plant. **b.** A vessel in which newly caught seafood is prepared for shipment and sale. **2.** A business establishment for commercial agents or factors in a foreign country. **3.** A source of prolific production. [LLat. *factōria,* mill, and Med.Lat. *factōria,* establishment for factors, both < Lat. *factor,* factor. See FACTOR.]

fac·to·tum (făk-tō′təm) *n.* An employee or assistant who serves in a wide range of capacities. [Med.Lat. *factōtum* : Lat. *fac,* sing. imper. of *facere,* to do; see **dhē-** in App. + Lat. *tōtum,* everything < neut. of *tōtus,* all; see **teutā-** in App.]

fac·tu·al (făk′chōō-əl) *adj.* **1.** Of the nature of fact; real. **2.** Of or containing facts. **—fac′tu·al′i·ty** (-ăl′ĭ-tē) *n.* **—fac′tu·al·ly** *adv.* **—fac′tu·al·ness** *n.*

fac·tu·al·ism (făk′chōō-ə-lĭz′əm) *n.* Devotion or adherence to fact. **—fac′tu·al·ist** *n.*

fac·ture (făk′chər) *n.* The manner in which something, esp. a work of art, is made. [Fr. < Lat. *factūra,* a working or making. See FEATURE.]

fac·u·la (făk′yə-lə) *n., pl.* **-lae** (-lē′) Any of various large bright spots or veined patches on the sun's photosphere, usu. near sunspots. [Lat., small torch, dim. of *fax, fac-,* torch.]

fac·ul·ta·tive (făk′əl-tā′tĭv) *adj.* **1.** Of or relating to a mental faculty. **2a.** Capable of occurring or not occurring; contingent. **b.** Not required or compulsory; optional. **3.** Granting permission or authority. **4.** *Biology* Capable of functioning under varying environmental conditions. **—fac′ul·ta′tive·ly** *adv.*

fac·ul·ty (făk′əl-tē) *n., pl.* **-ties 1.** An inherent power or ability. **2.** Any of the powers or capacities possessed by the human mind. **3.** The ability to perform or act. **4a.** Any of the divisions or comprehensive branches of learning at a college or university. **b.** The teachers and instructors within such a division. **c.** A body of teachers. **5.** All of the members of a learned profession. **6.** Authorization granted by authority; conferred power. **7.** *Archaic* An occupation; a trade. [ME *faculte* < OFr. < Lat. *facultās,* power, ability < *facilis,* easy. See **dhē-** in App.]

fad (făd) *n.* A fashion taken up enthusiastically for a brief period of time; a craze. [Poss. < *fidfad,* fussy person, fussy < FIDDLE-FAD-DLE.] **—fad′dism** *n.* **—fad′dist** *n.* **—fad′dy** *adj.*

fad·dish (făd′ĭsh) *adj.* **1.** Having the nature of a fad. **2.** Given to fads. **—fad′dish·ly** *adv.* **—fad′dish·ness** *n.*

fade (fād) *v.* **fad·ed, fad·ing, fades** *—intr.* **1.** To lose brightness, loudness, or brilliance gradually; dim. **2.** To lose freshness; wither. **3.** To lose strength or vitality; wane. **4.** To disappear gradually; vanish. See Syns at **disappear. 5.** *Sports* To swerve from a straight course, esp. as a slice. **6.** *Football* To move back from the scrimmage line. Used of a quarterback. *—tr.* **1.** To cause to lose brightness, freshness, or strength. **2.** *Games* To meet the bet of (an opposing player) in the game of dice. **3.** *Sports* To hit (a ball) with a fade. ❖ *n.* **1.** A gradual decrease or increase in the brightness or visibility of an image in cinema or television. **2.** A periodic reduction in the received strength of a radio transmission. **3.** *Sports* A moderate, usu. controlled slice, as in golf. ***—phrasal verbs:* fade in** To appear or become audible gradually. **fade out** To disappear or become inaudible gradually. [ME *faden* < OFr. *fader* < *fade*, faded, prob. < VLat. **fatidus*, alteration of Lat. *fatuus*, insipid.]

fade•a•way (fād′ə-wā′) *n.* The act or an instance of gradually diminishing in brightness, loudness, or strength until actual disappearance occurs.

fade-in or **fade•in** (fād′ĭn′) *n.* A gradual increase in the brightness of an image or the audibility of a sound, as in cinema.

fade•less (fād′lĭs) *adj.* Not fading or not subject to fading.

fade-out or **fade•out** (fād′out′) *n.* **1.** A gradual disappearance of an image or sound, as in cinema or radio. **2.** A gradual loss in reception of a radio or television signal, often generated by interference in transmission.

fad•ing (fā′dĭng) *n.* **1.** A waning; a decline. **2.** Fluctuation in the strength of radio signals because of variations in the transmission medium.

fa•do (fä′*th*o͞o, fäth′ō) *n., pl.* **-dos** A sad Portuguese folksong. [Port. < Lat. *fātum*, fate. See FATE.]

fa•e•na (fä-ā′nä) *n.* The series of final passes performed by a matador preparatory to killing a bull in a bullfight. [Sp., manual labor < Catalan *feyna* < Lat. *facienda*, things to be done, neut. pl. gerundive of *facere*, to do. See FACT.]

Fa•en•za (fä-ĕn′zə) A city of N-central Italy SW of Ravenna; noted for its richly colored pottery. Pop. 39,700.

fa•er•ie also **fa•er•y** (fā′ə-rē, fâr′ē) *n., pl.* **-ies 1.** A tiny mischievous imaginary being; a fairy. **2.** The land or realm of the fairies. [ME *faierie, fairie*. See FAIRY.] **—fa′er•ie** *adj.*

Faer•oe Islands or **Far•oe Islands** (fâr′ō) A group of volcanic islands in the N Atlantic Ocean between Iceland and the Shetland Is.

Faer•o•ese (fâr′ō-ēz′, -ēs′) *n.* Variant of **Faroese.**

Faf•nir (fäv′nər, -nîr′) *n. Mythology* The Norse dragon that guarded the treasure of the Nibelungs and was slain by Sigurd.

fag[1] (făg) *n.* **1a.** A student at a British public school required to perform menial tasks for a student in a higher class. **b.** A drudge. **2.** *Chiefly British* Fatiguing or tedious work; drudgery. ❖ *v.* **fagged, fag•ging, fags** *—intr.* **1.** To work to exhaustion; toil. **2.** To function as the servant of another student in a British public school. *—tr.* To exhaust; weary. [< *fag*, to droop (obsolete), perh. < ME *fagge*. See FAG END.]

fag[2] (făg) *n. Slang* A cigarette. [Short for FAG END.]

fag[3] (făg) *n. Offensive Slang* Used as a disparaging term for a homosexual man. [Short for FAGGOT[2].]

fag end *n.* **1.** The frayed end of a length of cloth or rope. **2a.** An inferior or worn-out remnant. **b.** The last part. [ME *fagge, fag*, broken thread in cloth.]

fag•got[1] (făg′ət) *n. & v.* Variant of **fagot.**

fag•got[2] (făg′ət) *n. Offensive Slang* Used as a disparaging term for a homosexual man. [Perh. < *faggot*, var. of FAGOT, bundle, lump, old woman.]

fag•ot also **fag•got** (făg′ət) *n.* **1.** A bundle of twigs, sticks, or branches bound together. **2.** A bundle of pieces of iron or steel to be welded or hammered into bars. ❖ *tr.v.* **-ot•ed, -ot•ing, -ots** also **-got•ed, -got•ing, -gots 1.** To bind into a fagot; bundle. **2.** To decorate with fagoting. [ME < OFr. < O Provençal, poss. < VLat. **facus* < Gk. *phakelos*, bundle.]

fag•ot•ing also **fag•got•ing** (făg′ə-tĭng) *n.* **1.** A method of decorating cloth by pulling out horizontal threads and tying the remaining vertical threads into hourglass-shaped bunches. **2.** A method of joining hemmed edges by crisscrossing thread over an open seam.

Fahd (fäd) b. 1922. King of Saudi Arabia (since 1982).

Fahr•en•heit (făr′ən-hīt′) *adj.* Of or relating to a temperature scale that registers the freezing point of water as 32° and the boiling point as 212° at one atmosphere of pressure. See table at **measurement.** [After Gabriel Daniel FAHRENHEIT.]

Fahr•en•heit (făr′ən-hīt′, fä′rən-), **Gabriel Daniel** 1686–1736. German-born physicist who invented the mercury thermometer (1714).

Fa•ial also **Fa•yal** (fə-yäl′, fä-) An island of the central Azores in the N Atlantic Ocean; noted for its abundant plant life.

fa•ience also **fa•ïence** (fī-äns′, -äNs′, fā-) *n.* **1.** Earthenware decorated with colorful glazes. **2.** A moderate to strong greenish blue. [Fr. *faïence*, after *Faïence* (Faenza), Italy.]

fail (fāl) *v.* **failed, fail•ing, fails** *—intr.* **1.** To prove deficient or lacking; perform ineffectively or inadequately. **2.** To be unsuccessful. **3.** To receive an academic grade below the acceptable minimum. **4.** To prove insufficient in quantity or duration; give out: *The water supply failed during the drought.* **5.** To decline, as in strength or effectiveness: *The light began to fail.* **6.** To cease functioning properly. **7.** To give way or be made otherwise useless as a result of excessive strain. **8.** To become bankrupt or insolvent. *—tr.* **1.** To disappoint or prove undependable to: *Our sentries failed us.* **2.** To abandon; forsake: *His strength failed him.* **3.** To omit to perform (an expected duty, for example). **4.** To leave (something) undone; neglect. **5a.** To receive an academic grade below the acceptable minimum in (a course, for example). **b.** To give such a grade to (a student). ❖ *n.* **1.** Failure to deliver securities to a purchaser within a specified time. **2.** Failure to receive the proceeds of a transaction, as in the sale of stock or securities, by a specified date. ***—idiom:* without fail** With no chance of failure; certainly. [ME *failen* < OFr. *faillir* < VLat. **fallīre*, var. of Lat. *fallere*, to deceive.]

failed (fāld) *adj.* Having undergone failure.

fail•ing (fā′lĭng) *n.* **1.** The act of a person or thing that fails; a failure. **2.** A minor fault. ❖ *adj.* Undergoing failure. ❖ *prep.* In the absence of; without.

faille (fīl, fāl) *n.* A slightly ribbed woven fabric of silk, cotton, or rayon. [Fr. < ONFr., cloth head covering worn by women in Flanders, poss. < MDu. *falie*, scarf.]

fail-safe (fāl′sāf′) *adj.* **1.** Capable of compensating automatically and safely for a failure, as of a mechanism or power source. **2.** Acting to discontinue a military attack on the occurrence of any of various predetermined conditions. **3.** Guaranteed not to fail. ❖ *n.* A fail-safe mechanism.

fail•ure (fāl′yər) *n.* **1.** The condition or fact of not achieving the desired end or ends. **2.** One that fails. **3.** The condition or fact of being insufficient or falling short: *a crop failure.* **4.** A cessation of proper functioning or performance. **5.** Nonperformance of what is requested or expected; omission. **6.** The act or fact of failing to pass a course, test, or assignment. **7.** A decline in strength or effectiveness. **8.** The act or fact of becoming bankrupt or insolvent. [Alteration of *failer*, default < AN < OFr. *faillir*, to fail. See FAIL.]

fain (fān) *adv.* **1.** Happily; gladly. **2.** *Archaic* Preferably; rather. ❖ *adj. Archaic* **1.** Ready; willing. **2.** Pleased; happy. **3.** Obliged or required. [ME < OE *fægen*, joyful, glad.]

fai•né•ant (fā′nā-äN′) *adj.* Given to doing nothing; idle. ❖ *n.* An irresponsible idler. [Fr., alteration of OFr. *faignant*, idler < pr. part. of *faindre, feindre*, to feign. See FEIGN.]

faint (fānt) *adj.* **faint•er, faint•est 1.** Lacking strength or vigor; feeble. **2.** Lacking conviction, boldness, or courage; timid. **3a.** Lacking brightness. **b.** Lacking clarity or distinctness. **4.** Likely to fall into a faint; dizzy and weak. ❖ *n.* An abrupt, usu. brief loss of consciousness, generally associated with failure of normal blood circulation. ❖ *intr.v.* **faint•ed, faint•ing, faints 1.** To fall into a faint. **2.** *Archaic* To weaken in purpose or spirit. [ME, deceitful, cowardly < OFr., p. part. of *feindre*, to feign. See FEIGN.] **—faint′er** *n.* **—faint′ly** *adv.* **—faint′ness** *n.*

faint-heart•ed (fānt′här′tĭd) *adj.* Deficient in conviction or courage; timid. **—faint′-heart′ed•ly** *adv.* **—faint′-heart′ed•ness** *n.*

fair[1] (fâr) *adj.* **fair•er, fair•est 1.** Of pleasing appearance, esp. because of a pure or fresh quality; comely. **2a.** Light in color, esp. blond: *fair hair.* **b.** Of light complexion: *fair skin.* **3.** Free of clouds or storms; clear and sunny. **4.** Free of blemishes or stains; clean and pure. **5.** Promising; likely. **6a.** Having or exhibiting a disposition that is free of favoritism or bias; impartial. **b.** Just to all parties; equitable: *a fair deal.* **7.** Being in accordance with relative merit or significance: *her fair share.* **8.** Consistent with rules, logic, or ethics. **9.** Moderately good; acceptable or satisfactory. **10.** Superficially true or appealing; specious. **11.** Lawful to hunt or attack: *fair game.* **12.** *Archaic* Free of all obstacles. ❖ *adv.* **1.** In a proper or legal manner: *playing fair.* **2.** Directly; straight. ❖ *tr.v.* **faired, fair•ing, fairs** To join (pieces) so as to be smooth, even, or regular. ❖ *n.* **1.** *Archaic* A beautiful or beloved woman. **2.** *Obsolete* Loveliness; beauty. ***—phrasal verb:* fair off** (or **up**) *Chiefly Southern US* To become clear. Used of weather. ***—idioms:* fair and square** Just and honest. **no fair** Something contrary to the rules. [ME < OE *fæger*, lovely, pleasant.] **—fair′ness** *n.*

SYNONYMS *fair, just, equitable, impartial, unprejudiced, unbiased, objective, dispassionate* These adjectives mean free from favoritism, self-interest, or preference in judgment. *Fair* is the most general: *a fair referee; a fair deal. Just* stresses conformity with what is legally or ethically right or proper: *"a just and lasting peace"* (Abraham Lincoln). *Equitable* implies justice dictated by reason, conscience, and a natural sense of what is fair: *an equitable distribution of gifts among the children. Impartial* emphasizes lack of favoritism: *"the cold neutrality of an impartial judge"* (Edmund Burke). *Unprejudiced* means without preconceived opinions or judgments: *an unprejudiced evaluation of the proposal. Unbiased* implies absence of preference or partiality: *gave an unbiased account of her family problems. Objective* implies detachment that permits impersonal observation and judgment: *an objective jury. Dispassionate* means free from or unaffected by strong emotions: *a dispassionate reporter.* See also Syns at **average.**

fair[2] (fâr) *n.* **1.** A gathering held at a specified time and place for the buying and selling of goods; a market. **2.** An exhibition, as of farm products, usu. accompanied by various competitions and entertainments: *a county fair.* **3.** An exhibition intended to inform people about a product or business opportunity: *a job fair.* **4.** An event, usu. for the benefit of a charity or public institution. [ME *faire* < OFr. *feire* < LLat. *fēria*, sing. of Lat. *fēriae*, holidays. See **dhēs-** in App.]

fair ball *n. Baseball* A batted ball that lands in the outfield, bounces past first or third base, comes to rest, or is touched by a fielder while within the foul lines.

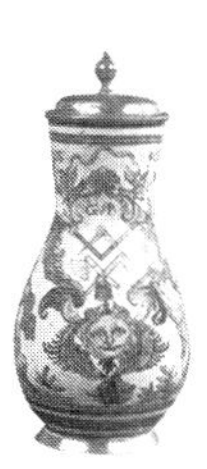

faience
c. 1750 Austrian jar

ă	pat	oi	boy
ā	pay	ou	out
âr	care	o͝o	took
ä	father	o͞o	boot
ĕ	pet	ŭ	cut
ē	be	ûr	urge
ĭ	pit	th	thin
ī	pie	*th*	this
îr	pier	hw	which
ŏ	pot	zh	vision
ō	toe	ə	about, item
ô	paw		

Stress marks:
′ (primary);
′ (secondary), as in
lexicon (lĕk′sĭ-kŏn′)

Fair·banks (fâr′băngks′) A city of central AK NNE of Anchorage; founded 1902. Pop. 30,224.

Fairbanks, Douglas 1883–1939. Amer. actor known for his roles in silent films such as *Robin Hood* (1922).

fair catch *n. Football* A catch of a kicked ball by a receiving player who has signaled the intention not to run with the ball and who may not be hit if making no attempt to advance the ball after catching it.

Fair·field (fâr′fēld′) A city of W CA NNE of Oakland; founded 1859. Pop. 96,178.

fair·ground (fâr′ground′) *n.* Open land where fairs or exhibitions are held.

fair-haired (fâr′hârd′) *adj.* **1.** Having blond hair. **2.** Favorite.

fair·ing¹ (fâr′ĭng) *n.* An auxiliary structure or the external surface of a vehicle, such as an aircraft, that reduces drag.

fair·ing² (fâr′ĭng) *n. Chiefly British* A gift, esp. one bought or given at a fair.

fair·ish (fâr′ĭsh) *adj.* Of moderately large size or good quality. **—fair′ish·ly** *adv.*

fair·lead (fâr′lēd′) also **fair·lead·er** (-lē′dər) *n. Nautical* A device such as a ring through which rigging is passed to hold it in place or prevent it from snagging or chafing.

fair·ly (fâr′lē) *adv.* **1a.** In a fair or just manner; equitably. **b.** Legitimately; suitably. **2.** Clearly; distinctly. **3.** Actually; fully. **4a.** Moderately; rather. **b.** To a reasonable degree. **5.** *Obsolete* **a.** Gently. **b.** Courteously.

fair market value *n.* The price, as of a service, at which both buyers and sellers agree to do business.

fair-mind·ed (fâr′mīn′dĭd) *adj.* Just and impartial; not prejudiced. **—fair′-mind′ed·ly** *adv.* **—fair′-mind′ed·ness** *n.*

Fair Oaks A locality E of Richmond VA where Union troops defeated the Confederates at the Battle of Seven Pines (May 31–Jun. 1, 1862).

fair play *n.* Conformity to established rules.

fair shake *n. Informal* A fair chance, as at achieving success.

fair-spo·ken (fâr′spō′kən) *adj.* Civil, courteous, and gentle in speech.

fair trade *n.* Trade that conforms to a fair-trade agreement.

fair-trade (fâr′trād′) *tr.v.* **-trad·ed, -trad·ing, -trades** To sell (a commodity) at a price consistent with a fair-trade agreement.

fair-trade agreement *n.* A commercial agreement under which distributors sell products of a given class at no less than a minimum price set by the manufacturer.

fair·way (fâr′wā′) *n.* **1.** A stretch of ground free of obstacles to movement. **2.** *Sports* The part of a golf course covered with short grass and extending from the tee to the putting green. **3.** *Nautical* **a.** A navigable deep-water channel in a river or harbor or along a coastline. **b.** The usual course taken by vessels through a harbor or coastal waters.

fair-weath·er (fâr′wĕth′ər) *adj.* **1.** Suitable or used only during fair weather: *fair-weather hiking gear.* **2.** Present and dependable only in good times: *fair-weather friends.*

Fair·weath·er (fâr′wĕth′ər) *,* **Mount** A peak, 4,666.5 m (15,300 ft), on the border between SE AK and W British Columbia, Canada.

fair·y (fâr′ē) *n., pl.* **-ies 1.** A tiny imaginary being in human form, depicted as clever, mischievous, and possessing magical powers. **2.** *Offensive Slang* Used as a disparaging term for a homosexual man. [ME *fairie*, fairyland, enchanted being < OFr. *faerie* < *fae, fairy* < VLat. *Fāta*, goddess of fate < Lat. *fātum*, fate. See FATE.]

fairy godmother *n.* A generous benefactor.

fair·y·land (fâr′ē-lănd′) *n.* **1.** The imaginary land of fairies. **2.** A charming enchanting place.

fairy ring *n.* A circle of mushrooms in a grassy area, marking the periphery of perennial underground mycelial growth.

fairy shrimp *n.* Any of various transparent freshwater crustaceans of the order Anostraca that lack a carapace and characteristically swim upside-down.

fairy tale *n.* **1.** A fanciful tale of legendary deeds and creatures, usu. intended for children. **2.** A fictitious fanciful story or explanation. **—fair′y-tale′** (fâr′ē-tāl′) *adj.*

Fai·sal also **Fei·sal** or **Fei·sul** (fī′səl) 1906?–75. King of Saudi Arabia (1964–75) who used oil revenue to increase industrialization and improve educational and medical facilities.

Fai·sa·la·bad (fī′sä-lə-bäd′) Formerly **Ly·all·pur** (lī′əl-pŏŏr′) A city of NE Pakistan W of Lahore; founded 1892. Pop. 1,104,209.

fait ac·com·pli (fā′tä-kôn-plē′, fĕt′ä-) *n., pl.* **faits ac·com·plis** (fā′tä-kôn-plē′, -plēz′, fĕt′ä-) An accomplished, presumably irreversible deed or fact. [Fr.]

faith (fāth) *n.* **1.** Confident belief in the truth, value, or trustworthiness of a person, idea, or thing. **2.** Belief that does not rest on logical proof or material evidence. **3.** Loyalty to a person or thing; allegiance. **4.** often **Faith** *Christianity* The theological virtue defined as secure belief in God and a trusting acceptance of God's will. **5.** The body of dogma of a religion: *the Muslim faith.* **6.** A set of principles or beliefs. **—idiom: in faith** Indeed; truly. [ME < AN *fed* < Lat. *fidēs.* See **bheidh-** in App.]

faith·ful (fāth′fəl) *adj.* **1.** Adhering firmly and devotedly, as to a person or idea; loyal. **2.** Engaging in sex only with one's spouse or only with one's partner in a sexual relationship. **3.** Having or full

of faith. **4.** Worthy of trust or belief; reliable. **5.** Consistent with truth or actuality: *a faithful reproduction.* ❖ *n., pl.* **faithful** or **-fuls 1.** The practicing members of a religious faith, esp. of Christianity or Islam. **2.** A steadfast adherent of a faith or cause. **—faith′ful·ly** *adv.* **—faith′ful·ness** *n.*

SYNONYMS *faithful, loyal, true, constant, fast, steadfast, staunch* These adjectives mean adhering firmly and devotedly to someone or something that elicits or demands one's fidelity. *Faithful* and *loyal* both suggest undeviating attachment, though *loyal* applies more often to political allegiance: *a faithful employee; a loyal citizen. True* implies steadiness, sincerity, and reliability: "I would be true, for there are those who trust me" (Howard Arnold Walter). *Constant* stresses uniformity and invariability: "But I am constant as the northern star" (Shakespeare). *Fast* suggests loyalty that is not easily deflected: *fast friends. Steadfast* strongly implies fixed unswerving loyalty: *a steadfast ally. Staunch* even more strongly suggests unshakable attachment or allegiance: "He lived and died a staunch loyalist" (Harriet Beecher Stowe).

faith healer *n.* One who treats disease with prayer. **—faith healing** *n.*

faith·less (fāth′lĭs) *adj.* **1.** Not true to duty or obligation; disloyal. **2.** Having no religious faith. **3.** Unworthy of faith or trust; unreliable. **—faith′less·ly** *adv.* **—faith′less·ness** *n.*

fai·tour (fā′tər) *n. Archaic* An impostor; a deceiver. [ME < AN < Lat. *factor*, maker. See FACTOR.]

fa·ji·ta (fə-hē′tə) *n.* A dish consisting of strips of marinated meat, poultry, or vegetables that are grilled over an open fire and served in a tortilla. Often used in the plural. [Am.Sp., dim. of *faja*, band, strip < Lat. *fascia*, band, bandage.]

fake¹ (fāk) *adj.* Having a false or misleading appearance; fraudulent. ❖ *n.* **1.** One that is not authentic or genuine; a sham. **2.** *Sports* A brief feint or aborted change of direction intended to mislead an opponent. ❖ *v.* **faked, fak·ing, fakes** *—tr.* **1.** To contrive and present as genuine; counterfeit. **2.** To simulate; feign. **3.** *Music* To improvise (a passage). **4.** *Sports* To deceive (an opponent) with a fake. Often used with *out.* *—intr.* **1.** To engage in feigning, simulation, or other deceptive activity. **2.** *Sports* To perform a fake. [?] **—fak′er** *n.* **—fak′er·y** (fā′kə-rē) *n.*

fake² (fāk) *n.* One loop or winding of a coiled rope or cable. ❖ *tr.v.* **faked, fak·ing, fakes** To coil (a rope or cable). [ME *faken*, to coil a rope.]

fake book *n.* A book or collection of information about songs, esp. their lyrics, melodies, and chord progressions.

fa·kir (fə-kîr′, fä-, fā-) *n.* **1.** A Muslim religious mendicant. **2.** A Hindu ascetic or religious mendicant, esp. one who performs feats of magic or endurance. [Ar. *faqīr* < *faqura*, to be poor.]

fa·la·fel or **fe·la·fel** (fə-lä′fəl) *n.* **1.** Ground spiced chickpeas shaped into balls and fried. **2.** A sandwich filled with such a mixture. [Ar. *falāfil*, pl. of *filfil*, pepper, prob. < Skt. *pippalī*. See PEPPER.]

Fa·lan·gist (fə-lăn′gĭst, fä′lăn′-) *n.* A member of the official ruling party of Spain after 1939. [Sp. *Falangista* < *Falange* (*Española*), (Sp.) Phalanx < Lat. *phalanx, phalang-.* See PHALANX.]

Fa·la·sha (fə-lä′shə, fä-) *n., pl.* **Falasha** or **-shas** *Often Offensive* An Ethiopian Jew. [Amharic *fälaša* < *fälaš*, migrant, active part. of *fälläsä*, to migrate.]

fal·cate (făl′kāt′) also **fal·cat·ed** (-kā′tĭd) *adj.* Curved and tapering to a point. [Lat. *falcātus* < *falx, falc-*, sickle.]

fal·chion (fôl′chən) *n.* **1.** A short broad sword with a convex cutting edge and a sharp point, used in medieval times. **2.** *Archaic* A sword. [ME *fauchoun* < OFr. *fauchon* < VLat. **falciō, falciōn-* < Lat. *falx, falc-*, sickle.]

fal·ci·form (făl′sə-fôrm′) *adj.* Curved or sickle-shaped; falcate. [Lat. *falx, falc-*, sickle + -FORM.]

fal·con (făl′kən, fôl′-, fô′kən) *n.* **1a.** Any of various birds of prey of the family Falconidae and esp. of the genus *Falco*, having a short curved beak and long pointed wings. **b.** Any of several birds of these or related species, trained for falconing. **c.** A female bird of this type. **2.** A small cannon in use from the 15th to the 17th century. [ME < OFr. *faucon, falcun* < LLat. *falcō, falcōn-.*]

fal·con·er (făl′kə-nər, fôl′-, fô′kə-) *n.* **1.** One that breeds and trains falcons. **2.** One who hunts with falcons.

fal·con·et (făl′kə-nĕt′, fôl′-, fô′kə-) *n.* **1.** A small or young falcon. **2.** Any of several small falcons, esp. of the genus *Microhierax* native to tropical Asia.

fal·con·gen·tle (făl′kən-jĕn′tl, fôl′-, fô′kən-) *n.* A female falcon, esp. a peregrine falcon. [ME *faucon gentil* < OFr. *faucon gentil*, noble falcon.]

fal·con·ry (făl′kən-rē, fôl′-, fô′kən-) *n.* **1.** Hunting of game with falcons. **2.** The art of training falcons for hunting.

fal·de·ral (făl′də-răl′) *n.* Variant of **folderol.**

fald·stool (fôld′stŏŏl′) *n.* **1.** A folding or small desk stool at which worshipers kneel to pray. **2.** A folding chair or stool, esp. one used by a bishop. **3.** A desk at which the litany is recited. [Partial transl. of Med.Lat. *faldistolium*, folding stool < Gmc. orig.]

Fa·lis·can (fə-lĭs′kən) *n.* **1.** A member of an ancient Italic people of southern Etruria. **2.** The language of this people, closely related to Latin. ❖ *adj.* Of or relating to the Faliscans or their language or culture. [< Lat. *Faliscus < Faleriī*, a city of ancient Etruria.]

falcon
peregrine falcon
Falco peregrinus

Fal•kirk (fôl′kûrk′) A burgh of central Scotland W of Edinburgh; site of Edward I's defeat of the Scots (1298). Pop. 37,800.

Falk•land Islands (fôk′lənd, fôlk′-) A group of islands in the S Atlantic Ocean E of the Strait of Magellan; controlled by Great Britain since the 1830s but also claimed by Argentina.

fall (fôl) *v.* **fell** (fĕl), **fall•en** (fô′lən), **fall•ing, falls** *—intr.* **1.** To drop or come down freely under the influence of gravity. **2.** To drop oneself to a lower or less erect position: *fell back in my chair.* **3a.** To lose an upright or erect position suddenly. **b.** To drop wounded or dead, esp. in battle. **4.** To go or come as if by falling: *Night fell quickly.* **5.** To come to rest; settle: *The light fell on my book.* **6.** To hang down: *The hair fell in ringlets.* **7.** To be cast down: *Her eyes fell.* **8.** To assume an expression of consternation or disappointment: *His face fell.* **9.** To undergo conquest or capture, esp. as the result of an armed attack. **10a.** To experience defeat or ruin. **b.** To lose office. **11.** To slope downward. **12a.** To lessen in amount or degree: *The air pressure is falling.* **b.** To decline in financial value. **c.** To lose weight: *The child fell off to 60 pounds.* **13.** To diminish in pitch or volume. **14a.** To give in to temptation; sin. **b.** *Theology* To lose primordial innocence and happiness. Used of humanity as a result of the Fall. **c.** To lose one's chastity. **15.** To pass into a particular state, condition, or situation: *fall in love.* **16.** To occur at a specified time. **17.** To occur at a specified place: *The stress falls on the last syllable.* **18.** To come, as by chance: *fell among a band of thieves.* **19a.** To be given by assignment or distribution: *The task fell to me.* **b.** To be given by right or inheritance. **20.** To be included within the range or scope of something. **21.** To come into contact; strike: *My gaze fell on him.* **22.** To come out; issue: *Compliments fell from their lips.* **23.** To apply oneself: *fell to work.* **24.** To be born. Used chiefly of lambs. *—tr.* To cut down (a tree); fell. ❖ *n.* **1.** The act or an instance of falling. **2.** A sudden drop from a relatively erect to a less erect position. **3.** Something that has fallen: *a fall of hail.* **4a.** An amount that has fallen. **b.** The distance that something falls. **5.** Autumn. **6. falls** (*used with a sing. or pl. verb*) A waterfall. **7.** A downward movement or slope. **8.** Any of several pendent articles of dress, esp.: **a.** A veil hung from a woman's hat and down the back. **b.** An ornamental cascade of lace or trimming attached to a dress, usu. at the collar. **c.** A woman's hairpiece with long free-hanging hair. **9a.** An overthrow; a collapse. **b.** Armed capture of a place under siege. **10.** A reduction in value, amount, or degree. **11.** A marked, often sudden decline in status, rank, or importance. **12a.** A moral lapse. **b.** A loss of chastity. **13.** often **Fall** *Theology* The loss of innocence and grace resulting from Adam's eating the forbidden fruit in the Garden of Eden. **14.** *Sports* **a.** The act of throwing or forcing a wrestling opponent down on his or her back. **b.** Any of various wrestling maneuvers so used. **15. falls** *Nautical* The apparatus used to hoist and transfer cargo or lifeboats. **16.** The end of a cable, rope, or chain that is pulled by the power source in hoisting. **17a.** The birth of an animal, esp. a lamb. **b.** All the animals born at one birth; a litter. **18.** A family of woodcock in flight. **19.** *Botany* The outer series of perianth in the irises and related plants. ***—phrasal verbs:*** **fall apart 1.** To break down; collapse. **2.** To suffer a nervous breakdown. **fall away 1.** To withdraw one's friendship and support. **2.** To become gradually diminished in size. **3.** To drift off an established course. **fall back 1.** To give ground; retreat. **2.** To recede. **fall behind 1.** To fail to keep up a pace; lag behind. **2.** To be financially in arrears. **fall down** To fail to meet expectations; lag in performance. **fall for 1.** To become infatuated with; start to love. **2.** To be deceived or swindled by. **fall in 1.** To take one's place in a military formation. **2.** To sink inward; cave in. **fall off 1.** To become less; decrease. **2.** *Nautical* To change course to leeward. **fall on** (or **upon**) **1.** To attack suddenly and viciously. **2.** To meet with; encounter. **fall out 1a.** To leave a barracks, for example, in order to take one's place in a military formation. **b.** To leave a military formation. **2.** To quarrel. **3.** To happen; occur. **4.** To be readily explainable; follow logically or naturally: *These facts fall out nicely from the new theory.* **fall through** To fail; miscarry. **fall to** To begin an activity energetically. ***—idioms:*** **fall back on** (or **upon**) **1.** To rely on. **2.** To resort to. **fall flat 1.** To fail miserably when attempting to achieve a result. **2.** To have no effect. **fall foul** (or **afoul**) **1.** *Nautical* To collide. Used of vessels. **2.** To clash. **fall into line** To adhere to established rules or predetermined courses of action. **fall in with 1.** To agree with or be in harmony with. **2.** To associate or begin to associate with. **fall on deaf ears** To go unheeded; be ignored completely. **fall over (oneself)** To display inordinate, typically effusive, enthusiasm. **fall short 1.** To fail to attain a specified amount, level, or degree. **2.** To prove inadequate. [ME *fallen* < OE *feallan.*]

Fal•la (fäl′yä), **Manuel de** 1876–1946. Spanish composer whose music draws heavily on folk songs and Spanish exoticism.

fal•la•cious (fə-lā′shəs) *adj.* **1.** Containing or based on a fallacy. **2.** Tending to mislead; deceptive. **—fal•la′cious•ly** *adv.*

fal•la•cy (făl′ə-sē) *n., pl.* **-cies 1.** A false notion. **2.** A statement or argument based on a false or invalid inference. **3.** Incorrectness of reasoning or belief; erroneousness. **4.** The quality of being deceptive. [Alteration of ME *fallace* < OFr. < Lat. *fallācia*, deceit < *fallāx, fallāc-*, deceitful < *fallere*, to deceive.]

fal•lal (fă-lăl′, făl′ăl′) *n.* A showy article of dress. [?] **—fal•lal′er•y** *n.*

fall•back (fôl′băk′) *n.* **1a.** Something to which one can resort or retreat. **b.** A retreat. **2.** Something that falls back: *the fallback of a huge explosion.* ❖ *adj.* Of, relating to, or constituting a resort or place of retreat.

fall•board (fôl′bôrd′, -bōrd′) *n.* The hinged cover protecting the keyboard of a piano.

fall•fish (fôl′fĭsh′) *n., pl.* **fallfish** or **-fish•es** A small silvery freshwater fish *(Semotilus corporalis)* of streams and rivers in eastern North America.

fall guy *n. Slang* **1.** A scapegoat. **2.** A gullible victim; a dupe.

fal•li•ble (făl′ə-bəl) *adj.* **1.** Capable of making an error. **2.** Tending or likely to be erroneous: *fallible hypotheses.* [ME < Med.Lat. *fallibilis* < Lat. *fallere*, to deceive.] **—fal′li•bil′i•ty, fal′li•ble•ness** *n.* **—fal′li•bly** *adv.*

fall•ing-out (fô′lĭng-out′) *n., pl.* **fall•ings-out** or **fall•ing-outs** A disagreement; a quarrel.

fall•ing rhythm (fô′lĭng) *n.* A rhythmic pattern in which the stress regularly occurs on the first syllable of each foot, as in *Jack and Jill went up the hill.*

falling star *n.* See **meteor.**

fall line *n.* **1.** A line connecting the waterfalls of nearly parallel rivers that marks a drop in land level. **2.** The natural line of descent, as for skiing, between two points on a slope.

fall•off (fôl′ôf′, -ŏf′) *n.* A reduction or decrease.

fal•lo•pi•an tube also **Fal•lo•pi•an tube** (fə-lō′pē-ən) *n.* Either of a pair of slender ducts through which ova pass from the ovaries to the uterus in humans and higher mammals. [After Gabriele *Fallopio* (1523–62), Italian anatomist.]

fall•out (fôl′out′) *n.* **1a.** The slow descent of minute particles of debris in the atmosphere following an explosion, esp. the descent of radioactive debris after a nuclear explosion. **b.** Such particles. **2.** An incidental result or side effect.

fal•low (făl′ō) *adj.* **1.** Plowed but left unseeded during a growing season: *fallow farmland.* **2.** Characterized by inactivity. ❖ *n.* **1.** Fallow land. **2.** The act of plowing land and leaving it unseeded. **3.** The condition or period of being unseeded. ❖ *tr.v.* **-lowed, -low•ing, -lows 1.** To plow (land) without seeding it afterward. **2.** To plow and till (land), esp. to eradicate or reduce weeds. [ME *falow* < OE *fealh*, fallow land.] **—fal′low•ness** *n.*

fallow deer *n.* A small Eurasian deer *(Dama dama)* having a yellowish-red coat spotted with white in summer and broad flattened antlers in the male. [Obsolete *fallow*, reddish-yellow < ME *falow, falwe* < OE *fealu.*]

Fall River A city of SE MA on the RI border WNW of New Bedford. Pop. 91,938.

false (fôls) *adj.* **fals•er, fals•est 1.** Contrary to fact or truth. **2.** Deliberately untrue. **3.** Arising from mistaken ideas. **4.** Intentionally deceptive. **5.** Not keeping faith; treacherous. **6.** Not genuine or real. **7.** Erected temporarily, as for support during construction. **8.** Resembling but not accurately or properly designated as such: *a false thaw in January.* **9.** *Music* Of incorrect pitch. **10.** Unwise; imprudent. ❖ *adv.* In a treacherous or faithless manner. [ME *fals* < OE, counterfeit, and < OFr., false, both < Lat. *falsus* < p. part. of *fallere*, to deceive.] **—false′ly** *adv.* **—false′ness** *n.*

false alarm *n.* **1.** An emergency alarm that is set off unnecessarily. **2.** A signal or warning that is groundless.

false arrest *n.* Unlawful or unjustifiable arrest.

false fruit *n.* **1.** See **accessory fruit. 2.** See **pome.**

false-heart•ed (fôls′här′tĭd) *adj.* Of a deceitful nature; treacherous. **—false′-heart′ed•ness** *n.*

false•hood (fôls′ho͝od′) *n.* **1.** An untrue statement; a lie. **2.** The practice of lying. **3.** Lack of conformity to truth.

false imprisonment *n.* Detention or imprisonment of a person contrary to the provisions of law.

false indigo *n.* **1.** A shrub *(Amorpha fruticosa)* of eastern North America having compound leaves and purplish flowers. **2.** A plant *(Baptisia australis)* of the southeast United States having compound leaves and deep blue or purplish flowers.

false-mem•o•ry syndrome (fôls′mĕm′ə-rē) *n.* The belief that one remembers events, esp. traumatic events, that have not actually occurred. Not in scientific use.

false miterwort *n.* See **foamflower.**

false pregnancy *n.* A condition marked by physical signs and symptoms of pregnancy in the absence of conception.

false pretense *n. Law* False representation of fact or circumstance, calculated to mislead.

false rib *n.* Any of the lower ribs that do not unite directly with the sternum.

false Solomon's seal *n.* Any of several plants of the genus *Smilacina*, native to North America and Asia and having a plumelike cluster of small greenish-white flowers.

false start *n.* **1.** An illegal racing start in which one of the competitors begins moving before the starting signal. **2.** A misguided or unsuccessful attempt to begin something. **—false′-start′** *v.*

fal•set•to (fôl-sĕt′ō) *n., pl.* **-tos 1.** A male voice in an upper register beyond its normal range. **2.** One who sings or talks in this register. [Ital., dim. of *falso*, false < Lat. *falsus.* See FALSE.] **—fal•set′to** *adv.*

fals•ie (fôl′sē) *n. Informal* Padding or a pad worn inside a brassiere to make the breasts appear larger. Often used in the plural.

fal•si•fy (fôl′sə-fī′) *v.* **-fied, -fy•ing, -fies** *—tr.* **1.** To state un-

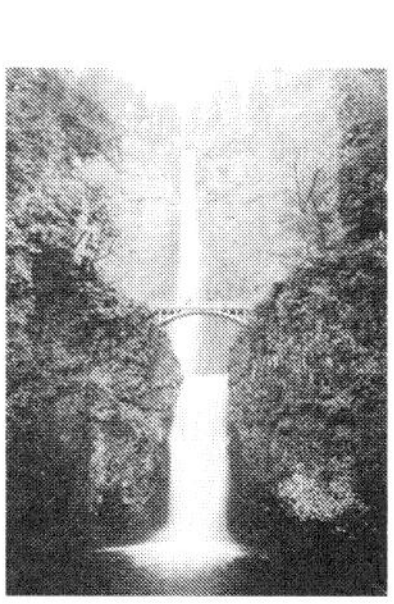

falls
Multnomah Falls, Columbia River Gorge, Oregon

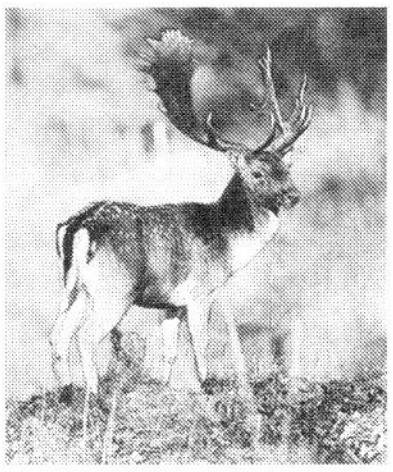

fallow deer
Dama dama

ă	pat	oi	boy
ā	pay	ou	out
âr	care	o͝o	took
ä	father	o͞o	boot
ĕ	pet	ŭ	cut
ē	be	ûr	urge
ĭ	pit	th	thin
ī	pie	*th*	this
îr	pier	hw	which
ŏ	pot	zh	vision
ō	toe	ə	about, item
ô	paw		

Stress marks:
′ (primary);
′ (secondary), as in
lexicon (lĕk′sĭ-kŏn′)

truthfully; misrepresent. **2a.** To make false by altering or adding to. **b.** To counterfeit; forge: *falsify a visa.* **3.** To declare or prove to be false. —*intr.* To make untrue statements; lie. [ME *falsifien* < OFr. *falsifier* < LLat. *falsificāre* : Lat. *falsus*, false; see FALSE + Lat. *-ficāre*, *-fy.*] —**fal′si•fi•ca′tion** (-fĭ-kā′shən) *n.* —**fal′si•fi′er** *n.*

fal•si•ty (fôl′sĭ-tē) *n.*, *pl.* **-ties 1.** The quality or condition of being false. **2.** Something false; a lie.

Fal•staff•i•an (fôl-stăf′ē-ən) *adj.* Characterized by joviality and conviviality. [After Sir John *Falstaff*, a character in *Henry IV* and *The Merry Wives of Windsor* by Shakespeare.]

Fal•ster (fäl′stər, fôl′-) An island of SE Denmark in the Baltic Sea off the S tip of Sjaelland.

falt•boat (fält′bōt′, fôlt′-) *n.* See **foldboat.** [Partial transl. of Ger. *Faltboot*, folding boat : *falten*, to fold (< MHGer. *valten* < OHGer. *faldan*) + *Boot*, boat.]

fal•ter (fôl′tər) *intr.v.* **-tered, -ter•ing, -ters 1.** To be unsteady in purpose or action, as from loss of courage or confidence; waver. **2.** To speak hesitatingly; stammer. **3a.** To move ineptly or haltingly; stumble. **b.** To operate or perform unsteadily or with a loss of effectiveness: *The engine faltered.* ❖ *n.* **1.** Unsteadiness in speech or action. **2.** A faltering sound. [ME *falteren*, to stagger, poss. < ON *faltrask*, to be puzzled, hesitate.] —**fal′ter•er** *n.* —**fal′ter•ing•ly** *adv.*

FAM *abbr.* Free and Accepted Masons

fame (fām) *n.* **1a.** Great renown. **b.** Public estimation; reputation. **2.** *Archaic* Rumor. ❖ *tr.v.* **famed, fam•ing, fames 1.** To make renowned or famous. **2.** *Archaic* To report to be. [ME < OFr. < Lat. *fāma.* See **bhā-** in App.]

famed (fāmd) *adj.* Having great fame. See Syns at **noted.**

fa•mil•ial (fə-mĭl′yəl) *adj.* **1.** Of or relating to a family. **2.** Occurring or tending to occur among members of a family, usu. by heredity: *familial traits; familial disease.*

fa•mil•iar (fə-mĭl′yər) *adj.* **1.** Often encountered or seen; common. **2.** Having fair knowledge; acquainted: *was familiar with those words.* **3.** Of established friendship; intimate. **4.** Natural and unstudied; informal. **5.** Taking undue liberties; presumptuous. **6.** Familial. **7.** Domesticated; tame. Used of animals. ❖ *n.* **1.** A close friend or associate. **2.** An attendant spirit, often taking animal form. **3.** One who performs domestic service in the household of a high official. **4.** A person who frequents a place. [ME < OFr. *familier* < Lat. *familiāris*, domestic < *familia*, family. See FAMILY.] —**fa•mil′iar•ly** *adv.*

fa•mil•iar•i•ty (fə-mĭl′yăr′ĭ-tē, -mĭl′ē-ăr′-) *n.*, *pl.* **-ties 1.** Considerable acquaintance with. **2.** Established friendship. **3a.** An excessively familiar or informal act; an impropriety. **b.** A sexual advance. **4.** The quality or condition of being familiar.

fa•mil•iar•ize (fə-mĭl′yə-rīz′) *tr.v.* **-ized, -iz•ing, -iz•es 1.** To make known, recognized, or familiar. **2.** To make acquainted with. —**fa•mil′iar•i•za′tion** (-yər-ĭ-zā′shən) *n.* —**fa•mil′iar•iz′er** *n.*

fam•i•ly (făm′ə-lē, făm′lē) *n.*, *pl.* **-lies 1a.** A fundamental social unit typically consisting of a parent or parents and their children. **b.** Two or more people who share goals and values, have commitments to one another, and reside usu. in the same place. **2.** All the members of a household under one roof. **3.** A group of persons sharing common ancestry. See Usage Note at **collective noun. 4.** Lineage, esp. distinguished lineage. **5.** A locally independent organized crime unit. **6a.** A group of like things; a class. **b.** A group of individuals derived from a common stock. **7.** *Biology* A taxonomic category of related organisms ranking below an order and above a genus. See table at **taxonomy. 8.** *Linguistics* A group of languages descended from the same parent language. **9.** *Mathematics* A set of functions or surfaces that can be generated by varying the parameters of a general equation. **10.** *Chemistry* A group of elements with similar chemical properties. **11.** *Chemistry* A vertical column in the periodic table of elements. ❖ *adj.* **1.** Of or relating to a family. **2.** Being suitable for a family. **3.** Of or relating to the practice of family medicine. [ME *familie* < Lat. *familia*, household < *famulus*, servant.]

family Bible *n.* A Bible with special pages to record births, deaths, and marriages.

family circle *n.* A section of theater seats that are less expensive than some others.

family leave *n.* An absence from work granted so that an employee can give care to a family member, such as a new baby.

family man *n.* **1.** A man having a wife and children. **2.** A man devoted to his family.

family medicine *n.* The branch of medicine that deals with provision of comprehensive health care to people of all ages, placing particular emphasis on the family unit.

family name *n.* See **surname** 1.

family planning *n.* The planned timing or prevention of pregnancy through the use of birth control.

family practice *n.* See **family medicine.**

family room *n.* A recreation room esp. for family use.

family style *adj.* Having food placed on the table at a sit-down meal so that participants serve themselves.

family tree *n.* **1.** A genealogical diagram of a family's ancestry. **2.** The ancestors and descendants of a family.

family values *pl.n.* The moral and social values traditionally

maintained and affirmed within a family.

fam•ine (făm′ĭn) *n.* **1.** A drastic wide-reaching food shortage. **2.** A drastic shortage; a dearth. **3.** Severe hunger; starvation. **4.** *Archaic* Extreme appetite. [ME < OFr. < *faim*, hunger < Lat. *famēs.*]

fam•ish (făm′ĭsh) *v.* **-ished, -ish•ing, -ish•es** —*tr.* **1.** To cause to endure severe hunger. **2.** To cause to starve to death. —*intr.* **1.** To endure severe deprivation, esp. of food. **2.** To undergo starvation and die. [ME *famishen*, alteration of *famen* < OFr. *afamer* < VLat. **affamāre* : Lat. *ad-*, *ad-* + Lat. *famēs*, hunger.] —**fam′ish•ment** *n.*

fa•mous (fā′məs) *adj.* **1.** Well or widely known. See Syns at **noted. 2.** First-rate; excellent. [ME < AN < Lat. *fāmōsus* < *fāma*, fame. See **bhā-** in App.] —**fa′mous•ness** *n.*

fa•mous•ly (fā′məs-lē) *adv.* **1.** In a way or to an extent that is well known: *famously well-made pizza.* **2.** With the result of becoming famous. **3.** Excellently; splendidly: *We got along famously.*

fam•u•lus (făm′yə-ləs) *n.*, *pl.* **-li** (-lī′) A private secretary or other close attendant. [Ger. < Lat.]

fan¹ (făn) *n.* **1.** A device for creating a current of air or a breeze, esp.: **a.** A machine using an electric motor to rotate thin rigid vanes to move air, as for cooling. **b.** A collapsible, usu. wedge-shaped device made of a light material. **2.** A machine for winnowing. **3.** Something resembling an open fan in shape: *a peacock's fan.* ❖ *v.* **fanned, fan•ning, fans** —*tr.* **1.** To move or cause a current of (air) with or as if with a fan. **2.** To direct a current of air or a breeze upon, esp. to cool. **3.** To stir (something) up by or as if by fanning: *fan a fire; fanned resentment.* **4.** To open (something) out into the shape of a fan. **5a.** To fire (an automatic gun) in a continuous sweep by keeping one's finger on the trigger. **b.** To fire (a nonautomatic gun) rapidly by chopping the hammer with the palm. **6.** To winnow. **7.** *Baseball* To strike out (a batter). —*intr.* **1.** To spread out like a fan: *The troops fanned out from the beachhead.* **2.** *Baseball* To strike out. [ME, winnowing fan < OE *fann* < Lat. *vannus.* See **wet-¹** in App.]

fan² (făn) *n.* An ardent devotee; an enthusiast. [Short for FANATIC.]

fa•nat•ic (fə-năt′ĭk) *n.* A person marked or motivated by an extreme unreasoning enthusiasm, as for a cause. ❖ *adj.* Fanatical. [Lat. *fānāticus*, inspired by orgiastic rites, relating to a temple < *fānum*, temple. See **dhēs-** in App.]

fa•nat•i•cal (fə-năt′ĭ-kəl) *adj.* Possessed with or motivated by excessive, irrational zeal. —**fa•nat′i•cal•ly** *adv.* —**fa•nat′i•cal•ness** *n.*

fa•nat•i•cism (fə-năt′ĭ-sĭz′əm) *n.* Excessive, irrational zeal.

fa•nat•i•cize (fə-năt′ĭ-sīz′) *v.* **-cized, -ciz•ing, -ciz•es** —*tr.* To make fanatical. —*intr.* To behave as a fanatic.

fan belt *n.* A taut rubber belt that transfers torque from the crankshaft to the shaft of the cooling fan on an engine.

fan•ci•er (făn′sē-ər) *n.* **1.** One who has a special enthusiasm for or interest in something. **2.** One who breeds a plant or an animal for those features held to be desirable.

fan•ci•ful (făn′sĭ-fəl) *adj.* **1.** Created in the fancy; unreal: *a fanciful story.* **2.** Tending to indulge in fancy: *a fanciful mind.* **3.** Showing invention or whimsy in design; imaginative. See Syns at **fantastic.** —**fan′ci•ful•ly** *adv.* —**fan′ci•ful•ness** *n.*

fan•cy (făn′sē) *n.*, *pl.* **-cies 1.** The mental faculty through which whims, visions, and fantasies are summoned up; imagination, esp. of a whimsical or fantastic nature. **2.** An image or a fantastic invention created by the mind. **3.** A capricious notion; a whim. **4.** A capricious liking or inclination. **5.** Critical sensibility; taste. **6.** Amorous or romantic attachment; love. **7a.** The enthusiasts of a sport or pursuit considered as a group. **b.** The sport or pursuit, such as boxing, engaging the interest of such a group. ❖ *adj.* **-ci•er, -ci•est 1.** Highly decorated. **2.** Arising in the fancy; capricious. **3.** Executed with skill; complex or intricate. **4.** Of superior grade; fine. **5.** Excessive or exorbitant. **6.** Bred for unusual qualities or special points. ❖ *tr.v.* **-cied, -cy•ing, -cies 1.** To visualize; imagine. **2.** To take a fancy to; like. **3.** To suppose; guess. [< ME *fantsy*, imagination, fantasy < *fantasie.* See FANTASY.] —**fan′ci•ly** *adv.* —**fan′ci•ness** *n.*

fancy dress *n.* A masquerade costume.

fan•cy-free (făn′sē-frē′) *adj.* **1.** Having no commitments or restrictions; carefree. **2.** Not in love or married; unattached.

fan•cy•work (făn′sē-wûrk′) *n.* Decorative needlework, such as embroidery.

fan•dan•go (făn-dăng′gō) *n.*, *pl.* **-gos 1.** An animated Spanish or Spanish-American dance in triple time. **2.** A piece of music for this dance. [Sp., poss. alteration of **fadango* < *fado* < Port., sad song. See FADO.]

fan•dom (făn′dəm) *n.* All the fans of a sport, activity, or famous person.

fan•fare (făn′fâr′) *n.* **1.** *Music* A loud flourish of brass instruments, esp. trumpets. **2.** A spectacular public display. [Fr., poss. of imit. orig.]

fan•far•o•nade (făn′făr-ə-nād′, -näd′) *n.* **1.** Bragging or blustering manner or behavior. **2.** A fanfare. [Fr. *fanfaronnade* < Sp. *fanfarronada*, bluster < *fanfarrón*, a braggart, perh. < Ar. *farfār*, talkative < *farfara*, to become agitated, become talkative.]

fan•fic (făn′fĭk′) *n. Informal* Fiction written by fans as an extension of an admired work, esp. a television show, often posted on the Internet or published in fanzines. [FAN² + FIC(TION).]

fang (făng) *n.* **1.** A long, pointed tooth, esp.: **a.** Any of the hollow or grooved teeth of a venomous snake with which it injects its poison. **b.** Any of the canine teeth of a carnivorous animal with which it seizes and tears its prey. **2.** A fanglike structure, esp. a chelicera of a venomous spider. **3.** The root of a tooth. [ME, booty, spoils, something seized < OE.] **—fanged** *adj.*

Fang (fäng, fäng, fän) *n., pl.* **Fang** or **Fangs 1.** A member of a people inhabiting Gabon, Equatorial Guinea, and Cameroon. **2.** The Bantu language of the Fang.

fan·ion (făn′yən) *n.* A small flag for marking a position, used esp. by surveyors or soldiers. [Fr., alteration of *fanillon*, dim. of *fanon*, maniple < OFr. < Frankish *fano.*]

fan·jet also **fan-jet** (făn′jĕt′) *n.* **1.** A jet engine that provides extra thrust by means of a ducted fan in its forward end that draws in extra air. **2.** An airplane with such an engine.

fan letter *n.* A piece of fan mail.

fan·light (făn′līt′) *n.* **1.** *Architecture* A half-circle window, often with sash bars arranged like the ribs of a fan. **2.** *Chiefly British* A transom.

fan mail *n.* Mail sent to a public figure by admirers.

Fan·nie Mae (făn′ē mā′) *n.* A security issued by the Federal National Mortgage Association and secured by a pool of federally insured and conventional mortgages. [Alteration of *F(ederal) N(ational) M(ortgage) A(ssociation).*]

fan·ny (făn′ē) *n., pl.* **-nies** *Slang* The buttocks. [Perh. < *Fanny*, a nickname for *Frances*.]

fanny pack *n.* A waist pack, esp. as worn with the pouch over the buttocks.

fan palm *n.* A palm tree having palmately divided fanlike leaves.

fan·tab·u·lous (făn-tăb′yə-ləs) *adj. Slang* Marvelously excellent. [Blend of FANTASTIC and FABULOUS.]

fan·tail (făn′tāl′) *n.* **1.** Any of a breed of domestic pigeons having a rounded fan-shaped tail. **2.** Any of several birds of the genus *Rhipidura* of eastern Asia and Australia, having a long fan-shaped tail. **3.** Any of a breed of goldfish having a wide fanlike double tail fin. **4.** A fanlike tail or end. **5.** *Nautical* The stern overhang of a ship. **—fan′tailed′** *adj.*

fan-tan (făn′tăn′) *n.* **1.** A Chinese betting game in which the players lay wagers on the number of counters that will remain when a hidden pile of them has been divided by four. **2.** A card game in which sevens and their equivalent are played in sequence and the first player out of cards wins. [Chin. *fān tān* : *fān*, turn, chance + *tān*, to spread out.]

fan·ta·sia (făn-tā′zhə, -zhē-ə, făn′tə-zē′ə) *n. Music* **1.** A free composition structured according to the composer's fancy. **2.** A medley of familiar themes, with variations and interludes. [Ital. < Lat. *phantasia*, fantasy. See FANTASY.]

fan·ta·sist (făn′tə-sĭst) *n.* One that creates a fantasy.

fan·ta·size (făn′tə-sīz′) *v.* **-sized, -siz·ing, -siz·es** *—tr.* To portray in the mind; imagine. *—intr.* To indulge in fantasies.

fan·tast (făn′tăst′) *n.* A visionary; a dreamer. [Ger. < Med.Lat. *phantasta* < Gk. *phantastēs*, boaster < *phantasiā*, imagination. See FANTASY.]

fan·tas·tic (făn-tăs′tĭk) also **fan·tas·ti·cal** (-tĭ-kəl) *adj.* **1.** Quaint or strange in form, conception, or appearance. **2a.** Unrestrainedly fanciful; extravagant. **b.** Bizarre, as in form or appearance; strange. **c.** Based on or existing only in fantasy; unreal. **3.** Wonderful or superb; remarkable. ❖ *n.* An eccentric person. [ME *fantastik*, imagined < OFr. *fantastique* < LLat. *phantasticus*, imaginary < Gk. *phantastikos*, able to create mental images < *phantazesthai*, to appear. See FANTASY.] **—fan′tas′ti·cal·i·ty** (-tĭ-kăl′ĭ-tē) *n.* **—fan·tas′ti·cal·ly** *adv.*

fan·tas·ti·cate (făn-tăs′tĭ-kāt′) *tr.v.* **-cat·ed, -cat·ing, -cates** To make fantastic. **—fan·tas′ti·ca′tion** *n.*

fan·ta·sy (făn′tə-sē, -zē) *n., pl.* **-sies 1.** The creative imagination; unrestrained fancy. **2.** Something, such as an invention, that is a creation of the fancy. **3.** A capricious or fantastic idea; a conceit. **4a.** Fiction characterized by highly fanciful or supernatural elements. **b.** An example of such fiction. **5a.** An imagined event or sequence of mental images usu. fulfilling a wish or psychological need. **b.** An unrealistic or improbable supposition. **6.** *Music* See **fantasia** 1. **7.** A coin issued esp. by a questionable authority and not intended for use as currency. **8.** *Obsolete* A hallucination. ❖ *tr.v.* **-sied, -sy·ing, -sies** To imagine; visualize. [ME *fantasie, fantsy* < OFr. *fantasie* < Lat. *phantasia* < Gk. *phantasiā*, appearance, imagination < *phantazesthai*, to appear < *phantos*, visible < *phainesthai, phan-*, to appear, passive of *phainein*, to show.]

fan·ta·sy·land (făn′tə-sē-lănd′, -zē-) *n.* A place conjured up by

the imagination, often populated by bizarre inhabitants.

Fan·te or **Fan·ti** (făn′tē, fän′-) *n., pl.* **Fante** or **Fanti** also **-tes** or **-tis 1.** A member of a people inhabiting Ghana. **2.** The variety of Akan spoken by this people.

fan·toc·ci·ni (făn′tə-chē′nē) *pl.n.* **1.** Puppets animated by moving wires or mechanical means. **2.** A show using such puppets. [Ital., pl. of *fantoccino*, dim. of *fantoccio*, puppet, augmentative of *fante*, child, short for *infante* < Lat. *īnfāns, infant-*, infant. See INFANT.]

fan·tod (făn′tŏd′) *n.* **1. fantods a.** A state of nervous irritability. **b.** Nervous movements caused by tension. **2.** An outburst of emotion; a fit. [?]

fan·tom (făn′təm) *n. & adj.* Variant of **phantom.**

fan vault *n.* A vault in which curving ribs radiate upward like a fan's ribs to form concave half cones that meet or nearly meet at the apex.

fan vaulting *n.* A series or system of fan vaults.

fan·wort (făn′wûrt′, -wôrt′) *n.* Any of several aquatic plants of the genus *Cabomba*, having fanlike submersed leaves and peltate floating leaves.

fan·zine (făn′zēn′) *n.* An amateur-produced magazine written for a subculture of enthusiasts devoted to a particular interest. [FAN² + (MAGA)ZINE.]

FAQ (făk) *n.* A list of frequently asked questions and their answers about a given subject. [f(requently) a(sked) q(uestions).]

far (fär) *adv.* **far·ther** (fär′thər), **far·thest** (fär′thĭst) or **fur·ther** (fûr′thər), **fur·thest** (fûr′thĭst) **1.** To, from, or at a considerable distance: *a cat that strayed far from home.* **2.** To a considerable degree; much: *felt far better yesterday.* **3.** Not at all; anything but: *far from a failure.* **4.** To an advanced point or stage: *a brilliant student who will go far.* ❖ *adj.* **farther, farthest** or **further, furthest 1a.** Being at considerable distance; remote: *a far country.* **b.** Going back a considerable extent in time: *the far past.* **2.** More distant than another: *the far corner.* **3.** Extensive or lengthy: *a far trek.* **4.** Far-seeing and comprehensive in thought or outlook. **5.** Marked by political views of the most advanced or extreme nature: *the far left.* **6.** Being on the right side of an animal or vehicle. **7.** Being the animal or vehicle on the right. **—idioms: by far** To the most extreme or evident degree. **far and away** By a great margin. **far and wide** Everywhere: *looked far and wide for him.* **far cry** A long way. **how far** To what degree, distance, or extent. **so far 1.** Up to the present moment. **2.** To a limited extent. **thus far** Up to this point; so far. [ME < OE *feor*. See **per¹** in App.]

far·ad (făr′əd, -ăd′) *n.* The unit of capacitance in the meter-kilogram-second system equal to the capacitance of a capacitor having a charge of one coulomb when a potential difference of one volt is applied.

far·a·day (făr′ə-dā′) *n.* The electric charge required to deposit or liberate 1 gram equivalent weight of a substance in electrolysis, approx. 9.6494 ×10⁴ coulombs.

Far·a·day (făr′ə-dā′, -dē), **Michael** 1791–1867. British physicist who discovered electromagnetic induction (1831).

Faraday effect *n.* The rotation of the plane of polarization of plane-polarized light passed through an isotropic medium in the direction of an applied magnetic field.

fa·rad·ic (fə-răd′ĭk) also **far·a·da·ic** (făr′ə-dā′ĭk) *adj.* Of, relating to, or using an intermittent asymmetrical alternating electric current produced by an induction coil.

far·a·dism (făr′ə-dĭz′əm) *n.* Faradization.

far·a·di·za·tion (făr′ə-dī-zā′shən) *n.* The application of faradic current to stimulate muscles and nerves.

far·a·dize (făr′ə-dīz′) *tr.v.* **-dized, -diz·ing, -diz·es** To treat or stimulate (a muscle or nerve) with faradic current.

far·an·dole (făr′ən-dōl′) *n.* **1.** A spirited circle dance of Provençal derivation. **2.** The music for this circle dance. [Fr. < Provençal *farandoulo*; akin to Sp. *farándula*, troupe of traveling comedians.]

far·a·way (făr′ə-wā′) *adj.* **1.** Very distant; remote. **2.** Abstracted; dreamy: *a faraway look.*

farce (färs) *n.* **1a.** A humorous play having a highly improbable plot and exaggerated characters. **b.** The branch of literature constituting such works. **c.** The broad or spirited humor characteristic of such works. **2.** A ludicrous empty show; a mockery: *The fixed election was a farce.* **3.** A seasoned stuffing, as for roasted turkey. ❖ *tr.v.* **farced, farc·ing, farc·es 1.** To pad or fill out (a speech, for example) with jokes or witticisms. **2.** To stuff, as for roasting. [ME *farse*, stuffing < OFr. *farce*, stuffing, interpolation, interlude < VLat. *farsa* < fem. of Lat. *farsus*, var. of *fartus*, p. part. of *farcīre*, to stuff.]

far·ceur (fär-sœr′) *n.* **1.** One who acts in or writes a farce. **2.** A comic; a wag. [Fr. < OFr. < *farcer*, to joke < *farce*, farce. See FARCE.]

far·ci or **far·cie** (fär-sē′) *adj.* Stuffed, esp. with finely ground meat: *mushrooms farci.* [Fr., p. part. of *farcir*, to stuff < OFr. < Lat. *farcīre*.]

far·ci·cal (fär′sĭ-kəl) *adj.* **1.** Of or relating to farce. **2a.** Resembling a farce; ludicrous. **b.** Ridiculously clumsy; absurd. **—far′ci·cal′i·ty** (-kăl′ĭ-tē), **far′ci·cal·ness** *n.* **—far′ci·cal·ly** *adv.*

far·cy (fär′sē) *n.* A chronic form of glanders that affects chiefly the skin and superficial lymph vessels. [ME *farsi, farsin* < OFr. *farcin* < Lat. *farcīmen*, sausage < *farcīre*, to stuff.]

fanlight

fan vaulting
ceiling of Washington
National Cathedral

far·del (fär′dl) *n.* **1.** A pack; a bundle. **2.** A burden. [ME < OFr., dim. of *farde*, package < Ar. *farda*, single piece, bundle < *farada*, to be separate.]

fare (fâr) *intr.v.* **fared, far·ing, fares 1.** To get along: *How are you faring?* **2.** To happen or develop: *How does it fare with you?* **3.** To travel; go. **4.** To dine; eat. ❖ *n.* **1.** A transportation charge, as for a bus. **2.** A passenger transported for a fee. **3.** Food and drink; diet: *simple fare.* [ME *faren* < OE *faran.* See **per-²** in App.] —**far′er** *n.*

Far East The countries and regions of E and SE Asia, esp. China, Japan, North Korea, South Korea, and Mongolia. —**Far Eastern** *adj.*

fare-thee-well (fâr′thē-wĕl′) *n.* **1.** A condition of utmost perfection. **2.** The most extreme degree. [< *fare thee well*, may it go well with you, goodbye.]

fare·well (fâr-wĕl′) *interj.* Used to express goodbye. ❖ *n.* **1.** An acknowledgment at parting; a goodbye. **2.** The act of departing or taking leave. [ME *fare wel* : *fare*, imper. of *faren*, to fare; see FARE + *wel*, well; see WELL².]

Fare·well (fâr-wĕl′, fär′wĕl′), **Cape** The S point of Greenland.

far·fal·le (fär-fäl′lā) *n.* Pasta in the shape of bow ties. [Ital., pl. of *farfalla*, butterfly, of imit. orig.]

far·fel or **far·fal** (fär′fəl) *n.* Noodles shaped like small grains or pellets. [Yiddish *farfl* < MHGer. *varveln.*]

far-fetched (fär′fĕcht′) *adj.* Not readily believable because of improbable elements therein: *a far-fetched excuse.*

far-flung (fär′flŭng′) *adj.* **1.** Remote; distant. **2.** Widely distributed; wide-ranging.

Far·go (fär′gō) A city of E ND on the Red R. E of Bismarck; founded 1871. Pop. 90,599.

far-gone (fär′gôn′, -gŏn′) *adj.* Very close to the end.

Fa·ri·da·bad (fə-rē′də-bäd′) A city of N-central India SSE of New Delhi. Pop. 330,864.

fa·ri·na (fə-rē′nə) *n.* Fine meal prepared from cereal grain and other plant products and often used as a cooked cereal. [ME < Lat. *farīna* < *far*, a kind of grain.]

far·i·na·ceous (fär′ə-nā′shəs) *adj.* **1.** Made from, rich in, or consisting of starch. **2.** Having a mealy or powdery texture. [< Lat. *farīnāceus*, mealy < *farīna*, farina. See FARINA.]

far·i·nose (fär′ə-nōs′) *adj.* **1.** Similar to or yielding farina. **2.** *Biology* Covered with mealy dust or powder. [LLat. *farīnōsus*, mealy < Lat. *farīna*, farina. See FARINA.]

far·kle·ber·ry (fär′kəl-bĕr′ē) *n.* A shrub or small tree (*Vaccinium arboreum*) of the southeast United States having hard black berries. [*farkle* (of unknown orig.) + BERRY.]

farm (färm) *n.* **1.** A tract of land cultivated for agricultural production. **2a.** A tract of land devoted to the raising and breeding of domestic animals. **b.** An area of water devoted to the raising, breeding, or production of an aquatic animal. **3.** An area of land devoted to storage or the emplacement of a group of devices. **4.** *Baseball* A minor-league club affiliated with a major-league club. **5.** *Obsolete* **a.** The system of leasing out the rights of collecting and retaining taxes in a certain district. **b.** A district so leased. ❖ *v.* **farmed, farm·ing, farms** —*tr.* **1.** To cultivate or produce a crop on. **2.** To pay a fixed sum in order to have the right to collect and retain profits from (a business, for example). **3.** To turn over (a business, for example) to another in return for a fixed sum. —*intr.* To engage in farming. —***phrasal verb:*** **farm out 1.** To send (work, for example) from a central point to be done elsewhere. **2.** *Baseball* To assign (a player) to a minor-league team. [ME, leased property < OFr. *ferme* < Med.Lat. *firma*, fixed payment < Lat. *firmāre*, to establish < *firmus*, firm.]

farm·er (fär′mər) *n.* **1.** One who works on or operates a farm. **2.** One who has paid for the right to collect and retain certain revenues or profits. **3.** A simple, unsophisticated person; a bumpkin.

Farmer, Fannie Merritt 1857–1915. Amer. cookery expert who edited the *Boston Cooking School Cook Book* (1896), later revised as the *Fannie Farmer Cookbook.*

Farmer, James Leonard 1920–99. Amer. civil rights leader who founded the Congress of Racial Equality (1942).

farmer cheese *n.* An unripened cheese similar to cottage cheese but drier and firmer in texture.

farm·er's lung (fär′mərz) *n.* An occupational disease affecting the lungs and characterized by shortness of breath caused by an allergic reaction to fungal spores in moldy hay dust.

farm hand *n.* A hired farm laborer.

farm·house (färm′hous′) *n.* A dwelling on a farm.

Far·ming·ton Hills (fär′mĭng-tən) A city of SE MI, a suburb of Detroit. Pop. 82,111.

farm·land (färm′lănd′, -lənd) *n.* Land suitable or used for farming.

farm·stead (färm′stĕd′) *n.* A farm, including its land and buildings.

farm·yard (färm′yärd′) *n.* An area surrounded by or adjacent to farm buildings.

far·o (fâr′ō) *n.* A card game in which the players lay wagers on the top card of the dealer's pack. [Alteration of PHARAOH.]

Far·oe Islands (fâr′ō) See **Faeroe Islands.**

Far·o·ese or **Faer·o·ese** (fâr′ō-ēz′, -ēs′) *n., pl.* **Faroese** or **Faeroese 1.** A member of the Scandinavian people inhabiting the Faeroe Islands. **2.** The North Germanic language spoken by

Fannie Farmer

the inhabitants of the Faeroe Islands. —**Fa′ro·ese′** *adj.*

far-off (fär′ôf′, -ŏf′) *adj.* Remote in space or time.

fa·ro·li·to (fär′ə-lē′tō, -tô) *n., pl.* **-tos** *New Mexico* See **luminaria 1.** [Sp., paper lantern, dim. of *farol*, lantern < *faro*, lighthouse < Lat. *pharus* < *Pharus*, Pharos.]

fa·rouche (fä-rōōsh′) *adj.* **1.** Fierce; wild. **2.** Sullen and withdrawn. [Fr. < OFr. *faroche*, alteration of *forasche* < LLat. *forāsticus*, belonging outside < Lat. *forās*, out of doors. See FOREIGN.]

Fa·rouk I also **Fa·ruk I** (fə-rōōk′) 1920–65. King of Egypt (1936–52) who was overthrown by a coup d'état.

far-out (fär′out′) *adj. Slang* Extremely unconventional.

far point *n.* The farthest point at which an object can be seen distinctly by the eye.

Far·quhar (fär′kwər), **George** 1678–1707. Irish playwright whose comedic works include *The Beaux' Stratagem* (1707).

far·rag·i·nous (fə-răj′ə-nəs) *adj.* Composed of a variety of substances. [< Lat. *farrāgō, farrāgin-*, medley. See FARRAGO.]

far·ra·go (fə-rä′gō, -rā′-) *n., pl.* **-goes** An assortment or a medley; a conglomeration. [Lat. *farrāgō*, mixed fodder, hodgepodge < *far, farr-*, a kind of grain.]

Far·ra·gut (făr′ə-gət), **David Glasgow** 1801–70. Amer. admiral who commanded Union ships on various Civil War missions, including the capture of New Orleans (1862).

Far·ra·khan (făr′ə-kän′), **Louis** Orig. Louis Eugene Wolcott. b. 1933. Amer. religious, cultural, and political leader. In 1997 he became the leader of the Nation of Islam.

far-reach·ing (fär′rē′chĭng) *adj.* Having a wide range, influence, or effect: *the far-reaching implications.*

Far·rell (făr′əl), **Eileen** b. 1920. Amer. soprano noted for her voice of exceptional power and clarity.

Farrell, James Thomas 1904–79. Amer. writer best known for his *Studs Lonigan* trilogy of novels (1932–35).

far·ri·er (făr′ē-ər) *n.* A person who shoes horses. [Obsolete Fr. *ferrier* < Lat. *ferrārius*, of iron, blacksmith < *ferrum*, iron.] —**far′ri·er·y** *n.*

far·row¹ (făr′ō) *n.* A litter of pigs. ❖ *v.* **-rowed, -row·ing, -rows** —*tr.* To give birth to (a litter of pigs). —*intr.* To produce a litter of pigs. [Ult. < OE *fearh*, pig. See **porko-** in App.]

far·row² (făr′ō) *adj.* Not pregnant. Used of a cow. [ME *ferow.*]

Fars (färz, färs) or **Far·si·stan** (fär′sĭ-stän′, -stän′) A historical region of S Iran along the Persian Gulf; roughly coextensive with ancient Pars, conquered by Arabs in the 7th cent.

far·see·ing (fär′sē′ĭng) *adj.* **1.** Prudent; foresighted. **2.** Able to see far; keen-sighted.

Far·si (fär′sē) *n., pl.* **-sis 1.** The modern Iranian language; Persian. **2a.** A native speaker of Farsi. **b.** A member of the predominant ethnic group of Iran. [Pers. *fārsī*, alteration (influenced by Ar. *Fāris*, Persia) of *pārsī* < MPers. *pārsīg.*]

far·sight·ed or **far-sight·ed** (fär′sī′tĭd) *adj.* **1.** Able to see distant objects better than objects at close range; hyperopic. **2.** Capable of seeing to a great distance. **3.** Planning prudently for the future; foresighted. —**far′sight′ed·ly** *adv.* —**far′sight′ed·ness** (fär′sī′tĭd-nĭs) *n.* See **hyperopia.**

fart (färt) *Vulgar Slang intr.v.* **fart·ed, fart·ing, farts 1.** To expel intestinal gas through the anus; break wind. **2.** To fool around; waste time. ❖ *n.* **1.** A discharge of intestinal gas. **2.** A person regarded as annoying or foolish. [ME *farten* < OE **feortan.* See **perd-** in App.]

far·ther (fär′thər) *Usage Problem adv.* A comparative of **far. 1.** To or at a more distant or remote point. **2.** To or at a more advanced point or stage: *I went no farther that day.* **3.** To a greater extent or degree: *carried the idea farther.* ❖ *adj.* A comparative of **far.** More distant; remoter. [ME, var. (influenced by *far*, far) of *further*; see FURTHER.]

USAGE NOTE *Farther* and *further* have been used interchangeably by many writers since the Middle English period. According to a rule of relatively recent origin, however, *farther* should be reserved for physical distance and *further* for advancement along a nonphysical dimension. Thus 74 percent of the Usage Panel prefers *farther* in the sentence *If you are planning to drive any farther than Ukiah, you'd better carry chains;* whereas 64 percent prefers *further* in the sentence *We won't be able to answer these questions until we are further along in our research.* In many cases, however, the distinction is not easy to draw.

far·ther·most (fär′thər-mōst′) *adj.* Most distant; farthest.

far·thest (fär′thĭst) *adj.* A superlative of **far.** Most remote or distant. ❖ *adv.* A superlative of **far. 1.** To or at the most distant or remote point. **2.** To or at the most advanced point or stage. **3.** By the greatest extent or degree. [ME *ferthest*, superl. of *farther*. See FARTHER.]

far·thing (fär′thĭng) *n.* **1.** A coin formerly used in Great Britain worth one fourth of a penny. **2.** Something of very little value. [ME *ferthing* < OE *fēorthung.* See **kʷetwer-** in App.]

far·thin·gale (fär′thĭn-gāl′, -thĭng-) *n.* A support, such as a hoop, worn beneath a skirt to extend it horizontally from the waist, used by European women in the 16th and 17th centuries. [Alteration of obsolete *verdynggale* < OFr. *verdugale* < OSpan. *verdugado* < *verdugo*, stick, shoot of a tree < *verde*, green < Lat. *viridis* < *virēre*, to be green.]

fart·lek (färt′lĕk) *n.* An athletic training technique, used esp. in running, in which periods of intense effort alternate with periods of less strenuous effort in a continuous workout. [Swed., speed play : *fart*, running, speed (< *fara*, to go, move < ON; see **per-**² in App.) + *lek*, play (< *leka*, to play < ON *leika*).]

Fa•ruk I (fə-ro͞ok′) See **Farouk I.**

Far West A region of the US orig. comprising all territories W of the Mississippi R.; now generally restricted to the area W of the Great Plains. —**Far Western** *adj.*

FAS *abbr.* **1.** fetal alcohol syndrome **2.** free alongside ship

fas•ces (făs′ēz′) *pl.n.* A bundle of rods bound around an ax with the blade projecting, carried before ancient Roman magistrates as an emblem of authority. [Lat. *fascēs*, pl. of *fascis*, bundle.]

fas•ci•a (făsh′ē-ə) *n., pl.* **fas•ci•ae** (făsh′ē-ē′, fā′shē-ē) **1.** *Anatomy* A sheet or band of fibrous tissue that envelops, separates, or binds together muscles, organs, and other soft structures of the body. **2.** A broad and distinct band of color. **3.** (*also* fā′shē-ə) *Architecture* A flat horizontal band or member between moldings, esp. in a classical entablature. **4.** (fā′shə) *Chiefly British* The dashboard of a motor vehicle. [Lat., band.] —**fas′ci•al** *adj.*

fas•ci•ate (făsh′ē-āt′) also **fas•ci•at•ed** (-ā′tĭd) *adj.* **1.** *Botany* Abnormally flattened or coalesced, as certain stems. **2.** *Zoology* Marked by broad bands of color, as certain insects. [Lat. *fasciātus* < *fascia*, band.]

fas•ci•a•tion (făs′ē-ā′shən, făsh′ē-) *n.* **1.** The act of binding up or fastening, as with bandages. **2.** The manner in which something is bound up or fastened. **3.** *Botany* An abnormal flattening or coalescence of stems, as in broccoli.

fas•ci•cle (făs′ĭ-kəl) *n.* **1.** A small bundle. **2.** One of the parts of a book published in separate sections. **3.** *Botany* A bundle or cluster of stems, flowers, or leaves. **4.** See **fasciculus.** [Lat. *fasciculus*, dim. of *fascis*, bundle.] —**fas′ci•cled** *adj.*

fas•cic•u•lar (fə-sĭk′yə-lər) *adj.* Of, relating to, or composed of fascicles. —**fas•cic′u•lar•ly** *adv.*

fas•cic•u•late (fə-sĭk′yə-lĭt) also **fas•cic•u•lat•ed** (-lā′tĭd) *adj.* Arranged in or formed of fascicles; fascicular. —**fas•cic′u•late•ly** *adv.* —**fas•cic′u•la′tion** *n.*

fas•ci•cule (făs′ĭ-kyo͞ol′) *n.* See **fascicle** 2.

fas•cic•u•lus (fə-sĭk′yə-ləs) *n., pl.* **-li** (-lī′) A bundle of anatomical fibers, as of muscle. [Lat., fascicle. See FASCICLE.]

fas•ci•nate (făs′ə-nāt′) *v.* **-nat•ed, -nat•ing, -nates** —*tr.* **1.** To hold an intense interest or attraction for. See Syns at **charm. 2.** To hold motionless; spellbind. **3.** *Obsolete* To bewitch. —*intr.* To be irresistibly charming or attractive. [Lat. *fascināre, fascināt-*, to cast a spell on < *fascinum*, an evil spell, a phallic-shaped amulet.]

fas•ci•nat•ing (făs′ə-nā′tĭng) *adj.* Possessing the power to charm or allure; captivating. —**fas′ci•nat′ing•ly** *adv.*

fas•ci•na•tion (făs′ə-nā′shən) *n.* **1.** The capability of eliciting intense interest or of being very attractive. **2.** The state of being intensely interested or attracted: *listened in fascination.* **3.** An attractive, intensely interesting quality or trait.

fas•ci•na•tor (făs′ə-nā′tər) *n.* **1.** One that fascinates. **2.** A woman's head scarf.

fas•cine (fă-sēn′, fə-) *n.* A cylindrical bundle of sticks bound together for use in construction, as of fortresses, earthworks, sea walls, or dams. [Fr. < Lat. *fascīna* < *fascis*, bundle.]

fas•cism (făsh′ĭz′əm) *n.* **1.** often **Fascism a.** A system of government marked by a totalitarian dictator, socioeconomic controls, suppression of the opposition, and usu. a policy of belligerent nationalism and racism. **b.** A political philosophy or movement based on or advocating such a system. **2.** Oppressive dictatorial control. [Ital. *fascismo* < *fascio*, group < LLat. *fascium* < Lat. *fascis*, bundle.]

fas•cist (făsh′ĭst) *n.* **1.** often **Fascist** An advocate or adherent of fascism. **2.** A reactionary or dictatorial person. ❖ *adj.* **1.** often **Fascist** Of, advocating, or practicing fascism. **2. Fascist** Of or relating to the Fascisti. [Ital. *fascista* < *fascio*, group. See FASCISM.] —**fas•cis′tic** (fə-shĭs′tĭk) *adj.*

Fa•scis•ti (fä-shē′stē) *pl.n.* The members of a political party that controlled Italy under Benito Mussolini from 1922 to 1943. [Ital., pl. of *fascista*, fascist. See FASCIST.]

fash•ion (făsh′ən) *n.* **1.** The prevailing style or custom, as in dress. **2.** Something, such as a garment, that is in the current mode. **3.** The style of the social elite. **4a.** Manner or mode; way. **b.** A personal, often idiosyncratic manner. See Syns at **method. 5.** Kind or variety; sort. **6.** Shape or form; configuration. ❖ *tr.v.* **-ioned, -ion•ing, -ions 1.** To give shape or form to; make. **2.** To train or influence into a particular state or character. **3.** To adapt, as to a purpose or occasion; accommodate. **4.** *Obsolete* To contrive. —***idiom:* after** (or **in**) **a fashion** In some way or other, esp. to a limited extent. [ME *facioun* < OFr. *façon*, appearance, manner < Lat. *factiō, factiōn-*, a making < *factus*, p. part. of *facere*, to make, do. See **dhē-** in App.] —**fash′ion•er** *n.*

fash•ion•a•ble (făsh′ə-nə-bəl) *adj.* **1.** Conforming to the current style; stylish. **2.** Associated with or frequented by persons of fashion. ❖ *n.* A stylish person. —**fash′ion•a•bil′i•ty, fash′ion•a•ble•ness** *n.* —**fash′ion•a•bly** *adv.*

fashion plate *n.* **1.** A person who consistently wears the latest fashions. **2.** An illustration of current styles in dress.

fast¹ (făst) *adj.* **fast•er, fast•est 1.** Acting, moving, or capable of acting or moving quickly; swift. **2a.** Accomplished in relatively little time: *a fast visit.* **b.** Acquired quickly with little effort and sometimes unscrupulously: *made a fast buck.* **3.** Quick to understand or learn: *a class for the faster students.* **4.** Indicating a time somewhat ahead of the actual time: *The clock is fast.* **5.** Adapted to or suitable for rapid movement. **6.** Designed for or compatible with a short exposure time: *fast film.* **7a.** Dissipated; wild: *a fast crowd.* **b.** Flouting moral standards; sexually promiscuous. **8.** Resistant, as to destruction or fading: *fast colors.* **9.** Firmly fixed or fastened: *a fast grip.* **10.** Fixed firmly in place; secure. **11.** Firm in loyalty: *fast friends* **12.** Lasting; permanent. **13.** Deep; sound: *in a fast sleep.* ❖ *adv.* **faster, fastest 1.** In a secure manner; tightly: *hold fast.* **2.** To a sound degree; deeply: *fast asleep.* **3.** In a rapid manner; quickly. **4.** In quick succession. **5.** Ahead of the correct or expected time. **6.** In a dissipated, immoderate way. **7.** *Archaic* Close by; near. [ME < OE *fæst*, firm, fixed.]

SYNONYMS *fast, rapid, swift, fleet, speedy, quick, hasty, expeditious* These adjectives refer to something marked by great speed. *Fast* and *rapid* are often used interchangeably, though *fast* is more often applied to the person or thing in motion, and *rapid* to the activity or movement involved: *a fast runner; rapid strides. Swift* suggests smoothness and sureness of movement (*a swift current*), and *fleet* lightness of movement (*The cheetah is the fleetest of animals*). *Speedy* refers to velocity (*a speedy train*) or to promptness or hurry (*a speedy resolution to the problem*). *Quick* most often applies to what takes little time or to what is prompt: *a quick snack; your quick reaction. Hasty* implies hurried action (*a hasty visit*) and often a lack of care or thought (*regretted the hasty decision*). *Expeditious* suggests rapid efficiency: *sent the package by the most expeditious means.* See also Syns at **faithful.**

fast² (făst) *intr.v.* **fast•ed, fast•ing, fasts 1.** To abstain from food. **2.** To eat very little or abstain from certain foods, esp. as a religious discipline. ❖ *n.* **1.** The act or practice of fasting. **2.** A period of fasting. [ME *fasten* < OE *fæstan.*]

fast•back (făst′băk′) *n.* An automobile designed with a curving downward slope from roof to rear.

fast•ball (făst′bôl′) *n. Baseball* A pitch thrown at the pitcher's maximum speed.

fas•ten (făs′ən) *v.* **-tened, -ten•ing, -tens** —*tr.* **1.** To attach firmly to something else, as by pinning or nailing. **2a.** To make fast or secure. **b.** To close, as by fixing firmly in place. **3.** To fix or direct steadily: *fastened her gaze on me.* **4.** To place; attribute. **5.** To impose (oneself) without welcome. —*intr.* **1.** To become attached, fixed, or joined. **2.** To take firm hold; cling fast. **3.** To focus steadily; concentrate. [ME *fastnen* < OE *fæstnian.*] —**fas′ten•er** *n.*

fas•ten•ing (făs′ə-nĭng) *n.* Something, such as a hook, used to attach one thing to another firmly.

fast food *n.* Inexpensive food, such as hamburgers, prepared and served quickly. —**fast′-food′** (făst′fo͞od′) *adj.*

fast-for•ward or **fast forward** (făst-fôr′wərd) *n.* **1a.** A function on a recording device, such as a videocassette player, that permits rapid advancement of the tape. **b.** The mechanism, such as a button, that activates this function. **2.** *Informal* A rapidly changing situation. —**fast•for′ward** *v.*

fas•tid•i•ous (fă-stĭd′ē-əs, fə-) *adj.* **1.** Possessing or displaying meticulous attention to detail. **2.** Difficult to please; exacting. **3.** Excessively scrupulous or sensitive, esp. in matters of taste or propriety. [ME, squeamish, particular, haughty < OFr. *fastidieux* < Lat. *fastīdiōsus* < *fastīdium*, squeamishness, haughtiness, prob. < *fastus*, disdain.] —**fas•tid′i•ous•ly** *adv.* —**fas•tid′i•ous•ness** *n.*

fas•tig•i•ate (fă-stĭj′ē-ĭt) also **fas•tig•i•at•ed** (-ē-ā′tĭd) *adj.* Having erect branches tapering toward the top, as in the Lombardy poplar. [Med.Lat. *fastīgiātus*, high < Lat. *fastīgium*, apex, height.] —**fas•tig′i•ate•ly** *adv.*

fas•tig•i•um (fă-stĭj′ē-əm) *n.* The period of maximum severity of a disease or fever. [Lat. *fastīgium*, apex, height.]

fast lane *n. Informal* A reckless, self-indulgent, and free-spending sphere of activity. —**fast′-lane′** (făst′lān′) *adj.*

fast•ness (făst′nĭs) *n.* **1.** The condition or quality of being fast, esp.: **a.** Firmness; security. **b.** Rapidity; swiftness. **2.** The quality or condition of color retention; colorfastness. **3a.** A secure or fortified place. **b.** A remote, secret place.

fast one *n. Informal* A shrewd trick or swindle; a deceitful or treacherous act.

fast-talk (făst′tôk′) *tr.v.* **-talked, -talk•ing, -talks** *Informal* To persuade, mislead, or obtain with a smooth line of talk: *fast-talked him out of his money.* —**fast′-talk′er** *n.*

fast track *n. Informal* The quickest and most direct route to achieve a goal, as in professional advancement. —**fast′-track′** (făst′trăk′) *adj. & v.* —**fast track′er** *n.*

fat (făt) *n.* **1a.** The ester of glycerol and fatty acids. **b.** Any of various organic compounds constituting the esters of glycerol and fatty acids. **c.** A mixture of such compounds occurring in organic tissue, esp. in the adipose tissue of animals and in the seeds, nuts, and fruits of plants. **d.** Animal tissue containing such substances. **e.** A solidified animal or vegetable oil. **2.** Obesity; corpulence. **3.** The best or richest part. **4.** Unnecessary excess. ❖ *adj.* **fat•ter, fat•test 1.** Having much or too much fat or flesh; plump or obese. **2.** Full of fat or oil; greasy. **3.** Abounding in desirable elements. **4.** Fertile or productive; rich. **5.** Having an abundance

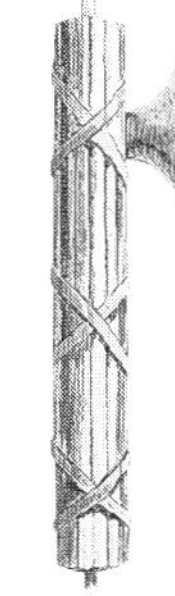

fasces
19th-century engraving

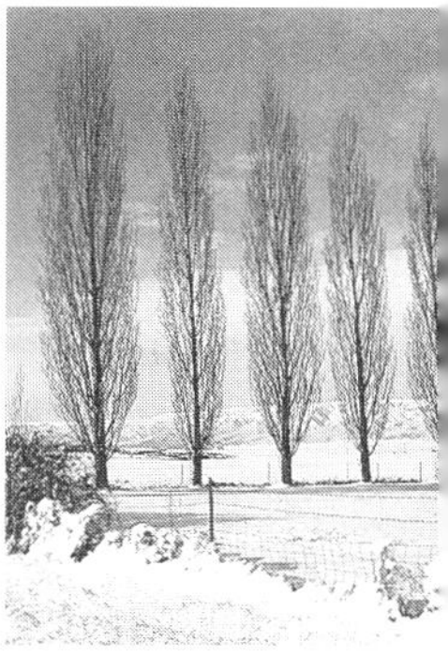

fastigiate
row of poplars in winter

ă pat	oi boy
ā pay	ou out
âr care	o͝o took
ä father	o͞o boot
ĕ pet	ŭ cut
ē be	ûr urge
ĭ pit	th thin
ī pie	*th* this
îr pier	hw which
ŏ pot	zh vision
ō toe	ə about, item
ô paw	

Stress marks:
′ (primary);
′ (secondary), as in
lexicon (lĕk′sĭ-kŏn′)

or amplitude; well-stocked. **6a.** Yielding profit or plenty; lucrative or rewarding. **b.** Prosperous; wealthy. **7a.** Thick; large. **b.** Puffed up; swollen. ❖ *tr. & intr.v.* **fat•ted, fat•ting, fats** To make or become fat; fatten. —*idiom:* **fat chance** *Slang* Very little or no chance. [ME < OE *fætt,* fatted. See **peiə-** in App.] —**fat′ly** *adv.* —**fat′ness** *n.*

SYNONYMS *fat, obese, corpulent, fleshy, portly, stout, pudgy, rotund, plump, chubby* These adjectives mean having an abundance and often an excess of flesh. *Fat* implies excessive weight and generally has negative connotations: *was getting fat and decided to exercise. Obese* and *corpulent* imply gross overweight: *"a woman of robust frame . . . though stout, not obese"* (Charlotte Brontë). *He was corpulent but surprisingly graceful. Fleshy* implies a not necessarily excessive abundance of flesh: *firm fleshy arms. Portly* refers to bulk combined with a stately or imposing bearing: *"a portly, rubicund man of middle age"* (Winston Churchill). *Stout* denotes a thickset, bulky figure: *a painting of stout peasants. Pudgy* means short and fat: *pudgy fingers. Rotund* suggests roundness of figure, often in a squat person: *"this pink-faced rotund specimen of prosperity"* (George Eliot). *Plump* and *chubby* apply to a pleasing fullness: *a plump toddler; chubby cheeks.*

fa•tal (fāt′l) *adj.* **1.** Causing or capable of causing death. **2.** Causing ruin or destruction; disastrous. **3.** Of decisive importance; fateful. **4.** Concerning or determining one's fate: *the fatal thread of life.* **5.** *Obsolete* Having been destined; fated. [ME, fateful < OFr. < Lat. *fātālis* < *fātum,* prophecy, doom. See **FATE.**]

fa•tal•ism (fāt′l-ĭz′əm) *n.* **1.** The doctrine that all events are predetermined and unalterable. **2.** Acceptance of this belief. —**fa′tal•ist** *n.* —**fa′tal•is′tic** *adj.* —**fa′tal•is′ti•cal•ly** *adv.*

fa•tal•i•ty (fā-tăl′ĭ-tē, fə-) *n., pl.* **-ties 1a.** A death resulting from an accident or a disaster. **b.** One killed in such an occurrence. **2.** The ability to cause death or disaster. **3.** The quality of being determined by fate. **4.** A decree made by fate; destiny. **5.** The quality of being doomed to disaster.

fatality rate *n.* See **death rate.**

fa•tal•ly (fāt′l-ē) *adv.* **1.** So as to cause death; mortally: *fatally injured.* **2.** So as to result in disaster or ruin. **3.** According to the decree of fate; inevitably.

fa•ta mor•ga•na (fä′tə môr-gä′nə) *n.* See **mirage** 1. [Ital., mirage, Morgan le Fay (< the belief that her witchcraft caused it) : *fata,* fairy (< VLat. *fāta,* goddess of fate; see **FAIRY**) + *Morgana,* Morgan (prob. < OIr. *Morrígain*).]

fat•back (făt′băk′) *n.* The strip of fat from the upper part of a side of pork, usu. dried and salt-cured.

fat body *n.* **1.** A food reserve of fatty tissue in the larval stages of certain insects. **2.** A mass of fatty tissue located near the genital glands in some amphibians, including the frogs.

fat cat *n. Slang* **1.** A wealthy and highly privileged person. **2.** A wealthy contributor to a political campaign.

fat cell *n.* Any of various cells found in adipose tissue that are specialized for the storage of fat.

Fat City or **fat city** *n. Slang* A condition or set of circumstances characterized by great prosperity.

fate (fāt) *n.* **1a.** The supposed force, principle, or power that predetermines events. **b.** The inevitable events predestined by this force. **2.** A final result or consequence; an outcome. **3.** Unfavorable destiny; doom. **4. Fates** *Greek & Roman Mythology* The three goddesses who control human destiny. Used with *the.* [ME < OFr. *fat* < Lat. *fātum,* prophecy, doom < neut. p. part. of *fārī,* to speak. See **bhā-** in App.]

fat•ed (fā′tĭd) *adj.* **1.** Governed by fate; predetermined. **2.** Condemned to death or destruction; doomed.

fate•ful (fāt′fəl) *adj.* **1.** Vitally affecting subsequent events; being of great consequence; momentous: *a fateful decision.* **2.** Controlled by or as if by fate; predetermined. **3.** Bringing death or disaster; fatal. **4.** Ominously prophetic; portentous: *a fateful sign.* —**fate′ful•ly** *adv.* —**fate′ful•ness** *n.*

fat farm *n. Informal* A spa or resort that specializes in weight loss.

fath. *abbr.* fathom

fat•head (făt′hĕd′) *n. Slang* A stupid person. —**fat′head′ed** *adj.* —**fat′head′ed•ly** *adv.* —**fat′head′ed•ness** *n.*

fa•ther (fä′thər) *n.* **1.** A man who begets or raises a child. **2.** A male parent of an animal. **3.** A male ancestor. **4.** A man who creates, originates, or founds something. **5.** An early form; a prototype. **6. Father a.** *Christianity* God. **b.** The first person of the Christian Trinity. **7.** An elderly or venerable man. Used as a title of respect. **8.** One of the leading men, as of a city. **9.** or **Father** A church father. **10a.** A Christian priest. **b.** Used as a title and form of address. ❖ *v.* **-thered, -ther•ing, -thers** —*tr.* **1.** To procreate (offspring) as the male parent. **2.** To act or serve as a father to (a child). **3.** To create, found, or originate. **4.** To acknowledge responsibility for. **5a.** To attribute the paternity, creation, or origin of. **b.** To assign falsely or unjustly; foist. —*intr.* To act or serve as a father. [ME *fader* < OE *fæder.* See **pəter-** in App.]

Father Christmas *n. Chiefly British* Santa Claus.

father confessor *n.* **1.** A priest who hears confessions. **2.** A person in whom one confides.

father figure *n.* An older man, often in a position of power or influence, who elicits the emotions usu. reserved for a father.

fa•ther•hood (fä′thər-hŏŏd′) *n.* **1.** The state of being a father.

2. The qualities of a father. **3.** Fathers considered as a group.

fa•ther-in-law (fä′thər-ĭn-lô′) *n., pl.* **fa•thers-in-law** (fä′thərz-) **1.** The father of one's husband or wife. **2.** *Archaic* A stepfather.

fa•ther•land (fä′thər-lănd′) *n.* **1.** One's native land. **2.** The land of one's ancestors.

fa•ther•less (fä′thər-lĭs) *adj.* **1.** Having no living father. **2.** Having no known father. —**fa′ther•less•ness** *n.*

fa•ther•ly (fä′thər-lē) *adj.* **1.** Of, like, or appropriate to a father. **2.** Showing the affection of a father. ❖ *adv.* In a manner befitting a father. —**fa′ther•li•ness** *n.*

Fa•ther's Day (fä′thərz) *n.* The third Sunday in June, observed in honor of fathers.

fath•om (făth′əm) *n.* A unit of length equal to 6 feet (1.83 meters), used principally in the measurement and specification of marine depths. ❖ *tr.v.* **-omed, -om•ing, -oms 1.** To penetrate to the meaning or nature of; comprehend. **2.** To determine the depth of; sound. [ME *fathme* < OE *fæthm,* outstretched arms.] —**fath′om•a•ble** *adj.*

Fa•thom•e•ter (fə-thŏm′ĭ-tər) A trademark used for a sonic depth finder.

fath•om•less (făth′əm-lĭs) *adj.* **1.** Too deep to be fathomed or measured. **2.** Too obscure or complicated to be understood. —**fath′om•less•ly** *adv.* —**fath′om•less•ness** *n.*

fa•tid•ic (fə-tĭd′ĭk) also **fa•tid•i•cal** (-ĭ-kəl) *adj.* Relating to or characterized by prophecy; prophetic. [Lat. *fātidicus : fātum,* prophecy, doom; see **FATE** + *dīcere,* to say; see **deik-** in App.]

fat•i•ga•ble (făt′ĭ-gə-bəl) *adj.* Subject to fatigue. [Fr. < OFr. < LLat. *fatīgābilis* < Lat. *fatīgāre,* to fatigue.] —**fat′i•ga•bil′i•ty** *n.*

fa•tigue (fə-tēg′) *n.* **1.** Physical or mental weariness due to exertion. **2.** Something, such as an effort or activity, that causes weariness. **3.** The weakening or failure of a material, such as metal or wood, from prolonged stress. **4a.** Manual or menial labor, such as barracks cleaning, assigned to soldiers. **b. fatigues** A military uniform for labor or field duty. ❖ *v.* **-tigued, -tigu•ing, -tigues** —*tr.* **1.** To tire with physical or mental exertion; weary. **2.** To create fatigue in (a metal or other material). —*intr.* To be or become fatigued. [Fr. < OFr. < *fatiguer,* to fatigue < Lat. *fatīgāre.*]

Fat•i•ma also **Fat•i•mah** (făt′ə-mə) 616?–633. Daughter of the Islamic prophet Muhammad; considered by Muslims to be one of the Four Perfect Women.

Fá•ti•ma (făt′ə-mə) A village of W-central Portugal NNE of Lisbon; a Christian pilgrimage site after the reported appearance of the Virgin Mary in 1917.

Fat•i•mid (făt′ə-mĭd′) also **Fat•i•mite** (-mīt′) A Muslim dynasty that ruled North Africa and parts of Egypt (909–1171).

fat•ling (făt′lĭng) *n.* A young animal, such as a lamb or calf, fattened for slaughter.

fat pine *n. Chiefly Southern US* **1.** See **longleaf pine. 2.** See **kindling.** See Regional Note at **kindling.**

fat•so (făt′sō) *n., pl.* **-soes** *Slang* A fat person.

fat-sol•u•ble (făt′sŏl′yə-bəl) *adj.* Soluble in fats or fat compounds.

fat•ten (făt′n) *v.* **-tened, -ten•ing, -tens** —*tr.* **1.** To make plump or fat. **2.** To fertilize (land). **3.** To increase the amount or substance of: *fatten one's bank account.* —*intr.* To grow fat or fatter. —**fat′ten•er** *n.*

fat•tish (făt′ĭsh) *adj.* Somewhat fat. —**fat′tish•ness** *n.*

fat•ty (făt′ē) *adj.* **-ti•er, -ti•est 1.** Containing or composed of fat: *fatty food.* **2.** Characteristic of fat; greasy. **3.** Derived from or chemically related to fat. ❖ *n., pl.* **-ties** *Informal* A fat person. —**fat′ti•ly** *adv.* —**fat′ti•ness** *n.*

fatty acid *n.* Any of a large group of monobasic acids, esp. those found in animal and vegetable fats and oils, having the general formula $C_nH_{2n+1}COOH$.

fa•tu•i•ty (fə-tōō′ĭ-tē, -tyōō′-, fă-) *n., pl.* **-ties 1.** Smug stupidity; utter foolishness. **2.** Something that is utterly stupid or silly. [Lat. *fatuitās* < *fatuus,* silly, foolish.]

fat•u•ous (făch′ōō-əs) *adj.* **1.** Vacuously, smugly, and unconsciously foolish. **2.** Delusive; unreal. [< Lat. *fatuus.*] —**fat′u•ous•ly** *adv.* —**fat′u•ous•ness** *n.*

fat•wa (făt′wä′) *n.* A legal opinion or ruling issued by an Islamic scholar. [Ar. *fatwā.*]

fat•wood (făt′wŏŏd′) *n. Chiefly Florida & Georgia* See **kindling.** See Regional Note at **kindling.**

fau•bourg (fō′bŏŏr′, -bōōrg′) *n.* A district lying outside the original city limits of a French-speaking city or a city with a French heritage. See Regional Note at **beignet.** [ME *faubourgh* < OFr. *faubourg,* alteration of *forsborc : fors,* outside (< Lat. *forīs;* see **dhwer-** in App.) + *borc,* town (< LLat. *burgus,* fort, of Gmc. orig.; see **bhergh-** in App.).]

REGIONAL NOTE In contemporary American English the word *faubourg,* a synonym for *suburb* borrowed from French, is virtually restricted to the city of New Orleans with its French background. Even there it is used not as a common noun like *suburb* but in combination in the names of various quarters of the city, for example, *Faubourg Sainte Marie.*

fau•ces (fô′sēz′) *pl.n.* *(used with a sing. or pl. verb)* The passage from the back of the mouth to the pharynx, bounded by the soft palate, the base of the tongue, and the palatine arches. [ME < Lat.

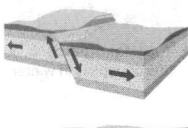
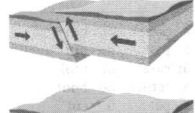

fault
top: normal fault
center: reverse fault
bottom: strike-slip fault

faucēs.] —fau′cal (-kəl), fau′cial (-shəl) adj.

fau·cet (fô′sĭt) n. A device for regulating the flow of a liquid from a reservoir such as a pipe or drum. See Regional Note at **andiron**. [ME < OFr. *fausset*, cask stopper < *fausser*, to break in < LLat. *falsāre*, to falsify < Lat. *falsus*, false. See FALSE.]

Faulk·ner (fôk′nər), **William** 1897–1962. Amer. writer whose works include *The Sound and the Fury* (1929). He won the 1949 Nobel Prize for literature. —**Faulk·ner′i·an** (fôk-nîr′ē-ən) adj.

fault (fôlt) n. **1a.** A character weakness, esp. a minor one. **b.** Something that impairs or detracts from physical perfection; a defect. **c.** A mistake; an error. **d.** A minor offense or misdeed. **2.** Responsibility for a mistake or offense; culpability. See Syns at **blame**. **3.** *Geology* A fracture in the continuity of a rock formation in which adjacent surfaces are displaced relative to each other along the plane of fracture. **4.** *Electronics* A defect, such as a short or ground, in a circuit or wiring. **5.** *Sports* A bad service, as in tennis. **6.** *Obsolete* A lack or deficiency. ❖ v. **fault·ed**, **fault·ing**, **faults** —tr. **1.** To find error or defect in; criticize or blame. **2.** *Geology* To produce a fault in; fracture. —intr. **1.** To commit a mistake or error. **2.** *Geology* To shift so as to produce a fault. —*idioms:* **at fault 1.** Deserving of blame; guilty. **2.** Confused and puzzled. **find fault** To seek, find, and complain about faults; criticize. **to a fault** To an excessive degree. [ME *faulte* < OFr. < VLat. **fallita* < var. of Lat. *falsa*, fem. p. part. of *fallere*, to deceive, fail.]

fault·find·ing (fôlt′fīn′dĭng) n. Petty or nagging criticism; carping. ❖ adj. Disposed to find fault. —**fault′find′er** n.

fault·less (fôlt′lĭs) adj. Being without fault. See Syns at **perfect**. —**fault′less·ly** adv. —**fault′less·ness** n.

fault·y (fôl′tē) adj. **-i·er, -i·est 1.** Containing a fault or defect; imperfect or defective. **2.** *Obsolete* Deserving of blame; guilty. —**fault′i·ly** adv. —**fault′i·ness** n.

faun (fôn) n. *Roman Mythology* Any of a group of rural deities represented as having the body of a man and the horns, ears, tail, and legs of a goat. [ME < OFr. < Lat. *Faunus*, Faunus.]

fau·na (fô′nə) n., pl. **-nas** or **-nae** (-nē′) **1.** (*used with a sing. or pl. verb*) Animals, esp. the animals of a region or period, considered as a group. **2.** A catalog of the animals of a specific region or period. [LLat. *Fauna*, sister of Faunus.] —**fau′nal** adj.

Fau·nus (fô′nəs) n. *Roman Mythology* A god of nature and fertility. [Lat.]

Fau·ré (fō-rā′), **Gabriel Urbain** 1845–1924. French composer chiefly noted for his songs and Requiem (1887).

Faust (foust) also **Faus·tus** (fou′stəs, fô′-) n. A magician and alchemist in German legend who sells his soul to the devil for power and knowledge. [Ger., after Johann Faust (1480?–1540?), German magician and alchemist.] —**Faust′i·an** (fou′stē-ən) adj.

faute de mieux (fōt də myœ′) adv. For lack of something better. [Fr.: *faute*, lack + *de*, of + *mieux*, better.]

fau·teuil (fō′tĭl, fō-tœ′yə) n. An upholstered armchair usu. having open sides. [Fr. < OFr. *faldestoel*, of Gmc. orig.]

fau·vism (fō′vĭz′əm) n. An early-20th-century movement in painting begun by a group of French artists and marked by the use of bold, distorted forms and vivid colors. [Fr. *fauvisme* < *fauve*, wild animal < *fauve*, wild < OFr. *falve*, reddish-yellow < Frankish **falw-*.] —**fau′vist** adj.

faux (fō) adj. Artificial; fake: *faux pearls*. [Fr. < OFr. *fals*. See FALSE.]

faux-na·ïf also **faux-naif** (fō-nä-ēf′) adj. Pretending innocent simplicity. [Fr.: *faux*, false + *naïf*, naive.]

faux pas (fō pä′) n., pl. **faux pas** (fō päz′) A social blunder. [Fr.: *faux*, false + *pas*, step.]

fa·va bean (fä′və) n. See **broad bean**. [Ital. *fava* < Lat. *faba*, broad bean. See bha-bhā- in App.]

fa·ve·la (fə-vĕl′ə) n. A shantytown or slum, esp. in Brazil. [Port., poss. < dim. of *favo*, honeycomb (< Lat. *favus*) or < *favelas*, prob. < pl. of *favela*, spurge (< *fava*, bean < Lat. *faba*; see bha-bhā- in App.).]

fa·ve·o·late (fə-vē′ə-lāt′) adj. Pitted with cavities or cells; honeycombed. [< NLat. *faveolus* : Lat. *favus*, honeycomb + (ALV)EOLUS.]

fa·vo·ni·an (fə-vō′nē-ən) adj. **1.** Of or relating to the west wind. **2.** Mild; benign. [Lat. *Favōniānus* < *Favōnius*, the west wind.]

fa·vor (fā′vər) n. **1.** A gracious, friendly, or obliging act that is freely granted. **2a.** Friendly or favorable regard; approval or support. **b.** A state of being held in such regard. **3.** Unfair partiality; favoritism. **4a.** A privilege or concession. **b. favors** Sexual privileges, esp. as granted by a woman. **5a.** Something given as a token of affection or remembrance. **b.** A small gift given to each guest at a party. **6.** Advantage; benefit. **7.** Behalf; interest. **8.** *Obsolete* A communication, esp. a letter. **9.** *Archaic* **a.** Aspect or appearance. **b.** Countenance; face. *Obsolete* A facial feature. ❖ v. **-vored**, **-vor·ing**, **-vors** —tr. **1.** To perform a kindness or service for; oblige. **2.** To treat or regard with friendship, approval, or support. **3.** To be partial to; indulge a liking for. **4.** To be or tend to be in support of. **5.** To make easier or more possible; facilitate. **6.** To treat with care; be gentle with. **7.** *Chiefly Southern US* To resemble in appearance: *She favors her father.* —intr. *Chiefly Southern US* To resemble another in appearance. —*idiom:* **in favor of 1.** In support of; approving. **2.** To the advantage of. **3.** Made out

to the benefit of. [ME < OFr. < Lat. < *favēre*, to be favorable.] —**fa′vor·er** n. —**fa′vor·ing·ly** adv.

REGIONAL NOTE When a Southerner *favors* a relative, he or she is not giving that person special privileges; rather, the Southerner looks like that relative. *Favor* can be either transitive—*She favors her father*—or intransitive with a compound subject: *She and her father favor.* This use of *favor* goes back to early modern English and derives from the noun *favor*, which was used from the 15th to the 19th century to mean "appearance, aspect; the countenance, face." This sense of the noun is now archaic, but the verb thrives in the English of the Southern United States.

fa·vor·a·ble (fā′vər-ə-bəl, fāv′rə-) adj. **1.** Advantageous; helpful. **2.** Encouraging; propitious: *a favorable diagnosis.* **3.** Manifesting approval; commendatory. **4.** Winning approval; pleasing. **5.** Granting what has been desired or requested: *a favorable reply.* **6.** Indulgent or partial. —**fa′vor·a·ble·ness** n. —**fa′vor·a·bly** adv.

SYNONYMS *favorable, propitious, auspicious, benign, conducive* These adjectives describe what is indicative of a successful outcome. *Favorable* can refer to what contributes to the attainment of a goal: *a favorable review. Propitious* implies a favorable tendency or inclination: "Miracles are propitious accidents" (George Santayana). *Auspicious* refers to what presages good fortune: *an auspicious beginning. Benign* applies to people or things that exert a beneficial influence: "I lingered round them, under that benign sky" (Emily Brontë). Something *conducive* leads or contributes to a result, often a desirable one: *a quiet place conducive to reading.*

fa·vored (fā′vərd) adj. **1.** Treated or thought of with kindness or partiality: *the favored child.* **2.** Endowed with special talents or advantages. **3.** Having an appearance of a specified kind. Often used in combination: *ill-favored.*

fa·vor·ite (fā′vər-ĭt, fāv′rĭt) n. **1a.** One enjoying special favor or regard. **b.** One trusted, indulged, or preferred above others, esp. by a superior: *a favorite of the boss.* **2.** A contestant or competitor regarded as most likely to win. ❖ adj. Preferred above all others; regarded with special favor. [Obsolete Fr. *favorit* < OItal. *favorito*, p. part. of *favorire*, to favor < *favore*, favor < Lat. *favor*. See FAVOR.]

favorite son n. **1.** A man favored for nomination as a presidential candidate by his own state delegates at a national political convention. **2.** A famous man viewed proudly by his hometown for his achievements.

fa·vor·it·ism (fā′vər-ĭ-tĭz′əm, fāv′rĭ-) n. **1.** A display of partiality toward a favored person or group. **2.** The state of being held in special favor.

fa·vour (fā′vər) n. & v. Chiefly British Variant of **favor**.

fa·vus (fā′vəs) n. A chronic skin infection, usu. of the scalp, caused by fungi of the genus *Trichophyton* and characterized by the development of thick yellow crusts. [Lat., honeycomb.]

Fawkes (fôks), **Guy** 1570–1606. English conspirator executed for his role in the Gunpowder Plot, an attempt to kill James I and blow up Parliament on Nov. 5, 1605.

fawn¹ (fôn) intr.v. **fawned, fawn·ing, fawns 1.** To exhibit affection or attempt to please, as a dog does by wagging its tail or whining. **2.** To seek favor or attention by flattery and obsequious behavior. [ME *faunen* < OE *fagnian*, to rejoice < *fagen, fægen*, glad.] —**fawn′er** n. —**fawn′ing·ly** adv.

fawn² (fôn) n. **1.** A young deer, esp. one less than a year old. **2.** A grayish yellow-brown to moderate reddish brown. [ME < OFr. *foun, faon, feon*, young animal < VLat. **fētō, *fētōn-* < Lat. *fētus*, offspring.]

fawn lily n. Any of several North American lilies of the genus *Erythronium*, esp. *E. californicum* of western North America, having nodding yellow flowers and mottled leaves.

fax (făks) n. **1.** A fax machine. **2.** A printed page or image transmitted or received by a fax machine. ❖ tr.v. **faxed, fax·ing, fax·es** To transmit (printed matter or an image) by a fax machine. [Shortening and alteration of FACSIMILE.]

fax machine n. A device that sends and receives printed pages or images over telephone lines by converting them to and from electronic signals.

fay¹ (fā) tr. & intr.v. **fayed, fay·ing, fays** To join or fit closely or tightly. [ME *feien* < OE *fēgan*.]

fay² (fā) n. A fairy or an elf. [ME *faie*, enchanted person or place < OFr. *fae*. See FAIRY.]

fay³ (fā) n. Archaic Faith. [ME *fai* < AN *fei, fed*. See FAITH.]

Fa·yal (fə-yäl′, fä-) See **Faial**.

Fay·ette·ville (fā′ĭt-vĭl′, -vəl) n. A city of S-central NC SSW of Raleigh; founded 1739. Pop. 121,015.

faze (fāz) tr.v. **fazed, faz·ing, faz·es** To disrupt the composure of; disconcert. [ME *fesen*, to drive away < OE *fēsian*.]

FB abbr. **1.** foreign body **2.** freight bill **3.** fullback

FBI abbr. Federal Bureau of Investigation

fc abbr. foot-candle

FCC abbr. Federal Communications Commission

F clef n. See **bass clef**.

FD abbr. **1.** fatal dose **2.** fire department **3.** focal distance

FDA abbr. Food and Drug Administration

FDIC abbr. Federal Deposit Insurance Corporation

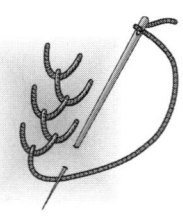

featherstitch

Fe The symbol for the element **iron** 1. [< Lat. *ferrum*, iron.]

fe·al·ty (fē′əl-tē) *n., pl.* **-ties 1a.** The fidelity owed by a vassal to his feudal lord. **b.** The oath of such fidelity. **2.** Faithfulness; allegiance. [ME *fealtye* < OFr. *fealte* < Lat. *fidēlitās*, faithfulness < *fidēlis*, faithful < *fidēs*, faith. See **bheidh-** in App.]

fear (fîr) *n.* **1a.** A feeling of agitation and anxiety caused by present or imminent danger. **b.** A state marked by this feeling. **2.** A feeling of disquiet or apprehension: *a fear of looking foolish.* **3.** Extreme reverence or awe, as toward a deity. **4.** A reason for dread or apprehension. ❖ *v.* **feared, fear·ing, fears** —*tr.* **1.** To be afraid or frightened of. **2.** To be uneasy or apprehensive about. **3.** To be in awe of; revere. **4.** To consider probable; expect: *I fear you are wrong.* **5.** *Archaic* To feel fear within (oneself). —*intr.* **1.** To be afraid. **2.** To be uneasy or apprehensive. [ME *fer* < OE *fǣr*, danger, sudden calamity.] —**fear′er** *n.*

SYNONYMS *fear, fright, dread, terror, horror, panic, alarm, consternation, trepidation* These nouns denote the agitation and anxiety caused by the presence or imminence of danger. *Fear* is the most general term: "*Fear is the parent of cruelty*" (J.A. Froude). *Fright* is sudden, usually momentary, great fear: *In my fright, I forgot to lock the door. Dread* is strong fear, especially of what one is powerless to avoid: *His dread of strangers kept him from socializing.* *Terror* is intense overpowering fear: "*And now at the dead hour of the night, amid the dreadful silence of that old house, so strange a noise as this excited me to uncontrollable terror*" (Edgar Allan Poe). *Horror* is a combination of fear and aversion or repugnance: *Murder arouses widespread horror. Panic* is sudden frantic fear, often groundless: *The fire caused a panic. Alarm* is fright aroused by the first realization of danger: *I watched with alarm as the boat began to sink. Consternation* is often paralyzing, characterized by confusion and helplessness: *consternation caused by the coup. Trepidation* is dread characteristically marked by trembling or hesitancy: "*They were . . . full of trepidation about things that were never likely to happen*" (John Morley).

Fear, Cape A promontory on Smith I. off the coast of SE NC at the mouth of the Cape Fear R.

fear·ful (fîr′fəl) *adj.* **1.** Causing or capable of causing fear; frightening. **2.** Experiencing fear; frightened. See Syns at **afraid**. **3.** Feeling or inclined to feel anxiety or apprehension; timid. **4.** Indicating anxiety, fear, or terror. **5.** Feeling reverence, dread, or awe. **6.** Extreme, as in degree or extent; dreadful. —**fear′ful·ly** *adv.* —**fear′ful·ness** *n.*

fear·less (fîr′lĭs) *adj.* Without fear; brave. See Syns at **brave**. —**fear′less·ly** *adv.* —**fear′less·ness** *n.*

fear·some (fîr′səm) *adj.* **1.** Causing or capable of causing fear. **2.** Fearful; timid. —**fear′some·ly** *adv.* —**fear′some·ness** *n.*

fea·si·ble (fē′zə-bəl) *adj.* **1.** Capable of being accomplished or brought about; possible. **2.** Used or dealt with successfully; suitable. **3.** Logical; likely. [ME *fesable* < OFr. *faisable* < *faire, fais-*, to do < Lat. *facere.* See **dhē-** in App.] —**fea′si·bil′i·ty, fea′si·ble·ness** *n.* —**fea′si·bly** *adv.*

feast (fēst) *n.* **1a.** A large elaborate meal, usu. for many persons; a banquet. **b.** A meal that is well prepared and abundantly enjoyed. **2.** A periodic religious festival. **3.** Something giving great pleasure or satisfaction. ❖ *v.* **feast·ed, feast·ing, feasts** —*tr.* To give a feast for; entertain or feed sumptuously. —*intr.* **1.** To partake of a feast; eat heartily. **2.** To experience something with gratification or delight. —*idiom:* **feast (one's) eyes on** To be delighted or gratified by the sight of. [ME *feste* < OFr. < VLat. **fēsta* < Lat., pl. of *fēstum* < *fēstus*, festive. See **dhēs-** in App.] —**feast′er** *n.*

Feast of Dedication *n. Judaism* See **Hanukkah.**

Feast of Lights *n. Judaism* See **Hanukkah.**

feat¹ (fēt) *n.* **1.** A notable act or deed, esp. an act of courage; an exploit. **2.** An act of skill, endurance, imagination, or strength; an achievement. **3.** *Obsolete* A specialized skill; a knack. [ME *fet* < AN < Lat. *factum* < neut. p. part. of *facere*, to make, do. See **dhē-** in App.]

feat² (fēt) *adj.* **feat·er, feat·est** *Archaic* **1.** Adroit; dexterous. **2.** Neat; trim. [ME *fet*, suitable < OFr. *fait* < Lat. *factus*, done, made. See FEATURE.] —**feat′ly** *adv.*

feath·er (fĕth′ər) *n.* **1.** One of the light flat growths forming the plumage of birds, consisting of slender parallel barbs forming a vane on either side of a horny, partly hollow shaft. **2. feathers** Plumage. **3. feathers** Clothing; attire. **4.** A feathery tuft or fringe of hair. **5.** Character, kind, or nature. **6.** Something small, trivial, or inconsequential. **7a.** A strip, wedge, or flange used as a strengthening part. **b.** A wedge or key that fits into a groove to make a joint. **8.** The vane of an arrow. **9.** A feather-shaped flaw, as in a precious stone. **10.** The wake made by a submarine's periscope. **11.** The act of feathering the blade of an oar in rowing. ❖ *v.* **-ered, -er·ing, -ers** —*tr.* **1.** To cover, dress, or decorate with or as if with feathers. **2.** To fit (an arrow) with a feather. **3a.** To thin, reduce, or fringe the edge of by cutting, shaving, or wearing away. **b.** To shorten and taper (hair) by cutting and thinning. **4.** To connect with a tongue-and-groove joint. **5.** To turn (an oar blade) almost horizontal as it is carried back after each stroke. **6a.** To alter the pitch of (a propeller) so that the chords of the blades are parallel with the line of flight. **b.** To alter the pitch of (the rotor of a helicopter) while in forward flight. **7.** To turn off (an

aircraft engine) while in flight. —*intr.* **1.** To grow feathers or become feathered. **2.** To move, spread, or grow in a manner suggestive of feathers. **3.** To feather an oar. **4.** To feather a propeller. —*idioms:* **feather in (one's) cap** An act or deed to one's credit; a distinctive achievement. **feather (one's) nest** To grow wealthy by taking advantage of one's position or property left in one's trust. **in fine** (or **good** or **high**) **feather** In excellent form, health, or humor. [ME *fether* < OE. See **pet-** in App.]

feather bed *n.* **1.** A mattress stuffed with feathers. **2.** A bed having a feather mattress.

feath·er·bed·ding (fĕth′ər-bĕd′ĭng) *n.* The practice of requiring an employer to hire superfluous workers or limit their production in keeping with a safety regulation or union rule. —**feath′er·bed′** *adj. & v.*

feath·er·brain (fĕth′ər-brān′) *n.* A silly, flighty, or empty-headed person. —**feath′er·brained′** *adj.*

feath·ered (fĕth′ərd) *adj.* **1.** Covered, provided, or adorned with feathers. **2.** Having feathering, as an animal's coat. **3.** Moving swiftly: *feathered feet.* **4.** Having the chords of propeller blades parallel to the line of flight.

feath·er·edge (fĕth′ər-ĕj′) *n.* **1.** A thin fragile edge, esp. a tapering edge of a board. **2.** See **deckle edge.**

feath·er·head (fĕth′ər-hĕd′) *n.* A featherbrain. —**feath′er·head′ed** *adj.*

feath·er·ing (fĕth′ər-ĭng) *n.* **1.** Plumage. **2.** The feathers fitted to an arrow. **3.** A fringe of hair on an animal's coat.

feather star *n.* Any of numerous crinoids of the genus *Antedon* and related genera, having a free-swimming stalkless adult stage with branched feathery arms.

feath·er·stitch (fĕth′ər-stĭch′) *n.* An embroidery stitch that produces a decorative zigzag line. —**feath′er·stitch′** *v.*

feath·er·weight (fĕth′ər-wāt′) *n.* **1a.** A professional boxer weighing more than 118 and not more than 126 pounds (approx. 53.5–57 kilograms), heavier than a bantamweight and lighter than a lightweight. **b.** A contestant in various other sports in a similar weight class. **2.** A person or thing of little weight or size. **3.** An insignificant person. —**feath′er·weight** *adj.*

feath·er·y (fĕth′ə-rē) *adj.* **1.** Covered with or consisting of feathers. **2.** Resembling or suggestive of a feather, as in form or lightness. —**feath′er·i·ness** *n.*

fea·ture (fē′chər) *n.* **1a.** Any of the distinct parts of the face, as the eyes, nose, or mouth. **b.** The overall appearance of the face. Often used in the plural. **2.** A distinctive quality or characteristic. **3.** *Linguistics* **a.** A property of linguistic units or forms, such as nasality. **b.** In generative linguistics, any of various abstract entities that combine to specify underlying properties of linguistic forms. **4a.** The main film presentation at a theater. **b.** A full-length film. **5.** A special attraction at an entertainment. **6.** A special article, story, or department in a newspaper or periodical. **7.** An item advertised or offered as particularly attractive. **8.** *Archaic* **a.** Outward appearance; form or shape. **b.** Physical beauty. ❖ *tr.v.* **-tured, -tur·ing, -tures 1.** To give special attention to; make prominent. **2.** To have or include as a prominent part or characteristic. **3.** To depict or outline the features of. **4.** *Informal* To picture mentally; imagine. [ME *feture* < OFr. *faiture* < Lat. *factūra*, a working or making < *factus*, p. part. of *facere*, to make, do. See **dhē-** in App.]

fea·tured (fē′chərd) *adj.* **1.** Given special prominence, attention, or publicity: *a featured item at a sale.* **2.** Having a specified kind of facial features. Often used in combination: *plain-featured.*

fea·ture·less (fē′chər-lĭs) *adj.* Lacking distinguishing characteristics or features: *the featureless landscape of the steppe.*

Feb. *abbr.* February

fe·bric·i·ty (fī-brĭs′ĭ-tē) *n.* The condition of having a fever. [Med.Lat. *febrĭcitās* < Lat. *febrĭcitāre*, to have a fever < *febris*, fever.]

fe·brif·ic (fī-brĭf′ĭk) *adj.* **1.** Producing fever. **2.** Having a fever; feverish. [Lat. *febris*, fever + –FIC.]

feb·ri·fuge (fĕb′rə-fyōōj′) *n.* An agent that reduces fever; an antipyretic. [Lat. *febris*, fever + –FUGE.] —**feb′ri·fuge** *adj.*

feb·rile (fĕb′rəl, fē′brəl) *adj.* Of, relating to, or characterized by fever; feverish. [LLat. *febrīlis* < Lat. *febris*, fever.]

Feb·ru·ar·y (fĕb′rōō-ĕr′ē, fĕb′yōō-) *n., pl.* **-ies** The second month of the year in the Gregorian calendar. See table at **calendar.** [ME *Februarie* < Lat. *Februārius (mēnsis)*, (month) of purification < *februa*, expiatory offerings, poss. of Sabine orig.]

USAGE NOTE Although the variant pronunciation (fĕb′yōō-ĕr′ē) is often censured because it doesn't reflect the spelling of the word, it is quite common in educated speech and is generally considered acceptable. The loss of the first *r* in this pronunciation can be accounted for by the phonological process known as dissimilation, by which similar sounds in a word tend to become less similar. Similarly, the word *barbiturate* is often pronounced (bär-bĭch′ə-wĭt), with loss of the second *r.*

fec. *abbr. Latin* fecit (he or she made or did it)

fe·cal (fē′kəl) *adj.* Of, relating to, or composed of feces.

fe·ces (fē′sēz) *pl.n.* (*used with a sing. or pl. verb*) Waste matter eliminated from the bowels; excrement. [ME < Lat. *faecēs*, pl. of *faex*, dregs.]

feck·less (fĕk′lĭs) *adj.* **1.** Feeble or ineffective. **2.** Careless and irresponsible. [Sc. *feck*, effect (alteration of EFFECT) + –LESS.] **—feck′less•ly** *adv.* **—feck′less•ness** *n.*

fec•u•lent (fĕk′yə-lənt) *adj.* Full of foul or impure matter; fecal. [ME < Lat. *faeculentus*, heavy with sediment < *faex*, *faec-*, dregs.] **—fec′u•lence** *n.*

fe•cund (fē′kənd, fĕk′ənd) *adj.* **1.** Productive of offspring or vegetation; fruitful. **2.** Intellectually productive. [ME < OFr. *fecond* < Lat. *fēcundus*.] **—fe•cun′di•ty** (fĭ-kŭn′dĭ-tē) *n.*

fe•cun•date (fē′kən-dāt′, fĕk′ən-) *tr.v.* **-dat•ed, -dat•ing, -dates 1.** To make fecund or fruitful. **2.** To impregnate; fertilize. [Lat. *fēcundāre*, *fēcundāt-* < *fēcundus*, fruitful.] **—fe′cun•da′tion** *n.*

fed (fĕd) *v.* Past tense and past participle of **feed.**

Fed *n. Informal* **1a.** The Federal Reserve System. **b.** The Federal Reserve Board. **2.** often **fed** A federal agent or official.

fed. *abbr.* **1.** federal **2.** federated **3.** federation

fe•da•yee (fĕ-dä′yē′, -dä′ē′, -dä′-) *n., pl.* **-yeen** (-yēn′, -ēn′) A commando or guerrilla, esp. an Arab commando operating in the Middle East. [Ar. *fidā'ī*, one who sacrifices himself < *fidā'*, sacrifice, ransom < *fadā*, sacrifice.]

fed•er•a•cy (fĕd′ər-ə-sē) *n., pl.* **-cies** *Archaic* An alliance; a confederacy. [Short for CONFEDERACY.]

fed•er•al (fĕd′ər-əl, fĕd′rəl) *adj.* **1.** Of, relating to, or being a form of government in which individual states recognize the sovereignty of a central authority but retain certain powers. **2.** Of or constituting a form of government in which sovereign power is divided between a central authority and a number of constituent political units. **3.** Of or relating to the central government of a federation as distinct from the governments of its member units. **4.** Favorable to or advocating federation. **5.** Relating to or formed by a treaty or compact between constituent political units. **6. Federal a.** Of, relating to, or supporting Federalism or the Federalist Party. **b.** Of, relating to, or loyal to the Union cause during the American Civil War. **7.** often **Federal** Of, relating to, or being the central government of the United States. **8. Federal** Relating to or characteristic of a style of architecture, furniture, and decoration produced in the United States esp. in the late 18th and early 19th centuries and characterized by adaptations of classical forms. ❖ *n.* **1. Federal a.** A supporter of the Union during the American Civil War, esp. a Union soldier. **b.** A Federalist. **2.** often **Federal** A federal agent or official. [< Lat. *foedus*, *foeder-*, league, treaty. See **bheidh-** in App.] **—fed′er•al•ly** *adv.*

federal district also **Federal District** *n.* An area that is reserved as the site of the national capital of a federation.

fed•er•al•ism (fĕd′ər-ə-lĭz′əm, fĕd′rə-) *n.* **1a.** A system of government in which power is divided between a central authority and constituent political units. **b.** Advocacy of such a system of government. **2. Federalism** The doctrine of the Federalist Party.

fed•er•al•ist (fĕd′ər-ə-lĭst, fĕd′rə-) *n.* **1.** An advocate of federalism. **2. Federalist** A member or supporter of the Federalist Party. **—fed′er•a•list** *adj.*

Federalist Party *n.* A US political party founded in 1787 to advocate the establishment of a strong federal government and the adoption by the states of the Constitution.

fed•er•al•ize (fĕd′ər-ə-līz′, fĕd′rə-) *tr.v.* **-ized, -iz•ing, -iz•es 1.** To unite in a federal union. **2.** To subject to the authority of a federal government; put under federal control. **—fed′er•al•i•za′tion** (-lĭ-zā′shən) *n.*

Federal Reserve System *n.* A US banking system that consists of 12 federal reserve banks, each one serving member banks within its own district.

fed•er•ate (fĕd′ə-rāt′) *v.* **-at•ed, -at•ing, -ates** *—tr.* To cause to join into a league, federal union, or similar association. *—intr.* To become united in such a union. ❖ *adj.* (fĕd′ər-ĭt, fĕd′rĭt) United in a federation. [Lat. *foederāre*, *foederāt-*, to ratify an agreement < *foedus*, *foeder-*, league, treaty. See **bheidh-** in App.]

fed•er•a•tion (fĕd′ə-rā′shən) *n.* **1.** The act of federating, esp. of states into a league or federal union. **2.** A league or association formed by federating, esp. a government or political body.

fed•er•a•tive (fĕd′ə-rā′tĭv, fĕd′ər-ə-, fĕd′rə-) *adj.* Forming, belonging to, or of the nature of a federation; federal. **—fed′er•a′tive•ly** *adv.*

Fed•Ex (fĕd′ĕks′) A trademark used for an express shipping service.

fe•do•ra (fĭ-dôr′ə, -dōr′ə) *n.* A soft felt hat with a fairly low crown creased lengthwise and a brim that can be turned up or down. [After *Fédora*, a play by Victorien Sardou.]

fed up *adj.* Unable or unwilling to put up with something any longer: *I resigned because I was fed up.*

fee (fē) *n.* **1.** A fixed sum charged, as by an institution or by law, for a privilege: *tuition fees.* **2.** A charge for professional services: *a surgeon's fee.* **3.** A tip; a gratuity. **4.** *Law* An inherited or heritable estate in land. **5a.** In feudal law, an estate in land granted by a lord to his vassal on condition of homage and service. **b.** The land so held. ❖ *tr.v.* **feed, fee•ing, fees 1.** To give a tip to. **2.** *Scots* To hire. ***—idiom:* in fee** *Law* In absolute and legal possession. [ME *fe* < OE *feoh*, cattle, goods, money, and < AN *fee*, fief (< OFr. *fie*, *fief*, of Gmc. orig.; akin to OE *feoh*; see **peku-** in App.).]

fee•ble (fē′bəl) *adj.* **-bler, -blest 1a.** Lacking strength; weak. **b.** Indicating weakness. **2.** Lacking vigor, force, or effectiveness; inadequate. [ME *feble* < OFr. < Lat. *flēbilis*, lamentable < *flēre*, to weep.] **—fee′ble•ness** *n.* **—fee′bly** *adv.*

fee•ble-mind•ed (fē′bəl-mīn′dĭd) *adj.* **1.** Deficient in intelligence. Not in scientific use. **2.** Lacking intelligent consideration and forethought: *a feeble-minded plan doomed to failure.* **3.** *Obsolete* Irresolute and weak-willed. **—fee′ble-mind′ed•ly** *adv.* **—fee′ble-mind′ed•ness** *n.*

feed (fēd) *v.* **fed** (fĕd), **feed•ing, feeds** *—tr.* **1a.** To give food or nourishment to: *feed the children.* **b.** To provide as food or nourishment: *fed fish to the cat.* **2a.** To be food for: *enough to feed a dozen.* **b.** To produce food for. **3a.** To provide for consumption, utilization, or operation: *feed data into a computer.* **b.** To supply with something essential for growth, maintenance, or operation: *rain feeding reservoirs.* **c.** To distribute (a local broadcast) to a larger audience or group of receivers by network or satellite. **4a.** To minister to; gratify. **b.** To support or promote; encourage. **5.** To supply as a cue: *feed lines to an actor.* **6.** *Sports* To pass a ball or puck to (a teammate), esp. to set up a scoring chance. *—intr.* **1.** To eat. **2.** To be nourished or supported: *an ego that feeds on flattery.* **3a.** To move steadily, as into a machine for processing. **b.** To be channeled; flow: *This road feeds into the freeway.* ❖ *n.* **1a.** Food for animals or birds. **b.** The amount of such food given at one time. **2.** *Informal* A meal, esp. a large one. **3.** The act of eating. **4a.** Material or an amount of material supplied, as to a machine or furnace. **b.** The act of supplying such material. **5a.** An apparatus that supplies material to a machine. **b.** The aperture through which such material enters a machine. **6a.** The transmission or conveyance of a local radio or television program, as by satellite, on the Internet, or by broadcast over a network of stations. **b.** A program or signal so transmitted or conveyed. ***—idiom:* off (one's) feed** Suffering a lack of appetite; sick. [ME *feden* < OE *fēdan*. See **pā-** in App.]

feed•back (fēd′băk′) *n.* **1a.** The return of a portion of the output of a process or system to the input, esp. when maintaining, controlling, or altering the system or process. **b.** The portion of the output so returned. **c.** Sound created when a transducer such as a microphone picks up sound from a speaker connected to an amplifier and regenerates it. **2.** The return of information about the result of a process or activity; an evaluative response.

feed•bag (fēd′băg′) *n.* A bag that fits over a horse's muzzle and holds feed.

feed•er (fē′dər) *n.* **1.** One that supplies food. **2.** One that is fed, esp. an animal being fattened for market. **3.** One that feeds materials into a machine for further processing. **4.** Something that contributes to the operation, maintenance, or supply of something else, esp.: **a.** A tributary stream. **b.** A branch line of a transport system, as of an airline or railroad. **5.** Any of the medium-voltage lines used to distribute electric power from a substation to consumers or to smaller substations. **6.** A transmission line between an antenna and a transmitter.

feed•ing frenzy (fē′dĭng) *n.* **1.** A period of intense or excited feeding, as by sharks. **2.** Excited activity by a group, esp. around a focal point: *reporters in a feeding frenzy around the actor.*

feed•lot (fēd′lŏt′) *n.* A plot of ground on which livestock are fattened for market.

feed•stock (fēd′stŏk′) *n.* Raw material required for an industrial process.

feed•stuff (fēd′stŭf′) *n.* Food for livestock; fodder.

feel (fēl) *v.* **felt** (fĕlt), **feel•ing, feels** *—tr.* **1a.** To perceive through the sense of touch: *feel a peach.* **b.** To perceive as a physical sensation: *feel the cold.* **2a.** To touch. **b.** To examine by touching. **3.** To test or explore with caution: *feel one's way in a new job.* **4a.** To undergo the experience of: *felt great joy.* **b.** To be aware of; sense: *felt the crowd's anger.* **c.** To be emotionally affected by. **5a.** To be persuaded of (something) on the basis of intuition, emotion, or other indefinite grounds: *I feel that what the informant says may well be true.* **b.** To believe; think: *She felt his answer to be evasive.* *—intr.* **1.** To experience sensations of touch. **2a.** To produce a particular sensation, esp. through the sense of touch: *The sheets felt smooth.* **b.** To produce a particular impression; appear to be; seem: *It feels good to be home.* See Usage Note at **well²**. **3.** To be conscious of a specified kind or quality of physical, mental, or emotional state: *felt content.* **4.** To seek or explore something by the sense of touch: *felt for the switch.* **5.** To have compassion. ❖ *n.* **1.** Perception by or as if by touch; sensation. **2.** The sense of touch. **3a.** An act or instance of touching or feeling. **b.** *Vulgar* An act or instance of sexual touching or fondling. **4.** The nature or quality of something as perceived by or as if by the sense of touch. **5.** Overall impression or effect; atmosphere. **6.** Intuitive awareness or natural ability: *has a feel for decorating.* ***—phrasal verbs:* feel out** To try cautiously or indirectly to ascertain the viewpoint or nature of. **feel up** *Vulgar* To touch or fondle (someone) sexually. ***—idioms:* feel in (one's) bones** To have an intuition of. **feel like** *Informal* To have an inclination or desire for. **feel like (oneself)** To sense oneself as being in one's normal state. [ME *felen* < OE *fēlan*.]

feel•er (fē′lər) *n.* **1.** Something, such as a hint or question, designed to elicit the attitudes or intentions of others. **2.** *Zoology* A sensory or tactile organ, such as an antenna.

feel•ing (fē′lĭng) *n.* **1a.** The sensation involving perception by touch. **b.** A sensation experienced through touch. **c.** A physical

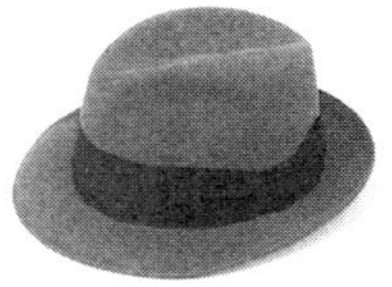

fedora

ă pat	oi boy		
ā pay	ou out		
âr care	ŏŏ took		
ä father	ōō boot		
ĕ pet	ŭ cut		
ē be	ûr urge		
ĭ pit	th thin		
ī pie	*th* this		
îr pier	hw which		
ŏ pot	zh vision		
ō toe	ə about,		
ô paw	item		

Stress marks:
′ (primary);
′ (secondary), as in
lexicon (lĕk′sĭ-kŏn′)

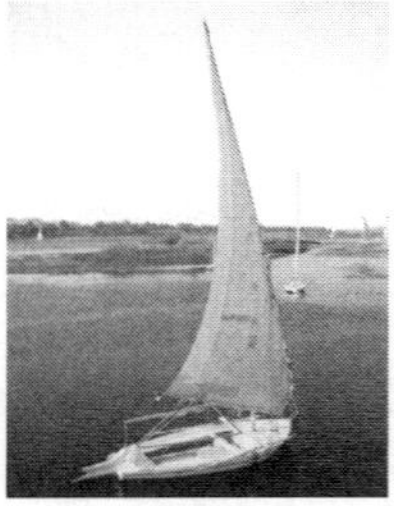

felucca
Nile River, Egypt

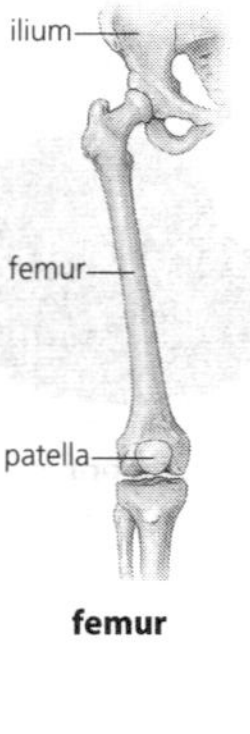

femur

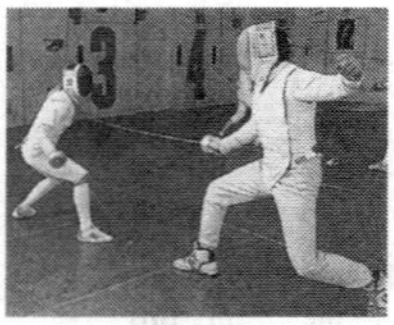

fencing

sensation: *a feeling of warmth.* **2.** An affective state, such as that resulting from emotions or desires: *a feeling of excitement.* **3.** An awareness or impression: *had the feeling he was being followed.* **4a.** An emotional state or disposition; an emotion: *expressed deep feeling.* **b.** A tender emotion; a fondness. **5a.** Capacity to experience the higher emotions; sensibility: *a man of feeling.* **b. feelings** Susceptibility to emotional response; sensibilities: *His feelings are easily hurt.* **6.** Opinion based more on emotion than on reason; sentiment. **7.** A general impression conveyed by a person, place, or thing. **8a.** Appreciative regard or understanding. **b.** Intuitive awareness or aptitude; a feel. ❖ *adj.* **1.** Having the ability to feel emotionally; sentient; sensitive. **2.** Easily moved emotionally; sympathetic. **3.** Expressive of sensibility or emotion: *a feeling glance.* **—feel′ing•ly** *adv.*

SYNONYMS *feeling, emotion, passion, sentiment* These nouns refer to complex and usually strong subjective human response. Although *feeling* and *emotion* are sometimes interchangeable, *feeling* is the more general and neutral: *"Poetry is the spontaneous overflow of powerful feelings: it takes its origin from emotion recollected in tranquillity"* (William Wordsworth). *Emotion* often implies the presence of excitement or agitation: *"Poetry is not a turning loose of emotion, but an escape from emotion"* (T.S. Eliot). *Passion* is intense compelling emotion: *"They seemed like ungoverned children inflamed with the fiercest passions of men"* (Francis Parkman). *Sentiment* often applies to a thought or opinion arising from or influenced by emotion. The word can also refer to delicate, sensitive, or higher feelings: *"The mystic reverence, the religious allegiance, which are essential to a true monarchy, are imaginative sentiments that no legislature can manufacture in any people"* (Walter Bagehot).

fee simple *n., pl.* **fees simple 1.** An estate in land of which the inheritor has unqualified ownership and power of disposition. **2.** Private ownership of real estate in which the owner has the right to control, use, and transfer the property at will.

fee splitting *n.* The practice of sharing fees with professional colleagues, such as physicians, for patient or client referrals.

feet (fēt) *n.* Plural of **foot.**

fee tail *n., pl.* **fees tail** An estate in land limited in inheritance to a particular class of heirs. [ME *fe taille* < AN *fee taile* : *fee,* fee; see FEE + OFr. *taile,* p. part. of *tailier,* to cut; see TAILOR.]

feign (fān) *v.* **feigned, feign•ing, feigns** *—tr.* **1a.** To give a false appearance of: *feign sleep.* **b.** To represent falsely; pretend to. **2.** To imitate so as to deceive: *feign another's voice.* **3.** To fabricate: *feigned an excuse.* **4.** *Archaic* To invent or imagine. *—intr.* To pretend; dissemble. [ME *feinen* < OFr. *feindre* < Lat. *fingere,* to shape, form. See **dheigh-** in App.]

feigned (fānd) *adj.* **1.** Not real; pretended: *feigned modesty.* **2.** Made-up; fictitious.

fei•jo•a (fā-zhô′ə, -jō′-, -hō′-) *n.* An evergreen shrub *(Acca sellowiana)* native to South America and cultivated as an ornamental and for its fruit. [NLat. *Feijoa,* former genus name, after João da Silva *Feijó* (1760–1824), Brazilian soldier and naturalist.]

Fei•ning•er (fī′nĭng-ər), **Lyonel Charles Adrian** 1871–1956. Amer.-born artist who developed a delicate geometric style with intersecting planes of translucent colors.

feint (fānt) *n.* **1.** A feigned attack designed to draw defensive action away from a target. **2.** A deceptive action to divert attention from one's real purpose. ❖ *v.* **feint•ed, feint•ing, feints** *—intr.* To make a feint. *—tr.* **1.** To deceive with a feint. **2.** To make a deceptive show of. [Fr. *feinte* < OFr. < p. part. of *feindre,* to feign. See FEIGN.]

Fei•sal (fī′səl) See **Faisal.**

feist (fīst) also **fice** (fīs) *n. Chiefly Southern US* A small mongrel dog. [Variant of obsolete *fist,* short for *fisting dog* < ME *fisting,* a blowing, breaking wind < OE *fīsting.*]

feist•y (fī′stē) *adj.* **-i•er, -i•est 1.** Touchy; quarrelsome. **2.** Full of spirit or pluck; frisky or spunky. See Regional Note at **andiron.** [< FEIST.] **—feist′i•ness** *n.*

Fei•sul (fī′səl) See **Faisal.**

fe•la•fel (fə-lä′fəl) *n.* Variant of **falafel.**

feld•spar (fĕld′spär′, fĕl′-) also **fel•spar** (fĕl′-) *n.* Any of a group of abundant rock-forming minerals occurring in igneous, sedimentary, and metamorphic rocks and consisting of silicates of aluminum with potassium, sodium, and calcium. [Partial transl. of obsolete Ger. *Feldspath* : *Feld,* field (< MHGer. *veld* < OHGer. *feld*; see **pelə-**[2] in App.) + *Spath,* spar.]

feld•spath•ic (fĕld-spăth′ĭk, fĕl-) *adj.* Of, relating to, or containing feldspar. [< obsolete Ger. *Feldspath,* feldspar. See FELDSPAR.]

fe•li•cif•ic (fē′lĭ-sĭf′ĭk) *adj.* Producing or intended to produce happiness. [Lat. *fēlīx, fēlīc-,* fortunate + -FIC.]

fe•lic•i•tate (fĭ-lĭs′ĭ-tāt′) *tr.v.* **-tat•ed, -tat•ing, -tates 1.** To offer congratulations to. **2.** *Archaic* To make happy. ❖ *adj. Obsolete* Made happy. [LLat. *fēlīcitāre, fēlīcitāt-,* to make happy < *fēlīx, fēlīc-,* fortunate.] **—fe•lic′i•ta′tor** *n.*

fe•lic•i•ta•tion (fĭ-lĭs′ĭ-tā′shən) *n.* Congratulations. Often used in the plural.

fe•lic•i•tous (fĭ-lĭs′ĭ-təs) *adj.* **1.** Admirably suited; apt: *a felicitous comparison.* **2.** Agreeably appropriate in manner or style: *a felicitous writer.* **3.** Happy or fortunate: *a felicitous life.* **—fe•lic′i•tous•ly** *adv.* **—fe•lic′i•tous•ness** *n.*

fe•lic•i•ty (fĭ-lĭs′ĭ-tē) *n., pl.* **-ties 1a.** Great happiness; bliss. **b.** An instance of this. **2.** A cause or source of happiness. **3a.** An appropriate and pleasing manner or style: *felicity of expression.* **b.** An instance of this. **4.** *Archaic* Good fortune. [ME *felicite* < OFr. *felicite* < Lat. *fēlīcitās* < *fēlīx, fēlīc-,* fortunate.]

fe•lid (fē′lĭd) *adj.* Feline. [< NLat. *Fēlidae,* family name < *Fēlis,* type genus < Lat. *fēlēs,* cat.] **—fe′lid** *n.*

fe•line (fē′līn′) *adj.* **1.** Of or belonging to the family Felidae, which includes the lions, tigers, jaguars, and cats; felid. **2.** Suggestive of a cat, as in suppleness or stealthiness. ❖ *n.* An animal of the family Felidae. [Lat. *fēlīnus* or LLat. *fēlīneus,* both < Lat. *fēlēs,* cat.] **—fe′line′ly** *adv.* **—fe′line′ness, fe•lin′i•ty** (fĭ-lĭn′ĭ-tē) *n.*

feline distemper *n.* See **distemper**[1] 1b.

feline leukemia virus *n.* A retrovirus, primarily affecting cats, that causes suppression of the immune system and leads to opportunistic infections or other diseases, such as leukemia.

fell[1] (fĕl) *tr.v.* **felled, fell•ing, fells 1a.** To make fall by striking; cut or knock down: *fell a tree.* **b.** To kill: *was felled by a bullet.* **2.** To sew or finish (a seam) with the raw edges flattened, turned under, and stitched down. ❖ *n.* **1.** The timber cut down in one season. **2.** A felled seam. [ME *fellen* < OE *fellan, fyllan.*] **—fell′a•ble** *adj.*

fell[2] (fĕl) *adj.* **1.** Inhumanly cruel; fierce. **2.** Capable of destroying; lethal. **3.** Dire; sinister. **4.** *Scots* Sharp and biting. ***—idiom:*** **at** (or **in**) **one fell swoop** All at once. [ME *fel* < OFr., nominative of *felon.* See FELON[1].] **—fell′ness** *n.*

fell[3] (fĕl) *n.* **1.** The hide of an animal; a pelt. **2.** A thin membrane beneath the hide. [ME *fel* < OE *fell.* See **pel-**[1] in App.]

fell[4] (fĕl) *n. Chiefly British* **1.** An upland stretch of open country; a moor. **2.** A barren or stony hill. [ME *fel* < ON *fell, fjall,* mountain, hill.]

fell[5] (fĕl) *v.* Past tense of **fall.**

fel•la (fĕl′ə) *n. Informal* A man or boy; a fellow.

fel•lah (fĕl′ə, fə-lä′) *n., pl.* **fel•la•hin** or **fel•la•heen** (fĕl′ə-hēn′, fə-lä-hēn′) A peasant or an agricultural laborer in an Arab country. [Ar. *fallāḥ* < *falaḥa,* to cultivate, till.]

fel•late (fə-lāt′) *v.* **-lat•ed, -lat•ing, -lates** *—tr.* To perform fellatio on. *—intr.* To engage in fellatio. [Lat. *fellāre, fellāt-,* to suck.] **—fel•la′tion** (-lā′shən) *n.* **—fel•la′tor** *n.*

fel•la•ti•o (fə-lā′shē-ō′, -shō′, fĕ-) *n.* Oral stimulation of the penis. [NLat. < Lat. *fellātus,* p. part. of *fellāre,* to suck.]

fell•er[1] (fĕl′ər) *n.* **1.** A lumberjack. **2.** One that fells seams.

fel•ler[2] (fĕl′ər) *n. Informal* A man or boy; a fellow.

Fel•li•ni (fə-lē′nē, fĕl-), **Federico** 1920–93. Italian filmmaker whose works include *La Dolce Vita* (1960).

fel•low (fĕl′ō) *n.* **1a.** A man or boy. **b.** *Informal* A boyfriend. **2.** A comrade or associate. **3a.** A person of equal rank or background; a peer. **b.** One of a pair; a mate. **4.** A member of a learned society. **5.** A graduate student receiving support for further study. **6.** *Chiefly British* **a.** An incorporated senior member of a college or university. **b.** A member of the governing body of a college or university. **7.** *Obsolete* A person of a lower social class. ❖ *adj.* Being of the same kind, group, occupation, society, or locality; sharing certain characteristics or interests. [ME *felau* < OE *fēolaga* < ON *fēlagi,* business partner, fellow < *fēlag,* partnership : *fē,* property, money; see **peku-** in App. + *lag,* a laying down; see **legh-** in App.]

WORD HISTORY The word *fellow* was borrowed into English from Old Norse *fēlagi,* meaning "a partner or shareholder of any kind." Old Norse *fēlagi* is derived from *fēlag,* "partnership," a compound made up of *fē,* "livestock, property, money" (related to English *fee*) and *lag,* "a laying in order" and "fellowship." The notion of putting one's property together lies behind the senses of *fēlagi* meaning "partner" and "consort." In Old Norse *fēlagi* also had the general sense "fellow, mate, comrade," as does *fellow.*

fellow feeling *n.* **1.** Sympathetic awareness of others; rapport. **2.** Community of interest.

fellow man also **fel•low•man** (fĕl′ō-măn′) *n.* Another human being.

fellow servant *n.* One of a group of employees working under such circumstances that the employer is not liable for injury to one worker resulting from the negligence of another.

fel•low•ship (fĕl′ō-shĭp′) *n.* **1a.** The condition of sharing similar interests, ideals, or experiences, as by reason of profession, religion, or nationality. **b.** The companionship of peers in a congenial atmosphere. **2.** A close association of friends or equals sharing similar interests. **3.** Friendship; comradeship. **4a.** The financial grant made to a fellow in a college or university. **b.** The status of having been awarded such a grant. **c.** A foundation established for the awarding of such a grant.

fellow traveler *n.* One who sympathizes with or supports the tenets and program of an organized group, such as the Communist Party, without being a member.

fel•ly (fĕl′ē) also **fel•loe** (fĕl′ō) *n., pl.* **-lies** also **-loes** The rim or a section of the rim of a wheel supported by spokes. [ME *felie, felwe* < OE *felg.*]

fel•on[1] (fĕl′ən) *n.* **1.** *Law* One who has committed a felony. **2.** *Archaic* An evil person. ❖ *adj. Archaic* Evil; cruel. [ME *feloun*

< OFr. *felon*, wicked, a wicked person < Med.Lat. *fellō, fellōn-*, poss. of Gmc. orig.]

fel·on² (fĕl′ən) *n.* A painful purulent infection at the end of a finger or toe in the area surrounding the nail. [ME *feloun*, prob. < Lat. *fel*, gall, bile. See **ghel-** in App.]

fe·lo·ni·ous (fə-lō′nē-əs) *adj.* **1.** *Law* Having the nature of, relating to, or concerning a felony: *felonious intent.* **2.** *Archaic* Evil; wicked. —**fe·lo′ni·ous·ly** *adv.* —**fe·lo′ni·ous·ness** *n.*

fel·o·ny (fĕl′ə-nē) *n., pl.* -**nies** *Law* **1.** One of several crimes, such as murder, rape, or burglary, punishable by a more stringent sentence than that given for a misdemeanor. **2.** Any of several crimes in early English law punishable by forfeiture of land or goods and by possible loss of life or a bodily part.

fel·sic (fĕl′sĭk) *adj.* Containing a group of light-colored silicate minerals that occur in igneous rocks. [FEL(DSPAR) + S(ILICA) + -IC.]

fel·site (fĕl′sīt′) *n.* A fine-grained light-colored igneous rock composed chiefly of feldspar and quartz. [FELS(PAR) + -ITE¹.] —**fel·sit′ic** (-sĭt′ĭk) *adj.*

fel·spar (fĕl′spär′) *n.* Variant of **feldspar.**

felt¹ (fĕlt) *n.* **1a.** A nonwoven fabric of matted compressed animal fibers, such as wool or fur, sometimes mixed with vegetable or synthetic fibers. **b.** A material resembling this fabric. **2.** Something made of this fabric. ❖ *adj.* Made of, relating to, or resembling felt. ❖ *v.* **felt·ed, felt·ing, felts** —*tr.* **1.** To make into felt. **2.** To cover with felt. **3.** To press or mat (something) together. —*intr.* To become like felt; mat together. [ME < OE. See **pel-²** in App.] —**felt′y** *adj.*

felt² (fĕlt) *v.* Past tense and past participle of **feel.**

felt·ing (fĕl′tĭng) *n.* **1.** The practice or process of making felt. **2.** The materials from which felt is made. **3.** Felted fabric.

fe·luc·ca (fə-lōō′kə, -lŭk′ə) *n.* A narrow, swift, lateen-rigged sailing vessel, such as that used in the Mediterranean Sea. [Ital. *feluca* < Ar. *falūka*, sloop < Gk. *epholkion*, small boat towed after a ship < *ephelkein*, to tow : *epi-*, *epi-* + *helkein*, to drag, pull.]

fem. *abbr.* **1.** female **2.** feminine

FEMA (fē′mə) *abbr.* Federal Emergency Management Agency

fe·male (fē′māl′) *adj.* **1a.** Of or denoting the sex that produces ova or bears young. **b.** Characteristic of or appropriate to this sex; feminine. **c.** Consisting of members of this sex. See Usage Note at **lady. 2.** *Botany* **a.** Relating to or being an organ, such as a pistil or an ovary, that produces seeds after fertilization. **b.** Bearing pistils but not stamens; pistillate. **3.** Having a recessed part, such as a slot, designed to receive a male part: *a female plug.* ❖ *n.* **1.** A member of the sex that produces ova or bears young. **2.** A woman or girl. **3.** *Botany* A plant having only pistillate flowers. [ME, alteration (influenced by *male*, male) of *femelle* < OFr. < Lat. *fēmella*, dim. of *fēmina*, woman.] —**fe′male·ness** *n.*

female circumcision *n.* Partial or complete removal of the clitoris, prepuce, or labia of a girl or young woman, as practiced among certain cultures.

female genital mutilation *n.* Female circumcision.

fem·i·nine (fĕm′ə-nĭn) *adj.* **1.** Of or relating to women or girls; female. **2.** Characterized by or possessing qualities generally attributed to a woman. **3.** Effeminate; womanish. **4.** *Grammar* Relating or belonging to the gender of words or forms that refer chiefly to females or to things grammatically classified as female. ❖ *n. Grammar* **1.** The feminine gender. **2.** A word or form of this gender. [ME < OFr. < Lat. *fēminīnus* < *fēmina*, woman.] —**fem′i·nine·ly** *adv.* —**fem′i·nine·ness** *n.*

feminine ending *n.* An extra unstressed syllable at the end of a line of verse. **2.** *Grammar* A final syllable or termination that marks or forms words in the feminine gender.

feminine rhyme *n.* A rhyme in which the final syllable is unstressed, as in *feather/heather.*

fem·i·nin·i·ty (fĕm′ə-nĭn′ĭ-tē) *n., pl.* -**ties 1.** The quality or condition of being feminine. **2.** A characteristic or trait traditionally held to be female. **3.** Women considered as a group. **4.** Effeminacy.

fem·i·nism (fĕm′ə-nĭz′əm) *n.* **1.** Belief in the social, political, and economic equality of the sexes. **2.** The movement organized around this belief.

fem·i·nist (fĕm′ə-nĭst) *n.* A person whose beliefs and behavior are based on feminism. —**fem′i·nist, fem′i·nis′tic** *adj.*

fem·i·nize (fĕm′ə-nīz′) *tr.v.* -**nized, -niz·ing, -niz·es 1.** To give a feminine appearance or character to. **2.** To cause (a male) to assume feminine characteristics. —**fem′i·ni·za′tion** (-nĭ-zā′shən) *n.*

femme (fĕm) *adj. Slang* Exhibiting stereotypical or exaggerated feminine traits. Used esp. of lesbians and gay men. ❖ *n.* **1.** *Slang* One who is femme. **2.** *Informal* A woman or girl. [Fr. < OFr. < Lat. *fēmina.*]

femme fa·tale (fĕm′ fə-tăl′, -täl′, făm′) *n., pl.* **femmes fa·tales** (fĕm′ fə-tăl′, -tälz′, -täl′, -tälz′, făm′) **1.** A seductive woman who leads men into dangerous situations. **2.** An alluring mysterious woman. [Fr. : *femme*, woman + *fatale*, deadly.]

fem·o·ral (fĕm′ər-əl) *adj.* Of, relating to, or located in the thigh or femur: *femoral artery.* [< Lat. *femur, femor-*, thigh.]

femto– *pref.* One quadrillionth (10⁻¹⁵): *femtovolt.* [< Dan. and Norw. *femten*, fifteen < ON *fimmtān.* See **penkwe** in App.]

fe·mur (fē′mər) *n., pl.* **fe·murs** or **fem·o·ra** (fĕm′ər-ə) **1a.** A

bone of the leg between the pelvis and knee in humans. **b.** A similar bone in the leg or hind limb of a vertebrate animal. **2.** The thick, most muscular segment of the insect leg, situated between the trochanter and the tibia. [Lat., thigh.]

fen (fĕn) *n.* Low, flat, swampy land; a bog or marsh. [ME < OE *fenn.*] —**fen′ny** *adj.*

fence (fĕns) *n.* **1.** A structure serving as an enclosure, a barrier, or a boundary, usu. made of posts or stakes joined by boards, wire, or rails. **2.** The sport of fencing. **3a.** One who receives and sells stolen goods. **b.** A place where such goods are received and sold. **4.** *Archaic* A means of defense; a protection. ❖ *v.* **fenced, fenc·ing, fenc·es** —*tr.* **1.** To enclose with or as if with a fence. **2.** To separate or close off by or as if by means of a fence. **3a.** To ward off; keep away. **b.** To defend. **4.** To sell (stolen goods) to a fence. —*intr.* **1.** To practice the sport of fencing. **2.** To use tactics similar to the parry and thrust of fencing. **3.** To avoid giving direct answers; hedge. **4.** To act as a conduit for stolen goods. —**idiom: on the fence** *Informal* Uncommitted or neutral. [ME *fens*, short for *defens*, defense. See DEFENSE.] —**fenc′er** *n.*

fence sitter *n. Informal* One who is neutral or indecisive in a controversy. —**fence′-sit′ting** (fĕns′sĭt′ĭng) *n.*

fenc·ing (fĕn′sĭng) *n.* **1.** The art or sport of using a foil, épée, or saber in attack and defense. **2.** Skillful repartee, esp. as a defense against having to give direct answers. **3.** Material, such as wire, stakes, and rails, used in building fences. **4.** A barrier or enclosure of fences.

fend (fĕnd) *v.* **fend·ed, fend·ing, fends** —*tr.* **1.** To ward off. Often used with *off.* **2.** *Archaic* To defend. —*intr.* **1.** To make an effort to resist: *fend against the cold.* **2.** To attempt to manage without assistance: *had to fend for ourselves until we were rescued.* [ME *fenden*, short for *defenden*, to defend. See DEFEND.]

fend·er (fĕn′dər) *n.* **1a.** A guard over each wheel of a motor vehicle, for example, that blocks the splashing of water or mud. **b.** A device at the front end of a locomotive or streetcar that pushes aside obstructions. **2.** A cushioning device on the side of a vessel or dock to absorb impact or friction. **3.** A screen or metal framework in front of a fireplace to keep hot coals and debris from falling out.

fend·er-bend·er or **fender bender** (fĕn′dər-bĕn′dər) *n. Informal* A collision involving motor vehicles that results in minor damage.

fe·nes·tra (fə-nĕs′trə) *n., pl.* -**trae** (-trē′) **1.** *Anatomy* A small opening, esp. in the medial wall of the middle ear. **2.** The opening in a bandage or cast for access or drainage. **3.** *Zoology* A transparent spot or marking, as on the wing of a butterfly. **4.** *Architecture* A windowlike opening. [Lat., window.] —**fe·nes′tral** *adj.*

fen·es·trat·ed (fĕn′ĭ-strā′tĭd) also **fen·es·trate** (fĕn′ĭ-strāt′, fĭ-nĕs′trāt′) *adj.* **1.** *Architecture* Having windows or windowlike openings. **2.** *Biology* Having fenestrae.

fen·es·tra·tion (fĕn′ĭ-strā′shən) *n.* **1.** The design and placement of windows in a building. **2.** An opening in the surface of a structure, as in a membrane. **3.** The surgical creation of an artificial opening in the bony part of the inner ear so as to improve or restore hearing.

feng shui (fŭng′ shwā′) *n.* The Chinese art or practice of positioning objects, esp. graves, buildings, and furniture, based on a belief in patterns of yin and yang and the flow of chi that have positive and negative effects. [Chin. (Mandarin) *fēng shuǐ*, wind (and) water : *fēng*, wind + *shuǐ*, water.]

Fe·ni·an (fē′nē-ən) *n.* **1.** One of a legendary group of heroic Irish warriors of the second and third centuries A.D. **2.** A member of a secret revolutionary organization formed in the United States in the mid-19th century and dedicated to the overthrow of British rule in Ireland. [< alteration of Ir.Gael. *fianna*, pl. of *fiann*, young warriors < OIr. *fianna*, pl. of *fian*.] —**Fe′ni·an** *adj.* —**Fe′ni·an·ism** *n.*

fen·nec (fĕn′ĭk) *n.* A small fawn-colored nocturnal fox (*Vulpes zerda*, formerly *Fennecus zerda*) of northern Africa. [Ar. *fanak.*]

fen·nel (fĕn′əl) *n.* **1.** A Eurasian plant (*Foeniculum vulgare*) having clusters of small yellow flowers and aromatic seeds used as flavoring. **2.** The edible seeds or stalks of this plant. [ME *fenel* < OE *fenol* < Lat. *fēnuculum*, var. of *faeniculum*, dim. of *faenum, fēnum*, hay.]

Fens (fĕnz) A lowland district of E England W and S of the Wash.

fen·u·greek (fĕn′yə-grēk′, fĕn′ə-) *n.* **1.** A cloverlike Eurasian plant (*Trigonella foenum-graecum*) having white flowers and pungent aromatic seeds used as flavoring. **2.** The seeds or leaves of this plant. [ME *fenigrek* < OFr. *fenegrec* < Lat. *fēnugraecum* < *fēnum Graecum* : *fēnum*, hay + *Graecum*, neut. of *Graecus*, Gk.; see GREEK.]

feoff·ee (fĕf-ē′, fē-fē′) *n.* One to whom a feoffment is granted. [AN *feoffé* < *feoffer*, to put in legal possession. See FEOFFMENT.]

feoff·er also **feof·for** (fĕf′ər, fē′fər) *n.* One who grants a feoffment. [AN *feoffour* < *feoffer*, to put in legal possession. See FEOFFMENT.]

feoff·ment (fĕf′mənt, fēf′-) *n. Law* A grant of lands as a fee. [ME *feffement* < AN *feoffement* < *feoffer*, to put in legal possession < OFr. *fief*, fief, fee. See FEE.]

FEPC *abbr.* Fair Employment Practices Commission

–fer *suff.* One that bears: *aquifer.* [Lat., bearer, bearing < *ferre*, to carry. See **bher-¹** in App.]

fennel
Foeniculum vulgare

fe·ral (fîr′əl, fĕr′-) *adj.* **1a.** Existing in a wild or untamed state. **b.** Having returned to an untamed state from domestication. **2.** Of or suggestive of a wild animal; savage: *a feral grin.* [< Lat. *fera,* wild animal < *ferus,* wild. See **ghwer-** in App.]

Fer·ber (fûr′bər), Edna 1887–1968. Amer. writer noted for her short stories and novels, including *So Big* (1924).

fer-de-lance (fĕr′dl-äns′, -äns′) *n., pl.* **fer-de-lance** A venomous tropical American pit viper (*Bothrops atrox*) having brown and grayish markings. [Fr. < *fer de lance,* spearhead : *fer,* iron + *de,* of + *lance,* spear.]

Fer·di·nand I[1] (fûr′dn-änd′) Known as "Ferdinand the Great." d. 1065. King of Castile (1035–65) and León (1037–65) who reconquered much of present-day Portugal from the Moors.

Fer·di·nand I[2] 1503–64. Holy Roman emperor (1558–64) and king of Bohemia and Hungary (1526–64) who ended the religious wars in Germany with the Peace of Augsburg (1555).

Ferdinand II 1578–1637. Holy Roman emperor (1619–37) and king of Bohemia (1617–19 and 1620–27) and Hungary (1618–25) who was a leader of the Counter Reformation.

Ferdinand III 1608–57. Holy Roman emperor (1637–57) and king of Hungary (1625–47) and Bohemia (1627–56) who signed the Peace of Westphalia (1648), ending the Thirty Years' War.

Ferdinand V 1452–1516. King of Castile and León (1474–1504) who ruled jointly with his wife, Isabella I; also king of Sicily (1468–1516) and Aragon (1479–1516) as Ferdinand II and of Naples (1504–16) as Ferdinand III.

fere (fîr) *n. Archaic* **1.** A companion. **2.** A spouse. [ME < OE *gefēra.* See **per-**[2] in App.]

Fer·ga·na also **Fer·gha·na** (fər-gä′nə) A city of E Uzbekistan E of Samarqand in the **Fergana Valley,** a densely populated agricultural and industrial region. Pop. 198,000.

fe·ri·a (fîr′ē-ə, fĕr′-) *n., pl.* **-ri·as** or **-ri·ae** (-ē-ē′) A weekday on a church calendar on which no feast is observed. [Med.Lat. *fēria,* ordinary day, weekday < LLat., feast day (used with ordinals to name the days of the week) < Lat. *fēriae,* religious festival, holidays. See **dhēs-** in App.] —**fe′ri·al** *adj.*

fe·rine (fîr′īn) *adj.* Untamed; feral. [Lat. *ferīnus* < *fera,* wild animal. See FERAL.]

fer·i·ty (fĕr′ĭ-tē) *n.* **1.** The state of being wild or untamed. **2.** The state of being savage; ferocity. [Lat. *feritās* < *ferus,* wild. See FERAL.]

Fer·mat (fĕr-mä′), Pierre de 1601–65. French mathematician who developed number theory and probability theory.

fer·ma·ta (fĕr-mä′tə) *n. Music* **1.** The prolongation of a tone, chord, or rest beyond its indicated time value. **2.** The sign indicating this prolongation. [Ital. < fem. p. part. of *fermare,* to stop < Lat. *firmāre,* to make firm < *firmus,* firm.]

Fer·mat's last theorem (fĕr-mäz′) *n.* The theorem that the equation $a^n + b^n = c^n$ has no solutions in positive integers *a, b, c* if *n* is an integer greater than 2. [After Pierre de FERMAT.]

fer·ment (fûr′mĕnt′) *n.* **1.** Something, such as a yeast, that causes fermentation. **2.** Fermentation. **3a.** A state of agitation or of turbulent change. **b.** An agent that precipitates such a state. ❖ *v.* (fər-mĕnt′) **-ment·ed, -ment·ing, -ments** —*tr.* **1.** To produce by or as if by fermentation. **2.** To cause to undergo fermentation. **3.** To make turbulent; excite or agitate. —*intr.* **1.** To undergo fermentation. **2.** To be in an agitated state; seethe. [ME < OFr. < Lat. *fermentum.*] —**fer·ment′a·bil′i·ty** *n.* —**fer·ment′a·ble** *adj.*

fer·men·ta·tion (fûr′mən-tā′shən, -mĕn-) *n.* **1.** Any of a group of chemical reactions that split complex organic compounds into relatively simple substances, esp. the anaerobic conversion of sugar to carbon dioxide and alcohol by yeast. **2.** Unrest; agitation.

fer·men·ta·tive (fər-mĕn′tə-tĭv) *adj.* **1a.** Causing fermentation. **b.** Capable of causing or undergoing fermentation. **2.** Relating to or of the nature of fermentation.

fer·ment·er (fər-mĕn′tər) *n.* **1.** An organism that causes fermentation. **2.** also **fer·men·tor** An apparatus used for fermentation.

fer·mi (fûr′mē, fĕr′-) *n., pl.* **-mis** A unit of length equal to one femtometer (10^{-15} meter). [After Enrico FERMI.]

Fer·mi (fĕr′mē), Enrico 1901–54. Italian-born Amer. physicist who won a 1938 Nobel Prize and produced the first controlled nuclear chain reaction (1942).

fer·mi·on (fûr′mē-ŏn′, fĕr′-) *n.* A particle, such as an electron, having half-integral spin and obeying statistical rules requiring that no two identical particles may occupy the same quantum state. [After Enrico FERMI.]

fer·mi·um (fûr′mē-əm, fĕr′-) *n. Symbol* **Fm** A synthetic radioactive metallic element whose most stable isotope is Fm 257 with a half-life of approx. 100 days. Atomic number 100. See table at **element.** [After Enrico FERMI.]

fern (fûrn) *n.* Any of numerous flowerless vascular plants having roots, stems, and fronds and reproducing by spores. [ME < OE *fearn.* See **per-**[2] in App.] —**fern′y** *adj.*

Fer·nan·do de No·ro·nha (fər-năn′dō də nə-rōn′yə, fər-nän′dōō də nô-rô′nyə) An island group in the Atlantic Ocean off the NE coast of Brazil; once used as a penal colony.

Fer·nan·do Po (fər-năn′dō pō′) See **Bioko.**

fern·er·y (fûr′nə-rē) *n., pl.* **-ies 1.** A place or container in which ferns are grown. **2.** A bed or collection of ferns.

fer·ninst (fər-nĭnst′) also **for·nent** (fər-nĕnt′) *prep. Chiefly Midland US* Opposite, near to, or against: *Their barn is ferninst the house.* [Dialectal *fornent, fornenst* : FORE + *anent, anenst* (< ME; see ANENT).]

fern seed *n.* The dustlike spores of ferns, once thought to be seeds and to be capable of making their possessor invisible.

fe·ro·cious (fə-rō′shəs) *adj.* **1.** Extremely savage; fierce. See Syns at **cruel. 2.** Marked by unrelenting intensity; extreme: *ferocious heat.* [< Lat. *ferōx, ferōc-,* fierce. See **ghwer-** in App.] —**fe·ro′cious·ly** *adv.* —**fe·ro′cious·ness** *n.*

fe·roc·i·ty (fə-rŏs′ĭ-tē) *n.* The state or quality of being ferocious; fierceness.

-ferous *suff.* Bearing; producing; containing: *carboniferous; sporiferous.* [—FER +-OUS.]

ferr- *pref.* Variant of **ferro-.**

Fer·ra·ra (fə-rär′ə, fĕ-rä′rä) A city of N Italy SW of Venice. Pop. 137,336.

fer·rate (fĕr′āt) *n.* See **ferrite** 1.

fer·re·dox·in (fĕr′ĭ-dŏk′sĭn) *n.* An iron-containing protein present in green plants and certain anaerobic bacteria that functions in electron transport reactions in biochemical processes, such as photosynthesis. [FER(RO)- + REDOX +-IN.]

fer·ret[1] (fĕr′ĭt) *n.* **1.** A weasellike mammal (*Mustela putorius furo*) often trained to hunt rats or rabbits. **2.** A black-footed ferret. ❖ *v.* **-ret·ed, -ret·ing, -rets** —*tr.* **1a.** To hunt (rabbits, for example) with ferrets. **b.** To drive out, as from a hiding place; expel. **2.** To uncover and bring to light by searching. Often used with *out.* **3.** To hound or harry persistently; worry. —*intr.* **1.** To engage in hunting with ferrets. **2.** To search intensively. [ME *furet, ferret* < OFr. *furet* < VLat. **fūrittus,* dim. of Lat. *fūr,* thief. See **bher-**[1] in App.] —**fer′ret·er** *n.* —**fer′ret·y** *adj.*

fer·ret[2] (fĕr′ĭt) also **fer·ret·ing** *n.* A narrow piece of tape used to bind or edge fabric. [Prob. alteration of Ital. *fioretti,* floss silk, pl. of *fioretto,* dim. of *fiore,* flower < Lat. *flōs, flōr-,* flower. See **bhel-** in App.]

ferri- *pref.* Iron, esp. ferric iron: *ferricyanide.* [< Lat. *ferrum,* iron.]

fer·ric (fĕr′ĭk) *adj.* Of, relating to, or containing iron, esp. with valence 3 or a valence higher than in a corresponding ferrous compound.

ferric oxide *n.* A dark red compound, Fe_2O_3, occurring naturally as hematite ore and rust and used in pigments and metal polishes and on magnetic tapes.

fer·ri·cy·a·nide (fĕr′ĭ-sī′ə-nīd′, fĕr′ĭ-) *n.* Any of various salts containing the negative trivalent radical $Fe(CN)_6$ and used in making blue pigments.

fer·rif·er·ous (fə-rĭf′ər-əs, fĕ-) *adj.* Containing or yielding iron.

Fer·ris wheel also **fer·ris wheel** (fĕr′ĭs) *n.* An amusement ride consisting of an upright rotating wheel having suspended seats that remain horizontal as the wheel revolves. [After George Washington Gale *Ferris* (1859–96), American engineer.]

fer·rite (fĕr′īt) *n.* **1.** Any of a group of ceramic, usu. ferromagnetic compounds of ferric oxide with other oxides, esp. such a compound with extremely high electrical resistivity that is used in computer memory elements, permanent magnets, and various solid-state devices. **2.** Iron uncombined with carbon, occurring commonly in steel, cast iron, and pig iron below 910°C.

fer·ri·tin (fĕr′ĭ-tĭn) *n.* An iron-containing protein complex, found principally in the intestinal mucosa, spleen, and liver, that functions as the primary form of iron storage in the body.

ferro- or **ferr-** *pref.* **1.** Iron: *ferromagnetic.* **2.** Ferrous iron: *ferrocyanide.* [< Lat. *ferrum,* iron.]

fer·ro·al·loy (fĕr′ō-ăl′oi′, -ə-loi′) *n.* Any of various alloys of iron and one or more other elements, such as manganese or silicon, used as a raw material in the production of steel.

fer·ro·con·crete (fĕr′ō-kŏn′krēt′, -kŏng′-, -kŏn-krēt′, -kŏng-) *n.* See **reinforced concrete.**

fer·ro·cy·a·nide (fĕr′ō-sī′ə-nīd′) *n.* A salt containing the negative tetravalent radical $Fe(CN)_6$, used in making blue pigments, blueprint paper, and ferricyanide.

fer·ro·e·lec·tric (fĕr′ō-ĭ-lĕk′trĭk) *adj.* Of or relating to a crystalline dielectric that develops a permanent electric polarization in an applied electric field. ❖ *n.* A ferroelectric substance. —**fer′ro·e·lec·tric′i·ty** (-ĭ-lĕk-trĭs′ĭ-tē, -ē′lĕk-) *n.*

fer·ro·mag·ne·sian (fĕr′ō-măg-nē′zhən, -shən) *adj.* Containing iron and magnesium.

fer·ro·mag·net (fĕr′ō-măg′nĭt) *n.* **1a.** A ferromagnetic substance. **b.** A substance with magnetic properties resembling those of iron. **2.** A ferromagnetic magnet.

fer·ro·mag·net·ic (fĕr′ō-măg-nĕt′ĭk) *adj.* Relating to or characteristic of substances such as iron that exhibit high magnetic permeability and magnetic hysteresis. —**fer′ro·mag′ne·tism** (-măg′nĭ-tĭz′əm) *n.*

fer·ro·man·ga·nese (fĕr′ō-măng′gə-nēz′, -nēs′) *n.* An alloy of iron and manganese used in the production of steel.

fer·ro·sil·i·con (fĕr′ō-sĭl′ĭ-kən, -kŏn′) *n.* An alloy of iron and silicon used in the production of carbon steel.

fer·ro·type (fĕr′ō-tīp′) *n.* **1.** A positive photograph made directly on an iron plate varnished with a thin sensitized film. **2.** The process by which such photographs are made.

fer·rous (fĕr′əs) *adj.* Of or containing iron, esp. with valence 2

or a valence lower than in a corresponding ferric compound.
ferrous oxide *n.* A powder, FeO, used in the manufacture of steel, heat-absorbing glass, and enamels.
ferrous sulfate *n.* A crystalline compound, $FeSO_4 \cdot 7H_2O$, used as a pigment, fertilizer, and feed additive, in sewage and water treatment, and in the treatment of anemia.
fer•ru•gi•nous (fə-ro͞o′jə-nəs, fĕ-) *adj.* **1.** Of, containing, or similar to iron. **2.** Having the color of iron rust; reddish-brown. [< Lat. *ferrūginus* < *ferrūgō, ferrūgin-*, iron rust < *ferrum*, iron.]
fer•rule (fĕr′əl) *n.* **1.** A metal ring or cap placed around a pole or shaft for reinforcement. **2.** A bushing used to secure a pipe joint. [Alteration of ME *verrele* < OFr. *virole* < Lat. *viriola*, dim. of *viriae*, bracelets.] **—fer′rule** *v.*
fer•ry (fĕr′ē) *v.* **-ried, -ry•ing, -ries** *—tr.* **1.** *Nautical* **a.** To transport (people, vehicles, or goods) by boat across a body of water. **b.** To cross (a body of water) by a ferry. **2a.** To deliver (a vehicle, esp. an aircraft) under its own power to its eventual user. **b.** To transport (people or goods) by vehicle, esp. by aircraft. *—intr.* To cross a body of water on or as if on a ferry. ❖ *n., pl.* **-ries 1.** *Nautical* **a.** A ferryboat. **b.** A place where passengers or goods are ferried. **2.** A franchise or legal right to operate a ferrying service for a fee. **3.** A service and route for ferrying an aircraft. [ME *ferien* < OE *ferian*. See **per-**[2] in App.]
fer•ry•boat (fĕr′ē-bōt′) *n.* A boat used to ferry passengers, vehicles, or goods.
fer•tile (fûr′tl) *adj.* **1.** *Biology* **a.** Capable of initiating, sustaining, or supporting reproduction. **b.** Capable of growing and developing; able to mature. **2.** *Botany* Bearing functional reproductive structures. **3.** Bearing or producing crops or vegetation abundantly; fruitful. **4.** Rich in material needed to sustain plant growth: *fertile soil.* **5.** Highly or continuously productive; prolific. **6.** *Physics* Capable of producing fissionable material. [ME *fertil* < OFr. *fertile* < Lat. *fertilis* < *ferre*, to bear. See **bher-**[1] in App.] **—fer′tile•ly** *adv.* **—fer′tile•ness** *n.*
Fertile Crescent A region of the Middle East across the N part of the Syrian Desert extending from the Nile Valley to the Tigris and Euphrates rivers.
fer•til•i•ty (fər-tĭl′ĭ-tē) *n.* **1.** The condition, quality, or degree of being fertile. **2.** The birthrate of a population.
fer•til•i•za•tion (fûr′tl-ĭ-zā′shən) *n.* **1.** The act or process of initiating biological reproduction by insemination or pollination. **2.** The union of male and female gametes to form a zygote. **3.** The act or process of applying a fertilizer. **—fer′til•i•za′tion•al** *adj.*
fer•til•ize (fûr′tl-īz′) *v.* **-ized, -iz•ing, -iz•es** *—tr.* **1.** To cause the fertilization of (an ovum, for example). **2.** To make (soil, for example) fertile. **3.** To spread fertilizer on. *—intr.* To spread fertilizer. **—fer′til•iz′a•ble** *adj.*
fer•til•iz•er (fûr′tl-ī′zər) *n.* Any of a large number of natural and synthetic materials, including manure and nitrogen, phosphorus, and potassium compounds, spread on or worked into soil to increase its capacity to support plant growth.
fer•ule (fĕr′əl) *n.* An instrument, such as a cane, used in punishing children. ❖ *tr.v.* **-uled, -ul•ing, -ules** To punish with a ferule. [ME *ferul*, fennel stalk < Lat. *ferula*, rod.]
fe•ru•lic acid (fə-ro͞o′lĭk) *n.* A compound, $C_{10}H_{10}O_4$, related to vanillin and obtained from certain plants. [< NLat. *Ferula*, plant genus < Lat. *ferula*, giant fennel.]
fer•ven•cy (fûr′vən-sē) *n., pl.* **-cies** The condition or quality of being fervent.
fer•vent (fûr′vənt) *adj.* **1.** Having or showing great emotion or zeal; ardent: *fervent protests; a fervent admirer.* **2.** Extremely hot; glowing. [ME < OFr. < Lat. *fervēns, fervent-*, pr. part. of *fervēre*, to boil.] **—fer′vent•ly** *adv.* **—fer′vent•ness** *n.*
fer•vid (fûr′vĭd) *adj.* **1.** Marked by great passion or zeal. **2.** Extremely hot; burning. [Lat. *fervidus* < *fervēre*, to boil.] **—fer′vid•ly** *adv.* **—fer′vid•ness** *n.*
fer•vor (fûr′vər) *n.* **1.** Great warmth and intensity of emotion. **2.** Intense heat. [ME *fervour* < OFr. < Lat. *fervor* < *fervēre*, to boil.]
fer•vour (fûr′vər) *n. Chiefly British* Variant of **fervor.**
Fès (fĕs) See **Fez.**
fes•cen•nine (fĕs′ə-nīn′, -nēn′) *adj.* Licentious; obscene. [Lat. *Fescennīnus*, of Fescennia, a town of ancient Etruria known for its licentious poetry.]
fes•cue (fĕs′kyo͞o) *n.* Any of various grasses of the genus *Festuca*, often cultivated as pasturage. [Alteration of ME *festu*, straw < OFr. < LLat. *festūcum* < Lat. *festūca.*]
fess[1] also **fesse** (fĕs) *n. Heraldry* A wide horizontal band forming the middle section of an escutcheon. [ME *fesse* < OFr. < Lat. *fascia*, band.]
fess[2] (fĕs) *intr.v.* **fessed, fess•ing, fess•es** *Informal* To admit to something; confess. Often used with *up.* [Short for CONFESS.]
fess point *n. Heraldry* The center point of an escutcheon.
fest (fĕst) *n.* A gathering or occasion characterized by a specified activity. Often used in combination: *a music fest; a chilifest.* [< Ger., festival < MHGer. < Lat. *fēstum.* See FEAST.]
fes•tal (fĕs′təl) *adj.* Of, relating to, or of the nature of a feast or festival; festive. [ME < OFr. < LLat. *fēstālis* < Lat. *fēstum*, feast. See FEAST.] **—fes′tal•ly** *adv.*
fes•ter (fĕs′tər) *v.* **-tered, -ter•ing, -ters** *—intr.* **1.** To generate pus; suppurate. **2.** To form an ulcer. **3.** To undergo decay; rot. **4a.** To be or become an increasing source of irritation or poisoning; rankle. **b.** To be subject to or exist in a condition of decline. *—tr.* To infect, inflame, or corrupt. ❖ *n.* A small festering sore or ulcer; a pustule. [ME *festren* < *festre*, fistula < OFr. < Lat. *fistula.*]
fes•ti•nate (fĕs′tə-nĭt) *adj.* Hasty. ❖ *intr.v.* (-nāt′) **-nat•ed, -nat•ing, -nates** To hasten. [Lat. *festīnātus*, p. part. of *festīnāre*, to hasten.] **—fes′ti•nate•ly** *adv.*
fes•ti•val (fĕs′tə-vəl) *n.* **1.** An occasion for feasting or celebration, esp. a day or time of religious significance that recurs at regular intervals. **2.** An often regularly recurring program of cultural performances, exhibitions, or competitions: *a film festival.* **3.** Revelry; conviviality. ❖ *adj.* Of, relating to, or suitable for a feast or festival; festive. [< ME, festive < OFr. < Med.Lat. *fēstivālis* < Lat. *fēstīvus* < *fēstus.* See **dhēs-** in App.]
fes•tive (fĕs′tĭv) *adj.* **1.** Of, relating to, or appropriate for a feast or festival. **2.** Merry; joyous. [Lat. *fēstīvus* < *fēstus.* See **dhēs-** in App.] **—fes′tive•ly** *adv.* **—fes′tive•ness** *n.*
fes•tiv•i•ty (fĕ-stĭv′ĭ-tē) *n., pl.* **-ties 1.** A joyous feast, holiday, or celebration; a festival. **2.** The pleasure, joy, and gaiety of a festival or celebration. **3. festivities** The proceedings or events of a festival.
fes•toon (fĕ-sto͞on′) *n.* **1.** A string or garland, as of flowers, suspended in a loop or curve between two points. **2.** A representation of such a string or garland, as in painting or sculpture. ❖ *tr.v.* **-tooned, -toon•ing, -toons 1.** To decorate with or as if with festoons; hang festoons on. **2.** To form or make into festoons. [Fr. *feston* < Ital. *festone* < *festa*, feast < VLat. **fēsta.* See FEAST.]
fes•toon•er•y (fĕ-sto͞o′nə-rē) *n., pl.* **-ies 1.** An arrangement of festoons. **2.** Festoons considered as a group.
fest•schrift (fĕst′shrĭft′) *n., pl.* **-schrif•ten** (-shrĭf′tən) or **-schrifts** A volume of learned articles or essays by colleagues and admirers, serving as a tribute or memorial esp. to a scholar. [Ger. : *Fest*, festival; see FEST + *Schrift*, writing (ult. < Lat. *scrībere*, to write; see **skrībh-** in App.).]
FET *abbr.* **1.** federal estate tax **2.** federal excise tax **3.** field-effect transistor
fet– *pref.* Variant of **feto–.**
fet•a (fĕt′ə, fā′tə) *n.* A white semisoft cheese usu. made of goat's or ewe's milk and often preserved in brine. [Mod.Gk. *(turi) pheta*, (cheese) slice < Ital. *fetta*, slice < **offetta*, dim. of **offa* < Lat. *offa*, morsel of food.]
fe•tal (fēt′l) *adj.* Of, relating to, characteristic of, or being a fetus.
fetal alcohol syndrome *n.* A complex of birth defects including craniofacial abnormalities, growth retardation, and mental retardation that occurs as a result of excessive alcohol consumption by the mother during pregnancy.
fetal position *n.* A position of the body at rest in which the spine is curved, the head is bowed forward, and the arms and legs are drawn in toward the chest.
fetch[1] (fĕch) *v.* **fetched, fetch•ing, fetch•es** *—tr.* **1.** To come or go after and take or bring back. **2a.** To cause to come. **b.** To bring in as a price. **c.** To interest or attract. **3a.** To draw in (breath); inhale. **b.** To bring forth (a sigh, for example) with obvious effort. **4.** *Informal* To deliver (a blow) by striking; deal. **5.** *Nautical* To arrive at; reach. *—intr.* **1a.** To go after something and return with it. **b.** To retrieve killed game. Used of a hunting dog. **2.** To take an indirect route. ❖ *n.* **1.** The act or an instance of fetching. **2.** A stratagem or trick. **3a.** The distance over which a wind blows. **b.** The distance traveled by waves with no obstruction. ***—phrasal verb:* fetch up 1.** To reach a stopping place or goal; end up. **2.** To make up (lost time, for example). **3.** To bring forth; produce. **4.** To bring to a halt; stop. [ME *fecchen* < OE *feccean.* See **ped-** in App.] **—fetch′er** *n.*
fetch[2] (fĕch) *n. Chiefly British* **1.** A ghost; an apparition. **2.** A doppelgänger. [?]
fetch•ing (fĕch′ĭng) *adj.* Very attractive; charming: *a fetching new hairstyle.* **—fetch′ing•ly** *adv.*
fete also **fête** (fāt, fĕt) *n.* **1.** A festival or feast. **2a.** An elaborate, often outdoor entertainment. **b.** An elaborate party. ❖ *tr.v.* **fet•ed, fet•ing, fetes** also **fêt•ed, fêt•ing, fêtes 1.** To celebrate or honor with a fete. **2.** To pay honor to. [Fr. *fête* < OFr. *feste.* See FEAST.]
feti– *pref.* Variant of **feto–.**
fe•ti•cide (fē′tĭ-sīd′) *n.* Intentional destruction of a human fetus. **—fe′ti•cid′al** (-sīd′l) *adj.*
fet•id also **foe•tid** (fĕt′ĭd, fē′tĭd) *adj.* Having an offensive odor. [ME < Lat. *fētidus* < *fētēre*, to stink.] **—fet′id•ly** *adv.* **—fet′id•ness** *n.*
fet•ish also **fet•ich** (fĕt′ĭsh, fē′tĭsh) *n.* **1.** An object that is believed to have magical or spiritual powers, esp. such an object associated with animistic or shamanistic religious practices. **2.** An object of unreasonably excessive attention or reverence. **3.** Something, such as a nonsexual part of the body, that arouses sexual desire and may become necessary for sexual gratification. **4.** An abnormally obsessive preoccupation or attachment; a fixation. [Fr. *fétiche* < Port. *feitiço*, artificial, charm < Lat. *factīcius*, artificial. See FACTITIOUS.]
fet•ish•ism also **fet•ich•ism** (fĕt′ĭ-shĭz′əm, fē′tĭ-) *n.* **1.** Worship of or belief in magical fetishes. **2.** Excessive attachment or regard. **3.** The displacement of sexual arousal or gratification to a fetish. **—fet′ish•ist** *n.* **—fet′ish•is′tic** *adj.* **—fet′ish•is′ti•cal•ly** *adv.*

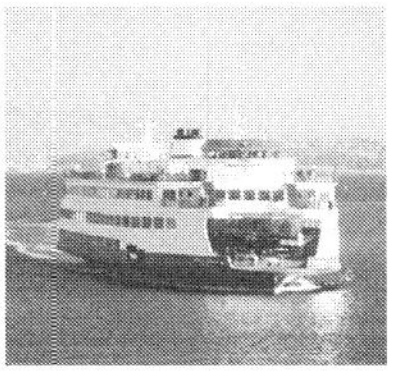

ferryboat
Seattle–Bainbridge Island ferry, Washington

ă	pat	oi	boy
ā	pay	ou	out
âr	care	o͝o	took
ä	father	o͞o	boot
ĕ	pet	ŭ	cut
ē	be	ûr	urge
ĭ	pit	th	thin
ī	pie	*th*	this
îr	pier	hw	which
ŏ	pot	zh	vision
ō	toe	ə	about, item
ô	paw		

Stress marks:
′ (primary);
′ (secondary), as in
lexicon (lĕk′sĭ-kŏn′)

feverfew
Chrysanthemum parthenium

fez

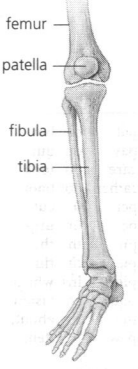

femur —
patella —
fibula —
tibia —

fibula

---

fet·ish·ize (fĕt′ĭ-shīz′) *tr.v.* **-ized, -iz·ing, -iz·es** To make a fetish of.

fet·lock (fĕt′lŏk′) *n.* **1a.** A projection on the lower part of the leg of a horse or related animal, above and behind the hoof. **b.** A tuft of hair on such a projection. **2.** The joint marked by such a projection. [ME *fitlok*. See **ped-** in App.]

feto- or **feti-** or **fet-** *pref.* Fetus; fetal: *fetology.* [< FETUS.]

fe·tol·o·gy (fē-tŏl′ə-jē) *n.* The medical study and treatment of the fetus, esp. within the uterus. —**fe·tol′o·gist** *n.*

fe·tor (fē′tər, -tôr′) also **foe·tor** (fē′tər) *n.* An offensive odor; a stench. [ME *fetoure* < Lat. *fētor* < *fetēre*, to stink.]

fe·to·scope (fē′tə-skōp′) *n.* **1.** A flexible fiberoptic device used to view a fetus in utero. **2.** A type of stethoscope used to listen to a fetal heartbeat. —**fe·tos′co·py** (fē-tŏs′kə-pē) *n.*

fet·ter (fĕt′ər) *n.* **1.** A chain or shackle for the ankles or feet. **2.** Something that restricts; a restraint. ❖ *tr.v.* **-tered, -ter·ing, -ters 1.** To put fetters on; shackle. **2.** To restrict the freedom of. [ME *feter* < OE. See **ped-** in App.]

fet·tle (fĕt′l) *n.* **1a.** Proper or sound condition. **b.** Mental or emotional state; spirits: *in fine fettle.* **2.** *Metallurgy* Loose sand or ore used to line the hearth of a reverberatory furnace in preparation for pouring molten metal. ❖ *tr.v.* **-tled, -tling, -tles** *Metallurgy* To line the hearth of (a reverberatory furnace) with fettle. [< ME *fetlen*, to make ready, poss. < OE *fetel*, girdle.]

fet·tling (fĕt′lĭng) *n. Metallurgy* Fettle.

fet·tuc·ci·ne (fĕt′ə-chē′nē) *n.* **1.** Pasta in narrow flat strips. **2.** A dish made with such strips of pasta. [Ital., pl. dim. of *fettuccia*, ribbon, poss. dim. of *fetta*, slice. See FETA.]

fettuccine Al·fre·do (ăl-frā′dō, äl-) *n.* A dish consisting of fettuccine in a rich cream sauce with Parmesan cheese. [After *Alfredo all'Augusteo*, a restaurant in Rome.]

fe·tus (fē′təs) *n., pl.* **-tus·es 1.** The unborn young of a viviparous vertebrate having a basic structural resemblance to the adult animal. **2.** In humans, the unborn young from the end of the eighth week after conception to the moment of birth, as distinguished from the earlier embryo. [ME < Lat. *fētus*, offspring.]

feud[1] (fyōōd) *n.* A bitter, often prolonged quarrel or state of enmity, esp. such a state of hostilities between two families or clans. ❖ *intr.v.* **feud·ed, feud·ing, feuds** To carry on or perpetuate a feud. [Alteration (prob. influenced by FEUD[2]) of ME *fede* < OFr. *faide*, of Gmc. orig.]

feud[2] (fyōōd) *n.* See **fee** 5a. [Med.Lat. *feudum*, of Gmc. orig. See **peku-** in App.]

feu·dal (fyōō′dl) *adj.* **1.** Of, relating to, or characteristic of feudalism. **2.** Of or relating to lands held in fee or to the holding of such lands. —**feu′dal·ly** *adv.*

feu·dal·ism (fyōō′dl-ĭz′əm) *n.* A political and economic system of Europe from the 9th to about the 15th century, based on the holding of all land in fief or fee and the resulting relation of lord to vassal and characterized by homage, legal and military service of tenants, and forfeiture. **2.** A political, economic, or social order resembling this medieval system. —**feu′dal·ist** *n.* —**feu′dal·is′tic** *adj.*

feu·dal·i·ty (fyōō-dăl′ĭ-tē) *n., pl.* **-ties 1.** The quality or state of being feudal. **2.** A feudal holding, system, or regime.

feu·dal·ize (fyōō′dl-īz′) *tr.v.* **-ized, -iz·ing, -iz·es** To make feudal. —**feu′dal·i·za′tion** (-ĭ-zā′shən) *n.*

feu·da·to·ry (fyōō′də-tôr′ē, -tōr′ē) *n., pl.* **-ries 1.** A person holding land by feudal fee; a vassal. **2.** A feudal fee. ❖ *adj.* **1.** Of, relating to, or characteristic of the feudal relationship between vassal and lord. **2.** Owing feudal homage or allegiance. [Med.Lat. *feudatōrius* < *feudātus*, p. part. of *feudāre*, to enfeoff < *feudum*, fee, fief. See FEUD[2].]

feud·ist[1] (fyōō′dĭst) *n.* A participant in a feud.

feud·ist[2] (fyōō′dĭst) *n.* A specialist in feudal law.

feuil·le·ton (fœ′yə-tôn′) *n.* **1a.** The part of a European newspaper given to light fiction, reviews, and articles of general entertainment. **b.** An article appearing in such a section. **2a.** A novel published in installments. **b.** A light popular work of fiction. **3.** A short literary essay or sketch. [Fr. < *feuillet*, sheet of paper, little leaf, dim. of *feuille*, leaf < OFr. *foille* < Lat. *folium*. See **bhel-** in App.] —**feuil′le·ton′ism** (-tôn′ĭz′əm, -tôN′nĭz′-) *n.* —**feuil′le·ton′ist** *n.* —**feuil′le·ton·is′tic** *adj.*

fe·ver (fē′vər) *n.* **1a.** Abnormally high body temperature. **b.** Any of various diseases characterized by fever. **2a.** A condition of heightened activity or excitement. **b.** A contagious, usu. short-lived enthusiasm or craze: *disco fever.* ❖ *v.* **-vered, -ver·ing, -vers** —*tr.* To effect fever in. —*intr.* To be or become feverish. [ME < OE *fefor* and < OFr. *fievre*, both < Lat. *febris.*]

fever blister *n.* See **cold sore.**

fe·ver·few (fē′vər-fyōō′) *n.* A Eurasian aromatic plant (*Chrysanthemum parthenium*) having buttonlike white-rayed flower heads. [ME *feverfu* < OE *feferfuge* and < AN *fevrefue*, both < LLat. *febrifugia : febris*, fever + *fuga*, flight.]

fe·ver·ish (fē′vər-ĭsh) *adj.* **1a.** Of, relating to, or resembling a fever. **b.** Having a fever or fever symptoms. **c.** Causing or tending to cause fever. **2.** Marked by intense agitation, emotion, or activity. —**fe′ver·ish·ly** *adv.* —**fe′ver·ish·ness** *n.*

fever pitch *n.* A state of extreme agitation or excitement.

fever tree *n.* Any of several trees of the southeast United States having leaves or bark used to allay fever.

fe·ver·weed (fē′vər-wēd′) *n.* Any of various plants considered to have medicinal properties.

fe·ver·wort (fē′vər-wûrt′, -wôrt′) *n.* See **horse gentian.**

few (fyōō) *adj.* **few·er, few·est 1.** Amounting to or consisting of a small number: *one of my few bad habits.* **2.** Being more than one but indefinitely small in number: *ate a few cookies.* ❖ *n.* (used with a pl. verb) **1.** An indefinitely small number of persons or things: *a few of the books.* **2.** An exclusive or limited number: *the discerning few.* ❖ *pron.* (used with a pl. verb) A small number of persons or things: "*For many are called, but few are chosen*" (Matthew 22:14). [ME *fewe* < OE *fēawe.*] —**few′ness** *n.*

fey (fā) *adj.* **1a.** Having or displaying an otherworldly, magical, or fairylike aspect or quality. **b.** Having visionary power; clairvoyant. **c.** Appearing touched or crazy, as if under a spell. **2.** *Scots* **a.** Fated to die soon. **b.** Full of the sense of approaching death. [ME *feie*, fated to die < OE *fǣge.*] —**fey′ly** *adv.* —**fey′ness** *n.*

Feyn·man (fīn′mən), **Richard Phillips** 1918–88. Amer. physicist who shared a 1965 Nobel Prize.

fez (fĕz) *n., pl.* **fez·zes** A man's felt cap in the shape of a flat-topped cone, usu. red with a black tassel hanging from the crown. [Fr. < Turk. *fes* < FEZ.]

Fez (fĕz) or **Fès** (fĕs) A city of N-central Morocco NE of Casablanca; orig. founded in the 9th cent. Pop. 564,000.

Fez·zan (fə-zăn′) A region of SW Libya; under Turkish control from the 16th cent. until 1912.

ff *abbr.* fortissimo

ff. *abbr.* **1.** folios **2.** following

FFA *abbr.* **1.** *Business* free from alongside **2.** Future Farmers of America

FG *abbr.* **1.** field goal **2.** fine grain

FHA *abbr.* **1.** Federal Housing Administration **2.** Future Homemakers of America

FHLBB *abbr.* Federal Home Loan Bank Board

FHLMC *abbr.* Federal Home Loan Mortgage Corporation

fhp or **f.hp.** *abbr.* friction horsepower

fi·a·cre (fē-ä′krə) *n.* A small hackney carriage. [Fr., after the Hôtel de St. *Fiacre* in Paris.]

fi·an·cé (fē′än-sā′, fē-än′sā′) *n.* A man to whom a woman is engaged to be married. [Fr. < p. part. of *fiancer*, to betroth < OFr. *fiancier* < *fiance*, trust < *fier*, to trust < VLat. **fīdāre* < Lat. *fīdere.* See **bheidh-** in App.]

fi·an·cée (fē′än-sā′, fē-än′sā′) *n.* A woman to whom a man is engaged to be married. [Fr., fem. of *fiancé*, fiancé. See FIANCÉ.]

fi·an·chet·to (fē′ən-kĕt′ō, -chĕt′ō) *n., pl.* **-chet·ti** (-kĕt′ē, -chĕt′ē) The development in chess of a bishop from its original position to the second square of the adjacent knight's file. ❖ *tr. & intr.v.* **-chet·toed, -chet·to·ing, -chet·tos** To develop as or set up a fianchetto. [Ital., dim. of *fianco*, flank < OItal. < OFr. *flanc.* See FLANK.]

fi·as·co (fē-ăs′kō, -ä′skō) *n., pl.* **-coes** or **-cos** A complete failure. [Fr. < Ital. *fare fiasco*, to make a bottle, fail < *fiasco*, bottle (perh. transl. of Fr. *bouteille*, bottle, error; used by the Fr. for linguistic errors committed by Ital. actors on the 18th-cent. Fr. stage) < LLat. *flascō.* See FLASK.]

fi·at (fē′ət, -ăt′, -ät′, fī′ăt′, -ət) *n.* **1.** An arbitrary order or decree. **2.** Authorization or sanction: *government fiat.* [Med.Lat. < Lat., let it be done, third pers. sing. pr. subjunctive of *fierī*, to become, to be done. See **bheuə-** in App.]

fiat money *n.* Legal tender, esp. paper currency, authorized by a government but not based on or convertible into gold or silver.

fib (fĭb) *n.* An insignificant or childish lie. ❖ *intr.v.* **fibbed, fib·bing, fibs** To tell a fib. [Perh. < obsolete and dialectal *fible-fable*, nonsense, redup. of FABLE.] —**fib′ber** *n.*

fi·ber (fī′bər) *n.* **1.** A threadlike object or structure. **2.** *Botany* One of the elongated thick-walled cells that give strength and support to plant tissue. **3.** *Anatomy* **a.** Any of the filaments constituting the extracellular matrix of connective tissue. **b.** Any of various elongated cells or threadlike structures, esp. a muscle fiber or a nerve fiber. **4a.** A natural or synthetic filament capable of being spun into yarn. **b.** Material made of such filaments. **5a.** Something that provides substance or texture. **b.** Essential character: "*stirred the deeper fibers of my nature*" (Oscar Wilde). **c.** Basic strength or toughness; fortitude. **6.** Coarse indigestible plant matter, consisting primarily of polysaccharides such as cellulose, that when eaten stimulates intestinal peristalsis. [Fr. *fibre* < OFr. < Lat. *fibra.*] —**fi′bered** *adj.*

fi·ber·board (fī′bər-bôrd′, -bōrd′) *n.* A building material composed of wood chips or plant fibers bonded together and compressed into rigid sheets.

fi·ber·fill (fī′bər-fĭl′) *n.* Lightweight synthetic fiber used as filling or insulation, as in comforters, pillows, and outerwear.

Fi·ber·glas (fī′bər-glăs′) A trademark used for a type of fiber-glass and for goods made of fiberglass.

fi·ber·glass (fī′bər-glăs′) *n.* A material consisting of extremely fine glass fibers, used in making yarns, fabrics, insulators, and structural objects or parts.

fi·ber·ize (fī′bə-rīz′) *tr.v.* **-ized, -iz·ing, -iz·es** To break into fibers. —**fi′ber·i·za′tion** (-bər-ĭ-zā′shən) *n.*

fiber optics *n.* (*used with a sing. verb*) **1.** The science or technology of light transmission through very fine flexible glass or plastic fibers. **2.** A bundle of optical fibers. —**fi′ber-op′tic, fi′ber·op′tik** *adj.*

fi·ber·scope (fī′bər-skōp′) *n.* A flexible fiber-optic instrument used to view an object or area, such as a body cavity, that would otherwise be inaccessible.

Fi·bo·nac·ci number (fē′bə-nä′chē) *n.* A number in the Fibonacci sequence.

Fibonacci sequence *n.* The sequence of numbers, 1, 1, 2, 3, 5, 8, 13, . . . , in which each successive number is equal to the sum of the two preceding numbers. [After Leonardo *Fibonacci* (died c. 1250), Italian mathematician.]

fibr– *pref.* Variant of **fibro–**.

fi·branne (fī′brän′) *n.* A linenlike fabric made of spun-rayon yarn. [Fr. < *fibre,* fiber. See FIBER.]

fi·bre (fī′bər) *n. Chiefly British* Variant of **fiber**.

fi·bril (fī′brəl, fĭb′rəl) *n.* **1.** A small slender fiber or filament. **2.** *Anatomy* Any threadlike fiber or filament, such as a myofibril, that is a constituent of a cell or larger structure. [NLat. *fibrilla,* dim. of Lat. *fibra,* fiber.] —**fi′bril·lar** (-lər), **fi′bril·lar′y** (-lĕr′ē) *adj.* —**fi′bril·lose′** (-lōs′) *adj.*

fib·ril·late (fĭb′rə-lāt′, fī′brə-) *intr. & tr.v.* **-lat·ed, -lat·ing, -lates** To undergo or cause to undergo fibrillation. [NLat. *fibrilla,* fibril; see FIBRIL + –ATE¹.]

fib·ril·la·tion (fĭb′rə-lā′shən, fī′brə-) *n.* **1.** The forming of fibers. **2a.** Rapid twitching of individual muscle fibers with little or no movement of the muscle as a whole. **b.** Rapid uncoordinated twitching that replaces the normal rhythmic contraction of the heart and may cause a lack of circulation and pulse.

fi·brin (fī′brĭn) *n.* An elastic insoluble protein produced by the action of thrombin on fibrinogen and forming a fibrous network in the coagulation of blood. —**fi′brin·ous** *adj.*

fi·brin·o·gen (fī-brĭn′ə-jən) *n.* A protein in the blood essential for coagulation that is converted to fibrin by thrombin in the presence of ionized calcium. —**fi·brin′o·gen′ic** (fī′brə-nŏj′ə-nəs) *adj.*

fi·brin·o·gen·ic (fī′brə-nō-jĕn′ĭk) *adj.* **1.** Of or relating to fibrinogen. **2.** Producing fibrin.

fi·bri·noid (fī′brə-noid′, fĭb′rə-) *adj.* Of or resembling fibrin. ❖ *n.* A homogenous acellular material similar to fibrin, found normally in the placenta and formed in connective tissue and in the walls of blood vessels in certain disease states.

fi·bri·nol·y·sin (fī′brə-nŏl′ĭ-sĭn) *n.* See **plasmin**.

fi·bri·nol·y·sis (fī′brə-nŏl′ĭ-sĭs) *n., pl.* **-ses** (-sēz′) The breakdown of fibrin, usu. by the enzymatic action of plasmin. —**fi′bri·no·lyt′ic** (-nə-lĭt′ĭk) *adj.*

fibro– or **fibr–** *pref.* Fiber, esp. fibrous tissue: *fibroma.* [< Lat. *fibra,* fiber.]

fi·bro·blast (fī′brə-blăst′) *n.* A cell that gives rise to connective tissue. —**fi′bro·blas′tic** *adj.*

fi·bro·car·ti·lage (fī′brō-kär′tl-ĭj) *n.* Cartilage that contains numerous thick bundles of collagen fibers.

fi·broid (fī′broid′) *adj.* Composed of or resembling fibrous tissue. ❖ *n.* A fibroma or myoma occurring esp. in the uterine wall.

fi·bro·in (fī′brō-ĭn) *n.* An insoluble protein that is the essential component of raw silk and spider web filaments.

fi·bro·ma (fī-brō′mə) *n., pl.* **-mas** or **-ma·ta** (-mə-tə) A benign, usu. enclosed neoplasm composed primarily of fibrous tissue. —**fi·brom′a·tous** (-brŏm′ə-təs, -brō′mə-) *adj.*

fi·bro·my·al·gi·a (fī′brō-mī-ăl′jē-ə, -jə) *n.* A syndrome marked by chronic pain in the muscles and soft tissues surrounding joints, fatigue, and tenderness at specific sites in the body.

fi·bro·pla·sia (fī′brə-plā′zhə, -zhē-ə) *n.* The formation of fibrous tissue, as normally occurs in the healing of wounds. —**fi′bro·plas′tic** (-plăs′tĭk) *adj.*

fi·bro·sis (fī-brō′sĭs) *n.* The formation of excessive fibrous tissue, as in a reparative or reactive process. —**fi·brot′ic** (-brŏt′ĭk) *adj.*

fi·bro·si·tis (fī′brə-sī′tĭs) *n.* **1.** Inflammatory hyperplasia of fibrous connective tissue, esp. surrounding the muscles, causing pain and stiffness. **2.** See **fibromyalgia**. [NLat. *fibrōsus,* fibrous (< Lat. *fibra,* fiber) + –ITIS.]

fi·brous (fī′brəs) *adj.* **1.** Having, consisting of, or resembling fibers. **2.** Full of sinews; tough. —**fi′brous·ly** *adv.* —**fi′brous·ness** *n.*

fi·bro·vas·cu·lar (fī′brō-văs′kyə-lər) *adj.* Having fibrous and vascular tissue, as in woody plant tissue.

fib·u·la (fĭb′yə-lə) *n., pl.* **-lae** (-lē′) or **-las** **1.** The outer and narrower of two bones of the human leg or the hind leg of an animal, between the knee and the ankle. **2.** A clasp or brooch used in ancient Greece and Rome to fasten clothing. [Lat. *fībula,* clasp < *fīgere,* to fasten.]

–fic *suff.* Causing; making: *soporific; febrific.* [Lat. *-ficus* < *fa-*

cere, to do. See **dhē–** in App.]

FICA *abbr.* Federal Insurance Contributions Act

–fication *suff.* Production; making: *jollification.* [Lat. *-ficātiō, -ficātiōn-* < *-ficātus,* p. part. of *-ficāre,* to make < *-ficus,* -fic.]

fice (fīs) *n. Chiefly Southern US* Variant of **feist**.

fiche (fēsh) *n.* A microfiche.

Fich·te (fĭk′tə, fĭkн′-), **Johann Gottlieb** 1762–1814. German philosopher who was an important influence on Hegel.

fich·u (fĭsh′ōō, fē-shōō′) *n.* A woman's triangular scarf of lightweight fabric, worn over the shoulders and crossed or tied in a loose knot at the breast. [Fr. < p. part. of *ficher,* to fix < VLat. *figicāre* < Lat. *fīgere.*]

fick·le (fĭk′əl) *adj.* Characterized by erratic changeableness or instability, esp. in affections or attachments; capricious. [ME *fikel* < OE *ficol,* deceitful.] —**fick′le·ness** *n.* —**fick′ly** *adv.*

fic·tile (fĭk′təl, -tīl′) *adj.* **1a.** Capable of being molded; plastic. **b.** Formed of a moldable substance, such as clay or earth. **2.** Of or relating to earthenware or pottery. [Lat. *fictilis,* made of clay < *fictus,* p. part. of *fingere,* to mold. See **dheigh–** in App.]

fic·tion (fĭk′shən) *n.* **1a.** An imaginative creation or a pretense that does not represent actuality but has been invented. **b.** The act of inventing such a creation or pretense. **2.** A lie. **3a.** A literary work whose content is produced by the imagination and is not necessarily based on fact. **b.** The category of literature comprising works of this kind, including novels and short stories. **4.** *Law* Something accepted as true without real justification. [ME *ficcioun* < OFr. *fiction* < Lat. *fictiō, fictiōn-* < *fictus,* p. part. of *fingere,* to form. See **dheigh–** in App.] —**fic′tion·al** *adj.* —**fic′tion·al·i·ty** (-shə-năl′ĭ-tē) *n.* —**fic′tion·al·ly** *adv.*

fic·tion·al·ize (fĭk′shə-nə-līz′) *tr.v.* **-ized, -iz·ing, -iz·es** To treat as or make into fiction. —**fic′tion·al·i·za′tion** (-lĭ-zā′shən) *n.*

fic·tion·eer (fĭk′shə-nîr′) *n.* One who writes fiction, esp. a prolific creator of commercial or pulp fiction.

fic·tion·ist (fĭk′shə-nĭst) *n.* A writer of fiction, esp. a novelist.

fic·tion·ize (fĭk′shə-nīz′) *tr.v.* **-ized, -iz·ing, -iz·es** To fictionalize. —**fic′tion·i·za′tion** (-shə-nĭ-zā′shən) *n.*

fic·ti·tious (fĭk-tĭsh′əs) *adj.* **1.** Of, relating to, or characterized by fiction; imaginary. **2a.** Accepted or assumed for the sake of convention. **b.** Adopted or assumed in order to deceive. **3.** Not genuinely believed or felt; sham. [< Lat. *ficticius* < *fictus,* p. part. of *fingere,* to form. See FICTION.] —**fic·ti′tious·ly** *adv.* —**fic·ti′tious·ness** *n.*

fictitious force *n.* See **pseudo-force**.

fic·tive (fĭk′tĭv) *adj.* **1.** Of, relating to, or able to engage in imaginative invention. **2.** Of, relating to, or being fiction; fictional. **3.** Not genuine; sham. —**fic′tive·ly** *adv.* —**fic′tive·ness** *n.*

fi·cus (fī′kəs) *n., pl.* **ficus** or **-cus·es** Any of numerous tropical trees, shrubs, or climbers of the genus *Ficus,* having pearlike fruit. [Lat. *ficus,* fig.]

fid (fĭd) *n.* A large tapering pin used to open the strands of a rope before splicing. [?]

–fid *suff.* Divided into parts or lobes: *pinnatifid.* [Lat. *-fidus* < *findere,* fid-, to split. See **bheid–** in App.]

fid·dle (fĭd′l) *n.* **1a.** A violin. **b.** A member of the violin family. **2.** *Nautical* A guardrail used on a table to prevent things from slipping off. **3.** *Informal* Nonsensical trifling matters: "*There are things that are important/beyond all this fiddle*" (Marianne Moore). **4.** The act or an instance of cheating or swindling; a fraud. ❖ *v.* **-dled, -dling, -dles** —*intr.* **1.** To play a violin. **2a.** To move one's fingers or hands in a nervous fashion. **b.** To occupy oneself in an aimless or desultory way. **c.** To meddle or tamper. **3.** To commit a fraud, esp. to steal from one's employer. —*tr.* **1.** To play (a tune) on a violin. **2.** To cheat or swindle. **3.** To alter or falsify (accounts, for example) for dishonest gain. —*phrasal verb:* **fiddle away** To waste or squander. [ME *fidle* < OE *fithele.*] —**fid′dler** *n.*

fid·dle-de-dee (fĭd′l-dē-dē′) *interj.* Used to express mild annoyance or impatience. [< FIDDLE.]

fid·dle-fad·dle (fĭd′l-făd′l) *n.* Nonsense. ❖ *intr.v.* **-dled, -dling, -dles** To fritter away one's time; dally. [Reduplication of FIDDLE.]

fid·dle-foot·ed (fĭd′l-fŏŏt′ĭd) *adj.* **1.** Excitable or nervous: *fiddle-footed ponies.* **2.** Inclined to roam or wander.

fid·dle·head (fĭd′l-hĕd′) *n.* **1.** *Nautical* A curved scroll-like ornamentation at the top of a ship's bow that resembles the neck of a violin. **2.** *Botany* The coiled young frond of any of various ferns, considered a delicacy when cooked.

fid·dle·neck (fĭd′l-nĕk′) *n.* **1.** A hairy annual herb (*Phacelia tanacetifolia*) of California, having large pinnately divided leaves and bluish flowers. **2.** See **amsinckia**.

fiddler crab *n.* Any of various burrowing crabs of the genus *Uca* of coastal areas, the male of which has a greatly enlarged anterior claw.

fid·dle·sticks (fĭd′l-stĭks′) *interj.* Used to express mild annoyance or impatience. [< pl. of *fiddlestick,* bow for playing a fiddle.]

fid·dling (fĭd′lĭng) *adj.* Trivial; petty.

fi·de·ism (fē′dā-ĭz-əm, fī′dē-) *n.* Reliance on faith alone rather than scientific reasoning or philosophy in questions of religion. [Prob. < Fr. *fidéisme* < Lat. *fidēs,* faith. See **bheidh–** in App.] —**fi′de·ist** *n.* —**fi′de·is′tic** *adj.*

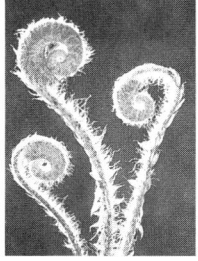

fiddlehead

fiddler crab
male fiddler crab

fi·del·i·ty (fĭ-dĕl′ĭ-tē, fī-) *n., pl.* **-ties 1.** Faithfulness to obligations, duties, or observances. **2.** Exact correspondence with fact or with a given quality, condition, or event; accuracy. **3.** The degree to which an electronic system accurately reproduces the sound or image of its input signal. [ME *fidelite* < OFr. < Lat. *fidelitās* < *fidēlis*, faithful < *fidēs*, faith. See **bheidh-** in App.]

fidg·et (fĭj′ĭt) *v.* **-et·ed, -et·ing, -ets** —*intr.* **1.** To behave or move nervously or restlessly. **2.** To play or fuss; fiddle: *He fidgeted with his notes.* —*tr.* To cause to behave or move nervously or restlessly. ❖ *n.* **1.** A condition of restlessness as manifested by nervous movements. Often used in the plural. **2.** One that fidgets. [< obsolete and dialectal *fidge*, to move restlessly, perh. < ME *fiken*, of Scand. orig.]

fidg·et·y (fĭj′ĭ-tē) *adj.* **1.** Tending to fidget. **2.** Creating unnecessary fuss. —**fidg′et·i·ness** *n.*

fi·do (fī′dō) *n., pl.* **-dos** A coin containing a minting error. [*f(reaks), i(rregulars), d(efects), o(ddities).*]

fi·du·cial (fĭ-dōō′shəl, -dyōō′-, fī-) *adj.* **1.** Based on or relating to faith or trust. **2.** Relating to or characteristic of a legal trust; fiduciary. **3.** Regarded or employed as a standard of reference, as in surveying. [LLat. *fidūciālis* < Lat. *fidūcia*, trust < *fidere*, to trust. See **bheidh-** in App.] —**fi·du′cial·ly** *adv.*

fi·du·ci·ar·y (fĭ-dōō′shē-ĕr′ē, -shə-rē, -dyōō′-, fī-) *adj.* **1a.** Of or relating to a holding of something in trust for another. **b.** Of or being a trustee or trusteeship. **c.** Held in trust. **2.** Of or consisting of fiat money. **3.** Of, relating to, or being a system of marking in the field of view of an optical instrument that is used as a reference point or measuring scale. ❖ *n., pl.* **-ies** One, such as a company director, that has a special relation of trust or responsibility in certain obligations to others. [Lat. *fidūciārius* < *fidūcia*, trust. See FIDUCIAL.]

fie (fī) *interj.* Used to express distaste or disapproval. [ME *fi* < OFr., of imit. orig.]

Fied·ler (fēd′lər), **Arthur** 1894–1979. Amer. conductor who was director of the Boston Pops Orchestra (1930–79).

fief (fēf) *n.* **1.** See **fee** 5a. **2.** A fiefdom. [Fr. < OFr. *feu, fief.* See FEE.]

fief·dom (fēf′dəm) *n.* **1.** The estate or domain of a feudal lord. **2.** Something that one person or group controls.

field (fēld) *n.* **1a.** A broad, level, open expanse of land. **b.** A meadow. **c.** A cultivated expanse of land, esp. one devoted to a particular crop: *a field of corn.* **d.** A portion of land or a geologic formation containing a specified natural resource. **e.** A wide unbroken expanse, as of ice. **2a.** A battleground. **b.** A battle. **c.** The scene or an area of military operations or maneuvers. **d.** A military area away from headquarters. **3a.** A background area, as on a flag, painting, or coin: *a blue insignia on a field of red.* **b.** *Heraldry* The background of a shield or one of the divisions of the background. **4.** *Sports* **a.** An area in which an athletic event takes place. **b.** The portion of a playing field having specific dimensions on which the action of a game takes place. **c.** All the contestants or participants in an event, esp. all except the favorite or the winner in a contest of more than two. **d.** The members of a team engaged in active play. **e.** The body of riders following a pack of hounds in hunting. **5a.** An area of human activity or interest. **b.** A topic, subject, or area of academic interest or specialization. **c.** Profession, employment, or business. **d.** An area or setting of practical activity or application outside an office, school, factory, or laboratory: *tested in the field.* **e.** An area or region where business activities are conducted. **6.** *Mathematics* A set of elements having two operations, designated addition and multiplication, satisfying the conditions that multiplication is distributive over addition, that the set is a group under addition, and that the elements with the exception of the additive identity form a group under multiplication. **7.** *Physics* A region of space in which a physical property, such as gravitational force, has a determinable value at every point. **8.** The usu. circular area in which the image is rendered by the lens system of an optical instrument. **9.** *Computer Science* **a.** A defined area of a storage medium, such as a set of bit locations, used to record a type of information consistently. **b.** An element of a database record in which one piece of information is stored. **c.** An interface element in a GUI that accepts the input of text. ❖ *adj.* **1.** Growing, cultivated, or living in fields or open land. **2.** Made, used, or carried on in the field: *field operations.* **3.** Working, operating, or active in the field: *field representatives of a firm.* ❖ *v.* **field·ed, field·ing, fields** —*tr.* **1.** *Sports* **a.** To retrieve (a ball) and perform the required maneuver, esp. in baseball. **b.** To place in the field to play: *field a team.* **2.** To give an unrehearsed response to: *fielded tough questions from the press.* **3a.** To place in competition. **b.** To put into action. **4.** *Computer Science* To enter (data) into a field. —*intr. Sports* To play as a fielder. —*idiom:* **take the field** To begin or resume activity, as in a sport. [ME < OE *feld.* See **pelə-²** in App.]

Field, Cyrus West 1819–92. Amer. financier who oversaw the laying of the transatlantic telegraph cable (1866).

Field, Eugene 1850–95. Amer. writer best known for his children's verse, esp. "Little Boy Blue."

field artillery *n.* Artillery other than antiaircraft artillery that is light enough to be mounted for use in the field.

field coil *n.* An electric coil around a field magnet used to generate a magnetic field, as in an electric motor.

field hockey

field day *n.* **1a.** A day set aside for sports or athletic competition. **b.** An outdoor meeting, social event, or festivity. **c.** A day for military exercises, maneuvers, or display. **2.** *Informal* A time of great pleasure, activity, or opportunity.

field-ef·fect transistor (fēld′ĭ-fĕkt′) *n.* A transistor in which the output current is controlled by a variable electric field.

field emission *n.* The emission of electrons from the surface of a conductor, caused by a strong electric field.

field·er (fēl′dər) *n.* One who plays a position on the field in a sport, esp. an outfielder in baseball.

field·er's choice (fēl′dərz) *Baseball* A play made on a ground ball in which the fielder chooses to put out an advancing base runner, thus allowing the batter to reach first base safely.

field event *n.* A throwing or jumping event of a track-and-field meet.

field·fare (fēld′fâr′) *n.* An Old World thrush (*Turdus pilaris*) having gray and reddish-brown plumage. [ME *feldfare* < OE *feldeware*, error for *feldefare* : perh. *felde*, field; see FIELD + *-fare*, goer (< *faran*, to go; see **per-²** in App.).]

field glass *n.* A portable binocular telescope without prisms used esp. for viewing distant objects. Often used in the plural.

field goal *n.* **1.** *Football* A score worth three points made on an ordinary down by place-kicking or drop-kicking the ball over the crossbar and between the goalposts. **2.** *Basketball* A basket in regulation play, worth two points or, if attempted from beyond a specified distance, three points.

field-grade officer (fēld′grād′) *n.* A military officer, such as a major, lieutenant colonel, or colonel, ranking above a captain and below a brigadier general.

field guide *n.* An illustrated book that provides descriptions of plants, animals, or other objects found in nature, such as minerals.

field hand *n.* An outdoor worker on a farm.

field hockey *n.* A game played on turf in which two opposing teams of players, using curved sticks, try to drive a ball into the opponents' goal.

field hospital *n.* A hospital established on a temporary basis to serve troops in a combat zone.

field house *n.* **1.** A building having locker rooms and storage and training facilities, located at an athletic field. **2.** A building having one or more areas for different athletic events and usu. grandstands for spectators.

Field·ing (fēl′dĭng), **Henry** 1707–54. British writer whose works include *Joseph Andrews* (1742) and *Tom Jones* (1749).

field-i·on microscope (fēld′ī′ən, -ī′ŏn) *n.* A microscope that produces an image of the atoms on a metal surface by means of ions formed in a high-voltage electric field.

field lens *n.* The lens positioned farthest from the eye in a compound eyepiece.

field magnet *n.* A magnet used to produce a magnetic field in an electrical device such as a generator or motor.

field marshal *n.* An officer in some European armies, usu. ranking just below the commander in chief.

field mouse *n.* Any of various small mice or voles, esp. of the genus *Microtus*, inhabiting meadows and fields and often causing damage to crops.

field officer *n.* See **field-grade officer.**

field of force *n., pl.* **fields of force** A region of space throughout which the force, such as an electric charge, produced by an agent, such as an electric field, is operative.

field of honor *n., pl.* **fields of honor 1.** The scene of a duel. **2.** A battlefield.

field of view *n., pl.* **fields of view** See **field** 8.

field of vision *n., pl.* **fields of vision** See **visual field.**

Fields (fēldz), **Dorothy** 1905–74. Amer. lyricist whose songs include "On the Sunny Side of the Street" (1930).

Fields, W.C. 1880–1946. Amer. entertainer whose films include *My Little Chickadee* (1940).

field·stone (fēld′stōn′) *n.* A stone occurring naturally in fields, often used as a building material.

field·strip (fēld′strĭp′) *tr.v.* **-stripped, -strip·ping, -strips** To disassemble (a weapon) for cleaning, repair, or inspection.

field-test (fēld′tĕst′) *tr.v.* **-test·ed, -test·ing, -tests** To test (a technique or product) under conditions of actual operation or use.

field theory *n.* **1.** An explicit mathematical description of physical phenomena that takes into account the effects of one or more fields. **2.** The study of fields and field extensions in algebra.

field trial *n.* **1.** A test for young untried hunting dogs to determine their competence in pointing and retrieving. Often used in the plural. **2.** A trial of a new product in actual use.

field trip *n.* A group excursion for firsthand observation.

field wind·ing (wīn′dĭng) *n.* See **field coil.**

field·work (fēld′wûrk′) *n.* **1.** A temporary military fortification erected in the field. **2.** Work done or firsthand observations made in the field. **3.** The collecting of sociological or anthropological data in the field. —**field′work′er** *n.*

fiend (fēnd) *n.* **1a.** An evil spirit; a demon. **b.** The Devil; Satan. A diabolically evil or wicked person. **2.** *Informal* One who is addicted to something: *a dope fiend.* **3.** *Informal* One who is completely absorbed in or obsessed with a given job or pastime. **4.** *In-*

formal One who is particularly adept at something. [ME < OE *fēond*.]

fiend·ish (fēn′dĭsh) *adj.* **1.** Of, relating to, or suggestive of a fiend; diabolical. **2.** Extremely wicked or cruel. **3.** Extremely bad, disagreeable, or difficult: *a fiendish blizzard; a fiendish problem.* —**fiend′ish·ly** *adv.* —**fiend′ish·ness** *n.*

fierce (fîrs) *adj.* **fierc·er, fierc·est 1.** Having a savage and violent nature; ferocious. See Syns at **cruel. 2.** Extremely severe or violent; terrible. **3.** Extremely intense or ardent: *fierce loyalty.* **4.** Strenuously active or resolute. **5.** *Informal* Very difficult or unpleasant: *a fierce exam.* **6.** Savage or threatening in appearance. [ME *fiers* < OFr. < Lat. *ferus.* See **ghwer-** in App.] —**fierce′ly** *adv.* —**fierce′ness** *n.*

fier·y (fîr′ē, fī′ə-rē) *adj.* **-i·er, -i·est 1a.** Consisting of or containing fire. **b.** Burning or glowing. **c.** Using or effected with fire. **d.** Easily ignited; flammable. **2.** Having the color of fire; brightly red: *fiery hair; a fiery sunset.* **3a.** Torridly hot. **b.** Feverishly hot and flushed. **c.** Being in an inflamed, usu. painful condition: *a fiery boil.* **4a.** Easily excited or emotionally volatile; tempestuous. **b.** Charged with emotion; spirited. [ME *firi* < *fir*, fire. See FIRE.] —**fier′i·ly** *adv.* —**fier′i·ness** *n.* —**fier′y** *adv.*

Fie·so·le (fyĕ′zō-lā, -lĕ), **Giovanni Angelica da** See Fra **Angelico.**

fi·es·ta (fē-ĕs′tə) *n.* A festival or religious holiday, esp. a saint's day celebrated in Spanish-speaking countries. [Sp. < VLat. *fĕsta.* See FEAST.]

fife (fīf) *n.* A small high-pitched transverse flute used primarily to accompany drums in a military or marching band. [Prob. Ger. *Pfeife* < MHGer. *pfife* < OHGer. *pfiffa* < VLat. *pīpa* < Lat. *pīpāre,* to chirp.] —**fife** *v.* —**fif′er** *n.*

Fife A region of E Scotland between the Firths of Forth and Tay; once a Pict kingdom.

fife rail *n.* A rail around the lower part of a ship's mast to which the belaying pins for the rigging are secured.

FIFO (fī′fō) *abbr.* first-in, first-out

fif·teen (fĭf-tēn′) *n.* **1.** The cardinal number equal to 14 + 1. **2.** The 15th in a set or sequence. [ME *fiftene* < OE *fīftēne.* See **pen-kʷe** in App.] —**fif·teen′** *adj. & pron.*

fif·teenth (fĭf-tēnth′) *n.* **1.** The ordinal number matching the number 15 in a series. **2.** One of 15 equal parts. —**fif·teenth′** *adv. & adj.*

fifth (fĭfth) *n.* **1.** The ordinal number matching the number five in a series. **2.** One of five equal parts. **3.** One fifth of a gallon or four fifths of a quart of liquor. **4.** *Music* **a.** A tone five degrees above or below a given tone in a diatonic scale. **b.** The interval between two such tones. **c.** The harmonic combination of two such tones. **d.** The dominant of a scale or key. **5. Fifth** The Fifth Amendment. Used with *the.* [ME < OE *fīfta.* See **penkʷe** in App.] —**fifth** *adv. & adj.* —**fifth′ly** *adv.*

Fifth Amendment *n.* An amendment to the Constitution of the United States, ratified in 1791, that deals with the rights of accused criminals by providing for due process of law, forbidding double jeopardy, and stating that no person may be forced to testify as a witness against himself or herself.

fifth column *n.* A clandestine subversive organization within a country furthering an invading enemy's aims. [Applied (1936) to rebel sympathizers in Madrid when it was being attacked by four columns of rebel troops.] —**fifth col′um·nism** (kŏl′əm-nĭz′əm) *n.* —**fifth columnist** *n.*

fifth disease *n.* A mild viral disease usu. of early childhood, characterized by fever, rash, and joint inflammation. [< its being fifth in frequency of rash-producing childhood diseases.]

fifth estate *n.* A class or group in society other than the nobility, the clergy, the middle class, and the press.

fifth force *n.* Any of the hypothetical forces purported to cause bits of matter to repel each other but not to be strong enough to counteract gravity.

fifth wheel *n.* **1a.** A wheel or portion of a wheel placed horizontally over the forward axle of a carriage to provide support and stability during turns. **b.** A similar device over the rear axle or axles of a tractor or pickup truck, serving as a coupling for a semitrailer. **2.** An additional wheel carried on a four-wheeled vehicle as a spare. **3.** An extra and unnecessary person or thing.

fif·ti·eth (fĭf′tē-ĭth) *n.* **1.** The ordinal number matching the number 50 in a series. **2.** One of 50 equal parts. —**fif′ti·eth** *adv. & adj.*

fif·ty (fĭf′tē) *n.* The cardinal number equal to 5 × 10. **2. fifties a.** A decade or the numbers from 50 to 59. **b.** often **Fifties** The decade from 50 to 59 in a century. **3.** A fifty-dollar bill. [ME *fifti* < OE *fiftig.* See **penkʷe** in App.] —**fif′ty** *adj. & pron.*

fif·ty-fif·ty (fĭf′tē-fĭf′tē) *adj.* **1.** Divided or shared in two equal portions. **2.** Equally likely or unlikely: *a fifty-fifty chance of winning.* —**fif′ty-fif′ty** *adv.*

fig¹ (fĭg) *n.* **1a.** Any of several Mediterranean trees or shrubs of the genus *Ficus,* widely cultivated for their edible fruit. **b.** The sweet pear-shaped fruit of this plant, having numerous tiny seedlike fruits. **2a.** Any of various plants bearing similar fruit. **b.** The fruit of such a plant. **3.** A trivial or contemptible amount: *didn't care a fig.* [ME < OFr. *figue* < O Provençal *figa* < VLat. *fīca* < Lat. *ficus.*]

fig² (fĭg) *n.* **1.** Dress; array. **2.** Physical condition; shape. [Perh.

< *fig,* dress up, var. of *feague,* to make a horse lively, prob. < Du. *vegen,* to brush < MDu. *vēghen.*]

fig. *abbr.* **1.** figurative **2.** figuratively **3.** figure

fight (fīt) *v.* **fought** (fôt), **fight·ing, fights** —*intr.* **1a.** To attempt to harm or gain power over an adversary by blows or with weapons. **b.** *Sports* To engage in boxing or wrestling. **2.** To engage in a quarrel; argue. **3.** To strive vigorously and resolutely. —*tr.* **1a.** To contend with physically or in battle. **b.** To wage or carry on (a battle). **c.** To contend for, by or as if by combat. **2a.** *Sports* To box or wrestle against in a ring. **b.** To participate in (a boxing match, for example). **3.** To set (a boxer, for example) in combat with another. **4.** To contend with or struggle against. See Syns at **oppose. 5.** To try to prevent the development or success of. **6.** To make (one's way) by struggle or striving. ❖ *n.* **1.** A confrontation between opposing groups in which each attempts to harm or gain power over the other, as with weapons. **2.** A quarrel or conflict. **3a.** A physical conflict between two or more individuals. **b.** *Sports* A boxing or wrestling match. **4.** A struggle to achieve an objective. See Syns at **conflict. 5.** The power or inclination to fight; pugnacity. —*phrasal verb:* **fight off** To defend against or drive back (a hostile force, for example). —*idioms:* **fight fire with fire** To combat one evil or one set of negative circumstances by reacting in kind. **fight shy of** To avoid meeting or confronting. [ME *fighten* < OE *feohtan, fihtan.*] —**fight′a·bil′i·ty** *n.* —**fight′a·ble** *adj.* —**fight′ing·ly** *adv.*

fight·er (fī′tər) *n.* **1.** One who fights, such as a soldier or boxer. **2.** A fast, maneuverable combat aircraft used to engage enemy aircraft. **3.** A pugnacious, unyielding, or determined person.

fight·er-bomb·er (fī′tər-bŏm′ər) *n.* A versatile aircraft capable of functioning as a fighter and a bomber, used chiefly in tactical and defensive operations.

fight·ing chance *n.* A chance to win but only with a struggle.

fight-or-flight reaction (fīt′ôr-flīt′) *n.* A set of physiological changes, such as elevated heart rate, initiated by the sympathetic nervous system in response to stress.

fig leaf *n.* **1.** A stylized representation of the leaf of a fig, used esp. to conceal genitals depicted in works of art. **2.** Something that serves as a usu. insufficient concealment.

fig marigold *n.* Any of various plants of the genus *Mesembryanthemum,* native to southern Africa and having thick fleshy leaves and variously colored flowers.

fig·ment (fĭg′mənt) *n.* Something invented, made up, or fabricated: *just a figment of the imagination.* [ME < Lat. *figmentum* < *fingere,* to form. See **dheigh-** in App.]

fig·ur·al (fĭg′yər-əl) *adj.* Of, relating to, consisting of, or forming a pictorial composition or design of human or animal figures.

fig·u·rant (fĭg′yə-ränt′, -ränt′, -rän′) *n.* **1.** A member of a corps de ballet who does not perform solos. **2.** A stage performer having no speaking part; a supernumerary. [Fr. < pr. part. of *figurer,* to represent < OFr. < Lat. *figūrāre,* to form < *figūra,* figure. See FIGURE.]

fig·u·ra·tion (fĭg′yə-rā′shən) *n.* **1.** The act of forming something into a particular shape. **2.** A shape, form, or outline. **3.** The act of representing with figures. **4.** A figurative representation. **5.** *Music* Ornamentation of a passage by embellishing and often repeating figures.

fig·u·ra·tive (fĭg′yər-ə-tĭv) *adj.* **1a.** Based on or making use of figures of speech; metaphorical. **b.** Containing many figures of speech; ornate. **2.** Represented by a figure or resemblance; symbolic or emblematic. **3.** Of or relating to artistic representation by means of animal or human figures. —**fig′u·ra·tive·ly** *adv.* —**fig′u·ra·tive·ness** *n.*

fig·ure (fĭg′yər) *n.* **1a.** A written or printed symbol representing something other than a letter, esp. a number. **b. figures** Mathematical calculations. **c.** An amount represented in numbers. **2a.** *Mathematics* A geometric form consisting of any combination of points, lines, or planes. **b.** The outline, form, or silhouette of a thing. **c.** The shape or form of a human body. **d.** An indistinct object or shape. **3a.** A person, esp. a well-known one. **b.** A person's public image or presence. **4.** Impression or appearance made. **5.** A person, animal, or object that symbolizes something. **6.** A pictorial or sculptural representation, esp. of the human body. **7a.** A diagram. **b.** A design or pattern, as in a textile. **8.** An illustration printed from an engraved plate or block. **9a.** A configuration or distinct group of steps in a dance. **b.** A pattern traced by a series of movements, as in ice skating. **10.** *Music* A brief melodic or harmonic unit often constituting the basis of a larger phrase or structure. **11.** *Logic* Any one of the forms that a syllogism can take, depending on the position of the middle term. ❖ *v.* **-ured, -ur·ing, -ures** —*tr.* **1.** *Mathematics* To calculate with numbers. **2.** To make a likeness of; depict. **3.** To adorn with a design or figures. **4.** *Music* **a.** To write a sequence of conventionalized numbers below or above (the bass line) to indicate harmony. **b.** To embellish with an ornamental pattern. **5.** *Informal* To conclude, believe, or predict: *I never figured that you'd go.* **b.** To consider or regard. —*intr.* **1.** *Mathematics* To calculate; compute. **2a.** To be or seem important or prominent. **b.** To be pertinent or involved. **3.** *Informal* To seem reasonable or expected: *It figures.* —*phrasal verbs:* **figure in** To include, as in making an account. **figure on** *Informal* **1.** To depend on. **2.** To take into considera-

fife

tion; expect. **3.** To plan. **figure out** *Informal* **1.** To discover or decide. **2.** To solve or decipher. [ME < OFr. < Lat. *figūra.* See **dheigh-** in App.] **—fig′ur•er** *n.*

fig•ured (fĭg′yərd) *adj.* **1.** Shaped or fashioned in a particular way. **2.** Decorated with a design; patterned. **3.** Represented, as in graphic art or sculpture; depicted.

figured bass (bās) *n.* See **continuo.** [< the numerals written underneath the notes.]

figure eight *n.* A form or representation, such as a knot or an ice-skating maneuver, that has the shape of the numeral 8.

fig•ure•head (fĭg′yər-hĕd′) *n.* **1.** A carved figure on the prow of a ship. **2.** A person given a position of nominal leadership but having no actual authority.

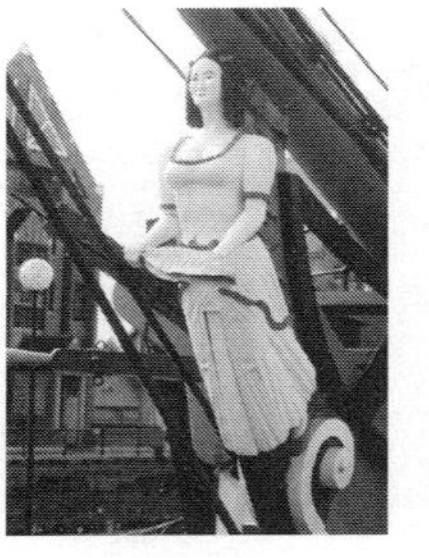

figurehead

figure of speech *n., pl.* **figures of speech** An expression that uses language in a nonliteral way, such as a metaphor or synecdoche, or in a structured or unusual way, such as anaphora or chiasmus, or that employs sounds, such as alliteration or assonance, to achieve a rhetorical effect.

figure skating *n.* Ice skating consisting of one or more planned sequences of required and optional spins, jumps, and dancelike maneuvers. **—figure skater** *n.*

fig•u•rine (fĭg′yə-rēn′) *n.* A small molded or sculptured figure; a statuette. [Fr. < Ital. *figurina,* dim. of *figura,* figure < Lat. *figūra.* See FIGURE.]

fig•wort (fĭg′wûrt′, -wôrt′) *n.* Any of various plants of the genus *Scrophularia,* having loose branching clusters of small greenish or purple flowers. [< FIG[1], piles (obsolete).]

Fi•ji (fē′jē) An island country of the SW Pacific Ocean comprising c. 320 islands; annexed by Great Britain in 1874 and gained independence in 1970. Cap. Suva. Pop. 784,000.

Fi•ji•an (fē′jē-ən, fĭ-jē′-) *n.* **1.** A native or inhabitant of Fiji. **2.** The Austronesian language of Fiji. **—Fi′ji•an** *adj.*

fi•la (fī′lə) *n.* Plural of **filum.**

fil•a•ment (fĭl′ə-mənt) *n.* **1.** A fine or thinly spun thread, fiber, or wire. **2.** *Botany* **a.** The stalk that bears the anther in a stamen. **b.** A chainlike series of cells, as in many algae. **3a.** A fine wire heated electrically to incandescence in an electric lamp. **b.** *Electronics* A high-resistance wire or ribbon forming the cathode in some thermionic tubes. [NLat. *fīlāmentum* < LLat. *fīlāre,* to spin < Lat. *fīlum,* thread.] **—fil′a•men′tous** (-mĕn′təs), **fil′a•men′ta•ry** (-mĕn′tə-rē, -mĕn′trē) *adj.*

fi•lar (fī′lər) *adj.* **1.** Of or relating to a thread. **2.** Having fine threads across the field of view for measuring small distances, as in a telescope eyepiece. [< Lat. *fīlum,* thread.]

fil•a•ree (fĭl′ə-rē′) *n.* See **alfilaria.** [Alteration of ALFILARIA.]

fi•lar•i•a (fə-lâr′ē-ə) *n., pl.* **-i•ae** (-ē-ē′) Any of various threadlike parasitic nematodes of the superfamily Filarioidea that live in the blood and lymphatic tissues and usu. develop as larvae in mosquitos and other biting insects. [NLat. *Fīlāria,* former genus name < Lat. *fīlum,* thread.] **—fi•lar′i•al** (-ē-əl), **fi•lar′i•an** (-ē-ən) *adj.*

fil•a•ri•a•sis (fĭl′ə-rī′ə-sĭs) *n., pl.* **-ses** (-sēz′) Disease caused by infestation of tissue with filariae. [FILAR(IA) + -IASIS.]

fil•a•ture (fĭl′ə-cho͝or′, -chər) *n.* **1.** The act or process of spinning, drawing, or twisting into threads. **2.** The act or process of reeling raw silk from cocoons. **3.** A reel used in drawing silk from cocoons. **4.** An establishment where silk is reeled. [Fr. < LLat. *fīlātus,* p. part. of *fīlāre,* to spin. See FILAMENT.]

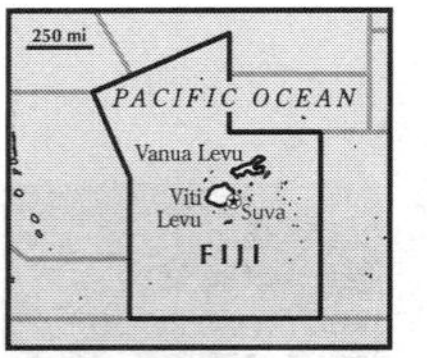

Fiji

fil•bert (fĭl′bərt) *n.* **1.** See **hazel** 1. **2.** See **hazelnut.** [ME < OFr. *(nois de) filbert,* (nut of) Philbert, after St. *Philibert* (died 684), whose feast day in late August coincides with the ripening of the nut.]

filch (fĭlch) *tr.v.* **filched, filch•ing, filch•es** To take (something, esp. something of little value) in a furtive manner; snitch. [ME *filchen.*] **—filch′er** *n.*

Filch•ner Ice Shelf (fĭlk′nər) An area of Antarctica at the head of Weddell Sea; first explored in 1912.

file[1] (fīl) *n.* **1.** A container, such as a cabinet or folder, for keeping papers in order. **2.** A collection of papers or published materials kept or arranged in convenient order. **3.** *Computer Science* A collection of related data or program records stored as a unit with a single name. **4a.** A line of persons, animals, or things positioned one behind the other. **b.** A line of troops or military vehicles so positioned. **5.** *Games* Any of the rows of squares that run forward and backward between players on a playing board in chess or checkers. **6.** *Archaic* A list or roll. ❖ *v.* **filed, fil•ing, files** *—tr.* **1.** To put or keep (papers, for example) in useful order for storage or reference. **2.** To enter (a legal document) on public official record. **3.** To send or submit (copy) to a newspaper. **4.** To carry out the first stage of (a lawsuit, for example): *filed charges.* *—intr.* **1.** To march or walk in a line. **2.** To put items in a file. **3.** To make application; apply: *file for a divorce.* **4.** To enter one's name in a political contest. ***—idiom:*** **on file** In or as if in a file for easy reference. [< ME *filen,* to put documents on file < OFr. *filer,* to spin thread, to put documents on a thread < LLat. *fīlāre,* to spin, draw out in a long line < Lat. *fīlum,* thread.]

file[2] (fīl) *n.* **1.** Any of several hardened steel tools with cutting ridges for forming, smoothing, or reducing esp. metallic surfaces. **2.** A nail file. **3.** *Chiefly British* A crafty or artful person. ❖ *tr.v.* **filed, fil•ing, files** To smooth, reduce, or remove with or as if with a file. [ME < OE *fīl.*]

file[3] (fīl) *tr.v.* **filed, fil•ing, files** *Archaic* To sully or defile. [ME *filen* < OE *fȳlan.* See **pŭ-** in App.]

fi•lé (fē′lā, fĭ-lā′) *n.* Powdered sassafras leaves used to thicken and season soups, stews, and gumbos. [Louisiana Fr. < Fr., p. part. of *filer,* to spin thread < OFr. See FILE[1].]

file•fish (fīl′fĭsh′) *n., pl.* **filefish** or **-fish•es** Any of various chiefly tropical marine fishes of the family Balistidae with a flat body and rough spiny scales.

file•name (fīl′nām′) *n.* The name of a computer file, often containing an extension that classifies it by type.

file server *n.* A computer that controls a central repository of data that can be downloaded or manipulated by a client.

fi•let[1] (fĭ-lā′, fĭl′ā′) *n.* A net or lace with a simple pattern of squares. [Fr. < OFr., dim. of *fil,* thread < Lat. *fīlum.* See FILE[1].]

fi•let[2] (fĭ-lā′, fĭl′ā′) *n.* Variant of **fillet** 2. ❖ *v.* Variant of **fillet** 2.

fi•let mi•gnon (fĭ-lā′ mēn-yôɴ′, fĭl′ā) *n., pl.* **fi•lets mi•gnons** (fĭ-lā′ mēn-yôɴ′, fĭl′ā) A small, round, very choice cut of beef from the loin. [Fr. : *filet,* fillet + *mignon,* dainty.]

File Transfer Protocol *n.* See **FTP.**

fil•i•al (fĭl′ē-əl, fē′lē-) *adj.* **1.** Of, relating to, or befitting a son or daughter. **2.** Having or assuming the relationship of child or offspring to parent. **3.** *Genetics* Of or relating to a generation or the sequence of generations following the parental generation. [ME < OFr. < LLat. *fīliālis* < Lat. *fīlius,* son.] **—fil′i•al•ly** *adv.*

fil•i•a•tion (fĭl′ē-ā′shən) *n.* **1.** The condition or fact of being the child of a certain parent. **2.** A line of descent; derivation. **3a.** The act or fact of forming a new branch, as of a society or language group. **b.** The branch thus formed.

fil•i•bus•ter (fĭl′ə-bŭs′tər) *n.* **1a.** The use of obstructionist tactics, esp. prolonged speechmaking, in order to delay legislative action. **b.** An instance of the use of this delaying tactic. **2.** An adventurer who engages in a private military action in a foreign country. ❖ *v.* **-tered, -ter•ing, -ters** *—intr.* **1.** To use obstructionist tactics in a legislative body. **2.** To take part in a private military action in a foreign country. *—tr.* To use a filibuster against (a legislative measure, for example). [< Sp. *filibustero,* freebooter < Fr. *flibustier* < Du. *vrijbuiter,* pirate. See FREEBOOTER.] **—fil′i•bus′ter•er** *n.*

fil•i•form (fĭl′ə-fôrm′, fī′lə-) *adj.* Having the form of or resembling a thread or filament. [Lat. *fīlum,* thread + -FORM.]

fil•i•gree (fĭl′ĭ-grē′) *n.* **1.** Delicate and intricate ornamental work made of gold, silver, or other fine twisted wire. **2a.** An intricate, delicate, or fanciful ornamentation. **b.** A design resembling such ornamentation. ❖ *tr.v.* **-greed, -gree•ing, -grees** To decorate with or as if with filigree. [Alteration of Fr. *filigrane* < Ital. *filigrana* : Lat. *fīlum,* thread + Lat. *grānum,* grain; see **g̥rə-no-** in App.]

fil•ing (fī′lĭng) *n.* **1.** A particle or shaving removed by a file. **2.** The act or an instance of using a file.

fil•i•o•pi•e•tis•tic (fĭl′ē-ō-pī′ĭ-tĭs′tĭk) *adj.* Of or relating to an often immoderate reverence for forebears or tradition. [Lat. *fīlius,* son + PIETISTIC.]

Fil•i•pi•na (fĭl′ə-pē′nə) *n.* A Filipino woman or girl. [Sp. *filipina,* fem. of *filipino,* Filipino. See FILIPINO.] **—Fil′i•pi′na** *adj.*

Fil•i•pi•no (fĭl′ə-pē′nō) *n., pl.* **-nos 1.** A native or inhabitant of the Philippines. **2.** The Austronesian language that is based on Tagalog, draws its lexicon from other Philippine languages, and is the official language of the Philippines. ❖ *adj.* Of or relating to the Philippines or its peoples, languages, or cultures. [Sp. *filipino* < *(Islas) Filipinas,* Philippine (Islands).]

fill (fĭl) *v.* **filled, fill•ing, fills** *—tr.* **1a.** To put into (a container, for example) as much as can be held: *fill a glass with milk.* **b.** To supply or provide to the fullest extent: *filled the mall with new stores.* **c.** To build up the level of (low-lying land) with material such as earth or gravel. **d.** To stop or plug up (an opening, for example). **e.** To repair a cavity in (a tooth). **f.** To add a foreign substance to (cloth or wood, for example). **2a.** To satiate, as with food and drink. **b.** To satisfy or meet; fulfill. See Syns at **satisfy. c.** To complete (something) by insertion or addition: *fill in the blanks.* **d.** To supply with material, such as writing. **3.** To supply as required: *fill a prescription.* **4a.** To place a person in: *fill a job vacancy.* **b.** To possess and discharge the duties of; hold. **5a.** To occupy the whole of; pervade. **b.** To spread throughout. **c.** To engage or occupy completely; make full: *a story that filled our hearts with joy.* **6.** To cover the surface of (an inexpensive metal) with a layer of precious metal. **7.** *Nautical* To cause (a sail) to swell. *—intr.* **1.** To become full. **2.** To swell. Used of a sail. ❖ *n.* **1.** An amount needed to make full, complete, or satisfied. **2.** Material for filling a container, cavity, or passage. **3a.** A built-up piece of land; an embankment. **b.** The material, such as gravel, used for this. ***—phrasal verbs:*** **fill in 1.** *Informal* To provide with information that is essential or newly acquired. **2.** To act as a substitute; stand in. **fill out 1.** To complete (a form, for example) by providing required information. **2.** To become or make more fleshy. ***—idioms:*** **fill (someone's) shoes** To assume someone's position or duties. **fill the bill** *Informal* To serve a particular purpose. [ME *fillen* < OE *fyllan.* See **pelə-**[1] in App.]

filled gold (fĭld) *n.* A relatively inexpensive metal such as brass with a surface layer of bonded gold.

filled milk *n.* Skim milk with vegetable oils added to substitute for butterfat.

fill•er (fĭl′ər) *n.* One that fills, as: **a.** Something added to augment weight or size or fill space. **b.** A composition, esp. a semisolid that hardens on drying, used to fill pores, cracks, or holes in construction surfaces before finishing. **c.** Tobacco used to form the body of a cigar. **d.** A short item used to fill space in a publication. **e.** Something used to fill time on radio or television. **f.** A sheaf of loose papers used to fill a notebook or binder. **g.** *Architecture* An element, such as a plate, used to fill the space between two supporting members.

fil•let (fĭl′ĭt) *n.* **1.** A narrow strip of ribbon or similar material, often worn as a headband. **2.** also **fi•let** (fĭ-lā′, fĭl′ā′) **a.** A strip or compact piece of boneless meat or fish, esp. the beef tenderloin. **b.** A boneless strip of meat rolled and tied, as for roasting. **3.** *Architecture* **a.** A thin flat molding used as separation between or ornamentation for larger moldings. **b.** A ridge between the indentations of a fluted column. **4.** A narrow decorative line impressed onto the cover of a book. **5.** *Heraldry* A narrow horizontal band placed in the lower fourth area of the chief. **6.** *Anatomy* A loop-shaped band of fibers, such as the lemniscus. ❖ *tr.v.* **-let•ed, -let•ing, -lets 1.** To bind or decorate with or as if with a fillet. **2.** also **fi•let** (fĭ-lā′, fĭl′ā′) To slice, bone, or make into fillets. [ME *filet* < OFr., dim. of *fil*, thread < Lat. *fīlum*.]

fill-in (fĭl′ĭn′) *n. Informal* **1.** One that serves as a substitute for another. **2.** A short informative summary.

fill•ing (fĭl′ĭng) *n.* **1.** An act or instance of filling. **2.** Something used to fill a space, cavity, or container. **3.** An edible mixture used to fill pastries, sandwiches, or cakes. See Regional Note at **frosting. 4.** The horizontal threads that cross the warp in weaving; weft.

filling station *n.* See **service station** 1.

fil•lip (fĭl′əp) *n.* **1.** A snap or light blow made by pressing a fingertip against the thumb and suddenly releasing it. **2.** An embellishment that excites or stimulates. **3.** One that is trivial or of little importance. ❖ *tr.v.* **-liped, -lip•ing, -lips 1.** To strike or propel rapidly by as or as if by a fillip. **2.** To stimulate or arouse. [Imit.]

Fill•more (fĭl′môr′, -mōr′), **Millard** 1800–74. The 13th President of the US (1850–53), who succeeded to office after the death of Zachary Taylor.

fil•ly (fĭl′ē) *n., pl.* **-lies 1.** A young female horse. **2.** *Informal* A lively high-spirited girl or young woman. [ME *filli* < ON *fylja*.]

film (fĭlm) *n.* **1.** A thin skin or membrane. **2.** A thin opaque abnormal coating on the cornea of the eye. **3.** A thin covering or coating: *a film of dust.* **4.** A thin flexible transparent sheet, as of plastic, used in wrapping or packaging. **5a.** A thin sheet or strip of flexible material, such as a cellulose derivative, coated with a photosensitive emulsion and used to make photographic negatives or transparencies. **b.** A sheet or strip of developed photographic negatives or transparencies. **6a.** A movie. **b.** Movies considered as a group. **7.** A coating of magnetic alloys on glass used in manufacturing computer storage devices. ❖ *v.* **filmed, film•ing, films** *—tr.* **1.** To cover with or as if with a film. **2.** To make a movie of or based on: *film a rocket launch.* *—intr.* **1.** To become coated or obscured with or as if with a film. **2.** To make or shoot scenes for a movie. [ME < OE *filmen.* See pel-¹ in App.]

film•dom (fĭlm′dəm) *n.* **1.** The movie industry. **2.** The people employed in the movie industry.

film•go•er (fĭlm′gō′ər) *n.* One who goes to see movies; a moviegoer. **—film′go′ing** *adj.*

fil•mi (fĭl′mē) *n.* Music composed for the Indian popular film industry, having melodies and vocal styles derived from Indian folk and classical music. [< Hindi *filmī*, cinematographic < *film*, film < E. FILM.]

film•ic (fĭl′mĭk) *adj.* Of, relating to, or characteristic of movies; cinematic. **—film′i•cal•ly** *adv.*

film•mak•er (fĭlm′mā′kər) *n.* One who directs or produces movies.

film•mak•ing (fĭlm′mā′kĭng) *n.* The making of movies.

film noir *n.* A movie characterized by low-key lighting, a bleak urban setting, and corrupt, cynical characters. **2.** The genre or style of such movies. [Fr. : *film*, film + *noir*, black.]

film•og•ra•phy (fĭl-mŏg′rə-fē) *n., pl.* **-phies** A comprehensive list of movies in a particular category, as of those by a given director or in a specific genre. **—film′og′ra•pher** *n.*

film•set•ting (fĭlm′sĕt′ĭng) *n.* Photocomposition.

film•strip (fĭlm′strĭp′) *n.* A length of film containing a series of photographs or other graphic matter prepared for still projection.

film•y (fĭl′mē) *adj.* **-i•er, -i•est 1.** Of, resembling, or consisting of film; gauzy. See Syns at **airy. 2.** Covered as or by a film; hazy. **—film′i•ly** *adv.* **—film′i•ness** *n.*

fi•lo (fē′lō, fī′-) *n.* Variant of **phyllo.**

fil•o•plume (fĭl′ə-plōōm′, fī′lə-) *n.* A hairlike feather having few or no barbs, usu. located between contour feathers. [Lat. *filum*, thread + PLUME.]

fi•lose (fī′lōs′) *adj.* **1.** Threadlike. **2.** Having or ending in a threadlike part or process. [Lat. *fīlum*, thread + −OSE¹.]

fi•lo•vi•rus (fē′lō-vī′rəs, fĭl′ō-) *n.* Any of a group of filamentous RNA viruses of the family Filoviridae that cause hemorrhagic fevers. [Lat. *fīlum*, thread + VIRUS.]

fils (fēs) *n.* Used to distinguish a son from his father when they have the same given name. [Fr. < Lat. *fīlius*, son.]

fil•ter (fĭl′tər) *n.* **1a.** A porous material through which a liquid or gas is passed to separate the fluid from suspended particles. **b.** A device containing such a material. **2a.** Any of various electric, electronic, acoustic, or optical devices that reject signals, vibrations, or radiations of certain frequencies while allowing others to pass. **b.** A colored glass or other transparent material used to select the wavelengths of light allowed to reach a photosensitive material. **3.** *Computer Science* A program or routine that blocks access to data that meet a particular criterion. ❖ *v.* **-tered, -ter•ing, -ters** *—tr.* **1.** To pass (a liquid or gas) through a filter. **2.** To remove by passing through a filter: *filters out sand.* **3.** *Computer Science* To use a filter to block access to (a website or Web content). *—intr.* **1.** To pass through or as if through a filter. **2.** To come or go gradually and in small groups. [ME *filtre* < OFr. < Med.Lat. *filtrum*, of Gmc. orig. See pel-² in App.] **—fil′ter•er** *n.* **—fil′ter•less** *adj.*

fil•ter•a•ble (fĭl′tər-ə-bəl, fĭl′trə-) also **fil•tra•ble** (-trə-bəl) *adj.* **1.** That can be filtered or separated by filtering. **2.** That can pass through a given pore size. **—fil′ter•a•bil′i•ty** *n.*

filterable virus *n.* A virus that is small enough to pass through a fine-pored filter, as of diatomite or porcelain.

filter bed *n.* A layer of sand or gravel on the bottom of a reservoir or tank, used to filter water or sewage.

filter feeder *n.* An aquatic animal, such as a clam or sponge, that feeds by filtering particulate organic material from water.

filter paper *n.* Porous paper suitable for use as a filter.

filth (fĭlth) *n.* **1a.** Foul or dirty matter. **b.** Disgusting garbage or refuse. **2.** A dirty or corrupt condition; foulness. **3.** Something, such as language, considered obscene, prurient, or immoral. [ME < OE *fȳlth.* See pŭ- in App.]

filth•y (fĭl′thē) *adj.* **-i•er, -i•est 1.** Covered or smeared with filth; disgustingly dirty. **2.** Obscene; scatological. **3.** Vile; nasty: *a filthy traitor.* **—filth′i•ly** *adv.* **—filth′i•ness** *n.*

fil•trate (fĭl′trāt′) *tr. & intr.v.* **-trat•ed, -trat•ing, -trates** To put or go through a filter. ❖ *n.* Material, esp. liquid, passed through a filter. [NLat. *filtrāre, filtrāt-*, to filter < Med.Lat. *filtrum*, filter. See FILTER.]

fil•tra•tion (fĭl-trā′shən) *n.* The act or process of filtering.

fi•lum (fī′ləm) *n., pl.* **-la** (-lə) A threadlike anatomical structure; a filament. [Lat. *fīlum*, thread.]

fim•bri•a (fĭm′brē-ə) *n., pl.* **-bri•ae** (-brē-ē′) A fringelike part or structure, as at the opening of the fallopian tubes. [LLat., fringe, back-formation < Lat. *fimbriae*, threads, fringe.] **—fim′bri•al** *adj.*

fim•bri•ate (fĭm′brē-ĭt, -āt′) also **fim•bri•at•ed** (-ā′tĭd) *adj.* Having fimbriae; fringed, as the edge of a petal. [Lat. *fimbriātus* < *fimbriae*, fringe.] **—fim′bri•a′tion** *n.*

fin¹ (fĭn) *n.* **1.** A membranous appendage extending from the body of a fish or other aquatic animal, for propelling, steering, or balancing the body in the water. **2.** Something resembling a fin, as: **a.** An airfoil used to stabilize an aircraft, missile, or projectile in flight. **b.** A thin projection attached to a surfboard for stability. **c.** A projecting vane for cooling, as on a radiator or an engine cylinder. **d.** See **tail fin** 2. **3.** See **flipper** 2. ❖ *v.* **finned, fin•ning, fins** *—tr.* To equip with fins. *—intr.* **1.** To emerge with the fins above water. **2.** To swim, as a fish. **3.** To lash the water with the fins. Used of a dying whale. [ME < OE *finn.*]

fin² (fĭn) *n. Slang* A five-dollar bill. [Yiddish *finf*, five < OHGer. *funf, finf.* See penk⁵e in App.]

Fin. *abbr.* **1.** Finland **2.** Finnish

fi•na•gle (fə-nā′gəl) *v.* **-gled, -gling, -gles** *Informal —tr.* **1.** To obtain or achieve by indirect, usu. deceitful methods: *finagle a day off.* **2.** To cheat; swindle. *—intr.* To use crafty, deceitful methods. [Prob. < dialectal *fainaigue*, to cheat.] **—fi•na′gler** *n.*

fi•nal (fī′nəl) *adj.* **1.** Forming or occurring at the end; last. **2.** Of or constituting the end result of a succession or process; ultimate. **3.** Not to be changed or reconsidered; unalterable. See Syns at **last¹.** ❖ *n.* Something that comes at or forms the end, esp. **a.** The last or one of the last of a series of contests. **b.** The last examination of an academic course. [ME < OFr. < Lat. *fīnālis* < *fīnis*, end.] **—fi′nal•ly** *adv.*

fi•na•le (fə-năl′ē, -näl′ē) *n.* The concluding part, esp. of a musical composition. [Ital. < Lat. *fīnālis*, final. See FINAL.]

fi•nal•ist (fī′nə-lĭst) *n.* A contestant in the final session of a competition.

fi•nal•i•ty (fī-năl′ĭ-tē, fə-) *n., pl.* **-ties 1.** The condition or fact of being final. **2.** A final, conclusive, or decisive act.

fi•nal•ize (fī′nə-līz′) *tr.v.* **-ized, -iz•ing, -iz•es** To put into final form; complete or conclude. **—fi′nal•i•za′tion** (-nə-lĭ-zā′shən) *n.* **—fi′nal•iz′er** *n.*

Millard Fillmore

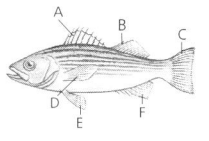

fin¹
fins of a typical bony fish
A. spinous dorsal fin
B. soft dorsal fin
C. caudal fin
D. pectoral fin
E. pelvic fin
F. anal fin

ă	pat	oi	boy
ā	pay	ou	out
âr	care	ŏŏ	took
ä	father	ōō	boot
ĕ	pet	ŭ	cut
ē	be	ûr	urge
ĭ	pit	th	thin
ī	pie	th	this
îr	pier	hw	which
ŏ	pot	zh	vision
ō	toe	ə	about,
ô	paw		item

Stress marks:
′ (primary);
′ (secondary), as in
lexicon (lĕk′sĭ-kŏn′)

finch
American goldfinch
Carduelis tristis

fi·nance (fə-năns′, fī-, fī′năns′) *n.* **1.** The science of the management of money and other assets. **2.** The management of money, banking, investments, and credit. **3. finances** Monetary resources; funds, esp. those of a government or corporate body. **4.** The supplying of funds or capital. ❖ *tr.v.* **-nanced, -nanc·ing, -nanc·es 1.** To provide or raise the funds or capital for. **2.** To supply funds to: *financing her through law school.* **3.** To furnish credit to. [ME *finaunce*, settlement, money supply < OFr. *finance*, payment < *finer*, to pay ransom < *fin*, end < Lat. *fīnis.*] —**fi·nance′a·ble** *adj.*

finance company *n.* A company that makes loans to clients.

fi·nan·cial (fə-năn′shəl, fī-) *adj.* Of, relating to, or involving finance, finances, or financiers. —**fi·nan′cial·ly** *adv.*

fin·an·cier (fĭn′ən-sîr′, fə-năn′-, fī′nən-) *n.* One who is occupied with or expert in large-scale financial affairs. [Fr. < OFr. < *finance*, payment. See FINANCE.]

fi·nas·ter·ide (fə-năs′tə-rīd′) *n.* A synthetic androgen inhibitor used esp. in the treatment of benign prostatic hyperplasia. [*fin*-(alteration of *(al)ph(a-reductase) in(hibitor)*) + *(az)aster(oid)*, steroid containing azine (alteration of AZO– + STEROID) + (AM)IDE.]

fin·back (fĭn′băk′) *n.* A rorqual, esp. *Balaenoptera physalus* of the Atlantic and Pacific coasts, that attains a length of about 21 meters (70 feet).

fin·ca (fĭng′kə, fēng′kä) *n.* A rural property, esp. a large farm or ranch, in Spanish America. [Am.Sp. < Sp., real estate < OSpan. *fincar*, to pitch tents, reside < VLat. *fīgicāre*, to fasten, attach < Lat. *fīgere.*]

finch (fĭnch) *n.* Any of various small birds of the family Fringillidae, including the goldfinches, sparrows, cardinals, grosbeaks, and canaries, having a short stout bill for cracking seeds. [ME < OE *finc.*]

find (fīnd) *v.* **found** (found), **find·ing, finds** —*tr.* **1.** To come upon, often by accident; meet with. **2.** To come upon or discover by searching or making an effort: *found the leak in the pipe.* **3.** To discover or ascertain through observation, experience, or study: *find the product of two numbers.* **4a.** To perceive to be, after experience or consideration: *found the book entertaining.* **b.** To experience or feel: *found comfort.* **5.** To recover (something lost): *found her keys.* **6.** To recover the use of; regain: *found my voice and replied.* **7.** To succeed in reaching; arrive at: *The dart found its mark.* **8.** To obtain or acquire by effort: *found the money by economizing.* **9.** To decide on and make a declaration about: *The jurors found him guilty.* **10.** To furnish; supply. **11a.** To bring (oneself) to an awareness of what one truly wishes to be and do in life. **b.** To perceive (oneself) to be in a specific place or condition: *found himself drawn to the stranger.* —*intr.* To come to a legal decision or verdict: *The jury found for the defendant.* ❖ *n.* **1.** The act of finding. **2.** Something that is found, esp. an unexpectedly valuable discovery: *a providential archaeological find.* —*phrasal verb:* **find out 1.** To ascertain (something), as by examination or inquiry. **2.** To detect the true nature or character of; expose. **3.** To detect and apprehend; catch. [ME *finden* < OE *findan.* See **pent-** in App.] —**find′a·ble** *adj.*

find·er (fīn′dər) *n.* **1.** One that finds. **2.** A viewfinder. **3.** A low-power wide-angle telescope fixed to one more powerful and pointed the same way for initially locating an object.

fin-de-siè·cle (făN′də-sē-ĕk′lə) *adj.* Of or characteristic of the last part of the 19th century, esp. regarding its artistic, effete sophistication. [Fr. : *fin*, end + *de*, of + *siècle*, cent.]

find·ing (fīn′dĭng) *n.* **1.** Something found. **2a.** A conclusion reached after examination or investigation: *a coroner's findings.* **b.** A statement or document containing an authoritative decision or conclusion. **3. findings** Small tools and materials used by an artisan.

fine[1] (fīn) *adj.* **fin·er, fin·est 1.** Of superior quality, skill, or appearance: *a fine day; a fine writer.* **2.** Very small in size, weight, or thickness: *fine type; fine paper.* **3a.** Free from impurities. **b.** *Metallurgy* Containing pure metal in a specified proportion or amount: *gold 21 carats fine.* **4.** Very sharp; keen: *a blade with a fine edge.* **5.** Thin; slender: *fine hairs.* **6.** Exhibiting careful and delicate artistry: *fine china.* See Syns at **delicate. 7.** Consisting of very small particles; not coarse: *fine dust.* **8a.** Subtle or precise. **b.** Able to make or detect effects of great subtlety or precision; sensitive. **9.** Trained to the highest degree of physical efficiency: *a fine racehorse.* **10.** Characterized by refinement or elegance. **11.** Satisfactory; acceptable: *Handing in your paper on Monday is fine.* **12.** Being in a state of satisfactory health; quite well: *I'm fine. And you?* **13.** Used as an intensive: *a fine mess.* ❖ *adv.* **1.** Finely. **2.** *Informal* Very well. ❖ *tr. & intr.v.* **fined, fin·ing, fines** To make or become finer, purer, or cleaner. [ME < OFr. < Lat. *fīnis*, end, supreme degree.] —**fine′ness** *n.*

fine[2] (fīn) *n.* **1.** A sum of money to be paid as a penalty for an offense. **2.** *Law* **a.** A forfeiture or penalty to be paid to the offended party in a civil action. **b.** An amicable settlement of a suit over land ownership. **3.** *Obsolete* An end; a termination. ❖ *tr.v.* **fined, fin·ing, fines** To require the payment of a fine from; impose a fine on. —*idiom:* **in fine 1.** In conclusion; finally. **2.** In summation; in brief. [ME *fin* < OFr., settlement, compensation < Med.Lat. *fīnis* < Lat., end.] —**fin′a·ble, fine′a·ble** *adj.*

fi·ne[3] (fē′nā) *n. Music* The end. [Ital. < Lat. *fīnis*, end.]

fine art (fīn) *n.* **1a.** Art produced or intended for beauty, not utility. **b.** Any of the art forms, such as music, used to create this art. Often used in the plural. **2.** Something requiring highly developed technique and skill: *the fine art of teaching.*

fine-drawn (fīn′drôn′) *adj.* **1.** Drawn out to a slender threadlike state. **2.** Subtly or precisely fashioned: *a fine-drawn theory.* **3.** Delicately formed: *fine-drawn features.*

fine-grained (fīn′grānd′) *adj.* Having a fine, smooth, even grain: *fine-grained wood.*

fine·ly (fīn′lē) *adv.* **1.** In a fine manner; splendidly. **2.** To a fine point; discriminatingly. **3.** In small pieces or parts: *finely chopped nuts.*

fine print (fīn) *n.* **1.** The part of a document, esp. a contract, containing qualifications or restrictions in small type or obscure language. **2.** Something presented so as to be ambiguous or obscure.

fin·er·y (fī′nə-rē) *n., pl.* **-ies** Elaborate adornment, esp. fine clothing and accessories.

fines herbes (fēn zĕrb′, fēn ĕrb′) *pl.n.* Finely chopped herbs, esp. parsley, chives, tarragon, and thyme, used together as a seasoning. [Fr. : *fines*, fem. pl. of *fin*, fine + *herbes*, pl. of *herbe*, herb.]

fine-spun (fīn′spŭn′) *adj.* **1.** Developed to extreme fineness or subtlety; elaborate. **2.** Developed to excessive fineness; overwrought.

fi·nesse (fə-nĕs′) *n.* **1.** Refinement and delicacy of performance, execution, or artisanship. **2.** Skillful subtle handling of a situation; tactful diplomatic maneuvering. **3.** A method of leading up to a tenace, as in bridge, to prevent an opponent from winning the trick with an intermediate card. **4.** A stratagem in which one appears to decline an advantage. ❖ *v.* **-nessed, -ness·ing, -ness·es** —*tr.* **1.** To accomplish by the use of finesse. **2.** To handle with a deceptive or evasive strategy. **3.** To play (a card) in a finesse. —*intr.* **1.** To use finesse. **2.** To make use of a finesse in cards. [Fr., fineness, subtlety < *fin*, fine. See FINE[1].]

fine structure (fīn) *n.* **1.** *Physics* The splitting of spectral lines caused by the magnetic moments of orbiting electrons in the atomic nucleus. **2.** *Biology* See **ultrastructure.**

fine-tooth comb (fīn′tōoth′) or **fine-toothed comb** (-tōoth′, -tōothd′) *n.* **1.** A comb with teeth set close together. **2.** A thorough method of searching or investigating in minute detail.

fine-tune (fīn′tōon′, -tyōon′) *tr.v.* **-tuned, -tun·ing, -tunes** To adjust minutely for optimal performance or effectiveness.

fin·fish (fĭn′fĭsh′) *n.* A true fish, as opposed to a shellfish.

fin·ger (fĭng′gər) *n.* **1.** One of the five digits of the hand, esp. one other than the thumb. **2.** The part of a glove designed to cover a finger. **3.** Something, such as an oblong peninsula, that resembles a digit of the hand. **4.** The length or width of a finger. **5.** A degree of participation; a share. **6.** An obscene gesture of defiance or derision made by pointing or jabbing the middle finger upward. Often used with *the.* ❖ *v.* **-gered, -ger·ing, -gers** —*tr.* **1.** To touch with the fingers; handle. **2.** *Music* **a.** To mark (a score) with indications of which fingers are to play the notes. **b.** To play (an instrument) by using the fingers in a particular order or way. **3.** *Slang* **a.** To inform on. **b.** To designate, esp. as an intended victim. —*intr.* **1.** To handle something with the fingers. **2.** *Music* To use the fingers in playing an instrument. —*idioms:* **have (or keep) (one's) fingers crossed** To hope for a successful or advantageous outcome. **put (one's) finger on** To remember; recall. **twist (or wrap) around (one's) little finger** To dominate utterly and effortlessly. [ME < OE. See **penkʷe** in App.] —**fin′ger·er** *n.* —**fin′ger·less** *adj.*

fin·ger·board (fĭng′gər-bôrd′, -bōrd′) *n. Music* A strip of wood on the neck of a stringed instrument against which the strings are pressed in playing.

finger bowl *n.* A bowl with water for rinsing the fingers at the table.

fin·ger·breadth (fĭng′gər-brĕdth′) *n.* The breadth of one finger.

fin·gered (fĭng′gərd) *adj.* Having a finger or fingers, esp. of a specific number or kind. Often used in combination.

finger hole *n. Music* Any of the holes on a wind instrument that cause a change in pitch when covered by a finger. **2.** A hole or opening for a finger, as in a bowling ball.

fin·ger·ing (fĭng′gər-ĭng) *n. Music* **1.** The technique used in playing an instrument with the fingers. **2.** The indication on a score of which fingers are to be used in playing.

Finger Lakes A group of 11 elongated glacial lakes in W-central NY.

fin·ger·ling (fĭng′gər-lĭng) *n.* A young or small fish, esp. a young salmon or trout.

finger millet *n.* An annual plant (*Eleusine coracana*) in the grass family, native to the Old World tropics.

fin·ger·nail (fĭng′gər-nāl′) *n.* The thin, horny, transparent plate covering the upper surface of the end of a finger.

fin·ger-paint (fĭng′gər-pānt′) *tr. & intr.v.* **-paint·ed, -paint·ing, -paints** To make by or engage in finger painting.

finger painting *n.* **1.** The technique of painting by applying color to paper with the fingers. **2.** A picture so made.

fin·ger·pick (fĭng′gər-pĭk′) *v.* **-picked, -pick·ing, -picks** —*intr.* To play a stringed instrument, such as the guitar, by plucking individual strings with the fingers. —*tr.* To play (a

fingerboard

stringed instrument) in this manner. **—fin′ger•pick′er** *n.*
finger pick *n.* A pointed, slightly curved plectrum worn on the fingertip, used in playing the guitar, for example.
fin•ger-point•ing (fĭng′gər-poin′tĭng) *n.* The act of blaming someone for something; the imputation of blame.
finger post *n.* A guidepost in the shape of a pointing hand.
fin•ger•print (fĭng′gər-prĭnt′) *n.* **1.** An impression on a surface of the curves formed by the ridges on a fingertip, esp. when made in ink and used as a means of identification. **2.** A distinctive or identifying mark or characteristic. **3a.** A DNA fingerprint. **b.** A chemical fingerprint. ❖ *tr.v.* **-print•ed, -print•ing, -prints 1.** To take the fingerprints of. **2.** To identify by means of a distinctive mark or characteristic.
fin•ger•spell•ing (fĭng′gər-spĕl′ĭng) *n.* Communication by means of a manual alphabet. **—fin′ger•spell′** *v.*
fin•ger•tip (fĭng′gər-tĭp′) *n.* The extreme end or tip of a finger. ***—idiom:*** **at (one's) fingertips** Readily available.
finger wave *n.* A wave set into dampened hair using only the fingers and a comb.
fin•i•al (fĭn′ē-əl) *n.* **1.** A sculptured ornament, often in the shape of a leaf or flower, at the top of a gable, pinnacle, or similar structure. **2.** An ornamental terminating part, as on a post or piece of furniture. [ME, last, finial, var. of *final.* See FINAL.]
fin•i•cal (fĭn′ĭ-kəl) *adj.* Finicky. [Prob. < FINE[1].] **—fin′i•cal•ly** *adv.* **—fin′i•cal•ness** *n.*
fin•ick•y (fĭn′ĭ-kē) *adj.* **-i•er, -i•est** Insisting capriciously on getting just what one wants; hard to please: *a finicky eater.* [< *finick,* a finical person < FINICAL.] **—fin′ick•i•ness** *n.*
fin•is (fĭn′ĭs, fī′nĭs, fē-nē′) *n.* The end; the conclusion. [ME < Lat. *fīnis.*]
fin•ish (fĭn′ĭsh) *v.* **-ished, -ish•ing, -ish•es** *—tr.* **1.** To arrive at or attain the end of. **2.** To bring to an end; terminate. **3.** To consume all of; use up. **4.** To bring to a desired or required state: *finish a painting.* **5.** To give (wood, for example) a desired or particular surface texture. **6.** To destroy; kill. **7.** To bring about the ruin of. *—intr.* **1.** To come to an end; stop. **2.** To reach the end of a task, course, or relationship. ❖ *n.* **1.** The final part; the conclusion. **2.** The reason for one's ruin; downfall. **3.** Something that completes, concludes, or perfects, esp.: **a.** The last treatment or coating of a surface. **b.** The surface texture produced by such a treatment or coating. **c.** A material used in surfacing or finishing. **4.** Completeness, thoroughness, refinement, or smoothness of execution; polish. [ME *finishen* < OFr. *finir, finiss-,* to complete < Lat. *fīnīre* < *fīnis,* end.] **—fin′ish•er** *n.*
fin•ished (fĭn′ĭsht) *adj.* **1.** Accomplished; expert; polished: *a finished artist.* **2.** Exhibiting much skill or polish. **3a.** Doomed to death or destruction. **b.** Having no more use, value, or potential.
fin•ish•ing school (fĭn′ĭ-shĭng) *n.* A private girls' school that stresses training in cultural subjects and social activities.
finishing touch *n.* A small change or addition that serves to complete something.
finish line *n.* A line that marks the end of a course for racing.
fi•nite (fī′nīt′) *adj.* **1a.** Having bounds; limited: *finite fuel reserves.* **b.** Existing, persisting, or enduring for a limited time only; impermanent. **2.** *Mathematics* **a.** Being neither infinite nor infinitesimal. **b.** Having a positive or negative numerical value; not zero. **c.** Having a limited number of elements. Used of a set. **3.** *Grammar* Of or relating to any of the forms of a verb that can occur on their own in a main clause and that can formally express distinctions in person, number, tense, mood, and voice, often by means of conjugation, as the verb *sees* in *She sees the sign.* ❖ *n.* A finite thing. [ME *finit* < Lat. *fīnītus,* p. part. of *fīnīre,* to limit < *fīnis,* end.] **—fi′nite′ly** *adv.* **—fi′nite′ness** *n.*
fin•i•tude (fĭn′ĭ-to͞od′, -tyo͞od′, fī′nĭ-) *n.* The quality or condition of being finite.
fink (fĭngk) *Slang n.* **1.** A contemptible person. **2.** An informer. **3.** A hired strikebreaker. ❖ *intr.v.* **finked, fink•ing, finks 1.** To inform against another person. **2.** To withhold promised support or participation. [?]
Fin•land (fĭn′lənd) A country of N Europe on the Gulf of Bothnia; gained independence from Russia in 1919. Cap. Helsinki. Pop. 5,095,000. **—Fin′land•er** *n.*
Finland, Gulf of An arm of the Baltic Sea bordering on Finland, Russia, and Estonia.
Fin•land•i•za•tion (fĭn′lən-də-zā′shən) *n.* **1.** The former policy of neutrality by non-Communist countries under the influence of the Soviet Union. **2.** The adoption of such a policy. **—Fin′land•ize′** *v.*
Fin•lay River (fĭn′lē) A river of N British Columbia, Canada, flowing c. 402 km (250 mi) to the Peace R.
Finn (fĭn) *n.* A native or inhabitant of Finland. [< Swed. *Finne.*]
fin•nan had•die (fĭn′ən hăd′ē) *n.* Smoked haddock. [< alteration of *Findon* or *Findhorn,* villages of NE Scotland.]
finned (fĭnd) *adj.* Having a fin, fins, or finlike parts. Often used in combination: *single-finned.*
Fin•nic (fĭn′ĭk) *adj.* Of or relating to Finland or the Finns. ❖ *n.* A branch of Finno-Ugric that includes Finnish, Estonian, and Lapp.
Finn•ish (fĭn′ĭsh) *adj.* Of or relating to Finland or its people, language, or culture. ❖ *n.* The Finno-Ugric language of the Finns.
Fin•no-U•gric (fĭn′ō-o͞o′grĭk, -yo͞o′-) also **Fin•no-U•gri•an** (-grē-ən) *n.* A subfamily of the Uralic language family that includes Finnish, Hungarian, and Estonian. ❖ *adj.* **1.** Of or relating to the Finns and the Ugrians. **2.** Of or relating to Finno-Ugric.
fin•ny (fĭn′ē) *adj.* **-ni•er, -ni•est 1.** Having a fin or fins. **2.** Resembling a fin; finlike. **3.** Of, relating to, or full of fish.
fi•no (fē′nō) *n., pl.* **-nos** A pale, very dry sherry. [Sp. *(jerez) fino,* dry (sherry) < *fino,* fine < Lat. *fīnis,* end, supreme degree.]
fi•noc•chi•o also **fi•no•chi•o** (fə-nō′kē-ō′) *n., pl.* **-os** A variety of fennel *(Foeniculum vulgare* var. *dulce)* whose blanched aromatic stalks are eaten as a vegetable. [Ital. < Lat. *fēniculum,* fennel, dim. of *faenum, fēnum,* hay.]
Fin•ster•aar•horn (fĭn′stər-är′hôrn′) A peak, 4,276.7 m (14,022 ft), of the Bernese Alps in S-central Switzerland.
fin whale *n.* See **finback.**
fiord (fyôrd, fyōrd) *n.* Variant of **fjord.**
fip•ple (fĭp′əl) *n.* **1.** A mouthpiece for certain wind instruments, such as a recorder, that channels the breath toward the sounding edge of a side opening. **2.** A similar object in an organ pipe. [?]
fipple flute *n.* A flute, such as a recorder, with a fipple.
fir (fûr) *n.* **1a.** Any of various evergreen trees of the genus *Abies,* having single flattened needles and erect cones with deciduous scales. **b.** Any of several similar or related trees, such as the Douglas fir. **2.** The wood of these trees. [ME *firre,* prob. of Scand. orig. See **perk^{w}u-** in App.] **—fir′ry** *adj.*
Fir•dau•si (fĭr-dou′sē) also **Fir•du•si** (fər-do͞o′-) Pen name of Abul Kasim Mansur. 940?–1020? Persian epic poet who wrote *Book of Kings* (1010), a history of Persia.
fire (fīr) *n.* **1a.** A chemical change that releases heat and light and is accompanied by flame, esp. the exothermic oxidation of a combustible substance. **b.** A burning fuel or other material: *a forest fire.* **2a.** Burning intensity of feeling; ardor. **b.** Enthusiasm. **3.** Luminosity or brilliance, as of a cut and polished gemstone. **4.** Liveliness and vivacity of imagination; brilliance. **5.** A severe test; a trial or torment. **6.** A fever or bodily inflammation. **7a.** The discharge of firearms or artillery: *heard the fire of cannon.* **b.** The launching of a missile, rocket, or similar ballistic body. **c.** Discharged bullets or other projectiles. **8.** Intense, repeated attack or criticism. ❖ *v.* **fired, fir•ing, fires** *—tr.* **1a.** To cause to burn; ignite. **b.** To light (something) up as if by fire. **2a.** To add fuel to (something burning). **b.** To maintain or fuel a fire in. **c.** To start (a fuel-burning engine). Often used with *up.* **3a.** To bake in a kiln: *fire pottery.* **b.** To dry by heating. **4.** To arouse the emotions of; make enthusiastic or ardent. Often used with *up.* **5a.** To discharge (a firearm, for example). **b.** To detonate (an explosive). **6a.** To propel (a projectile); launch (a missile). **b.** *Informal* To throw with force and speed; hurl. **c.** To utter or direct with insistence: *fired questions back.* **7.** *Games* To score (a number) in a game or contest. **8.** To discharge from a position; dismiss. *—intr.* **1.** To become ignited; flame up. **2a.** To become excited or ardent. **b.** To become angry or annoyed. **3.** To tend a fire. **4a.** To shoot a weapon: *aimed and fired at the target.* **b.** To detonate an explosive. **c.** To ignite fuel, as in an engine. **5.** *Informal* To project or hurl a missile: *The pitcher fired.* **6.** *Physiology* To generate an electrical impulse. Used of a neuron. **7.** To become yellowed or brown before reaching maturity, as grain. ***—phrasal verbs:*** **fire away** *Informal* To start to talk or ask questions. **fire off 1.** To utter or ask rapidly. **2.** To write and send (a letter, for example) in haste. ***—idioms:*** **on fire 1.** Ignited; ablaze. **2.** Filled with enthusiasm or excitement. **start (or light or build) a fire under** *Slang* To urge or goad to action. **under fire 1.** Exposed or subjected to enemy attack. **2.** Exposed or subjected to critical attack or censure. [ME *fir* < OE *fȳr.* See **pəwr̥** in App.] **—fire′a•ble** *adj.* **—fir′er** *n.*
fire alarm *n.* **1.** A device, such as a siren, used in announcing a fire. **2.** The signal, esp. the noise, produced by such a device.
fire and brimstone *n.* **1.** The punishment of hell. **2.** Homiletic rhetoric describing or warning of the punishment of hell.
fire ant *n.* Any of several ants of the genus *Solenopsis* of the southern United States and tropical America that can cause painful stings.
fire•arm (fīr′ärm′) *n.* A weapon, esp. a pistol or rifle, capable of firing a projectile and using an explosive as a propellant.
fire•ball (fīr′bôl′) *n.* **1.** A brilliantly burning sphere. **2.** An intensely luminous, hot spherical cloud of dust, gas, and vapor from a nuclear explosion. **3.** A meteor as bright or brighter than any planet. **4.** An energetic dynamic person.
fire•bird (fīr′bûrd′) *n.* Any of various birds, such as the Baltimore oriole, having bright scarlet or orange plumage.
fire blight *n.* A destructive disease of apple and pear trees, caused by a bacterium *(Erwinia amylovora)* that blackens the leaves and kills the branches.
fire•board (fīr′bôrd′, -bōrd′) *n.* *Upper Southern US* See **mantel** 2.
fire•boat (fīr′bōt′) *n.* A boat equipped to fight fires along waterfronts and on ships.
fire•bomb (fīr′bŏm′) *n.* A bomb used to start a fire; an incendiary bomb. **—fire′bomb′** *v.* **—fire′bomb′er** *n.*
fire•box (fīr′bŏks′) *n.* **1.** A chamber in which fuel is burned. **2.** A box containing a fire alarm.
fire•brand (fīr′brănd′) *n.* **1.** A person who stirs up trouble or kindles a revolt. **2.** A piece of burning wood.
fire•brat (fīr′brăt′) *n.* A small wingless insect *(Thermobia domestica)* inhabiting warm areas of buildings.

finial

Finland

ă	pat	oi	boy
ā	pay	ou	out
âr	care	o͝o	took
ä	father	o͞o	boot
ĕ	pet	ŭ	cut
ē	be	ûr	urge
ĭ	pit	th	thin
ī	pie	*th*	this
îr	pier	hw	which
ŏ	pot	zh	vision
ō	toe	ə	about, item
ô	paw		

Stress marks:
′ (primary);
′ (secondary), as in
lexicon (lĕk′sĭ-kŏn′)

fire escape

fire tower

fire•break (fīr′brāk′) *n.* A strip of land that has been cleared, plowed, or planted with fire-resistant vegetation to prevent a fire from spreading.

fire•brick (fīr′brĭk′) *n.* A refractory brick, usu. made of fire clay, used to line furnaces, fireboxes, chimneys, or fireplaces.

fire brigade *n.* An organized body of firefighters.

fire•bug (fīr′bŭg′) *n. Informal* An arsonist; a pyromaniac.

fire clay also **fire•clay** (fīr′klā′) *n.* A type of clay able to withstand intense heat, used to make firebricks, crucibles, and other objects that are exposed to high temperatures.

fire control *n.* The control of gunfire delivery on military targets.

fire•crack•er (fīr′krăk′ər) *n.* A small explosive charge and a fuse in a heavy paper casing, exploded to make noise.

fire•damp (fīr′dămp′) *n.* **1.** A combustible gas, chiefly methane, occurring naturally in mines from the decomposition of coal. **2.** The explosive mixture of firedamp and air.

fire department *n.* A department, esp. of a municipal government, whose purpose is preventing and putting out fires.

fire•dog (fīr′dôg′, -dŏg′) *n. Chiefly Southern US* See **andiron.** See Regional Note at **andiron.**

fire door *n.* A door made of fire-resistant material that can be closed to prevent the spread of fire.

fire•drake (fīr′drāk′) *n.* A fire-breathing dragon of Germanic mythology. [ME *firdrake* < OE *fȳrdraca* : *fȳr*, fire; see FIRE + *draca*, dragon; see DRAKE².]

fire drill *n.* An exercise in the use of firefighting equipment or the evacuation of a building in case of a fire.

fire-eat•er (fīr′ē′tər) *n.* **1.** A performer who pretends to swallow fire. **2.** A belligerent person or a militant partisan. —**fire′-eat′ing** *adj.*

fire engine *n.* Any of various large motor vehicles that carry firefighters and equipment to a fire and support extinguishing operations, as by pumping water.

fire escape *n.* A structure or device, such as an outside stairway, erected for emergency exit in the event of fire.

fire extinguisher *n.* A portable apparatus containing chemicals that can be discharged in a stream to extinguish a small fire.

fire•fight (fīr′fīt′) *n.* An exchange of gunfire.

fire•fight•er also **fire fighter** (fīr′fī′tər) *n.* A member of a fire department who fights fires. —**fire′fight′ing** *adj. & n.*

fire•flood (fīr′flŭd′) or **fire•flood•ing** (-flŭd′ĭng) *n.* A procedure for extracting additional oil from a well by injecting compressed air into the petroleum reservoir and burning some of the oil to increase the flow.

fire•fly (fīr′flī′) *n.* Any of various nocturnal beetles of the family Lampyridae, producing a flashing light in the abdomen. See Regional Note at **lightning bug.**

fire•guard (fīr′gärd′) *n.* **1.** A metal screen placed in front of an open fireplace to catch sparks. **2.** See **firebreak.**

fire•house (fīr′hous′) *n.* See **fire station.**

fire hydrant *n.* An upright pipe with a nozzle or spout for drawing water from a water main.

fire irons *pl.n.* Implements, such as tongs, a shovel, and a poker, used to tend a fireplace.

Fire Island A narrow barrier island off the S shore of Long I. in SE NY.

fire•light (fīr′līt′) *n.* The light from a fire, as in a fireplace.

fire•lock (fīr′lŏk′) *n.* See **flintlock** 2.

fire•man (fīr′mən) *n.* **1.** A firefighter. **2.** A man who tends fires; a stoker. **3.** An enlisted person in the US Navy who operates engineering machinery. **4.** *Baseball* A relief pitcher.

Fi•ren•ze (fē-rĕn′dzĕ) See **Florence.**

fire opal *n.* An opal with brilliant flamelike colors.

fire•place (fīr′plās′) *n.* **1.** An open recess for holding a fire at the base of a chimney; a hearth. **2.** A structure, usu. of stone or brick, for holding an outdoor fire.

fire•plug (fīr′plŭg′) *n.* See **fire hydrant.**

fire•pow•er (fīr′pou′ər) *n.* The capacity, as of a weapon, for delivering fire.

fire•proof (fīr′prōōf′) *adj.* Impervious or resistant to fire. ❖ *tr.v.* **-proofed, -proof•ing, -proofs** To make fireproof.

fire sale *n.* A sale of merchandise damaged by fire.

fire screen *n.* See **fireguard** 1.

fire ship *n.* A military vessel loaded with explosives and combustibles and set adrift among enemy ships or fortifications.

fire•side (fīr′sīd′) *n.* **1.** The area immediately surrounding a fireplace or hearth. **2.** A home. ❖ *adj.* At or as if at a fireside.

fire station *n.* A building for fire equipment and firefighters.

fire•stone (fīr′stōn′) *n.* **1.** A flint or pyrite used to strike a fire. **2.** A fire-resistant stone, such as certain sandstones.

fire•storm (fīr′stôrm′) *n.* **1.** A vast intense fire that generates and is fed by strong inrushing winds from all sides. **2.** An intense or violent response: *a firestorm of controversy.*

fire thorn *n.* Any of various thorny evergreen shrubs of the genus *Pyracantha,* native to Asia and having red or orange berries.

fire tower *n.* A tower in which a lookout for fires is posted.

fire•trap (fīr′trăp′) *n.* A building that can catch fire easily or is difficult to escape from in the event of fire.

fire truck *n.* See **fire engine.**

fire•wall (fīr′wôl′) *n.* **1.** A fireproof wall used as a barrier to prevent the spread of fire. **2.** *Computer Science* Any of a number of security schemes that prevent unauthorized users from gaining access to a network or that monitor transfers of information to and from the network.

fire•wa•ter (fīr′wô′tər, -wŏt′ər) *n. Slang* Strong liquor, esp. whiskey. [Transl. of Ojibwa *ishkodewaaboo,* whiskey.]

fire•weed (fīr′wēd′) *n.* **1.** Any of various plants of the genus *Epilobium,* esp. *E. angustifolium,* having long terminal spikelike flower clusters. **2.** Any of several weedy North American plants of the genus *Erechtites,* having small flowers grouped in discoid heads.

fire•wood (fīr′wŏŏd′) *n.* Wood used as fuel.

fire•work (fīr′wûrk′) *n.* **1a.** A device consisting of explosives and combustibles, set off to generate colored lights, smoke, and noise for amusement. **b. fireworks** A display of such devices. **2. fireworks a.** An exciting or spectacular display, as of musical virtuosity. **b.** A display of rage or fierce contention.

fir•ing (fīr′ĭng) *n.* **1.** The process of applying fire or heat, as in the hardening or glazing of ceramics. **2.** Fuel for fires. **3.** The act or an instance of dismissing someone from a job.

firing line *n.* **1.** The line of positions from which fire is directed at a target. **2.** The forefront of an activity; the vanguard.

firing pin *n.* The part of the bolt or breech of a firearm that strikes the primer and detonates the charge of a projectile.

firing squad *n.* **1.** A detachment assigned to shoot persons condemned to death. **2.** A detachment of soldiers chosen to fire a salute at a military funeral.

fir•kin (fûr′kĭn) *n.* **1.** A small wooden barrel or covered vessel. **2.** Any of several British units of capacity, usu. equal to about ¼ of a barrel or 9 gallons (34 liters). [ME *ferken, ferdekin,* prob. < MDu. **verdelkijn,* dim. of *veerdel,* one fourth : *veerde,* fourth; see kʷetwer- in App. + *deel,* part.]

firm¹ (fûrm) *adj.* **firm•er, firm•est 1.** Resistant to externally applied pressure. **2.** Marked by or indicating the tone and resiliency of healthy tissue. **3.** Securely fixed in place. **4.** Indicating or possessed of determination or resolution: *a firm voice.* **5.** Constant; steadfast: *a firm ally.* **6a.** Not subject to change; fixed and definite: *a firm offer.* **b.** Unfluctuating; steady. **7.** Strong and sure: *a firm grasp.* ❖ *tr. & intr.v.* **firmed, firm•ing, firms** To make or become firm. Often used with *up.* ❖ *adv.* **firmer, firmest** Without wavering; resolutely: *stand firm.* [ME *ferm* < OFr. < Lat. *firmus.*] —**firm′ly** *adv.* —**firm′ness** *n.*

firm² (fûrm) *n.* **1.** A commercial partnership of two or more persons, esp. when unincorporated. **2.** The name or designation under which a company transacts business. [Ital. *firma* < *firmare,* to ratify by signature < Med.Lat. *firmāre* < Lat., to confirm < *firmus,* firm.]

fir•ma•ment (fûr′mə-mənt) *n.* The vault or expanse of the heavens; the sky. [ME < OFr. < LLat. *firmāmentum* < Lat., support < *firmāre,* to strengthen. See FIRM².] —**fir′ma•ment′al** (-mĕn′tl) *adj.*

fir•mer chisel (fûr′mər) *n.* A chisel or gouge with a thin blade, used to finish and finish wood by hand. [Fr. *fermoir* < OFr., alteration of *formoir* < *former,* to form < Lat. *fōrmāre* < *fōrma,* form. See FORM.]

firm•ware (fûrm′wâr′) *n.* Software that is stored in ROM.

firn (fĭrn) *n.* Granular, partially consolidated snow that has passed through one summer melt season but is not yet glacial ice. [Ger. < Ger. dialectal, of last year < OHGer. *firni,* old.]

first (fûrst) *n.* **1.** The ordinal number matching the number one in a series. **2.** The one coming, occurring, or ranking before or above all others. **3.** The beginning; the outset: *at first.* **4.** *Music* The voice or instrument highest in pitch or carrying the principal part. **5.** The transmission gear or corresponding gear ratio used to produce the range of lowest drive speeds in a motor vehicle. **6.** The winning position in a contest. **7.** *Baseball* **a.** First base. **b.** A first baseman. ❖ *adj.* **1.** Corresponding in order to the number one. **2.** Coming before all others in order or location. **3.** Occurring or acting before all others in time; earliest. **4.** Ranking above all others, as in importance or quality; foremost. **5.** *Music* Being highest in pitch or carrying the principal part. **6.** Of, relating to, or being the transmission gear or corresponding gear ratio used to produce the range of lowest drive speeds in a motor vehicle. **7.** Being or related to a member of the US president's household: *first daughter Amy Carter.* ❖ *adv.* **1.** Before or above all others in time, order, rank, or importance. **2.** For the first time. **3.** Rather; preferably: *would die first.* **4.** In the first place; to begin with. See Usage Note at **firstly.** —**idiom: first off** (or **thing**) From the start; immediately. [ME < OE *fyrst.* See **per**¹ in App.]

first aid *n.* Emergency treatment administered to an injured or sick person before professional medical care is available. —**first′-aid′** (fûrst′ād′) *adj.*

first base *n.* **1.** *Baseball* **a.** The first of the bases in the infield, counterclockwise from home plate. **b.** The fielding position occupied by the first baseman. **2.** *Slang* The first stage or step toward completion or success.

first baseman *n. Baseball* The infielder near first base.

first•born (fûrst′bôrn′) *adj.* First in order of birth; born first. ❖ *n.* The firstborn child.

first class *n.* **1.** The first, highest, or best group in a system of classification. **2.** The most luxurious and expensive class of accommodations on a train or other conveyance. **3.** A class of mail including letters, post cards, and sealed packages.

first-class (fûrst′klăs′) *adj.* **1.** Being or belonging to the first, highest, or best group in a system of classification. **2.** Of the utmost excellence or highest quality; first-rate. —**first′ class′** *adv.*

first cousin *n.* See **cousin** 1.

first-de•gree burn (fûrst′dĭ-grē′) *n.* A mild burn that produces redness of the skin but no blistering.

first down *n. Football* **1.** The first in the series of four downs in which an offensive team must advance ten yards to retain possession of the ball. **2.** A gain of ten or more yards entitling the offensive team to a new series of downs.

first edition *n.* **1a.** The first published copies of a literary work printed from the same type and distributed at the same time. **b.** One such copy. **2.** The day's first press run of a newspaper.

first family also **First Family** *n.* **1.** A family having high social status, often because of descent. **2.** The family of the chief executive of a city, state, or country.

first finger *n.* See **index finger.**

first floor *n.* **1.** The ground floor of a building. **2.** *Chiefly British* The floor immediately above the ground floor.

first fruits also **first•fruits** (fûrst′frōōts′) *pl.n.* **1.** The first gathered fruits of a harvest, offered to God in gratitude. **2.** The first results of an undertaking.

first-gen•er•a•tion (fûrst′jĕn′ə-rā′shən) *adj.* **1.** Of or relating to one who has left one country and settled in another. **2.** Of or relating to one whose parents are immigrants. **3.** Of or relating to the first form or version available to users: *first-generation computers.*

first•hand (fûrst′hănd′) *adj.* Received from the original source: *firsthand information.* —**first′hand′** *adv.*

first-in, first-out (fûrst′ĭn′ fûrst′out′) *n.* A method of inventory accounting in which the oldest remaining items are assumed to have been the first sold.

first lady *n.* **1.** often **First Lady** The wife or hostess of the chief executive of a country, state, or city. **2.** The foremost woman of a specified profession or art.

first lieutenant *n.* **1.** A commissioned officer in the US Army, Air Force, and Marines ranking above second lieutenant and below captain. **2.** A lieutenant in the US Navy or Coast Guard, responsible for maintaining the ship's exterior and for management of the ship's deck.

first•ling (fûrst′lĭng) *n.* **1.** The first of a kind or category. **2.** A first-born offspring.

first•ly (fûrst′lē) *adv.* In the first place; to begin with.

USAGE NOTE It is well established that either *first* or *firstly* can be used to begin an enumeration: *Our objectives are, first* (or *firstly*), *to recover from last year's slump.* Any succeeding items should be introduced by words parallel to the form that is chosen, as in *first . . . second . . . third* or *firstly . . . secondly . . . thirdly.*

first mate *n.* An officer on a merchant ship ranking immediately below the captain.

first name *n.* A given name or the name that occurs first in a given name.

First Nation *n. Canadian* An organized aboriginal group or community in Canada, esp. any of the bands officially recognized by the Canadian government. —**First Nations** *adj.*

USAGE NOTE *First Nation* has gained wide acceptance in Canada since the early 1980s. Like *Native American* (which has little currency in Canada), *First Nation* provides a respectful alternative to *Indian,* a term that is more likely to be taken as directly offensive in Canada than it is in the United States. However, there are several differences between the Canadian and American expressions. *First Nation* is essentially a political term, promoted from within the indigenous community as a substitute for *band* in referring to any of the numerous aboriginal groups formally recognized by the Canadian government under the federal Indian Act of 1876. Unlike *Native American,* it is not a comprehensive term for all indigenous peoples of the Americas or even of Canada, and while it is often used loosely in referring to Indian groups or communities other than those specified in the 1876 Act, it specifically does not include non-Indian peoples such as the Inuit or the Métis. Although each recognized band or community is a *First Nation,* the term is more commonly used in the plural with a general collective sense, as in *a program designed for First Nations youth.* There is no related form for an individual who is a member of a First Nation; officially, such a person is known as a *status Indian.* See Usage Notes at **American Indian, Indian, Native American.**

first night *n.* **1.** The opening performance of a theatrical production. **2.** The performance presented on such a night.

first offender *n.* One convicted of a legal offense for the first time.

first papers *pl.n.* The documents first filed by one applying for US citizenship.

first person *n.* **1.** The grammatical category of forms that designate a speaker or writer referring to himself or herself. Examples of forms in the first person include English pronouns such as *I* and *we* and verb forms such as Spanish *hablo* "I speak." **2.** A discourse or literary style in which the narrator recounts his or her

own experiences or impressions using such forms.

first-rate (fûrst′rāt′) *adj.* Foremost in quality, rank, or importance. ❖ *adv. Informal* Very well; excellently.

first sergeant *n.* The senior noncommissioned officer of a US Army or Marine Corps unit, who is equivalent in rank to a master sergeant and performs administrative duties.

first strike *n.* A preemptive attack against an enemy, esp. one using nuclear weapons against an enemy armed with nuclear weapons. —**first′-strike′** (fûrst′strĭk′) *adj.*

first-string (fûrst′strĭng′) *adj.* **1.** Relating to or being a regular or starting member, as of a sports team, rather than a substitute. **2.** First-rate. —**first′-string′er** *n.*

first water *n.* **1.** The highest degree of quality or purity in diamonds or pearls. **2.** The foremost rank or quality. [Prob. transl. of Ar. *māʾ*, water, water luster.]

First World also **first world** *n.* During the Cold War, the industrialized capitalist nations of the world. —**First′-World′** (fûrst′wûrld′) *adj.*

First World War *n.* World War I.

firth (fûrth) *n. Scots* A long narrow inlet of the sea. [ME *furth* < ON *fjŏrdhr.* See **per-²** in App.]

fisc (fĭsk) *n.* The treasury of a kingdom or state. [Fr. < Lat. *fiscus,* money basket, treasury.]

fis•cal (fĭs′kəl) *adj.* **1.** Of or relating to government expenditures, revenues, and debt. **2.** Of or relating to finance or finances. [Fr. < Lat. *fiscālis < fiscus,* money basket, treasury.] —**fis′cal•ly** *adv.*

fiscal year *n.* A 12-month period for which an organization plans the use of its funds.

Fi•scher (fĭsh′ər), **Emil Hermann** 1852–1919. German chemist who won a 1902 Nobel Prize.

Fischer, Robert James Known as "Bobby." b. 1943. Amer. chess player who was world champion (1972–74).

fish (fĭsh) *n., pl.* **fish** or **fish•es 1.** Any of numerous cold-blooded aquatic vertebrates of the superclass Pisces, characteristically having fins, gills, and a streamlined body and including specifically: **a.** Any of the class Osteichthyes, having a bony skeleton. **b.** Any of the class Chondrichthyes, having a cartilaginous skeleton and including the sharks. **2.** The flesh of such animals used as food. **3.** Any of various primitive aquatic vertebrates of the class Cyclostomata, lacking jaws and including the lampreys and hagfishes. **4.** Any of various unrelated aquatic animals, such as the jellyfish, cuttlefish, or crayfish. **5.** *Informal* A person, esp. one considered deficient in something. ❖ *v.* **fished, fish•ing, fish•es** —*intr.* **1.** To catch or try to catch fish. **2.** To look for something by feeling one's way; grope. **3.** To seek something in a sly or indirect way. —*tr.* **1a.** To catch or try to catch (fish). **b.** To catch or try to catch fish in. **2.** To catch or pull as if fishing. —*phrasal verb:* **fish out** To deplete (a lake, for example) of fish by fishing. —*idioms:* **fish in troubled waters** To try to take advantage of a confused situation. **fish or cut bait** *Informal* To proceed with an activity or abandon it altogether. **like a fish out of water** Completely unfamiliar with one's surroundings or activity. **neither fish nor fowl** Having no specific characteristics; indefinite. **other fish to fry** *Informal* Other matters to attend to. [ME < OE *fisc.*]

Fish, Hamilton 1808–93. Amer. politician who served as US secretary of state (1869–77).

fish and chips *pl.n.* Fried fillets of fish and French-fried potatoes.

fish•bowl also **fish bowl** (fĭsh′bōl′) *n.* **1.** A transparent bowl for keeping live fish. **2.** *Informal* A place lacking in privacy.

fish cake *n.* A fried cake or patty of chopped fish, often mixed with potato, bread crumbs, or rice.

fish•er (fĭsh′ər) *n.* **1.** One that fishes, as a person or ship. **2a.** A carnivorous mammal (*Martes pennanti*) of northern North America having thick dark-brown fur. **b.** This fur.

fish•er•man (fĭsh′ər-mən) *n.* **1.** One who fishes as an occupation or for sport. **2.** A commercial fishing vessel.

fish•er•man's bend (fĭsh′ər-mənz) *n.* A knot used to secure the end of a line to a ring or spar, made by two turns with the end passed back under both.

fisherman's knot *n.* A knot used to join two lines, made by securing either end to the opposite standing part by an overhand knot.

fish•er•wom•an (fĭsh′ər-wŏŏm′ən) *n.* A woman who fishes as an occupation or for sport.

fish•er•y (fĭsh′ə-rē) *n., pl.* **-ies 1.** The industry or activity of catching, processing, or selling fish or other aquatic animals. **2.** A place where fish or other aquatic animals are caught. **3.** A fishing business. **4.** A fish hatchery. **5.** The legal right to fish in specified areas.

Fish•es (fĭsh′ĭz) *pl.n.* (*used with a sing. verb*) See **Pisces** 1, 2a.

fish•eye (fĭsh′ī′) *adj.* Of or being a wide-angle photographic lens that produces a circular image with foreshortening in the center and increasing distortion toward the periphery.

fish farm *n.* A commercial facility consisting of tanks or ponds in which fish are raised for food.

fish flour *n.* A flour made of dried and powdered fish.

fish fry *n.* **1.** A cookout or other meal at which fried fish is the main course. **2.** A piece of fried fish.

fish•gig (fĭsh′gĭg′) *n.* A pronged instrument that is used for spearing fish. [Alteration (influenced by FISH) of obsolete *fisgig*

fisheye
photograph taken with a fisheye lens

ă pat · oi boy
ā pay · ou out
âr care · ōō took
ä father · ōō boot
ĕ pet · ŭ cut
ē be · ûr urge
ĭ pit · th thin
ī pie · th this
îr pier · hw which
ŏ pot · zh vision
ō toe · ə about,
ô paw · item

Stress marks:
′ (primary);
′ (secondary); as in
lexicon (lĕk′sĭ-kŏn′)

< Sp. *fisga*, ult. < Lat. *fíxus*, fixed. See FIX.]

fish hawk n. See osprey 1.

fish•hook (fĭsh′hŏŏk′) n. A barbed metal hook used for catching fish.

fish•ing (fĭsh′ĭng) n. 1. The act, occupation, or sport of catching fish. 2. A place for catching fish.

fishing expedition n. An open-ended inquiry or investigation usu. with the unacknowledged purpose of uncovering politically damaging information, as about an opponent.

fishing rod n. A rod of wood, steel, or fiberglass used with a line to catch fish.

fish joint n. A joint formed by bolting a fishplate to each side of two abutting rails, timbers, or beams. [< FISH(PLATE).]

fish ladder n. A series of pools arranged like ascending steps at the side of a stream, enabling migrating fish to swim upstream around a dam or other obstruction.

fish•meal (fĭsh′mēl′) n. A nutritive mealy substance produced from fish or fish parts and used as animal feed and fertilizer.

fish•mon•ger (fĭsh′mŭng′gər, -mŏng′-) n. Chiefly British One that sells fish.

fish•net (fĭsh′nĕt′) n. 1. Netting used to catch fish. 2. A mesh fabric resembling such netting.

fish•plate (fĭsh′plāt′) n. A metal or wooden plate bolted to the sides of two abutting rails or beams, used esp. in the laying of railroad track. [Prob. < Fr. *fiche*, peg (< OFr.; see MICROFICHE) + PLATE.]

fish•pond (fĭsh′pŏnd′) n. A pond containing or stocked with fish.

fish protein concentrate n. A protein-rich flour or paste prepared from ground fish and added to foods as a supplement.

fish sauce n. See nuoc mam.

fish•skin disease (fĭsh′skĭn′) n. See ichthyosis.

fish stick n. An oblong piece of breaded fish fillet.

fish story n. Informal An implausible boastful story.

fish•tail (fĭsh′tāl′) adj. Resembling or suggestive of the tail of a fish in shape or movement. ❖ intr.v. **-tailed, -tail•ing, -tails** 1. To have the rear end of a forward-moving vehicle swerve from side to side out of control. 2. To swing the tail of an airplane from side to side in order to reduce speed.

fish•wife (fĭsh′wīf′) n., pl. **-wives** (-wīvz′) 1. A woman who sells fish. 2. A woman regarded as coarse and abusive.

fish•y (fĭsh′ē) adj. **-i•er, -i•est** 1. Resembling or suggestive of fish, as in odor. 2. Cold or expressionless. 3. Informal Inspiring doubt or suspicion. —**fish′i•ly** adv. —**fish′i•ness** n.

Fisk (fĭsk), **James** 1834–72. Amer. speculator who attempted to corner the gold market with Jay Gould (1869).

fissi– pref. 1. Fission: *fissiparous.* 2. Split; cleft: *fissipalmate.* [< Lat. *fissus*, p. part. of *findere*, to split. See **bheid–** in App.]

fis•sile (fĭs′əl, -īl′) adj. 1. Possible to split. 2. Physics Fissionable, esp. by neutrons. 3. Geology Easily split along close parallel planes. [Lat. *fissilis* < *fissus*, split. See FISSI–.] —**fis•sil′i•ty** (fĭ-sĭl′ĭ-tē) n.

fis•sion (fĭsh′ən) n. 1. The act or process of splitting into parts. 2. A nuclear reaction in which an atomic nucleus, esp. a heavy nucleus, splits into fragments, usu. two fragments of comparable mass, with the release of energy. 3. Biology An asexual reproductive process in which a unicellular organism divides into two or more independently maturing daughter cells. ❖ v. **-sioned, -sion•ing, -sions** —tr. To cause (an atom) to undergo fission. —intr. To undergo fission. [Lat. *fissiō, fissiōn-*, a cleaving < *fissus*, split. See FISSI–.] —**fis′sion•a•ble** adj. —**fis′sion•a•bil′i•ty** n.

fission bomb n. See atom bomb 1.

fis•si•pal•mate (fĭs′ə-păl′māt′) adj. Having lobed or partially webbed separated toes, as the feet of certain birds.

fis•sip•a•rous (fĭ-sĭp′ər-əs) adj. 1. Reproducing by biological fission. 2. Tending to break up into parts or break away from a main body; factious. —**fis•sip′a•rous•ly** adv. —**fis•sip′a•rous•ness** n.

fis•si•ped (fĭs′ə-pĕd′) adj. Having the toes separated from one another. ❖ n. A fissiped mammal.

fis•sure (fĭsh′ər) n. 1. A long narrow opening; a crack or cleft. 2. The process of splitting or separating; division. 3. A separation into subgroups or factions; a schism. 4. Anatomy A normal groove or furrow, as in the brain, that divides an organ into lobes or parts. 5. Medicine A break in a tissue, usu. where it joins a mucous membrane. ❖ intr. & tr.v. **-sured, -sur•ing, -sures** To form a crack or cleft or cause a crack or cleft in. [ME, cut < OFr. < Lat. *fissūra* < *fissus*, split. See FISSI–.]

fist (fĭst) n. 1. The hand closed tightly with the fingers bent against the palm. 2. Informal A grasp; a clutch: *had a fortune in his fist.* 3. Printing See index 3. ❖ tr.v. **fist•ed, fist•ing, fists** 1. To clench into a fist. 2. To grasp with the fist. 3. Vulgar To insert the fist into the rectum or vagina of (another) as a means of sexual stimulation. [ME < OE *fȳst.* See **penkʷe** in App.]

fist•fight (fĭst′fīt′) n. A fight with the bare fists.

fist•ful (fĭst′fŏŏl′) n., pl. **-fuls** The amount held by a fist.

fist•ic (fĭs′tĭk) adj. Of or relating to boxing or fighting with the fists.

fist•i•cuffs (fĭs′tĭ-kŭfs′) pl.n. 1. A fistfight. 2. The activity of fighting with the fists. [< fisty cuffs : fisty, with the fists (< FIST) + CUFF².] —**fist′i•cuff′er** n.

fish ladder
Rocky Reach Dam, Lake Entiat, Washington

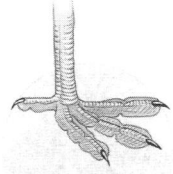

fissipalmate
American coot's foot

Ella Fitzgerald
photographed in 1954

fis•tu•la (fĭs′chə-lə) n., pl. **-las** or **-lae** (-lē′) An abnormal duct or passage resulting from injury, disease, or a congenital disorder that connects an abscess or hollow organ to the body surface or to another hollow organ. [ME < Lat.]

fis•tu•lous (fĭs′chə-ləs) also **fis•tu•lar** (-lər) adj. 1. Of or resembling a fistula. 2. Tubular and hollow, as the leaves of a scallion. 3. Made of or containing tubular parts.

fit¹ (fĭt) v. **fit•ted** or **fit, fit•ted, fit•ting, fits** —tr. **1a.** To be the proper size and shape for: *These shoes fit me.* **b.** To cause to be the proper size and shape: *He fitted the trousers by shortening them.* **c.** To measure for proper size: *She fitted me for a new jacket.* **2.** To be appropriate to; suit: *music that fits your mood.* **3.** To conform or agree with. **4.** To make suitable; adapt. See Syns at **adapt.** **5.** To make ready; prepare. **6.** To equip; outfit: *fit out a ship.* **7.** To provide a place or time for: *fit it in the box.* **8.** To insert or adjust so as to be properly in place. —intr. **1.** To be the proper size and shape. **2.** To be suited; belong: *fit in with us.* **3.** To be in harmony; agree. ❖ adj. **fit•ter, fit•test** **1.** Suited, adapted, or acceptable for a given circumstance or purpose. **2.** Appropriate; proper: *as seems fit.* **3.** Physically sound; healthy. **4.** Biology Successfully adapted to survive and produce viable offspring in a particular environment. ❖ n. **1.** The state, quality, or way of being fitted. **2.** The manner in which clothing fits. **3.** The degree of precision with which surfaces are adjusted or adapted to each other in a machine or collection of parts. —idioms: **fit to be tied** Roused to great anger or indignation; outraged. **fit to kill** Slang To an extreme or elaborate degree. [ME *fitten*, to be suitable, marshal troops.] —**fit′ly** adv. —**fit′ter** n.

fit² (fĭt) n. **1.** Medicine **a.** A seizure or convulsion, esp. one caused by epilepsy. **b.** The sudden appearance of a symptom such as coughing. **2.** A sudden outburst of emotion. **3.** A sudden period of vigorous activity. —idiom: **by (or in) fits and starts** With irregular intervals of action and inaction; intermittently. [ME, hardship, prob. < OE *fitt*, struggle.]

fit³ (fĭt) n. Archaic A section of a poem or ballad. [ME < OE.]

fitch (fĭch) n. **1.** See polecat 1a. **2.** The fur of this animal. [ME *fiche* < MDu. *vitsche, visse.*]

Fitch, John 1743–98. Amer. steamboat pioneer whose early designs (1787–90) received insufficient financial backing for large-scale production.

fitch•ew (fĭch′ōō) also **fitch•et** (-ĭt) n. Archaic The Old World polecat or its fur. [ME *ficheux*, poss. < Walloon *ficheau*, dim. of MDu. *vitsche, visse.*]

fit•ful (fĭt′fəl) adj. Occurring in or characterized by intermittent bursts, as of activity; irregular. See Syns at **periodic.** —**fit′ful•ly** adv. —**fit′ful•ness** n.

fit•ness (fĭt′nĭs) n. **1.** The state or condition of being fit. **2.** Good health or physical condition. **3.** The extent to which an organism is adapted to or able to produce offspring in a particular environment.

fit•ting (fĭt′ĭng) adj. Suiting a situation; appropriate. ❖ n. **1.** The trying on of clothes whose fit is being adjusted. **2.** A small detachable part, as for a machine. **3. fittings** Chiefly British Furnishings or fixtures. —**fit′ting•ly** adv. —**fit′ting•ness** n.

Fitz•ger•ald (fĭts-jĕr′əld), **Ella** 1917–96. Amer. jazz singer best known for her scat singing and her interpretations of the work of important songwriters.

Fitzgerald, F(rancis) Scott (Key) 1896–1940. Amer. writer whose works include *The Great Gatsby* (1925).

FitzGerald, Edward 1809–83. British poet and translator of *The Rubáiyát of Omar Khayyám* (1859).

Fiu•me (fyōō′mā, -mĕ) See Rijeka.

five (fīv) n. **1.** The cardinal number equal to 4 + 1. **2.** The fifth in a set or sequence. **3.** Something that has five parts, units, or members. **4.** A five-dollar bill. **5. fives** (*used with a sing. verb*) Sports One of several forms of handball originating in England, in which only the receiving side can score points. [ME < OE *fíf.* See **penkʷe** in App.] —**five** adj. & pron.

five-and-dime (fīv′ən-dīm′) n. See five-and-ten.

five-and-ten (fīv′ən-tĕn′) n. A retail store selling a wide variety of inexpensive articles. [Short for *five-and-ten-cent store.*]

Five Civilized Nations pl.n. The Cherokee, Chickasaw, Choctaw, Creek, and Seminole peoples.

five-fin•ger (fīv′fĭng′gər) n. Any of several plants having palmately compound leaves with five leaflets.

Five Forks A crossroads in SE VA SW of Petersburg where the last major Civil War battle was fought on Apr. 1, 1865.

five hole n. The space between a goalie's legs, as in ice hockey. [< the four corners of the goal being the other four holes.]

Five Nations pl.n. The original Iroquois confederacy of the Mohawk, Oneida, Onondaga, Cayuga, and Seneca peoples.

fiv•er (fī′vər) n. Informal **1.** A five-dollar bill. **2.** Chiefly British A five-pound note.

fix (fĭks) v. **fixed, fix•ing, fix•es** —tr. **1a.** To place securely; make stable or firm. **b.** To secure to another; attach. **2a.** To put into a stable or unalterable form. **b.** To make (a chemical) nonvolatile or stable. **c.** Biology To convert (nitrogen) into stable, biologically assimilable compounds. **d.** To kill and preserve (a specimen) intact for microscopic study. **e.** To prevent discoloration of (a photographic image) by washing or coating with a chemical preservative. **3.** To direct steadily: *fixed her eyes on the road.* **4.** To capture or hold: *fixed our attention.* **5a.** To set or place definitely; establish: *fixed her residence here.* **b.** To determine with accuracy; ascertain. **c.** To agree on; arrange. **6.** To assign; attribute: *fixing the blame.* **7a.** To correct or set right; adjust. **b.** To restore to proper condition or working order; repair. **8.** To make ready; prepare. **9.** To spay or castrate (an animal). **10.** *Informal* To take revenge upon; get even with. **11.** To influence the outcome or actions of by improper or unlawful means: *fix a jury.* —*intr.* **1.** To direct one's efforts or attention; concentrate: *fixed on the goal.* **2.** To become stable or firm; harden: *The plaster is fixing.* **3.** *Chiefly Southern US* To be on the verge of; to be making preparations for. Used in progressive tenses with the infinitive: *It's fixing to rain.* ❖ *n.* **1a.** The act of adjusting, correcting, or repairing. **b.** *Informal* Something that repairs or restores; a solution: *no easy fix.* **2.** The position, as of a ship or aircraft, determined by visual observations with the aid of equipment. **3.** A clear determination or understanding. **4.** An instance of arranging a special consideration, such as an exemption, or an illegal outcome, esp. by means of bribery. **5.** A difficult or embarrassing situation; a predicament. **6.** *Slang* An amount of something craved, esp. an intravenous injection of a narcotic. ***—phrasal verb:* fix up 1.** To improve the appearance or condition of; refurbish. **2.** To provide; equip. **3.** *Informal* To provide a companion on a date for. [ME *fixen* < *fix,* fixed in position < Lat. *fīxus,* p. part. of *fīgere,* to fasten.] **—fix′a•ble** *adj.*

REGIONAL NOTE *Fixing to* means "to be on the verge of or in preparation for (doing a given thing)," but like the modal auxiliaries, it has only a single invariant form, the present participle followed by the infinitive marker *to: They were fixing to leave without me.* Semantically, *fixing to* can refer only to events that immediately follow the speaker's point of reference.

fix•ate (fĭk′sāt′) *v.* **-at•ed, -at•ing, -ates** —*tr.* **1.** To make stable or stationary. **2.** To focus one's eyes or attention on. **3.** To command the attention of exclusively or repeatedly; preoccupy obsessively. **4.** *Psychology* **a.** To attach (oneself) immaturely or neurotically to a person or thing. **b.** In classical psychoanalysis, to cause (the libido) to be arrested at an early stage of psychosexual development. —*intr.* **1.** To focus the eyes or attention. **2.** *Psychology* **a.** To form a fixation. **b.** To be arrested at an early stage of psychosexual development.

fix•a•tion (fĭk-sā′shən) *n.* **1.** The act or process of fixing or fixating. **2.** An obsession. **3.** *Psychology* A strong attachment to a person or thing, esp. formed in childhood or infancy and manifested in immature or neurotic behavior throughout life.

fix•a•tive (fĭk′sə-tĭv) *n.* Something that fixes, protects, or preserves, esp.: **a.** A liquid preservative applied to artwork, such as charcoal drawings. **b.** A solution used to preserve and harden fresh tissue for microscopic examination. **c.** A liquid mixed with perfume to prevent rapid evaporation. **—fix′a•tive** *adj.*

fixed (fĭkst) *adj.* **1.** Firmly in position; stationary. **2.** Determined; established; set. **3.** Not subject to change or variation; constant: *a fixed income.* **4.** *Chemistry* **a.** Not readily evaporating; nonvolatile. **b.** Being in a stable, combined form. **5a.** Firmly, often dogmatically held. **b.** Persistently occurring in the mind; obsessive. **6.** Supplied, esp. with funds or needs. Often used in combination: *a well-fixed bachelor.* **7.** Illegally prearranged as to outcome. **—fix′ed•ly** (fĭk′sĭd-lē) *adv.* **—fix′ed•ness** *n.*

fixed annuity *n.* An annuity in which payments to the annuitant are unchanging over a specified period or over the annuitant's lifetime.

fixed head *n.* A stationary device, such as a tape-recording head, that reads and imprints information on a single track of magnetic tape.

fixed oil *n.* A nonvolatile oil, esp. a fatty oil of vegetable origin.

fixed-point (fĭkst′point′) *adj.* Of, relating to, or being a method of writing numbers with the decimal point located at a single unchanging position.

fixed star *n.* A star so distant from Earth that its position relative to other stars appears unchanging and its movements can be measured only over long periods of time.

fix•er (fĭk′sər) *n.* **1.** One that fixes. **2.** *Informal* A person who uses influence or makes arrangements for another, esp. improperly or unlawfully. **3.** A chemical preservative used to fix a photographic image.

fix•er-up•per (fĭk′sər-ŭp′ər) *n.* A dwelling badly in need of repair, usu. for sale at a low price.

fix•ings (fĭk′sĭngz) *pl.n. Informal* Accessories; trimmings.

fix•i•ty (fĭk′sĭ-tē) *n., pl.* **-ties 1.** The quality or condition of being fixed. **2.** Something fixed or immovable.

fix•ture (fĭks′chər) *n.* **1.** Something securely fixed in place. **2.** Something attached as a permanent appendage, apparatus, or appliance: *plumbing fixtures.* **3.** *Law* A chattel bound to realty. **4.** One invariably present in and long associated with a place. **5a.** The act or process of fixing. **b.** The condition of being fixed. [Variant of obsolete *fixure* < LLat. *fīxūra* < Lat. *fīxus,* fixed. See FIX.]

fizz (fĭz) *intr.v.* **fizzed, fizz•ing, fizz•es** To make a hissing or bubbling sound; effervesce. ❖ *n.* **1.** A fizzling sound. **2.** Effervescence. **3.** An effervescent beverage. [Imit.] **—fizz′y** *adj.*

fiz•zle (fĭz′əl) *intr.v.* **-zled, -zling, -zles 1.** To make a hissing or sputtering sound. **2.** *Informal* To fail or end weakly, esp. after a hopeful beginning. ❖ *n. Informal* A failure; a fiasco. [Prob. < obsolete *fise,* a breaking wind < ME, of Scand. orig.; akin to ON *fīsa,* to break wind.]

fjeld (fyĕld) *n.* A high barren plateau in the Scandinavian countries. [Dan. < ON *fjall.*]

fjord or **fiord** (fyôrd, fyōrd) *n.* A long, narrow, deep inlet of the sea between steep slopes. [Norw. < ON *fjördhr.* See **per-**[2] in App.]

fL *abbr.* foot-lambert

FL *abbr.* **1.** Florida **2.** focal length

fl. *abbr.* **1.** floor **2.** floruit **3.** fluid

Fla. *abbr.* Florida

flab (flăb) *n.* Soft fatty body tissue. [Back-formation < FLABBY.]

flab•ber•gast (flăb′ər-găst′) *tr.v.* **-gast•ed, -gast•ing, -gasts** To cause to be overcome with astonishment. [?]

flab•by (flăb′ē) *adj.* **-bi•er, -bi•est 1.** Lacking firmness; flaccid: *a flabby waist.* **2.** Lacking force or vitality; ineffectual: *flabby self-pity.* [Alteration of *flappy,* tending to flap < FLAP.] **—flab′bi•ly** *adv.* **—flab′bi•ness** *n.*

fla•bel•late (flə-bĕl′ĭt, flăb′ə-lāt′) also **fla•bel•li•form** (flə-bĕl′ə-fôrm′) *adj.* Fan-shaped. [Lat. *flābellum,* fan; see FLABELLUM + –ATE[1].]

fla•bel•lum (flə-bĕl′əm) *n., pl.* **-bel•la** (-bĕl′ə) A fan-shaped anatomical structure. [Lat. *flābellum,* fan, dim. of *flābra,* breeze < *flāre,* to blow.]

flac•cid (flăs′ĭd, flăk′sĭd) *adj.* **1.** Lacking firmness, resilience, or muscle tone: *flabby, wrinkled flesh.* **2.** Lacking vigor or energy: *flaccid management.* [Lat. *flaccidus* < *flaccus,* flabby.] **—flac•cid′i•ty** (-sĭd′ĭ-tē), **flac′cid•ness** *n.* **—flac′cid•ly** *adv.*

flack[1] (flăk) *Informal n.* A press agent; a publicist. ❖ *v.* **flacked, flack•ing, flacks** —*intr.* To act as a press agent. —*tr.* To act as a press agent for. [Perhaps after Gene *Flack,* movie press agent in the 1920s and 1930s.] **—flack′er•y** *n.*

flack[2] (flăk) *n.* Variant of **flak.**

flac•on (flăk′ən, -ŏn′) *n.* A small, often decorative bottle with a tight-fitting stopper or cap. [Fr. < OFr. See FLAGON.]

flag[1] (flăg) *n.* **1.** A piece of cloth, usu. rectangular, of distinctive color and design, used as a symbol, standard, signal, or emblem. **2.** National or other allegiance, as symbolized by a flag: *ships of the same flag.* **3.** A ship carrying the flag of an admiral; a flagship. **4.** A marking device attached to an object to attract attention or ease identification; a tab. **5.** The masthead of a newspaper. **6.** *Music* A cross stroke that halves the value of a note to which it is added. **7.** A distinctively shaped or marked tail, as of a dog. **8.** *Computer Science* A variable or memory location that stores true-or-false, yes-or-no information. ❖ *tr.v.* **flagged, flag•ging, flags 1.** To mark with a flag or flags for identification or ornamentation: *flag a page.* **2a.** To signal with or as if with a flag. **b.** To signal to stop: *flag a cab.* [?] **—flag′ger** *n.*

flag[2] (flăg) *n.* A plant, such as an iris, that has long sword-shaped leaves. [ME *flagge,* reed, of Scand. orig.]

flag[3] (flăg) *intr.v.* **flagged, flag•ging, flags 1.** To hang limply; droop. **2.** To decline in vigor or strength: *The conversation flagged.* [Poss. of Scand. orig.]

flag[4] (flăg) *n.* A flagstone. ❖ *tr.v.* **flagged, flag•ging, flags** To pave with slabs of flagstone. [ME *flagge,* piece of turf < ON *flaga,* slab of stone.]

Flag Day *n.* June 14, observed in commemoration of the adoption in 1777 of the official US flag.

flag•el•lant (flăj′ə-lənt, flə-jĕl′ənt) *n.* **1.** One who whips, esp. one who scourges oneself for religious discipline or public penance. **2.** One who seeks sexual gratification in beating or being beaten by another person. [Lat. *flagellāns, flagellant-* < pr. part. of *flagellāre,* to whip. See FLAGELLATE.] **—flag′el•lant** *adj.* **—flag′el•lant•ism** *n.*

fla•gel•lar (flə-jĕl′ər) *adj.* Of or relating to a flagellum.

flag•el•late (flăj′ə-lāt′) *tr.v.* **-lat•ed, -lat•ing, -lates 1.** To whip or flog; scourge. **2.** To punish or impel as if by whipping. ❖ *adj.* (-lĭt, -lāt′, flə-jĕl′ĭt) **1.** *Biology* Flagellated. **2.** Resembling a flagellum; whiplike. **3.** Relating to or caused by a flagellate organism. ❖ *n.* (-lĭt, -lāt′, flə-jĕl′ĭt) An organism, such as a euglena, having a flagellum. [Lat. *flagellāre, flagellāt-,* to whip < *flagellum,* dim. of *flagrum,* whip.]

flag•el•lat•ed (flăj′ə-lā′tĭd) *adj. Biology* Having a flagellum or flagella.

flag•el•la•tion (flăj′ə-lā′shən) *n.* **1.** The act or practice of flagellating. **2.** *Biology* The flagellar arrangement on an organism.

fla•gel•li•form (flə-jĕl′ə-fôrm′) *adj.* Long, thin, and tapering; whip-shaped: *flagelliform appendages.* [Lat. *flagellum,* little whip; see FLAGELLUM + –FORM.]

fla•gel•lin (flə-jĕl′ĭn) *n.* The chief protein component of bacterial flagella.

fla•gel•lum (flə-jĕl′əm) *n., pl.* **-gel•la** (-jĕl′ə) **1.** *Biology* A long threadlike appendage, esp. a whiplike extension of certain cells or unicellular organisms used for locomotion. **2.** A whip. [Lat., dim. of *flagrum,* whip.]

flag•eo•let (flăj′ə-lĕt′, -lā′) *n.* A small flutelike instrument with a cylindrical mouthpiece, four finger holes, and two thumbholes. [Fr., dim. of OFr. *flajol,* flute < VLat. **flābeolum,* poss. alteration of Lat. *flābellum,* dim. of *flābrum,* gust of wind < *flāre,* to blow.]

flag•ging[1] (flăg′ĭng) *adj.* **1.** Declining; weakening: *flagging*

F. Scott Fitzgerald
portrait by David Silvette
(1909–92)

fjord
Geirangerfjord, Norway

ă	pat	oi	boy
ā	pay	ou	out
âr	care	o͝o	took
ä	father	o͞o	boot
ĕ	pet	ŭ	cut
ē	be	ûr	urge
ĭ	pit	th	thin
ī	pie	*th*	this
îr	pier	hw	which
ŏ	pot	zh	vision
ō	toe	ə	about,
ô	paw		item

Stress marks:
′ (primary);
′ (secondary), as in
lexicon (lĕk′sĭ-kŏn′)

strength. **2.** Languid; drooping. **—flag′ging•ly** *adv.*

flag•ging² (flăg′ĭng) *n.* A pavement laid with flagstones.

fla•gi•tious (flə-jĭsh′əs) *adj.* **1.** Characterized by extremely brutal or cruel crimes; vicious. **2.** Infamous; scandalous. [ME *flagicious,* wicked < Lat. *flāgitiōsus* < *flāgitium,* shameful act, protest < *flāgitāre,* to importune, to demand vehemently.] **—fla•gi′tious•ly** *adv.* **—fla•gi′tious•ness** *n.*

flag•man (flăg′mən) *n.* One who signals with or carries a flag.

flag of convenience *n., pl.* **flags of convenience** A foreign flag under which a merchant vessel is registered for purposes of reducing operating costs or avoiding government regulations.

flag officer *n.* An officer in the navy or coast guard holding a rank higher than captain, such as rear admiral.

flag of truce *n., pl.* **flags of truce** A white flag shown to an enemy to request a conference or signal surrender.

flag•on (flăg′ən) *n.* **1.** A large vessel with a handle, spout, and often a lid, used for holding wine or other liquors. **2.** The quantity that a flagon can hold. [ME < OFr. *flacon* < LLat. *flascō, flascōn-,* bottle. See FLASK.]

flag•pole (flăg′pōl′) *n.* A pole on which a flag is raised. **—idiom: run (something) up the flagpole** *Slang* To test (a plan, for example) and then measure the response to it.

fla•grant (flā′grənt) *adj.* **1.** Conspicuously bad, offensive, or reprehensible: *a flagrant miscarriage of justice.* See Usage Note at **blatant. 2.** *Obsolete* Flaming; blazing. [Lat. *flagrāns, flagrant-,* pr. part. of *flagrāre,* to burn.] **—fla′gran•cy, fla′grance** *n.* **—fla′grant•ly** *adv.*

fla•gran•te de•lic•to (flə-grăn′tē dĭ-lĭk′tō) *adv.* **1.** In the very act of committing an offense; red-handed. **2.** In the act of having sex. [Med.Lat. *flagrante delictō,* while the crime is blazing : *flagrante,* ablative of *flagrāns,* blazing + *delictō,* ablative of *delictum,* offense.]

flag•ship (flăg′shĭp′) *n.* **1.** A ship that carries a fleet or squadron commander and bears the commander's flag. **2.** The chief one of a related group: *the flagship of a newspaper chain.*

Flag•stad (flăg′stăd′, flăg′stä′), **Kirsten Marie** 1895–1962. Norwegian soprano known for her performances in Wagnerian roles.

flag•staff (flăg′stăf′) *n.* See **flagpole.**

Flagstaff A city of N-central AZ N of Phoenix; site of Lowell Observatory (founded 1894). Pop. 52,894.

flag•stick (flăg′stĭk′) *n.* A removable pole with a flag marking each hole on the putting greens of a golf course.

flag•stone (flăg′stōn′) *n.* **1.** A flat slab of stone used as a paving material. **2.** An evenly layered sedimentary rock that can be split into paving stones.

flag-wav•ing (flăg′wā′vĭng) *n.* Excessive or fanatical patriotism; chauvinism. **—flag′-wav′er** *n.*

Fla•her•ty (flä′ər-tē, flā′-), **Robert Joseph** 1884–1951. Amer. explorer and documentary filmmaker whose works include *Nanook of the North* (1922).

flail (flāl) *n.* A manual threshing device consisting of a wooden handle or staff and a shorter free-swinging stick attached to its end. ❖ *v.* **flailed, flail•ing, flails** *—tr.* **1.** To beat or strike with or as if with a flail. **2.** To wave or swing vigorously; thrash: *flailed my arms to get their attention.* **3.** To thresh using a flail. *—intr.* **1.** To move vigorously or erratically; thrash about. **2.** To strike or lash out violently. **3.** To thresh grain. [ME < OE *flegil* and < OFr. *flaiel,* both < LLat. *flagellum,* threshing tool < Lat. *flagrum,* whip.]

flair (flâr) *n.* **1.** A natural talent or aptitude. **2.** Instinctive discernment; keenness. **3.** Distinctive elegance or style. [ME, fragrance < OFr. < *flairer,* to scent < LLat. *flāgrāre,* alteration of Lat. *frāgrāre,* to emit an odor.]

flak also **flack** (flăk) *n.* **1a.** Antiaircraft artillery. **b.** The bursting shells fired from such artillery: *planes that were hit by flak.* **2.** *Informal* **a.** Excessive or abusive criticism. **b.** Dissension; opposition. [Ger. < *Fl(ieger)a(bwehr)k(anone),* aircraft-defense gun.]

flake¹ (flāk) *n.* **1.** A flat thin piece or layer; a chip. **2.** *Archaeology* A stone fragment split off from a larger stone, serving esp. as a tool or blade. **3.** A small piece; a bit. **4.** A small crystalline bit of snow. **5.** *Slang* A somewhat eccentric person; an oddball. **6.** *Slang* Cocaine. ❖ *v.* **flaked, flak•ing, flakes** *—tr.* **1.** To remove a flake or flakes from; chip. **2.** To cover, mark, or overlay with or as if with flakes. *—intr.* **1.** To come off in flat thin pieces or layers. **—phrasal verb: flake out** *Slang* **1.** To fall asleep or collapse from fatigue or exhaustion. **2.** To act in an odd or eccentric manner. **3.** To lose interest or nerve. [ME.] **—flak′er** *n.*

flake² (flāk) *n.* A frame or platform for drying fish or produce. [ME *fleke* < ON *fleki,* hurdle, battle shield.]

flake²
stockfish drying in the sun

flake tool *n. Archaeology* A stone tool consisting of a flake that is often modified by further chipping or flaking.

flak jacket *n.* A bulletproof jacket or vest.

flak•y also **flak•ey** (flā′kē) *adj.* **-i•er, -i•est 1.** Made of or resembling flakes. **2.** Forming or tending to form flakes or thin crisp fragments: *flaky pastry.* **3.** *Slang* Somewhat eccentric; odd. **—flak′i•ly** *adv.* **—flak′i•ness** *n.*

flam¹ (flăm) *n. Informal* **1.** A lie or hoax; a deception. **2.** Nonsense; drivel. [Short for FLIMFLAM.]

flam² (flăm) *n. Music* A drumbeat consisting of two almost simultaneous strokes. [Prob. of imit. orig.]

flam•bé (fläm-bā′, flän-) *tr.v.* **-béed, -bé•ing, -bés** To drench

flamenco

with a liquor and ignite. ❖ *adj.* Served flaming in ignited liquor: *steak flambé.* [< Fr., p. part. of *flamber,* to flame < OFr. < *flambe,* flame. See FLAME.]

flam•beau (fläm′bō′) *n., pl.* **-beaux** (-bōz′) or **-beaus 1.** A lighted torch. **2.** A large ornamental candlestick. [Fr. < OFr. < *flambe,* flame. See FLAME.]

flam•boy•ant (fläm-boi′ənt) *adj.* **1.** Highly elaborate; ornate. **2.** Richly colored; resplendent. **3.** *Architecture* Of or having the wavy lines and flamelike forms of 15th- and 16th-century French Gothic architecture. **4.** Given to ostentatious or audacious display. See Syns at **showy.** ❖ *n.* See **royal poinciana.** [Fr. < OFr., pr. part. of *flamboyer,* to blaze < *flambe,* flame. See FLAME.] **—flam•boy′ance, flam•boy′an•cy** *n.* **—flam•boy′ant•ly** *adv.*

flame (flām) *n.* **1.** The hot glowing mixture of burning gases and fine suspended matter associated with rapid combustion. **2.** The condition of active blazing combustion: *burst into flame.* **3.** Something resembling a flame. **4.** A violent or intense passion. **5.** *Informal* A sweetheart. **6.** *Informal* An insulting criticism or remark meant to incite anger, as on a computer network. ❖ *v.* **flamed, flam•ing, flames** *—intr.* **1.** To burn brightly; blaze. **2.** To color or flash suddenly. **3.** *Informal* To make insulting criticisms or remarks, as on a computer network, to incite anger. *—tr.* **1.** To burn, ignite, or scorch (something) with a flame. **2.** *Informal* To insult or criticize provokingly, as on a computer network. **3.** *Obsolete* To excite; inflame. [ME < AN *flaumbe,* var. of OFr. *flambe < flamble < Lat. flammula,* dim. of *flamma.*] **—flam′er** *n.*

flame cell *n.* A hollow cell in the excretory system of certain invertebrates, including flatworms and rotifers, containing cilia that propel waste products into excretory tubules.

fla•men (flā′mən) *n., pl.* **fla•mens** or **flam•i•nes** (flăm′ə-nēz′) A priest, esp. of an ancient Roman deity. [ME *flamin* < Lat. *flāmen.*]

fla•men•co (flə-mĕng′kō) *n., pl.* **-cos 1a.** A dance style of the Andalusian Gypsies characterized by forceful, often improvised rhythms. **b.** A dance in this style. **2.** The guitar music that usu. accompanies a flamenco. [Sp., Flem. < MDu. *Vlāming,* Fleming.]

flame nettle *n.* See **coleus.**

flame•out (flām′out′) *n.* **1.** Failure of a jet aircraft engine due to the extinction of the flame in the combustion chamber. **2.** Sudden failure, esp. of one that has been successful.

flame•proof (flām′prōōf′) *adj.* Resistant to catching fire; flame-retardant. ❖ *tr.v.* **-proofed, -proof•ing, -proofs** To make flameproof.

flame-re•tar•dant (flām′rĭ-tär′dnt) *adj.* Resistant to catching fire. **—flame′-re•tar′dant** *n.*

flame•throw•er (flām′thrō′ər) *n.* A weapon that projects ignited incendiary fuel, such as napalm, in a steady stream.

flam•ing (flā′mĭng) *adj.* **1.** On fire; ablaze. **2.** Resembling a flame. **3.** Intense; ardent: *flaming passions.* **4.** *Informal* Used as an intensive: *a flaming fanatic.* **—flam′ing•ly** *adv.*

fla•min•go (flə-mĭng′gō) *n., pl.* **-gos** or **-goes 1.** Any of several large tropical wading birds of the family Phoenicopteridae, having reddish or pinkish plumage, long legs, and a long flexible neck. **2.** A moderate reddish orange. [Port. *flamengo* or Sp. *flamenco,* both prob. < O Provençal *flamenc < flama,* flame < Lat. *flamma.*]

Fla•min•i•an Way (flə-mĭn′ē-ən) An ancient Roman road, the principal artery between Rome and Cisalpine Gaul.

flam•ma•ble (flăm′ə-bəl) *adj.* Easily ignited and capable of burning rapidly; inflammable. See Usage Note at **inflammable.** [< Lat. *flammāre,* to set fire to < *flamma,* flame.] **—flam′ma•bil′i•ty** *n.* **—flam′ma•ble** *n.*

Flam•ma•rion (flə-măr′ē-ōN′), **Camille** 1842–1925. French astronomer who founded the French Astronomical Society (1887).

flam•y (flā′mē) *adj.* **-i•er, -i•est** Resembling a flame; flaming.

flan (flän, flăn, flăn) *n.* **1.** A tart filled with custard, fruit, or cheese. **2.** See **crème caramel. 3.** A metal disk to be stamped as a coin; a blank. [Fr. < OFr. *flaon* < LLat. *fladō, fladōn-,* flat cake, of Gmc. orig.]

Flan•ders (flăn′dərz) A historical region of NW Europe including parts of N France, W Belgium, and SW Netherlands along the North Sea.

flâ•ne•rie (flän-rē′, flä′nə-rē′) *n.* Aimless idling; dawdling. [Fr. < *flâner,* to idle about, stroll. See FLÂNEUR.]

flâ•neur (flä-nûr′) *n.* An aimless idler; a loafer. [Fr. < *flâner,* to idle about, stroll, of Gmc. orig. See pelə-² in App.]

flange (flănj) *n.* A protruding rim, edge, rib, or collar, as on a pipe shaft, used to strengthen an object, hold it in place, or attach it to another object. [Poss. var. of *flanch,* device at the side of an escutcheon, perh. < Fr. *flanche,* fem. of *flanc,* side. See FLANK.] **—flange** *v.*

flank (flăngk) *n.* **1.** The part of the body of a person or an animal between the last rib and the hip; the side. **2.** A cut of meat from the flank of an animal. **3.** A lateral part or side. **4a.** The right or left side of a military formation. **b.** The right or left side of a bastion. ❖ *tr.v.* **flanked, flank•ing, flanks 1.** To protect or guard the flank of. **2.** To menace or attack the flank of. **3.** To be placed or situated at the flank or side of. **4.** To put (something) on each side of. [ME < OE *flanc* < OFr., of Gmc. orig.]

flan•ken (fläng′kən) *n.* **1.** A cut of meat taken from the short ribs of beef. **2.** A dish prepared from this cut of beef by boiling or stewing, often served with horseradish. [Yiddish < Ger., pl. of *Flanke*, flank, side < Fr. *flanc* < OFr. See FLANK.]

flank•er (flăngʹkər) *n.* **1.** One that flanks, esp. a soldier positioned to protect the flank of a column of troops. **2.** *Football* A flankerback.

flank•er•back (flăngʹkər-băkʹ) *n. Football* A halfback stationed just behind the line of scrimmage and slightly wide of the formation, used chiefly as a pass receiver.

flan•nel (flănʹəl) *n.* **1.** A soft woven cloth of wool or a blend of wool and cotton or synthetics. **2. flannels a.** Outer clothing, esp. trousers, made of this cloth. **b.** Underclothing made of this cloth. **3.** Flannelette. [ME, a woolen cloth or garment, perh. var. of *flanyn*, sackcloth, prob. < OFr. *flaine*, a coarse wool.]

flannel cake *n.* See **pancake.**

flan•nel•ette (flănʹə-lĕtʹ) *n.* A soft cotton fabric with a nap.

flannel leaf *n.* See **mullein.**

Flan•ner (flănʹər), **Janet** Pen name Genêt. 1892–1978. Amer. journalist who was Paris correspondent for *The New Yorker* (1925–75).

flap (flăp) *n.* **1.** A flat, usu. thin piece attached at one side. **2.** A projecting or hanging piece usu. intended to double over and protect or cover: *the flap of an envelope.* **3a.** The act of waving or fluttering. **b.** The sound produced by this motion. **4.** A blow given with something flat; a slap. **5.** A control surface on the trailing edge of an aircraft wing, used primarily to increase lift or drag. **6.** Either of the folded ends of a book jacket that fit inside the front and back covers. **7.** *Medicine* Partially detached tissue used in surgical grafting or in covering the end of a bone after amputation. **8.** *Linguistics* A sound articulated by a single, quick touch of the tongue against the teeth or alveolar ridge, as (t) in *water.* **9.** *Informal* A commotion or disturbance. ❖ *v.* **flapped, flap•ping, flaps** —*tr.* **1.** To wave (the arms, for example) up and down. **2.** To cause to move or sway with a fluttering or waving motion. **3.** To hit with something broad and flat; slap. **4.** *Informal* To fling down; toss. —*intr.* **1.** To move or sway while fixed at one edge or corner; flutter. **2.** To wave arms or wings up and down. **3.** To fly by beating the air with the wings. **4.** *Informal* To become upset or flustered. [ME *flappe*, slap.]

flap•doo•dle also **flap-doo•dle** (flăpʹdo͞odʹl) *n. Slang* Foolish talk; nonsense. [?]

flap•er•on (flăpʹə-rŏnʹ) *n.* A control surface on an aircraft wing functioning both as a flap and as an aileron. [FLAP + (AIL)ERON.]

flap•jack (flăpʹjăkʹ) *n.* See **pancake.**

flap•pa•ble (flăpʹə-bəl) *adj. Informal* Easily excited or upset.

flap•per (flăpʹər) *n.* **1.** A broad flexible part, such as a flipper. **2.** A young woman, esp. one in the 1920s who showed disdain for convention. [Sense 2, Brit. slang, very young female prostitute, flapper, poss. < *flapper*, fledgling partridge or duck (< FLAP), or < dialectal *flap*, loose or flighty girl.]

flare (flâr) *v.* **flared, flar•ing, flares** —*intr.* **1.** To flame up with a bright wavering light. **2.** To burst into intense sudden flame. **3a.** To erupt or intensify suddenly: *Tempers flared.* **b.** To become suddenly angry. Used with *up.* **c.** To make a sudden angry verbal attack. Used with *out.* **4.** To expand or open outward in shape: *with nostrils flaring.* —*tr.* **1.** To cause to flame up. **2.** To signal with a blaze of light. ❖ *n.* **1.** A brief wavering blaze of light. **2.** A device that produces a bright light for signaling, illumination, or identification. **3.** An outbreak, as of emotion or activity. **4.** An expanding or opening outward. **5.** An unwanted reflection within an optical system or the resultant fogging of the image. **6.** A solar flare. **7a.** *Football* A quick pass to a back running toward the sideline. **b.** *Baseball* A fly ball hit a short distance into the outfield. **8.** *Medicine* An area of redness on the skin surrounding the primary site of infection or irritation. [?]

flare•back (flârʹbăkʹ) *n.* **1.** A flame produced in the breech of a gun by ignition of residual gases. **2.** A burst of something aimed back at its origin; a backfire.

flare-up (flârʹŭpʹ) *n.* **1.** A sudden outbreak of flame or light. **2.** An outburst or eruption: *a flare-up of anger.* **3.** A recurrence or an intensification: *a flare-up of rheumatism.*

flash (flăsh) *v.* **flashed, flash•ing, flash•es** —*intr.* **1.** To burst forth into or as if into flame. **2.** To give off light or be lighted in sudden or intermittent bursts. **3.** To appear or occur suddenly. **4.** To move or proceed rapidly. **5.** To hang up a phone line momentarily, as when using call waiting. **6.** *Slang* To think of or remember something suddenly. **7.** *Slang* To expose oneself in an indecent manner. —*tr.* **1a.** To cause (light) to appear suddenly or in intermittent bursts. **b.** To cause to burst into flame. **c.** To reflect (light). **d.** To cause to reflect light from (a surface). **2.** To make known or signal by flashing lights. **3.** To communicate or display at great speed. **4.** To exhibit briefly. **5.** To hang up (a phone line) momentarily, as when using call waiting. **6.** To display ostentatiously; flaunt. **7.** To fill suddenly with water. **8.** To cover with a thin protective layer. ❖ *n.* **1.** A sudden, brief, intense display of light. **2.** A sudden perception. **3.** A split second; an instant. **4.** A brief news dispatch or transmission. **5.** *Slang* Gaudy or ostentatious display. **6.** A flashlight. **7a.** Instantaneous illumination for photography. **b.** A device, such as a flashgun, used to produce such illumination. **8.** *Slang* The pleasurable sensation that accompanies the use of a drug; a rush. **9.** *Obsolete* The language or cant of thieves, tramps, or underworld figures. ❖ *adj.* **1.** Happening suddenly or very quickly: *flash freezing.* **2.** *Slang* Ostentatious; showy. **3.** Of or relating to figures of quarterly economic growth released by the government and subject to later revision. **4.** Of or relating to photography using instantaneous illumination. **5.** Of or relating to thieves, swindlers, and underworld figures. ***—idiom:* flash in the pan** One that promises great success but fails. [ME *flashen*, to splash, var. of *flasken*, of imit. orig.]

flash•back (flăshʹbăkʹ) *n.* **1a.** A literary or cinematic device in which an earlier event is inserted into a narrative. **b.** The episode or scene depicted by means of this device. **2.** An unexpected recurrence of the effects of a hallucinogenic drug after its original use. **3.** *Psychology* A recurring, intensely vivid mental image of a past traumatic experience.

flash•board (flăshʹbôrdʹ, -bōrdʹ) *n.* A board or structure of boards extending above a dam to increase its capacity.

flash•bulb or **flash bulb** (flăshʹbŭlbʹ) *n.* A glass bulb filled with aluminum or magnesium foil that is ignited to produce a short-duration high-intensity light flash for photography.

flash burn *n.* A burn resulting from brief exposure to intense radiation.

flash butt welding *n.* A technique for joining metal rail or pipe in which an electric current melts and welds the ends of the metal, yielding a strong smooth joint.

flash card also **flash•card** (flăshʹkärdʹ) *n.* A card printed with words or numbers and briefly displayed in a learning drill.

flash•cube (flăshʹkyo͞obʹ) *n.* A cube with four flashbulbs that attaches to a camera and rotates to an unused bulb when a picture is taken.

flash•er (flăshʹər) *n.* **1.** A device that automatically switches an electric lamp off and on, as in a commercial display sign. **2.** *Slang* One who engages in indecent exposure.

flash flood also **flash•flood** (flăshʹflŭdʹ) *n.* A sudden flood of great volume, usu. caused by a heavy rain.

flash-for•ward (flăshʹfôrʹwərd) *n.* **1.** A literary or cinematic device in which a future event is inserted into the narrative. **2.** The episode or scene depicted by means of this device.

flash•gun (flăshʹgŭnʹ) *n.* A dry-cell powered photographic apparatus that holds and electrically triggers a flashbulb.

flash•ing (flăshʹĭng) *n.* Sheet metal used to reinforce and weatherproof the joints and angles of a roof.

flash lamp *n.* An electric lamp for producing a high-intensity light of very short duration for use in photography.

flash•light (flăshʹlītʹ) *n.* **1.** A small portable lamp usu. powered by batteries. **2.** A brief brilliant flood of light from a photographic lamp. **3.** A bright light that flashes regularly.

flash memory *n.* A type of computer memory that retains its data when the power is turned off.

flash•o•ver (flăshʹōʹvər) *n.* **1.** An unintended electric arc, as between two conductors. **2.** The temperature at which all flammable material in an area will ignite simultaneously.

flash point also **flash•point** (flăshʹpointʹ) *n.* **1.** The lowest temperature at which the vapor of a combustible liquid can be made to ignite momentarily. **2.** The point at which eruption into significant action, creation, or violence occurs.

flash•tube also **flash tube** (flăshʹto͞obʹ) *n.* A gas discharge tube that emits a brief intense flash of light.

flash unit *n.* **1.** An electronic flash system containing both a power supply and a flashtube in a single compact unit. **2a.** See **flashgun. b.** A flashgun and reflector.

flash welding *n.* See **flash butt welding.**

flash•y (flăshʹē) *adj.* **-i•er, -i•est 1.** Cheap and showy; gaudy. **2.** Giving a momentary or superficial impression of brilliance. **—flashʹi•ly** *adv.* **—flashʹi•ness** *n.*

flask (flăsk) *n.* **1.** A small container having a narrow neck and usu. a cap, esp.: **a.** A flat, relatively thin container for liquor. **b.** A container for carrying gunpowder or shot. **c.** A vial or round long-necked vessel for laboratory use. **2.** A frame for holding a sand mold in a foundry. [ME, cask, keg < OFr. *flasque* < LLat. *flascō*, of Gmc. orig.]

flat[1] (flăt) *adj.* **flat•ter, flat•test 1.** Having a horizontal surface without a slope, tilt, or curvature. **2.** Having a smooth, even, level surface: *flat seams in the skirt.* **3.** Having a relatively broad surface in relation to thickness or depth. **4.** Stretched out or lying at full length along the ground; prone. **5.** Free of qualification; absolute. **6.** Fixed; unvarying: *a flat rate.* **7.** Lacking interest or excitement; dull. **8a.** Lacking in flavor. **b.** Having lost effervescence or sparkle. **9a.** Deflated. Used of a tire. **b.** Electrically discharged. Used of a storage battery. **10.** Of or relating to a horizontal line that displays no ups or downs and signifies the absence of physiological activity. **11.** Commercially inactive; sluggish. **12.** Unmodulated; monotonous: *a flat voice.* **13.** Lacking variety in tint or shading; uniform. **14.** Not glossy; mat: *flat paint.* **15.** *Music* **a.** Being below the correct pitch. **b.** Being one half step lower than the corresponding natural key: *the key of B flat.* **16.** Being the vowel *a* as pronounced in *bad* or *cat.* **17.** *Nautical* Having the edges pulled tight. Used of a sail. ❖ *adv.* **1a.** Level with the ground; horizontally. **b.** On or up against a flat surface; at full length. **2.** So as to be flat. **3a.** Directly; completely: *flat broke.* **b.** Exactly; precisely: *six minutes flat.* **4.** *Music* Below the intended pitch. **5.** *Business* Without interest charge. ❖ *n.* **1.** A flat surface or part. **2.** A stretch of level ground. Often used in the plural. **3.**

flamingo
Phoenicopterus ruber

ă	pat	oi	boy
ā	pay	ou	out
âr	care	o͝o	took
ä	father	o͞o	boot
ĕ	pet	ŭ	cut
ē	be	ûr	urge
ĭ	pit	th	thin
ī	pie	*th*	this
îr	pier	hw	which
ŏ	pot	zh	vision
ō	toe	ə	about, item
ô	paw		

Stress marks:
ʹ (primary);
ʹ (secondary), as in
lexicon (lĕkʹsĭ-kŏnʹ)

flat²

flavor of the month

flattop

A shallow frame or box for seeds or seedlings. **4.** A movable section of stage scenery, usu. consisting of a wooden frame and a decorated panel. **5.** A flatcar. **6.** A deflated tire. **7.** A shoe with a flat heel. **8.** A large flat piece of mail. **9.** A horse that competes in a flat race. **10.** *Music* **a.** A sign (♭) used to indicate that a note is to be lowered by a half step. **b.** A note that is lowered a half step. **11.** *Football* The area of the field to either side of an offensive formation. ❖ *v.* **flat·ted, flat·ting, flats** —*tr.* **1.** To make flat; flatten. **2.** *Music* To lower (a note) a semitone. —*intr. Music* To sing or play below the proper pitch. [ME < ON *flatr.*] —**flat′ly** *adv.* —**flat′ness** *n.*

flat² (flăt) *n.* **1.** An apartment on one floor of a building. **2.** *Archaic* A story in a house. [Alteration of Sc. *flet,* inner part of a house < ME < OE, floor, dwelling.]

flat·bed (flăt′běd′) *n.* **1.** An open truck bed or trailer with no sides, used to carry large objects. **2.** A railroad flatcar.

flatbed press *n.* A printing press in which the type, locked into a chase, is supported by a flat surface or bed and the paper is applied to the type either by a flat platen or by a cylinder against which the bed moves.

flatbed scanner *n.* An optical scanner in which the scanning head moves across a stationary page.

flat·boat (flăt′bōt′) *n.* A boat with a flat bottom and square ends used to transport freight on inland waterways.

flat·bot·tom (flăt′bŏt′əm) or **flat·bot·tomed** (-bŏt′əmd) *adj.* Having a flat bottom: *a flatbottom boat.*

flat·bread (flăt′brĕd′) *n.* Any of various breads made from usu. unleavened dough and baked in flat, often round loaves.

flat·car (flăt′kär′) *n.* A railroad freight car without sides or a roof.

flat-file database (flăt′fīl′) *n.* A database system in which each database contains only one file, which is not linked to any other file.

flat·fish (flăt′fĭsh′) *n., pl.* **flatfish** or **-fish·es** Any of numerous chiefly marine fishes of the order Pleuronectiformes, including the flounders, soles, and halibuts, having a laterally compressed body with both eyes on the upper side.

flat·foot (flăt′fŏŏt′) *n.* **1.** *pl.* **-feet** (-fēt′) A condition in which the arch of the foot is abnormally flat so that the entire sole makes contact with the ground. **2.** *pl.* **-foots a.** *Informal* A person with flat feet. **b.** *Slang* A police officer. ❖ *intr.v.* **-foot·ed, -foot·ing, -foots** To walk in a flat-footed manner.

flat-foot·ed (flăt′fŏŏt′ĭd) *adj.* **1.** Of or having flatfoot. **2a.** Steady on the feet. **b.** *Informal* Without reservation; forthright. **3.** Unable to react quickly; unprepared. —**flat′-foot′ed·ly** *adv.* —**flat′-foot′ed·ness** *n.*

Flat·head (flăt′hĕd′) *n., pl.* **Flathead** or **-heads 1a.** A member of a Native American people of western Montana and northern Idaho, now principally on Flathead Lake. **b.** The Salishan language of the Flathead. **2.** See **Interior Salish.** [Transl. of Fr. *Têtes-Plates,* flat heads, transl. of a name used by neighboring tribes (< the fact that the Flathead did not ornamentally taper the skull as neighboring peoples did).]

flathead catfish *n.* A large yellow and brown catfish (*Pylodictis olivaris*) that is common in streams of the Mississippi Valley and southeast United States.

Flathead River A river rising in SE British Columbia, Canada, and flowing c. 386 km (240 mi) across the MT border to **Flathead Lake** and the Clark Fork R.

flat·i·ron (flăt′ī′ərn) *n.* An iron for pressing clothes, esp. one that is heated externally, as on a hearth or stove.

flat·land (flăt′lănd′, -lənd) *n.* **1.** Land that varies little in elevation. **2. flatlands** A geographic area composed chiefly of land that varies little in elevation. —**flat′land′er** *n.*

flat·let (flăt′lĭt) *n. Chiefly British* An efficiency apartment.

flat·ling (flăt′lĭng) also **flat·lings** (-lĭngs) *adv. Chiefly British* With the flat side or edge of a sword.

flat out *adv. Informal* **1.** In a direct manner; bluntly: *told me the truth flat out.* **2.** At top speed: *running flat out.*

flat-out (flăt′out′) *adj. Informal* Thoroughgoing; out-and-out: *a flat-out deception.*

flat-pan·el display (flăt′păn′əl) *n.* A thin lightweight video display used in laptop and notebook computers and employing liquid crystals, electroluminescence, or a similar alternative to a cathode-ray tube.

flat pick *n.* A flat, often triangular plectrum, used in picking and strumming a guitar or similar instrument. —**flat′-pick′** (flăt′pĭk′) *v.* —**flat′-pick′er** *n.*

flat screen *n.* See **flat-panel display.**

flat silver *n.* Utensils made of silver or silver plate.

flat tax *n.* An income tax having a single rate for all taxpayers regardless of income level and type.

flat·ten (flăt′n) *v.* **-tened, -ten·ing, -tens** —*tr.* **1.** To make flat or flatter. **2.** To knock down; lay low. —*intr.* To become flat or flatter. —**flat′ten·er** *n.*

flat·ter¹ (flăt′ər) *v.* **-tered, -ter·ing, -ters** —*tr.* **1.** To compliment excessively and often insincerely, esp. in order to win favor. **2.** To please or gratify the vanity of. **3a.** To portray favorably: *a photograph that flatters its subject.* **b.** To show off becomingly or advantageously. —*intr.* To practice flattery. [ME *flateren* < OFr. *flater,* of Gmc. orig.] —**flat′ter·er** *n.* —**flat′ter·ing·ly** *adv.*

flat·ter² (flăt′ər) *n.* **1.** A flat-faced swage or hammer used by blacksmiths. **2.** A die plate for flattening metal into strips.

flat·ter·y (flăt′ə-rē) *n., pl.* **-ies 1.** The act or practice of flattering. **2.** Excessive or insincere praise.

flat·tish (flăt′ĭsh) *adj.* Somewhat flat.

flat·top (flăt′tŏp′) *n. Informal* **1.** An aircraft carrier. **2.** A short haircut in which the hair is brushed straight up and cropped flat across the top.

flat·u·lence (flăch′ə-ləns) *n.* **1.** The presence of excessive gas in the digestive tract. **2.** Self-importance; pomposity.

flat·u·len·cy (flăch′ə-lən-sē) *n.* Flatulence.

flat·u·lent (flăch′ə-lənt) *adj.* **1.** Of, afflicted with, or caused by flatulence. **2.** Inducing or generating flatulence. **3.** Pompous; bloated. [Fr. < Lat. *flātus,* a breaking wind. See FLATUS.] —**flat′u·lent·ly** *adv.*

fla·tus (flā′təs) *n.* Gas generated in or expelled from the digestive tract, esp. the stomach or intestines. [Lat. *flātus,* wind < *flāre,* to blow.]

flat·ware (flăt′wâr′) *n.* **1.** Tableware that is fairly flat and fashioned usu. of a single piece, as plates. **2.** Table utensils such as knives, forks, and spoons.

flat·wise (flăt′wīz′) also **flat·ways** (-wāz′) *adv.* With the flat side down or in contact with a surface.

flat·work (flăt′wûrk′) *n.* Laundry, such as sheets and linens, that can be ironed by a mangle rather than by hand.

flat·worm (flăt′wûrm′) *n.* Any of various parasitic and nonparasitic worms of the phylum Platyhelminthes, such as a tapeworm, having a flat, bilaterally symmetrical body.

Flau·bert (flō-bâr′), **Gustave** 1821–80. French writer known for his precise literary style. His works include *Madame Bovary* (1857). —**Flau·ber′tian** (-shən, -tē-ən) *adj.*

flaunt (flônt) *v.* **flaunt·ed, flaunt·ing, flaunts** —*tr.* **1.** To exhibit ostentatiously or shamelessly. **2.** *Usage Problem* To show contempt for; scorn. —*intr.* **1.** To parade oneself ostentatiously; show oneself off. **2.** To wave grandly. [?] —**flaunt′er** *n.* —**flaunt′ing·ly** *adv.*

> **USAGE NOTE** *Flaunt* as a transitive verb means "to exhibit ostentatiously": *She flaunted her wealth.* To *flout* is "to show contempt for": *He flouted the proprieties.* For some time now *flaunt* has been used in the sense "to show contempt for," even by educated users of English. This usage is still widely seen as erroneous and is best avoided.

flaunt·y (flôn′tē) *adj.* **-i·er, -i·est** Inclined to flaunt; ostentatious. —**flaunt′i·ly** *adv.* —**flaunt′i·ness** *n.*

flau·ta (flou′tä) *n.* A dish consisting of a tortilla rolled around a filling such as beef or cheese and usu. deep-fried. [Sp., flute, prob. < O Provençal *flaüt.* See FLUTE.]

flau·tist (flô′tĭst, flou′-) *n.* A flutist. [Ital. *flautista < flauto,* flute < O Provençal *flaüt.* See FLUTE.]

fla·va·none (flā′və-nōn′) *n.* A crystalline compound, $C_{15}H_{12}O_2$, derived from flavone. [FLAV(O)- + -AN(E) + -ONE.]

fla·ves·cent (flə-věs′ənt) *adj.* Turning yellow; yellowish. [Lat. *flāvēscēns, flāvēscent-,* pr. part. of *flāvēscere,* to turn yellow, inchoative of *flāvēre,* to be yellow < *flāvus,* yellow.]

fla·vin (flā′vĭn) also **fla·vine** (-vēn′) *n.* **1.** Any of various water-soluble yellow pigments, including riboflavin, found in plant and animal tissue as coenzymes of flavoprotein. **2.** A ketone, $C_{10}H_6N_4O_2$, found in various natural yellow pigments.

flavin adenine dinucleotide *n.* A coenzyme, $C_{27}H_{33}N_9O_{15}P_2$, that is a derivative of riboflavin and functions in certain oxidation-reduction reactions in the body.

fla·vine (flā′vēn′) *n.* A brownish-red crystalline powder, $C_{14}H_{15}N_3Cl_2$, used as an antiseptic.

flavin mononucleotide *n.* A derivative of riboflavin, $C_{17}H_{21}N_4O_9P$, that functions as a coenzyme of various flavoproteins in some bodily oxidation-reduction reactions.

flavo– or **flav–** *pref.* Yellow: *flavin.* **2.** Flavin: *flavoprotein.* [Lat. *flāvus,* yellow.]

fla·vone (flā′vōn′) *n.* A crystalline compound, $C_{15}H_{10}O_2$, the parent substance of a number of yellow pigments, occurring in primrose leaves, seed capsules, and stems.

fla·vo·noid (flā′və-noid′) *n.* Any of a large group of plant substances that includes the anthocyanins.

fla·vo·pro·tein (flā′vō-prō′tēn′, -tē-ĭn) *n.* Any of a group of enzymes containing flavin bound to protein and acting as dehydrogenation catalysts in biological reactions.

fla·vor (flā′vər) *n.* **1.** Distinctive taste; savor. **2.** A distinctive yet intangible quality felt to be characteristic of a given thing. **3.** A flavoring: *artificial flavors.* **4.** *Physics* The property that distinguishes the six quark varieties: up, down, strange, charmed, top, and bottom. **5.** *Archaic* Aroma; fragrance. ❖ *tr.v.* **-vored, -vor·ing, -vors** To give flavor to. [ME *flavour,* aroma < OFr. *flaor* < VLat. **flātor* < Lat. *flāre,* to blow.] —**fla′vor·er** *n.* —**fla′vor·less** *adj.* —**fla′vor·ous** (-əs), **fla′vor·some** (-səm) *adj.*

fla·vor·ful (flā′vər-fəl) *adj.* Full of flavor; savory.

fla·vor·ing (flā′vər-ĭng) *n.* A substance, such as an extract or spice, that imparts flavor.

fla·vor·ist (flā′vər-ĭst) *n.* One who blends artificially isolated chemicals to create the taste and smell of a particular food.

flavor of the month *n.* A person or thing that is currently but

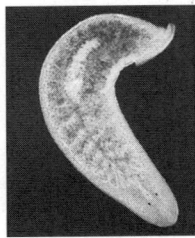

flatworm

temporarily popular; a trend.

fla•vour (flā′vər) *n. & v. Chiefly British* Variant of **flavor.**

flaw[1] (flô) *n.* **1.** An imperfection, often concealed, that impairs soundness: *a flaw in the crystal.* **2.** A defect or shortcoming in something intangible: *a character flaw.* **3.** A defect in a legal document that can render it invalid. ❖ *tr. & intr.v.* **flawed, flaw•ing, flaws** To make or become defective. [ME *flaue*, splinter, perh. < ON *flaga*, slab of stone.]

flaw[2] (flô) *n.* **1a.** A brief gust or blast of wind. **b.** A passing storm; a squall. **2.** *Obsolete* A burst of passion. [Prob. of Scand. orig.; akin to Swed. *flaga*, gust of wind.] **—flaw′y** *adj.*

flaw•less (flô′lĭs) *adj.* Being entirely without flaw or imperfection. See Syns at **perfect. —flaw′less•ly** *adv.* **—flaw′less•ness** *n.*

flax (flăks) *n.* **1a.** A widely cultivated plant, *Linum usitatissimum*, having blue flowers and seeds that yield linseed oil. **b.** The fine light-colored textile fiber obtained from the stems of this plant. **c.** Any of several similar plants. **2.** A pale grayish yellow. [ME < OE *fleax.* See **plek-** in App.]

flax•en (flăk′sən) *adj.* **1.** Made of or resembling flax. **2.** Having the pale grayish-yellow color of flax fiber: *flaxen braids.*

flax•seed (flăks′sēd′) *n.* The seed of flax, the source of linseed oil and emollient medicinal preparations.

flax•y (flăk′sē) *adj.* **-i•er, -i•est** Resembling flax.

flay (flā) *tr.v.* **flayed, flay•ing, flays 1.** To strip off the skin or outer covering of. **2.** To strip of money or goods; fleece. **3.** To whip or lash. **4.** To assail with stinging criticism; excoriate. [ME *flen* < OE *flēan.*] **—flay′er** *n.*

F layer *n.* **1.** The highest zone of the ionosphere, extending at night from about 190 to 400 kilometers (120 to 250 miles) and during the day from about 145 to 400 kilometers (90 to 250 miles) above the earth's surface. **2.** Either of two layers, the lower designated F_1 and the higher F_2, into which the F layer is divided during the day.

fl. dr. *abbr.* fluid dram

flea (flē) *n.* **1.** Any of various small wingless bloodsucking insects of the order Siphonaptera that have legs adapted for jumping and are parasitic on warm-blooded animals. **2.** Any of various small crustaceans that resemble or move like fleas, such as the water flea. ***—idiom:* a flea in (one's) ear** An annoying hint or a stinging rebuke. [ME *fle* < OE *flēah.*]

flea•bag (flē′băg′) *n. Informal* **1.** A seedy run-down hotel or other lodging place. **2.** An animal considered to be in poor condition.

flea•bane (flē′bān′) *n.* Any of various plants of the genus *Erigeron*, having many-rayed daisylike flower heads.

flea beetle *n.* Any of various small herbivorous beetles of the subfamily Alticinae that have hind legs adapted for jumping.

flea•bite (flē′bīt′) *n.* **1a.** The bite of a flea. **b.** The small red mark of a flea's bite. **2.** A trifling loss, inconvenience, or annoyance.

flea-bit•ten (flē′bĭt′n) *adj.* **1.** Covered with fleas or fleabites. **2.** *Informal* Seedy; dilapidated: *a flea-bitten couch.* **3.** Having a pale coat with reddish-brown flecks. Used of horses.

flea collar *n.* A collar, as for a cat or dog, containing a substance that repels or kills fleas.

flea market *n.* A market, usu. held outdoors, where antiques, used household goods, and curios are sold. [Transl. of Fr. *marché aux puces*, market with fleas.]

flea•pit (flē′pĭt′) *n. Chiefly British Slang* A cheap or squalid theater.

flèche (flĕsh, flāsh) *n.* A slender spire, esp. one on a church above the intersection of the nave and transepts. [Fr., arrow, flèche < OFr., arrow, of Gmc. orig. See **pleu-** in App.]

flé•chette (flā-shĕt′, flĕ-) *n.* A steel missile or dart dropped from an aircraft or fired from an artillery piece. [Fr., dim. of *flèche*, arrow. See FLÈCHE.]

fleck (flĕk) *n.* **1.** A tiny mark or spot. **2.** A small bit or flake. ❖ *tr.v.* **flecked, fleck•ing, flecks** To spot or streak. [Prob. < ME *flekked*, spotted; akin to ON *flekkr*, spot.]

flec•tion (flĕk′shən) *n.* Variant of **flexion** 1.

fledge (flĕj) *v.* **fledged, fledg•ing, fledg•es** *—tr.* **1.** To take care of (a young bird) until it can fly. **2.** To cover with or as if with feathers. **3.** To provide (an arrow) with feathers. *—intr.* To grow the plumage necessary for flight. [Prob. < obsolete *fledge*, feathered < ME *flegge* < OE **flycge.* See **pleu-** in App.]

fledg•ling also **fledge•ling** (flĕj′lĭng) *n.* **1.** A young bird that has recently fledged. **2.** A young or inexperienced person. ❖ *adj.* New and untried or inexperienced.

flee (flē) *v.* **fled** (flĕd), **flee•ing, flees** *—intr.* **1.** To run away, as from trouble or danger. **2.** To pass swiftly away; vanish: *"of time fleeing beneath him"* (William Faulkner). *—tr.* To flee from. [ME *flen* < OE *flēon.* See **pleu-** in App.] **—fle′er** *n.*

fleece (flēs) *n.* **1a.** The coat of wool of a sheep or similar animal. **b.** The wool shorn from a sheep at one time. **2.** A soft woolly covering or mass. **3.** Fabric with a soft deep pile. ❖ *tr.v.* **fleeced, fleec•ing, fleec•es 1.** To defraud of money or property; swindle. **2.** To shear the fleece from. **3.** To cover with or as if with fleece. [ME *fles* < OE *flēos.*] **—fleec′er** *n.*

fleec•y (flē′sē) *adj.* **-i•er, -i•est** Of, resembling, or covered with fleece: *fleecy clouds.* **—fleec′i•ly** *adv.* **—fleec′i•ness** *n.*

fleer (flîr) *intr.v.* **fleered, fleer•ing, fleers** To smirk or laugh in contempt or derision. ❖ *n.* A taunting, scoffing, or derisive look or gibe. [ME *flerien*, of Scand. orig.] **—fleer′ing•ly** *adv.*

fleet[1] (flēt) *n.* **1.** A number of warships operating together under one command. **2.** A group of vessels or vehicles, such as taxicabs, owned or operated as a unit. [ME *flete* < OE *flēot* < *flēotan*, to float. See **pleu-** in App.]

fleet[2] (flēt) *adj.* **fleet•er, fleet•est 1.** Moving swiftly; rapid or nimble. See Syns at **fast**[1]. **2.** Fleeting; evanescent. ❖ *v.* **fleet•ed, fleet•ing, fleets** *—intr.* **1.** To move or pass swiftly. **2.** To fade out; vanish. **3.** *Archaic* To flow. **4.** *Obsolete* To drift. *—tr.* **1.** To cause (time) to pass quickly. **2.** *Nautical* To alter the position of (tackle or rope, for example). [Prob. < ON *fljōtr.* V., ME *fleten*, to drift, float < OE *flēotan.* See **pleu-** in App.] **—fleet′ly** *adv.* **—fleet′ness** *n.*

Fleet Admiral *n.* See **Admiral of the Fleet.**

fleet•ing (flē′tĭng) *adj.* Passing quickly; ephemeral. **—fleet′ing•ly** *adv.*

Fleet Street *n.* British journalism. [After *Fleet Street* in central London, long the headquarters of many British newspapers.]

flei•shig (flā′shĭk) *adj.* Consisting of, prepared with, or relating to meat or meat products. [Yiddish *fleyshik* < *fleysh*, meat < MHGer. *vleisch* < OHGer. *fleisk*, flesh.]

Flem•ing (flĕm′ĭng) *n.* **1.** A native or inhabitant of the historical region of Flanders or of the region of Flanders in northern Belgium. **2.** A Belgian who is a native speaker of Flemish. [ME < MDu. *Vlāming.*]

Fleming, Sir **Alexander** 1881–1955. British bacteriologist who discovered penicillin in 1928 and shared a 1945 Nobel Prize.

Fleming, Ian Lancaster 1908–64. British writer noted for his spy novels featuring the secret agent James Bond.

Fleming, Peggy Gale b. 1948. Amer. figure skater who won the women's title at the 1968 Olympics.

Flem•ish (flĕm′ĭsh) *adj.* Of or relating to Flanders, the Flemings, or their language or culture. ❖ *n.* **1.** A group of Dutch dialects spoken in the southwestern Netherlands, northwest Belgium, and parts of northern France. **2.** (*used with a pl. verb*) The Flemings. [ME, prob. < MDu. *Vlaemisch.*]

Flens•burg (flĕnz′bûrg, flĕns′bŏŏrk′) A city of N Germany on **Flensburg Fjord,** an arm of the Baltic Sea at the Danish border; founded c. 1200. Pop. 86,873.

flense (flĕns) *tr.v.* **flensed, flens•ing, flens•es** To strip the blubber or skin from (a whale, for example). [Norw.] **—flens′er** *n.*

flesh (flĕsh) *n.* **1a.** The soft tissue of the body of a vertebrate, consisting mainly of skeletal muscle and fat. **b.** The surface or skin of the human body. **2.** The meat of animals as distinguished from the edible tissue of fish or fowl. **3.** *Botany* The pulpy, usu. edible part of a fruit or vegetable. **4.** Excess fatty tissue; plumpness. **5a.** The body as opposed to the mind or soul. **b.** The physical or carnal nature of humankind. **c.** Sensual appetites. **6.** Humankind in general; humanity. **7.** One's family; kin. **8.** Substance; reality. ❖ *v.* **fleshed, flesh•ing, flesh•es** *—tr.* **1.** To give substance or detail to; fill out: *fleshed out the story.* **2.** To clean (a hide) of adhering flesh. **3.** To encourage (a falcon, for example) to participate in the chase by feeding it flesh from a kill. **4.** To inure to battle or bloodshed. **5.** To plunge or thrust (a weapon) into flesh. *—intr.* To become plump or fleshy; gain weight. ***—idiom:* in the flesh 1.** Alive. **2.** In person; present. [ME < OE *flǣsc.*] **—flesh′less** *adj.*

flesh and blood *n.* **1.** Human nature or physical existence, together with its weaknesses. **2.** A person's blood relatives; kin. **3.** Substance and depth in artistic portrayal; lifelikeness.

flesh fly *n.* Any of various flies of the family Sarcophagidae whose larvae are parasitic in animal tissue or feed on carrion.

flesh•ly (flĕsh′lē) *adj.* **-li•er, -li•est 1.** Of or relating to the body; corporeal. See Syns at **bodily. 2.** Of, relating to, or inclined to carnality; sensual. **3.** Not spiritual; worldly. **4.** Tending to plumpness; fleshy. **—flesh′li•ness** *n.*

flesh•pot (flĕsh′pŏt′) *n.* **1.** A district or establishment offering sensual pleasures or entertainment. Often used in the plural. **2.** Physical or sensual gratification.

flesh wound (wo͞ond) *n.* A wound that penetrates the flesh but does not damage underlying bones or vital organs.

flesh•y (flĕsh′ē) *adj.* **-i•er, -i•est 1a.** Relating to, consisting of, or resembling flesh. **b.** Having abundant flesh; plump. See Syns at **fat. 2.** Having a juicy or pulpy texture. **3.** Fleshly; carnal. **—flesh′i•ness** *n.*

fleshy fruit *n.* A fruit that has a soft, pulpy wall.

fletch (flĕch) *tr.v.* **fletched, fletch•ing, fletch•es** To feather (an arrow). [Prob. back-formation < FLETCHER.]

fletch•er (flĕch′ər) *n.* One who makes arrows. [ME *fleccher* < OFr. *flechier* < *fleche*, arrow, of Gmc. orig. See **pleu-** in App.]

Fletcher, John 1579–1625. English playwright who collaborated with Francis Beaumont on romantic tragicomedies, including *The Maid's Tragedy* (1611).

fletch•ing (flĕch′ĭng) *n.* The feathers on an arrow.

fleur-de-lis or **fleur-de-lys** (flûr′də-lē′, flo͝or′-) *n., pl.* **fleurs-de-lis** or **fleurs-de-lys** (flûr′də-lēz′, flo͝or′-) **1.** An iris, esp. a white-flowered form of *Iris germanica.* **2.** *Heraldry* A device consisting of a stylized three-petaled iris flower, used as the armorial emblem of the kings of France. [ME *flour de lice* < OFr. *flor de lis* : *flor*, flower + *de*, of + *lis*, lily.]

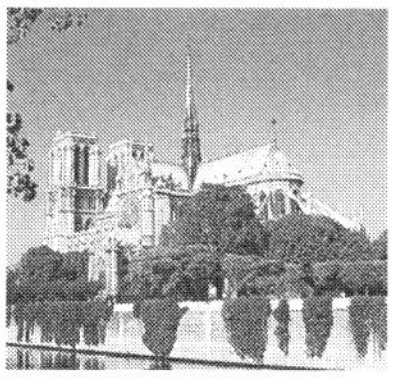

flèche
Notre Dame Cathedral, Paris

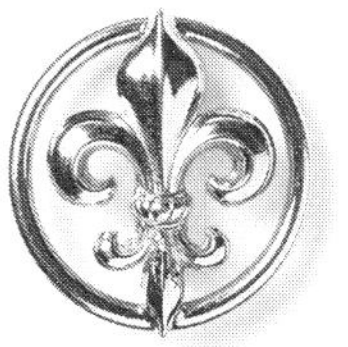

fleur-de-lis

ă	pat	oi	boy
ā	pay	ou	out
âr	care	o͝o	took
ä	father	o͞o	boot
ĕ	pet	ŭ	cut
ē	be	ûr	urge
ĭ	pit	th	thin
ī	pie	*th*	this
îr	pier	hw	which
ŏ	pot	zh	vision
ō	toe	ə	about,
ô	paw		item

Stress marks:
′ (primary);
′ (secondary), as in
lexicon (lĕk′sĭ-kŏn′)

Fleu·ry (flœ-rē′), **André Hercule de** 1653–1743. French prelate who served as prime minister (1726–43) to Louis XV.

flew (flōō) v. Past tense of **fly**[1].

flews (flōōz) pl.n. The pendulous corners of the upper lip of certain dogs, such as the bloodhound. [?]

flex (flĕks) v. **flexed, flex·ing, flex·es** —tr. 1. To bend (something pliant or elastic). 2a. To bend (a joint). b. To bend (a joint) repeatedly. 3a. To contract (a muscle, for example). b. To move by muscular control: *flexes his brow.* 4. To exhibit or show off the strength of. —intr. To bend. ❖ n. 1. *Chiefly British* Flexible insulated electric cord. 2. The act or an instance of flexing; a bending. 3. Pliancy; flexibility. —idiom: **flex (one's) muscles** *Informal* To exhibit or show off one's strength. [Lat. *flectere, flex-,* to bend.]

flex·a·gon (flĕk′sə-gŏn′) n. A paper construction that can be flexed along its folds to reveal and conceal its faces. [Blend of FLEX and HEXAGON.]

flexi– or **flex–** pref. Flexible: *flexitime.* [< FLEXIBLE.]

flex·i·ble (flĕk′sə-bəl) adj. 1a. Capable of being bent or flexed; pliable. b. Capable of being bent repeatedly without injury or damage. 2. Susceptible to influence or persuasion; tractable. 3. Responsive to change; adaptable. [< Lat. *flexibilis < flexus,* p. part. of *flectere,* to bend.] —flex′i·bil′i·ty, flex′i·ble·ness n. —flex′i·bly adv.

flex·ile (flĕk′səl, -sīl′) adj. Flexible.

flex·ion (flĕk′shən) n. 1. also **flec·tion** *Anatomy* a. The bending of a joint or limb by the action of flexors. b. The resulting condition of being bent. 2. A part that is bent. [Lat. *flexiō, flexiōn-,* a bending < *flexus,* p. part. of *flectere,* to bend.]

flex·i·time (flĕk′sĭ-tīm′) n. See **flextime**.

flex·og·ra·phy (flĕk-sŏg′rə-fē) n. A system of printing on a rotary press employing water-based ink, used esp. for printing on plastic or cardboard. —flex·og′ra·pher n. —flex′o·graph′ic (-sə-grăf′ĭk) adj. —flex′o·graph′i·cal·ly adv.

flex·or (flĕk′sər) n. A muscle that when contracted acts to bend a joint or limb in the body. [NLat. < Lat. *flexus,* p. part. of *flectere,* to bend.]

flex·time (flĕks′tīm′) n. A system by which employees may schedule their work, esp. their starting and finishing hours. [*flex(ible) time.*]

flex·u·ous (flĕk′shōō-əs) adj. Bending or winding alternately from side to side; sinuous. [< Lat. *flexuōsus < flexus,* a bending, a turning < p. part. of *flectere,* to bend.] —flex′u·os′i·ty (-ŏs′ĭ-tē) n. —flex′u·ous·ly adv.

flex·ure (flĕk′shər) n. 1. A curve, turn, or fold. 2. The act or an instance of bending or flexing; flexion. —flex′ur·al adj.

fley (flā) tr.v. **fleyed, fley·ing, fleys** *Scots* To frighten. [ME *fleien* < OE *flygan, flēgan.* See **pleu-** in App.]

flib·ber·ti·gib·bet (flĭb′ər-tē-jĭb′ĭt) n. A silly, scatterbrained, or garrulous person. [ME *flipergebet.*]

flic (flĭk) n. *Slang* A police officer, esp. in France. [Fr.]

flick[1] (flĭk) n. 1a. A light quick blow, jerk, or touch. b. The sound accompanying this motion. 2. A light splash, dash, or daub. ❖ v. **flicked, flick·ing, flicks** —tr. 1. To touch or hit with a light quick blow. 2. To cause to move with a light blow; snap. 3. To remove with a light quick blow. —intr. To twitch or flutter. [Imit.] —flick′a·ble adj.

flick[2] (flĭk) n. *Slang* A movie. [Short for FLICKER[1].]

flick·er[1] (flĭk′ər) v. **-ered, -er·ing, -ers** —intr. 1. To move waveringly; flutter. 2. To burn unsteadily. —tr. To cause to move waveringly. ❖ n. 1. A brief movement; a tremor. 2. An inconstant or wavering light. 3. A brief or slight sensation. 4. *Slang* A movie. [ME *flikeren,* to flutter < OE *flicerian.*]

flick·er[2] (flĭk′ər) n. Any of various large North American woodpeckers of the genus *Colaptes,* esp. *C. auratus,* the common flicker, which has a brown back, spotted breast, and white rump. [Perh. < FLICK[1].]

flied (flīd) intr.v. Past tense and past participle of **fly**[1] 7.

fli·er also **fly·er** (flī′ər) n. 1. One, such as an insect or bird, that flies with wings. 2. The pilot of an aircraft. 3. A passenger in an aircraft. 4. A pamphlet or circular for mass distribution. 5. A step in a straight stairway. 6. *Informal* A daring venture.

flies (flīz) v. Third person singular present tense of **fly**[1].

flight[1] (flīt) n. 1a. The motion of an object in or through a medium, esp. through the earth's atmosphere or through space. b. An instance of such motion. c. The distance covered in such motion. 2a. The act or process of flying through the air by means of wings. b. The ability to fly. 3. A swift passage or movement. 4. A scheduled airline run or trip. 5. A group, esp. of birds or aircraft, flying together. 6. A number of aircraft in the US Air Force forming a subdivision of a squadron. 7. A round of competition, as in a sports tournament. 8. An exuberant or transcendent effort or display: *flights of oratory.* 9. A series of stairs rising from one landing to another. ❖ intr.v. **flight·ed, flight·ing, flights** To migrate or fly in flocks. [ME < OE *flyht.* See **pleu-** in App.]

flight[2] (flīt) n. The act or an instance of running away; an escape. [ME < OE *flyht.* See **pleu-** in App.]

flight attendant n. One who assists aircraft passengers.

flight bag n. A lightweight flexible piece of luggage with zippered outside pockets.

flight deck n. 1. The upper deck of an aircraft carrier, used as a

runway. 2. An elevated compartment in certain aircraft, used by the pilot, copilot, and flight engineer.

flight engineer n. The crew member responsible for the mechanical performance of an aircraft in flight.

flight feather n. Any of the comparatively large stiff feathers of a bird's wing or tail that are necessary for flight.

flight·less (flīt′lĭs) adj. Incapable of flying. Used of certain birds, such as the penguin.

flight line n. The area of an airfield where aircraft are onloaded, offloaded, and serviced.

flight recorder n. A crashworthy device that records data about an aircraft's flight, such as the procedures of the pilot.

flight surgeon n. An air force physician who specializes in aeromedicine.

flight-test (flīt′tĕst′) tr.v. **-test·ed, -test·ing, -tests** To test (an aircraft, for example) during flight.

flight·wor·thy (flīt′wûr′thē) adj. Of, relating to, or being an aircraft that is fit to fly. —flight′wor′thi·ness n.

flight·y (flī′tē) adj. **-i·er, -i·est** 1a. Given to capricious or unstable behavior. b. Irresponsible or silly. 2. Easily excited; skittish. —flight′i·ly adv. —flight′i·ness n.

flim·flam (flĭm′flăm′) *Informal* n. 1. Nonsense; humbug. 2. A deception; a swindle. ❖ tr.v. **-flammed, -flam·ming, -flams** To swindle; cheat. [Prob. of Scand. orig.] —flim′flam′mer n. —flim′flam′mer·y n.

flim·sy (flĭm′zē) adj. **-si·er, -si·est** 1. Light, thin, and insubstantial. 2. Lacking solidity or strength. 3. Lacking plausibility; unconvincing. ❖ n., pl. **-sies** 1. Thin paper usu. used to make multiple copies. 2. Something written on this thin paper. [?] —flim′si·ly adv. —flim′si·ness n.

flinch (flĭnch) intr.v. **flinched, flinch·ing, flinch·es** 1. To start or wince involuntarily, as from surprise or pain. 2. To recoil, as from something unpleasant or difficult; shrink. ❖ n. An act or instance of flinching. [Obsolete Fr. *flenchir,* of Gmc. orig.] —flinch′er n. —flinch′ing·ly adv.

flin·ders (flĭn′dərz) pl.n. Bits, fragments, or splinters. [ME *flendris,* poss. of Scand. orig.; akin to Norw. *flindra,* splinter.]

Flinders Range A mountain range of S-central Australia E of Lake Torrens rising to 1,189.5 m (3,900 ft).

Flinders River An intermittent river of NE Australia flowing c. 837 km (520 mi) to the Gulf of Carpentaria.

fling (flĭng) v. **flung** (flŭng), **fling·ing, flings** —tr. 1. To throw with violence. See Syns at **throw**. 2. To put or send suddenly or unexpectedly. 3. To throw (oneself) into an activity with abandon and energy. 4. To cast aside; discard. —intr. To move quickly, violently, or impulsively. ❖ n. 1. The act of flinging. 2. A brief period of indulging one's impulses. See Syns at **binge**. 3. *Informal* A usu. brief attempt or effort. 4. A brief sexual or romantic relationship. [ME *flingen,* of Scand. orig. See **plāk-** in App.]

flint (flĭnt) n. 1. A hard fine-grained quartz that sparks when struck with steel. 2a. A piece of flint used to produce a spark. b. A cylinder of a spark-producing alloy, used in lighters to ignite the fuel. 3. A piece of flint used as a tool by early humans. 4. Something hard like flint. [ME < OE.]

Flint A city of SE-central MI NNW of Detroit; founded on the site of a fur-trading post est. in 1819. Pop. 124,943.

flint corn n. A variety of corn (*Zea mays* var. *indurata*) having small hard grains.

flint glass n. A soft, fusible, lustrous, brilliant lead-oxide optical glass with high refraction and low dispersion.

flint·head (flĭnt′hĕd′) n. See **wood ibis**.

flint·lock (flĭnt′lŏk′) n. 1. An obsolete gunlock in which a flint fixed in the hammer produces a spark that ignites the charge. 2. A firearm having this type of gunlock.

Flint River A river of W GA flowing c. 531 km (330 mi) to join the Chattahoochee R. and form the Apalachicola R.

flint·y (flĭn′tē) adj. **-i·er, -i·est** 1. Containing or composed of flint. 2. Unyielding; stern. —flint′i·ly adv. —flint′i·ness n.

flip (flĭp) v. **flipped, flip·ping, flips** —tr. 1. To throw or toss with a light brisk motion. 2. To toss in the air, imparting a spin. 3a. To turn over or around, esp. with a light quick motion. b. To turn through; leaf. 4. To strike quickly or lightly; flick. 5. To move or act on with a quick motion. —intr. 1. To turn over: *The canoe flipped over.* 2. To turn a somersault, esp. in the air. 3. To move in twists and turns. 4. To move quickly and lightly; snap: *The lid flipped open.* 5. To leaf; browse. 6. *Slang* a. To go crazy. Often used with *out.* b. To react strongly and esp. enthusiastically. ❖ n. 1. The act of flipping, esp.: a. A flick or tap. b. A short quick movement. c. A somersault. 2. *Informal* A reversal; a flipflop. 3. A mixed drink made with any of various alcoholic beverages and often beaten eggs. ❖ adj. **flip·per, flip·pest** *Informal* Marked by casual disrespect; impertinent. —idiom: **flip (one's) lid** *Slang* 1. To react strongly, as with anger or enthusiasm. 2. To go crazy. [Perh. imit.]

flip·book (flĭp′bŏŏk′) n. A small book consisting of a series of images that give the illusion of continuous movement when the edges of the pages are flipped quickly.

flip-flop (flĭp′flŏp′) n. 1. The movement or sound of repeated flapping. 2. A backward somersault or handspring. 3. *Informal* A reversal, as of a stand or position. 4. A backless, often foam rubber sandal held to the foot at the big toe by means of a thong. **5.** *Electronics* An electronic circuit or mechanical device capable of assuming either of two stable states, esp. a computer circuit used to store a single bit. **—flip′-flop′** *v.*

flip•pant (flĭp′ənt) *adj.* **1.** Marked by disrespectful levity or casualness; pert. **2.** *Archaic* Talkative; voluble. [Prob. < FLIP.] **—flip′pan•cy** *n.* **—flip′pant•ly** *adv.*

flip•per (flĭp′ər) *n.* **1.** A wide flat limb, as of a seal or whale, adapted for swimming. **2.** A rubber foot covering with a flat flexible part that extends forward from the toes, used in swimming.

flip side *n. Informal* **1.** The reverse side, as of a phonograph record. **2.** The opposite side.

flirt (flûrt) *v.* **flirt•ed, flirt•ing, flirts** *—intr.* **1.** To make playfully romantic or sexual overtures. **2.** To deal playfully, triflingly, or superficially with. **3.** To move abruptly or jerkily. *—tr.* **1.** To toss or flip suddenly. **2.** To move quickly. ❖ *n.* **1.** One given to flirting. **2.** An abrupt jerking movement. [?] **—flirt′y** *adj.*

flir•ta•tion (flûr-tā′shən) *n.* **1.** The practice of flirting. **2.** A superficial, usu. temporary romance. **3.** A brief involvement.

flir•ta•tious (flûr-tā′shəs) *adj.* **1.** Given to flirting. **2.** Full of playful allure. **—flir•ta′tious•ly** *adv.* **—flir•ta′tious•ness** *n.*

flit (flĭt) *intr.v.* **flit•ted, flit•ting, flits 1.** To move about rapidly and nimbly. **2.** To move quickly from one condition or location to another. ❖ *n.* **1.** A fluttering or darting movement. **2.** *Informal* An empty-headed, silly, often erratic person. [ME *flitten* < ON *flytja*, convey. See **pleu-** in App.] **—flit′ter** *n.*

flitch (flĭch) *n.* **1.** A salted and cured side of bacon. **2.** A longitudinal cut from a tree trunk. **3.** One of several planks secured together to form a single beam. [ME *flicche* < OE *flicce*.]

flit•ter (flĭt′ər) *intr.v.* **-tered, -ter•ing, -ters** To flutter. [Frequentative of FLIT.]

fliv•ver (flĭv′ər) *n. Slang* An automobile, esp. one that is small, inexpensive, and old. [?]

float (flōt) *v.* **float•ed, float•ing, floats** *—intr.* **1a.** To remain suspended within or on the surface of a fluid without sinking. **b.** To be suspended in or move through space as if supported by a liquid. **2.** To move from place to place, esp. at random. **3.** To move easily or lightly. **4.** *Economics* To find a value relative to other currencies solely in response to supply and demand. *—tr.* **1.** To cause to remain suspended without sinking or falling. **2a.** To put into the water; launch: *float a ship.* **b.** To start or establish (a business enterprise, for example). **3.** To flood (land), as for irrigation. **4.** *Economics* To allow (the exchange value of a currency) to float. **5.** To offer for consideration; suggest: *float an idea around the office.* **6.** To release (a security) for sale. **7.** To arrange for (a loan). **8.** To make the surface of (plaster, for example) level or smooth. **9.** *Computer Science* To convert (data) from fixed-point to floating-point notation. ❖ *n.* **1.** Something that floats, as: **a.** A raft. **b.** A buoy. **c.** A life preserver. **d.** A buoyant object, such as a cork, used to hold a net or fishing line afloat. **e.** A landing platform attached to a wharf and floating on the water. **f.** A floating ball attached to a lever to regulate the water level in a tank. **2.** *Biology* An air-filled sac or structure that aids in the flotation of an aquatic organism. **3.** A decorated exhibit or scene mounted on a mobile platform and pulled or driven in a parade. **4.** A sum of money representing checks that are outstanding. **5.** A tool for smoothing the surface of plaster or cement. **6.** A soft drink with ice cream floating in it. See Regional Note at **milk shake.** [ME *floten* < OE *flotian*. See **pleu-** in App.] **—float′a•ble** *adj.*

float•age (flō′tĭj) *n.* Variant of **flotage.**

float•a•tion (flō-tā′shən) *n.* Variant of **flotation.**

float•er (flō′tər) *n.* **1.** One that floats or is capable of floating. **2.** One who wanders; a drifter. **3.** An employee who is reassigned from job to job or shift to shift. **4.** One who votes illegally in different polling places. **5.** An insurance policy that protects property in transit or regularly subject to use in varying places. **6.** *Slang* A corpse found floating in a body of water. **7.** A speck in the visual field, usu. perceived to be moving, due to minute clumps of cells or proteins in the vitreous humor.

float•ing (flō′tĭng) *adj.* **1.** Buoyed on or suspended in or as if in a fluid. **2.** Not secured in place; unattached. **3.** Inclined to move or be moved about. **4.** *Economics* **a.** Available for use; in circulation. Used of capital. **b.** Short-term and usu. unfunded. Used of a debt. **5.** Designed or constructed to operate smoothly and without vibration. **6.** Of or relating to an organ of the body that is movable or out of normal position.

floating dock *n.* **1.** A structure that can be submerged to dock a ship and then raised to lift the ship from the water for repairs. **2.** A dock that can move up and down with the rise and fall of the water level.

float•ing-point (flō′tĭng-point′) *adj.* Of, relating to, or being a method of writing numbers with a mantissa representing the value of the digits and a characteristic indicating the power of the number base, such as 3×10^{-5}.

floating rib *n.* A false rib whose anterior end is unattached.

float•plane (flōt′plān′) *n.* An airplane equipped with one or more floats for landing on or taking off from a body of water.

floc (flŏk) *n.* A flocculent mass formed in a fluid through precipitation or aggregation of suspended particles.

floc•cose (flŏk′ōs) *adj. Botany* Covered with tufts of soft hair. [LLat. *floccōsus* < Lat. *floccus*, tuft of wool.]

floc•cu•late (flŏk′yə-lāt′) *v.* **-lat•ed, -lat•ing, -lates** *—tr.* **1.** To cause (soil) to form lumps or masses. **2.** To cause (clouds) to form fluffy masses. *—intr.* To form lumpy or fluffy masses. ❖ *n.* Something that has flocculated. **—floc′cu•la′tion** *n.*

floc•cule (flŏk′yo͞ol) *n.* A flocculus suspended in or precipitated from a solution. [NLat. *flocculus*. See FLOCCULUS.]

floc•cu•lent (flŏk′yə-lənt) *adj.* **1.** Having a fluffy or woolly appearance. **2.** *Chemistry* Made up of or containing woolly masses. **3.** *Zoology* Having a soft, waxy, and woollike covering, as certain insects. **—floc′cu•lence** *n.* **—floc′cu•lent•ly** *adv.*

floc•cu•lus (flŏk′yə-ləs) *n., pl.* **-li** (-lī′) **1.** A small fluffy mass or tuft. **2.** *Anatomy* Either of two small lobes on the lower posterior border of the cerebellum. **3.** *Astronomy* Any of various cloudlike masses of gases appearing as patches on the surface of the sun. [NLat., dim. of Lat. *floccus*, tuft of wool.]

flock[1] (flŏk) *n.* **1.** A group of animals that live, travel, or feed together. **2.** A group of people under the leadership of one person, esp. the members of a church. **3.** A large crowd or number. See Usage Note at **collective noun.** ❖ *intr.v.* **flocked, flock•ing, flocks** To congregate or travel in a flock or crowd. [ME *flok* < OE *floc*.]

flock[2] (flŏk) *n.* **1.** A tuft, as of fiber or hair. **2.** Waste wool or cotton used for stuffing furniture and mattresses. **3.** An inferior grade of wool added to cloth for extra weight. **4.** Pulverized wool or felt that is applied to paper, cloth, or metal to produce a texture or pattern. **5.** See **floccule.** ❖ *tr.v.* **flocked, flock•ing, flocks 1.** To stuff with flock. **2.** To texture or pattern with flock. [ME *flok* < OFr. *floc* < Lat. *floccus*, tuft of wool.]

Flod•den (flŏd′n) A hill of N England near the Scottish border; site of the Battle of Flodden Field (Sep. 9, 1513) in which the English defeated the Scots under James IV.

floe (flō) *n.* **1.** An ice floe. **2.** A segment that has separated from an ice floe. [Prob. < Norw. *flo*, layer < ON *flō*.]

flog (flŏg, flôg) *tr.v.* **flogged, flog•ging, flogs 1.** To beat severely with a whip or rod. **2.** *Informal* To publicize aggressively. [Perh. < alteration of Lat. *flagellāre*. See FLAGELLATE.] **—flog′ger** *n.*

flood (flŭd) *n.* **1.** An overflowing of water onto land that is normally dry. **2.** A flood tide. **3.** An abundant flow or outpouring. **4.** A floodlight. **5. Flood** In the Bible, the covering of the earth with water that occurred during the time of Noah. ❖ *v.* **flood•ed, flood•ing, floods** *—tr.* **1.** To cover or submerge with or as if with a flood; inundate. **2.** To fill with an abundance or an excess. *—intr.* **1.** To become inundated or submerged. **2.** To pour forth; overflow. [ME *flod* < OE *flōd*. See **pleu-** in App.]

flood•gate (flŭd′gāt′) *n.* **1.** A gate used to control the flow of a body of water. **2.** Something that restrains a flood or outpouring.

flood•light (flŭd′līt′) *n.* **1.** Artificial light in an intensely bright and broad beam. **2.** A unit that produces a beam of intense light; a flood. ❖ *tr.v.* **-light•ed** or **-lit** (-lĭt′), **-light•ing, -lights** To illuminate with a floodlight.

flood•plain also **flood plain** (flŭd′plān′) *n.* A plain bordering a river and subject to flooding.

flood tide also **flood•tide** (flŭd′tīd′) *n.* **1.** The incoming or rising tide; the period between low water and the succeeding high water. **2.** A climax or high point: *a flood tide of fears.*

flood•wall (flŭd′wôl′) *n.* A wall built along a shore or bank to protect an area from floods.

flood•wa•ter (flŭd′wô′tər, -wŏt′ər) *n.* The water of a flood. Often used in the plural.

flood•way (flŭd′wā′) *n.* A channel for an overflow of water caused by flooding.

floor (flôr, flōr) *n.* **1a.** The surface of a room on which one stands. **b.** The lower or supporting surface of a structure. **2a.** A story or level of a building. **b.** The occupants of such a story. **3.** A level surface or area used for a specified purpose. **4.** The surface of a structure on which vehicles travel. **5a.** The part of a legislative chamber or meeting hall where members are seated and from which they speak. **b.** The right to address an assembly, as granted under parliamentary procedure. **c.** The body of assembly members. **6.** The part of a room or building where the principal business or work takes place, esp.: **a.** The area of an exchange where securities are traded. **b.** The part of a retail store in which merchandise is displayed and sales are made. **c.** The area of a factory where the product is manufactured or assembled. **7.** The ground or lowermost surface, as of an ocean. **8.** A lower limit or base: *a pricing floor.* ❖ *tr.v.* **floored, floor•ing, floors 1.** To provide with a floor. **2.** *Informal* To press (the accelerator of a motor vehicle) to the floor. **3a.** To knock down. **b.** To stun; overwhelm. [ME *flor* < OE *flōr*. See **pelə-**[2] in App.] **—floor′er** *n.*

floor•age (flôr′ĭj, flōr′-) *n.* Floor space.

floor•board (flôr′bôrd′, flōr′bōrd′) *n.* **1.** A board in a floor. **2.** The floor of a motor vehicle.

floor•cloth (flôr′klôth′, -klŏth′, flōr′-) *n.* A piece of heavy canvas that has been primed, decorated, and varnished and is used as a floor covering.

floor exercise *n.* An event in competitive gymnastics that consists of various tumbling maneuvers on a mat.

floor•ing (flôr′ĭng, flōr′-) *n.* **1.** A floor. **2.** Material, such as lumber or tile, used in making floors.

floor lamp *n.* A tall lamp with a base that stands on the floor.

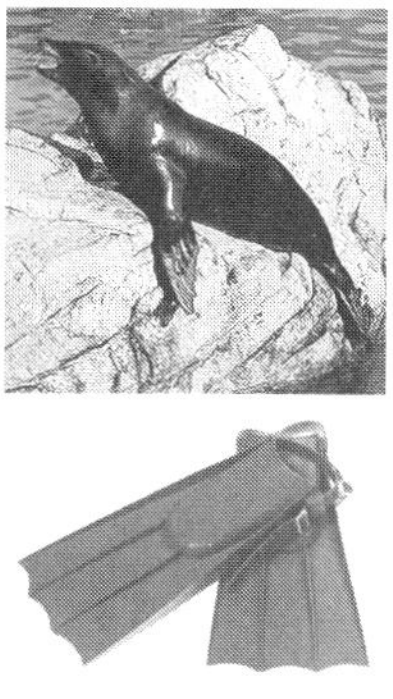

flipper
top: sea lion
bottom: swimming flippers

ă	pat	oi	boy
ā	pay	ou	out
âr	care	o͝o	took
ä	father	o͞o	boot
ĕ	pet	ŭ	cut
ē	be	ûr	urge
ĭ	pit	th	thin
ī	pie	*th*	this
îr	pier	hw	which
ŏ	pot	zh	vision
ō	toe	ə	about, item
ô	paw		

Stress marks:
′ (primary);
′ (secondary), as in
lexicon (lĕk′sĭ-kŏn′)

floor leader *n.* The member of a legislature chosen by fellow party members to direct the party's activities on the floor.

floor manager *n.* **1.** See **floorwalker. 2.** A person who directs from the floor, as at a political convention.

floor plan *n.* A scale diagram of a room or building drawn as if seen from above.

floor sample *n.* Merchandise sold at a reduced price because it has been a display or demonstration model.

floor·show (flôr′shō′, flōr′-) *n.* A series of entertainments presented in a nightclub.

floor·walk·er (flôr′wô′kər, flōr′-) *n.* A department store employee who supervises sales personnel and assists customers.

floo·zy also **floo·zie** (flōō′zē) *n., pl.* **-zies** *Slang* A woman regarded as tawdry or sexually promiscuous. [?]

flop (flŏp) *v.* **flopped, flop·ping, flops** —*intr.* **1.** To fall or lie down heavily and noisily. **2.** To move about loosely or limply. **3.** *Informal* To fail utterly. **4.** *Slang* To rest idly; lounge. **b.** To go to bed. —*tr.* To drop or lay (something) down heavily and noisily. ❖ *n.* **1.** The act of flopping. **2.** The sound made when flopping. **3.** *Informal* An utter failure. [Alteration of FLAP.] —**flop′per** *n.*

FLOP *abbr. Computer Science* floating-point operation

flop·house (flŏp′hous′) *n.* A cheap rundown hotel or boarding house.

flop·py (flŏp′ē) *adj.* **-pi·er, -pi·est** Tending to flop; loose and flexible. ❖ *n., pl.* **-pies** A floppy disk. —**flop′pi·ly** *adv.* —**flop′pi·ness** *n.*

floppy disk *n.* A flexible plastic disk coated with magnetic material and covered by a protective jacket, used primarily by computers to store data.

flo·ra (flôr′ə, flōr′ə) *n., pl.* **flo·ras** or **flo·rae** (flôr′ē, flōr′ē′) **1.** Plants considered as a group, esp. the plants of a particular country, region, or time. **2.** A treatise describing the plants of a region or time. **3.** The bacteria and other microorganisms that normally inhabit a body organ or part. [< FLORA.]

Flora *n. Roman Mythology* The goddess of flowers. [Lat. *Flōra* < *flōs, flōr-,* flower. See **bhel-** in App.]

flo·ral (flôr′əl, flōr′-) *adj.* Of, relating to, or suggestive of a flower: *a fabric with a floral pattern.* —**flo′ral·ly** *adv.*

floral cup *n.* A tubular or cup-shaped structure of a flower, bearing on its rim the sepals, petals, and stamens.

floral envelope *n.* The perianth of a flower.

floral tube *n.* A tube usu. formed by the basal fusion of the perianth and stamens, as in the flowers of the daffodil.

Flor·ence (flôr′əns, flōr′-) also **Fi·ren·ze** (fē-rĕn′dzĕ) A city of central Italy on the Arno R. E of Pisa; a powerful city-state during the Renaissance. Pop. 402,316.

Florence fennel *n.* See **finocchio.**

Flor·en·tine (flôr′ən-tēn′, -tīn′, flōr′-) *adj.* **1.** Of or relating to Florence, Italy. **2.** often **florentine** Having or characterized by a dull chased or rubbed finish. Used of gold. **3.** Prepared, cooked, or served with spinach. ❖ *n.* A native or inhabitant of Florence, Italy. [Lat. *Flōrentīnus < Flōrentia,* Florence, Italy.]

Flo·res (flôr′ĭs, -ĕz, flōr′-) An island of E Indonesia in the Lesser Sundas on the **Flores Sea,** between the E end of the Java Sea and the W end of the Banda Sea S of Sulawesi.

flo·res·cence (flô-rĕs′əns, flə-) *n.* A condition, time, or period of flowering. [NLat. *flōrēscentia* < Lat. *flōrēscēns, flōrēscent-,* pr. part. of *flōrēscere,* inchoative of *flōrēre,* to flower, bloom. See FLOURISH.] —**flo·res′cent** *adj.*

flo·ret (flôr′ĭt, -ĕt, flōr′-) *n.* **1.** A small or reduced flower, esp. one of the grasses and composite plants. **2.** Any of the tight, branched clusters of flower buds that together form a head of cauliflower or broccoli. [ME *flouret* < OFr. *florete,* dim. of *flor,* flower. See FLOWER.]

Flo·rey (flôr′ē, flōr′ē), Sir **Howard Walter** 1898–1968. Australian-born British pathologist who shared a 1945 Nobel Prize.

Flo·ri·a·nó·po·lis (flôr′ē-ə-nŏp′ə-lĭs, flōr-, flô′ryə-nô′pŏō-lēs′) A city of SE Brazil on an island just off the coast; linked to the mainland by a suspension bridge. Pop. 254,941.

flo·ri·at·ed also **flo·re·at·ed** (flôr′ē-ā′tĭd, flōr′-) *adj.* Decorated with floral designs. [< Lat. *flōs, flōr-,* flower. See **bhel-** in App.]

flo·ri·bun·da (flôr′ə-bŭn′də, flōr′-) *n.* Any of several hybrid roses bearing numerous single or double flowers. [NLat. *flōribunda,* fem. of *flōribundus,* blossoming freely < Lat. *flōs, flōr-,* flower. See FLOWER.]

flo·ri·cane (flôr′ĭ-kān′, flōr′-) *n.* The flowering and fruiting stem of a biennial plant, esp. of a bramble. [Lat. *flōs, flōr-,* flower; see FLOWER + CANE.]

flo·ri·cul·ture (flôr′ĭ-kŭl′chər, flōr′-) *n.* The cultivation of flowering and ornamental plants. [Lat. *flōs, flōr-,* flower; see FLOWER + CULTURE.] —**flo′ri·cul′tur·al** *adj.* —**flo′ri·cul′tur·al·ly** *adv.* —**flo′ri·cul′tur·ist** *n.*

flor·id (flôr′ĭd, flōr′-) *adj.* **1.** Flushed with rosy color; ruddy. **2.** Very ornate; flowery. **3.** *Archaic* Healthy. **4.** *Obsolete* Abounding in or covered with flowers. [Fr. *floride* < Lat. *flōridus < flōs, flōr-,* flower. See **bhel-** in App.] —**flo·rid′i·ty** (flə-rĭd′ĭ-tē, flô-), **flor′id·ness** *n.* —**flor′id·ly** *adv.*

Flor·i·da (flôr′ĭ-də, flōr′-) A state of the SE US bordering on the Atlantic Ocean and the Gulf of Mexico; admitted as the 27th state

in 1845. The region was ceded to the US by Spain in 1819. Cap. Tallahassee. Pop. 15,982,378. —**Flo·rid′i·an** (flə-rĭd′ē-ən), **Flor′i·dan** (-ĭd-n) *adj. & n.*

Florida, Straits of also **Florida Strait** A sea passage between Cuba and the Florida Keys, linking the Gulf of Mexico with the Atlantic Ocean.

Florida arrowroot *n.* See **coontie.**

Florida Keys A chain of coral and limestone islands and reefs extending c. 241 km (150 mi) from S of Miami to Key West.

flo·rif·er·ous (flô-rĭf′ər-əs) *adj.* Bearing flowers. [< Lat. *flōri- fer,* bearing flowers : *flōs, flōr-,* flower; see FLOWER + *-fer, -fer.*] —**flo·rif′er·ous·ly** *adv.* —**flo·rif′er·ous·ness** *n.*

flor·i·gen (flôr′ə-jən, flōr′-) *n.* A plant hormone that promotes flowering. [Lat. *flōs, flōr-,* flower; see **bhel-** in App. + –GEN.] —**flor′i·gen′ic** (-jĕn′ĭk) *adj.*

flor·i·le·gi·um (flôr′ə-lē′jē-əm, flōr′-) *n., pl.* **-gi·a** (-jē-ə) A collection of excerpts from written texts, esp. works of literature. [NLat. *flōrilegium,* flower-gathering (transl. of Gk. *anthologion,* flower-gathering, anthology) < Lat. *flōrilegus,* gathering flowers : *flōs, flōr-,* flower; see FLOWER + *legere,* to gather; see **leg-** in App.]

flor·in (flôr′ĭn, flōr′-) *n.* **1.** A guilder. **2.** A British coin worth two shillings. **3a.** A gold coin first issued at Florence, Italy, in 1252. **b.** Any of several gold coins similar to the Florentine florin, formerly used in Europe. [ME < OFr. < OItal. *fiorino < fiore,* flower < Lat. *flōs, flōr-,* flower. See **bhel-** in App.]

Flo·ri·o (flôr′ē-ō′, flōr′-), **John** 1553?–1625. English lexicographer noted for his Italian-English dictionary (1598).

flo·rist (flôr′ĭst, flōr′-, flŏr′-) *n.* One in the business of raising or selling flowers and ornamental plants. [Lat. *flōs, flōr-,* flower; see **bhel-** in App. + –IST.] —**flo′rist·ry** *n.*

flo·rist·ics (flô-rĭs′tĭks, flō-) *n.* (used with a sing. verb) The study of the number, distribution, and relationships of plant species in one or more areas.

–florous *suff.* Having a specified kind or number of flowers: *tubuliflorous.* [< LLat. *-flōrus* < Lat. *flōs, flōr-,* flower. See **bhel-** in App.]

flo·ru·it (flôr′yōō-ĭt, -ōō-, flōr′-) *n.* The period during which a person, school, or movement was most active or flourishing. [Lat. *flōruit,* third pers. sing. perfect t. of *flōrēre,* to flourish. See FLOURISH.]

Flo·ry (flôr′ē, flōr′ē), **Paul John** 1910–85. Amer. chemist who won a 1974 Nobel Prize.

floss (flôs, flŏs) *n.* **1.** Dental floss. **2.** Short or waste silk fibers, esp. from a silkworm cocoon. **3.** Soft, loosely twisted thread, as of silk, used in embroidery. **4.** A downy or silky fibrous substance, such as corn silk. ❖ *v.* **flossed, floss·ing, floss·es** —*tr.* To clean between (teeth) with dental floss. —*intr.* To use dental floss. [Perh. alteration of Fr. *floche,* tuft of wool < OFr. *floc, floche* < Lat. *floccus.*] —**floss′er** *n.*

floss·y (flô′sē, flŏs′ē) *adj.* **-i·er, -i·est 1.** Superficially stylish; slick: *flossy articles.* **2.** Of, relating to, or resembling floss. —**floss′i·ly** *adv.* —**floss′i·ness** *n.*

flo·tage also **float·age** (flō′tĭj) *n.* **1.** See **flotation** 1. **2.** Floating objects or material; flotsam.

flo·ta·tion also **float·a·tion** (flō-tā′shən) *n.* **1.** The act, process, or condition of floating. **2.** The act or an instance of launching or initiating, esp. one involving the floating of stocks or bonds. **3.** The process of separating different materials, esp. minerals, by agitating a pulverized mixture of the materials with water, oil, or chemicals. **4.** The capability, esp. of a vehicle tread or tire, to remain on top of a soft surface.

flotation device *n.* A life preserver.

flo·til·la (flō-tĭl′ə) *n.* **1a.** A small fleet. **b.** A fleet of small craft. **2.** A naval organizational unit of two or more squadrons of small warships. **3.** *Informal* A group of vehicles owned or operated as a unit. [Sp., dim. of *flota,* fleet < OFr. *flote* < ON *floti.* See **pleu-** in App.]

flot·sam (flŏt′səm) *n.* **1a.** Wreckage or cargo afloat after a shipwreck. **b.** Floating refuse or debris. **2.** Discarded odds and ends. **3.** Vagrant, usu. destitute people. [AN *floteson* < OFr. *floter,* to float, of Gmc. orig. See **pleu-** in App.]

> **USAGE NOTE** In maritime law, *flotsam* applies to wreckage or cargo left floating on the sea after a shipwreck. *Jetsam* applies to cargo or equipment thrown overboard (jettisoned) from a ship in distress and either sunk or washed ashore. The common phrase *flotsam and jetsam* is now used loosely to describe any objects found floating or washed ashore.

FLOTUS *abbr.* First Lady of the United States

flounce¹ (flouns) *n.* A strip of decorative, usu. gathered or pleated material attached by one edge, as on a garment. ❖ *tr.v.* **flounced, flounc·ing, flounc·es** To trim with a flounce. [Alteration of *frounce* < ME, pleat < OFr. *fronce,* of Gmc. orig.]

flounce² (flouns) *intr.v.* **flounced, flounc·ing, flounc·es 1a.** To move in a lively or bouncy manner. **b.** To move with exaggerated or affected motions. **2.** To move clumsily; flounder. ❖ *n.* The act of flouncing. [Poss. of Scand. orig.]

flounc·ing (floun′sĭng) *n.* **1.** Material used to make flounces. **2.** A flounce or an arrangement of flounces, as on a curtain.

floun·der¹ (floun′dər) *intr.v.* **-dered, -der·ing, -ders 1.** To make clumsy attempts to move or regain one's balance. **2.** To move or act clumsily and in confusion. See Syns at **blunder.** See Usage Note at **founder[1]**. ❖ *n.* The act of floundering. [Prob. alteration of FOUNDER[1].]

floun•der[2] (floun′dər) *n., pl.* **flounder** or **-ders** Any of various marine flatfishes of the families Bothidae and Pleuronectidae, which include important food fishes. [ME < AN *floundre,* of Scand. orig.]

flour (flou′ər, flour) *n.* **1.** A fine powdery foodstuff obtained by grinding and sifting the meal of a grain, esp. wheat, used chiefly in baking. **2.** Any of various similar finely ground or powdered foodstuffs, as of cassava, fish, or bananas. **3.** A soft fine powder. ❖ *tr.v.* **floured, flour•ing, flours 1.** To cover or coat with flour. **2.** To make into flour. [ME, flower, best of anything, flour. See FLOWER.] **—flour′y** *adj.*

flour•ish (flûr′ĭsh, flŭr′-) *v.* **-ished, -ish•ing, -ish•es** *—intr.* **1.** To grow well or luxuriantly; thrive. **2.** To do or fare well; prosper. **3.** To be in a period of highest productivity, excellence, or influence: *a poet who flourished in the tenth century.* **4.** To make bold, sweeping movements. *—tr.* To wield, wave, or exhibit dramatically. ❖ *n.* **1.** A dramatic or stylish movement, as of waving or brandishing. **2.** An embellishment or ornamentation: *many rhetorical flourishes.* **3.** An ostentatious act or gesture. **4.** *Music* A showy or ceremonious passage, such as a fanfare. [ME *florishen* < OFr. *florir, floriss-* < VLat. **flōrīre* < Lat. *flōrēre,* to bloom < *flōs, flōr-,* flower. See **bhel-** in App.] **—flour′ish•er** *n.*

flout (flout) *v.* **flout•ed, flout•ing, flouts** *—tr.* To show contempt for; scorn: *flouted convention.* See Usage Note at **flaunt.** *—intr.* To be scornful. ❖ *n.* A contemptuous action or remark; an insult. [Perh. < ME *flouten,* to play the flute < OFr. *flauter* < *flaute,* flute. See FLUTE.] **—flout′er** *n.* **—flout′ing•ly** *adv.*

flow (flō) *v.* **flowed, flow•ing, flows** *—intr.* **1a.** To move or run smoothly with unbroken continuity, as a fluid. **b.** To issue in a stream; pour forth: *Sap flowed from the gash in the tree.* **2.** To circulate, as the blood in the body. **3.** To move with a continual shifting of the component particles: *Wheat flowed into the bin.* **4.** To proceed steadily and easily: *The preparations flowed smoothly.* **5.** To exhibit a smooth or graceful continuity. **6.** To hang loosely and gracefully: *The cape flowed from his shoulders.* **7.** To rise. Used of the tide. **8.** To arise; derive: *Many conclusions flow from your argument.* See Syns at **stem[1]**. **9a.** To abound or teem. **b.** To stream copiously; flood: *Contributions flowed in.* **10.** To menstruate. **11.** To undergo plastic deformation without cracking or breaking. Used of rocks, metals, or minerals. *—tr.* **1.** To release as a flow. **2.** To cause to flow. ❖ *n.* **1a.** The act of flowing. **b.** The smooth motion characteristic of fluids. **2a.** A stream or current. **b.** A flood or overflow. **c.** A residual mass that has stopped flowing: *a hardened lava flow.* **3a.** A continuous output or outpouring. **b.** A continuous movement or circulation: *a flow of paperwork.* **4.** The amount that flows in a given period of time. **5.** The rising of the tide. **6.** Continuity and smoothness of appearance. **7.** A general movement or tendency. **8.** The sequence in which operations are performed. **9.** An apparent ease or effortlessness of performance. **10.** Menstrual discharge. [ME *flouen* < OE *flōwan.* See **pleu-** in App.] **—flow′ing•ly** *adv.*

flow•age (flō′ĭj) *n.* **1.** The act of flowing or overflowing. **2a.** The state of being flooded. **b.** A body of water formed by usu. deliberate flooding. **3.** An outflow or overflow. **4.** The gradual plastic deformation of a solid body, as by heat.

flow chart also **flow•chart** (flō′chärt′) *n.* A schematic representation of a sequence of operations.

flow•er (flou′ər) *n.* **1a.** The reproductive structure of some seed-bearing plants, characteristically having either specialized male or female organs or both male and female organs enclosed in an outer envelope of petals and sepals. **b.** Such a structure having showy or colorful parts; a blossom. **2.** A plant that is cultivated or appreciated for its blossoms. **3.** The condition or a time of having developed flowers. **4.** Something, such as an ornament, that resembles a flower in shape, fineness, or attractiveness. **5.** The period of highest development; the peak. **6.** The highest example or best representative. **7.** A natural development or outgrowth: *"His attitude was simply a flower of his general good nature"* (Henry James). **8. flowers** *Chemistry* A fine powder produced by condensation or sublimation of a compound. ❖ *v.* **-ered, -er•ing, -ers** *—intr.* **1.** To produce a flower or flowers; blossom. **2.** To develop naturally or fully; mature. *—tr.* To decorate with flowers or a floral pattern. [ME *flour* < OFr. *flor* < Lat. *flōs, flōr-.* See **bhel-** in App.] **—flow′er•er** *n.* **—flow′er•less** *adj.*

flow•er•age (flou′ər-ĭj) *n.* **1.** Flowers considered as a group. **2.** The process or state of flowering.

flower bug *n.* Any of a group of bugs in the family Anthocoridae, which feed on insects that infest flowers.

flower child *n. Informal* A hippie, esp. one advocating universal peace and love.

flow•er•et (flou′ər-ĭt, -ĕt) *n.* A small flower; a floret.

flower girl *n.* A young girl who carries flowers in a procession.

flower head *n.* **1.** A dense short compact cluster of sessile flowers, as of composite plants or clover. **2.** A very dense grouping of flower buds, as in broccoli and cauliflower.

flow•er•ing dogwood (flou′ər-ĭng) *n.* See **dogwood.**

flowering maple *n.* Any of various tropical plants of the genus *Abutilon,* having lobed leaves like those of the maple.

flowering plant *n.* A plant that produces flowers and fruit; an angiosperm.

flowering quince *n.* Any of several shrubs of the genus *Chaenomeles,* native to Asia and having spiny branches and red or pink flowers.

flower people *pl.n. Informal* Flower children.

flow•er•pot (flou′ər-pŏt′) *n.* A pot in which plants are grown.

flow•er•y (flou′ə-rē) *adj.* **-i•er, -i•est 1.** Of, relating to, or suggestive of flowers. **2.** Abounding in or covered with flowers. **3.** Full of ornate or grandiloquent expressions; highly embellished: *a flowery speech.* **—flow′er•i•ness** *n.*

flow meter *n.* An instrument for monitoring, measuring, or recording the rate of flow, pressure, or discharge of a fluid.

flown[1] (flōn) *v.* Past participle of **fly[1]**.

flown[2] (flōn) *adj. Archaic* Filled to excess. [Obs. p. part. of FLOW.]

flow•stone (flō′stōn′) *n.* A layered deposit of calcium carbonate on rock where water has flowed or dripped.

fl. oz. *abbr.* fluid ounce

flu (flo͞o) *n. Informal* Influenza. [Short for INFLUENZA.]

flub (flŭb) *Informal tr.v.* **flubbed, flub•bing, flubs** To botch; bungle. ❖ *n.* The act or an instance of botching or bungling. [?] **—flub′ber** *n.*

flub•dub (flŭb′dŭb′) *n. Informal* Pretentious nonsense; bunkum. [?]

fluc•tu•ate (flŭk′cho͞o-āt′) *v.* **-at•ed, -at•ing, -ates** *—intr.* **1.** To vary irregularly. **2.** To rise and fall in or as if in waves; undulate. *—tr.* To cause to fluctuate. [Lat. *flūctuāre, flūctuāt-* < *flūctus,* a flowing < p. part. of *fluere,* to flow.] **—fluc′tu•ant** (-ənt) *adj.* **—fluc′tu•a′tion** *n.*

flue[1] (flo͞o) *n.* **1.** A pipe, tube, or channel for conveying hot air, gas, steam, or smoke, as from a furnace or fireplace to a chimney. **2.** *Music* **a.** An organ pipe sounded by means of an air current striking a lip in the side of the pipe and causing the air within to vibrate. **b.** The lipped opening in such a pipe. [?]

flue[2] (flo͞o) *n.* A fishing net. [ME < MDu. *vlūwe.* See **pleu-** in App.]

flu•ent (flo͞o′ənt) *adj.* **1a.** Able to express oneself readily and effortlessly. **b.** Flowing effortlessly; polished: *fluent Russian.* **2.** Flowing or moving smoothly; graceful. **3.** Flowing or capable of flowing; fluid. [Lat. *fluēns, fluent-,* pr. part. of *fluere,* to flow.] **—flu′en•cy** *n.* **—flu′ent•ly** *adv.*

flue pipe *n. Music* An organ pipe with a lipped opening; a flue.

flue stop *n. Music* An organ stop controlling a set of flue pipes.

fluff (flŭf) *n.* **1.** Light down or fuzz, as on a young bird. **2.** Something having a very light, soft, or frothy consistency or appearance. **3.** Something of little substance or consequence, esp.: **a.** Light or superficial entertainment. **b.** Inflated or padded material. **4.** The nonrecyclable, nonmetal parts of a junked car. **5.** *Informal* An error, esp. in the delivery of lines, as by an actor. ❖ *v.* **fluffed, fluff•ing, fluffs** *—tr.* **1.** To make fluffy. **2.** *Informal* **a.** To ruin or mar by a mistake or blunder. **b.** To forget or botch (one's lines). *—intr.* **1.** To become fluffy. **2.** *Informal* To make an error, esp. in the delivery of lines. [?]

fluff•y (flŭf′ē) *adj.* **-i•er, -i•est 1a.** Of, relating to, or resembling fluff. **b.** Covered with fluff. **2.** Light and airy; soft: *a fluffy soufflé.* **3a.** Light or frivolous. **b.** Lacking depth or precision; fuzzy. **—fluff′i•ly** *adv.* **—fluff′i•ness** *n.*

flu•gel•horn or **flue•gel•horn** (flo͞o′gəl-hôrn′, flü′-) or **flü•gel•horn** (flü′-) *n.* A bugle with valves, similar to the cornet but having a wider bore. [Ger. *Flügelhorn,* flank horn (used to summon flanks in battle) : *Flügel,* wing, flank (< MHGer. *vlügel;* see **pleu-** in App.) + *Horn,* horn (< MHGer. < OHGer.; see **ker-[1]** in App.).] **—flü′gel•horn′ist** *n.*

flu•id (flo͞o′ĭd) *n.* A continuous amorphous substance whose molecules move freely past one another and that assumes the shape of its container; a liquid or gas. ❖ *adj.* **1.** Of, relating to, or characteristic of a fluid. **2.** Readily reshaped; pliable. **3.** Smooth and flowing; graceful. **4a.** Changing or tending to change; variable. **b.** Characterized by or allowing social mobility. **5.** Convertible into cash: *fluid assets.* [< ME, flowing < OFr. *fluide* < Lat. *fluidus* < *fluere,* to flow.] **—flu•id′i•ty** (-ĭd′ĭ-tē), **flu′id•ness** *n.* **—flu′id•ly** *adv.*

fluid dram *n.* A unit of volume or capacity in the apothecary system, equal to ⅛ of a fluid ounce (3.70 milliliters).

fluid drive *n.* An automotive transmission coupling that provides a smooth start, consisting of two separate turbines that rotate on the same axis in a surrounding liquid.

fluid dynamics *n.* (*used with a sing. verb*) The branch of science concerned with gases and liquids in motion.

flu•id•ex•tract (flo͞o′ĭd-ĕk′străkt′) *n.* A concentrated alcohol solution of a drug of such strength that each milliliter is the equivalent of one gram of the dry form of the drug.

flu•id•ic (flo͞o-ĭd′ĭk) *adj.* **1.** Of, relating to, or characteristic of a fluid. **2.** Relating to or controlled by fluidics.

flu•id•ics (flo͞o-ĭd′ĭks) *n.* (*used with a sing. verb*) The technology of using the flows and pressures of fluids in sensing, control, and information-processing systems with no moving parts.

flu•id•ize (flo͞o′ĭ-dīz′) *tr.v.* **-ized, -iz•ing, -iz•es 1.** To make fluid. **2.** To pulverize (a solid) so finely that it takes on most of the properties of a fluid. **—flu′id•i•za′tion** (-ĭ-dĭ-zā′shən) *n.*

fluid mechanics *n.* (*used with a sing. verb*) The branch of me-

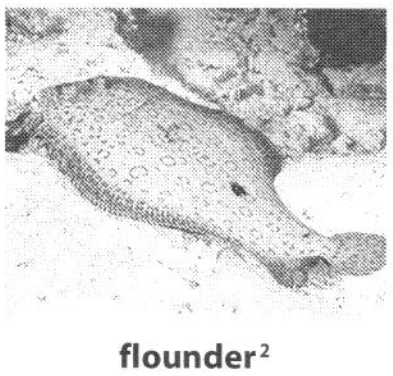

flounder[2]
peacock flounder
Bothus lunatus

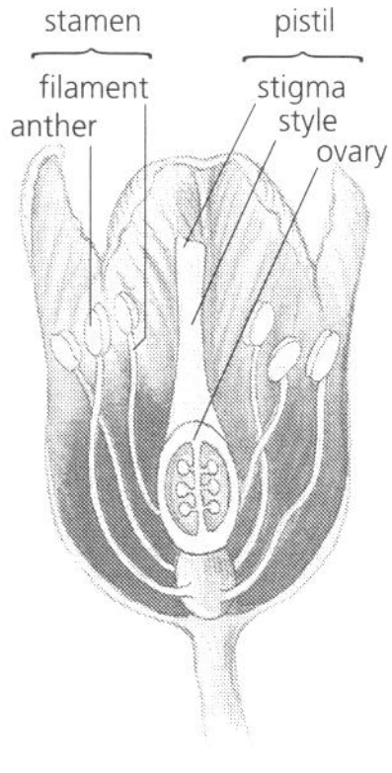
stamen
pistil
filament
anther
stigma
style
ovary

flower

ă	pat	oi	boy
ā	pay	ou	out
âr	care	o͝o	took
ä	father	o͞o	boot
ĕ	pet	ŭ	cut
ē	be	ûr	urge
ĭ	pit	th	thin
ī	pie	*th*	this
îr	pier	hw	which
ŏ	pot	zh	vision
ō	toe	ə	about, item
ô	paw		

Stress marks:
′ (primary);
′ (secondary), as in
lexicon (lĕk′sĭ-kŏn′)

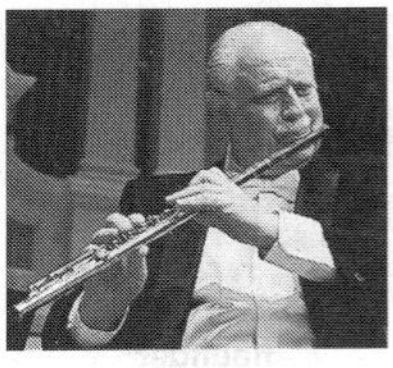

flute

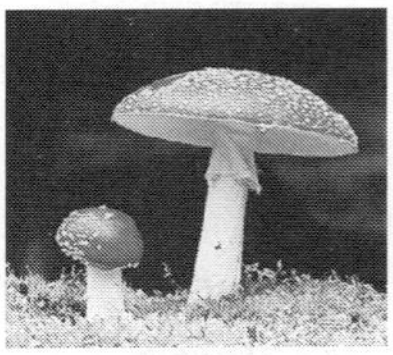

fly agaric
Amanita muscaria

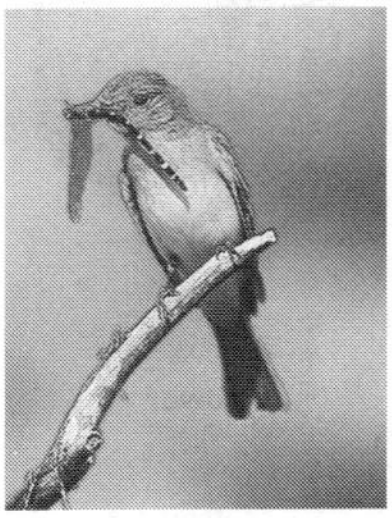

flycatcher
great crested flycatcher
Myiarchus crinitus

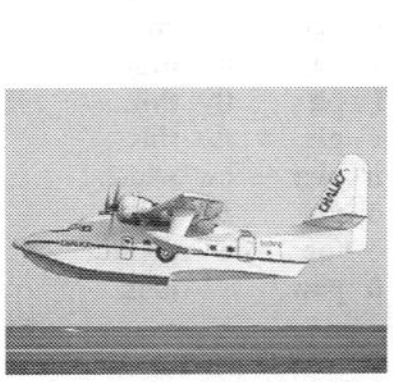

flying boat

chanics concerned with the properties of gases and liquids.

fluid ounce *n.* **1.** A unit of volume or capacity in the US Customary System, used in liquid measure, equal to 29.57 milliliters (1.804 cubic inches). **2.** A unit of volume or capacity in the British Imperial System, used in liquid and dry measure, equal to 28.41 milliliters (1.734 cubic inches).

fluke[1] (flo͞ok) *n.* **1.** Any of various flatfishes, esp. a flounder of the genus *Paralichthys.* **2.** See **trematode.** [ME < OE *flōc.* See **plāk-**[1] in App.]

fluke[2] (flo͞ok) *n.* **1.** *Nautical* The triangular blade at the end of an arm of an anchor, designed to catch in the ground. **2.** A barb or barbed head, as on an arrow. **3.** Either of the two horizontally flattened divisions of a whale's tail. [Poss. < FLUKE[1].]

fluke[3] (flo͞ok) *n.* **1.** A stroke of good luck. **2.** A chance occurrence; an accident. **3.** *Games* An accidentally good or successful stroke in billiards or pool. [?]

fluk•y also **fluk•ey** (flo͞o′kē) *adj.* **-i•er, -i•est 1.** Resulting from or depending on mere chance. **2.** Constantly shifting; uncertain. [< FLUKE[3].] **—fluk′i•ly** *adv.* **—fluk′i•ness** *n.*

flume (flo͞om) *n.* **1.** A narrow gorge, usu. with a stream flowing through it. **2.** An open artificial channel or chute carrying a stream of water, as for conveying logs. **3.** A small swimming pool designed with a propeller or pump to generate a current, allowing a swimmer to swim in place. [ME *flum,* river < OFr. < Lat. *flūmen* < *fluere,* to flow.]

flum•mer•y (flŭm′ə-rē) *n., pl.* **-ies 1.** Meaningless or deceptive language; humbug. **2a.** Any of several soft, sweet, bland foods, such as custard. **b.** A sweet gelatinous pudding made by straining boiled oatmeal or flour. **c.** A soft dessert of stewed, thickened fruit, often mixed with a grain such as rice. [Welsh *llymru,* soft jelly from sour oatmeal.]

flum•mox (flŭm′əks) *tr.v.* **-moxed, -mox•ing, -mox•es** *Informal* To confuse; perplex. [Prob. of E. dialectal orig.]

flung (flŭng) *v.* Past tense and past participle of **fling.**

flu•ni•traz•e•pam (flo͞o′nī-trăz′ə-păm) *n.* An illegal sedative drug, $C_{16}H_{12}FN_3O_3$, known for its use as a date-rape drug. [FLU(ORO)– + NITR(O)– + (DI)AZEPAM.]

flunk (flŭngk) *Informal v.* **flunked, flunk•ing, flunks** *—intr.* To fail, esp. in a course or an examination. *—tr.* **1.** To fail (an examination or course). **2.** To give a failing grade to. ❖ *n.* **1.** The act or an instance of flunking. **2.** A failing grade. ***—phrasal verb:* flunk out** To expel or be expelled from a school or course because of work below standard. [?] **—flunk′er** *n.*

flun•ky also **flun•key** (flŭng′kē) *n., pl.* **-kies** also **-keys 1.** A person of slavish or unquestioning obedience; a lackey. **2.** One who does menial or trivial work; a drudge. **3.** A liveried manservant. [Sc., perh. < FLANKER, an attendant at one's flank.] **—flun′ky•ism** *n.*

flu•or (flo͞o′ôr′, -ər) *n.* See **fluorite.** [NLat., mineral belonging to a group used as fluxes < Lat., a flowing < *fluere,* to flow.]

fluor– *pref.* Variant of **fluoro–.**

fluo•resce (flo͞o-rĕs′, flô-, flō-) *intr.v.* **-resced, -resc•ing, -resc•es** To undergo, produce, or show fluorescence. [Back-formation < FLUORESCENCE.] **—fluo•resc′er** *n.*

fluo•res•ce•in (flo͞o-rĕs′ē-ĭn, flô-, flō-) *n.* A compound, $C_{20}H_{12}O_5$, that exhibits intense fluorescence in alkaline solution and is used in medicine and to trace water flow.

fluo•res•cence (flo͞o-rĕs′əns, flô-, flō-) *n.* **1.** The emission of electromagnetic radiation, esp. of visible light, stimulated in a substance by the absorption of incident radiation and persisting only as long as the stimulating radiation is continued. **2.** The property of emitting such radiation. **3.** The radiation so emitted. [FLUOR(SPAR) + –ESCENCE.]

fluo•res•cent (flo͞o-rĕs′ənt, flô-, flō-) *adj.* **1a.** Of or relating to fluorescence. **b.** Exhibiting or produced by fluorescence: *fluorescent plankton.* **2.** Glowing as if with fluorescence; vivid: *fluorescent colors.* ❖ *n.* A fluorescent lamp.

fluorescent lamp *n.* A lamp that produces visible light by fluorescence, esp. a glass tube whose inner wall is coated with a material that fluoresces when an electrical current causes a vapor within the tube to discharge electrons.

fluor•i•date (flo͝or′ĭ-dāt′, flôr′-, flōr′-) *tr.v.* **-dat•ed, -dat•ing, -dates** To add a fluorine compound to (a drinking water supply, for example) for the purpose of reducing tooth decay. **—fluor′i•da′tion** *n.*

fluor•ide (flo͝or′īd′, flôr′-, flōr′-) *n.* A binary compound of fluorine with another element. [FLUOR(INE) + –IDE.]

fluor•i•na•tion (flo͝or′ĭ-nā′shən, flôr′-, flōr′-) *n.* A chemical reaction that introduces fluorine into a compound.

fluor•ine (flo͝or′ēn′, -ĭn, flôr′-, flōr′-) *n. Symbol* **F** A highly corrosive poisonous gaseous halogen element, the most reactive of all the elements, used in a wide variety of industrially important compounds. Atomic number 9; atomic weight 18.9984; melting point −223°C; boiling point −188.14°C; specific gravity of liquid 1.108 (at boiling point); valence 1. See table at **element.**

fluor•ite (flo͝or′īt′, flôr′-, flōr′-) *n.* A mineral, CaF_2, that is often fluorescent in ultraviolet light.

fluoro– or **fluor–** *pref.* **1.** Fluorine: *fluorosis.* **2.** Fluorescence: *fluoroscope.* [< FLUORINE and < FLUOR.]

fluor•o•car•bon (flo͝or′ō-kär′bən, flôr′-, flōr′-) *n.* An inert liquid or gaseous halocarbon compound in which fluorine replaces some or all hydrogen atoms, used in aerosol propellants and refrigerants and in making plastics and resins.

fluor•o•chem•i•cal (flo͝or′ō-kĕm′ĭ-kəl, flôr′-, flōr′-) *n.* A chemical compound containing fluorine, esp. a fluorocarbon.

fluor•o•chrome (flo͝or′ə-krōm′, flôr′-, flōr′-) *n.* Any of a group of fluorescent dyes used to stain biological specimens.

fluo•rog•ra•phy (flo͞o-rŏg′rə-fē, flô-, flō-) *n.* See **photofluorography.**

fluo•rom•e•ter (flo͞o-rŏm′ĭ-tər, flô-, flō-) *n.* An instrument to detect and measure fluorescence. **—fluo•rom′e•try** *n.*

fluor•o•scope (flo͝or′ə-skōp′, flôr′-, flōr′-) *n.* An x-ray device equipped with a fluorescent screen on which the internal structures of an optically opaque object may be continuously viewed as shadowy images. ❖ *tr.v.* **-scoped, -scop•ing, -scopes** To examine the interior of (an object) with a fluoroscope. **—fluor′o•scop′ic** (-skŏp′ĭk) *adj.*

fluo•ros•co•py (flo͞o-rŏs′kə-pē, flô-, flō-) *n., pl.* **-pies** Examination by means of a fluoroscope. **—fluo•ros′co•pist** *n.*

fluo•ro•sis (flo͞o-rō′sĭs, flô-, flō-) *n.* An abnormal condition caused by excessive intake of fluorine, characterized chiefly by mottling of the teeth. **—fluo•rot′ic** (-rŏt′ĭk) *adj.*

fluor•o•u•ra•cil (flo͝or′ō-yo͝or′ə-sĭl, flôr′-, flōr′-) *n.* An antineoplastic agent, $C_4H_3FN_2O_2$, used esp. in the treatment of cancers of the skin, breast, and digestive system.

flu•or•spar (flo͞o′ər-spär′, flo͝or′spär′) *n.* See **fluorite.**

flu•ox•e•tine hydrochloride (flo͞o′ŏk′sĭ-tēn′) *n.* An oral antidepressant that enhances the activity of serotonin in the central nervous system. [Prob. FLU(ORO)– + alteration of OXY– + T(OLYL) + (AM)INE.]

flur•ry (flûr′ē, flŭr′ē) *n., pl.* **-ries 1.** A brief light snowfall. **2a.** A sudden gust of wind. **b.** A stirring mass, as of dust; a shower. **3.** A sudden burst or commotion; a stir. **4.** A short period of active trading, as on a stock exchange. ❖ *v.* **-ried, -ry•ing, -ries** *—tr.* To agitate, stir, or confuse. *—intr.* To move or come down in a flurry. [Perh. < *flurr,* to scatter.]

flush[1] (flŭsh) *v.* **flushed, flush•ing, flush•es** *—intr.* **1.** To turn red, as from fever, embarrassment, or strong emotion; blush. **2.** To glow, esp. with a reddish color. **3.** To flow suddenly and abundantly, as from containment; flood. **4.** To be emptied or cleaned by a rapid flow of water, as a toilet. *—tr.* **1.** To cause to redden or glow. **2.** To excite or elate. **3a.** To clean, rinse, or empty with a rapid flow of a liquid, esp. water. **b.** To remove or eliminate by or as if by flushing. ❖ *n.* **1a.** A flooding flow or rush, as of water. **b.** The act of cleaning or rinsing by or as if by flushing. **2.** A blush or glow. **3a.** A reddening of the skin, as with fever or exertion. **b.** A brief sensation of heat over all or part of the body. **4.** A rush of strong feeling. **5.** A state of freshness or vigor. ❖ *adj.* **flush•er, flush•est 1.** Having a healthy reddish color; flushed. **2.** Having an abundant supply of money; affluent. **3.** Marked by abundance; plentiful. **4.** Swelling; overflowing. **5a.** Having surfaces in the same plane; even. **b.** Arranged with adjacent sides, surfaces, or edges close together. **c.** *Printing* Aligned evenly with a margin, as along an edge of a typeset page; not indented. **6.** Direct, straightforward, or solid. **7.** Designed to be emptied or cleaned by flushing. ❖ *adv.* **1.** So as to be even, in one plane, or aligned with a margin. **2.** Squarely or solidly. [Prob. < FLUSH[3], to dart out.] **—flush′er** *n.* **—flush′ness** *n.*

flush[2] (flŭsh) *n. Games* A hand in which all the cards are of the same suit but not in numerical sequence. [Fr. *flux, flus* < OFr. *flux* < Lat. *flūxus,* flux. See FLUX.]

flush[3] (flŭsh) *v.* **flushed, flush•ing, flush•es** *—tr.* **1.** To frighten (a game bird, for example) from cover. **2.** To drive or force into the open. *—intr.* To dart out or fly from cover. ❖ *n.* A bird or flock of birds that has been frightened from cover. [ME *flusshen.*]

Flush•ing (flŭsh′ĭng) **1.** A section of New York City in N Queens on W Long I.; site of two world's fairs (1939–40 and 1964–65). **2.** See **Vlissingen.**

flus•ter (flŭs′tər) *tr. & intr.v.* **-tered, -ter•ing, -ters** To make or become nervous or upset. ❖ *n.* A state of agitation, confusion, or excitement: *traffic that put the driver in a fluster.* [< ME *flostring,* agitation, prob. of Scand. orig. See **pleu-** in App.]

flute (flo͞ot) *n.* **1.** *Music* **a.** A high-pitched woodwind instrument consisting of a slender tube closed at one end with keys and finger holes on the side and an opening near the closed end across which the breath is blown. **b.** Any of various similar reedless woodwind instruments, such as the recorder. **2a.** *Architecture* A long, usu. rounded groove incised as a decorative motif on the shaft of a column, for example. **b.** A similar groove or furrow, as on a piece of furniture. **3.** A tall narrow wineglass. ❖ *v.* **flut•ed, flut•ing, flutes** *—tr.* **1.** *Music* To play (a tune) on a flute. **2.** To produce in a flutelike tone. **3.** To make flutes in (a column, for example). *—intr.* **1.** *Music* To play a flute. **2.** To sing, whistle, or speak with a flutelike tone. [ME *floute* < OFr. *flaute* < O Provençal *flaüt,* perh. a blend of *flaujol,* flageolet (< VLat. **flābeolum;* see FLAGEOLET) and *laut,* lute; see LUTE[1].] **—flut′er** *n.* **—flut′ey, flut′y** *adj.*

flut•ing (flo͞o′tĭng) *n.* **1a.** *Architecture* A decorative motif consisting of a series of uniform, usu. vertical flutes. **b.** The act of incising or making grooves. **2.** The grooves formed by narrow pleats in cloth.

flut•ist (flo͞o′tĭst) *n.* One who plays the flute.

flut•ter (flŭt′ər) *v.* **-tered, -ter•ing, -ters** *—intr.* **1.** To wave or flap rapidly in an irregular manner: *curtains that fluttered in the breeze.* **2a.** To fly by a quick light flapping of the wings. **b.** To flap the wings without flying. **3.** To move or fall in a manner suggestive of tremulous flight. **4.** To vibrate or beat rapidly or erratically. **5.** To move quickly in a nervous, restless, or excited fashion; flit. *—tr.* To cause to flutter. ❖ *n.* **1.** The act of fluttering. **2.** A condition of nervous excitement or agitation. **3.** A commotion; a stir. **4.** *Pathology* Abnormally rapid pulsation, esp. of the atria or ventricles of the heart. **5.** Rapid fluctuation in the pitch of a sound reproduction resulting from variations in the speed of the recording or reproducing equipment. **6.** *Chiefly British* A small bet; a gamble. [ME *floteren* < OE *floterian.* See **pleu-** in App.] **—flut′ter•er** *n.* **—flut′ter•y** *adj.*

flutter kick *n.* A swimming kick used in crawl and backstroke in which the legs are extended straight back and alternately moved up and down.

flu•vi•al (flo͞o′vē-əl) *adj.* **1.** Of, relating to, or inhabiting a river or stream. **2.** Produced by the action of a river or stream. [ME < Lat. *fluviālis* < *fluvius,* river < *fluere,* to flow.]

flu•vi•a•tile (flo͞o′vē-ə-tīl′) *adj.* Fluvial. [Fr. < Lat. *fluviātilis* < *fluvius,* river. See FLUVIAL.]

flux (flŭks) *n.* **1a.** A flow or flowing. **b.** A continued flow; a flood. **2.** The flowing in of the tide. **3.** *Medicine* The discharge of large quantities of fluid material from the body, esp. the discharge of watery feces from the intestines. **4.** *Physics* **a.** The rate of flow of fluid, particles, or energy through a given surface. **b.** See **flux density. c.** The lines of force of an electric or magnetic field. **5.** Constant or frequent change; fluctuation. **6.** *Chemistry & Metallurgy* A substance that aids, induces, or otherwise actively participates in fusing or flowing, as: **a.** A substance applied to a surface to be joined by welding, soldering, or brazing. **b.** A mineral added to the metals in a furnace to promote fusing. **c.** An additive that improves the flow of plastics during fabrication. **d.** A readily fusible glass or enamel used as a base in ceramic work. ❖ *v.* **fluxed, flux•ing, flux•es** *—tr.* **1.** To melt; fuse. **2.** To apply a flux to. *—intr.* **1.** To become fluid. **2.** To flow; stream. [ME < OFr. < Lat. *flūxus* < p. part. of *fluere,* to flow.]

flux density *n.* *Physics* Flux per unit area.

flux gate *n.* *Physics* A detector used to indicate the direction of the earth's magnetic field.

flux•ion (flŭk′shən) *n.* **1a.** A flow or flowing. **b.** Continual change. **2.** *Archaic* **a.** See **derivative** 3. **b. fluxions** Differential calculus. [Fr. < LLat. *flūxiō, flūxiōn-* < Lat. *flūxus,* flux. See FLUX.] **—flux′ion•al, flux′ion•ar′y** (flŭk′shə-nĕr′ē) *adj.* **—flux′ion•al•ly** *adv.*

fly[1] (flī) *v.* **flew** (flo͞o), **flown** (flōn), **fly•ing, flies** (flīz) *—intr.* **1.** To engage in flight, esp.: **a.** To move through the air by means of wings or winglike parts. **b.** To travel by air. **c.** To operate an aircraft or spacecraft. **2a.** To rise in or be carried through the air by the wind. **b.** To float or flap in the air. **3.** To move or be sent through the air with great speed. **4a.** To move with great speed; rush or dart. **b.** To flee; escape. **c.** To hasten; spring. **5.** To pass by swiftly. **6.** To be dissipated; vanish. **7.** *past tense and past participle* **flied** (flīd) *Baseball* To hit a fly ball. **8.** To undergo an explosive reaction; burst: *The dropped dish flew into pieces.* **9.** *Informal* To gain acceptance or approval; go over. *—tr.* **1a.** To cause to fly or float in the air. **b.** *Nautical* To operate under (a particular flag). **2a.** To pilot (an aircraft or spacecraft). **b.** To carry or transport in an aircraft or spacecraft. **c.** To pass over or through in flight. **d.** To perform in a spacecraft or aircraft. **3a.** To flee or run from. **b.** To avoid; shun. ❖ *n., pl.* **flies 1.** The act of flying; flight. **2a.** A fold of cloth that covers a fastening of a garment, esp. one on the front of trousers. **b.** The fastening or opening covered by such a fold. **3.** A flap that covers an entrance or forms a rooflike extension for a tent or the canopy of a vehicle. **4.** A flyleaf. **5.** *Baseball* A fly ball. **6a.** The span of a flag from the staff to the outer edge. **b.** The outer edge of a flag. **7.** A flywheel. **8. flies** The area directly over the stage of a theater, containing overhead lights, drop curtains, and equipment for raising and lowering sets. **9.** *Chiefly British* A one-horse carriage, esp. one for hire. ***—phrasal verb:*** **fly at** To attack fiercely; assault. ***—idioms:*** **fly high** To be elated. **fly off the handle** *Informal* To become suddenly enraged. **let fly 1.** To shoot, hurl, or release. **2.** To lash out; assault. **on the fly 1.** On the run; in a hurry. **2.** While in the air; in flight. [ME *flien* < OE *flēogan.* See **pleu-** in App.] **—fly′a•ble** *adj.*

fly[2] (flī) *n., pl.* **flies 1a.** Any of numerous two-winged insects of the order Diptera, esp. any of the family Muscidae, which includes the housefly. **b.** Any of various other flying insects, such as the caddis fly. **2.** A fishing lure simulating a fly. ***—idiom:*** **fly in the ointment** A detrimental circumstance or detail; a drawback. [ME *flie* < OE *flēoge.* See **pleu-** in App.]

fly[3] (flī) *adj.* **1.** *Chiefly British* Mentally alert; sharp. **2.** *Slang* Fashionable; stylish. [Prob. < FLY[1].]

fly agaric *n.* A poisonous mushroom *(Amanita muscaria)* usu. having a red or orange cap with white gills and patches.

fly ash *n.* Fine particulate ash sent up by the combustion of a solid fuel, such as coal, and discharged as an airborne emission or recovered as a byproduct for various commercial uses.

fly•a•way (flī′ə-wā′) *adj.* **1.** Made or worn loose or draped, as to allow or suggest fluttering in the wind. **2a.** Prepared for immediate flight. **b.** Designed for air travel. **3.** Given to frivolity; flighty.

fly ball *n.* *Baseball* A ball that is batted in a high arc.

fly•blow (flī′blō′) *n.* The egg or larva of a blowfly, usu. deposited on meat. ❖ *tr.v.* **-blew** (-blo͞o′), **-blown** (-blōn′), **-blow•ing, -blows 1.** To deposit flyblows on. **2.** To contaminate; taint.

fly•blown (flī′blōn′) *adj.* **1.** Contaminated with flyblows. **2a.** Tainted; corrupt. **b.** Dirty or rundown; squalid.

fly book *n.* A case for carrying flies for fishing.

fly•boy or **fly-boy** (flī′boi′) *n.* *Slang* A member of an air force, esp. a pilot.

fly bridge *n.* See **flying bridge.**

fly•by also **fly-by** (flī′bī′) *n., pl.* **-bys** A flight passing close to a specified target or position.

fly-by-night (flī′bī-nīt′) *Informal adj.* **1.** Unreliable or unscrupulous, esp. with regard to business dealings. **2.** Of an impermanent or insubstantial nature. ❖ *n.* also **fly-by-night•er** (-nī′tər) **1.** An unscrupulous or undependable person, esp. one who leaves secretly without paying creditors. **2.** Something shaky or impermanent.

fly-cast (flī′kăst′) *intr.v.* **-cast, -cast•ing, -casts** To cast artificial flies with a fly rod, as in fishing. **—fly′-cast′er** *n.*

fly•catch•er (flī′kăch′ər, -kĕch′-) *n.* **1.** Any of various Eurasian birds of the family Muscicapidae that feed on insects, usu. catching them in flight. **2.** Any of various similar American birds of the family Tyrannidae.

fly•er (flī′ər) *n.* Variant of **flier.**

fly-fish (flī′fĭsh′) *intr.v.* **-fish, -fish•ing, -fish•es** To fish using artificial flies for bait and usu. a fly rod for casting. **—fly′-fish′er•man, fly′-fish′er** *n.*

fly gallery *n.* A narrow elevated platform at the side of the stage in a theater, from which a stagehand works the ropes controlling equipment in the flies.

fly•ing (flī′ĭng) *adj.* **1.** Of or relating to aviation. **2.** Capable of or engaged in flight: *a flying mammal.* **3.** Situated, extending, or functioning in the air. **4a.** Swiftly moving; fleet. **b.** Done or performed swiftly in or as if in the air. **5.** Brief; hurried. **6.** Capable of swift deployment or response. **7.** *Nautical* Not secured by spars or stays. Used of a sail. ❖ *n.* **1.** Flight in an aircraft or spacecraft. **2.** The piloting or navigation of an aircraft or spacecraft. ***—idiom:*** **with flying colors** With complete or outstanding success.

flying boat *n.* A large seaplane that floats on its hull.

flying bomb *n.* See **robot bomb.**

flying bridge *n.* A small, usu. open platform located above the main bridge, as on a powerboat, equipped with a secondary set of navigational controls.

flying buttress *n.* An arched masonry support serving to bear thrust, as from a roof or vault, away from a main structure to an outer pier or buttress.

flying dragon *n.* See **flying lizard.**

Flying Dutchman *n.* **1.** A spectral ship said to appear in storms near the Cape of Good Hope. **2.** The captain of this ship, condemned to sail the seas until Judgment Day.

flying field *n.* A graded field on which airplanes may land and take off.

flying fish *n.* Any of various marine fishes of the family Exocoetidae, having enlarged winglike pectoral fins capable of sustaining it in brief gliding flight over the water.

flying fox *n.* Any of various fruit-eating bats of the suborder Megachiroptera, chiefly inhabiting tropical Africa, Asia, and Australia and having a foxlike muzzle and small pointed ears.

flying frog *n.* Either of two arboreal frogs *(Rhacophorus reinwardtii* or *R. nigropalmatus)* of southeast Asia, having toes connected by webbing and capable of making long leaps.

flying gurnard *n.* Any of various chiefly tropical marine fishes of the family Dactylopteridae, having greatly enlarged winglike pectoral fins that facilitate gliding through the water.

flying jib *n.* A light sail set forward of the outermost jib and attached to an extension of the jib boom.

flying lemur *n.* Either of two arboreal mammals, *Cynocephalus volans* of the Philippines or *C. variegatus* of southeast Asia, that are sustained in gliding leaps by a wide fur-covered membrane extending from each side of the body.

flying lizard *n.* Any of various small tropical Asian lizards of the genus *Draco,* having winglike membranes that enable it to glide through the air.

flying machine *n.* A machine designed for flight, esp. an early experimental type of aircraft.

flying mare *n.* A wrestling throw in which one grabs one's opponent's wrist, turns one's back to the opponent, and flips the opponent over one's shoulder onto the ground.

flying phalanger *n.* Any of several marsupials of the family Petauridae, esp. one of the genus *Petaurus,* of Australia, New Guinea, and Tasmania, having folds of skin between the forelegs and hind legs that enable it to glide through the air.

flying saucer *n.* Any of various unidentified flying objects of presumed extraterrestrial origin, typically described as luminous moving disks.

flying squad *n.* *Chiefly British* A small mobile unit, esp. of mo-

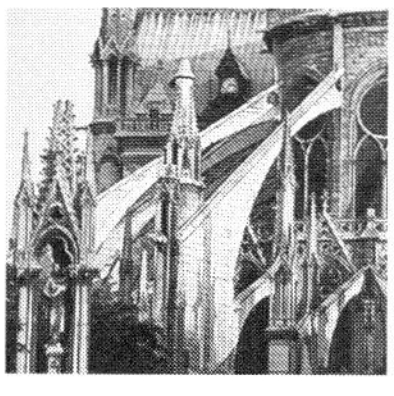

flying buttress
Notre Dame Cathedral, Paris

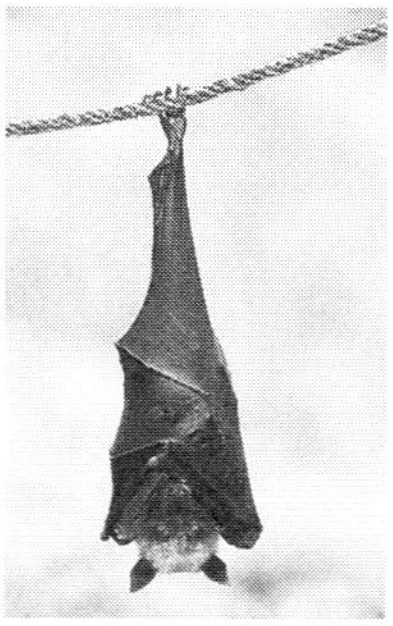

flying fox

ă	pat	oi	boy
ā	pay	ou	out
âr	care	o͝o	took
ä	father	o͞o	boot
ĕ	pet	ŭ	cut
ē	be	ûr	urge
ĭ	pit	th	thin
ī	pie	*th*	this
îr	pier	hw	which
ŏ	pot	zh	vision
ō	toe	ə	about,
ô	paw		item

Stress marks:
′ (primary);
′ (secondary), as in
lexicon (lĕk′sĭ-kŏn′)

torized police, capable of moving quickly into action.

flying squirrel *n.* Any of various nocturnal squirrels of the genera *Pteromys, Petaurista, Glaucomys,* and related genera, having membranes along each side of the body between the forelegs and hind legs that enable it to glide between trees.

flying start *n.* **1.** *Sports* A racing start in which the contestants are already moving when they cross the starting line. **2.** A quick or auspicious beginning.

flying wedge *n.* A moving wedge-shaped formation, as of police, used esp. for penetrating crowds.

fly·leaf (flī′lēf′) *n.* A blank or specially printed leaf at the beginning or end of a book.

fly·o·ver (flī′ō′vər) *n.* **1.** A flight over a specific location, usu. at low altitude, as by a formation of military aircraft. **2.** *Chiefly British* An overpass, as on a highway.

fly·pa·per (flī′pā′pər) *n.* Paper coated with a sticky, sometimes poisonous substance, used to catch flies.

Fly River A river, c. 1,046 km (650 mi), rising in W Papua New Guinea and flowing SE to the Gulf of Papua.

fly rod *n.* A long flexible fishing rod used in fly-fishing.

fly·sheet (flī′shēt′) *n.* A printed sheet or pamphlet; a handbill.

fly·speck (flī′spĕk′) *n.* **1.** A small dark speck or stain made by the excrement of a fly. **2.** A minute or insignificant spot. ❖ *tr.v.* **-specked, -speck·ing, -specks** **1.** To mark or foul with flyspecks. **2.** *Slang* To examine closely.

fly swat *n. Chiefly Southern US* See **fly swatter**.

fly swatter *n.* An implement used to kill insects, usu. consisting of a piece of plastic or wire mesh attached to a long handle.

fly·trap (flī′trăp′) *n.* **1.** A trap for catching flies. **2.** An insectivorous plant, such as the Venus flytrap.

fly-ty·ing (flī′tī′ing) *n.* The art or hobby of making artificial fishing flies. **—fly′-ti′er** (-tī′ər) *n.*

fly·way (flī′wā′) *n.* A seasonal route followed by birds migrating to and from their breeding areas.

fly·weight (flī′wāt′) *n.* **1.** A professional boxer weighing no more than 112 pounds (approx. 51 kilograms), lighter than a bantamweight. **2.** A contestant in various other sports in the lightest weight class. **—fly′weight′** *adj.*

fly·wheel (flī′hwēl′, -wēl′) *n.* **1.** A heavy-rimmed rotating wheel used to minimize variations in angular velocity and revolutions per minute, as in a machine subject to fluctuation in drive and load. **2.** An analogous device, esp. one used to regulate the speed of clockwork.

Fm The symbol for the element **fermium**.

FM *abbr.* **1.** field manual **2.** field marshal **3.** frequency modulation

fm. *abbr.* fathom

FMB *abbr.* Federal Maritime Board

FMS *abbr.* **1.** false-memory syndrome **2.** fibromyalgia syndrome

FN *abbr.* foreign national

fn. *abbr.* footnote

FNMA *abbr.* Federal National Mortgage Association

f-num·ber (ĕf′nŭm′bər) *n.* The ratio of the focal length of a lens or lens system to the effective diameter of its aperture. [F(OCAL LENGTH) + NUMBER.]

Fo (fō), **Dario** b. 1926. Italian playwright whose works include *Trumpets and Raspberries* (1981). He won the Nobel Prize for literature in 1997.

FO *abbr.* **1.** field-grade officer **2.** field order **3.** finance officer **4.** flight officer **5.** foreign office

foal (fōl) *n.* The young offspring of a horse or other equine animal, esp. one under a year old. ❖ *intr.v.* **foaled, foal·ing, foals** To give birth to a foal. [ME *fole* < OE *fola.*]

foam (fōm) *n.* **1a.** A mass of bubbles of air or gas in a matrix of liquid film, esp. an accumulation of fine frothy bubbles formed in or on the surface of a liquid, as from agitation or fermentation. **b.** A thick chemical froth, such as shaving cream. **2a.** Frothy saliva produced esp. as a result of physical exertion or a pathological condition. **b.** The frothy sweat of a horse or other equine animal. **3.** The sea. **4.** Any of various light porous semirigid or spongy materials used for thermal insulation or shock absorption. ❖ *v.* **foamed, foam·ing, foams** **—intr.** **1.** To produce or issue as foam; froth. **2.** To produce foam from the mouth, as from exertion or a pathological condition. **—tr.** **1.** To cause to produce foam. **2.** To cause to become foam. [ME *fom* < OE *fām.*]

foam·flow·er (fōm′flou′ər) *n.* A plant (*Tiarella cordifolia*) of eastern North America with small white flowers.

foam rubber *n.* A light firm spongy rubber made by beating air into latex and then curing it, used in upholstery and insulation.

foam·y (fō′mē) *adj.* **-i·er, -i·est** **1.** Of, consisting of, or resembling foam. **2.** Covered with foam. **—foam′i·ly** *adv.* **—foam′i·ness** *n.*

fob¹ (fŏb) *n.* **1.** A small pocket at the front waistline of a man's trousers or in the front of a vest, used esp. to hold a watch. **2a.** A short chain or ribbon attached to a pocket watch and worn hanging in front of the vest or waist. **b.** An ornament or seal attached to such a chain or ribbon. [Prob. of Gmc. orig.]

fob² (fŏb) *v.* **fobbed, fob·bing, fobs** *Archaic* To cheat or deceive (another). **—phrasal verb: fob off** **1.** To dispose of (goods) by fraud or deception; palm off. **2.** To put off or appease by deceitful or evasive means: *was fobbed off with promises.* [ME *fobben,* prob. < *fob,* trickster.]

focaccia

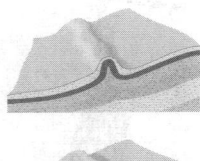

fold¹
top: isocline fold
center: overfold
bottom: recumbent fold

FOB *abbr.* free on board

fo·cac·ci·a (fə-kä′chē-ə, -chə, fō-) *n.* A flat Italian bread traditionally flavored with olive oil and salt and often topped with herbs, onions, or other items. [Ital., hearth-cake < VLat. *focācea* < var. of LLat. *focācia,* of the hearth, fem. of *focācius* < Lat. *focus,* hearth.]

fo·cal (fō′kəl) *adj.* **1.** Of or relating to a focus. **2.** Placed at or measured from a focus. **—fo′cal·ly** *adv.*

focal distance *n.* See **focal length**.

focal infection *n.* A bacterial infection localized in a specific part of the body that may spread to another part of the body.

fo·cal·ize (fō′kə-līz′) *tr. & intr.v.* **-ized, -iz·ing, -iz·es** **1.** To adjust or come to a focus. **2.** To bring or be brought to a focus; sharpen. **3.** To concentrate or be concentrated; localize. **—fo′cal·i·za′tion** (-kə-lĭ-zā′shən) *n.*

focal length *n.* The distance from the surface of a lens or mirror to its focal point.

focal point *n.* See **focus** 1a.

Foch (fôsh, fōsh), **Ferdinand** 1851–1929. French marshal and commander in chief of Allied forces during World War I.

fo′c's′le (fōk′səl) *n.* Variant of **forecastle**.

fo·cus (fō′kəs) *n., pl.* **-cus·es** or **-ci** (-sī′, -kī′) **1a.** A point at which rays of light or other radiation converge or from which they appear to diverge, as after refraction or reflection in an optical system. **b.** See **focal length**. **2a.** The distinctness or clarity of an image rendered by an optical system. **b.** The state of maximum distinctness or clarity of such an image: *in focus.* **c.** An apparatus used to adjust the focal length of an optical system in order to make an image distinct or clear. **3.** A center of interest or activity. See Syns at **center**. **4.** Close or narrow attention; concentration. **5.** A condition in which something can be clearly apprehended or perceived. **6.** *Pathology* The region of a localized bodily infection or disease. **7.** *Geology* The point of origin of an earthquake. **8.** *Mathematics* A fixed point whose relationship with a directrix determines a conic section. ❖ *v.* **-cused, -cus·ing, -cus·es** or **-cussed, -cus·sing, -cus·ses** **—tr.** **1.** To cause (light rays, for example) to converge on or toward a central point; concentrate. **2a.** To render (an object or image) in clear outline or sharp detail by adjustment of one's vision or an optical device; bring into focus. **b.** To adjust (a lens, for example) to produce a clear image. **3.** To direct toward a particular point or purpose. **—intr.** **1.** To converge on or toward a central point of focus; be focused. **2.** To adjust one's vision or an optical device so as to render a clear, distinct image. **3.** To concentrate attention or energy. [Lat., hearth.] **—fo′cus·er** *n.*

fod·der (fŏd′ər) *n.* **1.** Feed for livestock, esp. coarsely chopped hay or straw. **2.** Raw material, as for artistic creation. **3.** A consumable, often inferior item or resource that is in demand and usu. abundant supply. ❖ *tr.v.* **-dered, -der·ing, -ders** To feed with fodder. [ME < OE *fōdor.* See **pā-** in App.]

foe (fō) *n.* **1.** A personal enemy. **2.** An enemy in war. **3.** An adversary; an opponent: *a foe of tax reform.* See Syns at **enemy**. **4.** Something that opposes, injures, or impedes. [ME *fo* < OE *gefā* < *fāh,* hostile.]

foehn also **föhn** (fœn, fān) *n.* A warm dry wind coming off the lee slopes of a mountain range, esp. off the northern slopes of the Alps. [Ger. *Föhn* < MHGer. *phœnne* < OHGer. *phōno* < VLat. **faōnius* < Lat. *favōnius,* the west wind < *favēre,* to be favorable.]

foe·man (fō′mən) *n.* A foe in battle; an enemy.

foe·tal (fēt′l) *adj. Chiefly British* Variant of **fetal**.

foe·tid (fĕt′ĭd, fē′tĭd) *adj.* Variant of **fetid**.

foe·tor (fē′tər) *n.* Variant of **fetor**.

foe·tus (fē′təs) *n. Chiefly British* Variant of **fetus**.

fog¹ (fôg, fŏg) *n.* **1.** Condensed water vapor in cloudlike masses lying close to the ground and limiting visibility. **2a.** An obscuring haze, as of atmospheric dust. **b.** A mist or film clouding a surface, as of a window or lens. **3.** A cloud of vaporized liquid, esp. a chemical spray used in fighting fires. **4a.** A state of mental vagueness or bewilderment. **b.** Something that obscures or conceals; a haze. **5.** A blur on a developed photographic image. ❖ *v.* **fogged, fog·ging, fogs** **—tr.** **1.** To cover or envelop with or as if with fog. **2.** To cause to be obscured; cloud. **3.** To make vague, hazy, or confused. **4.** To obscure or dim (a photographic image). **—intr.** **1.** To be covered with or as if with fog. **2.** To be blurred, clouded, or obscured. **3.** To be dimmed or obscured. Used of a photographic image. [Perh. of Scand. orig.] **—fog′ger** *n.*

fog² (fôg, fŏg) *n.* **1.** A new growth of grass on a mowed or grazed field. **2.** Tall decaying grass left standing after the cutting or grazing season. [ME *fogge,* tall grass. See **pū-** in App.]

fog bank *n.* A dense mass of fog defined against clearer surrounding air, often as viewed from a distance at sea.

fog·bound (fôg′bound′, fŏg′-) *adj.* **1.** Immobilized by heavy fog. **2.** Enveloped or obscured by fog: *fogbound cliffs.*

fog·bow (fôg′bō′, fŏg′-) *n.* A faint arc-shaped light, similar to a rainbow, that sometimes appears in fog opposite the sun.

Fog·gia (fō′jə) A city of S Italy NE of Naples. Pop. 155,042.

fog·gy (fô′gē, fŏg′ē) *adj.* **-gi·er, -gi·est** **1a.** Full of or surrounded by fog. **b.** Resembling or suggestive of fog. **2.** Clouded or blurred by or as if by fog; vague: *a foggy memory.* **—fog′gi·ly** *adv.* **—fog′gi·ness** *n.*

Foggy Bottom *n.* The US Department of State. [< its location in a low-lying area of Washington DC near the Potomac R.]

fog•horn (fôg′hôrn′, fŏg′-) *n.* **1.** *Nautical* A horn for sounding warning signals in fog or darkness, used esp. on ships, buoys, and coastal installations. **2.** A booming insistent voice.

fo•gy also **fo•gey** (fō′gē) *n., pl.* **-gies** also **-geys** A person of stodgy or old-fashioned habits and attitudes. [Sc. *fogey.*] —**fo′gy•ish** *adj.* —**fo′gy•ism** *n.*

föhn (fœn, fān) *n.* Variant of **foehn.**

foi•ble (foi′bəl) *n.* **1.** A minor weakness or failing of character. **2.** The weaker section of a sword blade, from the middle to the tip. [Obsolete Fr. *foible,* weak point of a sword, weak < OFr. *feble,* weak. See FEEBLE.]

foil[1] (foil) *tr.v.* **foiled, foil•ing, foils 1.** To prevent from being successful; thwart. **2.** To obscure or confuse (a trail or scent) so as to evade pursuers. ❖ *n. Archaic* **1.** A repulse; a setback. **2.** The trail or scent of an animal. [ME *foilen,* to trample, defile, var. of *filen,* to defile. See FILE[3].]

foil[2] (foil) *n.* **1.** A thin flexible leaf or sheet of metal: *aluminum foil.* **2.** A thin layer of polished metal placed under a displayed gem to lend it brilliance. **3.** One that by contrast underscores or enhances the distinctive characteristics of another. **4.** The reflective metal coating on the back of a glass mirror. **5.** *Architecture* A curvilinear, often lobelike figure or space formed between the cusps of intersecting arcs, found esp. in Gothic tracery and Moorish ornament. **6a.** An airfoil. **b.** *Nautical* A hydrofoil. ❖ *tr.v.* **foiled, foil•ing, foils 1.** To cover or back with foil. **2.** To set off by contrast. [ME < OFr. *foille* < Lat. *folia,* pl. of *folium,* leaf. See **bhel-** in App.]

foil[3] (foil) *n.* **1.** A fencing sword having a usu. circular guard and a thin flexible four-sided blade with a button on the tip to prevent injury. **2.** The act or sport of fencing with such a sword. Often used in the plural. [?]

foin (foin) *Archaic intr.v.* **foined, foin•ing, foins** To thrust with a pointed weapon. ❖ *n.* A thrust with a pointed weapon. [ME *foinen,* ult. < Lat. *fuscina,* three-pronged spear.]

foi•son (foi′zən) *n.* **1.** *Scots* Physical strength or power. **2.** *Archaic* A plentiful harvest; abundance. **3. foisons** *Obsolete* Reserves of power; resources. [ME *foisoun* < OFr. *foison* < Lat. *fūsiō, fūsiōn-,* a pouring < *fūsus,* p. part. of *fundere,* to pour. See **gheu-** in App.]

foist (foist) *tr.v.* **foist•ed, foist•ing, foists 1.** To pass off as genuine, valuable, or worthy. **2.** To impose (something or someone unwanted) upon another by coercion or trickery. **3.** To insert fraudulently or deceitfully. [Prob. Du. dialectal *vuisten,* to take in hand < MDu. < *vuist,* fist. See **penkʷe** in App.]

Fo•kine (fô-kēn′, fō-), **Michel** 1880–1942. Russian-born Amer. choreographer whose works include *Petrouchka* (1916).

Fok•ker (fŏk′ər, fô′kər), **Anthony Herman Gerard** 1890–1939. Dutch-born Amer. aircraft designer.

fol. *abbr.* **1.** folio **2.** following

fo•la•cin (fō′lə-sĭn) *n.* See **folic acid.** [FOL(IC) AC(ID) + –IN.]

fo•late (fō′lāt′) *n.* **1.** A salt or ester of folic acid. **2.** See **folic acid.** [FOL(IC ACID) + –ATE[2].]

fold[1] (fōld) *v.* **fold•ed, fold•ing, folds** —*tr.* **1.** To bend over or double up so that one part lies on another part. **2.** To make compact by doubling or bending over parts. **3.** To bring from an extended to a closed position. **4.** To bring from a compact to an extended position; unfold. **5.** To place together and intertwine. **6.** To envelop or clasp; enfold. **7.** To blend (a light ingredient) into a heavier mixture with a series of gentle turns. **8a.** *Informal* To discontinue operating; close. **b.** *Games* To withdraw (one's hand) in defeat, as by laying cards face down on a table. **9.** *Geology* To form bends in (a stratum of rock). —*intr.* **1a.** To become folded. **b.** To be capable of being folded. **2.** *Informal* To close, esp. for lack of financial success; fail. **3.** *Games* To withdraw from a game in defeat. **4.** *Informal* **a.** To give in; buckle. **b.** To weaken or collapse from exertion. ❖ *n.* **1.** The act or an instance of folding. **2.** A part that has been folded over or against another. **3.** A line or mark made by folding; a crease. **4.** A coil or bend, as of rope. **5.** *Chiefly British* A hill or dale in undulating country. **6.** *Geology* A bend in a stratum of rock. **7.** *Anatomy* A crease or ridge apparently formed by folding, as of a membrane; a plica. [ME *folden* < OE *fealdan, faldan.*] —**fold′a•ble** *adj.*

fold[2] (fōld) *n.* **1.** A fenced enclosure for domestic animals, esp. sheep. **2.** A flock of sheep. **3a.** A group of people or institutions with common beliefs and aims. **b.** A religious congregation. ❖ *tr.v.* **fold•ed, fold•ing, folds** To place or keep (sheep, for example) in a fenced enclosure. [ME < OE *fald.*]

-fold *suff.* **1.** Divided into a specified number of parts: *fivefold.* **2.** Multiplied by a specified number: *fiftyfold.* [ME < OE *-feald, -fald.*]

fold•a•way (fōld′ə-wā′) *adj.* Designed to be folded up for easy storage: *a foldaway bed.* —**fold′a•way′** *n.*

fold•boat (fōld′bōt′) *n.* A small boat resembling a kayak, consisting of rubberized canvas stretched over a collapsible frame. [Transl. of Ger. *Faltboot.*]

fold•er (fōl′dər) *n.* **1.** One that folds or is folded, such as a booklet of one or more folded sheets of paper. **2.** A flexible cover folded in the center, used to hold loose paper.

fol•de•rol (fŏl′də-rŏl′) also **fal•de•ral** (făl′də-răl′) *n.* **1.** Foolishness; nonsense. **2.** A trifle; a gewgaw. [< a nonsense refrain in some old songs.]

fold•ing door (fōl′dĭng) *n.* A door with hinged or pleated sections that fold together when the door is opened.

folding money *n.* Paper money.

fold•out (fōld′out′) *n.* **1.** *Printing* A folded insert or section, as of a cover, whose full size exceeds that of the regular page. **2.** A piece or part, as of furniture, that folds out or down from a closed position. —**fold′out′** *adj.*

fold•up (fōld′ŭp′) *adj.* Designed to fold up, as for storage or carrying; collapsible. ❖ *n.* **1.** An object that folds up. **2.** *Informal* A complete failure or breakdown; a collapse.

fo•ley (fō′lē) *n.* **1.** A technical process by which sounds are created or altered for use esp. in a film or video. **2.** A person who creates or alters sounds using this process. [After Jack *Foley* (1891–1967), pioneering sound effect editor at Universal Studios in the 1930s.]

fo•li•a (fō′lē-ə) *n.* Plural of **folium.**

fo•li•a•ceous (fō′lē-ā′shəs) *adj.* **1.** Of, relating to, or resembling the leaf of a plant. **2.** Having leaves or leaflike structures. **3.** *Geology* Consisting of thin, leaflike layers, as of minerals. [< Lat. *foliāceus* < *folium,* leaf. See FOLIUM.]

fo•li•age (fō′lē-ĭj, fō′lĭj) *n.* **1a.** Plant leaves, esp. tree leaves, considered as a group. **b.** A cluster of leaves. **2.** An ornamental representation of leaves, stems, and flowers, esp. in architecture. [Alteration of ME *foilage* < OFr. *foillage* < *foille,* leaf. See FOIL[2].] —**fo′li•aged** *adj.*

fo•li•ar (fō′lē-ər) *adj.* Of or relating to a leaf or leaves. [NLat. *foliāris* < Lat. *folium,* leaf. See FOLIUM.]

fo•li•ate (fō′lē-ĭt, -āt′) *adj.* **1.** Of or relating to leaves. **2.** Shaped like a leaf. **3.** *Geology* Foliated. ❖ *v.* (-āt′) **-at•ed, -at•ing, -ates** —*tr.* **1.** To hammer or cut (metal) into thin leaf or foil. **2a.** To coat (glass, for example) with metal foil. **b.** To furnish or adorn with metal foil. **3.** To separate into thin layers or laminae. **4.** To decorate with foliage or foils. **5.** To number the leaves of (a manuscript, for example). —*intr.* **1.** To produce foliage. **2.** To split into thin leaflike layers or folia. [Lat. *foliātus,* bearing foliage < *folium,* leaf. See FOLIUM.]

-foliate *suff.* Having a specified kind or number of leaves: *trifoliate.* [< FOLIATE.]

fo•li•at•ed (fō′lē-ā′tĭd) *adj. Geology* Of or relating to rock in which structural and textural features are arranged in a planar manner.

fo•li•a•tion (fō′lē-ā′shən) *n.* **1.** The state of being in leaf. **2.** Decoration with sculpted or painted foliage. **3.** *Architecture* Decoration of an opening with cusps and foils, as in Gothic tracery. **4a.** The act, process, or product of forming metal into thin leaf or foil. **b.** The act or process of coating glass with metal foil. **5a.** The process of numbering consecutively the leaves of a book or manuscript. **b.** The leaves so numbered. **6.** *Geology* The layered structure common to metamorphic rocks.

fo•lic acid (fō′lĭk, fŏl′ĭk) *n.* A compound, $C_{19}H_{19}N_7O_6$, of the vitamin B complex group, occurring in green plants, fresh fruit, liver, and yeast. [Lat. *folium,* leaf; see FOLIUM + –IC.]

fo•lie à deux (fô-lē′ ä dœ′, fŏl′ē) *n.* A condition in which symptoms of a mental disorder occur simultaneously in two people who share a close association. [Fr. : *folie,* madness + *à,* between + *deux,* two.]

fo•li•o (fō′lē-ō′) *n., pl.* **-os 1a.** A large sheet of paper folded once in the middle, making two leaves or four pages of a book or manuscript. **b.** A book or manuscript of the largest common size, usu. about 38 centimeters (15 inches) in height, consisting of such folded sheets. **2a.** A leaf of a book numbered only on the front side. **b.** A number on such a leaf. **c.** A page number. **3.** *Accounting* A page in a ledger or two facing pages that are assigned a single number. ❖ *tr.v.* **-oed, -o•ing, -os** To number consecutively the pages or leaves of (a book, for example). [ME < LLat. *foliō,* ablative of *folium,* leaf of paper < Lat., leaf. See **bhel-** in App.]

-foliolate *suff.* Having a specified kind or number of leaflets: *bifoliolate.* [New Latin *foliolātus* < Fr. *foliole,* leaflet < LLat. *foliolum,* dim. of Lat. *folium,* leaf. See FOLIUM.]

fo•li•ose (fō′lē-ōs′) *adj.* **1.** Bearing numerous leaves; leafy. **2.** Of, relating to, or resembling a leaf. **3.** Of or relating to a lichen whose thallus is flat and leafy. [Lat. *foliōsus* < *folium,* leaf. See FOLIUM.]

fo•li•um (fō′lē-əm) *n., pl.* **-li•a** (-lē-ə) **1.** *Geology* A thin leaflike layer or stratum occurring esp. in metamorphic rock. **2.** *Mathematics* A plane cubic curve having a single loop, a node, and two ends asymptotic to the same line. [Lat., leaf. See **bhel-** in App.]

folk (fōk) *n., pl.* **folk** or **folks 1a.** The common people of a society or region considered esp. as the originators or carriers of the customs, beliefs, and arts that make up a distinctive culture. **b.** *Archaic* A nation; a people. **2. folks** *Informal* People in general. **3.** People of a specified group or kind. Often used in the plural. **4. folks** *Informal* **a.** The members of one's family or childhood household; one's relatives. **b.** One's parents. ❖ *adj.* Of, occurring in, or originating among the common people or folk. —***idiom:* just folks** *Informal* Down-to-earth, open-hearted. [ME < OE *folc.* See **pelə-**[1] in App.]

folk art also **folk-art** (fōk′ärt′) *n.* Art usu. reflecting the traditional culture of a nation or region, esp. everyday or festive items produced or decorated by unschooled artists. —**folk′-art′** *adj.* —**folk artist** *n.*

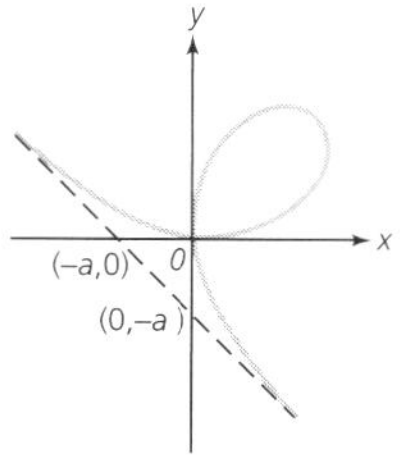

folium
folium of Descartes, a type of folium having the equation $x^3 + y^3 = 3axy$

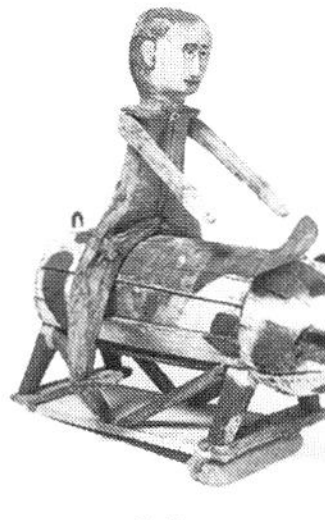

folk art
Killingsworth Image, Man on a Hog, c. 1890, by Clark Coe (1847–1919)

ă pat	oi boy
ā pay	ou out
âr care	o͝o took
ä father	o͞o boot
ĕ pet	ŭ cut
ē be	ûr urge
ĭ pit	th thin
ī pie	*th* this
îr pier	hw which
ŏ pot	zh vision
ō toe	ə about, item
ô paw	

Stress marks:
′ (primary);
′ (secondary), as in
lexicon (lĕk′sĭ-kŏn′)

Margot Fonteyn

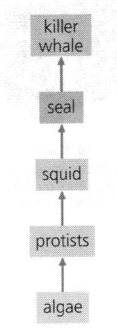

killer
whale

↑

seal

↑

squid

↑

protists

↑

algae

food chain
aquatic food chain diagram

---

folk etymology *n.* Change in the form of a word or phrase resulting from a mistaken assumption about its composition or meaning, as in *shamefaced* for earlier *shamfast*, "bound by shame."

folk·ie also **folk·y** (fō′kē) *n., pl.* **-ies 1.** A folk singer or musician. **2.** An enthusiast of folk music. ❖ *adj.* **-i·er, -i·est** Of, relating to, or in the style of folk music.

folk·ish (fō′kĭsh) *adj.* **1.** Of or characteristic of folk music, art, or literature. **2.** Simple or natural; folksy. —**folk′ish·ly** *adv.* —**folk′ish·ness** *n.*

folk·lore (fōk′lôr′, -lōr′) *n.* **1.** The traditional beliefs, myths, tales, and practices of a people, transmitted orally. **2.** The comparative study of folk knowledge and culture. **3a.** A body of widely accepted but usu. specious notions about a place, group, or institution. **b.** A popular but unfounded belief. —**folk′lor′ic** *adj.* —**folk′lor′ish** *adj.* —**folk′lor′ist** *n.* —**folk·lor·is′tic** *adj.*

folk·lor·is·tics (fōk′lô-rĭs′tĭks, -lō-) *n.* (used with a sing. verb) See **folklore** 2.

folk magic *n.* The practice of using charms, spells, or rituals to attempt to control natural or chance events or to influence the behavior or emotions of others.

folk medicine *n.* Traditional medicine as practiced by nonprofessional healers or embodied in local custom or lore, generally involving the use of natural and esp. herbal remedies.

folk·moot (fōk′mo͞ot′) or **folk·mote** (-mōt′) *n.* A general assembly of the people of a town, district, or shire in medieval England. [ME < OE *folcmōt : folc*, folk; see FOLK + *mōt*, meeting.]

folk music *n.* **1.** Music originating among the common people of a nation or region and spread about or passed down orally. **2.** Contemporary music in the style of traditional folk music. —**folk′-mu′sic** (fōk′myo͞o′zĭk) *adj.*

folk-rock or **folk rock** (fōk′rŏk′) *n.* A variety of music combining rock 'n' roll and folk music. —**folk′-rock′** *adj.*

folk·sing·er or **folk singer** (fōk′sĭng′ər) *n.* A singer of folksongs. —**folk singing** *n.*

folk song or **folk·song** (fōk′sông′, -sŏng′) *n.* **1.** A song of the folk music of a people or area. **2.** A song composed in the style of traditional folk music.

folk·sy (fōk′sē) *adj.* **-si·er, -si·est** *Informal* **1.** Simple and unpretentious in behavior. **2.** Characterized by informality and affability: *a friendly, folksy town.* **3.** Modest; low-key: *folksy humor.* [*folks*, pl. of FOLK + -Y¹.] —**folk′si·ly** *adv.* —**folk′si·ness** *n.*

folk·tale or **folk tale** (fōk′tāl′) *n.* A story or legend forming part of an oral tradition.

folk·way (fōk′wā′) *n.* A practice, custom, or belief shared by the members of a group as part of their common culture. Often used in the plural.

folk·y (fō′kē) *n. & adj.* Variant of **folkie**.

fol·li·cle (fōl′ĭ-kəl) *n.* **1.** *Anatomy* **a.** A small body cavity or sac. **b.** A cavity in the ovary containing a maturing ovum in its encasing cells. **c.** A crypt or minute cul-de-sac or lacuna. **2.** *Botany* A dry single-chambered fruit that splits along only one seam to release its seeds, as in larkspur. [Lat. *folliculus*, little bag, dim. of *follis*, bellows.]

follicle mite *n.* Any of various tiny mites of the genus *Demodex* that infest the hair follicles of mammals.

follicle stimulating hormone *n.* A gonadotropic hormone of the anterior pituitary gland that stimulates the growth of follicles in the ovary and induces the formation of sperm in the testis.

fol·lic·u·lar (fə-lĭk′yə-lər) *adj.* **1.** Relating to, having, or resembling a follicle or follicles. **2.** Affecting or growing out of a follicle or follicles.

fol·lic·u·late (fə-lĭk′yə-lĭt) also **fol·lic·u·lat·ed** (-lā′tĭd) *adj.* Having or consisting of a follicle or follicles.

fol·low (fōl′ō) *v.* **-lowed, -low·ing, -lows** —*tr.* **1.** To come or go after; proceed behind. **2a.** To go after in or as if in pursuit. **b.** To keep under surveillance. **3a.** To move along the course of; take. **b.** To go in the direction of; be guided by. **4.** To accept the guidance, command, or leadership of. **5.** To adhere to; practice. **6.** To take as a model or precedent; imitate. **7a.** To act in agreement or compliance with; obey. **b.** To keep to or stick to: *followed the recipe.* **8.** To engage in (a trade or occupation); work at. **9.** To come after in order, time, or position. **10.** To bring something about at a later time than or as a consequence of. **11.** To occur or be evident as a consequence of. **12a.** To watch or observe closely. **b.** To be attentive to; pay close heed to. **c.** To keep oneself informed of the course, progress, or fortunes of. **13.** To grasp the meaning or logic of; understand. —*intr.* **1.** To come, move, or take place after another person or thing in order or time. **2.** To occur or be evident as a consequence; result. **3.** To grasp the meaning or reasoning of something; understand. ❖ *n.* **1.** The act or an instance of following. **2.** *Games* A billiards shot in which the cue ball is struck above center so that it follows the path of the object ball after impact. —*phrasal verbs:* **follow along** To move or proceed in unison or in accord with an example. **follow through 1.** *Sports* To carry a stroke to natural completion after hitting or releasing a ball or other object. **2.** To carry an act, project, or intention to completion; pursue fully. **follow up 1.** To carry to completion; follow through on. **2.** To increase the effectiveness or enhance the success of by further action. —*idioms:* **as follows** As will be stated next. Used to introduce a specified enumeration, explanation, or command. **follow (one's) nose 1.** To move straight ahead or in a direct path. **2.** *Informal* To be guided by instinct. **follow suit 1.** *Games* To play a card of the same suit as the one led. **2.** To do as another has done; follow an example. [ME *folowen* < OE *folgian*.]

SYNONYMS *follow, succeed, ensue, result, supervene* These verbs mean to come after something or someone. *Follow*, which has the widest application, can refer to coming after in time or order, as a consequence or result, or by the operation of logic: *Night follows day.* To *succeed* is to come next after another, especially in planned order determined by considerations such as rank, inheritance, or election: *The heir apparent succeeded to the throne. Ensue* usually applies to what is a consequence or logical development: *After the government was toppled, chaos ensued. Result* implies that what follows is caused by what has preceded: *Failure to file an income tax return can result in a fine. Supervene*, in contrast, refers to something that is unexpected and often has little relation to what has preceded: "*A bad harvest supervened*" (Charlotte Brontë).

USAGE NOTE *As follows* (not *as follow*) is the established form of the idiom regardless of whether the noun that precedes it is singular or plural: *The regulations are as follows.*

fol·low·er (fōl′ō-ər) *n.* **1.** One who subscribes to the teachings or methods of another; an adherent: *a follower of Gandhi.* **2.** A servant; a subordinate. **3.** A fan; an enthusiast. **4.** One that imitates or copies another. **5.** A machine element moved by another machine element.

fol·low·er·ship (fōl′ō-ər-shĭp′) *n.* **1.** The act or condition of following a leader. **2.** A group of followers; a following.

fol·low·ing (fōl′ō-ĭng) *adj.* **1.** Coming next in time or order. **2.** Now to be enumerated: *The following people will report for duty.* **3.** Blowing in the same direction as the course of a ship or aircraft. Used of wind or seas. ❖ *n.* A group or gathering of admirers, adherents, or disciples. ❖ *prep.* Subsequent to; after.

following shot *n.* A shot in a movie in which the camera follows behind or along with a moving subject.

fol·low-on (fōl′ō-ŏn′, -ôn′) *adj.* Following as a related or consequent aspect or development. —**fol′low-on′** *n.*

follow shot *n.* **1.** A shot in a movie in which the camera follows the action of a subject from a fixed position. **2.** *Games* A follow in billiards.

fol·low-through or **fol·low·through** (fōl′ō-thro͞o′) *n.* **1.** The act or an instance of following through. **2.** *Sports* The concluding part of a stroke, as after a ball has been hit.

fol·low-up or **fol·low·up** (fōl′ō-ŭp′) *n.* **1.** The act or an instance of following up, as to review new developments. **2.** One that follows up, as to further an end. **3.** A news article or report adding information on a previously reported item. ❖ *adj.* Intended to follow up, as to reinforce or evaluate previous action.

fol·ly (fōl′ē) *n., pl.* **-lies 1.** A lack of good sense, understanding, or foresight. **2a.** An act or instance of foolishness. **b.** A costly undertaking having an absurd or ruinous outcome. **3. follies** (*used with a sing. or pl. verb*) An elaborate theatrical revue consisting of music, dance, and skits. **4.** *Obsolete* **a.** Perilously or criminally foolish action. **b.** Evil; wickedness. **c.** Lewdness; lasciviousness. [ME *folie* < OFr. < *fol*, foolish < LLat. *follis*, windbag, fool. See FOOL.]

Fol·som (fōl′səm) *adj.* Of or relating to a western North American culture flourishing east of the Rocky Mountains in the late Pleistocene Epoch and notable for its leaf-shaped flint projectile points. [After *Folsom*, a town of NE New Mexico.]

Fo·mal·haut (fō′məl-hôt′) *n.* The brightest star in the constellation Piscis Austrinus. [Ar. *fam al-ḥūt*, mouth of the fish, Fomalhaut : *fam*, mouth + *al-*, the + *ḥūt*, fish.]

fo·ment (fō-mĕnt′) *tr.v.* **-ment·ed, -ment·ing, -ments 1.** To promote the growth of; incite. **2.** To treat (the skin, for example) by fomentation. [ME *fomenten*, to apply warm liquids to the skin, ult. < Lat. *fōmentum*, poultice < *fovēre*, to warm.] —**fo·ment′er** *n.*

fo·men·ta·tion (fō′mən-tā′shən, -mĕn-) *n.* **1.** The act of fomenting; incitement. **2a.** A substance or material used as a warm moist medicinal compress; a poultice. **b.** The therapeutic application of warmth and moisture, as to relieve pain.

Fon (fŏn) *n., pl.* **Fon** or **Fons 1.** A member of a people of Benin and neighboring parts of Nigeria. **2.** The Gbe language of the Fon.

fond¹ (fŏnd) *adj.* **fond·er, fond·est 1.** Having a strong liking, inclination, or affection. **2.** Affectionate; tender: *a fond embrace.* **3.** Immoderately affectionate or indulgent; doting. **4.** Cherished; dear: *my fondest hopes.* **5.** *Archaic* Naively credulous or foolish. [ME *fonned*, foolish, prob. < p. part. of *fonnen*, to be foolish, prob. < *fonne*, fool.] —**fond′ly** *adv.*

fond² (fŏnd) *n.* The background of a design in lace. [Fr. < OFr. *fonds, fond* < Lat. *fundus*, bottom.]

Fon·da (fŏn′də), **Henry** 1905–82. Amer. actor noted for films such as *The Grapes of Wrath* (1940) and *On Golden Pond* (1981).

fon·dant (fŏn′dənt) *n.* **1.** A sweet creamy paste of sugar and flavorings that is used in candies and icings. **2.** A candy that contains or is made with this paste. [Fr. < pr. part. of *fondre*, to melt < Lat.

fundere, to pour. See **gheu-** in App.]

fon·dle (fŏn′dl) *v.* **-dled, -dling, -dles** —*tr.* **1.** To handle, stroke, or caress, usu. lovingly. **2.** *Obsolete* To treat with indulgence and solicitude; pamper. —*intr.* To show fondness or affection by caressing. [Frequentative of FOND¹, to show fondness for (obsolete).] —**fon′dler** *n.*

fond·ness (fŏnd′nĭs) *n.* **1.** Warm affection or liking. See Syns at **love. 2.** A strong inclination or preference; a taste: *a fondness for sweets.* **3.** *Archaic* Naive trustfulness; credulity.

fon·due also **fon·du** (fŏn-dōō′, -dyōō′) *n.* **1a.** A hot dish made of melted cheese and wine and eaten with bread. **b.** A similar dish, esp. one consisting of a melted sauce in which pieces of food, such as bread or meat, are dipped or cooked. **2.** A soufflé usu. made with cheese and bread crumbs. [Fr. < fem. p. part. of *fondre*, to melt. See FONDANT.] —**fon·due′** *v.*

Fon·se·ca (fôn-sā′kə, fôn-sĕ′kä), **Gulf of** An inlet of the Pacific Ocean in W Central America.

font¹ (fŏnt) *n.* **1.** A basin for holding baptismal water in a church. **2.** A receptacle for holy water; a stoup. **3.** The oil reservoir in an oil-burning lamp. **4.** An abundant source; a fount: *She was a font of wisdom.* [ME < OE < LLat. *fōns, font-* < Lat., fountain.] —**font′al** (fŏn′tl) *adj.*

font² (fŏnt) *n.* *Printing* A set of type of one size and face. [Fr. *fonte*, casting < OFr., ult. < Lat. *fundere*, to pour forth. See **gheu-** in App.]

Fon·taine·bleau (fŏn′tĭn-blō′, fôn-tĕn-blō′) A town of N France SE of Paris; site of the signing of the revocation of the Edict of Nantes (1685). Pop. 18,037.

Fon·tan·a (fŏn-tăn′ə) A city of S CA W of San Bernardino. Pop. 128,929.

fon·ta·nel also **fon·ta·nelle** (fŏn′tə-nĕl′) *n.* Any of the soft membranous gaps between the incompletely formed cranial bones of a fetus or infant. [ME *fontinel* < OFr. *fontanele*, dim. of *fontaine*, fountain. See FOUNTAIN.]

Fon·tanne (fŏn-tăn′), **Lynn** 1887?–1983. British-born Amer. actress who performed with her husband Alfred Lunt in many stage productions, including *Pygmalion* (1926).

Fon·teyn (fŏn-tān′), Dame **Margot** 1919–91. British ballerina noted for her portrayal of Aurora in *Sleeping Beauty.*

fon·ti·na (fŏn-tē′nə) *n.* A ripened cheese of variable texture and flavor, originally produced in Italy. [Ital.]

Foo·chow (fōō′jō′, -chou′) See **Fuzhou.**

food (fōōd) *n.* **1.** Material, usu. of plant or animal origin, that contains or consists of essential body nutrients, such as carbohydrates, fats, proteins, vitamins, or minerals, and is ingested and assimilated by an organism to produce energy, stimulate growth, and maintain life. **2.** A specified kind of nourishment. **3.** Nourishment eaten in solid form. **4.** Something that nourishes or sustains in a way suggestive of physical nourishment: *food for thought.* [ME *fode* < OE *fōda*. See **pā-** in App.]

food chain *n.* **1.** A succession of organisms in an ecological community that constitutes a continuation of food energy from one organism to another as each consumes a lower member and in turn is preyed upon by a higher member. **2.** *Informal* A competitive hierarchy.

food court *n.* An area, as in a mall, in which vendors sell food at stations around a common eating space.

food cycle *n.* See **food web.**

food·ie (fōō′dē) *n. Slang* A person who has an ardent or refined interest in food; a gourmet.

food poisoning *n.* **1.** An acute, often severe gastrointestinal disorder characterized by vomiting and diarrhea and caused by eating food contaminated with bacteria, esp. bacteria of the genus *Salmonella.* **2.** Poisoning caused by ingesting substances that contain natural toxins.

food processor *n.* An appliance consisting of a container housing interchangeable rotating blades and used for preparing foods, as by shredding, slicing, chopping, or blending.

food pyramid *n.* **1.** A graphic representation of the structure of a food chain, depicted as a broad-based pyramid formed by producers tapering to a point formed by end consumers. **2.** A diagrammatic representation of human nutritional needs depicted as a pyramid in which foods required in lesser amounts appear closer to the apex.

food stamp *n.* A stamp or coupon, issued by the government to people with low incomes, redeemable for food at stores.

food·stuff (fōōd′stŭf′) *n.* A substance that can be used or prepared for use as food.

food vacuole *n.* A vacuole in which phagocytized food is digested.

food web *n.* A complex of interrelated food chains in an ecological community.

foo·fa·raw (fōō′fə-rô′) *n.* **1.** Excessive or flashy ornamentation. **2.** A fuss over a trifling matter. [Prob. < Sp. *fanfarrón*, boaster; see FANFARONADE, and < Fr. *frou-frou*, rustling (of imit. orig.).]

fool (fōōl) *n.* **1.** One who is deficient in judgment, sense, or understanding. **2.** One who acts unwisely on a given occasion. **3.** One who has been tricked or made to appear ridiculous; a dupe. **4.** *Informal* A person with a talent or enthusiasm for a certain activity. **5.** A member of a royal or noble household who provided entertainment, as with jokes or antics; a jester. **6.** One who sub-

verts convention or orthodoxy or varies from social conformity in order to reveal spiritual or moral truth: *a holy fool.* **7.** A dessert made of stewed or puréed fruit mixed with cream or custard and served cold. **8.** *Archaic* A mentally deficient person. ❖ *v.* **fooled, fool·ing, fools** —*tr.* **1.** To deceive or trick; dupe. **2.** To confound or prove wrong; surprise, esp. pleasantly. —*intr.* **1.** *Informal* **a.** To speak or act facetiously or in jest; joke. **b.** To behave comically; clown. **c.** To feign; pretend. **2.** To engage in idle or frivolous activity. **3.** To toy, tinker, or mess. ❖ *adj. Informal* Foolish; stupid.
—*phrasal verbs:* **fool around** *Informal* **1.** To engage in idle or casual activity; putter. **2.** To engage in frivolous activity; make fun. **3.** To engage in casual, often promiscuous sexual acts. —*idiom:* **play** (or **act**) **the fool 1.** To act in an irresponsible or foolish manner. **2.** To behave in a playful or comical manner. [ME *fol* < OFr. < LLat. *follis*, windbag, fool < Lat. *follis*, bellows.]

fool·er·y (fōō′lə-rē) *n., pl.* **-ies 1.** Foolish behavior or speech. **2.** An instance of foolish behavior or speech; a jest.

fool·har·dy (fōōl′här′dē) *adj.* **-di·er, -di·est** Unwisely bold or daring; rash. [ME *folhardi* < OFr. *fol hardi* : *fol*, fool; see FOOL + *hardi*, bold; see HARDY¹.] —**fool′har′di·ly** *adv.* —**fool′har′di·ness** *n.*

fool·ish (fōō′lĭsh) *adj.* **1.** Lacking or exhibiting a lack of good sense or judgment; silly. **2.** Resulting from stupidity or misinformation; unwise: *a foolish decision.* **3.** Arousing laughter; absurd or ridiculous: *a foolish grin.* **4.** Immoderate or stubborn; unreasonable. **5.** Embarrassed; abashed. **6.** Insignificant; trivial. —**fool′ish·ly** *adv.* —**fool′ish·ness** *n.*

fool·proof (fōōl′prōōf′) *adj.* **1.** Designed so as to be impervious to human incompetence, error, or misuse: *a foolproof safety lock.* **2.** Effective; infallible: *a foolproof scheme.*

fools·cap (fōōlz′kăp′) *n.* **1.** *Chiefly British* A sheet of writing or printing paper measuring approx. 13 by 16 inches. A fool's cap. [< the original watermark of a fool's cap.]

fool's cap (fōōlz) *n.* **1.** A gaily decorated cap, usu. with a number of loose peaks tipped with bells, formerly worn by court jesters and clowns. **2.** See **dunce cap.**

fool's errand *n., pl.* **fools' errands** A fruitless mission or undertaking.

fool's gold *n.* See **pyrite.**

fool's paradise *n.* A state of delusive contentment or false hope.

fool's-pars·ley (fōōlz′pär′slē) *n.* A poisonous European weed (*Aethusa cynapium*) having finely divided leaves, umbels of small white flowers, and an unpleasant odor.

foot (fōōt) *n., pl.* **feet** (fēt) **1.** The lower extremity of the vertebrate leg that is in direct contact with the ground in standing or walking. **2.** A structure used for locomotion or attachment in an invertebrate animal, such as the muscular organ extending from the ventral side of a mollusk. **3.** Something suggestive of a foot in position or function, esp.: **a.** The lowest part; the bottom: *the foot of a page.* **b.** The end opposite the head, top, or front: *the foot of a bed.* **c.** The termination of the leg of a piece of furniture, esp. when shaped or modeled. **d.** The part of a sewing machine that holds down and guides the cloth. **e.** *Nautical* The lower edge of a sail. **f.** *Botany* The base of the sporophyte in mosses and liverworts. **4.** The inferior part or rank. **5.** The part of a stocking or high-topped boot that encloses the foot. **6a.** A manner of moving; a step. **b.** Speed or momentum, as in a race. **7.** (*used with a pl. verb*) Foot soldiers; infantry. **8.** A unit of poetic meter consisting of stressed and unstressed syllables, or of long and short syllables, in any of various set combinations. **9.** A unit of length in the US Customary and British Imperial systems equal to 12 inches (0.3048 meter). See table at **measurement. 10. foots** Sediment that forms during the refining of oil and other liquids; dregs. ❖ *v.* **foot·ed, foot·ing, foots** —*intr.* **1.** To go on foot; walk. Often used with *it: had to foot it to the store.* **2.** To dance. Often used with *it.* **3.** *Nautical* To make headway; sail. —*tr.* **1.** To go by foot over, on, or through; tread. **2.** To execute the steps of (a dance). **3.** To add up (a column of numbers) and write the sum at the bottom; total: *footed up the bill.* **4.** To pay; defray. **5.** To provide (a stocking, for example) with a foot. —*idioms:* **at** (someone's) **feet** Enchanted or fascinated by. **best foot forward** A favorable initial impression. **feet of clay** An underlying weakness or fault. **foot in the door** *Slang* **1.** An initial point of or opportunity for entry. **2.** A first step in working toward a goal. **have one foot in the grave** *Informal* To be on the verge of death. **on** (one's) **feet 1.** Standing up. **2.** Fully recovered, as after an illness. **3.** In a sound or stable operating condition. **4.** In an impromptu situation; extemporaneously. **on the right foot** In an auspicious manner. **on the wrong foot** In an inauspicious manner. [ME *fot* < OE *fōt.* See **ped-** in App.]

USAGE NOTE In Standard English, *foot* and *feet* have their own rules when they are used in combination with numbers to form expressions for units of measure: *a four-foot plank,* but not *a four feet plank*; also correct is *a plank four feet long* (or, less frequently, *four foot long*). When *foot* is combined with numbers greater than one to refer to simple distance, however, only the plural *feet* is used: *a ledge 20 feet* (not *foot*) *away.*

OUR LIVING LANGUAGE Some people in New England and the South use constructions such as *three foot* and *five mile* in place

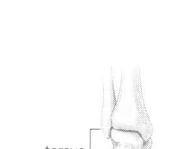

tarsus
metatarsus
phalanges

foot

ă	pat	oi	boy
ā	pay	ou	out
âr	care	ŏŏ	took
ä	father	ōō	boot
ĕ	pet	ŭ	cut
ē	be	ûr	urge
ĭ	pit	th	thin
ī	pie	th	this
îr	pier	hw	which
ŏ	pot	zh	vision
ō	toe	ə	about,
ô	paw		item

Stress marks:
′ (primary);
′ (secondary), as in
lexicon (lĕk′sĭ-kŏn′)

of Standard English *three feet* and *five miles* in certain contexts. Some speakers achieve this practice to measures of time, as in *He was gone three year*, though this is not as common. Interestingly, such constructions are used only if a specific numeral (other than *one*) precedes the noun. Thus, *She gave me four gallon of cider* can be heard in vernacular speech; however, no one would say *She gave me gallon of cider* for *She gave me gallons of cider*. This is because the numeral makes apparent the plural meaning that would not be specified if both the numeral and the plural form were omitted. See Note at **comparative.**

foot•age (fŏŏt′ĭj) *n.* **1.** Length, extent, or amount based on measurement in feet. **2a.** An amount or length of film or videotape. **b.** A shot or series of shots of a specified nature or subject: *news footage.*

foot-and-mouth disease (fŏŏt′n-mouth′) *n.* An acute, highly contagious degenerative but usu. nonfatal viral disease of cattle and other cloven-hoofed animals, characterized by fever and the eruption of vesicles around the mouth and hooves.

foot•bag (fŏŏt′băg′) *n.* **1.** A small round bag filled with plastic pellets or other material and used in games that require its being kept aloft with the feet. **2.** A game played with such a bag.

foot•ball (fŏŏt′bôl′) *n.* **1.** *Sports* **a.** A game played by two teams of 11 players each on a rectangular 100-yard-long field with goal lines and goal posts at either end, the object being to gain the ball and advance it in running or passing plays across the opponent's goal line or kick it between the opponent's goal posts. **b.** The inflated oval ball used in this game. **2.** *Chiefly British* **a.** Rugby. **b.** Soccer. **c.** The ball used in Rugby or soccer. **3.** *Informal* A problem or issue that is discussed but not settled. —**foot′ball′er** *n.*

foot•bath (fŏŏt′băth′, -bäth′) *n.* A small bath, such as a basin or shallow pool, for washing or disinfecting the feet.

foot•board (fŏŏt′bôrd′, -bōrd′) *n.* **1.** An upright board across the foot of a bedstead. **2.** A board or small raised platform on which to support or rest the feet, as in a carriage.

foot•boy (fŏŏt′boi′) *n.* A boy employed as a servant or page.

foot brake *n.* A brake operated by pressure of the foot on a pedal, as in an automobile or on a bicycle.

foot•bridge (fŏŏt′brĭj′) *n.* A bridge designed for pedestrians.

foot-can•dle (fŏŏt′kăn′dl) *n.* A unit of measure of the intensity of light falling on a surface, equal to one lumen per square foot and originally defined with reference to a standardized candle burning at one foot from a given surface.

foot•cloth (fŏŏt′klôth′, -klŏth′) *n. Archaic* A richly ornamented cloth draped over the back of a horse.

foot-drag•ging (fŏŏt′drăg′ĭng) *n.* Failure to take prompt or required action. —**foot′-drag′ger** *n.*

foot•ed (fŏŏt′ĭd) *adj.* Having feet or a foot: *a footed sofa.* Often used in combination: *web-footed; four-footed.*

foot•er (fŏŏt′ər) *n.* **1.** One that is an indicated number of feet in height or length. Often used in combination: *a six-footer.* **2.** Textual information, such as a title, date, or page number, positioned in the bottom margin of a page and usu. repeated throughout a document. **3.** See **footing** 4.

foot•fall (fŏŏt′fôl′) *n.* See **footstep** 1.

foot fault *n. Sports* A fault against the server, as in tennis, called for failure to keep both feet behind the base line.

foot•gear (fŏŏt′gîr′) *n.* Sturdy footwear, such as boots.

foot•hill (fŏŏt′hĭl′) *n.* A hill near the base of a mountain or mountain range.

foot•hold (fŏŏt′hōld′) *n.* **1.** A place providing support for the foot in climbing or standing. **2.** A firm or secure position that provides a base for further advancement.

foot•ing (fŏŏt′ĭng) *n.* **1.** Secure placement of the feet in standing or moving. **2a.** A surface or its condition with respect to its suitability for walking or running, esp. the condition of a racetrack. **b.** A secure place for the feet; a foothold. **3.** The act of moving on foot. **4.** *Architecture* The supporting base or groundwork of a structure, as for a wall. **5.** A basis or foundation. **6a.** Position or rank in relation to others; standing. **b.** Terms of social interaction. **7.** The act of making a foot, as for a stocking. **8.** The sum of a column of figures.

foot-lam•bert (fŏŏt′lăm′bərt) *n.* A unit of luminance equal to 1/π candela per square foot.

foo•tle (fŏŏt′l) *Informal intr.v.* **-tled, -tling, -tles** **1.** To waste time; trifle. **2.** To talk nonsense. ❖ *n.* Nonsense; foolishness. [Prob. var. of *footer*, to screw around < obsolete *footer*, an act of sexual intercourse < Fr. *foutre*, to have sexual intercourse < Lat. *futuere.*] —**foo′tler** *n.*

foot•less (fŏŏt′lĭs) *adj.* **1.** Having no feet. **2.** Lacking a firm support or basis; unsubstantial. **3.** *Informal* Not competent or skillful; inept. —**foot′less•ly** *adv.* —**foot′less•ness** *n.*

foot•lights (fŏŏt′līts′) *pl.n.* **1.** Lights placed in a row along the front of a stage floor. **2.** The theater as a profession.

foo•tling (fŏŏt′lĭng) *adj. Informal* **1.** Lacking importance or significance. **2.** Stupid; inept. [Pr. part. of FOOTLE.]

foot•lock•er (fŏŏt′lŏk′ər) *n.* A trunk for storing personal belongings, esp. one kept at the foot of a bed, as in a barracks.

foot•loose (fŏŏt′lōōs′) *adj.* Having no attachments or ties; free to do as one pleases.

foot•man (fŏŏt′mən) *n.* **1.** A man employed as a servant to wait

footrope

Forbidden City
The Hall of Supreme
Harmony

Betty Ford

at table, attend the door, and run various errands, as in a palace. **2.** *Archaic* A foot soldier; an infantryman.

foot•mark (fŏŏt′märk′) *n.* See **footprint** 1.

foot•note (fŏŏt′nōt′) *n.* **1.** A note at the bottom of a page of a book or manuscript that comments on or cites a reference for a designated part of the text. **2.** Something related to but of lesser importance than a larger work or occurrence. ❖ *tr.v.* **-not•ed, -not•ing, -notes** To furnish with or comment on in footnotes.

foot•pace (fŏŏt′pās′) *n.* **1.** A walking pace. **2.** A raised platform in a room, as for a lecturer; a dais.

foot•pad[1] (fŏŏt′păd′) *n.* A thief who preys on pedestrians. [FOOT + obsolete *pad*, highwayman (prob. < MDu., path; see **pent-** in App.).]

foot•pad[2] (fŏŏt′păd′) *n.* A plate or similar structure on the leg of a spacecraft that distributes weight and helps prevent sinking after landing.

foot•path (fŏŏt′păth′, -päth′) *n.* A path for pedestrians.

foot-pound (fŏŏt′pound′) *n.* A unit of work equal to the work required to raise a mass of one pound a distance of one foot.

foot-pound•al (fŏŏt′poun′dl) *n.* A unit of work equal to the work done by a force of one poundal acting through a distance of one foot.

foot-pound-sec•ond (fŏŏt′pound′sĕk′ənd) *adj.* Of or relating to the US Customary and British Imperial systems of measurement with base units of the foot, the pound, and the second.

foot•print (fŏŏt′prĭnt′) *n.* **1.** An outline or indentation left by a foot on a surface. **2.** The surface space occupied by a structure or device. **3.** An area within which a spacecraft is supposed to land. **4.** A designated area affected or covered by a device or phenomenon.

foot•race or **foot race** (fŏŏt′rās′) *n. Sports* A race run by contestants on foot. —**foot′rac′ing** *n.*

foot•rest (fŏŏt′rĕst′) *n.* A support on which to rest the feet.

foot•rope (fŏŏt′rōp′) *n. Nautical* **1.** A rope attached to the lower border of a sail. **2.** A rope, rigged beneath a yard, for sailors to stand on during the reefing or furling of a sail.

foot rot *n.* **1.** A bacterial infection of the feet in certain hoofed animals often resulting in loss of the hoof. **2.** A disease of plants in which the stem or trunk rots at its base.

foot•sie also **foot•sy** (fŏŏt′sē) *n. Informal* The flirtatious act of secretly touching the feet or legs of another with one's own, as under a table. —*idiom:* **play footsie with** **1.** To flirt with, esp. in secret. **2.** To cooperate or curry favor with in a sly or devious way. [< dim. of FOOT.]

foot•slog (fŏŏt′slŏg′) *intr.v.* **-slogged, -slog•ging, -slogs** To walk, march, or trudge, esp. over a long distance. —**foot′slog′ger** *n.*

foot soldier *n.* **1.** A soldier who fights on foot; an infantryman. **2.** One who performs necessary but basic, often mundane tasks.

foot•sore (fŏŏt′sôr′, -sōr′) *adj.* Having sore or tired feet, as from too much walking. —**foot′sore′ness** *n.*

foot•stalk (fŏŏt′stôk′) *n.* A supporting stalk, such as a peduncle or pedicel.

foot•stall (fŏŏt′stôl′) *n.* The pedestal, plinth, or base of a pillar, column, or statue.

foot•step (fŏŏt′stĕp′) *n.* **1a.** A step with the foot. **b.** The sound of a foot stepping. **2.** The distance covered by a step: *a footstep away.* **3.** See **footprint** 1. **4.** A step on which to go up or down. —*idiom:* **follow in (someone's) footsteps** To carry on the behavior, work, or tradition of.

foot•stone (fŏŏt′stōn′) *n.* A marking stone placed at the foot of a grave.

foot•stool (fŏŏt′stōōl′) *n.* A low stool for supporting the feet.

foot•wall (fŏŏt′wôl′) *n.* **1.** The mass of rock underlying a mineral deposit in a mine. **2.** The underlying block of a fault having an inclined fault plane.

foot•way (fŏŏt′wā′) *n.* A walk or path for pedestrians.

foot•wear (fŏŏt′wâr′) *n.* Attire, such as shoes, for the feet.

foot•work (fŏŏt′wûrk′) *n.* **1.** *Sports* The manner in which the feet are used or maneuvered, as in figure skating. **2.** Work that involves moving around on foot; legwork. **3.** *Informal* Skillful dealing or maneuvering; tactics.

foo•zle (fōō′zəl) *tr.v.* **-zled, -zling, -zles** To manage clumsily; bungle. ❖ *n.* The act of bungling, esp. a poor stroke in golf. [Perh. < Ger. dialectal *fuseln*, to work poorly or slowly.]

fop (fŏp) *n.* A man who is preoccupied with and often vain about his clothes and manners; a dandy. [ME, fool; prob. akin to ME *fob*, trickster, cheat. See FOB[2].]

fop•per•y (fŏp′ə-rē) *n., pl.* **-ies** **1.** Foolishness. **2.** The dress or manner of a fop.

fop•pish (fŏp′ĭsh) *adj.* Of, relating to, or characteristic of a fop; dandified. —**fop′pish•ly** *adv.* —**fop′pish•ness** *n.*

for (fôr; fər *when unstressed*) *prep.* **1a.** Used to indicate the object, aim, or purpose of an action or activity: *for sale.* **b.** Used to indicate a destination: *headed for town.* **2.** Used to indicate the object of a desire, intention, or perception: *a nose for news.* **3a.** Used to indicate the recipient or beneficiary of an action: *lunch for us.* **b.** On behalf of: *spoke for the members.* **c.** In favor of: *Were they for the proposal?* **d.** In place of: *a substitute for eggs.* **4a.** Used to indicate equivalence or equality: *ten dollars for a ticket.* **b.** Used to indicate correlation or correspondence: *two steps back for every step* *forward.* **5a.** Used to indicate amount, extent, or duration: *walked for miles; rained for an hour.* **b.** Used to indicate a specific time: *a date for two o'clock.* **c.** Used to indicate a number of attempts: *shot three for four from the foul line.* **6a.** As being: *take for granted.* **b.** Used to indicate an actual or implied listing or choosing: *For one thing, we can't afford it.* **7.** As a result of; because of: *jumped for joy.* **8.** Used to indicate appropriateness or suitability: *It is for the judge to decide.* **9.** Notwithstanding; despite. **10a.** As regards; concerning: *a stickler for neatness.* **b.** Considering the nature or usual character of: *spry for his age.* **c.** In honor of: *named for her grandmother.* ❖ *conj.* Because; since. [ME < OE. See **per**[1] in App.]

FOR *abbr.* free on rail

for– *pref.* Completely; excessively, esp. with destructive or detrimental effect: *forworn.* [ME < OE. See **per**[1] in App.]

fo•ra (fôr′ə, fōr′ə) *n.* A plural of **forum.**

for•age (fôr′ĭj, fŏr′-) *n.* **1.** Food for domestic animals; fodder. **2.** The act of looking or searching for food or provisions. ❖ *v.* **-aged, -ag•ing, -ag•es** —*intr.* **1.** To wander in search of food or provisions. **2.** To make a raid, as for food. **3.** To conduct a search; rummage. —*tr.* **1.** To collect forage from; strip of food or supplies. **2.** *Informal* To obtain by foraging: *foraged a snack.* [ME < OFr. *fourrage* < *forrer,* to forage < *feurre,* fodder, of Gmc. orig. See **pā-** in App.] **—for′ag•er** *n.*

For•a•ker (fôr′ə-kər, fŏr′-), **Mount** A peak, 5,307 m (17,400 ft), in the Alaska Range of S-central AK.

for•am (fôr′əm, fŏr′-) *n.* A foraminifer.

fo•ra•men (fə-rā′mən) *n., pl.* **-ram•i•na** (-răm′ə-nə) or **-ra•mens** An opening or orifice, as in a bone. [Lat. *forāmen,* an opening < *forāre,* to bore.] **—fo•ram′i•nal** (-răm′ə-nəl), **fo•ram′i•nous** (-nəs) *adj.*

foramen magnum *n.* The large orifice in the base of the skull through which the spinal cord passes to become the medulla oblongata. [NLat. *forāmen magnum* : Lat. *forāmen,* opening + Lat. *magnus,* large.]

foramen o•val•e (ō-văl′ē, -vā′lē, -vä′-) *n.* An opening in the septum between the atria of the heart, usu. present only in the fetus. [NLat. *forāmen ōvāle* : Lat. *forāmen,* opening + Med.Lat. *ōvāle,* neut. of *ōvālis,* oval.]

for•a•min•i•fer (fôr′ə-mĭn′ə-fər, fŏr′-) also **fo•ram•i•nif•er•an** (fə-răm′ə-nĭf′ər-ən) *n.* Any of the chiefly marine protozoans of the order Foraminifera, having a calcareous shell with perforations through which numerous pseudopods protrude. [< NLat. *Forāminifera,* order name : Lat. *forāmen, forāmin-,* an opening + Lat. *-fer,* -fer.] **—fo•ram′i•nif′er•ous** (fə-răm′ə-nĭf′ər-əs), **fo•ram′i•nif′er•al** *adj.*

for•as•much as (fôr′əz-mŭch′ əz) *conj.* Inasmuch as; since.

for•ay (fôr′ā′, fŏr′ā′, fôr′ā′) *n.* **1.** A sudden raid or military advance. **2.** A venture or an initial attempt, esp. outside one's usual area. ❖ *v.* **-ayed, -ay•ing, -ays** —*intr.* **1.** To make a raid. **2.** To make inroads, as for profit or adventure. —*tr. Archaic* To pillage for spoils. [ME *forrai* < *forraien,* to plunder, prob. back-formation < *forreour,* raider, plunderer < OFr. *forrier* < *forrer,* to forage. See FORAGE.]

forb (fôrb) *n.* A broad-leaved herb other than a grass, esp. one growing in a field, prairie, or meadow. [< Gk. *phorbē,* fodder < *pherbein,* to graze.]

for•bear[1] (fôr-bâr′) *v.* **-bore** (-bôr′, -bōr′), **-borne** (-bôrn′, -bōrn′), **-bear•ing, -bears** —*tr.* **1.** To refrain from; resist: *forbear replying.* **2.** To desist from; cease. **3.** *Obsolete* To avoid or shun. —*intr.* **1.** To hold back; refrain. **2.** To be tolerant or patient in the face of provocation. [ME *forberen* < OE *forberan,* to endure. See **bher-**[1] in App.] **—for•bear′er** *n.*

for•bear[2] (fôr′bâr′, fōr′-) *n.* Variant of **forebear.**

for•bear•ance (fôr-bâr′əns) *n.* **1.** The act of forbearing. **2.** Tolerance and restraint in the face of provocation; patience. See Syns at **patience. 3.** The quality of being forbearing. **4.** *Law* The act of a creditor who refrains from enforcing a debt when it falls due.

for•bid (fər-bĭd′, fôr-) *tr.v.* **-bade** (-băd′, -bād′) or **-bad** (-băd′), **-bid•den** (-bĭd′n) or **-bid, -bid•ding, -bids 1.** To command (someone) not to do something. **2.** To command against the doing or use of (something); prohibit. **3.** To have the effect of preventing; preclude: *Discretion forbids a reply.* [ME *forbidden, forbeden* < OE *forbēodan.* See **bheudh-** in App.] **—for•bid′dance** *n.* **—for•bid′der** *n.*

SYNONYMS *forbid, ban, enjoin, interdict, prohibit, proscribe* These verbs mean to refuse to allow: *laws that forbid speeding; banned smoking; was enjoined from broadcasting; interdict trafficking in drugs; rules that prohibit loitering; proscribed the importation of certain fruits.* **ANTONYM** *permit*

for•bid•den (fər-bĭd′n, fôr-) *adj. Physics* Having a low probability of occurrence. Used of quantum phenomena.

Forbidden City A walled enclosure of central Beijing, China, containing the palaces of former Ming and Qing dynasty emperors.

forbidden fruit *n.* An indulgence or a pleasure that is illegal or is believed immoral. [< the story of the fruit forbidden to Adam and Eve in Genesis 2:16–3:19.]

for•bid•ding (fər-bĭd′ĭng, fôr-) *adj.* **1.** Tending or threatening to impede progress. **2.** Unpleasant; disagreeable. **3.** Having a menacing aspect. **—for•bid′ding•ly** *adv.*

force (fôrs, fōrs) *n.* **1.** The capacity to do work or cause physical change; energy, strength, or active power. **2a.** Power made operative against resistance; exertion. See Syns at **strength. b.** The use of physical power or violence to compel or restrain. **3a.** Intellectual power or vigor, esp. as conveyed in writing or speech. **b.** Moral strength. **c.** A capacity for affecting the mind or behavior; efficacy. **d.** One that possesses such capacity: *the forces of evil.* **4a.** A body of persons or other resources organized or available for a certain purpose. **b.** A person or group capable of influential action. **5a.** Military strength. **b.** The entire military strength, as of a nation. Often used in the plural. **c.** A unit of a nation's military personnel, esp. one deployed into combat. **6.** *Law* Legal validity. **7.** *Physics* A vector quantity that tends to produce an acceleration of a body in the direction of its application. ❖ *tr.v.* **forced, forc•ing, forc•es 1.** To compel through pressure or necessity. **2a.** To gain by force or coercion. **b.** To move or effect against resistance or inertia. **c.** To inflict or impose relentlessly. **3a.** To put undue strain on. **b.** To increase or accelerate (a pace, for example) to the maximum. **c.** To produce with effort and against one's will: *force a smile.* **d.** To use (language) clumsily. **4a.** To move, open, or clear by force. **b.** To break down or open by force: *force a lock.* **5.** To rape. **6.** *Botany* To cause to grow or mature by artificially accelerating normal processes. **7.** *Baseball* **a.** To put (a runner) out on a force play. **b.** To allow (a run) to be scored by walking a batter with the bases loaded. **8.** *Games* To cause an opponent to play (a particular card). ***—idioms:* force (someone's) hand** To force to act or speak prematurely or unwillingly. **in force 1.** In full strength; in large numbers. **2.** In effect; operative. [ME < OFr. < Med.Lat. *fortia* < neut. pl. of Lat. *fortis,* strong. See **bhergh-** in App.] **—force′a•ble** *adj.* **—forc′er** *n.*

forced (fôrst, fōrst) *adj.* **1.** Imposed by force; involuntary: *forced labor.* **2.** Produced under strain; not spontaneous: *forced laughter.*

force-feed (fôrs′fēd′, fōrs′-) *tr.v.* **-fed** (-fĕd′), **-feed•ing, -feeds 1.** To compel to ingest food; feed forcibly, esp. by mechanical means. **2.** To force to assimilate.

force field *n.* See **field of force.**

force•ful (fôrs′fəl, fōrs′-) *adj.* Characterized by or full of force; effective: *forceful measures to reduce shoplifting.* **—force′ful•ly** *adv.* **—force′ful•ness** *n.*

force ma•jeure (fôrs′ mä-zhûr′, fōrs′) *n.* **1.** Superior or overpowering force. **2.** An unexpected or uncontrollable event. [Fr. : *force,* force + *majeure,* greater.]

force•meat (fôrs′mēt′, fōrs′-) *n.* Finely ground and highly spiced meat, fish, or poultry that is served alone or used in stuffing. [*force* (alteration of FARCE) + MEAT.]

force of habit *n.* Behavior that has become automatic through long practice or frequent repetition.

force-out (fôrs′out′, fōrs′-) *n. Baseball* The act or fact of putting out a base runner on a force play.

force play *n. Baseball* A play in which a runner is put out when forced by the batter to move to the next base.

for•ceps (fôr′səps, -sĕps) *n., pl.* **forceps 1.** A pincerlike instrument used for grasping, manipulating, or extracting, esp. such an instrument used by a surgeon. **2.** A pincerlike pair of movable posterior appendages in certain insects, such as earwigs. [Lat., fire tongs, pincers. See **g^wher-** in App.]

force pump *n.* A pump with a solid piston and valves used to raise a liquid or expel it under pressure.

forc•i•ble (fôr′sə-bəl, fōr′-) *adj.* **1.** Effected against resistance by using force: *The police used forcible restraint to subdue the assailant.* **2.** Characterized by force; powerful. **—forc′i•ble•ness** *n.* **—forc′i•bly** *adv.*

ford (fôrd, fōrd) *n.* A shallow place in a body of water where one can cross by walking or riding. ❖ *tr.v.* **ford•ed, ford•ing, fords** To cross (a body of water) at a ford. [ME < OE. See **per-**[2] in App.] **—ford′a•ble** *adj.*

Ford, Elizabeth Bloomer Known as "Betty." b. 1918. First Lady of the US (1974–77) who supported the Equal Rights Amendment, the arts, and programs for disabled children.

Ford, Ford Madox 1873–1939. British writer and editor noted for his novel *The Good Soldier* (1915).

Ford, Gerald Rudolph b. 1913. The 38th President of the US (1974–77), who was appointed Vice President on the resignation of Spiro Agnew (1973) and became President after Richard Nixon's resignation over the Watergate scandal.

Ford, Henry 1863–1947. Amer. automobile manufacturer who developed a gasoline-powered automobile (1893) and mass-produced the Model T (1908–27).

Ford[1]**, John** 1586–1639. English playwright whose works include *'Tis Pity She's a Whore* (1633).

Ford[2]**, John** 1895–1973. Amer. filmmaker whose motion pictures include *The Grapes of Wrath* (1940).

for•do also **fore•do** (fôr-dōō′, fōr-) *tr.v.* **-did** (-dĭd′), **-done** (-dŭn′), **-do•ing, -does** (-dŭz′) *Archaic* **1.** To bring to ruin; destroy. **2.** To exhaust utterly. [ME *fordon* < OE *fordōn* : *for-,* for- + *dōn,* to do; see **dhē-** in App.]

fore (fôr, fōr) *adj.* **1.** Located at or toward the front; forward. **2.** Earlier in order of occurrence; former. ❖ *n.* **1.** Something that is located at or toward the front. **2.** The front part. ❖ *adv.* **1.** At, toward, or near the front; forward. **2.** At an earlier time. ❖ *prep.* also **'fore** Before. ❖ *interj. Sports* Used by a golfer to warn those

Gerald Ford

Henry Ford
photographed in 1896 in his first automobile, the Quadricycle

ă	pat	oi	boy
ā	pay	ou	out
âr	care	ŏŏ	took
ä	father	ōō	boot
ĕ	pet	ŭ	cut
ē	be	ûr	urge
ĭ	pit	th	thin
ī	pie	*th*	this
îr	pier	hw	which
ŏ	pot	zh	vision
ō	toe	ə	about, item
ô	paw		

Stress marks:
′ (primary);
′ (secondary), as in
lexicon (lĕk′sĭ-kŏn′)

forehand

forelock¹

ahead that a ball is headed in their direction. —*idiom:* **to the fore** In, into, or toward a position of prominence. [ME, before-hand, before, in front of < OE. See **per¹** in App.]

fore– *pref.* **1.** Before; earlier: *foredoom.* **2.** In front of; front: *fore-deck.* [ME *for-*, *fore-* < OE < *fore*, in front. See **per¹** in App.]

fore and aft *adv.* **1a.** From the bow of a ship to the stern; lengthwise. **b.** In, at, or toward both ends of a ship. **2.** In or at the front and back.

fore-and-aft (fôr′ən-ăft′, fōr′-) *adj.* Parallel with the length of a structure, such as a ship or house; running lengthwise.

fore-and-aft•er (fôr′ən-ăf′tər, fōr′-) *n.* A sailing ship, such as a schooner, with a fore-and-aft rig.

fore-and-aft rig *n.* A rig on a sailing ship that has quadrilateral and triangular sails set to the fore-and-aft rig.

fore-and-aft sail *n.* A sail set along the fore-and-aft line of a vessel, having its luff attached to the mast.

fore•arm¹ (fôr-ärm′, fōr-) *tr.v.* **-armed, -arm•ing, -arms** To arm or prepare in advance of a conflict.

fore•arm² (fôr′ärm′, fōr′-) *n.* **1.** The part of the arm between the wrist and the elbow. **2.** The corresponding part of the foreleg in certain quadrupeds, such as a horse.

fore•bear also **for•bear** (fôr′bâr′, fōr′-) *n.* A person from whom one is descended; an ancestor. See Syns at **ancestor.** [ME *forbear* : *fore-*, fore- + *beer*, one who is (< *ben*, to be; see BE).]

fore•bode (fôr-bōd′, fōr-) *v.* **-bod•ed, -bod•ing, -bodes** —*tr.* **1.** To indicate the likelihood of; portend. **2.** To have a premonition of (a future misfortune). —*intr.* To prophesy or predict. —**fore•bod′er** *n.*

fore•bod•ing (fôr-bō′dĭng, fōr-) *n.* **1.** A sense of impending evil or misfortune. **2.** An evil omen; a portent. ❖ *adj.* Marked by or indicative of foreboding; ominous. —**fore•bod′ing•ly** *adv.*

fore•brain (fôr′brān′, fōr′-) *n.* **1.** The most anterior of the three primary regions of the embryonic brain. **2.** The segment of the adult brain that develops from the embryonic forebrain and includes the cerebrum, thalamus, and hypothalamus.

fore•cast (fôr′kăst′, fōr′-) *v.* **-cast** or **-cast•ed, -cast•ing, -casts** —*tr.* **1.** To estimate or calculate in advance, esp. to predict (weather conditions) by analysis of meteorological data. **2.** To serve as an advance indication of; foreshadow. —*intr.* To calculate or estimate something in advance; predict the future. ❖ *n.* A prediction, as of coming events. [ME *forecasten*, to plan beforehand : *fore-*, fore- + *casten*, to throw, calculate, prepare; see CAST.] —**fore•cast′a•ble** *adj.* —**fore′cast′er** *n.*

fore•cas•tle (fōk′səl, fôr′kăs′əl, fōr′-) also **fo′c′s′le** (fōk′səl) *n.* **1.** The section of the upper deck of a ship located at the bow forward of the foremast. **2.** A superstructure at the bow of a merchant ship where the crew is housed. [ME *forecastel* : *fore-*, fore- + *castel*, fortification; see CASTLE.]

fore-check (fôr′chĕk′, fōr′-) *intr.v.* **-checked, -check•ing, -checks** To check an ice-hockey opponent in the opponent's own defensive zone. —**fore′-check′er** *n.*

fore•close (fôr-klōz′, fōr-) *v.* **-closed, -clos•ing, -clos•es** —*tr.* **1a.** To deprive (a mortgagor) of the right to redeem mortgaged property, as when payments have not been made. **b.** To bar an equity or a right to redeem (a mortgage). **2.** To exclude or rule out; bar. **3.** To settle or resolve beforehand. —*intr.* To bar an equity or a right to redeem a mortgage. [ME *forclosen*, to exclude from an inheritance < OFr. *forclos*, shut out, p. part. of *forclore*, to exclude : *fors-*, outside (< Lat. *forīs*; see **dhwer-** in App.) + *clore*, to close (< Lat. *claudere*).] —**fore•clos′a•ble** *adj.*

fore•clo•sure (fôr-klō′zhər, fōr-) *n.* The act of foreclosing, esp. a legal proceeding by which a mortgage is foreclosed.

fore•court (fôr′kôrt′, fōr′kōrt′) *n.* **1.** A courtyard in front of a building. **2.** *Sports* The part of a court nearest the net or wall.

fore•deck (fôr′dĕk′, fōr′-) *n.* The forward part of the deck of a ship, usu. the main deck.

fore•do (fôr-dōo′, fōr-) *v.* Variant of **fordo.**

fore•doom (fôr-dōom′, fōr-) *tr.v.* **-doomed, -doom•ing, -dooms** To doom or condemn beforehand.

fore•fa•ther (fôr′fä′thər, fōr′-) *n.* An ancestor. See Syns at **ancestor.**

fore•feel (fôr-fēl′, fōr-) *tr.v.* **-felt** (-fĕlt′), **-feel•ing, -feels** To feel beforehand; have a premonition of.

fore•fend (fôr-fĕnd′, fōr-) *v.* Variant of **forfend.**

fore•fin•ger (fôr′fĭng′gər, fōr′-) *n.* See **index finger.**

fore•foot (fôr′fŏot′, fōr′-) *n.* **1.** Either of the front feet of a quadruped. **2.** The part of a ship where the prow joins the keel.

fore•front (fôr′frŭnt′, fōr′-) *n.* **1.** The foremost part or area. **2.** The position of most importance, prominence, or responsibility; the vanguard: *in the forefront of the movement.*

fore•gath•er (fôr-găth′ər, fōr-) *v.* Variant of **forgather.**

fore•go¹ (fôr-gō′, fōr-) *tr.v.* **-went** (-wĕnt′), **-gone** (-gôn′, -gŏn′), **-go•ing, -goes** (-gōz′) To precede, as in time or place. [ME *forgon* < OE *foregān* : *fore-*, fore- + *gān*, go; see **ghē-** in App.] —**fore•go′er** *n.*

fore•go² (fôr-gō′, fōr-) *v.* Variant of **forgo.**

fore•go•ing (fôr-gō′ĭng, fōr-, fôr′gō′ĭng, fōr′-) *adj.* Said, written, or encountered just before; previous.

fore•gone (fôr′gôn′, -gŏn′, fōr′-) *adj.* **1.** Having gone before; previous. **2.** *Usage Problem* Guaranteed as an outcome; assured. [P. part. of FOREGO¹.]

USAGE NOTE The widespread recent use of *foregone* to mean "assured," a truncation of the phrase *a foregone conclusion,* has not gained broad acceptance and is rejected by 80 percent of the Usage Panel.

foregone conclusion *n.* **1.** An end or result regarded as inevitable. See Usage Note at **foregone. 2.** A conclusion formed before consideration.

fore•ground (fôr′ground′, fōr′-) *n.* **1.** The part of a scene or picture nearest and in front of the viewer. **2.** See **forefront** 2. ❖ *tr.v.* **-ground•ed, -ground•ing, -grounds** To place in the foreground; call attention to.

fore•gut (fôr′gŭt′, fōr′-) *n.* **1.** The part of the embryonic vertebrate alimentary canal from which the pharynx, lungs, esophagus, stomach, liver, pancreas, and duodenum develop. **2.** The first part of the alimentary canal of an arthropod or annelid, which includes the buccal cavity, esophagus, crop, and gizzard.

fore•hand (fôr′hănd′, fōr′-) *adj.* **1.** Made or done with the hand moving palm forward: *a forehand tennis stroke.* **2.** *Obsolete* Taking place, done, or given beforehand; prior. ❖ *n.* **1.** A forehand stroke, as in tennis. **2.** The part of a horse in front of the rider. ❖ *adv.* With a forehand stroke or motion.

fore•hand•ed (fôr′hăn′dĭd, fōr′-) *adj.* **1.** Forehand, as in tennis. **2a.** Looking or planning ahead; circumspect. **b.** Having ample financial resources; well-off. —**fore′hand′ed•ly** *adv.* —**fore′hand′ed•ness** *n.*

fore•head (fôr′hĕd′, -ĭd, fōr′-) *n.* **1.** The part of the face between the eyebrows, the normal hairline, and the temples. **2.** The front part of something. [ME *forhed* < OE *forhēafod* : *for-*, fore- + *hēafod*, head; see HEAD.]

for•eign (fôr′ĭn, fōr′-) *adj.* **1.** Located away from one's native country. **2.** Of, characteristic of, or from a place other than the one being considered. **3.** Conducted or involved with other nations or governments; not domestic. **4.** Situated in an abnormal or improper place in the body and typically introduced from outside. **5.** Not natural; alien. **6.** Not germane; irrelevant. **7.** Subject to another political unit's jurisdiction. [ME *forein* < OFr. *forain* < LLat. *forānus*, on the outside < Lat. *forās*, outside. See **dhwer-** in App.] —**for′eign•ness** *n.*

foreign affairs *pl.n.* Affairs concerning international relations and national interests in foreign countries.

foreign aid *n.* Aid offered by one nation to another.

foreign bill *n.* A draft for a sum of money to be paid in another country.

for•eign-born (fôr′ĭn-bôrn′, fōr′-) *adj.* Foreign by birth; not native to the country in which one resides.

foreign correspondent *n.* A correspondent who sends news reports or commentary from a foreign country.

for•eign•er (fôr′ə-nər, fōr′-) *n.* **1.** One who is from a foreign country or place. **2.** One who is from outside a particular group or community; an outsider.

foreign exchange *n.* **1.** Transaction of international monetary business, as between different governments. **2.** Negotiable bills drawn in one country to be paid in another.

for•eign•ism (fôr′ī-nĭz′əm, fōr′-) *n.* A foreign idiom or custom.

foreign legion *n.* A unit of a nation's army that consists primarily of foreign volunteers, often tasked with fighting wars in colonies.

foreign minister *n.* A cabinet minister in charge of a nation's foreign affairs.

foreign mission *n.* **1.** A permanent diplomatic legation established in a foreign country. **2.** A religious group esp. of Christians sent to a foreign country for missionary service.

foreign office *n.* The governmental department in charge of foreign affairs in certain countries.

foreign policy *n.* The diplomatic policy of a nation in its interactions with other nations.

Foreign Service *n.* **1.** The diplomatic and consular staff of the United States. **2. foreign service** The diplomatic and consular personnel of a nation's foreign office.

fore•judge also **for•judge** (fôr-jŭj′, fōr-) *tr.v.* **-judged, -judg•ing, -judg•es** To judge beforehand without adequate examination or evidence; prejudge. —**fore•judg′ment** *n.*

fore•know (fôr-nō′, fōr-) *tr.v.* **-knew** (-nōō′, -nyōō′), **-known** (-nōn′), **-know•ing, -knows** To have foreknowledge of, esp. by supernatural means or through revelation.

fore•knowl•edge (fôr-nŏl′ĭj, fōr-, fôr′nŏl′-, fōr′-) *n.* Awareness of something before its existence or occurrence.

fore•la•dy (fôr′lā′dē, fōr′-) *n.* A forewoman.

fore•land (fôr′lənd, fōr′-) *n.* A projecting land mass.

fore•leg (fôr′lĕg′, fōr′-) *n.* Either of the front legs of a quadruped.

fore•limb (fôr′lĭm′, fōr′-) *n.* An anterior appendage, such as a leg, wing, or flipper.

fore•lock¹ (fôr′lŏk′, fōr′-) *n.* A lock of hair that grows from or falls on the forehead, esp. the part of a horse's mane that falls forward between the ears.

fore•lock² (fôr′lŏk′, fōr′-) *n.* A cotter pin; a linchpin.

fore•man (fôr′mən, fōr′-) *n.* **1.** A man who leads a work crew. **2.** A man who chairs and speaks for a jury. —**fore′man•ship′** *n.*

fore·mast (fôr′məst, -măst′, fōr′-) *n.* The forward mast on a sailing vessel.

fore·milk (fôr′mĭlk′, fōr′-) *n.* Colostrum.

fore·most (fôr′mōst′, fōr′-) *adj.* **1.** First in time or place. **2.** Ahead of all others, esp. in position or rank; paramount. ❖ *adv.* **1.** In the front or first position. **2.** So as to be most important. [Alteration of ME *formest,* first < OE. See **per**[1] in App.]

fore·moth·er (fôr′mŭth′ər, fōr′-) *n.* A woman ancestor.

fore·name (fôr′nām′, fōr′-) *n.* A name before one's surname; a first name.

fore·named (fôr′nāmd′, fōr′-) *adj.* Named previously.

fore·noon (fôr′nōōn′, fōr′-, fôr-nōōn′, fōr′-) *n.* The period of time between sunrise and noon; morning.

fo·ren·sic (fə-rĕn′sĭk, -zĭk) *adj.* **1.** Relating to, used in, or appropriate for courts of law or for public discussion or argumentation. **2.** Of, relating to, or used in debate or argument; rhetorical. **3.** Relating to the use of science and technology to establish facts or evidence in a court of law: *a forensic laboratory.* [< Lat. *forēnsis,* public, of a forum < *forum,* forum. See **dhwer-** in App.] —**fo·ren′si·cal·ly** *adv.*

forensic medicine *n.* The branch of medicine that interprets or establishes the facts in civil or criminal law cases.

fo·ren·sics (fə-rĕn′sĭks, -zĭks) *n.* (*used with a sing. verb*) **1.** The art or study of formal debate; argumentation. **2.** The use of science and technology to investigate and establish facts in a court of law.

fore·or·dain (fôr′ôr-dān′, fōr′-) *tr.v.* **-dained, -dain·ing, -dains** To determine or appoint beforehand; predestine. —**fore′or·dain′ment, fore·or′di·na′tion** (-ôr′dn-ā′shən) *n.*

fore·part (fôr′pärt′, fōr′-) *n.* **1.** The first or early part of a period of time. **2.** The anterior part, as of an object.

fore·paw (fôr′pô′, fōr′-) *n.* The paw of an animal's foreleg.

fore·peak (fôr′pēk′, fōr′-) *n.* The section of the hold of a ship that is within the angle made by the bow.

fore·per·son (fôr′pûr′sən, fōr′-) *n.* **1.** The chair and spokesperson for a jury. **2.** The leader of a work crew.

fore·play (fôr′plā′, fōr′-) *n.* Sexual stimulation preceding intercourse.

fore·quar·ter (fôr′kwôr′tər, fōr′-) *n.* **1.** The front section of a side of meat. **2.** The foreleg, shoulder, and adjacent lateral parts of an animal, esp. a horse.

fore·reach (fôr-rēch′, fōr-) *v.* **-reached, -reach·ing, -reach·es** *Nautical* —*tr.* To gain on or get ahead of (a sailing vessel). —*intr.* **1.** To forereach a sailing vessel. **2.** To continue moving forward after taking in sail, as when coming about.

fore·run (fôr-rŭn′, fōr-) *tr.v.* **-ran** (-răn′), **-run, -run·ning, -runs** **1.** To run before. **2.** To precede as an indication of what is to follow. **3.** To prevent from arriving or occurring.

fore·run·ner (fôr′rŭn′ər, fōr′-) *n.* **1a.** One that precedes, as in time; a predecessor. **b.** An ancestor; a forebear. **2a.** One that comes before and indicates the approach of another; a harbinger. **b.** A warning sign or symptom.

fore·said (fôr′sĕd′, fōr′-) *adj. Archaic* Aforesaid.

fore·sail (fôr′səl, -sāl′, fōr′-) *n. Nautical* **1.** The principal sail hung from the foreyard of a square-rigged vessel. **2.** The principal sail hung from the foremast of a fore-and-aft-rigged vessel. **3.** A triangular sail hung from the forestay of a cutter or sloop; a jib.

fore·see (fôr-sē′, fōr-) *tr.v.* **-saw** (-sô′), **-seen** (-sēn′), **-see·ing, -sees** To see or know beforehand: *foresaw the increase in unemployment.* —**fore·see′a·ble** *adj.* —**fore·se′er** *n.*

fore·shad·ow (fôr-shăd′ō, fōr-) *tr.v.* **-owed, -ow·ing, -ows** To present an indication or a suggestion of beforehand; presage. —**fore·shad′ow·er** *n.*

fore·sheet (fôr′shēt′, fōr′-) *n. Nautical* **1.** A sheet used in trimming a foresail. **2.** **foresheets** The space near the bow of an open boat.

fore·shock (fôr′shŏk′, fōr′-) *n.* A tremor that precedes an earthquake originating at approximately the same location.

fore·shore (fôr′shôr′, fōr′-) *n.* **1.** The area of a shore that lies between the average high tide and low tide marks. **2.** The part of a shore between the water and occupied or cultivated land.

fore·short·en (fôr-shôr′tn, fōr-) *tr.v.* **-ened, -en·ing, -ens** **1.** To shorten the lines of (an object) in a drawing or other representation so as to produce an illusion of projection or extension in space. **2.** To reduce the length of; curtail.

fore·show (fôr-shō′, fōr-) *tr.v.* **-showed, -shown** (-shōn′) or **-showed, -show·ing, -shows** To show in advance; prefigure.

fore·side (fôr′sīd′, fōr′-) *n.* The front or upper side or part.

fore·sight (fôr′sīt′, fōr′-) *n.* **1.** Perception of the significance and nature of events before they have occurred. **2.** Care in providing for the future; prudence. See Syns at **prudence.** **3.** The act of looking forward. —**fore′sight′ed, fore′sight′ful** *adj.* —**fore′sight′ed·ly** *adv.* —**fore′sight′ed·ness** *n.*

fore·skin (fôr′skĭn′, fōr′-) *n.* The loose fold of skin that covers the glans of the penis.

fore·speak (fôr-spēk′, fōr-) *tr.v.* **-spoke** (-spōk′), **-spo·ken** (-spō′kən), **-speak·ing, -speaks** **1.** To predict. **2.** To arrange for in advance.

for·est (fôr′ĭst, fōr′-) *n.* **1.** A dense growth of trees, plants, and underbrush covering a large area. **2.** Something that resembles a

large dense growth of trees, as in density. **3.** A defined area of land formerly set aside in England as a royal hunting ground. ❖ *tr.v.* **-est·ed, -est·ing, -ests** To plant trees on. [ME < OFr. < Med.Lat. *forestis (silva),* outside (forest) < Lat. *forīs,* outside. See **dhwer-** in App.] —**for·est′al, fo·res′tial** (fə-rĕs′chəl) *adj.* —**for′es·ta′tion** *n.*

fore·stage (fôr′stāj′, fōr′-) *n.* The part of a stage in front of the closed curtain.

fore·stall (fôr-stôl′, fōr-) *tr.v.* **-stalled, -stall·ing, -stalls** **1.** To delay, hinder, or prevent by taking precautionary measures. **2.** To deal with or think of beforehand; anticipate. **3.** To prevent or hinder normal sales in (a market) by buying up merchandise, discouraging persons from bringing their goods to market, or encouraging an increase in prices in goods already on sale. [ME *forestallen,* to waylay and rob < *forestal,* highway robbery, ambush < OE *foresteall* : *fore-,* fore- + *steall,* position; see **stel-** in App.] —**fore·stall′er** *n.* —**fore·stall′ment** *n.*

fore·stay (fôr′stā′, fōr′-) *n. Nautical* A stay extending from the head of the foremast to the bowsprit of a ship.

fore·stay·sail (fôr′stā′səl, -sāl′, fōr′-) *n. Nautical* A triangular sail set on the forestay.

for·est·er (fôr′ĭ-stər, fōr′-) *n.* **1.** One trained in forestry. **2.** One that inhabits a forest. **3.** Any of various chiefly black moths of the family Agaristidae.

Forester, C(ecil) S(cott) 1899–1966. British writer known esp. for his novels featuring Horatio Hornblower.

for·est·land (fôr′ĭst-lănd′, fōr′-) *n.* A section of land covered with forest or set aside for the cultivation of forests.

for·est·ry (fôr′ĭ-strē, fōr′-) *n.* **1a.** The science and art of cultivating, maintaining, and developing forests. **b.** The management of a forestland. **2.** A forestland.

fore·swear (fôr-swâr′, fōr-) *v.* Variant of **forswear.**

fore·taste (fôr′tāst′, fōr′-) *n.* **1.** An advance token or warning. **2.** A slight taste or sample in anticipation of something. ❖ *tr.v.* (fôr-tāst′, fōr′tāst′) **-tast·ed, -tast·ing, -tastes** To have an anticipatory taste of.

fore·tell (fôr-tĕl′, fōr-) *tr.v.* **-told** (-tōld′), **-tell·ing, -tells** To tell of or indicate beforehand; predict. —**fore·tell′er** *n.*

fore·thought (fôr′thôt′, fōr′-) *n.* **1.** Deliberation, consideration, or planning beforehand. **2.** Preparation or thought for the future. See Syns at **prudence.** —**fore′thought′ful** *adj.* —**fore′thought′ful·ly** *adv.* —**fore′thought′ful·ness** *n.*

fore·to·ken (fôr-tō′kən, fōr-) *tr.v.* **-kened, -ken·ing, -kens** To indicate or give warning of beforehand; presage. ❖ *n.* (fôr′tō′kən, fōr′-) An advance sign; a warning.

fore·top (fôr′tŏp′, fōr′-) *n.* **1.** (*also* -təp) *Nautical* A platform at the top of a ship's foremast. **2.** A forelock, esp. of a horse.

fore·top·gal·lant (fôr′tŏp-găl′ənt, -təp-, -tə-, fōr′-) *adj. Nautical* Of, relating to, or being the mast directly above the foretopmast.

fore·top·mast (fôr′tŏp′məst, -təp-măst′, fōr′-) *n. Nautical* The mast that is above the foretop.

fore·top·sail (fôr′tŏp′səl, -təp-, fōr′-) *n. Nautical* A sail hung from the foretopmast.

for·ev·er (fôr-ĕv′ər, fər-) *adv.* **1.** For everlasting time. **2.** At all times; incessantly. ❖ *n.* A seemingly very long time.

for·ev·er·more (fôr-ĕv′ər-môr′, -mōr′, fər-) *adv.* Forever.

fore·warn (fôr-wôrn′, fōr-) *tr.v.* **-warned, -warn·ing, -warns** To warn in advance.

fore·went (fôr-wĕnt′, fōr-) *v.* Past tense of **forego**[1].

fore·wing (fôr′wĭng′, fōr′-) *n.* Either of a pair of anterior wings of a four-winged insect.

fore·wom·an (fôr′wŏŏm′ən, fōr′-) *n.* **1.** A woman who leads a work crew. **2.** A woman who chairs and speaks for a jury.

fore·word (fôr′wərd, fōr′-) *n.* A preface or an introductory note, as for a book, esp. by a person other than the author.

fore·worn (fôr-wôrn′, fōr-wōrn′) *adj.* Variant of **forworn.**

fore·yard (fôr′yärd′, fōr′-) *n. Nautical* The lowest yard on a foremast, from which the foresail is hung.

for·feit (fôr′fĭt) *n.* **1.** Something surrendered or subject to surrender as punishment, as for a crime, for example. **2.** *Games* **a.** Something placed in escrow and then redeemed after payment of a fine. **b.** **forfeits** A game in which forfeits are demanded. **3.** A forfeiture. ❖ *adj.* Lost or subject to loss through forfeiture. ❖ *tr.v.* **-feit·ed, -feit·ing, -feits** **1.** To surrender, be deprived of, or give up the right to, as on account of a crime, for example. **2.** To subject to seizure as a forfeit. [ME *forfet,* crime, penalty < OFr. *forfait,* p. part. of *forfaire,* to commit a crime, act outside the law : *fors,* beyond; see **FORECLOSE** + *faire,* to do; see **FEASIBLE.**] —**for′feit·a·ble** *adj.* —**for′feit·er** *n.*

for·fei·ture (fôr′fĭ-chŏŏr′, -chər) *n.* **1.** The act of surrendering something as a forfeit. **2.** Something that is forfeited.

for·fend *also* **fore·fend** (fôr-fĕnd′, fōr-) *tr.v.* **-fend·ed, -fend·ing, -fends** **1a.** To keep or ward off; avert. **b.** *Archaic* To forbid. **2.** To defend or protect. [ME *forfenden* : *for-,* for- + *fenden,* to ward off; see **FEND.**]

for·gath·er *also* **fore·gath·er** (fôr-găth′ər, fōr-) *intr.v.* **-ered, -er·ing, -ers** **1.** To gather together; assemble. **2.** To meet another, esp. accidentally.

forge[1] (fôrj, fōrj) *n.* **1.** A furnace or hearth where metals are heated or wrought; a smithy. **2.** A workshop where pig iron is

forge[1]
forging a horseshoe

ă	pat	oi	boy
ā	pay	ou	out
âr	care	ŏŏ	took
ä	father	ōō	boot
ĕ	pet	ŭ	cut
ē	be	ûr	urge
ĭ	pit	th	thin
ī	pie	th	this
îr	pier	hw	which
ŏ	pot	zh	vision
ō	toe	ə	about,
ô	paw		item

Stress marks:
′ (primary);
′ (secondary), as in
lexicon (lĕk′sĭ-kŏn′)

transformed into wrought iron. ❖ *v.* **forged, forg•ing, forg•es** —*tr.* **1a.** To form (metal, for example) by heating in a forge and beating or hammering into shape. **b.** To form (metal) by a mechanical or hydraulic press. **2.** To give form or shape to, esp. by means of careful effort: *forge a relationship.* **3.** To reproduce for fraudulent purposes; counterfeit. —*intr.* **1.** To work at a forge or smithy. **2.** To make a forgery or counterfeit. [ME < OFr. < Lat. *fabrica* < *faber,* worker.] —**forge′a•bil′i•ty** *n.* —**forge′a•ble** *adj.* —**forg′er** *n.*

forge[2] (fôrj, fōrj) *intr.v.* **forged, forg•ing, forg•es 1.** To advance gradually but steadily: *forged ahead.* **2.** To advance with an abrupt increase of speed. [Prob. < FORGE[1].]

for•ger•y (fôr′jə-rē, fōr′-) *n., pl.* **-ies 1.** The act of forging, esp. the illegal production of something counterfeit. **2.** Something counterfeit, forged, or fraudulent.

for•get (fər-gĕt′, fôr-) *v.* **-got** (-gŏt′), **-got•ten** (-gŏt′n) or **-got, -get•ting, -gets** —*tr.* **1.** To be unable to remember (something). **2.** To treat with thoughtless inattention; neglect. **3.** To leave behind unintentionally. **4.** To fail to mention. **5a.** To banish from one's thoughts. **b.** *Informal* To disregard on purpose. Usu. used in the imperative: *Oh, forget it.* —*intr.* **1.** To cease remembering. **2.** To fail or neglect to become aware at the proper or specified moment: *forgot about my appointment.* ***—idiom:*** **forget (oneself)** To lose one's reserve, temper, or self-restraint. [ME *forgeten* < OE *forgietan.* See **ghend-** in App.] —**for•get′ter** *n.*

for•get•ful (fər-gĕt′fəl, fôr-) *adj.* **1.** Tending or likely to forget. **2.** Marked by neglectful or heedless failure to remember: *forgetful of one's responsibilities.* **3.** Causing one to be unable to remember. —**for•get′ful•ly** *adv.* —**for•get′ful•ness** *n.*

for•ge•tive (fôr′jĭ-tĭv, fōr′-) *adj. Archaic* Capable of imagining or inventing. [Poss. < FORGE[1] + *-tive* (as in INVENTIVE or CREATIVE).]

for•get-me-not (fər-gĕt′mē-nŏt′, fôr-) *n.* **1.** Any of various herbs of the genus *Myosotis,* having clusters of small blue flowers. **2.** Any of several similar or related plants.

for•get•ta•ble (fər-gĕt′ə-bəl, fôr-) *adj.* Fit or apt to be forgotten: *a very forgettable movie.*

for•give (fər-gĭv′, fôr-) *v.* **-gave** (-gāv′), **-giv•en** (-gĭv′ən), **-giv•ing, -gives** —*tr.* **1.** To excuse for a fault or an offense; pardon. **2.** To renounce anger or resentment against. **3.** To absolve from payment of (a debt, for example). —*intr.* To accord forgiveness. [ME *forgiven* < OE *forgiefan.* See **ghabh-** in App.] —**for•giv′a•ble** *adj.* —**for•giv′a•bly** *adv.* —**for•giv′er** *n.*

SYNONYMS *forgive, pardon, excuse, condone* These verbs mean to refrain from imposing punishment on an offender or demanding satisfaction for an offense. The first three can be used as conventional ways of offering apology. More strictly, to *forgive* is to grant pardon without harboring resentment: *"Children begin by loving their parents; as they grow older they judge them; sometimes they forgive them"* (Oscar Wilde). *Pardon* more strongly implies release from the liability for or penalty entailed by an offense: *All political prisoners were pardoned.* To *excuse* is to pass over a mistake or fault without demanding punishment or redress: *"There are some acts of injustice which no national interest can excuse"* (J.A. Froude). To *condone* is to overlook an offense, usually a serious one, and often suggests tacit forgiveness: *Failure to protest the policy may imply a willingness to condone it.*

---

for•give•ness (fər-gĭv′nĭs, fôr-) *n.* The act of forgiving.

for•giv•ing (fər-gĭv′ĭng, fôr-) *adj.* **1.** Inclined or able to forgive. **2.** Providing a margin for error or shortcomings. —**for•giv′ing•ly** *adv.* —**for•giv′ing•ness** *n.*

for•go also **fore•go** (fôr-gō′, fōr-) *tr.v.* **-went** (-wĕnt′), **-gone** (-gôn′, -gŏn′), **-go•ing, -goes** To abstain from; relinquish. [ME *forgon* < OE *forgān,* go away, forgo : *for-,* for- + *gān,* to go; see **ghē-** in App.] —**for•go′er** *n.*

fo•rint (fôr′ĭnt′) *n.* See table at **currency.** [Hung. < Ital. *fiorino,* florin. See FLORIN.]

for•judge (fôr-jŭj′, fōr-) *v.* Variant of **forejudge.**

fork (fôrk) *n.* **1.** A utensil with two or more prongs, used for eating or serving food. **2.** An implement with two or more prongs used for raising, carrying, piercing, or digging. **3a.** A bifurcation or separation into two or more branches or parts. **b.** The point at which such a bifurcation or separation occurs. **c.** One of the branches of such a bifurcation or separation. **4.** *Games* An attack by one chess piece on two pieces at the same time. ❖ *v.* **forked, fork•ing, forks** —*tr.* **1.** To raise, carry, pitch, or pierce with a fork. **2.** To give the shape of a fork to (one's fingers, for example). **3.** *Games* To launch an attack on (two chess pieces). **4.** *Informal* To pay. Used with *over, out,* or *up.* —*intr.* **1.** To divide into two or more branches. **2a.** To use a fork, as in working. **b.** To turn at or travel along a fork. [ME *forke,* digging fork < OE *forca* and < ONFr. *forque,* both < Lat. *furca.*] —**fork′er** *n.* —**fork′ful′** *n.*

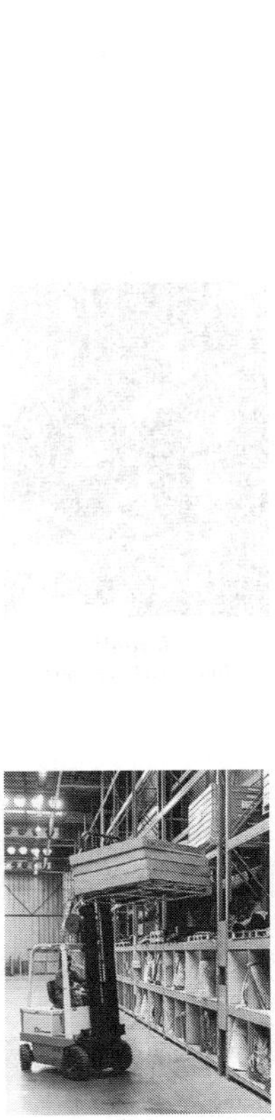

forklift

fork•ball (fôrk′bôl′) *n. Baseball* A pitch with the ball placed between the index and middle fingers so that the ball takes a sharp dip near home plate. —**fork′ball′er** *n.*

forked (fôrkt, fôr′kĭd) *adj.* **1.** Containing or characterized by a fork: *a forked river.* **2.** Shaped like or similar to a fork.

fork•lift (fôrk′lĭft′) *n.* A small industrial vehicle with a power-operated pronged platform that can be inserted under a load in order to lift and move it. —**fork′lift′** *v.*

fork•y (fôr′kē) *adj.* **-i•er, -i•est** Forked.

for•lorn (fər-lôrn′, fôr-) *adj.* **1a.** Appearing sad or lonely because deserted or abandoned. **b.** Forsaken or deprived: *forlorn of all hope.* **2.** Wretched or pitiful in appearance or condition: *forlorn roadside shacks.* **3.** Nearly hopeless; desperate. [ME *forloren,* p. part. of *forlesen,* to abandon < OE *forlēosan.* See **leu-** in App.] —**for•lorn′ly** *adv.* —**for•lorn′ness** *n.*

forlorn hope *n.* **1.** An arduous or nearly hopeless undertaking. **2.** An advance guard of troops sent on a hazardous mission. [By folk ety. < Du. *verloren hoop,* advance guard : *verloren,* p. part. of *verliezen,* to lose; see **leu-** in App. + *hoop,* troop.]

form (fôrm) *n.* **1a.** The shape and structure of an object. **b.** The body or outward appearance of a person or animal considered separately from the face or head; figure. **2a.** The essence of something. **b.** The mode in which a thing exists, acts, or manifests itself; kind. **3a.** Procedure as determined by regulation or custom. **b.** A fixed order of words or procedures, as for use in a ceremony; a formula. **4.** A document with blanks for the insertion of details or information. **5a.** Manners or conduct as governed by etiquette, decorum, or custom. **b.** Behavior according to a fixed or accepted standard: *bad form to be late.* **c.** Performance considered with regard to acknowledged criteria: *unusual form as a bowler.* **6a.** Proven ability to perform: *a musician in top form.* **b.** Fitness, as of an athlete, with regard to health or training. **c.** The past performance of a racehorse. **d.** A racing form. **7a.** Method of arrangement or manner of coordinating elements in literary or musical composition or in organized discourse: *in outline form.* **b.** A particular type or example of such arrangement: *The essay is a literary form.* **c.** The design, structure, or pattern of a work of art: *symphonic form.* **8a.** A mold for the setting of concrete. **b.** A model of the human figure or part of it used for displaying clothes. **c.** A proportioned model that may be adjusted for fitting clothes. **9.** A grade in a British secondary school or in some American private schools: *the sixth form.* **10a.** A linguistic form. **b.** The external aspect of words with regard to their inflections, pronunciation, or spelling. **11a.** *Chiefly British* A long seat; a bench. **b.** The resting place of a hare. **12.** *Botany* A subdivision of a variety usu. differing in one trivial characteristic. ❖ *v.* **formed, form•ing, forms** —*tr.* **1a.** To give form to; shape. **b.** To develop in the mind; conceive. **2a.** To shape or mold (dough, for example) into a particular form. **b.** To arrange oneself in. **c.** To organize or arrange. **d.** To fashion, train, or develop by instruction or precept. **3.** To come to have; develop or acquire. **4.** To constitute or compose a usu. basic element, part, or characteristic of. **5a.** To produce (a tense, for example) by inflection. **b.** To make (a word) by derivation or composition. **6.** To put in order; arrange. —*intr.* **1.** To become formed or shaped. **2.** To come into being by taking form; arise. **3.** To assume a specified form, shape, or pattern. [ME *forme* < Lat. *fōrma,* poss. (via Etruscan) < Gk. *morphē.*] —**form′a•bil′i•ty** *n.* —**form′a•ble** *adj.*

-form *suff.* Having the form of: *plexiform.* [NLat. *-fōrmis* < Lat. *fōrma,* form. See FORM.]

for•mal (fôr′məl) *adj.* **1a.** Relating to or involving outward form or structure. **b.** Being or relating to essential form or constitution: *a formal principle.* **2a.** Following or being in accord with accepted forms, conventions, or regulations: *a formal dinner.* **b.** Executed, carried out, or done in proper or regular form. **3a.** Characterized by strict observation of forms; methodical: *formal in their transactions.* **b.** Stiffly ceremonious: *a formal greeting.* **4.** Having the outward appearance but lacking in substance. ❖ *n.* Something, such as a gown, that is formal in nature. [ME < Lat. *fōrmālis* < *fōrma,* shape. See FORM.] —**for′mal•ly** *adv.* —**for′mal•ness** *n.*

for•mal•de•hyde (fôr-măl′də-hīd′) *n.* A colorless gaseous compound, HCHO, the simplest aldehyde, used in the synthesis of resins, as an embalming fluid, and in aqueous solution as a preservative and disinfectant. [FORM(IC ACID) + ALDEHYDE.]

for•ma•lin (fôr′mə-lĭn) *n.* An aqueous solution of formaldehyde that is 37 percent by weight. [Orig. a trademark.]

for•mal•ism (fôr′mə-lĭz′əm) *n.* **1.** Rigorous or excessive adherence to recognized forms, as in art. **2.** An instance of formalism. **3.** A method of aesthetic analysis that emphasizes structure and technique rather than content, as in literary works. —**for′mal•ist** *adj. & n.* —**for′mal•is′tic** *adj.* —**for′mal•is′ti•cal•ly** *adv.*

for•mal•i•ty (fôr-măl′ĭ-tē) *n., pl.* **-ties 1.** The quality or condition of being formal. **2.** Rigorous or ceremonious adherence to established forms, rules, or customs. **3.** An established form, rule, or custom, esp. one followed merely for the sake of procedure or decorum.

for•mal•ize (fôr′mə-līz′) *tr.v.* **-ized, -iz•ing, -iz•es 1.** To give a definite form or shape to. **2a.** To make formal. **b.** To give formal standing or endorsement to; make official by the observance of proper procedure. —**for′mal•iz′a•ble** *adj.* —**for′mal•i•za′tion** (-mə-lĭ-zā′shən) *n.* —**for′mal•iz′er** *n.*

formal logic *n.* The study of the properties of propositions and deductive reasoning by abstraction and analysis of the form rather than the content of propositions under consideration.

for•mal•wear (fôr′məl-wâr′) *n.* Attire, such as evening gowns and tuxedos, for wear on formal occasions.

For•man (fôr′mən, fōr′-), **Milos** b. 1932. Czech-born Amer.

filmmaker whose films include *Amadeus* (1984).

for•mant (fôr′mənt) *n.* Any of several frequency regions of relatively great intensity in a sound spectrum, which together determine the characteristic quality of a vowel sound. [Ger. < Lat. *fōrmāns, fōrmant-,* pr. part. of *fōrmāre,* to form < *fōrma,* form. See FORM.]

for•mat (fôr′măt′) *n.* **1.** A plan for the organization and arrangement of a specified production. **2.** The material form or layout of a publication. **3.** *Computer Science* **a.** The arrangement of data for storage or display. **b.** A method for achieving such an arrangement. ❖ *tr.v.* **-mat•ted, -mat•ting, -mats 1.** To plan or arrange in a specified form. **2.** *Computer Science* **a.** To divide (a disk) into marked sectors so that it may store data. **b.** To determine the arrangement of (data) for storage or display. [Fr., ult. < Lat. *fōrmātus,* p. part. of *fōrmāre,* to form < *fōrma,* form. See FORM.]

for•mate (fôr′māt′) *n.* A salt or ester of formic acid that contains the HCOO⁻ radical. [FORM(IC ACID) + -ATE².]

for•ma•tion (fôr-mā′shən) *n.* **1.** The act or process of forming something or of taking form. **2.** Something formed: *beautiful cloud formations.* **3.** The manner or style in which something is formed; structure. **4.** A specified arrangement or deployment, as of troops. **5.** *Geology* A primary stratigraphic unit consisting of a set of contemporaneous rocks sharing lithologic characteristics and origin, and sufficiently large to be useful in mapping. —**for•ma′tion•al** *adj.*

for•ma•tive (fôr′mə-tĭv) *adj.* **1.** Forming or capable of forming. **2a.** Susceptible to transformation by growth and development. **b.** *Biology* Capable of producing new cells or tissue. **3.** Of or relating to formation, growth, or development: *the formative stages of a plot.* **4.** *Linguistics* Relating to the formation or inflection of words. ❖ *n. Grammar* A derivational or inflectional affix. —**for′ma•tive•ly** *adv.*

form class *n.* A set of words that have one or more grammatical or syntactic characteristics in common.

form criticism *n.* A method of textual criticism, applied esp. to the Bible, for tracing the origin and history of certain passages through systematic study of the writings in terms of conventional literary forms.

form•er¹ (fôr′mər) *n.* **1.** One that forms; a maker or creator. **2.** A member of a school form.

form•er² (fôr′mər) *adj.* **1a.** Occurring earlier in time. **b.** Of, relating to, or taking place in the past. **2.** Coming before in place or order; foregoing. **3.** Being the first of two mentioned. **4.** Having been in the past: *a former ambassador.* [ME, comp. of *forme,* first < OE *forma.* See **per**¹ in App.]

USAGE NOTE Grammarians have often insisted that the phrases *the former* and *the latter* should be used only to refer to the first of two things and the second of two things, respectively, as in Ernest L. Thayer's "Casey at the Bat": "*But Flynn preceded Casey, as did also Jimmy Blake, and the former was a lulu and the latter was a fake.*" It is easy to find violations of this rule in the works of good writers; nonetheless, many readers feel uneasy when the words are used in enumerations of more than two things, just as they would feel uneasy over the similar incorrect use of a comparative in a sentence such as *Her boys are 7, 9, and 13; only the younger was born in California.*

for•mer•ly (fôr′mər-lē) *adv.* At an earlier time; once.

form-fit•ting (fôrm′fĭt′ĭng) *adj.* Snugly fitting the contours of the body: *formfitting jeans.*

form genus *n.* A classification, esp. of fossil plants, based on morphological resemblance.

for•mic (fôr′mĭk) *adj.* **1.** Of or relating to ants. **2.** Of, derived from, or containing formic acid. [< Lat. *formīca,* ant.]

For•mi•ca (fôr-mī′kə) A trademark for a variety of laminated plastic sheets of synthetic resin used esp. as a surface on tables and counters.

formic acid *n.* A colorless caustic fuming liquid, HCOOH, used in dyeing and finishing textiles and paper and in fumigants and insecticides. [< its natural occurrence in ants.]

for•mi•car•y (fôr′mĭ-kĕr′ē) *n., pl.* **-ies** A nest of ants; an anthill. [Med.Lat. *formīcārium* < Lat. *formīca,* ant.]

for•mi•civ•o•rous (fôr′mĭ-sĭv′ər-əs) *adj.* Feeding on ants. [Lat. *formīca,* ant + -VOROUS.]

for•mi•da•ble (fôr′mĭ-də-bəl, fôr-mĭd′ə-) *adj.* **1.** Arousing fear, dread, or alarm. **2.** Inspiring awe, admiration, or wonder. **3.** Difficult to undertake, surmount, or defeat: *a formidable challenge.* [ME < OFr. < Lat. *formīdābilis* < *formīdāre,* to fear < *formīdō,* fear.] —**for′mi•da•bil′i•ty, for′mi•da•ble•ness** *n.* —**for′mi•da•bly** *adv.*

form•less (fôrm′lĭs) *adj.* **1.** Having no definite form; shapeless. **2.** Lacking order. **3.** Having no material existence. —**form′less•ly** *adv.* —**form′less•ness** *n.*

form letter *n.* A usu. impersonal letter in a standardized format that may be sent to different people.

For•mo•sa (fôr-mō′sə) See **Taiwan.**

for•mu•la (fôr′myə-lə) *n., pl.* **-las** or **-lae** (-lē′) **1a.** An established form of words or symbols for use in a ceremony or procedure. **b.** An utterance of conventional notions or beliefs; a hackneyed expression. **2.** A method of doing or treating something

---

that relies on an established uncontroversial model or approach. **3.** *Chemistry* **a.** A symbolic representation of the composition or of the composition and structure of a compound. **b.** The compound so represented. **4a.** A prescription of ingredients in fixed proportion; a recipe. **b.** A liquid food for infants, containing most of the nutrients in human milk. **5.** *Mathematics* A statement, esp. an equation, of a rule, principle, or other factual relation. **6. Formula** *Sports* A set of specifications that determine a class of racing car. [Lat. *fōrmula,* dim. of *fōrma,* form. See FORM.] —**for′mu•la′ic** (-lā′ĭk) *adj.* —**for′mu•la′i•cal•ly** *adv.*

for•mu•la•rize (fôr′myə-lə-rīz′) *tr.v.* **-rized, -riz•ing, -riz•es** To express as or reduce to a formula; formulate. —**for′mu•la•ri•za′tion** (-lər-ĭ-zā′shən) *n.* —**for′mu•la•riz′er** *n.*

for•mu•lar•y (fôr′myə-lĕr′ē) *n., pl.* **-ies 1.** A book or other collection of stated and fixed forms, such as prayers. **2.** A statement expressed in formulas. **3.** A fixed form or pattern; a formula. **4.** A book containing a list of pharmaceutical substances, their formulas, uses, and methods of preparation.

for•mu•late (fôr′myə-lāt′) *tr.v.* **-lat•ed, -lat•ing, -lates 1a.** To state as or reduce to a formula. **b.** To express in systematic terms or concepts. **c.** To devise or invent: *formulate strategy.* **2.** To prepare according to a specified formula. —**for′mu•la′tion** *n.* —**for′mu•la′tor** *n.*

formula weight *n.* The sum of the atomic weights of all the atoms in a compound.

for•mu•lize (fôr′myə-līz′) *tr.v.* **-lized, -liz•ing, -liz•es** To formulate. —**for′mu•li•za′tion** (-lĭ-zā′shən) *n.* —**for′mu•liz′er** *n.*

form word *n.* See **function word.**

for•myl (fôr′mĭl′) *n.* The negative univalent radical HCO, characteristic of aldehydes. [FORM(IC ACID) + -YL.]

For•nax (fôr′năks′) *n.* A constellation in the Southern Hemisphere near Eridanus. [Lat. *fornāx,* furnace, oven. See **gʷher-** in App.]

for•nent (fər-nĕnt′) *prep.* *Chiefly Midland US* Variant of **fer-ninst.**

for•ni•cate (fôr′nĭ-kāt′) *intr.v.* **-cat•ed, -cat•ing, -cates** To engage in fornication. [LLat. *fornicārī, fornicāt-* < *fornix, fornic-,* vault, vaulted cellar, brothel. See **gʷher-** in App.] —**for′ni•ca′tor** *n.*

for•ni•ca•tion (fôr′nĭ-kā′shən) *n.* Sexual intercourse between partners who are not married to each other, esp. when considered as a sin.

WORD HISTORY The word *fornication* had a lowly beginning suitable to the low moral status of the act to which it refers. It ultimately comes from the Latin word *fornix,* "a vault, an arch," which by extension also referred to a vaulted cellar where prostitutes plied their trade. This sense of *fornix* in Late Latin yielded the verb *fornicārī,* "to commit fornication," from which was derived *fornicātiō,* "whoredom, fornication," the source of English *fornication.*

for•nix (fôr′nĭks) *n., pl.* **-ni•ces** (-nĭ-sēz′) An archlike anatomical structure or fold, such as the arched band of white matter located beneath the corpus callosum of the brain. [Lat., arch, vault. See **gʷher-** in App.]

For•rest (fôr′ĭst, fŏr′-), **Nathan Bedford** 1821–77. Amer. Confederate general who was the founder and first leader (1866–69) of the Ku Klux Klan.

for•sake (fôr-sāk′, fər-) *tr.v.* **-sook** (-sŏŏk′), **-sak•en** (-sā′kən), **-sak•ing, -sakes 1.** To give up (something held dear); renounce. **2.** To leave altogether; abandon. [ME *forsaken* < OE *forsacan.*]

for•sooth (fôr-sōōth′, fər-) *adv.* In truth; indeed. [ME *forsoth* < OE *forsōth : for,* for; see FOR + *sōth,* truth; see SOOTH.]

for•spent (fôr-spĕnt′, fər-) *adj. Archaic* Worn out, as from exertion; exhausted.

For•ster (fôr′stər), **E(dward) M(organ)** 1879–1970. British writer whose novels include *A Room with a View* (1908).

for•swear also **fore•swear** (fôr-swâr′, fōr-) *v.* **-swore** (fôr-swôr′, fōr-swōr′), **-sworn** (fôr-swôrn′, fōr-swōrn′), **-swear•ing, -swears** —*tr.* **1a.** To renounce or repudiate under oath. **b.** To renounce seriously. **2.** To disavow under oath; deny. **3.** To make (oneself) guilty of perjury. —*intr.* To swear falsely; commit perjury. [ME *forsweren* < OE *forswerian : for-,* wrongly; see FOR- + *swerian,* to swear; see SWEAR.]

for•syth•i•a (fôr-sĭth′ē-ə, -sĭf′thē-ə, fər-) *n.* Any of several Asian shrubs of the genus *Forsythia,* having early-blooming yellow flowers. [NLat. *Forsythia,* genus name, after William *Forsyth* (1737–1804), Scottish horticulturist.]

fort (fôrt, fōrt) *n.* **1.** A fortified place or position stationed with troops. **2.** A permanent army post. [ME, strength, stronghold < OFr., strong, strength < Lat. *fortis.* See **bhergh-** in App.]

For•ta•le•za (fôr′tl-ā′zə, -tə-lĕ′-) A city of NE Brazil NW of Natal; founded 1609. Pop. 1,765,794.

for•ta•lice (fôr′tə-lĭs) *n. Archaic* **1.** A defensive structure or position; a fortress. **2.** A small fort. [ME < Med.Lat. *fortalitia.* See FORTRESS.]

For•tas (fôr′təs), **Abraham** Known as "Abe." 1910–82. Amer. jurist; associate justice of the US Supreme Court (1965–69).

Fort Col•lins (fôrt kŏl′ĭnz, fōrt) A city of N CO NNE of Boulder. Pop. 118,652.

Fort-de-France (fôr-də-fräNs′) The cap. of Martinique, on the

forsythia

W coast on **Fort-de-France Bay,** an inlet of the Caribbean; settled by the French in 1762. Pop. 99,844.

for•te¹ (fôr′tā′, fôrt, fōrt) *n.* **1.** Something in which a person excels. **2.** The strong part of a sword blade, between the middle and the hilt. [Fr. *fort* < OFr., strong < Lat. *fortis.* See **bergh-** in App.]

USAGE NOTE USAGE NOTE The word *forte* has two competing pronunciations, an older one-syllable one like the word *fort,* and a more recent two-syllable one, (fôr′tā′). The second pronunciation has arisen under the mistaken impression that the word is the same as the well-known Italian musical term *forte.* In fact the word is originally from French *fort,* but the two-syllable pronunciation is widely accepted by educated speakers, and is preferred by 74 percent of the Usage Panel. The result is a delicate situation; speakers who are aware of the origin of the word may wish to continue to pronounce it as one syllable but at an increasing risk of puzzling their listeners.

for•te² (fôr′tā′) *Music adv. & adj.* In a loud forceful manner. ❖ *n.* A note, passage, or chord played forte. [Ital., strong, forte < Lat. *fortis.* See **bergh-** in App.]

for•te•pi•an•o (fôr′tā-pē-ăn′ō, -ä′nō) *n., pl.* **-os** Any of various precursors to the modern piano. [Ital., var. of *pianoforte.* See PI-ANOFORTE.]

for•te-pi•an•o (fôr′tā-pē-ăn′ō, -ä′nō) *adv. & adj. Music* In a loud, then suddenly soft manner. [Ital. : *forte,* loud; see FORTE² + *piano,* soft; see PIANO².]

forth (fôrth, fōrth) *adv.* **1.** Forward in time, place, or order; onward: *from this time forth.* **2.** Out into view: *put my ideas forth.* **3.** *Obsolete* Away from a specified place; abroad. ❖ *prep. Archaic* Out of; forth from. [ME < OE. See **per**¹ in App.]

Forth A river of S-central Scotland flowing c. 187 km (116 mi) to the **Firth of Forth,** an inlet of the North Sea.

forth•com•ing (fôrth-kŭm′ĭng, fōrth-) *adj.* **1.** About to appear or take place; approaching. **2a.** Available when required or as promised. **b.** Affable and outgoing: *a forthcoming person.* **c.** Candid and willing to cooperate. ❖ *n.* (fôrth′kŭm′ĭng, fōrth′-) The act or an instance of coming forth.

forth•right (fôrth′rīt′, fōrth′-) *adj.* **1.** Direct and without evasion; straightforward. **2.** *Archaic* Proceeding straight ahead. ❖ *adv.* **1a.** Directly ahead. **b.** Directly and frankly. **2.** *Archaic* At once. —**forth′right′ly** *adv.* —**forth′right′ness** *n.*

forth•with (fôrth-wĭth′, -wĭth′, fōrth-) *adv.* At once. [ME < *forth with,* along with, at the same time as.]

for•ti•eth (fôr′tē-ĭth) *n.* **1.** The ordinal number matching the number 40 in a series. **2.** One of 40 equal parts. —**for′ti•eth** *adv. & adj.*

for•ti•fi•ca•tion (fôr′tə-fĭ-kā′shən) *n.* **1a.** The science of fortifying. **b.** The act or process of fortifying. **2.** Something that serves to fortify, esp. military works erected to fortify a position or place.

for•ti•fied wine (fôr′tə-fīd′) *n.* Wine to which alcohol, usu. in the form of grape brandy, has been added.

for•ti•fy (fôr′tə-fī′) *v.* **-fied, -fy•ing, -fies** —*tr.* To make strong, as: **a.** To strengthen and secure (a position) with fortifications. **b.** To reinforce by adding material. **c.** To impart physical strength or endurance to; invigorate. **d.** To give emotional, moral, or mental strength to; encourage. **e.** To strengthen or enrich (food, for example), as by adding vitamins. —*intr.* To build fortifications. [ME *fortifien* < OFr. *fortifier* < LLat. *fortificāre* < Lat. *fortis,* strong. See **bergh-** in App.] —**for′ti•fi′a•ble** *adj.* —**for′ti•fi′er** *n.* —**for′ti•fy′ing•ly** *adv.*

for•tis (fôr′tĭs) *adj.* Articulated with relatively strong pressure of the airstream below the glottis, as in English (p) and (t) compared with (b) and (d). ❖ *n.* A fortis consonant. [Lat., strong. See FORT.]

for•tis•si•mo (fôr-tĭs′ə-mō′) *Music adv. & adj.* In a very loud manner. ❖ *n., pl.* **-mos** A note, chord, or passage played fortissimo. [Ital., superl. of *forte,* strong. See FORTE².]

for•ti•tude (fôr′tĭ-tōōd′, -tyōōd′) *n.* Strength of mind that allows one to endure pain or adversity with courage. [ME < Lat. *fortitūdō* < *fortis,* strong. See **bergh-** in App.] —**for′ti•tu′di•nous** (-tōōd′n-əs, -tyōōd′-) *adj.*

Fort-La•my (fôr-lä-mē′) See N′Djamena.

Fort Lau•der•dale (lô′dər-dāl′) A city of SE FL on the Atlantic coast N of Miami Beach. Pop. 152,397.

Fort Nelson A river, c. 418 km (260 mi), of NE British Columbia, Canada.

fort•night (fôrt′nīt′) *n.* A period of 14 days; two weeks. [Ult. < ME *fourtene night,* fourteen nights : OE *fēowertēne,* fourteen; see **kʷetwer-** in App. + OE *niht,* night; see **nokʷt-** in App.]

fort•night•ly (fôrt′nīt′lē) *adj.* Happening or appearing once in or every two weeks. ❖ *adv.* Once in a fortnight. ❖ *n., pl.* **-lies** A publication issued once every two weeks.

FOR•TRAN (fôr′trăn′) *n.* A high-level programming language for problems that can be expressed algebraically. [FOR(MULA) + TRAN(SLATION).]

for•tress (fôr′trĭs) *n.* A fortified place, esp. a large permanent military stronghold that often includes a town. [ME *fortresse* < OFr. < Med.Lat. *fortalitia* < Lat. *fortis,* strong. See **bergh-** in App.]

Fort Smith 1. A region of SW Northwest Terrs., Canada, including Great Slave Lake and most of Great Bear Lake. **2.** A city of W AR on the OK border WNW of Little Rock; founded as a military post in 1817. Pop. 80,268.

for•tu•i•tous (fôr-tōō′ĭ-təs, -tyōō′-) *adj.* **1.** Happening by accident or chance. **2.** *Usage Problem* Happening by a fortunate accident or chance. **b.** Lucky or fortunate. [< Lat. *fortuītus.* See **bher-**¹ in App.] —**for•tu′i•tous•ly** *adv.* —**for•tu′i•tous•ness** *n.*

USAGE NOTE USAGE NOTE In its best-established sense *fortuitous* means "happening by accident or chance," with no implication as to the desirability of the outcome. For decades, however, the word has often been used with particular reference to happy accidents, as in *The company's profits were the result of a fortuitous drop in the cost of paper.* This use may have arisen because *fortuitous* resembles both *fortunate* and *felicitous;* it is well established in the writing of reputable authors. More controversial is the use of *fortuitous* to mean simply "lucky or fortunate," which is still widely regarded as incorrect.

for•tu•i•ty (fôr-tōō′ĭ-tē, -tyōō′-) *n., pl.* **-ties 1.** A chance occurrence or event. **2.** The quality or condition of being fortuitous.

For•tu•na (fôr-tōō′nə, -tyōō′-) *n. Roman Mythology* The goddess of fortune. [Lat. *Fortūna.* See **bher-**¹ in App.]

for•tu•nate (fôr′chə-nĭt) *adj.* **1.** Bringing something good and unforeseen; auspicious. **2.** Having unexpected good fortune; lucky. ❖ *n.* One who has good fortune, esp. a wealthy person. [Lat. *fortūnātus* < *fortūna,* chance. See FORTUNE.] —**for′tu•nate•ly** *adv.* —**for′tu•nate•ness** *n.*

for•tune (fôr′chən) *n.* **1a.** The chance happening of fortunate or adverse events; luck. **b. fortunes** The turns of luck in the course of one's life. **c.** Success, esp. when at least partially resulting from luck. **2a.** A person's condition or standing in life determined by material possessions or financial wealth. **b.** Extensive amounts of material possessions or money; wealth. **c.** A large sum of money. **3.** often **Fortune** A hypothetical, often personified force or power that favorably or unfavorably governs the events of one's life. **4a.** Fate; destiny. **b.** A foretelling of one's destiny. ❖ *v.* **-tuned, -tun•ing, -tunes** —*tr.* **1.** *Archaic* To endow with wealth. **2.** *Obsolete* To ascribe or give good or bad fortune to. —*intr. Archaic* To occur by chance; happen. [ME < OFr. < Lat. *fortūna.* See **bher-**¹ in App.]

fortune cookie *n.* A cookie folded and baked around a slip of paper bearing a prediction of fortune or a maxim.

fortune hunter *n.* A person who seeks wealth, esp. through marriage.

for•tune•tell•er (fôr′chən-tĕl′ər) *n.* One who professes to predict future events. —**for′tune•tell′ing** *adj. & n.*

Fort Wayne A city of NE IN NE of Indianapolis; built on the site of a 17th-cent. French fort. Pop. 205,727.

Fort Worth A city of NE TX W of Dallas; on the site of a military post est. in the 1840s. Pop. 534,694.

for•ty (fôr′tē) *n., pl.* **-ties 1.** The cardinal number equal to 4 × 10. **2. forties a.** A decade or the numbers from 40 to 49. **b.** often **Forties** The decade from 40 to 49 in a century. [ME < OE *fēowertig.* See **kʷetwer-** in App.] —**for′ty** *adj. & pron.*

for•ty-five (fôr′tē-fīv′) *n.* **1.** A .45-caliber pistol. **2.** A phonograph record played at 45 revolutions per minute. —**for′ty-five′** *adj. & pron.*

for•ty-nin•er (fôr′tē-nī′nər) *n.* One who took part in the 1849 California gold rush.

forty winks *pl.n.* (*used with a sing. or pl. verb*) *Informal* A short nap.

fo•rum (fôr′əm, fōr′-) *n., pl.* **fo•rums** also **fo•ra** (fôr′ə, fōr′ə) **1a.** The public square or marketplace of an ancient Roman city that was the assembly place for judicial activity and public business. **b.** A public meeting place for open discussion. **c.** A medium of open discussion or voicing of ideas. **2.** A public meeting or presentation involving a discussion usu. among experts and often including audience participation. **3.** A court of law; a tribunal. [ME < Lat. See **dhwer-** in App.]

for•ward (fôr′wərd) *adj.* **1a.** At, near, or belonging to the front or forepart; fore. **b.** Located ahead or in advance. **2a.** Going, tending, or moving toward a position in front. **b.** *Sports* Advancing toward an opponent's goal. **c.** Moving in a prescribed direction or order for normal use: *forward rolling of the cassette tape.* **3a.** Ardently tending; eager: *a forward child.* **b.** Lacking restraint or modesty; presumptuous or bold. **4a.** Being ahead of current economic, political, or technological trends; progressive: *a forward concept.* **b.** Deviating radically from convention or tradition; extreme. **5.** Exceptionally advanced; precocious. **6.** Of, relating to, or done in preparation for the future. ❖ *adv.* or **for•wards** (-wərdz) **1.** Toward or tending to the front; frontward: *step forward.* **2.** Into consideration. **3.** In or toward the future. **4a.** In the prescribed direction or sequence for normal use. **b.** In an advanced position or a configuration registering a future time: *set the clock forward.* **c.** At or to a different time; earlier or later. ❖ *n. Sports* **1.** A player in certain games, such as basketball, who is part of the forward line of the offense. **2.** The position played by such a person. ❖ *tr.v.* **-ward•ed, -ward•ing, -wards 1.** To send on to a subsequent destination or address. **2.** To help advance; promote. See Syns at **advance.** [ME < OE *foreweard* : *fore-,* fore-

fortune cookie

+ -weard, -ward.] —**for′ward·ly** adv. —**for′ward·ness** n.

forward dive n. A dive in which the diver leaves the springboard or platform facing the open water and rotates the body forward.

for·ward·er (fôr′wər-dər) n. One that forwards, esp. an agent that helps received goods get to their destination.

for·ward-look·ing (fôr′wərd-lŏŏk′ĭng) adj. Concerned with or making provision for the future: forward-looking plans.

forward pass n. Football A pass thrown from behind the line of scrimmage toward the opponent's end line.

for·went (fôr-wĕnt′, fôr-) v. Past tense of **forgo.**

for·worn also **fore·worn** (fôr-wôrn′, fōr-wôrn′) adj. Archaic Worn-out.

for·zan·do (fôrt-sän′dō) adv., adj., & n. Variant of **sforzando.**

FOS abbr. free on steamer

fos·sa (fŏs′ə) n., pl. **fos·sae** (fŏs′ē′) Anatomy A small cavity or depression, as in a bone. [Lat., ditch < fem. p. part. of fodere, to dig.] —**fos′sate′** (fŏs′āt′) adj.

fosse also **foss** (fŏs) n. A ditch or moat. [ME < OFr. < Lat. fossa. See FOSSA.]

Fos·sey (fŏs′ē), **Dian** 1932–85. Amer. zoologist noted for her research on mountain gorillas.

fos·sick (fŏs′ĭk) v. **-sicked, -sick·ing, -sicks** Australian —intr. **1.** To search for gold, esp. by reworking washings or waste piles. **2.** To rummage or search around, esp. for a profit. —tr. To search for by or as if by rummaging. [E. dialectal, to find out, dig up.] —**fos′sick·er** n.

fos·sil (fŏs′əl) n. **1.** A remnant or trace of an organism of a past geologic age, such as a skeleton or leaf imprint, embedded and preserved in the earth's crust. **2.** One, such as a rigid theory, that is outdated or antiquated. **3.** Linguistics **a.** A word or morpheme that is used only in certain restricted contexts, as kempt in unkempt, but is otherwise obsolete. **b.** An archaic syntactic rule or pattern used only in idioms, as so be it. ❖ adj. **1.** Characteristic of or having the nature of a fossil. **2.** Being or similar to a fossil. **3.** Belonging to the past; antiquated. [< Lat. fossilis, dug up < fossus, p. part. of fodere, to dig.]

fossil fuel n. A hydrocarbon deposit, such as coal, derived from living matter of a previous geologic time and used for fuel.

fos·sil·if·er·ous (fŏs′ə-lĭf′ər-əs) adj. Containing fossils.

fos·sil·ize (fŏs′ə-līz′) v. **-ized, -iz·ing, -iz·es** —tr. **1.** To convert into a fossil. **2.** To make outmoded or inflexible with time; antiquate. —intr. To become a fossil. —**fos′sil·i·za′tion** (-sə-lĭ-zā′shən) n.

fos·so·ri·al (fŏ-sôr′ē-əl, -sōr′-) adj. Zoology Adapted for or used in burrowing or digging. [< LLat. fossōrius < Lat. fossus, p. part. of fodere, to dig.]

fos·ter (fô′stər, fŏs′tər) tr.v. **-tered, -ter·ing, -ters 1.** To bring up; nurture. See Syns at **nurture. 2.** To promote the growth and development of; cultivate. See Syns at **advance. 3.** To nurse; cherish. ❖ adj. **1.** Providing parental care and nurture to children not related through legal or blood ties. **2.** Receiving parental care and nurture from those not related to one through legal or blood ties. [ME fostren < OE *fōstrian, to nourish < fōstor, food, nourishing. See pā- in App.]

Foster, Stephen Collins 1826–64. Amer. songwriter whose works include "Oh! Susannah" (1848).

Fou·cault (fōō-kō′), **Jean Bernard Léon** 1819–68. French physicist who measured the velocity of light (1850).

Foucault, Michel 1926–84. French philosopher and historian whose works include Madness and Civilization (1961).

Foucault pendulum n. A simple pendulum suspended from a long wire whose plane of motion appears to turn clockwise in the Northern Hemisphere and counterclockwise in the Southern Hemisphere, demonstrating the axial rotation of the earth. [After Jean Bernard Léon FOUCAULT.]

fou·droy·ant (fōō-droi′ənt, fōō′drwä-yän′) adj. Dazzling or stunning in effect. [Fr. < pr. part. of foudroyer, to strike with lightning < foudre, lightning < OFr. fouldre < Lat. fulgur < fulgēre, to flash.]

fought (fôt) v. Past tense and past participle of **fight.**

foul (foul) adj. **foul·er, foul·est 1.** Offensive to the senses; revolting. **2.** Having an offensive odor; smelly. **3.** Rotten or putrid. **4a.** Full of dirt or mud; dirty. **b.** Full of impurities; polluted. **5.** Morally detestable; wicked. **6.** Of a vulgar or obscene nature. **7.** Very disagreeable or displeasing; horrid. **8.** Bad or unfavorable: foul weather. **9.** Violating accepted standards or rules; dishonorable. **10a.** Sports Contrary to the rules of a game or sport. **b.** Baseball Outside the foul lines. **11.** Entangled or twisted: a foul anchor. **12.** Clogged or obstructed; blocked: a foul ventilator shaft. **13.** Archaic Ugly; unattractive. ❖ n. **1a.** Sports An infraction or a violation of the rules of play. **b.** Baseball A foul ball. **2.** An entanglement or collision. **3.** An instance of clogging or obstructing. ❖ adv. In a foul manner. ❖ v. **fouled, foul·ing, fouls** —tr. **1.** To make dirty or foul; pollute. **2.** To bring into dishonor; besmirch. **3.** To clog or obstruct. **4.** To entangle or catch (a rope, for example). **5.** Nautical To encrust (a ship's hull) with foreign matter, such as barnacles. **6a.** Sports To commit a foul against. **b.** Baseball To hit (a ball) outside the foul lines. —intr. **1.** To become foul. **2a.** Sports To commit a foul. **b.** Baseball To foul a ball. **3.** To become entangled or twisted. **4.** To become clogged or obstructed. —**phrasal verbs: foul out** Sports To be put out of a

game for exceeding the number of permissible fouls. **foul up** To blunder or cause to blunder because of mistakes or poor judgment. [ME < OE fūl. See **pū-** in App.] —**foul′ly** adv. —**foul′ness** n.

fou·lard (fōō-lärd′) n. **1.** A lightweight twill or plain-woven fabric of silk or silk and cotton, usu. having a small printed design. **2.** An article of clothing, esp. a necktie or scarf, made of this fabric. [Fr.]

foul ball n. Baseball A batted ball that touches the ground outside of fair territory.

foul·brood (foul′brōōd′) n. A fatal disease of honeybee larvae.

foul line n. **1.** Baseball Either of two straight lines extending from the rear of home plate to the outer edge of the playing field and indicating the area in which a fair ball can be hit. **2.** Basketball A line 15 feet in front of each backboard from which players shoot foul shots. **3.** Sports A boundary limiting the permissible movements of a player, as in a field event.

foul·mouthed (foul′mouthd′, -moutht′) adj. Using abusive or obscene language.

foul play n. **1.** Unfair or treacherous action, esp. when violent.

foul shot n. Basketball An unobstructed shot from the foul line by a fouled player, worth one point if successful.

foul tip n. Baseball A pitched ball that is deflected slightly off the bat toward the catcher.

foul-up (foul′ŭp′) n. **1.** A condition of confusion caused by mistakes or poor judgment. **2.** A mechanical failure.

found[1] (found) tr.v. **found·ed, found·ing, founds 1.** To establish or set up, esp. with provision for continuing existence. **2.** To establish the foundation or basis of; base. [ME founden < OFr. fonder < Lat. fundāre < fundus, bottom.]

SYNONYMS found, create, establish, institute, organize These verbs mean to bring something into existence and set it in operation: founded a colony; created a trust fund; establishing a business; instituted an annual benefit concert; organizing a field trip.

found[2] (found) tr.v. **found·ed, found·ing, founds 1.** To melt (metal) and pour into a mold. **2.** To make (objects) by pouring molten material into a mold. [ME founden < OFr. fondre < Lat. fundere. See **gheu-** in App.]

found[3] (found) v. Past tense and past participle of **find.**

foun·da·tion (foun-dā′shən) n. **1.** The act of founding, esp. the establishment of an institution with provisions for future maintenance. **2.** The basis on which a thing stands, is founded, or is supported. **3a.** Funds for the perpetual support of an institution; an endowment. **b.** An institution founded and supported by an endowment. **4.** A foundation garment. **5.** A cosmetic base. [ME fundacioun < Lat. fundātiō, fundātiōn- < fundātus, p. part. of fundāre, to lay the groundwork for. See FOUND[1].] —**foun·da′tion·al** adj.

foundation garment n. A woman's supporting undergarment, such as a corset or girdle.

foun·der[1] (foun′dər) v. **-dered, -der·ing, -ders** —intr. **1.** To sink below the surface of the water. **2.** To cave in; sink. **3.** To fail utterly; collapse. **4.** To stumble, esp. to stumble and go lame. Used of horses. **5.** To become ill from overeating. Used of livestock. **6.** To be afflicted with laminitis. Used of horses. —tr. To cause to founder. ❖ n. See **laminitis.** [ME foundren, to sink to the ground < OFr. fondrer < VLat. *funderāre < *fundus, *funderē, bottom < Lat. fundus, fund-.]

USAGE NOTE The verbs founder and flounder are often confused. Founder means "to sink, fail utterly, collapse," while flounder means "to move clumsily, thrash about." Thus if John is foundering in Chemistry 1, he is failing it; but if he is floundering, he is struggling but may yet pull through.

found·er[2] (foun′dər) n. One who establishes something or formulates the basis for something.

Found·ing Father (foun′dĭng) n. **1.** A member of the convention that drafted the US Constitution in 1787. **2. founding father** A man who founds or establishes something.

found·ling (found′lĭng) n. An abandoned child of unknown parentage. [ME < found, p. part. of finden, to find. See FIND.]

found object n. A natural object or an artifact not intended as art, found and given aesthetic value. [Transl. of Fr. objet trouvé : objet, object + trouvé, p. part. of trouver, to find.]

foun·dry (foun′drē) n., pl. **-dries 1.** An establishment where metal is melted and poured into molds. **2a.** The skill or operation of founding. **b.** The castings made by founding.

fount[1] (fount) n. **1.** A fountain. **2.** One that initiates or dispenses; a source. [ME < OE and OFr. font, both < Lat. fons, font-.]

fount[2] (fount) n. Chiefly British Variant of **font**[2].

foun·tain (foun′tən) n. **1a.** An artificially created jet or stream of water. **b.** A structure, often decorative, from which a jet or stream of water issues. **2.** A spring, esp. the source of a stream. **3.** A reservoir or chamber containing a supply of liquid that can be siphoned off as needed. **4.** A soda fountain. **5.** A drinking fountain. **6.** A point of origin or dissemination; a source. ❖ intr. & tr.v. **-tained, -tain·ing, -tains** To flow or cause to flow like a fountain. [ME < OFr. fontaine < LLat. fontāna < Lat., fem. of fontānus, of a spring < fōns, font-, spring.]

foun·tain·head (foun′tən-hĕd′) n. **1.** A spring that is the source

foul line

fountain
Bethesda Fountain and its sculpture Angel of the Waters, 1873, by Emma Stebbins (1810–82), Central Park, New York City

ă	pat	oi	boy
ā	pay	ou	out
âr	care	ŏŏ	took
ä	father	ōō	boot
ĕ	pet	ŭ	cut
ē	be	ûr	urge
ĭ	pit	th	thin
ī	pie	th	this
îr	pier	hw	which
ŏ	pot	zh	vision
ō	toe	ə	about,
ô	paw		item

Stress marks:
′ (primary);
′ (secondary), as in
lexicon (lĕk′sĭ-kŏn′)

or head of a stream. **2.** A chief and copious source; an originator.

fountain pen *n.* A pen having a refillable or replaceable ink reservoir that feeds ink to the nib.

Fou·quet also **Fouc·quet** (foō-kā′), **Jean** 1420?–80? French artist noted for his book illuminations.

four (fôr, fōr) *n.* **1.** The cardinal number equal to 3 + 1. **2.** The fourth in a set or sequence. **3.** Something having four parts, units, or members, such as a four-cylinder engine. —*idiom:* **all fours** All four limbs of an animal or a person. [ME < OE *fēower*. See **kʷetwer-** in App.] —**four** *adj. & pron.*

four-by-four or **4 × 4** (fôr′bī-fôr′, fōr′bī-fōr′) *n.* **1.** A four-wheel-drive motor vehicle. **2.** A length of lumber that is 4 inches thick and 4 inches wide, or that is trimmed to slightly smaller dimensions.

four·chette (foōr-shĕt′) *n.* **1.** A narrow forked strip of material joining the front and back sections of the fingers of gloves. **2.** *Anatomy* A small band or fold of mucous membrane forming the posterior margin of the vulva and connecting the posterior ends of the labia majora. **3.** *Zoology* See **furcula.** [Fr. < OFr. *forchete*, fork, dim. of *forche*, pitchfork < Lat. *furca*.]

four-col·or (fôr′kŭl′ər, fōr′-) *adj.* Of or being an overprinting or photographic process in which three primary colors and black are transferred by four different plates or filters to a surface, reproducing the colors of the subject matter.

Four Corners A location in the SW US where the boundaries of CO, NM, AZ, and UT meet.

four-di·men·sion·al (fôr′dĭ-mĕn′shə-nəl, fōr′-) *adj.* Specified by or exhibiting four dimensions, such as the three spatial and single temporal dimensions of relativity theory.

four-eyed fish (fôr′īd′, fōr′-) *n.* Either of two freshwater fishes (*Anableps anableps* or *A. microlepis*) of tropical America having bulging eyes divided into an upper part for vision above the water and a lower part for vision below the water.

four eyes *n.* (*used with a sing. verb*) *Informal* One who wears eyeglasses.

four flush *n.* A five-card poker hand containing four cards in the same suit.

four-flush (fôr′flŭsh′, fōr′-) *intr.v.* **-flushed, -flush·ing, -flush·es 1.** *Games* To bluff in poker with a four flush. **2.** *Slang* To make empty claims; bluff. —**four′-flush′er** *n.*

four-foot·ed (fôr′foŏt′ĭd, fōr′-) *adj.* Having four feet.

four·gon (foōr-gôN′) *n., pl.* **-gons** (-gôN′, -gôNz′) A wagon for carrying baggage. [Fr.]

four·hand·ed (fôr′hăn′dĭd, fōr′-) *adj.* **1.** *Games* Involving or requiring four players. **2.** Designed for four hands.

4-H Club (fôr′āch′, fōr′-) *n.* A youth organization sponsored by the Department of Agriculture and offering instruction in agriculture and home economics. [< its four goals: to improve head, heart, hands, and health.]

Fou·rier (foōr′ē-ā′, foō-ryā′), **(François Marie) Charles** 1772–1837. French social theorist who propounded the reorganization of society into phalanxes. —**Fou′ri·er·ism** *n.* —**Fou′ri·er·ist, Fou′ri·er·ite′** (-ə-rīt′) *n.*

Fourier, Baron **Jean Baptiste Joseph** 1768–1830. French mathematician and physicist who formulated a method for analyzing periodic functions.

Fourier analysis *n.* The branch of mathematics concerned with the approximation of periodic functions by the Fourier series and with generalizations of such approximations to a wider class of functions.

Fourier series *n.* An infinite series whose terms are constants multiplied by sine and cosine functions and that can, if uniformly convergent, approximate a wide variety of functions. [After Baron Jean Baptiste Joseph FOURIER.]

Fou·rier's theorem (foōr′ē-āz′, foō-ryāz′) *n.* Any of a set of theorems stating that a function may be represented by a Fourier series provided that it meets certain, very general continuity and periodicity conditions.

four-in-hand (fôr′ĭn-hănd′, fōr′-) *n.* **1.** A team of four horses controlled by one driver. **2.** A vehicle drawn by four horses. **3.** A necktie tied in a slipknot with long ends left hanging one in front of the other.

four-leaf clover (fôr′lēf′, fōr′-) *n.* A clover leaf having four leaflets instead of three, considered an omen of good luck.

four-let·ter word (fôr′lĕt′ər, fōr′-) *n.* Any of several short English words generally regarded as vulgar or obscene.

four-o'clock (fôr′ō-klŏk′, fōr′-) *n.* Any of several plants of the genus *Mirabilis*, esp. *M. jalapa*, native to tropical America and having tubular flowers that open late in the afternoon.

401(k) (fôr′ō-wŭn-kā′, fōr′-) *n.* A retirement plan that allows an employee to put a percentage of earned wages into a tax-deferred investment account selected by the employer.

411 (fôr′wŭn′wŭn′, fōr′-) *n.* *Slang* Information or knowledge, esp. when acquired by word of mouth. [From *411*, a telephone number for telephone directory information.]

four·pen·ny nail (fôr′pĕn′ē, -pə-nē, fōr′-) *n.* A nail 1½ inches (3.8 centimeters) long.

four·plex (fôr′plĕks′, fōr′-) *adj.* **1.** Composed of four parts; fourfold; quadruple. **2.** Having four apartments, divisions, or floors. —**four′plex′** *n.*

four-post·er (fôr′pō′stər, fōr′-) *n.* A bed having tall corner

posts originally intended to support curtains or a canopy.

four·ra·gère (foōr′ə-zhâr′) *n.* An ornamental braided cord usu. looped around the left shoulder of a uniform. [Fr. < *fourrage*, forage < OFr. *forrage*. See FORAGE.]

four·score (fôr′skôr′, fōr′skōr′) *adj.* Four times twenty.

four·some (fôr′səm, fōr′-) *n.* **1.** A group of four persons or things, esp. two couples. **2a.** A game, esp. a golf match, played by four persons, usu. competing in pairs. **b.** The players in such a game. [ME *four-som* < OE *fēowra sum*, one of four : *fēowra*, genitive pl. of *fēower*, four; see FOUR + *sum*, one; see –SOME².]

four·square (fôr′skwâr′, fōr′-) *adj.* **1.** Having four equal sides and four right angles; square. **2.** Marked by firm unwavering conviction or expression; forthright. ❖ *adv.* In a forthright manner; squarely. ❖ *n.* A child's game in which a player stands in each of four squares in a two-by-two grid and must bounce a ball into another player's square without holding the ball or stepping out of bounds. —**four′square′ly** *adv.*

four-star (fôr′stär′, fōr′-) *adj.* Of superlative quality.

four·teen (fôr-tēn′, fōr-) *n.* **1.** The cardinal number equal to 13 + 1. **2.** The 14th in a set or sequence. **3.** Something having 14 parts, units, or members. [ME *fourtene* < OE *fēowertēne*. See **kʷetwer-** in App.] —**four·teen′** *adj. & pron.*

four·teenth (fôr-tēnth′, fōr-) *n.* **1.** The ordinal number matching the number 14 in a series. **2.** One of 14 equal parts. —**four·teenth′** *adv. & adj.*

fourth (fôrth, fōrth) *n.* **1.** The ordinal number matching the number four in a series. **2.** One of four equal parts. **3.** *Music* **a.** A tone four degrees above or below a given tone in a diatonic scale. **b.** The interval between two such tones. **c.** The harmonic combination of these tones. **d.** The subdominant of a scale or key. **4.** The transmission gear or gear ratio used to produce forward speeds next higher to those of third in a motor vehicle. **5. Fourth** The Fourth of July; Independence Day. Used with *the.* [ME *fourthe* < OE *fēortha*. See **kʷetwer-** in App.] —**fourth** *adv. & adj.*

fourth-class (fôrth′klăs′, fōrth′-) *n.* Of or being a class of mail consisting of merchandise and some printed matter weighing over eight ounces and not sealed against inspection. —**fourth′class′** *adv.*

fourth dimension *n.* Time regarded as a coordinate dimension and required by relativity theory, along with three spatial dimensions, to specify completely the location of any event.

fourth estate *n.* Journalists considered as a group; the press.

Fourth of July *n.* See **Independence Day.**

fourth wall *n.* The space separating the audience from the action of a theatrical performance, traditionally conceived of as an imaginary wall completing the enclosure of the stage.

Fourth World also **fourth world** *n.* The least-developed countries of the Third World. —**Fourth′-World′** (fôrth′wûrld′, fōrth′-) *adj.*

4WD *abbr.* four-wheel drive

four-wheel (fôr′hwēl′, -wēl′, fōr′-) or **four-wheeled** (-hwēld′, -wēld′) *adj.* **1.** Having or running on four wheels. **2.** Of or relating to four-wheel drive.

four-wheel drive *n.* An automotive drive system in which mechanical power is transmitted from the drive shaft to all four wheels.

four-wheel·er (fôr′hwē′lər, -wē′-, fōr′-) *n.* A small, one-person, four-wheel all-terrain motor vehicle with large tires.

fo·ve·a (fō′vē-ə) *n., pl.* **-ve·ae** (-vē-ē′) **1.** A small cuplike depression or pit in a bone or organ. **2.** The fovea centralis. [Lat., small pit.] —**fo′ve·al** (-əl), **fo′ve·ate′** (-āt′) *adj.* —**fo′ve·i·form′** (-ə-fôrm′) *adj.*

fovea cen·tra·lis (sĕn-trā′lĭs) *n.* A small depression near the center of the retina, constituting the area of most acute vision. [NLat. *fovea centrālis* : Lat. *fovea*, small pit + Lat. *centrālis*, central.]

fo·ve·o·la (fō-vē′ə-lə) *n., pl.* **-lae** (-lē′) or **-las** A small fovea. [NLat., dim. of Lat. *fovea*, small pit.]

fowl (foul) *n., pl.* **fowl** or **fowls 1.** Any of various birds of the order Galliformes, esp. the common domesticated chicken (*Gallus gallus*). **2a.** A bird, such as the turkey or pheasant, that is used as food or hunted as game. **b.** The flesh of such birds used as food. **3.** A bird of any kind. ❖ *intr.v.* **fowled, fowl·ing, fowls** To hunt, trap, or shoot wildfowl. [ME *foul* < OE *fugol*. See **pleu-** in App.] —**fowl′er** *n.*

Fow·ler (fou′lər), **Henry Watson** 1858–1933. British lexicographer who wrote *A Dictionary of Modern English Usage* (1926) and collaborated with his brother **Francis** (1870–1918) on *The King's English* (1906).

fowl·ing piece (fou′lĭng) *n.* A light shotgun for shooting birds and small animals.

fox (fŏks) *n.* **1.** *pl.* **fox·es** also **fox a.** Any of various carnivorous mammals of the genus *Vulpes* and related genera, related to the dogs and wolves and characteristically having upright ears, a pointed snout, and a long bushy tail. **b.** The fur of a fox. **2.** A crafty, sly, or clever person: *The old fox outwitted everyone.* **3.** *Slang* A sexually attractive person. **4.** *Archaic* A sword. ❖ *v.* **foxed, fox·ing, fox·es** —*tr.* **1.** To trick or fool by ingenuity or cunning; outwit. **2.** To baffle or confuse. **3.** To make (beer) sour by fermenting. **4.** To repair (a shoe) by attaching a new upper. **5.** *Obsolete* To intoxicate. —*intr.* **1.** To act slyly or craftily. **2.** To

four-o'clock
desert (or Colorado) four-
o'clock
Mirabilis multiflora

fox
red fox
Vulpes fulva

turn sour in fermenting. Used of beer. [ME < OE.]

Fox *n.*, *pl.* **Fox** or **Fox·es** **1.** A member of a Native American people formerly inhabiting various parts of southern Michigan, southern Wisconsin, northern Illinois, and eastern Iowa, with present-day populations in central Iowa and Oklahoma. **2.** The Algonquian language of the Fox. [Transl. of Fr. *Renards*, foxes, perh. transl. of Fox *wa·koše·haki*, foxes (name of a clan with the totem of a fox).]

Fox, George 1624–91. English religious leader who founded the Society of Friends, or Quakers (1647–48).

Fox, Vicente b. 1942. Mexican president (since 2000).

Fox, William 1879–1952. Hungarian-born Amer. motion-picture executive who founded his own film company (1915) and merged with 20th Century Pictures to form 20th Century Fox (1935).

Foxe (fŏks), **John** 1516–87. English martyrologist who wrote *The Book of Martyrs* (1563).

foxed (fŏkst) *adj.* Discolored with yellowish-brown stains: "*Their set of George Eliot was foxed and buckled by the rain*" (John Cheever). [Perh. < the color of foxes.]

fox·fire (fŏks′fīr′) *n.* A phosphorescent glow, esp. that produced by certain fungi found on rotting wood.

fox·glove (fŏks′glŭv′) *n.* **1.** Any of several herbs of the genus *Digitalis*, esp. *D. purpurea* of Europe, having a long cluster of large tubular pinkish-purple flowers and leaves that are the source of the drug digitalis. **2.** Any of several related plants. [< the resemblance of the flowers to the fingers of a glove.]

fox grape *n.* A wild grape (*Vitis labrusca*) of the eastern United States that bears purplish-black berries and is the source of many cultivated grape varieties.

fox·hole (fŏks′hōl′) *n.* A shallow pit dug by a soldier in combat for immediate refuge against enemy fire.

fox·hound (fŏks′hound′) *n.* Any of various medium-sized, short-haired hounds developed for fox hunting, esp. either of two breeds, the English foxhound and the American foxhound.

Fox River **1.** A river rising in SE WI and flowing c. 354 km (220 mi) SSW to the Illinois R. in NE IL. **2.** A river of central and E WI flowing c. 282 km (175 mi) to Green Bay.

fox·tail (fŏks′tāl′) *n.* Any of several grasses of the genus *Alopecurus*, having dense silky or bristly flowering spikes.

foxtail lily *n.* Eremurus.

fox terrier *n.* Any of various small wire-haired or smooth-coated terriers of a breed originating in England and having a white coat with dark markings.

fox·trot (fŏks′trŏt′) *intr.v.* **-trot·ted, -trot·ting, -trots** To dance the fox trot.

fox trot *n.* **1a.** A ballroom dance in 4/4 time with both slow and fast steps. **b.** The music for this dance. **2.** A slow broken gait of a horse, between a trot and a walk.

fox·y (fŏk′sē) *adj.* **-i·er, -i·est** **1a.** Of or resembling a fox. **b.** Slyly clever; crafty. **2.** Having a reddish-brown color. **3.** Discolored, as by age or decay; foxed. **4.** *Slang* Sensually attractive; sexy. **5.** Having a distinctive sharp flavor or aroma. **—fox′i·ly** *adv.* **—fox′i·ness** *n.*

foy (foi) *n.* *Scots* A farewell feast, drink, or gift, as at a wedding. [Du. dialectal *fooi* < MDu. *foye*, journey < OFr. *voie* < Lat. *via*, road. See **wegh-** in App.]

foy·er (foi′ər, foi′ā′, fwä′yā′) *n.* **1.** A lobby or anteroom, as of a hotel. **2.** An entrance hall; a vestibule. [Fr., social center < OFr. *foier*, fireplace, ult. < Lat. *focus*, fire.]

fp *abbr.* **1.** forte-piano **2.** freezing point

FPC *abbr.* **1.** Federal Power Commission **2.** fish protein concentrate **3.** Friends Peace Committee

fpl *abbr.* fireplace

fpm *abbr.* feet per minute

FPO *abbr.* fleet post office

fps *abbr.* **1.** feet per second **2.** foot-pound-second **3.** frames per second

Fr The symbol for the element **francium**.

fr. *abbr.* **1.** frame **2.** franc **3.** from

Fr. *abbr.* **1.** Ecclesiastical father (title) **2a.** France **b.** French **3.** Frau **4.** friar **5.** Friday

Fra (frä) *n.* *Roman Catholic Church* Used as a title for an Italian monk or friar; brother. [Ital., short for *frate*, brother < Lat. *frāter*. See **bhrāter-** in App.]

FRA *abbr.* Federal Railroad Administration

fra·cas (frā′kəs, frăk′əs) *n.* A noisy disorderly fight or quarrel; a brawl. [Fr. < Ital. *fracasso* < *fracassare*, to make an uproar.]

frac·tal (frăk′təl) *n.* A geometric pattern repeated at ever smaller scales to produce irregular shapes and surfaces and used esp. in computer modeling of irregular patterns and structures in nature. [Fr. < Lat. *frāctus*, p. part. of *frangere*, to break. See FRACTION.]

fract·ed (frăk′tĭd) *adj. Obsolete* Broken. [< Lat. *frāctus*, p. part. of *frangere*, to break. See FRACTION.]

frac·tion (frăk′shən) *n.* **1.** *Mathematics* An expression that indicates the quotient of two quantities, such as ⅓. **2.** A fragmentary piece; a fragment. **3.** A small part; a bit. **4.** A chemical component separated by fractionation. [ME *fraccioun*, a breaking < AN < LLat. *frāctiō*, *frāctiōn-* < Lat. *frāctus*, p. part. of *frangere*, to break. See **bhreg-** in App.]

frac·tion·al (frăk′shə-nəl) *adj.* **1.** Of, relating to, or constituting a fraction. **2.** Very small; insignificant. **3.** Being in fractions or pieces. **—frac′tion·al·ly** *adv.*

fractional currency *n.* Coin or paper currency in a denomination less than a standard monetary unit.

frac·tion·al·ize (frăk′shə-nə-līz′) *tr.v.* **-ized, -iz·ing, -iz·es** To divide into separate parts or sections. **—frac′tion·al·i·za′tion** (-lĭ-zā′shən) *n.*

frac·tion·ate (frăk′shə-nāt′) *tr.v.* **-at·ed, -at·ing, -ates** **1.** To divide or separate into parts; break up. **2.** To separate (a chemical compound) into components, as by distillation or crystallization. **—frac′tion·a′tion** *n.* **—frac′tion·a′tor** *n.*

frac·tion·ize (frăk′shə-nīz′) *tr. & intr.v.* **-ized, -iz·ing, -iz·es** To divide into parts or fractions. **—frac′tion·i·za′tion** (-shə-nĭ-zā′shən) *n.*

frac·tious (frăk′shəs) *adj.* **1.** Inclined to make trouble; unruly. **2.** Having a peevish nature; cranky. [< FRACTION, discord (obsolete).] **—frac′tious·ly** *adv.* **—frac′tious·ness** *n.*

frac·ture (frăk′chər) *n.* **1a.** The act or process of breaking. **b.** The condition of having been broken or ruptured. **2.** A break, rupture, or crack, esp. in bone or cartilage. **3.** *Mineralogy* **a.** The characteristic manner in which a mineral breaks. **b.** The characteristic appearance of the surface of a broken mineral. **4.** *Geology* A crack or fault in a rock. **❖** *v.* **-tured, -tur·ing, -tures** —*tr.* **1.** To cause to break. **2.** To disrupt or destroy as if by breaking. **3.** To abuse or misuse flagrantly, as by violating rules: *ignorant writers who fracture the language.* **4.** *Slang* To cause to laugh heartily. —*intr.* To undergo a fracture. See Syns at **break.** [ME < OFr. < Lat. *frāctūra* < *frāctus*, p. part. of *frangere*, to break. See **bhreg-** in App.]

frae (frā) *prep. Scots* From. [ME *fra* < ON *frā*. See **per**[1] in App.]

frag·ile (frăj′əl, -īl′) *adj.* **1.** Easily broken, damaged, or destroyed; frail. **2.** Lacking physical or emotional strength. **3.** Lacking substance; tenuous or flimsy. [Fr. < OFr. < Lat. *fragilis* < *frangere*, *frag-*, to break. See **bhreg-** in App.] **—frag′ile·ly** *adv.* **—fra·gil′i·ty** (frə-jĭl′ĭ-tē), **frag′ile·ness** *n.*

fragile X syndrome *n.* An inherited disorder characterized by mental retardation in males and caused by a defective gene on the X-chromosome.

frag·ment (frăg′mənt) *n.* **1.** A small part broken off or detached. **2.** An incomplete or isolated portion; a bit. **3.** A sentence fragment. **❖** *v.* (-mĕnt′) **-ment·ed, -ment·ing, -ments** —*tr.* To break or separate (something) into fragments. —*intr.* To become broken into fragments. [ME < Lat. *fragmentum* < *frangere*, *frag-*, to break. See **bhreg-** in App.]

frag·men·tal (frăg-mĕn′tl) *adj.* **1.** Fragmentary. **2.** *Geology* Consisting of broken rock, coal, or ore moved from its place of origin. **—frag·men′tal·ly** *adv.*

frag·men·tar·y (frăg′mən-tĕr′ē) *adj.* Consisting of small disconnected parts. **—frag′men·tar′i·ly** (-târ′ə-lē) *adv.* **—frag′men·tar′i·ness** *n.*

frag·men·ta·tion (frăg′mən-tā′shən, -mĕn-) *n.* **1.** The act or process of breaking into fragments. **2.** The scattering of the fragments of an exploding bomb or other projectile. **3.** The scattering of parts of a file throughout a disk, as when the operating system breaks up the file and fits it into the spaces left vacant by previously deleted files.

fragmentation bomb *n.* An aerial antipersonnel bomb that scatters shrapnel over a wide area upon explosion.

frag·men·tize (frăg′mən-tīz′) *tr. & intr.v.* **-tized, -tiz·ing, -tiz·es** To fragment. **—frag′men·tiz′er** *n.*

Fra·go·nard (frăg′ə-när′, frä-gô-), **Jean Honoré** 1732–1806. French artist best known for his rococo paintings of exotic landscapes and romantic scenes.

fra·grance (frā′grəns) *n.* **1.** The state or quality of having a pleasant odor. **2.** A sweet or pleasant odor; a scent. **3.** A substance, such as a perfume, designed to emit a pleasant odor.

fra·grant (frā′grənt) *adj.* Having a pleasant odor. [ME < Lat. *frāgrāns, frāgrant-*, p. part. of *frāgrāre*, to emit an odor.] **—fra′grant·ly** *adv.*

fraid·y cat (frā′dē) *n. Slang* A timid or fearful person. [Shortening of AFRAID + -Y[1].]

frail[1] (frāl) *adj.* **frail·er, frail·est** **1.** Physically weak; delicate. **2.** Not strong or substantial; slight: *frail evidence.* **3.** Easily broken or destroyed; fragile. **4.** Easily led astray; morally weak. [ME *frele* < OFr. < Lat. *fragilis* < *frangere*, *frag-*, to break. See **bhreg-** in App.] **—frail′ly** *adv.* **—frail′ness** *n.*

frail[2] (frāl) *n.* **1.** A rush basket for fruit, esp. dried fruit. **2.** The quantity of fruit that a frail can hold. [ME *fraiel* < OFr.]

frail·ty (frāl′tē) *n.*, *pl.* **-ties** **1.** The condition or quality of being

fractal

frail. **2.** A fault, esp. a moral weakness.

fraise (frāz) *n.* **1.** A defensive barrier of pointed inclined stakes or barbed wire. **2.** A ruff for the neck worn in the 16th century. [Fr. < OFr., mesentery (< its pleated shape) < (*feves*) *frasees*, shelled (beans) < Lat. (*faba*) *frēsa*, ground (bean), fem. p. part. of *frendere*, to crush. See FRENUM.]

frak•tur (fräk-tŏŏr′) *n.* A style of black letter formerly used in German manuscripts and printing. [Ger. < Lat. *frāctūra*, a breaking (< the curlicues). See FRACTURE.]

fram•be•sia (frăm-bē′zhə, -zhē-ə) *n.* See yaws. [NLat. < Fr. *framboise*, raspberry < OFr., of Gmc. orig.]

frame (frām) *v.* **framed, fram•ing, frames** —*tr.* **1.** To build by putting together the structural parts of; construct. **2.** To conceive or design. **3.** To arrange or adjust for a purpose: *a question framed to have one answer.* **4a.** To put into words; formulate. **b.** To form (words) silently with the lips. **5.** To enclose in or as if in a frame. **6.** *Informal* **a.** To make up evidence or contrive events so as to incriminate (a person) falsely. **b.** To prearrange (a contest) so as to ensure a desired fraudulent outcome; fix. —*intr.* **1.** *Archaic* To go; proceed. **2.** *Obsolete* To manage; contrive. ❖ *n.* **1.** Something composed of parts fitted and joined together. **2.** A structure that gives shape or support. **3a.** An open structure or rim for encasing, holding, or bordering. **b.** A closed, often rectangular border of drawn or printed lines. **4.** A pair of eyeglasses, excluding the lenses. Often used in the plural. **5.** The structure of a human or animal body; physique. **6.** A cold frame. **7.** A general structure or system. **8.** A general state or condition. **9.** A frame of reference. **10.** *Sports & Games* **a.** A round or period of play in some games, such as bowling and billiards. **b.** *Baseball* An inning. **11.** A single picture on a roll of movie film or videotape. **12.** The total area of a complete picture in television broadcasting. **13.** An individual drawing within a comic strip. **14.** *Computer Science* **a.** A rectangular segment within a browser's window that can be scrolled independently of other such segments. **b.** A single step in a sequence of programmed instructions. **15.** *Informal* A frame-up. **16.** *Obsolete* Shape; form. [ME *framen* < OE *framian*, to further < *fram*, forward. See FROM.] —**fram′a•ble, frame′a•ble** *adj.*

frame of reference *n., pl.* **frames of reference 1.** A set of coordinate axes in terms of which position or movement may be specified or with reference to which physical laws may be mathematically stated. **2.** A set of ideas in terms of which other ideas are interpreted or assigned meaning.

fram•er (frā′mər) *n.* **1.** One that frames. **2.** often **Framer** One of the people who wrote the US Constitution.

frame•shift (frām′shĭft′) *n.* A mutation in a DNA chain that occurs when the number of nucleotides inserted or deleted is not a multiple of three, so that every codon beyond the point of insertion or deletion is read incorrectly during translation.

frame-up (frām′ŭp′) *n. Informal* **1.** A scheme to incriminate an innocent person. **2.** A contest or deliberation the outcome of which is fraudulently prearranged.

frame•work (frām′wûrk′) *n.* **1.** A structure for supporting or enclosing something else, esp. the skeletal support of a physical construction. **2.** An external work platform; a scaffold. **3.** A fundamental structure, as for a written work. **4.** A set of assumptions, concepts, values, and practices that constitutes a way of viewing reality.

fram•ing (frā′mĭng) *n.* A frame, framework, or system of frames.

Fra•ming•ham (frā′mĭng-hăm′) A town of E-central MA WSW of Boston; settled in 1650. Pop. 66,910.

franc (frăngk) *n.* See table at **currency.** [ME *frank*, French gold coin < OFr. *franc* < Med.Lat. *Francōrum* (*rēx*), (king) of the Franks (< the legend on the first of these coins), genitive pl. *Francus*, Frank. See FRANK.]

France

France (frăns) A country of W Europe on the Atlantic Ocean and the English Channel; settled by the Franks after the retreat of the Romans. Cap. Paris. Pop. 54,334,871.

France (frăns, fräns), **Anatole** Pen name of Jacques Anatole François Thibault. 1844–1924. French critic and writer who won the 1921 Nobel Prize for literature.

Fran•ce•sca (frän-chĕs′kə, frän-), **Piero della** See **Piero della Francesca.**

Francesca da Ri•mi•ni (də rĭm′ə-nē, dä rē′mē-nē) d. c. 1285. Italian noblewoman who was murdered by her husband when he learned of her affair with his brother.

Francisco Franco

Franche-Com•té (fränsh-kôN-tā′) A historical region and former province of E France; first occupied by a Celtic tribe in the 4th cent. B.C. and part of France after 1676.

fran•chise (frăn′chīz′) *n.* **1.** A privilege or right officially granted a person or a group by a government, esp.: **a.** The constitutional or statutory right to vote. **b.** The establishment of a corporation's existence. **c.** The granting of certain rights and powers to a corporation. **d.** Legal immunity from servitude, certain burdens, or other restrictions. **2a.** Authorization granted to someone to sell a company's goods or services in a certain area. **b.** A business or group of businesses established or operated under such authorization. **3.** The territory or limits within which immunity, a privilege, or a right may be exercised. **4.** A professional sports team. ❖ *tr.v.* **-chised, -chis•ing, -chis•es** To grant a franchise to. [ME *fraunchise* < OFr. *franchise* < *franche*, fem. of

Francis of Assisi
fresco by Simone Martini
(c.1284–1344), St. Francis
Basilica, Assisi, Italy

frangipani

franc, free, exempt. See FRANK[1].]

fran•chis•ee (frăn′chī-zē′) *n.* One that is granted a franchise, as to market a company's goods in a certain local area.

fran•chis•er or **fran•chi•sor** (frăn′chī′zər) *n.* One that grants a franchise.

Fran•cis I (frăn′sĭs) 1494–1547. King of France (1515–47) who waged four wars against Holy Roman Emperor Charles V from 1521 to 1544.

Francis II 1768–1835. Last Holy Roman emperor (1792–1806) and emperor of Austria (1804–35) as Francis I, who was instrumental in the defeat of Napoleon (1813–15).

Fran•cis•can (frăn-sĭs′kən) *n. Roman Catholic Church* A member of an originally mendicant religious order founded by Saint Francis of Assisi in 1209 and dedicated to the virtues of humility and poverty. [NLat. *Franciscānus* < Med.Lat. *Franciscus* < St. FRANCIS OF ASSISI.] —**Fran•cis′can** *adj.*

Francis Ferdinand 1863–1914. Austrian archduke whose assassination precipitated World War I.

Francis Jo•seph I (jō′zəf, -səf, yō′zĕf) also **Franz Jo•sef I** (frănz jō′zəf, -səf, frănts, fränts yō′zĕf) 1830–1916. Emperor of Austria (1848–1916) and king of Hungary (1867–1916) whose ultimatum to Serbia led to World War I.

Francis of As•si•si (ə-sē′zē, -sē, ə-sĭs′ē), Saint. 1182?–1226. Italian Roman Catholic friar who founded the Franciscan order (1209) and was canonized in 1228.

Francis of Sales (sălz, säl), Saint. 1567–1622. French ecclesiastic who maintained that spiritual perfection is possible for people involved in secular pursuits.

fran•ci•um (frăn′sē-əm) *n. Symbol* **Fr** An extremely unstable radioactive element of the alkali metals, having approx. 19 isotopes, the most stable of which is Fr 223 with a half-life of 21 minutes. Atomic number 87; valence 1. See table at **element.** [After FRANCE.]

Franck (frängk, fränk), **César Auguste** 1822–90. French composer noted for his Symphony in D minor (1889).

Fran•co (frăng′kō, fräng′-), **Francisco** Known as "El Caudillo." 1892–1975. Spanish soldier and politician who directed the rebel armed forces that defeated the Republicans in the Spanish Civil War (1936–39) and ruled as dictator (1939–75).

Franco– *pref.* French: *Francophone.* [< LLat. *Francus*, a Frank. See FRANK.]

Fran•co-A•mer•i•can (frăng′kō-ə-mĕr′ĭ-kən) *n.* An American of French or French-Canadian descent. ❖ *adj.* **1.** Of or relating to the Franco-Americans. **2.** Of or relating to France and America: *Franco-American relations.*

fran•co•lin (frăng′kə-lĭn) *n.* Any of various Eurasian or African birds of the genus *Francolinus,* related to and resembling the quails and partridges. [Fr. < Ital. *francolino.*]

Fran•co•ni•a (frăng-kō′nē-ə, -kōn′yə, frän-) A region and former duchy of S Germany. —**Fran•co′ni•an** *adj. & n.*

Fran•co•phile (frăng′kə-fīl′) also **Fran•co•phil** (-fĭl′) *n.* One who admires France, its people, or its culture. —**Fran′co•phile** *adj.* —**Fran′co•phil′i•a** (-fĭl′ē-ə, -fēl′yə) *n.*

Fran•co•phobe (frăng′kə-fōb′) *n.* One who dislikes or fears France, its people, or its culture. —**Fran′co•phobe′, Fran′co•pho′bic** *adj.* —**Fran′co•pho′bi•a** *n.*

fran•co•phone or **fran•co•phone** (frăng′kə-fōn′) *n.* A French-speaking person, esp. in a region where two or more languages are spoken. ❖ *adj.* French-speaking. —**Fran′co•phon′ic** (-fŏn′ĭk) *adj.*

fran•gi•ble (frăn′jə-bəl) *adj.* Capable of being broken; breakable. See Syns at **fragile.** [ME < OFr. < Med.Lat. *frangibilis* < Lat. *frangere,* to break. See **bhreg-** in App.] —**fran′gi•bil′i•ty, fran′gi•ble•ness** *n.*

fran•gi•pan•i (frăn′jə-păn′ē, -pä′nē) *n., pl.* **-pan•is 1.** Any of various tropical American deciduous shrubs or trees of the genus *Plumeria,* having fragrant, funnel-shaped, variously colored flowers. **2.** A perfume derived from or similar in scent to frangipani flowers. **3.** also **fran•gi•pane** (frăn′jə-pān′) A creamy almond-flavored pastry filling. [Fr. *frangipane,* after Muzio *Frangipani,* 16th-cent. Italian marquis.]

Fran•glais (frän-glā′) *n.* French marked by many borrowings from English. [Blend of Fr. *français,* French (< OFr. *franceis* < *France,* France) and Fr. *anglais,* English (< OFr. *englois* < OE *Angul,* Angle < *Angli,* the Angles; see ANGLE).]

frank[1] (frăngk) *adj.* **frank•er, frank•est 1.** Open and sincere in expression; straightforward. **2.** Clearly manifest; evident. ❖ *tr.v.* **franked, frank•ing, franks 1a.** To put an official mark on (a piece of mail) so that it can be sent free of charge. **b.** To send (mail) free of charge. **2.** To place a stamp or mark on (a piece of mail) to show the payment of postage. **3.** To enable (a person) to come and go freely. ❖ *n.* **1a.** A mark or signature placed on a piece of mail to indicate the right to send it free of charge. **b.** The right to send mail free. **2.** A franked piece of mail. [ME, free < OFr. *franc* < LLat. *Francus,* Frank. See FRANK.] —**frank′ness** *n.*

SYNONYMS *frank, candid, outspoken, straightforward, open* These adjectives mean revealing or disposed to reveal one's thoughts freely and honestly. *Frank* implies forthrightness, sometimes to the point of bluntness: *"Be calm and frank, and confess at once all that weighs on your heart"* (Emily Brontë). *Can-*

did often suggests refusal to evade difficult or unpleasant issues: "Save, save, oh save me from the candid friend!" (George Canning). *Outspoken* usually implies bold lack of reserve: *an outspoken activist. Straightforward* denotes directness of manner and expression: "*George was a straightforward soul . . . . 'See here!' he said. 'Are you engaged to anybody?'*" (Booth Tarkington). *Open* suggests freedom from all trace of reserve or secretiveness: "*I will be open and sincere with you*" (Joseph Addison).

frank² (frăngk) *n. Informal* A frankfurter.

Frank (frăngk) *n.* A member of one of the Germanic tribes of the Rhine region in the early Christian era, esp. one of the Salian Franks who conquered Gaul after A.D. 500 and established an extensive empire. [ME < OE *Franca* and OFr. *Franc*, both < LLat. *Francus*, of Gmc. orig.]

Frank (frăngk, frängk), **Anne** 1929–45. German Jewish diarist who fled from Nazi Germany to Amsterdam with her family (1933) and kept a diary during her years in hiding (1942–44). The diary was published in 1947.

Frank·en·food (frăng′kən-fōōd′) *n. Slang* A genetically altered food, esp. a fruit or vegetable. [FRANKEN(STEIN) + FOOD.]

Frank·en·stein (frăng′kən-stīn′) *n.* **1.** An agency or creation that slips from the control of and ultimately destroys its creator. **2.** A monster having the appearance of a man. [From *Frankenstein*, the creator of the artificial monster in *Frankenstein* by Mary Wollstonecraft Shelley.]

Frank·en·thal·er (frăng′kən-thô′lər, -thŏl′ər), **Helen** b. 1928. Amer. abstract expressionist painter whose works include *The Human Edge* (1967).

Frank·fort (frăngk′fərt) The cap. of KY, in the N-central part NW of Lexington; chosen as capital in 1792. Pop. 27,741.

Frank·furt (frăngk′fərt, frängk′fōōrt′) **1.** also **Frankfurt am Main** (äm mīn′) A city of W-central Germany on the Main R.; founded in the 1st cent. B.C.; Pop. 659,803. **2.** also **Frankfurt an der O·der** (än dər ō′dər) A city of E Germany on the Oder R.; chartered 1253. Pop. 84,072.

frank·furt·er (frăngk′fər-tər) also **frank·furt** (frăngk′fər-tər) *n.* A sausage usu. of beef or beef and pork. [After FRANKFURT (am Main).]

Frankfurter, Felix 1882–1965. Austrian-born Amer. jurist; associate justice of the US Supreme Court (1939–62).

frank·in·cense (frăng′kĭn-sĕns′) *n.* An aromatic gum resin obtained from African and Asian trees of the genus *Boswellia* and used chiefly as incense and in perfumes. [ME *frank encens* < OFr. *franc encens : franc*, free, pure; see FRANK¹ + *encens*, incense; see INCENSE².]

Frank·ish (frăng′kĭsh) *adj.* Of or relating to the Franks or their language. ❖ *n.* The West Germanic language of the Franks.

frank·lin (frăng′klĭn) *n.* A medieval English freeholder of non-noble birth holding extensive property. [ME *frankelein* < AN *fraunclein* < *franc*. See FRANK¹.]

Franklin, Benjamin 1706–90. Amer. public official, writer, scientist, and printer who published *Poor Richard's Almanac* (1732–57).

Franklin, Sir John 1786–1847. British explorer who led a search for the Northwest Passage (1845–47).

Franklin, John Hope b. 1915. Amer. historian noted for works such as *From Slavery to Freedom* (1947).

frank·lin·ite (frăng′klĭ-nīt′) *n.* A black, slightly magnetic mineral of zinc, iron, and manganese, ZnFe$_2$O$_4$, that is a valuable source of zinc. [After *Franklin*, a borough of northern New Jersey.]

Franklin stove *n.* A cast-iron heating stove shaped like a fireplace but employing metal baffles to increase its heating efficiency. [After Benjamin FRANKLIN.]

Franklin tree *n.* A deciduous tree or shrub (*Franklinia alatamaha*) originally native to Georgia and having large white fragrant flowers and woody capsules.

frank·ly (frăngk′lē) *adv.* **1.** In a frank manner; candidly. **2.** In truth; honestly: *Frankly, I don't care.*

frank·pledge (frăngk′plĕj′) *n.* **1.** An Anglo-Saxon legal system in which units or tithings composed of ten households were formed, in each of which members were held responsible for one another's conduct. **2.** A member of a unit in frankpledge. [ME *frankplegge* < AN *frauncpledge : OFr. franc*, free, frank; see FRANK¹ + *plege*, pledge; see PLEDGE.]

fran·se·ri·a (frăn-sîr′ē-ə) *n.* Any of various herbs or shrubs of the genus *Franseria*, native to western North America. [NLat. *Franseria*, genus name, after Antonio Franseri, 18th-cent. Spanish botanist.]

fran·tic (frăn′tĭk) *adj.* **1.** Highly excited with strong emotion or frustration; frenzied. **2.** Characterized by rapid and disordered or nervous activity. **3.** *Archaic* Mad; insane. [ME *frantik* < OFr. *frenetique* < Lat. *phrenēticus*. See FRENETIC.] —**fran′ti·cal·ly**, **fran′tic·ly** *adv.*

Franz Jo·sef I (fränz jō′zəf, -səf, fränts, fränts yō′zĕf′) See **Francis Joseph I.**

Franz Josef Land (länd, länt) An archipelago in the Arctic Ocean N of Novaya Zemlya.

frap (frăp) *tr.v.* **frapped, frap·ping, fraps** *Nautical* **1.** To make secure by lashing. **2.** To take up the slack of; tighten. [ME *frapen*,

---

to strike < OFr. *fraper*. See FRAPPÉ.]

frappe (frăp) *n. Rhode Island & Southeastern Massachusetts* See **milk shake** 1. See Regional Note at **milk shake.** [Alteration of FRAPPÉ.]

frap·pé (fră-pā′, frăp) *n.* **1.** A frozen fruit-flavored mixture that is similar to sherbet and served as a dessert or appetizer. **2.** A beverage, usu. a liqueur, poured over shaved ice. [Fr. < p. part. of *frapper*, to strike, chill < OFr. *fraper*, to strike, prob. of imit. orig.]

Fra·ser (frā′zər), **James Earle** 1876–1953. Amer. sculptor whose works include the design for the buffalo nickel (1913).

Fraser River A river of British Columbia, Canada, flowing c. 1,368 km (850 mi) from the Rocky Mts. near the Alberta boundary to the Strait of Georgia at Vancouver.

frass (frăs) *n.* Debris or excrement produced by insects. [Ger., feed, result of eating, insect damage < MHGer. *vrâz* < OHGer. *frāz* < *frezzan*, to eat. See **ed-** in App.]

frat (frăt) *n. Informal* A college fraternity.

fra·ter·nal (frə-tûr′nəl) *adj.* **1a.** Of or relating to brothers. **b.** Showing comradeship; brotherly. **2.** Of or constituting a fraternity. **3.** *Biology* Of, relating to, or being a twin developed from two separately fertilized ova; dizygotic. [ME, ult. < Lat. *frāternus* < *frāter*, brother. See **bhrāter-** in App.] —**fra·ter′nal·ism** *n.* —**fra·ter′nal·ly** *adv.*

fra·ter·ni·ty (frə-tûr′nĭ-tē) *n., pl.* **-ties 1.** A body of people associated for a common purpose or interest, such as a guild. **2.** A group joined by similar backgrounds, occupations, interests, or tastes. **3.** A chiefly social organization of men students at a college or university. **4.** The quality or condition of being brothers; brotherliness. [ME *fraternite* < OFr. < Lat. *frāternitās* < *frāternus*, fraternal. See FRATERNAL.]

frat·er·nize (frăt′ər-nīz′) *intr.v.* **-nized, -niz·ing, -niz·es 1.** To associate with others in a brotherly or congenial way. **2.** To associate on friendly terms with an enemy or opposing group, often in violation of discipline or orders. [Ult. < Lat. *frāternus*, fraternal. See FRATERNAL.] —**frat′er·ni·za′tion** (-nĭ-zā′shən) *n.* —**frat′er·niz′er** *n.*

frat·ri·cide (frăt′rĭ-sīd′) *n.* **1.** The killing of one's brother or sister. **2.** One who has killed one's brother or sister. [ME < OFr. < Lat. *frātricīdium* and *frātricīda : frāter, frātr-*, brother; see **bhrāter-** in App. + *-cīdium* and *-cīda, -cide*.] —**frat′ri·cid′al** (-sīd′l) *adj.*

Frau (frou) *n., pl.* **Frau·en** (frou′ən) Used as a courtesy title in a German-speaking area before the surname or professional title of an adult woman. [Ger. < MHGer. *vrowe* < OHGer. *frouwa*. See **per**¹ in App.]

fraud (frôd) *n.* **1.** A deception deliberately practiced to secure unfair or unlawful gain. **2.** A piece of trickery; a trick. **3a.** One that defrauds; a cheat. **b.** One who assumes a false pose; an impostor. [ME *fraude* < OFr. < Lat. *fraus, fraud-*.]

fraud·u·lent (frô′jə-lənt) *adj.* **1.** Engaging in fraud; deceitful. **2.** Characterized by, constituting, or gained by fraud. [ME < OFr. < Lat. *fraudulentus < fraus, fraud-*, deceit.] —**fraud′u·lence** *n.* —**fraud′u·lent·ly** *adv.*

fraught (frôt) *adj.* **1.** Filled with a specified element or elements; charged. **2.** Marked by or causing distress; emotional. ❖ *n. Scots* Freight; cargo. [ME, p. part. of *fraughten*, to load < *fraght*, cargo; see FREIGHT, and < MDu. *vrachten*, to load (< *vracht*, freight).]

Fräu·lein (froi′līn′, frou′-) *n., pl.* **Fräulein 1.** Used as a courtesy title in a German-speaking area before the surname of a girl or sometimes an unmarried woman. **2.** *fräulein* Used as a form of address for a girl or young woman in a German-speaking area. **3.** *Chiefly British* A German governess. [Ger., dim. of *Frau*, woman. See FRAU.]

Fraun·ho·fer lines (froun′hō′fər) *pl.n.* A set of dark absorption lines appearing against the bright background of the continuous solar spectrum. [After Joseph von *Fraunhofer* (1787–1826), German physicist.]

frax·i·nel·la (frăk′sə-nĕl′ə) *n.* See **gas plant.** [NLat., dim. of Lat. *fraxinus*, ash tree.]

fray¹ (frā) *n.* **1.** A scuffle; a brawl. **2.** A heated dispute or contest. ❖ *tr.v.* **frayed, fray·ing, frays** *Archaic* **1.** To alarm; frighten. **2.** To drive away. [ME *frai*, shortening of *affrai*. See AFFRAY.]

fray² (frā) *v.* **frayed, fray·ing, frays** —*tr.* **1.** To strain; chafe. **2.** To wear away (the edges of fabric, for example) by rubbing. —*intr.* To become worn away or tattered along the edges. ❖ *n.* A frayed or threadbare spot or section on fabric. [ME *fraien*, to wear, bruise < OFr. *fraier*, to rub < Lat. *fricāre*.]

Fra·zer (frā′zər), **Sir James George** 1854–1941. British anthropologist noted for *The Golden Bough* (1890).

fraz·zle (frăz′əl) *Informal v.* **-zled, -zling, -zles** —*tr.* **1.** To wear away along the edges; fray. **2.** To exhaust physically or emotionally. —*intr.* **1.** To become worn away along the edges. **2.** To become exhausted physically or emotionally. ❖ *n.* **1.** A frayed or tattered condition. **2.** A condition of exhaustion. [Perh. a blend of FRAY² and dialectal *fazzle*, to unravel (< ME *facelyn*, to fray < *fasel*, frayed edge, prob. dim. of *fas*, rootlets < OE *fæs*).]

FRB *abbr.* Federal Reserve Board

freak¹ (frēk) *n.* **1.** A thing or occurrence that is markedly unusual or irregular. **2.** An abnormally formed organism, esp. a person or animal regarded as a curiosity or monstrosity. **3.** A sudden capri-

---

Anne Frank

Benjamin Franklin
c. 1778 portrait by Joseph-Siffred Duplessis
(1725–1802)

ă pat	oi boy
ā pay	ou out
âr care	ōō took
ä father	ōō boot
ĕ pet	ŭ cut
ē be	ûr urge
ĭ pit	th thin
ī pie	th this
îr pier	hw which
ŏ pot	zh vision
ō toe	ə about,
ô paw	item

Stress marks:
′ (primary);
′ (secondary), as in
lexicon (lĕk′sĭ-kŏn′)

Frederick II²
portrait by Anton Graff
(1736–1813)

cious turn of mind; a whim. **4.** *Slang* **a.** A drug user or addict. **b.** An eccentric or nonconformist person, esp. a member of a counterculture. **c.** An enthusiast. ❖ *adj.* Highly unusual or irregular: *a freak accident.* ❖ *intr. & tr.v.* **freaked, freak·ing, freaks** *Slang* **1.** To experience or cause to experience frightening hallucinations or feelings of paranoia, esp. as a result of taking a drug. **2.** To behave or cause to behave irrationally and uncontrollably. **3.** To become or cause to become greatly excited or upset. In all three senses, often used with *out.* [?]

freak² (frēk) *n.* A fleck or streak of color. ❖ *tr.v.* **freaked, freak·ing, freaks** To speckle or streak with color. [< FREAK¹.]

freak·ing (frē′kĭng) *adv. & adj. Slang* Used as an intensive: *Traffic was a freaking nightmare.* [Alteration of *frigging*, pr. part. of FRIG.]

freak·ish (frē′kĭsh) *adj.* **1.** Markedly unusual or abnormal; strange. **2.** Relating to or being a freak. **3.** Capricious or whimsical. —**freak′ish·ly** *adv.* —**freak′ish·ness** *n.*

freak-out or **freak·out** (frēk′out′) *n. Slang* **1.** An experience of frightening feelings or hallucinations, esp. as a result of taking a drug. **2.** An experience or scene of unrestrained excitement or irrational behavior. **3.** One having such an experience or participating in such a scene.

freak·y (frē′kē) *adj.* **-i·er, -i·est** **1.** Strange or unusual; freakish. **2.** *Slang* Frightening. —**freak′i·ly** *adv.*

freck·le (frĕk′əl) *n.* A small brownish spot on the skin, often turning darker or increasing in number upon exposure to the sun. ❖ *tr. & intr.v.* **-led, -ling, -les** To dot or become dotted with freckles or spots of color. [< ME *frakles*, freckles, alteration of *fraknes*, prob. of Scand. orig.] —**freck′ly** *adj.*

Fred·die Mac (frĕd′ē) *n.* A security issued by the Federal Home Loan Mortgage Corporation and secured by a pool of conventional home mortgages. [Alteration of *Fed(eral Home Loan) M(ortgage) C(ompany).*]

Fred·er·ick I (frĕd′rĭk, -ər-ĭk) Known as "Frederick Barbarossa." 1123?–90. Holy Roman emperor (1152–90) and king of Germany and Italy who conceded supremacy to Pope Alexander III (1177).

Frederick II¹ 1194–1250. Holy Roman emperor (1212–50) and king of Sicily (1198–1250) as Frederick I who led the Sixth Crusade (1228–29), capturing Jerusalem.

Frederick II² Known as "Frederick the Great." 1712–86. King of Prussia (1740–86) who waged the War of the Austrian Succession (1740–48) and the Seven Years' War (1756–63).

Frederick IX 1899–1972. King of Denmark (1947–72) who signed a constitutional amendment allowing the succession of a woman to the throne.

Fred·er·icks·burg (frĕd′rĭks-bûrg′, -ər-ĭks-) An independent city of NE VA N of Richmond; site of the Battle of Fredericksburg (Dec. 1862). Pop. 19,279.

Frederick William Known as "the Great Elector." 1620–88. Elector of Brandenburg (1640–88) who reorganized and rebuilt his domain after the Thirty Years' War.

Frederick William I 1688–1740. King of Prussia (1713–40) who diversified the economy of his dominion.

Frederick William II 1744–97. King of Prussia (1786–97) whose mismanaged reign was marked by a costly war with Revolutionary France (1792–95).

Frederick William III 1770–1840. King of Prussia (1797–1840) whose long turbulent reign included participation in the Napoleonic Wars.

Fred·er·ic·ton (frĕd′rĭk-tən, -ər-ĭk-) The cap. of New Brunswick, Canada, in the S-central part NW of St. John; founded 1783. Pop. 46,507.

free (frē) *adj.* **fre·er, fre·est** **1.** Not imprisoned or enslaved; being at liberty. **2.** Not controlled by obligation or the will of another. **3a.** Having political independence. **b.** Governed by consent and possessing or granting civil liberties. **c.** Not subject to arbitrary interference by a government: *a free press.* **4a.** Not affected or restricted by a given condition or circumstance. **b.** Not subject to a given condition; exempt. **5.** Not subject to external restraint. **6.** Not literal or exact: *a free translation.* **7a.** Costing nothing; gratuitous. **b.** Publicly supported. **8a.** Not occupied or used. **b.** Not taken up by scheduled activities. **9.** Unobstructed; clear. **10.** Unguarded in expression or manner; open; frank. **11.** Taking undue liberties; forward or overfamiliar. **12.** Liberal or lavish. **13.** Given, made, or done of one's own accord; voluntary or spontaneous. **14.** *Chemistry & Physics* **a.** Unconstrained; unconfined: *free expansion.* **b.** Not fixed in position; capable of relatively unrestricted motion: *a free electron.* **c.** Not chemically bound in a molecule: *free oxygen* **d.** Involving no collisions or interactions: *a free path.* **e.** Empty: *a free space.* **f.** Unoccupied: *a free energy level.* **15.** Not bound, fastened, or attached. **16.** *Linguistics* **a.** Being a form that can stand as an independent word, such as *boat* or *bring.* **b.** Being a vowel in an open syllable, as the *o* in *go.* ❖ *adv.* **1.** In a free manner; without restraint. **2.** Without charge. **3.** *Nautical* On a course other than close-hauled. ❖ *tr.v.* **freed, free·ing, frees** **1.** To set at liberty; make free. **2.** To relieve of a burden, obligation, or restraint. **3.** To remove obstructions or entanglements from; clear. —*idiom:* **for free** *Informal* Without charge. [ME *fre* < OE *frēo.* V., ME *freen* < OE *frēon*, to love, set free. See *prī-* in App.] —**free′ly** *adv.* —**free′ness** *n.*

free agent *n.* A professional athlete who is free to sign a contract with any team. —**free agency** *n.*

free alongside ship *adv. & adj.* Without charge to the purchaser for delivery to the point of loading aboard ship.

free·as·so·ci·ate (frē′ə-sō′shē-āt′, -sē-) *intr.v.* **-at·ed, -at·ing, -ates** To engage in free association.

free association *n.* **1.** A spontaneous, logically unconstrained and undirected association of ideas, emotions, and feelings. **2.** A psychoanalytic technique in which a patient's articulation of free associations is encouraged in order to reveal unconscious thoughts and emotions.

free·base or **free-base** (frē′bās′) *v.* **-based, -bas·ing, -bas·es** —*tr.* **1.** To purify (cocaine) by dissolving it in a heated solvent and separating and drying the precipitate. **2.** To use (freebase) by burning it and inhaling the fumes. —*intr.* To prepare or use freebase. ❖ *n.* Cocaine thus purified.

free·bie also **free·bee** (frē′bē) *n. Slang* An article or service given free. [< FREE.]

free·board (frē′bôrd′, -bōrd′) *n.* **1.** *Nautical* The distance between the water line and the freeboard deck of a ship. **2.** The distance between normal water level and the top of a structure, such as a dam, that impounds or restrains water. **3.** The distance between the ground and the undercarriage of an automobile. [Prob. ult. partial transl. of AN *franc bord*, land claimed outside the fence of a park or forest : *franc*, free + *bord*, border.]

freeboard deck *n.* A ship's uppermost deck that can be made watertight.

free·boot (frē′boot′) *intr.v.* **-boot·ed, -boot·ing, -boots** To act as a freebooter. [Back-formation < FREEBOOTER.]

free·boot·er (frē′boo′tər) *n.* A person who pillages and plunders, esp. a pirate. [Du. *vrijbuiter* < *vrijbuit*, plunder : *vrij*, free; see *prī-* in App. + *buit*, booty (< MDu. *būte*, or MLGer. orig.).]

free·born (frē′bôrn′) *adj.* **1.** Born as a free person, not as a slave or serf. **2.** Relating to or befitting a person born free.

free city *n.* A city governed as an autonomous political unit under international auspices.

freed·man (frēd′mən) *n.* A man freed from slavery.

free·dom (frē′dəm) *n.* **1.** The condition of being free of restraints. **2.** Liberty of the person from slavery, detention, or oppression. **3a.** Political independence. **b.** Exemption from the arbitrary exercise of authority in the performance of a specific action; civil liberty: *freedom of assembly.* **4.** Exemption from an unpleasant or onerous condition. **5.** The capacity to exercise choice; free will. **6.** Ease or facility of movement. **7.** Frankness or boldness; lack of modesty or reserve. **8a.** The right to unrestricted use; full access. **b.** The right of enjoying all the privileges of membership or citizenship. **9.** A right or the power to engage in certain actions without control or interference. [ME *fredom* < OE *frēodōm* : *frēo*, free; see FREE + *-dōm*, -dom.]

SYNONYMS *freedom, liberty, license* These nouns refer to the power to act, speak, or think without externally imposed restraints. *Freedom* is the most general term: "*In giving freedom to the slave, we assure freedom to the free*" (Abraham Lincoln). *Liberty* often stresses the power of free choice: "*liberty, perfect liberty, to think, feel, do just as one pleases*" (William Hazlitt). *License* sometimes denotes deliberate deviation from normally applicable rules or practices to achieve a desired effect: *poetic license.* Frequently, though, it denotes undue freedom: "*the intolerable license with which the newspapers break . . . the rules of decorum*" (Edmund Burke).

freedom of the seas *n.* **1.** The doctrine that ships of any nation may travel through international waters unhampered. **2.** The right of neutral shipping in wartime to trade at will except where blockades are established.

freedom rider *n.* One of a group of civil rights activists in the early 1960s who rode buses in the southern United States to challenge racial segregation. —**freedom ride** *n.*

freed·wom·an (frēd′woom′ən) *n.* A woman freed from slavery.

free energy *n.* **1.** A thermodynamic quantity that is the difference between the internal energy of a system and the product of its absolute temperature and entropy. **2.** A thermodynamic quantity that is the difference between the enthalpy and the product of the absolute temperature and entropy of a system.

free enterprise *n.* The freedom of private businesses to operate competitively for profit with minimal government regulation. —**free′en·ter·prise′** (frē′ĕn′tər-prīz′) *adj.*

free fall or **free-fall** (frē′fôl′) *n.* **1.** The fall of a body within the atmosphere without a drag-producing device. **2.** The ideal falling motion of a body that is subject only to the earth's gravitational field. **3.** Rapid uncontrolled decline. —**free′-fall′** (frē′fôl′) *v.*

free-fire zone (frē′fīr′) *n.* A battle area or combat zone without restrictions on the use of arms or explosives.

free flight *n.* Flight, as of an aircraft or spacecraft, after termination of powered flight.

free-float·ing (frē′flō′tĭng) *adj.* **1.** Not committed or decided. **2.** Experienced without an obvious basis or cause. **3.** Capable of free movement; not bound.

free-for-all (frē′fər-ôl′) *n.* A disorderly fight, argument, or competition in which everyone present participates.

free·form (frē'fôrm') *adj.* **1.** Having or characterized by a usu. flowing asymmetrical shape or outline. **2.** Characterized by an unconventional or variable form. —**free'form'** *adv.*

free·hand (frē'hănd') *adj.* Drawn by hand without the aid of tracing or drafting devices. —**free'hand'** *adv.*

free hand *n.* Freedom to do or decide as one sees fit.

free·hand·ed (frē'hăn'dĭd) *adj.* Openhanded; generous. See Syns at **liberal**. —**free'hand'ed·ly** *adv.*

free·heart·ed (frē'här'tĭd) *adj.* **1.** Unreserved; open. **2.** *Chiefly Southern & Northeastern US* Generous; liberal. —**free'heart'ed·ly** *adv.*

free·hold (frē'hōld') *n.* **1.** *Law* **a.** An estate held in fee or for life. **b.** The tenure by which such an estate is held. **2.** A tenure of an office or a dignity for life. [ME *frehold*, transl. of AN *fraunc tenement* : *fraunc*, free + *tenement*, possession.] —**free'hold'er** *n.*

free kick *n.* An unobstructed kick of a stationary ball, as in soccer, usu. awarded when the opposition commits a foul.

free·lance (frē'lăns') *n.* also **free lance** **1.** A person who sells services to employers without a long-term commitment to any of them. **2.** An uncommitted independent, as in politics. **3.** A medieval mercenary. ❖ *v.* **-lanced, -lanc·ing, -lanc·es** —*intr.* To work as a freelance. —*tr.* To produce and sell as a freelance. ❖ *adj.* Of, relating to, or working as a freelance. —**free'lanc'er** *n.*

free-liv·ing (frē'lĭv'ĭng) *adj.* **1.** Given to self-indulgence. **2.** *Biology* **a.** Living independently of another organism. **b.** Moving independently; not sessile.

free·load (frē'lōd') *intr.v.* **-load·ed, -load·ing, -loads** *Slang* To take advantage of the charity, generosity, or hospitality of others. —**free'load'er** *n.*

free love *n.* The belief in or practice of sexual relations without marriage and without formal obligations.

free lunch *n.* *Slang* Something acquired without due effort or without cost.

free·man (frē'mən) *n.* **1.** A person not in slavery or serfdom. **2.** One who possesses the rights or privileges of a citizen.

free market *n.* An economic market in which supply and demand are not regulated or are regulated with only minor restrictions.

free·mar·tin (frē'mär'tn) *n.* A sterile or otherwise sexually imperfect female calf, usu. born as the twin of a bull calf. [Perh. akin to Ir.Gael. *mart*, heifer.]

free·ma·son (frē'mā'sən) *n.* **1.** Freemason A member of the Free and Accepted Masons, an international fraternal and charitable organization with secret rites and signs. **2.** A member of a medieval guild of skilled itinerant masons.

free·ma·son·ry (frē'mā'sən-rē) *n.* **1.** Freemasonry The institutions, precepts, and rites of the Freemasons. **2.** Spontaneous fellowship and sympathy among a number of people.

free on board *adj. & adv.* Without charge to the purchaser for delivery on board or into a carrier at a specified point or location.

free port *n.* A port or an area of a port in which imported goods can be held or processed free of customs duties before reexport.

free radical *n.* An atom or group of atoms that has at least one unpaired electron and is therefore unstable and highly reactive.

free-range (frē'rānj') *adj.* Of, relating to, or produced by animals, esp. poultry, that range freely for food, rather than being confined in an enclosure: *free-range chickens.*

free rein *n.* Unlimited freedom to act or make decisions.

free ride *n.* *Slang* Something acquired without the ordinary effort or cost. —**free rider** *n.*

free·sia (frē'zhə, -zhē-ə, -zē-ə) *n.* Any of several plants of the genus *Freesia*, native to southern Africa and having one-sided flower clusters. [NLat. *Freesia*, genus name, after Friedrich Heinrich Theodor *Freese* (1795–1876), German physician.]

free silver *n.* The free coinage of silver, esp. at a fixed ratio to gold.

free soil *n.* US territory in which slavery was prohibited before the Civil War.

free-soil (frē'soil') *adj.* **1.** Prohibiting slavery. **2a.** Opposing the extension of slavery before the US Civil War. **b.** Free-Soil Of or being a US political party founded in 1848 to oppose the extension of slavery into US territories and the admission of slave states into the Union.

free speech *n.* The right to express any opinion in public without censorship or restraint by the government.

free spirit *n.* One who is not restrained, as by convention.

free-spo·ken (frē'spō'kən) *adj.* Candid in expression; outspoken.

free·stand·ing (frē'stăn'dĭng) *adj.* Standing or operating independently of anything else.

free·stone (frē'stōn') *n.* **1.** A stone, such as limestone, soft enough to be cut easily without shattering or splitting. **2.** A fruit, esp. a peach, that has a stone that does not adhere to the pulp. [ME *freston*, transl. of OFr. *franche pere*, high-grade stone.]

free·style (frē'stīl') *n.* **1a.** A swimming event or leg of an event in which the contestants may choose any stroke. **b.** The crawl. **2.** A competition, as in figure skating, in which any maneuver or movement is allowed and competitors are judged on their artistic expression, acrobatic skill, and athletic expertise. **3.** A style of wrestling in which all noninjurious holds or tactics are permitted. —**free'style'** *adv. & adj.* —**free'styl'er** *n.*

free-swim·ming (frē'swĭm'ĭng) *adj.* Able to swim freely; not sessile or attached. —**free'-swim'mer** *n.*

free-swing·ing (frē'swĭng'ĭng) *adj.* Bold and uninhibited.

free-think·er (frē'thĭng'kər) *n.* One who has rejected authority and dogma, esp. in religious thinking, in favor of rational thought and speculation. —**free'think'ing** *adj. & n.*

free thought *n.* Thought that rejects authority and dogma, esp. in religion; freethinking.

free throw *n.* See **foul shot**.

free-throw line (frē'thrō') *n.* See **foul line** 2.

Free·town (frē'toun') The cap. of Sierra Leone, in the W part on the Atlantic Ocean; settled in 1787. Pop. 469,776.

free trade *n.* Trade between nations without protective customs tariffs. —**free trader** *n.*

free verse *n.* Verse composed of variable, usu. unrhymed lines having no fixed metrical pattern. [Transl. of Fr. *vers libre* : *vers*, verse + *libre*, free.]

free·ware (frē'wâr') *n.* Software that is available for free, usu. over the Internet.

free·way (frē'wā') *n.* **1.** See **expressway**. **2.** A highway without tolls.

free·wheel (frē'hwēl', -wēl') *n.* also **free wheel** **1.** A power-transmission device that allows the drive shaft of a motor vehicle to continue turning when its speed is greater than that of the engine shaft. **2.** A clutch in the rear-wheel hub of a bicycle that permits the wheel to turn without pedal action. ❖ *intr.v.* **-wheeled, -wheel·ing, -wheels** **1.** To continue turning or spinning after disengagement from the drive mechanism. **2.** To live or move freely and sometimes aimlessly or irresponsibly. **3.** To operate independently or free of restraints.

free·wheel·ing (frē'hwē'lĭng, -wē'-) *adj.* **1a.** Free of restraints or rules in organization, methods, or procedure. **b.** Heedless of consequences; carefree. **2.** Relating to or equipped with a free wheel.

free·will (frē'wĭl') *adj.* Done of one's own accord; voluntary.

free will *n.* **1.** The ability or discretion to choose; free choice. **2.** The power of making free choices that are unconstrained by external circumstances or by an agency such as fate or divine will. [ME *fre wil*, transl. of LLat. *liberum arbitrium*.]

free world *n.* The countries of the world that have democratic and capitalistic or moderately socialistic systems rather than communist or totalitarian systems.

freeze (frēz) *v.* **froze** (frōz), **fro·zen** (frō'zən), **freez·ing, freez·es** —*intr.* **1a.** To pass from the liquid to the solid state by loss of heat. **b.** To acquire a surface or coat of ice from cold: *The lake froze over.* **2.** To become clogged or jammed because of the formation of ice. **3.** To be at that degree of temperature at which ice forms: *It may freeze tonight.* **4.** To be killed or harmed by cold or frost. **5.** To be or feel uncomfortably cold. **6.** To become fixed, stuck, or attached by or as if by frost. **7a.** To become motionless or immobile, as from surprise or attentiveness. **b.** To become unable to act or speak, as from fear. **8.** To become rigid and inflexible; solidify. —*tr.* **1a.** To convert into ice. **b.** To cause ice to form upon. **c.** To cause to congeal or stiffen from extreme cold. **2.** To preserve (foods, for example) by subjecting to freezing temperatures. **3.** To damage, kill, or make inoperative by cold or by the formation of ice. **4.** To make very cold; chill. **5.** To immobilize, as with fear or shock. **6.** To chill with an icy or formal manner. **7.** To stop the motion or progress of. **8a.** To fix (prices or wages, for example) at a given or current level. **b.** To prohibit further manufacture or use of. **c.** To prevent or restrict the exchange, withdrawal, liquidation, or granting of (assets, for example) by governmental action. **9a.** To photograph (a subject) in midaction so as to produce a still image. **b.** To stop (a moving film or videotape) at a particular image. **10.** To anesthetize by chilling. **11.** *Sports* To keep possession of (a ball or puck) so as to deny an opponent the opportunity to score. ❖ *n.* **1a.** The act of freezing. **b.** The state of being frozen. **2.** A spell of cold weather; a frost. **3.** A restriction that forbids a quantity from rising above a given or current level. —*phrasal verb:* **freeze out** To shut out or exclude, as by cold treatment. —*idiom:* **freeze (someone's) blood** To affect with terror or dread; horrify. [ME *fresen* < OE *frēosan*.] —**freez'a·ble** *adj.*

freeze-dry (frēz'drī') *tr.v.* **-dried, -dry·ing, -dries** To preserve (food, for example) by rapid freezing and drying in a high vacuum.

freeze-etch·ing (frēz'ĕch'ĭng) *n.* A method of specimen preparation for electron microscopy in which a replica is made from a sample that has been rapidly frozen and then fractured along natural planes of weakness to reveal its internal structure. —**freeze'-etch'** *v.*

freeze-frame or **freeze frame** (frēz'frām') *n.* **1.** A still picture in the course of a movie or television film, made by running a series of identical frames or by stopping a reel or videotape at one desired frame. **2.** A vivid, motionless scene or image.

freez·er (frē'zər) *n.* A thermally insulated compartment, cabinet, or room in which a subfreezing temperature is maintained for the rapid freezing and storing of perishable items, esp. food.

freezer burn *n.* Discoloration that appears on improperly or inadequately packaged frozen food, caused by evaporation of moisture.

freesia

ă pat	oi boy
ā pay	ou out
âr care	ŏŏ took
ä father	ōō boot
ĕ pet	ŭ cut
ē be	ûr urge
ĭ pit	th thin
ī pie	th this
îr pier	hw which
ŏ pot	zh vision
ō toe	ə about,
ô paw	item

Stress marks:
' (primary);
' (secondary), as in **lexicon** (lĕk'sĭ-kŏn')

French curve

French horn

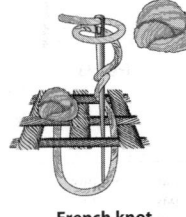

French knot

fret³
fret designs

freez·ing point (frē′zĭng) n. **1.** The temperature at which a liquid of specified composition solidifies under a specified pressure. **2.** The temperature at which the liquid and solid phases of a substance of specified composition are in equilibrium at atmospheric pressure.

free zone n. An area at a port or city where goods may be received and held without the payment of duty.

F region n. See **F layer** 1.

Frei·burg also **Frei·burg im Breis·gau** (frī′bûrg′ ĭm brīs′gou′, -boork′) A city of SW Germany near the Rhine R. at the edge of the Black Forest; founded 1120. Pop. 197,384.

freight (frāt) n. **1.** Goods carried by a vessel or vehicle, esp. by a commercial carrier; cargo. **2.** A burden; a load. **3a.** Commercial transportation of goods. **b.** The charge for transporting goods. **4.** A railway train carrying goods only. ❖ tr.v. **freight·ed, freight·ing, freights** **1.** To convey commercially as cargo. **2.** To load with goods to be transported. **3.** To load; charge. [ME fraught, freight < MDu. or MLGer. vracht, vrecht.]

freight·age (frā′tĭj) n. **1.** See **freight** 3. **2.** Cargo.

freight car n. A railroad car designed for carrying freight.

freight·er (frā′tər) n. **1.** A vehicle, esp. a ship, used for carrying freight. **2.** A shipper of cargo.

freight train n. A railroad train made up of an engine and freight cars.

frem·i·tus (frĕm′ĭ-təs) n., pl. **fremitus** A palpable vibration, as felt by the hand on the chest during coughing or speaking. [Lat., a murmuring < p. part. of fremere, to murmur.]

Fre·mont (frē′mŏnt′) A city of W CA on San Francisco Bay SE of Oakland. Pop. 203,413.

Fré·mont (frē′mŏnt′), **John Charles** 1813–90. Amer. soldier and politician who explored and mapped much of the American West and Northwest.

fre·na (frē′nə) n. A plural of **frenum**.

french (frĕnch) tr.v. **frenched, french·ing, french·es** **1.** To cut (green beans, for example) into thin strips before cooking. **2.** To trim fat or bone from (a chop, for example). **3.** or **French** Slang To give a French kiss to. [< FRENCH.]

French adj. **1.** Of, relating to, or characteristic of France or its people or culture. **2.** Of or relating to the French language. ❖ n. **1.** The Romance language of France, parts of Switzerland and Belgium, and other countries formerly under French influence or control. **2.** The people of France. **3.** Informal Coarse or vulgar language: Pardon my French. [ME < OE frencisc, Frankish < Franca, Frank. See FRANK.]

French, Daniel Chester 1850–1931. Amer. sculptor whose works include the seated marble figure of Abraham Lincoln at the Lincoln Memorial in Washington DC.

French bread n. Bread made with water, flour, and yeast and baked in long crusty loaves.

French bulldog n. Any of a breed of small muscular dogs developed in France from toy English bulldogs and native breeds.

French Cameroons A former French mandate (1922–46) and trust territory (1946–60) of W-central Africa.

French Canadian n. A Canadian of French descent. —**French′-Ca·na·di·an** (frĕnch′kə-nā′dē-ən) adj.

French chalk n. Chalk made of a soft white variety of talc, used for marking fabrics and for removing grease spots.

French chop n. A rib chop with the meat and fat trimmed from the end of the rib.

French cuff n. A wide cuff for a shirt sleeve that is folded back and fastened with a cuff link.

French curve n. A flat drafting instrument with curved edges and scroll-shaped cutouts, used as a guide in drawing curves when constructing graphs or making engineering drawings.

French door n. A door, usu. one of a pair, of light construction with glass panes extending for most of its length.

French dressing n. **1.** A salad dressing of oil, vinegar, and seasonings. **2.** A commercially prepared creamy salad dressing that is usu. pinkish in color and often sweet.

French Equatorial Africa Formerly **French Congo.** A former federation of W-central Africa (1910–58) comprising present-day Chad, Gabon, Congo, and Central African Republic.

French fry n. A thin strip of potato fried in deep fat. Often used in the plural.

French-fry (frĕnch′frī′) tr.v. **-fried, -fry·ing, -fries** To fry (potato strips, for example) in deep fat.

French Guiana A French overseas department of NE South America on the Atlantic Ocean; settled by the French after 1604. Cap. Cayenne. Pop. 72,012.

French harp n. South Midland US See **harmonica** 1.

French heel n. A curved, moderately high heel used on women's shoes.

French horn n. A valved brass wind instrument that produces a mellow tone from a long narrow tube that is coiled in a circle before ending in a flaring bell.

French·i·fy (frĕn′chə-fī′) tr.v. **-fied, -fy·ing, -fies** To make French in character or quality. —**French′i·fi·ca′tion** (-fĭ-kā′shən) n.

French kiss n. A kiss in which the tongue enters the partner's mouth. —**French′-kiss′** (frĕnch′kĭs′) v.

French knot n. A decorative embroidery stitch made by looping the thread two or more times around the needle, which is then inserted into the fabric.

French leave n. An informal, unannounced, or abrupt departure. [< the 18th-cent. Fr. custom of leaving without saying goodbye to the host or hostess.]

French·man (frĕnch′mən) n. A man who is a native or inhabitant of France.

French pastry n. Any of a wide variety of rich and elaborate pastries prepared in individual portions.

French Polynesia A French overseas island territory in the S-central Pacific Ocean; organized as a territory in 1903. Cap. Papeete. Pop. 166,753.

French provincial n. A style of architecture or furniture characteristic of the provinces in 17th- and 18th-century France.

French seam n. A seam stitched first on the right side and then turned in and stitched on the wrong side so that the raw edges are enclosed in the seam.

French telephone n. A telephone with the receiver and transmitter contained in a single unit.

French toast n. Sliced bread soaked in a batter of milk and egg and lightly fried.

French West Africa A former federation of W Africa (1895–1959) comprising present-day Benin, Burkina Faso, Côte d'Ivoire, Guinea, Mali, Mauritania, Niger, and Senegal.

French West Indies The French overseas departments of Guadeloupe and Martinique in the Lesser Antilles.

French window n. **1.** A pair or one of a pair of floor-length windows that open in the middle. **2.** A casement window.

French·wom·an (frĕnch′woŏm′ən) n. A woman who is a native or inhabitant of France.

Fre·neau (frĭ-nō′), **Philip Morin** 1752–1832. Amer. poet noted for his satirical attacks on the British.

fre·net·ic or **phre·net·ic** (frə-nĕt′ĭk) also **fre·net·i·cal** or **phre·net·i·cal** (-ĭ-kəl) adj. Wildly excited or active; frantic; frenzied. [ME frenetik, ult. < Gk. phrenītikos < phrenītis, brain disease < phrēn, mind.] —**fre·net′i·cal·ly** adv. —**fre·net′i·cism** (-ĭ-sĭz′əm) n.

fren·u·lum (frĕn′yə-ləm) n., pl. **-la** (-lə) **1.** A small frenum. **2.** A bristly structure on the hind wings of certain moths and butterflies that holds the forewings and hind wings together during flight. [NLat. frēnulum, dim. of Lat. frēnum, bridle. See FRENUM.]

fre·num (frē′nəm) n., pl. **-nums** or **-na** (-nə) A membranous fold of skin or mucous membrane that supports or restricts the movement of a part or organ. [Lat. frēnum, bridle < frendere, to grind. See ghrendh- in App.]

fren·zied (frĕn′zēd) adj. Affected with or marked by frenzy; frantic: a frenzied rush for the exits. —**fren′zied·ly** adv.

fren·zy (frĕn′zē) n., pl. **-zies** **1.** A state of violent mental agitation or wild excitement. **2.** Temporary madness or delirium. **3.** A mania; a craze. ❖ tr.v. **-zied, -zy·ing, -zies** To drive into a frenzy. [ME frenesie < OFr. < Med.Lat. phrenēsia < Lat. phrenēsis, back-formation < phrenēticus, delirious. See FRENETIC.]

Fre·on (frē′ŏn′) A trademark used for a variety of nonflammable gaseous or liquid fluorinated hydrocarbons used primarily in refrigeration and as aerosol propellants.

freq. abbr. **1.** frequency **2.** frequentative

fre·quence (frē′kwəns) n. Frequency. [ME, multitude < OFr. < Lat. frequentia. See FREQUENCY.]

fre·quen·cy (frē′kwən-sē) n., pl. **-cies** **1.** The property or condition of occurring at frequent intervals. **2.** Mathematics & Physics The number of times a specified phenomenon occurs within a specified interval, as: **a.** The number of repetitions of a complete sequence of values of a periodic function per unit variation of an independent variable. **b.** The number of complete cycles of a periodic process occurring per unit time. **c.** The number of repetitions per unit time of a complete waveform, as of an electric current. **3.** Statistics **a.** The number of measurements in an interval of a frequency distribution. **b.** The ratio of the number of times an event occurs in a series of trials of a chance experiment to the total number of trials. [Lat. frequentia, multitude < frequēns, frequent-, crowded, numerous, frequent.]

frequency distribution n. A set of intervals, usu. adjacent and of equal width, into which the range of a statistical distribution is divided, each associated with a frequency indicating the number of measurements in that interval.

frequency modulation n. The encoding of a carrier wave by variation of its frequency in accordance with an input signal.

fre·quent (frē′kwənt) adj. **1.** Occurring or appearing quite often or at close intervals. **2.** Habitual or regular: a frequent visitor. ❖ tr.v. (also frē-kwĕnt′) **-quent·ed, -quent·ing, -quents** To pay frequent visits to; be in or at often: frequent a restaurant. [ME, ample, profuse < OFr. < Lat. frequēns, frequent-, crowded, numerous, frequent.] —**fre′quen·ta′tion** n. —**fre′quent′er** (-kwĕn′tər) n. —**fre′quent·ness** n.

fre·quen·ta·tive (frē-kwĕn′tə-tĭv) Grammar adj. Expressing repeated action. ❖ n. A frequentative verb or verb form. [Lat. frequentātīvus < frequentātus, p. part. of frequentāre, to repeat < frequēns, frequent-, frequent.]

fre·quent·ly (frē′kwənt-lē) adv. At frequent intervals; often.

fres·co (frĕs′kō) n., pl. **-coes** or **-cos** **1.** The art of painting on fresh, moist plaster with pigments dissolved in water. **2.** A painting executed in this way. ❖ *tr.v.* **-coed, -co•ing, -coes** To paint in this way. [Ital., fresh (plaster), of Gmc. orig.] **—fres′co•er, fres′co•ist** *n.*

fresh (frĕsh) *adj.* **fresh•er, fresh•est 1.** New to one's experience; not encountered before. **2.** Novel; different: *a fresh slant on the problem.* See Syns at **new. 3.** Recently made, produced, or harvested; not stale or spoiled: *fresh bread.* **4.** Not preserved, as by canning or freezing: *fresh vegetables.* **5.** Not saline or salty: *fresh water.* **6.** Not yet used or soiled; clean: *a fresh sheet of paper.* **7.** Free from impurity or pollution; pure: *fresh air.* **8.** Additional; new: *fresh evidence.* **9.** Bright and clear; not dull or faded: *a fresh memory.* **10.** Having the glowing, unspoiled appearance of youth: *a fresh complexion.* **11.** Untried; inexperienced: *fresh recruits.* **12.** Having just arrived; straight: *fashions fresh from Paris.* **13.** Revived or reinvigorated; refreshed. **14.** Fairly strong; brisk: *a fresh wind.* **15.** *Informal* Bold and saucy; impudent. **16.** Having recently calved and therefore with milk. Used of a cow. **17.** *Slang* Excellent; first-rate. ❖ *adv.* Recently; newly. ❖ *n.* **1.** The early part. **2.** A freshet. [ME < OE *fersc,* pure, not salty, and < OFr. *freis* (fem. *fresche*), new, of Gmc. orig.] **—fresh′ly** *adv.* **—fresh′ness** *n.*

fresh•en (frĕsh′ən) *v.* **-ened, -en•ing, -ens** —*intr.* **1.** To become fresh, as in vigor or appearance. **2.** To become brisk; increase. Used of the wind. **3.** To lose saltiness. **4.** To calve and begin to produce milk. Used of a cow. —*tr.* **1.** To make fresh. **2.** To add to or strengthen (a drink). **—fresh′en•er** *n.*

fresh•et (frĕsh′ĭt) *n.* **1.** A sudden overflow of a stream resulting from a heavy rain or a thaw. **2.** A stream of fresh water that empties into a body of salt water.

fresh•man (frĕsh′mən) *n.* **1.** A student in the first-year class of a high school, college, or university. **2.** A beginner; a novice. See Usage Note at **man.**

fresh•wa•ter (frĕsh′wô′tər, -wŏt′ər) *adj.* **1.** Of, relating to, living in, or consisting of water that is not salty: *freshwater fish.* **2.** Situated away from the sea; inland. **3.** *Nautical* Accustomed to sailing on inland waters only: *a freshwater sailor.*

Fres•nel (frā-nĕl′), **Augustin Jean** 1788–1827. French physicist who investigated polarized light.

Fres•nel lens (frə-nĕl′) *n.* A thin optical lens consisting of concentric rings of segmental lenses, used in spotlights, overhead projectors, and headlights. [After Augustin Jean FRESNEL.]

Fres•no (frĕz′nō) A city of central CA SSE of Sacramento in the San Joaquin Valley. Pop. 427,652.

fret[1] (frĕt) *v.* **fret•ted, fret•ting, frets** —*tr.* **1.** To cause to be uneasy; vex. **2a.** To gnaw or wear away; erode. **b.** To produce a hole or worn spot in; corrode. **3.** To form (a passage or channel) by erosion. **4.** To disturb the surface of (water or a stream); agitate. —*intr.* **1.** To be vexed or troubled; worry. See Syns at **brood. 2.** To be worn or eaten away; become corroded. **3.** To move agitatedly. **4.** To gnaw with the teeth in the manner of a rodent. ❖ *n.* **1.** The act or an instance of fretting. **2.** A hole or worn spot made by abrasion or erosion. **3.** Irritation of mind; agitation. [ME *freten* < OE *fretan,* to devour. See **ed-** in App.]

fret[2] (frĕt) *n.* One of the ridges set across the fingerboard of a stringed instrument, such as a guitar. ❖ *tr.v.* **fret•ted, fret•ting, frets 1.** To provide with frets. **2.** To press (the strings of an instrument) against the frets. [?]

fret[3] (frĕt) *n.* **1.** An ornamental design consisting of repeated and symmetrical figures, often in relief, contained within a band or border. **2.** A headdress, worn by women of the Middle Ages, consisting of interlaced wire. ❖ *tr.v.* **fret•ted, fret•ting, frets** To provide with such a design or headdress. [ME, interlaced work < OFr. *frete.*]

fret•board (frĕt′bôrd′, -bōrd′) *n.* A fingerboard fitted with frets.

fret•ful (frĕt′fəl) *adj.* **1.** Inclined to be vexed or troubled; peevish. **2.** Marked by worry and distress; troublesome. **—fret′ful•ly** *adv.* **—fret′ful•ness** *n.*

fret saw *n.* A long narrow-bladed saw with fine teeth, used in making curved cuts in thin wood or metal.

fret•work (frĕt′wûrk′) *n.* Ornamental work consisting of three-dimensional frets; geometric openwork.

Freud (froid), **Anna** 1895–1982. Austrian-born British psychoanalyst who applied psychoanalysis to child therapy.

Freud, Sigmund 1856–1939. Austrian founder of psychoanalysis. **—Freud′i•an** *adj. & n.* **—Freud′i•an•ism** *n.*

Freudian slip *n.* A verbal mistake that is thought to reveal an unconscious belief, thought, or emotion.

Freund's adjuvant (froindz) *n.* A substance consisting of killed microorganisms, such as mycobacteria, in an oil and water emulsion that is administered to induce and enhance the formation of antibodies. [After Jules T. *Freund* (1890–1960), Hungarian-born American immunologist.]

Frey (frā) also **Freyr** (frâr) *n. Mythology* The Norse god who dispenses peace and prosperity; the brother of Freya. [ON *Freyr.* See **per**[1] in App.]

Frey•a also **Frey•ja** (frā′ə) *n. Mythology* The Norse goddess of love and beauty; the sister of Frey. [ON *Freyja* < *freyja,* lady. See **per**[1] in App.]

FRG *abbr.* Federal Republic of Germany

Fri. *abbr.* Friday

fri•a•ble (frī′ə-bəl) *adj.* Readily crumbled; brittle. [Lat. *friābilis* < *friāre,* to crumble.] **—fri′a•bil′i•ty, fri′a•ble•ness** *n.*

fri•ar (frī′ər) *n.* A member of a usu. mendicant Roman Catholic order. [ME *frere* < OFr. < Lat. *frāter,* brother. See **bhrāter-** in App.] **—fri′ar•ly** *adj.*

fri•ar's lantern (frī′ərz) *n.* See **ignis fatuus** 1.

fri•ar•y (frī′ə-rē) *n., pl.* **-ies** A monastery of friars.

frib•ble (frĭb′əl) *v.* **-bled, -bling, -bles** —*tr.* To waste (time, for example); fritter (something) away. —*intr.* To waste time; trifle. ❖ *n.* **1.** A frivolity; a trifle. **2.** A frivolous person. [?] **—frib′bler** *n.*

fric•an•deau (frĭk′ən-dō′) *n.* A cut of veal that has been larded and braised. [Fr. < *fricasser,* to fricassee. See FRICASSEE.]

fric•as•see (frĭk′ə-sē′, frĭk′ə-sē′) *n.* Poultry or meat cut into pieces and stewed in gravy. ❖ *tr.v.* **-seed, -see•ing, -sees** To prepare (poultry or meat) as a fricassee. [Fr. *fricassée* < OFr. < fem. p. part. of *fricasser,* to fricassee : prob. *frire,* to fry (< Lat. *frīgere,* to roast, fry) + *casser,* to break, crack (< Lat. *quassāre,* to shake, shatter; see SQUASH[2]) or VLat. **coāctiāre,* to press together (< Lat. *coāctus,* p. part. of *cōgere,* to drive or bring together; see COGENT).]

fric•a•tive (frĭk′ə-tĭv) *n.* A consonant, such as *f* or *s* in English, produced by the forcing of breath through a constricted passage. ❖ *adj.* Of, relating to, or being a fricative. [NLat. *fricātīvus* < Lat. *fricātus,* p. part. of *fricāre,* to rub.]

Frick (frĭk), **Henry Clay** 1849–1919. Amer. industrialist who bequeathed his art collection to New York City.

fric•tion (frĭk′shən) *n.* **1.** The rubbing of one object or surface against another. **2.** Conflict, as between persons having dissimilar ideas or interests; clash. **3.** *Physics* A force that resists the relative motion or tendency to such motion of two bodies in contact. [Lat. *frictiō, frictiōn-* < *frictus,* p. part. of *fricāre,* to rub.] **—fric′tion•al** *adj.* **—fric′tion•al•ly** *adv.*

friction match *n.* A match that ignites when struck on an abrasive surface.

friction tape *n.* A moisture-resistant adhesive tape, usu. made of cloth, used chiefly to insulate electrical conductors.

Fri•day (frī′dē, -dā′) *n.* The sixth day of the week. [ME *Fridai* < OE *Frīgedæg.* See **prī-** in App.] **—Fri′days** *adv.*

fridge (frĭj) *n. Informal* A refrigerator.

fried (frīd) *v.* Past tense and past participle of **fry**[1]. ❖ *adj. Slang* **1.** Drunk or intoxicated. **2.** Tired out; exhausted.

Frie•dan (frē-dăn′), **Betty Naomi** b. 1921. Amer. feminist who wrote *The Feminine Mystique* (1963).

Fried•man (frēd′mən), **Milton** b. 1912. Amer. economist who won a 1976 Nobel Prize.

friend (frĕnd) *n.* **1.** A person whom one knows, likes, and trusts. **2.** A person whom one knows; an acquaintance. **3.** A person with whom one is allied in a struggle or cause; a comrade. **4.** One who supports, sympathizes with, or patronizes a group, cause, or movement. **5. Friend** A member of the Society of Friends; a Quaker. ❖ *tr.v.* **friend•ed, friend•ing, friends** *Archaic* To befriend. [ME < OE *frēond.* See **prī-** in App.] **—friend′less** *adj.* **—friend′less•ness** *n.*

friend•ly (frĕnd′lē) *adj.* **-li•er, -li•est 1.** Of, relating to, or befitting a friend. **2.** Favorably disposed; not antagonistic. **3.** Warm; comforting. **4a.** User-friendly. **b.** *Informal* Easy to understand or use for a specified agent. ❖ *adv.* In the manner of a friend; amicably. ❖ *n., pl.* **-lies** *Informal* One fighting on or favorable to one's own side. **—friend′li•ly** *adv.* **—friend′li•ness** *n.*

friendly fire *n.* Discharge of a military weapon that injures or kills a member of one's own armed forces or an ally.

Friendly Islands See **Tonga.**

friend•ship (frĕnd′shĭp′) *n.* **1.** The quality or condition of being friends. **2.** A friendly relationship: *formed many new friendships.* **3.** Friendliness; good will: *friendship toward other nations.*

fri•er (frī′ər) *n.* Variant of **fryer.**

fries (frīz) *v.* Third person singular present tense of **fry**[1]. ❖ *n.* Plural of **fry**[1].

Frie•sian (frē′zhən) *n.* Variant of **Frisian.**

Fries•land (frēz′lənd, -lănd′, frēs′-) A region of N Europe on the North Sea between the Scheldt and Weser rivers; conquered by the Franks in the 8th cent.

frieze[1] (frēz) *n. Architecture* **1.** A plain or decorated horizontal part of an entablature between the architrave and cornice. **2.** A decorative horizontal band, as along the upper part of a wall. [Fr. *frise* < Med.Lat. *frisium, frigium,* embroidery < Lat. *Phrygium (opus),* Phrygian (work) < PHRYGIA.]

frieze[2] (frēz) *n.* **1.** A coarse shaggy woolen cloth with an uncut nap. **2.** A dense low-pile surface, as in carpeting, resembling such cloth. [ME *frise* < OFr. < Med.Lat. *(pannī) frīsiī,* woolen (garments) < pl. of *Frīsius,* Frisian.]

frig (frĭg) *v.* **frigged, frig•ging, frigs** *Vulgar Slang* —*tr.* **1.** To have sexual intercourse with. **2.** To perform an act of masturbation on. —*intr.* **1.** To have sexual intercourse. **2.** To masturbate. [ME, to quiver, poss. < OFr. *friquer,* to rub < Lat. *fricāre.*]

frig•ate (frĭg′ĭt) *n.* **1.** A warship larger than a destroyer and smaller than a cruiser, used primarily for escort duty. **2.** A high-speed medium-sized sailing war vessel of the 17th, 18th, and 19th centuries. [Fr. *frégate* < Ital. *fregata.*]

frigate bird *n.* Any of various tropical sea birds of the family Fregatidae that have long wings and dark plumage and character-

Sigmund Freud

frigate
replica of the mid-18th-century HMS *Rose*

ă	pat	oi	boy
ā	pay	ou	out
âr	care	ŏŏ	took
ä	father	ōō	boot
ĕ	pet	ŭ	cut
ē	be	ûr	urge
ĭ	pit	th	thin
ī	pie	*th*	this
îr	pier	hw	which
ŏ	pot	zh	vision
ō	toe	ə	about, item
ô	paw		

Stress marks:
′ (primary);
′ (secondary), as in
lexicon (lĕk′sĭ-kŏn′)

istically snatch food from other birds in flight.

Frigg (frĭg) also **Frig·ga** (frĭg′ə) *n. Mythology* The Norse goddess of the heavens and wife of Odin. [ON. See **prī-** in App.]

frig·ging (frĭg′ĭng) *adj. Vulgar Slang* Used as an intensive.

fright (frīt) *n.* 1. Sudden intense fear; alarm. See Syns at **fear.** 2. *Informal* Something extremely unsightly, alarming, or strange: *You look a fright.* ❖ *tr.v.* **fright·ed, fright·ing, frights** *Archaic* To frighten. [ME < OE *fyrhto, fryhto.* V., ME *frighten,* to frighten, be afraid < OE *fyrhtan.*]

fright·en (frīt′n) *v.* **-ened, -en·ing, -ens** —*tr.* 1. To fill with fear; alarm. 2. To drive or force by arousing fear: *The suspect was frightened into confessing.* —*intr.* To become afraid. —**fright′en·er** *n.* —**fright′en·ing·ly** *adv.*

fright·ful (frīt′fəl) *adj.* 1. Causing disgust or shock; horrifying. 2. Causing fright; terrifying. 3. *Informal* **a.** Excessive; extreme: *a frightful liar.* **b.** Disagreeable; distressing: *frightful weather.* —**fright′ful·ly** *adv.* —**fright′ful·ness** *n.*

fright wig *n.* A wig with hair, esp. long or frizzy hair, standing up from the surface.

frig·id (frĭj′ĭd) *adj.* 1. Extremely cold. See Syns at **cold.** 2. Lacking warmth of feeling. 3. Stiff and formal in manner: *a frigid refusal to a request.* 4. Persistently averse to sexual intercourse. [Lat. *frīgidus,* cold < *frīgus,* the cold.] —**fri·gid·i·ty** (frĭ-jĭd′ĭ-tē), **frig′id·ness** *n.* —**frig′id·ly** *adv.*

Frig·i·daire (frĭj′ĭ-dâr′) A trademark used for electric refrigerators and other household appliances.

Frigid Zone Either of two extreme latitude zones of the earth, the **North Frigid Zone,** between the North Pole and the Arctic Circle, or the **South Frigid Zone,** between the South Pole and the Antarctic Circle.

frig·o·rif·ic (frĭg′ə-rĭf′ĭk) also **frig·o·rif·i·cal** (-ĭ-kəl) *adj.* Causing coldness; chilling. [Lat. *frīgorificus : frīgus, frīgor-,* the cold + *-ficus,* -fic.]

fri·jol (frē-hōl′, frē′hōl′) also **fri·jo·le** (frē-hō′lē) *n., pl.* **fri·jo·les** (frē-hō′lēz, frē′hō′-) *Southwestern US* A bean cultivated and used for food. [Sp., var. of *fréjol* < OSpan. *frisol* < Catalan *fesol* < Lat. *phaseolus,* dim. of *phasēlus,* a type of legume < Gk. *phasēlos.*]

frill (frĭl) *n.* 1. A ruffled, gathered, or pleated border or projection, such as a fabric edge used to trim clothing. 2. A ruff of hair or feathers about the neck of an animal or a bird. 3. A wrinkling of the edge of a photographic film. 4. *Informal* Something that is desirable but not a necessity; a luxury. ❖ *v.* **frilled, frill·ing, frills** —*tr.* 1. To make into a ruffle or frill. 2. To add a ruffle or frill to. —*intr.* To become wrinkled along the edge. [?] —**frill′i·ness** *n.* —**frill′y** *adj.*

frilled lizard (frĭld) *n.* An Australian lizard (*Chlamydosaurus kingi*) having a membrane that can be extended from the neck when the mouth is opened.

Friml (frĭm′əl), **(Charles) Rudolf** 1879–1972. Czech-born Amer. composer whose works include *The Vagabond King* (1925).

fringe (frĭnj) *n.* 1. A decorative border or edging of hanging threads, cords, or strips, often attached to a separate band. 2. Something that resembles such a border or edging. 3. A marginal, peripheral, or secondary part. 4. Those members of a group or political party holding extreme views. 5. Any of the light or dark bands produced by the diffraction or interference of light. 6. A fringe benefit. ❖ *tr.v.* **fringed, fring·ing, fring·es** 1. To decorate with or as if with a fringe. 2. To serve as a fringe to. [ME *frenge* < OFr. < VLat. **frimbia,* alteration of LLat. *fimbria.* See FIMBRIA.] —**fring′y** *adj.*

fringe area *n.* A zone just outside of the range of a broadcasting station in which signals are weakened and distorted.

fringe benefit *n.* An employment benefit given in addition to one's wages or salary.

fringe tree *n.* A shrub or small tree (*Chionanthus virginicus*) of the southeast United States having drooping clusters of white flowers and dark blue fruit.

fring·ing reef (frĭn′jĭng) *n.* A coral reef formed close to a shoreline.

frip·per·y (frĭp′ə-rē) *n., pl.* **-ies** 1. Pretentious showy finery. 2. Pretentious elegance; ostentation. 3. Something trivial or nonessential. [Fr. *friperie* < OFr. *freperie,* old clothes < *felpe, frepe* < Med.Lat. *faluppa,* worthless material.]

Fris. *abbr.* Frisian

Fris·bee (frĭz′bē) A trademark used for a plastic disk-shaped toy that players throw and catch.

fri·sé (frē-zā′) *n.* See **frieze**[2]. [Fr. < p. part. of *friser,* to curl. See FRIZZ[1].]

fri·sée (frĭ-zā′) *n.* See **endive** 1a. [Fr. < fem. p. part. of *friser,* to curl. See FRIZZ[1].]

fri·sette also **fri·zette** (frĭ-zĕt′) *n.* A fringe of curled, often artificial hair, usu. worn on the forehead by a woman. [Fr. *frisette* < *friser,* to curl. See FRIZZ[1].]

fri·seur (frē-zûr′, -zœr′) *n.* A hairdresser; a coiffeur. [Fr. < *friser,* to curl. See FRIZZ[1].]

Fri·sian (frĭzh′ən, frē′zhən) also **Frie·sian** (frē′zhən) *n.* 1. A native or inhabitant of the Frisian Islands or Friesland. 2. The West Germanic language of the Frisians. [< Lat. *Frīsiī,* the Frisians, of Gmc. orig.] —**Fri′sian** *adj.*

Frisian Islands A chain of islands in the North Sea off the coast

frilled lizard
Chlamydosaurus kingi

of the Netherlands, Germany, and Denmark. The **West Frisian Islands** belong to the Netherlands; the **East Frisian Islands** and most of the **North Frisian Islands** are part of Germany; the other North Frisians are Danish.

frisk (frĭsk) *v.* **frisked, frisk·ing, frisks** —*intr.* To move about briskly and playfully; frolic. —*tr.* To search (a person) for something concealed by passing the hands quickly over clothes or through pockets. ❖ *n.* 1. An energetic playful movement; a gambol. 2. The act of frisking. [< ME *frisk,* lively < OFr. *frisque,* of Gmc. orig.] —**frisk′er** *n.*

frisk·y (frĭs′kē) *adj.* **-i·er, -i·est** Energetic, lively, and playful: *a frisky kitten.* —**frisk′i·ly** *adv.* —**frisk′i·ness** *n.*

fris·son (frē-sôN′) *n., pl.* **-sons** (-sôNz′, -sôN′) A moment of intense excitement; a shudder. [Fr. < OFr. *fricons,* pl. of *fricon,* a trembling < VLat. **frīctiō, *frīctiōn-* < Lat. *frīgere,* to be cold.]

frith (frĭth) *n. Scots* A firth. [Alteration of FIRTH.]

frit (frĭt) *n.* 1. The fused or partially fused materials used in making glass. 2. A vitreous substance used in making porcelain, glazes, or enamels. ❖ *tr.v.* **frit·ted, frit·ting, frits** To make into frit. [Ital. *fritta* < fem. p. part. of *friggere,* to fry < Lat. *frīgere,* to roast, fry.]

frit fly *n.* Any of several flies of the family Chloropidae, esp. *Oscinella frit,* with larvae destructive to cereal plants. [?]

frit·il·lar·y (frĭt′l-ĕr′ē) *n., pl.* **-ies** 1. Any of various bulbous plants of the genus *Fritillaria,* having nodding, often spotted or checkered flowers. 2. Any of various butterflies of the family Nymphalidae, having brownish wings marked with black or silvery spots on the underside. [NLat. *Fritillāria,* genus name < Lat. *fritillus,* dice box.]

frit·ta·ta (frĭ-tä′tə, frēt-tä′tə) *n.* An open-faced omelet with other ingredients, such as cheese or vegetables, mixed into the eggs rather than used as a filling. [Ital. < *fritto,* p. part. of *friggere,* to fry. See FRIT.]

frit·ter[1] (frĭt′ər) *tr.v.* **-tered, -ter·ing, -ters** 1. To reduce or squander little by little. 2. To break, tear, or cut into bits; shred. [Prob. < *fritter,* fragment, prob. alteration of *fitters* < *fitter,* to break into small pieces.]

frit·ter[2] (frĭt′ər) *n.* A small cake made of batter, often containing fruit, vegetables, or fish, sautéed or deep-fried. [ME *friture* < OFr. < LLat. *frīctūra* < Lat. *frīctus,* p. part. of *frīgere,* to roast, fry.]

fritz (frĭts) *n. Informal* A condition in which something does not work properly: *Our TV is on the fritz.* [Perh. < Ger. *Fritz,* dim. of the name *Friedrich.*]

Fri·u·li (frē′ə-lē′, frē-ōō′lē) A historical region and former duchy in present-day NE Italy and W Slovenia.

Fri·u·li-Ve·ne·zia Giu·lia (frē′ə-lē′və-nēt′sē-ə jōōl′yə, frē-ōō′lē-vĕ-nēt′syä) A region of NE Italy bounded by Austria in the N and Slovenia in the E; formed in 1947.

friv·ol (frĭv′əl) *intr.v.* **-oled, -ol·ing, -ols** or **-olled, -ol·ling, -ols** To behave frivolously. —**friv′ol·er** *n.*

fri·vol·i·ty (frĭ-vŏl′ĭ-tē) *n., pl.* **-ties** 1. The quality or condition of being frivolous. 2. A frivolous act or thing.

friv·o·lous (frĭv′ə-ləs) *adj.* 1. Unworthy of serious attention; trivial. 2. Inappropriately silly: *a frivolous purchase.* [ME, prob. < Lat. *frīvolus,* of little value, prob. < *friāre,* to crumble.] —**friv′o·lous·ly** *adv.* —**friv′o·lous·ness** *n.*

fri·zette (frĭ-zĕt′) *n.* Variant of **frisette**.

frizz[1] (frĭz) *tr. & intr.v.* **frizzed, frizz·ing, frizz·es** To form or be formed into small tight curls or tufts. ❖ *n.* 1. The condition of being frizzed. 2. A small tight curl or tuft. [Fr. *friser* < OFr., poss. < *frire, fris-,* to fry < Lat. *frīgere,* to roast, fry.] —**frizz′er** *n.*

frizz[2] (frĭz) *v.* **frizzed, frizz·ing, frizz·es** —*tr.* To fry or burn with a sizzling noise. —*intr.* To make a sizzling noise while frying or searing. [Poss. back-formation < FRIZZLE[1].]

friz·zle[1] (frĭz′əl) *v.* **-zled, -zling, -zles** —*tr.* 1. To fry (something) until crisp and curled: *frizzled the bacon.* 2. To scorch or sear with heat. —*intr.* To fry or sear with a sizzling noise. [Poss. blend of FRY[1] and SIZZLE.]

friz·zle[2] (frĭz′əl) *tr. & intr.v.* **-zled, -zling, -zles** To form or cause to be formed into small tight curls; frizz. ❖ *n.* A small tight curl. [?]

friz·zly (frĭz′lē) *adj.* **-zli·er, -zli·est** Tightly curled.

friz·zy (frĭz′ē) *adj.* **-zi·er, -zi·est** Tightly curled; frizzly. —**friz′zi·ly** *adv.* —**friz′zi·ness** *n.*

fro (frō) *adv.* Away; back: *moving to and fro.* ❖ *prep. Scots* From. [ME, prob. < ON *frā.* See **per**[1] in App.]

Fro·bish·er (frō′bĭ-shər, frŏb′ī-), **Sir Martin** 1535?–94. English explorer who voyaged to the Canadian Arctic (1576, 1577, and 1578) in search of the Northwest Passage.

Frobisher Bay An arm of the Atlantic Ocean extending into SE Baffin I. in Nunavut, Canada.

frock (frŏk) *n.* 1. A woman's dress. 2. A long loose outer garment, as that worn by artists; a smock. 3. A woolen garment formerly worn by sailors; a jersey. 4. A robe worn by monks, friars, and other clerics; a habit. ❖ *tr.v.* **frocked, frock·ing, frocks** 1. To clothe in a frock. 2. To invest with clerical office. [ME *frok,* a monk's habit < OFr. *froc* < Med.Lat. *froccus,* of Gmc. orig.]

frock coat *n.* A man's dress coat or suit coat with knee-length skirts.

froe also **frow** (frō) *n.* A cleaving tool having a heavy blade set at right angles to the handle. [Earlier *frower*, poss. < FROWARD, turned away (of the handle).]

Froe·bel also **Frö·bel** (frœ′bəl), **Friedrich Wilhelm August** 1782–1852. German educator who established the first kindergarten (1837).

frog (frôg, frŏg) *n.* **1.** Any of numerous tailless amphibians of the order Anura, characteristically having a smooth moist skin, webbed feet, and long hind legs adapted for leaping. **2.** A wedge-shaped horny prominence in the sole of a horse's hoof. **3.** A loop fastened to a belt to hold a tool or weapon. **4.** An ornamental looped braid or cord with a button or knot for fastening the front of a garment. **5.** A device on intersecting railroad tracks that permits wheels to cross the junction. **6.** A spiked or perforated device used to support stems in a flower arrangement. **7.** The nut of a violin bow. **8.** *Informal* Hoarseness or phlegm in the throat. **9.** *Offensive Slang* Used as a disparaging term for a French person. [ME *frogge* < OE *frogga*.]

frog·eye (frôg′ī′, frŏg′ī′) *n.* A plant disease caused by fungi and characterized by rounded spots on the leaves.

frog·fish (frôg′fĭsh′, frŏg′-) *n., pl.* **frogfish** or **-fish·es** Any of various bottom-dwelling fishes of the family Antennariidae, with a globose body and pectoral fins used for grasping.

frog·hop·per (frôg′hŏp′ər, frŏg′-) *n.* See **spittlebug**.

frog kick *n.* A swimming kick used in the breaststroke in which the knees are drawn up close to the hips and the feet are thrust outward and then drawn together.

frog·man (frôg′măn′, -mən, frŏg′-) *n.* A swimmer provided with breathing apparatus to execute underwater maneuvers.

frog spit *n.* **1.** A foamlike mat of small aquatic plants, such as green algae, on the surface of a pond. **2.** See **cuckoo spit**.

Frois·sart (froi′särt′, frwä-sär′), **Jean** 1333?–1405? French historian noted for his chronicles of the Hundred Years' War.

frol·ic (frŏl′ĭk) *n.* **1.** Gaiety; merriment: *fun and frolic.* **2.** A gay, carefree time. **3.** A playful antic. ❖ *intr.v.* **-icked, -ick·ing, -ics** **1.** To behave playfully and uninhibitedly; romp. **2.** To engage in merrymaking, joking, or teasing. ❖ *adj. Archaic* Merry. [< Du. *vrolijk,* merry < MDu. *vrolijc* : *vro,* happy + *-lijc,* -like.] **—frol′-ick·er** *n.*

frol·ic·some (frŏl′ĭk-səm) *adj.* Full of high-spirited fun.

from (frŭm, frŏm; frəm *when unstressed*) *prep.* **1a.** Used to indicate a specified place or time as a starting point: *walked home from the station; from six o'clock on.* See Usage Note at **whence.** **b.** Used to indicate a specified point as the first of two limits: *from grades four to six.* **2.** Used to indicate a source, cause, agent, or instrument: *a note from the teacher.* **3.** Used to indicate separation, removal, or exclusion: *keep someone from making a mistake.* **4.** Used to indicate differentiation: *know right from wrong.* **5.** Because of: *faint from hunger.* **—idiom: from away** *Chiefly Maine* Not native to a state or locality. [ME < OE *fram,* forward, from. See **per¹** in App.]

Fromm (frŏm, frŭm), **Erich** 1900–80. German-born Amer. psychoanalyst whose works include *Escape from Freedom* (1941).

frond (frŏnd) *n.* **1.** The leaf of a fern. **2.** A large compound leaf of a palm. **3.** A leaflike thallus, as of a seaweed or lichen. [Lat. *frōns, frond-,* foliage.] **—frond′ed** *adj.*

fron·des·cent (frŏn-dĕs′ənt) *adj.* Bearing, resembling, or having a profusion of leaves or fronds. **—fron·des′cence** *n.*

fron·dose (frŏn′dōs′) *adj.* **1.** Bearing fronds. **2.** Resembling a frond. [Lat. *frondōsus,* abounding in foliage < *frōns, frond-,* foliage.] **—fron′dose·ly** *adv.*

frons (frŏnz) *n., pl.* **fron·tes** (frŏn′tēz) The anterior, uppermost part of the head of an insect. [Lat. *frōns, front-.*]

front (frŭnt) *n.* **1.** The forward part or surface, as of a building. **2.** The area, location, or position directly before or ahead. **3.** A position of leadership or superiority. **4.** The forehead or face, esp. of a bird or other animal. **5a.** Demeanor or bearing, esp. in the presence of danger or difficulty. **b.** An outward, often feigned appearance or manner. **6a.** Land bordering a lake, river, or street. **b.** A promenade along the water at a resort. **7.** A detachable part of a man's dress shirt covering the chest; a dickey. **8a.** The most forward line of a combat force. **b.** The area of contact between opposing combat forces; a battlefront. **9.** *Meteorology* The interface between air masses of different temperatures or densities. **10.** A field of activity. **11a.** A group or movement uniting various individuals or organizations for the achievement of a common purpose; a coalition. **b.** A nominal leader lacking in real authority; a figurehead. **c.** An apparently respectable person, group, or business used as a cover for secret or illegal activities. **12.** *Archaic* **a.** The first part; the beginning. **b.** The face; the countenance. ❖ *adj.* **1.** Of, relating to, aimed at, or located in the front. **2.** *Linguistics* Produced at or toward the front of the mouth. Used of vowels such as that in *green.* ❖ *v.* **front·ed, front·ing, fronts** *—tr.* **1.** To look out on; face. **2.** To meet in opposition; confront. **3.** To provide a front for. **4.** To serve as a front for. **5.** *Music* To lead (a group of musicians). **6.** *Informal* To provide before payment. **7.** *Linguistics* **a.** To move (a word or phrase) to the beginning of a clause or sentence, as for emphasis. **b.** To cause (a vowel) to be pronounced farther toward the front of the oral cavity. *—intr.* **1.** To have a front; face onto something else: *property that fronts on the highway.* **2.** To provide a cover for secret or illegal activities. [ME < OFr. < Lat. *frōns, front-,* forehead, front.]

front. *abbr.* frontispiece

front·age (frŭn′tĭj) *n.* **1a.** The front part of a piece of property. **b.** The land between a building and the street. **c.** Land adjacent to something, such as a building, street, or body of water. **2.** The direction in which something faces.

fron·tal¹ (frŭn′tl) *adj.* **1.** Of, relating to, directed toward, or situated at the front: *a frontal attack.* **2.** *Anatomy* Of or relating to the forehead or frontal bone. **3.** Of or relating to a meteorological front. **—fron′tal·ly** *adv.*

fron·tal² (frŭn′tl) *n.* **1.** A drapery covering the front of an altar. **2.** The façade of a building. [ME *frontel* < OFr. < Med.Lat. *frontāle* < Lat. *frōns, front-,* forehead, front.]

frontal bone *n.* A cranial bone consisting of a vertical portion corresponding to the forehead and a horizontal portion that forms the roofs of the orbital and nasal cavities.

frontal lobe *n.* The largest and most anterior part of each cerebral hemisphere.

frontal lobotomy *n.* A prefrontal lobotomy.

front bench *n.* The first bench on either side of the aisle in a parliament, reserved for ministers and leaders of the principal political parties. **—front′-bench′er** (frŭnt′bĕnch′ər) *n.*

front·court (frŭnt′kôrt′, -kōrt′) *n. Basketball* **1.** The half of the court having the basket at which the offensive team shoots. **2.** The forwards and center on a team.

Fron·te·nac (frŏn′tə-năk′, frônt-näk′), **Comte de.** Title of **Louis de Buade.** 1620?–98. French colonial administrator who governed New France (1672–82 and 1689–98).

front-end (frŭnt′ĕnd′) *adj.* **1.** Relating to the initial phase of a project. **2.** Relating to the forward parts of a vehicle.

front-end load *n.* The amount deducted from early payments to a mutual fund for expenses such as sales commissions.

fron·ten·is (frŭn-tĕn′ĭs, frŏn′tĕn-ĭs) *n.* A Latin-American tennis game played on a three-walled court. [Am.Sp., blend of Sp. *frontón,* jai alai court; see FRONTON, and Sp. *tenis,* tennis (< E. TENNIS).]

fron·tes (frŏn′tēz) *n.* Plural of **frons.**

fron·tier (frŭn-tîr′, frŏn-, frŭn′tîr′, frŏn′-) *n.* **1a.** An international border. **b.** The area along an international border. **2.** A region just beyond or at the edge of a settled area. **3.** An undeveloped area or field for discovery or research. [ME *frountier* < OFr. *frontier* < *front,* forehead, front. See FRONT.]

fron·tiers·man (frŭn-tîrz′mən, frŏn-) *n.* A man who lives on the frontier.

fron·tiers·wom·an (frŭn-tîrz′wŏom′ən, frŏn-) *n.* A woman who lives on the frontier.

fron·tis·piece (frŭn′tĭ-spēs′) *n.* **1.** An illustration that faces or immediately precedes the title page of a book, book section, or magazine. **2.** *Architecture* **a.** A façade, esp. an ornamental façade. **b.** A small ornamental pediment, as on top of a door or window. **3.** *Archaic* A title page. [Alteration (influenced by PIECE) of Fr. *frontispice* < LLat. *frontispicium,* façade of a building : Lat. *frontis,* genitive of *frōns,* forehead, front + Lat. *specere,* to look at; see **spek-** in App.]

front·let (frŭnt′lĭt) *n.* **1.** An ornament or band worn on the forehead as a phylactery. **2.** The forehead of an animal. **3.** The forehead of a bird when of a different color or texture of plumage. **4.** An ornamental border for a frontal. [ME < OFr. *frontelet,* dim. of *frontel.* See FRONTAL².]

front·line also **front line** (frŭnt′līn′) *n.* **1.** A front or boundary, esp. one between military, political, or ideological positions. **2.** *Football* The linemen of a team. ❖ *adj.* or **front-line** **1.** Located or used at a military front. **2.** Of or relating to the most advanced or important position or activity in a field or undertaking. **3.** *Football* Of or relating to the frontline.

front·list (frŭnt′lĭst′) *n.* A publisher's list of new or current titles.

front-load (frŭnt′lōd′) *v.* **-load·ed, -load·ing, -loads** *—tr.* To concentrate costs or benefits of (a financial obligation or deal) in an early period. *—intr.* To concentrate costs or benefits in an early period.

front·man (frŭnt′măn′) *n.* also **front man 1.** A man who serves as a nominal leader but lacks real authority. **2.** *Music* A leading singer with a group.

front matter *n.* The material, such as the preface, frontispiece, and title page, preceding the text in a book.

front money *n.* Money paid in advance, as for contracted goods or services.

front nine *n.* The first half of an 18-hole golf course.

front office *n.* The executive or policymaking officers of an organization.

fron·to·gen·e·sis (frŭn′tō-jĕn′ĭ-sĭs) *n., pl.* **-ses** (-sēz′) Formation or intensification of a meteorological front.

fron·tol·y·sis (frŭn-tŏl′ĭ-sĭs) *n., pl.* **-ses** (-sēz′) Dissipation of a meteorological front.

fron·ton (frŏn′tŏn′, frŏn-tōn′) *n.* An arena for jai alai. [Sp. *frontón,* wall, fronton, augmentative of *frente,* forehead, face < OSpan. *fruente* < Lat. *frōns, front-.*]

front-page (frŭnt′pāj′) *adj.* Worthy of coverage on the front page of a newspaper. **—front′page′** *v.*

Front Range A range of the Rocky Mts. in N-central CO rising

Robert Frost
photographed c. 1960

front room *n.* See **living room.**

front-run·ner also **front-run·ner** (frŭnt′rŭn′ər) *n.* **1.** One that is leading in a race or other competition. **2.** A competitor who performs best when in the lead. —**front′-run′ning** *adj.*

front·ward (frŭnt′wərd) *adv. & adj.* Toward, to, or at the front. —**front′wards** *adv.*

front-wheel drive (frŭnt′hwēl′, -wēl′) *n.* An automotive drive system in which only the front pair of wheels receives power from the engine.

frore (frôr, frōr) *adj. Archaic* Extremely cold; frosty. [ME, p. part. of *fresen*, to freeze < OE *frēosan*.]

frosh (frŏsh) *n., pl.* **frosh** *Informal* A freshman, as in college. [Shortening and alteration of FRESHMAN (perh. influenced by Ger. *Frosch*, frog, grammar-school pupil).]

frost (frôst, frŏst) *n.* **1.** A deposit of minute ice crystals formed when water vapor condenses at a temperature below freezing. **2.** A temperature low enough to cause freezing. **3.** The process of freezing. **4.** A cold or icy manner. ❖ *v.* **frost·ed, frost·ing, frosts** —*tr.* **1.** To cover with frost. **2.** To damage or kill by frost. **3.** To cover (glass, for example) with a roughened or speckled surface. **4.** To cover or decorate with icing: *frost a cake.* **5.** *Slang* To anger or upset. —*intr.* To become covered with or as if with frost. [ME < OE.]

Frost, Robert Lee 1874–1963. Amer. poet whose works are often set in rural New England.

Frost·belt also **Frost Belt** (frôst′bĕlt′, frŏst′-) The N-central and NE US.

frost·bite (frôst′bīt′, frŏst′-) *n.* Injury or destruction of skin and underlying tissue, resulting from prolonged exposure to freezing temperatures. ❖ *tr.v.* **-bit** (-bĭt′), **-bit·ten** (-bĭt′n), **-bit·ing, -bites** To injure or damage by freezing.

frost boil *n. Upper Midwest* See **frost heave.**

frost-free (frôst′frē′, frŏst′-) *adj.* Requiring little or no defrosting: *a frost-free refrigerator.*

frost heave *n. New England* A section of ruptured pavement caused by the expansion of freezing water immediately under the road.

frost·ing (frô′stĭng, frŏs′tĭng) *n.* **1.** Icing, as on a cake. **2.** A roughened or speckled surface imparted to glass or metal.

REGIONAL NOTE Although the terms *frosting* and *icing* are both in widespread use, people in New England, the Upper Midwest, and the Western United States tend to put *frosting* on cake. In Pennsylvania, New Jersey, the Lower Midwest, and the South, the preferred term is *icing.* There is some overlap, especially in up-state New York, Michigan, and California, but the regions in which the two words predominate are surprisingly distinct. Some in the South call it *filling,* even when it goes on top.

frost line *n.* **1.** The depth to which frost penetrates the earth. **2.** The altitude below which frost does not occur, esp. in tropical regions.

frost·work (frôst′wûrk′, frŏst′-) *n.* **1.** The intricate patterns produced by frost, as on a windowpane. **2.** Artificially made ornamental patterns similar to those produced by frost, applied to the surface of metal or glass.

frost·y (frô′stē, frŏs′tē) *adj.* **-i·er, -i·est** **1.** Producing or characterized by frost; freezing. See Syns at **cold. 2.** Covered with or as if with frost. **3.** Silvery white; hoary. **4.** Cold in manner: *a frosty look.* —**frost′i·ly** *adv.* —**frost′i·ness** *n.*

froth (frôth, frŏth) *n.* **1.** A mass of bubbles in or on a liquid; foam. **2.** Salivary foam released as a result of disease or exhaustion. **3.** Something unsubstantial or trivial. **4.** A fit of resentment or vexation. ❖ *v.* (also frôth, frŏth) **frothed, froth·ing, froths** —*tr.* **1.** To cover with foam. **2.** To cause to foam. —*intr.* To exude or expel foam. [ME < ON *frodha.*]

froth·y (frô′thē, frŏth′ē) *adj.* **-i·er, -i·est** **1.** Made of, covered with, or resembling froth; foamy. **2.** Playfully frivolous in character or content. —**froth′i·ly** *adv.* —**froth′i·ness** *n.*

frot·tage (frô-täzh′) *n.* **1.** The act of rubbing against another person, as in a crowd, to attain sexual gratification. **2a.** A method of making a design by placing a piece of paper on top of an object and then rubbing over it, as with a pencil. **b.** A design so made. [Fr. < *frotter*, to rub < OFr. *froter.*]

frou·frou also **frou-frou** (frōō′frōō′) *n.* **1.** Fussy or showy dress or ornamentation. **2.** A rustling sound, as of silk. [Fr., of imit. orig.]

frow (frō) *n.* Variant of **froe.**

fro·ward (frō′wərd, -ərd) *adj.* Stubbornly contrary and disobedient; obstinate. —**fro′ward·ly** *adv.* —**fro′ward·ness** *n.*

Froward, Cape The S point of mainland South America, in S Chile on the Strait of Magellan.

frown (froun) *v.* **frowned, frown·ing, frowns** —*intr.* **1.** To wrinkle the brow, as in thought or displeasure. **2.** To regard something with disapproval or distaste. —*tr.* To express (disapproval, for example) by wrinkling the brow. ❖ *n.* A wrinkling of the brow in thought or displeasure; a scowl. [ME *frounen* < OFr. *froigner*, to turn up one's nose < *frogne*, grimace, of Celt. orig.] —**frown′er** *n.* —**frown′ing·ly** *adv.*

frows·ty (frou′stē) *adj.* **-ti·er, -ti·est** *Chiefly British* Having a stale smell; musty. [?]

frow·zy also **frow·sy** (frou′zē) *adj.* **-zi·er, -zi·est** also **-si·er, -si·est** **1.** Unkempt; slovenly. **2.** Having an unpleasant smell; musty. [?] —**frow′zi·ness** *n.*

froze (frōz) *v.* Past tense of **freeze.**

fro·zen (frō′zən) *v.* Past participle of **freeze.** ❖ *adj.* **1.** Made into, covered with, or surrounded by ice. **2.** Very cold. **3.** Preserved by freezing. **4a.** Rendered immobile. **b.** Immobile, as from pain or inflammation: *a frozen shoulder.* **5.** Expressive of cold unfriendliness or disdain. **6a.** Kept at a fixed level. **b.** Impossible to withdraw, sell, or liquidate.

FRS *abbr.* Federal Reserve System

frt. *abbr.* freight

fruc·tif·er·ous (frŭk-tĭf′ər-əs, frŏŏk-) *adj.* Bearing fruit. [Lat. *frūctifer* (*frūctus*, fruit; see FRUIT) + -OUS.]

fruc·ti·fi·ca·tion (frŭk′tə-fĭ-kā′shən, frŏŏk′-) *n.* **1.** The producing of fruit. **2.** A seed-bearing or spore-bearing structure.

fruc·ti·fy (frŭk′tə-fī′, frŏŏk′-) *v.* **-fied, -fy·ing, -fies** —*tr.* To make fruitful or productive. —*intr.* To bear fruit. [ME *fructifien*, to bear fruit < OFr. *fructifier* < Lat. *frūctificāre* : *frūctus*, fruit; see FRUIT + *-ficāre*, -fy.]

fruc·tose (frŭk′tōs′, frŏŏk′-) *n.* A very sweet sugar, $C_6H_{12}O_6$, found in fruits and honey and used as a food preservative and an intravenous nutrient. [Lat. *frūctus*, fruit; see FRUIT + -OSE².]

fruc·tu·ous (frŭk′chōō-əs, frŏŏk′-) *adj.* Fruitful; productive. [ME < OFr. < Lat. *frūctuōsus* < *frūctus*, fruit. See FRUIT.]

fru·gal (frōō′gəl) *adj.* **1.** Practicing or marked by economy, as in the expenditure of money or the use of material resources. See Syns at **sparing. 2.** Costing little; inexpensive. [Lat. *frūgālis*, virtuous, thrifty < *frūx, frūg-*, fruit, virtue.] —**fru·gal′i·ty** (frōō-găl′ĭ-tē), **fru′gal·ness** *n.* —**fru′gal·ly** *adv.*

fru·giv·o·rous (frōō-jĭv′ər-əs) *adj.* Feeding on fruit; fruit-eating. [Lat. *frūx, frūg-*, fruit + -VOROUS.]

fruit (frōōt) *n., pl.* **fruit** or **fruits 1a.** The ripened ovary or ovaries of a seed-bearing plant, together with accessory parts, containing the seeds. **b.** An edible, usu. sweet and fleshy form of such a structure. **c.** A part or an amount of such a plant product served as food. **2.** The fertile, often spore-bearing structure of a plant that does not bear seeds. **3.** A plant crop or product. **4.** Result; outcome. **5.** Offspring; progeny. **6.** A fruity aroma or flavor in a wine. **7.** *Offensive Slang* Used as a disparaging term for a homosexual man. ❖ *intr. & tr.v.* **fruit·ed, fruit·ing, fruits** To produce or cause to produce fruit. [ME < OFr. < Lat. *frūctus*, enjoyment, fruit < p. part. of *fruī*, to enjoy.]

fruit·age (frōō′tĭj) *n.* **1a.** The process, time, or condition of bearing fruit. **b.** A yield of fruit. **2.** A result or an effect.

fruit bat *n.* Any of various fruit-eating bats of the suborder Megachiroptera, inhabiting chiefly tropical and subtropical regions of Africa, Asia, and Australia.

fruit·cake (frōōt′kāk′) *n.* **1.** A spiced cake containing nuts and candied or dried fruits. **2.** *Slang* A crazy or eccentric person.

fruit cocktail *n.* A mixture of fresh or preserved fruits cut into pieces and served as an appetizer or dessert.

fruit fly *n.* **1.** Any of various flies of the family Drosophilidae, having larvae that feed on fruits and vegetables, esp. the common species *Drosophila melanogaster* often used in genetic research. **2.** Any of various flies of the family Tephritidae, having larvae that hatch in and damage plant tissue.

fruit·ful (frōōt′fəl) *adj.* **1a.** Producing fruit. **b.** Conducive to productivity; fertile: *fruitful soil.* **2.** Producing something in abundance; prolific. **3.** Producing results; profitable. —**fruit′ful·ly** *adv.* —**fruit′ful·ness** *n.*

fruit·ing body (frōō′tĭng) *n.* A specialized spore-producing structure, esp. of a fungus.

fru·i·tion (frōō-ĭsh′ən) *n.* **1.** Realization of something desired or worked for: *labor coming to fruition.* **2.** Enjoyment derived from use or possession. **3.** The condition of bearing fruit. [ME *fruicioun* < OFr. *fruicion* < LLat. *fruitiō, fruitiōn-*, enjoyment < Lat. *fruitus*, p. part. of *fruī*, to enjoy.]

fruit·less (frōōt′lĭs) *adj.* **1.** Producing no fruit. **2.** Unproductive of success: *a fruitless search.* See Syns at **futile.** —**fruit′less·ly** *adv.* —**fruit′less·ness** *n.*

fruit·let (frōōt′lĭt) *n.* **1.** A small fruit. **2.** *Botany* A single member of a multiple fruit.

fruit sugar *n.* See **fructose.**

fruit·wood (frōōt′wŏŏd′) *n.* The wood of any of several fruit-bearing trees, used esp. in cabinetmaking.

fruit·y (frōō′tē) *adj.* **-i·er, -i·est** **1.** Of, containing, or relating to fruit. **2.** Tasting or smelling richly of or as if of fruit. **3.** Excessively sentimental or sweet. **4.** *Slang* Crazy; eccentric. **5.** *Offensive Slang* Homosexual. —**fruit′i·ness** *n.*

fru·men·ta·ceous (frōō′mən-tā′shəs, -mĕn-) *adj.* Resembling or consisting of grain, esp. wheat. [< LLat. *frūmentāceus* < Lat. *frūmentum*, grain.]

fru·men·ty (frōō′mən-tē) also **fur·mi·ty** (fûr′mĭ-tē) *n., pl.* **-ties** Hulled wheat boiled in milk and flavored with sugar and spices. [ME *frumente* < OFr. *froumentee* < *froument*, grain < Lat. *frūmentum.*]

frump (frŭmp) *n.* **1.** A girl or woman regarded as dull, plain, or unfashionable. **2.** A person regarded as colorless and primly sedate. [Poss. short for ME *frumple*, wrinkle < MDu. *verrompelen*, to wrinkle : *ver-*, completely; see PER¹ in App. + *rompelen*, to

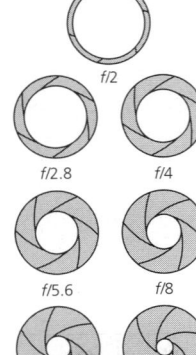

f/2

f/2.8   f/4

f/5.6   f/8

f/11   f/16

f-stop

wrinkle.] —**frump′i•ly** adv. —**frump′i•ness** n. —**frump′y** adj.

frump•ish (frŭm′pĭsh) adj. **1.** Dull or plain. **2.** Prim and sedate. —**frump′ish•ly** adv. —**frump′ish•ness** n.

Frun•ze (froon′zə) See **Bishkek.**

frus•trate (frŭs′trāt′) tr.v. **-trat•ed, -trat•ing, -trates 1a.** To prevent from accomplishing a purpose or fulfilling a desire; thwart. **b.** To cause feelings of discouragement or bafflement in. **2.** To make ineffectual or invalid; nullify. [ME frustraten < Lat. frūstrārī, frūstrāt- < frūstrā, in vain.] —**frus′trat′er** n. —**frus′trat′ing•ly** adv.

frus•tra•tion (frŭ-strā′shən) n. **1a.** The act of frustrating or an instance of being frustrated. **b.** The state of being frustrated. **2.** Something that serves to frustrate.

frus•tule (frŭs′chōōl, -tyōōl) n. The hard siliceous bivalve shell of a diatom. [Fr. < Lat. frūstulum, dim. of frūstum, piece broken off.]

frus•tum (frŭs′təm) n., pl. **-tums** or **-ta** (-tə) Mathematics The part of a solid between two parallel planes cutting the solid, esp. the section of a cone or pyramid between the base and a plane parallel to the base. [Lat. frūstum, piece broken off.]

fru•tes•cent (frōō-tĕs′ənt) adj. Relating to, resembling, or assuming the form of a shrub; shrubby. [Lat. frutex, shrub, bush + –ESCENT.] —**fru•tes′cence** n.

fru•ti•cose (frōō′tĭ-kōs′) adj. Resembling a shrub. [Lat. fruticōsus < frutex, frutic-, shrub, bush.]

fry[1] (frī) v. **fried** (frīd), **fry•ing, fries** (frīz) —tr. **1.** To cook over direct heat in hot oil or fat. **2.** Slang To destroy (electronic circuitry) with excessive heat or current. —intr. **1.** To be cooked in a pan over direct heat in hot oil or fat. **2.** Slang To undergo execution in an electric chair. ❖ n., pl. **fries** (frīz) **1.** A French fry. Often used in the plural. **2.** A dish of a fried food. **3.** A social gathering at which food is fried and eaten: a fish fry. [ME frien < OFr. frire < Lat. frīgere.]

fry[2] (frī) pl.n. **1a.** Small fish, esp. young, recently hatched fish. **b.** The young of certain other animals. **2.** Individuals, esp. young or insignificant persons. [ME fri, prob. < AN frie < frier, to rub < Lat. fricāre.]

Fry, Christopher b. 1907. British playwright whose works include A Phoenix Too Frequent (1946).

Frye (frī), **(Herman) Northrup** 1912–91. Canadian literary critic and theorist best known for Anatomy of Criticism (1957).

fry•er also **fri•er** (frī′ər) n. **1.** One that fries, as a deep utensil equipped with a basket for frying foods. **2.** A small young chicken suitable for frying.

fry•ing pan (frī′ĭng) n. A shallow long-handled pan used for frying food.

REGIONAL NOTE The terms frying pan and skillet are now virtually interchangeable in general use, but frying pan and fry pan were once New England terms. Skillet seems to have formerly been confined to the Midland section of the country, including the Upper South. The term spider, originally denoting a type of frying pan that had long legs to hold it up over the coals, spread from New England westward to the Upper Northern states and down the coast to the South Atlantic states. It is still well known in both these regions, although it is now considered old-fashioned. See Regional Note at **andiron.**

fry pan n. Chiefly Eastern, Southern, & Western US See **frying pan.** See Regional Note at **frying pan.**

FS abbr. **1.** Foreign Service **2.** Forest Service

FSH abbr. follicle stimulating hormone

FSLIC abbr. Federal Savings and Loan Insurance Corporation

f-stop (ĕf′stŏp′) n. **1.** A camera lens aperture setting that corresponds to an f-number. **2.** See **f-number.** [F(OCAL LENGTH) + STOP.]

FT abbr. full-time

ft. abbr. **1.** or **ft** foot **2.** Ft. fort

FTC abbr. Federal Trade Commission

ft-c abbr. foot-candle

fth. abbr. fathom

ft-lb abbr. foot-pound

FTP (ĕf′tē-pē′) n. A communications protocol governing the transfer of files from one computer to another over a network. ❖ v. **FTPed, FTP•ing, FTPs** —tr. To transfer (a file) using FTP. —intr. To transfer a file using FTP. [F(ILE) T(RANSFER) P(ROTOCOL).]

fu•bar (fōō′bär′) adj. Slang Utterly botched or confused. [f(ucked) u(p) b(eyond) a(ll) r(ecognition).]

fub•sy (fŭb′zē) adj. **-si•er, -si•est** Chiefly British Slang Somewhat fat and squat. [< obsolete fubs, chubby person.]

Fu•chou (fōō′jō′, -chou′) See **Fuzhou.**

fuch•sia (fyōō′shə) n. **1.** Any of various tropical shrubs or trees of the genus Fuchsia, cultivated for their drooping purplish, reddish, or white flowers. **2.** A strong vivid purplish red. [NLat. Fuchsia, genus name, after Leonhard Fuchs (1501–66), German botanist.] —**fuch′sia** adj.

fuch•sin (fyōōk′sĭn) also **fuch•sine** (-sĭn, -sēn′) n. A synthetic dyestuff, C20H19N3HCl, used to make a purple-red dye for coloring textiles and as a bacterial stain. [FUCHS(IA) + –IN.]

fuck (fŭk) Vulgar Slang v. **fucked, fuck•ing, fucks** —tr. **1.** To have sexual intercourse with. **2.** To take advantage of, betray, or

cheat; victimize. **3.** Used in the imperative as a signal of angry dismissal. —intr. **1.** To engage in sexual intercourse. **2.** To act wastefully or foolishly. **3.** To interfere; meddle. Often used with with. ❖ n. **1.** An act of sexual intercourse. **2.** A partner in sexual intercourse. **3.** A despised person. **4.** Used as an intensive. ❖ interj. Used to express extreme displeasure. —phrasal verbs: **fuck off 1.** Used in the imperative as a signal of angry dismissal. **2.** To spend time idly. **3.** To masturbate. **fuck over** To treat unfairly; take advantage of. **fuck up 1.** To bungle. **2.** To act carelessly, foolishly, or incorrectly. **3.** To cause to be intoxicated. [ME, attested in pseudo-Lat. fuccant, (they) fuck, deciphered from the coded form gxddbov.]

fuck•er (fŭk′ər) n. Vulgar Slang **1.** A despised person. **2.** One that engages in sexual intercourse.

fuck•ing (fŭk′ĭng) adv. & adj. Vulgar Slang Used as an intensive.

fuck•up (fŭk′ŭp′) n. Vulgar Slang **1.** One who acts carelessly or foolishly; a bungler. **2.** A blunder; a bungle.

fu•coid (fyōō′koid′) adj. Of or belonging to the order Fucales, which includes brown algae such as rockweed. ❖ n. A member of the order Fucales. [FUC(US) + –OID.]

fu•cus (fyōō′kəs) n. Any of various brown algae of the genus Fucus, which includes many of the rockweeds. [Lat. fūcus, seaweed, orchil < Gk. phūkos.]

fud•dle (fŭd′l) v. **-dled, -dling, -dles** —tr. **1.** To put into a state of confusion; befuddle. See Syns at **confuse. 2.** To make drunk; intoxicate. —intr. To drink; tipple. ❖ n. A state of confusion or intoxication. [?]

fud•dy-dud•dy (fŭd′ē-dŭd′ē) n., pl. **-dies** An old-fashioned, fussy person. [?]

fudge (fŭj) n. **1.** A soft rich candy made of sugar, milk, butter, and flavoring. **2.** Nonsense; humbug. ❖ v. **fudged, fudg•ing, fudg•es** —tr. **1.** To fake or falsify. **2.** To evade (an issue, for example); dodge. —intr. **1.** To act in an indecisive manner. **2a.** To exceed proper limits. **b.** To act dishonestly; cheat. [Poss. alteration of fadge, to fit.]

fudge factor n. A variable factor used in calculations or experiments that allows for a margin of error or produces a desired result.

fueh•rer (fyōōr′ər) n. Variant of **führer.**

fu•el (fyōō′əl) n. **1.** Something consumed to produce energy, esp.: **a.** A material such as coal, gas, or oil burned to produce heat or power. **b.** Fissionable material used in a nuclear reactor. **c.** Nutritive material metabolized by a living organism; food. **2.** Something that maintains or stimulates an activity or emotion. ❖ v. **-eled, -el•ing, -els** also **-elled, -el•ling, -els** —tr. **1.** To provide with fuel. **2.** To support or stimulate the activity or existence of. —intr. To take in fuel. [ME feuel < OFr. feuaile < VLat. *focālia, neut. pl. of *focālis, of the hearth < Lat. focus, hearth.] —**fu′el•er** n.

fuel cell n. An electrochemical cell in which the energy of a reaction between a fuel, such as hydrogen, and an oxidant, such as oxygen, is converted directly into electrical energy.

fu•el-ef•fi•cient (fyōō′əl-ĭ-fĭsh′ənt) adj. Using comparatively little fuel: fuel-efficient cars. —**fu′el-ef•fi′cien•cy** n.

fuel injection n. Any of several methods or mechanical systems by which a fuel is reduced to a fine spray and injected directly into the cylinders of an internal-combustion engine.

fuel oil n. A liquid or liquefiable petroleum product that is used to generate heat or power.

fuel rod n. A protective metal tube containing pellets of fuel for a nuclear reactor.

Fu•en•tes (fōō-ĕn′täs′, fwĕn′tĕs), **Carlos** b. 1928. Mexican writer whose works include The Death of Artemio Cruz (1962).

fug (fŭg) n. A heavy, stale atmosphere, esp. the musty air of a poorly ventilated room. [Perh. alteration of fogo, stench.]

fu•ga•cious (fyōō-gā′shəs) adj. **1.** Passing away quickly; evanescent. **2.** Botany Withering or dropping off early. [< Lat. fugāx, fugāc- < fugere, to flee.] —**fu•ga′cious•ly** adv. —**fu•ga′cious•ness, fu•gac′i•ty** (-găs′ĭ-tē) n.

-fuge suff. One that expels or drives away: vermifuge. [Fr. < NLat. -fugus, driving away, fleeing < Lat., fleeing (< fugere, to flee) and < Lat. fugāre, to drive away (< fuga, flight).]

Fug•ger (fōōg′ər) Family of German financiers, including **Johannes** (1348–1409) and his son **Jakob** (d. 1469).

fu•gi•tive (fyōō′jĭ-tĭv) adj. **1.** Running away or fleeing, as from the law. **2a.** Lasting only a short time; fleeting. **b.** Difficult to comprehend or retain; elusive. **c.** Given to change or disappearance; perishable: fugitive beauty. **d.** Of temporary interest: fugitive essays. **3.** Tending to wander; vagabond. ❖ n. **1.** One who flees; a refugee. **2.** Something fleeting or ephemeral. [ME fugitif < OFr. < Lat. fugitīvus < fugitus, p. part. of fugere, to flee.] —**fu′gi•tive•ly** adv. —**fu′gi•tive•ness** n.

fu•gle (fyōō′gəl) intr.v. **-gled, -gling, -gles** Archaic **1.** To act as a fugleman. **2.** To make signals.

fu•gle•man (fyōō′gəl-mən) n. **1.** A leader, esp. a political leader. **2.** Archaic A soldier who once served as a guide and model for his company. [Alteration of Ger. Flügelmann, file leader : Flügel, wing (< MHGer. vlügel; see **pleu-** in App.) + Mann, man (< MHGer. man < OHGer. man; see **man-**[1] in App.).]

fu•gu (fōō′gōō) n. Any of various poisonous fish related to the puffers that are used as food, esp. in Japan, after the poisonous

Carlos Fuentes

ă	pat	oi	boy
ā	pay	ou	out
âr	care	ōō	took
ä	father	ōō	boot
ĕ	pet	ŭ	cut
ē	be	ûr	urge
ĭ	pit	th	thin
ī	pie	th	this
îr	pier	hw	which
ŏ	pot	zh	vision
ō	toe	ə	about,
ô	paw		item

Stress marks:
′ (primary);
′ (secondary), as in
lexicon (lĕk′sĭ-kŏn′)

Mount Fuji

skin and organs have been removed. [J.]

fugue (fyōōg) *n.* **1.** *Music* An imitative polyphonic composition in which a theme or themes are stated successively in all of the voices of the contrapuntal structure. **2.** *Psychology* A pathological amnesiac condition during which one is apparently conscious of one's actions but has no recollection of them after returning to a normal state. [Ital. *fuga* (influenced by Fr. *fugue* < Ital. *fuga*) < Lat., flight.] —**fu′gal** (fyōō′gəl) *adj.* —**fu′gal·ly** *adv.* —**fugue** *v.* —**fugu′ist** (fyōō′gĭst) *n.*

füh·rer *also* **fueh·rer** (fyōōr′ər) *n.* A leader, esp. a tyrant. [Ger. < MHGer. *vüerer* < *vüeren*, to lead < OHGer. *fuoren*. See **per-²** in App.]

Fu·jay·rah (fə-jī′rə, fōō-jī′rä) A sheikdom of the United Arab Emirates on the Gulf of Oman. Pop. 32,191.

Fu·ji (fōō′jē), Mount *also* **Fu·ji·ya·ma** (fōō′jē-yä′mə, -mä) or **Fu·ji·no·ya·ma** (-nō-) or **Fu·ji·san** (-sän′) A dormant volcano, 3,778.6 m (12,389 ft), in central Honshu, Japan, WSW of Tokyo.

Fu·jian¹ (fōō′jyän′) *also* **Fu·kien** (-kyĕn′) A province of SE China on the East China Sea and the Taiwan Strait. Cap. Fuzhou. Pop. 30,048,224.

Fu·jian² (fōō′jyän′, fü′-) *also* **Fu·kien** (-kyĕn′) *n.* A variety of Chinese spoken in Fujian province, eastern Guangdong province, and Taiwan.

Fu·ji·sa·wa (fōō′jē-sä′wə, -wä) A city of E-central Honshu, Japan, a suburb of Tokyo. Pop. 362,088.

Fu·ku·o·ka (fōō′kōō-ō′kə, -kä) A city of NW Kyushu, Japan, on an inlet of the Sea of Japan. Pop. 1,268,626.

Fu·ku·ya·ma (fōō′kə-yä′mə, -kōō-yä′mä) A city of SW Honshu, Japan, on the Inland Sea E of Kure. Pop. 370,873.

-ful *suff.* **1a.** Full of: *playful.* **b.** Characterized by; resembling: *masterful.* **c.** Tending, given, or able to: *useful.* **2.** A quantity that fills: *armful.* [ME < OE < *full,* full. See FULL¹.]

USAGE NOTE The plurals of nouns ending in *-ful* are usually formed by pluralizing the suffix, not the base word: *cupfuls; glassfuls.*

Fu·la·ni (fōō′lä′nē, fōō-lä′-) *also* **Fu·la** (fōō′lə) *n., pl.* **Fulani** or **-nis** *also* **Fula** or **-las** **1.** A member of a pastoral, largely Muslim people inhabiting parts of West Africa from northern Nigeria to Mali and the Atlantic coast. **2.** The West Atlantic language of this people.

Ful·bright (fōōl′brīt′), **J(ames) William** 1905–95. Amer. politician who proposed the Fulbright Act (1946), establishing an exchange program for Amer. and foreign educators and students.

ful·crum (fōōl′krəm, fŭl′-) *n., pl.* **-crums** *or* **-cra** (-krə) **1.** The point or support on which a lever pivots. **2.** *Zoology* An anatomical structure that acts as a hinge or a point of support. **3.** An agent through which vital powers are exercised. [Lat., bedpost < *fulcīre,* to support.]

Ful·da (fōōl′də) A city of central Germany SSE of Kassel on the **Fulda River,** c. 217 km (135 mi). Pop. 57,180.

ful·fill *also* **ful·fil** (fōōl-fĭl′) *tr.v.* **-filled, -fill·ing, -fills** *also* **-fils** **1.** To bring into actuality; effect: *fulfilled their promises.* **2.** To carry out (an order, for example). **3.** To measure up to; satisfy: *fulfilled all requirements.* See Syns at **satisfy. 4.** To bring to an end; complete. [ME *fulfillen* < OE *fullfyllan : full,* full; see FULL¹ + *fyllan,* to fill; see FILL.] —**ful·fill′er** *n.* —**ful·fill′ment** *n.*

ful·gent (fōōl′jənt, fŭl′-) *adj.* Shining brilliantly; radiant: *"tower searchlights . . . as fulgent as half a billion candles"* (Nicholas Proffitt). [ME < Lat. *fulgēns, fulgent-,* pr. part. of *fulgēre,* to flash, shine.] —**ful′gent·ly** *adv.*

ful·gu·rant (fōōl′gyər-ənt, -gər-, fŭl′-) *adj.* Flashing like lightning; dazzlingly bright. [Lat. *fulgurāns, fulgurant-,* pr. part. of *fulgurāre,* to lighten. See FULGURATE.]

ful·gu·rate (fōōl′gyə-rāt′, -gə-, fŭl′-) *v.* **-rat·ed, -rat·ing, -rates** *—intr.* **1.** To emit flashes of lightning. *—tr.* **1.** To emit (light) in flashes. **2.** *Medicine* To destroy (abnormal tissue, for example) by electric current. [Lat. *fulgurāre, fulgurāt-* < *fulgur,* lightning.] —**ful′gu·ra′tion** *n.*

ful·gu·rite (fōōl′gyə-rīt′, -gə-, fŭl′-) *n.* A slender, usu. tubular glassy rock produced by lightning striking and then fusing dry sand. [Lat. *fulgur,* lightning + -ITE¹.]

ful·gu·rous (fōōl′gyər-əs, -gər-, fŭl′-) *adj.* **1.** Emitting flashes of lightning. **2.** Emitting flashes similar to lightning. [Lat. *fulgur,* lightning + -OUS.]

fu·lig·i·nous (fyōō-lĭj′ə-nəs) *adj.* **1.** Sooty. **2.** Colored by or as if by soot. [LLat. *fūlīginōsus* < Lat. *fūlīgō, fūlīgin-,* soot.] —**fu·lig′i·nous·ly** *adv.*

full¹ (fōōl) *adj.* **full·er, full·est** **1.** Containing all that is normal or possible: *a full pail.* **2.** Complete in every particular: *a full account.* **3.** *Baseball* **a.** Amounting to three balls and two strikes. Used of a count. **b.** Having base runners at first, second, and third base. **4a.** Of maximum or highest degree: *at full speed.* **b.** Being at the peak of development or maturity. **5.** Having a great deal or many: *full of errors.* **6.** Totally qualified, accepted, or empowered. **7a.** Rounded in shape; plump. **b.** Having or made with a generous amount of fabric. **8a.** Having an appetite completely satisfied, esp. for food or drink. **b.** Providing an abundance, esp. of food. **9.** Having depth and body; rich: *a full aroma.* **10.** Completely absorbed or preoccupied: *full of himself.* **11.** Possessing

both parents in common. ❖ *adv.* **1.** To a complete extent; entirely. **2.** Exactly; directly. ❖ *v.* **fulled, full·ing, fulls** *—tr.* To make (a garment) full, as by pleating or gathering. *—intr.* To become full. Used of the moon. ❖ *n.* **1.** The maximum or complete size or amount. **2.** The highest degree or state. [ME *ful* < OE *full.* See **pelə-¹** in App.] —**full′ness, ful′ness** *n.*

full² (fōōl) *tr.v.* **fulled, full·ing, fulls** To increase the weight and bulk of (cloth) by shrinking and beating or pressing. [ME *fullen* < OFr. *fouler* < VLat. **fullāre* < Lat. *fullō,* fuller.]

full·back (fōōl′băk′) *n.* **1.** *Football* **a.** An offensive backfield player whose position is behind the quarterback and halfbacks. **b.** The position of this player. **2.** *Sports* **a.** A defensive backfield player in field hockey, soccer, or Rugby. **b.** The position of this player.

full blood *n.* **1.** Relationship through the same set of parents. **2.** often **full-blood** or **full·blood** (fōōl′blŭd′) A person or animal of unmixed race or breed.

full-blood·ed (fōōl′blŭd′ĭd) *adj.* **1a.** Of unmixed ancestry; purebred. **b.** Related by way of having the same parents. **2a.** Not pale or anemic; florid or ruddy. **b.** Vigorous and vital. **3.** Complete in all respects. —**full′-blood′ed·ness** *n.*

full-blown (fōōl′blōn′) *adj.* **1.** Having blossomed or opened completely. **2.** Fully developed or matured. **3.** Having or displaying all the characteristics necessary for completeness.

full-bod·ied (fōōl′bŏd′ēd) *adj.* **1.** Having a rich and intense flavor or aroma: *a full-bodied wine.* **2.** Rich and intense.

full circle *adv.* Back to one's starting point.

full-court press (fōōl′kôrt′, -kōrt′) *n.* **1.** *Basketball* A defensive strategy in which one or two players harass the ball handler over the entire court. **2.** A strong, diversified effort.

full dress *n.* Attire appropriate for formal or ceremonial events.

full-dress (fōōl′drĕs′) *adj.* **1.** Of, appropriate for, or requiring full dress; formal. **2.** Complete or thorough.

full·er¹ (fōōl′ər) *n.* One that fulls cloth.

full·er² (fōōl′ər) *n.* **1.** A hammer used by a blacksmith for grooving or spreading iron. **2.** A groove made by such a hammer. [Poss. < FULL¹, to pleat.]

Fuller, Melville Weston 1833–1910. Amer. jurist; chief justice of the US Supreme Court (1888–1910).

Fuller, R(ichard) Buckminster 1895–1983. Amer. architect and inventor noted for designing the geodesic dome.

Fuller, (Sarah) Margaret 1810–50. Amer. writer and critic who wrote *Woman in the Nineteenth Century* (1845).

ful·ler·ene (fōōl′ə-rēn′) *n.* Any of various nearly spherical carbon molecules that constitute the third form of pure carbon after diamond and graphite. [After Richard Buckminster FULLER (< the resemblance of their configurations to his geodesic domes) + -ENE.]

full·er's earth (fōōl′ərz) *n.* A highly adsorbent claylike substance consisting of hydrated aluminum silicates, used formerly in fulling woolen cloth and now used in decolorizing oils and fats.

Ful·ler·ton (fōōl′ər-tən) A city of S CA SE of Los Angeles; founded 1887. Pop. 126,003.

full-fash·ioned (fōōl′făsh′ənd) *adj.* Knitted in a shape that conforms closely to body lines.

full-fledged (fōōl′flĕjd′) *adj.* **1.** Having reached full development; mature. **2.** Having full status or rank: *a full-fledged lawyer.* **3.** Having fully developed adult plumage.

full gainer *n.* A forward dive in which the diver executes a full back somersault before entering the water.

full house *n.* A poker hand containing three of a kind and a pair, ranked above a flush and below four of a kind.

full-length (fōōl′lĕngkth′, -lĕngth′, -lĕnth′) *adj.* **1.** Showing or fitted to the entire length, esp. of the human body: *a full-length mirror.* **2.** Of a normal or standard length: *a full-length novel.*

full moon *n.* **1.** The moon visible as a fully illuminated disk. **2.** The period of the month when such a moon occurs.

full-mouthed (fōōl′mouthd′, -moutht′) *adj.* **1.** Having a complete set of teeth. Used of cattle and other livestock. **2.** Uttered loudly or noisily.

full nelson *n.* A wrestling hold in which both hands are thrust under the opponent's arms from behind and then pressed against the back of the opponent's neck.

full rhyme *n.* See **perfect rhyme** 1.

full-scale (fōōl′skāl′) *adj.* **1.** Of actual or full size; not reduced. **2.** Employing all resources; not limited or partial.

full-ser·vice (fōōl′sûr′vĭs) *adj.* Associated with or offering complete service: *full-service banks.*

full-size (fōōl′sīz′) or **full-sized** (sīzd′) *adj.* **1.** Of the standard or normal size: *a full-size car.* **2a.** Measuring 54 by 75 inches. Used of a bed. **b.** Being of a size that will fit such a bed.

full stop *n.* **1.** A period indicating the end of a sentence. **2.** A complete halt, as one made by a motor vehicle.

full-time (fōōl′tīm′) *adj.* Employed for or involving a standard number of hours of working time. —**full′-time′** *adv.* —**full′-tim′er** *n.*

ful·ly (fōōl′ē) *adv.* **1.** Totally or completely. **2.** At least.

ful·mar (fōōl′mər, -mär′) *n.* **1.** A gull-like bird (*Fulmarus glacialis*) of Arctic regions having smoky gray plumage. **2.** Any of several similar or related birds. [Dialectal : prob. ON *fūll,* foul;

see **pŭ-** in App. + *măr*, mew; akin to OE *mǣw*.]

ful·mi·nant (fŏŏl′mə-nənt, fŭl′-) *adj.* **1.** Exploding or detonating. **2.** *Pathology* Occurring suddenly, rapidly, and with great severity or intensity. [Lat. *fulmināns, fulminant-*, pr. part. of *fulmināre*, to strike with lightning. See FULMINATE.]

ful·mi·nate (fŏŏl′mə-nāt′, fŭl′-) *v.* **-nat·ed, -nat·ing, -nates** —*intr.* **1.** To issue a thunderous verbal attack or denunciation. **2.** To explode or detonate. —*tr.* **1.** To issue (a denunciation, for example) thunderously. **2.** To cause to explode. ❖ *n.* An explosive salt of fulminic acid. [ME *fulminaten* < Lat. *fulmināre, fulmināt-*, to strike with lightning < *fulmen, fulmin-*, lightning that strikes.] —**ful′mi·na′tion** *n.* —**ful′mi·na′tor** *n.* —**ful′mi·na·to′ry** (-nə-tôr′ē, -tōr′ē) *adj.*

ful·mine (fŏŏl′mĭn, fŭl′-) *tr. & intr.v.* **-mined, -min·ing, -mines** *Archaic* To fulminate. [< Lat. *fulmināre*, to strike with lightning. See FULMINATE.]

ful·min·ic acid (fŏŏl-mĭn′ĭk, fŭl-) *n.* An unstable acid, HONC, that forms highly explosive salts. [Lat. *fulmen, fulmin-*, lightning that strikes + −IC.]

ful·some (fŏŏl′səm) *adj.* **1.** Offensively flattering or insincere. **2.** Offensive to the taste or sensibilities. **3.** *Usage Problem* Copious or abundant. [ME *fulsom*, abundant, well-fed, arousing disgust : *ful*, full; see FULL¹ + *-som*, adj. suff.; see SOME¹.] —**ful′some·ly** *adv.* —**ful′some·ness** *n.*

USAGE NOTE *Fulsome* once meant simply "abundant," as it still does in expressions like *fulsome praise.* Nowadays, though, *fulsome* often has a negative sense, "offensively flattering or insincere." It may therefore invite misunderstandings in contexts in which a deprecatory interpretation is possible, as in *I offer you my most fulsome apologies,* which leaves room for doubt as to the speaker's sincerity.

Ful·ton (fŏŏl′tən), **Robert** 1765–1815. Amer. engineer and inventor who produced the first practical steamboat, the *Clermont* (1807).

Fu Man·chu mustache (fŏŏ′ măn-chŏŏ′) *n.* A mustache with ends that hang downward toward or below the chin. [After *Fu Manchu,* character in novels by Sax Rohmer, pen name of Arthur Sarsfield Ward (1886–1959), British mystery writer.]

fu·ma·rate (fyŏŏ′mə-rāt′) *n.* A salt or ester of fumaric acid. [FUMAR(IC ACID) + −ATE².]

fu·mar·ic acid (fyŏŏ-măr′ĭk) *n.* An organic acid, C₄H₄O₄, found in living cells or synthesized and used in making dyes. [< NLat. *Fūmāria*, genus of herbaceous plants (< LLat. *fūmāria*, fumitory < Lat. *fūmus,* smoke) + −IC.]

fu·ma·role (fyŏŏ′mə-rōl′) *n.* A hole in a volcanic area from which hot smoke and gases escape. [Ital. *fumarola* < LLat. *fūmāriolum,* smoke hole, dim. of Lat. *fūmārium,* smoke chamber < *fūmus,* smoke.] —**fu′ma·rol′ic** (-rŏl′ĭk) *adj.*

fu·ma·to·ry (fyŏŏ′mə-tôr′ē, -tōr′ē) *adj.* Of or relating to smoke or fumigation. [< Lat. *fūmāre,* to smoke < *fūmus,* smoke.]

fum·ble (fŭm′bəl) *v.* **-bled, -bling, -bles** —*intr.* **1.** To touch or handle nervously or idly. **2.** To grope awkwardly to find or to accomplish something. **3.** To proceed awkwardly and uncertainly; blunder. **4a.** *Football* To drop a ball that is in play. **b.** *Baseball* To mishandle a ground ball. —*tr.* **1.** To touch or handle clumsily or idly. **2.** To make a mess of; bungle. See Syns at **botch. 3.** To feel or make (one's way) awkwardly. **4a.** *Football* To drop (a ball) while in play. **b.** *Baseball* To mishandle (a ground ball). ❖ *n.* **1.** The act or an instance of fumbling. **2.** *Sports* A ball that has been fumbled. [ME *fomelen,* to grope.] —**fum′bler** *n.*

fume (fyŏŏm) *n.* **1.** Vapor, gas, or smoke, esp. if irritating, harmful, or strong. **2.** A strong or acrid odor. **3.** A state of resentment or vexation. ❖ *v.* **fumed, fum·ing, fumes** —*tr.* **1.** To subject to or treat with fumes. **2.** To give off in or as if in fumes. —*intr.* **1.** To emit fumes. **2.** To rise in fumes. **3.** To feel or show resentment or vexation. [ME < OFr. *fum* < Lat. *fūmus.*]

fu·mi·gant (fyŏŏ′mĭ-gənt) *n.* A chemical compound used in its gaseous state as a pesticide or disinfectant. [Lat. *fūmigāns, fūmigant-*, pr. part. of *fūmigāre,* to smoke. See FUMIGATE.]

fu·mi·gate (fyŏŏ′mĭ-gāt′) *v.* **-gat·ed, -gat·ing, -gates** —*tr.* To subject to smoke or fumes, usu. in order to exterminate pests or disinfect. —*intr.* To employ smoke or fumes in order to exterminate or disinfect. [Lat. *fūmigāre, fūmigāt-*, to smoke : *fūmus,* smoke + *agere,* to drive, make; see **ag-** in App.] —**fu′mi·ga′tion** *n.* —**fu′mi·ga′tor** *n.*

fu·mi·to·ry (fyŏŏ′mĭ-tôr′ē, -tōr′ē) *n., pl.* **-ries** An herb (*Fumaria officinalis*) native to Eurasia and having spurred purplish flowers. [ME *fumetere* < OFr. *fumeterre* < Med.Lat. *fūmus terrae* : Lat. *fūmus,* smoke + Lat. *terrae,* genitive of *terra,* dry land, earth; see **ters-** in App.]

fun (fŭn) *n.* **1.** A source of enjoyment, amusement, or pleasure. **2.** Enjoyment; amusement: *have fun at the beach.* **3.** Playful, often noisy activity. ❖ *intr.v.* **funned, fun·ning, funs** *Informal* To behave playfully; joke. ❖ *adj. Informal* Amusing: *a fun day.* —*idiom:* **for** (or **in**) **fun** As a joke; playfully. [Poss. < *fon,* to make a fool of < ME *fonnen,* to fool, poss. < *fonne,* fool.]

USAGE NOTE The use of *fun* as an attributive adjective, as in *a fun time, a fun place,* most likely originated in a playful reanalysis of the use of the word in sentences such as *It is fun to ski,* where

fun has the syntactic function of adjectives such as *amusing* or *enjoyable.* The usage became popular in the 1950s and 1960s and may even have 19th-century antecedents, but it can still raise eyebrows among traditionalists. Writers may therefore want to avoid it in more formal contexts.

Fu·na·ba·shi (fŏŏ′nə-bä′shē, -nä-) A city of E-central Honshu, Japan, a suburb of Tokyo on Tokyo Bay. Pop. 539,740.

fu·nam·bu·list (fyŏŏ-năm′byə-lĭst) *n.* One who performs on a tightrope or a slack rope. [< Lat. *fūnambulus* : *fūnis,* rope + *ambulāre,* to walk; see **ambhi** in App.] —**fu·nam′bu·lism** *n.*

func·tion (fŭngk′shən) *n.* **1.** The action for which a person or thing is particularly fitted or employed. **2a.** Assigned duty or activity. **b.** A specific occupation or role. **3.** An official ceremony or a formal social occasion. **4.** Something closely related to another thing and dependent on it for its existence, value, or significance. **5.** *Mathematics* A rule of correspondence between two sets such that there is a unique element in the second set assigned to each element in the first set. **6.** *Biology* The physiological activity of an organ or body part. **7.** *Chemistry* The characteristic behavior of a chemical compound determined by its specific functional group. **8.** *Computer Science* A procedure within an application. ❖ *intr.v.* **-tioned, -tion·ing, -tions** To have or perform a function; serve. [Lat. *fūnctiō, fūnctiōn-*, performance, execution < *fūnctus,* p. part. of *fungī,* to perform, execute.] —**func′tion·less** *adj.*

SYNONYMS *function, duty, office, role* These nouns denote the actions and activities assigned to, required of, or expected of a person: *the function of a teacher; a bank clerk's duty; assumed the office of financial adviser; the role of a parent.*

func·tion·al (fŭngk′shə-nəl) *adj.* **1a.** Of or relating to a function. **b.** Of, relating to, or indicating a mathematical function or functions. **2.** Designed for or adapted to a particular function or use: *functional architecture.* **3.** Capable of performing; operative: *functional brakes.* **4.** *Pathology* Involving functions rather than a physiological or structural cause. ❖ *n.* A linear function on vectors whose values are scalars. —**func′tion·al·ly** *adv.*

functional group *n.* A group of atoms, such as a carboxyl group, that characterizes the properties of a family of organic compounds.

functional illiterate *n.* A person whose skills in reading and writing are insufficient for ordinary practical needs.

func·tion·al·ism (fŭngk′shə-nə-lĭz′əm) *n.* **1.** The doctrine that the function of an object should determine its design and materials. **2.** A doctrine stressing purpose, practicality, and utility. —**func′tion·al·ist** *adj. & n.*

func·tion·al·i·ty (fŭngk′shə-năl′ĭ-tē) *n.* **1.** The quality or capability of being functional. **2.** A useful function within a computer application or program.

functional shift *n.* A shift in the syntactic function of a word, as when a noun serves as a verb.

func·tion·ar·y (fŭngk′shə-nĕr′ē) *n., pl.* **-ies** One who holds an office or a trust or performs a particular function.

function key *n.* A key on a computer keyboard that activates a function within a given application, often in combination with another key.

function word *n.* A word, such as a preposition, that chiefly indicates a grammatical relationship.

func·tor (fŭngk′tər) *n.* **1.** One that performs an operation or a function. **2.** *Grammar* See **function word.** [NLat. *fūnctor* < Lat. *fūnctiō,* performance, function. See FUNCTION.]

fund (fŭnd) *n.* **1.** A source of supply; a stock: *a fund of goodwill.* **2a.** A sum of money or other resources set aside for a specific purpose: *a pension fund.* **b. funds** Available money; ready cash: *short on funds.* **3. funds** The stock of the British permanent national debt, considered as public securities. Used with *the.* **4.** An organization established to administer a sum of money. ❖ *tr.v.* **fund·ed, fund·ing, funds 1.** To provide money for paying off the interest or principal of (a debt). **2.** To convert into a long-term or floating debt with fixed interest payments. **3.** To place in a fund for accumulation. **4.** To furnish a fund for. [Lat. *fundus,* bottom, piece of land.]

fun·da·ment (fŭn′də-mənt) *n.* **1a.** The buttocks. **b.** The anus. **2.** The natural features of a land surface unaltered by humans. **3.** A foundation, as of a building. **4.** An underlying theoretical basis or principle. [ME *foundement* < OFr. *fondement* < Lat. *fundāmentum* < *fundāre,* to lay the foundation < *fundus,* bottom.]

fun·da·men·tal (fŭn′də-mĕn′tl) *adj.* **1a.** Of or relating to the foundation or base; elementary. **b.** Forming or serving as an essential component of a system or structure; central. **c.** Of great significance or entailing major change. **2.** *Physics* **a.** Of or relating to the component of lowest frequency of a periodic wave or quantity. **b.** Of or relating to the lowest possible frequency of a vibrating element or system. **3.** *Music* Having the root in the bass: *a fundamental chord.* ❖ *n.* **1.** An essential part of a system or object. **2.** The first harmonic in a harmonic series; the lowest harmonic. **3.** *Physics* The lowest frequency of a periodically varying quantity or a vibrating system. —**fun′da·men′tal·ly** *adv.*

fun·da·men·tal·ism (fŭn′də-mĕn′tl-ĭz′əm) *n.* **1.** A usu. religious movement or point of view characterized by a return to fundamental principles and by rigid adherence to them. **2a.** often

Fundamentalism An organized, militant Evangelical movement originating in the United States in the late 19th and early 20th century in opposition to Protestant Liberalism and secularism, insisting on the inerrancy of Scripture. **b.** Adherence to its theology. —**fun′da·men′tal·ist** *adj. & n.* —**fun′da·men′tal·ist′ic** *adj.*

fundamental particle *n.* See **elementary particle.**

fund·raise also **fund-raise** (fŭnd′rāz′) *intr.v.* **-raised, -rais·ing, -rais·es** To engage in fundraising.

fund·rais·er also **fund-rais·er** (fŭnd′rā′zər) *n.* **1.** One that raises funds. **2.** A social function held for raising funds.

fund·rais·ing or **fund-rais·ing** (fŭnd′rā′zĭng) *n.* The organized activity or an instance of soliciting money or pledges, as for political campaigns. —**fund′rais′ing** *adj.*

fun·dus (fŭn′dəs) *n., pl.* **-di** (-dī′) *Anatomy* The portion of a hollow organ opposite or farthest from its opening. [Lat., bottom.] —**fun′dic** *adj.*

Fun·dy (fŭn′dē), **Bay of** An inlet of the Atlantic Ocean in SE Canada between New Brunswick and Nova Scotia.

fu·ner·al (fyōō′nər-əl) *n.* **1a.** A ceremony or group of ceremonies held in connection with the burial or cremation of a dead person. **b.** *Archaic* The eulogy delivered or the sermon preached at such a ceremony. **2.** The burial procession accompanying a body to the grave. **3.** An end or a cessation of existence. **4.** *Slang* A source of concern or care. ❖ *adj.* Of, relating to, or resembling a funeral. [ME *funerelles,* funeral rites < OFr. *funerailles* < Med.Lat. *fūnerālia,* neut. pl. of *fūnerālis,* funereal < LLat. < Lat. *fūnus, fūner-,* death rites. See **dheuə-** in App.]

funeral director *n.* One whose business is to arrange for the burial or cremation of the dead and assist at the funeral rites and who is usu. an embalmer.

funeral home *n.* An establishment in which the dead are prepared for burial or cremation and in which wakes and funerals may be held.

fu·ner·ar·y (fyōō′nə-rĕr′ē) *adj.* Of or suitable for a funeral or burial. [Lat. *fūnerārius < fūnus, fūner-,* funeral. See **dheuə-** in App.]

fu·ne·re·al (fyōō-nîr′ē-əl) *adj.* **1.** Of or relating to a funeral. **2.** Appropriate for or suggestive of a funeral. [< Lat. *fūnereus < fūnus, fūner-,* death rites, funeral. See **dheuə-** in App.] —**fu·ne′re·al·ly** *adv.*

fun fair *n. Chiefly British* An amusement park.

fun·gal (fŭng′gəl) also **fun·gous** (-gəs) *adj.* **1.** Of, resembling, or characteristic of a fungus. **2.** Caused by a fungus.

fun·gi·ble (fŭn′jə-bəl) *adj.* **1.** *Law* Returnable or negotiable in kind or by substitution, as a quantity of grain for an equal amount of the same kind of grain. **2.** Interchangeable. ❖ *n.* Something that is exchangeable or substitutable. Often used in the plural. [Med.Lat. *fungibilis < Lat. fungī (vice),* to perform (in place of).] —**fun′gi·bil′i·ty** *n.*

fun·gi·cide (fŭn′jĭ-sīd′, fŭng′gĭ-) *n.* A chemical substance that destroys or inhibits the growth of fungi. —**fun′gi·cid′al** (-sīd′l) *adj.* —**fun′gi·cid′al·ly** *adv.*

fun·gi·form (fŭn′jə-fôrm′, fŭng′gə-) *adj.* Shaped like a mushroom. [FUNG(US) + -FORM.]

fun·gi·stat (fŭn′jĭ-stăt′, fŭng′gĭ-) *n.* A substance that inhibits the growth of fungi.

fun·giv·or·ous (fŭn-jĭv′ər-əs, fŭng-gĭv′-) *adj.* Feeding on fungi.

fun·go (fŭng′gō) *n., pl.* **-goes** *Baseball* A practice fly ball hit by a player who tosses the ball up and hits it on its way down with a long, thin, light bat. [?]

fun·goid (fŭng′goid′) *adj.* Of, relating to, resembling, or being a fungus. ❖ *n.* A fungus.

fun·gus (fŭng′gəs) *n., pl.* **fun·gi** (fŭn′jī, fŭng′gī) or **fun·gus·es** Any of numerous eukaryotic organisms of the kingdom Fungi, such as mushrooms, that lack chlorophyll and vascular tissue and range from a single cell to a body mass of branched filamentous hyphae that often produce specialized fruiting bodies. [Lat.; perh. akin to Gk. *spongos, sphongos,* sponge.]

fun house also **fun·house** (fŭn′hous′) *n.* A building or attraction in an amusement park or carnival that features devices intended to surprise, frighten, bewilder, or amuse.

fu·nic·u·lar (fyōō-nĭk′yə-lər, fə-) *adj.* **1.** Of, relating to, or like a rope or cord. **2.** Operated or moved by a cable. **3.** Of, relating to, or being a funiculus. ❖ *n.* A cable railway on a steep incline, esp. one with counterbalanced ascending and descending cars.

fu·nic·u·lus (fyōō-nĭk′yə-ləs, fə-) also **fu·ni·cle** (fyōō′nĭ-kəl) *n., pl.* **-li** (-lī′) also **-cles 1.** *Anatomy* A slender cordlike strand or band, esp.: **a.** A bundle of nerve fibers in a nerve trunk. **b.** One of three major divisions of white matter in the spinal cord, consisting of fasciculi. **c.** The umbilical cord. **2.** *Botany* A stalk connecting an ovule or a seed with the placenta. [Lat. *fūniculus,* slender rope, dim. of *fūnis,* rope.]

funk¹ (fŭngk) *n.* **1a.** A state of cowardly fright; a panic. **b.** A state of severe depression. **2.** A cowardly fearful person. ❖ *v.* **funked, funk·ing, funks** —*tr.* **1.** To shrink from in fright or dread. **2.** To be afraid of. —*intr.* To shrink in fright. [Prob. < obsolete Flem. *fonck,* disturbance, agitation.]

funk² (fŭngk) *n.* **1.** *Music* **a.** An earthy quality, as in jazz or soul. **b.** A type of popular music combining elements of jazz, blues,

furrow
furrows in a plowed field

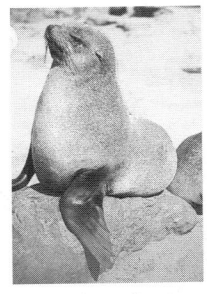
fur seal
Cape fur seal
Arctocephalus pusillus

and soul and characterized by syncopated rhythm and a heavy repetitive bass line. **2.** *Slang* An unsophisticated quality or atmosphere of a region or locality.

funk hole *n.* A dugout or similar place of shelter or refuge.

funk·y¹ (fŭng′kē) *adj.* **-i·er, -i·est** Frightened; panicky.

funk·y² (fŭng′kē) *adj.* **-i·er, -i·est 1a.** Having a moldy or musty smell: *funky cheese.* **b.** Having a strong, offensive, unwashed odor. **2.** Of or relating to funk music. **3.** *Slang* Earthy and uncomplicated; natural. **4.** *Slang* **a.** Marked by self-expression, originality, and modishness; unconventional. **b.** Outlandishly vulgar or eccentric in a humorous or tongue-in-cheek manner; campy. [< *funk,* strong smell, tobacco smoke, perh. < Fr. dialectal *funquer,* to give off smoke < OFr. *fungier* < Lat. *fūmigāre.* See FUMIGATE.] —**funk′i·ness** *n.*

fun·nel (fŭn′əl) *n.* **1a.** A conical utensil with a small hole or narrow tube at the apex, used to channel the flow of a substance, as into a small opening. **b.** Something resembling this utensil in shape. **2.** A shaft, flue, or stack for ventilation or the passage of smoke, esp. the smokestack of a ship or locomotive. ❖ *v.* **-neled, -nel·ing, -nels** or **-nelled, -nel·ling, -nels** —*intr.* **1.** To take the shape of a funnel. **2.** To move through or as if through a funnel. —*tr.* **1.** To cause to take the shape of a funnel. **2.** To cause to move through or as if through a funnel. [ME *fonel* < Provençal *fonilh* < LLat. *fundibulum* < Lat. *īnfundibulum < īnfundere,* to pour in. See INFUSE.]

fun·nel·form (fŭn′əl-fôrm′) *adj. Botany* Shaped like a funnel.

fun·ny (fŭn′ē) *adj.* **-ni·er, -ni·est 1a.** Causing laughter or amusement. **b.** Intended or designed to amuse. **2.** Strangely or suspiciously odd; curious. **3.** Tricky or deceitful. ❖ *n., pl.* **-nies** *Informal* **1.** A joke; a witticism. **2. funnies a.** Comic strips. **b.** The section of a newspaper containing comic strips. [< FUN.] —**fun′ni·ly** *adv.* —**fun′ni·ness** *n.*

funny bone *n. Informal* **1.** A point on the elbow where the ulnar nerve runs close to the surface and tingles sharply if knocked against the bone. **2.** A sense of humor.

funny book *n.* A comic book.

funny farm *n. Offensive Slang* A mental health facility or hospital.

funny money *n. Informal* **1.** Counterfeit currency. **2.** Money from an obscure or questionable source.

funny paper *n.* The section of a newspaper with comic strips.

fur (fûr) *n.* **1.** The thick coat of soft hair covering a mammal's skin. **2.** The hair-covered dressed pelt of such a mammal, used in the making of garments and as trimming or decoration. **3.** A garment made of or lined with the dressed pelt of a mammal. **4.** A coating similar to the pelt of a mammal. ❖ *tr.v.* **furred, fur·ring, furs 1.** To cover, line, or trim with fur. **2.** To provide fur garments for. **3.** To cover or coat as if with fur. **4.** To line (a wall or floor) with furring. [ME *furre,* prob. < *furren,* to line with fur < OFr. *forrer < forre, fuerre,* sheath, lining, of Gmc. orig. See **pā-** in App.]

fur. *abbr.* furlong

fu·ran (fyŏŏr′ăn′, fyŏŏ-răn′) *n.* **1.** One of a group of volatile heterocyclic organic compounds containing a ring of four carbon atoms and one oxygen atom, used in the synthesis of furfural. **2.** The simplest such compound, C_4H_4O. [FUR(FURAL) + -AN².]

fu·ra·nose (fyŏŏr′ə-nōs′) *n.* A sugar having a cyclic structure resembling that of furan.

fur·bear·er also **fur-bear·er** (fûr′bâr′ər) *n.* An animal with fur, esp. commercially valued for fur. —**fur′bear′ing** *adj.*

fur·be·low (fûr′bə-lō′) *n.* **1.** A ruffle or flounce on a garment. **2.** A piece of showy ornamentation. ❖ *tr.v.* **-lowed, -low·ing, -lows** To decorate with a ruffle or flounce. [Prob. alteration of Provençal *farbello, farbella,* fringe, perh. alteration of Ital. *faldella,* pleat, dim. of *falda,* flap, loose end, of Gmc. orig.]

fur·bish (fûr′bĭsh) *tr.v.* **-bished, -bish·ing, -bish·es 1.** To brighten by cleaning or rubbing; polish. **2.** To restore to attractive or serviceable condition. [ME *furbishen* < OFr. *fourbir, fourbiss- < Frankish *furbjan.*] —**fur′bish·er** *n.*

fur·cate (fûr′kāt′) *intr.v.* **-cat·ed, -cat·ing, -cates** To divide into branches; fork. ❖ *adj.* Divided into branches; forked. [LLat. *furcātus,* forked < Lat. *furca,* fork.] —**fur′cate·ly** *adv.* —**fur·ca′tion** *n.*

fur·cu·la (fûr′kyə-lə) *n., pl.* **-lae** (-lē′) *Zoology* A forked part or bone, such as a wishbone. [Lat., dim. of *furca,* fork.] —**fur′cu·lar** *adv.*

fur·fur (fûr′fər) *n., pl.* **-fu·res** (-fyə-rēz′) An epidermal scale, as that associated with dandruff. [Lat., bran, scales.]

fur·fu·ra·ceous (fûr′fə-rā′shəs, -fyə-) *adj.* **1.** Made of or covered with scaly particles, such as dandruff. **2.** Relating to or resembling bran. [< LLat. *furfurāceus,* branlike, scaly : Lat. *furfur,* bran + Lat. *-āceus, -aceous.*]

fur·fu·ral (fûr′fə-răl′, -fyə-) *n.* A sweet-smelling mobile liquid, C_4H_3OCHO, used as a solvent, in making resins, and as a fungicide. [FURFUR + -AL³.]

fur·fu·ran (fûr′fə-răn′, -fyə-) *n.* See **furan** 2. [FURFUR(AL) + -AN².]

fu·ri·o·so (fyŏŏr′ē-ō′sō, -zō) *adv. & adj. Music* In a tempestuous and vigorous manner. [Ital. < Lat. *furiōsus,* furious. See FURIOUS.]

fu·ri·ous (fyŏŏr′ē-əs) *adj.* **1.** Full of or characterized by extreme anger; raging. **2.** Suggestive of extreme anger in action or appearance; fierce. **3.** Full of activity; energetic or rapid. [ME < OFr. *furieus* < Lat. *furiōsus* < *furia*, fury. See FURY.] —**fu′ri•ous•ly** *adv.*

furl (fûrl) *v.* **furled, furl•ing, furls** —*tr.* To roll up and secure (a flag or sail, for example) to something else. —*intr.* To be or become rolled up. ❖ *n.* **1.** The act or an instance of rolling up. **2.** A single roll or a rolled section. [Perh. < Fr. *ferler* < OFr. *ferlier*, to fasten : *ferm*, firm; see FIRM[1] + *lier*, to bind (< Lat. *ligāre*).]

fur•long (fûr′lông′, -lŏng′) *n.* A unit for measuring distance, equal to ⅛ mile (201 meters). See table at **measurement.** [ME < OE *furlang* : *furh*, furrow + *lang*, long; see LONG[1].]

fur•lough (fûr′lō) *n.* **1a.** A leave of absence or vacation, esp. one granted to a member of the armed forces. **b.** A usu. temporary layoff from work. **c.** A leave of absence from prison granted to a prisoner. **2.** The papers or documents authorizing a leave. ❖ *tr.v.* **-loughed, -lough•ing, -loughs 1.** To grant a leave to. **2.** To lay off (workers). [Alteration of *vorloffe*, *furlogh* < Du. *verlof* < MDu.]

fur•mi•ty (fûr′mĭ-tē) *n.* Variant of **frumenty.**

fur•nace (fûr′nĭs) *n.* **1.** An enclosure in which energy in a nonthermal form is converted to heat, esp. such an enclosure in which heat is generated by the combustion of a suitable fuel. **2.** An intensely hot place. **3.** A severe test or trial. [ME < OFr. *fornais* < Lat. *fornāx*, *fornāc-*, oven. See **gʷher-** in App.]

fur•nish (fûr′nĭsh) *tr.v.* **-nished, -nish•ing, -nish•es 1.** To equip with what is needed, esp. to provide furniture for. **2.** To supply; give. [ME *furnisshen* < OFr. *fournir*, *fourniss-*, of Gmc. orig. See **per**[1] in App.] —**fur′nish•er** *n.*

fur•nish•ing (fûr′nĭ-shĭng) *n.* **1.** A piece of equipment necessary or useful for comfort or convenience. **2. furnishings** The furniture, appliances, and other movable articles in a home or other building. **3. furnishings** Wearing apparel and accessories.

fur•ni•ture (fûr′nĭ-chər) *n.* **1.** The movable articles in a room or establishment that make it fit for living or working. **2.** *Archaic* The necessary equipment for a saddle horse. [OFr. *fourniture* < *fournir*, to furnish. See FURNISH.]

Fur•ni•vall (fûr′nə-vəl), **Frederick James** 1825–1910. British philologist who proposed the *Oxford English Dictionary* (1857).

fu•ror (fyo͝or′ôr′, -ər) *n.* **1.** A general commotion; public disorder or uproar. **2.** Violent anger; frenzy. **3.** A fashion adopted enthusiastically by the public; a fad. **4.** A state of intense excitement or ecstasy. [ME *furour*, wrath, fury < OFr. *fureur* < Lat. *furor* < *furere*, to rage.]

fu•ro•re (fyo͞o-rô′rĭ) *n. Chiefly British* Variant of **furor** 1, 3. [Ital. < Lat. *furor*, frenzy. See FUROR.]

fu•ro•se•mide (fyo͞o-rō′sə-mīd′) *n.* A crystalline powder, $C_{12}H_{11}ClN_2O_5S$, used as a diuretic. [FUR(FURAL) + S(ULFO)– + *-emide* (alteration of AMIDE).]

furred (fûrd) *adj.* **1.** Bearing fur. **2.** Made, covered, or trimmed with fur. **3.** Wearing fur garments. **4.** Covered or coated as if with fur. **5.** Provided with furring, as a wall.

fur•ri•er (fûr′ē-ər) *n.* **1.** One that deals in furs. **2.** One whose occupation is the dressing, designing, cleaning, or repairing of furs. [Alteration (influenced by CLOTHIER) of ME *furrer* < AN *furrere* < OFr. *forrer*, to line with fur. See FUR.]

fur•ri•er•y (fûr′ē-ə-rē) *n., pl.* **-ies 1.** Fur garments and trimmings considered as a group. **2.** The business of a furrier.

fur•ring (fûr′ĭng) *n.* **1.** Trimming or lining made of fur. **2.** A furlike coating, as on the tongue. **3a.** The preparation of a wall, ceiling, or floor with strips of wood or metal to provide a level substratum for plaster, flooring, or another surface or to create an air space. **b.** Strips of material used in furring.

fur•row (fûr′ō, fŭr′ō) *n.* **1.** A long, narrow, shallow trench made in the ground by a plow. **2.** A rut, groove, or narrow depression. **3.** A deep wrinkle in the skin, as on the forehead. ❖ *v.* **-rowed, -row•ing, -rows** —*tr.* **1.** To make long, narrow, shallow trenches in; plow. **2.** To form grooves or deep wrinkles in. —*intr.* To become furrowed or wrinkled. [ME *forwe* < OE *furh.*]

fur•ry (fûr′ē, fŭr′ē) *adj.* **-ri•er, -ri•est 1.** Consisting of or similar to fur. **2a.** Covered with, wearing, or trimmed with fur. **b.** Covered with a furlike substance. **3.** Having a furlike quality, as in tone; fuzzy: *a furry voice.* —**fur′ri•ness** *n.*

fur seal *n.* Any of several eared seals of the genera *Callorhinus* or *Arctocephalus*, whose underfur is used in making garments.

fur•ther (fûr′*th*ər) *adj.* A comparative of **far. 1.** More distant in degree, time, or space. **2.** Additional. ❖ *adv.* A comparative of **far. 1.** To a greater extent; more. **2.** In addition; furthermore. **3.** At or to a more distant or advanced point. See Usage Note at **farther.** ❖ *tr.v.* **-thered, -ther•ing, -thers** To help the progress of; advance. See Syns at **advance.** [ME < OE *furthra* < *furthor*, farther. Adv., ME < OE *furthor.* See **per**[1] in App.] —**fur′ther•er** *n.*

fur•ther•ance (fûr′*th*ər-əns) *n.* The act of furthering, advancing, or helping forward.

fur•ther•more (fûr′*th*ər-môr′, -mōr′) *adv.* In addition.

fur•ther•most (fûr′*th*ər-mōst′) *adj.* Most distant or remote.

fur•thest (fûr′*th*ĭst) *adj.* A superlative of **far.** Most distant in degree, time, or space. ❖ *adv.* A superlative of **far. 1.** To the greatest extent or degree. **2.** At or to the most distant point in space or time. [ME < *further*, more distant. See FURTHER.]

fur•tive (fûr′tĭv) *adj.* **1.** Characterized by stealth; surreptitious. **2.** Expressive of hidden motives or purposes; shifty. [Fr. *furtif* < OFr. < Lat. *fūrtīvus* < *fūrtum*, theft < *fūr*, thief. See **bher-**[1] in App.] —**fur′tive•ly** *adv.* —**fur′tive•ness** *n.*

fu•run•cle (fyo͝or′ŭng′kəl) *n.* See **boil**[2]. [Lat. *fūrunculus*, knob on a vine that "steals" the sap, dim. of *fūr*, thief. See **bher-**[1] in App.] —**fu•run′cu•lar** (fyo͞o-rŭng′kyə-lər), **fu•run′cu•lous** (-ləs) *adj.*

fu•run•cu•lo•sis (fyo͞o-rŭng′kyə-lō′sĭs) *n.* A skin condition characterized by the development of recurring boils. [Lat. *fūrunculus*, furuncle; see FURUNCLE + –OSIS.]

fu•ry (fyo͝or′ē) *n., pl.* **-ries 1.** Violent anger; rage. See Syns at **anger. 2.** Violent, uncontrolled action; turbulence. **3. Furies** *Greek & Roman Mythology* The three winged goddesses, Alecto, Megaera, and Tisiphone, who pursue and punish doers of unavenged crimes. **4.** A woman regarded as angry or spiteful. [ME *furie* < OFr. < Lat. *furia* < *furere*, to rage.]

furze (fûrz) *n.* See **gorse.** [ME *furse* < OE *fyrs.*]

fu•sain (fyo͞o-zān′, fyo͞o′zān) *n.* **1a.** Fine charcoal in stick form, made from spindle tree wood. **b.** A sketch or drawing made with this charcoal. **2.** A dull dark gray, brittle, porous type of bituminous coal resembling charcoal. [Fr., spindle tree, charcoal made from its wood < VLat. **fūsāgō*, **fūsāgin-*, spindle < Lat. *fūsus.*]

Fu•san (fo͞o′sän′) See **Pusan.**

fu•sar•i•um (fyo͞o-zâr′ē-əm) *n., pl.* **-i•a** (-ē-ə) Any of various pathogenic fungi of the genus *Fusarium*, chiefly inhabiting temperate climates and infecting both plants and animals, including humans. [NLat. *Fūsārium*, genus name, poss. < Lat. *fūsus*, spindle (< its shape).]

fus•cous (fŭs′kəs) *adj.* Dark brownish-gray in color. [< Lat. *fuscus.*]

fuse[1] also **fuze** (fyo͞oz) *n.* **1.** A cord of readily combustible material that is lighted at one end to detonate an explosive at the other end. **2.** often **fuze** A mechanical or electrical mechanism used to detonate an explosive charge or a device such as a bomb or grenade. ❖ *tr.v.* **fused, fus•ing, fus•es** also **fuzed, fuz•ing, fuz•es** To equip with a mechanical or electrical fuse. [< Ital. *fuso*, spindle < Lat. *fūsus.*]

fuse[2] (fyo͞oz) *v.* **fused, fus•ing, fus•es** —*tr.* **1.** To liquefy or reduce to a plastic state by heating; melt. **2.** To mix (constituent elements) together by or as if by melting; blend. —*intr.* **1.** To become liquefied from heat. **2.** To become mixed or united by or as if by melting together. ❖ *n.* A safety device that protects an electric circuit from excessive current, consisting of or containing a metal element that melts when current exceeds a specific amperage, thereby opening the circuit. [Lat. *fundere*, *fūs-*, to melt. See **gheu-** in App.]

fused quartz (fyo͞ozd) *n.* See **quartz glass.**

fused sentence *n.* A sentence in which two or more independent clauses are not properly joined by a semicolon or conjunction.

fused silica *n.* See **quartz glass.**

fu•see also **fu•zee** (fyo͞o-zē′) *n.* **1.** A lucifer or a vesuvian. **2.** A colored flare used as a warning signal for trucks and railroad trains. **3.** A conical pulley with a spiral groove, used in a cord- or chain-winding clock to maintain even travel as the force of the mainspring lessens in unwinding. **4.** A combustible fuse for detonating explosives. [< Fr. *fusée*, spindle, rocket, flare, fuse < OFr., spindleful of thread < *fus*, spindle < Lat. *fūsus.*]

fu•se•lage (fyo͞o′sə-läzh′, -zə-) *n.* The central body of an aircraft, to which the wings and tail assembly are attached and which accommodates the crew, passengers, and cargo. [Fr. < *fuselé*, spindle-shaped < OFr. *fusel*, spindle < VLat. **fūsellus*, dim. of Lat. *fūsus.*]

Fu•sel•i (fyo͞o′zə-lē′), **Henry** 1741–1825. Swiss-born British painter whose works include *The Nightmare* (1781).

fu•sel oil (fyo͞o′zəl) *n.* An acrid, oily, poisonous liquid mixture of amyl alcohols, occurring in incompletely distilled alcoholic liquids and used as a solvent and in explosives and pure amyl alcohols. [Ger. *Fusel*, bad liquor < LGer.]

Fu•shun (fo͞o′sho͞on′) A city of NE China E of Shenyang. Pop. 1,388,011.

fu•si•ble (fyo͞o′zə-bəl) *adj.* Capable of being fused or melted by heating. —**fu′si•bil′i•ty** *n.*

fusible metal *n.* A metal alloy having a low melting point, used as solder and for safety plugs and fuses.

fu•si•form (fyo͞o′zə-fôrm′) *adj.* Tapering at each end; spindle-shaped. [Lat. *fūsus*, spindle + –FORM.]

fu•sil (fyo͞o′zəl) *n.* A light flintlock musket. [Fr., steel in a flintlock, firearm < OFr. *fuisil*, steel for a tinderbox < VLat. **focīlis (petra)*, fire-(stone) < LLat. *focus*, fire < Lat., hearth.]

fu•sile (fyo͞o′zəl, -zīl′) *adj. Archaic* **1.** Formed by melting or casting. **2.** Capable of being fused; fusible. [ME < Lat. *fūsilis* < *fūsus*, p. part. of *fundere*, to melt. See **gheu-** in App.]

fu•sil•ier also **fu•sil•eer** (fyo͞o′zə-lîr′) *n.* **1.** A soldier in any of certain British army regiments formerly armed with fusils. **2.** A soldier armed with a fusil. [Fr., musketeer < *fusil*, musket. See FUSIL.]

fu•sil•lade (fyo͞o′sə-läd′, -lād′, -zə-, fyo͞o′sə-läd′, -lād′, -zə-) *n.* **1.** A discharge from a number of firearms, fired simultaneously or in rapid succession. **2.** A rapid outburst or barrage, as of insults. ❖ *tr.v.* **-lad•ed, -lad•ing, -lades** To attack with a fusillade. [Fr. < *fusiller*, to shoot < *fusil*, firearm. See FUSIL.]

fu•sil•li (fyo͞o-sē′lē, -sĭl′ē) *n.* Pasta in short spirals or corkscrews.

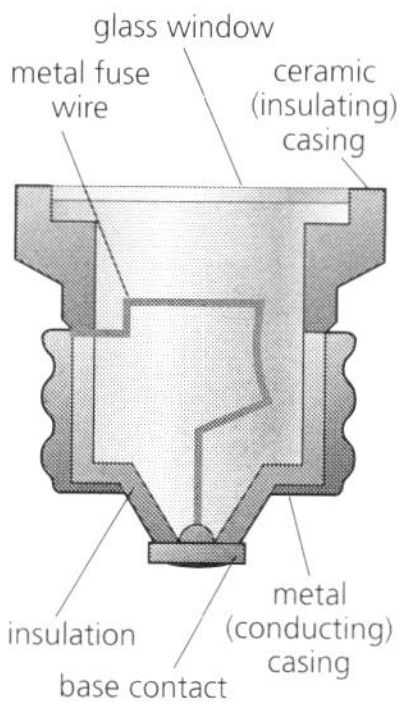
glass window
metal fuse wire
ceramic (insulating) casing
insulation
metal (conducting) casing
base contact

fuse[2]
electric plug fuse

ă	pat	oi	boy
ā	pay	ou	out
âr	care	o͝o	took
ä	father	o͞o	boot
ĕ	pet	ŭ	cut
ē	be	ûr	urge
ĭ	pit	th	thin
ī	pie	*th*	this
îr	pier	hw	which
ŏ	pot	zh	vision
ō	toe	ə	about, item
ô	paw		

Stress marks:
′ (primary);
′ (secondary), as in
lexicon (lĕk′sĭ-kŏn′)

[Ital. < pl. dim. of *fuso*, spindle < Lat. *fūsus*.]

Fu·sin (fōō′shĭn′) See **Fuxin.**

fu·sion (fyōō′zhən) *n.* **1.** The act or procedure of liquefying or melting by the application of heat. **2.** The liquid or melted state induced by heat. **3a.** The merging of different elements into a union: *fusion of metals in an alloy.* **b.** A union resulting from fusing: *a fusion of religion and politics.* **4.** *Physics* A nuclear reaction in which light nuclei combine to form a heavier nucleus with the release of energy. **5.** Music that blends jazz elements and the heavy repetitive rhythms of rock. **6.** A style of cooking that combines ingredients and techniques from very different cultures or countries. [Lat. *fūsiō, fūsiōn-* < *fūsus,* p. part. of *fundere,* to melt. See **gheu-** in App.]

fusion bomb *n.* A nuclear bomb, esp. a hydrogen bomb, that derives its released energy principally from fusion reactions.

fu·sion·ism (fyōō′zhə-nĭz′əm) *n.* The theory or practice of forming coalitions, esp. political ones. —**fu′sion·ist** *n.*

fuss (fŭs) *n.* **1.** Needlessly nervous or useless activity; commotion. **2a.** A state of excessive and unwarranted concern over an unimportant matter. **b.** An objection; a protest. **3.** A quarrel. **4.** A display of affectionate excitement and attention. ❖ *v.* **fussed, fuss·ing, fuss·es** —*intr.* **1.** To trouble or worry over trifles. **2.** To be excessively careful or solicitous. **3.** To get into or be in a state of nervous or useless activity; fidget. **4.** To object; complain. —*tr.* To disturb or vex with unimportant matters. [?] —**fuss′er** *n.*

fuss·budg·et also **fuss-bud·get** (fŭs′bŭj′ĭt) *n.* A person who fusses over trifles.

fuss·pot (fŭs′pŏt′) *n.* See **fussbudget.**

fuss·y (fŭs′ē) *adj.* **-i·er, -i·est 1.** Easily upset; given to bouts of ill temper. **2.** Paying great or excessive attention to personal tastes and appearance; fastidious. **3.** Calling for or requiring great attention to sometimes trivial details. **4.** Full of superfluous details. —**fuss′i·ly** *adv.* —**fuss′i·ness** *n.*

fus·tian (fŭs′chən) *n.* **1a.** A coarse sturdy cloth made of cotton and flax. **b.** Any of several thick twilled cotton fabrics, such as corduroy, having a short nap. **2.** Pretentious speech or writing; pompous language. ❖ *adj.* **1.** Made of or as if of fustian. **2.** Pompous, bombastic, and ranting. [ME < OFr. *fustaigne* < Med.Lat. *fūstānum, fūstiānum,* poss. < Lat. *fūstis,* wooden stick, club (transl. of Gk. *xulina* (*lina*), wood-linen, cotton), or from *El Fostat* (*El Fustat*), a section of Cairo, Egypt.]

fus·tic (fŭs′tĭk) *n.* **1.** A small dioecious tropical American tree (*Chlorophora tinctoria*) having wood that yields a yellow dyestuff. **2.** The wood of this plant. **3.** A dyestuff obtained from the wood of this plant. [ME *fustik* < OFr. *fustoc* < Ar. *fustuq* < Gk. *pistakē,* pistachio. See PISTACHIO.]

fus·ti·gate (fŭs′tĭ-gāt′) *tr.v.* **-gat·ed, -gat·ing, -gates 1.** To beat with a club; cudgel. **2.** To criticize harshly. [LLat. *fūstigāre, fūstigāt-* : Lat. *fūstis,* club + *agere,* to do; see **ag-** in App.] —**fus′ti·ga′tion** *n.*

fus·ty (fŭs′tē) *adj.* **-ti·er, -ti·est 1.** Smelling of mildew or decay; musty. **2.** Old-fashioned; antique. [ME < OFr. *fust,* piece of wood, wine cask < Lat. *fūstis,* stick, club.] —**fus′ti·ly** *adv.* —**fus′ti·ness** *n.*

fu·su·ma (fōō-sōō′mä) *n., pl.* **fusuma** A sliding partition of thick paper mounted in grooves on the floor and ceiling of a Japanese house and variously positioned to form rooms. [J.]

fut. *abbr.* **1.** future **2.** *Business* futures

fu·thark (fōō′thärk′) *n.* **1.** The common Germanic runic alphabet. **2.** also **fu·thorc** or **fu·thork** (-thôrk′) The Old English runic alphabet. [< the first six letters of the alphabet: *f, u, th, a, r, k* (or *c*).]

fu·tile (fyōōt′l, fyōō′tīl′) *adj.* **1.** Having no useful result. **2.** Trifling and frivolous; idle. [Lat. *fūtilis.* See **gheu-** in App.] —**fu′tile·ly** *adv.* —**fu′tile·ness** *n.*

SYNONYMS *futile, barren, bootless, fruitless, unavailing, useless, vain* These adjectives mean producing no result or effect: *a futile effort; a barren search; bootless entreaties; fruitless labors; an unavailing attempt; a useless discussion; vain regrets.* **ANTONYM** *useful*

fu·til·i·tar·i·an (fyōō-tĭl′ĭ-târ′ē-ən) *adj.* Holding or based on the view that human endeavor is futile. ❖ *n.* One who holds the view that human endeavor is futile. [FUTILIT(Y) + –ARIAN.] —**fu·til′i·tar′i·an·ism** *n.*

fu·til·i·ty (fyōō-tĭl′ĭ-tē) *n., pl.* **-ties 1.** The quality of having no useful result; uselessness. **2.** Lack of importance or purpose; frivolousness. **3.** A futile act.

fu·ton (fōō′tŏn) *n., pl.* **futon** or **-tons** A thin mattress of tufted cotton batting or similar material, placed on a floor or on a raised, foldable frame: *fu,* bed quilt (< M Chin. *phu*) + *ton,* round (< M Chin. *thuan*).]

fut·tock (fŭt′ək) *n.* One of the curved timbers that forms a rib in the frame of a ship. [ME *fottok,* perh. alteration of *fothok* : *fot,* foot; see FOOT + *hok,* hook; see HOOK.]

futtock plate *n. Nautical* An iron plate attached horizontally to

the top of the lower mast to secure the topmast rigging and the upper ends of the futtock shrouds.

futtock shroud *n. Nautical* One of the iron rods extending from a band on the lower mast to the futtock plate, used to brace the base of the topmast.

Fu·tu·na Islands (fə-tōō′nə, fōō-) also **Hoorn Islands** (hôrn, hōrn) An island group of the French overseas territory of Wallis and Futuna in the SW Pacific Ocean NE of Fiji; annexed by France in 1887.

fu·ture (fyōō′chər) *n.* **1.** The indefinite time yet to come. **2.** Something that will happen in time to come. **3.** A prospective or expected condition, esp. one considered with regard to growth, advancement, or development: *a business with no future.* **4.** **futures** *Business* Commodities or stocks bought or sold upon agreement of delivery in time to come. **5.** *Grammar* **a.** The form of a verb used in speaking of action that has not yet occurred or of states not yet in existence. **b.** A verb form in the future tense. ❖ *adj.* That is to be or to come; of or existing in later time. [ME < OFr. *futur* < Lat. *futūrus,* about to be. See **bheuə-** in App.]

fu·ture·less (fyōō′chər-lĭs) *adj.* Having no prospect or hope of success in one's future. —**fu′ture·less·ness** *n.*

future perfect *n.* A verb tense that expresses action completed by a specified time in the future, formed in English by combining *will have* or *shall have* with a past participle.

future shock *n.* A condition of distress and disorientation due to inability to cope with rapid societal and technological change. [After the book *Future Shock* by Alvin Toffler (born 1928).]

future tense *n.* A verb tense expressing future time.

fu·tur·ism (fyōō′chə-rĭz′əm) *n.* **1.** A belief that the meaning of life and one's personal fulfillment lie in the future. **2.** An artistic movement originating in Italy around 1910 whose aim was to express the energetic, dynamic, and violent quality of contemporary life. —**fu′tur·ist** *n.*

fu·tur·is·tic (fyōō′chə-rĭs′tĭk) *adj.* **1.** Of or relating to the future. **2a.** Of, characterized by, or expressing a vision of the future. **b.** Being ahead of the times; innovative or revolutionary. **3.** Of or relating to futurism. —**fu′tur·is′ti·cal·ly** *adv.*

fu·tur·ist·ics (fyōō′chə-rĭs′tĭks) *n.* (*used with a sing. verb*) Futurology.

fu·tu·ri·ty (fyōō-tōōr′ĭ-tē, -tyōōr′-, -chōōr′-) *n., pl.* **-ties 1.** The future. **2.** The quality or condition of being in or of the future. **3.** A future event or possibility. **4.** *Sports* A futurity race.

futurity race *n. Sports* A race for horses in which the competitors are entered at or before their birth.

fu·tur·ol·o·gy (fyōō′chə-rŏl′ə-jē) *n.* The study or forecasting of potential developments, as in science and society, based on current conditions and trends. —**fu′tur·o·log′i·cal** (-chər-ə-lŏj′ĭ-kəl) *adj.* —**fu′tur·ol′o·gist** *n.*

futz (fŭts) *intr.v.* **futzed, futz·ing, futz·es** *Slang* To waste time or effort on frivolities; fool. Often used with *around.* [Poss. blend of FUCK and PUTZ.]

Fu·xin also **Fu·sin** (fōō′shĭn′) A city of NE China WNW of Shenyang. Pop. 743,165.

fuze (fyōōz) *n. & v.* Variant of **fuse**[1].

fu·zee (fyōō-zē′) *n.* Variant of **fusee.**

Fu·zhou (fōō′jō′) also **Foo·chow** or **Fu·chou** (fōō′jō′, -chou′) A city of SE China on the Min R. delta; the cap. of Fujian province since the 10th cent. Pop. 1,395,739.

fuzz[1] (fŭz) *n.* A mass or coating of fine light fibers, hairs, or particles; down. ❖ *v.* **fuzzed, fuzz·ing, fuzz·es** —*tr.* **1.** To cover with fuzz. **2.** To make blurred or indistinct: *fuzzing up the details.* —*intr.* To become blurred or obscure. [Perh. back-formation < FUZZY.]

fuzz[2] (fŭz) *n. Slang* The police. [?]

fuzz·y (fŭz′ē) *adj.* **-i·er, -i·est 1.** Covered with fuzz. **2.** Of or resembling fuzz. **3.** Not clear; indistinct: *a fuzzy recollection.* **4.** Not coherent; confused: *a fuzzy plan.* [Perh. < LGer. *fussig,* spongy. See **pŭ-** in App.] —**fuzz′i·ly** *adv.* —**fuzz′i·ness** *n.*

fuzz·y·head·ed (fŭz′ē-hĕd′ĭd) *adj.* **1a.** Marked by unclear confused thinking. **b.** Giddy; silly. **2.** Having a head covered with fuzz. —**fuzz′y·head′ed·ness** *n.*

fuzzy logic *n.* A form of algebra employing a range of values from "true" to "false" that is used in decision-making with imprecise data.

FWB *abbr.* four-wheel brake

fwd *abbr.* forward

FWD *abbr.* **1.** four-wheel drive **2.** front-wheel drive

FX *abbr.* foreign exchange

FY *abbr.* fiscal year

–fy or **–ify** *suff.* Cause to become; make: *basify.* [ME *-fien* < OFr. *-fier* < Lat. *-ficāre, -ficārī* < *-ficus,* -fic.]

FYI *abbr.* for your information

fyke (fīk) *n.* A long bag-shaped fishing net held open by hoops. [Du. *fuik* < MDu. *fūke.*]

fyl·fot (fĭl′fŏt′) *n.* A swastika. [Orig. perh. a device for the foot of a painted window : FILL + FOOT.]

Fyn (fĭn, fün) An island of S-central Denmark W of Sjaelland.

Gg

g¹ or **G** (jē) *n., pl.* **g's** or **G's** also **gs** or **Gs 1.** The seventh letter of the modern English alphabet. **2.** Any of the speech sounds represented by the letter *g*. **3.** The seventh in a series. **4.** Something shaped like the letter G. **5.** *Music* **a.** The fifth tone in the scale of C major or the seventh tone in the relative minor scale. **b.** A key or scale in which G is the tonic.

g² *abbr.* **1.** acceleration of gravity **2.** gram

G¹ A trademark used for a movie rating indicating that admission will be granted to persons of all ages.

G² (jē) *n. Slang* One thousand dollars: *made 20 Gs on the deal.* [G(RAND), one thousand dollars.]

G³ The symbol for **conductance.**

G⁴ *abbr.* **1.** gauss **2.** genitive **3.** gravitational constant **4.** guanine

G. *abbr.* gulf

G8 (jēʹātʹ) *n.* The countries of Canada, France, Germany, Italy, Japan, Russia, the United Kingdom, and the United States. Representatives from these countries meet to discuss economic concerns. [G(roup of) 8.]

Ga¹ The symbol for the element **gallium.**

Ga² *abbr. Bible* Galatians

GA *abbr.* **1.** general agent **2.** general assembly **3.** general average **4.** also Ga. Georgia (US)

ga. *abbr.* gauge

gab (găb) *Slang intr.v.* **gabbed, gab·bing, gabs** To talk idly or incessantly, as about trivial matters. ❖ *n.* Idle talk; chatter. [ME *gabben,* to scoff, speak foolishly < ON *gabba,* to scoff.] —**gabʹber** *n.*

GABA *abbr.* gamma-aminobutyric acid

gab·ar·dine (găbʹər-dēn′, găbʹər-dēn′) *n.* **1.** A sturdy, tightly woven fabric of cotton, wool, or rayon twill. **2.** See **gaberdine** 1. **3.** *Chiefly British* A laborer's long loose smock; a gaberdine. [Alteration of GABERDINE.]

gab·ble (găbʹəl) *v.* **-bled, -bling, -bles** *—intr.* **1.** To speak rapidly or incoherently; jabber. **2.** To make rapid low muttering or quacking sounds, as a goose or duck. *—tr.* To utter rapidly or incoherently. ❖ *n.* **1.** Rapid, incoherent, or meaningless speech. **2.** The gabble of a goose or duck. [Prob. freq. of GAB.] —**gabʹbler** *n.*

gab·bro (găbʹrō) *n., pl.* **-bros** A usu. coarse-grained igneous rock composed chiefly of calcic plagioclase and pyroxene. [Ital., perh. < Lat. *glaber,* bald, beardless.] —**gab·broʹic** (gă-brōʹĭk) *adj.* —**gabʹbroid′** (găbʹroid′) *adj.*

gab·by (găbʹē) *adj.* **-bi·er, -bi·est** *Slang* Tending to talk excessively; garrulous. —**gabʹbi·ness** *n.*

ga·belle (gə-bĕlʹ) *n.* A tax, esp. the salt tax imposed in France before 1790. [ME *gabel* < OFr. < OItal. *gabella* < Ar. *qabāla,* tribute < *qabila,* to receive.]

gab·er·dine (găbʹər-dēn′, găbʹər-dēn′) *n.* **1.** A long coarse cloak or frock. **2.** *Chiefly British* A loose smock worn by laborers. **3.** See **gabardine** 1. [Obsolete Fr. *gauvardine* < OFr. *galvardine,* perh. < MHGer. *wallevart,* pilgrimage : *wallen,* to roam (< OHGer. *wallōn;* see **wel-** in App.) + *vart,* journey (< OHGer. < *faran,* to go; see **per-²** in App.).]

gab·fest (găbʹfĕst′) *n. Slang* **1.** An informal gathering or session for the exchange of news, opinions, and gossip. **2.** A long animated conversation or discussion.

ga·bi·on (gāʹbē-ən) *n.* **1.** A cylindrical wicker basket filled with earth and stones, formerly used in building fortifications. **2.** A hollow metal cylinder used esp. in constructing dams and foundations. [Fr. < Ital. *gabbione,* augmentative of *gabbia,* cage < Lat. *cavea.*]

ga·ble (gāʹbəl) *n.* **1a.** The generally triangular section of wall at the end of a pitched roof, occupying the space between the two slopes of the roof. **b.** The whole end wall of a building or wing having a pitched roof. **2.** A triangular, usu. ornamental architectural section, as one above an arched door or window. [ME *gable, gavel* < Norman Fr. *gable* (perh. of Celt. orig.) and < ON *gafl;* see **ghebh-el-** in App.] —**gaʹbled** *adj.*

Gable, (William) Clark 1901–60. Amer. actor whose films include *It Happened One Night* (1934).

gable roof *n.* See **pitched roof.**

Ga·bo (gäʹbō, -bə), **Naum** 1890–1977. Russian-born Amer. sculptor known for his experiments with constructivism.

Ga·bon (gă-bŏnʹ, -bônʹ) A country of W-central Africa on the Atlantic Ocean; achieved independence from France in 1960. Cap. Libreville. Pop. 1,283,000.

Ga·bor (gäʹbôr, gə-bôrʹ), **Dennis** 1900–79. Hungarian-born British physicist who won a 1971 Nobel Prize.

Ga·bo·ro·ne (gäʹbə-rōʹnĕ) The cap. of Botswana, in the SE

part; founded c. 1890. Pop. 133,468.

Ga·bri·el (gāʹbrē-əl) *n. Bible* An angel who explained signs from God and announced the conception, birth, and mission of Jesus to Mary.

gad¹ (găd) *intr.v.* **gad·ded, gad·ding, gads** To move about restlessly and with little purpose. See Syns at **wander.** [ME *gadden,* to hurry.] —**gadʹder** *n.*

gad² (găd) *n.* **1.** A pointed tool, such as a spike, used for breaking rock or ore. **2.** A goad, as for prodding cattle. ❖ *tr.v.* **gad·ded, gad·ding, gads** To break up (ore, for example) with a gad. [ME < ON *gaddr.*]

Gad¹ In the Bible, a son of Jacob and the forebear of one of the tribes of Israel.

Gad² *interj.* Used to express surprise or dismay. [Alteration of GOD.]

gad·a·bout (gădʹə-bout′) *n.* One who roams or roves about, as in search of amusement or social activity.

gad·fly (gădʹflī′) *n.* **1.** A persistent, irritating critic; a nuisance. **2.** One that acts as a provocative stimulus; a goad. **3.** Any of various flies, esp. of the family Tabanidae, that bite or annoy livestock and other animals. [GAD² + FLY².]

gadg·et (găjʹĭt) *n.* A small specialized mechanical or electronic device; a contrivance. [?] —**gadgʹet·y** *adj.*

gadg·e·teer (găj′ĭ-tîrʹ) *n.* A person who designs, builds, or delights in the use of gadgets.

gadg·et·ry (găjʹĭ-trē) *n.* **1.** Gadgets considered as a group. **2.** The design or construction of gadgets.

gad·jo (gäʹjō) *n., pl.* **gad·je** (-jə) *Offensive* Used as a disparaging term for one who is not Gypsy. [Romany, perh. < Prakrit **gājjha-,* domestic (as opposed to itinerant), ult. < Skt. *gṛhaḥ,* house. See **gher-** in App.]

ga·doid (gāʹdoid′, gădʹoid′) also **ga·did** (gāʹdĭd) *adj.* Of or belonging to the fish family Gadidae, which includes the cods and the hakes. ❖ *n.* A fish of the family Gadidae. [NLat. *Gadus,* fish genus (< Gk. *gados,* a kind of fish) + –OID.]

gad·o·lin·ite (gădʹl-ə-nīt′) *n.* A dark green or greenish-black silicate mineral, $Be_2FeY_2Si_2O_{10}$, containing several of the rare earths in combination with iron.

gad·o·lin·i·um (găd′l-ĭnʹē-əm) *n. Symbol* **Gd** A malleable, ductile metallic rare-earth element obtained from monazite and used in improving ferromagnetic characteristics of iron, cerium, and related alloys. Atomic number 64; atomic weight 157.25; melting point 1,312°C; boiling point approx. 3,000°C; specific gravity from 7.8 to 7.896; valence 3. See table at **element.** [After Johan Gadolin (1760–1852), Finnish chemist.]

ga·droon (gə-drōōnʹ) *n.* **1.** *Architecture* A band of convex molding carved with ornamental beading or reeding. **2.** An ornamental band, used esp. in silverwork, embellished with fluting, reeding, or another continuous pattern. [Fr. *godron* < OFr. *goderon,* perh. ult. < Lat. *guttus,* flask < *gutta,* drop.] —**ga·droonedʹ** *adj.*

Gads·den (gădzʹdən), **James** 1788–1858. Amer. diplomat and politician who negotiated the Gadsden Purchase.

Gadsden Purchase An area in extreme S NM and AZ S of the Gila R.; purchased by the US from Mexico in 1853.

gad·wall (gădʹwôl′) *n.* A North American duck *(Anas strepera)* having gray or brown plumage. [?]

gad·zooks (găd-zōōksʹ) *interj.* Used as a mild or ironic oath. [Perh. alteration of *God's hooks,* the nails of the crucifixion of Christ.]

Gae·a (jēʹə) also **Gai·a** (gāʹə) *n. Greek Mythology* The goddess of the earth, who bore and married Uranus.

Gael (gāl) *n.* **1.** A Gaelic-speaking Celt of Scotland, Ireland, or the Isle of Man. **2.** A Scottish Highlander. [Sc. Gael. *Gaidheal* and Ir. Gael. *Gaedheal,* both < OIr. *Goídil.* See GOIDELIC.]

Gael·ic (gāʹlĭk) *adj.* Of or relating to the Gaels or their culture or languages. ❖ *n.* **1.** Goidelic. **2.** A Goidelic language.

Gael·tacht (gālʹtəкнт) *n.* The collection of regions in Ireland where Irish Gaelic is spoken as a native language. [Ir.Gael. < *Gael,* a Gael. See GAEL.]

gaff (găf) *n.* **1.** A large iron hook attached to a pole or handle and used to land large fish. **2.** *Nautical* A spar attached to the mast and used to extend the upper edge of a fore-and-aft sail. **3a.** A sharp metal spur or spike fastened to the leg of a gamecock. **b.** A climbing hook used by telephone and electric line workers. **4.** *Slang* A trick or gimmick, esp. one used in a swindle or to rig a game. **5.** *Slang* Harshness of treatment; abuse. ❖ *tr.v.* **gaffed, gaf·fing, gaffs 1.** To hook or land (a fish) using a gaff. **2.** To equip (a gamecock) with a gaff. **3.** *Slang* **a.** To take in or defraud; swindle. **b.** To rig or fix in order to cheat. [ME *gaffe* < OFr. < O

gable
House of Seven Gables built c.1688 in Salem, Massachusetts

Gabon

Provençal *gaf* < *gafar*, to seize, of Gmc. orig. See **kap-** in App.]

gaff² (găf) *n. Chiefly British* **1.** A public place of entertainment, esp. a cheap or disreputable music hall or theater. **2.** *Slang* A house, building, or apartment, esp. where one resides. [?]

gaff³ (găf) *n.* Variant of **gaffe.**

gaffe also **gaff** (găf) *n.* **1.** A clumsy social error. **2.** A blatant mistake or misjudgment. [Fr. < OFr., hook. See GAFF¹.]

gaf•fer (găf′ər) *n.* **1.** An electrician in charge of lighting on a movie or television set. **2.** *Chiefly British* An old man or a rustic. **3.** *Chiefly British* A boss or foreman. [Prob. alteration (influenced by GRANDFATHER) of GODFATHER.]

gaff rig *n. Nautical* A rig with a fore-and-aft sail that has its upper edge supported by a gaff.

gaff-top•sail (găf′tŏp′səl, -sāl′) *n. Nautical* A light triangular or quadrilateral sail set above a gaff.

gag (găg) *n.* **1.** Something forced into or put over the mouth to prevent speaking or crying out. **2.** An obstacle to or a censoring of free speech. **3.** A device placed in the mouth to keep it open, as in dentistry. **4a.** A practical joke. **b.** A comic effect or remark. **5.** The act or an instance of gagging or choking. ❖ *v.* **gagged, gag•ging, gags** —*tr.* **1.** To prevent from speaking or crying out by using a gag. **2.** To stop or restrain from exercising free speech. **3.** To cause to choke, retch, or gag. **4.** To keep (the mouth) open by using a gag. **5.** To block off or obstruct (as a pipe). —*intr.* **1a.** To experience a regurgitative spasm in the throat, as from revulsion to a food. **b.** To retch or choke. **2.** To make jokes or quips. [< ME *gaggen*, to suffocate, perh. of imit. orig.]

ga•ga (gä′gä′) *adj. Informal* **1.** Silly; crazy. **2.** Completely absorbed, infatuated, or excited: *gaga over the album.* **3.** Senile; doddering. [Fr., old fool, gaga, of imit. orig.]

Ga•ga•rin (gə-gär′ĭn) **Yuri Alekseyevich** 1934–68. Soviet cosmonaut who was the first person to travel in space (1961).

gage¹ (gāj) *n.* **1.** Something deposited or given as security against an obligation; a pledge. **2.** Something, such as a glove, offered or thrown down as a pledge or challenge to fight. **3.** A challenge. ❖ *tr.v.* **gaged, gag•ing, gag•es** *Archaic* **1.** To pledge as security. **2.** To offer as a stake in a bet; wager. [ME < OFr., of Gmc. orig.]

gage² (gāj) *n.* Any of several varieties of plum. [After Sir William Gage (1656?–1727), English botanist.]

gage³ (gāj) *n. & v.* Variant of **gauge.**

Gage, Thomas 1721–87. British colonial administrator who served as governor of Massachusetts (1774–75).

gag•er (gā′jər) *n.* Variant of **gauger.**

gag•ger (găg′ər) *n.* One that gags.

gag•gle (găg′əl) *n.* **1.** A flock of geese. **2.** A cluster or group. [ME *gagel* < *gagelen*, to cackle, prob. of imit. orig.]

gag law *n.* A law intended to limit freedom of the press, as by instituting censorship. **2.** See **gag rule.**

gag•man (găg′măn′) *n.* **1.** A man employed to write jokes or comedy routines. **2.** A comedian who uses gags.

gag order *n. Law* A court order forbidding public reporting or commentary on a case currently before the court.

gag rule *n.* A rule limiting discussion or debate on an issue.

gahn•ite (gä′nīt′) *n.* A dark green to brown or black mineral, ZnAl₂O₄. [After Johan Gottlieb *Gahn* (1745–1818), Swedish mineralogist.]

Gai•a (gā′ə) *n.* Variant of **Gaea.**

gai•e•ty also **gay•e•ty** (gā′ĭ-tē) *n., pl.* **-ties** **1.** A state of joyful exuberance or merriment; vivacity. **2.** Merry or joyful activity; festivity. **3.** Bright color or showiness, as of dress; finery. [Fr. *gaieté* < *gai*, cheerful. See GAY.]

gai•jin (gī′jĕn′, -jĭn′) *n., pl.* **gaijin** A non-Japanese person. [J.: *gai,* outside, foreign (< M Chin. ŋwajh) + *jin,* person; see JINRIKSHA.]

Gail•lard Cut (gĭl-yärd′, gā′lärd′) Formerly **Cu•le•bra Cut** (kōō-lā′brə) An excavation, c. 13 km (8 mi) long and 14 m (45 ft) deep, that forms the SE section of the Panama Canal.

gail•lar•di•a (gə-lär′dē-ə) *n.* Any of several New World plants of the genus *Gaillardia* in the composite family, having red or yellow flower heads. [NLat. *Gaillardia,* genus name, after *Gaillard* de Marentonneau, 18th-cent. French botanist.]

gai•ly also **gay•ly** (gā′lē) *adv.* **1.** In a joyful, cheerful, or happy manner; merrily. **2.** With bright colors or trimmings; showily.

gain¹ (gān) *v.* **gained, gain•ing, gains** —*tr.* **1.** To come into possession or use of; acquire: *gained information about the enemy's plans.* **2.** To attain in competition or struggle; win: *gain control.* **3.** To obtain through effort or merit; achieve: *gain recognition.* **4.** To secure as profit or reward; earn: *gain a living.* **5a.** To manage to achieve an increase of: *The movement gained strength.* **b.** To increase by (a specific amount): *gained 15 pounds.* **6.** To come to; reach: *gained the summit.* See Syns at **reach.** **7.** To become fast by (a specified amount of time). Used of a timepiece. —*intr.* **1.** To increase; grow: *a painting that gained in value.* **2.** To become better; improve: *gaining in health.* **3.** To obtain a profit or advantage; benefit: *stood to gain politically.* **4a.** To close a gap; get closer: *gaining on the leader.* **b.** To increase a lead. **5.** To put on weight. **6.** To operate or run fast. Used of a timepiece. ❖ *n.* **1a.** Something gained or acquired: *territorial gains.* **b.** Progress; advancement. **2.** The act of acquiring; attainment. **3.** An increase in amount or degree. **4.** *Electronics* An increase in signal power, voltage, or current by an amplifier, expressed as the ratio of output

to input. —*idiom:* **gain time 1.** To run too fast. Used of a timepiece. **2.** To delay or prolong something until a desired event occurs. [< ME *gayne,* booty (< OFr. *gaigne,* gain, gain < *gaaignier,* to gain, of Gmc. orig.; see App.) and ME *gein,* advantage (< ON *gegn,* ready, and < OFr. *gain,* gain).]

gain² (gān) *n.* A notch or mortise cut into a board to receive another part. ❖ *tr.v.* **gained, gain•ing, gains 1.** To cut out a gain in. **2.** To join by or fit into a gain. [?]

gain•er (gā′nər) *n.* **1.** One that gains. **2.** *Sports* A dive in which the diver leaves the board facing forward, does a back somersault, and enters the water feet first.

Gaines•ville (gānz′vĭl′, -vəl) A city of N-central FL SW of Jacksonville. Pop. 95,447.

gain•ful (gān′fəl) *adj.* Providing a gain; profitable: *gainful employment.* —**gain′ful•ly** *adv.* —**gain′ful•ness** *n.*

gain•say (gān-sā′, gān′sā′) *tr.v.* **-said** (-sĕd′, -sĕd′), **-say•ing, -says** (-sāz′, -sĕz′) **1.** To declare false; deny. **2.** To oppose, esp. by contradiction. [ME *gainsayen* : *gain-,* against (< OE *gegn-*) + *sayen,* to say (< OE *secgan*; see SAY).] —**gain′say′er** *n.*

Gains•bor•ough (gānz′bûr′ō, -bər-ə), **Thomas** 1727–88. British painter whose works include *The Blue Boy* and *The Harvest Wagon* (both c. 1770).

'gainst also **gainst** (gĕnst, gānst) *prep. Informal* Against.

Gai•ser•ic (gī′zə-rĭk′) See **Genseric.**

gait (gāt) *n.* **1.** A particular way of moving on foot. **2.** Any of the ways by which a horse can move by lifting the feet in a different order or rhythm. **3.** Rate or manner of proceeding. ❖ *tr.v.* **gait•ed, gait•ing, gaits** To train (a horse) in a particular gait. [ME *gate* < ON *gata,* path. See **ghē-** in App.]

gait•ed (gā′tĭd) *adj.* Having a specified gait. Often used in combination: *smooth-gaited; slow-gaited.*

gai•ter (gā′tər) *n.* **1a.** A cloth or leather covering for the leg from the instep to the ankle or knee. **b.** A similar covering of lightweight fabric, used by skiers and hikers. **2.** An ankle-high shoe with elastic sides. **3.** An overshoe with a cloth top. **4.** A high tubular collar fitting closely around the neck, often worn by skiers. [Fr. *guêtre* < OFr. *guietre,* of Gmc. orig. See **wer-²** in App.]

Ga•ius (gā′əs, gī′-) also **Ca•ius** (kā′-, kī′-) fl. A.D. 130–180. Roman jurist noted esp. for his *Institutes.*

gal¹ (găl) *n. Informal* A girl. [Alteration of GIRL.]

gal² (găl) *n.* The centimeter-gram-second unit of acceleration, equal to one centimeter per second per second. [After GALILEO GALILEI.]

gal. *abbr.* gallon

Gal. *abbr. Bible* Galatians

ga•la (gā′lə, găl′ə, gä′lə) *n.* **1.** A festive occasion, esp. a lavish social event or entertainment. **2.** *Chiefly British* An athletic competition, esp. a swimming contest. ❖ *adj.* **1.** Marked by lavish or festive celebration: *a gala ball.* **2.** Characterized by sumptuous social pleasure. [Ital. and Fr., both ult. < OFr. *gale,* rejoicing < *galer,* to make merry. See GALLANT.]

ga•la•bi•a (jə-lä′bē-ə) *n.* Variant of **djellaba.**

ga•lac•tic (gə-lăk′tĭk) *adj.* **1.** Of or relating to a galaxy, esp. the Milky Way. **2.** Of enormous size; immense. **3.** Of, relating to, or causing the secretion of milk.

galactic equator *n.* The great circle of the celestial sphere that lies in the plane bisecting the band of the Milky Way, inclined at an angle of approx. 62° to the celestial equator.

galacto- or **galact–** *pref.* Milk: *galactose.* [< Gk. *galakto-* < *gala, galakt-,* milk. See **melg-** in App.]

ga•lac•tor•rhe•a (gə-lăk′tə-rē′ə) *n.* **1.** Excessive flow of milk from the breasts during lactation. **2.** Spontaneous milk flow not associated with childbirth or the nursing of an infant.

gal•ac•tos•am•ine (găl′ăk-tŏs′ə-mēn′, gə-lăk′-) *n.* An amino derivative of galactose commonly found in glycolipids.

ga•lac•tose (gə-lăk′tōs′) *n.* A monosaccharide, C₆H₁₂O₆, commonly occurring in lactose and in certain pectins, gums, and mucilages.

ga•lac•to•se•mi•a (gə-lăk′tə-sē′mē-ə) *n.* An inherited metabolic disorder marked by the deficiency of an enzyme needed for galactose metabolism. —**ga•lac′to•se′mic** *adj.*

ga•lac•to•side (gə-lăk′tə-sīd′) *n.* Any of a group of glycosides that yield galactose on hydrolysis.

ga•la•go (gə-lä′gō, -lā′-) *n., pl.* **-gos** See **bush baby.** [NLat. *Galago,* genus name, perh. < Wolof *golo,* monkey.]

ga•lah (gə-lä′) *n.* **1.** An Australian cockatoo (*Cacatua roseicapilla*) having pale blue-gray plumage and a pink breast. **2.** *Australian* A fool; an idiot. [Yuwaalaraay (Aboriginal language of SE Australia) *gilaa.*]

Gal•a•had (găl′ə-hăd′) *n.* **1.** In Arthurian legend, the Knight of the Round Table who succeeded in the quest for the Holy Grail. **2.** One considered noble, pure, or chivalrous.

ga•lan•gal (gə-lăng′gəl) *n.* **1.** A plant (*Alpinia officinarum*) of eastern Asia having pungent aromatic roots used medicinally and as seasoning. **2.** Its dried roots. [Variant of GALINGALE.]

gal•an•tine (găl′ən-tēn′) *n.* A dish of boned stuffed meat or fish, poached and served cold garnished with aspic. [ME *galauntine,* a kind of sauce < OFr. *galatine, galentine,* aspic, fish sauce < Med.Lat. *galentīnum,* prob. ult. < *gelāta,* jelly < fem. p. part. of Lat. *gelāre,* to freeze, coagulate. See GELATIN.]

ga•lan•ty show (gə-lăn′tē) *n.* A shadow play performed by cast-

Yuri Gagarin
photographed in 1961

Galileo Galilei

ing the shadows of miniature figures on a screen or wall. [Perh. < Ital. *galanti*, pl. of *galante*, a gallant < OFr. *galant*. See GALLANT.]

Ga•lá•pa•gos Islands (gə-lä′pə-gəs, -lăp′ə-) A group of volcanic islands lying along the equator in the Pacific Ocean about 1,045 km (650 mi) W of the mainland of Ecuador, to which they belong; famous for their rare species of fauna.

Gal•a•te•a (găl′ə-tē′ə) *n. Greek Mythology* **1.** A woman brought to life by Aphrodite from a statue carved by Pygmalion. **2.** A satellite of Neptune.

Ga•la•ţi (gä-läts′, -lät′sē) or **Ga•latz** (gä′läts′) A city of E Romania on the lower Danube R. NE of Bucharest; founded in the Middle Ages. Pop. 324,234.

Ga•la•tia (gə-lā′shə, -shē-ə) An ancient country of central Asia Minor in the region surrounding Ankara, Turkey; became a Roman province in 25 B.C. —**Ga•la′tian** *adj. & n.*

Ga•la•tians (gə-lā′shənz) *pl.n.* (*used with a sing. verb*) See table at **Bible.**

gal•a•vant (găl′ə-vănt′) *v.* Variant of **gallivant.**

ga•lax (gā′lăks′) *n.* A stemless evergreen perennial plant *(Galax urceolata)* of the eastern United States having glossy heart-shaped leaves and small white flowers in spikelike clusters. [NLat. *Galax*, genus name < Gk. *gala*, *galakt-*, milk. See GALAXY.]

gal•ax•y (găl′ək-sē) *n., pl.* **-ies 1a.** Any of numerous large-scale aggregates of stars, gas, and dust that constitute the universe, containing an average of 100 billion (10^{11}) solar masses and ranging in diameter from 1,500 to 300,000 light-years. **b.** often **Galaxy** The Milky Way. **2.** An assembly of brilliant, glamorous, or distinguished persons or things: *a galaxy of performers.* [ME *galaxie*, the Milky Way < LLat. *galaxiās* < Gk. < *gala*, *galakt-*, milk. See **melg-** in App.]

Gal•ba (găl′bə, gôl′-), **Servius Sulpicius** 3 B.C.–A.D. 69. Emperor of Rome (68–69) who was assassinated after naming an unpopular successor.

gal•ba•num (găl′bə-nəm, gôl′-) *n.* A bitter aromatic gum resin extracted from an Asiatic plant *(Ferula galbaniflua)* or any of several related plants and used in incense and medicinally. [ME < Lat. < Gk. *khalbanē*, of Semitic orig.; akin to Heb. *ḥelbənâ*.]

Gal•braith (găl′brāth′), **John Kenneth** b. 1908. Canadian-born Amer. economist, writer, and diplomat whose works include *The Affluent Society* (1955).

gale[1] (gāl) *n.* **1.** A very strong wind. **2.** Any wind with speeds of from 32 to 63 miles (51 to 102 kilometers) per hour, according to the Beaufort scale. **3.** A forceful outburst. **4.** *Archaic* A breeze. [?]

gale[2] (gāl) *n.* The sweet gale. [ME *gail* < OE *gagel*.]

ga•le•a (gā′lē-ə) *n., pl.* **-le•ae** (-lē-ē′) A helmet-shaped part, such as the upper petal of certain plants. [Lat., helmet.]

ga•le•ate (gā′lē-āt′) also **ga•le•at•ed** (-ā′tĭd) *adj.* **1.** *Biology* Having a galea. **2.** Helmet-shaped. [Lat. *galeātus*, p. part. of *galeāre*, to cover with a helmet < *galea*, helmet.]

Ga•len (gā′lən) A.D. 130?–200? Greek anatomist, physician, and writer whose theories formed the basis of European medicine until the Renaissance. —**Ga′len•ism** *n.* —**Ga′len•ist** *n.*

ga•le•na (gə-lē′nə) *n.* A gray mineral, essentially PbS, the principal ore of lead. [Lat. *galēna*, lead ore.]

ga•len•i•cal (gā-lĕn′ĭ-kəl, gə-) *n.* A medicinal preparation composed mainly of herbal or vegetable matter. ❖ *adj.* Of, relating to, or being a galenical. [After GALEN.]

Ga•li•bi (gə-lē′bē) *n., pl.* **Galibi** or **-bis 1.** A member of the Carib people of French Guiana. **2.** The language of the Galibi. [Carib, strong man, Galibi. See CANNIBAL.]

Ga•li•cia (gə-lĭsh′ə, -ē-ə) **1.** A historical region of central Europe in SE Poland and W Ukraine. An independent principality after 1087, it passed to Poland after World War I. The E portion was ceded to the USSR after World War II. **2.** (*often* gə-lē′sē-ə, gä-lē′thyä) A region and ancient kingdom of NW Spain on the Atlantic Ocean S of the Bay of Biscay; formerly a Goth kingdom and a Moorish stronghold. —**Ga•li′cian** *adj. & n.*

Gal•i•le•an also **Gal•i•lae•an** (găl′ə-lē′ən) *n.* **1.** A native or inhabitant of Galilee. **2.** A Christian. **3.** Jesus. ❖ *adj.* Of or relating to Galilee or its people.

gal•i•lee (găl′ə-lē′) *n.* A small chapel or porch at the western end of a medieval English church. [ME *galile* < ONFr. *galilee* < Med.Lat. *galilaea* < Lat. *Galilea*, Galilee.]

Galilee A region of N Israel; the center of Jesus's ministry.

Galilee, Sea of or **Lake Ti•be•ri•as** (tī-bîr′ē-əs) A freshwater lake of NE Israel drained by the Jordan R.

Ga•li•le•o Ga•li•lei (găl′ə-lā′ō găl′ə-lā′) 1564–1642. Italian astronomer and physicist who was the first to use a telescope to study the stars (1610). He was imprisoned by the Inquisition (1633) for advocating heliocentricity. —**Gal′i•le′an** *adj.*

gal•i•ma•ti•as (găl′ə-mā′shē-əs, -măt′ē-əs) *n.* Nonsense; gibberish. [Fr.]

gal•in•gale (găl′ĭn-gāl′) *n.* Any of various sedges of the genus *Cyperus*, esp. *C. longus* of Europe, having rough-edged leaves, reddish spikelets, and aromatic roots. [ME, a kind of root < OFr. *galingal* < Ar. *ḫulunjān* < Chin. (Mandarin) *Gāoliáng jiāng*, a kind of ginger : *Gāo liáng*, an area in Guangdong province + *jiāng*, ginger.]

gal•i•pot (găl′ə-pŏt′, -pō′) *n.* Crude turpentine obtained from a type of pine tree *(Pinus pinaster)* of southern Europe. [Fr.]

gall[1] (gôl) *n.* **1.** See **bile** 1. **2a.** Bitterness of feeling; rancor. **b.** Something bitter to endure. **3.** Outrageous insolence; effrontery. [ME < OE *gealla*, *galla*. See **ghel-** in App.]

gall[2] (gôl) *n.* **1.** A skin sore caused by friction and abrasion. **2a.** Exasperation; vexation. **b.** The cause of such vexation. ❖ *v.* **galled, gall•ing, galls** —*tr.* **1.** To make (the skin) sore by abrasion; chafe. **2.** To damage or break the surface of by or as if by friction; abrade. **3.** To irk or exasperate; vex. —*intr.* To become irritated, chafed, or sore. [ME *galle* < OE *gealla*, poss. < Lat. *galla*, nutgall.]

gall[3] (gôl) *n.* An abnormal swelling of plant tissue caused by insects, microorganisms, or external injury. [ME *galle* < OFr. < Lat. *galla*, nutgall.]

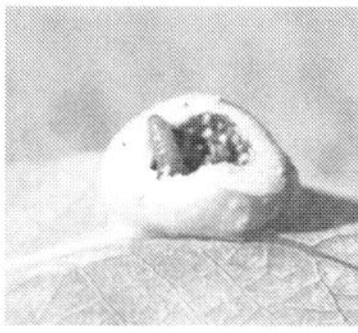

gall[3]
worm in gall

gal•lant (găl′ənt) *adj.* **1.** Smartly or boldly stylish; dashing: *a gallant hat.* **2a.** Unflinching in battle or action; valiant: *put up a gallant resistance.* **b.** Nobly or selflessly resolute. **3.** Stately; majestic. **4.** (gə-lănt′, -länt′) **a.** Courteously attentive esp. to women; chivalrous. **b.** Flirtatious; amorous. ❖ *n.* (gə-lănt′, -länt′, găl′ənt) **1.** A fashionable young man. **2a.** A man courteously attentive to women. **b.** A man who is a woman's lover. ❖ *v.* (gə-lănt′, -länt′) **-lant•ed, -lant•ing, -lants** —*tr.* To woo or pay court to (a lady). —*intr.* To play the gallant. [ME *galaunt* < OFr. *galant*, pr. part. of *galer*, to rejoice, of Gmc. orig.] —**gal′lant•ly** *adv.*

gal•lant•ry (găl′ən-trē) *n., pl.* **-ries 1.** Nobility of spirit or action; courage. **2.** Chivalrous attention toward women; courtliness. **3.** The act or an instance of gallant speech or behavior. **4.** *Archaic* A bold or stylish appearance.

Gal•la•tin (găl′ə-tĭn), **(Abraham Alfonse) Albert** 1761–1849. Swiss-born Amer. financier and politician who served as secretary of the treasury (1801–14).

Gallatin Range A section of the Rocky Mts. in NW WY and SW MT rising to 3,402.3 m (11,155 ft).

Gal•lau•det (găl′ə-dĕt′), **Thomas Hopkins** 1787–1851. Amer. educator who founded the first free school for the deaf and hearing-impaired (1817).

gall•blad•der also **gall bladder** (gôl′blăd′ər) *n.* A small muscular sac, located under the right lobe of the liver, in which bile secreted by the liver is stored until needed for digestion.

gal•le•ass (găl′ē-ăs′, -əs) *n. Nautical* A large, fast, heavily armed three-masted Mediterranean galley of the 16th and 17th centuries. [Fr. *galeasse* < OFr. < OItal. *galeaza*, augmentative of *galea*, galley < O Provençal or Catalan; see GALLEY.]

gal•lein (găl′ē-ĭn, găl′ēn′) *n.* A brown or metallic green dye, $C_{20}H_{12}O_7$, used as a pH indicator and in dyeing textiles. [GALL(IC ACID) + (PHTHAL)EIN.]

gal•le•on (găl′ē-ən, găl′yən) *n.* A large three-masted sailing ship with a square rig and usu. two or more decks, used from the 15th to the 17th century esp. by Spain as a merchant ship or warship. [Sp. *galeon* < OSpan., augmentative of *galea*, galley < OFr. *galie*. See GALLEY.]

gal•le•ri•a (găl′ə-rē′ə) *n.* A roofed passageway or indoor court usu. containing a variety of shops or businesses. [Ital. < OItal. < Med.Lat., gallery < var. of *galilaea*, galilee. See GALILEE.]

gal•ler•y (găl′ə-rē) *n., pl.* **-ies 1.** A roofed promenade, esp. one extending along the wall of a building and supported by arches or columns on the outer side. **2.** A long enclosed passage, such as a corridor. **3a.** A narrow balcony, usu. having a railing or balustrade, along the outside of a building. **b.** A projecting or recessed passageway along an upper story on the interior or exterior of a large building, generally marked by a colonnade or arcade. **c.** Such a passageway situated over the aisle of a church and opening onto the nave. **4.** *Southwestern Gulf States* See **veranda. 5a.** An upper section, often with a sloping floor, projecting from the rear or side walls of a theater or auditorium to provide additional seating. **b.** The seats in such a section, usu. cheaper than those on the main floor. **c.** The cheapest seats in a theater. **d.** The audience occupying a gallery. **6.** A large audience or group of spectators, as at a golf match. **7.** The general public, usu. considered undiscriminating or unsophisticated. **8a.** A building, institution, or room for the exhibition of artistic work. **b.** An establishment that displays and sells works of art. **c.** A photographer's studio. **9.** A collection; an assortment. **10a.** An underground tunnel or passageway, as in a cave. **b.** A passage made by a tunneling insect or animal. **11.** *Nautical* A platform or balcony at the stern or quarters of some early sailing ships. **12.** A decorative upright trimming or molding along the edge of a tabletop, tray, or shelf. [ME *galerie* < OFr. < ONFr. *galilee*, galilee. See GALILEE.] —**gal′ler•ied** *adj.*

galleon

gal•ley (găl′ē) *n., pl.* **-leys 1.** *Nautical* **a.** A large, usu. single-decked medieval ship of shallow draft, propelled by sails and oars and used as a merchant ship or warship in the Mediterranean. **b.** An ancient Mediterranean seagoing vessel propelled by oars. **c.** A large rowboat formerly used by British customs officers. **2.** The kitchen of an airliner, ship, or camper. **3.** *Printing* **a.** A long tray, usu. of metal, used for holding composed type. **b.** Galley proof. [ME *galei* < OFr. *galie* < O Provençal or Catalan *galea* < Med.Gk., prob. var. of Gk. *galeos*, shark, perh. < *galeē*, weasel.]

galley proof *n. Printing* A proof taken from composed type before page composition to allow for the correction of errors.

gall•fly (gôl′flī′) *n.* Any of various small insects, such as the gall wasp, that deposit their eggs on plant stems or in bark, causing the formation of galls in which their larvae grow.

ă	pat	oi	boy
ā	pay	ou	out
âr	care	ŏŏ	took
ä	father	ōō	boot
ĕ	pet	ŭ	cut
ē	be	ûr	urge
ĭ	pit	th	thin
ī	pie	*th*	this
îr	pier	hw	which
ŏ	pot	zh	vision
ō	toe	ə	about,
ô	paw		item

Stress marks:
′ (primary);
′ (secondary), as in
lexicon (lĕk′sĭ-kŏn′)

Gal·li·a (găl′ē-ä) See **Gaul**[2].

gal·liard (găl′yərd) *n.* **1.** A spirited dance popular in France in the 16th and 17th centuries. **2.** The triple-time music for this dance. ❖ *adj. Archaic* Spirited; lively; gay. [ME *gaillard* < OFr. *gaillart*, prob. of Celt. orig.]

Gal·lic (găl′ĭk) *adj.* Of or relating to Gaul or France; French. [Lat. *Gallicus* < *Gallus*, a Gaul.]

gal·lic acid (găl′ĭk, gô′lĭk) *n.* A crystalline compound, $C_7H_6O_5$, derived from tannin and used as a tanning agent and an ink dye and in photography and the manufacture of paper. [Fr. *acide gallique* < *galle*, plant gall. See GALL[3].]

Gal·li·can (găl′ĭ-kən) *adj.* **1.** Relating to or characteristic of Gallicanism. **2.** Gallic. ❖ *n.* A supporter of Gallicanism.

Gal·li·can·ism (găl′ĭ-kə-nĭz′əm) *n.* A movement originating among the French Roman Catholic clergy that favored the restriction of papal control and the individual administrative autonomy of nations.

Gal·li·cism (găl′ĭ-sĭz′əm) *n.* **1.** A French phrase or idiom appearing in another language. **2.** A characteristic French trait.

Gal·li·cize (găl′ĭ-sīz′) *tr. & intr.v.* **-cized, -ciz·ing, -ciz·es** To make or become French, as in form, character, or custom. —**Gal′li·ci·za′tion** (-sĭ-zā′shən) *n.*

gal·li·gas·kins (găl′ĭ-găs′kĭnz) *pl.n.* **1.** Loosely fitting hose or breeches worn in the 16th and 17th centuries. **2.** Loose trousers. **3.** *Chiefly British* Leggings. [Perh. alteration of Fr. *garguesques*, var. of *greguesques* < Sp. *gregüescos* < *griego*, Gk. < Lat. *Graecus*. See GREEK.]

gal·li·mau·fry (găl′ə-mô′frē) *n., pl.* **-fries** A jumble; a hodgepodge. [Fr. *galimafrée* < OFr. *galimafree*, sauce, ragout : prob. *galer*, to make merry; see GALLANT + *mafrer*, to gorge oneself (ult. of imit. orig.).]

gal·li·na·ceous (găl′ə-nā′shəs) *adj.* **1.** Of, belonging to, or characteristic of the order Galliformes, which includes the common domestic fowl. **2.** Relating to or resembling the domestic fowl. [< Lat. *gallīnāceus*, of poultry < *gallīna*, hen, fem. of *gallus*, cock.] —**gal′li·na′cean** *n.*

Gal·li·nas (gä-yē′näs), **Point** A cape of N Colombia, the northernmost point of South America.

gall·ing (gô′lĭng) *adj.* Causing extreme irritation or chagrin; vexing: *a galling delay.* —**gall′ing·ly** *adv.*

gal·li·nip·per (găl′ə-nĭp′ər) *n.* A large mosquito or other insect capable of inflicting a painful bite. [?]

gal·li·nule (găl′ə-nōōl′, -nyōōl′) *n.* Any of various wading and swimming birds of the family Rallidae, having dark iridescent plumage and a red bill tipped with yellow. [Lat. *gallīnula*, pullet, dim. of *gallīna*, hen. See GALLINACEOUS.]

Gal·lip·o·li (gə-lĭp′ə-lē) A narrow peninsula of NW Turkey extending between the Dardanelles and the Gulf of Saros; scene of heavy fighting (1915) between Allied and Turkish forces in World War I.

gal·li·pot (găl′ə-pŏt′) *n.* A small glazed earthenware jar formerly used by druggists for medicaments. [ME *galy pott* : prob. *galei*, galley; see GALLEY + *pott*, pot; see POT[1].]

gal·li·um (găl′ē-əm) *n. Symbol* **Ga** A rare metallic element that is liquid near room temperature, expands on solidifying, is found as a trace element in coal, bauxite, and other minerals, and is used in semiconductor technology. Atomic number 31; atomic weight 69.72; melting point 29.78°C; boiling point 2,403°C; specific gravity 5.907; valence 2, 3. See table at **element**. [< Lat. *gallus*, cock, punning transl. of surname of Paul Émile *Lecoq* de Boisbaudran (1838–1912), French chemist and element's discoverer : Fr. *le*, the + *coq*, rooster.]

gallium arsenide *n.* A crystalline compound, GaAs, used in transistors, solar cells, and semiconducting lasers.

gal·li·vant also **gal·a·vant** (găl′ə-vănt′) *intr.v.* **-vant·ed, -vant·ing, -vants** **1.** To roam about in search of pleasure or amusement. See Syns at **wander**. **2.** To play around amorously; flirt. [Perh. alteration of GALLANT.]

gal·li·wasp (găl′ə-wŏsp′, -wôsp′) *n.* Any of several long-bodied lizards of the genus *Diploglossus*, native to marshy regions of Central America and the West Indies. [?]

gall midge *n.* Any of various small mosquitolike flies of the family Cecidomyiidae, having larvae that mature in galls.

gall mite *n.* Any of various mites of the family Eriophyidae that produce galls on plants.

gall·nut (gôl′nŭt′) *n.* See **nutgall**.

gal·lo·glass or **gal·low·glass** (găl′ō-glăs′) *n.* An armed retainer or mercenary in the service of an Irish chieftain. [Ir.Gael. *gallóglach* : *gall*, foreigner + *oglach*, soldier (< *ōg* < OIr. *ōac*; see **yeu-** in App.).]

gal·lon (găl′ən) *n.* **1a.** A unit of volume in the US Customary System, used in liquid measure, equal to 4 quarts (3.785 liters). **b.** A unit of volume in the British Imperial System, used in liquid and dry measure, equal to 4 quarts (4.546 liters). See table at **measurement**. **2.** A container with a capacity of one gallon. [ME, a liquid measure < ONFr. *galon*.]

gal·lon·age (găl′ə-nĭj) *n.* An amount measured in gallons.

gal·loon (gə-lōōn′) *n.* A narrow band or braid used as trimming and commonly made of lace, metallic thread, or embroidery. [Fr. *galon* < OFr. *galonner*, to ribbon hair.]

gal·loot (gə-lōōt′) *n. Slang* Variant of **galoot**.

gal·lop (găl′əp) *n.* **1a.** A natural three-beat gait of a horse, faster than a canter, in which all four feet are off the ground at the same time during each stride. **b.** A fast running motion of other quadrupeds. **2.** A ride taken at a gallop. **3.** A rapid pace. ❖ *v.* **-loped, -lop·ing, -lops** —*tr.* **1.** To cause to gallop. **2.** To transport at or as if at a gallop. —*intr.* **1.** To ride a horse at a gallop. **2.** To move swiftly. [< ME *galopen*, to go at a gallop < OFr. *galoper*, of Gmc. orig.]

gal·lo·pade (găl′ə-pād′, -păd′) *n.* Variant of **galop**.

gal·lop·ing (găl′ə-pĭng) *adj.* **1.** Of or resembling a gallop, esp. in rhythm or rapidity. **2.** Developing at an accelerated rate and leading to death. Used of certain diseases.

Gal·lo·way (găl′ə-wā′) A region of SW Scotland. The **Mull of Galloway**, a promontory on a peninsula on its SW coast, is the southernmost point in Scotland.

gal·lows (găl′ōz) *n., pl.* **gallows** or **-lows·es** **1a.** A device usu. consisting of two upright posts supporting a crossbeam from which a noose is suspended and used for execution by hanging; a gallows tree. **b.** A similar structure used for supporting or suspending. **2.** Execution by hanging. [ME *galwes*, pl. of *galwe*, gallows < OE *gealga, galga*.]

gallows bird *n. Informal* One who is destined or deserves to be hanged.

gallows humor *n.* Humor about a grave or dire situation.

gallows tree *n.* A gallows.

gall·stone (gôl′stōn′) *n.* A small hard pathological concretion, composed chiefly of cholesterol, calcium salts, and bile pigments, formed in the gallbladder or in a bile duct.

Gal·lup (găl′əp), **George Horace** 1901–84. Amer. public-opinion analyst who accurately predicted the outcome of the 1936 presidential election.

gal·lus·es (găl′ə-sĭz) *pl.n.* Suspenders for trousers. [Variant of *gallowses*, var. of GALLOWS.]

gall wasp *n.* Any of various wasps of the family Cynipidae whose larvae produce galls on oaks and other plants.

Ga·lois theory (găl-wä′) *n.* The part of algebra concerned with the relation between solutions of a polynomial equation and the fields containing those solutions. It gives conditions under which the solutions can be expressed in terms of addition, subtraction, multiplication, and division, and in terms of the extraction of roots. [After Évariste *Galois* (1811–32), French mathematician.]

ga·loot also **gal·loot** (gə-lōōt′) *n. Slang* A person, esp. a clumsy or uncouth one. [?]

gal·op (găl′əp) also **gal·o·pade** or **gal·lo·pade** (găl′ə-pād′, -păd′) *n.* **1.** A lively dance in duple time, popular in the 19th century. **2.** The music for this dance. [Fr. < OFr., gallop < *galoper*, to gallop. See GALLOP.]

ga·lore (gə-lôr′, -lōr′) *adj.* In great numbers; in abundance. [Ir. Gael. *go leór*, enough : *go*, adv. particle + *leór*, enough (< OIr. *lour*, alteration of *roar*; see **wēro-** in App.).]

ga·losh (gə-lŏsh′) *n.* **1.** A waterproof overshoe. **2.** *Obsolete* A sturdy heavy-soled boot or shoe. [ME *galoche*, wooden soled shoe < OFr.]

galosh
pair of galoshes

Gals·wor·thy (gălz′wûr′thē), **John** 1867–1933. British writer who won the 1932 Nobel Prize for literature.

ga·lumph (gə-lŭmf′) *intr.v.* **-lumphed, -lumph·ing, -lumphs** To move or run clumsily or heavily. [Perh. blend of GALLOP and TRIUMPH.]

Gal·va·ni (găl-vä′nē, gäl-), **Luigi** 1737–98. Italian physiologist whose experiments stimulated research on electricity.

gal·van·ic (găl-văn′ĭk) *adj.* **1.** Of or relating to direct-current electricity, esp. when produced chemically. **2a.** Having the effect of an electric shock. **b.** Produced as if by an electric shock. [GALVAN(ISM) + -IC.] —**gal·van′i·cal·ly** *adv.*

galvanic cell *n.* See **primary cell**.

gal·va·nism (găl′və-nĭz′əm) *n.* **1.** Direct-current electricity, esp. when produced chemically. **2.** Therapeutic application of direct-current electricity, esp. the electric stimulation of nerves and muscle. [After Luigi GALVANI.]

gal·va·nize (găl′və-nīz′) *tr.v.* **-nized, -niz·ing, -niz·es** **1.** To stimulate or shock with an electric current. **2.** To arouse to awareness or action; spur. **3.** To coat (iron or steel) with rust-resistant zinc. —**gal′va·ni·za′tion** (-nĭ-zā′shən) *n.* —**gal′va·niz′er** *n.*

galvano– *pref.* Galvanism; galvanic: *galvanometer.*

gal·va·no·mag·net·ic (găl′və-nō-măg-nĕt′ĭk, găl-văn′ō-) *adj.* Of or relating to the generation of an electric field by a magnetic field in semiconductors and metals.

gal·va·nom·e·ter (găl′və-nŏm′ĭ-tər) *n.* An instrument used to detect, measure, and determine the direction of small electric currents by means of mechanical effects produced by a current-carrying coil in a magnetic field. —**gal′va·no·met′ric** (-nō-mĕt′rĭk), **gal′va·no·met′ri·cal** *adj.* —**gal′va·nom′e·try** *n.*

Gal·ves·ton (găl′vĭ-stən) A city of SE TX SSE of Houston on **Galveston Island** at the entrance to **Galveston Bay**, an arm of the Gulf of Mexico. Pop. 57,247.

Gal·way (gôl′wā′) A region of W-central Ireland bordering on **Galway Bay**, an inlet of the Atlantic. The city of **Galway** (pop. 37,835) was incorp. in the late 14th cent.

gal·yak (găl′yăk′) *n.* A flat glossy fur made from the pelt of a stillborn lamb or kid. [Russ. dialectal *golyak*, sheepskin coat of smooth fur < Russ. *golyĭ*, smooth, bald, naked.]

SENEGAL
50 mi
Banjul
GAMBIA
SENEGAL
GUINEA-BISSAU
ATLANTIC OCEAN

Gambia

gam¹ (găm) *n.* **1.** A social visit or friendly interchange, esp. between whalers or seafarers. **2.** A herd of whales or a social congregation of whalers, esp. at sea. ❖ *v.* **gammed, gam·ming, gams** —*intr.* To hold a visit, esp. while at sea. —*tr.* **1.** To visit with. **2.** To spend (time) talking or visiting. [Perh. short for GAMMON² or var. of GAME¹.]

gam² (găm) *n. Slang* A person's leg. [Prob. < Polari (theatrical argot) < Ital. *gamba* < LLat., hoof. See GAMBOL.]

gam– *pref.* Variant of **gamo–**.

Ga·ma (găm′ə, gä′mə), **Vasco da** 1460?–1524. Portuguese explorer and colonial administrator who was the first European to sail to India (1497–98).

ga·may (gă-mā′, găm′ā) *n.* Any of several related red grapes used for making red wines, esp. Beaujolais. [Fr., after *Gamay,* a village of E-central France.]

gam·ba (găm′bə, gäm′-) *n.* See **viola da gamba.**

gam·ba·do¹ (găm-bā′dō) *n., pl.* **-does** or **-dos 1.** A low leap of a horse in which all four feet leave the ground. **2.** A leaping or gamboling movement. [Alteration of Fr. *gambade* < Ital. *gambata* < OItal. See GAMBOL.]

gam·ba·do² (găm-bā′dō) *n., pl.* **-does** or **-dos 1.** Either of a pair of protective leather gaiters attached to a saddle. **2.** A rider's legging. [< Ital. *gamba,* leg < OItal. See GAMBOL.]

Gam·bi·a (găm′bē-ə) A country of W Africa on the Atlantic Ocean; gained independence from Great Britain in 1965. Cap. Banjul. Pop. 1,081,000. —**Gam′bi·an** *adj. & n.*

Gambia River A river of W Africa flowing c. 1,126 km (700 mi) from N Guinea to the Atlantic Ocean at Banjul.

gam·bier also **gam·bir** (găm′bîr) *n.* A resinous astringent extract obtained from the leaves of a woody vine *(Uncaria gambir)* of Malaysia and Indonesia, used medicinally and in tanning and dyeing. [Malay *gambir.*]

Gambier Islands An island group of French Polynesia in the S-central Pacific Ocean.

gam·bit (găm′bĭt) *n.* **1.** An opening in chess in which a minor piece, or pieces, is offered in exchange for a favorable position. **2.** A maneuver, stratagem, or ploy, esp. one used at an initial stage. **3.** A remark intended to open a conversation. [Ult. < Sp. *gambito* < Ital. *gambetto,* act of tripping someone up in wrestling < *gamba,* leg < OItal. See GAMBOL.]

USAGE NOTE Critics familiar with the nature of chess gambits have sometimes maintained that the word should not be used in an extended sense except to refer to maneuvers that involve the tactical sacrifice or loss of some advantage. But *gambit* is well established in the general sense of "maneuver" and in the related sense of "a remark intended to open a conversation."

gam·ble (găm′bəl) *v.* **-bled, -bling, -bles** —*intr.* **1a.** To bet on an uncertain outcome, as of a contest. **b.** To play a game of chance for stakes. **2.** To take a risk in the hope of gaining an advantage or a benefit. **3.** To engage in reckless or hazardous behavior. —*tr.* **1.** To put up as a stake in gambling; wager. **2.** To expose to hazard; risk. ❖ *n.* **1.** A bet, wager, or other gambling venture. **2.** An act or undertaking of uncertain outcome; a risk. [Perh. < obsolete *gamel,* to play games < ME *gamen, gamenen,* to play < OE *gamenian < gamen,* fun.] —**gam′bler** *n.*

gam·boge (găm-bōj′, -bōozh′) *n.* **1.** An orangish resin that is obtained from several trees of the genus *Garcinia* of south-central Asia and that yields a golden yellow pigment. **2.** A strong reddish yellow. [NLat. *cambugium, gambogium,* after CAMBODIA.] —**gam·boge′** *adj.*

gam·bol (găm′bəl) *intr.v.* **-boled, -bol·ing, -bols** or **-bolled, -bol·ling, -bols** To leap about playfully; frolic. ❖ *n.* A playful skipping or frolicking about. [Alteration of Fr. *gambade,* horse's jump < OFr., perh. < OItal. *gambata < gamba,* leg < LLat., hoof, perh. < Gk. *kampē,* bend.]

gam·brel (găm′brəl) *n.* **1.** The hock of a horse or other animal. **2.** A frame used by butchers for hanging carcasses by the legs. [Fr. dialectal *gamberel* < ONFr. < *gambe,* leg < LLat. *gamba,* hoof. See GAMBOL.]

gambrel roof *n.* A two-sided roof with a double slope on each side, the lower slope having the steeper pitch.

gam·bu·sia (găm-byōō′zhə) *n.* Any of various small livebearing fish of the genus *Gambusia* that feed on mosquito larvae and are often used in mosquito control. [NLat. *Gambusia,* genus name < Am.Sp. *gambusino.*]

game¹ (gām) *n.* **1.** An activity providing entertainment or amusement; a pastime. **2a.** A competitive activity or sport in which players contend with each other according to a set of rules. **b.** A single instance of such an activity. **c. games** An organized athletic program or contest. **d.** A period of competition or challenge. **3a.** The total number of points required to win a game. **b.** The score accumulated at any given time in a game. **4.** The equipment needed for playing certain games. **5.** A particular style or manner of playing a game. **6.** *Informal* **a.** An active interest or pursuit, esp. one involving competitive engagement or adherence to rules. **b.** A business or occupation; a line. **c.** An illegal activity; a racket. **7.** *Informal* **a.** Evasive, trifling, or manipulative behavior. **b.** A calculated strategy or approach; a scheme. **8.** *Mathematics* A model of a competitive situation that identifies interested parties and stipulates rules governing all aspects of the competition, used

in game theory. **9a.** Wild animals, birds, or fish hunted for food or sport. **b.** The flesh of these animals, eaten as food. **10a.** An object of attack, ridicule, or pursuit. **b.** Mockery; sport. ❖ *v.* **gamed, gam·ing, games** —*tr. Archaic* To waste or lose by gambling. —*intr.* To play for stakes; gamble. ❖ *adj.* **gam·er, gam·est 1.** Plucky and unyielding in spirit; resolute. **2.** Ready and willing. —*idiom:* **the only game in town** *Informal* The only alternative. [ME < OE *gamen.*] —**game′ly** *adv.* —**game′ness** *n.*

game² (gām) *adj.* **gam·er, gam·est** Crippled; lame. [?]

game bird *n.* A bird that is widely hunted for sport.

game·cock (gām′kŏk′) *n.* A rooster trained for cockfighting.

game fish *n.* See **sport fish.**

game·keep·er (gām′kē′pər) *n.* One who is employed to protect and maintain game birds and animals.

gam·e·lan (găm′ə-lăn′) *n.* An Indonesian orchestra composed mainly of tuned percussion instruments such as bamboo xylophones and gongs. [Javanese < O Javanese *gamĕlan,* percussion instrument, ensemble of percussion instruments < *gamĕl,* to play a percussion instrument.]

game law *n.* A regulation intended for the management or conservation of game animals.

game of chance *n.* A game in which the winner is determined by a chance event, as by drawing numbers.

game plan *n.* **1.** *Sports* The strategy devised before or used during an event. **2.** A strategy for reaching an objective.

game point *n.* **1.** A situation in a game, esp. tennis, in which one side or player needs only one point to win. **2.** The winning point in a game.

gam·er (gā′mər) *n.* One who plays a game, esp. a role-playing or computer game.

game show *n.* A television show in which contestants compete for prizes by playing games of knowledge or chance.

games·man·ship (gāmz′mən-shĭp′) *n.* **1.** The art or practice of using tactical maneuvers to further one's aims or better one's position. **2.** The use in a sport or game of aggressive, often dubious tactics, to win.

game·some (gām′səm) *adj.* Frolicsome; playful. —**game′some·ly** *adv.* —**game′some·ness** *n.*

game·ster (gām′stər) *n.* One who plays games, esp. a gambler.

gam·e·tan·gi·um (găm′ĭ-tăn′jē-əm) *n., pl.* **-gi·a** (-jē-ə) An organ or a cell in which gametes are produced. [GAMET(O)– + Gk. *angeion,* dim. of *angos,* vessel + –IUM.] —**gam′e·tan′gi·al** (-əl) *adj.*

gam·ete (găm′ēt′, gə-mēt′) *n.* A reproductive cell having the haploid number of chromosomes, esp. a mature sperm or egg capable of fusing with a gamete of the opposite sex to produce the fertilized egg. [NLat. *gameta* < Gk. *gametē,* wife and *gametēs,* husband < *gamein,* to marry < *gamos,* marriage.] —**ga·met′ic** (-mĕt′ĭk) *adj.*

gamete intrafallopian transfer *n.* A technique of assisted reproduction in which eggs and sperm are inserted directly into a woman's fallopian tubes.

game theory *n.* A mathematical method of decision-making in which a competitive situation is analyzed to determine the optimal course of action for an interested party.

gameto– or **gamet–** *pref.* Gamete: gametogenesis. [< NLat. *gameta,* gamete. See GAMETE.]

ga·me·to·cyte (gə-mē′tə-sīt′) *n.* A cell from which gametes develop by meiotic division, esp. a spermatocyte or an oocyte.

ga·me·to·gen·e·sis (gə-mē′tə-jĕn′ĭ-sĭs) *n.* The formation or production of gametes. —**ga·me′to·gen′ic, gam′e·tog′e·nous** (găm′ĭ-tŏj′ə-nəs) *adj.*

ga·me·to·phore (gə-mē′tə-fôr′, -fōr′) *n.* A structure, as in liverworts and mosses, on which gametangia are borne. —**ga·me′to·phor′ic** (-fôr′ĭk, -fōr′-) *adj.*

ga·me·to·phyte (gə-mē′tə-fīt′) *n.* The gamete-producing individual or phase of an organism such as a fungus or plant, characterized by alternation of generations. —**ga·me′to·phyt′ic** (-fĭt′ĭk) *adj.*

gam·ey (gā′mē) *adj.* Variant of **gamy.**

gam·ic (găm′ĭk) *adj.* Of or requiring fertilization to reproduce; sexual.

gam·in (găm′ĭn) *n.* An often homeless boy who roams about the streets; an urchin. [Fr.]

ga·mine (gă-mēn′, găm′ēn) *n.* **1.** An often homeless girl who roams about the streets; an urchin. **2.** A girl or woman of impish appeal. [Fr., fem. of *gamin,* gamin.]

gam·ing (gā′mĭng) *n.* **1.** Gambling. **2.** The playing of games, esp. video games.

gam·ma (găm′ə) *n.* **1.** The third letter of the Greek alphabet. **2.** The third item in a series or system of classification. **3.** A unit of magnetic intensity equal to one hundred thousandth (10^{-5}) of an oersted. **4.** A unit of mass equal to one millionth (10^{-6}) of a gram. **5.** *Chemistry* The third position from a designated carbon atom in an organic molecule at which an atom or radical may be substituted. [ME < Gk. < Phoenician **gaml,* throwstick (sense uncertain), third letter of the Phoenician alphabet.]

gam·ma-a·mi·no·bu·tyr·ic acid (găm′ə-ə-mē′nō-byōō-tîr′ĭk, -ăm′ə-) *n.* An amino acid, $C_4H_9NO_2$, that occurs in the central nervous system and is associated with the transmission of nerve impulses.

gambrel roof

gamelan

Indira Gandhi

Mahatma Gandhi

gantry
cargo lifted onto a
container ship

gamma correction *n.* A correction to the contrast of displayed images on a cathode ray-tube that compensates for the fact that the brightness of an image is not linearly related to the input voltage.

gamma globulin also **gam·ma·glob·u·lin** (găm′ə-glŏb′yə-lĭn) *n.* A protein fraction of blood serum containing numerous antibodies, used to immunize against bacterial and viral infectious diseases.

gam·ma-hy·drox·y·bu·ty·rate (găm′ə-hī-drŏk′sē-byōō′tə-rāt′) *n.* A compound similar in structure and function to gamma-aminobutyric acid, used illegally in synthetic form for its euphoric effects and known as a date-rape drug.

gamma ray *n.* Electromagnetic radiation emitted by radioactive decay and having energies in a range from ten thousand (10^4) to ten million (10^7) electron volts.

gam·ma-ray burst (găm′ə-rā′) *n.* A short-lived, localized, and intense burst of gamma radiation that originates outside the solar system from an unknown source.

gam·mer (găm′ər) *n. Chiefly British* An elderly woman. [Prob. alteration (influenced by GRANDMOTHER) of GODMOTHER.]

gam·mon¹ (găm′ən) *n.* A victory in backgammon reached before the loser has succeeded in removing a single piece. ❖ *tr.v.* **-moned, -mon·ing, -mons** To defeat in backgammon by scoring a gammon. [Prob. < ME *gamen, gammen*, game < OE *gamen.*]

gam·mon² (găm′ən) *Chiefly British n.* **1.** Misleading or nonsensical talk; humbug. **2. Gammon** See Shelta. ❖ *v.* **-moned, -mon·ing, -mons** —*tr.* To mislead by deceptive talk. —*intr.* To talk misleadingly or deceptively. [?] —**gam′mon·er** *n.*

gam·mon³ (găm′ən) *n.* **1.** A cured or smoked ham. **2.** The lower part of a side of bacon. [ME *gambon* < ONFr. < *gambe*, leg < LLat. *gamba*, hoof. See GAMBOL.]

gam·mon⁴ (găm′ən) *tr.v.* **-moned, -mon·ing, -mons** To fasten (a bowsprit) to the stem of a ship. [?]

gamo– or **gam–** *pref.* **1.** United; joined: *gamopetalous*. **2.** Sexual: *gamogenesis*. [Gk., marriage < *gamos.*]

gam·o·gen·e·sis (găm′ə-jĕn′ĭ-sĭs) *n.* Sexual reproduction. —**gam′o·ge·net′ic** (-jə-nĕt′ĭk) *adj.*

gam·o·pet·al·ous (găm′ə-pĕt′l-əs) *adj.* Having or being a corolla with partially or wholly fused petals.

gam·o·phyl·lous (găm′ə-fĭl′əs) *adj.* Having or being united leaves or leaflike parts.

gam·o·sep·al·ous (găm′ə-sĕp′ə-ləs) *adj.* Having or being united or partly united sepals.

–gamous *suff.* **1a.** Having a specified number of marriages: *monogamous*. **b.** Practicing a specified kind of marriage: *exogamous*. **2.** Having a specified kind of reproduction or reproductive organs: *heterogamous*. [< Gk. *-gamos < gamos*, marriage.]

Ga·mow (gä′mou, găm′ôf, -ôf), George 1904–68. Russian-born Amer. nuclear physicist known for his work on radioactivity and genetic information.

gamp (gămp) *n. Chiefly British* A large baggy umbrella. [After Mrs. Sarah Gamp, in *Martin Chuzzlewit* by Dickens.]

gam·ut (găm′ət) *n.* **1.** A complete range or extent. **2.** *Music* The entire series of recognized notes. [ME, the musical scale < Med.Lat. *gamma ut*, low G : *gamma*, lowest note of the medieval scale (< Gk., gamma; see GAMMA) + *ut*, first note of the lowest hexachord (after *ut*, first word in a Latin hymn to St. John the Baptist, the initial syllables of successive lines of which were sung to the notes of an ascending scale CDEFGA: *Ut* queant laxis resonare fibris *Mi*ra gestorum *fa*muli tuorum, *Sol*ve polluti *la*bii reatum, Sancte Iohannes).]

gam·y also **gam·ey** (gā′mē) *adj.* **-i·er, -i·est 1a.** Having the flavor or odor of game, esp. slightly spoiled game. **b.** Ill-smelling; rank. **2.** Showing an unyielding spirit; plucky. **3a.** Corrupt; tainted. **b.** Sordid; seamy. **c.** Sexually suggestive; racy. —**gam′i·ly** *adv.* —**gam′i·ness** *n.*

–gamy *suff.* **1.** Marriage: *exogamy*. **2.** Procreative or propagative union: *allogamy*. **3.** The possession of a specified manner of fertilization or specified reproductive organs: *apogamy*. [Gk. *-gamiā < gamos*, marriage.]

ga·nache (gə-näsh′) *n.* A rich icing of chocolate and cream heated and stirred together. [Fr.]

Gän·cä (gän-jä′) Formerly **Ki·ro·va·bad** (kĭ-rō′və-băd′, kyĭ′rə-və-bät′) A city of W Azerbaijan SE of Tbilisi. Pop. 261,000.

gan·der (găn′dər) *n.* **1.** A male goose. **2.** *Informal* A look or glance. **3.** *Informal* A simpleton; a ninny. [ME < OE *gandra*. See ghans- in App.]

Gan·dhi (gän′dē, găn′-), **Indira Nehru** 1917–84. Indian politician and prime minister (1966–77 and 1980–84).

Gandhi, Mohandas Karamchand Known as "Mahatma Gandhi." 1869–1948. Indian nationalist and spiritual leader who developed the practice of nonviolent disobedience that forced Great Britain to grant independence to India (1947).

gan·dy dancer (găn′dē) *n. Slang* **1.** A railroad worker. **2.** An itinerant laborer. [?]

ga·nef or **ga·nof** also **gon·if** (gä′nəf) *n.* A thief, scoundrel, or rascal. [Yiddish < Heb. *gannāb*, to steal.]

Ga·nesh (gə-nāsh′) also **Ga·ne·sha** (-nā′shə) *n. Hinduism* The god of wisdom and the remover of obstacles, depicted as a short fat man with an elephant's head. [Hindi *Gaṇeś < Skt. Gaṇeśaḥ < gaṇeśaḥ*, master of throngs : *gaṇaḥ*, throng, group of followers + *īśaḥ*, master (< *īṣṭe, īś-*, he rules over).]

gang¹ (găng) *n.* **1.** A group of criminals or hoodlums who band together for mutual protection and profit. **2.** A group of adolescents who band together, esp. a group of delinquents. **3.** *Informal* A group of people who associate regularly on a social basis. **4.** A group of laborers organized together on one job or under one supervisor. **5.** A matched or coordinated set, as of tools. **6a.** A pack of wolves or wild dogs. **b.** A herd, esp. of buffalo or elk. ❖ *v.* **ganged, gang·ing, gangs** —*intr.* To band together as a group or gang. —*tr.* **1.** To arrange or assemble into a group, as for simultaneous operation or production. **2.** To attack as an organized group. —*phrasal verb:* **gang up 1.** To join together in opposition or attack. **2.** To act together as a group. [ME, band of men < OE, journey, and ON *-gangr*, journey, group (as in *thjofa-gangr*, gang of thieves).]

gang² (găng) *n.* Variant of **gangue.**

gang·bang or **gang-bang** (găng′băng′) *n. Vulgar Slang* **1.** Rape or sexual intercourse involving one person and several others in succession. **2.** Sexual intercourse involving several partners. ❖ *v.* **-banged, -bang·ing, -bangs** —*intr. Vulgar Slang* To participate as an aggressor in a gangbang. **2.** *Slang* To participate in violent gang-related activities. —*tr. Vulgar Slang* To subject to a gangbang.

gang·bang·er (găng′băng′ər) *n.* **1.** *Slang* A member of a violent street gang. **2.** *Vulgar Slang* One who takes part as an aggressor in a gangbang.

gang·bus·ter (găng′bŭs′tər) *n. Slang* A law enforcement officer who breaks up organized criminal groups. —*idiom:* **like gangbusters** *Slang* With great impact, vigor, or zeal.

Gan·ges (găn′jēz′) also **Gan·ga** (gŭng′gə) A river of N India and Bangladesh rising in the Himalaya Mts. and flowing c. 2,510 km (1,560 mi) to the Bay of Bengal.

gang·land (găng′lănd′, -lənd) *n.* The underworld of organized criminal gangs. —**gang′land′** *adj.*

gan·gli·at·ed (găng′glē-ā′tĭd) also **gan·gli·ate** (-ĭt, -āt′) *adj.* Having ganglia.

gan·gling (găng′glĭng) *adj.* Awkwardly tall or long-limbed. [Perh. < dialectal *gang*, to go < ME *gangen* < OE *gangan*.]

gan·gli·on (găng′glē-ən) *n.,* pl. **-gli·a** (-glē-ə) or **-gli·ons 1.** A group of nerve cells forming a nerve center, esp. one located outside the brain or spinal cord. **2.** A center of power, activity, or energy. **3.** *Pathology* A benign cystic lesion resembling a tumor, occurring in a tendon sheath or joint capsule. [< Gk., cystlike tumor, nerve bundle.] —**gan′gli·on′ic** (-ŏn′ĭk) *adj.*

gan·gli·o·side (găng′glē-ə-sīd′) *n.* Any of a group of galactose-containing cerebrosides found in the surface membranes of nerve cells. [GANGLI(ON) + -OS(E)² + -IDE.]

gan·gly (găng′glē) *adj.* **-gli·er, -gli·est** Gangling.

gang·plank (găng′plăngk′) *n.* A board or ramp used as a removable footway between a ship and a pier. [< GANG¹, way (obsolete and dialectal).]

gang·plow (găng′plou′) *n.* A plow equipped with several blades that make parallel furrows.

gan·grel (găng′rəl) *n. Scots* A vagabond; a drifter. [ME, prob. < *gangen*, to go. See GANGLING.]

gan·grene (găng′grēn′, găng-grēn′) *n.* Death and decay of body tissue, often occurring in a limb, caused by insufficient blood supply and usu. following injury or disease. ❖ *tr. & intr.v.* **-grened, -gren·ing, -grenes** To affect or become affected with gangrene. [Med.Lat. *cancrēna* < Lat. *gangrēna* < Gk. *gangraina*.] —**gan′gre·nous** (găng′grə-nəs) *adj.*

gang·sta rap (găng′stə) also **gangster rap** *n.* A style of rap music associated with urban street gangs and characterized by violent and often misogynistic lyrics. [< African American Vernacular E. *gangsta*, gangster, alteration of GANGSTER.]

gang·ster (găng′stər) *n.* **1.** A member of an organized group of criminals. **2.** A member of a gang of antisocial, often criminal, young people. —**gang′ster·dom** *n.* —**gang′ster·ism** *n.*

gangue also **gang** (găng) *n.* Worthless rock or other material in which valuable minerals are found. [Fr. < Ger. *Gang*, lode < MHGer. *ganc* < OHGer. *gang*, a going.]

gang·way (găng′wā′) *n.* **1.** *Nautical* **a.** A passage along either side of a ship's upper deck. **b.** See gangplank. **c.** An opening in the bulwark of a ship through which passengers may board. **2.** A narrow passageway, as of boards laid on the ground. **3.** The main level of a mine. **4.** *Chiefly British* **a.** The aisle that divides the front and rear seating sections of the House of Commons. **b.** An aisle between seating sections, as in a theater. ❖ *interj.* Used to clear a passage through a crowded area. [< GANG¹, way, passage (obsolete, dial.).]

gan·is·ter also **gan·nis·ter** (găn′ĭ-stər) *n.* **1.** A fine-grained quartzite used to line refractory furnaces. **2.** A mixture of fire clay and ground quartz lining metallurgical furnaces. [?]

gan·ja (gän′jə) *n.* Marijuana, esp. of a highly resinous form prepared from the flowering tops and leaves of selected plants. [Hindi *gāmjhā*, hemp resin < Skt. *gāñjyā-*, of hemp < *gañjaḥ*, hemp, alteration of *gṛñjaḥ*.]

Gan Jiang (gän′ jyäng′) also **Kan River** (kän) A river of SE China flowing c. 885 km (550 mi) generally N to the Chang Jiang R. (Yangtze) N of Nanchang.

gan·net (găn′ĭt) *n.* Any of several large sea birds of the genus

Morus, esp. *M. bassanus* of northern Atlantic coastal regions, having white plumage with black wingtips. [ME *ganet* < OE *ganot.* See **ghans-** in App.]

ga·nof (gä′nəf) *n.* Variant of **ganef.**

gan·oid (gän′oid′) *adj.* Of, relating to, or characteristic of certain bony fishes, such as the gar, having armorlike scales of bony plates covered with layers of dentine and enamel. [< NLat. *Ganoideī,* subclass name < Gk. *ganos,* brightness < *ganusthai,* to rejoice.] —**gan′oid** *n.*

Gan·su (gän′sōo′) also **Kan·su** (kän′sōo′, gän′-) A province of N-central China; long a corridor for the Silk Road to Turkistan, India, and Persia. Cap. Lanzhou. Pop. 22,371,141.

gant·let[1] (gônt′lĭt, gänt′-) *n.* A section of double railroad tracks formed by the temporary convergence of two parallel tracks so that each set remains independent, affording passage at a narrow place without need of switching. ❖ *tr.v.* **-let·ed, -let·ing, -lets** To converge (railroad tracks) to form a gantlet. [Variant of GAUNTLET[2].]

gant·let[2] (gônt′lĭt, gänt′-) *n.* Variant of **gauntlet**[1].

gant·let[3] (gônt′lĭt, gänt′-) *n.* Variant of **gauntlet**[2].

gan·try (gän′trē) *n., pl.* **-tries 1.** A mount for a traveling crane consisting of a large archlike or bridgelike frame designed to move along a set of tracks. **2.** A similar spanning frame supporting a group of railway signals over several tracks. **3.** *Aerospace* A massive vertical frame structure used in assembling or servicing a rocket. **4.** A support for a barrel lying on its side. [ME *ganter, gauntre,* wooden stand for barrels < ONFr. *gantier,* wooden frame < Lat. *canthērius* < Gk. *kanthēlios,* pack ass < *kanthēlia,* panniers.]

Gan·y·mede (gän′ə-mēd′) *n.* **1.** *Greek Mythology* A beautiful boy carried away by Zeus to be the gods' cupbearer. **2.** A satellite of Jupiter. [Lat. *Ganymēdēs* < Gk. *Ganumēdēs.*]

GAO *abbr.* General Accounting Office

gaol (jäl) *n. & v. Chiefly British* Variant of **jail.**

Gao Xing·jian (gou′ shĭng′jyän′) b. 1940. Chinese-born novelist and playwright who won the 2000 Nobel Prize for literature.

gap (gäp) *n.* **1a.** An opening in a solid structure or surface; a cleft or breach: *a gap in the fence.* **b.** A break in a line of defense. **2.** An opening through mountains; a pass. **3.** A space between objects or points; an aperture: *a gap between his front teeth.* **4.** An interruption of continuity. **5a.** A conspicuous difference or imbalance; a disparity. **b.** A problematic situation resulting from such a disparity. **6.** A spark gap. **7.** *Computer Science* An absence of information on a recording medium, often used to signal the end of a segment of information. **8.** *Electronics* The distance between the head of a recording device and the surface of the recording medium. ❖ *v.* **gapped, gap·ping, gaps** —*tr.* To make an opening in. —*intr.* To be or become open. [ME < ON, chasm.]

gape (gāp, gäp) *intr.v.* **gaped, gap·ing, gapes 1.** To open the mouth wide; yawn. **2.** To stare wonderingly or stupidly, often with the mouth open. **3.** To open wide. ❖ *n.* **1.** The act or an instance of gaping. **2.** A large opening. **3.** *Zoology* The width of the space between the open jaws or mandibles of a vertebrate. **4. gapes** (*used with a sing. verb*) A disease of birds caused by gapeworms and resulting in obstructed breathing. **5. gapes** A fit of yawning. [ME *gapen* < ON *gapa.*]

gape·worm (gāp′wûrm′, gäp′-) *n.* A nematode worm (*Syngamus trachea*) that infects certain birds and causes gapes.

gap·ing (gā′pĭng) *adj.* Deep and wide open. —**gap′ing·ly** *adv.*

gap junction *n.* An intercellular network of protein channels that facilitates the cell-to-cell passage of ions, hormones, and neurotransmitters.

gar[1] *n.* **1.** Any of several ganoid fishes of the family Lepisosteidae of North and Central America, having long narrow jaws, an elongated body, and a long snout. **2.** A similar or related fish, such as the needlefish. [Short for GARFISH.]

gar[2] (gär) *tr.v.* **garred, gar·ring, gars** *Scots* To cause or compel. [ME *geren* < ON *gera,* to make.]

GAR *abbr.* Grand Army of the Republic

ga·rage (gə-räzh′, -räj′) *n.* **1.** A building or indoor space in which to park or keep a motor vehicle. **2.** A commercial establishment where cars are repaired, serviced, or parked. ❖ *tr.v.* **-raged, -rag·ing, -rag·es** To put or store in a garage. [Fr. < *garer,* to shelter < OFr. *garer, guerrer,* of Gmc. origin.] —**ga·rage′a·ble** *adj.*

garage sale *n.* A sale of used household belongings, typically held outdoors at the home of the seller.

ga·ram ma·sa·la (gä-räm′ mä-sä′lä) *n.* A seasoning made by blending dry-roasted, ground spices, such as black pepper, cumin, and cloves, used in the cooking of northern India. [Urdu *garm maṣāliḥ, garam masālā,* hot spices : *garm, garam,* hot, burning (< Pers. *garm* < MPers. < OPers. *garma-,* in *garma-pada,* entrance of the heat, month name; see **g**ʷ**her-** in App.) + *maṣāliḥ,* ingredients, mixture of spices (< Pers. *masālaḥ* < Ar. *maṣāliḥ,* pl. of *maṣlaha,* benefit < *ṣalaḥa,* to be good).]

Ga·rand (gə-rănd′, găr′ənd) *n.* See **M-1.** [After John Cantius *Garand* (1888–1974), Canadian-born American inventor.]

garb (gärb) *n.* **1.** A distinctive style or form of clothing; dress. **2.** An outward appearance; a guise. ❖ *tr.v.* **garbed, garb·ing, garbs** To cover with or as if with clothing; dress. [Obsolete Fr. *garbe,* grace < Ital. *garbo < garbare,* to please, of Gmc. origin.]

gar·bage (gär′bĭj) *n.* **1a.** Food wastes, as from a kitchen. **b.** Refuse; trash. **2.** A place or receptacle where rubbish is discarded. **3a.** Worthless or nonsensical matter; rubbish. **b.** Inferior or offensive literary or artistic material. [ME, offal from fowls.]

gar·ban·zo (gär-bän′zō) *n., pl.* **-zos** See **chickpea.** [Sp., alteration of OSpan. *arvanço,* perh. < Gk. *erebinthos.*]

gar·ble (gär′bəl) *tr.v.* **-bled, -bling, -bles 1.** To mix up or distort so as to make misleading or incomprehensible. **2.** To scramble (a signal or message), as by faulty transmission. **3.** *Archaic* To sort out; cull. ❖ *n.* The act or an instance of garbling. [ME *garbelen,* to clean spices < AN *garbeler,* to sift, and < Med.Lat. *garbellāre,* both < Ar. *ǵarbala,* to select < *ǵirbāl,* sieve < LLat. *crībellum,* dim. of Lat. *crībrum.* See **krei-** in App.] —**gar′bler** (-blər) *n.*

Gar·bo (gär′bō), **Greta** 1905–90. Swedish-born Amer. actress whose films include *Camille* (1937).

gar·board (gär′bôrd′, -bōrd′) *n.* The first range or strake of planks laid next to a ship's keel. [Obsolete Du. *gaarboord* : poss. Du. *gaar,* cooked, done (< MDu. *gaer*) + Du. *boord,* board (< MDu. *boort*).]

gar·boil (gär′boil′) *n. Archaic* Confusion; uproar. [Obsolete Fr. *garbouil,* ult. perh. < Lat. *bullīre,* to boil.]

Gar·ci·a (gär-sē′ə), **Jerome John** Known as "Jerry." 1942–95. Amer. musician who was the cofounder and lead guitarist of the folk-rock group the Grateful Dead (1965–95).

Gar·cí·a Lor·ca (gär-sē′ə lôr′kä), **Federico** 1898–1936. Spanish poet and playwright whose works include *Poet in New York* (1940).

Gar·cí·a Már·quez (gär-sē′ə mär′kəs, -kēs), **Gabriel** b. 1928. Colombian-born writer who won the 1982 Nobel Prize for literature.

Gar·cí·a Ro·bles (gär-sē′ə rō′bləs, -blěs), **Alfonso** 1911–91. Mexican diplomat who shared the 1982 Nobel Peace Prize.

gar·çon (gär-sôN′) *n., pl.* **-çons** (-sôN′) A waiter. [Fr. < OFr. *garçun,* servant, accusative of *gars,* boy, soldier, prob. of Gmc. orig.]

Gar·da (gär′də), **Lake** A lake of N Italy E of Milan.

gar·dant (gär′dnt) *adj. Heraldry* Variant of **guardant.**

gar·den (gär′dn) *n.* **1.** A plot of land for the cultivation of flowers, vegetables, herbs, or fruit. **2.** Grounds laid out with flowers, trees, and ornamental shrubs, used for recreation or display. Often used in the plural. **3.** A yard or lawn. **4.** A fertile, well-cultivated region. **5a.** An open-air establishment where refreshments are served. **b.** A large public auditorium or arena. ❖ *v.* **-dened, -den·ing, -dens** —*tr.* **1.** To cultivate (a plot) as a garden. **2.** To furnish with a garden. —*intr.* **1.** To plant or tend a garden. **2.** To work as a gardener. ❖ *adj.* **1.** Of, suitable to, or used in a garden. **2.** Provided with open areas and greenery. **3.** Garden-variety. —*idiom:* **lead (or take) down the garden path** To mislead or deceive (another). [ME *gardin* < ONFr. < *gart,* of Gmc. orig. See **gher-** in App.]

Garden, Alexander 1730?–91. Scottish-born Amer. naturalist and physician who contributed to the classification of New World plants.

garden apartment *n.* A unit in a low-rise apartment complex that includes open, usu. landscaped ground.

garden city *n.* A residential community combining a pleasant environment with low-density housing and open public land.

garden cress *n.* An annual herb (*Lepidium sativum*) of the mustard family, usu. grown as a salad plant.

gar·den·er (gärd′nər, gär′dn-ər) *n.* One who works in or tends a garden for pleasure or hire.

Garden Grove A city of S CA, a residential suburb of Long Beach and Los Angeles. Pop. 165,196.

garden heliotrope *n.* A widely cultivated valerian (*Valeriana officinalis*) having small fragrant flowers and strong-smelling rhizomes formerly used in medicine.

gar·de·nia (gär-dē′yə) *n.* **1.** Any of various shrubs or trees of the Old World tropics that belong to the genus *Gardenia,* esp. *G. jasminoides* native to China, having glossy evergreen leaves and large, fragrant, usu. white flowers. **2.** The flower of this plant. [NLat. *Gardenia,* genus name, after Alexander GARDEN.]

Garden of Eden *n.* See **Eden** 1.

gar·den·va·ri·e·ty (gärd′n-və-rī′ĭ-tē) *adj.* Common; unremarkable.

garde·robe (gärd′rōb′) *n. Archaic* **1a.** A chamber for storing clothes; a wardrobe. **b.** The contents of a wardrobe. **2.** A private chamber. [ME < OFr. : *garder,* to keep; see GUARD + *robe,* robe; see ROBE.]

Gard·ner (gärd′nər), **Erle Stanley** 1889–1970. Amer. lawyer and detective novelist best known for his character Perry Mason.

Gar·eth (gär′ĭth) *n.* In Arthurian legend, a nephew of King Arthur and one of the Knights of the Round Table.

Gar·field (gär′fēld′), **James Abram** 1831–81. The 20th President of the US (1881); assassinated by Charles Guiteau (1841–82), a frustrated office-seeker.

gar·fish (gär′fĭsh′) *n., pl.* **garfish** or **-fish·es** See **gar**[1]. [ME : *gare,* spear (< OE *gār*) + *fish,* fish; see FISH.]

gar·gan·tu·a (gär-găn′chōo-ə) *n.* A person of great size or stature and voracious physical or intellectual appetites. [After the hero of *Gargantua and Pantagruel* by François Rabelais.]

gar·gan·tu·an (gär-găn′chōo-ən) *adj.* Of immense size, volume, or capacity; gigantic.

Jerry Garcia
photographed in 1987

James A. Garfield
1881 portrait by Ole P.H.
Balling (1823–1906)

ă pat   oi boy
ā pay   ou out
âr care   ŏŏ took
ä father ōō boot
ĕ pet   ŭ cut
ē be   ûr urge
ĭ pit   th thin
ī pie   th this
îr pier   hw which
ŏ pot   zh vision
ō toe   ə about,
ô paw   item

Stress marks:
′ (primary);
′ (secondary), as in
lexicon (lěk′sĭ-kŏn′)

gar·get (gär'gĭt) *n.* Mastitis of domestic animals, esp. cattle. [Perh. < ME, throat < OFr. *gargate.*]

gar·gle (gär'gəl) *v.* **-gled, -gling, -gles** —*intr.* **1.** To force exhaled air through a liquid held in the back of the mouth, with the head tilted back, in order to cleanse or medicate the mouth or throat. **2.** To produce the sound of gargling when speaking or singing. —*tr.* **1.** To rinse or medicate by gargling. **2.** To circulate or apply by gargling. **3.** To utter with a gargling sound. ❖ *n.* **1.** A medicated solution for gargling. **2.** A gargling sound. [Fr. *gargouiller* < OFr.]

gar·goyle (gär'goil') *n.* **1.** A roof spout in the form of a grotesque or fantastic creature projecting from a gutter to carry rainwater clear of the wall. **2.** A grotesque ornamental figure or projection. **3.** A person of bizarre or grotesque appearance. [ME *gargoile* < OFr. *gargole, gargouille,* throat, waterspout.]

gar·i·bal·di (gär'ə-bôl'dē) *n., pl.* **-dis** **1.** A loose high-necked blouse styled after the red shirts worn by Garibaldi and his soldiers. **2.** A usu. bright orange damselfish (*Hypsypops rubicundus*) native to coastal marine waters of southern California. [After Giuseppe GARIBALDI.]

Gar·i·bal·di (gär'ə-bôl'dē, gä'rē-bäl'dē), **Giuseppe** 1807–82. Italian general whose conquests led to the formation of the kingdom of Italy (1861).

Ga·ri·fu·na (gä'rē-foo'nə) *n., pl.* **Garifuna** or **-nas** A member of a people of mixed Carib and African ancestry living along the Caribbean coast of Honduras, Guatemala, Belize, and Nicaragua. [Am.Sp. *Garífuna* < Proto-Carib **karipona,* Carib.]

gar·ish (gâr'ĭsh, găr'-) *adj.* **1a.** Marked by strident color or excessive ornamentation; gaudy. **b.** Loud and flashy. **2.** Glaring; dazzling. [?] —**gar'ish·ly** *adv.* —**gar'ish·ness** *n.*

gar·land (gär'lənd) *n.* **1a.** A wreath or festoon, esp. one of plaited flowers or leaves, worn on the body or draped as a decoration. **b.** A representation of such a wreath or festoon, used as an architectural ornament or heraldic device. **2.** A mark of honor or tribute; an accolade. **3.** An anthology, as of poems. ❖ *tr.v.* **-land·ed, -land·ing, -lands** **1.** To ornament or deck with a garland. **2.** To form into a garland. [ME < OFr. *garlande,* perh. of Gmc. orig.]

Garland A city of NE TX, a suburb of Dallas. Pop. 215,768.

Garland, (Hannibal) Hamlin 1860–1940. Amer. writer whose works include *Son of the Middle Border* (1917).

Garland, Judy 1922–69. Amer. actress and singer best known for her performance as Dorothy in *The Wizard of Oz* (1939).

garland chrysanthemum *n.* An annual Mediterranean herb (*Chrysanthemum coronarium*) of the composite family, with yellow flower heads and aromatic, bipinnately lobed leaves.

garland flower *n.* A European evergreen shrub (*Daphne cneorum*) having fragrant rose, pink, or white flowers grouped in dense terminal heads.

gar·lic (gär'lĭk) *n.* **1.** An onionlike plant (*Allium sativum*) of southern Europe having a bulb that separates into cloves with a strong distinctive odor and flavor. **2.** The bulb of this plant. ❖ *tr.v.* **-licked, -lick·ing, -licks** To season or flavor (a food) with garlic. [ME < OE *gärlēac : gär,* spear + *lēac,* leek.]

garlic chive *n.* See **Chinese chive.**

gar·lick·y (gär'lĭ-kē) *adj.* Containing, tasting of, or smelling of garlic.

gar·ment (gär'mənt) *n.* An article of clothing. ❖ *tr.v.* **-ment·ed, -ment·ing, -ments** To clothe; dress. [ME < OFr. *garnement* < *garnir,* to equip, of Gmc. orig.]

gar·ner (gär'nər) *tr.v.* **-nered, -ner·ing, -ners** **1.** To gather and store in or as if in a granary. **2.** To amass; acquire. ❖ *n.* **1.** A granary. **2.** An accumulation or collection of something. [ME < OFr. *garner, gerner,* granary < OFr. *gernier, grenier* < Lat. *grānārium.* See GRANARY.]

gar·net¹ (gär'nĭt) *n.* **1.** Any of several common aluminum or calcium silicate minerals occurring in two internally isomorphic series, $(Mg, Mn, Fe)_3Al_2Si_3O_{12}$ and $Ca_3(Cr, Al, Fe)_2Si_3O_{12}$, generally crystallized, colored red, brown, black, green, yellow, or white, and used as gemstones and abrasives. **2.** A dark to very dark red. [ME < OFr. *grenate* < *grenat,* pomegranate-red, prob. < Lat. *grānātum,* pomegranate < neut. of *grānātus,* seedy. See POMEGRANATE.]

gar·net² (gär'nĭt) *n. Nautical* A tackle for hoisting light cargo. [ME *garnet,* prob. < MDu. *garnāt.*]

gar·net·if·er·ous (gär'nĭ-tĭf'ər-əs) *adj.* Containing garnets.

gar·ni·er·ite (gär'nē-ə-rīt') *n.* A pale green or apple-green mineral, $(Ni, Mg)_3Si_2O_5(OH)_4$, used as a gemstone and as a nickel ore. [After Jules *Garnier,* 19th-cent. French geologist.]

gar·nish (gär'nĭsh) *tr.v.* **-nished, -nish·ing, -nish·es** **1a.** To enhance in appearance by adding decorative touches; embellish: *garnished the coat with a fur collar.* **b.** To decorate (prepared food or drink) with colorful or savory items. **2.** *Law* To garnishee. ❖ *n.* **1a.** Ornamentation; embellishment. **b.** An embellishment used to garnish a prepared food or drink. **2.** *Slang* An unwarranted fee, such as one extorted from a new prisoner by a jailer. [ME *garnishen* < OFr. *garnir, garniss-,* of Gmc. orig.]

gar·nish·ee (gär'nĭ-shē') *n.* A third party who has been notified that money or property in his or her hands but belonging to a defendant has been attached. ❖ *tr.v.* **-eed, -ee·ing, -ees** **1.** To seize by garnishment. **2.** To serve with a garnishment.

gargoyle

William Lloyd Garrison
19th-century engraving by
Hezekiah Wright Smith
(1828–?)

gar·nish·ment (gär'nĭsh-mənt) *n.* **1.** *Law* **a.** A legal proceeding whereby money or property due a debtor but in the possession of another is applied to the payment of the debt to the plaintiff. **b.** A court order directing a third party who holds money or property of a defendant to withhold it and appear in court. **2.** Ornamentation; embellishment.

gar·ni·ture (gär'nĭ-chər) *n.* Something that garnishes; an embellishment. [Fr. < OFr. < *garnir,* to garnish. See GARNISH.]

Ga·ronne (gä-rŏn') A river of SW France flowing c. 563 km (350 mi) to the Dordogne R. N of Bordeaux.

gar·pike (gär'pīk') *n.* See **gar¹** 2.

gar·ret (gär'ĭt) *n.* A room on the top floor of a house, typically under a pitched roof; an attic. [ME < OFr. *garite,* watchtower < *garir,* to defend, of Gmc. orig.]

Gar·rick (gär'ĭk), **David** 1717–79. British actor and theater manager noted for his Shakespearean roles.

gar·ri·son (gär'ĭ-sən) *n.* **1.** A military post, esp. one that is permanently established. **2.** The troops stationed at a military post. ❖ *tr.v.* **-soned, -son·ing, -sons** **1.** To assign (troops) to a military post. **2.** To supply (a post) with troops. **3.** To occupy as or convert into a military post. [ME *garison,* fortified place < OFr. < *garir,* to defend, of Gmc. orig.]

Garrison, William Lloyd 1805–79. Amer. abolitionist leader who founded and published *The Liberator* (1831–65), an antislavery journal.

garrison cap *n.* A soft cloth military cap without a visor.

Garrison finish *n.* A finish in a contest or race in which the winner comes from behind at the last moment. [After Edward Henry ("Snapper") *Garrison* (1868–1930), American jockey.]

gar·rote or **gar·rotte** (gə-rŏt', -rōt') *n.* **1a.** A method of execution in which a tightened iron collar is used to strangle or break the neck. **b.** The iron collar used for such an execution. **2a.** Strangulation, esp. in order to rob. **b.** A cord or wire for strangling. ❖ *tr.v.* **-rot·ed, -rot·ing, -rotes** or **-rot·ted, -rot·ting, -rottes** **1.** To execute by garrote. **2.** To strangle in order to rob. [Sp., cudgel, poss. < OFr. *garrot,* perh. < *garoquier,* to struggle.] —**gar·rot'er** *n.*

gar·ru·li·ty (gə-roo'lĭ-tē) *n.* Excessive talkativeness.

gar·ru·lous (gär'ə-ləs, găr'yə-) *adj.* **1.** Given to excessive and often trivial or rambling talk; tiresomely talkative. **2.** Wordy and rambling. [< Lat. *garrulus* < *garrīre,* to chatter.] —**gar'ru·lous·ly** *adv.* —**gar'ru·lous·ness** *n.*

gar·ter (gär'tər) *n.* **1a.** An elasticized band worn around the leg to hold up a stocking or sock. **b.** A suspender strap with a fastener attached to a girdle or belt to hold up a stocking or sock. **c.** An elasticized band worn around the arm to keep the sleeve pushed up. **2. Garter a.** The badge of the Order of the Garter. **b.** The order itself. **c.** Membership in the order. ❖ *tr.v.* **-tered, -ter·ing, -ters** **1.** To fasten and hold with a garter. **2.** To put a garter on. [ME, band to support socks < ONFr. *gartier* < *garet,* bend of the knee, prob. of Celt. orig.]

garter belt *n.* A flexible band of cloth worn around the waist to which garters are attached to hold up socks or stockings.

garter snake *n.* Any of various striped nonvenomous North and Central American snakes of the genus *Thamnophis.*

garth (gärth) *n.* **1.** A grassy quadrangle surrounded by cloisters. **2.** *Archaic* A yard, garden, or paddock. [ME, enclosed yard < ON *gardhr.* See **gher-** in App.]

Gar·vey (gär'vē), **Marcus (Moziah) Aurelius** 1887–1940. Jamaican Black nationalist who founded the Universal Negro Improvement Association (1914).

Gar·y (gâr'ē, găr'ē) A city of NW IN on Lake Michigan near the IL border; founded c. 1905. Pop. 102,746.

gas (găs) *n., pl.* **gas·es** or **gas·ses** **1a.** The state of matter distinguished from the solid and liquid states by relatively low density and viscosity and the spontaneous tendency to become distributed uniformly throughout any container. **b.** A substance in the gaseous state. **2.** A gaseous fuel, such as natural gas. **3.** Gasoline. **4.** The speed control of a gasoline engine. Used with *the: step on the gas.* **5.** A gaseous asphyxiant, irritant, or poison. **6.** A gaseous anesthetic, such as nitrous oxide. **7a.** Flatulence. **b.** Flatus. **8.** *Slang* Idle or boastful talk. **9.** *Slang* Someone or something exceptionally exciting or entertaining. ❖ *v.* **gassed, gas·sing, gas·es** or **gas·ses** —*tr.* **1.** To treat chemically with gas. **2.** To overcome, disable, or kill with poisonous fumes. —*intr.* **1.** To give off gas. **2.** *Slang* To talk excessively. —*phrasal verb:* **gas up** To supply a vehicle with gas or gasoline. [Du., an occult physical principle supposed in all bodies, alteration of Gk. *khaos,* chaos, empty space, coined by Jan Baptista van Helmont (1577–1644), Flem. chemist.]

gas·bag (găs'băg') *n.* **1.** An expansible bag for holding gas. **2.** *Slang* One given to empty or boastful talk.

gas burner *n.* A nozzle or jet on a fitting through which combustible gas is released to burn.

gas chamber *n.* A sealed enclosure in which condemned prisoners are executed by poison gas.

gas·con (găs'kən) *n.* A braggart. [< GASCON.]

Gascon *n.* A native or inhabitant of Gascony. ❖ *adj.* Of or relating to Gascony, the Gascons, or their language or culture. [Fr. < Lat. *Vascōnes,* the Basques.]

gas·con·ade (găs'kə-nād') *n.* Boastfulness; bravado. [Fr. *gas-*

connade < *Gascon*, Gascon. See GASCON.] —**gas′con•ade′** v. —**gas′con•ad′er** n.

Gasconade A river rising in the Ozark Plateau of S-central MO and flowing c. 426 km (265 mi) to the Missouri R. E of Jefferson City.

gas constant n. *Symbol* **R** *Physics* The constant of proportionality in the equation relating the product of the pressure and volume of a given number of moles of gas to the gas's absolute temperature, equal to 8.314 joules per kelvin.

Gas•co•ny (găs′kə-nē) A historical region and former province of SW France; settled orig. by Basque peoples and part of the French royal domain after 1607.

gas•e•ous (găs′ē-əs, găsh′əs) *adj.* **1.** Of, relating to, or existing as a gas. **2.** Lacking substance or concreteness; indefinite. **3.** Full of or containing gas; gassy. —**gas′e•ous•ness** n.

gas fitter n. One who installs or repairs gas pipes, fixtures, or appliances.

gas gangrene n. Gangrene occurring in a wound infected with bacteria of the genus *Clostridium,* esp. *C. perfringens,* and characterized by the presence of gas in the affected tissue.

gas-guz•zler (găs′gŭz′lər) n. *Informal* An automotive vehicle that gets relatively low gas mileage. —**gas′-guz′zling** *adj.*

gash (găsh) *tr.v.* **gashed, gash•ing, gash•es** To make a long deep cut in; slash deeply. ❖ n. **1.** A long deep cut. **2.** A deep flesh wound. [Alteration of ME *garsen,* to scarify < ONFr. *garser* < LLat. *charaxāre,* to scratch, engrave < Gk. *kharassein.*]

Gash•er•brum (gŭsh′ər-broōm′, -broōm′) A series of four peaks in the Karakoram Range of the Himalaya Mts. in N Kashmir. **Gasherbrum I** is the highest, at 8,073.4 m (26,470 ft), although **Gasherbrum IV,** 7,930 m (26,000 ft), has been called more difficult to climb than Everest. The other two peaks are 8,039.8 m (26,360 ft) and 7,957.5 m (26,090 ft).

gas•hold•er (găs′hōl′dər) n. A storage container for fuel gas, esp. a large, telescoping cylindrical tank.

gas•house (găs′hous′) n. See **gasworks.**

gas•i•form (găs′ə-fôrm′) *adj.* Having the form of gas; gaseous.

gas•i•fy (găs′ə-fī′) *tr. & intr.v.* **-fied, -fy•ing, -fies** To convert into or become gas. —**gas′i•fi′a•ble** *adj.* —**gas′i•fi•ca′tion** (-fĭ-kā′shən) n. —**gas′i•fi′er** n.

gas jet n. **1.** See **gas burner. 2.** The flame from a gas burner.

Gas•kell (găs′kəl), **Elizabeth Cleghorn Stevenson** 1810–65. British writer noted for her *Life of Charlotte Brontë* (1857) and her novels, including *Mary Barton* (1848).

gas•ket (găs′kĭt) n. **1.** Any of a wide variety of seals or packings used between matched machine parts or around pipe joints to prevent the escape of a gas or fluid. **2.** *Nautical* A cord or canvas strap used to secure a furled sail to a yard boom or gaff. [Perh. alteration of Fr. *garcette,* small cord, dim. of *garce,* girl < OFr., fem. of *gars,* boy, soldier. See GARÇON.]

gas•kin (găs′kĭn) n. **1.** The part of the hind leg of a horse or related animal between the stifle and the hock. **2. gaskins** *Obsolete* Galligaskins. [Prob. short for GALLIGASKINS.]

gas•light (găs′līt′) n. **1.** Light produced by burning illuminating gas. **2.** A gas burner or lamp.

gas-lit (găs′lĭt′) *adj.* Illuminated by gaslight.

gas log n. A gas burner shaped like a log for use in a fireplace.

gas main n. A major pipeline conveying gas to smaller pipes for distribution to consumers.

gas mask n. A respirator with a chemical air filter, worn over the face as protection against toxic gases and aerosols.

gas•o•hol (găs′ə-hôl′) n. A fuel consisting of a blend of ethyl alcohol and unleaded gasoline. [GAS(OLINE) + (ALC)OHOL.]

gas•o•line (găs′ə-lēn′, găs′ə-lēn′) n. A volatile mixture of flammable liquid hydrocarbons derived chiefly from crude petroleum and used as a fuel. [GAS + -OL(E) + -INE².]

gas•om•e•ter (gă-sŏm′ĭ-tər) n. **1.** An apparatus for measuring gases. **2.** See **gasholder.**

gasp (găsp) v. **gasped, gasp•ing, gasps** —*intr.* **1.** To draw in the breath sharply, as from shock. **2.** To breathe convulsively or laboriously. —*tr.* To utter in a breathless manner. ❖ n. A short convulsive intake or catching of the breath. [ME *gaspen, gaispen,* to gape, yawn < ON *geispa,* to yawn.]

Gas•par (găs′pər, -pär′) See **Caspar.**

Gas•pé (găs-pā′) A city of E Quebec, Canada, on **Gaspé Bay,** an inlet of the Gulf of St. Lawrence. Pop. 16,517.

Gaspé Peninsula A peninsula of E Quebec, Canada, between Chaleur Bay and the mouth of the St. Lawrence R.

gasp•er (găs′pər) n. *Chiefly British Slang* A cigarette.

gas plant n. A Eurasian plant (*Dictamnus albus*) having aromatic foliage and emitting a flammable vapor.

gas•ser (găs′ər) n. **1.** A well or drilling that yields natural gas. **2.** *Slang* Something highly entertaining or remarkable. **3.** *Slang* A talkative or boastful person.

gas station n. See **service station** 1.

gas•sy (găs′ē) *adj.* **-si•er, -si•est 1.** Containing or full of gas. **2.** Resembling gas. **3.** *Slang* Bombastic; boastful. —**gas′si•ness** n.

Gast•ar•beit•er (gäst′är-bī′tər) n. A guest worker, esp. one in Germany. [Ger. : *Gast,* guest (< MHGer. < OHGer.; see **ghos-ti-** in App.) + *Arbeiter,* worker (< *arbeiten,* to work < *Arbeit,* work < MHGer. *arebeit* < OHGer. *arabeit;* see **orbh-** in App.).]

gas•ter (găs′tər) n. The portion of the abdomen behind the peti-

ole in ants and other hymenopterous insects. [Gk. *gastēr,* belly.]

gas•trec•to•my (gă-strĕk′tə-mē) n., *pl.* **-mies** Surgical excision of part or all of the stomach.

gas•tric (găs′trĭk) *adj.* Of, relating to, or associated with the stomach.

gastric juice n. The watery acidic digestive fluid secreted by various glands in the mucous membrane of the stomach, consisting chiefly of hydrochloric acid, pepsin, rennin, and mucin.

gastric ulcer n. An ulcer in the stomach mucous membrane.

gas•trin (găs′trĭn) n. A hormone secreted by glands in the mucous membrane of the stomach that stimulates the production of gastric juice.

gas•tri•tis (gă-strī′tĭs) n. Chronic or acute inflammation of the stomach, esp. of the mucous membrane of the stomach.

gastro– or **gastr–** *pref.* **1a.** Belly: *gastropod.* **b.** Stomach: *gastritis.* **2.** Gastric: *gastrin.* [Gk. < *gastēr, gastr-,* belly.]

gas•troc•ne•mi•us (găs′trŏk-nē′mē-əs, găs′trə-) n., *pl.* **-mi•i** (-mē-ī′) The largest muscle of the calf of the leg, the action of which extends the foot and bends the knee. [NLat. *gastrocnēmius* < Gk. *gastroknēmiā,* calf of the leg : *gastro-,* belly (< its shape; see GASTRO- + *knēmē,* leg.]

gas•tro•en•ter•ic (găs′trō-ĕn-tĕr′ĭk) *adj.* Gastrointestinal.

gas•tro•en•ter•i•tis (găs′trō-ĕn′tə-rī′tĭs) n. Inflammation of the mucous membrane of the stomach and intestines.

gas•tro•en•ter•ol•o•gy (găs′trō-ĕn′tə-rŏl′ə-jē) n. The branch of medicine dealing with disorders of the stomach, intestines, and associated organs. —**gas′tro•en′ter•o•log′ic** (-ə-lŏj′ĭk), **gas′tro•en′ter•o•log′i•cal** *adj.* —**gas′tro•en′ter•ol′o•gist** n.

gas•tro•e•soph•a•ge•al (găs′trō-ĭ-sŏf′ə-jē′əl) *adj.* Of or relating to the stomach and esophagus.

gastroesophageal reflux n. A medical condition marked by the usu. persistent reflux of gastric fluids into the esophagus, causing chronic heartburn.

gas•tro•in•tes•ti•nal (găs′trō-ĭn-tĕs′tə-nəl) *adj.* Of or relating to the stomach and intestines.

gas•tro•lith (găs′trə-lĭth′) n. **1.** A pathological stony mass formed in the stomach. **2.** A small stone found in the stomach of some reptiles, fish, and birds that helps grind food.

gas•trol•o•gy (gă-strŏl′ə-jē) n. The medical study of the stomach and its diseases. —**gas′tro•log′i•cal, gas′tro•log′ic** *adj.* —**gas•trol′o•gist** n.

gas•tro•nome (găs′trə-nōm′) also **gas•tron•o•mer** (gă-strŏn′ə-mər) or **gas•tron•o•mist** (gă-strŏn′ə-mĭst) n. A connoisseur of good food and drink; a gourmet.

gas•tro•nom•ic (găs′trə-nŏm′ĭk) also **gas•tro•nom•i•cal** (-ĭ-kəl) *adj.* Of or relating to gastronomy. —**gas′tro•nom′i•cal•ly** *adv.*

gas•tron•o•my (gă-strŏn′ə-mē) n., *pl.* **-mies 1.** The art or science of good eating. **2.** A style of cooking. [Fr. *gastronomie* < Gk. *gastronomiā* : *gastro-, gastro-* + *-nomiā, -nomy.*]

gas•tro•pod (găs′trə-pŏd′) n. Any of various mollusks of the class Gastropoda, such as the snail, characteristically having a single, usu. coiled shell or no shell at all, a ventral muscular foot, and eyes and feelers. [< NLat. *Gastropoda,* class name : GASTRO– + *-poda, -pod.*] —**gas′tro•pod′, gas•trop′o•dan** (gă-strŏp′ə-dn), **gas•trop′o•dous** (-dəs) *adj.*

gas•tro•scope (găs′trə-skōp′) n. An endoscope that is inserted through the mouth to examine the interior of the stomach. —**gas′tro•scop′ic** (-skŏp′ĭk) *adj.* —**gas•tros′co•pist** (gă-strŏs′kə-pĭst) n. —**gas•tros′co•py** (-kə-pē) n.

gas•trot•o•my (gă-strŏt′ə-mē) n., *pl.* **-mies** Surgical incision into the stomach.

gas•tro•trich (găs′trə-trĭk) n. Any of various minute aquatic animals of the phylum Gastrotricha, having a wormlike ciliated body. [< NLat. *Gastrotricha,* phylum name : GASTRO– + Gk. *-trikhos, -trichous.*]

gas•tro•vas•cu•lar (găs′trō-văs′kyə-lər) *adj.* Having both a digestive and a circulatory function.

gas•tru•la (găs′trə-lə) n., *pl.* **-las** or **-lae** (-lē′) An embryo at the stage following the blastula, consisting of a hollow two-layered sac of ectoderm and endoderm surrounding an archenteron. [NLat. : Gk. *gastēr, gastr-,* belly + Lat. *-ula,* fem. dim. suff.] —**gas′tru•lar** (-lər) *adj.* —**gas′tru•late′** v. —**gas′tru•la′tion** n.

gas turbine n. An internal-combustion engine consisting of an air compressor, combustion chamber, and turbine wheel turned by the expanding products of combustion.

gas•works (găs′wûrks′) *pl.n.* (*used with a sing. verb*) A factory where gas for heating and lighting is produced.

gat¹ (găt) n. A narrow passage extending inland from a shore; a channel. [Prob. Du. < MDu.]

gat² (găt) n. *Slang* A pistol. [Short for GAT(LING GUN).]

gat³ (găt) v. *Archaic* A past tense of **get.**

gate¹ (găt) n. **1.** A structure that can be swung, drawn, or lowered to block an entrance or passageway. **2a.** An opening in a wall or fence for entrance or exit. **b.** The structure surrounding such an opening. **3a.** A means of access. **b.** A passageway, as in an airport, through which passengers proceed when boarding or leaving an airplane. **4.** A mountain pass. **5.** The total paid attendance or admission receipts at a public event. **6.** A device for controlling the passage of water or gas through a dam or conduit. **7.** The channel

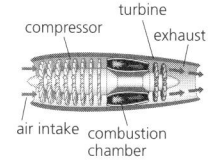

gas turbine
turbojet engine

ă	pat	oi	boy
ā	pay	ou	out
âr	care	oŏ	took
ä	father	oō	boot
ĕ	pet	ŭ	cut
ē	be	ûr	urge
ĭ	pit	th	thin
ī	pie	th	this
îr	pier	hw	which
ŏ	pot	zh	vision
ō	toe	ə	about,
ô	paw		item

Stress marks:
′ (primary);
′ (secondary), as in
lexicon (lĕk′sĭ-kŏn′)

through which molten metal flows into a shaped cavity of a mold. **8.** *Sports* A passage between two upright poles through which a skier must go in a slalom race. **9.** *Electronics* A logic gate. ❖ *tr.v.* **gat·ed, gat·ing, gates 1.** *Chiefly British* To confine (a student) to the grounds of a college as punishment. **2.** *Electronics* To select part of (a wave) for transmission, reception, or processing by magnitude or time interval. **3.** To furnish with a gate. —*idioms:* **get the gate** *Slang* To be dismissed or rejected. **give (someone) the gate** *Slang* **1.** To discharge from a job. **2.** To reject or jilt. [ME < OE *geat*.]

gate² (gāt) *n.* **1.** *Chiefly British* A particular way of acting. **2.** *Archaic* A path or way. [ME < ON *gata*. See **ghē-** in App.]

-gate *suff.* A scandal involving alleged illegal acts and often a cover-up, esp. by government officials: *Irangate.* [After WATERGATE.]

gâ·teau or **ga·teau** (gă-tō′, gä-) *n.*, *pl.* **-teaux** (-tō′) A cake or pastry, esp. a light, filled one. [Fr. < OFr. *gastel*, cake < Frankish **wastil*, food.]

gate·crash·er (gāt′krăsh′ər) *n. Slang* One who gains admittance, as to a party or concert, without being invited or without paying. —**gate′crash′** *v.*

gat·ed community (gā′tĭd) *n.* A residential area, often surrounded by a barrier that limits entry to residents and their guests.

gate·fold (gāt′fōld′) *n.* A foldout, esp. one that opens to double the page size.

gate·house (gāt′hous′) *n.* **1.** A lodge at the entrance to the driveway of an estate. **2.** A fortified structure built over the gateway to a city or castle. **3.** A building that houses the controls of a dam or canal lock.

gate·keep·er (gāt′kē′pər) *n.* **1.** One in charge of passage through a gate. **2.** One who monitors or oversees others.

gate-leg table (gāt′lĕg′) *n.* A drop leaf table with paired legs that swing out to support the leaves.

gate·post (gāt′pōst′) *n.* An upright post on which a gate is hung or against which it closes.

ga·ter (gā′tər) *n. Informal* Variant of **gator.**

Gates (gāts), **Horatio** 1728?–1806. Amer. Revolutionary general who won the Battle of Saratoga (1777).

Gates, William Henry ("Bill") b. 1955. Amer. computer software designer and business executive who cofounded Microsoft (1975), one of the world's largest computer software manufacturers.

Gates·head (gāts′hĕd′) A borough of NE England on the Tyne R. opposite Newcastle; dating probably to Saxon times. Pop. 202,850.

gate·way (gāt′wā′) *n.* **1.** An opening or structure framing an opening that may be closed by a gate. **2.** Something that serves as an entrance or a means of access. **3.** Software or hardware that enables communication between computer networks.

Gath (găth) An ancient city of Palestine ENE of Gaza; one of the five Philistine city-kingdoms and the home of Goliath.

gath·er (găth′ər) *v.* **-ered, -er·ing, -ers** —*tr.* **1.** To cause to come together; convene: *gathered the students around the exhibit.* **2a.** To accumulate (something) gradually; amass: *gathered dust.* **b.** To harvest or pick: *gather flowers.* **3.** To gain by a process of gradual increase: *gather speed.* **4.** To collect into one place; assemble. **5.** To pick up and enfold: *gathered the kittens into her arms.* **6.** *Printing* To arrange (signatures) in sequence for bookbinding. **7a.** To draw into small folds or puckers, as by pulling a thread through cloth. **b.** To contract and wrinkle (the brow). **8.** To bring closer to or draw about something else: *gathered the shawl about my shoulders.* **9.** To conclude; infer: *I gather that you've made your decision.* **10.** To summon up; muster: *gathered up his courage.* **11.** To attract or be a center of attraction for: *The parade gathered a large crowd.* —*intr.* **1.** To come together in a group; assemble: *A crowd gathered.* **2.** To accumulate: *Dark clouds are gathering.* **3.** To grow or increase by degrees. **4.** To come to a head, as a boil; fester. **5.** To forage for wild foodstuffs. ❖ *n.* **1a.** The act or an instance of gathering. **b.** A quantity gathered. **2.** A small fold or pucker made by gathering cloth. [ME *getheren, gaderen* < OE *gadrian*.] —**gath′er·er** *n.*

gatehouse
Meissen, Germany

SYNONYMS *gather, collect, assemble, accumulate, amass* These verbs mean to bring together in a group or aggregate. *Gather* is the most widely applicable: *gathered sticks for the fire. Collect* frequently refers to the careful selection of like or related things that become part of an organized whole: *collected stamps. Assemble* implies a definite and usually close relationship: *The curator is assembling Stone Age artifacts. Accumulate* applies to the increase of like or related things over an extended period: *They accumulated enough capital to invest. Amass* refers to the collection or accumulation of things, often valuable things, to form an imposing quantity: *Their families had amassed great fortunes.*

gath·er·ing (găth′ər-ĭng) *n.* **1a.** The action of one that gathers. **b.** That which is gathered or amassed; a collection or accumulation. **2.** An assembly of persons; a meeting. **3.** The collecting of food that grows wild, such as berries. **4.** A gather in cloth. **5.** A suppurated swelling; a boil or abscess.

Gat·i·neau (găt′n-ō′, gä-tē-nō′) A town of SW Quebec, Canada, NE of Hull near the mouth of the **Gatineau River,** which

Bill Gates
photographed in 1995

rises in the Laurentian Plateau and flows c. 386 km (240 mi) SW to the Ottawa R. Pop. 100,702.

Gat·ling gun (găt′lĭng) *n.* A machine gun having a cluster of barrels that are fired in sequence as the cluster is rotated. [After Richard Jordan *Gatling* (1818–1903), American firearms inventor.]

ga·tor or **ga·ter** (gā′tər) *n. Informal* An alligator.

GATT *abbr.* General Agreement on Tariffs and Trade

Ga·tún Lake (gə-tōōn′, gä-) An artificial lake of central Panama, a major link in the Panama Canal system.

gauche (gōsh) *adj.* Lacking social polish; tactless. [Fr., awkward < OFr. < *gauchir*, to turn aside, walk clumsily, of Gmc. orig.] —**gauche′ly** *adv.* —**gauche′ness** *n.*

gau·che·rie (gō′shə-rē′) *n.* **1.** An awkward or tactless act, manner, or expression. **2.** A lack of tact; awkwardness. [Fr. < *gauche,* gauche. See GAUCHE.]

gau·cho (gou′chō) *n.*, *pl.* **-chos 1.** A cowboy of the South American pampas. **2.** gauchos Calf-length pants with flared legs. [Am.Sp., prob. < Quechua *wáhcha,* vagabond.]

gaud (gôd) *n.* A gaudy or showy ornament or trinket. [ME *gaud, gaudi,* sing. of *gaudies,* large, ornamental beads on a rosary, trinkets < Med.Lat. *gaudia* < Lat., pl. of *gaudium,* joy (referring to the Joyful Mysteries of the Virgin Mary) < *gaudēre,* to rejoice.]

gaud·er·y (gô′də-rē) *n.*, *pl.* **-ies** Showy or gaudy decoration; ostentatious or pretentious show.

Gau·dí (gou′dē, gou-dē′), **Antonio** 1852–1926. Spanish architect whose most celebrated work is the façade of the Expiatory Church of the Holy Family in Barcelona.

gaud·y¹ (gô′dē) *adj.* **-i·er, -i·est** Showy in a tasteless or vulgar way. [Poss. < GAUDY² (influenced by GAUD).] —**gaud′i·ly** *adv.* —**gaud′i·ness** *n.*

gaud·y² (gô′dē) *n.*, *pl.* **-ies** *Chiefly British* A feast, esp. an annual university dinner. [ME *gaudi, gaud,* prank, trick, poss. < OFr. *gaudie,* merriment (< *gaudir,* to enjoy, make merry < Lat. *gaudēre,* to rejoice) and < Lat. *gaudium,* enjoyment, merry-making (< *gaudēre,* to rejoice).]

gauf·fer (gŏf′ər, gô′fər) *v. & n.* Variant of **goffer.**

Gau·ga·me·la (gô′gə-mē′lə) An ancient village of Assyria NE of Nineveh where Alexander the Great defeated the Persians under Darius III in 331 B.C.

gauge also **gage** (gāj) *n.* **1a.** A standard or scale of measurement. **b.** A standard dimension, quantity, or capacity. **2.** An instrument for measuring or testing. **3.** A means of estimating or evaluating; a test. **4a.** The distance between the two rails of a railroad. **b.** The distance between two wheels on an axle. **5.** The interior diameter of a shotgun barrel as determined by the number of lead balls of a size exactly fitting the barrel required to make one pound. **6.** The amount of plaster of Paris combined with common plaster to speed setting of the mixture. **7.** Thickness or diameter, as of sheet metal or wire. **8.** The fineness of knitted cloth as determined by the number of loops per 1½ inches. ❖ *tr.v.* **gauged, gaug·ing, gaug·es** also **gaged, gag·ing, gag·es 1.** To measure precisely. **2.** To determine the capacity, volume, or contents of. **3.** To evaluate or judge. **4.** To adapt to a specified measurement. **5.** To mix (plaster) in specific proportions. **6.** To chip or rub (bricks or stones) to size. [ME < ONFr., gauging rod, of Gmc. orig.] —**gauge′a·ble** *adj.*

gaug·er also **gag·er** (gā′jər) *n.* **1.** One that gauges. **2.** *Chiefly British* A revenue officer who inspects bulk goods subject to duty.

Gau·guin (gō-găn′), **(Eugène Henri) Paul** 1848–1903. French artist whose paintings include *Ia Orana Maria* (1891).

Gaul¹ (gôl) *n.* **1.** A Celt of ancient Gaul. **2.** A French person.

Gaul² (gôl) Formerly **Gal·li·a** (găl′ē-ä) An ancient region of W Europe S and W of the Rhine R., W of the Alps, and N of the Pyrenees, corresponding roughly to modern-day France and Belgium; conquered by Julius Caesar in the Gallic Wars (58–51 B.C.).

Gaul·ish (gô′lĭsh) *n.* The Celtic language of ancient Gaul.

Gaull·ism (gōl′ĭz′əm, gôl′-) *n.* **1.** The movement supporting Gen. Charles de Gaulle as leader of the French government in exile during World War II. **2.** The movement headed by Charles de Gaulle after World War II. —**Gaull′ist** *n.*

gaum (gôm) *tr.v.* **gaumed, gaum·ing, gaums** *Upper Southern US* To smudge or smear. [Perh. alteration of obsolete *gome,* grease, var. of *coom,* soot, mixture of dirt and axle grease, var. of CULM².]

gaunt (gônt) *adj.* **gaunt·er, gaunt·est 1.** Thin and bony; angular. See Syns at **lean². 2.** Emaciated and haggard; drawn. **3.** Bleak and desolate; barren. [ME, perh. < OFr. *gant,* poss. of Scand. orig.] —**gaunt′ly** *adv.* —**gaunt′ness** *n.*

gaunt·let¹ also **gant·let** (gônt′lĭt, gänt′-) *n.* **1.** A protective glove worn with medieval armor. **2.** A protective glove with a flared cuff, used in manual labor, in certain sports, and for driving. **3.** A challenge. **4.** A dress glove cuffed above the wrist. [ME < OFr. *gantelet,* dim. of *gant,* glove, of Gmc. orig.]

gaunt·let² also **gant·let** (gônt′lĭt, gänt′-) *n.* **1a.** A form of punishment or torture in which a person is forced to run between two lines of people armed to strike, as with sticks. **b.** The lines of people so arranged. **2.** An onslaught or attack from all sides. **3.** A severe trial; an ordeal. [Alteration (influenced by GAUNTLET¹) of *gantlope* < Swed. *gatlopp* : *gata,* lane (< ON; see **ghē-** in App.) + *lopp,* course, running (< MLGer. *lōp*.]

WORD HISTORY A perennial usage question is whether the spelling *gauntlet* is acceptable for both *gauntlet*[1] and *gauntlet*[2]. *Gauntlet*[1], as in *to throw down the gauntlet*, comes from the Old French word *gantelet*, a diminutive of *gant*, "glove." From the time of its appearance in Middle English (by 1449), the word has been spelled with an *au* as well as an *a*, still a possible spelling. But the other *gauntlet*, as in *to run the gauntlet*, is an alteration of the earlier English form *gantlope*, which came from the Swedish word *gatlopp*, a compound of *gata*, "lane," and *lopp*, "course." The English word was influenced by the spelling of the word *gauntlet*, "glove," and in 1676 we find the first recorded instance of the spelling *gauntlet* for this word, although *gantelope* is found as late as 1836. Although one could say that the *a* spelling is preferable because it reflects the Swedish source, in regard to a word that has been so altered in form, this seems a rather fine point.

gaur (gour) *n.* A large dark-coated wild ox *(Bos gaurus)* of southeast Asia. [Hindi < Skt. *gaurah*. See **gʷou-** in App.]

gauss (gous) *n., pl.* **gauss** or **gauss·es** The centimeter-gram-second unit of magnetic flux density, equal to one maxwell per square centimeter. [After Karl Friedrich GAUSS.]

Gauss, Karl Friedrich 1777–1855. German mathematician and astronomer known for his contributions to algebra, differential geometry, probability theory, and number theory.

Gauss·i·an distribution (gou′sē-ən) *n.* See **normal distribution.** [After Karl Friedrich GAUSS.]

Gau·ta·ma (gô′tə-mə, gou′-), **Siddhartha** See **Buddha**[1].

Gau·tier (gō-tyā′), **Théophile** 1811–72. French writer whose works include *Enamels and Cameos* (1852).

gauze (gôz) *n.* **1a.** A thin transparent fabric with a loose open weave. **b.** A thin, loosely woven surgical dressing, usu. made of cotton. **c.** A thin plastic or metal woven mesh. **2.** A mist or haze. [Fr. *gaze*, poss. < Sp. *gasa* < Ar. *qazz*, raw silk, poss. < Pers. *kazh*.] —**gauz′i·ly** *adv.* —**gauz′i·ness** *n.*

gauz·y (gô′zē) *adj.* **-i·er, -i·est** Resembling gauze in thinness or transparency. See Syns at **airy.** —**gauz′i·ly** *adv.* —**gauz′i·ness** *n.*

ga·vage (gə-väzh′) *n.* Introduction of nutritive material into the stomach by means of a tube. [Fr. < *gaver*, to force down the throat, ult. < OFr. *gave*, throat < VLat. **gaba.*]

gave (gāv) *v.* Past tense of **give.**

gav·el[1] (găv′əl) *n.* **1.** A small mallet used by a presiding officer or an auctioneer to signal for attention or order or mark the conclusion of a transaction. **2.** A maul used by masons in fitting stones. ❖ *tr.v.* **-eled, -el·ing, -els** also **-elled, -el·ling, -els** To bring about or compel by using a gavel. [?]

gav·el[2] (găv′əl) *n.* Tribute or rent in ancient and medieval England. [ME < OE *gafol.* See **ghabh-** in App.]

gav·el·kind (găv′əl-kīnd′) *n.* A former English system of land tenure that provided for the equal division of land among all qualified heirs. [ME *gavelkinde* : OE *gafol,* gavel; see GAVEL[2] + OE *gecynd,* kind; see KIND[2].]

ga·vi·al (gā′vē-əl) *n.* A large reptile *(Gavialis gangeticus)* of southern Asia, related to and resembling the crocodiles and having a long slender snout. [Fr. < Hindi *ghariyāl* < Skt. *ghaṇṭikaḥ,* alligator, gavial, prob. < *ghaṇṭā,* bell (< the bulbous end of its snout).]

ga·votte (gə-vŏt′) *n.* **1.** A French peasant dance of Baroque origin in moderately quick duple meter. **2.** Music for this dance. [Fr. < Provençal *gavoto* < *gavot,* native of the Alps, poss. < *gava,* crop of a bird < VLat. **gaba,* gullet, throat.]

GAW *abbr.* guaranteed annual wage

Ga·wain (gə-wān′, gä′wān′, gou′ən, gä′wən) *n.* A nephew of King Arthur and a Knight of the Round Table.

gawk (gôk) *n.* An awkward, loutish person; an oaf. ❖ *intr.v.* **gawked, gawk·ing, gawks** To stare or gape stupidly. [Perh. alteration of obsolete *gaw,* to gape < ME *gawen* < ON *gā,* to heed.] —**gawk′er** *n.*

gawk·y (gô′kē) *adj.* **-i·er, -i·est** Awkward; ungainly. —**gawk′i·ly** *adv.*

gay (gā) *adj.* **gay·er, gay·est 1.** Of, relating to, or having a sexual orientation to persons of the same sex. **2.** Showing or characterized by cheerfulness and lighthearted excitement; merry. **3.** Bright or lively, esp. in color. **4.** Given to social pleasures. **5.** Dissolute; licentious. ❖ *n.* **1.** A person whose sexual orientation is to persons of the same sex. **2.** A man whose sexual orientation is to men. [ME *gai* < OFr., poss. of Gmc. orig.] —**gay′ness** *n.*

USAGE NOTE The word *gay* is now standard in its use to refer to homosexuals, in large part because it is the term that most gay people prefer in referring to themselves. *Gay* is distinguished from *homosexual* primarily by the emphasis it places on the cultural and social aspects of homosexuality as opposed to sexual practice. Many writers reserve *gay* for males, but the word is also used to refer to both sexes; when the intended meaning is not clear in the context, the phrase *gay and lesbian* may be used. *Gay* can sometimes be regarded as objectionable when used as a noun to refer to particular individuals, as in *There were two gays on the panel;* here phrasing such as *gay members* should be used instead. But there is no objection to the use of the noun in the plural to refer collectively either to gay men or to gay men and lesbians, so

long as it is clear whether men alone or both men and women are being discussed. See Usage Note at **homosexual.**

Gay, John 1685–1732. English writer known esp. for his play *The Beggar's Opera* (1728).

Ga·ya (gə-yä′, gī′ə) A city of NE India S of Patna; a sacred area to Buddhist and Hindu pilgrims. Pop. 291,675.

ga·yal (gə-yäl′) *n.* A domesticated bovine mammal *(Bos frontalis)* of India and Myanmar (Burma), with thick pointed horns and a dark coat. [Bengali *gayāl,* prob. < Skt. *gauḥ,* ox. See **gʷou-** in App.]

gay·dar (gā′där) *n. Slang* The supposed ability to discern whether a person is homosexual. [Blend of GAY and RADAR.]

gay·e·ty (gā′ĭ-tē) *n.* Variant of **gaiety.**

gay feather *n.* See **blazing star** 2.

Gay-Lus·sac (gā′lə-săk′, -lü-săk′), **Joseph Louis** 1778–1850. French chemist and physicist who isolated boron (1809) and formulated a law of combining volumes of gases.

gay·ly (gā′lē) *adv.* Variant of **gaily.**

Ga·za (gä′zə, găz′ə, gā′zə) A city of SW Asia in the **Gaza Strip,** a narrow coastal area along the Mediterranean Sea adjoining Israel and Egypt. Part of the British mandate for Palestine (1917–48), the territory passed to Egypt in 1949 and was occupied by Israel in 1967. Limited autonomy was granted to Palestine in a 1993 Israeli-Palestinian accord. Pop. 118,272.

gaze (gāz) *intr.v.* **gazed, gaz·ing, gaz·es** To look steadily, intently, and with fixed attention. ❖ *n.* A steady fixed look. [ME *gasen,* prob. of Scand. orig.] —**gaz′er** *n.*

ga·ze·bo (gə-zā′bō, -zē′-) *n., pl.* **-bos** or **-boes 1.** A freestanding, roofed, usu. open-sided structure providing a shady resting place. **2.** A belvedere. [?]

gaze·hound (gāz′hound′) *n.* A dog, such as the Afghan hound or the greyhound, that hunts its prey by sight.

ga·zelle (gə-zĕl′) *n.* Any of various small swift antelopes of the genus *Gazella* and related genera of Africa and Asia, with a slender neck and annulate horns. [Fr. < OFr. < Ar. *gazāl.*]

ga·zette (gə-zĕt′) *n.* **1.** A newspaper. **2.** An official journal. **3.** *Chiefly British* An announcement in an official journal. ❖ *tr.v.* **-zet·ted, -zet·ting, -zettes** *Chiefly British* To announce or publish in an official journal or a newspaper. [Fr. < Ital. *gazzetta,* prob. < Ital. dialectal *gazeta,* a small coin.]

gaz·et·teer (găz′ĭ-tîr′) *n.* **1.** A geographic dictionary or index. **2.** *Archaic* A writer for a gazette; a journalist.

Ga·zi·an·tep (gä′zē-än-tĕp′) Formerly **Ain·tab** (īn-täb′) A city of S Turkey N of Aleppo, Syria; an ancient Hittite center. Pop. 716,000.

ga·zil·lion (gə-zĭl′yən) *n. Informal* An indefinitely large number. [On the model of MILLION, BILLION, etc.]

gaz·pa·cho (gə-spä′chō, gäz-pä′-) *n., pl.* **-chos** A chilled soup made with chopped tomatoes, cucumbers, onions, peppers, herbs, and sometimes bread. [Sp., prob. of Mozarabic orig.; akin to Sp. *caspicias,* remainders, worthless things.]

GB *abbr.* **1.** gigabyte **2.** Great Britain

Gbe (bĕ, gbĕ) *n.* A closely related group of Kwa languages, including Ewe and Fon, that are spoken in coastal Ghana, Togo, Benin, and Nigeria. [Gbe, language, voice.]

gcd *abbr.* greatest common divisor

gcf *abbr.* greatest common factor

G clef *n.* See **treble clef.**

GCT *abbr.* Greenwich Civil Time

Gd The symbol for the element **gadolinium.**

GD *abbr.* **1.** garbage disposal **2.** grand duchy

Gdańsk (gə-dänsk′, -dănsk′, -dĭnsk′) also **Dan·zig** (dăn′sĭg, dän′tsĭk) A city of N Poland on the **Gulf of Gdańsk,** an inlet of the Baltic Sea. The Treaty of Versailles (1919) declared Gdańsk a free city, although it came under Nazi control in 1935. It was liberated by the Russians in 1945 and subsequently restored to Poland. Pop. 465,395.

GDP *abbr.* gross domestic product

GDR *abbr.* German Democratic Republic

Gdy·ni·a (gə-dĭn′ē-ə, -dĭn′yə) A city of N Poland on the Gulf of Gdańsk NW of Gdańsk. Pop. 251,463.

Ge The symbol for the element **germanium.**

ge– *pref.* Variant of **geo–.**

ge·an·ti·cline (jē-ăn′tĭ-klīn′) *n.* A large upward fold of the earth's crust. —**ge·an′ti·cli′nal** *adj.*

gear (gîr) *n.* **1a.** A toothed machine part, such as a wheel or cylinder, that meshes with another toothed part to transmit motion or to change speed or direction. **b.** A complete assembly that performs a specific function in a larger machine. **c.** A transmission configuration for a specific ratio of engine to axle torque in a motor vehicle. **2.** Equipment used for a particular activity: *fishing gear.* **3a.** Clothing and accessories. **b.** Personal belongings, including clothing. **4.** The harness for a horse. **5.** *Nautical* **a.** A ship's rigging. **b.** A sailor's personal effects. ❖ *v.* **geared, gear·ing, gears** —*tr.* **1a.** To equip with gears. **b.** To connect by gears. **c.** To put into gear. **2.** To adjust or adapt so as to make suitable. **3.** To provide with gear; equip. —*intr.* **1.** To come into or be in gear. **2.** To become adjusted so as to fit or blend. —*phrasal verb:* **gear up** To get ready for a coming action or event. [ME *gere,* equipment < ON *gervi.*]

gazebo
Savannah, Georgia

ă	pat	oi	boy
ā	pay	ou	out
âr	care	ŏŏ	took
ä	father	ōō	boot
ĕ	pet	ŭ	cut
ē	be	ûr	urge
ĭ	pit	th	thin
ī	pie	*th*	this
îr	pier	hw	which
ŏ	pot	zh	vision
ō	toe	ə	about,
ô	paw		item

Stress marks:
′ (primary);
′ (secondary), as in
lexicon (lĕk′sĭ-kŏn′)

gear•box (gîr′bŏks′) *n.* **1.** See **transmission** 3. **2.** A protective casing for a system of gears.

gear•ing (gîr′ĭng) *n.* **1.** A system of gears and associated elements by which motion is transferred within a machine. **2.** The act or technique of providing with gears.

gear ratio *n.* The ratio of the speed of rotation of the powered gear of a gear train to that of the final or driven gear.

gear•shift (gîr′shĭft′) *n.* A mechanism for changing from one gear to another in a transmission.

gear train *n.* A system of interconnected gears.

gear•wheel also **gear wheel** (gîr′hwēl′, -wēl′) *n.* A wheel with a toothed rim.

Geat (gēt, yät) *n.* A member of an ancient Germanic people of southern Sweden conquered by the Swedes in the sixth century A.D. [OE *Gēat.*]

Ge•bel Mu•sa (jĕb′əl mōō′sə, -sä) See **Jebel Musa.**

geck•o (gĕk′ō) *n., pl.* **-os** or **-oes** Any of various usu. small tropical and subtropical lizards of the family Gekkonidae, having toes containing numerous suction cups that enable them to climb on vertical surfaces. [Javanese *ge'kok.*]

GED *abbr.* **1.** general equivalency diploma **2.** general educational development

Ged•des (gĕd′ēz), **Norman Bel** 1893–1958. Amer. designer who popularized the concept of streamlining.

gee[1] (jē) *n.* The letter *g.*

gee[2] (jē) *interj.* Used to command an animal pulling a load to turn to the right. ❖ *intr.v.* **geed, gee•ing, gees** To turn to the right.

gee[3] also **jee** (jē) *interj.* Used as a mild expletive or exclamation, as of surprise or sympathy. [Alteration of JESUS[1].]

gee[4] (jē) *n. Slang* A thousand dollars. [< GEE[1] < the first letter of GRAND.]

Gee•chee (gē′chē) *n.* **1.** *Southeastern US* **a.** The Gullah creole. **b.** A speaker of Gullah. **2.** *Offensive* Used as a disparaging term for a person who speaks a nonstandard local dialect, esp. in coastal Georgia and South Carolina. [Ultimately after the OGEECHEE River, along which distinct varieties of Black English were spoken.]

gee•gaw (jē′gô′, gē′-) *n.* Variant of **gewgaw.**

geek (gēk) *n. Slang* **1a.** A person regarded as foolish, inept, or clumsy. **b.** A person who is single-minded or accomplished in scientific or technical pursuits but is felt to be socially inept. **2.** A carnival performer whose show consists of bizarre acts, such as biting the head off a live chicken. [Perh. alteration of dialectal *geck,* fool < LGer. *gek* < MLGer.] **—geek′y** *adj.*

gecko
Tokay gecko
Gekko gecko

OUR LIVING LANGUAGE Our word *geek* is now chiefly associated with student and computer slang; one probably thinks first of a *computer geek.* In origin, however, it is one of the words American English borrowed from the vocabulary of the circus, which was a much more significant source of entertainment in the United States in the 19th and early 20th century than it is now. Large numbers of traveling circuses left a cultural legacy in various and sometimes unexpected ways. For example, Superman and other comic-book superheroes owe much of their look to circus acrobats, who were similarly costumed in capes and tights. The circus sideshow is the source of the word *geek,* "a performer who engaged in bizarre acts, such as biting the head off a live chicken." We also owe the word *ballyhoo* to the circus; its ultimate origin is unknown, but in the late 1800s it referred to a flamboyant free musical performance conducted outside a circus with the goal of luring customers to buy tickets to the inside shows. Other words and expressions with circus origins include *bandwagon* (coined by P.T. Barnum in 1855) and *Siamese twin.*

geese (gēs) *n.* Plural of **goose.**

gee whiz *interj.* Used to express mild surprise, amazement, or enthusiasm.

geez (jēz) *interj.* Used to express mild surprise, delight, dissatisfaction, or annoyance. [Shortening and alteration of JESUS[1].]

Ge'ez (gē-ĕz′, gŭ′əz) *n.* The Afro-Asiatic language of ancient Ethiopia that is still used as a liturgical language in the Christian Church in Ethiopia. [Ge'ez *go'əz,* Ethiopian.]

gee•zer (gē′zər) *n. Slang* An eccentric old man. [Prob. alteration of dialectal *guiser,* masquerader < ME *gysar* < *gysen,* to dress < *gyse, guise,* fashion < GUISE.]

ge•fil•te fish (gə-fĭl′tə) *n.* Finely chopped fish mixed with crumbs, eggs, and seasonings, cooked in a broth in oval-shaped cakes or balls, and usu. served chilled. [Yiddish : *gefilt,* p. part. of *filn,* to fill, stuff + *fish,* fish.]

ge•gen•schein (gā′gən-shīn′) *n.* A faint glowing spot in the sky, exactly opposite the position of the sun. [Ger. : *gegen,* against (< MHGer. < OHGer. *gegin*) + *Schein,* light (< MHGer. *schīn* < OHGer. *scīn* < *scīnan,* to shine).]

Ge•hen•na (gĭ-hĕn′ə) *n.* **1.** A place or state of torment or suffering. **2.** The abode of condemned souls; hell. [LLat. < Gk. *Geenna* < Heb. *gê' hinnōm,* poss. short for *gê' ben hinnōm,* valley of the son of Hinnom, a valley S of Jerusalem : *gê',* bound form of *gay',* valley + *hinnōm,* personal name.]

Geh•rig (gĕr′ĭg), **Henry Louis ("Lou")** 1903–41. Amer. baseball player who was a member of the New York Yankees (1925–39).

Gehr•y (gâr′ē, gär′ē), **Frank** b. 1929. Canadian-born Amer. ar-

geisha
Geisha Serving a Samurai,
woodblock print by Suzuki
Harunobu (1725?–1770)

chitect. His designs include the Guggenheim Museum Bilbao (1997).

Gei•ger counter (gī′gər) *n.* An instrument that detects and measures the intensity of radiation, consisting of a gas-filled tube through which charged particles pass, producing a voltage pulse which triggers a counter. [After Hans Wilhelm *Geiger* (1882–1945), German physicist.]

Gei•sel (gī′zəl), **Theodor Seuss** Pen name Dr. Seuss. 1904–91. Amer. writer and illustrator of children's books whose works include *The Cat in the Hat* (1957).

gei•sha (gā′shə, gē′-) *n., pl.* **geisha** or **-shas** One of a class of professional women in Japan trained from girlhood in conversation, dancing, and singing in order to entertain professional or social gatherings of men. [J. : *gei,* art (< M Chin. *ŋejh) + *sha,* person (< M Chin. *tšia²).]

gel (jĕl) *n.* **1.** A colloid in which the disperse phase has combined with the dispersion medium to produce a semisolid material. **2.** See **gelatin** 3. **3.** A jellylike substance used in styling hair. ❖ *v.* **gelled, gel•ling, gels** —*intr.* To become a gel. —*tr.* To apply a gel to (the hair). [Short for GELATIN.] **—gel′a•ble** *adj.*

ge•län•de•sprung (gə-lĕn′də-shprŏong′) *n.* A jump in skiing made from a crouching position with the use of both poles. [Ger. : *Gelände,* open field (< MHGer. *gelende* < OHGer. *gilanti* < *lant,* land) + *Sprung,* jump (< MHGer. *sprunc* < OHGer. < *springan,* to jump).]

gel•ate (jĕl′āt′) *intr.v.* **-at•ed, -at•ing, -ates** To gel.

gel•a•tin also **gel•a•tine** (jĕl′ə-tn) *n.* **1a.** A colorless or slightly yellow transparent brittle protein obtained from the skin, bones, and connective tissue of animals and used in foods, drugs, and photographic film. **b.** Any of various similar substances. **2.** A jelly made with gelatin. **3.** A thin sheet made of colored gelatin used in theatrical lighting. [Fr. *gélatine* < Ital. *gelatina,* dim. of *gelata,* jelly < fem. p. part. of *gelare,* to freeze < Lat. *gelāre.* See **gel-** in App.]

ge•lat•i•nize (jə-lăt′n-īz′, jĕl′ə-tn-īz′) *v.* **-nized, -niz•ing, -niz•es** —*tr.* To convert to gelatin or jelly. **2.** To coat with gelatin. —*intr.* To become gelatinous. **—ge•lat′i•ni•za′tion** (-lăt′n-ĭ-zā′shən) *n.*

ge•lat•i•nous (jə-lăt′n-əs) *adj.* **1.** Resembling gelatin; viscous. **2.** Of, relating to, or containing gelatin. **—ge•lat′i•nous•ly** *adv.* **—ge•lat′i•nous•ness** *n.*

ge•la•tion (jē-lā′shən) *n.* **1.** Solidification by cooling or freezing. **2.** The process of forming a gel. [Lat. *gelātiō, gelātiōn-* < *gelātus,* p. part. of *gelāre,* to freeze. See **gel-** in App.]

ge•la•to (jə-lä′tō, jē-) *n., pl.* **-ti** (-tē) An Italian ice cream or ice. [Ital. < p. part. of *gelare,* to freeze. See GELATIN.]

geld[1] (gĕld) *tr.v.* **geld•ed** or **gelt** (gĕlt), **geld•ing, gelds 1.** To castrate (a horse, for example). **2.** To deprive of strength or vigor; weaken. [ME *gelden* < ON *gelda.*]

geld[2] (gĕld) *n.* A tax paid to the crown by English landholders under Anglo-Saxon and Norman kings. [ME *geld* and Med.Lat. *geldum,* both < OE *geld, gield,* payment.]

Gel•der•land (gĕl′dər-lănd′, кнĕl′dər-länt′) A province and former duchy of E-central Netherlands; passed to the Hapsburgs (1543) and then to the Netherlands (1579).

geld•ing (gĕl′dĭng) *n.* A castrated animal, esp. a horse. [ME < ON *geldingr* < *gelda,* to geld.]

gel•id (jĕl′ĭd) *adj.* Very cold; icy. See Syns at **cold.** [Lat. *gelidus* < *gelu,* frost. See **gel-** in App.] **—ge•lid′i•ty** (jə-lĭd′ĭ-tē), **gel′id•ness** *n.* **—gel′id•ly** *adv.*

gel•ig•nite (jĕl′ĭg-nīt′) *n.* An explosive mixture composed of nitroglycerine, guncotton, wood pulp, and potassium nitrate. [GEL(ATIN) + Lat. *ignis,* fire + -ITE[1].]

Gell-Mann (gĕl′măn′), **Murray** b. 1929. Amer. physicist who won a 1969 Nobel Prize.

Gel•sen•kir•chen (gĕl′zən-kîr′kən, -кнən) A city of W-central Germany NE of Essen. Pop. 295,037.

gelt[1] (gĕlt) *n. Slang* Money. [Yiddish < MHGer. *gelt* < OHGer. *gelt,* recompense.]

gelt[2] (gĕlt) *v.* A past tense and a past participle of **geld**[1].

gem (jĕm) *n.* **1.** A pearl or mineral that has been cut and polished for use as an ornament. **2a.** Something valued for its beauty or perfection. **b.** A beloved or highly prized person. **3.** A type of muffin. ❖ *tr.v.* **gemmed, gem•ming, gems** To adorn with or as if with precious or semiprecious stones. [ME *gemme* < OFr. < Lat. *gemma.* See **gembh-** in App.]

Ge•ma•ra (gə-mär′ə, -môr′ə) *n.* The second part of the Talmud, consisting primarily of commentary on the Mishnah. [Aram. *gəmārā,* completion < *gamar,* to complete.] **—Ge•ma′ric** *adj.* **—Ge•ma′rist** *n.*

gem•i•nate (jĕm′ə-nāt′) *v.* **-nat•ed, -nat•ing, -nates** —*tr.* **1.** To double. **2.** To arrange in pairs. —*intr.* To occur in pairs. ❖ *adj.* (-nĭt, -nāt′) Forming a pair; doubled. ❖ *n.* (-nĭt, -nāt′) *Linguistics* A long or doubled consonant sound, such as the *nn* in the English word *thinness.* [Lat. *gemināre, gemināt-* < *geminus,* twin.] **—gem′i•na′tion** *n.*

Gem•i•ni (jĕm′ə-nī′, -nē′) *pl.n.* **1.** A constellation in the Northern Hemisphere containing the stars Castor and Pollux. **2a.** The third sign of the zodiac in astrology. **b.** *pl.* **-nis** One who is born under this sign. [ME < Lat. *Geminī,* pl. of *geminus,* twin.]

gem•ma (jĕm′ə) *n., pl.* **gem•mae** (jĕm′ē′) *Botany* An asexual budlike propagule, as in liverworts, capable of developing into a new individual; a bud. [Lat., bud. See **gembh-** in App.]

gem·mate (jĕm′āt′) *adj.* Having or reproducing by gemmae. ❖ *intr.v.* **-mat·ed, -mat·ing, -mates** To produce gemmae or reproduce by means of gemmae. [< Lat. *gemmātus*, p. part. of *gemmāre*, to bud < *gemma*, bud. See **gembh-** in App.] —**gem·ma′tion** (jĕ-mā′shən) *n.*

gem·mip·a·rous (jĕ-mĭp′ər-əs) *adj.* Reproducing by buds or gemmae. [Lat. *gemma*, bud; see GEMMA + –PAROUS.] —**gem·mip′a·rous·ly** *adv.*

gem·mule (jĕm′yōōl) *n.* **1.** A small gemma or similar structure, esp. a reproductive structure in some sponges. **2.** A hypothetical particle of heredity in the theory of pangenesis. [Fr. < Lat. *gemmula*, dim. of *gemma*, bud. See **gembh-** in App.] —**gem′mu·lif′er·ous** (jĕm′yōō-lĭf′ər-əs) *adj.*

gem·my (jĕm′ē) *adj.* **-mi·er, -mi·est 1.** Full of or set with gems. **2.** Glittering like a gem.

gem·ol·o·gy or **gem·mol·o·gy** (jĕ-mŏl′ə-jē) *n.* The study of gems. —**gem′o·log′i·cal** (jĕm′ə-lŏj′ĭ-kəl) *adj.* —**gem·ol′o·gist** *n.*

ge·mot also **ge·mote** (gə-mōt′) *n.* A public meeting or local judicial assembly in Anglo-Saxon England. [OE *gemōt* : *ge-*, collective pref.; see **kom** in App. + *mōt*, assembly.]

gems·bok (gĕmz′bŏk′) *n.* A large antelope (*Oryx gazella*) of southern Africa having long straight horns, a tufted tail, and distinctive black and white markings on the head. [Afr. < Du. < Ger. *Gemsbock* : *Gemse*, chamois (ult. < LLat. *camox*) + *Bock*, buck (< MHGer. *boc* < OHGer.).]

gem·stone (jĕm′stōn′) *n.* A precious or semiprecious stone that may be used as a jewel when cut and polished.

ge·müt·lich (gə-mōōt′lĭk, -mūt′lĬKH) *adj.* Warm and congenial; pleasant or friendly. [Ger. < MHGer. *gemüetlich* < *gemüete*, spirit, feelings < OHGer. *gimuoti* < *muot*, mind, spirit, joy.]

ge·müt·lich·keit (gə-mōōt′lĬKH-kīt′, -mūt′-) *n.* Warm friendliness; amicability. [Ger. < *gemütlich*, congenial. See GEMÜTLICH.]

gen. *abbr.* **1.** gender **2a.** general **b.** generally **3.** genitive **4.** genus

Gen. *abbr.* **1.** also **Gen** or **GEN** general **2.** *Bible* Genesis

–gen or **–gene** *suff.* **1.** Producer: *androgen.* **2.** One that is produced: *phosgene.* [Fr. *-gène* < Gk. *-genēs*, born. See **genə-** in App.]

gen·darme (zhän′därm′, zhän′därm′) *n.* **1.** A member of the French national police organization constituting a branch of the armed forces. **2.** *Slang* A police officer. [Fr. < OFr. *gent d'armes, gendarme*, sing. of *gens d'armes*, mounted soldiers, men-at-arms : *gens*, men (< Lat. *gentēs*, pl. of *gēns*, clan; see **genə-** in App.) + *de*, of (< Lat. *dē*; see DE–) + *armes*, pl. of *arme*, weapon; see ARM².]

gen·dar·me·rie (zhän-där′mə-rē) *n.* **1.** A body of French gendarmes. **2.** *Slang* A group of police officers. [Fr. < OFr., calvary < *gendarme*, mounted soldier. See GENDARME.]

gen·der (jĕn′dər) *n.* **1.** *Grammar* **a.** A grammatical category used in the classification of nouns, pronouns, adjectives, and, in some languages, verbs that may be arbitrary or based on characteristics such as sex or animacy and that determines agreement with or selection of modifiers, referents, or grammatical forms. **b.** One category of such a set. **c.** The classification of a word or grammatical form in such a category. **d.** The distinguishing form or forms used. **2.** Sexual identity, esp. in relation to society or culture. **3a.** The condition of being female or male; sex. **b.** Females or males considered as a group. ❖ *tr.v.* **-dered, -der·ing, -ders** To engender. [ME *gendre* < OFr. < Lat. *genus, gener-*. See **genə-** in App.] —**gen′der·less** *adj.*

USAGE NOTE Traditionally, *gender* has been used primarily to refer to the grammatical categories of "masculine," "feminine," and "neuter"; but in recent years the word has become well established in its use to refer to sex-based categories, as in *the politics of gender.* This usage is supported by the practice of many anthropologists, who reserve *sex* for reference to biological categories, while using *gender* to refer to social or cultural categories. According to this rule, one would say *The effectiveness of the medication depends on the sex of the patient,* but *In peasant societies, gender roles are more clearly defined.* This distinction, however, is by no means widely observed.

gen·dered (jĕn′dərd) *adj.* Having or making gender-based distinctions: *gendered behavior in children.*

gender gap or **gen·der-gap** (jĕn′dər-găp′) *n.* A disproportionate difference, as in attitudes, between the sexes.

gen·der·ize (jĕn′də-rīz′) *tr.v.* **-ized, -iz·ing, -iz·es** To categorize by gender: *genderize a mailing list by analyzing first names.*

gene (jēn) *n.* A hereditary unit consisting of a DNA sequence that occupies a specific location on a chromosome and determines a particular characteristic in an organism. [Ger. *Gen* < *gen-*, begetting (in words derived from Gk.). See **genə-** in App.]

ge·ne·al·o·gy (jē′nē-ŏl′ə-jē, -ăl′-) *n., pl.* **-gies 1.** A record or table of the descent of a person, family, or group from an ancestor or ancestors; a family tree. **2.** Direct descent from an ancestor; lineage or pedigree. **3.** The study or investigation of ancestry and family histories. [ME *genealogie* < OFr. < LLat. *geneālogia* < Gk. *geneālogiā* : *geneā*, family; see **genə-** in App. + *-logiā*, -logy.] —**ge′ne·a·log′i·cal** (-ə-lŏj′ĭ-kəl) *adj.* —**ge′ne·a·log′i·cal·ly** *adv.* —**ge′ne·al′o·gist** *n.*

gene amplification *n.* A cellular process characterized by the production of multiple copies of a particular gene or genes to amplify the phenotype that the gene confers on the cell.

gene flow *n.* Transfer of genes from one population to another of the same species, as by migration.

gene frequency *n.* The frequency of occurrence of an allele in relation to that of other alleles of the same gene in a population.

gene map *n.* See **genetic map.**

gene pool *n.* The collective genetic information contained within a population of sexually reproducing organisms.

gen·er·a (jĕn′ər-ə) *n.* Plural of **genus.**

gen·er·a·ble (jĕn′ər-ə-bəl) *adj.* Capable of being generated. [Lat. *generābilis* < *generāre*, to produce. See GENERATE.]

gen·er·al (jĕn′ər-əl) *adj.* **1.** Concerned with, applicable to, or affecting the whole or every member of a class or category: "*subduing all her impressions as a woman, to something more general*" (Virginia Woolf). **2.** Affecting or characteristic of the majority of those involved; prevalent: *general discontent.* **3.** Of or affecting the whole body: *general anesthesia.* **4.** Being usu. the case; true or applicable in most instances: *the general correctness of her decisions.* **5a.** Not limited in scope, area, or application: *as a general rule.* **b.** Not limited to or dealing with one class of things; diversified: *general studies.* **6.** Involving only the main features rather than precise details: *a general grasp of the subject.* **7.** Highest or superior in rank: *the general manager.* ❖ *n.* **1a.** A commissioned rank in the US Army, Air Force, or Marine Corps that is above lieutenant general. **b.** One who holds this rank or a similar rank in another military organization. **2.** A general officer. **3.** A statement, principle, or fact that embraces or is applicable to the whole. **4.** *Archaic* The public. —**idiom: in general** Generally. [ME < Lat. *generālis* < *genus, gener-*, kind. See **genə-** in App.] —**gen′er·al·ness** *n.*

SYNONYMS *general, common, generic, universal* These adjectives mean belonging to, relating to, or affecting the whole: *the general welfare; a common enemy; generic similarities; universal hopes.* **ANTONYM** *particular*

General American *n.* The variety of American English often considered typical of the United States, noted for the absence of phonological features that are associated with specific regions or social groups and for its use as a norm of pronunciation by national broadcasters.

general assembly *n.* **1.** A legislative body, esp. a US state legislature. **2. General Assembly** The principal deliberative body of the United Nations. **3.** The supreme governing body of some religious denominations.

General Court *n.* **1.** A legislative body having judicial powers in colonial New England. **2.** The state legislature of Massachusetts or New Hampshire.

general delivery *n.* **1.** A department of a post office that holds mail for addressees until picked up. **2.** Mail directed here.

general election *n.* An election involving all or most constituencies of a state or nation in the choice of candidates.

gen·er·al·is·si·mo (jĕn′ər-ə-lĭs′ə-mō′) *n., pl.* **-mos** The commander in chief of all the armed forces in certain countries. [Ital., superl. of *generale*, a general < Lat. *generālis*, general. See GENERAL.]

gen·er·al·ist (jĕn′ər-ə-lĭst) *n.* One who has broad general knowledge and skills in several areas.

gen·er·al·i·ty (jĕn′ə-răl′ĭ-tē) *n., pl.* **-ties 1.** The state or quality of being general. **2.** An observation or principle having general application; a generalization. **3.** An imprecise or vague statement or idea. **4.** The greater portion or number.

gen·er·al·i·za·tion (jĕn′ər-ə-lĭ-zā′shən) *n.* **1.** The act or an instance of generalizing. **2.** A principle, statement, or idea having general application.

gen·er·al·ize (jĕn′ər-ə-līz′) *v.* **-ized, -iz·ing, -iz·es** —*tr.* **1a.** To reduce to a general form, class, or law. **b.** To render indefinite or unspecific. **2a.** To infer from many particulars. **b.** To draw inferences or a general conclusion from. **3a.** To make generally or universally applicable. **b.** To popularize. —*intr.* **1a.** To form a concept inductively. **b.** To form general notions or conclusions. **2.** To deal in generalities; speak or write vaguely. **3.** *Medicine* To spread through the body. —**gen′er·al·iz′a·ble** *adj.*

gen·er·al·ized (jĕn′ər-ə-līzd′) *adj.* **1.** *Biology* Not specifically adapted to a particular environment or function; not specialized. **2.** Generally prevalent: *generalized discontent.* **3.** *Medicine* Spreading through or affecting the whole body.

gen·er·al·ly (jĕn′ər-ə-lē) *adv.* **1.** Popularly; widely: *generally known.* **2a.** As a rule; usually. **b.** For the most part. **3.** Without reference to particular instances or details.

general officer *n.* An officer in the US Army, Air Force, or Marine Corps ranking above colonel.

General of the Air Force *n.* The highest commissioned officer in the US Air Force.

General of the Army *n.* The highest commissioned officer in the US Army.

general paresis *n.* A brain disease occurring as a late consequence of syphilis, characterized by dementia, progressive muscular weakness, and paralysis.

general practitioner *n.* A physician whose practice covers a variety of medical problems in patients of all ages.

gemsbok
Oryx gazella

generator
hydroelectric generators at
the Grand Coulee Dam,
Washington

genet¹

gen•er•al-pur•pose (jĕn′ər-əl-pûr′pəs) *adj.* Designed for or suitable to more than one use; broadly useful.

general relativity *n.* The geometric theory of gravitation proposed by Albert Einstein, extending the theory of special relativity to accelerated frames of reference and introducing the principle that gravitational and inertial forces are equivalent.

general semantics *n.* (*used with a sing. verb*) A discipline developed by Alfred Korzybski that proposes to improve human behavioral responses by using words and symbols more critically.

gen•er•al•ship (jĕn′ər-əl-shĭp′) *n.* **1.** The rank, office, or tenure of a general. **2.** Leadership or skill in the conduct of a war. **3.** Skillful management or leadership.

general staff *n.* A group of military officers charged with assisting the commander of a division or higher unit in planning, coordinating, and supervising operations.

general store *n.* A retail store, usu. in a rural area, selling a wide variety of merchandise but not divided into departments.

gen•er•ate (jĕn′ə-rāt′) *tr.v.* **-at•ed, -at•ing, -ates** **1a.** To bring into being; give rise to: *generate a discussion.* **b.** To produce as a result of a chemical or physical process: *generate heat.* **2.** To engender (offspring); procreate. **3.** *Mathematics* To form (a geometric figure) by describing a curve or surface. **4.** *Computer Science* To produce (a specialized program) by instructing a computer to follow given parameters that select or complete parts of a general program. **5.** *Linguistics* To construct (a sentence, for example), as in generative grammar. [Lat. *generāre*, *generāt-*, to produce < *genus*, *gener-*, birth. See **genə-** in App.]

gen•er•a•tion (jĕn′ə-rā′shən) *n.* **1.** All of the offspring that are at the same stage of descent from a common ancestor. **2.** *Biology* A form or stage in the life cycle of an organism. **3.** The average interval of time between the birth of parents and the birth of their offspring. **4a.** A group of individuals born and living about the same time. **b.** A group of generally contemporaneous individuals regarded as having common cultural or social characteristics and attitudes. **5a.** A stage or period of sequential technological development and innovation. **b.** A class of objects derived from a preceding class: *a new generation of computers.* **6.** *Mathematics* The formation of a line or geometric figure by the movement of a point or line. **7.** The act or process of generating; origination, production, or procreation. —**gen•er•a′tion•al** *adj.* —**gen′er•a′tion•al•ly** *adv.*

generation gap *n.* A difference in values and attitudes between one generation and another.

Generation X *n.* The generation following the post–World War II baby boom, esp. people born in the US and Canada from the early 1960s to the late 1970s. [After *Generation X*, a novel by Douglas Coupland (born 1961), Canadian writer.]

Generation Y *n.* The generation following Generation X, esp. people born in the United States and Canada from the early 1980s to the late 1990s. [Modeled on GENERATION X.]

gen•er•a•tive (jĕn′ər-ə-tĭv, -ə-rā′-) *adj.* **1.** Having the ability to originate, produce, or procreate. **2.** Of or relating to the production of offspring. —**gen′er•a•tive•ly** *adv.* —**gen′er•a•tive•ness** *n.*

generative grammar *n.* A linguistic theory that attempts to describe a native speaker's tacit grammatical knowledge by a system of rules that can generate any grammatical sentence of a given language.

gen•er•a•tor (jĕn′ə-rā′tər) *n.* **1a.** One that generates, esp. a machine that converts mechanical energy into electrical energy. **b.** An apparatus that generates vapor or gas. **2.** A circuit that generates a specified waveform. **3.** *Mathematics* See **generatrix.** **4.** *Computer Science* A program that produces specific programs from the definition of an operation.

gen•er•a•trix (jĕn′ə-rā′trĭks) *n., pl.* **-er•a•tri•ces** (-ə-rā′trĭ-sēz′, -ər-ə-trī′sēz) A geometric element that generates a geometric figure, esp. a straight line that generates a surface by moving in a specified fashion.

ge•ner•ic (jə-nĕr′ĭk) *adj.* **1.** Relating to or descriptive of an entire group or class; general. See Syns at **general. 2.** *Biology* Of or relating to a genus. **3a.** Not having a brand name. **b.** Of or being a drug sold under or identified by its official nonproprietary or chemical name. **4.** *Grammar* Specifying neither masculine nor feminine gender: *a generic noun like* waitperson. ❖ *n.* **1.** A generic product or substance. **2.** A wine that is a blend of grape varieties and is named for no specific grape. [< Lat. *genus*, *gener-*, kind. See **genə-** in App.] —**ge•ner′i•cal•ly** *adv.*

gen•er•os•i•ty (jĕn′ə-rŏs′ĭ-tē) *n., pl.* **-ties 1.** Liberality in giving or willingness to give. **2.** Nobility of thought or behavior; magnanimity. **3.** Amplitude; abundance. **4.** A generous act. [ME *generosite* < OFr. < Lat. *generōsitās* < *generōsus*, generous. See GENEROUS.]

gen•er•ous (jĕn′ər-əs) *adj.* **1.** Liberal in giving or sharing. See Syns at **liberal. 2.** Characterized by nobility and forbearance in thought or behavior; magnanimous. **3.** Marked by abundance; ample. **4.** Having a rich bouquet and flavor. **5.** *Obsolete* Of noble lineage. [Fr. *genereux*, of noble birth, magnanimous < Lat. *generōsus*, of noble birth < *genus*, *gener-*, birth. See **genə-** in App.] —**gen′er•ous•ly** *adv.* —**gen′er•ous•ness** *n.*

Gen•e•see (jĕn′ĭ-sē′, jĕn′ĭ-sē′) A river rising in N PA and flowing c. 241 km (150 mi) to Lake Ontario.

gen•e•sis (jĕn′ĭ-sĭs) *n., pl.* **-ses** (-sēz′) **1.** The coming into being of something; the origin. See Syns at **beginning. 2. Genesis** See table at **Bible.** [Lat. < Gk. *gena-* in App.]

–genesis *suff.* Origin; production: *abiogenesis.* [NLat. < Lat. *genesis*, birth, origin. See GENESIS.]

gene-splic•ing (jēn′splī′sĭng) *n.* The process in which fragments of DNA from one or more different organisms are combined to form recombinant DNA.

gen•et¹ (jĕn′ĭt, jə-nĕt′) *n.* Any of several Old World carnivorous mammals of the genus *Genetta*, having a long ringed tail. [ME < OFr. *genete.*]

gen•et² (jĕn′ĭt) *n.* Variant of **jennet.**

Ge•net (zhə-nā′), **Jean** 1910–86. French writer who is best known for his absurdist plays, including *The Balcony* (1956).

Ge•nêt (zhə-nā′) See Janet **Flanner.**

Genêt or **Genet, Edmond Charles Edouard** Known as "Citizen Genêt." 1763–1834. French diplomat who attempted (1793) to draw the US into France's war against Great Britain and Spain.

gene therapy *n.* The treatment of usu. genetic disorders by introducing genetically engineered genes into a patient's cells.

ge•net•ic (jə-nĕt′ĭk) also **ge•net•i•cal** (-ĭ-kəl) *adj.* **1a.** Of or relating to genetics or genes. **b.** Affecting or determined by genes: *a genetic disorder.* **2.** Of, relating to, or influenced by the origin or development of something. **3.** *Linguistics* Of or relating to the relationship between or among languages that are descendants of the same language. [< Gk. *genetikos*, genitive < *genesis*, origin. See GENESIS.] —**ge•net′i•cal•ly** *adv.*

genetic code *n.* The nucleotide sequence in DNA or RNA that determines the amino acid sequence in the synthesis of proteins and is the basis of heredity. —**genetic coding** *n.*

genetic drift *n.* Random fluctuations in the frequency of the appearance of a gene in a small isolated population.

genetic engineering *n.* Scientific alteration of the structure of genetic material in a living organism, used, for example, to create bacteria that synthesize insulin. —**genetic engineer** *n.*

genetic fingerprint *n.* See DNA fingerprint.

ge•net•i•cist (jə-nĕt′ĭ-sĭst) *n.* One who specializes in genetics.

genetic load *n.* The difference in fitness between the theoretically most fit genotype within a population and the average genotype.

genetic map *n.* A graphic representation of the arrangement of genes or DNA sequences on a chromosome.

genetic marker *n.* A known DNA sequence associated with a particular gene or trait that is used to indicate the presence of that gene or trait.

ge•net•ics (jə-nĕt′ĭks) *n.* **1.** (*used with a sing. verb*) The branch of biology that deals with heredity, esp. the mechanisms of hereditary transmission and the variation of inherited characteristics among similar or related organisms. **2.** (*used with a pl. verb*) The genetic makeup of an individual, group, or class.

genetic screening *n.* The process of analyzing DNA samples to detect the presence of a gene or genes associated with an inherited disorder.

Ge•ne•va (jə-nē′və) A city of SW Switzerland located on Lake Geneva and bisected by the Rhone R.; a focal point of the Reformation. Pop. 170,861.

Geneva, Lake also **Lake Le•man** (lē′mən, lə-măn′) A lake on the Swiss-French border between the Alps and the Jura Mts.

Geneva bands *pl.n.* Two strips of white cloth that hang from the front of the collar of some clerical and academic robes.

Geneva Convention *n.* One of a series of agreements first formulated at an international convention held in Geneva, Switzerland, in 1864, establishing rules for the treatment of prisoners of war, the sick, and the wounded.

Geneva cross *n.* A red Greek or St. George's cross on a white ground, used as a symbol by the Red Cross and as a sign of neutrality. [After GENEVA, Switzerland.]

Geneva gown *n.* A loose black academic or clerical gown with wide sleeves. [After GENEVA, Switzerland.]

Ge•ne•van (jə-nē′vən) also **Gen•e•vese** (jĕn′ə-vēz′, -vēs′) *adj.* **1.** Of or relating to Geneva or its inhabitants. **2.** Of or relating to the teachings of John Calvin in Geneva; Calvinistic. ❖ *n.* **1.** A native or inhabitant of Geneva. **2.** A Calvinist.

Gen•ghis Khan (jĕng′gĭs kän′, gĕng′-) also **Jen•ghis Khan** or **Jen•ghiz Khan** (jĕn′gĭz kän′, -gĭs, jĕng′-) 1162?–1227. Mongol conqueror who united the Mongol tribes and forged an empire stretching from China to the Danube River and into Persia.

gen•ial¹ (jēn′yəl) *adj.* **1.** Having a pleasant or friendly disposition or manner. **2.** Conducive to life, growth, or comfort; mild: *"the genial sunshine . . . saturating his miserable body with its warmth"* (Jack London). **3.** *Obsolete* Relating to or marked by genius. **4.** *Obsolete* Of or relating to marriage; nuptial. [Lat. *genialis*, festive < *genius*, spirit of festivity. See **genə-** in App.] —**ge′ni•al′i•ty** (jē′nē-ăl′ĭ-tē), **gen′ial•ness** *n.* —**gen′ial•ly** *adv.*

ge•ni•al² (jĭ-nī′əl) *adj.* Of or relating to the chin. [< Gk. *geneion*, chin < *genus*, jaw.]

gen•ic (jē′nĭk, jĕn′ĭk) *adj.* Of, relating to, produced by, or being genes or a gene. —**gen′i•cal•ly** *adv.*

–genic *suff.* **1.** Producing; generating: *dysgenic.* **2.** Produced or generated by: *cryptogenic.* **3.** Suitable for production or reproduction by a specified medium: *photogenic.* [–GEN + –IC.]

ge·nic·u·late (jə-nĭk′yə-lĭt) also **ge·nic·u·lat·ed** (-lā′tĭd) *adj.* **1.** Bent abruptly, as a knee. **2.** Having kneelike joints; able to bend at an abrupt angle. [Lat. *geniculātus*, with bended knee < *geniculum*, dim. of *genū*, knee. See **genu-** in App.] —**ge·nic′u·late·ly** *adv.* —**ge·nic′u·la′tion** *n.*

ge·nie (jē′nē) *n.* **1.** A supernatural creature who does one's bidding when summoned. **2.** A jinni. [Fr. *génie*, spirit < Lat. *genius*, guardian spirit. See GENIUS.]

ge·ni·i (jē′nē-ī′) *n.* Roman Mythology Plural of **genius** 4.

gen·ip (jĕn′əp) *n.* **1a.** A tropical American tree (*Melicoccus bijugatus*) having small fruits with a green leathery rind and a juicy translucent pulp. **b.** The sweet edible fruit of this plant. **2.** See **genipap.** [Poss. alteration of GENIPAP.]

gen·i·pap (jĕn′ə-păp′) *n.* **1.** A tropical American evergreen tree (*Genipa americana*) having yellowish-white flowers and edible fruits used in preserves or drinks. **2.** The reddish-brown fruit of this plant. [Port. *genipapo* < Tupi *jenipapo* < *yandi-ipab*, genipap fruit.]

genit. *abbr.* genitive

gen·i·tal (jĕn′ĭ-tl) *adj.* **1.** Of or relating to biological reproduction. **2.** Of or relating to the genitalia. **3.** *Psychology* In psychoanalytic theory, of or relating to the final stage of psychosexual development, beginning in puberty, in which the genitals again become the focus of gratification and interest develops in relationships with persons of the opposite sex. ❖ *n.* A reproductive organ, esp. one of the external sex organs. Often used in the plural. [ME < Lat. *genitālis* < *genitus*, p. part. of *gignere*, to beget. See **genə-** in App.] —**gen′i·tal·ly** *adv.*

genital herpes *n.* A highly contagious, sexually transmitted viral infection of the genital and anal regions caused by herpes simplex and characterized by small clusters of painful lesions.

gen·i·ta·li·a (jĕn′ĭ-tā′lē-ə, -tăl′yə) *pl.n.* The genitals. [Lat. *genitālia*, pl. of *genitāle*, genital organ < neut. of *genitālis*, genital. See GENITAL.]

gen·i·tals (jĕn′ĭ-tlz) *pl.n.* The reproductive organs, esp. the external sex organs. [Transl. of Lat. *genitālia*. See GENITALIA.]

genital wart *n.* A wart typically found on the skin or mucous membranes of the anus and external genitals that is caused by a sexually transmitted human papillomavirus.

gen·i·ti·val (jĕn′ĭ-tī′vəl) *adj.* Of, relating to, or in the genitive case. —**gen′i·ti·val·ly** *adv.*

gen·i·tive (jĕn′ĭ-tĭv) *adj.* **1.** Of, relating to, or being the grammatical case expressing possession, measurement, or source. **2.** Of or relating to an affix or construction, such as a prepositional phrase, characteristic of the genitive case. ❖ *n.* **1.** The genitive case. **2.** A form or construction in this case. [ME *genitif* < Lat. *genetīvus* < *genitus*, p. part. of *gignere*, to beget. See **genə-** in App.]

gen·i·tor (jĕn′ĭ-tər) *n.* **1.** One who produces or creates. **2.** *Anthropology* A natural father or mother. [ME *genitour* < OFr. *genitor* < Lat. < *genitus*, p. part. of *gignere*, to beget. See **genə-** in App.]

gen·i·to·u·ri·nar·y (jĕn′ĭ-tō-yŏŏr′ə-nĕr′ē) *adj.* Of or relating to the genital and urinary organs or their functions.

gen·i·ture (jĕn′ĭ-chər) *n.* Birth; nativity. [Lat. *genitūra*, reproduction < *genitus*, p. part. of *gignere*, to beget. See **genə-** in App.]

gen·ius (jĕn′yəs) *n.*, *pl.* **-ius·es** **1a.** Extraordinary intellectual and creative power. **b.** A person of extraordinary intellect and talent. **c.** A person who has an exceptionally high intelligence quotient, typically above 140. **2a.** A strong natural talent, aptitude, or inclination. **b.** One who has such a talent or inclination. **3.** The prevailing spirit or distinctive character, as of a place, person, or era. **4.** *pl.* **ge·ni·i** (jĕ′nē-ī′) *Roman Mythology* A tutelary deity or guardian spirit of a person or place. **5.** A person who has great influence over another. **6.** A jinni in Muslim mythology. [ME, guardian spirit < Lat. See **genə-** in App.]

ge·ni·us lo·ci (jē′nē-əs lō′sī′, -kē, -kī) *n.* **1.** The distinctive atmosphere or pervading spirit of a place. **2.** The guardian deity of a place. [Lat. *genius locī* : *genius*, spirit + *locī*, genitive sing. of *locus*, place.]

Gennes (zhĕn), **Pierre-Gilles de** b. 1932. French physicist who won a 1991 Nobel Prize.

gen·o·a (jĕn′ō-ə) *n.* A large jib used on a sloop, overlapping the mainsail. [After GENOA.]

Genoa A city of NW Italy on the **Gulf of Genoa**, an arm of the Ligurian Sea. Pop. 675,659. —**Gen′o·ese′** (jĕn′ō-ēz′, -ēs′), **Gen′o·vese′** (-vēz′, -vēs′) *adj. & n.*

gen·o·cide (jĕn′ə-sīd′) *n.* The systematic and planned extermination of an entire national, racial, political, or ethnic group. [Gk. *genos*, race; see **genə-** in App. + -CIDE.] —**gen′o·cid′al** (-sīd′l) *adj.* —**gen′o·cid′al·ly** *adv.*

ge·nome (jē′nōm′) also **ge·nom** (-nōm′) *n.* **1.** The total genetic content contained in a haploid set of chromosomes in eukaryotes, in a single chromosome in bacteria, or in the DNA or RNA of viruses. **2.** An organism's genetic material. [GEN(E) + -OME.] —**ge·nom′ic** (-nōm′ĭk) *adj.*

genomic DNA *n.* The full complement of DNA contained in the genome of a cell or organism.

ge·no·mics (jə-nō′mĭks) *n.* (*used with a sing. verb*) The study of all of the nucleotide sequences in the chromosomes of an organism.

gen·o·type (jĕn′ə-tīp′, jē′nə-) *n.* **1.** The genetic makeup of an organism or a group of organisms. **2.** The combination of alleles located on homologous chromosomes that determines a specific characteristic or trait. [Gk. *genos*, race; see **genə-** in App. + Lat. *typus*, type; see TYPE.] —**gen′o·typ′ic** (-tīp′ĭk), **gen′o·typ′i·cal** *adj.* —**gen′o·typ′i·cal·ly** *adv.*

–genous *suff.* **1.** Producing; generating: *hematogenous*. **2.** Produced by or in a specified manner: *hypogenous*.

gen·re (zhän′rə) *n.* **1.** A type or class. **2a.** An established class or category of artistic composition, as in music or literature. **b.** A realistic style of painting that depicts scenes from everyday life. [Fr. < OFr., kind < Lat. *genus*, *gener-*. See **genə-** in App.]

gen·ro (gĕn′rō′) *n.*, *pl.* **-ros** Any of a group of elder male politicians in Japan who formerly advised the emperor. [J. *genrō* : *gen*, first (< M Chin. *ŋuan*) + *rō*, elder (< M Chin. *lawh*).]

gens (jĕnz) *n.*, *pl.* **gen·tes** (jĕn′tēz′) **1.** A patrilineal clan of ancient Rome composed of several families of the same name claiming a common ancestor and belonging to a common religious cult. **2.** *Anthropology* An exogamous patrilineal clan. [Lat. *gēns*. See **genə-** in App.]

Gen·ser·ic (jĕn′sə-rĭk′, gĕn′-) also **Gai·ser·ic** (gī′zə-) d. A.D. 477. King of the Vandals (428–477) who invaded Africa (429), captured Carthage (439), and sacked Rome (455).

gent¹ (jĕnt) *adj.* *Archaic* Graceful; elegant. [ME, noble, excellent < OFr., well-born < Lat. *genitus*, p. part. of *gignere*, to beget. See **genə-** in App.]

gent² (jĕnt) *n.* *Informal* A gentleman. [Short for GENTLEMAN.]

Gent (gĕnt, кнĕnt) See Ghent.

gen·ta·mi·cin (jĕn′tə-mī′sĭn) *n.* A broad-spectrum antibiotic derived from an actinomycete of the genus *Micromonospora* and used in its sulfate form to treat various infections. [Alteration of *gentamycin* : GENT(I)A(N VIOLET) + -MYCIN.]

gen·teel (jĕn-tēl′) *adj.* **1.** Refined in manner; well-bred and polite. **2.** Free from vulgarity or rudeness. **3.** Elegantly stylish. **4a.** Striving to convey a manner or appearance of refinement and respectability. See Syns at **polite.** **b.** Marked by affected and somewhat prudish refinement. [Fr. *gentil* < OFr. See GENTLE.] —**gen·teel′ly** *adv.* —**gen·teel′ness** *n.*

gen·teel·ism (jĕn-tēl′ĭz′əm) *n.* A word or expression thought by its user to be more refined than another.

gen·tian (jĕn′shən) *n.* **1.** Any of numerous plants of the genus *Gentiana*, characteristically having showy, variously colored flowers. **2.** The dried rhizome and roots of a yellow-flowered European gentian, *G. lutea*, sometimes used as a tonic. [ME *gencian* < OFr. *genciane* < Lat. *gentiāna*, perhaps after *Gentius*, 2nd-cent. B.C. king of Illyria.]

gentian violet *n.* A dye used as a biological stain and as a bactericide, fungicide, and anthelmintic.

gen·tile (jĕn′tīl′) *n.* often **Gentile** **1.** One who is not of the Jewish faith or is of a non-Jewish nation. **2.** A Christian. **3.** *Archaic* A pagan or heathen. **4.** *Mormon Church* A non-Mormon. ❖ *adj.* **1.** often **Gentile** Of or relating to a Gentile. **2.** Of or relating to a gens, tribe, or people. **3.** *Grammar* Expressing national or local origins. [ME *gentil* < LLat. *gentīlis*, pagan < Lat., of the same clan. See GENTLE.]

Gen·ti·le·schi (jĕn′tē-lĕs′kē), **Artemisia** 1593?–1652? Italian Renaissance painter whose works include self-portraits.

gen·ti·lesse (jĕn′tə-lĕs′) *n.* *Archaic* Refinement and courtesy resulting from good breeding. [ME < OFr. < *gentil*, noble. See GENTLE.]

gen·til·i·ty (jĕn-tĭl′ĭ-tē) *n.* **1.** The quality of being well-mannered; refinement. **2.** The condition of being born to the gentry. **3.** Persons of high social standing considered as a group. **4.** An attempt to convey or maintain the appearance of refinement and elegance. [ME *gentilete*, nobility of birth < OFr. < Lat. *gentīlitās* < *gentīlis*, of the same clan. See GENTLE.]

gen·tle (jĕn′tl) *adj.* **-tler, -tlest** **1.** Considerate or kindly in disposition; amiable and tender. **2.** Not harsh or severe; mild and soft. **3.** Easily managed or handled; docile. **4.** Not steep or sudden; gradual. **5a.** Of good family; wellborn. **b.** Suited to one of good breeding; refined and polite. **6.** *Archaic* Noble; chivalrous. ❖ *n.* *Archaic* One of good birth or relatively high station. ❖ *tr.v.* **-tled, -tling, -tles** **1.** To make less severe or intense. **2.** To soothe, as by stroking; pacify. **3.** To tame or break (a domestic animal, for instance). **4.** To raise to the status of a noble. [ME *gentil*, courteous, noble < OFr. < Lat. *gentīlis*, of the same clan < *gēns*, *gent-*, clan. See **genə-** in App.] —**gen′tle·ness** *n.* —**gen′tly** *adv.*

gen·tle·folk (jĕn′tl-fōk′) also **gen·tle·folks** (-fōks′) *pl.n.* Persons of good family and relatively high station.

gen·tle·man (jĕn′tl-mən) *n.* **1.** A man of gentle or noble birth or superior social position. **2.** A well-mannered and considerate man with high standards of proper behavior. See Usage Note at **lady. 3.** A man of independent means who does not need to have a wage-paying job. **4.** A man. **5. gentlemen** (-mən) Used as a form of address for a group of men. **6.** A manservant; a valet. —**gen′tle·man·ly** *adj.*

gen·tle·man-at-arms (jĕn′tl-mən-ət-ärmz′) *n.*, *pl.* **gen·tle·men-at-arms** (-mən-) One of a military corps of 40 gentlemen who attend the British sovereign on state occasions.

gentleman farmer *n.*, *pl.* **gentlemen farmers** A man of independent means who farms chiefly for pleasure.

gen·tle·man's agreement or **gen·tle·men's agreement** (jĕn'tl-mənz) *n.* An unwritten agreement guaranteed only by the pledged word or secret understanding of the participants.

gentleman's gentleman *n.* A manservant; a valet.

gen·tle·per·son (jĕn'tl-pûr'sən) *n.* A person of good breeding; a lady or a gentleman.

gen·tle·wom·an (jĕn'tl-wŏom'ən) *n.* **1.** A woman of gentle or noble birth or superior social position. **2.** A well-mannered and considerate woman with high standards of proper behavior. **3.** A woman personal attendant to a lady of rank.

gen·tri·fi·ca·tion (jĕn'trə-fĭ-kā'shən) *n.* The restoration or upgrading of deteriorated urban property esp. by middle-class or affluent people, often resulting in displacement of lower-income

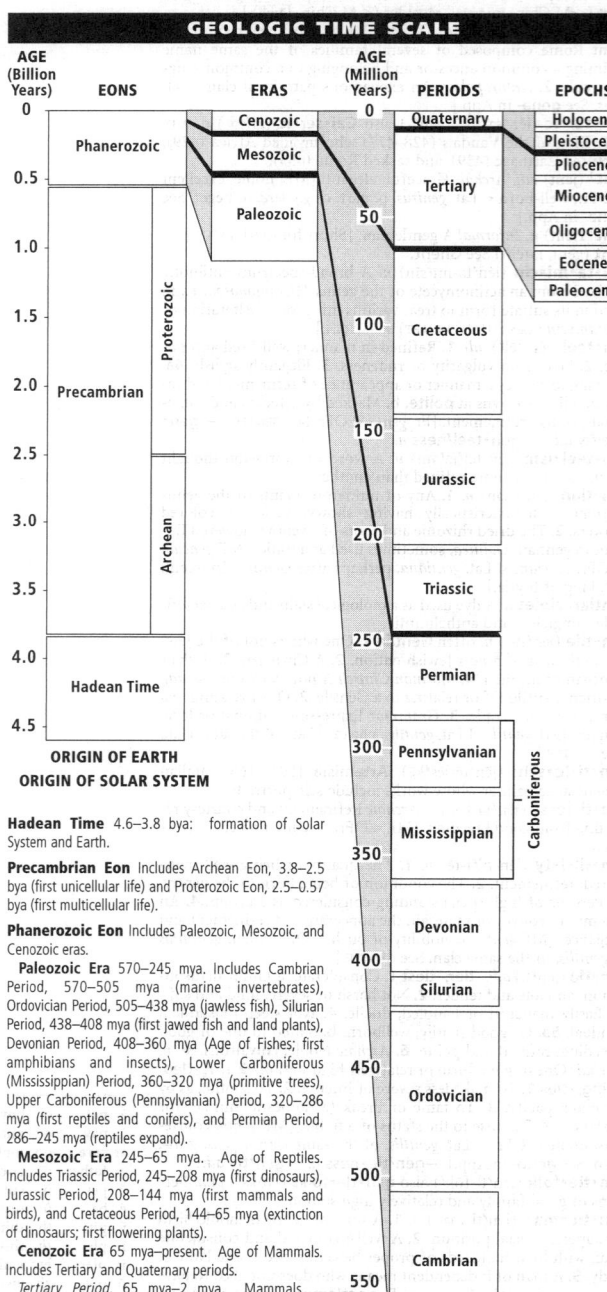

GEOLOGIC TIME SCALE

AGE (Billion Years)	EONS		ERAS	AGE (Million Years)	PERIODS		EPOCHS
0	Phanerozoic		Cenozoic	0	Quaternary		Holocene
							Pleistocene
			Mesozoic				Pliocene
0.5					Tertiary		Miocene
			Paleozoic	50			Oligocene
1.0							Eocene
		Proterozoic					Paleocene
1.5				100	Cretaceous		
2.0	Precambrian						
2.5				150			
					Jurassic		
3.0		Archean		200			
3.5					Triassic		
4.0				250			
	Hadean Time				Permian		
4.5				300	Pennsylvanian	Carboniferous	
				350	Mississippian		
				400	Devonian		
					Silurian		
				450	Ordovician		
				500			
				550	Cambrian		

ORIGIN OF EARTH
ORIGIN OF SOLAR SYSTEM

Hadean Time 4.6–3.8 bya: formation of Solar System and Earth.

Precambrian Eon Includes Archean Eon, 3.8–2.5 bya (first unicellular life) and Proterozoic Eon, 2.5–0.57 bya (first multicellular life).

Phanerozoic Eon Includes Paleozoic, Mesozoic, and Cenozoic eras.

Paleozoic Era 570–245 mya. Includes Cambrian Period, 570–505 mya (marine invertebrates), Ordovician Period, 505–438 mya (jawless fish), Silurian Period, 438–408 mya (first jawed fish and land plants), Devonian Period, 408–360 mya (Age of Fishes; first amphibians and insects), Lower Carboniferous (Mississippian) Period, 360–320 mya (primitive trees), Upper Carboniferous (Pennsylvanian) Period, 320–286 mya (first reptiles and conifers), and Permian Period, 286–245 mya (reptiles expand).

Mesozoic Era 245–65 mya. Age of Reptiles. Includes Triassic Period, 245–208 mya (first dinosaurs), Jurassic Period, 208–144 mya (first mammals and birds), and Cretaceous Period, 144–65 mya (extinction of dinosaurs; first flowering plants).

Cenozoic Era 65 mya–present. Age of Mammals. Includes Tertiary and Quaternary periods.

Tertiary Period, 65 mya–2 mya. Mammals expand. Includes following epochs: Paleocene (65–58 mya), Eocene (58–37 mya), Oligocene (37–24 mya), Miocene (24–5 mya), and Pliocene (5–2 mya).

Quaternary Period, 2 mya–present. Humans develop. Includes Pleistocene Epoch (2 mya–10,000 years ago) and Holocene Epoch (10,000 years ago to present).

Key
bya = billion years ago
mya = million years ago

people from their neighborhoods.

gen·tri·fy (jĕn'trə-fī') *tr.v.* **-fied, -fy·ing, -fies** To subject to gentrification. [GENTR(Y) + -FY.] —**gen'tri·fi'er** *n.*

gen·try (jĕn'trē) *n., pl.* **-tries 1.** People of gentle birth, good breeding, or high social position. **2.** An upper or ruling class. **b.** The class of English landowners ranking below the nobility. **3.** People of a particular class or group. [ME *gentri*, nobility of birth < OFr. *genterie*, var. of *genterise*, *gentilise* < *gentil*, noble. See GENTLE.]

gen·u·flect (jĕn'yə-flĕkt') *intr.v.* **-flect·ed, -flect·ing, -flects 1.** To bend the knee or touch one knee to the floor or ground, as in worship. **2.** To be servilely deferential; grovel. [LLat. *genūflectere* : Lat. *genū*, knee; see **genu-** in App. + Lat. *flectere*, to bend.] —**gen'u·flec'tion** (-flĕk'shən) *n.*

gen·u·ine (jĕn'yŏo-ĭn) *adj.* **1.** Possessing the alleged or apparent attribute or character: *genuine leather.* **2.** Not spurious or counterfeit; authentic. See Syns at **authentic. 3a.** Honestly felt or experienced. **b.** Actual; real. **4.** Free from hypocrisy or dishonesty; sincere. **5.** Being of pure or original stock: *a genuine Hawaiian.* [Lat. *genuīnus*, natural, poss. < alteration of *ingenuus*, native, freeborn. See INGENUOUS.] —**gen'u·ine·ly** *adv.* —**gen'u·ine·ness** *n.*

ge·nus (jē'nəs) *n., pl.* **gen·er·a** (jĕn'ər-ə) **1.** *Biology* A taxonomic category ranking below a family and above a species and usu. consisting of a group of species exhibiting similar characteristics. See table at **taxonomy. 2.** *Logic* A class of objects divided into subordinate species having certain common attributes. **3.** A class, group, or kind with common attributes. [Lat., kind. See **genə-** in App.]

Gen-X (jĕn'ĕks') *adj.* Of or relating to Generation X. —**Gen'-X'er** *n.*

Gen-Y (jĕn'wī') *adj.* Of or relating to Generation Y.

-geny *suff.* Production; generation; origin: *ontogeny.* [Gk. *-geneia* < *-genēs*, born. See **genə-** in App.]

geo- or **ge-** *pref.* **1.** Earth: *geocentric.* **2.** Geography: *geopolitical.* [Gk. *geō-* < *gē*, earth.]

ge·o·bot·a·ny (jē'ō-bŏt'n-ē) *n.* See **phytogeography.** —**ge'o·bo·tan'ic** (-bə-tăn'ĭk), **ge'o·bo·tan'i·cal** *adj.* —**ge'o·bo·tan'i·cal·ly** *adv.* —**ge'o·bot'a·nist** (bŏt'n-ĭst) *n.*

ge·o·cen·tric (jē'ō-sĕn'trĭk) *adj.* **1.** Relating to, measured from, or with respect to the center of the earth. **2.** Having the earth as a center. —**ge'o·cen'tri·cal·ly** *adv.*

ge·o·chem·is·try (jē'ō-kĕm'ĭ-strē) *n.* The chemistry of the composition and alterations of the solid matter of the earth or a celestial body. —**ge'o·chem'i·cal** (-ĭ-kəl) *adj.* —**ge'o·chem'i·cal·ly** *adv.* —**ge'o·chem'ist** *n.*

ge·o·chro·nol·o·gy (jē'ō-krə-nŏl'ə-jē) *n.* The chronology of the earth as determined by geologic events. —**ge'o·chron'o·log'ic** (-krŏn'ə-lŏj'ĭk), **ge'o·chron'o·log'i·cal** *adj.* —**ge'o·chro·nol'o·gist** *n.*

ge·o·chro·nom·e·try (jē'ō-krə-nŏm'ĭ-trē) *n.* Measurement of geologic time, as through isotopic radioactive decay. —**ge'o·chron'o·met'ric** (-krŏn'ə-mĕt'rĭk) *adj.*

ge·o·co·ro·na (jē'ō-kə-rō'nə) *n.* The outermost region of the earth's atmosphere, consisting chiefly of ionized hydrogen.

ge·ode (jē'ōd') *n.* A hollow, usu. spheroidal rock with crystals lining the inside wall. [Fr. *géode* < Lat. *geōdēs*, a precious stone < Gk., earthlike : *gē*, earth + *-ōdēs*, adj. suff.; see COLLODION.]

ge·o·des·ic (jē'ə-dĕs'ĭk, -dē'sĭk) *adj.* **1.** Of or relating to the geometry of curved surfaces and determining the shortest line between two points on such surfaces. **2.** Of or relating to geodesy. ❖ *n.* The shortest line between two points on any mathematically defined surface. [< GEODESY.]

geodesic dome *n.* A domed or vaulted structure of lightweight straight elements that form interlocking polygons.

ge·od·e·sy (jē-ŏd'ĭ-sē) *n.* The geologic science of the size and shape of the earth. [NLat. *geōdaesia* < Gk. *geōdaisia* : *geō-*, geo- + *daiesthai*, to divide; see **dā-** in App.] —**ge·od'e·sist** *n.*

ge·o·det·ic (jē'ə-dĕt'ĭk) also **ge·o·det·i·cal** (-ĭ-kəl) *adj.* Geodesic. —**ge'o·det'i·cal·ly** *adv.*

geodetic survey *n.* A survey of a large area of land in which corrections are made to account for the curvature of the earth.

geo·duck also **gwe·duc** (gōo'dŭk') *n.* A large edible clam (*Panope generosa*) of the Pacific coast of northwest North America. [< Puget Salish *gʷídəq*.]

ge·o·ec·o·nom·ics also **ge·o·ec·o·nom·ics** (jē'ō-ĕk'ə-nŏm'ĭks, -ē'kə-) *n.* (*used with a sing. verb*) **1.** The study of the relationship between politics and economics, esp. internationally. **2.** A governmental policy employing geoeconomics. **3.** The international economic and political factors relating to or influencing a nation or region. —**ge'o·ec'o·nom'ic** *adj.*

Geof·frey of Mon·mouth (jĕf'rē; mŏn'məth) 1100?–54. English prelate and chronicler whose *Historia Regum Britanniae* (c. 1139) is a source of Arthurian legend.

ge·o·graph·ic (jē'ə-grăf'ĭk) also **ge·o·graph·i·cal** (-ĭ-kəl) *adj.* **1.** Of or relating to geography. **2.** Concerning the topography of a specific region. —**ge'o·graph'i·cal·ly** *adv.*

Geographic Information System *n.* A computer application used to store, view, and analyze geographical information, esp. maps.

geographic mile *n.* A nautical mile.

ge·og·ra·phy (jē-ŏg′rə-fē) *n., pl.* **-phies 1.** The study of the earth and its features and of the distribution of life on the earth, including human life and the effects of human activity. **2.** The physical characteristics, esp. the surface features, of an area. **3.** A book on geography. **4.** An ordered arrangement of constituent elements. [Lat. *geōgraphia* < Gk. *geōgraphiā* : *geō-*, geo- + *-graphiā*, -graphy.] —**ge·og′ra·pher** *n.*

ge·oid (jē′oid′) *n.* The hypothetical surface of the earth that coincides everywhere with mean sea level. [Ger. < Gk. *geoeidēs*, earthlike : *gē*, earth + *-oeidēs*, -oid.] —**ge·oid′al** (-oid′l) *adj.*

geologic time *n.* The time covering the physical formation and development of Earth, esp. prior to human history.

ge·ol·o·gize (jē-ŏl′ə-jīz′) *intr.v.* **-gized, -giz·ing, -giz·es** To study geology or make geological investigations.

ge·ol·o·gy (jē-ŏl′ə-jē) *n., pl.* **-gies 1.** The scientific study of the origin, history, and structure of the earth. **2.** The structure of a specific region of the earth's crust. **3.** A book on geology. **4.** The scientific study of the origin, history, and structure of the solid matter of a celestial body. [Lat. *geōlogia*, study of earthly things : Gk. *geō-*, geo- + Gk. *-logiā*, -logy.] —**ge·o·log′ic** (jē′ə-lŏj′ĭk), **ge′o·log′i·cal** *adj.* —**ge′o·log′i·cal·ly** *adv.* —**ge·ol′o·gist** *n.*

geomagnetic equator *n.* The imaginary great circle on the earth's surface formed by the intersection of a plane passing through the earth's center perpendicular to the axis connecting the north and south magnetic poles.

geomagnetic storm *n.* See **magnetic storm.**

ge·o·mag·ne·tism (jē′ō-măg′nĭ-tĭz′əm) *n.* **1.** The magnetism of the earth. **2.** The study of the earth's magnetism. —**ge′o·mag·net′ic** (-nĕt′ĭk) *adj.*

ge·o·man·cy (jē′ə-măn′sē) *n.* Divination by means of lines and figures or by geographic features. [ME *geomancie*, ult. < L.Gk. *geōmanteia* : Gk. *geō-* + Gk. *manteia*, divination; see —MANCY.] —**ge′o·man′cer** *n.* —**ge′o·man′tic** (-tĭk) *adj.*

ge·o·met·ric (jē′ə-mĕt′rĭk) also **ge·o·met·ri·cal** (-rĭ-kəl) *adj.* **1a.** Of or relating to geometry and its methods and principles. **b.** Increasing or decreasing in a geometric progression. **2.** Using simple geometric forms such as circles and squares in design and decoration. **3.** Of or relating to properties in algebraic geometry involving algebraically closed fields. —**ge′o·met′ri·cal·ly** *adv.*

geometric isomer *n.* Any of a set of isomers that differ from one another because of a structural asymmetry about a molecular bond.

ge·o·met·ri·cize (jē′ə-mĕt′rĭ-sīz′) *tr.v.* **-cized, -ciz·ing, -ciz·es** To design or form in geometric patterns or figures.

geometric mean *n.* The *n*th root, usu. the positive *n*th root, of a product of *n* factors.

geometric pace *n.* See **pace**[1] 3a.

geometric progression *n.* A sequence, such as the numbers 1, 3, 9, 27, 81, in which each term is multiplied by the same factor in order to obtain the following term.

ge·o·met·rics (jē′ə-mĕt′rĭks) *n.* (*used with a pl. verb*) **1.** Geometric qualities or properties. **2.** A pattern or design characterized by the use of geometric figures.

geometric series *n.* An infinite series of the form $a + ax + ax^2 + ax^3 + \dots$

ge·om·e·trid (jē-ŏm′ĭ-trĭd) *n.* Any of various moths of the family Geometridae, having caterpillars commonly known as measuring worms that move by looping the body. [< NLat. *Geōmetridae*, family name < Lat. *geometrēs*, geometrician, land-measurer < Gk. < *geōmetrein*, to measure land. See GEOMETRY.] —**ge·om′e·trid** *adj.*

ge·om·e·trize (jē-ŏm′ĭ-trīz′) *v.* **-trized, -triz·ing, -triz·es** —*intr.* **1.** To study geometry. **2.** To apply the methods of geometry. —*tr.* **1.** To present in geometric form. **2.** To bring into conformance with the laws and principles of geometry.

ge·om·e·try (jē-ŏm′ĭ-trē) *n., pl.* **-tries 1a.** The mathematics of the properties, measurement, and relationships of points, lines, angles, surfaces, and solids. **b.** A system of geometry. **c.** A geometry restricted to a class of problems or objects. **d.** A book on geometry. **2a.** Configuration; arrangement. **b.** A surface shape. **3.** A physical arrangement suggesting geometric forms or lines. [ME *geometrie* < OFr. < Lat. *geōmetria* < Gk. *geōmetriā* < *geōmetrein*, to measure land : *gē*, earth + *metron*, measure; see **mē-**[1] in App.] —**ge·om′e·tri′cian** (-ŏm′ĭ-trĭsh′ən, jē′ə-mĭ-), **ge·om′e·ter** *n.*

ge·o·mor·phic (jē′ə-môr′fĭk) *adj.* Of or resembling the earth or its shape or surface configuration.

ge·o·mor·phol·o·gy (jē′ō-môr-fŏl′ə-jē) *n.* The study of the evolution and configuration of landforms. —**ge′o·mor′pho·log′ic** (-môr′fə-lŏj′ĭk), **ge′o·mor′pho·log′i·cal** (-ĭ-kəl) *adj.* —**ge′o·mor·phol′o·gist** *n.*

ge·oph·a·gy (jē-ŏf′ə-jē) *n.* The eating of earthy substances, such as clay. —**ge·oph′a·gism** *n.* —**ge·oph′a·gist** *n.*

ge·o·phone (jē′ə-fōn′) *n.* An electronic receiver designed to pick up seismic vibrations.

ge·o·phys·ics (jē′ō-fĭz′ĭks) *n.* (*used with a sing. verb*) The physics of the earth and its environment, including the physics of fields such as meteorology, oceanography, and seismology. —**ge′o·phys′i·cal** *adj.* —**ge′o·phys′i·cal·ly** *adv.* —**ge′o·phys′i·cist** (-ĭ-sĭst) *n.*

ge·o·phyte (jē′ə-fīt′) *n.* A perennial plant, such as a tulip, prop-agated by buds on underground bulbs, tubers, or corms.

ge·o·pol·i·tics (jē′ō-pŏl′ĭ-tĭks) *n.* (*used with a sing. verb*) **1.** The study of the relationship among politics and geography, demography, and economics, esp. with respect to the foreign policy of a nation. **2a.** A governmental policy employing geopolitics. **b.** A Nazi doctrine holding that the geographic, economic, and political needs of Germany justified its invasion and seizure of other lands. **3.** A combination of geographic and political factors relating to or influencing a nation or region. —**ge′o·po·lit′i·cal** (-pə-lĭt′ĭ-kəl) *adj.*

ge·o·pon·ic (jē′ə-pŏn′ĭk) *adj.* Of or relating to agriculture or farming. [Gk. *geōponikos* < *geōponein*, to till : *gē*, earth + *ponein*, to toil.]

ge·o·pon·ics (jē′ə-pŏn′ĭks) *n.* (*used with a sing. verb*) The study or science of agriculture.

ge·o·pres·sured (jē′ō-prĕsh′ərd) also **ge·o·pres·sur·ized** (jē′ō-prĕsh′ə-rīzd′) *adj.* Under high pressure within the earth.

Geor·die[1] (jôr′dē) *n. Chiefly British* **1.** A native or inhabitant of Newcastle upon Tyne, England, or its environs. **2.** Their dialect of English. [Sc., dim. of *George*.]

Geor·die[2] (jôr′dē) *n. Scots* A former British gold coin worth one pound and five pence; a guinea. [Sc., dim. of *George*, after Saint GEORGE.]

George (jôrj) *n.* **1.** A jeweled figure of Saint George killing the dragon, used as an insignia of the Knights of the Garter. **2.** An English coin during the reign of Henry VIII, imprinted with a figure of Saint George.

George, Saint. d. c. A.D. 303. Christian martyr and patron of England who according to legend slew a fearsome dragon.

George I[1] 1660–1727. Elector of Hanover (1698–1727) and king of Great Britain and Ireland (1714–27) who left the affairs of his country in the hands of Sir Robert Walpole.

George I[2] 1845–1913. King of Greece (1863–1913) who introduced a democratic constitution (1864).

George II[1] 1683–1760. King of Great Britain and Ireland and elector of Hanover (1727–60) who won the Battle of Dettingen (1743) in S-central present-day Germany.

George III 1738–1820. King of Great Britain and Ireland (1760–1820) and of Hanover (1815–20) whose policies fed American colonial discontent, leading to revolution in 1776.

George IV 1762–1830. King of Great Britain and Ireland and of Hanover (1820–30) who caused controversy when he attempted to divorce his estranged wife.

George V 1865–1936. King of Great Britain and Northern Ireland and emperor of India (1910–36) who gave up his German titles during World War I.

George V Coast also **George V Land** A section of the coastal area of Antarctica between Wilkes Land and Victoria Land; claimed by Australia.

George VI 1895–1952. King of Great Britain and Northern Ireland (1936–52) and emperor of India (1936–47) noted for his dedication to his duty, esp. during World War II.

George, Lake A glacial lake of NE NY in the foothills of the Adirondack Mts. S of Lake Champlain.

George River A river of NE Quebec, Canada, rising on the Quebec-Labrador border and flowing c. 563 km (350 mi) to Ungava Bay.

Geor·ges Bank (jôr′jĭz) A submerged sandbank in the Atlantic Ocean E of Cape Cod.

George·town (jôrj′toun′) **1.** also **George Town** The cap. of the Cayman Is., on Grand Cayman in the West Indies W of Jamaica. Pop. 7,617. **2.** The cap. of Guyana, in the N part on the Atlantic Ocean; founded by the British in 1781. Pop. 78,500. **3.** A section of W Washington DC; settled c. 1665 and annexed by Washington DC in 1878.

George Town 1. also **Pi·nang** or **Pe·nang** (pə-năng′, pē′năng′) A city of W Malaysia on Pinang I. in the Strait of Malacca. Pop. 250,578. **2.** See **Georgetown** 1.

geor·gette (jôr-jĕt′) *n.* A sheer strong silk or silklike clothing fabric with a dull, creped surface. [Orig. a trademark.]

Geor·gia (jôr′jə) **1.** A region and republic of Asia Minor in the Caucasus S of Russia; acquired by Russia between 1801 and 1829 and a constituent republic of the USSR from 1936 to 1991. Cap. Tbilisi. Pop. 5,450,000. **2.** A state of the SE US; admitted as one of the original Thirteen Colonies in 1788. Cap. Atlanta. Pop. 8,186,453.

Georgia, Strait of A channel between Vancouver I. and mainland British Columbia, Canada, and N WA linking Puget Sound with Queen Charlotte Sound.

Geor·gian (jôr′jən) *adj.* **1.** Of, relating to, or characteristic of the reigns of the four Georges who ruled Great Britain from 1714 to 1830. **2.** Of, relating to, or characteristic of the reign of George V of Great Britain. **3.** Of or relating to the US state of Georgia or its inhabitants. **4.** Of or relating to the country of Georgia or its people, language, or culture. ❖ *n.* **1.** A native or inhabitant of the US state of Georgia. **2a.** A native or inhabitant of the country of Georgia. **b.** The Kartvelian language of the Georgians.

Georgian Bay An extension of Lake Huron in SE Ontario, Canada.

geor·gic (jôr′jĭk) *adj.* also **geor·gi·cal** (-kəl) Of or relating to agriculture or rural life. ❖ *n.* A poem concerning farming or

geodesic dome

George III
c. 1767 portrait

Georgia

ă	pat	oi	boy
ā	pay	ou	out
âr	care	ŏŏ	took
ä	father	ōō	boot
ĕ	pet	ŭ	cut
ē	be	ûr	urge
ĭ	pit	th	thin
ī	pie	th	this
îr	pier	hw	which
ŏ	toe	zh	vision
ŏ	toe		about,
ô	paw		item

Stress marks:
′ (primary);
′ (secondary), as in
lexicon (lĕk′sĭ-kŏn′)

gerenuk
Litocranius walleri

German shepherd

Germany

rural life. [Lat. *geōrgicus* < Gk. *geōrgikos* < *geōrgos*, farmer : *geō-*, geo- + *ergon*, work; see **werg-** in App.]

ge·o·sci·ence (jē′ō-sī′əns) *n.* Any of the sciences, such as geology or geochemistry, that deals with the earth.

ge·o·sta·tion·ar·y (jē′ō-stā′shə-nĕr′ē) *adj.* 1. Of, relating to, or being a satellite that travels above Earth's equator from west to east at an altitude of approx. 35,900 kilometers (22,300 miles) and at a speed matching that of Earth's rotation, thus remaining stationary in relation to Earth. 2. Of, relating to, or being the orbit of such a satellite.

ge·o·strat·e·gy (jē′ō-străt′ə-jē) *n., pl.* **-gies** 1. The branch of geopolitics that deals with strategy. 2. The geopolitical and strategic factors that characterize a certain geographic area. 3. Governmental strategy based on geopolitics. —**ge′o·stra·te′gic** (-strə-tē′jĭk) *adj.* —**ge′o·strat′e·gist** *n.*

ge·o·stroph·ic (jē′ō-strŏf′ĭk) *adj.* Of or relating to the pseudo force caused by the earth's rotation. [GEO– + Gk. *strophē*, a turning; see STROPHE + –IC.] —**ge′o·stroph′i·cal·ly** *adv.*

ge·o·syn·chro·nous (jē′ō-sĭng′krə-nəs, -sĭn′-) *adj.* 1. Of or relating to an orbit that has a period of one sidereal day. 2. Geostationary. —**ge′o·syn′chro·nous·ly** *adv.*

ge·o·syn·cline (jē′ō-sĭn′klīn′) *n.* An extensive, usu. linear depression in the earth's crust. —**ge′o·syn·cli′nal** (-sĭn-klī′nəl) *adj.*

ge·o·tax·is (jē′ō-tăk′sĭs) *n.* Movement of a motile organism using the earth's gravity for orientation. —**ge′o·tac′tic** (-tĭk) *adj.* —**ge′o·tac′ti·cal·ly** *adv.*

ge·o·tec·ton·ic (jē′ō-tĕk-tŏn′ĭk) *adj.* Of or relating to the shape, structure, and arrangement of the rock masses resulting from structural deformation of the earth's crust.

ge·o·ther·mal (jē′ō-thûr′məl) also **ge·o·ther·mic** (-mĭk) *adj.* Of or relating to the internal heat of the earth.

ge·ot·ro·pism (jē-ŏt′rə-pĭz′əm) *n.* The growth of a living organism in response to gravity, as the downward growth of plant roots. —**ge′o·tro′pic** (jē′ə-trŏp′ĭk, -trōp′ĭk) *adj.*

ger. *abbr.* gerund

Ger. *abbr.* 1. German 2. Germany

ge·rah (gĭr′ə) *n.* An ancient Hebrew coin and unit of weight. [Heb. *gērâ*, grain, bean.]

ge·ra·ni·al (jə-rā′nē-əl) *n.* A structural isomer of citral obtained from the oxidation of geraniol. [GERANI(OL) + –AL³.]

ge·ra·ni·ol (jə-rā′nē-ôl′, -ōl′, -ŏl′) *n.* A fragrant pale yellow liquid alcohol, C₉H₁₇COH, derived chiefly from the oils of geranium and citronella and used in cosmetics and flavorings.

ge·ra·ni·um (jə-rā′nē-əm) *n.* 1. Any of various plants of the genus *Geranium,* having pink or purplish flowers. 2. Any of various chiefly southern African plants of the genus *Pelargonium,* having showy clusters of red, pink, or white flowers. 3. A strong to vivid red. [NLat. *Geranium,* genus name < Lat. *geranium,* cranesbill < Gk. *geranion,* dim. of *geranos,* crane.]

ge·rar·di·a (jə-rär′dē-ə) *n.* Any of various herbaceous, root-parasitizing, New World plants of the genus *Agalinus,* having large pink, purple, or white flowers. [NLat., after John *Gerard* (1545–1612), English botanist.]

ger·bil (jûr′bəl) *n.* Any of various mouselike rodents of the subfamily Gerbillinae of Africa and Asia Minor, having long hind legs and a long tail and often kept as pets. [Fr. *gerbille* < NLat. *Gerbillus,* genus name, dim. of *gerbō,* jerboa, var. of Med.Lat. *jerbōa.* See JERBOA.]

ge·rent (jîr′ənt) *n.* One that rules or manages. [< Lat. *gerēns, gerent-,* pr. part. of *gerere,* to manage.]

ger·e·nuk (gĕr′ə-nook′) *n.* An African gazelle (*Litocranius walleri*) having long legs, a long slender neck, and backward-curving horns in the male. [Somali *garanūg,* Waller's gazelle.]

ger·fal·con (jûr′făl′kən, -fôl′-, -fô′-) *n.* Variant of **gyrfalcon.**

ger·i·at·ric (jĕr′ē-ăt′rĭk) *adj.* 1. Of or relating to geriatrics. 2. Of or relating to the aged or the aging process. ❖ *n.* An aged person. [Back-formation < GERIATRICS.]

ger·i·a·tri·cian (jĕr′ē-ə-trĭsh′ən) also **ger·i·at·rist** (-ăt′rĭst) *n.* A physician who specializes in geriatrics.

ger·i·at·rics (jĕr′ē-ăt′rĭks) *n.* (*used with a sing. verb*) The branch of medicine that deals with the diagnosis and treatment of diseases and problems specific to the aged. [Gk. *gēras,* old age + –IATRICS.]

Gé·ri·cault (zhā-rē-kō′), (Jean Louis André) Théodore 1791–1824. French painter noted for his boldly colored, unorthodox works, such as *The Raft of the Medusa* (1819).

germ (jûrm) *n.* 1. *Biology* A small mass of protoplasm or cells from which a new organism or one of its parts may develop. 2. A seed, bud, or spore. 3. A microorganism, esp. a pathogen. 4. A possible basis of further growth or development. [ME *bud* < OFr. *germe* < Lat. *germen.* See **genə-** in App.]

ger·man¹ (jûr′mən) *n.* 1. An intricate dance for many couples. 2. A party for dancing at which this dance is featured. [Short for *German cotillion.*]

ger·man² (jûr′mən) *adj.* Having the same parents or the same grandparents on either the mother's or the father's side. Often used in combination: *a cousin-german.* [ME *germain* < OFr. < Lat. *germānus* < *germen,* offshoot. See **genə-** in App.]

German *adj.* 1. Of, relating to, or characteristic of Germany or its people. 2. Of or relating to the German language. ❖ *n.* 1a. A native or inhabitant of Germany. b. A person of German ancestry. 2. Any of the West Germanic languages and dialects spoken or originating in Germany, Austria, or Switzerland, esp. standard High German. [ME < Lat. *Germānus.*]

German cockroach *n.* A small light brown cockroach (*Blatella germanica*) that is a common household pest.

ger·man·der (jər-măn′dər) *n.* Any of various usu. aromatic plants of the genus *Teucrium,* with purplish or reddish flowers. [ME *germandre* < OFr. *germandree,* alteration of Med.Lat. *germandrea* < L.Gk. *khamandrua* < Gk. *khamaidrūs : khamai,* on the ground; see **dhghem-** in App. + *drūs,* oak; see **deru-** in App.]

ger·mane (jər-mān′) *adj.* Being both pertinent and fitting. [ME *germain,* having the same parents, closely connected. See GERMAN².] —**ger·mane′ly** *adv.*

German East Africa A former German protectorate of E Africa including much of what is now Tanzania, Rwanda, and Burundi.

Ger·ma·ni·a (jər-mā′nē-ə, -mān′yə) 1. An ancient region of central Europe N of the Danube and E of the Rhine. 2. A part of the Roman Empire W of the Rhine R. in present-day NE France and sections of Belgium and the Netherlands.

Ger·man·ic (jər-măn′ĭk) *adj.* 1a. Of, relating to, or characteristic of Germany or its people, language, or culture. b. Of or relating to the Teutons. c. Of or relating to the branch of the Indo-European language family that comprises North Germanic, West Germanic, and the extinct East Germanic. 2. Of or relating to a member of a German-speaking people. ❖ *n.* The Germanic branch of Indo-European.

Ger·man·ism (jûr′mə-nĭz′əm) *n.* 1. An attitude, custom, or feature that seems characteristically German. 2. A linguistic feature of German, esp. a German idiom or phrasing that appears in a language other than German. 3. Esteem for Germany and emulation of German ways.

Ger·man·ist (jûr′mə-nĭst) *n.* A specialist in the study of German or Germanic culture, literature, or language.

ger·ma·ni·um (jər-mā′nē-əm) *n.* *Symbol* **Ge** A brittle crystalline gray-white metalloid element, widely used as a semiconductor, as an alloying agent and catalyst, and in certain optical glasses. Atomic number 32; atomic weight 72.59; melting point 937.4°C; boiling point 2,830°C; specific gravity 5.323 (at 25°C); valence 2, 4. See table at **element.** [After GERMANIA.]

Ger·man·ize (jûr′mə-nīz′) *v.* **-ized, -iz·ing, -iz·es** —*tr.* 1. To give a German quality to. 2. *Archaic* To translate into German. —*intr.* To have or adopt German customs or attitudes. —**Ger′-man·i·za′tion** (-mə-nĭ-zā′shən) *n.* —**Ger′man·iz′er** *n.*

German measles *n.* (*used with a sing. or pl. verb*) See **rubella.**

Ger·man·o·phile (jər-măn′ə-fīl′) *n.* One who admires Germany, its people, and its culture. —**Ger′man·o·phile′** *adj.*

Ger·man·o·phobe (jər-măn′ə-fōb′) *n.* One who dislikes or fears Germany, its people, and its culture. —**Ger·man′o·phobe′** *adj.* —**Ger·man′o·pho′bi·a** *n.*

German shepherd *n.* Any of a breed of large dog developed in Germany, having a dense grayish to brownish or black coat and often trained to assist the police and guide the blind.

German shorthaired pointer *n.* Any of a breed of medium to large hunting dog, developed in Germany and having a short white and reddish coat.

German silver *n.* See **nickel silver.**

German Southwest Africa A former (1885–1919) German colony of SW Africa.

Ger·ma·ny (jûr′mə-nē) A country of N-central Europe bordered on the N by the Baltic and North seas; occupied since c. 500 B.C. by Germanic tribes and divided between **West Germany** and **East Germany** from 1949 to 1990. Cap. Berlin. Pop. 81,410,000.

germ cell *n.* An ovum or a sperm cell or one of its developmental precursors.

germ·free (jûrm′frē′) *adj.* Free of microorganisms.

ger·mi·cide (jûr′mĭ-sīd′) *n.* An agent that kills germs, esp. pathogenic microorganisms; a disinfectant. —**ger′mi·cid′al** (-sīd′l) *adj.*

ger·mi·nal (jûr′mə-nəl) *adj.* 1. Of, relating to, or having the nature of a germ cell. 2. Of, relating to, or occurring in the earliest stage of development. [Fr. < Lat. *germen, germin-,* seed. See **genə-** in App.] —**ger′mi·nal·ly** *adv.*

germinal disk *n.* A disklike region of cells from which the embryo develops in the fertilized ovum of many vertebrates.

germinal vesicle *n.* The enlarged nucleus of an oocyte before the end of meiosis.

ger·mi·nate (jûr′mə-nāt′) *v.* **-nat·ed, -nat·ing, -nates** —*tr.* To cause to sprout or grow. —*intr.* 1. To begin to sprout or grow. 2. To come into existence. [Lat. *germināre, germināt-,* to sprout < *germen, germin-,* seed. See **genə-** in App.] —**ger′mi·na′tion** *n.* —**ger′mi·na′tive** *adj.* —**ger′mi·na′tor** *n.*

germ layer *n.* Any of three cellular layers in the gastrula, the ectoderm, endoderm, or mesoderm, from which the organs and tissues of the body develop.

germ plasm *n.* 1. The cytoplasm of a germ cell, esp. that part containing the chromosomes. 2. Germ cells as distinguished from other body cells.

germ theory *n.* The doctrine holding that infectious diseases are caused by the activity of microorganisms within the body.

germ warfare *n.* The use of injurious microorganisms, such as bacteria or viruses, as weapons in warfare.

germ•y (jûr′mē) *adj.* **-i•er, -i•est** Full of germs. **—germ′i•ness** *n.*

Ge•ron•i•mo (jə-rŏn′ə-mō′) Orig. Goyathlay. 1829–1909. Chiricahua Apache leader who led a series of raids against settlements in the Southwest (1876–86).

ge•ron•tic (jə-rŏn′tĭk) *adj.* Of or relating to old age.

geronto– or **geront–** *pref.* Old age; aged one: *gerontology.* [Fr. *géronto-* < Gk. *geronta-* < *gerōn, geront-,* old man.]

ger•on•toc•ra•cy (jĕr′ən-tŏk′rə-sē) *n., pl.* **-cies 1.** Governmental rule by elders. **2.** A governing group of elders.

ger•on•tol•o•gy (jĕr′ən-tŏl′ə-jē) *n.* The study of the biological, psychological, and sociological phenomena associated with old age and aging. **—ge•ron′to•log′i•cal** (jə-rŏn′tə-lŏj′ĭ-kəl), **ge•ron′to•log′ic** (-lŏj′ĭk) *adj.* **—ger′on•tol′o•gist** *n.*

Ger•ry (gĕr′ē), **Elbridge** 1744–1814. Amer. politician who served as governor of MA (1810–11) and Vice President of the US (1813–14).

ger•ry•man•der (jĕr′ē-măn′dər, gĕr′-) *tr.v.* **-dered, -der•ing, -ders** To divide (a geographic area) into voting districts so as to give unfair advantage to one party in elections. ❖ *n.* **1.** The act, process, or an instance of gerrymandering. **2.** A district or configuration of districts differing widely in size or population because of gerrymandering. [After Elbridge GERRY + (SALA)MANDER (< the shape of an election district created while Gerry was governor of MA).]

Gersh•win (gûrsh′wĭn), **George** 1898–1937. Amer. composer whose works include *Rhapsody in Blue* (1924) and *Porgy and Bess* (1935), written with his brother **Ira** (1896–1983).

ger•und (jĕr′ənd) *n.* **1.** In Latin, a noun derived from a verb and having all case forms except the nominative. **2.** In other languages, a verbal noun analogous to the Latin gerund, such as the English form ending in *-ing.* [LLat. *gerundium* < Lat. *gerundum,* var. of *gerendum,* neut. gerundive of *gerere,* to carry on.] **—ge•run′di•al** (jə-rŭn′dē-əl) *adj.*

ge•run•dive (jə-rŭn′dĭv) *n.* A verbal adjective in Latin that in the nominative case expresses fitness or obligation and in other cases functions as a future passive participle. [ME *gerundif* < LLat. *gerundīvus* < *gerundium,* gerund. See GERUND.]

Ge•ry•on (jîr′ē-ən, gĕr′-) *n. Greek Mythology* A monster with three bodies that was slain by Hercules.

Ges•ner (gĕs′nər), **Konrad von** 1516–65. Swiss encyclopedist and naturalist whose *Historia Animalium* (1551–58) is considered the basis of modern zoology.

ges•ne•ri•ad (gĕs-nîr′ē-ăd′, jĕs-) *n.* Any of numerous tropical herbs or shrubs of the family Gesneriaceae, including African violets and gloxinia. [< NLat. *Gesneria,* type genus, after Konrad von GESNER.]

ges•so (jĕs′ō) *n., pl.* **-soes 1.** A preparation of plaster of Paris and glue used as a base for low relief or as a surface for painting. **2.** A surface of gesso. [Ital. < Lat. *gypsum,* gypsum. See GYPSUM.] **—ges′soed** *adj.*

gest or **geste** (jĕst) *n.* **1.** An adventure or exploit. **2a.** A verse romance or tale. **b.** A prose romance. [ME *geste.* See JEST.]

ge•stalt or **Ge•stalt** (gə-shtält′, -shtôlt′, -stält′, -stôlt′) *n., pl.* **-stalts** or **-stalt•en** (-shtält′n, -shtôlt′n, -stält′n, -stôlt′n) A physical, biological, psychological, or symbolic pattern of elements so unified that its properties cannot be derived from the sum of its parts. [Ger., shape < MHGer. < p. part. of *stellen,* to place < OHGer. See **stel-** in App.]

Ge•stalt•ist (gə-shtäl′tĭst, -shtôl′-, -stäl′-, -stôl′-) *n.* An adherent or a practitioner of Gestalt psychology.

Gestalt psychology *n.* The school or theory in psychology that considers psychological, physiological, and behavioral phenomena to be irreducible wholes rather than simple summations of discrete perceptual elements.

Ge•sta•po (gə-stä′pō, -shtä′-) *n.* **1.** The internal security police of Nazi Germany, known for its terrorist methods. **2. gestapo,** *pl.* **-pos** A police organization that employs terroristic methods to control a populace. [Ger. *Ge(heime) Sta(ats)po(lizei),* secret state police : *geheim,* secret + *Staat,* state + *Polizei,* police.] **—Ge•sta′po** *adj.*

ges•tate (jĕs′tāt′) *v.* **-tat•ed, -tat•ing, -tates** *—tr.* **1.** To carry within the uterus from conception to delivery. **2.** To conceive and develop in the mind. *—intr.* **1.** To gestate offspring. **2.** To develop gradually.

ges•ta•tion (jĕ-stā′shən) *n.* **1.** The period of development in the uterus from conception until birth; pregnancy. **2.** The conception and development of a plan or an idea in the mind. [LLat. *gestātiō, gestātiōn-* < Lat., a carrying < *gestātus,* p. part. of *gestāre,* freq. of *gerere,* to carry.] **—ges′ta•to′ry** (jĕs′tə-tôr′ē, -tōr′ē), **ges•ta′tion•al** *adj.*

ges•tic (jĕs′tĭk) *adj.* Relating to bodily movements or gestures, esp. in dancing. [< obsolete *gest,* bearing < Fr. *geste* < OFr. < Lat. *gestus.* See GESTURE.]

ges•tic•u•late (jĕ-stĭk′yə-lāt′) *v.* **-lat•ed, -lat•ing, -lates** *—intr.* To make gestures esp. while speaking, as for emphasis. *—tr.* To say or express by gestures. [Lat. *gesticulārī, gesticulāt-* < *gesticulus,* gesticulation, dim. of *gestus,* gesture, bearing. See GESTURE.] **—ges•tic′u•la′tive, ges•tic′u•la•to′ry** (-lə-tôr′ē, -tōr′ē) *adj.* **—ges•tic′u•la′tor** *n.*

ges•tic•u•la•tion (jĕ-stĭk′yə-lā′shən) *n.* **1.** The act of gesticulating. **2.** A deliberate vigorous motion or gesture.

ges•ture (jĕs′chər) *n.* **1.** A motion of the limbs or body made to express thought or to emphasize speech. **2.** The act of gesturing. **3.** An act or a remark made as a formality or a sign of intention or attitude. ❖ *v.* **-tured, -tur•ing, -tures** *—intr.* To make gestures. *—tr.* To show, express, or direct by gestures. [ME < Med.Lat. *gestūra,* bearing < Lat. *gestus,* p. part. of *gerere,* to behave.] **—ges′tur•al** *adj.* **—ges′tur•al•ly** *adv.* **—ges′tur•er** *n.*

ge•sund•heit (gə-zo͝ont′hīt′) *interj.* Used to wish good health to a person who has just sneezed. [Ger., health < MHGer. *gesuntheit* < *gesunt,* healthy < OHGer. *gisunt.*]

get (gĕt) *v.* **got** (gŏt), **got•ten** (gŏt′n) or **got, get•ting, gets** *—tr.* **1a.** To come into possession or use of; receive: *got a book for her birthday.* **b.** To meet with or incur: *got nothing but trouble for her efforts.* **2a.** To go after and obtain: *got breakfast in town.* **b.** To go after and bring: *Get me a pillow.* **c.** To purchase; buy: *get groceries.* **3a.** To acquire as a result of action or effort: *got information from the Internet.* **b.** To earn: *got high marks in math.* **c.** To accomplish or attain as a result of military action. **4.** To obtain by concession or request: *got permission to go.* **5a.** To arrive at; reach: *got home at 6:00.* **b.** To reach and board; catch: *got the bus.* **6.** To succeed in communicating with, as by telephone. **7.** To become affected with (an illness, for example) by infection or exposure: *get the flu.* **8a.** To be subjected to; undergo: *got a concussion.* **b.** To receive as retribution or punishment: *got six years in prison for tax fraud.* **c.** To sustain a stated injury to: *got my arm broken.* **9a.** To gain or have understanding of: *Do you get this question?* **b.** To learn (a poem, for example) by heart; memorize. **c.** To find or reach by calculating: *get a total.* **d.** To perceive by hearing: *I didn't get your name.* **10.** To procreate; beget. **11a.** To cause to become or be in a specified condition: *got the shirt clean.* **b.** To make ready; prepare: *get lunch for a crowd.* **c.** To cause to come or go: *got the car through traffic.* **d.** To cause to move or leave: *Get me out of here!* **12.** To cause to undertake or perform; prevail on: *got the baby to eat squash.* **13a.** To take, esp. by force; seize. **b.** *Informal* To overcome or destroy: *The ice storm got the rose bushes.* **c.** To evoke an emotional response or reaction in: *The sad movie got to me.* **d.** To annoy or irritate. **e.** To present a difficult problem to; puzzle. **f.** To take revenge on, esp. to kill in revenge for a wrong. **g.** *Informal* To hit or strike: *She got him on the chin.* **14.** *Baseball* To put out. **15.** To begin or start. Used with the present participle: *Let's get working.* **16a.** To have current possession of. Used in the present perfect form with the meaning of the present: *We've got cash.* **b.** *Nonstandard* To have current possession of. Used in the past tense form with the meaning of the present: *We got a nice house.* **c.** To have as an obligation. Used in the present perfect form with the meaning of the present: *I have got to leave early.* **d.** *Nonstandard* To have as an obligation. Used in the past tense with the meaning of the present: *I got to git me a huntin' dog.* *—intr.* **1a.** To become or grow to be: *got well.* **b.** To be successful in coming or going: *never got to Europe.* **2.** To be able or permitted: *got to work at home.* **3a.** To be successful in becoming: *The dog got loose.* **b.** Used with the past participle of transitive verbs as a passive voice auxiliary: *got stung.* **c.** To become drawn in, entangled, or involved: *got into debt.* **4.** *Informal* To depart immediately: *yelled at the dog to get.* **5.** To work for gain or profit; make money. ❖ *n.* **1a.** The act of begetting. **b.** Progeny; offspring. **2.** *Chiefly British Slang* A foolish or contemptible person. **3.** *Sports* A return, as in tennis, on a shot that seems impossible to reach. ***—phrasal verbs:* get about** To be out of bed and beginning to walk again, as after an illness. **get across 1.** To make understandable or clear: *got my point across.* **2.** To be convincing or understandable. **get after** To urge or scold. **get along 1.** To be or continue to be on harmonious terms: *gets along with the in-laws.* **2.** To manage or fare with reasonable success. **3a.** To make progress. **b.** To advance, esp. in years. **4.** To go away; leave. **get around 1.** To circumvent or evade: *got around the real issues.* **2.** *Informal* To convince or win over by flattering or cajoling. **3.** To travel from place to place: *gets around by bus.* **4.** To become known; circulate: *Word got around.* **get at 1.** To touch or reach successfully. **2.** To try to make understandable; hint at or suggest: *What are you getting at?* **3.** To discover or understand: *gets to the problem's cause.* **4.** *Informal* To influence by improper or illegal means. **get away 1.** To break free; escape. **2.** To leave or go away. **get back** To return to a person, place, or condition: *getting back to the subject.* **get by 1.** To pass or outstrip. **2.** To succeed at a level of minimal acceptability or with the minimal amount of effort. **3.** To succeed in managing; survive. **4.** To be unnoticed or ignored by. **get down 1.** To descend. **2.** To give one's attention. Often used with *to: Let's get down to work.* **3.** To exhaust, discourage, or depress. **4.** To swallow. **5.** To describe in writing. **6.** *Informal* To lose one's inhibitions; enjoy oneself wholeheartedly. **get in 1a.** To enter. **b.** To arrive. **2.** To become or cause to become involved. **3.** To become accepted, as in a club. **4.** To succeed in making or doing. **get into 1.** To become involved in. **2.** *Informal* To be interested in. **get off 1.** To start, as on a trip; leave. **2a.** To fire (a round of ammunition, for example). **b.** To write and send (a letter, for example). **3.** To escape, as from punishment. **4.** To obtain a release or lesser penalty for. **5.** *Slang* To act or speak with effrontery. **6.** *Slang* To have an orgasm. **7.** *Slang* **a.** To feel great

Geronimo

ă	pat	oi	boy
ā	pay	ou	out
âr	care	o͝o	took
ä	father	o͞o	boot
ĕ	pet	ŭ	cut
ē	be	ûr	urge
ĭ	pit	th	thin
ī	pie	*th*	this
îr	pier	hw	which
ŏ	pot	zh	vision
ō	toe	ə	about,
ô	paw		item

Stress marks:
′ (primary);
′ (secondary), as in
lexicon (lĕk′sĭ-kŏn′)

pleasure or gratification. **b.** To experience euphoria, as from taking a drug. **8.** To get permission to leave one's workplace. **get on 1.** To be or continue on harmonious terms. **2.** To manage or fare with reasonable success. **3a.** To make progress; continue. **b.** To advance in years. **4.** To acquire understanding or knowledge: *got on to the con game.* **get out 1a.** To leave or escape. **b.** To cause to leave or escape. **2.** To become known. **3.** To publish (a newspaper, for example). **get over 1.** To prevail against; overcome. **2.** To recover from. **3.** To get across. **get through 1.** To arrive at the end; finish or complete. **2a.** To succeed in making contact; reach. **b.** To make oneself understood. **get to 1a.** To begin. Used with the present participle: *got to reminiscing.* **b.** To start to deal with. **2.** To influence or affect, esp. adversely. **get together 1.** To bring together; gather. **2.** To come together. **3.** To arrive at an agreement. **get up 1a.** To arise from bed or rise to one's feet. **b.** To climb. **2.** To act as the creator or organizer of. **3.** To dress or adorn. **4.** To find within oneself: *trying to get up the nerve.* —*idioms:* **get around to** To find the time or occasion for. **get away with** To escape the consequences of: *got away with cheating.* **get back at** To take revenge on. **get cracking** To begin to work; get started. **get even** To obtain revenge. **get even with** To repay with an equivalent act, as for revenge. **get going** To make a beginning; get started. **get hold (or ahold) of 1.** To bring into one's grasp, possession, or control. **2.** To communicate with, especially by telephone. **get it** *Informal* To be punished or scolded. **get it on** *Slang* **1.** To become filled with energy or excitement. **2.** To engage in sexual intercourse. **get nowhere** To make no progress. **get (one's)** *Informal* To receive one's due punishment: *You are going to get yours!* **get on the stick** To begin to work. **get out of** To gain release from the obligation of. **get (someone's) goat** To make angry or vexed. **get somewhere** *Informal* To make progress. **get there** *Informal* To make progress or achieve success. **get wind of** To learn of: *got wind of the scheme.* [ME *geten* < ON *geta.* See **ghend-** in App.] —**get′a·ble**, **get′ta·ble** *adj.*

ge·ta (gĕt′ə, gĕ′tä) *n., pl.* **geta** or **ge·tas** A wooden-soled shoe worn by the Japanese. [J.]

get·a·way (gĕt′ə-wā′) *n.* **1.** The act or an instance of escaping: *made a quick getaway.* **2.** The start, as of a race. **3.** A place appropriate for a vacation.

get-go (gĕt′gō′) *n. Informal* The beginning; outset: *had trouble from the get-go.*

geth·sem·a·ne (gĕth-sĕm′ə-nē) *n.* An instance or a place of great suffering. [After GETHSEMANE.]

Gethsemane In the New Testament, a garden E of Jerusalem near the foot of the Mt. of Olives; scene of Jesus's agony and betrayal.

get·ter (gĕt′ər) *n.* A material added in small amounts during a chemical or metallurgical process to absorb impurities.

get-to·geth·er (gĕt′tə-gĕth′ər) *n. Informal* **1.** A meeting. **2.** A casual social gathering.

get-tough (gĕt′tŭf′) *adj. Informal* Marked by resoluteness, aggressiveness, or austerity: *a get-tough policy on crime.*

Get·tys·burg (gĕt′ēz-bûrg′) A town of S PA ESE of Chambersburg; site of a major Union victory in the Civil War (Jul. 1–3, 1863) and of Abraham Lincoln's Gettysburg Address (Nov. 19, 1863). Pop. 7,490.

get·up (gĕt′ŭp′) *n.* **1.** *Informal* An outfit or costume. **2.** *Printing* Arrangement and production style, as of a magazine.

get-up-and-go (gĕt′ŭp′ən-gō′) *n. Informal* Initiation of action motivated by energy and ambition.

get-well (gĕt′wĕl′) *adj.* Expressing wishes for one's recovery.

Getz (gĕts), **Stan** Orig. Stanley Gayetsky. 1927–91. Amer. tenor saxophonist who played in several big bands.

GeV *abbr.* giga-electron volt

gew·gaw (gyōō′gô′, gōō′-) also **gee·gaw** (jē′-, gē′-) *n.* A decorative trinket; a bauble. [ME *giuegaue.*]

Ge·würz·tra·mi·ner (gə-vōōrts′trə-mē′nər, -wûrts′-) *n.* **1.** A variety of grape used to make white wine. **2a.** A white table wine made from this grape and produced in the Alsace region of France. **b.** A similar wine produced elsewhere. [Ger. : *Gewürz,* spice (< MHGer. *gewirz,* collective of *wurz,* plant, root < OHGer.; see **wrād-** in App.) + *Traminer,* grape variety (< *Tramin,* winegrowing district of the S Tyrol).]

gey·ser (gī′zər) *n.* **1.** A natural hot spring that intermittently ejects a column of water and steam into the air. **2.** (gē′zər) *Chiefly British* A gas-operated hot-water heater. [After Icelandic *Geysir,* name of a hot spring of southwest Iceland < *geysa,* to gush < ON. See **gheu-** in App.]

gey·ser·ite (gī′zə-rīt′) *n.* A white or grayish opaline siliceous

Ghana

giant sequoia
Sequoiadendron giganteum

deposit formed around natural hot springs.

Ge·zer (gē′zər) An ancient city of Canaan on the coastal Plain of Sharon NW of Jerusalem.

Ge·zi·ra (jə-zîr′ə), **El** A region of E-central Sudan between the Blue Nile and the White Nile.

Gha·gha·ra (gä′gə-rä′) or **Gha·ghra** (gä′grə, -grä) also **Gog·ra** (gōg′rə, -rä) A river rising in SW Xizang (Tibet) and flowing c. 965 km (600 mi) to the Ganges R. in N India.

Gha·na (gä′nə) **1.** A medieval African kingdom in what is now E Senegal, SW Mali, and S Mauritania; probably founded in the 6th cent. A.D. **2.** A country of W Africa on the Gulf of Guinea; gained independence from Great Britain in 1957. Cap. Accra. Pop. 16,944,000. —**Gha′na·ian** (gä′nə-yən, gə-nā′ən), **Gha′ni·an** (gä′nē-ən) *adj. & n.*

gha·ri·al (gûr′ē-əl) *n.* See **gavial.**

ghar·ry (gär′ē, gä′rē) *n.* A horse-drawn carriage, used esp. in Egypt and India as a cab. [Hindi *gāṛī,* prob. ult. < Skt. *gartaḥ,* chariot.]

ghast·ly (găst′lē) *adj.* **-li·er, -li·est 1.** Inspiring shock, revulsion, or horror, as death does; terrifying: *a ghastly murder.* **2.** Suggestive of or resembling ghosts. **3.** Extremely unpleasant or bad: "*in the most abominable passage of his ghastly little book*" (Conor Cruise O'Brien). **4.** Very serious or great: *a ghastly error.* [Alteration of ME *gastli* < *gasten,* to terrify. See AGHAST.] —**ghast′li·ness** *n.* —**ghast′ly** *adv.*

ghat also **ghaut** (gôt, gät) *n.* **1.** A broad flight of steps leading down to the bank of a river in India, used esp. by bathers. [Hindi *ghāt* < Skt. *ghaṭṭaḥ,* prob. of Dravidian orig.; akin to Telugu *kaṭṭu, gaṭṭu,* dam embankment.]

Ghats (gôts) Two mountain ranges of S India separated by the Deccan Plateau into the **Eastern Ghats** along the Bay of Bengal and the **Western Ghats** along the Arabian Sea.

GHB *abbr.* gamma-hydroxybutyrate

ghee (gē) *n.* A clarified semifluid butter used esp. in Indian cooking. [Hindi *ghī* < Skt. *ghṛtam.* See **gʷher-** in App.]

Ghent (gĕnt) also **Gent** (gĕnt, кнĕnt) A city of W Belgium WNW of Brussels; founded in the 7th cent. Pop. 230,446.

gher·kin (gûr′kĭn) *n.* **1a.** A West Indian vine (*Cucumis anguria*) whose immature fruits are used for pickling. **b.** The fruit of this plant. **2.** A small cucumber, esp. one used for pickling. [Du. *gurken,* pl. of *gurk,* cucumber, short for *agurk,* poss. < Pol. *ogorek,* perh. < L.Gk. *angourion.*]

ghet·to (gĕt′ō) *n., pl.* **-tos** or **-toes 1.** A section of a city occupied by a minority group who live there esp. because of social, economic, or legal pressure. **2.** An often walled quarter in a European city to which Jews were restricted beginning in the Middle Ages. **3.** Something resembling the restriction or isolation of a ghetto. [Ital., after *Ghetto,* island near Venice where Jews were made to live in the 16th cent.]

ghetto blaster *n. Slang* A boom box.

ghet·to·ize (gĕt′ō-īz′) *tr.v.* **-ized, -iz·ing, -iz·es 1.** To set apart in or as if in a ghetto; isolate. **2.** To make into or similar to a ghetto. —**ghet′to·i·za′tion** (-īzā′shən) *n.*

Ghib·el·line (gĭb′ə-lēn′, -lĭn′, -līn) *n.* A member of the aristocratic political faction who fought during the Middle Ages for German imperial control of Italy, in opposition to the Guelphs and the papacy. [Ital. *Ghibellino* < MHGer. **wībeling,* name of a Hohenstaufen estate.]

Ghi·ber·ti (gē-bĕr′tē), **Lorenzo** 1378?–1455. Florentine sculptor known for his bronze panels *Gates of Paradise* (1425–52) for the baptistery of Florence Cathedral.

ghil·lie (gĭl′ē) *n.* Variant of **gillie.**

Ghir·lan·da·io also **Ghir·lan·da·jo** (gîr-län-dä′yō), **Domenico** Orig. Domenico Bigordi. 1449–94. Florentine painter whose narrative frescoes include *Scenes from the Life of Saint Francis* (1483–85).

ghost (gōst) *n.* **1.** The spirit of a dead person, esp. one believed to appear to living persons or to haunt former habitats. **2.** The center of spiritual life; the soul. **3.** A demon or spirit. **4.** A returning or haunting memory or image. **5a.** A slight or faint trace. **b.** The tiniest bit. **6.** A faint, false image, as: **a.** A secondary image on a television or radar screen caused by reflected waves. **b.** A displaced image in a photograph caused by the optical system of the camera. **7.** *Informal* A ghostwriter. **8a.** A nonexistent publication listed in bibliographies. **b.** A fictitious employee or business. ❖ *v.* **ghost·ed, ghost·ing, ghosts** —*intr.* **1.** *Informal* To engage in ghostwriting. **2.** To move noiselessly like a ghost. —*tr.* **1.** To haunt. **2.** *Informal* To ghostwrite. [ME *gost* < OE *gāst,* breath, spirit.] —**ghost′y** *adj.*

ghost dance *n.* Either of two group dances related to a messianic religious movement among late-19th-century Native American peoples of the Southwest and Great Plains.

ghost·ing (gō′stĭng) *n.* The appearance of one or more false images on a television screen.

ghost·ly (gōst′lē) *adj.* **-li·er, -li·est 1.** Of, relating to, or resembling a ghost or an apparition. **2.** Of or relating to the soul or spirit; spiritual. —**ghost′li·ness** *n.* —**ghost′ly** *adv.*

ghost story *n.* A story having supernatural or frightening elements, esp. a story featuring ghosts or spirits of the dead.

ghost town *n.* A once thriving town, esp. a boomtown of the American West, that has been completely abandoned.

ghost word *n.* A word that has come into a dictionary, grammar, or other scholarly work as a result of a misreading or misinterpretation, as by mistaking a typographical error for an actual word.

ghost•write (gōst′rīt′) *v.* **-wrote** (-rōt′), **-writ•ten** (-rĭt′n), **-writ•ing, -writes** —*intr.* To work as a ghostwriter. —*tr.* To write (a speech, for example) as a ghostwriter.

ghost•writ•er (gōst′rī′tər) *n.* One who writes for and gives credit of authorship to another.

ghoul (gōol) *n.* **1.** One who delights in the revolting, morbid, or loathsome. **2.** A grave robber. **3.** An evil spirit or demon in Muslim folklore believed to plunder graves and feed on corpses. [Ar. *ġūl* < *ġala*, to seize, snatch.] —**ghoul′ish** *adj.* —**ghoul′ish•ly** *adv.* —**ghoul′ish•ness** *n.*

GHQ *abbr.* general headquarters

GHz *abbr.* gigahertz

gi or **gi.** *abbr.* gill (liquid measure)

GI¹ (jē′ī′) *n.* An enlisted person in or a veteran of any of the US armed forces, esp. the army. ❖ *adj.* **1.** Relating to or characteristic of an enlisted person. **2.** Conforming to or in accordance with US military regulations or procedures. **3.** Issued by a US military supply department. [< abbr. of *galvanized iron* (applied to trash cans, etc.), later reinterpreted as *government issue*.]

GI² *abbr.* **1.** galvanized iron **2.** gastrointestinal **3.** general issue **4.** Government Issue

Gia•co•met•ti (jä-kə-mĕt′ē, -kō-mĕt′tē), **Alberto** 1901–66. Swiss sculptor and painter known for his sculptures of elongated figures, such as *Walking Man* (1960).

gi•ant (jī′ənt) *n.* **1a.** A person or thing of great size. **b.** A person or thing of extraordinary power or importance. **2a.** *Greek Mythology* One of a race of humanlike beings of enormous size, destroyed in battle with the Olympians. **b.** A being in folklore or myth similar to one of these beings. ❖ *adj.* Marked by great size, magnitude, or power. [ME < OFr. *geant, jaiant* < VLat. **gagās, gagant-* < Lat. *gigās* < Gk.]

giant anteater *n.* A large tropical American anteater (*Myrmecophaga tridactyla*) having an elongated snout, long sticky tongue, and shaggy tail.

gi•ant•ess (jī′ən-tĭs) *n.* A female giant.

gi•ant•ism (jī′ən-tĭz′əm) *n.* **1.** The quality or condition of being a giant. **2.** See **gigantism** 2.

Giant order *n.* See **Colossal order.**

giant panda *n.* See **panda** 1.

Gi•ant's Causeway (jī′ənts) A basaltic formation on the N coast of Northern Ireland consisting of thousands of columns forming three natural platforms.

giant schnauzer *n.* Any of a breed of dog developed in Germany, similar to but larger than the standard schnauzer.

giant sequoia *n.* A very tall coniferous evergreen tree (*Sequoiadendron giganteum*) of California having reddish wood.

giant slalom *n.* A downhill skiing race in which participants must pass between pairs of gates set along a course that is larger and often steeper than a slalom course.

giant star *n.* Any of a class of highly luminous, exceptionally massive stars.

giaour (jour) *n. Islam* A nonbeliever; an infidel. [Alteration of obsolete *gower, gour* < Turk. *gâvur* < Pers. *gabr*, Zoroastrian < Ar. *kāfir*, infidel < *kafr*, village < Aram. *kaprā*.]

gi•ar•di•a•sis (jē′är-dī′ə-sĭs) *n.* Intestinal infection with the protozoan *Giardia lamblia*. [After Alfred Mathieus *Girard* (1846–1908), French zoologist.]

gib¹ (gĭb) *n.* A plain or notched, often wedge-shaped piece of wood or metal designed to hold parts of a machine or structure in place or provide a bearing surface, usu. adjusted by a screw or key. ❖ *tr.v.* **gibbed, gib•bing, gibs** To fasten with a gib. [?]

gib² (gĭb) *n.* A male cat, esp. a castrated one. [ME, prob. short for the personal name *Gilbert*.]

Gib. *abbr.* Gibraltar

gib•ber (jĭb′ər) *intr.v.* **-bered, -ber•ing, -bers** To prattle and chatter unintelligibly. ❖ *n.* Unintelligible or foolish talk. [Prob. back-formation < GIBBERISH.]

gib•ber•el•lic acid (jĭb′ə-rĕl′ĭk) *n.* A hormone, $C_{19}H_{22}O_6$, obtained from the fungus *Gibberella fujikuroi* and used to promote plant growth. [< GIBBERELLIN.]

gib•ber•el•lin (jĭb′ə-rĕl′ĭn) *n.* Any of several plant hormones, such as gibberellic acid, used to promote stem elongation. [< NLat. *Gibberella (fujikoroī)*, fungus species (first source of gibberellin) < Lat. *gibberellus*, dim. of *gibber*, hump.]

gib•ber•ish (jĭb′ər-ĭsh) *n.* **1.** Unintelligible or nonsensical talk or writing. **2a.** Highly technical or esoteric language. **b.** Unnecessarily pretentious or vague language. [Prob. < *gibber*, to speak unintelligibly (of imit. orig.) + –ISH.]

gib•bet (jĭb′ĭt) *n.* **1.** A device used for hanging a person until dead; a gallows. **2.** An upright post with a crosspiece, forming a T-shaped structure from which executed criminals were formerly hung for public viewing. ❖ *tr.v.* **-bet•ed, -bet•ing, -bets** or **-bet•ted, -bet•ting, -bets** **1.** To execute by hanging on a gibbet. **2a.** To hang on a gibbet for public viewing. **b.** To expose to infamy or public ridicule. [ME *gibet* < OFr., dim. of *gibe*, staff, prob. < Frankish **gibb*, forked stick.]

gib•bon (gĭb′ən) *n.* Any of several small slender arboreal apes of the genus *Hylobates* of southeast Asia. [Fr.]

Gibbon, Edward 1737–94. British historian who wrote *The History of the Decline and Fall of the Roman Empire* (1776–88).

gib•bos•i•ty (gĭ-bŏs′ĭ-tē) *n., pl.* **-ties** **1.** The condition of being gibbous. **2.** A rounded hump or protuberance.

gib•bous (gĭb′əs) *adj.* **1a.** Characterized by convexity; protuberant. **b.** More than half but less than fully illuminated. Used of the moon or a planet. **2.** Having a hump; humpbacked. [ME, bulging < LLat. *gibbōsus*, hunch-backed < Lat. *gibbus*, hump.] —**gib′bous•ly** *adv.* —**gib′bous•ness** *n.*

Gibbs (gĭbz), **Josiah Willard** 1839–1903. Amer. mathematician and physicist who formulated the theoretical foundation of physical chemistry and developed vector analysis.

Gibbs free energy *n.* See **free energy** 2.

gibe also **jibe** (jīb) *v.* **gibed, gib•ing, gibes** also **jibed, jib•ing, jibes** —*intr.* To make taunting, heckling, or jeering remarks. —*tr.* To deride with gibes. ❖ *n.* A derisive remark. [Poss. < obsolete Fr. *giber*, to handle roughly, play < OFr.] —**gib′er** *n.*

Gib•e•on (gĭb′ē-ən) An ancient village of Palestine near Jerusalem. —**Gib′e•o•nite′** *n.*

gib•lets (jĭb′lĭts) *pl.n.* The edible heart, liver, or gizzard of a fowl. [< ME *gibelet* < OFr., game stew, perh. alteration of **giberet* < *gibier*, game.]

Gi•bral•tar¹ (jə-brôl′tər) A British colony at the NW end of the **Rock of Gibraltar**, a peninsula on the S-central coast of Spain in the **Strait of Gibraltar**, connecting the Mediterranean Sea and the Atlantic Ocean between Spain and N Africa. Gibraltar was captured by Arabs in 711 and passed to the Spanish in 1462; Great Britain took control in 1704. Pop. 31,874.

Gi•bral•tar² (jə-brôl′tər) *n.* An invincible stronghold.

Gibraltar fever *n.* See **brucellosis** 1.

Gib•ran (jə-brän′), **(Gibran)** Kahlil 1883–1931. Syrian-born Amer. mystic poet and painter best known for his prose poem *The Prophet* (1923).

Gib•son (gĭb′sən) *n.* A dry martini garnished with a small pickled onion. [< the name *Gibson*.]

Gibson, Althea b. 1927. Amer. tennis player who was the first African American to play at Wimbledon (1951), where she won singles and doubles titles in 1957 and 1958.

Gibson Desert A desert of W-central Australia bounded by the Great Sandy Desert and Great Victoria Desert.

Gibson girl *n.* The American young woman of the 1890s in idealized sketches by the American illustrator Charles Dana Gibson (1867–1944). ❖ *adj.* Of a clothing style marked by a high neck, puffed sleeves, and a tight waistline.

gid (gĭd) *n.* A disease of herbivores, esp. sheep, caused by larvae of the tapeworm *Multiceps multiceps* in the brain and marked by a staggering gait. [Back-formation < GIDDY.]

gid•dy (gĭd′ē) *adj.* **-di•er, -di•est** **1a.** Having a reeling lightheaded sensation; dizzy. **b.** Causing or capable of causing dizziness: *a giddy height*. **2.** Frivolous and lighthearted; flighty. ❖ *intr. & tr.v.* **-died, -dy•ing, -dies** To become or make giddy. [ME *gidi*, crazy < OE *gidig*. See **gheu(ə)-** in App.] —**gid′di•ly** *adv.* —**gid′di•ness** *n.*

gid•dy•up (gĭd′ē-ŭp′) also **gid•dy•ap** (-ăp′, -ŭp′) or **gid•dap** (gĭ-dăp′, -dŭp′) *interj.* Used to command a horse to go ahead or go at a faster pace. [Alteration of *get up*.]

Gide (zhēd), **André** 1869–1951. French writer who won the 1947 Nobel Prize for literature.

Gid•e•on¹ (gĭd′ē-ən) A Hebrew judge who opposed the Baal cult and defeated the Midianites.

Gid•e•on² (gĭd′ē-ən) *n.* A member of an interdenominational and international society known for placing Bibles in hotel rooms. [< *Gideons International*, after GIDEON¹.]

gie (gē) *v. Scots* Variant of **give.**

Giel•gud (gĭl′gōod′, gēl′-), Sir **(Arthur)** John 1904–2000. British actor and director noted for his Shakespearean productions.

GIF (jĭf, gĭf) A service mark used for a raster-based format for storing files of color graphics.

gift (gĭft) *n.* **1.** Something bestowed voluntarily and without compensation. **2.** The act, right, or power of giving. **3.** A talent, endowment, aptitude, or inclination. ❖ *tr.v.* **gift•ed, gift•ing, gifts** **1.** To present with as a gift. **2.** To endow with. [ME < ON. See **ghabh-** in App.]

gift•a•ble (gĭf′tə-bəl) *adj.* Appropriate for a gift. —**gift′a•ble** *n.*

gift certificate *n.* A certificate usu. presented as a gift that entitles the recipient to merchandise of an indicated cash value.

gift•ed (gĭf′tĭd) *adj.* **1.** Endowed with great natural ability, intelligence or talent: *a gifted pianist*. **2.** Revealing special talent. —**gift′ed•ly** *adv.* —**gift′ed•ness** *n.*

gift of tongues *n.* The ability or phenomenon to utter words or sounds of a language unknown to the speaker, esp. as an expression of religious ecstasy. [< Acts 2:4.]

gift-wrap (gĭft′răp′) *tr.v.* **-wrapped, -wrap•ping, -wraps** To wrap (a gift) in a decorative manner. ❖ *n.* Gift-wrapping.

gift-wrap•ping (gĭft′răp′ĭng) *n.* Decorative wrapping paper.

Gi•fu (gē′fōo′) A city of central Honshu, Japan, NNW of Nagoya; rebuilt after an earthquake in 1891. Pop. 409,558.

gig¹ (gĭg) *n.* **1.** A light two-wheeled carriage drawn by one horse. **2.** *Nautical* **a.** A long light ship's boat, usu. reserved for the ship's captain. **b.** A fast light rowboat. **3a.** An object that whirls. **b.**

Gibraltar¹
Rock of Gibraltar

Althea Gibson
at Wimbledon in 1957

ă pat	oi boy	
ā pay	ou out	
âr care	ōō took	
ä father	ōō boot	
ĕ pet	ŭ cut	
ē be	ûr urge	
ĭ pit	th thin	
ī pie	th this	
îr pier	hw which	
ŏ pot	zh vision	
ō toe	ə about,	
ô paw	item	

Stress marks:
′ (primary);
′ (secondary), as in
lexicon (lĕk′sĭ-kŏn′)

Dizzy Gillespie

Games A three-digit selection in a numbers game. ❖ *intr.v.* **gigged, gig·ging, gigs** To ride in a gig. [Perh. < obsolete *gig*, spinning top < ME *gyg-*, poss. of Scand. orig.]

gig² (gĭg) *n.* **1.** An arrangement of barbless hooks that is dragged through a school of fish to hook them in their bodies. **2.** A pronged spear for fishing or catching frogs. ❖ *v.* **gigged, gig·ging, gigs** —*tr.* To fish for or catch with a gig. —*intr.* To catch a fish or frog with a gig. [Short for FISHGIG.]

gig³ (gĭg) *Slang n.* A demerit given in the military. ❖ *tr.v.* **gigged, gig·ging, gigs** To give a military demerit to. [?]

gig⁴ (gĭg) *Slang n.* A job, esp. a booking for musicians. ❖ *intr.v.* **gigged, gig·ging, gigs** To work as a musician. [?]

gig⁵ (gĭg, jĭg) *n. Informal* A gigabyte.

giga– *pref.* **1.** One billion (10^9): *gigahertz.* **2.** 1,073,741,824 (2^{30}): *gigabyte.* [< Gk. *gigās*, giant.]

gig·a·bit (gĭg′ə-bĭt′, jĭg′-) *n. Computer Science* **1.** One billion bits. **2.** 1,073,741,824 (2^{30}) bits. See Usage Note at **megabyte.**

gig·a·byte (gĭg′ə-bīt′, jĭg′-) *n.* **1.** A unit of computer memory or data storage capacity equal to 1,024 megabytes (2^{30} bytes). **2.** One billion bytes. See Usage Note at **megabyte.**

gig·a·flop (gĭg′ə-flŏp′, jĭg′-) *n.* A measure of computing speed equal to one billion floating-point operations per second. [GIGA– + FLOP.]

gig·a·hertz (gĭg′ə-hûrtz′, jĭg′-) *n.* A unit of frequency equal to one billion (10^9) hertz.

gi·gan·tesque (jī′gän-tĕsk′) *adj.* Of enormous size or magnitude; huge. [Fr. < Ital. *gigantesco* < *gigante*, giant < Lat. *gigās*, *gigant-.* See GIANT.]

gi·gan·tic (jī-găn′tĭk) *adj.* **1.** Relating to or suggestive of a giant. **2a.** Exceedingly large of its kind: *a gigantic toadstool.* **b.** Very large or extensive: *a gigantic corporation.* [< Lat. *gigās*, *gigant-*, giant; see GIANT, or < Gk. *gigantikos* (< *gigās*, *gigant-*, giant).] —**gi·gan′ti·cal·ly** *adv.*

gi·gan·tism (jī-găn′tĭz′əm) *n.* **1.** The quality or state of being gigantic; abnormally large size. **2.** Excessive growth of the body or any of its parts.

gig·a·watt (gĭg′ə-wŏt′, jĭg′-) *n.* One billion (10^9) watts.

gig·gle (gĭg′əl) *v.* **-gled, -gling, -gles** —*intr.* To laugh with repeated short spasmodic sounds: *The clown's antics made me giggle.* —*tr.* To utter while giggling. ❖ *n.* A short spasmodic laugh. [Of imit. orig.] —**gig′gler** *n.* —**gig′gling·ly** *adv.* —**gig′gly** *adv.*

GIGO (gī′gō, gē′-) *n. Computer Science* An informal rule holding that the integrity of output is dependent on the integrity of input. [*g(arbage) i(n,) g(arbage) o(ut).*]

gig·o·lo (jĭg′ə-lō′, zhĭg′-) *n., pl.* **-los 1.** A man who has a continuing sexual relationship with and receives financial support from a woman. **2.** A man hired as a woman's escort or dancing partner. [Fr., perh. < *gigolette*, dancing girl, prostitute < *giguer*, to dance < *gigue*, fiddle < OFr. See GIGOT.]

gig·ot (jĭg′ət, zhē-gō′) *n.* **1.** A leg of mutton, lamb, or veal for cooking. **2.** A leg-of-mutton sleeve. [Fr. < OFr., dim. of *gigue*, fiddle < MHGer. *gīge* < OHGer. *gīga.*]

gigue (zhēg) *n.* See **jig**¹. [Fr., prob. < JIG.]

Gi·jón (hē-hōn′) A city of NW Spain on the Bay of Biscay W of Santander; of pre-Roman origin. Pop. 259,067.

Gi·ku·yu (gĭ-ko͞o′yo͞o) *n.* Variant of **Kikuyu.**

Gi·la monster (hē′lə) *n.* A black and orange venomous lizard (*Heloderma suspectum*) of the southwest United States and western Mexico. [After the GILA RIVER.]

Gila River A river rising in the mountains of W NM and flowing c. 1,014 km (630 mi) across S AZ to the Colorado R.

gil·bert (gĭl′bərt) *n.* The centimeter-gram-second electromagnetic unit of magnetomotive force, equal to $10^4/4\pi$ ampere-turn. [After William *Gilbert* (1544–1603), English physician.]

Gilbert, Cass 1859–1934. Amer. architect whose design of the 60-story Woolworth Building in New York City (1913) greatly influenced the development of the skyscraper.

Gilbert, Sir Humphrey 1539?–1583. English navigator who established in Newfoundland (1583) the first English colony in North America.

Gilbert, Sir William Schwenck 1836–1911. British playwright and lyricist known for his comic operas, including *H.M.S. Pinafore* (1878), written with composer Sir Arthur Sullivan.

Gilbert Islands A group of islands of W Kiribati in the central Pacific Ocean; made a British protectorate in 1892 and later became part of the **Gilbert and Ellice Islands Colony** (1915–76). Full independence was achieved in 1979.

gild¹ (gĭld) *tr.v.* **gild·ed** or **gilt** (gĭlt), **gild·ing, gilds 1.** To cover with or as if with a thin layer of gold. **2.** To give an often deceptively attractive or improved appearance to. **3.** *Archaic* To smear with blood. —*idiom:* **gild the lily 1.** To adorn unnecessarily something already beautiful. **2.** To make superfluous additions to what is already complete. [ME *gilden* < OE *gyldan.* See **ghel-** in App.] —**gild′er** *n.*

gild² (gĭld) *n.* Variant of **guild.**

gild·ing (gĭl′dĭng) *n.* **1.** The art or process of applying gilt to a surface. **2.** Gold leaf or a paint containing or simulating gold. **3.** Something used to give a superficially attractive appearance.

Gil·e·ad (gĭl′ē-əd) *n.* A mountainous region of ancient Palestine E of the Jordan R. in what is now NW Jordan.

Gil·ga·mesh (gĭl′gə-mĕsh′) *n. Mythology* The semidivine king

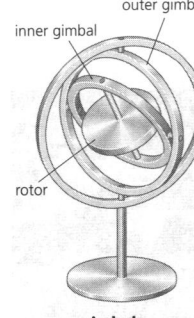

gimbal
supporting a two-degrees-of-freedom gyroscope

of Erech, a city of southern Babylonia, and hero of an epic that tells of a flood covering the earth.

gill¹ (gĭl) *n.* **1.** *Zoology* The respiratory organ of most aquatic animals that breathe water to obtain oxygen. **2a.** The wattle of a bird. Often used in the plural. **b. gills** *Informal* The area around the chin and neck. **3.** *Botany* One of the thin plates on the underside of the cap of a mushroom or similar fungus. ❖ *v.* **gilled, gill·ing, gills** —*tr.* To catch (fish) in a gill net. **2.** To gut or clean (fish). —*intr.* To become entangled in a gill net. Used of fish. —*idiom:* **to the gills** *Informal* As full as possible; completely. [ME *gile*, of Scand. orig.] —**gilled** *adj.*

gill² (jĭl) *n.* **1.** A unit of volume or capacity in the US Customary System, used in liquid measure, equal to ¼ of a pint or four ounces (118 milliliters). See table at **measurement. 2.** A unit of volume or capacity, used in dry and liquid measure, equal to ¼ of a British Imperial pint (142 milliliters). [ME *gille* < OFr., wine measure < LLat. *gillo*, vessel for cooling liquids.]

gill³ (gĭl) *n. Chiefly British* **1.** A ravine. **2.** A narrow stream. [ME *gille* < ON *gil.*]

gill⁴ also **jill** or **Gill** (jĭl) *n.* A girl or a sweetheart. Used esp. with *Jack.* [ME *gille* < *Gille*, a woman's name.]

gill arch (gĭl) *n.* **1.** One of several bony or cartilaginous arches on either side of the pharynx that support the gills in fish and amphibians. **2.** One of several corresponding arches in the embryo of a higher vertebrate.

gill cleft (gĭl) *n.* See **gill slit** 1.

Gilles de la Tour·ette syndrome (zhēl də lä too͞-rĕt′) *n.* See **Tourette's syndrome.**

Gil·les·pie (gə-lĕs′pē), **John Birks** Known as "Dizzy." 1917–93. Amer. jazz trumpeter, bandleader, and composer who was a key leader in the bop movement.

Gil·lette (jə-lĕt′), **King Camp** 1855–1932. Amer. inventor and manufacturer who developed the safety razor (c. 1895).

gill fungus (gĭl) *n.* A fleshy fungus having a cap with gills on the underside.

gil·lie also **ghil·lie** (gĭl′ē) *n., pl.* **-lies 1.** *Scots* A professional fishing and hunting guide. **2.** A low-cut sports shoe with fringed laces. [Sc. Gael. *gille*, boy < OIr. *gilla < gildae.*]

gill net (gĭl) *n.* A fishing net set vertically in the water so that fish swimming into it are entangled by the gills in its mesh. —**gill′net′** (gĭl′nĕt′) *v.* —**gill′net′ter** *n.*

gill slit (gĭl) *n.* **1.** One of several narrow external openings connecting with the pharynx, characteristic of sharks, through which water passes to the exterior, thereby bathing the gills. **2.** One of several rudimentary invaginations in the surface of the embryo, corresponding to the functional gill slits of aquatic species.

gil·ly·flow·er (jĭl′ē-flou′ər) *n.* **1.** The carnation or a similar plant of the genus *Dianthus.* **2.** Any of several plants, such as the wallflower, that have fragrant flowers. [Alteration (influenced by FLOWER) of ME *gilofre* < OFr. *gilofre, girofle*, clove < LLat. *gariofilum* < Gk. *karuophullon : karuon*, nut + *phullon*, leaf; see **bhel-** in App.]

Gil·man (gĭl′mən), **Charlotte Anna Perkins** 1860–1935. Amer. writer whose works include *Women and Economics* (1898), a plea for the economic independence of women.

Gil·son·ite (gĭl′sə-nīt′) A trademark for a natural black bitumen used in road construction and waterproof coatings.

gilt¹ (gĭlt) *v.* A past tense and a past participle of **gild¹.** ❖ *adj.* **1.** Covered with gold or gilt. **2.** Resembling gold, as in color or luster. ❖ *n.* **1.** A thin layer of gold or something simulating gold applied in gilding. **2.** Superficial brilliance or gloss. **3.** *Slang* Money.

gilt² (gĭlt) *n.* A young sow that has not farrowed. [ME, young sow < ON *gyltr.*]

gilt-edged (gĭlt′ĕjd′) also **gilt-edge** (-ĕj′) *adj.* **1.** Having gilded edges. **2.** Of the highest quality or value. **3.** Very wealthy.

gim·bal (gĭm′bəl, jĭm′-) *n.* A device consisting of two rings mounted on axes at right angles to each other so that an object will remain suspended in a horizontal plane between them regardless of any motion of its support. Often used in the plural. ❖ *tr.v.* **-baled, -bal·ing, -bals** or **-balled, -bal·ling, -bals** To supply with or support on gimbals. [Alteration of obsolete *gemel*, double ring. See GIMMAL.]

gim·crack (jĭm′krăk′) *n.* A cheap, showy, useless object. ❖ *adj.* Cheap and tasteless; gaudy. [Poss. alteration of ME *gibecrake*, small ornament.] —**gim′crack′er·y** *n.*

gim·el (gĭm′əl) *n.* The third letter of the Hebrew alphabet. [Heb. *gîmel* < alteration of Phoenician **gaml*, throwstick (sense uncertain), third letter of the Phoenician alphabet.]

gim·let (gĭm′lĭt) *n.* **1.** A small hand tool having a spiraled shank, a screw tip, and a cross handle and used for boring holes. **2.** A cocktail made with vodka or gin, sweetened lime juice, and sometimes effervescent water. ❖ *tr.v.* **-let·ed, -let·ing, -lets** To penetrate with or as if with a gimlet. ❖ *adj.* Having a penetrating or piercing quality. [ME < AN *guimbelet*, perh. < MDu. *wimmelkijn*, dim. of *wimmel*, auger.]

gim·let-eyed (gĭm′lĭt-īd′) *adj.* Having keen vision.

gim·mal (gĭm′əl, jĭm′-) *n.* **1.** A ring made of two or more interlocked rings. **2.** Any of various linkages allowing one part to rotate within another rotating part, used esp. in clockworks. [Alteration of obsolete *gemel* < ME, sing. of *gemelles*, twins < OFr., pl. of *jumel*, twin < Lat. *gemellus*, dim. of *geminus*, twin.]

ginger
Zingiber officinale

inner gimbal · outer gimbal · rotor

gim•mick (gĭm′ĭk) *n.* **1a.** A device used to cheat, deceive, or trick, esp. a mechanism to control a gambling apparatus. **b.** An innovative or unusual mechanical contrivance; a gadget. **2a.** An innovative stratagem or scheme employed esp. to promote a project. **b.** A significant feature that is obscured, misrepresented, or not readily evident; a catch. **3.** A small object whose name escapes one. ❖ *tr.v.* **-micked, -mick•ing, -micks 1.** To add gimmicks to; clutter with gadgets or attention-getting details. Often used with *up.* **2.** To change or affect by means of a gimmick. [?] **—gim′mick•y** *adj.*

gim•mick•ry (gĭm′ĭk-rē) *n., pl.* **-ries 1.** An array or abundance of gimmicks. **2.** The use of gimmicks.

gimp[1] (gĭmp) *n.* A narrow flat braid or rounded cord of fabric used for trimming. [Perh. < Fr. *guimpe.* See GUIMPE.]

gimp[2] (gĭmp) *Slang n.* **1.** A limp or a limping gait. **2.** A person who limps. ❖ *intr.v.* **gimped, gimp•ing, gimps** To walk with a limp. [?] **—gimp′y** *adj.*

gimp[3] (gĭmp) *n.* Spirit; pep. [?]

gin[1] (jĭn) *n.* A strong colorless alcoholic beverage made by distilling grain spirits and adding juniper berries or aromatics as flavoring. [Alteration of *geneva* < Du. *jenever,* ult. < Lat. *iūniperus.*] **—gin′ny** *adj.*

gin[2] (jĭn) *n.* **1.** Any of several machines or devices, esp.: **a.** A machine for hoisting or moving heavy objects. **b.** A pile driver. **c.** A snare or trap for game. **d.** A pump operated by a windmill. **2.** A cotton gin. ❖ *tr.v.* **ginned, gin•ning, gins 1.** To remove the seeds from (cotton) with a cotton gin. **2.** To trap in a gin. [ME < OFr., short for *engin,* skill. See ENGINE.]

gin[3] (jĭn) *n.* Gin rummy.

gin•ger (jĭn′jər) *n.* **1.** A plant *(Zingiber officinale)* of tropical southeast Asia having yellowish-green flowers and a pungent aromatic rhizome. **2.** The rhizome of this plant, often powdered and used as a spice. **3a.** Any of several related plants. **b.** Wild ginger. **4.** A strong brown. **5.** *Informal* Spirit and liveliness; vigor. ❖ *tr.v.* **-gered, -ger•ing, -gers 1.** To spice with ginger. **2.** *Informal* To make lively. [ME *gingivere* < OE *gingifer* and < OFr. *gingivre,* both < Med.Lat. *gingiber* < Lat. *zingiberi* < Gk. *zingiberis,* of M Indic orig. (akin to Pali *singiveram*) < a Dravidian source akin to Tamil *iñci,* ginger (of SE Asian orig.) + Tamil *vēr,* root.] **—gin′ger•y** *adj.*

ginger ale *n.* An effervescent sweetened soft drink flavored with ginger.

ginger beer *n.* A nonalcoholic drink similar to ginger ale but flavored with fermented ginger.

gin•ger•bread (jĭn′jər-brĕd′) *n.* **1a.** A molasses cake flavored with ginger. **b.** A molasses and ginger cookie cut in various shapes, sometimes elaborately decorated. **2a.** Elaborate ornamentation. **b.** Superfluous or tasteless embellishment, esp. in architecture. [ME *gingebred,* a stiff pudding, preserved ginger, alteration of OFr. *gingembrat,* ult. < Med.Lat. *gingiber,* ginger. See GINGER.] **—gin′ger•bread′, gin′ger•bread′y** *adj.*

gingerbread palm *n.* See **doom palm.**

gin•ger•ly (jĭn′jər-lē) *adv.* With great care or delicacy; cautiously. ❖ *adj.* Cautious; careful. [Poss. alteration of obsolete Fr. *gensor,* delicate < OFr., comp. of *gent,* gentle. See GENT[1].] **—gin′ger•li•ness** *n.*

gin•ger•root (jĭn′jər-ro͞ot′, -ro͝ot′) *n.* See **ginger** 2.

gin•ger•snap (jĭn′jər-snăp′) *n.* A flat brittle cookie spiced with ginger and sweetened with molasses.

ging•ham (gĭng′əm) *n.* A yarn-dyed cotton fabric woven in stripes, checks, plaids, or solid colors. [Du. *ginggang* < Malay.]

gin•gi•va (jĭn′jə-və, jĭn-jī′-) *n., pl.* **-vae** (-vē′) See **gum**[2]. [Lat. *gingīva.*]

gin•gi•val (jĭn′jə-vəl, jĭn-jī′-) *adj.* **1.** Of or relating to the gums. **2.** *Linguistics* Alveolar.

gin•gi•vec•to•my (jĭn′jə-vĕk′tə-mē) *n., pl.* **-mies** Surgical removal of gum tissue.

gin•gi•vi•tis (jĭn′jə-vī′tĭs) *n.* Inflammation of the gums.

Ging•rich (gĭng′grĭch), **Newton Leroy ("Newt")** b. 1943. Amer. politician who served as Speaker of the House from 1994 to 1999, when he resigned from Congress.

gink (gĭnk) *n. Slang* A man, esp. one regarded as foolish or contemptible. [?]

gink•go also **ging•ko** (gĭng′kō) *n., pl.* **-goes** also **-koes** A deciduous dioecious tree *(Ginkgo biloba)* native to China and having fan-shaped leaves and fleshy yellow seeds. [J. *ginkyō.*]

gin mill *n. Slang* A bar or saloon.

Gin•nie Mae (jĭn′ē mā′) *n.* A security issued by the Government National Mortgage Association and secured by mortgages serviced by certain federal agencies. [Alteration of *G(overnment) N(ational) M(ortgage) A(ssociation).*]

gin rummy *n.* A variety of rummy for two or more persons in which a player may win by matching all his or her cards or may end the game by melding with unmatched cards that add up to ten points or fewer.

Gins•berg (gĭnz′bərg), **Allen** 1926–97. Amer. poet and a leading figure of the Beat Generation whose works include *Howl* (1956).

Gins•burg (gĭnz′bərg), **Ruth Bader** b. 1933. Amer. jurist who was appointed an associate justice of the US Supreme Court in 1993.

gin•seng (jĭn′sĕng′) *n.* **1.** Any of several plants of the genus *Panax,* esp. *P. pseudoginseng* or *P. quinquefolius,* having small greenish flowers and forked roots believed to have medicinal properties. **2.** The roots of these plants. [Chin. (Mandarin) *rén shēn* : *rén,* man + *shēn,* ginseng.]

Gin•za (gĭn′zə) A shopping and entertainment district of Tokyo, Japan.

gin•zo (gĭn′zō) *n., pl.* **-zoes** *Offensive Slang* Used as a disparaging term for a person of Italian birth or descent. [?]

Gior•gio•ne (jôr-jō′nē, -nĕ) 1478?–1510. Italian painter and early master of the Venetian school whose ascribed works include *The Tempest* (c. 1505).

Giot•to (jŏt′ō, jōt′tō) Full name Giotto di Bondone. 1267?–1337. Florentine painter, architect, and sculptor renowned for his frescoes.

gip (jĭp) *v. & n. Slang* Variant of **gyp.**

Gip•sy (jĭp′sē) *n.* Variant of **Gypsy.**

gi•raffe (jə-răf′) *n., pl.* **-raffes** or **giraffe** An African ruminant *(Giraffa camelopardalis)* having a very long neck and legs, short horns, and a tan coat with orange-brown to black blotches, often reaching a height of 5 meters (16½ feet). [Fr. *girafe* < Ital. *giraffa* < Ar. dialectal *zirāfa,* prob. of African orig.] **—gi•raff′ish** *adj.*

gir•an•dole (jĭr′ən-dōl′) *n.* **1.** A composition or structure in radiating form or arrangement, such as a rotating display of fireworks. **2.** An ornamental branched candleholder, sometimes backed by a mirror. **3.** An earring that consists of a central piece with three smaller ornaments or stones hanging from it. [Fr. < Ital. *girandola* < *girare,* to turn < LLat. *gȳrāre.* See GYRATE.]

gir•a•sol (jĭr′ə-sôl′, -sōl′, -sŏl′) *n.* **1.** also **gir•o•sol** See **fire opal. 2.** also **gir•a•sole** See **Jerusalem artichoke** 2. [Ital. *girasole,* sunflower, opal : *girare,* to turn; see GIRANDOLE + *sole,* sun (< Lat. *sōl;* see **sāwel-** in App.).]

Gi•rau•doux (zhē-rō-do͞o′), **(Hippolyte) Jean** 1882–1944. French writer primarily known for his dramas, such as *Electra* (1937), that are based on Greek mythology or biblical stories.

gird[1] (gûrd) *v.* **gird•ed** or **girt** (gûrt), **gird•ing, girds** *—tr.* **1a.** To encircle with a belt or band. **b.** To fasten or secure (clothing, for example) with a belt or band. **c.** To surround. **2.** To equip or endow. **3.** To prepare (oneself) for action. *—intr.* To prepare for action. ***—idiom:* gird (up) (one's) loins** To summon up one's inner resources in preparation for action. [ME *girden* < OE *gyrdan.* See **gher-** in App.]

gird[2] (gûrd) *intr. & tr.v.* **gird•ed, gird•ing, girds** To jeer or jeer at. ❖ *n.* A sarcastic remark. [ME *girden,* to strike.]

gird•er (gûr′dər) *n.* A beam, as of wood or steel, used as a main horizontal support in a building or bridge.

gir•dle (gûr′dl) *n.* **1a.** A belt or sash worn around the waist. **b.** Something that encircles like a belt. **c.** An elasticized flexible undergarment worn over the waist and hips, esp. by women, to give the body a more slender appearance. **2.** A band made around the trunk of a tree by the removal of a strip of bark. **3.** The edge of a cut gem held by the setting. **4.** *Anatomy* The pelvic or pectoral girdle. ❖ *tr.v.* **-dled, -dling, -dles 1.** To encircle with or as if with a belt. **2.** To circle around. **3.** To remove a band of bark and cambium from the circumference of (a tree), usu. in order to kill it. [ME *girdel* < OE *gyrdel.* See **gher-**[1] in App.]

gird•ler (gûrd′lər) *n.* **1.** One that makes girdles. **2.** Any of several insects that chew bands around twigs or stems.

girl (gûrl) *n.* **1.** A female child. **2.** An immature or inexperienced woman, esp. a young woman. **3.** A daughter. **4.** *Informal* A grown woman: *a night out with the girls.* **5.** A female who comes from or belongs to a particular place: *a city girl.* **6.** *Offensive* A female servant, such as a maid. **7.** A female sweetheart. [ME *girle,* child, girl.] **—girl′hood′** *n.*

girl Friday *n. Informal* An efficient and faithful woman aide or employee. [GIRL + (MAN) FRIDAY.]

girl•friend (gûrl′frĕnd′) *n.* **1.** A favored female companion or sweetheart. **2.** A female friend.

Girl Guide *n.* A member of the Girl Guides, a British organization of young women and girls founded in 1910.

girl•ie also **girl•y** (gûr′lē) *adj. Informal* Featuring minimally clothed or naked women typically in pornographic contexts.

girl•ish (gûr′lĭsh) *adj.* Characteristic of or befitting a girl: *girlish charm.* **—girl′ish•ly** *adv.* **—girl′ish•ness** *n.*

Girl Scout *n.* A member of the Girl Scouts, an organization of young women and girls, founded in the United States in 1912 on the plan of the Girl Guides.

girn (gûrn) *intr.v.* **girned, girn•ing, girns** *Scots* **1.** To complain in a whining voice. **2.** To contort one's face, grimace. [ME *girnen,* var. of *grinnen, grennan.* See GRIN.] **—girn** *n.*

Gi•ronde[1] (jə-rŏnd′, zhē-RÔNd′) An estuary of SW France formed by the Garonne and Dordogne rivers and opening into the Bay of Biscay.

Gi•ronde[2] (jə-rŏnd′, zhĭ-) *n.* A moderate republican political party of Revolutionary France (1791–93). [After *Gironde,* a department of SW France.] **—Gi•rond′ist** *n.*

gir•o•sol (jĭr′ə-sôl′, -sōl′, -sŏl′) *n.* Variant of **girasol** 1.

girt[1] (gûrt) *v.* **girt•ed, girt•ing, girts** *—tr.* **1.** To gird. **2.** To secure with a girth. **3.** To measure the girth of. *—intr.* To measure in girth. [Variant of GIRD[1].]

girt[2] (gûrt) *v.* A past tense and a past participle of **gird**[1].

girth (gûrth) *n.* **1.** The distance around something; the circumfer-

ginkgo
Ginkgo biloba

giraffe
Masai giraffe
Giraffa camelopardalis tippelskirchi

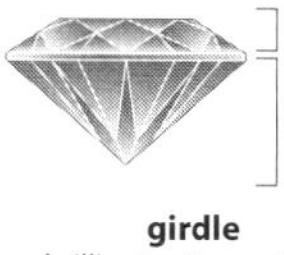
crown
girdle
pavilion

girdle
brilliant-cut gemstone

ă	pat	oi	boy
ā	pay	ou	out
âr	care	o͝o	took
ä	father	o͞o	boot
ĕ	pet	ŭ	cut
ē	be	ûr	urge
ĭ	pit	th	thin
ī	pie	*th*	this
îr	pier	hw	which
ŏ	pot	zh	vision
ō	toe	ə	about, item
ô	paw		

Stress marks:
′ (primary);
′ (secondary), as in
lexicon (lĕk′sĭ-kŏn′)

ence. **2.** Size; bulk. **3.** A strap around an animal's body that secures a load or saddle on its back; a cinch. ❖ *tr.v.* **girthed, girth•ing, girths 1.** To measure the circumference of. **2.** To encircle. **3.** To secure with a girth. [ME *gerth*, girth strap < ON *gjördh*, girdle. See **gher-** in App.]

GIS *abbr.* Geographic Information System

gi•sarme (gĭ-zärm′) *n.* A halberd with a two-sided blade, carried by medieval foot soldiers. [ME < OFr. *guisarme*, poss. < OHGer. *getīsarn* : *getan*, to weed + *īsarn*, iron; see **eis-** in App.]

Gis•card d'Es•taing (zhĭ-skär′ dĕs-tăng′, -tăɴ′), **Valéry** b. 1926. French politician who served as president (1974–81).

Gish (gĭsh), **Lillian Diana** 1893–1993. Amer. actress best known for her roles in silent films, such as *The Birth of a Nation* (1915). Her sister **Dorothy** (1898–1968) was also a film actress.

gis•mo (gĭz′mō) *n.* Variant of **gizmo.**

Gis•sing (gĭs′ĭng), **George Robert** 1857–1903. British writer whose works include *New Grub Street* (1891).

gist (jĭst) *n.* **1.** The central idea; the essence. **2.** *Law* The grounds for action in a suit. [< AN *(cest action) gist*, (this action) lies, third pers. sing. of *gesir*, to lie < Lat. *iacēre*.]

git (gĭt) *v. Regional* Variant of **get.**

gite (zhēt) *n.* A simple, usu. inexpensive rural vacation retreat, esp. in France. [Fr. *gîte*, lodging, lair < OFr. *giste* < fem. p. part. of *gesir*, to lie. See GIST.]

git•tern (gĭt′ərn) *n.* A guitar of the Middle Ages and Renaissance. [ME *giterne* < OFr. *guiterne* < Lat. *cithara*. See CITHARA.]

give (gĭv) *v.* **gave** (gāv), **giv•en** (gĭv′ən), **giv•ing, gives** —*tr.* **1.** To make a present of: *We gave her flowers for her birthday.* **2.** To place in the hands of; pass: *Give me the scissors.* **3a.** To deliver in exchange or recompense; pay: *gave five dollars for the book.* **b.** To let go for a price; sell: *gave the used car away for two thousand dollars.* **4a.** To administer: *give him medicine.* **b.** To convey by a physical action: *gave me a punch in the nose.* **c.** To inflict as punishment: *gave the child a spanking.* **d.** *Law* To accord by verdict: *A decision was given for the plaintiff.* **5a.** To bestow, esp. officially; confer: *The Bill of Rights gives us freedom of speech.* **b.** To accord or tender to another: *Give him your confidence.* **c.** To put temporarily at the disposal of: *gave me the cottage for a week.* **d.** To entrust to another, usu. for a specified reason: *gave me the keys for safekeeping.* **e.** To convey or offer for conveyance: *Give him my best.* **f.** *Law* To execute and deliver. Used esp. in the phrase *give bond.* **6a.** To endure the loss of; sacrifice: *gave his life for his country.* **b.** To devote or apply completely: *gives herself to her work.* **c.** To furnish or contribute: *gave his time to help others.* **d.** To offer in good faith; pledge: *gave me his word.* **7a.** To allot as a portion or share. **b.** To bestow (a name, for example). **c.** To attribute (blame, for example) to someone; assign. **d.** To award as due: *gave us first prize.* **8.** To emit or utter: *gave a muted response.* **9.** To submit for consideration, acceptance, or use: *give an opinion.* **10a.** To proffer to another: *gave the toddler my hand.* **b.** To consent to engage (oneself) in sexual intercourse with a man. **11a.** To perform for an audience: *give a recital.* **b.** To present to view: *gave the sign to begin.* **12a.** To offer as entertainment: *give a party.* **b.** To propose as a toast. **13a.** To be a source of; afford: *His remark gave offense.* **b.** To cause to catch or be subject to (a disease or bodily condition): *The draft gave me a cold.* **c.** To guide or direct, as by persuasion or behavior. Used with an infinitive phrase: *You gave me to imagine you approved of him.* **14a.** To yield or produce: *Cows give milk.* **b.** To bring forth or bear: *trees that give fruit.* **c.** To produce as a result of calculation: *5 × 12 gives 60.* **15a.** To manifest or show: *The scene gives evidence of tampering.* **b.** To carry out (a physical movement): *give a wink; give a start.* **16.** To permit one to have or take: *gave us an hour to finish.* **17.** To take an interest to the extent of: *"My dear, I don't give a damn"* (Margaret Mitchell). —*intr.* **1.** To make gifts or donations: *gives generously to charity.* **2a.** To yield to physical force. **b.** To collapse from force or pressure: *The roof gave under the weight of the snow.* **c.** To yield to change: *Both sides will have to give on some issues.* **3.** To afford access or a view; open: *The door gives onto the terrace.* **4.** *Slang* To be in progress; happen: *What gives?* ❖ *n.* **1.** Capacity or inclination to yield under pressure. **2.** The quality or condition of resilience; springiness. ***—phrasal verbs:*** **give away 1.** To make a gift of. **2.** To present (a bride) to the bridegroom at a wedding ceremony. **3a.** To reveal or make known, often accidentally. **b.** To betray. **give back** To return. **give in 1.** To hand in; submit: *She gave in her report.* **2.** To cease opposition; yield. **give of** To devote or contribute. **give off** To send forth; emit: *chemical changes that give off energy.* **give out 1.** To allow to be known; declare publicly. **2.** To send forth; emit. **3.** To distribute: *gave out the food.* **4.** To stop functioning; fail. **5.** To become used up or exhausted; run out. **give over 1.** To hand over; entrust. **2a.** To devote to a particular purpose or use. **b.** To surrender (oneself) completely; abandon. **3.** To cause an activity to stop: *ordered the combatants to give over.* **give up 1a.** To surrender: *The suspects gave themselves up.* **b.** To devote (oneself) completely. **2a.** To cease to do or perform. **b.** To desist from; stop: *gave up smoking.* **3.** To part with; relinquish: *gave up all hope.* **4a.** To lose hope for: *gave the cat up as lost.* **b.** To lose hope of seeing. **5.** To admit defeat. **6.** To abandon what one is doing or planning to do. ***—idioms:*** **give a good account of (oneself)** To behave or perform creditably. **give birth to 1.** To bear as offspring. **2.** To be the origin of. **give ground** To yield to a more powerful force; retreat. **give it to** *Informal* To punish or reprimand severely. **give or take** Plus or minus (a small specified amount). **give rise to** To be the cause or origin of; bring about. **give (someone) the eye** To look at admiringly or invitingly. **give the lie to 1.** To show to be inaccurate or untrue. **2.** To accuse of lying. **give up the ghost** To cease living or functioning; die. **give way 1a.** To retreat or withdraw. **b.** To yield the right of way: *gave way to oncoming cars.* **c.** To relinquish ascendancy or position. **2a.** To collapse from or as if from physical pressure: *The ladder gave way.* **b.** To yield to urging or demand; give in. **3.** To abandon oneself: *give way to hysteria.* [ME *given* < OE *giefan* and ON *gefa*; see **ghabh-** in App.]

glacier
Portage Glacier, Alaska

give•a•way (gĭv′ə-wā′) *n. Informal* **1.** The act or an instance of giving something away. **2.** Something given away at no charge. **3.** Something that accidentally exposes or betrays.

give•back (gĭv′băk′) *n.* **1.** A cutback in wages or benefits conceded by a union, as in exchange for other benefits. **2.** Something rebated or returned.

giv•en (gĭv′ən) *v.* Past participle of **give.** ❖ *adj.* **1a.** Specified; fixed. **b.** Granted as a supposition; acknowledged or assumed. **2.** Having a tendency; inclined. **3.** Bestowed as a gift; presented. **4.** *Law* Issued on a specified date. Used of legal documents. ❖ *n.* Something assumed or taken for granted.

given name *n.* A name given to a person at birth or at baptism, as distinguished from a surname.

giv•er (gĭv′ər) *n.* **1.** One that gives. **2.** A donor or contributor.

Gi•za (gē′zə) A city of N Egypt, a suburb of Cairo; near the site of the Great Pyramids and the Sphinx. Pop. 1,608,400.

giz•mo also **gis•mo** (gĭz′mō) *n., pl.* **-mos** A mechanical device or part whose name is forgotten or unknown. [?]

giz•zard (gĭz′ərd) *n.* **1.** A modified, thickly lined muscular pouch behind the stomach in birds, often containing ingested grit, that aids in the mechanical breakdown of food. **2.** A similar digestive organ in certain invertebrates. [Alteration of ME *giser* < OFr. < VLat. **gicērium* < Lat. *gigēria*, cooked entrails of poultry, prob. < Pers. *jigar*, liver. See **yĕkʷr̥** in App.]

Gjel•le•rup (gĕl′ə-ro͝op′), **Karl** 1857–1919. Danish writer who shared the 1917 Nobel Prize for literature.

Gk. *abbr.* Greek

gl. *abbr.* gloss (explanatory note)

gla•bel•la (glə-bĕl′ə) *n., pl.* **-bel•lae** (-bĕl′ē) The smooth area between the eyebrows. [NLat. < Lat. *glabellus*, hairless, dim. of *glaber*.] **—gla•bel′lar** *adj.*

gla•brous (glā′brəs) *adj.* Having no hairs, projections, or pubescence; smooth: *glabrous leaves.* [< Lat. *glaber, glabr-*, bald.]

gla•cé (glă-sā′) *adj.* **1.** Having a smooth glazed or glossy surface, such as certain silks or leathers. **2.** Coated with a sugar glaze; candied. ❖ *tr.v.* **-céed, -cé•ing, -cés 1.** To glaze. **2.** To candy. [Fr. < p. part. of *glacer*, to glaze, freeze < OFr., to freeze < Lat. *glaciāre*. See GLACIATE.]

gla•cial (glā′shəl) *adj.* **1a.** Of, relating to, or derived from a glacier. **b.** Suggesting the extreme slowness of a glacier. **2a.** often **Glacial** Characterized or dominated by glaciers. Used of a geologic epoch. **b.** Pleistocene. See table at **geologic time. 3.** Extremely cold; icy. See Syns at **cold. 4.** Having the appearance of ice. **5a.** Lacking warmth and friendliness. **b.** Coldly detached. [French < OFr., icy < Lat. *glaciālis* < *glaciēs*, ice. See **gel-** in App.] **—gla′cial•ly** *adv.*

glacial acetic acid *n.* Acetic acid that is at least 99.8 percent pure.

gla•ci•ate (glā′shē-āt′, -sē-) *tr.v.* **-at•ed, -at•ing, -ates 1a.** To cover with ice or a glacier. **b.** To subject to or affect by glacial action. **2.** To freeze. [Lat. *glaciāre, glaciāt-*, to freeze < *glaciēs*, ice. See **gel-** in App.] **—gla′ci•a′tion** *n.*

gla•cier (glā′shər) *n.* A huge mass of ice slowly flowing over a land mass, formed from compacted snow in an area where snow accumulation exceeds melting and sublimation. [Fr. < OFr., cold place < *glace*, ice < VLat. **glacia* < Lat. *glaciēs*. See **gel-** in App.] **—gla′ciered** *adj.*

Glacier Bay A narrow inlet of the Pacific Ocean in SE AK NW of Juneau; named for the surrounding mountain peaks with spectacular glaciers.

glacier meal *n.* See **rock flour.**

gla•ci•ol•o•gy (glā′shē-ŏl′ə-jē, -sē-) *n.* The scientific study of glaciers and their effects on the landscape. [GLACI(ER) + -LOGY.] **—gla′ci•o•log′ic** (-ə-lŏj′ĭk), **gla′ci•o•log′i•cal** *adj.* **—gla′ci•ol′o•gist** *n.*

gla•cis (glă-sē′, glăs′ē, glā′sĭs) *n., pl.* **glacis 1a.** A gentle slope; an incline. **b.** A slope extending down from a fortification. **2.** A neutral area separating conflicting forces. [Fr. < OFr. < *glacer*, to slide < *glace*, ice < VLat. **glacia* < Lat. *glaciēs*. See **gel-** in App.]

Glack•ens (glăk′ənz), **William James** 1870–1938. Amer. painter noted for his realistic street scenes and later impressionistic works.

glad[1] (glăd) *adj.* **glad•der, glad•dest 1a.** Experiencing or exhibiting joy and pleasure. **b.** Appreciative: *glad of the fire's warmth.* **2.** Providing joy and pleasure: *a glad occasion.* **3.** Very willing; pleased: *glad to help.* **4.** Bright and cheerful. **5.** *Archaic* Having a naturally cheerful disposition. ❖ *tr. & intr.v.* **glad•ded, glad•ding, glads** *Archaic* To gladden. [ME < OE *glæd*. See **ghel-** in App.] **—glad′ly** *adv.* **—glad′ness** *n.*

SYNONYMS *glad, happy, cheerful, lighthearted, joyful, joyous*
These adjectives mean being in or showing good spirits. *Glad* often refers to the feeling that results from the gratification of a wish or from satisfaction with immediate circumstances: *"Some folks rail against other folks, because other folks have what some folks would be glad of"* (Henry Fielding). *Happy* generally applies to a pleasurable feeling of contentment: *"Ask yourself whether you are happy, and you cease to be so"* (John Stuart Mill). *Cheerful* suggests characteristic good spirits: *a cheerful volunteer. Lighthearted* stresses the absence of care: *"He whistles as he goes, lighthearted wretch,/Cold and yet cheerful"* (William Cowper). *Joyful* and *joyous* suggest lively, often exultant happiness: *a joyful heart; joyous laughter.*

glad² (glăd) *n. Botany* A gladiolus.

glad·den (glăd′n) *v.* **-dened, -den·ing, -dens** —*tr.* To make glad. —*intr. Archaic* To be glad.

glade (glād) *n.* **1.** An open space in a forest. **2.** An everglade. [ME, perh. < *glad*, bright and shining. See GLAD¹.]

glad hand *n. Informal* A warm and hearty but often insincere welcome or greeting. —**glad′-hand** (glăd′hănd′) *v.* —**glad′-hand′er** *n.*

glad·i·ate (glăd′ē-āt, -ĭt, glā′dē-) *adj. Botany* Sword-shaped. [NLat. *gladiātus* < Lat. *gladius*, sword. See GLADIATOR.]

glad·i·a·tor (glăd′ē-ā′tər) *n.* **1.** A person, usu. a professional combatant, a captive, or a slave, trained to entertain the public by mortal combat with another person or a wild animal in the ancient Roman arena. **2.** A person engaged in a controversy or debate, esp. in public; a disputant. **3.** *Sports* A professional boxer. [ME < Lat. *gladiātor* < *gladius*, sword, of Celt. orig.] —**glad′i·a·to′ri·al** (-ə-tôr′ē-əl, -tōr′-) *adj.*

glad·i·o·lus (glăd′ē-ō′ləs) *n., pl.* **-li** (-lī, -lē) or **-lus·es 1.** also **glad·i·o·la** (-lə) Any of numerous chiefly African plants of the genus *Gladiolus*, having sword-shaped leaves and irregular flowers arranged in one-sided spikes. **2.** *Anatomy* The large middle section of the sternum. [ME *gladiol* < Lat. *gladiolus*, wild iris, dim. of *gladius*, sword. See GLADIATOR.]

glad rags *pl.n. Slang* Stylish clothes.

glad·some (glăd′səm) *adj.* Causing or showing gladness or joy. —**glad′some·ly** *adv.*

Glad·stone (glăd′stōn′, -stən) *n.* **1.** A light four-wheeled convertible carriage with two interior seats and exterior seats for a driver and footman. **2.** A Gladstone bag. [After William Ewart GLADSTONE.]

Gladstone, William Ewart 1809–98. British politician who served as prime minister four times between 1868 and 1894.

Gladstone bag *n.* A piece of light hand luggage consisting of two hinged compartments. [After William Ewart GLADSTONE.]

Glag·o·lit·ic (glăg′ə-lĭt′ĭk) also **Glag·o·lith·ic** (-lĭth′ĭk) *adj.* Belonging to or written in an alphabet attributed to Saint Cyril, formerly used in the writing of various Slavic languages. [< Serbo-Croatian *glagoljica* < *glagol*, word < O Church Slavonic *glagolŭ*.]

glair also **glaire** (glâr) *n.* **1.** The white of an egg. **2.** A sizing or glaze made of egg white. **3.** A viscous substance resembling egg white. [ME *glaire* < OFr. < VLat. *clāria* < Lat. *clārus*, clear. See kelə- in App.]

glaive (glāv) *n. Archaic* A sword, esp. a broadsword. [ME < OFr. < Lat. *gladius*. See GLADIATOR.]

Glå·ma (glô′mə) also **Glom·ma** (-mə, -mä) A river of E Norway flowing c. 587 km (365 mi) to the Skagerrak.

glam·or·ize also **glam·our·ize** (glăm′ə-rīz′) *tr.v.* **-ized, -iz·ing, -iz·es 1.** To make glamorous. **2.** To treat or portray in a romantic manner; idealize or glorify. —**glam′or·i·za′tion** (-ər-ĭ-zā′shən) *n.* —**glam′or·iz′er** *n.*

glam·or·ous also **glam·our·ous** (glăm′ər-əs) *adj.* Full of or characterized by glamour. —**glam′or·ous·ly** *adv.*

glam·our also **glam·or** (glăm′ər) *n.* **1.** An air of compelling charm, romance, and excitement, esp. when delusively alluring. **2.** *Archaic* A magic spell; enchantment. [Sc., magic spell, alteration of GRAMMAR (learning and magic being associated).]

USAGE NOTE Words such as *honor, vapor,* and *labor* usually end with *–or* in American English and *–our* in British English. The preferred spelling of *glamour,* however, is *–our.* The adjective is usually spelled *glamorous* in both American and British usage.

glance¹ (glăns) *v.* **glanced, glanc·ing, glanc·es** —*intr.* **1a.** To direct the gaze briefly: *glanced at the menu.* **b.** To move rapidly from one thing to another. Used of the eyes. **2.** To shine briefly; glint. **3.** To strike a surface at such an angle as to be deflected: *A pebble glanced off the windshield.* **4.** To make a passing reference; touch briefly. —*tr.* **1.** To strike (a surface) at an angle; graze. **2.** To cause to strike a surface at an angle: *glanced a stone off the wall.* ❖ *n.* **1.** A brief or cursory look: *gave the paper a glance before breakfast.* **2.** A quick flash of light; a gleam. **3.** An oblique movement following impact; a deflection. —*idiom:* **at first glance** On initial consideration. [ME *glauncen*, alteration (influenced by *glenten,* to shine) of *glacen* < OFr. *glacier,* to slide. See GLACIS.]

glance² (glăns) *n.* Any of various minerals that have a brilliant luster: *silver glance.* [Ger. *Glanz* < MHGer. *glanz* < OHGer., bright. See ghel- in App.]

glanc·ing (glăn′sĭng) *adj.* **1.** Oblique; slanting or deflected: *struck him a glancing blow.* **2.** Not straightforward; indirect. —**glanc′ing·ly** *adv.*

gland¹ (glănd) *n.* **1a.** A cell, a group of cells, or an organ that produces a secretion for use in or for elimination from the body. **b.** Any of various organs, such as lymph nodes, that resemble true glands but perform a nonsecretory function. **2.** *Botany* An organ or a structure that secretes a substance. [Fr. *glande* < OFr. *glandre,* alteration of Lat. *glandula,* dim. of *glāns,* gland-, acorn.]

gland² (glănd) *n.* A device designed to prevent a fluid from leaking past a moving machine part. [?]

glan·dered (glăn′dərd) *adj.* Affected with glanders.

glan·ders (glăn′dərz) *n.* (used with a sing. or pl. verb) A contagious, usu. fatal disease of horses, caused by the bacterium *Pseudomonas mallei* and symptomized by swollen lymph nodes, nasal discharge, and ulcers of the respiratory tract and skin. [ME *glaundres* < OFr. *glandres,* glandular swelling, pl. of *glandre,* gland. See GLAND¹.] —**glan′der·ous** *adj.*

glan·du·lar (glăn′jə-lər) *adj.* **1a.** Of, relating to, affecting, or resembling a gland or its secretion. **b.** Functioning as a gland. **2.** Having glands. **3a.** Innate; visceral. **b.** Carnal; sensual. [Fr. *glandulaire* < *glandule,* small gland < Lat. *glandula.* See GLAND¹.] —**glan′du·lar·ly** *adv.*

glandular fever *n.* See infectious mononucleosis.

glans (glănz) *n., pl.* **glan·des** (glăn′dēz) **1.** The glans penis. **2.** The glans clitoridis. [Lat. *glāns,* gland-, acorn, glans.]

glans cli·tor·i·dis (klĭ-tôr′ĭ-dĭs, klī-) *n.* The small mass of erectile tissue at the tip of the clitoris. [NLat. *glāns clītoridis* : Lat. *glāns,* glans + NLat. *clītoridis,* genitive of *clītoris,* clitoris.]

glans penis *n.* The head or tip of the penis. [NLat. *glāns pēnis* : Lat. *glāns,* glans + Lat. *pēnis,* genitive of *pēnis,* penis.]

glare¹ (glâr) *v.* **glared, glar·ing, glares** —*intr.* **1.** To stare fixedly and angrily. **2.** To shine intensely and blindingly. **3.** To be conspicuous; stand out obtrusively. —*tr.* To express by staring angrily. ❖ *n.* **1.** A fierce or angry stare. **2a.** An intense, blinding light. **b.** Garish or showy brilliance; gaudiness. [ME *glaren,* to glitter; akin to MLGer. *glaren,* to glisten. See ghel- in App.]

glare² (glâr) *n.* A sheet or surface of glassy and very slippery ice. [Prob. < GLARE¹.]

glar·ing (glâr′ĭng) *adj.* **1.** Shining intensely and blindingly. **2.** Tastelessly showy or bright; garish. **3.** Conspicuous; obvious. **4.** Staring with anger, fierceness, or hostility. —**glar′ing·ly** *adv.*

glar·y (glâr′ē) *adj.* **-i·er, -i·est** Dazzlingly bright; glaring.

Glas·gow (glăs′kō, -gō, glăz′-) A city of SW Scotland on the Clyde R.; founded in the late 6th cent. Pop. 681,470.

Glasgow, Ellen Anderson Gholson 1873?–1945. Amer. writer whose works include *In This Our Life* (1941).

glas·nost (gläs′nōst, -nôst) *n.* An official policy of the Soviet government emphasizing candor in discussion of social problems. [Russ. *glasnost′,* publicity, openness < obsolete *glas,* voice < O Church Slavonic *glasŭ.*]

glass (glăs) *n.* **1.** Any of a large class of materials that are typically made by silicates fusing with boric oxide, aluminum oxide, or phosphorus pentoxide, are generally hard, brittle, and transparent or translucent, and are considered to be supercooled liquids that form noncrystalline solids. **2.** Something usu. made of glass, esp.: **a.** A drinking vessel. **b.** A mirror. **c.** A barometer. **3a.** A window or windowpane. **b.** **glasses** A pair of lenses mounted in a light frame, used to correct faulty vision or protect the eyes. **c.** A binocular or field glass. Often used in the plural. **c.** A device, such as a monocle or spyglass, containing a lens or lenses and used as an aid to vision. **4.** The quantity contained in a drinking vessel; a glassful. **5.** Objects made of glass; glassware. ❖ *adj.* **1.** Made or consisting of glass. **2.** Fitted with panes of glass; glazed. ❖ *v.* **glassed, glass·ing, glass·es** —*tr.* **1a.** To enclose or encase with glass. **b.** To put into a glass container. **c.** To provide with glass or glass parts. **2.** To make glassy; glaze. **3a.** To see reflected, as in a mirror. **b.** To reflect. **4.** To scan (a tract of land, for example) with an optical instrument. —*intr.* **1.** To become glassy. **2.** To use an optical instrument, as in looking for game. [ME *glas* < OE *glæs.* See ghel- in App.]

Glass, Philip b. 1937. Amer. composer whose minimalist works include the opera *Einstein on the Beach* (1975).

glass blowing *n.* The art or process of shaping an object from molten glass by blowing air into it through a tube. —**glass blower** *n.*

glass ceiling *n.* An unacknowledged discriminatory barrier that prevents women and minorities from rising to positions of power or responsibility, as within a corporation.

glassed-in (glăst′ĭn′) *adj.* Enclosed by glass or panels of glass.

glass eel *n.* An eel in its transparent postlarval stage.

glass eye *n.* **1.** An artificial eye fashioned of glass. **2.** An eye whose iris is whitish, pale, or colorless.

glass·ful (glăs′fŏŏl′) *n.* The quantity that a glass can hold.

glass harmonica *n.* A musical instrument consisting of a set of graduated glass bowls on a rotating spindle that produce tones when a finger is pressed to their moistened rims.

glass·house (glăs′hous′) *n.* **1.** See glasswork 3. **2.** *Chiefly British* A greenhouse.

glass·ine (glă-sēn′) *n.* A nearly transparent resilient glazed paper resistant to the passage of light and air.

glass blowing

ă	pat	oi	boy
ā	pay	ou	out
âr	care	ŏŏ	took
ä	father	ōō	boot
ĕ	pet	ŭ	cut
ē	be	ûr	urge
ĭ	pit	th	thin
ī	pie	*th*	this
îr	pier	hw	which
ŏ	pot	zh	vision
ō	toe	ə	about,
ô	paw		item

Stress marks: ′ (primary);
′ (secondary), as in **lexicon** (lĕk′sĭ-kŏn′)

glass jaw *n.* Vulnerability of a boxer to a knockout punch.

glass·mak·er (glăs′mā′kər) *n.* One that makes glass. —**glass′·mak′ing** *n.*

glass noodle *n.* See **cellophane noodle.**

glass snake *n.* Any of several slender snakelike lizards of the genus *Ophisaurus,* having a tail that breaks or snaps off readily and later regenerates. [< the brittleness of its tail.]

glass·ware (glăs′wâr′) *n.* Objects, esp. containers, made of glass.

glass wool *n.* Fine-spun fibers of glass used esp. for insulation and in air filters.

glass·work (glăs′wûrk′) *n.* **1a.** The manufacture of glassware or glass. **b.** The cutting and fitting of glass panes; glaziery. **2.** See **glassware. 3.** glassworks (*used with a sing. verb*) An establishment where glass is manufactured.

glass·wort (glăs′wûrt′, -wôrt′) *n.* Any of various plants of the genus *Salicornia,* growing in salt marshes and having scalelike leaves. [< its former use in making glass.]

glass·y (glăs′ē) *adj.* -**i·er,** -**i·est 1.** Characteristic of or resembling glass. **2.** Lifeless; expressionless: *"the face changing to a demon's face with a fixed glassy grin"* (Katherine Anne Porter). —**glass′i·ly** *adv.* —**glass′i·ness** *n.*

Glas·ton·bur·y (glăs′tən-bĕr′ē) A municipal borough of SW England SSW of Bristol; traditional site of King Arthur's Isle of Avalon. Pop. 6,773.

Glas·we·gian (glăs-wē′jən, glăz-) *adj.* Of or relating to Glasgow, Scotland. ❖ *n.* A native or resident of Glasgow, Scotland. [GLAS(GOW) + (Gal)wegian, person from Galloway (< Med.Lat. *Galwidia,* Galloway, a region of SW Scotland).]

Glau·ber's salt (glou′bərz) *n.* A sodium sulfate, Na₂SO₄·10H₂O, used in paper and glass manufacturing and as a cathartic. [After Johann Rudolf *Glauber* (1604–68), German chemist.]

glau·co·ma (glou-kō′mə, glô-) *n.* Any of a group of eye diseases characterized by abnormally high intraocular fluid pressure, damaged optic disk, and partial to complete loss of vision. [Lat. *glaucōma,* cataract < Gk. *glaukōma < glaukos,* gray.] —**glau·co′ma·tous** (-kō′mə-təs) *adj.*

glau·co·nite (glô′kə-nīt′) *n.* A greenish clay mineral, a hydrous silicate of potassium, iron, aluminum, or magnesium, (K,Na)₂(Al,Fe,Mg)₂(Al,Si)₄O₁₀(OH)₂, found in greensand. [Ger. *Glaukonit* : Gk. *glaukon,* neut. of *glaukos,* gray + -ITE¹.] —**glau′co·nit′ic** (-nĭt′ĭk) *adj.*

glau·cous (glô′kəs) *adj.* **1.** Of a pale grayish or bluish green. **2.** *Botany* Covered with a grayish, bluish, or whitish coating that is easily rubbed off. [Lat. *glaucus* < Gk. *glaukos.*]

glaze (glāz) *n.* **1.** A thin smooth shiny coating. **2.** A thin glassy coating of ice. **3a.** A coating of material applied to ceramics before firing. **b.** A coating, as of syrup, applied to food. **c.** A transparent coating applied to the surface of a painting to modify the color tones. **4.** A glassy film, as one over the eyes. ❖ *v.* **glazed, glaz·ing, glaz·es** —*tr.* **1.** To fit, furnish, or secure with glass: *glaze a window.* **2.** To apply a glaze to: *glaze pottery.* **3.** To coat or cover thinly with ice. **4.** To give a smooth lustrous surface to. —*intr.* **1.** To be or become glazed or glassy: *His eyes glazed over from boredom.* **2.** To form a glaze. [< ME *glasen < glas,* glass < OE *glæs.* See **ghel-** in App.] —**glaz′er** *n.*

gla·zier (glā′zhər) *n.* One who cuts and fits glass. [ME *glasier < glas,* glass. See GLAZE.] —**gla′zier·y** (-zhə-rē) *n.*

glaz·ing (glā′zĭng) *n.* **1a.** Glasswork. **b.** Glass set or made to be set in frames. **2a.** A glaze. **b.** The act or process of applying a glaze.

Gla·zu·nov (glăz′ə-nôf′, -nôv′, glə-zoo-nôf′), Aleksandr Konstantinovich 1865–1936. Russian composer who worked with Rimski-Korsakov to complete Borodin's opera *Prince Igor* (1890).

gleam (glēm) *n.* **1.** A brief beam or flash of light. **2.** A steady but subdued shining; a glow. **3.** A brief or dim manifestation; a trace: *a gleam of intelligence.* ❖ *v.* **gleamed, gleam·ing, gleams** —*intr.* **1.** To emit a gleam; flash or glow: *"It shone with gold and gleamed with ivory"* (Edith Hamilton). **2.** To be manifested or indicated briefly or faintly. —*tr.* To cause to emit a flash of light. [ME *glem* < OE *glǣm.* See **ghel-** in App.] —**gleam′er** *n.*

glean (glēn) *v.* **gleaned, glean·ing, gleans** —*intr.* To glean grain. —*tr.* **1.** To gather (grain) left behind by reapers. **2.** To collect bit by bit. [ME *glenen* < OFr. *glener* < LLat. *glennāre,* prob. of Celt. orig.] —**glean′er** *n.*

glean·ings (glē′nĭngz) *pl.n.* Things collected bit by bit.

Glea·son (glē′sən), Herbert John Known as "Jackie." 1916–87. Amer. entertainer best remembered for his portrayal of Ralph Kramden on *The Honeymooners* (1952–57).

glebe (glēb) *n.* **1.** A plot of land belonging or yielding profit to an English parish church or an ecclesiastical office. **2.** *Archaic* The soil or earth; land. [Lat. *glēba,* clod.]

glede (glēd) *n.* Any of several birds of prey, esp. a European kite (*Milvus milvus*). [ME < OE *glida.* See **ghel-** in App.]

glee (glē) *n.* **1.** Jubilant delight; joy. **2.** *Music* A part song for three or more usu. male and unaccompanied voices that was popular in the 18th century. [ME *gle,* entertainment < OE *glēo.* See **ghel-²** in App.]

glee club *n.* A group of singers who perform usu. short pieces of choral music.

gleed (glēd) *n. Archaic* A glowing coal; an ember. [ME *glede* < OE *glēd.* See **ghel-** in App.]

glee·ful (glē′fəl) *adj.* Full of jubilant delight; joyful. —**glee′ful·ly** *adv.* —**glee′ful·ness** *n.*

glee·man (glē′mən) *n.* A medieval itinerant singer; a minstrel. [ME *gleman* < OE *glēoman* : *glēo,* minstrelsy; see **ghel-** in App. + *man,* man; see MAN.]

glee·some (glē′səm) *adj. Archaic* Gleeful.

gleet (glēt) *n.* **1.** Inflammation of the urethra resulting from chronic gonorrhea and characterized by a mucopurulent discharge. **2.** The discharge characteristic of gleet. [ME *glet,* slime < OFr. *glette* < Lat. *glittus,* sticky.] —**gleet′y** *adj.*

gleg (glĕg) *adj. Scots* Alert and quick to respond. [ME, clearsighted < ON *glöggr.* See **ghel-** in App.]

glen (glĕn) *n.* A small, secluded valley. [ME < Sc. Gael. *gleann* < OIr. *glenn.*]

Glen·dale (glĕn′dāl′) **1.** A city of S-central AZ, a suburb of Phoenix. Pop. 218,812. **2.** A city of S CA, a suburb of Los Angeles; located on part of the first Spanish land grant in the area (1784). Pop. 194,973.

Glen·dow·er (glĕn′dou′ər, glĕn-dou′-), Owen 1359?–1416? Welsh rebel who led a revolt against Henry IV (1400) and summoned a parliament (1405) before being crushed by English forces (1409).

Glen·gar·ry (glĕn-găr′ē) *n., pl.* -**ries** A woolen cap that is creased lengthwise and often has short ribbons at the back. [After *Glengarry,* a valley of central Scotland.]

Glenn (glĕn), **John Herschel, Jr.** b. 1921. Amer. politician who was the first US astronaut to orbit the earth (Feb. 20, 1962).

gley (glā) *n.* A sticky, bluish-gray subsurface layer of clay found in some waterlogged soils. [Russ. dialectal *gleĭ,* clay.]

gli·a (glē′ə, glī′ə) *n. (used with a sing. or pl. verb)* See **neuroglia.** [Short for NEUROGLIA.] —**gli′al** (glē′əl, glī′əl) *adj.*

gli·a·din (glī′ə-dĭn) *n.* Any of several simple proteins derived from rye or wheat gluten. [Ital. *gliadina* < Med.Gk. *glia,* glue. See ZOOGLEA.]

glial cell *n.* Any of the cells making up the neuroglia, esp. the astrocytes, oligodendroglia, and microglia.

glib (glĭb) *adj.* **glib·ber, glib·best 1a.** Performed with a natural offhand ease: *glib conversation.* **b.** Showing little thought, preparation, or concern. **2.** Marked by ease and fluency of speech or writing that often suggests or stems from insincerity, superficiality, or deceitfulness. [Poss. of LGer. orig. See **ghel-** in App.] —**glib′ly** *adv.* —**glib′ness** *n.*

glide (glīd) *v.* **glid·ed, glid·ing, glides** —*intr.* **1.** To move in a smooth, effortless manner: *a submarine gliding through the water.* See Syns at **slide. 2.** To move silently and furtively. **3.** To occur or pass imperceptibly. **4.** To fly without propulsion. Used of an aircraft. **5.** *Music* To blend one tone into the next; slur. **6.** *Linguistics* To articulate a glide in speech. —*tr.* To cause to move or pass smoothly, silently, or imperceptibly. ❖ *n.* **1.** The act of gliding. **2.** *Music* A slur. **3.** *Linguistics* **a.** The transitional sound made in passing between the articulatory positions of two speech sounds. **b.** See **semivowel.** [ME *gliden* < OE *glīdan.* See **ghel-** in App.]

glide path *n.* The path of descent of an aircraft, delineated by a radio beam that directs the pilot in landing the craft.

glid·er (glī′dər) *n.* **1.** A light aircraft that glides after being towed aloft or launched from a catapult. **2.** A swinging couch suspended from a vertical frame. **3.** A device that aids gliding.

glim (glĭm) *n.* **1.** A source of light, as a candle. **2.** The illumination given off by such a source. [Perh. short for GLIMMER.]

glim·mer (glĭm′ər) *n.* **1.** A dim or intermittent flicker or flash of light. **2.** A faint manifestation or indication; a trace. ❖ *intr.v.* -**mered, -mer·ing, -mers 1.** To emit a dim or intermittent light. **2.** To appear faintly or indistinctly. [ME *glimeren,* to glitter, glimmer. See **ghel-** in App.]

glimpse (glĭmps) *n.* **1.** A brief incomplete view or look. **2.** *Archaic* A brief flash of light. ❖ *v.* **glimpsed, glimps·ing, glimps·es** —*tr.* To obtain a brief incomplete view of. —*intr.* To look briefly; glance. [ME *glimsen,* to glisten, glance. See **ghel-** in App.] —**glimps′er** *n.*

Glin·ka (glĭng′kə, glyĕn′kə), **Mikhail Ivanovich** 1804–57. Russian composer known for operas such as *A Life for the Czar* (1836).

glint (glĭnt) *n.* **1.** A momentary flash of light; a sparkle. **2.** A faint or fleeting indication; a trace. ❖ *v.* **glint·ed, glint·ing, glints** —*intr.* To gleam or flash briefly. —*tr.* To cause to gleam or flash. [ME *glent,* of Scand. orig. See **ghel-** in App.]

glint·y (glĭn′tē) *adj.* -**i·er,** -**i·est 1.** Sparkling; glittery. **2.** Cheap and flashy.

gli·o·blas·to·ma (glē′ō-blă-stō′mə, glī′-) *n., pl.* -**mas** or -**ma·ta** (-mə-tə) A malignant tumor arising in glial cells of the brain. [GLI(A) + BLASTOMA.]

gli·o·ma (glē-ō′mə, glī-) *n., pl.* -**mas** or -**ma·ta** (-mə-tə) A tumor originating in the neuroglia of the brain or spinal cord. [GLI(A) + -OMA.]

glis·sade (glĭ-säd′, -sād′) *n.* **1.** A gliding step in ballet. **2.** A controlled slide used in descending a steep icy or snowy incline. ❖ *intr.v.* -**sad·ed, -sad·ing, -sades** To perform a glissade. [Fr. < *glisser,* to slide < OFr., poss. alteration of *glier,* to glide, of Gmc. orig. See **ghel-** in App.] —**glis·sad′er** *n.*

glis·san·do (glĭ-sän′dō) *n., pl.* -**di** (-dē) or -**dos** *Music* A rapid slide through a series of consecutive tones in a scalelike passage.

[Fr. *glissade*; see GLISSADE + *-ando*, as in ACCELERANDO.]

glis·ten (glĭs′ən) *intr.v.* **-tened, -ten·ing, -tens** To shine by reflection with a sparkling luster. ❖ *n.* A sparkling lustrous shine. [ME *glisnen* < OE *glisnian.* See **ghel-** in App.]

glis·ter (glĭs′tər) *intr.v.* **-tered, -ter·ing, -ters** To glisten. ❖ *n.* Glitter; brilliance. [ME *glisteren*, prob. < MDu. *glinsteren* or MLGer., alteration of *glinsteren.* See **ghel-** in App.]

glitch (glĭch) *n.* **1.** A minor malfunction, mishap, or technical problem; a snag: *a computer glitch.* **2.** A false or spurious electronic signal caused by a brief unwanted surge of electric power. **3.** *Astronomy* A sudden change in the period of rotation of a neutron star. [Prob. < Yiddish *glitsh*, a slip, lapse < *glitshn*, to slip < MHGer. *glitschen*, alteration of *glīten*, to glide < OHGer. *glītan.* See **ghel-** in App.] —**glitch′y** *adj.*

glit·ter (glĭt′ər) *n.* **1.** A sparkling or glistening light. **2.** Brilliant or showy, often superficial attractiveness. **3.** Small pieces of light-reflecting decorative material. ❖ *intr.v.* **-tered, -ter·ing, -ters 1a.** To sparkle brilliantly; glisten. **b.** To sparkle coldly or malevolently: *eyes that glittered.* **2.** To be brilliantly, often deceptively attractive. [ME *gliteren*, to sparkle < ON *glitra.* See **ghel-** in App.] —**glit′ter·ing·ly** *adv.* —**glit′ter·y** *adj.*

glit·te·ra·ti (glĭt′ə-rä′tē) *pl.n. Informal* Highly fashionable celebrities; the smart set. [Blend of GLITTER and LITERATI.]

glitz (glĭts) *Informal n.* Ostentatious showiness; flashiness. ❖ *tr.v.* **glitz·ed, glitz·ing, glitz·es** To invest with an ostentatiously showy quality. [Back-formation < *glitzy*, flashy, showy, prob. < Ger. *glitzern*, to glitter < MHGer. *glitzen*, to shine < OHGer. *glīzan.* See **ghel-** in App.] —**glitz′i·ness** *n.* —**glitz′y** *adj.*

Gli·wi·ce (glĭ-vēt′sə, glē-vē′tsĕ) A city of S-central Poland WNW of Katowice; chartered 1276. Pop. 214,762.

gloam (glōm) *n. Archaic* Twilight; gloaming.

gloam·ing (glō′mĭng) *n.* Twilight; dusk. [ME *gloming* < OE *glōmung* < *glōm*, dusk. See **ghel-** in App.]

gloat (glōt) *intr.v.* **gloat·ed, gloat·ing, gloats** To feel or express great, often malicious pleasure or self-satisfaction. ❖ *n.* **1.** The act of gloating. **2.** A feeling of gloating. [Perh. of Scand. orig. See **ghel-** in App.] —**gloat′er** *n.*

glob (glŏb) *n.* **1.** A small drop; a globule. **2.** A soft thick lump or mass: *globs of red mud.* [ME *globbe*, large mass < Lat. *globus*, globular mass.]

glob·al (glō′bəl) *adj.* **1.** Having the shape of a globe; spherical. **2.** Of, relating to, or involving the entire earth; worldwide. **3.** Comprehensive; total. **4.** *Computer Science* Of or relating to an entire program, document, or file. —**glob′al·ly** *adv.*

glob·al·ism (glō′bə-lĭz′əm) *n.* A policy in which the world is seen as the appropriate sphere for a state's influence. —**glob′al·ist** *n.*

glob·al·ize (glō′bə-līz′) *tr.v.* **-ized, -iz·ing, -iz·es** To make global or worldwide in scope or application. —**glob′al·i·za′tion** (-lĭ-zā′shən) *n.* —**glob′al·iz′er** *n.*

Global Positioning System *n.* A system that determines latitude and longitude by calculating the time difference for signals from different satellites to reach a receiver on Earth.

global village *n.* The entire world and its inhabitants.

global warming *n.* An increase in the average temperature of the earth's atmosphere, esp. a sustained increase sufficient to cause climatic change.

globe (glōb) *n.* **1.** A body with the shape of a sphere, esp. a representation of the earth in the form of a hollow ball. **2a.** The earth. **b.** A planet. **3.** A spherical or bowllike container, esp. a glass cover for a light bulb. **4.** A sphere emblematic of sovereignty; an orb. ❖ *intr. & tr.v.* **globed, glob·ing, globes** To assume the shape of or form into a sphere. [ME < OFr. < Lat. *globus.*]

globe·fish (glōb′fĭsh′) *n., pl.* **globefish** or **-fish·es** Any of various fishes, esp. the ocean sunfish or puffer, having or capable of assuming a globular shape.

globe·flow·er (glōb′flou′ər) *n.* Any of several plants of the genus *Trollius*, having globose, usu. yellow flowers.

globe·trot (glōb′trŏt′) *intr.v.* **-trot·ted, -trot·ting, -trots** To travel far and often, esp. for pleasure. —**globe′trot′ter** *n.*

glo·bin (glō′bĭn) *n.* The protein constituent of hemoglobin and myoglobin.

glo·boid (glō′boid′) *adj.* Having a globelike shape; spheroid. ❖ *n.* a globe-shaped object.

glo·bose (glō′bōs′) *also* **glo·bous** (-bəs) *adj.* Spherical; globular. —**glo·bose′ly** *adv.* —**glo′bose′ness, glo·bos′i·ty** (-bŏs′ĭ-tē) *n.*

glob·u·lar (glŏb′yə-lər) *adj.* **1.** Having the shape of a globe or globule; spherical. **2.** Consisting of globules. **3.** Worldwide; global. —**glob′u·lar·ly** *adv.* —**glob′u·lar·ness** *n.*

glob·ule (glŏb′yōol) *n.* A small spherical mass, esp. a small drop of liquid. [Fr. < Lat. *globulus*, dim. of *globus*, sphere.]

glob·u·lif·er·ous (glŏb′yə-lĭf′ər-əs) *adj.* Composed of or producing globules.

glob·u·lin (glŏb′yə-lĭn) *n.* Any of a class of proteins found extensively in plant and animal tissue that are soluble in dilute salt solution and insoluble in pure water. [GLOBUL(E) + -IN.]

glo·chid·i·um (glō-kĭd′ē-əm) *n., pl.* **-i·a** (-ē-ə) **1.** The parasitic larva of certain freshwater mussels of the family Unionidae, having hooks for attaching to the external parts of a host fish. **2.** also **glo·chid** (glō′kĭd) A minute barbed hair or bristle on certain

plants, such as the prickly pear. [NLat. *glōchidium* : Gk. *glōkhīs*, barb of an arrow + Lat. *-idium*, diminutive suff. (< Gk. *-idion*).] —**glo·chid′i·ate** (-ĭt, -āt′) *adj.*

glock·en·spiel (glŏk′ən-spēl′, -shpēl′) *n.* A percussion instrument with a series of metal bars tuned to the chromatic scale and played with two light hammers. [Ger. : *Glocken*, pl. of *Glocke*, bell (< MHGer. < OHGer. *glocka*, of imit. orig.) + *Spiel*, play; see SPIEL.]

glogg (glŏg) *also* **glögg** (glœg) *n.* A hot punch made of red wine, brandy, and sherry with almonds, raisins, and orange peel. [Swed. *glögg*, alteration of *glödgat* (*vin*), mulled (wine) < p. part. of *glödga*, to mull < *glöd*, ember < ON *glodh.* See **ghel-** in App.]

glom (glŏm) *Slang v.* **glommed, glom·ming, gloms** —*tr.* **1.** To steal. **2.** To seize; grab. **3.** To look or stare at. —*intr.* To seize upon or latch on to something. ❖ *n.* A glimpse; a look. [Prob. < Sc. *glam*, to snatch at.]

glom·er·ate (glŏm′ər-ĭt) *adj.* Formed into a compact rounded mass; tightly clustered. [Lat. *glomerātus*, p. part. of *glomerāre*, to wind into a ball < *glomus*, *glomer-*, ball.]

glom·er·ule (glŏm′ə-rōol) *n.* **1.** *Botany* A compact cymose cluster of flowers. **2.** *Anatomy* A glomerulus. [NLat. *glomerulus.* See GLOMERULUS.] —**glo·mer′u·late** (glō-mĕr′yə-lĭt) *adj.*

glo·mer·u·lo·ne·phri·tis (glō-mĕr′yə-lō-nə-frī′tĭs) *n.* A form of nephritis characterized by inflammation of the renal glomeruli. [GLOMERUL(US) + NEPHRITIS.]

glo·mer·u·lus (glō-mĕr′yə-ləs) *n., pl.* **-li** (-lī′) *Anatomy* **1.** A small cluster or mass of blood vessels or nerve fibers. **2.** A tuft of capillaries situated within a Bowman's capsule in the vertebrate kidney that filters waste products from the blood. [NLat., dim. of Lat. *glomus*, *glomer-*, ball.]

Glom·ma (glô′mə, -mä) See **Glåma.**

gloom (glōom) *n.* **1a.** Partial or total darkness; dimness. **b.** A partially or totally dark place, area, or location. **2a.** An atmosphere of melancholy or depression. **b.** A state of melancholy or depression. ❖ *v.* **gloomed, gloom·ing, glooms** —*intr.* **1.** To be or become dark, shaded, or obscure. **2.** To feel, appear, or act despondent, sad, or mournful. —*tr.* **1.** To make dark, shaded, or obscure. **2.** *Archaic* To make despondent; sadden. [Prob. < ME *gloumen*, to become dark.]

gloom·y (glōo′mē) *adj.* **-i·er, -i·est 1.** Partially or totally dark, esp. dismal and dreary: *a damp, gloomy day.* **2.** Showing or filled with gloom. **3a.** Causing or producing gloom; depressing. **b.** Marked by hopelessness; very pessimistic. —**gloom′i·ly** *adv.* —**gloom′i·ness** *n.*

glop (glŏp) *n. Slang* **1.** A soft soggy mixture, as of food. **2.** Something, such as a piece of writing, that is judged worthless. [Imit. of the sound of mushy food being dished out.] —**glop** *v.* —**glop′py** *adj.*

Glo·ri·a (glôr′ē-ə, glōr′-) *n.* **1a.** A Latin doxology beginning with the words *Gloria Patri.* **b.** A Latin doxology beginning with the words *Gloria in excelsis Deo.* **c.** A musical setting for either of these doxologies. **2. gloria** A halo or nimbus. [ME < LLat. *Glōria* < Lat. *glōria*, glory.]

glo·ri·fy (glôr′ə-fī′, glōr′-) *tr.v.* **-fied, -fy·ing, -fies 1.** To give glory, honor, or high praise to; exalt. **2.** To cause to be or seem more glorious or excellent than is actually the case. **3.** To give glory to, esp. through worship. [ME *glorifien* < OFr. *glorefier* < Lat. *glōrificāre* : *glōria*, glory + *-ficāre*, -fy.] —**glo′ri·fi·ca′tion** (-fĭ-kā′shən) *n.* —**glo′ri·fi′er** *n.*

glo·ri·ole (glôr′ē-ōl′, glōr′-) *n.* See **glory** 8. [Fr. < Lat. *glōriola*, dim. of *glōria*, glory.]

glo·ri·ous (glôr′ē-əs, glōr′-) *adj.* **1.** Having or deserving glory; famous. **2.** Conferring or advancing glory: *a glorious achievement.* **3.** Characterized by great beauty and splendor; magnificent: *a glorious sunset.* **4.** Delightful; wonderful. —**glo′ri·ous·ly** *adv.* —**glo′ri·ous·ness** *n.*

glo·ry (glôr′ē, glōr′ē) *n., pl.* **-ries 1.** Great honor, praise, or distinction accorded by common consent; renown. **2.** Something conferring honor or renown. **3.** A highly praiseworthy asset. **4.** Adoration, praise, and thanksgiving offered in worship. **5.** Majestic beauty and splendor; resplendence. **6.** The splendor and bliss of heaven; perfect happiness. **7.** A height of achievement, enjoyment, or prosperity. **8.** A halo, nimbus, or aureole. ❖ *v.* **-ried, -ry·ing, -ries** To rejoice triumphantly; exult. [ME *glorie* < OFr. < Lat. *glōria.*]

gloss¹ (glôs, glŏs) *n.* **1.** A surface shininess or luster. **2.** A cosmetic that adds shine or luster. **3.** A superficially or deceptively attractive appearance. ❖ *v.* **glossed, gloss·ing, gloss·es** —*tr.* **1.** To give a bright sheen or luster to. **2.** To make attractive or acceptable by deception or superficial treatment: *glossed over my errors.* —*intr.* To become shiny or lustrous. [Perh. of Scand. orig.; akin to Icel. *glossi*, a spark. See **ghel-** in App.]

gloss² (glôs, glŏs) *n.* **1a.** A brief explanatory note or translation usu. inserted in the margin or between lines of a text or manuscript. **b.** A collection of such notes; a glossary. **2.** An extensive commentary, often accompanying a text or publication. **3.** A purposefully misleading interpretation or explanation. ❖ *tr.v.* **glossed, gloss·ing, gloss·es 1.** To provide (an expression or a text) with a gloss or glosses. **2.** To give a false interpretation to. [ME *glose* < OFr. < Med.Lat. *glōsa* < LLat. *glōssa*, foreign word requiring explanation < Gk., tongue, language.] —**gloss′er** *n.*

glos·sa (glô′sə, glŏs′ə) *n., pl.* **glos·sae** (glô′sē, glŏs′ē) or **glos·sas 1.** *Anatomy* The tongue. **2.** *Zoology* A tonguelike structure in the labium of an insect. [Gk. *glôssa,* tongue.]

glos·sal (glô′səl, glŏs′əl) *adj.* Of or relating to the tongue.

glos·sa·ry (glô′sə-rē, glŏs′ə-) *n., pl.* **-ries** A list of often difficult or specialized words with their definitions, often placed at the back of a book. [ME *glosarie* < LLat. *glōssārium* < *glōssa,* foreign word. See GLOSS².] —**glos·sar′i·al** (glô-sâr′ē-əl, glŏ-) *adj.* —**glos′sa·rist** *n.*

glos·si·tis (glô-sī′tĭs, glŏ-) *n.* Inflammation of the tongue. —**glos·sit′ic** (-sĭt′ĭk) *adj.*

glos·sog·ra·phy (glô-sŏg′rə-fē, glŏ-) *n.* The compilation of glosses or glossaries. —**glos·sog′ra·pher** *n.*

glos·so·la·li·a (glô′sə-lā′lē-ə, glŏs′ə-) *n.* **1.** Fabricated and meaningless speech, esp. when associated with a trance state or certain schizophrenic syndromes. **2.** See **gift of tongues.** [NLat. : Gk. *glôssa,* tongue + Gk. *lalein,* to babble.]

gloss·y (glô′sē, glŏs′ē) *adj.* **-i·er, -i·est 1.** Having a smooth shiny lustrous surface: *glossy satin.* **2.** Superficially and often speciously attractive; showy. ❖ *n., pl.* **-ies 1.** A photographic print on smooth shiny paper. **2.** *Chiefly British* A popular magazine printed on smooth-coated stock. —**gloss′i·ly** *adv.* —**gloss′i·ness** *n.*

glot·tal (glŏt′l) *adj.* Relating to or articulated in the glottis.

glottal stop *n.* A speech sound produced by closure of the glottis, followed by an explosive release.

glot·tis (glŏt′ĭs) *n., pl.* **-tis·es** or **glot·ti·des** (glŏt′ĭ-dēz′) **1.** The opening between the vocal cords at the upper part of the larynx. **2.** The vocal apparatus of the larynx. [Gk. *glôttis* < *glôtta, glôssa,* tongue.]

glove (glŭv) *n.* **1a.** A fitted covering for the hand with a separate sheath for each finger and the thumb. **b.** A gauntlet. **2.** *Sports* Any of various coverings for the hand designed to provide protection or improve the grip, as: **a.** An oversized leather glove used for catching baseballs. **b.** A glove made of leather and fabric having padding on the back and extending over the wrist, used in hockey and lacrosse. **c.** A boxing glove. **d.** A close-fitting leather glove used to improve the grip, as in golf. ❖ *v.* **gloved, glov·ing, gloves** —*tr.* **1.** To furnish with gloves. **2.** To cover with or as if with a glove. —*intr.* To don gloves, as before surgery. [ME < OE *glōf.*]

glove box *n.* **1.** See **glove compartment. 2.** An enclosed workspace equipped with gloved openings that allow manipulation in the interior, designed to prevent contamination.

glove compartment *n.* A small dashboard storage container.

glow (glō) *intr.v.* **glowed, glow·ing, glows 1.** To shine brightly and steadily, esp. without a flame. **2a.** To have a bright, warm, usu. reddish color. **b.** To flush; blush. **3.** To be exuberant or radiant: *glowing with pride.* ❖ *n.* **1.** A light produced by a body heated to luminosity; incandescence. **2.** Brilliance or warmth of color, esp. redness. **3.** A sensation of physical warmth. **4.** A warm feeling, as of pleasure or well-being. [ME *glouen* < OE *glōwan.* See **ghel-** in App.]

glow·er (glou′ər) *intr.v.* **-ered, -er·ing, -ers** To look or stare angrily or sullenly. ❖ *n.* An angry or sullen look or stare. [ME *gloren,* prob. of Scand. orig. See **ghel-** in App.] —**glow′er·ing·ly** *adv.*

glow plug *n.* An electric heating element in a diesel engine that facilitates starting by preheating the air in a cylinder.

glow·worm (glō′wûrm′) *n.* Any of various luminous female beetles or beetle larvae of the families Phengodidae and Lampyridae, esp. the larva or wingless female of a firefly.

glox·in·i·a (glŏk-sĭn′ē-ə) *n.* Any of several tropical South American plants of the genus *Sinningia,* esp. *S. speciosa,* having showy, variously colored flowers. [NLat. *Gloxinia,* genus name of a related plant, after Benjamin Peter *Gloxin,* 18th-cent. German botanist.]

gloze (glōz) *v.* **glozed, gloz·ing, gloz·es** —*tr.* To minimize or underplay; gloss: *glozed over the embarrassing part.* —*intr. Archaic* To use flattery or cajolery. [ME *glosen,* to interpret, explain away < OFr. *gloser* < *glose,* gloss. See GLOSS².]

glu·ca·gon (glōō′kə-gŏn′) *n.* A pancreatic hormone that stimulates an increase in blood sugar levels. [Prob. GLUC(O)- + Gk. *agōn,* pr. part. of *agein,* to lead, drive; see **ag-** in App.]

Gluck (glŏŏk), **Christoph Willibald** 1714–87. German operatic composer whose works include *Orfeo ed Euridice* (1762).

gluco– or **gluc–** *pref.* Glucose: *glucagon.* [< GLUCOSE.]

glu·co·cor·ti·coid (glōō′kō-kôr′tĭ-koid′) *n.* Any of a group of corticoids, such as cortisone, that are involved in carbohydrate, protein, and fat metabolism and have anti-inflammatory properties.

glu·co·ne·o·gen·e·sis (glōō′kō-nē′ə-jĕn′ĭ-sĭs) *n.* The formation of glucose, esp. by the liver, from noncarbohydrates, such as proteins and fats.

glu·co·sa·mine (glōō-kō′sə-mēn′, glōō′kō-) *n.* An amino derivative of glucose, $C_6H_{13}NO_5$, that is a component of many polysaccharides and is the basic structural unit of chitin.

glu·cose (glōō′kōs′) *n.* **1.** A monosaccharide sugar, $C_6H_{12}O_6$, common in most plant and animal tissue, that is the major energy source of the body. **2.** A colorless to yellowish syrupy mixture of dextrose, maltose, dextrins, and water, used in confectionary, al-

coholic fermentation, tanning, and treating tobacco. [Fr. < Gk. *glukos,* sweet.]

glu·co·side (glōō′kə-sīd′) *n.* A glycoside containing glucose. —**glu′co·sid′ic** (-sĭd′ĭk) *adj.* —**glu′co·sid′i·cal·ly** *adv.*

glue (glōō) *n.* **1a.** A strong liquid adhesive obtained by boiling collagenous animal parts such as bones, hides, and hooves into hard gelatin and then adding water. **b.** Any of various similar adhesives, such as paste. **2.** An adhesive force or factor. ❖ *tr.v.* **glued, glu·ing, glues 1.** To stick or fasten with or as if with glue. **2.** To fasten on something attentively: *Our eyes were glued to the stage.* [ME *glu* < OFr. < LLat. *glūs, glūt-* < Lat. *glūten.*] —**glu′ey** *adj.* —**glu′i·ness** *n.*

glum (glŭm) *adj.* **glum·mer, glum·mest 1.** Moody and melancholy; dejected. **2.** Gloomy; dismal. ❖ *n.* **1.** The quality or state of being glum or an instance of it. **2. glums** *Chiefly British* The blues. [Prob. akin to ME *gloumen,* to become dark. See GLOOM.] —**glum′ly** *adv.* —**glum′ness** *n.*

glume (glōōm) *n.* One of the two chaffy basal bracts of a grass spikelet. [Lat. *glūma,* husk.] —**glu·ma·ceous** (glōō-mā′shəs) *adj.*

glu·on (glōō′ŏn) *n.* A hypothetical massless, neutral elementary particle believed to mediate the strong interaction that binds quarks together. [GLU(E) + -ON¹.]

glut (glŭt) *v.* **glut·ted, glut·ting, gluts** —*tr.* **1.** To fill beyond capacity, esp. with food; satiate. **2.** To supply (a market) with goods in excess of demand. —*intr.* To eat or indulge to excess. ❖ *n.* An oversupply. [ME *glotten,* prob. < OFr. *glotoiier,* to eat greedily < Lat. *gluttīre.*]

glu·ta·mate (glōō′tə-māt′) *n.* A salt or ester of glutamic acid, esp. one that functions as a neurotransmitter. [GLUTAM(IC ACID) + -ATE².]

glu·tam·ic acid (glōō-tăm′ĭk) *n.* A nonessential amino acid, $C_5H_9NO_4$, common in plant and animal tissue and having monosodium glutamate as a salt. [GLUT(EN) + AM(IDE) + -IC.]

glu·ta·mine (glōō′tə-mēn′) *n.* A nonessential amino acid, $C_5H_{10}N_2O_3$, common in plant and animal tissue and produced commercially for use in research. [GLUT(EN) + AMINE.]

glu·ta·thi·one (glōō′tə-thī′ōn′) *n.* A polypeptide, $C_{10}H_{17}N_3O_6S$, of glycine, cystine, and glutamic acid that occurs widely in plant and animal tissues and is important in biological oxidation-reduction reactions. [GLUTA(MINE) + THI(O)- + -ONE.]

glute (glōōt) *n. Slang* A gluteus muscle. Often used in the plural.

glu·ten (glōōt′n) *n.* A mixture of plant proteins occurring in cereal grains, used as an adhesive and as a flour substitute. [Fr. < Lat. *glūten,* glue.] —**glu′ten·ous** *adj.*

glu·teth·i·mide (glōō-tĕth′ə-mīd′) *n.* A nonbarbiturate hypnotic drug, $C_{13}H_{15}NO_2$. [GLUTE(N) + THI(O)- + (A)MIDE.]

glu·te·us (glōō′tē-əs, glōō-tē′-) *n., pl.* **glu·te·i** (glōō′tē-ī′, glōō-tē′ī′) Any of the three large muscles of each buttock, esp. the gluteus maximus, that extend, abduct, and rotate the thigh. [NLat. *glūteus* < Gk. *gloutos,* buttock.] —**glu′te·al** *adj.*

gluteus max·i·mus (măk′sə-məs) *n., pl.* **glutei max·i·mi** (măk′sə-mī′) The largest and outermost gluteus. [NLat. *glūteus maximus : glūteus,* gluteus + Lat. *maximus,* greatest.]

glu·ti·nous (glōōt′n-əs) *adj.* Of the nature of or resembling glue; sticky. [ME < Lat. *glūtinōsus* < *glūten, glūtin-,* glue.] —**glu′ti·nous·ly** *adv.* —**glu′ti·nos′i·ty** (-ŏs′ĭ-tē) *n.*

glut·ton (glŭt′n) *n.* **1.** A person who eats or consumes immoderately. **2.** A person with an inordinate capacity to receive or withstand something. **3.** See **wolverine.** [ME *glotoun* < OFr. *gloton* < Lat. *gluttō, gluttōn-.*]

glut·ton·ous (glŭt′n-əs) *adj.* **1.** Given to or marked by gluttony. **2.** Indulging in something, such as an activity, to excess; voracious. —**glut′ton·ous·ly** *adv.*

glut·ton·y (glŭt′n-ē) *n., pl.* **-ies** Excess in eating or drinking.

gly·ce·mic index (glī-sē′mĭk) *n.* A numerical index given to a carbohydrate-rich food that is based on the average increase in blood glucose levels occurring after the food is eaten. [< *glycemia,* presence of glucose in the blood : GLYC(O)- + -EM(IA) + -IC.]

glyc·er·al·de·hyde (glĭs′ə-răl′də-hīd′) *n.* A sweet colorless crystalline solid, $C_3H_6O_3$, that is an intermediate compound in carbohydrate metabolism. [GLYCER(IN) + ALDEHYDE.]

gly·cer·ic acid (glī-sĕr′ĭk) *n.* A colorless syrupy acid, $C_3H_6O_4$, obtained from oxidation of glycerol. [GLYCER(IN) + -IC.]

glyc·er·ide (glĭs′ə-rīd′) *n.* An ester of glycerol and fatty acids, found in plant oils and animal fats. [GLYCER(IN) + -IDE.]

glyc·er·in also **glyc·er·ine** (glĭs′ər-ĭn) *n.* Glycerol. [Fr. *glycérine* < Gk. *glukeros,* sweet.]

glyc·er·ol (glĭs′ə-rôl′, -rōl′) *n.* A syrupy sweet colorless or yellowish liquid, $C_3H_8O_3$, obtained from the saponification of fats and oils and used as a solvent and sweetener and in dynamite and cosmetics. [GLYCER(IN) + -OL¹.]

glyc·er·yl (glĭs′ər-əl) *n.* A trivalent radical, CH_2CHCH_2, of glycerol. [GLYCER(IN) + -YL.]

gly·cine (glī′sēn′, -sĭn) *n.* A sweet-tasting crystalline nonessential amino acid, $C_2H_5NO_2$, that is the principal amino acid occurring in sugar cane. [GLYC(O)- + -INE².]

glyco– or **glyc–** *pref.* **1.** Sugar: *glycoprotein.* **2.** Glycogen: *glycogenesis.* [< Gk. *glukus,* sweet.]

gly·co·gen (glī′kə-jən) *n.* A polysaccharide, $(C_6H_{10}O_5)_n$, that is the main form of carbohydrate storage in animals and occurs pri-

gloxinia
Sinningia speciosa

marily in the liver and muscle tissue. **—gly′co·gen′ic** (-jĕn′ĭk) *adj.*

gly·co·gen·e·sis (glī′kə-jĕn′ĭ-sĭs) *n.* The formation or synthesis of glycogen. [GLYCO– + –GENESIS.] **—gly′co·ge·net′ic** (-jə-nĕt′ĭk) *adj.*

gly·col (glī′kôl′, -kōl′, -kŏl′) *n.* **1.** Ethylene glycol. **2.** Any of various alcohols containing two hydroxyl groups.

gly·col·ic acid (glī-kŏl′ĭk) *n.* A colorless crystalline compound, $C_2H_4O_3$, found in sugar beets and unripe grapes and used in leather processing.

gly·co·lip·id (glī′kə-lĭp′ĭd) *n.* A lipid that contains one or more carbohydrate groups.

gly·col·y·sis (glī-kŏl′ə-sĭs) *n.* The ATP-generating metabolic process that occurs in nearly all living cells by which carbohydrates and sugars, typically glucose, are converted in a series of steps to pyruvic acid. **—gly′co·lyt′ic** *adj.*

gly·co·pro·tein (glī′kō-prō′tēn′, -tē-ĭn) *n.* Any of a group of conjugated proteins that contain a carbohydrate as the nonprotein component.

gly·cos·a·mi·no·gly·can (glī′kōs-ə-mē′nō-glī′kăn) *n.* Any of a group of polysaccharides that contain amino sugars and often form complexes with proteins. [GLYC(O)– + (HEX)OS(E) + AMIN(E) + *glycan*, polysaccharide (GLYC(O)– + –AN²).]

gly·co·side (glī′kə-sīd′) *n.* Any of a group of organic compounds, common in plants, that yield a sugar on hydrolysis. [*glycose*, a monosaccharide (var. of GLUCOSE) + –IDE.] **—gly′co·sid′ic** (-sĭd′ĭk) *adj.*

gly·co·su·ri·a (glī′kə-so͝or′ē-ə, -sho͝or′-) *n.* Excess sugar in the urine, often associated with diabetes mellitus. [*glycose*, a monosaccharide (var. of GLUCOSE) + –URIA.] **—gly′co·su′ric** *adj.*

glyph (glĭf) *n.* **1.** *Architecture* A vertical groove, esp. in a Doric column or frieze. **2.** A symbolic figure that is usu. engraved or incised. **3.** A symbol, such as a stylized figure or arrow on a public sign, that imparts information nonverbally. [Gk. *gluphē*, carving < *gluphein*, to carve.] **—glyph′ic** *adj.*

gly·phos·ate (glī-fŏs′āt) *n.* A white compound, $C_3H_8NO_5P$, soluble in water, and used as a broad-spectrum herbicide. [GLY(CINE) + PHOS(PH)ATE.]

glyp·tic (glĭp′tĭk) *adj.* Of or relating to engraving or carving, esp. on precious stones. [Gk. *gluptikos* < *gluptos*, carved < *gluphein*, to carve.]

glyp·tics (glĭp′tĭks) *n.* (*used with a sing. verb*) The art of engraving or carving, esp. on precious stones; glyptography.

glyp·to·graph (glĭp′tə-grăf′) *n.* An engraved inscription on a precious stone. [Gk. *gluptos*, carved; see GLYPTIC + –GRAPH.] **—glyp·tog′ra·pher** (-tŏg′rə-fər) *n.* **—glyp′to·graph′ic** (-tə-grăf′ĭk), **glyp′to·graph′i·cal** *adj.* **—glyp·tog′ra·phy** *n.*

GM *abbr.* **1.** general manager **2.** grand master (chess)

gm. *abbr.* gram

G-man (jē′măn′) *n.* An agent of the Federal Bureau of Investigation. [G(OVERNMENT) + MAN.]

GMAT *abbr.* **1.** Graduate Management Admissions Test **2.** Greenwich Mean Astronomical Time

GMO *abbr.* genetically modified organism

GMP (jē′ĕm-pē′) *n.* A nucleotide composed of guanine, ribose, and one phosphate group, formed by the breakdown of GTP during protein synthesis. [G(UANOSINE) M(ONO)P(HOSPHATE).]

GMT *abbr.* Greenwich Mean Time

GMW *abbr.* gram molecular weight

Gn *abbr. Bible* Genesis

gnar also **gnarr** (när) *intr.v.* **gnarred, gnar·ring, gnars** To snarl; growl. [Imit.]

gnarl¹ (närl) *intr.v.* **gnarled, gnarl·ing, gnarls** To snarl; growl. [Frequentative of GNAR.]

gnarl² (närl) *n.* A protruding knot on a tree. ❖ *tr.v.* **gnarled, gnarl·ing, gnarls** To make knotted; twist. **—gnarl′y** *adj.*

gnarled (närld) *adj.* **1.** Having gnarls; knotty or misshapen. **2.** Morose or peevish; crabbed. **3.** Rugged and roughened, as from old age. [Prob. var. of *knarled* < *knarl*, knot, alteration of ME *knarre*, knot in wood. See KNAR.]

gnash (năsh) *tr.v.* **gnashed, gnash·ing, gnash·es 1.** To grind or strike (the teeth, for example) together. **2.** To bite (something) by grinding the teeth. [Alteration of ME *gnasten*, *gnaisten*, poss. of Scand. orig.] **—gnash** *n.*

gnat (năt) *n.* Any of various small biting two-winged flies, such as a punkie or black fly. [ME < OE *gnæt*.]

gnat·catch·er (năt′kăch′ər, -kĕch′-) *n.* Any of several tiny North American birds of the genus *Polioptila*, having bluish-gray and white plumage.

gnath·ic (năth′ĭk) *adj.* Of or relating to the jaw. [Gk. *gnathos*, jaw + –IC.]

gna·thite (nā′thīt′, năth′īt′) *n.* A jawlike appendage of an arthropod. [Gk. *gnathos*, jaw + –ITE¹.]

–gnathous *suff.* Having a specified kind of jaw: *metagnathous*. [NLat. *-gnathus* < Gk. *-gnathos* < *gnathos*, jaw.]

gnaw (nô) *v.* **gnawed, gnaw·ing, gnaws** *—tr.* **1a.** To bite, chew on, or erode with the teeth. **b.** To produce by gnawing: *gnaw a hole.* **c.** To erode or diminish gradually as if by gnawing. **2.** To afflict or worry persistently: *fear that constantly gnawed me.* *—intr.* **1.** To bite or chew persistently. **2.** To cause erosion or gradual diminishment. **3.** To cause persistent worry or pain. [ME *gnauen* < OE *gnagan*.] **—gnaw′er** *n.*

gneiss (nīs) *n.* A banded or foliated metamorphic rock, usu. of the same composition as granite. [Ger. *Gneis*, prob. alteration of MHGer. *ganeist*, spark (< its appearance) < OHGer. *gneista*.] **—gneiss′ic** (nī′sĭk), **gneiss′ose′** (nī′sōs′) *adj.*

GNMA *abbr.* Government National Mortgage Association

gnoc·chi (nyō′kē, nyŏk′ē) *pl.n.* Small dumplings made of flour, semolina, or potatoes and served with grated cheese or a sauce. [Ital., pl. of *gnocco*, prob. alteration of *nocchio*, knot in wood.]

gnome¹ (nōm) *n.* **1.** One of a fabled race of dwarflike creatures who live underground and guard treasure hoards. **2.** In the occult philosophy of Paracelsus, a being that has earth as its element. [Fr. < NLat. *gnomus*.] **—gnom′ish** *adj.*

gnome² (nōm) *n.* A pithy saying that expresses a general truth; a maxim. [Gk. *gnōmē* < *gignōskein*, to know. See **gnō-** in App.]

gno·mic (nō′mĭk) *adj.* Marked by aphorisms; aphoristic.

gno·mon (nō′mŏn′, -mən) *n.* **1.** An object, such as the style of a sundial, that projects a shadow used as an indicator. **2.** The geometric figure that remains after a parallelogram has been removed from a similar but larger parallelogram with which it shares a corner. [Lat. *gnōmōn* < Gk., interpreter, pointer of a sundial < *gignōskein*, to know. See **gnō-** in App.] **—gno·mon′ic, gno·mon′i·cal** *adj.*

gno·sis (nō′sĭs) *n.* Intuitive apprehension of spiritual truths, an esoteric form of knowledge sought by the Gnostics. [Gk. *gnōsis*, knowledge < *gignōskein*, to know. See **gnō-** in App.]

Gnos·tic (nŏs′tĭk) *adj.* **1. gnostic** Of, relating to, or possessing intellectual or spiritual knowledge. **2.** Of or relating to Gnosticism. ❖ *n.* A believer in Gnosticism. [LLat. *Gnōsticus*, a Gnostic < L.Gk. *Gnōstikos* < Gk. *gnōstikos*, concerning knowledge < *gnōsis*, knowledge. See GNOSIS.]

Gnos·ti·cism (nŏs′tĭ-sĭz′əm) *n.* The doctrines and practices of several pre-Christian pagan, Jewish, and early Christian sects in which it was held that a secret knowledge could secure release for the soul from imprisonment in the material body.

gno·to·bi·ot·ics (nō′tō-bī-ŏt′ĭks) *n.* (*used with a sing. verb*) The study of organisms or environmental conditions that have been rendered free of bacteria or contaminants or into which a known microorganism or contaminant has been introduced. [Gk. *gnōtos*, known; see **gnō-** in App. + *biotics*, study of living organisms.] **—gno′to·bi·ot′ic** *adj.*

GNP *abbr.* gross national product

GnRH *abbr.* gonadotropin-releasing hormone

gnu (no͞o, nyo͞o) *n.* Either of two large African antelopes (*Connochaetes gnou* or *C. taurinus*) having a mane and beard, a long tail, and curved horns. [Prob. < Du. *gnoe* < Xhosa *i-ngu*, white-tailed gnu < San *!nu*, black wildebeest.]

go¹ (gō) *v.* **went** (wĕnt), **gone** (gôn, gŏn), **go·ing, goes** (gōz) *—intr.* **1.** To move or travel; proceed: *will go by bus; went from door to door.* **2.** To move away from a place; depart: *Go before I cry.* **3a.** To pursue a certain course: *go through diplomatic channels.* **b.** To resort to another, as for aid. **4a.** To extend between two points or in a certain direction; run: *curtains that go from the ceiling to the floor.* **b.** To give entry; lead: *a stairway that goes to the attic.* **5.** To function properly: *The car won't go.* **6a.** To have currency. **b.** To pass from one person to another; circulate: *Wild rumors were going around the office.* **7.** To pass as the result of a sale: *The gold watch went to the highest bidder.* **8.** *Informal* Used as an intensifier when joined by *and* to a coordinate verb: *She went and complained.* **9.** Used in the progressive tense with an infinitive to indicate future intent or expectation: *I am going to read.* **10a.** To continue to be in a certain condition or continue an activity: *go barefoot.* **b.** To come to be in a certain condition: *go mad.* **c.** To continue to be in effect or operation: *a lease with one year to go.* **d.** To carry out an action to a certain point or extent: *went to great expense.* **11.** To be called; be known: *He goes by Billy.* **12a.** To be customarily located; belong: *The fork goes to the left of the plate.* **b.** To be capable of entering or fitting: *Will the suitcase go in the trunk?* **13a.** To pass into someone's possession: *Her estate went to her niece.* **b.** To be allotted: *How much of your salary goes for rent?* **14.** To be a contributing factor: *It goes to show us how much can be done.* **15a.** To have a particular form: *as the saying goes.* **b.** To be such, by and large: *well behaved, as dogs go.* **16a.** To extend in time: *The house goes back to the 1800s.* **b.** To pass by; elapse. **17a.** To be used up. **b.** To be discarded or abolished: *All luxuries will have to go.* **18a.** To become weak; fail: *His hearing has started to go.* **b.** To come apart; break up: *The dam is about to go.* **19.** To cease living; die. **20a.** To happen or develop; fare: *How are things going?* **b.** To have a successful outcome. **21.** To be suitable or appropriate as an accessory or accompaniment. **22a.** To have authority: *Whatever I say, goes.* **b.** To be valid, acceptable, or adequate. **23.** *Informal* To excrete waste from the bladder or bowels. **24.** *Informal* To begin an act: *Here goes!* **25.** *Obsolete* To walk. *—tr.* **1.** To proceed or move according to: *free to go my way.* **2.** To traverse: *Only two of the runners went the entire distance.* **3.** To engage in: *go swimming.* **4.** *Informal* **a.** To bet: *go $20 on the black horse.* **b.** To bid: *I'll go $500 on the vase.* **5.** *Informal* **a.** To take on the responsibility or obligation for: *go bail for a client.* **b.** To participate to (a given extent). **6.** To amount to; weigh. **7.** To have as a record: *went 3 for 4 against their pitcher.* **8.** *Informal* To enjoy. **9.** *Informal* To say or utter. Used chiefly in

glyph
tortoise crossing, Mojave Desert, California

gnu
brindled gnu
Connochaetes taurinus

ă	pat	oi	boy
ā	pay	ou	out
âr	care	o͝o	took
ä	father	o͞o	boot
ĕ	pet	ŭ	cut
ē	be	ûr	urge
ĭ	pit	th	thin
ī	pie	*th*	this
îr	pier	hw	which
ŏ	pot	zh	vision
ō	toe	ə	about, item
ô	paw		

Stress marks:
′ (primary);
′ (secondary), as in
lexicon (lĕk′sĭ-kŏn′)

verbal narration. ❖ *n., pl.* **goes 1.** The act or an instance of going. **2.** An attempt; an effort: *had a go at acting.* **3.** The time or period of an activity. **4.** *Informal* Energy; vitality. **5.** *Informal* **a.** The go-ahead. **b.** often **Go** The starting point. **c.** *Informal* A situation in which planned operations can be effectuated. ❖ *adj. Informal* Functioning correctly and ready for action: *All systems are go.* —**phrasal verbs: go about** To set about to do; undertake. **go along** To cooperate. **go around 1.** To satisfy a demand or requirement: *just enough food to go around.* **2.** To go here and there; move from place to place. **3.** To have currency: *rumors going around.* **go at 1.** To attack, esp. with energy. **2.** To approach; undertake. **go by 1.** To elapse; pass: *as time goes by.* **2.** To pay a short visit. **go down 1a.** To drop below the horizon; set: *The sun went down.* **b.** To fall to the ground. **c.** To sink. **d.** To experience defeat or ruin. **2.** To admit of easy swallowing. **3.** To decrease in price or value. **4.** *Chiefly British* To leave a university. **5.** *Slang* To occur; happen. **6a.** To be accepted or tolerated. **b.** To come to be remembered in posterity. **go for 1.** *Informal* To have a special liking for. **2.** To attack. **3.** To pass for or serve as: *a couch that also goes for a bed.* **go in 1.** To take part in a cooperative venture. **2.** To make an approach, as before an attack. **go into 1.** To discuss or investigate: *The book goes into all the details.* **2.** To undertake as a profession or course of study. **go off 1.** To undergo detonation; explode. **2.** To make a noise; sound: *The siren went off at noon.* **3.** To leave. **4.** *Informal* To adhere to the expected course of events or the expected plan. **go on** To take place; happen. **2a.** To continue. **b.** To keep on doing (something). **c.** To proceed: *She went on to become a senator.* **3.** *Informal* To talk volubly. **go out 1.** To become extinguished. **2a.** To go outdoors; leave one's residence. **b.** To take part in social life outside the home. **3.** To become unfashionable. **4.** To undergo structural collapse: *The bridge went out.* **go over 1.** To gain acceptance or approval. **2.** To examine. **go through 1.** To examine carefully. **2.** To experience: *went through agony.* **3.** To perform: *went through the sonata.* **go under 1.** To suffer defeat or destruction; fail. **2.** To lose consciousness. **go up 1.** To increase in price or value. **2.** *Chiefly British* To go to a university. **go with** To date regularly. —**idioms: go all the way** *Slang* To engage in sex. **go back on** To fail to honor or keep. **go begging** To be in little or no demand. **go belly up** *Informal* To undergo total financial failure. **go bust** *Informal* To undergo financial collapse. **go by the board** To be discarded or ignored. **go down on** *Vulgar Slang* To perform oral sex on. **go down the line** To provide strong support. **go fly a kite** *Informal* To cease being an annoyance. Often used in the imperative. **go for broke** *Informal* To commit or expend all of one's resources toward a goal. **go for it** *Informal* To expend all one's resources toward an end or purpose. **go in for 1.** To have interest in. **2.** To take part in. **go it alone** To undertake a project, trip, or responsibility by oneself. **go off the deep end** To behave hysterically or very recklessly. **go one better** To surpass or outdo by one degree. **go out for** To seek to become a participant in: *go out for varsity soccer.* **go out of (one's) way** To inconvenience oneself in doing something beyond what is required. **go out the window** *Informal* To become insignificant or inoperative. **go places** *Informal* To be on the way to success. **go steady** To date someone exclusively. **go the distance** To carry a course of action through to completion. **go to pieces 1.** To lose one's self-control. **2.** To suffer the loss of one's health. **go to the mat** *Informal* To fight or dispute until one side or another is victorious. **go to town** *Informal* **1.** To work or perform efficiently and rapidly. **2.** To be highly successful. **go up in flames** (or **smoke**) To be utterly destroyed. **go without saying** To be self-evident. **on the go** Constantly busy or active. **to go** To be taken out, as restaurant food or drink. [ME *gon* < OE *gān.* See **ghē-** in App.]

USAGE NOTE *Go* has long been used to describe the production of nonlinguistic noises, as in *The cow goes "moo."* In recent years, however, many speakers have begun to use *go* informally to report speech, as in *Then he goes, "You think you're real smart, don't you?"* This usage parallels the quotation introducers *be all* and *be like.* But unlike these other expressions, which can indicate thoughts or attitudes, the quotational use of *go* is largely restricted to dialogue related in the narrative present, especially when the narrator wishes to mimic the accent or intonation of the original speaker.

---

go² (gō) *n.* A Japanese game for two, played on a board ruled with 19 vertical and 19 horizontal lines. [J. < M Chin. *gi.*]
go·a (gō′ə) *n.* A Tibetan gazelle (*Procapra picticaudata*) having backward-curving horns in the male. [Tibetan *dgoba.*]
Go·a (gō′ə) A state of west-central India on the Malabar Coast; formerly a Portuguese colony (1510–1961).
goad (gōd) *n.* **1.** A long pointed stick used to prod animals. **2.** An agent or means of prodding or urging; a stimulus. ❖ *tr.v.* **goad·ed, goad·ing, goads** To prod or urge with or as if with a long pointed stick. [ME *gode* < OE *gād.*]
go-a·head (gō′ə-hĕd′) *Informal n.* **1.** Permission to proceed. **2.** Energetic assertiveness.
goal (gōl) *n.* **1.** The purpose toward which effort is directed; an objective. See Syns at **intention. 2.** *Sports* **a.** The finish line of a race. **b.** A structure or zone into or over which players try to advance a ball or puck. **c.** The score awarded for such an act. **3.** *Lin-*

guistics **a.** A noun or noun phrase referring to the place to which something moves. **b.** See **patient** 2. [ME *gol,* boundary, poss. < OE **gāl,* barrier.]
goal·ie (gō′lē) *n.* See **goalkeeper.**
goal·keep·er (gōl′kē′pər) *n.* A player assigned to protect the goal in various sports.
goal kick *n.* In soccer, a free kick awarded to the defensive team when the ball has been driven out of bounds over the goal line by an opponent.
goal line *n.* **1.** *Sports* A line crossing either end of a playing area, on which a goal is positioned. **2.** *Football* A line crossing either end of the playing field over which the ball must be moved to score a touchdown.
goal·post or **goal post** (gōl′pōst′) *n.* **1.** One of a pair of posts usu. joined with a crossbar and set at each end of a playing field to form a goal. **2.** A post or a pair of posts supporting a crossbar and either supporting or extending into the uprights of a goal, as in football.
goal·tend·er (gōl′tĕn′dər) *n.* See **goalkeeper.**
goal·tend·ing (gōl′tĕn′dĭng) *n.* **1.** *Sports* The act of protecting a goal, as in hockey. **2.** *Basketball* An illegal play in which a player deflects a ball on its downward path to the basket or already on the rim of the basket.
goat (gōt) *n.* **1.** Any of various hollow-horned bearded ruminants of the genus *Capra,* esp. any of the forms of *C. hircus,* raised for wool, milk, and meat. **2.** A lecherous man. **3.** A scapegoat. **4. Goat** See **Capricorn.** [ME *got* < OE *gāt.*] —**goat′ish** *adj.*
goat antelope *n.* Any of various wild ruminants of the family Bovidae, such as the chamois, resembling both goats and antelopes.
goat·ee (gō-tē′) *n.* A small chin beard trimmed into a point. [Alteration of *goaty* < GOAT (< its resemblance to a goat's beard).]
goat·fish (gōt′fĭsh′) *n., pl.* **goatfish** or **-fish·es** Any of various brightly colored fishes of the family Mullidae, having two sensory barbels on the chin.
goats·beard also **goat's-beard** (gōts′bîrd′) *n.* **1.** Any of several Eurasian species of the genus *Tragopogon,* esp. *T. pratensis,* widely naturalized in eastern North America and having dandelionlike flower heads. **2.** A genus (*Aruncus*) of dioecious plants, native to the north temperate and subarctic zones, having a large panicle of small white flowers.
goat·skin (gōt′skĭn′) *n.* **1.** The skin of a goat. **2.** Leather made from a goatskin. **3.** A container made from a goatskin.
goat·suck·er (gōt′sŭk′ər) *n.* Any of various chiefly nocturnal, insectivorous birds of the family Caprimulgidae, such as the nighthawk or the whippoorwill. [Transl. of Gk. *aigothēlās* : *aigo-,* goat + *-thēlās,* sucker (< the belief that the bird sucked milk from goats).]
gob¹ (gŏb) *n.* **1.** A small mass or lump. **2.** *Informal* A large quantity. Often used in the plural. [ME *gobbe,* prob. < OFr. *gobe,* mouthful < *gober,* to gulp, of Celt. orig.]
gob² (gŏb) *n. Slang* The mouth. [Perh. < Scottish and Ir.Gael.]
gob³ (gŏb) *n. Slang* A sailor. [Prob. shortening of earlier *gobshite,* wad of expectorated chewing tobacco, sailor. See GOBSHITE.]
gob·bet (gŏb′ĭt) *n.* **1.** A piece or chunk, esp. of raw meat. **2.** A bit or morsel. **3.** A small amount of liquid; a drop. [ME *gobet* < OFr., dim. of *gobe,* mouthful. See GOB¹.]
gob·ble¹ (gŏb′əl) *v.* **-bled, -bling, -bles** —*tr.* **1.** To devour in large greedy gulps. **2.** To take greedily; grab: *gobbled up the tickets.* —*intr.* To eat greedily or rapidly. [Frequentative of ME *gobben,* to drink greedily, prob. < *gobbe,* lump, mouthful. See GOB¹.]
gob·ble² (gŏb′əl) *n.* The guttural chortling sound of a male turkey. [Imit.] —**gob′ble** *v.*
gob·ble·dy·gook also **gob·ble·de·gook** (gŏb′əl-dē-gook′) *n.* Unclear, wordy jargon. [Imit. of the gobbling of a turkey.]
gob·bler (gŏb′lər) *n.* A male turkey.
Go·be·lin (gō′bə-lĭn, gŏb′ə-) *n.* A tapestry of a kind woven at the Gobelin works in Paris, France, noted for rich pictorial design.
go-be·tween (gō′bĭ-twēn′) *n.* One who acts as an intermediary or messenger between two sides.
Go·bi (gō′bē) A desert of SE Mongolia and N China.
gob·let (gŏb′lĭt) *n.* **1.** A drinking vessel, such as a glass, with a stem and base. **2.** *Archaic* A drinking bowl without handles. [ME *gobelet* < OFr., dim. of *gobel,* cup, prob. of Celt. orig.]
goblet cell *n.* Any of the mucus-secreting epithelial cells found in mucous membranes, as in the intestinal and respiratory tracts. [< its shape.]
gob·lin (gŏb′lĭn) *n.* A grotesque elfin creature of folklore, thought to work mischief or evil. [ME *gobelin* < Norman Fr. **gobelin,* a ghost in Évreux in the 12th cent.]
gob·shite (gŏb′shīt′) *n. Chiefly British Slang* A person regarded as mean or contemptible. [Perh. ult. < obsolete *gobshite,* wad of expectorated chewing tobacco or tobacco juice : GOB² + dialectal *shite,* excrement (< ME *shiten,* to defecate < OE **scītan*).]
go·by (gō′bē) *n., pl.* **goby** or **-bies** Any of numerous small spiny-finned fishes of the family Gobiidae, usu. having united pelvic fins forming a suction disk. [Lat. *gōbius,* gudgeon < Gk. *kōbios.*]
go-by (gō′bī′) *n. Informal* An intentional slight; a snub.
go-cart (gō′kärt′) *n.* **1.** A small wagon for children to ride in,

drive, or pull. **2.** also **go-kart** (-kärt′) See **kart. 3.** A small frame on casters designed to help support a child learning to walk. **4.** A handcart. **5.** A stroller.

go cup *n. Chiefly Southern US* A plastic cup provided for a patron who wishes to take an alcoholic beverage outdoors.

god (gŏd) *n.* **1. God a.** A perfect being conceived as the creator of the universe, and worshiped in monotheistic religions. **b.** The force, effect, or a manifestation or aspect of this being. **2.** A being of supernatural powers or attributes, believed in and worshiped by a people, esp. a male deity. **3.** An image of such a being. **4.** One that is worshiped, idealized, or followed. **5.** A very handsome man. **6.** A powerful ruler or despot. [ME < OE. See **gheu(ə)-** in App.]

Go·dard (gō-där′), **Jean Luc** b. 1930. French filmmaker known for innovative films such as *Breathless* (1959).

Go·da·va·ri (gō-dä′və-rē) A river of central India flowing c. 1,448 km (900 mi) to the Bay of Bengal.

God-aw·ful (gŏd′ô′fəl) *adj. Slang* Extremely trying; atrocious.

god·child (gŏd′chīld′) *n.* A person for whom another serves as sponsor, as at baptism.

god·damn also **God·damn** (gŏd′dăm′) *interj.* Used to express extreme displeasure, anger, or surprise. ❖ *n.* Damn. ❖ *tr. & intr.v.* **-damned, -damn·ing, -damns** To damn.

god·damned (gŏd′dămd′) or **god·damn** (-dăm′) *adj.* Damned. —**god·damned′,** or **god′damn′** *adv.*

God·dard (gŏd′ərd), **Robert Hutchings** 1882–1945. Amer. physicist who developed the first successful liquid-fueled rocket (1926).

god·daugh·ter (gŏd′dô′tər) *n.* A female godchild.

god·dess (gŏd′ĭs) *n.* **1.** A female being of supernatural powers or attributes, believed in and worshiped by a people. **2.** often **Goddess** A female being believed to be the source of life and being and worshiped as the principal deity in various religions. Used with *the.* **3.** An image of such a being. **4.** Something worshiped or idealized. **5.** A woman of great beauty or grace.

Gö·del (gœd′l), **Kurt** 1906–78. Czech-born Amer. mathematician and logician best known for his proof that the consistency of a mathematical system in which the truths of arithmetic can be expressed cannot be proven from within that system (1931).

go-dev·il (gō′dĕv′əl) *n.* **1.** A logging sled. **2.** A railway handcar. **3.** A jointed tool for cleaning an oil pipeline and disengaging obstructions. **4.** An iron dart dropped into an oil well to explode a charge of dynamite.

god·fa·ther (gŏd′fä′thər) *n.* **1.** A man who sponsors a person, as at baptism. **2.** One that has a relationship to another person or to something that is the equivalent of being a baptismal sponsor. **3.** *Slang* The leader of an organized crime family. ❖ *tr.v.* **-thered, -ther·ing, -thers** To serve as or as if a godfather to.

god·for·sak·en also **God·for·sak·en** (gŏd′fər-sā′kən) *adj.* **1.** Located in a dismal or remote area. **2.** Desolate; forlorn.

God·frey of Bouil·lon (gŏd′frē; boo-yôɴ′) 1061?–1100. French leader of the First Crusade (1096–99).

god·head (gŏd′hĕd′) *n.* **1.** Divinity; godhood. **2. Godhead a.** The Christian God, esp. the Trinity. **b.** The essential and divine nature of God, regarded abstractly. [ME *godhode, godhede* < OE *godhād* : *god,* god; see GOD + *-hād,* -hood.]

god·hood (gŏd′hood′) *n.* The quality or state of being a god.

god·less (gŏd′lĭs) *adj.* **1.** Recognizing or worshiping no god. **2.** Wicked, impious, or immoral. —**god′less·ly** *adv.* —**god′less·ness** *n.*

god·like (gŏd′līk′) *adj.* Resembling or of the nature of a god or God; divine. —**god′like′ness** *n.*

god·ling (gŏd′lĭng) *n.* A minor god.

god·ly (gŏd′lē) *adj.* **-li·er, -li·est 1.** Having great reverence for God; pious. **2.** Divine. —**god′li·ness** *n.*

god·moth·er (gŏd′mŭth′ər) *n.* **1.** A woman who sponsors a person, as at baptism. **2.** One that has a relationship to another person or to something that is the equivalent of being a baptismal sponsor. ❖ *tr.v.* **-ered, -er·ing, -ers** To serve as or as if a godmother to.

go·down (gō′doun′) *n.* In India and East Asia, a warehouse, esp. one at a dockside. [Alteration (influenced by DOWN¹) of Malay *godong,* prob. of Dravidian orig.; akin to Kannada *gaḍaṅgu,* storehouse, godown.]

god·par·ent (gŏd′pâr′ənt, -păr′-) *n.* A godfather or a godmother.

God's acre (gŏdz) *n.* A churchyard or burial ground.

god·send (gŏd′sĕnd′) *n.* Something wanted or needed that comes or happens unexpectedly. [Alteration of ME *goddes sand,* God's message : *goddes,* genitive of *God,* God; see GOD + *sand,* message (< OE).]

god·son (gŏd′sŭn′) *n.* A male godchild.

God·speed (gŏd′spēd′) *n.* Success or good fortune. [ME *God spede (you),* may God prosper (you) : *God,* god; see GOD + *spede,* third pers. sing. pr. subjunctive of *speden,* to prosper (< OE *spēdan* < *spēd,* success).]

Godt·håb (gŏd′hôp′) or **Nuuk** (nook) The cap. of Greenland, on the SW coast of the island on **Godthåb Fjord;** founded 1721. Pop. 10,559.

Go·du·nov (gōōd′n-ôf′, gŏd′-, gə-dōō-nôf′), **Boris Fyodorovich** 1551?–1605. Czar of Russia (1598–1605) whose reign was

---

marked by the colonization of Siberia.

God·win (gŏd′wĭn), **William** 1756–1836. British writer and political theorist whose most important work is *Enquiry Concerning Political Justice* (1793).

Godwin Aus·ten (ô′stən), **Mount** See **K2.**

god·wit (gŏd′wĭt′) *n.* Any of various large shore birds of the genus *Limosa,* with a slender, slightly upturned bill. [?]

Goeb·bels (gœ′bəls), **(Paul) Joseph** 1897–1945. German Nazi propaganda minister (1933–45) who led propaganda attacks on the Jews and other groups.

go·er (gō′ər) *n.* One that goes, esp. a person who goes to a specified place frequently or regularly. Often used in combination: *beachgoer; clubgoer.*

Goe·ring (gĕr′ĭng, gûr′-, gœ′rĭng), **Hermann Wilhelm** See Hermann Wilhelm **Göring.**

goes (gōz) *v.* Third person singular present tense of **go**¹.

Goe·thals (gō′thəlz), **George Washington** 1858–1928. Amer. army officer who directed the construction of the Panama Canal (1907–14).

Goe·the (gœ′tə), **Johann Wolfgang von** 1749–1832. German writer renowned for his two-part dramatic poem *Faust* (published 1808 and 1832). —**Goe′the·an** (-tē-ən) *adj.*

goe·thite (gō′thīt′, gœ′tīt′) *n.* A brown mineral, HFeO₂, a common constituent of rust.

go·fer also **go-fer** (gō′fər) *n. Slang* An employee who runs errands in addition to regular duties. [Alteration of *go for* < that person's having to go for or after things.]

gof·fer also **gauf·fer** (gŏf′ər, gō′fər) *tr.v.* **-fered, -fer·ing, -fers** To press ridges or narrow pleats into (a frill, for example). ❖ *n.* **1.** An iron used for goffering. **2.** Ridges or pleats produced in this manner. [Fr. *gaufrer,* to emboss < OFr. < *gaufre,* honeycomb, waffle, of Gmc. orig. See **webh-** in App.]

Gog and Ma·gog (gŏg; mā′gŏg) *pl.n.* In Judeo-Christian tradition, the satanic powers who wage war against God and the righteous at the end of the world.

go-get·ter (gō′gĕt′ər, -gĕt′-) *n. Informal* An enterprising person.

gog·gle (gŏg′əl) *v.* **-gled, -gling, -gles** *—intr.* **1.** To stare with wide and bulging eyes. **2.** To roll or bulge. Used of the eyes. *—tr.* To roll or bulge (the eyes). ❖ *n.* **1.** A stare or leer. **2. goggles** A pair of tight-fitting eyeglasses, often tinted or having side shields, worn to protect the eyes. [ME *gogelen,* to squint.] —**gog′gly** *adj.*

gog·gle-eyed (gŏg′əl-īd′) *adj.* Having prominent or rolling eyes.

Gogh, Vincent van (gō, gôĸʜ, ĸʜôĸʜ) See Vincent **van Gogh.**

go-go¹ (gō′gō′) *adj. Informal* Of or relating to discotheques or to their music and dancing. [< À GOGO.]

go-go² (gō′gō′) *adj. Informal* Marked by assertive action. [Intensive redup. of GO¹.]

Go·gol (gō′gəl, gō′gôl), **Nikolai Vasilievich** 1809–52. Russian writer whose works include the novel *Dead Souls* (1842).

Gog·ra (gŏg′rə, -rä) See **Ghaghara.**

Goi·â·ni·a (goi-än′ē-ə, -ä′nē-ə) A city of S-central Brazil SW of Brasília. Pop. 920,840.

Goi·del·ic (goi-dĕl′ĭk) *n.* A subdivision of the Insular Celtic languages that includes Irish Gaelic, Scottish Gaelic, and Manx. ❖ *adj.* **1.** Of or relating to the Gaels. **2.** Of or relating to Goidelic. [< OIr. *Goidil,* Gael, poss. < O Welsh *-guoidel, Gwyddel.*]

go·ing (gō′ĭng) *n.* **1.** Departure. **2.** The condition underfoot as it affects walking or riding. **3.** *Informal* Progress toward a goal; headway. ❖ *adj.* **1.** Working; running. **2.** In full operation; flourishing. **3.** Current; prevailing. **4.** To be found; available. —*idiom:* **going on** Approaching.

go·ing-o·ver (gō′ĭng-ō′vər) *n., pl.* **go·ings-o·ver** (-ĭngz-) *Informal* **1.** An examination; an inspection. **2a.** A severe beating. **b.** A severe reprimand.

go·ings-on (gō′ĭngz-ŏn′, -ôn′) *pl.n. Informal* Actions or behavior, esp. when regarded with disapproval.

goi·ter (goi′tər) *n.* A noncancerous enlargement of the thyroid gland, visible as a swelling at the front of the neck, that is often associated with iodine deficiency. [Fr. *goitre* < Provençal *goitron* < VLat. **gutturiō, gutturiōn-,* throat < Lat. *guttur.*] —**goi′trous** (-trəs) *adj.*

go-kart (gō′kärt′) *n.* Variant of **go-cart** 2.

Go·lan Heights (gō′län′) A region between NE Israel and SW Syria NE of the Sea of Galilee; captured by Israel in the 1967 Arab-Israeli War and formally annexed in 1981.

Gol·con·da (gŏl-kŏn′də) A ruined city of S-central India W of Hyderabad; cap. of an ancient kingdom (fl. 1364–1512) and later one of the five Muslim kingdoms of the Deccan.

gold (gōld) *n.* **1a.** *Symbol* **Au** A soft yellow malleable metallic element, occurring in veins and alluvial deposits. A good thermal and electrical conductor, it is used as an international monetary standard, in jewelry, for decoration, and as a plated coating on a wide variety of electrical and mechanical components. Atomic number 79; atomic weight 196.967; melting point 1,063.0°C; boiling point 2,966.0°C; specific gravity 19.32; valence 1, 3. See table at **element. b.** Coinage made of this element. **c.** A gold standard. **2.** Money; riches. **3.** A light olive-brown to dark yellow or a moderate strong to vivid yellow. **4.** Something regarded as having great value or goodness: *a heart of gold.* **5a.** A medal made

goggles
skiers wearing goggles

ă	pat	oi	boy
ā	pay	ou	out
âr	care	ŏŏ	took
ä	father	ōō	boot
ĕ	pet	ŭ	cut
ē	be	ûr	urge
ĭ	pit	th	thin
ī	pie	th	this
îr	pier	hw	which
ŏ	pot	zh	vision
ō	toe	ə	about,
ô	paw		item

Stress marks:
′ (primary);
′ (secondary), as in
lexicon (lĕk′sĭ-kŏn′)

golden retriever

goldenseal
Hydrastis canadensis

goldfinch
male American goldfinch
Carduelis tristis

of gold, awarded for first place in a competition: *won 9 golds in 13 events.* **b.** A gold record. ❖ *adj.* Having the color of gold. [ME < OE. See **ghel-** in App.]

gold·beat·ing (gōld′bē′tĭng) *n.* The act, process, or art of beating sheets of gold into gold leaf. —**gold′beat′er** *n.*

gold beetle *n.* See **gold bug** 1.

Gold·berg (gōld′bûrg), **Arthur Joseph** 1908–90. Amer. jurist and diplomat; associate justice of the US Supreme Court (1962–65) and a delegate to the United Nations (1965–68).

Goldberg, Reuben ("Rube") Lucius 1883–1970. Amer. cartoonist noted for his diagrams of complicated impractical contraptions designed to effect comparatively simple results.

gold·brick (gōld′brĭk′) *Slang n.* A person, esp. a soldier, who avoids assigned duties or work; a shirker. ❖ *v.* **-bricked, -brick·ing, -bricks** —*intr.* To shirk one's assigned duties or responsibilities. —*tr.* To cheat; swindle. —**gold′brick′er** *n.*

gold brick *n.* A bar of gilded cheap metal that appears to be genuine gold. **2.** A fraudulent worthless substitute.

gold bug *n.* **1.** Any of several North American beetles, esp. *Metriona bicolor,* with a golden luster. **2.** A supporter of the gold standard. **3.** A gold speculator or purchaser.

gold coast *n. Informal* **1.** A rich neighborhood. **2.** The executive suite or suites in a company's headquarters. [After the GOLD COAST.]

Gold Coast 1. A section of coastal W Africa along the Gulf of Guinea on the S shore of Ghana; named for the large quantities of gold formerly sold there. **2.** A former British colony (1874–1957) on the Gold Coast, now part of Ghana.

gold digger *n. Informal* A woman who seeks money and expensive gifts from men.

gold·en (gōl′dən) *adj.* **1.** Of, relating to, made of, or containing gold. **2a.** Having the color of gold or a yellow color suggestive of gold. **b.** Lustrous; radiant. **c.** Suggestive of gold, as in richness or splendor. **3.** Of the greatest value or importance; precious. **4.** Marked by peace, prosperity, and often creativeness. **5.** Very favorable or advantageous; excellent. **6.** Having a promising future; seemingly assured of success. **7.** Of or relating to a 50th anniversary. —**gold′en·ly** *adv.* —**gold′en·ness** *n.*

golden age *n.* **1.** A period of great peace, prosperity, and happiness. **2.** *Greek & Roman Mythology* The first age of the world, a prosperous era during which people lived in ideal happiness.

golden aster *n.* Any of various North American plants of the genus *Chrysopsis,* having yellow rayed flower heads.

golden bantam *n.* A variety of corn having large bright yellow kernels on a relatively small ear.

golden calf *n.* **1.** A golden image of a sacrificial calf fashioned by Aaron and worshiped by the Israelites. **2a.** Money as an object of worship; mammon. **b.** The subject of intense veneration.

golden club *n.* An aquatic plant (*Orontium aquaticum*) of the eastern United States having a clublike golden-yellow spadix.

golden eagle *n.* A large eagle (*Aquila chrysaetos*) of mountainous areas of the Northern Hemisphere having dark plumage with brownish-yellow feathers on the back of the head and neck.

gol·den·eye (gōl′dən-ī′) *n.* **1.** Either of two yellow-eyed diving ducks (*Bucephala clangula* or *B. islandica*) of northern regions. **2.** Any of various lacewings of the family Chrysopidae having yellow or copper-colored eyes.

Golden Fleece *n. Greek Mythology* The fleece of the golden ram, stolen by Jason and the Argonauts from Colchis.

Golden Gate A strait in W CA connecting the Pacific Ocean and San Francisco Bay; first sighted by Sir Francis Drake in 1579.

golden glow *n.* A tall plant (*Rudbeckia laciniata*) cultivated for its large yellow many-rayed double flower heads.

Golden Horde *n.* The Mongol army that swept over eastern Europe in the 13th century and established a suzerain in Russia. [< the golden tent of their commander.]

Golden Horn An inlet of the Bosporus in NW Turkey forming the harbor of Istanbul.

golden mean *n.* The ethical midpoint between unethical extremes.

golden oldie *n.* A recording, movie, or other form of entertainment that was very popular in the past.

golden parachute *n. Slang* An agreement guaranteeing a key executive lucrative severance benefits when a company changes hands through management shifts.

golden pheasant *n.* A brilliantly colored pheasant (*Chrysolophus pictus*) of Tibet and western China.

golden retriever *n.* A retriever of a breed originating in Scotland, having a dense coat of golden hair.

gold·en·rod (gōl′dən-rŏd′) *n.* Any of numerous chiefly North American plants of the genus *Solidago,* having clusters of small yellow flower heads that bloom in late summer or fall.

golden rule *n.* The biblical teaching of treating others as one would be treated.

gold·en·seal (gōl′dən-sēl′) *n.* A woodland plant (*Hydrastis canadensis*) of eastern North America having small greenish-white flowers and a yellow root formerly used medicinally.

golden section *n.* A ratio, observed esp. in the fine arts, between the two dimensions of a plane figure or the two divisions of a line such that the smaller is to the larger as the larger is to the sum of the two, a ratio of roughly three to five.

gold·field (gōld′fēld′) *n.* An area containing abundant deposits of gold or gold ore.

gold-filled (gōld′fĭld′) *adj.* Made of a hard base metal with an outer layer of gold.

gold·finch (gōld′fĭnch′) *n.* **1.** Any of several American finches of the genus *Carduelis,* esp. *C. tristis,* of which the male has yellow plumage with a black forehead, wings, and tail. **2.** A Eurasian finch (*Carduelis carduelis*) having dark plumage marked with yellow and a red face.

gold·fish (gōld′fĭsh′) *n., pl.* **goldfish** or **-fish·es** An Asian freshwater fish (*Carassius auratus*), having brassy or reddish coloring and bred as an aquarium fish.

gold foil *n.* Gold rolled or beaten into sheets somewhat thicker than gold leaf.

Gold·ing (gōl′dĭng), **William Gerald** 1911–93. British writer noted for his dark novels, such as *The Lord of the Flies* (1954), who won the 1983 Nobel Prize for literature.

gold leaf *n.* Gold beaten into extremely thin sheets used esp. for gilding.

Gold·man (gōld′mən), **Emma** 1869–1940. Russian-born Amer. anarchist who advocated opposition to military conscription and was deported to the Soviet Union in 1919.

gold mine *n. Informal* A rich or plentiful source of something desired.

Gol·do·ni (gŏl-dō′nē), **Carlo** 1707–93. Italian dramatist whose plays include *The Mistress of the Inn* (1753).

gold rush *n.* **1.** A rush of migrants to an area where gold has been discovered. **2.** Headlong pursuit of wealth and success.

gold·smith (gōld′smĭth′) *n.* **1.** An artisan who fashions objects of gold. **2.** A trader or dealer in gold articles.

Goldsmith, Oliver 1730?–74. British writer renowned for his novel *The Vicar of Wakefield* (1766).

gold standard *n.* A monetary standard under which the basic unit of currency is equal in value to and exchangeable for a specified amount of gold.

gold·stone (gōld′stōn′) *n.* An aventurine with gold-colored inclusions.

gold·thread (gōld′thrĕd′) *n.* Any of several plants of the genus *Coptis,* having white flowers and slender yellow roots.

Gold·wa·ter (gōld′wô′tər, -wŏt′ər), **Barry Morris** 1909–98. Amer. politician who ran unsuccessfully for President in 1964.

Gold·wyn (gōld′wĭn), **Samuel** 1882–1974. Polish-born Amer. film producer who joined with Louis B. Mayer to form Metro-Goldwyn-Mayer (1925).

go·lem (gō′ləm) *n.* In Jewish folklore, an artificially created human supernaturally endowed with life. [Heb. *gōlem,* lump, clod, fool < *gālam,* to wrap up.]

golf (gŏlf, gôlf) *n.* A game played on an outdoor course with a series of 9 or 18 holes spaced far apart, the object being to propel a small ball with the use of various clubs into each hole with as few strokes as possible. ❖ *intr.v.* **golfed, golf·ing, golfs** To play this game. [ME.] —**golf′er** *n.*

golf club *n.* **1.** One of a set of clubs having a slender shaft and a head of wood or iron, used in golf. **2.** An organization of golfers.

golf course *n.* A large tract of land laid out for golf.

Gol·gi apparatus (gôl′jē) *n.* A network of membranous vesicles present in most living cells that functions in the formation of cellular secretions. [After Camillo *Golgi* (1844?–1926), Italian histologist.]

gol·go·tha (gŏl′gə-thə) *n.* A place or occasion of great suffering. [After GOLGOTHA.]

Gol·go·tha (gŏl′gə-thə, gŏl-gŏth′ə) See **Calvary**[1].

gol·iard (gōl′yərd, -yärd′) *n.* A wandering student in medieval Europe, noted for writing and singing ribald and satirical Latin songs. [ME < OFr., glutton, goliard < *gole,* throat < Lat. *gula.*] —**gol·iar′dic** (gōl-yär′dĭk) *adj.*

Go·li·ath[1] (gə-lī′əth) In the Bible, a giant Philistine warrior who was slain by David with a stone and sling.

go·li·ath[2] (gə-lī′əth) *n.* A person or thing of colossal power or achievement. [After GOLIATH[1].]

gol·li·wog or **gol·li·wogg** (gŏl′ē-wŏg′) *n.* A doll fashioned in grotesque caricature of a Black male. [After *Golliwog,* a character in books by Florence Upton (died 1922).]

gol·ly (gŏl′ē) *interj.* Used to express mild surprise or wonder. [Alteration of GOD.]

gom·been (gŏm-bēn′) *n. Irish* Usury. [Ir.Gael. *gaimbín,* dim. of *gamba,* smidgen, lump.]

Go·mel (gō′məl, -myĕl) See **Homyel′**.

Go·mor·rah[1] (gə-môr′ə, -mŏr′ə) An ancient city of Palestine near Sodom, possibly covered by the waters of the Dead Sea. According to the Bible, the city was destroyed by fire because of its wickedness.

Go·mor·rah[2] (gə-môr′ə, -mŏr′ə) *n.* A wicked place. [After GOMORRAH[1].]

Gom·pers (gŏm′pərz), **Samuel** 1850–1924. British-born Amer. labor leader who served as president of the American Federation of Labor (1886–1924, except 1895).

gon– *pref.* Variant of **gono–**.

–gon *suff.* A figure having a specified kind or number of angles: *isogon.* [Gk. *-gōnon* < neut. of *gōnos,* angled < *gōniā,* angle. See **genu-** in App.]

go·nad (gō′năd′) *n.* An organ in animals that produces gametes, esp. a testis or ovary. [NLat. *gonas, gonad-* < Gk. *gonos,* procreation, genitals. See **genə-** in App.] **—go·nad′al** (gō-năd′l), **go·nad′ic** *adj.*

go·nad·o·trop·ic (gō-năd′ə-trŏp′ĭk, -trō′pĭk) also **go·nad·o·troph·ic** (-trŏf′ĭk, -trō′fĭk) *adj.* Acting on or stimulating the gonads: *a gonadotropic hormone.*

go·nad·o·tro·pin (gō-năd′ə-trō′pĭn, -trŏp′ĭn) also **go·nad·o·tro·phin** (-trō′fĭn) *n.* A hormone that stimulates the growth and activity of the gonads.

Go·na·ïves (gō′nə-ēv′, gô-nä-) A city of W Haiti on an arm of the Caribbean Sea NNW of Port-au-Prince. Haitian independence was proclaimed here in 1804. Pop. 34,209.

Gon·court (gôn-kŏor′), **Edmond Louis Antoine Huot de** 1822–96. French writer who collaborated with his brother **Jules Alfred Huot de Goncourt** (1830–70) on works such as *Madame Gervaisais* (1869).

Gond (gŏnd) *n.* A member of a Dravidian people inhabiting central India.

Gon·dar (gŏn′dər, -där′) also **Gon·der** (-dər) A town of NW Ethiopia on Lake Tana; an early cap. of Ethiopia that flourished c. 1630 to c. 1860. Pop. 85,941.

Gon·di (gŏn′dē) *n.* The Dravidian language of the Gonds.

gon·do·la (gŏn′dl-ə, gŏn-dō′lə) *n.* **1.** *Nautical* **a.** A lightweight narrow barge with ends that curve up into a point and often a small cabin in the middle, propelled with a single oar from the stern. **b.** A flatbottom riverboat. **2.** A gondola car. **3.** A basket, enclosure, or instrument sling suspended from and carried aloft by a balloon. **4.** An enclosed structure suspended from a cable, used for conveying passengers, as to and from a ski slope. [Ital. < OItal. *gondula.*]

gondola car *n.* An open railroad freight car with low sides.

gon·do·lier (gŏn′dl-îr′) *n.* *Nautical* One who propels a gondola. [Fr. < Ital. *gondoliere* < *gondola,* gondola. See GONDOLA.]

Gond·wa·na·land (gŏnd-wä′nə-lănd′) *n.* The supercontinent of the Southern Hemisphere that, according to the theory of plate tectonics, broke up into India, Australia, Antarctica, Africa, and South America. [After *Gondwana,* a region of central India < GOND.]

gone (gôn, gŏn) *v.* Past participle of **go¹.** ❖ *adj.* **1.** Being away from a place; absent or departed. **2.** Past; bygone. **3.** Advanced beyond hope or recall. **4.** Dying or dead. **5.** Ruined; lost. **6.** Carried away; absorbed. **7.** Used up; exhausted. **8.** *Slang* Infatuated. **9.** *Slang* Pregnant.

gon·er (gô′nər, gŏn′ər) *n.* *Slang* One ruined or doomed.

gon·fa·lon (gŏn′fə-lŏn′, -lən) *n.* A banner suspended from a crosspiece, esp. in an ecclesiastical procession or as the ensign of a medieval Italian republic. [Ital. *gonfalone,* of Gmc. orig. See **gwhen-** in App.]

gon·fa·lon·ier (gŏn′fə-lə-nîr′) *n.* The bearer of a gonfalon. [Fr. < Ital. *gonfaloniere* < *gonfalone.* See GONFALON.]

gong (gông, gŏng) *n.* **1.** A rimmed metal disk that produces a loud sonorous tone when struck with a padded mallet. **2.** A usu. saucer-shaped bell that is struck with a mechanically operated hammer. ❖ *intr.v.* **gonged, gong·ing, gongs** To make the sound of a gong. [Malay.]

Gon·gor·ism (gông′gə-rĭz′əm) *n.* A florid literary style employing puns and conceits. [After Luis de *Góngora y Argote* (1561–1627), Spanish poet.] **—Gon·gor·is′tic** (-rĭs′tĭk) *adj.*

go·nid·i·um (gō-nĭd′ē-əm) *n.,* pl. **-i·a** (-ē-ə) **1.** An asexually produced reproductive cell found in certain algae. **2.** An algal cell filled with chlorophyll, formed in the thallus of a lichen. [NLat. < Gk. *gonos,* seed. See GONO–.] **—go·nid′i·al** *adj.*

gon·if (gä′nəf) *n.* Variant of **ganef.**

go·ni·om·e·ter (gō′nē-ŏm′ĭ-tər) *n.* **1.** An optical instrument for measuring the angles between crystal faces. **2.** An electronic instrument for determining the angular direction of incoming radio signals. [Gk. *gōnia,* angle; see **genu-** in App. + –METER.] **—go′ni·o·met′ric** (-nē-ə-mĕt′rĭk), **go′ni·o·met′ri·cal** *adj.* **—go′ni·om′e·try** *n.*

go·ni·on (gō′nē-ŏn′) *n.* The outer point on either side of the lower jaw at which the jawbone angles upward. [Fr. < Gk. *gōnia,* angle. See **genu-** in App.]

gon·na (gŭn′ə) *Informal* Contraction of *going to: We're gonna win.*

Gonne (gŏn, gŭn), **Maud** 1865–1953. Irish patriot and actress who was a leader of the Irish independence movement.

gono– or **gon–** *pref.* Sexual; reproductive: *gonophore.* [Gk. < *gonos,* seed, procreation. See **genə-** in App.]

gon·o·coc·cus (gŏn′ə-kŏk′əs) *n.,* pl. **-coc·ci** (-kŏk′sī′, -kŏk′ī′) The bacterium *Neisseria gonorrhoeae,* the causative agent of gonorrhea. **—gon′o·coc′cal** (-kŏk′əl), **gon′o·coc′cic** (-kŏk′ĭk, -kŏk′sĭk) *adj.*

go-no-go (gō-nō′gō) *adj.* Of, relating to, or involving a mandatory decision to continue or halt a course of action.

gon·o·phore (gŏn′ə-fôr′, -fōr′) *n.* A structure bearing or consisting of a reproductive organ or part. **—gon′o·pho′ric** (-fôr′ĭk, -fōr′-), **go·noph′o·rous** (-nŏf′ər-əs) *adj.*

gon·o·pore (gŏn′ə-pôr′, -pōr′) *n.* A reproductive aperture or pore, esp. of certain insects and worms.

gon·or·rhe·a (gŏn′ə-rē′ə) *n.* A sexually transmitted disease

caused by gonococcal bacteria, affecting the mucous membrane chiefly of the genital and urinary tracts and sometimes marked by purulent discharge and painful or difficult urination, esp. in men, but often without symptoms in women. [Gk. *gonorrhoia,* flow of seed (< the mistaken belief that the discharge contained semen) : *gono-, gono-* + *-rhoia, -rrhea.*] **—gon′or·rhe′al, gon′or·rhe′ic** *adj.*

–gony *suff.* Generation; reproduction; manner of origin: *heterogony.* [Lat. *-gonia* < Gk. *-goneia* < *gonos,* offspring. See **genə-** in App.]

gon·zo (gŏn′zō) *adj. Slang* **1.** Using an exaggerated, highly subjective style, esp. in journalism. **2.** Bizarre; unconventional. [Perh. Ital., simpleton (perh. short for *Borgonzone,* Burgundian) or Sp. *ganso,* dullard, goose (of Gmc. orig.; see **ghans-** in App.).]

goo (gōo) *n. Informal* **1.** A sticky wet viscous substance. **2.** Sentimental drivel. [Perh. short for BURGOO.]

goo·ber (gōo′bər) *n. Chiefly Southern US* See **peanut** 2. [Of Bantu orig.; akin to Kongo or Kimbundu *n-guba.*]

Most Southerners recognize the terms *goober* and *goober pea* as other names for the peanut. *Goober* is related to Kongo or Kimbundu *n-guba,* "peanut." The word is especially interesting as one of a small stock of African language borrowings brought over by slaves. In this category are *gumbo* ("okra"), which is of Bantu origin, and *yam,* which is of West African origin. The noun *cooter* is related to the Mandingo word *kuta* and the Tshiluba word *nkudu,* both meaning "turtle."

goober pea *n. Chiefly Southern US* See **peanut** 2. See Regional Note at **goober.**

good (gŏod) *adj.* **bet·ter** (bĕt′ər), **best** (bĕst) **1.** Being positive or desirable in nature; not bad or poor: *a good experience; good news from the hospital.* **2a.** Having the qualities that are desirable or distinguishing in a particular thing: *a good exterior paint; a good joke.* **b.** Serving the desired purpose or end; suitable. **3a.** Not spoiled or ruined: *The milk is still good.* **b.** In excellent condition; sound: *a good tooth.* **4a.** Superior to the average; satisfactory: *a good student.* **b.** Used formerly to refer to the US Government grade of meat higher than standard and lower than choice. **5a.** Of high quality: *good books.* **b.** Discriminating: *good taste.* **6.** Worthy of respect; honorable: *ruined the family's good name.* **7.** Attractive; handsome: *good looks.* **8.** Beneficial to health; salutary: *a good night's rest.* **9.** Competent; skilled: *a good machinist.* **10.** Complete; thorough: *a good workout.* **11a.** Reliable; sure: *a good investment.* **b.** Valid or true: *a good reason.* **c.** Genuine; real: *a good dollar bill.* **12a.** In effect; operative: *a warranty good for two years.* **b.** Able to continue in a specified activity: *I'm good for another game.* **13a.** Able to pay or contribute: *is good for the money that I lent her.* **b.** Able to elicit a specified reaction: *good for a laugh.* **14a.** Ample; substantial: *a good income.* **b.** Bountiful: *a good table.* **15.** Full: *It is a good mile from here.* **16a.** Pleasant; enjoyable: *had a good time at the party.* **b.** Propitious; favorable: *good weather; a good omen.* **17a.** Of moral excellence; upright: *a good person.* **b.** Benevolent; kind: *a good heart.* **c.** Loyal; staunch: *a good Republican.* **18a.** Well-behaved; obedient: *a good child.* **b.** Socially correct; proper: *good manners.* **19.** *Sports* **a.** Landing within bounds or within a particular area of a court and therefore in play. **b.** Passing between the uprights of the goal and therefore scoring, as a field goal in football. **20.** Used to form exclamatory phrases expressing surprise or dismay: *Good grief!* ❖ *n.* **1a.** Something that is good. **b.** A good, valuable, or useful part or aspect. **2.** Welfare; benefit: *the common good.* **3.** Goodness; virtue. **4. goods a.** Commodities; wares. **b.** Portable personal property. **c.** (*used with a sing. or pl. verb*) Fabric; material. **5. goods** *Slang* Incriminating information or evidence. ❖ *adv. Informal* Well. **—idioms: good as** Practically; nearly. **but good** *Informal* Used as an intensive: *The pipe started to leak but good.* **for good** Permanently; forever: *I'm moving to England for good.* **good and** *Informal* Very; thoroughly: *good and ready.* **no good** *Informal* **1.** Worthless. **2.** Futile; useless. **to the good 1.** For the best; advantageous. **2.** In an advantageous financial position. [ME < OE *gōd.*]

Good is properly used as an adjective with linking verbs such as *be, seem,* or *appear: The future looks good.* It should not be used as an adverb with other verbs: *The car runs well* (not *good*). See Usage Note at **well².**

Good·all (gŏod′ôl), **Jane** b. 1934. English zoologist noted for her study of chimpanzee behavior and for her conservation work.

Good Book *n.* The Christian Bible.

good·bye or **good-bye** also **good-by** (gŏod-bī′) *interj.* Used to express an acknowledgment of parting. ❖ *n.,* pl. **-byes** also **-bys** **1.** An acknowledgment at parting, esp. by saying "goodbye." **2.** An act of parting or leave-taking: *many sad goodbyes.* [Alteration of *God be with you.*]

good faith *n.* Compliance with what is decent and honest.

good·fel·low·ship (gŏod′fĕl′ō-shĭp′) *n.* Pleasant sociability; comradeship.

good-for-noth·ing (gŏod′fər-nŭth′ĭng) *n.* A person of little worth or usefulness. ❖ *adj.* Having little worth; useless.

Good Friday *n.* The Friday before Easter, observed by Christians in commemoration of the crucifixion of Jesus. [< GOOD, pious, holy (obsolete).]

gondola
top: the Grand Canal, Venice, Italy
bottom: Jackson Hole Ski Area, Grand Teton National Park, Wyoming

goose
greylag goose
Anser anser

gooseberry
Ribes uva-crispa

Mikhail Gorbachev

Berry Gordy, Jr.

good·heart·ed (gŏŏd′här′tĭd) *adj.* Kind and generous. —**good′heart′ed·ly** *adv.* —**good′heart′ed·ness** *n.*

Good Hope, Cape of A promontory on the SW coast of South Africa S of Cape Town; first circumnavigated by Bartolomeu Dias in 1488.

good·hu·mored (gŏŏd′hyōō′mərd) *adj.* Cheerful; amiable. —**good′-hu′mored·ly** *adv.* —**good′-hu′mored·ness** *n.*

good·ie (gŏŏd′ē) *n.* Variant of **goody**[1].

good·look·ing (gŏŏd′lŏŏk′ĭng) *adj.* Of a pleasing or attractive appearance; handsome. —**good′-look′er** *n.*

good·ly (gŏŏd′lē) *adj.* **-li·er, -li·est 1.** Good-looking. **2.** Quite large; considerable. —**good′li·ness** *n.*

good·man (gŏŏd′mən) *n. Archaic* **1a.** The male head of a household. **b.** A husband. **2. Goodman** Used formerly as a courtesy title before the surname of a man not of noble birth.

Goodman, Benjamin David ("Benny") 1909–86. Amer. clarinetist whose band, formed in 1934, introduced swing.

good nature *n.* A cheerful, obliging disposition.

good-na·tured (gŏŏd′nā′chərd) *adj.* Having an easygoing, cheerful disposition. —**good′-na′tured·ly** *adv.* —**good′-na′tured·ness** *n.*

good·ness (gŏŏd′nĭs) *n.* **1.** The state or quality of being good. **2.** The beneficial part. ❖ *interj.* Used to express mild surprise.

good offices *pl.n.* Beneficial acts performed for another, esp. acts performed by a mediator in a dispute.

good old boy also **good ol′ boy** or **good ole boy** (ōl) *n. Slang* A man having qualities held to be stereotypic of certain Southern white males, such as a relaxed manner, strong loyalty to family and friends, and often an intolerant point of view.

Good Samaritan *n.* A compassionate person who helps others. [After the Samaritan passerby in the biblical parable who alone aided a man beaten and robbed (Luke 10:30–37).]

good-sized (gŏŏd′sīzd′) *adj.* Of a fairly large size.

good-tem·pered (gŏŏd′tĕm′pərd) *adj.* Having an even temper; not easily irritated. —**good′-tem′pered·ly** *adv.*

good·wife (gŏŏd′wīf′) *n., pl.* **-wives** (-wīvz′) *Archaic* **1.** The female head of a household. **2. Goodwife** Used formerly as a courtesy title before the surname of a married woman not of noble birth.

good·will also **good will** (gŏŏd′wĭl′) *n.* **1.** A kind or friendly attitude; benevolence. **2.** Cheerful acquiescence or willingness. **3.** A good relationship, as of a business with its customers.

good·y[1] (gŏŏd′ē) *Informal interj.* Used to express delight. ❖ *n.* also **good·ie** *pl.* **-ies** Something attractive or delectable, esp. something sweet to eat.

good·y[2] (gŏŏd′ē) *n., pl.* **good·ies** *Archaic* A goodwife. [Shortening and alteration of GOODWIFE.]

Good·year (gŏŏd′yîr′), **Charles** 1800–60. Amer. inventor who developed vulcanized rubber (1839).

good·y-good·y (gŏŏd′ē-gŏŏd′ē) *adj.* Affectedly sweet, good, or virtuous. —**good′y-good′y** *n.*

goody two-shoes (tōō′shōōz′) *n., pl.* **goody two-shoes** *Informal* A goody-goody. [After the title character in *The History of Little Goody Two-Shoes*, a nursery tale.]

goo·ey (gŏŏ′ē) *adj.* **-i·er, -i·est** Sticky and viscous.

goof (gŏŏf) *Slang n.* **1.** An incompetent, foolish, or stupid person. **2.** A careless mistake; a slip. ❖ *v.* **goofed, goof·ing, goofs** —*intr.* **1.** To make a silly mistake; blunder. **2.** To waste or kill time. **3.** To tease or make fun of someone. —*tr.* To spoil, as through clumsiness; bungle. Usu. used with *up.* [Poss. alteration of dialectal *goff,* fool < obsolete Fr. *goffe,* stupid.]

goof·ball (gŏŏf′bôl′) *Slang n.* **1.** A foolish, incompetent, or stupid person. **2.** A barbiturate or tranquilizer pill. ❖ *adj.* Silly or outlandish.

goof-off (gŏŏf′ôf′, -ŏf′) *Slang* One who shirks work or responsibility.

goof·y (gŏŏ′fē) *adj.* **-i·er, -i·est** *Slang* Silly; ridiculous: *a goofy hat.* —**goof′i·ly** *adv.* —**goof′i·ness** *n.*

goo·gol (gŏŏ′gôl′) *n.* The number 10 raised to the power 100 (10^{100}), written out as the numeral 1 followed by 100 zeros. [Coined at the age of nine by Milton Sirotta, nephew of Edward Kasner (1878–1955), Amer. mathematician.]

goo·gol·plex (gŏŏ′gôl-plĕks′) *n.* The number 10 raised to the power googol, written out as the numeral 1 followed by 10^{100} zeros. [GOOGOL + -*plex,* as in DUPLEX.]

goo-goo (gŏŏ′gŏŏ′) *adj. Slang* Amorous or loving, often humorously so: *made goo-goo eyes at her.* [Perh. alteration of GOGGLE.]

gook[1] (gŏŏk, gŏŏk) *n.* Variant of **guck**.

gook[2] (gŏŏk) *Offensive Slang* Used as a disparaging term for a person of East Asian birth or descent. [Perh. alteration of earlier *goo-goo,* native inhabitant of the Philippines, Pacific islander.]

goom·bah (gŏŏm′bä, gōōm′-) *n. Slang* A companion or associate, esp. an older friend who acts as a patron, protector, or adviser. [Prob. alteration of Ital. *compare,* godfather < Med.Lat. *compater.* See COMPADRE.]

goon (gōōn) *n. Slang* **1.** A thug hired to intimidate or harm opponents. **2.** A stupid or oafish person. [Prob. ult. short for GOONEY, simpleton.]

goo·ney also **goo·ny** (gōō′nē) *n., pl.* **-neys** also **-nies** An albatross, esp. the black-footed albatross. [?]

goop (gōōp) *n. Slang* A sticky wet viscous substance. [Perh. alteration of GOO.] —**goop′y** *adj.*

goos·an·der (gōō-săn′dər) *n. Chiefly British* A fish-eating duck (*Mergus merganser*), the male of which has a glossy greenish-black head and a white body. [?]

goose (gōōs) *n., pl.* **geese** (gēs) **1a.** Any of various water birds of the family Anatidae, esp. of the genera *Anser* and *Branta,* usu. having a shorter neck than that of a swan and a shorter, more pointed bill than that of a duck. **b.** The female goose. **c.** The flesh of a goose used as food. **2.** *Informal* A silly person. **3.** *pl.* **goos·es** A tailor's pressing iron with a long curved handle. **4.** *Slang* A poke, prod, or pinch between or on the buttocks. ❖ *tr.v.* **goosed, goos·ing, goos·es** *Slang* **1.** To poke, prod, or pinch (a person) between or on the buttocks. **2.** To move to action, spur. **3.** To give a spurt of fuel to (an engine, for example). [ME *gos* < OE *gōs.* See **ghans-** in App.]

goose barnacle *n.* Any of various barnacles of the genus *Lapas,* having a fleshy stalk that attaches to rocks or floating objects.

goose·ber·ry (gōōs′bĕr′ē, -bə-rē, gōōz′-) *n.* **1a.** A European shrub (*Ribes uva-crispa*) with green flowers and edible berries. **b.** The fruit of this plant. **2.** Any of several plants with similar fruit. [*goose* (prob. shortening and alteration by folk-ety. of Fr. *groseille,* gooseberry; see GROSSULARITE) + BERRY.]

gooseberry gourd *n.* See **gherkin** 1.

goose bumps *pl.n.* Momentary roughness of the skin caused by erection of the papillae in response to cold or fear.

goose egg *n. Slang* **1.** Zero, esp. as a score. **2.** A swelling or lump, esp. one caused by a blow.

goose·fish (gōōs′fĭsh′) *n., pl.* **goosefish** or **-fish·es** Any of several anglerfishes of the genus *Lophius,* such as *L. americanus* of North American Atlantic waters.

goose flesh *n.* See **goose bumps**.

goose·foot (gōōs′fŏŏt′) *n., pl.* **-foots** Any of various weeds of the genus *Chenopodium,* having small greenish flowers.

goose grass *n.* See **silverweed**.

goose·neck (gōōs′nĕk′) *n.* A slender curved object or part, such as the shaft of certain lamps. —**goose′necked′** *adj.*

gooseneck barnacle *n.* See **goose barnacle**.

goose pimples *pl.n.* See **goose bumps**.

goose step *n.* A military parade step executed by swinging the legs sharply from the hips and keeping the knees locked. —**goose′-step′** *v.*

goos·y also **goos·ey** (gōō′sē) *adj.* **-i·er, -i·est** **1.** Relating to or resembling a goose. **2.** Foolish or scatterbrained.

GOP *abbr.* Grand Old Party (Republican Party)

go·pher (gō′fər) *n.* **1.** Any of various short-tailed burrowing rodents of the family Geomyidae of North America, having fur-lined external cheek pouches. **2.** Any of various ground squirrels of the genus *Citellus* of North American prairies. **3.** Any of several burrowing tortoises of the genus *Gopherus,* esp. *G. polyphemus* of the southeast United States. [Prob. short for earlier *megopher,* gopher tortoise, of unknown orig.]

gopher snake *n.* See **bull snake**.

Go·rakh·pur (gôr′ək-pŏŏr′, gôr′-) A city of N India E of Lucknow; founded c. 1400. Pop. 290,814.

Gor·ba·chev (gôr′bə-chôf′, -chŏf′, gər-bə-chôf′), **Mikhail Sergeyevich** b. 1931. Soviet politician who served as general secretary of the Communist Party (1985–91) and president of the USSR (1989–91). He won the 1990 Nobel Peace Prize.

Gor·di·an knot (gôr′dē-ən) *n.* **1.** An exceedingly complicated problem. **2.** An intricate knot tied by King Gordius of Phrygia and cut by Alexander the Great with his sword after hearing that whoever undid it would be the next ruler of Asia.

Gor·di·mer (gôr′də-mər), **Nadine** b. 1923. South African writer whose works include *Burger's Daughter* (1979). She won the 1991 Nobel Prize for literature.

Gor·don (gôr′dn), **Charles George** 1833–85. British army officer who commanded the Chinese force that quashed the Taiping Rebellion (1863–64).

Gordon setter *n.* A medium-sized hunting dog of a Scottish breed that has a silky black-and-tan coat. [After Alexander, 4th Duke of *Gordon* (1745?–1827).]

Gor·dy (gôr′dē), **Berry, Jr.** b. 1929. Amer. music producer who founded Motown Records (1959).

gore[1] (gôr, gōr) *tr.v.* **gored, gor·ing, gores** To pierce or stab with a horn or tusk. [ME *goren,* prob. < *gore,* spear < OE *gār.*]

gore[2] (gôr, gōr) *n.* **1.** A triangular or tapering piece of cloth forming a part of something, as in a skirt. **2.** A small triangular piece of land. ❖ *tr.v.* **gored, gor·ing, gores 1.** To provide with a gore. **2.** To cut into a gore. [ME < OE *gāra.*]

gore[3] (gôr, gōr) *n.* Blood, esp. coagulated blood from a wound. [ME, filth < OE *gor.*]

Gore, Albert, Jr. Known as "Al." b. 1948. Vice President of the US (1993–2001).

Gore-Tex (gôr′tĕks, gōr′-) A trademark used for a water-repellant, breathable laminated fabric used in outerwear and shoes.

Go·rey (gôr′ē, gōr′ē), **Edward** 1925–2000. Amer. writer and illustrator whose works include *Amphigorey* (1972).

Gor·gas (gôr′gəs), **William Crawford** 1854–1920. Amer. army surgeon who suppressed yellow fever in Havana (1898) and the Panama Canal Zone (1904–13).

gorge (gôrj) *n.* **1.** A deep narrow passage with steep rocky sides;

a ravine. **2.** A narrow entrance into the outwork of a fortification. **3.** The throat; the gullet. **4.** The crop of a hawk. **5.** An instance of gluttonous eating. **6.** The contents of the stomach; something swallowed. **7.** A mass obstructing a narrow passage. **8.** The seam on the front of a coat or jacket where the lapel and the collar are joined. ❖ *v.* **gorged, gorg•ing, gorg•es** *—tr.* **1.** To stuff with food; glut. **2.** To devour greedily. *—intr.* To eat gluttonously. [ME, throat < OFr. < LLat. *gurga*, perh. < Lat. *gurges*, whirlpool, abyss.] **—gorg′er** *n.*

gor•geous (gôr′jəs) *adj.* **1a.** Dazzlingly beautiful or magnificent. **b.** Characterized by magnificence or virtuosic brilliance. **2.** *Informal* Wonderful; delightful. [ME *gorgeouse*, prob. < OFr. *gorgias*, jewelry-loving, elegant < *gorge*, throat. See GORGE.] **—gor′geous•ly** *adv.* **—gor′geous•ness** *n.*

gor•get (gôr′jĭt) *n.* **1.** A piece of armor protecting the throat. **2.** An ornamental collar. **3.** The scarflike part of a wimple covering the neck and shoulders. **4.** A band or patch of distinctive color on the throat of an animal. [ME < OFr. *gorgete*, dim. of *gorge*, throat. See GORGE.]

Gor•gon (gôr′gən) *n.* **1.** *Greek Mythology* Any of three sisters who had snakes for hair and eyes that turned the beholder into stone. **2. gorgon** A woman regarded as ugly or terrifying. [ME < Lat. *Gorgō*, *Gorgon-* < Gk. < *gorgos*, terrible.] **—Gor•go′ni•an** (-gō′nē-ən) *adj.*

gor•go•ni•an (gôr-gō′nē-ən) *n.* Any of various corals of the order Gorgonacea, having a flexible, horny, often branching skeleton. [< Lat. *gorgonia*, coral < *Gorgō*, *Gorgon-*, Gorgon. See GORGON.] **—gor•go′ni•an** *adj.*

gor•gon•ize (gôr′gə-nīz′) *tr.v.* **-ized, -iz•ing, -iz•es** To have a paralyzing or stupefying effect on.

Gor•gon•zo•la (gôr′gən-zō′lə) *n.* A pungent blue-veined pressed Italian cheese made of cow's milk. [After *Gorgonzola*, a town of northern Italy.]

go•ril•la (gə-rĭl′ə) *n.* **1.** The largest of the anthropoid apes *(Gorilla gorilla)*, native to the forests of equatorial Africa and having a stocky body and coarse dark brown or black hair. **2.** *Slang* **a.** A brutish man. **b.** A thug. [NLat. < Gk. *Gorillai*, a tribe of hairy women, perh. of African orig.]

Gö•ring also **Goe•ring** (gĕr′ĭng, gûr′-, gœ′rĭng), **Hermann Wilhelm** 1893–1946. German Nazi politician responsible for the buildup of German air forces.

Gor•ky or **Gor•ki** (gôr′kē) See **Nizhniy Novgorod.**

Gorky, Arshile 1904–48. Armenian-born Amer. painter whose works include *The Liver Is the Cock's Comb* (1944).

Gorky also **Gorki, Maksim** also **Maxim** 1868–1936. Russian writer whose works include *The Life of Klim Samgin* (1925–36), an unfinished cycle of novels.

Gor•lov•ka (gôr′ləf-kə) See **Horlivka.**

gorm (gôrm) *n. Upper Southern US* Variant of **gaum.**

gor•mand•ize (gôr′mən-dīz′) *v.* **-ized, -iz•ing, -iz•es** *—intr.* To eat gluttonously; gorge. *—tr.* To devour (food) gluttonously. [< GOURMANDISE.] **—gor′mand•iz′er** *n.*

gorm•less (gôrm′lĭs) *adj. Chiefly British* Lacking intelligence and vitality; dull. [< dialectal *gawm*, sense < ME *gome*, notice < ON *gaumr.*]

go-round (gō′round′) *n.* An argument; a go-around.

gorp (gôrp) *n.* A mixture of high-energy foods, such as nuts and dried fruit, eaten as a snack. [?]

gorse (gôrs) *n.* Any of several spiny shrubs of the genus *Ulex*, esp. *U. europaeus*, native to Europe and having fragrant yellow flowers and black pods. [ME *gorst, gors* < OE.]

go•ry (gôr′ē, gōr′ē) *adj.* **-ri•er, -ri•est 1.** Covered or stained with gore; bloody. **2.** Full of or marked by bloodshed and violence. **—gor′i•ly** *adv.* **—gor′i•ness** *n.*

gosh (gŏsh) *interj.* Used to express mild surprise or delight. [Alteration of GOD.]

gos•hawk (gŏs′hôk′) *n.* **1.** A large hawk *(Accipiter gentilis)* having rounded wings, a long tail, and gray or brown plumage. **2.** Any of several similar or related hawks. [ME *goshauk* < OE *gōshafoc* : *gōs*, goose; see GOOSE + *hafoc*, hawk; see HAWK[1].]

Go•shen (gō′shən) A region of ancient Egypt on the E delta of the Nile R.; inhabited by the Israelites from the time of Jacob until the Exodus.

Go•siute (gō′sho͞ot) *n., pl.* **Gosiute** or **-siutes 1.** A member of a Native American people inhabiting an area southwest of Great Salt Lake. **2.** The Uto-Aztecan language of this people, a dialect of Shoshone.

gos•ling (gŏz′lĭng) *n.* **1.** A young goose. **2.** A naive or inexperienced young person. [ME, var. of *gesling* < ON *gæslingr*, dim. of *gās*, goose. See **ghans-** in App.]

gos•pel (gŏs′pəl) *n.* **1.** often **Gospel** The proclamation of redemption preached by Jesus and the Apostles, which is the central content of Christian revelation. **2a. Gospel** *Bible* One of the first four New Testament books, describing the life, teaching, death, and resurrection of Jesus. **b.** A similar narrative. **3.** often **Gospel** A lection from any of the four Gospels included as part of a religious service. **4.** A teaching or doctrine of a religious teacher. **5.** *Music* Gospel music. **6.** Something, such as an idea, accepted without question. ❖ *adj.* **1.** often **Gospel** Of or in accordance with the Gospel. **2.** Of or relating to gospel music. [ME < OE *gōdspel* (ult. transl. of Gk. *euangelion*) : *gōd*, good + *spel*, news.]

gos•pel•er also **gos•pel•ler** (gŏs′pə-lər) *n.* **1.** One who teaches or professes faith in a gospel. **2.** One who reads or sings the Gospel as part of a church service.

gospel music *n.* A kind of Christian music based on American folk music, marked by strong rhythms and elaborated refrains, and incorporating elements of spirituals, blues, and jazz.

gospel side also **Gospel side** *n.* The left side of an altar or a chancel as the congregation faces it.

gos•port (gŏs′pôrt′, -pōrt′) *n.* A flexible speaking tube used for one-way communication between individual compartments or cockpits of an airplane. [After GOSPORT.]

Gosport A municipal borough of S England W of Portsmouth; an embarkation point for the invasion of France in 1944. Pop. 77,400.

gos•sa•mer (gŏs′ə-mər) *n.* **1.** A soft sheer gauzy fabric. **2.** Something delicate, light, or flimsy. **3.** A fine film of cobwebs often seen floating in the air or caught on bushes or grass. ❖ *adj.* Sheer, light, delicate, or tenuous. See Syns at **airy.** [ME *gossomer* : *gos*, goose; see GOOSE + *somer*, summer (prob. < the abundance of gossamer during early autumn when geese are in season); see SUMMER[1].] **—gos′sa•mer•y** *adj.*

gos•san (gŏs′ən, gŏz-) *n.* An oxidized, iron-bearing portion of a mineral vein overlying a sulfide deposit. [Cornish *gossen* < *gōs*, blood < O Cornish *guit.*]

gos•sip (gŏs′əp) *n.* **1.** Rumor or talk of a personal, sensational, or intimate nature. **2.** A person who habitually spreads gossip. **3.** Trivial, chatty talk or writing. **4.** A close friend or companion. **5.** *Chiefly British* A godparent. ❖ *intr.v.* **-siped, -sip•ing, -sips** To engage in or spread gossip. [ME *godsib, gossip*, godparent < OE *godsibb* : *god*, god; see GOD + *sibb*, kinsman; see **s(w)e-** in App.] **—gos′sip•er** *n.* **—gos′sip•ry** *n.* **—gos′sip•y** *adj.*

gos•sip•mon•ger (gŏs′əp-mŭng′gər, -mŏng′-) *n.* One who relates gossip.

gos•sy•pol (gŏs′ə-pôl′, -pōl′, -pŏl′) *n.* A toxic pigment, $C_{30}H_{30}O_8$, obtained from cottonseed oil and detoxified by heating, that inhibits sperm production. [NLat. *Gossypium*, genus name (< Lat. *gossypion*, cotton plant) + -OL[1].]

got (gŏt) *v.* Past tense and a past participle of **get.**

Gö•ta Canal (yœ′tə) A system of rivers, lakes, and canals of S Sweden extending from the Kattegat at the mouth of the **Göta River,** c. 93 km (58 mi), to the Baltic Sea.

got•cha (gŏch′ə) *interj.* Used to indicate understanding or to signal the fact of having caught or defeated another. ❖ *n.* A game or endeavor in which one party seeks to catch another out, as in a mistake or lie. [Contraction of *got you.*]

Gö•te•borg (yœ′tə-bôr′ē) A city of SW Sweden on the Göta Canal; founded 1604. Pop. 424,085.

goth (gŏth) *n.* **1.** A style of rock music, noted esp. for somber or ethereal tones and lugubrious lyrics. **2.** A performer or follower of this style of music. [< GOTHIC (< a view of Goth. styles or genres as dark or gloomy).]

Goth *n.* A member of a Germanic people who invaded the Roman Empire in the early Christian era. [< ME *Gothes*, Goths < LLat. *Gothī*, of Gmc. orig.; akin to OE *Gota* and ON *Goti*, Goth.]

Go•tha (gō′thə, -tä) A city of central Germany W of Erfurt. The *Almanach de Gotha*, a record of Europe's aristocratic and royal houses, was first published here in 1763. Pop. 57,662.

Goth•am (gŏth′əm) New York City. The nickname was popularized by Washington Irving in *Salmagundi*, a series of satirical sketches (1807–08). **—Goth′am•ite′** (-ə-mīt′) *n.*

Goth•ic (gŏth′ĭk) *adj.* **1a.** Of or relating to the Goths or their language. **b.** Germanic; Teutonic. **2.** Of or relating to the Middle Ages; medieval. **3a.** Of or relating to an architectural style prevalent in western Europe from the 12th through the 15th century and marked by pointed arches, rib vaulting, and a developing emphasis on verticality and the impression of height. **b.** Of or relating to an architectural style derived from medieval Gothic. **4.** Of or relating to painting or other art forms prevalent in northern Europe from the 12th through the 15th century. **5.** often **gothic** Of or relating to a style of fiction that emphasizes the grotesque, mysterious, and desolate. **6. gothic** Barbarous; crude. ❖ *n.* **1.** The extinct East Germanic language of the Goths. **2.** Gothic art or architecture. **3.** often **gothic** *Printing* **a.** See **black letter. b.** See **sans serif. 4.** A gothic novel. **—Goth′i•cal•ly** *adv.*

Gothic arch *n.* A pointed arch, esp. one with a jointed apex.

Goth•i•cism (gŏth′ĭ-sĭz′əm) *n.* **1.** The use or imitation of Gothic style. **2.** A barbarous or crude manner or style.

Goth•i•cize also **goth•i•cize** (gŏth′ĭ-sīz′) *tr.v.* **-cized, -ciz•ing, -ciz•es** To make Gothic.

Gothic revival *n.* An architectural style imitating elements of Gothic design, popular in Europe and North America from the late 18th to the beginning of the 20th century.

Got•land (gŏt′lənd, gôt′lŭnd) An island region of SE Sweden in the Baltic Sea, including **Gotland Island.**

got•ta (gŏt′ə) *Informal* Contraction of *got to: I gotta go home.*

got•ten (gŏt′n) *v.* A past participle of **get.**

göt•ter•däm•mer•ung or **Göt•ter•däm•mer•ung** (gŏt′ər-dăm′ə-rŭng′, gœt′ər-dĕm′ə-ro͝ong′) *n.* A turbulent ending of a regime or an institution. [After *Götterdämmerung*, an opera by Richard Wagner < Ger., twilight of the gods : Ger. *Götter-*, genitive pl. of *Gott*, god (< MHGer. *got* < OHGer.; see **gheu(ə)-** in

gorilla
Western lowland gorilla

Gothic
façade of the Cathedral of Notre Dame, Amiens, France

Gothic revival
House of Lords at Parliament, London

ă	**pat**	oi	**boy**
ā	**pay**	ou	**out**
âr	**care**	o͝o	**took**
ä	**father**	o͞o	**boot**
ĕ	**pet**	ŭ	**cut**
ē	**be**	ûr	**urge**
ĭ	**pit**	th	**thin**
ī	**pie**	*th*	**this**
îr	**pier**	hw	**which**
ŏ	**pot**	zh	**vision**
ō	**toe**	ə	**about,**
ô	**paw**		**item**

Stress marks:
′ (primary);
′ (secondary), as in
lexicon (lĕk′sĭ-kŏn′)

App.) + Ger. *Dämmerung,* twilight (ult. < OHGer. *demar,* twilight).]

Göt·tin·gen (gœt′ĭng-ən) A city of central Germany NE of Kassel; noted for its university. Pop. 132,454.

Gott·schalk (gŏch′ôk′, gŏt′shôk), **Louis Moreau** 1829–69. Amer. composer whose works include *The Dying Poet* (1864).

gouache (gwäsh, gōō-äsh′) *n.* **1a.** A method of painting with opaque watercolors mixed with a preparation of gum. **b.** An opaque pigment used when painting in this way. **2.** A painting executed in this manner. [Fr. < Ital. *guazzo* < Lat. *aquātiō,* watering < *aquātus,* p. part. of *aquārī,* to fetch water < *aqua,* water. See **ak^w-ā-** in App.]

Gou·da (gōō′də, gou′-) *n.* A mild close-textured cheese made from whole or partially skimmed milk. [After *Gouda,* a city in the W Netherlands.]

Gou·dy (gou′dē), **Frederic William** 1865–1947. American printer and designer of more than 90 typefaces.

gouge (gouj) *n.* **1.** A chisel with a rounded troughlike blade. **2a.** A scooping or digging action, as with such a chisel. **b.** A groove or hole scooped with or as if with such a chisel. **3.** *Informal* A large amount, as of money, exacted or extorted. ❖ *tr.v.* **gouged, goug·ing, goug·es 1.** To cut or scoop out with or as if with a gouge: "*He began to gouge a small pattern in the sand with his cane*" (Vladimir Nabokov). **2a.** To force out the eye of (a person) with one's thumb. **b.** To thrust one's thumb into the eye of. **3.** *Informal* To extort from. **4.** *Slang* To swindle. [ME < OFr. < LLat. *gubia,* var. of *gulbia,* of Celt. orig.] —**goug′er** *n.*

gou·lash (gōō′läsh′, -läsh′) *n.* **1.** A stew of beef or veal and vegetables, seasoned mainly with paprika. **2.** A mixture of many different elements; a hodgepodge. [Hung. *gulyás (hús),* herdsman's (meat), goulash < *gulya,* herdsman.]

Gould (gōōld), **Jay** 1836–92. Amer. financier who with James Fisk caused the financial panic of Sep. 24, 1869, with an attempt to corner the gold market.

Gould, Stephen Jay b. 1941. Amer. evolutionary biologist, writer, and historian of science. He developed the theory of punctuated equilibrium with Niles Eldredge (b. 1943) in 1972.

Gou·nod (gōō′nō, gōō-nō′), **Charles François** 1818–93. French composer whose operas include *Faust* (1859).

gou·ra·mi (gōō-rä′mē, gŏŏr′ə-) *n.,* pl. **-mis** Any of various freshwater fishes of the family Anabantidae of southeast Asia, capable of breathing air. [Malay *gurami,* carp, of Javanese orig.]

gourd (gôrd, gōrd, gōōrd) *n.* **1.** Any of several trailing or climbing plants related to the pumpkin, squash, and cucumber and bearing fruits with a hard rind. **2a.** The fruit of a gourd, often of unusual shape. **b.** The dried and hollowed-out shell of such a fruit, often used as a drinking utensil. [ME *gourde* < AN, ult. < Lat. *cucurbita.*]

gourde (gōōrd) *n.* See table at **currency.** [Haitian < fem. of Fr. *gourd,* dull < LLat. *gurdus,* blunt < Lat., dullard.]

gour·mand (gōōr-mänd′, gōōr′mənd) *n.* **1.** A lover of good food. **2.** A gluttonous eater. See Usage Note at **gourmet.** [ME *gourmant,* glutton < OFr. *gormant.*]

gour·man·dise (gōōr′mən-dēz′) *n.* A taste and relish for good food. [ME *gromandise,* gluttony < OFr. *gormandise < gormant,* glutton.]

gour·met (gōōr-mā′, gōōr′mā′) *n.* A connoisseur of fine food and drink. ❖ *adj.* Of or relating to fine food and drink: *a gourmet meal.* [Fr. < OFr., alteration of *groumet,* servant, valet in charge of wines < ME *grom,* boy, valet.]

> **USAGE NOTE** A *gourmet* is a person with discriminating taste in food and wine, as is a *gourmand. Gourmand* can also mean one who enjoys food in great quantities. An *epicure* is much the same as a *gourmet,* but the word may sometimes carry overtones of excessive refinement.

gout (gout) *n.* **1.** A disorder of uric-acid metabolism occurring chiefly in males, characterized by painful inflammation of the joints, esp. of the feet and hands, resulting from deposition of urate crystals around the joints. **2.** A large blob or clot: "*and makes it bleed great gouts of blood*" (Oscar Wilde). [ME *goute* < OFr., drop, gout < Med.Lat. *gutta,* drop (< ascribing gout to drops of morbid humors).] —**gout′i·ness** *n.* —**gout′y** *adj.*

Gov. *abbr.* governor

gov·ern (gŭv′ərn) *v.* **-erned, -ern·ing, -erns** —*tr.* **1.** To make and administer the public policy and affairs of; exercise sovereign authority in. **2.** To control the speed or magnitude of; regulate: *a valve that governs fuel intake.* **3.** To control the actions or behavior of. **4.** To keep under control; restrain. **5.** To exercise a deciding or determining influence on. **6.** *Grammar* To require (a specific morphological form) of accompanying words. —*intr.* **1.** To exercise political authority. **2.** To have or exercise a determining influence. [ME *governen* < OFr. *governer* < Lat. *gubernāre* < Gk. *kubernān.*] —**gov′ern·a·ble** *adj.*

Go·ver·na·dor Va·la·da·res (gŭv′ər-nə-dôr′ väl′ə-där′ĭs, gô′vĭr-nä-dôr′ vä′lä-där′ĭs) A city of E Brazil NE of Belo Horizonte. Pop. 230,403.

gov·er·nance (gŭv′ər-nəns) *n.* **1.** The act, process, or power of governing; government. **2.** The state of being governed.

gov·ern·ess (gŭv′ər-nĭs) *n.* A woman employed to educate and

train the children of a private household. [ME *governesse,* short for *governouresse* < OFr. *governeresse,* fem. of *governeor,* governor < Lat. *gubernātor.* See GUBERNATORIAL.]

gov·ern·ment (gŭv′ərn-mənt) *n.* **1.** The act or process of governing, esp. the control and administration of public policy in a political unit. **2.** The office, function, or authority of a governing individual or body. **3.** Exercise of authority in a political unit; rule. **4.** The agency or apparatus through which a governing individual or body functions and exercises authority. **5.** A governing body or organization, as: **a.** The ruling political party or coalition in a parliamentary system. **b.** The cabinet in a parliamentary system. **c.** The persons who make up a governing body. **6.** A system or policy by which a political unit is governed. **7.** Management or administration of an organization, business, or institution. **8.** Political science. **9.** *Grammar* The influence of a word over the morphological inflection of another word in a phrase or sentence. —**gov′ern·men′tal** (-mĕn′tl) *adj.* —**gov′ern·men′tal·ly** *adv.*

> **USAGE NOTE** In American usage *government* always takes a singular verb. In British usage *government,* in the sense of a governing group of officials, takes a plural verb: *The government are divided.* See Usage Note at **collective noun.**

gov·er·nor (gŭv′ər-nər) *n.* **1.** A person who governs, esp.: **a.** The chief executive of a state in the United States. **b.** An official appointed to govern a colony or territory. **c.** A member of a governing body. **2.** The manager or administrative head of an organization, business, or institution. **3.** A military commandant. **4.** *Chiefly British* Used as a form of polite address for a man. **5.** A feedback device on a machine or engine that provides automatic control, as of speed.

gov·er·nor-gen·er·al (gŭv′ər-nər-jĕn′ər-əl) *n.,* pl. **gov·er·nors-gen·er·al** or **gov·er·nor-gen·er·als** A governor who has jurisdiction over subordinate governors. —**gov′er·nor-gen′er·al·ship′** *n.*

gov·er·nor·ship (gŭv′ər-nər-shĭp′) *n.* The office, term, or jurisdiction of a governor.

Gov·er·nors Island (gŭv′ər-nərz) An island of SE NY in Upper New York Bay S of Manhattan; a residence for British colonial governors in the 17th and 18th cent.

govt. *abbr.* government

gow·an (gou′ən) *n. Scots* A yellow or white wildflower, esp. the Old World daisy. [Prob. alteration of ME *gollan,* a plant with yellow flowers; akin to ON *gullinn,* golden < *gull,* gold. See **ghel-** in App.]

Gow·er (gou′ər, gôr′, gōr′), **John** 1325?–1408. English poet whose allegorical works include *Vox Clamantis* (1382?–84).

gown (goun) *n.* **1.** A long loose flowing garment, such as a robe. **2.** A long, usu. formal dress for a woman. **3.** A robe or smock worn in hospitals as a guard against contamination. **4.** A distinctive outer robe worn on ceremonial occasions, as by scholars. **5.** The faculty and student body of a university: *town and gown.* ❖ *v.* **gowned, gown·ing, gowns** —*tr.* To clothe (oneself or another) with a gown. —*intr.* To dress in a gown. [ME *goune* < OFr. < LLat. *gunna,* leather garment.]

gowns·man (gounz′mən) *n.* One who wears a distinctive gown as a mark of profession or office.

goy (goi) *n.,* pl. **goy·im** (goi′ĭm) or **goys** *Often Offensive* A non-Jewish person; a gentile. [Yiddish < Heb. *gôy,* Jew ignorant of Judaism, non-Jew.] —**goy′ish** *adj.*

Go·ya y Lu·ci·en·tes (goi′ə ē lōō-syĕn′tĕs, gô′yä ē lōō-thyĕn′tĕs), **Francisco José de** 1746–1828. Spanish painter and etcher whose works include *The Third of May 1808* (1814).

GP *abbr.* general practitioner

GPA *abbr.* grade point average

gpd *abbr.* gallons per day

gpm *abbr.* gallons per minute

GPO *abbr.* **1.** general post office **2.** Government Printing Office

G-pro·tein (jē′prō′tēn′, -tēn′) *n.* Any of a class of proteins involved in cell metabolism that act as intermediaries between hormone receptors and effector molecules. [*G*(*TP-binding regulatory*) *protein.*]

gps *abbr.* gallons per second

GPS *abbr.* Global Positioning System

GQ *abbr.* general quarters

gr. *abbr.* **1.** grade **2.** grain (measurement) **3.** gram **4.** gravity **5.** great **6.** gross

Gr. *abbr.* **1.** Greece **2.** Greek

Graaf·i·an follicle (grä′fē-ən, gräf′ē-) *n.* Any of the fluid-filled vesicles in the mammalian ovary containing a maturing ovum. [After Regnier de *Graaf* (1641–73), Dutch physician and anatomist.]

grab¹ (grăb) *v.* **grabbed, grab·bing, grabs** —*tr.* **1.** To take or grasp suddenly. **2.** To capture or restrain; arrest. **3.** To obtain or appropriate unscrupulously or forcibly. **4.** To take hurriedly: *grabbed my hat and left.* **5.** *Slang* To capture the attention of: *a plot that grabs the reader.* —*intr.* To make a grasping or snatching motion. ❖ *n.* **1.** Sudden seizure of something or someone; a snatch. **2.** One that is grabbed. **3.** A mechanical device for gripping an object. —*idiom:* **up for grabs** *Slang* Available for anyone to take or win. [Obsolete Du. or LGer. *grabben* < MDu. or

Francisco Goya
detail from a
c. 1815 self-portrait

MLGer.] **—grab′ba•ble** *adj.* **—grab′ber** *n.*

grab² (grăb) *n.* A usu. two-masted, square-rigged Arab coastal vessel. [Ar. *ġurāb*, raven, swift galley.]

grab bag *n.* **1.** A container filled with articles, such as gifts, to be drawn unseen. **2.** *Slang* A miscellaneous collection.

grab•ble (grăb′əl) *intr.v.* **-bled, -bling, -bles 1.** To feel around with the hands; grope. **2.** To fall down; sprawl. [Prob. < Du. *grabbelen* < MDu., freq. of *grabben*, to grab.] **—grab′bler** *n.*

grab•by (grăb′ē) *adj.* **-bi•er, -bi•est** *Informal* **1.** Acquisitive or greedy. **2.** Attracting attention; striking. **—grab′bi•ness** *n.*

gra•ben (grä′bən) *n.* A usu. elongated depression between geologic faults. [Ger. *Graben* < MHGer. *grabe*, trench < OHGer. *grabo* < *graban*, to dig.]

Grac•chi (grăk′ī) See **Gracchus.**

Grac•chus (grăk′əs), **Tiberius Sempronius** 163–133 B.C. Roman social reformer who with his brother **Gaius Sempronius Gracchus** (153–121 B.C.), known together as "the Gracchi," initiated reforms to aid farmers.

grace (grās) *n.* **1.** Seemingly effortless beauty or charm of movement, form, or proportion. **2.** A characteristic or quality pleasing for its charm or refinement. **3.** A sense of fitness or propriety. **4a.** A disposition to be generous or helpful; goodwill. **b.** Mercy; clemency. **5.** A favor rendered by one who need not do so; indulgence. **6.** A temporary immunity or exemption; a reprieve. **7. Graces** *Greek & Roman Mythology* Three sister goddesses who dispense charm and beauty. **8a.** Divine love and protection bestowed freely on people. **b.** *Christianity* The state of being protected or sanctified by the favor of God. **9.** A short prayer said before or after a meal. **10. Grace** Used with *His, Her,* or *Your* as a title and form of address for a duke, duchess, or archbishop. **11.** *Music* An appoggiatura, trill, or other musical ornament. ❖ *tr.v.* **graced, grac•ing, grac•es 1.** To honor or favor. **2.** To give beauty, elegance, or charm to. **3.** *Music* To embellish with grace notes. ***—idioms:*** **in the bad graces of** Out of favor with. **in the good graces of** In favor with. **with bad grace** In a grudging manner. **with good grace** In a willing manner. [ME < OFr. < Lat. *grātia* < *grātus*, pleasing.]

grace cup *n.* **1.** A cup used at the end of a meal, usu. after grace, for the final toast. **2.** The final toast of a meal.

grace•ful (grās′fəl) *adj.* Showing grace of movement, form, or proportion. **—grace′ful•ly** *adv.* **—grace′ful•ness** *n.*

grace•less (grās′lĭs) *adj.* **1.** Lacking grace; clumsy. **2.** Having or exhibiting no sense of propriety or decency. **3.** Inferior or clumsy in treatment or performance: *a graceless production of the play.* **—grace′less•ly** *adv.* **—grace′less•ness** *n.*

grace note *n.* *Music* A note, esp. an appoggiatura, added as an embellishment.

grace period *n.* **1.** A period in which a debt may be paid without accruing interest or penalty. **2.** A period in which an insurance policy is effective though the premium is past due.

grac•ile (grăs′əl, -īl′) *adj.* **1.** Gracefully slender. **2.** Graceful. [Lat. *gracilis.*] **—gra•cil′i•ty** (grə-sĭl′ĭ-tē) *n.*

gra•ci•o•so (grä′sē-ō′sō) *n., pl.* **-sos** A clown or buffoon in Spanish comedies. [Sp. < Lat. *grātiōsus.* See GRACIOUS.]

gra•cious (grā′shəs) *adj.* **1.** Marked by kindness and warm courtesy. **2.** Marked by tact and propriety. **3.** Of a merciful or compassionate nature. **4.** Condescendingly courteous; indulgent. **5.** Marked by charm or beauty; graceful. **6.** Marked by elegance and good taste. **7.** *Archaic* Enjoying favor or grace; acceptable or pleasing. ❖ *interj.* Used to express surprise or mild emotion. [ME < OFr. *gracieus* < Lat. *grātiōsus* < *grātia*, good will. See GRACE.] **—gra′cious•ly** *adv.* **—gra′cious•ness** *n.*

grack•le (grăk′əl) *n.* **1.** Any of several American blackbirds of the family Icteridae, esp. of the genus *Quiscalus,* having iridescent blackish plumage. **2.** Any of several Asian mynas of the genus *Gracula.* [NLat. *Grācula*, genus name < Lat. *grāculus*, jackdaw.]

grad (grăd) *n.* *Informal* **1.** A graduate of a school or college. **2.** A student studying for a graduate degree, such as a PhD.

grad. *abbr.* gradient

gra•date (grā′dāt′) *v.* **-dat•ed, -dat•ing, -dates** *—intr.* To pass imperceptibly from one degree, shade, or tone to another. *—tr.* **1.** To cause to gradate. **2.** To arrange in or according to grades. [Back-formation < GRADATION.]

gra•da•tion (grā-dā′shən) *n.* **1a.** A series of gradual successive stages; a systematic progression. **b.** A degree or stage in such a progression. **2.** A passing by barely perceptible degrees from one tone or shade, as of color, to another. **3.** The act of gradating or arranging in grades. **4.** *Linguistics* See **ablaut.** [Lat. *gradātiō, gradātiōn-* < *gradus*, step. See GRADE.] **—gra•da′tion•al** *adj.* **—gra•da′tion•al•ly** *adv.*

grade (grād) *n.* **1.** A stage or degree in a process. **2.** A position in a scale of size, quality, or intensity: *a poor grade of lumber.* **3.** An accepted level or standard. **4.** A set whose members fall in the same specified limits; a class. **5a.** A level of academic development in a school: *learned fractions in the fourth grade.* **b.** A group of students at such a level: *The third grade has recess at 10:30.* **c. grades** Elementary school. **6.** A number, letter, or symbol indicating a student's level of accomplishment: *a passing grade in history.* **7.** A government service rank. **8.** The degree of inclination of a slope: *the steep grade of the mountain road.* **9.** A slope or gradual inclination, esp. of a road or railroad track: *slowed the truck when he approached the grade.* **10.** The level at which the ground surface meets the foundation of a building. **11.** A domestic animal produced by crossbreeding purebred stock with ordinary stock. **12.** *Linguistics* A degree of ablaut. ❖ *v.* **grad•ed, grad•ing, grades** *—tr.* **1.** To arrange in steps or degrees. **2.** To arrange in a series or according to a scale. **3a.** To determine the quality of (academic work, for example); evaluate: *graded the book reports.* **b.** To give a grade to (a student, for example). **4.** To level or smooth to a desired or horizontal gradient: *bulldozers graded the road.* **5.** To gradate. **6.** To improve the quality of (livestock) by crossbreeding with purebred stock. *—intr.* **1.** To hold a certain rank or position. **2.** To change or progress gradually: *piles of gravel that grade from coarse to fine.* [Fr. < Lat. *gradus.* See **ghredh-** in App.] **—grad′a•ble** *adj.*

grade crossing *n.* An intersection of railroad tracks, roads, walkways, or a combination of these at the same level.

grade point *n.* A point assigned to a course credit that corresponds to the letter grade made in a course.

grade point average *n.* The average grade of a student, the grade points earned divided by the number of credits taken.

grad•er (grā′dər) *n.* **1.** One that grades, esp.: **a.** One who grades students' work. **b.** A piece of heavy equipment used to level or smooth road or other surfaces to the desired gradient. **2.** A student in a specified class in an elementary, middle, or secondary school. Often used in combination: *tenth graders.*

grade school *n.* See **elementary school. —grade′-school′er** (grād′sko͞o′lər) *n.*

gra•di•ent (grā′dē-ənt) *n.* **1.** A rate of inclination; a slope. **2.** An ascending or descending part; an incline. **3.** The rate at which a physical quantity, such as temperature or pressure, changes from one endpoint value to another in response to changes in a given variable, esp. distance. **4.** *Mathematics* A vector having coordinate components that are the partial derivatives of a function with respect to its variables. **5.** *Biology* A series of progressively changing differences in the growth rate, metabolism, or physiological activity of a cell, organ, or organism. [Perh. GRADE + *-ient*, as in QUOTIENT.]

gra•din (grād′n) also **gra•dine** (grā′dēn′, grə-dēn′) *n.* One of a series of steps or tiered seats, as in an amphitheater. [Fr. < Ital. *gradino*, dim. of *grado*, step < Lat. *gradus.* See GRADE.]

grad school *n.* *Informal* Graduate school.

grad•u•al (grăj′o͞o-əl) *adj.* Advancing or progressing by regular or continuous degrees. ❖ *n.* *Roman Catholic Church* **1.** The liturgical book containing the chants for the Mass. **2.** A biblical text sung between the Epistle and the Gospel of the Mass. [ME, having steps < Med.Lat. *graduālis* < Lat. *gradus*, step; see GRADE. N., ME < Med.Lat. *graduāle*, the part of the service sung by the choir from the altar steps, gradual < neut. of *graduālis.*] **—grad′u•al•ly** *adv.* **—grad′u•al•ness** *n.*

grad•u•al•ism (grăj′o͞o-ə-lĭz′əm) *n.* **1.** The belief in or the policy of advancing toward a goal by gradual, often slow stages. **2.** *Biology* The view that speciation proceeds by imperceptibly small, cumulative steps over long periods of time rather than by abrupt, major changes. **—grad′u•al•ist** *n.* **—grad′u•al•is′tic** *adj.*

grad•u•ate (grăj′o͞o-āt′) *v.* **-at•ed, -at•ing, -ates** *—intr.* **1.** To be granted an academic degree or diploma. **2a.** To change gradually or by degrees. **b.** To advance to a new level of skill, achievement, or activity. *—tr.* **1a.** To grant an academic degree or diploma to. **b.** *Usage Problem* To receive an academic degree from. **2.** To arrange or divide into categories, steps, or grades. **3.** To divide into marked intervals, esp. for use in measurement. ❖ *n.* (-ĭt) **1.** One who has received an academic degree or diploma. **2.** A graduated container, such as a beaker. ❖ *adj.* (-ĭt) **1.** Possessing an academic degree or diploma. **2.** Of, intended for, or relating to studies beyond a bachelor's degree. [ME *graduaten*, to confer a degree < Med.Lat. *graduārī, graduāt-*, to take a degree < Lat. *gradus*, step. See GRADE.] **—grad′u•a′tor** *n.*

USAGE NOTE The verb *graduate* has long denoted the action of conferring an academic degree or diploma; accordingly the action of receiving a degree should be expressed in the passive, as in *She was graduated from Yale in 2000.* This usage is still current, if old-fashioned, and is acceptable to 78 percent of the Usage Panel. In general usage, however, it has largely yielded to the much more recent active pattern: *She graduated from Yale in 2000.* This pattern is acceptable to 89 percent of the Panel; it has the advantage of ascribing the accomplishment to the student, rather than to the institution. When the institution's responsibility or accomplishment is emphasized, however, the older pattern may be preferable, as in *The university graduated more computer science majors in 1997 than in the entire previous decade.* • The transitive use of *graduate,* as in *She graduated Yale in 1980,* was unacceptable to 77 percent of the Usage Panel.

grad•u•ate school (grăj′o͞o-ĭt) *n.* An institution of higher learning that grants master's degrees or doctorates or both.

grad•u•a•tion (grăj′o͞o-ā′shən) *n.* **1a.** Conferral or receipt of an academic degree or diploma marking completion of studies. **b.** A ceremony at which degrees or diplomas are conferred. **2a.** A division or interval on a graduated scale. **b.** A mark indicating the boundary of such an interval. **3.** An arrangement in or a division into stages or degrees.

gradin
Roman amphitheater, Alexandria, Egypt

ă	pat	oi	boy
ā	pay	ou	out
âr	care	o͝o	took
ä	father	o͞o	boot
ĕ	pet	ŭ	cut
ē	be	ûr	urge
ĭ	pit	th	thin
ī	pie	*th*	this
îr	pier	hw	which
ŏ	pot	zh	vision
ō	toe	ə	about, item
ô	paw		

Stress marks:
′ (primary);
′ (secondary), as in
lexicon (lĕk′sĭ-kŏn′)

Graeco– *pref.* Variant of **Greco–**.

Graf (gräf, gräf), **Stephanie Maria ("Steffi")** b. 1969. German tennis player who in 1988 won the Grand Slam (Wimbledon, French, US, and Australian titles) and an Olympic gold medal.

graf·fi·ti (grə-fēʹtē) *n.* (*used with a sing. or pl. verb*) Plural of **graffito**. [Ital., pl. of *graffito*. See GRAFFITO.]

graf·fi·tist (grə-fēʹtĭst) *n.* One who produces graffiti.

graf·fi·to (grə-fēʹtō) *n.*, *pl.* **-ti** (-tē) A drawing or inscription made on a wall or other surface. Often used in the plural with a singular verb. [Ital., dim. of *graffio*, a scratching, scribble, prob. < *graffiare*, to scratch, scribble, prob. ult. < Lat. *graphium*, stylus < Gk. *grapheion, graphion < graphein*, to write. See **gerbh–** in App.]

> **USAGE NOTE** *Graffiti* is a plural noun in Italian. As a loanword in English it is much more common than the singular *graffito*, and is mainly used as a singular noun in much the same way *data* is. Using the etymologically correct singular *graffito* to refer to a particular drawing or inscription, as in *a bold graffito on the wall*, may sound pedantic outside of an archaeological context. There is no substitute for the singular use of *graffiti* as a mass noun referring to wall drawings in general or the related social phenomenon, as in *Graffiti is a major problem for the Transit Authority Police*; it is justified by both utility and widespread precedent.

graft¹ (grăft) *v.* **graft·ed, graft·ing, grafts** —*tr.* **1a.** To unite (a shoot or bud) with a growing plant by insertion or by placing in close contact. **b.** To join (a plant or plants) by such union. **2.** To transplant or implant (living tissue, for example) surgically to replace a damaged part or compensate for a defect. **3.** To join or unite closely. —*intr.* **1.** To make a graft. **2.** To be or become joined. ❖ *n.* **1a.** A detached shoot or bud united or to be united with a growing plant. **b.** The union or point of union of a detached shoot or bud with a growing plant by insertion or attachment. **c.** A plant produced by such union. **2a.** Material that is surgically grafted, esp. living tissue or an organ. **b.** The procedure of grafting such material. **c.** The configuration or condition resulting from such a procedure. [ME *graften*, alteration of *graffen*, prob. < OFr. *grafier* < *graffe*, stylus (< its shape) < Lat. *graphium*, stylus; see GRAFFITO. N., ME *grafte*, alteration of *graffe* < OFr.] —**graftʹer** *n.*

graft² (grăft) *n.* **1.** Unscrupulous use of one's position for profit or advantages; extortion. **2.** Money or an advantage gained by unscrupulous means. ❖ *tr. & intr.v.* **graft·ed, graft·ing, grafts** To gain by or practice graft. [?] —**graftʹer** *n.*

graft·age (grăfʹtĭj) *n.* The process of making a plant graft.

graft-ver·sus-host disease (grăftʹvûrʹsəs-hōstʹ, -səz-) *n.* A pathological condition in which cells from the transplanted tissue of a donor initiate an immunologic attack on the cells and tissue of the recipient.

Gra·ham (grāʹəm, grăm), **Martha** 1894–1991. Amer. choreographer whose works include *Clytemnestra* (1958).

Graham, William Franklin ("Billy") b. 1918. Amer. religious leader who has led evangelical tours throughout the world.

graham cracker (grăm, grāʹəm) *n.* A slightly sweet, usu. rectangular cracker made with whole-wheat flour. [< GRAHAM FLOUR.]

graham flour (grăm, grāʹəm) *n.* Whole-wheat flour. [After Sylvester *Graham* (1794–1851), American cleric and social reformer.]

Gra·hame (grāʹəm), **Kenneth** 1859–1932. British writer known esp. for *The Wind in the Willows* (1908).

Gra·ham Land (grāʹəm, grăm) A region of Antarctica near the tip of the Antarctic Peninsula; part of the British Antarctic Territory and also claimed by Argentina and Chile.

Gra·ian Alps (grāʹən, grīʹən) A section of the W Alps between SE France and NW Italy rising to 4,063.5 m (13,323 ft).

grail (grāl) *n.* **1. Grail** A cup or plate that, according to medieval legend, was used by Jesus at the Last Supper and that later became the object of many chivalrous quests. **2.** often **Grail** The object of a prolonged endeavor. [ME *greal* < OFr. *graal* < Med.Lat. *gradālis*, flat dish.]

grain (grān) *n.* **1a.** A small, dry, one-seeded fruit of a cereal grass, having the fruit and the seed walls united. **b.** The fruits of cereal grasses esp. after having been harvested, considered as a group. **2a.** A cereal grass: *Wheat is grown in Kansas.* **b.** Cereal grasses considered as a group: *grain that grows along the river.* **3a.** A relatively small discrete particulate or crystalline mass: *a grain of sand.* **b.** A small amount or the smallest amount possible: *not a grain of sense.* **4.** Aerospace A mass of solid propellant. **5.** A unit of weight in the US Customary System, an avoirdupois unit equal to 0.002285 ounce (0.065 gram). **6.** The arrangement, direction, or pattern of the fibrous tissue in wood. **7a.** The side of a hide or piece of leather from which the hair or fur has been removed. **b.** The pattern or markings on this side of leather. **8.** The pattern produced, as in stone, by the arrangement of particulate constituents. **9.** The relative size of the particles composing a substance or pattern: *a coarse grain.* **10.** A painted, stamped, or printed design that imitates the pattern found in wood, leather, or stone. **11.** The direction or texture of fibers in a woven fabric. **12.** A state of fine crystallization. **13a.** Basic temperament or nature; disposition. **b.** An essential quality or characteristic. **14.** Archaic Color; tint. ❖ *v.* **grained, grain·ing, grains** —*tr.* **1.** To cause to

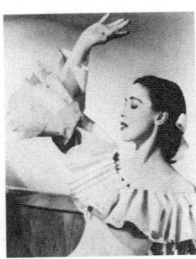

Martha Graham
performing in
Appalachian Spring

Grand Canal
Venice, Italy

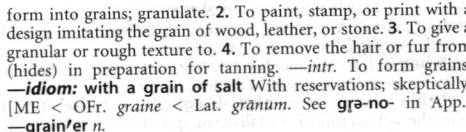

form into grains; granulate. **2.** To paint, stamp, or print with a design imitating the grain of wood, leather, or stone. **3.** To give a granular or rough texture to. **4.** To remove the hair or fur from (hides) in preparation for tanning. —*intr.* To form grains. —*idiom:* **with a grain of salt** With reservations; skeptically. [ME < OFr. *graine* < Lat. *grānum*. See **grə-no–** in App.] —**grainʹer** *n.*

grain alcohol *n.* See **alcohol** 1.

Grain Coast A historical region of W Africa along the Atlantic coast, roughly coextensive with present-day Liberia.

grain elevator *n.* A building equipped with mechanical lifting devices and used for storing grain.

grains of paradise (grānz) *pl.n.* **1.** The pungent aromatic seeds of a tropical African plant (*Aframomum melegueta*) used medicinally and in beverages. **2.** The seeds of cardamom.

grain·y (grāʹnē) *adj.* **-i·er, -i·est** **1.** Made of or resembling grain; granular. **2.** Resembling the grain of wood. **3.** Having a granular appearance. Used of photographs and film. —**grainʹi·ness** *n.*

gram¹ (grăm) *n.* A metric unit of mass equal to one thousandth (10^{-3}) of a kilogram. See table at **measurement**. [Fr. *gramme* < LLat. *gramma*, a small weight < Gk., something written, small weight. See **gerbh–** in App.]

gram² (grăm) *n.* **1.** Any of several plants, such as the chickpea, bearing seeds used as food in tropical Asia. **2.** The seeds of such a plant. [Obsolete Port. < Lat. *grānum*. See **grə-no–** in App.]

–gram *suff.* **1.** Something written or drawn; a record: *cardiogram*. **2.** A direct mail solicitation or personally delivered message or gift: *candygram*. [Gk. *-gramma < gramma*, letter; see **gerbh–** in App. Sense 2 < TELEGRAM.]

gra·ma also **gram·ma** (gräʹmə, grămʹə) *n.* Any of various pasture grasses of the genus *Bouteloua* of western North America and South America. [Am.Sp. < Sp., Bermuda grass, quitch grass < Lat. *grāmen, grāmin-*, grass.]

gram atom *n.* One mole of atoms of an element.

gram-a·tom·ic mass (grămʹə-tŏmʹĭk) *n.* The mass of one mole of atoms of an element.

gram calorie *n.* See **calorie** 1.

gram equivalent *n.* The amount of a substance whose weight in grams is numerically equal to its equivalent weight.

gra·mer·cy (grə-mûrʹsē, grămʹər-) *interj.* Archaic Used to express surprise or gratitude. [ME *gramerci* < OFr. *grand merci* : *grand*, great; see GRAND + *merci*, thanks; see MERCY.]

gram·i·ci·din (grămʹĭ-sīdʹn) *n.* An antibiotic produced by the soil bacterium *Bacillus brevis* and used against certain gram-positive bacteria. [GRAM(-POSITIVE) + –CID(E) + –IN.]

gra·min·e·ous (grə-mĭnʹē-əs) *adj.* **1.** Of, relating to, or characteristic of grasses. **2.** Of or belonging to the grass family. [< Lat. *grāmineus*, grassy < *grāmen, grāmin-*, grass.]

gram·i·niv·o·rous (grămʹə-nĭvʹər-əs) *adj.* Feeding on grasses. [Lat. *grāmen, grāmin-*, grass + –VOROUS.]

gram·ma¹ (grămʹə) *n.* Informal A grandmother. [Alteration of GRANDMA.]

gram·ma² (gräʹmə, grămʹə) *n.* Variant of **grama**.

gram·mar (grămʹər) *n.* **1a.** The study of how words and their component parts combine to form sentences. **b.** The study of structural relationships in language or in a language. **2a.** The system of inflections, syntax, and word formation of a language. **b.** The system of rules of a language, viewed as a mechanism for generating all sentences possible in that language. **3a.** A normative or prescriptive set of rules setting forth a standard of usage. **b.** Writing or speech judged with regard to such a set of rules. **4.** A book containing the morphologic, syntactic, and semantic rules for a specific language. **5a.** The basic principles of an area of knowledge: *the grammar of music.* **b.** A book dealing with such principles. [ME *gramere* < OFr. *gramaire*, alteration of Lat. *grammatica* < Gk. *grammatikē* < fem. of *grammatikos*, of letters < *gramma, grammat-*, letter. See **gerbh–** in App.]

gram·mar·i·an (grə-mârʹē-ən) *n.* A specialist in grammar.

grammar school *n.* **1.** See **elementary school**. **2.** Chiefly British A secondary or preparatory school. **3.** A school stressing the study of classical languages.

gram·mat·i·cal (grə-mătʹĭ-kəl) *adj.* **1.** Of or relating to grammar. **2.** Conforming to the rules of grammar: *a grammatical sentence.* [LLat. *grammaticalis* < Lat. *grammaticus* < Gk. *grammatikos*, of letters. See GRAMMAR.] —**gram·mat·i·cal·i·ty** (-kălʹĭ-tē) *n.* —**gram·matʹi·cal·ly** *adv.*

gram·ma·tol·o·gy (grămʹə-tŏlʹə-jē) *n.* The study and science of systems of graphic script. [< Gk. *gramma, grammat-*, letter. See GRAMMAR.] —**gram·ma·to·logʹic** (-tə-lŏjʹĭk), **gram·ma·to·logʹi·cal** *adj.* —**gram·ma·tolʹo·gist** *n.*

gramme (grăm) *n.* Chiefly British Variant of **gram¹**.

gram-mo·lec·u·lar weight (grămʹmə-lĕkʹyə-lər) *n.* See **mole⁵** 2.

gram molecule *n.* See **mole⁵** 1.

Gram·my (grămʹē) *n.* A trademark for an award for excellence in the creation and production of musical recordings.

gram-neg·a·tive or **Gram-neg·a·tive** (grămʹnĕgʹə-tĭv) *adj.* Of, relating to, or being a bacterium that does not retain the violet stain used in Gram's method.

gram·o·phone (grămʹə-fōnʹ) *n.* A record player; a phonograph. [Orig. a trademark.]

gramp (grămp) *or* **gramps** (grămps) *n. Informal* A grandfather. [Short for GRAMPA.]

gram·pa (grăm′pə) *n. Informal* A grandfather. [Alteration of GRANDPA.]

Gram·pi·an Mountains (grăm′pē-ən) A mountain range of central Scotland extending NE to SW and forming a natural barrier between the Highlands and the Lowlands.

gram-pos·i·tive *or* **Gram-pos·i·tive** (grăm′pŏz′ĭ-tĭv) *adj.* Of, relating to, or being a bacterium that retains the violet stain used in Gram's method.

gram·pus (grăm′pəs) *n.* **1.** A cetacean (*Grampus griseus*) related to and resembling the dolphins but lacking a beaklike snout. **2.** Any of various similar cetaceans, such as the killer whale. [Alteration of ME *graspeis* < OFr. *craspois, graspeis* < Med.Lat. *crassus piscis, craspiscis* : Lat. *crassus*, fat + Lat. *piscis*, fish.]

Gram·sci (grăm′shē), **Antonio** 1891–1937. Italian political leader and theorist who helped establish the Italian Communist party (1921).

Gram's method (grămz) *n.* A staining technique used to classify bacteria in which a bacterial specimen is stained with crystal violet, then treated with an iodine solution, decolorized with alcohol, and counterstained with safranine. [After Hans C.J. Gram (1853–1938), Danish physician.]

gra·na (grā′nə) *n.* Plural of **granum**.

Gra·na·da (grə-nä′də, grä-nä′thä) A city of S Spain SE of Córdoba; founded by the Moors in the 8th cent. and captured by Castilian troops in 1492. Pop. 256,7841.

gran·a·dil·la (grăn′ə-dĭl′ə, -dē′yə) *n.* **1.** Any of various tropical American passionflowers, esp. *Passiflora quadrangularis*. **2.** The egg-shaped fruit of such a plant. [Sp., dim. of *granada*, pomegranate < Lat. *grānātum* < neut. of *grānātus*, seedy. See POMEGRANATE.]

Gra·na·dos (grə-nä′dōs, grä-nä′thōs), **Enrique** 1867–1916. Spanish composer whose works include *Goyescas* (1912–14).

gran·a·ry (grăn′ə-rē, grā′nə-) *n., pl.* **-ries 1.** A building for storing threshed grain. **2.** A region yielding much grain. [Lat. *grānārium* < *grānum*, grain. See **grə-no-** in App.]

Gran Cha·co (grän′ chä′kō) A lowland plain of central South America divided among Paraguay, Bolivia, and Argentina.

grand (grănd) *adj.* **grand·er, grand·est 1.** Large and impressive in size, scope, or extent; massive. **2a.** Rich and sumptuous. **b.** Of a solemn, stately, or splendid nature. **3a.** Dignified or noble in appearance or effect. **b.** Noble or admirable in conception or intent. **c.** Lofty or sublime in character: *the grand style of the great orators.* **4.** Wonderful or very pleasing. **5.** Having higher rank than others of the same category. **6.** Having more importance than others; principal. **7.** Of a haughty or pretentious nature. **8.** Including or covering all units or aspects: *the grand total.* ❖ *n.* **1.** A grand piano. **2.** *pl.* **grand** *Slang* A thousand dollars. [ME < OFr. < Lat. *grandis.*] —**grand′ly** *adv.* —**grand′ness** *n.*

SYNONYMS *grand, magnificent, imposing, stately, majestic, august, grandiose* These adjectives mean strikingly large in size, scope, or extent. Both *grand* and *magnificent* apply to what is physically or aesthetically impressive. *Grand* implies dignity, sweep, or eminence: *a grand hotel lobby with marble floors. Magnificent* suggests splendor, sumptuousness, and grandeur: *a magnificent cathedral. Imposing* describes what impresses by virtue of its size, bearing, or power: *mountain peaks of imposing height. Stately* refers principally to what is dignified and handsome: *a stately oak. Majestic* suggests lofty dignity or nobility: *the majestic Alps. August* describes what inspires solemn reverence or awe: *the august presence of royalty. Grandiose* often suggests pretentiousness, affectation, or pompousness: *grandiose ideas.*

gran·dad·dy (grăn′dăd′ē) *n.* Variant of **granddaddy**.

gran·dam (grăn′dăm′, -dəm) *also* **gran·dame** (-dām′, -dăm, -dəm) *n.* **1.** The mother of one's father or mother; a grandmother. **2.** An old woman. [ME *grandame* < OFr. *grant-dame* : *dame*, lady; see DAME + *grant, grand*, great; see GRAND.]

grand·aunt (grănd′ănt′, -änt′) *n.* See **great-aunt**.

grand·ba·by (grănd′bā′bē, grăn′-) *n., pl.* **-bies** *Informal* A grandchild.

Grand Ba·ha·ma (bə-hä′mə) An island of the Bahamas in the Atlantic Ocean E of West Palm Beach FL.

Grand Banks An extensive area of shoals in the W Atlantic Ocean off SE Newfoundland, Canada.

Grand Canal 1. An inland waterway, c. 1,609 km (1,000 mi), of E China extending from Tianjin to Hangzhou; begun in the 6th to 5th cent. B.C. and completed in the 13th cent. A.D. **2.** The principal waterway of Venice, Italy.

Grand Canary The chief island of the Canary Is. in the Atlantic Ocean ESE of Tenerife I.

Grand Canyon A gorge of the Colorado R. in NW AZ up to 1.6 km (1 mi) deep, from 6.4 to 29 km (4 to 18 mi) wide, and more than 321.8 km (200 mi) long.

Grand Cayman See **Cayman Islands**.

grand·child (grănd′chīld′, grăn′-) *n.* A child of one's son or daughter.

Grand Coulee A gorge, c. 48 km (30 mi), of N-central WA, carved by the Columbia R.

grand·dad (grăn′dăd′) *n. Informal* A grandfather.

grand·dad·dy *also* **gran·dad·dy** (grăn′dăd′ē) *n., pl.* **-dies** *Informal* A grandfather.

grand·daugh·ter (grăn′dô′tər) *n.* A daughter of one's son or daughter.

grand duchess *n.* **1.** The wife or widow of a grand duke. **2.** A woman who is the sovereign of a grand duchy. **3.** The daughter or granddaughter of a czar in the male line. **4.** Used as the title for such a noblewoman.

grand duchy *n.* A territory ruled by a grand duke or grand duchess.

grand duke *n.* **1.** A nobleman who is the sovereign of a grand duchy. **2.** A son or grandson of a czar in the male line. **3.** Used as the title for such a nobleman.

Gran·de (grăn′də, grän′dī), **Rio** A river, c. 1,046 km (650 mi), flowing from SE Brazil to the Paranaíba R.

grande dame (gränd′ dăm′, gränd′ däm′) *n., pl.* **grandes dames** *also* **grand dames** (gränd′ dăm′, gränd′ däm′) **1.** A highly respected elderly or middle-aged woman. **2.** A respected woman having extensive experience in her field. [Fr.]

gran·dee (grăn-dē′) *n.* **1a.** A nobleman of the highest rank in Spain or Portugal. **b.** Used as the title for such a nobleman. **2.** A person of eminence or high rank. [Sp. *grande* < Lat. *grandis*, great.]

Grande-Terre (gränd′târ′, gränd-) An island of E Guadeloupe in the Leeward Is. of the West Indies.

gran·deur (grăn′jər, -jŏŏr′) *n.* **1.** The quality or condition of being grand; magnificence. **2.** Nobility or greatness of character. [ME < OFr. < *grand*, great < Lat. *grandis*.]

Grand Falls See **Churchill Falls**.

grand·fa·ther (grănd′fä′thər, grăn′-) *n.* **1.** The father of one's mother or father. **2.** A forefather; an ancestor. ❖ *tr.v.* **-thered, -ther·ing, -thers** To exempt (one already involved in an activity or business) from new regulations.

grandfather clause *n.* **1.** A provision in a statute exempting those already involved in a regulated activity from the new regulations in the statute. **2.** A clause in the constitutions of several southern states before 1915, intended to disfranchise African Americans by exempting from stringent voting requirements all lineal descendants of persons registered before 1867.

grandfather clock *n.* A pendulum clock enclosed in a tall narrow cabinet. [From the song *My Grandfather's Clock* by Henry Clay Work (1832–84), American songwriter.]

grand·fa·ther·ly (grănd′fä′thər-lē, grăn′-) *adj.* **1.** Characteristic of or befitting a grandfather. **2.** Having the qualities of a grandfather.

Grand Forks A city of E ND on the Red R. N of Fargo; est. as a fur-trading post in 1801. Pop. 49,321.

Grand Gui·gnol (grän gē-nyôl′) *n.* Drama emphasizing the horrifying or macabre. [After Le *Grand Guignol*, a theater in Paris.]

gran·dil·o·quent (grăn-dĭl′ə-kwənt) *adj.* Pompous or bombastic. [< Lat. *grandiloquus* : *grandis*, great + *loquī*, to speak.] —**gran·dil′o·quence** *n.* —**gran·dil′o·quent·ly** *adv.*

gran·di·ose (grăn′dē-ōs′, grăn′dē-ōs′) *adj.* **1.** Marked by greatness of scope or intent. See Syns at **grand**. **2.** Marked by feigned or affected grandeur; pompous. [Fr. < Ital. *grandioso* < *grande*, great < Lat. *grandis*.] —**gran′di·ose′ly** *adv.* —**gran′di·os′i·ty** (-ŏs′ĭ-tē), **gran′di·ose′ness** *n.*

gran·di·o·so (grän′dē-ō′sō, -zō, grän′-) *adv. & adj. Music* In a grand and noble style. [Ital. See GRANDIOSE.]

grand jury *n.* A jury of 12 to 23 persons convened in private session to evaluate accusations against persons charged with crime and determine whether a bill of indictment is warranted.

grand·kid (grănd′kĭd′, grăn′-) *n. Informal* A grandchild.

Grand Lama *n.* Either of two high lamas of Tibetan Buddhism, the Dalai Lama or the Panchen Lama.

grand larceny *n.* The theft of property of a value exceeding the amount constituting petit larceny.

grand·ma (grănd′mä′, grăn′-, grăm′mä′, grăm′ə) *n. Informal* A grandmother.

grand mal (grăn′ măl′, măl′, grănd′) *n.* A severe form of epilepsy characterized by seizures involving spasms and loss of consciousness. [Fr. : *grand*, great + *mal*, illness.]

Grand Ma·nan Island (mə-năn′) An island of S New Brunswick, Canada, in the Bay of Fundy separated from the coast of ME by **Grand Manan Channel**.

grand master *or* **grand·mas·ter** (grănd′măs′tər) *n.* **1.** A chess player regarded as having the highest level of ability. **2.** A person of the highest competence or accomplishment in a field.

grand·moth·er (grănd′mŭth′ər, grăn′-) *n.* **1.** The mother of one's father or mother. **2.** A female ancestor.

grand·moth·er·ly (grănd′mŭth′ər-lē, grăn′-) *adj.* **1.** Characteristic of or befitting a grandmother. **2.** Having the qualities of a grandmother.

grand·neph·ew (grănd′nĕf′yōō, grăn′-) *n.* A son of one's nephew or niece.

grand·niece (grănd′nēs′, grăn′-) *n.* A daughter of one's nephew or niece.

grand opera *n.* **1.** A serious or tragic opera for which the entire text is set to music. **2.** A lavishly produced opera.

grand·pa (grănd′pä′, grăn′-, grăm′pä′, grăm′pə) *n. Informal* A grandfather.

Grand Canyon

grandfather clock

ă pat	oi boy
ā pay	ou out
âr care	ŏŏ took
ä father	ōō boot
ĕ pet	ŭ cut
ē be	ûr urge
ĭ pit	th thin
ī pie	th this
îr pier	hw which
ŏ pot	zh vision
ō toe	ə about,
ô paw	item

Stress marks:
′ (primary);
′ (secondary), as in
lexicon (lĕk′sĭ-kŏn′)

grand·par·ent (grănd′pâr′ənt, -păr′-, grăn′-) *n.* A parent of one's mother or father; a grandmother or grandfather. —**grand′par′ent·hood′** *n.*

grand piano *n.* A piano having the strings strung in a horizontal harp-shaped frame supported usu. on three legs.

Grand Prairie A city of NE TX between Dallas and Fort Worth. Pop. 127,427.

Grand Prix (grän′ prē′) *n., pl.* **Grand Prix** (prēz′, prē′) Any of several competitive international road races for sports cars of specific engine size over an exacting, usu. risky course. [Fr., short for *Grand Prix de Paris,* orig. an international horserace established in 1863 at Longchamp in Paris.]

Grand Rapids (grănd) A city of W-central MI on the Grand R. WNW of Lansing. Pop. 197,800.

Grand River 1. A river rising in SE IA and flowing c. 483 km (300 mi) across NW MO to the Missouri R. **2.** A river of S MI flowing c. 418 km (260 mi) to Lake Michigan.

grand·sire (grănd′sīr′, grăn′-) also **grand·sir** (-sər) *n. Archaic* **1.** A grandfather. **2.** A male ancestor; a forefather. **3.** An old man.

grand slam *n.* **1.** The winning of all the tricks during the play of one hand in bridge and other whist-derived card games. **2.** *Sports* The winning of all the major or specified events, esp. on a professional circuit. **3.** *Baseball* A home run hit when three runners are on base.

grand·son (grănd′sŭn′, grăn′-) *n.* A son of one's son or daughter.

grand·stand (grănd′stănd′, grăn′-) *n.* **1.** A roofed stand for spectators at a stadium or racetrack. **2.** The spectators or audience at an event. ❖ *intr.v.* **-stand·ed, -stand·ing, -stands** To perform ostentatiously so as to impress an audience. —**grand′stand′er** *n.*

Grand Te·ton (tē′tŏn′, tĕt′n) A mountain, 4,198.6 m (13,766 ft), of the Teton Range in NW WY.

grand tour *n.* **1.** A comprehensive tour or survey. **2.** An extended tour of continental Europe formerly considered a finishing course for young English gentlemen.

Grand Turk The chief island of the Turks and Caicos Is. in the Atlantic Ocean SE of the Bahamas. The town of **Grand Turk** (pop. 3,146) is the cap. of the island group.

grand·un·cle (grănd′ŭng′kəl) *n.* See **great-uncle.**

grand unified theory *n. Physics* A theory of elementary forces that views the weak, strong, electromagnetic, and gravitational interactions as low-energy manifestations of a single unified interaction.

grange (grānj) *n.* **1.** **Grange** *Chiefly Northeastern US* **a.** An association of farmers founded in the United States in 1867. **b.** One of the branch lodges of this association. **2.** *Chiefly British* A farm, esp. the residence and outbuildings of a gentleman farmer. **3.** *Archaic* A granary. [ME, granary < OFr. < VLat. *grānica* < Lat. *grānum,* seed. See **grə-no-** in App.]

grang·er (grān′jər) *n.* **1.** *Chiefly Upper Midwest* A farmer. **2.** **Granger** *Chiefly Northeastern US* A member of the Grange.

grani– *pref.* Grain; seed: *granivorous.* [Lat. *grāni-* < *grānum,* seed. See **grə-no-** in App.]

gra·ni·ta (grə-nē′tə) *n.* A granular dessert ice with a sugar-syrup base, usu. flavored with fruit purée, coffee, or wine. [Ital. < fem. part. of *granire,* to make grainy, granulate. See **GRANITE.**]

gran·ite (grăn′ĭt) *n.* **1.** A common, coarse-grained, hard igneous rock consisting chiefly of quartz, orthoclase or microcline, and mica, used for building. **2.** Unyielding endurance; steadfastness. [Ital. *granito* < p. part. of *granire,* to make grainy < *grano,* grain < Lat. *grānum,* seed. See **grə-no-** in App.] —**gra·nit′ic** (grə-nĭt′ĭk, grə-), **gran′it·oid′** (grăn′ĭ-toid′) *adj.*

gran·ite·ware (grăn′ĭt-wâr′) *n.* **1.** Iron utensils with a mottled enamel resembling granite. **2.** Earthenware with a speckled glaze resembling granite.

gra·niv·o·rous (grə-nĭv′ər-əs) *adj.* Feeding on grain and seeds.

gran·ny or **gran·nie** (grăn′ē) *n., pl.* **-nies 1.** *Informal* A grandmother. **2.** *Informal* A fussy person. **3.** *Chiefly Southern US* See **midwife** 1. [Short for **GRANDMOTHER** or **GRANDAM.**]

granny knot *n.* A knot resembling a square knot but with the second tie crossed incorrectly. [So called in contempt.]

Granny Smith *n.* A variety of apple having green skin and tart, tough flesh. [After Maria Ann *Smith* (died 1870), Australian woman to whom its development is attributed.]

grano– *pref.* Granite: *granolith.* [Ger. < *Granit,* granite < Ital. *granito.* See **GRANITE.**]

gra·no·la (grə-nō′lə) *n.* Rolled oats and various ingredients, such as nuts. [Orig. a trademark.]

gran·o·lith (grăn′ə-lĭth′) *n.* A paving stone of crushed granite and cement. —**gran′o·lith′ic** *adj.*

gran·o·phyre (grăn′ə-fīr′) *n.* A fine-grained granite porphyry having a groundmass with irregular intergrowths of quartz and feldspar. [Ger. *Granophyr: grano-,* grano- + *(Por)phyr,* porphyry (< Med.Lat. *porphyrium;* see **PORPHYRY.**)]

grant (grănt) *tr.v.* **grant·ed, grant·ing, grants 1.** To consent to the fulfillment of. **2.** To accord as a favor, prerogative, or privilege. **3a.** To bestow; confer: *grant aid.* **b.** To transfer (property) by a deed. **4.** To concede; acknowledge. ❖ *n.* **1.** The act of granting. **2a.** Something granted. **b.** A giving of funds for a specific purpose. **3.** *Law* **a.** A transfer of property by deed. **b.** The prop-

erty so transferred. **c.** The deed by which the property is so transferred. **4.** One of several tracts of land in New Hampshire, Maine, and Vermont originally granted to an individual or a group. [ME *granten* < OFr. *granter,* var. of *creanter* < VLat. **crēdentāre,* to assure < Lat. *crēdēns, crēdent-,* pr. part. of *crēdere,* to believe. See **kerd-** in App.] —**grant′a·ble** *adj.* —**grant′er** *n.*

Grant, Cary 1904–86. British-born Amer. actor whose films include *The Philadelphia Story* (1940).

Grant, Ulysses Simpson 1822–85. The 18th President of the US (1869–77) and a Civil War general. After his victorious Vicksburg campaign (1862–63) he was made commander in chief of the Union Army (1864) and accepted the surrender of Gen. Robert E. Lee at Appomattox (1865).

grant·ee (grăn-tē′) *n. Law* One to whom a grant is made.

grant-in-aid (grănt′ĭn-ād′) *n., pl.* **grants-in-aid** (grănts′-) **1.** A giving of federal funds to a state or local government to subsidize a public project. **2.** A giving of funds to an institution or a person in order to subsidize a project or program.

gran·tor (grăn′tər, -tôr′) *n. Law* One that makes a grant.

gran·u·lar (grăn′yə-lər) *adj.* **1.** Composed of or appearing to be composed of granules or grains. **2.** Having a grainy texture. **3.** *Biology* Containing granules: *granular cells.* —**gran′u·lar′i·ty** (-lăr′ĭ-tē) *n.* —**gran′u·lar·ly** *adv.*

gran·u·late (grăn′yə-lāt′) *v.* **-lat·ed, -lat·ing, -lates** —*tr.* **1.** To form into grains or granules. **2.** To make rough and grainy. —*intr.* To become granular or grainy. —**gran′u·la·tive** *adj.* —**gran′u·la·tor** *n.*

gran·u·la·tion (grăn′yə-lā′shən) *n.* **1a.** The act or process of granulating. **b.** The condition or appearance of being granulated. **2a.** Small fleshy beadlike outgrowths of new capillaries on the surface of a wound that is healing. **b.** The formation of these protuberances. **3.** The transient brilliant granular markings on the photosphere of the sun.

gran·ule (grăn′yōōl) *n.* **1.** A small grain or pellet; a particle. **2.** *Geology* A rock fragment larger than a sand grain and smaller than a pebble, between 2 and 4 millimeters in diameter. **3.** *Astronomy* One of the transient brilliant markings on the photosphere of the sun. **4.** *Biology* A cellular or cytoplasmic particle, esp. one that stains readily. [LLat. *grānulum,* dim. of Lat. *grānum,* grain. See **grə-no-** in App.]

gran·u·lite (grăn′yə-līt′) *n.* A fine-grained metamorphic rock often banded in appearance and composed chiefly of feldspar and quartz. —**gran′u·lit′ic** (-lĭt′ĭk) *adj.*

gran·u·lo·cyte (grăn′yə-lō-sīt′) *n.* Any of a group of white blood cells having cytoplasmic granules.

gran·u·lo·ma (grăn′yə-lō′mə) *n., pl.* **-mas** or **-ma·ta** (-mə-tə) A mass of inflamed granulation tissue, usu. associated with infections. —**gran′u·lo′ma·tous** (-mə-təs) *adj.*

gran·u·lose (grăn′yə-lōs′) *adj.* Having a surface covered with granules.

gra·num (grā′nəm) *n., pl.* **-na** (-nə) A stacked chlorophyll-containing structure within a chloroplast that is the site of the light reactions of photosynthesis. [Lat. *grānum,* seed. See **GRAIN.**]

Gran·ville-Bar·ker (grăn′vĭl-bär′kər), **Harley** 1877–1946. British actor, playwright, and theater manager known for his Shakespearean criticism.

grape (grāp) *n.* **1.** Any of numerous woody vines of the genus *Vitis,* bearing edible berries and cultivated in many species and varieties. **2.** The fleshy smooth-skinned purple, red, or green berry of a grape, eaten raw or dried as a raisin and used in winemaking. **3.** A dark violet to dark grayish purple. **4.** Grapeshot. [ME < OFr., bunch of grapes, hook, of Gmc. orig.] —**grap′ey, grap′y** *adj.*

grape fern *n.* Any of various ferns of the genus *Botrychium,* having a fertile frond bearing grapelike clusters of spore cases.

grape·fruit (grāp′frōōt′) *n.* **1.** A tropical or semitropical evergreen (*Citrus paradisi*) cultivated for its edible fruit. **2.** Its large round fruit having juicy, somewhat acid pulp.

grape hyacinth *n.* Any of various Eurasian plants of the genus *Muscari,* having rounded, usu. blue flowers.

grape·shot (grāp′shŏt′) *n.* A cluster of small iron balls formerly used as a cannon charge.

grape sugar *n.* Dextrose obtained from grapes.

grape·vine (grāp′vīn′) *n.* **1.** A vine on which grapes grow. **2a.** The informal transmission of information, gossip, or rumor. **b.** A source of confidential information.

graph¹ (grăf) *n.* **1.** A diagram that shows the relation, often functional, between two sets of numbers as a set of points having coordinates determined by the relation. **2.** A pictorial device, such as a pie chart, used to illustrate quantitative relationships. ❖ *tr.v.* **graphed, graph·ing, graphs 1.** To represent by a graph. **2.** To plot (a function) on a graph. [Short for *graphic formula.*]

graph² (grăf) *n.* **1.** The spelling of a word. **2.** Any of the possible forms of a grapheme. **3.** A written character that represents a phoneme, syllable, word, or other expression and cannot be further analyzed. [Gk. *graphē,* writing. See **GRAPHIC.**]

–graph *suff.* **1.** Something written or drawn: *monograph.* **2.** An instrument for writing, drawing, or recording: *seismograph.* [Fr. *-graphe* < LLat. *-graphus* < Gk. *-graphos* < *graphein,* to write. See **gerbh-** in App.]

graph·eme (grăf′ēm′) *n.* **1.** A letter of an alphabet. **2.** All of the

Ulysses S. Grant

letters and letter combinations that represent a phoneme, as *f, ph,* and *gh* for the phoneme /f/. [GRAPH² + –EME.] **—gra•phe′mic** (grə-fē′mĭk) *adj.* **—gra•phe′mi•cal•ly** *adv.*

–grapher *suff.* One who writes about a specified subject or in a specified manner: *stenographer.* [< LLat. *-graphus* < Gk. *-graphos* < *graphein,* to write. See **gerbh-** in App.]

graph•ic (grăf′ĭk) *adj.* also **graph•i•cal** (-ĭ-kəl) **1a.** Of or relating to written representation. **b.** Of or relating to pictorial representation. **2.** Of, relating to, or represented by or as if by a graph. **3a.** Described in vivid detail. **b.** Clearly outlined or set forth. **4.** Of or relating to the graphic arts. **5.** Of or relating to graphics. **6.** *Geology* Having crystals resembling printed characters. ❖ *n.* **1.** A work of graphic art. **2.** A pictorial device used for illustration, as a slide. **3.** A graphic display generated by a computer or an imaging device. [Lat. *graphicus* < Gk. *graphikos* < *graphē,* writing < *graphein,* to write. See **gerbh-** in App.] **—graph′i•cal•ly** *adv.* **—graph′ic•ness** *n.*

SYNONYMS *graphic, lifelike, realistic, vivid* These adjectives mean strikingly sharp and accurate: *a graphic account of the battle; a lifelike portrait; a realistic description; a vivid recollection.*

graphical user interface *n.* See **GUI.**

graphic arts *pl.n.* **1.** The visual arts and associated techniques involving the application of lines and strokes to a two-dimensional surface. **2.** The visual arts and associated techniques in which images are made by blocks, plates, or type.

graphic novel *n.* A novel whose narrative is related through both text and art, often in comic-strip form.

graph•ics (grăf′ĭks) *n.* **1a.** (*used with a sing. verb*) The making of drawings in accordance with the rules of mathematics. **b.** (*used with a pl. verb*) Calculations from such drawings. **2.** (*used with a sing. or pl. verb*) See **graphic arts** 2. **3.** *Computer Science* **a.** (*used with a sing. or pl. verb*) The pictorial representation of data, as in computer-aided design, typesetting, and video games. **b.** (*used with a sing. verb*) The process by which a computer displays data pictorially.

graph•ite (grăf′īt′) *n.* A soft, gray to black, hexagonally crystallized allotrope of carbon with a metallic luster, used in lead pencils, lubricants, and coatings and fabricated into a variety of forms such as molds and electrodes. [Gk. *graphein,* to write; see **gerbh-** in App. + –ITE¹.] **—gra•phit′ic** (grə-fĭt′ĭk) *adj.*

graph•i•tize (grăf′ĭ-tīz′) *tr.v.* **-tized, -tiz•ing, -tiz•es 1.** To convert into graphite, as by heating. **2.** To coat or impregnate with graphite. **—graph′i•ti•za′tion** (-tĭ-zā′shən) *n.*

gra•phol•o•gy (grə-fŏl′ə-jē) *n.* The study of handwriting, esp. for analyzing character. [Gk. *graphē,* writing; see GRAPHIC + –LOGY.] **—gra•phol′o•gist** *n.*

graph paper *n.* Paper ruled usu. into small squares of equal size for use in drawing charts, graphs, or diagrams.

–graphy *suff.* **1.** Writing or representation produced in a specified manner or by a specified process: *photography.* **2a.** Writing about a specified subject: *oceanography.* **b.** Representation of a specified object: *phonography.* [Lat. *-graphia* < Gk. *-graphia* < *graphein,* to write. See **gerbh-** in App.]

grap•nel (grăp′nəl) *n.* **1.** *Nautical* A small anchor with three or more flukes, esp. for anchoring a small vessel. **2.** See **grapple** 1a. [ME *grapenel,* prob. ult. < OFr. *grapin,* hook, dim. of *grape.* See GRAPE.]

grap•pa (grä′pə) *n.* An Italian brandy distilled from the pomace of grapes used in winemaking. [Ital. < Ital. dialectal, grape stalk, brandy, of Gmc. orig.]

grap•ple (grăp′əl) *n.* **1a.** An iron shaft with claws at one end, usu. thrown by a rope and used for grasping and holding, esp. of an enemy ship alongside. **b.** *Nautical* See **grapnel** 1. **2.** The act of grappling. **3a.** A contest in which the participants attempt to clutch or grip each other. **b.** A struggle for superiority or dominance. ❖ *v.* **-pled, -pling, -ples** —*tr.* **1.** To seize and hold, as with a grapple. **2.** To seize firmly, as with the hands. —*intr.* **1.** To hold onto something with or as if with a grapple. **2.** To use a grapple or similar device. **3.** To struggle in or as if in wrestling. [ME *grapel* < OFr. *grapil,* dim. of *grape,* hook. See GRAPE.] **—grap′pler** *n.*

grap•pling (grăp′lĭng) *n.* **1.** See **grapple** 1a. **2.** *Nautical* See **grapnel** 1.

grappling hook *n.* See **grapple** 1a.

grappling iron *n.* See **grapple** 1a.

grap•to•lite (grăp′tə-līt′) *n.* Any of numerous extinct colonial marine animals chiefly of the orders Dendroidea and Graptoloidea of the late Cambrian to the early Mississippian periods, whose fossils help date Paleozoic rocks. [Gk. *graptos,* written (< *graphein,* to write; see GRAPHIC) + –LITE.]

grap•y (grā′pē) *adj.* **-i•er, -i•est** Variant of **grapey.**

GRAS *abbr.* generally recognized as safe (US Food and Drug Administration label)

Gras•mere (grăs′mîr′) A lake of NW England in the Lake District. Dove Cottage, in the former village of **Grasmere,** was the home of William Wordsworth from 1799 to 1808.

grasp (grăsp) *v.* **grasped, grasp•ing, grasps** —*tr.* **1.** To take hold of or seize firmly with or as if with the hand. **2.** To clasp firmly with or as if with the hand. **3.** To take hold of intellectually; comprehend. See Syns at **apprehend.** —*intr.* **1.** To make a motion of seizing, snatching, or clutching. **2.** To show eager and prompt willingness or acceptance. ❖ *n.* **1.** The act of grasping. **2a.** A firm hold or grip. **b.** An embrace. **3.** The ability or power to seize or attain; reach. **4.** Understanding; comprehension. [ME *graspen.*]

grasp•ing (grăs′pĭng) *adj.* Exceedingly eager for material gain; avaricious. **—grasp′ing•ly** *adv.* **—grasp′ing•ness** *n.*

grass (grăs) *n.* **1a.** The grass family. **b.** The members of the grass family considered as a group. **2.** Any of various plants having slender leaves characteristic of the grass family. **3.** An expanse of ground covered with grass or similar plants. **4.** Grazing land; pasture. **5.** *Slang* Marijuana. **6.** *Electronics* Small variations in amplitude of an oscilloscope display caused by electrical noise. ❖ *v.* **grassed, grass•ing, grass•es** —*tr.* **1a.** To cover with grass. **b.** To grow grass on. **2.** To feed (livestock) with grass. —*intr.* **1.** To become covered with grass. **2.** To graze. [ME *gras* < OE *græs.*]

Grass (gräs), **Günter Wilhelm** Born 1927. German writer best known for his novel *The Tin Drum* (1959). He won the 1999 Nobel Prize for literature.

Grasse (grăs, gräs) A town of SE France W of Nice; long noted for its perfume industry. Pop. 42,077.

Grasse, Comte **François Joseph Paul de** 1722?–88. French naval officer who during the American Revolution commanded the French fleet in Chesapeake Bay.

grass family *n.* A large and widespread family of plants, the Gramineae (or Poaceae), characterized by usu. hollow stems, sheath-forming leaves, and minute flowers arranged in spikelets and including wheat, rice, and plants for fodder.

grass green *n.* A moderate yellow-green to strong or dark yellowish-green. **—grass′-green′** (grăs′grēn′) *adj.*

grass•hop•per (grăs′hŏp′ər) *n.* **1.** Any of numerous orthopteran insects of the families Locustidae (or Acrididae) and Tettigoniidae, often destructive to plants and typically having long hind legs adapted for jumping. **2.** A light, usu. unarmed airplane for liaison and scouting. **3.** A cocktail consisting of crème de menthe, crème de cacao, and cream.

grasshopper
lubber grasshopper

grass•land (grăs′lănd′) *n.* An area, such as a prairie or meadow, of grass or grasslike vegetation.

Gras•so (grăs′ō, grä′sō), **Ella Tambussi** 1919–81. Amer. public official who served as governor of CT (1975–81).

grass•plot (grăs′plŏt′) *n. Eastern US* See **parking** 3. See Regional Note at **parking.**

grass roots *pl.n.* (*used with a sing. or pl. verb*) **1.** People or society at a local level instead of the political center. **2.** The groundwork or source. **—grass′-roots′** (grăs′ro͞ots′, -ro͝ots′) *adj.*

grass snake *n.* Any of several greenish nonvenomous snakes, esp. *Natrix natrix* of Europe.

grass tree *n.* Any of several woody-stemmed Australian plants of the genus *Xanthorrhoea,* having grasslike leaves and white flowers.

grass widow *n.* **1.** A divorced or separated woman. **2.** A woman whose husband is temporarily absent. **3.** An abandoned mistress. **4.** The mother of a child born out of wedlock.

grass widower *n.* **1.** A divorced or separated man. **2.** A man whose wife is temporarily absent.

grass•y (grăs′ē) *adj.* **-i•er, -i•est 1.** Covered with or abounding in grass. **2.** Resembling or suggestive of grass.

grate¹ (grāt) *v.* **grat•ed, grat•ing, grates** —*tr.* **1.** To reduce to fragments, shreds, or powder by rubbing against an abrasive surface. **2.** To cause to make a harsh grinding or rasping sound through friction: *grated her teeth.* **3.** To irritate or annoy persistently. **4.** *Archaic* To rub or wear away. —*intr.* **1.** To make a harsh rasping sound by or as if by scraping or grinding. **2.** To cause irritation or annoyance: *grates on my nerves.* ❖ *n.* A harsh rasping sound made by scraping or rubbing. [ME *graten* < OFr. *grater,* to scrape, of Gmc. orig.]

grate² (grāt) *n.* **1.** A framework of parallel or latticed bars for blocking an opening. **2.** A framework of metal bars used to hold fuel or food in a stove, furnace, or fireplace. **3.** A fireplace. **4.** A perforated iron plate or screen for sieving and grading crushed ore. ❖ *tr.v.* **grat•ed, grat•ing, grates** To equip with a grate. [ME < Med.Lat. *grāta,* alteration of Lat. *crātis,* wickerwork.]

grate²
window grate

grate•ful (grāt′fəl) *adj.* **1.** Appreciative of benefits; thankful. **2.** Expressing gratitude. **3.** Affording pleasure or comfort; agreeable. [< obsolete *grate,* pleasing < Lat. *grātus.*] **—grate′ful•ly** *adv.* **—grate′ful•ness** *n.*

grat•er (grā′tər) *n.* One that grates, as an implement with sharp-edged slits and perforations on which to grate foods.

Gra•tian (grā′shən, -shē-ən) A.D. 359–383. Emperor of Rome (367–383) who ruled jointly (from 379) with Theodosius I.

grat•i•fi•ca•tion (grăt′ə-fĭ-kā′shən) *n.* **1a.** The act of gratifying. **b.** The state of being gratified. **2.** An instance or a cause of being gratified. **3.** *Archaic* **a.** A reward. **b.** A gratuity.

grat•i•fy (grăt′ə-fī′) *tr.v.* **-fied, -fy•ing, -fies 1.** To please or satisfy. **2.** To give what is desired to; indulge. **3.** *Archaic* To reward. [ME *gratifien,* to favor < Lat. *grātificārī* : *grātus,* pleasing + *-ficārī,* -fy.] **—grat′i•fi′er** *n.* **—grat′i•fy′ing** *adj.*

gra•tin (grät′n, grăt′n, grä-tăɴ′) *n.* A top crust consisting of browned crumbs and butter, often with grated cheese. [Fr. < obsolete *grater,* to scratch, scrape < OFr. See GRATE¹.]

grat•ing (grā′tĭng) *n.* **1.** A grate set in a window or door or used as a partition. **2.** A diffraction grating.

ă	pat	oi	boy
ā	pay	ou	out
âr	care	o͝o	took
ä	father	o͞o	boot
ĕ	pet	ŭ	cut
ē	be	ûr	urge
ĭ	pit	th	thin
ī	pie	*th*	this
îr	pier	hw	which
ŏ	pot	zh	vision
ō	toe	ə	about,
ô	paw		item

Stress marks:
′ (primary);
′ (secondary), as in
lexicon (lĕk′sĭ-kŏn′)

grat·is (grăt′ĭs, grä′tĭs, grä′-) *adv. & adj.* Without charge. [ME < Lat. *grātīs*, alteration of *grātiīs*, out of kindness, free, ablative pl. of *grātia*, kindness.]

grat·i·tude (grăt′ĭ-tōōd′, -tyōōd′) *n.* The state of being grateful; thankfulness. [ME < OFr., prob. < LLat. *grātitūdō* < Lat. *grātus*, pleasing.]

Grat·tan (grăt′n), **Henry** 1746–1820. Irish politician and orator who opposed the union of Ireland with England (1800).

gra·tu·i·tous (grə-tōō′ĭ-təs, -tyōō′-) *adj.* **1.** Given or granted without return or recompense; unearned. **2.** Given or received without cost or obligation; free. **3.** Unnecessary or unwarranted; unjustified. [< Lat. *grātuītus*.] —**gra·tu′i·tous·ly** *adv.* —**gra·tu′i·tous·ness** *n.*

gra·tu·i·ty (grə-tōō′ĭ-tē, -tyōō′-) *n., pl.* -**ties** A favor or gift, usu. of money, given in return for service. [Fr. *gratuité* < OFr. *gratuite* < Med.Lat. *grātuītās*, prob. < Lat. *grātuītus*, voluntary. See GRATUITOUS.]

grat·u·late (grăch′ə-lāt′) *Archaic tr.v.* -**lat·ed**, -**lat·ing**, -**lates** To congratulate. [Lat. *grātulārī*, *grātulāt*- < *grātārī*, to rejoice with < *grātus*, pleasing. See GRATEFUL.] —**grat′u·la·to′ry** (-lə-tôr′ē, -tōr′ē) *adj.*

grau·pel (grou′pəl) *n.* See **snow pellet.** [Ger. *Graupel*, dim. of *Graupe*, hulled grain, prob. of Slav. orig.]

gra·va·men (grə-vā′mən) *n., pl.* -**va·mens** or -**vam·i·na** (-văm′ə-nə) *Law* The most substantial part of a charge or an accusation. [Med.Lat. *gravāmen*, injury, accusation < LLat., encumbrance, obligation < Lat. *gravāre*, to burden < *gravis*, heavy. See GRAVE².]

grave¹ (grāv) *n.* **1a.** An excavation for the interment of a corpse. **b.** A place of burial. **2.** Death or extinction. [ME < OE *græf*.]

grave² (grāv) *adj.* **grav·er**, **grav·est** **1.** Requiring serious thought; momentous. **2.** Fraught with danger or harm. **3.** Dignified and somber in conduct or character. See Syns at **serious**. **4.** Somber or dark in hue. **5.** (*also* gräv) *Linguistics* **a.** Written with or modified by the mark (`), as the *è* in *Sèvres*. **b.** Of or referring to a phonetic feature that distinguishes sounds made at the periphery of the vocal tract, as in labial consonants and back vowels. [Fr. < OFr. < Lat. *gravis*. See gʷerə- in App.] —**grave′ly** *adv.* —**grave′ness** *n.*

grave³ (grāv) *tr.v.* **graved**, **grav·en** (grā′vən) *or* **graved, grav·ing, graves** **1.** To sculpt or carve; engrave. **2.** To stamp or impress deeply; fix permanently. [ME *graven* < OE *grafan*.]

grave⁴ (grāv) *tr.v.* **graved, grav·ing, graves** To clean and coat (the bottom of a wooden ship) with pitch. [ME *graven*.]

gra·ve⁵ (grä′vā) *adj. & adj. Music* In a slow and solemn manner. [Ital. < Lat. *gravis*, heavy. See GRAVE².]

grave accent (grāv, gräv) *n.* A mark (`) indicating: **a.** A vowel that is open or lax, such as *è* in French *père*. **b.** A falling pitch of a vowel or syllable, as in Chinese. **c.** An absence of pitch, as in Ancient Greek. **d.** Secondary stress. **e.** An *e* that is pronounced, as in *belovèd*, esp. for the sake of meter in English poetry.

grave·dig·ger (grāv′dĭg′ər) *n.* One that digs graves.

grav·el (grăv′əl) *n.* **1.** An unconsolidated mixture of rock fragments or pebbles. **2.** *Pathology* The sandlike granular material of urinary calculi. ❖ *tr.v.* -**eled**, -**el·ing**, -**els** *or* -**elled**, -**el·ling**, -**els** **1.** To apply a surface of rock fragments or pebbles to. **2.** To confuse; perplex. **3.** *Informal* To irritate. [ME < OFr. *gravele*, dim. of *grave*, pebbly shore, of Celt. orig.]

grav·el-blind (grăv′əl-blīnd′) *adj.* Having minimal vision.

grav·el·ly (grăv′ə-lē) *adj.* **1.** Of, full of, or covered with gravel. **2.** Having a harsh rasping sound: *a gravelly voice.*

grav·en image (grā′vən) *n.* An idol or fetish carved in wood or stone.

grav·er (grā′vər) *n.* **1.** One who carves or engraves. **2.** See **burin** 1, 3.

grave robber (grāv) *n.* One who plunders valuables from tombs or graves or steals corpses after burial, as for illicit dissection.

Graves (gräv′) A region of SW France in the Garonne R. valley; known for its fine table wines.

Graves (grāvz), **Robert Ranke** 1895–1985. British writer and critic whose works include *The White Goddess* (1948).

Graves′ disease (grāvz) *n.* A condition usu. caused by excessive production of thyroid hormone and marked by an enlarged thyroid gland, protruding eyeballs, and nervousness. [After Robert James *Graves* (1797–1853), Irish physician.]

Graves·end (grāvz′ĕnd′) A municipal borough of SE England on the Thames R. E of London. Pop. 96,300.

grave·side (grāv′sīd′) *n.* The area beside a grave.

grave·site (grāv′sīt′) *n.* A place used for graves or a grave.

grave·stone (grāv′stōn′) *n.* A tombstone.

grave·yard (grāv′yärd′) *n.* **1.** A burial ground; a cemetery. **2.** A place where worn-out or obsolete equipment or objects are kept: *an automobile graveyard.*

graveyard shift *n.* **1.** A work shift that runs during the early morning hours. **2.** The workers on such a shift.

grav·id (grăv′ĭd) *adj.* Carrying developing young or eggs. [Lat. *gravidus* < *gravis*, heavy. See gʷerə- in App.] —**gra·vid′i·ty** (grə-vĭd′ĭ-tē), **grav′id·ness** *n.* —**grav′id·ly** *adv.*

gra·vim·e·ter (grā-vĭm′ĭ-tər, grăv′ə-mē′-) *n.* **1.** An instrument used to measure specific gravity. **2.** An instrument used to measure variations in a gravitational field. [Fr. *gravimètre* : Lat. *gravis*, heavy; see GRAVITY + Fr. *-mètre*, -meter.] —**gra·vim′e·try** (grā-vĭm′ĭ-trē, grə-)

grav·i·met·ric (grăv′ə-mĕt′rĭk) *also* **grav·i·met·ri·cal** (-rĭ-kəl) *adj.* **1.** Of or relating to measurement by weight. **2.** Of or relating to measurement of variations in a gravitational field.

grav·ing dock (grā′vĭng) *n.* A dry dock where the hulls of ships are repaired and maintained.

grav·i·sphere (grăv′ĭ-sfîr′) *n.* The spherical region of space dominated by the gravitational field of a celestial body.

grav·i·tas (grăv′ĭ-täs′) *n.* Seriousness, as in demeanor or treatment. [Lat. *gravitās*, heaviness, seriousness. See GRAVITY.]

grav·i·tate (grăv′ĭ-tāt′) *intr.v.* -**tat·ed**, -**tat·ing**, -**tates** **1.** To move in response to gravitation. **2.** To move downward. **3.** To be attracted by or as if by an irresistible force. [NLat. *gravitāre*, *gravitāt*- < Lat. *gravitās*, heaviness. See GRAVITY.] —**grav′i·tat′er** *n.* —**grav′i·ta′tive** *adj.*

grav·i·ta·tion (grăv′ĭ-tā′shən) *n.* **1.** *Physics* **a.** The natural phenomenon of attraction between physical objects with mass or energy. **b.** The act or process of moving due to gravitation. **2.** A movement toward a source of attraction: *gravitation to the suburbs.* —**grav′i·ta′tion·al** *adj.* —**grav′i·ta′tion·al·ly** *adv.*

gravitational collapse *n.* **1.** The implosion of a star or other celestial body due to its own gravity, resulting in a body many times smaller and denser than the original. **2.** The process by which stars, star clusters, and galaxies form from interstellar gas under the influence of gravity.

gravitational constant *n.* The constant in Newton's law of gravitation that yields the force one body exerts on another when multiplied by the product of the masses of the two bodies and divided by the square of the distance between them. It equals 6.67 × 10⁻¹¹ $m^3kg^{-1}s^{-2}$.

gravitational interaction *n. Physics* A weak, fundamental attraction between two physical objects, esp. elementary particles.

gravitational lens *n.* A massive celestial object, such as a galaxy, whose gravity bends the light of a more distant object, often distorting its image.

gravitational wave *n.* A hypothetical wave that propagates the force of gravity and travels at the speed of light.

grav·i·ti·no (grăv′ĭ-tē′nō) *n.* A hypothetical particle postulated in supersymmetry theory to be the fermion related to the graviton. [GRAVIT(ON) + (NEUTR)INO.]

grav·i·ton (grăv′ĭ-tŏn′) *n.* A hypothetical particle postulated to be the quantum of gravitational interaction and presumed to be very stable and to have zero charge and rest mass. [GRAVIT(ATION) + -ON¹.]

grav·i·ty (grăv′ĭ-tē) *n.* **1.** *Physics* **a.** The force of attraction exerted by a celestial body upon objects at or near its surface, tending to draw them toward the center of the body. **b.** The force of attraction between any two massive bodies, directly proportional to the product of their masses and inversely proportional to the square of the distance between them. **c.** Gravitation. **2.** Grave consequence; seriousness or importance. **3.** Solemnity or dignity of manner. [Fr. *gravité*, heaviness < OFr. < Lat. *gravitās* < *gravis*, heavy. See gʷerə- in App.]

gravity wave *n.* See **gravitational wave.**

grav·lax (grăv′läks) *n.* Raw, thinly sliced, cured salmon seasoned with dill. [Swed. : *grava*, to bury (orig. cured in the ground) + *lax*, salmon; see **laks-** in App.]

gra·vure (grə-vyŏŏr′) *n.* **1a.** A method of printing with etched plates or cylinders; intaglio printing. **b.** Photogravure. **2a.** A plate used in the process of gravure. **b.** A reproduction produced by gravure. [Fr. < *graver*, to engrave < OFr., of Gmc. orig.]

gra·vy (grā′vē) *n., pl.* -**vies 1a.** The juices from cooking meat. **b.** A sauce made from these juices. **2.** *Slang* **a.** Money or benefit easily or illicitly gained. **b.** Payment or benefit in excess of what is expected or required. [ME *grave* < OFr., poss. a misreading of *grane*, stew, sauce < Lat. *grānātus*, having many seeds. See POMEGRANATE.]

gravy train *n. Slang* An occupation or other source of income that requires little effort while yielding considerable profit.

gray¹ *also* **grey** (grā) *adj.* **gray·er**, **gray·est** *also* **grey·er**, **grey·est 1.** Of or relating to an achromatic color of any lightness between the extremes of black and white. **2a.** Dull or dark. **b.** Lacking cheer; gloomy. **3a.** Having gray hair; hoary. **b.** Old or venerable. **4.** Intermediate in character or position, as between differing views on a subject. ❖ *n.* **1.** A gray color. **2.** An object or animal of the color gray. **3.** *often* **Gray a.** A member of the Confederate Army. **b.** The Confederate Army. ❖ *v.* **grayed, gray·ing, grays** *also* **greyed, grey·ing, greys** —*intr.* **1.** To become gray. **2.** To become old; age. **3.** To include a large or increasing proportion of old people: *The town's population is graying.* —*tr.* To make gray. [ME *grei* < OE *græg*.] —**gray′ly** *adv.* —**gray′ness** *n.*

gray² (grā) *n.* The SI unit for the energy absorbed from ionizing radiation, equal to one joule per kilogram. [After Louis Harold *Gray* (1905–65), British radiobiologist.]

Gray, Asa 1810–88. Amer. botanist who greatly enlarged and improved the description of North American flora.

Gray, Thomas 1716–71. British poet whose most famous work is *Elegy Written in a Country Churchyard* (1751).

gray·beard (grā′bîrd′) *n.* An old man.

gray eminence *n.* See **éminence grise.**

gray•fish (grā′fĭsh′) *n., pl.* **grayfish** or **-fish•es** See **dogfish** 1.

gray•ish (grā′ĭsh) *adj.* Somewhat gray.

gray jay *n.* A bird *(Perisoreus canadensis)* of North American conifer forests, having gray plumage.

gray•lag also **grey•lag** (grā′lăg′) *n.* A wild gray goose *(Anser anser)* of Europe. [Poss. GRAY[1] + LAG[1], lingering behind (obsolete) < its being the last of the geese to leave England on its annual migration.]

gray•ling (grā′lĭng) *n., pl.* **grayling** or **-lings** Any of several edible freshwater fishes of the genus *Thymallus* of the Northern Hemisphere, having a large dorsal fin.

gray•mail (grā′māl′) *n.* A defensive tactic in an espionage trial whereby the accused threatens to reveal secrets unless charges are dropped. [GRAY[1] + (BLACK)MAIL.]

gray market *n.* The business of buying or selling at prices below those set by an official regulatory agency. [GRAY[1] + (BLACK) MARKET.]

gray matter *n.* **1.** Brownish-gray nerve tissue, esp. of the brain and spinal cord, composed of nerve cell bodies and their dendrites and some supportive tissue. **2.** *Informal* Intellect.

gray mullet *n.* See **mullet** 1.

Grays Peak (grāz) A mountain, 4,352.4 m (14,270 ft), in the Front Range of the Rocky Mts. in central CO.

gray squirrel *n.* A common squirrel *(Sciurus carolinensis)* of eastern North America having grayish or blackish fur.

gray•wacke (grā′wăk′, -wăk′ə) *n.* Any of various dark gray sandstones that contain shale. [Partial transl. of Ger. *Grauwacke* : *grau*, gray + *Wacke*, rock (< MHGer. < OHGer. *waggo*, boulder; see **wegh-** in App.).]

gray•wa•ter (grā′wô′tər, -wŏt′ər) *n.* Wastewater from household baths and washing machines that is recycled esp. for use in gardening or for flushing toilets.

gray whale *n.* A grayish-black whalebone whale *(Eschrichtius robustus)* of northern Pacific waters, with white blotches.

gray wolf *n.* A large, tawny gray wolf *(Canis lupus)* once found throughout northern North America and Eurasia.

Graz (gräts) A city of SE Austria on the Mur R. SSW of Vienna; probably founded in the 12th cent. Pop. 237,810.

graze[1] (grāz) *v.* **grazed, graz•ing, graz•es** *—intr.* To feed on growing grasses and herbage. *—tr.* **1.** To feed on (herbage) in a field or on pastureland. **2.** To feed on the herbage of (a piece of land). **3.** To afford herbage for the feeding of. **4.** To put (livestock) out to feed. **5.** To tend (feeding livestock) in a pasture. [ME *grasen* < OE *grasian* < *græs*, grass.] **—graze′a•ble, graz′a•ble** *adj.* **—graz′er** *n.*

graze[2] (grāz) *v.* **grazed, graz•ing, graz•es** *—tr.* **1.** To touch lightly in passing; brush. **2.** To scrape or scratch slightly; abrade. *—intr.* To graze something in passing. ❖ *n.* **1.** The act of grazing a surface. **2.** A minor scratch or abrasion. [Perh. < GRAZE[1].]

gra•zier (grā′zhər) *n.* A person who grazes cattle. [ME *grasier* < *grasen*, to graze. See GRAZE[1].]

gra•zi•o•so (grät′sē-ō′sō, -zō) *adv. & adj. Music* In a graceful smooth manner. [Ital. < Lat. *grātiōsus*, gracious, agreeable. See GRACIOUS.]

Gr. Brit. *abbr.* Great Britain

grease (grēs) *n.* **1.** Soft or melted animal fat, esp. after rendering. **2.** A thick oil or viscous substance, esp. a lubricant. **3a.** The oily substance present in raw wool; suint. **b.** Raw wool that has not been cleansed of suint. **4.** *Slang* Something, such as money, that facilitates the attainment of a goal. ❖ *tr.v.* (grēs, grēz) **greased, greas•ing, greas•es 1.** To coat, lubricate, smear, or soil with grease. **2.** To facilitate the progress of. **3.** *Slang* To kill. ***—idiom:* grease (someone's) palm** (or **hand**) *Slang* To bribe. [ME *grese* < AN *grece* < VLat. **crassia* < Lat. *crassus*, fat, thick.] **—grease′less** *adj.* **—grease′proof′** *adj.*

grease gun *n.* A hand-powered pump used to force grease under pressure into bearings.

grease monkey *n. Slang* A mechanic, esp. one who works on motor vehicles or aircraft.

grease•paint also **grease paint** (grēs′pānt′) *n.* Theatrical makeup, esp. a preparation of grease mixed with colorings.

grease pencil *n.* A pencil of hard grease mixed with colorings, used esp. for marking on glossy or glazed surfaces.

greas•er (grē′sər, -zər) *n.* **1.** One who greases. **2.** *Slang* A tough young man, esp. a working-class white person much involved with motorcycles or cars. **3.** *Offensive Slang* Used as a disparaging term for a Latin American, esp. a Mexican.

grease•wood (grēs′wo͝od′) *n.* A spiny shrub *(Sarcobatus vermiculatus)* of western North America having small alternate leaves, white stems, and small greenish flowers.

greas•y (grē′sē, -zē) *adj.* **-i•er, -i•est 1.** Coated or soiled with grease. **2.** Containing grease, esp. too much. **3.** Like grease in slickness or slipperiness. **—greas′i•ly** *adv.* **—greas′i•ness** *n.*

REGIONAL NOTE In the North and West, *greasy* is pronounced with an (s) sound; in the Midlands and South, it is pronounced with a (z). This (s)/(z) distinction marks a clear division between major dialect regions of the United States. The (z) pronunciation is so stable and so characteristic of Southern dialects that dialect scholars use it to trace the migration of Southern speakers into other dialect areas, such as Colorado, Oregon, and California.

greasy spoon *n. Slang* A small, inexpensive, often unsanitary restaurant.

great (grāt) *adj.* **great•er, great•est 1.** Very large in size. **2.** Larger in size than others of the same kind. **3.** Large in quantity or number: *A great throng attended the rally.* See Syns at **large. 4.** Extensive in time or distance: *a great delay.* **5.** Remarkable or outstanding in magnitude, degree, or extent: *a great crisis.* **6.** Of outstanding significance or importance: *a great work of art.* **7.** Chief or principal: *the great house on the estate.* **8.** Superior in quality or character; noble: *"For he was great, ere fortune made him so"* (John Dryden). **9.** Powerful; influential: *a great nation.* **10.** Eminent; distinguished: *a great leader.* **11.** Grand; aristocratic. **12.** *Informal* Enthusiastic. **13.** *Informal* Very skillful: *great at algebra.* **14.** *Informal* Very good; first-rate: *had a great time at the dance.* **15.** Being one generation removed from the relative specified. Often used in combination: *a great-granddaughter.* **16.** *Archaic* Pregnant. ❖ *n.* **1.** *pl.* **greats** or **great** One that is great. **2.** *Music* A division of organs, usu. containing the most powerful ranks of pipes. ❖ *adv. Informal* Very well: *got along great with the teacher.* [ME *grete* < OE *grēat*, thick, coarse.] **—great′ly** *adv.* **—great′ness** *n.*

Great Abaco The largest island of the Abaco and Cays group in the N Bahamas.

Great Alföld See **Alföld.**

great ape *n.* Any of various anthropoid apes of the family Pongidae, which includes the chimpanzees and gorillas.

great auk *n.* A large flightless sea bird *(Pinguinus impennis)* once common on northern Atlantic coasts but now extinct.

great-aunt or **great aunt** (grāt′ănt′, -änt′) *n.* A sister of one's grandparent.

Great Australian Bight A wide bay of the Indian Ocean on the S coast of Australia.

Great Barrier Reef The largest coral reef in the world, c. 2,011 km (1,250 mi) long, off the NE coast of Australia.

Great Basin A desert region of the W US comprising most of NV and parts of UT, CA, ID, WY, and OR.

Great Bear *n.* See **Ursa Major.**

Great Bear Lake A lake of NW mainland Northwest Terrs., Canada. The **Great Bear River,** c. 113 km (70 mi), flows W from the lake to the Mackenzie R.

great blue heron *n.* An American heron *(Ardea herodias)* with blue-gray plumage, a white head, and a dark crest.

Great Britain 1. An island off the W coast of Europe comprising England, Scotland, and Wales. **2.** See **United Kingdom.**

great circle *n.* **1.** A circle described by the intersection of the surface of a sphere with a plane passing through the center of the sphere. **2.** A segment of such a circle representing the shortest distance between two terrestrial points.

great•coat (grāt′kōt′) *n.* A heavy overcoat.

Great Dane *n.* Any of various large strong dogs of a breed developed in Germany, having a short smooth coat and a narrow head.

great divide *n.* **1.** A large or major watershed of a landmass. **2.** A major point of division, esp. death.

Great Divide See **Continental Divide.**

Great Dividing Range A chain of mountains curving along the E coast of Australia.

great•en (grāt′n) *tr. & intr.v.* **-ened, -en•ing, -ens** *Archaic* To make or become great or greater.

great•er also **Great•er** (grā′tər) *adj.* Of, relating to, or being a city together with its populous suburbs.

Greater Antilles An island group of the N West Indies including Cuba, Jamaica, Hispaniola, and Puerto Rico.

greater omentum *n.* A fold of the peritoneum, passing from the stomach to the transverse colon.

great•est common divisor (grā′tĭst) *n.* The largest number that divides evenly into each of a given set of numbers.

Great Falls A city of central MT on the Missouri R. NNE of Helena. Pop. 56,690.

great•heart•ed (grāt′här′tĭd) *adj.* **1.** Noble or courageous in spirit. **2.** Generous; magnanimous. **—great′heart′ed•ly** *adv.* **—great′heart′ed•ness** *n.*

great horned owl *n.* A large North American owl *(Bubo virginianus)* with prominent ear tufts and brownish plumage.

Great Indian Desert See **Thar Desert.**

Great Lakes A group of five freshwater lakes of central North America between the US and Canada, including Lakes Superior, Huron, Erie, Ontario, and Michigan; first sighted by French traders in the early 17th cent.

great laurel *n.* See **rosebay** 1.

Great Miami River See **Miami River.**

Great Ouse River See **Ouse River** 1.

Great Pee Dee See **Pee Dee.**

Great Plains A vast grassland region of central North America E of the Rocky Mts.

Great Power *n.* One of the nations having great political, social, and economic influence in international affairs.

Great Pyrenees *n.* Any of a breed of large heavy-boned dogs having a thick white coat and developed to guard sheep.

Great Rift Valley A geologic depression of SW Asia and E Africa extending from the Jordan R. valley to Mozambique.

great blue heron
Ardea herodias

Great Dane

ă	pat	oi	boy
ā	pay	ou	out
âr	care	o͝o	took
ä	father	o͞o	boot
ĕ	pet	ŭ	cut
ē	be	ûr	urge
ĭ	pit	th	thin
ī	pie	*th*	this
îr	pier	hw	which
ŏ	pot	zh	vision
ō	toe	ə	about, item
ô	paw		

Stress marks:
′ (primary);
′ (secondary), as in
lexicon (lĕk′sĭ-kŏn′)

Great Russian *n.* A Russian. Used formerly in distinguishing ethnic Russians from other constituent peoples of the Soviet Union or the Russian Empire. [Transl. of Russ. *Velikorusskiĭ* : *velikiĭ,* great + *russkiĭ,* Russ.]

Great Saint Bernard Pass An Alpine pass, 2,473.6 m (8,110 ft), on the Italian-Swiss border.

Great Salt Lake A shallow body of salt water of NW UT between the Wasatch Range and the **Great Salt Lake Desert.**

Great Sandy Desert A vast arid area of NW Australia N of the Gibson Desert.

great seal *n.* The principal seal of a government or state, with which official documents are stamped.

great skua *n.* A predatory gull-like sea bird *(Catharacta skua)* of northern regions, having brownish plumage.

Great Slave Lake A lake of S Northwest Terrs., Canada.

Great Smoky Mountains A range of the Appalachians on the NC–TN border rising to 2,026.1 m (6,643 ft).

Great Spirit *n.* The principal deity in the religion of many Native American peoples.

great-un·cle or **great uncle** (grāt'ŭng'kəl) *n.* A brother of one's grandparent.

Great Victoria Desert An arid region of S-central Australia.

Great Vowel Shift *n.* A series of phonetic changes in Early Modern English that raised the Middle English low and mid long vowels, so that (ä) became (ā), for example, while the high long vowels became diphthongs.

Great Wall of China A line of fortifications extending c. 2,414 km (1,500 mi) across N China; built in the 3rd cent. B.C.

Great War *n.* World War I.

great white shark *n.* A shark *(Carcharodon carcharias)* of temperate and tropical waters that grows to about 7 meters (23 feet) and feeds regularly on marine mammals.

greave (grēv) *n.* Leg armor worn below the knee. Often used in the plural. [Sing. of ME *greves* < OFr., shins.]

greaves (grēvz) *pl.n.* *(used with a sing. or pl. verb)* The unmelted residue from rendered animal fat. [< LGer. *greven.*]

grebe (grēb) *n.* Any of various swimming and diving birds of the family Podicipedidae, having a pointed bill and lobed fleshy membranes along each toe. [Fr. *grèbe.*]

Gre·cian (grē'shən) *adj.* ❖ *n.* A native or inhabitant of Greece. [< Lat. *Graecia,* Greece < *Graecus,* Greek. See GREEK.]

Gre·cism (grē'sĭz'əm) *n.* **1.** The style or spirit of Greek culture, art, or thought. **2.** Something done in imitation of Greek style or spirit. **3.** An idiom of the Greek language.

Gre·cize (grē'sīz') *tr.v.* **-cized, -ciz·ing, -ciz·es** To make Greek or Hellenic in form or style. [Fr. *gréciser* < LLat. *graecizāre* < Gk. *graikizein,* to speak Greek < *Graikos,* Greek.]

Grec·o (grĕk'ō), **El** Orig. Doménikos Theotokópoulos. 1541–1614. Greek-born Spanish painter of religious works characterized by elongated human figures and deep shadows.

Greco– or **Graeco–** *pref.* Greek; Greek: *Greco-Roman.* [< Lat. *Graecus,* Greek. See GREEK.]

Grec·o·Ro·man (grĕk'ō-rō'mən, grē'kō-) *adj.* Of or relating to both Greece and Rome: *Greco-Roman mythology.*

gree (grē) *n. Scots* Superiority; preeminence. [ME *gre* < OFr., step < Lat. *gradus.* See GRADE.]

Greece (grēs) A country of SE Europe on the S Balkan Peninsula and including numerous islands in the Mediterranean, Aegean, and Ionian seas. One of the most important centers of early civilization, it was ruled by the Ottoman Turks from the 15th cent. until its independence in 1829. Cap. Athens. Pop. 9,740,417.

greed (grēd) *n.* An excessive desire to acquire or possess more than one needs or deserves, esp. of material wealth.

greed·y (grē'dē) *adj.* **-i·er, -i·est 1.** Having greed. **2.** Wanting to eat or drink more than one can reasonably consume; gluttonous. **3.** Extremely eager or desirous. [ME *gredi* < OE *grǣdig.*] **—greed'i·ly** *adv.* **—greed'i·ness** *n.*

Greek (grēk) *n.* **1a.** The Indo-European language of the Greeks. **b.** Greek language and literature from the middle of the eighth century B.C. to the end of the third century A.D., esp. the Attic Greek of the fifth and fourth centuries B.C. **2a.** A native or inhabitant of Greece. **b.** A person of Greek ancestry. **3.** *Informal* A member of a fraternity or sorority with a name composed of Greek letters. **4.** *Informal* Something unintelligible. ❖ *adj.* Of or relating to Greece or its people, language, or culture. [ME *Grek* < OE *Grēcas,* the Greeks < Lat. *Graecus,* Greek < Gk. *Graikos,* tribal name.]

Greek Catholic *n.* **1.** A member of the Eastern Orthodox Church. **2.** A member of a Uniat church.

Greek Church *n.* The Eastern Orthodox Church.

Greek cross *n.* A cross formed by two bars of equal length crossing in the middle at right angles to each other.

Greek fire *n.* An incendiary preparation first used by the Byzantine Greeks to set fire to enemy ships.

Greek Orthodox Church *n.* The state church of Greece, an autonomous part of the Eastern Orthodox Church.

Greek Revival *n.* An architectural style imitating elements of ancient Greek temple design, popular in the United States and Europe in the first half of the 19th century.

Gree·ley (grē'lē), **Horace** 1811–72. Amer. journalist and politician who founded and edited the *New York Tribune* (1841–72).

green (grēn) *n.* **1.** The hue of the portion of the visible spectrum between yellow and blue, evoked in the human observer by radiant energy with wavelengths of approx. 490 to 570 nanometers; any of a group of colors whose hue is that of the emerald or somewhat less yellow than that of growing grass; one of the additive or light primaries; one of the psychological primary hues. **2.** Something green in color. **3. greens** Green growth or foliage, esp.: **a.** The branches and leaves of plants used for decoration. **b.** Leafy plants or plant parts eaten as vegetables. **4.** A grassy lawn or plot, esp.: **a.** A common. **b.** *Sports* A putting green. **5. greens** A green uniform. **6.** *Slang* Money. **7. Green** A supporter of a social and political movement that espouses global environmental protection, social responsibility, and nonviolence. ❖ *adj.* **green·er, green·est 1.** Of the color green. **2.** Abounding in or covered with green growth or foliage. **3.** Made with green or leafy vegetables. **4.** Characterized by mild or temperate weather. **5.** Youthful; vigorous. **6.** Not mature or ripe; young. **7.** Brand-new; fresh. **8.** Not yet fully processed, esp.: **a.** Not aged: *green wood.* **b.** Not cured or tanned: *green pelts.* **9.** Lacking training or experience. **10a.** Lacking sophistication or worldly experience; naive. **b.** Easily duped or deceived; gullible. **11.** Having a sickly or unhealthy pallor indicative of nausea or jealousy, for example. **12.** Supporting or beneficial to environmentalism. ❖ *tr. & intr.v.* **greened, green·ing, greens** To make or become green. **—idiom: green around** (or **about) the gills** Pale or sickly in appearance. [ME *grene* < OE *grēne.* N., sense 7, transl. of Ger. *(die) Grünen,* (the) Greens < *grün,* green.] **—green'ly** *adv.* **—green'ness** *n.*

Green, William 1873–1952. Amer. labor leader who was president of the American Federation of Labor (1924–52).

green alga *n.* Any of the numerous algae of the division Chlorophyta having chlorophyll unmasked by other pigments.

Gree·na·way (grē'nə-wā'), **Catherine ("Kate")** 1846–1901. British artist and writer noted for her children's books, such as *Under the Window* (1879).

green·back (grēn'băk') *n.* A note of US currency.

Green Bay A city of E WI on **Green Bay,** an arm of Lake Michigan; founded 1634. Pop. 102,313.

green bean *n.* See **string bean** 1.

green·belt (grēn'bĕlt') *n.* A belt of recreational parks, farmland, or uncultivated land surrounding a community.

Green Beret *n.* A member of the US Army Special Forces.

green·bri·er (grēn'brī'ər) *n.* See **catbrier.**

green card *n.* A card issued by the US government to aliens, allowing them to work legally in the United States.

green corn *n.* Young, tender ears of sweet corn.

green dragon *n.* A tuberous plant *(Arisaema dracontium)* of eastern North America having minute flowers at the base of a spadix projecting from a narrow green spathe.

Greene (grēn), **(Henry) Graham** 1904–91. British writer whose novels include *The Power and the Glory* (1940).

Greene, Nathanael 1742–86. Amer. Revolutionary general noted for his campaigns in the S colonies.

green·er·y (grē'nə-rē) *n., pl.* **-ies 1a.** Green foliage; verdure. **b.** Greenery used as decoration. **2.** A place where plants are grown.

green-eyed (grēn'īd') *adj.* Jealous.

green-eyed monster *n.* Jealousy. [< the association of envy with the color green.]

green·field (grēn'fēld') *n.* A piece of undeveloped, usu. rural property that is considered as a site for urban expansion.

green·finch (grēn'fĭnch') *n.* A common Eurasian finch *(Carduelis chloris)* having green and yellow plumage.

green·fly (grēn'flī') *n.* A green aphid commonly occurring as a destructive pest of various cultivated plants.

green·gage (grēn'gāj') *n.* A variety of plum *(Prunus domestica)* having yellowish-green skin and sweet flesh. [GREEN + gage (after Sir William *Gage* (1656?–1727), English botanist).]

green·gro·cer (grēn'grō'sər) *n. Chiefly British* A retail seller of fresh fruits and vegetables. **—green'gro'cer·y** *n.*

green·head (grēn'hĕd') *n.* A male mallard duck.

green·heart (grēn'härt') *n.* **1a.** A tropical American tree *(Ocotea rodioei)* having greenish dark durable wood. **b.** Any of various similar trees. **2.** The wood of any of these trees.

green·horn (grēn'hôrn') *n.* **1.** An inexperienced or immature person, esp. one easily deceived. **2.** A newcomer, esp. one unfamiliar with a place or group. [ME *greene horn,* horn of a newly slaughtered animal.]

green·house (grēn'hous') *n.* A structure, primarily of glass, in which temperature and humidity can be controlled for the cultivation or protection of plants.

greenhouse effect *n.* **1.** The phenomenon whereby the earth's atmosphere traps solar radiation, caused by the presence of gases such as carbon dioxide that allow incoming sunlight to pass through but absorb heat radiated back from the earth's surface. **2.** A similar retention of solar radiation.

greenhouse gas *n.* Any of the atmospheric gases that contribute to the greenhouse effect.

green·ing[1] (grē'nĭng) *n.* **1.** Restoration of vitality or freshness; rejuvenation. **2.** Support or advocacy of the Green movement.

green·ing[2] (grē'nĭng) *n.* Any of several varieties of green-skinned apples.

green·ish (grē'nĭsh) *adj.* Somewhat green.

great seal
Great Seal of the United
States of America

Great Wall of China

Greece

Green·land (grēn′lənd, -lǎnd′) An island of Denmark in the N Atlantic Ocean off NE Canada; discovered by Eric the Red in the 10th cent. —**Green·land′ic** (-lǎn′dǐk) *adj.*

Greenland Sea A section of the S Arctic Ocean off the E coast of Greenland.

Greenland spar *n.* See **cryolite.**

green·let (grēn′lǐt) *n.* Any of various small greenish birds of the genus *Hylophilus* of Central and South America.

green light *n.* **1.** The green-colored light that signals traffic to proceed. **2.** *Informal* Permission to proceed.

green·ling (grēn′lǐng) *n.* Any of various northern Pacific marine food fishes of the family Hexagrammidae.

green·mail (grēn′māl′) *n.* An antitakeover maneuver in which the target firm purchases the raider's stock at a price above that available to other stockholders. [GREEN, money + (BLACK)MAIL.] —**green′mail′er** *n.*

green manure *n.* A growing crop, such as clover or grass, that is plowed under the soil to improve fertility.

green monkey *n.* See **vervet.**

Green Mountains A range of the Appalachian Mts. extending from S Quebec, Canada, through VT to W MA and rising to 1,339.9 m (4,393 ft).

green·ock·ite (grē′nə-kīt′) *n.* A yellow to brown or red mineral, CdS, the only ore of cadmium. [After Charles Murray Cathcart, 2nd Earl *Greenock* (1783–1859).]

green onion *n.* An immature onion; a scallion.

Gree·nough (grē′nō′), **Horatio** 1805–52. Amer. sculptor whose principal work is the neoclassical statue of George Washington at the Smithsonian Institution in Washington DC.

green pepper *n.* The unripened green fruit of a bell pepper.

green plover *n.* See **lapwing.**

green revolution *n.* A significant increase in agricultural productivity due to the use of high-yield varieties of grains, pesticides, and improved management techniques.

Green River 1. A river rising in central KY and flowing c. 595 km (370 mi) to the Ohio R. near Evansville IN. **2.** A river, c. 1,175 km (730 mi), rising in W WY and flowing through NW CO and E UT to the Colorado R.

green·room (grēn′rōōm′, -rŏŏm′) *n.* An offstage waiting room or lounge for performers, as in a theater.

green·sand (grēn′sǎnd′) *n.* A sand or sediment having a dark greenish color caused by the presence of glauconite.

Greens·bor·o (grēnz′bûr′ə, -bûr′ō) A city of N-central NC E of Winston-Salem; settled in 1749. Pop. 223,891.

green·shank (grēn′shǎngk′) *n.* A European wading bird (*Tringa nebularia*) having greenish legs and a long bill.

green·sick·ness (grēn′sǐk′nǐs) *n.* See **chlorosis** 2.

greens·keep·er (grēnz′kē′pər) *n.* One who is responsible for the maintenance of a golf course.

green snake *n.* Any of several slender yellow-green nonvenomous North American snakes of the genus *Opheodrys.*

green soap *n.* A translucent yellowish-green soap made chiefly from vegetable oils and used to treat skin disorders.

Green·span (grēn′spǎn′), **Alan** b. 1926. Amer. economist who was appointed chairman of the board of governors of the Federal Reserve System in 1987.

green·stick fracture (grēn′stǐk′) *n.* A partial bone fracture in which the bone is bent but broken only on one side.

green·stone (grēn′stōn′) *n.* Any of various altered basic igneous rocks colored green by chlorite, hornblende, or epidote.

green·strip (grēn′strǐp′) *n.* A strip of land planted with fire-resistant vegetation to retard the spread of wildfires.

green·sward (grēn′swôrd′) *n.* Grassy green ground; turf.

green·wash (grēn′wŏsh′, -wôsh′) *n.* **1.** The dissemination of misleading information by an organization to conceal its abuse of the environment in order to present a positive public image. **2.** The information so disseminated. [GREEN + (WHITE)WASH.]

green tea *n.* Tea made from unfermented dried leaves.

green thumb *n.* An extraordinary ability to make plants grow.

green turtle *n.* A large marine turtle (*Chelonia mydas*) having greenish flesh that is prized as food, esp. in turtle soup.

Green·wich 1. (grĭn′ĭch, grĭn′ĭj) A borough of Greater London in SE England on the Thames R. It is the site of the original Royal Observatory, through which passes the prime meridian, or longitude 0°. Pop. 214,836. **2.** (grĕn′ĭch, grĭn′-, grĕn′wĭch′) A town of SW CT on Long Island Sound; settled in 1640. Pop. 61,101.

Green·wich Mean Time (grĕn′ĭch, grĭn′ĭj) *n.* See **universal time.**

Greenwich time *n.* See **universal time.**

Green·wich Village (grĕn′ĭch, -ĭj, grĭn′-) A section of lower Manhattan in New York City; noted as an artists' and writers' community since the early 1900s.

green-winged teal (grĕn′wĭngd′) *n.* A small freshwater duck (*Anas crecca*) with an iridescent green speculum in the male.

green·wood (grĕn′wŏŏd′) *n.* A wood or forest with green foliage.

Greer (grĭr), **Germaine** b. 1939. Australian feminist best known for her book *The Female Eunuch* (1970).

greet (grēt) *tr.v.* **greet·ed, greet·ing, greets 1.** To salute or welcome in a friendly and respectful way. **2.** To receive with a specified reaction. **3.** To be perceived by: *A din greeted our ears.* [ME

greten < OE *grētan.*] —**greet′er** *n.*

greet·ing (grē′tĭng) *n.* A word or gesture of welcome or salutation.

greeting card *n.* A folded card with a greeting or another sentiment, usu. for a special occasion or holiday.

greg·a·rine (grĕg′ə-rīn′) *n.* Any of various sporozoan protozoans of the order Gregarinida that are parasitic within the digestive tracts of various invertebrates including arthropods and annelids. [< NLat. *Gregārīna,* type genus < Lat. *gregārius,* of a flock. See GREGARIOUS.] —**greg′a·rine** *adj.*

gre·gar·i·ous (grĭ-gâr′ē-əs) *adj.* **1.** Seeking and enjoying the company of others; sociable. **2.** Tending to move in or form a group with others of the same kind. **3.** *Botany* Growing in groups that are close together but not densely clustered or matted. [< Lat. *gregārius,* of a flock < *grex, greg-,* flock.] —**gre·gar′i·ous·ly** *adv.* —**gre·gar′i·ous·ness** *n.*

Gre·go·ri·an calendar (grĭ-gôr′ē-ən, -gōr′-) *n.* The solar calendar used in most of the world, sponsored by Pope Gregory XIII in 1582 to correct the Julian calendar. See table at **calendar.**

Gregorian chant *n. Roman Catholic Church* An unaccompanied, monophonic liturgical chant. [After St. GREGORY I.]

Greg·o·ry I (grĕg′ə-rē), Saint. Known as "Gregory the Great." 540?–604. Pope (590–604) who sponsored the missionary expedition of Saint Augustine to Britain (596).

Gregory VII Orig. Hildebrand. 1020?–85. Pope (1073–85) who sought to establish papal supremacy.

Gregory XIII 1502–85. Pope (1572–85) who sponsored the adoption of the Gregorian calendar (1582).

Gregory, Lady Isabella Augusta Persse 1852–1932. Irish playwright who was a founder (1899) and director (1904–32) of the Abbey Theater.

Gregory of Nys·sa (nĭs′ə), Saint. A.D. 335?–394? Eastern theologian who led the conservative faction during the Trinitarian controversy.

Gregory of Tours (tŏŏr, tôr), Saint. 538–594. Frankish prelate and historian who wrote a history of the 6th-cent. Franks.

greige (grā, grāzh) *adj.* Not bleached or dyed; unfinished. Used of textiles. [Fr. *grège* < Ital. *(seta) greggia,* raw (silk) < *greggio,* gray, of Gmc. orig.]

grei·sen (grī′zən) *n.* A granitic rock composed chiefly of quartz and mica. [Ger. < *greissen,* to split.]

grem·lin (grĕm′lĭn) *n.* **1.** An imaginary gnomelike creature to whom mechanical problems, esp. in aircraft, are attributed. **2.** A maker of mischief. [Perh. blend of Ir. *gruaimín,* bad-tempered little guy (< MIr. *gruaim,* gloom) and GOBLIN.]

Gre·na·da (grə-nā′də) A country in the Windward Is. of the West Indies comprising the island of **Grenada** and the S Grenadines; achieved independence from Great Britain in 1974. Cap. St. George's. Pop. 92,000.

gre·nade (grə-nād′) *n.* **1.** A small bomb or explosive missile that is detonated by a fuse and thrown by hand or shot from a rifle or launcher. **2.** A glass container filled with a chemical that is dispersed when the container is thrown and broken. [Fr. < OFr. *(pome) grenate,* pomegranate. See POMEGRANATE.]

gren·a·dier (grĕn′ə-dîr′) *n.* **1a.** A member of the British Grenadier Guards, the first regiment of the royal household infantry. **b.** A soldier in a special corps or regiment. **c.** A soldier equipped with grenades. **2.** Any of various deep-sea fishes of the family Macrouridae, having a long tapering tail and no tail fin. [Fr. < *grenade,* grenade, from GRENADE.]

gren·a·dine (grĕn′ə-dēn′, grĕn′ə-dēn′) *n.* **1.** A thick sweet syrup made from pomegranates and used as a flavoring, esp. in beverages. **2.** A thin, loosely woven fabric of silk, cotton, or synthetic fiber. [Fr. < *grenade,* pomegranate < OFr. *grenate.* See POMEGRANATE.]

Gren·a·dines (grĕn′ə-dēnz′) An archipelago in the Windward Is. of the E Caribbean. The S islands are part of Grenada; the others are part of St. Vincent and the Grenadines.

Gren·del (grĕn′dl) *n.* The male monster, descended from Cain, slain by Beowulf in the Old English epic *Beowulf.*

Gre·no·ble (grə-nō′bəl, -nôbl′) A city of SE France on the Isère R. SSW of Chambéry. Pop. 150,815.

Gren·ville (grĕn′vĭl′, -vəl), **George** 1712–70. British political leader who served as prime minister (1763–65).

Gresh·am (grĕsh′əm), **Sir Thomas** 1519–79. English financier who is traditionally credited with Gresham's law.

Gresh·am's law (grĕsh′əmz) *n.* The theory holding that if two kinds of money in circulation have the same denominational value but different intrinsic values, the money with higher intrinsic value will be hoarded and driven out of circulation by the other money. [After Sir Thomas GRESHAM.]

gres·so·ri·al (grĕ-sôr′ē-əl, -sōr′-) *adj.* Adapted for walking or having limbs adapted for walking. Used of flightless birds. [< NLat. *gressōrius* < Lat. *gressus,* step < p. part. of *gradī,* to walk. See **ghredh-** in App.]

Gret·na Green (grĕt′nə) A village of S Scotland on the English border; formerly noted as a site of runaway marriages.

Gretz·ky (grĕt′skē), **Wayne** b. 1961. Canadian hockey player who became the NHL's all-time leading scorer in 1989 and the all-time leading scorer in North American professional hockey in 1999.

greenhouse effect
Energy radiated by the sun converts to heat when it reaches the earth. Some heat is reflected back through the atmosphere, while some is absorbed by atmospheric gases and radiated back to the earth.

atmosphere

heat

earth

Alan Greenspan

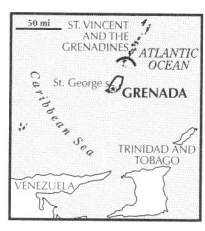

Grenada

ă	pat	oi	boy
ā	pay	ou	out
âr	care	ŏŏ	took
ä	father	ōō	boot
ĕ	pet	ŭ	cut
ē	be	ûr	urge
ĭ	pit	th	thin
ī	pie	th	this
îr	pier	hw	which
ŏ	pot	zh	vision
ō	toe	ə	about,
ô	paw		item

Stress marks:
′ (primary);
′ (secondary), as in
lexicon (lĕk′sĭ-kŏn′)

Greuze (grœz), **Jean Baptiste** 1725–1805. French painter of moralistic genre works.

grew (grōō) *v.* Past tense of **grow**.

grey (grā) *adj., n.,* & *v.* Variant of **gray**[1].

Grey, Charles. 2nd Earl Grey. 1764–1845. British politician who as prime minister (1830–34) implemented the abolition of slavery throughout the British Empire.

Grey, Lady Jane 1537–54. Queen of England for nine days (1553) who was beheaded for treason.

Grey, Zane 1875–1939. Amer. writer of Western adventure novels, including *Riders of the Purple Sage* (1912).

grey·hen (grā′hĕn′) *n.* The female of the black grouse.

grey·hound (grā′hound′) *n.* Any of a breed of tall slender dog, having a smooth coat, a narrow head, and long legs and capable of running swiftly.

grey·lag (grā′lăg′) *n.* Variant of **graylag**.

grib·ble (grĭb′əl) *n.* Any of several small wood-boring marine isopod crustaceans of the genus *Limnoria,* esp. *L. lignorum.* [Poss. dim. of GRUB.]

grid (grĭd) *n.* **1a.** A framework of crisscrossed or parallel bars; a grating or mesh. **b.** A cooking surface of parallel metal bars; a gridiron. **2.** Something resembling a grid. **3.** A pattern of regularly spaced horizontal and vertical lines forming squares on a map, a chart, an aerial photograph, or an optical device, used for locating points. **4.** *Electricity* **a.** An interconnected system for the distribution of electricity or electromagnetic signals over a wide area, esp. a network of high-tension cables and power stations. **b.** A corrugated or perforated conducting plate in a storage battery. **c.** A network or coil of fine wires located between the plate and the filament in an electron tube. **5.** *Football* The gridiron. **6.** *Sports* The starting positions of cars on a racecourse. **7.** *Printing* A device in a photocomposition machine on which the characters used in composition are etched. [Short for GRIDIRON.] —**grid′ded** *adj.*

grid·der (grĭd′ər) *n.* A football player.

grid·dle (grĭd′l) *n.* A flat metal surface used for cooking by dry heat. [ME *gridel,* gridiron < ONFr. *gredil* < Lat. *crāticula,* dim. of *crātis,* hurdle, lattice.] —**grid′dle** *v.*

grid·dle·cake (grĭd′l-kāk′) *n.* See **pancake**.

grid·i·ron (grĭd′ī′ərn) *n.* **1.** *Football* **a.** The field of play. **b.** The game itself. **2.** A metal structure high above the stage of a theater, from which ropes or cables are strung to scenery and lights. **3a.** A flat framework of parallel metal bars for broiling meat or fish. **b.** An object resembling a griddle. [ME *gridirne,* alteration of *gridere,* alteration of *gridel.* See GRIDDLE.]

grid·lock (grĭd′lŏk′) *n.* **1.** A traffic jam in which no vehicular movement is possible. **2.** A complete lack of movement or progress. —**grid′lock′** *v.* —**grid′locked′** *adj.*

grief (grēf) *n.* **1.** Deep mental anguish, as from bereavement. **2.** A source of deep mental anguish. **3.** Annoyance or frustration. **4.** Trouble or difficulty. **5.** *Archaic* A grievance. [ME < OFr. < *grever,* to harm. See GRIEVE.]

Grieg (grēg, grĭg), **Edvard Hagerup** 1843–1907. Norwegian composer known for his works incorporating folk music.

griev·ance (grē′vəns) *n.* **1a.** An actual or supposed circumstance regarded as just cause for complaint. **b.** A complaint or protestation based on a grievance. **2.** Indignation or resentment stemming from feeling wronged. **3.** *Obsolete* **a.** The act of inflicting hardship or harm. **b.** The cause of hardship or harm. [ME *grevaunce* < OFr. *grevance* < *grever,* to harm. See GRIEVE.]

grieve (grēv) *v.* **grieved, griev·ing, grieves** —*tr.* **1.** To cause to be sorrowful; distress. **2.** To mourn or sorrow for. **3.** *Archaic* To hurt or harm. —*intr.* To experience or express grief. [ME *greven* < OFr. *grever,* to harm < Lat. *gravāre* < *gravis,* heavy. See gʷerə- in App.] —**griev′er** *n.* —**griev′ing·ly** *adv.*

SYNONYMS *grieve, lament, mourn, sorrow* These verbs mean to feel, show, or express grief, sadness, or regret: *grieved over the loss; lamenting over declining standards; mourns for lost hopes; sorrowed by the level of poverty.* **ANTONYM** *rejoice*

---

griev·ous (grē′vəs) *adj.* **1.** Causing grief, pain, or anguish. **2.** Serious or dire; grave: *a grievous crime.* —**griev′ous·ly** *adv.* —**griev′ous·ness** *n.*

grif·fin also **grif·fon** or **gryph·on** (grĭf′ən) *n.* A fabulous beast with the head and wings of an eagle and the body of a lion. [ME *griffoun* < OFr. *griffon* < *grif* < Lat. *grўpus, grўphus,* var. of *grўps, grўph-* < Gk. *grūps.*]

Grif·fith (grĭf′ĭth), **D(avid Lewelyn) W(ark)** 1875–1948. Amer. filmmaker whose works include *The Birth of a Nation* (1915).

grif·fon (grĭf′ən) *n.* **1.** Any of a breed of dog originating in Belgium and having a short bearded muzzle. **2.** Any of various wirehaired hunting dogs of a breed originating in the Netherlands in the late 19th century. **3.** Variant of **griffin.** [Fr. < OFr. See GRIFFIN.]

grift (grĭft) *Slang n.* **1.** Money made by grifting. **2.** A swindle or confidence game. ❖ *v.* **grift·ed, grift·ing, grifts** —*intr.* To engage in swindling or cheating. —*tr.* To obtain by grifting. [Perh. alteration of GRAFT[2].] —**grift′er** *n.*

grig (grĭg) *n.* A lively, bright person. [ME, dwarf.]

gri·gri also **gris-gris** (grē′grē) *n., pl.* **gri·gris** also **gris-gris** (grē′grē) An African charm, fetish, or amulet. [Fr., of West African orig.; akin to Balanta (Niger-Congo language of Guinea-Bissau and Senegal) *grigri,* amulet.]

grill (grĭl) *tr.v.* **grilled, grill·ing, grills 1.** To broil on a gridiron. **2.** To torture or afflict as if by broiling. **3.** *Informal* To question relentlessly; cross-examine. **4.** To mark or emboss with a gridiron. ❖ *n.* **1.** A cooking surface of parallel metal bars; a gridiron. **2.** Food cooked by broiling or grilling. **3.** A grillroom. **4.** A series of marks grilled or embossed on a surface. **5.** Variant of **grille.** [Fr. *griller* < *gril,* gridiron < OFr. *greille* < Lat. *crāticula.* See GRIDDLE.] —**grill′er** *n.*

grill·age (grĭl′ĭj) *n.* A network or frame of timber or steel serving as a foundation, usu. on wet or soft ground. [Fr. < OFr., trellis < *greille,* gridiron. See GRILL.]

grille also **grill** (grĭl) *n.* **1.** A grating used as a screen, divider, barrier, or decorative element, as in a window. **2.** An opening covered with a grating. [Fr. < OFr. *greille.* See GRILL.]

grill·er·y (grĭl′ə-rē) *n., pl.* **-ies** A grillroom; a grill.

grill·room (grĭl′rōōm′, -rŏŏm′) *n.* A place where grilled foods are served to customers.

grill·work (grĭl′wûrk′) *n.* Material formed into a grille.

grilse (grĭls) *n., pl.* **grilse** A young Atlantic salmon first returning to fresh or brackish waters. [< ME *grills,* (pl.).]

grim (grĭm) *adj.* **grim·mer, grim·mest 1.** Unrelenting; rigid. **2.** Uninviting or unnerving in aspect; forbidding. **3.** Ghastly; sinister. **4.** Dismal; gloomy. **5.** Ferocious; savage. [ME < OE, fierce, severe.] —**grim′ly** *adv.* —**grim′ness** *n.*

grim·ace (grĭm′ĭs, grĭ-mās′) *n.* A sharp contortion of the face expressive of pain, contempt, or disgust. [Fr. < OFr. *grimache,* alteration of *grimuche,* prob. < Frankish **grīma,* mask.] —**grim′ace** *v.* —**grim′ac·er** *n.*

gri·mal·kin (grĭ-môl′kĭn, -măl′-) *n.* **1.** A cat, esp. an old female cat. **2.** An ill-tempered old woman. [Variant of *graymalkin* : GRAY[1] + obsolete *malkin,* lower-class woman (< *Malkin,* dim. of the personal name *Matilda*).]

grime (grīm) *n.* Black dirt or soot, esp. that clinging to or ingrained in a surface. [ME *grim*; akin to MDu. *grīme.*] —**grime** *v.*

Grim·ké (grĭm′kē), **Sarah Moore** 1792–1873. Amer. feminist and abolitionist who with her sister **Angelina Emily Grimké** (1805–79) campaigned publicly against slavery.

Grimm (grĭm), **Jakob Ludwig Karl** 1785–1863. German philologist and folklorist who formulated Grimm's Law (1819) and with his brother **Wilhelm Karl** (1786–1859) compiled *Grimm's Fairy Tales* (1812–15).

Grimm's Law (grĭmz) *n.* A formula showing how Indo-European stops changed in Germanic, stating that Indo-European *p, t,* and *k* became Germanic *f, th,* and *h; b, d,* and *g* became *p, t,* and *k;* and *bh, dh,* and *gh* became *b, d,* and *g.* [After Jakob Ludwig Karl GRIMM.]

Grim Reaper *n.* The personification of death as a cloaked man or skeleton carrying a scythe.

grim·y (grī′mē) *adj.* **-i·er, -i·est** Covered or smudged with grime. —**grim′i·ly** *adv.* —**grim′i·ness** *n.*

grin (grĭn) *v.* **grinned, grin·ning, grins** —*intr.* To smile broadly, often baring the teeth, as in amusement or embarrassment. —*tr.* To express with a grin. ❖ *n.* **1.** The act of grinning. **2.** The facial expression in grinning. [ME *grennen,* to grimace < OE *grennian.*] —**grin′ner** *n.* —**grin′ning·ly** *adv.*

grind (grīnd) *v.* **ground** (ground), **grind·ing, grinds** —*tr.* **1a.** To crush, pulverize, or reduce to powder by friction, esp. by rubbing between two hard surfaces. **b.** To shape, sharpen, or refine with friction: *grind a lens.* **2.** To rub (two surfaces) together harshly; gnash: *grind the teeth.* **3.** To bear down on harshly; crush. **4.** To oppress or weaken gradually. **5a.** To operate by turning a crank. **b.** To produce or process by turning a crank. **6.** To produce mechanically or without inspiration: *grinds out work.* **7.** To instill or teach by persistent repetition. —*intr.* **1.** To grind something. **2.** To become crushed, pulverized, or powdered by friction. **3.** To move with noisy friction; grate. **4.** *Informal* To devote oneself to study or work: *grinding away at math.* **5.** *Slang* To rotate the pelvis erotically, as in the manner of a stripteaser. ❖ *n.* **1.** The act of grinding. **2.** A crunching or grinding noise. **3.** A specific grade or degree of pulverization, as of coffee beans. **4.** *Informal* A laborious task, routine, or study. **5.** *Informal* A student who works or studies excessively. **6.** *Slang* An erotic rotation of the pelvis. [ME *grinden* < OE *grindan.* See ghrendh- in App.] —**grind′ing·ly** *adv.*

grind·er (grīn′dər) *n.* **1.** One that grinds, esp.: **a.** One who sharpens cutting edges. **b.** A mechanical device that grinds. **2.** A molar. **3.** **grinders** *Informal* The teeth. **4.** *New England & Sacramento* See **submarine** 2. See Regional Note at **submarine**.

grind·stone (grīnd′stōn′) *n.* **1.** A revolving stone disk used for grinding, polishing, or sharpening tools. **2.** A millstone. —*idiom:* **put (one's) nose to the grindstone** To work in earnest.

grin·ga (grĭng′gə) *n. Offensive Slang* Used as a disparaging term for a foreign woman in Latin America, esp. an American or English woman. [Sp., fem. of *gringo,* gringo. See GRINGO.]

grin·go (grĭng′gō) *n., pl.* **-gos** *Offensive Slang* Used as a disparaging term for a foreigner in Latin America, esp. an American or English person. [Sp., foreign, foreign language, gibberish, prob. alteration of *griego,* Gk. < Lat. *Graecus.* See GREEK.]

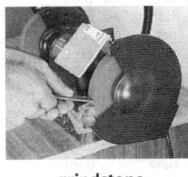

grindstone

gri•ot (grē-ō′, grē′ō, grē′ŏt) *n.* A storyteller in western Africa who perpetuates the oral tradition of a village or family. [Fr., alteration of *guiriot*, perh. ult. < Port. *criado*, servant < Lat. *creātus*, one trained < p. part. of *creāre*, to bring up. See CREATE.]

grip[1] (grĭp) *n.* **1a.** A tight hold; a firm grasp. **b.** The pressure or strength of such a grasp. **c.** A manner of grasping and holding. **2a.** Intellectual hold; understanding: *a good grip on French history.* **b.** Ability to function properly or well; competence: *getting a grip on the new technique.* **c.** Mental or emotional composure: *lost his grip after he was fired.* **3a.** A mechanical device that grasps and holds. **b.** A part, such as a handle, that is designed to be grasped and held. **4.** A suitcase or valise. **5a.** A stagehand who helps in shifting scenery. **b.** A member of a film crew who adjusts sets, lighting, and props and sometimes assists the camera operator. ❖ *v.* **gripped, grip•ping, grips** —*tr.* **1.** To secure and maintain a grip on; seize firmly. **2.** To hold the interest or attention of. —*intr.* To maintain a secure grasp. [ME < OE *gripe*, grasp and *gripa*, handful.] **—grip′per** *n.* **—grip′ping•ly** *adv.*

grip[2] (grĭp) *n.* Variant of **grippe.**

gripe (grīp) *v.* **griped, grip•ing, gripes** —*intr.* **1.** *Informal* To complain naggingly or petulantly; grumble. **2.** To have sharp pains in the bowels. —*tr.* **1.** *Informal* To irritate; annoy. **2.** To cause sharp pain in the bowels of. **3.** To grasp; seize. **4.** To oppress or afflict. ❖ *n.* **1.** *Informal* A complaint. **2. gripes** Sharp spasmodic pains in the bowels. **3.** A firm hold; a grasp. **4.** A grip; a handle. [ME *gripen*, to seize < OE *grīpan*.] **—grip′er** *n.*

grippe also **grip** (grĭp) *n.* See **influenza** 1. [Fr. < OFr., claw, quarrel < *gripper*, to seize, grasp < Frankish **grīpan*.] **—grip′py** *adj.*

grip•sack (grĭp′săk′) *n.* A small suitcase.

Gris (grēs), **Juan** 1887–1927. Spanish painter whose works include *Homage to Picasso* (1912).

gri•saille (grĭ-zī′, -zāl′) *n.* **1.** A style of monochromatic painting in shades of gray, used esp. to depict relief sculpture. **2.** A painting or design in this style. **3a.** Vitrifiable glass paint. **b.** A lacy pattern painted on light glass with grisaille and fired. [Fr. < *gris*, gray < OFr. < Frankish **grīs*.]

gris•e•o•ful•vin (grĭz′ē-ə-fŭl′vĭn) *n.* An antibiotic, $C_{17}H_{17}ClO_6$, used to treat ringworm and other fungal infections. [NLat. *(Pēnĭcillium) grīseofulvum*, species of penicillium : Med.Lat. *grīseus*, griseous; see GRISEOUS + Lat. *fulvum*, neut. of *fulvus*, tawny; see **ghel-** in App.]

gris•e•ous (grĭz′ē-əs, grĭs′-) *adj.* Mottled with gray, esp. bluish gray; grizzled. [Med.Lat. *grīseus*, of Gmc. orig.]

gris-gris (grē′grē) *n.* Variant of **grigri.**

gris•ly (grĭz′lē) *adj.* **-li•er, -li•est** Repugnant; gruesome. [ME *grisli* < OE *grislīc*.] **—gris′li•ness** *n.*

gri•son (grī′sən, grĭz′ən) *n.* Either of two small carnivorous mammals *(Galictis vittata* or *G. cuja)* of Central and South America having grizzled fur, a slender body, and short legs. [Fr. < OFr., gray fur < *gris*, gray. See GRISAILLE.]

grist (grĭst) *n.* **1.** Grain or a quantity of grain for grinding. **2.** Ground grain. ***—idiom:* grist for (one's) (or the) mill** Something that can be used to advantage. [ME < OE *grīst*. See **ghrendh-** in App.]

gris•tle (grĭs′əl) *n.* Cartilage, esp. in meat. [ME < OE.]

gris•tly (grĭs′lē) *adj.* **-tli•er, -tli•est 1.** Composed of or containing gristle. **2.** Resembling gristle. **—gris′tli•ness** *n.*

grist•mill (grĭst′mĭl′) *n.* A mill for grinding grain.

grit (grĭt) *n.* **1.** Minute rough granules, as of sand. **2.** The texture or fineness of sand or stone used in grinding. **3.** A coarse hard sandstone used in grindstones and millstones. **4.** *Informal* Indomitable spirit; pluck. ❖ *v.* **grit•ted, grit•ting, grits** —*tr.* **1.** To clamp (the teeth) together. **2.** To cover or treat with grit. —*intr.* To make a grinding noise. [ME *gret*, sand < OE *grēot*.]

grith (grĭth) *n.* Protection or sanctuary provided by Old English law to persons in certain circumstances, as when in a church. [ME < OE < ON *gridh*, domicile, asylum.]

grits (grĭts) *pl.n.* (*used with a sing. or pl. verb*) **1.** A ground, usu. white meal of dried and hulled corn kernels that is boiled and eaten. **2.** Coarsely ground grain, esp. corn. [Alteration of ME *grutta*, coarse meal < OE *grytta*, pl. of *grytt*.]

grit•ty (grĭt′ē) *adj.* **-ti•er, -ti•est 1.** Containing, covered with, or resembling grit. **2.** Showing resolution and fortitude; plucky. **—grit′ti•ly** *adv.* **—grit′ti•ness** *n.*

griv•et (grĭv′ĭt) *n.* See **vervet.** [Fr.]

griz•zle (grĭz′əl) *tr. & intr.v.* **-zled, -zling, -zles** To make or become gray. ❖ *n.* **1a.** The color of a grizzled animal. **b.** A grizzled animal. **2.** *Archaic* Gray hair. ❖ *adj.* **1.** Gray. **2.** Grizzled. [< ME *grisel*, gray < OFr., dim. of *gris*, gray. See GRISAILLE.]

griz•zled (grĭz′əld) *adj.* **1.** Streaked with or partly gray. **2.** Having fur or hair streaked or tipped with gray.

griz•zly (grĭz′lē) *adj.* **-zli•er, -zli•est** Grayish or flecked with gray. ❖ *n., pl.* **-zlies** A grizzly bear.

grizzly bear *n.* The brown bear of northwest North America, now considered a subspecies *(Ursus arctos* subsp. *horribilis).*

gro. *abbr.* gross

groan (grōn) *v.* **groaned, groan•ing, groans** —*intr.* **1.** To voice a deep inarticulate sound, as of pain. **2.** To make a sound expressive of stress or strain. —*tr.* To utter or express by groaning. ❖ *n.* The sound made in groaning. [ME *gronen* < OE *grānian*.] **—groan′er** *n.* **—groan′ing•ly** *adv.*

groat (grōt) *n.* An English silver coin worth four pence, used from the 14th to the 17th century. [ME *grot* < MDu. *groot*, a thick large coin, transl. of Med.Lat. *(dēnārius) grossus*.]

groats (grōts) *pl.n.* (*used with a sing. or pl. verb*) Hulled, usu. crushed grain, esp. oats. [ME *grotes* < OE *grotan*.]

gro•cer (grō′sər) *n.* A seller of foodstuffs and various household supplies. [ME, wholesaler < AN *grosser* < Med.Lat. *grossārius*, *grocerius* < LLat. *grossus*, thick.]

gro•cer•y (grō′sə-rē) *n., pl.* **-ies 1.** A store selling groceries. **2. groceries** Commodities sold by a grocer.

Grod•no (grôd′nō, -nə) See **Hrodna.**

grog (grŏg) *n.* An alcoholic liquor, esp. rum diluted with water. [After O *Grog*, nickname of Edward Vernon (1684–1757), British admiral who ordered that grog be served his sailors < GROGRAM (< his wearing a grogram cloak).]

grog•gy (grŏg′ē) *adj.* **-gi•er, -gi•est** Unsteady and dazed; shaky. [< GROG.] **—grog′gi•ly** *adv.* **—grog′gi•ness** *n.*

grog•ram (grŏg′rəm, grō′grəm) *n.* A coarse, often stiffened fabric made of silk, mohair, wool, or a blend of these fibers. [Alteration of Fr. *gros grain*, coarse texture. See GROSGRAIN.]

groin (groin) *n.* **1.** *Anatomy* The crease or hollow at the junction of the inner part of each thigh with the trunk, together with the adjacent region and often including the external genitals. **2.** *Architecture* The curved edge at the junction of two intersecting vaults. **3.** A small jetty extending from a shore to protect a beach against erosion or trap shifting sands. ❖ *tr.v.* **groined, groin•ing, groins** To provide or build with groins. [Alteration of ME *grinde*, perh. < OE *grynde*, abyss, hollow.]

groin vault *n.* See **cross vault.**

grok (grŏk) *tr.v.* **grok•ked, grok•king, groks** *Slang* To understand profoundly through intuition or empathy. [Coined by Robert A. Heinlein (1907–88) in his *Stranger in a Strange Land.*]

grom•met (grŏm′ĭt) also **grum•met** (grŭm′-) *n.* **1a.** A reinforced eyelet, as in cloth, through which a fastener may be passed. **b.** A small metal or plastic ring used to reinforce a grommet. **2.** *Nautical* A loop of rope or metal used for securing the edge of a sail to its stay. [Prob. < obsolete Fr. *gromette*, chain joining the ends of a bit < OFr. < *gourmer*, to bridle.]

grom•well (grŏm′wəl, -wĕl′) *n.* See **puccoon** 1. [Alteration of ME *gromil* < OFr. : *gro-*, of unknown meaning + *mil*, millet (< Lat. *milium*; see MILLET).]

Gro•my•ko (grə-mē′kō, grō-), **Andrei Andreyevich** 1909–89. Soviet politician who served as ambassador to the US (1943–46) and the United Nations (1946–48).

Gro•ning•en (grō′nĭng-ən, KHrō′-) A city of NE Netherlands NNE of Apeldoorn. Pop. 170,287.

groom (grōōm, grŏŏm) *n.* **1.** A person employed to take care of horses. **2.** A bridegroom. **3.** One of several officers in an English royal household. **4.** *Archaic* **a.** A man. **b.** A male servant. ❖ *v.* **groomed, groom•ing, grooms** —*tr.* **1.** To care for the appearance of; to make neat and trim. **2.** To clean and brush (an animal). **3.** To remove dirt and parasites from the skin, fur, or feathers of: *baboons grooming each other.* **4.** To prepare, as for a specific purpose. **5.** *Sports* To prepare (a trail) for skiers, as by leveling moguls. —*intr.* To care for one's appearance. [ME *grom*. N., sense 2, short for BRIDEGROOM.] **—groom′er** *n.*

grooms•man (grōōmz′mən, grŏŏmz′-) *n.* A man who attends the bridegroom at a wedding.

groove (grōōv) *n.* **1.** A long narrow furrow or channel. **2.** The spiral track cut into a phonograph record for the stylus to follow. **3.** *Slang* A settled routine. **4.** *Slang* A situation or an activity that one enjoys or to which one is well suited. **5.** *Slang* A very pleasurable experience. ❖ *v.* **grooved, groov•ing, grooves** —*tr.* To cut a groove or grooves in. —*intr. Slang* **1a.** To take great pleasure or satisfaction; enjoy oneself. **b.** To be pleasurably excited. **2.** To react or interact harmoniously. ***—idiom:* in the groove** *Slang* Performing exceptionally well. [ME *groof*, mining shaft, prob. < MDu. *groeve*, ditch.]

groov•y (grōō′vē) *adj.* **-i•er, -i•est** *Slang* Very pleasing; wonderful. **—groov′i•ness** *n.*

grope (grōp) *v.* **groped, grop•ing, gropes** —*intr.* **1.** To reach about uncertainly; feel one's way. **2.** To search blindly or uncertainly. —*tr.* **1.** To make (one's way) by reaching about uncertainly. **2.** *Slang* To handle or fondle for sexual pleasure. ❖ *n.* The act or an instance of groping. [ME *gropen* < OE *grāpian*.] **—grop′er** *n.* **—grop′ing•ly** *adv.*

Gro•pi•us (grō′pē-əs), **Walter Adolph** 1883–1969. German-born Amer. architect and founder of the Bauhaus school of design.

gros•beak (grōs′bēk′) *n.* Any of various finches of the family Fringillidae of Europe and America, having a thick conical bill. [Partial transl. of Fr. *grosbec* : *gros*, thick, large (< OFr.; see GROSS) + *bec*, beak.]

gros•grain (grō′grān′) *n.* **1.** A closely woven silk or rayon fabric with narrow horizontal ribs. **2.** A ribbon made of this fabric. [Fr. *gros grain*, coarse texture : *gros*, coarse, thick (< OFr.; see GROSS) + *grain*, texture, grain (< OFr. *graine*, grain, seed; see GRAIN).]

gross (grōs) *adj.* **gross•er, gross•est 1a.** Exclusive of deductions; total. See Syns at **whole. b.** Unmitigated in any way; utter. **2.** Glaringly obvious; flagrant. **3a.** Brutishly coarse, as in behavior; crude. **b.** Offensive; disgusting. **c.** Lacking sensitivity or dis-

Walter Gropius
with his design for the 1922 *Chicago Tribune* competition

ă pat	oi boy
ā pay	ou out
âr care	ŏŏ took
ä father	ōō boot
ĕ pet	ŭ cut
ē be	ûr urge
ĭ pit	th thin
ī pie	*th* this
îr pier	hw which
ŏ pot	zh vision
ō toe	ə about, item
ô paw	

Stress marks:
′ (primary);
′ (secondary), as in
lexicon (lĕk′sĭ-kŏn′)

cernment; unrefined. **d.** Carnal; sensual. **4a.** Overweight; corpulent. **b.** Dense; profuse. **5.** Broad; general: *gross outlines.* ❖ *n.* **1.** *pl.* **gross•es** The gross amount or body, as of income. **2.** *pl.* **gross** A group of 144 items; 12 dozen. ❖ *tr.v.* **grossed, gross•ing, gross•es** To earn as a gross income or profit. —*phrasal verb:* **gross out** *Slang* To fill with disgust; nauseate. [ME, large < OFr. *gros* < LLat. *grossus,* thick. N., sense 2, ME *grosse* < OFr. *grosse (douzain),* large (dozen), fem. of *gros.*] —**gross′er** *n.* —**gross′ly** *adv.* —**gross′ness** *n.*

gross anatomy *n.* The study of the organs, parts, and structures of a body that are visible to the naked eye.

gross domestic product *n.* The total market value of all the goods and services produced within the borders of a nation during a specified period.

gross national product *n.* The total market value of all the goods and services produced by a nation in a specified period.

gross-out (grōs′out′) *n. Slang* Something that disgusts.

gros•su•la•rite (grŏs′yə-lə-rīt′) also **gros•su•lar** (-lər) *n.* A pale green, pink, brown, or black garnet, $Ca_3Al_2(SiO_4)_3$, occurring alone or as a constituent of the common garnet. [Ger. *Grossularit* < NLat. *Grossulària,* former genus of gooseberry (< the color of some garnets) < Fr. *groseille,* gooseberry < OFr. *grosele,* < Gmc. orig.]

Gros Ventre (grō′ vänt′) *n., pl.* **Gros Ventre** or **Gros Ventres** (vänt′) **1.** See **Atsina. 2.** See **Hidatsa.** [Fr., big belly : *gros,* big + *ventre,* belly (< an indigenous sign-language gesture designating this people that suggested a big belly).]

Grosz (grōs), **George** 1893–1959. German-born Amer. artist known for his biting antimilitaristic caricatures of the 1920s.

grot (grŏt) *n.* A grotto. [Fr. *grotte* < Ital. *grotta.* See GROTTO.]

gro•tesque (grō-tĕsk′) *adj.* **1.** Marked by ludicrous or incongruous distortion, as of appearance. **2.** Outlandish or bizarre, as in character. See Syns at **fantastic. 3.** Of, relating to, or being the grotesque style in art or a work executed in this style. ❖ *n.* **1.** One that is grotesque. **2a.** A style of painting, sculpture, and ornamentation in which natural forms and monstrous figures are intertwined in bizarre or fanciful combinations. **b.** A grotesque work of art. [< Fr., a fanciful style of decorative art < Ital. *grottesca* < fem. of *grottesco,* of a grotto < *grotta,* grotto. See GROTTO.] —**gro•tesque′ly** *adv.* —**gro•tesque′ness** *n.*

gro•tes•que•ry also **gro•tes•que•rie** (grō-tĕs′kə-rē) *n., pl.* **-ries 1.** Grotesqueness. **2.** Something grotesque.

Gro•ti•us (grō′shē-əs, -shəs), **Hugo** Orig. Huig de Groot. 1583–1645. Dutch jurist and politician known for *Of the Law of War and Peace* (1625).

grot•to (grŏt′ō) *n., pl.* **-toes** or **-tos 1.** A small cave or cavern. **2.** An artificial structure or excavation made to resemble a cave or cavern. [Alteration of Ital. *grotta* < VLat. **grupta* < Lat. *crypta,* vault. See CRYPT.]

grot•ty (grŏt′ē) *adj.* **-ti•er, -ti•est** *Chiefly British Slang* Very unpleasant; miserable. [Alteration of GROTESQUE.] —**grot′ti•ness** *n.*

grouch (grouch) *n.* **1.** A habitually complaining or irritable person. **2.** A grumbling or sulky mood. ❖ *intr.v.* **grouched, grouch•ing, grouch•es** To grumble or sulk. [< ME *grucchen,* to grumble, complain. See GRUDGE.]

grouch•y (grou′chē) *adj.* **-i•er, -i•est** Tending to grouch; peevish or grumpy. —**grouch′i•ly** *adv.* —**grouch′i•ness** *n.*

ground¹ (ground) *n.* **1a.** The solid surface of the earth. **b.** The floor of a body of water, esp. the sea. **2.** Soil; earth. **3.** An area of land designated for a particular purpose. Often used in the plural. **4.** The land surrounding or forming part of a house or another building. Often used in the plural. **5.** An area or position that is contested in or as if in battle. **6.** Something that serves as a foundation or means of attachment for something else. **7.** A surrounding area; a background. **8.** The foundation for an argument, belief, or action; a basis. Often used in the plural. **9.** The underlying condition prompting an action; a cause. Often used in the plural. **10.** An area of reference or discussion; a subject. **11. grounds** The sediment at or from the bottom of a liquid. **12.** *Electricity* **a.** A large conducting body, such as the earth, used as an arbitrary zero of potential. **b.** A conducting object, such as a wire, connected to such a position of zero potential. ❖ *v.* **ground•ed, ground•ing, grounds** —*tr.* **1.** To place on or cause to touch the ground. **2.** To provide a basis for (a theory, for example); justify. **3.** To supply with basic information; instruct in fundamentals. **4a.** To prevent (an aircraft or pilot) from flying. **b.** *Informal* To restrict (someone) esp. to a certain place as a punishment. **5.** *Electricity* To connect (an electric circuit) to a ground. **6.** *Nautical* To run (a vessel) aground. **7a.** *Baseball* To hit (a ball) onto the ground. **b.** *Football* To throw (a ball) to the ground in order to stop play and avoid being tackled behind the line of scrimmage. —*intr.* **1.** To touch or reach the ground. **2.** *Baseball* To hit a ground ball. **3.** *Nautical* To run aground. —*phrasal verb:* **ground out** *Baseball* To be put out by hitting a ground ball that is fielded and thrown to first base. —*idioms:* **drive (or run) into the ground** To belabor (a subject). **from the ground up** From the most basic level to the highest level; completely. **off the ground** Under way, as if in flight. **on (one's) own ground** In a situation where one has knowledge or competence. [ME < OE *grund.*]

ground² (ground) *v.* Past tense and past participle of **grind.**

ground ball also **ground·ball** (ground′bôl′) *n. Baseball* A batted ball that rolls or bounces along the ground.

ground bass (bās) *n.* A musical line in the bass that is repeated throughout the composition.

ground beetle *n.* See **carabid.**

ground·break·er (ground′brā′kər) *n.* One that is original or innovative.

ground·break·ing (ground′brā′kĭng) *n.* The act or ceremony of breaking ground to begin a construction project. ❖ *adj.* **1.** Of, relating to, or being a ceremony of breaking ground. **2.** Characterized by originality and innovation.

ground cedar *n.* See **ground pine.**

ground cherry *n.* Any of various chiefly New World plants of the genus *Physalis,* having small globose fleshy fruit enclosed in a papery bladderlike persistent calyx.

ground cloth *n.* **1.** A waterproof cover used to protect an area of ground, such as a baseball field. **2.** A waterproof sheet placed under camp bedding as a protection against moisture.

ground-con·trolled approach (ground′kən-trōld′) *n.* A control mode in which an aircraft is talked down for landing through the use of surveillance and precision approach radar.

ground cover also **ground·cov·er** (ground′kŭv′ər) *n.* **1.** Small plants other than saplings, such as mosses and undershrubs, growing on a forest floor; undergrowth. **2a.** A low-growing dense growth of plants, such as pachysandra, planted as ornament or to prevent soil erosion in areas where turf is difficult to grow, as in deep shade. **b.** A plant used for such a growth.

ground crew *n.* A team of mechanics and technicians that maintain and service aircraft on the ground.

ground-ef·fect machine (ground′ĭ-fĕkt′) *n.* See **air-cushion vehicle.** [< *ground effect,* a peculiarity of certain aircraft when landing, in which a cushion of air directed off the wings prevents touchdown.]

ground·er (groun′dər) *n. Baseball* A ground ball.

ground·fish (ground′fĭsh′) *n., pl.* **groundfish** or **-fish·es** A bottom-dwelling fish, esp. a commercially valuable marine species such as cod.

ground floor *n.* **1.** The floor of a building at or nearest ground level. **2.** *Informal* The beginning of a venture, esp. as a position of advantage.

ground glass *n.* **1.** Glass that has been ground or etched to create a roughened nontransparent surface. **2.** Glass that has been ground into fine particles, as for use as an abrasive.

ground hemlock *n.* A low-growing yew (*Taxus canadensis*) of northeast North America.

ground·hog also **ground hog** (ground′hôg′, -hŏg′) *n.* See **woodchuck.** See Regional Note at **woodchuck.**

Groundhog Day *n.* February 2, on which according to popular legend the groundhog emerges from its burrow, prompting the prediction of an early spring if it does not see its shadow or six more weeks of winter if it does.

ground ivy *n.* A creeping or trailing aromatic plant (*Glechoma hederacea*) having rounded scalloped leaves and small purplish flowers.

ground·keep·er (ground′kē′pər) *n.* Variant of **groundskeeper.**

ground·less (ground′lĭs) *adj.* Having no ground or foundation; unsubstantiated. —**ground′less·ness** *n.*

ground level *n.* See **ground state.**

ground·ling (ground′lĭng) *n.* **1a.** A plant or an animal living on or near the ground. **b.** A bottom fish. **2.** A person with uncultivated tastes. **3.** A spectator in the cheap standing-room section of an Elizabethan theater.

ground loop *n.* A sharp horizontal turn made by an aircraft on the ground when taxiing, landing, or taking off.

ground·mass (ground′măs′) *n.* The fine-grained crystalline base of porphyritic rock in which larger crystals are embedded.

ground meristem *n.* The tissue at the tip of a growing stem or root that differentiates into the pith and cortex.

ground·nut (ground′nŭt′) *n.* **1a.** A climbing vine (*Apios americana*) of eastern North America having compound leaves and small edible tubers. **b.** Any of several plants having underground tubers or nutlike parts. **c.** The tuber or nutlike part of such a plant. **2.** *Chiefly British & South Atlantic US* A peanut.

ground·out (ground′out′) *n. Baseball* A play in which a batter grounds out.

ground pine *n.* A club moss, esp. *Lycopodium obscurum* or *L. complanatum* or a similar species.

ground plan *n.* **1.** A plan of a floor of a building drawn as if seen from overhead. **2.** A preliminary plan or strategy.

ground plum *n.* **1.** A perennial plant (*Astragalus crassicarpus*) of the central and western United States having compound leaves and plumlike edible fruit. **2.** The fruit of this plant.

ground rent *n. Chiefly British* Rent paid for land to be used chiefly for building.

ground robin *n.* See **towhee** 1.

ground rule *n.* **1.** *Sports* A rule governing the playing of a game on a particular field, course, or court. **2.** A basic rule of procedure or behavior. Often used in the plural.

ground rule double *n. Baseball* A double awarded to a batter when a batted ball bounces and goes over, strikes and goes over, or is touched by a player and goes over an outfield wall.

ground•sel[1] (ground'səl, groun'-) *n.* Any of various plants of the genus *Senecio,* having rayed, usu. yellow flower heads. [ME *groundeswille* < OE *grundeswylige,* alteration of *gundeswilge* : *gund,* pus + *swelgan,* to swallow (used in reducing abscesses).]

ground•sel[2] (ground'səl, groun'-) *n.* Variant of **groundsill.**

ground sheet *n.* See **ground cloth.**

ground•side (ground'sīd') *n.* The part of an airport used for operations unrelated to the departure and arrival of aircraft.

ground•sill (ground'sĭl') also **ground•sel** (ground'səl, groun'-) *n.* The horizontal timber nearest the ground in the frame of a building.

grounds•keep•er (groundz'kē'pər) also **ground•keep•er** (ground'-) *n.* One who maintains grounds, as of an estate.

ground sloth *n.* Any of various massive extinct edentates, esp. of the genus *Megatherium,* inhabiting South America during the Pleistocene Epoch.

ground speed also **ground•speed** (ground'spēd') *n.* The speed of an airborne aircraft relative to the ground it traverses in a given period of time.

ground squirrel *n.* Any of several burrowing or terrestrial squirrels of the genus *Citellus* or *Spermophilus.*

ground state *n.* The state of least possible energy in a physical system, as of elementary particles.

ground stroke *n.* A swing of a tennis racquet at a ball that has bounced from the ground.

ground substance *n.* **1.** The intercellular material in which the cells and fibers of connective tissue are embedded. **2.** See **hyaloplasm.**

ground•swell (ground'swĕl') *n.* **1.** A sudden gathering of force, as of public opinion. **2.** A broad deep undulation of the ocean, often caused by a distant storm or an earthquake.

ground water also **ground•wa•ter** (ground'wô'tər, -wŏt'ər) *n.* Water beneath the earth's surface, often between saturated soil and rock, that supplies wells and springs.

ground wave *n.* A radio wave traveling along the earth's surface.

ground•work (ground'wûrk') *n.* A foundation; a basis.

ground zero *n.* **1.** The target of a projectile, such as a missile or bomb. **2.** The site directly below, directly above, or at the point of detonation of a nuclear weapon. **3.** The center of rapid or intense development or change. **4.** The starting point or most basic level.

group (gro͞op) *n.* **1.** An assemblage of persons or objects gathered or located together; an aggregation. **2.** Two or more figures that make up a unit or design, as in sculpture. **3.** A number of individuals or things considered together because of similarities. **4.** *Linguistics* A category of related languages that is less inclusive than a family. **5a.** A military unit consisting of two or more battalions and a headquarters. **b.** A unit of two or more squadrons in the US Air Force, smaller than a wing. **6.** A class or collection of related objects or entities, as: **a.** Two or more atoms behaving or regarded as behaving as a single chemical unit. **b.** A column in the periodic table of the elements. **c.** A stratigraphic unit, esp. a unit of two or more formations deposited during a single geologic era. **7.** *Mathematics* A set with a binary associative operation such that the operation admits an identity element and each element of the set has an inverse element for the operation. ❖ *adj.* Of, relating to, constituting, or being a member of a group. ❖ *v.* **grouped, group•ing, groups** *—tr.* To place or arrange in a group. *—intr.* To belong to or form a group. [Fr. *groupe* < Ital. *gruppo,* prob. of Gmc. orig.]

USAGE NOTE *Group* as a collective noun can be followed by a singular or plural verb. It takes a singular verb when those making up the group are considered collectively: *The group is here.* It takes a plural verb when those constituting the group are considered individually: *The group were divided in their sympathies.* See Usage Note at **collective noun.**

grou•per (gro͞o'pər) *n., pl.* **grouper** or **-pers** Any of various often large food and game fishes of the genera *Epinephelus, Mycteroperca,* and related genera. [Port. *garupa.*]

group home *n.* A small supervised residential facility, as for mentally ill people.

group•ie (gro͞o'pē) *n. Slang* A fan, esp. a young woman, who follows a rock group around on tours.

group•ing (gro͞o'pĭng) *n.* **1.** The act or process of uniting into groups. **2.** People or things united into a group.

group insurance *n.* Insurance purchased by a group of persons, such as the employees of a company, often at a reduced individual rate.

group practice *n.* **1.** The practice of health care by an association of professionals who share premises and other resources. **2.** An association engaged in group practice.

group theory *n.* The branch of mathematics concerned with groups and the description of their properties.

group therapy *n.* A form of psychotherapy in which several clients guided by a therapist confront their problems together. **—group therapist** *n.*

group•think (gro͞op'thĭngk') *n.* The act or practice of reasoning or decision-making by a group, esp. when characterized by uncritical acceptance or conformity to prevailing points of view.

group•ware (gro͞op'wâr') *n.* Software that integrates work on a single project by several users at separated sites.

grouse[1] (grous) *n., pl.* **grouse** or **grous•es** Any of various plump chickenlike game birds of the family Tetraonidae, chiefly of the Northern Hemisphere and having mottled brown or grayish plumage. [?]

grouse[2] (grous) *Informal intr.v.* **groused, grous•ing, grous•es** To complain; grumble. ❖ *n.* A cause for complaint; a grievance. [Perh. < Fr. dialectal *groucer* < OFr. *grouchier.* See GRUDGE.] **—grous'er** *n.*

grout (grout) *n.* **1a.** A thin mortar used to fill cracks and crevices in masonry. **b.** A thin plaster for finishing walls and ceilings. **2.** *Chiefly British* Sediment; lees. Often used in the plural. ❖ *tr.v.* **grout•ed, grout•ing, grouts** To fill or finish with grout. [ME, grain used for making malt, mud < OE *grūt,* coarse meal.] **—grout'er** *n.*

grove (grōv) *n.* **1.** A small wood or stand of trees lacking dense undergrowth. **2.** A group of trees planted and cultivated for fruit or nut production: *an orange grove.* [ME < OE *grāf.*]

grov•el (grŏv'əl, grŭv'-) *intr.v.* **-eled, -el•ing, -els** also **-elled, -el•ling, -els 1.** To behave in a servile or demeaning manner; cringe. **2.** To lie flat or crawl on one's belly, as in humility or submission: *The dog groveled at its owner's feet.* **3.** To give oneself over to base pleasures: *"Have we not groveled here long enough, eating and drinking like mere brutes?"* (Walt Whitman). [Back-formation < obsolete *groveling,* prone, face downward < ME : *(on) grufe,* face downward (< ON *ā grūfu* < *grūfa,* to grovel) + *-ling,* adv. suff.; see –LING[2].] **—grov'el•er** *n.*

grow (grō) *v.* **grew** (gro͞o), **grown** (grōn), **grow•ing, grows** *—intr.* **1.** To increase in size by a natural process. **2a.** To expand; gain: *The business grew.* **b.** To increase in amount or degree; intensify: *Suspense grew.* **3.** To develop and reach maturity. **4.** To be capable of growth; thrive. **5.** To become attached by or as if by the process of growth. **6.** To come into existence from a source; spring up. **7.** To come to be by a gradual process or by degrees; become. *—tr.* **1.** To cause to grow; raise: *grow tulips.* **2.** To develop (something) to develop or increase by a natural process. **3.** *Usage Problem* To cause to increase or expand. **—phrasal verbs: grow into 1.** To develop so as to become. **2.** To develop or change so as to fit. **grow on** (or **upon**) **1.** To become gradually more evident to. **2.** To become gradually more pleasurable or acceptable to. **grow up** To become an adult. **—idiom: grow out of** To develop or come into existence from. [ME *growen* < OE *grōwan.*] **—grow'er** *n.* **—grow'ing•ly** *adv.*

USAGE NOTE In recent times, a new transitive sense of *grow* has come into being, "to cause to expand," used especially in business contexts. This usage does not find much favor among the Usage Panel; 80 percent rejected the phrase *grow our business.* But the Panel is more accepting of the phrase *grow our way:* 48 percent accept *We've got to grow our way out of this recession.*

grow•ing pains (grō'ĭng) *pl.n.* **1.** Limb and joint pains in children or adolescents, often wrongly attributed to rapid growth. **2.** Emotional difficulties during adolescence. **3.** Problems in the initiation or enlargement of an enterprise.

growl (groul) *n.* **1.** The low guttural menacing sound made by an animal. **2.** A gruff surly utterance. ❖ *v.* **growled, growl•ing, growls** *—intr.* **1.** To emit a low guttural sound or utterance. **2.** To speak in an angry or surly manner. *—tr.* To utter by growling. [ME *groule, grollen,* to rumble, growl, prob. < OFr. *grouler,* of Gmc. orig.] **—growl'y** *adj.*

grow lamp *n.* See **grow light.**

growl•er (grou'lər) *n.* **1.** One, such as a dog, that growls. **2.** A small iceberg. **3.** *Informal* A container, such as a pail, used for carrying beer. **4.** *Electricity* An electromagnetic device with two poles, used for magnetizing, demagnetizing, and finding short-circuited coils.

grow light *n.* A fluorescent lamp that emits a spectrum of light similar to that of the sun, used to grow plants indoors.

grown (grōn) *v.* Past participle of **grow.** ❖ *adj.* **1.** Having full growth; mature: *a grown woman.* **2.** Produced or cultivated in a certain way or place: *locally grown produce.*

grown•up also **grown-up** (grōn'ŭp') *n.* An adult.

grown-up (grōn'ŭp') *adj.* **1.** Of, characteristic of, or intended for adults: *a grown-up discussion.* **2.** Having or showing maturity in outlook, attitude, or appearance: *a grown-up attitude toward work.*

growth (grōth) *n.* **1a.** The process of growing. **b.** Full development; maturity. **2.** Development from a lower or simpler to a higher or more complex form; evolution. **3.** An increase, as in size or strength; extension or expansion: *population growth.* **4.** Something that grows or has grown. **5.** *Pathology* An abnormal mass of tissue, such as a tumor, growing in or on a living organism. **6.** A result of growth; a product. ❖ *adj.* Expected to have higher-than-average increases in revenues and returns: *a growth stock.*

growth factor *n.* A substance that affects the growth of a cell or organism.

growth fund *n.* A mutual fund that offers long-term capital appreciation.

growth hormone *n.* Any of various natural or synthetic substances, including human growth hormone and plant auxins, that

grouse[1]
spruce grouse
Dendragapus canadensis

ă	pat	oi	boy
ā	pay	ou	out
âr	care	o͝o	took
ä	father	o͞o	boot
ĕ	pet	ŭ	cut
ē	be	ûr	urge
ĭ	pit	th	thin
ī	pie	th	this
îr	pier	hw	which
ŏ	pot	zh	vision
ō	toe	ə	about,
ô	paw		item

Stress marks:
′ (primary);
′ (secondary), as in
lexicon (lĕk'sĭ-kŏn')

regulate the growth of an organism.

growth ring *n.* A growth layer in secondary xylem seen in a cross section.

Groz·ny or **Groz·nyy** (grôz′nē) The cap. of Chechnya in SW Russia. Its 1993 pop. was 393,000.

grub (grŭb) *v.* **grubbed, grub·bing, grubs** —*tr.* **1.** To dig up by or as if by the roots. **2.** To clear of roots and stumps by digging: *grubbed a small plot.* **3.** *Slang* To obtain by importunity. —*intr.* **1.** To dig in the earth: *grub for potatoes.* **2a.** To search laboriously by or as if by digging; rummage. **b.** To toil arduously; drudge: *grub for a living.* ❖ *n.* **1.** The thick wormlike larva of certain beetles and other insects. **2.** A drudge. **3.** *Slang* Food. [ME *grubben* < OE *grybban*.] —**grub′ber** *n.*

grub·by (grŭb′ē) *adj.* **-bi·er, -bi·est 1.** Dirty; grimy: *grubby clothes.* **2.** Infested with grubs. **3.** Contemptible; despicable: *grubby treatment.* —**grub′bi·ly** *adv.* —**grub′bi·ness** *n.*

grub·stake (grŭb′stāk′) *n.* Supplies or funds advanced to a mining prospector or a person starting a business in return for a promised share of the profits. ❖ *tr.v.* **-staked, -stak·ing, -stakes** To supply with a grubstake. —**grub′stak′er** *n.*

Grub Street *n.* The world of impoverished writers and literary hacks. [After *Grub Street,* London.]

grudge (grŭj) *tr.v.* **grudged, grudg·ing, grudg·es 1.** To be reluctant to give or admit. **2.** To resent for having; begrudge. ❖ *n.* A deep-seated resentment or rancor. [ME *gruggen, grucchen* < OFr. *grouchier.*] —**grudg′er** *n.*

grudg·ing (grŭj′ĭng) *adj.* Reluctant; unwilling. —**grudg′ing·ly** *adv.*

gru·el (grōō′əl) *n.* **1.** A thin watery porridge. **2.** *Chiefly British* Severe punishment. [ME < OFr., of Gmc. orig.]

gru·el·ing also **gru·el·ling** (grōō′ə-lĭng, grōō′lĭng) *adj.* Physically or mentally demanding to the point of exhaustion: *a grueling campaign.* —**gru′el·ing·ly** *adv.*

grue·some (grōō′səm) *adj.* Causing horror and repugnance; frightful and shocking. [Obsolete *grue,* to shudder (< ME *gruen* < MDu. *grūwen* or MLGer. *gruwen*) + -SOME[1].] —**grue′some·ly** *adv.* —**grue′some·ness** *n.*

gruff (grŭf) *adj.* **gruff·er, gruff·est 1.** Brusque or stern in manner or appearance. **2.** Hoarse; harsh: *a gruff voice.* [Du. *grof* < MDu. or MLGer.] —**gruff′ly** *adv.* —**gruff′ness** *n.*

grum·ble (grŭm′bəl) *v.* **-bled, -bling, -bles** —*intr.* **1.** To complain in a surly manner; mutter discontentedly. **2.** To rumble or growl. —*tr.* To express in a grumbling discontented manner. ❖ *n.* **1.** A muttered complaint. **2.** A rumble; a growl. [Prob. Du. *grommelen,* to mutter < MDu., freq. of *grommen.*] —**grum′bler** *n.* —**grum′bly** *adj.*

grum·met (grŭm′ĭt) *n.* Variant of **grommet.**

grump (grŭmp) *n.* **1.** A cranky complaining person. **2.** A fit of ill temper. Often used in the plural. ❖ *intr.v.* **grumped, grump·ing, grumps 1.** To mutter complaints. **2.** To behave in a grumpy manner. [?]

grump·y (grŭm′pē) *adj.* **-i·er, -i·est** Surly and peevish; cranky. —**grump′i·ly** *adv.* —**grump′i·ness** *n.*

Grü·ne·wald (grōō′nə-wôld′, grü′nə-vält′), **Matthias** d. 1528. German painter noted for his religious scenes.

grunge (grŭnj) *n.* **1.** *Informal* Filth; dirt. **2.** Rock music that incorporates elements of punk rock and heavy metal, often expressing a bleak or nihilistic outlook. [Back-formation < GRUNGY.]

grun·gy (grŭn′jē) *adj.* **-gi·er, -gi·est** *Informal* In a dirty, rundown, or inferior condition: *grungy old jeans.* [?]

grun·ion (grŭn′yən) *n.* A small fish (*Leuresthes tenuis*) of coastal waters of California and Mexico. [Perh. < Sp. *gruñón,* grumbler < *gruñir,* to grumble, grunt < Lat. *grunnīre, grundīre,* to grunt.]

grunt (grŭnt) *v.* **grunt·ed, grunt·ing, grunts** —*intr.* **1.** To utter a deep guttural sound, as a hog does. **2.** To utter a sound similar to a grunt, as in disgust. —*tr.* To utter or express with a deep guttural sound: *grunted approval.* ❖ *n.* **1.** A deep guttural sound. **2.** Any of various chiefly tropical marine fishes of the family Haemulidae that, upon removal from the water, produce grunting sounds by rubbing together tooth plates in the throat. **3.** *Slang* An infantryman in the US military, esp. in the Vietnam War. **4.** *Slang* One who performs routine or mundane tasks. **5.** *New England* A dessert made by stewing fruit topped with pieces of biscuit dough, which steam as the fruit cooks. [ME *grunten* < OE *grunnettan;* prob. akin to *grunnian,* to make a loud noise, grunt, of imit. orig.] —**grunt′er** *n.* —**grunt′ing·ly** *adv.*

Grus (grŭs, grōōs) *n.* A constellation in the Southern Hemisphere near Indus and Phoenix. [Lat. *grūs,* crane.]

Gru·yère (grōō-yâr′, grē-) *n.* A nutty, pale yellow, firm cheese made from cow's milk. [Fr., after *Gruyère,* a district of west-central Switzerland.]

gr. wt. *abbr.* gross weight

gryph·on (grĭf′ən) *n.* Variant of **griffin.**

GS *abbr.* **1.** general staff **2.** ground speed

GSA *abbr.* **1.** General Services Administration **2.** Girl Scouts of America

GSC *abbr.* general staff corps

GSO *abbr.* general staff officer

G spot *n.* An area around the female urethra and on the roof of the vagina postulated to enhance sexual arousal. [First described

by Ernst *G(räfenberg)* (1881–1957), German obstetrician and gynecologist.]

GST *abbr.* Greenwich sidereal time

G-string (jē′strĭng′) *n.* **1.** A narrow loincloth supported by a waistband; a breechcloth. **2.** A similar garment, usu. decorated, worn esp. by stripteasers. [?]

G-suit (jē′sōōt′) *n.* A flight garment worn by astronauts and jet pilots that presses on the lower body to maintain the blood supply to the brain during rapid vertical acceleration.

gt. *abbr. Pharmacology* gutta

Gt. Brit. *abbr.* Great Britain

GTC *abbr.* good till canceled

gtd. *abbr.* guaranteed

GTP (jē′tē-pē′) *n.* A nucleotide composed of guanine, ribose, and three phosphate groups that is necessary for the synthesis of RNA and proteins. [G(UANOSINE) T(RI)P(HOSPHATE).]

GTS *abbr.* gas turbine ship

gtt. *abbr. Pharmacology* guttae

GU *abbr.* **1.** genitourinary **2.** Guam

gua·ca·mo·le (gwä′kə-mō′lē) *n.* A thick paste of mashed avocado, often combined with citrus juice, onion, and seasonings and usu. served as a dip or in salads. [Am.Sp. < Nahuatl *ahuacamolli : ahuacatl,* avocado + *molli,* sauce, paste.]

gua·cha·ro (gwä′chə-rō′) *n., pl.* **-ros** A fruit-eating nocturnal bird (*Steatornis caripensis*) of South America. [Am.Sp. *guácharo* < *guacho,* vagabond < Quechua *wáhcha,* poor person, orphan.]

Gua·da·la·ja·ra (gwŏd′l-ə-här′ə, gwä′dä-lä-hä′rä) A city of W-central Mexico WNW of Mexico City. Pop. 1,626,152.

Gua·dal·ca·nal (gwŏd′l-kə-näl′) A volcanic island in the Solomon Is. of the W Pacific Ocean; occupied by the Japanese in World War II and captured by the Allies in Feb. 1943.

Gua·dal·qui·vir (gwä′dəl-kwĭv′ər, gwä′thäl-kē-vēr′) A river of S Spain flowing c. 644 km (400 mi) to the Gulf of Cádiz.

Gua·da·lupe Hi·dal·go (gwäd′l-ōōp′ hĭ-däl′gō, gwä′dä-lōō′pĕ ē-däl′gō) Officially **Gus·ta·vo A. Ma·de·ro** (gōō-stä′vō ä′ mə-dâr′ō, mä-dĕ′rō) A city of S-central Mexico, a suburb of Mexico City; site of the treaty ending the Mexican War (1848). Pop. 88,537.

Gua·da·lupe Mountains (gwŏd′l-ōōp′, gwŏd′l-ōō′pē) A range of S NM and W TX rising to **Guadalupe Peak,** 2,668.4 m (8,749 ft), in TX.

Guadalupe River A river of SE TX flowing c. 102 km (250 mi) to the San Antonio R.

Gua·de·loupe (gwŏd′l-ōōp′, gwŏd′l-ōōp′) An overseas department of France comprising Grande-Terre and Basse-Terre and smaller islands in the Leeward Is. of the West Indies; first colonized in 1635. Cap. Basse-Terre. Pop. 421,000.

Gua·di·a·na (gwä-dyä′nə, -thyä′nä) A river rising in S-central Spain and flowing c. 821 km (510 mi) partly along the Spanish-Portuguese border to the Gulf of Cádiz.

guai·a·col (gwī′ə-kôl′, -kōl′) *n.* An oily aromatic substance, $C_7H_8O_2$, derived from guaiacum or wood creosote and used chiefly as an expectorant and antiseptic. [GUAIAC(UM) + -OL[2].]

guai·a·cum (gwī′ə-kəm) *n.* **1.** A tree of the genus *Guaiacum;* a lignum vitae. **2.** also **guai·ac** (gwī′ăk′) **a.** The wood of a guaiacum. **b.** A greenish-brown resin obtained from this tree. [NLat. < Sp. *guayacán* < Taino.]

Guam (gwäm) An unincorporated US territory, the largest of the Mariana Is. in the W Pacific Ocean; ceded by Spain 1898. Cap. Agana. Pop. 156,974. —**Gua·ma′ni·an** (gwä-mä′nē-ən) *adj. & n.*

guan (gwän) *n.* Any of several large game birds of the family Cracidae, native to the jungles of tropical America and related to the curassows. [Am.Sp., of South American Indian orig.]

gua·na·ba·na (gwə-nä′bə-nə) *n.* See **soursop.** [Am.Sp. *guanábana* < Taino.]

Gua·na·ba·ra Bay (gwä′nə-bär′ə) An inlet of the Atlantic Ocean on the SE coast of Brazil.

gua·na·co (gwä-nä′kō) *n., pl.* **-cos** or **guanaco** A reddishbrown South American ruminant mammal (*Lama guanicoe*) related to the domesticated llama. [Sp. < Quechua *huanaco.*]

Guang·dong (gwäng′dông′) also **Kwang·tung** (kwäng′tŏŏng′, gwäng′dŏŏng′) A province of SE China on the South China Sea; part of China since c. 200 B.C. Cap. Guangzhou. Pop. 62,829,236.

Guang·xi Zhuang·zu (gwäng′shē′ jwäng′dzōō′) also **Kwang·si Chuang** (kwäng′sē′ chwäng′) An autonomous region of S China on the Vietnamese border. Cap. Nanning. Pop. 42,245,765.

Guang·zhou (gwäng′jō′) also **Kwang·chow** (kwäng′chō′) Formerly **Can·ton** (kăn′tŏn′, kăn′tŏn′) A city of S China on a delta near the South China Sea; cap. of Guangdong province. Pop. 3,918,010.

gua·ni·dine (gwä′nĭ-dēn′) *n.* A strongly alkaline crystalline compound, $NHC(NH_2)_2$, formed by the oxidation of guanine and found in the urine as a normal product of protein metabolism. [GUAN(INE) + -ID(E) + -INE[2].]

gua·nine (gwä′nēn′) *n.* A purine base, $C_5H_5N_5$, that is an essential constituent of both RNA and DNA. [< GUANO, in which it is found.]

gua·no (gwä′nō) *n., pl.* **-nos 1.** A substance composed chiefly of the dung of sea birds or bats, accumulated along certain coastal areas or in caves and used as fertilizer. **2.** Any of various similar substances. [Sp. < Quechua *huanu*, dung.]

gua·no·sine (gwä′nə-sēn′, -sĭn) *n.* A nucleoside, C₁₀H₁₃N₅O₅, that is a major constituent of DNA and RNA. [GUAN(INE) + (RIB)OSE) + -INE².]

guanosine mon·o·phos·phate (mŏn′ō-fŏs′fāt′) *n.* GMP.

guanosine triphosphate *n.* GTP.

Guan·tá·na·mo (gwän-tä′nə-mō′) A city of SE Cuba N of **Guantánamo Bay,** an inlet of the Caribbean Sea and site of a US naval station (since 1903). Pop. 206,311.

gua·nyl·ic acid (gwä-nĭl′ĭk) *n.* See GMP. [GUAN(INE) + -YL + -IC.]

Gua·po·ré (gwä′pə-rā′, -pōō-rĕ′) A river of South America rising in W Brazil and flowing c. 1,609 km (1,000 mi) partly along the Brazil-Bolivia border to the Mamoré R.

guar (gwär) *n.* An annual plant *(Cyamopsis tetragonolobus)* adapted to semiarid regions and grown as a forage crop and for its seeds, from which guar gum is obtained. [Hindi *guār* < Skt. *gopālī,* a kind of cucumber, short for *gopālakarkaṭī,* cowherder's cucumber < *gopālaḥ,* cowherd : *gauḥ,* cow; see g*ʷou*- in App. + *pālayati,* he brings across safely, protects (var. of *pārayati;* see per-² in App.).]

gua·ra·ni (gwä′rə-nē′) *n., pl.* **guarani** or **-nis** See table at **currency.** [Sp. *guaraní,* Guarani. See GUARANI.]

Guarani *n., pl.* **Guarani** or **-nis 1.** A member of a South American Indian people of Paraguay, northern Argentina, and southern Brazil. **2.** The Tupi-Guaranian language of this people. [Sp. *guaraní,* of South American Indian orig.]

guar·an·tee (gär′ən-tē′) *n.* **1.** Something that assures a particular outcome or condition. **2a.** A promise or assurance that attests to the quality or durability of a product or service. **b.** A pledge that something will be performed in a specified manner. **3a.** A guaranty by which one person assumes responsibility for another's debts or responsibilities. **b.** A guaranty for the execution, completion, or existence of something. **4.** A guarantor. ❖ *tr.v.* **-teed, -tee·ing, -tees 1.** To assume responsibility for the debt, default, or miscarriage of. **2.** To assume responsibility for the quality or performance of. **3.** To undertake to do, accomplish, or ensure (something) for another. **4.** To make certain. **5.** To furnish security for. **6.** To express or declare with conviction. [Alteration of ME *garant,* warranty < OFr. See GUARANTY.]

guar·an·tor (gär′ən-tôr′, gär′ən-tər) *n.* One, such as a person or corporation, that makes or gives a guarantee or guaranty.

guar·an·ty (gär′ən-tē) *n., pl.* **-ties 1.** An agreement by which one person assumes the responsibility of assuring payment or fulfillment of another's debts or obligations. **2a.** Something given as security for the execution, completion, or existence of something else. **b.** The act of providing such security. **3a.** A guarantee, as for a product or service. **b.** A guarantee to perform something in a specified way. **4.** A guarantee serving to assure a particular outcome or condition. **5.** A guarantor. ❖ *tr.v.* **-tied, -ty·ing, -ties** To guarantee. [AN *guarantie* < OFr. < *garant, guarant,* warrant, of Gmc. orig.]

guard (gärd) *v.* **guard·ed, guard·ing, guards** —*tr.* **1.** To protect from harm by or as if by watching over. See Syns at **defend. 2.** To watch over so as to prevent escape or violence. **3.** *Sports* To keep (an opposing player) from scoring or playing efficiently. **4.** To maintain control over, as to prevent indiscretion. **5.** To supervise entry or exit through (a door, for example). **6.** To furnish (a device or object) with a protective piece. **7.** *Archaic* To escort. —*intr.* **1.** To take precautions. **2.** To serve as a guard. ❖ *n.* **1.** One who protects, keeps watch, or acts as a sentinel. **2.** One who supervises prisoners. **3.** An honor guard. **4.** *Chiefly British* A railway employee in charge of a train. **5.** *Football* One of the two offensive linemen on either side of the center. **6.** *Basketball* Either of the two players normally positioned in the backcourt who initiate offensive plays. **7.** *Sports* A defensive position or stance, as in boxing or fencing. **8a.** The act or duty of guarding. **b.** Protection; watch. **9.** Something that gives protection; a safeguard. **10.** A device or an attachment that prevents injury, damage, or loss, esp.: **a.** An attachment or a covering put on a machine to protect the operator or a part of the machine. **b.** A device on a foil, sword, or knife that protects the hand. **c.** A padded covering worn to protect a body part from injury. **d.** A small chain or band attached to a watch or bracelet to prevent loss. **11.** *Electronics* A signal that prevents accidental activation of a device or ambiguous interpretation of data. —*idioms.* **off (one's) guard** Not alert; unprepared. **on (one's) guard** Alert and watchful; cautious. **stand guard 1.** To keep watch. **2.** To act as a sentinel. [ME *garden* < OFr. *garder, guarder,* of Gmc. orig.] —**guard′er** *n.*

guar·dant also **gar·dant** (gär′dnt) *adj. Heraldry* Positioned so that the head is turned toward the viewer. Used of an animal. [Obsolete Fr. < OFr. *guardant, gardant,* pr. part. of *garder,* to guard. See GUARD.]

guard cell *n.* One of the paired epidermal cells that control the opening and closing of a stoma in plant tissue.

guard·ed (gär′dĭd) *adj.* **1.** Protected; defended. **2.** Watched over; supervised. **3.** Cautious; restrained: *guarded optimism.* —**guard′ed·ly** *adv.* —**guard′ed·ness** *n.*

guard hair *n.* Any of the long coarse hairs forming a layer that covers and protects the soft underfur of certain mammals.

guard·house (gärd′hous′) *n.* **1.** A building that accommodates

a military guard. **2.** A jail for the detention of military personnel guilty of minor offenses or awaiting court-martial.

guard·i·an (gär′dē-ən) *n.* **1.** One that guards, watches over, or protects. **2.** *Law* One who is legally responsible for the care and management of the person or property of an incompetent or a minor. **3.** A superior in a Franciscan monastery. [Ult. < OFr. *garder,* to guard. See GUARD.] —**guard′i·an·ship′** *n.*

WORD HISTORY It is no accident that one kind of *guardian* is a *ward:* both words have the same etymological source. *Guardian* is a borrowing from Old French, where it is derived from the verb *guarder* or *garder,* "to guard," the source also of English *guard.* This Old French verb was itself borrowed from a Germanic word reconstructed as *wardaz* and meaning "a protector, guard." Old French did not have words beginning with (w), and the closest it could come to approximating this sound was (gw), spelled *gu.* In time this came to be pronounced simply (g), as in modern English and modern French. English never had a problem with the sound (w), however, and the Germanic word *wardaz* developed in Old English into *weard,* which became *ward* in the modern language. English has several other doublets of similar origin, such as *guile/wile* and *guise/wise,* where both come from the same Germanic source but the one beginning with *gu* was borrowed into French first before then making its way into English.

Guatemala

guard·rail (gärd′rāl′) *n.* A protective railing, as on stairs.

guard·room (gärd′room′, -room′) *n.* **1.** A room used by guards on duty. **2.** A room in which military prisoners are confined.

guards·man (gärdz′mən) *n.* **1.** A person who acts as a guard. **2.** A member of the National Guard. **3.** *Chiefly British* A soldier in a regiment of household guards.

guar gum *n.* A mucilage made from the seeds of the guar plant and used as a thickener in foods and pharmaceuticals.

Guar·ne·ri (gwär-nér′ē, -nyér′ē) Family of Italian violin makers, including **Andrea** (1626?–98) and his grandson **Giuseppe** (1687?–1745).

Guar·ne·ri·us (gwär-nâr′ē-əs, -nĭr′-) *n.* A violin made by a member of the Guarneri family.

Gua·rul·hos (gwä-rool′lyoos) A city of SE Brazil, a suburb of São Paulo. Pop. 786,355.

Gua·te·ma·la (gwä′tə-mä′lə) **1.** A country of N Central America; inhabited by a Mayan civilization for more than a thousand years before the Spanish conquest in 1524. Guatemala achieved independence in 1839. Cap. Guatemala. Pop. 10,322,000. **2.** also **Guatemala City** The cap. of Guatemala, in the S-central part; founded 1776. Pop. 1,675,589. —**Gua′te·ma′lan** *adj. & n.*

gua·va (gwä′və) *n.* **1.** Any of various tropical American shrubs and trees of the genus *Psidium,* esp. *P. guajava,* having white flowers and edible fruit. **2.** The fruit of this plant having sweet, pinkish flesh. [Sp. *guayaba,* perh. of Arawakan orig.]

Gua·vi·a·re (gwäv-yär′ē, -yä′rĕ) A river of central and E Colombia flowing c. 1,046 km (650 mi) to the Orinoco R.

gua·ya·ber·a (gwī′ə-bĕr′ə) *n.* A light open-necked cotton shirt, often with large pockets and pleats down the front. [Am.Sp.]

Gua·ya·quil (gwī′ə-kēl′) A city of W Ecuador near the **Gulf of Guayaquil,** an inlet of the Pacific Ocean; founded 1535. Pop. 1,508,444.

Guay·na·bo (gwī-nä′bō) A city of NE Puerto Rico, a suburb of San Juan. Pop. 78,806.

gua·yu·le (gwī-ōō′lē) *n.* A shrub *(Parthenium argentatum)* of the southwest United States and Mexico. [Am.Sp. < Nahuatl *cuauhuli* : *cuahuitl,* tree + *uli,* latex gum.]

gu·ber·na·to·ri·al (gōō′bər-nə-tôr′ē-əl, -tôr′-, gyōō′-) *adj.* Of or relating to a governor. [< Lat. *gubernātor,* governor < *gubernāre,* to govern. See GOVERN.]

guck (gŭk, gook) also **gook** (gook, gook) *n. Slang* A thick messy substance, such as sludge. [Poss. G(OO) + (M)UCK.]

gudg·eon¹ (gŭj′ən) *n.* **1a.** A small Eurasian freshwater fish *(Gobio gobio)* related to the carp and used for bait. **b.** Any of various similar or related fishes. **2.** *Slang* One who is easily duped. [ME *gojoun* < OFr. *goujon* < Lat. *gōbiō, gōbiōn-,* var. of *gōbius.* See GOBY.]

gudg·eon² (gŭj′ən) *n.* **1.** A metal pivot or journal at the end of a shaft or an axle, around which a wheel or other device turns. **2.** The socket of a hinge into which a pin fits. **3.** A metal pin that joins two pieces of stone. [ME *gudyon* < OFr. *gojon,* peg, dim. of *gouge,* gouge < VLat. **gubius,* var. of LLat. *gubia.* See GOUGE.]

gudgeon pin *n.* See **wrist pin.**

Gud·run (gōōd′rōōn′) also **Guth·run** (gōōth′-) *n. Mythology* The daughter of the king of the Nibelungs and wife of Sigurd, later of Atli, in the *Volsunga Saga.*

guel·der rose (gĕl′dər) *n.* A Eurasian shrub *(Viburnum opulus)* having clusters of white flowers and small red fruit. [After *Guelderland* (Gelderland), the Netherlands.]

Guelph¹ (gwĕlf) A city of S Ontario, Canada, W of Toronto. Pop. 95,821.

Guelph² also **Guelf** (gwĕlf) *n.* A member of a faction in medieval Italy that supported the pope and the city-states against the German emperors and the Ghibellines. [Ital. *Guelfo* < MHGer. *Welf,* the founder of a German princely family.]

Guen·e·vere (gwĕn′ə-vîr′) *n.* Variant of **Guinevere.**

gue·non (gə-nŏn′) *n.* Any of various African monkeys, primar-

ă	pat	oi	boy
ā	pay	ou	out
âr	care	oo	took
ä	father	oo	boot
ĕ	pet	ŭ	cut
ē	be	ûr	urge
ĭ	pit	th	thin
ī	pie	th	this
îr	pier	hw	which
ŏ	pot	zh	vision
ō	toe	ə	about,
ô	paw		item

Stress marks:
′ (primary);
′ (secondary), as in
lexicon (lĕk′sĭ-kŏn′)

gueridon

Guernsey²

Che Guevara
photographed in 1961

guide dog

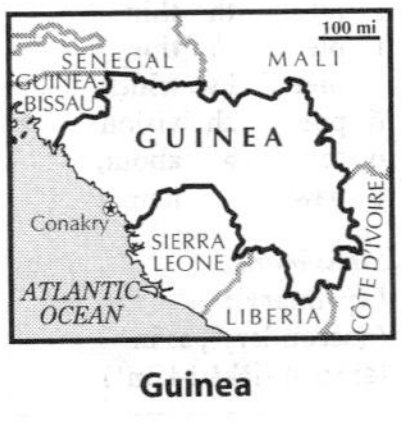

Guinea

ily of the genus *Cercopithecus,* having a long tail. [Fr.]

guer•don (gûr′dn) *n.* A reward; recompense. ❖ *tr.v.* **-doned, -don•ing, -dons** To reward. [ME < OFr. < Med.Lat. *widerdōnum,* alteration of OHGer. *widarlōn* : *widar,* back, against + *lōn,* reward.]

gue•ri•don (gĕr′ĭ-dŏn′, gā-rē-dôN′) *n.* A small round table. [Fr. *guéridon* < the proper name *Guéridon.*]

Guer•ni•ca (gwâr′nĭ-kə, gĕr-nē′kä) also **Guernica y Lu•no** (ē lo͞o′nō) A town in the Basque region of N-central Spain NE of Bilbao. Its Apr. 1937 bombing by German planes during the Spanish Civil War inspired one of Picasso's most famous paintings. Pop. 12,100.

Guern•sey¹ (gûrn′zē) An island of S Great Britain, one of the Channel Is. in the English Channel off NW France.

Guern•sey² (gûrn′zē) *n., pl.* **-seys** Any of a breed of brown and white dairy cattle originally developed on the island of Guernsey and noted for producing a rich golden milk.

guer•ril•la or **gue•ril•la** (gə-rĭl′ə) *n.* A member of an irregular, usu. indigenous military unit operating in small bands to undermine the enemy. [Sp., raiding party, dim. of *guerra,* war, of Gmc. orig.]

guerrilla theater *n.* See **street theater.**

guess (gĕs) *v.* **guessed, guess•ing, guess•es** —*tr.* **1a.** To predict (a result or event) without sufficient information. **b.** To assume or assert (a fact) without sufficient information. **2.** To form a correct estimate or conjecture of. **3.** To suppose; think. —*intr.* **1.** To make an estimate or conjecture. **2.** To estimate or conjecture correctly. ❖ *n.* **1.** An act or instance of guessing. **2.** A conjecture arrived at by guessing. [ME *gessen,* prob. of Scand. orig. See **ghend-** in App.] —**guess′er** *n.*

guess•ti•mate (gĕs′tə-mĭt) *n. Informal* An estimate based on conjecture. [Blend of GUESS and ESTIMATE.] —**guess′ti•mate′** (-māt′) *v.*

guess•work (gĕs′wûrk′) *n.* **1.** The process of making guesses. **2.** An estimate or judgment made by guessing.

guest (gĕst) *n.* **1.** One who is a recipient of hospitality at the home or table of another. **2.** One to whom entertainment or hospitality has been extended by another, as at a party. **3.** One who patronizes a restaurant, hotel, or other establishment. **4.** A distinguished visitor to whom the hospitality of an institution, city, or government is extended. **5.** A visiting performer, speaker, or contestant, as on a radio program. **6.** *Zoology* A commensal organism, esp. an insect that lives in the nest or burrow of another species. ❖ *v.* **guest•ed, guest•ing, guests** —*tr.* To entertain as a guest. —*intr.* To appear as a guest. ❖ *adj.* **1.** Provided for guests. **2.** Participating as a guest: *a guest conductor.* [ME *gest* < ON *gestr.* See **ghos-ti-** in App.]

guest•house (gĕst′hous′) *n.* **1.** A small house or cottage adjacent to a main house, used for lodging guests. **2.** A bed-and-breakfast.

guest worker *n.* A foreigner who is permitted to work in a country on a temporary basis, as for farm labor. [Transl. of Ger. *Gastarbeiter.* See GASTARBEITER.]

Gue•va•ra (gə-vär′ə, gĕ-vä′rä), **Ernesto** Known as "Che." 1928–67. Argentine-born Cuban revolutionary leader who was Fidel Castro's chief lieutenant in the Cuban revolution (1956–59) and later served as minister of industry (1961–65).

guff (gŭf) *n. Slang* **1.** Nonsense; baloney. **2.** Insolent talk; back talk. [Perh. imit.]

guf•faw (gə-fô′) *n.* A hearty boisterous burst of laughter. ❖ *intr.v.* **-fawed, -faw•ing, -faws** To laugh heartily and boisterously. [Prob. imit.]

GUI (go͞o′ē) *n.* An interface for issuing commands to a computer utilizing a pointing device that manipulates and activates graphical images on a monitor. [G(RAPHICAL) U(SER) I(NTERFACE).]

Gui•an•a (gē-ăn′ə, -ä′nə, gī-) A region of NE South America including SE Venezuela, part of N Brazil, and French Guiana, Suriname, and Guyana.

Guiana Highlands A mountainous tableland region of N South America extending from SE Venezuela into Guyana and N Brazil.

guid•ance (gīd′ns) *n.* **1.** The act or process of guiding. **2.** Counseling, such as that provided for students about vocational and educational matters. **3.** Any of various processes for guiding a vehicle by means of built-in equipment.

guide (gīd) *n.* **1a.** One who shows the way by leading, directing, or advising. **b.** One who serves as a model for others, as in a course of conduct. **2.** A person employed to conduct others and give information. **3a.** Something, such as a pamphlet, that offers basic information or instruction. **b.** A guidebook. **4a.** Something that serves to direct or indicate. **b.** A device, such as a ruler or bar, that serves as an indicator or a regulator. **5.** A soldier stationed at the right or left of a column of marchers to control alignment, show direction, or mark the point of pivot. ❖ *v.* **guid•ed, guid•ing, guides** —*tr.* **1.** To serve as a guide for; conduct. **2.** To direct the course of; steer. **3.** To exert control or influence over. **4.** To supervise the training or education of. —*intr.* To serve as a guide. [ME < OFr. < O Provençal *guida* < *guidar,* to guide, of Gmc. orig. See **weid-** in App.] —**guid′a•ble** *adj.* —**guid′er** *n.*

guide•book (gīd′bo͝ok′) *n.* A handbook of directions and other information, esp. for travelers or tourists.

guid•ed missile (gī′dĭd) *n.* A self-propelled missile that can be guided while it is in flight.

guide dog *n.* A dog that has been specially trained to guide a visually impaired or blind person.

guide•line (gīd′līn′) *n.* A statement or other indication of policy or procedure by which to determine a course of action.

guide•post (gīd′pōst′) *n.* **1.** A post with a sign giving directions for travelers, usu. placed at a crossroad. **2.** Something that serves as a guide or an example; a guideline.

guide•word (gīd′wûrd′) *n.* A word or term that appears at the top of each page or column in a reference book, such as a dictionary, to indicate the first or last entry.

Gui•do d'A•rez•zo (gwē′dō dä-rĕt′sō) or **Guido A•re•ti•no** (är′ĕ-tē′nō) 990?–1050. Benedictine monk who devised the four-line staff, thereby allowing precise musical notation.

gui•don (gī′dŏn′, gīd′n) *n.* **1.** A small flag or pennant carried as a standard by a military unit. **2.** A soldier bearing such a flag or pennant. [Fr. < OFr. < OItal. *guidone* < *guidare,* to guide < O Provençal *guidar.* See GUIDE.]

Gui•enne or **Guy•enne** (gē-ĕn′) A historical region and former province of SW France; part of England from 1152 to 1453.

guild also **gild** (gĭld) *n.* **1.** An association of persons of the same trade or pursuits, formed to protect mutual interests and maintain standards. **2.** A similar association, as of artisans, in medieval times. [ME *gild* < ON *gildi,* payment, guild.]

guil•der (gĭl′dər) *n.* See table at **currency.** [ME *gilder,* alteration of MDu. *gulden,* golden. See **ghel-** in App.]

guild•hall (gĭld′hôl′) *n.* **1.** The meeting hall of a guild. **2.** A town hall.

guilds•man (gĭldz′mən) *n.* **1.** A member of a guild. **2.** An advocate of guild socialism.

guild socialism *n.* An English socialist doctrine of the early 20th century according to which industry would be owned by the state but managed by guilds of workers.

guile (gīl) *n.* **1.** Treacherous cunning; skillful deceit. **2.** *Obsolete* A trick or stratagem. ❖ *tr.v.* **guiled, guil•ing, guiles** *Archaic* To beguile; deceive. [ME < OFr., of Gmc. orig.] —**guile′ful** *adj.* —**guile′ful•ly** *adv.*

guile•less (gīl′lĭs) *adj.* Free of guile; artless. See Syns at **naive.**

Gui•lin (gwē′lĭn′) also **Kwei•lin** (kwā′-) A city of SE China NW of Guangzhou; orig. founded in the 6th cent. A.D. Pop. 557,346.

Guil•lain-Bar•ré Syndrome (gē-yăn′bə-rā′) *n.* A temporary inflammation of the nerves, causing pain, weakness, and paralysis in the extremities and often progressing to the chest and face. [After Georges *Guillain* (1876–1961) and Jean Alexandre *Barré* (1880–1967), French neurologists.]

guil•le•met (gĭl′ə-mĕt′, gē-ə-mĕ′) *n.* Either of a pair of punctuation marks («) or (») used in some languages to mark the beginning and end of a quotation. [Fr., dim. of *Guillaume,* William (the name of its supposed inventor).]

guil•le•mot (gĭl′ə-mŏt′) *n.* Any of several auks of the genus *Cepphus,* having black plumage with white markings. [Fr., dim. of the personal name *Guillaume.*]

guil•loche (gĭ-lōsh′, gē-yōsh′) *n. Architecture* An ornamental border formed of two or more curved bands that interlace to repeat a circular design. [Fr., tool used in making the ornamentation.]

guil•lo•tine (gĭl′ə-tēn′, gē′ə-) *n.* **1.** A device consisting of a heavy blade held aloft between upright guides and dropped to behead the victim below. **2.** An instrument, such as a paper cutter, similar in action to a guillotine. ❖ *tr.v.* **-tined, -tin•ing, -tines 1.** To behead with a guillotine. **2.** To cut with or as if with a guillotine. [Fr., after Joseph Ignace *Guillotin* (1738–1814), French physician.]

guilt (gĭlt) *n.* **1.** The fact of being responsible for the commission of an offense. See Syns at **blame. 2.** *Law* Culpability for a crime or lesser breach of regulations that carries a legal penalty. **3a.** Remorseful awareness of having done something wrong. **b.** Self-reproach for supposed inadequacy or wrongdoing. **4.** Guilty conduct; sin. [ME *gilt* < OE *gylt,* crime.]

guilt•less (gĭlt′lĭs) *adj.* Free of guilt; innocent.

guilt trip *n. Informal* A usu. prolonged feeling of guilt or culpability.

guilt-trip (gĭlt′trĭp′) *tr.v.* **-tripped, -trip•ping, -trips** *Informal* To make or try to make (someone) feel guilty.

guilt•y (gĭl′tē) *adj.* **-i•er, -i•est 1.** Responsible for or chargeable with a reprehensible act; culpable. **2.** *Law* Adjudged to have committed a crime. **3.** Suffering from or prompted by a sense of guilt: *a guilty conscience.* **4.** Hinting at or entailing guilt: *a guilty smirk.* —**guilt′i•ly** *adv.* —**guilt′i•ness** *n.*

guimpe (gămp, gĭmp) *n.* **1.** A blouse worn under a jumper. **2.** A yoke insert for a low-necked dress. **3.** A starched cloth covering the neck and shoulders as part of a nun's habit. **4.** See **gimp¹.** [Fr. < OFr. *guimple* < OHGer. *wimpal.* See **weip-** in App.]

guin•ea (gĭn′ē) *n.* **1a.** A gold coin issued in England from 1663 to 1813 and worth one pound and one shilling. **b.** The sum of one pound and one shilling. **2.** *Offensive Slang* Used as a disparaging term for a person of Italian birth or descent. [After the GUINEA coast of Africa, the source of the gold from which it was first made.]

Guinea 1. A historical region of W Africa extending along the coast from Gambia to Angola. **2.** A country of W Africa on the Atlantic Ocean; a French colony from 1898 until 1958. Cap. Conakry. Pop. 6,501,000. —**Guin′e·an** *adj. & n.*

Guinea, Gulf of A broad inlet of the Atlantic Ocean formed by the great bend in the W-central coast of Africa.

Guin·ea-Bis·sau (gĭn′ē-bĭ-sou′) A country of W Africa on the Atlantic Ocean; achieved independence from Portugal in 1974. Cap. Bissau. Pop. 1,050,000.

guinea fowl *n.* Any of several pheasantlike birds of the family Numididae native to Africa, esp. a domesticated species *(Numida meleagris)* having blackish plumage marked with small white spots. [After the GUINEA coast of Africa.]

guinea hen *n.* See **guinea fowl**.

guinea pig *n.* **1.** Any of various small short-eared domesticated rodents of the genus *Cavia,* having no visible tail and often kept as pets and used as experimental animals. **2.** *Informal* A person who is used as a subject for experimentation or research. [Perh. alteration (influenced by GUINEA, used as a name for any faraway unknown country) of GUIANA.]

guinea worm *n.* A long nematode worm *(Dracunculus medinensis)* of tropical Asia and Africa that is a subcutaneous parasite of humans and other mammals. [After the GUINEA coast of Africa.]

Guin·e·vere (gwĭn′ə-vîr′) also **Guen·e·vere** (gwĕn′-) *n.* The wife of King Arthur and lover of Lancelot.

Guin·ness (gĭn′is), Sir **Alec** 1914–2000. British actor whose films include *The Bridge on the River Kwai* (1957).

gui·pure (gĭ-poŏr′, -pyoŏr′) *n.* **1.** A coarse large-patterned lace without a net ground. **2.** See **gimp**[1]. [Fr. < OFr. < *guiper,* to cover with silk, of Gmc. orig.]

gui·ro (gwē′rō, gwĭr′ō) *n., pl.* **-ros** A Latin American percussion instrument made of a hollow gourd with a grooved or serrated surface, played by scraping with a stick or rod. [Am.Sp. *güiro* < Taino.]

guise (gīz) *n.* **1.** Outward appearance or aspect; semblance. **2.** False appearance; pretense: *under the guise of friendship.* **3.** Mode of dress; garb. **4.** *Obsolete* Custom; habit. [ME, manner, fashion < OFr., of Gmc. orig. See **weid-** in App.]

Guise (gēz), 2nd Duke. Title of François de Lorraine. 1519–63. French general and politician who suppressed the Huguenots.

Guise (gēz), 3rd Duke. Title of Henri de Lorraine. 1550–88. French military leader who helped plan the massacre of Huguenots on Saint Bartholomew's Day, 1572.

gui·tar (gĭ-tär′) *n.* A musical instrument having a large flat-backed sound box, a long fretted neck, and usu. six strings, played by strumming or plucking. [Fr. *guitare* < Sp. *guitarra* < alteration of Gk. *kitharā,* cithara.] —**gui·tar′ist** *n.*

gui·tar·fish (gĭ-tär′fĭsh′) *n., pl.* **guitarfish** or **-fish·es** Any of several marine fishes of the family Rhinobatidae, having a guitar-shaped body and related to the skates and rays.

Gui·yang (gwē′yäng′) also **Kwei·yang** (kwā′-) A city of SW China ENE of Kunming; cap. of Guizhou. Pop. 1,664,709.

Gui·zhou (gwē′jō′) also **Kwei·chow** (kwā′chō′) A province of SE China; passed under Chinese suzerainty in the 10th cent. Cap. Guiyang. Pop. 32,391,066.

Gu·ja·rat (goŏ′jə-rät′, goŏj′ə-) A region of W India bordering on the Arabian Sea; annexed by the Moguls in 1572.

Gu·ja·ra·ti (goŏ′jə-rä′tē, goŏj′ə-) *n., pl.* **Gujarati** or **-tis 1.** The Indic language of Gujarat. **2.** A native or inhabitant of Gujarat.

Guj·ran·wa·la (goŏj′rən-wä′lə, goŏj′-) A city of NE Pakistan N of Lahore; a center of Sikh influence. Pop. 658,753.

gu·lag also **Gu·lag** (goŏ′läg) *n.* **1.** A network of forced labor camps in the Soviet Union. **2.** A forced labor camp or prison, esp. for political dissidents. [Russ. *Gulag* < *G(lavnoe) u(pravlenie ispravitel′no-trudovykh) lag(ereĭ),* Chief Administration of (Correctional Labor) Camps.]

gu·lar (goŏ′lər, gyoŏ′-) *adj.* Of, relating to, or located on the throat. [Lat. *gula,* throat + –AR.]

gulch (gŭlch) *n.* A small ravine, esp. one cut by a torrent. [Perh. < dialectal *gulch,* (of land) to sink in < ME *gulchen,* to spew.]

gul·den (goŏl′dən, goŏl′-) *n., pl.* **-dens** or **gulden** A guilder. [ME < Du. *gulden (florijn),* golden (florin) < MDu. See **ghel-** in App.]

gules (gyoŏlz) *n.* *Heraldry* The color red, indicated on a blazon by vertical lines. [ME *goules* < OFr., red fur neckpiece, pl. of *gole,* throat < Lat. *gula.*]

gulf (gŭlf) *n.* **1.** A large area of a sea or ocean partially enclosed by land. **2.** A deep wide chasm; an abyss. **3.** A wide gap, as in understanding. **4.** Something, such as a whirlpool, that draws down or engulfs. ❖ *tr.v.* **gulfed, gulf·ing, gulfs** To engulf. [ME *goulf* < OFr. *golfe* < OItal. *golfo* < LLat. *colpus, colfus* < Gk. *kolpos,* bosom, gulf.]

Gulf Intracoastal Waterway An inland waterway of bays, canals, and rivers from NW FL to Brownsville TX, approx. 1,770 km (1,100 mi) long.

Gulf of For names of actual gulfs, see the specific element of the name; for example, **Mexico, Gulf of**.

Gulf States 1. The countries bordering the Persian Gulf in SW Asia, including Iran, Iraq, Kuwait, Saudi Arabia, Bahrain, Qatar, United Arab Emirates, and Oman. **2.** The states of the S US with coastlines on the Gulf of Mexico, including FL, AL, MS, LA, and TX.

Gulf Stream A warm ocean current of the N Atlantic Ocean off

E North America flowing from the Gulf of Mexico through the Straits of Florida to the North Atlantic Drift.

Gulf War *n.* A war fought in 1991 in which a coalition of countries led by the United States destroyed much of the military capability of Iraq and drove the Iraqi army out of Kuwait.

Gulf War syndrome *n.* A complex of symptoms affecting some veterans of the Gulf War and including fatigue, headache, and joint pain, attributed to reactions to prophylactic medications, infectious diseases, or exposure to pesticides or other chemicals.

gulf·weed also **gulf weed** (gŭlf′wĕd′) *n.* Any of several brownish seaweeds of the genus *Sargassum* of tropical Atlantic waters, having round air sacs. [After the *Gulf* of MEXICO.]

gull[1] (gŭl) *n.* Any of various chiefly coastal aquatic birds of the family Laridae, having long wings, webbed feet, and usu. gray and white plumage. [ME *gulle,* poss. of Brythonic orig.]

gull[2] (gŭl) *n.* A person who is easily tricked or cheated; a dupe. ❖ *tr.v.* **gulled, gull·ing, gulls** To deceive or cheat. [Prob. < *gull,* to swallow (obsolete) < ME *golen,* to pretend to swallow < *golc,* throat, gorge. See GULLET.]

Gul·lah (gŭl′ə) *n.* **1.** One of a group of people of African ancestry inhabiting the Sea Islands and coastal areas of South Carolina, Georgia, and northern Florida. **2.** The creolized language of the Gullahs, based on English but including elements and features from several African languages. [Perh. alteration of ANGOLA or < *Gola,* a people of Sierra Leone and Liberia.]

gul·let (gŭl′ĭt) *n.* **1.** The esophagus. **2.** The throat. **3.** *Zoology* An invagination into the cytoplasm of some ciliates for food intake. [ME *golet* < OFr. *goulet* < *goule,* throat < Lat. *gula.*]

gul·li·ble (gŭl′ə-bəl) *adj.* Easily deceived or duped. [< GULL[2].] —**gul′li·bil′i·ty** *n.* —**gul′li·bly** *adv.*

Gul·li·ver (gŭl′ə-vər) *n.* An Englishman who travels to imaginary lands such as Lilliput and Brobdingnag in Jonathan Swift's satire *Gulliver's Travels* (1726).

gull·wing (gŭl′wĭng′) *adj.* Hinged at the top so as to swing upward. Used of a type of automobile door.

gul·ly[1] (gŭl′ē) *n., pl.* **-lies** A deep ditch or channel cut in the earth by running water after a prolonged downpour. ❖ *v.* **-lied, -ly·ing, -lies** —*tr.* To wear a deep ditch or channel in. —*intr.* To form a deep ditch or channel. [Perh. alteration of ME *golet,* throat, channel. See GULLET.]

gul·ly[2] (gŭl′ē) *n., pl.* **-lies** *Chiefly British* A large knife. [Short for dialectal *gully knife* : *gully* (prob. alteration of ME *golet,* throat; see GULLET) + KNIFE.]

gulp (gŭlp) *v.* **gulped, gulp·ing, gulps** —*tr.* **1.** To swallow greedily or rapidly in large amounts. **2.** To choke back by or as if by swallowing. —*intr.* **1.** To choke or gasp, as in gulping liquid. **2.** To swallow air audibly, as in nervousness. ❖ *n.* **1.** The act of gulping. **2.** A large amount gulped at one time. [< ME *gulpen* or < Flem. or Du. *gulpen.*] —**gulp′er** *n.*

gum[1] (gŭm) *n.* **1a.** Any of various viscous substances exuded by certain plants and trees that dry into water-soluble noncrystalline brittle solids. **b.** A similar plant exudate, such as a resin. **c.** Any of various adhesives made from such exudates or other sticky substances. **2.** A substance resembling gum, as in stickiness. **3a.** Any of various trees of the genera *Eucalyptus, Liquidambar,* or *Nyssa* that are sources of gum. **b.** The wood of such a tree; gumwood. **4.** Chewing gum. ❖ *v.* **gummed, gum·ming, gums** —*tr.* To cover, smear, seal, fill, or fix in place with or as if with gum. —*intr.* **1.** To exude or form gum. **2.** To become sticky or clogged. —*phrasal verb:* **gum up** To ruin or bungle. [ME *gomme* < OFr. < LLat. *gumma,* var. of Lat. *gummi, cummi* < Gk. *kommi,* perh. < Egypt. *kmj-t.*]

gum[2] (gŭm) *n.* The firm connective tissue covered by mucous membrane that envelops the alveolar arches of the jaw and surrounds the bases of the teeth. ❖ *tr.v.* **gummed, gum·ming, gums** To chew (food) with toothless gums. [ME *gome* < OE *gōma,* palate, jaw.]

gum ammoniac *n.* See **ammoniac**[2].

gum arabic *n.* A gum exuded by various African trees of the genus *Acacia,* esp. *A. senegal,* used in making candy, medicine, and mucilage. [GUM[1] + ARABIC.]

gum·ball (gŭm′bôl′) *n.* A small ball of chewing gum with a colored sugar coating.

gum band *n.* *Pennsylvania* See **rubber band**. [Transl. of Ger. *Gummiband : Gummi,* rubber, gum; see GUMMITE + *Band,* band (< MHGer. < OHGer.; see **bhendh-** in App.).]

REGIONAL NOTE Many Pennsylvanians are only a generation or two removed from German-speaking homes. Naturally, the English spoken in Pennsylvania would feature words borrowed directly from German. *Gum band,* the western Pennsylvania equivalent for *rubber band,* is derived from German *Gummiband,* "rubber band." *Smearcase,* a Pennsylvania term for cottage cheese, is from *Schmierkäse,* "soft cheese that can be 'smeared,' or spread." In the expression *The smearcase is all,* the word *all* comes from German *alle,* meaning "finished."

gum benjamin *n.* See **benzoin** 1.

gum benzoin *n.* See **benzoin** 1.

gum·bo (gŭm′bō) *n., pl.* **-bos 1.** *Chiefly Southern US* See **okra** 1. See Regional Note at **goober**. **2.** A soup or stew thickened with okra pods. **3.** *Chiefly Mississippi Valley & Western US* A fine silty

Guinea-Bissau

guinea fowl
helmeted guinea fowl
Numida meleagris

gullwing

ă	pat	oi	boy
ā	pay	ou	out
âr	care	oŏ	took
ä	father	oō	boot
ĕ	pet	ŭ	cut
ē	be	ûr	urge
ĭ	pit	th	thin
ī	pie	*th*	this
îr	pier	hw	which
ŏ	pot	zh	vision
ō	toe	ə	about,
ô	paw		item

Stress marks:
′ (primary);
′ (secondary), as in
lexicon (lĕk′sĭ-kŏn′)

soil that forms an unusually sticky mud when wet. [Louisiana Fr. *gombo*, of Bantu orig.; akin to Tshiluba *ki-ngumbo*, okra.]

gum•boil (gŭm′boil′) *n.* A small boil or abscess on the gum, often resulting from tooth decay.

gum•drop (gŭm′drŏp′) *n.* A small candy made of sweetened gum arabic or gelatin and coated with granulated sugar.

gum•ma (gŭm′ə) *n., pl.* **gum•mas** or **gum•ma•ta** (gŭm′ə-tə) A rubbery granuloma with a necrotic center and an inflamed fibrous capsule, characteristic of an advanced stage of syphilis. [NLat. < LLat., gum. See GUM[1].]

gum•mite (gŭm′īt) *n.* A mixture of several uranium oxides, silicates, and salts occurring naturally in the oxidation and hydration of uraninite. [Ger. *Gummit* < *Gummi*, gum < MHGer. < Med.Lat. < Lat. See GUM[1].]

gum•mo•sis (gŭ-mō′sĭs) *n.* The pathological formation of patches of gum on certain plants, resulting from attack by insects or microorganisms or from adverse weather. [Lat. *gummi*, gum; see GUM[1] + -OSIS.]

gum•mous (gŭm′əs) also **gum•mose** (-ōs′) *adj.* Made of or resembling gum.

gum•my (gŭm′ē) *adj.* **-mi•er, -mi•est** **1.** Consisting of or containing gum. **2.** Covered or clogged with or as if with gum. **3.** Sticky and viscid; gumlike. —**gum′mi•ness** *n.*

gump•tion (gŭmp′shən) *n. Informal* **1.** Boldness of enterprise; initiative or aggressiveness. **2.** Guts; spunk. **3.** Common sense. [Sc.]

gum resin *n.* A mixture of gum and resin that exudes from some plants or trees.

gum•shoe (gŭm′shōō′) *n.* **1.** A sneaker or rubber overshoe. **2.** *Slang* An investigator, esp. a detective. ❖ *intr.v.* **-shoed, -shoe•ing, -shoes** *Slang* **1.** To work as a detective. **2.** To move about stealthily; sneak.

gum tree *n.* See **gum**[1] 3.

gum•wood (gŭm′wŏod′) *n.* The wood of a gum tree.

gun (gŭn) *n.* **1.** A weapon consisting of a metal tube from which a projectile is fired at high velocity. **2.** A cannon with a long barrel and a relatively low angle of fire. **3.** A portable firearm, such as a rifle or revolver. **4.** A device that can project something, such as grease, under pressure or at great speed. **5.** A discharge of a firearm or cannon as a signal or salute. **6.** One, such as a hunter, who carries or uses a gun. **7a.** A person skilled in the use of a gun. **b.** A professional killer: *a hired gun.* **8.** The throttle of an engine, as of an automobile. ❖ *v.* **gunned, gun•ning, guns** —*tr.* **1.** To shoot (a person). **2.** To open the throttle of (an engine) so as to accelerate. **3.** *Maine* To hunt (game). —*intr.* To hunt with a gun. —*phrasal verb:* **gun for** **1.** To pursue relentlessly so as to overcome or destroy. **2.** To go after in earnest; set out to obtain. —*idioms:* **go great guns** To proceed or perform with great speed, skill, or success. **under the gun** Under great pressure or under threat. [ME *gonne*, cannon, short for *Gunilda*, woman's name applied to a siege engine < ON *Gunnhildr*, woman's name : *gunnr*, war; see gʷhen- in App. + *hildr*, war.]

gun•boat (gŭn′bōt′) *n.* A small armed vessel.

gunboat diplomacy *n.* Diplomacy involving intimidation by threat or use of military force.

gun carriage *n.* A frame or structure upon which a gun is mounted for firing or maneuvering.

gun control *n.* Regulation of the sale and use of firearms.

gun•cot•ton (gŭn′kŏt′n) *n.* See **nitrocellulose.**

gun dog *n.* A dog trained or bred to assist hunters.

gun•fight (gŭn′fīt′) *n.* A duel or battle with firearms. —**gun′-fight′er** *n.*

gun•fire (gŭn′fīr′) *n.* The firing of guns.

gun•flint (gŭn′flĭnt′) *n.* The piece of flint used to strike the igniting spark in a flintlock.

gung ho or **gung-ho** (gŭng′hō′) *adj. Slang* Extremely enthusiastic and dedicated. [Earlier *Gung Ho*, motto of certain US marine forces in Asia in World War II < Chin. (Mandarin) *gōnghé*, to work together (short for *gōngyèhézuòshè*, Chinese Industrial Cooperative Society) : *gōng*, work + *hé*, together.]

gun•ite (gŭn′īt) *n.* A concrete mixture sprayed over steel reinforcements in light construction. [Orig. a trademark.]

gunk (gŭngk) *n. Informal* A thick greasy substance. [After *Gunk*, a trademark for a degreasing solvent.]

gun•lock (gŭn′lŏk′) *n.* A device for igniting the charge of a firearm.

gun•man (gŭn′mən) *n.* **1.** A man armed with a gun, esp. an

armed criminal or a killer. **2.** A man skilled in the use of a gun.

gun•met•al (gŭn′mĕt′l) *n.* **1.** An alloy of copper with 10 percent tin. **2.** Metal used for guns. **3.** A dark gray.

gun moll *n. Slang* The girlfriend of a gangster. [Obsolete Brit. slang *gun*, thief (short for *ganef*; see GANEF) + MOLL.]

Gun•nar (gŏon′är′, -ər) *n. Mythology* The husband of Brynhild and the brother of Gudrun in the *Volsunga Saga.*

gun•nel[1] (gŭn′əl) *n.* Any of various small elongated fishes of the family Pholidae, common in northern seas. [?]

gun•nel[2] (gŭn′əl) *n.* Variant of **gunwale.**

gun•ner (gŭn′ər) *n.* **1.** A member of the armed forces who operates a gun. **2.** A warrant officer in the US Marine Corps having charge of ordnance. **3.** *Chiefly British* An artillery soldier, esp. a private. **4.** One who hunts with a gun.

gun•ner•y (gŭn′ə-rē) *n.* **1.** The science dealing with the techniques and procedures of operating guns. **2.** The use of guns.

gunnery sergeant *n.* A noncommissioned officer in the US Marine Corps ranking above staff sergeant and below master sergeant and first sergeant.

gun•ning (gŭn′ing) *n. Maine* The sport of hunting.

gun•ny (gŭn′ē) *n.* A coarse heavy fabric made of jute or hemp, used esp. for bags or sacks. [Hindi *gonī* < Skt., sack, prob. fem. of Pali *gona*-, ox. See gʷou- in App.]

gun•ny•sack (gŭn′ē-săk′) *n. Midwestern & Western US* A bag or sack made of gunny.

gun•play (gŭn′plā′) *n.* A shooting of guns to inflict harm.

gun•point (gŭn′point′) *n.* The point of a gun. —*idiom:* **at gunpoint** Under or as if under the threat of being shot.

gun•pow•der (gŭn′pou′dər) *n.* Any of various explosive powders used to propel projectiles from guns, esp. a black mixture of potassium nitrate, charcoal, and sulfur.

gunpowder tea *n.* A Chinese green tea, each leaf of which is rolled into a pellet.

gun•room (gŭn′rōom′, -rŏom′) *n.* The quarters of midshipmen and junior officers on a British warship.

gun•run•ner (gŭn′rŭn′ər) *n.* One that smuggles firearms and ammunition. —**gun′run′ning** *n.*

gun•sel (gŭn′səl) *n. Slang* A hoodlum or other criminal, esp. one who carries a gun. [Perh. alteration (influenced by GUN) of Yiddish *gendzl*, gosling, dim. of *gandz*, goose < MHGer. *gans* < OHGer. See ghans- in App.]

gun•ship (gŭn′shĭp′) *n.* An armed aircraft, such as a helicopter, that is used to support troops and provide fire cover.

gun•shot (gŭn′shŏt′) *n.* **1.** The shooting of a gun. **2.** The range of a gun: *within gunshot.* **3.** Shot fired from a gun.

gun-shy (gŭn′shī′) *adj.* **1.** Afraid of loud noise, such as that of gunfire. **2.** Extremely distrustful or wary.

gun•sling•er (gŭn′slĭng′ər) *n.* One who is armed with a gun, esp. an outlaw. —**gun′sling′ing** *n.*

gun•smith (gŭn′smĭth′) *n.* One that makes or repairs firearms.

gun•stock (gŭn′stŏk′) *n.* The handle of a gun.

Gun•ter (gŭn′tər) *n.* **Edmund** 1581–1626. English astronomer and mathematician who invented a surveying chain and introduced the terms *cosine* and *cotangent.*

Gun•ter's chain (gŭn′tərz) *n.* See **chain** 8a. [After Edmund GUNTER.]

Gun•ther (gŏon′tər) *n. Mythology* A king of Burgundy and the husband of Brunhild in the *Nibelungenlied.*

Gun•tur (gŏon-tŏor′) A city of SE India ESE of Hyderabad; founded by the French in the 18th cent. Pop. 471,051.

gun•wale also **gun•nel** (gŭn′əl) *n. Nautical* The upper edge of the side of a vessel. [So called because guns were on it.]

Guo•yu (gwô′yōō′) also **Kuo•yu** (kwô′-) *n.* See **Mandarin** 4. [Chin. (Mandarin) : *guó*, nation, country + *yǔ*, language.]

gup•py (gŭp′ē) *n., pl.* **-pies** A small live-bearing freshwater fish (*Poecilia reticulata* or *Lebistes reticulatus*) native to the Caribbean and popular in home aquariums. [After R.J. Lechmere *Guppy* (1836–1916), clergyman in Trinidad.]

Gup•ta (gŏop′tə, gōop′-) A Hindu dynasty that ruled most of northern India (320?–520?) and under which the arts flourished and a unified code of laws was promulgated.

gur•gi•ta•tion (gûr′jĭ-tā′shən) *n.* A whirling or surging motion, as of water. [LLat. *gurgitāre*, to engulf (< Lat. *gurges, gurgit-*, whirlpool) + -ATION.]

gur•gle (gûr′gəl) *v.* **-gled, -gling, -gles** —*intr.* **1.** To flow in a broken irregular current with a bubbling sound. **2.** To make a sound similar to this. —*tr.* To express or pronounce with a gurgle. [< ME *gurguling*, gurgle < Med.Lat. **gurgulāre*, to gurgle < Lat. *gurguliō*, gullet.] —**gur′gle** *n.*

Gur•kha (gŏor′kə) *n.* **1.** A member of a Rajput ethnic group predominant in Nepal. **2.** A Gurkha in the British or Indian armies. [Nepalese < Skt. *gurakṣaḥ*, cowherd : Skt. *gauḥ*, cow + Skt. *rakṣati*, he guards.]

gur•nard (gûr′nərd) *n., pl.* **-nards** or **gurnard** **1.** Any of various marine fishes of the family Triglidae, having fanlike pectoral fins and an armored head, and including the sea robins. **2.** The flying gurnard. [ME < OFr. *gornart* < *gronir*, to grunt < Lat. *grunnīre*.]

gur•ney (gûr′nē) *n., pl.* **-neys** A metal stretcher with wheeled legs. [Probably after J. Theodore *Gurney*, American inventor who patented a type of wheeled horse-drawn cab in 1883.]

gu•ru (gŏor′ōō, gŏo-rōo′) *n., pl.* **-rus** **1.** *Hinduism & Tibetan*

Buddhism a. A personal spiritual leader. **b.** A spiritual teacher and leader, considered by disciples to have absolute authority. **2a.** A teacher and guide in spiritual and philosophical matters. **b.** A trusted counselor and adviser; a mentor. **3.** A recognized leader in a field. [Hindi < Skt. *guruḥ* < *guru-*, heavy, venerable. See **g^werə-** in App.]

gush (gŭsh) *v.* **gushed, gush·ing, gush·es** —*intr.* **1.** To flow forth suddenly in great volume. **2.** To issue in a sudden and abundant flow, as of tears. **3.** To make an excessive display of sentiment or enthusiasm. —*tr.* To emit abundantly; pour forth. ❖ *n.* **1.** A sudden copious outflow: *a gush of tears.* **2.** Excessively demonstrative language or behavior. [ME *gushen,* perh. < Scandinavian orig. See **gheu-** in App.]

gush·er (gŭsh′ər) *n.* One that gushes, esp. an abundantly flowing gas or oil well.

gush·y (gŭsh′ē) *adj.* **-i·er, -i·est** Marked by excessive displays of sentiment or enthusiasm. —**gush′i·ly** *adv.* —**gush′i·ness** *n.*

gus·set (gŭs′ĭt) *n.* **1.** A triangular insert, as in the seam of a garment, for added strength or expansion. **2.** A triangular metal bracket used to strengthen a joist. **3.** A piece of mail or plate armor protecting the joints in a suit of armor. [ME < OFr. *gousset,* perh. dim. of *gousse,* pod, husk.]

gus·sy (gŭs′ē) *tr.v.* **-sied, -sy·ing, -sies** *Slang* To dress or decorate elaborately. [Perh. < Australian slang *gussie,* an effeminate man, dim. of the personal name *Augustus.*]

gust[1] (gŭst) *n.* **1.** A strong, abrupt rush of wind. **2.** A sudden burst, as of rain or smoke. **3.** An outburst of emotion. ❖ *intr.v.* **gust·ed, gust·ing, gusts** To blow in gusts. [Prob. < ON *gustr.* See **gheu-** in App.]

gust[2] (gŭst) *n.* **1.** *Archaic* Relish; gusto. **2.** *Obsolete* **a.** The sense of taste. **b.** Personal taste or inclination; liking. [ME *guste,* taste < Lat. *gustus.* See GUSTO.]

gus·ta·tion (gŭ-stā′shən) *n.* The act or faculty of tasting. [Lat. *gustātiō, gustātiōn-,* an appetizer < *gustātus,* p. part. of *gustāre,* to taste. See **geus-** in App.]

gus·ta·to·ry (gŭs′tə-tôr′ē, -tōr′ē) also **gus·ta·tive** (-tə-tĭv) *adj.* Of or relating to the sense of taste.

Gus·ta·vo A. Ma·de·ro (gōō-stä′vō ä′ mə-dâr′ō, mä-dĕ′rō) See **Guadalupe Hidalgo.**

Gus·ta·vus I (gŭs-tā′vəs, -tä′-) 1496–1560. King of Sweden (1523–60) who established Lutheranism as the state religion.

Gustavus II Known as "Gustavus Adolphus." 1594–1632. King of Sweden (1611–32) drawn into the Thirty Years' War by his desire to assure Swedish control of the Baltic States.

Gustavus III 1746–92. King of Sweden (1771–92) who waged war against Russia (1788–90).

Gustavus IV 1778–1837. King of Sweden (1792–1809) whose loss of Swedish possessions to France and Russia led to his dethronement.

Gustavus V 1858–50. King of Sweden (1907–50) who kept Sweden neutral through both World Wars.

Gustavus VI 1882–1973. King of Sweden (1950–73) who was the last Swedish monarch with real political power.

gus·to (gŭs′tō) *n., pl.* **-toes 1.** Vigorous enjoyment; zest. **2.** Individual taste. **3.** *Archaic* Artistic style. [Ital. < Lat. *gustus,* taste. See **geus-** in App.]

gust·y (gŭs′tē) *adj.* **-i·er, -i·est 1.** Blowing in or marked by gusts: *a gusty storm.* **2.** Characterized by sudden outbursts. —**gust′i·ly** *adv.* —**gust′i·ness** *n.*

gut (gŭt) *n.* **1a.** The intestine. **b.** The embryonic digestive tube. **2. guts** The bowels; entrails; viscera. **3.** *Slang* **a.** Innermost emotional or visceral response. **b. guts** The essential components or inner working parts. **4. guts** *Slang* **a.** Courage; fortitude. **b.** Nerve; audacity. **5.** *Slang* A gut course. **6.** A thin tough cord made from the intestines of animals, usu. sheep, used as strings for musical instruments or as surgical sutures. **7.** A narrow passage or channel. **8.** Fibrous material taken from the silk gland of a silkworm before it spins a cocoon, used for fishing tackle. ❖ *tr.v.* **gut·ted, gut·ting, guts 1.** To remove the intestines or entrails of; eviscerate. **2.** To extract essential or major parts of. **3.** To destroy the interior of. ❖ *adj. Slang* Arousing or involving basic emotions; visceral. —*idiom:* **gut it out** *Slang* To show pluck and perseverance in the face of opposition or adversity. [< ME *guttes,* entrails < OE *guttas.* See **gheu-** in App.] —**gut′ty** *adj.*

GUT *abbr.* grand unified theory

gut·buck·et (gŭt′bŭk′ĭt) *n.* **1.** An early type of jazz characterized by a strong beat and rollicking delivery, similar to barrelhouse. **2.** A homemade bass instrument. [< *gutbucket bass,* homemade bass instrument made from a bucket.]

gut course *n. Slang* An undemanding academic course of study. [Poss. < GUT, to extract, excerpt.]

Gu·ten·berg (gōōt′n-bûrg′), **Johann** or **Johannes** 1400?–68? German printer who is considered the inventor of movable type, using it to print the *Mazarin Bible* (c. 1455).

Guth·rie (gŭth′rē), **Woodrow Wilson ("Woody")** 1912–67. Amer. folk singer and composer whose songs include "This Land Is Your Land" (1940).

Guth·run (gōōth′rōōn′) *n.* Variant of **Gudrun.**

gut·less (gŭt′lĭs) *adj. Slang* **1.** Lacking courage or drive. **2.** Lacking substance; weak. —**gut′less·ness** *n.*

guts·y (gŭt′sē) *adj.* **-i·er, -i·est** *Slang* **1.** Marked by courage or

daring; plucky. **2.** Robust and uninhibited; lusty: *"the gutsy . . . intensity of her musical involvement"* (Judith Crist). —**guts′i·ly** *adv.* —**guts′i·ness** *n.*

gut·ta (gŭt′ə) *n., pl.* **gut·tae** (gŭt′ē′) **1.** *Architecture* One of a series of small ornaments in the shape of truncated cones used on a Doric entablature. **2.** *Pharmacology* A drop, as of liquid medicine. [ME < Lat., drop.]

gut·ta-per·cha (gŭt′ə-pûr′chə) *n.* A substance derived from the latex of any of several tropical trees of the genera *Palaquium* and *Payena,* used as an electrical insulator and in golf balls. [Malay *getah perca* : *getah,* sap + *perca,* strip of cloth (< Hindi *pārca* < Pers. *pārche,* prob. dim. of *pāre* < MPers. *pārang*).]

gut·tate (gŭt′āt′) also **gut·tat·ed** (-ā′tĭd) *adj.* **1.** Having or resembling drops. **2.** Spotted as if by drops. [Lat. *guttātus,* speckled < *gutta,* drop.]

gut·ta·tion (gŭ-tā′shən) *n.* The exudation of water from leaves as a result of root pressure.

gut·ter (gŭt′ər) *n.* **1.** A channel at the edge of a street or road for carrying off surface water. **2.** A trough fixed under or along the eaves for draining rainwater from a roof. **3.** A furrow or groove formed by running water. **4.** A trough or channel for carrying something off, such as that on either side of a bowling alley. **5.** *Printing* The white space formed by the inner margins of two facing pages. **6.** A degraded and squalid class or state of human existence. ❖ *v.* **-tered, -ter·ing, -ters** —*tr.* **1.** To form gutters or furrows in. **2.** To provide with gutters. —*intr.* **1.** To flow in channels or rivulets. **2.** To melt away through the side of the hollow formed by a burning wick. Used of a candle. **3.** To burn low and unsteadily; flicker. ❖ *adj.* Befitting the lowest class of human life; vulgar, sordid, or unprincipled. [ME *goter, guter* < OFr. *gotier* < *gote,* drop < Lat. *gutta.*]

REGIONAL NOTE The channels along the edge of a roof for carrying away rainwater (normally referred to in the plural) are variously known as *eaves troughs* or, less commonly, *eaves spouts* in parts of New England, the Great Lakes states, and, for the former, the West; *spouting* or *rainspouts* in eastern Pennsylvania and the Delmarva Peninsula; and *gutters* from Virginia southward. Historically, along the Atlantic coast, the transition points have marked unusually clear boundaries for the three major dialect areas—Northern, Midland, and Southern—traditionally acknowledged by scholars of American dialects. Nowadays, however, Southern *gutters* has become widely established as the standard US term. See Regional Note at **andiron.**

gut·ter·snipe (gŭt′ər-snīp′) *n.* **1.** A street urchin. **2.** A person of the lowest class.

gut·tur·al (gŭt′ər-əl) *adj.* **1.** Of or relating to the throat. **2.** Having a harsh grating quality, as some sounds made in the back of the mouth. **3.** *Linguistics* Velar. [Fr. < NLat. *gutturālis* < Lat. *guttur,* throat.] —**gut′tur·al·ism, gut′tur·al′i·ty** (-ə-răl′ĭ-tē), **gut′tur·al·ness** *n.* —**gut′tur·al·ly** *adv.*

gut·tur·al·ize (gŭt′ər-ə-līz′) *tr.v.* **-ized, -iz·ing, -iz·es 1.** To pronounce in a guttural manner. **2.** *Linguistics* To velarize. —**gut′tur·al·i·za′tion** (-ə-lĭ-zā′shən) *n.*

guy[1] (gī) *n.* A rope, cord, or cable used to steady, guide, or secure something. ❖ *tr.v.* **guyed, guy·ing, guys** To steady, guide, or secure with a guy. [Partly < ME *gie,* guide, guy (< OFr. *guie* < *guier,* to guide; see **weid-** in App.) and partly < LGer.; akin to Du. *gei,* brail.]

guy[2] (gī) *n.* **1.** *Informal* A man; a fellow. **2. guys** *Informal* Persons of either sex. **3.** *Chiefly British* A person of odd or grotesque appearance or dress. **4.** often **Guy** An effigy of Guy Fawkes paraded through English towns and burned on Guy Fawkes Day. ❖ *tr.v.* **guyed, guy·ing, guys** To hold up to ridicule; mock. [After Guy FAWKES.]

Guy·a·na (gī-ăn′ə, -ä′nə) Formerly **British Gui·a·na** (gē-ăn′ə, -ä′nə, gī-) A country in NE South America on the Atlantic Ocean; a British colony from 1814 until 1966. Cap. Georgetown. Pop. 825,000. —**Guy′a·nese′** (-nēz′, -nēs′) *adj. & n.*

Guy·enne (gē-ĕn′) See **Guienne.**

Guy Fawkes Day (gī′ fôks′) *n.* November 5, observed in England to commemorate the foiling of the attempt led by Guy Fawkes in 1605 to blow up the king and Parliament in retaliation for increasing repression of Roman Catholics.

guy·ot (gē′ō) *n.* A flat-topped submarine mountain. [After Arnold Henri *Guyot* (1807–84), American geologist.]

guz·zle (gŭz′əl) *v.* **-zled, -zling, -zles** —*tr.* **1.** To drink greedily or habitually. **2.** To consume to excess. —*intr.* To drink, esp. alcoholic beverages, greedily or habitually. [?] —**guz′zler** *n.*

GVW *abbr.* gross vehicular weight

GW *abbr.* gigawatt

Gwa·li·or (gwä′lē-ôr′) A city of N-central India S of Agra. Pop. 690,765.

gwe·duc (gōō′ē-dŭk′) *n.* Variant of **geoduck.**

gwine (gwīn) *v. Chiefly Southern & South Midland US* A present participle of **go.** [African American Vernacular E., alteration of *going.*]

Gwyn or **Gwynne** (gwĭn), **Eleanor ("Nell")** 1650?–87. English actress who was the lover of Charles II after c. 1668.

gybe (jīb) *v. & n.* Variant of **jibe**[1].

gym (jĭm) *n. Sports* **1.** A gymnasium. **2.** A course in physical edu-

Johann Gutenberg

Guyana

cation. **3.** A metal frame supporting equipment used in outdoor play.

gym·kha·na (jĭm-kä′nə) *n.* **1.** Any of various meets at which contests are held to test the skill of the competitors, as in equestrianship or gymnastics. **2.** The place where such an event is held. [Prob. alteration of Hindi *gĕṁd-khānā*, racket court : *gĕṁd*, ball (of Dravidian orig.) + *khānā*, house (< Pers. *khāna*, var. *khān*; see KHAN²).]

gym·na·si·um (jĭm-nā′zē-əm) *n., pl.* **-si·ums** or **-si·a** (-zē-ə) **1.** *Sports* A room or building equipped for indoor sports. **2.** (gĭm-nä′zē-ŏŏm′) An academic high school in some central European countries, esp. Germany, that prepares students for the university. [Lat., school < Gk. *gumnasion* < *gumnazein*, to exercise naked < *gumnos*, naked.]

gym·nast (jĭm′năst′, -nəst) *n.* A person who is trained and skilled in gymnastics. [Fr. *gymnaste* < Gk. *gumnastēs*, athletic trainer < *gumnazein*, to exercise. See GYMNASIUM.]

gym·nas·tic (jĭm-năs′tĭk) *adj.* Of or relating to gymnastics. **—gym·nas′ti·cal·ly** *adv.*

gym·nas·tics (jĭm-năs′tĭks) *n.* **1a.** (*used with a pl. verb*) Physical exercises designed to develop and display strength, balance, and agility, esp. those performed on or with specialized apparatus. **b.** (*used with a sing. verb*) The art or practice of such exercises. **2.** (*used with a pl. verb*) **a.** Complex intellectual or artistic exercises. **b.** *Informal* Feats of physical agility.

gym·nos·o·phist (jĭm-nŏs′ə-fĭst) *n.* One of an ancient sect of Hindu ascetics who wore little or no clothing and were devoted to mystical contemplation. [ME *gumnosophist* < sing. of Lat. *gymnosophistae* < Gk. *gumnosophistai* : *gumnos*, naked + *sophistēs*, expert; see SOPHIST.]

gym·no·sperm (jĭm′nə-spûrm′) *n.* A plant, such as a cycad or conifer, whose seeds are not enclosed within an ovary. [< NLat. *Gymnospermae*, class name < Gk. *gumnospermos* : *gumnos*, naked + *sperma*, seed; see SPERM¹.] **—gym′no·sper′mous** *adj.* **—gym′no·sper′my** *n.*

gyn. *abbr.* gynecology

gyn– *pref.* Variant of gyno–.

gy·nan·dro·morph (jī-năn′drə-môrf′, gī-, jĭ-) *n.* An organism having both male and female characteristics, esp. an insect exhibiting a mixture of male and female tissues or sex organs. **—gy·nan′dro·mor′phic, gy·nan′dro·mor′phous** *adj.* **—gy·nan′dro·mor′phism, gy·nan′dro·mor′phy** *n.*

gy·nan·drous (jī-năn′drəs, gī-, jĭ-) *adj.* Having the stamens and pistil united to form a column, as in orchids.

gyn·ar·chy (jĭn′är′kē, jī′när′-, jĭ-) *n., pl.* **-chies** Government by women. **—gyn·ar′chic** *adj.*

–gyne *suff.* Female reproductive organ: *trichogyne*. [< Gk. *gunē*, woman. See gʷen- in App.]

gyneco– or **gynec–** *pref.* Woman: *gynecology*. [Gk. *gunaiko-* < *gunē, gunaik-*, woman. See GYNO–.]

gyn·e·coc·ra·cy (jĭn′ĭ-kŏk′rə-sē, gī′-nĭ-, jĭ′-) or **gy·noc·ra·cy** (jī-nŏk′rə-sē, gī-, jĭ-) *n., pl.* **-cies 1.** Government by women. **2.** A society ruled by women. [Gk. *gunaikokratiā* : *gunē, gunaik-*, woman; see gʷen- in App. + *-kratiā*, -cracy.]

gyn·e·coid (jĭn′ĭ-koid′, gī′nĭ-, jĭ′-) *adj.* Characteristic of a woman.

gy·ne·col·o·gy (gī′nĭ-kŏl′ə-jē, jĭn′ĭ-, jī′nĭ-, jĭ′nĭ-) *n.* The branch of medicine dealing with health care for women, esp. the diagnosis and treatment of disorders affecting the reproductive organs. **—gy′ne·co·log′i·cal** (-kə-lŏj′ĭ-kəl), **gy′ne·co·log′ic** *adj.* **—gy′ne·col′o·gist** *n.*

gyn·e·co·mas·ti·a (jĭn′ĭ-kō-măs′tē-ə, gī′nĭ-, jĭ′-) *n.* Abnormal enlargement of the breasts in a male.

gyno– or **gyn–** *pref.* **1.** Woman: *gynarchy*. **2.** Female reproductive organ; pistil: *gynophore*. [< Gk. *gunē*, woman. See gʷen- in App.]

gy·noe·ci·um (jī-nē′sē-əm, gī-, jĭ-) *n., pl.* **-ci·a** (-sē-ə) The female reproductive organ of a flower; the pistil or pistils considered as a group. [NLat., alteration of Lat. *gynaecēum*, women's apartments < Gk. *gunaikeion* < neut. of *gunaikeios*, of women < *gunē, gunaik-*, woman. See gʷen- in App.]

gyn·o·gen·e·sis (jĭn′ə-jĕn′ĭ-sĭs, gī′nə-, jī′-) *n.* Parthenogenesis in which the egg is activated by sperm but without fusion of the egg and sperm nuclei. **—gy′no·ge·net′ic** (-jə-nĕt′ĭk) *adj.*

gy·no·pho·bi·a (gī′nə-fō′bē-ə, jĭn′ə-, jī′nə-) *n.* **1.** Fear of or contempt for women. **2.** Behavior based on such an attitude or feeling. **—gy′no·phobe′** *n.* **—gy′no·pho′bic** (-fō′bĭk) *adj.*

gyn·o·phore (jĭn′ə-fôr′, -fōr′, gī′nə-, jī′-) *n.* The stalk of a pistil. **—gyn′o·phor′ic** (-fôr′ĭk, -fōr′-) *adj.*

–gynous *suff.* **1.** Of, relating to, or having a specified number or kind of females: *heterogynous*. **2a.** Of, relating to, or situated in a specified place with respect to female plant organs: *epigynous*. **b.** Having a specified number or kind of female plant organs: *protogynous*. [< NLat. *-gynus* < Gk. *gunē*, woman. See gʷen- in App.]

–gyny *suff.* **1.** The state or condition of having a specified number of women or females: *monogyny*. **2a.** The condition of being situated in a specified place with respect to female plant organs: *epigyny*. **b.** The condition of having a specified number or kind of female plant organs: *protogyny*. [< Gk. *gunē*, woman. See gʷen- in App.]

gyo·za (gyō′zə, gyô′zä′) *n.* A pocket of dough that is stuffed, as with minced pork or shrimp, and fried. [J.]

gyp also **gip** (jĭp) *Slang tr.v.* **gypped, gyp·ping, gyps** also **gipped, gip·ping, gips** To deprive (another) of something by fraud; cheat or swindle. ❖ *n.* **1.** A fraud or swindle. **2.** One who defrauds. [Prob. short for GYPSY.] **—gyp′per** *n.*

gyp·sif·er·ous (jĭp-sĭf′ər-əs) *adj.* Containing gypsum.

gyp·soph·i·la (jĭp-sŏf′ə-lə) *n.* Any of various plants of the genus *Gypsophila*, having small white or pink flowers, as baby's breath. [NLat. *Gypsophila*, genus name : Gk. *gupsos*, chalk; see GYPSUM + Gk. *philos*, loving; see –PHILE.]

gyp·so·phile (jĭp′sə-fīl′) *n.* A plant living in gypsiferous soil. [GYPS(UM) + –PHILE.]

gyp·sum (jĭp′səm) *n.* A widespread colorless, white, or yellowish mineral, $CaSO_4 \cdot 2H_2O$, used in plaster of Paris, Portland cement, and wallboard. [ME *gipsum* < Lat. *gypsum* < Gk. *gupsos*, prob. of Semitic orig.; akin to Ar. *jibs, jiṣṣ*.]

gypsum board *n.* See **plasterboard.**

Gyp·sy also **Gip·sy** (jĭp′sē) *n., pl.* **-sies 1.** A member of a traditionally Romany-speaking people that arrived in Europe in migrations from northern India around the 14th century, now also living in the Americas and Australia. **2.** See **Romany** 2. **3. gypsy** One inclined to a nomadic, unconventional way of life. **4.** A person who moves from place to place as required for employment. [Alteration of ME *gypcian*, short for *Egipcien* (so called because they were thought to have come from Egypt).]

gypsy cab *n.* A taxicab that is licensed only to respond to calls but often cruises the streets for passengers.

gypsy moth *n.* A European moth (*Lymantria dispar*) having hairy caterpillars that feed on foliage.

gy·ral (jī′rəl) *adj.* **1.** Moving in a circle or spiral; gyratory. **2.** Of or relating to a gyrus. **—gy′ral·ly** *adv.*

gy·rate (jī′rāt′) *intr.v.* **-rat·ed, -rat·ing, -rates 1.** To revolve around a fixed point or axis. **2.** To move in a spiral or spirallike course. **3.** To oscillate or vary, esp. in a repetitious pattern. ❖ *adj. Biology* In rings; coiled or convoluted. [LLat. *gȳrāre, gȳrāt-* < Lat. *gȳrus*, circle. See GYRE.] **—gy·ra′tion** *n.* **—gy′ra′tor** *n.*

gy·ra·to·ry (jī′rə-tôr′ē, -tōr′ē) *adj.* Having a circular or spiral motion.

gyre (jīr) *n.* **1.** A circular or spiral form; a vortex. **2.** A circular or spiral motion, esp. a circular ocean current. ❖ *intr.v.* **gyred, gyr·ing, gyres** To whirl. [Lat. *gȳrus* < Gk. *gūros*.]

gy·rene (jī-rēn′) *n. Slang* A member of the US Marine Corps. [Perh. alteration of GI¹ + (MA)RINE.]

gyr·fal·con also **ger·fal·con** (jûr′făl′kən, -fôl′-, -fô′-) *n.* A large falcon (*Falco rusticolus*) of Arctic regions, having color phases that range from black to gray to white. [ME *girfaucoun* < OFr. *girfaut, gerfaucon* : OHGer. *gīr*, vulture + OFr. *faucon*, falcon; see FALCON.]

gy·ri (jī′rī′) *n.* Plural of **gyrus.**

gy·ro¹ (jī′rō) *n., pl.* **-ros 1.** A gyroscope. **2.** A gyrocompass.

gy·ro² (jī′rō, jē′-, yĕr′-) *n., pl.* **-ros** A sandwich made usu. of sliced roasted lamb, onion, and tomato on pita bread. [< Mod.Gk. *guros*, a turning < Gk. *gūros*, circle (< the turning spit).]

gyro– *pref.* **1.** Spinning: *gyromagnetic*. **2.** Circle; spiral: *gyroplane*. **3.** Gyroscopic: *gyrostabilizer*. [Gk. *guro-*, circular < *guros*, circle.]

gy·ro·com·pass (jī′rō-kŭm′pəs, -kŏm′-) *n.* A compass with a motorized gyroscope whose angular momentum interacts with the force produced by the earth's rotation to maintain a north-south orientation of the gyroscopic spin axis.

gy·ro horizon (jī′rō) *n.* See **artificial horizon.** [*gyro(scopic) horizon*.]

gy·ro·mag·net·ic (jī′rō-măg-nĕt′ĭk) *adj.* Of or relating to the magnetic properties of a spinning charged particle.

gyromagnetic ratio *n.* The ratio of the magnetic moment of a system to its angular momentum.

gy·ro pilot (jī′rō) *n.* An automatic pilot incorporating a gyroscope that maintains a preset course and altitude.

gy·ro·plane (jī′rə-plān′) *n.* An aircraft, such as a helicopter, equipped with wings that rotate about an approximately vertical axis.

gy·ro·scope (jī′rə-skōp′) *n.* A device consisting of a spinning mass, typically a disk or wheel, mounted on a base so that its axis can turn freely in any direction and thereby maintain its orientation regardless of any movement of the base. **—gy′ro·scop′ic** (-skŏp′ĭk) *adj.* **—gy′ro·scop′i·cal·ly** *adv.*

gy·ro·sta·bi·liz·er (jī′rō-stā′bə-lī′zər) *n.* An instrument having a heavy gyroscope whose axis spins in a vertical plane to reduce the rolling of a ship or aircraft.

gy·ro·stat (jī′rə-stăt′) *n.* A gyroscope consisting of a rotating wheel in a rigid case. **—gy′ro·stat′ic** *adj.*

gy·rus (jī′rəs) *n., pl.* **-ri** (-rī′) Any of the prominent rounded elevated convolutions on the surfaces of the cerebral hemispheres. [Lat. *gȳrus*, circle. See GYRE.]

GySgt *abbr.* gunnery sergeant

Gyum·ri (gē-ŏŏm′rē, gyŏŏm-rē′) A city of NW Armenia SSE of Tbilisi; known as Leninakan from 1924–90. Pop. 206,600.

gyve (jīv) *Archaic n.* A shackle or fetter, esp. for the leg. ❖ *tr.v.* **gyved, gyv·ing, gyves** To shackle or fetter. [< ME *gives, gyves*.]

Hh

h¹ or **H** (āch) *n., pl.* **h's** or **H's** also **hs** or **Hs** **1.** The eighth letter of the modern English alphabet. **2.** Any of the speech sounds represented by the letter *h.* **3.** The eighth in a series. **4.** Something shaped like the letter H.

h² The symbol for **Planck's constant.**

h³ *abbr.* **1.** height **2.** hour

H¹ **1.** The symbol for the element **hydrogen. 2.** The symbol for **enthalpy.**

H² *abbr.* **1.** *Physics* Hamiltonian **2.** *Physics* henry **3.** high **4.** *Baseball* hit **5.** hot **6.** humidity

h. *abbr.* **1.** hard **2.** husband

ha¹ also **hah** (hä) *interj.* Used to express surprise, wonder, triumph, puzzlement, or pique.

ha² *abbr.* **1.** hectare **2.** *Latin* hoc anno (this year) **3.** hour angle

Haa·kon VII (hô′kən, -kōōn′) 1872–1957. King of Norway (1905–57) who headed the exiled government in London during the Nazi occupation of his country (1940–45).

Haar·lem (här′ləm) A city of W Netherlands near the North Sea W of Amsterdam; chartered 1245. Pop. 149,764.

Ha·bak·kuk¹ (hăb′ə-kŭk′, -kōōk′, hə-băk′ək) A Hebrew prophet of the late 7th cent. B.C. [Heb. *ḥăbaqqûq;* perh. akin to Akkadian *ḥabbaququ,* a type of plant.]

Ha·bak·kuk² (hăb′ə-kŭk′, -kōōk′, hə-băk′ək) *n.* See table at **Bible.** [After HABAKKUK¹.]

ha·ba·ne·ra (hä′bə-nâr′ə, ä′bə-) *n.* **1.** A slow Cuban dance. **2.** The music for this dance, in duple time. [Sp. *(danza) habanera,* (dance) of Havana, fem. of *habanero < (La) Habana,* Havana, Cuba.]

hab. corp. *abbr.* habeas corpus

ha·be·as corpus (hā′bē-əs) *n.* **1.** One of a variety of writs that may be issued to bring a party before a court or judge, serving to release the party from unlawful restraint. **2.** The right of a citizen to obtain such a writ. [ME < Med.Lat. *habeās corpus,* produce the body (< the opening words of the writ) : Lat. *habeās,* second pers. sing. pr. subjunctive of *habēre,* to have + Latin *corpus,* body.]

Ha·ber (hä′bər), **Fritz** 1868–1934. German chemist who won a 1918 Nobel Prize.

hab·er·dash·er (hăb′ər-dăsh′ər) *n.* **1.** A dealer in men's furnishings. **2.** *Chiefly British* A dealer in sewing notions and small wares. [ME, perh. < AN *hapertas,* petty wares.]

hab·er·dash·er·y (hăb′ər-dăsh′ə-rē) *n., pl.* **-ies** **1.** A haberdasher's shop. **2.** The goods sold by a haberdasher.

hab·er·geon (hăb′ər-jən) also **hau·ber·geon** (hô′-) *n.* **1.** A short sleeveless coat of mail. **2.** A hauberk. [ME < OFr. *hauberjon < hauberc,* hauberk. See HAUBERK.]

hab·ile (hăb′īl) *adj.* Generally able or adroit; handy. [ME *habil* < OFr. *habile* < Lat. *habilis < habēre,* to handle. See **ghabh-** in App.]

ha·bil·i·ment (hə-bĭl′ə-mənt) *n.* **1a.** The special dress associated with an occasion or office. Often used in the plural. **b.** Clothes. Often used in the plural. **2.** habiliments Characteristic furnishings or equipment; trappings. [ME *habilement* < OFr. *habillement < habiller,* to clothe, alteration of *abiller,* to prepare, strip a tree of its branches : *a-,* toward (< Lat. *ad-;* see AD-) + *bille,* log; see BILLET².]

ha·bil·i·tate (hə-bĭl′ĭ-tāt′) *v.* **-tat·ed, -tat·ing, -tates** **—***tr.* **1.** To clothe. **2.** To fit out or equip (a mine) for operation. **3.** *Obsolete* To impart an ability or capacity to. **—***intr.* To qualify oneself for a post or office. [Med.Lat. *habilitāre, habilitāt-,* to enable < Lat. *habilis,* able. See HABILE.] **—ha·bil′i·ta′tion** *n.*

hab·it (hăb′ĭt) *n.* **1a.** A recurrent, often unconscious pattern of behavior acquired through frequent repetition. **b.** An established disposition of the mind or character. **2.** Customary manner or practice. **3.** An addiction, esp. to a narcotic drug. **4.** Physical constitution. **5.** Characteristic appearance, form, or manner of growth, esp. of a plant or crystal. **6a.** A distinctive dress or costume, esp. of a religious order. **b.** The outfit typically worn by a horseback rider. ❖ *tr.v.* **-it·ed, -it·ing, -its** To clothe; dress. [ME, clothing < OFr., clothing, behavior, custom < Lat. *habitus < p.* part. of *habēre,* to have. See **ghabh-** in App.]

SYNONYMS *habit, practice, custom, usage* These nouns denote patterns of behavior established by continual repetition. *Habit* applies to a behavior or practice so ingrained in an individual that it is often done without conscious thought: *a habit of interrupting. Practice* often denotes a chosen pattern of behavior: *"You will find it a very good practice always to verify your references, sir"* (Martin Joseph Routh). *Custom* is established by long practice and especially by accepted conventions: *"No written law has ever been more binding than unwritten custom supported by popular opinion"* (Carrie Chapman Catt). *Usage* refers to an accepted standard for a group that regulates individual behavior: *"laws . . . corrected, altered, and amended by acts of parliament and common usage"* (William Blackstone).

hab·it·a·ble (hăb′ĭ-tə-bəl) *adj.* Suitable to inhabit. [ME < OFr. < Lat. *habitābilis < habitāre,* to dwell, freq. of *habēre,* to have. See **ghabh-** in App.] **—hab′it·a·bil′i·ty** *n.* **—hab′it·a·bly** *adv.*

hab·i·tant (hăb′ĭ-tənt) *n.* **1.** An inhabitant. **2.** also **ha·bi·tan** (ä′bē-tän′) An inhabitant of French descent living in Canada, esp. Quebec, or in Louisiana. [ME < OFr. < pr. part. of *habiter,* to dwell < Lat. *habitāre.* See HABITABLE.]

hab·i·tat (hăb′ĭ-tăt′) *n.* **1.** The environment in which an organism normally lives or occurs. **2.** The place in which a person or thing is most likely to be found. **3.** A structure that affords a controlled living environment in inhospitable locations, such as the ocean floor. [Lat., it dwells, third pers. sing. pr. of *habitāre,* to dwell. See HABITABLE.]

hab·i·ta·tion (hăb′ĭ-tā′shən) *n.* **1.** The act of inhabiting or the state of being inhabited. **2a.** A natural environment or locality. **b.** A place of abode; a residence. [ME *habitacioun* < Lat. *habitātiō, habitātiōn- < habitātus,* p. part. of *habitāre,* to dwell. See HABITABLE.]

hab·it-form·ing (hăb′ĭt-fôr′mĭng) *adj.* **1.** Capable of leading to physiological or psychological dependence: *a habit-forming drug.* **2.** Tending to become habitual.

ha·bit·u·al (hə-bĭch′ōō-əl) *adj.* **1a.** Of the nature of a habit: *habitual lying.* **b.** Being such by force of habit: *a habitual liar.* **2.** Established by long use. See Syns at **usual. 3.** *Grammar* Designating an action or state that lasts for or is repeated over an extended duration, expressed in English by such means as the simple present tense (*She works downtown*) and the phrase *used to* (*A factory used to be located at that intersection*). **—ha·bit′u·al·ly** *adv.*

ha·bit·u·ate (hə-bĭch′ōō-āt′) *v.* **-at·ed, -at·ing, -ates** **—***tr.* To accustom by frequent repetition or prolonged exposure. **—***intr.* **1.** To cause physiological or psychological habituation, as to a drug. **2.** *Psychology* To experience habituation. [< ME, accustomed < LLat. *habituātus,* p. part. of *habituārī,* to be in a condition < Lat. *habitus,* condition, habit. See HABIT.]

ha·bit·u·a·tion (hə-bĭch′ōō-ā′shən) *n.* **1.** The process of habituating or the state of being habituated. **2a.** Physiological tolerance to a drug resulting from repeated use. **b.** Psychological dependence on a drug. **3.** *Psychology* The decline of a conditioned response following repeated exposure to the conditioned stimulus.

hab·i·tude (hăb′ĭ-tōōd′, -tyōōd′) *n.* A habitual tendency or way of behaving. [ME < Lat. *habitūdō,* condition < *habitus.* See HABIT.]

ha·bit·u·é (hə-bĭch′ōō-ā′, hə-bĭch′ōō-ā′) *n.* One who frequents a particular place, esp. a place offering a specific pleasurable activity. [Fr. < p. part. of *habituer,* to frequent < OFr. < LLat. *habituārī,* to be in a state. See HABITUATE.]

hab·i·tus (hăb′ĭ-təs) *n., pl.* **habitus** The physical and constitutional characteristics of an individual, esp. as related to the tendency toward a certain disease. [Lat., state. See HABIT.]

ha·boob (hə-bōōb′) *n.* A violent sandstorm or dust storm, occurring chiefly in Arabia, North Africa, and India. [Ar. *habūb,* strong wind < *habba,* to blow.]

Habs·burg (hăps′bûrg′, häps′bōōrk′) See **Hapsburg.**

ha·ček (hä′chĕk′) *n.* A diacritical mark (ˇ) that is used over certain letters, such as č, to indicate quality of pronunciation. [Czech *háček,* dim. of *hák,* hook < MHGer. *hāken* < OHGer. *hāko.*]

Ha·chi·o·ji (hä′chē-ō′jĕ) A city of E-central Honshu, Japan, W of Tokyo. Pop. 488,187.

ha·chure (hă-shōōr′, hăsh′ōōr) *n.* One of the short lines used on maps to shade or to indicate topography. ❖ *tr.v.* (hă-shōōr′) **-chured, -chur·ing, -chures** To make hatching on (a map). [Fr. < OFr. < *hacher,* to crosshatch. See HATCH³.]

ha·ci·en·da (hä′sē-ĕn′də, ä′sē-) *n.* **1.** A large estate or plantation in Spanish-speaking countries. **2.** The house of the owner of such an estate. [Sp. < Lat. *facienda,* things to be done < neut. pl. of *facere,* to do. See **dhē-** in App.]

hack¹ (hăk) *v.* **hacked, hack·ing, hacks** **—***tr.* **1.** To cut or chop with repeated and irregular blows. **2.** To break up the surface of (soil). **3a.** *Informal* To alter (a computer program). **b.** To gain access to (a computer file or network) without authorization. **4.** *Slang* To cut or mutilate as if by hacking. **5.** *Slang* To cope with successfully; manage. **—***intr.* **1.** To chop or cut something by hacking. **2.** *Informal* **a.** To write or refine computer programs skillfully. **b.** To use programming skills to gain access to a file or

ă	pat	oi	boy
ā	pay	ou	out
âr	care	ōō	took
ä	father	ōō	boot
ē	be	ûr	urge
ĭ	pit	th	thin
ī	pie	th	this
îr	pier	hw	which
ŏ	pot	zh	vision
ō	toe	ə	about,
ô	paw		item

Stress marks:
′ (primary);
′ (secondary), as in
lexicon (lĕk′sĭ-kŏn′)

network. **3.** To cough roughly or harshly. ❖ *n.* **1.** A rough irregular cut made by hacking. **2.** A tool, such as a hoe, used for hacking. **3.** A blow made by hacking. **4.** A short dry cough. [ME *hacken* < OE *-haccian.* V., intr., sense 2, back-formation < HACKER¹.] —**hack′a•ble** *adj.*

hack² (hăk) *n.* **1.** A horse used for riding or driving; a hackney. **2.** A worn-out horse for hire; a jade. **3a.** One who undertakes distasteful tasks for money or reward; a hireling. **b.** A writer hired to produce hack writing. **4.** A carriage or hackney for hire. **5.** *Informal* **a.** A taxicab. **b.** See **hackie.** ❖ *v.* **hacked, hack•ing, hacks** —*tr.* **1.** To let out (a horse) for hire. **2.** To make banal or hackneyed with indiscriminate use. —*intr.* **1.** To drive a taxicab for a living. **2.** To work as a hack writer. **3.** To ride on horseback at an ordinary pace. ❖ *adj.* **1.** By, characteristic of, or being routine or commercial writing. **2.** Hackneyed; banal. [Short for HACKNEY.]

hack•a•more (hăk′ə-môr′, -mōr′) *n.* A simple bridle with an adjustable noseband and no bit, used esp. in breaking horses. [Alteration of Sp. *jáquima,* halter < OSpan. *xaquima* < Ar. *šakīma,* bit of a bridle < *šakama,* to bridle.]

hack•ber•ry (hăk′bĕr′ē) *n.* **1.** Any of various trees or shrubs of the genus *Celtis,* having inconspicuous flowers and small, usu. ovoid drupes. **2.** The fruit of such a plant. **3.** The soft yellowish wood of these trees or shrubs. [Alteration of obsolete *hagberry, hegberry* : *hag-, heg-,* hackberry (< ON *heggr*) + BERRY.]

hack•but (hăk′bŭt′) *n.* See **harquebus.** [Fr. *haquebute* < OFr. *hacquebute,* alteration of MDu. *hakebus.* See HARQUEBUS.] —**hack′but•eer′** (-bə-tîr′), **hack′but′ter** *n.*

hack•er¹ (hăk′ər) *n. Informal* **1a.** One who is proficient at using or programming a computer; a computer buff. **b.** One who illegally enters another's electronic system, as to gain secret information. **2.** One who demonstrates poor or mediocre ability, esp. in a sport. [Prob. < HACK¹ or < *hacker,* amateurish player.]

WORD HISTORY Computer programmers started using the word *hacker* in the 1960s as a positive term for a person of skillful programming ability. The usage probably derives from *hack,* meaning "to chop," or from *hacker,* "an amateurish player, as at golf." As time went on, *hacker* became less positive, however. Already in the 1960s, engineering students at such universities as Cal Tech used the related noun *hack* to mean "an ingenious prank." Among the pranks that some computer programmers would engage in, of course, were break-ins into other computer systems. As such break-ins attracted national attention, the media seized upon the word *hacker* as the label for the perpetrators—a usage that many programmers object to because they know it used to be a term of praise.

hack•er² (hăk′ər) *n.* See **hackie.**

hack•ie (hăk′ē) *n.* A taxicab driver.

hack•le¹ (hăk′əl) *n.* **1.** Any of the long slender feathers on the neck of a bird, esp. a male domestic fowl. **2. hackles** The erectile hairs along the back of the neck of an animal, esp. of a dog. **3a.** A tuft of cock feathers trimming an artificial fishing fly. **b.** An artificial fishing fly so trimmed. ❖ *tr.v.* **-led, -ling, -les** To trim (an artificial fishing fly) with a hackle. —*idiom:* **get (one's) hackles up** To be extremely insulted or irritated. [ME *hakell,* plumage, poss. < OE *hacele,* cloak.]

hack•le² (hăk′əl) *v.* **-led, -ling, -les** —*tr.* To chop roughly; mangle by hacking. —*intr.* To hack. [Frequentative of HACK¹.]

hack•ly (hăk′lē) *adj.* Nicked or notched; jagged. [< HACKLE².]

hack•ma•tack (hăk′mə-tăk′) *n.* See **balsam poplar.** [Earlier *hakmantak, hacmontac,* perh. < Western Abenaki.]

hack•ney (hăk′nē) *n., pl.* **-neys** **1.** often **Hackney** A horse of a breed developed in England, having a gait characterized by pronounced flexion of the knee. **2.** A trotting horse suited for routine riding or driving; a hack. **3.** A coach or carriage for hire. ❖ *tr.v.* **-neyed, -ney•ing, -neys** **1.** To cause to become banal and trite through overuse. **2.** To hire out; let. **3.** Banal; trite. **2.** Having been hired. [ME *hakenei,* probably after *Hakenei,* Hackney, a borough of London.]

hack•neyed (hăk′nēd) *adj.* Overfamiliar through overuse.

hack•saw (hăk′sô′) *n.* A saw having a tough fine-toothed blade, used for cutting metal. [Alteration of ME *hagge-saue,* a kind of saw : *haggen,* to cut, chop; see HAGGLE + *sawe,* saw; see SAW¹.] —**hack′saw′** *v.*

Hack′y Sack (hăk′ē săk′) A trademark used for a footbag.

had (hăd) *v.* Past tense and past participle of **have.**

ha•dal (hăd′l) *adj.* Of or relating to the deepest regions of the ocean, below about 6,000 meters (20,000 feet). [Fr. < *Hadès,* Hades < Gk. *Haidēs.* See **weid-** in App.]

had•dock (hăd′ək) *n., pl.* **haddock** or **-docks** A food fish (*Melanogrammus aeglefinus*) of northern Atlantic waters, related to and resembling the cod. [ME *haddok.*]

hade (hād) *n. Geology* The angle of inclination from the vertical of a vein, fault, or lode. [?]

Ha•de•an Time (hā-dē′ən, hā′dē-) *n.* The period of time during which Earth formed, from the start of the solar system (4.6 billion years ago) until accretion, impact, and cooling led to stable Earth-Moon orbits and the formation of the earliest rocks on Earth (3.8 billion years ago). See table at **geologic time.** [After HADES (from the intense heat during part of this period).]

Ha•des (hā′dēz) *n.* **1.** *Greek Mythology* **a.** The god of the netherworld and dispenser of earthly riches. **b.** This netherworld kingdom, the abode of the shades of the dead. **2.** also **hades** Hell. [Gk. *Haidēs.* See **weid-** in App.]

ha•dith (hə-dēth′) *n., pl.* **hadith** or **-diths** *Islam* **1a.** A report of the sayings or actions of Muhammad or his companions, together with the tradition of its chain of transmission. **b.** The collective body of these traditions. **2.** See **Sunna** 1. [Ar. *ḥadīṯ,* report, news, tradition < *ḥaddaṯa,* to report < *ḥadaṯa,* to be new.]

hadj (hăj) *n.* Variant of **haj.**

hadj•i (hăj′ē) *n.* Variant of **haji.**

had•n't (hăd′nt) Contraction of *had not.*

Ha•dri•an (hā′drē-ən) Orig. Publius Aelius Hadrianus. A.D. 76–138. Emperor of Rome (117–138) who during his visit to Britain (122) ordered the construction of Hadrian's Wall.

Ha•dri•an's Wall (hā′drē-ənz) An ancient Roman wall that marked the N defensive boundary of Roman Britain.

had•ron (hăd′rŏn′) *n.* Any of a class of subatomic particles that are composed of quarks and take part in the strong interaction. [Gk. *hadros,* thick + –ON¹.] —**had•ron′ic** *adj.*

had•ro•saur (hăd′rə-sôr′) *n.* Any of various amphibious dinosaurs of the genus *Anatosaurus* and related genera that had webbed feet and a ducklike bill. [NLat. *Hadrosaurus,* genus name : Gk. *hadros,* thick; see HADRON + *sauros,* lizard.]

hadst (hădst) *v. Archaic* A second person singular past tense of **have.**

hae (hā, hă) *tr.v.* **haed, haen** (hān, hăn), **hae•ing, haes** *Scots* To have.

Haeck•el (hĕk′əl), **Ernst Heinrich** 1834–1919. German philosopher and naturalist who developed the maxim "Ontogeny recapitulates phylogeny."

Haeck•el's law (hĕk′əlz) *n.* See **biogenetic law.** [After Ernst Heinrich HAECKEL.]

haem– also **haema–** or **haemo–** *pref.* Variants of **hemo–.**

haemat– or **haemato–** *pref.* Variants of **hemato–.**

–haemia *suff.* Variant of **–emia.**

haen (hān, hăn) *v. Scots* Past participle of **hae.**

haet (hāt) *n. Scots* A minute amount; a jot. [Sc., contraction of *hae it,* take it.]

ha•fiz (hä′fĭz) *n. Islam* **1.** One who has memorized the Koran. **2.** Used as a title of respect for such a person. [Ar. *ḥāfiẓ,* guardian, hafiz, active part. of *ḥafiẓa,* to guard, memorize.]

Ha•fiz (hä-fēz′, -fĕz′) fl. 14th cent. Persian poet whose sensuous verses are interpreted allegorically by Sufic Muslims.

haf•ni•um (hăf′nē-əm) *n.* **Symbol Hf** A metallic element found with zirconium and used in nuclear reactor control rods and in tungsten alloys in filaments. Atomic number 72; atomic weight 178.49; melting point 2,220°C; boiling point 5,400°C; specific gravity 13.3; valence 4. See table at **element.** [After *Hafnia,* Med.Lat. name for Copenhagen, Denmark.]

haft (hăft) *n.* A handle or hilt, esp. of a tool or weapon. ❖ *tr.v.* **haft•ed, haft•ing, hafts** To fit into or equip with a hilt or handle. [ME < OE *hæft.* See **kap–** in App.]

haf•ta•rah or **haf•to•rah** (häf′tä-rä′, häf-tôr′ə, -tōr′ə) *n.* Variants of **haphtarah.**

hag¹ (hăg) *n.* **1.** An old woman considered ugly or frightful. **2a.** A witch; a sorceress. **b.** *Obsolete* A female demon. **3.** A hagfish. [ME *hagge,* perh. short for OE *hægtesse,* witch.] —**hag′gish** *adj.* —**hag′gish•ly** *adv.* —**hag′gish•ness** *n.*

hag² (hăg) *n. Chiefly British* **1.** A boggy area; a quagmire. **2.** A spot in boggy land that is softer or more solid than the surrounding area. **3.** A cutting in a peat bog. [ME, gap, chasm, of Scand. orig.; akin to ON *högg.*]

Hag. *abbr. Bible* Haggai

Ha•gar (hā′gər, -gär) In the Bible, the Egyptian servant of Abraham's wife, Sarah, and the mother of Ishmael.

Ha•gen (hä′gən) A city of W-central Germany NE of Cologne; chartered 1746. Pop. 214,877.

hag•fish (hăg′fĭsh′) *n., pl.* **hagfish** or **-fish•es** Any of various primitive eel-shaped marine fishes of the family Myxinidae, having a jawless sucking mouth equipped with rasping teeth with which it bores into and feeds on other fishes.

Hag•ga•dah also **Hag•ga•da** (hä′gä-dä′, hə-gä′də, -gô′də) *n., pl.* **-doth** (-dôt′, -dōt′, -dōs, -dəz) *Judaism* **1.** Traditional Jewish literature, esp. the nonlegal part of the Talmud. **2.** The book containing the story of the Exodus and the ritual of the Seder, read at the Passover Seder. [Heb. *haggādâ,* narration, telling < *higgîd,* to narrate, tell.]

hag•gad•ic also **Hag•gad•ic** (hə-gäd′ĭk, -gä′dĭk, -gô′dĭk) *adj. Judaism* Of or relating to the Haggadah.

hag•ga•dist (hə-gä′dĭst, -gô′-) *n. Judaism* **1.** A haggadic writer. **2.** A student of haggadic literature.

Hag•ga•i¹ (hăg′ē-ī′, hăg′ī) A Hebrew prophet of the 6th cent. B.C. [Heb. *ḥaggay,* born on a feast day (sense uncertain) < *ḥag,* pilgrimage feast < *ḥāgag,* to make a pilgrimage.]

Haggai² *n.* See table at **Bible.** [After HAGGAI¹.]

hag•gard (hăg′ərd) *adj.* **1a.** Appearing worn and exhausted; gaunt. **b.** Wild or distraught in appearance. **2.** Wild and intractable. Used of a hawk in falconry. ❖ *n.* An adult hawk captured for training. [Fr. *hagard,* wild < OFr., wild hawk, raptor, perh. of Gmc. orig.] —**hag′gard•ly** *adv.* —**hag′gard•ness** *n.*

Hadrian

Haggard, Sir **(Henry) Rider** 1856–1925. British writer whose novels include *King Solomon's Mines* (1885).

hag·gis (hăg′ĭs) *n.* A Scottish dish consisting of the minced heart, lungs, and liver of a sheep or calf mixed with suet, onion, oatmeal, and seasonings and boiled in the stomach of the slaughtered animal. [ME *hagese*; perh. akin to *haggen*, to chop. See HAGGLE.]

hag·gle (hăg′əl) *v.* **-gled, -gling, -gles** —*intr.* **1.** To bargain, as over the price of something; dicker. **2.** To argue in an attempt to come to terms. —*tr.* **1.** To cut (something) in a crude manner; hack. **2.** *Archaic* To harass or worry by wrangling. ❖ *n.* An instance of bargaining or arguing. [Frequentative of dialectal *hag*, to chop, hack < ME *haggen* < ON *höggva*.] —**hag′gler** *n.*

hag·i·ar·chy (hăg′ē-är′kē, hā′jē-) *n., pl.* **-chies** Government by people considered to be holy, such as priests or saints.

hagio– or **hagi–** *pref.* **1.** Saint: *hagiography*. **2.** Holy: *hagioscope*. [Gk. *hagios*, holy.]

hag·i·oc·ra·cy (hăg′ē-ŏk′rə-sē, hā′jē-) *n., pl.* **-cies** See **hagiarchy.**

Hag·i·og·ra·pha (hăg′ē-ŏg′rə-fə, hā′jē-) *pl.n.* (*used with a sing. or pl. verb*) *Bible* The Writings. [LLat. < L.Gk. < neut. pl. of *hagiographos*, written by inspiration, scriptural : Gk. *hagio-*, hagio- + Gk. *-graphos*, written < *graphein*, to write; see –GRAPH.]

hag·i·og·ra·phy (hăg′ē-ŏg′rə-fē, hā′jē-) *n., pl.* **-phies 1.** Biography of saints. **2.** A worshipful or idealizing biography. —**hag′i·og′ra·pher** *n.* —**hag′i·o·graph′ic** (-ə-grăf′ĭk), **hag′i·o·graph′i·cal** *adj.*

hag·i·ol·o·gy (hăg′ē-ŏl′ə-jē, hā′jē-) *n., pl.* **-gies 1.** Literature dealing with the lives of saints. **2.** A collection of sacred writings. **3.** An authoritative list of saints. —**hag′i·o·log′ic** (-ə-lŏj′ĭk), **hag′i·o·log′i·cal** *adj.* —**hag′i·ol′o·gist** *n.*

hag·i·o·scope (hăg′ē-ə-skōp′, hā′jē-) *n.* A small opening in an interior wall of a church, enabling those in the transept to view the main altar. —**hag′i·o·scop′ic** (-skŏp′ĭk) *adj.*

hag·ride (hăg′rīd′) *tr.v.* **-rode** (-rōd′), **-rid·den** (-rĭd′n), **-rid·ing, -rides** To torment or harass, esp. with worry or dread.

Hague (hāg), **The.** Officially 's **Gra·ven·ha·ge** (skrä′vən-hä′gə, sкнrä′vən-hä′кнə) The de facto cap. of the Netherlands, in the W part near the North Sea. Pop. 444,392.

hah (hä) *interj.* Variant of **ha**[1].

ha-ha[1] (hä′hä′) also **haw-haw** (hô′hô′) *interj.* Used to express amusement or scorn.

ha-ha[2] (hä′hä′) also **haw-haw** (hô′hô′) *n.* See **sunk fence.** [Fr., exclamation of surprise, ha-ha (because it cannot be seen until closely approached).]

Hahn (hän), **Otto** 1879–1968. German chemist who won a 1944 Nobel Prize.

Hah·ne·mann (hä′nə-mən, -män′), **(Christian Friedrich) Samuel** 1755–1843. German founder of homeopathy.

Hai·da (hī′də) *n., pl.* **Haida** or **-das 1.** A member of a Native American people inhabiting the Queen Charlotte Islands of British Columbia, Canada, and Prince of Wales Island in Alaska. **2.** Any or all of the Haida language varieties. [Haida *ḥà·t'e·*, the people < *ḥà·ta·*, *ḥà·da·*, to be human.] —**Hai′dan** *adj.*

Hai·fa (hī′fə) A city of NW Israel on the **Bay of Haifa,** an inlet of the Mediterranean Sea; probably founded in the 3rd cent. A.D. Pop. 248,200.

Haig (hāg), **Douglas.** 1st Earl Haig. 1861–1928. British field marshal who led British forces in France in World War I.

Haight-Ash·bu·ry (hāt′ăsh′bĕr-ē, -bə-rē) A section of central San Francisco; a gathering place for hippies and followers of the drug culture in the 1960s.

Hai·kou (hī′kou′, -kō′) A city of S China on Hainan I. in the South China Sea; cap. of Hainan province. Pop. 410,050.

hai·ku (hī′kōō) *n., pl.* **haiku** also **-kus 1.** A Japanese lyric verse form having three unrhymed lines of five, seven, and five syllables, traditionally invoking an aspect of nature or the seasons. **2.** A poem written in this form. [J. : *hai*, amusement (< M Chin. *baij*, *pha·j*) + *ku*, sentence (< M Chin. *kuəh*).]

hail[1] (hāl) *n.* **1.** Precipitation in the form of spherical or irregular pellets of ice larger than 5 millimeters (0.2 inch) in diameter. **2.** Something with the force and quantity of a shower of ice. ❖ *v.* **hailed, hail·ing, hails** —*intr.* **1.** To precipitate in pellets of ice. **2.** To fall like hailstones. —*tr.* To pour (something) down or forth. [ME < OE *hægel*.]

hail[2] (hāl) *v.* **hailed, hail·ing, hails** —*tr.* **1a.** To salute or greet. **b.** To greet or acclaim enthusiastically. **2.** To call out or yell in order to catch the attention of. —*intr.* To signal or call to a passing ship as a greeting or identification. ❖ *n.* **1.** The act of greeting or acclaiming. **2.** A shout made to catch someone's attention or to greet. **3.** Hailing distance. ❖ *interj.* Used to express a greeting or tribute. —*phrasal verb:* **hail from** To come or originate from. [ME *heilen* < (*wæs*) *hæil*, (be) healthy. See WASSAIL.] —**hail′er** *n.*

hail·er (hā′lər) *n.* **1.** One that greets, acclaims, or catches someone's attention. **2.** A bullhorn.

Hai·le Se·las·sie (hī′lē sə-lăs′ē, -lä′sē) Title of Ras Tafari Makonnen. 1892–1975. Emperor of Ethiopia (1930–74) who was deposed in a military coup.

hail-fel·low (hāl′fĕl′ō) also **hail-fel·low-well-met** (-wĕl′mĕt′) *adj.* Heartily friendly and congenial. [< the obs. greeting *hail, fellow!*] —**hail′-fel′low** *n.*

Hail Mary *n., pl.* **Hail Marys 1.** *Roman Catholic Church* A prayer based on the greetings of Gabriel and Saint Elizabeth to the Virgin Mary. **2.** *Football* A long pass thrown in desperation, esp. near the end of a game.

hail·stone (hāl′stōn′) *n.* A pellet of hail.

hail·storm (hāl′stôrm′) *n.* A storm with hail.

haim·ish (hā′mĭsh) *adj. Slang* Warm and comfortable; homey; folksy. [Yiddish *heymish* < MHGer. *heimisch* < OHGer. *heimisc* < *heim*, home. See **tkei-** in App.]

Hai·nan (hī′nän′) An island and province of S China in the South China Sea separated from Leizhou Peninsula by a narrow strait. Cap. Haikou. Pop. 6,557,482.

Hai·naut (hā-nō′, ĕ-nō′) A historical region of SW Belgium and N France.

haint (hānt) *n. Chiefly Southern US* Variant of **haunt** 2.

hain't (hānt) *Nonstandard* Variant of **ain't.**

Hai·phong (hī′fŏng′) A city of NE Vietnam on the Red R. delta near the Gulf of Tonkin; heavily bombed by US forces during the Vietnam War. Pop. 783,133.

hair (hâr) *n.* **1a.** Any of the cylindrical, keratinized, often pigmented filaments characteristically growing from the epidermis of a mammal. **b.** A growth of such filaments, as that covering the scalp of a human. **2.** A filamentous projection or bristle similar to a hair, such as an epidermal process of a plant. **3.** Fabric made from the hair of certain animals. **4a.** A minute distance or narrow margin. **b.** A precise or exact degree. [ME *her* < OE *hǽr*.]

hair·ball (hâr′bôl′) *n.* A small mass of hair in the stomach or intestine of an animal, such as a cat, that accumulates each time the animal licks its coat.

hair·brained (hâr′brānd′) *adj. Usage Problem* Harebrained. See Usage Note at **harebrained.** [Variant of HAREBRAINED.]

hair·breadth (hâr′brĕdth′) *adj.* Extremely close: *a hairbreadth escape.* ❖ *n.* Variant of **hairsbreadth.**

hair·brush (hâr′brŭsh′) *n.* A brush for the hair.

hair cell *n.* A cell in the organ of Corti having fine hairlike processes.

hair·cloth (hâr′klôth′, -klŏth′) *n.* A wiry fabric woven esp. from horsehair or camel's hair.

hair·cut (hâr′kŭt′) *n.* **1.** The act or an instance of cutting the hair. **2.** A style in which hair is cut. —**hair′cut′ter** *n.* —**hair′cut′ting** *adj. & n.*

hair·do (hâr′dōō′) *n., pl.* **-dos** A hairstyle.

hair·dress·er (hâr′drĕs′ər) *n.* One who cuts or arranges hair.

hair·dress·ing (hâr′drĕs′ĭng) *n.* **1.** The occupation of a hairdresser. **2.** The act of dressing or arranging the hair. **3.** A cosmetic or medicinal preparation for dressing the hair.

haired (hârd) *adj.* Having a specified kind of hair. Often used in combination: *a longhaired cat; a shorthaired dog.*

hair follicle *n.* A tubular infolding of the epidermis containing the root of a hair.

hair·less (hâr′lĭs) *adj.* Having little or no hair.

hair·line (hâr′lĭn′) *n.* **1.** The outline of the growth of hair on the head, esp. across the front. **2.** A very slender line. **3.** *Printing* **a.** A very fine line on a typeface. **b.** A style of type using such lines. **4a.** A textile design having thin threadlike stripes. **b.** A fabric with such stripes. ❖ *adj.* Resembling a hair or a fine line: *a hairline fracture.*

hair·net (hâr′nĕt′) *n.* A mesh for holding the hair in place.

hair·piece (hâr′pēs′) *n.* A covering or bunch of human or artificial hair used to conceal baldness or shape a coiffure.

hair·pin (hâr′pĭn′) *n.* **1.** A thin strip of metal or other material bent in the shape of a long U, used to secure a hairdo or headdress. **2.** Something shaped like a hairpin.

hair-rais·ing (hâr′rā′zĭng) *adj.* Causing excitement, terror, or thrills.

hairs·breadth or **hair's-breadth** (hârz′brĕdth′) also **hair·breadth** (hâr′-) *n.* A small space, distance, or margin.

hair seal *n.* Any of various seals of the family Phocidae, having a stiff hairlike coat and ears visible only as small indentations.

hair shirt *n.* A coarse haircloth garment worn next to the skin by religious ascetics as penance.

hair space *n.* **1.** The narrowest of the metal spaces used for separating words or letters. **2.** A similar narrow space used in formatting text.

hair·split·ting (hâr′splĭt′ĭng) *n.* The making of unreasonably fine distinctions. —**hair′split′ter** *n.* —**hair′split′ting** *adj.*

hair spray or **hair·spray** (hâr′sprā′) *n.* A sticky, quick-drying liquid sprayed on the hair to keep it in place.

hair·spring (hâr′sprĭng′) *n.* A fine coiled spring that regulates the movement of the balance wheel in a watch or clock.

hair·streak (hâr′strēk′) *n.* Any of numerous butterflies of the subfamily Theclinae, having transverse streaks on the underside of the wings and hairlike projections on the hind wings.

hair stroke *n.* A very fine line in writing or printing.

hair·style (hâr′stīl′) *n.* A style in which hair is cut and arranged. —**hair′styl′ing** *n.* —**hair′styl′ist** *n.*

hair trigger *n.* A gun trigger adjusted to respond to a very slight pressure.

hair-trig·ger (hâr′trĭg′ər) *adj.* Responding to the slightest provocation or stimulation: *a hair-trigger temper.*

hair·worm (hâr′wûrm′) *n.* **1.** Any of various slender, parasitic nematode worms of the genus *Trichostrongylus*, which infest cat-

ă pat   oi boy
ā pay   ou out
âr care   ōō took
ä father   ōō boot
ĕ pet   ŭ cut
ē be   ûr urge
ĭ pit   th thin
ī pie   th this
îr pier   hw which
ŏ toe   ə about,
ô paw   item

Stress marks:
′ (primary);
′ (secondary), as in
lexicon (lĕk′sĭ-kŏn′)

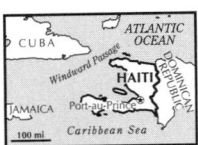

Haiti

haku

tle, sheep, and related animals. **2.** See **horsehair worm.**

hair·y (hâr′ē) *adj.* **-i·er, -i·est 1.** Covered with hair or hairlike projections. **2.** Consisting of or resembling hair. **3.** *Slang* Fraught with difficulties: *a hairy escape.* —**hair′i·ness** *n.*

Hai·ti (hā′tē) A country of the West Indies comprising the W part of Hispaniola and two offshore islands; became independent in 1804 following a slave revolt led by Toussaint L'Ouverture. Cap. Port-au-Prince. Pop. 7,041,000. **2.** See **Hispaniola.**

Hai·tian (hā′shən, -tē-ən) *adj.* Of or relating to Haiti or its people or culture. ❖ *n.* **1.** A native or inhabitant of Haiti. **2.** Haitian Creole.

Haitian Creole *n.* A language spoken by the majority of Haitians, based on French and various African languages.

haj or **hadj** also **hadj** (hăj) *n., pl.* **haj·es** or **hadj·es** also **hadj·es** *Islam* A pilgrimage to Mecca during Dhu'l Hijja, made as an objective of the religious life of a Muslim. [Ar. *ḥajj* < *ḥajja,* to perform the annual Meccan pilgrimage.]

haj·i or **haj·ji** also **hadj·i** (hăj′ē) *n., pl.* **haj·is** or **haj·jis** also **hadj·is** *Islam* **1.** One who has made a pilgrimage to Mecca. **2.** Often used as a form of address for one who has made such a pilgrimage. [Pers. *ḥājī* < Ar. *ḥajj,* pilgrim, active part. of *ḥajja,* to perform the Meccan pilgrimage.]

hake (hāk) *n., pl.* **hake** or **hakes** Any of various marine food fishes of the genera *Merluccius* and *Urophycis,* related to and resembling the cod. [ME, poss. < OE *haca,* hook (< the shape of its lower jaw).]

Ha·ken·kreuz (hä′kən-kroits′) *n.* A swastika. [Ger. : *Haken,* hook (< MHGer. *hāken;* see HACEK) + *Kreuz,* cross (< MHGer. *kriuze;* see KREUZER).]

ha·kim¹ also **ha·keem** (hä′kēm) *n., pl.* **-kims** also **-keems** A Muslim physician. [Ar. *ḥakīm,* wise, wise man < *ḥakama,* to judge, decide.]

ha·kim² (hä′kĭm) *n., pl.* **-kims** A male Muslim ruler, provincial governor, or judge. [Ar. *ḥākim,* active part. of *ḥakama,* to decide, govern.]

Hak·luyt (hăk′lŏŏt′), **Richard** 1552?–1616. English geographer noted for *Principal Navigations, Voyages, and Discoveries of the English Nation* (1589).

Ha·ko·da·te (hä′kō-dä′tĕ) A city of SW Hokkaido, Japan, on Tsugaru Strait. Pop. 304,286.

ha·ku (hä′kōō) *n. Hawaii* A crown made of fresh flowers. [Hawaiian < *haku,* to put in order, make a wreath.]

hal– *pref.* Variant of **halo–.**

Ha·la·cha or **Ha·la·khah** also **Ha·la·kah** (hä′lä-кнä′, hä-lä′кнə, -lō′-) *n. Judaism* The legal part of Talmudic literature, an interpretation of the scriptural laws. [Heb. *hălākâ,* rule, tradition < *hālak,* to go.] —**Ha·lak′ic** (hə-läk′ĭk, -lä′кнĭk) *adj.*

ha·lal (hə-läl′) *Islam n.* Meat from animals slaughtered in the manner prescribed by the shari'a. ❖ *adj.* **1.** Of or being such meat. **2.** In accordance with or permitted under the shari'a. [Ar. *ḥalāl,* legally permissible < *ḥalla,* to free, be permissible.]

ha·la·tion (hā-lā′shən) *n.* **1.** A blurring or spreading of light around bright areas on a photographic image. **2.** A glow around a bright object on a television screen. [< HALO.]

hal·berd (hăl′bərd, hôl′-) *n.* A weapon of the 15th and 16th centuries having an axlike blade and a steel spike mounted on the end of a long shaft. [Fr. *hallebarde* < OFr. *alabarde* < OItal. *alabarda* < MHGer. *helmbarde, halmbarte* : *helm,* handle + *barte,* ax (< OHGer. *barta;* see **bhardh-ā-** in App.).] —**hal′ber·dier** (-bər-dîr′) *n.*

hal·cy·on (hăl′sē-ən) *n.* **1.** A kingfisher, esp. one of the genus *Halcyon.* **2.** A fabled bird, identified with the kingfisher, believed to be able to calm the wind and the waves while it nested on the sea during the winter solstice. ❖ *adj.* **1.** Calm and peaceful; tranquil. **2.** Prosperous; golden: *halcyon years.* [ME *alcioun* < Lat. *alcyōn, halcyōn* < Gk. *halkuōn,* a mythical bird, kingfisher, alteration (influenced by *hals,* salt, sea, and *kuōn,* conceiving) of *alkuōn.*]

Hal·dol (hăl′dôl′, -dŏl′, -dōl′) A trademark used for haloperidol.

hale¹ (hāl) *adj.* **hal·er, hal·est** Free from infirmity or illness; sound. See Syns at **healthy.** [ME < OE *hāl.* See **kailo-** in App.] —**hale′ness** *n.*

hale² (hāl) *t.v.* **haled, hal·ing, hales 1.** To compel to go. **2.** *Archaic* To pull, draw, drag, or hoist. [ME *halen,* to pull, drag < OFr. *haler,* of Gmc. orig. See **kela-** in App.]

Hale, Edward Everett 1822–1909. Amer. Unitarian cleric and writer whose works include the story "The Man Without a Country" (1863). His sister **Lucretia Peabody Hale** (1820–1900) was a writer of children's books.

Hale, George Ellery 1868–1938. Amer. astrophysicist who invented the spectroheliograph (1891).

Hale, Nathan 1755–76. Amer. Revolutionary soldier who was hanged by the British as a spy.

Hale, Sarah Josepha Buell 1788–1879. Amer. writer and editor of *Godey's Lady's Book* (1837–77).

Ha·le·a·ka·la Crater (hä′lē-ä′kə-lä′) A volcanic crater, 829.6 m (2,720 ft) deep, of E Maui, HI.

Ha·ley (hā′lē), **Alex** 1921–92. Amer. writer best known for *Roots* (1976), a fictionalized chronicle tracing his family history back to its African origins.

half (hăf, häf) *n., pl.* **halves** (hăvz, hävz) **1a.** One of two equal parts that together make a whole. **b.** One part approximately equal to the remaining part. **2.** *Informal* A 50-cent piece. **3.** *Sports* **a.** One of the two periods into which certain games are divided. **b.** A halfback. **c.** *Chiefly British* A school term; a semester. **5.** Half an hour. ❖ *adj.* **1a.** Being one of two equal parts. **b.** Being approximately a half. **2.** Partial or incomplete. ❖ *adv.* **1.** To the extent of exactly or nearly half. **2.** Not completely or sufficiently; partly. —*idioms:* **by half 1.** By a considerable extent. **2.** By an excessive amount. **by halves** In a reluctant manner; unenthusiastically. **half again as many** (or **much**) One-and-a-half times more; 50 percent more. **in half** Into halves. **not half** Not at all. **not the half of** Only a fraction or a small part of. [ME < OE *healf.*]

half-and-half (hăf′ənd-hăf′, häf′ənd-häf′) *adj.* Being half one thing and half another. ❖ *adv.* In equal portions. ❖ *n.* **1.** A mixture of two things in equal portions, esp. milk and cream. **2.** *Chiefly British* A blend of malt liquors, esp. porter and ale.

half-assed (hăf′ăst′, häf′ăst′) *adj. Vulgar Slang* **1.** Not well planned or executed. **2.** Incompetent. —**half′-assed′** *adv.*

half·back (hăf′băk′, häf′-) *n.* **1.** *Football* One of the players positioned near the flanks behind the line of scrimmage. **2.** *Sports* One of several players stationed behind the forward line, as in soccer or Rugby.

half-baked (hăf′bākt′, häf′-) *adj.* **1.** Only partly baked. **2.** *Informal* Insufficiently thought out; ill-conceived. **3.** *Informal* Exhibiting a lack of common sense: *a half-baked visionary.*

half binding *n.* A bookbinding in which the back and often the corners of the volume are bound in a material differing from the rest of the cover.

half blood also **half-blood** (hăf′blŭd′, häf′-) *n.* **1a.** The relationship between people having one parent in common. **b.** A person in such a relationship. **2.** *Often Offensive* A person having parents of different races, esp. a person of Native American and white parentage. **3.** A half-blooded domestic animal.

half-blood·ed (hăf′blŭd′ĭd, häf′-) *adj.* **1.** Having only one parent in common. **2.** Having one pedigreed parent and one of unknown or mixed ancestry. Used of animals.

half boot *n.* A low boot extending just above the ankle.

half-breed (hăf′brēd′, häf′-) *n. Offensive* A person having parents of different races, esp. a person of Native American and white parentage. ❖ *adj.* Half-blooded; hybrid. Used of animals.

half brother *n.* A brother to whom one is biologically related through one parent only.

half-caste (hăf′kăst′, häf′käst′) *Offensive n.* A person of mixed racial descent. ❖ *adj.* Of mixed racial descent.

half-cell (hăf′sĕl′, häf′-) *n.* Either of the two connected parts of an electrochemical cell, consisting of one electrode in a conductive fluid.

half cock *n.* The position of the hammer of a firearm when it is locked halfway up so that the trigger cannot be pulled.

half·cocked (hăf′kŏkt′, häf′-) *adj.* **1.** *Informal* Inadequately or poorly prepared: *a halfcocked plan.* **2.** Being at the position of half cock. Used of a firearm. —**half′cocked′** *adv.*

half-crown (hăf′kroun′, häf′-) *n.* A coin formerly used in Great Britain, worth two shillings and sixpence.

half-dol·lar (hăf′dŏl′ər, häf′-) *n.* A US silver 50-cent coin.

half gainer *n.* A dive in which the diver springs from the board facing forward, rotates in a half backward somersault, and enters the water headfirst, facing the board.

half·heart·ed (hăf′här′tĭd, häf′-) *adj.* Exhibiting or feeling little interest or enthusiasm; uninspired. —**half′heart′ed·ly** *adv.*

half hitch *n.* A knot or hitch made by looping a rope or strap around an object and then back around itself, bringing the end of the rope through the loop.

half-hour (hăf′our′, häf′-) *n.* **1.** A period of 30 minutes. **2.** The middle point of an hour. —**half′-hour′ly** *adv. & adj.*

half-length (hăf′lĕngkth′, -lĕngth′, lĕnth′, häf′-) *n.* A portrait that shows only the upper half and hands of a person. ❖ *adj.* Of or relating to a half-length. **2.** Of half the full length.

half-life (hăf′līf′, häf′-) *n.* **1.** *Physics* The time required for half the nuclei in a sample of a specific isotopic species to undergo radioactive decay. **2.** *Biology* **a.** The time required for half the quantity of a drug or other substance deposited in a living organism to be metabolized or eliminated normally. **b.** The time required for the radioactivity of material taken in by a living organism to be halved from its initial value.

half-light (hăf′līt′, häf′-) *n.* The soft subdued light seen at dusk or dawn or in dimly lit interiors.

half-line or **half line** (hăf′līn′, häf′-) *n.* See **ray¹** 4.

half-mast (hăf′măst′, häf′mäst′) *n.* The position about halfway up a mast or pole at which a flag is flown as a symbol of mourning or a signal of distress. ❖ *t.v.* **-mast·ed, -mast·ing, -masts** To place (a flag) halfway up a mast or pole.

half-moon (hăf′mōōn′, häf′-) *n.* **1.** The moon when only half its disk is illuminated. **2.** Something shaped like a crescent.

half nelson *n.* A wrestling hold with one arm under the opponent's arm from behind to the back of the neck.

half note *n. Music* A note worth one half of a whole note.

half-o·pen interval (hăf′ō′pən, häf′-) *n.* A set of numbers representing all the numbers between a pair of given numbers and including either of the endpoints.

Alex Haley

half note
from *Fra Jacopino* (1614) by
Girolamo Frescobaldi
(1583–1643)
A. half note
B. quarter note

half·pen·ny (hā′pə-nē, hāp′nē) n., pl. **half·pence** (hā′pəns) or **half·pen·nies 1a.** A British coin worth one half of a new penny. **b.** A British coin worth one half of an old penny, no longer in circulation. **2.** The sum of one half of a penny.

half-pint (hāf′pīnt′, hāf′-) n. Slang A small person or animal.

half·pipe or **half pipe** (hāf′pīp′, hāf′-) n. A smooth-surfaced structure shaped like a trough and used for stunts in sports such as in-line skating and snowboarding.

half relief n. Sculptural relief composed of modeled forms that project approximately halfway from the background.

half rhyme n. See **off rhyme**.

half shell n. Either of the halves of a shell of a bivalve, such as an oyster.

half sister n. A sister to whom one is biologically related through one parent only.

half-slip (hāf′slip′, hāf′-) n. A woman's skirtlike undergarment that hangs from the waist.

half sole n. A shoe sole that extends from the shank to the toe.

half-sole (hāf′sōl′, hāf′-) tr.v. **-soled, -sol·ing, -soles** To fit or repair with a half sole.

half-staff (hāf′stāf′, hāf′stäf′) n. See **half-mast**.

half step n. **1.** Music See **semitone**. **2.** A marching step of 15 inches (38 centimeters) at quick time and 18 inches (46 centimeters) at double time.

half-tim·bered (hāf′tim′bərd, hāf′-) also **half-tim·ber** (-bər) adj. Having a wooden framework, often exposed, with plaster, brick, stone, or other masonry filling the spaces.

half·time (hāf′tīm′, hāf′-) n. The intermission between halves in games of certain sports, such as basketball and football.

half title n. The title of a book at the top of the first page of the text or on a full page preceding the main title page.

half·tone (hāf′tōn′, hāf′-) n. **1.** A tone or value halfway between a highlight and a dark shadow. **2a.** A picture in which gradations of light are obtained by photographing the subject through a fine screen. **b.** A picture made by such a process. **3.** Music See **semitone**.

half-track (hāf′trāk′, hāf′-) n. A lightly armored military motor vehicle having continuous tracks in the rear for power and conventional wheels in front for steering.

half-truth (hāf′trōōth′, hāf′-) n. A statement, esp. one intended to deceive, that omits some facts.

half volley n. A stroke in certain sports in which the ball is hit immediately after it bounces off the ground.

half·way (hāf′wā′, hāf′-) adj. **1.** Midway between two points or conditions. **2.** Reaching or including only half or a portion; partial: halfway measures. —**half′way′** adv.

halfway house n. **1.** A rehabilitation center, esp. for people who have left an institution. **2.** A stopping place that marks the midpoint of a journey.

half-wit (hāf′wit′, hāf′-) n. Slang A foolish or stupid person. —**half′-wit′ted** adj. —**half′-wit′ted·ly** adv.

hal·i·but (hāl′ə-bət, hōl′-) n., pl. **halibut** or **-buts** Any of several large edible flatfishes of the genus Hippoglossus and related genera of northern Atlantic or Pacific waters. [ME : hali, holi, holy (< its being eaten on holy days); see HOLY + butte, flatfish (< MDu.; see bhau- in App.).]

Hal·i·car·nas·sus (hāl′ī-kär-nās′əs) An ancient Greek city of SW Asia Minor on the Aegean Sea; site of the tomb of King Mausolus, one of the Seven Wonders of the World.

hal·ide (hāl′īd′, hā′līd′) n. A chemical compound of a halogen with a more electropositive element or group.

hal·i·dom (hāl′ī-dəm) n. Obsolete **1.** Something considered holy. **2.** A sanctuary. [ME < OE hāligdōm : hālig, holy; see HOLY + -dōm, -dom.]

Hal·i·fax (hāl′ə-fāks′) **1.** The cap. of Nova Scotia, Canada, in the S-central part on the Atlantic Ocean; founded 1749. Pop. 113,910. **2.** A borough of NE England NE of Manchester. Pop. 192,560.

hal·ite (hāl′īt′, hā′līt′) n. **1.** A colorless or white mineral, NaCl, occurring as cubic crystals and found in dried lakebeds in arid climates, used as table salt. **2.** Rock salt.

hal·i·to·sis (hāl′ī-tō′sīs) n. The condition of having stale or foul-smelling breath. [Lat. hālitus, breath; akin to hālāre, to breathe + −OSIS.]

hall (hōl) n. **1.** A corridor or passageway in a building. **2.** A large entrance room or vestibule in a building; a lobby. **3a.** A building for public gatherings or entertainments. **b.** The large room in which such events are held. **4.** A building used for the meetings, entertainments, or living quarters of a social or religious organization. **5a.** A building belonging to a school, college, or university that provides classroom, dormitory, or dining facilities. **b.** A large room in such a building. **c.** Chiefly British A meal served in such a building. **6.** The main house on a landed estate. **7a.** The castle or house of a medieval monarch or noble. **b.** The principal room in such a hall. [ME halle, large residence < OE heall. See kel- in App.]

Hall, Charles Francis 1821–71. Amer. explorer who led three expeditions (1860–62, 1864–69, and 1871) to the Arctic.

Hall, Granville Stanley 1844–1924. Amer. psychologist who founded child psychology.

hal·lah (КНä′lə, hä′-) n. Variant of **challah**.

Hal·le (hä′lə) A city of central Germany WNW of Leipzig; first mentioned in the 9th cent. Pop. 295,372.

Hal·lel (hä-lāl′, hāl′əl) n. Judaism A chant of praise consisting of Psalms 113 through 118, recited on certain holidays. [Heb. hallēl, song of praise < hillēl, to praise.]

hal·le·lu·jah (hāl′ə-lōō′yə) interj. Used to express praise or joy. ❖ n. **1.** An exclamation of "hallelujah." **2.** Music A composition expressing praise and based on the word "hallelujah." [Heb. halălûyāh, praise Yahweh : hallalu, masc. pl. imper. of hillēl, to praise + Yāh, Yahweh (short for Yahweh).]

Hal·ley (hāl′ē), **Edmund** or **Edmond** 1656–1742. English astronomer who first applied Newton's laws of motion to predict correctly the period of a comet (1705).

Hal·ley's comet (hāl′ēz, hā′lēz) n. A comet last observed from Earth in 1986, having a period of 76 years. [After Edmund HALLEY.]

hal·liard (hāl′yərd) n. Variant of **halyard**.

hall·mark (hōl′märk′) n. **1.** A mark indicating quality or excellence. **2.** A mark used in England to stamp gold and silver articles that meet established standards of purity. **3.** A conspicuous feature or characteristic. ❖ tr.v. **-marked, -mark·ing, -marks** To stamp (gold and silver articles) with a hallmark. [After Goldsmith's Hall in London, England.]

Hall of Fame n., pl. **Halls of Fame 1.** A group of persons judged outstanding, as in a sport or profession. **2.** A building housing memorial items honoring illustrious persons. —**Hall′ of Fam′er** n.

hal·loo (hə-lōō′) also **hal·loa** (-lō′) interj. **1.** Used to catch someone's attention. **2.** Used to urge on hounds in a hunt. ❖ n., pl. **-loos** also **-loas** A shout or call of "halloo." ❖ v. **-looed, -loo·ing, -loos** also **-loaed, -loa·ing, -loas** —intr. To shout "halloo." —tr. **1.** To urge on or pursue by calling "halloo" or shouting. **2.** To call out to. **3.** To shout or yell (something). [Alteration of obsolete holla, stop! See HELLO.]

hal·low (hāl′ō) tr.v. **-lowed, -low·ing, -lows 1.** To make or set apart as holy. **2.** To respect or honor greatly; revere. [ME halwen < OE hālgian. See kailo- in App.]

hal·lowed (hāl′ōd) adj. **1.** Sanctified; consecrated. **2.** Highly venerated; sacrosanct.

Hal·low·een also **Hal·low·e'en** (hāl′ə-wēn′, hōl′-) n. October 31, celebrated by children going door to door in costume begging treats and playing pranks. [Short for All Hallow Even : ALLHALLOW(MAS) + EVEN².]

Hal·low·mas also **Hal·low·mass** (hāl′ō-məs, -mās′) n. Archaic All Saints' Day. [Short for ALLHALLOWMAS.]

Hall·statt (hāl′stät′, häl′shtät′) adj. Of or relating to a dominant Iron Age culture of central and western Europe, probably chiefly Celtic, that flourished from approx. 900 to 500 B.C. [After the type site at Hallstatt in northern Austria.]

hal·lu·ci·nate (hə-lōō′sə-nāt′) v. **-nat·ed, -nat·ing, -nates** —intr. To undergo hallucination. —tr. **1.** To cause to have hallucinations. **2.** To experience as a hallucination. [Lat. hallūcinārī, hallūcināt-, to dream, be deceived, var. of ālūcinārī.] —**hal·lu′ci·na′tor** n.

hal·lu·ci·na·tion (hə-lōō′sə-nā′shən) n. **1a.** A visual, auditory, olfactory, or other sensory experience that seems real but lacks an external stimulus. **b.** The sensation or visual image caused by such an experience. **2.** A false or mistaken idea; a delusion. —**hal·lu′ci·na′tion·al, hal·lu′ci·na′tive** adj.

hal·lu·ci·na·to·ry (hə-lōō′sə-nə-tôr′ē, -tōr′ē) adj. **1.** Of or characterized by hallucination. **2.** Inducing hallucination.

hal·lu·ci·no·gen (hə-lōō′sə-nə-jən) n. A substance that induces hallucination. [HALLUCIN(ATION) + −GEN.] —**hal·lu′cin·o·gen′ic** (-jĕn′ĭk) adj.

hal·lu·ci·no·sis (hə-lōō′sə-nō′sīs) n. An abnormal condition or mental state characterized by hallucination.

hal·lux (hāl′əks) n., pl. **hal·lu·ces** (hāl′yə-sēz′, hāl′ə-) **1.** The innermost or first digit on the hind foot of certain mammals. **2.** A homologous digit of a bird, a reptile, or an amphibian. [Med. Lat. hallux, hallus, blend of Lat. allus, hallus, thumb, and Lat. hallex, big toe.]

hall·way (hōl′wā′) n. **1.** A corridor in a building. **2.** An entrance hall.

Hal·ma·he·ra (hāl′mə-hĕr′ə, häl′mä-hē′rä) An island of E Indonesia in the Moluccas E of Sulawesi.

ha·lo (hā′lō) n., pl. **-los** or **-loes 1a.** A circular band of colored light around a light source, as around the sun, caused by the refraction and reflection of light by ice particles suspended in the intervening atmosphere. **b.** Something resembling this band. **2.** A luminous ring or disk of light surrounding sacred figures in religious paintings; a nimbus. **3.** The aura of majesty or glory surrounding a person or thing that is regarded with reverence, awe, or sentiment. ❖ v. **-loed, -lo·ing, -loes** To encircle with or as if with a halo. [Med. Lat. halō < accusative of Lat. halōs < Gk. halōs, threshing floor, disk of or around the sun or moon.]

halo– or **hal–** pref. **1.** Salt: halophyte. **2.** Halogen: halocarbon. [Fr. < Gk. < hals, hal-, salt, sea. See sal– in App.]

hal·o·bac·te·ri·um (hāl′ō-bāk-tîr′ē-əm) n., pl. **-te·ri·a** (-tîr′ē-ə) Any of various rod-shaped, halophilic, red or purple archaea of the genus Halobacterium, some species of which produce bacteriorhodopsin.

Halley's comet

ă pat   oi boy
ā pay   ou out
âr care   ōō took
ä father   ōō boot
ĕ pet   ŭ cut
ē be   ûr urge
ĭ pit   th thin
ī pie   th this
îr pier   hw which
ŏ pot   zh vision
ō toe   ə about,
ô paw   item

Stress marks:
′ (primary);
′ (secondary), as in
lexicon (lĕk′sĭ-kŏn′)

hamadryas
Papio hamadryas

hamantasch

Alexander Hamilton
detail from an 1806 portrait
by John Trumbull

hal·o·car·bon (hăl′ə-kär′bən) *n.* A compound, such as a fluorocarbon, of carbon and one or more halogens.

hal·o·cline (hăl′ə-klīn′) *n.* A vertical gradient in ocean salinity.

hal·o·gen (hăl′ə-jən) *n.* Any of the chemically related elements fluorine, chlorine, bromine, iodine, and astatine. —**ha·log′e·nous** (hă-lŏj′ə-nəs) *adj.*

hal·o·ge·nate (hăl′ə-jə-nāt′) *tr.v.* **-nat·ed, -nat·ing, -nates** To treat or combine with a halogen. —**hal′o·ge·na′tion** *n.*

hal·o·per·i·dol (hăl′ō-pĕr′ĭ-dôl′, -dŏl′, -dōl′) *n.* A tranquilizer, $C_{21}H_{23}ClFNO_2$, used esp. in the treatment of psychotic disorders. [HALO– + (PI)PERID(INE) + –OL¹.]

hal·o·phile (hăl′ə-fīl′) *n.* An organism that requires a salty environment. —**hal′o·phil′ic** (-fĭl′ĭk), **ha·loph′i·lous** (hă-lŏf′ə-ləs) *adj.*

hal·o·phyte (hăl′ə-fīt′) *n.* A plant adapted to saline environments. —**hal′o·phyt′ic** (-fĭt′ĭk) *adj.*

hal·o·thane (hăl′ə-thān′) *n.* A colorless nonflammable liquid, $C_2HBrClF_3$, used as an inhalant anesthetic. [HALO– + (E)THANE.]

Hals (hälz, häls), **Frans** 1580?–1666. Dutch painter of genre scenes and portraits, such as *The Laughing Cavalier* (1624).

Hal·sey (hôl′zē), **William Frederick** 1882–1959. Amer. naval officer during World War II.

halt¹ (hôlt) *n.* A suspension of movement or progress, esp. a temporary one. ❖ *v.* **halt·ed, halt·ing, halts** —*tr.* To cause to stop: *hopes to halt tax fraud.* —*intr.* To stop; pause: *halted for lunch.* See Syns at **stop.** [Ger., sing. imper. of *halten,* to stop < MHGer. < OHGer. *haltan.*]

halt² (hôlt) *intr.v.* **halt·ed, halt·ing, halts** **1.** To proceed or act with uncertainty; waver. **2.** To be defective or hesitant, as in logic or in expression. **3.** To limp or hobble. ❖ *adj. Archaic* Lame; crippled. [ME *halten,* to limp < OE *healtian.*]

hal·ter¹ (hôl′tər) *n.* **1.** A device made of rope or leather straps used to lead or secure an animal by the head. **2a.** A rope with a noose used for execution by hanging. **b.** Death or execution by hanging. **3.** A woman's top that ties behind the neck and across the back. ❖ *tr.v.* **-tered, -ter·ing, -ters** **1.** To put a halter on. **2.** To control with or as if with a halter. **3.** To hang (someone). [ME < OE *hælftre.*]

hal·ter² (hôl′tər, hăl′-) *n., pl.* **-ter·es** (-tîr′ēz) Either of the small clublike balancing organs that are the rudimentary hind wings of flies and other dipterous insects. [Lat. *halter,* lead weights used in leaping exercises < sing. of Gk. *halteres* < *hallesthai,* to jump. See **sel-** in App.]

halt·ing (hôl′tĭng) *adj.* **1.** Hesitant or wavering. **2.** Imperfect; defective. **3.** Limping; lame. —**halt′ing·ly** *adv.*

hal·vah or **hal·va** (häl-vä′, häl′vä) *n.* A confection consisting of crushed sesame seeds in a binder of honey. [Turk. *helva* < Ar. *ḥalwā* < *ḥaluwa,* to be sweet.]

halve (hăv, häv) *tr.v.* **halved, halv·ing, halves** **1.** To divide (something) into two equal parts. **2.** To lessen or reduce by half. **3.** *Informal* To share (something) equally. **4.** *Sports* To play (a golf game or hole) using the same number of strokes as one's opponent. [ME *halven* < *half,* half. See HALF.]

halves (hăvz, hävz) *n.* Plural of **half.**

hal·yard also **hal·liard** (hăl′yərd) *n. Nautical* A line used to raise or lower a sail, flag, or yard. [Alteration (influenced by YARD¹) of ME *halier* < *halen,* to pull. See HALE².]

ham (hăm) *n.* **1.** The thigh of the hind leg of certain animals, esp. a hog. **2.** A cut of meat from the thigh of a hog. **3.** The back of the knee. **4.** The back of the thigh. **5. hams** The buttocks. **6.** A performer who overacts or exaggerates. **7.** A licensed amateur radio operator. ❖ *v.* **hammed, ham·ming, hams** —*intr.* To overact. —*tr.* To exaggerate or overdo (a dramatic role, for example). [ME *hamme* < OE *hamm.*]

Ham (hăm) In the Bible, a son of Noah and the brother of Japheth and Shem.

Ha·ma or **Ha·mah** (hä′mä) A city of W Syria SSW of Aleppo; frequently mentioned in the Bible as Hamath. Pop. 273,000.

Ham·a·dan (hăm′ə-dăn′, -dän′) A city of W Iran WSW of Tehran; captured by Alexander in 330 B.C. Pop. 406,070.

ham·a·dry·ad (hăm′ə-drī′əd) *n., pl.* **-ads** or **-a·des** (-ə-dēz′) **1.** *Greek & Roman Mythology* A nymph who lives as long as the tree of which she is the spirit lives. **2.** See **king cobra.** [ME *amadriad* < Lat. *Hamadryas, Hamadryad-* < Gk. *Hamadruas* : *hama,* together with; see **sem-¹** in App. + *Druas,* dryad (< *drūs,* oak; see **deru-** in App.).]

ham·a·dry·as (hăm′ə-drī′əs) *n.* A baboon (*Papio hamadryas*) of northern Africa and Arabia, the adult male of which has a heavy mane. [Lat., hamadryad. See HAMADRYAD.]

ha·mal also **ham·mal** (hə-mäl′) *n.* A porter or bearer in certain Muslim countries. [Ar. *ḥammāl* < *ḥamala,* to carry.]

Ha·ma·ma·tsu (hä′mə-mät′sōō) A city of S Honshu, Japan, ESE of Nagoya. Pop. 560,660.

Ha·man (hā′mən) In the Bible, a Persian minister who was hanged for plotting the destruction of the Jews.

ha·man·tasch (hä′mən-täsh′) *n., pl.* **-tasch·en** A triangular pastry with a filling such as preserves or poppy seeds. [Yiddish *homentash* : *Homen,* Haman + *tash,* pocket (< MHGer. *tasche* < OHGer. *tasca*).]

ha·mar·ti·a (hä′mär-tē′ə) *n.* A character flaw, esp. one leading to tragedy. [Gk. < *hamartanein,* to miss the mark, err.]

ha·mate (hā′māt′) *Anatomy adj.* Hooked at the tip. ❖ *n.* A small hook-shaped carpal bone of the wrist. [Lat. *hāmātus* < *hāmus,* hook.]

Ham·burg (hăm′bûrg′, hăm′bŏŏrg′, -bŏŏrk′) A city of N Germany on the Elbe R. NE of Bremen; formed an alliance with Lübeck (1241) that became the basis for the Hanseatic League. Pop. 1,702,887.

ham·burg·er (hăm′bûr′gər) also **ham·burg** (-bûrg′) *n.* **1a.** Ground meat, usu. beef. **b.** A patty of such meat. **2.** A sandwich made with a patty of ground meat usu. in a roll or bun. [Short for *Hamburger steak,* after HAMBURG.]

hame (hām) *n.* One of the two curved pieces of a harness that fits around the neck of a draft animal and to which the traces are attached. [ME < MDu. See **tkei-** in App.]

Ha·mer (hā′mər), **Fannie Lou** 1917–77. Amer. civil rights activist who was imprisoned for challenging Mississippi's discriminatory voting laws (1962).

ham-fist·ed (hăm′fĭs′tĭd) *adj.* Ham-handed.

ham-hand·ed (hăm′hăn′dĭd) *adj.* **1.** Lacking dexterity or skill; clumsy. **2.** Lacking social grace or tact. **3.** Having unusually large hands.

Ham·hung (hăm′hŏŏng′) A city of E-central North Korea NE of Pyongyang. Pop. 775,000.

Ha·mil·car Bar·ca (hə-mĭl′kär′ bär′kə, hăm′əl-) 270?–228? B.C. Carthaginian general who led the Carthaginian forces during the final years of the First Punic War (264–241).

Ham·il·ton (hăm′əl-tən) **1.** The cap. of Bermuda, on Bermuda I.; founded 1790. Pop. 1,100. **2.** A city of SE Ontario, Canada, at the W end of Lake Ontario SW of Toronto. Pop. 322,352.

Hamilton, Alexander 1755?–1804. Amer. politician who was first US secretary of the treasury (1789–95). He was mortally wounded in a duel with his political rival Aaron Burr. —**Ham′il·to′ni·an** (-tō′nē-ən) *adj. & n.*

Hamilton, Edith 1867–1963. German-born Amer. classicist whose works include *The Greek Way* (1930).

Hamilton, Lady Emma Lyon 1765?–1815. British socialite who became Horatio Nelson's lover in 1798.

Hamilton, Mount A peak, 1,285 m (4,213 ft), of W CA E of San Jose; site of Lick Observatory.

Ham·il·to·ni·an (hăm′əl-tō′nē-ən) *n.* A mathematical function that can be used to generate the equations of motion of a dynamic system, often equal to the sum of the kinetic and potential energies of the system expressed in terms of the system's coordinates and momenta. [After Sir William R. *Hamilton* (1805–65), Irish mathematician.]

Hamilton Inlet A deep inlet of the N Atlantic Ocean in SE Labrador connecting with Lake Melville.

Ham·ite (hăm′īt′) *n.* A member of a group of peoples of northern and northeast Africa, including the Berbers, Tuaregs, and the ancient Egyptians and their descendants. [After HAM.]

Ha·mit·ic (hă-mĭt′ĭk) *adj.* Of or relating to the Hamites or their languages or cultures. ❖ *n.* A presumed language family formerly thought to include Egyptian and the Berber, Cushitic, and Chadic languages.

Ham·i·to-Se·mit·ic (hăm′ĭ-tō-sə-mĭt′ĭk) *n.* Afro-Asiatic. No longer in technical use. [HAMIT(IC) + SEMITIC.]

ham·let (hăm′lĭt) *n.* A small village. [ME *hamelet* < OFr., dim. of *hamel,* dim. of *ham,* village, of Gmc. orig. See **tkei-** in App.]

Hamm (hăm, häm) A city of W-central Germany in the Ruhr district SSE of Münster; founded c. 1226. Pop. 182,390.

ham·mal (hə-mäl′) *n.* Variant of **hamal.**

Ham·mar·skjöld (hăm′ər-shōld′, -shəld, hä′mär-shœld′), **Dag Hjalmar Agné Carl** 1905–61. Swedish political leader and secretary-general of the United Nations (1953–61) who won the 1961 Nobel Peace Prize posthumously.

ham·mer (hăm′ər) *n.* **1.** A hand tool consisting of a handle with a head of metal or other heavy rigid material that is attached at a right angle, used for striking or pounding. **2.** A tool or device similar to a hammer. **a.** The part of a gunlock that hits the primer or firing pin or explodes the percussion cap and causes the gun to fire. **b.** *Music* One of the padded wooden pieces of a piano that strikes the strings. **c.** A part of an apparatus that strikes a gong or bell, as in a clock. **3.** *Anatomy* See **malleus. 4.** *Sports* A metal ball weighing 16 pounds (7.2 kilograms) and having a long wire or wooden handle by which it is thrown in track-and-field competition. **5.** A small mallet used by auctioneers. ❖ *v.* **-mered, -mer·ing, -mers** —*tr.* **1.** To hit, esp. repeatedly, with or as if with a hammer; pound. **2.** To beat into a shape with or as if with a hammer. **3.** To put together, fasten, or seal, particularly with nails, by hammering. **4.** To force upon by constant repetition. **5a.** To defeat soundly. **b.** To inflict a heavy loss or damage on. —*intr.* **1.** To deal repeated blows with or as if with a hammer; pummel: *"Wind hammered at us violently in gusts"* (Thor Heyerdahl). **2.** To undergo beating in the manner of a hammer. **3.** *Informal* To keep at something continuously. —**idiom: under the hammer** For sale at an auction. [ME *hamer* < OE *hamor.* See **ak-** in App.] —**ham′mer·er** *n.*

hammer and sickle *n.* An emblem of the Communist movement signifying the alliance of workers and peasants.

hammer and tongs *adv.* With tremendous energy or effort.

ham·mer·beam (hăm′ər-bēm′) *n.* A short horizontal beam

projecting inward at the top of an interior wall, used as an attachment for rafters.

ham·mered (hăm′ərd) *adj.* **1.** Shaped or worked with a metalworker's hammer and often showing the marks of these tools. **2.** *Slang* Drunk or intoxicated.

hammered dulcimer or **hammer dulcimer** *n.* A musical instrument with wire strings of graduated lengths stretched over a sound box, played by striking with two padded hammers.

Ham·mer·fest (hăm′ər-fĕst′, hä′mər-) A town of N Norway on an island in the Arctic Ocean; the northernmost town of Europe. Pop. 7,208.

ham·mer·head (hăm′ər-hĕd′) *n.* **1.** The head of a hammer. **2.** Any of several predatory sharks of the genus *Sphyrna*, having a head with a fleshy extension on each side with the eyes at the ends. **3.** A wading bird (*Scopus umbretta*) of Africa and southwest Asia having a large bladelike bill and a long backward-pointing crest. **4.** An African fruit bat (*Hypsignathus monstrosus*), the male of which has an enlarged head.

ham·mer·kop (hăm′ər-kŏp′) *n.* See **hammerhead** 3. [Partial transl. of Afr. *hamerkop* : *hamer*, hammer + *kop*, head (< MDu., prob. < LLat. *cuppa*, drinking vessel, cup).]

ham·mer·lock (hăm′ər-lŏk′) *n.* **1.** A wrestling hold in which the opponent's arm is pulled behind the back and twisted upward. **2.** Overwhelming dominance that is difficult if not impossible to overcome.

Ham·mer·stein (hăm′ər-stīn′, -stēn′), **Oscar** 1846?–1919. German-born Amer. operatic manager. His grandson **Oscar Hammerstein II** (1895–1960), a lyricist, collaborated with Richard Rodgers on musicals such as *Oklahoma!* (1943).

ham·mer·stone (hăm′ər-stōn′) *n. Archaeology* A stone or cobble used as a pounding or pecking tool.

ham·mer·toe (hăm′ər-tō′) *n.* A toe, usu. the second, that is permanently flexed downward, resulting in a clawlike shape.

Ham·mett (hăm′ĭt), **Dashiell** 1894–1961. Amer. writer of detective fiction, including *The Maltese Falcon* (1930).

ham·mock[1] (hăm′ək) *n.* A hanging, easily swung length of canvas or heavy netting suspended between two trees or other supports and used as a seat or bed. [Sp. *hamaca* < Taino.]

ham·mock[2] (hăm′ək) *n.* Variant of **hummock** 2.

Ham·mond (hăm′ənd) A city of NW IN on the IL border W of Gary. Pop. 83,048.

Ham·mu·ra·bi (hăm′ə-rä′bē, hä′mŏŏ-) also **Ham·mu·ra·pi** (-bē, -pē) d. 1750 B.C. Babylonian king (1792–1750) who codified the laws of Mesopotamia and Sumeria.

ham·my (hăm′ē) *adj.* **-mi·er, -mi·est** Marked by overacting; affectedly humorous or dramatic. —**ham′mi·ly** *adv.* —**ham′mi·ness** *n.*

ham·per[1] (hăm′pər) *tr.v.* **-pered, -per·ing, -pers** To prevent the free movement or progress of. ❖ *n. Nautical* Necessary but encumbering equipment on a ship. [ME *hamperen.*]

ham·per[2] (hăm′pər) *n.* A large basket, usu. with a cover. [ME, alteration of AN *hanaper* < OFr. *hanepier*, a case for holding goblets < *hanap*, goblet, of Gmc. orig.]

Hamp·shire (hămp′shĭr, -shər) *n.* **1.** A large sheep of a breed originating in England. **2.** A pig of a breed developed in the United States, having a black body with a white beltlike band. [After *Hampshire*, a county of southern England.]

Hamp·ton (hămp′tən) An independent city of SE VA opposite Norfolk on **Hampton Roads,** the outlet of three rivers into Chesapeake Bay; settled in 1610. Pop. 146,437.

Hampton, Lionel b. 1913. Amer. musician who was the first to use the vibraphone as a jazz instrument.

Hampton, Wade 1818–1902. Amer. Confederate general who later served as US senator (1879–91) for SC.

ham·ster (hăm′stər) *n.* A small Eurasian rodent of the subfamily Cricetinae, esp. *Mesocricetus auratus*, often kept as a pet. [Ger. < MHGer. *hamster*, perh. < OHGer. *hamustro*, of Slav. orig.]

ham·string (hăm′strĭng′) *n.* **1.** Any of the tendons at the rear hollow of the human knee. **2.** Any of the three muscles constituting the back of the upper leg that serve to flex the knee joint and extend the hip joint. Often used in the plural. **3.** The large tendon in the back of the hock of a quadruped. ❖ *tr.v.* **-strung** (-strŭng′), **-string·ing, -strings** **1.** To cut the hamstring of and thereby cripple. **2.** To destroy or hinder the efficiency of; frustrate.

Ham·sun (hăm′sən, -sŏŏn′), **Knut** Pen name of Knut Pedersen. 1859–1952. Norwegian writer who won the 1920 Nobel Prize for literature.

ham·u·lus (hăm′yə-ləs) *n., pl.* **-li** (-lī′) A small hooklike projection or process. [Lat. *hāmulus*, dim. of *hāmus*, hook.]

ham·za also **ham·zah** (hăm′zə, häm′zä) *n.* A sign in Arabic orthography used for a glottal stop, transliterated in English as an apostrophe. [Ar. < *hamaza*, to urge on, goad.]

Han[1] (hän) *n., pl.* **Han** or **Hans** A member of the principal ethnic group of China, constituting about 93 percent of the population. [Chin. (Mandarin) *Hàn.*]

Han[2] (hän) A Chinese dynasty (206 B.C.–A.D. 220) noted for unifying and expanding its national territory. [Chin. (Mandarin) *Hàn.*]

Han Chinese *n.* See **Han**[1].

Han·cock (hăn′kŏk′), **John** 1737–93. Amer. politician who was

president of the Continental Congress (1775–77) and the first to sign the Declaration of Independence.

Hancock, Winfield Scott 1824–86. Amer. Civil War general who was victorious in the Gettysburg Campaign (1863).

hand (hănd) *n.* **1a.** The terminal part of the human arm located below the forearm, used for grasping and holding and consisting of the wrist, palm, four fingers, and an opposable thumb. **b.** A homologous or similar part in other animals, as the terminal part of the forelimb in certain vertebrates. **2.** A unit of length equal to 4 inches (10.2 centimeters), used esp. to specify the height of a horse. **3.** Something suggesting the shape or function of the human hand, esp.: **a.** Any of the rotating pointers used as indexes on the face of a mechanical clock. **b.** A pointer, as on a gauge or dial. **4.** *Printing* See **index** 3. **5.** Lateral direction indicated according to the way in which one is facing: *at my right hand.* **6a.** A style or individual sample of writing. **b.** A signature: *put my hand to the contract.* **7.** A round of applause to signify approval. **8.** Physical assistance; help: *gave me a hand with the bags.* **9. hands** *Sports* A handball in soccer. **10.** *Games* **a.** The cards held in a card game by a given player at any time; the deal. **b.** The number of cards dealt each player; the deal. **c.** A player or participant in a card game. **d.** A portion of a game during which all the cards dealt out are played: *a hand of poker.* **11a.** One who performs manual labor. **b.** One who is part of a group or crew: *the ship's hands.* **12.** A participant, often a specialist, in an activity. **13a.** The degree of immediacy of a source of information; degree of reliability: *heard the gossip third hand.* **b.** The strength or force of one's position. **14a.** Possession, ownership, or keeping. Often used in the plural. **b.** Power; jurisdiction; care. Often used in the plural. **15a.** Involvement or participation. **b.** An influence or effect. **c.** Evidence of craft or artistic skill. **16.** An aptitude or ability: *I tried my hand at decorating.* **17.** The aesthetic feel or tactile quality of something, such as a fabric, that indicates its fineness, texture, and durability. **18.** A manner or way of performing something: *a light hand with makeup.* **19a.** Permission or a promise, esp. a pledge to wed. **b.** A commitment or agreement, esp. when sealed by a handshake. ❖ *tr.v.* **hand·ed, hand·ing, hands** **1.** To give or pass with or as if with the hands; transmit. **2.** To aid, direct, or conduct with the hands. **3.** *Nautical* To roll up and secure (a sail); furl. **4.** *Sports* **a.** To give (the ball) directly to a teammate, as in football. Often used with *off.* **b.** To carry, strike, or propel (the ball) with the hand or arm in violation of the rules in soccer. **—phrasal verbs:** **hand down 1.** To bequeath as an inheritance to one's heirs. **2.** To make and pronounce an official decision, esp. a court verdict. **hand on** To turn over to another. **hand out 1.** To distribute freely; disseminate. **2.** To administer or deal out. **hand over** To release or relinquish to another. **—idioms: at hand 1.** Close by; near. **2.** Soon in time; imminent. **at the hand (or hands) of** Performed by someone or through the agency of someone. **by hand** Performed manually. **hand and foot** With concerted, never-ending effort. **hand in (or and) glove** On intimate terms or in close association. **hand in hand** In cooperation; jointly. **hand it to** *Informal* To give credit to. **hand over fist** At a tremendous rate: *made money hand over fist.* **hands down 1.** With no trouble; easily. **2.** Unquestionably. **in hand 1.** Under control. **2.** Accessible at the present time. **3.** Under consideration. **4.** In preparation. **off (one's) hands** No longer under one's jurisdiction, within one's responsibility, or in one's care. **on hand 1.** Available. **2.** About to happen; imminent. **on (or upon) (one's) hands** In one's possession, often as an imposed responsibility or burden. **on the one hand** As one point of view; from one standpoint. **on the other hand** As another point of view; from another standpoint. **out of hand 1.** Out of control. **2.** At once; immediately. **3.** Over and done with; finished. **4.** Uncalled for or improper; indiscreet. **to hand 1.** Nearby. **2.** In one's possession. [ME < OE.] —**hand′er** *n.*

Hand, (Billings) Learned 1872–1961. Amer. jurist who was an influential federal judge (1924–51).

Han·dan also **Han·tan** (hän′dän′) A city of E-central China SSW of Beijing. Pop. 1,769,315.

hand ax also **hand·ax** (hănd′ăks′) *n.* **1.** A short-handled ax; a hatchet. **2.** A cutting or chopping tool, esp. of the early Paleolithic Period, typically consisting of a stone that has been flaked on one or both sides to produce a sharp edge.

hand·bag (hănd′băg′) *n.* **1.** A woman's purse. **2.** A piece of small hand luggage.

hand·ball (hănd′bôl′) *n.* **1a.** A game played by two or more players who hit a ball against a wall with one of their hands, usu. gloved. **b.** The small rubber ball used. **2.** A violation of the rules in soccer in which a player other than the goalie inside the penalty area carries, strikes, or propels the ball with the hand or arm.

hand·bar·row (hănd′băr′ō) *n.* A flat rectangular tray or cart with carrying poles at each end, used in transporting loads.

hand bell *n.* A small bell having a handle, esp. one of a set of bells tuned to different pitches.

hand·bill (hănd′bĭl′) *n.* A flier distributed by hand.

hand·blown also **hand-blown** (hănd′blōn′) *adj.* Formed or shaped with a hand-held blowpipe: *handblown goblets.*

hand·book (hănd′bŏŏk′) *n.* **1.** A concise manual or reference book providing specific information or instruction about a subject or place. **2.** *Games* **a.** A book in which off-track bets are re-

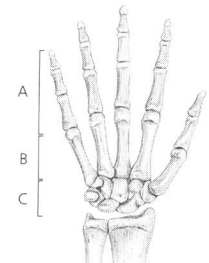

hand
A. phalanges
B. metacarpus
C. carpus

ă pat	oi boy
ā pay	ou out
âr care	ŏŏ took
ä father	ōō boot
ĕ pet	ŭ cut
ē be	ûr urge
ĭ pit	th thin
ī pie	th this
îr pier	hw which
ŏ pot	zh vision
ō toe	ə about,
ô paw	item

Stress marks:
′ (primary);
′ (secondary), as in
lexicon (lĕk′sĭ-kŏn′)

corded. **b.** A place where off-track bets are taken.
hand brake *n.* See **emergency brake.**
hand·breadth (hănd′brĕdth′) also **hand's-breadth** or **hand's breadth** (hăndz′-) *n.* A linear measurement approximating the width of the palm of the hand, from 2½ to 4 inches (6.25 to 10 centimeters).
hand·car (hănd′kär′) *n.* A small open railroad car propelled by a hand pump or a small motor.
hand·cart (hănd′kärt′) *n.* A small, usu. two-wheeled cart pulled or pushed by hand.
hand·clap (hănd′klăp′) *n.* A beating together of the palms of the hands, as to indicate applause.
hand·clasp (hănd′klăsp′) *n.* The act of clasping the hand of another, esp. in friendship.
hand·craft (hănd′krăft′) *n.* Variant of **handicraft.** ❖ *tr.v.* (hănd-krăft′) **-craft·ed, -craft·ing, -crafts** To fashion or make by hand: *handcrafts wooden toys for children.* —**hand′craft′er** *n.* —**hand′crafts′man·ship′, hand′craft′man·ship** *n.*
hand·cuff (hănd′kŭf′) *n.* A restraining device consisting of a pair of strong connected hoops that can be tightened and locked about the wrists and used on one or both arms of a prisoner in custody; a manacle. Often used in the plural. ❖ *tr.v.* **-cuffed, -cuff·ing, -cuffs 1.** To restrain with or as if with handcuffs. **2.** To render ineffective or impotent.

handcar

hand·ed (hăn′dĭd) *adj.* **1.** Of or relating to dexterity, preference, or size with respect to a hand or hands. Often used in combination: *one-handed.* **2.** Relating to a specified number of people. Often used in combination. **3.** *Chemistry* Of or relating to the mirror-image structure of a chiral molecule.
hand·ed·ness (hăn′dĭd-nĭs) *n.* **1.** A preference for using one hand as opposed to the other. **2.** *Chemistry & Physics* The property that distinguishes an asymmetric from its mirror image but not from a rotated object.
Han·del (hăn′dl), **George Frederick** 1685–1759. German-born composer whose works include the *Messiah* (1742). —**Han·del′i·an** (hăn-dē′lē-ən, -dēl′ē-ən) *adj.*
hand·fast (hănd′făst′) *n. Archaic* A handclasp used to signify a pledge, such as a contract or marriage. [< ME *hondfast,* p. part. of *hondfesten,* to betroth < ON *handfesta,* to strike a bargain : *hönd,* hand + *festa,* to fasten.]
hand·ful (hănd′fool′) *n., pl.* **-fuls 1.** The amount that a hand can hold. **2.** A small, undefined number or quantity. **3.** *Informal* One that is difficult to control or handle.
hand glass *n.* **1.** A small magnifying glass held in the hand. **2.** A mirror with a handle.
hand·grip (hănd′grĭp′) *n.* **1.** A grip of or by the hand. **2.** Something, such as a handle, that is suited to a grip by the hand. **3.** **handgrips** Hand-to-hand combat.
hand·gun (hănd′gŭn′) *n.* A firearm used with one hand.
hand·hold (hănd′hōld′) *n.* **1.** A grip of or by the hand. **2.** Something that one can hold onto for support.
hand·hold·ing (hănd′hōl′dĭng) *n.* Strong personal support and reassurance, esp. to alleviate tension and anxiety.
hand·i·cap (hăn′dē-kăp′) *n.* **1.** *Sports & Games* **a.** A race or contest in which contestants are given advantages or compensations to equalize the chances of winning. **b.** Such an advantage or penalty. **2.** A physical or mental disability. See Syns at **disadvantage. 3.** A hindrance. ❖ *tr.v.* **-capped, -cap·ping, -caps 1.** *Sports & Games* To assign handicaps or a handicap to (a contestant). **2.** To cause to be at a disadvantage; impede. [< obsolete *hand in cap,* a game in which forfeits were held in a cap.]
hand·i·capped (hăn′dē-kăpt′) *adj.* Physically or mentally disabled: *a pool equipped for handicapped swimmers.* ❖ *n.* (used with *a pl. verb*) People with a physical or mental disability considered as a group.

USAGE NOTE Although *handicapped* is widely used in both law and everyday speech to refer to people having physical or mental disabilities, those described by the word tend to prefer the expressions *disabled* or *people with disabilities.* The term *handicapped* may imply an inequality in functioning, while *disability* implies functioning equally but in different ways. The word *handicapped,* therefore, is best reserved to describe a disabled person who is unable to function owing to some property of the environment. Thus people with a physical disability requiring a wheelchair may or may not be *handicapped,* depending on whether wheelchair ramps are made available to them.

hand organ

hand·i·cap·per (hăn′dē-kăp′ər) *n. Sports & Games* **1.** One who assigns handicaps. **2.** One who predicts the winners in a horse-race, esp. one who publishes such predictions as a guide.
hand·i·craft (hăn′dē-krăft′) also **hand·craft** (hănd′krăft′) *n.* **1.** Skill and facility with the hands. **2.** A craft or occupation requiring skilled use of the hands. **3.** Work produced by skilled hands. [ME *handecraft* < OE *handcræft* : *hand,* hand + *cræft,* craft.]
Han·dies Peak (hăn′dēz) A mountain, 4,284.6 m (14,048 ft), in the San Juan Mts. of SW CO.
hand·i·ly (hăn′dĭ-lē, -dl-ē) *adv.* **1.** In an easy manner. **2.** In a convenient manner.
hand·i·work (hăn′dē-wûrk′) *n.* **1.** Work performed by hand. **2.** The product of a person's efforts and actions. [ME *handiwerk*

< OE *handgeweorc* : *hand,* hand + *geweorc,* work (*ge-,* collective pref.; see **kom** in App. + *weorc,* work; see WORK).]
hand·ker·chief (hăng′kər-chĭf, -chēf′) *n., pl.* **-chiefs** also **-chieves** (-chĭvz, -chēvz′) **1.** A small square of cloth used esp. for wiping the nose or mouth. **2.** A large piece of cloth worn as a decorative article; a scarf.
han·dle (hăn′dl) *v.* **-dled, -dling, -dles** —*tr.* **1.** To touch, lift, or hold with the hands. **2.** To operate with the hands; manipulate. **3.** To deal with or have responsibility for; conduct. See Syns at **treat. 4.** To cope with or dispose of. **5a.** To direct, execute, or dispose of. **b.** To manage, administer to, or represent. **6.** To deal or trade in the purchase or sale of. —*intr.* To act or function in a given way while in operation. ❖ *n.* **1.** A part that is designed to be held or operated with the hand. **2.** An opportunity or a means for achieving a purpose. **3.** Understanding or control: *has a handle on the situation.* **4.** *Slang* A person's name. **5.** *Games* The total amount of money bet on an event or over a set period of time. [ME *handelen* < OE *handlian.*]
han·dle·bar (hăn′dl-bär′) *n.* A cylindrical, straight or curved steering bar, as on a bicycle. Often used in the plural.
handlebar mustache *n.* A long curved mustache resembling the curved ends of a handlebar.
han·dler (hănd′lər) *n.* **1.** One that handles or directs something or someone: *the mayor's campaign handlers; handlers of food in a restaurant.* **2a.** One who trains or exhibits an animal, such as a dog. **b.** One who acts as the trainer or second of a boxer.
han·dling (hănd′lĭng) *n.* **1.** A touching, feeling, or manipulating with the hands. **2.** The process of packing and distributing merchandise. **3.** The way in which something is handled or taken care of: *a situation requiring delicate handling.*
hand·made (hănd′mād′) *adj.* Made or prepared by hand rather than by machine.
hand·maid (hănd′mād′) also **hand·maid·en** (-mād′n) *n.* **1.** A woman attendant or servant. **2.** often **handmaiden** Something that accompanies or is attendant on another.
hand-me-down (hănd′mē-doun′) *adj.* **1.** Handed down to one person after use by another. **2.** Of inferior quality; shabby. ❖ *n.* Something passed on from one person to another.
hand·off (hănd′ôf′, -ŏf′) *n.* **1.** *Football* The act or an instance of handing the ball to a teammate during a play. **2.** *Sports* The act or an instance of handing a baton to a teammate in a relay race.
hand organ *n. Music* A barrel organ operated by turning a crank by hand.
hand·out (hănd′out′) *n.* **1.** Food, clothing, or money given to the needy. **2.** A folder or leaflet circulated free of charge. **3.** A sheet or sheets of paper containing topical information for distribution, as at a lecture or meeting. **4.** A prepared news or publicity release.
hand·pick (hănd′pĭk′) *tr.v.* **-picked, -pick·ing, -picks 1.** To gather or pick by hand. **2.** To select personally. —**hand′picked′** *adj.*
hand press *n.* A printing press operated by hand.
hand·print (hănd′prĭnt′) *n.* An outline or indentation left by a hand.
hand puppet *n.* A puppet operated by hand.
hand·rail (hănd′rāl′) *n.* A narrow railing to be grasped with the hand for support.
hand·saw (hănd′sô′) *n.* A small saw operated by one hand.
hand's-breadth or **hand's breadth** (hăndz′brĕdth′) *n.* Variant of **handbreadth.**
hand·sel (hănd′səl) also **han·sel** (hăn′-) *Chiefly British n.* **1.** A gift to express good wishes at the beginning of a new year or enterprise. **2.** The first money or barter taken in, as by a new business, esp. when considered good luck. **3a.** A first payment. **b.** A specimen or foretaste of what is to come. ❖ *tr.v.* **-seled, -sel·ing, -sels** or **-selled, -sel·ling, -sels 1.** To give a handsel to. **2.** To launch with a ceremonial gesture or gift. **3.** To do or use the first time. [ME *hanselle* < OE *handselen,* a handing over (*hand,* hand + *selen,* gift) and < ON *handsal,* legal transfer (*hand* + *sal,* a giving).]
hand·set (hănd′sĕt′) *n.* The part of a telephone containing the receiver and transmitter and often a dial or push buttons.
hand·shake (hănd′shāk′) *n.* **1.** The grasping of hands by two people, as in greeting or leave-taking. **2.** *Computer Science* An exchange of signals to ensure synchronization between two devices when communications begin.
hands-off (hăndz′ôf′, -ŏf′) *adj.* Marked by nonintervention.
hand·some (hăn′səm) *adj.* **-som·er, -som·est 1.** Pleasing and dignified in form or appearance. **2.** Generous or copious: *a handsome reward.* See Syns at **liberal. 3.** Marked by or requiring skill or dexterity. **4.** Appropriate or fitting. **5.** Large: *a handsome price.* [ME *handsom,* handy : *hand,* hand (< OE) + *-som,* n. suff.; see –SOME¹.] —**hand′some·ly** *adv.* —**hand′some·ness** *n.*
hands-on (hăndz′ŏn′, -ôn′) *adj.* Involving active participation; applied, as opposed to theoretical.
hand·spike (hănd′spīk′) *n.* A bar used as a lever. [Alteration of Du. *handspaak* : *hand,* hand (< MDu. *hant*) + *spaak,* spoke (< MDu. *spāke,* stick).]
hand·spring (hănd′sprĭng′) *n.* A gymnastic feat in which the body is flipped forward or backward from an upright position, landing first on the hands and then on the feet.]

hand·stand (hănd′stănd′) *n.* The act of balancing on the hands with one's feet in the air.

hand-to-hand (hănd′tə-hănd′) *adj.* Being at close quarters: *hand-to-hand combat.* —**hand to hand** *adv.*

hand-to-mouth (hănd′tə-mouth′) *adj.* Having or providing only the bare essentials: *a hand-to-mouth existence.* —**hand to mouth** *adv.*

hand truck *n.* A two-wheeled cart for moving heavy objects by hand, consisting of a vertical framework with handles at the top and a metal blade at the bottom.

hand·work (hănd′wûrk′) *n.* Work done by hand rather than by machine.

hand·wo·ven (hănd′wō′vən) *adj.* **1.** Woven on a hand-operated loom. **2.** Woven by hand: *handwoven baskets.*

hand·write (hănd′rīt′) *tr.v.* **-wrote** (-rōt′), **-writ·ten** (-rĭt′n), **-writ·ing,** **-writes** To write by hand. [Back-formation < *handwritten,* written by hand.]

hand·writ·ing (hănd′rī′tĭng) *n.* **1.** Writing done with the hand. **2.** The writing characteristic of a particular person.

hand·y (hăn′dē) *adj.* **-i·er, -i·est 1.** Skillful in using one's hands; manually adroit. See Syns at **dexterous. 2.** Readily accessible. **3.** Useful; convenient. **4.** Easy to use or handle: *a handy book.* —**hand′i·ness** *n.*

Handy, W(illiam) C(hristopher) 1873–1958. Amer. composer whose works include "The Memphis Blues" (1911).

hand·y·man also **handy man** (hăn′dē-măn′) *n.* A man who does odd jobs or various small tasks.

hang (hăng) *v.* **hung** (hŭng), **hang·ing, hangs** —*tr.* **1.** To fasten from above with no support from below; suspend. **2.** To suspend or fasten so as to allow free movement at or about the point of suspension: *hang a door.* **3.** *past tense and past participle* **hanged** (hăngd) **a.** To execute by suspending by the neck. **b.** Used to express exasperation or disgust: *Hang it all!* **4.** To fix or attach at an appropriate angle: *hang a scythe to its handle.* **5.** To alter the hem of (a garment) so as to fall evenly at a specified height. **6.** To furnish, decorate, or appoint by suspending objects around or about. **7.** To hold or incline downward; let droop. **8a.** To attach to a wall: *hang wallpaper.* **b.** To display by attaching to a wall or other structure. **9.** *Informal* To give (a nickname or label) to someone. **10.** To deadlock (a jury) by failing to render a unanimous verdict. **11.** *Baseball* To throw (a pitch) in such a manner as to fail to break. **12.** *Computer Science* To cause (a computer system) to halt so that input devices do not function. —*intr.* **1.** To be attached from above with no support from below. **2.** To die as a result of hanging. **3.** To remain suspended or poised over a place or an object; hover. **4.** To attach oneself as a dependent or an impediment; cling. **5.** To incline downward; droop. **6.** To depend. **7.** To pay strict attention. **8.** To remain unresolved or uncertain. **9.** To fit the body in loose lines. **10.** To be on display, as in a gallery. **11.** *Baseball* To fail to break or move in the intended way, as a curve ball. **12.** To be imminent; loom. **13.** To be or become burdensome. **14.** *Computer Science* To be halted, as a computer system, so that input devices do not function. **15a.** To spend one's free time in a certain place. Often used with *around* or *out.* **b.** To pass time idly; loiter. Often used with *around* or *out.* **c.** To keep company; see socially. Often used with *around* or *out.* ❖ *n.* **1.** The way in which something hangs. **2.** A downward inclination or slope. **3.** Particular meaning or significance. **4.** *Informal* The proper method for doing or using something: *got the hang of it.* **5.** A suspension of motion; a slackening. —*phrasal verbs:* **hang back** To be averse; hold back. **hang in** *Informal* To persevere. **hang off** To hold back; be averse. **hang on 1.** To cling tightly to something. **2.** To continue persistently; persevere. **3.** To keep a telephone connection open. **4.** To wait for a short period of time. **hang together 1.** To stand united; stick together. **2.** To make sense as a unity; cohere. **hang up 1.** To suspend on a hook or hanger. **2a.** To replace (a telephone receiver) on its base or cradle. **b.** To end a telephone conversation. **3a.** To delay or impede; hinder. **b.** To become halted or snagged. **c.** *Informal* To have or cause to have emotional difficulties or inhibitions. —*idioms:* **hang a left** *Informal* To make a left turn, as in an automobile. **hang a right** *Informal* To make a right turn, as in an automobile. **hang fire 1.** To delay. **2.** To be slow in firing, as a gun. **hang in there** *Informal* To persevere despite difficulties; persist. **hang it up** *Informal* To give up; quit. **hang loose** *Slang* To stay calm or relaxed. **hang on to** To hold firmly; keep fast. **hang tough** *Informal* To remain firmly resolved. [ME *hongen* < OE *hangian,* to be suspended, and < *hōn,* to hang.]

USAGE NOTE *Hanged,* as a past tense and a past participle of *hang,* is used in the sense of "to put to death by hanging." A majority of the Usage Panel objects to *hung* used in this sense. In all other senses of the word, *hung* is the preferred form as past tense and past participle.

han·gar (hăng′ər, hăng′gər) *n.* A shelter esp. for housing or repairing aircraft. [Fr. < OFr. *hangard,* of Gmc. orig. See **tkei-** in App.]

Hang·chow or **Hang·chou** (hăng′chou′, häng′jō′) See **Hangzhou.**

hang·dog (hăng′dôg′, -dŏg′) *adj.* **1.** Shamefaced or guilty. **2.** Downcast; intimidated. ❖ *n.* A sneaky or despicable person.

hang·er (hăng′ər) *n.* **1.** One who hangs something. **2.** A contrivance on which something hangs or by which something is hung, as: **a.** A device around which a garment is draped for hanging from a hook or rod. **b.** A loop or strap by which something is hung. **3.** A bracket on the spring shackle of a motor vehicle, designed to hold it to the chassis. **4.** A decorative strip of cloth hung on a garment or wall. **5.** A short sword that may be hung from a belt.

hang·er-on (hăng′ər-ŏn′, -ôn′) *n., pl.* **hang·ers-on** (hăng′ərz-) A sycophant; a parasite.

hang-glide (hăng′glīd′) *intr.v.* **-glid·ed, -glid·ing, -glides** To fly by means of a hang glider.

hang glider *n.* **1.** A kitelike device from which a harnessed rider hangs while gliding from a height. **2.** Its rider.

hang·ing (hăng′ĭng) *n.* **1.** Execution on a gallows. **2.** Something, such as a tapestry, that is hung. **3.** A descending slope or an inclination. ❖ *adj.* **1.** Situated on a sharp declivity. **2.** Projecting downward; overhanging. **3.** Suited for holding something that hangs. **4a.** Deserving death by hanging. **b.** Disposed to inflict severe sentences.

hanging indention *n.* Indention of every line in a paragraph except the first.

hanging valley *n.* A tributary valley that joins a main valley where the latter has been deepened, usu. by glacial erosion, resulting in a steep drop between the two valley floors.

hanging wall *n. Geology* **1.** The mass of rock overlying a mineral deposit in a mine. **2.** The overlying block of a fault having an inclined fault plane.

hang·man (hăng′mən) *n.* A man employed to execute condemned prisoners by hanging.

hang·nail (hăng′nāl′) *n.* A small piece of dead skin at the side or the base of a fingernail that is partly detached from the rest of the skin. [Alteration of AGNAIL.]

hang·out (hăng′out′) *n. Slang* A frequently visited place.

hang·o·ver (hăng′ō′vər) *n.* **1.** Unpleasant physical effects following the heavy use of alcohol. **2.** A letdown, as after a period of excitement. **3.** A vestige; a holdover.

hang·tag (hăng′tăg′) *n.* A tag attached to a piece of merchandise giving information about its composition, care, and use.

Han·gul (häng′gool) *n.* The alphabetic system of writing used in Korea, invented in the 15th century. [Korean *Hangŭl,* great writing : *han,* great + *kŭl,* writing.]

hang-up (hăng′ŭp′) *n. Informal* **1.** A psychological or emotional difficulty or inhibition. **2.** An obstacle to smooth progress or development.

Hang·zhou (häng′jō′) also **Hang·chow** or **Hang·chou** (häng′chou′, häng′jō′) A city of E China at the head of **Hangzhou Bay,** an inlet of the East China Sea; founded 606 and the cap. of Zhejiang province. Pop. 1,250,000.

hank (hăngk) *n.* **1.** A coil or loop. **2.** *Nautical* A ring or clip by which a jib or staysail is attached to its stay. **3.** A looped bundle, as of yarn. [ME < ON *hǫnk.*]

han·ker (hăng′kər) *intr.v.* **-kered, -ker·ing, -kers** To have a strong, often restless desire. [Perh. < Du. dialectal *hankeren.*] —**han′ker·er** *n.*

han·kie also **han·ky** (hăng′kē) *n., pl.* **-kies** *Informal* A handkerchief.

han·ky-pan·ky (hăng′kē-păng′kē) *n. Slang* **1.** Devious or mischievous activity. **2.** Illicit sexual activity. [Alteration of *hokey-pokey,* alteration of HOCUS-POCUS.]

Han·na (hăn′ə), **Marcus Alonzo ("Mark")** 1837–1904. Amer. financier and politician who managed the 1896 and 1900 presidential campaigns of William McKinley.

Han·ni·bal¹ (hăn′ə-bəl) 247–183? B.C. Carthaginian general who crossed the Alps in 218 with c. 35,000 men and routed Roman armies at Lake Trasimeno (217) and Cannae (216).

Han·ni·bal² (hăn′ə-bəl) A city of NE MO on the Mississippi R. NW of St. Louis; boyhood home of Mark Twain. Pop. 17,757.

Ha·noi (hă-noi′, hə-) The cap. of Vietnam, in the N part on the Red R.; cap. of French Indochina (after 1887) and of North Vietnam (1954–75). Pop. 1,089,760.

Han·o·ver¹ (hăn′ō′vər) British ruling family (1714–1901).

Han·o·ver² or **Han·no·ver** (hăn′ō′vər, hä-nō′-) **1.** A former kingdom and province of NW Germany; an electorate of the Holy Roman Empire from 1692 to 1805. **2.** A city of NW Germany SE of Bremen; chartered 1241. Pop. 514,010.

Han·o·ve·ri·an (hăn′ō-vîr′ē-ən) *adj.* **1.** Of, relating to, or characteristic of the royal family of Hanover. **2.** Of, belonging to, or characteristic of the kingdom or province of Hanover.

Han River (hän) A river, c. 1,126 km (700 mi), of E-central China flowing to the Chang Jiang (Yangtze River).

Han·sard (hăn′sərd) *n.* The official report of the proceedings and debates of a legislature in the Commonwealth of Nations, esp. of the British or Canadian parliament. [After Luke *Hansard* (1752–1828), British printer.]

Hans·ber·ry (hănz′bĕr-ē), **Lorraine** 1930–65. Amer. playwright known esp. for *A Raisin in the Sun* (1959).

hanse (hăns) *n.* A medieval merchant guild or trade association. [ME < OFr. < MLGer. < OHGer. *hansa,* military troop.] —**han′se·at′ic** (hăn′sē-ăt′ĭk) *adj.*

Han·se·at·ic League (hăn′sē-ăt′ĭk) A former economic and

hang glider

Lorraine Hansberry

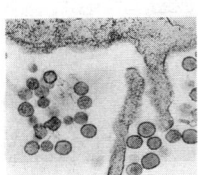

hantavirus
transmission electron
micrograph

defensive confederation of free towns in N Germany and neighboring areas; reached the height of its power in the 14th cent. and held its last official assembly in 1669.

han•sel (hăn**′**səl) *n. & v.* Variant of **handsel.**

Han•sen's disease (hăn**′**sənz) *n.* See **leprosy.** [After Gerhard Henrik Armauer *Hansen* (1841–1912), Norwegian physician.]

han•som (hăn**′**səm) *n.* A two-wheeled covered carriage with the driver's seat above and behind. [After Joseph Aloysius *Hansom* (1803–82), British architect.]

hant (hănt) *n. Chiefly Southern US* Variant of **haunt** 2.

Han•tan (hän**′**dän**′**) See **Handan.**

han•ta•vi•rus (hăn**′**tə-vī**′**rəs) *n.* Any of a group of viruses carried by rodents that cause epidemic hemorrhagic fever and severe respiratory infections in humans. [After the *Hantan* River, South Korea.]

Ha•nuk•kah or **Ha•nu•kah** also **Cha•nu•kah** (кнä**′**nə-kə, hä**′**-) *n. Judaism* An eight-day festival beginning on the 25th of Kislev, commemorating the victory in 165 B.C. of the Maccabees over Antiochus Epiphanes (c. 215–164 B.C.) and the rededication of the Temple at Jerusalem. [Heb. *hǎnukkâ,* dedication < *hānak,* to dedicate.]

hao•le (hou**′**lē, -lā) *n. Hawaii* A white person. [Hawaiian, foreign, foreigner.]

hap (hăp) *n.* **1.** Fortune; chance. **2.** A happening; an occurrence. ❖ *intr.v.* **happed, hap•ping, haps** To happen. [ME < ON *happ.*]

ha•pax le•go•me•non (hā**′**păks**′** lĭ-gŏm**′**ə-nŏn**′**) *n., pl.* **ha•pax le•go•me•na** (-nə) A word or form that occurs only once in the recorded corpus of a language. [Gk. : *hapax,* once + *legomenon,* neut. sing. passive part. of *legein,* to say.]

ha•pen•ny (hā**′**pə-nē, hāp**′**nē) *n., pl.* **-nies** *Chiefly British* A halfpenny. [Alteration of HALFPENNY.]

hap•haz•ard (hăp-hăz**′**ərd) *adj.* Dependent upon or characterized by mere chance. See Syns at **chance.** ❖ *adv.* By chance; casually. —**hap•haz′ard•ly** *adv.* —**hap•haz′ard•ness** *n.*

haph•ta•rah also **haf•ta•rah** or **haf•to•rah** (häf**′**tä-rä**′**, häf-tôr**′**ə, -tōr**′**ə) *n., pl.* **-ta•roth** or **-to•roth** or **-to•rot** or **-to•ros** (-tä-rōt**′**, -rōs**′**, -tôr**′**ōt**′**, -ōs**′**, -tōr**′**-) *Judaism* A selection from the Prophets, read in synagogue services on the Sabbath following each lesson from the Torah. [Mishnaic Heb. *haptārâ,* conclusion < *hiptîr,* to conclude, dismiss, derived stem of Heb. *pātar,* to separate, discharge.]

hap•less (hăp**′**lĭs) *adj.* Luckless; unfortunate. —**hap′less•ly** *adv.* —**hap′less•ness** *n.*

hap•lite (hăp**′**līt**′**) *n.* Variant of **aplite.**

hap•loid (hăp**′**loid**′**) *adj.* **1.** Having the same number of sets of chromosomes as a germ cell or half as many as a somatic cell. **2.** Having a single set of chromosomes. ❖ *n.* An organism having haploid cells. [< Gk. *haploos,* single; see **sem-**¹ in App. + –OID.] —**hap′loi′dy** (-loi**′**dē) *n.*

hap•lol•o•gy (hăp-lŏl**′**ə-jē) *n.* The loss of one of two identical or similar adjacent syllables in a word, as in *idolatry* from Latin *īdōlolatrīa.* [Gk. *haploos,* single, simple; see HAPLOID + –LOGY.]

hap•lont (hăp**′**lŏnt**′**) *n.* An organism with haploid somatic cells but a diploid zygote, as in many algae and fungi. [Gk. *haploos,* single, simple; see HAPLOID + –ONT.]

hap•lo•sis (hăp-lō**′**sĭs) *n.* Meiotic reduction of the diploid number of chromosomes by one half, resulting in haploidy. [Gk. *haploos,* single, simple; see HAPLOID + –OSIS.]

hap•ly (hăp**′**lē) *adv.* By chance or accident.

hap•pen (hăp**′**ən) *intr.v.* **-pened, -pen•ing, -pens** **1a.** To come to pass. **b.** To come into being. **2.** To take place or occur by chance. **3.** To come upon something by chance. **4.** To come or go casually; make an appearance: *He happened by.* [ME *happenen* < *hap,* chance. See HAP.]

hap•pen•chance (hăp**′**ən-chăns**′**) *n.* A happenstance.

hap•pen•ing (hăp**′**ə-nĭng) *n.* **1.** Something that takes place. See Syns at **occurrence.** **2.** An improvised spectacle or performance, esp. one involving the audience.

hap•pen•stance (hăp**′**ən-stăns**′**) *n.* A chance circumstance. [HAPPEN + (CIRCUM)STANCE.]

hap•pi coat (hăp**′**ē) *n.* A Japanese jacket made of cotton or similar material and having an open front, often fastened with ties. [J. *happi* : *han,* half (< M Chin. *panh*) + *pi,* to wear (< M Chin. *bi?, phi*).]

hap•py (hăp**′**ē) *adj.* **-pi•er, -pi•est** **1.** Characterized by good luck; fortunate. **2.** Enjoying, showing, or marked by pleasure, satisfaction, or joy. See Syns at **glad**¹. **3.** Well-adapted; felicitous. **4.** Cheerful; willing. **5a.** Characterized by a spontaneous or obsessive inclination to use something. Often used in combination: *trigger-happy.* **b.** Inordinately enthusiastic about or involved with. Often used in combination: *clothes-happy.* [ME < *hap,* luck. See HAP.] —**hap′pi•ly** *adv.* —**hap′pi•ness** *n.*

hap•py-go-luck•y (hăp**′**ē-gō-lŭk**′**ē) *adj.* Taking things easily; carefree.

happy hour *n.* A period during which a bar or lounge serves drinks at reduced prices or free hors d'oeuvres.

happy hunting ground *n.* **1.** An afterlife conceived as a paradise in which hunting is plentiful and game unlimited. **2.** A place or situation of abundant opportunity.

Haps•burg also **Habs•burg** (hăps**′**bûrg**′**, häps**′**boŏork**′**) A royal German family that supplied rulers to various European states from the late Middle Ages to the early 20th cent.

hap•ten (hăp**′**tĕn**′**) also **hap•tene** (-tēn**′**) *n.* An antibody-specific substance that cannot induce antibody formation unless bound to a carrier protein or other molecule. [Ger. : Gk. *haptein,* to fasten + Ger. -*en,* n. suff. (< Gk. -*ēnē,* -ene).] —**hap•ten′ic** *adj.*

hap•tic (hăp**′**tĭk) *adj.* Of or relating to the sense of touch; tactile. [Gk. *haptikos* < *haptesthai,* to grasp, touch.]

hap•to•glo•bin (hăp**′**tə-glō**′**bĭn) *n.* A plasma protein that binds free hemoglobin in the bloodstream. [Gk. *haptein,* to bind, fasten + (HEMO)GLOBIN.]

ha•ra-ki•ri (här**′**ĭ-kîr**′**ē, hä**′**rē-) also **ha•ri-ka•ri** (här**′**ē-kär**′**ē, hä**′**rē-kär**′**ē) *n., pl.* **-ris** See **seppuku.** [J. *harakiri : hara,* abdomen, bowels + *kiri,* to cut.]

ha•rangue (hə-răng**′**) *n.* **1.** A long pompous speech, esp. one delivered before a gathering. **2.** A speech or piece of writing characterized by strong feeling or expression; a tirade. ❖ *v.* **-rangued, -rangu•ing, -rangues** —*tr.* To deliver a harangue to. —*intr.* To deliver a harangue. [ME *arang,* a speech to an assembly < OFr. *harangue* < OItal. *aringa* < *aringare,* to speak in public, prob. < *aringo, arringa,* public square, meeting place, of Gmc. orig. See **koro-** in App.] —**ha•rangu′er** *n.*

Ha•rap•pa (hə-răp**′**ə) A locality in the Indus R. valley of the Punjab in Pakistan; site of archaeological finds dating to the 3rd millennium B.C.

Ha•ra•re (hə-rär**′**ā) The cap. of Zimbabwe, in the NE part; founded by the British in 1890. Its name was changed from Salisbury in 1982. Pop. 1,189,103.

ha•rass (hə-răs**′**, hăr**′**əs) *tr.v.* **-rassed, -rass•ing, -rass•es** **1.** To irritate or torment persistently. **2.** To wear out; exhaust. **3.** To impede and exhaust (an enemy) by repeated attacks or raids. [Fr. *harasser,* poss. < OFr. *harer,* to set a dog on < *hare,* interj. used to set a dog on, of Gmc. orig.] —**ha•rass′er** *n.* —**ha•rass′ment** *n.*

SYNONYMS *harass, harry, hound, badger, pester, plague* These verbs mean to trouble persistently or incessantly. *Harass* and *harry* imply systematic persecution by besieging with repeated annoyances, threats, or demands: *The landlord harassed tenants who were behind in their rent. A rude customer harried the clerk. Hound* suggests unrelenting pursuit to gain a desired end: *Reporters hounded the celebrity.* To *badger* is to nag or tease persistently: *The child badgered his parents for toys.* To *pester* is to inflict a succession of petty annoyances: "*How she would have pursued and pestered me with questions*" (Charlotte Brontë). *Plague* refers to an affliction likened to an epidemic disease: "*As I have no estate, I am plagued with no tenants or stewards*" (Henry Fielding).

USAGE NOTE In a recent survey 50 percent of the Usage Panel preferred a pronunciation of *harass* with stress on the first syllable, while 50 percent preferred stress on the second syllable. Educated speakers are therefore evenly divided on the pronunciation of this word.

Har•bin (här**′**bĭn**′**) A city of NE China N of Jilin; cap. of Heilongjiang province. Pop. 3,597,404.

har•bin•ger (här**′**bĭn-jər) *n.* One that indicates or foreshadows what is to come. ❖ *tr.v.* **-gered, -ger•ing, -gers** To signal the approach of; presage. [ME *herbengar,* one sent to arrange lodgings < OFr. *herbergeor* < *herberger,* to lodge < *herberge,* lodging, of Gmc. orig. See **koro-** in App.]

har•bor (här**′**bər) *n.* **1.** A sheltered part of a body of water deep enough to provide anchorage for ships. **2.** A place of shelter; a refuge. ❖ *tr.v.* **-bored, -bor•ing, -bors** **1.** To give shelter to: *harbor refugees.* **2.** To provide a place, home, or habitat for. **3.** To entertain or nourish (a thought or feeling): *harbor a grudge.* [ME *herberwe,* prob. < OE *hereboerg,* lodging. See **koro-** in App.] —**har′bor•er** *n.*

har•bor•age (här**′**bər-ĭj) *n.* **1.** Shelter and anchorage for ships. **2.** Shelter; refuge.

har•bor•mas•ter (här**′**bər-măs**′**tər) *n.* An officer who oversees and enforces the regulations of a harbor.

harbor seal *n.* A hair seal (*Phoca vitulina*) of coastal waters of the Northern Hemisphere having a spotted coat.

har•bour (här**′**bər) *n. & v. Chiefly British* Variant of **harbor.**

hard (härd) *adj.* **hard•er, hard•est** **1.** Resistant to pressure; not readily penetrated. **2a.** Physically toughened; rugged. **b.** Mentally toughened; strong-minded. **3a.** Requiring great effort or endurance. **b.** Performed with or marked by great diligence or energy. **c.** Difficult to resolve, accomplish, or finish. **d.** Difficult to understand or impart. **4a.** Intense in force or degree. **b.** Inclement: *a hard winter.* **5a.** Stern or strict in nature or comportment. **b.** Resistant to persuasion or appeal; obdurate. **c.** Making few concessions. **6a.** Difficult to endure. **b.** Oppressive or unjust in nature or effect. **c.** Lacking compassion or sympathy; callous. **7a.** Harsh or severe in effect or intention: *said some hard things.* **b.** Bitter; resentful. **8a.** Causing damage or premature wear. **b.** Bad; adverse: *hard luck.* **9.** Proceeding or performing with force, vigor, or persistence; assiduous. **10a.** Real and unassailable: *hard evidence.* **b.** Definite; firm. **c.** Close; penetrating: *a hard look at the situation.* **d.** Free from illusion or bias; practical. **e.** Using or based on data that are readily quantified or verified. **11a.** Marked by sharp outline or definition; stark. **b.** Lacking in delicacy, shading, or nuance. **12.** Hardcore. **13.** Being a turn in a specific direction at an angle more than about three other possible routes. **14a.** Metallic, as opposed to paper. Used of currency. **b.** Backed by bullion rather than by credit. Used of currency. **c.** High and stable. Used of prices. **15.** Erect; tumid. Used of a penis. **16a.** Having high alcoholic content; intoxicating. **b.** Rendered alcoholic by fermentation; fermented. **17.** Containing dissolved salts. Used of water. **18.** *Linguistics* Velar, as *c* in *cake* or *g* in *log*, as opposed to palatal or soft. **19.** *Physics* Of relatively high energy; penetrating: *hard x-rays.* **20.** High in gluten content. **21.** *Chemistry* Resistant to biodegradation. **22.** Physically addictive. Used of certain illegal drugs, such as heroin. **23.** Resistant to blast, heat, or radiation. Used esp. of nuclear weapons. ❖ *adv.* **1.** With strenuous effort; intently. **2.** With great force, vigor, or energy. **3.** In such a way as to cause great damage or hardship. **4.** With great distress, grief, or bitterness. **5.** Firmly; securely. **6.** Toward or into a solid condition: *concrete that sets hard within a day.* **7.** Near in space or time; close. **8.** *Nautical* Completely; fully: *hard alee.* —*idioms:* **hard and fast** Defined, fixed, and invariable. **hard of hearing** Having a partial loss of hearing. **hard put** Undergoing great difficulty. **hard up** *Informal* In need; poor. [ME < OE *heard.*]

hard-ass (härd′ăs′) *n. Vulgar Slang* One who inflexibly follows or enforces rules. —**hard′-assed′** (-ăst′) *adj.*

hard·back (härd′băk′) *adj. & n.* Hardcover.

hard·ball (härd′bôl′) *n.* **1.** Baseball. **2.** *Informal* The use of any means, however ruthless, to attain an objective.

hard-bit·ten (härd′bĭt′n) *adj.* Toughened by experience.

hard·board (härd′bôrd′, -bōrd′) *n.* A construction board made by compressing fibers of wood chips usu. with a binder.

hard-boiled (härd′boild′) *adj.* **1.** Cooked by boiling in the shell to a solid consistency. Used of eggs. **2.** Callous; unfeeling. **3.** Unsentimental and practical; tough.

hard·bound (härd′bound′) *adj. & n.* Hardcover.

hard coal *n.* See **anthracite.**

hard core *n.* **1.** The most dedicated, loyal faction of a group or organization. **2.** An intractable core or nucleus of a society, esp. one resistant to improvement or change. **3.** often **hard·core** (härd′kôr′, -kōr′) A form of exceptionally harsh punk rock.

hard·core also **hard-core** (härd′kôr′, -kōr′) *adj.* **1.** Intensely loyal; die-hard: *a hardcore golfer.* **2.** Stubbornly resistant to improvement or change. **3.** Extremely graphic or explicit.

hard court *n.* A tennis court with a hard surface, such as asphalt or sometimes clay, rather than grass. —**hard′court′** (härd′kôrt′, -kōrt′) *adj.*

hard·cov·er (härd′kŭv′ər) *adj.* Bound in cloth, cardboard, or leather rather than paper. Used of books. ❖ *n.* A hardcover book.

hard disk *n.* A rigid magnetic disk fixed within a drive unit and used for storing computer data.

hard drive or **hard disk drive** *n.* A disk drive that reads data stored on hard disks.

Har·de·ca·nute or **Har·di·ca·nute** (här′dĭ-kə-nōōt′, -nyōōt′) 1019?-42. King of England (1040-42) and of Denmark (1035-42) who claimed the English throne after the death of Harold I.

hard·edge (härd′ĕj′) *n.* A form of abstract painting characterized by clearly defined geometric shapes.

hard-edged (härd′ĕjd′) *adj.* Inclined to hold a position; severe.

hard·en (härd′n) *v.* **-ened, -en·ing, -ens** —*tr.* **1.** To make hard or harder. **2.** To enable to withstand physical or mental hardship. **3.** To make unfeeling, unsympathetic, or callous. **4.** To make sharp, as in outline. —*intr.* **1.** To become hard or harder. **2.** To rise and become stable. Used of prices. **3.** To become inured.

hard·en·er (härd′n-ər) *n.* One that hardens, esp. a substance added to varnish or paint to give it a harder finish.

hard·en·ing (härd′n-ĭng) *n.* **1.** The act or process of becoming hard or harder. **2.** Something that hardens, as a substance added to iron to yield steel. **3.** Gradual exposure of plants to cold weather.

hardening of the arteries *n.* Arteriosclerosis.

hard-fist·ed (härd′fĭs′tĭd) *adj.* Tightfisted; stingy.

hard·hack (härd′hăk′) *n.* A downy plant (*Spiraea tomentosa*) of eastern North America having small rose-purple flowers.

hard-hand·ed (härd′hăn′dĭd) *adj.* **1.** Having hands calloused or hardened by work. **2.** Oppressive; tyrannical.

hard·hat or **hard-hat** (härd′hăt′) *n.* **1a.** A lightweight protective helmet, usu. of metal or reinforced plastic, worn by workers in industrial settings. **b.** *Informal* A construction worker. **2.** *Slang* An extremely patriotic or conservative person. —**hard′hat′** *adj.*

hard·head (härd′hĕd′) *n.* **1.** A shrewd tough person. **2.** A stubborn unmovable person. **3.** *pl.* **hardhead** or **-heads** Any of several fishes having a bony head, esp. the Atlantic croaker.

hard·head·ed (härd′hĕd′ĭd) *adj.* **1.** Stubborn; willful. **2.** Realistic; pragmatic. —**hard′head′ed·ly** *adv.* —**hard′head′ed·ness** *n.*

hard·heart·ed (härd′här′tĭd) *adj.* Lacking in feeling or compassion; pitiless and cold. —**hard′heart′ed·ly** *adv.* —**hard′heart′ed·ness** *n.*

hard-hit (härd′hĭt′) *adj.* Badly or adversely affected.

hard-hit·ting (härd′hĭt′ĭng) *adj.* Effective; forceful.

Har·di·ca·nute (här′dĭ-kə-nōōt′, -nyōōt′) See **Hardecanute.**

har·di·hood (här′dē-hŏŏd′) *n.* **1.** Boldness and daring. **2.** Impudence or insolence.

Har·ding (här′dĭng), **Florence Mabel King** 1860-1924. First Lady of the US (1921-23).

Harding, Warren Gamaliel 1865-1923. The 29th President of the US (1921-23), who made several misguided appointments that led to a corrupt administration.

hard knocks *pl.n. Informal* The practical experiences of life, including hardships and disappointments.

hard labor *n.* Compulsory physical labor coincident with a prison term imposed as punishment for a crime.

hard line *n.* A firm, uncompromising policy or position. —**hard′-line′** *adj.* —**hard′-lin′er** *n.*

hard·ly (härd′lē) *adv.* **1.** Barely; just. **2.** To almost no degree; almost not. **3.** Probably or almost surely not. **4.** With severity; harshly. **5.** With great difficulty; painfully. [ME *hardli* < OE *heardlīce,* harshly < *heard,* hard.]

hard maple *n.* See **sugar maple.**

hard·ness (härd′nĭs) *n.* **1.** The quality or condition of being hard. **2.** The relative resistance of a mineral to scratching, as measured by the Mohs scale. **3.** The relative resistance of a metal or other material to denting, scratching, or bending.

hard-nosed (härd′nōzd′) *adj.* Hardheaded.

hard-on (härd′ŏn′, -ôn′) *n. Vulgar Slang* An erection of the penis.

hard palate *n.* The bony anterior portion of the palate.

hard·pan (härd′păn′) *n.* **1.** A layer of hard subsoil or clay. **2.** Hard unbroken ground. **3.** A foundation; bedrock.

hard-pressed (härd′prĕst′) *adj.* Experiencing great difficulty or distress: *financially hard-pressed.*

hard rock *n.* A style of rock 'n' roll characterized by a harsh, amplified sound and loud, distorted electric guitars.

hard rubber *n.* Ebonite.

hard sauce *n.* A creamy sauce of butter and sugar with rum, brandy, or vanilla flavoring, served with some desserts.

hard·scrab·ble (härd′skrăb′əl) *adj.* Earning a bare subsistence; marginal. ❖ *n.* Barren or marginal farmland.

hard sell *n. Informal* **1.** Aggressive, high-pressure selling or promotion. **2.** A difficult sales prospect.

hard-set (härd′sĕt′) *adj.* Fixed; rigid.

hard-shell (härd′shĕl′) *n.* A hard-shell clam or hard-shell crab. ❖ *adj.* also **hard-shelled** (-shĕld′) **1.** Having a thick, heavy, or hardened shell. **2.** Uncompromising; confirmed.

hard-shell clam *n.* See **quahog.**

hard-shell crab *n.* A crab, esp. an edible marine crab, with a fully hardened shell.

hard·ship (härd′shĭp′) *n.* **1.** Extreme privation; suffering. **2.** A cause of privation or suffering. See Syns at **difficulty.**

hard·stand (härd′stănd′) *n.* A hard-surfaced area for parking aircraft or ground vehicles.

hard·tack (härd′tăk′) *n.* A hard biscuit or bread made with flour and water.

hard·top (härd′tŏp′) *n.* An automobile designed to look like a convertible but having a rigidly fixed hard top.

hard·ware (härd′wâr′) *n.* **1.** Metal goods and utensils such as locks, tools, and cutlery. **2a.** *Computer Science* A computer and the associated physical equipment directly involved in the performance of data-processing or communications functions. **b.** Machines and other physical equipment directly involved in performing an industrial, technological, or military function. **3.** *Informal* Weapons, esp. military weapons.

hard-wire (härd′wīr′) *tr.v.* **-wired, -wir·ing, -wires 1.** To connect (electronic components, for example) by electrical wires or cables. **2.** To implement (a capability) through logic circuitry that is permanently connected within a computer and not subject to change by programming. **3.** To determine or put into effect by physiological or neurological mechanisms; make automatic or innate.

hard·wood (härd′wŏŏd′) *n.* **1.** The wood of a dicotyledonous tree. **2.** A dicotyledonous tree.

har·dy[1] (här′dē) *adj.* **-di·er, -di·est 1.** Being in robust and sturdy good health. See Syns at **healthy. 2.** Courageous; intrepid. **3.** Brazenly daring; audacious. **4.** Capable of surviving unfavorable conditions, such as cold weather. Used esp. of cultivated plants. [ME < OFr. *hardi,* p. part. of *hardir,* make hard, em-

hardhat

Warren G. Harding

ă pat	oi boy
ā pay	ou out
âr care	ŏŏ took
ä father	ōō boot
ĕ pet	ŭ cut
ē be	ûr urge
ĭ pit	th thin
ī pie	th this
îr pier	hw which
ŏ pot	zh vision
ō toe	ə about,
ô paw	item

Stress marks:
′ (primary),
′ (secondary), as in
lexicon (lĕk′sĭ-kŏn′)

hare

harlequin bug
Murgantia histrionica

harp
top: musical instrument
bottom: for a lampshade

bolden, of Gmc. orig.] —**har′di·ly** *adv.* —**har′di·ness** *n.*

har·dy² (här′dē) *n., pl.* **-dies** A square-shanked chisel that fits into a square hole in an anvil. [Prob. < HARD.]

Hardy, Oliver 1892–1957. Amer. comedian famous for his slapstick routines with Stan Laurel.

Hardy, Thomas 1840–1928. British writer whose works include *Tess of the d'Urbervilles* (1891).

hare (hâr) *n.* Any of various mammals of the family Leporidae, esp. of the genus *Lepus,* similar to rabbits but having longer ears and legs and giving birth to active, furred young. ❖ *intr.v.* **hared, har·ing, hares** To move hurriedly, as if hunting a swift quarry. [ME < OE *hara.*]

hare and hounds *n.* A game in which one group leaves a trail of paper scraps for a pursuing group to follow.

hare·bell (hâr′bĕl′) *n.* A perennial plant (*Campanula rotundifolia*) having bell-shaped, blue or white flowers.

hare·brained (hâr′brānd′) *adj.* Foolish; flighty.

> **USAGE NOTE** The first part of the compound *harebrained* is often misspelled *hair* in the belief that the meaning of the word is "with a hair-sized brain" rather than "with no more sense than a hare."

Ha·re Krish·na (hä′rē krĭsh′nə) *n.* **1.** A chant to the Hindu god Krishna. **2.** *Informal* **a.** A member of the International Society for Krishna Consciousness, founded in the United States in 1966. **b.** The society itself. [< the chant *Hare Krishna* : Skt. *Hare,* vocative of *Hariḥ,* a name of Vishnu (< *hari-,* yellow-green, tawny yellow; see **ghel-** in App.) + Skt. *Kṛṣṇa,* vocative of *Kṛṣṇaḥ,* Krishna; see KRISHNA¹.]

hare·lip (hâr′lĭp′) *n.* A cleft lip. Not in scientific use.

har·em (hâr′əm, här′-) *n.* **1.** A house or a section of a house reserved for women members of a Muslim household. **2.** The women occupying such a place. **3.** A group of women sexual partners for one man. [Turk. < Ar. *ḥarīm,* forbidden place < *ḥarama,* to prohibit.]

Har·greaves (här′grēvz′), **James** d. 1778. British inventor of the spinning jenny (c. 1764; patented 1770).

har·i·cot (här′ĭ-kō′) *n.* The edible pod or seed of any of several beans, esp. the kidney bean. [Fr., poss. alteration of Nahuatl *ayacotli.*]

Har·i·jan (här′ĭ-jən) *n., pl.* **Harijan** or **-jans** An Untouchable. [Skt. *harijanaḥ,* person of Hari, child of God (coined as a euphemism for Untouchable by Mohandas K. Gandhi in 1931) : *Hariḥ,* Hari (Vishnu); see HARE KRISHNA + *janaḥ,* person, child; see **genə-** in App.]

ha·ri·ka·ri (här′ē-kär′ē, här′ē-kăr′ē) *n.* Variant of **hara-kiri.**

Ha·ri Rud (hä′rē rōōd′) A river, c. 1,126 km (700 mi), of NW Afghanistan, NE Iran, and S Turkmenistan.

ha·ris·sa (hä-rē′sə) *n.* A spicy North African sauce made from chili peppers, garlic, cumin, and other seasonings. [Ar. *harīsa,* dish of pounded meat and bulgur < *harasa,* to pound.]

hark (härk) *intr.v.* **harked, hark·ing, harks** To listen attentively. —*idiom:* **hark back** To return to a previous point, as in a narrative. [ME *harken, herken* < OE **heorcian.*]

har·ken (här′kən) *v.* Variant of **hearken.**

Har·lan (här′lən), **John Marshall** 1833–1911. Amer. jurist; associate justice of the US Supreme Court (1877–1911). His grandson **John Marshall Harlan** (1899–1971) also served as an associate justice of the Court (1955–71).

Har·lem (här′ləm) A section of New York City in N Manhattan bordering on the Harlem and East rivers; est. as the settlement of Nieuw Haarlem in 1658. —**Har′lem·ite** *n.*

Harlem River A channel in New York City separating the N end of Manhattan I. from the Bronx and with Spuyten Duyvil Creek connecting the Hudson and East rivers.

har·le·quin (här′lĭ-kwĭn, -kĭn) *n.* **1. Harlequin** A buffoon of the commedia dell'arte, traditionally presented in a mask and parti-colored tights. **2.** A clown; a buffoon. ❖ *adj.* Having a pattern of brightly colored diamond shapes. [Obsolete Fr. < OFr. *Herlequin, Hellequin,* a demon, perh. < ME *Herleking < OE *Herla cyning,* King Herla, a mythical figure identified with Woden.]

har·le·quin·ade (här′lĭ-kwə-nād′) *n.* **1.** A comedy or pantomime featuring Harlequin. **2.** Clowning or buffoonery. [Obsolete Fr. < *harlequin,* harlequin. See HARLEQUIN.]

harlequin bug *n.* A brightly colored stinkbug (*Murgantia histrionica*) that is destructive to some cruciferous plants.

har·lot (här′lət) *n.* A woman prostitute. [ME, vagabond, lecher, harlot < OFr. *arlot, herlot,* vagabond.] —**har′lot·ry** (-lə-trē) *n.*

Har·low (här′lō), **Jean** 1911–37. Amer. actress whose films include *Hell's Angels* (1930) and *Red Dust* (1932).

harm (härm) *n.* **1.** Physical or psychological injury or damage. **2.** Wrong; evil. ❖ *tr.v.* **harmed, harm·ing, harms** To do harm to. [ME < OE *hearm.*]

har·mat·tan (här′mə-tăn′, här-măt′n) *n.* A dry dusty wind that blows along the northwest coast of Africa. [Akan (Twi) *haramata,* poss. < Ar. *ḥarām,* evil thing < *ḥarama,* to prohibit.]

harm·ful (härm′fəl) *adj.* Causing or capable of causing harm; injurious. —**harm′ful·ly** *adv.* —**harm′ful·ness** *n.*

harm·less (härm′lĭs) *adj.* **1.** Not causing or incapable of causing harm. **2.** Not intended to harm or offend; inoffensive. **3.** Free

from loss or legal liability: *held harmless if the other parties defaulted.* —**harm′less·ly** *adv.*

har·mon·ic (här-mŏn′ĭk) *adj.* **1a.** Of or relating to harmony. **b.** Pleasing to the ear. **c.** Characterized by harmony. **2.** Of or relating to harmonics. **3.** Integrated in nature. ❖ *n.* **1a.** Any of a series of musical tones whose frequencies are integral multiples of the frequency of a fundamental tone. **b.** A tone produced on a stringed instrument by lightly touching an open or stopped vibrating string so that both segments vibrate. **2. harmonics** (*used with a sing. verb*) The theory or study of the physical properties and characteristics of musical sound. **3.** *Physics* A wave whose frequency is a whole-number multiple of that of another. [Lat. *harmonicus* < Gk. *harmonikos* < *harmoniā,* harmony. See HARMONY.] —**har·mon′i·cal·ly** *adv.*

har·mon·i·ca (här-mŏn′ĭ-kə) *n. Music* **1.** A small rectangular instrument consisting of a row of free reeds set back in air holes, played by exhaling or inhaling. **2.** A glass harmonica. **3.** An instrument consisting of tuned strips of metal or glass fixed to a frame and struck with a hammer. [Alteration of obsolete *armonica,* glass harmonica < Ital., fem. of *armonico,* harmonious < Lat. *harmonicus,* harmonic. See HARMONIC.]

harmonic analysis *n.* The study of functions given by a Fourier series or analogous representations, such as periodic functions and functions on topological groups.

harmonic mean *n.* The reciprocal of the arithmetic mean of the reciprocals of a specified set of numbers.

harmonic motion *n.* A periodic vibration, as of a violin string, in which the motions are symmetrical about a region of equilibrium.

harmonic progression *n.* A sequence of quantities whose reciprocals form an arithmetic progression.

harmonic series *n.* **1.** *Mathematics* A series whose terms are in harmonic progression, esp. the series $1 + \frac{1}{2} + \frac{1}{3} + \frac{1}{4} + \ldots$. **2.** *Music* A series of tones consisting of a fundamental tone and the consecutive harmonics produced by it.

har·mo·ni·ous (här-mō′nē-əs) *adj.* **1.** Exhibiting accord in feeling or action. **2.** Having component elements pleasingly or appropriately combined: *a harmonious blend of architectural styles.* **3.** Characterized by harmony of sound; melodious. —**har·mo′ni·ous·ly** *adv.* —**har·mo′ni·ous·ness** *n.*

har·mo·nist (här′mə-nĭst) *n.* One skilled in harmony. —**har′mo·nis′tic** *adj.* —**har′mo·nis′ti·cal·ly** *adv.*

har·mo·ni·um (här-mō′nē-əm) *n. Music* A keyboard instrument having free metal reeds actuated by a bellows. [Fr. < *harmonie,* harmony < OFr. See HARMONY.]

har·mo·nize (här′mə-nīz′) *v.* **-nized, -niz·ing, -niz·es** —*tr.* **1.** To bring into agreement or harmony. **2.** To provide harmony for (a melody). —*intr.* **1.** To be in or come into agreement; be harmonious. **2.** To sing or play in harmony. —**har′mo·ni·za′tion** (-nĭ-zā′shən) *n.* —**har′mo·niz′er** *n.*

har·mo·ny (här′mə-nē) *n., pl.* **-nies** **1.** Agreement in feeling or opinion; accord. **2.** A pleasing combination of elements in a whole. See Syns at **proportion.** **3.** *Music* **a.** The study of the structure, progression, and relation of chords. **b.** Simultaneous combination of notes in a chord. **c.** The structure of a work or passage as considered from the point of view of its chordal characteristics and relationships. **d.** A combination of sounds considered pleasing to the ear. **4.** A collation of parallel passages, esp. from the Gospels, with a commentary. [ME *armonie* < OFr. < Lat. *harmonia* < Gk. *harmoniā,* articulation, agreement, harmony < *harmos,* joint.]

Harms·worth (härmz′wûrth′), **Alfred Charles William.** Viscount Northcliffe. 1865–1922. British newspaper publisher who founded the *Daily Mail* (1896) and the *Daily Mirror* (1903).

har·ness (här′nĭs) *n.* **1.** The gear or tackle, other than a yoke, with which a draft animal pulls a vehicle or implement. **2.** Something resembling such gear or tackle, as the straps used to hold a parachute to the body. **3.** A device that raises and lowers the warp threads on a loom. **4.** *Archaic* Armor for a man or horse. ❖ *tr.v.* **-nessed, -ness·ing, -ness·es** **1a.** To put a harness on (a draft animal). **b.** To fasten by the use of a harness. **2.** To bring under control and direct the force of. —*idiom:* **in harness** On duty or at work. [ME *harnes* < OFr. *harneis,* of Gmc. orig. See **nes-¹** in App.]

harness race *n.* A horserace between pacers or trotters harnessed to sulkies. —**harness racing** *n.*

Har·old I (här′əld) Known as "Harold Harefoot." d. 1040. King of England (1035–40) who was the illegitimate son of Canute and claimed the English throne after his father's death.

Harold II 1022?–66. King of England (1066) who was killed fighting the invasion of William the Conqueror.

Ha·roun al-Ra·schid (hä-rōōn′ äl-rä-shēd′) See **Harun al-Rashid.**

harp (härp) *n.* **1.** *Music* **a.** Any of various instruments having a usu. triangular frame with strings of graded lengths that are played by plucking with the fingers. **b.** *Informal* A harmonica. **2.** Something, such as a pair of vertical supports for a lampshade, that resembles a harp. ❖ *intr.v.* **harped, harp·ing, harps** To play a harp. —*phrasal verb:* **harp on** To talk or write about to an excessive, tedious degree. [ME < OE *hearpe* and < OFr. *harpe,* of Gmc. orig.] —**harp′er** *n.* —**harp′ist** *n.*

Har·pers Ferry (här′pərz) A locality of extreme NE WV; scene of John Brown's rebellion (1859), in which he briefly seized the US arsenal.

har·poon (här-pōōn′) n. A spearlike weapon with a barbed head used in hunting whales and large fish. ❖ tr.v. **-pooned, -poon·ing, -poons** To strike, kill, or capture with or as if with a harpoon. [Prob. < Du. harpoen < MDu. < OFr. harpon, poss. < harpe, clamp, claw < Lat. harpa, sickle < Gk. harpē.] —**har·poon′er** n.

harp seal n. An earless seal (Pagophilus groenlandicus) of the North Atlantic and Arctic oceans. [< the shape of the markings on its shoulders and sides.]

harp·si·chord (härp′sĭ-kôrd′, -kôrd′) n. A keyboard instrument whose strings are plucked with quills or plectrums. [Alteration of obsolete Fr. harpechorde < Ital. arpicordo : arpa, harp (< Lat. harpa, of Gmc. orig.) + corda, string (< Lat. chorda < Gk. khordē).] —**harp′si·chord′ist** n.

Har·py (här′pē) n., pl. **-pies 1.** Greek Mythology One of several monsters with the head and trunk of a woman and the tail, wings, and talons of a bird. **2. harpy** A predatory person. **3. harpy** A woman held to be shrewish.

har·que·bus (här′kə-bəs, -kwə-) also **ar·que·bus** (är′-) n. A heavy portable matchlock gun invented during the 15th century. [Obsolete Fr. harquebuse < OFr., alteration of MDu. hakebus : hake, hook + busse, gun (< Lat. buxis, box; see BOX¹).]

har·ri·dan (hăr′ĭ-dn) n. A woman regarded as scolding and vicious. [Poss. < Fr. haridelle, gaunt woman, old horse, nag.]

har·ri·er¹ (hăr′ē-ər) n. **1.** One that harries. **2.** Any of various slender narrow-winged hawks of the genus Circus that prey on small animals. [Sense 2, alteration (influenced by HARRY) of obsolete harrower < HARROW².]

har·ri·er² (hăr′ē-ər) n. **1.** Any of a breed of small hound used to hunt hares and rabbits. **2.** A cross-country runner. [ME hairer, eirer, poss. alteration of OFr. errier, wanderer < errer, to wander. See ERR.]

Har·ri·man (hăr′ə-mən), **Edward Henry** 1848–1909. Amer. railway magnate who joined J.P. Morgan and James J. Hill to form the Northern Securities Company.

Harriman, (William) Averell 1891–1986. Amer. financier who served as ambassador to the USSR (1943–46).

Har·ris (hăr′ĭs), **Benjamin** fl. 1673–1713. English publisher and journalist in Massachusetts whose Publick Occurrences was the first newspaper printed in America (1690).

Harris, Joel Chandler 1848–1908. Amer. writer and journalist who wrote Uncle Remus: His Songs and His Sayings (1880).

Harris, Zellig Sabbatai 1909–92. Ukrainian-born Amer. linguist who developed mathematical linguistics and pioneered an effort to understand speech and writing in social context.

Har·ris·burg (hăr′ĭs-bûrg′) The cap. of PA, in the SE-central part WNW of Philadelphia. Pop. 48,950.

Har·ri·son¹ (hăr′ĭ-sən), **Benjamin** 1726–91. Amer. Revolutionary leader who served in the Continental Congress (1774–78).

Har·ri·son² (hăr′ĭ-sən), **Benjamin** 1833–1901. The 23rd President of the US (1889–93); the first Pan-American conference took place (1889) during his administration.

Harrison, George 1943–2001. British singer and songwriter whose best-known compositions include "My Sweet Lord."

Harrison, William Henry 1773–1841. The 9th President of the US (1841); died of pneumonia after one month in office.

har·row¹ (hăr′ō) n. A farm implement consisting of a heavy frame with sharp teeth or upright disks, used to break up and even off plowed ground. ❖ tr.v. **-rowed, -row·ing, -rows 1.** To break up and level with a harrow. **2.** To inflict great distress or torment on. [ME harwe.] —**har′row·er** n.

har·row² (hăr′ō) tr.v. **-rowed, -row·ing, -rows** Archaic To plunder; sack. [ME herwen, var. of harien. See HARRY.]

Harrow A borough of NE Greater London; site of the public school Harrow (founded 1571). Pop. 206,632

har·row·ing (hăr′ō-ĭng) adj. Extremely distressing.

har·rumph (hə-rŭmf′) intr.v. **-rumphed, -rumph·ing, -rumphs 1.** To make a show of clearing one's throat. **2.** To offer usu. brief critical comments. [Imit.] —**har·rumph′** n.

har·ry (hăr′ē) tr.v. **-ried, -ry·ing, -ries 1.** To disturb or distress by or as if by repeated attacks; harass. See Syns at harass. **2.** To raid, as in war; sack or pillage. [ME harien < OE hergian. See koro- in App.]

harsh (härsh) adj. **harsh·er, harsh·est 1.** Unpleasantly coarse and rough to the touch. **2.** Disagreeable to the senses, esp. to the sense of hearing. **3.** Extremely severe or exacting; stern. **4.** Unpleasant or uncomfortable: a harsh wilderness. [ME harsk, of Scand. orig.] —**harsh′ly** adv. —**harsh′ness** n.

harsh·en (här′shən) tr. & intr.v. **-ened, -en·ing, -ens** To make or become harsh.

hars·let (här′slĭt) n. Variant of haslet.

hart (härt) n., pl. **harts** or **hart** A male deer, esp. a male red deer over five years old. [ME < OE heorot. See ker-¹ in App.]

Hart, Lorenz Milton 1895–1943. Amer. lyricist whose songs include "My Funny Valentine" and "Blue Moon."

Hart, Moss 1904–61. Amer. playwright, librettist, and director whose collaborations with George S. Kaufman include The Man Who Came to Dinner (1939).

Harte (härt), **(Francis) Bret** 1836–1902. Amer. writer whose works include "The Luck of Roaring Camp" (1868).

har·te·beest (här′tə-bēst′, härt′bēst′) n., pl. **-beests** or **hartebeest** Any of various large reddish-brown African antelopes of the genus Alcelaphus, having ringed outward-curving horns. [Obsolete Afr. < MDu., var. of hertebeest : hert, deer; see ker-¹ in App. + beest, beast (< OFr. beste; see BEAST).]

Hart·ford (härt′fərd) The cap. of CT, in the N-central part on the Connecticut R.; settled 1635–36 by Massachusetts colonists on the site of a Dutch trading post. Pop. 121,578.

Har·tle·pool (härt′lē-pōōl′, här′tl-) A borough of NE England on the North Sea SSE of Newcastle. Pop. 94,600.

harts·horn (härts′hôrn′) n. **1.** The antler of a hart, formerly used as a source of ammonia and in smelling salts. **2.** Ammonium carbonate.

hart's-tongue (härts′tŭng′) n. A European evergreen fern (Phyllitis scolopendrium) with narrow undivided fronds. [< the shape of its fronds.]

har·um-scar·um (hâr′əm-skâr′əm, hăr′əm-skâr′əm) adj. Lacking a sense of responsibility; reckless. ❖ adv. With abandon; recklessly. [Perh. alteration of hare 'em, scare 'em : hare, to frighten + SCARE.]

Ha·run al-Ra·shid or **Ha·roun al-Ra·schid** (hä-rōōn′ äl-rä-shēd′) also **Harun ar-Ra·shid** (är′-) 763?–809. Caliph of Baghdad (786–809) noted for the splendor of his court.

ha·rus·pex (hə-rŭs′pĕks′, hăr′ə-spĕks′) also **a·rus·pex** (ə-rŭs′pĕks′) n., pl. **ha·rus·pi·ces** (hə-rŭs′pĭ-sēz′) also **a·rus·pi·ces** (ə-rŭs′pĭ-sēz′) A priest in ancient Rome who practiced divination by the inspection of the entrails of animals. [Lat.]

Har·vard (här′vərd), **John** 1607–38. Amer. cleric and philanthropist who left his library and half his estate to the college in Cambridge MA that now bears his name.

Harvard, Mount A peak, 4,398.1 m (14,420 ft), in the Sawatch Range of the Rocky Mts. in central CO.

har·vest (här′vĭst) n. **1.** The act or process of gathering a crop. **2a.** The crop that ripens or is gathered in a season. **b.** The amount or measure of the crop gathered in a season. **c.** The time or season of such gathering. **3.** The result or consequence of an activity. ❖ v. **-vest·ed, -vest·ing, -vests** —tr. **1a.** To gather (a crop). **b.** To take or kill (fish, for example) for food, sport, or population control. **c.** To extract from a culture or body, esp. for transplantation: harvested bone marrow. **2.** To gather a crop from. **3.** To receive (the benefits or consequences of an action). —intr. To gather a crop. [ME < OE hærfest. See kerp- in App.] —**har′vest·a·ble** adj. —**har′vest·a·bil′i·ty** n.

har·vest·er (här′vĭ-stər) n. **1.** One who gathers a crop. **2.** A machine for harvesting crops; a reaper.

harvest fly n. Any of several cicadas of the genus Tibicen.

harvest home n. **1.** The completion of a harvest. **2a.** The time of completing a harvest. **b.** A festival held at this time. **c.** A song sung at this time.

har·vest·man (här′vĭst-mən) n. **1.** A man who harvests. **2.** See daddy longlegs 1.

harvest mite n. See chigger 1.

harvest moon n. The full moon that occurs nearest the autumnal equinox.

Har·vey (här′vē), **William** 1578–1657. English physician and anatomist who discovered human blood circulation (1628).

Harz Mountains (härts) A mountain range of central Germany extending c. 97 km (60 mi) between the Weser and the Elbe and rising to 1,142.8 m (3,747 ft).

has (hăz) v. Third person singular present tense of **have.**

has-been (hăz′bĭn′) n., pl. **has-beens** Informal One that is no longer famous, popular, successful, or useful.

Has·dru·bal (hăz′drŏŏ′bəl, hăz-drōō′-) d. 207 B.C. Carthaginian general who was defeated by Roman forces (207) during the Second Punic War.

ha·sen·pfef·fer (hä′zən-fĕf′ər, -sən-) n. A highly seasoned stew of marinated rabbit meat. [Ger. : Hase, rabbit (< MHGer. < OHGer. haso) + Pfeffer, pepper (< OHGer. pfeffar < Lat. piper; see PEPPER).]

hash¹ (hăsh) n. **1.** A dish of chopped meat, potatoes, and sometimes vegetables, usu. browned. **2a.** A jumble; a hodgepodge. **b.** Informal A mess. **3.** A reworking or restatement of familiar material. ❖ tr.v. **hashed, hash·ing, hash·es 1.** To chop into pieces; mince. **2.** Informal To make a mess of; mangle. **3.** Informal To discuss carefully; review: hash over plans. —**idiom:** settle (someone's) hash Slang To silence or subdue. [Variant of ME hache < OFr., p. part. of hacher, hachier, to chop up < hache, ax, of Gmc. orig. See HATCHET.]

hash² (hăsh) n. Slang Hashish.

hash browns pl.n. Chopped cooked potatoes, fried until brown.

Hash·e·mite also **Hash·i·mite** (hăsh′ə-mīt′) n. A member of a princely Arab family claiming direct descent from the prophet Muhammad. [< Ar. hāšimī < hāšima, to destroy, smash.]

hash house n. Slang A cheap restaurant.

hash·ish (hăsh′ēsh′, -ĭsh, hă-shēsh′, hä-) also **hash·eesh** (hăsh′ēsh′, hă-shēsh′, hä-) n. A purified resin prepared from the female cannabis plant and smoked or chewed as a narcotic or intoxicant. [Ar. hašīš, hemp, dried grass < hašša, to mow.]

hash mark n. **1.** A service stripe on the sleeve of an enlisted per-

Benjamin Harrison²

William Henry Harrison

ă	pat	oi	boy
ā	pay	ou	out
âr	care	ŏŏ	took
ä	father	ōō	boot
ĕ	pet	ŭ	cut
ē	be	ûr	urge
ĭ	pit	th	thin
ī	pie	th	this
îr	pier	hw	which
ŏ	pot	zh	vision
ō	toe	ə	about,
ô	paw		item

Stress marks:
′ (primary);
′ (secondary), as in
lexicon (lĕk′sĭ-kŏn′)

son's uniform. **2.** *Football* A mark in either of two series placed on the field perpendicular to the yard lines and used for spotting the ball. [Alteration of HATCH³.]

hash slinger *n. Slang* One who prepares food in a cheap restaurant.

Ha•sid or **Has•sid** also **Chas•sid** (кнӓ′sĭd, khô′-, hä′-) *n., pl.* **Ha•si•dim** or **Has•si•dim** also **Chas•si•dim** (кнӓ-sē′dĭm, кнô-, hä-) A member of a Jewish mystic movement founded in the 18th century in eastern Europe that reacted against Talmudic learning. [< Heb. *ḥāsîd*, pious < *ḥāsad*, to be kind.] —**Ha•si′dic** *adj.* —**Ha•si′dism** *n.*

has•let (hăs′lĭt, hāz′-) also **hars•let** (här′slĭt) *n.* The edible viscera of an animal, esp. hog viscera. [ME *hastelet* < OFr., dim. of *haste*, roast meat, spit, perh. < Lat. *hasta*, spear, or, of Gmc. orig.]

has•n't (hăz′ənt) Contraction of *has not.*

hasp (hăsp) *n.* A metal fastener with a hinged slotted part that fits over a staple and is secured by a pin, bolt, or padlock. ❖ *tr.v.* **hasped, hasp•ing, hasps** To close or lock with a hasp. [ME < OE *hæsp, hæpse.*]

Has•sam (hăs′əm), **(Frederick) Childe** 1859–1935. Amer. painter whose works include *Rainy Day in Boston* (1885).

has•si•um (hăs′ē-əm) *n. Symbol* **Hs** An artificially produced radioactive element with atomic number 108 whose most long-lived isotopes have mass numbers of 264 and 265 with half-lives of 0.08 millisecond and 2 milliseconds, respectively. See table at **element.** [< Med.Lat. *Hassia*, Hesse (Ger. state containing Darmstadt, where the element was first synthesized).]

has•sle (hăs′əl) *Informal n.* **1.** An argument or fight. **2.** Trouble; bother. ❖ *v.* **-sled, -sling, -sles** —*intr.* To argue or fight. —*tr.* To bother or harass. [?]

has•sock (hăs′ək) *n.* **1.** A thick cushion used as a footstool or for kneeling. **2.** A dense clump of grass. [ME *hassok*, clump of grass < OE *hassuc.*]

hast (hăst) *v. Archaic* Second person singular present tense of **have.**

has•tate (hăs′tāt′) *adj. Botany* Having the shape of an arrowhead but with the basal lobes pointing outward at right angles. [< Lat. *hasta*, spear.] —**has′tate•ly** *adv.*

haste (hāst) *n.* **1.** Rapidity of action or motion. **2.** Overeagerness to act. **3.** Rash or headlong action; precipitateness. ❖ *intr. & tr.v.* **hast•ed, hast•ing, hastes** To hasten or cause to hasten. —*idiom:* **make haste** To move or act swiftly; hurry. [ME < OFr., of Gmc. orig.]

SYNONYMS *haste, celerity, dispatch, expedition, hurry, speed* These nouns denote rapidity or promptness of movement or activity: *left in haste; a legal system known for celerity; advanced with all possible dispatch; progressed with great expedition; worked without hurry; drove with excessive speed.* **ANTONYM** *deliberation*

---

has•ten (hā′sən) —*intr.* **-tened, -ten•ing, -tens** To move or act swiftly. —*tr.* **1.** To cause to hurry. **2.** To speed up; accelerate: *fanned the paint to hasten drying.*

Has•tings (hā′stĭngz) A borough of SE England on the English Channel at the entrance to the Strait of Dover; near the site of William the Conqueror's victory over the Saxons (Oct. 14, 1066). Pop. 75,900.

Hastings, Warren 1732–1818. British colonial administrator who served as governor-general of India (1773–85).

hast•y (hā′stē) *adj.* **-i•er, -i•est** **1.** Characterized by speed; rapid. See Syns at **fast¹.** **2.** Done or made too quickly to be accurate or wise; rash. **3.** Easily angered; irritable. —**hast′i•ly** *adv.* —**hast′i•ness** *n.*

hasty pudding *n.* **1.** Cornmeal mush served with maple syrup, brown sugar, or other sweetening. **2.** *Chiefly British* A mush made with flour or oatmeal.

hat (hăt) *n.* **1.** A covering for the head, esp. one with a shaped crown and brim. **2a.** A head covering of distinctive color and shape worn as a symbol of office. **b.** The office symbolized by the wearing of such a head covering. **3.** A role or office symbolized by or as if by the wearing of different hats: *wears many hats.* ❖ *tr.v.* **hat•ted, hat•ting, hats** To supply or cover with a hat. —*idioms:* **at the drop of a hat** At the slightest pretext or provocation. **hat in hand** In a humble manner; humbly. **take (one's) hat off to** To respect, admire, or congratulate. **talk through (one's) hat** **1.** To talk nonsense. **2.** To bluff. **throw (or toss) (one's) hat into the ring** To enter a political race as a candidate for office. **under (one's) hat** As a secret or in confidence. [ME < OE *hæt, hætt.*]

hat•band (hăt′bănd′) *n.* A band of ribbon or cloth worn on a hat just above the brim.

hat•box (hăt′bŏks′) *n.* A box or case for a hat.

hatch¹ (hăch) *n.* **1a.** An opening, as in the deck of a ship, in the roof or floor of a building, or in an aircraft. **b.** The cover for such an opening. **c.** A hatchway. **d.** *Nautical* A ship's compartment. **2.** The hinged rear door of a hatchback. **3.** A floodgate. —*idiom:* **down the hatch** *Slang* Drink up. Often used as a toast. [ME, small door < OE *hæc, hæcc.*]

hatch² (hăch) *v.* **hatched, hatch•ing, hatch•es** —*intr.* To emerge from or break out of an egg. —*tr.* **1.** To produce (young) from an egg. **2.** To cause (an egg or eggs) to produce young. **3.** To devise or originate, esp. in secret. ❖ *n.* **1.** The act or an in-**

Hatshepsut
granite sculpture, c. 15th
century B.C.

stance of hatching. **2.** The young hatched at one time; a brood. [ME *hacchen* < OE **hæccan.*] —**hatch′er** *n.*

hatch³ (hăch) *tr.v.* **hatched, hatch•ing, hatch•es** To shade by drawing or etching fine parallel or crossed lines on. ❖ *n.* A fine line used in hatching. [ME *hachen*, to engrave, carve < OFr. *hacher, hachier*, to crosshatch, cut up. See HASH¹.]

hatch•back (hăch′băk′) *n.* An automobile having a sloping back with a hinged rear door that opens upward.

hat•check (hăt′chĕk′) *n.* A room for checking hats and other outer garments.

hatch•el (hăch′əl) *n.* A comb for separating flax fibers. ❖ *tr.v.* **-eled, -el•ing, -els** also **-elled, -el•ling, -els** To separate (flax fibers) with a hatchel. [ME *hechel*, poss. < OE **hecel*; akin to MDu. *hekel.*]

hatch•er•y (hăch′ə-rē) *n., pl.* **-ies** A place where eggs, esp. those of fish or poultry, are hatched.

hatch•et (hăch′ĭt) *n.* **1.** A small short-handled ax for use in one hand. **2.** A tomahawk. [ME *hachet* < OFr. *hachete*, dim. of *hache*, ax, of Gmc. orig.; akin to OHGer. *happa*, sickle.]

hatchet face *n.* A thin face with sharp features. —**hatch′et-faced′** (hăch′ĭt-fāst′) *adj.*

hatchet job *n. Slang* A crude or ruthless effort usu. ending in destruction: *did a hatchet job on the mayor's reputation.*

hatchet man *n. Slang* **1.** A man hired to commit murder. **2.** One assigned to carry out a ruthless task or a vicious or unscrupulous order.

hatch•ing (hăch′ĭng) *n.* **1.** Fine lines used in graphic arts to show shading. **2.** The process of decorating with such lines.

hatch•ling (hăch′lĭng) *n.* A newly hatched bird, amphibian, fish, or reptile.

hatch•ment (hăch′mənt) *n. Heraldry* A panel bearing the coat of arms of a deceased person. [Alteration of *hachement, achiment* < ACHIEVEMENT, escutcheon.]

hatch•way (hăch′wā′) *n.* A passage or an opening leading to a hold, compartment, or cellar.

hate (hāt) *v.* **hat•ed, hat•ing, hates** —*tr.* **1a.** To feel hostility or animosity toward. **b.** To detest. **2.** To feel dislike or distaste for: *hates washing dishes.* —*intr.* To feel hatred. ❖ *n.* **1.** Intense animosity or dislike; hatred. **2.** An object of detestation or hatred. [ME *haten* < OE *hete.*] —**hat′er** *n.*

hate crime *n.* A crime motivated by prejudice against a social group.

hate•ful (hāt′fəl) *adj.* **1.** Eliciting or deserving hatred. **2.** Feeling or showing hatred; malevolent. —**hate′ful•ly** *adv.* —**hate′ful•ness** *n.*

hate•mon•ger (hāt′mŭng′gər, -mŏng′-) *n.* One who incites others to hatred or prejudice.

hate speech *n.* Bigoted speech attacking or disparaging a social or ethnic group or a member of such a group.

hath (hăth) *v. Archaic* Third person singular present tense of **have.**

Hath•a•way (hăth′ə-wā′), **Anne** 1556?–1623. The wife of William Shakespeare who married the playwright in 1582.

ha•tha yoga (hŭt′ə, hä′thə) *n.* A form of yogic exercise that emphasizes specific postures in combination with controlled breathing. [Skt. *haṭhayogaḥ : haṭhaḥ*, violence, force (< forcing the mind to withdraw from the outside world by the use of difficult postures) + *yogaḥ*, union, yoga; see YOGA.]

hat•pin (hăt′pĭn′) *n.* A long straight pin usu. with an ornamental head, used to secure a hat to the wearer's hair.

ha•tred (hā′trĭd) *n.* Intense animosity or hostility. [ME : *hate*, hate; see HATE + *-rede*, condition (< OE *-rǣden*).]

Hat•shep•sut (hăt-shĕp′sōōt′) also **Hat•shep•set** (-sĕt′) d. c. 1482 B.C. Queen of Egypt (1503–1482) who assumed the title of pharaoh while serving as regent for Thutmose III.

hat•ter (hăt′ər) *n.* One whose occupation is the manufacture, selling, or repair of hats.

Hat•ter•as Island (hăt′ər-əs) A long barrier island off the E coast of NC between Pamlico Sound and the Atlantic Ocean, with **Cape Hatteras** projecting from the SE part.

hat trick *n.* **1.** Three goals scored by one player in one game, as in ice hockey. **2.** Three wickets taken in cricket by a bowler in three consecutive balls. **3.** Three consecutive wins or outstanding accomplishments by the same individual. [< the hat traditionally awarded for this in cricket.]

hau•ber•geon (hô′bər-jən) *n.* Variant of **habergeon.**

hau•berk (hô′bərk) *n.* A long tunic made of chain mail. [ME < OFr. *hauberc*, of Gmc. orig. See *kʷel-* in App.]

haugh•ty (hô′tē) *adj.* **-ti•er, -ti•est** Scornfully and condescendingly proud. See Syns at **proud.** [< ME *haut* < OFr. *haut, halt*, alteration (influenced by Frankish *hōh*) of Lat. *altus*, high.] —**haugh′ti•ly** *adv.* —**haugh′ti•ness** *n.*

haul (hôl) *v.* **hauled, haul•ing, hauls** —*tr.* **1.** To pull or drag forcibly; tug. See Syns at **pull.** **2.** To transport, as with a truck or cart. **3.** *Informal* To compel to go, esp. for trial. **4.** *Nautical* To change the course of (a ship), esp. to sail closer into the wind. —*intr.* **1.** To pull; tug. **2.** To provide transportation; cart. **3a.** To shift direction. **b.** To change one's mind. **4.** *Nautical* To change the course of a ship. ❖ *n.* **1.** The act of pulling or dragging. **2.** The act of transporting or carting. **3.** A distance, esp. over which something is pulled or transported. **4.** Something pulled or transported; a load. **5.** Everything collected or acquired by a single effort; the take. —**phrasal verbs: haul off** *Informal* **1.** To draw back slightly, as to prepare an action. **2.** To shift operations to a new place; to move away. **haul up** To come to a halt. [ME *haulen* < OFr. *haler*, of Gmc. orig. See **kela-** in App.] —**haul′er** *n.*

haul•age (hô′lĭj) *n.* **1.** The act or process of hauling. **2.** A charge made for hauling.

haulm (hôm) *n. Chiefly British* The stems of peas, beans, potatoes, or grasses. [ME *halm*, straw < OE *healm.*]

haunch (hônch, hŏnch) *n.* **1.** The hip, buttock, and upper thigh in humans and animals. **2.** The loin and leg of a four-footed animal, esp. as used for food. **3.** *Architecture* Either of the sides of an arch, curving down from the apex to an impost. [ME *haunche* < OFr. *hanche* < Frankish **hanka.*]

haunt (hônt, hŏnt) *v.* **haunt•ed, haunt•ing, haunts** —*tr.* **1.** To inhabit, visit, or appear to in the form of a ghost or other supernatural being. **2.** To visit often; frequent. **3.** To come continually to the mind of; obsess. **4.** To be continually present in; pervade. —*intr.* To recur or visit often, esp. as a ghost. ❖ *n.* **1.** A place much frequented. **2.** also **hant** (hănt) or **haint** (hānt) *Chiefly Southern US* A ghost or other supernatural being. [ME *haunten*, to frequent < OFr. *hanter*. See **tkei-** in App.] —**haunt′er** *n.*

haunt•ing (hôn′tĭng, hŏn′-) *adj.* Continually recurring to the mind; unforgettable. —**haunt′ing•ly** *adv.*

Haupt•mann (houpt′män′, houp′-), **Gerhart** 1862–1946. German writer known esp. for his plays, such as *The Weavers* (1892), who won the 1912 Nobel Prize for literature.

Hau•sa (hou′sə, -zə) *n., pl.* **Hausa** or **Hau•sas 1.** A member of a predominantly Muslim people in northern Nigeria and southern Niger. **2.** The Chadic language of the Hausa. [Hausa *hāusáawáa*, pl. of *bàhàusèe*, a Hausa.]

haus•frau (hous′frou′) *n.* A housewife. [Ger. : *Haus*, house (< MHGer. *hūs* < OHGer.) + *Frau*, wife; see FRAU.]

Hauss•mann (hous′mən, ōs-män′), Baron **Georges Eugène** 1809–91. French public official who planned and oversaw the rebuilding of Paris during the reign of Napoleon III.

haus•tel•lum (hô-stĕl′əm) *n., pl.* **haus•tel•la** (hô-stĕl′ə) A portion of the proboscis that in many insects is adapted for sucking. [NLat., dim. of Lat. *haustrum*, scoop on a water wheel < *haurīre*, to draw up.]

haus•to•ri•um (hô-stôr′ē-əm, -stōr′-) *n., pl.* **haus•to•ri•a** (hô-stôr′ē-ə, -stōr′-) A specialized food-absorbing structure of a parasitic plant. [NLat. *haustōrium* < Lat. *haustus*, absorption < p. part. of *haurīre*, to draw up.]

haut•boy also **haut•bois** (hō′boi′, ō′boi′) *n., pl.* **-boys** also **-bois** (-boiz′) An oboe. [Fr. *hautbois* < OFr. : *haut*, high; see HAUGHTY + *bois*, wood (of Gmc. orig.).]

haute (ōt) *adj.* Fashionably elegant. [< such phrases as HAUTE COUTURE.]

haute couture *n.* **1.** The leading establishments or designers for the creation of exclusive fashions. **2a.** The creation of these fashions. **b.** The fashions created. [Fr. : *haute*, fem. of *haut*, high, elegant + *couture*, sewing.]

haute cuisine *n.* **1.** Elaborate or skillfully prepared food, esp. of France. **2.** The characteristic manner or style of preparing such food. [Fr. : *haute*, fem. of *haut*, high, elegant + *cuisine*, cooking.]

haute é•cole (ā-kôl′) *n.* The art, techniques, or practice of equestrianship. [Fr. : *haute*, high, advanced + *école*, school.]

hau•teur (hō-tûr′, ō-tœr′) *n.* Haughtiness in bearing and attitude; arrogance. [Fr. < OFr. < *haut*, high. See HAUGHTY.]

haut monde also **haute monde** (ō mônd′) *n.* Fashionable society. [Fr. : *haut*, high + *monde*, world, society.]

Ha•van•a[1] (hə-văn′ə) The cap. of Cuba, in the NW part on the Gulf of Mexico; founded on its present site in 1519. Pop. 2,160,368. —**Ha•van′an** *adj. & n.*

Ha•van•a[2] (hə-văn′ə) *n.* A cigar made in Cuba, esp. one of fine quality. [After HAVANA[1].]

Ha•var•ti (hə-vär′tē) *n.* A mild, semisoft, pale yellow cheese of Danish origin. [After *Havarti*, experimental farm in Denmark where it was developed.]

Ha•va•su•pai (hä′və-sōō′pī) *n., pl.* **Havasupai** or **-pais 1** A member of a Native American people inhabiting an area southeast of the Grand Canyon. **2.** The Yuman language of the Havasupai. [Prob. Mohave *havasu-pay*, blue-green (water) person : *havasu-*, blue-green (water) + *-pay*, person.]

have (hăv) *v.* **had** (hăd), **hav•ing, has** (hăz) —*tr.* **1a.** To be in possession of: *has a nice car.* **b.** To possess as a characteristic, quality, or function: *has a beard.* **c.** To possess or contain as a constituent part: *a car that has air bags.* **2.** To occupy a particular relation to others: *has many disciples.* **3.** To possess knowledge of or facility in: *has some Spanish.* **4.** To hold in the mind; entertain: *had doubts.* **5.** To use or exhibit in action: *have compassion.* **6a.** To come into possession of; acquire: *not a single copy of the book to be had.* **b.** To receive; get: *had a letter from my cousin.* **c.** To accept; take: *I'll have some peas.* **7a.** To suffer from: *have defective vision.* **b.** To be subject to the experience of: *had a difficult winter.* **8a.** To cause to do something, as by persuasion or compulsion: *had my assistant run the errand.* **b.** To cause to be in a specified place or state: *had the neighbors over; had everyone fascinated.* **9.** To permit; allow: *won't have that kind of behavior.* **10.** To carry on, perform, or execute: *have an argument.* **11a.** To place at a disadvan-

tage: *With new evidence, we had our opponents.* **b.** *Informal* To get the better of, esp. by trickery or deception: *was had by the swindler.* **c.** *Informal* To influence by dishonest means; bribe: *an official who could not be had.* **12a.** To procreate (offspring). **b.** To give birth to; bear. **13.** To partake of: *have lunch.* **14.** To be obliged to; must: *We have to go.* **15.** To engage in sexual intercourse with. —*aux.* Used with a past participle to form the present perfect, past perfect, and future perfect tenses indicating completed action: *has gone for good; had lost my temper; will have finished by then.* ❖ *n.* One enjoying esp. material wealth. —**phrasal verbs: have at** To attack. **have on 1.** To wear. **2.** To be scheduled for. —**idioms: had better** (or **best**) *Usage Problem* To be wise or obliged to; should or must. **have done with** To stop; cease. **have had it** *Informal* **1.** To have endured all that one can. **2.** To be in a state beyond remedy, repair, or salvage. **3.** To have done everything that is possible or that will be permitted. **have it 1.** To assert; maintain: *Rumor has it that he quit.* **2.** To think and act with respect to (something being considered). **have it in for (someone)** To intend to harm, esp. because of a grudge. **have it out** To settle decisively, esp. by means of an argument or a discussion. **have (something) coming** To deserve what one receives. **have to do with** To be concerned or associated with. [ME *haven* < OE *habban.* See **kap-** in App.]

Ha•vel (hä′fəl) A river, c. 346 km (215 mi), of E Germany flowing through Berlin to the Elbe R.

Ha•vel (hä′vəl), **Václav** b. 1936. Czech writer and politician whose plays include *The Garden Party* (1969). He served as president from 1989 to 1992.

have•lock (hăv′lŏk′, -lək) *n.* A cloth covering for a cap, having a flap to cover and protect the back of the neck. [After Sir Henry *Havelock* (1795–1857), British soldier.]

ha•ven (hā′vən) *n.* **1.** A harbor or anchorage; a port. **2.** A place of refuge or rest; a sanctuary. ❖ *tr.v.* **-vened, -ven•ing, -vens** To put into or provide with a haven. [ME < OE *hæfen.* See **kap-** in App.]

have-not (hăv′nŏt′) *n.* One enjoying little or no material wealth.

have•n't (hăv′ənt) Contraction of *have not.*

hav•er•sack (hăv′ər-săk′) *n.* A bag carried over one shoulder to transport supplies, as on a hike. [Fr. *havresac* < obsolete Ger. *Habersack* : Ger. dialectal *Haber*, oats (< MHGer. *habere* < OHGer. *habaro*) + Ger. *Sack*, bag (< MHGer. *sac* < OHGer. < Lat. *saccus*; see SACK[1]).]

Ha•ver•sian canal (hə-vûr′zhən) *n.* Any of the interconnecting vascular channels in bone tissue. [After Clopton *Havers* (1650?–1702), English physician and anatomist.]

Haversian system *n.* A structural unit of bone consisting of a Haversian canal and corresponding lamellae of compact bone.

hav•oc (hăv′ək) *n.* **1.** Widespread destruction; devastation. **2.** Disorder or chaos. ❖ *tr.v.* **-ocked, -ock•ing, -ocs** To destroy or pillage. [ME *havok* < AN *(crier) havok*, (to cry) havoc, var. of OFr. *havot*, plundering, of Gmc. orig.]

haw[1] (hô) *n.* An utterance used by a speaker who is fumbling for words. ❖ *intr.v.* **hawed, haw•ing, haws** To fumble in speaking. [Imit.]

haw[2] (hô) *n.* **1.** The fruit of a hawthorn. **2.** A hawthorn or similar tree or shrub. [ME < OE *haga.*]

haw[3] (hô) *n.* **1.** A nictitating membrane, esp. of a domesticated animal. **2.** An inflamed condition of this membrane. [?]

haw[4] (hô) *interj.* Used to command an animal pulling a load to turn to the left. ❖ *intr.v.* **hawed, haw•ing, haws** To turn left.

Ha•wai•i or **Ha•wai′i** (hə-wä′ē, -wī′ē, -vä′ē) A state of the US in the central Pacific Ocean comprising the Hawaiian Is.; admitted as the 50th state in 1959. Cap. Honolulu. Pop. 1,211,537.

Ha•wai•i-A•leu•tian Standard Time (hə-wä′ē-ə-lōō′shən, -wī′ē-) *n.* Standard time in the tenth time zone west of Greenwich, England, reckoned at 150° west and used, for example, in Hawaii and the western Aleutian Islands.

Ha•wai•ian or **Ha•wai′ian** (hə-wä′yən) *n.* **1a.** See Native Hawaiian. **b.** A native or inhabitant of the Hawaiian Islands, the state of Hawaii, or Hawaii Island. **2.** The Polynesian language of Hawaii. —**Ha•wai′ian** *adj.*

Hawaiian goose *n.* See nene.

Hawaiian guitar *n.* An electric guitar consisting of a long fretted neck and six to eight steel strings that are plucked while being pressed with a movable steel bar.

Hawaiian Islands *Formerly* **Sandwich Islands.** A group of volcanic and coral islands in the central Pacific Ocean coextensive with the state of HI. Settled by Polynesians in the 6th cent. A.D. and visited by Capt. James Cook in 1778, the islands were ruled by native monarchs from 1795 until 1893, when Queen Liliuokalani was deposed. Petitions for annexation by the US were approved in 1898.

Hawaiian shirt *n.* A colorfully patterned short-sleeved sport shirt. [< the fact that the style originated in Hawaii.]

Hawaii Island The largest and southernmost of the Hawaiian Is.,

Václav Havel
photographed in 1990

Stephen Hawking

the top of an enormous submarine mountain.

Hawaii Standard Time n. Hawaii-Aleutian Standard Time.

ha•wa•la (hə-wä′lə) n. **1.** An agreement or binding arrangement, primarily in Islamic societies, in which a financial obligation between two parties is settled by transferring it to a third party, as when money owed by a debtor to a creditor is paid by a person who owes the debtor money. **2.** An informal system for the transfer of money based on such arrangements. [Ar. *ḥawāla,* bill of exchange, check < *ḥāla,* to change.]

Ha•wash River (hä′wäsh′) See **Awash River.**

haw•finch (hô′fĭnch′) n. **1.** A thick-billed Eurasian bird (*Coccothraustes coccothraustes*) having brown, white, and black plumage. **2.** Any of various similar birds. [HAW² + FINCH.]

haw-haw¹ (hô′hô′) interj. Variant of **ha-ha¹.**

haw-haw² (hô′hô′) n. Variant of **ha-ha².**

hawk¹ (hôk) n. **1.** Any of various birds of prey of the order Falconiformes, esp. of the genera *Accipiter* and *Buteo,* having a short hooked bill and strong claws for seizing. **2.** Any of various similar birds of prey. **3.** A person who preys on others; a shark. **4a.** One who demonstrates an aggressive or combative attitude. **b.** A person who favors military action to carry out foreign policy. ❖ intr.v. **hawked, hawk•ing, hawks 1.** To hunt with trained hawks. **2.** To swoop and strike in the manner of a hawk. [ME *hauk* < OE *hafoc.* See **kap-** in App.] —**hawk′ish** adj.

hawk² (hôk) v. **hawked, hawk•ing, hawks** —intr. To hawk goods. —tr. To peddle (goods) aggressively, esp. by calling out.

hawk³ (hôk) v. **hawked, hawk•ing, hawks** —intr. To clear or attempt to clear the throat by or as if by coughing up phlegm. —tr. To clear the throat of (phlegm). ❖ n. An audible effort to clear the throat by expelling phlegm. [Imit.]

hawk•er (hô′kər) n. One who sells goods aggressively, esp. by calling out. [ME *hauker,* prob. < MLGer. *höker* < *hōken,* to peddle, bend, bear on the back.]

hawk-eyed (hôk′īd′) adj. Having very keen eyesight.

Haw•king (hô′kĭng), **Stephen William** b. 1942. British theoretical physicist noted for his research into the origin of the universe.

Hawking radiation n. A form of radiation believed to emanate from black holes, arising from the creation of pairs of subatomic particles in the space adjacent to the black hole, with one particle falling into the black hole and the other radiating away. The energy lost to such radiated particles is believed to cause the eventual disappearance of the black hole. [After Stephen William HAWKING.]

Haw•kins (hô′kĭnz), **Coleman Randolph** 1901?–69. Amer. jazz musician who established the saxophone as a leading jazz instrument.

hawk•moth or **hawk moth** (hôk′môth′, -môth′) n. Any of various thick-bodied, slender-winged moths of the family Sphingidae that, in their adult stage, suck nectar through an extended proboscis.

hawks•bill (hôks′bĭl′) n. A tropical sea turtle (*Eretmochelys imbricata*) valued as a source of tortoiseshell.

hawk•weed (hôk′wēd′) n. Any of numerous plants of the genus *Hieracium,* having dandelionlike flower heads.

Haw•orth (hou′ərth, härth) A village of N England WNW of Bradford; home of the Brontë sisters.

Haw River A river, c. 209 km (130 mi), rising in N-central NC and flowing SE to join the Deep R. and form the Cape Fear R.

hawse (hôz) n. **1.** The part of a ship where the hawseholes are located. **2.** A hawsehole. **3.** The space between the bows and anchors of an anchored ship. **4.** The arrangement of a ship's anchor cables when both starboard and port anchors are secured. [ME *hals,* forward curve of a strake, prob. < ON *hāls,* neck, ship's bow. See k°el- in App.]

hawse•hole (hôz′hōl′) n. An opening in the bow of a ship through which a cable or hawser is passed.

hawse•er (hô′zər) n. A cable or rope used in mooring or towing a ship. [ME < AN *haucer* < OFr. *haucier,* to hoist < VLat. *altiāre,* alteration of LLat. *altāre* < Lat. *altus,* high.]

haw•thorn (hô′thôrn′) n. Any of various usu. thorny trees or shrubs of the genus *Crataegus,* having white or pinkish flowers and reddish fruits. [ME < OE *hagathorn : haga,* haw + *thorn,* thorn.]

Haw•thorne (hô′thôrn′), **Nathaniel** 1804–64. Amer. writer whose novels include *The Scarlet Letter* (1850).

hay (hā) n. **1.** Grass or other plants, such as clover or alfalfa, cut and dried for fodder. **2.** *Slang* A trifling amount of money. ❖ v. **hayed, hay•ing, hays** —intr. To mow and cure grass and herbage for hay. —tr. **1.** To make (grass) into hay. **2.** To feed with hay. [ME < OE *hīeg.*] —**hay′er** n.

hay•cock (hā′kŏk′) n. *Chiefly British* A conical mound of hay.

Hay•den (hād′n), **Robert** 1913–80. Amer. poet whose works include *Heart-Shape in the Dust* (1940).

Haydn (hīd′n), **Franz Joseph** 1732–1809. Austrian composer who wrote numerous symphonies and string quartets as well as operas and concertos.

Hay•ek (hī′ək, -ěk′), **Friedrich August von** 1899–1992. Austrian-born British economist who shared a 1974 Nobel Prize.

Hayes (hāz), **Helen** 1900–93. Amer. actress acclaimed for performances on stage, as in *Victoria Regina* (1935–39), and in film.

Hayes, Rutherford Birchard 1822–93. The 19th President of the

US (1877–81). He won the controversial election of 1876 by one electoral vote.

Hayes River A river, c. 483 km (300 mi), of E Manitoba, Canada, flowing NE to Hudson Bay.

hay fever n. An allergic reaction, usu. to airborne pollen, of the upper respiratory tract and the eyes, characterized by nasal discharge, sneezing, and itchy watery eyes.

hay•fork (hā′fôrk′) n. **1.** A hand tool for pitching hay. **2.** A machine-operated fork for moving hay.

hay•loft (hā′lôft′, -lŏft′) n. A loft for storing hay.

hay•mak•er (hā′mā′kər) n. *Slang* A powerful blow with the fist.

hay•mow (hā′mou′) n. **1.** See **hayloft. 2.** The hay stored in a hayloft. **3.** *Archaic* A haystack.

hay•rack (hā′răk′) n. **1.** A rack from which livestock feed. **2a.** A rack fitted to a wagon for carrying hay. **b.** A wagon fitted with such a rack.

hay•rick (hā′rĭk′) n. See **haystack.**

hay•ride (hā′rīd′) n. A recreational ride in a large wagon or other vehicle piled with hay.

Hay River A river of NW Canada rising in NE British Columbia and flowing c. 853 km (530 mi) across NW Alberta to Great Slave Lake in S Northwest Terrs.

hay•seed (hā′sēd′) n. **1.** Grass seed shaken out of hay. **2.** Pieces of chaff or straw that fall from hay. **3.** *Slang* A bumpkin.

hay•stack (hā′stăk′) n. A large stack of hay, esp. as left in a field to dry.

Hay•ward (hā′wərd) A city of W CA SE of Oakland. Pop. 140,030.

hay•wire (hā′wīr′) n. Wire used in baling hay. ❖ adj. *Informal* **1.** Mentally confused or erratic; crazy. **2.** Not functioning properly; broken. [Adj. < the use of baling wire for makeshift repairs.]

Hay•wood (hā′wŏŏd′), **William Dudley** Known as "Big Bill." 1869–1928. Amer. labor leader who helped found the Industrial Workers of the World (1905).

Hay•worth (hā′wûrth′), **Rita** 1918–87. Amer. actress and dancer whose films include *Gilda* (1946).

haz•ard (hăz′ərd) n. **1.** A chance; an accident. **2.** A chance of being injured or harmed; danger. **3.** A possible source of danger. **4.** A dice game similar to craps. **5.** An obstacle found on a golf course. ❖ tr.v. **-ard•ed, -ard•ing, -ards 1.** To expose to danger or harm. See Syns at **endanger. 2.** To venture (something); dare. [ME *hasard,* dice game < OFr., poss. < OSpan. *azar,* poss. < Ar. *az-zahr,* the gaming die : *al-,* the + *zahr,* gaming die.]

haz•ard•ous (hăz′ər-dəs) adj. **1.** Marked by danger; perilous. **2.** Depending on chance; risky. —**haz′ard•ous•ly** adv. —**haz′ard•ous•ness** n.

hazardous waste n. Waste material, such as nuclear or industrial waste, that is potentially opaque to the environment and harmful to humans and other living organisms.

haze¹ (hāz) n. **1a.** Atmospheric moisture, dust, smoke, and vapor that diminishes visibility. **b.** A partially opaque covering. **2.** A vague or confused state of mind. ❖ intr.v. **hazed, haz•ing, haz•es** To become misty or hazy; blur.

haze² (hāz) tr.v. **hazed, haz•ing, haz•es 1.** To persecute or harass with meaningless, difficult, or humiliating tasks. **2.** To initiate, as into a college fraternity, by exacting humiliating performances from or playing rough practical jokes upon. [Perh. < obsolete *haze,* to frighten < obsolete Fr. *haser,* to annoy < OFr.] —**haz′er** n.

ha•zel (hā′zəl) n. **1.** Any of various shrubs or small trees of the genus *Corylus,* esp. the European species *C. avellana* or the American species *C. americana,* bearing edible nuts. **2.** A hazelnut. **3.** A light brown or yellowish brown. [ME *hasel* < OE *hæsel.*] —**ha′zel** adj.

ha•zel•nut (hā′zəl-nŭt′) n. The edible nut of a hazel, having a hard smooth brown shell.

Haz•litt (hăz′lĭt, hāz′-), **William** 1778–1830. British essayist whose works include *The Spirit of the Age* (1825).

haz•y (hā′zē) adj. **-i•er, -i•est 1.** Marked by the presence of haze; misty. **2.** Unclear, confused, or uncertain: *had only a hazy idea of what was meant.* [?] —**haz′i•ly** adv. —**haz′i•ness** n.

haz•zan (кнä′zən) n. Variant of **chazan.**

Hb abbr. **1.** *Bible* Habakkuk **2.** hemoglobin

HB abbr. **1.** Brinell hardness number **2.** halfback

H-bomb (āch′bŏm′) n. A hydrogen bomb.

HC abbr. **1.** hardcover **2.** hazardous cargo **3.** Holy Communion **4.** House of Commons

h.c. abbr. *Latin* Honoris causa (by reason of honor)

hcf abbr. highest common factor

HCG abbr. human chorionic gonadotropin

HDL abbr. high-density lipoprotein

HDPE abbr. high-density polyethylene

hdqrs. abbr. headquarters

HDTV abbr. high-definition television

hdwe. abbr. hardware

he¹ (hē) pron. **1a.** Used to refer to the man or boy previously mentioned or implied. **b.** Used to refer to a male animal. **2.** *Usage Problem* Used to refer to a person whose gender is unspecified or unknown: *"He who desires but acts not, breeds pestilence"* (William Blake). ❖ n. A male person or animal: *Is the cat a he?* [ME < OE *hē.* See **ko-** in App.]

hawkmoth
hummingbird hawkmoth
Macroglossum stellatarum

USAGE NOTE Traditionally the pronouns *he, him,* and *his* have been used as generic or gender-neutral singular pronouns, as in *A novelist should write about what he knows best* and *No one seems to take any pride in his work anymore.* Since the early 20th century, however, this usage has come under increasing criticism for reflecting and perpetuating gender stereotyping, and the analysis of the masculine pronouns *he, his,* and *him* as generic is linguistically doubtful. *He* cannot be used to refer to the members of any group containing both men and women, contrary to what we would expect of a truly gender-neutral term. There is something plainly disconcerting about sentences such as *Each of the stars of* As Good As It Gets [i.e., Jack Nicholson and Helen Hunt] *won an Academy Award for his performance.* In this case, the use of *his* forces the reader to envision a single male who stands as the representative member of the group, a picture that is at odds with the image that comes to mind when we picture the stars of *As Good As It Gets.* Thus *he* is not really a gender-neutral pronoun; rather, it refers to a male who is to be taken as the representative member of the group referred to by its antecedent. • Many people now routinely construct their remarks to avoid generic *he,* usually using one of two strategies: changing to the plural, so *they* is used (which is often the easiest solution), or using compound and coordinate forms such as *he/she* or *he or she* (which can be cumbersome in sustained use). In some cases, the generic pronoun can simply be dropped or changed to an article with no change in meaning. The phrase *a writer who draws on personal experience for material* is complete as it stands and requires no pronoun before the word *material.* • Not surprisingly, the opinion of the Usage Panel in such matters is mixed. While 37 percent actually prefer the generic *his* in the sentence *A taxpayer who fails to disclose the source of ______ income can be prosecuted under the new law,* 46 percent prefer a coordinate form like *his or her;* 7 percent felt that no pronoun was needed in the sentence; 2 percent preferred an article, usually *the;* and another 2 percent overturned tradition by advocating the use of generic *her,* a strategy that brings the politics of language to the reader's notice. Thus a clear majority of the Panel prefers something other than *his.* The writer who chooses to use generic *he* and its inflected forms in the face of the strong trend away from that usage may be viewed as deliberately calling attention to traditional gender roles or may simply appear to be insensitive. See Usage Notes at **any, anyone, each, every, neither, one.**

he² (hā) *n.* The fifth letter of the Hebrew alphabet. [Heb. *hē*, of Phoenician orig.]

He The symbol for the element **helium.**

HE *abbr.* **1.** Her (or His) Excellency **2.** high explosive **3.** His Eminence

head (hĕd) *n.* **1a.** The uppermost or forwardmost part of the body of a vertebrate, containing the brain and the eyes, ears, nose, mouth, and jaws. **b.** The analogous part of an invertebrate organism. **c.** The length or height of such a part. **2.** The seat of the faculty of reason; intelligence, intellect, or mind. **3.** Mental ability or aptitude: *has a good head for math.* **4.** Freedom of choice or action. **5.** *Slang* **a.** A habitual drug user. Often used in combination: *a dopehead.* **b.** An enthusiast. Often used in combination: *a chilihead.* **6.** A person considered foolish or contemptible. Often used in combination: *a chowderhead.* **7.** A portrait or representation of a person's head. **8.** The side of a coin having the principal design, often the profile of a political leader's head. Often used in the plural with a singular verb. **9.** *Informal* A headache. **10a.** An individual; a person: *charged five dollars a head.* **b.** *pl.* **head** A single animal: *20 head of cattle.* **11.** A person who leads, rules, or is in charge. **12.** The foremost or leading position. **13.** A headwaiter. **14a.** The difference in depth of a liquid at two given points. **b.** The measure of pressure at the lower point expressed in terms of this difference. **c.** The pressure exerted by a liquid or gas. **d.** The liquid or gas exerting the pressure. **15.** The froth or foam that rises to the top in pouring an effervescent liquid, such as beer. **16.** The tip of an abscess, boil, or pimple, in which pus forms. **17.** A turning point; a crisis: *bring matters to a head.* **18a.** A projection, weight, or fixture at the end of an elongated object: *the head of a pin.* **b.** The working end of a tool or implement. **c.** The part of an explosive device that carries the explosive; a warhead. **d.** The part of a stringed instrument where the strings are wound. **19.** *Anatomy* The proximal end of a long bone. **20a.** An attachment to or part of a machine that holds or contains the operative device. **b.** The magnetic head of a tape recorder or VCR. **c.** The device in a magnetic disk or tape drive that enables it to read data from and write data to the disk or tape. **21.** A rounded compact mass, as of leaves or buds: *a head of cabbage.* **22.** *Botany* A flower head. **23.** The uppermost part; the top. **24.** The end considered the most important: *the head of the table.* **25.** Either end of an object, such as a drum, whose two ends are interchangeable. **26.** *Nautical* **a.** The forward part of a vessel. **b.** The top part or upper edge of a sail. **27.** A toilet, esp. on a ship. **28.** A passage or gallery in a coal mine. **29.** *Printing* **a.** The top of a book or of a page. **b.** A headline or heading. **c.** A distinct topic or category. **30.** Headway; progress. **31.** *Linguistics* The word in a construction that has the same grammatical function as the construction as a whole and that determines relationships of concord to other parts of the construction or sentence in which the construction occurs. **32.** *Vulgar Slang* Oral sex. ❖ *adj.* **1.** Of, relating to, or intended for the head. Often used in combination: *headwrap.* **2.** Foremost in rank or importance. **3.** Placed at the top or the front. **4.** *Slang* Of, relating to, or for drugs or drug users. ❖ *v.* **head•ed, head•ing, heads** —*tr.* **1.** To be in charge of; lead: *headed the committee.* **2.** To be in the first or foremost position of. **3.** To aim, point, or turn in a certain direction. **4.** To remove the head or top of. **5.** *Sports* To hit (a soccer ball) in the air with one's head. **6.** To provide with a head: *head each column with a number.* —*intr.* **1.** To proceed or go in a certain direction. **2.** To form a head, as lettuce or cabbage. **3.** To originate, as a stream or river; rise. ***—phrasal verb:*** **head off** To block the progress or completion of; intercept. ***—idioms:*** **head and shoulders above** Far superior to. **head over heels 1.** Rolling, as in a somersault. **2.** Completely; hopelessly. **keep (one's) head** To remain calm; remain in control of oneself. **lose (one's) head** To lose one's poise or self-control. **off (or out of) (one's) head** Insane; crazy. **over (one's) head 1.** Beyond one's comprehension. **2.** Beyond one's financial means. **put heads together** To consult and plan together. [ME < OE *hēafod.* See **kaput-** in App.]

head•ache (hĕd′āk′) *n.* **1.** A pain in the head. **2.** *Informal* Something that causes annoyance or trouble.

head•band (hĕd′bănd′) *n.* **1.** A band worn around the head. **2.** *Printing* An ornamental strip at the top of a page or beginning of a chapter or paragraph. **3.** *Printing* A cloth band attached to the top of the spine of a book.

head•board (hĕd′bôrd′, -bōrd′) *n.* A board or panel that forms the head, as of a bed.

head•cheese (hĕd′chēz′) *n.* A jellied loaf or sausage made from chopped and boiled parts of the feet, head, and sometimes the tongue and heart of an animal, usu. a hog.

head cold *n.* A common cold mainly affecting the mucous membranes of the nasal passages, characterized by congestion, headache, and sneezing.

head count or **head•count** (hĕd′kount′) *n.* **1.** The act of counting people in a particular group. **2.** The number of people counted in this way.

head•dress (hĕd′drĕs′) *n.* **1.** A covering or ornament for the head. **2.** A hairdo; a coiffure.

head•ed (hĕd′ĭd) *adj.* **1.** Growing or grown into a head. **2.** Having a head or heading. **3.** Having a specified kind or number of heads. Often used in combination: *three-headed Cerberus.* **4.** Having a mentality of a certain type. Often used in combination: *a cool-headed pilot.*

head•er (hĕd′ər) *n.* **1.** One that fits a head on an object. **2.** One that removes a head from an object, esp. a machine that reaps and gathers the heads of grain. **3.** A pipe that connects two or more smaller pipes. **4.** A beam that crosses and supports the ends of joists, studs, or rafters. **5.** A brick or stone laid at a right angle to the face of a wall so that only its short end is showing. **6.** *Informal* A headlong dive or fall. **7.** *Sports* A pass or shot made in soccer by heading the ball. **8.** Textual information positioned in the top margin of a page and usu. repeated throughout a document. **9.** A raised tank or hopper that maintains a constant pressure or supply to a system, esp. the small tank that supplies water to a central heating system.

head•first (hĕd′fûrst′) also **head•fore•most** (-fôr′mōst′, -məst, -fōr′-) *adv.* **1.** With the head leading; headlong. **2.** Impetuously; brashly. —**head′first′** *adj.*

head•ful (hĕd′fo͝ol′) *n. Informal* **1.** A relatively great amount of knowledge. **2.** An amount that covers the surface of the head, usu. except for the face: *a headful of auburn curls.*

head gate *n.* **1.** A control gate upstream of a lock or canal. **2.** A floodgate that controls the flow of water, as in a ditch.

head•gear (hĕd′gîr′) *n.* **1.** A covering for the head. **2.** The part of a harness that fits about a horse's head. **3.** The rigging for hauling or lifting located at the head of a mine shaft.

head•hunt•ing (hĕd′hŭn′tĭng) *n.* **1.** The custom of cutting off and preserving the heads of enemies as trophies. **2.** *Slang* The process of attempting to remove influence and power from enemies, esp. political enemies. **3.** *Informal* The business of recruiting personnel, esp. executive personnel, as for a corporation. —**head′hunt′** *v.* & *n.* —**head′hunt′er** *n.*

head•ing (hĕd′ĭng) *n.* **1.** The title, subtitle, or topic that stands at the top or beginning, as of a paragraph, letter, or chapter. **2.** The course or direction of a ship or aircraft. **3a.** A gallery or drift in a mine. **b.** The end of a gallery or drift.

head•lamp (hĕd′lămp′) *n.* See **headlight** 1.

head•land (hĕd′lənd, -lănd′) *n.* **1.** A point of land, usu. high, extending out into a body of water; a promontory. **2.** The unplowed land at the end of a plowed furrow.

head•less (hĕd′lĭs) *adj.* **1a.** Formed without a head. **b.** Decapitated. **2.** Lacking a leader or director. **3.** Lacking intelligence and prudence; stupid or foolish. —**head′less•ness** *n.*

head•light (hĕd′līt′) *n.* **1.** A light with a reflector and lens mounted on the front of a vehicle. **2.** A lamp mounted on a miner's or spelunker's hard hat.

head•line (hĕd′līn′) *n.* **1.** The title or caption of a newspaper article, usu. set in large type. **2.** An important or sensational piece of news. Often used in the plural. **3.** A line at the head of a page

Rutherford B. Hayes

haystack

headdress
Balinese dancer with floral headdress

ă	pat	oi	boy
ā	pay	ou	out
âr	care	o͝o	took
ä	father	o͞o	boot
ĕ	pet	ŭ	cut
ē	be	ûr	urge
ĭ	pit	th	thin
ī	pie	*th*	this
îr	pier	hw	which
ŏ	pot	zh	vision
ō	toe	ə	about,
ô	paw		item

Stress marks:
′ (primary);
′ (secondary), as in
lexicon (lĕk′sĭ-kŏn′)

or passage giving information such as the title, author, and page number. ❖ *tr.v.* **-lined, -lin·ing, -lines** **1.** To supply (a page or passage) with a headline. **2a.** To present or promote as a headliner. **b.** To serve as the headliner of.

head·lin·er (hĕd′lī′nər) *n.* A performer who receives prominent billing.

head·lock (hĕd′lŏk′) *n.* A hold in which one wrestler encircles the other's head and locks it with the arm and body.

head·long (hĕd′lông′, -lŏng′) *adv.* **1.** With the head leading; headfirst. **2.** In an impetuous manner; rashly. **3.** At breakneck speed or with uncontrolled force. ❖ *adj.* (hĕd′lông′, -lŏng′) **1.** Done with the head leading; headfirst. **2.** Impetuous; rash. **3.** Uncontrollably forceful or fast. **4.** *Archaic* Steep; sheer. [< ME *(bi)hedlong*, alteration of *(bi) hedling* : *hed*, head; see HEAD + *-ling*, in a specified direction; see -LING².]

head·man (hĕd′măn′, -măn′) *n.* **1.** The chief man esp. of a tribal or traditional village. **2.** A headsman.

head·mas·ter (hĕd′măs′tər) *n.* A man who is the principal of a school, usu. a private school.

head·mis·tress (hĕd′mĭs′trĭs) *n.* A woman who is the principal of a school, usu. a private school.

head·most (hĕd′mōst′, -məst) *adj.* Leading; foremost.

head-on (hĕd′ŏn′, -ôn′) *adv.* **1.** With the head or front first. **2.** In open conflict; in direct opposition. ❖ *adj.* **1.** Facing forward; frontal. **2.** With the front end foremost.

head·phone (hĕd′fōn′) *n.* A receiver, as for a telephone, radio, or stereo, held to the ear by a headband.

head·piece (hĕd′pēs′) *n.* **1.** A protective covering for the head. **2.** A set of headphones; a headset. **3.** See **headstall**. **4.** An ornamental design, esp. at the top of a page. **5.** The seat of intelligence; brains.

head·pin (hĕd′pĭn′) *n.* *Sports* The foremost pin in an arrangement of bowling pins.

head·quar·ter (hĕd′kwôr′tər) *v.* **-tered, -ter·ing, -ters** *Usage Problem* —*tr.* To provide with headquarters. —*intr.* To establish headquarters.

> **USAGE NOTE** The verb *headquarter* occurs in both transitive and intransitive senses: *The magazine has headquartered him* (or *He headquarters*) *in a building that houses many foreign journalists.* Although ample citational evidence exists for these usages, a majority of the Usage Panel found them unacceptable in formal writing. Writers who wish to avoid criticism should consider using alternative expressions, for example: *The magazine has just assigned him to* (or *has stationed him in*) *Europe. He will make his headquarters in Paris.*

head·quar·ters (hĕd′kwôr′tərz) *pl.n.* (*used with a sing. or pl. verb*) **1.** The offices of a commander, as of a military unit, from which orders are issued. **2.** A center of operations or administration. See Syns at **center**.

> **USAGE NOTE** The noun *headquarters* is used with either a singular or a plural verb. The plural is more common: *The corporation's headquarters are in Boston.* But the singular is sometimes preferred when reference is to authority rather than to physical location: *Division headquarters has approved the plans.*

head·race (hĕd′rās′) *n.* A watercourse that feeds water into a mill, water wheel, or turbine.

head·rest (hĕd′rĕst′) *n.* **1.** A support for the head, as at the back of a chair. **2.** A cushion attached to the top of the back of an automotive vehicle's seat, esp. to prevent whiplash.

head·room (hĕd′rōōm′, -rŏŏm′) *n.* **1.** Space above one's head; clearance. **2.** *Electronics* The capacity of an amplifier to reproduce unusually strong signals without distortion.

head·sail (hĕd′səl, -sāl′) *n.* *Nautical* A sail, such as a jib, set forward of a foremast.

head·set (hĕd′sĕt′) *n.* **1.** A pair of headphones. **2.** A pair of headphones with a voice transmitter attached.

head·ship (hĕd′shĭp′) *n.* **1.** The position or office of a head or leader; primacy or command. **2.** *Chiefly British* The position of a headmaster or headmistress.

head·shrink·er (hĕd′shrĭng′kər) *n.* **1.** A headhunter who dries and shrinks the heads of enemies. **2.** *Slang* A psychiatrist, esp. a psychoanalyst.

heads·man (hĕdz′mən) *n.* A public executioner who beheads condemned prisoners.

head·spring (hĕd′sprĭng′) *n.* A fountainhead; a source.

head·stall (hĕd′stôl′) *n.* The section of a bridle that fits over a horse's head.

head·stand (hĕd′stănd′) *n.* A position in which one supports oneself vertically on one's head with one's hands.

head start *n.* **1.** *Sports* A start before other contestants in a race. **2.** An early start that confers an advantage.

head·stock (hĕd′stŏk′) *n.* A nonmoving part of a machine or power tool that supports a revolving part, such as the spindle of a lathe.

head·stone (hĕd′stōn′) *n.* **1.** A memorial stone set at the head of a grave. **2.** also **head stone** *Architecture* See **keystone** 1.

head·stream (hĕd′strēm′) *n.* A stream that is a source of a river.

head·strong (hĕd′strông′, -strŏng′) *adj.* **1.** Stubbornly and often recklessly willful. See Syns at **obstinate, unruly**. **2.** Result-

ing from willfulness and obstinacy.

heads up (hĕdz) *interj.* Used as a warning to watch out for a potential source of danger, as at a construction site.

heads-up (hĕdz′ŭp′) *adj.* Showing an alert competent style. *n.* *Informal* Information or notification, esp. in advance: *gave me the heads-up on the new security measures.*

head-to-head (hĕd′tə-hĕd′) *adv. & adj.* **1.** In direct confrontation or conflict at close quarters. **2.** Arranged in a line with the heads adjacent to each other. **3.** Running close together in the same direction; neck and neck.

head·wait·er (hĕd′wā′tər) *n.* The supervisor of the waiters and waitresses in a restaurant, often responsible for taking reservations and seating guests.

head wall *n.* A steep slope or precipice rising at the head of a valley or glacial cirque.

head·wa·ter (hĕd′wô′tər, -wŏt′ər) *n.* The water from which a river rises; a source. Often used in the plural.

head·way (hĕd′wā′) *n.* **1.** Forward movement or the rate of forward movement, esp. of a ship. **2.** Progress toward a goal. **3.** The clear vertical space beneath a ceiling or archway; clearance. **4.** The distance in time or space that separates two vehicles traveling the same route.

head·wind or **head wind** (hĕd′wĭnd′) *n.* A wind blowing directly against the course of an aircraft or ship.

head·word (hĕd′wûrd′) *n.* A word, phrase, or name, usu. set in boldface or other distinctive type, that serves as the heading for an entry in a reference work.

head·work (hĕd′wûrk′) *n.* Mental activity or work; thought.

head·y (hĕd′ē) *adj.* **-i·er, -i·est** **1a.** Intoxicating or stupefying. **b.** Tending to upset the mind or the balance of senses. **c.** Serving to exhilarate. **2a.** Impetuous and rash. **b.** Domineering; overbearing. **3.** Swift and violent; headlong: *a heady current.* **4.** Showing intelligence and good judgment; prudent. **5.** Suffering from a headache. —**head′i·ly** *adv.* —**head′i·ness** *n.*

heal (hēl) *v.* **healed, heal·ing, heals** —*tr.* **1.** To restore to health or soundness; cure. See Syns at **cure**. **2.** To set right; repair. **3.** To restore (a person) to spiritual wholeness. —*intr.* To become whole and sound; return to health. [ME *helen* < OE *hǣlan.* See **kailo-** in App.] —**heal′a·ble** *adj.*

heal·er (hē′lər) *n.* One that heals or attempts to heal, esp. a faith healer.

health (hĕlth) *n.* **1.** The overall condition of an organism at a given time. **2.** Soundness, esp. of body or mind; freedom from disease or abnormality. **3.** A condition of optimal well-being. **4.** A wish for someone's good health, often expressed as a toast. [ME *helthe* < OE *hǣlth.* See **kailo-** in App.]

health care also **health·care** (hĕlth′kâr′) *n.* The prevention, treatment, and management of illness and the preservation of well-being through the services offered by the medical and allied health professions. —**health′-care′, health′care** *adj.*

health food *n.* A food believed to be beneficial to health, esp. a food grown organically and free of chemical additives.

health·ful (hĕlth′fəl) *adj.* **1.** Conducive to good health; salutary. **2.** Healthy. See Usage Note at **healthy**. —**health′ful·ly** *adv.* —**health′ful·ness** *n.*

health insurance *n.* Insurance against expenses incurred through illness of the insured.

health maintenance organization *n.* An HMO.

health spa *n.* A business establishment with equipment and facilities for exercising and improving physical fitness.

health·y (hĕl′thē) *adj.* **-i·er, -i·est** **1.** Possessing good health. **2.** Conducive to good health; healthful. **3.** Indicative of sound rational thinking or frame of mind. **4.** Sizable; considerable. —**health′i·ly** *adv.* —**health′i·ness** *n.*

> **SYNONYMS** *healthy, sound, wholesome, hale, robust, well, hardy, vigorous* These adjectives mean being in or indicative of good physical or mental health. *Healthy* stresses the absence of disease and often implies energy and strength: *a rosy, healthy infant.* *Sound* emphasizes freedom from injury, imperfection, or impairment: "The man with the toothache thinks everyone happy whose teeth are sound" (George Bernard Shaw). *Wholesome* suggests appealing healthiness and well-being: "Exercise develops wholesome appetites" (Louisa May Alcott). *Hale* stresses freedom from infirmity, especially in elderly persons, while *robust* emphasizes healthy strength and ruggedness: "He is pretty well advanced in years, but hale, robust, and florid" (Tobias Smollett). *Well* indicates absence of or recovery from sickness: *Stay home from work if you're not well.* *Hardy* implies robust and sturdy good health: *hardy mountaineers.* *Vigorous* suggests healthy, active energy and strength: *a vigorous old man who jogged every day.*

> **USAGE NOTE** Some language critics have insisted since the 1880s that a distinction should be made between *healthy* ("possessing good health") and *healthful* ("conducive to good health"). But citational evidence clearly indicates that *healthy* and *healthful* have shared the meaning "conducive to good health" since at least the mid-16th century. Therefore, both *healthy* and *healthful* are correct in these contexts: *a healthy (healthful) climate; a healthful (healthy) diet.* Few readers are likely to appreciate a distinction made between these two words.

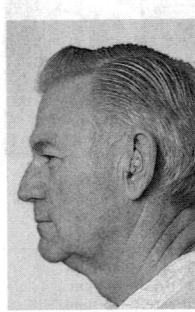

hearing aid

heap (hēp) *n.* **1.** A group of things placed or thrown one on top of the other. **2.** *Informal* A great deal; a lot. Often used in the plural: *heaps of homework.* **3.** *Slang* An old or run-down car. ❖ *tr.v.* **heaped, heap•ing, heaps 1.** To put or throw in a pile. **2.** To fill completely or to overflowing. **3.** To bestow in abundance or lavishly. [ME < OE *hēap.*]

hear (hîr) *v.* **heard** (hûrd), **hear•ing, hears** —*tr.* **1.** To perceive (sound) by the ear. **2.** To learn by hearing; be told by others. **3a.** To listen to attentively. **b.** To listen to in an official, professional, or formal capacity. **c.** To listen to and consider favorably. **d.** To attend or participate in: *hear Mass.* —*intr.* **1.** To be capable of perceiving sound. **2.** To receive news or information; learn. **3.** To consider, permit, or consent to something. Used only in the negative: *I won't hear of your going!* ***—phrasal verb:*** **hear from 1.** To get a letter, telephone call, or transmitted communication from. **2.** To be reprimanded by. ***—idiom:*** **hear, hear** Used to express approval. [ME *hearen,* OE *hīeran.* See **kous-** in App.] —**hear′er** *n.*

hear•ing (hîr′ĭng) *n.* **1.** The sense by which sound is perceived; the capacity to hear. **2.** Range of audibility; earshot. **3.** An opportunity to be heard. **4.** *Law* **a.** A preliminary examination of an accused person. **b.** The trial of an equity case. **5.** A session at which testimony is taken from witnesses. ❖ *adj.* Able to hear.

hearing aid *n.* A small electronic sound amplifier worn in or behind the ear that compensates for impaired hearing.

hear•ing-im•paired (hîr′ĭng-ĭm-pârd′) *adj.* **1.** Having a diminished or defective sense of hearing, but not deaf; hard of hearing. **2.** Completely incapable of hearing; deaf. ❖ *n.* (*used with a pl. verb*) Persons who are deficient in hearing or are deaf.

hear•ken also **har•ken** (här′kən) *v.* **-kened, -ken•ing, -kens** —*intr.* To listen attentively; give heed. —*tr. Archaic* To listen to; hear. [ME *herknen* < OE *hercnian.* See **kous-** in App.]

Hearn (hûrn), **Lafcadio** 1850–1904. Greek-born Amer. writer whose works include *Chita* (1887).

hear•say (hîr′sā′) *n.* **1.** Unverified information received from another. **2.** *Law* Evidence based on the reports of others and therefore generally not admissible as testimony.

hearse (hûrs) *n.* **1.** A vehicle for conveying a coffin to a church or cemetery. **2.** *Roman Catholic Church* A triangular candelabrum used at Tenebrae. **3.** A framelike structure over a coffin or tomb on which to hang epitaphs. [ME *herse,* a harrow-shaped structure for holding candles over a coffin < OFr. *herce* < Med.Lat. *hercia* < Lat. *hirpex, hirpic-,* harrow, prob. < Oscan *hirpus,* wolf (alluding to its teeth).]

Hearst (hûrst), **William Randolph** 1863–1951. Amer. newspaper and magazine publisher who built the world's largest publishing empire, comprising 28 major newspapers.

heart (härt) *n.* **1.** *Anatomy* **a.** The chambered muscular organ in vertebrates that pumps blood through the entire circulatory system. **b.** A similarly functioning structure in invertebrates. **2.** The area that is the approximate location of the heart in the body; the breast. **3a.** The vital center and source of one's being, emotions, and sensibilities. **b.** The repository of one's deepest and sincerest feelings and beliefs. **c.** The seat of the intellect or imagination. **4a.** Emotional constitution, basic disposition, or character. **b.** One's prevailing mood or current inclination. **5a.** Capacity for sympathy or generosity; compassion. **b.** Love; affection: *won my heart.* **6a.** Courage; resolution; fortitude. **b.** The firmness of will or the callousness required to carry out an unpleasant task or responsibility. **7.** A person esteemed or admired as lovable, loyal, or courageous: *a dear heart.* **8a.** The central or innermost physical part of a place or region. See Syns at **center. b.** The core of a plant, fruit, or vegetable. **9.** The most important or essential part. **10.** A conventional two-lobed, usu. red or pink representation of the heart. **11.** *Games* **a.** A red heart-shaped figure on certain playing cards. **b.** A playing card with this figure. **c. hearts** (*used with a sing. or pl. verb*) The suit of cards represented by this figure. **d.** A card game in which the object is either to avoid hearts when taking tricks or to take all the hearts. ❖ *tr.v.* **heart•ed, heart•ing, hearts** *Archaic* To encourage; hearten. ***—idioms:*** **at heart** In one's deepest feelings; fundamentally. **by heart** Learned by rote; memorized. **do (one's) heart good** To lift one's spirits; make one happy. **from the bottom** (or **depths**) **of (one's) heart** With the deepest appreciation; most sincerely. **have (one's) heart in (one's) mouth** To be extremely frightened or anxious. **have (one's) heart in the right place** To be well-intentioned. **heart and soul** Completely; entirely. **in (one's) heart of hearts** In the seat of one's truest feelings. **lose (one's) heart to** To fall in love with. **near** (or **close to**) **(one's) heart** Loved by or important to one. **steal (someone's) heart** To win one's affection or love. **take to heart** To take seriously and be affected or troubled by. **to (one's) heart's content** To one's entire satisfaction, without limitation. **wear (one's) heart on (one's) sleeve** To show one's feelings clearly by one's behavior. **with all (one's) heart 1.** With great willingness or pleasure. **2.** With the deepest feeling or devotion. **with half a heart** In a halfhearted manner. [ME *hert* < OE *heorte.* See **kerd-** in App.]

heart•ache (härt′āk′) *n.* Emotional anguish; sorrow.

heart attack *n.* Sudden interruption or insufficiency of blood supply to the heart typically resulting from occlusion or obstruction of a coronary artery and often marked by severe chest pain.

heart•beat (härt′bēt′) *n.* **1.** A single complete pulsation of the heart. **2.** A vital force or driving impulse. **3.** An instant: *was ready in a heartbeat.*

heart block *n.* A condition in which the atria and ventricles of the heart contract independently as a result of faulty transmission of the impulses that control the heartbeat.

heart•break (härt′brāk′) *n.* Overwhelming sorrow, grief, or disappointment.

heart•break•er (härt′brā′kər) *n.* **1.** One that causes sorrow, grief, or disappointment. **2.** *Sports & Games* A narrow or last-minute defeat.

heart•break•ing (härt′brā′kĭng) *adj.* **1.** Causing overwhelming grief or distress. **2.** Producing a strong emotional reaction. —**heart′break′ing•ly** *adv.*

heart•bro•ken (härt′brō′kən) *adj.* Suffering from or exhibiting overwhelming sorrow, grief, or disappointment. —**heart′bro′ken•ly** *adv.* —**heart′bro′ken•ness** *n.*

heart•burn (härt′bûrn′) *n.* A burning sensation, usu. near the sternum, caused by the reflux of acidic stomach fluids into the lower end of the esophagus.

heart disease *n.* A structural or functional abnormality of the heart that impairs its normal functioning.

heart•en (här′tn) *tr.v.* **-ened, -en•ing, -ens** To give strength, courage, or hope to; encourage.

heart failure *n.* **1.** Cessation of normal heart function. **2.** The inability of the heart to pump adequately, resulting in shortness of breath and edema in the lower extremities.

heart•felt (härt′fĕlt′) *adj.* Deeply or sincerely felt; earnest.

hearth (härth) *n.* **1.** The brick, stone, or cement floor of a fireplace, usu. extending into a room. **2.** Family life; the home. **3.** *Metallurgy* **a.** The lowest part of a blast furnace or cupola, from which the molten metal flows. **b.** The bottom of a reverberatory furnace, where ore is exposed to the flame. **4.** The fireplace or brazier of a blacksmith's forge. [ME *herth* < OE *heorth.*]

hearth•stone (härth′stōn′) *n.* **1.** Stone used in the construction of a hearth. **2.** Family life; the home. **3.** A soft stone or composition of pipe clay and pulverized stone used for scouring and whitening hearths or doorsteps.

heart•i•ly (här′tl-ē) *adv.* **1.** With warmth and sincerity; cordially: *She greeted us heartily.* **2.** Thoroughly; completely: *wished heartily that they would leave.* **3.** With zest or enthusiasm. **4.** With great appetite or enjoyment.

heart•land (härt′lănd′) *n.* A central region, esp. one that is politically, economically, or militarily vital to a nation, region, or culture.

heart•less (härt′lĭs) *adj.* **1.** Devoid of compassion or feeling; pitiless. **2.** *Archaic* Devoid of courage or enthusiasm; spiritless. —**heart′less•ly** *adv.* —**heart′less•ness** *n.*

heart-lung machine (härt′lŭng′) *n.* An apparatus through which blood is temporarily diverted, esp. during heart surgery, to oxygenate it and pump it throughout the body.

heart-rend•ing or **heart•rend•ing** (härt′rĕn′dĭng) *adj.* Causing anguish or deep distress; arousing deep sympathy.

hearts•ease also **heart's-ease** (härts′ēz′) *n.* **1.** Peace of mind. **2.** A hybrid plant derived from crossing certain species of the genus *Viola* and having small spurred flowers.

heart•sick (härt′sĭk′) *adj.* Profoundly disappointed; despondent. —**heart′sick′ness** *n.*

heart•string (härt′strĭng′) *n.* **1. heartstrings** The deepest feelings or affections. **2.** One of the nerves or tendons formerly believed to brace and sustain the heart.

heart•throb (härt′thrŏb′) *n.* **1.** A pulsation of the heart; a heartbeat. **2a.** Sentimental or tender emotion. **b.** Infatuation. **3a.** A sweetheart. **b.** The object of one's infatuation.

heart-to-heart (härt′tə-härt′) *adj.* Candid; frank. ❖ *n.* An intimate conversation in private.

heart•warm•ing or **heart-warm•ing** (härt′wôr′mĭng) *adj.* Causing gladness and tender feelings.

heart•wood (härt′wo͝od′) *n.* The older, nonliving central wood of a tree or woody plant, usu. dark in color.

heart•worm (härt′wûrm′) *n.* **1.** A filarial worm (*Dirofilaria immitis*) transmitted by mosquitoes and parasitic in the heart and associated blood vessels of dogs and other canids. **2.** The condition resulting from infestation with the heartworm.

heart•y (här′tē) *adj.* **-i•er, -i•est 1.** Expressed warmly, exuberantly, and unrestrainedly. **2.** Complete or thorough; unequivocal. **3.** Vigorous; robust. **4a.** Enjoying or requiring much food: *a hearty appetite.* **b.** Providing abundant nourishment. ❖ *n., pl.* **-ies 1.** A good fellow; a comrade. **2.** A sailor. —**heart′i•ness** *n.*

heat (hēt) *n.* **1.** *Physics* **a.** A form of energy associated with the motion of atoms and capable of being transmitted by conduction, convection, or radiation. **b.** The transfer of energy between bodies as a result of a difference in temperature or a change in phase. **2.** The sensation or perception of such energy as warmth or hotness. **3.** An abnormally high bodily temperature. **4a.** The condition of being hot. **b.** A degree of warmth or hotness: *The burner was on low heat.* **5a.** The warming of a room or building by a furnace or another source of energy. **b.** A furnace or other source of warmth in a room or building. **6.** A hot season; a spell of hot weather. **7a.** Intensity, as of passion, emotion, color, appearance, or effect. **b.** The most intense or active stage. **c.** A burn-

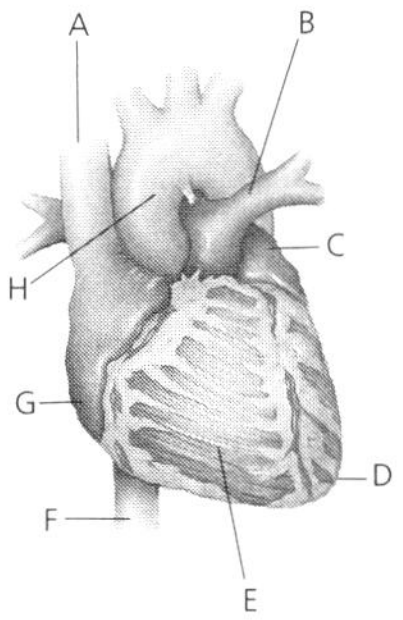

heart
A. superior vena cava
B. pulmonary artery
C. left atrium
D. left ventricle
E. right ventricle
F. inferior vena cava
G. right atrium
H. aorta

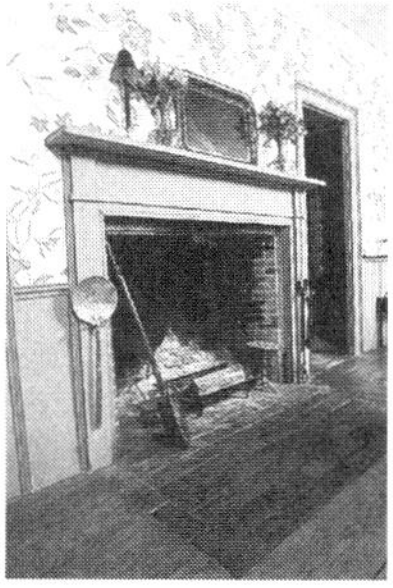

hearth

ă	pat	oi	boy
ā	pay	ou	out
âr	care	o͝o	took
ä	father	o͞o	boot
ĕ	pet	ŭ	cut
ē	be	ûr	urge
ĭ	pit	th	thin
ī	pie	*th*	this
îr	pier	hw	which
ŏ	pot	zh	vision
ō	toe	ə	about, item
ô	paw		

Stress marks:
′ (primary);
′ (secondary), as in
lexicon (lĕk′sĭ-kŏn′)

ing sensation in the mouth produced by spicy flavoring. **8.** Estrus. **9.** One of a series of efforts or attempts. **10a.** *Sports & Games* One round of several in a competition, such as a race. **b.** A preliminary contest held to determine finalists. **11.** *Informal* Pressure; stress. **12.** *Slang* **a.** An intensification of police activity in pursuing criminals. **b.** The police. **13.** *Slang* Adverse comments or hostile criticism. **14.** *Slang* A firearm, esp. a pistol. ❖ *v.* **heat·ed, heat· ing, heats** —*tr.* **1.** To make warm or hot. **2.** To excite the feelings of; inflame. **3.** To increase the molecular or kinetic energy of (an object). —*intr.* **1.** To become warm or hot. **2.** To become excited emotionally or intellectually. —*phrasal verb:* **heat up** *Informal* To become acute or intense. [ME *hete* < OE *hætu*.]

heat capacity *n.* The amount of heat required to raise the temperature of a substance or a system by one degree.

heat·ed (hē′tĭd) *adj.* Angry; vehement; impassioned. —**heat′ed·ly** *adv.*

heat·er (hē′tər) *n.* **1.** An apparatus that heats or provides heat. **2.** One who heats something or tends a heating apparatus. **3.** *Slang* A pistol.

heat exchanger *n.* A device used to transfer heat from one fluid to another without direct contact of the fluids.

heat exhaustion *n.* A condition caused by exposure to heat, resulting in the depletion of body fluids and causing weakness, dizziness, nausea, and often collapse.

heath (hēth) *n.* **1.** Any of various usu. low-growing evergreen shrubs of the genus *Erica* and related genera, native to Europe and South Africa and having small colorful urn-shaped flowers. **2.** An extensive tract of uncultivated open land covered with herbage and low shrubs; a moor. [ME, uncultivated land < OE *hæth*.]

Heath, Edward Richard George b. 1916. British politician who served as prime minister (1970–74).

hea·then (hē′thən) *n., pl.* **-thens** or **heathen 1a.** One who adheres to a religion that does not acknowledge the God of Judaism, Christianity, or Islam. **b.** Such persons considered as a group. **2a.** One who is regarded as irreligious, uncivilized, or unenlightened. **b.** Such persons considered as a group. [ME *hethen* < OE *hæthen.*] —**hea′then** *adj.* —**hea′then·dom, hea′then·ism, hea′then·ry** *n.*

hea·then·ish (hē′thə-nĭsh) *adj.* **1.** Of or having to do with heathens. **2.** Uncouth; barbarous.

heath·er (hĕth′ər) *n.* **1.** A low-growing Eurasian evergreen shrub (*Calluna vulgaris*) having small, bell-shaped, pinkish-purple flowers. **2.** See **heath** 1. **3.** A grayish purple to purplish red. [Alteration (influenced by HEATH) of ME *hather*, prob. < OE **hæddre.*] —**heath′er** *adj.*

heath·er·y (hĕth′ə-rē) *adj.* **1.** Of, relating to, or resembling heather. **2.** Flecked with various colors.

heath hen *n.* A now extinct subspecies of the prairie chicken (*Tympanuchus cupido* subsp. *cupido*) of North America.

heat index *n.* A measurement of the air temperature in relation to the relative humidity, used as an indicator of the perceived temperature.

heat lightning *n.* Intermittent flashes of light near the horizon, usu. seen on a hot summer evening, unaccompanied by thunder and thought to be cloud reflections of distant lightning.

heat of combustion *n.* The amount of heat released per unit mass or unit volume of a substance when the substance is completely burned.

heat prostration *n.* See **heat exhaustion.**

heat pump *n.* A device that warms or cools a building by transferring heat from a relatively low-temperature reservoir to one at a higher temperature.

heat rash *n.* An inflammatory skin condition caused by obstruction of the sweat gland ducts, resulting from exposure to high heat and humidity and characterized by red papules and an itching or prickling sensation.

heat shield *n.* A barrier that prevents the heating of a space or an object, esp. a protective structure on a spacecraft or missile that dissipates heat on atmospheric reentry.

heat sink *n.* **1.** An environment capable of absorbing heat from an object with which it is in thermal contact. **2.** A protective device that absorbs and dissipates excess heat.

heat stroke *n.* A severe condition resulting from prolonged exposure to heat and characterized by cessation of sweating and high fever that can lead to loss of consciousness and coma.

heat-treat (hēt′trēt′) *tr.v.* **-treat·ed, -treat·ing, -treats** To treat (metal, for example) by alternate heating and cooling in order to produce desired characteristics, such as increased hardness; temper. —**heat treater** *n.* —**heat treatment** *n.*

heat wave *n.* A period of unusually hot weather.

heave (hēv) *v.* **heaved, heav·ing, heaves** —*tr.* **1.** To raise or lift, esp. with great effort or force. See Syns at **lift. 2a.** To throw (a heavy object) with great effort; hurl. **b.** To throw or toss. **3.** To utter with effort or pain. **4.** To vomit (something). **5.** *past tense and past participle* **hove** (hōv) *Nautical* **a.** To raise or haul up by means of a rope, line, or cable. **b.** To move (a ship) in a certain direction or into a certain position by hauling. **6.** To make rise or swell: *the wind heaving waves.* **7.** *Geology* To displace or move (a vein, lode, or stratum, for example). —*intr.* **1.** To rise up or swell, as if pushed up; bulge. **2.** To rise and fall in turn, as waves. **3.** To

gag or vomit. **4.** *past tense and past participle* **hove** *Nautical* **a.** To move in a certain direction or to a specified position. **b.** To pull at or haul a rope or cable. **c.** To push at a capstan bar or lever. ❖ *n.* **1.** The effort of heaving. **2.** An act of hurling; a throw, esp. when considered in terms of distance. **3.** *Geology* A horizontal dislocation, as of a rock stratum, at a fault. **4.** An upward movement. **5.** The act or an instance of gagging or vomiting. **6. heaves** (*used with a sing. or pl. verb*) A pulmonary disease of horses that is characterized by respiratory irregularities, such as coughing, and is noticeable esp. after exercise or in cold weather. —*phrasal verb:* **heave to** *Nautical* **1.** To turn a sailing ship so that its bow heads into the wind and the ship lies motionless except for drifting, in order to meet a storm. **2.** To turn an engine-powered vessel in a similar situation so that its bow heads into the seas while proceeding at low speed. [ME *heven* < OE *hebban.* See **kap-** in App.] —**heav′er** *n.*

heave ho *interj.* Used as a command to sailors to pull on a rope or cable.

heave-ho (hēv′hō′) *n. Slang* Dismissal, as from one's job.

heav·en (hĕv′ən) *n.* **1.** The sky or universe as seen from earth; the firmament. Often used in the plural. **2.** *Christianity* **a.** often **Heaven** The abode of God, the angels, and the souls of those who are granted salvation. **b.** An eternal state of communion with God; everlasting bliss. **3.** Any of the places in or beyond the sky conceived of as domains of divine beings in various religions. **4a. Heaven** God: *Heaven help you!* **b. heavens** Used in various phrases to express surprise: *Good heavens!* **5.** The celestial powers; the gods. Often used in the plural. **6.** A condition or place of great happiness, delight, or pleasure: *The lake was heaven.* —*idiom:* **move heaven and earth** To do everything possible to bring about something desired. [ME *heven* < OE *heofon.* See **ak-** in App.]

heav·en·ly (hĕv′ən-lē) *adj.* **1.** Sublime; delightful; enchanting. **2.** Of or relating to the firmament; celestial. **3.** Of or relating to the abode of God; divine. —**heav′en·li·ness** *n.*

heav·en-sent (hĕv′ən-sĕnt′) *adj.* Occurring at an opportune time; providential.

heav·en·ward (hĕv′ən-wərd) *adv. & adj.* Toward, to, or in heaven. —**heav′en·wards** (-wərdz) *adv.*

heav·i·er-than-air (hĕv′ē-ər-thən-âr′) *adj.* Of, relating to, or being an aircraft heavier than the air it displaces.

heav·i·ly (hĕv′ə-lē) *adv.* **1.** With a great weight or burden. **2.** Very slowly and with difficulty; laboriously. **3.** Greatly or severely: *heavily in debt.*

Heav·i·side layer (hĕv′ē-sīd′) *n.* See **E layer.** [After Oliver Heaviside (1850–1925), British physicist.]

heav·y (hĕv′ē) *adj.* **-i·er, -i·est 1.** Having relatively great weight. **2.** Having relatively high density; having a high specific gravity. **3a.** Large, as in number or quantity. **b.** Large in yield or output: *heavy rainfall.* **4.** Of great intensity: *heavy activity.* **5a.** Having great power or force. **b.** Violent; rough: *heavy seas.* **6a.** Equipped with massive armaments and weapons. **b.** Large enough to fire powerful shells. **7a.** Indulging to a great degree. **b.** Involved or participating on a large scale. **8.** Of great import or seriousness; grave. **9a.** Having considerable thickness: *a heavy coat.* **b.** Broad or coarse: *drew the face with heavy lines.* **10a.** Dense; thick: *a heavy fog.* **b.** Slow to dissipate; strong: *a heavy scent.* **c.** Too dense or rich to digest easily. **d.** Insufficiently leavened: *heavy bread.* **e.** Full of clay and readily saturated: *heavy soil.* **11a.** Weighed down; burdened: *trees heavy with plums.* **b.** Emotionally weighed down; despondent. **c.** Marked by or exhibiting weariness. **d.** Sad or painful: *heavy news.* **12a.** Hard to do or accomplish; arduous. **b.** Not easily borne; oppressive. **13.** Lacking vitality; deficient in vivacity or grace. **14.** Sharply inclined; steep: *a heavy grade.* **15.** Having a large capacity or designed for rough work. **16.** Of, relating to, or involving the large-scale production of basic products, such as steel. **17.** Of or relating to a serious dramatic role. **18.** *Physics* Of or relating to an isotope with an atomic mass greater than the average mass of that element. **19.** Loud; sonorous. **20.** *Linguistics* Of, relating to, or being a syllable ending in a long vowel or in a vowel plus two consonants. **21.** *Slang* **a.** Of great significance or profundity. **b.** Very popular or important. ❖ *adv.* **-i·er, -i·est** Heavily. ❖ *n., pl.* **-ies 1a.** A serious or tragic role in a play. **b.** An actor playing such a role. **2.** *Slang* A villain in a story or play. **3.** *Slang* A mobster. **4.** *Slang* One that is very important or influential. [ME *hevi* < OE *hefig.* See **kap-** in App.] —**heav′i·ness** *n.*

heav·y-dut·y (hĕv′ē-dōō′tē, -dyōō′-) *adj.* Made to withstand hard use or wear.

heav·y-foot·ed (hĕv′ē-fŏŏt′ĭd) *adj.* Having a ponderous, lumbering gait.

heav·y-hand·ed (hĕv′ē-hăn′dĭd) *adj.* **1.** Clumsy; awkward. **2.** Tactless; indiscreet. **3.** Oppressive; harsh. —**heav′y-hand′ed· ness** *n.*

heav·y-heart·ed (hĕv′ē-här′tĭd) *adj.* Melancholy; depressed; sad. —**heav′y-heart′ed·ly** *adv.* —**heav′y-heart′ed·ness** *n.*

heavy hitter *n. Informal* A person who is important or influential.

heavy hydrogen *n.* An isotope of hydrogen with mass number greater than 1; deuterium or tritium.

heav·y-lad·en (hĕv′ē-lād′n) *adj.* **1.** Loaded with great weight. **2.** Burdened with grievous cares.

heavy lifting n. Slang Serious or difficult activities or work.

heavy metal n. **1.** A metal with a specific gravity greater than about 5.0, esp. one that is poisonous, such as lead or mercury. **2.** Music Very loud, brash rock music, often with shouted, violent lyrics.

heav•y•set (hĕv′ē-sĕt′) adj. Having a stout or compact build.

heavy spar n. See **barite**.

heavy water n. An isotopic form of water, esp. deuterium oxide, that consists chiefly of molecules containing heavy hydrogen and is used as a moderator in certain nuclear reactors.

heav•y•weight (hĕv′ē-wāt′) n. **1.** One of above average weight. **2a.** A professional boxer in the heaviest weight class, usu. weighing more than 190 pounds (85.5 kilograms). **b.** A contestant in other sports in the heaviest weight class. **3.** Informal A person of great importance or influence. —**heav′y•weight′** adj.

Heb. abbr. **1.** Hebrew **2.** Bible Hebrews

heb•do•mad (hĕb′də-mād′) n. **1.** A group of seven. **2.** A period of seven days; a week. [Lat. hebdomas, hebdomad-, the number seven < Gk. < hebdomos, seventh < hepta, seven. See **septm̥** in App.]

heb•dom•a•dal (hĕb-dŏm′ə-dəl) adj. Weekly.

He•be (hē′bē) n. Greek Mythology The goddess of youth and spring, cupbearer to the Olympian gods.

He•bei (hŭ′bā′) also **Ho•pei** or **Ho•peh** (hō′pā′, hŭ′bā′) A province of NE China bordering on the Bo Hai. Cap. Shijiazhuang. Pop. 61,082,439.

he•be•phre•ni•a (hē′bə-frē′nē-ə, -frĕn′ē-) n. A type of schizophrenia characterized by senseless laughter, delusions, hallucinations, and regressive behavior. [Gk. hēbē, youth + –PHRENIA.] —**he′be•phren′ic** (-frĕn′ĭk) adj.

heb•e•tate (hĕb′ĭ-tāt′) tr.v. **-tat•ed, -tat•ing, -tates** To make obtuse or dull. [Lat. hebetāre, hebetāt- < hebes, hebet-, blunt.] —**heb′e•ta′tion** n. —**heb′e•ta′tive** adj.

heb•e•tude (hĕb′ĭ-tood′, -tyood′) n. Dullness of mind; mental lethargy. [LLat. hebetūdō < Lat. hebes, hebet-, dull.] —**heb′e•tu′di•nous** (-tood′n-əs, -tyood′-) adj.

He•bra•ic (hĭ-brā′ĭk) also **He•bra•i•cal** (-ĭ-kəl) adj. Of, relating to, or characteristic of the Hebrews or their language or culture. [ME Ebraik < LLat. Hebrāicus < Gk. Hebraikos < Hebraios. See HEBREW.] —**He•bra′i•cal•ly** adv.

He•bra•ism (hē′brā-ĭz′əm) n. **1.** A manner or custom characteristic of the Hebrews. **2.** A linguistic feature typical of Hebrew occurring esp. in another language. **3.** The culture, spirit, or character of the Hebrew people. **4.** Judaism.

He•bra•ist (hē′brā′ĭst) n. A scholar who specializes in the study of Hebrew. —**He′bra•is′tic, He′bra•is′ti•cal** adj.

He•bra•ize (hē′brā-īz′) v. **-ized, -iz•ing, -iz•es** —tr. To make Hebraic in form or idiom. —intr. To use or adopt Hebraisms. —**He′bra•i•za′tion** (-ī-zā′shən) n.

He•brew (hē′broo) n. **1.** A member or descendant of a Semitic people claiming descent from Abraham, Isaac, and Jacob; an Israelite; a Jew. **2a.** The Semitic language of the ancient Hebrews. **b.** Any of the later forms of this language, esp. Modern Hebrew. **3.** Hebrews (used with a sing. verb) See table at **Bible**. [ME Ebreu < OFr. < Lat. Hebraeus, Hebraic < Gk. Hebraios < Aram. 'ibrāy < Heb. 'ibrî.] —**He′brew** adj.

Hebrew Bible n. The Hebrew Scriptures.

Hebrew Scriptures pl.n. The Torah, the Prophets, and the Writings, forming the covenant between God and the Jewish people that is the foundation and Bible of Judaism while constituting for Christians the Old Testament. See table at **Bible**.

Heb•ri•des (hĕb′rĭ-dēz′) also **Western Islands** An island group of W Scotland in the Atlantic Ocean, divided into the **Inner Hebrides**, near the mainland, and the **Outer Hebrides**, to the NW. —**Heb′ri•de′an** adj. & n.

He•bron (hĕb′rən, -rŏn′, hē′brən) A city of the West Bank SSW of Jerusalem; according to the Bible, the burial place of Abraham and Sarah. Pop. 79,089.

Hec•a•te or **Hek•a•te** (hĕk′ə-tē, hĕk′ĭt) n. Greek Mythology An ancient fertility goddess who later became associated with Persephone as queen of Hades and protector of witches.

hec•a•tomb (hĕk′ə-tōm′) n. **1.** A large sacrifice or slaughter. **2.** A sacrifice to the ancient Greek and Roman gods, originally 100 oxen or cattle. [Lat. hecatombē < Gk. hekatombē : hekaton, hundred; see **dekm̥** in App. + -bē, oxen; see **gʷou-** in App.]

Hecht (hĕkt), **Ben** 1894–1964. Amer. writer of short stories, novels, and dramas, including The Front Page (1928), written with Charles MacArthur.

heck (hĕk) interj. Used as a mild oath. ❖ n. Slang Used as an intensive: was crowded as heck. [Alteration of HELL.]

heck•le (hĕk′əl) tr.v. **-led, -ling, -les 1.** To try to embarrass or annoy (someone speaking or performing in public), as with questions or objections. **2.** To comb (flax or hemp) with a hatchel. [ME hekelen, to comb with a hatchel < hekel, hatchel < MDu.] —**heck′ler** n.

hec•tare (hĕk′târ′) n. A metric unit of area equal to 100 ares (2.471 acres).

hec•tic (hĕk′tĭk) adj. **1.** Characterized by intense activity, confusion, or haste. **2.** Medicine Of, relating to, or being a fever that fluctuates during the day, as in tuberculosis. **3.** Consumptive; feverish. **4.** Flushed. [ME etik, recurring, consumptive < OFr. etique

< LLat. hecticus < Gk. hektikos < hexis, habit < ekhein, to be in a certain condition. See **segh-** in App.]

hecto– or **hect–** pref. One hundred (10²): hectare. [Fr., alteration of Gk. hekaton, hundred. See **dekm̥** in App.]

hec•to•graph (hĕk′tə-grăf′) n. A machine employing a glycerin-coated layer of gelatin in order to make copies of typed or written material. —**hec′to•graph′** v. —**hec′to•graph′ic** adj. —**hec′to•graph′i•cal•ly** adv.

hec•to•li•ter (hĕk′tə-lē′tər) n. A metric unit of volume equal to 100 liters.

hec•tor (hĕk′tər) n. A bully. ❖ v. **-tored, -tor•ing, -tors** —tr. To bully in a blustering way. —intr. To behave like a bully; swagger. [Lat. Hectōr, Hector < Gk. Hektōr.]

Hector n. Greek Mythology A Trojan prince, the eldest son of Priam and Hecuba, killed by Achilles in Homer's Iliad.

Hec•u•ba (hĕk′yə-bə) n. Greek Mythology The wife of Priam and mother of Hector, Paris, and Cassandra in Homer's Iliad.

he'd (hēd) **1.** Contraction of he had. **2.** Contraction of he would.

hed•dle (hĕd′l) n. One of a set of parallel cords or wires in a loom used to separate and guide the warp threads and make a path for the shuttle. [Prob. alteration of ME helde < OE hefeld. See **kap-** in App.]

hedge (hĕj) n. **1.** A row of closely planted shrubs or low-growing trees forming a fence or boundary. **2.** A line of people or objects forming a barrier. **3a.** A means of protection or defense, esp. against financial loss. **b.** A securities transaction that reduces the risk on an existing investment position. **4.** An intentionally noncommittal or ambiguous statement. **5.** A word or phrase, such as possibly or I think, that weakens the certainty of a statement. ❖ v. **hedged, hedg•ing, hedg•es** —tr. **1.** To enclose or bound with or as if with hedges. **2.** To hem in, hinder, or restrict with or as if with a hedge. **3.** To minimize or protect against the loss of by counterbalancing one transaction against another. —intr. **1.** To plant or cultivate hedges. **2.** To take compensatory measures so as to counterbalance possible loss. **3.** To avoid making a clear direct response or statement. [ME < OE hecg.] —**hedg′er** n. —**hedg′y** adj.

hedge fund n. An investment company that uses high-risk techniques, such as borrowing money and selling short, in an effort to make extraordinary capital gains.

hedge•hog (hĕj′hôg′, -hŏg′) n. **1.** Any of several small insectivorous mammals of the family Erinaceidae of Europe, Africa, and Asia, covered with dense erectile spines and rolling into a ball for protection. **2.** Any of several spiny animals, such as the porcupine, that are similar to the hedgehog. **3.** A well fortified military position. **4.** An obstacle used against tanks and landing craft, consisting of three crossed iron bars welded or bolted together.

hedge•hop (hĕj′hŏp′) intr.v. **-hopped, -hop•ping, -hops** To fly an airplane close to the ground, rising above objects as they appear, as in spraying crops. —**hedge′hop′per** n.

hedge•row (hĕj′rō′) n. A row of bushes, shrubs, or trees forming a hedge.

Hed•jaz (hē-jăz′) See **Hejaz**.

he•don•ic (hĭ-dŏn′ĭk) adj. **1.** Of, relating to, or marked by pleasure. **2.** Of or relating to hedonism or hedonists. [Gk. hēdonikos < hēdonē, pleasure. See **swād-** in App.]

he•don•ics (hĭ-dŏn′ĭks) n. (used with a sing. verb) **1.** The branch of psychology that studies pleasant and unpleasant sensations and states of mind. **2.** Philosophy The branch of ethics that deals with the relation of pleasure to duty.

he•don•ism (hēd′n-ĭz′əm) n. **1.** Pursuit of or devotion to pleasure, esp. to the pleasures of the senses. **2.** Philosophy The ethical doctrine holding that only what is pleasant or has pleasant consequences is intrinsically good. **3.** Psychology The doctrine holding that behavior is motivated by the desire for pleasure and the avoidance of pain. [Gk. hēdonē, pleasure; see **swād-** in App. + –ISM.] —**he′don•ist** n. —**he′don•is′tic** adj. —**he′don•is′ti•cal•ly** adv.

–hedral suff. Having a specified kind or number of surfaces: dihedral. [< –HEDRON.]

–hedron suff. A crystal or geometric figure having a specified kind or number of surfaces: heptahedron. [NLat. < Gk. -edron, neut. of -edros, -sided < hedrā, face. See **sed-** in App.]

hee•bie-jee•bies (hē′bē-jē′bēz) pl.n. Slang Uneasiness or nervousness; the jitters. [Coined by William De Beck (1890–1942), American cartoonist, in his comic strip Barney Google.]

heed (hēd) v. **heed•ed, heed•ing, heeds** —tr. To pay attention to; listen to and consider. —intr. To pay attention. ❖ n. Close attention; notice. [ME heden < OE hēdan.]

heed•ful (hēd′fəl) adj. Paying close attention; mindful. See Syns at **careful**. —**heed′ful•ly** adv.

heed•less (hēd′lĭs) adj. Marked by or paying little heed; unmindful or thoughtless. —**heed′less•ness** n.

hee-haw (hē′hô′) n. **1.** The braying sound made by a donkey. **2.** Informal A noisy laugh; a guffaw. ❖ intr.v. **-hawed, -haw•ing, -haws 1.** To bray. **2.** Informal To guffaw. [Imit.]

heel[1] (hēl) n. **1a.** The rounded posterior portion of the human foot under and behind the ankle. **b.** The corresponding part of the hind foot of other vertebrates. **c.** A similar anatomical part, such as the fleshy rounded base of the human palm. **2a.** The part, as of a sock, shoe, or stocking, that covers the heel of the human

helicon

foot. **b.** The built-up portion of a shoe or boot, supporting the heel. **3.** One of the crusty ends of a loaf of bread. **4.** The lower or rearward part, as: **a.** The part of the head of a golf club where it joins the shaft. **b.** The end of a violin bow where the handle is located. **5.** *Nautical* **a.** The lower end of a mast. **b.** The after end of a ship's keel. **6.** *Botany* The basal end of a plant cutting or tuber used in propagation. **7.** Oppression; tyranny. **8.** *Informal* A dishonorable man; a cad. ❖ *v.* **heeled, heel·ing, heels** —*tr.* **1a.** To furnish with a heel or heels. **b.** To repair or replace the heels, as for shoes. **2.** *Slang* To furnish, esp. with money. **3.** To arm (a gamecock) with gaffs. **4.** To press or strike with the heel. —*intr.* To follow at one's heels. —*idioms:* **down at the heels 1.** Having one's shoe heels worn down. **2.** Shabby; rundown; poor. **lay by the heels** To put in fetters or shackles; imprison. **on** (or **upon**) **the heels of 1.** Directly behind. **2.** Immediately following. **out at the heel** (or **heels**) **1.** Having holes in one's socks or shoes. **2.** Rundown; shabby; seedy. **take to** (one's) **heels** To run away; flee. **to heel 1.** Close behind. **2.** Under discipline or control. [ME < OE *hēla*.]

heel² (hēl) *intr. & tr.v.* **heeled, heel·ing, heels** To tilt or cause to tilt to one side. ❖ *n.* A tilt, as of a boat, to one side. [Alteration of ME *helden* < OE *hieldan*.]

heel-and-toe (hēl′ən-tō′) *adj.* Characterized by a stride in which the heel of one foot touches ground before the toe of the other foot is lifted, as in walking races.

heel·ball (hēl′bôl′) *n.* A wax colored with lampblack that is used to stain and polish the edges of the soles and heels of shoes or to take rubbings of brass or stone inscriptions.

heel·er (hē′lər) *n.* **1.** One who heels shoes. **2.** *Informal* A ward heeler.

heel·piece (hēl′pēs′) *n.* A piece made for or serving as the heel of a shoe or stocking.

heel·tap (hēl′tăp′) *n.* **1.** A layer of leather or wood added to raise the heel of a shoe; a lift. **2.** A small amount of liquor remaining in a container or drinking vessel.

He·fei also **Ho·fei** (hŭ′fā′) A city of E-central China W of Nanjing; cap. of Anhui province. Pop. 1,099,523.

heft (hĕft) *n.* Weight; heaviness; bulk. ❖ *v.* **heft·ed, heft·ing, hefts** —*tr.* **1.** To lift (something) in order to judge or estimate its weight. **2.** To hoist (something); heave. —*intr.* To have a given weight; weigh. [ME < *heven*, to lift. See HEAVE.]

heft·y (hĕf′tē) *adj.* **-i·er, -i·est 1.** Of considerable weight; heavy. **2.** Rugged and powerful. **3.** *Informal* Of considerable size or amount. —**heft′i·ly** *adv.* —**heft′i·ness** *n.*

He·gel (hā′gəl), **Georg Wilhelm Friedrich** 1770–1831. German idealist philosopher whose works include *Encyclopedia of the Philosophical Sciences* (1817).

He·ge·li·an·ism (hā-gā′lē-ə-nĭz′əm, hĭ-jē′-) *n.* The monist, idealist philosophy of Hegel in which the dialectic of thesis, antithesis, and synthesis is used as an analytic tool to approach a higher unity or a new thesis. —**He·ge′li·an** *adj. & n.*

he·gem·o·ny (hĭ-jĕm′ə-nē, hĕj′ə-mō′nē) *n., pl.* **-nies** The predominant influence, as of a state, region, or group, over another or others. [Gk. *hēgemoniā* < *hēgemōn*, leader < *hēgeisthai*, to lead.] —**heg′e·mon′ic** (hĕj′ə-mŏn′ĭk) *adj.* —**he·gem′o·nism** *n.* —**he·gem′o·nist** *adj. & n.*

> **USAGE NOTE** *Hegemony* may be stressed on either the first or second syllable, though 72 percent of the Usage Panel prefers the latter.

he·gi·ra also **he·ji·ra** (hĭ-jī′rə, hĕj′ər-ə) *n.* **1.** A flight to escape danger. **2.** also **Hegira** The flight of Muhammad from Mecca to Medina in 622, marking the beginning of the Muslim era. [Med. Lat. < Ar. *hijra*, emigration, flight < *hajara*, to depart.]

Hei·deg·ger (hī′dĕg′ər, -dī-gər), **Martin** 1889–1976. German philosopher whose works, including *Being and Time* (1927), greatly influenced Sartre and other existentialists.

Hei·del·berg (hīd′l-bûrg′, -bĕrk′) A city of SW Germany on the Neckar R. NNW of Stuttgart; first mentioned in the 12th cent. Pop. 139,429.

Heidelberg man *n.* An early member of an extinct human species, considered closely related to *Homo erectus,* chiefly known from a jawbone found near Heidelberg in 1907.

heif·er (hĕf′ər) *n.* A young cow, esp. one that has not given birth to a calf. [ME < OE *hēahfore : hēah-,* of unknown meaning + *fearr,* calf.]

Hei·fetz (hī′fĭts), **Jascha** 1901–87. Russian-born Amer. violinist considered among the world's best at the age of 13.

heigh-ho (hī′hō′, hā′-) *interj.* Used to express fatigue, mild surprise, boredom, disappointment, or sometimes exultation.

height (hīt) *n.* **1a.** The distance from the base of something to the top. **b.** Elevation above a given level, as of the sun or a star above the horizon; altitude. **2a.** The condition or attribute of being relatively or sufficiently high or tall. **b.** Stature, esp. of the human body. **3.** The highest or uppermost point; the summit or apex. **4a.** The highest or most advanced degree; the zenith. **b.** The point of highest intensity; the climax. **5.** An eminence, such as a hill or mountain. Often used in the plural. **6a.** A high point or position. **b.** *Obsolete* High rank, estate, or degree. **7a.** *Archaic* Loftiness of mind. **b.** *Obsolete* Arrogance; hauteur. [ME < OE *hēhthu, hēahthu.*]

height·en (hīt′n) —*tr.* **-ened, -en·ing, -ens 1.** To raise or increase the quantity or degree of; intensify. **2.** To make high or higher; raise. —*intr.* **1.** To rise or increase in quantity or degree; intensify. **2.** To become high or higher; rise. —**height′en·er** *n.*

height-to-pa·per (hīt′tə-pā′pər) *n. Printing* The height of type from foot to face, standardized at 0.9186 inch (2.333 centimeters).

Hei·long·jiang (hā′lông′jyäng′) also **Hei·lung·kiang** (hā′lŏong′kyäng′) A province of extreme NE China bordering on Russia. Cap. Harbin. Pop. 35,214,873.

Hei·long Jiang (hā′lông′ jyäng′) See **Amur River.**

Heim·lich maneuver (hīm′lĭk′, -lĭкн′) *n.* An emergency technique used to eject an object, such as food, from the trachea of a choking person, employing a firm upward thrust just below the rib cage to force air from the lungs. [After Henry Jay *Heimlich* (born 1920), American surgeon.]

Hei·ne (hī′nə), **Heinrich** 1797–1856. German writer primarily noted for his romantic poems.

hei·nie (hī′nē) *n. Slang* The buttocks. [Alteration of HINDER².]

hei·nous (hā′nəs) *adj.* Grossly wicked or reprehensible; abominable. [ME < OFr. *haineus* < *haine,* hatred < *hair,* to hate < Frankish **hatjan.*] —**hei′nous·ness** *n.*

heir (âr) *n.* **1.** One who inherits or is entitled by law or by the terms of a will to inherit the estate of another. **2.** One who succeeds or is in line to succeed to a hereditary rank, title, or office. **3.** One who receives or is expected to receive a heritage, as of ideas, from a predecessor. [ME < AN < Lat. *hērēs.* See **ghē-** in App.]

heir apparent *n., pl.* **heirs apparent** An heir whose right to inheritance is indefeasible by law provided he or she survives an ancestor.

heir·dom (âr′dəm) *n.* **1.** Succession by right of blood; heirship. **2.** An inheritance.

heir·ess (âr′ĭs) *n.* A woman who is an heir, esp. to great wealth. See Usage Note at **-ess.**

heir·loom (âr′lōōm′) *n.* A valued possession passed down in a family through succeeding generations. [ME *heirlome : heir,* heir; see HEIR + *lome,* implement; see LOOM².]

heir presumptive *n., pl.* **heirs presumptive** An heir whose claim can be defeated by the birth of a closer relative before the death of the ancestor.

heir·ship (âr′shĭp′) *n.* **1.** The condition of being an heir. **2.** Right to inheritance; heirdom.

Hei·sen·berg (hī′zən-bûrg′, -bĕrk′), **Werner Karl** 1901–76. German physicist who won a 1932 Nobel Prize.

heist (hīst) *Slang tr.v.* **heist·ed, heist·ing, heists 1.** To steal. **2.** To hold up; rob. ❖ *n.* A robbery; a burglary. [Alteration of HOIST.]

He·jaz also **Hed·jaz** (hē-jăz′) A region in NW Saudi Arabia on the Gulf of Aqaba and the Red Sea.

he·ji·ra (hĭ-jī′rə, hĕj′ər-ə) *n.* Variant of **hegira.**

Hek·a·te (hĕk′ə-tē, hĕk′ĭt) *n.* Variant of **Hecate.**

Hel (hĕl) *n. Mythology* **1.** The Norse goddess of death and the underworld; the daughter of Loki. **2.** The Norse underworld of the dead not killed in battle. [ON. See **kel-** in App.]

He·La cell (hē′lə) *n.* Any of the cells of the first continuously cultured human carcinoma strain, obtained from cancerous cervical tissue and used to study cellular processes. [After *He(nrietta) La(cks),* who donated such cells in 1951.]

held (hĕld) *v.* Past tense and past participle of **hold¹.**

hel·den·te·nor also **Hel·den·te·nor** (hĕl′dən-tə-nôr′, -nōr′) *n.* **1.** A dramatic tenor voice well suited for heroic roles, as in Wagnerian opera. **2.** A person with such a voice. [Ger. : *Held,* hero (< MHGer. *helt* < OHGer. *helid*) + *Tenor,* tenor (< Ital. *tenore;* see TENOR).]

Hel·en (hĕl′ən) *n. Greek Mythology* The daughter of Zeus and Leda and wife of Menelaus whose abduction by Paris caused the Trojan War. [Gk. *Helenē.* See **wel-** in App.]

Hel·e·na (hĕl′ə-nə) The cap. of MT, in the W-central part NNE of Butte; founded 1864. Pop. 25,780.

He·lene (hə-lēn′) *n.* A satellite of Saturn. [< Gk. *Helenē,* Amazon who battled Achilles.]

Hel·go·land (hĕl′gō-länd′, -länt′) An island of NW Germany, one of the North Frisian Is. in **Helgoland Bay,** an inlet of the North Sea SW of Jutland.

heli-¹ *pref.* Helicopter; heliport. [< HELICOPTER.]

heli-² *pref.* Variant of **helio-.**

he·li·a·cal (hĭ-lī′ə-kəl) *adj.* Of or relating to the sun, esp. rising and setting with the sun. [< LLat. *hēliacus* < Gk. *hēliakos* < *hēlios,* sun. See **sāwel-** in App.] —**he·li′a·cal·ly** *adv.*

hel·i·cal (hĕl′ĭ-kəl, hē′lĭ-) *adj.* **1.** Of or having the shape of a helix; spiral. **2.** Having a shape approximating that of a helix. —**hel′i·cal·ly** *adv.*

hel·i·ces (hĕl′ĭ-sēz′, hē′lĭ-) *n.* A plural of **helix.**

helico- or **helic-** *pref.* Helix; spiral: *helicoid.* [Gk. *heliko-* < *helix, helik-,* spiral. See HELIX.]

hel·i·coid (hĕl′ĭ-koid′, hē′lĭ-) *adj.* Arranged in or having the approximate shape of a flattened coil or spiral. ❖ *n. Mathematics* A surface in the form of a coil or screw. [Gk. *helikoeidēs : helix, helik-,* spiral; see HELIX + *-oeidēs,* -oid.]

hel·i·con (hĕl′ĭ-kŏn′, -kən) *n.* A large spiral brass tuba that fits

heliport
on an offshore oil-drilling
platform

around the player's shoulder. [Prob. < Gk. *helix, helik-,* spiral. See **wel-** in App.]

Helicon A mountain, 1,749.2 (5,735 ft), of central Greece; legendary abode of the Muses.

hel·i·cop·ter (hĕl′ĭ-kŏp′tər) *n.* An aircraft that derives its lift from blades that rotate about an approximately vertical central axis. ❖ *intr. & tr.v.* **-tered, -ter·ing, -ters** To go or transport by helicopter. [Fr. *hélicoptère* : Gk. *helix, helik-,* spiral; see HELIX + Gk. *pteron,* wing; see -PTER-.]

helio- or **heli-** *pref.* Sun: *heliocentric.* [Gk. *hēlio- < hēlios,* sun. See **sāwel-** in App.]

he·li·o·cen·tric (hē′lē-ō-sĕn′trĭk) also **he·li·o·cen·tri·cal** (-trĭ-kəl) *adj.* **1.** Relating to, measured from, or with respect to the center of the sun. **2.** Having or regarding the sun as a center. **—he′li·o·cen·tric′i·ty** (-sĕn-trĭs′ĭ-tē) *n.*

He·li·o·gab·a·lus (hē′lē-ə-găb′ə-ləs, -lē-ō-) also **El·a·gab·a·lus** (ĕl′ə-) A.D. 204–222. Emperor of Rome (218–222) who was killed during an insurrection.

he·li·o·graph (hē′lē-ə-grăf′) *n.* **1.** A device for transmitting messages by reflecting sunlight with movable mirrors. **2.** A device for photographing the sun. ❖ *v.* **-graphed, -graph·ing, -graphs** *—tr.* To send (a message) by heliograph. *—intr.* To send a heliograph. **—he′li·og′ra·pher** (-ŏg′rə-fər) *n.* **—he′li·o·graph′ic** *adj.* **—he′li·og′ra·phy** (-ŏg′rə-fē) *n.*

he·li·ol·a·try (hē′lē-ŏl′ə-trē) *n.* Worship of the sun.

he·li·om·e·ter (hē′lē-ŏm′ĭ-tər) *n.* A telescope equipped to measure small angular distances between celestial bodies. **—he′li·o·met′ric** (-ə-mĕt′rĭk), **he′li·o·met′ri·cal** *adj.* **—he′li·o·met′ri·cal·ly** *adv.* **—he′li·om′e·try** *n.*

he·li·o·pause (hē′lē-ə-pôz′) *n.* The boundary of the solar system, where the outgoing solar wind meets the incoming plasma from interstellar space.

He·li·op·o·lis (hē′lē-ŏp′ə-lĭs) **1.** An ancient city of N Egypt in the Nile R. delta; center of worship of the sun god Ra until the rise of Thebes (c. 2100 B.C.). **2.** See **Baalbek.**

He·li·os (hē′lē-ŏs′) *n. Greek Mythology* The sun god, son of Hyperion, depicted as driving his chariot across the sky daily.

he·li·o·stat (hē′lē-ə-stăt′) *n.* An instrument in which a mirror is automatically moved so that it reflects sunlight in a constant direction.

he·li·o·tax·is (hē′lē-ō-tăk′sĭs) *n.* The movement of an organism in response to the light of the sun. **—he′li·o·tac′tic** (-tăk′tĭk) *adj.*

he·li·o·ther·a·py (hē′lē-ō-thĕr′ə-pē) *n., pl.* **-pies** Medical therapy involving exposure to sunlight.

he·li·o·trope (hē′lē-ə-trōp′) *n.* **1a.** Any of several Peruvian plants of the genus *Heliotropium,* esp. *H. arborescens,* having small, highly fragrant, purplish flowers. **b.** The garden heliotrope. **c.** Any of various plants that turn toward the sun. **2.** See **bloodstone. 3.** A moderate, light, or brilliant violet to moderate or deep reddish purple. [ME *elitrope* (< OE *eliotropus*) and Fr. *héliotrope,* both < Lat. *hēliotropium* < Gk. *hēliotropion* : *hēlio-,* helio- + *tropos,* turn; see TROPE.] **—he′lio·trope′** *adj.*

he·li·ot·ro·pism (hē′lē-ŏt′rə-pĭz′əm) *n.* Growth or orientation of a sessile organism, esp. a plant, toward or away from the light of the sun. **—he′li·o·trop′ic** (-ə-trŏp′ĭk) *adj.*

he·li·o·type (hē′lē-ə-tīp′) *n.* **1.** A photomechanically produced plate for pictures or type made by exposing a gelatin film under a negative, hardening it with chrome alum, and printing directly from it. **2.** also **he·li·o·typ·y** (-tī′pē) The process of producing a heliotype. **—he′li·o·typ′ic** (-tĭp′ĭk) *adj.*

he·li·o·zo·an (hē′lē-ə-zō′ən) *n.* Any of various aquatic protozoans of the order Heliozoa, having numerous spindlelike pseudopods that radiate from a central cell mass. [< NLat. *Hēliozōa,* class name : HELIO– (< their shape) + -zōa, pl. of -zōon, -zoon.] **—he′li·o·zo′ic** (-zō′ĭk) *adj.*

hel·i·pad (hĕl′ĭ-păd′) *n.* See **heliport.**

hel·i·port (hĕl′ə-pôrt′, -pōrt′) *n.* A place for helicopters to land and take off. [HELI(COPTER) + (AIR)PORT.]

hel·i·ski·ing (hĕl′ĭ-skē′ĭng) *n.* Downhill skiing on glaciers or remote mountains reached by helicopter. [HELI(COPTER) + *skiing,* gerund of SKI.]

he·li·um (hē′lē-əm) *n. Symbol* **He** An inert gaseous element occurring in natural gas and used as a component of artificial atmospheres and laser media, a refrigerant, and a lifting gas for balloons. Atomic number 2; atomic weight 4.0026; boiling point −268.9°C; density at 0°C 0.1785 gram per liter. See table at **element.** [< Gk. *hēlios,* sun (so called because its existence was deduced from the solar spectrum). See **sāwel-** in App.]

he·lix (hē′lĭks) *n., pl.* **-lix·es** or **hel·i·ces** (hĕl′ĭ-sēz′, hē′lĭ-) **1.** *Mathematics* A three-dimensional curve that lies on a cylinder or cone, so that its angle to a plane perpendicular to the axis is constant. **2.** A spiral form or structure. **3.** *Anatomy* The folded rim of skin and cartilage around most of the outer ear. **4.** *Architecture* A volute on a Corinthian or Ionic capital. [Lat. < Gk. See **wel-** in App.]

hell (hĕl) *n.* **1a.** often **Hell** The abode of condemned souls and devils in some religions; the place of eternal punishment for the wicked after death, presided over by Satan. **b.** A state of separation from God. **2.** The abode of the dead, identified with the Hebrew Sheol and the Greek Hades; the underworld. **3a.** A situation

or place of evil, misery, discord, or destruction. **b.** Torment; anguish. **4a.** The powers of darkness and evil. **b.** *Informal* One that causes trouble, agony, or annoyance. **5.** A sharp scolding. **6.** *Informal* Excitement, mischievousness, or high spirits. **7a.** A tailor's receptacle for discarded material. **b.** *Printing* A hellbox. **8.** *Informal* Used as an intensive: *a hell of a job.* **9.** *Archaic* A gambling house. ❖ *intr.v.* **helled, hell·ing, hells** *Informal* To behave riotously; carouse. ❖ *interj.* Used to express anger, disgust, or impatience. **—idioms: for the hell of it** For no particular reason; on a whim. **hell on** *Informal* **1.** Damaging or destructive to. **2.** Unpleasant to or painful for. **hell or (or and) high water** Troubles or difficulties of whatever magnitude. **hell to pay** Great trouble. **like hell 1.** Used as an intensive: *ran like hell.* **2.** Used to express strong contradiction or refusal: *He says he went.—Like hell he did!* [ME *helle* < OE. See **kel-** in App.]

he'll (hĕl) Contraction of *he will.*

hel·la·cious (hĕ-lā′shəs) *adj.* **1.** Distasteful and repellant. **2.** *Slang* Extraordinary; remarkable. [HELL + *-acious* (as in AUDACIOUS).]

Hel·las (hĕl′əs) The Greek name for Greece.

hell·bend·er (hĕl′bĕn′dər) *n.* A large aquatic salamander (*Cryptobranchus alleganiensis*) of the eastern and central United States.

hell·bent or **hell-bent** (hĕl′bĕnt′) *adj.* Impetuously or recklessly determined to do or achieve something.

hell·box (hĕl′bŏks′) *n. Printing* A receptacle for broken or discarded type.

hell·cat (hĕl′kăt′) *n. Informal* **1.** A woman regarded as bad-tempered and evil. **2.** A woman who practices sorcery.

Hel·le (hĕl′ē) *n. Greek Mythology* The daughter of a Greek king who, while fleeing with her brother from their stepmother, drowned in the Hellespont, thereafter named for her.

hel·le·bore (hĕl′ə-bôr′, -bōr′) *n.* **1.** Any of various, usu. poisonous Eurasian plants of the genus *Helleborus.* **2.** Any of various plants of the genus *Veratrum,* esp. *V. viride* of North America, having large leaves and greenish flowers and yielding a toxic alkaloid used medicinally. [ME *ellebre* < OFr. < Lat. *elleborus* < Gk. *helleboros* : perh. *hellos,* fawn + *-boros,* eaten (< *bibrōskein,* to eat).]

Hel·lene (hĕl′ēn) also **Hel·le·ni·an** (hĕ-lē′nē-ən) *n.* A Greek. [Gk. *Hellēn.*]

Hel·len·ic (hĕ-lĕn′ĭk) *adj.* Of or relating to the ancient Hellenes, their language, or their history; Greek. ❖ *n.* The branch of Indo-European that consists only of Greek.

Hel·le·nism (hĕl′ə-nĭz′əm) *n.* **1.** An idiom or custom peculiar to the Greeks. **2.** The civilization and culture of ancient Greece. **3.** Admiration for and adoption of Greek ideas, style, or culture.

Hel·le·nist (hĕl′ə-nĭst) *n.* **1.** One in Hellenistic times who adopted the Greek language and culture, esp. a Jew of the Diaspora. **2.** A devotee or student of Greek civilization, language, or literature.

Hel·le·nis·tic (hĕl′ə-nĭs′tĭk) also **Hel·le·nis·ti·cal** (-tĭ-kəl) *adj.* **1.** Of or relating to the Hellenists. **2.** Of or relating to post-classical Greek history and culture from the death of Alexander the Great to the accession of Augustus. **3.** Relating to or in the style of the Greek art or architecture of this period.

Hel·le·nize (hĕl′ə-nīz′) *v.* **-nized, -niz·ing, -niz·es** *—intr.* To adopt Greek ways and speech; become Greek. *—tr.* To make Greek in character, culture, or civilization. **—Hel′le·ni·za′tion** (-nĭ-zā′shən) *n.* **—Hel′le·niz′er** *n.*

hell·er (hĕl′ər) *n.* A person who behaves recklessly or wildly.

Hel·les·pont (hĕl′ĭ-spŏnt′) See **Dardanelles.**

hell·fire (hĕl′fīr′) *n.* The fire of hell, considered as punishment for sinners.

hell-for-leath·er (hĕl′fər-lĕth′ər) *adv. & adj. Informal* At breakneck speed.

Hell Gate A narrow channel of the East R. in New York City between Manhattan and Long I.

hell·gram·mite (hĕl′grə-mīt′) *n.* The large brownish aquatic larva of the dobsonfly, often used as fishing bait. [?]

hell·hole (hĕl′hōl′) *n.* **1.** A place of extreme wretchedness or squalor. **2.** *Obsolete* The pit of hell.

hell·hound (hĕl′hound′) *n.* **1.** A devilish person; a fiend. **2.** *Greek Mythology* Cerberus.

hel·lion (hĕl′yən) *n. Informal* A mischievous, troublesome, or unruly person. [Prob. alteration (influenced by HELL) of dialectal *hallion,* worthless person.]

hell·ish (hĕl′ĭsh) *adj.* **1.** Of, resembling, or worthy of hell; fiendish. **2.** Highly unpleasant: *hellish weather.* **—hell′ish·ly** *adv.* **—hell′ish·ness** *n.*

Hell·man (hĕl′mən), **Lillian** 1905–84. Amer. playwright whose works include *The Little Foxes* (1939).

hel·lo (hĕ-lō′, hə-) *interj.* Used to greet someone, answer the telephone, or express surprise. ❖ *n., pl.* **-los** A calling or greeting of "hello." ❖ *intr.v.* **-loed, -lo·ing, -loes** To call "hello." [Alteration of *hallo,* alteration of obsolete *holla,* stop!, perh. < OFr. *hola* : *ho,* ho! + *la,* there (< Lat. *illāc,* that way).]

hell-rais·er (hĕl′rā′zər) *n.* A rowdy or troublesome person.

helm[1] (hĕlm) *n.* **1.** *Nautical* The steering gear of a ship, esp. the tiller or wheel. **2.** A position of leadership or control. ❖ *tr.v.* **helmed, helm·ing, helms** To take the helm of; steer or direct. [ME < OE *helma.*]

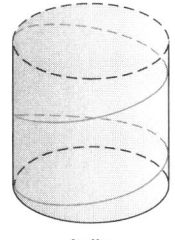

helix
circular helix in a right circular cylinder

hellbender
Cryptobranchus alleganiensis

helm² (hĕlm) *Archaic n.* A helmet. [ME < OE. See **kel-** in App.] —**helm** *v.*

Hel·mand (hĕl′mənd) A river rising in the Hindu Kush and flowing c. 1,287 km (800 mi) to the Iranian border.

hel·met (hĕl′mĭt) *n.* **1a.** A protective head covering made of hard material, such as leather, metal, or plastic. **b.** The headgear with a glass mask worn by deep-sea divers. **c.** A pith helmet; a topi. **d.** A head covering, such as a balaclava, shaped like a helmet. **2.** A piece of armor, usu. made of metal, designed to protect the head. **3.** *Botany* The hood-shaped sepal or corolla of some flowers. ❖ *tr. & intr.v.* **-met·ed, -met·ing, -mets** To provide with or put on a helmet. [ME < OFr., dim. of *helme,* of Gmc. orig. See **kel-¹** in App.]

Helm·holtz (hĕlm′hōlts′), **Hermann Ludwig Ferdinand von** 1821–94. German physicist and physiologist who formulated the mathematical law of the conservation of energy (1847).

hel·minth (hĕl′mĭnth′) *n.* A worm, esp. a parasitic roundworm or tapeworm. [Fr. *helminthe* < Gk. *helmins, helminth-.* See **wel-** in App.]

hel·min·thi·a·sis (hĕl′mĭn-thī′ə-sĭs) *n., pl.* **-ses** (-sēz′) A disease caused by infestation with parasitic worms.

hel·min·thic (hĕl-mĭn′thĭk) *adj.* **1.** Of or relating to worms, esp. parasitic worms. **2.** Tending to expel worms; anthelmintic. ❖ *n.* An agent that expels or destroys parasitic worms.

hel·min·thol·o·gy (hĕl′mĭn-thŏl′ə-jē) *n.* The study of worms, esp. parasitic worms. —**hel′min·thol′o·gist** *n.*

helms·man (hĕlmz′mən) *n.* A person who steers a ship. —**helms′man·ship′** *n.*

Hé·lo·ise (ĕl′ə-wēz′, ā-lô-ēz′) 1098?–1164. French philosopher, writer, and religious figure who was the lover and wife of Peter Abelard.

hel·ot (hĕl′ət) *n.* **1. Helot** One of a class of serfs in ancient Sparta, neither a slave nor a free citizen. **2.** A person in servitude; a serf. [< Gk. *Heilōtes,* pl. of *Heilōs, Heilōt-.*]

hel·ot·ism (hĕl′ə-tĭz′əm) *n.* **1.** A system under which a nominally free social class or a minority is permanently oppressed and degraded. **2.** A type of symbiosis, as among certain ants, in which one species is subservient to another.

hel·ot·ry (hĕl′ə-trē) *n.* **1.** The condition of serfdom. **2.** Helots considered as a group.

help (hĕlp) *v.* **helped, help·ing, helps** —*tr.* **1.** To give assistance to; aid. **2.** To contribute to the furtherance of; promote. **3.** To give relief to: *help the needy.* **4.** To ease; relieve: *medication to help your cold.* **5.** To change for the better; improve. **6.** To refrain from; avoid or resist. Used with *can* or *cannot: couldn't help laughing.* **7.** To wait on, as in a store or restaurant. —*intr.* To be of service; give assistance. ❖ *n.* **1a.** The act or an instance of helping. **b.** Aid or assistance. **2.** Relief; remedy. **3.** One that helps. **4.** A person employed to help, esp. a farm worker or domestic servant. **5.** Such employees considered as a group. Often used with *the.* —**idiom: help (oneself) to 1.** To serve or provide oneself with. **2.** *Informal* To take (something) without asking permission. [ME *helpen* < OE *helpan.*]

> **USAGE NOTE** Many people commonly use *help* in the sense conveyed in the sentence *Don't change it any more than you can help* (that is, "any more than you have to"). Some grammarians condemn this usage on the grounds that *help* in this sense means "avoid" and logically requires a negative. But the expression is a well-established idiom. See Usage Note at **cannot.**

help·er (hĕl′pər) *n.* One that helps; an assistant.

helper T cell also **helper cell** *n.* Any of the T cells that release lymphokines that function in the activation of B cells and killer T cells.

help·ful (hĕlp′fəl) *adj.* Providing assistance; useful. —**help′ful·ly** *adv.*

help·ing (hĕl′pĭng) *n.* A single portion of food.

help·less (hĕlp′lĭs) *adj.* **1.** Unable to help oneself; powerless. **2.** Lacking support or protection. **3.** Impossible to control; involuntary. —**help′less·ly** *adv.* —**help′less·ness** *n.*

help·mate (hĕlp′māt′) *n.* A helper and companion, esp. a spouse. [Prob. alteration of HELPMEET.]

help·meet (hĕlp′mēt′) *n.* A helpmate. [< misunderstanding of the phrase *an help meet for him,* a helper fit for him (Adam), in Genesis 2:18, referring to Eve.]

Hel·sing·ør (hĕl′sĭng-ûr′, -cer′) also **El·si·nore** (ĕl′sə-nôr′, -nōr′) A city of E Denmark N of Copenhagen on N Sjaelland I.; setting for Shakespeare's *Hamlet.* Pop. 56,161.

Hel·sin·ki (hĕl′sĭng′kē, hĕl-sĭng′-) The cap. of Finland, in the S part on the Gulf of Finland; founded 1550. Pop. 505,051.

hel·ter-skel·ter (hĕl′tər-skĕl′tər) *adv.* **1.** In disorderly haste; pell-mell. **2.** Haphazardly. ❖ *adj.* **1.** Carelessly hurried and confused. **2.** Haphazard. ❖ *n.* **1.** Turmoil; confusion. [?]

helve (hĕlv) *n.* A handle of a tool, as an ax. [ME < OE *hielfe.*]

Hel·ve·tia (hĕl-vē′shə, -shē-ə) An ancient region of central Europe between the Alps and the Jura Mts.; named by the Romans for its predominantly Celtic inhabitants.

Hel·ve·tian (hĕl-vē′shən) *adj.* **1.** Of or relating to Helvetia or the Helvetii. **2.** Swiss. ❖ *n.* **1.** One of the Helvetii. **2.** A Swiss. [< Lat. *Helvētius* < *Helvētiī,* Helvetii.]

Hel·ve·ti·i (hĕl-vē′shē-ī′) *pl.n.* A Celtic people inhabiting western Switzerland during the time of Julius Caesar. [Lat. *Helvētiī.*]

hem¹ (hĕm) *n.* **1.** An edge or border on a piece of cloth, esp. a finished edge made by folding an edge under and stitching it down. **2.** The height or level of the bottom edge of a skirt, dress, or coat; a hemline. ❖ *tr.v.* **hemmed, hem·ming, hems 1.** To fold back and stitch down the edge of. **2.** To surround and shut in; enclose. [ME < OE.] —**hem′mer** *n.*

hem² (hĕm) *n.* A short cough or clearing of the throat made esp. to gain attention, warn another, hide embarrassment, or fill a pause in speech. ❖ *intr.v.* **hemmed, hem·ming, hems 1.** To utter a hem. **2.** To hesitate in speech. —**idiom: hem and haw** To be hesitant and indecisive; equivocate. [< ME *heminge,* coughing, of imit. orig.]

hem- or **hema-** *pref.* Variants of **hemo-.**

he·ma·cy·tom·e·ter (hē′mə-sī-tŏm′ĭ-tər) *n.* An instrument for counting blood cells in a measured volume of blood.

he·mag·glu·ti·nate (hē′mə-glōōt′n-āt′) *tr.v.* **-nat·ed, -nat·ing, -nates** To cause agglutination of red blood cells. —**he′mag·glu′ti·na′tion** *n.*

he·mag·glu·ti·nin (hē′mə-glōōt′n-ĭn) *n.* A substance, such as an antibody, that causes agglutination of red blood cells. [HEMAGGLUTIN(ATE) + -IN.]

he·mal (hē′məl) *adj.* **1.** Of or relating to the blood or blood vessels. **2.** Relating to or located on the side of the body that contains the heart and principal blood vessels.

he-man (hē′măn′) *n. Informal* A strong virile man.

he·man·gi·o·ma (hĭ-măn′jē-ō′mə) *n., pl.* **-mas** also **-ma·ta** (-mə-tə) A benign skin lesion consisting of dense, usu. elevated masses of dilated blood vessels.

he·ma·te·in (hē′mə-tē′ĭn, hē′mə-tēn′) *n.* A reddish-brown crystalline compound, $C_{16}H_{12}O_6$, used as an indicator and a biological stain.

he·mat·ic (hĭ-măt′ĭk) *adj.* Of, relating to, resembling, containing, or acting on blood. ❖ *n.* A hematinic. [Gk. *haimatikos* < *haima, haimat-,* blood.]

he·ma·tin (hē′mə-tĭn) *n.* A blue to blackish-brown compound, $C_{34}H_{32}N_4O_4$·FeOH, formed in the decomposition of hemoglobin.

he·ma·tin·ic (hē′mə-tĭn′ĭk) *adj.* **1.** Acting to increase the amount of hemoglobin in the blood. **2.** Of, relating to, or derived from hematin. ❖ *n.* A hematinic drug.

he·ma·tite (hē′mə-tīt′) *n.* A black or blackish-red to brick-red mineral, Fe_2O_3, the chief ore of iron. [ME *emathite, ematites* < Lat. *haematītēs* < Gk. *(lithos) haimatītēs,* bloodlike (stone) < *haima, haimat-,* blood.]

hemato- or **hemat-** also **haemat-** or **haemato-** *pref.* Blood: *hematology.* [Gk. *haimato-* < *haima, haimat-,* blood.]

he·ma·to·blast (hē′mə-tə-blăst′, hĭ-măt′ə-) *n.* An immature blood cell. —**he′ma·to·blas′tic** *adj.*

he·ma·to·crit (hĭ-măt′ə-krĭt′) *n.* **1.** The percentage by volume of packed red blood cells in a given sample of blood after centrifugation. **2.** A centrifuge used to determine the volume of blood cells and plasma in a given sample of blood. [HEMATO- + Gk. *kritēs,* judge (< *krīnein,* to judge; see **krei-** in App.).]

he·ma·tog·e·nous (hē′mə-tŏj′ə-nəs) *adj.* **1.** Producing blood. **2.** Originating in or spread by the blood.

he·ma·tol·o·gy (hē′mə-tŏl′ə-jē) *n.* The science encompassing the medical study of the blood and blood-producing organs. —**he′ma·to·log′ic** (-tə-lŏj′ĭk), **he′ma·to·log′i·cal** *adj.* —**he′ma·to·log′i·cal·ly** *adv.* —**he′ma·tol′o·gist** *n.*

he·ma·to·ma (hē′mə-tō′mə) *n., pl.* **-mas** or **-ma·ta** (-mə-tə) A localized swelling filled with blood resulting from a break in a blood vessel.

he·ma·to·poi·e·sis (hē′mə-tō-poi-ē′sĭs, hĭ-măt′ə-) also **he·mo·poi·e·sis** (hē′mə-poi-ē′sĭs) *n.* Formation of blood or blood cells in the body. —**he′ma·to·poi·et′ic** (-ĕt′ĭk) *adj.*

he·ma·tox·y·lin (hē′mə-tŏk′sə-lĭn) *n.* A yellow or red crystalline compound, $C_{16}H_{14}O_6$·3H_2O, that is used in dyes, inks, and stains. [NLat. *Haematoxylon,* a genus of plants (Gk. *haimato-,* hemato- + Gk. *xylon,* wood) + -IN.]

he·ma·to·zo·on (hē′mə-tə-zō′ŏn′, hĭ-măt′ə-) *n., pl.* **-zo·a** (-zō′ə) A parasitic protozoan or similar organism found in blood. —**he′ma·to·zo′al, he′ma·to·zo′ic** *adj.*

he·ma·tu·ri·a (hē′mə-tŏōr′ē-ə, -tyŏōr′-) *n.* The presence of blood in the urine. —**he′ma·tu′ric** *adj.*

heme (hēm) *n.* The deep red nonprotein ferrous component of hemoglobin, $C_{34}H_{32}FeN_4O_4$. [Short for HEMATIN.]

he·mel·y·tron (hē-mĕl′ĭ-trŏn′) *n., pl.* **-tra** (-trə) One of the forewings of a hemipterous insect, having a thick membranous apex. [HEM(I)- + ELYTRON.]

hem·er·a·lo·pi·a (hĕm′ər-ə-lō′pē-ə) *n.* A visual defect characterized by the inability to see as clearly in bright light as in dim. [NLat. < Gk. *hēmeralōps,* suffering from hemeralopia : *hēmera,* day + *alaos,* blind + *ōps,* eye; see NYCTALOPIA.] —**hem′er·a·lop′ic** (-lŏp′ĭk) *adj.*

hem·er·o·cal·lis (hĕm′ər-ə-kăl′ĭs) *n.* See **day lily.** [NLat. < Gk. *hēmerokalles,* a lily : *hēmera,* day + *kallos,* beauty.]

hemi- *pref.* **1.** Half: *hemihedral.* **2.** Partial; partially: *hemiparasite.* [Gk. *hēmi-.*]

-hemia *suff.* Variant of **-emia.**

hem·i·al·gi·a (hĕm′ē-ăl′jē-ə, -jə) *n.* Pain affecting one half of the body.

he·mic (hē′mĭk) *adj.* Of or relating to the blood.

hem·i·cel·lu·lose (hĕm′ĭ-sĕl′yə-lōs′, -lōz′) *n.* Any of several polysaccharides more complex than a sugar and less complex than cellulose, found in plant cell walls.

hem·i·chor·date (hĕm′ĭ-kôr′dāt′, -dĭt) *n.* Any of various wormlike marine animals of the phylum Hemichordata, having a primitive notochord. —**hem′i·chor′date** *adj.*

hem·i·cy·cle (hĕm′ĭ-sī′kəl) *n.* **1.** A semicircle. **2.** A semicircular structure or arrangement. [Fr. *hémicycle* < Lat. *hēmicyclium* < Gk. *hēmikuklion* : *hēmi-*, hemi- + *kuklos*, circle; see CYCLE.]

hem·i·dem·i·sem·i·qua·ver (hĕm′ē-dĕm′ē-sĕm′ē-kwā′vər) *n.* *Chiefly British* A sixty-fourth note.

hem·i·he·dral (hĕm′ĭ-hē′drəl) *adj.* Exhibiting only half the faces required for complete symmetry. Used of a crystal.

hem·i·hy·drate (hĕm′ĭ-hī′drāt′) *n.* A hydrate in which the molecular ratio of water molecules to anhydrous compound is 1:2. —**hem′i·hy′drat′ed** *adj.*

hem·i·me·tab·o·lous (hĕm′ē-mə-tăb′ə-ləs) also **hem·i·met·a·bol·ic** (-mĕt′ə-bŏl′ĭk) *adj.* Undergoing a metamorphosis that lacks a pupal stage. Used of certain insects. —**hem′i·me·tab′o·lism** (-ə-lĭz′əm) *n.*

hem·i·mor·phic (hĕm′ĭ-môr′fĭk) *adj.* Asymmetrical at the axial ends. Used of a crystal.

hem·i·mor·phite (hĕm′ĭ-môr′fīt′) *n.* A usu. white or colorless mineral, Zn₄Si₂O₇(OH)₂·H₂O, an important ore of zinc.

he·min (hē′mĭn) *n.* The reddish-brown crystalline chloride of heme, C₃₄H₃₂N₄O₄FeCl, produced when hemoglobin reacts with glacial acetic acid and sodium chloride in a test for the presence of blood.

Hem·ing·way (hĕm′ĭng-wā′), **Ernest Miller** 1899–1961. Amer. writer whose works include *For Whom the Bell Tolls* (1940). He won the 1954 Nobel Prize for literature.

hem·i·par·a·site (hĕm′ĭ-păr′ə-sīt′) *n.* **1.** A plant, such as mistletoe, that obtains nourishment from its host but also photosynthesizes. **2.** An organism that can live independently or as a parasite. —**hem′i·par′a·sit′ic** (-sĭt′ĭk) *adj.*

hem·i·ple·gia (hĕm′ĭ-plē′jə, -jē-ə) *n.* Paralysis in only one side of the body. —**hem′i·ple′gic** (-plē′jĭk) *adj. & n.*

he·mip·ter·an (hĭ-mĭp′tər-ən) *adj.* Hemipterous. ❖ *n.* also **he·mip·ter·on** (-tə-rŏn′) A hemipterous insect; a true bug.

he·mip·ter·ous (hĭ-mĭp′tər-əs) *adj.* Of or belonging to the insect order Hemiptera, including the suborders Heteroptera and Homoptera, marked by piercing or sucking mouthparts and two pairs of wings.

hem·i·sphere (hĕm′ĭ-sfîr′) *n.* **1a.** A half of a sphere bounded by a great circle. **b.** A half of a symmetrical, approximately spherical object as divided by a plane of symmetry. **2.** Either half of the celestial sphere as divided by the ecliptic, the celestial equator, or the horizon. **3.** Either the northern or southern half of the earth as divided by the equator or the eastern or western half as divided by a meridian. **4.** *Anatomy* Either of the lateral halves of the cerebrum; a cerebral hemisphere. —**hem′i·spher′ic** (-sfîr′ĭk, -sfĕr′-), **hem′i·spher′i·cal** *adj.* —**hem′i·spher′i·cal·ly** *adv.*

hem·i·stich (hĕm′ĭ-stĭk′) *n.* **1.** A half line of verse, esp. when separated rhythmically from the rest of the line by a caesura. **2.** An incomplete or imperfect line of verse. [Lat. *hēmistichium* < Gk. *hēmistikhion* : *hēmi-*, hemi- + *stikhos*, line; see **steigh-** in App.]

hem·line (hĕm′līn′) *n.* **1.** The bottom edge of a skirt, dress, or coat. **2.** The height of a hem from the floor.

hem·lock (hĕm′lŏk′) *n.* **1a.** Any of various coniferous evergreen trees of the genus *Tsuga* of North America and eastern Asia, having small cones and short flat leaves with two white bands underneath. **b.** The wood of such trees. **2a.** Any of several poisonous plants of the genera *Conium* and *Cicuta*, such as the poison hemlock. **b.** A poison obtained from the poison hemlock. [ME *hemlok*, poison hemlock < OE *hymlice*, *hemlic*.]

hemo– or **hema–** or **hem–** also **haemo–** or **haema–** or **haem–** *pref.* Blood: *hemocyte.* [Gk. *haimo-* < *haima*.]

he·mo·chro·ma·to·sis (hē′mə-krō′mə-tō′sĭs) *n.* A hereditary disorder of iron metabolism in which iron accumulates in the body tissues.

he·mo·coel (hē′mə-sēl′) *n.* A cavity or series of spaces between the organs of most arthropods and mollusks through which the blood circulates.

he·mo·cy·a·nin (hē′mō-sī′ə-nĭn) *n.* A bluish, copper-containing protein with an oxygen-carrying function similar to that of hemoglobin, present in the blood of certain mollusks and arthropods.

he·mo·cyte (hē′mə-sīt′) *n.* A cellular component of the blood, esp. of an invertebrate.

he·mo·di·al·y·sis (hē′mō-dī-ăl′ĭ-sĭs) *n., pl.* **-ses** (-sēz′) A procedure for removing metabolic waste products or toxic substances from the bloodstream by dialysis.

he·mo·dy·nam·ics (hē′mə-dī-năm′ĭks) *n.* (*used with a sing. verb*) The study of the forces involved in the circulation of blood. —**he′mo·dy·nam′ic** *adj.*

he·mo·flag·el·late (hē′mō-flăj′ə-lāt′, -lĭt, -flə-jĕl′ĭt) *n.* A flagellate protozoan that is parasitic in the blood.

he·mo·glo·bin (hē′mə-glō′bĭn) *n.* The iron-containing respiratory pigment in red blood cells of vertebrates, consisting of

about 6 percent heme and 94 percent globin. [Ult. short for *hematinoglobulin* : HEMATIN + GLOBULIN.]

he·mo·glo·bi·nu·ri·a (hē′mə-glō′bə-nŏŏr′ē-ə, -nyŏŏr′-) *n.* The presence of hemoglobin in the urine. —**he′mo·glo′bi·nu′ric** *adj.*

he·mo·lymph (hē′mə-lĭmf′) *n.* The circulatory fluid of certain invertebrates, analogous to lymph in other invertebrates.

he·mol·y·sin (hī-mŏl′ĭ-sĭn, hē′mə-lī′-) *n.* An agent or substance, such as an antibody, that causes hemolysis.

he·mol·y·sis (hī-mŏl′ĭ-sĭs, hē′mə-lī′sĭs) *n.* The destruction or dissolution of red blood cells, with subsequent release of hemoglobin. —**he′mo·lyt′ic** (hē′mə-lĭt′ĭk) *adj.* —**he′mo·lyze′** (hē′mə-līz′) *v.*

hemolytic anemia *n.* Anemia resulting from the lysis of red blood cells, as in certain inherited blood disorders.

he·mo·phil·i·a (hē′mə-fĭl′ē-ə, -fēl′yə) *n.* Any of several sex-linked blood-coagulation disorders in which the blood fails to clot normally because of a defective clotting factor.

he·mo·phil·i·ac (hē′mə-fĭl′ē-ăk′, -fēl′lē-) *n.* A person, almost exclusively a male, who is affected with hemophilia.

he·mo·phil·ic (hē′mə-fĭl′ĭk) *adj.* **1.** Of, relating to, or affected by hemophilia. **2.** Growing well in blood or in a culture containing blood. Used of certain bacteria.

he·mo·pho·bi·a (hē′mə-fō′bē-ə) *n.* An abnormal fear of blood. —**he′mo·pho′bic** *adj.*

he·mo·poi·e·sis (hē′mə-poi-ē′sĭs) *n.* Variant of **hematopoiesis.**

he·mop·ty·sis (hī-mŏp′tĭ-sĭs) *n.* The expectoration of blood. [HEMO– + Gk. *ptusis*, a spitting (< *ptuein*, to spit).]

hem·or·rhage (hĕm′ər-ĭj) *n.* **1.** Excessive discharge of blood from the blood vessels; profuse bleeding. **2.** A copious loss of something valuable: *a hemorrhage of profit.* ❖ *v.* **-rhaged, -rhag·ing, -rhag·es** —*intr.* **1.** To bleed copiously. **2.** To undergo a rapid and sudden loss. —*tr.* To lose (something valuable) rapidly and in quantity. [Ult. < Gk. *haimorrhagiā* : *haimo-*, hemo- + *-rrhagiā*, -rrhagia.] —**hem′or·rhag′ic** (hĕm′ə-răj′ĭk) *adj.*

hemorrhagic fever *n.* Any of a group of viral infections often transmitted to humans by arthropods or rodents and characterized by high fever, petechiae, and internal bleeding, usu. leading to hypotension and shock.

hemorrhagic measles *n.* (*used with a sing. verb*) See **black measles.**

hem·or·rhoid (hĕm′ə-roid′) *n.* **1.** An itching or painful mass of dilated veins in swollen anal tissue. **2. hemorrhoids** The pathological condition in which hemorrhoids occur. [Ult. < Gk. *haimorrhoïdes*, pl. of *haimorrhoïs* < *haimorrhoos*, flowing with blood : *haimo-*, hemo- + *rhein*, to flow; see **sreu-** in App.]

hem·or·rhoi·dal (hĕm′ə-roid′l) *adj.* **1.** Of or relating to hemorrhoids. **2.** Supplying the region of the rectum and anus. Used of certain arteries.

hem·or·rhoi·dec·to·my (hĕm′ə-roi-dĕk′tə-mē) *n., pl.* **-mies** Surgical removal of hemorrhoids.

he·mo·sid·er·in (hē′mō-sĭd′ər-ĭn) *n.* A protein that stores iron in the body, derived chiefly from the hemoglobin released during hemolysis.

he·mo·sta·sis (hē′mə-stā′sĭs, hē-mŏs′tə-) also **he·mo·sta·sia** (hē′mə-stā′zhə, -zhē-ə, -zē-ə) *n.* **1.** The stoppage of bleeding or hemorrhage. **2.** The stoppage of blood flow through a blood vessel or body part.

he·mo·stat (hē′mə-stăt′) *n.* **1.** An agent that stops bleeding. **2.** A clamplike instrument used to compress a blood vessel to reduce or arrest the flow of blood during surgery.

he·mo·stat·ic (hē′mə-stăt′ĭk) *adj.* Acting to arrest bleeding or hemorrhage. ❖ *n.* A hemostatic device or agent. [HEMO– + Gk. *statikos*, causing to stop; see STATIC.]

hemp (hĕmp) *n.* **1.** Cannabis. **2.** The tough, coarse fiber of the cannabis plant, used to make cordage. **3a.** Any of various plants similar to cannabis, esp. one yielding a similar fiber. **b.** The fiber of such a plant. [ME < OE *hænep*.]

hemp agrimony *n.* An Old World plant (*Eupatorium cannabinum*) having clusters of small reddish-purple flower heads.

hemp·en (hĕm′pən) *adj.* Of, relating to, or resembling hemp.

hemp nettle *n.* Any of various Eurasian plants of the genus *Galeopsis,* having bristly stems and flowers with two lips.

hem·stitch (hĕm′stĭch′) *n.* **1.** A decorative stitch usu. bordering a hem, made by drawing out several parallel threads and catching together the cross threads in uniform groups. **2.** Needlework using this stitch. ❖ *tr.v.* **-stitched, -stitch·ing, -stitch·es** To embroider with hemstitches.

hen (hĕn) *n.* **1.** A female bird, esp. the adult female of the domestic fowl. **2.** The female of certain aquatic animals, such as an octopus or lobster. **3.** *Slang* A woman, esp. a fussy or nosy old woman. [ME < OE. See **kan-** in App.] —**hen′nish** *adj.* —**hen′ny·ly** *adv.* —**hen′nish·ness** *n.*

He·nan (hŭ′nän′) also **Ho·nan** (hō′-) A province of E-central China; site of many Stone Age remains. Cap. Zhengzhou. Pop. 85,509,535.

hen-and-chick·ens (hĕn′ən-chĭk′ənz) *n., pl.* **hens-and-chick·ens** (hĕnz′-) Any of several plants having many runners or off-shoots, esp. the houseleek.

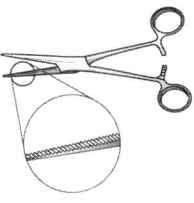

hemostat
straight hemostat

ă	pat	oi	boy
ā	pay	ou	out
âr	care	ŏŏ	took
ä	father	ōō	boot
ĕ	pet	ŭ	cut
ē	be	ûr	urge
ĭ	pit	th	thin
ī	pie	th	this
îr	pier	hw	which
ŏ	pot	zh	vision
ō	toe	ə	about,
ô	paw		item

Stress marks:
′ (primary);
′ (secondary), as in
lexicon (lĕk′sĭ-kŏn′)

henbane
Hyoscyamus niger

hen·bane (hĕn′bān′) *n.* A poisonous Eurasian plant (*Hyoscyamus niger*) having an unpleasant odor, sticky leaves, and funnel-shaped flowers and serving as a source of hyoscyamine.

hen·bit (hĕn′bĭt′) *n.* A Eurasian plant (*Lamium amplexicaule*) having toothed opposite leaves and small white or purplish-red flowers with two lips. [HEN + BIT¹.]

hence (hĕns) *adv.* **1a.** For this reason; therefore: *handmade and hence expensive.* **b.** From this source: *They grew up in the Sudan, hence their interest in Nubian art.* **2.** From this time; from now. **3a.** From this place; away from here: *Get you hence!* **b.** From this life. [ME *hennes,* from *here* < *henne* (< OE *heonan;* see **ko-** in App.) + *-es,* adv. suff.; see *-s*³.]

hence·forth (hĕns′fôrth′) *adv.* From this time forth.

hence·for·ward (hĕns-fôr′wərd) *adv.* Henceforth.

hench·man (hĕnch′mən) *n.* **1.** A loyal and trusted follower or subordinate. **2.** A person who supports a political figure chiefly from selfish interests. **3.** A member of a criminal gang. **4.** *Obsolete* A page to a person of high rank. [ME *hengsman, henshman,* servant to a person of rank : *hengest,* horse (< OE) + *man,* man; see MAN.]

hen·coop (hĕn′kōōp′) *n.* A coop or cage for poultry.

hen·dec·a·syl·lab·ic (hĕn-dĕk′ə-sĭ-lăb′ĭk) *adj.* Containing 11 syllables. ❖ *n.* A verse of 11 syllables. [< Lat. *hendecasyllabus,* a line of 11 syllables < Gk. *hendekasullabos* : *hendeka,* eleven (*hen,* neut. of *heis,* one; see SEM-¹ in App. + *deka,* ten; see DECADE) + *sullabē,* syllable; see SYLLABLE.] —**hen·dec′a·syl′la·ble** (-sĭl′ə-bəl) *n.*

Hen·der·son (hĕn′dər-sən) A city of SE NV SE of Las Vegas; founded 1942. Pop. 175,381.

Henderson, Fletcher Hamilton 1897–1952. Amer. jazz pianist, composer, and bandleader.

hen·di·a·dys (hĕn-dī′ə-dĭs) *n.* A figure of speech in which two words joined by a conjunction express a notion normally expressed by an adjective and a substantive, such as *grace and favor* instead of *gracious favor.* [LLat. < Gk. *hen dia duoin,* one by means of two : *hen,* neut. of *heis,* one; see SEM-¹ in App. + *dia,* through + *duoin,* genitive of *duō,* two; see DWO- in App.]

Hen·drix (hĕn′drĭks), **Jimi** 1942–70. Amer. musician whose innovative electric guitar playing greatly influenced the development of rock music.

hen·e·quen also **hen·e·quin** (hĕn′ĭ-kwĭn) *n.* **1.** A tropical American plant (*Agave fourcroydes*) having large sword-shaped leaves that yield a fiber used in making rope. **2.** This fiber. [Sp. *henequén,* perh. of Arawakan orig.]

Heng·yang (hŭng′yäng′) A city of SE China SSW of Wuhan. Pop. 1,814,936.

hen harrier *n.* See **northern harrier.**

Hen·ie (hĕn′ē), **Sonja** 1912–69. Norwegian-born figure skater who won ten world championships (1927–36).

Hen·ley (hĕn′lē) or **Hen·ley-on-Thames** (-ŏn-tĕmz′, -ôn-) A municipal borough of S-central England W of London; site of an annual rowing regatta (est. 1839). Pop. 10,976.

hen·na (hĕn′ə) *n.* **1a.** A tree or shrub (*Lawsonia inermis*) of the Middle East having fragrant white or reddish flowers. **b.** A reddish-orange dyestuff prepared from the leaves of this plant. **2.** A moderate or strong reddish brown to strong brown. ❖ *tr.v.* **-naed, -na·ing, -nas** To dye (hair, for example) with henna. [Ar. *ḥinnā′;* akin to *ḥana′a,* to become green.] —**hen′na** *adj.*

hen·ner·y (hĕn′ə-rē) *n., pl.* **-ies 1.** A poultry farm. **2.** See **hen-coop.**

hen·o·the·ism (hĕn′ō-thē-ĭz′əm) *n.* Belief in one god without denying the existence of others. [Gk. *heno-,* one (< *hen,* neut. of *heis;* see SEM-¹ in App.) + Gk. *theos,* god; see DHĒS- in App. + -ISM.] —**hen′o·the′ist** *n.* —**hen′o·the·is′tic** *adj.*

hen·peck (hĕn′pĕk′) *tr.v.* **-pecked, -peck·ing, -pecks** *Informal* To dominate or nag (one's husband).

Hen·ri (hĕn′rē), **Robert** 1865–1929. Amer. painter and member of the Ashcan School.

hen·ry (hĕn′rē) *n., pl.* **-ries** or **-rys** The unit of inductance in which an induced electromotive force of one volt is produced when the current is varied at the rate of one ampere per second. [After Joseph HENRY.]

Henry I Known as "Henry Beauclerc." 1068–1135. King of England (1100–35) who conquered Normandy (1106).

Henry II¹ 1133–89. King of England (1154–89) who founded the Plantagenet royal line.

Henry II² 1519–59. King of France (1547–59) who regained Calais from the English (1558).

Henry III¹ 1207–72. King of England (1216–72) whose reign was marred by opposition led by Simon de Montfort.

Henry III² 1551–89. King of France (1574–89) who helped plot the Saint Bartholomew's Day Massacre (1572).

Henry IV¹ 1050–1106. Holy Roman emperor and king of Germany (1056–1106) who vied with Pope Gregory VII.

Henry IV² Known as "Henry Bolingbroke." 1366?–1413. King of England (1399–1413) and founder of the Lancastrian line.

Henry IV³ Known as "Henry of Navarre." 1553–1610. King of France (1589–1610) who founded the Bourbon royal line and gave rights to French Protestants in the Edict of Nantes (1598).

Henry V¹ 1081–1125. Holy Roman emperor and king of Germany (1106–25).

Sonja Henie

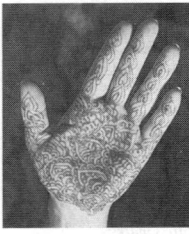

henna
tattoos made with henna dye

Henry V² 1387–1422. King of England (1413–22) who defeated the French at Agincourt (1415).

Henry VI 1421–71. King of England (1422–61 and 1470–71) who was captured at the Battle of Barnet and murdered in the Tower of London.

Henry VII Known as "Henry Tudor." 1457–1509. King of England (1485–1509) and founder of the Tudor line.

Henry VIII 1491–1547. King of England (1509–47) whose divorce from Catherine of Aragon compelled him to break from the Catholic Church by the Act of Supremacy (1534).

Henry, Cape A promontory of SE VA at the entrance to Chesapeake Bay E of Norfolk.

Henry, Joseph 1797–1878. Amer. physicist who conducted extensive studies of electromagnetic phenomena.

Henry, O. See William Sydney **Porter.**

Henry, Patrick 1736–99. Amer. Revolutionary leader and orator who spurred the creation of the Virginia militia with his words "Give me liberty, or give me death" (1775).

Henry the Navigator 1394–1460. Prince of Portugal who established an observatory and school of navigation and directed voyages that expanded Portugal's colonial empire.

hens-and-chick·ens (hĕnz′ən-chĭk′ənz) *n.* Plural of **hen-and-chickens.**

Hen·son (hĕn′sən), **Jim** 1936–90. Amer. puppeteer and creator of the Muppets, including Kermit the Frog and Big Bird.

Henson, Matthew Alexander 1866–1955. Amer. explorer who accompanied Peary on seven Arctic expeditions, including the 1909 expedition that claimed to have first reached the North Pole.

hent (hĕnt) *tr.v.* **hent·ed, hent·ing, hents** *Obsolete* To take hold of; seize. [ME *henten* < OE *hentan.*]

hep (hĕp) *adj. Slang* Variant of **hip².**

hep·a·rin (hĕp′ər-ĭn) *n.* A glycosaminoglycan found esp. in lung and liver tissue, able to prevent the clotting of blood and used to treat thrombosis. [LLat. *hēpar,* liver (< Gk.; see YĒK°ʳ in App.) + -IN.]

he·pat·ic (hĭ-păt′ĭk) *adj.* **1.** Of, relating to, or resembling the liver. **2.** Acting on or occurring in the liver. ❖ *n.* A drug that acts on the liver. [ME *epatic* < OFr. *hepatique* < Lat. *hēpaticus* < Gk. *hēpatikos* < *hēpar, hēpat-,* liver. See YĒK°ʳ in App.]

he·pat·i·ca (hĭ-păt′ĭ-kə) *n.* Any of several woodland plants of the genus *Hepatica,* esp. *H. americana* of eastern North America, having three-lobed leaves and white or lavender flowers. [ME *epatica,* liverwort < Med.Lat. *hēpatica* < fem. of Lat. *hēpaticus,* of the liver. See HEPATIC.]

hepatic duct *n.* The main excretory duct of the liver, which joins the cystic duct to form the common bile duct.

hep·a·ti·tis (hĕp′ə-tī′tĭs) *n., pl.* **-tit·i·des** (-tĭt′ĭ-dēz′) Inflammation of the liver, usu. caused by a virus and characterized by jaundice, fever, liver enlargement, and abdominal pain.

hepatitis A *n.* Hepatitis caused by an RNA virus that is transmitted by ingestion of infected food and water, usu. having milder symptoms than hepatitis B.

hepatitis B *n.* Hepatitis caused by a DNA virus that is transmitted by contact with contaminated blood or blood products, sometimes leading to chronic liver disease.

hepatitis C *n.* Hepatitis caused by an RNA virus that is transmitted by contact with contaminated blood or blood products, esp. by the injection of illegal drugs.

hepato– or **hepat–** *pref.* Liver: *hepatitis.* [Gk. *hēpato-* < *hēpar,* *hēpat-,* liver. See YĒK°ʳ in App.]

hep·a·to·cyte (hĕp′ə-tə-sīt′, hĭ-păt′ə-) *n.* A parenchymal cell of the liver.

hep·a·to·ma (hĕp′ə-tō′mə) *n., pl.* **-mas** or **-ma·ta** (-mə-tə) A usu. cancerous tumor occurring in the liver.

hep·a·to·meg·a·ly (hĕp′ə-tə-mĕg′ə-lē, hĭ-păt′ə-) *n.* Abnormal enlargement of the liver.

hep·a·to·tox·ic·i·ty (hĕp′ə-tō-tŏk-sĭs′ĭ-tē, hĭ-păt′ō-) *n.* **1.** The quality or condition of being toxic or destructive to the liver. **2.** The capacity of a substance to have damaging effects on the liver. —**hep′a·to·tox′ic** (-tŏk′sĭk) *adj.*

hep·a·to·tox·in (hĕp′ə-tō-tŏk′sĭn, hĭ-păt′ō-) *n.* A substance capable of causing damage to the liver.

Hep·burn (hĕp′bûrn′), **Audrey** 1929–93. Belgian-born Amer. actress whose films include *Breakfast at Tiffany's* (1961).

Hepburn, Katharine Houghton b. 1909. Amer. actress whose films include *The African Queen* (1951).

hep·cat (hĕp′kăt′) *n. Slang* A performer or devotee of swing and jazz, esp. during the 1940s.

He·phaes·tus (hĭ-fĕs′təs) *n. Greek Mythology* The god of fire and metalworking.

Hep·ple·white (hĕp′əl-hwīt′, -wīt′) *adj.* Of, relating to, or being an English style of furniture of the late 18th century, marked by its graceful lines and concave curves and the shield or heart backs of its chairs. [After George HEPPLEWHITE.]

Hepplewhite, George d. 1786. British cabinetmaker known for his elegant designs.

hepta– or **hept–** *pref.* Seven: *heptarchy.* [Gk. < *hepta,* seven. See SEPTM̥ in App.]

hep·tad (hĕp′tăd′) *n.* A group or series of seven. [Gk. *heptas, heptad-,* the number seven < *hepta,* seven. See SEPTM̥ in App.]

hep•ta•gon (hĕp′tə-gŏn′) *n.* A polygon having seven sides. [Lat. *heptagōnum* < Gk. *heptagōnos*, having seven angles : *hepta-*, hepta- + *-gōnos*, angled; see –GON.] —**hep•tag′o•nal** (-tăg′ə-nəl) *adj.*

hep•ta•he•dron (hĕp′tə-hē′drən) *n., pl.* **-drons** or **-dra** (-drə) A polyhedron with seven faces. —**hep′ta•he′dral** (-drəl) *adj.*

hep•tam•e•ter (hĕp-tăm′ĭ-tər) *n.* **1.** A metrical unit consisting of seven feet. **2.** A line of verse with seven metrical feet.

hep•tane (hĕp′tān′) *n.* A volatile flammable liquid hydrocarbon, C_7H_{16}, obtained in the fractional distillation of petroleum and used as a standard for octane ratings, an anesthetic, and a solvent.

hep•tar•chy (hĕp′tär′kē) *n., pl.* **-chies 1a.** Government by seven persons. **b.** A state governed by seven persons. **2.** often **Heptarchy** The informal confederation of Anglo-Saxon kingdoms from the fifth to the ninth century, consisting of Kent, Sussex, Wessex, Essex, Northumbria, East Anglia, and Mercia.

hep•ta•stich (hĕp′tə-stĭk′) *n.* A stanza or strophe consisting of seven lines.

Hep•ta•teuch (hĕp′tə-to͞ok′, -tyo͞ok′) *n. Bible* The first seven books of the Old Testament. [Gk. *heptateukhos*, volume containing seven books : *hepta-*, hepta- + *teukhos*, case for papyrus rolls, book.]

hep•tath•lon (hĕp-tăth′lən, -lŏn′) *n.* A track-and-field event usu. for women that includes the 200-meter and 800-meter runs, 100-meter hurdles, shot put, javelin throw, high jump, and long jump. [HEPT(A)– + (DEC)ATHLON.]

Hep•worth (hĕp′wûrth′), Dame **Barbara** 1903–75. British sculptor known esp. for her abstract works in stone and in bronze.

her (hər, ər; hûr *when stressed*) *adj.* The possessive form of **she.** Used as a modifier before a noun: *her skill.* ❖ *pron.* The objective case of **she. 1a.** Used as the direct object of a verb: *saw her at work.* **b.** Used as the indirect object of a verb: *gave her a round of applause.* **2.** Used as the object of a preposition: *addressed to her.* **3.** *Informal* Used as a predicate nominative: *It's her.* **4.** *Nonstandard* Used reflexively as the indirect object of a verb: *She got her a new job.* See Note at **me.** ❖ *n.* A female: *The dog is a her.* See Usage Notes at **be, I**[1]. [ME < OE *hire.* See **ko-** in App.]

He•ra (hîr′ə) also **He•re** (hîr′ē) *n. Greek Mythology* The goddess of women, marriage, and childbirth; the wife and sister of Zeus.

Her•a•cle•a (hĕr′ə-klē′ə) An ancient Greek city of S Italy near the Gulf of Taranto.

Her•a•cles or **Her•a•kles** (hĕr′ə-klēz′) *n. Greek & Roman Mythology* Variants of **Hercules** 1.

Her•a•cli•tus (hĕr′ə-klī′təs) fl. 500 B.C. Early Greek philosopher who maintained that strife and change are natural conditions of the universe. —**Her′a•cli′te•an** (-tē-ən) *adj.*

Her•a•cli•us (hĕr′ə-klī′əs, hĭ-răk′lē-) 575?–641. Emperor of the Byzantine Empire (610–641).

her•ald (hĕr′əld) *n.* **1.** A person who heralds important news; a messenger. **2.** One that gives a sign or indication of something to come; a harbinger. **3.** An official whose specialty is heraldry. **4a.** An official formerly charged with making royal proclamations and bearing messages of state between sovereigns. **b.** An official who formerly made proclamations and conveyed challenges at a tournament. ❖ *tr.v.* **-ald•ed, -ald•ing, -alds** To proclaim; announce. [ME < AN, of Gmc. orig. See **koro-** in App.]

he•ral•dic (hə-răl′dĭk) *adj.* Of or relating to heralds or heraldry. —**he•ral′di•cal•ly** *adv.*

her•ald•ry (hĕr′əl-drē) *n., pl.* **-ries 1a.** The profession, study, or art of devising, granting, and blazoning arms, tracing genealogies, and determining rank or protocol. **b.** The study of the history and description of armorial bearings and their accessories. **2.** Armorial ensigns or similar insignia. **3.** Pomp and ceremony, esp. attended with armorial trappings; pageantry. —**her′ald•ist** *n.*

herb (ûrb, hûrb) *n.* **1.** A plant whose stem does not produce woody persistent tissue and usu. dies after each growing season. **2.** Any of various often aromatic plants used esp. in medicine or as seasoning. **3.** *Slang* Marijuana. [ME *herbe* < OFr. *erbe* < Lat. *herba.*] —**herb′y** *adj.*

her•ba•ceous (hûr-bā′shəs, ûr-) *adj.* **1.** Relating to or characteristic of an herb. **2.** Green and leaflike in appearance or texture. [< Lat. *herbāceus* < *herba*, herb.]

herb•age (ûr′bĭj, hûr′-) *n.* **1.** Herbaceous plant growth, esp. grass or similar vegetation for pasturage. **2.** The fleshy, often edible parts of plants. [ME < OFr. *erbage* < *erbe.* See HERB.]

herb•al (ûr′bəl, hûr′-) *adj.* Of, relating to, or containing herbs. ❖ *n.* A book about plants and herbs, esp. those useful to people.

herb•al•ism (ûr′bə-lĭz′əm, hûr′-) *n.* **1.** Herbal medicine. **2.** The business of growing, collecting, and distributing herbal products. —**herb′al•ist** *n.*

herbal medicine *n.* **1.** The use of medicinal herbs to promote health or healing. **2.** A plant-based preparation used for its medicinal properties.

her•bar•i•um (hûr-bâr′ē-əm, ûr-) *n., pl.* **-i•ums** or **-i•a** (-ē-ə) **1.** A collection of dried plants mounted, labeled, and systematically arranged for scientific study. **2.** A place or institution keeping such a collection. [LLat. *herbārium* < Lat. *herbārius*, one skilled in herbs < Lat. *herba*, herb, vegetation.]

herb bennet *n.* A Eurasian herb *(Geum urbanum)* having having a root valued for its astringent properties and for its essential oil. [ME *herbe benet* < AN < Med.Lat. *herba benedicta* : Lat. *herba*, herb + Lat. *benedicta*, fem. p. part. of *benedīcere*, to bless; see BENEDICTION.]

herb doctor *n.* One who practices healing with herbs.

herbed (ûrbd, hûrbd) *adj.* Flavored with herbs.

Her•bert (hûr′bərt), **George** 1593–1633. English metaphysical poet whose works include "The Collar" (1633).

Herbert, Victor 1859–1924. Amer. composer known for his comic operas, including *Babes in Toyland* (1903).

her•bi•cide (hûr′bĭ-sīd′, ûr′-) *n.* A chemical substance used to destroy or inhibit the growth of plants, esp. weeds. —**her′bi•cid′al** (-sīd′l) *adj.*

her•bi•vore (hûr′bə-vôr′, -vōr′, ûr′-) *n.* An animal that feeds chiefly on plants. [< NLat. *Herbivora*, former mammalian group < neut. pl. of *herbivorus*, plant-eating : Lat. *herba*, vegetation + Lat. *-vorus*, -vorous.] —**her•biv′o•rous** (hûr-bĭv′ər-əs, ûr-) *adj.*

herb Paris *n.* A European plant *(Paris quadrifolia)* having a whorl of four leaves and a solitary yellow or greenish flower. [Prob. Med.Lat. *herba paris*, herb of a pair (perh. a reference to the two pairs of leaves on the whorl) : Lat. *herba*, herb + Lat. *paris*, genitive of *pār*, equal; see PAR.]

herb Robert *n.* A Eurasian herb *(Geranium robertianum)* having small reddish-purple flowers.

Her•cu•la•ne•um (hûr′kyə-lā′nē-əm) An ancient city of S-central Italy on the Bay of Naples; destroyed by the eruption of Mt. Vesuvius (A.D. 79).

Her•cu•le•an (hûr′kyə-lē′ən, hûr-kyo͞o′lē-) *adj.* **1.** often **herculean** Of unusual size, power, or difficulty. **2.** *Greek & Roman Mythology* **a.** Of or relating to Hercules. **b.** Resembling Hercules.

Her•cu•les (hûr′kyə-lēz′) *n.* **1.** also **Her•a•cles** or **Her•a•kles** (hĕr′ə-klēz′) *Greek & Roman Mythology* The son of Zeus and Alcmene, a hero of great strength who performed 12 labors demanded by the Argive king Eurystheus. **2.** A constellation in the Northern Hemisphere near Lyra and Corona Borealis. [Lat. *Herculēs* < Gk. *Hēraklēs* : *Hērā*, Hera + *kleos*, fame; see **kleu-** in App.]

Her•cu•les' club (hûr′kyə-lēz) *n.* **1.** A tree or shrub *(Aralia spinosa)* of the southeast United States having prickly, bipinnately compound leaves. **2.** A spiny shrub or tree *(Zanthoxylum clava-herculis)* of the central and southeast United States having pinnately compound leaves. [After the spiny club of Hercules.]

herd (hûrd) *n.* **1a.** A group of a single kind of domestic animal kept together for a purpose. **b.** A number of wild animals of one species that remain together as a group. **2a.** A large number of people; a crowd. **b.** The multitude of common people regarded as a mass. ❖ *v.* **herd•ed, herd•ing, herds** —*intr.* To come together in a herd. —*tr.* **1.** To gather, keep, or drive (animals) in a herd. **2.** To tend (sheep or cattle). **3.** To gather and place into a group or mass. [ME < OE *heord.*]

herd•er (hûr′dər) *n.* **1.** One who tends or drives a herd. **2.** An owner or a breeder of livestock.

her•dic (hûr′dĭk) *n.* A small horse-drawn cab with two wheels, side seats, and an entrance at the back, used in the 19th century. [After Peter *Herdic* (1824–88), American inventor.]

herds•man (hûrdz′mən) *n.* A herder.

here (hîr) *adv.* **1.** At or in this place: *Stop here for a rest.* **2.** At this time; now. **3.** At or on this point, detail, or item: *Here I disagree.* **4.** In the present life or condition. **5.** To this place; hither: *Come here.* ❖ *adj.* **1.** Used for emphasis after the demonstrative pronoun *this* or *these* or after a noun modified by the demonstrative adjective *this* or *these*: *these tires here.* **2.** *Nonstandard* Used for emphasis between a demonstrative adjective and a noun: *this here word.* ❖ *interj.* Used to respond to a roll call, attract attention, command an animal, or rebuke, admonish, or concur. ❖ *n.* **1.** This place. **2.** The present time or state: *in the here and now.* —***idiom:*** **neither here nor there** Unimportant and irrelevant. [ME < OE *hēr.* See **ko-** in App.]

He•re (hîr′ē) *n.* Variant of **Hera.**

here•a•bout (hîr′ə-bout′) also **here•a•bouts** (-bouts′) *adv.* In this general vicinity; around here.

here•af•ter (hîr-ăf′tər) *adv.* **1.** Immediately following this in time, order, or place; after this. **2.** In a future time or state: *hope to succeed hereafter.* ❖ *n.* The afterlife.

here•by (hîr-bī′) *adv.* By virtue of this; by this means.

her•e•dit•a•ment (hĕr′ĭ-dĭt′ə-mənt) *n.* Heritable property. [ME < Med.Lat. *hērēditāmentum* < LLat. *hērēditāre*, to inherit < Lat. *hērēs, hērēd-*, heir. See **ghē-** in App.]

he•red•i•tar•i•an (hə-rĕd′ĭ-târ′ē-ən) *n.* One who supports hereditarianism. —**he•red′i•tar′i•an** *adj.*

he•red•i•tar•i•an•ism (hə-rĕd′ĭ-târ′ē-ə-nĭz′əm) *n.* The doctrine or school regarding heredity as the primary determinant of intelligence and behavior independent of environment.

he•red•i•tar•y (hə-rĕd′ĭ-tĕr′ē) *adj.* **1.** *Law* **a.** Descending from an ancestor to a legal heir; passing down by inheritance. **b.** Having title or possession through inheritance. **2.** Transmitted or capable of being transmitted genetically from parent to offspring: *a hereditary disease.* **3a.** Appearing in or typical of successive generations. **b.** Learned from ancestors: *a hereditary prejudice.* **4.** Ancestral; traditional. **5.** Of or relating to heredity or inheritance. [ME < Lat. *hērēditārius* < *hērēditās*, inheritance. See HEREDITY.] —**he•red′i•tar′i•ly** (-târ′ə-lē) *adv.* —**he•red′i•tar′i•ness** *n.*

he•red•i•tist (hə-rĕd′ĭ-tĭst) *n.* A hereditarian.

Henry VIII
portrait by Hans Holbein the Younger

Katharine Hepburn

ă	pat	oi	**boy**
ā	pay	ou	**out**
âr	**care**	o͝o	**took**
ä	father	o͞o	**boot**
ĕ	pet	ŭ	cut
ē	be	ûr	**urge**
ĭ	pit	th	**thin**
ī	pie	*th*	this
îr	**pier**	hw	**which**
ŏ	pot	zh	vision
ō	toe	ə	about, item
ô	paw		

Stress marks:
′ (primary);
′ (secondary), as in
lexicon (lĕk′sĭ-kŏn′)

he•red•i•ty (hə-rĕd′ĭ-tē) *n., pl.* **-ties 1.** The genetic transmission of traits from parent to offspring. **2.** The sum of traits and potentialities transmitted genetically to an individual organism. [Fr. *hérédité* < OFr. *heredite*, inheritance < Lat. *hērēditās* < *hērēs*, *hērēd-*, heir. See **ghē-** in App.]

Here•ford (hûr′fərd, hĕr′ə-fərd) *n.* Any of a breed of beef cattle developed in England and having a reddish coat with white markings. [After *Hereford*, a former county of western England.]

here•in (hîr-ĭn′) *adv.* In or into this.

here•in•af•ter (hîr′ĭn-ăf′tər) *adv.* In a following part of this document, statement, or book.

here•in•be•fore (hîr′ĭn-bĭ-fôr′, -fōr′) *adv.* In a preceding part of this document, statement, or book.

here•in•to (hîr-ĭn′tōō) *adv.* Into this matter, circumstance, situation, or place.

here•of (hîr-ŭv′, -ŏv′) *adv.* Of this.

here•on (hîr-ŏn′, -ôn′) *adv.* On this; hereupon.

He•re•ro (hə-râr′ō, hĕr′ə-rō′) *n., pl.* **Herero** or **-ros 1.** A member of a pastoral people inhabiting Namibia and Botswana. **2.** The Bantu language of this people.

Hereford

he•re•si•arch (hə-rē′zē-ärk′, hĕr′ī-särk-) *n.* The originator or chief proponent of a heresy or heretical movement. [LLat. *haeresiarcha* < L.Gk. *hairesiarkhēs* : Gk. *hairesis*, sect; see **HERESY** + Gk. *-arkhēs*, -arch.]

her•e•sy (hĕr′ī-sē) *n., pl.* **-sies 1a.** An opinion or a doctrine at variance with established religious beliefs, esp. dissension from Christian dogma by a church member. **b.** Adherence to such an opinion or doctrine. **2a.** A controversial or unorthodox opinion or doctrine, as in politics, philosophy, or science. **b.** Adherence to such an opinion. [ME *heresie* < OFr. < LLat. *haeresis* < L.Gk. *hairesis* < Gk., a choosing, faction < *haireisthai*, to choose, middle voice of *hairein*, to take.]

her•e•tic (hĕr′ī-tĭk) *n.* One holding controversial opinions, esp. contrary to the accepted dogma of Christianity. ❖ *adj.* Heretical. [ME *heretik* < OFr. *heretique* < LLat. *haereticus* < Gk. *hairetikos*, able to choose, factious < *hairetos*, chosen < *haireisthai*, to choose. See **HERESY.**]

he•ret•i•cal (hə-rĕt′ī-kəl) *adj.* **1.** Of or relating to heresy or heretics. **2.** Marked by, revealing, or approaching departure from established beliefs or standards. **—he•ret′i•cal•ly** *adv.*

here•to (hîr-tōō′) *adv.* To this document, matter, or proposition.

here•to•fore (hîr′tə-fôr′, -fōr′) *adv.* Up to the present time; before this; previously.

here•un•to (hîr-ŭn′tōō) *adv.* Hereto.

here•up•on (hîr′ə-pŏn′, -pôn′) *adv.* **1.** Immediately after this. **2.** At or on this.

here•with (hîr-wĭth′, -wĭth′) *adv.* **1.** Along with this. **2.** By this means; hereby.

her•i•ot (hĕr′ē-ət) *n.* A tribute or service rendered to a feudal lord on the death of a tenant. [ME < OE *heregeatu* : *here*, army; see **koro-** in App. + *geatwe*, equipment, arms.]

her•i•ta•ble (hĕr′ī-tə-bəl) *adj.* **1.** Capable of being passed from one generation to the next; hereditary. **2.** Capable of inheriting or passing by inheritance. [ME < OFr. < *heriter*, to inherit < LLat. *hērēditāre*. See **INHERIT.**] **—her′i•ta•bil′i•ty** *n.* **—her′i•ta•bly** *adv.*

her•i•tage (hĕr′ī-tĭj) *n.* **1.** Property that is or can be inherited; an inheritance. **2.** Something passed down from preceding generations; a tradition. **3.** The status acquired through birth; a birthright. [ME < OFr. < *eritier*, heir < Med.Lat. *hērēditārius* < Lat., inherited. See **HEREDITARY.**]

her•i•tor (hĕr′ī-tər) *n.* An inheritor. [Alteration of ME *heriter* < AN < Med.Lat. *hērēditārius*. See **HEREDITARY.**]

He•riz (hîr′ēz, -ĕs) *n.* A strong, finely woven Persian rug that has patterns of flowers, garlands, and trees. [Alteration of *Heris*, a town of Iran.]

herk•y-jerk•y (hûr′kē-jûr′kē) *adj.* Spasmodic, irregular, and unpredictable, as in movement. [Reduplication of JERKY[1].]

herm (hûrm) also **her•ma** (hûr′mə) *n., pl.* **herms** also **-mae** (-mī) A bust, usu. of Hermes mounted on a rectangular stone post, used as a boundary marker in ancient Greece. [Lat. *hermēs*, *herma* < Gk. *hermēs* < *Hermēs*, Hermes.]

Her•man (hûr′mən), **Woodrow Charles** ("Woody") 1913–87. Amer. jazz musician and bandleader.

her•maph•ro•dite (hər-măf′rə-dīt′) *n.* **1.** An organism, such as an earthworm, having both male and female reproductive organs. **2.** A person or animal exhibiting hermaphroditism. [ME *hermofrodite* < Med.Lat. *hermofrodītus* < Lat. *Hermaphrodītus*. See **HERMAPHRODITUS.**] **—her•maph′ro•dit′ic** (-dĭt′ĭk) *adj.* **—her•maph′ro•dit′i•cal•ly** *adv.*

hermaphrodite brig *n. Nautical* A two-masted vessel with a square-rigged foremast and a schooner-rigged mainmast.

her•maph•ro•dit•ism (hər-măf′rə-dī-tĭz′əm) also **her•maph•ro•dism** (-rə-dĭz′əm) *n.* **1.** An anomalous condition in humans and animals in which both male and female reproductive organs and secondary sexual characteristics are present in the same individual. **2.** The presence of both male and female reproductive organs in a plant or animal, as in an earthworm.

Her•maph•ro•di•tus (hər-măf′rə-dī′təs) *n. Greek Mythology* The son of Hermes and Aphrodite, who became united in one

body with the nymph Salmacis. [Lat. *Hermaphrodītus* < Gk. *Hermaphrodītos* : *Hermēs*, Hermes + *Aphroditē*, Aphrodite; see **APHRODITE.**]

her•me•neu•tic (hûr′mə-nōō′tĭk, -nyōō′-) also **her•me•neu•ti•cal** (-tĭ-kəl) *adj.* Interpretive; explanatory. [Gk. *hermēneutikos* < *hermēneutēs*, interpreter < *hermēneuein*, to interpret < *hermēneus*, interpreter.] **—her′me•neu′ti•cal•ly** *adv.*

her•me•neu•tics (hûr′mə-nōō′tĭks, -nyōō′-) *n. (used with a sing. or pl. verb)* The theory and methodology of interpretation, esp. of scriptural text. **—her′me•neu′tist** *n.*

Her•mes (hûr′mēz) *n. Greek Mythology* The gods' messenger and the god of commerce, invention, cunning, and theft.

Hermes Tris•me•gis•tus (trĭs′mə-jĭs′təs, trĭz′-) *n. Mythology* Hermes as identified with the Egyptian god Thoth, the legendary author of works on alchemy, astrology, and magic. [Med.Lat. *Hermēs Trismegistus* < Gk. *Hermēs trismegistos* : *Hermēs*, Hermes + *trismegistos*, thrice greatest (*tris*, thrice; see **trei-** in App. + *megistos*, greatest; see **meg-** in App.).]

her•met•ic (hər-mĕt′ĭk) also **her•met•i•cal** (-ĭ-kəl) *adj.* **1.** Completely sealed, esp. against the escape or entry of air. **2.** Impervious to outside interference or influence. **3.** often **Hermetic a.** *Mythology* Of or relating to Hermes Trismegistus or the works ascribed to him. **b.** Having to do with the occult sciences, esp. alchemy; magical. [NLat. *hermēticus*, alchemical < Med.Lat. *Hermēs (Trismegistus)*. See **HERMES TRISMEGISTUS.**] **—her•met′i•cal•ly** *adv.*

her•mit (hûr′mĭt) *n.* **1.** One who has withdrawn from society and lives alone; a recluse. **2.** A spiced cookie made with molasses, raisins, and nuts. [ME *heremite* < OFr. < Med.Lat. *herēmīta* < LLat. *erēmīta* < LGk. *erēmītēs* < Gk. *erēmiā*, desert < *erēmos*, solitary.] **—her•mit′ic, her•mit′i•cal** *adj.* **—her•mit′i•cal•ly** *adv.*

her•mit•age (hûr′mĭ-tĭj) *n.* **1a.** The habitation of a hermit or group of hermits. **b.** A monastery or abbey. **2.** A place where one can live in seclusion; a retreat. **3.** The condition or way of life of a hermit. [ME < OFr. *hermitage* < *heremite*, hermit. See **HERMIT.**]

hermit crab *n.* Any of various crabs of the order Decapoda that protect their unarmored abdomens by taking over the empty shells of snails or other univalve mollusks.

hermit thrush *n.* A North American bird *(Catharus guttatus)* with brown plumage, a spotted breast, and a reddish tail.

Her•mon (hûr′mən), **Mount** A peak, 2,815.8 m (9,232 ft), of the Anti-Lebanon Range on the Syria-Lebanon border; traditionally considered the site of Jesus's transfiguration.

Her•mo•sil•lo (ĕr′mō-sē′ō) A city of NW Mexico near the Gulf of CA W of Chihuahua; est. c. 1700. Pop. 297,175.

hern (hûrn) *n.* A heron. [Variant of HERON.]

Her•ne (hĕr′nə) A city of W-central Germany in the Ruhr district ENE of Essen. Pop. 180,539.

her•ni•a (hûr′nē-ə) *n., pl.* **-ni•as** or **-ni•ae** (-nē-ē′) The protrusion of an organ or other structure through the wall that normally contains it; a rupture. [ME < Lat.] **—her′ni•al** *adj.*

her•ni•ate (hûr′nē-āt′) *intr.v.* **-at•ed, -at•ing, -ates** To protrude through a ruptured body wall. **—her′ni•a′tion** *n.*

he•ro (hîr′ō) *n., pl.* **-roes 1.** In mythology and legend, a man, often of divine ancestry, who is endowed with great courage and strength, celebrated for bold exploits, and favored by the gods. **2.** A person noted for feats of courage or nobility of purpose, esp. one who has risked or sacrificed his or her life. **3.** A person noted for special achievement in a particular field: *the heroes of medicine.* **4.** The principal male character in a novel, poem, or dramatic presentation. **5.** *Chiefly New York City* See **submarine** 2. See Regional Note at **submarine.** [Ult. < Gk. *hērōs.*]

He•ro[1] (hîr′ō) *n. Greek Mythology* A priestess of Aphrodite beloved by Leander.

He•ro[2] (hē′rō, hîr′ō) or **He•ron** (hē′rŏn′) 1st cent. A.D. Alexandrian scientist who devised a formula for determining the area of a triangle.

Her•od (hĕr′əd) Known as "the Great." 73?–4 B.C. King of Judea (40–4) who according to the Bible attempted to kill the infant Jesus by ordering the death of all children under the age of two in Bethlehem.

Herod An•ti•pas (ăn′tĭ-păs′, -pəs) d. c. A.D. 40. Ruler of Judea and tetrarch in Galilee (4 B.C.–A.D. 40).

He•ro•di•as (hĭ-rō′dē-əs) d. c. A.D. 39. The niece and second wife of Herod Antipas and the mother of Salome.

He•rod•o•tus (hĭ-rŏd′ə-təs) Known as "the Father of History." 5th cent. B.C. Greek historian whose writings are the earliest known examples of narrative history.

he•ro•ic (hĭ-rō′ĭk) *adj.* also **he•ro•i•cal** (-ĭ-kəl) **1.** Of, relating to, or resembling the heroes of literature, legend, or myth. **2.** Having, showing, or characteristic of the qualities appropriate to a hero; courageous. **3a.** Impressive in size or scope; grand. **b.** Of a size or scale that is larger than life. ❖ *n.* **1.** A line of heroic verse.

hermit crab

2. heroics Heroic behavior or action. **3. heroics** Melodramatic behavior or language. —**he·ro′i·cal·ly** *adv.*

heroic couplet *n.* A verse unit consisting of two rhymed lines in iambic pentameter.

heroic drama *n.* Restoration tragedy or tragicomedy in heroic couplets and marked by exoticism, bombastic rhetoric, and exaggerated characters.

heroic meter *n.* See **heroic verse.**

heroic stanza *n.* A stanza consisting of four lines in iambic pentameter rhyming *abab* or *aabb.*

heroic verse *n.* One of several verse forms traditionally used in epic and dramatic poetry, esp.: **a.** The dactylic hexameter in Greek and Latin. **b.** The iambic pentameter in English. **c.** The alexandrine in French.

her·o·in (hĕr′ō-ĭn) *n.* An odorless, bitter crystalline compound, $C_{17}H_{17}NO(C_2H_3O_2)_2$, that is derived from morphine and is a highly addictive narcotic. [Ger., orig. a trademark.]

her·o·ine (hĕr′ō-ĭn) *n.* **1.** A woman noted for courage and daring action. **2.** A woman noted for special achievement in a particular field. **3.** The principal female character in a novel, poem, or dramatic presentation. See Usage Note at **hero.** [Lat. *hērōīnē, hērōīna* < Gk. *hērōīnē,* fem. of *hērōs,* hero. See HERO.]

her·o·in·ism (hĕr′ō-ĭn-ĭz′əm) *n.* Addiction to heroin.

her·o·ism (hĕr′ō-ĭz′əm) *n.* **1.** Heroic conduct or behavior. **2.** Heroic characteristics or qualities; courage.

her·on (hĕr′ən) *n.* Any of various wading birds of the family Ardeidae, having a long neck, long legs, a long pointed bill, and usu. white, gray, or bluish-gray plumage. [ME < OFr., of Gmc. orig.]

He·ron (hĕr′ŏn) See **Hero².**

her·on·ry (hĕr′ən-rē) *n., pl.* **-ries** A place where herons nest and breed.

hero worship *n.* Intense or excessive admiration for a hero or a person regarded as a hero.

he·ro-wor·ship (hîr′ō-wûr′shĭp) *tr.v.* **-shiped, -ship·ing, -ships** or **-shipped, -ship·ping, -ships 1.** To revere as an ideal. **2.** To adulate. —**he′ro-wor′ship·er** *n.*

her·pes (hûr′pēz) *n.* Any of several viral diseases causing the eruption of vesicles on the skin or mucous membranes, esp. herpes simplex or herpes zoster. [ME < Lat. *herpēs* < Gk. < *herpein,* to creep.] —**her·pet′ic** (hər-pĕt′ĭk) *adj.*

herpes simplex *n.* **1.** A recurrent viral disease caused by the herpes simplex virus, type one, and marked by the eruption of vesicles on the mouth, lips, or face. **2.** A recurrent viral disease caused by the herpes simplex virus, type two, and marked by the eruption of vesicles on the genitals. [NLat. *herpēs simplex.*]

her·pes·vi·rus (hûr′pēz-vī′rəs) *n., pl.* **-rus·es** Any of a group of DNA-containing animal viruses that form characteristic inclusion bodies within the nuclei of host cells and cause diseases such as chickenpox and herpes simplex.

herpes zoster *n.* See **shingles.** [NLat. *herpēs zōstēr* : Lat. *herpēs,* herpes + Gk. *zōstēr,* girdle.]

her·pe·tol·o·gy (hûr′pĭ-tŏl′ə-jē) *n.* The branch of zoology that deals with reptiles and amphibians. [Gk. *herpeton,* reptile (< *herpein,* to creep) + –LOGY.] —**her′pe·to·log′ic** (-tə-lŏj′ĭk), **her′pe·to·log′i·cal** *adj.* —**her′pe·tol′o·gist** *n.*

Herr (hĕr) *n., pl.* **Her·ren** (hĕr′ən) Used as a male courtesy title in a German-speaking area, prefixed to a surname or professional title. [Ger. < MHGer. *hērre* < OHGer. *hērro,* lord, master, alteration of *hēriro,* older, more venerable, comp. of *hēr,* proud, holy, splendid, noble.]

Her·rick (hĕr′ĭk), **Robert** 1591–1674. English Cavalier poet whose works include "Delight in Disorder" (1648).

her·ring (hĕr′ĭng) *n., pl.* **herring** or **-rings** Any of various fishes of the family Clupeidae, esp. a commercially important food fish (*Clupea harengus*) of Atlantic and Pacific waters. [ME *hering* < OE *hæring.*]

her·ring·bone (hĕr′ĭng-bōn′) *n.* **1a.** A decorative pattern of rows of slanted parallel lines with the direction of the slant alternating row by row. **b.** A twilled fabric woven in this pattern. **2.** *Sports* A method of climbing a ski slope with the tips of the skis pointed outward. ❖ *v.* **-boned, -bon·ing, -bones** —*tr.* To arrange or decorate with a herringbone pattern. —*intr.* **1.** To produce a herringbone pattern. **2.** *Sports* To ascend a ski slope with the ski tips pointed outward.

herring gull *n.* A common seagull (*Larus argentatus*) of the Northern Hemisphere having gray and white plumage with black wing tips.

hers (hûrz) *pron.* (*used with a sing. or pl. verb*) Used to indicate the one or ones belonging to her: *Whose hat? Hers.* [ME *hires, hirs : hire,* her; see HER + *-es,* possessive suff.; see *-'s.*]

Her·schel (hûr′shəl) Family of British astronomers, including Sir **William** (1738–1822), who discovered Uranus (1781); his sister **Caroline** (1750–1848), who published a star catalog; and his son Sir **John Frederick William** (1792–1871), who conducted research on light, photography, and astrophysics.

her·self (hûr-sĕlf′) *pron.* **1.** That one identical with her: **a.** Used reflexively as the direct or indirect object of a verb or the object of a preposition: *She bought herself a car.* **b.** Used for emphasis: *She herself was certain.* **c.** Used in an absolute construction: *In office herself, she helped him get a job.* **2.** Her normal or healthy condition or state: *She's feeling herself again.* [ME *hire self* < OE *hire self.*]

selfre, dative of *hēo self* : *hēo,* she; see SHE + *self,* self; see SELF.]

her·sto·ry (hûr′stə-rē) *n., pl.* **-sto·ries** History considered from a feminist viewpoint or emphasizing the actions of women. [Blend of HER and HISTORY (under an interpretation of the latter as "his story").]

hertz (hûrts) *n., pl.* **hertz** A unit of frequency equal to one cycle per second. [After Heinrich Rudolf HERTZ.]

Hertz (hûrts, hĕrts), **Heinrich Rudolf** 1857–94. German physicist who was the first to produce radio waves artificially.

Hertz·i·an wave (hûrt′sē-ən, hĕrt′-) *n.* An electromagnetic wave, usu. of radio frequency, produced by the oscillation of electricity in a conductor. [After Heinrich Rudolf HERTZ.]

Hertz·sprung-Rus·sell diagram (hĕrts′sprŭng-rŭs′əl) *n.* A graph of the absolute magnitude of stars plotted against their surface temperature or color, used in the study of stellar evolution. [After Ejnar *Hertzsprung* (1873–1967), Danish astronomer, and Henry Norris RUSSELL.]

Herz·berg (hûrts′bûrg′), **Gerhard** 1904–99. German-born Canadian physicist who won a 1971 Nobel Prize for chemistry.

Her·ze·go·vi·na (hĕrt′sə-gō′vē-nə, -gō-vē′-, hûrt′-) The S region of Bosnia and Herzegovina; conquered by Serbs in the 13th cent. and joined with Bosnia since the 15th cent. —**Her′ze·go·vi′ni·an** *adj.* & *n.*

Her·zl (hĕrt′səl), **Theodor** 1860–1904. Hungarian-born Austrian who organized the Zionist World Congress (1897).

Her·zog (hûrt′sôg, hĕrt′sōкн), **Chaim** 1918–97. Irish-born Israeli politician who served as president (1983–93).

he's (hēz) **1.** Contraction of *he is: He's going.* **2.** Contraction of *he has: He's been there.*

Hesh·van also **Hesh·wan** (кнĕsh′vən, -vän) *n.* The second month of the year in the Jewish calendar. See table at **calendar.** [Heb. *ḥešwān,* short for *marḥeswān* < Akkadian *araḥsamnu, waraḥsamnu,* a month name : *arḥu, warḥu,* month + *samnu,* eighth (< *samāne,* eight).]

He·si·od (hē′sē-əd, hĕs′ē-) fl. 8th cent. B.C. Greek poet whose epics include *Works and Days* and *Theogony.*

hes·i·tan·cy (hĕz′ĭ-tən-sē) *n., pl.* **-cies 1.** The state or quality of being hesitant. **2.** An instance of hesitating.

hes·i·tant (hĕz′ĭ-tənt) *adj.* Inclined or tending to hesitate.

hes·i·tate (hĕz′ĭ-tāt′) *intr.v.* **-tat·ed, -tat·ing, -tates 1a.** To be slow to act, speak, or decide. **b.** To pause in uncertainty; waver. **2.** To be reluctant. **3.** To speak haltingly; falter. [Lat. *haesitāre, haesitāt-,* to hesitate, freq. of *haerēre,* to hold fast.] —**hes′i·tat′er** *n.* —**hes′i·tat′ing·ly** *adv.*

hes·i·ta·tion (hĕz′ĭ-tā′shən) *n.* **1.** The act or an instance of hesitating. **2.** The state of being hesitant. **3.** A pause or faltering in speech.

Hes·pe·ri·an (hĕ-spîr′ē-ən) *adj.* Of or relating to the west. [< Lat. *Hesperius* < Gk. *hesperios* < *hesperos,* evening. See **wespero-** in App.]

Hes·per·i·des (hĕ-spĕr′ĭ-dēz′) *pl.n. Greek Mythology* **1.** The nymphs who together with a dragon watch over a garden in which golden apples grow. **2.** (*used with a sing. verb*) A garden at the western end of the earth, in which golden apples grow. [Gk. < pl. of *hesperis,* fem. of *hesperios,* of the evening, western. See HESPERIAN.] —**Hes′per·id′i·an, Hes′per·id′e·an** (hĕs′pə-rĭd′ē-ən) *adj.*

hes·per·i·din (hĕ-spĕr′ĭ-dĭn) *n.* A crystalline compound, $C_{28}H_{34}O_{15}$, occurring in citrus fruit. [HESPERID(IUM) + –IN.]

hes·per·id·i·um (hĕs′pə-rĭd′ē-əm) *n., pl.* **-i·a** (-ē-ə) A berry having a leathery rind and juicy pulp divided into segments, as a citrus fruit. [NLat. < HESPERIDES, land of golden apples.]

Hes·per·us (hĕs′pər-əs) *n.* The planet Venus as the evening star. [ME < Lat. < Gk. *hesperos.* See HESPERIAN.]

Hess (hĕs), **(Walter Richard) Rudolf** 1894–1987. German Nazi leader who at the Nuremburg trials (1946) was sentenced to life imprisonment for war crimes.

Hess, Walter Rudolf 1881–1973. Swiss physiologist who shared a 1949 Nobel Prize.

Hesse (hĕs) A region and former grand duchy of W-central Germany; divided after 1567 into four regions ruled by various branches of the Hesse family.

Hes·se (hĕs′ə), **Hermann** 1877–1962. German-born Swiss writer whose works include *Siddhartha* (1922). He won the 1946 Nobel Prize for literature.

Hes·sian (hĕsh′ən) *adj.* Of or relating to Hesse or its inhabitants. ❖ *n.* **1.** A native or inhabitant of Hesse. **2.** A German mercenary in the British army in America during the Revolutionary War. **3.** A mercenary soldier.

Hessian boot *n.* A man's high tasseled boot introduced into England by Hessians in the 19th century.

Hessian fly *n.* A small fly (*Mayetiola destructor*) having larvae that infest and destroy wheat and other grain plants.

hes·so·nite (hĕs′ə-nīt′) *n.* Variant of **essonite.**

hest (hĕst) *n. Archaic* Command; behest. [ME, alteration of *hes* < OE *hǣs.* See **kei-²** in App.]

Hes·ti·a (hĕs′tē-ə) *n. Greek Mythology* The goddess of the hearth and the daughter of Cronus and Rhea.

he·tae·ra (hĭ-tîr′ə) also **he·tai·ra** (-tīr′ə) *n., pl.* **-tae·rae** (-tîr′ē) or **-tae·ras** also **-tai·rai** (-tīr′ī′) or **-tai·ras** An ancient Greek courtesan, esp. one of a special class of cultivated female

herringbone

ă	pat	oi	boy
ā	pay	ou	out
âr	care	oo	took
ä	father	oo	boot
ĕ	pet	ŭ	cut
ē	be	ûr	urge
ĭ	pit	th	thin
ī	pie	th	this
îr	pier	hw	which
ŏ	pot	zh	vision
ō	toe	ə	item
ô	paw		

Stress marks:
′ (primary);
′ (secondary), as in
lexicon (lĕk′sĭ-kŏn′)

companions. [Gk. *hetairā*, fem. of *hetairos*, companion. See **s(w)e-** in App.] —**he•tae′ric** *adj.*

het•er•o (hĕt′ə-rō′) *n., pl.* **-os** *Informal* A heterosexual person. —**het′er•o** *adj.*

hetero– *or* **heter–** *pref.* **1.** Other; different: *heterochromatic.* **2.** Containing different kinds of atoms: *heterocyclic.* [Gk. < *heteros,* other. See **sem-**[1] in App.]

het•er•o•at•om (hĕt′ə-rō-ăt′əm) *n.* An atom other than carbon in the structure of a heterocyclic compound.

het•er•o•cer•cal (hĕt′ə-rō-sûr′kəl) *adj.* Relating to, having, or being a tail fin in which the upper lobe is larger than the lower, as in sharks. [HETERO– + Gk. *kerkos,* tail + –AL[1].]

het•er•o•chro•mat•ic (hĕt′ə-rō-krō-măt′ĭk) *adj.* **1.** Of or characterized by different colors. **2.** Consisting of different wavelengths or frequencies. **3.** Of or relating to heterochromatin. —**het′er•o•chro′ma•tism** (-krō′mə-tĭz′əm) *n.*

het•er•o•chro•ma•tin (hĕt′ə-rō-krō′mə-tĭn) *n.* Tightly coiled chromosomal material that stains deeply during interphase and is believed to be genetically inactive.

het•er•o•cy•clic (hĕt′ə-rō-sī′klĭk, -sĭk′lĭk) *adj.* Containing more than one kind of atom joined in a ring. —**het′er•o•cy′cle** (-sī′kəl) *n.* —**het′er•o•cy′clic** *n.*

het•er•o•cyst (hĕt′ər-ə-sĭst′) *n.* A large transparent cell that occurs along the filaments of certain cyanobacteria.

het•er•o•dox (hĕt′ər-ə-dŏks′) *adj.* **1.** Not in agreement with accepted beliefs, esp. church doctrine or dogma. **2.** Holding unorthodox opinions. [Gk. *heterodoxos : hetero-,* hetero- + *doxa,* opinion (< *dokein,* to think; see **dek-** in App.).]

het•er•o•dox•y (hĕt′ər-ə-dŏk′sē) *n., pl.* **-ies 1.** The condition or quality of being heterodox. **2.** A heterodox opinion.

het•er•o•dyne (hĕt′ər-ə-dīn′) *adj.* Having alternating currents of two different frequencies that are combined to produce two new frequencies, the sum and difference of the original frequencies. ❖ *tr.v.* **-dyned, -dyn•ing, -dynes** To combine (a radio frequency wave) with a locally generated wave of different frequency in order to produce a new frequency equal to the sum or difference of the two. [HETERO– + *-dyne,* power, frequency (< Gk. *dunamis,* power; see DYNAMIC).]

het•er•oe•cious (hĕt′ə-rē′shəs) *adj.* Spending different stages of a life cycle on different, usu. unrelated hosts. Used of parasites such as tapeworms. [HETERO– + Gk. *oikiā,* house; see **weik-** in App. + –OUS.] —**het′er•oe′cism** (-sĭz′əm) *n.*

het•er•o•gam•ete (hĕt′ə-rō-găm′ēt′, -gə-mēt′) *n.* Either of two conjugating gametes that differ in structure or behavior.

het•er•o•ga•met•ic (hĕt′ə-rō-gə-mĕt′ĭk) *adj.* **1.** Producing dissimilar gametes, such as human males, who produce spermatozoa bearing X-chromosomes or Y-chromosomes. **2.** Of or relating to heterogametes.

het•er•og•a•mous (hĕt′ə-rŏg′ə-məs) *adj.* **1.** *Biology* **a.** Reproducing by the fusion of unlike gametes. **b.** Heterogonous. **2.** *Botany* Bearing male and female flowers.

het•er•og•a•my (hĕt′ə-rŏg′ə-mē) *n.* **1.** Alternation of sexual and parthenogenic generations, as in some aphids. **2.** The state or condition in which conjugating gametes are dissimilar in structure and size as well as in function. —**het′er•o•gam′ic** (-rō-găm′ĭk) *adj.*

het•er•o•ge•ne•i•ty (hĕt′ə-rō′jə-nē′ĭ-tē) *n.* The quality or state of being heterogeneous.

het•er•o•ge•ne•ous (hĕt′ə-rə-jē′nē-əs, -jēn′yəs) *adj.* **1.** also **het•er•og•e•nous** (hĕt′ə-rŏj′ə-nəs) Consisting of dissimilar elements or parts; not homogeneous. See Syns at **miscellaneous. 2.** Completely different; incongruous. [< Med.Lat. *heterogeneus* < Gk. *heterogenēs : hetero-,* hetero- + *genos,* kind, race; see **genə-** in App.] —**het′er•o•ge′ne•ous•ly** *adv.* —**het′er•o•ge′ne•ous•ness** *n.*

het•er•og•e•nous[1] (hĕt′ə-rŏj′ə-nəs) also **het•er•o•gen•ic** (-rō-jĕn′ĭk) *adj.* Not arising within the body; derived from another individual or species. —**het′er•og′e•ny** *n.*

het•er•og•e•nous[2] (hĕt′ə-rŏj′ə-nəs) *adj.* Variant of **heterogeneous** 1.

het•er•og•o•nous (hĕt′ə-rŏg′ə-nəs) *adj.* Characterized by the alternation of sexual and parthenogenic generations. [HETERO– + –GON(Y) + –OUS.] —**het′er•og′o•ny** *n.*

het•er•o•graft (hĕt′ə-rō-grăft′) *n.* A type of tissue graft in which the donor and recipient are of different species.

het•er•o•kar•y•on (hĕt′ər-ə-kăr′ē-ŏn′, -ən) *n.* A cell having two or more genetically different nuclei. [HETERO– + KARY(O)– + –ON[1].] —**het′er•o•kar′y•ot′ic** (-ŏt′ĭk) *adj.*

het•er•o•lec•i•thal (hĕt′ə-rō-lĕs′ə-thəl) *adj. Embryology* Having the yolk unevenly distributed throughout the egg. [HETERO– + Gk. *lekithos,* egg yolk + –AL[1].]

het•er•ol•o•gous (hĕt′ə-rŏl′ə-gəs) *adj.* **1.** Derived from a different species: *a heterologous graft.* **2.** Of or relating to cytologic or histological elements not normally occurring in a body part. **3.** Immunologically related but not identical. Used of certain cells and antiserums. [HETERO– + Gk. *logos,* word, relation; see –LOGY + –OUS.] —**het′er•ol′o•gous•ly** *adv.*

het•er•ol•o•gy (hĕt′ə-rŏl′ə-jē) *n.* Lack of correspondence between body parts, as in structure, due to different origins.

het•er•ol•y•sis (hĕt′ə-rŏl′ĭ-sĭs, -ə-rō-lĭ′sĭs) *n., pl.* **-ses** (-sēz′) **1.** *Biology* Dissolution of cells or proteins in one species by the action of lysins or enzymes of another. **2.** *Chemistry* An organic reaction in which the breaking of bonds leads to the formation of ion pairs. —**het′er•o•lyt′ic** (-ə-rō-lĭt′ĭk) *adj.*

het•er•om•er•ous (hĕt′ə-rŏm′ər-əs) *adj.* Having unequal or differing parts within the same structure or similar structures.

het•er•o•mor•phic (hĕt′ə-rō-môr′fĭk) *adj.* **1.** Having different forms at different periods of the life cycle. **2.** Nonstandard in size or structure. —**het′er•o•mor′phism** *n.*

het•er•on•o•mous (hĕt′ə-rŏn′ə-məs) *adj.* **1.** Subject to external or foreign laws or domination; not autonomous. **2.** *Biology* Differing in development or manner of specialization. [HETERO– + Gk. *nomos,* law; see –NOMY + –OUS.] —**het′er•on′o•mous•ly** *adv.*

het•er•o•nym (hĕt′ər-ə-nĭm′) *n.* One of two or more words with identical spellings but different meanings and pronunciations, such as *row* (a series arranged in a line), pronounced (rō), and *row* (a fight), pronounced (rou).

het•er•on•y•mous (hĕt′ə-rŏn′ə-məs) *adj.* **1.** Having the nature of or relating to a heteronym. **2.** Being different names or terms but having correspondence or relationship, as *mother* and *daughter.* [< L.Gk. *heterōnumos* < Gk., with a different denominator : Gk. *hetero-,* hetero- + Gk. *onoma,* name; see **nō-men-** in App.]

het•er•oph•o•ny (hĕt′ə-rŏf′ə-nē) *n.* The simultaneous playing or singing of two or more versions of a melody. —**het′er•o•phon′ic** (-ə-rə-fŏn′ĭk) *adj.*

het•er•o•phyl•lous (hĕt′ə-rō-fĭl′əs) *adj.* Having dissimilar leaves on one plant. —**het′er•o•phyl′ly** *n.*

het•er•o•phyte (hĕt′ə-rə-fīt′) *n.* A plant, as a parasite, that feeds on other organisms. —**het′er•o•phyt′ic** (-fĭt′ĭk) *adj.*

het•er•o•plas•ty (hĕt′ər-ə-plăs′tē) *n., pl.* **-ties** The surgical grafting of tissue from one individual or species to another. —**het′er•o•plas′tic** *adj.*

het•er•o•ploid (hĕt′ər-ə-ploid′) *adj.* Having a chromosome number that is not a whole-number multiple of the haploid chromosome number for that species. —**het′er•o•ploid′** *n.* —**het′er•o•ploi′dy** *n.*

het•er•op•ter•ous (hĕt′ə-rŏp′tər-əs) *adj.* Of or belonging to the hemopterous insect suborder Heteroptera, which includes the true bugs, marked by differing forewings and hind wings.

het•er•o•sex•ism (hĕt′ə-rō-sĕk′sĭz′əm) *n.* Discrimination or prejudice against lesbians or gay men by heterosexual people. —**het′er•o•sex′ist** *adj. & n.*

het•er•o•sex•u•al (hĕt′ə-rō-sĕk′shōō-əl) *adj.* **1.** Sexually oriented to persons of the opposite sex. **2.** Of or relating to different sexes. ❖ *n.* A heterosexual person. —**het′er•o•sex′u•al•ly** *adv.*

het•er•o•sex•u•al•i•ty (hĕt′ə-rō-sĕk′shōō-ăl′ĭ-tē) *n.* **1.** Sexual orientation to persons of the opposite sex. **2.** Sexual activity with another of the opposite sex.

het•er•o•sis (hĕt′ə-rō′sĭs) *n.* See **hybrid vigor.** [L.Gk. *heterōsis,* alteration, alteration of Gk. *heteroiōsis < heteroioun,* to alter < *heteroios,* different in kind < *heteros,* other. See HETERO–.] —**het′er•ot′ic** (-rŏt′ĭk) *adj.*

het•er•o•spo•rous (hĕt′ə-rə-spôr′əs, -spôr′-, hĕt′ə-rŏs′pər-əs) *adj.* Producing two types of spores differing in size and sex. —**het′er•o•spo′ry** *n.*

het•er•o•tax•is (hĕt′ə-rō-tăk′sĭs) also **het•er•o•tax•y** (hĕt′ər-ə-tăk′sē) or **het•er•o•tax•i•a** (hĕt′ə-rō-tăk′sē-ə) *n., pl.* **-tax•es** (-tăk′sēz) also **-tax•ies** or **-tax•i•as** Abnormal structural arrangement, as of body parts. —**het′er•o•tac′tic** (-tăk′tĭk), **het′er•o•tac′tous** (-tăk′təs) *adj.*

het•er•o•thal•lic (hĕt′ə-rō-thăl′ĭk) *adj.* Producing male and female gametangia in different structures or plants, as in some algae and fungi. [HETERO– + Gk. *thallos,* young shoot; see THALLO–.] —**het′er•o•thal′lism** *n.*

het•er•o•pi•a (hĕt′ə-rə-tō′pē-ə) also **het•er•ot•o•py** (hĕt′ə-rŏt′ə-pē) *n.* The occurrence of an organ, portion of an organ, or other tissue in an abnormal anatomic location.

het•er•o•top•ic (hĕt′ə-rō-tŏp′ĭk) *adj.* **1.** *Medicine* Occurring in an abnormal anatomic location: *heterotopic bone formation.* **2.** *Ecology* Occurring in a number of different habitats.

het•er•o•troph (hĕt′ə-rō-trŏf′, -trŏf′) *n.* An organism that cannot synthesize its own food and is dependent on complex organic substances for nutrition. [HETERO– + Gk. *trophos,* feeder; see –TROPHY.] —**het′er•o•troph′ic** (hĕt′ə-rō-trŏf′ĭk, -trŏf′ĭk) *adj.* —**het′er•o•troph′i•cal•ly** *adv.* —**het′er•ot′ro•phy** (-ə-rŏt′rə-fē) *n.*

het•er•o•typ•ic (hĕt′ə-rō-tĭp′ĭk) also **het•er•o•typ•i•cal** (-ĭ-kəl) *adj.* **1.** *Biology* Of, relating to, or being the reduction division of meiosis. **2.** Of a different type or form.

het•er•o•zy•go•sis (hĕt′ə-rō-zī-gō′sĭs) *n.* **1.** The formation of a zygote by the union of genetically different gametes. **2.** The condition of being a heterozygote.

het•er•o•zy•gote (hĕt′ə-rō-zī′gōt′) *n.* An organism that has different alleles at a particular gene locus on homologous chromosomes.

het•er•o•zy•gous (hĕt′ər-ə-zī′gəs) *adj.* **1.** Having different alleles at one or more corresponding chromosomal loci. **2.** Of or relating to a heterozygote. —**het′er•o•zy•gos′i•ty** (-ə-rō-zī-gŏs′ĭ-tē) *n.*

heth (кнĕt, кнĕs) *n.* The eighth letter of the Hebrew alphabet. [Heb. *ḥêt,* of Phoenician orig.]

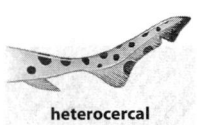

heterocercal
leopard shark's tail

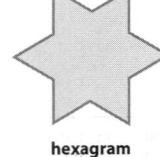

hexagram

het·man (hĕt′mən) *n., pl.* **-mans** See **ataman.** [Ukrainian *het-man* < Pol. *hetman* < Ger. dialectal *hötmann, hetmann,* captain; akin to Ger. *Hauptmann* < MHGer. *houbetman* : *houbet,* head (< OHGer. *houbit;* see **kaput-** in App.) + *man,* man (< OHGer.; see FUGLEMAN).]

heu·land·ite (hyōō′lən-dīt′) *n.* A white, red, or yellow zeolite mineral, CaO·Al₂O₃·6SiO₂·5H₂O. [After Henry *Heuland,* 19th-cent. British mineralogist.]

heu·ris·tic (hyōō-rĭs′tĭk) *adj.* **1.** Of or relating to a usu. speculative formulation guiding the investigation or solution of a problem. **2.** Of, relating to, or constituting an educational method in which students learn through their own investigations. **3.** *Computer Science* Relating to or using a problem-solving technique in which the most appropriate solution is selected at successive stages of a program for use in the next step of the program. ❖ *n.* **1.** A heuristic method or process. **2. heuristics** (*used with a sing. verb*) The study and application of heuristic methods and processes. [< Gk. *heuriskein,* to find.] **—heu·ris′ti·cal·ly** *adv.*

hew (hyōō) *v.* **hewed, hewn** (hyōōn) or **hewed, hew·ing, hews** —*tr.* **1.** To make or shape with or as if with an ax: *hew a path.* **2.** To cut down with an ax; fell: *hew an oak.* **3.** To strike or cut; cleave. —*intr.* **1.** To cut something by repeated blows, as of an ax. **2.** To adhere or conform strictly; hold. [ME *hewen* < OE *hēawan.*] **—hew′er** *n.*

HEW *abbr.* Department of Health, Education, and Welfare

hex¹ (hĕks) *n.* **1.** An evil spell; a curse. **2.** One that brings bad luck. ❖ *tr.v.* **hexed, hex·ing, hex·es** **1.** To put a hex on. **2.** To bring or wish bad luck to. [Penn. Dutch < Ger. *hexen,* to hex < *Hexe,* witch < MHGer. *hecse* < OHGer. *hagzissa.*] **—hex′er** *n.*

hex² (hĕks) *adj.* Hexagonal. Used of hardware.

hexa– or **hex–** *pref.* **1.** Six: *hexagram.* **2.** Containing six atoms, molecules, or groups: *hexose.* [Gk. < *hex,* six. See **s(w)eks** in App.]

hex·a·chlo·ro·eth·ane (hĕk′sə-klôr′ō-ĕth′ān′, -klôr′-) also **hex·a·chlor·eth·ane** (-klôr-ĕth′ān′, -klôr-) *n.* A colorless crystalline compound, Cl₃CCCl₃, used as a camphor substitute and in explosives and veterinary medicine.

hex·a·chlo·ro·phene (hĕk′sə-klôr′ə-fēn′, -klôr′-) *n.* A white powder, (C₆HCl₃OH)₂CH₂, used as a disinfectant and an antibacterial agent in soaps. [HEXA– + CHLORO– + PHEN(OL).]

hex·a·chord (hĕk′sə-kôrd′) *n.* A sequence of six tones with a semitone between the third and fourth tones, the others being whole tones, that was used in medieval music. [Med.Lat. *hexachordum* < Lat. *hexachordos,* having six strings or stops : Gk. *hexa-,* hexa- + Gk. *-khordos,* string, note (< *khordē*).]

hex·ad (hĕk′săd′) *n.* A group or series of six. [LLat. *hexas, hexad-,* the number six < Gk. < *hex,* six. See **s(w)eks** in App.] **—hex·ad′ic** (hĕk-săd′ĭk) *adj.*

hex·a·dec·i·mal (hĕk′sə-dĕs′ə-məl) *adj.* **1.** Of, relating to, or based on the number 16: *the hexadecimal number system.* **2.** Of or relating to sixteenths. ❖ *n.* A sixteenth.

hex·a·gon (hĕk′sə-gŏn′) *n.* A polygon having six sides. [Lat. *hexagōnum* < Gk. *hexagōnos,* having six angles : *hexa-,* hexa- + *-gōnos,* angled; see -GON.]

hex·ag·o·nal (hĕk-săg′ə-nəl) *adj.* **1.** Having six sides. **2.** Containing or shaped like a hexagon. **3.** *Mineralogy* Having three equal axes intersecting at angles of 60° in one plane and one axis of variable length that is perpendicular to the others. **—hex·ag′o·nal·ly** *adv.*

hex·a·gram (hĕk′sə-grăm′) *n.* **1.** A six-pointed star formed by extending each of the sides of a regular hexagon into equilateral triangles. **2.** A figure of six lines or sides.

hex·a·he·dron (hĕk′sə-hē′drən) *n.* A polyhedron, such as a cube, that has six faces. [Gk. *hexaedron* < neut. of *hexaedros,* having six sides : *hexa-,* hexa- + *-edros,* sided; see -HEDRON.] **—hex′a·he′dral** (-drəl) *adj.*

hex·am·er·ous (hĕk-săm′ər-əs) *adj.* **1.** Having six similar parts or divisions. **2.** *Botany* Having flower parts in sets of six. **—hex·am′er·ous·ly** *adv.*

hex·am·e·ter (hĕk-săm′ĭ-tər) *n.* **1.** A line of verse consisting of six metrical feet. **2.** In classical prosody, a line in which the first four feet are either dactylic or spondaic, the fifth is dactylic, and the sixth is spondaic. [Lat. < Gk. *hexametros,* having six metrical feet : *hexa-,* hexa- + *metron,* meter; see METER¹.] **—hex′a·met′ric** (hĕk′sə-mĕt′rĭk) *adj.* **hex′a·me′tri·cal** (-rĭ-kəl) *adj.*

hex·a·meth·yl·ene·tet·ra·mine (hĕk′sə-mĕth′ə-lēn-tĕt′rə-mēn′) *n.* See **methenamine.**

hex·ane (hĕk′sān′) *n.* A flammable liquid, C₆H₁₄, derived from the fractional distillation of petroleum and used as a solvent and a working fluid in some thermometers.

hex·a·pod (hĕk′sə-pŏd′) *n.* A six-legged arthropod of the class Insecta (formerly Hexapoda); an insect. ❖ *adj.* **1.** Of or belonging to the class Insecta. **2.** Having six legs or feet. [< NLat. *Hexapoda,* class name : Gk. *hexa-,* hexa- + NLat. *-poda,* -pod.] **—hex·ap′o·dous** (hĕk-săp′ə-dəs) *adj.*

Hex·a·teuch (hĕk′sə-tōōk′, -tyōōk′) *n. Bible* The first six books of the Old Testament. [HEXA– + (PENTA)TEUCH.]

hex·o·san (hĕk′sə-săn′) *n.* Any of several polysaccharides that have the general formula (C₆H₁₀O₅)ₙ and form a hexose on hydrolysis.

hex·ose (hĕk′sōs′) *n.* Any of various simple sugars, such as glucose, that have six carbon atoms per molecule.

---

hex sign *n.* Any of various round signs with designs thought to be magical, painted on barns to ward off evil.

hex·yl (hĕk′səl) *n.* The hydrocarbon radical, C₆H₁₃, having valence 1.

hex·yl·re·sor·ci·nol (hĕk′səl-rĭ-zôr′sə-nôl′, -nōl′, -nŏl′) *n.* A yellowish-white crystalline phenol, C₆H₁₃C₆H₃(OH)₂, used as an antiseptic and anthelmintic.

hey (hā) *interj.* Used to attract attention or express surprise, appreciation, wonder, or pleasure.

REGIONAL NOTE Originally just an exclamation, *hey* is nowadays also used as a greeting. As a short colloquial version of *How are you?* it seems to be replacing its close kin *hi* in many situations. *Hey* once had a distinctly Southern flavor but has become common throughout the United States.

hey·day (hā′dā′) *n.* The period of greatest popularity, success, or power; prime. [Perh. alteration of *heyda,* exclamation of pleasure, prob. alteration of ME *hey, hey.*]

Hey·er·dahl (hā′ər-däl′, hī′-), **Thor** b. 1914. Norwegian ethnologist and explorer who led the Kon Tiki expedition (1947) on a raft across the Pacific Ocean from Peru to Tuamotu to demonstrate that Polynesians may be of South American origin.

Hey·ward (hā′wərd), **(Edwin) DuBose** 1885–1940. Amer. writer best known for the novel *Porgy* (1925).

Hez·e·ki·ah (hĕz′ĭ-kī′ə) also **Ez·e·ki·as** (ĕz′ĭ-kī′əs) fl. 715?–686? B.C. King of Judah who according to the Bible sought to abolish idolatry and restore worship of Jehovah.

Hf The symbol for the element **hafnium.**

HF *abbr.* high frequency

hf. *abbr.* half

hg *abbr.* hemoglobin

Hg The symbol for the element **mercury** 1. [< NLat. *hydrargyrum,* mercury < Lat. *hydrargyrus* < Gk. *hudrarguros* : *hudr-, hudro-,* hydro- + *arguros,* silver; see LITHARGE.]

HG *abbr.* High German

HGH *abbr.* human growth hormone

hgt. *abbr.* height

hgwy. *abbr.* highway

HH *abbr.* **1.** Her (or His) Highness **2.** His Holiness

hhd *abbr.* hogshead

HHD *abbr. Latin* Humanitatum Doctor (Doctor of Humanities)

HHFA *abbr.* Housing and Home Finance Agency

H-hour (āch′our′) *n.* See **zero hour.** [*H* (abbr. of HOUR) + HOUR.]

HHS *abbr.* Department of Health and Human Services

hi (hī) *interj. Informal* Used to express greeting. See Regional Note at **hey.**

HI *abbr.* **1.** Hawaii **2.** high intensity **3.** humidity index

H.I. *abbr.* Hawaiian Islands

Hi·a·le·ah (hī′ə-lē′ə) A city of SE FL NW of Miami; noted esp. for its racetrack. Pop. 226,419.

hiatal hernia *n.* A hernia in which part of the stomach protrudes through the esophageal opening of the diaphragm.

hi·a·tus (hī-ā′təs) *n., pl.* **-tus·es** or **hiatus** 1. A gap or interruption in space, time, or continuity; a break. **2.** *Linguistics* A slight pause between two adjacent vowels in consecutive syllables, as in *naive.* **3.** *Anatomy* A separation, aperture, fissure, or short passage in an organ or body part. [Lat. *hiātus* < p. part. of *hiāre,* to gape.] **—hi·a′tal** (-āt′l) *adj.*

hiatus hernia *n.* See **hiatal hernia.**

Hi·a·wa·tha (hī′ə-wŏth′ə, -wô′thə, hē′ə-) fl. 1570. Onondagan leader credited with organizing the Iroquois confederacy.

Hib *abbr. Haemophilus influenzae* type b

hi·ba·chi (hĭ-bä′chē) *n., pl.* **-chis** A portable charcoal-burning brazier with a grill, used chiefly for cooking. [J. : *hi,* fire + *bachi,* bowl (< M Chin. *pat, puat,* Buddhist monk's begging bowl < Skt. *pātram,* cup, bowl; see pō(i)- in App.).]

hi·ber·nac·u·lum (hī′bər-năk′yə-ləm) *n., pl.* **-la** (-lə) *Biology* **1.** A protective covering or structure in which an organism remains dormant for the winter. **2.** The shelter of a hibernating animal. [Lat. *hībernāculum,* winter residence < *hībernāre,* to winter < *hībernus,* of winter. See **ghei-** in App.]

hi·ber·nal (hī-bûr′nəl) *adj.* Of or relating to winter. [Lat. *hībernālis* < *hībernus,* wintry. See HIBERNACULUM.]

hi·ber·nate (hī′bər-nāt′) *intr.v.* **-nat·ed, -nat·ing, -nates** **1.** To pass the winter in a dormant or torpid state. **2.** To be in an inactive or dormant state or period. [Lat. *hībernāre, hībernāt-,* to winter < *hībernus,* relating to winter. See **ghei-** in App.] **—hi′ber·na′tion** *n.* **—hi′ber·na′tor** *n.*

Hi·ber·ni·a (hī-bûr′nē-ə) The Latin and poetic name for the island of Ireland. **—Hi·ber′ni·an** *adj. & n.*

Hi·ber·no-Eng·lish (hī-bûr′nō-ĭng′glĭsh) *n.* See **Irish English.**

hi·bis·cus (hī-bĭs′kəs) *n.* Any of various chiefly tropical shrubs or trees of the genus *Hibiscus,* having large showy flowers with numerous stamens united into a tube surrounding the style. [NLat. *Hibīscus,* genus name < LLat. *hibiscus,* var. of Lat. *hibīscum,* marsh mallow, perh. of Celt. orig.]

Hib vaccine (hĭb) *n.* A conjugate vaccine administered to immunize children against infection by a rod-shaped, gram-negative bacterium, *Haemophilus influenzae* type b, capable of causing severe illness.

hic·cup also **hic·cough** (hĭk′əp) *n.* **1a.** A spasm of the dia-

hex sign

hibiscus

ă	pat	oi	boy
ā	pay	ou	out
âr	care	ōō	took
ä	father	ōō	boot
ĕ	pet	ŭ	cut
ē	be	ûr	urge
ĭ	pit	th	thin
ī	pie	th	this
îr	pier	hw	which
ŏ	pot	zh	vision
ō	toe	ə	about,
ô	paw		item

Stress marks:
′ (primary);
′ (secondary), as in
lexicon (lĕk′sĭ-kŏn′)

phragm resulting in a rapid involuntary inhalation stopped by the sudden closure of the glottis and accompanied by a sharp distinctive sound. **b. hiccups** An attack of these spasms. Often used with *the*. **2.** The sound made by such a spasm or a sound resembling it. ❖ *intr.v.* **-cupped, -cup·ping, -cups** also **-coughed, -cough·ing, -coughs 1.** To make a hiccup or a sound like a hiccup. **2.** To have a hiccup attack. [Imit.]

hick (hĭk) *Informal n.* A person regarded as gullible or provincial. ❖ *adj.* Provincial; unsophisticated: *a hick town.* [After *Hick*, a nickname for *Richard* < ME *Hikke*.]

hick·ey (hĭk′ē) *n., pl.* **-eys** *Informal* **1.** A device or contrivance; a gadget. **2a.** A reddish mark on the skin caused by amorous kissing, biting, or sucking. **b.** A pimple. **3.** A pipe-bending apparatus. **4.** A threaded electrical fitting used to connect a fixture to an outlet box. [?]

Hick·ok (hĭk′ŏk′), **James Butler** Known as "Wild Bill." 1837–76. Amer. frontier scout and marshal noted for his legendary exploits against outlaws.

hick·o·ry (hĭk′ə-rē) *n., pl.* **-ries 1.** Any of several chiefly North American deciduous trees of the genus *Carya*, having compound leaves and hard smooth stones or nuts, each containing an edible seed and surrounded by a four-valved husk. **2a.** The hard, tough, heavy wood of such a tree. **b.** A walking stick or switch made from such wood. [Short for Virginia Algonquian *pocohiquara*, pressed hickory nut drink.]

Hicks (hĭks), **Edward** 1780–1849. Amer. painter of primitive works, notably *The Peaceable Kingdom.*

hi·dal·go (hĭ-dăl′gō, ē-thäl′-) *n., pl.* **-gos** A member of the minor nobility in Spain. [Sp., alteration of *hijo dalgo* < OSpan. *fijo dalgo* : *fijo*, son (< Lat. *fīlius*; see **dhē(i)-** in App.) + *de*, of (< Lat. *dē*; see **de-**) + *algo*, something, possession (< Lat. *aliquō*, ablative of *aliquid* : *alius*, some; see **al-** in App. + *quid*, something; see **kʷo-** in App.).]

Hi·dal·go y Co·stil·la (ē-däl′gō ē kō-stē′yä), **Miguel** 1753–1811. Mexican priest and revolutionary who initiated (1810) a revolt against Spanish rule.

Hi·dat·sa (hē-dät′sä) *n., pl.* **Hidatsa** or **-sas 1** A member of a Native American people living along the Missouri River in western North Dakota. **2.** Their Siouan language. [Hidatsa, people of the willows.]

hid·den·ite (hĭd′n-īt′) *n.* A transparent emerald-green variety of spodumene, used as a gemstone. [After William Earl *Hidden* (1832–1918), American mineralogist.]

hide¹ (hīd) *v.* **hid** (hĭd), **hid·den** (hĭd′n) or **hid, hid·ing, hides** —*tr.* **1.** To put or keep out of sight; secrete. **2.** To prevent the disclosure or recognition of; conceal. **3.** To cut off from sight; cover up. **4.** To avert (one's gaze), esp. in shame or grief. —*intr.* **1.** To keep oneself out of sight. **2.** To seek refuge. —*phrasal verb:* **hide out** To be in hiding, as from a pursuer. [ME *hiden* < OE *hȳdan.* See **(s)keu-** in App.]

SYNONYMS *hide, conceal, secrete, cache, screen, cloak* These verbs mean to keep from the sight or knowledge of others. *Hide* and *conceal* are the most general and are often used interchangeably: *I used a throw rug to hide* (or *conceal*) *the stain. I smiled to hide* (or *conceal*) *my feelings. Secrete* and *cache* involve concealment in a place unknown to others; *cache* often implies storage for later use: *The lioness secreted her cubs in the grass. The mountain climbers cached their food in a cave.* To *screen* is to shield or block from the view of others: *Tall shrubs screen the home.* To *cloak* is to conceal something by masking or disguising it: *"On previously cloaked issues, the Soviets have suddenly become forthcoming"* (John McLaughlin). See also Syns at **block.**

hide² (hīd) *n.* The skin of an animal, esp. the skin or pelt of a large animal. ❖ *tr.v.* **hid·ed, hid·ing, hides** To beat severely; flog. —*idiom:* **hide nor hair** A trace; a vestige: *haven't seen hide nor hair of them.* [ME < OE *hȳd.* See **(s)keu-** in App.]

hide³ (hīd) *n.* An old English measure of land, usu. the amount held adequate for one free family and its dependents. [ME < OE *hīd.* See **kei-¹** in App.]

hide-and-seek (hīd′n-sēk′) or **hide-and-go-seek** (hīd′n-gō-sēk′) *n.* A children's game in which a player tries to catch others who are hiding.

hide·a·way (hīd′ə-wā′) *n.* **1.** A place of concealment; a hideout. **2.** A secluded or isolated place.

hide·bound (hīd′bound′) *adj.* **1.** Stubbornly prejudiced, narrow-minded, or inflexible. **2.** Having abnormally dry stiff skin that adheres closely to the underlying flesh. Used of domestic animals such as cattle. **3.** Having the bark so contracted and unyielding as to hinder growth. Used of trees.

hid·e·ous (hĭd′ē-əs) *adj.* **1.** Repulsive, esp. to the sight; revoltingly ugly. **2.** Offensive to moral sensibilities. [ME, var. of *hidous* < AN < OFr. *hide, hisde*, fear, poss. of Gmc. orig.] —**hid′e·ous·ly** *adv.* —**hid′e·ous·ness, hid′e·os′i·ty** (-ŏs′ĭ-tē) *n.*

hide·out (hīd′out′) *n.* A place of shelter or concealment.

hid·ey-hole (hīd′ē-hōl′) *n. Informal* A secluded hideaway.

hi·dro·sis (hĭ-drō′sĭs, hī-) *n., pl.* **-ses** (-sēz) **1.** The formation and excretion of sweat. **2.** Sweat, esp. in excessive or abnormal amounts. [Gk. *hidrōsis*, sweating < *hidrōs*, sweat. See **sweid-** in App.] —**hi·drot′ic** (-drŏt′ĭk) *adj.*

hie (hī) *intr. & tr.v.* **hied, hie·ing** or **hy·ing** (hī′ĭng), **hies** To go

quickly; hasten. [ME *hien* < OE *hīgian*, to strive.]

hi·e·mal (hī′ə-məl) *adj.* Of or relating to winter. [Lat. *hiemālis* < *hiems*, winter. See **ghei-** in App.]

hi·er·arch (hī′ə-rärk′, hī′rärk′) *n.* One who occupies a position of authority in a religious or other hierarchy. [< ME *jerarchis*, hierarchs < Med.Lat. *hierarcha*, dignitary, prelate < Gk. *hierarkhēs*, high priest : *hieros*, holy; see **eis-** in App. + *-arkhēs*, -arch.]

hi·er·ar·chi·cal (hī′ə-rär′kĭ-kəl, hī-rär′-) or **hi·er·ar·chic** (-kĭk) or **hi·er·ar·chal** (-rär′kəl) *adj.* Of or relating to a hierarchy. —**hi′er·ar′chi·cal·ly** *adv.*

hi·er·ar·chize (hī′ə-rär-kīz′, hī′rär-) *tr.v.* **-chized, -chiz·ing, -chiz·es** To arrange in a hierarchy. —**hi′er·ar·chi·za′tion** (-kī-zā′shən) *n.*

hi·er·ar·chy (hī′ə-rär′kē, hī-rär′-) *n., pl.* **-chies 1.** A body of persons having authority. **2a.** Categorization of a group of people according to ability or status. **b.** The group so categorized. **3.** A series in which each element is graded or ranked. **4a.** A body of clergy organized into successive ranks or grades. **b.** Religious rule by a group of ranked clergy. **5.** One of the divisions of angels. [ME *ierarchie* < OFr. < Med.Lat. *hierarchia* < Gk. *hierarkhiā*, rule of a high priest < *hierarkhēs*, high priest. See HIERARCH.]

hi·er·at·ic (hī′ə-rät′ĭk, hī-rät′-) *adj.* **1.** Of or associated with sacred persons or offices; sacerdotal. **2.** Constituting or relating to a simplified cursive style of Egyptian hieroglyphics. **3.** Extremely formal or stylized, as in a work of art. [Lat. *hierāticus* < Gk. *hierātikos* < *hierāteia*, priesthood < *hierāsthai*, to be a priest < *hiereus*, priest < *hieros*, holy. See **eis-** in App.] —**hi′er·at′i·cal·ly** *adv.*

hiero– or **hier–** *pref.* Sacred; holy: *hierology.* [Gk. < *hieros*, holy. See **eis-** in App.]

hi·er·oc·ra·cy (hī′ə-rŏk′rə-sē, hī-rŏk′-) *n., pl.* **-cies** Government by the clergy; ecclesiastical rule. —**hi′er·o·crat′ic** (hī′ər-ə-krăt′ĭk, hī′rə-krăt′-), **hi′er·o·crat′i·cal** *adj.*

hi·er·o·dule (hī′ər-ə-dool′, -dyool′) *n.* A slave serving in an ancient temple, as in Greece or Anatolia, in the service of a specific deity. [LLat. *hierodūlus* < Gk. *hierodoulos* : *hieron*, temple < neut. of *hieros*, holy; see **eis-** in App. + *doulos*, slave.] —**hi′er·o·du′lic** (-doo′lĭk, -dyoo′-) *adj.*

hi·er·o·glyph (hī′ər-ə-glĭf′, hī′rə-) *n.* **1.** A symbol used in hieroglyphic writing. **2.** Something that suggests a hieroglyph.

hi·er·o·glyph·ic (hī′ər-ə-glĭf′ĭk, hī′rə-) also **hi·er·o·glyph·i·cal** (-ĭ-kəl) *adj.* **1a.** Of, relating to, or being a system of writing, such as that of ancient Egypt, in which pictorial symbols are used to represent meaning or sounds or a combination of them. **b.** Written with such symbols. **2.** Difficult to read or decipher. ❖ *n.* **1a.** A hieroglyph. **b.** Hieroglyphic writing, esp. that of the ancient Egyptians. Often used in the plural with a singular or plural verb. **2.** Something, such as illegible writing, that resembles a hieroglyph. [Fr. *hiéroglyphique* < LLat. *hieroglyphicus* < Gk. *hierogluphikos* : *hieros*, holy; see **eis-** in App. + *gluphē*, carving (< *gluphein*, to carve).] —**hi′er·o·glyph′i·cal·ly** *adv.*

Hieroglyphic Luvian *n.* A dialect of Luvian found in documents and inscriptions in an indigenous hieroglyphic script from the late second and early first millennia B.C. in Anatolia and northern Syria.

hi·er·ol·o·gy (hī′ə-rŏl′ə-jē, hī-rŏl′-) *n., pl.* **-gies** The sacred literature of a people.

hi·er·o·phant (hī′ər-ə-fănt′, hī′rə-, hī-ĕr′ə-fənt) *n.* **1.** An ancient Greek priest who interpreted sacred mysteries, esp. the Eleusinian mysteries. **2.** An interpreter of sacred mysteries or arcane knowledge. **3.** One who explains or makes a commentary. [LLat. *hierophanta* < Gk. *hierophantēs* : *hieros*, holy; see **eis-** in App. + *-phantēs*, one who shows (< *phainein*, *phan-*, to show; see **bhā-¹** in App.).] —**hi′er·o·phan′tic** *adj.*

hi·fa·lu·tin (hī′fə-loot′n) *adj.* Variant of **highfalutin.**

hi-fi (hī′fī′) *n., pl.* **-fis** *Informal* **1.** High fidelity. **2.** An electronic system for reproducing high-fidelity sound from radio or recordings. [HI(GH) + FI(DELITY).] —**hi′-fi′** *adj.*

Hi·ga·shi·o·sa·ka (hē-gä′shē-ō-sä′kä) A city of S Honshu, Japan, a suburb of Osaka. Pop. 515,375.

Hig·gin·son (hĭg′ən-sən), **Thomas Wentworth Storrow** 1823–1911. Amer. writer and soldier who led the first Black Union Army regiment (1862–64).

hig·gle (hĭg′əl) *intr.v.* **-gled, -gling, -gles** To haggle. [Prob. alteration of HAGGLE.] —**hig′gler** *n.*

hig·gle·dy-pig·gle·dy (hĭg′əl-dē-pĭg′əl-dē) *adv.* In utter disorder or confusion. ❖ *adj.* Topsy-turvy; jumbled. [?]

Higgs boson (hĭgz) *n.* A hypothetical, massive subatomic particle with zero electric charge and zero spin, whose existence would explain the masses of the elementary particles. [After Peter Ware *Higgs* (born 1929), British physicist.]

high (hī) *adj.* **high·er, high·est 1a.** Having a relatively great elevation; extending far upward: *a high mountain.* **b.** Extending a specified distance upward. **2.** Far or farther from a reference point: *too high in the offensive zone to take a shot.* **3a.** Being at or near the peak or culminating stage: *high summer.* **b.** Advanced in development or complexity. **c.** Far removed in time; remote: *high antiquity.* **4a.** Slightly spoiled or tainted; gamy. Used of meat. **b.** Having a bad smell; malodorous. **5a.** Having a pitch corresponding to a relatively large number of sound wave cycles per second: *the high tones of a flute.* **b.** Raised in pitch; not soft or hushed: *a high voice.* **6.** Situated relatively far from the equator. **7a.** Of great

importance. **b.** Eminent in rank or status. **c.** Serious; grave. **d.** Constituting a climax; crucial. **e.** Characterized by lofty or stirring events or themes: *high drama.* **8.** Lofty or exalted in quality or character: *high morals.* **9a.** Greater than usual or expected, as in quantity, magnitude, cost, or degree. **b.** Favorable: *a high opinion of himself.* **10.** Of great force or violence: *high winds.* **11a.** Filled with excitement or euphoria. **b.** *Slang* Intoxicated by alcohol or a drug, such as marijuana. **12.** Luxurious; extravagant. **13.** *Linguistics* Of or relating to vowels produced with part of the tongue close to the palate, as in the vowel of *tree.* **14.** Of, relating to, or being the gear configuration, as in an automotive transmission, that produces the greatest vehicular speed with respect to engine speed. ❖ *adv.* **higher, highest 1.** At, in, or to a lofty position, level, or degree. **2.** In an extravagant or luxurious way. ❖ *n.* **1.** A lofty place or region. **2.** A high level or degree. **3.** The high gear of a transmission. **4.** A center of high atmospheric pressure; an anticyclone. **5.** *Slang* An intoxicated or euphoric condition induced by or as if by a drug. —*idioms:* **high and dry 1.** In a position of helplessness; stranded. **2.** *Nautical* Out of water. Used of a ship, for example. **high and low** Here and there; everywhere. **on high 1.** High in the sky. **2.** In heaven. **3.** In a position of authority. [ME < OE *hēah.*] —**high′ly** *adv.*

high-and-might•y (hī′ən-mī′tē) *adj.* Marked by arrogance; haughty and overbearing. —**high and mighty** *adv. & n.*

high•ball (hī′bôl′) *n.* **1.** A cocktail served in a tall glass and consisting of liquor mixed with water or a carbonated beverage. **2a.** A railroad signal indicating full speed ahead. **b.** A high-speed train. ❖ *intr.v.* **-balled, -ball•ing, -balls** *Slang* To move ahead at full speed.

high bar *n.* See **horizontal bar.**

high beam *n.* The beam of a vehicle's headlight that provides long-range illumination.

high•bind•er (hī′bīn′dər) *n.* **1.** A corrupt politician. **2.** A member of a Chinese-American secret society of paid assassins and blackmailers. [After the *Highbinders,* a group of ruffians in New York City c. 1806.]

high blood pressure *n.* Hypertension.

high•born (hī′bôrn′) *adj.* Of noble birth.

high•boy (hī′boi′) *n.* A tall chest of drawers usu. divided into two sections and supported on four legs.

high•bred (hī′brĕd′) *adj.* Of superior breed or stock.

high•brow (hī′brou′) *adj.* also **high•browed** (-broud′) Of, relating to, or being highly cultured or intellectual. ❖ *n.* One who has or affects a high degree of culture or learning.

high•bush cranberry (hī′boŏsh′) *n.* See **cranberry bush.**

high•chair (hī′châr′) *n.* A very young child's feeding chair that has long legs, a footrest, and a usu. detachable tray.

High-Church (hī′chûrch′) *adj.* Of or relating to a group in the Anglican Church that maintains traditional definitions of authority, the episcopacy, and the sacraments.

high-class (hī′klăs′) *adj.* Of superior quality; first-class.

high comedy *n.* Comedy of a sophisticated and witty nature, often satirizing genteel society.

high commissioner *n.* **1.** A chief commissioner or one of high rank. **2.** A chief representative of the government of one country who is assigned to an ambassadorial post in another.

high-con•cept (hī′kŏn′sĕpt′) *adj.* Designed to appeal to a mass audience, as by incorporating popular, glamorous features.

high-count (hī′kount′) *adj.* Having a large number of warp and filling threads per square inch. Used of a woven fabric.

high court *n.* See **Supreme Court** 2.

high-def•i•ni•tion television (hī′dĕf′ə-nĭsh′ən) *n.* A television system that has twice the standard number of scanning lines per frame and so produces greater detail.

high-den•si•ty (hī′dĕn′sĭ-tē) *adj.* Having a high concentration: *high-density urban areas.*

high-density lipoprotein *n.* A complex of lipids and proteins that transports cholesterol in the blood, high levels of which may decrease the risk of developing heart disease.

high-end (hī′ĕnd′) *adj. Informal* Sophisticated and discerning: *the high-end consumer.*

high-en•er•gy (hī′ĕn′ər-jē) *adj.* **1.** Of or relating to elementary particles with energies exceeding hundreds of thousands of electron volts. **2.** Yielding a large amount of energy in a chemical reaction. **3.** Vigorous; dynamic.

high•er criticism (hī′ər) *n.* Critical study of biblical texts to ascertain their history and meaning. —**higher critic** *n.*

higher education *n.* Education beyond the secondary level.

higher law *n.* A moral or religious principle that takes precedence over the constitutions or statutes of society.

high•er-up (hī′ər-ŭp′) *n. Informal* One who has a rank, position, or status superior to others.

high•est common factor (hī′ĭst) *n.* See **greatest common divisor.**

high explosive *n.* An explosive that combusts nearly instantaneously, thereby producing a violent shattering effect.

high•fa•lu•tin or **hi•fa•lu•tin** (hī′fə-loōt′n) also **high•fa•lu•ting** (-loŏt′n, -loō′tĭng) *adj. Informal* Pompous or pretentious. [?]

high fashion *n.* **1.** See **high style. 2.** Haute couture.

high fidelity *n.* The electronic reproduction of sound, esp. from broadcast or recorded sources, with minimal distortion. —**high′-fi•del′i•ty** (hī′fī-dĕl′ĭ-tē, -fī-) *adj.*

high-five (hī′fīv′) *n. Slang* A gesture, as of greeting, in which one person slaps an upraised palm against that of another.

high-fli•er also **high-fli•er** (hī′flī′ər) *n.* **1.** One who is extravagant or extreme in manner or opinions. **2.** A stock that sells well above its normal value.

high-flown (hī′flōn′) *adj.* **1.** Exceedingly lofty or exalted. **2.** Highly pretentious or inflated: *high-flown rhetoric.*

high-fly•ing (hī′flī′ĭng) *adj.* **1.** Rising to a great height. **2.** Unusually extravagant, affected, or ambitious.

high frequency *n.* A radio frequency in the range between 3 and 30 megahertz.

High German *n.* **1.** German as indigenously spoken and written in central and southern Germany. **2.** The standard variety of German used as the official language in Germany and Austria and as one of the official languages in Switzerland. [Transl. of Ger. *Hochdeutsch* : *hoch,* high (< the mountainous terrain of the area where it originated) + *Deutsch,* German.]

high-grade (hī′grād′) *adj.* Of superior grade or quality.

high-hand•ed (hī′hăn′dĭd) *adj.* Arrogant in manner; overbearing. —**high′hand′ed•ly** *adv.* —**high′hand′ed•ness** *n.*

high hat *n.* **1.** See **top hat. 2.** also **hi hat** *Music* A pair of cymbals positioned to be worked by a foot pedal.

high-hat (hī′hăt′) *Informal tr.v.* **-hat•ted, -hat•ting, -hats** To treat in a condescending or supercilious manner. ❖ *adj.* Snobbish; haughty.

High Holy Day *n. Judaism* **1.** Rosh Hashanah or Yom Kippur. **2. High Holy Days** The period from Rosh Hashanah to the end of Yom Kippur.

high horse *n. Informal* A mood or attitude of stubborn arrogance or contempt.

high•jack (hī′jăk′) *Informal v. & n.* Variant of **hijack.**

high jinks or **hi•jinks** (hī′jĭnks′) *pl.n.* Playful, often noisy and rowdy activity, usu. involving mischievous pranks.

high jump *n.* **1.** A jump for height made over a horizontal bar in a track-and-field contest. **2.** A contest in which high jumps are made. —**high jumper** *n.*

high•land (hī′lənd) *n.* **1.** Elevated land. **2. highlands** A mountainous or hilly section of a country. —**high′land** *adj.* —**high′land•er** *n.*

Highland fling *n.* A lively folk dance originating in the Highlands of Scotland.

High•lands (hī′ləndz) A region of central and N Scotland including the Grampian Mts. —**High′land** *adj.* —**High′land•er** *n.*

high-lev•el (hī′lĕv′əl) *adj.* **1.** Situated or occurring high above the ground or other reference point. **2.** Being high on a scale or in relation to a standard. **3.** *Computer Science* Of, relating to, or being a programming language, such as BASIC, in which each instruction corresponds to several instructions in machine language.

high•life or **high life** (hī′līf′) *n.* **1.** *Informal* An extravagant or luxurious style of living. **2.** Popular West African dance music that combines African rhythms and Western-style pop melodies.

high•light (hī′līt′) *n.* **1.** A strongly illuminated area or spot in a drawing, painting, or photograph. **2.** An esp. significant or interesting detail or event. ❖ *tr.v.* **-light•ed, -light•ing, -lights 1.** To give a highlight to (the subject of a painting, for example). **2a.** To make prominent; emphasize. **b.** To be a highlight of. **3.** To mark (text) with a highlighter.

high•light•er (hī′lī′tər) *n.* **1.** A usu. fluorescent marker used to mark important passages of text. **2.** A cosmetic for emphasizing areas of the face, such as the eyes or cheekbones.

high-low (hī′lō′) *n.* **1.** A poker game in which both high and low hands can win. **2.** A signal chiefly in bridge for one's partner to lead a suit.

High Mass *n. Roman Catholic Church* A form of Mass, now obsolete, in which the celebrant was assisted by a deacon and a subdeacon and accompanied by acolytes, a thurifer, and a choir.

high-mind•ed (hī′mīn′dĭd) *adj.* Marked by elevated ideals or conduct; noble. —**high′-mind′ed•ly** *adv.* —**high′mind′ed•ness** *n.*

high muckamuck also **high muckety-muck** *n. Slang* An important, often overbearing person. [< Chinook Jargon *hayo makamak,* plenty to eat.]

high•ness (hī′nĭs) *n.* **1.** The quality or condition of being high. **2. Highness** Used with *His, Her,* or *Your* as a title and form of address for a prince or princess: *Her Royal Highness.*

high noon *n.* **1.** Exactly noon. **2.** The highest or most advanced stage or period: *the high noon of her creativity.*

high-oc•tane (hī′ŏk′tān′) *adj.* **1.** Having a high octane number and thus good antiknock properties and high efficiency: *high-octane gas.* **2.** *Slang* High-powered; dynamic.

high-pass filter (hī′păs′) *n.* A filter designed to transmit only those electromagnetic frequencies above a certain value.

high-pitched (hī′pĭcht′) *adj.* **1.** High in pitch, as a voice or musical tone. **2.** Steeply sloped, as a roof. **3.** Marked by or indicating intense emotion: *a high-pitched debate.*

high place *n.* In early Semitic religions, a place of worship built usu. on top of a hill.

high-pow•ered (hī′pou′ərd) also **high-pow•er** (-pou′ər) *adj.*

highboy

high jump

ă	pat	oi	boy
ā	pay	ou	out
âr	care	oō	took
ä	father	oō	boot
ĕ	pet	ŭ	cut
ē	be	ûr	urge
ĭ	pit	th	thin
ī	pie	*th*	this
îr	pier	hw	which
ŏ	pot	zh	vision
ō	toe	ə	about,
ô	paw		item

Stress marks:
′ (primary);
′ (secondary), as in
lexicon (lĕk′sĭ-kŏn′)

Having great power or energy; dynamic.

high-pres·sure (hī′prĕsh′ər) *adj.* **1.** Of or relating to pressures higher than normal, esp. higher than atmospheric pressure. **2.** *Informal* **a.** Using aggressive, persistent persuasive tactics. **b.** Full of or imposing great stress or tension.

high priest *n.* **1.** A chief priest, esp. of the ancient Levitical priesthood in Judaism. **2.** *Mormon Church* A priest of the Melchizedek order. **3.** The head or chief proponent, as of a movement. —**high priesthood** *n.*

high priestess *n.* **1.** A chief priestess, as of a pagan religion. **2.** The female head or chief proponent, as of a movement.

high relief *n.* Sculptural relief in which the modeled forms project from the background by at least half their depth.

high-res (hī′rĕz′) *adj. Informal* High-resolution.

high-res·o·lu·tion (hī′rĕz′ə-lōō′shən) *adj.* **1.** Relating to an image that has fine detail. **2.** *Computer Science* **a.** Relating to an output device that produces images that contain a large number of dots per unit area and are therefore sharp and detailed. **b.** Relating to a raster-based image that contains a large number of pixels per unit of area.

high-rise (hī′rīz′) *adj.* **1.** Being a high-rise. **2.** Of, relating to, or marked by multistoried buildings: *a high-rise district.* ❖ *n.* or **high rise** A multistoried building equipped with elevators.

high-risk (hī′rĭsk′) *adj.* **1.** Of, relating to, or marked by risk. **2.** Being particularly subject to potential danger or hazard.

high road also **high·road** (hī′rōd′) *n.* **1a.** The easiest or surest path or course. **b.** The most positive, diplomatic, or ethical course. **2.** *Chiefly British* A main road; a highway.

high roller *n. Slang* **1.** One that spends or invests freely, rashly, or extravagantly. **2.** One who gambles rashly or for high stakes. —**high′-roll′ing** (hī′rō′lĭng) *adj.*

high school *n.* A secondary school that usu. includes grades 9 through 12 or 10 through 12. —**high′-school′** (hī′skōōl′) *adj.* —**high school′er** *n.*

high seas *pl.n.* The open waters of an ocean or a sea beyond the limits of the territorial jurisdiction of a country: *piracy on the high seas.*

high sign *n. Informal* An often prearranged secret sign or signal intended esp. to warn or inform.

high-sound·ing (hī′soun′dĭng) *adj.* Pretentiously impressive; pompous: *high-sounding oratory.*

high-speed (hī′spēd′) *adj.* **1.** Operated or designed for operation at high speed. **2.** Taking place at high speed: *a high-speed chase.* **3.** Having a speed of 50 to 500 frames per second to record events that occur too rapidly for usual photography.

high-spir·it·ed (hī′spîr′ĭ-tĭd) *adj.* **1.** Having a proud or unbroken spirit: *a high-spirited horse.* **2.** Vivacious; lively. —**high′-spir′it·ed·ly** *adv.* —**high′-spir′it·ed·ness** *n.*

high stick *n.* A hockey stick carried so that the blade is above a specified illegal height, shoulder height in professional play. —**high′-stick′ing** (hī′stĭk′ĭng) *n.*

high street *n. Chiefly British* A main street.

high-strung (hī′strŭng′) *adj.* Very nervous and easily excited.

high style *n.* The latest in fashion or design, usu. intended for an exclusive clientele. —**high′-style′** (hī′stīl′) *adj.*

hight (hīt) *adj. Archaic* Named or called. [ME, p. part. of *highten, hihten,* to call, be called < *hehte, hight,* p. t. of *hoten* < OE *hātan.* See **kei-²** in App.]

high·tail (hī′tāl′) *intr.v.* **-tailed, -tail·ing, -tails** *Slang* To go as fast as possible, esp. in fleeing: *hightailed out of town.* —*idiom:* **hightail it** To hurry or flee. [< those animals that raise their tails when fleeing.]

high tea *n. Chiefly British* A fairly substantial meal that includes tea and is served in the late afternoon or early evening.

high tech *Informal n.* **1.** High technology. **2.** A style of interior decoration marked by the use of industrial materials, equipment, or design.

high-tech also **hi-tech** (hī′tĕk′) *adj. Informal* Of, relating to, or resembling high technology.

high technology *n.* Technology that involves highly advanced or specialized systems or devices. —**high′-tech′nol′o·gy** (hī′tĕk-nŏl′ə-jē) *adj.*

high-ten·sion (hī′tĕn′shən) *adj.* Having a high voltage.

high-test (hī′tĕst′) *adj.* **1.** Of or relating to highly volatile high-octane gasoline. **2.** Meeting exacting requirements.

high tide *n.* **1a.** The tide at its fullest, when the water reaches its highest level. **b.** The time at which this tide occurs. **2.** A point of culmination; a climax.

high-toned (hī′tōnd′) *adj.* **1.** Intellectually, morally, or socially superior. **2.** *Informal* Pretentiously elegant or fashionable.

high-tops (hī′tŏps′) *pl.n.* Sneakers or athletic shoes that lace up to the ankle.

high treason *n.* Treason against one's country or sovereign.

high water *n.* **1.** See **high tide** 1. **2.** The state of a body of water that has reached its highest level. —**high′-wa′ter** (hī′wô′tər, -wŏt′ər) *adj.*

high-water mark *n.* **1.** A mark indicating the highest level reached by a body of water. **2.** The highest point, as of achievement; the apex.

high·way (hī′wā′) *n.* A main public road, esp. one connecting towns and cities.

high·way·man (hī′wā′mən) *n.* A man who holds up and robs travelers on a road.

highway patrol *n.* A state law enforcement organization whose police officers patrol the public highways.

highway robbery *n.* **1.** Robbery usu. of travelers on or near a public road. **2.** *Informal* The exaction of an exorbitantly high price or fee. —**highway robber** *n.*

high wire *n.* A tightrope for aerialists that is stretched very high above the ground. —**high′-wire′** (hī′wīr′) *adj.*

HIH *abbr.* Her (or His) Imperial Highness

hi hat *n.* Variant of **high hat** 2.

hi·jab (hĭ-jäb′) *n.* **1.** The headscarf worn by Muslim women, sometimes including a veil that covers the face except for the eyes. **2.** The institution of protection of women in some Islamic societies through veiling or seclusion. [Ar. *ḥijāb,* curtain, veil < *ḥajaba,* to cover.]

hi·jack also **high·jack** (hī′jăk′) *Informal tr.v.* **-jacked, -jack·ing, -jacks 1a.** To stop and rob (a vehicle in transit). **b.** To steal (goods) from a vehicle in transit. **c.** To seize control of (a moving vehicle) by use of force, esp. to reach an alternate destination. **2a.** To steal from as if by hijacking. **b.** To swindle or subject to extortion. ❖ *n.* An act or an instance of hijacking. [Prob. back-formation < *highjacker,* perh. < *jacker,* holdup man < JACK, to jack-light.] —**hi′jack′er** *n.*

hi·jinks (hī′jĭngks′) *pl.n.* Variant of **high jinks.**

hike (hīk) *v.* **hiked, hik·ing, hikes** —*intr.* **1.** To go on an extended walk for pleasure or exercise. **2.** To rise, esp. to rise upward out of place: *My coat had hiked up in the back.* —*tr.* **1.** To increase or raise in amount, esp. abruptly. **2.** To pull or raise with a sudden motion; hitch: *hiked up her socks.* **3.** *Football* To snap (the ball). ❖ *n.* **1.** A long walk or march. **2.** An abrupt increase or rise. **3.** *Football* See **snap** 13. —*phrasal verb:* **hike out** To sit facing the sail and lean far backward and over the side of a heeling sailboat to counterbalance the heel. —*idiom:* **take a hike** *Slang* To leave because one is unwanted. [?] —**hik′er** *n.*

hi·la (hī′lə) *n.* Plural of **hilum.**

hi·lar·i·ous (hĭ-lâr′ē-əs, -lăr′-, hī-) *adj.* Characterized by or causing great merriment. [Lat. *hilaris,* cheerful; see HILARITY + –IOUS.] —**hi·lar′i·ous·ly** *adv.* —**hi·lar′i·ous·ness** *n.*

hi·lar·i·ty (hĭ-lâr′ĭ-tē, -lăr′-, hī-) *n.* Great merriment. [ME *hilarite,* good spirits < OFr. < Lat. *hilaritās* < *hilaris,* cheerful < Gk. *hilaros.*]

Hil·de·brand (hĭl′də-brănd′) See **Gregory VII.**

Hil·de·gard von Bing·en (hĭl′də-gärd′ vŏn bĭng′ən, fôn) 1098–1178. German nun, poet, and composer who set her poems to music and wrote works on medicine and natural history.

hill (hĭl) *n.* **1.** A well-defined natural elevation smaller than a mountain. **2.** A small heap, pile, or mound. **3a.** A mound of earth piled around and over a plant. **b.** A plant thus covered. **4.** An incline, esp. of a road; a slope. **5. Hill a.** Capitol Hill. **b.** The US Congress. ❖ *tr.v.* **hilled, hill·ing, hills 1.** To form into a hill, pile, or heap. **2.** To cover (a plant) with a mound of soil. —*idiom:* **over the hill** *Informal* Past one's prime. [ME *hil* < OE *hyll.*] —**hill′er** *n.*

Hill, Ambrose Powell 1825–65. Amer. Confederate officer whose charge began the Battle of Gettysburg (1863).

Hill, J(ames) J(erome) 1838–1916. Amer. railroad magnate who promoted the Great Northern Railway.

Hil·la·ry (hĭl′ə-rē), Sir **Edmund Percival** b. 1919. New Zealand explorer who in 1959 with Tenzing Norgay first attained the summit of Mt. Everest.

hill·bil·ly (hĭl′bĭl′ē) *n., pl.* **-lies** *Informal* A person from the backwoods or a remote mountain area. [HILL + *Billy,* a nickname for *William.*]

Hil·lel (hĭl′ĕl, -āl, hē-lĕl′) fl. 1st cent. B.C.–A.D. 1st cent. Palestinian rabbi who influenced the interpretation of Judaic law.

hill myna *n.* A starling (*Gracula religiosa*) native to Europe and North America that is able to mimic human speech.

hill·ock (hĭl′ək) *n.* **1.** A small hill. **2.** *Biology* A small protuberance or elevation, as from an organ, tissue, or structure. [ME *hillok* < *hil,* hill. See HILL.] —**hill′ock·y** *adj.*

hill·side (hĭl′sīd′) *n.* The side or slope of a hill, situated between the foot and the summit.

hill·top (hĭl′tŏp′) *n.* The crest or top of a hill.

hill·y (hĭl′ē) *adj.* **-i·er, -i·est 1.** Having many hills. **2.** Similar to a hill; steep. —**hill′i·ness** *n.*

Hi·lo (hē′lō) A city of HI on the E coast of Hawaii I. on **Hilo Bay,** an inlet of the Pacific Ocean; settled in the 1820s. Pop. 40,759.

hilt (hĭlt) *n.* The handle of a weapon or tool. —*idiom:* **to the hilt** To the limit; completely. [ME < OE.]

Hil·ton (hĭl′tən), **James** 1900–54. British novelist whose works include *Lost Horizon.*

Hilton Head Island An island off the S coast of SC in the Sea Is. of the Atlantic Ocean.

hi·lum (hī′ləm) *n., pl.* **-la** (-lə) **1a.** The scar on a seed, such as a bean, indicating the point of attachment to the funiculus. **b.** The nucleus of a starch grain. **2.** The area through which ducts, nerves, or blood vessels enter and leave an organ or gland. [Lat. *hīlum,* trifle.] —**hi′lar** (-lər) *adj.*

Hil·ver·sum (hĭl′vər-səm) A city of central Netherlands SE of Amsterdam. Pop. 84,379.

high relief
Robert Gould Shaw and the 54th Regiment Memorial, by Augustus Saint-Gaudens, Boston, Massachusetts

hijab

Hildegard von Bingen

him (hĭm) *pron.* The objective case of **he. 1.** Used as the direct object of a verb: *They saw him.* **2.** Used as the indirect object of a verb: *They offered him a ride.* **3.** Used as the object of a preposition: *This call is for him.* **4.** *Informal* Used as a predicate nominative: *It's him.* See Usage Note at **it¹. 5.** *Nonstandard* Used reflexively as the indirect object of a verb: *He bought him some new clothes.* See Note at **me.** ❖ *n.* A male: *The dog is a him.* [ME < OE, dative sing. of *hē,* he. See **ko-** in App.]

HIM *abbr.* Her (or His) Imperial Majesty

Him·a·la·ya Mountains (hĭm′ə-lā′ə, hĭ-mäl′yə) or **Him·a·la·yas** (-əs, -yəs) A mountain system of S-central Asia extending c. 2,414 km (1,500 mi) through Kashmir, N India, S Tibet, Nepal, Sikkim, and Bhutan. —**Him′a·la′yan** *adj. & n.*

Hi·ma·li·a (hə-mā′lē-ə, hī-māl′yə) *n.* A satellite of Jupiter. [Gk. *Himaliā,* nymph who bore three sons to Zeus, prob. < *himaliā,* abundance of wheat meal, fem. of *himalios,* abundant.]

hi·ma·ti·on (hĭ-măt′ē-ŏn′) *n.,* *pl.* **-i·a** (-ē-ə) A rectangular cloak worn in ancient Greece. [Gk. *hīmation,* dim. of *hīma,* hīmat-, garment, var. of *heima < hennunai,* to clothe. See **wes-²** in App.]

Hi·me·ji (hē′mĕ-jē′, hē-mĕ′jē) A city of SW Honshu, Japan, WNW of Kobe. Pop. 463,197.

Himm·ler (hĭm′lər), **Heinrich** 1900–45. German Nazi leader who directed the Nazi elite forces, the SS (1929–45), and coordinated the operation of the concentration and extermination camps (1941–45).

him·self (hĭm-sĕlf′) *pron.* **1.** That one identical with him: **a.** Used reflexively as the direct or indirect object of a verb or the object of a preposition: *He praised himself.* **b.** Used for emphasis: *He himself came.* **c.** Used in an absolute construction: *In the black himself, he could help his cousin.* **2.** His normal or healthy condition or state: *He's feeling himself again.* See Usage Note at **myself.** [ME < OE *himselfum* : *him,* him; see HIM + *selfum,* dative of *self,* self; see SELF.]

Him·yar·ite (hĭm′yə-rīt′) *n.* **1.** A member of an ancient tribe of southwest Arabia. **2.** The Semitic language of the ancient Himyarites. [After *Himyar,* a legendary king of Yemen.] —**Him′yar·ite, Him′yar·it′ic** (-rĭt′ĭk) *adj.*

hin (hĭn) *n.* A unit of liquid measure used by the ancient Hebrews, equal to about five liters. [ME < Med.Lat. < Gk. < Heb. *hîn,* of Egypt. orig.]

Hi·na·ya·na (hē′nə-yä′nə) *n.* *Often Offensive* Theravada Buddhism. [Skt. *hīnayānam,* lesser vehicle (as contrasted with *Mahāyānam,* greater vehicle; see MAHAYANA) : *hīna-,* inferior; see **ghē-** in App. + *yānam,* vehicle, way; see **ei-** in App.] —**Hi′na·ya′nist** *n.*

hind¹ (hīnd) *also* **hind·er** (hīn′dər) *adj.* Located at or toward the back or rear; posterior: *an animal's hind legs.* [ME *hinde,* short for *bihinde,* behind < OE *bihindan.* See **ko-** in App.]

hind² (hīnd) *n.* **1.** A female red deer. **2.** Any of several fishes of the genus *Epinephelus* of Atlantic waters, related to the groupers. [ME < OE.]

hind³ (hīnd) *n.* **1.** *Chiefly British* A farm laborer, esp. a skilled worker. **2.** *Archaic* A country bumpkin; a rustic. [Alteration of ME *hine,* household servants, poss. < OE *hīne,* genitive of *hīgan,* *hīwan,* members of a household. See **kei-¹** in App.]

Hind. *abbr.* **1.** Hindi **2.** Hindustani

hind·brain (hīnd′brān′) *n.* **1.** The portion of the embryonic brain from which the metencephalon and myelencephalon develop. **2.** The lower or hind region of the adult brain comprising the pons and medulla oblongata.

Hin·de·mith (hĭn′də-mĭth, -mĭt), **Paul** 1895–1963. German composer of chamber music, instrumental works, and operas.

Hin·den·burg (hĭn′dən-bûrg′, -bŏŏrk′), **Paul von** 1847–1934. German politician who was president of the Weimar Republic (1925–34).

hin·der¹ (hĭn′dər) *v.* **-dered, -der·ing, -ders** —*tr.* **1.** To be or get in the way of. **2.** To obstruct or delay the progress of. —*intr.* To interfere with action or progress. [ME *hindren* < OE *hindrian.* See **ko-** in App.] —**hin′der·er** *n.*

hind·er² (hīn′dər) *adj.* Variant of **hind¹.**

hind·gut (hīnd′gŭt′) *n.* The caudal portion of the embryonic alimentary canal in vertebrates.

Hin·di (hĭn′dē) *n.* **1.** A group of Indic dialects of northern India. **2.** The literary and official language of northern India, based on these dialects. [Hindi *Hindī < Hind,* India < Pers. < OPers. *Hinduš,* Sind < Skt. *sindhuh,* river.] —**Hin′di** *adj.*

Hin·di-Ur·du (hĭn′dē-ŏŏr′dŏŏ, -ûr′-) *n.* Hindi and Urdu, viewed as essentially the same language with respect to their grammar and core vocabulary, though widely divergent in their literary forms.

hind limb *n.* A posterior appendage, such as a leg or wing.

hind·most (hīnd′mōst′) *also* **hind·er·most** (hīn′dər-) *adj.* Farthest to the rear; last.

hind·quar·ter (hīnd′kwôr′tər) *n.* **1.** The posterior portion of a side of beef, lamb, veal, or mutton, including a hind leg and one or two ribs. **2. hindquarters** The posterior part of a quadruped, adjacent to the hind legs.

hin·drance (hĭn′drəns) *n.* **1a.** The act of hindering. **b.** The condition of being hindered. **2.** One that hinders. [ME *hindraunce,* harm < *hindren,* to hinder. See HINDER¹.]

hind·sight (hīnd′sīt′) *n.* **1.** Perception of the significance and

nature of events after they have occurred. **2.** The rear sight of a firearm.

Hin·du (hĭn′dŏŏ) *adj.* **1.** Of or relating to Hinduism. **2.** Of or relating to the Hindus or their culture. ❖ *n.* An adherent of Hinduism. [Pers. *Hindū < Hind,* India. See HINDI.]

Hindu calendar *n.* The lunisolar calendar of Hindu religious life, dating in its classic form from the fourth century A.D.

Hin·du·ism (hĭn′dŏŏ-ĭz′əm) *n.* A diverse body of religion, philosophy, and culture native to India, marked esp. by a belief in reincarnation and a supreme being of many forms and natures.

Hindu Kush (kŏŏsh, kŭsh) A mountain range of SW Asia extending more than 805 km (500 mi) from N Pakistan to NE Afghanistan and rising to 7,695.2 m (25,230 ft).

Hin·du·stan (hĭn′dŏŏ-stän′, -stăn′) A historical region of India considered at various times to include only the upper Ganges R. plateau or all of N India from the Himalaya Mts. to the Deccan Plateau and from the Punjab to Assam. The term has also been applied to the entire Indian subcontinent.

Hin·du·sta·ni (hĭn′dŏŏ-stä′nē, -stăn′ē) *n.* A group of Indic dialects that function as a lingua franca throughout much of northern and central India, including the spoken form of Hindi-Urdu. ❖ *adj.* Of or relating to Hindustan, its people, or the Hindustani language.

Hines (hīnz), **Earl** ("Fatha") 1905–83. Amer. jazz pianist who first gained wide recognition in the 1920s.

hinge (hĭnj) *n.* **1a.** A jointed or flexible device that allows the turning or pivoting of a part, such as a door, on a stationary frame. **b.** A similar structure or part. **2.** A small folded paper rectangle gummed on one side, used esp. to fasten stamps in an album. **3.** A point or circumstance on which subsequent events depend. ❖ *v.* **hinged, hing·ing, hing·es** —*tr.* **1.** To attach by or equip with or as if with hinges or a hinge. **2.** To consider or make (something) dependent on something else; predicate. —*intr.* To be contingent on a single factor; depend. [ME *henge.*]

hinge joint *n.* A joint, such as the elbow, in which a convex part of one bone fits into a concave part of another.

hin·ny (hĭn′ē) *n.,* *pl.* **-nies** The hybrid offspring of a male horse and a female donkey. [Alteration of Lat. *hinnus < Gk. ginnos, innos.*]

Hin·shel·wood (hĭn′shəl-wŏŏd′, -chəl-), Sir **Cyril Norman** 1897–1967. British chemist who shared a 1956 Nobel Prize.

hint (hĭnt) *n.* **1.** A slight indication or intimation: *a hint of scandal.* **2a.** A brief or indirect suggestion; a tip. **b.** A statement conveying information in an indirect fashion; a clue. **3.** A barely perceptible amount: *a hint of color.* **4.** *Archaic* An occasion; an opportunity. ❖ *v.* **hint·ed, hint·ing, hints** —*tr.* To indicate or make known in an indirect manner. —*intr.* To give a hint. See Syns at **suggest.** [Prob. < ME *hinten, henten,* to catch, grasp < OE *hentan.*] —**hint′er** *n.*

hin·ter·land (hĭn′tər-lănd′) *n.* **1.** The land next to and inland from a coast. **2a.** A region remote from urban areas; backcountry. **b.** A region far from metropolitan culture. [Ger. : *hinter,* behind (< MHGer. < OHGer. *hintar*; see **ko-** in App.) + *Land,* land (< MHGer. *lant* < OHGer.).]

hip¹ (hĭp) *n.* **1a.** The laterally projecting prominence of the pelvis or pelvic region from the waist to the thigh. **b.** A homologous posterior part in quadrupeds. **c.** The hip joint. **2.** *Architecture* The external angle formed by the meeting of two adjacent sloping sides of a roof. [ME < OE *hype.*]

hip² (hĭp) *also* **hep** (hĕp) *adj.* **hip·per, hip·pest** *also* **hep·per, hep·pest** *Slang* **1.** Keenly aware of, knowledgeable about, or interested in the latest developments. **2.** Very fashionable or stylish. [Perh. < Wolof *hipi, hepi,* to open one's eyes, be aware.] —**hip** *n.* & *v.* —**hip′ly** *adv.*

hip³ (hĭp) *n.* A rose hip. [ME *hipe* < OE *hēope.*]

hip⁴ (hĭp) *interj.* Usu. used to begin a cheer: *Hip, hip, hooray!*

hip·bone (hĭp′bōn′) *n.* Either of two large flat bones each forming one of the lateral halves of the pelvis and consisting of the fused ilium, ischium, and pubis.

hip boot *n.* A very high boot extending to the hips.

hip-hop (hĭp′hŏp′) *n.* **1.** A popular urban youth culture, closely associated with rap music and with the style and fashions of African-American inner-city residents. **2.** Rap music. ❖ *adj.* Of or characteristic of hip-hop culture. [Prob. HIP² + HOP¹.]

hip-hug·gers (hĭp′hŭg′ərz) *pl.n.* Tight-fitting pants whose waistline rests at hip level.

hip joint *n.* The ball-and-socket joint formed by the head of the femur and the cup-shaped cavity of the hipbone.

Hip·par·chus¹ (hĭ-pär′kəs) d. 514 B.C. Athenian tyrant (527–514) who ruled with his brother Hippias.

Hip·par·chus² (hĭ-pär′kəs) fl. 2nd cent. B.C. Greek astronomer who mapped the earliest known star chart.

hipped¹ (hĭpt) *adj.* Having hips, esp. of a given kind. Often used in combination: *slim-hipped; large-hipped.*

hipped² (hĭpt) *adj. Slang* Interested or preoccupied to a great degree. [Prob. < *hip,* to make aware < HIP².]

hipped³ (hĭpt) *adj. Chiefly British* Melancholy; depressed. [Shortening and alteration of HYPOCHONDRIAC.]

hipped roof *n.* Variant of **hip roof.**

Hip·pi·as (hĭp′ē-əs) d. 490 B.C. Athenian tyrant (527–510) who governed with his brother Hipparchus until 514, and he was

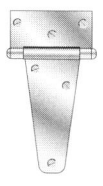

hinge
left: strap hinge
right: T-hinge

ă pat	oi boy	
ā pay	ou out	
âr care	ŏŏ took	
ä father	ŏō boot	
ĕ pet	ŭ cut	
ē be	ûr urge	
ĭ pit	th thin	
ī pie	th this	
îr pier	hw which	
ŏ pot	zh vision	
ō toe	ə about,	
ô paw	item	

Stress marks:
′ (primary);
′ (secondary), as in
lexicon (lĕk′sĭ-kŏn′)

hip·pie also **hip·py** (hĭp′ē) *n., pl.* **-pies** A person who rejects many of the conventional standards and customs of society, esp. one who advocates extreme liberalism. [< HIP².]

hip·po (hĭp′ō) *n., pl.* **-pos** A hippopotamus.

Hippo also **Hippo Re·gi·us** (rē′jē-əs) An ancient city of NW Africa in present-day NE Algeria S of Annaba.

hip·po·cam·pus (hĭp′ə-kăm′pəs) *n., pl.* **-pi** (-pī′) A ridge in the floor of each lateral ventricle of the brain that consists mainly of gray matter and has a central role in memory processes. [LLat., a sea horse with a horse's forelegs and a dolphin's tail (< its shape in cross section) < Gk. *hippokampos* : *hippos*, horse; see **ekwo-** in App. + *kampos*, sea monster.] —**hip′po·cam′pal** (-pəl) *adj.*

hip·po·cras (hĭp′ə-krăs′) *n.* A cordial made from spiced wine, formerly used as a medicine. [ME *ipocras* < OFr. *ypocras, hypocras* < alteration of *Hippocras,* Hippocrates.]

Hip·poc·ra·tes (hĭ-pŏk′rə-tēz′) Called "the Father of Medicine." 460?–377? B.C. Greek physician who laid the foundations of modern medicine. —**Hip′po·crat′ic** (hĭp′ə-krăt′ĭk) *adj.*

Hippocratic oath *n.* An oath of ethical professional behavior sworn by many new physicians, inaccurately attributed to Hippocrates.

Hip·po·crene (hĭp′ə-krēn′, hĭp′ə-krē′nē) *Greek Mythology* A fountain on Mount Helicon, Greece, sacred to the Muses and a source of poetic inspiration. [Lat. *Hippocrēnē* < Gk. *Hippokrēnē* : *hippos,* horse (the myth that Pegasus's hoof created it); see **ekwo-** in App. + *krēnē,* fountain.]

hip·po·drome (hĭp′ə-drōm′) *n.* **1.** *Sports* An arena for equestrian shows. **2.** An open-air stadium with an oval course for horse and chariot races in ancient Greece and Rome. [Fr. < OFr. *ypodrome* < Lat. *hippodromos* < Gk. : *hippos,* horse; see **ekwo-** in App. + *dromos,* racecourse.]

hip·po·griff also **hip·po·gryph** (hĭp′ə-grĭf′) *n. Mythology* A monster having the wings, claws, and head of a griffin and the body and hindquarters of a horse. [Fr. *hippogriffe* < Ital. *ippogrifo* : Gk. *hippos,* horse; see **ekwo-** in App. + Ital. *grifo,* griffin (< Lat. *grȳphus;* see GRIFFIN).]

Hip·pol·y·ta (hĭ-pŏl′ĭ-tə) *n. Greek Mythology* A queen of the Amazons who was defeated by Hercules.

Hip·pol·y·tus (hĭ-pŏl′ĭ-təs) *n. Greek Mythology* A son of Hippolyta and Theseus who was killed by Poseidon.

Hip·pom·e·nes (hĭ-pŏm′ə-nēz′) *n. Greek Mythology* The suitor who tricked and thereby outran Atalanta.

hip·po·pot·a·mus (hĭp′ə-pŏt′ə-məs) *n., pl.* **-mus·es** or **-mi** (-mī′) **1.** A large, chiefly aquatic African herbivorous mammal (*Hippopotamus amphibius*) having thick skin, short legs with four toes, and a broad wide-mouthed muzzle. **2.** The pygmy hippopotamus. [Lat. < Gk. *hippopotamos* : *hippos,* horse; see **ekwo-** in App. + *potamos,* river; see **pet-** in App.]

hip·py (hĭp′ē) *n.* Variant of **hippie**.

hip roof or **hipped roof** *n.* A four-sided roof having sloping ends and sides.

hip·ster (hĭp′stər) *n. Slang* One who is esp. interested in the latest trends and tastes.

hip·ster·ism (hĭp′stə-rĭz′əm) *n. Slang* **1.** The quality or condition of being hip. **2.** The lifestyle characteristic of hipsters.

hi·ra·ga·na (hîr′ə-gä′nə) *n.* A cursive kana used for polite, informal, or casual writing. [J. : *hira,* ordinary, plain + *kana,* kana; see KANA.]

Hi·ra·ka·ta (hē′rä-kä′tä, hē-rä′kä-tä′) A city of S Honshu, Japan, a suburb of Osaka. Pop. 396,867.

hir·cine (hûr′sīn′, -sĭn) *adj.* Of or characteristic of a goat, esp. in strong odor. [ME *hircyne* < Lat. *hircīnus* < *hircus,* goat.]

hire (hīr) *v.* **hired, hir·ing, hires** —*tr.* **1a.** To engage the services of (a person) for a fee; employ: *hired a new clerk.* **b.** To engage the temporary use of for a fee; rent. **2.** To grant the services of or the temporary use of for a fee. —*intr.* To obtain work: *hired on today.* ❖ *n.* **1a.** The act of hiring. **b.** The condition or fact of being hired. **2a.** Payment for services; wages. **b.** Payment for the use of something. **3.** *Informal* One hired. [ME *hiren* < OE *hȳrian.*] —**hir′a·ble, hire′a·ble** *adj.* —**hir′er** *n.*

hired gun (hīrd) *n. Slang* **1.** One hired to kill another person. **2.** One hired to fight for or protect another.

hired hand *n.* **1.** A paid employee, esp. on a farm or ranch. **2.** *Informal* A paid employee.

hire·ling (hīr′lĭng) *n.* One who works solely for compensation, esp. one who performs tasks considered menial or offensive.

hire purchase *n. Chiefly British* Purchase of a commodity on an installment plan.

hir·ing hall (hīr′ĭng) *n.* A union-operated placement center where jobs are allotted to applicants according to a set order.

Hi·ro·hi·to (hîr′ō-hē′tō) 1901–89. Emperor of Japan (1926–89) who advocated the Japanese government's unconditional surrender that ended World War II (1945).

Hi·ro·shi·ge (hîr′ō-shē′gā, hĭ-rô′shĕ′gĕ), **Ando** 1797–1858. Japanese artist known for his color woodblock prints.

Hi·ro·shi·ma (hîr′ə-shē′mə, hĭ-rō′shə-mə) A city of SW Honshu, Japan, on the Inland Sea W of Osaka; destroyed by US forces in World War II with the first atomic bomb used in warfare (Aug. 6, 1945). Pop. 1,102,047.

hir·sute (hûr′sōōt′, hîr′-, hər-sōōt′) *adj.* **1.** Covered with hair;

hippopotamus
Hippopotamus amphibius

Hirohito
photographed in the 1940s

hairy. **2.** *Botany* Covered with stiff or coarse hairs. [Lat. *hirsūtus,* hairy, bristly.] —**hir′sute′ness** *n.*

hir·sut·ism (hûr′sōō-tĭz′əm, hîr′-, hər-sōō′-) *n.* Heavy growth of hair, often in abnormal distribution.

hir·u·din (hîr-ōōd′n, hîr′ə-dən, -yə-) *n.* A substance extracted from the buccal glands of leeches and used as an anticoagulant. [Orig. a trademark < Lat. *hirūdō,* leech.]

his (hĭz) *adj.* The possessive form of **he**¹. Used as a modifier before a noun: *his boots.* ❖ *pron.* (*used with a sing. or pl. verb*) Used to indicate the one or ones belonging to him: *If you can't find your hat, take his.* [ME < OE. See **ko-** in App.]

His·pan·ic (hĭ-spăn′ĭk) *adj.* **1.** Of or relating to Spain or Spanish-speaking Latin America. **2.** Of or relating to a Spanish-speaking people or culture. ❖ *n.* **1.** A Spanish-speaking person. **2.** A US citizen or resident of Latin-American or Spanish descent. [Lat. *Hispānicus* < *Hispānia,* Spain.]

USAGE NOTE Though often used interchangeably in American English, *Hispanic* and *Latino* are not identical terms. *Hispanic* has the broader reference, potentially encompassing all Spanish-speaking peoples in both hemispheres. *Latino* refers more exclusively to persons or communities of Latin-American origin. • For a certain segment of the Spanish-speaking population, *Latino* is a term of ethnic pride and *Hispanic* a label that borders on the offensive. According to this view, *Hispanic* lacks the authenticity and cultural resonance of *Latino,* with its Spanish sound and its ability to show the feminine form *Latina* when used of women. Furthermore, *Hispanic*—the term used by government agencies—is said to bear the stamp of an Anglo establishment far removed from the concerns of the Spanish-speaking community. These views are strongly held by some but are by no means universal, and the division in usage seems as related to geography as it is to politics, with *Latino* widely preferred in California and *Hispanic* the more usual term in Florida and Texas. Even in these regions, however, usage is often mixed, and it is not uncommon to find both terms used by the same writer or speaker. See Usage Note at **Chicano**.

Hispanic American *n.* **1.** A US citizen or resident of Hispanic descent. **2.** A Spanish American. —**His·pan′ic-A·mer′i·can** (hĭ-spăn′ĭk-ə-mĕr′ĭ-kən) *adj.*

His·pan·i·cize (hĭ-spăn′ĭ-sīz′) *tr.v.* **-cized, -ciz·ing, -ciz·es 1.** To make Spanish in form, style, or character. **2.** To bring under Hispanic influence or control. —**His·pan′i·ci·za′tion** (-sĭ-zā′shən) *n.*

His·pan·io·la (hĭs′pən-yō′lə) An island of the West Indies E of Cuba, divided between Haiti and the Dominican Republic.

His·pa·nism (hĭs′pə-nĭz′əm) or **His·pan·i·cism** (hĭ-spăn′ĭ-sĭz′əm) *n.* A Spanish word, phrase, or linguistic feature occurring in another language.

His·pa·nist (hĭs′pə-nĭst) *n.* A specialist in Spanish language or literature or in the languages and literatures of Spain, Portugal, and Latin America.

His·pa·no (hĭ-spăn′ō, -spä′nō) *n., pl.* **-nos 1.** A native or resident of Spanish descent in the southwest United States. **2.** A Hispanic. [Short for *Hispano-American* < Sp. *hispano,* Sp. < Lat. *Hispānus* < *Hispānī,* the Spaniards.]

Hispano– *pref.* Spanish; Hispanic: *Hispanophile.* [< Lat. *Hispānus.* See HISPANO.]

his·pid (hĭs′pĭd) *adj.* Covered with stiff or rough hairs; bristly: *hispid stems.* [Lat. *hispidus.*] —**his·pid′i·ty** (hĭ-spĭd′ĭ-tē) *n.*

hiss (hĭs) *n.* **1.** A sharp sibilant sound similar to a sustained *s.* **2.** An expression of disapproval, contempt, or dissatisfaction conveyed by a hiss. ❖ *v.* **hissed, hiss·ing, hiss·es** —*intr.* To make a hiss. —*tr.* **1.** To utter with a hiss. **2.** To express (a negative view or reaction) by hissing. [ME *hissen,* to hiss, of imit. orig.] —**hiss′er** *n.*

Hiss, Alger 1904–96. Amer. public official who was accused of espionage at the height of the Communist scare and was convicted of perjury (1950) in a controversial case.

his·self (hĭz-sĕlf′) *pron. Chiefly Southern & South Midland US* Himself.

OUR LIVING LANGUAGE Speakers of some vernacular American dialects, particularly in the South, may use the possessive reflexive form *hisself* instead of *himself* (as in *He cut hisself shaving*) and *theirselves* or *theirself* for *themselves* (as in *They found theirselves alone*). These forms reflect the tendency of speakers of vernacular dialects to regularize irregular patterns found in the corresponding standard variety. In Standard English, the pattern of reflexive pronoun forms shows slightly irregular patterning; all forms but two are composed of the possessive form of the pronoun and *-self* or *-selves,* as in *myself* or *ourselves.* The exceptions are *himself* and *themselves,* which are formed by attaching the suffix *-self/-selves* to the object forms of *he* and *they* rather than their possessive forms. Speakers who use *hisself* and *theirselves* are smoothing out the pattern's inconsistencies by applying the same rule to all forms in the set. *Hisself* and *theirselves* have origins in British English and are still prevalent today in vernacular speech in England.

hiss·y¹ (hĭs′ē) *adj.* **-si·er, -si·est** Characterized by or making a hissing sound.

his·sy² (hĭs′ē) n., pl. **-sies** Chiefly Southern & South Midland US See **tantrum**. [Short for HISSY FIT.]

hissy fit n. Chiefly Southern US See **tantrum**. [< HISSY¹.]

his·tam·i·nase (hĭ-stăm′ə-nās′, -năz′, hĭs′tə-mə-) n. An enzyme that catalyzes the inactivation of histamine and is found in the digestive system.

his·ta·mine (hĭs′tə-mēn′, -mĭn) n. A physiologically active amine, $C_5H_9N_3$, found in plant and animal tissue and released in humans as part of an allergic reaction. [HIST(IDINE) + AMINE.] —**his′ta·min′ic** (-mĭn′ĭk) adj.

his·ti·dine (hĭs′tĭ-dēn′, -dĭn) n. An essential amino acid, $C_6H_9N_3O_2$, important for the growth and repair of tissues. [HIST(O)– + –ID(E) + –INE².]

his·ti·o·cyte (hĭs′tē-ə-sīt′) n. A relatively inactive immobile macrophage found in normal connective tissue. [Gk. histion, web, dim. of histos; see **stā-** in App. + –CYTE.]

histo– or **hist–** pref. Body tissue: histogenesis. [< Gk. histos, web. See **stā-** in App.]

his·to·chem·is·try (hĭs′tō-kĕm′ĭ-strē) n. The study of the chemical composition of body cells and tissues. —**his′to·chem′i·cal** (-ĭ-kəl) adj. —**his′to·chem′i·cal·ly** adv.

his·to·com·pat·i·bil·i·ty (hĭs′tō-kəm-păt′ə-bĭl′ĭ-tē) n., pl. **-ties** A state in which the absence of immunological interference permits the grafting of tissue or the transfusion of blood without rejection. —**his′to·com·pat′i·ble** adj.

his·to·gen·e·sis (hĭs′tō-jĕn′ĭ-sĭs) n. The formation and development of body tissues. —**his′to·ge·net′ic** (-jə-nĕt′ĭk), **his′to·gen′ic** (-jĕn′ĭk) adj. —**his′to·ge·net′i·cal·ly, his′to·gen′i·cal·ly** adv.

his·to·gram (hĭs′tə-grăm′) n. A bar graph of a frequency distribution in which the widths of the bars are proportional to the classes into which the variable has been divided and the heights of the bars are proportional to the class frequencies. [Gk. histos, mast, web; see **stā-** in App. + –GRAM.]

his·tol·o·gy (hĭ-stŏl′ə-jē) n., pl. **-gies** 1. The anatomical study of the microscopic structure of animal and plant tissues. 2. The microscopic structure of tissue. —**his′to·log′i·cal** (hĭs′tə-lŏj′ĭ-kəl), **his′to·log′ic** adj. —**his′to·log′i·cal·ly** adv. —**his·tol′o·gist** n.

his·tol·y·sis (hĭ-stŏl′ĭ-sĭs) n. The breakdown and disintegration of organic tissue. —**his′to·lyt′ic** (hĭs′tə-lĭt′ĭk) adj. —**his′to·lyt′i·cal·ly** adv.

his·tone (hĭs′tōn′) n. Any of several small basic proteins most commonly found in association with the DNA in the chromatin of eukaryotes.

his·to·pa·thol·o·gy (hĭs′tō-pə-thŏl′ə-jē, -pă-) n. The study of the microscopic anatomical changes in diseased tissue. —**his′to·path′o·log′ic** (-păth′ə-lŏj′ĭk), **his′to·path′o·log′i·cal** adj. —**his′to·pa·thol′o·gist** n.

his·to·phys·i·ol·o·gy (hĭs′tō-fĭz′ē-ŏl′ə-jē) n. The branch of physiology that deals with the structure and function of tissues. —**his′to·phys′i·o·log′ic** (-ē-ə-lŏj′ĭk), **his′to·phys′i·o·log′i·cal** (-ĭ-kəl) adj.

his·to·plas·mo·sis (hĭs′tō-plăz-mō′sĭs) n., pl. **-ses** (-sēz) A disease caused by the inhalation of spores of the fungus Histoplasma capsulatum, most often asymptomatic but occasionally producing acute pneumonia or an influenzalike illness.

his·to·ri·an (hĭ-stôr′ē-ən, -stŏr′-) n. 1. A writer, student, or scholar of history. 2. One who writes or compiles a chronological record of events; a chronicler.

his·tor·ic (hĭ-stôr′ĭk, -stŏr′-) adj. 1. Having importance in or influence on history. 2. Historical.

his·tor·i·cal (hĭ-stôr′ĭ-kəl, -stŏr′-) adj. 1a. Of or relating to the character of history. b. Based on or concerned with events in history. c. Used in the past: historical costumes. 2. Important or famous in history. 3. Diachronic. —**his·tor′i·cal·ly** adv. —**his·tor′i·cal·ness** n.

historical linguistics n. (used with a sing. verb) The study of linguistic change over time in language or in a particular language or language family.

historical materialism n. A major tenet in the Marxist theory of history that regards material economic forces as the base on which sociopolitical institutions and ideas are built.

historical present n. The present tense used in the narration of events set in the past.

historical school n. A school of theorists, as in law or economics, stressing the influence of historical conditions.

his·tor·i·cism (hĭ-stôr′ĭ-sĭz′əm, -stŏr′-) n. 1. A theory that events are determined or influenced by conditions beyond human control. 2. A theory that stresses the significant influence of history as a criterion of value. 3. Art & Architecture The deliberate use or revival of historical styles in contemporary works. 4. Philosophy The view that historical periods should be studied without imposing anachronistic categories of evaluation. —**his·tor′i·cist** adj. & n.

his·to·ric·i·ty (hĭs′tə-rĭs′ĭ-tē) n. Historical authenticity.

his·tor·i·cize (hĭ-stôr′ĭ-sīz′, -stŏr′-) v. **-cized, -ciz·ing, -ciz·es** —tr. 1. To make or make appear historical. —intr. To use historical details or materials. —**his′tor′i·ci·za′tion** (-sī-zā′shən) n.

his·to·ried (hĭs′tə-rēd) adj. Having an interesting history.

his·to·ri·og·ra·pher (hĭ-stôr′ē-ŏg′rə-fər, -stŏr′-) n. 1. A specialist in historiography. 2. A historian, esp. one designated by a group or public institution.

his·to·ri·og·ra·phy (hĭ-stôr′ē-ŏg′rə-fē, -stŏr′-) n. 1. The principles and methodology of historical research and presentation. 2. The writing of history based on the analysis and selection of sources. 3. A body of historical literature. [Fr. historiographie < OFr. < Gk. historiographiā : historiā, history; see HISTORY + -graphiā, -graphy.] —**his′to·ri·o·graph′ic** (-ē-ə-grăf′ĭk), **his′to·ri·o·graph′i·cal** (-ĭ-kəl) adj.

his·to·ry (hĭs′tə-rē) n., pl. **-ries** 1. A narrative of events; a story. 2a. A chronological record of events, as of the development of a people, often including an explanation of or commentary on those events. b. A formal written account of related natural phenomena. c. A record of a patient's medical background. d. An established record or pattern of behavior. 3. The discipline that records and analyzes past events. 4a. The events forming the subject matter of a historical account. b. The aggregate of past events or human affairs: throughout history. c. Something that belongs to the past. d. An interesting past. e. Slang One that is no longer worth consideration: Why worry about him? He's history! 5. A drama based on historical events. [ME histoire < OFr. < Lat. historia < Gk. historiā < historein, to inquire < histōr, learned man. See **weid-** in App.]

his·tri·on·ic (hĭs′trē-ŏn′ĭk) also **his·tri·on·i·cal** (-ĭ-kəl) adj. 1. Of or relating to actors or acting. 2. Excessively dramatic or emotional; affected. [LLat. histriōnicus < Lat. histriō, histriōn-, actor, prob. of Etruscan orig.]

his·tri·on·ics (hĭs′trē-ŏn′ĭks) n. 1. (used with a pl. verb) Theatrical arts or performances. 2. (used with a sing. or pl. verb) Exaggerated emotional behavior calculated for effect.

hit (hĭt) v. **hit, hit·ting, hits** —tr. 1a. To come into contact with forcefully; strike. b. To reach with or as if with a blow: The bullet hit him. 2a. To cause to come into contact: She hit her hand against the wall. b. To deal a blow to. c. To strike with a missile. 3. To press or push (a key or button, for example). 4. Sports a. To reach with a propelled object: hit him with a pass. b. To score in this way: hit a basket. c. To perform (a shot or maneuver) successfully. d. To propel with a stroke or blow. 5. Baseball a. To execute (a base hit) successfully. b. To bat against (a pitcher or kind of pitch) successfully. 6a. To affect, esp. adversely: The flu hit him hard. b. To be affected by (a negative development): Their marriage hit a bad patch. 7. To arise suddenly in the mind; occur to: It hit him that she was serious. 8a. Informal To go to or arrive at: We hit the beach early. b. Informal To attain or reach: Sales hit a new high. c. To produce or represent accurately: trying to hit the right note. 9. Games To deal cards to. 10. Slang To give a drink of liquor or a dose of a narcotic to. —intr. 1. To strike or deal a blow. 2a. To come into contact with something; collide. b. To attack. c. To happen or occur: The storm hit at dawn. 3. To achieve or find something desired or sought: hit on the answer. 4. Baseball To bat. 5. To ignite a mixture of air and fuel in the cylinders. Used of an internal-combustion engine. ❖ n. 1a. A collision or impact. b. A successfully executed shot, blow, thrust, or throw. 2. A successful or popular venture: a Broadway hit. 3. Computer Science a. A match of data in a search string against data that one is searching. b. A connection made to a website. 4. An apt or effective remark. 5. Baseball A base hit. 6. Slang a. A dose of a narcotic drug. b. A puff of a cigarette or a pipe. 7. Slang A murder carried out usu. by a member of an underworld syndicate. —**phrasal verbs: hit on** Slang To pay unsolicited and usu. unwanted sexual attention to. **hit up** Slang To approach and ask (someone) for something, esp. for money. —**idioms: hit it big** Slang To be successful. **hit it off** Informal To get along well together. **hit the books** Informal To study, esp. with concentrated effort. **hit the bottle** Slang To engage in drinking alcoholic beverages. **hit the ground running** Informal To begin a venture with great energy, involvement, and competence. **hit the hay** (or **sack**) Slang To go to bed. **hit the jackpot** To become highly and unexpectedly successful, esp. to win a great deal of money. **hit the nail on the head** To be absolutely right. **hit the road** Slang To set out, as on a trip; leave. **hit the roof** (or **ceiling**) Slang To express anger, esp. vehemently. **hit the spot** To give total or desired satisfaction, as food or drink. [ME hitten < OE hyttan < ON hitta.] —**hit′ta·ble** adj.

hit-and-miss (hĭt′n-mĭs′) adj. Sometimes succeeding and sometimes not.

hit-and-run (hĭt′n-rŭn′) adj. 1. Being or involving the driver of a motor vehicle who leaves the scene of an accident, esp. one in which a pedestrian or another vehicle has been struck. 2. Baseball Relating to or being a play in which a base runner starts to run on the pitch and the batter attempts to hit the ball to protect the runner. 3. Involving or designed for swift action or effect.

hitch (hĭch) v. **hitched, hitch·ing, hitch·es** —tr. 1. To fasten or catch temporarily with or as if with a loop, hook, or noose. 2. To connect or attach, as to a vehicle. 3. To move or raise by pulling or jerking: hitch up one's suspenders. 4. Informal To hitchhike. 5. Slang To marry: get hitched. —intr. 1. To move haltingly; hobble. 2. To become entangled, snarled, or fastened. 3. Informal To hitchhike. ❖ n. 1. Any of various knots used as a temporary fastening. 2. A device used to connect one thing to another. 3. A short jerking motion; a tug. 4. A hobble or limp. 5. An impedi-

Adolf Hitler
photographed in 1934

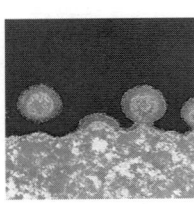

HIV
transmission electron
micrograph of viruses
budding from a T cell

hoarfrost
leaves covered with
hoarfrost

ment or delay: *a hitch in our plans.* **6.** A term of service, esp. of military service. **7.** *Informal* A free ride obtained along a road. [Prob. < ME *hytchen, icchen,* to move, jerk.] —**hitch′er** *n.*

Hitch·cock (hĭch′kŏk′), Sir **Alfred Joseph** 1899–1980. British director known for suspense films such as *The 39 Steps* (1935) and *Psycho* (1960).

hitch·hike (hĭch′hīk′) *v.* **-hiked, -hik·ing, -hikes** —*intr.* To travel by hitchhiking rides. —*tr.* To solicit or get (a free ride) along a road. —**hitch′hike′** *n.* —**hitch′hik′er** *n.*

hitch·ing post (hĭch′ĭng) *n.* A post to which an animal, esp. a horse, is hitched.

hi-tech (hī′tĕk′) *adj.* Variant of **high-tech.**

hith·er (hĭth′ər) *adv.* To or toward this place: *Come hither.* ❖ *adj.* Located on the near side. —*idiom:* **hither and thither** (or **yon**) In or to many places; here and there: *ran hither and yon.* [ME < OE *hider.* See **ko-** in App.]

hith·er·most (hĭth′ər-mōst′) *adj.* Nearest to this place or side.

hith·er·to (hĭth′ər-tōō′, hĭth′ər-tōō′) *adv.* Until this time.

hith·er·ward (hĭth′ər-wərd) also **hith·er·wards** (-wərdz) *adv.* Hither.

Hit·ler (hĭt′lər), **Adolf** Known as "Der Führer." 1889–1945. Austrian-born founder of the German Nazi Party, chancellor of the Third Reich (1933–45), and absolute dictator (1934–45). —**Hit·ler′i·an** (hĭt-lîr′ē-ən) *adj.* —**Hit′ler·ism** (hĭt′lə-rĭz′əm) —**Hit′ler·ite′** (-lə-rīt′) *adj. & n.*

hit list *n. Slang* **1.** A list of potential murder victims. **2.** A list designating a target, as for attack, coercion, or elimination.

hit man *n. Slang* **1.** A man hired by a crime syndicate as a professional killer. **2.** A hatchet man.

hit-or-miss (hĭt′ər-mĭs′) *adj.* Marked by a lack of care, accuracy, or organization; random. —**hit or miss** *adv.*

hit parade *n.* **1.** A ranked group or listing of the currently most popular songs. **2.** A collection or listing of the most popular or excellent items or people of a certain kind.

hit squad *n. Slang* **1.** A squad or team of hired executioners. **2.** A group of political terrorists.

hit·ter (hĭt′ər) *n.* **1.** One who hits or strikes something. **2.** *Baseball* A batter.

Hit·tite (hĭt′īt′) *n.* **1.** A member of an ancient people living in Anatolia and northern Syria about 2000–1200 B.C. **2.** The Indo-European language of the Hittites. ❖ *adj.* Of or relating to the Hittites, their language, or their culture. [< Heb. *hittī* < Akkadian *ḫatti* < Hittite *Ḫatti,* land of the Hattians (an indigenous people).]

HIV (āch′ī-vē′) *n.* A retrovirus that causes AIDS by infecting helper T cells of the immune system. [H(UMAN) I(MMUNODEFICIENCY) V(IRUS).]

hive (hīv) *n.* **1a.** A structure for housing bees, esp. honeybees. **b.** A colony of bees living in such a structure. **2.** A place swarming with activity. ❖ *v.* **hived, hiv·ing, hives** —*tr.* **1.** To collect into a hive. **2.** To store (honey) in a hive. **3.** To store up; accumulate. —*intr.* **1.** To enter and occupy a beehive. **2.** To live closely with many others. —*phrasal verb:* **hive off** To set apart from a group. [ME < OE *hȳf.*]

hives (hīvz) *pl.n.* (*used with a sing. or pl. verb*) A skin condition characterized by intensely itching welts and caused by an allergic reaction, an infection, or a nervous condition. [?]

hl *abbr.* hectoliter

HL *abbr.* House of Lords

HLA (āch′ĕl-ā′) *n.* The class of major histocompatibility antigens in humans. [H(*uman*) L(*eukocyte*) A(*ntigen*).]

HM *abbr.* Her (or His) Majesty

HMO (āch′ĕm-ō′) *n.* A corporation financed by insurance premiums whose physicians and staff provide health care to enrolled members and their families. [H(EALTH) M(AINTENANCE) O(RGANIZATION).]

Hmong (hmông) *n., pl.* **Hmong** or **Hmongs** **1.** A member of a people inhabiting the mountainous regions of southern China and adjacent areas. **2.** The Miao-Yao language of the Hmong.

HMS *abbr.* Her (or His) Majesty's Ship

ho¹ (hō) *interj.* Used to express surprise or joy, to attract attention to something sighted, or to urge onward: *Land ho!*

ho² (hō) *n., pl.* **hos** *Slang* A prostitute. [African American Vernacular E., alteration of WHORE.]

Ho¹ The symbol for the element **holmium.**

Ho² *abbr. Bible* Hosea

hoa·gie also **hoa·gy** (hō′gē) *n., pl.* **-gies** *Chiefly Pennsylvania & New Jersey* See **submarine** 2. See Regional Note at **submarine.** [Alteration of *hoggy.*]

hoar (hôr, hōr) *adj.* Hoary. ❖ *n.* Hoarfrost. [ME *hor* < OE *hār.*]

hoard (hôrd, hōrd) *n.* A hidden fund or supply stored for future use; a cache. ❖ *v.* **hoard·ed, hoard·ing, hoards** —*intr.* To gather or accumulate a hoard. —*tr.* **1.** To accumulate a hoard of. **2.** To keep hidden or private. [ME *hord* < OE. See **(s)keu-** in App.] —**hoard′er** *n.*

hoard·ing (hôr′dĭng, hōr′-) *n.* **1.** A temporary wooden fence around a building or structure under construction or repair. **2.** *Chiefly British* A billboard. [Obsolete *hoard, hourd* < Fr. dialectal *hourd,* fence, scaffold, hurdle < OFr., of Gmc. orig.]

hoar·frost (hôr′frôst′, -frŏst′, hōr′-) *n.* Frozen dew that forms a white coating on a surface.

hoarse (hôrs, hōrs) *adj.* **hoars·er, hoars·est** **1.** Rough or grating in sound: *a hoarse cry.* **2.** Having or characterized by a husky grating voice. [ME *hos, hors* < OE *hās, *hārs.*] —**hoarse′ly** *adv.* —**hoarse′ness** *n.*

hoars·en (hôr′sən, hōr′-) *tr. & intr.v.* **-ened, -en·ing, -ens** To make or become hoarse.

hoar·y (hôr′ē, hōr′ē) *adj.* **-i·er, -i·est** **1.** Gray or white with or as if with age. **2.** Covered with grayish hair or pubescence: *hoary leaves.* **3.** So old as to inspire veneration; ancient. —**hoar′i·ly** *adv.* —**hoar′i·ness** *n.*

hoary alyssum *n.* An annual European herb (*Berteroa incana*) of the mustard family, having silvery foliage.

hoat·zin (wät-sēn′) *n.* A crested brownish bird (*Opisthocomus hoazin*) of tropical South America. [Am.Sp. *hoazín* < Nahuatl *uatzin,* pheasant or small game bird.]

hoax (hōks) *n.* **1.** An act intended to deceive or trick. **2.** Something that has been established or accepted by fraudulent means. ❖ *tr.v.* **hoaxed, hoax·ing, hoax·es** To deceive or cheat with a hoax. [Perh. alteration of HOCUS.] —**hoax′er** *n.*

hob¹ (hŏb) *n.* **1.** A shelf or projection at the back or side of a fireplace, used for keeping food or utensils warm. **2.** A tool used for cutting the teeth of machine parts.

hob² (hŏb) *n.* **1.** *Chiefly British* A hobgoblin, sprite, or elf. **2.** Mischievous behavior. [< ME *Hob,* a nickname for *Robert.*]

Ho·bart (hō′bärt′) A city of SE Tasmania, Australia, on an inlet of the Tasman Sea. Pop. 47,920.

Hob·be·ma (hŏb′ə-mə, hô′bə-mä), **Meindert** 1638–1709. Dutch landscape painter whose works include *The Hermitage, St. Petersburg* (1663).

Hobbes (hŏbz), **Thomas** 1588–1679. English political philosopher and political theorist best known for his book *Leviathan* (1651). —**Hobbes′i·an** *adj.*

Hobb·ism (hŏb′ĭz′əm) *n.* A political theory promulgated by Thomas Hobbes, advocating absolute monarchy as the means of guaranteeing a stable civil society.

hob·ble (hŏb′əl) *v.* **-bled, -bling, -bles** —*intr.* To walk or move along haltingly or with difficulty; limp. —*tr.* **1.** To put a device around the legs of (a horse, for example) to hamper but not prevent movement. **2.** To cause to limp. **3.** To hamper the action or progress of; impede. ❖ *n.* **1.** A hobbling walk or gait. **2.** A device, such as a rope or strap, used to hobble an animal. **3.** *Archaic* An awkward situation. [ME *hobblen,* of LGer. orig.] —**hob′bler** *n.*

hob·ble·bush (hŏb′əl-bŏosh′) *n.* A deciduous shrub (*Viburnum alnifolium*) of eastern North America having flat clusters of white flowers.

hob·ble·de·hoy (hŏb′əl-dē-hoi′) *n., pl.* **-hoys** A gawky adolescent boy. [?]

hobble skirt *n.* A long skirt, popular between 1910 and 1914, so narrow below the knees that it restricted normal stride.

hob·by¹ (hŏb′ē) *n., pl.* **-bies** An activity or interest pursued outside one's regular occupation, primarily for pleasure. [ME *hobi, hobyn,* small horse, hobby horse, perh. < *Hobin, Hobby,* nickname for *Robert.*] —**hob′by·ist** *n.*

hob·by² (hŏb′ē) *n., pl.* **-bies** Any of several small falcons of the genus *Falco,* formerly used for catching small birds or game. [ME *hobi* < OFr. *hobe, hobel.*]

hob·by·horse (hŏb′ē-hôrs′) *n.* **1a.** A child's riding toy that consists of a long stick with an imitation horse's head on one end. **b.** See **rocking horse.** **2a.** A figure of a horse worn attached to a mummer's waist. **b.** One who wears such a figure. **3a.** A favorite hobby. **b.** A topic that one frequently brings up or dwells on.

hob·gob·lin (hŏb′gŏb′lĭn) *n.* **1.** An ugly mischievous elf or goblin. **2.** An object or a source of fear, dread, or harassment.

hob·nail (hŏb′nāl′) *n.* A short nail with a thick head used to protect the soles of shoes or boots. [HOB¹, peg, projection (obsolete) + NAIL.] —**hob′nailed′** *adj.*

hob·nob (hŏb′nŏb′) *intr.v.* **-nobbed, -nob·bing, -nobs** To associate familiarly. [< the phrase (*drink*) *hob or nob,* (toast) one another alternately < obsolete and dialectal *hab nab,* have or have not : prob. ME *habbe,* have + ME *nabbe* (contraction of *ne habbe,* have not : OE *ne,* not; see NOT + *habbe,* have).]

ho·bo (hō′bō) *n., pl.* **-boes** or **-bos** **1.** One who wanders from place to place without a permanent home or a means of livelihood. **2.** A migrant worker. ❖ *intr.v.* **-boed, -bo·ing, -boes** To live or wander like a vagrant. [?]

Hob·son's choice (hŏb′sənz) *n.* An apparently free choice that offers no real alternative. [After Thomas *Hobson* (1544?–1630), English keeper of a livery stable, from his requirement that customers take the horse nearest the stable door or none.]

Ho Chi Minh (hō′ chē′ mĭn′) 1890–1969. Vietnamese leader and first president of North Vietnam (1954–69).

Ho Chi Minh City Formerly **Sai·gon** (sī-gŏn′) A city of S Vietnam near the South China Sea; cap. of South Vietnam (1954–75). Pop. 3,015,743.

hock¹ (hŏk) *n.* **1a.** The tarsal joint of the hind leg of a digitigrade quadruped, such as a horse, corresponding to the human ankle but bending in the opposite direction. **b.** A joint in the leg of a domestic fowl similar to the hock of a quadruped. **2.** A small cut of meat, esp. ham, from the front or hind leg directly above the foot. ❖ *tr.v.* **hocked, hock·ing, hocks** To disable by cutting the tendons of the hock; hamstring. [ME < OE *hōh,* heel.]

hock² (hŏk) *n. Chiefly British* Rhine wine. [Short for obsolete *Hockamore,* alteration of Ger. *Hochheimer* < *Hochheim,* a town of W-central Germany.]

hock³ (hŏk) *Slang tr.v.* **hocked, hock·ing, hocks** To pawn. ❖ *n.* **1.** The state of being pawned: *put the diamonds in hock.* **2.** The state of being in debt. [Prob. < Du. *hok,* prison.]

hock·ey (hŏk′ē) *n.* **1.** Ice hockey. **2.** Field hockey. **3.** Street hockey. [?]

hockey stick *n.* A long-handled stick with one curved end that is used in hockey.

Hock·ney (hŏk′nē), **David** b. 1937. British painter and printmaker known esp. for his highly personal realistic style.

hock·shop (hŏk′shŏp′) *n. Slang* A pawnshop.

ho·cus (hō′kəs) *tr.v.* **-cused, -cus·ing, -cus·es** or **-cussed, -cus·sing, -cus·ses 1.** To fool or deceive; hoax. **2.** To infuse (food or drink) with a drug. [Short for HOCUS-POCUS.]

ho·cus-po·cus (hō′kəs-pō′kəs) *n.* **1.** Nonsense words or phrases used as a formula by quack conjurers. **2.** A trick performed by a magician or juggler; sleight-of-hand. **3.** Foolishness or empty pretense used esp. to disguise deception or chicanery. ❖ *tr.v.* **-cused, -cus·ing, -cus·es** or **-cussed, -cus·sing, -cus·ses** To play tricks on; deceive. [Poss. < alteration of Lat. *hoc est corpus (meum),* this is (my) body (words used in the Eucharist).]

hod (hŏd) *n.* **1.** A trough carried over the shoulder for transporting loads. **2.** A coal scuttle. [Perh. alteration of dialectal *hot* < ME, pannier < OFr. *hotte,* of Gmc. orig.]

Ho·dei·da (hō-dā′də) See **Al Hudaydah.**

hodge·podge (hŏj′pŏj′) *n.* A mixture of dissimilar ingredients; a jumble. [Alteration of ME *hochepot* < OFr., stew. See HOTCH-POTCH.]

Hodg·kin (hŏj′kĭn), Sir **Alan Lloyd** 1914–98. British physiologist who shared a 1963 Nobel Prize.

Hodgkin, Dorothy Mary Crowfoot 1910–94. Egyptian-born British chemist who won a 1964 Nobel Prize.

Hodg·kin's disease (hŏj′kĭnz) *n.* A type of malignant lymphoma marked by enlargement of the lymph nodes, spleen, and liver. [After Thomas *Hodgkin* (1798–1866), British physician.]

hoe (hō) *n.* A tool with a flat blade attached approximately at a right angle to a long handle, used for weeding or cultivating. ❖ *v.* **hoed, hoe·ing, hoes** —*tr.* To weed, cultivate, or dig up with a hoe. —*intr.* To work with a hoe. [ME *howe* < OFr. *houe,* of Gmc. orig. See **kau-** in App.] —**ho′er** *n.*

hoe·cake (hō′kāk′) *n. Chiefly Southern US* See **johnnycake.** [Poss. because it was sometimes baked on the blade of a hoe.]

hoe·down (hō′doun′) *n.* **1.** A square dance. **2.** The music for a square dance. **3.** A social gathering at which square dancing takes place.

Ho·fei (hŭ′fā′) See **Hefei.**

Hoff·mann (hŏf′mən, hôf′män′), **Roald** b. 1937. Polish-born Amer. chemist who shared a 1981 Nobel Prize.

Hof·mann (hŏf′mən, hôf′män′), **Hans** 1880–1966. German-born Amer. artist whose schools helped develop abstract expressionism.

Hof·manns·thal (hôf′mäns-täl′, hôf′-), **Hugo von** 1874–1929. Austrian writer who wrote lyric poems and plays, including *Death and the Fool* (1893).

Hof·stadt·er (hôf′stät′ər), **Robert** 1915–90. Amer. physicist who shared a 1961 Nobel Prize.

hog (hôg, hŏg) *n.* **1a.** Any of various mammals of the family Suidae, including the domesticated pig and wild species, such as the boar. **b.** A domesticated pig, esp. one weighing over 54 kilograms (120 pounds). **2a.** A self-indulgent, gluttonous, or filthy person. **b.** One that uses too much of something. **3a.** *Chiefly British* A young sheep before it has been shorn. **b.** The wool from this sheep. **4.** *Slang* A big, heavy motorcycle. ❖ *v.* **hogged, hog·ging, hogs** —*tr.* **1.** *Informal* To take more than one's share of. **2.** To cause (the back) to arch like a hog's. **3.** To cut (a horse's mane) short and bristly. **4.** To shred (waste wood, for example) by machine. —*intr. Nautical* To arch upward in the middle. Used of a ship's keel. —*idiom:* **on** (or **off**) **the hog** *Slang* In a lavish or extravagant manner. [ME < OE *hogg,* poss. of Celt. orig. See **sū-** in App.]

ho·gan (hō′gän′, -gən) *n.* A one-room Navajo structure traditionally built with the entrance facing east, used as a dwelling or for ceremonial purposes. [Navajo *hooghan.*]

Ho·gan (hō′gən), **William Benjamin ("Ben")** 1912–97. Amer. golfer who won the US Open championship (1948, 1950, 1951, and 1953) and the PGA championship (1948).

Ho·garth (hō′gärth′), **William** 1697–1764. British artist whose satirical paintings attacked the contradiction of luxury and squalor in society. —**Ho·garth′i·an** *adj.*

hog·back (hôg′băk′, hŏg′-) *n.* A sharp ridge with steeply sloping sides, produced by erosion of the broken edges of highly tilted strata.

hog cholera *n.* A highly infectious, often fatal viral disease of swine, characterized by fever, loss of appetite, and diarrhea.

hog·fish (hôg′fĭsh′, hŏg′-) *n., pl.* **hogfish** or **-fish·es 1.** A colorful fish (*Lachnolaimus maximus*) of warm Atlantic waters, having a long snout in the adult male. **2.** See **pigfish.**

hogg (hôg, hŏg) *n. Chiefly British* Variant of **hog** 3.

hog·gish (hô′gĭsh, hŏg′ĭsh) *adj.* **1.** Coarsely self-indulgent or

gluttonous. **2.** Filthy. —**hog′gish·ness** *n.*

Hog·ma·nay (hŏg′mə-nā′, hŏg′mə-nā′) *n. Scots* **1.** The eve of New Year's Day, on which children traditionally beg for presents. **2.** A present requested or given this day. [?]

hog·nose snake (hŏg′nōz′, hŏg′-) *n.* Any of several thick-bodied, nonvenomous North American snakes of the genus *Heterodon,* having an upturned snout.

hog peanut *n.* A North American vine (*Amphicarpaea bracteata*) having pinkish or white flowers and bearing three-seeded pods and basal or underground one-seeded pods.

hogs·head (hôgz′hĕd′, hŏgz′-) *n.* **1.** Any of various units of volume or capacity ranging from 63 to 140 gallons (238 to 530 liters), esp. a unit of capacity used in liquid measure in the United States equal to 63 gallons (238 liters). **2.** A large barrel or cask with this capacity.

hog·tie (hôg′tī′, hŏg′-) *tr.v.* **-tied, -tie·ing** or **-ty·ing, -ties 1.** To tie together the feet or legs of. **2.** *Informal* To impede or disrupt in movement or action.

hog·wash (hôg′wŏsh′, -wôsh′, hŏg′-) *n.* **1.** Worthless, false, or ridiculous speech or writing. **2.** Garbage fed to hogs; swill.

hog·weed (hôg′wēd′, hŏg′-) *n.* Any of certain coarse weedy plants of the genera *Ambrosia, Erigeron,* or *Heracleum.*

hog-wild (hôg′wīld′, hŏg′-) *adj. Informal* **1.** So wildly excited as to be irrational or devoid of good judgment. **2.** Wildly enthusiastic. —**hog′-wild′** *adv.*

Ho·hen·stau·fen (hō′ən-shtou′fən) Family of German rulers of the Holy Roman Empire (1138–1208 and 1215–54) and Sicily (1194–1268).

Ho·hen·zol·lern (hō′ən-zŏl′ərn, -tsôl′-) German royal family who ruled Brandenburg, Prussia, and the German Empire (1415–1918).

Hoh·hot (hō′hōt′) also **Hu·he·hot** (hōō′hə-) A city of N China WNW of Beijing; cap. of Nei Monggol (Inner Mongolia) autonomous region. Pop. 938,470.

Ho·ho·kam (hə-hō′kəm) *n., pl.* **Hohokam** or **-kams 1.** A Native American culture flourishing from about the 3rd century B.C. to the mid-15th century A.D. in south-central Arizona, noted for an extensive system of irrigation canals. **2.** A member of this culture. [< Papago *huhugam,* those who are gone < *huhug,* to perish, disappear.]

ho hum (hō′hŭm′) *interj.* Used to express boredom, weariness, or contempt.

ho-hum (hō′hŭm′) *adj. Informal* Boring and dull; routine.

hoicks (hoiks) *interj.* Variant of **yoicks.**

hoi pol·loi (hoi′ pə-loi′) *n.* The common people; the masses. [Gk., the many : *hoi,* masc. pl. of *ho,* the; see **so-** in App. + *polloi,* pl. of *polus,* many; see **pelǝ-¹** in App.]

USAGE NOTE In Greek, *hoi polloi* means literally "the many," and by extension "the masses." This is also its meaning in English. Sometimes, though, it is improperly understood to mean "the elite," perhaps because it sounds like *hoity-toity.*

---

hoi·sin sauce (hoi′sĭn, hoi-sĭn′) *n.* A thick sweet pungent sauce used in Chinese cooking. [Chin. (Cantonese) *hoisin,* seafood, equivalent to Chin. (Mandarin) *hăi,* ocean + Chin. (Mandarin) *xiān,* fresh, delicacy.]

hoist (hoist) *v.* **hoist·ed, hoist·ing, hoists** —*tr.* **1.** To raise or haul up with or as if with a mechanical apparatus. See Syns at **lift. 2.** To raise (a glass, for example) to one's mouth in order to drink. —*intr.* To become raised or lifted. ❖ *n.* **1.** An apparatus for lifting heavy or cumbersome objects. **2.** The act of hoisting; a lift. **3.** *Nautical* **a.** The height or vertical dimension of a flag or of any square sail other than a course. **b.** A group of flags raised together as a signal. [Alteration of dialectal *hoise,* perh. var. of ME *hisse,* heave!, poss. < MDu. *hissen,* to haul.] —**hoist′er** *n.*

hoi·ty-toi·ty (hoi′tē-toi′tē) *adj.* **1.** Pretentiously self-important; pompous. **2.** Given to frivolity or silliness. [< redup. of dialectal *hoit,* to romp; perh. akin to HOYDEN.]

Ho·kan (hō′kən) *n.* A proposed grouping of a number of Native American language families of western North America. [< Atsugewi (California) *hoqi,* two.]

hoke (hōk) *tr.v.* **hoked, hok·ing, hokes** *Slang* To give an impressive but artificial or false quality to. [< HOKUM.]

hok·ey (hō′kē) *adj.* **-i·er, -i·est** *Slang* **1.** Mawkishly sentimental; corny. **2.** Noticeably contrived; artificial. —**hok′i·ly** *adv.* —**hok′i·ness, hok′ey·ness** *n.*

Hok·kai·do (hŏ-kī′dō, hô′kī-dō′) An island of Japan N of Honshu; became part of Japan in the medieval period (c. 1600) and was called Yezo or Ezo until 1868.

hok·ku (hō′kōō) *n., pl.* **hokku** A haiku. [J. : *hotsu,* to start, give rise to (< M Chin. *puat*) + *ku,* phrase, haiku; see HAIKU.]

ho·kum (hō′kəm) *n.* **1.** Something apparently impressive or legitimate but actually untrue or insincere; nonsense. **2.** A stock technique for eliciting a desired response from an audience. [Perh. HO(CUS-POCUS) + (BUN)KUM.]

Ho·ku·sai (hō′kōō-sī′, hō′kōō-sī′) 1760–1849. Japanese artist noted for his historical scenes and landscapes.

holo- *pref.* Variant of **holo-.**

ho·lan·dric (hō-lăn′drĭk, hô-) *adj.* Relating to a trait encoded by a gene or genes specific to the Y-chromosome and therefore occurring only in males. [HOL(O)- + ANDR(O)- + -IC.]

hogan

ă	pat	oi	boy
ā	pay	ou	out
âr	care	ōō	took
ä	father	ōō	boot
ĕ	pet	ŭ	cut
ē	be	ûr	urge
ĭ	pit	th	thin
ī	pie	th	this
îr	pier	hw	which
ŏ	pot	zh	vision
ō	toe	ə	about,
ô	paw		item

Stress marks:
′ (primary);
′ (secondary), as in
lexicon (lĕk′sĭ-kŏn′)

Billie Holiday

Hol•arc•tic (hō-lärk′tĭk, -lär′tĭk, hŏ-) *adj.* Of, relating to, or being the zoogeographic region that is divided into Nearctic and Palearctic regions.

Hol•bein (hōl′bīn, hôl′-), **Hans** Known as "the Elder." 1465?–1524. German painter whose religious works include the altarpiece of the Augsburg Cathedral (1493). His son **Hans** (1497?–1543), known as "the Younger," is noted for his religious paintings and portraits such as *Anne of Cleves* (1539).

hold[1] (hōld) *v.* **held** (hĕld), **hold•ing, holds** —*tr.* **1a.** To have and keep in one's grasp. **b.** To aim or direct; point. **c.** To keep from falling or moving; support. **d.** To sustain the pressure of. **2a.** To keep from departing or getting away. **b.** To keep in custody. **c.** To retain (one's attention or interest). **d.** To avoid letting out or expelling: *held her breath.* **3a.** To be filled by; contain: *a box holding all his notebooks.* **b.** To be capable of holding: *a jug that holds a gallon.* **c.** To have as a chief characteristic or quality. **d.** To have in store: *what the future holds.* **4a.** To have and maintain in one's possession. **b.** To have as a responsible position or a privilege. **c.** To have in recognition of achievement or superiority: *holds our respect.* **5a.** To maintain control over: *The dam held the floodwaters.* **b.** To maintain occupation of by force or coercion. **c.** To withstand the efforts or advance of (an opposing team, for example). **d.** To maintain in a given condition, situation, or action: *held the crowd spellbound.* **6a.** To impose control or restraint on; curb: *She held her temper.* **b.** To stop the movement or progress of. **c.** To reserve or keep back from use: *Please hold two tickets.* **d.** To defer the immediate handling of. **7a.** To be the legal possessor of. **b.** To bind by a contract. **c.** To adjudge or decree. **d.** To make accountable; obligate: *held me to my promise.* **8a.** To keep in the mind or convey as a judgment, conviction, or point of view. **b.** To assert or affirm, esp. formally. **c.** To regard in a certain way: *I hold you in high esteem.* **9a.** To cause to take place; carry on: *hold a yard sale.* **b.** To assemble for and conduct the activity of; convene. **10a.** To carry or support (the body or a body part) in a certain position. **b.** To cover (the ears or the nose, for example) esp. for protection. —*intr.* **1a.** To maintain a grasp or grip on something. **b.** To stay securely fastened. **2a.** To maintain a desired or accustomed position or condition. **b.** To withstand stress, pressure, or opposition. **3.** To continue in the same direction. **4.** To be valid, applicable, or true. **5.** To have legal right or title. Often used with *of* or *from.* **6.** To halt an intended action. Often used in the imperative. **7.** To stop the countdown during a missile or spacecraft launch. **8.** *Slang* To have in one's possession illicit or illegally obtained material or goods, esp. narcotics. ❖ *n.* **1a.** The act or a means of grasping. **b.** A manner of grasping an opponent, as in wrestling or aikido. **2.** Something that may be grasped or gripped, as for support. **3.** A control or adjustor on a television that keeps the screen image in proper position. **4.** A telephone service that allows one to temporarily interrupt a call without severing the connection. **5a.** A bond or force that attaches or restrains, or by which something is affected or dominated. **b.** Complete control. **c.** Full understanding. **6.** *Music* **a.** The sustaining of a note longer than its indicated time value. **b.** The symbol designating this pause; a fermata. **7a.** A direction or indication that something is to be reserved or deferred. **b.** A temporary halt, as in a countdown. **8a.** A prison cell. **b.** The state of being in confinement; custody. **9.** *Archaic* A fortified place; a stronghold. ***—phrasal verbs:*** **hold back 1.** To retain in one's possession or control. **2.** To impede the progress of. **3.** To restrain oneself. **hold down 1.** To limit. **2.** To fulfill the duties of (a job): *holds down two jobs.* **hold forth** To talk at great length. **hold off 1.** To keep at a distance; resist. **2.** To stop or delay doing something. **hold on 1.** To maintain one's grip; cling. **2.** To continue to do something; persist. **3.** To wait for something wanted or requested, esp. to keep a telephone connection open. **hold out 1.** To present or proffer as something attainable. **2.** To continue to be in supply or service; last. **3.** To continue to resist. **4.** To refuse to reach or satisfy an agreement. **hold over 1a.** To postpone or delay. **b.** To keep in a position or state from an earlier period of time. **2.** To continue a term of office past the usual length of time. **3.** To prolong the engagement of: *The film was held over for weeks.* **hold to** To remain loyal or faithful to. **hold up 1.** To obstruct or delay. **2.** To rob while armed, often at gunpoint. **3.** To offer or present as an example. **4.** To continue to function without losing force or effectiveness; cope. **hold with** To agree with; support. ***—idioms:*** **get hold of 1.** To come into possession of; find. **2.** To communicate with, as by telephone. **3.** To gain control of. Often used reflexively: *Get hold of yourself!* **hold a candle to** To compare favorably with. **hold (one's) end up** To fulfill one's part of an agreement; do one's share. **hold (one's) own** To do reasonably well despite difficulty or criticism. **hold out on (someone)** To withhold something from. **hold (someone's) feet to the fire** To pressure (someone) to consent to or undertake something. **hold sway** To have a controlling influence; dominate. **hold the bag** *Informal* **1.** To be left with empty hands. **2.** To be forced to assume total responsibility when it ought to have been shared. **hold the fort** *Informal* **1.** To assume responsibility, esp. in another's absence. **2.** To maintain a secure position. **hold the line** To maintain the existing position or state of affairs. **hold the phone** *Slang* To stop doing what one is engaged in doing. Often used in the imperative. **hold water** To stand up to critical examination. **no holds barred** Without limits or restraints. **on hold 1.** Into a state of temporary interruption without total disconnection during a telephone call. **2.** *Informal* Into a state of delay or indeterminate suspension. [ME *holden* < OE *healdan.*]

hold[2] (hōld) *n.* The lower interior part of a ship or airplane where cargo is stored. [Alteration (influenced by HOLD[1]) of ME *hole,* husk, hull of a ship < OE *hulu.* See **kel-** in App.]

hold•all (hōld′ôl′) *n.* A container for holding or carrying miscellaneous items, esp. a traveling case or bag.

hold•back (hōld′băk′) *n.* **1a.** The act of holding back. **b.** Something held back. **2.** A device that retains or restrains. **3.** A strap or an iron catch between the shaft and the harness on a drawn wagon, allowing the horse to stop or back up.

hold-down (hōld′doun′) *n.* **1a.** The act of holding down. **b.** A limit or restraint. **2.** Something, such as a clamp, used to hold an object in place.

hold•en (hōl′dən) *v. Archaic* A past participle of **hold**[1].

hold•er (hōl′dər) *n.* **1.** One that holds, as: **a.** One that possesses something; an owner: *the holder of farmland.* **b.** One, esp. a tenant, that occupies or controls something. **c.** *Law* One that legally possesses and is entitled to the payment of a check, bill, or promissory note. **2.** A device for holding.

hold•fast (hōld′făst′) *n.* **1.** Any of various devices used to fasten something securely. **2.** *Biology* An organ or structure of attachment, esp. the basal rootlike formation by which certain seaweeds or other algae are attached to a substrate.

hold•ing (hōl′dĭng) *n.* **1a.** Land rented or leased from another. **b.** Legally owned property, such as land, capital, or stocks. Often used in the plural. **2. holdings** The collection of books and other reading materials at a library. **3.** *Law* A court ruling, esp. a ruling on a point of law raised in an official proceeding. **4.** *Sports* Illegal obstruction of the movements of an opponent. ❖ *adj.* **1.** Tending to impede or delay progress: *a holding action.* **2.** Designed for usu. short-term storage or retention.

holding company *n.* A company controlling partial or complete interest in another company or other companies.

holding pattern *n.* **1.** A usu. circular pattern flown by aircraft awaiting clearance to land at an airport. **2.** *Informal* A state of waiting or delay; a static situation.

hold•out (hōld′out′) *n.* One that withholds agreement or consent upon which progress is contingent.

hold•o•ver (hōld′ō′vər) *n.* One that is held over from an earlier time.

hold•up (hōld′ŭp′) *n.* **1.** An interruption or a delay. **2.** An armed robbery.

hole (hōl) *n.* **1.** A hollowed place in something solid; a cavity or pit. **2a.** An opening or perforation: *a hole in the clouds; a hole in my shirt.* **b.** *Sports* An opening in a defensive formation. **c.** A fault or flaw: *holes in the argument.* **3.** A deep place in a body of water. **4.** An animal's hollowed-out habitation, such as a burrow. **5.** An ugly, squalid, or depressing dwelling. **6.** A deep or isolated place of confinement; a dungeon. **7.** An awkward situation; a predicament. **8.** *Sports* **a.** The small pit into which a golf ball must be hit. **b.** One of the divisions of a golf course, from tee to cup. **9.** *Physics* A vacant position in a crystal left by the absence of an electron, esp. a position in a semiconductor that acts as a carrier of positive electric charge. ❖ *v.* **holed, hol•ing, holes** —*tr.* **1.** To put a hole in. **2.** To put or propel into a hole. —*intr.* To make a hole in something. ***—phrasal verbs:*** **hole out** *Sports* To hit a golf ball into the hole. **hole up 1.** To hibernate in or as if in a hole. **2.** *Informal* To take refuge in or as if in a hideout. ***—idiom:*** **in the hole 1.** Having a score below zero. **2.** In debt. **3.** At a disadvantage. [ME < OE *hol.* See **kel-** in App.]

hole-and-cor•ner (hōl′ən-kôr′nər) *adj.* Being in a secret place; conducted secretly.

hole card *n.* **1.** A card in stud poker that remains face-down until the showdown. **2.** *Informal* Something held in reserve until it can be used advantageously.

hole in one *n., pl.* **holes in one** The driving of a golf ball from the tee into the hole in a single stroke.

hole in the wall *n., pl.* **holes in the wall** A small, very modest, often out-of-the-way place.

hol•ey (hō′lē) *adj.* **-i•er, -i•est** Having holes or full of holes.

Hol•guín (ŏl-gēn′) A city of E Cuba NNW of Santiago de Cuba. Pop. 239,000.

hol•i•day (hŏl′ĭ-dā′) *n.* **1.** A day free from work that one may spend at leisure, esp. a day on which general business activity halts to celebrate a particular event. **2.** A religious feast day; a holy day. **3.** *Chiefly British* A vacation. ❖ *intr.v.* **-dayed, -day•ing, -days** *Chiefly British* To pass a holiday or vacation. [ME *holidai,* holy day < OE *hāligdæg* : *hālig,* holy; see HOLY + *dæg,* day.]

Holiday, Eleanora ("Billie") 1915–59. Amer. singer who was the leading female jazz vocalist of her time.

hol•i•day•mak•er (hŏl′ĭ-dā-mā′kər) *n. Chiefly British* One who goes on vacation.

ho•li•er-than-thou (hō′lē-ər-*th*ən-thou′) *adj.* Exhibiting an attitude of superior virtue; self-righteously pious.

ho•li•ness (hō′lē-nĭs) *n.* **1.** The state or quality of being holy; sanctity. **2. Holiness** *Roman Catholic Church* Used with *His* or *Your* as a title and form of address for a pope.

Hol·in·shed (hŏl′ən-shĕd′, -ĭnz-hĕd′) also **Hol·lings·head** (-ĭngz-hĕd′), **Raphael** d. c. 1580. English historian whose *Chronicles of England, Scotland, and Ireland* (1577) was used extensively by Shakespeare and other Elizabethan dramatists.

ho·lism (hō′lĭz′əm) *n.* **1.** The theory that living matter or reality is made up of organic or unified wholes that are greater than the simple sum of their parts. **2.** Holistic medicine. —**ho′list** *n.*

ho·lis·tic (hō-lĭs′tĭk) *adj.* **1.** Of, relating to, or involving holistic medicine. **2a.** Emphasizing the importance of the whole and the interdependence of its parts. **b.** Concerned with wholes rather than analysis or separation into parts. —**ho·lis′ti·cal·ly** *adv.*

holistic medicine *n.* An approach to medical care that emphasizes the study of all aspects of a person's health and often combines traditional and alternative medical therapies.

hol·land (hŏl′ənd) *n.* A cotton or linen fabric, usu. sized or glazed, used esp. for window shades, bookbinding, and upholstery. [ME *holand*, after *Holand* (Holland), a former province of the Netherlands < MDu.]

Holland See **Netherlands**.

hol·lan·daise sauce (hŏl′ən-dāz′) *n.* A rich creamy sauce made of butter, egg yolks, and lemon juice or vinegar. [< Fr. *(sauce) Hollandaise*, Holland-style < *Hollande*, Holland.]

hol·ler[1] (hŏl′ər) *v.* **-lered, -ler·ing, -lers** —*intr.* **1.** To yell or shout. **2.** *Informal* To complain. —*tr.* To shout out (words or phrases). See Syns at **shout.** ❖ *n.* **1.** A yell or shout; a call. **2.** *Informal* A complaint or gripe. [< obsolete *hollo*, hail!, stop! See HELLO.]

hol·ler[2] (hŏl′ər) *adj., v., & n.* Upper Southern US Variant of **hollow.**

REGIONAL NOTE One feature of Upper Southern English and specifically of Appalachian English is its pronunciation of the final unstressed syllable in words such as *hollow*, *window*, and *potato* as (-ər). *Holler*, *winder*, and *tater* are merely variant pronunciations reflected in spelling. As a noun, *holler* has the specific meaning in the Appalachians of "a small valley between mountains."

Hol·ler·ith (hŏl′ə-rĭth′), **Herman** 1860–1929. Amer. inventor who founded the company that became IBM (1924).

Hollerith card *n.* See **punch card**.

Hollerith code *n.* A code used for recording alphanumeric information on punch cards.

Hol·li·day (hŏl′ĭ-dā′), **Judith Tuvim ("Judy")** 1922–65. Amer. comedian best remembered for her performance in the play (1946–50) and film (1950) *Born Yesterday.*

Hol·lings·head (hŏl′ĭngz-hĕd′), **Raphael** See Raphael **Holinshed.**

hol·low (hŏl′ō) *adj.* **-er, -est 1.** Having a cavity, gap, or space within: *a hollow wall.* **2.** Deeply indented or concave; sunken. **3.** Without substance or character: *a hollow person.* **4.** Devoid of truth or validity; specious. **5.** Having a reverberating, sepulchral sound: *hollow footsteps.* ❖ *n.* **1.** A cavity, gap, or space. **2.** An indented or concave surface or area. **3.** A void; an emptiness. **4.** A small valley between mountains. ❖ *v.* **-lowed, -low·ing, -lows** —*tr.* **1.** To make hollow: *hollow out a pumpkin.* **2.** To scoop or form by making concave. —*intr.* To become hollow or empty. [ME *holwe, holowe* < *holgh*, hole, burrow < OE *holh.* See **kel-** in App.] —**hol′low·ly** *adv.* —**hol′low·ness** *n.*

hol·low·ware (hŏl′ō-wâr′) *n.* Items of usu. metal tableware, such as bowls and pitchers, that serve as containers or receptacles.

hol·ly (hŏl′ē) *n., pl.* **-lies 1a.** Any of numerous trees or shrubs of the genus *Ilex*, usu. having red berries and evergreen leaves with spiny margins. **b.** Branches of these plants, traditionally used for Christmas decoration. **2.** Any of various similar or related plants. [ME *holin, holi* < OE *holen.*]

Holly, Charles Hardin Known as "Buddy." 1938–59. Amer. singer, guitarist, and songwriter who greatly influenced the development of rock 'n' roll.

hol·ly·hock (hŏl′ē-hŏk′) *n.* A tall plant (*Alcea rosea*) native to the Middle East and widely cultivated for its showy clusters of very large, variously colored flowers. [ME *holihocke*, marsh mallow : *holi*, holy; see HOLY + *hoc*, mallow (< OE).]

holly oak *n.* See **holm oak**.

Hol·ly·wood[1] (hŏl′ē-wood′) **1.** A district of Los Angeles CA; long a film and entertainment center. **2.** A city of SE FL on the Atlantic Ocean N of Miami Beach. Pop. 139,357.

Hol·ly·wood[2] (hŏl′ē-wood′) *n.* **1.** The US film industry. **2.** Flashy vulgarity associated with the US film industry. ❖ *adj.* **1.** Of or relating to the US film industry. **2.** Flashy and vulgar.

hollywood bed *n.* A mattress on a box spring supported by a metal frame or attached low legs, often with an upholstered headboard.

holm (hōm, hōlm) *n. Chiefly British* An island in a river. [ME < ON *hólmr.*]

Holmes (hōmz, hōlmz), **Oliver Wendell** 1809–94. Amer. physician and writer of humorous conversational pieces, including *The Autocrat of the Breakfast Table* (1858).

Holmes, Oliver Wendell, Jr. 1841–1935. Amer. jurist; associate justice of the US Supreme Court (1902–32).

hol·mic (hŏl′mĭk) *adj.* Relating to trivalent holmium.

hol·mi·um (hŏl′mē-əm) *n. Symbol* **Ho** A soft malleable rare-earth element that is found in monazite and other rare-earth minerals. Atomic number 67; atomic weight 164.930; melting point 1,461°C; boiling point 2,600°C; specific gravity 8.803; valence 3. See table at **element**. [From *Holmia* (Stockholm).]

holm oak *n.* A Mediterranean evergreen tree (*Quercus ilex*) whose leaves are dark green on top and yellow or white underneath. [ME *holm*, alteration of *holin*, holly. See HOLLY.]

holo– or **hol–** *pref.* Whole; entire; entirely: *holoblastic.* [Gk. < *holos*, whole. See **sol–** in App.]

hol·o·blas·tic (hŏl′ə-blăs′tĭk, hō′lə-) *adj. Embryology* Exhibiting cleavage in which the entire egg separates into individual blastomeres. —**hol′o·blas′ti·cal·ly** *adv.*

hol·o·caust (hŏl′ə-kôst′, hō′lə-) *n.* **1.** Great destruction resulting in the extensive loss of life, esp. by fire. **2a.** Holocaust The genocide of European Jews and others by the Nazis during World War II. **b.** A massive slaughter. **3.** A sacrificial offering that is consumed entirely by flames. [ME, burnt offering < OFr. *holocauste* < Lat. *holocaustum* < Gk. *holokauston* < neut. of *holokaustos*, burnt whole : *holo-*, holo- + *kaustos*, burnt (< *kaiein*, to burn).] —**hol′o·caus′tal, hol′o·caus′tic** *adj.*

USAGE NOTE *Holocaust* has a secure place in the language when it refers to the massive destruction of humans by other humans. Ninety-nine percent of the Usage Panel accepts its use in the phrase *nuclear holocaust*, and 60 percent accepts the sentence *As many as two million people may have died in the holocaust that followed the Khmer Rouge takeover in Cambodia.* But when the word, with its associations with genocide, is used to refer to death brought about by natural causes, the percentage of the Panel accepting drops sharply. Only 31 percent of the Panel approves the sentence *In East Africa five years of drought have brought about a holocaust in which millions have died.* This suggests that other figurative usages, such as *the huge losses in the Savings and Loan holocaust,* may be viewed as overblown or in poor taste. • When capitalized, *Holocaust* refers specifically to the destruction of Jews and other Europeans by the Nazis and may also encompass the Nazi persecution of Jews that preceded the outbreak of the war.

Hol·o·cene (hŏl′ə-sēn′, hō′lə-) *adj.* Of or belonging to the geologic time of the more recent of the two epochs of the Quaternary Period, beginning at the end of the last Ice Age, and characterized by the development of human civilizations. See table at **geologic time.** ❖ *n.* The Holocene Epoch or its deposits.

hol·o·crine (hŏl′ə-krĭn, -krīn′, -krēn′, hō′lə-) *adj.* Of or relating to a gland whose output consists of disintegrated secretory cells along with the secretory product itself. [HOLO- + Gk. *krīnein*, to separate; see ENDOCRINE.]

hol·o·en·zyme (hŏl′ō-ĕn′zīm′, hō′lō-) *n.* An active complex enzyme consisting of an apoenzyme and a coenzyme.

ho·log·a·mous (hə-lŏg′ə-məs) *adj.* Of or relating to an organism whose germ cells morphologically resemble its somatic cells.

hol·o·gram (hŏl′ə-grăm′, hō′lə-) *n.* **1.** The pattern produced on a photosensitive medium that has been exposed by holography and then photographically developed. **2.** The photosensitive medium so treated.

hol·o·graph (hŏl′ə-grăf′, hō′lə-) *n.* **1.** A document written wholly in the handwriting of the person whose signature it bears. **2.** See **hologram**.

hol·o·graph·ic (hŏl′ə-grăf′ĭk, hō′lə-) also **hol·o·graph·i·cal** (-ĭ-kəl) *adj.* **1.** Of or relating to holography or holograms. **2.** also **hol·o·graph** (hŏl′ə-grăf′, hō′lə-) Of or being a document written wholly in the handwriting of the person whose signature it bears. —**hol′o·graph′i·cal·ly** *adv.*

ho·log·ra·phy (hō-lŏg′rə-fē) *n.* A method of producing a three-dimensional image of an object by recording on a photographic plate or film the pattern of interference formed by a split laser beam and then illuminating the pattern. —**ho·log′ra·pher** *n.*

hol·o·gyn·ic (hŏl′ə-jĭn′ĭk, -gī′nĭk, hō′lə-) *adj.* Passing to successive generations only in females: *a hologynic trait.*

hol·o·he·dral (hŏl′ə-hē′drəl, hō′lə-) *adj.* Having the required planes for complete symmetry in a given crystal system.

hol·o·me·tab·o·lism (hŏl′ō-mə-tăb′ə-lĭz′əm, hō′lə-) *n.* See **complete metamorphosis.** —**hol′o·me·tab′o·lous** *adj.* —**hol′o·me·tab′o·lous·ly** *adv.*

Ho·lon (hō-lôn′, KHô-lôn′) A city of W-central Israel near Tel Aviv–Yafo; est. 1941. Pop. 162,800.

hol·o·phras·tic (hŏl′ə-frăs′tĭk, hō′lə-) *adj.* **1.** Polysynthetic. **2.** Of or relating to the stage of child language development characterized by the use of single-word utterances. [HOLO- + Gk. *phrastikos*, expressive (< *-phrastos*, speakable, thought of < *phrazein*, to show).]

hol·o·plank·ton (hŏl′ə-plăngk′tən, hō′lə-) *n.* Plankton that remains free-swimming through all stages of its life cycle.

hol·o·thu·ri·an (hŏl′ə-thoor′ē-ən, hō′lə-) *n.* Any of various echinoderms of the class Holothuroidea, which includes the sea cucumbers. [< Lat. *holothūria*, water polyp < Gk. *holothourion.*] —**hol′o·thu′ri·an** *adj.*

hol·o·type (hŏl′ə-tīp′, hō′lə-) *n.* The specimen or element used as the basis of the first published description of a taxonomic group. —**hol′o·typ′ic** (-tĭp′ĭk) *adj.*

Oliver Wendell Holmes

ă pat	oi boy
ā pay	ou out
âr care	ŏŏ took
ä father	ŏŏ boot
ĕ pet	ŭ cut
ē be	ûr urge
ĭ pie	th thin
ĭ pie	*th* this
îr pier	hw which
ŏ pot	zh vision
ō toe	ə about,
ô paw	item

Stress marks:
′ (primary);
′ (secondary); as in
lexicon (lĕk′sĭ-kŏn′)

hol·o·zo·ic (hŏl′ə-zō′ĭk, hō′lə-) *adj.* Obtaining nourishment by the ingestion of organic material, as animals do.

holp (hōlp) *v. Archaic* A past tense of **help.**

hol·pen (hōl′pən) *v. Archaic* A past participle of **help.**

Holst (hōlst), **Gustav Theodore** 1874–1934. English composer whose works include the orchestral suite *The Planets* (1914–16).

Hol·stein¹ (hōl′stīn, -stēn′) A region and former duchy of N Germany at the base of the Jutland Peninsula.

Hol·stein² (hōl′stīn, -stēn′) *n.* Any of a breed of black and white dairy cattle developed in Friesland. [After HOLSTEIN¹.]

Hol·stein-Frie·sian (hōl′stīn-frēzhən, -stēn-) *n.* A Holstein.

hol·ster (hōl′stər) *n.* **1.** A case, usu. of leather, shaped to hold a pistol snugly and designed to be attached to a belt, strap, or saddle. **2.** A belt with loops or slots for carrying small tools or other equipment. ❖ *tr.v.* **hol·stered, hol·ster·ing, hol·sters** To put (a gun, for example) in a holster. [Prob. Du., alteration of *holfter, hulfter* < MHGer. *hulffter,* case, sheath, quiver, covering < *hulft* < OHGer. See **kel-** in App.] —**hol′stered** *adj.*

Holstein²

holt (hōlt) *n. Archaic* A wood or grove; a copse. [ME < OE.]

ho·ly (hō′lē) *adj.* **-li·er, -li·est 1.** Of, derived from, or associated with a divine power; sacred. **2.** Regarded with or worthy of worship or veneration. **3.** Living according to a strict or highly moral religious or spiritual system; saintly. **4.** Specified or set apart for a religious purpose: *a holy place.* **5.** Solemnly undertaken; sacrosanct: *a holy pledge.* **6.** Regarded with or deserving special respect or reverence. **7.** *Informal* Used as an intensive. [ME *holi* < OE *hālig.* See **kailo-** in App.] —**ho′li·ly** *adv.* —**ho′li·ness** *n.*

Holy Ark *n. Judaism* The cabinet in a synagogue in which the scrolls of the Torah are kept.

Holy Communion *n.* The sacrament of the Eucharist received by a congregation.

Holy Cross, Mount of the A peak, 4,271.5 m (14,005 ft), in the Sawatch Range of the Rocky Mts. in W-central CO.

holy day also **ho·ly·day** (hō′lē-dā′) *n.* A day specified for religious observance.

holy day of obligation *n. Roman Catholic Church* A feast on which the faithful are obliged to hear Mass and abstain from servile work.

Holy Father *n. Roman Catholic Church* Used as a title and form of address for the pope.

Holy Ghost *n. Christianity* The Holy Spirit. [ME *holi gost,* holy spirit < OE *hālig gāst* (transl. of Lat. *spīritus sānctus*) : *hālig,* holy; see HOLY + *gāst,* spirit.]

Holy Grail *n.* See **grail** 1.

Holy Innocents′ Day *n. Ecclesiastical* December 28, observed in commemoration of the slaughter of male infants in Bethlehem when Herod the Great tried to kill Jesus.

Holy Island or **Lin·dis·farne** (lĭn′dĭs-färn′) An island off the coast of NE England near the Scottish border; site of a monastery founded by Saint Aidan (d. 651) in 635.

Holy Land The biblical region of Palestine.

Holy Office *n. Roman Catholic Church* A Roman congregation of the Curia that deals with protection of the faith and morals.

holy of holies *n.* **1.** *Judaism* The sanctuary inside the tabernacle in the Temple of Jerusalem, in which the Ark of the Covenant was kept. **2.** *Eastern Orthodox Church* The bema or sanctuary in a church. **3.** A place of awe. [Transl. of LLat. *sānctum sānctōrum,* neut. sing. and neut. genitive pl. of *sānctus,* holy (ult. transl. of Heb. *qōdeš haq-qodāšim*).]

holy oil *n. Ecclesiastical* **1.** See **chrism** 1. **2.** Olive oil blessed by a bishop and used to anoint the sick and in sacramentals.

holy order also **Holy Order** *n. Ecclesiastical* **1.** The sacrament or rite of ordination. Often used in the plural. **2.** The rank of an ordained Christian minister or priest. Often used in the plural. **3.** See **major order.**

Holy Roller *n. Offensive* Used as a disparaging term for a member of a religious denomination in which spiritual fervor is expressed by shouts and violent body movements.

Holy Roman Empire A loosely federated European political entity that began with the papal coronation of the German king Otto I as the first emperor in 962 and lasted until Francis II′s renunciation of the title in 1806.

Holy Saturday *n.* The Saturday before Easter.

Holy Scriptures *pl.n.* See **Scripture** 2.

Holy See *n. Roman Catholic Church* **1.** The see of the bishop of Rome. **2.** The authority, jurisdiction, and governmental functions associated with the papacy.

Holy Spirit *n. Christianity* The third person of the Trinity.

ho·ly·stone (hō′lē-stōn′) *n.* A piece of soft sandstone used for scouring the wooden decks of a ship. ❖ *tr.v.* **-stoned, -ston·ing, -stones** To scrub or scour with a piece of holystone. [Perh. < a sailor′s kneeling position while scouring with the stone.]

Holy Synod *n.* The governing body of any of the Eastern Orthodox churches.

Holy Thursday *n.* **1.** See **Maundy Thursday. 2.** See **Ascension Day.**

holy war also **Holy War** *n.* A war deemed to have a religious or high moral purpose, as to extend or defend a religion.

holy water *n.* Water blessed by a priest and used esp. for religious purposes.

Holy Week *n.* The week before Easter.

holster

holy writ *n.* **1.** often **Holy Writ** The Bible. **2.** *Informal* A document held to be the most authoritative of its kind.

hom– *pref.* Variant of **homo–.**

hom·age (hŏm′ĭj, ŏm′-) *n.* **1.** Ceremonial acknowledgment by a vassal of allegiance to a feudal lord. **2.** Special honor or respect shown or expressed publicly. [ME < OFr., prob. < *omne, homme,* man < Lat. *homō, homin-.* See **dhghem-** in App.]

hom·ag·er (hŏm′ə-jər, ŏm′-) *n.* A vassal who paid homage to a feudal lord.

hom·bre¹ (ŏm′brā′, ŏm′brĕ) *n. Slang* A man; a fellow. [Sp. < OSpan. *omne* < Lat. *homō, homin-.* See **dhghem-** in App.]

hom·bre² (hŏm′bər, ŏm′-) *n.* Variant of **ombre.**

Hom·burg also **hom·burg** (hŏm′bûrg′) *n.* A man′s felt hat having a soft dented crown and a shallow, slightly rolled brim. [After *Bad Homburg,* Germany.]

home (hōm) *n.* **1.** A place where one lives; a residence. **2.** The physical structure within which one lives, such as a house. **3.** A dwelling place together with the social unit that occupies it; a household. **4a.** An environment offering security and happiness. **b.** A valued place regarded as a refuge or place of origin. **5.** The place, such as a town, where one was born or has lived for a long period. **6.** The native habitat, as of a plant. **7.** The place where something is discovered, founded, developed, or promoted; a source. **8.** A headquarters; a home base. **9a.** *Baseball* Home plate. **b.** *Games* Home base. **10.** An institution where people are cared for. ❖ *adj.* **1a.** Of or relating to a home, esp. to one′s household or house: *home cooking.* **b.** Taking place in the home. **2.** Of, relating to, or being a place of origin or headquarters. **3.** *Sports* Relating to or played at a team′s place of origin. ❖ *adv.* **1.** At, to, or toward the direction of home. **2.** On or into the point at which something is directed. **3.** To the center or heart of something; deeply. ❖ *v.* **homed, hom·ing, homes** —*intr.* **1.** To go or return to one′s residence or base of operations. **2.** To be guided to a target automatically, as by means of radio waves. **3.** To move or lead toward a goal: *homing in on the truth.* —*tr.* To guide (a missile or aircraft) to a target automatically. —*idioms:* **at home 1.** Available to receive visitors. **2.** Comfortable and relaxed; at ease. **3.** Feeling an easy competence and familiarity. **home free** Out of jeopardy; assured of success. [ME < OE *hām.* See **tkei-** in App.]

home base *n.* **1a.** An objective toward which players of certain games, such as backgammon, progress. **b.** *Baseball* Home plate. **2.** A base of operations; a headquarters.

home·bod·y (hōm′bŏd′ē) *n., pl.* **-ies** One whose interests center on the home.

home·bound¹ (hōm′bound′) *adj.* Moving homeward.

home·bound² (hōm′bound′) *adj.* Restricted or confined to home.

home·boy (hōm′boi′) *n. Slang* **1.** A male friend or acquaintance from one′s neighborhood or hometown. **2.** A fellow male gang member.

home·bred (hōm′brĕd′) *adj.* Raised, bred, or reared at home.

home·brew or **home-brew** (hōm′brōō′) *n.* An alcoholic beverage, esp. beer, that is made at home. —**home′brewed′** *adj.*

home·com·ing (hōm′kŭm′ĭng) *n.* **1.** A coming to or returning home. **2.** An annual event at schools, colleges, and universities for visiting graduates.

home economics *n.* (used with a sing. or pl. verb) The science and art of home management. —**home economist** *n.*

home front *n.* The civilian population or the civilian activities of a country at war.

home fry *n.* A piece of sliced or chopped potato pan-fried until brown and crisp. Often used in the plural.

home·girl (hōm′gûrl′) *n. Slang* **1.** A female friend or acquaintance from one′s neighborhood or hometown. **2.** A fellow female gang member.

home·grown (hōm′grōn′) *adj.* **1.** Raised or grown at home. **2.** Originating in or characteristic of a locality.

home·land (hōm′lănd′) *n.* **1.** One′s native land. **2.** A state, region, or territory identified with a particular people or ethnic group. **3.** Any of the ten regions designated by South Africa in the 1970s as semiautonomous territorial states for the Black population. They were dissolved and reincorporated into South Africa by the 1994 constitution.

home·less (hōm′lĭs) *adj.* Having no home or haven. ❖ *n.* (used with a pl. verb) People without homes considered as a group. Often used with *the.* —**home′less·ness** *n.*

home·ly (hōm′lē) *adj.* **-li·er, -li·est 1.** Not attractive or good-looking. **2.** Lacking elegance or refinement: *homely furniture.* **3.** Of a simple or unpretentious nature; plain: *homely truths.* **4.** Typical of the home or of home life. —**home′li·ness** *n.*

home·made (hōm′mād′) *adj.* **1.** Made or prepared in the home. **2.** Made by oneself. **3.** Crudely or simply made.

home·mak·er (hōm′mā′kər) *n.* One who manages a household, esp. as one′s main daily activity. —**home′mak′ing** *n.*

homeo– or **homoio–** *pref.* Like; similar; homeostasis. [Gk. *homoio–* < *homoios* < *homos,* same. See **sem-¹** in App.]

ho·me·o·box gene (hō′mē-ə-bŏks′) *n.* One of a group of genes with a shared nucleotide segment that are involved in the formation of bodily segmentation during embryologic development. [*homeo(tic gene),* developmental control gene in which it is found (< Gk. *homoiōsis,* resemblance < *homoioun,* to make like

< *homoios*, like; see HOMEO–) + BOX[1] (because its DNA sequence is short and when written can be enclosed by a box on paper).]

ho•me•o•mor•phism (hō′mē-ə-môr′fĭz′əm) *n.* **1.** *Chemistry* A close similarity in the crystal forms of unlike compounds. **2.** *Mathematics* A one-to-one correspondence between the points of two geometric figures that is continuous in both directions. —**ho′me•o•mor′phous** *adj.*

ho•me•op•a•thy (hō′mē-ŏp′ə-thē) *n., pl.* **-thies** A system for treating disease based on the administration of minute doses of a drug that in massive amounts produces symptoms in healthy individuals similar to those of the disease itself. —**ho′me•o•path′** (-ə-păth′) *n.* —**ho′me•op′a•thist** *n.* —**ho′me•o•path′ic** *adj.* —**ho′me•o•path′i•cal•ly** *adv.*

ho•me•o•sta•sis (hō′mē-ō-stā′sĭs) *n.* The ability or tendency of an organism or cell to maintain internal equilibrium by adjusting its physiological processes. —**ho′me•o•stat′ic** (-stăt′ĭk) *adj.*

ho•me•o•therm (hō′mē-ə-thûrm′) *n.* A homeothermic organism; an endotherm. —**ho′me•o•ther′my** (-mē) *n.* —**ho′me•o•ther′mic** (-mĭk) *adj.*

home•own•er (hōm′ō′nər) *n.* A person who owns a home. —**home′own′er•ship′** *n.*

home page or **home page** (hōm′pāj′) *n.* The opening or main page of a website, usu. for greeting visitors and providing site or owner information.

home plate *n. Baseball* The base at which a batter stands when hitting and which a base runner must touch in order to score.

home port also **home•port** (hōm′pôrt′, -pōrt′) *n.* **1.** The port in which a vessel is registered or permanently based. **2.** The port from which a merchant vessel primarily operates, regardless of its registry.

hom•er¹ (hō′mər) *n.* **1.** *Baseball* A home run. **2.** A homing pigeon. —**hom′er** *v.*

ho•mer² (hō′mər) *n.* A unit of capacity used by the ancient Hebrews, equal to 10 ephahs (about 10 bushels) or 10 baths (about 100 gallons). [Heb. *ḥōmer*, heap, homer.]

Homer fl. 850 B.C. Greek epic poet and the traditional author of the *Iliad* and the *Odyssey.*

Homer, Winslow 1836–1910. Amer. painter known for his realistic seascapes, such as *Eight Bells* (1886).

home range *n.* The geographic area to which an organism normally confines its activity.

Ho•mer•ic (hō-mĕr′ĭk) *adj.* **1.** Of, relating to, or characteristic of Homer, his works, or his subject matter. **2.** Heroic in proportion, degree, or character; epic. —**Ho•mer′i•cal•ly** *adv.*

Homeric simile *n.* See **epic simile.**

home•room (hōm′rōōm′, -rōom′) *n.* A school classroom to which a group of pupils is required to report each day.

home rule *n.* The principle or practice of self-government in the internal affairs of a dependent country or other political unit.

home run *n. Baseball* A hit that allows the batter to make a complete circuit of the diamond and score a run.

home•school or **home-school** (hōm′skōōl′) *v.* **-schooled, -school•ing, -schools** —*tr.* To instruct (a pupil, for example) in an educational program outside of established schools, esp. in a home. —*intr.* To provide educational instruction in a homeschool. ❖ *n.* A school operated outside established educational institutions, esp. in a home. —**home′school′er** *n.*

home•sick (hōm′sĭk′) *adj.* Acutely longing for one's family or home. —**home′sick′ness** *n.*

home•spun (hōm′spŭn′) *adj.* **1.** Spun or woven in the home. **2.** Made of a homespun fabric. **3.** Simple and homely; unpretentious. ❖ *n.* **1.** A plain, coarse, usu. woolen cloth made of homespun yarn. **2.** A similar fabric made on a power loom.

home stand *n.* A succession of games played esp. by a baseball team at the team's home field or court.

home•stead (hōm′stĕd′) *n.* **1.** A house, esp. a farmhouse, with adjoining buildings and land. **2.** *Law* Property claimed as a householder's home and protected by law from forced sale to meet debts. **3.** Land claimed by a settler or squatter, esp. under the Homestead Act. **4.** The place where one's home is. ❖ *v.* **-stead•ed, -stead•ing, -steads** —*intr.* To settle and farm land, esp. under the Homestead Act. —*tr.* To claim and settle (land) as a homestead. —**home′stead′er** *n.*

Homestead Act *n.* An act passed by Congress in 1862 promising ownership of a 160-acre tract of public land to a citizen or head of a family who had resided on and cultivated the land for five years after the initial claim.

homestead law *n.* Any of several laws passed in most states exempting a householder's homestead from attachment or forced sale to meet general debts.

home•stretch (hōm′strĕch′) *n.* **1.** The portion of a racetrack from the last turn to the finish line. **2.** *Informal* The final stages of an undertaking.

home study *n.* A course of study in which instruction is offered at home, usu. by mail.

home•town (hōm′toun′) *n.* The town or city of one's birth, rearing, or main residence.

home truth *n.* A central or basic truth, esp. one that is discomforting to acknowledge.

home video *n.* **1.** A videotape recorded on a personal recorder. **2.** The business of providing videotapes for home viewing.

home•ward (hōm′wərd) *adv. & adj.* Toward or at home. —**home′wards** (-wərdz) *adv.*

home•work (hōm′wûrk′) *n.* **1.** Work, such as schoolwork, that is done at home. **2.** Preparatory or preliminary work.

hom•ey¹ also **hom•y** (hō′mē) *adj.* **-i•er, -i•est** *Informal* Having a feeling of home; comfortable; cozy. —**hom′ey•ness** *n.*

hom•ey² (hō′mē) *n. Slang* A homeboy or homegirl.

hom•i•cid•al (hŏm′ĭ-sīd′l, hō′mĭ-) *adj.* **1.** Of or relating to homicide. **2.** Capable of or conducive to homicide.

hom•i•cide (hŏm′ĭ-sīd′, hō′mĭ-) *n.* **1.** The killing of one person by another. **2.** A person who kills another person. [ME < OFr. < Lat. *homicidium* and *homicida : homō*, person; see **dhghem-** in App. + *-cīdium* and *-cīda*, -cide.]

hom•i•let•ic (hŏm′ə-lĕt′ĭk) also **hom•i•let•i•cal** (-ĭ-kəl) *adj.* **1.** Relating to or of the nature of a homily. **2.** Relating to homiletics. [LLat. *homīlēticus* < Gk. *homīlētikos*, of conversation < *homīlētos*, conversation < *homīlein*, to converse with < *homīlos*, crowd. See HOMILY.]

hom•i•let•ics (hŏm′ə-lĕt′ĭks) *n.* (*used with a sing. verb*) The art of preaching.

hom•i•ly (hŏm′ə-lē) *n., pl.* **-lies** **1.** A sermon, esp. on a scriptural text. **2.** A tedious moralizing lecture or admonition. **3.** An inspirational saying or platitude. [ME *omelie* < OFr. < LLat. *homīlia* < Gk. *homīlia*, discourse < *homīlos*, crowd. See **sem-¹** in App.] —**hom′i•list** *n.*

hom•ing pigeon (hō′mĭng) *n.* A pigeon trained to return to its home roost.

hom•i•nid (hŏm′ə-nĭd) *n.* A primate of the family Hominidae, of which *Homo sapiens* is the only extant species. [< NLat. Hominidae, family name < Lat. *homō, homin-*, man. See **dhghem-** in App.] —**hom′i•nid** *adj.*

hom•i•ni•za•tion (hŏm′ə-nī-zā′shən) *n.* The evolutionary process leading to the human characteristics that distinguish hominids from other primates. [Lat. *homō, homin-*, man; see HOMO¹ + –IZATION.]

hom•i•noid (hŏm′ə-noid′) *adj.* **1.** Of or belonging to the superfamily Hominoidea, which includes apes and humans. **2.** Resembling a human. ❖ *n.* A member of the Hominoidea. [< NLat. Hominoīdea, superfamily name : *Homō*, type genus (< Lat. *homō, homin-*, man; see HOMO¹) + *-oīdea*, resembling, neut. pl. of *-oīdēs*, resembling (< Gk. *-oeidēs*, -oid).]

hom•i•ny (hŏm′ə-nē) *n.* Hulled and dried kernels of corn. [Short for Virginia Algonquian *uskatahomen*.]

hominy grits *pl.n.* Grits, esp. eaten as a breakfast food. See Regional Note at **pone.**

hom•mos (hŏom′əs, hŭm′-) *n.* Variant of **hummus.**

ho•mo¹ (hō′mō) *n.* A member of the genus *Homo*, which includes the extinct and extant species of humans. [Lat. *homō*, man. See **dhghem-** in App.]

ho•mo² (hō′mō) *n., pl.* **-mos** *Offensive Slang* Used as a disparaging term for a gay man or lesbian. [Short for HOMOSEXUAL.]

homo– or **hom–** *pref.* Same; like: *homophone.* [Gk. < *homos*, same. See **sem-¹** in App.]

ho•mo•cen•tric (hō′mə-sĕn′trĭk, hŏm′ə-) *adj.* Having the same center.

ho•mo•cer•cal (hō′mə-sûr′kəl, hŏm′ə-) *adj.* Relating to, being, or characterized by a tail fin having two symmetrical lobes extending from the end of the vertebral column, as in most bony fishes. [HOMO– + Gk. *kerkos*, tail > –AL¹.]

ho•mo•chro•mat•ic (hō′mə-krō-măt′ĭk, hŏm′ə-) *adj.* Of or characterized by one color; monochromatic.

ho•mo•cys•te•ine (hō′mə-sĭs′tə-ēn′, -ĭn, -tē-) *n.* An amino acid important in cellular metabolism and protein synthesis that may contribute to an increased risk of heart disease when present in higher than normal concentrations. [*homo-*, homologous with (< HOMOLOGOUS) + CYSTEINE.]

ho•moe•cious (hō-mē′shəs, hō-) *adj.* Of or being a parasite that spends its entire life cycle on the same host. [HOMO– + Gk. *oikiā*, house; see HETEROECIOUS + –OUS.]

Homo e•rec•tus (ĭ-rĕk′təs) *n.* An extinct species of humans, regarded as an ancestor of *Homo sapiens.* [NLat. *Homō ērēctus*, species name : Lat. *homō*, man + Lat. *ērēctus*, upright.]

ho•mo•e•rot•ic (hō′mō-ĭ-rŏt′ĭk) *adj.* **1.** Of or concerning homosexual love and desire. **2.** Arousing such desire.

ho•mo•e•rot•i•cism (hō′mō-ĭ-rŏt′ĭ-sĭz′əm) also **ho•mo•er•o•tism** (-ĕr′ə-tĭz′əm) *n.* A homoerotic quality or theme.

ho•mo•ga•met•ic (hō′mō-gə-mĕt′ĭk) *adj.* Producing gametes that contain only one type of sex chromosome.

ho•mog•a•mous (hō-mŏg′ə-məs) *adj.* **1.** Having one kind of flower on the same plant. **2.** Having stamens and pistils that mature simultaneously.

ho•mog•e•nate (hə-mŏj′ə-nāt′, -nĭt, hō-) *n.* Something that has been homogenized. [HOMOGEN(IZE) + –ATE².]

ho•mo•ge•ne•i•ty (hō′mə-jə-nē′ĭ-tē, -nā′-, hŏm′ə-) *n., pl.* **-ties** The state or quality of being homogeneous.

ho•mo•ge•ne•ous (hō′mə-jē′nē-əs, -jēn′yəs) *adj.* **1.** Of the same or similar nature or kind. **2.** Uniform in structure or composition. **3.** *Mathematics* Consisting of terms of the same degree or elements of the same dimension. [< Med.Lat. *homogeneus* < Gk. *homogenēs : homo-*, homo- + *genos*, kind; see HETEROGENEOUS.] —**ho′mo•ge′ne•ous•ness** *n.*

homeomorphism

homogeneous

Homer

homocercal
swordfish tail

ă	pat	oi	boy
ā	pay	ou	out
âr	care	ōō	took
ä	father	ōō	boot
ĕ	pet	ŭ	cut
ē	be	ûr	urge
ĭ	pit	th	thin
ī	pie	th	this
îr	pier	hw	which
ŏ	pot	zh	vision
ō	toe	ə	about,
ô	paw		item

Stress marks:
′ (primary);
′ (secondary), as in
lexicon (lĕk′sĭ-kŏn′)

ho·mog·e·nize (hə-mŏj′ə-nīz′, hō-) v. **-nized, -niz·ing, -niz·es** —tr. **1.** To make homogeneous. **2a.** To reduce to particles and disperse throughout a fluid. **b.** To make uniform in consistency, esp. to make (milk) so by emulsifying the fat content. —intr. To become homogenized. [< HOMOGENEOUS.] —**ho·mog′e·ni·za′tion** (-nĭ-zā′shən) n. —**ho·mog′e·niz′er** n.

ho·mog·e·nous[1] (hə-mŏj′ə-nəs, hō-) adj. Of or exhibiting homogeny.

ho·mog·e·nous[2] (hə-mŏj′ə-nəs, hō-) adj. Homogeneous. [Alteration of HOMOGENEOUS (prob. influenced by HOMOGENIZE).]

ho·mog·e·ny (hə-mŏj′ə-nē, hō-) n., pl. **-nies** Similarity of structure between organs or parts of common descent, regardless of function. [Gk. homogeneia, community of orig. < homogenēs, of the same race, kind. See HOMOGENEOUS.]

ho·mo·graft (hō′mə-grăft′, hŏm′ə-) n. See **allograft.**

hom·o·graph (hŏm′ə-grăf′, hō′mə-) n. One of two or more words that have the same spelling but differ in origin, meaning, and sometimes pronunciation. —**hom′o·graph′ic** adj.

Homo hab·i·lis (hăb′ə-ləs) n. An extinct species of humans considered to be an ancestor of modern humans and the earliest hominid to make tools. [NLat. Homō habilis, species name : Lat. homō, man + Lat. habilis, skillful.]

homoio- pref. Variant of **homeo-.**

Ho·moi·ou·si·an (hō′moi-ōō′sē-ən, -zē-) n. A member of a Christian sect in the fourth century A.D. that held that Jesus and God the Father were similar but not the same in substance. [< Gk. homoiousios, of similar substance : homoio-, homeo- + ousiā, substance (< ousa, fem. pr. part. of einai, to be; see es- in App.).]

ho·mo·lec·i·thal (hō′mə-lĕs′ə-thəl) adj. Having a yolk that is evenly distributed throughout: a homolecithal egg. [HOMO- + Gk. lekithos, egg yolk + −AL[1].]

ho·mol·o·gate (hə-mŏl′ə-gāt′, hō-) tr.v. **-gat·ed, -gat·ing, -gates** Scots To approve, esp. to confirm officially. [Med.Lat. homologāre, homologāt- < Gk. homologein, to agree < homologos, agreeing. See HOMOLOGOUS.] —**ho·mol′o·ga′tion** n.

ho·mo·log·i·cal (hō′mə-lŏj′ĭ-kəl, hŏm′ə-) also **ho·mo·log·ic** (-lŏj′ĭk) adj. Homologous. —**ho′mo·log′i·cal·ly** adv.

ho·mol·o·gize (hə-mŏl′ə-jīz′, hō-) tr.v. **-gized, -giz·ing, -giz·es** **1.** To make homologous. **2.** To show to be homologous. —**ho·mol′o·giz′er** n.

ho·mol·o·gous (hə-mŏl′ə-gəs, hō-) adj. **1.** Corresponding or similar in position, value, structure, or function. **2.** Biology Similar in structure and evolutionary origin, though not necessarily in function, as the flippers of a seal and the hands of a human. **3.** Relating to the correspondence between an antigen and its antibody. **4.** Genetics Having the same morphology and linear sequence of gene loci as another chromosome. **5.** Chemistry Belonging to or being a series of organic compounds each successive member of which differs from the preceding by a constant increment, esp. by a CH_2 group. [< Gk. homologos, agreeing : homo-, homo- + logos, word, proportion; see leg- in App.]

hom·o·lo·graph·ic (hŏm′ə-lə-grăf′ĭk) adj. Maintaining the ratio of parts. [Gk. homalos, even; see sem-[1] in App. + GRAPHIC.]

homolographic projection n. A map projection reproducing the ratios of areas as they exist on the earth's surface.

hom·o·logue also **hom·o·log** (hŏm′ə-lôg′, -lŏg′, hō′mə-) n. Something homologous. [Fr. < Gk. homologon, neut. of homologos, agreeing. See HOMOLOGOUS.]

ho·mol·o·gy (hə-mŏl′ə-jē, hō-) n., pl. **-gies** **1.** The quality or condition of being homologous. **2.** A homologous relationship or correspondence. **3.** Chemistry **a.** The relation of the elements of a periodic family or group. **b.** The relation of the organic compounds in a homologous series. **4.** Mathematics A topological classification of configurations into distinct types that imposes an algebraic structure on families of geometric figures. [Gk. homologiā, agreement < homologos, agreeing. See HOMOLOGOUS.]

ho·mol·o·sine projection (hō-mŏl′ə-sīn′, -sĭn, hə-) n. A map of the earth's surface based on sinusoidal curves, with the ocean areas distorted so that the continents appear with minimal distortion. [HOMOLO(GRAPHIC) + SINE.]

ho·mo·mor·phism (hō′mə-môr′fĭz′əm, hŏm′ə-) n. **1.** Biology Similarity of external form or appearance but not of structure or origin. **2.** Zoology A resemblance in form between an animal's immature and adult stages. **3.** Mathematics A transformation from one set into another that preserves algebraic operations. —**ho·mo·mor′phic, ho′mo·mor′phous** adj.

hom·o·nym (hŏm′ə-nĭm′, hō′mə-) n. **1.** One of two or more words that have the same sound and often the same spelling but differ in meaning, such as bank (embankment) and bank (place where money is kept). **2a.** A word used to designate several different things. **b.** A namesake. **3.** Biology A taxonomic name identical to one previously applied to a different species or genus and therefore unacceptable in its new use. [Lat. homōnymum < Gk. homōnumon < neut. of homōnumos, homonymous. See HOMONYMOUS.] —**hom′o·nym′ic** adj.

ho·mon·y·mous (hō-mŏn′ə-məs, hə-) adj. **1.** Having the same name. **2.** Of the nature of a homonym; homonymic. [< Lat. homōnymus < Gk. homōnumos : homo-, homo- + onuma, name; see nŏ-men- in App.] —**ho·mon′y·mous·ly** adv.

ho·mon·y·my (hō-mŏn′ə-mē, hə-) n., pl. **-mies** The quality or condition of being homonymous.

Ho·mo·ou·si·an (hō′mō-ōō′sē-ən, -zē-) n. A Christian supporting the Council of Nicaea's Trinitarian definition of Jesus as consubstantial with God the Father. [LLat. homoūsiānus < homoūsius, of same substance < Gk. homoousios : homo-, homo- + ousiā, substance; see HOMOIOUSIAN.]

ho·mo·phile (hō′mə-fīl′) adj. **1.** Gay or lesbian. **2.** Actively concerned with the rights of gay men or lesbians. —**ho′mo·phile′** n.

ho·mo·pho·bi·a (hō′mə-fō′bē-ə) n. **1.** Fear of or contempt for lesbians and gay men. **2.** Behavior based on such a feeling. [HOMO(SEXUAL) + −PHOBIA.] —**ho′mo·phobe′** n. —**ho′mo·pho′bic** adj.

hom·o·phone (hŏm′ə-fōn′, hō′mə-) n. One of two or more words, such as night and knight, that are pronounced the same but differ in meaning, origin, and sometimes spelling. —**ho·moph′o·nous** (hō-mŏf′ə-nəs) adj.

ho·mo·phon·ic (hŏm′ə-fŏn′ĭk, hō′mə-) adj. **1.** Sounding alike. **2.** Having or characterized by a single melodic line with accompaniment. [< Gk. homophōnos : homo-, homo- + phōnē, sound; see PHONE[2].]

ho·moph·o·ny (hō-mŏf′ə-nē) n., pl. **-nies** **1.** The quality or condition of being homophonic. **2.** Homophonic music.

ho·mo·phy·ly (hō′mə-fī′lē, hŏm′ə-; hō-mŏf′ə-lē) n., pl. **-lies** Zoology Resemblance arising from common ancestry. [HOMO− + PHYL(UM) + −Y[2].] —**ho′mo·phyl′ic** (-fĭl′ĭk) adj.

ho·mo·plas·tic (hō′mə-plăs′tĭk, hŏm′ə-) adj. **1.** Of, relating to, or exhibiting homoplasy. **2.** Of, relating to, or derived from a different individual of the same species.

ho·mo·pla·sy (hō′mə-plā′sē, -plăs′ē, hŏm′ə-) n. Correspondence between parts or organs due to evolutionary convergence.

ho·mop·ter·an (hō-mŏp′tər-ən) n. A homopterous insect. [< NLat. Homoptera, order name : Gk. homo-, homo- + Gk. pteron, wing; see −PTER-.] —**ho·mop′ter·an** adj.

ho·mop·ter·ous (hō-mŏp′tər-əs) adj. Of or belonging to the order Homoptera, which includes the cicadas and scale insects and is characterized by sucking mouthparts. [< NLat. Homoptera, order name. See HOMOPTERAN.]

hom·or·gan·ic (hŏm′ôr-găn′ĭk) adj. Articulated in the same area of the vocal tract, as (t) and (n).

Homo sa·pi·ens (sā′pē-ənz, -ĕnz′) n. The modern species of humans, the only extant species of the primate family Hominidae. [NLat. Homō sapiēns, species name : Lat. homō, man + Lat. sapiēns, wise, rational, pr. part. of sapere, to be wise.]

ho·mo·sex·u·al (hō′mə-sĕk′shōō-əl, -mō-) adj. Of, relating to, or having a sexual orientation to persons of the same sex. ❖ n. A homosexual person; a gay man or a lesbian.

USAGE NOTE Many people now avoid using homosexual because of the emphasis this term places on sexuality. Indeed, the words gay and lesbian, which imply cultural and social matters more than sexual ones, are frequently better choices. Homosexual is most objectionable when used as a noun; here gay man and gay woman or lesbian and their plural forms are called for. It is generally unobjectionable when used adjectivally, as in a homosexual relationship, although gay, lesbian, or same-sex are also available for adjectival use. See Usage Note at **gay.**

ho·mo·sex·u·al·i·ty (hō′mə-sĕk′shōō-ăl′ĭ-tē, -mō-) n. **1.** Sexual orientation to persons of the same sex. **2.** Sexual activity with another of the same sex.

ho·mo·spo·rous (hō′mə-spôr′əs, -spōr′-, hŏm′ə-, hō-mŏs′pər-əs) adj. Producing spores of one kind only. —**ho′mo·spo′ry** n.

ho·mo·tax·is (hō′mō-tăk′sĭs, hŏm′ō-) n. Similarity of stratigraphic arrangement and fossils in noncontemporaneous or widely separated geologic deposits.

ho·mo·thal·lic (hō′mō-thăl′ĭk, hŏm′ō-) adj. Having male and female reproductive structures on the same thallus. [HOMO− + Gk. thallos, young shoot; see THALLO− + −IC.] —**ho′mo·thal′lism** n.

ho·mo·zy·go·sis (hō′mō-zī-gō′sĭs, -mə-, hŏm′ə-) n. The union of genetically identical gametes, resulting in the formation of a homozygote. —**ho′mo·zy·got′ic** (-gŏt′ĭk) adj.

ho·mo·zy·gote (hō′mō-zī′gōt′, -mə-, hŏm′ə-) n. A homozygous organism.

ho·mo·zy·gous (hō′mō-zī′gəs, -mə-, hŏm′ə-) adj. Having the same alleles at a particular gene locus on homologous chromosomes. —**ho′mo·zy·gos′i·ty** (-gŏs′ĭ-tē) n. —**ho′mo·zy′gous·ly** adv.

Homs (hômz, hôms) A city of W-central Syria N of Damascus; birthplace of the emperor Heliogabalus. Pop. 558,000.

ho·mun·cu·lus (hō-mŭng′kyə-ləs, hə-) n., pl. **-li** (-lī′) **1.** A diminutive human. **2.** A miniature, fully formed individual believed by adherents of the early biological theory of preformation to be present in the sperm cell. [Lat., dim. of homō, man. See dhghem- in App.] —**ho·mun′cu·lar** adj.

hom·y (hō′mē) adj. Variant of **homey.**

Ho·myel′ (hō′myĕl′) or **Go·mel** (gō′məl, -myĕl) A city of E Belarus SE of Minsk; first mentioned in 1142. Pop. 503,000.

Hon. abbr. **1.** honorable (title) **2.** hon. honorary

ho·nan also **Ho·nan** (hō′năn′) n. A pongee fabric of even color made originally from silk produced by the silkworms of Henan (formerly Honan), China.

Honan See Henan.

hon·cho (hŏn′chō) n., pl. **-chos** Slang One who is in charge; a manager or leader. [J. hanchō, squad leader : han, squad (< M Chin. pa·n, arrangement, class) + chō, chief (< M Chin. triᴀŋ).]
—**hon′cho** v.

Hon·du·ras (hŏn-door′əs, -dyoor′-) A country of N Central America; colonized by the Spanish in the early 1500s and proclaimed its independence in 1821. Cap. Tegucigalpa. Pop. 5,770,000. —**Hon·du′ran** adj. & n.

Honduras, Gulf of An inlet of the W Caribbean Sea bordering on Belize, Honduras, and Guatemala.

hone¹ (hōn) n. **1.** A fine-grained whetstone for giving a keen edge to a cutting tool. **2.** A tool with a rotating abrasive tip for enlarging holes to precise dimensions. ❖ tr.v. **honed, hon·ing, hones 1.** To sharpen on a fine-grained whetstone. **2.** To perfect or make more intense or effective: honed her skills. —**phrasal verb: hone in 1.** To move or advance toward a target or goal. Often used with on. **2.** To direct one's attention; focus. Often used with on. [ME < OE hān, stone. Hone in, alteration of home in.]

hone² (hōn) intr.v. **honed, hon·ing, hones** Informal **1.** To whine or moan. **2.** To hanker; yearn. [Obsolete Fr. hoigner < OFr., perh. < hon, cry of discontent.]

Hon·eg·ger (hŏn′ĭ-gər, hō′nĕg′ər, ô-nĕ-gĕr′), Arthur 1892–1955. French-born Swiss composer whose works include Pacific 231 (1923).

hon·est (ŏn′ĭst) adj. **1.** Marked by or displaying integrity; upright. **2.** Not deceptive or fraudulent; genuine. **3.** Equitable; fair. **4a.** Truthful; not false. **b.** Sincere; frank. **5a.** Of good repute; respectable. **b.** Without affectation; plain. **6.** Virtuous; chaste. [ME < OFr. honeste < Lat. honestus, honorable < honor (earlier honōs), perh. < hon, cry of discontent.]

honest broker n. A neutral agent, as in mediation.

hon·est·ly (ŏn′ĭst-lē) adv. **1.** In an honest manner. **2.** Used as an intensive: I honestly don't care. ❖ interj. Used to express mild disapproval or dismay: Honestly! Look at this mess!

hon·es·ty (ŏn′ĭ-stē) n., pl. **-ties 1.** The quality or condition of being honest; integrity. **2.** Truthfulness; sincerity. **3.** Archaic Chastity. **4.** Botany A European plant (Lunaria annua) having round, flat, papery, silver-white seedpods.

hone·wort (hōn′wûrt′, -wôrt′) n. An eastern North American perennial plant (Cryptotaenia canadensis) having umbels of small whitish flowers. [Perh. obsolete dialectal hone, a swelling (< its use in treating tumors) + WORT¹.]

hon·ey (hŭn′ē) n., pl. **-eys 1a.** A sweet yellowish or brownish viscid fluid produced by various bees from the nectar of flowers and used as food. **b.** A similar substance made by certain other insects. **2.** A sweet substance, such as nectar. **3.** Sweetness; pleasantness. **4.** Sugary or ingratiating words; flattery. **5.** Informal Sweetheart; dear. **6.** Informal Something remarkably fine. ❖ tr.v. **-eyed** or **-ied** (hŭn′ēd), **-ey·ing, -eys 1.** To sweeten with or as if with honey. **2.** To cajole with sweet talk. [ME honi < OE hunig.]

honey badger n. See ratel.

honey bear n. See kinkajou.

hon·ey·bee (hŭn′ē-bē′) n. Any of several honey-producing social bees of the genus Apis, esp. A. mellifera, raised for honey and beeswax.

hon·ey·ber·ry (hŭn′ē-bĕr′ē) n. See genip 1.

hon·ey·comb (hŭn′ē-kōm′) n. **1.** A beeswax structure of hexagonal thin-walled cells made by honeybees to hold honey and larvae. **2.** Something resembling this structure in configuration or pattern. ❖ tr.v. **-combed, -comb·ing, -combs 1.** To fill with holes or compartments; riddle. **2.** To form in or cover with a pattern like that of a honeycomb.

hon·ey·creep·er (hŭn′ē-krē′pər) n. **1.** Any of various small tropical American birds of the family Coerebidae, having a curved bill adapted for sucking nectar from flowers. **2.** Any of several similar birds of the family Drepanididae of Hawaii.

hon·ey·dew (hŭn′ē-doo′, -dyoo′) n. **1.** A sweet sticky substance excreted by various insects, esp. aphids, on plant leaves. **2.** A sweet exudate similar to honeydew on plant leaves. **3.** A honeydew melon.

honeydew melon n. A kind of melon (Cucumis melo) having a smooth whitish rind and green flesh.

hon·ey·eat·er (hŭn′ē-ē′tər) n. Any of various birds of the family Meliphagidae of Australia, having a long extensible tongue adapted for sucking nectar from flowers.

hon·eyed (hŭn′ēd) adj. also **hon·ied 1.** Containing, full of, or sweetened with honey. **2.** Ingratiating; sugary: honeyed words. **3.** Sweet; dulcet: a honeyed voice.

hon·ey·guide also **honey guide** (hŭn′ē-gīd′) n. Any of various tropical Old World birds of the family Indicatoridae, some species of which lead to the nests of wild honeybees in their own quest for food.

honey locust n. Any of several trees of the genus Gleditsia, esp. G. triacanthos, having deciduous compound leaves, small flowers in racemes, and large indehiscent pods.

honey mesquite n. See mesquite a.

hon·ey·moon (hŭn′ē-moon′) n. **1.** A holiday or trip taken by a newly married couple. **2.** An early harmonious period in a relationship. ❖ intr.v. **-mooned, -moon·ing, -moons** To go on a honeymoon. [Perh. < a comparison with the moon, which wanes as soon as it is full, to the affections of a newly married couple.] —**hon′ey·moon′er** n.

hon·ey·suck·le (hŭn′ē-sŭk′əl) n. **1.** Any of various shrubs or vines of the genus Lonicera, having opposite leaves, fragrant, usu. paired tubular flowers, and small berries. **2.** Any of various similar or related plants. [ME honysoukel, alteration of honisouke < OE hunīsūce : hunig, honey + sūcan, to suck; see SUCK.]

Hong Ha (hông′ hä′) See Red River 2.

hon·gi (hông′gē) New Zealand intr.v. **-gied, -gi·ing, -ies** To greet another or exchange greetings in Maori fashion by touching or pressing noses together. ❖ n. The act or an instance of making such a greeting. [Maori.]

Hong Kong (hŏng′kŏng′, -kŏng′, hông′kông′, -kông′) An administrative region of SE China SE of Guangzhou, including Hong Kong Island and adjacent areas. A former British crown colony, Hong Kong was an important center of international commerce and banking for most of the 20th century. It reverted to Chinese sovereignty in 1997. Cap. Victoria. Pop. 6,061,000.

Hong·shui He also **Hung·shui He** (hŏong′shwā′ hŭ′) A river rising in SW China and flowing c. 1,448 km (900 mi) to the Xiang Jiang.

Ho·ni·a·ra (hō′nē-är′ə) The cap. of the Solomon Is., on the NW coast of Guadalcanal. Pop. 35,288.

hon·ied (hŭn′ēd) v. A past tense and a past participle of **honey.** ❖ adj. Variant of **honeyed.**

honk (hôngk, hŏngk) n. **1.** The raucous resonant sound typical of a wild goose. **2a.** A sound like a goose's honk. **b.** The sound of a motor vehicle horn. ❖ v. **honked, honk·ing, honks** —intr. To emit a honk. —tr. To cause (a horn) to produce a honk. [Imit.] —**honk′er** n.

hon·ky or **hon·kie** also **hon·key** (hông′kē, hŏng′-) n., pl. **-kies** also **-keys** Offensive Slang Used as a disparaging term for a white person. [Poss. blend of Wolof honq, red, pink, of light complexion, and HUNKY.]

hon·ky-tonk (hông′kē-tôngk′, hŏng′kē-tŏngk′) n. A cheap, noisy bar or dance hall. ❖ adj. **1.** Of or relating to such a bar or dance hall; tawdry. **2.** Of, relating to, or being a type of ragtime played on a tinny-sounding piano or in a honky-tonk. ❖ intr.v. **-tonked, -tonk·ing, -tonks** To visit honky-tonks. [Perh. < HONK.]

Hon·o·lu·lu (hŏn′ə-loo′loo, hō′nō-) The cap. of HI, on the SE coast of Oahu; first settled in 1816. Pop. 371,657.

hon·or (ŏn′ər) n. **1.** High respect, as for special merit; esteem. **2a.** Good name; reputation. **b.** A source or cause of credit. **3a.** Glory or recognition; distinction. **b.** A mark, token, or gesture of respect or distinction. **c.** A military decoration. **d.** A title conferred for achievement. **4.** High rank. **5.** The dignity accorded to position. **6.** Great privilege: May I have the honor of this dance? **7.** Honor Used with His, Her, or Your as a title and term of address for certain officials: Her Honor the Mayor. **8a.** Principled uprightness of character; personal integrity. **b.** A code of integrity, dignity, and pride, chiefly among men, maintained in some societies, as in feudal Europe, by force of arms. **c.** A woman's chastity or reputation for chastity. **9. honors** Social courtesies offered to guests. **10. honors** a. Special recognition for unusual academic achievement. **b.** A program of advanced study for exceptional students. **11.** Sports The right of being first at the tee in golf. **12.** Games **a.** Any of the four or five highest cards in each suit, esp. in bridge. **b. honors** A bonus score, esp. in bridge, awarded for having certain honor cards in one's hand. ❖ tr.v. **-ored, -or·ing, -ors 1.** To hold in respect; esteem. **b.** To show respect for. **c.** To bow to (another dancer) in square dancing. **2.** To confer distinction on. **3.** To accept or pay as valid. —**idiom: honor bound** Under an obligation enforced by the personal integrity of the one obliged. [ME < OFr. < Lat.] —**hon′or·er** n.

hon·or·a·ble (ŏn′ər-ə-bəl) adj. **1.** Deserving or earning honor and respect. **2.** Bringing distinction or recognition: honorable service. **3.** Possessing and characterized by honor. **4.** Consistent with honor or good name. **5.** Distinguished; illustrious. **6.** Attended by marks of recognition and honor. **7.** Honorable **a.** Used as a title of respect for certain high government officials. **b.** Used as a courtesy title for the children of barons and viscounts and the younger sons of earls. **c.** Used in the House of Commons as a title of respect for members. —**hon′or·a·ble·ness** n. —**hon′or·a·bly** adv.

honorable discharge n. Discharge from the armed forces with a commendable record.

honorable mention n. A citation to one who has performed well in a competition but has not been awarded a prize.

hon·o·rar·i·um (ŏn′ə-râr′ē-əm) n., pl. **-i·ums** or **-i·a** (-ē-ə) A payment given to a professional person for services for which fees are not required. [Lat. honōrārium < neut. of honōrārius, honorary < honor, honor.]

hon·or·ar·y (ŏn′ə-rĕr′ē) adj. **1.** Held or given as a mark of honor, esp. conferred as an honor without the usual adjuncts. **2a.** Holding an office or title given as an honor, without payment. **b.** Voluntary. **3.** Relying on honor and not legally enforceable, as a duty.

hon·or·ee (ŏn′ə-rē′) n. The recipient of an honor.

honor guard n. A group of people serving as an escort or performing drill exhibitions on ceremonial occasions.

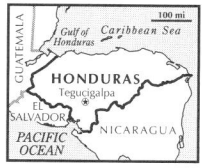

Honduras

honeycomb

ă	pat	oi	boy
ā	pay	ou	out
âr	care	oo	took
ä	father	oo	boot
ĕ	pet	ŭ	cut
ē	be	ûr	urge
ĭ	pit	th	thin
ī	pie	th	this
îr	pier	hw	which
ŏ	pot	zh	vision
ō	toe	ə	about,
ô	paw		item

Stress marks:
′ (primary);
′ (secondary), as in
lexicon (lĕk′sĭ-kŏn′)

hoop skirt

Herbert Hoover

hon·or·if·ic (ŏn′ə-rĭf′ĭk) *adj.* Conferring or showing respect or honor. ❖ *n.* A title, phrase, or grammatical form conveying respect, used esp. for a social superior. [Lat. *honōrificus* : *honor, honōr-,* honor + *-ficus, -fic.*] **—hon′or·if′i·cal·ly** *adv.*

Ho·no·ri·us (hō-nôr′ē-əs), **Flavius** A.D. 384–423. Roman emperor of the West (395–423).

honor roll *n.* A list of names of people worthy of honor, esp.: **a.** A list of students who have earned high grades during a specified period. **b.** A list of people who have served in the armed forces.

honor society *n.* An organization to which students are admitted in recognition of academic achievement.

honor system *n.* A system under which persons are trusted without supervision in situations that might allow for dishonesty.

hon·our (ŏn′ər) *n. & v. Chiefly British* Variant of **honor.**

Hon·shu (hŏn′shōō) An island of central Japan between the Sea of Japan and the Pacific Ocean.

hooch[1] also **hootch** (hōōch) *n. Slang* **1.** Alcoholic liquor, esp. inferior or bootleg liquor. **2.** Marijuana. [Short for *hoochinoo* < *Hoochinoo,* a Tlingit village where illegal liquor was distilled < Tlingit *xutsnuuwú.*]

hooch[2] also **hootch** (hōōch) *n. Slang* A dwelling, esp. a thatched hut. [Alteration of J. *uchi,* inside, interior.]

hood[1] (hōōd) *n.* **1.** A loose pliable covering for the head and neck, often attached to a robe or jacket. **2.** An ornamental draping of cloth hung from the shoulders of an academic or ecclesiastical robe. **3.** A sack placed over the head of a falcon to keep it quiet. **4a.** A metal cover or cowl for a hearth or stove. **b.** A carriage top. **c.** The hinged metal lid over the engine of a motor vehicle. **5.** *Zoology* An expanded part, crest, or marking on or near the head of an animal. ❖ *tr.v.* **hood·ed, hood·ing, hoods** To supply or cover with a hood. [ME *hod* < OE *hōd.*]

hood[2] (hōōd) *n. Slang* A person given to violence, esp. for criminal ends. [Short for HOODLUM.]

hood[3] or **'hood** (hōōd) *n. Slang* A neighborhood, usu. in the inner city. [African American Vernacular E., short for NEIGHBORHOOD.]

Hood, John Bell 1831–79. Amer. Confederate soldier who commanded the Atlanta Campaign (1864).

Hood, Mount A volcanic peak, 3,426.7 m (11,235 ft), in the Cascade Range of NW OR.

Hood, Thomas 1799–1845. British poet and editor whose verses include "The Song of the Shirt" (1843).

–hood *suff.* **1a.** Condition; state; quality: *manhood.* **b.** An instance of a specified state or quality: *falsehood.* **2.** A group sharing a specified state or quality: *sisterhood.* [ME *-hed, -hode* < OE *-hǣde, -hād.*]

hood·ed (hōōd′ĭd) *adj.* **1.** Covered with or having a hood. **2.** Shaped like a hood or cowl. **3.** *Zoology* **a.** Having coloration or a crest suggesting a hood. **b.** Having elastic skin at the neck that when distended resembles a hood, as that of the cobra.

hooded seal *n.* A seal (*Cystophora cristata*) of northern seas, having a grayish spotted coat and an inflatable hoodlike or bladderlike pouch near the nose.

hood·lum (hōōd′ləm, hŏōd′-) *n.* **1.** A gangster; a thug. **2.** A tough, aggressive or violent youth. [?]

hood·mold (hōōd′mōld′) *n.* See **dripstone** 1.

hoo·doo (hōō′dōō) *n., pl.* **-doos 1a.** Magic healing and control, esp. in African-based folk medicine in the United States and the Caribbean. **b.** A practitioner of hoodoo. **2.** Voodoo. **3a.** Bad luck. **b.** One that brings bad luck. **4.** *Geology* A column of eccentrically shaped rock, produced by differential weathering. ❖ *tr.v.* **-dooed, -doo·ing, -doos 1.** To practice hoodoo on; affect with a charm or curse. **2.** To bring bad luck to. [Of West African orig., poss. < VOODOO.] **—hoo′doo·ism** *n.*

hood·wink (hōōd′wĭngk′) *tr.v.* **-winked, -wink·ing, -winks 1.** To take in by deceptive means; deceive. **2.** *Archaic* To blindfold. **3.** *Obsolete* To conceal. **—hood′wink′er** *n.*

hoo·ey (hōō′ē) *n. Slang* Nonsense. [?]

hoof (hōōf, hŏōf) *n., pl.* **hooves** (hōōvz, hŏōvz) or **hoofs 1a.** The horny sheath covering the toes or lower part of the foot of a mammal of the orders Perissodactyla and Artiodactyla, such as an ox. **b.** The foot of such an animal, esp. a horse. **2.** *Slang* The human foot. ❖ *v.* **hoofed, hoof·ing, hoofs** *—tr.* To trample with the hooves. *—intr. Slang* **1.** To dance, esp. professionally. **2.** To go on foot; walk. **—idioms: hoof it** *Slang* **1.** To walk. **2.** To dance. **on the hoof** Not yet butchered; alive. Used esp. of cattle. [ME *hof* < OE *hōf.*]

hoof-and-mouth disease (hōōf′ən-mouth′, hŏōf′-) *n.* See **foot-and-mouth disease.**

hoof·bound (hōōf′bound′, hŏōf′-) *adj.* Afflicted with drying and contraction of the hoof, resulting in lameness. Used of a horse.

hoofed (hōōft, hŏōft) *adj.* Having hooves; ungulate.

hoof·er (hōō′fər, hŏō′fər) *n. Slang* A professional dancer, esp. a tap dancer.

Hoogh·ly (hōō′glē) See **Hugli.**

hoo-ha or **hoo-hah** (hōō′hä′) *n. Slang* **1.** A fuss; a disturbance. **2.** A chortle or laugh. [Perh. < Yiddish *hu-ha,* to-do, uproar.]

hook (hŏōk) *n.* **1a.** A curved or sharply bent device, usu. of metal, used to catch, pull, suspend, or fasten something. **b.** A fishhook. **2.** Something shaped like a hook, esp.: **a.** A curved or barbed plant or animal part. **b.** A short angled or curved line on a letter. **c.** A sickle. **3a.** A sharp bend or curve, as in a river. **b.** A point or spit of land with a sharply curved end. **4.** A means of catching or ensnaring; a trap. **5.** *Slang* **a.** A means of attracting interest or attention; an enticement. **b.** *Music* A catchy motif or refrain. **6.** *Sports* **a.** A short swinging blow in boxing delivered with a crooked arm. **b.** The course of a ball that curves in a direction away from the dominant hand of the player propelling it, as to the left of a right-handed player. **c.** A stroke that sends a ball on such a course. ❖ *v.* **hooked, hook·ing, hooks** *—tr.* **1a.** To catch, suspend, or connect with a hook. **b.** *Informal* To snare. **c.** *Slang* To steal; snatch. **2.** To fasten by or as if by a hook. **3.** To pierce or gore with or as if with a hook. **4.** *Slang* **a.** To take strong hold of; captivate. **b.** To cause to become addicted. **5.** To make (a rug) by looping yarn through canvas with a hook. **6.** *Sports* **a.** To hit with a hook in boxing. **b.** To hit (a ball) in a hook. **c.** To impede the progress of (an opponent in ice hockey) by holding or restraining the player with one's stick, in violation of the rules. *—intr.* **1.** To bend like a hook. **2.** To be fastened by means of a hook or a hook and eye. **3.** *Slang* To work as a prostitute. **—phrasal verb: hook up 1.** To assemble or wire (a mechanism). **2.** To connect a mechanism and a source of power. **3.** *Informal* To meet or associate: *hooked up after class.* **—idioms: by hook or by crook** By whatever means possible, fair or unfair. **get the hook** *Slang* To be unceremoniously dismissed or terminated. **hook, line, and sinker** *Informal* Without reservation; completely. **off the hook** *Informal* Freed, as from blame or a vexatious obligation. **on (one's) own hook** By one's own efforts. [ME *hok* < OE *hōc.*]

hook·ah (hŏōk′ə) *n.* An Eastern smoking pipe having a long tube passing through an urn of water that cools the smoke. [Hindi *huqqā* < Ar. *ḥuqqa,* small box, the hookah's water urn < *ḥaqqa,* to be suitable.]

hook and eye *n.* **1.** A clothes fastener consisting of a small blunt metal hook that is inserted in a corresponding loop or eyelet. **2.** A latch consisting of a hook that is inserted in a screw eye.

hook-and-lad·der truck (hŏōk′ən-lăd′ər) *n.* A fire engine equipped with extension ladders and hooked poles.

Hooke (hŏōk), **Robert** 1635–1703. English physicist who formulated the theory of planetary movement.

hooked (hŏōkt) *adj.* **1.** Bent or angled like a hook. **2.** Having a hook. **3.** Made by hooking yarn: *a hooked rug.* **4.** *Slang* **a.** Captivated by or devoted to a custom or thing. **b.** Addicted to a narcotic. **—hook′ed·ness** (hŏōk′ĭd-nĭs) *n.*

hook·er[1] (hŏōk′ər) *n.* **1.** A single-masted fishing smack used off the coast of Ireland. **2.** An old worn-out or clumsy ship. [Du. *hoeker* < MDu. *hoeckboot* : *hoec,* fishhook + *boot,* boat.]

hook·er[2] (hŏōk′ər) *n.* **1.** One that hooks. **2.** *Slang* A prostitute.

Hooker, Joseph Known as "Fighting Joe." 1814–79. Amer. Union army officer who was defeated by Robert E. Lee at Chancellorsville (1863).

Hooker, Richard 1554?–1600. English theologian whose *Laws of Ecclesiastical Polity* (1594) contributed to the formation of Anglican theology.

Hooker, Thomas 1586?–1647. English-born Amer. colonizer and cleric who founded Hartford in Connecticut (1636).

hook·nose (hŏōk′nōz′) *n.* An aquiline nose. **—hook′nosed′** *adj.*

Hook of Holland A cape and harbor of SW Netherlands on the North Sea W of Rotterdam.

hook shot *n. Basketball* A shot made by arcing the far hand upward while being positioned or moving sideways to the basket.

hook·up (hŏōk′ŭp′) *n.* **1.** A system of electrical circuits or equipment designed to operate together. **2a.** A configuration of mechanical parts or devices providing a link between a supply source and a user. **b.** A plan or schematic drawing of such a system or configuration. **3.** *Informal* A linkage or connection, often between unlikely associates or factors.

hook·worm (hŏōk′wûrm′) *n.* Any of numerous small parasitic nematode worms of the family Ancylostomatidae, having a hooked mouthpart with which it fastens itself to the intestinal walls of its host, causing ancylostomiasis.

hookworm disease *n.* See **ancylostomiasis.**

hook·y (hŏōk′ē) *n. Informal* Absence without leave; truancy: *play hooky from school.* [Perh. < *hook it,* to make off.]

hoo·li·gan (hōō′lĭ-gən) *n.* A tough and aggressive or violent youth. [?] **—hoo′li·gan·ism** *n.*

hoop (hōōp, hŏōp) *n.* **1.** A circular band of metal or wood put around a cask or barrel to bind the staves together. **2.** A large wooden, plastic, or metal ring, esp. one used as a toy. **3.** One of the lightweight circular supports for a hoop skirt. **4.** A circular ringlike earring. **5.** One of a pair of circular frames used to hold material taut for needlework. **6.** *Basketball* **a.** The basket. **b.** also **hoops** The game of basketball. **7.** *Sports* A croquet wicket. ❖ *tr.v.* **hooped, hoop·ing, hoops 1.** To hold together or support with or as if with a hoop. **2.** To encircle. **—idiom: jump (or go) through the hoop** To undergo a rigorous trial or examination. [ME *hop.*]

hoop·er (hōō′pər, hŏōp′ər) *n.* A maker or repairer of barrels and tubs; a cooper.

hoop·la (hōōp′lä′, hŏōp′-) *n. Informal* **1a.** Boisterous, jovial commotion or excitement. **b.** Extravagant publicity. **2.** Talk intended to mislead or confuse. [Perh. < Fr. *houp-là,* upsy-daisy! : *houp* (of imit. orig.) + *là,* here; see VOILÀ.]

hoo•poe (hōō′pōō, -pō) *n.* Any of several Old World birds, esp. *Upupa epops,* having a fanlike crest and a slender downward-curving bill. [Alteration (influenced by Lat. *ūpupa*) of obsolete *hoop* < Fr. *huppe* < OFr. < VLat. **ūppa,* alteration of Lat. *upupa, ūpupa,* of imit. orig.]

hoop skirt *n.* A long full skirt belled out with a series of connected circular supports.

hoop snake *n.* Any of several snakes said to grasp the tail in the mouth and move with a rolling hooplike motion.

hoo•ray (hōō-rā′, hə-) *interj., n.,* & *v.* Variant of **hurrah.**

Hoorn Islands (hôrn, hōrn) See **Futuna Islands.**

hoose•gow (hōōs′gou′) *n. Slang* A jail. [Sp. *juzgado,* tribunal, courtroom < p. part. of *juzgar,* to judge < Lat. *iūdicāre* < *iūdex, iūdic-,* judge. See JUDGE.]

Hoo•sier (hōō′zhər) *n.* Used as a nickname for a native or resident of Indiana. [?]

WORD HISTORY We know where Hoosiers come from: Indiana. But where does the name *Hoosier* come from? That is less easy to answer. The first recorded instance of *Hoosier* meaning "Indiana resident" is dated 1826; however, it seems possible that senses of the word recorded later in the *Dictionary of Americanisms,* including "a big, burly, uncouth specimen or individual; a frontiersman, countryman, rustic," reflect the kind of use this word had before it settled down in Indiana. As a nickname, *Hoosier* was but one of a variety of disparaging terms arising in the early 19th century for the inhabitants of particular states. For example, Texans were called *Beetheads,* Alabamans were *Lizards,* Nebraskans were *Bug-eaters,* South Carolinians were *Weasels,* and Pennsylvanians were *Leatherheads.* People in Missouri might have had it worst of all—they were called *Pukes.* Originally, these names were probably taken up by people living in neighboring states, but belittled residents adopted them in a spirit of defiant pride, much as American colonists turned the derisive term *Yankee* into a moniker for their spirit of rebellion. Today, most of these frontier nicknames have disappeared from the landscape; some survive as nicknames for the sports teams of state universities, such as the North Carolina *Tarheels* and the Ohio *Buckeyes*—fighting words only on the playing field.

---

hoot[1] (hōōt) *v.* **hoot•ed, hoot•ing, hoots** —*intr.* **1.** To utter the hoot of an owl. **2.** To make a loud raucous cry, esp. of derision or contempt. —*tr.* **1.** To shout down or drive off with jeers. **2.** To express or convey by hooting. ❖ *n.* **1a.** The characteristic cry of an owl. **b.** A sound suggesting the cry of an owl, esp. the sound of a horn. **2.** A cry of scorn or derision. **3.** *Informal* One that is hilariously funny. —*idiom:* **not give** (or **care**) **a hoot** To be completely indifferent or unconcerned. [ME *houten,* of imit. orig.]

hoot[2] (hōōt, ōōt) also **hoots** (hōōts, ōōts) *interj. Scots* Used to express annoyance or objection.

hootch[1] (hōōch) *n.* Variant of **hooch**[1].

hootch[2] (hōōch) *n.* Variant of **hooch**[2].

hootch•y-kootch•y (hōō′chē-kōō′chē) *n., pl.* **-kootch•ies** A deliberately sensual form of belly dance, typically part of a carnival. [?]

hoot•en•an•ny (hōōt′n-ăn′ē) *n., pl.* **-nies 1.** An informal performance by folk singers, typically with participation by the audience. **2.** *Informal* An unidentified or unidentifiable gadget. [?]

hoot•er (hōō′tər) *n.* **1.** One that hoots, esp. an owl. **2. hooters** *Vulgar Slang* A woman's breasts.

hoot owl (hōōt) *n.* Any of various owls having a hooting cry.

Hoo•ver (hōō′vər), **Herbert Clark** 1874–1964. The 31st President of the US (1929–33), whose fiscal policies failed to stem the effects of the crash of 1929.

Hoover, J(ohn) Edgar 1895–1972. Amer. director of the FBI (1924–72) remembered for his vigorous anti-Communist campaign after World War II.

Hoover, Lou Henry 1874–1944. First Lady of the US (1929–33).

Hoo•ver•ville (hōō′vər-vĭl′) *n.* A crudely built camp put up usu. on the edge of a town to house the destitute during the depression of the 1930s. [After Herbert Clark HOOVER.]

hooves (hōōvz, hōōvz) *n.* A plural of **hoof.**

hop[1] (hŏp) *v.* **hopped, hop•ping, hops** —*intr.* **1a.** To move with light bounding skips or leaps. **b.** *Informal* To move quickly or busily. **2.** To jump on one foot. **3.** To make a quick trip, esp. in an airplane. **4.** To travel or move often from place to place. —*tr.* **1.** To move over by hopping: *hop a ditch.* **2.** *Informal* To jump aboard: *hop a train.* ❖ *n.* **1a.** A light springy jump or leap, esp. on one foot. **b.** A rebound: *The ball took a bad hop.* **2.** *Informal* A dance or dance party. **3a.** A short distance. **b.** A short trip, esp. by air. **4.** A free ride; a lift. —*idioms:* **hop, skip, and** (a) **jump** A short distance. **hop to it** To begin an activity or a task quickly and energetically. [ME *hoppen* < OE *hoppian.*]

hop[2] (hŏp) *n.* **1.** A twining vine (*Humulus lupulus*) having lobed leaves and green female flowers arranged in conelike spikes. **2. hops** The dried ripe flowers of this plant, containing a bitter aromatic oil and used in brewing beer to prevent bacterial action and add the characteristic bitter taste. **3.** *Slang* Opium. ❖ *tr.v.* **hopped, hop•ping, hops** To flavor with hops. —*phrasal verb:* **hop up** *Slang* **1.** To increase the power or energy of: *hop*

up *a car.* **2.** To stimulate with or as if with a narcotic. [ME *hoppe* < MDu.]

HOP *abbr.* high oxygen pressure

hop clover *n.* A Eurasian clover (*Trifolium agrarium*) or one of its relatives, having yellow flower heads that resemble hops when withered.

hope (hōp) *v.* **hoped, hop•ing, hopes** —*intr.* **1.** To wish for something with expectation of its fulfillment. **2.** *Archaic* To have confidence; trust. —*tr.* **1.** To look forward to with confidence or expectation. **2.** To expect and desire. ❖ *n.* **1.** A wish or desire accompanied by confident expectation of its fulfillment. **2.** Something hoped for or desired: *Success is our hope.* **3.** A source of or reason for hope. **4.** often **Hope** *Christianity* The theological virtue defined as the desire and search for a future good, difficult but not impossible to attain with God's help. **5.** *Archaic* Trust; confidence. —*idiom:* **hope against hope** To hope with little reason or justification. [ME *hopen* < OE *hopian.*] —**hop′er** *n.*

Hope, Bob b. 1903. British-born Amer. entertainer known esp. for his films and variety shows.

hope chest *n.* A chest traditionally used by a young woman for clothing and household goods in anticipation of marriage.

hope•ful (hōp′fəl) *adj.* **1.** Having or manifesting hope. **2.** Inspiring hope; promising. ❖ *n.* A person who aspires to success or who shows promise of succeeding, esp. as a political candidate: *presidential hopefuls.* —**hope′ful•ness** *n.*

hope•ful•ly (hōp′fə-lē) *adv.* **1.** In a hopeful manner. **2.** *Usage Problem* It is to be hoped.

USAGE NOTE Writers who use *hopefully* as a sentence adverb, as in *Hopefully, the measures will be adopted,* should be aware that the usage is unacceptable to many critics, including a large majority of the Usage Panel. But it is not easy to explain why critics dislike this use of *hopefully.* It is justified by analogy to the unexceptionable uses of many other adverbs, as in *Mercifully, the play was brief.* The wide acceptance of the usage reflects popular recognition of its usefulness; there is no precise substitute. Someone who says *Hopefully, the treaty will be ratified* makes a hopeful prediction about the fate of the treaty, whereas someone who says *I hope* (or *We hope* or *It is hoped*) *the treaty will be ratified* expresses a bald statement about what is desired. Only the latter could be continued with a clause such as *but it isn't likely.* • Even though the usage is well established, critics appear to have become more adamant in their opposition. Only 34 percent of the Panel accepted the usage of *hopefully* in our 1999 survey, down from 44 percent in 1969. By contrast, 82 percent in the 1999 survey accepted the comparable use of *mercifully* as a sentence adverb. Thus it is not the use of sentence adverbs per se that bothers the Panel; rather, the specific use of *hopefully* in this way has become a shibboleth.

Ho•pei or **Ho•peh** (hō′pā′, hŭ′bä′) See **Hebei.**

hope•less (hōp′lĭs) *adj.* **1.** Having no hope; despairing. **2.** Offering no hope; bleak. **3.** Incurable. **4.** Having no possibility of solution; impossible. —**hope′less•ly** *adv.* —**hope′less•ness** *n.*

hope•less•ness (hōp′lĭs-nĭs) *n.* The condition or quality of being hopeless.

Hope•well (hōp′wĕl′, -wəl) *n.* An early Native American culture centered in the Ohio River valley from about the second century B.C. to the fourth century A.D., noted for extensive earthworks and large burial mounds. [After the owner of a farm in Ross County, Ohio.]

hop•head (hŏp′hĕd′) *n. Slang* A drug addict. [HOP[2] + HEAD.]

hop hornbeam *n.* Any of several deciduous trees of the genus *Ostrya,* esp. *O. virginiana* of eastern North America, having fruit clusters resembling hops.

Ho•pi (hō′pē) *n., pl.* **Hopi** or **-pis 1** A member of a Pueblo people occupying a number of mesa-top pueblos on reservation land in northeast Arizona. **2.** The Uto-Aztecan language of the Hopi. [Hopi *hópi,* peaceable, Hopi.]

Hop•kins (hŏp′kĭnz), **Gerard Manley** 1844–89. British poet known for his posthumously published works, including "The Wreck of the Deutschland."

Hopkins, Johns 1795–1873. Amer. financier whose bequest funded the creation of the Baltimore hospital and university that bear his name.

Hop•kin•son (hŏp′kĭn-sən), **Francis** 1737–91. Amer. Revolutionary leader known for his satires against the British.

hop•lite (hŏp′līt′) *n.* A heavily armed foot soldier of ancient Greece. [Gk. *hoplītēs* < *hoplon,* armor.]

hop•per (hŏp′ər) *n.* **1.** One that hops. **2a.** A usu. funnel-shaped container in which materials, such as grain, are stored for later dispensation. **b.** *Informal* A place in which something is held for later use or consideration. **c.** A freight car with a door in the floor through which materials are unloaded. [Sense 2 < the shaking motion of grain hoppers as grain is passed through.]

Hopper, Edward 1882–1967. Amer. painter famous for his realist style in works such as *Nighthawks* (1942).

Hopper, Grace Murray 1906–92. Amer. mathematician and computer programmer who developed programming languages and is credited with inventing the first compiler.

hop•per•grass (hŏp′ər-grăs′) *n. Chiefly Southern US* See **grasshopper** 1. See Regional Note at **everwhere.**

hopper

Grace Murray Hopper
photographed in 1985

ă pat	oi boy
ā pay	ou out
âr care	ŏŏ took
ä father	ōō boot
ĕ pet	ŭ cut
ē be	ûr urge
ĭ pit	th thin
ī pie	th this
îr pier	hw which
ŏ pot	zh vision
ō toe	ə about,
ô paw	item

Stress marks:
′ (primary);
′ (secondary), as in
lexicon (lĕk′sĭ-kŏn′)

hop·sack·ing (hŏp′săk′ĭng) also **hop·sack** (-săk′) *n.* A loosely woven coarse fabric of cotton or wool used in clothing. [< its being used for bags by hop growers.]

hop·scotch (hŏp′skŏch′) *n.* A children's game in which players toss an object into numbered spaces drawn on the ground and then hop or jump through the spaces to retrieve the object. ❖ *intr.v.* **-scotched, -scotch·ing, -scotch·es** To move in or as if in irregular jumps. [HOP¹ + SCOTCH¹, a score, line.]

hor. *abbr.* horizontal

ho·ra also **ho·rah** (hôr′ə, hōr′ə) *n.* A traditional round dance of Romania and Israel. [Mod.Heb. *hôrâ* < Rom. *horă* < Turk. *hora*, perh. < Mod.Gk. *khoro,* accusative of *khoros,* round dance < Gk. See **gher-** in App.]

Hor·ace (hôr′əs, hŏr′-) Orig. Quintus Horatius Flaccus. 65–8 B.C. Roman lyric poet noted for his *Odes* and *Satires.* —**Ho·ra′tian** (hə-rā′shən) *adj.*

ho·ra·ry (hôr′ə-rē, hŏr′-) *adj.* **1.** An hour or hours. **2.** Occurring once an hour; hourly. [Med.Lat. *hōrārius* < Lat. *hōra,* hour. See HOUR.]

Horatian ode *n.* An ode with a fixed stanzaic pattern.

horde (hôrd, hōrd) *n.* **1.** A large group or crowd; a swarm. **2a.** A nomadic Mongol tribe. **b.** A nomadic tribe or group. [Ult. (via Pol. *horda*) < NW Turkic *ordī,* residence, court < O Turkic *ordu.*]

hore·hound (hôr′hound′, hōr′-) *n.* **1a.** An aromatic Eurasian plant (*Marrubium vulgare*) in the mint family, having square stems and opposite leaves covered with white pubescence and yielding a bitter extract used in flavoring and as a cough remedy. **b.** A candy or preparation flavored with horehound. **2.** Any of similar plants, such as the black horehound. [ME, alteration of *horhune* < OE *hārehūne* : *hār,* hoary + *hūne,* a plant.]

ho·ri·zon (hə-rī′zən) *n.* **1.** The apparent intersection of the earth and sky as seen by an observer. **2.** *Astronomy* **a.** The sensible horizon. **b.** The celestial horizon. **c.** The limit of the theoretically possible universe. **3.** The range of one's knowledge, experience, or interest. **4.** *Geology* **a.** A specific position in a stratigraphic column, such as the location of one or more fossils, that serves to identify the stratum. **b.** A specific layer of soil or subsoil in a vertical cross section of land. [ME *orizon* < OFr. < Lat. *horizōn* < Gk. *horizōn (kuklos),* limiting (circle), horizon < pr. part. of *horizein,* to limit < *horos,* boundary.]

hor·i·zon·tal (hôr′ĭ-zŏn′tl, hŏr′-) *adj.* **1.** Of, relating to, or near the horizon. **2a.** Parallel to or in the plane of the horizon. **b.** At right angles to a vertical line. **3.** Occupying or restricted to the same level in a hierarchy. ❖ *n.* Something, such as a plane, that is horizontal. [Fr. < Lat. *horizōn, horizont-,* horizon. See HORIZON.] —**hor′i·zon·tal′i·ty** (-zən-tăl′ĭ-tē) *n.* —**hor′i·zon·tal·ly** *adv.*

horizontal bar *n.* A gymnastics apparatus consisting of a single bar mounted approximately eight feet above the ground and used for swinging maneuvers.

horizontal union *n.* See **craft union.**

Hor·liv·ka (hôr′lŭv-kə, -lēw-) or **Gor·lov·ka** (gôr′ləf-kə) A city of SE Ukraine in the Donets Basin N of Donetsk. Pop. 336,100.

hor·mone (hôr′mōn′) *n.* **1a.** A substance, usu. a peptide or steroid, produced by one tissue and conveyed by the bloodstream to another to effect physiological activity, such as growth. **b.** A synthetic compound that acts like a hormone in the body. **2.** Any of various similar substances in plants and insects that regulate development. [< Gk. *hormōn,* pr. part. of *hormān,* to urge on < *hormē,* impulse. See **er-** in App.] —**hor·mon′al** (-mō′nəl), **hor·mon′ic** (-mŏn′ĭk) *adj.* —**hor·mon′al·ly** *adv.*

hormone replacement therapy *n.* The administration of estrogen and progestin to women to relieve the symptoms of menopause, prevent osteoporosis, and reduce the risk of heart disease.

Hor·muz (hôr′mŭz′, hôr-mōōz′), **Strait of** also **Strait of Or·muz** (ôr-mōōz′, ôr′mŭz′) A strategic waterway linking the Persian Gulf with the Gulf of Oman.

horn (hôrn) *n.* **1.** One of the hard, usu. permanent structures projecting from the head of certain mammals, such as sheep, consisting of a bony core covered with a sheath of keratinous material. **2.** A hard protuberance, such as an antler, that is similar to or suggestive of a horn. **3a.** The hard smooth keratinous material forming the outer covering of the horns of cattle or related animals. **b.** A natural or synthetic substance resembling this material. **4.** A container made from a horn. **5.** Something shaped like a horn, esp.: **a.** Either of the ends of a crescent moon. **b.** The point of an anvil. **c.** The pommel of a saddle. **d.** A device for projecting sound waves, as in a loudspeaker. **e.** An electromagnetic transmission antenna with a circular or rectangular cross section. **6.** *Music* **a.** A wind instrument made of an animal horn. **b.** A brass wind instrument, such as a tuba. **c.** A French horn. **d.** A wind instrument, such as a saxophone, used in a jazz band. **7a.** A usu. electrical signaling device that produces a loud resonant sound: *a car horn.* **b.** Any of various noisemakers operated by blowing or by squeezing a hollow rubber bulb. **8.** *Slang* A telephone. ❖ *intr.v.* **horned, horn·ing, horns** To join without being invited; intrude. Used with *in.* —*idioms:* **blow** (or **toot**) **(one's) own horn** *Informal* To brag or boast about oneself. **draw** (or **haul** or **pull) in (one's) horns** *Informal* **1.** To restrain oneself; draw back. **2.** To retreat from a previously taken position, view, or stance. **3.** To economize. **on the horns of a dilemma** Faced

hornbill
great hornbill
Buceros bicornis

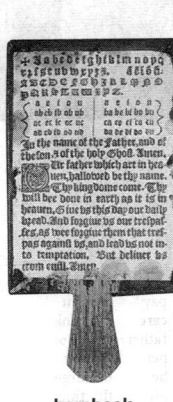

hornbook
17th-century English
hornbook

with two equally undesirable alternatives. [ME < OE. See **ker-¹** in App.] —**horn** *adj.* —**horn′ist** *n.*

Horn, Cape A headland of extreme S Chile in the Tierra del Fuego archipelago; first rounded by the Dutch in 1616.

horn·beam (hôrn′bēm′) *n.* **1.** Any of various trees of the genus *Carpinus,* having smooth grayish bark and hard whitish wood. **2.** The wood of one of these trees.

horn·bill (hôrn′bĭl′) *n.* Any of various tropical Old World birds of the family Bucerotidae, having a very large bill often surmounted by an enlarged protuberance at the base.

horn·blende (hôrn′blĕnd′) *n.* The most common mineral in the amphibole group, $CaNa(Mg,Fe)_4(Al,Fe,Ti)_3Si_6O_{22}(OH,F)_2$, usu. green to black, and common in igneous and metamorphic rocks. [Ger. : *Horn,* horn (< MHGer. *horn* < OHGer.; see **ker-¹** in App.) + *Blende,* blende; see BLENDE.]

horn·book (hôrn′bŏŏk′) *n.* **1.** A one-page primer protected by a transparent sheet of horn, once used to teach children to read. **2.** A text teaching basic skills or introducing a subject.

Horne (hôrn), **Lena** b. 1917. Amer. singer and actress.

Horne, Marilyn b. 1934. Amer. operatic soprano.

horned (hôrnd) *adj.* Having a horn, horns, or a hornlike growth.

horned lizard *n.* Any of several lizards of the genus *Phrynosoma* of western North America and Central America, with hornlike projections on the head, and a flat spiny body.

horned owl *n.* Any of various owls with characteristic ear tufts that resemble horns.

horned toad *n.* See **horned lizard.**

horned viper *n.* A venomous African snake (*Cerastes cornutus*) having a hornlike projection above each eye.

hor·net (hôr′nĭt) *n.* Any of various large stinging wasps of the family Vespidae, chiefly of the genera *Vespa* and *Vespula,* characteristically building large papery nests. [ME *hornet,* alteration of *hernet* < OE *hyrnet.* See **ker-¹** in App.]

hor·nets' nest (hôr′nĭts) *n.* A violent or highly contentious situation.

Hor·ney (hôr′nī), **Karen Danielsen** 1885–1952. German-born Amer. psychoanalyst who emphasized environmental and cultural factors in the development of neurosis.

horn·fels (hôrn′fĕlz′) *n., pl.* **hornfels** A fine-grained metamorphic rock composed of quartz, feldspar, mica, and other minerals, formed by the action of intrusive rock upon sedimentary rock, esp. shale. [Ger. : *Horn,* horn; see HORNBLENDE + *Fels,* rock, cliff (< MHGer. *vels* < OHGer. *felis*).]

horn fly *n.* A small black European fly (*Haematobia irritans*) that sucks blood from cattle, usu. at the base of the horn.

horn·ing (hôr′nĭng) *n.* Upstate New York, Northern Pennsylvania, & Western New England See **shivaree.**

hor·ni·to (hôr-nē′tō) *n., pl.* **-tos** A low mound of volcanic origin, sometimes emitting smoke or vapor. [Sp., dim. of *horno,* oven < Lat. *furnus.* See **gʷʰer-** in App.]

horn of plenty *n., pl.* **horns of plenty** See **cornucopia** 1.

horn·pipe (hôrn′pīp′) *n.* **1.** A musical instrument with a single reed, finger holes, and a bell and mouthpiece made of horn. **2a.** A spirited British folk dance originally accompanied by this instrument. **b.** The music accompanying such a dance.

horn-rims (hôrn′rĭmz′) *pl.n.* Eyeglasses with frames made of horn or a hornlike material, such as tortoiseshell. [Prob. backformation < *horn-rimmed (glasses).*]

horn·swog·gle (hôrn′swŏg′əl) *tr.v.* **-gled, -gling, -gles** *Chiefly Northern & Western US* To bamboozle; deceive. [?]

horn·tail (hôrn′tāl′) *n.* Any of various sawflies of the family Siricidae, the female of which has a long stout ovipositor.

horn·worm (hôrn′wûrm′) *n.* The larva of the hawk moth, having a hornlike posterior segment.

horn·wort (hôrn′wûrt′, -wôrt′) *n.* Any of several submerged plants of the genus *Ceratophyllum,* forming branched masses in quiet water and having finely dissected whorled leaves. [< the appearance of the branched stems.]

horn·y (hôr′nē) *adj.* **-i·er, -i·est 1.** Having horns or hornlike projections. **2.** Made of horn or a similar substance. **3.** Tough and calloused: *horny skin.* **4.** *Vulgar Slang* **a.** Desirous of sexual activity. **b.** Sexually aroused. [Sense 4 < HORN, an erection.] —**horn′i·ness** *n.*

hor·o·loge (hôr′ə-lōj′, hŏr′-) *n.* A device, such as a clock, for telling time. [ME *orloge* < OFr. < Lat. *hōrologium* < Gk. *hōrologion,* hour, season; see **yēr-** in App. + *legein,* to speak; see **leg-** in App.]

hor·o·log·ic (hôr′ə-lŏj′ĭk, hŏr′-) also **hor·o·log·i·cal** (-ĭ-kəl) *adj.* Of or relating to horology or a horologe.

ho·rol·o·gist (hô-rŏl′ə-jĭst) also **ho·rol·o·ger** (-jər) *n.* One who practices or is skilled in horology.

Hor·o·lo·gi·um (hôr′ə-lō′jē-əm, hŏr′-) *n.* A constellation in the Southern Hemisphere near Hydrus, Eridanus, and Reticulum. [Lat. *hōrologium,* horologe. See HOROLOGE.]

ho·rol·o·gy (hô-rŏl′ə-jē) *n.* **1.** The science of measuring time. **2.** The art of making timepieces. [Gk. *hōrā,* hour, season; see **yēr-** in App. + -LOGY.]

hor·o·scope (hôr′ə-skōp′, hŏr′-) *n.* **1a.** The aspect of the planets and stars at a given moment, as of a person's birth, used by astrologers. **b.** A diagram of the signs of the zodiac based on such an aspect. **2.** An astrological forecast, as of a person's future, based on such a diagram. [Fr. < OFr. < Lat. *hōroscopus* < Gk. *hō-roskopos* : *hōrā*, hour, season; see **yēr-** in App. + *skopos*, observer; see **spek-** in App.]

Ho·ro·witz (hôr′ə-wĭts, hŏr′-), **Vladimir** 1904–89. Russian-born Amer. pianist noted for his interpretations of Chopin and Liszt.

hor·ren·dous (hô-rĕn′dəs, hə-) *adj.* Hideous; dreadful. [< Lat. *horrendus* < gerundive of *horrēre*, to tremble.] **—hor·ren′dous·ly** *adv.*

hor·rent (hôr′ənt, hŏr′-) *adj. Archaic* Covered with bristles; bristling. [Lat. *horrēns, horrent-*, pr. part. of *horrēre*, to tremble, bristle.]

hor·ri·ble (hôr′ə-bəl, hŏr′-) *adj.* **1.** Arousing or tending to arouse horror; dreadful. **2.** Very unpleasant; disagreeable. [ME < OFr. < Lat. *horribilis* < *horrēre*, to tremble.] **—hor′ri·ble·ness** *n.* **—hor′ri·bly** *adv.*

hor·rid (hôr′ĭd, hŏr′-) *adj.* **1.** Causing horror; dreadful. **2.** Extremely disagreeable; offensive. **3.** *Archaic* Bristling; rough. [Alteration (influenced by Lat. *horridus*, bristling) of ME *horred*, p. part. of *horren*, to bristle < Lat. *horrēre*, to tremble, bristle.] **—hor′rid·ly** *adv.* **—hor′rid·ness** *n.*

hor·rif·ic (hô-rĭf′ĭk, hŏ-) *adj.* Causing horror; terrifying. [Lat. *horrificus* : *horrēre*, to tremble + *-ficus*, *-fic.*] **—hor·rif′i·cal·ly** *adv.*

hor·ri·fy (hôr′ə-fī′, hŏr′-) *tr.v.* **-fied, -fy·ing, -fies** **1.** To cause to feel horror. **2.** To cause unpleasant surprise; shock. [Lat. *horrificāre* < *horrificus*, horrific. See HORRIFIC.] **—hor′ri·fi·ca′tion** (-fĭ-kā′shən) *n.*

hor·rip·i·la·tion (hô-rĭp′ə-lā′shən, hŏ-) *n.* The bristling of the body hair, as from fear; goose bumps. [LLat. *horripilātiō, horripilātiōn-* < Lat. *horripilātus*, p. part. of *horripilāre*, to bristle with hairs : *horrēre*, to tremble + *pilāre*, to grow hair (< *pilus*, hair).] **—hor·rip′i·late′** *v.*

hor·ror (hôr′ər, hŏr′-) *n.* **1.** An intense painful feeling of repugnance and fear. See Syns at **fear. 2.** Intense dislike; abhorrence. **3.** A cause of horror. **4.** *Informal* Something unpleasant, ugly, or disagreeable. **5.** **horrors** *Informal* Intense nervous depression or anxiety. Often used with *the.* [ME *horrour* < OFr. *horreur* < Lat. *horror* < *horrēre*, to tremble.]

horror show *n. Informal* **1.** A situation or example of great horror. **2.** Something provoking great dismay or disgust.

hors de com·bat (ôr′ də kôⁿ-bä′) *adv. & adj.* Out of action; disabled. [Fr. : *hors*, out + *de*, of + *combat*, combat.]

hors d'oeuvre (ôr dûrv′) *n., pl.* **hors d'oeuvres** (ôr dûrvz′) or **hors d'oeuvre** An appetizer served before a meal. [Fr. *hors d'œuvre*, outside + *de*, of + *œuvre*, (the main) work.]

horse (hôrs) *n.* **1a.** A large hoofed mammal (*Equus caballus*) having a short-haired coat, a long mane, and a long tail, domesticated for riding and for drawing or carrying loads. **b.** An adult male horse; a stallion. **c.** Any of various equine mammals, such as certain extinct forms that are related ancestrally to the modern horse. **2.** A frame or device, usu. with four legs, used for supporting or holding. **3.** *Sports* A vaulting horse. **4.** *Slang* Heroin. **5.** Horsepower. Often used in the plural. **6.** Cavalry. **7.** *Geology* **a.** A block of rock interrupting a vein and containing no minerals. **b.** A displaced rock caught along a fault. ❖ *v.* **horsed, hors·ing, hors·es** —*tr.* **1.** To provide with a horse. **2.** To haul or hoist energetically. —*intr.* To be in heat. Used of a mare. ❖ *adj.* **1.** Of or relating to horses. **2.** Mounted on horses. **3.** Drawn or operated by a horse. **4.** Larger or cruder than others of its kind. —*phrasal verb:* **horse around** *Informal* To indulge in horseplay or frivolous activity. —*idioms:* **a horse of another (or different) color** Another matter entirely; something else. **beat (or flog) a dead horse 1.** To continue to pursue a hopeless cause. **2.** To dwell tiresomely on a decided matter. **on (one's) high horse** Disdainfully self-righteous. **hold (one's) horses** To restrain oneself. **the horse's mouth** A source of information regarded as original or unimpeachable. [ME < OE *hors.*]

horse·back (hôrs′băk′) *n.* **1.** The back of a horse. **2.** A natural ridge; a hogback. ❖ *adv. & adj.* On the back of a horse.

horse bean *n.* See **broad bean.**

horse chestnut *n.* **1.** Any of several trees of the genus *Aesculus,* esp. the European species *A. hippocastanum,* having opposite, palmately compound leaves, erect flower clusters, and spiny or smooth capsules containing large brown seeds. **2.** The seed of any of these plants. [Perh. < having once been used to cure cough in horses.]

horse·feath·ers (hôrs′fĕth′ərs) *Slang n.* (*used with a sing. verb*) Nonsense; foolishness. ❖ *interj.* Used to express disagreement or exasperation. [Alteration of HORSESHIT.]

horse·flesh (hôrs′flĕsh′) *n.* **1.** The flesh of a horse. **2.** Horses considered as a group, esp. for driving, riding, or racing.

horse·fly also **horse fly** (hôrs′flī′) *n.* Any of numerous large flies of the family Tabanidae, the females of which suck the blood of various mammals.

horse gentian *n.* Any of various plants of the genus *Triosteum,* having small purplish-brown flowers and leathery fruit.

horse·hair (hôrs′hâr′) *n.* **1.** The hair of a horse, esp. from the mane or tail. **2.** Cloth made from the hair of horses.

horsehair worm *n.* Any of various aquatic worms of the phylum Nematomorpha, the larvae of which are parasitic within insects.

horse·hide (hôrs′hīd′) *n.* **1.** The hide of a horse. **2.** Leather made from the hide of a horse.

horse latitudes *pl.n.* Either of two belts of latitudes located over the oceans at about 30° to 35° north and south, having high barometric pressure, calms, and light changeable winds. [Poss. < Sp. *golfo de las yeguas*, mares' sea.]

horse·laugh (hôrs′lăf′, -läf′) *n. Informal* A loud coarse laugh; a guffaw.

horse·leech (hôrs′lēch′) *n.* Any of several large leeches of the genus *Haemopis.*

horse·less carriage (hôrs′lĭs) *n.* An automobile.

horse mackerel *n.* **1.** See **saurel** 1. **2.** Any of several tunas or related fishes.

horse·man (hôrs′mən) *n.* **1a.** A man who rides a horse. **b.** A man skilled in equitation. **2.** A man who breeds and raises horses.

horse·man·ship (hôrs′mən-shĭp′) *n.* The skill of riding horses; equitation.

horse·mint (hôrs′mĭnt′) *n.* **1.** A perennial aromatic eastern North American plant (*Monarda punctata*) having opposite leaves and yellowish flowers with purple spots. **2.** A Eurasian wild mint (*Mentha longifolia*) having long opposite leaves and dense spikelike clusters of flowers.

horse nettle *n.* A prickly-stemmed plant (*Solanum carolinense*) of eastern and central North America having purplish or white star-shaped flowers and yellowish berries.

horse opera *n.* A film or other theatrical work about the American West; a western.

horse·play (hôrs′plā′) *n.* Rowdy or rough play.

horse·play·er (hôrs′plā′ər) *n.* One who regularly bets on horse-races.

horse·pow·er (hôrs′pou′ər) *n., pl.* **horsepower 1.** A unit of power in the US Customary System, equal to 745.7 watts or 33,000 foot-pounds per minute. **2.** The power of a horse in pulling. **3.** *Informal* Effective strength: *political horsepower.*

horse·race or **horse race** (hôrs′rās′) *n.* **1.** A contest in which horses ridden by jockeys are raced. **2.** A closely fought contest or competition. **—horse′rac′ing** *n.*

horse·rad·ish (hôrs′răd′ĭsh) *n.* **1a.** A Eurasian plant (*Armoracia rusticana*) in the mustard family, having a pungent root, large basal leaves, and white flowers. **b.** The roots of this plant. **2a.** A sharp condiment made from the grated roots of this plant. **b.** Any of various pungent condiments resembling horseradish, such as wasabi.

horse sense *n. Informal* Common sense; gumption.

horse·shit (hôrs′shĭt′, hôrsh′-) *n.* **1.** *Vulgar* Horse feces. **2.** *Vulgar Slang* Meaningless or insincere talk or action. ❖ *interj. Vulgar Slang* Used to express disagreement or exasperation.

horse·shoe (hôrs′shoo′, hôrsh′-) *n.* **1.** A flat U-shaped metal plate fitted and nailed to the bottom of a horse's hoof for protection. **2.** A U-shaped object similar to a horseshoe. **3.** **horseshoes** (*used with a sing. verb*) A game in which players toss horseshoes at a stake. ❖ *tr.v.* **-shoed, -shoe·ing, -shoes** To fit with horseshoes.

horseshoe crab *n.* Any of various marine arthropods of the class Merostomata, esp. *Limulus polyphemus* or *Xiphosura polyphemus* of eastern North America, having a large rounded body and a stiff pointed tail.

Horseshoe Falls See **Canadian Falls.**

horse·tail (hôrs′tāl′) *n.* Any of various nonflowering plants of the genus *Equisetum,* having a jointed hollow stem and narrow, sometimes much reduced leaves.

horse-trad·ing (hôrs′trā′dĭng) *n.* Negotiation characterized by hard bargaining and shrewd exchange. **—horse trade** *n.* **—horse′-trade′** *v.* **—horse trader** *n.*

horse·weed (hôrs′wēd′) *n.* A weedy North American plant (*Erigeron canadensis*) having narrow leaves and numerous small white or greenish flower heads grouped in panicles.

horse·whip (hôrs′hwĭp′, -wĭp′) *n.* A whip used to control a horse. ❖ *tr.v.* **-whipped, -whip·ping, -whips** To beat with or as if with a horsewhip.

horse·wom·an (hôrs′woom′ən) *n.* **1a.** A woman who rides a horse. **b.** A woman skilled in equitation. **2.** A woman who breeds and raises horses.

horst (hôrst) *n.* A mass of the earth's crust that lies between two faults and is higher than the surrounding land. [Ger. < MHGer. *hurst*, thicket < OHGer.]

hors·y also **hors·ey** (hôr′sē) *adj.* **-i·er, -i·est 1.** Of, relating to, or resembling horses or a horse. **2.** Devoted to horses and horsemanship: *the horsy set.* **3.** Large and clumsy: *a horsy bureau.* **—hors′i·ly** *adv.* **—hors′i·ness** *n.*

hor·ta·tive (hôr′tə-tĭv) *adj.* Hortatory. [LLat. *hortātīvus* < Lat. *hortātus*, p. part. of *hortārī*, to exhort.]

hor·ta·to·ry (hôr′tə-tôr′ē, -tōr′ē) *adj.* Marked by exhortation or strong urging: *a hortatory speech.* [LLat. *hortātōrius* < Lat. *hortātus*, exhorted. See HORTATIVE.]

hor·ti·cul·ture (hôr′tĭ-kŭl′chər) *n.* **1.** The science or art of cultivating fruits, vegetables, flowers, or ornamental plants. **2.** The cultivation of a garden. [Lat. *hortus*, garden; see **gher-** in App. + (AGRI)CULTURE.] **—hor′ti·cul′tur·al** *adj.* **—hor′ti·cul′tur·al·ly** *adv.* **—hor′ti·cul′tur·ist** *n.*

Hor·ton River (hôr′tn) A river, c. 443 km (275 mi), of N North-

Lena Horne

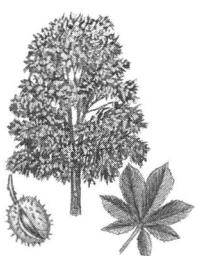

horse chestnut
Aesculus hippocastanum

ă	pat	oi	boy
ā	pay	ou	out
âr	care	ŏŏ	took
ä	father	ōō	boot
ĕ	pet	ŭ	cut
ē	be	ûr	urge
ĭ	pit	th	thin
ī	pie	th	this
îr	pier	hw	which
ŏ	pot	zh	vision
ō	toe	ə	about,
ô	paw		item

Stress marks:
′ (primary);
′ (secondary), as in
lexicon (lĕk′sĭ-kŏn′)

west Terrs., Canada, flowing into Franklin Bay, an inlet of the Beaufort Sea.

Ho·rus (hôr′əs, hōr′-) *n. Mythology* The ancient Egyptian god of the sun, son of Osiris and Isis.

Hos. *abbr. Bible* Hosea

ho·san·na also **ho·san·nah** (hō-zăn′ə) *interj.* Used to express praise or adoration to God. ❖ *n.* **1.** A cry of "hosanna." **2.** A shout of fervent and worshipful praise. [ME *osanna* < OE < LLat. *ōsanna* < Gk. *hōsanna* < Heb. *hôšaʿ-nā′*, deliver us : *hôšaʿ*, second pers. sing. imper. of *hôšîaʿ*, to save + *-nā′*, injunctive particle.]

hose (hōz) *n., pl.* **hose** or **hos·es 1.** *pl.* **hose** Stockings; socks. Used only in the plural. **2.** *pl.* **hose a.** Close-fitting breeches or leggings reaching up to the hips and fastened to a doublet, formerly worn by men. Used only in the plural. **b.** Breeches reaching down to the knees. Used only in the plural. **3.** *pl.* **hos·es** A flexible tube for conveying liquids or gases under pressure. ❖ *tr.v.* **hosed, hos·ing, hos·es 1.** To water, drench, or wash with a hose: *hosed down the deck.* **2.** *Slang* To attack and kill (someone), typically by use of a firearm. [ME, a stocking < OE *hosa*, leg covering. See **(s)keu-** in App.]

Ho·se·a¹ (hō-zē′ə, -zā′ə) A Hebrew prophet of the 8th cent. B.C. [Heb. *hôšēaʿ*, salvation < *hôšîaʿ*, to save.]

Ho·se·a² (hō-zē′ə, -zā′ə) *n.* See table at **Bible.** [After HOSEA¹.]

ho·sel (hō′zəl) *n.* The socket or neck in the head of a golf club into which the shaft is inserted. [Dim. of HOSE.]

ho·sey (hō′zē) *intr.v.* **-seyed, -sey·ing, -seys** *New England* To choose sides for a children's game. [Perh. < Fr. *(je) choisis*, (I) choose, first pers. sing. pr. of *choisir*, to choose < OFr. See CHOICE.]

ho·sier·y (hō′zhə-rē) *n.* **1.** Socks and stockings; hose. **2.** *Chiefly British* Stockings, socks, and underclothing. [< *hosier*, stocking maker < ME < *hose*, stocking; see HOSE.]

hos·pice (hŏs′pĭs) *n.* **1.** A shelter or lodging, as for travelers, esp. one maintained by a monastic order. **2.** A program or facility that provides palliative care and attends to the needs of the terminally ill. [Fr. < OFr. < Lat. *hospitium*, hospitality < *hospes, hospit-*, host. See **ghos-ti-** in App.]

hos·pi·ta·ble (hŏs′pĭ-tə-bəl, hŏ-spĭt′ə-bəl) *adj.* **1.** Disposed to treat guests with warmth and generosity. **2.** Indicative of cordiality toward guests: *a hospitable act.* **3.** Having an open mind; receptive. **4.** Favorable to growth and development; agreeable. [Obsolete Fr. < Med.Lat. **hospitābilis* < Lat. *hospitāre*, to put up as a guest < *hospes, hospit-*, guest, host. See **ghos-ti-** in App.] —**hos′pi·ta·bly** *adv.*

hos·pi·tal (hŏs′pĭ-tl, -pĭt′l) *n.* **1.** An institution that provides care and treatment for the sick or the injured. **2.** *Chiefly British* A charitable institution, such as an orphanage. **3.** A repair shop for specified items: *a doll hospital.* **4.** *Archaic* A hospice for travelers or pilgrims. [ME, hospice < OFr. *ospital* < Med.Lat. *hospitāle* < neut. of Lat. *hospitālis*, of a guest < *hospes, hospit-*, guest. See **ghos-ti-** in App.]

Hos·pi·tal·er also **Hos·pi·tal·ler** (hŏs′pĭt′l-ər) *n.* **1.** A member of a military religious order founded among crusaders in 12th-century Jerusalem to care for sick and needy pilgrims. **2.** A member of any of several religious orders who care for sick or needy persons. [ME *Hospiteler* < OFr. *hospitalier* < Med.Lat. *hospitālārius*, giver of hospitality < *hospitāle*, hospice. See HOSPITAL.]

Hos·pi·ta·let (hŏs′pĭt-l-ĕt′, ŏs′pē-tä-lĕt′) A city of NE Spain, a suburb of Barcelona. Pop. 272,578.

hos·pi·tal·ist (hŏs′pĭt-l-ĭst) *n.* A physician, usu. an internist, who specializes in the care of hospitalized patients.

hos·pi·tal·i·ty (hŏs′pĭ-tăl′ĭ-tē) *n., pl.* **-ties 1.** Cordial and generous reception of or disposition toward guests. **2.** An instance of such treatment. [ME *hospitalite* < OFr. < Lat. *hospitālitās* < *hospitālis*, of a guest. See HOSPITAL.]

hos·pi·tal·i·za·tion (hŏs′pĭ-tl-ĭ-zā′shən) *n.* **1a.** The act of placing a person in a hospital as a patient. **b.** The condition of being hospitalized. **2.** Insurance that fully or partially covers a patient's hospital expenses.

hos·pi·tal·ize (hŏs′pĭt-l-īz′) *tr.v.* **-ized, -iz·ing, -iz·es** To place in a hospital for treatment, care, or observation.

host¹ (hōst) *n.* **1.** One who receives or entertains guests in a social or official capacity. **2.** A person who manages an inn or hotel. **3.** One that furnishes facilities and resources for a function or event. **4.** The emcee or interviewer on a radio or television program. **5.** *Biology* The animal or plant on which or in which another organism lives. **6.** *Medicine* The recipient of a transplanted tissue or organ. **7.** *Computer Science* A computer containing data or programs that another computer can access by network or modem. ❖ *tr.v.* **host·ed, host·ing, hosts** *Usage Problem* To serve as host to or at. [ME, host, guest < OFr. < Lat. *hospes, hospit-*. See **ghos-ti-** in App.]

host² (hōst) *n.* **1.** An army. **2.** A great number; a multitude. [ME < OFr. < LLat. *hostis* < Lat., enemy. See **ghos-ti-** in App.]

host³ also **Host** (hōst) *n. Ecclesiastical* The consecrated bread of the Eucharist. [ME < Lat. *hostia*, sacrifice.]

hos·ta (hŏs′tə, hôs′tə) *n.* See **plantain lily.** [NLat. *Hosta*, genus name, after Nicolaus Thomas *Host* (1761–1834), Austrian botanist.]

hos·tage (hŏs′tĭj) *n.* **1.** A person held by one party in a conflict as security that specified terms will be met by the opposing party. **2.** One that serves as security against an implied threat. **3.** One that is manipulated by the demands of another. [ME < OFr., prob. < *host*, guest, host. See HOST¹.]

hos·tel (hŏs′təl) *n.* **1.** An inexpensive lodging place for travelers, esp. young travelers. **2.** An inn; a hotel. ❖ *intr.v.* **-teled, -tel·ing, -tels** To stay at hostels while traveling. [ME, lodging < OFr. < Med.Lat. *hospitāle*, inn. See HOSPITAL.]

hos·tel·er (hŏs′tə-lər) *n.* **1.** A traveler who stays at hostels. **2.** *Archaic* An innkeeper.

hos·tel·ry (hŏs′təl-rē) *n., pl.* **-ries** An inn; a hotel. [ME *hostelrie* < OFr. *hostelerie* < *hostel*, lodging, inn. See HOSTEL.]

host·ess (hō′stĭs) *n.* **1.** A woman who receives or entertains guests in a social or official capacity. **2.** A woman who manages an inn or hotel. **3.** A woman who is the emcee or interviewer on a radio or television program. **4.** A woman who is employed to greet and assist patrons, as in a restaurant. **5.** A woman who is employed to dance with customers in a dance hall or nightclub. See Usage Note at **-ess.**

hos·tile (hŏs′təl, -tīl′) *adj.* **1.** Of, relating to, or characteristic of an enemy: *hostile acts.* **2.** Feeling or showing enmity or ill will; antagonistic. **3.** Unfavorable to health or well-being; inhospitable or adverse: *a hostile climate.* ❖ *n.* **1.** An antagonistic person or thing. **2.** An enemy in warfare. [Lat. *hostīlis* < *hostis*, enemy. See **ghos-ti-** in App.] —**hos′tile·ly** *adv.*

hostile takeover *n.* An acquisition of a firm despite resistance by the target firm's management and board of directors.

hos·til·i·ty (hŏ-stĭl′ĭ-tē) *n., pl.* **-ties 1.** The state of being hostile; antagonism or enmity. **2a.** A hostile act. **b. hostilities** Acts of war; overt warfare.

hos·tler (hŏs′lər, ŏs′-) also **os·tler** (ŏs′-) *n.* **1.** One who is employed to tend horses, esp. at an inn. **2.** One who services a large vehicle or engine, such as a locomotive. [ME < AN *hostiler* < OFr. *hostel*, lodging. See HOSTEL.]

hot (hŏt) *adj.* **hot·ter, hot·test 1a.** Having or giving off heat; capable of burning. **b.** Being at a high temperature. **2.** Being at or exhibiting a temperature higher than normal or desirable: *a hot forehead.* **3.** Causing a burning sensation, as in the mouth; spicy. **4a.** Charged or energized with electricity. **b.** Radioactive, esp. to a dangerous degree. **5a.** Marked by intensity of emotion; ardent or fiery. **b.** Having or displaying great enthusiasm; eager. **6a.** *Informal* Arousing intense interest, excitement, or controversy. **b.** *Informal* Marked by excited activity or energy. **c.** Violent; raging. **7.** *Slang* Sexually excited or exciting. **8.** *Slang* Recently stolen. **b.** Wanted by the police. **9.** Close to a successful solution or conclusion: *hot on the trail.* **10.** *Informal* **a.** Most recent; new or fresh. **b.** Currently very popular or successful. **c.** Requiring immediate action or attention: *a hot opportunity.* **11.** *Slang* Very good or impressive. Often used in the negative: *I'm not so hot at math.* **12.** *Slang* Funny or absurd. **13.** *Slang* **a.** Performing with great skill and daring: *a hot drummer.* **b.** Having or characterized by repeated successes: *a hot goal scorer.* **c.** Fast and responsive: *a hot sports car.* **d.** Unusually lucky. **14.** *Music* Of, relating to, or being an emotionally charged style of performance marked by strong rhythms and improvisation. **15.** Bold and bright. ❖ *n.* **hots** *Slang* Strong sexual attraction or desire. ❖ *adv.* **1.** In a hot manner; hotly. **2.** While hot. ❖ *tr.v.* **hot·ted, hot·ting, hots** *Informal* To cause to increase in intensity or excitement. Often used with *up.* —*idioms:* **hot and bothered** *Informal* In a state of agitated excitement; flustered. **hot and heavy** *Informal* **1.** Passionate or intense. **2.** Characterized by or engaging in amorous or sexual activity. **hot to trot** *Slang* **1.** Sexually avid; lascivious. **2.** Ready and willing; eager. **hot under the collar** *Informal* Angry. **make it hot for** *Slang* To make things uncomfortable or dangerous for. [ME < OE *hāt*.] —**hot′ness** *n.*

hot air *n. Slang* Empty, exaggerated talk.

hot·bed (hŏt′bĕd′) *n.* **1.** An environment conducive to vigorous growth or development, esp. of something undesirable: *a hotbed of intrigue.* **2.** A glass-covered bed of heated soil, used for the germination of seeds or for protecting tender plants.

hot-blood·ed (hŏt′blŭd′ĭd) *adj.* Easily excited or aroused. —**hot′-blood′ed·ness** *n.*

hot·box (hŏt′bŏks′) *n.* An axle or journal box, as on a railway car, that has become overheated by excessive friction.

hot·cake also **hot cake** (hŏt′kāk′) *n.* See **pancake.** —*idiom:* **go (or sell) like hotcakes** *Informal* To be disposed of quickly; be in great demand.

hotch (hŏch) *intr.v.* **hotched, hotch·ing, hotch·es** *Scots* To fidget. [ME, perh. < OFr. *hocher*, to shake, poss. of Gmc. orig.]

hotch·potch (hŏch′pŏch′) *n.* A hodgepodge. [ME *hochepoche*, alteration of *hochepot*, legal pooling of properties < OFr., mixture, stew : *hocher*, to shake together; see HOTCH + *pot*, pot.]

hot cross bun *n.* A sweet bun marked on top with a cross of frosting, traditionally eaten during Lent.

hot dog or **hot·dog** (hŏt′dôg′, -dŏg′) *n.* **1.** A frankfurter, esp. one served hot in a roll. **2.** *Slang* One who performs showy, often

Horus

Harry Houdini

dangerous stunts, as in skiing or surfing. ❖ *interj. Informal* Used to express delight or enthusiasm.

hot-dog (hŏt′dôg′, -dŏg′) *intr.v.* **-dogged, -dog•ging, -dogs** *Slang* To perform daring stunts or ostentatious maneuvers, as while surfing. —**hot′-dog′ger** *n.*

ho•tel (hō-tĕl′) *n.* An establishment that provides lodging and usu. meals and other services for travelers and other paying guests. [Fr. *hôtel* < OFr. *hostel*, hostel. See HOSTEL.]

ho•te•lier (ō′təl-yā′, hō′-) *n.* A manager or owner of a hotel. [Fr. *hôtelier* < OFr. *hostilier* < *hostel*, inn. See HOSTEL.]

ho•tel•keep•er (hō-tĕl′kē′pər) *n.* See **hotelier.**

hot flash *n.* **1.** A sudden brief sensation of heat, caused by a transient dilation of the blood vessels of the skin. **2.** *Slang* A brief important piece of news or other information.

hot•foot (hŏt′fo͝ot′) *intr.v.* **-foot•ed, -foot•ing, -foots** *Informal* To go in haste. Often used with *it.* ❖ *adv.* In haste. ❖ *n., pl.* **-foots** The practical joke of lighting a match secretly inserted between the sole and upper of a victim's shoe.

hot•head (hŏt′hĕd′) *n.* A quick-tempered or impetuous person.

hot•head•ed (hŏt′hĕd′ĭd) *adj.* **1.** Easily angered; quick-tempered. **2.** Impetuous; rash. —**hot′head′ed•ness** *n.*

hot•house (hŏt′hous′) *n.* **1.** A heated greenhouse for plants that require an even, relatively warm temperature. **2.** An environment conducive to vigorous growth or development; a hotbed. ❖ *adj.* **1.** Grown in a hothouse: *a hothouse orchid.* **2.** Delicate and sensitive, as if from growing up in a protective environment. ❖ *tr.v.* **-housed, -hous•ing, -hous•es** To cultivate in a hothouse.

hot line or **hot•line** (hŏt′līn′) *n.* **1.** A direct and immediate telephone linkup, esp. between heads of government, as for use in a crisis. **2.** A telephone line that gives quick and direct access to a source of information or help.

hot•link (hŏt′lĭngk′) *n.* **1.** A connection between two files that automatically updates one whenever the other is updated. **2.** See **link**[1] 7.

hot•ly (hŏt′lē) *adv.* In an intense or fiery way: *a hotly contested will.*

hot metal *n. Printing* Type cast from molten metal.

hot money *n.* Money moved by its owner quickly from one form or investment to another.

hot pants *pl.n.* Very brief tight shorts worn by women.

hot pepper *n.* **1.** The pungent fruit of any of several varieties of *Capsicum annuum* or *C. frutescens.* **2.** See **pepper** 4.

hot plate *n.* **1.** An electrically heated plate for cooking or warming food. **2.** A tabletop cooking device with burners.

hot pot *n. Chiefly British* A stew of lamb or beef and potatoes cooked in a tightly covered pot.

hot potato *n. Informal* A problem that is so controversial or sensitive that those handling it risk unpleasant consequences.

hot rod also **hot-rod** (hŏt′rŏd′) *n. Slang* An automobile that has been rebuilt or modified to increase its speed and acceleration. —**hot′-rod′** *v.* —**hot rodder, hot′-rod′der** *n.*

hot seat *n.* **1.** *Slang* The electric chair. **2.** *Informal* A position in which one is subjected to extreme stress or discomfort.

hot•shot (hŏt′shŏt′) *n.* **1.** *Slang* A person of impressive skill and daring, esp. one who is highly successful and self-assured. **2.** A nonstop freight train. —**hot′shot′** *adj.*

hot spot also **hot•spot** (hŏt′spŏt′) *n.* **1.** An area in which there is dangerous unrest or hostile action. **2.** *Informal* A lively and popular place, such as a nightclub. **3.** An area of intense heat, radiation, or activity.

hot spring *n.* A natural spring that produces warm water.

hot stuff *n. Slang* **1.** One that is exceptionally good, interesting, or exciting. **2.** One who is sexually aroused or arousing.

Hot•ten•tot (hŏt′n-tŏt′) *n., pl.* **Hottentot** or **-tots** *Often Offensive* **1.** A Khoikhoin. **2.** Any of the Khoikhoin group of languages. [Afr.]

hot ticket *n. Slang* One that is extremely popular.

hot•tish (hŏt′ĭsh) *adj.* Somewhat hot.

hot toddy *n.* A drink consisting of whiskey, brandy, or other liquor mixed with hot water, sugar, and spices.

hot tub *n.* A very large tub filled with hot water in which one or more bathers may soak.

hot war *n.* Armed open conflict between nations or factions.

hot water *n.* Trouble; difficulty: *is in political hot water.*

hot-wa•ter bottle (hŏt′wô′tər, -wŏt′ər) *n.* A stoppered container, usu. made of plastic or rubber, filled with hot water and applied to a part of the body for warmth.

hot-wire (hŏt′wīr′) *tr.v.* **-wired, -wir•ing, -wires** *Informal* To start the engine of (an automobile, for example) without a key, as by short-circuiting the ignition system.

hou•dah (hou′də) *n.* Variant of **howdah.**

Hou•dan (ho͞o′dăn′) *n.* A domesticated fowl characterized by black-and-white plumage and a V-shaped comb. [Fr., after *Houdan*, a village of N-central France.]

Hou•di•ni (ho͞o-dē′nē), **Harry** Originally Ehrich Weiss. 1874–1926. Amer. magician known for his spectacular escapes.

Hou•don (ho͞o′dŏn′, o͞o-dôN′), **Jean Antoine** 1741–1828. French sculptor noted esp. for his statue of Washington.

Hough•ton (hōt′n), **Henry Oscar** 1823–95. Amer. publisher who founded (1852) the printing office that became the Houghton Mifflin Company.

hound (hound) *n.* **1a.** A domestic dog of any of various breeds commonly used for hunting, characteristically having drooping ears, a short coat, and a deep resonant voice. **b.** A dog. **2.** A contemptible person; a scoundrel. **3a.** One who eagerly pursues something: *a gossip hound.* **b.** A devotee or enthusiast. ❖ *tr.v.* **hound•ed, hound•ing, hounds 1.** To pursue relentlessly and tenaciously. See Syns at **harass. 2.** To urge insistently; nag. [ME < OE *hund.* See **kwon-** in App.] —**hound′er** *n.*

hound's-tongue (houndz′tŭng′) *n.* Any of several Eurasian plants of the genus *Cynoglossum*, having hairy leaves, small red-dish-purple flowers, and prickly, clinging fruit.

hounds•tooth check or **hound's-tooth check** (houndz′to͞oth′) *n.* A textile design of small broken checks.

hour (our) *n.* **1.** One of the 24 equal parts of a day. **2a.** One of the points on a timepiece marking off 12 or 24 successive intervals of 60 minutes, from midnight to noon and noon to midnight or from midnight to midnight. **b.** The time of day indicated by a 12-hour clock. **c. hours** The time of day determined on a 24-hour basis. **3.** A unit of measure of longitude or right ascension, equal to 15° or 1⁄24 of a great circle. **4a.** A customary or fixed time: *the dinner hour.* **b. hours** A set period of time for a specified activity: *banking hours.* **5a.** A particular time. **b.** A significant time. **c.** The present time. **6a.** The work that can be accomplished in an hour. **b.** The distance that can be traveled in an hour. **7a.** A single session of a school day or class. **b.** A credit hour. **8. hours** *Ecclesiastical* The canonical hours. [ME < OFr. *houre* < Lat. *hōra* < Gk. *hōrā*, season, time. See **yēr-** in App.]

hour angle *n.* The angular distance, measured westward along the celestial equator, between the celestial meridian of the observer and the hour circle passing through a celestial body.

hour circle *n.* A great circle passing through the poles of the celestial sphere and intersecting the celestial equator at right angles.

hour•glass (our′glăs′) *n.* An instrument for measuring time, consisting of two glass chambers connected by a narrow neck and containing a quantity of a flowing substance that trickles from the upper chamber to the lower in a fixed amount of time. ❖ *adj.* Shaped like an hourglass: *an hourglass design.*

hour hand *n.* The short hand on a clock or watch that indicates hours.

hou•ri (ho͝or′ē, ho͞o′rē) *n., pl.* **-ris 1.** A voluptuous, alluring woman. **2.** One of the beautiful virgins of the Koranic paradise. [Fr. < Pers. *ḥūrī* < Ar. *ḥūrīya*, nymph, houri < *ḥūr*, pl. of *'aḥwaru*, possessing *ḥawar*, intense whiteness of the sclera contrasting with deep blackness of the iris of the eye.]

hour•long or **hour-long** (our′lông′, -lŏng′) *adj.* Lasting an hour: *an hourlong television episode.*

hour•ly (our′lē) *adj.* **1.** Occurring every hour: *hourly chimes.* **2.** Frequent; continual. **3.** By the hour as a unit: *hourly pay.* ❖ *adv.* **1.** At or during every hour. **2.** Frequently; continually. ❖ *n., pl.* **-lies** *Informal* An employee paid by the hour.

Hou•sa•ton•ic (ho͞o′sə-tŏn′ĭk) A river rising in W MA and flowing c. 209 km (130 mi) to Long Island Sound.

house (hous) *n., pl.* **hous•es** (hou′zĭz, -sĭz) **1a.** A structure serving as a dwelling for one or more persons, esp. for a family. **b.** A household or family. **2.** Something, such as a burrow or shell, that serves as a shelter or habitation for a wild animal. **3.** A dwelling for a group of people, such as students, who live together as a unit. **4.** A building that functions as the primary shelter or location of something. **5a.** A facility, such as a theater or restaurant, that provides entertainment or food for the public. **b.** The audience or patrons of such an establishment. **6a.** A commercial firm. **b.** A publishing company. **c.** A gambling casino. **d.** *Slang* A house of prostitution. **7.** A residential college within a university. **8a.** often **House** A legislative or deliberative assembly. **b.** The hall or chamber in which such an assembly meets. **c.** A quorum of such an assembly. **9.** often **House** A family line, esp. of a royal or noble family: *the House of Orange.* **10a.** One of the 12 parts into which the heavens are divided in astrology. **b.** The sign of the zodiac indicating the seat or station of a planet in the heavens. ❖ *v.* (houz) **housed, hous•ing, hous•es** —*tr.* **1.** To provide living quarters for. **2.** To shelter, keep, or store in or as if in a house. **3.** To contain; harbor. **4.** To fit into a socket or mortise. **5.** *Nautical* To secure or stow safely. —*intr.* **1.** To reside; dwell. **2.** To take shelter. ***—idioms:* on the house** At the expense of the establishment; free. **put (or set) (one's) house in order** To organize one's affairs in a sensible, logical way. [ME *hous* < OE *hūs.*]

House, Eddie James Known as "Son." 1902–88. Amer. singer and guitarist. During the 1940s he made many blues recordings for the Library of Congress.

house arrest *n.* Confinement to one's quarters, rather than prison, by administrative or judicial order.

house•boat (hous′bōt′) *n.* A barge designed and equipped for use as a dwelling or cruiser.

house•boy (hous′boi′) *n.* A male servant in a house.

house•break (hous′brāk′) *tr.v.* **-broke** (-brōk′), **-bro•ken** (-brō′kən), **-break•ing, -breaks 1.** To train to have excretory habits that are acceptable for indoor living: *housebreak a puppy.* **2.** To subdue; tame. ❖ *n.* Burglary of a dwelling.

house•break•ing (hous′brā′kĭng) *n.* The act of unlawfully breaking into and entering another's house. —**house′break′er** *n.*

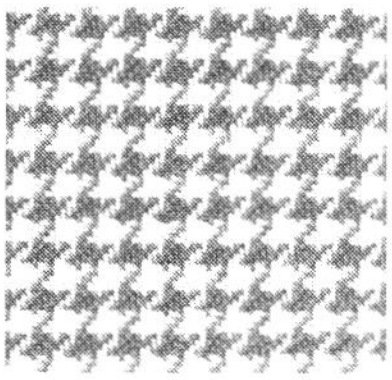

houndstooth check

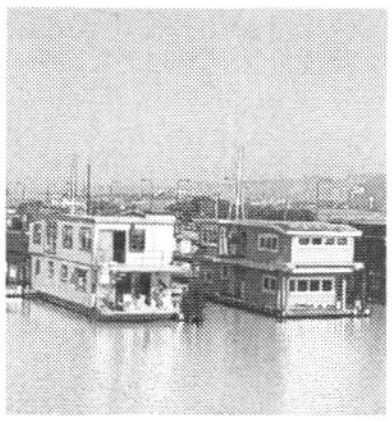

houseboat

ă	**pat**	oi	**boy**
ā	**pay**	ou	**out**
âr	**care**	o͝o	**took**
ä	**father**	o͞o	**boot**
ĕ	**pet**	ŭ	**cut**
ē	**be**	ûr	**urge**
ĭ	**pit**	th	**thin**
ī	**pie**	*th*	**this**
îr	**pier**	hw	**which**
ŏ	**pot**	zh	**vision**
ō	**toe**	ə	**about, item**
ô	**paw**		

Stress marks:
′ (primary);
′ (secondary), as in
lexicon (lĕk′sĭ-kŏn′)

house·bro·ken (hous′brō′kən) *adj.* **1.** Trained to have excretory habits that are appropriate for indoor living: *The dog is housebroken.* **2.** Trained to be docile or compliant.

house call *n.* A professional visit made to a home, esp. by a physician.

house·carl (hous′kärl′) *n.* A member of the bodyguard or household troops of a Danish or Anglo-Saxon king or noble.

house·clean·ing (hous′klē′nǐng) *n.* **1.** The cleaning and tidying of a house and its contents. **2.** *Informal* Removal of unwanted personnel, methods, or policies in an effort at reform or improvement. —**house′clean′** *v.* —**house′clean′er** *n.*

house·coat (hous′kōt′) *n.* A woman's garment, usu. long and loose, used for informal wear at home.

house detective *n.* A detective employed by an establishment, such as a hotel, to prevent theft or misconduct.

house·dress (hous′drĕs′) *n.* A simple washable dress worn for housework.

house finch *n.* See **linnet** 2.

house·fly (hous′flī′) *n.* A widely distributed fly (*Musca domestica*) that frequents human dwellings, breeds in moist or decaying organic matter, and transmits many diseases.

house·ful (hous′fool′) *n.* The amount or number that a house can hold or accommodate: *a houseful of furniture.*

house·guest (hous′gĕst′) *n.* A person who stays in a home as a guest.

house·hold (hous′hōld′) *n.* **1a.** A domestic unit consisting of the members of a family who live together along with nonrelatives. **b.** The living spaces and possessions belonging to such a unit. **2.** A person or group of people occupying a single dwelling: *nonfamily households.* ❖ *adj.* **1.** Of, relating to, or used in a household. **2.** Commonly known; familiar. [ME *houshold* : *hous,* house; see HOUSE + *hold,* possession, holding (< OE < *healdan,* to hold; see HOLD¹).]

household arts *pl.n.* The crafts practiced in households, esp. in earlier times.

house·hold·er (hous′hōl′dər) *n.* **1.** One who occupies or owns a house. **2.** The head of a household.

household word *n.* Someone or something widely known.

house·hus·band (hous′hŭz′bənd) *n.* A married man who manages the household as his main occupation. [HOUSE(WIFE) + HUSBAND.]

house·keep·er (hous′kē′pər) *n.* **1.** One who is employed to perform or direct the domestic tasks in a household. **2.** A housewife. **3.** An employee of an establishment, such as an inn or hotel, who performs or coordinates housekeeping tasks.

house·keep·ing (hous′kē′pǐng) *n.* **1.** Performance or management of household tasks. **2.** Management and maintenance of the property and equipment of an institution or organization. **3.** Routine tasks and procedures carried out in the functioning of an operation or a system. —**house′keep′** *v.*

hou·sel (hou′zəl) *Archaic n.* The Eucharist. ❖ *tr.v.* **-seled, -sel·ing, -sels** To administer the Eucharist to. [ME < OE *hūsel,* sacrifice, Eucharist.]

house·leek (hous′lēk′) *n.* Any of various Old World plants of the genus *Sempervivum,* esp. *S. tectorum,* having a basal rosette of leaves and a cluster of pinkish or purplish flowers.

house·lights (hous′līts′) *pl.n.* The lights that illuminate the audience section of a concert hall, theater, or auditorium.

house·maid (hous′mād′) *n.* A woman or girl employed to do housework.

house·maid's knee (hous′mādz′) *n.* Bursitis in the knee.

house·man (hous′măn′, -mən) *n.* A man employed for cleaning, maintenance, and other general work in a house or hotel.

house martin *n.* An Old World bird (*Delichon urbica*) having blue-black plumage, white underparts, and a forked tail.

house·mas·ter (hous′măs′tər) *n.* A male teacher in charge of a residence hall at a school.

house·mate (hous′māt′) *n.* One who shares a house with another.

house·moth·er (hous′mŭth′ər) *n.* A woman employed as a houseparent.

house mouse *n.* A gray or brownish-gray mouse (*Mus musculus*) that lives in or near buildings and often carries disease.

house music *n.* A style of disco music with a heavy bass beat, initially popularized in underground all-night parties held in abandoned warehouses. [After (*The Ware*)*house,* nightclub in Chicago where it was first popularized.]

House of Burgesses *n.* The lower house of the legislature in colonial Virginia.

house of cards *n., pl.* **houses of cards** A flimsy structure, arrangement, or situation that is in danger of collapsing or failing.

House of Commons *n.* The lower house of Parliament in the United Kingdom and Canada.

house of correction *n., pl.* **houses of correction** An institution for persons convicted of minor criminal offenses.

House of Delegates *n.* The lower house of the state legislature in Maryland, Virginia, and West Virginia.

House of Lords *n.* The upper house of Parliament in the United Kingdom, made up of members of the nobility and high-ranking clergy.

house of prostitution *n., pl.* **houses of prostitution** An estab-

Sam Houston

lishment in which the services of prostitutes are available on the premises.

House of Representatives *n.* The lower house of the US Congress and of most state legislatures.

house organ *n.* A periodical published by a business organization for its employees or clients.

house·par·ent (hous′pâr′ənt, -pǎr′-) *n.* One who supervises a residence, such as a dormitory, for young people.

house party *n.* A party at which guests stay overnight or for several days in a residence, such as the home of the host.

house physician *n.* **1.** A physician, esp. an intern or resident, who cares for hospitalized patients under the supervision of the surgical and medical staff of a hospital. **2.** A physician employed by a hotel or another establishment.

house·plant (hous′plǎnt′) *n.* Any of a wide variety of plants grown indoors, often for decorative purposes.

house-proud (hous′proud′) *adj.* Proud of one's house or its furnishings or upkeep.

house-rais·ing (hous′rā′zǐng) *n.* The construction of a house or its framework by a group of friends or neighbors.

house·room (hous′rōōm′, -rŏōm′) *n.* Space or accommodation in or as if in a house.

house sitter *n.* One who lives in and cares for a house while the usual occupant is away. —**house′sit′** (hous′sǐt′) *v.*

house snake *n.* See **milk snake.**

house sparrow *n.* A small bird (*Passer domesticus*) native to the Old World but widely naturalized and having brown and gray plumage with a black throat in the adult male.

house·top (hous′tŏp′) *n.* The roof of a house. —**idiom: shout (or proclaim) from the housetops** To make known publicly.

house·train *also* **house-train** (hous′trān′) *tr.v.* **-trained, -train·ing, -trains** *Chiefly British* To housebreak.

house·wares (hous′wârz′) *pl.n.* Cooking utensils and other articles used in a household, esp. in the kitchen.

house·warm·ing (hous′wôr′mǐng) *n.* A celebration of the occupancy of a new home.

house·wife (hous′wīf′) *n., pl.* **-wives** (-wīvz′) **1.** A woman who manages the household as her main occupation. **2.** (hŭz′ǐf) A small container for sewing equipment. [ME *houswif* : *hous,* house; see HOUSE + *wif,* wife; see WIFE.]

house·wife·ly (hous′wīf′lē) *adj.* Of, relating to, or suited to a housewife; domestic. —**house′wife′li·ness** *n.*

house·wif·er·y (hous′wī′fə-rē, -wīf′rē) *n.* The function or duties of a housewife; housekeeping.

house·work (hous′wûrk′) *n.* The tasks, such as cleaning and cooking, performed in housekeeping. —**house′work′er** *n.*

hous·ing¹ (hou′zǐng) *n.* **1a.** Buildings or other shelters in which people live. **b.** A place to live; a dwelling. **2.** Provision of lodging or shelter. **3.** Something that covers, protects, or supports, esp.: **a.** A frame, bracket, or box for holding or protecting a mechanical part: *a wheel housing.* **b.** An enclosing frame in which a shaft revolves. **4.** A hole, groove, or slot in a piece of wood into which another piece is inserted. **5.** A niche for a statue.

hous·ing² (hou′zǐng) *n.* **1.** An ornamental or protective covering for a saddle. **2.** Trappings for a horse. Often used in the plural. [< ME *house* < OFr. *houce* < Med.Lat. *hucia, hulcia, hultia,* protective covering, of Gmc. orig. See **kel-** in App.]

housing development *n.* A group of houses or apartment buildings on a site, usu. under a single management.

housing project *n.* A publicly funded and administered housing development, usu. for low-income families.

Hous·man (hous′mən), **A(lfred) E(dward)** 1859–1936. British poet whose works include *A Shropshire Lad* (1896).

Hous·ton (hyōō′stən) A city of SE TX NW of Galveston connected with Galveston Bay and the Gulf of Mexico by the **Houston Ship Channel;** founded 1836. Pop. 1,953,631. —**Hous·to′ni·an** (hyōō-stō′nē-ən) *n.*

Houston, Samuel ("Sam") 1793–1863. Amer. general who was president of the Republic of Texas (1836–38 and 1841–44).

hove (hōv) *tr.v.* Past tense and past participle of **heave** 5. ❖ *intr.v.* Past tense and past participle of **heave** 4.

hov·el (hŭv′əl, hŏv′-) *n.* **1.** A small miserable dwelling. **2.** An open low shed. [ME, hut.]

hov·er (hŭv′ər, hŏv′-) *intr.v.* **-ered, -er·ing, -ers** **1.** To remain floating, suspended, or fluttering in the air: *gulls hovering over the waves.* **2.** To remain or linger in or near a place. **3.** To remain in an uncertain state; waver. ❖ *n.* The act or state of hovering. [ME *hoveren,* freq. of *hoven.*] —**hov′er·er** *n.* —**hov′er·ing·ly** *adv.*

hov·er·craft (hŭv′ər-krǎft′, hŏv′-) *n.* See **air-cushion vehicle.**

HOV lane (āch′ō-vē′) *n.* An expressway lane restricted to vehicles with at least a set minimum of occupants, usu. two. [h(*igh*-)o(*ccupancy*) v(*ehicle*) lane.]

how (hou) *adv.* **1.** In what manner or way; by what means: *How does this machine work?* **2.** In what state or condition: *How are you today?* **3.** To what extent, amount, or degree: *How bad was it?* **4.** For what reason or purpose; why: *How is it that he left early?* **5.** With what meaning: *How should I take that remark?* **6.** By what name: *How is she called?* **7.** By what measure; in what units: *How do you sell this corn?* **8.** What. Usu. used in requesting that something be said again: *How's that again?* **9.** Used as an intensive: *How we laughed!* ❖ *conj.* **1.** The manner or way in which. **2.** That.

3. In whatever way or manner; however: *Cook it how you please.* ❖ *n.* A manner or method of doing something. —*idioms:* **and how** *Informal* Most certainly; you bet. **how about** What is your thought, feeling, or desire regarding. **how about that** *Informal* Used rhetorically to express surprise or wonder at or approval for something. **how come** *Informal* How is it that; why. **how so** How is it so. [ME *howe* < OE *hū.* See **k**ʷ**o-** in App.]

How·ard (houʹərd), **Catherine** 1520?–42. Queen of England as the fifth wife of Henry VIII (1540–42); executed for adultery.

Howard, Henry. 1st Earl of Surrey. 1517?–47. English poet and soldier noted for his sonnets.

how·be·it (hou-bēʹĭt) *adv.* Be that as it may; nevertheless. ❖ *conj. Obsolete* Although.

how·dah also **hou·dah** (houʹdə) *n.* A seat, usu. fitted with a canopy and railing, placed on the back of an elephant or a camel. [Urdu *haudah* < Ar. *hawdaj,* litter, sedan chair < *hadaja,* to shuffle along, totter.]

how·dy (houʹdē) *interj.* Used to express a greeting. [< *how do ye,* how do you do.]

Howe (hou), **Elias** 1819–67. Amer. inventor and manufacturer who designed early sewing machines (1845 and 1846).

Howe, Julia Ward 1819–1910. Amer. writer who was active in the women's suffrage movement and wrote "Battle Hymn of the Republic" (published 1862).

Howe, Richard. Earl Howe. 1726–99. British admiral who conducted naval operations in America (1776–78).

Howe, Sir William. 5th Viscount Howe. 1729–1814. British general in America who defeated George Washington in a number of battles but could not force a surrender.

How·ells (houʹəlz), **William Dean** 1837–1920. Amer. writer and editor (1871–81) of the *Atlantic Monthly.*

how·ev·er (hou-ĕvʹər) *adv.* **1.** In whatever manner or way: *However he did it, it was very clever.* **2.** To whatever degree or extent. **3.** In what way. Used as an intensive of *how: However did you get here so soon?* **4.** In spite of that; nevertheless; yet: *The book is expensive; however, it's worth it.* **5.** On the other hand; by contrast. ❖ *conj.* **1.** In whatever manner or way: *Dress however you like.* **2.** *Archaic* Notwithstanding that; although.

USAGE NOTE Although some grammarians have insisted that *however* should not be used to begin a sentence, this rule has been ignored by a number of reputable writers. Forty-two percent of Usage Panelists say they do not follow the rule in their own writing, 19 percent say they observe it only sometimes, and 36 percent say they usually observe it. • When meaning "nevertheless" or "by contrast" and not coming at the end of a sentence, *however* should be followed by a comma in writing (*However, he didn't make it*), and unless it begins a sentence it should be preceded by punctuation too—by a semicolon if it begins its clause (*I thought he would come; however, he didn't make it*), otherwise by another comma (*He, however, didn't make it*). See Usage Notes at **but, whatever.**

how·it·zer (houʹĭt-sər) *n.* A relatively short cannon that delivers shells at a medium muzzle velocity, usu. by a high trajectory. [Du. *houwitser* < Ger. *Haubitze,* alteration of obsolete *haufnitz,* catapult < O Czech *haufnice,* prob. < *haufný,* catapult that slung many stones at once : *hauf,* group, heap (prob. < MHGer. *hūfe* < OHGer. *hūfo*) + *-ný,* n. suff.]

howl (houl) *v.* **howled, howl·ing, howls** —*intr.* **1.** To utter a long, mournful, plaintive sound. **2.** To cry or wail loudly, as in pain. **3.** *Slang* To laugh heartily. **4.** *Slang* To go on a spree. —*tr.* To express or utter with a howl. See Syns at **shout.** ❖ *n.* **1.** A long wailing cry. **2.** A loud derisive call. **3.** *Slang* Something uproariously funny or absurd. —*phrasal verb:* **howl down** To drown out or silence by loud derisive calls. [ME *houlen.*]

howl·er (houʹlər) *n.* **1.** One that howls. **2.** A howler monkey. **3.** *Slang* A laughably stupid blunder.

howler monkey *n.* Any of several monkeys of the genus *Alouatta* of tropical America, having a long prehensile tail and an extremely loud howling call.

howl·ing (houʹlĭng) *adj.* **1.** Marked by the sound of howling. **2.** Desolate; wild. **3.** *Slang* Very great; tremendous.

Howl·in' Wolf (houʹlĭn) Pseudonym of Chester Arthur Burnett. 1910–76. Amer. blues singer and musician noted for the baying cries that characterized his singing style.

How·rah (houʹrə, -rä) A city of E India on the Hugli R. opposite Calcutta. Pop. 950,435.

how·so·ev·er (houʹsō-ĕvʹər) *adv.* **1.** To whatever degree or extent. **2.** By whatever means.

how-to (houʹtoōʹ) *Informal adj.* Offering practical advice and detailed instruction in an activity. ❖ *n., pl.* **how-tos** Something, such as a book or learning situation, that provides practical advice and detailed instruction in an activity.

hoy[1] (hoi) *n.* **1.** A small sloop-rigged coasting ship. **2.** A heavy barge used for freight. [ME *hoie* < MDu. *hoey, hoede.*]

hoy[2] (hoi) *interj.* Used to attract attention.

hoy·a (hoiʹə) *n.* Any of several evergreen climbing vines or shrubs of the genus *Hoya,* having opposite simple leaves and axillary umbellate flower clusters. [NLat. *Hoya,* genus name, after Thomas *Hoy* (1750?–1822), British gardener.]

hoy·den (hoidʹn) *n.* A high-spirited or boisterous girl. ❖ *adj.*

High-spirited; boisterous. [< earlier *hoyden,* a rude youth, prob. < Du. *heiden,* heathen, boor < MDu. *heiden,* heathen.]

Hoyle (hoil) *n.* A reference book of rules for card games and other indoor games. —*idiom:* **according to Hoyle** In accord with the prescribed rules or regulations. [After Edmond *Hoyle* (1672?–1769), British writer on games.]

hp *abbr.* horsepower

HP *abbr.* high pressure

HPV *abbr.* human papillomavirus

HQ *abbr.* headquarters

HR *abbr.* **1.** heart rate **2.** House of Representatives **3.** home rule **4.** home run **5.** human resources

hr. *abbr.* hour

Hr. *abbr.* Herr

H. Rept. *abbr.* House Report

H. Res. *abbr.* House Resolution

HRH *abbr.* Her (or His) Royal Highness

Hrod·na (hrôdʹnə) or **Grod·no** (grôdʹnō, -nə) A city of W Belarus on the Neman R. near the Polish border. Pop. 247,000.

Hrolf (rôlf, hrôlf) See **Rollo.**

HRT *abbr.* hormone replacement therapy

hryv·nia (hrĭvʹnyä) See table at **currency.** [Ukrainian, prob. < Russ. *grivnya,* var. of *grivna,* pendant worn from the neck, obsolete Russ. unit of currency < *griva,* mane.]

Hs The symbol for the element **hassium.**

HS *abbr.* high school

HSH *abbr.* Her (or His) Serene Highness

Hsian (shyän) See **Xi'an.**

Hsiang Kiang (shyängʹ kyängʹ) See **Xiang Jiang.**

Hsin·king (shĭnʹgĭngʹ) See **Changchun.**

HST *abbr.* **1.** Hawaii-Aleutian Standard Time **2.** hypersonic transport

ht *abbr.* height

HT *abbr.* **1.** halftime **2.** high-tension **3.** high tide

HTLV-I (āchʹtē-ĕlʹvē-wŭnʹ) *n.* A retrovirus associated with certain leukemias and lymphomas and with demyelinating diseases such as multiple sclerosis. [H(UMAN) T(-CELL) L(YMPHOTROPIC) V(IRUS) I.]

HTLV-III (āchʹtē-ĕlʹvē-thrēʹ) *n.* HIV. [H(UMAN) T(-CELL) L(YM-PHOTROPIC) V(IRUS) III.]

HTML (āchʹtē-ĕm-ĕlʹ) *n.* A markup language used to structure text and multimedia documents and to set up hypertext links between documents. [H(yper)t(ext) M(arkup) L(anguage).]

Hts. *abbr.* heights

HTTP or **http** (āchʹtē-tē-pēʹ) *n.* A protocol used to request and transmit files over the Internet or other computer network. [H(yper)t(ext) T(ransfer) P(rotocol).]

HUAC (hyōōʹăkʹ) *abbr.* House Un-American Activities Committee

Huai·nan (hwīʹnänʹ) A city of E-central China WNW of Nanjing. Pop. 1,228,052.

Hua·la·pai or **Wa·la·pai** (wäʹlə-pīʹ) *n., pl.* **Hualapai** or **-pais** or **Walapai** or **-pais 1.** A member of a Native American people inhabiting northwest Arizona south of the Grand Canyon. **2.** The Yuman language of the Hualapai. [Mohave *hwa·lʹapay,* pine person : *hwa·lʹa,* pine + *-pay,* person.]

Hual·la·ga (wä-yäʹgä) A river rising in W-central Peru and flowing c. 1,126 km (700 mi) to the Marañón R.

Huang He (hwängʹ hĕʹ) also **Hwang Ho** (hōʹ) or **Yellow River** A river of N China rising in the Kunlun Mts. and flowing c. 4,827 km (3,000 mi) to the Bo Hai.

hua·ra·che (wə-räʹchē, hə-) *n.* A flat-heeled sandal with an upper of woven leather strips. [Am.Sp. *huarache, guarache* < Tarascan *huarache,* straw sandal.]

Huás·car (wäsʹkärʹ) d. 1532. Incan emperor who fought with his brother Atahualpa over the division of the empire and was assassinated after the Spanish conquest.

Huas·ca·rán (wäsʹkə-ränʹ, -kä-) An extinct volcano, 6,770.4 m (22,198 ft), in the Andes of W-central Peru.

Huay·na Ca·pac (wīʹnä kä-päkʹ) d. 1525. Incan emperor (1493–1525) under whom the empire reached its greatest extent.

hub (hŭb) *n.* **1.** The center part of a wheel, fan, or propeller. **2.** A center of activity or interest; a focal point. See Syns at **center.** [Prob. alteration of HOB[1].]

Hub·bard (hŭbʹərd), **Mount** A peak, 4,559.8 m (14,950 ft), in the Coast Mts. of SE AK.

hubbard squash *n. Northern & Western US* A variety of winter squash. [< the surname *Hubbard.*]

Hub·ble (hŭbʹəl), **Edwin Powell** 1889–1953. Amer. astronomer who discovered (1929) that the velocities of nebulae increase with distance.

hub·ble-bub·ble (hŭbʹəl-bŭbʹəl) *n.* **1.** An uproar; a hubbub. **2.** See **hookah.** [Reduplication and alteration of BUBBLE.]

Hub·ble's constant (hŭbʹəlz) *n.* A ratio expressing the rate of apparent expansion of the universe, equal to the velocity at which a typical galaxy is receding from Earth divided by its distance from Earth. [After Edwin Powell HUBBLE.]

hub·bub (hŭbʹŭb) *n.* **1.** Loud noise; din. See Syns at **noise. 2.** Confusion; tumult. [Prob. of Ir.Gael. orig.]

hub·by (hŭbʹē) *n., pl.* **-bies** *Informal* A husband. [Alteration of HUSBAND.]

Julia Ward Howe
photographed in 1908

huarache
pair of huaraches

ă pat   oi boy
ā pay   ou out
âr care   ōō took
ä father   ōō boot
ĕ pet   ŭ cut
ē be   ûr urge
ĭ pit   *th* thin
ī pie   *th* this
îr pier   hw which
ŏ pot   zh vision
ō toe   ə about,
ô paw   item

Stress marks:
ʹ (primary);
ʹ (secondary), as in
lexicon (lĕkʹsĭ-kŏnʹ)

hub•cap (hŭb′kăp′) *n.* A round covering over the hub of the wheel of a motor vehicle.

Hu•bei (hōō′bā′) also **Hu•pei** or **Hu•peh** (-pā′) A province of E-central China. Cap. Wuhan. Pop. 53,969,210.

Hu•bel (hyōō′bəl), **David** b. 1926. Amer. neurobiologist who shared a 1981 Nobel Prize.

Hu•bli-Dhar•war (hōōb′lē-där-wär′) A city of SW India NW of Bangalore; est. 1961. Pop. 648,298.

hu•bris (hyōō′brĭs) also **hy•bris** (hī′-) *n.* Overbearing pride or presumption; arrogance. [Gk., excessive pride, wanton violence. See ud- in App.] —**hu•bris′tic** (-brĭs′tĭk) *adj.* —**hu•bris′tic•al•ly** *adv.*

huck•a•back (hŭk′ə-băk′) *n.* A coarse absorbent cotton or linen fabric used esp. for toweling. [?]

huck•le•ber•ry (hŭk′əl-bĕr′ē) *n.* **1.** Any of various New World shrubs of the genus *Gaylussacia*, related to the blueberries. **2.** The glossy, blackish, many-seeded edible berry of these plants. [Prob. alteration of *hurtleberry*, whortleberry. See WHORTLEBERRY.]

huck•ster (hŭk′stər) *n.* **1.** One who sells wares or provisions in the street; a peddler or hawker. **2.** One who uses aggressive, showy, and sometimes devious methods to promote or sell a product. **3.** *Informal* One who writes advertising copy, esp. for radio or television. ❖ *v.* **-stered, -ster•ing, -sters** —*tr.* **1.** To sell; peddle. **2.** To promote or attempt to sell in an overaggressive or showy manner. **3.** To haggle over; deal in. —*intr.* To engage in haggling. [ME, prob. of LGer. orig.; akin to MDu. *hokester*.] —**huck′ster•ism** *n.*

HUD *abbr.* Department of Housing and Urban Development

Hud•ders•field (hŭd′ərz-fēld′) A borough of N-central England NE of Manchester. Pop. 125,800.

hud•dle (hŭd′l) *n.* **1.** A densely packed group or crowd, as of people or animals. **2.** *Football* A brief gathering of a team's players behind the line of scrimmage. **3.** A small private conference or meeting. ❖ *v.* **-dled, -dling, -dles** —*intr.* **1.** To crowd together, as from cold or fear. **2.** To draw or curl one's limbs close to one's body; crouch. **3.** *Football* To gather in a huddle. **4.** *Informal* To gather together for conference or consultation. —*tr.* **1.** To cause to crowd together. **2.** To draw (oneself) together in a crouch. **3.** *Chiefly British* To arrange, do, or make hastily or carelessly. [Poss. < LGer. *hudeln*, to crowd together. See (s)keu- in App.] —**hud′dler** *n.*

Hu•di•bras•tic (hyōō′də-brăs′tĭk) *adj.* Of or relating to a style of mock-heroic verse composed in rhymed iambic pentameter couplets. [After *Hudibras*, a satiric epic by Samuel Butler.]

Hud•son (hŭd′sən), **Henry** d. 1611. English navigator and first European to explore the Hudson R. (1609).

Hudson, William Henry 1841–1922. British naturalist and writer whose works include *Green Mansions* (1904).

Hudson Bay An inland sea of E-central Canada connected to the Atlantic Ocean by **Hudson Strait**, lying between S Baffin I. and N Quebec; explored and named by Henry Hudson in 1610.

Hudson River A river rising in the Adirondack Mts. of NE NY and flowing c. 507 km (315 mi) to Upper New York Bay at New York City.

Hudson River school *n.* A group of American landscape painters active from about 1825 to 1875 whose works depict the beauty of areas such as the Hudson River Valley.

Hudson seal *n.* Muskrat fur treated to resemble seal. [After HUDSON (BAY).]

hue (hyōō) *n.* **1.** The property of colors by which they can be perceived as ranging from red through yellow, green, and blue, as determined by the dominant wavelength of the light. **2.** A particular gradation of color; a shade or tint. **3.** Color. **4.** Appearance; aspect. [ME, color, form < OE *hīw, hēo*.]

Hue (hwā) A city of central Vietnam near the South China Sea NW of Da Nang. Pop. 219,149.

hue and cry *n.* **1.** A public clamor, as of protest or demand. **2a.** The pursuit of a felon with loud shouts to alert others who were then legally obliged to give chase. **b.** The loud outcry formerly used in such a pursuit. [ME *hew and cri*, partial transl. of AN *hu e cri : hu*, outcry, clamor (< OFr. *huer*, to shout, of imit. orig.) + *e*, and + *cri*, cry (< OFr. *crier*, to cry; see CRY).]

hued (hyōōd) *adj.* Having a given hue, aspect, or character. Often used in combination: *rosy-hued; dark-hued.*

Huel•va (wĕl′və, -vä) A city of SW Spain near the Gulf of Cádiz; founded by Carthaginians. Pop. 144,053.

huff (hŭf) *n.* A fit of anger or annoyance; a pique. ❖ *v.* **huffed, huff•ing, huffs** —*intr.* **1.** To puff; blow. **2.** To make empty threats; bluster. **3.** To react indignantly; take offense. **4.** *Slang* To inhale the fumes of a volatile substance so as to become intoxicated. —*tr.* **1.** To cause to puff up; inflate. **2.** To treat insolently; bully. **3.** To anger; annoy. **4.** *Slang* To inhale the fumes of a (volatile substance) so as to become intoxicated. [Imit. of puffing.]

hula

huff•ish (hŭf′ĭsh) *adj.* **1.** Peevish; sulky. **2.** Arrogant; insolent. —**huff′ish•ly** *adv.* —**huff′ish•ness** *n.*

huff•y (hŭf′ē) *adj.* **-i•er, -i•est 1.** Easily offended; touchy. **2.** Irritated or annoyed; indignant. **3.** Arrogant; haughty. —**huff′i•ly** *adv.* —**huff′i•ness** *n.*

hug (hŭg) *v.* **hugged, hug•ging, hugs** —*tr.* **1.** To clasp or hold closely, esp. in the arms, as in affection; embrace. **2.** To hold steadfastly; cherish. **3.** To stay close to. —*intr.* To embrace or

cling together closely. ❖ *n.* **1.** A close affectionate embrace. **2.** A crushing embrace, as in wrestling. [Prob. of Scand. orig.; akin to ON *hugga*, to comfort.] —**hug′ga•ble** *adj.* —**hug′ger** *n.*

huge (hyōōj) *adj.* **hug•er, hug•est 1.** Of exceedingly great size, extent, or quantity; tremendous. **2.** Of exceedingly great scope or nature. [ME < OFr. *ahuge*.] —**huge′ly** *adv.* —**huge′ness** *n.*

huge•ous (hyōō′jəs) *adj.* Huge.

hug•ger-mug•ger (hŭg′ər-mŭg′ər) *n.* **1.** Disorderly confusion; muddle. **2.** Secrecy; concealment. ❖ *adj.* **1.** Disorderly; jumbled. **2.** Secret; clandestine. ❖ *v.* **-gered, -ger•ing, -gers** —*tr.* To keep secret; conceal. —*intr.* To act in a secretive manner. [?] —**hug′ger-mug′ger** *adv.* —**hug′ger-mug′ger•y** *n.*

Hugh Ca•pet (hyōō′ kā′pĭt, kăp′ĭt, kä-pā′) See **Capet.**

Hughes (hyōōz), **Charles Evans** 1862–1948. Amer. jurist; associate justice (1910–16) and chief justice (1930–41) of the Supreme Court.

Hughes, Howard Robard 1905–76. Amer. industrialist, film producer, and aviator who broke the airplane speed record (1935) and flew around the world in record time (1938).

Hughes, (James) Langston 1902–67. Amer. writer whose works include *The Ways of White Folks* (1934).

Hughes, Ted 1930–98. British poet whose work is noted for its violence, passion, and natural imagery.

Hu•gli or **Hoogh•ly** (hōō′glē) A channel, c. 257 km (160 mi), of the Ganges R. in E India between Calcutta and the Bay of Bengal.

Hu•go (hyōō′gō, ü-gō′), **Victor Marie** 1802–85. French writer whose novels include *The Hunchback of Notre Dame* (1831) and *Les Misérables* (1862).

Hu•gue•not (hyōō′gə-nŏt′) *n.* A French Protestant of the 16th and 17th centuries. [Fr. < OFr. *huguenot*, member of a Swiss political movement, ult. < MHGer. *eitgenōz*, confederate : *eit*, oath (< OHGer. *eid*) + *genōz*, companion (< OHGer. *ginōz*).] —**Hu′gue•not′ic** *adj.* —**Hu′gue•not′ism** *n.*

huh (hŭ) *interj.* Used to express interrogation, surprise, contempt, or indifference.

Hu•he•hot (hōō′hā-hōt′) See **Hohhot.**

Hui (hwē) also **Hwei** (hwē), *n., pl.* **Hui** or **Huis** also **Hwei** or **Hweis** A member of a Muslim people of northwest China, descended chiefly from the Han. [Chin. (Mandarin) *Huí*.]

huit•la•co•che (wēt′lä-kō′chä) *n.* Variant of **cuitlacoche.**

Hui•tzi•lo•poch•tli (wē′tsə-lō-pōch′tlē) *n. Mythology* The tutelary deity of the Aztecs and a manifestation of the sun god Tezcatlipoca. [Nahuatl : *huizilin*, hummingbird + *opochtli*, left-hand side.]

Hui•zing•a (hī′zĭng-ə, hou′zĭng-ᴋʜᴀ), **Johan** 1872–1945. Dutch historian noted for *The Waning of the Middle Ages* (1919).

hu•la (hōō′lə) also **hu•la-hu•la** (hōō′lə-hōō′lə) *n.* A Polynesian dance characterized by undulating hips and miming movements of the arms and hands. [Hawaiian.]

Hu•la-Hoop (hōō′lə-hōōp′) A trademark used for a light plastic hoop that is whirled around the body by the hips.

hulk (hŭlk) *n.* **1.** *Nautical* **a.** A heavy unwieldy ship. **b.** The hull of an old, unseaworthy, or wrecked ship. **c.** An old or unseaworthy ship used as a prison or warehouse. Often used in the plural. **2.** One that is bulky, clumsy, or unwieldy. **3.** A wrecked or abandoned shell of a usu. large object, such as a vehicle. ❖ *intr.v.* **hulked, hulk•ing, hulks 1.** To appear as a massive or towering form; loom. **2.** To move clumsily. [ME < OE *hulc* < Med.Lat. *hulcus*, prob. < Gk. *holkas*, merchant ship, ship that is towed < *holkos*, machine for hauling ships < *helkein*, to pull.]

hulk•ing (hŭl′kĭng) also **hulk•y** (hŭl′kē) *adj.* Unwieldy or bulky; massive.

hull (hŭl) *n.* **1a.** The dry outer covering of a fruit, seed, or nut; a husk. **b.** The enlarged calyx of a fruit, such as a strawberry, that is usu. green and easily detached. **2a.** *Nautical* The frame or body of a ship, exclusive of masts, engines, or superstructure. **b.** The main body of various other large vehicles, such as a tank or airship. **3.** The outer casing of a rocket, guided missile, or spaceship. ❖ *tr.v.* **hulled, hull•ing, hulls** To remove the hulls of (fruit or seeds). [ME *hulle*, husk < OE *hulu*. See kel- in App.] —**hull′er** *n.*

Hull also **King•ston-up•on-Hull** (kĭng′stən-ə-pŏn-hŭl′, -pôn-) A borough of NE-central England on the N shore of the Humber estuary at the influx of the **Hull River.** Pop. 267,889.

Hull, Cordell 1871–1955. Amer. public official who as secretary of state (1933–44) laid the groundwork for the founding of the United Nations.

hul•la•ba•loo also **hul•la•bal•loo** (hŭl′ə-bə-lōō′) *n., pl.* **-loos** Great noise or excitement; uproar. [Alteration of obsolete *holloballo*, prob. < *holla*, hello. See HELLO.]

hul•lo (hə-lō′) *interj., n., & v. Chiefly British* Variant of **hello.**

Hulse (hŭls), **Russell Alan** b. 1950. Amer. physicist who shared a 1993 Nobel Prize.

hum (hŭm) *v.* **hummed, hum•ming, hums** —*intr.* **1a.** To emit a continuous low droning sound like that of the speech sound (m) when prolonged. **b.** To give forth the hum of a bee on the wing; buzz. **c.** To give forth a low continuous drone blended of many sounds. **2.** To be in a state of busy activity. **3.** To hum a tune. —*tr.* **1.** To sing (a tune) without opening the lips or forming words. **2.** *Baseball* To throw or pitch (a ball) very fast. ❖ *n.* **1.** The sound produced by humming. **2.** The act of humming. ❖ *interj.* Used to indicate hesitation, surprise, or displeasure. [ME *hummen*, of imit. orig.] —**hum′ma•ble** *adj.*

hu•man (hyōō′mən) *n.* **1.** A member of the genus *Homo* and esp. of the species *H. sapiens.* **2.** A person: *the extraordinary humans who explored Antarctica.* ❖ *adj.* **1.** Of, relating to, or characteristic of humans. **2.** Having or showing those positive aspects of nature and character regarded as distinguishing humans from other animals. **3.** Subject to or indicative of the weaknesses, imperfections, and fragility associated with humans: *The mistake shows he's only human.* **4.** Having the form of a human. **5.** Made up of humans. [ME *humain* < OFr. < Lat. *hūmānus.* See **dhghem-** in App.] —**hu′man•hood′** *n.* —**hu′man•ness** *n.*
human being *n.* A human.
human chorionic gonadotropin *n.* A placental hormone that maintains the corpus luteum during pregnancy.
hu•mane (hyōō-mān′) *adj.* **1.** Characterized by kindness, mercy, or compassion: *a humane judge.* **2.** Marked by an emphasis on humanistic values and concerns. [ME *humain,* human. See HUMAN.] —**hu•mane′ly** *adv.* —**hu•mane′ness** *n.*

SYNONYMS *humane, compassionate, humanitarian, merciful* These adjectives mean marked or motivated by concern with the alleviation of suffering: *a humane physician; compassionate toward impoverished people; released the prisoner for humanitarian reasons; is merciful to the repentant.* **ANTONYM** *inhumane*

human ecology *n.* See **ecology** 2, 3.
human engineering *n.* See **ergonomics** 1.
human factors engineering *n.* See **ergonomics** 1.
human growth hormone *n.* A polypeptide hormone secreted by the pituitary gland that promotes growth and regulates cellular metabolism.
human immunodeficiency virus *n.* HIV.
hu•man•ism (hyōō′mə-nĭz′əm) *n.* **1.** A system of thought centering on humans and their values, capacities, and worth and de-emphasizing religious beliefs. **2.** Concern with the interests, needs, and welfare of humans. **3.** The study of the humanities; learning in the liberal arts. **4. Humanism** The major intellectual movement of the European Renaissance arising from the revival of classical learning and emphasizing secularism and critical modes of thought.
hu•man•ist (hyōō′mə-nĭst) *n.* **1.** A believer in the principles of humanism. **2.** One who is concerned with or displays humanism. **3a.** A classical scholar. **b.** A student of the liberal arts. **4. Humanist** A Renaissance scholar devoted to Humanism. —**hu′man•is′tic** *adj.* —**hu′man•is′ti•cal•ly** *adv.*
hu•man•i•tar•i•an (hyōō-măn′ĭ-târ′ē-ən) *n.* One who is devoted to the promotion of human welfare and the advancement of social reforms. ❖ *adj.* Of or characteristic of a humanitarian or humanitarianism. See Syns at **humane.**
hu•man•i•tar•i•an•ism (hyōō-măn′ĭ-târ′ē-ə-nĭz′əm) *n.* **1.** Concern for human welfare, esp. as manifested through philanthropy. **2.** The belief that the sole moral obligation of humankind is the improvement of human welfare. **3.** *Theology* The doctrine holding that Jesus was human only and not divine.
hu•man•i•ty (hyōō-măn′ĭ-tē) *n., pl.* **-ties 1.** Humans considered as a group; the human race. **2.** The condition or quality of being human; humanness. **3.** The quality of being humane; benevolence. **4.** A humane characteristic, attribute, or act. **5. humanities a.** The languages and literatures of ancient Greece and Rome; the classics. **b.** Those branches of knowledge, such as literature and art, that are concerned with human thought and culture; the liberal arts. [ME *humanite* < OFr. < Lat. *hūmānitās* < *hūmānus,* human. See HUMAN.]
hu•man•ize (hyōō′mə-nīz′) *tr.v.* **-ized, -iz•ing, -iz•es 1.** To portray or endow with human characteristics or attributes; make human. **2.** To imbue with humaneness or humanity. —**hu′man•i•za′tion** (-mə-nī-zā′shən) *n.* —**hu′man•iz′er** *n.*
hu•man•kind (hyōō′mən-kīnd′) *n.* The human race.
hu•man•ly (hyōō′mən-lē) *adv.* **1.** In a human way. **2.** Within the scope of human means, capabilities, or powers. **3.** According to human experience or knowledge.
human nature *n.* The sum of qualities and traits shared by all humans.
hu•man•oid (hyōō′mə-noid′) *adj.* Having human characteristics or form. ❖ *n.* A being having human form. **2.** See **android.**
human pap•il•lo•ma•vi•rus (păp′ə-lō′mə-vī′rəs) *n.* Any of various strains of papovavirus that cause warts, with some strains thought to be a causative factor in certain cancers, esp. of the female genitals.
human rights *pl.n.* The basic rights and freedoms of all humans, often held to include the right to life and liberty, freedom of thought and expression, and equality before the law.
human T-cell lym•pho•trop•ic virus I (tĕ′sĕl′ lĭm′fə-trŏp′ĭk, -trŏf′pĭk) *n.* HTLV-I.
human T-cell lymphotropic virus III *n.* HTLV-III.
Hum•ber (hŭm′bər) An estuary of the Trent R. and Ouse R. in NE-central England; navigable for large vessels as far inland as Hull.
hum•ble (hŭm′bəl) *adj.* **-bler, -blest 1.** Marked by meekness or modesty in behavior, attitude, or spirit; not arrogant or prideful. **2.** Showing deferential or submissive respect: *a humble apology.* **3.** Low in rank, quality, or station; unpretentious or lowly. ❖ *tr.v.* **-bled, -bling, -bles 1.** To curtail or destroy the pride of; humili-

ate. **2.** To cause to be meek or modest in spirit. **3.** To give a lower condition or station to; abase. See Syns at **degrade.** [ME < OFr. < Lat. *humilis,* low, lowly < *humus,* ground. See **dhghem-** in App.] —**hum′ble•ness** *n.* —**hum′bler** *n.* —**hum′bly** *adv.*
hum•ble•bee (hŭm′bəl-bē′) *n.* A bumblebee. [ME *humbulbe :* poss. MDu. *hummel* + ME *be, bee,* bee; see BEE¹.]
humble pie *n.* A pie formerly made from the edible organs of a deer or hog. —**idiom: eat humble pie** To be forced to apologize abjectly or admit one's faults in humiliating circumstances. [Alteration (influenced by HUMBLE) of obsolete *umble pie :* ME *umbles,* edible animal organs (alteration of *numbles* < Norman Fr. *nombles* < OFr., loin of veal, prob. < alteration of Lat. *lumbulus,* dim. of *lumbus,* loin) + PIE¹.]
Hum•boldt (hŭm′bōlt′, hōōm′bōlt′), Baron **(Friedrich Heinrich) Alexander von** 1769–1859. German naturalist and writer who advanced the science of ecology.
Humboldt Bay (hŭm′bōlt′) A sheltered inlet of the Pacific Ocean in NW CA.
Humboldt Current *n.* A cold ocean current flowing north along the western coast of South America. [After Baron Friedrich Heinrich Alexander von HUMBOLDT.]
Humboldt Peak A mountain, 4,289.5 m (14,064 ft), in the Sangre de Cristo Mts. of S-central CO.
Humboldt River A river rising in NE NV and meandering c. 467 km (290 mi) to the **Humboldt Sink,** a lake in W NV.
hum•bug (hŭm′bŭg′) *n.* **1.** Something intended to deceive; a hoax or fraud. **2.** A person who claims to be other than what he or she is; an impostor. **3.** Nonsense; rubbish. **4.** Pretense; deception. ❖ *interj.* Used to express disbelief or disgust. ❖ *v.* **-bugged, -bug•ging, -bugs** —*tr.* To deceive or trick. —*intr.* To practice deception or trickery. [?] —**hum′bug′ger** *n.* —**hum′bug′ger•y** *n.*
hum•ding•er (hŭm′dĭng′ər) *n. Slang* One that is extraordinary or remarkable. [?]
hum•drum (hŭm′drŭm′) *adj.* Lacking variety or excitement; dull. See Syns at **boring.** ❖ *n.* Monotonous talk or routine. [Prob. < HUM.]
Hume (hyōōm), **David** 1711–76. Scottish philosopher and historian who argued that human knowledge comes from sense experience.
Hume, John b. 1937. Politician of Northern Ireland who shared the 1998 Nobel Peace Prize.
hu•mec•tant (hyōō-mĕk′tənt) *n.* A humectant substance. ❖ *adj.* Promoting retention of moisture. [< Lat. *hūmectāns, hūmectānt-,* pr. part. of *hūmectāre,* to moisten < *hūmectus,* moist < *hūmēre,* to be moist.]
hu•mer•al (hyōō′mər-əl) *adj.* **1.** Of, relating to, or located in the region of the humerus or the shoulder. **2.** Relating to or being a body part analogous to the humerus.
humeral veil *n. Roman Catholic Church* A vestment resembling a shawl worn over the shoulders during certain rituals.
hu•mer•us (hyōō′mər-əs) *n., pl.* **-mer•i** (-mə-rī′) The long bone of the arm or forelimb, extending from the shoulder to the elbow. [Lat., upper arm.]
hu•mic (hyōō′mĭk) *adj.* Of or derived from humus.
hu•mid (hyōō′mĭd) *adj.* Containing or characterized by a high amount of water or water vapor: *humid air.* See Syns at **wet.** [ME < Lat. *hūmidus < hūmēre,* to be moist.] —**hu′mid•ly** *adv.*
hu•mid•i•fi•er (hyōō-mĭd′ə-fī′ər) *n.* A device for increasing the humidity in a room, greenhouse, or other enclosure.
hu•mid•i•fy (hyōō-mĭd′ə-fī′) *tr.v.* **-fied, -fy•ing, -fies** To make humid. —**hu•mid′i•fi•ca′tion** (-fĭ-kā′shən) *n.*
hu•mid•i•stat (hyōō-mĭd′ĭ-stăt′) *n.* An instrument designed to indicate or control the relative humidity of the air.
hu•mid•i•ty (hyōō-mĭd′ĭ-tē) *n.* **1.** Dampness, esp. of the air. **2.** Relative humidity. [ME *humidite* < OFr. < Med.Lat. *hūmiditās* < Lat. *hūmidus,* humid. See HUMID.]
hu•mi•dor (hyōō′mĭ-dôr′) *n.* A container designed for storing cigars or other tobacco products at a constant level of humidity. [< HUMID (on the model of CUSPIDOR).]
hu•mi•fi•ca•tion (hyōō′mə-fĭ-kā′shən) *n.* The formation of humus.
hu•mil•i•ate (hyōō-mĭl′ē-āt′) *tr.v.* **-at•ed, -at•ing, -ates** To lower the pride, dignity, or self-respect of. See Syns at **degrade.** [LLat. *humiliāre, humiliāt-,* to humble < *humilis,* humble. See HUMBLE.]
hu•mil•i•a•tion (hyōō-mĭl′ē-ā′shən) *n.* **1.** The act of humiliating; degradation. **2.** The state of being humiliated or disgraced; shame. **3.** A humiliating condition or circumstance.
hu•mil•i•ty (hyōō-mĭl′ĭ-tē) *n.* The quality or condition of being humble. [ME *humilite* < OFr. < LLat. *humilitās < humilis,* humble. See HUMBLE.]
hu•mi•ture (hyōō′mĭ-chər) *n.* See **heat index.** [HUMI(DITY) + (TEMPERA)TURE.]
hum•mer (hŭm′ər) *n.* **1.** One that hums. **2.** *Informal* A hummingbird. **3.** *Baseball* A fastball.
Hummer A trademark used for a durable wide-bodied vehicle with four-wheel drive.
hum•ming•bird (hŭm′ĭng-bûrd′) *n.* Any of numerous New World birds of the family Trochilidae, usu. very small and having brilliant iridescent plumage, a slender bill, and wings that can

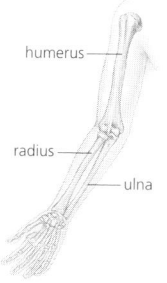

humerus

hummingbird
calliope hummingbird
Stellula calliope

ă	pat	oi	boy
ā	pay	ou	out
âr	care	ōō	took
ä	father	ōō	boot
ĕ	pet	ŭ	cut
ē	be	ûr	urge
ĭ	pit	th	thin
ī	pie	*th*	this
îr	pier	hw	which
ŏ	pot	zh	vision
ō	toe	ə	about,
ô	paw		item

Stress marks:
′ (primary);
′ (secondary), as in
lexicon (lĕk′sĭ-kŏn′)

beat rapidly, enabling the bird to hover.

hum•mock (hŭm′ək) *n.* **1.** A low mound or ridge of earth; a knoll. **2.** also **ham•mock** (hăm′ək) A tract of forested land that rises above an adjacent marsh in the southern United States. **3.** A ridge or hill of ice in an ice field. [?] —**hum′mock•y** *adj.*

hum•mus also **hum•us** or **hom•mos** (hŏom′əs, hŭm′-) *n.* A mixture of mashed chickpeas, tahini, oil, lemon juice, and garlic, eaten esp. as a dip. [Colloquial Ar. ḥummuṣ, chickpea, var. of Ar. ḥimmaṣ, ḥimmiṣ.]

hu•mon•gous (hyōō-mŏng′gəs, -mŭng′-) or **hu•mun•gous** (-mŭng′-) *adj. Slang* Extremely large; enormous. [Perh. blend of HUGE and MONSTROUS or TREMENDOUS.]

hu•mor (hyōō′mər) *n.* **1.** The quality that makes something laughable or amusing; funniness. **2.** That which is intended to induce laughter or amusement. **3.** The ability to perceive, enjoy, or express what is amusing, comical, incongruous, or absurd. **4.** One of the four fluids of the body, blood, phlegm, choler, and black bile, whose relative proportions were thought in ancient and medieval physiology to determine disposition and general health. **5.** *Physiology* **a.** A body fluid, such as blood, lymph, or bile. **b.** Aqueous humor. **c.** Vitreous humor. **6.** Disposition or temperament. **7.** An often temporary state of mind; a mood. **8a.** A sudden, unanticipated whim. See Syns at **mood**[1]. **b.** Capricious or peculiar behavior. ❖ *tr.v.* **-mored, -mor•ing, -mors** **1.** To comply with the wishes or ideas of; indulge. **2.** To adapt or accommodate oneself to. —*idiom:* **out of humor** In a bad mood; irritable. [ME, fluid < OFr. *umor* < Lat. *ūmor*, *hūmor*.]

hu•mor•al (hyōō′mər-əl) *adj.* **1.** Relating to body fluids, esp. serum. **2.** Of or arising from any of the body humors.

humoral immunity *n.* Immunity resulting from the transformation of B cells into plasma cells that secrete antibodies to a specific antigen.

hu•mor•esque (hyōō′mə-rĕsk′) *n. Music* A whimsical or fanciful composition. [Ger. *Humoreske* < *Humor*, humor < E. HUMOR.]

hu•mor•ist (hyōō′mər-ĭst) *n.* **1.** A person with a good sense of humor. **2.** A performer or writer of humorous material.

hu•mor•less (hyōō′mər-lĭs) *adj.* **1.** Lacking a sense of humor. **2.** Said or done without humor. —**hu′mor•less•ly** *adv.* —**hu′mor•less•ness** *n.*

hu•mor•ous (hyōō′mər-əs) *adj.* **1.** Full of or characterized by humor; funny. **2.** Employing or showing humor; witty. **3.** *Archaic* Given to moods or whims; capricious. **4.** *Obsolete* Damp; moist. —**hu′mor•ous•ly** *adv.* —**hu′mor•ous•ness** *n.*

hu•mour (hyōō′mər) *n. & v. Chiefly British* Variant of **humor**.

hump (hŭmp) *n.* **1.** A rounded mass or protuberance, such as the fleshy structure on the back of a camel or of some cattle. **2.** A deformity of the back in humans caused by an abnormal convex curvature of the upper spine. **3.** *Vulgar Slang* The act or an instance of having sexual intercourse. **4a.** A low mound of earth; a hummock. **b.** A mountain range. **5.** *Chiefly British* A fit of depression; an emotional slump. ❖ *v.* **humped, hump•ing, humps** —*tr.* **1.** To bend or round into a hump; arch. **2.** *Slang* **a.** To exert (oneself). **b.** To carry, esp. on the back. **3.** *Vulgar Slang* To engage in sexual intercourse with. —*intr.* **1.** *Slang* To exert oneself. **2.** *Slang* To hurry. **3.** *Vulgar Slang* To engage in sexual intercourse. —*idiom:* **over the hump** Past the worst or most difficult part or stage. [Prob. of LGer. orig.] —**humped** (hŭmpt) *adj.*

hump•back (hŭmp′băk′) *n.* **1.** See **hunchback**[1]. **2.** A humped upper back. **3.** A humpback whale. —**hump′backed**′ *adj.*

humpback salmon *n.* See **pink salmon**.

humpback whale *n.* A baleen whale (*Megaptera novaeangliae*) having a rounded back and long knobby flippers.

humpback whale
Megaptera novaeangliae

Hum•per•dinck (hōōm′pər-dĭngk′, hŭm′-), **Engelbert** 1854–1921. German composer who wrote the fairy tale opera *Hansel and Gretel* (1893).

humph (hŭmf, həmf) *interj.* Used to express doubt, displeasure, or contempt.

Hum•phrey (hŭm′frē, hŭmp′-), **Hubert Horatio** 1911–78. Vice President of the US (1965–69).

hump•y (hŭm′pē) *adj.* **-i•er, -i•est** **1.** Covered with or containing humps. **2.** Resembling a hump.

hu•mu•hu•mu•nu•ku•nu•ku•a•pu•a•a (hōō′mōō-hōō′mōō-nōō′kōō-nōō-kōō-ä′pōō-ä′ä′) *n., pl.* **humuhumunukunukuapuaa** or **-as** Either of two triggerfishes, *Rhinecanthus aculeatus* or *R. rectangulus*, native to the outer reefs of Hawaii. [Hawaiian *humuhumu-nukunuku-ā-pua'a*, trigger fish with a blunt snout like a pig's : *humuhumu*, small trigger fish (< redup. of Proto-Polynesian **sumu*, trigger fish) + *nukunuku*, small snout, redup. of *nuku*, snout + *ā*, like + *pua'a*, pig.]

hu•mun•gous (hyōō-mŭng′gəs) *adj.* Variant of **humongous**.

hu•mus[1] (hyōō′məs) *n.* An organic substance of decayed vegetable or animal matter that provides plants nutrients and increases soil water retention. [Lat., soil. See **dhghem-** in App.]

hum•us[2] (hōōm′əs, hŭm′-) *n.* Variant of **hummus**.

Hum•vee (hŭm′vē′) A trademark used for a durable wide-bodied military vehicle with four-wheel drive.

Hun (hŭn) *n.* **1.** A member of a nomadic pastoralist people who invaded Europe in the fourth and fifth centuries A.D. and were defeated in 455. **2.** often **hun** A barbarous or destructive person. **3.** *Offensive Slang* Used as a disparaging term for a German.

[< LLat. *Hunnī*, the Huns < Turki *Hunyü*.]

Hu•nan (hōō′nän′) A province of SE-central China; under Chinese rule since the 3rd cent. B.C. Cap. Changsha. Pop. 60,659,754.

hunch (hŭnch) *n.* **1.** An intuitive feeling or a premonition. **2.** A hump. **3.** A lump or chunk. **4.** A push or shove. ❖ *v.* **hunched, hunch•ing, hunch•es** —*tr.* **1.** To bend or draw up into a hump. **2.** To push or shove. —*intr.* **1.** To assume a crouched or cramped posture. **2.** To thrust oneself forward. [?]

hunch•back (hŭnch′băk′) *n.* **1.** One whose back is hunched due to abnormal convex curvature of the upper spine. **2.** An abnormally curved or hunched back. **3.** Kyphosis. —**hunch′backed**′ *adj.*

hun•dred (hŭn′drĭd) *n., pl.* **hundred** or **-dreds** **1.** The cardinal number equal to 10×10 or 10^2. **2.** The number in the third position left of the decimal point in an Arabic numeral. **3.** A one-hundred-dollar bill. **4. hundreds** The numbers between 100 and 999. **5.** An administrative division of some counties in England and the United States. [ME < OE. See **dekm** in App.] —**hun′dred** *adj.*

hun•dredth (hŭn′drĭdth) *n.* **1.** The ordinal number matching the number 100 in a series. **2.** One of 100 equal parts. —**hun′dredth** *adj.*

hun•dred•weight (hŭn′drĭd-wāt′) *n., pl.* **hundredweight** or **-weights** **1.** A unit of weight in the US Customary System equal to 100 pounds (45.36 kilograms). **2.** A unit of weight in the British Imperial System equal to 112 pounds (50.80 kilograms).

hung (hŭng) *v.* Past tense and a past participle of **hang**. See Usage Note at **hang**. ❖ *adj.* **1.** *Vulgar Slang* Having large genitals. Used of males. **2.** *Slang* **a.** Anxious; nervous. **b.** Overly involved or preoccupied.

Hung. *abbr.* **1.** Hungarian **2.** Hungary

Hun•gar•i•an (hŭng-gâr′ē-ən) *adj.* Of or relating to Hungary or its people, language, or culture. ❖ *n.* **1.** A native or inhabitant of Hungary. **2.** The Finno-Ugric language of the Magyars that is the official language of Hungary.

Hun•ga•ry (hŭng′gə-rē) A country of central Europe. An independent kingdom (until 1526) and later part of the Ottoman Empire and then the dual monarchy of Austria-Hungary (1867–1918), Hungary came under Communist rule in 1949. A new constitution, guaranteeing free multiparty elections, was adopted in 1989. Cap. Budapest. Pop. 10,261,000.

hun•ger (hŭng′gər) *n.* **1a.** A strong desire or need for food. **b.** The discomfort, weakness, or pain caused by a prolonged lack of food. **2.** A strong desire or craving. ❖ *v.* **-gered, -ger•ing, -gers** —*intr.* **1.** To have a need or desire for food. **2.** To have a strong desire or craving. —*tr.* To cause to experience hunger; make hungry. [ME < OE *hungor*.]

hunger strike *n.* A voluntary fast undertaken as a means of protest, as by a prisoner. —**hunger striker** *n.*

hung jury *n.* A jury that is unable to agree on a verdict.

hung-over also **hung over** or **hung•o•ver** (hŭng′ō′vər) *adj.* Suffering from a hangover.

hun•gry (hŭng′grē) *adj.* **-gri•er, -gri•est** **1.** Experiencing a desire or need for food. **2.** Extremely desirous; avid. **3.** Characterized by or expressing hunger or craving. **4.** Lacking richness or fertility. [ME *hungri* < OE *hungrig* < *hungor*, hunger.] —**hun′gri•ly** *adv.* —**hun′gri•ness** *n.*

Hung•shui He (hōong′shwä′ hŭ′) See **Hongshui He**.

hung up *adj. Informal* **1.** Delayed; hindered: *motorists hung up in traffic*. **2.** also **hung-up** (hŭng′ŭp′) Anxious; nervous. **3.** Overly involved or preoccupied.

hunk (hŭngk) *n.* **1.** *Informal* A large piece; a chunk. **2.** *Slang* A man with a well-developed physique considered sexually attractive. [Perh. < Flem. *hunke*, a piece of food.]

hun•ker (hŭng′kər) *intr.v.* **-kered, -ker•ing, -kers** **1.** To squat close to the ground; crouch. Often used with *down*: *hunkered down to avoid the icy wind*. **2.** To take shelter, settle in, or hide out. Often used with *down*. **3.** To hold stubbornly to a position. Often used with *down*. ❖ *n.* **hunkers** The haunches. [Perh. of Scand. orig.]

Hunk•pa•pa (hŭngk′pä′pä) *n., pl.* **Hunkpapa** or **-pas** A member of a Native American people constituting a subdivision of the Teton Sioux.

hun•ky (hŭng′kē) *n., pl.* **-kies** *Offensive Slang* Used as a disparaging term for a person, esp. a laborer, from east-central Europe. [Prob. shortening and alteration of BOHUNK.]

hun•ky-do•ry (hŭng′kē-dôr′ē, -dôr′ē) *adj. Slang* Perfectly satisfactory; fine. [Prob. alteration of *hunky*, safe, all right < obsolete *hunk*, goal < Du. *honk* < Frisian *hunk*.]

Hun•nish (hŭn′ĭsh) *adj.* **1.** Of, relating to, or characteristic of the Huns. **2.** often **hunnish** Barbarous; destructive.

hunt (hŭnt) *v.* **hunt•ed, hunt•ing, hunts** —*tr.* **1.** To pursue or lie in wait for (game) for food or sport. **2.** To search through (an area) for prey: *hunted the ridges*. **3.** To make use of (hounds, for example) in pursuing game. **4.** To pursue intensively so as to capture or kill. **5.** To seek out; search for. **6.** To drive out forcibly, esp. by harassing; chase away. —*intr.* **1.** To pursue game. **2.** To make a search; seek. **3.** *Engineering* **a.** To oscillate about a selected value. Used of a machine, instrument, or system. **b.** To swing back and forth; oscillate. Used of an indicator on a display or instrument panel. ❖ *n.* **1.** The act or sport of hunting. **2a.** A hunt-

ing expedition or outing, usu. with horses and hounds. **b.** Those taking part in such an expedition or outing. **3.** A diligent search or pursuit. [ME *hunten* < OE *huntian*.]

Hunt, (James Henry) Leigh 1784–1859. British writer and editor of the *Examiner* (1806–21).

Hunt, Richard Morris 1827–95. Amer. architect who designed an extension of the US Capitol (1855).

Hunt, (William) Holman 1827–1910. British painter who with Rossetti and Millais founded the Pre-Raphaelite Brotherhood.

hunt-and-peck (hŭn′ən-pĕk′) *n.* A slow method of typing in which an untrained typist finds each key before striking it.

hunt•er (hŭn′tər) *n.* **1.** One who hunts game. **2.** A dog bred or trained for use in hunting. **3.** A horse, typically a strong fast jumper, that has been bred or trained for use in hunting. **4.** One who searches for or seeks something.

hunt•er-gath•er•er (hŭn′tər-găth′ər-ər) *n.* A member of a people subsisting on food obtained by hunting and foraging.

hunt•ing (hŭn′tĭng) *n.* **1.** The activity or sport of pursuing game. **2.** The act of conducting a search for something: *house hunting.* **3.** *Electronics* The periodic variation in speed of a synchronous motor with respect to the current.

Hun•ting•ton (hŭn′tĭng-tən), **Collis Potter** 1821–1900. Amer. transportation executive who built the W section of the first US transcontinental railroad (completed 1869).

Huntington, Samuel 1731–96. Amer. Revolutionary leader who was president of the Continental Congress (1779–81 and 1783) and a signer of the Declaration of Independence.

Huntington Beach A city of S CA on the Pacific Ocean SE of Long Beach. Pop. 189,594.

Hun•ting•ton's chorea (hŭn′tĭng-tənz) *n.* A rare inherited disease of the central nervous system characterized by progressive dementia, abnormal posture, and involuntary movements. [After George *Huntington* (1851?–1916), American physician.]

hunt•ress (hŭn′trĭs) *n.* A woman who hunts.

hunts•man (hŭnts′mən) *n.* **1.** A man who hunts. **2.** A man who manages the hounds in the hunting field.

Hunts•ville (hŭnts′vĭl′) A city of N AL ENE of Decatur; settled in 1805. Pop. 158,216.

Hu•nya•di or **Hu•nya•dy** (hōōn′yä-dē, -yô-), **János** 1387?–1456. Hungarian general and nationalist leader who fought to protect Hungary from Turkish conquest (1437–56).

Hu•pei or **Hu•peh** (hōō′pā′) See **Hubei.**

hur•dle (hûr′dl) *n.* **1.** *Sports* **a.** A light portable barrier over which competitors must leap in certain races. **b. hurdles** A race in which a series of such barriers must be jumped without the competitors' breaking stride. **c.** A leaping step made off one foot as means of maximizing spring at the end of an approach, as to a dive. **2.** An obstacle or difficulty to be overcome. **3.** *Chiefly British* A portable framework made of intertwined branches or wattle and used for temporary fencing. **4.** *Chiefly British* A frame or sledge on which condemned persons were dragged to execution. ❖ *v.* **-dled, -dling, -dles** —*tr.* **1.** To leap over (a barrier) in or as if in a race. **2.** To overcome or deal with successfully; surmount. —*intr.* To leap over a barrier or other obstacle. [ME *hurdel,* portable fence panel < OE *hyrdel.*] —**hur′dler** *n.*

hur•dy-gur•dy (hûr′dē-gûr′dē, hûr′dē-gûr′dē) *n., pl.* **-dies 1.** A medieval stringed instrument played by turning a rosined wheel with a crank and depressing keys connected to tangents on the strings. **2.** Any instrument, such as a barrel organ, played by turning a crank. [Imit.]

hurl (hûrl) *v.* **hurled, hurl•ing, hurls** —*tr.* **1.** To throw with great force; fling. See Syns at **throw. 2.** To send with great vigor; thrust. **3.** To throw down; overthrow. **4.** To utter vehemently. **5.** *Slang* To vomit (the contents of the stomach). —*intr.* **1.** To move with great speed, force, or violence; hurtle. **2.** To throw something with force. **3.** *Slang* To vomit. **4.** *Baseball* To pitch the ball. [ME *hurlen.*] —**hurl** *n.* —**hurl′er** *n.*

hurl•ing (hûr′lĭng) *n.* An Irish game resembling lacrosse played with a broad-bladed netless stick.

hurl•y-bur•ly (hûr′lē-bûr′lē) *n., pl.* **-lies** Noisy confusion; tumult. [Alteration and redup. of *hurling,* gerund of HURL.]

Hu•ron (hyŏōr′ən, -ŏn′) *n., pl.* **Huron** or **-rons 1.** A member of a Native American confederacy formerly inhabiting southeast Ontario around Lake Simcoe, with small present-day populations in Quebec and northeast Oklahoma, where they are known as Wyandot. **2.** The Iroquoian language of the Huron. [Fr., boor, Huron < OFr. *hure,* bristling hair.]

Huron, Lake The second largest of the Great Lakes, between SE Ontario, Canada, and E MI.

hur•rah (hōō-rä′, -rô′, hə-) also **hoo•ray** or **hur•ray** (-rā′) *interj.* Used as an exclamation of pleasure, approval, elation, or victory. ❖ *n.* **1.** A shout of "hurrah." **2.** Excitement; fanfare. ❖ *v.* **-rahed, -rah•ing, -rahs** also **-rayed, -ray•ing, -rays** —*tr.* To applaud, cheer, or approve by shouting "hurrah." —*intr.* To shout "hurrah." [Alteration of HUZZAH.]

hur•ri•cane (hûr′ĭ-kān′, hûr′-) *n.* **1.** A tropical cyclone originating in the equatorial regions of the Atlantic Ocean or Caribbean Sea, traveling north, northwest, or northeast from its point of origin, and usu. involving heavy rains. **2.** A wind with a speed greater than 74 miles (119 kilometers) per hour. **3.** Something resembling a hurricane in force or speed. [Sp. *huracán* < Taino *hu-*

rákan; akin to Arawak *kulakani,* thunder.]

hurricane deck *n.* The upper deck on a passenger steamship.

hurricane lamp *n.* A lamp with a candle, oiled wick, or electric bulb protected by a glass chimney.

hur•ried (hûr′ēd, hûr′-) *adj.* **1a.** Moving or acting rapidly. **b.** Required to move or act more rapidly; rushed. **2.** Done in great haste. —**hur′ried•ly** *adv.* —**hur′ried•ness** *n.*

hur•ry (hûr′ē, hûr′-) *v.* **-ried, -ry•ing, -ries** —*intr.* To move or act with speed or haste. —*tr.* **1.** To cause to move or act with speed or haste. **2.** To cause to move or act with undue haste; rush. **3.** To speed the progress or completion of; expedite. ❖ *n., pl.* **-ries 1.** The act or an instance of hurrying; hastened progress. **2.** Activity or motion that is often unduly hurried; haste. See Syns at **haste. 3.** The need or wish to hurry; a condition of urgency. [Poss. ME *horien,* perh. var. of *harien,* to harass. See HARRY.] —**hur′ri•er** *n.*

hur•ry-scur•ry also **hur•ry-skur•ry** (hûr′ē-skûr′ē, hûr′ē-skûr′ē) *intr.v.* **-ried, -ry•ing, -ries** To move or act with undue hurry and confusion. ❖ *n., pl.* **-ries** Confused haste; agitation. [Reduplication of HURRY.] —**hur′ry-scur′ry** *adj.*

Hur•ston (hûr′stən), **Zora Neale** 1901?–60. Amer. writer whose works include *Their Eyes Were Watching God* (1937).

hurt (hûrt) *v.* **hurt, hurt•ing, hurts** —*tr.* **1a.** To cause injury or pain to: *The fall hurt my back.* **b.** To cause damage to: *The frost hurt the crops.* **2.** To cause mental or emotional suffering to; distress. **3.** To be detrimental to; hinder or impair: *The scandal hurt his chances for success.* —*intr.* **1a.** To have or produce a feeling of pain or discomfort. **2a.** To cause distress or damage. **b.** To have an adverse effect. **3.** *Informal* To experience distress, esp. of a financial kind; be in need: *does not hurt for money.* ❖ *n.* **1.** Something that hurts; a pain, injury, or wound. **2.** Mental suffering; anguish. **3.** A wrong; harm. [ME *hurten,* poss. < OFr. *hurter,* to bang into, perh. of Gmc. orig.] —**hurt′er** *n.*

hurt•ful (hûrt′fəl) *adj.* Causing injury or suffering; damaging. —**hurt′ful•ly** *adv.* —**hurt′ful•ness** *n.*

hur•tle (hûr′tl) *v.* **-tled, -tling, -tles** —*intr.* To move with or as if with great speed: *A train hurtled past.* —*tr.* To fling with great force; hurl. [ME *hurtlen,* to collide, freq. of *hurten,* to knock against, damage. See HURT.]

hurt•less (hûrt′lĭs) *adj.* **1.** Causing no hurt; harmless. **2.** Having no hurt; unhurt.

Hus or **Huss** (hŭs, hōōs), **Jan** or **John** 1372?–1415. Czech religious reformer who was excommunicated (1409) for attacking the corruption of the clergy.

Hu•sain or **Hu•sayn** (hōō-sān′) See **Hussein.**

hus•band (hŭz′bənd) *n.* **1.** A man joined to a woman in marriage; a male spouse. **2.** *Chiefly British* A manager or steward, as of a household. **3.** *Archaic* A prudent thrifty manager. ❖ *tr.v.* **-band•ed, -band•ing, -bands 1.** To use sparingly or economically; conserve: *husband one's energy.* **2.** *Archaic* To find a husband for. [ME *huseband* < OE *hūsbōnda* < ON *hūsbōndi* : *hūs,* house + *bōndi, būandi,* householder, pr. part. of *būa,* to dwell; see **bheuə-** in App.]

WORD HISTORY The English word *husband,* even though it is a basic kinship term, is not a native English word. It comes ultimately from the Old Norse word *hūsbōndi,* meaning "master of a house," which was borrowed into Old English as *hūsbōnda.* The master of the house was usually a spouse as well, of course, and it would seem that the main modern sense of *husband* arises from this overlap. When the Norsemen settled in Anglo-Saxon England, they would often marry Anglo-Saxon women; it was then natural to refer to the husband using the Norse word for the concept, and to refer to the wife with her Anglo-Saxon (Old English) designation, *wīf,* "woman, wife" (Modern English *wife*). Interestingly, Old English did have a feminine word related to Old Norse *hūsbōndi* that meant "mistress of a house," namely, *hūsbonde.* Had this word survived into Modern English, it would have sounded identical to *husband*—surely leading to ambiguities.

---

hus•band•man (hŭz′bənd-mən) *n.* One whose occupation is husbandry; a farmer.

hus•band•ry (hŭz′bən-drē) *n.* **1a.** The act or practice of cultivating crops and breeding and raising livestock; agriculture. **b.** The application of scientific principles to agriculture, esp. to animal breeding. **2.** Careful management or conservation of resources; economy. [ME *husbondri* < *huseband,* husband. See HUSBAND.]

hush (hŭsh) *v.* **hushed, hush•ing, hush•es** —*tr.* **1.** To make silent or quiet. **2.** To calm; soothe. **3.** To keep from public knowledge; suppress mention of. Often used with *up.* —*intr.* To be or become silent or still. ❖ *n.* A silence or stillness, esp. after noise. ❖ *adj. Archaic* Silent; quiet. [Prob. back-formation < ME *husht,* silent, of imit. orig.]

hush-hush (hŭsh′hŭsh′) *adj. Informal* Secret; confidential.

hush money *n. Informal* A bribe paid to keep a secret.

hush puppy or **hush•pup•py** (hŭsh′pŭp′ē) *n.* A small cake of cornmeal fried in deep fat. [Perh. < their use as snacks for dogs to quiet them while a meal was being eaten.]

husk (hŭsk) *n.* **1.** The outer membranous or green envelope of some fruits or seeds, as that of a walnut or an ear of corn. **2.** A

hurricane lamp

Zora Neale Hurston
1938 photograph by Carl
Van Vechten (1880–1964)

ă	pat	oi	boy
ā	pay	ou	out
âr	care	ōō	took
ä	father	ōō	boot
ĕ	pet	ŭ	cut
ē	be	ûr	urge
ĭ	pit	th	thin
ī	pie	*th*	this
îr	pier	hw	which
ŏ	pot	zh	vision
ō	toe	ə	about,
ô	paw		item

Stress marks:
′ (primary)
′ (secondary), as in
lexicon (lĕk′sĭ-kŏn′)

Hussein

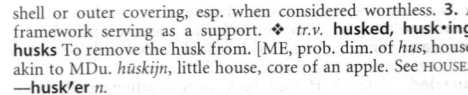

shell or outer covering, esp. when considered worthless. **3.** A framework serving as a support. ❖ *tr.v.* **husked, husk·ing, husks** To remove the husk from. [ME, prob. dim. of *hus,* house; akin to MDu. *hūskijn,* little house, core of an apple. See HOUSE.] —**husk′er** *n.*

husk·ing bee (hŭs′kĭng) *n.* See **cornhusking** 2.

husk tomato *n.* See **ground cherry.**

husk·y¹ (hŭs′kē) *adj.* **-i·er, -i·est 1.** Hoarse or rough in quality: *a husky voice.* **2a.** Resembling a husk. **b.** Containing husks. [< HUSK.] —**husk′i·ly** *adv.*

husk·y² (hŭs′kē) *adj.* **-i·er, -i·est 1.** Strongly built; burly. **2.** Heavily built. ❖ *n., pl.* **-ies** A husky person. [Perh. < HUSK.]

hus·ky³ also **hus·kie** (hŭs′kē) *n., pl.* **-kies 1.** often **Husky** or **Huskie** A dog of a breed developed in Siberia for pulling sleds and having a dense, variously colored coat. **2.** A similar dog of Arctic origin. [Prob. < alteration of ESKIMO.]

Huss, John See Jan **Hus.**

hus·sar (hə-zär′, -sär′) *n.* **1.** A horseman of the Hungarian light cavalry organized during the 15th century. **2.** A member of any similar European unit. [Hung. *huszár* < Serbian *husar,* highwayman < OItal. *corsaro.* See CORSAIR.]

Hus·sein or **Hu·sain** or **Hu·sayn** (hoo-sān′) 1935–99. King of Jordan (1953–99) who lost control of W Jordan in the Arab-Israeli War (1967).

Hussein, Saddam b. 1937. Iraqi military and political leader (since 1979) who waged war against Iran over a territorial dispute (1980–88) and invaded and occupied Kuwait (1990–91).

Hus·serl (hoos′ərl, -ĕrl), **Edmund** 1859–1938. Austrian-born German philosopher and mathematician who helped develop phenomenology.

hus·sy (hŭz′ē, hŭs′ē) *n., pl.* **-sies 1.** A woman considered brazen or immoral. **2.** A girl considered saucy or impudent. [Alteration of ME *houswif,* housewife : *hous,* house; see HOUSE + *wif,* woman; see WIFE.]

hust·ings (hŭs′tĭngz) *pl.n.* (*used with a sing. or pl. verb*) **1.** A place where political campaign speeches are made. **b.** The activities involved in political campaigning. **2.** *Chiefly British* A court formerly held in some English cities and still held infrequently in London. **3.** *Chiefly British* **a.** A platform on which candidates for Parliament formerly stood to address the electors. **b.** The proceedings of a parliamentary election. [< ME *husting,* court of common pleas < OE *hūsting,* court < ON *hūsthing* : *hūs,* house + *thing,* assembly.]

hus·tle (hŭs′əl) *v.* **-tled, -tling, -tles** —*tr.* **1.** To push or convey in a hurried or rough manner: *hustled him out of the room.* **2.** To cause or urge to proceed quickly; hurry: *hustled the board into action.* **3.** *Slang* **a.** To sell or get by questionable or aggressive means. **b.** To pressure into buying or doing something. **c.** To misrepresent one's skill in (a game or activity) in order to deceive someone. —*intr.* **1.** To move or act energetically or rapidly. **2.** To push or force one's way. **3.** To act aggressively, esp. in business dealings. **4.** *Slang* **a.** To obtain something by deceitful or illicit means. **b.** To solicit customers. Used of a pimp or prostitute. **c.** To misrepresent one's ability in a game or activity in order to deceive someone. ❖ *n.* **1.** The act or an instance of jostling or shoving. **2.** Energetic activity or effort; drive. **3.** *Slang* An illicit or unethical way of doing business or obtaining money; a fraud or deceit. [Du. *husselen,* to shake < MDu. *hustelen,* freq. of *hutsen.*] —**hus′tler** *n.*

Hus·ton (hyoo′stən), **John** 1906–87. Amer. filmmaker whose works include *The African Queen* (1951).

hut (hŭt) *n.* **1.** A crude or makeshift dwelling or shelter; a shack. **2.** A temporary structure for sheltering troops. ❖ *tr. & intr.v.* **hut·ted, hut·ting, huts** To shelter or take shelter in a hut. [Fr. *hutte,* of Gmc. orig. See (s)keu- in App.]

hutch (hŭch) *n.* **1.** A pen or coop for small animals, esp. rabbits. **2.** A cupboard with drawers for storage and usu. open shelves on top, often used for dishes. **3.** A chest or bin for storage. **4.** A hut. [ME *huche,* chest < OFr. < Med.Lat. *hūtica,* poss. of Gmc. orig.]

Hutch·in·son (hŭch′ĭn-sən), **Anne** 1591–1643. English-born Amer. colonist who was banished from Boston (1637) for her religious beliefs.

Hutchinson, Thomas 1711–80. Amer. colonial official who served as governor of Massachusetts (1771–74).

Hutch·in·son-Gil·ford syndrome (hŭch′ĭn-sən-gĭl′fərd) *n.* See **progeria.** [After Sir Jonathan *Hutchinson* (1828–1913) and Hastings *Gilford* (1861–1941), British physicians.]

hut·ment (hŭt′mənt) *n.* An encampment of huts.

Hut·ter·ite (hŭt′ə-rīt′, hoot′-) *n.* A member of an Anabaptist sect originating in Moravia and now living communally in parts of Canada and the northwest United States. [After Jakob *Hutter* (died 1536), Moravian Anabaptist leader.]

Hut·ton (hŭt′n), **James** 1726–97. Scottish physician and geologist whose ideas, presented in *A Theory of the Earth* (1785), form the basis of modern geology.

Hu·tu (hoo′too′) *n., pl.* **-tu** or **-tus** A member of a Bantu people inhabiting Rwanda and Burundi.

hutz·pah (кноot′spə, hoot′-) *n.* Variant of **chutzpah.**

Hux·ley (hŭks′lē), **Aldous Leonard** 1894–1963. British writer whose best-known work is *Brave New World* (1932).

Huxley, Andrew Fielding b. 1917. British physiologist who

shared a 1963 Nobel Prize for research on nerve cells.

Huxley, Thomas Henry 1825–95. British biologist who championed Darwin's theory of evolution in works such as *Zoological Evidences as to Man's Place in Nature* (1863).

Hu Yao·bang (hoo′ you′bäng′) also **Hu Yao-pang** (-päng′) 1915–89. Chinese politician who served as general secretary of the Communist Party (1980–89).

Huy·gens (hī′gənz, hoi′gĕns), **Christiaan** 1629–95. Dutch physicist who discovered Saturn's rings (1655) and pioneered the use of the pendulum in clocks (1657).

Huy·gens' principle (hī′gənz) *n.* The principle that any point on a wave front of light may be regarded as the source of secondary waves and that the surface that is tangent to the secondary waves can be used to determine the future position of the wave front. [After Christiaan HUYGENS.]

huz·zah also **huz·za** (hə-zä′) *interj.* Used to express joy, encouragement, or triumph. ❖ *n.* **1.** A shout of "huzzah." **2.** A cheer. [Perh. var. of ME *hisse,* heave! See HOIST.]

HV *abbr.* **1.** high velocity **2.** high voltage

HW *abbr.* **1.** high water **2.** hot water

Hwang Ho (hwäng′ hō′) See **Huang He.**

Hwei (hwā) *n.* Variant of **Hui.**

hwy. *abbr.* highway

hy·a·cinth (hī′ə-sĭnth) *n.* **1a.** A bulbous Mediterranean plant (*Hyacinthus orientalis*) having narrow leaves and variously colored, usu. fragrant flowers, with a funnel-shaped perianth. **b.** Any of several similar or related plants, such as the grape hyacinth. **2.** *Greek Mythology* A plant that sprang from the blood of the slain Hyacinthus. **3.** A deep purplish blue to vivid violet. **4a.** A reddish or cinnamon-colored variety of transparent zircon, used as a gemstone. **b.** A blue precious stone, perhaps the sapphire, known in antiquity. [Lat. *hyacinthus* < Gk. *huakinthos,* wild hyacinth.] —**hy′a·cin′thine** (-sĭn′thĭn, -thĭn′) *adj.*

hyacinth bean *n.* A vine (*Dolichos lablab*) of the Old World tropics, having edible pods and seeds.

Hy·a·cin·thus (hī′ə-sĭn′thəs) *n. Greek Mythology* A beautiful young man loved but accidentally killed by Apollo, from whose blood Apollo caused the hyacinth to grow.

Hy·a·des (hī′ə-dēz′) *pl.n.* **1.** *Greek Mythology* The five daughters of Atlas and sisters of the Pleiades, placed by Zeus among the stars. **2.** A cluster of stars in the constellation Taurus. [Lat. < Gk. *Huades,* prob. < *hūs,* pig. See **sū**- in App.]

hy·ae·na (hī-ē′nə) *n.* Variant of **hyena.**

hy·a·lin (hī′ə-lĭn) also **hy·a·line** (-lĭn, -lĭn′) *n.* **1.** *Physiology* The uniform matrix of hyaline cartilage. **2.** *Pathology* A translucent product of some degenerative skin conditions. [Gk. *hualos,* glass + -IN.]

hy·a·line (hī′ə-lĭn, -lĭn′) *adj.* Resembling glass, as in translucence or transparency; glassy. ❖ *n.* Something translucent or transparent. [LLat. *hyalinus* < Gk. *hualinos,* of glass < *hualos,* glass.]

hyaline membrane disease *n.* See **respiratory distress syndrome.**

hy·a·lite (hī′ə-līt′) *n.* A clear colorless opal. [Gk. *hualos,* glass + -ITE¹.]

hy·a·loid (hī′ə-loid′) *adj.* Glassy or transparent in appearance; hyaline. [Gk. *hualoeidēs* : *hualos,* glass + *-oeidēs,* -oid.]

hy·a·lo·plasm (hī′ə-lō-plăz′əm) *n.* The clear fluid portion of cytoplasm as distinguished from the granular and netlike components. [Gk. *hualos,* glass + -PLASM.]

hy·a·lu·ron·ic acid (hī′ə-loo-rŏn′ĭk) *n.* A gellike aminoglycan that is found in the tissue space, the synovial fluid of joints, and the vitreous humor of the eyes and acts as a binding, lubricating, and protective agent. [Gk. *hualos,* glass + Gk. *ouron,* urine.]

hy·brid (hī′brĭd) *n.* **1.** *Genetics* The offspring of genetically dissimilar parents or stock, esp. the offspring produced by breeding plants or animals of different varieties, species, or races. **2a.** Something of mixed origin or composition. **b.** Something, such as a computer or power plant, having two kinds of components that produce the same or similar results. **3.** A word whose elements are derived from different languages. [Lat. *hibrida, hybrida,* mongrel.] —**hy′brid·ism, hy·brid′i·ty** (hī-brĭd′ĭ-tē) *n.* —**hy′brid·ist** *n.*

hy·brid·ize (hī′brĭ-dīz′) *v.* **-ized, -iz·ing, -iz·es** To produce or cause to produce hybrids; crossbreed. —*intr.* **1.** To produce a hybrid; crossbreed. **2.** To form base pairs between complementary regions of two strands of DNA that were not originally paired. —*tr.* To cause to produce a hybrid; crossbreed. —**hy′brid·i·za′tion** (-brĭ-dĭ-zā′shən) *n.* —**hy′brid·iz′er** *n.*

hy·brid·o·ma (hī′brĭ-dō′mə) *n.* A cell formed in the laboratory from the fusion of an antibody-producing lymphocyte and a non-antibody producing tumor cell, such as a myeloma cell, capable of producing a specific antibody.

hybrid vigor *n.* Increased vigor or other superior qualities arising from the crossbreeding of genetically different plants or animals.

hy·bris (hī′brĭs) *n.* Variant of **hubris.**

hy·da·thode (hī′də-thōd′) *n.* A water-excreting microscopic epidermal structure in many plants. [Gk. *hudōr, hudat-,* water; see **wed**- in App. + *hodos,* way, road.]

hy·da·tid (hī′də-tĭd) *n.* **1.** A cyst formed as a result of infestation by larvae of the tapeworm *Echinococcus granulosus.* **2.** The

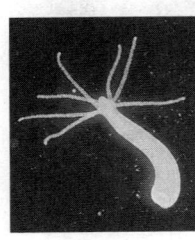
hydra
green hydra
Chlorohydra viridissima

encysted larva of *E. granulosus*. [Gk. *hudatis, hudatid-*, watery vesicle < *hudōr, hudat-*, water. See **wed-** in App.]

Hyde (hīd), Douglas 1860–1949. Irish nationalist and writer who was president of Ireland (1938–45).

Hyde, Edward. 1st Earl of Clarendon. 1609–74. English politician who was adviser to Charles I during the Civil War.

Hyde Park A large public park in W-central London, England, famous for its soapbox orators.

Hy·der·a·bad (hī′dər-ə-bäd′, -bäd′, hī′drə-) **1.** A city of S-central India ESE of Mumbai (Bombay); founded 1589. Pop. 2,964,638. **2.** A city of S Pakistan on the Indus R. NE of Karachi; founded 1768. Pop. 751,529.

hydr– *pref.* Variant of **hydro–**.

hy·dra (hī′drə) *n., pl.* **-dras** or **-drae** (-drē) Any of several small freshwater polyps of the genus *Hydra* and related genera, having a naked cylindrical body and an oral opening surrounded by tentacles. [NLat. *Hydra*, genus name < Lat. *Hydra*, Hydra. See HYDRA.]

Hydra *n.* **1.** *Greek Mythology* The many-headed serpent that was slain by Hercules. **2.** A constellation in the equatorial region of the southern sky near Cancer, Libra, and Centaurus. **3.** A persistent or multifaceted problem. [ME *Idra* < Lat. *Hydra* < Gk. *Hudrā*, Hydra, a water serpent. See **wed-** in App.]

hy·dra-head·ed (hī′drə-hĕd′ĭd) *adj.* Having many facets or aspects, esp. difficult or intractable ones.

hy·dran·gea (hī-drān′jə, -drăn′-) *n.* Any of various shrubs of the genus *Hydrangea*, having opposite leaves and large white, pink, or blue flowers. [NLat. *Hydrangĕa*, genus name : HYDR(O)- + Gk. *angeion*, vessel; see ANGIO-.]

hy·drant (hī′drənt) *n.* A fire hydrant.

hy·dranth (hī′drănth′) *n.* A feeding zooid in a hydroid colony, having an oral opening surrounded by tentacles. [HYDR(A) + Gk. *anthos*, flower.]

hy·dras·tine (hī-drăs′tēn′, -tĭn) *n.* A poisonous white alkaloid, $C_{21}H_{21}NO_6$, obtained from the root of the goldenseal and formerly used locally to treat inflammation of mucous membranes. [NLat. *Hydrastis*, plant genus + -INE².]

hy·drate (hī′drāt′) *n.* A solid compound containing water molecules combined in a definite ratio as an integral part of the crystal. ❖ *v.* **-drat·ed, -drat·ing, -drates** —*tr.* **1.** To rehydrate. **2.** To supply water to (a person, for example) in order to restore or maintain fluid balance. —*intr.* To become a hydrate. —**hy·dra′tion** *n.* —**hy′dra·tor** *n.*

hy·drat·ed (hī′drā′tĭd) *adj.* Chemically combined with water, esp. existing in the form of a hydrate.

hy·drau·lic (hī-drô′lĭk) *adj.* **1.** Of, involving, moved by, or operated by a fluid, esp. water, under pressure. **2.** Able to set and harden under water, as Portland cement. **3.** Of or relating to hydraulics. [Lat. *hydraulicus* < Gk. *hudraulikos* < *hudraulis*, water organ : *hudro-, hudr-*, hydro- + *aulos*, pipe, flute.] —**hy·drau′li·cal·ly** *adv.*

hydraulic press *n.* A machine in which a large force is exerted on the larger of two pistons in a pair of hydraulically coupled cylinders by a small force applied to the smaller piston.

hydraulic ram *n.* **1.** A water pump in which the downward flow of naturally running water is intermittently halted by a valve so that the flow is forced upward through an open pipe into a reservoir. **2.** The large piston of a hydraulic press.

hy·drau·lics (hī-drô′lĭks) *n.* (*used with a sing. verb*) The science and technology of the mechanics of fluids.

hy·dra·zine (hī′drə-zēn′, -zĭn) *n.* A fuming corrosive hygroscopic liquid, H_2NNH_2, used in jet and rocket fuels.

hy·dric (hī′drĭk) *adj.* Relating to, characterized by, or requiring considerable moisture.

hy·dride (hī′drīd′) *n.* A compound of hydrogen with another, more electropositive element or group.

hy·dri·od·ic acid (hī′drē-ŏd′ĭk) *n.* A clear colorless or pale yellow aqueous solution of hydrogen iodide, HI, that is a strong acid and reducing agent.

hy·dro (hī′drō) *adj.* Hydroelectric. ❖ *n., pl.* **-dros 1.** Hydroelectric power. **2.** A hydroelectric power plant.

hydro– or **hydr–** *pref.* **1a.** Water: *hydroelectric.* **b.** Liquid: *hydrodynamics.* **2.** Hydrogen: *hydrochloride.* [Gk. *hudro-, hudr-* < *hudōr.* See **wed-** in App.]

hy·dro·bi·ol·o·gy (hī′drō-bī-ŏl′ə-jē) *n.* The biological study of bodies of water. —**hy′dro·bi·ol′o·gist** *n.*

hy·dro·bro·mic acid (hī′drə-brō′mĭk) *n.* A highly acidic and corrosive aqueous solution of hydrogen bromide, HBr, used in the manufacture of bromides.

hy·dro·car·bon (hī′drə-kär′bən) *n.* Any of numerous organic compounds, such as benzene, that contain only carbon and hydrogen. —**hy′dro·car′bo·na′ceous** (-bə-nā′shəs), **hy′dro·car·bon′ic** (-bŏn′ĭk), **hy′dro·car′bon·ous** (-bə-nəs) *adj.*

hy·dro·cast (hī′drə-kăst′) *n.* The process of gathering data on water samples simultaneously from different depths by using water-collection bottles that are wired together.

hy·dro·cele (hī′drə-sēl′) *n.* A pathological accumulation of serum in a body cavity, esp. in the scrotum. [Lat. *hydrocēle* < Gk. *hudrokēlē* : *hudro-*, hydro- + *kēlē*, tumor; see -CELE¹.]

hy·dro·ceph·a·lus (hī′drō-sĕf′ə-ləs) also **hy·dro·ceph·a·ly** (-lē) *n.* A usu. congenital condition in which an abnormal accu-

mulation of fluid in the cerebral ventricles causes enlargement of the skull and compression of the brain, destroying much of the neural tissue. [NLat. < Gk. *hudrokephalon* : *hudro-*, hydro- + *kephalē*, head; see ghebh-el- in App.] —**hy′dro·ce·phal′ic** (-sə-făl′ĭk), **hy′dro·ceph′a·loid′** (-loid′), **hy′dro·ceph′a·lous** (-ləs) *adj.*

hy·dro·chlo·ric acid (hī′drə-klôr′ĭk, -klōr′-) *n.* A fuming, poisonous, highly acidic aqueous solution of hydrogen chloride, HCl, used in industry and found in the stomach in dilute form.

hy·dro·chlo·ride (hī′drə-klôr′īd′, -klōr′-) *n.* A compound resulting or regarded as resulting from the reaction of hydrochloric acid with an organic base.

hy·dro·col·loid (hī′drə-kŏl′oid′) *n.* A substance that forms a gel with water. —**hy′dro·col·loid′al** (-kə-loid′l) *adj.*

hy·dro·cor·ti·sone (hī′drə-kôr′tĭ-sōn′, -zōn′) *n.* **1.** A steroid hormone, $C_{21}H_{30}O_5$, produced by the adrenal cortex, that regulates carbohydrate metabolism and maintains blood pressure. **2.** A preparation of this hormone used to treat inflammatory conditions and adrenal failure.

hy·dro·crack·ing (hī′drə-krăk′ĭng) *n.* A process by which the hydrocarbon molecules of petroleum are broken into simpler molecules, as of gasoline, by the addition of hydrogen under high pressure and in the presence of a catalyst.

hy·dro·cy·an·ic acid (hī′drō-sī-ăn′ĭk) *n.* An aqueous solution of hydrogen cyanide.

hy·dro·dy·nam·ic (hī′drō-dī-năm′ĭk) also **hy·dro·dy·nam·i·cal** (-ĭ-kəl) *adj.* **1.** Of or relating to hydrodynamics. **2.** Of, relating to, or operated by the force of liquid in motion. —**hy′dro·dy·nam′i·cal·ly** *adv.*

hy·dro·dy·nam·ics (hī′drō-dī-năm′ĭks) *n.* **1.** (*used with a sing. verb*) The scientific study of the dynamics of fluids in motion. **2.** (*used with a pl. verb*) The dynamics of fluids in motion. —**hy′dro·dy·nam′i·cist** (-ĭ-sĭst) *n.*

hy·dro·e·lec·tric (hī′drō-ĭ-lĕk′trĭk) *adj.* **1.** Generating electricity by conversion of the energy of running water. **2.** Of or using electricity so generated. —**hy′dro·e·lec′tri·cal·ly** *adv.* —**hy′dro·e·lec·tric′i·ty** (-ĭ-lĕk-trĭs′ĭ-tē) *n.*

hy·dro·fluor·ic acid (hī′drō-flŏŏr′ĭk, -flôr′-, -flōr′-) *n.* A corrosive poisonous aqueous solution of hydrogen fluoride, HF, widely used as a fluorinating agent.

hy·dro·foil (hī′drə-foil′) *n.* **1.** A winglike structure attached to the hull of a boat that raises all or part of the hull out of the water when the boat is moving forward, thus reducing drag. **2.** A boat equipped with hydrofoils.

hy·dro·form·ing (hī′drə-fôr′mĭng) *n.* A process in which naphthas are converted to high-octane aromatics in the presence of hydrogen and a catalyst under pressure and heat.

hy·dro·gen (hī′drə-jən) *n. Symbol* **H** A colorless, highly flammable gaseous element, the most abundant in the universe, used in ammonia and methanol synthesis, in petroleum refining, in the hydrogenation of organic materials, and as a reducing atmosphere. Atomic number 1; atomic weight 1.00794; melting point −259.14°C; boiling point −252.8°C; density at 0°C 0.08987 gram per liter; valence 1. See table at **element.** [Fr. *hydrogène* : Gk. *hudro-*, hydro- + Fr. *-gène*, -gen.] —**hy·drog′e·nous** (-drŏj′ə-nəs) *adj.*

hy·dro·gen·ate (hī′drə-jə-nāt′, hī-drŏj′ə-) *tr.v.* **-at·ed, -at·ing, -ates** To combine with or subject to the action of hydrogen, esp. to combine (an unsaturated oil) with hydrogen.

hydrogen bomb *n.* An explosive weapon of enormous destructive power caused by the fusion of the nuclei of various hydrogen isotopes in the formation of helium nuclei.

hydrogen bond *n.* A chemical bond in which a hydrogen atom of one molecule is attracted to an electronegative atom, esp. a nitrogen, oxygen, or flourine atom, usu. of another molecule.

hydrogen bromide *n.* An irritating colorless gas, HBr, used in the manufacture of barbiturates and synthetic hormones.

hydrogen chloride *n.* A colorless, pungent gas, HCl, that forms hydrochloric acid when dissolved in water and is used in the manufacture of plastics.

hydrogen cyanide *n.* A colorless, volatile, extremely poisonous flammable liquid, HCN, miscible in water and used in the manufacture of dyes, fumigants, and plastics.

hydrogen fluoride *n.* A colorless fuming corrosive liquid or a highly soluble corrosive gas, HF, used in making hydrofluoric acid and as a reagent, catalyst, and fluorinating agent.

hydrogen iodide *n.* A corrosive colorless suffocating gas, HI, used to manufacture hydriodic acid.

hy·dro·gen·ol·y·sis (hī′drə-jə-nŏl′ĭ-sĭs) *n.* The breaking of a chemical bond by reaction with hydrogen.

hydrogen peroxide *n.* A colorless, heavy, strongly oxidizing liquid, H_2O_2, used principally in aqueous solution as a mild antiseptic, a bleaching agent, and a reagent.

hydrogen sulfide *n.* A colorless flammable poisonous gas, H_2S, having a characteristic rotten-egg odor.

hy·dro·ge·ol·o·gy (hī′drō-jē-ŏl′ə-jē) *n.* The branch of geology that deals with the occurrence, distribution, and effect of ground water. —**hy′dro·ge·ol′o·gist** *n.*

hy·drog·ra·phy (hī-drŏg′rə-fē) *n., pl.* **-phies 1.** The scientific description and analysis of the physical conditions, boundaries, flow, and related characteristics of the earth's surface waters. **2.**

Hydra
Hercules slaying the Hydra, from a c. fifth-century B.C. vase

hydrofoil

ă	pat	oi	boy
ā	pay	ou	out
âr	care	ŏŏ	took
ä	father	ōō	boot
ĕ	pet	ŭ	cut
ē	be	ûr	urge
ĭ	pit	th	thin
ī	pie	*th*	this
îr	pier	hw	which
ŏ	pot	zh	vision
ō	toe	ə	about,
ô	paw		item

Stress marks:
′ (primary);
′ (secondary), as in
lexicon (lĕk′sĭ-kŏn′)

The mapping of bodies of water. —**hy·drog'ra·pher** *n.* —**hy'dro·graph'ic** (hī'drə-grăf'ĭk) *adj.*

hy·droid (hī'droid') *n.* **1.** Any of numerous characteristically colonial hydrozoan cnidarians having a polyp rather than a medusoid form as the dominant stage of the life cycle. **2.** The asexual polyp in the life cycle of a hydrozoan. ❖ *adj.* Of, relating to, or characteristic of a hydroid. [HYDR(A) + −OID.]

hy·dro·ki·net·ic (hī'drō-kə-nĕt'ĭk, -kī-) also **hy·dro·ki·net·i·cal** (-ĭ-kəl) *adj.* **1.** Of or relating to hydrokinetics. **2.** Of or relating to the kinetic energy and motion of fluids.

hy·dro·ki·net·ics (hī'drō-kə-nĕt'ĭks, -kī-) *n.* (*used with a sing. verb*) The scientific study of fluids in motion.

hydrologic cycle *n.* See **water cycle.**

hy·drol·o·gy (hī-drŏl'ə-jē) *n.* The scientific study of the properties, distribution, and effects of water on the earth's surface, in the soil and underlying rocks, and in the atmosphere. —**hy'dro·log'ic** (-drə-lŏj'ĭk), **hy'dro·log'i·cal** *adj.* —**hy'dro·log'i·cal·ly** *adv.* —**hy·drol'o·gist** *n.*

hy·drol·y·sate (hī-drŏl'ĭ-sāt', hī'drə-lĭ'-) also **hy·drol·y·zate** (-zāt') *n.* A product of hydrolysis.

hy·drol·y·sis (hī-drŏl'ĭ-sĭs) *n.* Decomposition of a chemical compound by reaction with water, such as the dissociation of a dissolved salt. —**hy'dro·lyte'** (-līt') *n.* —**hy'dro·lyt'ic** (-drə-lĭt'ĭk) *adj.*

hy·dro·lyze (hī'drə-līz') *tr. & intr.v.* **-lyzed, -lyz·ing, -lyz·es** To subject to or undergo hydrolysis. —**hy'dro·lyz'a·ble** *adj.* —**hy'dro·ly·za'tion** (-lĭ-zā'shən) *n.*

hy·dro·mag·net·ics (hī'drō-măg-nĕt'ĭks) *n.* (*used with a sing. verb*) See **magnetohydrodynamics.** —**hy'dro·mag·net'ic** *adj.*

hy·dro·man·cy (hī'drə-măn'sē) *n.* Divination by the observation of water. [ME *ydromancy* < OFr. *ydromancie* < Lat. *hydromantīa* < Gk. *hudromanteia* : *hudro-*, hydro- + *manteia*, -mancy; see −MANCY.]

hy·dro·me·chan·ics (hī'drō-mĭ-kăn'ĭks) *n.* (*used with a sing. verb*) The scientific study of the mechanics of fluids or the laws of equilibrium and motion concerning fluids. —**hy'dro·me·chan'i·cal** *adj.*

hy·dro·me·du·sa (hī'drō-mĭ-dōō'sə, -dyōō'-) *n., pl.* **-sas** or **-sae** (-sē) A hydrozoan in the medusoid stage of its life cycle.

hy·dro·mel (hī'drə-mĕl') *n.* A mixture of water and honey that becomes mead when fermented. [ME *ydromel* < OFr. < Lat. *hydromeli* < Gk. *hudromeli* : *hudro-*, hydro- + *meli*, honey; see **melit-** in App.]

hy·dro·met·al·lur·gy (hī'drō-mĕt'l-ûr'jē) *n.* The treatment of metal or the separation of metal from ores and ore concentrates by liquid processes.

hy·dro·me·te·or (hī'drō-mē'tē-ər, -ôr') *n.* A precipitation product, such as rain, snow, fog, or clouds, formed from the condensation of water vapor in the atmosphere.

hy·dro·me·te·or·ol·o·gy (hī'drō-mē'tē-ə-rŏl'ə-jē) *n.* The study of hydrologic problems, such as flood control and irrigation. —**hy'dro·me'te·or·ol'o·gist** *n.*

hy·drom·e·ter (hī-drŏm'ĭ-tər) *n.* An instrument used to determine specific gravity, esp. a sealed graduated tube, weighted at one end, that sinks in a fluid to a depth used as a measure of the fluid's specific gravity. —**hy'dro·met'ric** (hī'drə-mĕt'rĭk), **hy'dro·met'ri·cal** *adj.* —**hy'dro·met'ri·cal·ly** *adv.* —**hy·drom'e·try** *n.*

hy·dron·ic (hī-drŏn'ĭk) *adj.* Of or relating to a heating or cooling system that transfers heat by circulating a fluid through a closed system of pipes. [HYDR(O)− + *-onic* (as in ELECTRONIC).]

hy·dro·ni·um (hī-drō'nē-əm) *n.* A hydrated hydrogen ion, H_3O^+. [HYDR(O)− + (AMM)ONIUM.]

hy·drop·a·thy (hī-drŏp'ə-thē) *n., pl.* **-thies** Use of water as a therapeutic treatment for disease. —**hy'dro·path'ic** (hī'drə-păth'ĭk), **hy'dro·path'i·cal** *adj.* —**hy'drop'a·thist, hy'dro·path'** *n.*

hy·dro·phane (hī'drə-fān') *n.* An opal that is almost opaque when dry but transparent when wet. —**hy·droph'a·nous** (hī-drŏf'ə-nəs) *adj.*

hy·dro·phil·ic (hī'drə-fĭl'ĭk) *adj.* Having an affinity for water; readily absorbing or dissolving in water. —**hy'dro·phile'** (-fīl') *n.* —**hy'dro·phil'i·ty** (-fə-lĭs'ĭ-tē) *n.*

hy·droph·i·lous (hī-drŏf'ə-ləs) *adj.* *Botany* **1.** Growing or thriving in water. **2.** Pollinated by water, as the flowers of hornwort. —**hy'droph'i·ly** *n.*

hy·dro·pho·bi·a (hī'drə-fō'bē-ə) *n.* **1.** An abnormal fear of water. **2.** Rabies.

hy·dro·pho·bic (hī'drə-fō'bĭk) *adj.* **1.** Repelling, tending not to combine with, or incapable of dissolving in water. **2.** Of or exhibiting hydrophobia. —**hy'dro·pho·bic'i·ty** (-bĭs'ĭ-tē) *n.*

hy·dro·phone (hī'drə-fōn') *n.* An electrical instrument for detecting or monitoring sound under water.

hy·dro·phyte (hī'drə-fīt') *n.* A plant adapted to grow in water. —**hy'dro·phyt'ic** (-fĭt'ĭk) *adj.*

hy·dro·plane (hī'drə-plān') *n.* **1.** A motorboat designed to skim the surface at high speeds. **2.** See **hydrofoil** 2. **3.** A horizontal rudder on a submarine. ❖ *intr.v.* **-planed, -plan·ing, -planes** **1.** To drive or ride in a hydroplane. **2a.** To skim along on the surface of the water. **b.** To be or go out of control by skimming along the surface of a wet road. Used of a motor vehicle.

hy·dro·pon·ics (hī'drə-pŏn'ĭks) *n.* (*used with a sing. verb*) Cultivation of plants in nutrient solution rather than in soil. [HYDRO− + (GEO)PONICS.] —**hy'dro·pon'ic** *adj.* —**hy'dro·pon'i·cal·ly** *adv.* —**hy'dro·pon'i·cist** (-ĭ-sĭst) *n.*

hy·dro·pow·er (hī'drə-pou'ər) *n.* Hydroelectric power.

hy·dro·qui·none (hī'drō-kwĭ-nōn', -kwĭn'ōn') also **hy·dro·quin·ol** (-kwĭn'ôl', -ōl') *n.* A white crystalline compound, $C_6H_4(OH)_2$, used as a photographic developer, an antioxidant, a stabilizer, and a reagent.

hy·dro·scope (hī'drə-skōp') *n.* An optical device used for viewing objects far below the surface of water. —**hy'dro·scop'ic** (-skŏp'ĭk) *adj.*

hy·dro·sol (hī'drə-sôl', -sŏl', -sōl') *n.* A colloid with water as the dispersing medium. —**hy'dro·sol'ic** (-sŏl'ĭk) *adj.*

hy·dro·space (hī'drə-spās') *n.* The regions beneath the ocean's surface, considered as an area to be studied.

hy·dro·sphere (hī'drə-sfîr') *n.* **1.** The waters of the earth's surface as distinguished from those of the lithosphere and the atmosphere. **2.** The water vapor in the earth's atmosphere. —**hy'dro·spher'ic** (-sfîr'ĭk, -sfĕr'-) *adj.*

hy·dro·stat·ic (hī'drə-stăt'ĭk) also **hy·dro·stat·i·cal** (-ĭ-kəl) *adj.* Of or relating to hydrostatics.

hy·dro·stat·ics (hī'drə-stăt'ĭks) *n.* (*used with a sing. verb*) The scientific study of fluids at rest and under pressure.

hy·dro·sul·fite (hī'drə-sŭl'fīt') *n.* A salt of hyposulfurous acid.

hy·dro·sul·fu·rous acid (hī'drō-sŭl-fyŏor'əs, -sŭl'fər-əs) *n.* See **hyposulfurous acid.**

hy·dro·tax·is (hī'drə-tăk'sĭs) *n.* Movement of an organism in response to moisture. —**hy'dro·tac'tic** (-tăk'tĭk) *adj.*

hy·dro·ther·a·peu·tics (hī'drə-thĕr'ə-pyōō'tĭks) *n.* (*used with a sing. verb*) Hydrotherapy. —**hy'dro·ther'a·peu'tic** *adj.*

hy·dro·ther·a·py (hī'drə-thĕr'ə-pē) *n., pl.* **-pies** External use of water in the medical treatment of certain diseases.

hy·dro·ther·mal (hī'drə-thûr'məl) *adj.* **1.** Of or relating to hot water. **2.** *Geology* **a.** Of or relating to hot magmatic emanations rich in water. **b.** Of or relating to the rocks, ore deposits, and springs produced by such emanations.

hy·dro·tho·rax (hī'drə-thôr'ăks', -thôr'-) *n.* Accumulation of serous fluid in one or both pleural cavities.

hy·drot·ro·pism (hī-drŏt'rə-pĭz'əm) *n.* Growth or movement in a sessile organism toward or away from water. —**hy'dro·tro'pic** (hī'drə-trō'pĭk, -trŏp'ĭk) *adj.*

hy·drous (hī'drəs) *adj.* Containing water, esp. water of crystallization or hydration.

hy·drox·ide (hī-drŏk'sīd') *n.* A chemical compound containing the hydroxyl group.

hy·drox·y (hī-drŏk'sē) *adj.* Containing the hydroxyl group.

hy·drox·y·a·pa·tite (hī-drŏk'sē-ăp'ĭ-tīt') *n.* The principal bone salt, $Ca_5(PO_4)_3OH$, which provides the compressional strength of vertebrate bone.

hy·drox·yl (hī-drŏk'sĭl) *n.* The univalent radical or group OH, a characteristic component of bases, certain acids, phenols, alcohols, carboxylic and sulfonic acids, and amphoteric compounds. [HYDROX(O)− + OX(YGEN) + −YL.] —**hy'drox·yl'ic** (hī'drŏk-sĭl'ĭk) *adj.*

hy·drox·yl·a·mine (hī-drŏk'sə-lə-mēn', hī'drŏk-sĭl'ə-mēn', -sə-lăm'ĭn) *n.* A colorless crystalline compound, NH_2OH, that is used as a reducing agent and in organic synthesis.

hy·drox·yl·ate (hī-drŏk'sə-lāt') *tr.v.* **-at·ed, -at·ing, -ates** To introduce hydroxyl into (a compound). —**hy·drox'y·la'tion** *n.*

hy·drox·zo·an (hī'drə-zō'ən) *n.* Any of numerous cnidarians of the class Hydrozoa, including the freshwater hydras, hydroids, and siphonophores. [< NLat. *Hydrozoa*, class name : HYDRO− + −*zōa* (pl. of -*zōon*, -zoon).] —**hy'dro·zo'an** *adj.*

Hy·drus (hī'drəs) *n.* A constellation in the Southern Hemisphere near Tucana and Mensa. [Lat. < Gk. *hudros*, water snake. See **wed-** in App.]

hy·e·na also **hy·ae·na** (hī-ē'nə) *n.* Any of several carnivorous mammals of the family Hyaenidae of Africa and Asia, which feed as scavengers and have powerful jaws and relatively short hind limbs. [ME *hiena* < OFr. *hiene* < Lat. *hyaena* < Gk. *huaina*, fem. of *hūs*, swine (< its bristly mane like a hog's). See **sū-** in App.]

hy·e·tal (hī'ĭ-tl) *adj.* Of or relating to rain or rainy regions. [< Gk. *hūetos*, rain.]

Hy·gei·a (hī-jē'ə) *n.* *Greek Mythology* The goddess of health.

hy·giene (hī'jēn') *n.* **1.** The science that deals with the promotion and preservation of health. **2.** Conditions and practices that serve to promote or preserve health: *personal hygiene.* [Fr. *hygiène* and NLat. *hygieina*, both < Gk. *hugieinē* (*tekhnē*), (art) of health, fem. of *hugiēs*, healthy. See **gʷei-** in App.] —**hy'gien'ist** (hī-jē'nĭst, hī'jē'-, hī-jĕn'ĭst) *n.*

hy·gi·en·ic (hī'jē-ĕn'ĭk, hī-jĕn'-, -jē'nĭk) *adj.* **1.** Of or relating to hygiene. **2.** Tending to promote or preserve health. **3.** Sanitary. —**hy'gi·en'i·cal·ly** *adv.*

hy·gi·en·ics (hī'jē-ĕn'ĭks, hī-jĕn'-, -jē'nĭks) *n.* (*used with a sing. verb*) See **hygiene** 1.

hygro– *pref.* Moisture; humidity: *hygroscope.* [< Gk. *hugros*, wet, moist.]

hy·grom·e·ter (hī-grŏm'ĭ-tər) *n.* Any of several instruments that measure atmospheric humidity. —**hy'gro·met'ric** (hī'grə-mĕt'rĭk) *adj.* —**hy·grom'e·try** *n.*

hyena
spotted hyena
Crocuta crocuta

hy·gro·scope (hī′grə-skōp′) *n.* An instrument that indicates changes in atmospheric humidity.

hy·gro·scop·ic (hī′grə-skōp′ĭk) *adj.* Readily absorbing moisture, as from the atmosphere. —**hy′gro·scop′i·cal·ly** *adv.* —**hy′gro·sco·pic′i·ty** (-skŏ-pĭs′ĭ-tē) *n.*

hy·gro·stat (hī′grə-stăt′) *n.* See **humidistat.**

hy·ing (hī′ĭng) *v.* A present participle of **hie.**

Hyk·sos (hĭk′sōs, -sōs) *pl.n.* A Semitic people who invaded Egypt and ruled it during the 17th and 16th centuries B.C.

hy·lo·zo·ism (hī′lə-zō′ĭz′əm) *n.* The philosophical doctrine holding that all matter has life, which is a property or derivative of matter. [Gk. *hūlē*, matter + Gk. *zōē*, life; see **gⁱeiə-** in App. + –ISM.] —**hy′lo·zo′ic** *adj.* —**hy′lo·zo′ist** *n.*

hy·men (hī′mən) *n.* A tissue that partly or completely occludes the external vaginal orifice. [LLat. *hymen* < Gk. *humēn*, thin skin, membrane. See **syū-** in App.] —**hy′men·al** *adj.*

Hymen *n.* Greek Mythology The god of marriage.

hy·me·ne·al (hī′mə-nē′əl) *adj.* Of or relating to a wedding or marriage. ❖ *n.* **1.** A wedding song or poem. **2.** hymeneals Archaic A wedding; nuptials. [< Lat. *hymenaeus*, wedding song, wedding < Gk. *humenaios* < *Humēn*, Hymen < *humēn*, membrane. See HYMEN.] —**hy′me·ne′al·ly** *adv.*

hy·me·ni·um (hī-mē′nē-əm) *n., pl.* **-ni·a** (-nē-ə) or **-ni·ums** The spore-bearing layer of the fruiting body of certain fungi. [NLat. < Gk. *humenion*, dim. of *humēn*, membrane. See HYMEN.] —**hy·me′ni·al** (-əl) *adj.*

hy·me·nop·ter·an (hī′mə-nŏp′tər-ən) also **hy·me·nop·ter·on** (-tə-rŏn′) *n.* Any of the insects of the order Hymenoptera, including bees and ants, often living in complex social groups and usu. having two pairs of wings. [< NLat. *Hymenoptera*, order name < Gk. *humenopteros*, membrane-winged : *humēn*, membrane; see HYMEN + *pteron*, wing; see –PTER-.] —**hy′me·nop′ter·an, hy′me·nop′ter·ous** (-tər-əs) *adj.*

Hy·met·tus (hī-mĕt′əs) A mountain ridge, rising to c. 1,028 m (3,370 ft), in E-central Greece near Athens.

hymn (hĭm) *n.* **1.** A song of praise or thanksgiving to God or a deity. **2.** A song of praise or joy; a paean. ❖ *v.* **hymned, hymn·ing, hymns** —*tr.* To praise, glorify, or worship in or as if in a hymn. —*intr.* To sing hymns. [ME *imne* < OFr. *ymne* < Lat. *hymnus*, song of praise < Gk. *humnos*.]

hym·nal (hĭm′nəl) *n.* A collection of church hymns. [ME *himnale* < Med.Lat. *hymnāle* < Lat. *hymnus*, hymn. See HYMN.]

hymnal stanza *n.* See **common measure.**

hym·na·ry (hĭm′nə-rē) *n.* See **hymnal.**

hymn·book or **hymn book** (hĭm′bŏŏk′) *n.* See **hymnal.**

hym·no·dy (hĭm′nə-dē) *n., pl.* **-dies 1.** The singing of hymns. **2.** The composing or writing of hymns. **3.** The hymns of a particular period or church. [Med.Lat. *hymnōdia* < Gk. *humnōidiā* : *humnos*, hymn + *ōidē*, song.] —**hym′no·dist** (-dĭst) *n.*

hym·nol·o·gy (hĭm-nŏl′ə-jē) *n.* **1.** Hymnody. **2.** The study of hymns. [Gk. *humnologiā*, singing of hymns : *humnos*, hymn + *logos*, saying; see –LOGY.] —**hym′no·log′ic** (hĭm′nə-lŏj′ĭk), **hym′no·log′i·cal** (-ĭ-kəl) *adj.* —**hym·nol′o·gist** *n.*

hy·oid (hī′oid′) *adj.* Of or relating to the hyoid. ❖ *n.* A U-shaped bone at the base of the tongue, supporting the muscles of the tongue. [NLat. *hyoīdēs*, the hyoid bone < Gk. *huoeidēs*, shaped like the letter upsilon : *hū*, upsilon + *-oeidēs*, -oid.]

hy·o·scine (hī′ə-sēn′) *n.* See **scopolamine.** [Ger. *Hyoscin* < NLat. *Hyoscyamus*, henbane genus < Gk. *huoskuamos*, henbane : *huos*, genitive of *hūs*, swine; see **sū-** in App. + *kuamos*, bean.]

hy·o·scy·a·mine (hī′ə-sī′ə-mēn′) *n.* A poisonous white crystalline alkaloid, C₁₇H₂₃NO₃, isometric with atropine and having similar uses but more potent effects. [NLat. *Hyoscyamus*, henbane genus; see HYOSCINE + –INE².]

hyp. *abbr.* **1.** hypotenuse **2.** hypothesis **3.** hypothetical

hyp– *pref.* Variant of **hypo–.**

hyp·a·bys·sal (hĭp′ə-bĭs′əl, hī′pə-) *adj.* Geology Solidifying chiefly as a minor intrusion, esp. as a dike or sill, before reaching the earth's surface. Used of rocks.

hy·pae·thral also **hy·pe·thral** (hī-pē′thrəl) *adj.* Wholly or partly open to the sky. [< Lat. *hypaethrus* < Gk. *hupaithros* : *hupo*, under; see HYPO– + *aithēr*, sky, air.]

hy·pan·thi·um (hī-păn′thē-əm) *n., pl.* **-thi·a** (-thē-ə) The structure of a flower on which the sepals, petals, and stamens are borne, as in the flowers of the rose or cherry. [NLat. : HYP(O)– + Gk. *anthos*, flower.] —**hy·pan′thi·al** *adj.*

Hy·pa·tia (hī-pā′shə, -shē-ə) A.D. 370?–415. Neo-Platonist philosopher, mathematician, and astronomer who lived and taught in Alexandria.

hype¹ (hīp) Slang *n.* **1.** Excessive publicity and the ensuing commotion: *the hype surrounding the murder trial.* **2.** Exaggerated or extravagant claims made esp. in advertising or promotional material. **3.** An advertising or promotional ploy. **4.** Something deliberately misleading; a deception. ❖ *tr.v.* **hyped, hyp·ing, hypes** To publicize or promote, esp. by extravagant, inflated, or misleading claims. [Partly < *hype*, a swindle (perh. < HYPER–) and partly < HYPE(RBOLE).]

hype² (hīp) Slang *n.* **1.** A hypodermic injection, syringe, or needle. **2.** A drug addict. ❖ *tr.v.* **hyped, hyp·ing, hypes** To stimulate with or as if with a hypodermic injection.

hyped-up (hīpt′ŭp′) *adj.* Slang Stimulated with or as if with a hypodermic injection.

hy·per (hī′pər) *adj.* Slang **1.** Having a very excitable or nervous temperament; high-strung. **2.** Emotionally stimulated or overexcited. [Short for HYPERACTIVE.]

hyper– *pref.* **1.** Over; above; beyond: *hypercharge.* **2.** Excessive; excessively: *hypercritical.* **3.** Existing in more than three dimensions: *hyperspace.* **4.** Linked or arranged nonsequentially: *hypertext.* [Gk. *huper-* < *huper*, over, beyond. See **uper** in App.]

hy·per·ac·id (hī′pər-ăs′ĭd) *adj.* Excessively acidic. —**hy′per·a·cid′i·ty** (-ə-sĭd′ĭ-tē) *n.*

hy·per·ac·tive (hī′pər-ăk′tĭv) *adj.* **1.** Highly or excessively active. **2a.** Having behavior characterized by overactivity. **b.** Having attention deficit disorder. Not in scientific use. —**hy′per·ac′tive·ly** *adv.* —**hy′per·ac·tiv′i·ty** (-ăk-tĭv′ĭ-tē) *n.*

hy·per·aes·the·sia (hī′pər-ĭs-thē′zhə) *n.* Variant of **hyperesthesia.**

hy·per·bar·ic (hī′pər-băr′ĭk) *adj.* Of, relating to, producing, operating, or occurring at pressures higher than normal atmospheric pressure. —**hy′per·bar′i·cal·ly** *adv.*

hy·per·ba·ton (hī-pûr′bə-tŏn′) *n.* A figure of speech, such as anastrophe, using deviation from normal or logical word order to produce an effect. [Gk. *huperbaton* < neut. of *huperbatos*, transposed < *huperbainein*, to step over : *huper-*, over, across; see HYPER– + *bainein*, to step; see **gⁱā-** in App.]

hy·per·bo·la (hī-pûr′bə-lə) *n., pl.* **-las** (-ləz) or **-lae** (-lē) A plane curve having two branches, formed by the intersection of a plane with both halves of a right circular cone at an angle parallel to the axis of the cone. [NLat. < Gk. *huperbolē*, a throwing beyond, excess (< the relationship between the line joining the vertices of a conic and the line through its focus and parallel to its directrix). See HYPERBOLE.]

hy·per·bo·le (hī-pûr′bə-lē) *n.* A figure of speech in which exaggeration is used for emphasis or effect, as in *That book weighs a ton.* [Lat. *hyperbolē* < Gk. *huperbolē*, excess < *huperballein*, to exceed : *huper*, beyond; see HYPER– + *ballein*, to throw; see **gⁱelə-** in App.] —**hy·per′bo·lize′** *v.*

hy·per·bol·ic (hī′pər-bŏl′ĭk) also **hy·per·bol·i·cal** (-ĭ-kəl) *adj.* **1.** Of, relating to, or employing hyperbole. **2.** Mathematics **a.** Of, relating to, or resembling a hyperbola. **b.** Of or relating to a geometry in which two or more lines can be drawn through any point in a plane and not intersect a given line in the plane. **c.** Of or relating to a hyperbolic function. —**hy′per·bol′i·cal·ly** *adv.*

hyperbolic function *n.* Any of a set of six functions related to the hyperbola in a manner analogous to the relationship of the trigonometric functions to the circle, including the hyperbolic sine, the hyperbolic cosine, and the hyperbolic tangent.

hyperbolic paraboloid *n.* A surface of which all sections parallel to one coordinate plane are hyperbolas and all sections parallel to another coordinate plane are parabolas.

hy·per·bo·lism (hī-pûr′bə-lĭz′əm) *n.* **1.** The use of hyperbole. **2.** An instance of hyperbole.

hy·per·bo·loid (hī-pûr′bə-loid′) *n.* Either of two quadric surfaces generated by rotating a hyperbola about either of its main axes and having plane sections that are hyperbolas, ellipses, or circles.

Hy·per·bo·re·an (hī′pər-bôr′ē-ən, -bōr′-, -bə-rē′ən) *n.* Greek Mythology An inhabitant of a perpetually warm and sunny land north of the source of the north wind. ❖ *adj.* **1.** Of or relating to the Hyperboreans. **2.** hyperborean a. Of or relating to the far north; Arctic. **b.** Very cold; frigid. [< Lat. *Hyperboreus* < *Hyperboreī*, the Hyperboreans < Gk. *Huperboreoi* : *huper-*, hyper- + *boreios*, northern, or *Boreās*, the north wind, the north.]

hy·per·cat·a·lec·tic (hī′pər-kăt′l-ĕk′tĭk) *adj.* Having an extra syllable or syllables at the end of a metrically complete line of verse or in a metrical foot. [Ult. < Gk. *huperkatalēktikos* : *huper-*, hyper- + *katalēktikos*, incomplete; see CATALECTIC.] —**hy′per·cat′a·lex′is** (-kăt′l-ĕk′sĭs) *n.*

hy·per·charge (hī′pər-chärj′) *n.* Symbol Y A quantum number equal to the sum of the strangeness and the baryon number of a particle.

hy·per·cor·rect (hī′pər-kə-rĕkt′) *adj.* Of, relating to, or characterized by hypercorrection. —**hy′per·cor·rect′ly** *adv.* —**hy′per·cor·rect′ness** *n.*

hy·per·cor·rec·tion (hī′pər-kə-rĕk′shən) *n.* **1.** A construction or pronunciation produced by mistaken analogy with standard usage out of a desire to be correct, as in the substitution of *I* for *me* in *on behalf of my parents and I.* **2.** The production of such a construction or pronunciation.

hy·per·crit·i·cal (hī′pər-krĭt′ĭ-kəl) *adj.* Excessively critical; captious. —**hy′per·crit′ic** *n.* —**hy′per·crit′i·cal·ly** *adv.* —**hy′per·crit′i·cism** (-ĭ-sĭz′əm) *n.*

hy·per·drive (hī′pər-drīv′) *n.* **1.** A fictional device allowing a spaceship to travel faster than the speed of light, esp. by passing through hyperspace. **2.** Informal A state of heightened activity or concentration. [HYPER(SPACE) + DRIVE.]

hy·per·e·mi·a (hī′pə-rē′mē-ə) *n.* An increase in the quantity of blood flow to a body part; engorgement. —**hy′per·e′mic** (-mĭk) *adj.*

hy·per·es·the·sia also **hy·per·aes·the·sia** (hī′pər-ĭs-thē′zhə) *n.* An abnormal or pathological increase in sensitivity to sen-

ă	pat	oi	boy
ā	pay	ou	out
âr	care	ŏŏ	took
ä	father	ŏŏ	boot
ĕ	pet	ŭ	cut
ē	be	ûr	urge
ĭ	pit	th	thin
ī	pie	th	this
îr	pier	hw	which
ŏ	pot	zh	vision
ō	toe	ə	about,
ô	paw		item

Stress marks:
′ (primary);
′ (secondary), as in
lexicon (lĕk′sĭ-kŏn′)

sory stimuli, as of the ear to sound. —**hy•per•es•thet′ic** (-thĕt′ĭk) *adj.*

hy•per•eu•tec•tic (hī′pər-yōō-tĕk′tĭk) *adj.* Having the minor component present in a larger amount than in the eutectic composition of the same components.

hy•per•ex•ten•sion (hī′pər-ĭk-stĕn′shən) *n.* Extension of a bodily joint beyond its normal range of motion. —**hy′per•ex•tend′** (-ĭk-stĕnd′) *v.*

hy•per•fic•tion (hī′pər-fĭk′shən) *n.* **1.** A work of fiction written and presented as an electronic hypertext document, esp. one that allows variations in plot development. **2.** The category of literature comprising such works.

hy•per•fine structure (hī′pər-fīn′) *n.* Any of the spectral lines formed from the splitting of broader spectral lines as a result of the interaction between the magnetic moments of electrons and atomic nuclei.

hy•per•gly•ce•mi•a (hī′pər-glī-sē′mē-ə) *n.* The presence of an abnormally high concentration of glucose in the blood. —**hy′per•gly•ce′mic** (-mĭk) *adj.*

hy•per•gol•ic (hī′pər-gŏl′ĭk) *adj.* **1.** Of or relating to a rocket propellant consisting of fuel and an oxidizer that ignite spontaneously on contact. **2.** Using such a fuel. [< Ger. *Hypergol,* a hypergolic fluid propellant : < *hyper-,* extreme (< Gk. *huper-;* see HYPER–) + Gk. *ergon,* work; see ERG.] —**hy′per•gol** (hī′pər-gôl′, -gŏl′, -gōl′) *n.* —**hy′per•gol′i•cal•ly** *adv.*

hy•per•in•su•lin•ism (hī′pər-ĭn′sə-lə-nĭz′əm) *n.* An abnormally high level of insulin in the blood, resulting in hypoglycemia.

Hy•pe•ri•on (hī-pîr′ē-ən) *n.* **1.** *Greek Mythology* A Titan, the son of Gaea and Uranus and the father of Helios. **2.** A satellite of Saturn. [Gk. *Hyperiōn.*]

hy•per•ka•le•mi•a (hī′pər-kā-lē′mē-ə) *n.* An abnormally high concentration of potassium ions in the blood. [HYPER– + NLat. *kalium,* potassium; see HYPOKALEMIA + –EMIA.]

hy•per•ker•a•to•sis (hī′pər-kĕr′ə-tō′sĭs) *n., pl.* **-ses** (-sēz) Hypertrophy of the cornea or the horny layer of the skin. —**hy′per•ker•a′tot′ic** (-tŏt′ĭk) *adj.*

hy•per•ki•ne•sia (hī′pər-kə-nē′zhə, -kī-) also **hy•per•ki•ne•sis** (-sĭs) *n.* **1.** An abnormal increase in muscular activity. **2.** Hyperactivity, esp. in children. [HYPER– + Gk. *kīnēsis,* movement (< *kīnein,* to move; see kei-² in App.) + –IA¹.] —**hy′per•ki•net′ic** (-nĕt′ĭk) *adj.*

hy•per•link (hī′pər-lĭngk′) *n.* See **link¹.** ❖ *v.* **-linked, -link•ing, -links** —*tr.* To make a hypertext link (in an electronic document or file). —*intr.* To follow a hypertext link to an electronic document or file. [HYPER(TEXT) + LINK¹.]

hy•per•mar•ket (hī′pər-mär′kĭt) *n.* A large commercial establishment combining a department store and a supermarket.

hy•per•met•ric (hī′pər-mĕt′rĭk) *adj.* Having one or more syllables in addition to those found in a standard metrical unit or line of verse. —**hy′per•me′ter** (hī-pûr′mĭ-tər) *n.*

hy•per•me•tro•pi•a (hī′pər-mĭ-trō′pē-ə) *n.* See **hyperopia.** [Gk. *hupermetros,* beyond measure (*huper-,* hyper- + *metron,* measure; see METER²) + –OPIA.] —**hy′per•me•tro′pic** (-trŏp′ĭk, -trōp′ĭk) *adj.*

hy•perm•ne•sia (hī′pərm-nē′zhə) *n.* Exceptionally exact or vivid memory, esp. as associated with certain mental illnesses. [HYPER– + (A)MNESIA.] —**hy′perm•ne′sic** (-zĭk, -sĭk) *adj.*

hy•per•on (hī′pə-rŏn′) *n.* A semistable or unstable baryon with mass greater than the neutron.

hy•per•o•pi•a (hī′pə-rō′pē-ə) *n.* An abnormal condition of the eye in which vision is better for distant objects than for near objects. —**hy′per•ope′** (hī′pə-rōp′) *n.* —**hy′per•o′pic** (-ō′pĭk, -ŏp′ĭk) *adj.*

hy•per•os•to•sis (hī′pər-ŏ-stō′sĭs) *n., pl.* **-ses** (-sēz) Excessive or abnormal thickening or growth of bone tissue. [HYPER– + OST(EO)– + –OSIS.] —**hy′per•os•tot′ic** (-ŏ-stŏt′ĭk) *adj.*

hy•per•pig•men•ta•tion (hī′pər-pĭg′mən-tā′shən) *n.* Excess pigmentation, esp. of the skin.

hy•per•pi•tu•i•ta•rism (hī′pər-pĭ-tōō′ĭ-tə-rĭz′əm, -tyōō′-) *n.* **1.** Pathologically excessive production of anterior pituitary hormones, esp. growth hormones. **2.** The condition resulting from an excess of pituitary hormones. —**hy′per•pi•tu′i•tar′y** (-tĕr′ē) *adj.*

hy•per•pla•sia (hī′pər-plā′zhə) *n.* An abnormal increase in the number of cells in an organ or a tissue with consequent enlargement. —**hy′per•plas′tic** (-plăs′tĭk) *adj.*

hy•per•ploid (hī′pər-ploid′) *adj.* Having a chromosome number greater than but not an exact multiple of the normal euploid number. —**hy′per•ploid′** *n.* —**hy′per•ploi′dy** *n.*

hy•perp•ne•a (hī′pərp-nē′ə, hī′pər-nē′ə) *n.* Abnormally deep or rapid breathing. [HYPER– + Gk. *pnoiā, -pnoia,* breath, breathing (< *pnein,* to breathe).] —**hy′perp•ne′ic** (-ĭk) *adj.*

hy•per•py•rex•i•a (hī′pər-pī-rĕk′sē-ə) *n.* Abnormally high fever. —**hy′per•py•rex′i•al, hy′per•py•ret′ic** (-rĕt′ĭk) *adj.*

hy•per•sen•si•tive (hī′pər-sĕn′sĭ-tĭv) *adj.* Highly or excessively sensitive. —**hy′per•sen′si•tive•ness, hy′per•sen′si•tiv′i•ty** (-tĭv′ĭ-tē) *n.*

hy•per•sex•u•al (hī′pər-sĕk′shōō-əl) *adj.* Excessively interested or involved in sexual activity. —**hy′per•sex′u•al′i•ty** (-sĕk′shōō-ăl′ĭ-tē) *n.*

hy•per•son•ic (hī′pər-sŏn′ĭk) *adj.* Of, relating to, or capable of speed equal to or exceeding five times the speed of sound.

hy•per•space (hī′pər-spās′) *n.* **1.** Space that has four or more dimensions. **2.** A fictional space in which laws of physics may be circumvented.

hy•per•sthene (hī′pərs-thēn′) *n.* A green, brown, or black splintery cleavable pyroxene mineral, (Fe,Mg)₂Si₂O₆. [Fr. *hypersthène : hyper-,* extreme (< Gk. *huper-;* see HYPER–) + Gk. *sthenos,* strength; see segh- in App.] —**hy′per•sthen′ic** (-thĕn′ĭk) *adj.*

hy•per•ten•sion (hī′pər-tĕn′shən) *n.* **1.** Arterial disease in which chronic high blood pressure is the primary symptom. **2.** Abnormally high blood pressure.

hypertensive (hī′pər-tĕn′sĭv) *adj.* **1.** Of or characterized by hypertension. **2.** Causing an increase in blood pressure. ❖ *n.* **1.** A person with or susceptible to hypertension. **2.** A drug that causes an increase in blood pressure.

hy•per•text (hī′pər-tĕkst′) *n.* A computer-based text retrieval system that enables a user to access particular locations in webpages or other electronic documents by clicking on links within specific webpages or documents.

hy•per•ther•mi•a (hī′pər-thûr′mē-ə) *n.* Unusually high body temperature. —**hy′per•ther′mal** *adj.*

hy•per•thy•roid (hī′pər-thī′roid′) *adj.* Of, relating to, or affected with hyperthyroidism.

hy•per•thy•roid•ism (hī′pər-thī′roi-dĭz′əm) *n.* **1.** Pathologically excessive production of thyroid hormones. **2.** The condition resulting from excessive activity of the thyroid gland.

hy•per•to•ni•a (hī′pər-tō′nē-ə) *n. Pathology* The state of being hypertonic.

hy•per•ton•ic (hī′pər-tŏn′ĭk) *adj.* **1.** *Pathology* Having extreme muscular or arterial tension. **2.** *Chemistry* Having the higher osmotic pressure of two solutions. —**hy′per•to•nic′i•ty** (-tə-nĭs′ĭ-tē, -tō-) *n.*

hy•per•tro•phy (hī-pûr′trə-fē) *n., pl.* **-phies** A nontumorous enlargement of an organ or tissue due to an increase in the size rather than the number of constituent cells. ❖ *intr. & tr.v.* **-phied, -phy•ing, -phies** To grow or cause to grow abnormally large. —**hy′per•tro′phic** (-trŏf′fĭk, -trōf′fĭk) *adj.*

hy•per•ven•ti•late (hī′pər-vĕn′tl-āt′) *v.* **-lat•ed, -lat•ing, -lates** —*intr.* **1.** To breathe abnormally fast or deeply so as to effect hyperventilation. **2.** To breathe in this manner as from excitement or anxiety. —*tr.* To subject to hyperventilation.

hy•per•ven•ti•la•tion (hī′pər-vĕn′tl-ā′shən) *n.* Abnormally fast or deep respiration, which results in the loss of carbon dioxide from the blood.

hy•per•vi•ta•min•o•sis (hī′pər-vī′tə-mə-nō′sĭs) *n., pl.* **-ses** (-sēz) Any of various abnormal conditions produced by excessive intake of a vitamin.

hy•pes•the•sia (hī′pĭs-thē′zhə) *n.* Variant of **hypoesthesia.**

hy•pe•thral (hī-pē′thrəl) *adj.* Variant of **hypaethral.**

hy•pha (hī′fə) *n., pl.* **-phae** (-fē) Any of the threadlike filaments forming the mycelium of a fungus. [NLat. < Gk. *huphē,* web. See webh- in App.] —**hy′phal** *adj.*

hy•phen (hī′fən) *n.* A punctuation mark (-) used between the parts of a compound word or name or between the syllables of a word, esp. when divided at the end of a line of text. ❖ *tr.v.* **-phened, -phen•ing, -phens** To hyphenate. [LLat. < Gk. *huphen,* a sign indicating a compound or two words which are to be read as one < *huph′ hen,* in one : *hupo,* under; see HYPO– + *hen,* neut. of *heis,* one; see sem-¹ in App.]

hy•phen•ate (hī′fə-nāt′) *tr.v.* **-at•ed, -at•ing, -ates** To divide or connect (syllables, word elements, or names) with a hyphen. ❖ *n.* **hy•phen•ate** (-nĭt′, -nāt′) One who performs more than one job or function: *auditioned actor-models and other hyphenates.* —**hy′phen•a′tion** *n.*

hy•phen•at•ed (hī′fə-nā′tĭd) *adj.* **1.** Having a hyphen. **2.** *Often Offensive* Of or relating to naturalized US citizens or their descendants or culture.

hyp•na•gog•ic also **hyp•no•gog•ic** (hĭp′nə-gŏj′ĭk, -gō′jĭk) *adj.* **1.** Inducing sleep; soporific. **2.** Of or relating to the state of intermediate consciousness that precedes sleep. [Fr. *hypnagogique :* Gk. *hupnos,* sleep; see HYPNO– + Gk. *agōgos,* leading (< *agein,* to lead; see ag- in App.).]

hypno– or **hypn–** *pref.* **1.** Sleep: *hypnophobia.* **2.** Hypnosis: *hypnoanalysis.* [< Gk. *hupnos,* sleep. See swep- in App.]

hyp•no•a•nal•y•sis (hĭp′nō-ə-năl′ĭ-sĭs) *n., pl.* **-ses** (-sēz′) The use of hypnosis in conjunction with psychoanalytic techniques.

hyp•no•gen•e•sis (hĭp′nō-jĕn′ĭ-sĭs) *n.* The process of inducing or entering sleep or a hypnotic state. —**hyp′no•ge•net′ic** (-jə-nĕt′ĭk) *adj.* —**hyp′no•ge•net′i•cal•ly** *adv.*

hyp•noid (hĭp′noid′) also **hyp•noi•dal** (hĭp-noid′l) *adj.* Of or resembling hypnosis or sleep.

hyp•no•pe•di•a (hĭp′nə-pē′dē-ə) *n.* See **sleep-learning.** [HYPNO– + Gk. *paideia,* education; see ENCYCLOPEDIA.]

hyp•no•pho•bi•a (hĭp′nə-fō′bē-ə) *n.* An abnormal fear of falling asleep. —**hyp′no•pho′bic** *adj.*

hyp•no•pom•pic (hĭp′nə-pŏm′pĭk) *adj.* Of or relating to the partially conscious state that precedes complete awakening from sleep. [< HYPNO– + Gk. *pompē,* a sending away; see POMP.]

Hyp•nos (hĭp′nŏs′) *n. Greek Mythology* The god of sleep.

hyp•no•sis (hĭp-nō′sĭs) *n., pl.* **-ses** (-sēz) **1.** An artificially induced altered state of consciousness, marked by heightened suggestibility and receptivity to direction. **2.** Hypnotism. **3.** A sleep-like condition.

hyp•no•ther•a•py (hĭp′nō-thĕr′ə-pē) *n., pl.* **-pies** Therapy based on or using hypnosis.

hyp•not•ic (hĭp-nŏt′ĭk) *adj.* **1a.** Of or relating to hypnosis. **b.** Of or relating to hypnotism. **2.** Inducing or tending to induce sleep; soporific. ❖ *n.* **1a.** A person who is hypnotized. **b.** A person who can be hypnotized. **2.** An agent that causes sleep; a soporific. [Fr. *hypnotique* < LLat. *hypnōticus*, inducing sleep < Gk. *hupnōtikos* < *hupnoun*, to put to sleep < *hupnos*, sleep. See **swep-** in App.] —**hyp•not′i•cal•ly** *adv.*

hyp•no•tism (hĭp′nə-tĭz′əm) *n.* **1.** The theory or practice of inducing hypnosis. **2.** The act of inducing hypnosis. —**hyp′no•tist** *n.*

hyp•no•tize (hĭp′nə-tīz′) *tr.v.* **-tized, -tiz•ing, -tiz•es 1.** To put into a state of hypnosis. **2.** To fascinate by or as if by hypnosis. —**hyp′no•tiz′a•ble** *adj.* —**hyp′no•ti•za′tion** (-tĭ-zā′shən) *n.* —**hyp′no•tiz′er** *n.*

hy•po¹ (hī′pō) *n.* See **sodium thiosulfate.** [Short for *hyposulfite.*]

hy•po² (hī′pō) *Informal n., pl.* **-pos 1.** A hypodermic syringe. **2.** A hypodermic injection. ❖ *tr.v.* **-poed, -po•ing, -pos** To stimulate by or as if by hypodermic injection. [Short for HYPODERMIC.]

hypo– or **hyp–** *pref.* **1.** Below; beneath; under: *hypodermic.* **2.** Less than normal; deficient: *hypoesthesia.* **3.** In the lowest state of oxidation: *hypoxanthine.* [Gk. *hupo-* < *hupo*, under, beneath. See **upo** in App.]

hy•po•al•ler•gen•ic (hī′pō-ăl′ər-jĕn′ĭk) *adj.* Having a decreased tendency to provoke an allergic reaction.

hy•po•bar•ic (hī′pō-băr′ĭk) *adj.* Below normal pressure. —**hy′po•bar′ism** *n.*

hy•po•blast (hī′pə-blăst′) *n.* See **endoderm.** —**hy′po•blas′tic** *adj.*

hy•po•cal•ce•mi•a (hī′pō-kăl-sē′mē-ə) *n.* An abnormally low concentration of calcium in the blood.

hy•po•caust (hī′pə-kôst′) *n.* A space under the floor of an ancient Roman building where heat from a furnace was accumulated to heat a room or a bath. [Lat. *hypocaustum* < Gk. *hupokauston* < *hupokaiein*, to light a fire beneath : *hupo-*, hypo- + *kaiein*, to burn.]

hy•po•cen•ter (hī′pə-sĕn′tər) *n.* The surface position directly beneath the center of a nuclear explosion. —**hy′po•cen′tral** (-sĕn′trəl) *adj.*

hy•po•chlo•rite (hī′pə-klôr′īt′, -klōr′-) *n.* A salt or ester of hypochlorous acid.

hy•po•chlo•rous acid (hī′pə-klôr′əs, -klōr′-) *n.* A weak unstable acid, HOCl, occurring only in solution and used as a bleach, an oxidizer, a deodorant, and a disinfectant.

hy•po•chon•dri•a (hī′pə-kŏn′drē-ə) *n.* The conviction that one is or is likely to become ill, persisting despite medical evidence to the contrary. [LLat., abdomen < Gk. *hupokhondria*, pl. of *hupokhondrion*, abdomen (held to be the seat of melancholy) < neut. of *hupokhondrios*, under the cartilage of the breastbone : *hupo-*, hypo- + *khondros*, cartilage; see **ghrendh-** in App.]

hy•po•chon•dri•ac (hī′pə-kŏn′drē-ăk′) *n.* A person affected with hypochondria. ❖ *adj.* **1.** Relating to or affected with hypochondria. **2.** *Anatomy* Relating to or located in the hypochondrium. —**hy′po•chon•dri′a•cal** (-kŏn-drī′ə-kəl) *adj.*

hy•po•chon•dri•a•sis (hī′pə-kən-drī′ə-sĭs) *n., pl.* **-ses** (-sēz′) See **hypochondria.** [HYPOCHONDR(IA) + –IASIS.]

hy•po•chon•dri•um (hī′pə-kŏn′drē-əm) *n., pl.* **-dri•a** (-drē-ə) The upper lateral region of the abdomen, marked by the lower ribs. [NLat. < Gk. *hupokhondrion*, abdomen. See HYPOCHONDRIA.]

hy•poc•o•rism (hī-pŏk′ə-rĭz′əm, hī′pə-kôr′īz′əm, -kōr′-) *n.* **1.** A name of endearment; a pet name. **2.** The use of such names. [LLat. *hypocorisma* < Gk. *hupokorisma* < *hupokorizesthai*, to call by endearing names : *hupo-*, beneath, secretly; see HYPO- + *korizesthai*, to caress (< *koros*, boy, or *korē*, girl; see **ker-²** in App.).] —**hy′po•co•ris′tic** (hī′pə-kə-rĭs′tĭk) *adj. & n.* —**hy′po•co•ris′ti•cal•ly** *adv.*

hy•po•cot•yl (hī′pə-kŏt′l) *n.* The part of the axis of a plant embryo or seedling plant that is below the cotyledons. [HYPO- + COTYL(EDON).]

hy•poc•ri•sy (hĭ-pŏk′rĭ-sē) *n., pl.* **-sies 1.** The practice of professing beliefs, feelings, or virtues that one does not hold or possess; falseness. **2.** An act or instance of such falseness. [ME *ipocrisie* < OFr. < LLat. *hypocrisis*, play-acting, pretense < Gk. *hupokrisis* < *hupokrīnesthai*, to play a part, pretend : *hupo-*, hypo- + *krīnesthai*, to explain, middle voice of *krīnein*, to decide, judge; see **krei-** in App.]

hyp•o•crite (hĭp′ə-krĭt′) *n.* A person given to hypocrisy. [ME *ipocrite* < OFr. < LLat. *hypocrita* < Gk. *hupokritēs*, actor < *hupokrīnesthai*, to play a part, pretend. See HYPOCRISY.]

hyp•o•crit•i•cal (hĭp′ə-krĭt′ĭ-kəl) *adj.* **1.** Characterized by hypocrisy. **2.** Being a hypocrite. —**hyp′o•crit′i•cal•ly** *adv.*

hy•po•cy•cloid (hī′pō-sī′kloid′) *n.* The plane locus of a point fixed on a circle that rolls on the inside circumference of a fixed circle.

hy•po•der•mal (hī′pə-dûr′məl) *adj.* **1.** Of or relating to the hypodermis. **2.** Lying below the epidermis.

hy•po•der•mic (hī′pə-dûr′mĭk) *adj.* **1.** Of or relating to the layer just beneath the epidermis. **2.** Relating to the hypodermis. **3.** Injected in or beneath the skin. ❖ *n.* **1.** A hypodermic injection. **2.** A hypodermic needle. **3.** A hypodermic syringe. —**hy′po•der′mi•cal•ly** *adv.*

hypodermic needle *n.* **1.** A hollow needle used with a hypodermic syringe. **2.** A hypodermic syringe including the needle.

hypodermic syringe *n.* A piston syringe that is fitted with a hypodermic needle for giving injections.

hy•po•der•mis (hī′pə-dûr′mĭs) *also* **hy•po•derm** (hī′pə-dûrm′) *n.* **1.** An epidermal layer of cells that secretes an overlying chitinous cuticle, as in arthropods. **2.** *Botany* A layer of cells lying immediately below the epidermis. **3.** *Anatomy* A subcutaneous layer of tissue containing a number of cells.

hy•po•es•the•sia (hī′pō-ĭs-thē′zhə) *also* **hy•pes•the•sia** (hī′pĭs-) *n.* Partial loss of sensation; diminished sensibility.

hy•po•eu•tec•tic (hī′pō-yoō-tĕk′tĭk) *adj. Chemistry* Having the minor component present in a smaller amount than in the eutectic composition of the same components.

hy•po•gas•tri•um (hī′pə-găs′trē-əm) *n., pl.* **-tri•a** (-trē-ə) The lowest of the abdomen's three median regions. [NLat. < Gk. *hypogastrion* : *hupo-*, hypo- + *gastēr, gastr-*, belly.] —**hy′po•gas′tric** *adj.*

hy•po•ge•al (hī′pə-jē′əl) *also* **hy•po•ge•an** (-ən) *or* **hy•po•ge•ous** (-əs) *adj.* **1.** Located under the earth's surface. **2.** *Botany* Of or relating to seed germination in which the cotyledons remain below the surface of the ground. [< Lat. *hypogēus* < Gk. *hupogeios* : *hupo-*, hypo- + *gē*, earth.]

hy•po•gene (hī′pə-jēn′) *adj.* Formed or situated below the earth's surface. Used of rocks.

hy•pog•e•nous (hī-pŏj′ə-nəs) *adj. Botany* Growing on a lower surface of a structure, as fungi on leaves.

hy•po•ge•um (hī′pə-jē′əm) *n., pl.* **-ge•a** (-jē′ə) **1.** A subterranean chamber of an ancient building. **2.** An ancient subterranean burial chamber, such as a catacomb. [Lat. *hypogēum* < Gk. *hupogeion* < neut. of *hupogeios*, underground. See HYPOGEAL.]

hy•po•glos•sal (hī′pə-glŏs′əl) *adj.* **1.** Of or relating to the area under the tongue. **2.** Of or relating to the hypoglossal nerve. [HYPO- + Gk. *glōssa*, tongue.]

hypoglossal nerve *n.* Either of the 12th pair of cranial nerves that innervate the muscles of the tongue.

hy•po•gly•ce•mi•a (hī′pō-glī-sē′mē-ə) *n.* An abnormally low level of glucose in the blood.

hy•po•gly•ce•mic (hī′pō-glī-sē′mĭk) *adj.* **1.** Of or relating to hypoglycemia. **2.** Lowering the concentration of glucose in the blood: *a hypoglycemic drug.*

hy•pog•y•nous (hī-pŏj′ə-nəs) *adj.* Having the floral parts, such as sepals, petals, and stamens, borne on the receptacle beneath the ovary. —**hy′pog′y•ny** (-nē) *n.*

hy•po•ka•le•mi•a (hī′pō-kā-lē′mē-ə) *n.* An abnormally low concentration of potassium ions in the blood. [HYPO- + NLat. *kalium*, potassium (< Med.Lat. *kali*, alkali, potassium < Ar. *qily*, ashes, lye, potash; see ALKALI) + –EMIA.]

hy•po•lim•ni•on (hī′pə-lĭm′nē-ŏn′, -ən) *n.* The layer of water in a thermally stratified lake that lies below the thermocline, is noncirculating, and remains perpetually cold. [HYPO- + Gk. *limnē*, lake, pool.] —**hy′po•lim•net′ic** (-lĭm-nĕt′ĭk), **hy′po•lim′ni•al** *adj.*

hy•po•ma•ni•a (hī′pō-mā′nē-ə, -mān′yə) *n.* A mild state of mania, esp. as a phase of a manic-depressive cycle. —**hy′po•man′ic** (-măn′ĭk) *adj.*

hy•po•nas•ty (hī′pə-năs′tē) *n., pl.* **-ties** An upward bending of leaves or other plant parts, resulting from growth of the lower side. —**hy′po•nas′tic** *adj.*

hy•po•na•tre•mi•a (hī′pō-nə-trē′mē-ə) *n.* A deficiency of sodium in the blood. [HYPO- + NLat. *natrium*, sodium (< Fr. *natron*, natron; see NATRON) + –EMIA.]

hy•po•phos•phite (hī′pō-fŏs′fīt′) *n.* A salt of hypophosphorous acid.

hy•po•phos•pho•rous acid (hī′pō-fŏs′fər-əs, -fŏs-fôr′əs, -fōr′-) *n.* A clear colorless or slightly yellow liquid, H₃PO₂, used as a reducing agent.

hy•poph•y•sis (hī-pŏf′ĭ-sĭs) *n., pl.* **-ses** (-sēz′) See **pituitary gland.** [NLat. < Gk. *hupophusis*, attachment underneath < *hupophuein*, to grow up beneath : *hupo-*, hypo- + *phuein*, to make grow; see **bheuə-** in App.] —**hy•poph′y•si′al** (-sē′əl), **hy•poph′y•se′al** (hī-pŏf′ī-sē′əl, -zē′-, hī′pə-fĭz′ē-əl) *adj.*

hy•po•pi•tu•i•ta•rism (hī′pō-pĭ-tōō′ĭ-tə-rĭz′əm, -tyōō′-) *n.* **1.** Deficient or diminished production of pituitary hormones. **2.** The condition resulting from a deficiency in pituitary hormone, esp. growth hormone, marked by dwarfism in children and by decreased activity of the thyroid, adrenal, or gonadal glands. —**hy′po•pi•tu′i•tar′y** (-tĕr′ē) *adj.*

hy•po•pla•sia (hī′pō-plā′zhə, -zhē-ə) *n.* Incomplete or arrested development of an organ or a part. —**hy′po•plas′tic** (-plăs′tĭk) *adj.*

hy•po•ploid (hī′pō-ploid′) *adj.* Having a chromosome number lower by only a few chromosomes than the normal diploid number. —**hy′po•ploi′dy** *n.*

hy•po•pne•a (hī-pŏp′nē-ə, hī′pō-nē′ə) *n.* Abnormally slow shallow breathing. [HYPO- + Gk. *pnoiā, -pnoia*, breath, breathing

ă	pat	oi	boy
ā	pay	ou	out
âr	care	oŏ	took
ä	father	oō	boot
ĕ	pet	ŭ	cut
ē	be	ûr	urge
ĭ	pit	th	thin
ī	pie	th	this
îr	pier	hw	which
ŏ	pot	zh	vision
ō	toe	ə	about,
ô	paw		item

Stress marks:
′ (primary);
′ (secondary), as in
lexicon (lĕk′sĭ-kŏn′)

hyposensitivity

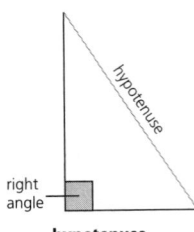

right angle

hypotenuse

(< *pnein*, to breathe).] —**hy′pop•ne′ic** *adj.*

hy•po•sen•si•tiv•i•ty (hī′pō-sĕn′sĭ-tĭv′ĭ-tē) *n., pl.* **-ties** Less than the normal ability to respond to stimuli. —**hy′po•sen′si•tive** *adj.*

hy•po•sen•si•tize (hī′pō-sĕn′sĭ-tīz′) *tr.v.* **-tized, -tiz•ing, -tiz•es** To make less sensitive, as to an allergen; desensitize. —**hy′po•sen′si•ti•za′tion** (-tĭ-zā′shən) *n.*

hy•pos•ta•sis (hī-pŏs′tə-sĭs) *n., pl.* **-ses** (-sēz′) **1.** *Philosophy* The substance, essence, or underlying reality. **2.** *Christianity* **a.** Any of the persons of the Trinity. **b.** The essential person of Jesus in which his human and divine natures are united. **3.** Something hypostatized. **4a.** A settling of solid particles in a fluid. **b.** Something that settles to the bottom of a fluid; sediment. **5.** *Medicine* The settling of blood in the lower part of an organ or the body as a result of decreased blood flow. **6.** *Genetics* A condition in which the action of one gene conceals or suppresses the action of another gene that is not its allele but that affects the same part or biochemical process in an organism. [LLat. < Gk. *hupostasis* : *hupo-*, hypo- + *stasis*, a standing; see **stā-** in App.] —**hy′po•stat′ic** (hī′pə-stăt′ĭk), **hy′po•stat′i•cal** *adj.* —**hy′po•stat′i•cal•ly** *adv.*

hy•pos•ta•tize (hī-pŏs′tə-tīz′) *tr.v.* **-tized, -tiz•ing, -tiz•es** To ascribe material existence to. [< Gk. *hupostatos*, placed under, substantial < *huphistasthai*, to stand under, exist : *hupo*, beneath; see HYPO– + *histasthai*, middle voice of *histanai*, to set, place; see EPISTASIS.] —**hy′pos′ta•ti•za′tion** (-tĭ-zā′shən) *n.*

hy•po•style (hī′pə-stīl′) *adj.* Having a roof or ceiling supported by rows of columns. ❖ *n.* A hypostyle building. [< Gk. *hupostūlos*, resting upon pillars : *hupo-*, hypo- + *stūlos*, pillar; see **stā-** in App.]

hy•po•sul•fu•rous acid (hī′pō-sŭl-fyōōr′əs, -sŭl′fər-əs) *n.* An unstable acid, $H_2S_2O_4$, known only in aqueous solution and used as a bleaching and reducing agent.

hy•po•tax•is (hī′pə-tăk′sĭs) *n. Grammar* The dependent subordinate relationship of clauses and connectives. [Gk. *hupotaxis*, subjection < *hupotassein*, to arrange under : *hupo-*, hypo- + *tassein*, tag-, to arrange.] —**hy′po•tac′tic** (-tăk′tĭk) *adj.*

hy•po•ten•sion (hī′pə-tĕn′shən) *n.* Abnormally low blood pressure.

hy•po•ten•sive (hī′pə-tĕn′sĭv) *adj.* **1.** Of or characterized by hypotension. **2.** Causing a reduction in blood pressure. ❖ *n.* A person with or susceptible to hypotension.

hy•pot•e•nuse (hī-pŏt′n-ōōs′, -yōōs′) also **hy•poth•e•nuse** (-pŏth′ə-nōōs′, -nyōōs′) *n.* The side of a right triangle opposite the right angle. [Lat. *hypotēnūsa* < Gk. *hupoteinousa* < fem. pr. part. of *hupoteinein*, to stretch or extend under : *hupo-*, hypo- + *teinein*, to stretch; see **ten-** in App.]

hy•po•thal•a•mus (hī′pō-thăl′ə-məs) *n.* The part of the brain below the thalamus, forming the major portion of the ventral region of the diencephalon and regulating bodily temperature and other autonomic activities. —**hy′po•tha•lam′ic** (-thə-lăm′ĭk) *adj.*

hy•poth•e•cate (hī-pŏth′ĭ-kāt′) *tr.v.* **-cat•ed, -cat•ing, -cates** To pledge (property) as security or collateral for a debt without transfer of title or possession. [Med.Lat. *hypothēcāre, hypothēcāt-* < Lat. *hypothēca*, pledge, deposit < Gk. *hupothēkē* < *hupotithenai*, to give as a pledge, suppose. See HYPOTHESIS.] —**hy•poth′e•ca′tion** *n.* —**hy•poth′e•ca′tor** *n.*

hy•po•ther•mal (hī′pō-thûr′məl) *adj.* Of, relating to, or being mineral deposits formed at great depths and high temperatures.

hy•po•ther•mi•a (hī′pə-thûr′mē-ə) *n.* Abnormally low body temperature. [HYPO– + Gk. *thermē*, heat; see gʷher- in App. + –IA[1].] —**hy′po•ther′mic** (-mĭk) *adj.*

hy•poth•e•sis (hī-pŏth′ĭ-sĭs) *n., pl.* **-ses** (-sēz′) **1.** A tentative explanation for an observation or phenomenon that can be used as the basis for an investigation. **2.** Something taken to be true for the purpose of argument or investigation; an assumption. **3.** The antecedent of a conditional statement. [Lat., subject for a speech < Gk. *hupothesis*, proposal, supposition < *hupotithenai*, *hupothe-*, to suppose : *hupo-*, hypo- + *tithenai*, to place; see **dhē-** in App.]

hy•poth•e•size (hī-pŏth′ĭ-sīz′) *v.* **-sized, -siz•ing, -siz•es** —*tr.* To assert as a hypothesis. —*intr.* To form a hypothesis.

hy•po•thet•i•cal (hī′pə-thĕt′ĭ-kəl) *adj.* also **hy•po•thet•ic** (-thĕt′ĭk) **1.** Of, relating to, or based on a hypothesis. **2a.** Suppositional; uncertain. **b.** Conditional; contingent. ❖ *n.* A hypothetical circumstance, condition, scenario, or situation. [< Gk. *hupothetikos* < *hupothetos*, placed under, supposed < *hupotithenai*, to suppose. See HYPOTHESIS.] —**hy′po•thet′i•cal•ly** *adv.*

hy•po•thy•roid (hī′pō-thī′roid′) *adj.* Affected by or manifesting hypothyroidism.

hy•po•thy•roid•ism (hī′pō-thī′roi-dĭz′əm) *n.* **1.** Insufficient production of thyroid hormones. **2.** Any of various pathological conditions resulting from severe thyroid insufficiency, including myxedema and a congenital form that is marked by dwarfed stature and mental retardation.

hy•po•ton•ic (hī′pō-tŏn′ĭk) *adj.* **1.** *Pathology* Having less than normal tone or tension, as of muscles or arteries. **2.** *Chemistry* Having the lower osmotic pressure of two fluids. —**hy′po•to•nic′i•ty** (-tə-nĭs′ĭ-tē) *n.*

hy•po•xan•thine (hī′pō-zăn′thēn′) *n.* A white powder, $C_5H_4N_4O$, that is an intermediate in the metabolism of animal purines.

hy•pox•e•mi•a (hī′pŏk-sē′mē-ə) *n.* Insufficient oxygenation of the blood.

hy•pox•i•a (hī-pŏk′sē-ə, hī-) *n.* Deficiency in the amount of oxygen reaching body tissues. —**hy•pox′ic** *adj.*

hypso– or **hyps–** *pref.* Height: *hypsometer*. [< Gk. *hupsos*, height, top. See **upo** in App.]

hyp•sog•ra•phy (hĭp-sŏg′rə-fē) *n., pl.* **-phies 1a.** The scientific study of the earth's topologic configuration above sea level, esp. the measurement and mapping of land elevations. **b.** A representation or description of the earth's topologic features above sea level. **2.** Hypsometry. —**hyp′so•graph′ic** (hĭp′sə-grăf′ĭk), **hyp′so•graph′i•cal** *adj.*

hyp•som•e•ter (hĭp-sŏm′ĭ-tər) *n.* An instrument using atmospheric pressure to determine land elevations.

hyp•som•e•try (hĭp-sŏm′ĭ-trē) *n.* The measurement of elevation relative to sea level. —**hyp′so•met′ric** (hĭp′sə-mĕt′rĭk), **hyp′so•met′ri•cal** *adj.* —**hyp•som′e•trist** *n.*

hy•ra•co•there (hī′rə-kō-thîr′) *n.* A small herbivorous mammal of the genus *Hyracotherium* (syn. *Eohippus*) from the Eocene Epoch of the Northern Hemisphere, having four-toed front feet and three-toed hind feet and identified in some taxonomical schemes as an ancestor of the modern horse. [NLat. *Hyracotherium*, genus name : *hyrax, hyrac-*, hyrax (< some shared skeletal characteristics); see HYRAX + Gk. *thērion*, wild beast; see TREACLE.]

hy•rax (hī′răks) *n., pl.* **-rax•es** or **-ra•ces** (-rə-sēz′) Any of several herbivorous mammals of the family Procaviidae of Africa and adjacent Asia, resembling rodents but more closely related to the hoofed mammals. [NLat. < Gk. *hurax*, shrew mouse.]

hy•son (hī′sən) *n.* A type of Chinese green tea with twisted leaves. [Chin. (Mandarin) *xī chūn* : *xī*, warm, sunny + *chūn*, springlike.]

hys•sop (hĭs′əp) *n.* **1.** A woody Eurasian plant (*Hyssopus officinalis*) having spikes of small blue flowers and aromatic leaves used in perfumery and as a condiment. **2.** Any of several similar or related plants. **3.** An unidentified plant mentioned in the Bible as the source of twigs used for sprinkling in certain Hebraic purificatory rites. [ME *ysope* < OE *ȳsōpe* < Lat. *hȳsōpum, hyssōpus* < Gk. *hussōpos*, prob. of Semitic orig.; akin to Aram. *'ezobā*.]

hys•ter•ec•to•my (hĭs′tə-rĕk′tə-mē) *n., pl.* **-mies** Surgical removal of part or all of the uterus. —**hys′ter•ec′to•mize′** (-mīz′) *v.*

hys•ter•e•sis (hĭs′tə-rē′sĭs) *n., pl.* **-ses** (-sēz) The lagging of an effect behind its cause, as when the change in magnetism of a body lags behind changes in the magnetic field. [Gk. *husterēsis*, a shortcoming < *husterein*, to come late < *husteros*, late. See **ud-** in App.] —**hys′ter•et′ic** (-rĕt′ĭk) *adj.*

hys•ter•i•a (hī-stĕr′ē-ə, -stĭr′-) *n.* **1.** Excessive or uncontrollable emotion, such as fear or panic. **2.** A mental disorder marked by excitability and sometimes by amnesia or a physical deficit, such as paralysis, without an organic cause. [NLat. : HYSTER(IC) + –IA[1].]

hys•ter•ic (hī-stĕr′ĭk) *n.* **1.** A person suffering from hysteria. **2.** **hysterics** (*used with a sing. or pl. verb*) **a.** A fit of uncontrollable laughing or crying. **b.** An attack of hysteria. ❖ *adj.* Hysterical. [< Lat. *hystericus*, hysterical < Gk. *husterikos* < *husterā*, womb (< the former idea that disturbances in the womb caused hysteria).]

hys•ter•i•cal (hī-stĕr′ĭ-kəl) *adj.* **1.** Of, characterized by, or arising from hysteria. **2.** Having or prone to having hysterics. **3.** *Informal* Extremely funny. —**hys•ter′i•cal•ly** *adv.*

hystero– or **hyster–** *pref.* **1.** Uterus: *hysterectomy*. **2.** Hysteria: *hysteroid*. [< Gk. *husterā*, womb.]

hys•ter•o•gen•ic (hĭs′tə-rō-jĕn′ĭk) *adj.* Inducing hysteria.

hys•ter•oid (hĭs′tə-roid′) *adj.* Resembling hysteria.

hys•ter•on prot•er•on (hĭs′tə-rŏn′ prŏt′ə-rŏn′) *n.* **1.** A figure of speech in which the natural or rational order of its terms is reversed, as in *bred and born* instead of *born and bred*. **2.** The logical fallacy of assuming as true and using as a premise a proposition that is yet to be proved. [LLat. < Gk. *husteron proteron*, latter first : *husteron*, neut. sing. of *husteros*, latter, later; see **ud-** in App. + *proteron*, neut. sing. of *proteros*, former; see **per**[1] in App.]

hys•ter•ot•o•my (hĭs′tə-rŏt′ə-mē) *n., pl.* **-mies** Surgical incision of the uterus, as in a cesarean section.

Hz *abbr.* hertz

I i

i¹ or **I** (ī) *n.*, *pl.* **i's** or **I's** also **is** or **Is 1.** The ninth letter of the modern English alphabet. **2.** Any of the speech sounds represented by the letter *i*. **3.** The ninth in a series. **4.** Something shaped like the letter I.

i² *n.* The symbol for **imaginary unit.**

I¹ (ī) *pron.* Used to refer to oneself as speaker or writer. ❖ *n.*, *pl.* **I's** The self; the ego. [ME < OE *ic*. See **eg** in App.]

USAGE NOTE The question of when to use nominative forms of the personal pronouns (for example, *I, she, they*) and when to use objective forms (for example, *me, her, them*) has always created controversy among grammarians and uncertainty among speakers and writers. When pronouns are joined with other nouns or pronouns by *and* or *or*, there is a widespread tendency to use the objective form even when the phrase is the subject of the sentence: *Robert and her are not speaking to each other.* This usage is natural in colloquial speech, but the nominative forms should be used in formal speech and writing: *John and she will be giving the talk.* • When pronouns joined by a conjunction occur as the object of a preposition such as *between, according to,* or *like*, many people use the nominative form where the traditional grammatical rule would require the objective; they say *between you and I* rather than *between you and me* and so forth. Such constructions are best avoided. The objective form sounds most natural when the pronoun is not grammatically related to an accompanying verb or preposition. Thus, in response to the question *"Who cut down the cherry tree?"* we more colloquially say *"Me,"* even though some grammarians have argued that *I* must be correct here by analogy to the form *"I did."* See Usage Notes at **be, but, we.**

I² **1.** The symbol for the element **iodine 1. 2.** *Electricity* The symbol for **current 4. 3.** also **i** The symbol for the Roman numeral 1.
I³ *abbr.* **1.** incomplete **2.** interstate **3.** isospin
i. *abbr.* **1.** *Economics* interest **2.** intransitive
I. *abbr.* **1.** island **2.** isle
–i– Used as a connective to join word elements: *setiform*. [ME < OFr. < Lat., stem vowel of nouns and adjectives used in combination.]
IA or **Ia.** *abbr.* Iowa
i.a. *abbr.* in absentia
–ia¹ *suff.* **1.** Disease; pathological or abnormal condition: *anoxia*. **2.** Territory; country: *Australia*. [NLat. < Lat. *-ia* and Gk. *-iā*, n. suff.]
–ia² *suff.* Things derived from, relating to, or belonging to: *personalia*. [Lat., neut. pl. of *-ius*, and Gk., neut. pl. of *-ios*, n. and adj. suffixes.]
–ial *suff.* Of, relating to, or characterized by: *baronial*. [ME < OFr. < Lat. *-iālis*.]
i•amb (ī'ămb', ī'ăm') also **i•am•bus** (ī-ăm'bəs) *n.*, *pl.* **i•ambs** also **-bus•es** or **-bi** (-bī') A metrical foot consisting of an unstressed syllable followed by a stressed syllable or a short syllable followed by a long syllable. [Fr. *iambe* < Lat. *iambus* < Gk. *iambos*.]
i•am•bic (ī-ăm'bĭk) *adj.* Consisting of iambs or characterized by their predominance: *iambic pentameter.* ❖ *n.* **1.** An iamb. **2.** A verse, stanza, or poem written in iambs. Often used in the plural.
–ian *suff.* **1.** Of, relating to, or resembling: *Bostonian*. **2.** One relating to, belonging to, or resembling: *academician*. [ME *-ien, -ian* < OFr. *-ien* < Lat. *-iānus*, adj. and n. suff.]
–iana *suff.* Variant of **–ana.**
I•ap•e•tus (ī-ăp'ĭ-təs, ē-ăp'-) *n.* **1.** *Greek Mythology* A Titan who was the father of Prometheus and Atlas and an ancestor of the human race. **2.** A satellite of Saturn. [Lat. *Iapetus* < Gk. *Iapetos*.]
IAS *abbr.* indicated air speed
Ia•și (yăsh, yä'shē) A city of NE Romania NNE of Bucharest; cap. of the country until 1861. Pop. 337,643.
–iasis *suff.* A pathological condition characterized or produced by: *taeniasis*. [NLat. *-iāsis* < Gk., n. suff.]
–iatric *suff.* Of or relating to a specified kind of medical practice, treatment, or healing: *geriatric*. [< Gk. *iātrikos*, medical < *iātros*, physician < *iāsthai*, to heal.]
–iatrics *suff.* Medical treatment: *pediatrics*. [< –IATRIC.]
i•at•ro•gen•ic (ī-ăt'rə-jĕn'ĭk) *adj.* Induced in a patient by a physician's activity, manner, or therapy. [Gk. *iātros*, physician; see –IATRIC + –GENIC.] —**i•at'ro•gen'i•cal•ly** *adv.*
–iatry *suff.* Medical treatment: *psychiatry*. [Gk. *-iātreia*, art of healing < *iātros*, physician. See –IATRIC.]
ib. *abbr.* ibidem
I•ba•dan (ē-bäd'n, ē-bä'dän) A city of SW Nigeria NNW of

Lagos; founded in the 1830s. Pop. 1,009,400.
I•ba•gué (ē-bä-gě') A city of W-central Colombia W of Bogotá. Pop. 280,638.
I-beam (ī'bēm') *n.* A steel joist or girder with short flanges and a cross section formed like the letter I.

I-beam

I•be•ri•a (ī-bîr'ē-ə) **1.** An ancient country of Transcaucasia roughly equivalent to the E part of present-day Georgia; became a Byzantine province in the 6th cent. A.D. **2.** See **Iberian Peninsula.**
I•be•ri•an (ī-bîr'ē-ən) *adj.* **1.** Of or relating to ancient Iberia in Transcaucasia or its peoples, languages, or cultures. **2.** Of or relating to the Iberian Peninsula or its peoples, languages, or cultures. ❖ *n.* **1.** A native or inhabitant of ancient Iberia in Transcaucasia. **2a.** A native or inhabitant of the Iberian Peninsula. **b.** A member of one of the ancient peoples that inhabited the Iberian Peninsula. **3.** Any of the languages of these peoples.
Iberian Peninsula also **I•be•ri•a** (ī-bîr'ē-ə) A peninsula of SW Europe separated from the rest of Europe by the Pyrenees and from Africa by the Strait of Gibraltar.
I•ber•ville (ē-bĕr-vēl'), **Pierre Le Moyne.** Sieur d'Iberville. 1661–1706. Canadian-born French explorer who established settlements in what is now S LA.
i•bex (ī'bĕks) *n.*, *pl.* **ibex** or **i•bex•es** Any of several wild goats of the genus *Capra*, esp. *C. ibex*, native to mountainous regions of Eurasia and northern Africa and having long, ridged, backward-curving horns. [Lat.]
I•bib•i•o (ī-bĭb'ē-ō) *n.*, *pl.* **Ibibio** or **-os 1.** A member of a people of southeast Nigeria. **2.** The Benue-Congo language of the Ibibio, closely related to Efik.
i•bi•dem (ĭb'ĭ-dĕm', ĭ-bī'dəm) *adv.* In the same place. Used in footnotes and bibliographies to refer to the reference cited just before. [Lat. *ibīdem*. See **i-** in App.]
–ibility *suff.* Variant of **–ability.**
i•bis (ī'bĭs) *n.*, *pl.* **ibis** or **i•bis•es 1.** Any of various storklike wading birds of the family Threskiornithidae of temperate and tropical regions, having a slender downward-curving bill. **2.** The wood ibis. [ME *ibin* < Lat. *ībis* < Gk. < Egypt. *hbj*.]
I•bi•za also **I•vi•za** (ē-bē'sə, ē-vē'thä) A Spanish island of the Balearic Is. in the W Mediterranean Sea SW of Majorca.
I•bi•zan hound (ī-bē'zən, -zän) *n.* A swift slender hunting dog bred primarily in the Balearic Islands and having a short, solid or spotted red and white or tawny coat. [After IBIZA.]
–ible *suff.* Variant of **–able.**
Ibn Rushd (ĭb'ən rōosht') See **Averroës.**
Ibn Sa•ud (sä-ōod'), **Abdul Aziz** 1880?–1953. Arab leader who was the first king of Saudi Arabia (1932–53).
I•bo (ē'bō) *n.* Variant of **Igbo.**
Ib•sen (ĭb'sən, ĭp'-), **Henrik** 1828–1906. Norwegian playwright whose works include *Peer Gynt* (1867) and *A Doll's House* (1879). —**Ib•sen'i•an** (-sē'nē-ən, -sĕn'ē-) *adj.*
i•bu•pro•fen (ī'byōō-prō'fən) *n.* A nonsteroidal anti-inflammatory medication, $C_{13}H_{18}O_2$, used esp. in the treatment of arthritis and commonly taken as an analgesic and antipyretic. [Alteration of chemical name *i(so)bu(tyl)phen(yl) pro(pionic acid)*.]
IC *abbr.* integrated circuit
–ic *suff.* **1.** Of, relating to, or characterized by: *seismic*. **2.** Having a valence higher than that of a specified element in compounds or ions named with adjectives ending in *–ous*: *sulfuric acid*. **3.** One relating to or characterized by: *academic*. [ME < OFr. *-ique* < Lat. *-icus* and Gk. *-ikos.*]
ICAO *abbr.* International Civil Aviation Organization
I•car•i•a (ī-kâr'ē-ə, ĭ-kâr'-) See **Ikaria.**
Ic•a•rus (ĭk'ər-əs) *n.* *Greek Mythology* The son of Daedalus who in escaping from Crete on wings made for him by his father flew so close to the sun that the wax fastening his wings melted and he fell into the Aegean Sea. [Lat. *Īcarus* < Gk. *Īkaros*.]
ICBM *abbr.* intercontinental ballistic missile
ICC *abbr.* **1.** Indian Claims Commission **2.** International Chamber of Commerce **3.** Interstate Commerce Commission
ice (īs) *n.* **1.** Water frozen solid. **2.** A surface, layer, or mass of frozen water. **3.** Something resembling frozen water. **4.** A frozen dessert consisting of water, sugar, and a liquid flavoring. **5.** Cake frosting; icing. **6.** *Slang* A pebbly white form of methamphetamine that is smoked and is considered highly addictive. **7.** *Slang* Diamonds. **8.** *Sports* The playing field in ice hockey; the rink. **9.** Extreme unfriendliness or reserve. **10.** *Slang* A payment over the listed price of a ticket for a public event. ❖ *v.* **iced, ic•ing, ic•es** —*tr.* **1.** To coat or slick with solidly frozen water. **2.** To cause to become ice; freeze. **3.** To chill by setting in or as if in ice. **4.** To cover or decorate (a cake, for example) with a sugar coating. **5.**

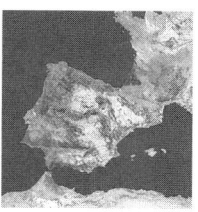
Iberian Peninsula

ibex
Capra ibex

Slang To ensure of victory, as in a game; clinch. **6.** *Sports* To shoot (the puck) from one's defensive half of an ice hockey rink across the opponent's goal line outside of the goal. **7.** *Slang* To kill; murder. —*intr.* To turn into or become coated with ice; freeze. —*idioms:* **on ice** *Slang* **1.** In reserve or readiness. **2.** Held incommunicado. **on thin ice** In a precarious position. [ME *is* < OE *īs.*]

ICE *abbr.* **1.** internal-combustion engine **2.** International Cultural Exchange

Ice. *abbr.* **1.** Iceland **2.** Icelandic

ice age *n.* **1.** A cold period marked by extensive glaciation. **2. Ice Age** The most recent glacial period, which occurred during the Pleistocene Epoch.

ice ax *n.* A pickax having a sharp point or spike at the bottom of the handle, used by mountaineers for climbing on ice.

ice ax

ice bag *n.* See **ice pack** 2.

ice barrier *n.* A section of the Antarctic ice shelf beyond the coastline, resting partly on the ocean floor.

ice·berg (īs′bûrg′) *n.* **1.** A massive floating body of ice broken away from a glacier. **2.** *Informal* A cold aloof person. [Partial transl. of Du. *ijsberg* < MDu. *ijsbergh* : *ijs*, ice + *bergh*, mountain; see **bhergh-** in App.]

iceberg lettuce *n.* A crisp round compact head of lettuce with light green, tightly folded leaves. [< its pale color.]

ice·blink (īs′blĭngk′) *n.* **1.** A yellowish glare in the sky over an ice field. **2.** A coastal ice cliff.

ice blue *n.* A very pale blue.

ice·boat (īs′bōt′) *n.* **1.** A boatlike vehicle set on sharp runners, used for sailing on ice. **2.** See **icebreaker** 1.

ice·bound (īs′bound′) *adj.* Locked in or covered over by ice.

ice·box (īs′bŏks′) *n.* **1.** An insulated chest or box into which ice is placed to cool and preserve food. **2.** A refrigerator.

ice·break·er (īs′brā′kər) *n.* **1.** *Nautical* A sturdy ship built to break a passage through icebound waters. **2.** A protective pier or dock apron used as a buffer against floating ice. **3a.** Something done or said to relax an unduly formal atmosphere or situation. **b.** A beginning; a start. —**ice′break′ing** *n.*

ice bucket *n.* **1.** A small insulated container with a lid, used for holding ice. **2.** A similar container without a lid, used to cool bottles placed inside it.

ice·cap or **ice cap** (īs′kăp′) *n.* An extensive dome-shaped or platelike perennial cover of ice and snow that spreads out from a center and covers a large area, esp. of land.

ice-cold (īs′kōld′) *adj.* Extremely cold.

ice cream *n.* A dessert food prepared from a frozen mixture of milk products, sugar, and flavorings, containing a minimum of 10 percent milk fat.

ice-cream cone *n.* **1.** A conical wafer used to hold a scoop of ice cream. **2.** A cone with ice cream in it.

ice-cream parlor *n.* An establishment serving ice cream.

ice-cream social *n. Chiefly Upper Northern US* A picnic featuring ice cream, often held for the purpose of raising money for charity.

ice-cream soda *n.* A refreshment consisting of scoops of ice cream in a mixture of soda water and syrup.

iced (īst) *adj.* **1.** Covered over with ice. **2.** Chilled with ice. **3.** Decorated or coated with icing.

ice·fall (īs′fôl′) *n.* **1.** The part of a glacier resembling a frozen waterfall flowing down a steep slope. **2.** An ice avalanche.

ice field *n.* A large level expanse of floating ice that is more than eight kilometers (five miles) in its greatest dimension.

ice floe *n.* A flat expanse of floating ice smaller than an ice field.

ice fog *n.* A fog of ice particles.

ice foot *n.* A belt or ledge of ice along Arctic shorelines.

ice-free (īs′frē′) *adj.* **1.** Free of ice and passable: *an ice-free river.* **2.** Lacking obstructive ice: *an ice-free period.*

ice hockey *n.* A game played on ice in which two opposing teams of skaters, using sticks with usu. curved blades, try to drive a puck into the opponent's goal.

ice·house (īs′hous′) *n.* A place where ice is made, stored, or sold.

Icel. *abbr.* **1.** Iceland **2.** Icelandic

Ice·land (īs′lənd) An island country in the North Atlantic near the Arctic Circle; gained independence from Denmark in 1944. Cap. Reykjavík. Pop. 266,000. —**Ice′land·er** *n.*

Ice·land·ic (īs-lăn′dĭk) *adj.* Of or relating to Iceland or its people, language, or culture. ❖ *n.* The North Germanic language of Iceland.

Iceland moss *n.* A brittle grayish-brown Arctic lichen (*Cetraria islandica*) sometimes used as a food or in medicine.

Iceland spar *n.* A doubly refracting transparent calcite used in optical instruments.

ice·mak·er (īs′mā′kər) *n.* A machine, often built into a refrigerator, that freezes water into ice cubes.

ice·man (īs′măn′) *n.* **1.** A man who cuts, sells, or delivers ice. **2.** *Slang* A hired killer.

ice milk *n.* A dessert food prepared from a frozen mixture of milk products, sugar, and flavorings.

ice-mi·nus (īs′mī′nəs) *adj.* Of or relating to a strain of genetically altered bacteria that are applied to crop plants to inhibit the formation of frost.

ice needle *n.* A long thin ice crystal floating high in the atmosphere under certain conditions of temperature and humidity.

icebreaker
Russian nuclear-powered icebreaker

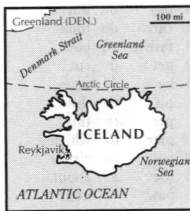

Iceland

I·ce·ni (ī-sē′nī′) *pl.n.* An ancient Celtic tribe of eastern Britain who under Queen Boudicca fought unsuccessfully against the Romans about A.D. 60. [Lat. *Icenī.*] —**I·ce′nic** (-nĭk) *adj.*

ice pack *n.* **1.** A floating mass of compacted ice fragments. **2.** A folded sac filled with crushed ice and applied to parts of the body to reduce pain and inflammation.

ice pick *n.* A pointed awl for chipping or breaking ice.

ice plant *n.* A succulent annual (*Mesembryanthemum crystallinum*) native to southern Africa and having fleshy leaves and stems covered with glistening papillae.

ice point *n.* The temperature, equal to 0°C (32°F), at which pure water and ice are in equilibrium in a mixture at 1 atmosphere of pressure.

ice show *n.* An entertainment consisting of figure skating, ice dancing, acrobatic stunts, and buffoonery performed on ice.

ice skate *n.* A shoe or light boot with a metal runner or blade fitted to the sole, used for skating on ice. —**ice′-skate′** (īs′skāt′) *v.* —**ice skater** *n.*

ice storm *n.* A storm in which snow or rain freezes on contact, forming a coat of ice on the surfaces it touches.

ice water *n.* **1.** Very cold or chilled water, esp. for drinking, often with ice in it. **2.** Melted ice.

ICFTU *abbr.* International Confederation of Free Trade Unions

I·chi·ka·wa (ē-chē′kä-wä′) A city of E-central Honshu, Japan, a suburb of Tokyo. Pop. 447,165.

I Ching (ē jĭng′) *n.* An ancient Chinese book consisting of 64 interrelated hexagrams that were originally used for divination, with commentaries attributed to Confucius. [Chin. (Mandarin) *Yì Jīng*, Book of Changes : *yì*, change + *jīng*, classic, book.]

ich·neu·mon (ĭk-nōō′mən, -nyōō′-) *n.* **1.** A large mongoose (*Herpestes ichneumon*) of Africa and southern Europe having a gray coat and black tail tufts. **2.** The ichneumon fly. [Lat. *ichneumōn*, weasel, ichneumon fly < Gk. *ikhneumōn* < *ikhneuein*, to track < *ikhnos*, track.]

ichneumon fly *n.* Any of various wasplike insects of the family Ichneumonidae, whose larvae are parasitic on the larvae of other insects.

ich·nite (ĭk′nīt′) also **ich·no·lite** (-nō-līt′) *n.* A fossilized footprint. [Gk. *ikhnos*, track + –ITE.]

ich·nog·ra·phy (ĭk-nŏg′rə-fē) *n., pl.* **-phies** **1.** The art or process of drawing ground plans. **2.** A ground plan of a building. [Lat. *ichnographia* : Gk. *ikhnos*, track + Gk. *-graphiā*, -graphy.]

ich·nol·o·gy (ĭk-nŏl′ə-jē) *n.* The branch of paleontology dealing with the study of fossilized evidence of the activities of organisms, such as footprints and burrows. [Gk. *ikhnos*, footprint + –LOGY.]

i·chor (ī′kôr′, ī′kər) *n.* **1.** *Greek Mythology* The rarefied fluid running in the veins of the gods. **2.** *Pathology* A watery acrid discharge from a wound or ulcer. [ME *icor* < LLat. *īchōr* < Gk. *īkhōr*.] —**i′chor·ous** (ī′kər-əs) *adj.*

ich·thy·ic (ĭk′thē-ĭk) *adj.* Of or characteristic of fishes.

ichthyo- or **ichthy–** *pref.* Fish: *ichthyophagous.* [Lat. < Gk. *ikhthuo-* < *ikhthūs*, fish.]

ich·thy·o·fau·na (ĭk′thē-ə-fô′nə) *n.* The fish of a particular region.

ich·thy·oid (ĭk′thē-oid′) *n.* A fish or fishlike vertebrate. —**ich′-thy·oid**, **ich′thy·oi′dal** (ĭk′thē-oid′l) *adj.*

ich·thy·ol·o·gy (ĭk′thē-ŏl′ə-jē) *n.* The branch of zoology that deals with the study of fishes. —**ich′thy·o·log′ic** (-ə-lŏj′ĭk), **ich′thy·o·log′i·cal** *adj.* —**ich′thy·ol′o·gist** *n.*

ich·thy·oph·a·gous (ĭk′thē-ŏf′ə-gəs) *adj.* Feeding on fish.

ich·thy·or·nis (ĭk′thē-ôr′nĭs) *n.* Any of various extinct birds of the genus *Ichthyornis* that existed during the Cretaceous Period. [NLat. *Ichthyornis*, genus name : ICHTHY(O)- + Gk. *ornis*, bird.]

ich·thy·o·saur (ĭk′thē-ə-sôr′) also **ich·thy·o·sau·rus** (ĭk′thē-ə-sôr′əs) *n., pl.* **-saurs** also **-sau·ri** (-sôr′ī′) Any of various extinct marine reptiles of the order Ichthyosauria of the Triassic Period to the Cretaceous Period, having a porpoiselike head and an elongated toothed snout. [< NLat. *ichthyosaurus* : Gk. *ikhthuo-*, ichthyo- + Gk. *sauros*, lizard.]

ich·thy·o·sis (ĭk′thē-ō′sĭs) *n.* A congenital, often hereditary skin disease marked by dry thickened scaly skin.

–ician *suff.* One who practices; a specialist: *technician.* [ME < OFr. *-icien* < *-ique*, n. suff.; see –IC n. suff., adj. and n. suff.; see –IAN.]

i·ci·cle (ī′sĭ-kəl) *n.* **1.** A tapering spike of ice formed by the freezing of dripping or falling water. **2.** *Informal* An aloof or emotionally unresponsive person. [ME *isikel* : *is*, *ise*, ice; see ICE + *ikel*, icicle (< OE *gicel*; see **yeg-** in App.).]

icicle plant *n.* See **fig marigold.** [< its glistening papillae.]

ic·ing (ī′sĭng) *n.* **1.** A sweet glaze made of sugar, butter, water, and egg whites or milk, used to cover or decorate baked goods. See Regional Note at **frosting.** **2.** *Sports* A minor rule violation in ice hockey in which a player ices the puck, and the puck is not played by the goalie. —**idiom: icing on the cake** An additional benefit to something already good.

ICJ *abbr.* International Court of Justice

ick·y (ĭk′ē) *adj.* **-i·er, -i·est** *Informal* **1.** Disagreeably sticky. **2.** Offensive; distasteful. [< *ick*, expression of disgust.] —**ick′i·ly** *adv.* —**ick′i·ness** *n.*

ICMP *abbr.* Internet Control Message Protocol

i·con *n.* **1.** also **i·kon** (ī′kŏn′) **a.** An image; a representation. **b.** A representation or picture of a sacred or sanctified Christian personage, traditional to the Eastern Church. **2.** An important, enduring symbol. **3.** The object of great attention and devotion; an idol. **4.** *Computer Science* A picture on a screen representing a specific file, directory, window, option, or program. [Gk. *eikōn* < *eikenai*, to be like, seem.]

i•con•ic (ī-kŏn′ĭk) *adj.* **1.** Of, relating to, or characteristic of an icon. **2.** Conventional or formulaic. Used of memorial statues and busts. **—i′co•nic′i•ty** (ī′kə-nĭs′ĭ-tē) *n.*

icono– or **icon–** *pref.* Image; icon: *iconolatry.* [Med.Gk. *eikono-* < *eikōn*, image, icon < Gk., likeness. See ICON.]

i•con•o•clasm (ī-kŏn′ə-klăz′əm) *n.* The beliefs, practices, or doctrine of an iconoclast. [Back-formation < ICONOCLAST.]

i•con•o•clast (ī-kŏn′ə-klăst′) *n.* **1.** One who attacks and seeks to overthrow traditional or popular ideas or institutions. **2.** One who destroys sacred religious images. [Fr. *iconoclaste* < Med.Gk. *eikonoklastēs*, smasher of religious images : *eikono-*, icono- + Gk. *-klastēs*, breaker (< *klān*, *klas-*, to break).] **—i•con′o•clas′tic** *adj.*

i•co•nog•ra•phy (ī′kə-nŏg′rə-fē) *n., pl.* **-phies 1a.** Pictorial illustration of a subject. **b.** The collected representations illustrating a subject. **2.** A set of specified or traditional symbolic forms associated with the theme of a stylized work of art. **3.** A treatise or book dealing with iconography. [LLat. *īconographia*, description < Med.Gk. *eikonographiā* : *eikono-*, icono- + Gk. *-graphiā*, -graphy.] **—i′co•nog′ra•pher** *n.* **—i•con′o•graph′ic** (ī-kŏn′ə-grăf′ĭk), **i•con′o•graph′i•cal** *adj.*

i•co•nol•a•try (ī′kə-nŏl′ə-trē) *n.* Worship of icons or images. **—i′co•nol′a•ter** *n.* **—i•con•o•lat′ric** (ī′kŏn-ə-lăt′rĭk) *adj.*

i•co•nol•o•gy (ī′kə-nŏl′ə-jē) *n.* The branch of art history that deals with the description, analysis, and interpretation of icons or iconic representations. **—i•con′o•log′i•cal** (ī-kŏn′ə-lŏj′ĭ-kəl) *adj.* **—i′co•nol′o•gist** *n.*

i•con•o•scope (ī-kŏn′ə-skōp′) *n.* An early form of a television-camera tube, equipped for rapid scanning of a photoactive mosaic. [Orig. a trademark.]

i•co•nos•ta•sis (ī′kə-nŏs′tə-sĭs) *n., pl.* **-ses** (-sēz′) The screen with icons that divides the sanctuary from the nave of an Eastern Orthodox church. [< Med.Gk. *eikonostasion*, shrine : *eikono-*, icono- + Gk. *stasis*, a standing; see **stā-** in App.]

i•co•sa•he•dron (ī-kō′sə-hē′drən, ī-kŏs′ə-) *n., pl.* **-drons** or **-dra** (-drə) A polyhedron having 20 faces. [Gk. *eikosaedron* : *eikosi*, twenty; see **wīkm̥tī** in App. + *-edron*, -hedron.] **—i•co′sa•he′dral** (-drəl) *adj.*

ICRC *abbr.* International Committee of the Red Cross

–ics *suff.* **1.** Science, art, study, or knowledge of, or skill in: *photonics.* **2.** Actions, activities, or practices of: *athletics.* **3.** Qualities or operations of: *mechanics.* [–IC + –S¹ (transl. of Gk. *-ika* < neut. pl. of *-ikos*, adj. suff.)]

ic•ter•ic (ĭk-tĕr′ĭk) *adj.* **1.** Relating to or affected with jaundice. **2.** Used to treat jaundice. ❖ *n.* A remedy for jaundice. [Lat. *ictericus* < Gk. *ikterikos* < *ikteros*, jaundice.]

ic•ter•us (ĭk′tər-əs) *n.* See **jaundice.** [NLat. < Gk. *ikteros.*]

Ic•ti•nus (ĭk-tī′nəs) fl. 5th cent. B.C. Greek architect and the chief designer of the Parthenon at Athens.

ic•tus (ĭk′təs) *n., pl.* **ictus** or **-tus•es 1.** *Medicine* A sudden attack, blow, stroke, or seizure. **2.** The accent that falls on a stressed syllable in a line of scanned verse. [Lat., stroke < p. part. of *īcere*, to strike.]

ICU *abbr.* intensive care unit

ic•y (ī′sē) *adj.* **ic•i•er, ic•i•est 1.** Containing or covered with ice. **2.** Bitterly cold. See Syns at **cold. 3a.** Resembling ice. **b.** Chilling in manner. **—ic′i•ly** *adv.* **—ic′i•ness** *n.*

id (ĭd) *n.* In Freudian theory, the unconscious part of the psyche that serves as the source of instinctual impulses and demands immediate satisfaction of primitive needs. [NLat. (transl. of Ger. *Es*, a special use of *es*, it, as a psychoanalytic term) < Lat., it. See **i-** in App.]

ID¹ (ī′dē′) *Informal n.* A form of identification, esp. an ID card. ❖ *tr.v.* **ID'ed, ID'ing, ID's** To check the identification of, esp. in order to verify legal age; card.

ID² *abbr.* **1. Id.** Idaho **2.** identification **3.** Intelligence Department

id. *abbr.* idem

–id *suff.* Body; particle: *chromatid.* [Lat. *-is*, *-id-*, fem. patronymic suff. < Gk.]

I'd (īd) **1.** Contraction of *I had.* **2.** Contraction of *I would.*

I•da (ī′də), **Mount** A peak, 2,457.7 m (8,058 ft), of central Crete; associated with the worship of Zeus in ancient times.

I•da•ho (ī′də-hō′) A state of the NW US; admitted as the 43rd state in 1890. The region was held jointly by Great Britain and the US from 1818 to 1846. Cap. Boise. Pop. 1,293,953. **—I′da•ho′an** *adj. & n.*

Idaho Falls A city of SE ID NNE of Pocatello. Pop. 50,730.

'Id al-Fitr also **Eid al-Fitr** (ĭd əl-fĭt′ər) *n. Islam* A festival that ends the fast of Ramadan. [Ar. *'īd al-fiṭr*, Feast of Breaking the Fast : *'īd*, feast (< Aram. *'ed*, day of assembly < *'ad*, to fix a time) + *al-*, the + *fiṭr*, breaking the fast (< *faṭara*, to split, break, break the fast).]

ID card *n.* A card, often bearing a photograph, that gives identifying data, such as name and age, about a person.

–ide *suff.* **1.** Group of related chemical compounds: *diglyceride, monosaccharide.* **2.** Binary compound: *sodium chloride, hydrogen cyanide.* **3.** Chemical element with properties similar to another: *actinide, lanthanide.* [< (OX)IDE.]

i•de•a (ī-dē′ə) *n.* **1.** Something, such as a thought, that potentially or actually exists in the mind because of mental activity. **2.** An opinion, conviction, or principle. **3.** A plan, scheme, or method. **4.** The gist of a specific situation; significance. **5.** A notion; a fancy. **6.** *Music* A theme or motif. **7.** *Philosophy* **a.** In the philosophy of Plato, an archetype of which a corresponding being in phenomenal reality is an imperfect replica. **b.** In the philosophy of Kant, a transcendent but nonempirical concept of reason. **c.** In the philosophy of Hegel, absolute truth; the complete and ultimate product of reason. **8.** *Obsolete* A mental image of something remembered. [ME < Lat. < Gk. See **weid-** in App.]

SYNONYMS *idea, thought, notion, concept, conception* These nouns refer to what is formed or represented in the mind as the product of mental activity. *Idea* has the widest range: *"Human history is in essence a history of ideas"* (H.G. Wells). *Thought* is distinctively intellectual and thus stresses contemplation and reasoning: *"Language is the dress of thought"* (Samuel Johnson). *Notion* often refers to a vague, general, or even fanciful idea: *"She certainly has some notion of drawing"* (Rudyard Kipling). *Concept* and *conception* are applied to mental formulations on a broad scale: *no concept of time; ancient conceptions of divinity.*

i•de•al (ī-dē′əl, ī-dēl′) *n.* **1.** A conception of something in its absolute perfection. **2.** One seen as a standard or model of perfection or excellence. **3.** An ultimate object of endeavor; a goal. **4.** An honorable or worthy principle or aim. ❖ *adj.* **1a.** Of, relating to, or embodying an ideal. **b.** Conforming to an ultimate form or standard of perfection or excellence. **2.** Considered the best of its kind. **3.** Completely or highly satisfactory. **4a.** Existing only in the mind; imaginary. **b.** Lacking practicality or the possibility of realization. **5.** Of, relating to, or consisting of ideas or mental images. **6.** *Philosophy* **a.** Existing as an archetype or pattern, esp. as a Platonic idea. **b.** Of or relating to idealism. [< ME, of divine archetypes < LLat. *ideālis* < Lat. *idea*, idea. See IDEA.]

i•de•al•ism (ī-dē′ə-lĭz′əm) *n.* **1.** The act or practice of envisioning things in an ideal form. **2.** Pursuit of one's ideals. **3.** Idealized treatment of a subject in literature or art. **4.** *Philosophy* The theory that the object of external perception consists of ideas.

i•de•al•ist (ī-dē′ə-lĭst) *n.* **1.** One whose conduct is influenced by ideals that often conflict with practical considerations. **2.** One who is unrealistic and impractical; a visionary. **3.** An artist or writer whose work shows idealism. **4.** An adherent of any system of philosophical idealism.

i•de•al•is•tic (ī-dē′ə-lĭs′tĭk) *adj.* Of, relating to, or having the nature of an idealist or idealism. **—i′de•al•is′ti•cal•ly** *adv.*

i•de•al•i•ty (ī′dē-ăl′ĭ-tē) *n., pl.* **-ties 1.** The state or quality of being ideal. **2.** Existence in idea only.

i•de•al•ize (ī-dē′ə-līz′) *v.* **-ized, -iz•ing, -iz•es** *—tr.* **1.** To regard as ideal. **2.** To make or envision as ideal. *—intr.* **1.** To render something as an ideal. **2.** To conceive an ideal. **—i•de′al•i•za′tion** (-ə-lĭ-zā′shən) *n.* **—i•de′al•iz′er** *n.*

i•de•al•ly (ī-dē′ə-lē) *adv.* **1.** In conformity with an ideal; perfectly. **2.** In theory or imagination; theoretically.

i•de•ate (ī′dē-āt′) *v.* **-at•ed, -at•ing, -ates** *—tr.* To form an idea of; imagine or conceive. *—intr.* To conceive mental images; think. **—i′de•a′tion** *n.* **—i′de•a′tion•al** *adj.*

i•dée fixe (ē-dā fēks′) *n., pl.* **i•dées fixes** (ē-dā fēks′) A fixed idea; an obsession. [Fr. : *idée*, idea + *fixe*, fixed.]

i•dem (ī′dĕm′) *pron.* Something that has been mentioned previously; the same. [Lat. < *id*, it. See **i-** in App.]

i•den•tic (ī-dĕn′tĭk) *adj.* **1.** Being or constituting a diplomatic action or language in which governments agree to use the same forms in their relations with other governments. **2.** Identical. [Med.Lat. *identicus*, identical. See IDENTICAL.]

i•den•ti•cal (ī-dĕn′tĭ-kəl) *adj.* **1.** Being the same. **2.** Exactly equal and alike. **3.** Having such a close similarity or resemblance as to be essentially equal or interchangeable. **4.** *Biology* Of or relating to a twin or twins developed from the same fertilized ovum and having the same genetic makeup and closely similar appearance; monozygotic. [< Med.Lat. *identicus* < LLat. *identitās*, identity. See IDENTITY.] **—i•den′ti•cal•ly** *adv.* **—i•den′ti•cal•ness** *n.*

USAGE NOTE Either *with* or *to* is acceptable after *identical.*

identical rhyme *n.* **1.** Repetition of the same word in the rhyme position. **2.** See **rime riche.**

i•den•ti•fi•ca•tion (ī-dĕn′tə-fĭ-kā′shən) *n.* **1a.** The act of identifying. **b.** The state of being identified. **2.** Proof or evidence of identity. **3.** *Psychology* A person's association with the qualities, traits, or views of another person or group.

identification card *n.* An ID card.

i•den•ti•fy (ī-dĕn′tə-fī′) *v.* **-fied, -fy•ing, -fies** *—tr.* **1.** To establish the identity of. **2.** To ascertain the origin, nature, or characteristics of. **3.** *Biology* To determine the taxonomic classification of (an organism). **4.** To consider as identical or united; equate. **5.** To associate or affiliate (oneself) closely with a person or group. *—intr.* To establish an identification with another or others. [Med.Lat. *identificāre*, to make to resemble : LLat. *identitās*, identity; see IDENTITY + Lat. *-ficāre*, -fy.] **—i•den′ti•fi′a•ble** *adj.* **—i•den′ti•fi′a•bly** *adv.* **—i•den′ti•fi′er** *n.*

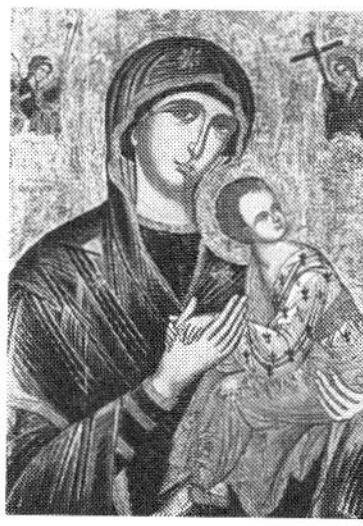

icon
Cretan icon of Mary and Jesus

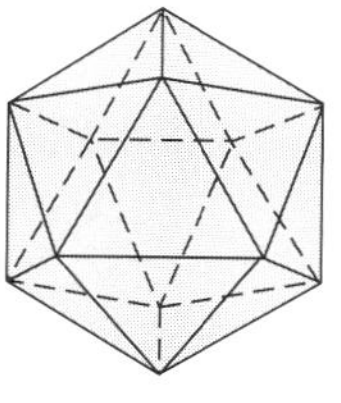

icosahedron

ă	pat	oi	boy
ā	pay	ou	out
âr	care	o͝o	took
ä	father	o͞o	boot
ĕ	pet	ŭ	cut
ē	be	ûr	urge
ĭ	pit	th	thin
ī	pie	*th*	this
îr	pier	hw	which
ŏ	pot	zh	vision
ō	toe	ə	about,
ô	paw		item

Stress marks:
′ (primary);
′ (secondary), as in
lexicon (lĕk′sĭ-kŏn′)

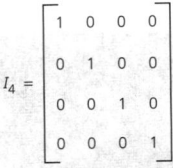

$$I_4 = \begin{bmatrix} 1 & 0 & 0 & 0 \\ 0 & 1 & 0 & 0 \\ 0 & 0 & 1 & 0 \\ 0 & 0 & 0 & 1 \end{bmatrix}$$

identity matrix

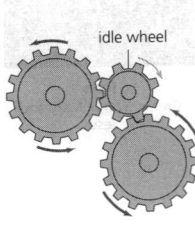

idle wheel

idle wheel

Ignatius of Loyola

i·den·ti·ty (ī-dĕn′tĭ-tē) *n., pl.* **-ties 1.** The set of characteristics by which a thing is recognized or known. **2.** The set of behavioral or personal traits by which an individual is recognizable as a member of a group. **3.** The quality or condition of being the same as something else. **4.** The distinct personality of an individual regarded as a persisting entity; individuality. **5.** Information, such as an identification number, used to establish or prove a person's individuality, as in providing access to a credit account. **6.** *Mathematics* **a.** An equation that is satisfied by any number that replaces the letter for which the equation is defined. **b.** Identity element. [Fr. *identité* < OFr. *identite* < LLat. *identitās* < Lat. *idem*, the same < *id*, it. See **i-** in App.]

identity crisis *n.* **1.** A psychosocial state or condition of disorientation and role confusion occurring esp. in adolescents as a result of conflicting pressures and expectations and often producing acute anxiety. **2.** An analogous state of confusion occurring in a social structure, such as a corporation.

identity element *n.* The element of a set of numbers that when combined with another number in a particular operation leaves that number unchanged. For example, 0 is the identity element under addition for the real numbers.

identity function *n. Mathematics* The function whose output is identical to its input.

identity matrix *n.* A square matrix with 1's along the diagonal from upper left to lower right and 0's in all other positions.

identity politics *n.* (*used with a sing. or pl. verb*) Political attitudes or positions that focus on the concerns of social groups identified mainly on the basis of gender, race, ethnicity, or sexual orientation.

identity sign *n. Mathematics* The symbol (≡), used to designate identity rather than equality.

ideo– *pref.* Idea: *ideography.* [Fr. *idéo-* < Gk. *idea*, form, idea. See **weid-** in App.]

id·e·o·gram (ĭd′ē-ə-grăm′, ī′dē-) *n.* **1.** A character or symbol representing an idea or thing without expressing the pronunciation of the words for it, as in many traffic signs. **2.** See **logogram**. **3.** A graphic symbol, such as &. —**id′e·o·gram·mat′ic** (-grə-măt′ĭk) *adj.*

id·e·o·graph (ĭd′ē-ə-grăf′) *n.* See **ideogram** 1. —**id′e·o·graph′ic** *adj.* —**id′e·o·graph′i·cal·ly** *adv.*

id·e·og·ra·phy (ĭd′ē-ŏg′rə-fē, ī′dē-) *n.* **1.** The representation of ideas by graphic symbols. **2.** The use of ideograms to express ideas.

i·de·o·log·i·cal (ī′dē-ə-lŏj′ĭ-kəl, ĭd′ē-) also **i·de·o·log·ic** (-lŏj′ĭk) *adj.* **1.** Of or relating to ideology. **2.** Of or concerned with ideas.

i·de·o·logue (ī′dē-ə-lôg′, -lŏg′, ĭd′ē-) *n.* An advocate of a particular ideology. [Fr. *idéologue*, back-formation < *idéologie*, ideology. See IDEOLOGY.]

i·de·ol·o·gy (ī′dē-ŏl′ə-jē, ĭd′ē-) *n., pl.* **-gies 1.** The body of ideas reflecting the social needs and aspirations of an individual, group, class, or culture. **2.** A set of doctrines or beliefs that form the basis of a political, economic, or other system. —**i′de·ol′o·gist** *n.*

i·de·o·mo·tor (ī′dē-ə-mō′tər, ĭd′ē-) *adj. Psychology* Of or relating to an unconscious or involuntary body movement made in response to a thought rather than to a sensory stimulus.

ides (īdz) *pl.n.* (*used with a sing. or pl. verb*) The 15th day of March, May, July, or October or the 13th day of the other months in the ancient Roman calendar. [ME < OFr. < Lat. *īdūs.*]

idio– *pref.* One's own; private; personal: *idiolect.* [Gk. < *idios*, personal, private. See **s(w)e-** in App.]

id·i·o·blast (ĭd′ē-ə-blăst′) *n.* A plant cell that differs noticeably in form from neighboring cells. —**id′i·o·blas′tic** *adj.*

id·i·o·cy (ĭd′ē-ə-sē) *n., pl.* **-cies 1.** Extreme folly or stupidity. **2.** A foolish or stupid utterance or deed. **3.** *Psychology* Profound mental retardation. Not in scientific use. [< IDIOT.]

id·i·o·graph·ic (ĭd′ē-ō-grăf′ĭk) *adj.* Relating to or concerned with discrete or unique facts or events.

id·i·o·lect (ĭd′ē-ə-lĕkt′) *n.* One individual's speech considered linguistically unique among speakers of the same language or dialect. [IDIO- + (DIA)LECT.] —**id′i·o·lec′tal, id′i·o·lec′tic** *adj.*

id·i·om (ĭd′ē-əm) *n.* **1.** A speech form or an expression of a given language that is peculiar to itself grammatically or cannot be understood from the individual meanings of its elements, as in *keep tabs on.* **2.** The specific grammatical, syntactic, and structural character of a given language. **3.** Regional speech or dialect. **4a.** A specialized vocabulary used by a group; jargon. **b.** A style or manner of expression peculiar to a given people. **5.** A style of artistic expression characteristic of a particular individual, school, period, or medium. [LLat. *idiōma, idiōmat-* < Gk. < *idiousthai*, to make one's own < *idios*, own, personal, private. See **s(w)e-** in App.]

id·i·o·mat·ic (ĭd′ē-ə-măt′ĭk) *adj.* **1a.** Peculiar to or characteristic of a given language. **b.** Characterized by proficient use of idiomatic expressions: *speaks idiomatic English.* **2.** Resembling or having the nature of an idiom. **3.** Using many idioms. **4.** Peculiar to or characteristic of a given group. —**id′i·o·mat′i·cal·ly** *adv.*

id·i·o·path·ic (ĭd′ē-ə-păth′ĭk, ĭd′ē-ō-) *adj.* Of, relating to, or being a disease having no known cause.

id·i·op·a·thy (ĭd′ē-ŏp′ə-thē) *n.* A disease of unknown origin or cause. [NLat. *idiopathīa*, primary disease < Gk. *idiopatheia* : *idio-*, idio- + *-patheia*, -pathy.]

id·i·o·syn·cra·sy (ĭd′ē-ō-sĭng′krə-sē) *n., pl.* **-sies 1.** A structural or behavioral characteristic peculiar to an individual or group. **2.** A physiological or temperamental peculiarity. **3.** An unusual individual reaction to food or a drug. [Gk. *idiosunkrāsia* : *idio-*, idio- + *sunkrāsis*, mixture, temperament (*sun-*, syn- + *krāsis*, a mixing).] —**id′i·o·syn·crat′ic** (-sĭn-krăt′ĭk) *adj.* —**id′i·o·syn·crat′i·cal·ly** *adv.*

id·i·ot (ĭd′ē-ət) *n.* **1.** A foolish or stupid person. **2.** A person of profound mental retardation having a mental age below three years. Not in scientific use. [ME, ignorant person < OFr. *idiote* < Lat. *idiōta* < Gk. *idiōtēs*, private person, layman < *idios*, own, private. See **s(w)e-** in App.]

idiot box *n. Slang* A television.

id·i·ot·ic (ĭd′ē-ŏt′ĭk) *adj.* **1.** Showing foolishness or stupidity. **2.** Exhibiting idiocy. —**id′i·ot′i·cal·ly** *adv.*

idiot savant *n., pl.* **idiot savants** A mentally retarded person who exhibits extraordinary ability in a highly specialized area, such as mathematics or music. [Fr. : *idiot*, idiot + *savant*, learned.]

id·i·o·type (ĭd′ē-ə-tīp′) *n.* A set of one or more antigenic determinants specific to the region of an immunoglobulin molecule that can vary in its amino acid structure.

i·dle (īd′l) *adj.* **i·dler, i·dlest 1a.** Not employed or busy: *idle carpenters.* See Syns at **inactive. b.** Avoiding work or employment; lazy. **c.** Not in use or operation: *idle hands.* **2.** Lacking substance, value, or basis. ❖ *v.* **i·dled, i·dling, i·dles** —*intr.* **1.** To pass time without working or while avoiding work. **2.** To move lazily and without purpose. **3.** To run at a slow speed or out of gear. Used of a motor vehicle. —*tr.* **1.** To pass (time) without working or while avoiding work; waste. **2.** To make or cause to be unemployed or inactive. **3.** To cause (a motor, for example) to idle. ❖ *n.* **1.** A state of idling. Used of a motor vehicle. **2.** A mechanism for regulating the speed at which an engine runs at rest. [ME *idel* < OE *īdel.*] —**i′dle·ness** *n.* —**i′dler** (īd′lər) *n.* —**i′dly** *adv.*

idle character *n.* An alphanumeric or digital character that is transmitted over a communications line but does not appear in the output of the receiving terminal.

idle pulley also **idler pulley** *n.* A pulley on a shaft that rests on or presses against a drive belt to guide it or take up slack.

idle wheel *n.* **1.** A gear, wheel, or roller interposed between two similar parts to convey motion from one to the other without change in speed or direction of motion. **2.** See **idle pulley.**

i·do·crase (ī′də-krās′, -krāz′, ĭd′ə-) *n.* See **vesuvianite.** [Fr. < Gk. *eidos*, form; see **weid-** in App. + *krāsis*, mixture.]

i·dol (īd′l) *n.* **1a.** An image used as an object of worship. **b.** A false god. **2.** One that is adored, often blindly or excessively. **3.** Something visible but without substance. [ME < OFr. *idole* < LLat. *īdōlum* < Gk. *eidōlon*, phantom, idol < *eidos*, form. See **weid-** in App.]

i·dol·a·ter or **i·dol·a·tor** (ī-dŏl′ə-tər) *n.* **1.** One who worships idols. **2.** One who blindly or excessively admires or adores another. [ME *idolatre* < OFr. < Lat. *īdōlolatrēs* < Gk. *eidōlolatrēs* : *eidōlon*, idol; see IDOL + *-latrēs*, worshiper.]

i·dol·a·trous (ī-dŏl′ə-trəs) *adj.* **1.** Of or constituting idolatry. **2.** Given to blind or excessive devotion to something. —**i·dol′a·trous·ly** *adv.* —**i·dol′a·trous·ness** *n.*

i·dol·a·try (ī-dŏl′ə-trē) *n., pl.* **-tries 1.** Worship of idols. **2.** Blind or excessive devotion to something. [ME *idolatrie* < OFr. < Lat. *īdōlolatrīa* < Gk. *eidōlolatreiā* : *eidōlon*, idol; see IDOL + *latreiā*, service.]

i·dol·ize (īd′l-īz′) *tr.v.* **-ized, -iz·ing, -iz·es 1.** To regard with idolatrous devotion. See Syns at **revere**[1]. **2.** To worship as an idol. —**i·dol′i·za′tion** (-ī-zā′shən) *n.* —**i·dol′iz′er** *n.*

IDP *abbr.* **1.** integrated data processing **2.** international driving permit

i·dyll also **i·dyl** (īd′l) *n.* **1a.** A short poem or prose piece depicting a rural or pastoral scene, usu. in idealized terms. **b.** A narrative poem treating an epic or romantic theme. **2.** A scene or event of a simple and tranquil nature. **3a.** A carefree episode or experience: *a summer idyll in France.* **b.** A romantic interlude. [Lat. *īdyllium* < Gk. *eidullion*, dim. of *eidos*, form, figure. See **weid-** in App.]

i·dyl·lic (ī-dĭl′ĭk) *adj.* **1.** Of or having the nature of an idyll. **2.** Simple and carefree: *an idyllic vacation.* —**i·dyl′li·cal·ly** *adv.*

i·dyl·list (īd′l-ĭst) *n.* A writer of idylls.

IE *abbr.* **1.** Indo-European **2.** industrial engineer **3.** industrial engineering

i.e. *abbr. Latin* id est (that is)

–ie *suff.* Variant of **-y**[3].

Ie·per (yā′pər) also **Y·pres** (ē′prə) A city of W Belgium near the French border S of Ostend; site of three World War I battles (1914, 1915, and 1917). Pop. 35,235.

if (ĭf) *conj.* **1a.** In the event that: *If I were to go, I would be late.* **b.** Granting that: *If that is true, what next?* **c.** On the condition that: *She will sing only if paid.* **2.** Although possibly; even though: *a handsome if useless trinket.* **3.** Whether: *Ask if he plans to come.* **4.** Used to introduce an exclamatory clause, indicating a wish: *If they had only come!* ❖ *n.* A possibility, condition, or stipulation:

no ifs, ands, or buts. [ME < OE *gif.* See **i-** in App.]

IF *abbr.* intermediate frequency

I•fe (ē′fā) A city of SW Nigeria E of Ibadan; center of a powerful Yoruba kingdom until the late 17th cent. Pop. 209,100.

iff *abbr.* if and only if

if•fy (ĭf′ē) *adj.* **-fi•er, -fi•est** *Informal* Doubtful; uncertain.

If•ni (ēf′nē) A former Spanish possession (1860–1969) on the Atlantic coast of SW Morocco.

IFO *abbr.* identified flying object

I formation *n. Football* An offensive formation in which the running backs line up in single file behind the center and the quarterback.

IFR *abbr.* instrument flight rules

–ify *suff.* Variant of **-fy.**

Ig *abbr.* immunoglobulin

IG *abbr.* inspector general

Ig•bo (ĭg′bō) also **I•bo** (ē′bō) *n., pl.* **Igbo** or **-bos** also **Ibo** or **-bos 1.** A member of a people inhabiting southeast Nigeria. **2.** The Benue-Congo language of the Igbo.

igg (ĭg) *tr.v.* **igged, igg•ing, iggs** To ignore.

ig•loo (ĭg′lōō) *n., pl.* **-loos** An Inuit or Eskimo dwelling, esp. a dome-shaped dwelling built of blocks of packed snow. [Inuit *iglu,* house.]

Ig•na•tius (ĭg-nā′shəs), Saint. d. c. A.D. 110. Bishop of Antioch who was martyred during the reign of Trajan.

Ignatius of Loy•o•la (loi-ō′lə), Saint. 1491–1556. Spanish ecclesiastic who founded the Jesuits.

ig•ne•ous (ĭg′nē-əs) *adj.* **1.** Of, relating to, or characteristic of fire. **2.** *Geology* **a.** Formed by solidification from a molten state. Used of rocks. **b.** Of or relating to rock so formed; pyrogenic. [< Lat. *igneus < ignis,* fire.]

ig•nim•brite (ĭg′nĭm-brīt′) *n.* A volcanic rock formed by the welding together of tuffs from an explosive volcanic eruption. [Lat. *ignis,* fire + *imber, imbr-,* rain + **-ITE**[1].]

ig•nis fat•u•us (ĭg′nĭs făch′ōō-əs) *n., pl.* **ig•nes fat•u•i** (ĭg′nēz făch′ōō-ī′) **1.** A phosphorescent light over swampy ground at night, possibly from spontaneous combustion of gases emitted by rotting organic matter. **2.** Something that misleads or deludes; an illusion. [Med.Lat. : Lat. *ignis,* fire + Lat. *fatuus,* foolish.]

ig•nite (ĭg-nīt′) *v.* **-nit•ed, -nit•ing, -nites 1a.** To cause to burn. **b.** To set fire to. **2.** To subject to great heat, esp. to make luminous by heat. **3.** To arouse the passions of; excite: *The insults ignited my anger.* —*intr.* **1.** To begin to burn. **2.** To begin to glow. [LLat. *ignīre, ignīt- <* Lat. *ignis,* fire.] —**ig•nit′a•ble, ig•nit′i•ble** *adj.* —**ig•nit′er, ig•nit′tor** *n.*

ig•ni•tion (ĭg-nĭsh′ən) *n.* **1.** The raising of a substance to its ignition point, as by electric current. **2a.** An electrical system, typically powered by a battery or magneto, that provides the spark to ignite the fuel mixture in an internal-combustion engine. **b.** A switch that activates this system.

ignition point *n.* The minimum temperature at which a substance will continue to burn without additional external heat.

ig•ni•tron (ĭg-nī′trŏn′, ĭg′nī-) *n.* A single-anode, mercury-vapor rectifier in which current passes as an arc between an anode and cathode, consisting of pools of mercury, used in power rectification. [IGNI(TE) + **-TRON**.]

ig•no•ble (ĭg-nō′bəl) *adj.* **1.** Not noble in quality, character, or purpose; base or mean. **2.** Not of the nobility; common. [ME, of

---

low birth < OFr. < Lat. *ignōbilis* : *i-, in-,* not; see **IN-**[1] + *nōbilis, gnōbilis,* noble; see **NOBLE.**] —**ig′no•bil′i•ty** (-bĭl′ĭ-tē), **ig•no′ble•ness** *n.* —**ig•no′bly** *adv.*

ig•no•min•i•ous (ĭg′nə-mĭn′ē-əs) *adj.* **1.** Marked by shame or disgrace. **2.** Deserving disgrace or shame; despicable. **3.** Degrading; debasing: *an ignominious task.* —**ig′no•min′i•ous•ly** *adv.* —**ig′no•min′i•ous•ness** *n.*

ig•no•min•y (ĭg′nə-mĭn′ē, -mə-nē) *n., pl.* **-ies 1.** Great personal dishonor or humiliation. **2.** Shameful or dishonorable action, conduct, or character. [Fr. *ignominie <* OFr. < Lat. *ignōminia* : *i-, in-,* not; see **IN-**[1] + *nōmen, nōmin-,* name, reputation (influenced by *gnōscere,* to know); see **nō-men-** in App.]

ig•no•ra•mus (ĭg′nə-rā′məs) *n., pl.* **-mus•es** An ignorant person. [Ult. < Lat. *ignōrāmus,* we do not know, first pers. pl. pr. t. of *ignōrāre,* to be ignorant. See IGNORE.]

ig•no•rance (ĭg′nər-əns) *n.* The condition of being uneducated, unaware, or uninformed.

ig•no•rant (ĭg′nər-ənt) *adj.* **1.** Lacking education or knowledge. **2.** Showing or arising from a lack of education or knowledge: *an ignorant mistake.* **3.** Unaware or uninformed. [ME *ignoraunt* < OFr. *ignorant <* Lat. *ignōrāns, ignōrant-,* pr. part. of *ignōrāre,* to be ignorant, not to know. See **gnō-** in App.] —**ig′no•rant•ly** *adv.*

ig•nore (ĭg-nôr′, -nōr′) *tr.v.* **-nored, -nor•ing, -nores** To refuse to pay attention to; disregard. [Fr. *ignorer <* OFr. < Lat. *ignōrāre.* See **gnō-** in App.] —**ig•nor′a•ble** *adj.* —**ig•nor′er** *n.*

I•go•rot (ĭg′ə-rŏt′, ē′gə-) *n., pl.* **Igorot** or **-rots 1.** A member of any of several peoples of the mountains of northern Luzon in the Philippines. **2.** Any of the Austronesian languages of the Igorot.

i•gua•na (ĭ-gwä′nə) *n.* Any of various large tropical American lizards of the family Iguanidae, often having spiny projections along the back. [Sp. < Arawak *iwana.*]

i•guan•o•don (ĭ-gwä′nə-dŏn′) *n.* Any of various large dinosaurs of the genus *Iguanodon,* of the Jurassic and Cretaceous periods. [NLat. *Iguanodōn,* genus name : IGUANA + **-ODON**.]

I•gua•zú (ē′gwə-zōō′) or **I•gua•çú** (-sōō′) A river of S Brazil flowing c. 1,199 km (745 mi) to the Paraná R. at the **Iguazú Falls,** a series of cataracts averaging 61 m (200 ft) high.

ihp or **i.hp.** *abbr.* indicated horsepower

ih•ram (ē-räm′) *n. Islam* **1.** The sacred dress of Muslim pilgrims, consisting of two lengths of white cotton. **2.** The state of ritual purity of Muslims in wearing this dress for pilgrimage or for other acts of worship, esp. the daily worship. [Ar. *'iḥrām,* prohibition, ihram, infinitive of *'aḥrama,* to enter the state of ihram < *ḥarama,* to prohibit.]

IHS *abbr.* Jesus (Greek ΙΗΣΟΥΣ with S for sigma)

Ijs•sel or **IJs•sel** (ī′səl) A river, c. 113 km (70 mi) of E Netherlands flowing from the Lower Rhine R. to the Ijsselmeer.

Ijs•sel•meer or **IJs•sel•meer** (ī′səl-mâr′, -mâr′) A shallow dike-enclosed lake of NW Netherlands; formed from the Zuider Zee by the construction of two dams (completed 1932).

I•ka•ri•a (ē′kä-rē′ä) also **I•car•i•a** (ĭ-kâr′ē-ə, ī-kâr′-) An island of SE Greece in the Aegean Sea W of Samos.

i•kat (ē′kät) *n.* **1.** A technique for weaving fabric using tie-dyed threads to create an intricate design. **2.** The fabric so created. [Malay, tying, binding.]

i•ke•ba•na (ē′kĕ-bä′nä, ĭk′ə-) *n.* The Japanese art of formal flower arrangement with special regard shown to balance, harmony, and form. [J. : *ikeru,* to arrange + *hana,* flower.]

Ikh•na•ton (ĭk-nät′n) See **Akhenaton.**

i•kon (ī′kŏn′) *n.* Variant of **icon** 1.

IL *abbr.* Illinois

il-[1] *pref.* Variant of **in-**[1].

il-[2] *pref.* Variant of **in-**[2].

IL-1 *abbr.* interleukin-1

IL-2 *abbr.* interleukin-2

IL-3 *abbr.* interleukin-3

ILA *abbr.* International Longshoremen's Association

i•lang-i•lang (ē′läng-ē′läng) *n.* Variant of **ylang-ylang.**

–ile[1] *suff.* Of, relating to, or capable of: *audile.* [ME < OFr. < Lat. *-ilis, -īlis.*]

–ile[2] *suff.* A division of a specified size in the range of a statistic: *percentile.* [Prob. < **-ILE**[1].]

il•e•ac[1] (ĭl′ē-ăk′) *adj.* Of, relating to, or having the nature of ileus.

il•e•ac[2] (ĭl′ē-ăk′) *adj.* Of, relating to, or involving the ileum.

Île-de-France (ēl′də-fräns′) A historical region and former province of N-central France in the Paris basin; became the nucleus of the crown lands in 987 with the choice of Hugh Capet, Count of Paris, as the French king.

il•e•i•tis (ĭl′ē-ī′tĭs) *n.* Inflammation of the ileum.

il•e•os•to•my (ĭl′ē-ŏs′tə-mē) *n., pl.* **-mies** Surgical construction of an artificial excretory opening through the abdominal wall into the ileum. [ILE(UM) + **-STOMY**.]

il•e•um (ĭl′ē-əm) *n., pl.* **-e•a** (-ē-ə) The terminal portion of the small intestine extending from the jejunum to the cecum. [LLat. *ileum,* groin, flank, var. of Lat. *ilia.*] —**il′e•al** *adj.*

il•e•us (ĭl′ē-əs) *n.* Intestinal obstruction causing colic, vomiting, and constipation. [Lat. *ileus <* Gk. *eileos < eilein,* to squeeze, hold in check. See **wel-** in App.]

i•lex (ī′lĕks′) *n.* Any of various trees or shrubs of the genus *Ilex;*

---

iguana

ikebana

ă	pat	oi	boy
ā	pay	ou	out
âr	care	ōō	took
ä	father	ōō	boot
ĕ	be	ûr	urge
ē	pit	th	thin
ī	pie	th	this
î	pier	hw	which
ŏ	pot	zh	vision
ō	toe	ə	about,
ô	paw		item

Stress marks:
′ (primary);
′ (secondary); as in
lexicon (lĕk′sĭ-kŏn′)

holly. [ME, holm oak < Lat. *īlex*.]

ILGWU *abbr.* International Ladies' Garment Workers' Union

I·li (ē′lē′) A river, c. 1,287 km (800 mi), of NW China and SE Kazakhstan flowing into Lake Balkhash.

il·i·ac (ĭl′ē-ăk′) *adj.* Of, relating to, or situated near the ilium.

Il·i·ad (ĭl′ē-əd, -ăd′) *n.* The older of the two surviving ancient Greek epic poems, traditionally ascribed to Homer, that begins with the wrathful withdrawal of Achilles from the fighting in the Trojan War and ends after his return to slay Hector.

Il·i·on (ĭl′ē-ŏn, -ŏn′) See **Troy** 1.

il·i·um (ĭl′ē-əm) *n., pl.* **-i·a** (-ē-ə) The uppermost and widest of the three bones constituting either of the lateral halves of the pelvis. [LLat. *ilium*, groin, flank, var. of Lat. *īlia*.]

Ilium See **Troy** 1.

ilk[1] (ĭlk) *n.* Type or kind: *people of that ilk.* ❖ *pron. Scots* The same. Used following a name to indicate that the one named resides in an area bearing the same name: *Duncan of that ilk.* [ME *ilke*, same < OE *ilca*. See **i-** in App.]

ilk[2] (ĭlk) *adj.* Variant of **ilka**.

il·ka (ĭl′kə) also **ilk** (ĭlk) *adj. Scots* Each; every. [ME *ilk a*, each one : *ilk* (var. of *ech*, each; see EACH) + *a*, one, a; see A[2].]

ill (ĭl) *adj.* **worse** (wûrs), **worst** (wûrst) **1.** Not healthy; sick. **2.** Not normal; unsound. **3.** Resulting in suffering; harmful or distressing. **4a.** Resulting from or suggestive of evil intentions. **b.** Ascribing an objectionable quality. **c.** Hostile or unfriendly. **5.** Not favorable; unpropitious. **6.** Not measuring up to recognized standards of excellence, as of conduct. ❖ *adv.* **worse**, **worst 1.** In a sickly or unsound manner; not well. **2.** Scarcely or with difficulty. ❖ *n.* **1.** Evil; sin. **2.** Disaster, distress, or harm. **3.** Something that causes suffering; trouble. **4.** Something that reflects in an unfavorable way on one. **—idiom: ill at ease** Anxious or unsure; uneasy. [ME < ON *illr*, bad.]

ill. *abbr.* **1.** illustrated **2.** illustration

Ill. *abbr.* Illinois

I'll (īl) Contraction of *I will.*

ill-ad·vised (ĭl′əd-vīzd′) *adj.* Performed, carried out, or done without wise counsel or careful deliberation. **—ill′-ad·vis′ed·ly** (-vī′zĭd-lē) *adv.*

Il·lam·pu (ē-yäm′pōō) A peak, 6,366.3 m (20,873 ft), in the Andes of W Bolivia NW of La Paz.

il·la·tion (ĭ-lā′shən) *n.* **1.** The act of inferring or drawing conclusions. **2.** A conclusion drawn; a deduction. [LLat. *illātiō, illātiōn-* < Lat. *illātus,* p. part. of *inferre,* to carry in, infer : *in-,* in; see IN-[2] + *lātus,* brought; see **telə-** in App.]

il·la·tive (ĭl′ə-tĭv, ĭ-lā′-) *adj.* **1.** Of, relating to, or of the nature of an illation. **2.** Expressing or preceding an inference. Used of a word. ❖ *n.* **1.** A word or phrase, such as *hence,* that expresses an inference. **2.** See **illation** 2. **—il′la·tive·ly** *adv.*

ill-be·ing (ĭl′bē′ĭng) *n.* Lack of prosperity, happiness, or health.

ill-bred (ĭl′brĕd′) *adj.* **1.** Badly brought up; impolite and crude. **2.** Not thoroughbred; underbred. Used of animals.

il·le·gal (ĭ-lē′gəl) *adj.* **1.** Prohibited by law. **2.** Prohibited by official rules. **3.** Unacceptable to or not performable by a computer. ❖ *n.* An illegal immigrant. **—il·le′gal·ly** *adv.*

il·le·gal·i·ty (ĭl′ē-găl′ĭ-tē) *n., pl.* **-ties 1.** The quality or state of being illegal. **2.** An illegal act.

il·leg·i·ble (ĭ-lĕj′ə-bəl) *adj.* Not legible or decipherable. **—il·leg′i·bil′i·ty, il·leg′i·ble·ness** *n.* **—il·leg′i·bly** *adv.*

il·le·git·i·ma·cy (ĭl′ĭ-jĭt′ə-mə-sē) *n.* **1.** The quality or condition of being illegitimate. **2.** Bastardy.

il·le·git·i·mate (ĭl′ĭ-jĭt′ə-mĭt) *adj.* **1.** Against the law; illegal. **2.** Born out of wedlock. **3.** *Grammar* Not in correct usage. **4.** Incorrectly deduced; illogical. **5.** *Biology* Unacceptable as a scientific name because of contradiction to the international rules of nomenclature. **—il′le·git′i·mate·ly** *adv.*

ill-e·quipped (ĭl′ĭ-kwĭpt′) *adj.* Poorly or inadequately equipped.

ill-fat·ed (ĭl′fā′tĭd) *adj.* Destined for misfortune; doomed. **2.** Marked by or causing misfortune; unlucky.

ill-fa·vored (ĭl′fā′vərd) *adj.* **1.** Having an ugly or unattractive face. **2.** Objectionable; offensive.

ill feeling *n.* A feeling of animosity or rancor.

ill-found·ed (ĭl′foun′dĭd) *adj.* Having no factual basis.

ill-got·ten (ĭl′gŏt′n) *adj.* Obtained in an evil manner or by dishonest means: *ill-gotten gains.*

ill health *n.* Poor health; sickness.

ill humor *n.* An irritable state of mind; surliness.

ill-hu·mored (ĭl′hyōō′mərd) *adj.* Irritable; surly.

il·lib·er·al (ĭ-lĭb′ər-əl) *adj.* **1.** Narrow-minded; bigoted. **2.** *Archaic* Ungenerous, mean, or stingy. **3.** *Archaic* Lacking liberal culture. **b.** Ill-bred; vulgar. **—il·lib′er·al·ism** *n.* **—il·lib′er·al′i·ty** (-ə-răl′ĭ-tē), **il·lib′er·al·ness** *n.* **—il·lib′er·al·ly** *adv.*

il·lic·it (ĭ-lĭs′ĭt) *adj.* Not sanctioned by custom or law; unlawful. [Lat. *illicitus : in-,* not; see IN-[1] + *licitus,* lawful; see LICIT.] **—il·lic′it·ly** *adv.* **—il·lic′it·ness** *n.*

Il·li·ma·ni (ē′yē-mä′nē) A mountain, 6,461.1 m (21,184 ft), in the Andes of W Bolivia E of La Paz.

il·lim·it·a·ble (ĭ-lĭm′ĭ-tə-bəl) *adj.* Impossible to limit or circumscribe; limitless. See Syns at **infinite**. **—il·lim′it·a·bil′i·ty, il·lim′it·a·ble·ness** *n.* **—il·lim′it·a·bly** *adv.*

Il·li·noi·an (ĭl′ə-noi′ən) *adj.* Of or relating to the third glacial stage of the Pleistocene in North America. [After ILLINOIS[2].]

Il·li·nois[1] (ĭl′ə-noi′) *n., pl.* **Illinois 1.** A member of a confederacy of Native American peoples formerly inhabiting southern Wisconsin, northern Illinois, and parts of eastern Iowa and Missouri, with present-day descendants mostly in Oklahoma. **2.** The Algonquian language of the Illinois. [Fr., of Algonquian orig.]

Il·li·nois[2] (ĭl′ə-noi′) A state of the N-central US; admitted as the 21st state in 1818. Cap. Springfield. Pop. 12,419,293. **—Il′li·nois′an** (-noi′ən) *adj. & n.*

Illinois River A river rising in NE IL and flowing c. 439 km (273 mi) to the Mississippi R. in W-central IL.

Illinois Waterway A system of rivers and canals of N and W IL, linking Lake Michigan with the Mississippi R.

il·liq·uid (ĭ-lĭk′wĭd) *adj.* **1.** Not readily converted into cash. **2.** Lacking cash or liquid assets. **—il′li·quid′i·ty** *n.*

il·lit·er·a·cy (ĭ-lĭt′ər-ə-sē) *n., pl.* **-cies 1.** The state of being unable to read and write. **2.** An error, as in speech, made by or thought typical of an illiterate. **3.** The condition or quality of being ignorant or unknowledgeable in a particular subject or field.

il·lit·er·ate (ĭ-lĭt′ər-ĭt) *adj.* **1a.** Unable to read and write. **b.** Having little or no formal education. **2a.** Inferior to an expected standard of familiarity with language and literature. **b.** Violating prescribed standards of speech or writing. **3.** Ignorant of the fundamentals of a given art or branch of knowledge. **—il·lit′er·ate** *n.* **—il·lit′er·ate·ly** *adv.* **—il·lit′er·ate·ness** *n.*

ill-man·nered (ĭl′măn′ərd) *adj.* Lacking or indicating a lack of good manners; rude. **—ill′-man′nered·ly** *adv.*

ill nature *n.* A disagreeable or malevolent disposition.

ill-na·tured (ĭl′nā′chərd) *adj.* **1.** Having an ill nature. **2.** Spiteful; nasty. **—ill′-na′tured·ness** *n.*

ill·ness (ĭl′nĭs) *n.* **1a.** Poor health resulting from disease of body or mind; sickness. **b.** A disease. **2.** *Obsolete* Evil; wickedness.

il·log·ic (ĭ-lŏj′ĭk) *n.* A lack of logic.

il·log·i·cal (ĭ-lŏj′ĭ-kəl) *adj.* **1.** Contradicting or disregarding the principles of logic. **2.** Without logic; senseless. **—il·log′i·cal′i·ty** (-kăl′ĭ-tē), **il·log′i·cal·ness** *n.* **—il·log′i·cal·ly** *adv.*

ill-sort·ed (ĭl′sôr′tĭd) *adj.* Badly matched.

ill-starred (ĭl′stärd′) *adj.* Ill-fated; unlucky.

ill-tem·pered (ĭl′tĕm′pərd) *adj.* Having a bad temper; irritable. **—ill′-tem′pered·ly** *adv.*

ill-timed (ĭl′tīmd′) *adj.* Done or occurring at an inappropriate time; untimely.

ill-treat (ĭl′trēt′) *tr.v.* **-treat·ed, -treat·ing, -treats** To treat unkindly or harshly; maltreat. **—ill′-treat′ment** *n.*

il·lume (ĭ-lōōm′) *tr.v.* **-lumed, -lum·ing, -lumes** To illuminate. [Short for ILLUMINE, prob. on the model of French verbs in *-lumer,* to light up, such as *allumer,* to light up.]

il·lu·mi·nance (ĭ-lōō′mə-nəns) *n.* See **illumination** 7.

il·lu·mi·nant (ĭ-lōō′mə-nənt) *n.* Something that gives off light. [Lat. *illūmināns, illūminant-,* pr. part. of *illūmināre,* to illuminate. See ILLUMINATE.]

il·lu·mi·nate (ĭ-lōō′mə-nāt′) *v.* **-nat·ed, -nat·ing, -nates** *—tr.* **1.** To provide or brighten with light. **2.** To decorate or hang with lights. **3.** To make understandable; clarify. **4.** To enlighten intellectually or spiritually; enable to understand. **5.** To endow with fame or splendor; celebrate. **6.** To adorn (a page of a book, for example) with designs, miniatures, or lettering in brilliant colors or precious metals. **7.** To expose to or reveal by radiation. *—intr.* **1.** To become lighted; glow. **2.** To provide intellectual or spiritual enlightenment and understanding. **3.** To be exposed to or revealed by radiation. ❖ *n.* (-nĭt) One who has or professes to have an unusual degree of enlightenment. [ME *illuminaten* < Lat. *illūmināre, illūmināt- : in-,* in; see IN-[2] + *lūmināre,* to light up (< *lūmen, lūmin-,* light; see **leuk-** in App.).] **—il·lu′mi·nat′ing·ly** *adv.*

il·lu·mi·na·ti (ĭ-lōō′mə-nä′tē) *pl.n.* **1.** People claiming to have enlightenment in a subject. **2. Illuminati** Any of various groups claiming special religious enlightenment. [Lat. *illūminātī,* pl. of *illūminātus,* p. part. of *illūmināre,* to illuminate. See ILLUMINATE.]

il·lu·mi·na·tion (ĭ-lōō′mə-nā′shən) *n.* **1a.** The act of illuminating. **b.** The state of being illuminated. **2.** A source of light. **3.** Decorative lighting. **4.** Intellectual or spiritual enlightenment. **5.** Clarification; elucidation. **6a.** The art or act of decorating a text with designs, miniatures, or lettering. **b.** An example of this art. **7.** *Physics* The luminous flux per unit area at any point on a surface exposed to incident light.

il·lu·mi·na·tive (ĭ-lōō′mə-nā′tĭv) *adj.* Of, causing, or capable of causing illumination.

il·lu·mi·na·tor (ĭ-lōō′mə-nā′tər) *n.* **1.** One that illuminates, esp. a device for producing, concentrating, or reflecting light. **2.** One who illuminates manuscripts or other objects.

il·lu·mine (ĭ-lōō′mĭn) *tr.v.* **-mined, -min·ing, -mines** To give light to; illuminate. [ME *illuminen* < OFr. *illuminer* < Lat. *illūmināre.* See ILLUMINATE.] **—il·lu′min·a·ble** *adj.*

il·lu·mi·nism (ĭ-lōō′mə-nĭz′əm) *n.* **1.** Belief in or proclamation of a special personal enlightenment. **2. Illuminism** The ideas and principles of various groups of Illuminati. [Fr. *illuminisme* < *illuminé,* an illuminist < p. part. of *illuminer,* to illuminate < OFr. See ILLUMINE.] **—il·lu′mi·nist** *n.*

illus. *abbr.* **1.** illustrated **2.** illustration

ill-us·age (ĭl′yōō′sĭj, -zĭj) *n.* Bad treatment; ill-use.

illumination
detail from an 11th-century illuminated manuscript

ill-use (ĭl′yōōz′) tr.v. **-used, -us·ing, -us·es** To maltreat. ❖ n. (ĭl′yōōs′) Unjust or poor treatment; ill-usage.

il·lu·sion (ĭ-lōō′zhən) n. **1a.** An erroneous perception of reality. **b.** An erroneous concept or belief. **2.** The condition of being deceived by an illusion. **3.** Something, such as a fantastic plan, that causes an erroneous belief or perception. **4.** Illusionism in art. **5.** A fine transparent cloth, used for dresses or trimmings. [ME < OFr. < LLat. *illūsiō, illūsiōn-* < Lat., a mocking, irony < *illūsus,* p. part. of *illūdere,* to mock : *in-,* against; see IN-² + *lūdere,* to play.] **—il·lu′sion·al, il·lu′sion·ar′y** (-zhə-nĕr′ē) *adj.*

il·lu·sion·ism (ĭ-lōō′zhə-nĭz′əm) n. **1.** *Philosophy* The doctrine that the material world is an immaterial product of the senses. **2.** The use of illusionary techniques in art or decoration. **—il·lu′-sion·is′tic** *adj.* **—il·lu′sion·is′ti·cal·ly** *adv.*

il·lu·sion·ist (ĭ-lōō′zhə-nĭst) n. **1.** *Philosophy* An adherent of the doctrine of illusionism. **2.** An artist whose work is marked by illusionism. **3.** A magician or ventriloquist.

il·lu·sive (ĭ-lōō′sĭv) *adj.* Illusory. **—il·lu′sive·ly** *adv.* **—il·lu′sive·ness** *n.*

il·lu·so·ry (ĭ-lōō′sə-rē, -zə-rē) *adj.* Produced by, based on, or having the nature of an illusion; deceptive.

il·lus·trate (ĭl′ə-strāt′, ĭ-lŭs′trāt′) v. **-trat·ed, -trat·ing, -trates** *—tr.* **1a.** To clarify, as by examples. **b.** To clarify by serving as an example or comparison. **2.** To provide (a publication) with explanatory or decorative features. **3.** *Obsolete* To illuminate. *—intr.* To present a clarification, example, or explanation. [Lat. *illūstrāre, illūstrāt-* : *in-,* in; see IN-² + *lūstrāre,* to make bright; see leuk- in App.] **—il·lus′trat′a·ble** *adj.* **—il·lus·tra′tor** *n.*

il·lus·tra·tion (ĭl′ə-strā′shən) n. **1a.** The act of clarifying or explaining. **b.** The state of being clarified or explained. **2.** Material used to clarify or explain. **3.** Visual matter used to clarify or decorate a text. **4.** *Obsolete* Illumination. **—il′lus·tra′tion·al** *adj.*

il·lus·tra·tive (ĭ-lŭs′trə-tĭv, ĭl′ə-strā′tĭv) *adj.* Acting or serving as an illustration. **—il·lus′tra·tive·ly** *adv.*

il·lus·tri·ous (ĭ-lŭs′trē-əs) *adj.* **1.** Well known and very distinguished; eminent. See Syns at **noted. 2.** *Obsolete* Shining brightly. [< Lat. *illūstris < illūstrāre,* to give glory to, shine upon. See ILLUSTRATE.] **—il·lus′tri·ous·ly** *adv.* **—il·lus′tri·ous·ness** *n.*

il·lu·vi·ate (ĭ-lōō′vē-āt′) *intr.v.* **-at·ed, -at·ing, -ates** To undergo illuviation. [Back-formation < ILLUVIATION.]

il·lu·vi·a·tion (ĭ-lōō′vē-ā′shən) n. The deposition in an underlying soil layer of colloids, soluble salts, and mineral particles leached out of an overlying soil layer. [*illuvial,* resulting from illuviation (IN-² + *-luvial,* relating to the action of flowing water, as in ALLUVIAL) + -ATION.]

ill will n. Unfriendly feeling; enmity.

ill-wish·er (ĭl′wĭsh′ər) n. One who wishes another no good.

il·ly (ĭl′lē) *adv.* Badly; ill: *"Beauty is jealous, and illy bears the presence of a rival"* (Thomas Jefferson).

Il·lyr·i·a (ĭ-lîr′ē-ə) also **Il·lyr·i·cum** (-ĭ-kəm) An ancient region of the Balkan Peninsula on the Adriatic coast; became the Roman province of Illyricum after 33 B.C. and was later coextensive with the Illyrian Provinces (1809–15) and the kingdom of Illyria, a division of Austria (1816–49).

Il·lyr·i·an (ĭ-lîr′ē-ən) *adj.* Of or relating to ancient Illyria or its peoples, languages, or cultures. ❖ n. **1.** A member of one of the ancient peoples that inhabited Illyria. **2.** An extinct Indo-European language spoken in Illyria.

il·men·ite (ĭl′mə-nīt′) n. A lustrous black to brownish titanium ore, essentially FeTiO₃. [After the *Ilmen* Mountains, a range of the southern Ural Mountains.]

ILO *abbr.* International Labor Organization

I·lo·ca·no also **I·lo·ka·no** (ē′lō-kä′nō) *n., pl.* **Ilocano** or **-nos** also **Ilokano** or **-nos 1.** A member of an agricultural people of northern Luzon in the Philippines. **2.** The Austronesian language of the Ilocano. ❖ *adj.* Of or relating to the Ilocano or their language or culture. [Sp. *Ilócano* < Ilocano *Ilóko,* people who live along the shore (unattested sense), Ilocano; perh. akin to *luĕk,* cove.]

I·lo·i·lo (ē′lō-ē′lō) A city of SE Panay, Philippines, on **Iloilo Strait,** an inlet of the Sulu Sea. Pop. 302,200.

I·lo·rin (ē′lə-rēn′, ĭ-lôr′ən) A city of SW Nigeria NNE of Lagos; cap. of a Yoruba kingdom c. 1800–25. Pop. 355,400.

ILS *abbr.* instrument landing system

im-¹ *pref.* Variant of in-¹.

im-² *pref.* Variant of in-².

I'm (īm) I am.

in present-day Scots English and Irish English. It is rare in the United States, and when it does occur, it tends to be used in first person singular contexts and in contracted form: speakers do not say *I am forgot* but *I'm forgot.* Forms such as *we're* for *we've* or *they're* for *they've* are rare, but they do occur in the vernacular of the Lumbee.

im·age (ĭm′ĭj) n. **1.** A reproduction of a person or object, esp. a sculptured likeness. **2.** *Physics* An optically or electronically formed representative reproduction of an object, esp. an optical reproduction formed by a lens or mirror. **3.** One that closely or exactly resembles another; a double. **4a.** The public's opinion or concept of something. **b.** The character projected to the public, as by a person, esp. as interpreted by the mass media. **5.** A personification of something specified. **6.** A mental picture of something not real or present. **7a.** A vivid description or representation. **b.** A figure of speech, esp. a metaphor or simile. **c.** A concrete representation, as in art, that expresses or evokes something else. **8.** *Mathematics* A set of values of a function corresponding to a given subset of a domain. **9.** *Computer Science* An exact replica of the contents of a storage device, such as a hard disk, stored on a second storage device, such as a network server. **10.** *Obsolete* An apparition. ❖ *tr.v.* **-aged, -ag·ing, -ag·es 1.** To make or produce a likeness of. **2.** To mirror or reflect. **3.** To symbolize or typify. **4.** To picture mentally; imagine. **5.** To describe, esp. so as to evoke a mental picture of. **6.** *Computer Science* **a.** To print (a file) using a laser printer, direct-to-plate press, or similar device. **b.** To transmit (an exact replica of the contents of a storage device) to another storage device. **7.** To render visually, as by magnetic resonance imaging. [ME < OFr. < Lat. *imāgō.* See aim- in App.] **—im′ag·er** *n.*

im·age-mak·er (ĭm′ĭj-mā′kər) n. One who uses the techniques of advertising or public relations to create a favorable view, as of an institution. **—im′age-mak′ing** *n.*

image orthicon n. See **orthicon.**

im·age·ry (ĭm′ĭj-rē) *n., pl.* **-ries 1.** A set of mental pictures or images. **2a.** The use of vivid or figurative language to represent objects, actions, or ideas. **b.** The use of expressive or evocative images in art, literature, or music. **c.** A group or body of related images, as in a poem. **3a.** Representative images, esp. statues or icons. **b.** The art of making them. **4.** *Psychology* A technique in behavior therapy in which the patient uses pleasant fantasies to relax and counteract anxiety.

i·mag·i·na·ble (ĭ-măj′ə-nə-bəl) *adj.* Conceivable in the imagination. **—i·mag′i·na·bil′i·ty** *n.* **—i·mag′i·na·bly** *adv.*

i·ma·gi·nal (ĭ-măj′gə-nəl, ĭ-mā′-) *adj.* Of, relating to, or having the form of an insect imago.

i·mag·i·nar·y (ĭ-măj′ə-nĕr′ē) *adj.* **1.** Having existence only in the imagination; unreal. **2.** *Mathematics* **a.** Of, relating to, or being the coefficient of the imaginary unit in a complex number. **b.** Of, relating to, involving, or being an imaginary number. ❖ *n., pl.* **-ies** *Mathematics* An imaginary number. **—i·mag′i·nar′i·ly** *adv.* **—i·mag′i·nar′i·ness** *n.*

imaginary number n. A complex number in which the imaginary part is not zero.

imaginary unit n. The square root of −1.

i·mag·i·na·tion (ĭ-măj′ə-nā′shən) n. **1a.** The formation of a mental image of something that is neither perceived as real nor present to the senses. **b.** The mental image so formed. **c.** The ability or tendency to form such images. **2.** The ability to confront and deal with reality creatively; resourcefulness. **3.** A traditional or widely held belief or opinion. **4.** *Archaic* **a.** An unrealistic idea or notion; a fancy. **b.** A plan or scheme. **—i·mag′i·na′tion·al** *adj.*

i·mag·i·na·tive (ĭ-măj′ə-nə-tĭv, -nā′tĭv) *adj.* **1.** Having a lively or creative imagination. **2.** Created by, indicative of, or characterized by imagination or creativity. **3.** Tending to indulge in the fanciful or in make-believe. **4.** Having no truth. **—i·mag′i·na·tive·ly** *adv.* **—i·mag′i·na·tive·ness** *n.*

i·mag·ine (ĭ-măj′ĭn) v. **-ined, -in·ing, -ines** *—tr.* **1.** To form a mental picture or image of. **2.** To think; conjecture. **3.** To have a notion of or about without adequate foundation; fancy. *—intr.* **1.** To employ the imagination. **2.** To guess; conjecture. [ME *imaginen* < OFr. *imaginer* < Lat. *imāgināri < imāgō, imāgin-,* image. See aim- in App.] **—i·mag′in·er** *n.*

im·ag·ing (ĭm′ĭ-jĭng) n. The visual representation of an object, such as a body part or celestial body, for the purpose of medical diagnosis or data collection, using any of a variety of usu. computerized techniques, such as ultrasonography or spectroscopy. **2.** *Psychology* The use of mental images to influence bodily processes.

im·a·gism also **Im·a·gism** (ĭm′ə-jĭz′əm) n. A literary movement launched by British and American poets early in the 20th century that advocated the use of free verse, common speech patterns, and concrete images. **—im′a·gist** *n.* **—im′a·gis′tic** *adj.* **—im′a·gis′ti·cal·ly** *adv.*

i·ma·go (ĭ-mā′gō, ĭ-mä′-) *n., pl.* **-goes** or **-gi·nes** (-gə-nēz′) **1.** An insect in the sexually mature adult stage of complete metamorphosis. **2.** *Psychology* An often idealized image of a person, usu. a parent, formed in childhood and persisting unconsciously into adulthood. [Lat. *imāgō, imāgin-,* image. See aim- in App.]

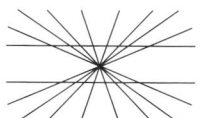

illusion
top: In a Hering figure, straight horizontal rules appear curved.
bottom: In Gestalt theory boxes, a gray box against a black background appears lighter than the same gray box against a white background.

ă	pat	oi	boy
ā	pay	ou	out
âr	care	ŏŏ	took
ä	father	ōō	boot
ĕ	pet	ŭ	cut
ē	be	ûr	urge
ĭ	pit	th	thin
ī	pie	th	this
îr	pier	hw	which
ŏ	pot	zh	vision
ō	toe	ə	about,
ô	paw		item

Stress marks:
′ (primary);
′ (secondary), as in
lexicon (lĕk′sĭ-kŏn′)

i·mam also **I·mam** (ĭ-mäm′) n. Islam **1a.** In law and theology, the caliph who is successor to Muhammad as the lawful temporal leader of the Islamic community. **b.** The male prayer leader in a mosque. **c.** The Muslim worshiper who leads the recitation of prayer when two or more worshipers are present. **2a.** A male spiritual and temporal leader regarded by Shiites as a descendant of Muhammad divinely appointed to guide humans. **b.** An earthly representative of the 12 such leaders recognized by Imamites. **3.** A male ruler claiming descent from Muhammad and exercising authority in an Islamic state. **4a.** Any one of the founders of the four schools of law and theology. **b.** An authoritative scholar who founds a school of law or theology. **5.** Used as a title for an imam. [Ar. *'imām*, leader, imam < *'amma*, to lead.]

i·mam·ate (ĭ-mä′māt′) n. Islam The office of a ruling imam.

I·mam·ite (ĭ-mä′mīt′) n. A member of the largest branch of Shiism, marked by recognition of a hereditary line of 12 divinely appointed imams.

i·ma·ret (ĭ-mä′rĕt) n. An inn or hostel for pilgrims in Turkey. [Turk. < Ar. *'imāra*, building < *'amara*, to build.]

im·bal·ance (ĭm-băl′əns) n. A lack of balance, as in distribution or functioning. —**im·bal′anced** adj.

im·be·cile (ĭm′bə-sĭl, -səl) n. **1.** A stupid or silly person; a dolt. **2.** A person whose mental acumen is well below par. **3.** A person of moderate to severe mental retardation having a mental age of from three to seven years. The term is no longer in scientific use and is now considered offensive. ❖ adj. also **im·be·cil·ic** (ĭm′bə-sĭl′ĭk) **1.** Stupid; silly. **2.** Well below par in mental acumen. [< obsolete Fr. *imbécille*, weak, feeble < OFr. < Lat. *imbecillus* : *in-*, not; see IN-¹ + poss. *bacillum*, staff, dim. of *baculum*, rod.]

im·be·cil·i·ty (ĭm′bə-sĭl′ĭ-tē) n., pl. **-ties 1a.** Great stupidity or foolishness. **b.** Something stupid or foolish, such as an act. **2.** Psychology The state or condition of being an imbecile; moderate or severe mental retardation.

im·bed (ĭm-bĕd′) v. Variant of **embed**.

im·bibe (ĭm-bīb′) v. **-bibed, -bib·ing, -bibes** —tr. **1.** To drink. **2.** To absorb or take in as if by drinking. **3.** To receive and absorb into the mind. **4.** Obsolete To permeate; saturate. —intr. To drink alcoholic beverages. [ME *embiben*, to soak up, saturate < Lat. *imbibere*, to drink in, imbibe : *in-*, in; see IN-² + *bibere*, to drink; see **pō(i)-** in App.] —**im·bib′er** n.

im·bi·bi·tion (ĭm′bə-bĭsh′ən) n. **1.** The act of imbibing. **2.** Chemistry Absorption of fluid by a solid or colloid that causes swelling.

im·bri·cate (ĭm′brĭ-kĭt) adj. Having regularly arranged, overlapping edges, as roof tiles or fish scales. ❖ v. **-cat·ed, -cat·ing, -cates** —tr. To overlap in a regular pattern. —intr. To be arranged with regular overlapping edges. [Lat. *imbricātus*, covered with roof tiles < *imbrex*, *imbric-*, roof tile < *imber*, *imbr-*, rain.] —**im′bri·ca′tion** n.

imbricate
imbricated roof tiles

im·bro·glio (ĭm-brōl′yō) n., pl. **-glios 1a.** A difficult or intricate situation; an entanglement. **b.** A confused or complicated disagreement. **2.** A confused heap; a tangle. [Ital. < OItal. < *imbrogliare*, to tangle, confuse : *in-*, in (< Lat.; see IN-²) + *brogliare*, to mix, stir (prob. < OFr. *brooiller*, *brouiller*; see BROIL².).]

im·brue (ĭm-brōō′) also **em·brue** (ĕm-) tr.v. **-brued, -bru·ing, -brues 1.** To saturate. **2.** To stain. [ME *embrewen* < OFr. *embreuver* < VLat. **imbiberāre* : Lat. *in-*, in; see IN-² + LLat. *biber*, beverage (< Lat. *bibere*, to drink; see BEVERAGE).]

im·brute (ĭm-brōōt′) tr. & intr.v. **-brut·ed, -brut·ing, -brutes** To make or become brutal.

im·bue (ĭm-byōō′) tr.v. **-bued, -bu·ing, -bues 1.** To inspire or influence thoroughly; pervade. **2.** To permeate or saturate. **3.** To stain or dye deeply. [ME *enbuen*, *imbeuen* < Lat. *imbuere*, to moisten, stain.]

IMF abbr. International Monetary Fund

IMHO abbr. in my humble opinion

im·id·az·ole (ĭm′ĭ-dăz′ōl′) n. An organic crystalline base, C₃H₄N₂, that is an inhibitor of histamine. [IMID(E) + AZOLE.]

im·ide (ĭm′īd′) n. A compound derived from ammonia and containing the bivalent NH group combined with a bivalent acid group or two monovalent acid groups. [Alteration of AMIDE.] —**i·mid′ic** (ə-mĭd′ĭk, ĭ-mĭd′-) adj.

im·i·do (ĭm′ĭ-dō′) adj. Of or relating to imides or an imide. [< *imido-* < IMIDE.]

im·ine (ĭm′ēn′, -ĭn, ĭ-mēn′) n. A compound derived from ammonia and containing the bivalent NH group combined with a bivalent nonacid group. [Alteration of AMINE.]

im·i·no (ĭm′ə-nō′) adj. Of or relating to imines or an imine. [< *imino-* < IMINE.]

i·mip·ra·mine (ĭ-mĭp′rə-mēn′) n. A tricyclic compound, C₁₉H₂₄N₂, used to treat depression and enuresis. [IMI(NO) + PR(OPYL) + AMINE.]

imit. abbr. **1.** imitation **2.** imitative

im·i·ta·ble (ĭm′ĭ-tə-bəl) adj. **1.** That can be imitated. **2.** Worthy of imitation.

im·i·tate (ĭm′ĭ-tāt′) tr.v. **-tat·ed, -tat·ing, -tates 1.** To use or follow as a model. **2a.** To copy the actions, appearance, mannerisms, or speech of; mimic: *amused friends by imitating the teachers*. **b.** To copy or use the style of: *brushwork that imitates Rembrandt*. **3.** To copy exactly; reproduce. **4.** To appear like;

resemble. [Lat. *imitārī*, *imitāt-*. See **aim-** in App.] —**im′i·ta′tor** n.

SYNONYMS *imitate, copy, mimic, ape, parody, simulate* These verbs mean to follow something or someone taken as a model. To *imitate* is to act like or follow a pattern or style set by another: *"Art imitates Nature"* (Richard Franck). To *copy* is to duplicate an original as precisely as possible: *"spent a laborious life-time in Rome, copying the Old Masters for a generation which lacked the facile resource of the camera"* (Edith Wharton). To *mimic* is to make a close imitation, often with an intent to ridicule: *mimicked their dialect*. To *ape* is to follow another's lead slavishly but often with an absurd result: *"Those* [superior] *states of mind do not come from aping an alien culture"* (John Russell). To *parody* is either to imitate with comic effect or to attempt a serious imitation and fail: *"All these peculiarities* [of Samuel Johnson's literary style] *have been imitated by his admirers and parodied by his assailants"* (Thomas Macaulay). To *simulate* is to feign or falsely assume the appearance or character of something: *"I . . . lay there simulating death"* (W.H. Hudson).

im·i·ta·tion (ĭm′ĭ-tā′shən) n. **1.** The act or an instance of imitating. **2.** Something derived or copied from an original. **3.** Music Repetition of a phrase or melody often with variations in key, rhythm, and voice. ❖ adj. Made to resemble another, usu. superior material. —**im′i·ta′tion·al** adj.

im·i·ta·tive (ĭm′ĭ-tā′tĭv) adj. **1.** Of or involving imitation. **2.** Not original; derivative. **3.** Tending to imitate. **4.** Onomatopoeic. —**im′i·ta′tive·ly** adv. —**im′i·ta′tive·ness** n.

im·mac·u·la·cy (ĭ-măk′yə-lə-sē) n. The quality or condition of being immaculate.

im·mac·u·late (ĭ-măk′yə-lĭt) adj. **1.** Impeccably clean; spotless. See Syns at **clean. 2.** Free from stain or blemish; pure. **3.** Free from fault or error. **4.** Having no markings. [ME *immaculat* < Lat. *immaculātus* : *in-*, not; see IN-¹ + *maculātus*, p. part. of *maculāre*, to blemish (< *macula*, spot).] —**im·mac′u·late·ly** adv. —**im·mac′u·late·ness** n.

Immaculate Conception n. Roman Catholic Church **1.** The doctrine that the Virgin Mary was conceived free from original sin. **2.** The feast of the Immaculate Conception, celebrated on December 8.

im·ma·nent (ĭm′ə-nənt) adj. **1.** Existing or remaining within; inherent. **2.** Restricted entirely to the mind; subjective. [LLat. *immanēns*, *immanent-*, pr. part. of *immanēre*, to remain in : Lat. *in-*, in; see IN-² + Lat. *manēre*, to remain.] —**im′ma·nence**, **im′ma·nen·cy** n. —**im′ma·nent·ly** adv.

im·ma·nent·ism (ĭm′ə-nən-tĭz′əm) n. Any of various religious theories postulating that a deity, mind, or spirit is immanent in the world and in the individual. —**im′ma·nent·ist** adj. & n.

im·ma·te·ri·al (ĭm′ə-tîr′ē-əl) adj. **1.** Of no importance or relevance; inconsequential or irrelevant. **2.** Having no material body or form. —**im′ma·te′ri·al·ly** adv. —**im′ma·te′ri·al·ness** n.

im·ma·te·ri·al·ism (ĭm′ə-tîr′ē-ə-lĭz′əm) n. A metaphysical doctrine denying the existence of matter. —**im′ma·te′ri·al·ist** adj. & n.

im·ma·te·ri·al·i·ty (ĭm′ə-tîr′ē-ăl′ĭ-tē) n., pl. **-ties 1.** The state or quality of being immaterial. **2.** Something immaterial.

im·ma·te·ri·al·ize (ĭm′ə-tîr′ē-ə-līz′) tr.v. **-ized, -iz·ing, -iz·es** To render immaterial.

im·ma·ture (ĭm′ə-tyoͅor′, -toͅor′, -choͅor′) adj. **1.** Not fully grown or developed. **2.** Marked by or suggesting a lack of maturity. [Lat. *immātūrus* : *in-*, not; see IN-¹ + *mātūrus*, mature.] —**im′ma·ture′ly** adv. —**im′ma·tur′i·ty**, **im′ma·ture′ness** n.

im·meas·ur·a·ble (ĭ-mĕzh′ər-ə-bəl) adj. **1.** Impossible to measure. See Syns at **incalculable. 2.** Vast; limitless. —**im·meas′ur·a·bil′i·ty**, **im·meas′ur·a·ble·ness** n. —**im·meas′ur·a·bly** adv.

im·me·di·a·cy (ĭ-mē′dē-ə-sē) n., pl. **-cies 1.** The state or quality of being immediate. **2.** Lack of an intervening or mediating agency; directness: *the immediacy of TV*. **3.** Something immediate in importance.

im·me·di·ate (ĭ-mē′dē-ĭt) adj. **1.** Occurring at once; instant. **2a.** Of or near the present time. **b.** Of or relating to the present time and place; current. **3.** Close at hand; near. See Syns at **close. 4.** Next in line or relation. **5.** Directly apprehended or perceived. **6.** Acting or occurring without the interposition of another agency or object; direct. [ME *immediat* < OFr. < LLat. *immediātus* : Lat. *in-*, not; see IN-¹ + Lat. *mediātus*, p. part. of *mediāre*, to be in the middle; see MEDIATE.] —**im·me′di·ate·ness** n.

im·me·di·ate·ly (ĭ-mē′dē-ĭt-lē) adv. **1.** Without delay. **2.** With no intermediary; directly. ❖ conj. As soon as; directly.

im·med·i·ca·ble (ĭ-mĕd′ĭ-kə-bəl) adj. Incurable.

Im·mel·mann (ĭm′əl-mən, -män′) n. A maneuver in which an airplane first completes half a loop and then half a roll in order to gain altitude and change flight direction simultaneously. [After Max *Immelmann* (1890–1916), German aviator.]

im·me·mo·ri·al (ĭm′ə-môr′ē-əl, -mōr′-) adj. Exceeding the limits of memory, tradition, or recorded history. —**im′me·mo′ri·al·ly** adv.

im·mense (ĭ-mĕns′) adj. **1.** Extremely large; huge. **2.** Boundless or immeasurable in size or extent. **3.** Informal Surpassingly good; excellent. [ME < OFr. < Lat. *immēnsus* : *in-*, not; see IN-¹ + *mēnsus*, p. part. of *mētīrī*, to measure; see **mē-¹** in App.] —**im·**

mense′ly *adv.* —**im•mense′ness** *n.*

im•men•si•ty (ĭ-mĕn′sĭ-tē) *n., pl.* **-ties 1.** The quality or state of being immense. **2.** Something immense.

im•men•sur•a•ble (ĭ-mĕn′shər-ə-bəl) *adj.* Immeasurable.

im•merge (ĭ-mûrj′) *intr.v.* **-merged, -merg•ing, -merg•es** To submerge or disappear in or as if in a liquid. [Lat. *immergere.* See IMMERSE.] —**im•mer′gence** *n.*

im•merse (ĭ-mûrs′) *tr.v.* **-mersed, -mers•ing, -mers•es 1.** To cover completely in a liquid; submerge. **2.** To baptize by submerging in water. **3.** To engage wholly or deeply; absorb: *immersed in study.* [< ME *immersed,* embedded deeply < Lat. *immersus,* p. part. of *immergere,* to immerse : *in-,* in; see IN-² + *mergere,* to dip.]

im•mers•i•ble (ĭ-mûr′sə-bəl) *adj.* Capable of being completely immersed in water without suffering damage.

im•mer•sion (ĭ-mûr′zhən, -shən) *n.* **1a.** The act or an instance of immersing. **b.** The state of being immersed. **2.** Baptism performed by submerging a person in water. **3.** *Astronomy* The obscuring of a celestial body by another or by the shadow of another.

im•mesh (ĭm-mĕsh′) *v.* Variant of **enmesh.**

im•mi•grant (ĭm′ĭ-grənt) *n.* **1.** A person who leaves one country to settle permanently in another. **2.** A plant or animal that establishes itself where it previously did not exist. —**im′mi•grant** *adj.*

im•mi•grate (ĭm′ĭ-grāt′) *v.* **-grat•ed, -grat•ing, -grates** —*intr.* To enter and settle in a land to which one is not native. See Usage Note at **migrate.** —*tr.* To send or introduce as immigrants. [Lat. *immigrāre, immigrāt-,* to go into : *in-,* in; see IN-² + *migrāre,* to depart.] —**im′mi•gra′tion** *n.* —**im′mi•gra′tion•al** *adj.*

im•mi•nence (ĭm′ə-nəns) *n.* **1.** The quality or condition of being about to occur. **2.** Something about to occur.

im•mi•nen•cy (ĭm′ə-nən-sē) *n., pl.* **-cies** Imminence.

im•mi•nent (ĭm′ə-nənt) *adj.* About to occur; impending. [Ult. < Lat. *imminēns, imminent-,* pr. part. of *imminēre,* to overhang : *in-,* in; see IN-² + *-minēre,* to jut, threaten.] —**im′mi•nent•ly** *adv.* —**im′mi•nent•ness** *n.*

im•mis•ci•ble (ĭ-mĭs′ə-bəl) *adj.* That cannot undergo mixing or blending. —**im•mis′ci•bil′i•ty** *n.* —**im•mis′ci•bly** *adv.*

im•mit•i•ga•ble (ĭ-mĭt′ĭ-gə-bəl) *adj.* That cannot be mitigated: *immitigable circumstances.* —**im•mit′i•ga•bil′i•ty** *n.* —**im•mit′i•ga•bly** *adv.*

im•mit•tance (ĭ-mĭt′ns) *n.* Electrical impedance or admittance. [IM(PEDANCE) + (AD)MITTANCE.]

im•mix (ĭ-mĭks′) *tr.v.* **-mixed, -mix•ing, -mix•es** To commingle; blend. [Ult. < Lat. *immixtus,* p. part. of *immiscēre,* to blend : *in-,* in; see IN-² + *miscēre,* to mix; see meik- in App.] —**im•mix′ture** (-mĭks′chər) *n.*

im•mo•bile (ĭ-mō′bəl, -bēl′, -bīl′) *adj.* **1.** Immovable; fixed. **2.** Not moving; motionless. —**im•mo•bil′i•ty** (-bĭl′ĭ-tē) *n.*

im•mo•bi•lize (ĭ-mō′bə-līz′) *tr.v.* **-lized, -liz•ing, -liz•es 1.** To render immobile. **2.** To fix the position of (a joint or fractured limb), as with a cast. **3.** To impede movement or use of: *A storm immobilized us.* **4.** *Economics* **a.** To withdraw (specie) from circulation and reserve as security for other money. **b.** To convert (floating capital) into fixed capital. —**im•mo′bi•li•za′tion** (-lĭ-zā′shən) *n.* —**im•mo′bi•liz′er** *n.*

im•mod•er•a•cy (ĭ-mŏd′ər-ə-sē) *n., pl.* **-cies 1.** The quality or state of being immoderate. **2.** Something immoderate.

im•mod•er•ate (ĭ-mŏd′ər-ĭt) *adj.* Exceeding normal or appropriate bounds; extreme: *immoderate spending.* See Syns at **excessive.** [ME < Lat. *immoderātus* : *in-,* not; see IN-¹ + *moderātus,* p. part. of *moderārī,* to moderate; see med- in App.] —**im•mod′er•ate•ly** *adv.* —**im•mod′er•ate•ness, im•mod′er•a′tion** *n.*

im•mod•est (ĭ-mŏd′ĭst) *adj.* **1.** Lacking modesty. **2a.** Offending against sexual mores in conduct or appearance; indecent: *immodest dress.* **b.** Not properly restrained in expression or self-assertion; boastful: *immodest claims.* **3.** Arrogant. [Lat. *immodestus* : *in-,* not; see IN-¹ + *modestus,* moderate, modest; see med- in App.] —**im•mod′est•ly** *adv.* —**im•mod′es•ty** *n.*

im•mo•late (ĭm′ə-lāt′) *tr.v.* **-lat•ed, -lat•ing, -lates 1.** To kill as a sacrifice. **2.** To kill (oneself) by fire. **3.** To destroy. [Lat. *immolāre, immolāt-,* to sacrifice, sprinkle with sacrificial meal : *in-,* on; see IN-² + *mola,* meal, millstone; see melə- in App.] —**im′mo•la′tion** *n.* —**im′mo•la′tor** *n.*

im•mor•al (ĭ-môr′əl, -mŏr′-) *adj.* Contrary to established moral principles. —**im•mor′al•ly** *adv.*

im•mor•al•ist (ĭ-môr′ə-lĭst, -mŏr′-) *n.* An advocate of immorality.

im•mor•al•i•ty (ĭm′ô-răl′ĭ-tē, ĭm′ə-) *n., pl.* **-ties 1.** The quality or condition of being immoral. **2.** An immoral act or practice.

im•mor•tal (ĭ-môr′tl) *adj.* **1.** Not subject to death. **2.** Never to be forgotten; everlasting: *immortal words.* **3.** Of or relating to immortality. **4.** *Biology* Capable of indefinite growth or division. Used of cells in culture. ❖ *n.* **1.** One not subject to death. **2.** One whose fame is enduring. [ME < OFr. *immortel* < Lat. *immortālis.* See mer- in App.] —**im•mor′tal•ly** *adv.*

im•mor•tal•i•ty (ĭm′ôr-tăl′ĭ-tē) *n.* **1.** The quality or condition of being immortal. **2.** Endless life or existence. **3.** Enduring fame.

im•mor•tal•ize (ĭ-môr′tl-īz′) *tr.v.* **-ized, -iz•ing, -iz•es** To make immortal. —**im•mor′tal•i•za′tion** (-ĭ-zā′shən) *n.*

im•mor•telle (ĭm′ôr-tĕl′) *n.* Any of various plants, such as species of the genera *Helichrysum* and *Erythrina,* having flowers of lasting color. [Fr. < fem. of *immortel,* immortal < OFr. See IMMORTAL.]

im•mo•tile (ĭ-mōt′l, ĭ-mōt′īl′) *adj.* Not moving or lacking the ability to move. —**im′mo•til′i•ty** (-tĭl′ĭ-tē) *n.*

im•mov•a•ble (ĭ-mōō′və-bəl) *adj.* **1a.** Impossible to move. **b.** Incapable of movement. **2.** Unalterable: *immovable plans.* **3.** Unyielding in principle, purpose, or adherence; steadfast. **4.** Incapable of being moved emotionally. ❖ *n.* One that cannot move or be moved. —**im•mov′a•bil′i•ty, im•mov′a•ble•ness** *n.* —**im•mov′a•bly** *adv.*

im•mune (ĭ-myōōn′) *adj.* **1.** Not subject to an obligation imposed on others; exempt: *immune from taxation.* **2.** Not affected by a given influence; unresponsive: *immune to persuasion.* **3.** *Immunology* **a.** Of, relating to, or having resistance to infection by a specific pathogen. **b.** Of or relating to antibodies or lymphocytes capable of reacting to specific antigens. ❖ *n.* An individual that is immune to a particular infection. [ME < Lat. *immūnis.*]

immune reaction *n.* The reaction due to the recognition and binding of an antigen by its specific antibody or by a previously sensitized lymphocyte.

immune response *n.* An integrated bodily response to an antigen, esp. one mediated by lymphocytes and involving an immune reaction.

immune system *n.* The integrated body system of organs, tissues, cells, and cell products that identifies nonself and neutralizes potentially pathogenic organisms or substances.

im•mu•ni•ty (ĭ-myōō′nĭ-tē) *n., pl.* **-ties 1.** The quality or condition of being immune. **2.** *Immunology* Inherited, acquired, or induced resistance to infection by a specific pathogen. **3.** *Law* **a.** Exemption from legal duties, penalties, or liabilities, granted to a group. **b.** Exemption from legal prosecution, often granted a witness in exchange for testimony.

im•mu•nize (ĭm′yə-nīz′) *tr.v.* **-nized, -niz•ing, -niz•es 1.** To render immune. **2.** To produce immunity in, as by inoculation. **3.** *Law* To grant immunity from prosecution: *immunize a witness.* —**im′mu•ni•za′tion** (-nĭ-zā′shən) *n.*

immuno– *pref.* Immune; immunity: *immunoelectrophoresis.* [< IMMUNE.]

im•mu•no•as•say (ĭm′yə-nō-ăs′ā, ĭ-myōō′-) *n.* A laboratory technique that makes use of the binding between an antigen and its homologous antibody in order to identify and quantify the specific antigen or antibody in a sample.

im•mu•no•chem•is•try (ĭm′yə-nō-kĕm′ĭ-strē, ĭ-myōō′-) *n.* The chemistry of immunologic phenomena. —**im′mu•no•chem′i•cal** (-ĭ-kəl) *adj.*

im•mu•no•com•pe•tent (ĭm′yə-nō-kŏm′pĭ-tənt, ĭ-myōō′-) *adj.* Having the normal bodily capacity to develop an immune response following exposure to an antigen. —**im′mu•no•com′pe•tence** *n.*

im•mu•no•de•fi•cien•cy (ĭm′yə-nō-dĭ-fĭsh′ən-sē, ĭ-myōō′-) *n., pl.* **-cies** An inability to develop a normal immune response. —**im′mu•no•de•fi′cient** *adj.*

im•mu•no•di•ag•no•sis (ĭm′yə-nō-dī′əg-nō′sĭs, ĭ-myōō′-) *n., pl.* **-ses** (-sēz) See serodiagnosis.

im•mu•no•e•lec•tro•pho•re•sis (ĭm′yə-nō-ĭ-lĕk′trə-fə-rē′sĭs, ĭ-myōō′-) *n.* The separation and identification of proteins based on differences in electrical charge and reactivity with antibodies.

im•mu•no•fluo•res•cence (ĭm′yə-nō-flōō-rĕs′əns, -flô-, -flō-) *n.* Any of various techniques that use antibodies chemically linked to a fluorescent dye to identify or quantify antigens in a tissue sample. —**im′mu•no•fluo•res′cent** *adj.*

im•mu•no•ge•net•ics (ĭm′yə-nō-jə-nĕt′ĭks) *n.* (*used with a sing. verb*) **1.** The study of the interrelation between immunity to disease and genetic makeup. **2.** The branch of immunology that deals with the molecular and genetic bases of the immune response. —**im′mu•no•ge•net′ic** *adj.* —**im′mu•no•ge•net′i•cist** (-ĭ-sĭst) *n.*

im•mu•no•gen•ic (ĭm′yə-nō-jĕn′ĭk, ĭmyōō′-) *adj.* Capable of inducing an immune response; antigenic.

im•mu•no•glob•u•lin (ĭm′yə-nō-glŏb′yə-lĭn, ĭ-myōō′-) *n.* Any of the classes of large glycoproteins, esp. IgA, IgD, IgE, IgG, and IgM, that are secreted by plasma cells and function as antibodies in the immune response by binding to specific antigens.

im•mu•nol•o•gy (ĭm′yə-nŏl′ə-jē) *n.* The branch of biomedicine concerned with the structure and function of the immune system, innate and acquired immunity, the bodily distinction of self from nonself, and laboratory techniques involving the interaction of antigens with specific antibodies. —**im′mu•no•log′ic** (-nə-lŏj′ĭk), **im′mu•no•log′i•cal** —**im′mu•no•log′i•cal•ly** *adv.* —**im′mu•nol′o•gist** *n.*

im•mu•no•sup•pres•sion (ĭm′yə-nō-sə-prĕsh′ən, ĭ-myōō′-) *n.* Suppression of the immune response, as by drugs, in order to prevent the rejection of grafts or transplants or control autoimmune diseases. —**im′mu•no•sup•pres′sant** (-prĕs′ənt) *n.* —**im′mu•no•sup•pressed′** (-prĕst′) *adj.* —**im′mu•no•sup•pres′sive** *adj.*

im•mu•no•ther•a•py (ĭm′yə-nō-thĕr′ə-pē, ĭ-myōō′-) *n., pl.* **-pies** Treatment of disease by inducing, enhancing, or suppressing an immune response. —**im'mu·no·ther'a·peu'tic** (-pyōō'tĭk) *adj.* —**im'mu·no·ther'a·pist** *n.*

im·mu·no·tox·in (ĭm'yə-nō-tŏk'sĭn, ĭ-myōō'-) *n.* A hybrid molecule formed by binding a toxin to a monoclonal antibody, used to destroy tumor cells.

im·mure (ĭ-myŏŏr') *tr.v.* **-mured, -mur·ing, -mures** 1. To confine within or as if within walls; imprison. 2. To build into a wall. 3. To entomb in a wall. [Med.Lat. *immūrāre* : Lat. *in-*, in; see IN-¹ + Lat. *mūrus*, wall.] —**im·mure'ment** *n.*

im·mu·ta·ble (ĭ-myōō'tə-bəl) *adj.* Not subject or susceptible to change. —**im·mu'ta·bil'i·ty, im·mu'ta·ble·ness** *n.* —**im·mu'ta·bly** *adv.*

imp (ĭmp) *n.* 1. A mischievous child. 2. A small demon. 3. *Obsolete* A graft. ❖ *tr.v.* **imped, imp·ing, imps** 1. To graft (new feathers) onto the wing of a trained falcon or hawk to repair damage or increase flying capacity. 2. To furnish with wings. [ME *impe*, scion, sprig, offspring < OE *impa*, young shoot < *impian*, to graft, ult. < Med.Lat. *impotus*, graft < Gk. *emphutos*, grafted < *emphuein*, to implant : *en-*, in; see EN-² + *phuein*, to make grow; see bheuə- in App.]

imp. *abbr.* 1. imperative 2. imperfect 3. imperial 4a. import b. imported 5. imprimatur

im·pact (ĭm'păkt') *n.* 1. The striking of one body against another; collision. 2. The force or impetus transmitted by a collision. 3. The effect or impression of one thing on another. 4. The power of making a strong, immediate impression. ❖ *v.* (ĭm-păkt') **-pact·ed, -pact·ing, -pacts** —*tr.* 1. To pack firmly together. 2. To strike forcefully. 3. *Usage Problem* To have an effect or impact on. —*intr. Usage Problem* To have an effect or impact. [< Lat. *impāctus*, p. part. of *impingere*, to push against. See IMPINGE.] —**im·pac'tion** *n.*

> **USAGE NOTE** The use of *impact* as a verb meaning "to have an effect" often has a big impact on readers. Eighty-four percent of the Usage Panel disapproves of the construction *to impact on*, as in the phrase *social pathologies that impact heavily on a community*; and fully 95 percent disapproves of the use of *impact* as a transitive verb in the sentence *Companies have used disposable techniques that have a potential for impacting our health.* • Why this usage provokes such a strong response is unclear, for it has been in the language since at least 1935. It may be that its frequent appearance in the jargon-riddled remarks of politicians, military officials, and financial analysts continues to make people suspicious. But *impact* has by now become so common in corporate and institutional contexts that younger speakers appear to regard it as wholly standard and straightforward usage. It seems likely, then, that the usage will eventually be no more objectionable than the use of *contact* as a verb. See Usage Note at **contact.**

im·pact·ed (ĭm-păk'tĭd) *adj.* 1. Wedged together at the broken ends. Used of a fractured bone. 2. Placed in the alveolus and prohibiting eruption into a normal position. Used of a tooth. 3. Wedged or packed in, so as to fill or block an organ or a passage.

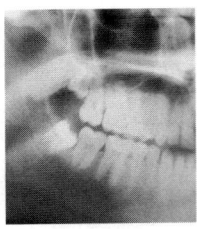

impacted
x-ray of an impacted
wisdom tooth in the lower
jaw

im·pair (ĭm-pâr') *tr.v.* **-paired, -pair·ing, -pairs** To cause to diminish, as in strength or quality: *An injury impaired my hearing.* [ME *empairen* < OFr. *empeirer* < VLat. *impēiōrāre* : Lat. *in-*, causative pref.; see IN-² + LLat. *pēiōrāre*, to worsen (< Lat. *pēior*, worse; see ped- in App.).] —**im·pair'ment** *n.*

im·paired (ĭm-pârd') *adj.* 1. Diminished, damaged, or weakened: *an impaired sense of smell.* 2. Functioning poorly or incompetently: *an impaired driver.* 3. Having a physical or mental disability: *an impaired child.* ❖ *n.* (*used with a pl. verb*) People who have a physical or mental disability considered as a group.

im·pa·la (ĭm-pä'lə) *n.* A reddish African antelope (*Aepyceros melampus*) noted for its leaping ability and having ridged curved horns in the male. [Zulu *im-pàla* : *im-*, n. pref. + *-pàla*, impala.]

im·pale (ĭm-pāl') *tr.v.* **-paled, -pal·ing, -pales** 1a. To pierce with a sharp stake or point. b. To torture or kill by impaling. 2. To render helpless as if by impaling. [Med.Lat. *impālāre* : Lat. *in-*, in; see IN-² + Lat. *pālus*, stake.] —**im·pale'ment** *n.* —**im·pal'er** *n.*

impala
black-faced impala
Aepyceros melampus petersi

im·pal·pa·ble (ĭm-păl'pə-bəl) *adj.* 1. Not perceptible to the touch; intangible. 2. Difficult to perceive or grasp by the mind. —**im·pal'pa·bil'i·ty** *n.* —**im·pal'pa·bly** *adv.*

im·pan·el (ĭm-păn'əl) also **em·pan·el** (ĕm-) *tr.v.* **-eled, -el·ing, -els** or **-elled, -el·ling, -els** *Law* To enroll (a jury) upon a panel or list. [ME *empanellen* < AN *empaneller* : *en-*, in (< Lat. *in-*; see IN-²) + *panel*, piece of paper listing jurors, jury; see PANEL.] —**im·pan'el·ment** *n.*

im·par·i·ty (ĭm-păr'ĭ-tē) *n., pl.* **-ties** Inequality; disparity. [LLat. *imparitās* < Lat. *impār*, not equal : *in-*, not; see IN-¹ + *pār*, equal; see perə- in App.]

im·part (ĭm-pärt') *tr.v.* **-part·ed, -part·ing, -parts** 1. To grant a share of; bestow. 2. To make known; disclose. 3. To pass on; transmit: *impart a forward motion.* [Ult. < Lat. *impertīre* : *in-*, in; see IN-² + *partīre*, to share (< *pars, part-*, part; see perə- in App.).]

im·par·tial (ĭm-pär'shəl) *adj.* Not partial or biased; unprejudiced. See Syns at **fair**¹. —**im'par·ti·al'i·ty** (-shē-ăl'ĭ-tē), **im·par'tial·ness** *n.* —**im·par'tial·ly** *adv.*

im·part·i·ble (ĭm-pär'tə-bəl) *adj.* Not partible; indivisible.

im·pass·a·ble (ĭm-păs'ə-bəl) *adj.* Impossible to pass, cross, or overcome. —**im·pass'a·bil'i·ty** *n.* —**im·pass'a·bly** *adv.*

im·passe (ĭm'păs') *n.* 1. A road or passage having no exit; a cul-de-sac. 2. A situation in which no progress can be made; a deadlock or a stalemate. [Fr. : *in-*, not (< Lat. *in-*; see IN-¹) + *passe*, a passing (< OFr. < *passer*, to pass; see PASS).]

im·pas·si·ble (ĭm-păs'ə-bəl) *adj.* 1. Not subject to suffering or pain. 2. Unfeeling; impassive. —**im·pas·si·bil'i·ty** *n.* —**im·pas'si·bly** *adv.*

im·pas·sion (ĭm-păsh'ən) *tr.v.* **-sioned, -sion·ing, -sions** To arouse the passions of. [Ital. *impassionare* : *in-*, in (< Lat.; see IN-²) + *passione*, passion (< Lat. *passiō, passiōn-*, emotion; see PASSION).]

im·pas·sioned (ĭm-păsh'ənd) *adj.* Full of passion; fervent.

im·pas·sive (ĭm-păs'ĭv) *adj.* 1. Devoid of or not subject to emotion. 2. Revealing no emotion; expressionless. 3. *Archaic* Incapable of physical sensation. 4. Motionless; still. [IN-¹ + PASSIVE, suffering (obsolete).] —**im·pas'sive·ly** *adv.* —**im·pas'sive·ness, im·pas·siv'i·ty** *n.*

im·paste (ĭm-pāst') *tr.v.* **-past·ed, -past·ing, -pastes** 1. To enclose with or as if with a paste or crust. 2. To paint by applying thick layers of pigment.

im·pas·to (ĭm-păs'tō, -pä'stō) *n., pl.* **-tos** 1. The application of thick layers of pigment to a canvas or other surface in painting. 2. The paint so applied. [Ital. < *impastare*, to make into a paste : *in-*, in (< Lat.; see IN-²) + *pasta*, paste (< LLat.; see PASTE¹).]

im·pa·tience (ĭm-pā'shəns) *n.* The quality or condition of being impatient.

im·pa·tiens (ĭm-pā'shənz, -shəns) *n.* Any of various plants of the genus *Impatiens*, which includes the jewelweed. [Lat. *impatiēns*, impatient (so called because the ripe pods burst open when touched). See IMPATIENT.]

im·pa·tient (ĭm-pā'shənt) *adj.* 1. Unable to wait patiently or tolerate delay; restless. 2. Unable to endure irritation or opposition; intolerant: *impatient of criticism.* 3. Expressing or produced by impatience. 4. Restively eager or desirous; anxious. [Ult. < Lat. *impatiēns, impatient-* : *in-*, not; see IN-¹ + *patiēns*, pr. part. of *patī*, to suffer, endure; see PATIENT.] —**im·pa'tient·ly** *adv.*

im·peach (ĭm-pēch') *tr.v.* **-peached, -peach·ing, -peach·es** 1a. To accuse. b. To charge (a public official) with improper conduct in office before a proper tribunal. 2. To challenge the validity of; try to discredit: *impeach one's credibility.* [ME *empechen*, to impede, accuse < AN *empecher* < LLat. *impedicāre*, to entangle : Lat. *in-*, in; see IN-² + Lat. *pedica*, fetter; see ped- in App.] —**im·peach'er** *n.* —**im·peach'ment** *n.*

im·peach·a·ble (ĭm-pē'chə-bəl) *adj.* 1. Capable of being impeached: *impeachable mayors.* 2. Warranting impeachment: *impeachable offenses.* —**im·peach'a·bil'i·ty** *n.*

im·pearl (ĭm-pûrl') *tr.v.* **-pearled, -pearl·ing, -pearls** 1. To form (something) into pearls. 2. To adorn with or as if with pearls.

im·pec·ca·ble (ĭm-pĕk'ə-bəl) *adj.* 1. Flawless; perfect. See Syns at **perfect**. 2. Incapable of sin or wrongdoing. [Lat. *impeccābilis* : *in-*, not; see IN-¹ + *peccāre*, to sin; see ped- in App.] —**im·pec'ca·bil'i·ty** *n.* —**im·pec'ca·bly** *adv.*

im·pe·cu·ni·ous (ĭm'pĭ-kyōō'nē-əs) *adj.* Lacking money; penniless. See Syns at **poor**. [IM-¹ + *pecunious*, rich (< ME < OFr. *pecunios* < Lat. *pecūniōsus* < *pecūnia*, money, wealth; see peku- in App.).] —**im'pe·cu'ni·ous·ly** *adv.* —**im'pe·cu'ni·ous·ness, im'pe·cu'ni·os'i·ty** (-ŏs'ĭ-tē) *n.*

im·ped·ance (ĭm-pēd'ns) *n.* Symbol **Z** 1. A measure of the total opposition to current flow in an alternating current circuit, usu. represented in complex notation as $Z = R + iX$, where R is the ohmic resistance, X is the reactance, and i is the imaginary unit. 2. An analogous measure of resistance to an alternating effect, as the resistance to vibration of the medium in sound transmission.

impedance matching *n.* The optimization of power transfer in a system by equalizing the impedance of a load and the internal impedance of the power source.

im·pede (ĭm-pēd') *tr.v.* **-ped·ed, -ped·ing, -pedes** To retard or obstruct the progress of. [Lat. *impedīre*. See ped- in App.] —**im·ped'er** *n.*

im·ped·i·ment (ĭm-pĕd'ə-mənt) *n.* 1. Something that impedes; a hindrance or obstruction. 2. An organic defect preventing clear articulation: *a speech impediment.* 3. *Law* Something that obstructs the making of a legal contract. [ME < OFr. < Lat. *impedīmentum* < *impedīre*, to impede. See IMPEDE.] —**im·ped'i·men'tal** (-mĕn'tl), **im·ped'i·men'ta·ry** (-mĕn'tə-rē) *adj.*

im·ped·i·men·ta (ĭm-pĕd'ə-mĕn'tə) *pl.n.* Objects, such as provisions or baggage, that impede or encumber. [Lat. *impedīmenta*, pl. of *impedīmentum*, impediment. See IMPEDIMENT.]

im·pel (ĭm-pĕl') *tr.v.* **-pelled, -pel·ling, -pels** 1. To urge to action through moral pressure; drive. 2. To drive forward; propel. [ME *impellen* < Lat. *impellere* : *in-*, against; see IN-² + *pellere*, to drive; see pel-² in App.]

im·pel·ler (ĭm-pĕl'ər) *n.* 1. One that impels, as a rotating device moving fluid under pressure. 2. A rotor or rotor blade.

im·pend (ĭm-pĕnd') *intr.v.* **-pend·ed, -pend·ing, -pends** 1. To be about to occur: *Her retirement is impending.* 2. To threaten to happen; menace. 3. *Archaic* To jut out; hang suspended. [Lat. *im-*

pendēre : in-, over; see IN-² + pendēre, to hang.]

im·pen·e·tra·bil·i·ty (ĭm-pĕn′ĭ-trə-bĭl′ĭ-tē) n. 1. The quality or condition of being impenetrable. 2. The inability of two bodies to occupy the same space at the same time.

im·pen·e·tra·ble (ĭm-pĕn′ĭ-trə-bəl) adj. 1. Impossible to penetrate or enter. 2. Impossible to understand; incomprehensible. 3. Impervious to sentiment or argument. —im·pen′e·tra·ble·ness n. —im·pen′e·tra·bly adv.

im·pen·i·tent (ĭm-pĕn′ĭ-tənt) adj. Not penitent; unrepentant. —im·pen′i·tence n. —im·pen′i·tent n. —im·pen′i·tent·ly adv.

im·per·a·tive (ĭm-pĕr′ə-tĭv) adj. 1. Expressing a command or plea; peremptory. 2. Having the power or authority to command or control. 3. Grammar Of, relating to, or being the mood that expresses a command or request. 4. Impossible to deter or evade; pressing. See Syns at **urgent**. ❖ n. 1a. A command; an order. b. An obligation; a duty. 2. A rule, principle, or instinct that compels a certain behavior: imperatives of survival. 3. Grammar a. The imperative mood. b. A verb in the imperative. [ME imperatif, relating to the imperative mood < OFr. < LLat. imperatīvus < Lat. imperātus, p. part. of imperāre, to command. See EMPEROR.] —im·per′a·tive·ly adv. —im·per′a·tive·ness n.

im·pe·ra·tor (ĭm′pə-rä′tôr′, -tər) n. 1. An army commander in the Roman Republic. 2. The supreme power of the Roman emperor. 3. The head of state and supreme commander of the Roman Empire, in whose name all victories were won. [Lat. imperātor. See EMPEROR.] —im·per′a·to′ri·al (ĭm-pĕr′ə-tôr′ē-əl, -tōr′-) adj.

im·per·cep·ti·ble (ĭm′pər-sĕp′tə-bəl) adj. 1. Impossible or difficult to perceive by the mind or senses: an imperceptible drop in temperature. 2. So subtle, slight, or gradual as to be barely perceptible. —im′per·cep′ti·bil′i·ty, im′per·cep′ti·ble·ness n. —im′per·cep′ti·bly adv.

im·per·cep·tive (ĭm′pər-sĕp′tĭv) adj. Lacking perception; not perceptive. —im′per·cep′tive·ness, im′per·cep·tiv′i·ty n.

im·per·cip·i·ent (ĭm′pər-sĭp′ē-ənt) adj. Imperceptive.

im·per·fect (ĭm-pûr′fĭkt) adj. 1. Not perfect. 2. Grammar Of or being the tense of a verb that shows, usu. in the past, an action or a condition as incomplete, continuous, or coincident with another action. 3. Botany Having either stamens or a pistil only. Used of a flower. 4. Law Not legally enforceable: an imperfect contract. ❖ n. 1. A flawed but usable piece of merchandise, usu. sold at a discount. 2. Grammar a. The imperfect tense. b. A verb in the imperfect. —im·per′fect·ly adv. —im·per′fect·ness n.

imperfect fungus n. Any of various fungi of the order Fungi Imperfecti, which reproduce only by asexual means.

im·per·fec·tion (ĭm′pər-fĕk′shən) n. 1. The quality or state of being imperfect. 2. Something imperfect; a defect or flaw.

im·per·fec·tive (ĭm′pər-fĕk′tĭv) adj. Of, related to, or being the aspect expressing the action denoted by the verb without regard to its beginning or completion. ❖ n. 1. The imperfective aspect. 2. A verb in this tense.

im·per·fo·rate (ĭm-pûr′fər-ĭt) adj. 1. Having no opening; not perforated. 2. Not separated by rows of perforations: imperforate stamps. 3. Medicine Lacking a normal opening: an imperforate anus. ❖ n. An imperforate stamp.

im·pe·ri·al (ĭm-pîr′ē-əl) adj. 1. Of or suggestive of an empire or sovereign, esp. an emperor or empress. 2. Ruling over extensive territories or over colonies or dependencies. 3a. Having supreme authority; sovereign. b. Regal; majestic. 4. Outstanding in size or quality. 5. Of or belonging to the British Imperial System of weights and measures. ❖ n. 1. An emperor or empress. 2. The top of a carriage. 3. Something outstanding in size or quality. 4. A variable size of paper, usu. 23 by 33 inches (55.8 by 83.8 centimeters). 5. A pointed beard grown from the lower lip and chin. [ME < OFr. < Lat. imperiālis < imperium, command. See EMPIRE. N., sense 5, after the beard of Napoleon III.] —im·pe′ri·al·ly adv.

im·pe·ri·al·ism (ĭm-pîr′ē-ə-lĭz′əm) n. 1. The policy of extending a nation's authority by territorial acquisition or by establishing economic and political hegemony over other nations. 2. The system, policies, or practices of such a government. —im·pe′ri·al·ist n. & adj. —im·pe′ri·al·is′tic adj. —im·pe′ri·al·is′ti·cal·ly adv.

imperial moth n. A large New World moth (Eacles imperialis) having yellow wings with purplish or brownish markings.

Imperial Valley A fertile irrigated region of SE CA and NE Baja California, Mexico.

im·per·il (ĭm-pĕr′əl) tr.v. -iled, -il·ing, -ils or -illed, -il·ling, -ils To put into peril. See Syns at **endanger**. —im·per′il·ment n.

im·pe·ri·ous (ĭm-pîr′ē-əs) adj. 1. Arrogantly domineering or overbearing. 2. Urgent; pressing. 3. Obsolete Regal; imperial. [< Lat. imperiōsus < imperium, imperium. See EMPIRE.] —im·pe′ri·ous·ly adv. —im·pe′ri·ous·ness n.

im·per·ish·a·ble (ĭm-pĕr′ĭsh-ə-bəl) adj. Not perishable: imperishable food. —im·per′ish·a·bil′i·ty, im·per′ish·a·ble·ness n. —im·per′ish·a·bly adv.

im·pe·ri·um (ĭm-pîr′ē-əm) n., pl. -pe·ri·a (-pîr′ē-ə) 1. Absolute rule; supreme power. 2. A sphere of power or dominion; an empire. [Lat. See EMPIRE.]

im·per·ma·nent (ĭm-pûr′mə-nənt) adj. Not lasting; not per-

manent. —im·per′ma·nence, im·per′ma·nen·cy n.

im·per·me·a·ble (ĭm-pûr′mē-ə-bəl) adj. Impossible to permeate: an impermeable border. —im·per′me·a·bil′i·ty, im·per′me·a·ble·ness n. —im·per′me·a·bly adv.

im·per·mis·si·ble (ĭm′pər-mĭs′ə-bəl) adj. Not permitted; not permissible: impermissible behavior. —im′per·mis′si·bil′i·ty n. —im′per·mis′si·bly adv.

im·per·son·al (ĭm-pûr′sə-nəl) adj. 1. Lacking personality; not being a person: an impersonal force. 2a. Showing no emotion or personality. b. Having no personal reference or connection. c. Not responsive to or expressive of human personalities: an impersonal corporation. 3. Grammar a. Of, relating to, or being a verb expressing the action of an unspecified or expletive subject, as it snowed. b. Indefinite. Used of pronouns. —im·per′son·al′i·ty (-sə-nǎl′ĭ-tē) n. —im·per′son·al·ly adv.

im·per·son·al·ize (ĭm-pûr′sə-nə-līz′) tr.v. -ized, -iz·ing, -iz·es To make impersonal.

im·per·son·ate (ĭm-pûr′sə-nāt′) tr.v. -at·ed, -at·ing, -ates 1. To assume the character or appearance of, esp. fraudulently: impersonate a police officer. 2. To imitate the appearance, voice, or manner of; mimic. 3. Archaic To embody; personify. —im·per′son·a′tion n. —im·per′son·a′tor n.

im·per·ti·nence (ĭm-pûr′tn-əns) n. 1. The quality or condition of being impertinent, esp.: a. Insolence. b. Irrelevance. 2. An impertinent act or statement.

im·per·ti·nen·cy (ĭm-pûr′tn-ən-sē) n., pl. -cies Impertinence.

im·per·ti·nent (ĭm-pûr′tn-ənt) adj. 1. Exceeding the limits of propriety or good manners; improperly forward or bold. 2. Not pertinent; irrelevant. [ME, irrelevant < OFr. < LLat. impertinēns, impertinent- : Lat. in-, not; see IN-¹ + Lat. pertinēns, pertinent; see PERTINENT.] —im·per′ti·nent·ly adv.

im·per·turb·a·ble (ĭm′pər-tûr′bə-bəl) adj. Unshakably calm and collected. —im′per·turb′a·bil′i·ty, im′per·turb′a·ble·ness n. —im′per·turb′a·bly adv.

im·per·vi·ous (ĭm-pûr′vē-əs) adj. 1. Impossible to penetrate. 2. Impossible to affect. —im·per′vi·ous·ly adv. —im·per′vi·ous·ness n.

im·pe·ti·go (ĭm′pĭ-tī′gō) n., pl. -gos A contagious bacterial skin infection, usu. of children, that is characterized by the eruption of superficial pustules and the formation of thick yellow crusts, commonly on the face. [ME < Lat. impetīgō < impetere, to attack. See IMPETUS.] —im′pe·tig′e·nous (-tĭj′ə-nəs) adj.

im·pet·u·os·i·ty (ĭm-pĕch′ōō-ŏs′ĭ-tē) n., pl. -ties 1. The quality or condition of being impetuous. 2. An impetuous act.

im·pet·u·ous (ĭm-pĕch′ōō-əs) adj. 1. Marked by sudden and forceful energy or emotion; impulsive and passionate. 2. Having or marked by violent force: impetuous waves. [ME, violent < OFr. impetueux < LLat. impetuōsus < Lat. impetus, impetus. See IMPETUS.] —im·pet′u·ous·ly adv. —im·pet′u·ous·ness n.

im·pe·tus (ĭm′pĭ-təs) n., pl. -tus·es 1. An impelling force; an impulse. 2. The force or energy associated with a moving body. 3a. Something that incites; a stimulus. b. Increased activity in response to a stimulus: The deadline gave impetus to the work. [ME impetous < Lat. impetus < impetere, to attack : in-, against; see IN-² + petere, to go towards, seek; see pet- in App.]

im·pi·e·ty (ĭm-pī′ĭ-tē) n., pl. -ties 1. The quality or state of being impious. 2. An impious act. 3. Undutifulness.

im·pinge (ĭm-pĭnj′) —intr. -pinged, -ping·ing, -ping·es 1. To collide or strike. 2. To encroach; trespass: impinged on my privacy. 3. Usage Problem To have a negative or harmful effect. —tr. To encroach upon. [Lat. impingere : in-, against; see IN-² + pangere, to fasten.] —im·pinge′ment n. —im·ping′er n.

> **USAGE NOTE** The use of impinge meaning "to encroach; trespass," as in Americans dislike any policy that impinges on their liberty, is unobjectionable. However, when impinge is used more loosely to mean "to have a negative or harmful effect," the Usage Panel is split. Only 47 percent of the Panel found the following sentence to be acceptable: What the recovered diary revealed about the villagers directly impinged on the lives of people living there many years later.

im·pi·ous (ĭm′pē-əs, ĭm-pī′-) adj. 1. Lacking reverence; not pious. 2. Lacking due respect or dutifulness: impious toward one's parents. [< Lat. impius : in-, not; see IN-¹ + pius, dutiful.] —im′pi·ous·ly adv. —im′pi·ous·ness n.

imp·ish (ĭm′pĭsh) adj. Of or befitting an imp; mischievous. —imp′ish·ly adv. —imp′ish·ness n.

im·plac·a·ble (ĭm-plăk′ə-bəl, -plā′kə-) adj. Impossible to placate or appease: implacable foes. —im·plac′a·bil′i·ty, im·plac′a·ble·ness n. —im·plac′a·bly adv.

im·plant (ĭm-plănt′) v. -plant·ed, -plant·ing, -plants —tr. 1. To set in firmly, as into the ground: implant fence posts. 2. To establish securely, as in the mind; instill. 3. Medicine a. To insert or embed (an object or a device) surgically. b. To graft or insert (a tissue) within the body. —intr. Embryology To become attached to and embedded in the uterine lining. Used of a fertilized egg. ❖ n. (ĭm′plănt′) Something implanted, esp. surgically: a dental implant. [ME implanten < Med.Lat. implantāre : Lat. in-, into; see IN-² + Lat. plantāre, to plant (< planta, a shoot; see PLANT).] —im·plant′a·ble adj.

im·plan·ta·tion (ĭm′plăn-tā′shən) n. 1a. The act or an instance

imperial moth
Eacles imperialis

ă	pat	oi	boy
ā	pay	ou	out
âr	care	ōō	took
ä	father	ōō	boot
ĕ	pet	ŭ	cut
ē	be	ûr	urge
ĭ	pit	th	thin
ī	pie	th	this
îr	pier	hw	which
ŏ	pot	zh	vision
ō	toe	ə	about,
ô	paw		item

Stress marks:
′ (primary);
′ (secondary), as in
lexicon (lĕk′sĭ-kŏn′)

of implanting. **b.** The condition of being implanted. **2.** *Embryology* The process by which a fertilized egg implants in the uterine lining.

im·plau·si·ble (ĭm-plô′zə-bəl) *adj.* Difficult to believe; not plausible. —**im·plau′si·bil′i·ty** *n.* —**im·plau′si·bly** *adv.*

im·plead (ĭm-plēd′) *tr.v.* **-plead·ed, -plead·ing, -pleads** To sue in court in response to an earlier pleading. [ME *empleden* < AN *empleder*, var. of OFr. *emplaider* : *en-*, intensive pref. (< Lat. *in-*; see IN-²) + *plaidier*, to plead; see PLEAD.]

im·ple·ment (ĭm′plə-mənt) *n.* **1.** A tool or instrument used in doing work: *hoes, spades, and other gardening implements.* **2.** An article used to outfit or equip. **3.** A means of achieving an end; an instrument or agent. ❖ *tr.v.* (-mĕnt′) **-ment·ed, -ment·ing, -ments** **1.** To put into practical effect; carry out: *implement the plan.* **2.** To supply with implements. [ME, supplementary payment < OFr. *emplement*, act of filling < LLat. *implēmentum* < Lat. *implēre*, to fill up : *in-*, intensive pref.; see IN-² + *plēre*, to fill; see **pelə-¹** in App.] —**im′ple·men·ta′tion** (-mən-tā′shən, -mĕn-) *n.* —**im′ple·ment′er, im′ple·men′tor** *n.*

im·pli·cate (ĭm′plĭ-kāt′) *tr.v.* **-cat·ed, -cat·ing, -cates** **1.** To involve or connect intimately or incriminatingly. **2.** To have as a consequence or an inference; imply. **3.** *Linguistics* To convey, imply, or suggest by implicature. **4.** *Archaic* To interweave or entangle; entwine. [ME, to convey a truth in a fable < Lat. *implicāre, implicāt-*, to entangle, unite : *in-*, in; see IN-² + *plicāre*, to fold; see **plek-** in App.]

im·pli·ca·tion (ĭm′plĭ-kā′shən) *n.* **1.** The act of implicating or the condition of being implicated. **2.** The act of implying or the condition of being implied. **3.** Something that is implied, esp.: **a.** An indirect indication; a suggestion. **b.** An implied meaning; implicit significance. **c.** An inference. See Usage Note at **infer.** —**im′pli·ca′tive** *adj.* —**im′pli·ca′tive·ly** *adv.*

im·plic·a·ture (ĭm-plĭk′ə-chər) *n.* **1.** The aspect of meaning that a speaker conveys, implies, or suggests without directly expressing. Although the utterance *"Can you pass the salt?"* is literally a request for information about one's ability to pass salt, the understood implicature is a request for salt. **2.** The process by which such a meaning is conveyed, implied, or suggested. In saying *"Some dogs are mammals,"* the speaker conveys by implicature that not all dogs are mammals.

im·plic·it (ĭm-plĭs′ĭt) *adj.* **1.** Implied or understood though not directly expressed. **2.** Contained in the nature of something though not readily apparent. **3.** Having no doubts or reservations; unquestioning. [Lat. *implicitus*, var. of *implicātus*, p. part. of *implicāre*, to entangle. See IMPLICATE.] —**im·plic′it·ly** *adv.* —**im·plic′it·ness** *n.*

implicit differentiation *n.* The process of computing the derivative of an implicit function.

implicit function *n.* A function whose relation to the variable is given by an equation for which the function has not been solved explicitly. In the equation $x^2 + y^2 = 1$, y is an implicit function of x.

im·plode (ĭm-plōd′) *v.* **-plod·ed, -plod·ing, -plodes** —*intr.* **1.** To collapse inward violently. —*tr.* **1.** To cause to implode. **2.** To demolish (a building) by causing to implode. [IN-² + (EX)PLODE.]

im·plore (ĭm-plôr′, -plōr′) *v.* **-plored, -plor·ing, -plores** —*tr.* **1.** To appeal to in supplication; beseech: *implored the judge for mercy.* **2.** To beg for urgently: *implored her mercy.* —*intr.* To make an earnest appeal. [Lat. *implōrāre* : *in-*, toward; see IN-² + *plōrāre*, to weep.] —**im′plo·ra′tion** *n.* —**im·plor′er** *n.* —**im·plor′ing·ly** *adv.*

im·plo·sion (ĭm-plō′zhən) *n.* **1.** A violent collapse inward. **2.** Violent compression. **3.** The controlled imploding of a building whose structural members are weakened and broken by explosives. **4.** *Linguistics* The pronunciation of an implosive. [IN-² + (EX)PLOSION.]

im·plo·sive (ĭm-plō′sĭv) *n.* A stop consonant pronounced with the breath drawn in. —**im·plo′sive** *adj.*

im·ply (ĭm-plī′) *tr.v.* **-plied, -ply·ing, -plies** **1.** To involve by logical necessity; entail. **2.** To express or indicate indirectly: *His tone implied disapproval.* See Syns at **suggest.** See Usage Note at **infer.** **3.** *Obsolete* To entangle. [ME *implien* < OFr. *emplier*, to enfold < Lat. *implicāre*. See IMPLICATE.]

im·po·lite (ĭm′pə-līt′) *adj.* Not polite; discourteous. [Lat. *impolītus*, unpolished, inelegant : *in-*, not; see IN-¹ + *polītus*, p. part. of *polīre*, to polish; see POLISH.] —**im′po·lite′ly** *adv.* —**im′po·lite′ness** *n.*

im·pol·i·tic (ĭm-pŏl′ĭ-tĭk) *adj.* Not wise or expedient; not politic: *an impolitic speech.* —**im·pol′i·tic·ly** *adv.*

im·pon·der·a·ble (ĭm-pŏn′dər-ə-bəl) *adj.* That cannot undergo precise evaluation: *imponderable problems.* —**im·pon′der·a·ble** *n.* —**im·pon′der·a·bil′i·ty, im·pon′der·a·ble·ness** *n.* —**im·pon′der·a·bly** *adv.*

im·port (ĭm-pôrt′, -pōrt′, ĭm′pôrt′, -pōrt′) *v.* **-port·ed, -port·ing, -ports** —*tr.* **1.** To bring or carry in from an outside source, esp. from abroad for trade or sale. **2.** *Computer Science* To receive (data) into one program from another. **3.** To carry or hold the meaning of; signify: *high inflation importing hard times.* **4.** To imply. **5.** *Archaic* To have importance for. —*intr.* To be significant. See Syns at **count¹.** ❖ *n.* (ĭm′pôrt′, -pōrt′) **1.** Something imported. **2.** The act or occupation of importing goods or mate-

implosion

rials. **3.** Meaning; signification. See Syns at **meaning. 4.** Importance; significance. [ME *importen*, to convey a meaning < Med.Lat. *importāre* and < OFr. *importer*, to cause, both < Lat. *importāre*, to carry in, cause : *in-*, into; see IN-² + *portāre*, to carry; see **per-²** in App.] —**im·port′a·bil′i·ty** *n.* —**im·port′a·ble** *adj.* —**im·port′er** *n.*

im·por·tance (ĭm-pôr′tns) *n.* **1.** The quality or condition of being important; significance. **2.** Personal status; standing. **3.** *Obsolete* An important matter. **4.** *Obsolete* Meaning; import. **5.** *Obsolete* Importunity.

im·por·tant (ĭm-pôr′tnt) *adj.* **1.** Strongly affecting the course of events or the nature of things; significant. **2.** Having or suggesting a consciousness of high position or authority; authoritative. **3.** *Obsolete* Importunate. [ME < OFr. < Med.Lat. *importāns, important-*, pr. part. of *importāre*, to mean < Lat., to import. See IMPORT.] —**im·por′tant·ly** *adv.*

> **USAGE NOTE** Some critics have objected to the use of the phrase *more importantly* in place of *more important* as a means of introducing an assertion. But both forms are widely used by reputable writers, and there is no obvious reason for preferring one or the other.

im·por·ta·tion (ĭm′pôr-tā′shən, -pōr-) *n.* **1a.** The act or business of importing. **b.** The condition or process of being imported. **2.** Something imported; an import.

im·por·tu·nate (ĭm-pôr′chə-nĭt) *adj.* Troublesomely urgent or persistent in requesting: *an importunate beggar.* —**im·por′tu·nate·ly** *adv.* —**im·por′tu·nate·ness** *n.*

im·por·tune (ĭm′pôr-tōōn′, -tyōōn′, ĭm-pôr′chən) *v.* **-tuned, -tun·ing, -tunes** —*tr.* **1.** To beset with insistent or repeated requests; entreat pressingly. **2.** *Archaic* To ask for urgently or repeatedly. **3.** To annoy; vex. —*intr.* To plead or urge irksomely, often persistently. ❖ *adj.* Importunate. [Fr. *importuner* < OFr. *importun*, inopportune < Lat. *importūnus* : *in-*, not; see IN-¹ + *portus*, port, refuge; see **per-²** in App.] —**im′por·tune′ly** *adv.* —**im′por·tun′er** *n.*

im·por·tu·ni·ty (ĭm′pôr-tōō′nĭ-tē, -tyōō′-) *n., pl.* **-ties** **1.** An importunate request. **2.** The quality of being importunate.

im·pose (ĭm-pōz′) *v.* **-posed, -pos·ing, -pos·es** —*tr.* **1.** To establish or apply as compulsory; levy: *impose a tax.* **2.** To apply or make prevail by or as if by authority: *impose a peace settlement.* See Syns at **dictate. 3.** To obtrude or force (oneself, for example) on another or others. **4.** *Printing* To arrange (type or plates) on an imposing stone. **5.** To offer or circulate fraudulently; pass off. —*intr.* To take unfair advantage: *imposed on their generosity.* [ME *imposen* < OFr. *imposer*, alteration (influenced by *poser*, to put, place) of Lat. *impōnere*, to place upon : *in-*, on; see IN-² + *pōnere*, to place; see **apo-** in App.] —**im·pos′er** *n.*

im·pos·ing (ĭm-pō′zĭng) *adj.* Impressive, as in power. See Syns at **grand.** —**im·pos′ing·ly** *adv.*

imposing stone *n.* A stone or metal slab on which material to be printed is arranged.

im·po·si·tion (ĭm′pə-zĭsh′ən) *n.* **1.** The act of imposing or the condition of being imposed. **2.** Something imposed, such as a tax or a fraud. **3.** A burdensome or unfair demand, as upon someone's time. **4.** *Printing* The arrangement of printed matter to form a sequence of pages.

im·pos·si·bil·i·ty (ĭm-pŏs′ə-bĭl′ĭ-tē) *n., pl.* **-ties** **1.** The state or quality of being impossible. **2.** Something impossible.

im·pos·si·ble (ĭm-pŏs′ə-bəl) *adj.* **1.** Incapable of existing or occurring. **2.** Not capable of being accomplished. **3.** Unacceptable; intolerable. **4.** Extremely difficult to deal with or tolerate. —**im·pos′si·bly** *adv.*

im·post¹ (ĭm′pōst′) *n.* **1.** Something, such as a tax, that is imposed. **2.** *Sports* The weight a horse must carry in a handicap race. [Obsolete Fr. < OFr. < Med.Lat. *impostum* < Lat., neut. of *impostus*, var. of *impositus*, p. part. of *impōnere*, to place upon. See IMPOSE.]

im·post² (ĭm′pōst′) *n.* The uppermost part of a column or pillar supporting an arch. [Fr. *imposte* < Ital. *imposta* < Lat., fem. p. part. of *impōnere*, to place upon. See IMPOSE.]

im·pos·tor or **im·pos·ter** (ĭm-pŏs′tər) *n.* One who engages in deception under an assumed name or identity. [Fr. *imposteur* < Lat. *impostor*, one who assigns a name < *impostus*, var. of *impositus*, p. part. of *impōnere*, to place upon. See IMPOSE.]

im·pos·ture (ĭm-pŏs′chər) *n.* The act or instance of engaging in deception under an assumed name or identity. [Fr. < OFr. < LLat. *impostūra* < Lat. *impostus*, var. of *impositus*, p. part. of *impōnere*, to place upon. See IMPOSE.]

im·po·tence (ĭm′pə-təns) also **im·po·ten·cy** (-tən-sē) *n.* **1.** The quality or condition of being impotent. **2.** See **erectile dysfunction.**

im·po·tent (ĭm′pə-tənt) *adj.* **1.** Lacking physical strength or vigor; weak. **2.** Lacking in power, as to act effectively; helpless. **3a.** Incapable of sexual intercourse, often because unable to achieve or sustain an erection. **b.** Sterile. Used of males. **4.** *Obsolete* Lacking self-restraint. —**im′po·tent·ly** *adv.*

im·pound (ĭm-pound′) *tr.v.* **-pound·ed, im·pound·ing, im·pounds** **1.** To confine in or as if in a pound: *impound stray dogs.* **2.** To seize and retain in legal custody. **3.** To set aside in a fund rather than spend as prescribed. **4.** To accumulate and store in a reservoir. —**im•pound′ment** *n.* —**im•pound′er** *n.*

im•pov•er•ish (ĭm-pŏv′ər-ĭsh, -pŏv′rĭsh) *tr.v.* **-ished, -ish•ing, -ish•es** **1.** To reduce to poverty; make poor. **2.** To deprive of natural richness or strength: *impoverish the soil by overuse.* See Syns at **deplete.** [ME *empoverishen* < OFr. *empovrir, empoveriss- : en-,* causative pref.; see EN-² + *povre,* poor (< Lat. *pauper*).] —**im•pov′er•ish•ment** *n.*

im•pov•er•ished (ĭm-pŏv′ər-ĭsht, -pŏv′rĭsht) *adj.* **1.** Reduced to poverty; poverty-stricken. See Syns at **poor.** **2.** Deprived of natural richness or strength; limited or depleted.

im•prac•ti•ca•ble (ĭm-prăk′tĭ-kə-bəl) *adj.* **1.** Impossible to do or carry out. **2.** Unfit for passage: *roads impracticable in winter.* **3.** *Archaic* Unmanageable; intractable. —**im•prac′ti•ca•bil′i•ty, im•prac′ti•ca•ble•ness** *n.* —**im•prac′ti•ca•bly** *adv.*

USAGE NOTE *Impracticable* applies to a course of action that is impossible to carry out; *impractical,* though it can be used in this way, also can be weaker in sense, suggesting that the course of action would yield an insufficient return or would have little practical value. A plan for a new stadium might be *impracticable* if the site is too marshy for safe construction; but if the site is too remote for patrons to attend games easily, the plan would be *impractical.* See Usage Note at **practicable.**

im•prac•ti•cal (ĭm-prăk′tĭ-kəl) *adj.* **1.** Unwise to implement or maintain in practice. **2.** Incapable of dealing efficiently with practical matters, esp. finances. **3.** Not a part of experience, fact, or practice; theoretical. **4.** Impracticable. See Usage Note at **impracticable.** —**im•prac′ti•cal′i•ty** (-kăl′ĭ-tē), **im•prac′ti•cal•ness** *n.*

im•pre•cate (ĭm′prĭ-kāt′) *tr.v.* **-cat•ed, -cat•ing, -cates** To invoke evil upon; curse. [Lat. *imprecārī, imprecāt- : in-,* towards; see IN-² + *precārī,* to pray, ask; see prek- in App.] —**im′pre•ca′tor** *n.* —**im′pre•ca•to′ry** (-kə-tôr′ē, -tōr′ē) *adj.*

im•pre•ca•tion (ĭm′prĭ-kā′shən) *n.* **1.** The act of imprecating. **2.** A curse.

im•pre•cise (ĭm′prĭ-sīs′) *adj.* Not precise. —**im′pre•cise′ly** *adv.* —**im′pre•ci′sion** (-sĭzh′ən) *n.*

im•preg•na•ble¹ (ĭm-prĕg′nə-bəl) *adj.* **1.** Impossible to capture or enter by force: *an impregnable fortress.* **2.** Difficult or impossible to attack, challenge, or refute with success: *an impregnable argument.* [ME *imprenable* < OFr. : *in-,* not (< Lat. *in-;* see IN-¹) + *prenable, pregnauble,* pregnable; see PREGNABLE.] —**im•preg′na•bly** *adv.*

im•preg•na•ble² (ĭm-prĕg′nə-bəl) *adj.* Capable of being impregnated. [IMPREGN(ATE) + -ABLE.]

im•preg•nate (ĭm-prĕg′nāt) *tr.v.* **-nat•ed, -nat•ing, -nates** **1.** To make pregnant; inseminate. **2.** To fertilize (an ovum, for example). **3.** To fill throughout; saturate. **4.** To permeate or imbue. ❖ *adj.* (also -nĭt) Saturated or filled. [Prob. < LLat. *im•praegnātus,* pregnant : Lat. *in-,* in; see IN-² + Lat. *praegnātus,* var. of *praegnās,* pregnant. See PREGNANT¹.] —**im′preg•na′tion** *n.* —**im′preg•na′tor** *n.*

im•pre•sa (ĭm-prā′zə) *n.* An emblem or device with a motto. [Ital., undertaking, impresa. See IMPRESARIO.]

im•pre•sa•ri•o (ĭm′prĭ-sär′ē-ō′, -sär′-) *n., pl.* **-os** **1.** One who sponsors or produces entertainment, esp. the director of an opera company. **2.** A manager; a producer. [Ital. < *impresa,* undertaking < fem. p. part. of *imprendere,* to undertake < VLat. **imprēndere.* See EMPRISE.]

im•press¹ (ĭm-prĕs′) *tr.v.* **-pressed, -press•ing, -press•es** **1.** To affect strongly, often favorably. **2.** To produce or attempt to produce a vivid impression or image of. **3.** To mark or stamp with or as if with pressure. **4.** To apply with pressure; press. ❖ *n.* (ĭm′prĕs′) **1.** The act of impressing. **2.** A mark or pattern produced by or as if by impressing. **3.** A stamp or seal meant to be impressed. [ME *impressen,* to imprint < OFr. *empresser* < Lat. *impressus,* p. part. of *imprimere : in-,* in; see IN-² + *premere,* press.]

im•press² (ĭm-prĕs′) *tr.v.* **-pressed, -press•ing, -press•es** **1.** To compel (a person) to serve in a military force. **2.** To seize (property) by force or authority; confiscate. ❖ *n.* (ĭm′prĕs) Impressment. [IN-² + PRESS² (influenced by IMPREST, advance on a soldier's pay (obsolete)).]

im•press•i•ble (ĭm-prĕs′ə-bəl) *adj.* Susceptible to impressions; malleable: *impressible young minds.* —**im•press′i•bil′i•ty** *n.* —**im•press′i•bly** *adv.*

im•pres•sion (ĭm-prĕsh′ən) *n.* **1.** An effect, feeling, or image retained as a consequence of experience. **2.** A vague notion, remembrance, or belief. **3.** A mark produced on a surface by pressure. **4.** The act or process of impressing. **5.** *Printing* **a.** All the copies of a publication printed at one time from the same set of type. **b.** A single copy of such a printing. **6.** A humorous imitation of the voice and mannerisms of a celebrity. **7.** An initial or single coat of color or paint. **8.** *Dentistry* An imprint of the teeth and surrounding tissues, used as a mold to make dentures, inlays, or plastic models.

im•pres•sion•a•ble (ĭm-prĕsh′ə-nə-bəl) *adj.* **1.** Readily or easily influenced; suggestible. **2.** Capable of receiving an impression; plastic: *impressionable plaster.* —**im•pres′sion•a•bil′i•ty** *n.*

im•pres•sion•ism (ĭm-prĕsh′ə-nĭz′əm) *n.* **1.** often **Impressionism** A theory or style of painting originating in France dur-

ing the 1870s, marked by concentration on the immediate visual impression produced by a scene and by the use of unmixed primary colors and small strokes to simulate reflected light. **2.** A literary style marked by the use of details and mental associations to evoke subjective and sensory impressions rather than objective reality. **3.** *Music* A style of the late 19th and early 20th centuries, using somewhat vague harmony and rhythm to evoke a mood, place, and natural phenomena. **4.** The practice of expressing or developing one's subjective response to art or experience.

im•pres•sion•ist (ĭm-prĕsh′ə-nĭst) *n.* **1.** An artist, composer, or writer who practices or upholds impressionism. **2.** An entertainer who does impressions. ❖ *adj.* Impressionistic, esp. in painting.

im•pres•sion•is•tic (ĭm-prĕsh′ə-nĭs′tĭk) *adj.* **1.** Of, relating to, or practicing impressionism. **2.** Of, relating to, or predicated on impression as opposed to reason or fact. **3.** Impressionable. —**im•pres′sion•is′ti•cal•ly** *adv.*

im•pres•sive (ĭm-prĕs′ĭv) *adj.* Making a strong or vivid impression; striking or remarkable: *an impressive ceremony.* —**im•pres′sive•ly** *adv.* —**im•pres′sive•ness** *n.*

im•press•ment (ĭm-prĕs′mənt) *n.* The act or policy of seizing people or property for public service or use.

im•pres•sure (ĭm-prĕsh′ər) *n. Archaic* A mark produced by pressure; an impression.

im•prest (ĭm-prĕst′) *n.* An advance or a loan of funds, esp. for services rendered to a government. [< obsolete Ital. *impresto,* loan < p. part. of *imprestare,* to lend : *in-,* toward (< Lat.; see IN-²) + *prestare,* to lend (< Lat. *praestāre,* to give < *praestō,* at hand; see ghes- in App.).]

im•pri•ma•tur (ĭm′prə-mä′tŏŏr, -mä′tər) *n.* **1.** Official approval or license to print or publish, esp. under conditions of censorship. **2a.** Official approval; sanction. **b.** A mark of official approval. [< NLat. *imprimātur,* let it be printed, third pers. sing. pr. subjunctive passive of Lat. *imprimere,* to imprint. See IM-PRESS¹.]

im•pri•mis (ĭm-prī′mĭs) *adv.* In the first place. [ME *in primis* < Lat. *in prīmīs : in,* among; see IN-² + *prīmīs,* ablative pl. of *prīmus,* first; see per¹ in App.]

im•print (ĭm-prĭnt′) *tr.v.* **-print•ed, -print•ing, -prints** **1.** To produce (a mark or pattern) on a surface by pressure. **2.** To produce a mark on (a surface) by pressure. **3.** To impart a strong or vivid impression of: "We imprint our own ideas onto acts" (Ellen Goodman). **4.** To fix firmly, as in the mind. ❖ *n.* (ĭm′prĭnt′) **1.** A mark or pattern produced by imprinting. **2.** A distinguishing influence or effect. **3.** A publisher's name, often with the date, address, and edition, printed at the bottom of a title page of a publication. [ME *emprenten* < OFr. *empreinter < empreinte,* impression < fem. p. part. of *empreindre,* to print < Lat. *imprimere,* to impress. See IMPRESS¹.]

im•print•ing (ĭm′prĭn′tĭng) *n.* A learning process by which a newborn or very young animal establishes a behavior pattern of recognition and attraction to another animal of its own kind or to a substitute identified as the parent.

im•pris•on (ĭm-prĭz′ən) *tr.v.* **-oned, -on•ing, -ons** To put in or as if in prison; confine. [ME *emprisonen* < OFr. *emprisoner : en-,* in (< Lat. *in-;* see IN-²) + *prison,* prison; see PRISON.] —**im•pris′on•a•ble** *adj.* —**im•pris′on•ment** *n.*

im•prob•a•bil•i•ty (ĭm-prŏb′ə-bĭl′ĭ-tē) *n., pl.* **-ties** **1.** The quality or condition of being improbable. **2.** Something improbable.

im•prob•a•ble (ĭm-prŏb′ə-bəl) *adj.* Unlikely to take place or be true. —**im•prob′a•ble•ness** *n.* —**im•prob′a•bly** *adv.*

im•pro•bi•ty (ĭm-prō′bĭ-tē) *n.* Lack of probity; dishonesty. [ME *improbite,* shameless persistence < OFr., dishonesty < Lat. *im-probitās < improbus,* dishonest : *in-,* not; see IN-¹ + *probus,* honest, good; see per¹ in App.]

im•promp•tu (ĭm-prŏmp′tŏŏ, -tyŏŏ) *adj.* **1.** Prompted by the occasion rather than being planned in advance. **2.** Spoken, performed, done, or composed with little or no preparation; extemporaneous: *impromptu remarks.* ❖ *adv.* With little or no preparation; extemporaneously. ❖ *n.* **1.** Something impromptu, such as a speech. **2.** *Music* A short composition, esp. for the piano, including extemporaneous passages. [Fr. < Lat. *in prōmptū,* at hand : *in,* in; see IN-² + *prōmptū,* ablative of *prōmptus,* readiness < p. part. of *prōmere,* to bring forth; see PROMPT.]

im•prop•er (ĭm-prŏp′ər) *adj.* **1.** Not suited to circumstances or needs; unsuitable. **2.** Not in keeping with conventional mores; indecorous. **3.** Not consistent with established truth, fact, or rule; incorrect. **4.** Irregular or abnormal. —**im•prop′er•ly** *adv.* —**im•prop′er•ness** *n.*

improper fraction *n.* A fraction in which the numerator is larger than or equal to the denominator.

improper integral *n.* An integral having at least one nonfinite limit or an integrand that becomes infinite between the limits of integration.

im•pro•pri•e•ty (ĭm′prə-prī′ĭ-tē) *n., pl.* **-ties** **1.** The quality or condition of being improper. **2.** An improper act. **3.** An improper or unacceptable usage in speech or writing.

im•prov (ĭm′prŏv′) *n. Informal* **1.** Improvisation: *practiced improv in acting class.* **2.** An improvisation: *a funny improv about looking for a job.*

im•prove (ĭm-prŏŏv′) *v.* **-proved, -prov•ing, -proves** —*tr.* **1.**

ă	pat	oi	boy
ā	pay	ou	out
âr	care	ŏŏ	took
ä	father	ōō	boot
ĕ	pet	ŭ	cut
ē	be	ûr	urge
ĭ	pit	th	thin
ī	pie	th	this
îr	pier	hw	which
ŏ	pot	zh	vision
ō	toe	ə	about,
ô	paw		item

Stress marks:
′ (primary);
′ (secondary), as in
lexicon (lĕk′sĭ-kŏn′)

To raise to a more desirable or more excellent quality or condition; make better. **2.** To increase the productivity or value of (land or property). **3.** To put to good use; use profitably. —*intr.* **1.** To become better. **2.** To make beneficial additions or changes. [ME *improwen*, to enclose land for cultivation < AN *emprouwer*, to turn to profit : OFr. *en-*, causative pref. (< Lat. *in-*; see IN—²) + OFr. *prou*, profit (< LLat. *prōde*, advantageous; see PROUD).]

im·prove·ment (ĭm-prōōv′mənt) *n.* **1a.** The act or process of improving. **b.** The state of being improved. **2.** A change or addition that improves.

im·prov·i·dent (ĭm-prŏv′ĭ-dənt) *adj.* **1.** Not providing for the future; thriftless. **2.** Rash; incautious. —**im·prov′i·dence** *n.* —**im·prov′i·dent·ly** *adv.*

im·prov·i·sa·tion (ĭm-prŏv′ĭ-zā′shən, ĭm′prə-vī–) *n.* **1.** The act of improvising. **2.** Something improvised, esp. a musical passage or a dramatic skit. —**im·prov′i·sa′tion·al** *adj.*

im·prov·i·sa·tor (ĭm-prŏv′ĭ-zā′tər) *n.* One who improvises.

im·prov·i·sa·to·ry (ĭm-prŏv′ĭ-zə-tôr′ē, -tōr′ē, ĭm′prə-vī′-) also **im·prov·i·sa·to·ri·al** (ĭm-prŏv′ĭ-zə-tôr′ē-əl, -tōr′-) *adj.* **1.** Made up without preparation; improvised. **2.** Of or relating to improvisation: *improvisory skill.*

im·pro·vise (ĭm′prə-vīz′) *v.* **-vised, -vis·ing, -vis·es** —*tr.* **1.** To invent, compose, or perform with little or no preparation. **2.** To play or sing (music) extemporaneously. **3.** To make or provide from available materials. —*intr.* **1.** To invent, compose, or perform something extemporaneously. **3.** To improvise music. **3.** To make do with whatever materials are at hand. [Fr. *improviser* < Ital. *improvvisare* < *improvviso*, unforeseen < Lat. *imprōvīsus* : *in-*, not; see IN—¹ + *prōvīsus*, p. part. of *prōvidēre*, to foresee; see PROVIDE.] —**im′pro·vis′er** *n.*

im·pru·dence (ĭm-prōōd′ns) *n.* **1.** The quality or condition of being imprudent. **2.** An imprudent act.

im·pru·dent (ĭm-prōōd′nt) *adj.* Unwise or indiscreet; not prudent.

im·pu·dence (ĭm′pyə-dəns) also **im·pu·den·cy** (-dən-sē) *n.* **1.** The quality of being impudent. **2.** Impudent behavior.

im·pu·dent (ĭm′pyə-dənt) *adj.* **1.** Marked by offensive boldness; insolent. **2.** *Obsolete* Immodest. [ME < Lat. *impudēns, impudent- : in-*, not; see IN—¹ + *pudēns*, pr. part. of *pudēre*, to be ashamed.] —**im′pu·dent·ly** *adv.*

im·pu·dic·i·ty (ĭm′pyōō-dĭs′ĭ-tē) *n.* Immodesty; shamelessness. [LLat. *impudīcitās* < Lat. *impudīcus*, immodest : *in-*, not; see IN—¹ + *pudīcus*, modest (< *pudēre*, to be ashamed).]

im·pugn (ĭm-pyōōn′) *tr.v.* **-pugned, -pugn·ing, -pugns** To attack as false or questionable; challenge in argument: *impugn an opponent's record.* [ME *impugnen* < OFr. *impugner* < Lat. *impugnāre : in-*, against; see IN—² + *pugnāre*, to fight.] —**im·pugn′a·ble** *adj.* —**im·pugn′er** *n.*

im·pu·is·sance (ĭm-pyōō′ĭ-səns, ĭm-pwĭs′əns) *n.* Lack of power or effectiveness; weakness. [ME *impuissaunce* < OFr. *im-puissance : in-*, not; see IN—¹ + *puissance*, power; see PUISSANCE.] —**im·pu′is·sant** *adj.*

im·pulse (ĭm′pŭls′) *n.* **1a.** An impelling force; an impetus. **b.** The motion produced by such a force. **2.** A sudden wish or urge that prompts an unpremeditated act or feeling; an abrupt inclination. **3.** A motivating force or tendency. **4.** *Electronics* A surge of electrical power in one direction. **5.** *Physics* The product obtained by multiplying the average value of a force by the time during which it acts, equal to the change in momentum produced by the force in this time interval. **6.** *Physiology* The electrochemical transmission of a signal along a nerve fiber that produces an excitatory or inhibitory response at a target tissue, such as a muscle. ❖ *adj.* Marked by impulsiveness or acting on impulse. [Lat. *impulsus* < p. part. of *impellere*, to impel. See IMPEL.]

im·pul·sion (ĭm-pŭl′shən) *n.* **1.** The act of impelling or the condition of being impelled. **2.** An impelling force; a thrust. **3.** Motion produced by an impelling force; momentum. **4.** A wish or urge from within; an impulse.

im·pul·sive (ĭm-pŭl′sĭv) *adj.* **1.** Inclined to act on impulse rather than thought. **2.** Motivated by or resulting from impulse: *impulsive generosity.* **3.** Having force or power to impel or incite; forceful. **4.** *Physics* Acting within brief time intervals. Used esp. of a force. —**im·pul′sive·ly** *adv.* —**im·pul′sive·ness, im′pul·siv′i·ty** *n.*

im·pu·ni·ty (ĭm-pyōō′nĭ-tē) *n., pl.* **-ties** Exemption from punishment, penalty, or harm. [Lat. *impūnitās* < *impūne*, without punishment : *in-*, not; see IN—¹ + *poena*, penalty (< Gk. *poinē*; see kʷei- in App.).]

im·pure (ĭm-pyōōr′) *adj.* **-pur·er, -pur·est** **1.** Not pure or clean; contaminated. **2.** Not purified by religious rite; unclean. **3.** Immoral or sinful. **4.** Mixed with another, usu. inferior substance; adulterated. **5.** Being a composite of more than one color or mixed with black or white. **6.** Deriving from more than one source, style, or convention; eclectic. —**im·pure′ly** *adv.* —**im·pure′ness** *n.*

im·pu·ri·ty (ĭm-pyōōr′ĭ-tē) *n., pl.* **-ties** **1.** The quality or condition of being impure, esp.: **a.** Contamination or pollution. **b.** Lack of consistency or homogeneity; adulteration. **c.** A state of immorality; sin. **2.** Something that renders something else impure; an inferior component or additive.

im·put·a·ble (ĭm-pyōō′tə-bəl) *adj.* Possible to impute or as-

cribe; attributable. —**im·put′a·bly** *adv.*

im·pu·ta·tion (ĭm′pyōō-tā′shən) *n.* **1.** The act of imputing or attributing. **2.** Something imputed or attributed. —**im·pu′ta·tive** (ĭm-pyōō′tə-tĭv) *adj.* —**im·pu′ta·tive·ly** *adv.*

im·pute (ĭm-pyōōt′) *tr.v.* **-put·ed, -put·ing, -putes** **1.** To relate to a particular cause or source; attribute the fault or responsibility to: *imputed the rocket failure to a faulty gasket.* **2.** To assign as a characteristic; credit: *the gracefulness so often imputed to cats.* [ME *imputen* < OFr. *emputer* < Lat. *imputāre : in-*, in; see IN—² + *putāre*, to settle an account.]

in¹ (ĭn) *prep.* **1a.** Within the limits, bounds, or area of: *in the garden.* **b.** From the outside to a point within; into: *threw the pin in the cup.* **2.** To or at a situation or condition of: *in debt.* **3a.** Having the activity, occupation, or function of: *work in politics.* **b.** During the act or process of: *tripped in running.* **4a.** With the arrangement or order of: *fabric that fell in luxuriant folds.* **b.** After the style or form of: *a poem in couplets.* **5.** With the characteristic, attribute, or property of: *a man in an overcoat.* **6a.** By means of: *paid in cash.* **b.** Made with or through the medium of: *written in German.* **7.** With the aim or purpose of: *in pursuit.* **8.** With reference to: *six inches in depth.* **9.** Used to indicate the second and larger term of a ratio or proportion: *one in ten.* ❖ *adv.* **1.** To or toward the inside: *knocked and came in.* **2.** To or toward a destination or goal: *closed in.* **3.** *Sports* So as to score, as by crossing home plate in baseball: *runs driven in.* **4.** Within a place, as of business or residence: *The boss stayed in.* **5.** So as to be available or under one's control: *The evidence is now in.* **6.** So as to include or incorporate: *Fold in the egg whites.* **7.** So as to occupy a position of success or favor: *was voted in.* **8.** In a particular relationship: *got in bad with their supervisor.* ❖ *adj.* **1.** Located inside; inner. **2.** Incoming; inward: *the in bus.* **3.** Holding office; having power: *the in party.* **4.** *Informal* **a.** Currently fashionable: *the in thing to wear.* **b.** Concerned with or attuned to the latest fashions: *the in crowd.* **5.** Relating to, understandable to, or coming from an exclusive group: *an in reference.* ❖ *n.* **1.** One with position, influence, or power. **2.** *Informal* Influence; power. —*idioms:* **in for** Guaranteed to get or have. **in on** Informed about; participating in: *in on the scheme.* **in that** For the reason that. [ME < OE. See **en** in App.]

in² or **in.** *abbr.* inch

In The symbol for the element **indium.**

IN *abbr.* Indiana

in—¹ or **il—** or **im—** or **ir—** *pref.* Not: *inarticulate.* Before *l, in-* is usu. assimilated to *il-*; before *r* to *ir-*; and before *b, m,* and *p* to *im-*. [ME < OFr. < Lat. See **ne** in App.]

in—² or **il—** or **im—** or **ir—** *pref.* **1.** In; into; within: *inundation.* Before *l, in-* is usu. assimilated to *il-*; before *r* to *ir-*; and before *b, m,* and *p* to *im-*. **2.** Variant of **en—¹**. [ME < OE (< *in,* in; see IN¹) and < OFr. (< Lat. < *in,* in, within; see **en** in App.).]

-in *suff.* **1.** Neutral chemical compound, esp.: **a.** Neutral carbohydrate: *inulin.* **b.** Protein or protein derivative: *albumin.* **c.** Lipid or lipid derivative: *lecithin.* **d.** Enzyme: *pancreatin.* **e.** Glycoside: *chitin.* **2.** A pharmaceutical: *rifampin.* **3.** An antibiotic: *penicillin.* **4.** Antigen: *tuberculin.* **5.** Variant of **-ine²** 1. [Variant of **-INE²**.]

in·a·bil·i·ty (ĭn′ə-bĭl′ĭ-tē) *n.* Lack of ability or means.

in ab·sen·tia (ĭn ăb-sĕn′shə, -shē-ə) *adv.* While or although not present; in absence. [Lat. *in absentiā*.]

in·ac·ces·si·ble (ĭn′ăk-sĕs′ə-bəl) *adj.* Not accessible; unapproachable: *inaccessible executives.* —**in′ac·ces′si·bil′i·ty** *n.* —**in′ac·ces′si·bly** *adv.*

in·ac·cu·ra·cy (ĭn-ăk′yər-ə-sē) *n., pl.* **-cies** **1.** The quality or condition of being inaccurate. **2.** An instance of being inaccurate; an error.

in·ac·cu·rate (ĭn-ăk′yər-ĭt) *adj.* Mistaken or incorrect; not accurate. —**in·ac′cu·rate·ly** *adv.* —**in·ac′cu·rate·ness** *n.*

in·ac·tion (ĭn-ăk′shən) *n.* Lack or absence of action.

in·ac·ti·vate (ĭn-ăk′tə-vāt′) *tr.v.* **-vat·ed, -vat·ing, -vates** To render inactive. —**in·ac′ti·va′tion** *n.*

in·ac·tive (ĭn-ăk′tĭv) *adj.* **1.** Not active or tending to be active. **2a.** Not functioning or operating; out of use: *inactive machinery.* **b.** Not being in continuous use or operation: *an inactive account.* **3.** Retired from duty or service. **4.** *Chemistry* Not readily participating in chemical reactions; inert. **5.** *Biology* Marked by the absence or reduction of activity, such as the ability to cause infection. **6.** *Medicine* Quiescent. Used esp. of a disease. **7.** *Physics* Showing no optical activity in polarized light. —**in·ac′tive·ly** *adv.* —**in·ac′tiv′i·ty, in·ac′tive·ness** *n.*

SYNONYMS *inactive, idle, inert, passive, dormant* These adjectives mean not involved in or disposed to movement or activity. *Inactive* simply indicates absence of activity: *retired but not inactive.* *Idle* refers to persons who are not doing anything or are not busy (*employees who were idle because of the strike*); it also refers to what is not in use or operation (*idle machinery*). *Inert* describes things powerless to move themselves or to produce a desired effect; applied to persons, it implies lethargy or sluggishness, especially of mind or spirit: *"The Honorable Mrs. Jamieson . . . was fat and inert, and very much at the mercy of her old servants"* (Elizabeth C. Gaskell). *Passive* implies being reactive instead of proactive: *"in an hour like this, when the mind has a passive sensibility, but no active strength"* (Nathaniel Hawthorne). *Dormant* refers principally to a state of suspended activity but often implies the possibility of renewal: *dormant feelings of affection.*

in·ad·e·qua·cy (ĭn-ăd′ĭ-kwə-sē) *n., pl.* **-cies 1.** The quality or condition of being inadequate. **2.** An instance of being inadequate; a failing or lack.

in·ad·e·quate (ĭn-ăd′ĭ-kwĭt) *adj.* Not adequate to fulfill a need or requirement; insufficient. —**in·ad′e·quate·ly** *adv.*

in·ad·mis·si·ble (ĭn′əd-mĭs′ə-bəl) *adj.* Not admissible. —**in′ad·mis′si·bil′i·ty** *n.* —**in′ad·mis′si·bly** *adv.*

in·ad·ver·tence (ĭn′əd-vûr′tns) *n.* **1.** The quality or habit of being inadvertent. **2.** An instance of being inadvertent; an oversight or slip. [ME < OFr. < Med.Lat. *inadvertentia* : Lat. *in-*, not; see IN-[1] + Med.Lat. *advertentia*, advertence (< Lat. *advertēns, advertent-*, pr. part. of *advertere*, to turn toward; see ADVERSE.)]

in·ad·ver·ten·cy (ĭn′əd-vûr′tn-sē) *n., pl.* **-cies** Inadvertence.

in·ad·ver·tent (ĭn′əd-vûr′tnt) *adj.* **1.** Not duly attentive. **2.** Marked by unintentional lack of care. —**in′ad·ver′tent·ly** *adv.*

in·ad·vis·a·ble (ĭn′əd-vī′zə-bəl) *adj.* Not recommended; unwise. —**in′ad·vis′a·bil′i·ty** *n.*

in ae·ter·num (ē-tûr′nəm) *adv.* To eternity; forever. [Lat. *in*, in + *aeternum*, all the time to come < neut. accusative of *aeternus*, eternal.]

in·al·ien·a·ble (ĭn-āl′yə-nə-bəl, -ā′lē-ə-) *adj.* That cannot be transferred to another or others: *inalienable rights.* —**in·al′ien·a·bil′i·ty** *n.* —**in·al′ien·a·bly** *adv.*

in·al·ter·a·ble (ĭn-ôl′tər-ə-bəl) *adj.* Impossible to alter. —**in·al′ter·a·bil′i·ty** *n.* —**in·al′ter·a·bly** *adv.*

in·am·o·ra·ta (ĭn-ăm′ə-rä′tə) *n., pl.* **-tas** A woman with whom one is in love or has an intimate relationship. [Ital. *innamorata*, fem. of *innamorato*, inamorato. See INAMORATO.]

in·am·o·ra·to (ĭn-ăm′ə-rä′tō) *n., pl.* **-tos** A man with whom one is in love or has an intimate relationship. [Ital. *innamorato* < p. part. of *innamorare*, to enamor : *in-*, into (< Lat.; see IN-[2]) + *amore*, love (< Lat. *amor* < *amāre*, to love).]

in-and-in (ĭn′ənd-ĭn′) *adv.* Repeatedly within the same or closely related stocks: *breeding in-and-in.* —**in′-and-in′** *adj.*

in·ane (ĭn-ān′) *adj.* **-an·er, -an·est** One that lacks sense or substance: *inane comments.* [Lat. *inānis.*] —**in·ane′ly** *adv.*

in·an·i·mate (ĭn-ăn′ə-mĭt) *adj.* **1.** Not having the qualities associated with active, living organisms. **2.** Not animated or energetic; dull. **3.** *Grammar* Belonging to the class of nouns that stand for nonliving things. —**in·an′i·mate·ly** *adv.* —**in·an′i·mate·ness** *n.*

in·a·ni·tion (ĭn′ə-nĭsh′ən) *n.* **1.** Exhaustion, as from lack of nourishment. **2.** The condition or quality of being empty. [ME *inanisioun*, emptiness < OFr. *inanicion*, exhaustion from hunger < LLat. *inānītiō, inānītiōn-*, emptiness < *inānītus*, p. part. of *inānīre*, to make empty < Lat. *inānis*, empty.]

in·an·i·ty (ĭn-ăn′ĭ-tē) *n., pl.* **-ties 1.** The condition or quality of being inane. **2.** Something empty of meaning or sense.

I·nan·na (ĭ-nä′nä) *n. Mythology* The chief Sumerian goddess, associated with fertility, the natural world, and war. [Sumerian *in-an-ak*, lady of the sky : *in*, var. of *nin*, lady + *an*, sky + *-ak*, genitive suff.]

in an·tis (ăn′tĭs) *adj.* **1.** Having a recessed portico with a row of columns between the antae, as in some Greek temples. **2.** Of or being the portico or columns in such an arrangement. [< Lat. *in antīs*, among the pilasters : *in*, in + *antīs*, ablative of *antae*, pilasters, antae.]

in·ap·peas·a·ble (ĭn′ə-pē′zə-bəl) *adj.* Difficult or impossible to appease: *inappeasable resentment.*

in·ap·pe·tence (ĭn-ăp′ĭ-təns) also **in·ap·pe·ten·cy** (-tən-sē) *n.* Lack of appetite. —**in·ap′pe·tent** *adj.*

in·ap·pli·ca·ble (ĭn-ăp′lĭ-kə-bəl, ĭn′ə-plĭk′ə-) *adj.* Not applicable: *inapplicable rules.* —**in·ap′pli·ca·bil′i·ty** *n.* —**in·ap′pli·ca·bly** *adv.*

in·ap·po·site (ĭn-ăp′ə-zĭt) *adj.* Not pertinent; unsuitable. —**in·ap′po·site·ly** *adv.* —**in·ap′po·site·ness** *n.*

in·ap·pre·cia·ble (ĭn′ə-prē′shə-bəl) *adj.* Too small to be noticed or make a significant difference; negligible: *inappreciable fluctuations in temperature.* —**in′ap·pre′cia·bly** *adv.*

in·ap·pre·cia·tive (ĭn′ə-prē′shə-tĭv, -shē-ā′tĭv, -shē-ə-) *adj.* Feeling or showing no appreciation; unappreciative. —**in′ap·pre′cia·tive·ly** *adv.*

in·ap·proach·a·ble (ĭn′ə-prō′chə-bəl) *adj.* Not approachable: *a cold, inapproachable person.* —**in′ap·proach′a·bil′i·ty** *n.* —**in′ap·proach′a·bly** *adv.*

in·ap·pro·pri·ate (ĭn′ə-prō′prē-ĭt) *adj.* Unsuitable or improper. —**in′ap·pro′pri·ate·ly** *adv.* —**in′ap·pro′pri·ate·ness** *n.*

in·apt (ĭn-ăpt′) *adj.* **1.** Inappropriate: *inapt remarks.* **2.** Inept: *inapt work.* —**in·apt′ly** *adv.* —**in·apt′ness** *n.*

in·ap·ti·tude (ĭn-ăp′tĭ-tood′, -tyood′) *n.* **1.** Lack of talent or ability. **2.** The quality or state of being inappropriate.

in·ar·gu·a·ble (ĭn-är′gyoo-ə-bəl) *adj.* Not arguable. —**in·ar′gu·a·bly** *adv.*

I·na·ri (ĭn′ə-rē, ē′när′ē), **Lake** A lake of N Finland with an outlet to the Arctic Ocean.

in·ar·tic·u·late (ĭn′är-tĭk′yə-lĭt) *adj.* **1.** Uttered without the use of normal words or syllables; incomprehensible as speech or language. **2.** Unable to speak; speechless: *inarticulate with shock.* **3.** Unable to speak with clarity or eloquence. **4.** Going unexpressed: *inarticulate sorrow.* **5.** *Biology* Not having joints or segments. —**in′ar·tic′u·late·ly** *adv.* —**in′ar·tic′u·late·ness, in′ar·tic′u·la·cy** (-lə-sē) *n.*

in·ar·tis·tic (ĭn′är-tĭs′tĭk) *adj.* **1.** Not conforming to the principles or criteria of art: *"Never would she resort to the inartistic expedient of modifying her work to suit the popular taste"* (Edith Wharton). **2.** Lacking taste or interest in art. —**in′ar·tis′tic·al·ly** *adv.*

in·as·much as (ĭn′əz-mŭch′) *conj.* **1.** Because of the fact that; since. **2.** To the extent that; insofar as.

in·at·ten·tion (ĭn′ə-tĕn′shən) *n.* Lack of attention, notice, or regard.

in·at·ten·tive (ĭn′ə-tĕn′tĭv) *adj.* Exhibiting a lack of attention; not attentive. —**in′at·ten′tive·ly** *adv.* —**in′at·ten′tive·ness** *n.*

in·au·di·ble (ĭn-ô′də-bəl) *adj.* Impossible to hear. —**in·au′di·bil′i·ty** *n.* —**in·au′di·bly** *adv.*

in·au·gu·ral (ĭn-ô′gyər-əl, -gə-) *adj.* **1.** Of, relating to, or characteristic of an inauguration. **2.** Initial; first: *the inaugural issue of a magazine.* ❖ *n.* **1.** An inauguration. **2.** A speech given by a person being formally inducted into office.

in·au·gu·rate (ĭn-ô′gyə-rāt′, -gə-) *tr.v.* **-rat·ed, -rat·ing, -rates 1.** To induct into office by a formal ceremony. **2.** To cause to begin, esp. officially or formally. **3.** To open or begin use of with a ceremony; dedicate. [Lat. *inaugurāre, inaugurāt-*, to consecrate by augury < in-, intensive pref.; see IN-[2] + *augurāre*, to augur (< *augur*, soothsayer; see **aug-** in App.).] —**in·au′gu·ra·tor** *n.*

in·au·gu·ra·tion (ĭn-ô′gyə-rā′shən, -gə-) *n.* **1.** Formal induction into office. **2.** A formal beginning or introduction.

in·aus·pi·cious (ĭn′ô-spĭsh′əs) *adj.* Not favorable; not auspicious. —**in′aus·pi′cious·ness** *n.*

in·au·then·tic (ĭn′ô-thĕn′tĭk) *adj.* Not genuine or authentic. —**in′au·then·tic′i·ty** (-tĭs′ĭ-tē) *n.*

in between *prep. & adv.* Between.

in-be·tween (ĭn′bĭ-twēn′) *adj.* Intermediate: *an in-between age.* ❖ *n.* An intermediate.

in·board (ĭn′bôrd′, -bōrd′) *adj.* **1.** *Nautical* Within the hull or toward the center of a vessel. **2.** Relatively close to the fuselage of an aircraft: *the inboard engines.* ❖ *n. Nautical* A motor on the inside of the hull of a boat. —**in′board′** *adv.*

in·born (ĭn′bôrn′) *adj.* **1.** Possessed by an organism at birth. **2.** Inherited or hereditary.

in·bound[1] (ĭn′bound′) *adj.* Bound or headed inward.

in·bound[2] (ĭn′bound′) *v.* **-bound·ed, -bound·ing, -bounds** *Basketball* —*tr.* To put (the ball) into play by passing it from out of bounds to a teammate on the court. —*intr.* To execute an inbounds pass.

in·bounds (ĭn′boundz′) *adj.* **1.** *Basketball* Involving putting the ball into play by passing it from out of bounds to a teammate on the court. **2.** *Sports* Within the designated boundaries.

in·breathe (ĭn′brēth′) *tr.v.* **-breathed, -breath·ing, -breathes** To breathe (something) in; inhale.

in·bred (ĭn′brĕd′) *adj.* **1.** Produced by inbreeding. **2.** Fixed in the character or disposition as if inherited; deep-seated.

in·breed (ĭn′brēd′) *tr.v.* **-bred** (-brĕd′), **-breed·ing, -breeds 1.** To breed by the continued mating of closely related individuals, esp. to preserve desirable traits in a stock. **2.** To breed or develop within; engender. —**in′breed′er** *n.*

in·breed·ing (ĭn′brē′dĭng) *n.* **1.** The breeding of related individuals within an isolated or a closed group of organisms or people. **2.** The inbreeding of closely related individuals.

in·built (ĭn′bĭlt′) *adj.* Built-in; inherent.

Inc. *abbr.* incorporated

In·ca also **In·ka** (ĭng′kə) *n., pl.* **Inca** or **-cas** also **Inka** or **-kas 1a.** A member of the group of Quechuan peoples of highland Peru who established an empire from northern Ecuador to central Chile before the Spanish conquest. **b.** A ruler or high-ranking member of the Inca empire. **2.** A member of any of the peoples ruled by the Incas. [Sp. < Quechua *inka*, ruler, man of royal lineage.]

in·cal·cu·la·ble (ĭn-kăl′kyə-lə-bəl) *adj.* **1a.** Impossible to calculate: *a mass of incalculable figures.* **b.** Too great to be calculated or reckoned: *incalculable wealth.* **2.** Impossible to foresee; unpredictable. —**in·cal′cu·la·bil′i·ty, in·cal′cu·la·ble·ness** *n.* —**in·cal′cu·la·bly** *adv.*

SYNONYMS *incalculable, countless, immeasurable, incomputable, inestimable, infinite, innumerable, measureless* These adjectives mean being greater than can be calculated or reckoned: *incalculable riches; countless hours; an immeasurable distance; an incomputable amount; jewels of inestimable value; an infinite number of reasons; innumerable difficulties; measureless power.* **ANTONYM** *calculable*

in·ca·les·cent (ĭn′kə-lĕs′ənt) *adj.* Growing hotter or more ardent. [Lat. *incalēscēns, incalēscent-*, pr. part. of *incalēscere*, to grow warm : *in-*, intensive pref.; see IN-[2] + *calēscere*, to grow warm, inchoative of *calēre*, to be warm.] —**in′ca·les′cence** *n.*

in cam·er·a (kăm′ər-ə) *adv.* **1.** In secret; privately. **2.** *Law* In private with a judge rather than in open court. [NLat. *in camerā* :

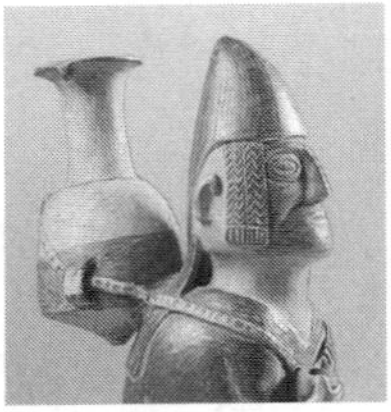

Incan
c. 15th-century ceramic effigy

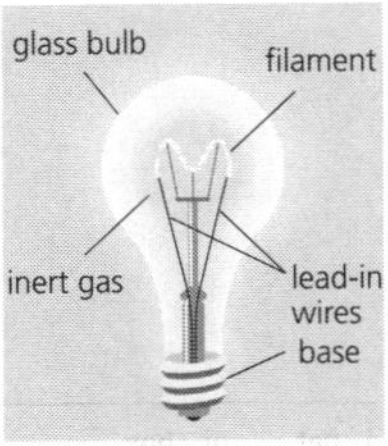
glass bulb
filament
inert gas
lead-in wires
base

incandescent lamp

Lat. *in*, in + LLat. *camerā*, ablative of *camera*, chamber.]

In•can also **In•kan** (ĭng′kən) *adj.* Of or relating to the Inca, their civilization, or their language. ❖ *n.* **1.** An Inca. **2.** Quechua.

in•can•desce (ĭn′kən-dĕs′) *tr. & intr.v.* **-desced, -desc•ing, -desc•es** To make or become incandescent. [Lat. *incandēscere*, to glow : *in-*, intensive pref.; see IN–[2] + *candēscere*, to glow, inchoative of *candēre*, to shine.]

in•can•des•cence (ĭn′kən-dĕs′əns) *n.* **1.** The emission of visible light by a hot object. **2.** The light emitted by such an object. **3.** A high degree of emotion, intensity, or brilliance.

in•can•des•cent (ĭn′kən-dĕs′ənt) *adj.* **1.** Emitting visible light as a result of being heated. **2.** Shining brilliantly; very bright. See Syns at **bright. 3.** Characterized by ardent emotion, intensity, or brilliance. **—in′can•des′cent•ly** *adv.*

incandescent lamp *n.* An electric lamp in which a filament is heated to incandescence by an electric current.

in•can•ta•tion (ĭn′kăn-tā′shən) *n.* **1.** Ritual recitation of charms or spells to produce a magic effect. **2a.** A formula used in ritual recitation; a charm or spell. **b.** A conventionalized utterance repeated without thought or aptness. [ME *incantacioun* < OFr. *incantation* < LLat. *incantātiō, incantātiōn-*, spell < Lat. *incantātus*, p. part. of *incantāre*, to enchant. See ENCHANT.] **—in′can•ta′tion•al** *adj.* **—in•can′ta•to′ry** (-tə-tôr′ē, -tōr′ē) *adj.*

in•ca•pa•ble (ĭn-kā′pə-bəl) *adj.* **1a.** Lacking the necessary ability, capacity, or power: *incapable of love.* **b.** Unable to perform adequately; incompetent. **2.** *Usage Problem* Not susceptible to action or treatment: *a feat incapable of duplication.* See Usage Note at **able. 3.** *Law* Lacking legal qualifications or requirements; ineligible. **—in•ca′pa•bil′i•ty, in•ca′pa•ble•ness** *n.* **—in•ca′pa•bly** *adv.*

in•ca•pac•i•tant (ĭn′kə-păs′ĭ-tənt) *n.* A device or substance, such as tear gas, used to incapacitate individuals temporarily.

in•ca•pac•i•tate (ĭn′kə-păs′ĭ-tāt′) *tr.v.* **-tat•ed, -tat•ing, -tates 1.** To deprive of strength or ability; disable. **2.** To make legally ineligible; disqualify. **—in′ca•pac′i•ta′tion** *n.*

in•ca•pac•i•ty (ĭn′kə-păs′ĭ-tē) *n., pl.* **-ties 1.** Inadequate strength or ability; lack of capacity. **2.** A defect or handicap; a disability. **3.** *Law* Something that renders one incapable.

in•car•cer•ate (ĭn-kär′sə-rāt′) *tr.v.* **-at•ed, -at•ing, -ates 1.** To put into jail. **2.** To shut in; confine. [Med.Lat. *incarcerāre, incarcerāt-* : Lat. *in-*, in; see IN–[2] + Lat. *carcer*, prison.] **—in•car′cer•a′tion** *n.* **—in•car′cer•a′tor** *n.*

in•car•na•dine (ĭn-kär′nə-dīn′, -dēn′, -dĭn) *adj.* **1.** Of a fleshy pink color. **2.** Blood-red. ❖ *tr.v.* **-dined, -din•ing, -dines** To make incarnadine, esp. to redden. [Fr. *incarnadin* < Ital. *incarnadino*, var. of *incarnadino*, dim. of *incarnato* : *in-*, in (< Lat.; see IN–[2]) + *carne*, flesh (< Lat. *carō, carn-*; see INCARNATE).]

in•car•nate (ĭn-kär′nĭt) *adj.* **1a.** Invested with bodily nature and form: *an incarnate spirit.* **b.** Embodied in human form; personified: *a villain who is evil incarnate.* **2.** Incarnadine. ❖ *tr.v.* (-nāt′) **-nat•ed, -nat•ing, -nates 1a.** To give bodily, esp. human, form to. **b.** To personify. **2.** To realize in action or fact; actualize. [ME < LLat. *incarnātus*, p. part. of *incarnāre*, to make flesh : Lat. *in-*, causative pref.; see IN–[2] + Lat. *carō, carn-*, flesh; see **sker-**[1] in App.] **—in•car′na′tor** *n.*

in•car•na•tion (ĭn′kär-nā′shən) *n.* **1a.** The act of incarnating. **b.** The condition of being incarnated. **2. Incarnation** *Christianity* The doctrine that the Son of God was conceived in the womb of Mary and that Jesus is true God and true man. **3.** A bodily manifestation of a supernatural being. **4.** One believed to personify a given abstract quality or idea. **5.** A period of time passed in a given bodily form or condition: *hopes for a better life in another incarnation.*

in•cau•tious (ĭn-kô′shəs) *adj.* Not cautious; rash. **—in•cau′tious•ly** *adv.* **—in•cau′tious•ness** *n.*

Ince (ĭns), **Thomas Harper** 1882–1924. Amer. film director, producer, and screenwriter.

in•cen•di•ar•y (ĭn-sĕn′dē-ĕr′ē) *adj.* **1a.** Causing or capable of causing fire. **b.** Of or containing chemicals that produce intensely hot fire when exploded: *an incendiary bomb.* **c.** Of or involving arson. **2.** Tending to inflame; inflammatory: *an incendiary speech.* ❖ *n., pl.* **-ies 1.** An arsonist. **2.** An incendiary device. **3.** One who creates or stirs up factionalism or sedition; an agitator. [ME < Lat. *incendiārius* < *incendium*, fire < *incendere*, to set on fire.] **—in•cen′di•a•rism** (-ə-rĭz′əm) *n.*

in•cense[1] (ĭn-sĕns′) *tr.v.* **-censed, -cens•ing, -cens•es** To cause to be extremely angry; infuriate. [ME *encensen* < OFr. *incenser* < LLat. *incēnsāre*, to sacrifice, burn < Lat. *incēnsus*, p. part. of *incendere*, to set on fire.]

in•cense[2] (ĭn′sĕns′) *n.* **1a.** An aromatic substance, such as wood or a gum, that is burned to produce a pleasant odor. **b.** The smoke or odor produced by the burning of such a substance. **2.** A pleasant smell. **3.** Flattering or fawning attention; homage. ❖ *tr.v.* **-censed, -cens•ing, -cens•es 1.** To perfume with incense. **2.** To burn incense to, as a ritual offering. [ME *encens* < OFr. < Lat. *incēnsum* < neut. p. part. of *incendere*, to set on fire.]

incense cedar *n.* Any of several coniferous evergreen trees of the genera *Calocedrus* and *Libocedrus*, having flattened branches with scalelike leaves.

in•cen•tive (ĭn-sĕn′tĭv) *n.* Something, such as a reward or punishment, that induces action or motivates effort. ❖ *adj.* Serving to induce or motivate. [ME < LLat. *incentīvum* < neut. of *incentīvus*, inciting < Lat., setting the tune < *incentus*, p. part. of *incinere*, to sound : *in-*, intensive pref.; see IN–[2] + *canere*, to sing; see **kan-** in App.]

in•cen•tiv•ize (ĭn-sĕn′tə-vīz′) *tr.v.* **-ized, -iz•ing, -iz•es** To offer incentives or an incentive to; motivate.

in•cept (ĭn-sĕpt′) *tr.v.* **-cept•ed, -cept•ing, -cepts** To take in; ingest. [Lat. *incipere, incept-*, to begin, take up. See INCEPTION.] **—in•cep′tor** *n.*

in•cep•tion (ĭn-sĕp′shən) *n.* The beginning of something, such as an undertaking; a commencement. [ME *incepcion* < Lat. *inceptiō, inceptiōn-* < *inceptus*, p. part. of *incipere*, to begin, take up : *in-*, in; see IN–[2] + *capere*, to take; see **kap-** in App.]

in•cep•tive (ĭn-sĕp′tĭv) *adj.* **1.** Incipient; beginning. **2.** *Grammar* Inchoative. ❖ *n. Grammar* An inchoative verb.

in•cer•ti•tude (ĭn-sûr′tĭ-to͞od′, -tyo͞od′) *n.* **1.** Uncertainty. **2.** Absence of confidence; doubt. **3.** Insecurity or instability.

in•ces•sant (ĭn-sĕs′ənt) *adj.* Continuing without interruption. See Syns at **continual.** [ME *incessaunte* < LLat. *incessāns, incessant-* : Lat. *in-*, not; see IN–[1] + Lat. *cessāns*, pr. part. of *cessāre*, to stop; see CEASE.] **—in•ces′san•cy** *n.* **—in•ces′sant•ly** *adv.*

in•cest (ĭn′sĕst′) *n.* **1.** Sexual relations between persons so closely related that their marriage is illegal or forbidden by custom. **2.** The statutory crime of sexual relations with such a relative. [ME < Lat. *incestum* < neut. of *incestus*, impure, unchaste : *in-*, not; see IN–[1] + *castus*, pure, chaste.]

in•ces•tu•ous (ĭn-sĕs′cho͞o-əs) *adj.* **1.** Of, involving, or suggestive of incest. **2.** Having committed incest. **3.** Improperly intimate or interconnected. **—in•ces′tu•ous•ly** *adv.* **—in•ces′tu•ous•ness** *n.*

inch[1] (ĭnch) *n.* **1.** A unit of length in the US Customary and British Imperial systems, equal to 1⁄12 of a foot (2.54 centimeters). See table at **measurement. 2.** A fall, as of rain or snow, sufficient to cover a surface to the depth of one inch. **3.** A unit of atmospheric pressure that is equal to the pressure exerted by a one-inch column of mercury at the earth's surface at a temperature of 0°C. **4.** A very small degree or amount: *won't budge an inch.* ❖ *intr. & tr.v.* **inched, inch•ing, inch•es** To move or cause to move slowly or by small degrees. ***—idioms:* every inch** In every respect; entirely. **inch by inch** Very gradually or slowly. **within an inch of** Almost to the point of. [ME < OE *ynce* < Lat. *ūncia*, one twelfth of a unit. See **oi-no-** in App.]

inch[2] (ĭnch) *n. Scots* A small island. [ME < Sc. Gael. *innis* < OIr. *inis.*]

inch•er (ĭn′chər) *n.* Something measuring a specified number of inches. Often used in combination: *an 18-incher.*

inch•meal (ĭnch′mēl′) *adv.* Little by little; gradually. [INCH[1] + (PIECE)MEAL.]

in•cho•ate (ĭn-kō′ĭt) *adj.* **1.** In an initial or early stage; incipient. **2.** Imperfectly formed or developed: *a vague, inchoate idea.* [Lat. *inchoātus*, p. part. of *inchoāre*, to begin, alteration of *incohāre* : *in-*, in; see IN–[2] + *cohum*, strap from yoke to harness.] **—in•cho′ate•ly** *adv.* **—in•cho′ate•ness** *n.*

in•cho•a•tive (ĭn-kō′ə-tĭv) *adj.* **1.** Beginning; initial. **2.** *Grammar* Of or being a verb or verbal form that designates the beginning of an action, state, or event. **—in•cho′a•tive** *n.* **—in•cho′a•tive•ly** *adv.*

In•chon (ĭn′chŏn′) A city of NW South Korea on an inlet of the Yellow Sea SW of Seoul. Pop. 2,116,794.

inch•worm (ĭnch′wûrm′) *n.* See **measuring worm.**

in•ci•dence (ĭn′sĭ-dəns) *n.* **1.** The act or an instance of happening; occurrence. **2.** Extent or frequency of occurrence: *a high incidence of malaria.* **3.** *Physics* **a.** The arrival of radiation or a projectile at a surface. **b.** Angle of incidence.

in•ci•dent (ĭn′sĭ-dənt) *n.* **1.** A definite and separate occurrence; an event. See Syns at **occurrence. 2.** A usu. minor event or condition subordinate to another. **3.** Something contingent on or related to something else. **4.** An occurrence or event that interrupts normal procedure or precipitates a crisis: *an international incident.* ❖ *adj.* **1.** Tending to arise or occur as a result or accompaniment. **2.** Related to or dependent on another thing. **3.** *Physics* Falling upon or striking a surface: *incident radiation.* [ME < OFr., apt to happen, an incident < Lat. *incidēns, incident-*, pr. part. of *incidere*, to happen : *in-*, on; see IN–[2] + *cadere*, to fall.]

in•ci•den•tal (ĭn′sĭ-dĕn′tl) *adj.* **1.** Occurring or likely to occur as an unpredictable or minor accompaniment. **2.** Of a minor, casual, or subordinate nature: *incidental expenses.* ❖ *n.* A minor accompanying item or expense.

in•ci•den•tal•ly (ĭn′sĭ-dĕn′tl-ē) *adv.* **1.** As a minor or subordinate matter: *a lawyer and incidentally a musician.* **2.** (*also* -dĕnt′lē) Apart from the main subject; parenthetically.

incidental music *n.* Music accompanying the action or dialogue of a drama or filling intervals between scenes or acts.

in•cin•er•ate (ĭn-sĭn′ə-rāt′) *v.* **-at•ed, -at•ing, -ates** *—tr.* To cause to burn to ashes. *—intr.* To burn completely. [Med.Lat. *incinerāre, incinerāt-* : Lat. *in-*, causative pref.; see IN–[2] + Lat. *cinis, ciner-*, ashes.] **—in•cin′er•a′tion** *n.*

in•cin•er•a•tor (ĭn-sĭn′ə-rā′tər) *n.* One that incinerates, esp. an apparatus, such as a furnace, for burning waste.

in•cip•i•ent (ĭn-sĭp′ē-ənt) *adj.* Beginning to exist or appear: *detecting incipient tumors.* [Lat. *incipiēns, incipient-*, pr. part. of *in-*

cipere, to begin. See INCEPTION.] —**in•cip′i•en•cy, in•cip′i•ence** *n.*

in•ci•pit (ĭn′sĭ-pĭt′, ĭng′kĭ-) *n.* The beginning or opening words of the text of a medieval manuscript or early printed book. [< Lat., third pers. sing. pr. t. of *incipere*, to begin. See INCEPTION.]

in•cise (ĭn-sīz′) *tr.v.* **-cised, -cis•ing, -cis•es 1.** To cut into, as with a sharp instrument: *incised the tablet with chisels.* **2a.** To engrave (designs, writing, or other marks into a surface; carve. **b.** To engrave designs, writing, or other marks into. [Fr. *inciser* < OFr. *enciser* < VLat. *incisāre*, freq. of Lat. *incīdere, incīs-* : *in-*, in; see IN-² + *caedere*, to cut.]

in•cised (ĭn-sīzd′) *adj.* **1.** Cut into a surface; engraved. **2.** Made with or as if with a sharp instrument. **3.** Deeply and sharply cut: *the incised margin of a leaf.*

in•ci•sion (ĭn-sĭzh′ən) *n.* **1.** The act of incising. **2.** *Medicine* **a.** A cut into a body tissue or organ, esp. during surgery. **b.** The scar resulting from such a cut. **3.** A notch, as in the edge of a leaf. **4.** The condition or quality of being incisive.

in•ci•sive (ĭn-sī′sĭv) *adj.* Penetrating, clear, and sharp, as in expression. —**in•ci′sive•ly** *adv.* —**in•ci′sive•ness** *n.*

in•ci•sor (ĭn-sī′zər) *n.* A tooth for cutting or gnawing, located at the front of the mouth along the apex of the dental arch.

in•cite (ĭn-sīt′) *tr.v.* **-cit•ed, -cit•ing, -cites** To provoke and urge on: *inciting workers to strike.* [ME *encyten* < OFr. *enciter* < Lat. *incitāre*, to urge forward : *in-*, intensive pref.; see IN-² + *citāre*, to stimulate, freq. of *ciēre*, to put in motion; see **kei-²** in App.] —**in•cite′ment** *n.* —**in•cit′er** *n.* —**in•ci′ta′tion** *n.*

in•ci•vil•i•ty (ĭn′sĭ-vĭl′ĭ-tē) *n., pl.* **-ties 1.** The quality or condition of being uncivil. **2.** An uncivil or discourteous act.

incl. *abbr.* **1.** including **2.** inclusive

in•clem•ent (ĭn-klĕm′ənt) *adj.* **1.** Stormy: *inclement weather.* **2.** Showing no clemency; unmerciful. —**in•clem′en•cy** *n.* —**in•clem′ent•ly** *adv.*

in•clin•a•ble (ĭn-klī′nə-bəl) *adj.* **1.** Having a specified tendency or disposition; inclined. **2.** Favorably disposed; amenable.

in•cli•na•tion (ĭn′klə-nā′shən) *n.* **1.** The act of inclining or the state of being inclined; a bend or tilt. **2a.** A deviation or the degree of deviation from the horizontal or vertical; a slant. **b.** An inclined surface; a slope. **3.** A tendency toward a certain condition. **4.** A characteristic disposition to do, prefer, or favor one thing rather than another; a propensity.

in•cline (ĭn-klīn′) *v.* **-clined, -clin•ing, -clines** —*intr.* **1.** To deviate from the horizontal or vertical; slant. **2.** To be disposed to a certain preference, opinion, or course of action. **3.** To lower or bend the head or body, as in a nod or bow. —*tr.* **1.** To cause to lean, slant, or slope. **2.** To influence to have a certain tendency; dispose. **3.** To bend or lower in a nod or bow. ❖ *n.* (ĭn′klīn′) An inclined surface; a slope or gradient. [ME *enclinen* < OFr. *encliner* < Lat. *inclīnāre* : *in-*, into, toward; see IN-² + *-clīnāre*, to lean; see **klei-** in App.] —**in•clin′er** *n.*

SYNONYMS incline, bias, dispose, predispose These verbs mean to influence or be influenced toward a particular attitude or course of action: *inclined to believe her; is biased in his favor; were disposed to admire him; predisposed to studying.* See also Syns at **slant.**

in•clined (ĭn-klīnd′) *adj.* **1.** Sloping, slanting, or leaning. **2.** Having a preference, disposition, or tendency.

inclined plane *n.* A plane set at an angle to the horizontal, esp. to raise or lower a load by rolling or sliding.

in•cli•nom•e•ter (ĭn′klə-nŏm′ĭ-tər) *n.* **1.** An instrument used to determine the angle of the earth's magnetic field in respect to the horizontal plane. **2.** An instrument for showing the inclination of an aircraft or ship relative to the horizontal. **3.** See clinometer.

in•close (ĭn-klōz′) *v.* Variant of **enclose.**

in•clude (ĭn-klōōd′) *tr.v.* **-clud•ed, -clud•ing, -cludes 1.** To take in as a part, element, or member. **2.** To contain as a secondary or subordinate element. **3.** To consider with or place into a group, class, or total. [ME *includen* < Lat. *inclūdere*, to enclose : *in-*, in; see IN-² + *claudere*, to close.] —**in•clud′a•ble, in•clud′i•ble** *adj.*

USAGE NOTE Some writers have insisted that *include* be used only when it is followed by a partial list of the contents of the referent of the subject. Accordingly, one could write *New England includes Connecticut and Rhode Island,* but one must use *comprise* or *consist of* when a full enumeration is provided: *New England comprises Connecticut, Rhode Island, Massachusetts, Vermont, New Hampshire, and Maine.* However, this restriction is too strong; *include* does not rule out the possibility of a complete listing. Thus the sentence *The bibliography should include all the journal articles you have used* does not mean that the bibliography must contain something other than journal articles, though it does leave that possibility open. When one wants to make clear that the listing is exhaustive, however, the use of *comprise* or *consist of* will avoid ambiguity. See Usage Note at **comprise.**

in•clud•ed (ĭn-klōō′dĭd) *adj.* **1.** *Botany* Not protruding beyond a surrounding part, as stamens that do not project from a corolla. **2.** *Mathematics* Formed by and between two intersecting straight lines: *an included angle.*

in•clu•sion (ĭn-klōō′zhən) *n.* **1.** The act of including or the state of being included. **2.** Something included. **3.** *Geology* A solid, liquid, or gaseous foreign body enclosed in a mineral or rock. **4.** *Biology* A nonliving mass, such as fat, in the cytoplasm of a cell. **5.** *Computer Science* A logical operation that assumes the second statement of a pair is true if the first one is true. [Lat. *inclūsiō, inclūsiōn-* < *inclūsus*, p. part. of *inclūdere*, to enclose. See INCLUDE.] —**in•clu′sion•ar′y** (-zhə-nĕr′ē) *adj.*

inclusion body *n.* An abnormal structure in a cell nucleus or cytoplasm having characteristic staining properties and associated esp. with certain viral infections, such as rabies.

in•clu•sive (ĭn-klōō′sĭv) *adj.* **1.** Taking a great deal or everything within its scope; comprehensive. **2.** Including the specified extremes or limits and the area between them. **3.** Of, relating to, or being a first person plural pronoun that includes the addressee. —**in•clu′sive•ly** *adv.* —**in•clu′sive•ness** *n.*

inclusive of *prep.* Taking into consideration; including.

in•co•er•ci•ble (ĭn′kō-ûr′sə-bəl) *adj.* Difficult or impossible to coerce or control forcibly: *incoercible rebel leaders.*

in•cog•i•tant (ĭn-kŏj′ĭ-tənt) *adj.* Thoughtless; inconsiderate. [Lat. *incōgitāns, incōgitant-* : *in-*, not; see IN-¹ + *cōgitāns*, pr. part. of *cōgitāre*, to think; see COGITATE.]

in•cog•ni•ta (ĭn′kŏg-nē′tə, ĭn-kŏg′nĭ-tə) *adv. & adj.* With one's identity disguised or concealed. Used of a woman. [Ital., fem. of *incognito.* See INCOGNITO.] —**in′cog•ni′ta** *n.*

in•cog•ni•to (ĭn′kŏg-nē′tō, ĭn-kŏg′nĭ-tō′) *adv. & adj.* With one's identity is disguised or concealed. ❖ *n., pl.* **-tos 1.** One whose identity is disguised or concealed. **2.** The condition of having a disguised or concealed identity. [Ital. < Lat. *incognitus*, unknown : *in-*, not; see IN-¹ + *cognitus*, p. part. of *cognōscere*, to learn, recognize; see COGNITION.]

in•cog•ni•zant (ĭn-kŏg′nĭ-zənt) *adj.* Lacking knowledge or awareness; unaware. —**in•cog′ni•zance** (-zəns) *n.*

in•co•her•ence (ĭn′kō-hîr′əns) *n.* **1.** The condition or quality of being incoherent. **2.** Something incoherent. —**in′co•her′en•cy** *n.*

in•co•her•ent (ĭn′kō-hîr′ənt) *adj.* **1.** Lacking cohesion, connection, or harmony; not coherent. **2.** Unable to think or express one's thoughts in a clear or orderly manner. —**in′co•her′ent•ly** *adv.* —**in′co•her′ent•ness** *n.*

in•com•bus•ti•ble (ĭn′kəm-bŭs′tə-bəl) *adj.* Incapable of burning. ❖ *n.* An incombustible object or material. —**in′com•bus′ti•bil′i•ty** *n.* —**in′com•bus′ti•bly** *adv.*

in•come (ĭn′kŭm′) *n.* **1.** The amount of money or its equivalent received during a period of time for labor or services, from the sale of goods or property, or as profit from financial investments. **2.** The act of coming in; entrance. [ME, arrival, entrance < *incomen*, to come in < OE *incuman* : *in*, in; see IN¹ + *cuman*, to come; see COME.]

income fund *n.* An investment company whose main objective is to achieve current income for its owners.

income tax *n.* A tax levied on net personal or business income.

in•com•ing (ĭn′kŭm′ĭng) *adj.* **1.** Coming in or about to come in: *incoming trains.* **2.** About to assume an office or position: *the incoming governor.* ❖ *n.* **1.** The act of coming in; arrival. **2.** Income; revenue. Often used in the plural.

in•com•men•su•ra•ble (ĭn′kə-mĕn′sər-ə-bəl, -shər-) *adj.* **1a.** Impossible to measure or compare. **b.** Lacking a common quality on which to make a comparison. **2.** *Mathematics* **a.** Having no common measure or number of which all the given lengths or measures are integral multiples. **b.** Having an irrational ratio. ❖ *n.* One that is incommensurable. —**in′com•men′su•ra•bil′i•ty** *n.* —**in′com•men′su•ra•bly** *adv.*

in•com•men•su•rate (ĭn′kə-mĕn′sər-ĭt, -shər-) *adj.* **1a.** Not commensurate; disproportionate: *a reward incommensurate with their efforts.* **b.** Inadequate. **2.** Incommensurable. —**in′com•men′su•rate•ly** *adv.* —**in′com•men′su•rate•ness** *n.*

in•com•mode (ĭn′kə-mōd′) *tr.v.* **-mod•ed, -mod•ing, -modes** To cause to be inconvenienced; disturb. [Fr. *incommoder* < OFr. < Lat. *incommodāre* < *incommodus*, inconvenient : *in-*, not; see IN-¹ + *commodus*, convenient; see COMMODIOUS.]

in•com•mo•di•ous (ĭn′kə-mō′dē-əs) *adj.* Inconvenient or uncomfortable, as by not affording sufficient space. —**in′com•mo′di•ous•ly** *adv.* —**in′com•mo′di•ous•ness** *n.*

in•com•mod•i•ty (ĭn′kə-mŏd′ĭ-tē) *n., pl.* **-ties 1.** Inconvenience. **2.** Something inconvenient.

in•com•mu•ni•ca•ble (ĭn′kə-myōō′nĭ-kə-bəl) *adj.* **1.** Impossible to be transmitted; not communicable. **2.** Incommunicative. —**in′com•mu′ni•ca•bil′i•ty** *n.* —**in′com•mu′ni•ca•bly** *adv.*

in•com•mu•ni•ca•do (ĭn′kə-myōō′nĭ-kä′dō) *adv. & adj.* Without the means or right of communicating with others. [Sp. *incomunicado*, p. part. of *incomunicar*, to deny communication : *in-*, not (< Lat.; see IN-¹) + *comunicar*, to communicate (< Lat. *commūnicāre*; see COMMUNICATE).]

in•com•mu•ni•ca•tive (ĭn′kə-myōō′nĭ-kə-tĭv, -kā′tĭv) *adj.* Not disposed to be forthcoming or communicative; uncommunicative. —**in′com•mu′ni•ca•tive•ly** *adv.* —**in′com•mu′ni•ca•tive•ness** *n.*

in•com•mut•a•ble (ĭn′kə-myōō′tə-bəl) *adj.* **1.** Not able to be exchanged for one another. **2.** That cannot be changed; unalterable. —**in′com•mut′a•bil′i•ty** *n.* —**in′com•mut′a•bly** *adv.*

ă	pat	oi	boy
ā	pay	ou	out
âr	care	ŏŏ	took
ä	father	ōō	boot
ĕ	pet	ŭ	cut
ē	be	ûr	urge
ĭ	pit	th	thin
ī	pie	th	this
îr	pier	hw	which
ŏ	pot	zh	vision
ō	toe	ə	about,
ô	paw		item

Stress marks:
′ (primary);
′ (secondary), as in
lexicon (lĕk′sĭ-kŏn′)

in·com·pa·ra·ble (ĭn-kŏm′pər-ə-bəl) *adj.* **1.** Being such that comparison is impossible. **2.** So outstanding as to be beyond comparison; unsurpassed. —**in′com·pa·ra·bil′i·ty,** **in·com′pa·ra·ble·ness** *n.* —**in·com′pa·ra·bly** *adv.*

in·com·pat·i·bil·i·ty (ĭn′kəm-păt′ə-bĭl′ĭ-tē) *n., pl.* **-ties 1.** The state or quality of being incompatible. **2. incompatibilities** Mutually exclusive or antagonistic qualities or things.

in·com·pat·i·ble (ĭn′kəm-păt′ə-bəl) *adj.* **1.** Incapable of associating or blending or of being associated or blended because of disharmony, incongruity, or antagonism. **2.** Impossible to be held simultaneously by one person: *the incompatible offices of prosecutor and judge.* **3.** *Logic* That cannot be simultaneously true; mutually exclusive. **4.** *Medicine* **a.** Producing an undesirable effect when combined with a particular substance. **b.** Not immunologically compatible. ❖ *n.* One that is incompatible. —**in′com·pat′i·ble·ness** *n.* —**in′com·pat′i·bly** *adv.*

in·com·pe·tent (ĭn-kŏm′pĭ-tənt) *adj.* **1.** Not qualified in legal terms: *incompetent to stand trial.* **2.** Inadequate for or unsuited to a particular purpose or application. **3.** Devoid of qualities requisite for effective conduct or action. ❖ *n.* An incompetent person. —**in·com′pe·tence,** **in·com′pe·ten·cy** *n.* —**in·com′pe·tent·ly** *adv.*

in·com·plete (ĭn′kəm-plēt′) *adj.* **1.** Not complete. **2.** *Football* Not caught in bounds or intercepted: *an incomplete pass* —**in′com·plete′ly** *adv.* —**in′com·plete′ness, in′com·ple′tion** *n.*

in·com·pli·ant (ĭn′kəm-plī′ənt) *adj.* Not willing to comply; unyielding. —**in′com·pli′ance, in′com·pli′an·cy** *n.*

in·com·pre·hen·si·ble (ĭn′kŏm-prī′sə-bəl, ĭn-kŏm′-) *adj.* **1a.** Difficult or impossible to understand; unintelligible. **b.** Impossible to know or fathom. **2.** *Archaic* Having no limits; boundless. —**in′com·pre·hen′si·bil′i·ty, in′com·pre·hen′si·ble·ness** *n.* —**in′com·pre·hen′si·bly** *adv.*

in·com·pre·hen·sion (ĭn′kŏm-prī-hĕn′shən, ĭn-kŏm′-) *n.* Lack of comprehension or understanding.

in·com·pre·hen·sive (ĭn′kŏm-prī-hĕn′sĭv, ĭn-kŏm′-) *adj.* Limited in scope; not all-inclusive. —**in′com·pre·hen′sive·ly** *adv.* —**in′com·pre·hen′sive·ness** *n.*

in·com·press·i·ble (ĭn′kəm-prĕs′ə-bəl) *adj.* Impossible to compress; resisting compression.

in·com·put·a·ble (ĭn′kəm-pyōō′tə-bəl) *adj.* Impossible to compute or be computed; incalculable. See Syns at **incalculable.** —**in′com·put′a·bil′i·ty** *n.*

in·con·ceiv·a·ble (ĭn′kən-sē′və-bəl) *adj.* **1.** Impossible to comprehend or grasp fully: *inconceivable folly.* **2.** So unlikely or surprising as to have been thought impossible; unbelievable: *an inconceivable victory.* —**in′con·ceiv′a·bil′i·ty, in′con·ceiv′a·ble·ness** *n.* —**in′con·ceiv′a·bly** *adv.*

in·con·cin·ni·ty (ĭn′kən-sĭn′ĭ-tē) *n.* Lack of congruity or harmony; unsuitability.

in·con·clu·sive (ĭn′kən-klōō′sĭv) *adj.* Not conclusive. —**in′con·clu′sive·ly** *adv.* —**in′con·clu′sive·ness** *n.*

in·con·den·sa·ble also **in·con·den·si·ble** (ĭn′kən-dĕn′sə-bəl) *adj.* Difficult or impossible to condense: *an incondensable judicial opinion.* —**in′con·den′sa·bil′i·ty** *n.*

in·con·dite (ĭn-kŏn′dīt, -dĭt′) *adj.* Badly constructed; crude. [Lat. *inconditus : in-,* not; see IN-¹ + *conditus,* p. part. of *condere,* to put together; see **dhē-** in App.] —**in·con′dite·ly** *adv.*

in·con·form·i·ty (ĭn′kən-fôr′mĭ-tē) *n.* Lack of conformity; disagreement.

in·con·gru·ent (ĭn-kŏng′grōō-ənt, ĭn′kŏn-grōō′ənt) *adj.* **1.** Not congruent. **2.** Incongruous. —**in·con′gru·ence** *n.* —**in·con′gru·ent·ly** *adv.*

in·con·gru·i·ty (ĭn′kŏn-grōō′ĭ-tē) *n., pl.* **-ties 1.** Lack of congruence. **2.** The state or quality of being incongruous. **3.** Something incongruous.

in·con·gru·ous (ĭn-kŏng′grōō-əs) *adj.* **1.** Lacking in harmony; incompatible. **2.** Not in agreement, as with principles; inconsistent. **3.** Not in keeping with what is correct, proper, or logical; inappropriate. —**in·con′gru·ous·ly** *adv.* —**in·con′gru·ous·ness** *n.*

in·con·se·quent (ĭn-kŏn′sĭ-kwənt) *adj.* **1.** Having no importance or significance. **2.** Inconsistent or illogical. **3.** Proceeding without a natural or logical sequence; haphazard. —**in·con′se·quence** *n.* —**in·con′se·quent·ly** *adv.*

in·con·se·quen·tial (ĭn-kŏn′sĭ-kwĕn′shəl, ĭn′kŏn-) *adj.* **1.** Lacking importance. **2.** Not following from premises or evidence; illogical. ❖ *n.* A triviality. —**in·con′se·quen′ti·al′i·ty** (-kwĕn′shē-ăl′ĭ-tē) *n.* —**in·con′se·quen′tial·ly** *adv.*

in·con·sid·er·a·ble (ĭn′kən-sĭd′ər-ə-bəl) *adj.* Too small or unimportant to merit attention or consideration; trivial. —**in′con·sid′er·a·ble·ness** *n.* —**in′con·sid′er·a·bly** *adv.*

in·con·sid·er·ate (ĭn′kən-sĭd′ər-ĭt) *adj.* **1.** Thoughtless of others; heedless. **2.** Not well considered or carefully thought out; ill-advised. —**in′con·sid′er·ate·ly** *adv.* —**in′con·sid′er·ate·ness** *n.* —**in′con·sid′er·a′tion** (-ā′shən) *n.*

in·con·sis·tence (ĭn′kən-sĭs′təns) *n.* Inconsistency.

in·con·sis·ten·cy (ĭn′kən-sĭs′tən-sē) *n., pl.* **-cies 1.** The state or quality of being inconsistent. **2.** Something inconsistent.

in·con·sis·tent (ĭn′kən-sĭs′tənt) *adj.* **1.** Displaying or marked by a lack of consistency, esp.: **a.** Not regular or predictable; er-

ratic: *inconsistent behavior.* **b.** Lacking in correct logical relation; contradictory: *inconsistent statements.* **c.** Not in agreement or harmony; incompatible. **2.** *Mathematics* Not solvable by the same set of values for the unknowns. Used of two or more equations or inequalities. —**in′con·sis′tent·ly** *adv.*

in·con·sol·a·ble (ĭn′kən-sō′lə-bəl) *adj.* Impossible or difficult to console; despondent. —**in′con·sol′a·bil′i·ty, in′con·sol′a·ble·ness** *n.* —**in′con·sol′a·bly** *adv.*

in·con·so·nant (ĭn-kŏn′sə-nənt) *adj.* Lacking harmony, agreement, or compatibility; discordant. —**in·con′so·nance** *n.* —**in·con′so·nant·ly** *adv.*

in·con·spic·u·ous (ĭn′kən-spĭk′yōō-əs) *adj.* Not readily noticeable. —**in′con·spic′u·ous·ly** *adv.* —**in′con·spic′u·ous·ness** *n.*

in·con·stan·cy (ĭn-kŏn′stən-sē) *n., pl.* **-cies 1.** The state or quality of being eccentrically variable or fickle. **2.** An instance of being eccentrically variable or fickle.

in·con·stant (ĭn-kŏn′stənt) *adj.* **1.** Changing or varying, esp. often and without discernible pattern or reason. **2.** Fickle; faithless. —**in·con′stant·ly** *adv.*

in·con·sum·a·ble (ĭn′kən-sōō′mə-bəl) *adj.* That cannot be consumed: "*I have an . . . inconsumable passion for truth and love*" (Mahatma Gandhi). —**in′con·sum′a·bly** *adv.*

in·con·test·a·ble (ĭn′kən-tĕs′tə-bəl) *adj.* Impossible to contest; unquestionable. —**in′con·test′a·bil′i·ty** *n.* —**in′con·test′a·bly** *adv.*

in·con·ti·nence (ĭn-kŏn′tə-nəns) *n.* The quality or state of being incontinent.

in·con·ti·nent (ĭn-kŏn′tə-nənt) *adj.* **1.** Not restrained; uncontrolled: *incontinent rage.* **2.** Lacking normal voluntary control of excretory functions. **3.** Lacking sexual restraint; unchaste. —**in·con′ti·nent·ly** *adv.*

in·con·trol·la·ble (ĭn′kən-trō′lə-bəl) *adj.* Being such that control is impossible: *incontrollable rage.*

in·con·tro·vert·i·ble (ĭn-kŏn′trə-vûr′tə-bəl, ĭn′kŏn-) *adj.* Impossible to dispute; unquestionable. —**in·con′tro·vert′i·bil′i·ty** *n.* —**in·con′tro·vert′i·bly** *adv.*

in·con·ven·ience (ĭn′kən-vēn′yəns) *n.* **1.** The state or quality of being inconvenient. **2.** Something inconvenient. ❖ *tr.v.* **-ienced, -ienc·ing, -ienc·es** To cause inconvenience to; trouble: *The snow inconvenienced the travelers.*

in·con·ven·ient (ĭn′kən-vēn′yənt) *adj.* Not convenient, esp.: **a.** Not accessible; hard to reach. **b.** Not suited to one's comfort, purpose, or needs. **c.** Inopportune: *Next Tuesday is inconvenient for us.* —**in′con·ven′ient·ly** *adv.*

in·con·vert·i·ble (ĭn′kən-vûr′tə-bəl) *adj.* **1.** Not redeemable for money in coin. **2.** Not able to be legally exchanged for another currency. —**in′con·vert′i·bil′i·ty, in′con·vert′i·ble·ness** *n.* —**in′con·vert′i·bly** *adv.*

in·con·vin·ci·ble (ĭn′kən-vĭn′sə-bəl) *adj.* Not convincible.

in·co·or·di·nate (ĭn′kō-ôr′dn-ĭt, -āt′) *adj.* Lacking coordination; uncoordinated. —**in′co·or′di·nate·ly** *adv.*

in·co·or·di·na·tion (ĭn′kō-ôr′dn-ā′shən) *n.* Lack of coordination, esp. of normal voluntary and harmonious control of muscular movement.

in·cor·po·rate (ĭn-kôr′pə-rāt′) *v.* **-rat·ed, -rat·ing, -rates** —*tr.* **1.** To unite (one thing) with something else already in existence. **2.** To admit as a member to a corporation or similar organization. **3.** To cause to merge or combine together into a united whole. **4.** To cause to form into a legal corporation: *incorporate a business.* **5.** To give substance or material form to; embody. —*intr.* **1.** To become united or combined into an organized body. **2.** To become or form a legal corporation. ❖ *adj.* (-pər-ĭt) **1.** Combined into one united body; merged. **2.** Formed into a legal corporation. [ME *incorporate* < LLat. *incorporāre, incorporāt-,* to form into a body : Lat. *in-,* causative pref.; see IN-² + Lat. *corpus, corpor-,* body; see CORPUS.] —**in·cor′po·ra·ble** (-pər-ə-bəl) *adj.* —**in·cor′po·ra′tion** *n.* —**in·cor′po·ra′tive** *adj.* —**in·cor′po·ra′tor** *n.*

in·cor·po·rat·ed (ĭn-kôr′pə-rā′tĭd) *adj.* **1.** United into one body; combined. **2.** Formed into or organized and maintained as a legal corporation.

in·cor·po·re·al (ĭn′kôr-pôr′ē-əl, -pōr′-) *adj.* **1.** Lacking material form or substance. **2.** *Law* Of or relating to property or an asset that does not have value in material form, as a right or patent. —**in′cor·po′re·al′i·ty** (-ăl′ĭ-tē) *n.* —**in′cor·po′re·al·ly** *adv.*

in·cor·po·re·i·ty (ĭn-kôr′pə-rē′ĭ-tē) *n.* The state or quality of being incorporeal; immateriality.

in·cor·rect (ĭn′kə-rĕkt′) *adj.* **1.** Not correct; erroneous or wrong. **2.** Defective; faulty. **3.** Improper; inappropriate. —**in′cor·rect′ly** *adv.* —**in′cor·rect′ness** *n.*

in·cor·ri·gi·ble (ĭn-kôr′ĭ-jə-bəl, -kŏr′-) *adj.* **1.** Incapable of being corrected or reformed. **2.** Firmly rooted; ineradicable: *incorrigible habits.* **3.** Difficult or impossible to control: *an incorrigible child.* ❖ *n.* One that cannot be corrected or reformed. [ME < Lat. *incorrigibilis : in-,* not; see IN-¹ + *corrigere,* to correct; see CORRECT.] —**in·cor′ri·gi·bil′i·ty, in·cor′ri·gi·ble·ness** *n.* —**in·cor′ri·gi·bly** *adv.*

in·cor·rupt (ĭn′kə-rŭpt′) *adj.* **1.** Free of corruption or immorality. **2.** Not decayed; unspoiled. **3.** Free of errors or faults.

—in•cor•rupt•ly *adv.* —in•cor•rupt•ness *n.*

in•cor•rupt•i•ble (ĭn′kə-rŭp′tə-bəl) *adj.* **1.** Incapable of being morally corrupted. **2.** Not subject to corruption or decay. —in′cor•rupt′i•bil′i•ty *n.* —in′cor•rupt′i•bly *adv.*

in•crease (ĭn-krēs′) *v.* **-creased, -creas•ing, -creas•es** —*intr.* **1.** To become greater or larger. **2.** To multiply; reproduce. —*tr.* To make greater or larger. ❖ *n.* (ĭn′krēs′) **1.** The act or process of increasing. **2.** The amount or rate by which something is increased. **3.** *Obsolete* Reproduction and spread; propagation. —*idiom:* on the increase Increasing, esp. in frequency of occurrence. [ME *encresen* < OFr. *encreistre, encreiss-* < Lat. *incrēscere* : *in-*, intensive pref.; see IN-[2] + *crēscere*, to grow; see ker-[2] in App.] —in•creas′a•ble *adj.* —in•creas′er *n.* —in•creas′ing•ly *adv.*

SYNONYMS *increase, expand, enlarge, extend, augment, multiply* These verbs mean to make or become greater or larger. *Increase* sometimes suggests steady growth: *"No machines will increase the possibilities of life. They only increase the possibilities of idleness"* (John Ruskin). To *expand* is to increase in size, area, volume, bulk, or range: *He inhaled deeply, expanding his chest. Enlarge* refers to expansion in size, extent, capacity, or scope: *The landowner enlarged her property by repeated purchases.* To *extend* is to lengthen in space or time or to broaden in range: *The transit authority extended the subway line into the next town. Augment* usually applies to what is already developed or well under way: *She augmented her collection of books each month.* To *multiply* is to increase in number, usually by propagation or procreation: *"May thy days be multiplied!"* (Sir Walter Scott).

in•cre•ate (ĭn′krē-āt′, ĭn-krē′ĭt) *adj.* Existing without having been created. [ME *increat* < LLat. *increātus* : Lat. *in-*, not; see IN-[1] + Lat. *creātus*, p. part. of *creāre*, to create; see CREATE.]

in•cred•i•ble (ĭn-krĕd′ə-bəl) *adj.* **1.** So implausible as to elicit disbelief. **2.** Astonishing. —in•cred′i•bil′i•ty, in•cred′i•ble•ness *n.* —in•cred′i•bly *adv.*

in•cre•du•li•ty (ĭn′krĭ-dōō′lĭ-tē, -dyōō′-) *n.* The state or quality of being incredulous; disbelief.

in•cred•u•lous (ĭn-krĕj′ə-ləs) *adj.* **1.** Skeptical; disbelieving. **2.** Expressive of disbelief: *an incredulous stare.* —in•cred′u•lous•ly *adv.* —in•cred′u•lous•ness *n.*

in•cre•ment (ĭn′krə-mənt, ĭng′-) *n.* **1.** The process of increasing in number, size, quantity, or extent. **2.** Something added or gained. **3.** A slight, often barely perceptible augmentation. **4.** One of a series of regular additions or contributions: *accumulating a fund by increments.* **5.** *Mathematics* A small positive or negative change in the value of a variable. [ME < Lat. *incrēmentum* < *incrēscere*, to increase. See INCREASE.] —in′cre•men′tal (-mĕn′tl) *adj.* —in′cre•men′tal•ly *adv.*

in•cre•men•tal•ism (ĭn′krə-mĕn′tl-ĭz′əm) *n.* Social or political gradualism. —in′cre•men′tal•ist *n.*

in•cres•cent (ĭn-krĕs′ənt) *adj.* Showing an ever larger lighted surface; waxing: *the increscent moon.* [Lat. *incrēscēns, incrēscent-*, pr. part. of *incrēscere*, to increase. See INCREASE.]

in•cre•tion (ĭn-krē′shən) *n.* **1.** The process of internal secretion characteristic of endocrine glands. **2.** The product of this process; a hormone. [IN-[2] + (SE)CRETION.]

in•crim•i•nate (ĭn-krĭm′ə-nāt′) *tr.v.* **-nat•ed, -nat•ing, -nates** **1.** To accuse of a crime or other wrongful act. **2.** To cause to appear guilty of a crime or fault; implicate. [LLat. *incrīmināre, incrīmināt-* : Lat. *in-*, causative pref.; see IN-[2] + Lat. *crīmen, crīmin-*, crime; see CRIME.] —in•crim′i•na′tion *n.* —in•crim′i•na•to′ry (-nə-tôr′ē, -tōr′ē) *adj.*

in•crust (ĭn-krŭst′) *v.* Variant of encrust.

in•crust•a•tion (ĭn′krŭ-stā′shən) also en•crust•a•tion (ĕn′-) *n.* **1a.** The act of encrusting. **b.** The state of being encrusted. **2.** A crust or coating: *an incrustation of salt on the window.* **3a.** A decorative technique in which a contrasting material is applied to a surface as an inlay or overlay. **b.** A material so applied. **4.** *Biology* A coating of hardened exudate or other material on a body or body part; a scale or scab.

in•cu•bate (ĭn′kyə-bāt′, ĭng′-) *v.* **-bat•ed, -bat•ing, -bates** —*tr.* **1.** To sit on (eggs) to provide heat, promote embryonic development, and hatch the young; brood. **2.** To maintain (living tissue or a chemical system, for example) at suitable conditions for growth and development or for a particular reaction. **3.** To form or consider slowly and protectively, as if hatching: *incubated the idea for a while.* —*intr.* **1.** To brood eggs. **2.** To develop and hatch. **3.** To undergo incubation. [Lat. *incubāre, incubāt-*, to lie down on : *in-*, on; see IN-[2] + *cubāre*, to lie down.] —in′cu•ba′tive *adj.*

in•cu•ba•tion (ĭn′kyə-bā′shən, ĭng′-) *n.* **1a.** The act of incubating. **b.** The state of being incubated. **2.** *Pathology* The development of an infection from the entrance of the pathogen into the body until the appearance of signs or symptoms. **3.** *Medicine* The maintenance of an infant in an incubator. —in′cu•ba′tion•al *adj.*

in•cu•ba•tor (ĭn′kyə-bā′tər, ĭng′-) *n.* **1.** An apparatus in which the environment can be controlled, often used for growing bacterial cultures, hatching eggs artificially, or providing suitable conditions for a chemical or biological reaction. **2.** *Medicine* An apparatus for controlling the temperature, humidity, and oxygen

level surrounding an infant. **3.** An environment that is conducive to development, as of new ideas.

in•cu•bus (ĭn′kyə-bəs, ĭng′-) *n., pl.* **-bus•es** or **-bi** (-bī′) **1.** An evil spirit supposed to descend upon and have sexual intercourse with women as they sleep. **2.** A nightmare. **3.** An oppressive or nightmarish burden. [ME < LLat., alteration of Lat. *incubō* < *incubāre*, to lie down on. See INCUBATE.]

in•cu•des (ĭng-kyōō′dēz) *n.* Plural of incus.

in•cul•cate (ĭn-kŭl′kāt′, ĭn′kŭl-) *tr.v.* **-cat•ed, -cat•ing, -cates** **1.** To impress (something) upon the mind of another by frequent instruction or repetition; instill: *inculcating sound principles.* **2.** To teach (others) by frequent instruction or repetition; indoctrinate. [Lat. *inculcāre, inculcāt-*, to force upon : *in-*, on; see IN-[2] + *calcāre*, to trample (< *calx, calc-*, heel).] —in′cul•ca′tion *n.* —in•cul′ca•tor *n.*

in•cul•pa•ble (ĭn-kŭl′pə-bəl) *adj.* Free of guilt; blameless.

in•cul•pate (ĭn-kŭl′pāt′, ĭn′kŭl-) *tr.v.* **-pat•ed, -pat•ing, -pates** To incriminate. [Lat. *inculpāre, inculpāt-* : *in-*, on; see IN-[2] + *culpāre*, to blame (< *culpa*, fault).] —in′cul•pa′tion *n.* —in•cul′pa•to′ry (-pə-tôr′ē, -tōr′ē) *adj.*

in•cult (ĭn-kŭlt′) *adj.* Not cultured; coarse. [Lat. *incultus* : *in-*, not; see IN-[1] + *cultus*, p. part. of *colere*, to till; see kʷel-[1] in App.]

in•cum•ben•cy (ĭn-kŭm′bən-sē) *n., pl.* **-cies** **1.** The quality or condition of being incumbent. **2.** Something incumbent; an obligation. **3a.** The holding of an office or ecclesiastical benefice. **b.** The term of an office or benefice.

in•cum•bent (ĭn-kŭm′bənt) *adj.* **1.** Imposed as an obligation or duty; obligatory: *It was incumbent on me to help.* **2.** Lying, leaning, or resting on something else. **3.** Currently holding a specified office. ❖ *n.* A person who holds an office or ecclesiastical benefice. [ME, holder of an office < Med.Lat. *incumbēns, incumbent-* < Lat., pr. part. of *incumbere*, to lean upon : *in-*, on; see IN-[2] + *-cumbere*, to recline.] —in•cum′bent•ly *adv.*

in•cu•na•ble (ĭn-kyōō′nə-bəl) *n.* An incunabulum. [Fr. < NLat. *incūnābulum*. See INCUNABULUM.]

in•cu•nab•u•lum (ĭn′kyə-năb′yə-ləm, ĭng′-) *n., pl.* **-la** (-lə) **1.** A book printed before 1501. **2.** An artifact of an early period. [NLat. *incūnābulum* < sing. of Lat. *incūnābula*, swaddling clothes : *in-*, in; see IN-[2] + *cūnābula*, infancy (< *cūnae*, cradle; see kei-[1] in App.).] —in′cu•nab′u•lar (-lər) *adj.*

in•cur (ĭn-kûr′) *tr.v.* **-curred, -cur•ring, -curs** **1.** To acquire or come into (something usu. undesirable); sustain: *incurred heavy losses during the recession.* **2.** To become subject to as a result of one's actions; bring upon oneself: *incur the anger of a friend.* [ME *incurren* < OFr. *encorir* < Lat. *incurrere*, to run upon : *in-*, on; see IN-[2] + *currere*, to run.]

in•cur•a•ble (ĭn-kyōōr′ə-bəl) *adj.* **1.** Impossible to cure: *an incurable disease.* **2.** Impossible to alter, as in disposition or habits: *an incurable optimist.* —in•cur′a•bil′i•ty, in•cur′a•ble•ness *n.* —in•cur′a•ble *n.* —in•cur′a•bly *adv.*

in•cu•ri•ous (ĭn-kyōōr′ē-əs) *adj.* Lacking curiosity; uninterested. —in′cu•ri•os′i•ty (-ŏs′ĭ-tē), in•cu′ri•ous•ness *n.* —in•cu′ri•ous•ly *adv.*

in•cur•rent (ĭn-kûr′ənt, -kûr′-) *adj.* Affording passage to an inflowing current. [Lat. *incurrēns, incurrent-*, pr. part. of *incurrere*, to run upon. See INCUR.]

in•cur•sion (ĭn-kûr′zhən, -shən) *n.* **1.** A raid or invasion into foreign territory. **2.** The act of entering another's territory or domain. **3.** The act of entering or running into. [ME < OFr. < Lat. *incursio, incursiōn-* < *incursus*, p. part. of *incurrere*, to run upon. See INCUR.]

in•cur•vate (ĭn-kûr′vāt′, ĭn′kûr-) *tr.v.* **-vat•ed, -vat•ing, -vates** To cause to bend into an inward curve. ❖ *adj.* Curved inward. —in′cur•va′tion *n.* —in•cur′va•ture′ (-və-chōōr′, -chər) *n.*

in•curve (ĭn-kûrv′, ĭn′kûrv′) *tr. & intr.v.* **-curved, -curv•ing, -curves** To cause to bend or to bend into an inward curve. ❖ *n.* (ĭn′kûrv′) An inward curve. [ME *incurven*, to twist, distort < Lat. *incurvāre*, to curve in, be crooked : *in-*, in; see IN-[2] + *curvus*, curve; see CURVE.]

in•cus (ĭn′kəs) *n., pl.* **in•cu•des** (ĭng-kyōō′dēz) **1.** An anvil-shaped bone between the malleus and the stapes in the mammalian middle ear. **2.** A thunderhead. [Lat. *incūs, incūd-*, anvil < *incūsus*, p. part. of *incūdere*, to forge with a hammer : *in-*, intensive pref.; see IN-[2] + *cūdere*, to beat, forge.]

in•cuse (ĭn-kyōōz′, -kyōōs′) *adj.* Formed by hammering, stamping, or pressing: *an incuse design on a coin.* [Lat. *incūdere, incūs-*, to forge with a hammer. See INCUS.]

ind. *abbr.* **1a.** independence **b.** independent **2.** index **3a.** industrial **b.** industry

Ind. *abbr.* **1.** India **2.** Indian **3.** Indiana **4.** Indies

in•da•mine (ĭn′də-mēn′) *n.* Any of a group of organic bases forming unstable bluish or greenish salts and used in making dyes. [IND(IGO) + AMINE.]

in•debt•ed (ĭn-dĕt′ĭd) *adj.* Morally, socially, or legally obligated to another; beholden. [ME *endetted* < OFr. *endette*, p. part. of *endetter*, to oblige : *en-*, causative pref.; see EN-[1] + *dette*, debt; see DEBT.]

in•debt•ed•ness (ĭn-dĕt′ĭd-nĭs) *n.* **1.** The state of being indebted. **2.** Something owed to another.

in•de•cen•cy (ĭn-dē′sən-sē) *n., pl.* **-cies** **1.** The state or quality

incubator
students observing chicks
hatching in an incubator

of being unseemly or immodest. **2.** Something indecent.

in·de·cent (ĭn-dē′sənt) *adj.* **1.** Offensive to good taste; unseemly. **2.** Offensive to public morals; immodest. —**in·de′cent·ly** *adv.*

indecent assault *n.* Sexual assault.

indecent exposure *n.* The exposure of one's body, esp. one's genitals, in public, in a way considered offensive.

in·de·ci·pher·a·ble (ĭn′dĭ-sī′fər-ə-bəl) *adj.* Impossible to decipher. —**in′de·ci′pher·a·bil′i·ty** *n.* —**in′de·ci′pher·a·bly** *adv.*

in·de·ci·sion (ĭn′dĭ-sĭzh′ən) *n.* Reluctance or an inability to make up one's mind; irresolution.

in·de·ci·sive (ĭn′dĭ-sī′sĭv) *adj.* **1.** Prone to or characterized by indecision; irresolute. **2.** Inconclusive: *an indecisive battle.* **3.** Not clearly defined; indefinite: *indecisive boundaries.* —**in′de·ci′sive·ly** *adv.* —**in′de·ci′sive·ness** *n.*

in·de·clin·a·ble (ĭn′dĭ-klī′nə-bəl) *adj.* **1.** Without grammatical inflection. **2.** Of or being a word that lacks grammatical inflection though belonging to a form class whose members are usu. inflected.

in·de·com·pos·a·ble (ĭn-dē′kəm-pō′zə-bəl) *adj.* That cannot be separated into components: *indecomposable matter.*

in·dec·o·rous (ĭn-dĕk′ər-əs) *adj.* Lacking propriety or good taste. —**in·dec′o·rous·ly** *adv.* —**in·dec′o·rous·ness** *n.*

in·de·cor·um (ĭn′dĭ-kôr′əm, -kōr′-) *n.* **1.** Lack of propriety or good taste; impropriety. **2.** An instance of such behavior.

in·deed (ĭn-dēd′) *adv.* **1.** Without a doubt; certainly: *very cold indeed.* **2.** In fact; in reality. ❖ *interj.* Used to express surprise, skepticism, or irony. [ME *in dede,* in fact : *in,* in; see IN[1] + *dede,* deed, fact; see DEED.]

indef. *abbr.* indefinite

in·de·fat·i·ga·ble (ĭn′dĭ-făt′ĭ-gə-bəl) *adj.* Incapable or seemingly incapable of being fatigued; tireless. [Obsolete Fr. *indéfatigable* < Lat. *indēfatigābilis* : < *in-,* not; see IN[1] + *dēfatigāre,* to tire out (*dē-,* intensive pref.; see DE- + *fatīgāre,* to weary).] —**in′de·fat′i·ga·bil′i·ty,** **in′de·fat′i·ga·ble·ness** *n.* —**in′de·fat′i·ga·bly** *adv.*

in·de·fea·si·ble (ĭn′dĭ-fē′zə-bəl) *adj.* That cannot be annulled or made void: *an indefeasible claim.* —**in′de·fea′si·bil′i·ty** *n.* —**in′de·fea′si·bly** *adv.*

in·de·fec·ti·ble (ĭn′dĭ-fĕk′tə-bəl) *adj.* **1.** Having the ability to resist decay or failure; lasting. **2.** Having no flaw or defect; perfect. —**in′de·fec′ti·bil′i·ty** *n.* —**in′de·fec′ti·bly** *adv.*

in·de·fen·si·ble (ĭn′dĭ-fĕn′sə-bəl) *adj.* **1.** Inexcusable; unpardonable. **2.** Invalid; untenable. **3.** Vulnerable to physical attack. —**in′de·fen′si·bil′i·ty,** **in′de·fen′si·ble·ness** *n.* —**in′de·fen′si·bly** *adv.*

in·de·fin·a·ble (ĭn′dĭ-fī′nə-bəl) *adj.* Impossible to define, describe, or analyze. ❖ *n.* One that is indefinable. —**in′de·fin′a·bil′i·ty,** **in′de·fin′a·ble·ness** *n.* —**in′de·fin′a·bly** *adv.*

in·def·i·nite (ĭn-dĕf′ə-nĭt) *adj.* Not definite, esp.: **a.** Unclear; vague. **b.** Lacking precise limits. **c.** Uncertain; undecided. —**in·def′i·nite·ly** *adv.* —**in·def′i·nite·ness** *n.*

indefinite article *n.* An article, such as English *a* or *an,* that does not fix the identity of the noun modified.

indefinite integral *n. Mathematics* A function whose derivative is a given function.

indefinite pronoun *n.* A pronoun, such as English *any* or *some,* that does not specify the identity of its object.

in·de·his·cent (ĭn′dĭ-hĭs′ənt) *adj. Botany* Not splitting open at maturity: *indehiscent fruit.* —**in′de·his′cence** *n.*

in·del·i·ble (ĭn-dĕl′ə-bəl) *adj.* **1.** Impossible to remove, erase, or wash away; permanent: *indelible ink.* **2.** Making a mark not easily erased or washed away: *an indelible pen.* **3.** Unable to be forgotten; memorable: *an indelible memory.* [Alteration of earlier *indeleble,* Lat. *indēlēbilis* : *in-,* not; see IN[1] + *dēlēbilis,* capable of being effaced (< *dēlēre,* to wipe out).] —**in·del′i·bil′i·ty,** **in·del′i·ble·ness** *n.* —**in·del′i·bly** *adv.*

in·del·i·ca·cy (ĭn-dĕl′ĭ-kə-sē) *n., pl.* **-cies 1.** The quality or condition of being indelicate. **2.** Something indelicate.

in·del·i·cate (ĭn-dĕl′ĭ-kĭt) *adj.* **1.** Offensive to established standards of propriety; improper. **2.** Marked by a lack of good taste; coarse. **3.** Lacking in consideration for the feelings of others; tactless. —**in·del′i·cate·ly** *adv.* —**in·del′i·cate·ness** *n.*

in·dem·ni·fi·ca·tion (ĭn-dĕm′nə-fĭ-kā′shən) *n.* **1a.** The act of indemnifying. **b.** The condition of being indemnified. **2.** Something that indemnifies; a compensation for loss.

in·dem·ni·fy (ĭn-dĕm′nə-fī′) *tr.v.* **-fied,** **-fy·ing,** **-fies 1.** To protect against damage, loss, or injury; insure. **2.** To make compensation to for damage, loss, or injury suffered. [Lat. *indemnis,* uninjured (*in-,* not; see IN[1] + *damnum,* harm, damage entailing liability) + -FY.] —**in·dem′ni·fi′er** *n.*

in·dem·ni·ty (ĭn-dĕm′nĭ-tē) *n., pl.* **-ties 1.** Security against damage, loss, or injury. **2.** A legal exemption from liability for damages. **3.** Compensation for damage, loss, or injury suffered. [ME *indempnite* < AN < LLat. *indemnitās* < Lat. *indemnis,* uninjured. See INDEMNIFY.]

in·de·mon·stra·ble (ĭn′dĭ-mŏn′strə-bəl) *adj.* Impossible to prove or demonstrate. —**in′de·mon′stra·ble·ness,** **in′de·mon′stra·bil′i·ty** *n.* —**in′de·mon′stra·bly** *adv.*

in·dene (ĭn′dēn′) *n.* An organic liquid, C_9H_8, obtained from coal tar and used in preparing synthetic resins. [IND(OLE) + -ENE.]

in·dent[1] (ĭn-dĕnt′) *v.* **-dent·ed,** **-dent·ing,** **-dents** —*tr.* **1.** To set (the first line of a paragraph, for example) in from the margin. **2a.** To cut or tear (a document with two or more copies) along an irregular line so that the parts can later be matched for establishing authenticity. **b.** To draw up (a document) in duplicate or triplicate. **3a.** To notch or serrate the edge of; make jagged. **b.** To make notches, grooves, or holes in (wood, for example) for the purpose of mortising. **c.** To fit or join together by or as if by mortising. **4.** *Chiefly British* To order (goods) with an indent. —*intr.* **1.** To make or form an indentation. **2.** *Chiefly British* To draw up or order an indent. ❖ *n.* (ĭn-dĕnt′, ĭn′dĕnt′) **1.** The act of indenting or the condition of being indented. **2.** A blank space before the beginning of an indented line. **3.** An indenture. **4.** *Chiefly British* An official requisition or purchase order for goods. [ME *endenten,* to notch < AN and OFr. *endenter,* both < Med.Lat. *indentāre* : Lat. *in-,* in; see IN[2] + Lat. *dēns, dent-,* tooth; see **dent-** in App.]

in·dent[2] (ĭn-dĕnt′) *tr.v.* **-dent·ed,** **-dent·ing,** **-dents 1.** To make a dent in. **2.** To impress (a design, for example); stamp. ❖ *n.* (ĭn-dĕnt′, ĭn′dĕnt′) An indentation.

in·den·ta·tion (ĭn′dĕn-tā′shən) *n.* **1a.** The act of indenting. **b.** The condition of being indented. **2.** The blank space between a margin and the beginning of an indented line. **3.** A notch or jagged cut in an edge. **4.** A recess, as in a border or coastline.

in·den·tion (ĭn-dĕn′shən) *n.* **1a.** The act of indenting. **b.** The condition of being indented. **2.** The blank space between a margin and the beginning of an indented line. **3.** *Archaic* An indentation or dent.

in·den·ture (ĭn-dĕn′chər) *n.* **1.** A contract binding one party into the service of another for a specified term. Often used in the plural. **2a.** A document in duplicate having indented edges. **b.** A deed or legal contract executed between two or more parties. **c.** An official or authenticated inventory, list, or voucher. **3.** Indentation. ❖ *tr.v.* **-tured,** **-tur·ing,** **-tures 1.** To bind into the service of another by indenture. **2.** *Archaic* To form a small depression in (a surface). [ME *endenture,* a written agreement < AN < *endenter,* to indent (< the matching notches on multiple copies of the documents). See INDENT[1].]

in·de·pen·dence (ĭn′dĭ-pĕn′dəns) *n.* **1.** The state or quality of being independent. **2.** *Archaic* Sufficient income for comfortable self-support; a competence.

Independence A city of W MO, a suburb of Kansas City. Pop. 113,288.

Independence Day *n.* July 4, celebrated in the United States to commemorate the adoption in 1776 of the Declaration of Independence.

in·de·pen·den·cy (ĭn′dĭ-pĕn′dən-sē) *n., pl.* **-cies 1.** Independence. **2.** An independent territory or state. **3. Independency** The Independent movement in 17th-century England.

in·de·pen·dent (ĭn′dĭ-pĕn′dənt) *adj.* **1.** Not governed by a foreign power; self-governing. **2.** Free from the influence, guidance, or control of another or others; self-reliant. **3.** Not determined or influenced by someone or something else; not contingent. **4.** often **Independent** Affiliated or loyal to no one political party or organization. **5.** Not dependent on or affiliated with a larger or controlling group or system: *an independent film.* **6a.** Not relying on others for support, care, or funds; self-supporting. **b.** Providing or being sufficient income to enable one to live without working. **7.** *Mathematics* **a.** Not dependent on other variables. **b.** Of or relating to a system of equations no one of which can be derived from another equation in the system. **8. Independent** Of or relating to the 17th-century English Independents. ❖ *n.* **1.** often **Independent** One that is independent, esp. a voter, officeholder, or political candidate not committed to a political party. **2. Independent** A member of a movement in England in the 17th century advocating the political and religious independence of individual congregations. **3. Independent** *Chiefly British* A Congregationalist. —**in′de·pen′dent·ly** *adv.*

independent clause *n.* See **main clause.**

independent living *n.* A living arrangement that maximizes independence and self-determination, esp. of disabled persons living in a community instead of in a medical facility.

independent variable *n.* **1.** *Mathematics* A variable whose value determines the value of other variables. **2.** *Statistics* A manipulated variable in an experiment or study whose presence or degree determines the change in the dependent variable.

in-depth (ĭn′dĕpth′) *adj.* Detailed; thorough.

in·de·scrib·a·ble (ĭn′dĭ-skrī′bə-bəl) *adj.* Impossible to describe adequately. —**in′de·scrib′a·bil′i·ty,** **in′de·scrib′a·ble·ness** *n.* —**in′de·scrib′a·bly** *adv.*

in·de·struc·ti·ble (ĭn′dĭ-strŭk′tə-bəl) *adj.* Impossible to destroy. —**in′de·struc′ti·bil′i·ty** *n.* —**in′de·struc′ti·bly** *adv.*

in·de·ter·min·a·ble (ĭn′dĭ-tûr′mə-nə-bəl) *adj.* **1.** Impossible to fix or measure. **2.** Impossible to settle or decide: *indeterminable questions.* —**in′de·ter′min·a·bly** *adv.*

in·de·ter·mi·na·cy (ĭn′dĭ-tûr′mə-nə-sē) *n.* The state or quality of being indeterminate.

in·de·ter·mi·nate (ĭn′dĭ-tûr′mə-nĭt) *adj.* **1a.** Not precisely determined, determinable, or established. **b.** Not precisely fixed, as to extent, size, nature, or number. **c.** Lacking clarity or precision, as in meaning; vague. **d.** Not fixed or known in advance: *an indeterminate future.* **e.** Not leading up to a definite result or ending. **2.** *Botany* Continuing to grow at the apex and not terminating in a flower. —**in′de·ter′mi·nate·ly** *adv.* —**in′de·ter′mi·nate·ness,** *or* **in′de·ter′mi·na′tion** (-nā′shən) *n.*

indeterminate vowel *n.* A mid-central neutral vowel; schwa.

in·de·ter·min·ism (ĭn′dĭ-tûr′mə-nĭz′əm) *n.* **1.** Unpredictability. **2.** *Philosophy* The doctrine that there are some events, particularly some human actions or decisions, which have no cause. —**in′de·ter′min·ist** *n.* —**in′de·ter′min·is′tic** *adj.*

in·dex (ĭn′dĕks′) *n., pl.* **-dex·es** *or* **-di·ces** (-dĭ-sēz′) **1.** Something that serves to guide, point out, or facilitate reference, esp.: **a.** An alphabetized list of names, places, and subjects in a printed work, giving the page or pages on which each item is mentioned. **b.** A thumb index. **c.** A table, file, or catalog. **d.** *Computer Science* A list of keywords associated with a record or document, used esp. as an aid in searching for information. **2.** Something that reveals or indicates; a sign. **3.** A character (☞) used in printing to call attention to a particular paragraph or section. **4.** An indicator or pointer, as on a scientific instrument. **5a.** *Mathematics* A number or symbol, often written as a subscript or superscript to a mathematical expression, indicating an operation to be performed, an ordering relation, or a use of the associated expression. **b.** A number derived from a formula, used to characterize a set of data. **6.** *Index Roman Catholic Church* A list formerly published by Church authority, restricting or forbidding the reading of certain books. ❖ *tr.v.* **-dexed, -dex·ing, -dex·es 1.** To furnish with an index: *index a book.* **2.** To enter in an index. **3.** To indicate or signal. **4.** To adjust through indexation. [ME, forefinger < Lat. See **deik-** in App.] —**in′dex′er** *n.*

in·dex·a·tion (ĭn′dĕk-sā′shən) *n.* The automatic adjustment of an economic variable, such as wages, taxes, or pension benefits, to a cost-of-living index, so that the variable rises or falls in accordance with the rate of inflation.

index finger *n.* The finger next to the thumb.

index fossil *n.* The fossil remains of an organism that lived in a particular geologic age, used to identify or date the rock or rock layer in which it is found.

index fund *n.* A mutual fund that keeps a portfolio of stocks designed to match the performance of a stock market or one of its sectors as measured by an index of selected stocks.

in·dex·i·cal (ĭn-dĕk′sĭ-kəl) *adj.* **1.** Of or having the function of an index. **2.** *Linguistics* Deictic. ❖ *n.* A deictic word or element.

index of refraction *n.* The ratio of the speed of light in a vacuum to the speed of light in a given medium.

In·di·a (ĭn′dē-ə) **1.** A peninsula and subcontinent of S Asia S of the Himalaya Mts. **2.** A country of S Asia; site of one of the oldest civilizations in the world, centered in the Indus R. valley c. 2500 to 1500 B.C. India gained independence from Great Britain in 1947. Cap. New Delhi. Pop. 918,570,000.

India ink *n.* **1.** A black pigment made from lampblack mixed with a binding agent and molded into cakes or sticks. **2.** A liquid ink made from this pigment.

In·di·a·man (ĭn′dē-ə-mən) *n.* A large merchant ship formerly used on trade routes to India.

In·di·an (ĭn′dē-ən) *adj.* **1.** Of or relating to India or the East Indies or to their peoples, languages, or cultures. **2.** Of or relating to any of the American Indian peoples. ❖ *n.* **1.** A native or inhabitant of India or the East Indies. **2a.** An American Indian. **b.** Any of the languages of the American Indians. See Usage Note at **Native American. 3.** See **Indus²**.

USAGE NOTE Assuming that he had reached the Indies, Columbus called the people on the islands his ships visited "indios," or "Indians," and the misnomer has stuck ever since. It is natural that people have proposed alternative names, whether to avoid confusion between the inhabitants of America and India or to indicate respect for the original occupants of the American continents. Thus *Native American* has become widely established in American English, being acceptable in all contemporary contexts and preferred in many. However, the acceptance of *Native American* has not brought about the demise of *Indian,* despite persistent criticism. Unlike *Negro,* which was quickly stigmatized once *black* became preferred, *Indian* never fell out of favor with a large segment of the American population. It is firmly rooted in English in such common terms as *Plains Indian, French and Indian War,* and *Indian Territory* as well as in numerous plant and place names. In locutions of this kind there is no possibility of substitution. • The charge that *Indian* is an offensive term—hopelessly tainted by the ignorant or romantic stereotypes of popular American culture—can be answered, at least in part, by pointing to the continuing use of this term among American Indians themselves. Indeed, Indian authors and those sympathetic to Indian causes often prefer it for its unpretentious familiarity as well as its emotional impact, as in this passage from the Kiowa writer N. Scott Momaday's memoir *The Names* (1976): "*It was about this time that* [my mother] *began to see herself as an Indian. That dim native heritage became a fascination and a cause for her.*" See Usage Notes at **American Indian, First Nation, Native American.**

In·di·an·a (ĭn′dē-ăn′ə) A state of the N-central US; admitted as the 19th state in 1816. The area was controlled by France until 1763 and by Great Britain until 1783. The Indiana Territory was formed in 1800. Cap. Indianapolis. Pop. 6,080,485. —**In′di·an′an, In′di·an′i·an** *adj.* & *n.*

In·di·an·ap·o·lis (ĭn′dē-ə-năp′ə-lĭs) The cap. of IN, in the central part; settled in 1820. Pop. 791,926.

Indian bean *n.* See **catalpa.**

Indian bread *n.* Any of various edible plants, such as the breadroot, once used by certain Native American peoples for food.

Indian club *n.* A bottle-shaped wooden club swung in the hand for gymnastic exercise.

Indian corn *n.* See **corn¹** 1.

Indian currant *n.* See **coralberry.**

Indian file *n.* See **single file.** —**Indian file** *adv.*

Indian giver *n. Offensive* One who gives something to another and then takes or demands the gift back.

Indian hemp *n.* Cannabis.

Indian licorice *n.* See **rosary pea.**

Indian mallow *n.* See **flowering maple.**

Indian meal *n.* See **cornmeal.**

Indian mustard *n.* An annual plant (*Brassica juncea*) in the mustard family, having yellow flowers and oil-rich seeds.

Indian Ocean A body of water extending from S Asia to Antarctica and from E Africa to SE Australia.

Indian paintbrush *n.* Any of various partly parasitic plants of the genus *Castilleja,* having spikes of flowers surrounded by showy, brightly colored bracts.

Indian pipe *n.* A waxy white or sometimes pinkish saprophytic woodland plant (*Monotropa uniflora*) having scalelike leaves and a solitary nodding flower.

Indian pony *n.* A small hardy horse of western North America, often used for crossbreeding.

Indian pudding *n. New England* A pudding consisting of milk, cornmeal, egg, and molasses baked for several hours in a heavy casserole. [< INDIAN (MEAL).]

Indian red *n.* An iron oxide used as a paint and pigment. [Because earths containing the pigment are found in the East Indies.]

Indian River A lagoon extending c. 265 km (165 mi) along the coast of E-central FL.

Indian summer *n.* **1.** A period of mild weather occurring in late autumn. **2.** A pleasant, tranquil, or flourishing period occurring near the end of something.

Indian Territory A region of the S-central US mainly in present-day OK; set aside by the government as a homeland for forcibly displaced Native Americans in 1834.

Indian tobacco *n.* A poisonous North American plant (*Lobelia inflata*) having light blue to white flowers and rounded seedpods enclosed by an inflated persistent calyx.

Indian turnip *n. Upper Northern & Midland US* See **jack-in-the-pulpit.**

Indian wrestling *n.* **1.** A form of wrestling in which two opponents, lying supine in reversed position, lock their adjacent arms, raise and lock their adjacent legs, and attempt to force the other's leg down. **2.** A form of wrestling in which two opponents stand facing each other with usu. right hands interlocked and the outsides of their adjacent feet set together and attempt to unbalance each other.

India paper *n.* **1.** A thin uncoated delicate paper made of vegetable fiber, used esp. for taking impressions of engravings. **2.** See **Bible paper.**

India rubber *n.* See **rubber¹** 1.

In·dic (ĭn′dĭk) *adj.* **1.** Of or relating to India or its peoples or cultures. **2.** Of or relating to the branch of the Indo-European language family comprising Sanskrit, the Prakrits, and their modern descendants, such as Hindi-Urdu. ❖ *n.* The Indic branch of Indo-European.

indic. *abbr.* indicative

in·di·can (ĭn′dĭ-kăn′) *n.* **1.** A potassium salt, $C_8H_6NO_4SK$, in sweat and urine, formed by the conversion of tryptophan to indole by intestinal bacteria. **2.** A glucoside, $C_{14}H_{17}NO_6$, occurring in the indigo plant and a source of indigo dye. [Lat. *indicum,* indigo; see INDIGO + -AN².]

in·di·cant (ĭn′dĭ-kənt) *n.* Something, such as a typographical device, that serves to indicate.

in·di·cate (ĭn′dĭ-kāt′) *tr.v.* **-cat·ed, -cat·ing, -cates 1.** To show the way to or the direction of; point out. **2.** To serve as a sign, symptom, or token of; signify. **3.** To suggest or demonstrate the necessity, expedience, or advisability of. **4.** To state or express briefly: *indicated his wishes in a letter.* [Lat. *indicāre, indicāt-,* to show < *index,* forefinger, indicator. See **deik-** in App.] —**in′di·ca·to′ry** (-kə-tôr′ē, -tōr′ē) *adj.*

in·di·ca·tion (ĭn′dĭ-kā′shən) *n.* **1.** The act of indicating. **2.** Something that serves to indicate; a sign. **3.** Something indicated as necessary or expedient. **4.** The degree indicated by a measuring instrument.

in·dic·a·tive (ĭn-dĭk′ə-tĭv) *adj.* **1.** Serving to indicate. **2.** *Grammar* Of, relating to, or being the mood of the verb used in ordinary objective statements. ❖ *n. Grammar* **1.** The indicative mood. **2.** A verb in this mood. —**in·dic′a·tive·ly** *adv.*

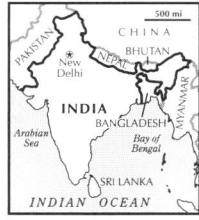

India

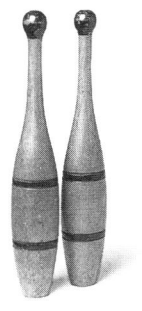

Indian club
pair of Indian clubs

ă	pat	oi	boy
ā	pay	ou	out
âr	care	ŏŏ	took
ä	father	ōō	boot
ĕ	pet	ŭ	cut
ē	be	ûr	urge
ĭ	pit	th	thin
ī	pie	th	this
îr	pier	hw	which
ŏ	pot	zh	vision
ō	toe	ə	about,
ô	paw		item

Stress marks:
′ (primary);
′ (secondary), as in
lexicon (lĕk′sĭ-kŏn′)

in·di·ca·tor (ĭn′dĭ-kā′tər) *n.* **1.** One that indicates, esp.: **a.** A pointer or index. **b.** An instrument used to monitor the operation or condition of an engine, electrical network, or other physical system; a meter or gauge. **c.** The needle, dial, or other registering device on such an instrument. **2.** *Chemistry* Any of various substances, such as litmus, that indicate the presence or concentration of another substance or the degree of a reaction by means of a characteristic change, esp. in color. **3.** A plant or animal whose existence in an area is indicative of specific environmental conditions. **4.** Any of various statistical values that together provide an indication of the condition or direction of the economy.

indicator species *n.* **1.** A species whose presence, absence, or relative well-being in a given environment is indicative of the health of its ecosystem as a whole. **2.** A species used to locate another, less visible species.

in·di·ces (ĭn′dĭ-sēz′) *n.* A plural of **index.**

in·di·cia (ĭn-dĭsh′ə, -dĭsh′ē-ə) *pl.n.* **1.** Identifying marks; indications. **2.** Markings on bulk mailings used as a substitute for stamps or cancellations. [Lat., pl. of *indicium*, sign < *index, indic-,* indicator. See INDEX.]

in·dict (ĭn-dīt′) *tr.v.* **-dict·ed, -dict·ing, -dicts** **1.** To accuse of wrongdoing; charge. **2.** *Law* To make a formal accusation or indictment against (a party) by the findings of a jury, esp. a grand jury. [Alteration of ME *enditen.* See INDITE.] —**in′dict·ee′** (ĭn′dī-tē′) *n.* —**in·dict′er, in·dict′or** *n.*

in·dict·a·ble (ĭn-dī′tə-bəl) *adj.* **1.** Capable of being indicted: *indictable for the crime.* **2.** Making one liable to indictment.

in·dic·tion (ĭn-dĭk′shən) *n.* A 15-year cycle used as a chronological unit in ancient Rome and incorporated in some medieval systems. [ME *indiccioun* < LLat. *indictiō, indictiōn-,* proclamation, period of 15 years < Lat. *indictus,* p. part. of *indīcere,* to proclaim : *in-,* toward; see IN-² + *dīcere,* to say; see INDITE.]

in·dict·ment (ĭn-dīt′mənt) *n.* **1a.** The act of indicting. **b.** The condition of being indicted. **2.** *Law* A written statement charging a party with committing an offense, drawn up by a prosecuting attorney and found and presented by a grand jury.

in·die (ĭn′dē) *n. Informal* **1.** One, such as a studio or producer, that is unaffiliated with a larger or more commercial organization. **2.** An artistic work produced by an independent company or group. [IND(EPENDENT) + -Y¹.] —**in′die** *adj.*

In·dies (ĭn′dēz) **1.** See **East Indies. 2.** See **West Indies.**

in·dif·fer·ence (ĭn-dĭf′ər-əns, -dĭf′rəns) *n.* The state or quality of being indifferent.

in·dif·fer·en·cy (ĭn-dĭf′ər-ən-sē, -dĭf′rən-) *n. Archaic* Indifference.

in·dif·fer·ent (ĭn-dĭf′ər-ənt, -dĭf′rənt) *adj.* **1.** Having no particular interest or concern; apathetic: *indifferent to the sufferings of others.* **2.** Having no marked feeling for or against. **3.** Not mattering one way or the other. **4.** Characterized by a lack of partiality; unbiased. **5.** Being neither too much nor too little; moderate. **6.** Being neither good nor bad; mediocre. See Syns at **average. 7.** Being neither right nor wrong. **8.** Not active or involved; neutral: *an indifferent chemical in a reaction.* **9.** *Biology* Undifferentiated, as cells or tissue. —**in·dif′fer·ent·ly** *adv.*

in·dif·fer·ent·ism (ĭn-dĭf′ər-ən-tĭz′əm, -dĭf′rən-) *n.* The belief that all religions are equally valid.

in·di·gen (ĭn′dĭ-jən, -jēn′) also **in·di·gene** (-jən, -jēn′) *n.* One that is native or indigenous to an area. [Fr. *indigène,* native, a native < Lat. *indigena.* See **genə-** in App.]

in·di·gence (ĭn′dĭ-jəns) *n.* Poverty; neediness.

in·dig·e·nous (ĭn-dĭj′ə-nəs) *adj.* **1.** Originating and living or occurring naturally in an area or environment. **2.** Intrinsic; innate. [< Lat. *indigena,* a native. See INDIGEN.] —**in·dig′e·nous·ly** *adv.* —**in·dig′e·nous·ness** *n.*

in·di·gent (ĭn′dĭ-jənt) *adj.* **1.** Experiencing want or need; impoverished. See Syns at **poor. 2.** *Archaic* Lacking or deficient. ❖ *n.* A needy or destitute person. [ME < OFr. < Lat. *indigēns, indigent-,* pr. part. of *indigēre,* to need : *indu-,* in; see **en** in App. + *egēre,* to lack.] —**in′di·gent·ly** *adv.*

in·di·gest·ed (ĭn′dĭ-jĕs′tĭd, -dī-) *adj.* **1.** Not digested; undigested: *indigested food.* **2.** *Archaic* **a.** Not carefully thought over or considered. **b.** Formless or shapeless.

in·di·gest·i·ble (ĭn′dĭ-jĕs′tə-bəl, -dī-) *adj.* Difficult or impossible to digest: *an indigestible meal.* —**in′di·gest′i·bil′i·ty** *n.* —**in′di·gest′i·bly** *adv.*

in·di·ges·tion (ĭn′dĭ-jĕs′chən, -dī-) *n.* **1.** Inability to digest or difficulty in digesting something, esp. food. **2.** Discomfort or illness resulting from this inability or difficulty.

In·di·gir·ka (ĭn′dĭ-gîr′kə) A river of NE Russia flowing c. 1,789 km (1,112 mi) to the East Siberian Sea.

in·dign (ĭn-dīn′) *adj.* **1.** *Archaic* Unworthy. **2.** *Obsolete* Shameful; disgraceful. [ME *indigne* < OFr. < Lat. *indignus* : *in-,* not; see IN-¹ + *dignus,* worthy.]

in·dig·nant (ĭn-dĭg′nənt) *adj.* Characterized by or filled with indignation. [Lat. *indignāns, indignant-,* pr. part. of *indignārī,* to be indignant < *indignus,* unworthy.] —**in·dig′nant·ly** *adv.*

in·dig·na·tion (ĭn′dĭg-nā′shən) *n.* Anger aroused by something unjust, mean, or unworthy. See Syns at **anger.** [ME *indignacioun* < OFr. *indignation* < Lat. *indignātiō, indignātiōn-* < *indignātus,* p. part. of *indignārī,* to regard as unworthy < *indignus,* unworthy.]

in·dig·ni·ty (ĭn-dĭg′nĭ-tē) *n., pl.* **-ties** **1.** Humiliating, degrad-

ing, or abusive treatment. **2.** A source of offense, as to a person's pride or sense of dignity; an affront. **3.** *Obsolete* Lack of dignity or honor. [Fr. *indignité* < OFr. < Lat. *indignitās* < *indignus,* unworthy.]

in·di·go (ĭn′dĭ-gō′) *n., pl.* **-gos** or **-goes** **1a.** Any of various shrubs or herbs of the genus *Indigofera* in the pea family, having odd-pinnate leaves and usu. red or purple flowers in axillary racemes. **b.** A blue dye obtained from these plants or produced synthetically. **2.** Any of several related plants, esp. those of the genera *Amorpha* or *Baptisia.* **3.** The hue of that portion of the visible spectrum lying between blue and violet, evoked in the human observer by radiant energy with wavelengths of approximately 420 to 450 nanometers; a dark blue to grayish purple blue. [Sp. *indigo* and Du. *indigo* (< Port. *endego*), both < Lat. *indicum* < Gk. *Indikon (pharmakon),* Indian (dye), neut. of *Indikos,* of India < *Indiā,* India < *Indos,* the Indus River < OPers. *Hinduš,* Sind. See HINDI.] —**in′di·go′** *adj.*

indigo bunting *n.* A finch (*Passerina cyanea*) of North and Central America, the male of which has deep blue plumage.

indigo snake *n.* A nonvenomous bluish-black snake (*Drymarchon corais*) of southern North America.

in·dig·o·tin (ĭn-dĭg′ə-tĭn, ĭn′dĭ-gō′-) *n.* A dark blue crystalline compound, $C_{16}H_{10}N_2O_2$, the principal coloring matter of indigo. [INDIGO + -IN.]

in·di·rect (ĭn′dĭ-rĕkt′, -dī-) *adj.* **1.** Diverging from a direct course; roundabout. **2a.** Not proceeding straight to the point or object. **b.** Not forthright and candid; devious. **3.** Not directly planned for; secondary: *indirect benefits.* **4.** Reporting the words of another with the changes necessary to bring the original statement into grammatical conformity with the sentence in which it is included: *indirect discourse.* **5.** *Logic* Involving, relating to, or being the proof of a statement by the demonstration of the impossibility or absurdity of the statement's negation. **6.** Being a free kick in soccer by which a goal cannot be scored without the ball being touched by a second player. —**in′di·rect′ly** *adv.* —**in′di·rect′ness** *n.*

in·di·rec·tion (ĭn′dĭ-rĕk′shən, -dī-) *n.* **1.** The quality or state of being indirect. **2a.** Lack of straightforwardness; deviousness. **b.** A devious act or statement. **3.** Lack of direction; aimlessness.

indirect lighting *n.* Illumination by reflected or diffused light.

indirect object *n.* An object indirectly affected by the action of a verb, as *me* in *Sing me a song* and *turtles* in *He feeds turtles lettuce.*

indirect tax *n.* A tax levied on goods or services that is ultimately paid by consumers in the form of higher prices.

in·dis·cern·i·ble (ĭn′dĭ-sûr′nə-bəl, -zûr′-) *adj.* Difficult or impossible to discern or perceive; imperceptible. —**in′dis·cern′i·bly** *adv.*

in·dis·ci·pline (ĭn-dĭs′ə-plĭn) *n.* Lack of discipline or restraint. —**in·dis′ci·plined** *adj.*

in·dis·creet (ĭn′dĭ-skrēt′) *adj.* Lacking discretion; injudicious. —**in′dis·creet′ly** *adv.* —**in′dis·creet′ness** *n.*

in·dis·crete (ĭn′dĭ-skrēt′) *adj.* Not divided or divisible into separate parts: *layers that were fused into an indiscrete mass.*

in·dis·cre·tion (ĭn′dĭ-skrĕsh′ən) *n.* **1.** Lack of discretion; injudiciousness. **2.** An indiscreet act or remark.

in·dis·crim·i·nate (ĭn′dĭ-skrĭm′ə-nĭt) *adj.* **1.** Not making or based on careful distinctions; unselective. **2.** Random; haphazard. **3.** Confused; chaotic. **4.** Unrestrained or wanton; profligate: *indiscriminate spending.* —**in′dis·crim′i·nate·ly** *adv.* —**in′dis·crim′i·nate·ness** *n.* —**in′dis·crim′i·na′tive** *adj.*

in·dis·crim·i·nat·ing (ĭn′dĭ-skrĭm′ə-nā′tĭng) *adj.* Not discriminating: *an indiscriminating judgment.*

in·dis·crim·i·na·tion (ĭn′dĭ-skrĭm′ə-nā′shən) *n.* Lack of discrimination or judgment.

in·dis·pens·a·ble (ĭn′dĭ-spĕn′sə-bəl) *adj.* **1.** Not to be dispensed with; essential. **2.** Obligatory; unavoidable. ❖ *n.* One that is indispensable. —**in′dis·pens′a·bil′i·ty, in′dis·pens′a·ble·ness** *n.* —**in′dis·pens′a·bly** *adv.*

SYNONYMS *indispensable, essential, necessary, needful, requisite* These adjectives indicate a pressing need: *foods indispensable to good nutrition; funds essential to the project; necessary tools and materials; provided them with all things needful; lacking the requisite qualifications.*

---

in·dis·pose (ĭn′dĭ-spōz′) *tr.v.* **-posed, -pos·ing, -pos·es** **1.** To make averse; disincline. **2.** To cause to be or feel ill; sicken. **3.** To render unfit; disqualify.

in·dis·posed (ĭn′dĭ-spōzd′) *adj.* **1.** Mildly ill. **2.** Averse; disinclined: *was clearly indisposed to grant their request.*

in·dis·po·si·tion (ĭn-dĭs′pə-zĭsh′ən) *n.* **1.** Disinclination; unwillingness. **2.** A minor ailment.

in·dis·put·a·ble (ĭn′dĭ-spyōō′tə-bəl) *adj.* Beyond dispute or doubt; undeniable: *indisputable evidence.* —**in′dis·put′a·bly** *adv.*

in·dis·sol·u·ble (ĭn′dĭ-sŏl′yə-bəl) *adj.* **1.** Permanent; binding: *an indissoluble contract.* **2.** Impossible to dissolve, disintegrate, or decompose. —**in′dis·sol′u·bil′i·ty, in′dis·sol′u·ble·ness** *n.* —**in′dis·sol′u·bly** *adv.*

in·dis·tinct (ĭn′dĭ-stĭngkt′) *adj.* **1.** Not clearly or sharply delineated: *indistinct shapes in the gloom.* **2.** Faint; dim. **3a.** Hazy; vague: *an indistinct memory.* **b.** Difficult to understand or make out.

Indonesia

—in′dis·tinct′ly adv. **—in′dis·tinct′ness** n.

in·dis·tinc·tive (ĭn′dĭ-stĭngk′tĭv) adj. Lacking distinguishing qualities; not distinctive. **—in′dis·tinc′tive·ly** adv. **—in′dis·tinc′tive·ness** n.

in·dis·tin·guish·a·ble (ĭn′dĭ-stĭng′gwĭ-shə-bəl) adj. **1.** Not distinguishable, esp.: **a.** Impossible to differentiate or tell apart. **b.** Impossible to discern; imperceptible. **2.** Difficult to understand or make out; vague: *indistinguishable speech.* **—in′dis·tin′guish·a·ble·ness, in′dis·tin′guish·a·bil′i·ty** n. **—in′dis·tin′guish·a·bly** adv.

in·dite (ĭn-dīt′) tr.v. **-dit·ed, -dit·ing, -dites 1.** To write; compose. **2.** To set down in writing. **3.** *Obsolete* To dictate. [ME *enditen* < OFr. *enditer* < VLat. *indictāre* : Lat. *in-*, toward; see IN⁻² + Lat. *dictāre*, to compose, to say habitually, freq. of *dīcere*, to say; see **deik-** in App.] **—in·dit′er** n.

in·di·um (ĭn′dē-əm) n. Symbol **In** A soft malleable metallic element found primarily in ores of zinc used as a plating and in some semiconductor compounds. Atomic number 49; atomic weight 114.82; melting point 156.61°C; boiling point 2,080°C; specific gravity 7.31; valence 1, 2, 3. See table at **element.** [IND(IGO) + -IUM (< the indigo blue lines in its spectrum).]

in·di·vid·u·al (ĭn′də-vĭj′ōō-əl) adj. **1a.** Of or relating to an individual, esp. a single human: *individual consciousness.* **b.** By or for one person. **2.** Existing as a distinct entity; separate: *individual drops of rain.* **3a.** Distinctive; individualistic. **b.** Special; particular. **c.** Serving to identify or set apart. ❖ n. **1a.** A single human considered apart from a society or community. **b.** A human regarded as unique. **c.** A person distinguished from others by a special quality. **d.** A person. **2.** A single animal or plant as distinguished from a species, community, or group. **3.** A member of a collection or set; a specimen. [ME, single, indivisible < OFr. < Med.Lat. *indīviduālis* < Lat. *indīviduus* : *in-*, not; see IN⁻¹ + *dīviduus*, divisible (< *dīvidere*, to divide).] **—in′di·vid′u·al·ly** adv.

> **USAGE NOTE** The noun *individual* is used to refer to an individual person as opposed to a larger social group or as distinguished from others by some special quality: *"This is not only a crisis of individuals, but also of a society"* (Raymond Williams). Critics have objected, however, to use of the word to mean "a person" where no larger contrast is implied, as in *Two individuals were arrested.* This usage is common in official statements. Writers wishing to avoid the formal or even pretentious tone that it can convey may wish to use *person* and *people* instead, neutral terms that are appropriate in almost any context.

in·di·vid·u·al·ism (ĭn′də-vĭj′ōō-ə-lĭz′əm) n. **1a.** Belief in the primary importance of the individual and in the virtues of self-reliance and personal independence. **b.** Acts or an act based on this belief. **2a.** A doctrine of freedom from government regulation in the pursuit of personal economic goals. **b.** The doctrine that the interests of the individual should take precedence over the interests of the state or social group. **3a.** The quality of being an individual; individuality. **b.** An individual characteristic; a quirk.

in·di·vid·u·al·ist (ĭn′də-vĭj′ōō-ə-lĭst) n. **1.** One that asserts individuality by independence of thought and action. **2.** An advocate of individualism. **—in′di·vid′u·al·is′tic** adj. **—in′di·vid′u·al·is′ti·cal·ly** adv.

in·di·vid·u·al·i·ty (ĭn′də-vĭj′ōō-ăl′ĭ-tē) n., pl. **-ties 1a.** The aggregate of qualities and characteristics that distinguish one person or thing from others; character. **b.** An individual or distinguishing feature. **2.** The quality or state of being individual; singularity. **3.** A single, distinct entity. **4.** *Archaic* Indivisibility.

in·di·vid·u·al·ize (ĭn′də-vĭj′ōō-ə-līz′) tr.v. **-ized, -iz·ing, -iz·es 1.** To give individuality to. **2.** To consider or treat individually; particularize. **3.** To modify to suit a particular individual. **—in′di·vid′u·al·i·za′tion** (-ə-lĭ-zā′shən) n.

individual retirement account n. An investment account in which a person can set aside income up to a specified amount each year and usu. deduct the contributions from taxable income, with the contributions and interest being tax-deferred until retirement.

in·di·vid·u·ate (ĭn′də-vĭj′ōō-āt′) tr.v. **-at·ed, -at·ing, -ates 1.** To give individuality to; individualize. **2.** To form into a separate distinct entity.

in·di·vid·u·a·tion (ĭn′də-vĭj′ōō-ā′shən) n. **1.** The act or process of individuating, esp. the process by which social individuals become differentiated. **2.** The condition of being individuated; individuality. **3.** *Philosophy* **a.** The development of the individual from the general or universal. **b.** The distinction or determination of the individual within the general or universal. **4.** *Embryology* Formation of distinct organs or structures in adjacent tissues.

in·di·vis·i·ble (ĭn′də-vĭz′ə-bəl) adj. **1.** Incapable of undergoing division. **2.** *Mathematics* Incapable of being divided without a remainder. **—in′di·vis′i·ble·ness, in′di·vis′i·bil′i·ty** n. **—in′di·vis′i·bly** adv.

Indo– pref. **1.** India; East Indies: *Indochina.* **2.** Indo-European: *Indo-Hittite.* [Gk. < *Indos*, the Indus R.. See INDIGO.]

In·do-Ar·y·an (ĭn′dō-âr′ē-ən, -ăr′-) adj. **1.** Of, relating to, or being a member of an Indic-speaking people. **2.** Of or relating to the Indic branch of Indo-European. ❖ n. **1.** A member of an Indic-speaking people. **2.** See **Indic.**

In·do·chi·na (ĭn′dō-chī′nə) **1.** A peninsula of SE Asia comprising Vietnam, Laos, Cambodia, Thailand, Myanmar (Burma), and the mainland territory of Malaysia. **2.** The former French colonial empire (c. 1862–1954) in SE Asia. **—In′do·chi′nese′** (-nēz′, -nēs′) adj. & n.

in·doc·ile (ĭn-dŏs′əl) adj. Resistant to authority or discipline; recalcitrant. **—in′do·cil′i·ty** (ĭn′dŏ-sĭl′ĭ-tē, -dō-) n.

in·doc·tri·nate (ĭn-dŏk′trə-nāt′) tr.v. **-nat·ed, -nat·ing, -nates 1.** To instruct in a body of doctrine or principles. **2.** To imbue with a partisan or ideological point of view. **—in·doc′tri·na′tion** n.

In·do-Eu·ro·pe·an (ĭn′dō-yŏŏr′ə-pē′ən) n. **1a.** A family of languages consisting of most of the languages of Europe as well as those of Iran, the Indian subcontinent, and other parts of Asia. **b.** Proto-Indo-European. **2.** A member of any of the peoples speaking an Indo-European language. **—In′do-Eu′ro·pe′an** adj. **—In′do-Eu′ro·pe′an·ist** n.

In·do-Ger·man·ic (ĭn′dō-jər-măn′ĭk) n. See **Indo-European 1. —In′do-Ger·man′ic** adj.

In·do-Hit·tite (ĭn′dō-hĭt′īt′) n. **1.** The Indo-European language family considered from the viewpoint that Proto-Indo-European as traditionally reconstructed is the sister and not the ancestor of Anatolian. **2.** The hypothetical parent language of Indo-European and Anatolian.

In·do-I·ra·ni·an (ĭn′dō-ĭ-rā′nē-ən) n. **1.** A branch of the Indo-European language family that comprises the Indic and Iranian languages. **2.** A member of any of the peoples speaking an Indo-Iranian language. **—In′do-I·ra′ni·an** adj.

in·dole (ĭn′dōl′) n. **1.** A crystalline compound, C_8H_7N, obtained from coal tar or various plants and produced by the bacterial decomposition of tryptophan in the intestine. **2.** A derivative of this compound. [IND(IGO) + -OLE.]

in·dole·a·ce·tic acid (ĭn′dō-lə-sē′tĭk) n. A plant hormone, $C_{10}H_9NO_2$, that stimulates growth.

in·dole·bu·tyr·ic acid (ĭn′dōl-byōō-tîr′ĭk) n. A synthetic compound, $C_{12}H_{13}NO_2$, used to regulate plant growth.

in·do·lence (ĭn′də-ləns) n. Habitual laziness; sloth.

in·do·lent (ĭn′də-lənt) adj. **1a.** Disinclined to exert oneself; habitually lazy. **b.** Conducive to inactivity or laziness; lethargic. **2a.** Causing little or no pain. **b.** Slow to heal, grow, or develop; inactive. [LLat. *indolēns, indolent-*, painless : Lat. *in-*, not; see IN⁻¹ + Lat. *dolēns*, pr. part. of *dolēre*, to feel pain.] **—in′do·lent·ly** adv.

in·do·meth·a·cin (ĭn′dō-mĕth′ə-sĭn) n. A nonsteroidal anti-inflammatory drug, $C_{19}H_{16}ClNO_4$, used esp. in the treatment of arthritis. [INDO(LE) + METH(YL) + AC(ETIC ACID) + -IN.]

in·dom·i·ta·ble (ĭn-dŏm′ĭ-tə-bəl) adj. Incapable of being overcome or subdued; unconquerable. [LLat. *indomitābilis* : Lat. *in-*, not; see IN⁻¹ + Lat. *domitāre*, to tame, freq. of *domāre*, to subdue.] **—in·dom′i·ta·bil′i·ty, in·dom′i·ta·ble·ness** n. **—in·dom′i·ta·bly** adv.

In·do·ne·sia (ĭn′də-nē′zhə, -shə, -dō-) Formerly **Dutch East Indies.** A country of SE Asia in the Malay Archipelago; achieved full independence from the Netherlands in 1949. Cap. Jakarta. Pop. 192,217,000.

In·do·ne·sian (ĭn′də-nē′zhən, -shən) n. **1.** A native or inhabitant of Indonesia. **2.** A native or inhabitant of the Malay Archipelago. **3.** A subfamily of Austronesian that includes Malay, Tagalog, and the languages of Indonesia. **4.** A dialect of Malay that is the official language of Indonesia. ❖ adj. Of or relating to Indonesia, the Indonesians, or their languages or cultures.

in·door (ĭn′dôr′, -dōr′) adj. **1.** Of, situated in, or intended for use in the interior of a building. **2.** Carried on within doors.

in·doors (ĭn-dôrz′, -dōrz′) adv. In or into a house or building.

in·do·phen·ol (ĭn′dō-fē′nôl, -nōl, -nŏl) n. Any of various synthetic blue or green dyes. [IND(IGO) + PHENOL.]

In·dore (ĭn-dôr′, -dōr′) A city of W-central India NNE of Mumbai (Bombay); founded 1715. Pop. 1,091,674.

in·dorse (ĭn-dôrs′) v. Variant of **endorse.**

In·dra (ĭn′drə) n. *Hinduism* A principal Vedic deity associated with rain and thunder.

in·draft (ĭn′drăft′) n. **1.** An inward flow or current, as of air. **2.** A pulling or drawing inward.

in·drawn (ĭn′drôn′) adj. **1.** Drawn in or inward: *an indrawn gasp.* **2.** Introverted; withdrawn.

in·dri (ĭn′drē) n., pl. **-dris** A large arboreal lemur (*Indri indri*) of Madagascar having large eyes and a rudimentary tail. [Prob. < misunderstanding of Malagasy *indry*, lo!]

in·dri·co·there (ĭn′drə-kō-thîr′) n. A very large extinct land mammal (*Indricotherium transouralicum*) of the Oligocene and Miocene epochs, related to the rhinoceros, and thought to have been the largest and heaviest land mammal ever to have lived. [NLat. *Indricothērium*, genus name : Russ. *indrik*, fabulous beast in Russian folklore (prob. < alteration of ORuss. *inŭrogŭ*, unicorn : *inŭ*, one; see **oi-no-** in App. + *rogŭ*, horn) + Gk. *thērion*, wild beast; see THERACLE.]

in·du·bi·ta·ble (ĭn-dōō′bĭ-tə-bəl, -dyōō′-) adj. Too apparent to be doubted; unquestionable. **—in·du′bi·ta·bly** adv.

in·duce (ĭn-dōōs′, -dyōōs′) tr.v. **-duced, -duc·ing, -duc·es 1.** To lead or move, as to a course of action, by influence or persuasion. **2.** To bring about or stimulate; cause: *a drug used to induce labor.* **3.** To infer by inductive reasoning. **4.** *Physics* **a.** To produce

indri
Indri indri

ă pat   oi boy
ā pay   ou out
âr care   ŏŏ took
ä father   ōō boot
ĕ pet   ŭ cut
ē be   ûr urge
ĭ pit   th thin
ī pie   th this
îr pier   hw which
ŏ pot   zh vision
ō toe   ə about,
ô paw   item

Stress marks:
′ (primary);
′ (secondary), as in
lexicon (lĕk′sĭ-kŏn′)

(an electric current or a magnetic charge) by induction. **b.** To produce (radioactivity, for example) artificially by bombardment, as with neutrons. **5.** *Biochemistry* To initiate or increase the production of (an enzyme or other protein) at the level of genetic transcription. **6.** *Genetics* To cause an increase in the transcription of the RNA of (a gene). [ME *inducen* < OFr. *inducer* < Lat. *indūcere* : *in-*, in; see IN-² + *dūcere*, to lead; see deuk- in App.] —**in•duc′i•ble** *adj.*

in•duce•ment (ĭn-do͞os′mənt, -dyo͞os′-) *n.* **1.** Something that helps bring about an action or a desired result; an incentive. **2.** The act or process of inducing; inducement of sleep.

in•duc•er (ĭn-do͞o′sər, -dyo͞o′-) *n.* **1.** One that induces, esp. a substance that is capable of activating transcription from specific genes within a cell. **2.** A part or structure in an embryo that influences the differentiation of another part.

in•duct (ĭn-dŭkt′) *tr.v.* **-duct•ed, -duct•ing, -ducts** **1.** To place ceremoniously or formally in an office or position; install. **2a.** To admit as a member; receive. **b.** To admit to military service. **c.** To introduce, as to new experience or knowledge; initiate. **3.** *Physics* To induce. [ME *inducten* < Lat. *indūcere, induct-.* See INDUCE.]

in•duc•tance (ĭn-dŭk′təns) *n.* **1.** The property of an electric circuit by which an electromotive force is induced in it as the result of a changing magnetic flux. **2.** A circuit element in which electromotive force is generated by electromagnetic induction.

in•duct•ee (ĭn′dŭk-tē′) *n.* One who is inducted, esp. a person newly admitted to military service.

in•duc•tion (ĭn-dŭk′shən) *n.* **1a.** The act or an instance of inducting. **b.** A ceremony or formal act by which a person is inducted, as into office. **2.** *Electricity* **a.** The generation of electromotive force in a closed circuit by a varying magnetic flux through the circuit. **b.** The charging of an isolated conducting object by momentarily grounding it while a charged body is nearby. **3.** *Logic* **a.** The process of deriving general principles from particular facts or instances. **b.** A conclusion reached by this process. **4.** *Mathematics* A method of proving a theorem involving an integral parameter by which the theorem is verified for the smallest admissible value of the integer and it is then proven that if the theorem is true for any value of the integer, it is true for the next greater value. **5.** The act or process of inducing or bringing something about. **6.** Presentation of material in support of an argument or proposition. **7.** A preface or prologue. **8.** *Biochemistry* The process of initiating or increasing the production of an enzyme or other protein at the level of genetic transcription. **9.** *Embryology* The change in form or shape caused by the action of one tissue of an embryo on adjacent tissues.

induction coil *n.* A transformer in which an interrupted low-voltage direct current in the primary is converted into an intermittent high-voltage current in the secondary.

in•duc•tive (ĭn-dŭk′tĭv) *adj.* **1.** Of, relating to, or using logical induction: *inductive reasoning.* **2.** *Electricity* Of or arising from inductance. **3.** Causing or influencing; inducing. **4.** Introductory. —**in•duc′tive•ly** *adv.* —**in•duc′tive•ness** *n.*

inductive statistics *n.* (*used with a sing. verb*) The branch of statistics that deals with generalizations, predictions, estimations, and decisions from data initially presented.

in•duc•tor (ĭn-dŭk′tər) *n.* One that inducts, esp. a device that functions by or introduces inductance into a circuit.

in•due (ĭn-do͞o′, -dyo͞o′) *v.* Variant of **endue.**

in•dulge (ĭn-dŭlj′) *v.* **-dulged, -dulg•ing, -dulg•es** —*tr.* **1.** To yield to the desires and whims of; humor. **2a.** To yield to; gratify. **b.** To allow (oneself) unrestrained gratification. **3.** *Roman Catholic Church* To grant an ecclesiastical indulgence or dispensation to. —*intr.* **1.** To indulge oneself: *eyed the desserts but didn't indulge.* **2.** To engage or take part, esp. freely or avidly. [Lat. *indulgēre.* See dlegh- in App.] —**in•dulg′er** *n.*

in•dul•gence (ĭn-dŭl′jəns) *n.* **1a.** The act or an instance of indulging; gratification. **b.** The state of being indulgent. **2a.** The act of indulging in something. **b.** Something indulged in. **3.** Liberal or lenient treatment; tolerance. **4.** Self-indulgence. **5a.** Something granted as a favor or privilege. **b.** Permission to extend the time of payment or performance. **c.** Patient attention. **6.** *Roman Catholic Church* The remission of temporal punishment still due for a sin that has been sacramentally absolved. ❖ *tr.v.* **-genced, -genc•ing, -genc•es** *Roman Catholic Church* To attach an indulgence to.

in•dul•gent (ĭn-dŭl′jənt) *adj.* Showing, characterized by, or given to indulgence; lenient. —**in•dul′gent•ly** *adv.*

in•dult (ĭn-dŭlt′) *n. Roman Catholic Church* A faculty granted by the pope to deviate from the common law of the Church. [ME < Med.Lat. *indultum* < LLat., concession, gift < Lat., neut. p. part. of *indulgēre*, to be kind.]

in•du•pli•cate (ĭn-do͞o′plĭ-kĭt, -dyo͞o′-) *adj. Botany* Having the edges folded or turned inward.

in•du•rate (ĭn′də-rāt′, -dyə-) *v.* **-rat•ed, -rat•ing, -rates** —*tr.* **1.** To make hard; harden. **2.** To inure, as to hardship. **3.** To make callous or obdurate. —*intr.* **1.** To grow hard; harden. **2.** To become firmly fixed or established. ❖ *adj.* (ĭn′do͞o-rĭt, -dyə-) Hardened; obstinate; unfeeling. [Lat. *indūrāre, indūrāt-* : *in-*, intensive pref.; see IN-² + *dūrus*, hard; see deru- in App.] —**in′du•ra′tive** *adj.*

in•du•ra•tion (ĭn′də-rā′shən, -dyə-) *n.* **1.** The quality or condi-

tion of being hardened. **2.** The act or process of becoming hardened. **3.** *Pathology* The hardening of a normally soft tissue or organ, as because of inflammation.

In•dus¹ (ĭn′dəs) A river of S-central Asia rising in SW Xizang (Tibet) and flowing c. 3,057 km (1,900 mi) through N India and Pakistan to the Arabian Sea. Its valley was the site of an advanced civilization lasting c. 2500–1500 B.C.

In•dus² (ĭn′dəs) *n.* A constellation in the Southern Hemisphere near Tucana and Pavo. [Lat. *Indus*, an Indian < Gk. *Indos*, the Indus River, an Indian. See INDIGO.]

indus. *abbr.* **1.** industrial **2.** industry

in•du•si•um (ĭn-do͞o′zē-əm, -zhē-, -dyo͞o′-) *n., pl.* **-si•a** (-zē-ə, -zhē-ə) An enclosing membrane, as that covering the sorus of a fern. [Lat., tunic, perh. alteration of Gk. *endusis*, dress < *enduein*, put on : *en-*, in; see EN-² + *duein*, to sink.]

in•dus•tri•al (ĭn-dŭs′trē-əl) *adj.* **1.** Of, relating to, or resulting from industry. **2.** Having highly developed industries: *an industrial nation.* **3.** Employed, required, or used in industry. ❖ *n.* **1.** A firm engaged in industry. **2.** A stock or bond issued by an industrial enterprise. **3.** A person employed in industry. **4.** A style of rock music marked by harsh rhythms, little melody, and nihilistic lyrics. —**in•dus′tri•al•ly** *adv.*

industrial arts *n.* (*used with a sing. verb*) A subject of study aimed at developing the manual and technical skills required to work with tools and machinery.

industrial disease *n.* Occupational disease.

industrial engineering *n.* The branch of engineering that is concerned with the efficient production of industrial goods. —**industrial engineer** *n.*

in•dus•tri•al•ism (ĭn-dŭs′trē-ə-lĭz′əm) *n.* An economic and social system based on large-scale industries.

in•dus•tri•al•ist (ĭ-dŭs′trē-ə-lĭst) *n.* One who owns, directs, or has a substantial financial interest in an industrial enterprise.

in•dus•tri•al•ize (ĭn-dŭs′trē-ə-līz′) *v.* **-ized, -iz•ing, -iz•es** —*tr.* **1.** To develop industry in. **2.** To organize (the production of something) as an industry. —*intr.* To become industrial. —**in•dus′tri•al•i•za′tion** (-ə-lĭ-zā′shən) *n.*

industrial park *n.* An area usu. located on the outskirts of a city and zoned for a group of industries and businesses.

industrial psychology *n.* The branch of applied psychology that is concerned with efficient management of an industrial labor force. —**industrial psychologist** *n.*

industrial relations *pl.n.* Relations between the management of an industrial enterprise and its employees.

industrial revolution also **Industrial Revolution** *n.* The complex of radical socioeconomic changes brought about by the extensive mechanization of production.

in•dus•tri•al-strength (ĭn-dŭs′trē-əl-strĕngkth′, -strĕngth′, -strĕnth′) *adj.* Extremely strong, durable, or concentrated.

industrial union *n.* A labor union to which all the workers of a particular industry can belong regardless of occupation.

in•dus•tri•ous (ĭn-dŭs′trē-əs) *adj.* **1.** Assiduous in work or study; diligent. **2.** *Obsolete* Skillful; clever. —**in•dus′tri•ous•ly** *adv.* —**in•dus′tri•ous•ness** *n.*

in•dus•try (ĭn′də-strē) *n., pl.* **-tries** **1.** Commercial production and sale of goods. **2.** A specific branch of manufacture and trade: *the textile industry.* See Syns at **business. 3.** The sector of an economy made up of manufacturing enterprises. **4.** Industrial management. **5.** Energetic devotion to a task or an endeavor; diligence. **6.** Ongoing work or study associated with a specified subject or figure. **7.** *Archaeology* **a.** A collection of artifacts or tools made from a specified material: *a Mesolithic bone industry.* **b.** A standardized tradition of toolmaking associated with a specified tool or culture. [ME *industrie*, skill < OFr. < Lat. *industria*, diligence < fem. of *industrius*, diligent.]

WORD HISTORY A clear indication of the way in which human effort has been harnessed as a force for the commercial production of goods and services is the change in meaning of the word *industry.* Coming from the Latin word *industria*, meaning "diligent activity directed to some purpose," and its descendant, Old French *industrie*, with the senses "activity," "ability," and "a trade or occupation," our word (first recorded in 1475) originally meant "skill," "a device," and "diligence" as well as "a trade." Over the course of the Industrial Revolution, as more and more human effort became involved in producing goods and services for sale, the last sense of *industry* as well as the slightly newer sense "systematic work or habitual employment" grew in importance, to a large extent taking over the word. We can even speak now of the Shakespeare industry, rather like the garment industry.

in•dwell (ĭn-dwĕl′) *v.* **-dwelt** (-dwĕlt′), **-dwell•ing, -dwells** —*intr.* **1.** To exist as an animating or divine inner spirit, force, or principle. **2.** To be located or implanted inside something. —*tr.* **1.** To inhabit or reside within. —**in•dwell′er** *n.*

–ine¹ *suff.* **1.** Of or relating to: *Benedictine.* **2.** Made of; resembling: *opaline.* [ME *-in, -ine* < OFr. < Lat. *-īnus, -īna*, adj. suff., and < Lat. *-inus*, adj. suff. (< Gk. *-inos*.)]

–ine² *suff.* **1.** also **–in** A chemical substance, esp.: **a.** Halogen: *bromine.* **b.** Basic compound: *amine.* **c.** Alkaloid: *quinine.* **2.** Amino acid: *glycine.* **3.** A mixture of compounds: *gasoline.* **4.** Commer-

industrial park
Hempfield Industrial Park,
Lancaster County,
Pennsylvania

cial material: *glassine.* [Ult. < Lat. -*īnus* and -*inus,* adj. suffixes; see –INE¹.]

in•e•bri•ant (ĭn-ē′brē-ənt) *adj.* Serving to intoxicate. ❖ *n.* An intoxicant.

in•e•bri•ate (ĭn-ē′brē-āt′) *tr.v.* **-at•ed, -at•ing, -ates 1.** To make drunk; intoxicate. **2.** To exhilarate or stupefy as if with alcohol. ❖ *adj.* (-ĭt) Intoxicated. ❖ *n.* (-ĭt) An intoxicated person. [Lat. *inēbriāre, inēbriāt-* : *in-,* intensive pref.; see IN–² + *ēbriāre,* to intoxicate (< *ēbrius,* drunk).] —**in•e′bri•a′tion** *n.*

in•e•bri•at•ed (ĭn-ē′brē-ā′tĭd) *adj.* Exhilarated or stupefied by or as if by alcohol; intoxicated.

in•e•bri•e•ty (ĭn′ĭ-brī′ĭ-tē) *n.* Intoxication; drunkenness.

in•ed•i•ble (ĭn-ĕd′ə-bəl) *adj.* Unfit to be eaten; not edible. —**in•ed′i•bil′i•ty** *n.* —**in•ed′i•bly** *adv.*

in•ed•it•ed (ĭn-ĕd′ĭ-tĭd) *adj.* **1.** Not edited. **2.** Not published.

in•ed•u•ca•ble (ĭn-ĕj′ə-kə-bəl) *adj.* Incapable of being educated. —**in•ed′u•ca•bil′i•ty** *n.*

in•ef•fa•ble (ĭn-ĕf′ə-bəl) *adj.* **1.** Incapable of being expressed; indescribable or unutterable. **2.** Not to be uttered; taboo. [ME < OFr. < Lat. *ineffābilis* : *in-,* not; see IN–¹ + *effābilis,* utterable (< *effārī,* to utter : *ex-, ex-* + *fārī,* to speak; see **bhā-** in App.).] —**in•ef′fa•bil′i•ty** *n.* —**in•ef′fa•bly** *adv.*

in•ef•face•a•ble (ĭn′ĭ-fā′sə-bəl) *adj.* Impossible to efface; indelible. —**in′ef•face′a•bil′i•ty** *n.* —**in′ef•face′a•bly** *adv.*

in•ef•fec•tive (ĭn′ĭ-fĕk′tĭv) *adj.* **1.** Not producing an intended effect; ineffectual. **2.** Inadequate; incompetent. —**in′ef•fec′tive•ly** *adv.* —**in′ef•fec′tive•ness** *n.*

in•ef•fec•tu•al (ĭn′ĭ-fĕk′chōō-əl) *adj.* **1a.** Insufficient to produce a desired effect: *an ineffectual effort.* **b.** Useless; worthless. **2.** Lacking forcefulness or effectiveness; weak: *an ineffectual ruler.* —**in′ef•fec′tu•al′i•ty** (-ăl′ĭ-tē), **in′ef•fec′tu•al•ness** *n.* —**in′ef•fec′tu•al•ly** *adv.*

in•ef•fi•ca•cious (ĭn-ĕf′ĭ-kā′shəs) *adj.* Not capable of producing a desired effect or result; ineffective. —**in•ef′fi•ca′cious•ly** *adv.* —**in•ef′fi•ca′cious•ness** *n.*

in•ef•fi•ca•cy (ĭn-ĕf′ĭ-kə-sē) *n.* The state or quality of being incapable of producing a desired effect.

in•ef•fi•cien•cy (ĭn′ĭ-fĭsh′ən-sē) *n., pl.* **-cies 1.** The quality, condition, or fact of being inefficient. **2.** An inefficient act, design, or procedure.

in•ef•fi•cient (ĭn′ĭ-fĭsh′ənt) *adj.* **1.** Not efficient, as: **a.** Lacking the ability or skill to perform effectively; incompetent. **b.** Not producing the intended result; ineffective. **2.** Wasteful of time, energy, or materials. —**in′ef•fi′cient•ly** *adv.*

in•e•gal•i•tar•i•an (ĭn′ĭ-găl′ĭ-târ′ē-ən) *adj.* Marked by or accepting of social, economic, or political inequality.

in•e•las•tic (ĭn′ĭ-lăs′tĭk) *adj.* Lacking elasticity; unyielding or unadaptable. See Syns at **stiff.** —**in′e•las•tic′i•ty** (-ĭ-lă-stĭs′ĭ-tē) *n.*

inelastic collision *n.* A collision between two particles in which part of their kinetic energy is transformed to another form of energy, the total amount of energy remaining the same.

in•el•e•gance (ĭn-ĕl′ĭ-gəns) *n.* Lack of refinement or polish.

in•el•e•gant (ĭn-ĕl′ĭ-gənt) *adj.* Lacking refinement or polish; not elegant. —**in•el′e•gant•ly** *adv.*

in•el•i•gi•ble (ĭn-ĕl′ĭ-jə-bəl) *adj.* **1.** Disqualified by law, rule, or provision. **2.** Unworthy of being chosen; unfit. —**in•el′i•gi•ble** *n.* —**in•el′i•gi•bly** *adv.*

in•el•o•quent (ĭn-ĕl′ə-kwənt) *adj.* Lacking eloquence. —**in•el′o•quence** *n.* —**in•el′o•quent•ly** *adv.*

in•e•luc•ta•ble (ĭn′ĭ-lŭk′tə-bəl) *adj.* Not to be avoided or escaped; inevitable. [Lat. *inēluctābilis* : *in-,* not; see IN–¹ + *ēluctābilis,* penetrable (< *ēluctārī,* to struggle out of : *ex-, ex-* + *luctārī,* to struggle).] —**in′e•luc′ta•bil′i•ty** *n.* —**in′e•luc′ta•bly** *adv.*

in•ept (ĭn-ĕpt′) *adj.* **1.** Not apt or fitting; inappropriate. **2a.** Displaying a lack of judgment, sense, or reason; foolish. **b.** Bungling or clumsy; incompetent. [Lat. *ineptus* : *in-,* not; see IN–¹ + *aptus,* suitable; see APT.] —**in•ept′ly** *adv.* —**in•ept′ness** *n.*

in•ep•ti•tude (ĭn-ĕp′tĭ-tōōd′, -tyōōd′) *n.* **1.** The quality of being inept; ineptness. **2.** An inept act or remark.

in•e•qual•i•ty (ĭn′ĭ-kwŏl′ĭ-tē) *n., pl.* **-ties 1a.** The condition of being unequal. **b.** An instance of being unequal. **2a.** Lack of equality, as of opportunity. **b.** Social or economic disparity: *the growing inequality between rich and poor.* **3.** Lack of smoothness or regularity; unevenness. **4.** Variability; changeability. **5.** *Mathematics* An algebraic expression showing that a quantity is greater than or less than another quantity. **6.** *Astronomy* A deviation from uniformity in the motion of a celestial body.

in•eq•ui•ta•ble (ĭn-ĕk′wĭ-tə-bəl) *adj.* Not equitable; unfair. —**in•eq′ui•ta•bly** *adv.*

in•eq•ui•ty (ĭn-ĕk′wĭ-tē) *n., pl.* **-ties 1.** Injustice; unfairness. **2.** An instance of injustice or unfairness.

in•e•rad•i•ca•ble (ĭn′ĭ-răd′ĭ-kə-bəl) *adj.* Incapable of being eradicated. —**in′e•rad′i•ca•bly** *adv.*

in•er•ran•cy (ĭn-ĕr′ən-sē) *n.* Freedom from error or untruths.

in•er•rant (ĭn-ĕr′ənt) *adj.* **1.** Incapable of erring; infallible. **2.** Containing no errors.

in•ert (ĭn-ûrt′) *adj.* **1.** Unable to move or act. **2.** Sluggish in action or motion; lethargic. See Syns at **inactive. 3.** *Chemistry* Not readily reactive with other elements. **4.** *Pharmacology* Having no therapeutic action. [Lat. *iners, inert-* : *in-,* not; see IN–¹ + *ars,* skill.]

—**in•ert′ly** *adv.* —**in•ert′ness** *n.*

inert gas *n.* See **noble gas.**

in•er•tia (ĭ-nûr′shə) *n.* **1.** *Physics* The tendency of a body at rest to remain at rest or of a body moving in a straight line to continue moving in a straight line unless acted on by an outside force. **2.** Resistance or disinclination to motion, action, or change: *bureaucratic inertia.* [Lat., idleness < *iners, inert-,* inert. See INERT.] —**in•er′tial** *adj.* —**in•er′tial•ly** *adv.*

inertial guidance *n.* Guidance of an aircraft or spacecraft in which gyroscopic and accelerometer data are used by a computer to maintain a predetermined course.

in•es•cap•a•ble (ĭn′ĭ-skā′pə-bəl) *adj.* Impossible to escape or avoid; inevitable. —**in′es•cap′a•bly** *adv.*

in•es•sen•tial (ĭn′ĭ-sĕn′shəl) *adj.* **1.** Not essential; unessential. **2.** Without essence. ❖ *n.* Something that is not essential. —**in′es•sen′ti•al′i•ty** (-shē-ăl′ĭ-tē) *n.*

in•es•ti•ma•ble (ĭn-ĕs′tə-mə-bəl) *adj.* **1.** Impossible to estimate or compute. See Syns at **incalculable. 2.** Of immeasurable value; invaluable. —**in•es′ti•ma•bly** *adv.*

in•ev•i•ta•ble (ĭn-ĕv′ĭ-tə-bəl) *adj.* **1.** Impossible to avoid or prevent. **2.** Invariably occurring or appearing; predictable. —**in•ev′i•ta•bil′i•ty** *n.* —**in•ev′i•ta•bly** *adv.*

in•ex•act (ĭn′ĭg-zăkt′) *adj.* **1.** Not strictly accurate; not exact: *an inexact quotation.* **2.** Not rigorous or meticulous: *an inexact method.* —**in′ex•act′ly** *adv.* —**in′ex•act′ness** *n.*

in•ex•act•i•tude (ĭn′ĭg-zăk′tĭ-tōōd′, -tyōōd′) *n.* Lack of exactitude; inexactness.

in•ex•cus•a•ble (ĭn′ĭk-skyōō′zə-bəl) *adj.* Impossible to excuse or justify; unpardonable: *inexcusable behavior.* —**in′ex•cus′a•ble•ness** *n.* —**in′ex•cus′a•bly** *adv.*

in•ex•haust•i•ble (ĭn′ĭg-zô′stə-bəl) *adj.* **1.** That cannot be depleted or used up. **2.** Never wearying; tireless: *an inexhaustible campaigner.* —**in′ex•haust′i•bil′i•ty, in′ex•haust′i•ble•ness** *n.* —**in′ex•haust′i•bly** *adv.*

in•ex•is•tent (ĭn′ĭg-zĭs′tənt) *adj.* Having no existence; nonexistent. —**in′ex•is′tence** *n.*

in•ex•o•ra•ble (ĭn-ĕk′sər-ə-bəl) *adj.* Incapable of being persuaded by entreaty; relentless: *inexorable doom.* [Lat. *inexōrābilis* : *in-,* not; see IN–¹ + *exōrābilis,* pliant (< *exōrāre,* to prevail upon : *ex-,* intensive pref.; see EX– + *ōrāre,* to argue).] —**in•ex′o•ra•bil′i•ty, in•ex′o•ra•ble•ness** *n.* —**in•ex′o•ra•bly** *adv.*

in•ex•pe•di•ent (ĭn′ĭk-spē′dē-ənt) *adj.* Not expedient; inadvisable: *an inexpedient tactic.* —**in′ex•pe′di•ence, in′ex•pe′di•en•cy** *n.* —**in′ex•pe′di•ent•ly** *adv.*

in•ex•pen•sive (ĭn′ĭk-spĕn′sĭv) *adj.* Not high in price; cheap. —**in′ex•pen′sive•ly** *adv.* —**in′ex•pen′sive•ness** *n.*

in•ex•pe•ri•ence (ĭn′ĭk-spîr′ē-əns) *n.* **1.** Lack of experience. **2.** Lack of the knowledge gained from experience. —**in′ex•pe′ri•enced** *adj.*

in•ex•pert (ĭn-ĕk′spûrt′, ĭn′ĭk-spûrt′) *adj.* Not expert; unskilled. —**in•ex′pert•ly** *adv.* —**in•ex′pert′ness** *n.*

in•ex•pi•a•ble (ĭn-ĕk′spē-ə-bəl) *adj.* **1.** Impossible to expiate or atone for: *inexpiable crimes.* **2.** *Obsolete* Implacable. —**in•ex′pi•a•bly** *adv.*

in•ex•plain•a•ble (ĭn′ĭk-splā′nə-bəl) *adj.* Difficult or impossible to explain; inexplicable. —**in′ex•plain′a•bly** *adv.*

in•ex•pli•ca•ble (ĭn-ĕk′splĭ-kə-bəl, ĭn′ĭk-splĭk′ə-bəl) *adj.* Difficult or impossible to account for. —**in′ex′pli•ca•bil′i•ty, in•ex′pli•ca•ble•ness** *n.* —**in′ex′pli•ca•bly** *adv.*

in•ex•plic•it (ĭn′ĭk-splĭs′ĭt) *adj.* Not explicit; indefinite.

in•ex•press•i•ble (ĭn′ĭk-sprĕs′ə-bəl) *adj.* Impossible to express; indescribable: *felt inexpressible grief.* —**in′ex•press′i•bil′i•ty, in′ex•press′i•ble•ness** *n.* —**in′ex•press′i•bly** *adv.*

in•ex•pres•sive (ĭn′ĭk-sprĕs′ĭv) *adj.* **1.** Lacking expression; blank. **2.** Devoid of emotion or style; flat or dull. —**in′ex•pres′sive•ly** *adv.* —**in′ex•pres′sive•ness** *n.*

in•ex•pug•na•ble (ĭn′ĭk-spŭg′nə-bəl, -spyōō′nə-) *adj.* **1.** Impossible to overcome or overthrow by force. **2.** Impossible to put aside or drive away: *inexpugnable dislike.* [ME < OFr. < Lat. *inexpugnābilis* : *in-,* not; see IN–¹ + *expugnābilis,* capable of being overcome (< *expugnāre* : *ex-,* completely; see EX– + *pugnāre,* to fight; see IMPUGN.] —**in′ex•pug•na•bil′i•ty** *n.* —**in′ex•pug′na•bly** *adv.*

in•ex•ten•si•ble (ĭn′ĭk-stĕn′sə-bəl) *adj.* Not extensible.

in ex•ten•so (ĭn ĕk-stĕn′sō) *adv.* At full length. [Lat. *in extēnsō* : *in,* at (extēnsō, ablative of *extēnsus,* stretch.]

in•ex•tin•guish•a•ble (ĭn′ĭk-stĭng′gwĭ-shə-bəl) *adj.* Difficult or impossible to extinguish. —**in′ex•tin′guish•a•bly** *adv.*

in•ex•tir•pa•ble (ĭn′ĭk-stûr′pə-bəl) *adj.* Difficult or impossible to eradicate or destroy.

in ex•tre•mis (ĭn ĕk-strē′mĭs) *adv.* **1.** At the point of death. **2.** In grave or extreme circumstances. [Lat. *in extrēmīs* : *in,* in + *extrēmīs,* ablative pl. of *extrēmus,* extreme.]

in•ex•tri•ca•ble (ĭn-ĕk′strĭ-kə-bəl, ĭn′ĭk-strĭk′ə-bəl) *adj.* **1a.** So intricate or entangled as to make escape impossible: *an inextricable maze.* **b.** Difficult or impossible to disentangle or untie. **c.** Too involved or complicated to solve. **2.** Unavoidable; inescapable: *bound together by an inextricable fate.* —**in•ex′tri•ca•bil′i•ty, in•ex′tri•ca•ble•ness** *n.* —**in•ex′tri•ca•bly** *adv.*

inf. *abbr.* **1.** infantry **2.** inferior **3.** infinitive **4.** infinity

in•fal•li•ble (ĭn-făl′ə-bəl) *adj.* **1.** Incapable of erring. **2.** Incapa-

ă	pat	oi	boy
ā	pay	ou	out
âr	care	ŏŏ	took
ä	father	ōō	boot
ĕ	pet	ŭ	cut
ē	be	ûr	urge
ĭ	pit	th	thin
ī	pie	th	this
îr	pier	hw	which
ŏ	pot	zh	vision
ō	toe	ə	about,
ô	paw		item

Stress marks:
′ (primary);
′ (secondary), as in
lexicon (lĕk′sĭ-kŏn′)

ble of failing; certain. **3.** *Roman Catholic Church* Incapable of error in expounding doctrine on faith or morals. —**in•fal′li•bil′i•ty, in•fal′li•ble•ness** *n.* —**in•fal′li•bly** *adv.*

in•fa•mous (ĭn′fə-məs) *adj.* **1.** Having an exceedingly bad reputation; notorious: *an infamous traitor.* **2.** Causing or deserving infamy; heinous: *an infamous deed.* **3.** *Law* **a.** Punishable by severe measures, such as death or long imprisonment. **b.** Convicted of a crime that carries such a punishment. [ME *infamis* < Lat. *īnfāmis* : *in-*, not; see IN-¹ + *fāma*, renown, fame; see **bhā-** in App.] —**in′fa•mous•ly** *adv.* —**in′fa•mous•ness** *n.*

in•fa•my (ĭn′fə-mē) *n., pl.* **-mies 1.** Evil fame or reputation. **2.** The condition of being infamous. **3.** An evil or criminal act that is publicly known. [ME *infamie*, dishonor < OFr. < Lat. *īnfāmia* < *īnfāmis*, infamous. See INFAMOUS.]

in•fan•cy (ĭn′fən-sē) *n., pl.* **-cies 1.** The earliest period of childhood, esp. before the ability to walk has been acquired. **2.** The state of being an infant. **3.** An early stage of existence. **4.** *Law* The state or period of being a minor.

in•fant (ĭn′fənt) *n.* **1.** A child in infancy. **2.** *Law* A person under the legal age of majority; a minor. ❖ *adj.* **1.** Of or being in infancy. **2.** Intended for infants or young children. **3.** Newly begun or formed. [ME < OFr. *enfant* < Lat. *īnfāns*, *īnfant-* < *īnfāns*, not able to speak, young : *in-*, not; see IN-¹ + *fāns*, pr. part. of *fārī*, to speak; see **bhā-** in App.]

in•fan•ta (ĭn-fän′tə, -fän′-) *n.* A daughter of a Spanish or Portuguese king. [Sp. and Port., fem. of *infante*, infante; see INFANTE.]

in•fan•te (ĭn-fän′tē, -fän′tā) *n.* A son of a Spanish or Portuguese king other than the heir to the throne. [Sp. and Port., both < Lat. *īnfāns, īnfant-*, infant. See INFANT.]

in•fan•ti•cide (ĭn-fän′tĭ-sīd′) *n.* **1.** The act of killing an infant. **2.** The practice of killing newborn infants. **3.** One who kills an infant. [LLat. *īnfanticīdium*, the killing of a child and *īnfanticīda*, killer of a child : Lat. *īnfāns, īnfant-*, infant; see INFANT + Lat. *-cīdium* and *-cīda*, -cide.] —**in•fan′ti•cid′al** (-sīd′l) *adj.*

in•fan•tile (ĭn′fən-tīl′, -tĭl) *adj.* **1.** Of or relating to infants or infancy. **2.** Displaying or suggesting a lack of maturity; childish: *infantile behavior.* [ME *infantil* < Lat. *īnfantīlis* < *īnfāns, īnfant-*, infant. See INFANT.]

infantile autism *n.* See **poliomyelitis.**

infantile paralysis *n.* See **poliomyelitis.**

in•fan•til•ism (ĭn′fən-tl-ĭz′əm, ĭn-făn′tl-) *n.* **1.** A state of arrested development in an adult, characterized by retention of infantile mentality and accompanied by stunted growth and sexual immaturity and often by dwarfism. **2a.** Marked immaturity, as in behavior or character: **b.** An infantile act or remark.

in•fan•til•ize (ĭn′fən-tl-īz′, ĭn-făn′-) *tr.v.* **-ized, -iz•ing, -iz•es 1.** To reduce to an infantile state or condition. **2.** To treat or condescend to as if still a young child. —**in•fan′til•i•za′tion** (-ĭ-zā′shən) *n.*

in•fan•tine (ĭn′fən-tīn′, -tĭn) *adj.* Infantile; childish.

in•fan•try (ĭn′fən-trē) *n., pl.* **-tries 1.** The branch of an army made up of units trained to fight on foot. **2.** Soldiers armed and trained to fight on foot. **3.** A unit of such soldiers. [Fr. *infanterie* < OFr. < OItal. *infanteria* < *infante*, youth, foot soldier < Lat. *īnfāns, īnfant-*, infant. See INFANT.]

infantry fighting vehicle *n.* A heavily armed, armored combat vehicle, having tracks or wheels and often amphibious capability, used to transport infantry into battle and support them there.

in•fan•try•man (ĭn′fən-trē-mən) *n.* A soldier in the infantry.

infant school *n. Chiefly British* A kindergarten.

in•farct (ĭn′färkt′, ĭn-färkt′) *n.* An area of tissue that undergoes necrosis as a result of obstruction of local blood supply. [< Lat. *īnfarctus*, p. part. of *īnfarcīre*, to cram : *in-*, in; see IN-² + *farcīre*, to stuff.] —**in•farct′ed** *adj.*

in•farc•tion (ĭn-färk′shən) *n.* **1.** The formation or development of an infarct. **2.** An infarct.

in•fat•u•ate (ĭn-făch′ōō-āt′) *tr.v.* **-at•ed, -at•ing, -ates 1.** To inspire with unreasoning love or attachment. **2.** To cause to behave foolishly. ❖ *adj.* (-ĭt, -āt′) Infatuated. [Lat. *īnfatuāre, īnfatuāt-* : *in-*, causative pref.; see IN-² + *fatuus*, foolish.]

in•fat•u•at•ed (ĭn-făch′ōō-ā′tĭd) *adj.* Possessed by an unreasoning passion or attraction. —**in•fat′u•at′ed•ly** *adv.*

in•fat•u•a•tion (ĭ-făch′ōō-ā′shən) *n.* **1.** A foolish, unreasoning, or extravagant passion or attraction. **2.** An object of extravagant, short-lived passion.

in•fau•na (ĭn-fô′nə) *n.* Aquatic animals that live in the substrate of a body of water. [IN-² + FAUNA.]

in•fea•si•ble (ĭn-fē′zə-bəl) *adj.* Not feasible; impracticable. —**in•fea′si•bil′i•ty** *n.*

in•fect (ĭn-fĕkt′) *tr.v.* **-fect•ed, -fect•ing, -fects 1.** To contaminate with a pathogen. **2.** To communicate a pathogen or disease to. **3.** To invade and produce infection in. **4.** To contaminate or corrupt. **5.** To affect in a contagious way. [ME *infecten*, to afflict with disease < Lat. *īnficere, īnfect-*, to stain, infect : *in-*, in; see in- in App. + *facere*, to do; see **dhē-** in App.]

in•fec•tion (ĭn-fĕk′shən) *n.* **1a.** Invasion by and multiplication of pathogenic microorganisms in a body tissue. **b.** An instance of being infected. **c.** An agent or a contaminated substance responsible for one's becoming infected. **d.** The pathological state resulting from having been infected. **2.** An infectious disease. **3a.** Moral contamination or corruption. **b.** Ready communication of

an emotion or attitude by contact or example.

in•fec•tious (ĭn-fĕk′shəs) *adj.* **1.** Capable of causing infection. **2.** Caused by or capable of being transmitted by infection. **3.** Easily or readily communicated: *an infectious laugh.* —**in•fec′tious•ly** *adv.* —**in•fec′tious•ness** *n.*

infectious enterohepatitis *n.* See **blackhead** 2.

infectious hepatitis *n.* See **hepatitis A.**

infectious mononucleosis *n.* An acute infectious disease caused by Epstein-Barr virus and characterized by fever, swollen lymph nodes, sore throat, and lymphocyte abnormalities.

in•fec•tive (ĭn-fĕk′tĭv) *adj.* Capable of producing infection; infectious. —**in•fec′tive•ness, in′fec•tiv′i•ty** *n.*

in•fe•lic•i•tous (ĭn′fĭ-lĭs′ĭ-təs) *adj.* **1.** Inappropriate; ill-chosen: *an infelicitous remark.* **2.** Not happy; unfortunate. —**in′fe•lic′i•tous•ly** *adv.*

in•fe•lic•i•ty (ĭn′fĭ-lĭs′ĭ-tē) *n., pl.* **-ties 1.** The quality or condition of being infelicitous. **2.** Something inappropriate or unpleasing. [ME *infelicite* < Lat. *īnfēlīcitās* < *īnfēlīx, īnfēlīc-*, unhappy : *in-*, not; see IN-¹ + *fēlīx*, happy.]

in•fer (ĭn-fûr′) *v.* **-ferred, -fer•ring, -fers** —*tr.* **1.** To conclude from evidence or premises. **2.** To reason from circumstance; surmise. **3.** To lead to as a consequence or conclusion: "*Socrates argued that a statue inferred the existence of a sculptor*" (Academy). **4.** *Usage Problem* To hint; imply. —*intr.* To draw inferences. [Lat. *īnferre*, to bring in, adduce : *in-*, in; see IN-² + *ferre*, to bear; see **bher-¹** in App.] —**in•fer′a•ble** *adj.* —**in•fer′a•bly** *adv.* —**in•fer′rer** *n.*

USAGE NOTE The traditional distinction between *imply* and *infer* is a useful one. When we say that a speaker or sentence implies something, we mean that it is conveyed or suggested without being stated outright: *When the mayor said that she would not rule out a business tax increase, she implied* (not *inferred*) *that some taxes might be raised.* Inference, on the other hand, is the activity performed by a reader or interpreter in drawing conclusions that are not explicit in what is said: *When the mayor said that she would not rule out a tax increase, we inferred that she had been consulting with some new financial advisers, since her old advisers were in favor of tax reductions.*

in•fer•ence (ĭn′fər-əns) *n.* **1a.** The act or process of deriving logical conclusions from premises known or assumed to be true. **b.** The act of reasoning from factual knowledge or evidence. **2a.** Something inferred. **b.** *Usage Problem* A hint or suggestion. See Usage Note at **infer.**

in•fer•en•tial (ĭn′fə-rĕn′shəl) *adj.* **1.** Of, relating to, or involving inference. **2.** Derived or capable of being derived by inference. —**in′fer•en′tial•ly** *adv.*

in•fe•ri•or (ĭn-fîr′ē-ər) *adj.* **1.** Low or lower in order, degree, or rank. **2a.** Low or lower in quality, value, or estimation: *felt inferior to his older sibling.* **b.** Second-rate; poor. **3.** Situated under or beneath. **4.** *Botany* Located below the perianth and other floral parts. Used of an ovary. **5.** *Anatomy* Located beneath or directed downward. **6.** *Printing* Set below the normal line of type; subscript. **7.** *Astronomy* **a.** Orbiting between the earth and the sun. **b.** Lying below the horizon. ❖ *n.* **1.** A person lower in rank, status, or accomplishment than another. **2.** *Printing* An inferior character, such as the number 2 in CO_2. [ME < Lat. *īnferior*, comp. of *īnferus*, low. See **ṇdher-** in App.] —**in•fe′ri•or′i•ty** (-ôr′ĭ-tē, -ŏr′-) *n.* —**in•fe′ri•or•ly** *adv.*

inferiority complex *n.* A persistent sense of inadequacy or a tendency to self-diminishment.

in•fer•nal (ĭn-fûr′nəl) *adj.* **1a.** Of or relating to a lower world of the dead. **b.** Of or relating to hell. **2.** Fiendish; diabolical: *infernal instruments of war.* **3.** Abominable; awful. [ME < OFr. < LLat. *īnfernālis* < *īnfernus*, hell < Lat., lower, underground.] —**in•fer′nal•ly** *adv.*

infernal machine *n.* An explosive device designed to harm or destroy, esp. with criminal intent.

in•fer•no (ĭn-fûr′nō) *n., pl.* **-nos 1.** A place or condition suggestive of hell. **2.** A place of fiery heat or destruction. [Ital., hell < LLat. *īnfernus*. See INFERNAL.]

in•fer•tile (ĭn-fûr′tl) *adj.* **1.** Not fertile; unproductive or barren. **2.** Incapable of producing offspring; sterile.

in•fer•til•i•ty (ĭn′fər-tĭl′ĭ-tē) *n.* **1.** Absent or diminished fertility. **2.** The persistent inability to conceive a child.

in•fest (ĭn-fĕst′) *tr.v.* **-fest•ed, -fest•ing, -fests 1.** To inhabit or overrun in numbers large enough to be harmful, threatening, or obnoxious. **2.** To live as a parasite in or on: *livestock infested with tapeworms.* [ME *infesten*, to distress < OFr. *infester* < Lat. *īnfestāre* < *īnfestus*, hostile.] —**in′fes•ta′tion** *n.* —**in•fest′er** *n.*

in•fib•u•late (ĭn-fĭb′yə-lāt′) *tr.v.* **-lat•ed, -lat•ing, -lates** To close off or obstruct the genitals of, so as to prevent sexual intercourse. [Lat. *īnfībulāre, īnfībulāt-*, to clasp with a brooch, infibulate : *in-*, on; see IN-² + *fībula*, brooch, clasp; see FIBULA.] —**in•fib′u•la′tion** *n.*

in•fi•del (ĭn′fĭ-dəl, -dĕl′) *n.* **1.** An unbeliever with respect to a particular religion, esp. Christianity or Islam. **2.** One who has no religious beliefs. **3.** One who doubts or rejects a particular doctrine, system, or principle. [ME *infidele* < OFr. < Lat. *īnfidēlis*, disloyal : *in-*, not; see IN-¹ + *fidēlis*, faithful (< *fidēs*, faith; see **bheidh-** in App.).]

in·fi·del·i·ty (ĭn′fĭ-dĕl′ĭ-tē) n., pl. **-ties 1a.** Unfaithfulness to a sexual partner, esp. a spouse. **b.** An act of sexual unfaithfulness. **2.** Lack of loyalty. **3.** Lack of religious belief.

in·field (ĭn′fēld′) n. **1.** Baseball **a.** The area of the field bounded by home plate and first, second, and third bases. **b.** The defensive positions of first base, second base, third base, and shortstop considered as a unit. **2.** The area inside a racetrack or running track. **3.** A field located near a farmhouse.

in·field·er (ĭn′fēl′dər) n. Baseball An infield player.

in·fight·ing (ĭn′fī′tĭng) n. **1.** Contentious rivalry or disagreement among members of a group or organization. **2.** Sports Fighting or boxing at close range. —**in′fight′er** n.

in·fil·trate (ĭn-fĭl′trāt′, ĭn′fĭl-) v. **-trat·ed, -trat·ing, -trates** —tr. **1a.** To pass (troops, for example) surreptitiously into enemy-held territory. **b.** To penetrate with hostile intent. **2.** To enter or take up positions in gradually or surreptitiously, as for espionage. **3.** To cause (a liquid, for example) to permeate by passing through interstices or pores. **4.** To permeate (a porous substance) with a liquid or gas. —intr. To gain entrance gradually or surreptitiously. ❖ n. One that infiltrates, esp. an abnormal substance that accumulates gradually in cells or body tissues. —**in·fil′tra·tive** (-trə-tĭv) adj. —**in·fil′tra·tor** n.

in·fil·tra·tion (ĭn′fĭl-trā′shən) n. **1.** The act or process of infiltrating. **2.** The state of being infiltrated. **3.** Something that infiltrates.

infin. abbr. infinitive

in·fi·nite (ĭn′fə-nĭt) adj. **1.** Having no boundaries or limits. **2.** Immeasurably great or large; boundless: infinite importance. **3.** Mathematics **a.** Existing beyond or being greater than any arbitrarily large value. **b.** Unlimited in spatial extent. **c.** Of or relating to a set capable of being put into one-to-one correspondence with a proper subset of itself. ❖ n. Something infinite. [ME infinit < OFr. < Lat. īnfīnītus : in-, not; see IN–¹ + fīnītus, finite < p. part. of fīnīre, to limit; see FINITE.] —**in′fi·nite·ly** adv. —**in′fi·nite·ness** n.

SYNONYMS infinite, boundless, eternal, illimitable, sempiternal These adjectives mean being without beginning or end: infinite wisdom; boundless ambition; eternal beauty; illimitable space; sempiternal truth. See also Syns at **incalculable. ANTONYM** finite

USAGE NOTE Infinite is sometimes grouped with absolute terms such as unique, absolute, and omnipotent, since in its strict mathematical sense infiniteness is an absolute property; some infinite sets are smaller than others, but they are no less infinite. In nontechnical usage infinite is often used metaphorically to refer to an unimaginably large degree or amount, and here comparison or modification of the word is unexceptionable: Nothing could give me more infinite pleasure than to see you win. See Usage Note at **unique.**

in·fin·i·tes·i·mal (ĭn′fĭn-ĭ-tĕs′ə-məl) adj. **1.** Immeasurably or incalculably minute. **2.** Mathematics Capable of having values approaching zero as a limit. ❖ n. **1.** An infinitesimal amount or quantity. **2.** Mathematics An infinitesimal function or variable. [< NLat. īnfīnītēsimus, infinite in rank < Lat. īnfīnītus, infinite. See INFINITE.] —**in′fin·i·tes′i·mal·ly** adv.

infinitesimal calculus n. Differential and integral calculus.

in·fin·i·ti·val (ĭn′fĭn-ĭ-tī′vəl) adj. Relating to the infinitive.

in·fin·i·tive (ĭn-fĭn′ĭ-tĭv) n. A verb form that functions as a substantive while retaining certain verbal characteristics and that in English may be preceded by to, as in We want to go too, or may also occur without to, as in We may finish today. See Usage Note at **split infinitive.** [< ME infinitif, of an infinitive < OFr. < LLat. īnfīnītīvus, unlimited, indefinite, infinitive < Lat. īnfīnītus, infinite. See INFINITE.]

in·fin·i·tude (ĭn-fĭn′ĭ-tōōd′, -tyōōd′) n. **1.** The state or quality of being infinite. **2.** An immeasurably large quantity, number, or extent.

in·fin·i·ty (ĭn-fĭn′ĭ-tē) n., pl. **-ties 1.** The quality or condition of being infinite. **2.** Unbounded space, time, or quantity. **3.** An indefinitely large number or amount. **4.** Mathematics The limit that a function f is said to approach at x = a when f(x) is larger than any preassigned number for all x sufficiently near a. **5a.** A range in relation to an optical system in which light rays reflected from objects may be regarded as parallel. **b.** A distance setting, as on a camera, beyond which the entire field is in focus.

in·firm (ĭn-fûrm′) adj. **1.** Weak in body, esp. from old age or disease; feeble. **2.** Lacking firmness of will, character, or purpose; irresolute. **3.** Not strong or stable; shaky. [ME infirme < OFr. < Lat. īnfirmus : in-, not; see IN–¹ + firmus, strong, firm.] —**in·firm′ly** adv.

in·fir·ma·ry (ĭn-fûr′mə-rē) n., pl. **-ries** A place for the care of the infirm, sick, or injured, esp. a small hospital or dispensary in an institution. [ME infirmarie < Med.Lat. īnfirmāria < Lat. īnfirmus, infirm. See INFIRM.]

in·fir·mi·ty (ĭn-fûr′mĭ-tē) n., pl. **-ties 1.** A bodily ailment or weakness, esp. one brought on by old age. **2.** Frailty; feebleness. **3.** A condition or disease producing weakness. **4.** A failing or defect in a person's character.

in·fix (ĭn-fĭks′) tr.v. **-fixed, -fix·ing, -fix·es 1.** To fix in the mind; instill. **2.** Linguistics To insert (a morphological element) into the body of a word. ❖ n. (ĭn′fĭks′) Linguistics An inflectional or derivational element appearing in the body of a word. [Ult. < Lat. īnfīxus, p. part. of īnfīgere, to fasten in : in-, in; see IN–² + fīgere, to fasten.]

in flagrante delicto adv. Flagrante delicto. [NLat. in flagrante dēlictō : Lat. in, in; see IN–² + Med.Lat. flagrante dēlictō, while the crime is blazing; see FLAGRANTE DELICTO.]

in·flame (ĭn-flām′) v. **-flamed, -flam·ing, -flames** —tr. **1.** To arouse to passionate feeling or action. **2.** To make more violent; intensify. **3a.** To cause (the skin) to redden or grow hot. **b.** To turn red or make glow: Great bonfires inflamed the night. **4.** To produce inflammation in (a tissue or organ). **5.** To set on fire; kindle. —intr. **1.** To become excited or aroused. **2.** To be affected by inflammation. **3.** To catch fire. [Ult. < Lat. īnflammāre : in-, intensive pref.; see IN–² + flammāre, to set on fire (< flamma, flame; see **bhel-¹** in App.).] —**in·flam′er** n.

in·flam·ma·ble (ĭn-flăm′ə-bəl) adj. **1.** Easily ignited and capable of burning rapidly; flammable. **2.** Quickly or easily aroused to strong emotion; excitable. [Ult. < Lat. īnflammāre, to inflame. See INFLAME.] —**in·flam′ma·bil′i·ty** n. —**in·flam′ma·ble** n. —**in·flam′ma·bly** adv.

USAGE NOTE Historically, flammable and inflammable mean the same thing. However, the presence of the prefix in– has misled many people into assuming that inflammable means "not flammable" or "noncombustible." Use flammable to avoid ambiguity.

in·flam·ma·tion (ĭn′flə-mā′shən) n. **1.** The act of inflaming or the state of being inflamed. **2.** A localized protective reaction of tissue to irritation, injury, or infection, characterized by pain, redness, swelling, and sometimes loss of function.

in·flam·ma·to·ry (ĭn-flăm′ə-tôr′ē, -tōr′ē) adj. **1.** Arousing passion or strong emotion, such as anger. **2.** Characterized or caused by inflammation. —**in·flam′ma·to′ri·ly** adv.

inflammatory bowel disease n. Either of two chronic disorders of the gastrointestinal tract, esp. Crohn's disease or an ulcerative form of colitis, characterized by inflammation of the intestine and resulting in abdominal cramping and persistent diarrhea.

in·flat·a·ble (ĭn-flā′tə-bəl) adj. Designed to be filled with air or gas before use: an inflatable mattress. ❖ n. An object that can be filled with air or gas, esp.: **a.** A small rubber boat or raft. **b.** A large helium or hot-air balloon.

inflatable
Macy's Thanksgiving Day
Parade, New York City

in·flate (ĭn-flāt′) v. **-flat·ed, -flat·ing, -flates** —tr. **1.** To fill (something) with air or gas so as to make it swell. **2a.** To enlarge or amplify unduly or improperly; aggrandize. **b.** To raise or expand abnormally or improperly. See Syns at **exaggerate. 3.** To cause (a currency or an economy) to undergo inflation. —intr. To become inflated. [ME inflaten < Lat. īnflāre, īnflāt- : in-, in; see IN–² + flāre, to blow.] —**in·fla′tor, in·flat′er** n.

in·flat·ed (ĭn-flā′tĭd) adj. **1.** Filled or expanded by gas or air. **2.** Unduly enlarged or aggrandized; swollen: an inflated estimate. **3.** Full of empty or pretentious language; bombastic. **4.** Raised or expanded to abnormal levels: an inflated economy. **5.** Hollow and enlarged: an inflated calyx.

in·fla·tion (ĭn-flā′shən) n. **1.** The act of inflating or the state of being inflated. **2.** A persistent increase in the level of consumer prices or a persistent decline in the purchasing power of money, caused by an increase in available currency and credit beyond the proportion of available goods and services.

in·fla·tion·ar·y (ĭn-flā′shə-nĕr′ē) adj. Of, associated with, or tending to cause inflation: inflationary prices.

inflationary universe n. A model of the universe in which the early universe undergoes a period of exponentially rapid expansion, resulting in the high degree of homogeneity of the present-day universe.

in·fla·tion·ist (ĭn-flā′shə-nĭst) n. An advocate of deliberate inflation achieved by increasing available currency and credit. —**in·fla′tion·ism** n. —**in·fla′tion·ist** adj.

in·flect (ĭn-flĕkt′) v. **-flect·ed, -flect·ing, -flects** —tr. **1.** To alter (the voice) in tone or pitch; modulate. **2.** Grammar To alter (a word) by inflection. **3.** To turn from a course or a specified alignment; bend. —intr. Grammar **1.** To be modified by inflection. **2.** To give all of the inflected forms of a word; to provide a paradigm. [ME inflecten, to bend down < Lat. īnflectere : in-, in; see IN–² + flectere, to bend.] —**in·flec′tive** adj. —**in·flec′tor** n.

in·flec·tion (ĭn-flĕk′shən) n. **1.** The act of inflecting or the state of being inflected. **2.** Alteration in pitch or tone of the voice. **3.** Grammar **a.** An alteration of the form of a word by the addition of an affix or by changing the form of the base to indicate grammatical features such as number, person, mood, or tense. **b.** An affix indicating such a grammatical feature, as the –s in the English plural noun form books. **c.** The paradigm of a word. **d.** A pattern of forming paradigms. **4.** A turning or bending away from a course or position of alignment. —**in·flec′tion·al** adj. —**in·flec′tion·al·ly** adv.

in·flexed (ĭn-flĕkst′) adj. Bent or curved inward or downward, as petals. [< Lat. īnflexus, p. part. of īnflectere, to bend. See INFLECT.]

in·flex·i·ble (ĭn-flĕk′sə-bəl) adj. **1.** Not easily bent; stiff or rigid. See Syns at **stiff. 2.** Incapable of being changed; unalterable. **3.** Unyielding in purpose, principle, or temper; immovable. —**in·**

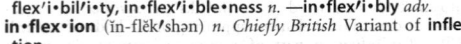

flex′i•bil′i•ty, in•flex′i•ble•ness n. —in•flex′i•bly adv.

in•flex•ion (ĭn-flĕk′shən) n. Chiefly British Variant of inflection.

in•flict (ĭn-flĭkt′) tr.v. -flict•ed, -flict•ing, -flicts 1. To deal or mete out (something punishing or burdensome); impose. 2. To afflict. [Lat. īnflīgere, īnflīct-: in-, on; see IN-² + flīgere, to strike.] —in•flict′er, in•flic′tor n.

in•flic•tion (ĭn-flĭk′shən) n. 1. The act or process of imposing or meting out something unpleasant. 2. Something, such as punishment, that is inflicted. —in•flic′tive adj.

in-flight (ĭn′flīt′) adj. 1. Occurring, carried out, or present while in flight. 2. Provided or offered during a flight.

in•flo•res•cence (ĭn′flə-rĕs′əns) n. 1a. A characteristic arrangement of flowers on a stem. b. A flower cluster. 2. A flowering. [NLat. īnflōrēscentia < LLat. īnflōrēscēns, īnflōrēscent-, pr. part. of īnflōrēscere, to begin to flower : Lat. in-, intensive pref.; see IN-² + Lat. flōrēscere, to begin to blossom; see FLORESCENCE.] —in′flo•res′cent adj.

in•flow (ĭn′flō′) n. 1. The act or process of flowing in or into. 2. Something that flows in or into: a freshwater inflow.

in•flu•ence (ĭn′flōō-əns) n. 1. A power affecting a person, thing, or course of events, esp. without direct or apparent effort. 2. Power to sway or affect based on prestige, wealth, ability, or position. 3a. A person who exerts influence: You are a bad influence on me. b. An effect or change produced by influence. 4. In astrology, a factor or group of factors determining one's tendencies and characteristics, believed to be caused by the positions of the stars and planets at the time of one's birth. ❖ tr.v. -enced, -enc•ing, -enc•es 1. To produce an effect on by imperceptible or intangible means; sway. 2. To affect the nature, development, or condition of; modify. —idiom: under the influence Intoxicated, esp. with alcohol. [ME < OFr. < Med.Lat. īnfluentia, influx < Lat. īnfluēns, īnfluent-, pr. part. of īnfluere, to flow in : in-, in; see IN-² + fluere, to flow.] —in′flu•ence•a•ble adj. —in′flu•enc•er n.

in•flu•ent (ĭn′flōō-ənt, ĭn-flōō′-) adj. Flowing in or into. ❖ n. 1. An inflow, esp. a tributary. 2. Ecology A nondominant organism in a community that modifies it in an important way. [ME < Lat. īnfluēns, īnfluent-, pr. part. of īnfluere, to flow in. See INFLUENCE.]

in•flu•en•tial (ĭn′flōō-ĕn′shəl) adj. Having or exercising influence. ❖ n. One that is of considerable importance or influence: policy influentials. —in′flu•en′tial•ly adv.

in•flu•en•za (ĭn′flōō-ĕn′zə) n. 1. An acute contagious viral infection characterized by inflammation of the respiratory tract and by fever, chills, muscular pain, and prostration. 2. Any of various viral infections of domestic animals characterized generally by fever and respiratory involvement. [Ital. < Med.Lat. īnfluentia, influence (so called apparently < the belief that epidemics were due to the influence of the stars). See INFLUENCE.] —in′flu•en′zal adj.

in•flux (ĭn′flŭks′) n. 1. A flowing in: an influx of capital. 2. A mass arrival or incoming: an influx of visitors. [LLat. īnflūxus < Lat., p. part. of īnfluere, to flow in. See INFLUENCE.]

in•fo (ĭn′fō) n. Informal Information.

in•fold (ĭn-fōld′) v. -fold•ed, -fold•ing, -folds —intr. To fold inward. —tr. To enfold. —in•fold′er n. —in•fold′ment n.

in•fo•mer•cial (ĭn′fə-mûr′shəl) n. A television program that provides information about a product or service; a commercial having the format of a regular program. [INFO(RMATION) + (COM)MERCIAL.]

in•form (ĭn-fôrm′) v. -formed, -form•ing, -forms —tr. 1a. To impart information to; make aware of something. b. To acquaint (oneself) with knowledge of a subject. 2. To give form or character to; imbue with a quality or an essence. 3. To be a pervasive presence in; animate. 4. Obsolete To form (the mind or character) by teaching or training. —intr. 1. To give or provide information. 2. To disclose confidential or incriminating information to an authority. [ME enfourmen, informen < OFr. enfourmer < Lat. īnfōrmāre : in-, in; see IN-² + fōrmāre, to fashion (< fōrma, form).]

in•for•mal (ĭn-fôr′məl) adj. 1. Not formal or ceremonious; casual. 2. Not being in accord with prescribed regulations or forms; unofficial. 3. Suited for everyday wear or use. 4. Being more appropriate for use in the spoken language than in the written language. —in•for′mal•ly adv.

in•for•mal•i•ty (ĭn′fôr-măl′ĭ-tē) n., pl. -ties 1. The state or quality of being informal. 2. An informal act.

in•for•mant (ĭn-fôr′mənt) n. 1a. One that gives information. b. One who informs against others; an informer. 2. One who furnishes linguistic or cultural information to a researcher.

in•for•mat•ics (ĭn′fər-măt′ĭks) n. (used with a sing. verb) Information science. [INFORMAT(ION) + -ICS.]

in•for•ma•tion (ĭn′fər-mā′shən) n. 1. Knowledge derived from study, experience, or instruction. 2. Knowledge of a specific event or situation; intelligence or news. 3. A collection of facts or data: statistical information. 4. The act of informing or the condition of being informed; communication of knowledge: for the information of our passengers. 5. Computer Science Processed, stored, or transmitted data. 6. A numerical measure of the uncertainty of an experimental outcome. 7. Law A formal accusation of a crime made by a public officer rather than by grand jury indictment. —in′for•ma′tion•al adj.

information age n. The period beginning around 1970 and noted for the abundant publication, consumption, and manipulation of information, esp. by computers and computer networks.

information science n. The science that is concerned with the gathering, manipulation, classification, storage, and retrieval of recorded knowledge.

information superhighway n. The global information and communications network that includes the Internet and other networks and switching systems such as telephone and cable television networks.

information technology n. The development, installation, and implementation of computer systems and applications.

information theory n. The theory of the probability of transmission of messages with specified accuracy when the bits of information constituting the messages are subject, with certain probabilities, to transmission errors and noise.

in•for•ma•tive (ĭn-fôr′mə-tĭv) adj. Serving to inform; providing or disclosing information; instructive. —in•for′ma•tive•ly adv. —in•for′ma•tive•ness n.

in•for•ma•to•ry (ĭn-fôr′mə-tôr′ē, -tôr′ē) adj. Informative.

in•formed (ĭn-fôrmd′) adj. 1. Possessing, displaying, or based on reliable information. 2. Knowledgeable; educated.

informed consent n. Consent by a patient to a surgical or medical procedure or participation in a clinical study after understanding the medical facts and the risks involved.

in•form•er (ĭn-fôr′mər) n. An informant, esp. one who informs against others, often for compensation.

infra– pref. Inferior to, below, or beneath: infrasonic. [< Lat. īnfrā, below. See ņdher- in App.]

in•fra•class (ĭn′frə-klăs′) n. A taxonomic category of related organisms ranking below a subclass and above an order.

in•fract (ĭn-frăkt′) tr.v. -fract•ed, -fract•ing, -fracts To infringe; violate. [Lat. īnfringere, īnfrāct-, to destroy. See INFRINGE.] —in•frac′tor n.

in•frac•tion (ĭn-frăk′shən) n. The act or an instance of infringing; a violation. See Syns at breach.

in•fra dig (ĭn′frə dĭg′) adj. Beneath one's dignity. [Short for Lat. īnfrā dignitātem : īnfrā, below + dignitātem, dignity.]

in•fra•hu•man (ĭn′frə-hyōō′mən) adj. Of a lower order than humans; subhuman. —in′fra•hu′man n.

in•fran•gi•ble (ĭn-frăn′jə-bəl) adj. 1. Difficult or impossible to break or separate into parts. 2. Inviolable: infrangible human rights. [LLat. īnfrangibilis : Lat. in-, not; see IN-¹ + Lat. frangere, to break; see bhreg- in App.] —in•fran′gi•bil′i•ty, —in•fran′gi•bly adv.

in•fra•red (ĭn′frə-rĕd′) adj. 1. Of or relating to the range of invisible radiation wavelengths from about 750 nanometers, just longer than red in the visible spectrum, to 1 millimeter, on the border of the microwave region. 2. Generating, using, or sensitive to infrared radiation. ❖ n. Infrared light or the infrared part of the spectrum.

in•fra•son•ic (ĭn′frə-sŏn′ĭk) adj. Generating or using waves or vibrations with frequencies below that of audible sound.

in•fra•sound (ĭn′frə-sound′) n. Vibrations of the air with frequencies below that of human hearing.

in•fra•struc•ture (ĭn′frə-strŭk′chər) n. 1. An underlying base or foundation, esp. for an organization or a system. 2. The basic facilities, services, and installations needed for the functioning of a community or society, such as transportation and communications systems.

in•fre•quent (ĭn-frē′kwənt) adj. 1. Not occurring regularly; occasional or rare: an infrequent guest. 2. Situated or placed at rather wide intervals, as in time or space. —in•fre′quence, in•fre′quen•cy n. —in•fre′quent•ly adv.

in•fringe (ĭn-frĭnj′) v. -fringed, -fring•ing, -fring•es —tr. 1. To transgress or exceed the limits of; violate: infringe a contract. 2. Obsolete To defeat; invalidate. —intr. To encroach on someone or something. [Lat. īnfringere, to destroy : in-, intensive pref.; see IN-² + frangere, to break; see bhreg- in App.] —in•fring′er n.

in•fringe•ment (ĭn-frĭnj′mənt) n. 1. A violation, as of a law, regulation, or agreement; a breach. 2. An encroachment, as of a right or privilege. See Syns at breach.

in•fruc•tes•cence (ĭn′frŭk-tĕs′əns) n. The fruiting stage of an inflorescence. [Fr. : Lat. in-, in; see IN-² + Lat. frūctus, fruit; see FRUIT.]

in•fun•dib•u•li•form (ĭn′fən-dĭb′yə-lə-fôrm′) adj. Shaped like a funnel.

in•fun•dib•u•lum (ĭn′fən-dĭb′yə-ləm) n., pl. -la (-lə) Any of various funnel-shaped body passages, openings, or parts, esp. a. The stalk of the pituitary gland. b. The calyx of a kidney. c. The ovarian opening of a fallopian tube. [Lat., funnel < īnfundere, to pour in. See INFUSE.] —in′fun•dib′u•lar (-lər), in′fun•dib′u•late′ (-lāt′, -lĭt) adj.

in•fu•ri•ate (ĭn-fyŏŏr′ē-āt′) tr.v. -at•ed, -at•ing, -ates To make furious; enrage. ❖ adj. Archaic Furious. [Med.Lat. īnfuriāre, īnfuriāt-: Lat. in-, intensive pref.; see IN-² + Lat. furiāre, to enrage (< furia, fury; see FURY).] —in•fu′ri•at′ing•ly adv. —in•fu′ri•a′tion n.

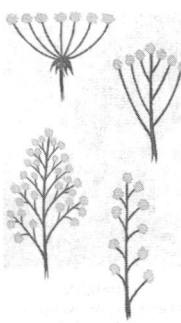

inflorescence
top left to right: umbel and corymb
bottom left to right: panicle and raceme

infundibuliform
petunia blossom

ingot
gold ingot

in•fuse (ĭn-fyo͞oz′) *tr.v.* **-fused, -fus•ing, -fus•es 1.** To put into or introduce as if by pouring. **2.** To fill or cause to be filled with something. **3.** *Chemistry* To steep or soak without boiling in order to extract soluble elements or active principles. **4.** To flavor or scent (a liquid) by steeping ingredients in it. **5.** To introduce (a solution) into the body through a vein for therapeutic purposes. [ME *infusen* < OFr. *infuser* < Lat. *īnfundere, īnfūs-* : *in-*, in; see IN–[2] + *fundere*, to pour; see **gheu-** in App.] **—in•fus′er** *n.* **—in•fus′i•bil′i•ty** *n.* **—in•fus′i•ble** *adj.*

in•fu•sion (ĭn-fyo͞o′zhən) *n.* **1.** The act or process of infusing. **2.** Something infused or introduced. **3.** The liquid product obtained by infusing: *an infusion of medicinal herbs.* **4a.** Introduction of a solution into the body through a vein for therapeutic purposes. **b.** The solution so introduced.

-ing[1] *suff.* **1.** Used to form the present participle of verbs: *seeing.* **2.** Used to form adjectives resembling present participles but not derived from verbs: *swashbuckling.* [ME, alteration (influenced by *-inge*, noun or gerund suff.; see –ING[2]) of *-ende, -inde* < OE *-ende*, pr.part. suff.]

-ing[2] *suff.* **1a.** Action, process, or art: *dancing.* **b.** An instance of an action, process, or art: *a gathering.* **2.** An action or process connected with a specified thing: *berrying.* **3a.** Something necessary to perform an action or process: *mooring.* **b.** The result of an action or process: *a drawing.* **c.** Something connected with a specified thing or concept: *siding; offing.* [ME < OE *-ung, -ing.*]

-ing[3] *suff.* One having a specified quality or nature: *sweeting.* [ME < OE, belonging to, descended from.]

in•gath•er (ĭn′găth′ər) *v.* **-ered, -er•ing, -ers** *—tr.* To gather in; collect. *—intr.* To come together in a central place.

Inge (ĭnj), **William** 1913–73. Amer. playwright whose dramas include *Picnic* (1953).

in•gen•ious (ĭn-jēn′yəs) *adj.* **1.** Marked by inventive skill and imagination. **2.** Having or arising from an inventive or cunning mind; clever: *an ingenious scheme.* See Syns at **clever. 3.** *Obsolete* Having genius; brilliant. [ME < OFr. *ingenios* < Lat. *ingeniōsus* < *ingenium*, inborn talent. See **genə-** in App.] **—in•gen′ious•ly** *adv.* **—in•gen′ious•ness** *n.*

in•gé•nue also **in•ge•nue** (ăN′zhə-no͞o′) *n.* **1.** A naive, innocent girl or young woman. **2a.** The role of an ingénue in a dramatic production. **b.** An actress playing such a role. [Fr., fem. of *ingénu*, guileless < Lat. *ingenuus*, ingenuous. See INGENUOUS.]

in•ge•nu•i•ty (ĭn′jə-no͞o′ĭ-tē, -nyo͞o′-) *n., pl.* **-ties 1.** Inventive skill or imagination; cleverness. **2.** Imaginative and clever design or construction. **3.** An ingenious or imaginative contrivance. **4.** *Obsolete* Ingenuousness. [Lat. *ingenuitās*, frankness (influenced by INGENIOUS) < *ingenuus*, ingenuous. See INGENUOUS.]

in•gen•u•ous (ĭn-jĕn′yo͞o-əs) *adj.* **1.** Lacking in cunning, guile, or worldliness; artless. **2.** Openly straightforward or frank; candid. See Syns at **naive. 3.** *Obsolete* Ingenious. [< Lat. *ingenuus*, honest, freeborn. See **genə-** in App.] **—in•gen′u•ous•ly** *adv.* **—in•gen′u•ous•ness** *n.*

in•gest (ĭn-jĕst′) *tr.v.* **-gest•ed, -gest•ing, -gests** To take or absorb (food) into the body. [Lat. *ingerere, ingest-* : *in-*, in; see IN–[2] + *gerere*, to carry.] **—in•gest′i•ble** *adj.* **—in•ges′tion** *n.* **—in•ges′tive** *adj.*

in•ges•ta (ĭn-jĕs′tə) *pl.n.* Ingested matter, esp. food taken into the body through the mouth. [NLat. < neut. pl. of Lat. *ingestus*, p. part. of *ingerere*, to carry in. See INGEST.]

in•gle (ĭng′gəl) *n.* **1.** An open fire in a fireplace. **2.** A fireplace. [Perh. Sc. Gael. *aingeal*, fire, light.]

in•gle•nook (ĭng′gəl-no͝ok′) *n.* **1.** A nook or corner beside an open fireplace. **2.** A bench, esp. either of two facing benches, placed in a nook or corner beside a fireplace.

In•gle•wood (ĭng′gəl-wo͝od′) A city of S CA, a suburb of Los Angeles. Pop. 112,580.

in•glo•ri•ous (ĭn-glôr′ē-əs, -glōr′-) *adj.* **1.** Ignominious; disgraceful. **2.** Not famous or renowned; obscure. **—in•glo′ri•ous•ly** *adv.* **—in•glo′ri•ous•ness** *n.*

in•go•ing (ĭn′gō′ĭng) *adj.* Going in; entering.

in•got (ĭng′gət) *n.* **1.** A mass of metal cast in a standard shape for convenient storage or shipment. **2.** A casting mold for metal. [ME, mold for casting metal : prob. *in-*, in; see IN–[2] + OE *goten*, p. part. of *geotan*, to pour, or perh. < OFr. *lingot*, metal ingot (interpreted as *l'ingot* : *le*, the + **ingot*, ingot).]

ingot iron *n.* A bar of iron that contains small quantities of other elements.

in•grain (ĭn-grān′) *tr.v.* **-grained, -grain•ing, -grains 1.** To fix deeply or indelibly, as in the mind. **2.** *Archaic* To dye or stain into the fiber of. ❖ *adj.* (ĭn′grān′) **1.** Deep-seated; ingrained. **2.** Made of predyed fibers; thoroughly dyed. **3.** Made of fiber or yarn dyed before weaving, as a rug. ❖ *n.* (ĭn′grān′) **1.** Yarn or fiber dyed before manufacture. **2.** An ingrain rug or carpet. [Variant of ENGRAIN.]

in•grained (ĭn-grānd′) *adj.* **1.** Firmly established; deep-seated. **2.** Worked deeply into the texture or fiber.

in•grate (ĭn′grāt′) *n.* An ungrateful person. [< ME *ingrat*, ungrateful < OFr. < Lat. *ingrātus* : *in-*, not; see IN–[1] + *grātus*, pleasing, thankful.]

in•gra•ti•ate (ĭn-grā′shē-āt′) *tr.v.* **-at•ed, -at•ing, -ates** To bring (oneself, for example) into another's favor, esp. deliberately. [Perh. < Ital. *ingraziare* < *in grazia*, into favor < Lat. *in grātiam* : *in*, in; see IN–[2] + *grātiam*, accusative of *grātia*, favor (< *grātus*, pleasing).] **—in•gra′ti•a′tion** *n.* **—in•gra′ti•a•to′ry** (-shē-ə-tôr′ē, -tōr′ē) *adj.*

in•gra•ti•at•ing (ĭn-grā′shē-ā′tĭng) *adj.* **1.** Pleasing; agreeable. **2.** Calculated to please or win favor. **—in•gra′ti•at′ing•ly** *adv.*

in•grat•i•tude (ĭn-grăt′ĭ-to͞od′, -tyo͞od′) *n.* Lack of gratitude.

in•gre•di•ent (ĭn-grē′dē-ənt) *n.* An element in a mixture or compound; a constituent. See Syns at **element.** [ME < Lat. *ingrediēns, ingredient-*, pr. part. of *ingredī*, to enter. See INGRESS.]

In•gres (ăN′grə), **Jean Auguste Dominique** 1780–1867. French painter best known for his historical works.

in•gress (ĭn′grĕs′) *n.* **1.** also **in•gres•sion** (ĭn-grĕsh′ən) A going in or entering. **2.** Right or permission to enter. **3.** A means or place of entering. [ME *ingresse* < Lat. *ingressus* < p. part. of *ingredī*, to enter : *in-*, in; see IN–[2] + *gradī*, to step; see **ghredh-** in App.]

in•gres•sive (ĭn-grĕs′ĭv) *adj.* **1.** Of, relating to, or involving ingress. **2.** *Grammar* Inchoative. **3.** *Linguistics* Of or being a speech sound produced with an inhalation of breath. **—in•gres′sive** *n.* **—in•gres′sive•ness** *n.*

in-group (ĭn′gro͞op′) *n.* A group of people united by common beliefs, attitudes, or interests and usu. excluding outsiders.

in•grow•ing (ĭn′grō′ĭng) *adj.* Growing inward or into, esp. into the flesh.

in•grown (ĭn′grōn′) *adj.* **1.** Grown abnormally into the flesh. **2.** Inbred; innate. **3.** Insular; self-contained.

in•growth (ĭn′grōth′) *n.* **1.** The act of growing inward or into. **2.** Something that grows inward or into.

in•gui•nal (ĭng′gwə-nəl) *adj.* Of, relating to, or located in the groin. [Lat. *inguinālis* < *inguen, inguin-*, groin.]

in•gur•gi•tate (ĭn-gûr′jĭ-tāt′) *tr.v.* **-tat•ed, -tat•ing, -tates** To swallow greedily or in excessive amounts; gulp. [Lat. *ingurgitāre, ingurgitāt-* : *in-*, in; see IN–[2] + *gurges, gurgit-*, throat, whirlpool.] **—in•gur′gi•ta′tion** *n.*

In•gush (ĭn′go͞osh, ĭng′-) *n., pl.* **Ingush** or **-gush•es 1.** A native or inhabitant of Ingushetia. **2.** The Caucasian language of the Ingush.

In•gu•she•ti•a (ĭn′go͞o-shē′tē-ə, ĭng′-) An autonomous republic of SW Russia in the N Caucasus W of Chechnya.

in•hab•it (ĭn-hăb′ĭt) *v.* **-it•ed, -it•ing, -its** *—tr.* **1.** To live or reside in. **2.** To be present in; fill. *—intr. Archaic* To dwell. [ME *enhabiten* < OFr. *enhabiter* < Lat. *inhabitāre* : *in-*, in; see IN–[2] + *habitāre*, to dwell, freq. of *habēre*, to have; see **ghabh-** in App.] **—in•hab′it•a•bil′i•ty** *n.* **—in•hab′it•a•ble** *adj.* **—in•hab′i•ta′tion** *n.* **—in•hab′it•er** *n.*

in•hab•i•tan•cy (ĭn-hăb′ĭ-tən-sē) *n., pl.* **-cies** Occupancy.

in•hab•i•tant (ĭn-hăb′ĭ-tənt) *n.* One that inhabits a place, esp. as a permanent resident: *the inhabitants of a village.*

in•hab•it•ed (ĭn-hăb′ĭ-tĭd) *adj.* Having inhabitants; lived in.

in•ha•lant (ĭn-hā′lənt) *adj.* Used in or for inhaling. ❖ *n.* **1.** Something inhaled. **2.** A medication or other compound in vapor or aerosol form, taken by inhalation.

in•ha•la•tion (ĭn′hə-lā′shən) *n.* **1.** The act or an instance of inhaling. **2.** An inhalant.

in•ha•la•tor (ĭn′hə-lā′tər) *n.* **1.** See **respirator** 1. **2.** See **inhaler** 2.

in•hale (ĭn-hāl′) *v.* **-haled, -hal•ing, -hales** *—tr.* **1.** To draw (air or smoke, for example) into the lungs by breathing; inspire. **2.** *Informal* To consume rapidly or eagerly; devour. *—intr.* **1.** To breathe in; inspire. **2.** To draw smoke into the lungs; puff. [Lat. *inhālāre*, to breathe upon : *in-*, in; see IN–[2] + *hālāre*, to breathe.]

in•hal•er (ĭn-hā′lər) *n.* **1.** One that inhales. **2.** A device that produces a vapor to ease breathing or is used to medicate by inhalation.

in•har•mon•ic (ĭn′här-mŏn′ĭk) *adj.* Not harmonic; discordant.

in•har•mo•ni•ous (ĭn′här-mō′nē-əs) *adj.* **1.** Not in harmony; discordant. **2.** Not in accord or agreement. **—in′har•mo′ni•ous•ly** *adv.* **—in′har•mo′ni•ous•ness** *n.*

in•har•mo•ny (ĭn-här′mə-nē) *n., pl.* **-nies 1.** Lack of harmony; discord. **2.** An instance of such discord.

in•here (ĭn-hîr′) *intr.v.* **-hered, -her•ing, -heres** To be inherent or innate. [Lat. *inhaerēre* : *in-*, in; see IN–[2] + *haerēre*, to stick.] **—in•her′ence** (-hîr′əns, -hĕr′-), **in•her′en•cy** *n.*

in•her•ent (ĭn-hîr′ənt, -hĕr′-) *adj.* Existing as an essential constituent or characteristic; intrinsic. [Lat. *inhaerēns, inhaerent-*, pr. part. of *inhaerēre*, to inhere. See INHERE.] **—in•her′ent•ly** *adv.*

in•her•it (ĭn-hĕr′ĭt) *v.* **-it•ed, -it•ing, -its** *—tr.* **1a.** To receive (property or a title, for example) from an ancestor by legal succession or will. **b.** To receive by bequest or as a legacy. **2.** To receive or take over from a predecessor. **3.** *Biology* To receive (a characteristic) from one's parents by genetic transmission. **4.** To gain (something) as one's right or portion. *—intr.* To hold or take possession of an inheritance. [ME *enheriten* < OFr. *enheriter*, to make heir to < LLat. *inhērēditāre* : Lat. *in-*, in; see IN–[2] + LLat. *hērēditāre* (< Lat. *hērēs, hērēd-*, heir; see **ghē-** in App.).] **—in•her′i•tor** *n.*

in•her•it•a•ble (ĭn-hĕr′ĭ-tə-bəl) *adj.* **1.** That can be inherited. **2.** Having the right to inherit or the capability of inheriting. **—in•her′it•a•bil′i•ty** *n.*

in•her•i•tance (ĭn-hĕr′ĭ-təns) *n.* **1a.** The act of inheriting. **b.** Something inherited or to be inherited. **2.** Something regarded as

Jean Auguste Dominique Ingres
self-portrait, painted in 1804 and re-painted in 1850

ă	pat	oi	boy
ā	pay	ou	out
âr	care	o͝o	took
ä	father	o͞o	boot
ĕ	pet	ŭ	cut
ē	be	ûr	urge
ĭ	pit	th	thin
ī	pie	*th*	this
îr	pier	hw	which
ŏ	pot	zh	vision
ō	toe	ə	about, item
ô	paw		

Stress marks:
′ (primary);
′ (secondary), as in
lexicon (lĕk′sĭ-kŏn′)

inkstand
used at the signing of the US Constitution, Independence Hall, Philadelphia, Pennsylvania

inky cap

inlay
section of the floor of St. Mark's Basilica, Venice, Italy

a heritage. **3.** *Biology* **a.** The process of genetic transmission of characteristics from parents to offspring. **b.** A characteristic so inherited. **c.** The sum of characteristics genetically transmitted from parents to offspring.

inheritance tax *n.* A tax imposed on the privilege of receiving property by inheritance or legal succession and assessed on the value of the property received.

in•hib•in (ĭn-hĭb′ĭn) *n.* A peptide hormone that acts to inhibit secretion of follicle stimulating hormone from the pituitary gland.

in•hib•it (ĭn-hĭb′ĭt) *tr.v.* **-it•ed, -it•ing, -its 1.** To hold back; restrain. **2.** To prohibit; forbid. **3.** *Psychology* To suppress or restrain (an impulse, for example) consciously or unconsciously. **4a.** *Chemistry* To prevent or decrease the rate of (a reaction). **b.** *Biology* To decrease, limit, or block the action or function of (an enzyme, for example). [ME *inhibiten*, to forbid < Lat. *inhibēre*, *inhibit-*, to restrain, forbid : *in-*, in; see IN–[2] + *habēre*, to hold; see **ghabh-** in App.] **—in•hib′it•a•ble** *adj.* **—in•hib′i•tive, in•hib′i•to′ry** (-tôr′ē, -tōr′ē) *adj.*

in•hi•bi•tion (ĭn′hə-bĭsh′ən, ĭn′ə-) *n.* **1.** The act of inhibiting or the state of being inhibited. **2.** Something that restrains, blocks, or suppresses. **3.** *Psychology* Conscious or unconscious restraint of a behavioral process, a desire, or an impulse. **4a.** *Chemistry* The condition in which or the process by which a reaction is inhibited. **b.** *Biology* The condition in which or the process by which an enzyme, for example, is inhibited.

in•hib•i•tor also **in•hib•it•er** (ĭn-hĭb′ĭ-tər) *n.* One that inhibits, as a substance that retards or stops a chemical reaction.

in•hold•ing (ĭn′hōl′dĭng) *n.* A privately owned parcel of land within the boundaries of a federal preserve. **—in′hold′er** *n.*

in•ho•mo•ge•ne•i•ty (ĭn-hō′mə-jə-nē′ĭ-tē, -nā′-, hŏm′ə-) *n., pl.* **-ties 1.** Lack of homogeneity. **2.** Something that is not homogeneous or uniform.

in•hos•pi•ta•ble (ĭn-hŏs′pĭ-tə-bəl, ĭn′hŏ-spĭt′ə-bəl) *adj.* **1.** Displaying no hospitality; unfriendly. **2.** Unfavorable to life or growth; hostile: *the barren, inhospitable desert.* **—in•hos′pi•ta•ble•ness** *n.* **—in•hos′pi•ta•bly** *adv.*

in•hos•pi•tal•i•ty (ĭn′hŏs-pĭ-tăl′ĭ-tē) *n.* Lack of hospitality or friendliness.

in-house (ĭn′hous′) *adj.* Conducted within, coming from, or being within an organization or group. **—in′-house′** *adv.*

in•hu•man (ĭn-hyo͞o′mən) *adj.* **1a.** Lacking kindness, pity, or compassion; cruel. See Syns at **cruel. b.** Deficient in emotional warmth; cold. **2.** Not suited for human needs: *an inhuman environment.* **3.** Not of ordinary human form; monstrous. **—in•hu′man•ly** *adv.* **—in•hu′man•ness** *n.*

in•hu•mane (ĭn′hyo͞o-mān′) *adj.* Lacking pity or compassion. **—in′hu•mane′ly** *adv.*

in•hu•man•i•ty (ĭn′hyo͞o-măn′ĭ-tē) *n., pl.* **-ties 1.** Lack of pity or compassion. **2.** An inhuman or cruel act.

in•hume (ĭn-hyo͞om′) *tr.v.* **-humed, -hum•ing, -humes** To place in a grave; bury. [Fr. *inhumer* < OFr. < Lat. *inhumāre* : *in-*, in; see IN–[2] + *humus*, earth; see **dhghem-** in App.] **—in′hu•ma′tion** *n.* **—in•hum′er** *n.*

in•im•i•cal (ĭ-nĭm′ĭ-kəl) *adj.* **1.** Injurious or harmful in effect; adverse. **2.** Unfriendly; hostile. [LLat. *inimīcālis* < Lat. *inimīcus*, enemy. See ENEMY.] **—in•im′i•cal•ly** *adv.*

in•im•i•ta•ble (ĭ-nĭm′ĭ-tə-bəl) *adj.* Defying imitation; matchless. [ME < Lat. *inimitābilis* : *in-*, not; see IN–[1] + *imitābilis*, imitable (< *imitārī*, to imitate; see **aim-** in App.).] **—in•im′i•ta•bil′i•ty, in•im′i•ta•ble•ness** *n.* **—in•im′i•ta•bly** *adv.*

in•i•on (ĭn′ē-ən) *n.* The most prominent projecting point of the occipital bone at the base of the skull. [Gk. *īnion*, occipital bone < *īs*, *īn-*, sinew, fiber.]

in•iq•ui•tous (ĭ-nĭk′wĭ-təs) *adj.* Characterized by iniquity; wicked. **—in•iq′ui•tous•ly** *adv.* **—in•iq′ui•tous•ness** *n.*

in•iq•ui•ty (ĭ-nĭk′wĭ-tē) *n., pl.* **-ties 1.** Gross immorality or injustice; wickedness. **2.** A grossly immoral act; a sin. [ME *iniquite* < OFr. < Lat. *inīquitās* < *inīquus*, unjust, harmful : *in-*, not; see IN–[1] + *aequus*, equal.]

in•i•tial (ĭ-nĭsh′əl) *adj.* **1.** Of, relating to, or occurring at the beginning; first: *took the initial step toward peace.* **2.** Being the first letter or letters of a word. ❖ *n.* **1a.** The first letter of a proper name. **b. initials** The first letter of each word of a person's complete name considered as a unit. **2.** The first letter of a word. **3.** A large, often highly decorated letter set at the beginning of a chapter, verse, or paragraph. ❖ *tr.v.* **-tialed, -tial•ing, -tials** also **-tialled, -tial•ling, -tials** To mark or sign with initials, esp. for purposes of authorization or approval. [Lat. *initiālis* < *initium*, beginning. See **ei-** in App.] **—in•i′tial•ly** *adv.*

in•i•tial•ism (ĭ-nĭsh′ə-lĭz′əm) *n.* An abbreviation consisting of the first letter or letters of words in a phrase (for example, *IRS* for *Internal Revenue Service*), syllables or components of a word (*TNT* for *trinitrotoluene*), or a combination of words and syllables (*ESP* for *extrasensory perception*) and pronounced by spelling out the letters one by one rather than as a solid word.

in•i•tial•ize (ĭ-nĭsh′ə-līz′) *tr.v.* **-ized, -iz•ing, -iz•es** *Computer Science* **1.** To set (a starting value of a variable). **2.** To prepare (a computer or printer) for use; boot. **3.** To format (a storage medium, such as a disk). **—in•i′tial•i•za′tion** (-shə-lĭ-zā′shən) *n.* **—in•i′tial•iz′er** *n.*

initial rhyme *n.* See **beginning rhyme.**

in•i•ti•ate (ĭ-nĭsh′ē-āt′) *tr.v.* **-at•ed, -at•ing, -ates 1.** To set going by taking the first step; begin: *initiated trade with developing nations.* **2.** To introduce to a new field, interest, skill, or activity. **3.** To admit into membership, as with ritual. ❖ *adj.* (-ĭt) **1.** Initiated or admitted, as to membership. **2a.** Instructed in esoteric knowledge. **b.** Introduced to something new. ❖ *n.* (-ĭt) **1.** One who is being or has been initiated. **2.** One who has been introduced to or has attained knowledge in a particular field. [Lat. *initiāre*, *initiāt-* < *initium*, beginning. See **ei-** in App.] **—in•i′ti•a′tor** *n.*

in•i•ti•a•tion (ĭ-nĭsh′ē-ā′shən) *n.* **1a.** The act or an instance of initiating. **b.** The process of being initiated. **c.** The condition of being initiated. **2.** A ceremony, test, or period of instruction marking admission, as to an organization. **3.** The condition of being knowledgeable.

in•i•tia•tive (ĭ-nĭsh′ə-tĭv) *n.* **1.** The power or ability to begin or follow through energetically with a plan or task; enterprise and determination. **2.** A beginning or introductory step; an opening move. **3a.** The power or right to introduce a new legislative measure. **b.** The right and procedure by which citizens can propose a law by petition and ensure its submission to the electorate. ❖ *adj.* **1.** Of or relating to initiation. **2.** Used to initiate; initiatory. ***—idiom:* on (one's) own initiative** Without prompting or direction from others; on one's own. **—in•i′tia•tive•ly** *adv.*

in•i•ti•a•to•ry (ĭ-nĭsh′ē-ə-tôr′ē, -tōr′ē) *adj.* **1.** Introductory; initial. **2.** Tending or used to initiate.

in•ject (ĭn-jĕkt′) *tr.v.* **-ject•ed, -ject•ing, -jects 1.** To force or drive (a fluid) into something. **2a.** *Medicine* To introduce (a drug, for example) into a body part, esp. by a syringe. **b.** To treat by means of injection: *injected the patient with digitalis.* **3.** To introduce into conversation or consideration. **4.** To place into an orbit, trajectory, or stream. [Lat. *inicere*, *iniect-*, to throw in : *in-*, in; see IN–[2] + *iacere*, to throw.] **—in•jec′tor** *n.*

in•ject•a•ble (ĭn-jĕk′tə-bəl) *adj.* That can be injected. Used of a drug. **—in•ject′a•ble** *n.*

in•jec•tion (ĭn-jĕk′shən) *n.* **1.** The act of injecting. **2.** Something injected, esp. a dose of medicine injected into the body.

in-joke (ĭn′jōk′) *n. Informal* A joke originated or appreciated by the members of a particular group.

in•ju•di•cious (ĭn′jo͞o-dĭsh′əs) *adj.* Lacking or showing a lack of judgment or discretion; unwise. **—in′ju•di′cious•ly** *adv.* **—in′ju•di′cious•ness** *n.*

in•junc•tion (ĭn-jŭngk′shən) *n.* **1.** The act or an instance of enjoining; a command, directive, or order. **2.** *Law* A court order prohibiting a party from a specific course of action. [ME *injunccion* < LLat. *iniūnctiō*, *iniūnctiōn-* < Lat. *iniūnctus*, p. part. of *iniungere*, to enjoin : *in-*, in; see IN–[2] + *iungere*, to join; see **yeug-** in App.] **—in•junc′tive** *adj.*

in•jure (ĭn′jər) *tr.v.* **-jured, -jur•ing, -jures 1.** To cause physical harm to; hurt. **2.** To cause damage to; impair. **3.** To cause distress to; wound. **4.** To commit an injustice or offense against; wrong. [ME *injuren*, to wrong < OFr. *injurier* < Lat. *iniūriārī* < *iniūria*, a wrong. See INJURY.] **—in′jur•er** *n.*

in•ju•ri•ous (ĭn-jo͝or′ē-əs) *adj.* **1.** Causing or tending to cause injury; harmful. **2.** Slanderous; libelous. **—in•ju′ri•ous•ly** *adv.* **—in•ju′ri•ous•ness** *n.*

in•ju•ry (ĭn′jə-rē) *n., pl.* **-ries 1.** Damage or harm. **2.** A particular form of hurt, damage, or loss. **3.** *Law* Violation of the rights of another party for which legal redress is available. **4.** *Obsolete* An insult. [ME *injurie* < AN < Lat. *iniūria*, a wrong, injustice < fem. of *iniūrius*, unjust : *in-*, not; see IN–[1] + *iūs*, *iūr-*, law.]

in•jus•tice (ĭn-jŭs′tĭs) *n.* **1.** Violation of another's rights or of what is right; lack of justice. **2.** A specific unjust act; a wrong. [ME < OFr. < Lat. *iniūstitia* < *iniūstus*, unjust : *in-*, not; see IN–[1] + *iūstus*, just; see JUST[1].]

ink (ĭngk) *n.* **1.** A pigmented liquid or paste used esp. for writing or printing. **2.** A dark liquid ejected for protection by most cephalopods. **3.** *Informal* Coverage in the print media; publicity. ❖ *tr.v.* **inked, ink•ing, inks 1.** To mark, coat, or stain with ink. **2.** *Informal* To append one's signature to (a contract, for example). [ME *inke* < OFr. *enque* < LLat. *encaustum*, purple ink < Gk. *enkauston*, painted in encaustic < *enkaiein*, to paint in encaustic, burn in. See ENCAUSTIC.] **—ink′er** *n.* **—ink′i•ness** *n.* **—ink′y** *adj.*

In•ka (ĭng′kə) *n.* Variant of **Inca.**

In•kan (ĭng′kən) *adj. & n.* Variant of **Incan.**

ink•ber•ry (ĭngk′bĕr′ē) *n.* **1.** A North American shrub *(Ilex glabra)* having black berrylike fruit. **2.** Its fruit.

ink•blot (ĭngk′blŏt′) *n.* **1.** A blotted pattern of spilled ink. **2.** A pattern resembling an inkblot used in inkblot tests.

inkblot test *n.* A psychological test in which a subject's interpretation of inkblots is analyzed.

ink•horn (ĭngk′hôrn′) *n.* A small container made of horn or a similar material, formerly used to hold ink for writing. ❖ *adj.* Affectedly or ostentatiously learned; pedantic.

ink-jet printer (ĭngk′jĕt′) *n.* A printer that forms an image by using electromagnetic fields to guide electrically charged ink streams onto the page.

in•kle (ĭng′kəl) *n.* **1.** A colored linen tape woven on a simple narrow loom and used for trimmings. **2.** The yarn or thread used in making this tape. [?]

in·kling (ĭng′klĭng) n. **1.** A slight hint or indication. **2.** A slight understanding or vague idea or notion. [Prob. alteration of ME *(a) ningkiling*, (a) hint, suggestion, poss. alteration of *nikking* < *nikken*, to mark a text for correction < *nik*, notch, tally, perh. < var. of OFr. *niche*, niche. See NICHE.]

ink·stand (ĭngk′stănd′) n. **1.** A tray or rack for pens and bottles of ink. **2.** See **inkwell**.

ink·well (ĭngk′wĕl′) n. A small reservoir for ink.

inky cap n. Any of various mushrooms of the genus *Coprinus*, having gills that dissolve into a dark liquid after the spores mature.

in·lace (ĭn-lās′) v. Variant of **enlace**.

in·laid (ĭn′lād′) adj. **1.** Set into a surface in a decorative pattern. **2.** Decorated with a pattern set into a surface.

in·land (ĭn′lənd) adj. **1.** Of, relating to, or located in the interior part of a country or region. **2.** *Chiefly British* Operating or applying within the borders of a country or region; domestic. ❖ adv. In, toward, or into the interior of a country or region. ❖ n. (-lănd′, -lənd) The interior of a country or region. —**in′land·er** n.

Inland Empire (ĭn′lənd, -lănd′) A region of the NW US between the Cascade Range and the Rocky Mts. comprising E WA, E OR, N ID, and W MT.

Inland Passage See **Inside Passage**.

Inland Sea An arm of the Pacific Ocean in S Japan between Honshu, Shikoku, and Kyushu.

in-law (ĭn′lô′) n. A relative by marriage. [Back-formation < such compounds as MOTHER-IN-LAW.]

in·lay (ĭn′lā′, ĭn-lā′) tr.v. **-laid** (-lād′), **-lay·ing**, **-lays 1a.** To set (pieces of wood, for example) into a surface to form a design. **b.** To decorate by setting in such designs. **2.** To insert (a photograph, for example) within a mat in a book. ❖ n. **1a.** Contrasting material set into a surface in pieces to form a design. **b.** A design, pattern, or decoration made by inlaying. **2.** *Dentistry* A solid filling fitted to a cavity in a tooth and cemented into place. —**in·lay′er** n.

in·let (ĭn′lĕt′, -lĭt) n. **1a.** A recess, such as a bay or cove, along a coast. **b.** A stream or bay leading inland, as from the ocean; an estuary. **c.** A narrow passage of water, as between two islands. **d.** A drainage passage, as to a culvert. **2.** An opening providing a means of entrance or intake. [IN¹ + LET¹.]

in·li·er (ĭn′lī′ər) n. An area or formation of older rocks completely surrounded by younger layers. [IN¹ + (OUT)LIER.]

in-line skate (ĭn′lĭn′) n. A roller skate whose wheels are arranged in a straight line. —**in-line skating** n.

in lo·co pa·ren·tis (ĭn lō′kō pə-rĕn′tĭs) adv. In the position or place of a parent. [Lat. *in locō parentis*.]

in·ly (ĭn′lē) adv. **1.** In an inward manner; inwardly. **2.** With thorough knowledge or understanding.

in·ly·ing (ĭn′lī′ĭng) adj. Located farther in: *inlying streams*.

in·mate (ĭn′māt′) n. A resident of a dwelling that houses a number of occupants, esp. a person confined to an institution.

in me·di·as res (ĭn mē′dē-əs rās′) adv. In or into the middle of a sequence of events, as in a literary narrative. [Lat. *in mediās rēs*.]

in me·mo·ri·am (ĭn′ mə-môr′ē-əm, -mōr′-) prep. In memory of; as a memorial to. Used esp. in epitaphs. [< Lat. *in memoriam*, to the memory (of).]

in·mi·grate (ĭn′mĭ′grāt) intr.v. **-grat·ed**, **-grat·ing**, **-grates** To move into a different region of the same country or territory. —**in′mi′grant** (ĭn′mĭ′grənt) n.

in·most (ĭn′mōst′) adj. Farthest within; innermost.

inn (ĭn) n. **1.** A public lodging house serving food and drink to travelers; a hotel. **2.** A tavern or restaurant. **3.** *Chiefly British* Formerly, a residence hall for students, esp. law students, in London. [ME < OE. See **en** in App.]

Inn A river of E Switzerland, W Austria, and SE Germany flowing c. 515 km (320 mi) to the Danube R.

in·nards (ĭn′ərdz) pl.n. *Informal* **1.** Internal bodily organs; viscera. **2.** The inner parts, as of a machine. [Alteration of *inwards*, pl. of INWARD.]

in·nate (ĭ-nāt′, ĭn′āt′) adj. **1.** Possessed at birth; inborn. **2.** Possessed as an essential characteristic; inherent. **3.** Of or produced by the mind rather than learned through experience: *innate knowledge*. [ME *innat* < Lat. *innātus*, p. part. of *innāscī*, to be born in : *in-*, in; see IN-² + *nāscī*, to be born; see **genə-** in App.] —**in·nate′ly** adv. —**in·nate′ness** n.

in·ner (ĭn′ər) adj. **1.** Located or occurring farther inside: *an inner room*. **2.** Less apparent; deeper: *inner meaning*. **3.** Of or relating to the mind or spirit. **4.** More exclusive, influential, or important. [ME < OE *innera*. See **en** in App.] —**in′ner** n. —**in′ner·ly** adv. & adj. —**in′ner·ness** n.

inner city n. The usu. older, central part of a city, esp. when characterized by crowded impoverished neighborhoods. —**in′ner-cit′y** (ĭn′ər-sĭt′ē) adj.

in·ner-di·rect·ed (ĭn′ər-dĭ-rĕk′tĭd, -dī-) adj. Guided in thought and behavior by one's own set of values.

inner ear n. The portion of the ear located within the temporal bone that is involved in both hearing and balance and includes the semicircular canals, vestibule, and cochlea.

Inner Hebrides See **Hebrides**.

Inner Light n. In Quaker doctrine, a divine presence in the human soul believed to be an enlightening and guiding force.

Inner Mongolia See **Nei Monggol**.

in·ner·most (ĭn′ər-mōst′) adj. **1.** Situated or occurring farthest within. **2.** Most intimate: *innermost feelings*. ❖ n. The part situated farthest in.

inner planet n. Any of the four planets, Mercury, Venus, Earth, and Mars, whose orbits are closest to the sun.

inner product n. See **scalar product**.

in·ner·sole (ĭn′ər-sōl′) n. See **insole**.

in·ner·spring (ĭn′ər-sprĭng′) adj. Having numerous coil springs enclosed by a padded cover: *an innerspring mattress*.

inner tube n. A flexible airtight hollow ring, usu. made of rubber, inside a pneumatic tire for holding compressed air.

in·ner·vate (ĭ-nûr′vāt′, ĭn′ər-) tr.v. **-vat·ed**, **-vat·ing**, **-vates 1.** To supply (an organ or a body part) with nerves. **2.** To stimulate (a nerve, muscle, or body part) to action. —**in′ner·va′tion** n. —**in′ner·va′tion·al** (-vā′shə-nəl) adj.

in·nerve (ĭ-nûrv′) tr.v. **-nerved**, **-nerv·ing**, **-nerves** To give nervous energy to; stimulate.

In·ness (ĭn′ĭs), **George** 1825–94. Amer. painter whose works include *Rainbow after a Storm* (1869).

in·ning (ĭn′ĭng) n. **1a.** *Baseball* One of nine periods of a game, in which each team has a turn at bat as limited by three outs. **b. innings** (*used with a sing. verb*) *Sports* The period in cricket during which one team is at bat. **2.** An opportunity to act or speak out; a chance for accomplishment. Often used in the plural with a singular or plural verb. **3.** The reclamation of flooded or marshy land. [ME *innynge*, a getting in < OE *innung*, gerund of *innian*, to put in < *in*, in. See IN¹.]

inn·keep·er (ĭn′kē′pər) n. One who owns or manages an inn or hotel.

in·no·cence (ĭn′ə-səns) n. **1.** The state, quality, or virtue of being innocent, as: **a.** Freedom from sin, moral wrong, or guilt through lack of knowledge of evil. **b.** Guiltlessness of a specific legal crime or offense. **c.** Freedom from guile, cunning, or deceit; simplicity or artlessness. **d.** Lack of worldliness or sophistication; naiveté. **e.** Lack of knowledge or understanding. **f.** Freedom from harmfulness; inoffensiveness. **2.** One that is innocent. **3.** *Botany* See **blue-eyed Mary**.

in·no·cen·cy (ĭn′ə-sən-sē) n., pl. **-cies 1.** Innocence. **2.** An innocent quality or action.

in·no·cent (ĭn′ə-sənt) adj. **1.** Uncorrupted by evil, malice, or wrongdoing; sinless. **2a.** Not guilty of a specific crime or offense; legally blameless. **b.** Within, allowed by, or sanctioned by the law; lawful. **3a.** Not dangerous or harmful; innocuous. **b.** Candid; straightforward. **4a.** Not experienced or worldly; naive. **b.** Betraying or suggesting no deception or guile; artless. **5a.** Not exposed to or familiar with something specified; ignorant. **b.** Unaware. **6.** Lacking, deprived, or devoid of something. ❖ n. **1.** A person, esp. a child, who is free of evil or sin. **2.** A simple, guileless, inexperienced, or unsophisticated person. **3.** A very young child. [ME < OFr. < Lat. *innocēns, innocent-* : *in-*, not; see IN-¹ + *nocēns*, pr. part. of *nocēre*, to harm; see **nek-** in App.] —**in′no·cent·ly** adv.

Innocent III 1161–1216. Pope (1198–1216) whose reign was marked by the Fourth Crusade.

in·noc·u·ous (ĭ-nŏk′yōō-əs) adj. **1.** Having no adverse effect; harmless. **2.** Not likely to offend or provoke to strong emotion; insipid. [< Lat. *innocuus* : *in-*, not; see IN-¹ + *nocuus*, harmful (< *nocēre*, to harm; see **nek-** in App.).] —**in·noc′u·ous·ly** adv. —**in·noc′u·ous·ness** n.

in·nom·i·nate (ĭ-nŏm′ə-nĭt) adj. **1.** Having no name. **2.** Anonymous. [LLat. *innōminātus* : Lat. *in-*, not; see IN-¹ + Lat. *nōminātus*, p. part. of *nōmināre*, to name; see NOMINATE.]

innominate bone n. See **hipbone**.

in·no·vate (ĭn′ə-vāt′) v. **-vat·ed**, **-vat·ing**, **-vates** —tr. To begin or introduce (something new) for or as if for the first time. —intr. To begin or introduce something new. [Fr. *innover* < OFr. < Lat. *innovāre, innovāt-*, to renew : *in-*, intensive pref.; see IN-² + *novāre*, to make new (< *novus*, new; see **newo-** in App.).] —**in′no·va′tor** n. —**in′no·va′to·ry** (-və-tôr′ē, -tōr′ē) adj.

in·no·va·tion (ĭn′ə-vā′shən) n. **1.** The act of introducing something new. **2.** Something newly introduced. —**in′no·va′tion·al** adj.

in·no·va·tive (ĭn′ə-vā′tĭv) adj. Marked by or given to innovations. —**in′no·va′tive·ness** n.

Inns·bruck (ĭnz′brŏŏk′, ĭns′-) A city of SW Austria WSW of Salzburg; settled c. 1180. Pop. 118,112.

Inns of Court (ĭnz) pl.n. **1.** The four legal societies in England having the exclusive right to confer the title of barrister on law students. **2.** The buildings housing the Inns of Court.

In·nu (ĭn′ōō) n., pl. **Innu** also **In·nus** A member of an Algonquian people comprising the Montagnais and Naskapi. [Montagnais and Naskapi, people.]

in·nu·en·do (ĭn′yōō-ĕn′dō) n., pl. **-does** An indirect or subtle, usu. derogatory implication in expression; an insinuation. [< Lat. *innuendō*, by hinting, ablative of *innuendum*, gerund of *innuere*, to nod to : *in-*, in; to, toward; see IN-² + -*nuere*, to nod.]

In·nu·it (ĭn′yōō-ĭt) n. Variant of **Inuit**.

in·nu·mer·a·ble (ĭ-nōō′mər-ə-bəl, ĭ-nyōō′-) adj. Too numerous to be counted; numberless. See Syns at **incalculable**. —**in·**

in-line skate
pair of in-line skates

ă	pat	oi	boy
ā	pay	ou	out
âr	care	ŏŏ	took
ä	father	ōō	boot
ĕ	pet	ŭ	cut
ē	be	ûr	urge
ĭ	pit	th	thin
ī	pie	th	this
îr	pier	hw	which
ŏ	pot	zh	vision
ō	toe	ə	about,
ô	paw		item

Stress marks:
′ (primary),
′ (secondary), as in
lexicon (lĕk′sĭ-kŏn′)

nu'mer·a·ble·ness *n.* —in·nu'mer·a·bly *adv.*

in·nu'mer·ate (ĭ-nōō'mər-ĭt, -nyōō'-) *adj.* Unfamiliar with mathematical concepts and methods. ❖ *n.* One who is innumerate. —in·nu'mer·a·cy *n.*

in·nu'mer·ous (ĭ-nōō'mər-əs) *adj.* Innumerable. [< Lat. *innumerus* : *in-*, not; see IN-¹ + *numerus*, number; see NUMBER.]

in·ob·ser·vance (ĭn'əb-zûr'vəns) *n.* **1.** Lack of heed or attention; disregard. **2.** Nonobservance, as of a law or custom. —in'ob·ser'vant *adj.*

in·ob·tru·sive (ĭn'əb-trōō'sĭv) *adj.* Not noticeable; unobtrusive.

in·oc·u·la·ble (ĭ-nŏk'yə-lə-bəl) *adj.* **1.** Susceptible to a disease spread by inoculation. **2.** That can be used in an inoculation. **3.** Transmissible by inoculation. —in·oc'u·la·bil'i·ty *n.*

in·oc·u·lant (ĭ-nŏk'yə-lənt) *n.* See inoculum.

in·oc·u·late (ĭ-nŏk'yə-lāt') *tr.v.* -lat·ed, -lat·ing, -lates **1.** To introduce a serum, vaccine, or antigenic substance into (the body), esp. to produce or boost immunity to a specific disease. **2.** To communicate a disease to (a living organism) by transferring its causative agent into the organism. **3.** To implant microorganisms or infectious material into (a culture medium). **4.** To safeguard as if by inoculation; protect. **5.** To introduce an idea or attitude into the mind of. [ME *inoculaten*, to graft a scion < Lat. *inoculāre*, *inoculāt-* : *in-*; see IN-² + *oculus*, eye, bud; see okʷ- in App.] —in·oc'u·la'tive *adj.* —in·oc'u·la'tor *n.*

in·oc·u·la·tion (ĭ-nŏk'yə-lā'shən) *n.* The act or an instance of inoculating, esp. inoculating the body.

in·oc·u·lum (ĭ-nŏk'yə-ləm) *n.*, *pl.* -la (-lə) or -lums The material used in an inoculation. [NLat. < Lat. *inoculāre*, to graft a scion. See INOCULATE.]

in·o·dor·ous (ĭn-ō'dər-əs) *adj.* Having no odor.

in·of·fen·sive (ĭn'ə-fĕn'sĭv) *adj.* **1.** Giving no offense; unobjectionable. **2.** Causing no harm; harmless. —in'of·fen'sive·ly *adv.* —in'of·fen'sive·ness *n.*

I·nö·nü (ĭn'ə-nōō', ĭ-nœ-nü') **Ismet** 1884–1973. Turkish politician who served as president (1938–50).

Ismet Inönü
photographed in 1963

in·op·er·a·ble (ĭn-ŏp'ər-ə-bəl, -ŏp'rə-) *adj.* **1.** Not functioning. **2.** Unsuitable for surgery. —in·op'er·a·bil'i·ty *n.* —in·op'er·a·bly *adv.*

in·op·er·a·tive (ĭn-ŏp'ər-ə-tĭv, -ŏp'rə-) *adj.* **1.** Not working or functioning. **2.** No longer in force, countermanded: *earlier instructions now inoperative.* —in·op'er·a·tive·ness *n.*

in·o·per·cu·late (ĭn'ō-pûr'kyə-lĭt) *adj.* Lacking an operculum. —in'o·per'cu·late *n.*

in·op·por·tune (ĭn-ŏp'ər-tōōn', -tyōōn') *adj.* Inappropriate or ill-timed; not opportune. —in·op'por·tune'ly *adv.* —in·op'por·tune'ness *n.*

in·or·di·nate (ĭn-ôr'dn-ĭt) *adj.* **1.** Exceeding reasonable limits; immoderate. See Syns at **excessive**. **2.** Not regulated; disorderly. [ME *inordinat* < Lat. *inōrdinātus*, disordered : *in-*, not; see IN-¹ + *ōrdinātus*, p. part. of *ōrdināre*, to set in order (< *ōrdō*, *ōrdin-*, order; see **ar-** in App.).] —in·or'di·na·cy, in·or'di·nate·ness *n.* —in·or'di·nate·ly *adv.*

in·or·gan·ic (ĭn'ôr-găn'ĭk) *adj.* **1a.** Involving no organic life or the products of organic life. **b.** Not composed of organic matter. **2.** *Chemistry* Of or relating to compounds not containing hydrocarbon groups. **3.** Not arising in normal growth. **4.** Lacking system or structure. —in'or·gan'i·cal·ly *adv.*

in·os·cu·late (ĭn-ŏs'kyə-lāt') *v.* -lat·ed, -lat·ing, -lates —*tr.* **1.** To unite (blood vessels, nerve fibers, or ducts) by small openings. **2.** To make continuous; blend. —*intr.* **1.** To open into one another. **2.** To unite so as to be continuous; blend. [IN-² + Lat. *ōsculāre*, *ōsculāt-*, to provide with an opening (< *ōsculum*, dim. of *ōs*, mouth; see **ōs-** in App.).] —in·os'cu·la'tion *n.*

in·o·si·tol (ĭ-nō'sĭ-tôl', -tōl', ĭ-nŏ'-) *n.* Any of nine isomeric alcohols, $C_6H_{12}O_6 \cdot 2H_2O$, esp. one found in plant and animal tissue and classified as a member of the vitamin B complex. [Gk. *īs*, *īn-*, sinew + -OS(E)² + -IT(E)² + -OL¹.]

in·o·tro·pic (ē'nə-trō'pĭk, -trŏp'ĭk, ī'nə-) *adj.* Affecting the contraction of muscle, esp. heart muscle: *an inotropic drug.* [Gk. *īs*, *īn-*, tendon, sinew + -TROPIC.]

in·pa·tient (ĭn'pā'shənt) *n.* One admitted to a hospital or clinic for treatment that requires at least one overnight stay. —in'pa'tient *adj.*

in per·so·nam (ĭn' pər-sō'nəm) *adv. & adj. Law* Against a person rather than against property. Used of an action or judgment. [LLat. *in persōnam*.]

in pet·to (ĭn pĕt'ō) *adv. & adj. Roman Catholic Church* In secret or private. Used of appointments of cardinals by the pope undisclosed in consistory. [Ital. : *in*, in + *petto*, breast.]

in·phase (ĭn'fāz') *adj.* Having the same electrical phase.

in pos·se (ĭn pŏs'ē) *adv. & adj. Law* In potential but not in actuality. [Med.Lat. : Lat. *in*, in + Lat. *posse*, to be able.]

in pro·pri·a per·so·na (ĭn prō'prē-ə pər-sō'nə) *adv.* In one's own person, esp. without representation by an attorney. [Med. Lat. *in propriā persōnā* : Lat. *in*, in + *propriā*, fem. ablative sing. of *proprius*, one's own + *persōnā*, ablative of *persōna*, person.]

in·put (ĭn'pŏŏt') *n.* **1.** Something put into a system or expended in its operation to achieve output or a result, esp.: **a.** Energy, work, or power used to drive a machine. **b.** Current, electromotive force, or power supplied to an electric circuit, network, or device. **c.** *Computer Science* Information put into a communications system for transmission or into a computer system for processing. **d.** *Computer Science* A position, terminal, or station at which input enters a system. **e.** Any of the items, including materials, equipment, and funds, required for production. **2a.** The act of putting in; infusion: *a steady input of fuel.* **b.** An amount put in. **3.** *Usage Problem* **a.** Contribution of information or a comment or viewpoint. **b.** Information in general. ❖ *tr.v.* -put·ted or -put, -put·ting, -puts *Computer Science* To enter (data or a program) into a computer.

input device *n.* A device, such as a keyboard, used to enter information into a computer.

in·quest (ĭn'kwĕst') *n.* **1.** *Law* **a.** A judicial inquiry into a matter usu. held before a jury, esp. into the cause of a death. **b.** A jury making such an inquiry. **c.** The finding based on such an inquiry. **2.** An investigation or inquiry. [ME *enqueste* < OFr. < VLat. **inquaesīta*, thing inquired into, alteration of Lat. *inquīsīta*, fem. p. part. of *inquīrere*, to inquire into. See INQUIRE.]

in·qui·e·tude (ĭn-kwī'ĭ-tōōd', -tyōōd') *n.* A state of restlessness or uneasiness; disquietude. [ME, disturbance < LLat. *inquiētūdō*, restlessness < Lat. *inquiētus*, restless : *in-*, not; see IN-¹ + *quiētus*, quiet; see QUIET.]

in·qui·line (ĭn'kwə-lĭn', -lĭn, ĭng'-) *n.* An animal that characteristically lives commensally in the nest or burrow of an animal of another species. ❖ *adj.* Being or living as an inquiline. [Lat. *inquilīnus*, lodger, tenant : *in-*, in; see IN-² + *colere*, to inhabit; see kʷel- in App.] —in'qui·lin·ism (-lə-nĭz'əm), in'qui·lin'i·ty (-lĭn'ĭ-tē) *n.* —in'qui·lin'ous (-lĭn'nəs) *adj.*

in·quire (ĭn-kwīr') also en·quire (ĕn-) *v.* -quired, -quir·ing, -quires —*intr.* **1.** To seek information by asking a question. **2.** To make an inquiry or investigation. —*tr.* **1.** To ask about. **2.** To ask. See Syns at **ask**. —*phrasal verb:* **inquire after** To ask about the health or condition of. [ME *enquiren* < OFr. *enquerre* < VLat. **inquaerere*, alteration of Lat. *inquīrere* : *in-*, into; see IN-² + *quaerere*, to seek.] —in·quir'er *n.* —in·quir'ing·ly *adv.*

in·quir·y (ĭn-kwīr'ē, ĭn'kwīr'ē, ĭn'kwə-rē, ĭng'-) also en·quir·y (ĕn-kwīr'ē, ĕn'kwə-rē, ĭn'-) *n.*, *pl.* -ies **1.** The act of inquiring. **2.** A question; a query. **3.** A close examination of a matter in a search for information or truth.

in·qui·si·tion (ĭn'kwĭ-zĭsh'ən, ĭng'-) *n.* **1.** The act of inquiring into a matter; an investigation. **2.** *Law* **a.** An inquest. **b.** The verdict of a judicial inquiry. **3a. Inquisition** A tribunal formerly held in the Roman Catholic Church to suppress heresy. **b.** An investigation that violates the privacy or rights of individuals. **c.** A rigorous harsh interrogation. [ME *inquisicioun* < OFr. *inquisicion* < Lat. *inquīsītiō*, *inquīsītiōn-* : *in-*, into; part. of *inquīrere*, to inquire. See INQUIRE.] —in'qui·si'tion·al *adj.*

in·quis·i·tive (ĭn-kwĭz'ĭ-tĭv) *adj.* **1.** Inclined to investigate; eager for knowledge. **2.** Unduly curious and inquiring. See Syns at **curious**. —in·quis'i·tive·ly *adv.* —in·quis'i·tive·ness *n.*

in·quis·i·tor (ĭn-kwĭz'ĭ-tər) *n.* One who inquires or makes an inquisition, esp. an excessively rigorous or harsh questioner.

in·quis·i·to·ri·al (ĭn-kwĭz'ĭ-tôr'ē-əl, -tōr'-) *adj.* **1.** Of, relating to, or having the function of an inquisitor. **2.** *Law* **a.** Relating to a trial in which one party acts as both prosecutor and judge. **b.** Relating to a criminal proceeding conducted in secrecy. —in·quis'i·to'ri·al·ly *adv.*

in re (ĭn rā', rē') *prep. Law* In the matter or case of; in regard to. [Lat. *in rē* : *in*, in + *rē*, ablative of *rēs*, thing, matter.]

in rem (ĭn rĕm') *adv. & adj. Law* Against a thing, such as property, status, or a right, rather than against a person. Used of an action or judgment. [LLat. : Lat. *in*, against + Lat. *rem*, accusative of *rēs*, thing, matter.]

in-res·i·dence (ĭn-rĕz'ĭ-dəns) *adj.* Associated in an official specified position with an organization such as a university or college. Often used in combination: *artist-in-residence.*

INRI *abbr. Latin* Iesus Nazarenus Rex Iudaeorum (Jesus of Nazareth, King of the Jews)

in·ro (ĭn'rō) *n.*, *pl.* inro A small, usu. ornamented box that hangs from the waist of a kimono and holds small objects such as cosmetics, perfumes, or medicines. [J. *inrō* : *in*, stamp, seal (< M Chin. *ʔin*) + -*rō*, seclusion, case (< M Chin. *ləwŋ*).]

in·road (ĭn'rōd') *n.* **1.** An invasion; a raid. **2.** An advance, esp. at another's expense; an encroachment. Often used in the plural. [IN¹ + ROAD, riding, raid (obsolete).]

in·rush (ĭn'rŭsh') *n.* A sudden rushing in; an influx. —in'rush'ing *adj. & n.*

INS *abbr.* **1.** Immigration and Naturalization Service **2.** International News Service

insessorial
foot of a chickadee

ins. *abbr.* **1.** inches **2.** inspector **3.** insurance

in•sal•i•vate (ĭn-săl′ə-vāt′) *tr.v.* **-vat•ed, -vat•ing, -vates** To mix (food) with saliva in chewing. —**in•sal′i•va′tion** *n.*

in•sa•lu•bri•ous (ĭn′sə-lōō′brē-əs) *adj.* Not promoting health; unwholesome. —**in′sa•lu′bri•ous•ly** *adv.* —**in′sa•lu′bri•ty** *n.*

ins and outs (ĭnz; outs) *pl.n.* **1.** The intricate details of a situation, decision, or process. **2.** The windings of a way.

in•sane (ĭn-sān′) *adj.* **1a.** Mentally ill. **b.** Deranged; disturbed. **c.** Intended for use by the mentally ill or deranged. **2.** Immoderate; wild: *insane jealousy.* **3.** Very foolish; absurd: *insane risks.* [Lat. *īnsānus* : *in-*, not; see IN-¹ + *sānus*, sane, healthy.] —**in•sane′ly** *adv.* —**in•sane′ness** *n.*

in•san•i•tar•y (ĭn-săn′ĭ-tĕr′ē) *adj.* So unclean as to be a likely cause of disease.

in•san•i•ty (ĭn-săn′ĭ-tē) *n., pl.* **-ties 1.** Mental illness or derangement. **2.** *Law* **a.** Unsoundness of mind sufficient to render a person unfit to maintain a contractual or other legal relationship or to warrant commitment to a mental health facility. **b.** In most criminal jurisdictions, a degree of mental malfunctioning sufficient to relieve the accused of legal responsibility for the act committed. **3a.** Extreme foolishness; folly. **b.** Something extremely foolish.

in•sa•tia•ble (ĭn-sā′shə-bəl, -shē-ə-) *adj.* Impossible to satiate or satisfy. —**in•sa′tia•bil′i•ty, in•sa′tia•ble•ness** *n.* —**in•sa′tia•bly** *adv.*

in•sa•ti•ate (ĭn-sā′shē-ĭt) *adj.* Insatiable. —**in•sa′ti•ate•ly** *adv.* —**in•sa′ti•ate•ness** *n.*

in•scribe (ĭn-skrīb′) *tr.v.* **-scribed, -scrib•ing, -scribes 1a.** To write, print, carve, or engrave (words or letters) on or in a surface. **b.** To mark or engrave (a surface) with words or letters. **2.** To enter (a name) on a list or in a register. **3a.** To sign one's name or write a brief message in or on (a gift book, for example). **b.** To dedicate to someone. **4.** *Mathematics* To draw (one figure) within another figure so that every vertex of the enclosed figure touches the outer figure. [Lat. *īnscrībere* : *in-*, in, on; see IN-² + *scrībere*, to write; see **skrībh-** in App.] —**in•scrib′er** *n.*

in•scrip•tion (ĭn-skrĭp′shən) *n.* **1.** The act or an instance of inscribing. **2.** A marking, such as the wording on a coin, that is inscribed. **3.** A piece of material, such as a stone tablet, that is inscribed. **4.** An enrollment or a registration of names. **5a.** A short signed message in a book or on a photograph given as a gift. **b.** The usu. informal dedication of a book or an artistic work. [ME *inscripcioun*, statement giving the author or title of a book < Lat. *īnscrīptiō, īnscrīptiōn-* < *īnscrīptus*, p. part. of *īnscrībere*, to inscribe. See INSCRIBE.] —**in•scrip′tion•al, in•scrip′tive** *adj.* —**in•scrip′tive•ly** *adv.*

in•scru•ta•ble (ĭn-skrōō′tə-bəl) *adj.* Difficult to fathom or understand; impenetrable. See Syns at **mysterious.** —**in•scru′ta•bil′i•ty, in•scru′ta•ble•ness** *n.* —**in•scru′ta•bly** *adv.*

in•seam (ĭn′sēm′) *n.* **1.** The inside seam of a pant leg. **2.** The length or measurement of such a seam.

in•sect (ĭn′sĕkt′) *n.* **1a.** Any of numerous usu. small arthropod animals of the class Insecta, having an adult stage characterized by three pairs of legs and a body segmented into head, thorax, and abdomen and usu. having two pairs of wings. **b.** Any of various similar arthropod animals, such as spiders, centipedes, or ticks. **2.** An insignificant or contemptible person. [Lat. *īnsectum* < neut. p. part. of *īnsecāre*, to cut up (transl. of Gk. *entomon*, segmented, cut up, insect) : *in-*, in; see IN-² + *secāre*, to cut; see **sek-** in App.] —**in•sect′** (ĭn′sĕk-tī′vəl) *adj.*

in•sec•tar•y (ĭn′sĕk′tə-rē, ĭn-sĕk′-) or **in•sec•tar•i•um** (ĭn′sĕk-târ′ē-əm) *n., pl.* **-tar•ies** or **-tar•i•a** (-târ′ē-ə) A place for keeping, breeding, or observing living insects.

in•sec•ti•cide (ĭn-sĕk′tĭ-sīd′) *n.* A chemical substance used to kill insects. —**in•sec′ti•cid′al** (-sīd′l) *adj.* —**in•sec′ti•cid′al•ly** *adv.*

in•sec•ti•vore (ĭn-sĕk′tə-vôr′, -vōr′) *n.* **1.** Any of various small, principally nocturnal mammals of the order Insectivora, characteristically feeding chiefly on insects. **2.** An organism that feeds mainly on insects. [NLat. *Insectivora*, order name : Lat. *īnsectum*, insect; see INSECT + Lat. *-vora*, neut. pl. of *-vorus*, -vorous.]

in•sec•tiv•o•rous (ĭn′sĕk-tĭv′ər-əs) *adj.* **1.** Feeding on insects. **2.** *Botany* Capable of trapping and absorbing insects.

in•se•cure (ĭn′sĭ-kyŏŏr′) *adj.* **1.** Not sure or certain; doubtful: *an insecure future.* **2.** Inadequately guarded or protected; unsafe. **3.** Not firm or fixed; unsteady. **4a.** Lacking emotional stability; troubled. **b.** Lacking self-confidence; plagued by anxiety. —**in′se•cure′ly** *adv.* —**in′se•cure′ness** *n.* —**in′se•cu′ri•ty** (-kyŏŏr′ĭ-tē) *n.*

in•sel•berg (ĭn′səl-bûrg′, -zəl-) *n.* See **monadnock.** [Ger. : *Insel*, island (< MHGer. *insule* < alteration of OHGer. *isila*, prob. < VLat. **īsula*; see ISLE) + *Berg*, mountain (< MHGer. *berc* < OHGer. *berg*; see **bhergh-** in App.).]

in•sem•i•nate (ĭn-sĕm′ə-nāt′) *tr.v.* **-nat•ed, -nat•ing, -nates 1.** To introduce or inject semen into the reproductive tract of (a female). **2.** To sow seed in. [Lat. *īnsēmināre, īnsēmināt-*, to implant, impregnate : *in-*, in; see IN-² + *sēmen*, to plant (< *sēmen, sēmin-*, seed; see SEMEN).] —**in•sem′i•na′tion** *n.* —**in•sem′i•na′tor** *n.*

in•sen•sate (ĭn-sĕn′sāt′, -sĭt) *adj.* **1a.** Lacking sensation or awareness; inanimate. **b.** Unconscious. **2.** Lacking sensibility; un-

feeling. **3a.** Lacking sense or the power to reason. **b.** Foolish; witless. —**in•sen′sate•ly** *adv.* —**in•sen′sate•ness** *n.*

in•sen•si•ble (ĭn-sĕn′sə-bəl) *adj.* **1a.** Imperceptible; inappreciable. **b.** Very small or gradual. **2a.** Having lost consciousness, esp. temporarily; unconscious. **b.** Not invested with sensation; inanimate. **c.** Devoid of physical sensation or the power to react, as to pain or cold; numb. **3a.** Unaware; unmindful. **b.** Not emotionally responsive; indifferent. **4.** Lacking meaning; unintelligible. —**in•sen′si•bil′i•ty, in•sen′si•ble•ness** *n.* —**in•sen′si•bly** *adv.*

in•sen•si•tive (ĭn-sĕn′sĭ-tĭv) *adj.* **1.** Not physically sensitive; numb. **2a.** Lacking in sensitivity to the feelings or circumstances of others; unfeeling. **b.** Lacking in responsiveness: *insensitive to the customers.* —**in•sen′si•tive•ly** *adv.* —**in•sen′si•tiv′i•ty, in•sen′si•tive•ness** *n.*

in•sen•tient (ĭn-sĕn′shənt) *adj.* Devoid of sensation or consciousness; inanimate. —**in•sen′tience** *n.*

in•sep•a•ra•ble (ĭn-sĕp′ər-ə-bəl, -sĕp′rə-) *adj.* **1.** Impossible to separate or part. **2.** Very closely associated; constant. —**in•sep′a•ra•bil′i•ty, in•sep′a•ra•ble•ness** *n.* —**in•sep′a•ra•ble** *n.* —**in•sep′a•ra•bly** *adv.*

in•sert (ĭn-sûrt′) *tr.v.* **-sert•ed, -sert•ing, -serts 1.** To put or set into, between, or among. **2.** To put or introduce into the body of something; interpolate. **3.** To place into an orbit, trajectory, or stream. ❖ *n.* (ĭn′sûrt′) Something inserted or intended for insertion. [Lat. *īnserere, īnsert-* : *in-*, in; see IN-² + *serere*, to join.] —**in•sert′er** *n.*

in•ser•tion (ĭn-sûr′shən) *n.* **1.** The act or process of inserting. **2.** Something inserted. **3.** *Anatomy* The point or mode of attachment of a skeletal muscle to the bone or other body part that it moves. **4.** *Genetics* The addition, as by mutation, of one or more nucleotides to a chromosome. —**in•ser′tion•al** *adj.*

in-ser•vice (ĭn′sûr′vĭs) *adj.* **1.** Of, relating to, or being a full-time employee. **2.** Taking place or continuing while one is a full-time employee.

in•ses•so•ri•al (ĭn′sĕ-sôr′ē-əl, -sōr′-) *adj.* Perching or adapted for perching. [< NLat. *Inessōrēs*, the perchers (former order name) < Lat. *īnsessus*, p. part. of *īnsidēre*, to sit upon. See INSIDIOUS.]

in•set (ĭn′sĕt′, ĭn-sĕt′) *tr.v.* **-set, -set•ting, -sets 1.** To set in; insert. **2.** To furnish with an inset. ❖ *n.* (ĭn′sĕt′) **1.** Something set in, as: **a.** A small map or illustration set within a larger one. **b.** A leaf or group of pages inserted into a publication. **c.** A piece of material set into a garment as decoration or trim. **2a.** An inflow, as of water. **b.** A channel.

in•shore (ĭn′shôr′, -shōr′) *adv. & adj.* **1.** Close to a shore. **2.** Toward or coming toward a shore.

in•shrine (ĭn-shrīn′) *v.* Variant of **enshrine.**

in•side (ĭn-sīd′, ĭn′sīd′) *n.* **1a.** An inner or interior part. **b.** Inward character, perceptions, or feelings. **2.** An inner side or surface. **3.** The part away from the edge; the middle part. **4. insides** *Informal* **a.** The inner organs; entrails. **b.** The inner parts or workings. **5.** *Slang* Confidential or secret information. ❖ *adj.* **1.** Inner; interior. **2.** Relating to, known to, or coming from an exclusive group. **3.** *Baseball* Passing on the side of home plate nearer the batter. Used of a pitch. ❖ *adv.* **1.** Into or in the interior; within. **2.** On the inner side. **3.** *Slang* In prison. ❖ *prep.* **1.** Within: *We'll be there inside an hour.* **2a.** On the inner side or part of. **b.** Into the interior of. —**idioms: inside out 1.** With the inner surface turned out; reversed. **2.** *Informal* As completely as possible; thoroughly. **on the inside** In a position of confidence or influence.

inside job *n. Slang* A crime perpetrated by or with the help of a person working for or trusted by the victim.

inside of *prep.* Within; inside.

In•side Passage (ĭn′sīd′) also **In•land Passage** (ĭn′lənd) A natural protected waterway extending c. 1,529 km (950 mi) from Puget Sound to Skagway AK.

in•sid•er (ĭn-sī′dər) *n.* **1.** An accepted member of a group. **2.** One who has special knowledge or access to information.

insider trading *n.* The illegal buying or selling of securities on the basis of information that is unavailable to the public.

inside track *n.* **1.** *Informal* An advantageous position. **2.** *Sports* The inside path in a curved racetrack.

in•sid•i•ous (ĭn-sĭd′ē-əs) *adj.* **1.** Working or spreading harmfully in a subtle or stealthy manner. **2.** Intended to entrap; treacherous. **3.** Beguiling but harmful; alluring. [< Lat. *īnsidiōsus* < *īnsidiae*, ambush < *īnsidēre*, to sit upon, lie in wait for : *in-*, in, on; see IN-² + *sedēre*, to sit; see **sed-** in App.] —**in•sid′i•ous•ly** *adv.* —**in•sid′i•ous•ness** *n.*

in•sight (ĭn′sīt′) *n.* **1.** The capacity to discern the true nature of a situation; penetration. **2.** The act or outcome of grasping the inward nature of things or of perceiving in an intuitive manner.

in•sight•ful (ĭn-sīt′fəl, ĭn′sīt′-) *adj.* Showing or having insight; perceptive. —**in•sight′ful•ly** *adv.* —**in•sight′ful•ness** *n.*

in•sig•ni•a (ĭn-sĭg′nē-ə) also **in•sig•ne** (-nē) *n., pl.* **insignia** or **-ni•as 1.** A badge of office, rank, membership, or nationality; an emblem. **2.** A distinguishing sign. [Lat. *īnsignia*, pl. of *īnsigne*, badge of office, mark < neut. of *īnsignis*, distinguished, marked : *in-*, in; see IN-² + *signum*, sign; see **sek**ʷ-¹ in App.]

in•sig•nif•i•cance (ĭn′sĭg-nĭf′ĭ-kəns) *n.* The quality or state of being insignificant.

insignia
insignia of a US submarine officer

in·sig·nif·i·can·cy (ĭn′sĭg-nĭf′ĭ-kən-sē) n., pl. **-cies 1.** Insignificance. **2.** One that is insignificant.

in·sig·nif·i·cant (ĭn′sĭg-nĭf′ĭ-kənt) adj. **1.** Not significant, esp.: **a.** Lacking in importance; trivial. **b.** Lacking power, position, or value; worthy of little regard. **c.** Small in size or amount. **2.** Having little or no meaning. —**in′sig·nif′i·cant·ly** adv.

in·sin·cere (ĭn′sĭn-sîr′) adj. Not sincere; hypocritical. —**in′sin·cere′ly** adv. —**in′sin·cer′i·ty** (-sĕr′ĭ-tē) n.

in·sin·u·ate (ĭn-sĭn′yoō-āt′) v. **-at·ed, -at·ing, -ates** —tr. **1.** To introduce or otherwise convey (a thought, for example) gradually and insidiously. See Syns at **suggest. 2.** To introduce or insert (oneself) by subtle and artful means. —intr. To make insinuations. [Lat. *īnsinuāre, īnsinuāt-* : *in-*, in; see IN-² + *sinuāre*, to curve (< *sinus*, curve).] —**in·sin′u·a′tive** adj. —**in·sin′u·a′tor** n. —**in·sin′u·a·tor′y** (-yoō-ə-tôr′ē, -tōr′ē) adj.

in·sin·u·at·ing (ĭn-sĭn′yoō-ā′tĭng) adj. **1.** Provoking gradual doubt or suspicion; suggestive. **2.** Artfully contrived to gain favor or confidence; ingratiating. —**in·sin′u·at′ing·ly** adv.

in·sin·u·a·tion (ĭn-sĭn′yoō-ā′shən) n. **1.** The act, process, or practice of insinuating. **2.** Something insinuated, esp. an artfully indirect, often derogatory suggestion.

in·sip·id (ĭn-sĭp′ĭd) adj. **1.** Lacking flavor or zest; not tasty. **2.** Lacking qualities that excite, stimulate, or interest; dull. [Fr. *insipide* < LLat. *īnsipidus* : Lat. *in-*, not; see IN-¹ + Lat. *sapidus*, savory (< *sapere*, to taste).] —**in·si·pid′i·ty** (ĭn′sĭ-pĭd′ĭ-tē), **in·sip′id·ness** n. —**in·sip′id·ly** adv.

in·sip·i·ence (ĭn-sĭp′ē-əns) n. Archaic Lack of wisdom. [ME < OFr. < Lat. *īnsipientia* < *īnsipiēns, īnsipient-*, not wise : *in-*, not; see IN-¹ + *sapiēns*, wise; see SAPIENT.]

in·sist (ĭn-sĭst′) v. **-sist·ed, -sist·ing, -sists** —intr. To be firm in a demand or course; refuse to yield. —tr. To assert or demand (something) vehemently and persistently: *We insist that you come along.* [Lat. *īnsistere*, to persist : *in-*, on; see IN-² + *sistere*, to stand; see stā- in App.] —**in·sis′tence, in·sis′ten·cy** n. —**in·sist′er** n. —**in·sist′ing·ly** adv.

in·sis·tent (ĭn-sĭs′tənt) adj. **1.** Firm in asserting a demand or an opinion; unyielding. **2.** Demanding attention or a response: *insistent hunger.* **3.** Repetitive and persistent. —**in·sis′tent·ly** adv.

in si·tu (ĭn sē′toō, sī′-, sĭch′oō) adv. & adj. In the original position. [Lat. *in situ* : *in*, in + *situ*, ablative of *situs*, place.]

in·snare (ĭn-snâr′) v. Variant of **ensnare.**

in·so·bri·e·ty (ĭn′sə-brī′ĭ-tē) n. Lack of sobriety; intemperance, esp. in drinking.

in·so·cia·ble (ĭn-sō′shə-bəl) adj. Not sociable. —**in·so′cia·bil′i·ty** n. —**in·so′cia·bly** adv.

in·so·far (ĭn′sō-fär′) adv. To such an extent.

insofar as conj. To the extent that.

insol. abbr. insoluble

in·so·late (ĭn′sō-lāt′, ĭn-sō′-) tr.v. **-lat·ed, -lat·ing, -lates** To expose to sunlight. [Lat. *īnsōlāre, īnsōlāt-* : *in-*, in; see IN-² + *sōl*, sun; see sāwel- in App.]

in·so·la·tion (ĭn′sō-lā′shən) n. **1a.** The act or an instance of exposing to sunlight. **b.** Therapeutic exposure to sunlight. **2.** See **sunstroke. 3a.** The solar radiation striking Earth or another planet. **b.** The rate of delivery of solar radiation per unit of horizontal surface.

in·sole (ĭn′sōl′) n. **1.** The inner sole of a shoe or boot. **2.** An extra strip of material put inside a shoe for comfort or protection.

in·so·lence (ĭn′sə-ləns) n. **1.** The quality or condition of being insolent. **2.** An instance of such behavior or speech.

in·so·lent (ĭn′sə-lənt) adj. **1.** Presumptuous and insulting in manner or speech; arrogant. **2.** Audaciously rude or disrespectful; impertinent. [ME < Lat. *īnsolēns, īnsolent-*, immoderate, arrogant : *in-*, not; see IN-¹ + *solēns*, pr. part. of *solēre*, to be accustomed.] —**in′so·lent** n. —**in′so·lent·ly** adv.

in·sol·u·ble (ĭn-sŏl′yə-bəl) adj. **1.** That cannot be dissolved. **2.** Difficult or impossible to solve or explain; insolvable. —**in·sol′u·bil′i·ty, in·sol′u·ble·ness** n. —**in·sol′u·ble** n. —**in·sol′u·bly** adv.

in·solv·a·ble (ĭn-sŏl′və-bəl) adj. Impossible to solve; having no solution. —**in·solv′a·bil′i·ty** n. —**in·solv′a·bly** adv.

in·sol·ven·cy (ĭn-sŏl′vən-sē) n., pl. **-cies 1.** The condition of being insolvent. **2.** An instance of being insolvent.

in·sol·vent (ĭn-sŏl′vənt) adj. **1a.** Unable to meet debts or discharge liabilities; bankrupt. **b.** Insufficient to meet all debts, as an estate or fund. **2.** Of or relating to bankrupt persons or entities. ❖ n. A bankrupt.

in·som·ni·a (ĭn-sŏm′nē-ə) n. Chronic inability to fall asleep or remain asleep for a length of time. [Lat. *īnsomnia* < *īnsomnis*, sleepless : *in-*, not; see IN-¹ + *somnus*, sleep; see swep- in App.]

in·som·ni·ac (ĭn-sŏm′nē-ăk′) n. One who suffers from insomnia. ❖ adj. Having or causing insomnia.

in·so·much as (ĭn′sō-mŭch′) conj. **1.** To such extent or degree as. **2.** Inasmuch; since.

insomuch that conj. With the result that; so.

in·sou·ci·ant (ĭn-soō′sē-ənt, ăn′soō-syäN′) adj. Marked by blithe unconcern; nonchalant. [Fr. : *in-*, not (< OFr.; see IN-¹) + *souciant*, pr. part. of *soucier*, to trouble (< OFr. < VLat. *sollicitāre*, alteration of Lat. *sollicitāre*, to vex; see SOLICIT).] —**in·sou′ci·ance** n. —**in·sou′ci·ant·ly** adv.

in·soul (ĭn-sōl′) v. Variant of **ensoul.**

insp. abbr. **1.** inspected **2.** inspector

in·spect (ĭn-spĕkt′) tr.v. **-spect·ed, -spect·ing, -spects 1.** To examine carefully and critically, esp. for flaws. **2.** To review or examine officially. [< Lat. *īnspicere, īnspect-* : *in-*, intensive pref.; see IN-² + *specere*, to look at; see spek- in App.] —**in·spec′tive** adj.

in·spec·tion (ĭn-spĕk′shən) n. **1.** The act of inspecting. **2.** Official examination or review. —**in·spec′tion·al** adj.

in·spec·tor (ĭn-spĕk′tər) n. **1.** One who is appointed or employed to inspect something. **2.** A police officer ranking next below superintendent. —**in·spec′to·ral, in′spec·to′ri·al** (-tôr′ē-əl, -tōr′-) adj. —**in·spec′tor·ship′** n.

in·spec·tor·ate (ĭn-spĕk′tər-ĭt) n. **1.** The office or duties of an inspector. **2.** A staff of inspectors. **3.** An inspector's district.

inspector general n., pl. **inspectors general** An officer with general investigative powers within a civil, military, or other organization.

in·sphere (ĭn-sfîr′) v. Variant of **ensphere.**

in·spi·ra·tion (ĭn′spə-rā′shən) n. **1a.** Stimulation of the mind or emotions to a high level of feeling or activity. **b.** The condition of being so stimulated. **2.** An agency, such as a person or work of art, that moves the intellect or emotions or prompts action or invention. **3.** Something, such as a sudden creative act, that is inspired. **4.** The quality of inspiring or exalting. **5.** Divine guidance or influence exerted directly on the mind and soul. **6.** The act of drawing in, esp. the inhalation of air into the lungs.

in·spi·ra·tion·al (ĭn′spə-rā′shə-nəl) adj. **1.** Of or relating to inspiration. **2.** Providing or intended to convey inspiration. **3.** Resulting from inspiration. —**in′spi·ra′tion·al·ly** adv.

in·spi·ra·tor (ĭn′spə-rā′tər) n. **1.** A device by which a gas, vapor, or air is drawn in, as to a combustion system. **2.** One who inspires or motivates others. [Lat. *īnspīrāre*, to breathe into; see INSPIRE + -ATOR.]

in·spir·a·to·ry (ĭn-spīr′ə-tôr′ē, -tōr′ē) adj. **1.** Of, relating to, or used for the drawing in of air. **2.** Intended or used to motivate or inspire.

in·spire (ĭn-spīr′) v. **-spired, -spir·ing, -spires** —tr. **1.** To affect, guide, or arouse by divine influence. **2.** To fill with enlivening or exalting emotion. **3a.** To stimulate to action; motivate. **b.** To affect or touch. **4.** To bring forth; elicit or arouse. **5.** To be the cause or source of; bring about. **6.** To draw in (air) by inhaling. **7.** Archaic **a.** To breathe on. **b.** To breathe life into. —intr. **1.** To stimulate energies, ideals, or reverence. **2.** To inhale. [ME *enspiren* < OFr. *enspirer* < Lat. *īnspīrāre* : *in-*, into; see IN-² + *spīrāre*, to breathe.] —**in·spir′er** n.

in·spired (ĭn-spīrd′) adj. Of such surpassing brilliance or excellence as to suggest divine inspiration: *an inspired musician.* —**in·spir′ed·ly** (-spī′rĭd-lē, -spīrd′lē) adv.

in·spir·ing (ĭn-spīr′ĭng) adj. Tending to arouse or exalt: *an inspiring eulogy.* —**in·spir′ing·ly** adv.

in·spir·it (ĭn-spīr′ĭt) tr.v. **-it·ed, -it·ing, -its** To instill courage or life into; animate. —**in·spir′it·ing·ly** adv.

in·spis·sate (ĭn-spĭs′āt′, ĭn′spĭ-sāt′) intr. & tr.v. **-sat·ed, -sat·ing, -sates** To undergo thickening or cause to thicken, as by boiling or evaporation; condense. [< LLat. *īnspissāre, īnspissāt-*, to thicken : Lat. *in-*, causative pref.; see IN-² + Lat. *spissus*, thick.] —**in·spis·sa′tion** n. —**in·spis′sa·tor** n.

inst. abbr. **1.** instant **2.** institute **3.** institution

in·sta·bil·i·ty (ĭn′stə-bĭl′ĭ-tē) n., pl. **-ties 1.** Lack of physical stability; unsteadiness. **2.** The quality or condition of being erratic or undependable: *political instability.*

in·stall also **in·stal** (ĭn-stôl′) tr.v. **-stalled, -stall·ing, -stalls** also **-stals 1.** To connect or set in position and prepare for use. **2.** To induct into an office, rank, or position: *install the new governor.* **3.** To settle in an indicated place or condition; establish. [ME *installen*, to place in office < OFr. *installer* < Med.Lat. *īnstallāre* : *in-*, in (< Lat.; see IN-²) + *stallum*, stall, place; see stel- in App.] —**in·stall′er** n.

in·stal·la·tion (ĭn′stə-lā′shən) n. **1a.** The act of installing. **b.** The state of being installed. **2.** A system of machinery or other apparatus set up for use. **3.** A permanent military base.

in·stall·ment¹ also **in·stal·ment** (ĭn-stôl′mənt) n. **1.** One of a number of successive payments in settlement of a debt. **2a.** A portion of something, such as a publication, issued at intervals. **b.** A chapter or part of a literary work presented serially. [Alteration of obsolete *estallment* < AN < OFr. *estaler*, to place, fix < *estal*, place, of Gmc. orig. See stel- in App.]

in·stall·ment² also **in·stal·ment** (ĭn-stôl′mənt) n. See **installation 1.**

installment plan n. A credit system by which payment for merchandise is made in installments over a fixed period.

in·stance (ĭn′stəns) n. **1a.** An example that is cited to prove or invalidate a contention or illustrate a point. **b.** A case or an occurrence. **2.** Law A legal proceeding or process; a suit. **3.** A step in a process or series of events. **4a.** A suggestion or request. **b.** Archaic Urgent solicitation. **5.** Obsolete An impelling motive. ❖ tr.v. **-stanced, -stanc·ing, -stanc·es 1.** To offer as an example; cite. **2.** To demonstrate or show by an example; exemplify. —**idiom: for instance** As an example; for example. [ME *instaunce* < OFr. *instance*, request, instant, and < Med.Lat. *īnstantia*, example, both < Lat., presence < *īnstāns, īnstant-*, present. See INSTANT.]

in·stan·cy (ĭn′stən-sē) n., pl. **-cies 1.** The quality or condition of being insistent; urgency. **2.** Immediacy of occurrence.

in·stant (ĭn′stənt) n. **1.** A period ot time so short as to be almost imperceptible. **2.** A particular or precise time. **3.** The current month. **4.** A food or beverage designed for quick preparation. ❖ adj. **1.** Occurring at once; immediate. **2.** Imperative; urgent. **3.** Now under consideration; present. **4a.** Commercially prepared or processed for quick and easy final preparation. **b.** Readily soluble in water. **c.** Appearing, done, or taking place with or as if with maximum quickness and ease. ❖ adv. At once; instantly. [ME < OFr. < Lat. *īnstāns*, *īnstant-*, present, pr. part. of *īnstāre*, to approach : *in-*, on; see IN-² + *stāre*, to stand; see *stā-* in App.] —**in′stant·ness** n.

in·stan·ta·ne·ous (ĭn′stən-tā′nē-əs) adj. **1.** Occurring or completed without perceptible delay. **2.** Done or made as quickly or directly as possible. **3.** Present or occurring at a specific instant. [< Med.Lat. *īnstantāneus* < Lat. *īnstāns*, *īnstant-*, present. See INSTANT.] —**in·stan′ta·ne′i·ty** (ĭn-stăn′tə-nē′ĭ-tē, ĭn′stən-) n. —**in·stan·ta′ne·ous·ly** adv. —**in·stan′ta·ne·ous·ness** n.

in·stan·ter (ĭn-stăn′tər) adv. Instantly. [Med.Lat. < Lat., urgently < *īnstāns*, *īnstant-*, present. See INSTANT.]

in·stan·ti·ate (ĭn-stăn′shē-āt′) tr.v. **-at·ed, -at·ing, -ates** To represent (an abstract concept) by a concrete or tangible example. [Lat. *īnstantia*, example; see INSTANCE + -ATE¹.] —**in·stan′ti·a′tion** n. —**in·stan′tia·tive** (-stăn′shə-tĭv) adj.

in·stant·ly (ĭn′stənt-lē) adv. **1.** At once. **2.** With insistence; urgently. ❖ conj. Chiefly British As soon as.

instant replay n. **1a.** The recording and immediate playback of part of a live television broadcast, as of a sports play. **b.** The part so recorded and replayed. **2.** Informal Something repeated directly or soon after its original occurrence.

in·star¹ (ĭn-stär′) tr.v. **-starred, -star·ring, -stars** To stud with or as if with stars.

in·star² (ĭn′stär′) n. A stage of an insect or other arthropod between molts. [NLat. *īnstar* < Lat., image, form.]

in·state (ĭn-stāt′) tr.v. **-stat·ed, -stat·ing, -states** To establish in office; install.

in·stau·ra·tion (ĭn′stô-rā′shən) n. **1.** Renovation; restoration. **2.** The institution or establishment of something. [Lat. *īnstaurātiō*, *īnstaurātiōn-* < *īnstaurātus*, p. part. of *īnstaurāre*, to renew. See *stā-* in App.]

in·stead (ĭn-stĕd′) adv. **1.** In the place of something previously mentioned; as a substitute or an equivalent. **2.** In preference; as an alternative. [< ME *in sted of*, in place of : *in*, in; see IN¹ + *stede*, place; see STEAD + *of*, of; see OF.]

instead of prep. In place of; rather than.

in·step (ĭn′stĕp′) n. **1.** The arched middle part of the human foot between the toes and the ankle. **2.** The part of a shoe or stocking covering the instep. [ME.]

in·sti·gate (ĭn′stĭ-gāt′) tr.v. **-gat·ed, -gat·ing, -gates 1.** To urge on; goad. **2.** To stir up; foment. [Lat. *īnstīgāre*, *īnstīgāt-*.] —**in′sti·ga′tion** n. —**in′sti·ga′tive** adj. —**in′sti·ga′tor** n.

in·still also **in·stil** (ĭn-stĭl′) tr.v. **-stilled, -still·ing, -stills** also **-stils 1.** To introduce by gradual, persistent efforts; implant. **2.** To pour in (medicine, for example) drop by drop. [ME *instillen* < Lat. *īnstīllāre* : *in-*, into; see IN-² + *stīllāre*, to drip, drop (< *stīlla*, drop).] —**in′stil·la′tion** (ĭn′stə-lā′shən) n. —**in·still′er** n. —**in·still′ment** n.

in·stinct (ĭn′stĭngkt′) n. **1.** An inborn pattern of behavior that is characteristic of a species and is often a response to specific environmental stimuli: *the spawning instinct.* **2.** A powerful motivation or impulse. **3.** An innate capability or aptitude. ❖ adj. (ĭn-stĭngkt′) **1.** Deeply filled or imbued: *words instinct with love.* **2.** Obsolete Impelled from within. [ME < Lat. *īnstīnctus*, impulse < p. part. of *īnstinguere*, to incite : *in-*, intensive pref.; see IN-² + *stinguere*, to prick.]

in·stinc·tive (ĭn-stĭngk′tĭv) adj. **1.** Of, relating to, or prompted by instinct. **2.** Arising from impulse; spontaneous and unthinking. —**in·stinc′tive·ly** adv.

in·stinc·tu·al (ĭn-stĭngk′chōō-əl) adj. Of, relating to, or derived from instinct. —**in·stinc′tu·al·ly** adv.

in·sti·tute (ĭn′stĭ-tōōt′, -tyōōt′) tr.v. **-tut·ed, -tut·ing, -tutes 1a.** To establish, organize, and set in operation. **b.** To initiate; begin. See Syns at **found¹. 2.** To establish or invest in an office or a position. ❖ n. **1a.** Something instituted, esp. an authoritative rule or precedent. **b. institutes** A digest of the principles or rudiments of a particular subject, esp. a legal abstract. **2.** An organization founded to promote a cause: *a cancer research institute.* **3a.** An educational institution, esp. for technical subjects. **b.** The building or buildings housing such an institution. **4.** An intensive workshop or seminar on a specific subject. [ME *instituten* < Lat. *īnstituere*, *īnstitūt-*, to establish : *in-*, in; see IN-² + *statuere*, to set up; see *stā-* in App.] —**in′sti·tut′er, in′sti·tu′tor** n.

in·sti·tu·tion (ĭn′stĭ-tōō′shən, -tyōō′-) n. **1.** The act of instituting. **2a.** A custom, practice, relationship, or behavioral pattern of importance in a community or society. **b.** Informal One long associated with a specified place, position, or function. **3a.** An established organization or foundation, as one dedicated to education or culture. **b.** The building or buildings housing an institution. **c.** A place for the care of persons who are destitute, disabled, or mentally ill.

in·sti·tu·tion·al (ĭn′stĭ-tōō′shə-nəl, -tyōō′-) adj. **1.** Of or relating to an institution or institutions. **2.** Organized as or forming an institution: *institutional religion.* **3.** Characteristic or suggestive of an institution, esp. in being uniform, dull, or unimaginative. **4.** Of or relating to the principles or institutes of a subject such as law. —**in′sti·tu′tion·al·ly** adv.

in·sti·tu·tion·al·ism (ĭn′stĭ-tōō′shə-nə-lĭz′əm, -tyōō′-) n. **1.** Adherence to or belief in established forms, esp. belief in organized religion. **2.** Use of public institutions for the care of those who are physically or mentally disabled, criminally delinquent, or incapable of independent living. —**in′sti·tu′tion·al·ist** n.

in·sti·tu·tion·al·ize (ĭn′stĭ-tōō′shə-nə-līz′, -tyōō′-) tr.v. **-ized, -iz·ing, -iz·es 1a.** To make into, treat as, or give the character of an institution to. **b.** To make part of a structured and usu. well-established system. **2.** To place (a person) in the care of an institution. —**in′sti·tu′tion·al·i·za′tion** (-lĭ-zā′shən) n.

instr. abbr. **1.** instructor **2.** instrument **3.** instrumental

in·stroke (ĭn′strōk′) n. An inward stroke, esp. a piston stroke moving away from the crankshaft.

in·struct (ĭn-strŭkt′) v. **-struct·ed, -struct·ing, -structs** —tr. **1.** To provide with knowledge, esp. in a methodical way. See Syns at **teach. 2.** To give orders to; direct. —*intr.* To serve as an instructor. [ME *instructen* < Lat. *īnstruere*, *īnstrūct-*, to prepare, instruct : *in-*, on; see IN-² + *struere*, to build.]

in·struc·tion (ĭn-strŭk′shən) n. **1.** The act, practice, or profession of instructing. **2a.** Imparted knowledge. **b.** An imparted or acquired item of knowledge; a lesson. **3.** Computer Science A sequence of bits that tells a computer to perform a particular operation. **4a.** An authoritative direction to be obeyed; an order. Often used in the plural. **b. instructions** Detailed directions on procedure. —**in·struc′tion·al** adj.

in·struc·tive (ĭn-strŭk′tĭv) adj. Conveying knowledge or information. —**in·struc′tive·ly** adv. —**in·struc′tive·ness** n.

in·struc·tor (ĭn-strŭk′tər) n. **1.** One who instructs; a teacher. **2.** A college or university teacher who ranks below an assistant professor. —**in·struc′tor·ship′** n.

in·stru·ment (ĭn′strə-mənt) n. **1.** A means by which something is done; an agency. **2.** One used by another to accomplish a purpose; a dupe. **3.** An implement used to facilitate work: *a scalpel and other surgical instruments.* **4.** A device for recording, measuring, or controlling, esp. such a device functioning as part of a control system. **5.** Music A device for playing or producing music. **6.** A legal document, such as a deed or will. ❖ tr.v. (-mĕnt′) **-ment·ed, -ment·ing, -ments 1.** To provide or equip with instruments. **2.** Music To compose or arrange for performance. **3.** To address a legal document to. [ME < OFr. < Lat. *īnstrūmentum*, tool, implement < *instruere*, to prepare. See INSTRUCT.]

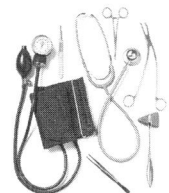

instrument
variety of medical
instruments

in·stru·men·tal (ĭn′strə-mĕn′tl) adj. **1.** Serving as a means or agency; implemental: *instrumental in solving the crime.* **2.** Of, relating to, or accomplished with an instrument or tool. **3.** Music Performed on or written for an instrument. **4.** Grammar Of or being a case used typically to express means, agency, or accompaniment. **5.** Of or relating to instrumentalism. ❖ n. **1a.** Grammar The instrumental case. **b.** A word or form in the instrumental case. **2.** Music A composition for one or more instruments. —**in′stru·men′tal·ly** adv.

in·stru·men·tal·ism (ĭn′strə-mĕn′tl-ĭz′əm) n. A pragmatic theory that ideas are instruments that guide action, their validity being determined by the success of the action.

in·stru·men·tal·ist (ĭn′strə-mĕn′tl-ĭst) n. **1.** Music One who plays an instrument. **2.** An advocate or student of instrumentalism. —**in′stru·men′tal·ist** adj.

in·stru·men·tal·i·ty (ĭn′strə-mĕn-tăl′ĭ-tē) n., pl. **-ties 1.** The state or quality of being instrumental. **2.** A means; an agency. **3.** A subsidiary branch, as of a government, by means of which functions or policies are carried out.

in·stru·men·ta·tion (ĭn′strə-mĕn-tā′shən) n. **1.** The application or use of instruments. **2.** Music **a.** The study and practice of arranging music for instruments. **b.** The arrangement or orchestration resulting from such practice. **c.** A list of instruments used in an orchestration. **3a.** The study, development, and manufacture of instruments, as for scientific or industrial use. **b.** Instruments for a specific purpose. **4.** Instrumentality.

instrument board n. See **instrument panel**.

instrument flying n. Aircraft navigation by reference to instruments only.

instrument landing n. An aircraft landing made by means of instruments and ground-based radio equipment only.

instrument panel n. A mounted array of instruments used to operate a machine, as in an aircraft.

in·sub·or·di·nate (ĭn′sə-bôr′dn-ĭt) adj. Not submissive to authority: *insubordinate behavior.* —**in′sub·or′di·nate** n. —**in′sub·or′di·nate·ly** adv. —**in′sub·or·di·na′tion** n.

in·sub·stan·tial (ĭn′səb-stăn′shəl) adj. **1.** Lacking substance or reality. **2a.** Not firm or solid; flimsy. **b.** Delicate; fine. **3.** Negligible in size or amount. —**in′sub·stan′ti·al′i·ty** (-shē-ăl′ĭ-tē) n.

in·suf·fer·a·ble (ĭn-sŭf′ər-ə-bəl, -sŭf′rə-) adj. Difficult or impossible to endure; intolerable. —**in·suf′fer·a·bly** adv.

in·suf·fi·cien·cy (ĭn′sə-fĭsh′ən-sē) n., pl. **-cies 1.** The quality or state of being insufficient, esp.: **a.** Moral or mental incompetence. **b.** Inadequate supply: *an insufficiency of funds.* **c.** Inability of a body part or organ to function normally: *cardiac insufficiency.* **2.** A failing; an inadequacy.

in•suf•fi•cient (ĭn′sə-fĭsh′ənt) *adj.* Not sufficient; inadequate. —**in′suf•fi′cient•ly** *adv.*

in•suf•flate (ĭn′sə-flāt′, ĭn-sŭf′lāt′) *tr.v.* **-flat•ed, -flat•ing, -flates 1.** To blow or breathe into or on. **2.** To treat medically by blowing a powder, gas, or vapor into a bodily cavity. [Lat. *īnsufflāre, īnsufflāt-* : *in-*, into; see IN–[2] + *sufflāre*, to inflate; see SOUFFLÉ.] —**in′suf•fla′tor** *n.*

in•suf•fla•tion (ĭn′sə-flā′shən) *n.* **1.** The act or an instance of insufflating. **2.** *Ecclesiastical* A ritual act of breathing on baptismal water or on the one being baptized.

in•su•lant (ĭn′sə-lənt, ĭns′yə-) *n.* A material used for insulation; an insulator.

insulation
installing wall insulation

in•su•lar (ĭn′sə-lər, ĭns′yə-) *adj.* **1a.** Of, relating to, or constituting an island. **b.** Living or located on an island. **2a.** Suggestive of the isolated life of an island. **b.** Circumscribed and detached in outlook and experience; narrow or provincial. **3.** *Anatomy* Of or relating to isolated tissue or an island of tissue. [Fr. *insulaire* < LLat. *īnsulāris* < Lat. *īnsula*, island.] —**in′su•lar•ism, in′su•lar′i•ty** (-lăr′ĭ-tē) *n.* —**in′su•lar•ly** *adv.*

Insular Celtic *n.* A branch of the Celtic languages comprising those spoken or having originated in the British Isles and divided into the Goidelic and Brittonic groups.

in•su•late (ĭn′sə-lāt′, ĭns′yə-) *tr.v.* **-lat•ed, -lat•ing, -lates 1.** To cause to be in a detached or isolated position. **2.** To prevent the passage of heat, electricity, or sound into or out of, esp. by surrounding with a nonconducting material. [Lat. *īnsula*, island + –ATE[1].]

in•su•la•tion (ĭn′sə-lā′shən, ĭns′yə-) *n.* **1.** The act of insulating or the state of being insulated. **2.** A material or substance used in insulating: *soundproof cork insulation.*

in•su•la•tive (ĭn′sə-lā′tĭv, ĭns′yə-) *adj.* Serving to insulate or keep safe: *the insulative value of an animal's fur.*

in•su•la•tor (ĭn′sə-lā′tər, ĭns′yə-) *n.* **1.** A material that insulates, esp. a nonconductor of sound, heat, or electricity. **2.** A device that insulates.

in•su•lin (ĭn′sə-lĭn) *n.* **1.** A hormone secreted by the islets of Langerhans and regulating the metabolism of carbohydrates and fats, esp. the conversion of glucose to glycogen. **2.** Any of various pharmaceutical preparations containing this hormone, used to treat diabetes mellitus (type I). [NLat. *īnsula*, island (of Langerhans) (< Lat., island) + –IN.]

insulin shock *n.* Acute hypoglycemia usu. resulting from an overdose of insulin and characterized by sweating, trembling, dizziness, and if left untreated, convulsions and coma.

in•sult (ĭn-sŭlt′) *v.* **-sult•ed, -sult•ing, -sults** —*tr.* **1a.** To treat with gross insensitivity, insolence, or rudeness. **b.** To affront or demean. **2.** *Obsolete* To make an attack on. —*intr. Archaic* **1.** To behave arrogantly. **2.** To give offense; offend. ❖ *n.* (ĭn′sŭlt′) **1.** An offensive action or remark. **2.** A traumatic bodily injury or event. [Ult. < Lat. *īnsultāre*, to leap at, insult, freq. of *īnsilīre*, to leap upon : *in-*, on; see IN–[2] + *salīre*, to leap.] —**in•sult′er** *n.* —**in•sult′ing•ly** *adv.*

in•su•per•a•ble (ĭn-so͞o′pər-ə-bəl) *adj.* Impossible to overcome; insurmountable. —**in•su′per•a•bil′i•ty, in•su′per•a•ble•ness** *n.* —**in•su′per•a•bly** *adv.*

in•sup•port•a•ble (ĭn′sə-pôr′tə-bəl, -pōr′-) *adj.* **1.** Not endurable; intolerable: *insupportable anguish.* **2.** Lacking grounds or defense; unjustifiable: *an insupportable claim.* —**in′sup•port′a•ble•ness** *n.* —**in′sup•port′a•bly** *adv.*

in•sup•press•i•ble (ĭn′sə-prĕs′ə-bəl) *adj.* Impossible to suppress or control; irrepressible. —**in′sup•press′i•bly** *adv.*

in•sur•ance (ĭn-sho͝or′əns) *n.* **1a.** The act, business, or system of insuring. **b.** The state of being insured. **c.** A means of being insured. **2a.** Coverage by a contract binding a party to indemnify another against specified loss in return for premiums paid. **b.** The sum or rate for which such a contract insures something. **c.** The periodic premium paid for this coverage. **3.** A protective measure.

intarsia
designed by Antonio and Paolo Mola; the Palazzo Ducale, Mantua, Italy

in•sure (ĭn-sho͝or′) *v.* **-sured, -sur•ing, -sures** —*tr.* **1a.** To provide or arrange insurance for: *companies insuring homeowners.* **b.** To acquire or have insurance for: *insured her car for theft.* **2.** To make sure, certain, or secure. See Usage Note at **assure.** —*intr.* To buy or sell insurance. [ME *ensuren*, to assure < OFr. *enseurer*, poss. var. of *assurer*. See ASSURE.] —**in•sur′a•bil′i•ty** *n.* —**in•sur′a•ble** *adj.*

in•sured (ĭn-sho͝ord′) *n., pl.* **insured** or **-sureds** One who has or is covered by an insurance policy.

in•sur•er (ĭn-sho͝or′ər) *n.* One that insures, esp. an insurance underwriter.

in•sur•gence (ĭn-sûr′jəns) *n.* The action or an instance of rebellion; an insurrection.

in•sur•gen•cy (ĭn-sûr′jən-sē) *n., pl.* **-cies 1.** The quality or circumstance of being rebellious. **2.** An instance of rebellion.

in•sur•gent (ĭn-sûr′jənt) *adj.* **1.** Rising in revolt against established authority, esp. a government. **2.** Rebelling against the leadership of a political party. ❖ *n.* One who is insurgent. [Lat. *īnsurgēns, īnsurgent-*, pr. part. of *īnsurgere*, to rise up : *in-*, intensive pref.; see IN–[2] + *surgere*, to rise; see SURGE.] —**in•sur′gent•ly** *adv.*

in•sur•mount•a•ble (ĭn′sər-moun′tə-bəl) *adj.* Impossible to surmount; insuperable. —**in′sur•mount′a•bil′i•ty, in′sur•mount′a•ble•ness** *n.* —**in′sur•mount′a•bly** *adv.*

in•sur•rec•tion (ĭn′sə-rĕk′shən) *n.* The act or an instance of open revolt against civil authority or a constituted government. [ME < OFr. < LLat. *īnsurrēctiō, īnsurrēctiōn-* < Lat. *īnsurrēctus*, p. part. of *īnsurgere*, to rise up. See INSURGENT.] —**in′sur•rec′tion•al** *adj.* —**in′sur•rec′tion•ar′y** (-shə-nĕr′ē) *adj. & n.* —**in′sur•rec′tion•ism** *n.* —**in′sur•rec′tion•ist** *n.*

in•sus•cep•ti•ble (ĭn′sə-sĕp′tə-bəl) *adj.* Not susceptible. —**in•sus•cep′ti•bil′i•ty** *n.* —**in′sus•cep′ti•bly** *adv.*

int. *abbr.* **1.** intercept **2.** interest **3.** interim **4.** interior **5.** interjection **6.** intermediate **7.** internal **8.** international **9.** interval **10.** intransitive

in•tact (ĭn-tăkt′) *adj.* **1.** Remaining sound, entire, or uninjured; not impaired in any way. **2.** Having all physical parts, esp.: **a.** Having the hymen unbroken. **b.** Not castrated. [ME < Lat. *intāctus* : *in-*, not; see IN–[1] + *tāctus*, p. part. of *tangere*, to touch; see **tag-** in App.] —**in•tact′ly** *adv.* —**in•tact′ness** *n.*

in•ta•glio (ĭn-tăl′yō, -täl′-) *n., pl.* **-glios 1a.** A figure or design carved into or beneath the surface of hard metal or stone. **b.** The art or process of carving a design in this manner. **2.** A gemstone carved in intaglio. **3.** Printing done with a plate bearing an image in intaglio. **4.** A die incised so as to produce a design in relief. [Ital. < *intagliare*, to engrave : *in-*, in (< Lat.; see IN–[2]) + *tagliare*, to cut (< VLat. **talliāre* < LLat. *tāliāre*; see TAILOR).]

in•take (ĭn′tāk′) *n.* **1.** An opening by which a fluid is admitted into a container or conduit. **2a.** The act of taking in. **b.** The quantity taken in. **c.** Something, esp. energy, taken in.

in•tan•gi•ble (ĭn-tăn′jə-bəl) *adj.* **1.** Incapable of being perceived by the senses. **2.** Incapable of being realized or defined. **3.** Incorporeal. ❖ *n.* **1.** Something intangible, esp. an asset that cannot be perceived by the senses. Often used in the plural: *intangibles such as goodwill and dedication.* **2.** *Law* Incorporeal property such as bank deposits, stocks, bonds, and promissory notes. Often used in the plural. —**in•tan′gi•bil′i•ty, in•tan′gi•ble•ness** *n.* —**in•tan′gi•bly** *adv.*

in•tar•si•a (ĭn-tär′sē-ə) *n.* **1.** A decorative inlaid pattern in a surface, esp. a mosaic in wood. **2.** A knitted design resembling a mosaic that is visible on both sides of a fabric. **3.** The art or practice of making intarsias. [Ger. < Ital. *intarsio* < *intarsiare*, to inlay : *in-*, in (< Lat.; see IN–[2]) + *tarsia*, inlaid mosaic work (< Ar. *tarṣīʿ*, inlaying, setting, infinitive of *raṣṣaʿa*, to inlay, derived stem of *raṣiʿa*, to adhere).]

in•te•ger (ĭn′tĭ-jər) *n. Mathematics* **1.** A member of the set of positive whole numbers {1, 2, 3 . . . }, negative whole numbers (−1, −2, −3 . . .), and zero (0). **2.** A complete unit or entity. [< Lat., whole, complete. See **tag-** in App.]

in•te•gra•ble (ĭn′tĭ-grə-bəl) *adj. Mathematics* Capable of undergoing integration or of being integrated.

in•te•gral (ĭn′tĭ-grəl, ĭn-tĕg′rəl) *adj.* **1.** Essential or necessary for completeness; constituent: *A kitchen is integral to a house.* **2.** Possessing everything essential; entire. **3.** (ĭn′tĭ-grəl) *Mathematics* **a.** Expressed or expressible as or in terms of integers. **b.** Expressed as or involving integrals. ❖ *n.* **1.** A complete unit; a whole. **2.** (ĭn′tĭ-grəl) *Mathematics* **a.** A number computed by a limiting process in which the domain of a function is divided into arbitrarily small units, the value of the function at a point in each unit is multiplied by the linear or areal measurement of that unit, and all such products are summed. **b.** A definite integral. **c.** An indefinite integral. [ME < OFr. < Med.Lat. *integrālis*, making up a whole < Lat. *integer*, complete. See INTEGER.] —**in′te•gral′i•ty** (-grăl′ĭ-tē) *n.* —**in′te•gral•ly** *adv.*

integral calculus *n.* The study of integration and its uses, such as in finding volumes, areas, and solutions of differential equations.

integral domain *n. Mathematics* A commutative ring with identity where the product of nonzero elements cannot be zero.

in•te•grand (ĭn′tĭ-grănd′) *n.* A function to be integrated. [< Lat. *integrandus*, gerundive of *integrāre*, to integrate. See INTEGRATE.]

in•te•grant (ĭn′tĭ-grənt) *adj.* Constituting part of a whole; integral.

in•te•grate (ĭn′tĭ-grāt′) *v.* **-grat•ed, -grat•ing, -grates** —*tr.* **1.** To make a whole by bringing all parts together; unify. **2a.** To join with something else; unite. **b.** To make part of a larger unit. **3a.** To open to people of all races or ethnic groups without restriction; desegregate. **b.** To admit (a racial or ethnic group) to equal membership in an institution or society. **4.** *Mathematics* **a.** To calculate the integral of. **b.** To perform integration on. **5.** *Psychology* To bring about the integration of (personality traits). —*intr.* To become integrated or undergo integration. [< ME, intact < Lat. *integrātus*, p. part. of *integrāre*, to make whole < *integer*, complete. See **tag-** in App.] —**in′te•gra′tive** *adj.*

in•te•grat•ed circuit (ĭn′tĭ-grā′tĭd) *n.* A complex set of electronic components and their interconnections that are etched or imprinted on a chip of semiconducting material.

in•te•gra•tion (ĭn′tĭ-grā′shən) *n.* **1a.** The act or process of integrating. **b.** The state of becoming integrated. **2.** The bringing of people of different racial or ethnic groups into unrestricted and equal association, as in society or an organization; desegregation. **3.** *Psychology* The organization of the psychological or social traits and tendencies of a personality into a harmonious whole.

4. *Mathematics* The process of computing an integral; the inverse of differentiation. **5.** *Electronics* The process of placing more than one integrated circuit on a single chip.

in•te•gra•tion•ist (ĭn′tĭ-grā′shə-nĭst) *n.* One who advocates or works for social integration. **—in′te•gra′tion•ist** *adj.*

in•te•gra•tor (ĭn′tĭ-grā′tər) *n.* **1.** One that integrates. **2.** An instrument for mechanically calculating definite integrals.

in•teg•ri•ty (ĭn-tĕg′rĭ-tē) *n.* **1.** Steadfast adherence to a strict ethical code. **2.** The state of being unimpaired; soundness. **3.** The quality or condition of being whole or undivided; completeness. [ME *integrite* < OFr. < Lat. *integritās*, soundness < *integer*, whole, complete. See **tag-** in App.]

in•teg•u•ment (ĭn-tĕg′yo͞o-mənt) *n.* **1.** A natural outer covering, such as the membrane enclosing an organ. **2.** *Botany* The envelope of an ovule. [Lat. *integumentum* < *integere*, to cover : *in-*, on; see IN–[2] + *tegere*, to cover; see **(s)teg-** in App.] **—in•teg′u•men′ta•ry** (-mĕn′tə-rē, -mĕn′trē) *adj.*

in•tel•lect (ĭn′tl-ĕkt′) *n.* **1a.** The ability to learn and reason; the capacity for knowledge and understanding. **b.** The ability to think abstractly or profoundly. **2.** A person of great intellectual ability. [ME < OFr. *intellecte* < Lat. *intellēctus*, perception < p. part. of *intellegere*, to perceive. See INTELLIGENT.]

in•tel•lec•tion (ĭn′tl-ĕk′shən) *n.* **1.** The act or process of using the intellect; thinking or reasoning. **2.** A thought or an idea. [ME *intelleccioun*, understanding < Lat. *intellēctiō*, *intellēctiōn-*, synecdoche < *intellēctus*, intellect. See INTELLECT.]

in•tel•lec•tive (ĭn′tl-ĕk′tĭv) *adj.* Of, relating to, or generated by the intellect. **—in′tel•lec′tive•ly** *adv.*

in•tel•lec•tu•al (ĭn′tl-ĕk′cho͞o-əl) *adj.* **1a.** Of or relating to the intellect. **b.** Rational rather than emotional. **2.** Appealing to or engaging the intellect. **3a.** Having or showing intellect, esp. to a high degree. See Syns at **intelligent. b.** Given to activities or pursuits that require exercise of the intellect. ❖ *n.* An intellectual person. [ME < OFr. *intellectuel* < LLat. *intellēctuālis* < Lat. *intellēctus*, intellect. See INTELLECT.] **—in′tel•lec′tu•al′i•ty** (-ăl′ĭ-tē), **in′tel•lec′tu•al•ness** *n.* **—in′tel•lec′tu•al•ly** *adv.*

in•tel•lec•tu•al•ism (ĭn′tl-ĕk′cho͞o-ə-lĭz′əm) *n.* **1.** Exercise or application of the intellect. **2.** Devotion to exercise or development of the intellect. **—in′tel•lec′tu•al•ist** *n.* **—in′tel•lec′tu•al•is′tic** *adj.*

in•tel•lec•tu•al•i•za•tion (ĭn′tl-ĕk′cho͞o-ə-lĭ-zā′shən) *n. Psychology* **1.** The act or process of intellectualizing. **2.** Excessive reasoning as an unconscious means of protecting oneself from the anxiety of confronting painful fears or problems.

in•tel•lec•tu•al•ize (ĭn′tl-ĕk′cho͞o-ə-līz′) *tr.v.* **-ized, -iz•ing, -iz•es 1.** To furnish a rational structure or meaning for. **2.** To avoid psychological insight into (an emotional problem) by intellectual analysis. **—in′tel•lec′tu•al•iz′er** *n.*

intellectual property *n.* A product of the intellect that has commercial value, including copyrighted property such as literary works, and ideational property, such as patents and business methods.

in•tel•li•gence (ĭn-tĕl′ə-jəns) *n.* **1a.** The capacity to acquire and apply knowledge. **b.** The faculty of thought and reason. **c.** Superior powers of mind. **2.** An intelligent incorporeal being. **3.** Information; news. **4a.** Secret information, esp. about an enemy. **b.** An agency, staff, or office gathering intelligence. **c.** Espionage agents, organizations, and activities considered as a group.

intelligence quotient *n.* The ratio of tested mental age to chronological age, usu. expressed as a quotient multiplied by 100.

in•tel•li•genc•er (ĭn-tĕl′ə-jən-sər, -jĕn′-) *n.* **1.** One who conveys information. **2.** A secret agent, an informer, or a spy.

in•tel•li•gent (ĭn-tĕl′ə-jənt) *adj.* **1.** Having intelligence. **2.** Having a high degree of intelligence; mentally acute. **3.** Showing sound judgment and rationality. **4.** Appealing to the intellect; intellectual. **5.** *Computer Science* Having certain data storage and processing capabilities. [Lat. *intelligēns*, *intelligent-*, pr. part. of *intellegere*, *intelligere*, to perceive : *inter-*, inter- + *legere*, to choose; see **leg-** in App.] **—in•tel′li•gen′tial** (-jĕn′shəl) *adj.* **—in•tel′li•gent•ly** *adv.*

SYNONYMS *intelligent, bright, brilliant, knowing, quick-witted, smart, intellectual* These adjectives mean having or showing mental keenness. *Intelligent* usually implies the ability to cope with new problems and to use the power of reasoning and inference effectively: *The intelligent math students excelled in calculus. Bright* implies quickness or ease in learning: *The bright child learned the alphabet quickly. Brilliant* suggests unusually impressive mental acuteness: *"The dullard's envy of brilliant men is always assuaged by the suspicion that they will come to a bad end"* (Max Beerbohm). *Knowing* implies the possession of knowledge, information, or understanding: *Knowing collectors bought all the auctioned paintings. Quick-witted* suggests mental alertness and prompt response: *quick-witted emergency medical staff. Smart* refers to quick intelligence and often a ready capability for taking care of one's own interests: *Smart lawyers can effectively manipulate juries. Intellectual* implies the capacity to grasp difficult or abstract concepts: *intellectual philosophers.*

in•tel•li•gent•si•a (ĭn-tĕl′ə-jĕnt′sē-ə, -gĕnt′-) *n.* The intellectual elite of a society. [Russ. *intelligentsiya* < Lat. *intelligentia*, intelligence < *intelligēns*, *intelligent-*, intelligent. See INTELLIGENT.]

in•tel•li•gi•ble (ĭn-tĕl′ĭ-jə-bəl) *adj.* **1.** Capable of being understood. **2.** Capable of being apprehended by the intellect alone. [ME < OFr. < Lat. *intellegibilis*, *intelligibilis* < *intellegere*, to perceive. See INTELLIGENT.] **—in•tel′li•gi•bil′i•ty, in•tel′li•gi•ble•ness** *n.* **—in•tel′li•gi•bly** *adv.*

in•tem•per•ance (ĭn-tĕm′pər-əns, -prəns) *n.* **1.** Lack of temperance, as in the indulgence of an appetite or a passion. **2.** Excessive use of alcoholic beverages.

in•tem•per•ate (ĭn-tĕm′pər-ĭt, -prĭt) *adj.* Not temperate or moderate; excessive, esp. in the use of alcoholic beverages. **—in•tem′per•ate•ly** *adv.* **—in•tem′per•ate•ness** *n.*

in•tend (ĭn-tĕnd′) *v.* **-tend•ed, -tend•ing, -tends** *—tr.* **1.** To have in mind; plan: *We intend to go.* **2a.** To design for a specific purpose. **b.** To have in mind for a particular use. **3.** To signify or mean. *—intr.* To have a design or purpose in mind. [ME *entenden* < OFr. *entendre* < Lat. *intendere* : *in-*, toward; see IN–[2] + *tendere*, to stretch; see **ten-** in App.]

in•ten•dance (ĭn-tĕn′dəns) *n.* **1.** The function of an intendant; management. **2.** An administrative office or district.

in•ten•dan•cy (ĭn-tĕn′dən-sē) *n., pl.* **-cies 1.** The position or function of an intendant. **2.** Intendants considered as a group. **3.** The district supervised by an intendant.

in•ten•dant (ĭn-tĕn′dənt) *n.* **1.** An administrative official serving a French, Spanish, or Portuguese monarch. **2.** A district administrator in some countries of Latin America. [Fr. < OFr., administrator < Lat. *intendēns*, *intendent-*, pr. part. of *intendere*, to intend. See INTEND.]

in•tend•ed (ĭn-tĕn′dĭd) *adj.* **1.** Deliberate; intentional. **2.** Prospective; future. ❖ *n. Informal* A person whom one intends to marry; a fiancé or fiancée. **—in•tend′ed•ly** *adv.*

in•tend•ing (ĭn-tĕn′dĭng) *adj.* Purposing to become or be; prospective.

in•tend•ment (ĭn-tĕnd′mənt) *n.* The true meaning or intention of something, esp. of a law.

in•ten•er•ate (ĭn-tĕn′ə-rāt′) *tr.v.* **-at•ed, -at•ing, -ates** To make tender; soften. [IN–[2] + Lat. *tener*, tender; see TENDER[1] + –ATE[1].] **—in•ten′er•a′tion** *n.*

in•tense (ĭn-tĕns′) *adj.* **-tens•er, -tens•est 1.** Possessing or displaying a distinctive feature to an extreme degree. **2.** Extreme in degree, strength, or size. **3.** Involving or showing strain or extreme effort. **4a.** Deeply felt; profound. **b.** Tending to feel deeply. [ME < OFr. < Lat. *intēnsus*, p. part. of *intendere*, to stretch, intend. See INTEND.] **—in•tense′ly** *adv.* **—in•tense′ness** *n.*

USAGE NOTE The meanings of *intense* and *intensive* overlap considerably but are often subtly distinct. When used to describe human feeling or activity, *intense* often suggests a strength or concentration that arises from inner dispositions. *Intensive* is frequently applied when the strength or concentration of an activity is imposed from without. *Mark's intense study of German* suggests that Mark himself was responsible for the concentrated activity, whereas *Mark's intensive study of German* suggests that the program in which Mark was studying was designed to cover a great deal of material in a brief period.

in•ten•si•fi•er (ĭn-tĕn′sə-fī′ər) *n. Grammar* See **intensive.**

in•ten•si•fy (ĭn-tĕn′sə-fī′) *v.* **-fied, -fy•ing, -fies** *—tr.* **1.** To make intense or more intense. **2.** To increase the contrast of (a photographic image). *—intr.* To become intense or more intense. **—in•ten′si•fi•ca′tion** (-fĭ-kā′shən) *n.*

in•ten•sion (ĭn-tĕn′shən) *n.* **1.** The state or quality of being intense; intensity. **2.** The act of becoming intense or more intense; intensification. **3.** *Logic* The sum of the attributes contained in a term. [Lat. *intēnsiō*, *intēnsiōn-* < *intēnsus*, stretched. See INTENSE.] **—in•ten′sion•al** *adj.*

in•ten•si•ty (ĭn-tĕn′sĭ-tē) *n., pl.* **-ties 1.** Exceptionally great concentration, power, or force. **2.** *Physics* The amount or degree of strength of electricity, light, heat, or sound per unit area or volume. **3a.** The strength of a color, esp. the degree to which it lacks its complementary color. **b.** See **saturation** 5.

in•ten•sive (ĭn-tĕn′sĭv) *adj.* **1.** Of, relating to, or marked by intensity. See Usage Note at **intense. 2.** *Grammar* Tending to emphasize or intensify. **3.** Possessing or requiring to a high degree. Often used in combination: *research-intensive.* **4.** Relating to or being a method esp. of land cultivation intended to increase the productivity of a fixed area by means of an increase in capital and labor. **5.** *Physics* Having the same value for any subdivision of a thermodynamic system: *intensive pressure.* ❖ *n. Grammar* A linguistic element, such as the adverb *extremely*, that provides force or emphasis. **—in•ten′sive•ly** *adv.* **—in•ten′sive•ness** *n.*

intensive care *n.* Continuous and closely monitored health care that is provided to critically ill patients.

intensive care unit *n.* A specialized section of a hospital containing the equipment and staff to provide intensive care.

in•tent (ĭn-tĕnt′) *n.* **1.** Something that is intended; an aim or purpose. See Syns at **intention. 2.** *Law* The state of one's mind at the time one carries out an action. **3.** Meaning; purport. ❖ *adj.* **1.** Firmly fixed; concentrated. **2.** Having the attention applied; engrossed. **3.** Having the mind and will on a specific purpose. ***—idiom:* for (or to) all intents and purposes** In every practical sense; practically. [ME *entent* < OFr. < Med.Lat. *intentus* < Lat.,

ă pat	oi boy
ā pay	ou out
âr care	o͝o took
ä father	o͞o boot
ĕ pet	ŭ cut
ē be	ûr urge
ĭ pit	th thin
ī pie	*th* this
îr pier	hw which
ŏ pot	zh vision
ō toe	ə about, item
ô paw	

Stress marks:
′ (primary);
′ (secondary), as in
lexicon (lĕk′sĭ-kŏn′)

an extending < *intentus*, attentive to < p. part. of *intendere*, to direct attention. See INTEND.] —**in·tent′ly** *adv.* —**in·tent′ness** *n.*

in·ten·tion (ĭn-tĕn′shən) *n.* **1.** A course of action that one intends to follow. **2a.** An aim that guides action; an objective. **b. intentions** Purpose with respect to marriage. **3.** *Medicine* The process by which or the manner in which a wound heals. **4.** *Archaic* Import; meaning. [Ult. < Lat. *intentiō, intentiōn-* < *intentus,* intent < p. part. of *intendere,* to direct attention. See INTEND.]

SYNONYMS *intention, intent, purpose, goal, end, aim, object, objective* These nouns refer to what one plans to do or achieve. *Intention* signifies a course of action that one proposes to follow: *It is my intention to take a vacation next month. Intent* more strongly implies deliberateness: *The executor complied with the testator's intent. Purpose* strengthens the idea of resolution or determination: *"His purpose was to discover how long these guests intended to stay"* (Joseph Conrad). *Goal* may suggest an idealistic or long-term purpose: *set a goal to raise ten million dollars. End* suggests a long-range goal: *will use any means to achieve that end. Aim* stresses the direction one's efforts take in pursuit of an end: *The aim of most students is to graduate.* An *object* is an end that one tries to carry out: *The object of chess is to capture your opponent's king. Objective* often implies that the end or goal can be reached: *The report outlines the committee's objectives.*

in·ten·tion·al (ĭn-tĕn′shə-nəl) *adj.* **1.** Done deliberately; intended: *an intentional slight.* See Syns at **voluntary. 2.** Having to do with intention. —**in·ten′tion·al·ly** *adv.*

in·ten·tion·al·i·ty (ĭn-tĕn′shə-năl′ĭ-tē) *n., pl.* **-ties 1.** The state of having or being formed by an intention. **2.** *Philosophy* The property of being about or directed toward a subject, as inherent in conscious states, beliefs, or creations of the mind.

in·ter (ĭn-tûr′) *tr.v.* **-terred, -ter·ring, -ters** To place in a grave or tomb; bury. [Ult. < Med.Lat. *interrāre* : Lat. *in-*, in; see IN-[2] + Lat. *terra,* earth; see **ters-** in App.]

inter. *abbr.* intermediate

inter– *pref.* **1.** Between; among: *international.* **2.** In the midst of; within: *intertropical.* **3.** Mutual; mutually: *interrelate.* **4.** Reciprocal; reciprocally: *intermingle.* [ME *entre-, inter-* < OFr. *entre-* < Lat. *inter-* < *inter.* See **en** in App.]

in·ter·a·bang (ĭn-tĕr′ə-băng′) *n.* Variant of **interrobang.**

in·ter·act (ĭn′tər-ăkt′) *intr.v.* **-act·ed, -act·ing, -acts** To act on each other: *Students learn by interacting.*

in·ter·ac·tion (ĭn′tər-ăk′shən) *n.* **1a.** The act or process of interacting. **b.** The state of undergoing interaction. **2.** *Physics* Any of four fundamental ways in which bodies can influence each other, classified as strong, weak, electromagnetic, and gravitational.

in·ter·ac·tive (ĭn′tər-ăk′tĭv) *adj.* **1.** Acting or capable of acting on each other. **2.** *Computer Science* Of or relating to a program that responds to user activity. **3.** Of, relating to, or being a form of television entertainment in which the viewer participates directly. —**in′ter·ac′tive·ly** *adv.*

in·ter a·li·a (ĭn′tər ā′lē-ə, ä′lē-ə) *adv.* Among other things. [Lat.]

inter a·li·os (ā′lē-ōs′, ä′lē-ōs′) *adv.* Among other persons. [Lat. *inter aliōs* : *inter,* among + *aliōs,* masc. accusative pl. of *alius,* other.]

in·ter·a·tom·ic (ĭn′tər-ə-tŏm′ĭk) *adj.* Occurring, operating, or situated between atoms.

in·ter·breed (ĭn′tər-brēd′) *v.* **-bred** (-brĕd′), **-breed·ing, -breeds** —*intr.* **1.** To breed with another kind or species; hybridize. **2.** To breed within a narrow range or with closely related types or individuals; inbreed. —*tr.* To cause to interbreed.

in·ter·ca·lar·y (ĭn-tûr′kə-lĕr′ē, ĭn′tər-kăl′ə-rē) *adj.* **1a.** Inserted in the calendar to make the calendar year correspond to the solar year. Used of a day or month. **b.** Having such a day or month inserted. Used of a year. **2.** Inserted between other elements or parts; interpolated. [Lat. *intercalārius, intercalāris* < *intercalāre,* to intercalate. See INTERCALATE.]

in·ter·ca·late (ĭn-tûr′kə-lāt′) *tr.v.* **-lat·ed, -lat·ing, -lates 1.** To insert (a day or month) in a calendar. **2.** To insert, interpose, or interpolate. [Lat. *intercalāre, intercalāt-* : *inter-,* inter- + *calāre,* to proclaim; see **kelə-** in App.] —**in′ter·ca·la′tion** *n.* —**in·ter′ca·la′tive** *adj.*

in·ter·cede (ĭn′tər-sēd′) *intr.v.* **-ced·ed, -ced·ing, -cedes 1.** To plead on another's behalf. **2.** To act as mediator in a dispute. [Lat. *intercēdere,* to intervene : *inter-,* inter- + *cēdere,* to go.] —**in′ter·ced′er** *n.*

in·ter·cel·lu·lar (ĭn′tər-sĕl′yə-lər) *adj.* *Biology* Located among or between cells: *intercellular fluid.*

in·ter·cept (ĭn′tər-sĕpt′) *tr.v.* **-cept·ed, -cept·ing, -cepts 1.** To stop, deflect, or interrupt the progress or intended course of. **2.** *Sports* **a.** To gain possession of (an opponent's pass), as in football or basketball. **b.** To gain possession of a pass made by (an opponent), esp. in football. **3.** *Mathematics* To include or bound (a part of a space or curve) between two points or lines. **4.** *Archaic* To prevent. **5.** *Obsolete* To cut off from access or communication. ❖ *n.* (ĭn′tər-sĕpt′) **1.** *Mathematics* The coordinate of a point at which a line, curve, or surface intersects an axis. **2a.** The interception of a missile by another missile or an aircraft by another aircraft. **b.** Interception of a radio transmis-

sion. **3.** An interceptor. [ME *intercepten* < Lat. *intercipere, intercept-* : *inter-, inter-* + *capere,* to seize; see **kap-** in App.] —**in′ter·cep′tive** *adj.*

in·ter·cep·tion (ĭn′tər-sĕp′shən) *n.* **1.** The act of intercepting or the state of being intercepted. **2.** Something that is intercepted. **3.** *Sports* An intercepted pass.

in·ter·cep·tor also **in·ter·cept·er** (ĭn′tər-sĕp′tər) *n.* One that intercepts, esp. a plane or missile designed to intercept enemy aircraft.

in·ter·ces·sion (ĭn′tər-sĕsh′ən) *n.* **1.** Entreaty in favor of another, esp. a prayer or petition to God in behalf of another. **2.** Mediation in a dispute. [ME < OFr. < Lat. *intercessiō, intercessiōn-,* intervention < *intercessus,* p. part. of *intercēdere,* to intervene. See INTERCEDE.] —**in′ter·ces′sion·al** *adj.* —**in′ter·ces′sor** (-sĕs′ər) *n.* —**in′ter·ces′so·ry** *adj.*

in·ter·change (ĭn′tər-chānj′) *v.* **-changed, -chang·ing, -chang·es** —*tr.* **1.** To switch each (of two things) into the place of the other. **2.** To give and receive mutually; exchange. **3.** To cause to succeed each other in a series or pattern; alternate. —*intr.* **1.** To change places with each other. **2.** To succeed each other; alternate. ❖ *n.* (ĭn′tər-chānj′) **1.** The act or process of interchanging. **2.** A highway intersection designed to permit traffic to move freely from one road to another without crossing another line of traffic. —**in′ter·chang′er** *n.*

in·ter·change·a·ble (ĭn′tər-chān′jə-bəl) *adj.* That can be interchanged. —**in′ter·change′a·bil′i·ty, in′ter·change′a·ble·ness** *n.* —**in′ter·change′a·bly** *adv.*

in·ter·clav·i·cle (ĭn′tər-klăv′ĭ-kəl) *n.* A bone located in front of the sternum and between the clavicles in certain vertebrates, such as reptiles and amphibians. —**in′ter·cla·vic′u·lar** (-klə-vĭk′yə-lər) *adj.*

in·ter·coast·al (ĭn′tər-kōs′təl) *adj.* Relating to, involving, or connecting two or more coastlines: *intercoastal trade.*

in·ter·col·le·giate (ĭn′tər-kə-lē′jĭt, -jē-ĭt) *adj.* Involving or representing two or more colleges.

in·ter·co·lum·ni·a·tion (ĭn′tər-kə-lŭm′nē-ā′shən) *n.* **1.** The open spaces between the columns in a colonnade. **2.** The system by which intercolumniation is determined.

in·ter·com (ĭn′tər-kŏm′) *n.* An electronic intercommunication system, as between two rooms.

in·ter·com·mu·ni·cate (ĭn′tər-kə-myōō′nĭ-kāt′) *intr.v.* **-cat·ed, -cat·ing, -cates 1.** To communicate with each other. **2.** To be connected or adjoined, as rooms. —**in′ter·com·mu′ni·ca′tion** *n.* —**in′ter·com·mu′ni·ca′tive** (-kā′tĭv, -kə-tĭv) *adj.*

in·ter·com·mun·ion (ĭn′tər-kə-myōōn′yən) *n.* **1.** Communion, relationship, or association between persons or groups. **2.** The practice by which Christians of different denominations can receive Communion at one another's services or at a common service.

in·ter·con·nect (ĭn′tər-kə-nĕkt′) *v.* **-nect·ed, -nect·ing, -nects** —*intr.* To be connected with each other. —*tr.* To connect reciprocally: *interconnected theories.* —**in′ter·con·nect′ed·ness** *n.* —**in′ter·con·nect′i·ble, in′ter·con·nect′a·ble** *adj.* —**in′ter·con·nec′tion** *n.*

in·ter·con·ti·nen·tal (ĭn′tər-kŏn′tə-nĕn′tl) *adj.* **1.** Extending or taking place between or among continents. **2.** Having the capability of traveling from one continent to another.

in·ter·con·ver·sion (ĭn′tər-kən-vûr′zhən, -shən) *n.* Mutual conversion. —**in′ter·con·vert′** *v.* —**in′ter·con·vert′i·bil′i·ty** *n.* —**in′ter·con·vert′i·ble** *adj.*

in·ter·cool·er (ĭn′tər-kōō′lər) *n.* A device for cooling a fluid between successive heating stages. —**in′ter·cool′** *v.*

in·ter·cos·tal (ĭn′tər-kŏs′təl) *adj.* Located or occurring between the ribs. ❖ *n.* An intercostal space, muscle, or part. [NLat. *intercostālis* : INTER- + Lat. *costa,* rib.]

in·ter·course (ĭn′tər-kôrs′, -kōrs′) *n.* **1.** Dealings or communications between persons or groups. **2.** Sexual intercourse. [ME *entercours,* commercial dealings < OFr. *entrecours* < Lat. *intercursus,* a running between, interposition < p. part. of *intercurrere,* to mingle with : *inter-,* inter- + *currere,* to run.]

in·ter·crop (ĭn′tər-krŏp′) *v.* **-cropped, -crop·ping, -crops** —*intr.* To grow more than one crop in the same field, esp. in alternating rows or sections. —*tr.* To plant (a crop) in the same field with another. —**in′ter·crop′** *n.*

in·ter·cul·tur·al (ĭn′tər-kŭl′chər-əl) *adj.* Of, relating to, involving, or representing different cultures.

in·ter·cur·rent (ĭn′tər-kûr′ənt, -kŭr′-) *adj.* Occurring at the same time as and usu. altering the course of another disease. [Lat. *intercurrēns, intercurrent-,* pr. part. of *intercurrere,* to mingle with. See INTERCOURSE.]

in·ter·cut (ĭn′tər-kŭt′) *tr.v.* **-cut, -cut·ting, -cuts** To interweave (two separate, usu. concurrent scenes) in a film; crosscut. —**in′ter·cut′** *adj.*

in·ter·de·nom·i·na·tion·al (ĭn′tər-də-nŏm′ə-nā′shə-nəl) *adj.* Of or involving different religious denominations.

in·ter·den·tal (ĭn′tər-dĕn′tl) *adj.* **1.** Located or made for use between the teeth. **2.** Pronounced with the tip of the tongue between the teeth, as (*th*) in *that.* ❖ *n.* An interdental consonant.

in·ter·de·part·men·tal (ĭn′tər-dē′pärt-mĕn′tl) *adj.* Involving or representing different departments, as of a business.

in·ter·de·pen·dent (ĭn′tər-dĭ-pĕn′dənt) *adj.* Mutually de-

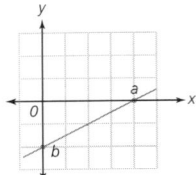
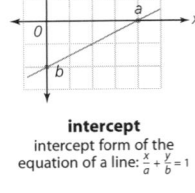

intercept
intercept form of the
equation of a line: $\frac{x}{a} + \frac{y}{b} = 1$

intercrop
wheat, corn, and alfalfa

pendent. —**in′ter•de•pen′dence, in′ter•de•pen′den•cy** n.

in•ter•dict (ĭn′tər-dĭkt′) tr.v. **-dict•ed, -dict•ing, -dicts 1.** To prohibit or place under an ecclesiastical or legal sanction. **2.** To forbid or deny, esp. authoritatively. See Syns at **forbid. 3a.** To cut or destroy (a line of communication) by firepower so as to halt an enemy's advance. **b.** To confront and halt the activities, advance, or entry of. ❖ *n.* (ĭn′tər-dĭkt′) **1.** *Law* A prohibition by court order. **2.** *Roman Catholic Church* An ecclesiastical censure that excludes a person or district from participation in most sacraments and from Christian burial. [Ult. < Lat. *interdīcere, interdict-*, to forbid : *inter-*, inter- + *dīcere*, to say; see **deik-** in App.] —**in′ter•dic′tion** n. —**in′ter•dic′tive, in′ter•dic′to•ry** (-dĭk′tə-rē) adj. —**in′ter•dic′tive•ly** adv. —**in′ter•dic′tor** n.

in•ter•dis•ci•pli•nar•y (ĭn′tər-dĭs′ə-plə-nĕr′ē) adj. Of, relating to, or involving two or more academic disciplines that are usu. considered distinct.

in•ter•est (ĭn′trĭst, -tər-ĭst, -trĕst′) n. **1a.** A state of curiosity or concern about or attention to something. **b.** Something, such as a subject, that evokes this mental state. **2.** Regard for one's own benefit or advantage; self-interest. Often used in the plural. **3a.** A right, claim, or legal share. **b.** Something in which such a right, claim, or share is held. **c.** A person or group of persons holding such a right, claim, or share. **4.** Involvement with or participation in something. **5a.** A charge for a loan, usu. a percentage of the amount loaned. **b.** An excess or bonus beyond what is expected or due. **6a.** An interest group. **b.** The particular cause supported by an interest group. ❖ *tr.v.* **-est•ed, -est•ing, -ests 1.** To arouse the curiosity or hold the attention of. **2.** To cause to become involved or concerned with. **3.** *Obsolete* To concern or affect. —**idiom: in the interest (or interests) of** To the advantage of; for the sake of. [ME < OFr. < Lat., it is of importance, third pers. sing. pr. t. of *interesse*, to be between, take part in : *inter-*, inter- + *esse*, to be; see **es-** in App.]

in•ter•est•ed (ĭn′trĭ-stĭd, -tər-ĭ-stĭd, -tə-rĕs′tĭd) adj. **1.** Having or showing curiosity, fascination, or concern. **2.** Possessing a right, claim, or stake. See Usage Note at **disinterested.** —**in′ter•est•ed•ly** adv. —**in′ter•est•ed•ness** n.

interest group n. A group of persons working on behalf of or strongly supporting a particular cause. —**in′ter•est-group′** (ĭn′trĭst-group′, -tər-ĭst, -trĕst-) adj.

in•ter•est•ing (ĭn′trĭ-stĭng, -tər-ĭ-stĭng, -tə-rĕs′tĭng) adj. Arousing or holding the attention; absorbing. —**in′ter•est•ing•ly** adv.

in•ter•face (ĭn′tər-fās′) n. **1.** A surface forming a common boundary between adjacent regions, bodies, substances, or phases. **2.** A point at which independent systems or diverse groups interact. **3.** *Computer Science* **a.** The point of interaction or communication between a computer and any other entity, such as a printer or human operator. **b.** The layout of an application's graphic or textual controls in conjunction with the way the application responds to user activity. ❖ *v.* (ĭn′tər-fās′) **-faced, -fac•ing, -fac•es** —tr. **1.** To join by means of an interface. **2.** To serve as an interface for. —intr. **1.** To serve as an interface or become interfaced. **2.** *Usage Problem* To interact or coordinate smoothly.

USAGE NOTE The verb *interface*, referring in computer science to the interaction between a computer and another system, has been recently extended to other interactions, such as between departments in an organization. The Usage Panel has been unable to muster much enthusiasm for this generalized usage, with 37 percent of Panelists accepting it when it designates the interaction between people, and only 22 percent accepting it when the interaction is between a corporation and the public or between various communities in a city. Many Panelists complain that *interface* is pretentious and jargony. Certainly, it has no shortage of acceptable synonyms; *cooperate, deal, exchange information, interact,* and *work* present themselves as ready substitutes.

---

in•ter•fac•ing (ĭn′tər-fā′sĭng) n. Material inserted between the layers of a garment to thicken or stiffen it.

in•ter•faith (ĭn′tər-fāth′) adj. Of, relating to, or involving persons of different religious faiths: *an interfaith marriage.*

in•ter•fas•cic•u•lar cambium (ĭn′tər-fə-sĭk′yə-lər) n. The cambium arising between the vascular bundles.

in•ter•fere (ĭn′tər-fîr′) intr.v. **-fered, -fer•ing, -feres 1.** To be or create a hindrance or obstacle. **2.** *Sports* To perform an act of interference. **3.** To intervene or intrude in the affairs of others; meddle. **4.** To strike one hoof against the opposite hoof or leg while moving. Used of a horse. **5.** *Physics & Electronics* To cause interference. [ME *enterferen* < OFr. *s'entreferer*, to strike one another : *entre-*, between (< Lat. *inter-*; see **INTER−**) + *ferir*, to strike (< Lat. *ferīre*).] —**in′ter•fer′er** n. —**in′ter•fer′ing•ly** adv.

SYNONYMS *interfere, meddle, tamper* These verbs mean to intervene unasked in the affairs of others, often impudently or indiscreetly. *Interfere* implies action that seriously hampers, hinders, or frustrates: *"Romantics of all ages can recall occasions when lust interfered with reason"* (Christine Gorman). *Meddle* stresses unwanted, unwarranted, or unnecessary intrusion: *"wholly unacquainted with the world in which they are so fond of meddling"* (Edmund Burke). To *tamper* is to interfere by making unsought,

---

unwelcome, and often destructive changes or by trying to influence another improperly: *"persons accused of . . . tampering with ballot boxes"* (James Bryce).

in•ter•fer•ence (ĭn′tər-fîr′əns) n. **1a.** The act or an instance of hindering, obstructing, or impeding. **b.** Something that hinders, obstructs, or impedes. **2a.** *Sports* Illegal obstruction or hindrance of an opposing player, as of a receiver in football. **b.** *Football* The legal blocking of defensive tacklers to protect and make way for the ball carrier. **3.** *Physics* The variation of wave amplitude that occurs when waves of the same or different frequency come together. **4.** *Electronics* **a.** The inhibition or prevention of clear reception of broadcast signals. **b.** The distorted portion of a received signal. **5.** The negative or distorting effect that new learning can have on previous learning or that previous learning can have on new learning. —**in′ter•fer•en′tial** (-fə-rĕn′shəl) adj.

in•ter•fe•rom•e•ter (ĭn′tər-fə-rŏm′ĭ-tər) n. Any of several optical, acoustic, or radio frequency instruments that use interference phenomena between waves to determine wavelengths, wave velocities, and small distances and thicknesses. —**in′ter•fer′o•met′ric** (-fîr′ə-mĕt′rĭk) adj. —**in′ter•fer′o•met′ri•cal•ly** adv. —**in′ter•fe•rom′e•try** n.

in•ter•fer•on (ĭn′tər-fîr′ŏn′) n. Any of a group of glycoproteins usu. produced in response to infection by a virus that act to prevent viral replication and have the ability to induce resistance to viral antigens. [INTERFER(E) + −ON³.]

in•ter•fer•tile (ĭn′tər-fûr′tl) adj. Capable of interbreeding. —**in′ter•fer•til′i•ty** (-fûr-tĭl′ĭ-tē) n.

in•ter•fluve (ĭn′tər-flōōv′) n. The region of higher land between two rivers that are in the same drainage system. [Back-formation < INTERFLUVIAL.] —**in′ter•flu′vi•al** adj.

in•ter•ga•lac•tic (ĭn′tər-gə-lăk′tĭk) adj. Being or occurring between galaxies. —**in′ter•ga•lac′ti•cal•ly** adv.

in•ter•gen•er•a•tion•al (ĭn′tər-jĕn′ə-rā′shə-nəl) adj. Being or occurring between generations.

in•ter•gla•cial (ĭn′tər-glā′shəl) adj. Occurring between glacial epochs. ❖ *n.* A comparatively short period of warmth during an overall period of glaciation.

in•ter•gov•ern•men•tal (ĭn′tər-gŭv′ərn-mĕn′tl) adj. Being or occurring between two or more governments or divisions of a government. —**in′ter•gov′ern•men′tal•ly** adv.

in•ter•grade (ĭn′tər-grād′) intr.v. **-grad•ed, -grad•ing, -grades** To merge into each other in a series of stages, forms, or types. ❖ *n.* (ĭn′tər-grād′) A transitional stage, form, or type. —**in′ter•gra•da′tion** (-grā-dā′shən) n.

in•ter•im (ĭn′tər-ĭm) n. An interval of time between one event, process, or period and another. ❖ *adj.* Belonging to, serving during, or taking place during an interim; temporary: *an interim agreement.* [< Lat., in the meantime. See **en** in App.]

in•ter•i•on•ic (ĭn′tər-ī-ŏn′ĭk) adj. Located or occurring between ions.

in•te•ri•or (ĭn-tîr′ē-ər) adj. **1.** Of, relating to, or located on the inside; inner. **2.** Of or relating to one's mental or spiritual being. **3.** Situated away from a coast or border; inland. ❖ *n.* **1.** The internal portion or area. **2.** One's mental or spiritual life. **3.** The inland part of a political or geographic entity. **4.** The internal affairs of a country or nation. **5.** A representation of the inside of a building or room, as in a photograph. [Ult. Lat., comp. adj. of *inter*, between. See **en** in App.] —**in•te′ri•or′i•ty** (-ôr′ē-tē, -ŏr′-) n. —**in•te′ri•or•ly** adv.

interior angle n. **1.** Any of the four angles formed between two straight lines intersected by a third straight line. **2.** The angle formed inside a polygon by two adjacent sides.

interior decoration n. The planning and execution of the layout, decoration, and furnishing of an architectural interior. —**interior decorator** n.

in•te•ri•or•ize (ĭn-tîr′ē-ə-rīz′) tr.v. **-ized, -iz•ing, -iz•es** To cause (feelings, for example) to become an interior or internal part of one's mental or spiritual being; internalize.

interior monologue n. A passage of writing presenting a character's inner thoughts and emotions directly.

Interior Salish n. A group of Salish-speaking Native American peoples in parts of British Columbia, northern Washington, northern Idaho, and western Montana.

interj. abbr. interjection

in•ter•ject (ĭn′tər-jĕkt′) tr.v. **-ject•ed, -ject•ing, -jects** To insert between other elements; interpose. [Lat. *intericere, interiect-* : *inter-*, inter- + *iacere*, to throw.] —**in′ter•jec′tor** n. —**in′ter•jec′to•ry** (-jĕk′tə-rē) adj.

in•ter•jec•tion (ĭn′tər-jĕk′shən) n. **1.** A sudden short utterance; an ejaculation. **2a.** The part of speech that usu. expresses emotion and is capable of standing alone. **b.** Any of the words belonging to this part of speech, such as *Ugh!* or *Wow!* —**in′ter•jec′tion•al** adj. —**in′ter•jec′tion•al•ly** adv.

in•ter•lace (ĭn′tər-lās′) v. **-laced, -lac•ing, -lac•es** —tr. **1.** To connect by or as if by lacing together; interweave. **2.** To intersperse; intermix: *interlaced lies with truth.* —intr. To intertwine. —**in′ter•lace′ment** n.

In•ter•la•ken (ĭn′tər-lä′kən, ĭn′tər-lä′-) A town of central Switzerland SE of Bern in the Bernese Alps. Pop. 4,852.

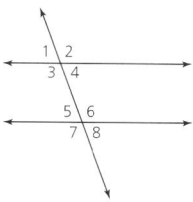

interior angle
Angles 3, 4, 5, and 6 are interior angles; angles 3 and 6 and angles 4 and 5 are alternate interior angles.

ă	pat	oi	boy
ā	pay	ou	out
âr	care	ŏŏ	took
ä	father	ōō	boot
ĕ	pet	ŭ	cut
ē	be	ûr	urge
ĭ	pit	th	thin
ī	pie	th	this
îr	pier	hw	which
ŏ	pot	zh	vision
ō	toe	ə	about,
ô	paw		item

Stress marks:
′ (primary);
′ (secondary), as in
lexicon (lĕk′sĭ-kŏn′)

in·ter·lam·i·nate (ĭn′tər-lăm′ə-nāt′) *tr.v.* **-nat·ed, -nat·ing, -nates** 1. To insert between layers. 2. To arrange in alternating layers. —**in′ter·lam′i·na′tion** *n.*

in·ter·lard (ĭn′tər-lärd′) *tr.v.* **-lard·ed, -lard·ing, -lards** To insert something foreign into. [ME *interlarden*, to mix fat into < OFr. *entrelarder* : *entre-*, between (< Lat. *inter-*; see INTER–) + *larder*, to lard (< *lard*, lard; see LARD).]

in·ter·leaf (ĭn′tər-lēf′) *n., pl.* **-leaves** (-lēvz′) A blank leaf inserted between the regular pages of a book.

in·ter·leave (ĭn′tər-lēv′) *tr.v.* **-leaved, -leav·ing, -leaves** To provide with interleaves or an interleaf.

in·ter·leu·kin-1 (ĭn′tər-lōō′kĭn-wŭn′) *n.* Either of two proteins, released by macrophages and other cells, that induce the production of interleukin-2 by helper T cells and stimulate the inflammatory response. [INTER– + Gk. *leukos*, white; see LEUKO– + –IN.]

in·ter·leu·kin-2 (ĭn′tər-lōō′kĭn-tōō′) *n.* A lymphokine released by helper T cells in response to an antigen and interleukin-1 that stimulates the proliferation of helper T cells.

in·ter·leu·kin-3 (ĭn′tər-lōō′kĭn-thrē′) *n.* A lymphokine released by helper T cells that stimulates the growth of blood stem cells and lymphoid cells such as macrophages.

in·ter·line¹ (ĭn′tər-līn′) *tr.v.* **-lined, -lin·ing, -lines** To insert between printed or written lines. —**in′ter·lin′e·a′tion** (-lĭn′ē-ā′shən) *n.*

in·ter·line² (ĭn′tər-līn′) *tr.v.* **-lined, -lin·ing, -lines** To fit (a garment) with an interlining.

in·ter·lin·e·ar (ĭn′tər-lĭn′ē-ər) *adj.* 1. Inserted between the lines of a text. 2. Written or printed with different languages or versions in alternating lines.

in·ter·lin·ing (ĭn′tər-lī′nĭng) *n.* An extra lining between the outer fabric and regular lining of a garment.

in·ter·link (ĭn′tər-lĭngk′) *tr.v.* **-linked, -link·ing, -links** To link together or join (one) with another: *interlinked policies.*

in·ter·lock (ĭn′tər-lŏk′) *v.* **-locked, -lock·ing, -locks** —*tr.* 1. To unite or join closely as by hooking or dovetailing. 2. To connect together (parts of a mechanism, for example) so that individual parts affect each other in motion or operation. —*intr.* To become interlocked. ❖ *n.* (ĭn′tər-lŏk′) 1. A mechanical device that prevents a component from functioning when another component is functioning or situated in a particular way, as on an assembly line. 2. A stretchy fabric knitted with interlocking stitches by alternating sets of needles on a circular knitting machine.

in·ter·lo·cu·tion (ĭn′tər-lō-kyōō′shən) *n.* Speech between two or more persons; conversation. [Lat. *interlocūtiō, interlocūtiōn-* < *interlocūtus*, p. part. of *interloquī*, to interrupt : *inter-*, inter- + *loquī*, to speak.]

in·ter·loc·u·tor (ĭn′tər-lŏk′yə-tər) *n.* One who takes part in a conversation, often formally or officially.

in·ter·loc·u·to·ry (ĭn′tər-lŏk′yə-tôr′ē, -tōr′ē) *adj. Law* Pronounced or decided during the course of an action or suit and temporary or provisional in nature.

in·ter·lop·er (ĭn′tər-lō′pər) *n.* 1. One that interferes with the affairs of others, often for selfish reasons; a meddler. 2. One that intrudes in a place, situation, or activity: *"When these interlopers choke out native species, ecologists see a danger signal"* (William K. Stevens). 3. *Archaic* **a.** One that trespasses on a trade monopoly. **b.** A ship or other vessel used in such trade. [INTER– + prob. MDu. *lōper*, runner (< *lōpen*, to run).] —**in′ter·lope′** *v.*

in·ter·lude (ĭn′tər-lōōd′) *n.* 1. An intervening episode, feature, or period of time. 2a. A short farcical entertainment performed between the acts of a medieval mystery or morality play. **b.** A 16th-century genre of comedy derived from this. **c.** An entertainment between the acts of a play. 3. *Music* A short piece inserted between the parts of a longer composition. [Ult. < Med.Lat. *interlūdium* : Lat. *inter-*, inter- + Lat. *lūdus*, play.]

in·ter·lu·nar (ĭn′tər-lōō′nər) *adj.* Of or relating to the four-day period between the old and new moon.

in·ter·mar·ry (ĭn′tər-măr′ē) *intr.v.* **-ried, -ry·ing, -ries** 1. To marry a member of another group. 2. To be bound together by the marriages of members. 3. To marry within one's family, tribe, or clan. —**in′ter·mar′riage** (-măr′ĭj) *n.*

in·ter·med·dle (ĭn′tər-mĕd′l) *intr.v.* **-dled, -dling, -dles** To interfere in the affairs of others; meddle. [ME *entermedlen* < OFr. *entremedler* : *entre-*, between (< Lat. *inter-*; see INTER–) + *medler*, to mix; see MEDDLE.] —**in′ter·med′dler** *n.*

in·ter·me·di·ar·y (ĭn′tər-mē′dē-ĕr′ē) *adj.* 1. Existing or occurring between; intermediate. 2. Acting as a mediator or an agent between persons or things. ❖ *n., pl.* **-ies** 1. One that acts as a mediator. 2. One that acts as an agent between persons or things; a means. 3. An intermediate state or stage. [Prob. Fr. *intermédiaire* < Lat. *intermedius*, intermediate. See INTERMEDIATE.]

in·ter·me·di·ate (ĭn′tər-mē′dē-ĭt) *adj.* Lying or occurring between two extremes or in a middle position or state: *an intermediate school.* ❖ *n.* 1. One that is in a middle position or state. 2. An intermediary. 3. *Chemistry* A substance formed as a necessary stage in the manufacture of a desired end product. 4. An automobile that is smaller than a full-sized model but larger than a compact. ❖ *intr.v.* (-āt′) **-at·ed, -at·ing, -ates** 1. To act as an intermediary; mediate. 2. To intervene. [ME < Med.Lat. *intermediātus* < LLat. *intermedius* : Lat. *inter-*, inter- + Lat. *medius*, mid-

dle; see medhyo- in App.] —**in′ter·me′di·a·cy** *n.* —**in′ter·me′di·ate·ly** *adv.* —**in′ter·me′di·ate·ness** *n.* —**in′ter·me′di·a′tion** *n.* —**in′ter·me′di·a′tor** *n.*

in·ter·me·di·ate care *n.* 1. A level of medical care in a hospital that is intermediate between intensive and basic care. 2. A level of care in a facility for the chronically ill or disabled that usu. involves less intensive care than that offered at a hospital or skilled nursing facility.

intermediate host *n.* An organism in or on which a parasite develops to an adult but not sexually mature stage.

intermediate vector boson *n.* Either of the two bosons, the W boson or the Z boson, that are quanta of the weak interaction.

in·ter·me·din (ĭn′tər-mēd′n) *n.* See melanocyte-stimulating hormone. [NLat. *(pars) intermed(ia)*, middle part of the hypophysis < fem. of LLat. *intermedius*. See INTERMEDIATE + –IN.]

in·ter·ment (ĭn-tûr′mənt) *n.* The act or ritual of interring.

in·ter·mez·zo (ĭn′tər-mĕt′sō, -mĕd′zō) *n., pl.* **-zos** or **-zi** (-sē, -zē) 1. A brief entertainment between two acts of a play; an entr'acte. 2. *Music* **a.** A short movement separating the major sections of a lengthy composition or work. **b.** An independent instrumental composition similar to such a movement. [Ital. < Lat. *intermedius*, intermediate. See INTERMEDIATE.]

in·ter·mi·na·ble (ĭn-tûr′mə-nə-bəl) *adj.* 1. Being or seeming to be without an end; endless. See Syns at **continual.** 2. Tiresomely long; wearisome. —**in·ter′mi·na·bil′i·ty** *n.* —**in·ter′mi·na·bly** *adv.*

in·ter·min·gle (ĭn′tər-mĭng′gəl) *tr. & intr.v.* **-gled, -gling, -gles** To mix or become mixed together.

in·ter·mis·sion (ĭn′tər-mĭsh′ən) *n.* 1. The act of intermitting or the state of being intermitted. 2. A respite or recess. 3. The period between the acts of a theatrical or musical performance. See Syns at **pause.** [Ult. < Lat. *intermissiō, intermissiōn-* < *intermissus*, p. part. of *intermittere*, to interrupt. See INTERMIT.]

in·ter·mit (ĭn′tər-mĭt′) *intr. & tr.v.* **-mit·ted, -mit·ting, -mits** To suspend or cause to suspend activity temporarily or periodically. [Lat. *intermittere* : *inter-*, inter- + *mittere*, to let go.] —**in′ter·mit′ter** *n.*

in·ter·mit·tent (ĭn′tər-mĭt′nt) *adj.* 1. Stopping and starting at intervals. See Syns at **periodic.** 2. Alternately containing and empty of water: *an intermittent lake.* —**in′ter·mit′tence** *n.* —**in′ter·mit′tent·ly** *adv.*

intermittent current *n.* A periodically interrupted unidirectional electric current.

in·ter·mix (ĭn′tər-mĭks′) *tr. & intr.v.* **-mixed, -mix·ing, -mix·es** To mix or become mixed together. [Ult. < Lat. *intermixtus*, p. part. of *intermiscēre*, to mix together : *inter-*, inter- + *miscēre*, to mix; see MIX.]

in·ter·mod·al (ĭn′tər-mōd′l) *adj.* Relating to transportation by more than one means of conveyance, as by truck and rail.

in·ter·mod·u·la·tion (ĭn′tər-mŏj′ə-lā′shən) *n.* Modulation of the frequencies of electromagnetic waves resulting from their interaction as they are transmitted through a nonlinear electronic system.

in·ter·moun·tain (ĭn′tər-moun′tən) *adj.* Located between mountains or mountain systems, esp. lying between the Rocky Mountains and the Sierra Nevada or Cascade Range in the western United States.

in·tern also **in·terne** (ĭn′tûrn′) *n.* **1a.** An advanced student or a recent graduate undergoing supervised practical training. **b.** A recent medical school graduate who works as a physician in a hospital under supervision before beginning a residency program. 2. One who is interned. ❖ *v.* **-terned, -tern·ing, -terns** —*intr.* To train or serve as an intern. —*tr.* (*also* ĭn-tûrn′) To confine, esp. in wartime. ❖ *adj.* (ĭn-tûrn′) *Archaic* Internal. [Fr. *interne* < Lat. *internus*, internal. See INTERNAL.] —**in′tern·ship′** *n.*

in·ter·nal (ĭn-tûr′nəl) *adj.* 1. Of, relating to, or located within the limits or surface; inner. 2. Residing in or dependent on essential nature; intrinsic: *internal contradictions.* 3. Located, acting, or effective within the body. 4. Of or relating to mental or spiritual nature. 5. Of or relating to the domestic affairs of a nation, group, or business. [ME *internall* < OFr. *internel* < Med.Lat. *internālis* < Lat. *internus* < *inter*, within. See **en** in App.] —**in′ter·nal′i·ty** (-năl′ĭ-tē) *n.* —**in·ter′nal·ly** *adv.*

in·ter·nal-com·bus·tion engine (ĭn-tûr′nəl-kəm-bŭs′chən) *n.* An engine in which fuel is burned within the engine rather than in an external furnace.

internal ear *n.* See inner ear.

internal energy *n. Symbol* U The total kinetic and potential energy associated with the motions and relative positions of the molecules of an object, excluding the kinetic or potential energy of the object as a whole.

in·ter·nal·ize (ĭn-tûr′nə-līz′) *tr.v.* **-ized, -iz·ing, -iz·es** To make internal, personal, or subjective, esp. to make an integral part of one's attitudes or beliefs. —**in·ter′nal·i·za′tion** (-lī-zā′shən) *n.*

internal medicine *n.* The branch of medicine that deals with the diagnosis and nonsurgical treatment of diseases affecting the internal organs of the body, esp. in adults.

internal respiration *n.* The metabolic process by which living cells absorb oxygen and release carbon dioxide.

internal rhyme *n.* Rhyme that occurs within a line of verse, as in "the grains beyond age, the dark veins of her mother" (Dylan Thomas).

in·ter·na·tion·al (ĭn′tər-năsh′ə-nəl) *adj.* **1.** Of, relating to, or involving two or more nations: *international affairs.* **2.** Extending across or transcending national boundaries. ❖ *n.* **International** Any of several international socialist organizations formed during the late 19th and early 20th centuries. —**in′ter·na′tion·al′i·ty** (-shə-năl′ĭ-tē) *n.* —**in′ter·na′tion·al·ly** *adv.*

international candle *n.* See **candle** 2a.

International Date Line *n.* An imaginary line through the Pacific Ocean roughly corresponding to 180° longitude, to the east of which, by international agreement, the calendar date is one day earlier than to the west.

in·ter·na·tion·al·ism (ĭn′tər-năsh′ə-nə-lĭz′əm) *n.* **1.** The condition or quality of being international in character, principles, or concern. **2.** Cooperation among nations, esp. in politics and economics. —**in′ter·na′tion·al·ist** *n.*

in·ter·na·tion·al·ize (ĭn′tər-năsh′ə-nə-līz′) *tr.v.* **-ized, -iz·ing, -iz·es 1.** To make international. **2.** To put under international control. —**in′ter·na′tion·al·i·za′tion** (-lĭ-zā′shən) *n.*

international law *n.* A set of rules generally regarded and accepted as binding in relations between states and nations.

international Morse code *n.* A form of Morse code having no spaces between the dot and dash elements, commonly used in telegraphy outside the United States and Canada.

International Phonetic Alphabet *n.* A phonetic alphabet and diacritic marks sponsored by the International Phonetic Association to provide a uniform and universally understood system for transcribing the speech sounds of all languages.

international pitch *n.* A sound wave frequency of 440 cycles per second, assigned to the A above middle C.

international relations *pl.n.* **1.** (*used with a sing. verb*) The branch of political science that is concerned with the foreign affairs of and relations among countries. **2.** (*used with a pl. verb*) Foreign affairs; relations among countries.

International Style *n.* A modernist style of architecture, characterized by unadorned geometric forms, open interiors, and the use of glass, steel, and concrete.

International System *n.* A complete coherent system of units used for scientific work, in which the fundamental quantities are length, time, electric current, temperature, luminous intensity, amount of substance, and mass.

international unit *n.* **1.** The quantity of a biologically active substance, such as a vitamin, required to produce a specific response. **2.** A unit of potency for similarly active substances, based on this quantity and accepted as an international standard.

in·terne (ĭn′tûrn′, ĭn-tûrn′) *n., v., & adj.* Variant of **intern.**

in·ter·nec·ine (ĭn′tər-nĕs′ēn′, -īn, -nē′sīn′) *adj.* **1.** Of or relating to struggle within a nation, organization, or group. **2.** Mutually destructive; ruinous or fatal to both sides. **3.** Characterized by bloodshed or carnage. [Lat. *internecīnus,* destructive, var. of *internecīvus* < *internecāre,* to slaughter : *inter-,* intensive pref.; see INTER– + *nex, nec-,* death; see **nek-** in App.]

WORD HISTORY *Internecine,* first recorded in English in 1663, meant "fought to the death, deadly, destructive," coming as it did from Latin *internecīnus,* a variant of *internecīvus,* "fought to the death, murderous," ultimately derived from *necāre,* "to kill." Its present-day meaning, "relating to internal struggle," arose by mistake. Samuel Johnson, inserting the word in his dictionary of 1755, thought that *inter–* meant "mutual" and so defined it as "endeavoring mutual destruction." In fact, in this word the prefix was an intensifier meaning "all the way, to the death." But due to Johnson's influence, his definition set the word incorrectly on its present course, and when *internecine* was further extended simply to mean "relating to internal struggle," the original error was compounded. However, the ultimate arbiter of language is how people use it, and what was once compounded error has long since become acceptable practice.

in·tern·ee (ĭn′tûr-nē′) *n.* One who is interned or confined, esp. in wartime.

In·ter·net (ĭn′tər-nĕt′) *n.* An interconnected system of networks that connects computers around the world via the TCP/IP protocol.

in·ter·net·work (ĭn′tər-nĕt′wûrk′) *n.* An interconnected system of networks, esp. computer networks.

in·ter·neu·ron (ĭn′tər-nŏor′ŏn′, -nyŏor′-) *n.* A nerve cell found entirely within the central nervous system that acts as a link between sensory neurons and motor neurons. —**in′ter·neu′ro·nal** (-nŏor′ə-nəl, -nyŏor′-, -nŏo-rŏ′-, -nyŏo-) *adj.*

in·ter·nist (ĭn-tûr′nĭst) *n.* A physician specializing in internal medicine. [INTERN(AL MEDICINE) + –IST.]

in·tern·ment (ĭn-tûrn′mənt) *n.* **1.** The act of interning or confining, esp. in wartime. **2.** The state of being interned.

in·ter·node (ĭn′tər-nōd′) *n.* A section or part between two nodes, as of a nerve or stem. —**in′ter·nod′al** (-nōd′l) *adj.*

in·ter nos (ĭn′tər nōs′) *adv. & adj.* Between ourselves. [Lat. *inter nōs : inter,* among + *nōs,* us.]

in·ter·nu·cle·ar (ĭn′tər-nōo′klē-ər, -nyōo′klē-ər) *adj.* Located

ed or occurring between nuclei.

in·ter·nun·cial (ĭn′tər-nŭn′shəl, -sē-əl) *adj.* Linking two neurons in a neuronal pathway. [INTERNUNCI(O) + –AL¹.]

in·ter·nun·ci·o (ĭn′tər-nŭn′sē-ō′, -nōon′-) *n., pl.* **-os 1.** A Vatican diplomatic envoy or representative ranking just beneath a nuncio. **2.** A messenger or an agent; a go-between. [Ital. *internunzio* < Lat. *internūntius,* mediator : *inter-,* inter- + *nūntius,* messenger.]

in·ter·o·cep·tor (ĭn′tər-ō-sĕp′tər) *n.* A specialized sensory nerve receptor that receives and responds to stimuli originating from within the body. [INTER(IOR) + (RE)CEPTOR.]

in·ter·of·fice (ĭn′tər-ô′fĭs, -ŏf′ĭs) *adj.* Transmitted or occurring between offices, esp. within one organization.

in·ter·pen·e·trate (ĭn′tər-pĕn′ĭ-trāt′) *v.* **-trat·ed, -trat·ing, -trates** —*intr.* To become mixed or united by penetration: *planes that interpenetrate in a painting.* —*tr.* **1.** To penetrate reciprocally: *The streams interpenetrate each other at the rapids.* **2.** To penetrate thoroughly; permeate or pervade.

in·ter·per·son·al (ĭn′tər-pûr′sə-nəl) *adj.* Relating to, occurring among, or involving several people. —**in′ter·per′son·al·ly** *adv.*

in·ter·phase (ĭn′tər-fāz′) *n.* The stage of a cell between two successive mitotic or meiotic divisions. —**in′ter·phase′** *v.*

in·ter·plan·e·tar·y (ĭn′tər-plăn′ĭ-tĕr′ē) *adj.* Existing or occurring between planets.

in·ter·play (ĭn′tər-plā′) *n.* Reciprocal action and reaction; interaction. ❖ *intr.v.* **-played, -play·ing, -plays** To act or react on each other; interact.

in·ter·plead (ĭn′tər-plēd′) *intr.v.* **-plead·ed, -plead·ing, -pleads** *Law* To submit one's claim to the process of interpleader. [ME *enterpleden* < AN *enterpleder* : *enter-,* between (< Lat. *inter-*; see INTER–) + *pleder,* to plead (var. of OFr. *plaidier;* see PLEAD).]

in·ter·plead·er (ĭn′tər-plē′dər) *n. Law* A procedure to determine which of two parties making the same claim against a third party is the rightful claimant. [AN *enterpleder,* to interplead, interpleader. See INTERPLEAD.]

in·ter·po·late (ĭn-tûr′pə-lāt′) *v.* **-lat·ed, -lat·ing, -lates** —*tr.* **1.** To insert or introduce between other elements or parts. **2a.** To insert (material) into a text. **b.** To insert into a conversation. **3.** To change or falsify (a text) with new or incorrect material. **4.** *Mathematics* To estimate a value of (a function or series) between two known values. —*intr.* To make insertions or additions. [Lat. *interpolāre, interpolāt-,* to touch up, refurbish < *interpolis,* refurbished. See **pel-**² in App.] —**in·ter′po·la′tion** *n.* —**in·ter′po·la′tive** *adj.* —**in·ter′po·la′tor** *n.*

in·ter·pose (ĭn′tər-pōz′) *v.* **-posed, -pos·ing, -pos·es** —*tr.* **1a.** To insert or introduce between parts. **b.** To place (oneself) between others or things. **2.** To introduce or interject (a comment, for example) during discourse or a conversation. **3.** To exert (influence or authority) in order to interfere or intervene: *interpose one's veto.* —*intr.* **1.** To come between things. **2.** To come between the parties in a dispute; intervene. **3.** To insert a remark, question, or argument. [Fr. < OFr. *interposer,* to intervene, alteration (influenced by *poser,* to put, place) of Lat. *interpōnere,* to put between : *inter-,* inter- + *pōnere,* to put; see **apo-** in App.] —**in′ter·pos′al** *n.* —**in′ter·pos′er** *n.* —**in′ter·po·si′tion** (-pə-zĭsh′ən) *n.*

in·ter·pret (ĭn-tûr′prĭt) *v.* **-pret·ed, -pret·ing, -prets** —*tr.* **1.** To explain the meaning of. **2.** To conceive the significance of; construe. **3.** To present or conceptualize the meaning of by means of art or criticism. **4.** To translate orally. —*intr.* **1.** To offer an explanation. **2.** To serve as an interpreter for speakers of different languages. [Ult. < Lat. *interpretārī < interpres, interpret-,* negotiator, explainer.] —**in·ter′pret·a·bil′i·ty, in·ter′pret·a·ble·ness** *n.* —**in·ter′pret·a·ble** *adj.*

in·ter·pre·ta·tion (ĭn-tûr′prĭ-tā′shən) *n.* **1.** The act or process of interpreting. **2.** A result of interpreting. **3a.** An explanation by a critic of a work of literature, painting, or other art form; an exegesis. **b.** A performer's version of a song, for example. —**in·ter′·pre·ta′tion·al** *adj.*

in·ter·pret·er (ĭn-tûr′prĭ-tər) *n.* **1.** An oral translator. **2.** One who gives or expounds an interpretation. **3.** *Computer Science* A program that translates an instruction into a machine language and executes it before the next instruction.

in·ter·pre·tive (ĭn-tûr′prĭ-tĭv) *also* **in·ter·pre·ta·tive** (-tā′tĭv) *adj.* Relating to or marked by interpretation; explanatory. —**in·ter′pre·tive·ly** *adv.*

in·ter·pu·pil·lar·y (ĭn′tər-pyōo′pə-lĕr′ē) *adj.* Occurring between the pupils of the eyes: *interpupillary distance.*

in·ter·ra·cial (ĭn′tər-rā′shəl) *adj.* Relating to, involving, or representing different races: *an interracial marriage.*

in·ter·re·gion·al (ĭn′tər-rē′jə-nəl) *adj.* Of, involving, or connecting two or more regions.

in·ter·reg·num (ĭn′tər-rĕg′nəm) *n., pl.* **-nums** *or* **-na** (-nə) **1.** The interval of time between the end of a sovereign's reign and the accession of a successor. **2.** A period of temporary suspension of the usual functions of government or control. **3.** A gap in continuity. [Lat. : *inter-,* inter- + *rēgnum,* reign; see REIGN.] —**in′ter·reg′nal** (-nəl) *adj.*

in·ter·re·late (ĭn′tər-rĭ-lāt′) *tr. & intr.v.* **-lat·ed, -lat·ing,**

International Style
the Villa Savoye, Poissy, France, 1928–31, by Le Corbusier

intersection

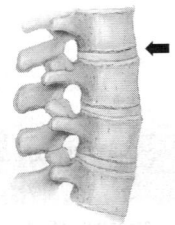
intervertebral disk
profile of lumbar
intervertebral disks

-lates To place in or come into mutual relationship. —**in′ter•re•lat′ed•ness** *n.* —**in′ter•re•la′tion•ship′** *n.*

in•ter•ro•bang also **in•ter•a•bang** (ĭn-tĕr′ə-băng′) *n.* A punctuation mark in the form of a question mark superimposed on an exclamation point, used to end a simultaneous question and exclamation. [INTERRO(GATION POINT) + BANG[1], exclamation point (printers' slang).]

interrog. *abbr.* interrogative

in•ter•ro•gate (ĭn-tĕr′ə-gāt′) *tr.v.* -gat•ed, -gat•ing, -gates 1. To examine by questioning formally or officially. See Syns at **ask.** 2. *Computer Science* To transmit a signal for setting off an appropriate response. [ME *enterrogate* < Lat. *interrogāre, interrogāt-* : *inter-*, in the presence of; see INTER– + *rogāre*, to ask; see **reg-** in App.] —**in′ter•ro•ga′tion** *n.* —**in′ter•ro•ga′tion•al** *adj.* —**in•ter′ro•ga′tor** *n.*

interrogation point *n.* See **question mark.**

in•ter•rog•a•tive (ĭn′tə-rŏg′ə-tĭv) *adj.* 1. Interrogatory. 2. Of, relating to, or being an element or construction used to ask a question: *an interrogative adverb.* ❖ *n.* 1. A word or form used to ask a question. 2. A sentence or expression that asks a question. —**in′ter•rog′a•tive•ly** *adv.*

in•ter•rog•a•to•ry (ĭn′tə-rŏg′ə-tôr′ē, -tōr′ē) *adj.* Asking a question; of the nature of a question. ❖ *n., pl.* -ries *Law* A formal or written question, as to a witness, usu. requiring an answer under oath. —**in′ter•rog′a•to′ri•ly** *adv.*

in•ter•rupt (ĭn′tə-rŭpt′) *v.* -rupt•ed, -rupt•ing, -rupts —*tr.* 1. To break the continuity or uniformity of. 2. To hinder or stop the action or discourse of (someone) by breaking in on. —*intr.* To break in on an action or discourse. ❖ *n. Computer Science* 1. A signal to a computer that stops the execution of a running program so that another action can be performed. 2. A circuit that conveys a signal stopping the execution of a running program. [Ult. < Lat. *interruptus,* p. part. of *interrumpere,* to break off : *inter-*, inter- + *rumpere,* to break; see **reup-** in App.] —**in′ter•rupt′i•ble** *adj.* —**in′ter•rup′tion** *n.* —**in′ter•rup′tive** *adj.*

in•ter•rupt•er (ĭn′tə-rŭp′tər) *n.* 1. One that interrupts. 2. *Electronics* A device that periodically and automatically opens and closes an electric circuit, producing pulses.

in•ter•scho•las•tic (ĭn′tər-skə-lăs′tĭk) *adj.* Being between or among schools. —**in′ter•scho•las′ti•cal•ly** *adv.*

in•ter se (ĭn′tər sĕ′, sā′) *adv. & adj.* Between or among themselves. [Lat. *inter sē* : *inter,* between + *sē,* themselves.]

in•ter•sect (ĭn′tər-sĕkt′) *v.* -sect•ed, -sect•ing, -sects —*tr.* 1. To cut across or through. 2. To form an intersection with; cross. —*intr.* 1. To cut across or overlap each other. 2. To form an intersection; cross. [Lat. *intersecāre, intersect-* : *inter-*, inter- + *secāre,* to cut; see **sek-** in App.]

in•ter•sec•tion (ĭn′tər-sĕk′shən) *n.* 1. The act, process, or result of intersecting. 2. A place where things, esp. roads, intersect. 3. *Mathematics* **a.** The point or locus of points where one line, surface, or solid crosses another. **b.** A set that contains elements shared by two or more given sets.

in•ter•ses•sion (ĭn′tər-sĕsh′ən) *n.* The time between two academic sessions or semesters. —**in′ter•ses′sion•al** *adj.*

in•ter•sex (ĭn′tər-sĕks′) *n.* An intersexual individual.

in•ter•sex•u•al (ĭn′tər-sĕk′shōō-əl) *adj.* 1. Existing or occurring between the sexes. 2. *Biology* Having both male and female sexual characteristics. ❖ *n.* An intersexual person. —**in′ter•sex′u•al′i•ty** (-ăl′ĭ-tē) *n.* —**in′ter•sex′u•al•ly** *adv.*

in•ter•space (ĭn′tər-spās′) *tr.v.* -spaced, -spac•ing, -spac•es To make or occupy a space between. ❖ *n.* A space between two things; an interval. —**in′ter•spa′tial** (-spā′shəl) *adj.*

in•ter•spe•cif•ic (ĭn′tər-spĭ-sĭf′ĭk) *adj.* Arising or occurring between species.

in•ter•sperse (ĭn′tər-spûrs′) *tr.v.* -spersed, -spers•ing, -spers•es 1. To distribute among other things at intervals. 2. To supply or diversify with things distributed at intervals. [< Lat. *interspergere, interspers-* : *inter-*, inter- + *spargere,* to scatter.] —**in′ter•spers′ed•ly** (-spûr′sĭd-lē) *adv.* —**in′ter•sper′sion** (-spûr′zhən, -shən) *n.*

in•ter•state (ĭn′tər-stāt′) *adj.* Involving, existing between, or connecting two or more states. ❖ *n.* One of a system of highways connecting the major cities of the 48 contiguous United States.

in•ter•stel•lar (ĭn′tər-stĕl′ər) *adj.* Between or among the stars: *interstellar gases.*

in•ter•stice (ĭn-tûr′stĭs) *n., pl.* -stic•es (-stĭ-sēz′, -sĭz) A space, esp. a small or narrow one, between things or parts. [ME < OFr. < Lat. *interstitium* < *interstitium,* p. part. of *intersistere,* to pause, make a break : *inter-*, inter- + *sistere,* to cause to stand, set up; see **stā-** in App.]

in•ter•sti•tial (ĭn′tər-stĭsh′əl) *adj.* 1. Relating to, occurring in, or affecting interstices. 2. *Anatomy* Relating to or situated in the small narrow spaces between tissues or parts of an organ: *interstitial cells.* —**in′ter•sti′tial•ly** *adv.*

in•ter•tex•tu•al (ĭn′tər-tĕks′chōō-əl) *adj.* Relating to or deriving meaning from the interdependent ways in which texts stand in relation to each other. —**in′ter•tex′tu•al′i•ty** (-ăl′ĭ-tē) *n.* —**in′ter•tex′tu•al•ly** *adv.*

in•ter•tex•ture (ĭn′tər-tĕks′chər) *n.* 1. The act of interweaving or the state of being interwoven. 2. Something interwoven.

[< Lat. *intertextus,* p. part. of *intertexere,* to interweave : *inter-*, inter- + *texere,* to weave; see TEXT.]

in•ter•tid•al (ĭn′tər-tīd′l) *adj.* Of, relating to, or being the region between the high tide mark and the low tide mark. —**in′ter•tid′al•ly** *adv.*

in•ter•ti•tle (ĭn′tər-tīt′l) *n.* A printed portion of narration or dialogue flashed on the screen between the scenes of a silent film.

in•ter•tri•bal (ĭn′tər-trī′bəl) *adj.* Existing or occurring between tribes.

in•ter•trop•i•cal (ĭn′tər-trŏp′ĭ-kəl) *adj.* 1. Between or within the tropics. 2. Of or relating to the tropics.

in•ter•twine (ĭn′tər-twīn′) *tr. & intr.v.* -twined, -twin•ing, -twines To join or become joined by twining together. —**in′ter•twine′ment** *n.*

in•ter•twist (ĭn′tər-twĭst′) *tr. & intr.v.* -twist•ed, -twist•ing, -twists To intertwine.

in•ter•ur•ban (ĭn′tər-ûr′bən) *adj.* Relating to or connecting urban areas: *an interurban railroad.*

in•ter•val (ĭn′tər-vəl) *n.* 1. A space between two objects, points, or units. 2. The amount of time between two specified instants, events, or states. 3. One of a series of distances covered at regular time increments with intermittent periods of rest in an athletic workout. 4. *Mathematics* **a.** A set of numbers consisting of all the numbers between a pair of given numbers along with either, both, or none of the endpoints. **b.** A closed interval. **c.** An open interval. **d.** A half-open interval. **e.** A line segment representing the set of numbers in an interval. 5. *Chiefly British* An intermission, as between acts of a play. 6. *Music* The difference, usu. expressed in the number of steps, between two pitches. [ME *intervalle* < OFr. < Lat. *intervallum* : *inter-*, inter- + *vallum,* rampart.] —**in′ter•val′ic, in′ter•val′lic** *adj.*

in•ter•vale (ĭn′tər-vəl) *n. New England* A tract of low-lying land, esp. along a river. [Variant of INTERVAL.]

in•ter•vene (ĭn′tər-vēn′) *intr.v.* -vened, -ven•ing, -venes 1. To come, appear, or lie between two things. 2. To come or occur between two periods or points of time. 3. To occur as an extraneous or unplanned circumstance. 4a. To involve oneself in a situation so as to alter or hinder an action or development. **b.** To interfere, usu. through force or threat of force, in the affairs of another nation. 5. *Law* To enter into a suit as a third party for one's own interests. [Lat. *intervenīre* : *inter-*, inter- + *venīre,* to come; see **gʷā-** in App.] —**in′ter•ve′nor, in′ter•ven′er** *n.* —**in′ter•ven′tion** (-vĕn′shən) *n.* —**in′ter•ven′tion•al** *adj.*

in•ter•ven•tion•ism (ĭn′tər-vĕn′shə-nĭz′əm) *n.* The policy or practice of intervening, esp.: **a.** The policy of intervening in the affairs of another sovereign state. **b.** The use of government power to control or influence domestic economic activity. —**in′ter•ven′tion•ist** *n.*

in•ter•ver•te•bral (ĭn′tər-vûr′tə-brəl, -vûr-tē′-) *adj.* Located between vertebrae. —**in′ter•ver′te•bral•ly** *adv.*

intervertebral disk *n.* A broad disk of fibrocartilage situated between adjacent vertebrae of the spinal column.

in•ter•view (ĭn′tər-vyōō′) *n.* 1. A formal meeting in person, esp. one arranged for the assessment of the qualifications of an applicant. 2a. A conversation, such as one conducted by a reporter, in which facts or statements are elicited from another. **b.** An account or a reproduction of such a conversation. ❖ *v.* -viewed, -view•ing, -views —*tr.* To obtain an interview from. —*intr.* To have an interview: *interviewed for the job.* [Fr. *entrevue* < OFr. < fem. p. part. of *entrevoir,* to see : *entre-*, between (< Lat. *inter-*; see INTER–) + *voir,* to see (< Lat. *vidēre;* see **weid-** in App.).] —**in′ter•view′a•ble** *adj.* —**in′ter•view•ee′** *n.* —**in′ter•view′er** *n.*

in•ter vi•vos (ĭn′tər vē′vōs, vī′-) *adj. Law* Between living persons: *an inter vivos trust.* [Lat. *inter vīvōs* : *inter,* among + *vīvōs,* masc. accusative pl. of *vīvus,* a living being.]

in•ter•vo•cal•ic (ĭn′tər-vō-kăl′ĭk) *adj.* Occurring between vowels.

in•ter•weave (ĭn′tər-wēv′) *v.* -wove (-wōv′), -wo•ven (-wō′vən), -weav•ing, -weaves —*tr.* 1. To weave together. 2. To blend together; intermix. —*intr.* To intertwine.

in•tes•tate (ĭn-tĕs′tāt′, -tĭt) *adj. Law* 1. Having made no legal will. 2. Not disposed of by a legal will. ❖ *n.* One who dies without a legal will. —**in•tes′ta•cy** (-tə-sē) *n.*

in•tes•ti•nal (ĭn-tĕs′tə-nəl) *adj.* Of, relating to, or constituting the intestine: *intestinal bacteria.* —**in•tes′ti•nal•ly** *adv.*

intestinal fortitude *n.* Courage; endurance.

in•tes•tine (ĭn-tĕs′tĭn) *n.* The portion of the alimentary canal extending from the stomach to the anus and, in humans and other mammals, consisting of two segments, the small intestine and the large intestine. Often used in the plural. ❖ *adj.* Internal; civil: *intestine affairs.* [ME < OFr. *intestin* < Lat. *intestīna,* intestines < neut. pl. of *intestīnus,* internal < *intus,* within. See **en** in App.]

in•ti•fa•da also **in•ti•fa•dah** (ĭn′tə-fä′də) *n.* An uprising among Palestinian Arabs of the Gaza Strip and West Bank, beginning in 1987, in protest against Israeli occupation of these territories. [Ar. *intifāḍa,* shudder, awakening, uprising < *intifāḍa,* to be shaken, wake up, derived stem of *nafaḍa,* to shake.]

in•ti•ma (ĭn′tə-mə) *n., pl.* -mae (-mē′) or -mas *Anatomy* The innermost membrane of an organ or part, esp. the inner lining of

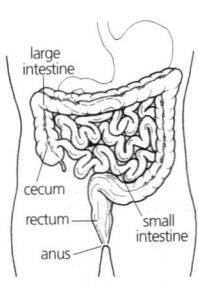
intestine

large
intestine

cecum

rectum

small
intestine

anus

an artery, vein, or lymphatic vessel. [Lat. < fem. of *intimus*, innermost. See **en** in App.] —**in′ti•mal** *adj.*

in•ti•ma•cy (ĭn′tə-mə-sē) *n.*, *pl.* **-cies 1.** The condition of being intimate. **2.** An instance of being intimate.

in•ti•mate[1] (ĭn′tə-mĭt) *adj.* **1.** Marked by close acquaintance, association, or familiarity. **2.** Relating to or indicative of one's deepest nature. **3.** Essential; innermost. **4.** Marked by informality and privacy. **5.** Very personal; private. **6.** Of or involved in a sexual relationship. ❖ *n.* A close friend or confidant. [Lat. *intimātus*, p. part. of *intimāre*, to make familiar with. See INTIMATE[2].] —**in′ti•mate•ly** *adv.* —**in′ti•mate•ness** *n.*

in•ti•mate[2] (ĭn′tə-māt′) *tr.v.* **-mat•ed, -mat•ing, -mates 1.** To make known subtly and indirectly; hint. See Syns at **suggest. 2.** To announce; proclaim. [Lat. *intimāre*, *intimāt-*, to make known < *intimus*, innermost. See **en** in App.] —**in′ti•mat′er** *n.* —**in′ti•ma′tion** *n.*

in•time (ăn-tēm′) *adj.* Intimate; private: *an intime dining corner.* [Fr. < OFr. < Lat. *intimus*, innermost. See INTIMATE[2].]

in•tim•i•date (ĭn-tĭm′ĭ-dāt′) *tr.v.* **-dat•ed, -dat•ing, -dates 1.** To make timid; fill with fear. **2.** To coerce or inhibit by or as if by threats. [Med.Lat. *intimidāre*, *intimidāt-* : Lat. *in-*, causative pref.; see IN—[2] + Lat. *timidus*, timid; see TIMID.] —**in•tim′i•dat′ing•ly** *adv.* —**in•tim′i•da′tion** *n.* —**in•tim′i•da′tor** *n.*

in•tinc•tion (ĭn-tĭngk′shən) *n. Ecclesiastical* The administration of the Eucharist by dipping the host into the wine and thus offering both simultaneously to the communicant. [LLat. *intīnctiō*, *intīnctiōn-*, a dipping in < Lat. *intīnctus*, p. part. of *intingere*, to dip in : *in-*, in; see IN—[2] + *tingere*, to moisten.]

in•tine (ĭn′tēn′) *n.* The innermost wall of a spore or pollen grain. [Ger. < Lat. *intus*, within. See **en** in App.]

in•ti•tule (ĭn-tĭch′ool) *tr.v.* **-uled, -ul•ing, -ules** *Chiefly British* To give a designation or title to (a legislative act, for example). [Ult. < LLat. *intitulāre* : Lat. *in-*, in; see IN—[2] + LLat. *titulāre*, to entitle < *titulus*, title).]

intl. *abbr.* international

in•to (ĭn′too) *prep.* **1.** To the inside or interior of. **2a.** To the activity or occupation of: *went into banking.* **b.** To the condition, state, or form of: *changed into a butterfly.* **c.** So as to be in or be included in: *entering into an agreement.* **d.** *Informal* Interested in or involved with: *into jogging.* **3.** To a point within the limits of a period of time or extent of space. **4.** In the direction of; toward. **5.** Against: *crashed into a tree.* **6.** As a divisor of: *3 goes into 9 three times.*

in•tol•er•a•ble (ĭn-tŏl′ər-ə-bəl) *adj.* Impossible to tolerate or endure; unbearable: *intolerable agony.* —**in•tol′er•a•bil′i•ty, in•tol′er•a•ble•ness** *n.* —**in•tol′er•a•bly** *adv.*

in•tol•er•ance (ĭn-tŏl′ər-əns) *n.* **1.** The quality or condition of being intolerant; lack of tolerance. **2.** *Medicine* Extreme sensitivity or allergy to a substance: *lactose intolerance.*

in•tol•er•ant (ĭn-tŏl′ər-ənt) *adj.* Not tolerant, esp.: **a.** Unwilling to tolerate differences in opinions or beliefs, esp. religious beliefs. **b.** Opposed to the inclusion or participation of those different from oneself, esp. those of a different racial, ethnic, or social background. **c.** Unable or unwilling to endure or support: *intolerant of interruptions.* —**in•tol′er•ant•ly** *adv.*

in•to•nate (ĭn′tə-nāt′) *tr.v.* **-nat•ed, -nat•ing, -nates 1.** To intone. **2.** To utter with a particular tone of voice. [Med.Lat. *intonāre*, *intonāt-*. See INTONE.]

in•to•na•tion (ĭn′tə-nā′shən, -tō-) *n.* **1a.** The act of intoning or chanting. **b.** An intoned utterance. **2.** A manner of producing tones, esp. with regard to accurate pitch. **3.** *Linguistics* The use of pitch to convey syntactic information: *a questioning intonation.* **4.** A use of pitch characteristic of a speaker or dialect. **5.** *Music* The opening phrase of a plainsong composition sung as a solo. —**in′to•na′tion•al** *adj.*

in•tone (ĭn-tōn′) *v.* **-toned, -ton•ing, -tones** —*tr.* **1.** To recite in a singing tone. **2.** To utter in a monotone. —*intr.* **1.** To speak with a singing tone or with a particular intonation. **2.** *Music* To sing a plainsong intonation. [Ult. < Med.Lat. *intonāre* : Lat. *in-*, in; see IN—[2] + Lat. *tonus*, tone; see TONE.] —**in•tone′ment** *n.* —**in•ton′er** *n.*

in to•to (ĭn tō′tō) *adv.* Totally; altogether: *He accepted her ideas in toto.* [Lat. *in tōtō* : *in*, in + *tōtō*, ablative of *tōtus*, all.]

in•tox•i•cant (ĭn-tŏk′sĭ-kənt) *n.* An agent that intoxicates, esp. an alcoholic beverage. —**in•tox′i•cant** *adj.*

in•tox•i•cate (ĭn-tŏk′sĭ-kāt′) *v.* **-cat•ed, -cat•ing, -cates** —*tr.* **1.** To stupefy or excite by the action of a drug or alcohol. **2.** To stimulate or excite: *The sea breeze intoxicated him.* **3.** To poison. —*intr.* To cause stupefaction, stimulation, or excitement by or as if by a chemical substance. [ME, to poison < Med.Lat. *intoxicāre*, *intoxicāt-* : Lat. *in-*, in; see IN—[2] + LLat. *toxicāre*, to smear with poison (< Lat. *toxicum*, poison; see TOXIC).] —**in•tox′i•cat′ing•ly** *adv.* —**in•tox′i•ca′tion** *n.* —**in•tox′i•ca′tive** *adj.* —**in•tox′i•ca′tor** *n.*

intr. *abbr.* intransitive

intra– *pref.* Within: *intraocular.* [Lat. *intrā–* < *intrā*. See **en** in App.]

in•tra-ar•te•ri•al (ĭn′trə-är-tîr′ē-əl) *adj.* Within an artery.

in•tra-a•tom•ic (ĭn′trə-ə-tŏm′ĭk) *adj.* Within an atom.

in•tra•car•di•ac (ĭn′trə-kär′dē-ăk′) *adj.* Within the heart.

in•tra•cel•lu•lar (ĭn′trə-sĕl′yə-lər) *adj.* Occurring or situated

within a cell or cells. —**in′tra•cel′lu•lar•ly** *adv.*

In•tra•coas•tal Waterway (ĭn′trə-kōs′təl) A system of artificial and natural channels and canals along the Atlantic and Gulf coasts of the E and SE US.

in•tra•cer•e•bral (ĭn′trə-sə-rē′brəl, -sĕr′ə-) *adj.* Occurring or situated within the cerebrum. —**in′tra•cer′e•bral•ly** *adv.*

in•tra•cra•ni•al (ĭn′trə-krā′nē-əl) *adj.* Occurring or situated within the cranium. —**in′tra•cra′ni•al•ly** *adv.*

in•trac•ta•ble (ĭn-trăk′tə-bəl) *adj.* **1.** Difficult to manage or govern; stubborn. See Syns at **unruly. 2.** Difficult to mold or manipulate: *intractable materials.* **3.** Difficult to alleviate, remedy, or cure: *intractable pain.* —**in•trac′ta•bil′i•ty, in•trac′ta•ble•ness** *n.* —**in•trac′ta•bly** *adv.*

in•tra•cu•ta•ne•ous (ĭn′trə-kyoō-tā′nē-əs) *adj.* Within the skin; intradermal. —**in′tra•cu•ta′ne•ous•ly** *adv.*

in•tra•day (ĭn′trə-dā′) *adj.* Occurring within a single day.

in•tra•der•mal (ĭn′trə-dûr′məl) *adj.* Within or between the layers of the skin. —**in′tra•der′mal•ly** *adv.*

intradermal test *n.* A test for hypersensitivity or allergy in which some of the suspected allergen is injected into the skin.

in•tra•dos (ĭn′trə-dŏs′, -dō′, ĭn-trā′dŏs′, -dōs′) *n.*, *pl.* **-dos** (-dōz′) or **-dos•es** (-dōs′ĭz) *Architecture* The inner curve of an arch. [Fr. : *intra-*, within (< Lat. *intrā-*; see INTRA—) + *dos*, back (< OFr. < Lat. *dorsum*).]

intrados
semicircular arch

in•tra•fal•lo•pi•an (ĭn′trə-fə-lō′pē-ən) *adj.* Located or occurring within the fallopian tubes.

in•tra•ga•lac•tic (ĭn′trə-gə-lăk′tĭk) *adj.* Occurring or situated within the space of a galaxy.

in•tra•mo•lec•u•lar (ĭn′trə-mə-lĕk′yə-lər) *adj.* Within a molecule. —**in′tra•mo•lec′u•lar•ly** *adv.*

in•tra•mu•ral (ĭn′trə-myoor′əl) *adj.* **1.** Existing or carried on within the bounds of an institution, esp. a school: *intramural athletics.* **2.** *Anatomy* Occurring or situated within the wall of a cavity or organ. —**in′tra•mu′ral•ly** *adv.*

in•tra•mus•cu•lar (ĭn′trə-mŭs′kyə-lər) *adj.* Within a muscle: *an intramuscular injection.* —**in′tra•mus′cu•lar•ly** *adv.*

in•tra•na•sal (ĭn′trə-nā′zəl) *adj.* Within the nose.

in•tra•net (ĭn′trə-nĕt′) *n.* A privately maintained computer network that can be accessed only by authorized persons.

in•tran•si•gent also **in•tran•si•geant** (ĭn-trăn′sə-jənt, -zə-) *adj.* Refusing to moderate a position, esp. an extreme one; uncompromising. [Fr. *intransigeant* < Sp. *intransigente* : *in-*, not (< Lat.; see IN—[1]) + *transigir*, pr. part. of *transigir*, to compromise (< Lat. *trānsigere*, to come to an agreement : *trāns-*, trans- + *agere*, to drive; see **ag-** in App.).] —**in•tran′si•gence, in•tran′si•gen•cy** *n.* —**in•tran′si•gent** *n.* —**in•tran′si•gent•ly** *adv.*

in•tran•si•tive (ĭn-trăn′sĭ-tĭv, -zĭ-) *adj.* Being a verb or verb construction that does not require or cannot take a direct object. ❖ *n.* An intransitive verb. —**in•tran′si•tive•ly** *adv.* —**in•tran′si•tive•ness, in•tran′si•tiv′i•ty** *n.*

in•tra•nu•cle•ar (ĭn′trə-noo′klē-ər, -nyoo′-) *adj.* Situated or occurring within the nucleus of an atom or cell.

in•tra•oc•u•lar (ĭn′trə-ŏk′yə-lər) *adj.* Situated or occurring within the eyeball: *intraocular pressure.*

in•tra•per•son•al (ĭn′trə-pûr′sə-nəl) *adj.* Existing or occurring within the individual self or mind. —**in′tra•per′son•al•ly** *adv.*

in•tra•pre•neur (ĭn′trə-prə-nûr′) *n.* A person in a large corporation empowered to create new products without being constrained by standard procedures. [Blend of *intra–* and (ENTRE)PRENEUR.]

in•tra•psy•chic (ĭn′trə-sī′kĭk) *adj.* Existing or taking place within the mind or psyche. —**in′tra•psy′chi•cal•ly** *adv.*

in•tra•spe•cif•ic (ĭn′trə-spĭ-sĭf′ĭk) also **in•tra•spe•cies** (-spē′shēz, -sēz) *adj.* Arising or occurring within a species.

in•tra•state (ĭn′trə-stāt′) *adj.* Relating to or existing within the boundaries of a state.

in•tra•u•ter•ine (ĭn′trə-yoo′tər-ĭn, -tə-rīn′) *adj.* Occurring or situated within the uterus.

intrauterine device *n.* A birth control device, such as a plastic loop, that is inserted into the uterus to prevent implantation.

in•trav•a•sa•tion (ĭn-trăv′ə-sā′shən) *n.* Entry of foreign matter into a blood vessel. [INTRA— + (EXTRA)VASATION.]

in•tra•vas•cu•lar (ĭn′trə-văs′kyə-lər) *adj.* Within blood vessels or a blood vessel. —**in′tra•vas′cu•lar•ly** *adv.*

in•tra•ve•nous (ĭn′trə-vē′nəs) *adj.* Within or administered into a vein. ❖ *n.* A drug, nutrient solution, or other substance administered into a vein. —**in′tra•ve′nous•ly** *adv.*

in•tra•vi•tal (ĭn′trə-vīt′l) *adj.* Occurring in or performed on a living organism: *intravital staining.* —**in′tra•vi′tal•ly** *adv.*

in•treat (ĭn-trēt′) *v.* Variant of **entreat.**

in•trench (ĭn-trĕnch′) *v.* Variant of **entrench.**

in•trep•id (ĭn-trĕp′ĭd) *adj.* Resolutely courageous; fearless. See Syns at **brave.** [Lat. *intrepidus* : *in-*, not; see IN—[1] + *trepidus*, alarmed.] —**in′tre•pid′i•ty** (-trə-pĭd′ĭ-tē), **in•trep′id•ness** *n.* —**in•trep′id•ly** *adv.*

in•tri•ca•cy (ĭn′trĭ-kə-sē) *n.*, *pl.* **-cies 1.** The condition or quality of being intricate; complexity. **2.** Something intricate.

in•tri•cate (ĭn′trĭ-kĭt) *adj.* **1.** Having many complexly arranged elements; elaborate. **2.** Solvable or comprehensible only with painstaking effort. See Syns at **complex.** [ME < Lat. *intrīcātus*, p.

part. of *intrīcāre*, to entangle, perplex : *in-*, in; see IN–[2] + *trīcae*, perplexities, wiles.] —**in′tri•cate•ly** *adv.* —**in′tri•cate•ness** *n.*

in•trigue (ĭn′trēg′, ĭn-trēg′) *n.* **1a.** A secret or underhand scheme; a plot. **b.** The practice of or involvement in such schemes. **2.** A clandestine love affair. ❖ *v.* (ĭn-trēg′) **-trigued, -trigu•ing, -trigues** —*intr.* To engage in secret or underhand schemes; plot. —*tr.* **1.** To effect through such schemes. **2.** To arouse the interest or curiosity of. [< Fr. *intriguer*, to plot < Ital. *intrigare*, to plot < Lat. *intrīcāre*, to entangle. See INTRICATE.] —**in•trigu′er** *n.* —**in′trigu′ing•ly** *adv.*

USAGE NOTE The introduction of the verb *intrigue* to mean "to arouse the interest or curiosity of" was initially resisted by writers on usage as an unneeded French substitute for available English words such as *interest, fascinate,* or *puzzle,* but it now appears to be well established. Seventy-eight percent of the Usage Panel accepts it in the sentence *The special-quota idea intrigues some legislators, who have asked a Washington think tank to evaluate it,* whereas only 52 percent accepted it in a 1968 survey.

in•trin•sic (ĭn-trĭn′zĭk, -sĭk) *adj.* **1.** Of or relating to the essential nature of a thing; inherent. **2.** *Anatomy* Situated within or belonging solely to the organ or body part on which it acts. Used of certain nerves and muscles. [ME *intrinsique*, inner < OFr. *intrinseque* < LLat. *intrīnsecus*, inward < Lat., inwardly. See **en** in App.] —**in•trin′si•cal•ly** *adv.*

intrinsic factor *n.* A substance that is secreted by the gastric mucous membrane and is essential for the absorption of vitamin B_{12} in the intestines.

in•tro (ĭn′trō′) *n., pl.* **-tros** *Informal* An introduction.

intro– *pref.* **1.** In; into: *introjection.* **2.** Inward: *introvert.* [Lat. *intrō-* < *intrō*, to the inside. See **en** in App.]

in•tro•duce (ĭn′trə-do͞os′, -dyo͞os′) *tr.v.* **-duced, -duc•ing, -duc•es 1a.** To present (someone) by name to another in order to establish an acquaintance. **b.** To present (a performer, for example) to the public for the first time. **2.** To bring forward (a plan, for example) for consideration. **3.** To provide with a beginning knowledge or first experience of something: *introduced me to weightlifting.* **4a.** To bring in and establish in a new place or environment. **b.** To bring into currency, use, or practice; originate. **5.** To put inside or into; insert or inject. **6.** To open or begin; preface. [ME *introducen*, to bring into < Lat. *intrōdūcere* : *intrō-*, within; see **en** in App. + *dūcere*, to lead; see **deuk-** in App.] —**in′tro•duc′er** *n.* —**in′tro•duc′i•ble** *adj.*

in•tro•duc•tion (ĭn′trə-dŭk′shən) *n.* **1.** The act or process of introducing or the state of being introduced. **2.** A means, such as a personal letter, of presenting one person to another. **3.** Something recently introduced; an innovation. **4.** Something presented in beginning or introducing something, esp.: **a.** A preface, as to a book. **b.** *Music* A short preliminary passage in a larger movement or work. **c.** A basic introductory text or course of study. [Ult. < Lat. *intrōductiō, intrōductiōn-* < *intrōductus*, p. part. of *intrōdūcere*, to bring in. See INTRODUCE.]

in•tro•duc•to•ry (ĭn′trə-dŭk′tə-rē) *adj.* **1.** Of, relating to, or constituting an introduction. **2.** Serving to introduce. —**in′tro•duc′to•ri•ly** *adv.*

in•tro•gres•sion (ĭn′trə-grĕsh′ən) *n.* Infiltration of the genes of one species into the gene pool of another through repeated backcrossing of an interspecific hybrid with one of its parents. [< Lat. *intrōgressus*, p. part. of *intrōgredī*, to step in : *intrō-*, intro- + *gradī*, to step; see INGRESS.] —**in′tro•gres′sive** (-grĕs′ĭv) *adj.*

in•tro•it also **In•tro•it** (ĭn′trō′ĭt, -troit′, ĭn-trō′ĭt) *n.* **1.** A hymn or psalm sung at the opening of a Christian service, esp. in the Anglican Church. **2.** *Roman Catholic Church* The beginning of the Mass, usu. consisting of an antiphon, a psalm verse, and the Gloria Patri. [Ult. < Med.Lat. *introitus*, sung passage at entrance of celebrant < Lat., entrance < p. part. of *introīre*, to enter : *intrō-*, in; see **en** in App. + *īre*, to go; see **ei-** in App.]

in•tro•ject (ĭn′trə-jĕkt′) *tr.v.* To incorporate (characteristics of a person or object) into one's own psyche unconsciously. [Back-formation < INTROJECTION < Ger. *Introjektion* : Lat. *intrō-*, intro- + Lat. *-iectiō, -iectiōn-*, throwing (< *iactus*, p. part. of *iacere*, to throw; see INJECT).] —**in′tro•jec′tion** *n.*

in•tro•mis•sion (ĭn′trə-mĭsh′ən) *n.* The act or process of intromitting; introduction or admission. [Med.Lat. *intrōmissiō, intrōmissiōn-*, usurpation < Lat. *intrōmissus*, p. part. of *intrōmittere*, to intromit. See INTROMIT.] —**in′tro•mis′sive** (-mĭs′ĭv) *adj.*

in•tro•mit (ĭn′trə-mĭt′) *tr.v.* **-mit•ted, -mit•ting, -mits** To cause or permit to enter; introduce or admit. [ME *intromitten*, to deal illegally with others < Lat. *intrōmittere*, to send in, let into : *intrō-*, in; see **en** in App. + *mittere*, to send.] —**in′tro•mit′tent** *adj.* —**in′tro•mit′ter** *n.*

in•tron (ĭn′trŏn) *n.* A segment of a gene situated between exons that does not function in coding for protein synthesis. [*intra(genic)*, within a gene (INTRA– + GENIC) + –ON[1].]

in•trorse (ĭn′trôrs′) *adj. Botany* Facing inward; turned toward the axis. Used esp. of anthers. [Lat. *intrōrsus*, contraction of *intrōversus*, inwards : *intrō-*, to the inside; see **en** in App. + *versus*, p. part. of *vertere*, to turn; see **wer-**[2] in App.]

introrse
close-up of a wood lily

in•tro•spect (ĭn′trə-spĕkt′, ĭn′trə-spĕkt′) *intr.v.* **-spect•ed, -spect•ing, -spects** To engage in introspection. [Lat. *intrōspicere, intrōspect-*, to look into : *intrō-*, within; see **en** in App. + *specere*, to look at; see **spek-** in App.] —**in′tro•spec′tive** *adj.* —**in′tro•spec′tive•ly** *adv.* —**in′tro•spec′tive•ness** *n.*

in•tro•spec•tion (ĭn′trə-spĕk′shən) *n.* Contemplation of one's own thoughts, feelings, and sensations; self-examination. —**in′tro•spec′tion•al** *adj.*

in•tro•ver•sion (ĭn′trə-vûr′zhən, -shən) *n.* **1.** Preoccupation with or interest in oneself or one's own interests. **2.** A turning inward, as of an organ. —**in′tro•ver′sive** (-vûr′sĭv) *adj.*

in•tro•vert (ĭn′trə-vûrt′, ĭn′trə-vûrt′) *tr.v.* **-vert•ed, -vert•ing, -verts 1.** To turn or direct inward. **2.** To concentrate (one's interests) upon oneself. ❖ *n.* (ĭn′trə-vûrt′) An introverted person. [INTRO– + Lat. *vertere*, to turn; see **wer-**[2] in App.]

in•tro•vert•ed (ĭn′trə-vûr′tĭd) *adj.* Marked by introversion; shy or retiring.

in•trude (ĭn-tro͞od′) *v.* **-trud•ed, -trud•ing, -trudes** —*tr.* **1.** To put or force in inappropriately, esp. without invitation, fitness, or permission: *intruded opinion into a factual report.* **2.** *Geology* To thrust (molten rock) into preexisting rock. —*intr.* To come in rudely or inappropriately; enter as an improper or unwanted element. [ME *intruden* < Lat. *intrūdere, intrūs-*, to thrust in : *in-*, in; see IN–[2] + *trūdere*, to thrust.] —**in•trud′er** *n.*

in•tru•sion (ĭn-tro͞o′zhən) *n.* **1.** The act of intruding or the state of being intruded on. **2.** An inappropriate or unwelcome addition. **3.** *Geology* **a.** The intruding of molten rock. **b.** The rock mass produced by an intrusive process.

in•tru•sive (ĭn-tro͞o′sĭv, -zĭv) *adj.* **1.** Intruding or tending to intrude. **2.** *Geology* Of or relating to igneous rock that is forced while molten into cracks or between other layers of rock. **3.** *Linguistics* Of or relating to epenthesis. —**in•tru′sive•ly** *adv.* —**in•tru′sive•ness** *n.*

in•trust (ĭn-trŭst′) *v.* Variant of **entrust.**

in•tu•bate (ĭn′to͞o-bāt′, -tyo͞o-) *tr.v.* **-bat•ed, -bat•ing, -bates** To insert a tube into (a hollow organ or body passage). —**in′tu•ba′tion** *n.* —**in′tu•ba′tion•al** *adj.*

in•tu•it (ĭn-to͞o′ĭt, -tyo͞o′-) *tr.v.* **-it•ed, -it•ing, -its** *Usage Problem* To know intuitively. [Back-formation < INTUITION.]

USAGE NOTE The verb *intuit* is well established in reputable writing, but some critics have objected to it. Only 34 percent of the Usage Panel accepts it in the sentence *Claude often intuits my feelings about things long before I am really aware of them myself.* The source of the objections most likely lies in the fact that the verb is often used in reference to more trivial sorts of insight than would be permitted by a full appreciation of the traditional meaning of *intuition.* In this connection, a greater percentage of the Panel, 46 percent, accepts *intuit* in the sentence *Mathematicians sometimes intuit the truth of a theorem long before they are able to prove it.*

in•tu•i•tion (ĭn′to͞o-ĭsh′ən, -tyo͞o-) *n.* **1a.** The act or faculty of knowing or sensing without the use of rational processes; immediate cognition. **b.** Knowledge gained by the use of this faculty; a perceptive insight. **2.** A sense of something not evident or deducible; an impression. [ME *intuicioun*, insight < LLat. *intuitiō, intuitiōn-*, a looking at < Lat. *intuitus*, a look < p. part. of *intuērī*, contemplate : *in-*, on; see IN–[2] + *tuērī*, to look at.] —**in′tu•i′tion•al** *adj.* —**in′tu•i′tion•al•ly** *adv.*

in•tu•i•tion•ism (ĭn′to͞o-ĭsh′ə-nĭz′əm, -tyo͞o-) *n. Philosophy* **1.** The theory that truth or certain truths are known by intuition rather than reason. **2.** The theory that external objects of perception are immediately known to be real by intuition. **3.** The theory that ethical principles are known to be valid through intuition. —**in′tu•i′tion•ist** *n.*

in•tu•i•tive (ĭn-to͞o′ĭ-tĭv, -tyo͞o′-) *adj.* **1.** Of, relating to, or arising from intuition. **2.** Known or perceived through intuition. **3.** Possessing or demonstrating intuition. —**in•tu′i•tive•ly** *adv.* —**in•tu′i•tive•ness** *n.*

in•tu•mesce (ĭn′to͞o-mĕs′, -tyo͞o-) *intr.v.* **-mesced, -mesc•ing, -mesc•es 1.** To swell or expand; enlarge. **2.** To bubble up, esp. due to heating. [Lat. *intumēscere* : *in-*, intensive pref.; see IN–[2] + *tumēscere*, to begin to swell, inchoative of *tumēre*, to swell.]

in•tu•mes•cence (ĭn′to͞o-mĕs′əns, -tyo͞o-) *n.* **1.** The act or process of swelling or the condition of being swollen. **2.** A swollen organ or body part. —**in′tu•mes′cent** *adj.*

in•tus•sus•cept (ĭn′tə-sə-sĕpt′) *tr.v.* **-cept•ed, -cept•ing, -cepts** To take within, as in telescoping one part of the intestine into another; invaginate.

in•tus•sus•cep•tion (ĭn′tə-sə-sĕp′shən) *n.* **1.** Invagination, esp. an infolding of one part of the intestine into another. **2.** *Biology* Assimilation of new substances into the existing components of living tissue. [Med.Lat. *intussusceptiō, intussusceptiōn-*, a taking in, admission < *intussusceptus*, p. part. of *intussuscipere*, to take in : Lat. *intus*, within; see **en** in App. + Lat. *suscipere*, to take up (*sub-*, sub- + *capere*, to take; see **kap-** in App.).]

In•u•it also **In•nu•it** (ĭn′yo͞o-ĭt) *n., pl.* **Inuit** or **-its** also **Innuit** or **-its 1.** A member of a group of Eskimoan peoples inhabiting the Arctic from northern Alaska eastward to eastern Greenland, particularly those of Canada. **2a.** The family of languages spoken by the Inuit. **b.** Any of those languages. See Usage Note at **Eskimo.** [Inuit, pl. of *Inuk*, human being, Eskimo.]

in•u•lase (ĭn′yə-lās′) *n.* An enzyme that catalyzes the conversion of inulin to fructose. [INUL(IN) + –ASE.]

in·u·lin (ĭn′yə-lĭn) *n.* A polysaccharide with the general formula ($C_6H_{10}O_5$)$_n$ that is found in the roots of various composite plants and yields fructose when hydrolyzed. [NLat. *Inula*, plant genus (< Lat. *inula*, elecampane < Gk. *helenion*; see ELECAMPANE) + -IN.]

in·unc·tion (ĭn-ŭngk′shən) *n.* **1.** The process of applying and rubbing in an ointment. **2.** The act of anointing, as in a ceremony. [ME, anointing < Lat. *inūnctiō, inūnctiōn-* < *inūnctus*, p. part. of *inunguere*, to anoint : *in-*, on; see IN-² + *unguere*, to smear.]

in·un·date (ĭn′ŭn-dāt′, ĭn′ən-) *tr.v.* **-dat·ed, -dat·ing, -dates 1.** To cover with water, esp. floodwaters. **2.** To overwhelm as if with a flood; swamp: *inundated with work.* [Lat. *inundāre, inundāt-* : *in-*, in; see IN-² + *undāre*, to surge (< *unda*, wave; see **wed-** in App.).] —**in′un·da′tion** *n.* —**in·un′da·to·ry** (-də-tôr′ē, -tōr′ē) *adj.*

I·nu·pi·aq (ĭ-nōō′pē-äk′, -äk′, -nyōō′-) *n., pl.* **Inupiaq** or **-aqs** or **I·nu·pi·at** (-ät′, -ät′) or **-ats 1.** A member of a group of Eskimoan peoples inhabiting the northwest and northern coastal areas of Alaska. **2.** The language of the Inupiaq. See Usage Note at **Eskimo.** [Inupiaq *iñupiaq,* original person : *iñuk,* person + *-pia-,* real + *-q,* sing. suff.]

in·ure *also* **en·ure** (ĭn-yŏor′) *tr.v.* **-ured, -ur·ing, -ures** To habituate to something undesirable, esp. by prolonged subjection; accustom. [ME, back-formation < *enured,* customary < *in ure* : *in,* in; see IN-¹ + *ure,* use (< OFr. *euvre, uevre,* work < Lat. *opera,* activity associated with work).] —**in·ure′ment** *n.*

in·urn (ĭn-ûrn′) *tr.v.* **-urned, -urn·ing, -urns 1.** To put in an urn. **2.** To bury or entomb; inter.

in u·ter·o (ĭn yōō′tə-rō) *adv. & adj.* In the uterus. [NLat. *in uterō.*]

in·u·tile (ĭn-yōōt′l, -yōō′tĭl′) *adj.* Lacking in utility or serviceability; not useful. [ME < OFr. < Lat. *inūtilis* : *in-,* not; see IN-¹ + *ūtilis,* useful; see UTILE.] —**in·u′tile·ly** *adv.* —**in·u′til·i·ty** (ĭn′yōō-tĭl′ĭ-tē) *n.*

I·nu·vik (ĭ-nōō′vĭk) A region of NW Northwest Terrs., Canada.

inv. *abbr.* **1a.** invented **b.** inventor **2.** invoice

in vac·u·o (ĭn văk′yōō-ō′) *adv.* **1.** In a vacuum. **2.** In isolation; without reference to related evidence. [NLat. *in vacuō.*]

in·vade (ĭn-vād′) *v.* **-vad·ed, -vad·ing, -vades** —*tr.* **1.** To enter by force in order to conquer or pillage. **2.** To encroach or intrude on; violate. **3.** To overrun as if by invading; infest: *"About 1917 the shipworm invaded the harbor of San Francisco"* (Rachel Carson). **4.** To enter and permeate, esp. harmfully. —*intr.* To make an invasion. [ME < OFr. *invader* < Lat. *invādere* : *in-,* in; see IN-² + *vādere,* to go.] —**in·vad′er** *n.*

in·vag·i·nate (ĭn-văj′ə-nāt′) *tr. & intr.v.* **-nat·ed, -nat·ing, -nates 1.** To enclose or become enclosed in or as if in a sheath. **2.** To turn or become turned inward. **3.** To infold or become infolded so as to form a hollow space within a previously solid structure, as in the formation of a gastrula from a blastula. [Med.Lat. *invāgināre, invāgināt-* : Lat. *in-,* in; see IN-² + Lat. *vāgīna,* sheath.]

in·vag·i·na·tion (ĭn-văj′ə-nā′shən) *n.* **1.** The act or process of invaginating or the condition of being invaginated. **2.** An invaginated organ or part. **3.** The infolding of a portion of the outer layer of a blastula in the formation of a gastrula.

in·va·lid¹ (ĭn′və-lĭd) *n.* One who is incapacitated by a chronic illness or disability. ❖ *adj.* **1.** Incapacitated by illness or injury. **2.** Of, relating to, or intended for invalids. ❖ *tr.v.* **-lid·ed, -lid·ing, -lids 1.** To incapacitate physically. **2.** *Chiefly British* To release or exempt from duty because of ill health. [< INVALID² (influenced by Fr. *invalide,* sickly, infirm).]

in·val·id² (ĭn-văl′ĭd) *adj.* **1.** Not legally or factually valid; null: *an invalid license.* **2.** Falsely based or reasoned; faulty: *an invalid argument.* [Lat. *invalidus,* weak : *in-,* not; see IN-¹ + *validus,* strong (< *valēre,* to be strong).] —**in′va·lid′i·ty** (-və-lĭd′ĭ-tē) *n.* —**in·val′id·ly** *adv.*

in·val·i·date (ĭn-văl′ĭ-dāt′) *tr.v.* **-dat·ed, -dat·ing, -dates** To make invalid; nullify. —**in·val′i·da′tion** *n.* —**in·val′i·da′tor** *n.*

in·va·lid·ism (ĭn′və-lĭ-dĭz′əm) *n.* The condition of being incapacitated by an illness or disability.

in·val·u·a·ble (ĭn-văl′yōō-ə-bəl) *adj.* Of inestimable value; priceless: *invaluable help.* —**in·val′u·a·ble·ness** *n.* —**in·val′u·a·bly** *adv.*

in·var·i·a·ble (ĭn-vâr′ē-ə-bəl) *adj.* Not changing or subject to change; constant. —**in·var′i·a·bil′i·ty, in·var′i·a·ble·ness** *n.* —**in·var′i·a·bly** *adv.*

in·var·i·ant (ĭn-vâr′ē-ənt) *adj.* **1.** Not varying; constant. **2.** *Mathematics* Unaffected by a designated operation, as a transformation of coordinates. ❖ *n.* An invariant quantity, function, configuration, or system. —**in·var′i·ance** *n.*

in·va·sion (ĭn-vā′zhən) *n.* **1.** The act of invading, esp. the entrance of an armed force into a territory to conquer. **2.** A large-scale onset of something injurious or harmful, such as a disease. **3.** An intrusion or encroachment. [ME *invasioun* < OFr. *invasion* < LLat. *invāsiō, invāsiōn-* < *invāsus,* p. part. of *invādere,* to invade. See INVADE.]

in·va·sive (ĭn-vā′sĭv) *adj.* **1.** Of, engaging in, or given to armed aggression. **2.** Marked by the tendency to spread, esp. into healthy tissue: *an invasive carcinoma.* **3.** Of or relating to a medical procedure in which a part of the body is entered, as by incision. **4.** Tending to intrude or encroach, as upon privacy. —**in·va′sive·ly** *adv.* —**in·va′sive·ness** *n.*

in·vec·tive (ĭn-vĕk′tĭv) *n.* **1.** Denunciatory or abusive language; vituperation. **2.** Denunciatory or abusive expression or discourse. [< ME *invectif,* denunciatory < OFr. < LLat. *invectīvus,* reproachful, abusive < Lat. *invectus,* p. part. of *invehī,* to inveigh against. See INVEIGH.] —**in·vec′tive** *adj.* —**in·vec′tive·ly** *adv.* —**in·vec′tive·ness** *n.*

in·veigh (ĭn-vā′) *intr.v.* **-veighed, -veigh·ing, -veighs** To give vent to angry disapproval; protest vehemently. [Lat. *invehī,* to attack with words, inveigh against, passive of *invehere,* to carry in : *in-,* in; see IN-² + *vehere,* to carry; see **wegh-** in App.] —**in·veigh′er** *n.*

in·vei·gle (ĭn-vā′gəl, -vē′-) *tr.v.* **-gled, -gling, -gles 1.** To win over by coaxing, flattery, or artful talk. **2.** To obtain by cajolery: *inveigle a free museum pass.* [ME *envegle,* alteration of OFr. *aveugler,* to blind < *aveugle,* blind < VLat. **aboculus* : Lat. *ab-,* away from; see AB-¹ + Lat. *oculus,* eye (prob. transl. of Gaulish *exsops* : *exs-,* from + *ops,* eye); see **okʷ-** in App.] —**in·vei′gle·ment** *n.* —**in·vei′gler** *n.*

in·vent (ĭn-vĕnt′) *tr.v.* **-vent·ed, -vent·ing, -vents 1.** To produce or contrive (something previously unknown) by ingenuity or imagination. **2.** To make up; fabricate. [Lat. *invenīre, invent-,* to find : *in-,* on, upon; see IN-² + *venīre,* to come; see **gʷā-** in App.] —**in·vent′i·ble** *adj.* —**in·ven′tor** *n.*

in·ven·tion (ĭn-vĕn′shən) *n.* **1.** The act or process of inventing. **2.** A new device, method, or process developed from study and experimentation. **3.** A mental fabrication, esp. a falsehood. **4.** Skill in inventing; inventiveness. **5.** *Music* A short composition developing a single theme contrapuntally. **6.** A discovery; a finding. [Ult. < Lat. *inventiō, inventiōn-,* inventiveness < *inventus,* p. part. of *invenīre,* to find. See INVENT.] —**in·ven′tion·al** *adj.*

in·ven·tive (ĭn-vĕn′tĭv) *adj.* **1.** Of, relating to, or characterized by invention. **2.** Adept or skillful at inventing; creative. —**in·ven′tive·ly** *adv.* —**in·ven′tive·ness** *n.*

in·ven·to·ry (ĭn′vən-tôr′ē, -tōr′ē) *n., pl.* **-ries 1a.** A detailed itemized record of things in one's possession, esp. a periodic survey of all goods and materials in stock. **b.** The process of making such a record. **c.** The items listed in such a record. **d.** The quantity of goods and materials on hand; stock. **2.** An evaluation or a survey, as of resources. ❖ *tr.v.* **-ried, -ry·ing, -ries 1.** To make an inventory of. **2.** To include in an inventory. [ME *inventorie* < Med.Lat. *inventōrium,* alteration of LLat. *inventārium* < Lat. *inventus,* p. part. of *invenīre,* to find. See INVENT.] —**in·ven′to·ri·al** *adj.* —**in·ven′to·ri·al·ly** *adv.*

in·ve·rac·i·ty (ĭn′və-răs′ĭ-tē) *n., pl.* **-ties 1.** Lack of veracity; untruthfulness. **2.** An untruth; a falsehood.

in·ver·ness *also* **In·ver·ness** (ĭn′vər-nĕs′) *n.* **1.** A long loose overcoat with a detachable cape having a round collar. **2.** The cape of such an overcoat. [After INVERNESS.]

Inverness A burgh of N Scotland on the Moray Firth; chartered c. 1200. Pop. 40,010

in·verse (ĭn-vûrs′, ĭn′vûrs′) *adj.* **1.** Reversed in order, nature, or effect. **2.** *Mathematics* Of or relating to an inverse or an inverse function. **3.** *Archaic* Turned upside down; inverted. ❖ *n.* (ĭn′vûrs′, ĭn-vûrs′) **1.** Something that is opposite, as in sequence; the reverse. **2.** *Mathematics* One of a pair of elements in a set whose result under the operation of the set is the identity element, esp.: **a.** The reciprocal of a given quantity. **b.** The negative of a given quantity. [ME < Lat. *inversus,* p. part. of *invertere,* to invert. See INVERT.] —**in·verse′ly** *adv.*

inverse function *n.* *Mathematics* A function whose relation to a given function is such that their composite is the identity function.

in·ver·sion (ĭn-vûr′zhən, -shən) *n.* **1a.** The act of inverting. **b.** The state of being inverted. **2.** An interchange of position of adjacent objects in a sequence, esp. a change in normal word order, such as the placement of a verb before its subject. **3.** *Music* A rearrangement of tones in which: **a.** the upper and lower voices are transposed. **b.** each interval in a single melody is applied in the opposite direction. **c.** the notes of a chord are rearranged such that the bass has a different pitch. **4.** *Psychology* **a.** The taking on of the gender role of the opposite sex. **b.** In the theory of Sigmund Freud, homosexuality. Not in scientific use. **5.** *Chemistry* Conversion of a compound in which the direction of optical rotation is reversed, as from the dextrorotatory to the levorotatory form. **6.** *Meteorology* An atmospheric condition in which the air temperature rises with increasing altitude, holding surface air down and preventing dispersion of pollutants. **7.** *Genetics* A chromosomal defect in which a segment of the chromosome breaks off and reattaches in the reverse direction. [Lat. *inversiō, inversiōn-* < *inversus,* p. part. of *invertere,* to invert. See INVERT.]

in·vert (ĭn-vûrt′) *v.* **-vert·ed, -vert·ing, -verts** —*tr.* **1.** To turn inside out or upside down. **2.** To reverse the position, order, or condition of. **3.** To subject to inversion. —*intr.* To be subjected to inversion. ❖ *n.* (ĭn′vûrt′) **1.** Something inverted. **2.** *Psychology* **a.** One who takes on the gender role of the opposite sex. **b.** In the theory of Sigmund Freud, a homosexual person. Not in scientific use. [Lat. *invertere* : *in-,* in; see IN-² + *vertere,* to turn; see **wer-²** in App.] —**in·vert′i·ble** *adj.*

in·ver·tase (ĭn-vûr′tās′, ĭn′vər-tās′, -tāz′) *n.* An enzyme that catalyzes the hydrolysis of sucrose into glucose and fructose.

in·ver·te·brate (ĭn-vûr′tə-brĭt, -brāt′) *adj.* **1.** Lacking a backbone or spinal column; not vertebrate. **2.** Of or relating to invertebrates. ❖ *n.* An invertebrate animal.

in·vert·ed comma *n.* Chiefly British A quotation mark.

inverted mordent *n.* See pralltriller.

in·vert·er (ĭn-vûr′tər) *n.* **1.** One that inverts or produces inversion. **2.** A device used to convert direct current into alternating current.

invert sugar *n.* A mixture of equal parts of glucose and fructose resulting from the hydrolysis of sucrose.

in·vest (ĭn-vĕst′) *v.* **-vest·ed, -vest·ing, -vests** —*tr.* **1.** To commit (money or capital) in order to gain a financial return. **2a.** To spend or devote for future advantage or benefit. **b.** To devote morally or psychologically, as to a purpose; commit. **3.** To endow with authority or power. **4.** To install in office with ceremony. **5.** To endow with an enveloping or pervasive quality. **6.** To clothe; adorn. **7.** To cover completely; envelop. **8.** To surround with troops or ships; besiege. —*intr.* To make investments or an investment. [Ult. < Lat. *investīre,* to clothe, surround : *in-,* in; see IN-² + *vestīre,* to clothe (< *vestis,* clothes; see wes-² in App.).] —**in·vest′a·ble** *adj.* —**in·ves′tor** *n.*

in·ves·ti·gate (ĭn-vĕs′tĭ-gāt′) *v.* **-gat·ed, -gat·ing, -gates** —*tr.* To observe or inquire into in detail; examine systematically. —*intr.* To make a detailed inquiry or systematic examination. [Lat. *investīgāre, investīgāt- : in-,* in; see IN-² + *vestīgāre,* to track (< *vestīgium,* footprint).] —**in·ves′ti·ga·ble** (-gə-bəl) *adj.* —**in·ves′ti·ga·to′ry** (-gə-tôr′ē, -tōr′ē) *adj.*

in·ves·ti·ga·tion (ĭn-vĕs′tĭ-gā′shən) *n.* **1.** The act or process of investigating. **2.** A detailed inquiry or systematic examination. —**in·ves′ti·ga′tion·al** *adj.*

in·ves·ti·ga·tive (ĭn-vĕs′tĭ-gā′tĭv) *adj.* **1.** Of or relating to investigation. **2.** Marked by or engaged in investigation; uncovering and reporting hidden information.

in·ves·ti·ga·tor (ĭn-vĕs′tĭ-gā′tər) *n.* One, esp. a detective, who investigates. —**in·ves′ti·ga·to′ri·al** (-gə-tôr′ē-əl, -tōr′-) *adj.*

in·ves·ti·ture (ĭn-vĕs′tə-chŏŏr′, -chər) *n.* **1.** The act or ceremony of conferring the authority and symbols of a high office. **2.** An adornment or cover. [ME < Med.Lat. *investītūra* < Lat. *investīre,* to clothe. See INVEST.]

in·vest·ment (ĭn-vĕst′mənt) *n.* **1.** The act of investing. **2.** An amount invested. **3.** A property or possession acquired for future financial benefit. **4.** A commitment, as of time. **5.** A military siege. **6.** *Archaic* **a.** A garment; a vestment. **b.** An outer covering.

investment bank *n.* A financial institution that deals primarily with raising capital, corporate mergers and acquisitions, and securities trades.

in·vet·er·ate (ĭn-vĕt′ər-ĭt) *adj.* **1.** Firmly and long established; deep-rooted. **2.** Persisting in an ingrained habit; habitual. [ME < Lat. *inveterātus,* p. part. of *inveterāre,* to grow old, endure : *in-,* causative pref.; see IN-² + *vetus, veter-,* old; see wet-² in App.] —**in·vet′er·a·cy** (-ər-ə-sē), **in·vet′er·ate·ness** *n.* —**in·vet′er·ate·ly** *adv.*

in·vi·a·ble (ĭn-vī′ə-bəl) *adj.* Unable to survive or develop normally: *an inviable newborn calf.* —**in·vi·a·bil′i·ty** *n.*

in·vid·i·ous (ĭn-vĭd′ē-əs) *adj.* **1.** Tending to rouse ill will, animosity, or resentment: *invidious accusations.* **2.** Containing or implying a slight; discriminatory: *invidious policies.* **3.** Envious. [Lat. *invidiōsus,* envious, hostile < *invidia,* envy. See ENVY.] —**in·vid′i·ous·ly** *adv.* —**in·vid′i·ous·ness** *n.*

in·vig·or·ate (ĭn-vĭg′ə-rāt′) *tr.v.* **-at·ed, -at·ing, -ates** To impart vigor, strength, or vitality to; animate. [Poss. obsolete *invigor* (< Fr. *envigorer* < OFr. *envigourer : en-,* in; see IN-² + *vigour,* vigor; see VIGOR) + -ATE¹.] —**in·vig′or·at′ing·ly** *adv.* —**in·vig′or·a′tion** *n.* —**in·vig′or·a′tor** *n.*

in·vin·ci·ble (ĭn-vĭn′sə-bəl) *adj.* Incapable of being overcome or defeated; unconquerable. —**in·vin′ci·bil′i·ty, in·vin′ci·ble·ness** *n.* —**in·vin′ci·bly** *adv.*

in·vi·o·la·ble (ĭn-vī′ə-lə-bəl) *adj.* **1.** Secure from violation or profanation. **2.** Impregnable to assault or trespass; invincible. —**in·vi′o·la·bil′i·ty, in·vi′o·la·ble·ness** *n.* —**in·vi′o·la·bly** *adv.*

in·vi·o·late (ĭn-vī′ə-lĭt) *adj.* Not violated or profaned; intact. [ME < Lat. *inviolātus : in-,* not; see IN-¹ + *violātus,* p. part. of *violāre,* to violate; see VIOLATE.] —**in·vi′o·la·cy** (-lə-sē), **in·vi′o·late·ness** *n.* —**in·vi′o·late·ly** *adv.*

in·vis·cid (ĭn-vĭs′ĭd) *adj.* Having no viscosity.

in·vis·i·ble (ĭn-vĭz′ə-bəl) *adj.* **1.** Impossible to see; not visible. **2.** Not accessible to view; hidden. **3.** Not easily noticed or detected; inconspicuous. **4.** Not published in financial statements: *an invisible asset.* —**in·vis′i·ble** *n.* —**in·vis′i·bil′i·ty, in·vis′i·ble·ness** *n.* —**in·vis′i·bly** *adv.*

invisible hand *n.* An economic principle, first postulated by Adam Smith, holding that the greatest benefit to a society is brought about by individuals acting freely in a competitive marketplace in the pursuit of their own self-interest.

invisible ink *n.* Ink that is colorless and invisible until treated by a chemical, heat, or special light.

in·vi·ta·tion (ĭn′vĭ-tā′shən) *n.* **1.** The act of inviting. **2.** A request for someone's presence or participation. **3.** An allurement or enticement. **4.** See altar call.

in·vi·ta·tion·al (ĭn′vĭ-tā′shə-nəl) *adj.* Restricted to invited participants. ❖ *n.* An invitational event, esp. a sports tournament.

in·vi·ta·to·ry (ĭn-vī′tə-tôr′ē, -tōr′ē) *adj.* Constituting or containing an invitation.

in·vite (ĭn-vīt′) *tr.v.* **-vit·ed, -vit·ing, -vites** **1.** To ask for the presence or participation of. **2.** To request formally. **3.** To welcome; encourage. **4.** To tend to bring on; provoke. **5.** To entice; tempt. ❖ *n.* (ĭn′vīt′) *Informal* An invitation. [Fr. *inviter* < OFr. < Lat. *invītāre.* See weiə- in App.]

in·vi·tee (ĭn′vī-tē′) *n.* One that is invited.

in·vit·ing (ĭn-vī′tĭng) *adj.* Attractive; tempting: *an inviting dessert.* —**in·vit′ing·ly** *adv.*

in vi·tro (ĭn vē′trō) *adv. & adj.* In an artificial environment outside the living organism: *in vitro fertilization.* [NLat. *in vitrō* : Lat. *in,* in + Lat. *vitrō,* ablative of *vitrum,* glass.]

in vi·vo (vē′vō) *adv. & adj.* Within a living organism. [NLat. *in vīvō.*]

in·vo·cate (ĭn′və-kāt′) *tr.v.* **-cat·ed, -cat·ing, -cates** *Archaic* To invoke. [Lat. *invocāre, invocāt-,* to invoke. See INVOKE.]

in·vo·ca·tion (ĭn′və-kā′shən) *n.* **1.** The act or an instance of invoking, esp. an appeal to a higher power for assistance. **2.** A prayer or other formula used in invoking. **3a.** The act of conjuring up a spirit by incantation. **b.** An incantation used in conjuring. [ME *invocacion* < OFr. < Lat. *invocātiō, invocātiōn-* < *invocātus,* p. part. of *invocāre,* to invoke. See INVOKE.] —**in′vo·ca′tion·al** *adj.*

in·voc·a·to·ry (ĭn-vŏk′ə-tôr′ē, -tōr′ē) *adj.* Of or having the nature of an invocation.

in·voice (ĭn′vois′) *n.* **1.** A detailed list of goods shipped or services rendered, with an account of all costs; an itemized bill. **2.** The goods or services itemized in an invoice. ❖ *tr.v.* **-voiced, -voic·ing, -voic·es** **1.** To make an invoice of (goods or services). **2.** To send an invoice to; bill. [Alteration of obsolete *invoyes,* pl. of *invoy,* invoice < Fr. *envoi,* a sending, shipment < *envoyer,* to send. See ENVOY¹.]

in·voke (ĭn-vōk′) *tr.v.* **-voked, -vok·ing, -vokes** **1.** To call on (a higher power) for assistance, support, or inspiration. **2.** To appeal to or cite in support or justification. **3.** To call for earnestly; solicit. **4.** To summon with incantations; conjure. **5.** To resort to; use or apply. **6.** *Computer Science* To activate or start (a program, for example). [ME *envoken* < OFr. *invoquer* < Lat. *invocāre : in-,* in; see IN-² + *vocāre,* to call; see wek^w- in App.] —**in·vok′er** *n.*

in·vo·lu·cel (ĭn-vŏl′yə-sĕl′) *n.* A secondary involucre, as at the base of an umbel within a compound umbel. [NLat. *involūcellum,* dim. of *involūcrum,* involucre. See INVOLUCRUM.]

in·vo·lu·cre (ĭn′və-lōō′kər) *n.* A series of bracts beneath or around a flower or flower cluster. [Fr. < Lat. *involūcrum,* wrapper, envelope. See INVOLUCRUM.] —**in′vo·lu′cral** (-krəl), **in′vo·lu′crate** (-krĭt, -krāt′) *adj.*

in·vo·lu·crum (ĭn′və-lōō′krəm) *n., pl.* **-cra** (-krə) An enveloping sheath or envelope. [NLat. *involūcrum* < Lat., wrapper, envelope < *involvere,* to enwrap. See INVOLVE.]

in·vol·un·tar·y (ĭn-vŏl′ən-tĕr′ē) *adj.* **1.** Acting or done without or against one's will. **2.** Not subject to control of the volition. —**in·vol′un·tar′i·ly** (-târ′ə-lē) *adv.* —**in·vol′un·tar′i·ness** *n.*

in·vo·lute (ĭn′və-lōōt′) *adj.* **1.** Intricate; complex. **2.** *Botany* **a.** Having the margins rolled inward. **b.** Having whorls that obscure the axis or other volutions, as the shell of a cowrie. ❖ *intr.v.* **-lut·ed, -lut·ing, -lutes** **1.** To curl inward. **2.** To return to a normal or former condition. ❖ *n.* The curve traced by a point on a taut inextensible string as it unwinds from another curve. [Lat. *involūtus,* p. part. of *involvere,* to enwrap. See INVOLVE.] —**in′vo·lute′ly** *adv.*

in·vo·lu·tion (ĭn′və-lōō′shən) *n.* **1.** The act of involving. **b.** The state of being involved. **2.** Intricacy; complexity. **3.** Something that is intricate or complex. **4.** *Mathematics* An operation, such as negation, which, when applied to itself, returns the original number. **5.** *Embryology* The ingrowth and curling inward of a group of cells, as in the formation of a gastrula from a blastula. **6.** *Medicine* **a.** A decrease in size of an organ, as of the uterus after childbirth. **b.** A progressive decline or degeneration of normal physiological function, caused by the aging process. [Lat. *involūtiō, involūtiōn-* < *involūtus,* p. part. of *involvere,* to enwrap. See INVOLVE.] —**in′vo·lu′tion·al** *adj.*

in·volve (ĭn-vŏlv′) *tr.v.* **-volved, -volv·ing, -volves** **1.** To contain as a part; include. **2.** To have as a necessary feature or consequence; entail. **3.** To engage as a participant; embroil. **4a.** To connect closely and often incriminatingly; implicate. **b.** To influence or affect. **5.** To occupy or engage the interest of. **6.** To make complex or intricate; complicate. **7.** To wrap; envelop. **8.** *Archaic* To wind or coil about. [ME *involven* < Lat. *involvere,* to enwrap : *in-,* in; see IN-² + *volvere,* to roll, turn; see wel- in App.] —**in·volve′ment** *n.* —**in·volv′er** *n.*

in·volved (ĭn-vŏlvd′) *adj.* **1.** Complicated; intricate. See Syns at **complex. 2.** Curled inward; coiled or involute. **3.** Confused; tangled. **4.** Connected by participation or association. **5a.** Emotionally committed. **b.** Having a sexual relationship. —**in·volv′ed·ly** (-vŏl′vĭd-lē) *adv.*

in·vul·ner·a·ble (ĭn-vŭl′nər-ə-bəl) *adj.* **1.** Immune to attack;

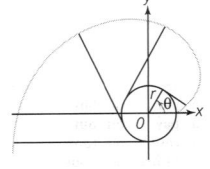

involute
$x = r \cos\theta + r\theta \sin\theta$
$y = r \sin\theta - r\theta \cos\theta$

impregnable. **2.** Impossible to damage, injure, or wound. —**in·vul′ner·a·bil′i·ty, in·vul′ner·a·ble·ness** *n.* —**in·vul′ner·a·bly** *adv.*

in·ward (ĭn′wərd) *adj.* **1.** Located inside; inner. **2.** Directed or moving toward the interior. **3.** Of, relating to, or being in the mind. **4.** Intimate; familiar. ❖ *adv.* also **in·wards** (-wərdz) **1.** Toward the inside, center, or interior. **2.** Toward the mind or the self: *looked inward.* ❖ *n.* **1.** An inner or central part. **2.** An inner essence or spirit. **3. inwards** Entrails; innards. [ME < OE *inweard.* See **wer-²** in App.]

inward dive A dive in which the diver, standing on the end of the board or platform with the back to the water, leaps up and rotates forward.

in·ward·ly (ĭn′wərd-lē) *adv.* **1.** On or in the inside; within. **2.** Privately; to oneself.

in·ward·ness (ĭn′wərd-nĭs) *n.* **1.** Intimacy; familiarity. **2.** Preoccupation with one's own thoughts or feelings; introspection.

in·weave (ĭn-wēv′) *tr.v.* -**wove** (-wōv′), -**wo·ven** (-wō′vən), -**weav·ing, -weaves** To weave into a fabric or design.

in·wrought (ĭn-rôt′, ĭn′rôt′) *adj.* **1.** Worked or woven in: *an inwrought design.* **2.** Having an inwrought decorative pattern.

in-your-face (ĭn′yoŏr′fās′, -yôr′-, -yōr′-, -yər-) *adj.* Marked by or done in a bold, defiant, or aggressive manner: *in-your-face advertising.*

I·o (ī′ō, ē′ō) *n.* **1.** *Greek Mythology* A young woman whom Zeus loved and Hera transformed into a heifer. **2.** A satellite of Jupiter. [Lat. *Īō* < Gk.]

I/O *abbr.* input/output

IOC *abbr.* International Olympic Committee

i·o·date (ī′ə-dāt′) *tr.v.* -**dat·ed, -dat·ing, -dates** To combine, impregnate, or treat with iodine. ❖ *n.* (-dāt′, -dĭt) A salt of iodic acid. —**i′o·da′tion** *n.*

i·od·ic acid (ī-ŏd′ĭk) *n.* A crystalline powder, HIO₃, used as an astringent and disinfectant. [Fr. *iodique* < *iode,* iodine. See IODINE.]

i·o·dide (ī′ə-dīd′) *n.* A compound of iodine with a more electropositive element or group.

i·o·dine (ī′ə-dīn′, -dĭn, -dēn′) *n. Symbol* **I** **1.** A poisonous halogen element having compounds used as germicides, antiseptics, and food supplements, with radioactive isotopes, esp. I 131, used in thyroid disease diagnosis and therapy. Atomic number 53; atomic weight 126.9045; melting point 113.5°C; boiling point 184.35°C; specific gravity (solid, at 20°C) 4.93; valence 1, 3, 5, 7. See table at **element. 2.** A liquid containing iodine dissolved in ethyl alcohol, used as an antiseptic for wounds. [Fr. *iode,* iodine (< Gk. *ioeidēs,* violet-colored : *ion,* violet + -*oeidēs,* -oid) + -INE².]

i·o·dize (ī′ə-dīz′) *tr.v.* -**dized, -diz·ing, -diz·es** To treat or combine with iodine or an iodide: *iodize salt.* —**i′o·di·za′tion** (-dĭ-zā′shən) *n.*

iodo– or **iod–** *pref.* Iodine: *iodoform.* [< Fr. *iode,* iodine. See IODINE.]

i·o·do·form (ī-ō′də-fôrm′, ī-ŏd′ə-) *n.* A crystalline iodine compound, CHI₃, used as an antiseptic. [IODO- + FORM(YL).]

i·o·do·phor (ī-ō′də-fôr′) *n.* A substance consisting of iodine and a solubilizing agent that releases free iodine when in solution. [IODO- + -PHOR(E).]

i·o·dop·sin (ī′ə-dŏp′sĭn) *n.* A violet light-sensitive pigment found in the retinal cones of the eye.

i·o moth (ī′ō, ē′ō) *n.* A large yellowish North American moth (*Automeris io*) having a prominent eyelike spot on each hind wing. [After Io, who was tormented by gadflies sent by Hera as a punishment (< the stinging spines of its larvae).]

i·on (ī′ən, ī′ŏn′) *n.* An atom or a group of atoms that has acquired a net electric charge by gaining or losing one or more electrons. [Gk. *ion,* something that goes, neut. pr. part. of *ienai,* to go. See **ei-** in App.]

Ion. *abbr.* Ionic

–ion *suff.* **1a.** Action or process: *completion.* **b.** Result of an action or process: *indention.* **2.** State or condition: *dehydration.* [ME < OFr. < Lat. -*iō,* -*iōn-,* n. suff.]

I·o·na (ī-ō′nə) An island of W Scotland in the S Inner Hebrides.

ion engine *n.* A rocket engine that develops thrust by expelling ions rather than gaseous combustion products.

Io·nes·co (ē′ə-něs′kō, yə-), **Eugène** 1912–93. Romanian-born French dramatist whose plays include *Rhinoceros* (1959).

ion exchange *n.* A reversible chemical reaction between an insoluble solid and a solution during which ions may be interchanged, used in water softening, for example.

I·o·ni·a (ī-ō′nē-ə) An ancient region of W Asia Minor along the Aegean Sea; colonized by Greeks before 1000 B.C.

I·o·ni·an (ī-ō′nē-ən) *n.* **1.** A native or inhabitant of Ionia. **2.** One of a Hellenic people of Mycenaean origin that inhabited Attica, the Peloponnesus along the Saronic Gulf, Euboea, the Cyclades, and Ionia. —**I·o′ni·an** *adj.*

Ionian Islands A chain of islands of W Greece in the Ionian Sea; ceded to Greece by Great Britain in 1864.

Ionian Sea An arm of the Mediterranean Sea between W Greece and S Italy.

i·on·ic (ī-ŏn′ĭk) *adj.* Of, containing, or involving ions.

I·on·ic *adj.* **1.** Of or relating to Ionia or the Ionians. **2.** *Architecture* Of or belonging to the Ionic order: *a building with Ionic columns.*

❖ *n.* The ancient Greek dialect of Ionia.

ionic bond *n.* A chemical bond between two ions with opposite charges, characteristic of salts.

Ionic order *n.* One of the three main orders of classical Greek architecture, characterized by two opposed volutes in the capital.

ionic propulsion *n.* Propulsion by the reactive thrust of a high-speed beam of similarly charged ions from an ion engine.

i·on·i·za·tion (ī′ə-nī-zā′shən) *n.* **1.** The formation of or separation into ions by heat, electrical discharge, radiation, or chemical reaction. **2.** The state of being ionized.

ionization chamber *n.* A gas-filled enclosure containing two electrodes that measures the amount of radiation passing through the enclosure by the degree of ionization caused.

ionization potential *n.* The energy required to remove completely an electron from its atom.

i·on·ize (ī′ə-nīz′) *tr. & intr.v.* -**ized, -iz·ing, -iz·es** To convert or be converted into ions. —**i′on·iz′er** *n.*

i·on·iz·ing radiation (ī′ə-nī′zĭng) *n.* High-energy radiation, such as a stream of x-rays, capable of ionizing the substances through which it passes.

ion microscope *n.* A field-ion microscope.

i·o·none (ī′ə-nōn′) *n.* A liquid, C₁₃H₂₀O, having a strong odor of violets and used in perfumes. [Orig. a trademark.]

i·on·o·phore (ī-ŏn′ə-fôr, -fōr′) *n.* Any of a group of organic compounds facilitating ion transport across the cell membrane.

i·on·o·sphere (ī-ŏn′ə-sfîr′) *n.* A region of the earth's atmosphere extending from a height of 70 kilometers (43 miles) to 400 kilometers (250 miles) above the surface, where ionization caused by solar radiation affects the transmission of radio waves. —**i·on′o·spher′ic** (-sfîr′ĭk, -sfĕr′-) *adj.*

ion propulsion *n.* See **ionic propulsion.**

ion rocket *n.* **1.** A rocket using ionic propulsion. **2.** See **ion engine.**

ion trap *n.* A device, such as a magnet, used to prevent ions in an electron beam from striking other apparatus.

i·o·ta (ī-ō′tə) *n.* **1.** The ninth letter of the Greek alphabet. **2.** A very small amount; a bit. [Lat. *iōta* < Gk. < Phoenician *yōd,* hand, tenth letter of the Phoenician alphabet.]

i·o·ta·cism (ī-ō′tə-sĭz′əm) *n.* In Greek, the pronunciation of certain letters, like eta and upsilon, as iota (ē) because of a regular sound change. [LLat. *iōtacismus* < Gk. *iōtakismos* < *iōta,* iota. See IOTA.]

IOU (ī′ō-yōō′) *n.* A promise to pay a debt, esp. a signed paper stating the amount owed and often bearing the letters IOU. [< pronunciation of *I owe you.*]

–ious *suff.* Having; having the qualities of; full of: *bilious.* [ME, partly < Lat. -*ius* and partly < OFr. -*ieus,* -*ieux* (< Lat. -*iōsus*).]

I·o·wa¹ (ī′ə-wə) *n., pl.* **Iowa** or **-was** **1.** A member of a Native American people formerly inhabiting parts of Iowa and southwest Minnesota, with present-day descendants in Nebraska, Kansas, and Oklahoma. **2.** The Siouan language of the Iowa. [< Fr. *ayoés,* ult. < Dakota *ayúxba.*]

I·o·wa² (ī′ə-wə) A state of the N-central US; admitted as the 29th state in 1846. Cap. Des Moines. Pop. 2,926,324. —**I′o·wan** *adj. & n.*

Iowa City A city of E IA SSE of Cedar Rapids. Pop. 62,220.

Iowa River A river rising in N IA and flowing c. 529 km (329 mi) SE to the Mississippi R.

IP *abbr.* Internet Protocol

IPA *abbr.* **1.** International Phonetic Alphabet **2.** International Phonetic Association **3.** isopropyl alcohol

ip·e·cac (ĭp′ĭ-kăk′) also **ip·e·cac·u·an·ha** (ĭp′ĭ-kăk′yōō-än′ə) *n.* **1a.** A low-growing tropical American shrub (*Cephaelis ipecacuanha*) having roots and rhizomes that yield emetine. **b.** The dried roots and rhizomes of this shrub. **2.** A medicinal preparation made from this shrub and used as an emetic. [Short for Port. *ipecacuanha* < Tupi *ipekaaguéne* : *ipeh,* low + *kaâ,* leaves + *guéne,* vomit.]

Iph·i·ge·ni·a (ĭf′ə-jə-nī′ə, -nē′ə) *n. Greek Mythology* The daughter of Clytemnestra and Agamemnon who was offered as a sacrifice by Agamemnon but rescued by Artemis.

ipm *abbr.* inches per minute

IPO *abbr.* Business initial public offering

I·poh (ē′pō) A city of W Malaysia NNW of Kuala Lumpur. Pop. 382,633.

i·pro·ni·a·zid (ī′prə-nī′ə-zĭd) *n.* A compound, C₉H₁₃N₃O, used as an antidepressant and formerly used to treat tuberculosis. [I(SO)PRO(PYL ALCOHOL) + NI(COTINE) + AZ(O)- + -ID.]

ips *abbr.* inches per second

ip·se dix·it (ĭp′sē dĭk′sĭt) *n.* An unsupported assertion, usu. by a person of standing; a dictum. [Lat. *ipse dīxit,* he himself said (it) : *ipse,* he himself + *dīxit,* third pers. sing. perfect t. of *dīcere,* to say.]

ip·si·lat·er·al (ĭp′sə-lăt′ər-əl) *adj.* Located on or affecting the same side of the body. [Alteration of Lat. *ipse,* self + LATERAL.] —**ip′si·lat′er·al·ly** *adv.*

ip·sis·si·ma ver·ba (ĭp-sĭs′ə-mə vûr′bə) *pl.n.* The very words, of a quote. [NLat.]

ip·so fac·to (ĭp′sō făk′tō) *adv.* By the fact itself; by that very fact. [NLat. *ipsō factō.*]

io moth
Automeris io

Ionic order
Ionic order capital

ă	pat	oi	boy
ā	pay	ou	out
âr	care	ōō	took
ä	father	ōō	boot
ĕ	pet	ŭ	cut
ē	be	ûr	urge
ĭ	pit	th	thin
ī	pie	*th*	this
îr	pier	hw	which
ŏ	pot	zh	vision
ō	toe	ə	about,
ô	paw		item

Stress marks:
′ (primary);
′ (secondary), as in
lexicon (lĕk′sĭ-kŏn′)

Iran

Iraq

ip·so ju·re (joŏr′ē) *adv.* By the law itself. [NLat. *ipsō iūre.*]

Ips·wich (ĭp′swĭch′) A borough of E England near the North Sea NE of London. Pop. 114,806.

IQ *abbr.* intelligence quotient

i.q. *abbr. Latin idem quod* (the same as)

I·qa·lu·it (ĭ-kăl′ōō-ĭt, ē-kăl′ōō-ēt) The cap. of Nunavut, Canada, on Baffin I. in Frobisher Bay; it became the cap. in 1999. Pop. 4,220.

I·qui·tos (ĭ-kē′tōs, ē-kē′-) A city of NE Peru on the Amazon R. NE of Lima. Pop. 293,100.

Ir The symbol for the element **iridium.**

IR *abbr.* 1. information retrieval 2. infrared

Ir. *abbr.* Irish

ir-¹ *pref.* Variant of **in-¹.**

ir-² *pref.* Variant of **in-².**

IRA *abbr.* 1. Individual Retirement Account 2. Irish Republican Army

I·rá·kli·on (ĭ-rä′klē-ôn′) also **Can·di·a** (kăn′dē-ə) A city of S Greece on the N coast of Crete; founded by Saracens in the 9th cent. Pop. 102,398.

I·ran (ĭ-rän′, ĭ-răn′) Formerly **Per·sia** (pûr′zhə, -shə) A country of SW Asia; first inhabited c. 4000 B.C. and officially called Iran since 1935. Cap. Tehran. Pop. 59,778,000.

I·ran·gate (ĭ-răn′găt′, ĭ-rän′-) *n.* A scandal occurring during the Reagan administration in which members of the executive branch sold weapons to Iran and illegally used the profits to continue funding an army of rebels in Nicaragua.

I·ra·ni·an (ĭ-rä′nē-ən, ĭ-rā′-) *adj.* Of or relating to Iran or its people, language, or culture. ❖ *n.* 1. A native or inhabitant of Iran. 2. A branch of the Indo-European language family that includes Persian, Kurdish, Pashto, and other languages of Iran, Afghanistan, and western Pakistan.

I·raq (ĭ-răk′, ĭ-räk′) A country of SW Asia; site of a number of flourishing ancient Mesopotamian civilizations and independent since 1921. Cap. Baghdad. Pop. 19,925,000.

I·ra·qi (ĭ-răk′ē, ĭ-rä′kē) *adj.* Of or relating to Iraq or its people, language, or culture. ❖ *n., pl.* **-qis** 1. A native or inhabitant of Iraq. 2. The modern dialect of Arabic spoken in Iraq.

i·ras·ci·ble (ĭ-răs′ə-bəl, ĭ-răs′-) *adj.* 1. Prone to outbursts of temper; easily angered. 2. Characterized by or resulting from anger. [ME < OFr. < LLat. *īrāscibilis* < Lat. *īrāscī,* to be angry < *īra,* anger. See **eis-** in App.] —**i·ras′ci·bil′i·ty,** **i·ras′ci·ble·ness** *n.* —**i·ras′ci·bly** *adv.*

i·rate (ī-rāt′, ī′rāt′) *adj.* 1. Extremely angry; enraged. 2. Characterized or occasioned by anger: *an irate phone call.* [Lat. *īrātus,* p. part. of *īrāscī,* to be angry < *īra,* anger. See **eis-** in App.] —**i·rate′ly** *adv.* —**i·rate′ness** *n.*

Ir·bil (îr′bĭl) See **Arbil.**

IRBM *abbr.* intermediate-range ballistic missile

IRC (ī′är-sē′) *n.* An international computer network of Internet servers, using its own protocol through which individual users can hold real-time online conversations. [*I(nternet) R(elay) C(hat).*]

ire (īr) *n.* Anger; wrath. See Syns at **anger.** [ME < OFr. < Lat. *īra.* See **eis-** in App.]

Ire. *abbr.* Ireland

ire·ful (īr′fəl) *adj.* Full of ire; wrathful. —**ire′ful·ly** *adv.*

Ire·land¹ (īr′lənd) An island in the N Atlantic Ocean W of Great Britain; joined Great Britain in 1801 but after 1921 was split into the independent Irish Free State (now Ireland) and Northern Ireland, which is allied with Great Britain.

Ire·land² (īr′lənd) Formerly **Irish Free State** also **Eir·e** (âr′ə, ī′rə, âr′ē, ī′rē) A country occupying most of the island of Ireland. Est. as the Irish Free State in 1922, Ireland became Eire in 1937 and the Republic of Ireland in 1949. Cap. Dublin. Pop. 3,571,000.

i·ren·ic (ī-rĕn′ĭk, ī-rē′nĭk) also **i·ren·i·cal** (-ĭ-kəl, -nĭ-kəl) *adj.* Promoting peace; conciliatory. [Gk. *eirēnikos* < *eirēnē,* peace.] —**i·ren′i·cal·ly** *adv.*

I·ri·an Ja·ya (îr′ē-än′ jä′yə, jĭ′ə) A province of Indonesia occupying the W half of New Guinea and about 12 offshore islands.

irid. *abbr.* iridescent

ir·i·da·ceous (ĭr′ĭ-dā′shəs) *adj.* Of or belonging to the iris family. [< NLat. *Iridācea,* iris family < *Īris, Īrid-,* type genus < Lat. *īris, iris.* See IRIS.]

ir·i·dec·to·my (ĭr′ĭ-dĕk′tə-mē, ĭ′rĭ-) *n., pl.* **-mies** Surgical removal of part of the iris of the eye.

ir·i·des·cent (ĭr′ĭ-dĕs′ənt) *adj.* 1. Producing a display of lustrous rainbowlike colors: *iridescent plumage.* 2. Brilliant, lustrous, or colorful in effect or appearance: *"The prelude was as iridescent as a prism in a morning room"* (Carson McCullers). —**ir′i·des′-cence** *n.*

ir·i·dic (ĭ-rĭd′ĭk, ī-rĭd′-) *adj.* Of or relating to the iris of the eye.

ir·i·di·um (ĭ-rĭd′ē-əm) *n. Symbol* **Ir** A hard, brittle, corrosion-resistant metallic element occurring in platinum ores and used principally to harden platinum and in high-temperature furnaces, electrical contacts, and wear-resistant bearings. Atomic number 77; atomic weight 192.2; melting point 2,410°C; boiling point 4,130°C; specific gravity 22.42 (at 17°C); valence 3, 4. See table at **element.** [Lat. *īris, īrid-,* rainbow (< the colors produced by dissolving it in hydrochloric acid); see IRIDO- + -IUM.]

irido- or **irid-** *pref.* 1. Rainbow: *iridescent.* 2. Iris of the eye: *iridectomy.* [Lat. *īris, īrid-,* rainbow < Gk.]

ir·i·dol·o·gy (ĭr′ĭ-dŏl′ə-jē, ī′rĭ-) *n.* The study of the iris of the eye, esp. as associated with disease. —**ir′i·dol′o·gist** *n.*

ir·i·dos·mine (ĭr′ĭ-dŏz′mēn) See **osmiridium.** [IRID(O)- + OSM(IUM) + -INE².]

i·ris (ī′rĭs) *n., pl.* **i·ris·es** or **i·ri·des** (ī′rĭ-dēz′, ĭr′ĭ-) 1. The pigmented round contractile membrane of the eye that regulates the amount of light entering the eye. 2. Any of numerous plants of the genus *Iris,* having narrow sword-shaped leaves and variously colored flowers. 3. A rainbow or rainbowlike display of colors. 4. An iris diaphragm. [ME, iris (the plant) < Lat. *īris, īrid-,* rainbow, iris (the plant) < Gk., rainbow, brightly-colored gemstone, iris of the eye.]

Iris *n. Greek Mythology* The goddess of the rainbow and messenger of the gods. [Lat. *Īris* < Gk. < *īris,* rainbow.]

iris diaphragm *n.* A device with a variable diameter, used on cameras to regulate the amount of light admitted to a lens.

I·rish (ī′rĭsh) *adj.* Of Ireland, its people, language, or culture. ❖ *n.* 1. (*used with a pl. verb*) The people of Ireland. 2a. See **Irish Gaelic.** b. See **Irish English.** 3. *Informal* Fieriness of temper or passion; high spirit. [ME < OE *Īras,* the Irish. See **peiə-** in App.]

Irish coffee *n.* A beverage of sweetened hot coffee and Irish whiskey, topped with whipped cream.

Irish elk *n.* A large extinct European deer of the genus *Megaceros* of the Pliocene and Pleistocene Epochs.

Irish English *n.* English as spoken by the Irish.

Irish Free State See **Ireland².**

Irish Gaelic *n.* The Goidelic language of Ireland.

I·rish·ism (ī′rĭsh-ĭz′əm) *n.* An Irish idiom or custom.

I·rish·man (ī′rĭsh-mən) *n.* A man of Irish birth or ancestry.

Irish moss *n.* An edible North Atlantic seaweed (*Chondrus crispus*) that yields a mucilaginous substance used medicinally and in preparing jellies.

I·rish·ry (ī′rĭsh-rē) *n., pl.* **-ries** 1. The Irish people, esp. those of Celtic descent. 2a. Irish character. b. An Irish trait, custom, or locution; an Irishism.

Irish Sea An arm of the N Atlantic Ocean between Ireland and Great Britain.

Irish setter *n.* Any of a breed of setters having a silky reddish-brown or red and white coat.

Irish stew *n.* A stew of meat and vegetables.

Irish terrier *n.* Any of a breed of terriers having a wiry reddish-brown coat.

Irish whiskey *n.* Whiskey made by the distillation of barley.

Irish wolfhound *n.* Any of an ancient breed of large powerful dogs having a rough, shaggy coat.

I·rish·wom·an (ī′rĭsh-woŏm′ən) *n.* A woman of Irish birth or ancestry.

i·ri·tis (ī-rī′tĭs) *n.* Inflammation of the iris of the eye. [IR(IS) + -ITIS.] —**i·rit′ic** (ī-rĭt′ĭk) *adj.*

irk (ûrk) *tr.v.* **irked, irk·ing, irks** To be irritating, wearisome, or vexing to. [ME *irken,* to weary, poss. < ON *yrkja,* to work, make verses, harangue. See **werg-** in App.]

irk·some (ûrk′səm) *adj.* Causing annoyance, weariness, or vexation; tedious: *irksome restrictions.* See Syns at **boring.** —**irk′some·ly** *adv.* —**irk′some·ness** *n.*

Ir·kutsk (îr-kōotsk′) A city of S-central Russia near the S end of Lake Baikal. Pop. 629,747.

IRO *abbr.* International Refugee Organization

i·ron (ī′ərn) *n.* 1. *Symbol* **Fe** A lustrous, malleable, ductile, magnetic or magnetizable metallic element occurring abundantly in ores such as hematite and magnetite and used alloyed in a wide range of important structural materials. Atomic number 26; atomic weight 55.845; melting point 1,535°C; boiling point 2,750°C; specific gravity 7.874 (at 20°C); valence 2, 3, 4, 6. See table at **element.** 2. An implement made of iron alloy or similar metal, esp. a heated bar used to brand, curl hair, or cauterize. 3. Great hardness or strength; firmness. 4. *Sports* Any of a series of golf clubs having a bladelike metal head and numbered from one to nine in order of increasing loft. 5. A metal appliance with a handle and a weighted flat bottom, used when heated to press wrinkles from fabric. 6. A harpoon. 7. **irons** Fetters; shackles. 8. A pill or other medication containing iron and taken as a dietary supplement. ❖ *adj.* 1. Made of or containing iron. 2. Very hard and strong. 3. Strong, healthy, and capable of great endurance. 4. Inflexible; unyielding. 5. Holding tightly; very firm. ❖ *v.* **i·roned, i·ron·ing, i·rons** —*tr.* **1a.** To press and smooth with a heated iron. **b.** To remove (creases) by pressing. **2.** To put into irons; fetter. **3.** To fit or clad with iron. —*intr.* To iron clothes. —*phrasal verb:* **iron out** To settle through discussion or compromise; work out. —*idioms:* **in irons** *Nautical* Lying head to the wind and unable to turn either way. **iron in the fire** An undertaking in progress. [ME *iren* < OE *īren.* See **eis-** in App.]

Iron Age *n.* The period in cultural development after the Bronze Age in Asia, Europe, and Africa, marked by the introduction of iron metallurgy. In Europe it began around the eighth century B.C.

iron blue *n.* Any of various light-resistant and heat-resistant, semitransparent blue pigments of powerful tinctorial strength, esp. used in permanent industrial finishes, ink, and artists' colors.

Ireland²

iris

i·ron·bound (ī′ərn-bound′) *adj.* **1.** Bound with iron. **2.** Rigid and unyielding. **3.** Bound with rocks and cliffs.

i·ron·clad (ī′ərn-klăd′) *adj.* **1.** Sheathed with iron plates for protection. **2.** Rigid; fixed: *an ironclad rule.* ❖ *n.* A 19th-century warship having sides armored with metal plates.

iron curtain *n.* **1.** often **Iron Curtain** The military, political, and ideological barrier existing between the Soviet bloc and western Europe from 1945 to 1990. **2.** A barrier that prevents free exchange of ideas and information.

iron fist *n.* Rigorous or despotic control. —**i′ron·fist′ed** (ī′ərn-fĭs′tĭd) *adj.*

Iron Gate A narrow gorge of the Danube R. on the border of Serbia and Romania; created by a gap between the Carpathian and Balkan mountains.

iron gray *n.* A dark gray with a slightly greenish tinge.

iron hand *n.* Rigorous or despotic control. —**i′ron·hand′ed** (ī′ərn-hăn′dĭd) *adj.* —**i′ron·hand′ed·ness** *n.*

iron horse *n.* *Informal* A railroad locomotive.

i·ron·ic (ī-rŏn′ĭk) also **i·ron·i·cal** (ī-rŏn′ĭ-kəl) *adj.* **1.** Characterized by or constituting irony. **2.** Given to the use of irony. **3.** Poignantly contrary to what was expected or intended. —**i·ron′i·cal·ly** *adv.* —**i·ron′i·cal·ness** *n.*

> **USAGE NOTE** The words *ironic, irony,* and *ironically* are sometimes used of events and circumstances that might better be described as simply "coincidental" or "improbable," in that they suggest no particular lessons about human vanity or folly. Thus 78 percent of the Usage Panel rejects the use of *ironically* in the sentence *In 1969 Susie moved from Ithaca to California where she met her husband-to-be, who, ironically, also came from upstate New York.* By contrast, 73 percent accepted the sentence *Ironically, even as the government was fulminating against American policy, American jeans and videocassettes were the hottest items in the stalls of the market,* where the incongruity can be seen as an example of human inconsistency.

i·ron·ing (ī′ər-nĭng) *n.* **1.** The act or process of pressing clothes with an iron. **2.** Clothing ironed or to be ironed.

ironing board *n.* A long narrow padded board, often with collapsible supporting legs, on which to iron.

i·ro·nist (ī′rə-nĭst) *n.* A notable user of irony, esp. a writer.

i·ron·ize (ī′rə-nīz′) *v.* -**ized,** -**iz·ing,** -**iz·es** —*tr.* To make ironic in effect. —*intr.* To use irony. [IRON(IC) + -IZE.]

iron lung *n.* An airtight metal tank that encloses all of the body except the head and forces the lungs to inhale and exhale through regulated changes in air pressure.

iron maiden *n.* A medieval instrument of torture consisting of an iron frame in the form of a person in which the victim was enclosed and impaled on interior spikes.

i·ron·man (ī′ərn-măn′) *n.* A male athlete of remarkable endurance or durability.

i·ron·mon·ger (ī′ərn-mŭng′gər, -mŏng′-) *n. Chiefly British* A hardware merchant.

i·ron·mon·ger·y (ī′ərn-mŭng′gə-rē, -mŏng′-) *n., pl.* -**ies** *Chiefly British* **1.** Ironware. **2.** The shop or business of an ironmonger.

iron oxide *n.* Any of various oxides of iron, such as ferric oxide or ferrous oxide.

iron pyrites *n.* See **pyrite.**

i·ron·smith (ī′ərn-smĭth′) *n.* One that makes iron articles; a blacksmith.

i·ron·stone (ī′ərn-stōn′) *n.* **1.** A hard white pottery. **2.** A rock containing enough iron to permit commercial extraction; an iron ore.

i·ron·ware (ī′ərn-wâr′) *n.* Iron utensils and ironwork.

i·ron·weed (ī′ərn-wēd′) *n.* Any of various plants of the genus *Vernonia,* having alternate leaves and purplish flower clusters.

i·ron·wom·an (ī′ərn-woom′ən) *n.* A female athlete of remarkable endurance or durability.

i·ron·wood (ī′ərn-wood′) *n.* **1.** Any of numerous trees, such as the hornbeam and the hop hornbeam, that have very hard wood. **2.** The wood of any of these trees.

i·ron·work (ī′ərn-wûrk′) *n.* Work in iron, such as gratings.

i·ron·work·er (ī′ərn-wûr′kər) *n.* **1.** A construction worker who builds steel structures. **2.** One who is employed in an ironworks. **3.** One who makes iron articles.

i·ron·works (ī′ərn-wûrks′) *pl.n.* (*used with a sing. or pl. verb*) A building or establishment where iron is smelted or where heavy iron products are made.

i·ro·ny (ī′rə-nē, ī′ər-) *n., pl.* -**nies** **1a.** The use of words to express something different from and often opposite to their literal meaning. **b.** An expression or utterance marked by irony. **c.** A literary style employing irony for humorous or rhetorical effect. **2a.** Incongruity between what might be expected and what actually occurs. **b.** An occurrence, result, or circumstance notable for such incongruity. See Usage Note at **ironic. 3.** Dramatic irony. **4.** Socratic irony. [Fr. *ironie* < OFr. < Lat. *īrōnīa* < Gk. *eirōneia,* feigned ignorance < *eirōn,* dissembler, prob. < *eirein,* to say. See **wer-**[1] in App.]

Ir·o·quoi·an (ĭr′ə-kwoi′ən) *n.* **1.** A family of North American Indian languages of the eastern part of Canada and the United States that includes Cayuga, Mohawk, Oneida, Onondaga, Sen-

eca, Tuscarora, Cherokee, Erie, Huron, and Wyandot. **2.** A member of an Iroquoian-speaking people. ❖ *adj.* Of or constituting the Iroquoian language family.

Ir·o·quois (ĭr′ə-kwoi′) *n., pl.* **Iroquois** (-kwoi′, -kwoiz′) **1a.** A Native American confederacy inhabiting New York State and composed of the Mohawk, Oneida, Onondaga, Cayuga, Seneca, and, after 1722, Tuscarora peoples. **b.** A member of this confederacy or of any of its peoples. **2.** Any or all of the languages of the Iroquois. [?] —**Ir′o·quois′** *adj.*

ir·ra·di·ant (ĭ-rā′dē-ənt) *adj.* Sending forth radiant light. —**ir·ra′di·ance,** **ir·ra′di·an·cy** *n.*

ir·ra·di·ate (ĭ-rā′dē-āt′) *v.* -**at·ed,** -**at·ing,** -**ates** —*tr.* **1a.** To expose to radiation. **b.** To treat with radiation. **2.** To shed light on; illuminate. **3.** To manifest in a manner suggesting the emission of light; radiate. —*intr. Archaic* **1.** To send forth rays; radiate. **2.** To become radiant. [Lat. *irradiāre, irradiāt-,* to illuminate : *in-,* on; see IN-[2] + *radiāre,* to shine; see RADIATE.] —**ir·ra′di·a′tive** *adj.* —**ir·ra′di·a′tor** *n.*

ir·ra·di·a·tion (ĭ-rā′dē-ā′shən) *n.* **1.** The act of exposing or the condition of being exposed to radiation. **2.** The use or application of ionizing radiation, esp. in medical treatment and food preservation.

ir·rad·i·ca·ble (ĭ-răd′ĭ-kə-bəl) *adj.* Impossible to uproot or destroy; ineradicable. [Med.Lat. *irrādīcābilis* : Lat. *in-,* not; see IN-[1] + Lat. *rādīx, rādīc-,* root; see ERADICATE.] —**ir·rad′i·ca·bly** *adv.*

ir·ra·tion·al (ĭ-răsh′ə-nəl) *adj.* **1a.** Not endowed with reason. **b.** Affected by loss of usual or normal mental clarity; incoherent, as from shock. **c.** Marked by a lack of accord with reason or sound judgment: *an irrational dislike.* **2a.** Being a syllable in Greek and Latin prosody whose length does not fit the meter. **b.** Being a metric foot containing such a syllable. **3.** *Mathematics* Of or relating to an irrational number. ❖ *n. Mathematics* An irrational number. —**ir·ra′tion·al·ly** *adv.* —**ir·ra′tion·al·ness** *n.*

ir·ra·tion·al·ism (ĭ-răsh′ə-nə-lĭz′əm) *n.* **1.** Irrational thought, expression, or behavior; irrationality. **2.** Belief in instinct or other nonrational forces rather than reason.

ir·ra·tion·al·i·ty (ĭ-răsh′ə-năl′ĭ-tē) *n., pl.* -**ties** **1.** The state or quality of being irrational. **2.** Something irrational.

irrational number *n.* Any real number that cannot be expressed as a ratio between two integers.

Ir·ra·wad·dy (ĭr′ə-wä′dē) A river of Myanmar (Burma) flowing c. 1,609 km (1,000 mi) to the Bay of Bengal.

ir·re·claim·a·ble (ĭr′ĭ-klā′mə-bəl) *adj.* Impossible to reclaim: *irreclaimable wasteland.* —**ir′re·claim′a·bil′i·ty,** **ir′re·claim′a·ble·ness** *n.* —**ir′re·claim′a·bly** *adv.*

ir·re·con·cil·a·ble (ĭ-rĕk′ən-sī′lə-bəl, ĭ-rĕk′ən-sī′-) *adj.* Impossible to reconcile. ❖ *n.* **1.** A person, esp. a group member who will not compromise, adjust, or submit. **2.** One of two or more irreconcilable ideas or beliefs. —**ir·rec′on·cil′a·bil′i·ty** *n.* —**ir·rec′on·cil′a·bly** *adv.*

ir·re·cov·er·a·ble (ĭr′ĭ-kŭv′ər-ə-bəl) *adj.* Impossible to recover; irreparable: *irrecoverable losses.* —**ir′re·cov′er·a·ble·ness** *n.* —**ir′re·cov′er·a·bly** *adv.*

ir·re·cu·sa·ble (ĭr′ĭ-kyōō′zə-bəl) *adj.* Not subject to challenge or objection: *an irrecusable premise.* [Fr. *irrécusable* < LLat. *irrecūsābilis* : Lat. *in-,* not; see IN-[1] + LLat. *recūsābilis,* deserving of rejection (< Lat. *recūsāre,* to refuse; see RECUSE).] —**ir′re·cu′sa·bly** *adv.*

ir·re·deem·a·ble (ĭr′ĭ-dē′mə-bəl) *adj.* **1.** That cannot be bought back or paid off: *irredeemable sales.* **2.** Not convertible into coin. **3.** Impossible to remedy. **4.** Impossible to redeem or reform: *irredeemable evil.* —**ir′re·deem′a·bly** *adv.*

ir·re·den·tist (ĭr′ĭ-dĕn′tĭst) *n.* One who advocates the recovery of land culturally or historically related to one's nation but now under foreign control. [Ital. *irredentista* < (*Italia*) *irredenta,* unredeemed (Italy), Italian-speaking areas subject to other countries : *in-,* not (< Lat.; see IN-[1]) + *redenta,* fem. of *redento,* redeemed (< Lat. *redemptus,* p. part. of *redimere,* to redeem; see REDEEM).] —**ir′re·den′tism** *n.* —**ir′re·den′tist** *adj.*

ir·re·duc·i·ble (ĭr′ĭ-dōō′sə-bəl, -dyōō′-) *adj.* Impossible to reduce to a desired, simpler, or smaller form or amount. —**ir′re·duc′i·bil′i·ty,** **ir′re·duc′i·ble·ness** *n.* —**ir′re·duc′i·bly** *adv.*

ir·ref·ra·ga·ble (ĭ-rĕf′rə-gə-bəl) *adj.* Impossible to refute or controvert; indisputable. [LLat. *irrefrāgābilis* : Lat. *in-,* not; see IN-[1] + Lat. *refrāgārī,* to oppose, resist; see **bhreg-** in App.] —**ir·ref′ra·ga·bil′i·ty** *n.* —**ir·ref′ra·ga·bly** *adv.*

ir·re·fran·gi·ble (ĭr′ĭ-frăn′jə-bəl) *adj.* **1.** Impossible to break; indestructible: *irrefrangible cookware.* **2.** *Physics* That cannot be refracted. —**ir′re·fran′gi·bly** *adv.*

ir·ref·u·ta·ble (ĭ-rĕf′yə-tə-bəl, ĭr′ĭ-fyōō′-) *adj.* Impossible to refute or disprove; incontrovertible: *irrefutable arguments.* —**ir·ref′u·ta·bil′i·ty** *n.* —**ir·ref′u·ta·bly** *adv.*

ir·re·gard·less (ĭr′ĭ-gärd′lĭs) *adv. Nonstandard* Regardless. [Perh. blend of IRRESPECTIVE and REGARDLESS.]

> **USAGE NOTE** Many mistakenly believe *irregardless* to be correct in formal style, when in fact it is chiefly used in nonstandard speech or casual writing. It was coined in the US in the early 20th century and has been roundly condemned because of the logical absurdity of combining the negative *ir–* prefix and *–less* suffix

Irish setter

ironwork
wrought iron fence with
corn motif

ă	pat	oi	boy
ā	pay	ou	out
âr	care	ōō	took
ä	father	ōō	boot
ĕ	be	ŭ	cut
ē	be	ûr	urge
ĭ	pit	th	thin
ī	pie	th	this
îr	pier	hw	which
ŏ	pot	zh	vision
ō	toe	ə	about,
ô	paw		item

Stress marks:
′ (primary);
′ (secondary), as in
lexicon (lĕk′sĭ-kŏn′)

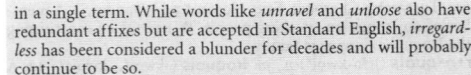

irrigate
flood irrigation of a
vineyard

Isabella I
detail from a retable,
c. 1500

734

irregular
Iseult

in a single term. While words like *unravel* and *unloose* also have redundant affixes but are accepted in Standard English, *irregardless* has been considered a blunder for decades and will probably continue to be so.

ir·reg·u·lar (ĭ-rĕgʹyə-lər) *adj.* **1.** Contrary to rule, accepted order, or general practice. **2.** Not conforming to legality, moral law, or social convention. **3.** Not straight, uniform, or symmetrical. **4.** Of uneven rate, occurrence, or duration. **5.** Deviating from a type; atypical. **6.** *Botany* Having differing floral parts, as of a zygomorphic flower. **7.** Falling below the manufacturer's standard or usual specifications; imperfect. **8.** *Grammar* Departing from the usual pattern of inflection, derivation, or word formation, as the plural noun *children.* **9.** Not belonging to a permanent organized military force. ❖ *n.* **1.** One that is irregular. **2.** A soldier who is not part of a regular military force. —**ir·regʹu·lar·ly** *adv.*

ir·reg·u·lar·i·ty (ĭ-rĕgʹyə-lărʹĭ-tē) *n., pl.* **-ties 1.** The quality or state of being irregular. **2.** Something irregular: *found the firm's books riddled with irregularities.* **3.** Constipation.

ir·rel·a·tive (ĭ-rĕlʹə-tĭv) *adj.* **1.** Having no correlative relationship; unconnected. **2.** Irrelevant. —**ir·relʹa·tive·ly** *adv.*

ir·rel·e·van·cy (ĭ-rĕlʹə-vən-sē) *n., pl.* **-cies** Irrelevance.

ir·rel·e·vant (ĭ-rĕlʹə-vənt) *adj.* Unrelated to the matter being considered. —**ir·relʹe·vance** *n.* —**ir·relʹe·vant·ly** *adv.*

ir·re·li·gion (ĭrʹĭ-lĭjʹən) *n.* Hostility or indifference to religion.

ir·re·li·gious (ĭrʹĭ-lĭjʹəs) *adj.* Hostile or indifferent to religion; ungodly. —**irʹre·liʹgious·ly** *adv.* —**irʹre·liʹgious·ness** *n.*

ir·re·me·a·ble (ĭ-rēʹmē-ə-bəl) *adj. Archaic* Affording no possibility of return. [Lat. *irremeabilis : in-*, not; see IN–[1] + *remeāre*, to return (*re-*, re- + *meāre*, to go).]

ir·re·me·di·a·ble (ĭrʹĭ-mēʹdē-ə-bəl) *adj.* Impossible to remedy, correct, or repair. —**irʹre·meʹdi·a·bly** *adv.*

ir·re·mis·si·ble (ĭrʹĭ-mĭsʹə-bəl) *adj.* Not remissible; unpardonable. —**irʹre·misʹsi·blʹi·ty** *n.* —**irʹre·misʹsi·bly** *adv.*

ir·re·mov·a·ble (ĭrʹĭ-mōōʹvə-bəl) *adj.* Impossible to remove. —**irʹre·movʹa·blʹi·ty** *n.* —**irʹre·movʹa·bly** *adv.*

ir·rep·a·ra·ble (ĭ-rĕpʹər-ə-bəl) *adj.* Impossible to repair, rectify, or amend. —**ir·repʹa·ra·bilʹi·ty, ir·repʹa·ra·ble·ness** *n.* —**ir·repʹa·ra·bly** *adv.*

ir·re·peal·a·ble (ĭrʹĭ-pēʹlə-bəl) *adj.* Impossible to repeal.

ir·re·place·a·ble (ĭrʹĭ-plāʹsə-bəl) *adj.* Impossible to replace: *irreplaceable antiques.* —**irʹre·placeʹa·bilʹi·ty, irʹre·placeʹa·ble·ness** *n.* —**irʹre·placeʹa·bly** *adv.*

ir·re·press·i·ble (ĭrʹĭ-prĕsʹə-bəl) *adj.* Difficult or impossible to control or restrain. —**irʹre·pressʹi·bilʹi·ty, irʹre·pressʹi·ble·ness** *n.* —**irʹre·pressʹi·bly** *adv.*

ir·re·proach·a·ble (ĭrʹĭ-prōʹchə-bəl) *adj.* Perfect or blameless in every respect; faultless. —**irʹre·proachʹa·bilʹi·ty, irʹre·proachʹa·ble·ness** *n.* —**irʹre·proachʹa·bly** *adv.*

ir·re·sis·ti·ble (ĭrʹĭ-zĭsʹtə-bəl) *adj.* **1.** Impossible to resist. **2.** Having an overpowering appeal. —**ir·reʹsisʹti·bilʹi·ty, irʹre·sisʹti·ble·ness** *n.* —**irʹre·sisʹti·bly** *adv.*

ir·re·sol·u·ble (ĭrʹĭ-zŏlʹyə-bəl) *adj.* Impossible to resolve: *irresoluble conflicts.*

ir·res·o·lute (ĭ-rĕzʹə-lōōtʹ) *adj.* Unsure of how to act; undecided. **2.** Lacking in resolution; indecisive. —**ir·resʹo·luteʹly** *adv.* —**ir·resʹo·luteʹness, ir·resʹo·luʹtion** *n.*

ir·re·solv·a·ble (ĭrʹĭ-zŏlʹvə-bəl) *adj.* **1.** Irresoluble. **2.** Impossible to separate into component parts; irreducible.

ir·re·spec·tive (ĭrʹĭ-spĕkʹtĭv) *adj. Archaic* Characterized by disregard; heedless. —**irʹre·specʹtive·ly** *adv.*

irrespective of *prep.* Without consideration of; regardless of.

ir·res·pi·ra·ble (ĭ-rĕsʹpər-ə-bəl, ĭrʹĭ-spīrʹ-) *adj.* Not fit for breathing; not respirable.

ir·re·spon·si·ble (ĭrʹĭ-spŏnʹsə-bəl) *adj.* **1.** Marked by a lack of responsibility: *irresponsible claims.* **2.** Not responsible; unreliable or untrustworthy. **3.** *Law* Mentally or financially unfit for responsibility. **4.** Not accountable to a higher authority. ❖ *n.* **1.** One with no sense of responsibility. **2.** *Law* One who is mentally or financially unfit for responsibility. **3.** One who is unlikely to be called to account by a higher authority. —**irʹre·sponʹsi·bilʹi·ty, irʹre·sponʹsi·ble·ness** *n.* —**irʹre·sponʹsi·bly** *adv.*

ir·re·spon·sive (ĭrʹĭ-spŏnʹsĭv) *adj.* **1.** Not responsive, as to treatment or stimuli. **2.** Not responding or answering readily. —**irʹre·sponʹsive·ly** *adv.* —**irʹre·sponʹsive·ness** *n.*

ir·re·triev·a·ble (ĭrʹĭ-trēʹvə-bəl) *adj.* Difficult or impossible to retrieve or recover. —**ir·reʹtrievʹa·ble·ness, irʹre·trievʹa·bilʹi·ty** *n.* —**irʹre·trievʹa·bly** *adv.*

ir·rev·er·ence (ĭ-rĕvʹər-əns) *n.* **1.** Lack of reverence or due respect. **2.** A disrespectful act or remark.

ir·rev·er·ent (ĭ-rĕvʹər-ənt) *adj.* **1.** Lacking reverence; disrespectful. **2.** Critical of what is generally accepted or respected; satirical. —**ir·revʹer·entʹly** *adv.*

ir·re·vers·i·ble (ĭrʹĭ-vûrʹsə-bəl) *adj.* Impossible to reverse: *an irreversible action.* —**ir·reʹversʹi·bilʹi·ty, irʹre·versʹi·ble·ness** *n.* —**irʹre·versʹi·bly** *adv.*

ir·rev·o·ca·ble (ĭ-rĕvʹə-kə-bəl) *adj.* Impossible to retract or revoke: *an irrevocable decision.* —**ir·revʹo·ca·bilʹi·ty, ir·revʹo·ca·ble·ness** *n.* —**ir·revʹo·ca·bly** *adv.*

ir·ri·ga·ble (ĭrʹĭ-gə-bəl) *adj.* That can be irrigated.

ir·ri·gate (ĭrʹĭ-gātʹ) *v.* **-gat·ed, -gat·ing, -gates** —*tr.* **1.** To supply (dry land) with water by means of ditches, pipes, or streams. **2.** To wash out (a body cavity or wound) with water or a medicated fluid. **3.** To make fertile or vital as if by watering. —*intr.* To irrigate land. [Lat. *irrigāre, irrigāt- : in-*, in; see IN–[2] + *rigāre*, to water.] —**irʹri·gaʹtion** *n.* —**irʹri·gaʹtion·al** *adj.* —**irʹri·gaʹtor** *n.*

ir·ri·ta·bil·i·ty (ĭrʹĭ-tə-bĭlʹĭ-tē) *n., pl.* **-ties 1.** The quality or state of being irritable; testiness or petulance. **2.** *Pathology* Abnormal or excessive sensitivity of a body organ or part to a stimulus. **3.** *Physiology* The capacity to respond to stimuli.

ir·ri·ta·ble (ĭrʹĭ-tə-bəl) *adj.* **1.** Easily irritated or annoyed. **2.** *Pathology* Abnormally sensitive to a stimulus. **3.** *Physiology* Capable of responding to stimuli. [Ult. < Lat. *irrītābilis < irrītāre*, to irritate.] —**irʹri·ta·ble·ness** *n.* —**irʹri·ta·bly** *adv.*

irritable bowel syndrome *n.* A disorder characterized by the spontaneous occurrence of abnormally strong and frequent contractions of the intestines, causing abdominal pain and often diarrhea.

ir·ri·tant (ĭrʹĭ-tənt) *adj.* Causing irritation, esp. physical irritation. ❖ *n.* A source of irritation.

ir·ri·tate (ĭrʹĭ-tātʹ) *v.* **-tat·ed, -tat·ing, -tates** —*tr.* **1.** To make impatient or angry; annoy. **2.** To chafe or inflame. **3.** *Physiology* To cause an activity or response in (an organ or tissue), as by application of a stimulus. —*intr.* To be a cause of impatience or anger. [Lat. *irrītāre, irrītāt-.*] —**irʹri·tatʹing·ly** *adv.* —**irʹri·taʹtor** *n.*

ir·ri·ta·tion (ĭrʹĭ-tāʹshən) *n.* **1a.** The act of irritating. **b.** The condition of being irritated; vexation. **2.** Something that irritates. **3.** A condition of inflammation, soreness, or irritability of a body organ or part. **4.** The elicitation of activity or response in an organ or tissue.

ir·ri·ta·tive (ĭrʹĭ-tāʹtĭv) *adj.* Involving irritation.

ir·ro·ta·tion·al (ĭrʹō-tāʹshə-nəl) *adj.* Involving no rotation.

ir·rupt (ĭ-rŭptʹ) *intr.v.* **-rupt·ed, -rupt·ing, -rupts 1.** To break or burst in. **2.** *Ecology* To increase rapidly and irregularly in number. [Lat. *irrumpere, irrupt- : in-*, in; see IN–[2] + *rumpere*, to break; see reup- in App.] —**ir·rupʹtion** *n.*

ir·rup·tive (ĭ-rŭpʹtĭv) *adj.* **1.** Irrupting or tending to irrupt. **2.** *Geology* Intrusive.

IRS *abbr.* Internal Revenue Service

Ir·tysh or **Ir·tish** (ĭr-tĭshʹ) A river of NW China, E Kazakhstan, and central Russia flowing c. 4,264 km (2,650 mi) to the Ob R.

Ir·vine (ûrʹvīn) A city of S CA SE of Santa Ana. Pop. 143,072.

Ir·ving (ûrʹvĭng) A town of NE TX, a suburb of Dallas. Pop. 191,615.

Irving, John b. 1942. Amer. writer whose novels include *The World According to Garp* (1978).

Irving, Washington 1783–1859. Amer. writer best remembered for his stories "Rip Van Winkle" and "The Legend of Sleepy Hollow" in *The Sketch Book* (1819–20).

is (ĭz) *v.* Third person singular present indicative of **be.** [ME < OE. See **es-** in App.]

Is. *abbr. Bible* **1.** Isaiah **2a.** island **b.** islands **3.** isle

is– *pref.* Variant of **iso–.**

Isa. *abbr. Bible* Isaiah

I·saac (īʹzək) In the Bible, the son of Abraham and Sarah who was offered as a sacrifice to God.

Is·a·bel·la I (ĭzʹə-bĕlʹə) Known as "Isabella the Catholic." 1451–1504. Queen of Castile (1474–1504) whose marriage in 1469 to Ferdinand V of Castile and León (later Ferdinand II of Aragon) marked the beginning of a unified Spanish state.

I·sa·iah[1] (ī-zāʹə, ī-zīʹə) A Hebrew prophet of the 8th cent. B.C. [LLat. *Īsaïās* < Heb. *yəšaʻyāhû*, salvation of Yahweh : *yēšaʻ*, salvation + *yāhû*, Yahweh.]

I·sa·iah[2] (ī-zāʹə, ī-zīʹə) *n.* See table at **Bible.** [After ISAIAH[1].]

i·sal·lo·bar (ī-sălʹō-bärʹ) *n.* A line on a weather map connecting places having equal changes in atmospheric pressure within a given period of time. [IS(O)– + ALLO– + Gk. *baros*, weight; see gʷerə- in App.]

–isation *suff.* Variant of **–ization.**

ISBN *abbr.* International Standard Book Number

is·che·mi·a (ĭ-skēʹmē-ə) *n.* A decrease in the blood supply to a body organ, tissue, or part caused by constriction or obstruction of the blood vessels. [NLat. *ischaemia* < Gk. *iskhaimos*, a stopping of the blood : *iskhein*, to keep back; see **segh-** in App. + *haima*, blood.] —**is·cheʹmic** *adj.*

Is·chi·a (ĭsʹkē-ə, ēʹskyä) An island of S Italy in the Tyrrhenian Sea at the entrance to the Bay of Naples.

is·chi·um (ĭsʹkē-əm) *n., pl.* **-chi·a** (-kē-ə) The lowest of the three major bones that constitute each half of the pelvis. [Lat., hip joint < Gk. *ischion*.] —**isʹchi·al** (-əl) *adj.*

ISDN *abbr.* Integrated Services Digital Network

–ise *suff.* Variant of **–ize.**

I·se Bay (ēʹsä, ēʹsĕʹ) An arm of the Pacific Ocean on the S-central coast of Honshu, Japan.

is·en·tro·pic (īʹsən-trōʹpĭk, -trŏpʹĭk) *adj.* Without change in entropy; at constant entropy. [IS(O)– + ENTROP(Y) + –IC.]

I·sère (ē-zârʹ) A river of SE France rising in the Graian Alps and flowing c. 290 km (180 mi) to the Rhone R.

I·seult (ĭ-sōōltʹ) also **I·sol·de** (ĭ-sōlʹdə, ĭ-zōlʹ-) *n.* In Arthurian legend, an Irish princess who married the king of Cornwall and had a love affair with his knight Tristan.

Is·fa·han (ĭs′fə-hän′) See Esfahan.

–ish *suff.* **1.** Of, relating to, or being: *Swedish.* **2a.** Characteristic of: *girlish.* **b.** Having the usu. undesirable qualities of: *childish.* **3.** Approximately; somewhat: *greenish.* **4.** Tending toward; preoccupied with: *selfish.* [ME < OE *-isc.*]

Ish·er·wood (ĭsh′ər-wŏŏd′), **Christopher William Bradshaw** 1904–86. British-born Amer. writer best known for his works about Berlin in the early 1930s.

I·shim (ĭ-shĭm′) A river, c. 1,818 km (1,130 mi), rising in the steppe region of Kazakhstan and flowing to the Irtysh R. in S-central Russia.

Ish·ma·el¹ (ĭsh′mē-əl, -mā-) In the Bible, the son of Abraham and Hagar who was cast out after the birth of Isaac.

Ish·ma·el² (ĭsh′mē-əl, -mā-) *n.* An outcast. [After ISHMAEL¹.]

Ish·ma·el·ite (ĭsh′mē-ə-līt′, -mā-) *n.* **1.** A descendant of Ishmael. **2.** An outcast. —**Ish′ma·el·it·ism** *n.*

Ish·tar (ĭsh′tär′) *n. Mythology* The chief Babylonian and Assyrian goddess, associated with love, fertility, and war. [Akkadian *Ištar,* akin to Phoenician *'aštart,* Astarte.]

Is·i·dore of Seville (ĭz′ĭ-dôr′, -dōr′), Saint. 560?–636. Spanish ecclesiastic who wrote the encyclopedia *Etymologiae.*

i·sin·glass (ī′zən-glăs′, ī′zĭng-) *n.* **1.** A transparent, almost pure gelatin prepared from the air bladder of the sturgeon and certain other fishes and used as an adhesive and a clarifying agent. **2.** Mica in thin transparent sheets. [By folk ety. (influenced by GLASS) < obsolete Du. *huizenblas* < MDu. *hûsblase : hûs,* sturgeon + *blase,* bladder.]

I·sis¹ (ī′sĭs) *n. Mythology* An ancient Egyptian goddess of fertility, the sister and wife of Osiris.

I·sis² (ī′sĭs) The upper Thames R. in S-central England in the vicinity of Oxford. The name is used locally and in literature.

Is·ken·de·run (ĭs-kĕn′də-rōōn′, -kĕn′dĕ-rŏŏn′) Formerly **Al·ex·an·dret·ta** (ăl′ĭg-zăn-drĕt′ə) A city of S Turkey on an inlet of the E Mediterranean Sea; founded by Alexander the Great c. 333 B.C. Pop. 156,800.

Isl. *abbr.* island

Is·lam (ĭs-läm′, ĭz-, ĭs′läm′, ĭz′-) *n.* **1.** A monotheistic religion characterized by the acceptance of the doctrine of submission to God and of Muhammad as the chief and last prophet of God. **2a.** The people or nations that practice Islam; the Muslim world. **b.** The civilization developed by the Muslim world. [Ar. *'islām,* submission < *'aslama,* to surrender, resign oneself < Syriac *'ašlem,* to make peace, surrender, derived stem of *šlem,* to be complete.] —**Is·lam′ic** *adj.*

Is·lam·a·bad (ĭs-lä′mə-bäd′, ĭz-läm′ə-bäd′) The cap. of Pakistan, in the NE part NE of Rawalpindi; replaced Karachi as the cap. in 1967. Pop. 201,000.

Islamic calendar *n.* The lunar calendar used by Muslims reckoned from the year of the Hegira in A.D. 622. See table at **calendar.**

Is·la·mi·cist (ĭs-lä′mĭ-sĭst, ĭz-) *n.* **1.** A specialist in the study of Islam. **2.** A member or supporter of an Islamic revivalist movement; an Islamist.

Is·lam·ism (ĭs′lə-mĭz′əm, ĭz′-) *n.* **1.** An Islamic revivalist movement, often characterized by moral conservatism, literalism, and the attempt to implement Islamic values in all spheres of life. **2.** The religious faith, principles, or cause of Islam. —**Is·lam′ist** (-lä′mĭst) *n.*

Is·lam·ize (ĭs′lə-mīz′, ĭz′-) *tr.v.* **-ized, -iz·ing, -iz·es 1.** To convert to Islam. **2.** To cause to conform to Islamic law or precepts. —**Is·lam·i·za′tion** (-lə-mĭ-zā′shən) *n.*

is·land (ī′lənd) *n.* **1.** A land mass, esp. one smaller than a continent, entirely surrounded by water. **2.** Something resembling an island, esp. in being isolated or surrounded, as: **a.** An unattached kitchen counter providing easy access from all sides. **b.** A raised curbed area, often used to delineate rows of parking spaces or lanes of traffic. **c.** The superstructure of a ship, esp. an aircraft carrier. **3.** *Anatomy* A cluster of cells differing in structure or function from those in the surrounding tissue. ❖ *tr.v.* **-land·ed, -land·ing, -lands** To make into or as if into an island; insulate. [Alteration (influenced by ISLE) of ME *ilond* < OE *īegland : īg, īeg,* island; see **akʷ-ā-** in App. + *land,* land.]

is·land·er (ī′lən-dər) *n.* An inhabitant of an island.

is·lands of Lang·er·hans (ī′ləndz; läng′ər-häns′) *pl.n.* See **islets of Langerhans.**

Is·lay (ī′lä, ī′lə) An island of the S Inner Hebrides of W Scotland.

isle (īl) *n.* An island, esp. a small one. [ME *ile* < OFr. *isle* < Lat. *īnsula.*]

Isle of For names of actual isles, see the specific element of the name; for example, **Wight, Isle of.**

Isle Roy·ale (roi′əl) An island of N MI in Lake Superior near the coast of Ontario; named by French fur traders in 1671.

is·let (ī′lĭt) *n.* A very small island.

is·lets of Lang·er·hans (ī′lĭts; läng′ər-häns′) *pl.n.* Irregular clusters of endocrine cells scattered throughout the tissue of the pancreas that secrete insulin and glucagon. [After Paul *Langerhans* (1847–88), German pathologist.]

ism (ĭz′əm) *n. Informal* A distinctive doctrine, system, or theory. [< –ISM.]

–ism *suff.* **1.** Action; process; practice: *terrorism.* **2.** Characteristic behavior or quality: *heroism.* **3a.** State; condition; quality: *pauperism.* **b.** State or condition due to an excess of something specified: *strychninism.* **4.** Distinctive or characteristic trait: *Latinism.* **5a.** Doctrine; theory; system of principles: *pacifism.* **b.** An attitude of prejudice against a given group: *racism.* [ME *-isme* < OFr. < Lat. *-ismus* < Gk. *-ismos,* n. suff.]

Is·ma·i·li (ĭs′mä-ē′lē) also **Is·ma·i·li·an** (-ē′lē-ən) *n.* **-lis** also **-li·ans** A member of a branch of Shiism that follows a living imam and is noted for esoteric philosophy. [Ar. *isma'īlī,* after *Isma'īl* (died 760), son of the sixth imam, Jafar (700?–765).]

Is·ma·i·li·a (ĭz′mä-ə-lē′ə, ĭs′-) A city of NE Egypt on the Suez Canal; founded in 1863. Pop. 255,000.

is·n't (ĭz′ənt) Contraction of *is not.*

ISO (ī′ĕs-ō′) *n.* An organization, the International Organization for Standardization, that sets standards in many businesses and technologies, including computing and communications. [< Gk. *īsos,* equal.]

iso– or **is–** *pref.* **1.** Equal; uniform: *isobar.* **2.** Isomeric: *isopropyl.* [Gk. *īso–* < *īsos,* equal.]

i·so·ag·glu·ti·na·tion (ī′sō-ə-glōōt′n-ā′shən) *n.* The agglutination of the red blood cells of an individual by antibodies in the serum of another individual of the same species.

i·so·ag·glu·ti·nin (ī′sō-ə-glōōt′n-ĭn) *n.* An isoantibody normally present in the serum of an individual that causes isoagglutination.

i·so·an·ti·bod·y (ī′sō-ăn′tĭ-bŏd′ē) *n., pl.* **-ies** See **alloantibody.**

i·so·an·ti·gen (ī′sō-ăn′tĭ-jən) *n.* See **alloantigen.** —**i′so·an′ti·gen′ic** (-jĕn′ĭk) *adj.*

i·so·bar (ī′sə-bär′) *n.* **1.** A line on a weather map connecting points of equal atmospheric pressure. **2.** Any of two or more kinds of atoms having the same atomic mass but different atomic numbers. [ISO- + Gk. *baros,* weight; see **gʷerə-** in App.] —**i′so·bar′ic** (-bâr′ĭk, -băr′-) *adj.*

i·so·chro·mat·ic (ī′sə-krō-măt′ĭk) *adj.* **1.** Having the same color or wavelength. Used of light. **2.** Orthochromatic.

i·soch·ro·nal (ī-sŏk′rə-nəl) or **i·soch·ro·nous** (-nəs) *adj.* **1.** Equal in duration. **2.** Marked by or occurring at equal intervals of time. [< NLat. *īsochronus* < Gk. *īsokhronos : īso-,* iso- + *khronos,* time.] —**i·soch′ro·nal·ly** *adv.* —**i·soch′ro·nism** *n.* —**i·soch′ro·nize** *tr.v.*

i·soch·ro·ous (ī-sŏk′rō-əs) *adj.* Having the same color throughout. [Gk. *īsokhroos : īso-,* iso- + *khrōs,* flesh, color.]

i·so·cli·nal (ī′sə-klī′nəl) or **i·so·clin·ic** (-klĭn′ĭk) *adj.* Having the same magnetic inclination or dip. ❖ *n.* See **isoclinic line.** —**i′so·cli′nal·ly** *adv.*

i·so·cline (ī′sə-klīn′) *n. Geology* An anticline or syncline in which the rock beds of the two sides are nearly parallel.

isoclinic line *n.* A line on a map connecting points of equal magnetic inclination.

I·soc·ra·tes (ī-sŏk′rə-tēz′) 436–338 B.C. Athenian rhetorician whose letters are a valuable source of Greek thought.

i·so·di·a·met·ric (ī′sō-dī′ə-mĕt′rĭk) *adj.* Having equal diameters or axes.

i·so·dy·nam·ic (ī′sō-dī-năm′ĭk) *adj.* **1.** Having equal force or strength. **2.** Connecting points of equal magnetic intensity.

i·so·e·lec·tric (ī′sō-ĭ-lĕk′trĭk) *adj.* Having equal electric potential.

i·so·e·lec·tron·ic (ī′sō-ĭ-lĕk-trŏn′ĭk, -ē′lĕk-) *adj.* Having equal numbers of electrons or the same electronic configuration.

i·so·en·zyme (ī′sō-ĕn′zīm′) *n.* Any of the chemically distinct forms of an enzyme that perform the same biochemical function. —**i′so·en′zy′mic** *adj.*

i·so·fla·vone (ī′sō-flā′vōn′) *n.* One of a family of phytoestrogens found chiefly in soybeans that is under investigation for its preventive health benefits.

i·so·gam·ete (ī′sō-găm′ēt′, -gə-mēt′) *n.* A gamete that has the same size and structure as the one with which it unites.

i·sog·a·my (ī-sŏg′ə-mē) *n.* Reproduction by the fusion or conjugation of isogametes. —**i·sog′a·mous** *adj.*

i·sog·e·nous (ī-sŏj′ə-nəs) *adj.* Having the same or similar origin, as parts derived from the same embryonic tissue.

i·so·gloss (ī′sə-glôs′, -glŏs′) *n.* A geographic boundary line delimiting the area in which a given linguistic feature occurs. [ISO- + Gk. *glōssa,* language; tongue.] —**i′so·gloss′al** *adj.*

i·so·gon (ī′sə-gŏn′) *n.* A polygon whose angles are equal. —**i′so·gon′ic, i·sog′o·nal** (ī-sŏg′ə-nəl) *adj.*

isogonic line *n.* A line on a map connecting points of equal magnetic declination.

i·so·gram (ī′sə-grăm′) *n.* See **isoline.**

i·so·hel (ī′sō-hĕl′) *n.* A line drawn on a map connecting points that receive equal amounts of sunlight. [ISO- + Gk. *hēlios,* sun; see **sāwel-** in App.]

i·so·hy·et (ī′sō-hī′ĭt) *n.* A line drawn on a map connecting points that receive equal amounts of rainfall. [ISO- + Gk. *huetos,* rain.]

i·so·la·ble (ī′sə-lə-bəl) also **i·so·lat·a·ble** (-lā′tə-bəl) *adj.* Possible to isolate: *isolable viruses.*

i·so·late (ī′sə-lāt′) *tr.v.* **-lat·ed, -lat·ing, -lates 1.** To set apart or cut off from others. **2.** To place in quarantine. **3.** *Chemistry* To

Isis¹
Isis suckling her son Horus

ă	pat	oi	boy
ā	pay	ou	out
âr	care	ŏŏ	took
ä	father	ōō	boot
ĕ	pet	ŭ	cut
ē	be	ûr	urge
ĭ	pit	th	thin
ī	pie	th	this
îr	pier	hw	which
ŏ	pot	zh	vision
ō	toe	ə	about,
ô	paw		item

Stress marks:
′ (primary);
′ (secondary), as in
lexicon (lĕk′sĭ-kŏn′)

extract (the pure form of a substance) from a mixture. **4.** To render free of external influence; insulate. **5.** *Biology* To separate (a pure strain) from a mixed bacterial or fungal culture. **6.** *Electricity* **a.** To set apart (a component or circuit, for instance) from a source of electricity. **b.** To insulate or shield. ❖ *adj.* (-lĭt, -lāt′) Solitary; alone. ❖ *n.* (-lĭt, -lāt′) **1.** One that has been isolated. **2.** *Biology* An isolated strain, as of bacteria. **3.** A language isolate. —**i′so·la′tor** *n.*

i·so·lat·ed (ī′sə-lā′tĭd) *adj.* Separated from others; solitary. [< Fr. *isolé* < Ital. *isolato* < Lat. *īnsulātus*, made into an island < *īnsula*, island.]

i·so·la·tion (ī′sə-lā′shən) *n.* **1.** The act of isolating. **2.** The quality or condition of being isolated.

i·so·la·tion·ism (ī′sə-lā′shə-nĭz′əm) *n.* A national policy of abstaining from political or economic relations with other countries. —**i′so·la′tion·ist** *n.*

I·sol·de (ĭ-sōl′də, ĭ-zōl′-) *n.* Variant of **Iseult.**

i·so·leu·cine (ī′sə-lōō′sēn) *n.* An essential amino acid, $C_6H_{13}NO_2$, that is isomeric with leucine.

i·so·line (ī′sə-līn) *n.* A line on a map, chart, or graph connecting points of equal value.

i·so·mag·net·ic (ī′sō-măg-nĕt′ĭk) *adj.* Of, relating to, or being lines connecting points of equal magnetic force.

i·so·mer (ī′sə-mər) *n.* **1.** *Chemistry* Any of two or more substances that are composed of the same elements in the same proportions but differ in properties because of differences in the arrangement of atoms. **2.** *Physics* Any of two or more nuclei with the same mass number and atomic number but different energy states and radioactive properties. [Gk. *īsomeros*, having equal share : *īso-*, iso- + *meros*, part, share.] —**i′so·mer′ic** (-mĕr′ĭk) *adj.* —**i′so·mer′i·cal·ly** *adv.*

i·som·er·ase (ī-sŏm′ə-rās′) *n.* One of a group of enzymes that catalyzes the conversion of one isomer into another.

i·som·er·ism (ī-sŏm′ə-rĭz′əm) *n.* **1.** The existence of isomers. **2.** The complex of phenomena characteristic of or attributable to isomers. **3.** The state or condition of being an isomer.

i·som·er·ize (ī-sŏm′ə-rīz′) *v.* **-ized, -iz·ing, -iz·es** —*tr.* To cause to change into an isomeric form. —*intr.* To become changed into an isomeric form. —**i·som′er·i·za′tion** (-ər-ĭ-zā′shən) *n.*

i·som·er·ous (ī-sŏm′ər-əs) *adj.* **1.** Having an equal number of parts, as organs or markings. **2.** Having or being floral whorls with equal numbers of parts.

i·so·met·ric (ī′sə-mĕt′rĭk) also **i·so·met·ri·cal** (-rĭ-kəl) *adj.* **1.** Of or exhibiting equality in dimensions or measurements. **2.** Of or being a crystal system of three equal axes lying at right angles to each other. **3.** *Physiology* Of or involving muscular contraction against resistance in which the length of the muscle remains the same. ❖ *n.* A line connecting isometric points. [Gk. *īsometros*, of equal measure : *īso-*, iso- + *metron*, measure; see **mē-**[1] in App.]

i·so·met·rics (ī′sə-mĕt′rĭks) *n.* (*used with a sing. or pl. verb*) Exercise or a system of exercises in which isometric muscular contraction is used to strengthen and tone muscles.

i·so·me·tro·pi·a (ī′sō-mĭ-trō′pē-ə) *n.* Equality of refraction in both eyes. [Gk. *īsometros*, isometric; see ISOMETRIC + -OPIA.]

i·som·e·try (ī-sŏm′ĭ-trē) *n.* **1.** Equality of measure. **2.** Equality of elevation above sea level. **3.** *Mathematics* A function between metric spaces which preserves distances, such as a rotation or translation in a plane.

i·so·morph (ī′sə-môrf′) *n.* An object, organism, or substance exhibiting isomorphism.

i·so·mor·phic (ī′sə-môr′fĭk) *adj.* **1.** *Biology* Having a similar structure or appearance but being of different ancestry. **2.** Related by an isomorphism.

i·so·mor·phism (ī′sə-môr′fĭz′əm) *n.* **1.** *Biology* Similarity in form, as in organisms of different ancestry. **2.** *Mathematics* A one-to-one correspondence between two sets such that an operation on elements of one set corresponds to the analogous operation on their images in the other set. **3.** A close similarity in the crystalline structure of two or more substances of similar chemical composition. —**i′so·mor′phous** *adj.*

i·so·ni·a·zid (ī′sə-nī′ə-zĭd) *n.* A crystalline antibacterial compound, $C_6H_7N_3O$, used in the treatment of tuberculosis. [*isoni-*(*cotinic acid*), isomer of nicotinic acid (ISO- + NICOTINIC ACID) + (*hydr*)*azid*(*e*) (HYDR(O)- + AZ(O)- + -IDE).]

i·so·oc·tane (ī′sō-ŏk′tān′) *n.* A flammable liquid, $(CH_3)_3CHCH_2C(CH_3)_3$, used to determine octane numbers.

i·so·pi·es·tic (ī′sō-pī-ĕs′tĭk, -pē-) *adj.* Marked by or indicating equal pressure; isobaric. ❖ *n.* See **isobar** 1. [ISO- + Gk. *piestos*, able to be compressed (< *piezein*, to press tight; see **sed-** in App.) + -IC.]

i·so·pod (ī′sə-pŏd′) *n.* Any of numerous crustaceans of the order Isopoda, characterized by a flattened body bearing seven pairs of legs. [< NLat. *Īsopoda*, order name : ISO- + NLat. -*poda*, -pod.]

i·so·prene (ī′sə-prēn′) *n.* A colorless volatile liquid, C_5H_8, used chiefly to make synthetic rubber. [ISO- + PR(OPYL)ENE.] —**i′so·pre′noid** (-prē′noid′) *adj.*

i·so·pro·pyl alcohol (ī′sə-prō′pəl) *n.* A clear colorless flammable mobile liquid, $(CH_3)_2CHOH$, used in antifreeze compounds, in lotions and cosmetics, and as a solvent.

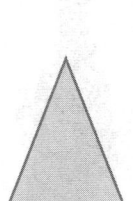

isosceles
isosceles triangle

Israel[2]

i·sos·ce·les (ī-sŏs′ə-lēz′) *adj.* *Mathematics* Having two equal sides. [LLat. *īsosceles* < Gk. *īsoskelēs* : *īso-*, iso- + *skelos*, leg.]

i·so·seis·mic (ī′sə-sīz′mĭk) also **i·so·seis·mal** (-məl) *adj.* Of or exhibiting equal intensity of earthquake shock.

i·sos·mot·ic (ī′sŏz-mŏt′ĭk, -sŏs-) *adj.* Of or exhibiting equal osmotic pressure.

i·so·spin (ī′sə-spĭn′) *n.* A quantum number related to the number of charge states of a baryon or meson. [ISO(TOPIC) + SPIN.]

i·sos·ta·sy (ī-sŏs′tə-sē) *n.* Equilibrium in the earth's crust such that the forces tending to elevate landmasses balance the forces tending to depress landmasses. [ISO- + Gk. *stasis*, a standstill; see **stā-** in App. + -Y[2].] —**i′so·stat′ic** (ī′sō-stăt′ĭk) *adj.* —**i′so·stat′i·cal·ly** *adv.*

i·so·therm (ī′sə-thûrm′) *n.* A line drawn on a weather map or chart linking all points of equal or constant temperature.

i·so·ther·mal (ī′sə-thûr′məl) *adj.* **1.** Of, relating to, or indicating equal or constant temperatures. **2.** Of or being changes of pressure and volume at constant temperature. **3.** Of or relating to an isotherm. ❖ *n.* An isotherm.

i·so·tone (ī′sə-tōn′) *n.* One of two or more atoms whose nuclei have the same number of neutrons but different numbers of protons. [Alteration of ISOTOPE (with *n* for *neutron* replacing *p* as though for *proton*).]

i·so·ton·ic (ī′sə-tŏn′ĭk) *adj.* **1.** Of equal tension. **2.** Isosmotic. **3.** Having the same concentration of solutes as the blood. **4.** *Physiology* Of or involving muscular contraction in which the muscle stays under relatively constant tension while changing length. [ISO- + Gk. *tonos*, tension; see TONE + -IC.] —**i′so·ton′i·cal·ly** *adv.* —**i′so·to·nic′i·ty** (-tə-nĭs′ĭ-tē) *n.*

i·so·tope (ī′sə-tōp′) *n.* One of two or more atoms having the same atomic number but different mass numbers. [ISO- + Gk. *topos*, place (the isotopes of a chemical element occupying the same position in the periodic table of elements).] —**i′so·top′ic** (-tŏp′ĭk) *adj.* —**i′so·top′i·cal·ly** *adv.*

isotopic spin *n.* An isospin.

i·so·tro·pic (ī′sə-trō′pĭk, -trŏp′ĭk) *adj.* Identical in all directions; invariant with respect to direction. —**i·sot′ro·py** (ī-sŏt′rə-pē), **i·sot′ro·pism** (-pĭz′əm) *n.*

i·so·type (ī′sə-tīp′) *n.* **1.** A biological specimen that is a duplicate of a holotype. **2.** Any of the subclasses of immunoglobulins defined by the chemical characteristics and antigen specificity of their invariable molecular regions. —**i′so·typ′ic** (-tĭp′ĭk) *adj.*

i·so·zyme (ī′sə-zīm′) *n.* An isoenzyme. [ISO- + (EN)ZYME.]

ISP *abbr.* Internet service provider

Isr. *abbr.* **1.** Israel **2.** Israeli

Is·ra·el[1] (ĭz′rē-əl) *n.* **1.** *Bible* **a.** Jacob. **b.** The descendants of Jacob. **2.** *Judaism* The Hebrew people, regarded as the chosen people of God by the covenant of Jacob. [ME < OE < Lat. < Gk. *Israēl* < Heb. *yiśrā'ēl*, God has striven, God has saved : *yiśrā*, he has striven, saved + *'ēl*, God.]

Is·ra·el[2] (ĭz′rē-əl) **1.** An ancient kingdom of SW Asia founded by Saul c. 1025 B.C. After 933 it split into the Northern Kingdom, or kingdom of Israel, and the kingdom of Judah to the S. **2.** A country of SW Asia on the E Mediterranean Sea; created in 1948 on recommendation of the United Nations. Cap. Jerusalem. Pop. 5,383,000.

Is·rae·li (ĭz-rā′lē) *n.*, *pl.* **-lis** A native or inhabitant of modern-day Israel. —**Is·rae′li** *adj.*

Is·ra·el·ite (ĭz′rē-ə-līt′) *n.* **1.** A native or inhabitant of ancient Israel. **2.** A descendant of Jacob; a Jew. **3.** A member of a people regarded as the chosen people of God. **4.** A Jew not descended from the tribe of Levi and not a priest. ❖ *adj.* also **Is·ra·el·it·ic** (ĭz′rē-ə-lĭt′ĭk) Of or relating to ancient Israel, the ancient Israelites, or their culture.

Is·sa·char (ĭs′ə-kär′) In the Bible, a son of Jacob and Leah and the forebear of one of the tribes of Israel.

is·sei (ĭs′sā′) *n.*, *pl.* **issei** or **-seis** A Japanese immigrant, esp. one to the United States. [J. : *ichi*, one, first (< M Chin. *ʔjit*) + *sei*, generation (< M Chin. *shiaj*).]

ISSN *abbr.* International Standard Serial Number

is·su·a·ble (ĭsh′ōō-ə-bəl) *adj.* **1.** Authorized for issue or to be issued: *issuable currency.* **2.** Open to debate or litigation. **3.** That can be accrued: *issuable profits.*

is·su·ance (ĭsh′ōō-əns) *n.* **1.** The act of issuing. **2.** An issue.

is·su·ant (ĭsh′ōō-ənt) *adj.* **1.** *Heraldry* Being an animal with only the upper part depicted. **2.** *Archaic* Emerging.

is·sue (ĭsh′ōō) *n.* **1a.** The act or an instance of flowing, passing, or giving out. **b.** The act of circulating, distributing, or publishing by an office or official group. **2.** Something produced, published, or offered, as: **a.** An item or set of items, as stamps or coins, made available at one time by an office or bureau. **b.** A single copy of a periodical. **c.** A distinct set of copies of an edition of a book distinguished from others by print variations. **d.** A final result or conclusion, as a solution to a problem. **e.** Proceeds from estates or fines. **3.** Something proceeding from a specified source. **4a.** A point or matter of discussion, debate, or dispute. **b.** A matter of public concern. **c.** A misgiving, objection, or complaint. **d.** The essential point; crux. **e.** A culminating point leading to a decision. **5.** *Informal* A personal problem or emotional disorder. **6.** A place of egress; an outlet. **7.** *Pathology* **a.** A discharge, as of blood or pus. **b.** A lesion, wound, or ulcer producing such a discharge. **8.** *Archaic* Termination; close. ❖ *v.* **-sued, -su•ing, -sues** —*intr.* **1.** To go or come out. **2.** To accrue as proceeds or profit. **3.** To be born or be descended. **4.** To be circulated or published. **5.** To spring or proceed from a source. See Syns at **stem**[1]. **6.** To terminate or result. —*tr.* **1.** To cause to flow out; emit. **2.** To circulate or distribute in an official capacity. **3.** To publish. ***—idioms:*** **at issue 1.** In question; in dispute. **2.** At variance; in disagreement. **join issue 1.** To enter into controversy. **2.** *Law* To submit an issue for decision. **take issue** To take an opposing point of view; disagree. [ME < OFr. *eissue, issue* < VLat. **exūta*, alteration of Lat. *exita*, fem. p. part. of *exīre*, to go out : *ex-*, ex- + *īre*, to go; see **ei-** in App.] **—is′su•er** *n.*

Is•sus (ĭs′əs) An ancient town of SE Asia Minor; site of Alexander the Great's defeat of Darius III of Persia (333 B.C.).

Is•syk-Kul (ĭs′ĭk-ko͝ol′, -kœl′) A lake of NE Kyrgyzstan in the Tien Shan near the NW Chinese border.

-ist *suff.* **1a.** One that performs a specified action: *lobbyist.* **b.** One that produces, makes, operates, plays, or is connected with a specified thing: *novelist.* **2.** A specialist in a specified art, science, or skill: *biologist.* **3.** An adherent or advocate of a specified doctrine, theory, or school of thought: *anarchist.* **4.** One that is characterized by a specified trait or quality: *romanticist.* [ME *-iste* < OFr. < Lat. *-istēs, -ista* < Gk. *-istēs*, agent n. suff.]

Is•tan•bul (ĭs′tăn-bo͞ol′, -tän-, ĭ-stän′bo͞ol) Formerly **Con•stan•ti•no•ple** (kŏn′stăn-tə-nō′pəl) A city of NW Turkey on both sides of the Bosporus at its entrance into the Sea of Marmara. Founded c. 660 B.C. as Byzantium, it was renamed Constantinople in A.D. 330 by Constantine the Great. Istanbul was chosen as the official name in 1930. Pop. 7,615,500.

Isth. *abbr.* isthmus

isth•mi•an (ĭs′mē-ən) *adj.* **1.** Of, relating to, or forming an isthmus. **2.** Of or relating to the Isthmus of Corinth, esp. to the ancient Pan-Hellenic games held there.

isth•mus (ĭs′məs) *n., pl.* **-mus•es** or **-mi** (-mī′) **1.** A strip of land connecting two larger masses of land. **2.** *Anatomy* **a.** A strip of tissue joining two larger organs or parts of an organ. **b.** A narrow passage connecting two larger cavities. [Lat. < Gk. *isthmos.*]

is•tle also **ix•tle** (ĭs′lē, ĭst′-) *n.* See **pita**[2] 1. [Am.Sp. *ixtle* < Nahuatl *ixtli*, fibrous stem.]

Is•tri•a (ĭs′trē-ə) A peninsula of NW Croatia projecting into the Adriatic Sea; conquered by Rome in the 2nd cent. A.D. **—Is′tri•an** *adj. & n.*

it (ĭt) *pron.* **1.** Used to refer to that one previously mentioned. Used of a nonhuman entity; an animate being whose sex is unspecified, unknown, or irrelevant; a group of objects or individuals; an action; or an abstraction. **2.** Used as the subject of an impersonal verb: *It is snowing.* **3a.** Used as an anticipatory subject or object: *Is it certain that they will win?* **b.** Used as an anticipatory subject to emphasize a term that is not itself a subject: *It was on Friday that all the snow fell.* **4.** Used to refer to a general condition or state of affairs: *She couldn't stand it.* **5.** Used to refer to a crucial situation, culmination, or cause of impatience: *That's it! We're finally finished. That's it! I won't tolerate any more foolishness.* **6.** *Informal* Used to refer to something that is the best, the most desirable, or without equal: *He thinks he's it.* ❖ *n. Games* A player, as in tag, who attempts to find or catch the other players. [ME < OE *hit.* See **ko-** in App.]

OUR LIVING LANGUAGE *"I told Anse it likely won't be no need."* This quotation from William Faulkner's *As I Lay Dying* demonstrates a use of *it* that occurs in some vernacular varieties of American speech. *It* is used instead of Standard English *there* when *there* functions as a so-called existential—that is, when *there* indicates the mere existence of something rather than a physical location, as in *It was nothing I could do.* Existential *it* is hardly a recent innovation—it appears in Middle English; in Elizabethan English, as in Marlowe's *Edward II: "Cousin, it is no dealing with him now"*; and in modern American literature as well. Although most British and American varieties no longer have this historical feature, it still occurs in some Southern-based dialects and in African American Vernacular English. • In some American vernacular dialects, particularly in the South (including the Appalachian and Ozark mountains), speakers may pronounce *it* as *hit* in stressed positions, especially at the beginning of a sentence, as in *Hit's cold out here!* This pronunciation is called a *relic dialect feature* because it represents the retention of an older English form. In fact, *hit* is the original form of the third person singular neuter pronoun and thus can be traced to the beginnings of the Old English period (c. 449–1100). Early in the history of English, speakers began to drop the *h* from *hit,* particularly in unaccented positions, as in *I saw it yesterday.* Gradually, *h* also came to be lost in accented positions, although *hit* persisted in socially prestigious speech well into the Elizabethan period. Some relatively isolated dialects in Great Britain and the United States have retained *h.* But even in such places, *h* tends to be retained only in accented words. Thus, we might hear *Hit's the one I want* side by side with *I took it back to the store.* Nowadays, *hit* is fading even in the most isolated dialect communities and occurs primarily among older speakers.

IT *abbr.* information technology

It. *abbr.* **1.** Italian **2.** Italy

ITA *abbr.* initial teaching alphabet

it•a•col•u•mite (ĭt′ə-kŏl′yə-mīt′) *n.* A variety of sandstone that is flexible when cut into thin slabs. [After *Itacolumi* (Itacolomi), a mountain of east-central Brazil.]

ital. *abbr.* **1.** italic **2.** italics

Ital. *abbr.* **1.** Italian **2.** Italy

I•tal•ian (ĭ-tăl′yən) *adj.* Of or relating to Italy or its people, language, or culture. ❖ *n.* **1a.** A native or inhabitant of Italy. **b.** A person of Italian descent. **2.** The Romance language of the Italians and an official language of Switzerland. [ME < Lat. *Italiānus* < *Italia*, Italy.]

I•tal•ian•ate (ĭ-tăl′yə-nāt′, -nĭt) *adj.* Italian in character.

Italian East Africa A former federation (1936–41) of Italian-held territories in E Africa, including Ethiopia, Eritrea, and part of present-day Somalia.

I•tal•ian•ism (ĭ-tăl′yə-nĭz′əm) *n.* **1.** An Italian idiom or custom. **2.** A quality characteristic of Italy or its people.

I•tal•ian•ize (ĭ-tăl′yə-nīz′) *v.* **-ized, -iz•ing, -iz•es** —*tr.* To give an Italian aspect to. —*intr.* To adopt Italian speech or ways. **—I•tal′ian•i•za′tion** (-yə-nĭ-zā′shən) *n.*

Italian sandwich *n. Chiefly Maine* See **submarine** 2.

Italian Somaliland A former Italian colony of E Africa; part of Italian East Africa after 1936.

Italian sonnet *n.* See **Petrarchan sonnet.**

I•tal•ic (ĭ-tăl′ĭk, ī-tăl′-) *adj.* **1.** Of or relating to ancient Italy or its peoples or cultures. **2.** Of or relating to the branch Indo-European that includes Latin, Faliscan, Oscan, Umbrian, and the Romance languages. **3. italic** Of or being a style of printing type patterned on a Renaissance script with the letters slanting to the right. ❖ *n.* **1.** The Italic branch of Indo-European. **2.** Italic print or typeface. Often used in the plural. [Lat. *Italicus* < *Italia*, Italy.]

I•tal•i•cism (ĭ-tăl′ĭ-sĭz′əm) *n.* An Italianism, esp. a word or idiom borrowed from or suggestive of Italian.

i•tal•i•cize (ĭ-tăl′ĭ-sīz′, ī-tăl′-) *tr.v.* **-cized, -ciz•ing, -ciz•es 1.** To print in italic type. **2.** To underscore (written matter) with a single line to indicate italics. **3.** To emphasize. **—i•tal′i•ci•za′tion** (-sĭ-zā′shən) *n.*

It•a•ly (ĭt′l-ē) **1.** A peninsula of S Europe projecting into the Mediterranean between the Tyrrhenian and Adriatic seas. **2.** A country of S Europe comprising the peninsula of Italy, Sardinia, Sicily, and several smaller islands; settled by Ligurian peoples and later by Etruscans (before 800 B.C.), who were supplanted by the Latin Romans by 270 B.C. Cap. Rome. Pop. 57,193,000.

I•tas•ca (ī-tăs′kə) A lake of NW MN; identified in 1832 as the source of the Mississippi R.

itch (ĭch) *n.* **1.** An irritating skin sensation causing a desire to scratch. **2.** Any of various skin disorders, such as scabies, marked by intense irritation and itching. **3.** A restless desire or craving for something: *an itch to travel.* ❖ *v.* **itched, itch•ing, itch•es** —*intr.* **1a.** To feel, have, or produce an itch. **b.** To have a desire to scratch. **2.** To have a persistent, restless craving. —*tr.* **1.** To cause to itch. **2.** To scratch (an itch). [ME *yicche* < OE *gicce* < *giccan*, to itch.]

itch mite *n.* A parasitic mite *(Sarcoptes scabiei)* that burrows into the skin and causes scabies.

itch•y (ĭch′ē) *adj.* **-i•er, -i•est 1.** Having or causing an itching sensation. **2.** Restless or nervous. **—itch′i•ness** *n.*

it'd (ĭt′əd) **1.** Contraction of *it had.* **2.** Contraction of *it would.*

-ite[1] *suff.* **1.** Native or resident of: *New Jerseyite.* **2a.** Descendant of: *Levite.* **b.** Adherent or follower of: *Luddite.* **3.** A part of an organ, body, or bodily part: *somite.* **4a.** Rock; mineral: *graphite.* **b.** Fossil: *trilobite.* **5a.** Product: *metabolite.* **b.** A commercial product: *ebonite.* [ME < OFr. < Lat. *-ītēs, -īta* < Gk. *-ītēs.*]

-ite[2] *suff.* A salt or ester of an acid named with an adjective ending in *-ous*: *sulfite.* [Alteration of -ATE[2].]

i•tem (ī′təm) *n.* **1.** A single article or unit in a collection, enumeration, or series. **2.** A clause of a document, such as a bill. **3.** An entry in an account. **4a.** A bit of information; a detail. **b.** A short piece in a newspaper or magazine. **5.** A romantically involved couple. ❖ *adv.* Also; likewise. Used to introduce each article in an enumeration or list. ❖ *tr.v.* **i•temed, i•tem•ing, i•tems** *Archaic* To compute. [< ME, also, moreover < Lat. See **i-** in App.]

SYNONYMS *item, detail, particular* These nouns denote an individual, often specialized element of a whole: *a list with numerous items; discussed the details of their trip; gave the particulars of the accident.*

i•tem•ize (ī′tə-mīz′) *v.* **-ized, -iz•ing, -iz•es** —*tr.* **1.** To place or include on a list of items: *itemized her expenses on the form.* **2.** To list the items of: *itemized the expense account.* —*intr.* To list deductions from taxable income on a tax return. **—i′tem•i•za′tion** (ī′tə-mĭ-zā′shən) *n.* **—i′tem•iz′er** *n.*

item veto *n.* See **line-item veto.**

it•er•ance (ĭt′ər-əns) *n.* Iteration.

it•er•ant (ĭt′ər-ənt) *adj.* Marked by iteration; repeating.

it•er•ate (ĭt′ə-rāt′) *tr.v.* **-at•ed, -at•ing, -ates** To say or perform again; repeat. See Syns at **repeat.** [Lat. *iterāre, iterāt-* < *iterum*, again. See **i-** in App.]

it•er•a•tion (ĭt′ə-rā′shən) *n.* **1.** The act or an instance of iterating; repetition. **2.** *Mathematics* A computational procedure in which a cycle of operations is repeated, often to approximate the

issuant

Italy

ă	pat	oi	boy
ā	pay	ou	out
âr	care	o͝o	took
ä	father	o͞o	boot
ĕ	pet	ŭ	cut
ē	be	ûr	urge
ĭ	pit	th	thin
ī	pie	*th*	this
îr	pier	hw	which
ŏ	pot	zh	vision
ō	toe	ə	about, item
ô	paw		

Stress marks:
′ (primary);
′ (secondary), as in
lexicon (lĕk′sĭ-kŏn′)

desired result more closely. **3.** *Computer Science* **a.** The process of repeating a set of instructions a specified number of times or until a specific result is achieved. **b.** One cycle of a set of instructions to be repeated.

it·er·a·tive (ĭt′ə-rā′tĭv, -ər-ə-tĭv) *adj.* **1.** Characterized by or involving repetition, recurrence, reiteration, or repetitiousness. **2.** *Grammar* Frequentative.

I·tha·ki (ē-thä′kē) also **Ith·a·ca** (ĭth′ə-kə) An island of W Greece in the Ionian Is.; traditional home of Odysseus.

ith·y·phal·lic (ĭth′ĭ-făl′ĭk) *adj.* **1.** Of or relating to the phallus carried in the ancient festival of Bacchus. **2.** Having the penis erect. Used of graphic and sculptural representations. **3.** Lascivious; salacious. [LLat. *ithyphallicus* < Gk. *ithuphallikos* < *ithuphallos*, erect phallus : *ithus*, straight + *phallos*, phallus.]

i·tin·er·an·cy (ī-tĭn′ər-ən-sē, ĭ-tĭn′-) also **i·tin·er·a·cy** (-ə-sē) *n.*, *pl.* **-cies** A state or system of itinerating, esp. in the role or office of public speaker, minister, or judge.

i·tin·er·ant (ī-tĭn′ər-ənt, ĭ-tĭn′-) *adj.* Traveling from place to place, esp. to perform work or a duty. ❖ *n.* One who is itinerant. [LLat. *itinerāns, itinerant-*, pr. part. of *itinerārī*, to travel < Lat. *iter, itiner-*, journey. See **ei-** in App.]

i·tin·er·ar·y (ī-tĭn′ə-rĕr′ē, ĭ-tĭn′-) *n.*, *pl.* **-ies** **1.** A route or proposed route of a journey. **2.** An account or record of a journey. **3.** A guidebook for travelers. ❖ *adj.* **1.** Of or relating to a journey or route. **2.** Traveling from place to place; itinerant. [Ult. < LLat. *itinerārius*, of traveling < Lat. *iter, itiner-*, journey. See **ei-** in App.]

i·tin·er·ate (ī-tĭn′ə-rāt′, ĭ-tĭn′-) *intr.v.* **-at·ed, -at·ing, -ates** To travel around. [LLat. *itinerārī, itinerāt-* < Lat. *iter, itiner-*, journey. See ITINERARY.] —**i·tin′er·a′tion** *n.*

-itious *suff.* Relating to or characterized by: *cementitious*. [< Lat. *-icius* and *-īcius*, adj. suffixes.]

-itis *suff.* **1.** Inflammation or disease of: *laryngitis*. **2.** Excessive preoccupation with, indulgence in, reliance on, or possession of the qualities of: *televisionitis*. [Gk. *-itis* < fem. of *-ītēs*, adj. suff. (orig. modifying feminine noun *nostos*, disease).]

it'll (ĭt′l) Contraction of *it will.*

ITO *abbr.* International Trade Organization

its (ĭts) *adj.* The possessive form of **it.** Used as a modifier before a noun: *The airline canceled its early flight to New York.* [Alteration of *it's* : IT + -'s.]

> **USAGE NOTE** *Its,* the possessive form of the pronoun *it,* is never written with an apostrophe. The contraction *it's* (for *it is* or *it has*) is always written with an apostrophe.

it's (ĭts) **1.** Contraction of *it is.* **2.** Contraction of *it has.* See Usage Note at **its.**

it·self (ĭt-sĕlf′) *pron.* **1.** That one identical with it: **a.** Used reflexively as the direct or indirect object of a verb or the object of a preposition: *The cat scratched itself.* **b.** Used for emphasis: *The trouble is in the machine itself.* **c.** Used in an absolute construction: *Itself no great poem, it still reveals talent.* **2.** Its normal or healthy condition or state: *The car is acting itself again.*

I·tsu·ku·shi·ma (ĭt′sōō-kōō′shĭ-mə) An island of SW Japan in the Inland Sea SW of Hiroshima.

it·ty-bit·ty (ĭt′ē-bĭt′ē) also **it·sy-bit·sy** (ĭt′sē-bĭt′sē) *adj. Informal* Very small. [Prob. alteration of *little bit.*]

It·u·rae·a (ĭch′ə-rē′ə) An ancient country of NE Palestine; first inhabited by Arabians and later controlled by Judea and Rome. —**It′u·rae′an** *adj. & n.*

I·tur·bi·de (ē′tōōr-bē′dä), **Agustín de** 1783–1824. Mexican revolutionary who established Mexican independence from Spain (1821) and served as emperor (1822–23).

Agustín de Iturbide
19th-century engraving

-ity *suff.* State; quality: *abnormality.* [ME *-itie* < OFr. *-ite* < Lat. *-itās,* var. of *-tās, -ty.*]

IU *abbr.* international unit

IUD *abbr.* intrauterine device

-ium *suff.* Chemical element or group: *californium.* [NLat., neut. n. suff. < Gk. *-ion.*]

IV[1] (ī′vē′) *n.* An apparatus for providing intravenous injections. [< I(NTRA)V(ENOUS).]

IV[2] *abbr.* **1.** intravenous **2.** intravenously

I·van III Va·sil·ie·vich (ī′vən, ē-vän′; ə-sĭl′yə-vĭch′) Known as "Ivan the Great." 1440–1505. Grand duke of Muscovy (1462–1505) who laid the foundations for Russian unity.

Ivan IV Vasilievich Known as "Ivan the Terrible." 1530–84. The first czar of Russia (1547–84), who conducted unsuccessful wars against Sweden and Livonia.

I·va·no-Fran·kivs′k (ī-vä′nō-fräng-kĭvsk′, ē-vä′nō-fräng-kĕwsk′) or **I·va·no-Fran·kovsk** (-kôvsk′, -kôfsk′) A city of SW Ukraine SW of Kiev; chartered 1662. Pop. 230,400.

I·va·no·vo (ī-vä′nə-və) A city of W-central Russia NE of Moscow. Pop. 474,000.

-ive *suff.* Performing or tending toward a specified action: *de-*

ivory-billed woodpecker
Campephilus principalis
illustration from *Birds of America* by John James Audubon

monstrative. [ME < OFr. < Lat. *-īvus,* adj. suff.]

I've (īv) Contraction of *I have.*

Ives (īvz), **Charles Edward** 1874–1954. Amer. composer whose works include the Third Symphony (1904–11).

Ives, James Merritt 1824–95. Amer. lithographer best known for his works with Nathaniel Currier.

IVF *abbr.* in vitro fertilization

i·vied (ī′vēd) *adj.* Overgrown or cloaked with ivy.

I·vi·za (ē-bē′sə, ē-vē′thä) See **Ibiza.**

I·vo·ri·an (ī-vôr′ē-ən, ī-vōr′-) or **I·voir·i·an** (ē-vwär′ē-ən) *n.* A native or inhabitant of Côte d'Ivoire. —**I·vo′ri·an, I·voir′i·an** *adj.*

i·vo·ry (ī′və-rē, īv′rē) *n.*, *pl.* **-ries** **1a.** A hard smooth yellowish-white substance obtained from the tusks of the elephant. **b.** A similar substance forming the tusks or teeth of certain other mammals. **2.** A tusk, esp. an elephant's tusk. **3.** An article made of ivory. **4.** A substance resembling ivory. **5.** A pale or grayish yellow to yellowish white. **6a.** *Music* Piano keys. Often used in the plural. **b.** *Games* Dice. Often used in the plural. **c.** *Slang* The teeth. Often used in the plural. [ME *ivorie* < OFr. *ivoire, ivurie* < Lat. *eboreus,* of ivory < *ebur, ebor-,* ivory < Coptic *ebou,* elephant < Egypt. *'bw.*] —**i′vo·ry** *adj.*

i·vo·ry-billed woodpecker (ī′və-rē-bĭld′, īv′rē-) *n.* A large, extinct woodpecker (*Campephilus principalis*) of the southern United States and Cuba having black plumage, white wing patches, and an ivory-colored bill.

ivory black *n.* A black pigment prepared from charred ivory.

Ivory Coast or **Côte d'I·voire** (kōt′ dē-vwär′) **1.** See **Côte d'I·voire. 2.** A section of coastal W Africa along the Gulf of Guinea roughly corresponding to present-day Côte d'Ivoire.

ivory nut *n.* The seed of the ivory palm, having bony endosperm that is used as a substitute for true ivory.

ivory palm *n.* A stemless unarmed dioecious palm (*Phytelephas macrocarpa*) native to Brazil and Peru.

ivory tower *n.* A place or attitude of retreat, esp. preoccupation with lofty, remote, or intellectual considerations. [Transl. of Fr. *tour d'ivoire* : *tour,* tower + *de,* of + *ivoire,* ivory.]

i·vy (ī′vē) *n.*, *pl.* **i·vies** Any of several woody climbing or trailing evergreen plants of the genus *Hedera* native to the Old World, esp. *H. helix,* having palmately lobed leaves and root-bearing young stems. [ME *ivi* < OE *ĩfig.*]

Ivy League *n.* An association of eight universities and colleges in the northeast United States, comprising Brown, Columbia, Cornell, Dartmouth, Harvard, Princeton, the University of Pennsylvania, and Yale. [< the ivy-covered older college buildings.] —**Ivy Leaguer** *n.*

IW *abbr.* **1.** index word **2.** inside width **3.** isotopic weight

I·wa·ki (ĭ-wä′kē) A city of E Honshu, Japan, on the Pacific Ocean NNE of Tokyo. Pop. 359,098.

i·wis also **y·wis** (ĭ-wĭs′) *adv. Archaic* Certainly; assuredly. [ME < OE *gewis,* certain. See **weid-** in App.]

I·wo (ē′wō) A city of SW Nigeria ENE of Ibadan; cap. of a Yoruba sultanate from the 17th to the 19th cent. Pop. 255,100.

I·wo Ji·ma (ē′wə jē′mə, ē′wō) The largest of the Volcano Is. of Japan in the NW Pacific Ocean E of Taiwan.

IWW *abbr.* Industrial Workers of the World

Ix·i·on (ĭk-sī′ən, ĭk′sē-ŏn′) *n. Greek Mythology* A king of Thessaly who committed parricide and attempted to rape Hera and was punished by Zeus by being bound to a perpetually revolving wheel in Hades.

ix·tle (ĭs′tlē, ĭst′-) *n.* Variant of **istle.**

I·yar also **Iy·yar** (ē-yär′, ē′yär′) *n.* The eighth month of the year in the Jewish calendar. See table at **calendar.** [Heb. *'iyyār* < Akkadian *ayyaru,* name of a month corresponding to parts of April and May, perh. < *ayyaru,* blossom.]

-ization or **-isation** *suff.* Action, process, or result of doing or making: *colonization.* [-IZ(E) + -ATION.]

-ize or **-ise** *suff.* **1a.** To cause to be or to become: *dramatize.* **b.** To cause to conform to or resemble: *Hellenize.* **c.** To treat as: *idolize.* **2a.** To treat or affect with: *anesthetize.* **b.** To subject to: *tyrannize.* **3.** To treat according to or practice the method of: *pasteurize.* **4.** To become; become like: *materialize.* **5.** To perform, engage in, or produce: *botanize.* [ME *-isen* < OFr. *-iser* < LLat. *-izāre* < Gk. *-izein,* v. suff.]

I·zet·be·go·vić (ī′zĕt-bĕg′ə-vĭch), **Alija** b. 1925. Bosnian lawyer and politician who was elected president of Bosnia and Herzegovina in 1990.

I·zhevsk (ē-zhĕfsk′, ē-zhĭfsk′) Formerly **U·sti·nov** (ōō-stĭn′ôf) A city of W-central Russia NE of Kazan. Pop. 652,424.

Iz·mir (ĭz-mîr′) Formerly **Smyr·na** (smûr′nə) A city of W Turkey on the **Gulf of Izmir,** an inlet of the Aegean Sea; settled during the Bronze Age. Pop. 1,985,300.

iz·zard (ĭz′ərd) *n. Informal* The letter *z.* [Prob. var. of Sc. *ezed,* var. of ZED.]

Jj

j¹ or **J** (jā) *n.*, *pl.* **j's** or **J's** also **js** or **Js** **1.** The tenth letter of the modern English alphabet. **2.** Any of the speech sounds represented by the letter *j*. **3.** The tenth in a series. **4.** Something shaped like the letter J.

j² or **J** *Electricity* The symbol for **current density** 1.

J *abbr.* **1.** *Games* jack **2.** or **j** joule

J. *abbr.* **1.** Japanese **2.** judge **3.** justice

JA *abbr.* **1.** joint account **2.** judge advocate

jab (jăb) *v.* **jabbed, jab·bing, jabs** —*tr.* **1.** To poke or thrust abruptly: *jabbed a knife into the log.* **2.** To stab or pierce. **3.** To punch (someone) with short blows. —*intr.* **1.** To make an abrupt poking or thrusting motion. **2.** To deliver a quick punch. ❖ *n.* **1.** A quick stab or blow. **2.** *Sports* A short straight punch in boxing. [Variant of JOB².]

Jab·al·pur (jŭb′əl-poor′) also **Jub·bul·pore** (-pôr′, -pōr′) A city of central India SSE of Delhi. Pop. 741,927.

jab·ber (jăb′ər) *v.* **-bered, -ber·ing, -bers** —*intr.* To talk rapidly, unintelligibly, or idly. —*tr.* To utter rapidly or unintelligibly. ❖ *n.* Rapid or babbling talk. [ME *javeren*, of imit. orig.] —**jab′ber·er** *n.*

jab·ber·wock·y (jăb′ər-wŏk′ē) *n.* Nonsensical speech or writing. [After "*Jabberwocky*," a nonsense poem by Lewis Carroll.]

jab·i·ru (jăb′ə-roo′) *n.* A large tropical American stork (*Jabiru mycteria*) having white plumage with a pink band at the neck and a naked head. [Port. and Am.Sp. *jabirú* < Tupi.]

jab·o·ran·di (jăb′ə-răn-dē′, -răn′dē) *n.*, *pl.* **-dis 1.** Either of two tropical American shrubs (*Pilocarpus jaborandi* or *P. microphyllus*) whose dried leaves yield the medicinal alkaloid pilocarpine. **2.** The dried leaves of these plants. [Port. and Am.Sp. < Tupi, one that spits.]

ja·bot (zhă-bō′, jăb′ō) *n.* An ornamental cascade of ruffles or frills down the front of a garment. [Fr., crop of a bird, jabot, perh. of Celt. orig.]

ja·bo·ti·ca·ba (zhə-boo′tĭ-kä′bə) *n.* A Brazilian shrub (*Myrciaria cauliflora*) cultivated for its purplish-black fruits, which are borne directly on its trunk and larger branches. [Port. < Tupi *iauoti kaua*, having branches tipped with black fruit.]

ja·cal (hä-käl′) *n.*, *pl.* **-ca·les** (-kä′lās) or **-cals** A thatch-roofed hut made of wattle and daub found in Mexico and the southwest United States. [Am.Sp. < Nahuatl *xahcalli* : *xamitl, xam-, xah-,* adobe + *calli,* house.]

jac·a·mar (jăk′ə-mär′) *n.* Any of various tropical American birds of the family Galbulidae, having iridescent plumage and a long bill. [Fr., poss. of Tupian orig.]

ja·ça·na (zhä′sə-nä′) also **ja·ca·na** (-kə-) *n.* Any of several tropical water birds of the family Jacanidae, having long toes for walking on floating vegetation. [Port. *jaçanã* < Tupi *jaçanam, jaçanã,* one that cries out.]

jac·a·ran·da (jăk′ə-răn′də) *n.* **1.** Any of several tropical American trees or shrubs of the genus *Jacaranda* having pinnately compound leaves and pale purple flowers. **2.** The wood of this tree or a wood similar to it. [Port. *jacarandá* < Tupi, having a hard core, hard branch.]

ja·cinth (jā′sĭnth, jăs′ĭnth) *n.* See **hyacinth** 1a. [ME *jacinte,* ult. < Lat. *hyacinthus.* See HYACINTH.]

jack (jăk) *n.* **1.** often **Jack** *Informal* A man; a fellow. **2a.** One who does odd or heavy jobs; a laborer. **b.** One who works in a specified manual trade. Often used in combination: *a lumberjack.* **c.** **Jack** A sailor; a tar. **3.** *Games* A playing card showing the figure of a servant or soldier and ranking below a queen. **4.** *Games* **a.** **jacks** (*used with a sing.* or *pl. verb*) A game played with small six-pointed metal pieces and a small ball, the object being to pick up the pieces in various combinations. **b.** One of the metal pieces so used. **5.** *Sports* A pin used in some games of bowling. **6a.** A usu. portable device for raising heavy objects, as by means of a lever. **b.** A wooden wedge for cleaving rock. **7.** *Nautical* **a.** A support or brace, esp. the iron crosstree on a topgallant masthead. **b.** A small flag flown at the bow of a ship. **8.** The male of certain animals, esp. the ass. **9.** Any of several food and game fishes of the family Carangidae, found in tropical and temperate seas. **10.** A jackrabbit. **11.** A socket that accepts a plug at one end and attaches to electric circuitry at the other. **12.** *Slang* Money. **13.** Applejack. **14.** *Slang* A small or worthless amount: *You don't know jack about that.* ❖ *v.* **jacked, jack·ing, jacks** —*tr.* **1.** To hunt or fish for with a jacklight. **2a.** To move or hoist by or as if by using a jack: *jacked up the car.* **b.** To raise (something) to a higher level: *jacked up the price.* —*intr.* To hunt or fish for quarry by using a jacklight. —*phrasal verb:* **jack off** *Vulgar Slang* To masturbate. [< the name *Jack* < ME *Jakke,* poss. < OFr. *Jacques* < LLat. *Iaco-*

bus; see JACOB. N., sense 14, short for JACK SHIT.] —**jack′er** *n.*

jack·al (jăk′əl, -ôl′) *n.* **1.** Any of several doglike mammals of the genus *Canis* of Africa and southern Asia that are mainly foragers. **2a.** An accomplice or a lackey who aids in the commission of base or disreputable acts. **b.** One who performs menial tasks for another. [Turk. *chakāl* < Pers. *shaghāl* < M Indic *shagāl* < Skt. *śṛgālaḥ.*]

jack·a·napes (jăk′ə-nāps′) *n.* **1.** A conceited or impudent person. **2.** A mischievous child. **3.** *Archaic* A monkey or an ape. [< ME *Jack Napis,* nickname of William de la Pole, 4th Earl and 1st Duke of Suffolk (1396–1450).]

jack·ass (jăk′ăs′) *n.* **1.** A male ass or donkey. **2.** A foolish or stupid person; a blockhead.

jack bean *n.* A tropical American annual plant (*Canavalia ensiformis*) having long pods with edible seeds.

jack·boot also **jack-boot** (jăk′boot′) *n.* **1.** A stout military boot that extends above the knee. **2.** A person who uses bullying tactics, esp. to force compliance. **3.** The spirit sustaining and motivating a militaristic or totalitarian regime or system.

jack·boot·ed also **jack-boot·ed** (jăk′boo′tĭd) *adj.* **1.** Wearing jackboots. **2.** Cruelly and violently oppressive.

jack cheese *n.* Monterey jack. [After David *Jacks,* 19th-cent. California landowner.]

jack crevalle *n.* See **crevalle jack.**

jack·daw (jăk′dô′) *n.* A Eurasian bird (*Corvus monedula*) related to the crows.

jack·et (jăk′ĭt) *n.* **1.** A short coat usu. extending to the hips. **2.** An outer covering or casing, esp.: **a.** The skin of a potato. **b.** The dust jacket of a book or phonograph record. **c.** An insulation covering, as for a steam pipe. **d.** An open envelope or folder for filing papers. **e.** The outer metal shell or case of a bullet. ❖ *tr.v.* **-et·ed, -et·ing, -ets** To supply or cover with a jacket. [ME *jaket* < OFr. *jaquet,* dim. of *jaque,* short jacket, tunic < *jacques,* nickname for Fr. peasants (< the name *Jacques;* see JACK), or < Catalan *jaco* (perh. < Ar. *šakk,* mailcoat).] —**jack′et·ed** *adj.*

Jack Frost *n.* Frost or cold weather personified.

jack·fruit (jăk′froot′) *n.* **1.** A tropical Asian tree (*Artocarpus heterophyllus*) having large edible fruits, unisexual flowers, and fine-grained durable wood. **2.** The fruit of this tree. [Port. *jaca* (< Malayalam *cakkai*) + FRUIT.]

jack·ham·mer (jăk′hăm′ər) *n.* A hand-held machine for drilling rock and breaking up pavement, operated by compressed air. —**jack′ham′mer** *v.*

jack-in-the-box (jăk′ĭn-thə-bŏks′) *n.*, *pl.* **jack-in-the-box·es** or **jacks-in-the-box** (jăks′-) A toy consisting of a clownlike puppet that springs out of a box when the lid is activated.

jack-in-the-pul·pit (jăk′ĭn-thə-pool′pĭt, -pul′-) *n.*, *pl.* **jack-in-the-pulpits** An eastern North American tuberous herb (*Arisaema triphyllum*) having a striped leaflike spathe with a bent blade.

jack·knife (jăk′nīf′) *n.* **1.** A large clasp knife. **2.** *Sports* A dive in the pike position, in which the diver straightens out to enter the water hands first. ❖ *v.* **-knifed, -knif·ing, -knifes** —*tr.* **1.** To fold or double (something or oneself) like a jackknife. **2.** To cut or stab with a jackknife. —*intr.* **1.** To bend or fold up like a jackknife. **2.** To form a 90° angle.

jack·leg (jăk′lĕg′) *adj.* **1.** Lacking skill or training; incompetent. Used esp. of lawyers or preachers. **2.** Unscrupulous or dishonest. **3.** Makeshift; temporary. ❖ *n.* **1.** An unskilled or unscrupulous itinerant worker. **2.** A strikebreaker. [Perh. JACK + (BLACK)LEG.]

jack·light (jăk′līt′) *n.* A light used as a lure in night hunting or fishing. —**jack′light′** *v.*

jack mackerel *n.* A common food and game fish (*Trachurus symmetricus*) of Pacific coastal waters.

jack-of-all-trades (jăk′əv-ôl′trādz′) *n.*, *pl.* **jacks-of-all-trades** (jăks′-) A person who can do many kinds of work.

jack-o′-lan·tern (jăk′ə-lăn′tərn) *n.*, *pl.* **jack-o′-lanterns 1.** A lantern made from a hollowed pumpkin with a carved face, usu. displayed on Halloween. **2.** See **ignis fatuus.** [< earlier *Jack-with-a-lantern,* man with a lantern, will-o′-the-wisp.]

jack pine *n.* An evergreen tree (*Pinus banksiana*) of northern North America with soft wood and short twisted needles.

jack·plane (jăk′plān′) *n.* A bench plane for rough surfacing, usu. slightly over one foot in length.

jack·pot (jăk′pŏt′) *n.* **1a.** The accumulated stakes in a kind of poker that requires one to hold a pair of jacks or better in order to open the betting. **b.** A cumulative pool. **2.** A top prize or reward.

jack·rab·bit (jăk′răb′ĭt) *n.* or **jack rabbit** Any of several large long-eared long-legged hares of the genus *Lepus.* ❖ *intr.v.* **-bit·**

jabot
portrait of Francis, Earl of Huntingdon, by Sir Joshua Reynolds

jaçana
African jaçana
Actophilornis africanus

ă	pat	oi	boy
ā	pay	ou	out
âr	care	ŏŏ	took
ä	father	ōō	boot
ĕ	pet	ŭ	cut
ē	be	ûr	urge
ĭ	pit	th	thin
ī	pie	*th*	this
îr	pier	hw	which
ŏ	pot	zh	vision
ō	toe	ə	about,
ô	paw		item

Stress marks:

′ (primary);

′ (secondary), as in

lexicon (lĕk′sĭ-kŏn′)

Andrew Jackson
1845 portrait by George Peter Alexander Healy (1813–94)

Jesse Jackson

Cheddi Jagan

jaguar
Panthera onca

jai alai

ed, -bit•ing, -bits To move or begin to move rapidly or suddenly. [JACK(ASS) (< its long ears) + RABBIT.] **—jack′rab′bit** *adj.*

Jack Russell terrier *n.* A terrier originating in England, having a small sturdy body, straight legs, and a smooth, mostly white coat that has brown or black markings. [After the Reverend John *Russell* (1795–1883), English clergyman who bred the strain.]

jack•screw (jăk′skro͞o′) *n.* A jack operated by a screw.

jack•shaft (jăk′shăft′) *n.* A short shaft that transmits motion from a motor to a machine, esp. in an automobile.

jack shit *n. Vulgar Slang* A small or worthless amount.

jack•snipe (jăk′snīp′) *n., pl.* **jacksnipe** or **-snipes 1.** An Old World wading bird *(Limnocryptes minima)* having brownish plumage and a long bill. **2.** Any of several similar New World wading birds.

Jack•son (jăk′sən) The cap. of MS, in the W-central part; chosen as cap. in 1821. Pop. 184,256.

Jackson, Andrew Known as "Old Hickory." 1767–1845. The seventh President of the US (1829–37), who objected to the right of individual states to nullify federal laws. **—Jack•so′ni•an** (jăk-sō′nē-ən) *adj. & n.* **—Jack•so′ni•a•nism** *n.*

Jackson, Helen (Maria Fiske) Hunt 1830–85. Amer. writer best known for *Ramona* (1884).

Jackson, Jesse Louis b. 1941. Amer. civil rights leader who directed national antidiscrimination efforts (1966–77).

Jackson, Mahalia 1911–72. Amer. singer whose recordings popularized gospel music.

Jackson, Thomas Jonathan Known as "Stonewall." 1824–63. Amer. Confederate general who commanded troops at Bull Run (1861 and 1862) and directed the Shenandoah Valley campaign (1862).

Jackson Hole A fertile valley of NW WY in the Rocky Mts. E of the Teton Range.

Jack•son•ville (jăk′sən-vĭl′) A city of NE FL on the St. Johns R. near the Atlantic Ocean and the GA border; settled in 1816. Pop. 735,617.

jack•stay (jăk′stā′) *n. Nautical* **1.** A stay used to steady a mast against the forward strain of a gaff. **2.** A rope, rod, or batten along the upper side of a yard, to which a sail is fastened.

jack•stone (jăk′stōn′) *n.* **1. jackstones** *(used with a sing. verb)* The game of jacks. **2.** One of the pieces used in jacks.

jack•straw (jăk′strô′) *n.* **1. jackstraws** *(used with a sing. verb)* A game played with a pile of straws or thin sticks, the object being to remove a single stick without disturbing the others. **2.** One of the straws or sticks used in this game.

jack-tar also **Jack-tar** (jăk′tär′) *n.* A sailor.

Ja•cob (jā′kəb) In the Bible, the son of Isaac whose sons became the progenitors of the 12 tribes of Israel. [LLat. *Iacōbus* < Gk. *Iakōb* < Heb. *ya'ăqōb*, (God) has protected.]

Jac•o•be•an (jăk′ə-bē′ən) *adj.* Of or having to do with the reign of James I of England or his times. ❖ *n.* A prominent figure during this period. [< NLat. *Iacobaeus* < Lat. *Iacōbus*, James, Jacob.]

Jac•o•bin (jăk′ə-bĭn) *n.* **1.** A radical or extreme leftist. **2.** A radical republican during the French Revolution. **3.** A Dominican friar. [ME, Dominican friar < Fr. < OFr. *(frere) jacobin* (transl. of Med.Lat. *(frāter) Iacōbīnus*, Jacobinic brother < *Iacōbus*, James, after the church of St. *Jacques* in Paris, near which the friars built their first convent). Sense 2 < the fact that the Jacobins first met in the convent.] **—Jac′o•bin′ic, Jac′o•bin′i•cal** *adj.* **—Jac′o•bin•ism** *n.* **—Jac′o•bin•ize′** (-bĭ-nīz′) *v.*

Jac•o•bite (jăk′ə-bīt′) *n.* A supporter of James II of England or the Stuart pretenders after 1688. [< Lat. *Iacōbus*, James. See JACOB.] **—Jac′o•bit′i•cal** (-bĭt′ĭ-kəl) *adj.* **—Jac′o•bit•ism** (-bī-tĭz′əm) *n.*

Ja•cobs (jä′kəbz), **Aletta** 1854–1929. Dutch physician who opened the world's first birth control clinic in Amsterdam in 1882.

Jacob's ladder *n.* **1.** *Nautical* A rope or chain ladder with rigid rungs. **2.** Any of various plants of the genus *Polemonium*, esp. *P. caeruleum*, having alternate, pinnately compound leaves with numerous leaflets. [< the ladder seen by the biblical patriarch Jacob in a dream (Genesis 28:12).]

jac•o•net (jăk′ə-nĕt′) *n.* A lightweight cotton cloth resembling lawn used for clothing and bandages. [< Urdu *jagannāthī*, after *Jagannath* (Puri), a town of eastern India.]

jac•quard also **Jac•quard** (jăk′ärd′, jə-kärd′) *n.* **1.** A fabric with an intricately woven pattern. **2.** The loom or method employed in the weaving of a figured fabric. [After Joseph Marie JACQUARD.] **—jac′quard′** *adj.*

Jac•quard (jăk′ärd′, jə-kärd′, zhä-kär′), **Joseph Marie** 1752–1834. French inventor of the jacquard loom (1801), the first automatic loom able to weave complex patterns.

Jac•que•rie (zhä-krē′) *n.* **1.** The uprising of the French peasants against the nobility in 1358. **2. jacquerie** A peasant revolt, esp. a bloody one. [Fr. < OFr. *jacquerie*, peasantry < *jacques*, peasant. See JACKET.]

jac•ti•ta•tion (jăk′tĭ-tā′shən) *n.* **1.** A false boasting or claim. **2.** Extreme restlessness or tossing in bed. [Med.Lat. *iactitātiō*, *iactitātiōn-*, false declaration < Lat. *iactitātus*, p. part. of *iactitāre*, to utter, freq. of *iactāre*, to boast, freq. of *iacere*, to throw.]

Ja•cuz•zi (jə-ko͞o′zē, jă-) A trademark used for a whirlpool bath or a device that swirls water in a bath.

jade¹ (jād) *n.* **1.** Either of two distinct minerals, nephrite and jadeite, that are generally pale green or white and are used mainly as gemstones or in carving. **2.** A carving made of jade. **3.** Jade green. [Fr. *(le) jade*, (the) jade, alteration of *(l')ejade* < Sp. *(piedra de) ijada*, flank (stone) (< the belief that it cured renal colic) < VLat. **īliāta* < Lat. *īlia*, pl. of *īlium*, flank.] **—jade** *adj.*

jade² (jād) *v.* **jad•ed, jad•ing, jades** *—tr.* To wear out, as by overuse or overindulgence. *—intr.* To become weary or spiritless. ❖ *n.* **1.** A broken-down or useless horse; a nag. **2.** A woman regarded as disreputable or shrewish. [ME *iade*, cart-horse, nag; akin to Swed. dialectal *jälda*, mare, poss. of Finno-Ugric orig.]

jad•ed (jā′dĭd) *adj.* **1.** Worn-out; wearied. **2.** Dulled by surfeit; sated. **3.** Cynically or pretentiously callous. **—jad′ed•ly** *adv.* **—jad′ed•ness** *n.*

jade•ite (jā′dīt′) *n.* A rare, valuable, usu. emerald to light green mineral, $NaAlSi_2O_6$, used as a gem and in carving.

jae•ger (yā′gər) *n.* **1.** *(also* jā′gər) Any of several Arctic and Boreal sea birds of the genus *Stercorarius* that harass smaller birds for their food. **2.** A huntsman or hunting attendant. [Ger. *Jäger*, hunter, jaeger, ult. < OHGer. *jagōn*, to hunt.]

Jaf•fa (jăf′ə, yä′fə) See **Yafo.**

Jaff•na (jăf′nə) A city of N Sri Lanka on Palk Strait; center of an ancient Tamil culture until 1617. Pop. 129,000.

jag¹ (jăg) *n.* **1.** A sharp projection; a barb. **2a.** A hanging flap along the edge of a garment. **b.** A slash or slit in a garment exposing material of a different color. ❖ *tr.v.* **jagged, jag•ging, jags 1.** To cut jags in; notch. **2.** To cut unevenly. **3.** *Scots* To jab sharply; prick. [ME *jagge.*] **—jag′ger** *n.*

jag² (jăg) *n.* **1.** *Slang* **a.** A bout of drinking or drug use. **b.** A period of overindulgence in an activity; a spree: *a crying jag.* See Syns at **binge. 2.** A small load or portion. [?]

JAG *abbr.* judge advocate general

Ja•gan (jā′gən), **Cheddi Berret** 1918–97. Guyanese politician who served as president (1992–97).

Jag•a•tai (jăg′ə-tī′) or **Chag•a•tai** (chăg′-) d. 1242. Mongol ruler who succeeded his father, Genghis Khan.

jag•ged (jăg′ĭd) *adj.* **1.** Marked by irregular projections and indentations on the edge or surface. **2.** Having a rough or harsh quality. **—jag′ged•ly** *adv.* **—jag′ged•ness** *n.*

jag•ger•y (jăg′ə-rē) *n.* Unrefined sugar made from palm sap. [Port. dialectal *jágara*, ult. < Skt. *śarkarā*, sugar, grit.]

jag•gy (jăg′ē) *adj.* **-gi•er, -gi•est** Jagged or serrated.

jag•uar (jăg′wär′, jăg′yo͞o-är′) *n.* A large feline mammal *(Panthera onca)* of Central and South America, closely related to the leopard and having a tawny coat spotted with black rosettes. [Sp. and Port. < Guarani *jaguá, yaguar*, dog.]

jag•ua•run•di also **jag•ua•ron•di** (jăg′wə-rŭn′dē) *n., pl.* **-dis** A long-tailed grayish-brown wildcat *(Felis yagouaroundi)* of tropical America. [Sp. and Port. < Guarani *jaguarundi, yaguarundi*, var. of *jaguá, yaguar*, dog.]

Jah (jä) *n.* In Rastafarianism, God or Jehovah. [Heb. *yāh.*]

Jah•veh (yä′vā, -vĕ) or **Jah•weh** (-wā, -wĕ) *n.* Variants of **Yahweh.**

jai a•lai (hī′ lī′, hī′ ə-lī′, hī′ ə-lī′) *n.* A court game in which players use a long hand-shaped basket strapped to the wrist to propel a ball against a wall. [Sp. < Basque : *jai*, festival + *alai*, joyous.]

jail (jāl) *n.* **1.** A place for the confinement of persons in lawful detention, esp. persons awaiting trial under local jurisdiction. **2.** Detention in a jail. ❖ *tr.v.* **jailed, jail•ing, jails** To detain in or as if in a jail. [ME *jaiole* (< OFr.) and ME *gaiol, gaol* (< ONFr. *gaiole*), both < VLat. **gaviola* < Lat. **caveola*, dim. of *cavea*, cage, hollow.]

jail•bait (jāl′bāt′) *n. Slang* A person below the age of consent with whom sexual intercourse can constitute statutory rape.

jail•bird (jāl′bûrd′) *n. Informal* A prisoner or an ex-convict.

jail•break (jāl′brāk′) *n.* An escape from jail.

jail•er also **jail•or** (jā′lər) *n.* A keeper of a jail.

jail•house (jāl′hous′) *n.* A place for confining prisoners; a jail.

Jain (jīn) also **Jai•na** (jī′nə) *n.* A believer or follower of Jainism. [Hindi *jaina* < Skt. *jaina-*, relating to the saints < *jinaḥ*, saint, victor < *jayati*, he conquers.]

Jain•ism (jī′nĭz′əm) *n.* An ascetic religion of India, founded in the sixth century B.C., that teaches the immortality and transmigration of the soul and denies the existence of a perfect or supreme being. **—Jain′ist** *adj.*

Jai•pur (jī′po͝or′) A city of NW India SSW of Delhi; founded 1728. Pop. 1,458,483.

Ja•kar•ta or **Dja•kar•ta** (jə-kär′tə) Formerly **Ba•ta•vi•a** (bə-tā′vē-ə) The cap. of Indonesia, on the NE coast of Java; founded c. 1619 by the Dutch. Pop. 8,259,266.

jake (jāk) *adj. Slang* Suitable or satisfactory; fine. [?]

jakes (jāks) *pl.n. (used with a sing. or pl. verb) Chiefly British* A latrine; a privy. [Perh. < Fr. *Jacques*, James, Jack.]

Ja•kob-Creutz•feldt disease (yä′kôp-kroits′fĕlt) *n.* See **Creutzfeldt-Jakob disease.**

Ja•kob•son (yä′kəb-sən), **Roman** 1896–1982. Russian-born Amer. linguist and founder of modern structural linguistics and modern phonology.

jal•ap (jăl′əp, jä′ləp) *n.* **1.** A twining eastern Mexican vine *(Ipomoea purga* syn. *I. jalapa)* having tuberous roots that are dried and powdered for use as a cathartic. **2.** Any of several similar or related plants. **3.** The dried roots of these plants. [Fr. < Am.Sp. *jalapa*, short for *(purga de) Jalapa*, (purgative of) Jalapa, after JA-LAPA.]

Ja·la·pa (hə-lä′pə, hä-lä′pä) A city of E-central Mexico E of Mexico City; built on the site of a pre-Columbian city. Pop. 279,451.

ja·la·pe·ño (hä′lə-pān′yō) n., pl. **-ños 1.** A cultivar of the tropical pepper *Capsicum annuum* having a very pungent green or red fruit used in cooking. **2.** The fruit of this plant. [Am.Sp. *(chile) jalapeño*, (chile) of Jalapa, after JALAPA.]

ja·lop·y (jə-lŏp′ē) n., pl. **-ies** Informal An old dilapidated motor vehicle, esp. an automobile. [?]

jal·ou·sie (jăl′ə-sē) n. A blind or shutter having adjustable horizontal slats. [Fr. < *jalousie*, jealousy < OFr. *gelosie* < *gelos*, jealous. See JEALOUS.]

jam¹ (jăm) v. **jammed, jam·ming, jams** —tr. **1.** To drive or wedge forcibly into a tight position. **2.** To activate or apply (a brake) suddenly. Often used with *on*: *jam on the brakes on.* **3.** To cause (moving parts, for example) to lock into an unworkable position. **4a.** To pack (items, for example) to excess; cram. **b.** To fill (something) to excess. **5.** To block, congest, or clog. **6.** To crush or bruise. **7.** *Electronics* To interfere with or prevent the clear reception of (broadcast signals). —intr. **1.** To become wedged or stuck. **2.** To become inoperable. **3.** To force one's way into or through a limited space. **4.** *Music* To participate in a jam session. ❖ n. **1.** The act of jamming or the condition of being jammed. **2.** A crush or congestion of people or things in a limited space. **3.** A trying situation; a predicament. [?] —**jam′ma·ble** adj. —**jam′mer** n.

jam² (jăm) n. A preserve made from whole fruit boiled to a pulp with sugar. [Poss. < JAM¹.] —**jam′my** adj.

Ja·mai·ca (jə-mā′kə) An island country in the Caribbean Sea S of Cuba; gained independence from Great Britain in 1962. Cap. Kingston. Pop. 2,496,000. —**Ja·mai′can** adj. & n.

jamb also **jambe** (jăm) n. **1.** One of a pair of vertical posts or pieces that together form the sides of a door, for example. **2.** A projecting mass or columnar part. [ME *jambe* < OFr., leg, jamb < LLat. *gamba*, horse's hock, leg. See GAMBOL.]

jam·ba·lay·a (jŭm′bə-lī′ə) n. A spicy Creole dish consisting mainly of rice cooked with shrimp, oysters, ham, or chicken. [Louisiana Fr. < Provençal *jambalaia.*]

jam·beau (jăm′bō) n., pl. **-beaux** (-bōz) A piece of armor for the leg below the knee. [ME, prob. < ONFr. **jambeau* < OFr. *jambe*, leg, jamb. See JAMB.]

jam·bo·ree (jăm′bə-rē′) n. **1.** A noisy celebration. **2.** A large assembly, esp. of Boy Scouts or Girl Scouts. **3.** A mass gathering or assembly, as of a political party. [?]

James (jāmz) n. See table at **Bible.** [Ult. < LLat. *Iacomus*, var. of *Iacobus*, Iacob, Jacob. See JACOB.]

James¹, Saint. Known as "the Great." d. A.D. 44. One of the 12 Apostles, the son of Zebedee and brother of John.

James², Saint. Known as "the Less." d. c. A.D. 62. Christian leader traditionally regarded as the author of the Epistle of James.

James³, Saint. fl. 1st cent. A.D. One of the 12 Apostles.

James I 1566–1625. King of England (1603–25) and of Scotland as James VI (1567–1625) whose belief in the divine right of kings led to the English Civil War.

James II 1633–1701. King of England, Scotland, and Ireland (1685–88). The last Stuart king to rule both England and Scotland, he was overthrown by his son-in-law William of Orange.

James, C(yril) L(ionel) R(obert) 1901–89. Trinidadian author and historian noted esp. for *The Black Jacobins: Toussaint L'Ouverture and the San Domingo Revolution* (1938).

James, Henry 1843–1916. Amer. writer whose works include *The Bostonians* (1886) and *The Golden Bowl* (1904).

James, Jesse 1847–82. Amer. outlaw who led a group of armed brigands that for 15 years robbed banks and trains.

James, William 1842–1910. Amer. psychologist and philosopher whose works include *The Varieties of Religious Experience* (1902).

James Bay The S arm of Hudson Bay, in E-central Canada between NE Ontario and W Quebec.

James·i·an (jām′zē-ən) adj. **1.** Of, relating to, or characteristic of William James, his philosophy, or his teachings. **2.** Of, relating to, or characteristic of Henry James or his writings.

James River 1. A river rising in central ND and flowing c. 1,142 km (710 mi) across SD to the Missouri R. **2.** A river rising in central VA and flowing c. 547 km (340 mi) to Chesapeake Bay.

James·town (jāmz′toun′) **1.** The cap. of St. Helena in the S Atlantic Ocean. Pop. 1,516. **2.** A former village of SE VA. The first permanent English settlement in America, it was founded in May 1607.

Ja·mi·son (jā′mĭ-sən), **Judith** b. 1944. Amer. dancer and choreographer who became director of the Alvin Ailey American Dance Theater in 1989.

jam·mies (jăm′ēz) pl.n. Informal Pajamas. [Shortening and alteration of PAJAMAS.]

jam·min′ (jăm′ən) adj. Slang Excellent; first-rate. [< JAM¹.]

Jam·mu (jŭm′ōō) A city of N India near the Pakistan border S of Srinagar. Pop. 206,135.

Jammu and Kashmir A former princely state of N India and Pakistan; annexed by British India in 1846 and partitioned after

fierce fighting (1947–49). Both India and Pakistan have continued to claim jurisdiction over the whole territory.

Jam·na·gar (jăm-nŭg′ər) A city of W India on the Gulf of Kutch SW of Ahmadabad; founded 1540. Pop. 341,637.

jam-pack (jăm′păk′) tr.v. **-packed, -pack·ing, -packs** Informal To crowd to capacity: *The room was jam-packed.*

jam session n. **1.** An informal gathering of musicians to play improvised or unrehearsed music. **2.** Informal An impromptu discussion.

Jam·shed·pur (jăm′shĕd-pōŏr′) A city of E India WNW of Calcutta. Pop. 460,577.

jam-up (jăm′ŭp′) n. A congested situation; a jam.

Jan. abbr. January

Ja·ná·ček (yä′nə-chĕk′), **Leoš** 1854–1928. Czech composer whose works include *Jenůfa* (1904).

Jane Doe (jān) n. **1.** Used as a name in legal proceedings to designate an unknown or unidentified woman or girl. **2.** An average or ordinary woman.

jan·gle (jăng′gəl) v. **-gled, -gling, -gles** —intr. To make a harsh metallic sound. —tr. **1.** To cause to make a harsh discordant sound. **2.** To have an irritating effect on: *The noise jangled my nerves.* ❖ n. A harsh metallic sound. [ME *janglen*, to chatter < OFr. *jangler*, prob. of Gmc. orig.] —**jan′gler** n.

jan·is·sar·y (jăn′ĭ-sĕr′ē) also **jan·i·zar·y** (-zĕr′ē) n., pl. **-ies 1.** A member of a group of elite, highly loyal supporters. **2.** A soldier in an elite Turkish guard organized in the 14th century and abolished in 1826. [Fr. *janissaire*, ult. < Ottoman Turk. *yañi cheri*, new army : *yañi*, new + *cheri*, special troops (ult. < MPers. *chēr*, brave, victorious).]

jan·i·tor (jăn′ĭ-tər) n. **1.** One who attends to the maintenance or cleaning of a building. **2.** A doorman. [Lat. *iānitor*, doorkeeper < *iānua*, door < *iānus*, archway. See ei- in App.] —**jan′i·to′ri·al** (-tôr′ē-əl, -tōr′-) adj.

Jan May·en Island (yän mī′ən) An island in the Greenland Sea between Norway and Greenland; annexed by Norway in 1929.

Jan·sen (jăn′sən, yän′-), **Cornelis** 1585–1638. Dutch theologian and founder of the Jansenist movement, whose adherents included Blaise Pascal and Jean Racine.

Jan·sen·ism (jăn′sə-nĭz′əm) n. The theological principles of Cornelis Jansen, which emphasize predestination, deny free will, and maintain that human nature is incapable of good. —**Jan′sen·ist** n. —**Jan′sen·is′tic** adj.

Jan·u·ar·y (jăn′yōō-ĕr′ē) n., pl. **-ies** The first month of the year in the Gregorian calendar. See table at **calendar.** [Ult. < Lat. *Iānuārius (mēnsis)*, (month) of Janus < *Iānus*, Janus. See ei- in App.]

Ja·nus (jā′nəs) n. **1.** *Roman Mythology* The god of gates and doorways, depicted with two faces looking in opposite directions. **2.** A satellite of Saturn. [Lat. *Iānus* < *iānus*, archway. See ei- in App.]

Ja·nus-faced (jā′nəs-fāst′) adj. Hypocritical.

Janus word n. A word having opposite or contradictory meanings, as *sanction* or *cleave.*

Jap (jăp) n. Offensive Slang Used as a disparaging term for a person of Japanese birth or descent.

JAP (jăp) n. Offensive Slang A Jewish-American girl or woman regarded as being pampered or overindulged. [J(ewish) A(merican) P(rincess).]

ja·pan (jə-păn′) n. **1.** A black enamel or lacquer used to produce a durable glossy finish. **2.** An object decorated with this substance. ❖ tr.v. **-panned, -pan·ning, -pans 1.** To decorate with japan. **2.** To coat with a glossy finish. [After JAPAN.]

Japan A country of Asia on an archipelago off the NE coast of the mainland; traditionally settled c. 660 B.C. Cap. Tokyo. Pop. 124,961,000.

Japan, Sea of An enclosed arm of the W Pacific Ocean between Japan and the Asian mainland.

Japan clover n. An annual plant (*Lespedeza striata*) of China and Japan having compound leaves with many leaflets.

Japan Current n. A warm ocean current flowing northeast from the Philippine Sea past southeast Japan to the North Pacific.

Jap·a·nese (jăp′ə-nēz′, -nēs′) adj. Of or relating to Japan or its people, language, or culture. ❖ n., pl. **Japanese 1a.** A native or inhabitant of Japan. **b.** A person of Japanese ancestry. **2.** The language of the Japanese.

Japanese andromeda n. An ornamental shrub (*Pieris japonica*) native to Japan and having small white flowers.

Japanese beetle n. A metallic green and brown beetle (*Popillia japonica*) native to eastern Asia, the larvae and adults of which damage various crop plants in North America.

Japanese cedar n. An eastern Asian coniferous evergreen tree (*Cryptomeria japonica*) having curved, spirally arranged leaves and cultivated as an ornamental and timber tree.

Japanese clover n. See **Japan clover.**

Japanese iris n. A Japanese ornamental plant (*Iris kaempferi*) having large, variously colored showy flowers.

Japanese ivy n. See **Boston ivy.**

Japanese maple n. An eastern Asian shrub or tree (*Acer palmatum*) cultivated for its decorative, often reddish foliage.

Japanese quail n. See **coturnix.**

Japanese quince n. A Chinese ornamental shrub (*Chaenomeles*

Jamaica

Japan

ă	pat	oi	boy
ā	pay	ou	out
âr	care	ŏŏ	took
ä	father	ōō	boot
ĕ	pet	ŭ	cut
ē	be	ûr	urge
ĭ	pit	th	thin
ī	pie	*th*	this
îr	pier	hw	which
ŏ	pot	zh	vision
ō	toe	ə	about,
ô	paw		item

Stress marks:
′ (primary);
′ (secondary), as in
lexicon (lĕk′sĭ-kŏn′)

speciosa) having spiny branches and red or white flowers.

Japanese radish *n.* See **daikon**.

Japanese river fever *n.* See **scrub typhus**.

Japanese spurge *n.* See **pachysandra**.

Jap·a·nize (jăp′ə-nīz′) *tr. & intr.v.* **-nized, -niz·ing, -niz·es** To make or become Japanese in form, idiom, style, or character. —**Jap′a·ni·za′tion** (-nĭ-zā′shən) *n.*

Japan wax *n.* A pale yellow solid wax obtained from the berries of plant species of the genus *Rhus.*

jape (jāp) *v.* **japed, jap·ing, japes** —*intr.* To joke or quip. —*tr.* To make sport of. ❖ *n.* A joke or quip. [ME *japen,* prob. < OFr. *japer,* to yap, chatter, nag, of imit. orig.] —**jap′er** *n.* —**jap′er·y** *n.*

Ja·pheth (jā′fĭth′, jăf′ĭth) In the Bible, a son of Noah and the brother of Shem and Ham.

Ja·phet·ic (jə-fĕt′ĭk) *adj.* Of or relating to Japheth or his descendants.

ja·pon·i·ca (jə-pŏn′ĭ-kə) *n.* An ornamental shrub (*Chaenomeles japonica*) native to Japan and cultivated for its red flowers. [NLat., species name < *Japonia,* Japan.]

Jap·o·nism (jăp′ə-nĭz′əm) *n.* **1.** Something characteristically Japanese. **2.** The influence of Japan on European art, esp. in impressionism. [Fr. *japonisme* < *Japon,* Japan.]

Ja·pu·rá (zhä′pŏŏ-rä′) A river rising in SW Colombia and flowing *c.* 2,816 km (1,750 mi) to the Amazon R.

jar[1] (jär) *n.* **1.** A cylindrical glass or earthenware vessel with a wide mouth and usu. no handles. **2.** The amount that a jar can hold. **3.** *Chiefly British* A glass of beer. ❖ *tr.v.* **jarred, jar·ring, jars** To put into a jar. [ME *jarre,* a liquid measure < OFr. (< Provençal *jarra*) and < Med.Lat. *jarra,* both < Ar. *jarra,* earthen jar < *jarra,* to draw, pull.] —**jar′ful′** *n.*

jar[2] (jär) *v.* **jarred, jar·ring, jars** —*intr.* **1.** To make or utter a harsh sound. **2.** To be disturbing or irritating; grate: *The noise jarred on my nerves.* **3.** To shake or shiver from impact. **4.** To clash or conflict. —*tr.* **1.** To bump or cause to move or shake from impact. **2.** To startle or unsettle; shock. ❖ *n.* **1.** A jolt; a shock. **2.** Harsh or grating sound; discord. [Perh. of imit. orig.] —**jar′ring·ly** *adv.*

jar·di·nière (jär′dn-îr′, zhär′dn-yâr′) *n.* **1.** A large decorative stand or pot for plants or flowers. **2.** Finely cut vegetables usu. blanched and served as a garnish. [Fr. < fem. of *jardinier,* gardener < OFr. < *jardin,* garden. See GARDEN.]

jar·gon (jär′gən) *n.* **1.** Nonsensical, incoherent, or meaningless talk. **2.** A hybrid language or dialect; a pidgin. **3.** The specialized or technical language of a trade, for example. **4.** Speech or writing having unusual or pretentious vocabulary, convoluted phrasing, and vague meaning. ❖ *intr.v.* **-goned, -gon·ing, -gons** To speak in or use jargon. [ME *jargoun* < OFr. *jargon,* prob. of imit. orig.] —**jar′gon·ist, jar′gon·eer′** *n.* —**jar′gon·is′tic** *adj.*

jar·gon·ize (jär′gə-nīz′) *v.* **-ized, -iz·ing, -iz·es** —*tr.* To translate into jargon. —*intr.* To talk or write jargon.

jarl (yärl) *n.* A medieval Scandinavian chieftain or nobleman. [ON.]

Jarls·berg (yärlz′bûrg′) A trademark used for a mild, pale yellow, hard Norwegian cheese with large holes.

jar·rah (jăr′ə) *n.* An Australian tree (*Eucalyptus marginata*) widely grown for its hard red-brown wood. [Nyungar (Aboriginal language of SW Australia) *jarilʸ.*]

Jar·rell (jə-rĕl′), **Randall** 1914–65. Amer. poet and critic whose works include *Little Friend, Little Friend* (1945).

Jar·rett (jăr′ĭt), **Keith** b. 1945. Amer. pianist and composer best known for his solo jazz improvisations.

Jas. *abbr.* Bible James

jas·mine (jăz′mĭn) *also* **jes·sa·mine** (jĕs′ə-mĭn) *n.* **1a.** Any of several vines or shrubs of the genus *Jasminum,* native chiefly to Asia and having usu. compound leaves and often fragrant white or yellow flowers. **b.** A perfume obtained from these plants. **2.** See **Carolina jasmine**. **3.** Any of several plants or shrubs having fragrant flowers. **4.** A light to brilliant yellow. [Fr. *jasmin* < OFr. *jassemin* < Ar. *yasmīn* < Pers. *yasmīn, yāsman* < MPers. *yāsman.*]

Ja·son (jā′sən) *n. Greek Mythology* The husband of Medea and leader of the Argonauts who went in quest of the Golden Fleece.

jas·per (jăs′pər) *n.* An opaque cryptocrystalline variety of quartz that may be red, yellow, or brown. [ME *jaspre* < AN < Lat. *iaspis, iaspid-* < Gk. < Pers. *yašm, yašb* < Ar. *yašb;* akin to Heb. *yāšpê,* perh. < blend of Akkadian *yašpu,* chalcedony (sense uncertain) and Akkadian *ašpû,* jasper (perh. of Sumerian orig.).]

Jas·pers (yäs′pərs), **Karl Theodor** 1883–1969. German psychiatrist, philosopher, and theologian who was a founder of modern existentialism.

jasper ware *or* **jas·per·ware** (jăs′pər-wâr′) *n.* A white stoneware often colored by metallic oxides and having raised white designs.

Jat (jät) *n.* A member of a peasant caste residing in the Punjab and other areas of northern India and Pakistan. [Hindi *jāṭ;* prob. akin to Skt. *Jartikaḥ,* tribal name.]

ja·to (jā′tō) *n., pl.* **-tos 1.** An aircraft takeoff aided by an auxiliary jet or rocket. **2.** An auxiliary jet-producing unit providing additional thrust for a takeoff. [*j(et-)a(ssisted) t(ake)o(ff).*]

jaun·dice (jôn′dĭs, jän′-) *n.* **1.** Yellowish tissue discoloration, as of the skin, that occurs as a symptom of various diseases that af-

fect the processing of bile. **2.** A state or feeling of negativity or bitterness arising esp. from world-weariness. ❖ *tr.v.* **-diced, -dic·ing, -dic·es 1.** To affect with jaundice. **2.** To affect with the negativity or bitterness of jaundice. [ME *jaundis* < OFr. *jaunice* < *jaune, jalne,* yellow < Lat. *galbinus,* yellowish.]

jaun·diced (jôn′dĭst, jän′-) *adj.* **1.** Affected with jaundice. **2.** Yellow or yellowish. **3.** Affected by or exhibiting envy, prejudice, or hostility.

jaunt (jônt, jänt) *n.* A short trip or excursion, usu. for pleasure; an outing. ❖ *intr.v.* **jaunt·ed, jaunt·ing, jaunts** To make a short journey. [?]

jaun·ty (jôn′tē, jän′-) *adj.* **-ti·er, -ti·est 1.** Having a buoyant or self-confident air; brisk. **2.** Crisp and dapper in appearance. **3.** *Archaic* **a.** Stylish. **b.** Genteel. [Fr. *gentil,* nice < OFr., noble. See GENTLE.] —**jaun′ti·ly** *adv.* —**jaun′ti·ness** *n.*

Jau·rès (zhô-rĕs′), **Jean** 1859–1914. French journalist and leader of the French Socialist Party before World War I.

Jav. *abbr.* Javanese

ja·va (jä′və, jăv′ə) *n. Informal* Brewed coffee. [After JAVA[1].]

Java[1] An island of Indonesia separated from Borneo by the **Java Sea,** an arm of the W Pacific Ocean.

Java[2] A trademark used for a programming language designed to develop applications, esp. ones for the Internet, that can operate on different platforms.

Java man *n.* Pithecanthropus.

Jav·a·nese (jăv′ə-nēz′, -nēs′, jä′və-) *adj.* Of or relating to Java or its people, language, or culture. ❖ *n., pl.* **Javanese 1.** A native or inhabitant of Java, esp. a member of the Javanese-speaking majority. **2.** The Austronesian language of the principal ethnic group of Java. [JAVA[1] + *-nese* (as in JAPANESE).]

Ja·va·rí (zhä′və-rē′) A river rising in E Peru and flowing *c.* 965 km (600 mi) to the Amazon R.

Java sparrow *n.* A small grayish bird (*Padda oryzivora*) native to tropical Asia and often kept as a cage bird.

jave·lin (jăv′lĭn, jăv′ə-) *n.* **1.** A light spear thrown with the hand and used as a weapon. **2.** *Sports* **a.** A metal or metal-tipped spear thrown for distance in track and field competitions. **b.** The athletic field event in which a javelin is thrown. [ME < OFr. *javeline,* dim. of *javelot,* of Celt. orig.]

ja·ve·li·na (hä′və-lē′nə) *n.* See **collared peccary**. [Alteration of Sp. *jabalina,* fem. of *jabalí, jabalín,* wild boar < Ar. (*ḥinzīr*) *jabalī,* mountain (swine) < *jabal,* mountain.]

Ja·velle water *also* **Ja·vel water** (zhə-vĕl′) *n.* An aqueous solution of potassium or sodium hypochlorite, used as a disinfectant and bleaching agent. [Transl. of Fr. *eau de Javel,* after *Javel,* a former town of north-central France.]

jaw (jô) *n.* **1a.** Either of two bony or cartilaginous structures that in most vertebrates form the framework of the mouth and hold the teeth. **b.** The mandible or maxilla or the part of the face covering these bones. **c.** Any of various structures of invertebrates that have an analogous function to vertebrate jaws. **2.** Either of two opposed hinged parts in a mechanical device. **3. jaws** The walls of a pass, canyon, or cavern. **4. jaws** A dangerous situation or confrontation. **5.** *Slang* **a.** Impudent argument or back talk. **b.** A conversation or chat. ❖ *intr.v.* **jawed, jaw·ing, jaws** *Slang* **1.** To talk vociferously; jabber. **2.** To talk; converse. [ME *jawe,* perh. < OFr. *joue,* cheek.] —**jaw′less** *adj.*

jaw·bone (jô′bōn′) *n.* A bone of the jaw, esp. the bone of the lower jaw. ❖ *v.* **-boned, -bon·ing, -bones** *Slang* —*tr.* To try to influence or pressure through strong persuasion. —*intr.* To urge compliance with official wishes or guidelines.

jaw·break·er (jô′brā′kər) *n.* **1.** A very hard candy. **2.** *Slang* A word that is difficult to pronounce. **3.** A machine that crushes rock or ore. —**jaw′break′ing** *adj.*

jawless fish *n.* Any of several eellike marine and freshwater fishes that lack a jaw and constitute the subphylum Agnatha, including the lampreys.

Jaws of Life A trademark used for a pneumatic pincerlike metal device that is inserted into the body of a wrecked vehicle and opened to provide access to people trapped inside.

jay[1] (jā) *n.* The letter *j.*

jay[2] (jā) *n.* **1.** Any of various often crested birds of the genera *Garrulus, Cyanocitta, Aphelocoma,* and related genera within the family Corvidae, often having a loud harsh call. **2.** A very talkative person; a chatterbox. [ME *jai* < OFr. < LLat. *gāius, gāia,* perh. < Lat. *Gāius,* personal name.]

Jay, John 1745–1829. Amer. diplomat and jurist; first chief justice of the US Supreme Court (1789–95).

jay·bird (jā′bûrd′) *n.* See **jay**[2] 1.

Jay·cee (jā′sē′) *n.* A member of a junior chamber of commerce.

jay·hawk·er (jā′hô′kər) *n.* **1.** One of the free-soil guerrillas in Kansas and Missouri during the border disputes of 1854 to 1859. **2.** A Unionist guerrilla. **3. Jayhawker** *Informal* A native or resident of Kansas. [< *jayhawk,* a fictitious bird.]

jay·vee (jā′vē′) *n.* **1.** Junior varsity. **2.** A member of a junior varsity. —**jay′vee′** *adj.*

jay·walk (jā′wôk′) *intr.v.* **-walked, -walk·ing, -walks** To cross a street illegally or in a reckless manner. [< JAY[2], inexperienced person.] —**jay′walk′er** *n.*

jazz (jăz) *n.* **1.** *Music* **a.** A style of music, native to America and characterized by strong but flexible rhythms, with solo and en-

javelin

semble improvisations on basic tunes and chord patterns. **b.** Big band dance music. **2.** *Slang* **a.** Animation; enthusiasm. **b.** Nonsense. **c.** Miscellaneous, unspecified things. ❖ *v.* **jazzed, jazz·ing, jazz·es** —*tr.* **1.** *Music* To play in a jazz style. **2.** *Slang* **a.** To utter exaggerations or lies to. **b.** To give great pleasure to; excite. —*intr. Slang* To exaggerate or lie. —**phrasal verb: jazz up** *Slang* To make more interesting; enliven. [Earlier *jaz, jazz,* pep, vim, vigor (baseball slang).] —**jazz'er** *n.*

jazz·fu·sion (jăz-fyōō′zhən) *n.* See **fusion** 5.

jazz·man (jăz′măn′, -mən) *n.* A jazz musician or composer.

jazz-rock (jăz′rŏk′) *n.* See **fusion** 5.

jazz·y (jăz′ē) *adj.* **-i·er, -i·est 1.** Resembling jazz in form or nature; rhythmical. **2.** *Slang* Showy; flashy: *a jazzy car.* —**jazz'i·ly** *adv.* —**jazz'i·ness** *n.*

Jb *abbr. Bible* Job

J-bar (jā′bär′) *n.* A J-shaped bar, suspended from overhead cables, by which a skier is towed uphill.

J.C. *abbr.* **1.** Jesus Christ **2.** Julius Caesar **3.** jurisconsult

JCD *abbr. Latin* Juris Canonici Doctor (Doctor of Canon Law)

JCS *abbr.* Joint Chiefs of Staff

jct. *abbr.* junction

Jd *abbr. Bible* Jude

JD *abbr.* **1.** *Latin* Juris Doctor (Doctor of Law) **2.** Justice Department **3.** juvenile delinquent

Jdt. *abbr. Bible* Judith

Je *abbr. Bible* Jeremiah

jeal·ous (jĕl′əs) *adj.* **1.** Fearful or wary of being supplanted; apprehensive of losing affection or position. **2a.** Resentful or bitter in rivalry; envious: *jealous of the success of others.* **b.** Inclined to suspect rivalry. **3.** Having to do with or arising from feelings of envy, apprehension, or bitterness. **4.** Vigilant in guarding something. **5.** Intolerant of disloyalty or infidelity; autocratic. [ME *jelous* < OFr. *gelos,* jealous, zealous < VLat. **zēlōsus* < LLat. *zēlus,* zeal. See ZEAL.] —**jeal'ous·ly** *adv.* —**jeal'ous·ness** *n.*

SYNONYMS *jealous, covetous, envious* These adjectives mean resentfully or painfully desirous of another's advantages: *jealous of her success; covetous of his possessions; envious of their art collection.*

jeal·ous·y (jĕl′ə-sē) *n., pl.* **-ies 1.** A jealous attitude or disposition. **2.** Close vigilance.

jean (jēn) *n.* **1.** A heavy strong twilled cotton, used in making uniforms and work clothes. **2. jeans** Pants made usu. of jean or denim. [Short for obsolete *jene (fustian),* Genoan (fustian) < ME *jene, gene* < OFr. *Genes,* Genoa.]

Jeanne d'Arc (zhän därk′) See **Joan of Arc.**

Je·bel Mu·sa also **Ge·bel Mu·sa** (jĕb′əl mōō′sə, -sä) A mountain, 851 m (2,790 ft), of N Morocco on the Strait of Gibraltar.

Jed·dah (jĕd′ə) See **Jidda.**

jee (jē) *interj.* Variant of **gee**[3].

jeep (jēp) *n.* A small durable motor vehicle with four-wheel drive, used by the US Army during and after World War II. [Prob. pronunciation of the letters *GP,* designation for this vehicle in the manufacturer's parts numbering system : *G(overnment)* + *P,* designator for 80-inch wheelbase reconnaissance car.]

Jeep A trademark used for a civilian motor vehicle.

jee·pers (jē′pərz) *interj.* Used to express surprise or annoyance. [Alteration of JESUS[1].]

jeer (jîr) *v.* **jeered, jeer·ing, jeers** —*intr.* To speak or shout derisively; mock. —*tr.* To abuse vocally; taunt: *jeered the speaker.* ❖ *n.* A jeering remark or shout. [?] —**jeer'er** *n.*

jeez (jēz) *interj.* Used to express surprise or annoyance. [Alteration of JESUS[1].]

Jef·fers (jĕf′ərz), **(John) Robinson** 1887–1962. Amer. poet whose works include *Tamar and Other Poems* (1924).

Jef·fer·son (jĕf′ər-sən), **Thomas** 1743–1826. The third President of the US (1801–09), who drafted the Declaration of Independence (1776). —**Jef'fer·so'ni·an** (jĕf′ər-sō′nē-ən) *adj. & n.* —**Jef'fer·so'ni·an·ism** *n.*

Jefferson City The cap. of MO, in the central part on the Missouri R.; chosen as cap. in 1821. Pop. 39,636.

Jefferson River A river, c. 402 km (250 mi), of SW MT.

je·had (jĭ-häd′) *n.* Variant of **jihad.**

Je·hosh·a·phat (jə-hŏsh′ə-făt′, -hŏs′-) or **Je·hos·a·phat** (-hŏs′-) 9th cent. B.C. King of Judah who formed an alliance with the kingdom of Israel.

Je·ho·vah (jĭ-hō′və) *n.* God, esp. in Christian translations of the Old Testament. [Blend of the letters of the Tetragrammaton and, with modification, the vowels of ADONAI.]

Je·ho·vah's Witness (jĭ-hō′vəz) *n.* A member of a religious denomination founded in the United States during the late 19th century in which the imminent approach of the millennium is preached and war and organized governmental authority in matters of conscience are strongly opposed.

Je·hu (jē′hyōō) 9th cent. B.C. Israeli king proverbially known for his swift chariot driving.

je·june (jə-jōōn′) *adj.* **1.** Not interesting; dull. **2.** Lacking maturity; childish. **3.** Lacking in nutrition. [< Lat. *iēiūnus,* meager, dry, fasting.] —**je·june'ly** *adv.* —**je·june'ness** *n.*

je·ju·num (jə-jōō′nəm) *n., pl.* **-na** (-nə) The section of the small intestine between the duodenum and the ileum. [ME < Med.Lat. *iēiūnum (intestīnum),* fasting (intestine) (in dissection always being found empty), neut. of Lat. *iēiūnus.*]

Je·kyll and Hyde (jĕk′əl, jē′kəl; hīd′) *n. Informal* One who has a dual personality that alternates between phases of good and evil behavior. [After *The Strange Case of Dr. Jekyll and Mr. Hyde* by Robert Louis Stevenson.]

jell (jĕl) *v.* **jelled, jell·ing, jells** —*intr.* **1.** To become firm or gelatinous; congeal. **2.** To take shape or fall into place; crystallize. —*tr.* **1.** To cause to become firm or gelatinous. **2.** To cause to take shape; make clear and definite; crystallize. [Prob. back-formation < JELLY.]

jel·la·ba (jə-lä′bə) *n.* Variant of **djellaba.**

Jel·li·coe (jĕl′ĭ-kō′), **John Rushworth.** 1st Earl Jellicoe. 1859–1935. British naval officer who commanded the fleet that fought the Germans at Jutland (1916).

jel·lied (jĕl′ēd) *adj.* **1.** Chilled or otherwise congealed into jelly. **2.** Coated with jelly. **3.** Prepared or cooked in or with jelly.

jel·li·fy (jĕl′ə-fī′) *intr. & tr.v.* **-fied, -fy·ing, -fies** To become or make into jelly.

Jell-O (jĕl′ō) A trademark used for a gelatin dessert.

jel·ly (jĕl′ē) *n., pl.* **-lies 1.** A soft, semisolid food substance with a resilient consistency, esp. one made of fruit juice containing pectin boiled with sugar. **2.** Something, such as a petroleum ointment, having this consistency. **3.** A shapeless, pulpy mass. **4.** Something, such as a body part, that has suddenly become limp or enervated: *so frightened his knees turned to jelly.* ❖ *v.* **-lied, -ly·ing, -lies** —*tr.* To cause to have the consistency of jelly. —*intr.* To acquire the consistency of jelly. [ME *gelee* < OFr. < VLat. **gelāta* < Lat., fem. p. part. of *gelāre,* to freeze. See **gel-** in App.]

jel·ly·bean (jĕl′ē-bēn′) *n.* A small ovoid candy with a hardened sugar coating over a chewy center.

jel·ly·fish (jĕl′ē-fĭsh′) *n., pl.* **jellyfish** or **-fish·es 1a.** Any of numerous marine cnidarians of the class Scyphozoa, existing as a gelatinous, tentacled, often bell-shaped medusa for most of its life cycle. **b.** Any of various similar or related coelenterates. **2.** *Informal* One who lacks force of character; a weakling.

jel·ly·roll (jĕl′ē-rōl′) *n.* A thin sheet of sponge cake layered with jelly and then rolled up.

jem·my (jĕm′ē) *n. & v. Chiefly British* Variant of **jimmy.**

Je·na (yā′nə) A city of central Germany SW of Leipzig; site of Napoleon I's defeat of the Prussians (1806). Pop. 100,093.

je ne sais quoi (zhə′ nə sā kwä′, sĕ) *n.* A quality or attribute that is difficult to describe or express. [Fr. : *je,* I + *ne,* not + *sais,* know + *quoi,* what.]

Jen·ghis Khan or **Jen·ghiz Khan** (jĕn′gĭz kän′, -gĭs, jĕng′-) See **Genghis Khan.**

Jen·ner (jĕn′ər), **Edward** 1749–1823. British physician who discovered that smallpox could be prevented by inoculation with the substance from cowpox lesions.

jen·net also **gen·et** (jĕn′ĭt) *n.* A small Spanish saddle horse. [ME *genet* < OFr. < Catalan *ginet,* of Ar. or Berber orig.]

jen·ny (jĕn′ē) *n., pl.* **-nies 1.** The female of certain animals, esp. the donkey and the wren. **2.** A spinning jenny. [< the name *Jenny.*]

jeop·ard·ize (jĕp′ər-dīz′) *tr.v.* **-ized, -iz·ing, -izes** To expose to loss or injury; imperil. See Syns at **endanger.**

jeop·ard·y (jĕp′ər-dē) *n., pl.* **-ies 1.** Risk of loss or injury; peril or danger. **2.** *Law* A defendant's risk or danger of conviction when put on trial. [ME *juperti* < OFr. *jeu-parti,* even game, uncertainty : *jeu,* game (< Lat. *iocus,* joke, game) + *parti,* p. part. of *partir,* to divide (< Lat. *partīre* < *pars, part-,* part; see PART).]

Je·qui·tin·hon·ha (zhə-kēt′n-yōn′yə, zhĭ-kwē′tĭ-nyō′nyä) A river of E Brazil flowing c. 805 km (500 mi) to the Atlantic Ocean.

Jer. *abbr. Bible* Jeremiah

jer·bo·a (jər-bō′ə) *n.* Any of various small nocturnal rodents of the family Dipodidae of Asia and northern Africa, having long hind legs. [Med.Lat. *jerboa* < Ar. *jarbū'.*]

jer·e·mi·ad (jĕr′ə-mī′əd) *n.* A literary work or speech expressing a bitter lament or a righteous prophecy of doom. [Fr. *jérémiade,* after *Jérémie,* Jeremiah, author of *The Lamentations* < LLat. *Ieremiās.* See JEREMIAH[1].]

Jer·e·mi·ah[1] (jĕr′ə-mī′ə) A Hebrew prophet of the 7th and 6th cent. B.C. [LLat. *Ieremiās* < Heb. *yirməyāhû,* Yahweh has established : *yirm,* he has established + *yāhû,* Yahweh.]

Jer·e·mi·ah[2] (jĕr′ə-mī′ə) *n.* See table at **Bible.** [After JEREMIAH[1].]

Je·rez (hĕ-rĕs′, -rĕth′) also **Jerez de la Fron·te·ra** (dĕ lä frōn-tĕ′rä, thĕ) A city of SW Spain NE of Cádiz; held by the Moors from 711 to 1264. Pop. 183,316.

Jer·i·cho (jĕr′ĭ-kō′) An ancient city of Palestine near the NW shore of the Dead Sea.

jerk[1] (jûrk) *v.* **jerked, jerk·ing, jerks** —*tr.* **1.** To give a sudden quick thrust, push, pull, or twist to. **2.** To throw or toss with a quick abrupt motion. **3.** To utter abruptly or sharply: *jerked out a sob.* **4.** To make and serve (ice-cream sodas, for example) at a soda fountain. **5.** *Sports* To press (a weight) overhead from shoulder height in a quick motion. —*intr.* **1.** To move in sudden abrupt motions; jolt. **2.** To make spasmodic motions. ❖ *n.* **1.** A sudden abrupt motion, such as a yank. **2.** A jolting or lurching motion. **3.** *Physiology* A sudden reflexive muscular movement. **4. jerks** Involuntary convulsive twitching often re-

Thomas Jefferson

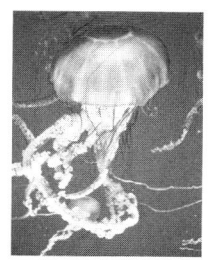
jellyfish
West Coast stinging nettle
Chrysaora fuscescens

jewel box

sulting from excitement. Often used with *the*. **5.** *Slang* A foolish, rude, or contemptible person. **6.** *Sports* A lift in which the weight is heaved overhead from shoulder height with a quick motion. —*phrasal verbs:* **jerk off** *Vulgar Slang* To masturbate. **jerk around** To take unfair advantage of, deceive, or manipulate. [?] —**jerk′er** *n.* —**jerk′ing•ly** *adv.*

jerk² (jûrk) *tr.v.* **jerked, jerk•ing, jerks** To cut (meat) into long strips and dry in the sun or cure by exposing to smoke. ❖ *adj.* Being or relating to a method of barbecuing meat that has been seasoned and wrapped in leaves of the allspice tree: *jerk chicken.* [Back-formation < JERKY².]

jer•kin (jûr′kĭn) *n.* **1.** A hip-length collarless and sleeveless jacket, worn over a doublet by men esp. in the 16th century. **2.** A short close-fitting, often sleeveless coat or jacket. [?]

jerk•wa•ter (jûrk′wô′tər, -wŏt′ər) *adj. Informal* **1.** Remote, small, and insignificant: *a jerkwater town.* **2.** Contemptibly trivial: *jerkwater notions.* [< *jerkwater*, a branch-line train, so called because its small boiler had to be refilled often, requiring train crews to "jerk" or draw water from streams.]

jerk•y¹ (jûr′kē) *adj.* **-i•er, -i•est 1.** Marked by jerks or jerking. **2.** *Slang* Foolish. —**jerk′i•ly** *adv.* —**jerk′i•ness** *n.*

jerk•y² (jûr′kē) *n.* Jerked meat. [Alteration of CHARQUI.]

jer•o•bo•am (jĕr′ə-bō′əm) *n.* A wine bottle holding ⅘ of a gallon (3.03 liters). [After *Jeroboam I* (died c. 901 B.C.), king of northern Israel.]

Je•rome (jə-rōm′), Saint. 340?–420? Latin scholar who produced the *Vulgate*, a Latin translation of the Bible.

Jer•ry (jĕr′ē) *n., pl.* **-ries** *Chiefly British Slang* A German, esp. a German soldier. [Alteration of GERMAN.]

jer•ry-build (jĕr′ē-bĭld′) *tr.v.* **-built** (-bĭlt′), **-build•ing, -builds** To build shoddily and cheaply. [< dialectal *jerry*, defective, perh. < the name *Jerry*.] —**jer′ry-build′er** *n.*

jer•ry-rig (jĕr′ē-rĭg′) *tr.v.* **-rigged, -rig•ging, -rigs** To jury-rig. [Alteration (influenced by JERRY-BUILD) of JURY-RIG.]

jer•sey (jûr′zē) *n., pl.* **-seys 1a.** A soft plain-knitted fabric. **b.** A garment made of this fabric. **2.** A close-fitting knitted pullover. **3.** often **Jersey** Any of a breed of fawn-colored dairy cattle developed on the island of Jersey. [After JERSEY.]

Jersey The largest of the Channel Is. in the English Channel; annexed by the Normans in 933 and autonomous since 1204.

Jersey City A city of NE NJ on the Hudson R. opposite Lower Manhattan; settled by the Dutch before 1650. Pop. 240,055.

Je•ru•sa•lem (jə-rōō′sə-ləm, -zə-) The cap. of Israel, in the E-central part in the West Bank; occupied as early as the 4th millennium B.C. Jerusalem is considered a holy city by Jews, Muslims, and Christians. Pop. 561,900.

Jerusalem artichoke *n.* **1.** A North American sunflower (*Helianthus tuberosus*) having yellow rayed flower heads and edible tubers. **2.** The edible tuber of this plant. [By folk ety. < Ital. *girasole,* sunflower. See GIRASOL.]

Jerusalem cherry *n.* An Old World ornamental shrub (*Solanum pseudocapsicum*) having inedible scarlet or yellow fruit.

Jerusalem oak *n.* **1.** A sticky Old World weed (*Chenopodium botrys*) having lobed leaves and a turpentinelike odor. **2.** See wormseed 1.

Jerusalem thorn *n.* A spiny tropical American tree (*Parkinsonia aculeata*) having bipinnately compound leaves.

Jes•per•sen (yĕs′pər-sən), **(Jens) Otto (Harry)** 1860–1943. Danish philologist noted for his contributions to phonetics and the teaching of languages.

jess (jĕs) *n.* A short strap fastened around the leg of a hawk or other bird, to which a leash may be fastened. ❖ *tr.v.* **jessed, jess•ing, jess•es** To put jesses or a jess on (a hawk, for example). [ME *ges* < OFr., pl. of *jet,* something thrown, ult. < Lat. *iactus,* p. part. of *iacere,* to throw.]

jes•sa•mine (jĕs′ə-mĭn) *n.* Variant of **jasmine.**

Jes•se (jĕs′ē) The father of King David and progenitor of the line of Jesus.

jest (jĕst) *n.* **1.** A playful or amusing act; a prank. **2.** A frolicsome or frivolous mood: *spoken in jest.* **3.** An object of ridicule. **4.** A witty remark. ❖ *v.* **jest•ed, jest•ing, jests** —*intr.* **1.** To act or speak playfully. **2.** To make witty remarks. **3.** To utter scoffs; gibe. —*tr.* To make fun of; ridicule. [ME *geste,* tale < OFr. < Lat. *gesta,* deeds < neut. pl. p. part. of *gerere,* to perform.] —**jest′ing•ly** *adv.*

jest•er (jĕs′tər) *n.* **1.** One given to jesting. **2.** A fool or buffoon at medieval courts.

Jes•u•it (jĕzh′ōō-ĭt, jĕz′ōō-, -yōō-) *n.* **1.** *Roman Catholic Church* A member of the Society of Jesus. **2.** often **jesuit** One given to subtle casuistry. [Fr. *Jésuite* < *Jésus,* Jesus < LLat. *Iēsus.* See JESUS¹.] —**Jes′u•it′i•cal** *adj.* —**Jes′u•it′i•cal•ly** *adv.*

Jes•u•it's bark (jĕzh′ōō-ĭts, jĕz′ōō-, -yōō-) *n.* See **cinchona** 2. [First known to Europeans through Jesuit missions in Peru.]

Je•sus¹ (jē′zəs) A teacher and prophet whose life and teachings form the basis of Christianity. Christians believe Jesus to be Son of God and the Christ. [ME < LLat. *Iēsus* < Gk. *Iēsous* < Heb. *yēšûă‘* < *yəhôšûă‘,* Joshua. See JOSHUA¹.]

Je•sus² (jē′zəs) Called "son of Sirach." fl. 3rd cent. B.C. The author of the Apocryphal book of Ecclesiasticus.

jet¹ (jĕt) *n.* **1.** A dense black coal that takes a high polish and is used for jewelry. **2.** A deep black. ❖ *adj.* **1.** Made of or resembling

jet. **2.** Black as coal; jet-black: *jet hair.* [ME < AN *geet* < Lat. *gagātēs* < Gk., after *Gagas,* a town of Lycia.]

jet² (jĕt) *n.* **1a.** A high-velocity fluid stream forced out of a small-diameter opening or nozzle. **b.** An outlet used for emitting such a stream. **c.** Something emitted in or as if in a high-velocity fluid stream. **2a.** A jet-propelled vehicle, esp. an aircraft. **b.** A jet engine. ❖ *v.* **jet•ted, jet•ting, jets** —*intr.* **1.** To travel by jet aircraft. **2.** To move very quickly. —*tr.* To propel outward or squirt, as under pressure. [Fr. < OFr. < *jeter,* to spout forth, throw < VLat. **iectāre,* alteration of Lat. *iactāre,* freq. of *iacere,* to throw.]

jet-black (jĕt′blăk′) *adj.* Deep black. [< JET¹.]

jet boat *n.* A boat propelled by a powerful jet of water.

je•té (zhə-tā′) *n.* A leap in ballet in which the weight is transferred from one foot to the other. [Fr. < p. part. of *jeter,* to throw < OFr. See JET².]

jet engine *n.* An engine that develops thrust by ejecting a jet, esp. of gaseous combustion products.

jet-fight•er or **jet fighter** (jĕt′fī′tər) *n.* A jet-propelled fighter aircraft.

jet•foil (jĕt′foil′) *n.* A passenger-carrying hydrofoil that is propelled by a jet engine. [JET² + (HYDRO)FOIL.]

jet lag also **jet•lag** (jĕt′lăg′) *n.* A temporary disruption of body rhythms typically caused by high-speed travel across several time zones in a jet aircraft. —**jet′-lagged′** *adj.*

jet•lin•er (jĕt′lī′nər) *n.* A large passenger jet airplane.

jet•port (jĕt′pôrt′, -pōrt′) *n.* An airport for jet aircraft.

jet-pro•pelled (jĕt′prə-pĕld′) *adj.* Driven by jet propulsion.

jet propulsion *n.* Propulsion derived from the rearward expulsion of matter in a jet stream, esp. by jet engines.

jet•sam (jĕt′səm) *n.* **1.** Cargo or equipment thrown overboard to lighten a ship in distress. **2.** Discarded cargo or equipment found washed ashore. See Usage Note at **flotsam. 3.** Discarded odds and ends. [< earlier *jetson,* alteration of ME *jetteson,* a throwing overboard. See JETTISON.]

jet set *n.* An international social set made up of wealthy people who travel from one fashionable place to another. —**jet′-set′** (jĕt′sĕt′), **jet′-set′ting** *adj.* —**jet setter** *n.*

Jet Ski A trademark used for a personal watercraft.

jet stream *n.* **1.** A high-speed meandering wind current, generally from a westerly direction at speeds often exceeding 400 kilometers (250 miles) per hour at altitudes of 15 to 25 kilometers (10 to 15 miles). **2.** A high-speed stream; a jet.

jet•ti•son (jĕt′ĭ-sən, -zən) *tr.v.* **-soned, -son•ing, -sons 1.** To cast overboard or off. **2.** *Informal* To discard (something) as unwanted or burdensome. ❖ *n.* **1.** The act of discarding or casting overboard. **2.** Jetsam. [< ME *jetteson,* throwing goods overboard to lighten ship < AN *getteson* < VLat. **iectātiō, *iectātiōn-* < **iectātus,* p. part. of **iectāre,* to throw. See JET².]

jet•ty¹ (jĕt′ē) *n., pl.* **-ties 1.** A structure, such as a pier, that projects into a body of water to influence the current or protect a harbor, for example. **2.** A wharf. [ME *getti, jettie* < OFr. *jetee* < fem. p. part. of *jeter,* to project, throw. See JET².]

jet•ty² (jĕt′ē) *adj.* **1.** Resembling jet, as in texture. **2.** Of the color jet; black. —**jet′ti•ness** *n.*

jew (jōō) *tr.v.* **jewed, jew•ing, jews** *Offensive* **1.** To bargain shrewdly or unfairly with. Often used with *down.* **2.** To haggle so as to reduce (a price). Often used with *down.* [< Jews' supposedly extortionate practices as moneylenders in the M Ages.]

Jew (jōō) *n.* **1.** An adherent of Judaism as a religion or culture. **2.** A member of the widely dispersed people originally descended from the ancient Hebrews and sharing an ethnic heritage based on Judaism. **3.** A native or inhabitant of the ancient kingdom of Judah. [ME *Jeu* < OFr. *giu* < Lat. *Iūdaeus* < Gk. *Ioudaios* < Aram. *yəhudāy* < Heb. *yəhûdî,* inhabitant of Judah, after *yəhûdâ,* Judah.]

USAGE NOTE It is widely recognized that the attributive use of the noun *Jew,* in phrases such as *Jew lawyer* or *Jew ethics,* is both offensive and vulgar. In such contexts *Jewish* is the only acceptable possibility. But some people have become so wary of this construction that they avoid any use of the noun, a practice that carries risks of its own. In a sentence such as *There are now several Jews on the council,* which is unexceptionable, the substitution of a circumlocution like *Jewish people* or *persons of Jewish background* may unwittingly suggest an unwarranted and hence suspect delicacy.

jew•el (jōō′əl) *n.* **1a.** A precious stone; a gem. **b.** A small natural or artificial gem used as a bearing in a watch. **2.** A costly ornament of precious metal or gems. **3.** One that is treasured or esteemed. ❖ *tr.v.* **-eled, -el•ing, -els** or **-elled, -el•ling, -els 1.** To adorn with jewels. **2.** To fit with jewels. [ME *juel* < AN, perh. < VLat. **iocāle* < neut. of Lat. *iocālis,* of play < Lat. *iocus,* joke.]

jewel box *n.* **1.** A usu. lined box or case for holding jewelry. **2.** A hinged plastic case designed to hold a compact disk.

jew•el•er also **jew•el•ler** (jōō′ə-lər) *n.* One that makes, repairs, or deals in jewelry.

jew•el•fish (jōō′əl-fĭsh′) *n., pl.* **jewelfish** or **-fish•es** A small, brilliantly colored freshwater fish (*Hemichromis bimaculatus*) of tropical Africa, popular in home aquariums.

jew•el•ry (jōō′əl-rē) *n.* Ornaments, such as bracelets or rings, made of precious metals set with gems or imitation gems.

jew•el•weed (jōō′əl-wēd′) *n.* Any of several plants of the genus *Impatiens* having yellowish spurred flowers and seedpods that dehisce into five valves when mature.

Jew•ess (jōō′ĭs) *n. Offensive* A Jewish woman or girl.

Jew•ett (jōō′ĭt), **Sarah Orne** 1849–1909. Amer. writer whose works include *The Country of the Pointed Firs* (1896).

jew•fish (jōō′fĭsh′) *n., pl.* **jewfish** or **-fish•es** Any of several large marine fishes of the family Serranidae, esp. the grouper *Epinephelus itajara* of tropical waters.

Jew•ish (jōō′ĭsh) *adj.* Of or relating to the Jews or their culture or religion. See Usage Note at **Jew.** —**Jew′ish•ly** *adv.* —**Jew′ish•ness** *n.*

Jewish calendar *n.* The lunisolar calendar used to mark the events of the Jewish year, dating the creation of the world to 3761 B.C. See table at **calendar.**

Jew•ry (jōō′rē) *n.* 1. The Jewish people. 2. A section of a medieval city inhabited by Jews.

Jew's harp also **jew's harp** (jōōz) *n.* A small musical instrument consisting of a lyre-shaped metal frame held between the teeth and a projecting steel tongue that is plucked to produce a soft twanging sound. [?]

jez•e•bel (jĕz′ə-bĕl′, -bəl) *n.* An evil and scheming woman. [After JEZEBEL.]

Jez•e•bel (jĕz′ə-bĕl′) fl. 9th cent. B.C. Phoenician princess and queen of Israel, who according to the Bible encouraged idolatry.

jg *abbr.* junior grade

Jg or **Jgs** *abbr. Bible* Judges

Jhan•si (jän′sē) A city of N-central India SSE of Delhi. Pop. 300,850

Jhe•lum (jā′ləm) A river, c. 772 km (480 mi), of N India and NE Pakistan; one of the five rivers of the Punjab.

JHVH or **JHWH** (yōōd′hä′väv′hä′, yä′wä, yä′wĕ) *n.* Variants of YHWH.

Jia•ling also **Chia-ling** (jyä′lĭng′) or **Kia•ling** (kyä′-, jyä′-) A river, c. 965 km (600 mi), of central China flowing to the Chang Jiang (Yangtze River) at Chongqing.

Jia•mu•si (jyä′mōō′sē′) also **Chia•mus•su** (-mōō′sōō′) or **Kia•mu•sze** (kyä′mōō′sōō′) A city of NE China ENE of Harbin. Pop. 744,584.

Jiang•su (jyäng′sōō′) also **Kiang•su** (kyäng′-) A province of E China bordering on the Yellow Sea. Cap. Nanjing. Pop. 67,056,519.

Jiang•xi (jyäng′shē′) also **Kiang•si** (kyäng′-) A province of SE China. Cap. Nanchang. Pop. 37,710,281.

Jiang Ze•min (jyäng′ dzə-mĕn′) Born 1926. Chinese politician who has served as president and head of the ruling Communist Party since 1989.

jib¹ (jĭb) *n.* **1.** *Nautical* A triangular sail stretching from the foretopmast head to the jib boom and in small craft from the foremost mast to the bowsprit or stem. **2a.** The arm of a mechanical crane. **b.** The boom of a derrick.

jib² (jĭb) *intr.v.* **jibbed, jib•bing, jibs** To stop short and turn restively from side to side; balk. [?] —**jib′ber** *n.*

jib boom *n. Nautical* A spar forming a continuation of the bowsprit.

jibe¹ also **gybe** (jĭb) *Nautical v.* **jibed, jib•ing, jibes** also **gybed, gyb•ing, gybes** —*intr.* To shift a fore-and-aft sail from one side of a vessel to the other while sailing before the wind so as to sail on the opposite tack. —*tr.* To cause (a sail) to jibe. ❖ *n.* The act of jibing. [Alteration (perh. influenced by JIB¹) of *gybe* < obsolete Du. *gijben.*]

jibe² (jĭb) *intr.v.* **jibed, jib•ing, jibes** *Informal* To be in accord; agree: *Your figures jibe with mine.* [?]

jibe³ (jĭb) *v. & n.* Variant of **gibe.**

ji•ca•ma (hē′kə-mə, hĭk′ə-) *n.* A crisp sweet turnip-shaped root vegetable (*Pachyrhizus erosus*) eaten raw in salads or cooked in stews. [Am.Sp. *jicama* < Nahuatl *xīcamatl.*]

Ji•ca•ril•la (hē′kə-rē′yə, -rēl′yə) *n., pl.* **Jicarilla** or **-las** A member of an Apache tribe formerly inhabiting southeast Colorado and northern New Mexico and ranging eastward to the Great Plains, with a present-day population in northern New Mexico. [Am.Sp. (*Apaches de la*) *Jicarilla,* (Apaches of the) Jicarilla, prob. dim. of *jícara,* chocolate-cup (< the shape of a local hill), perh. < Nahuatl *xicalli,* gourd.]

Jid•da (jĭd′ə) or **Jed•dah** (jĕd′ə) A city of W-central Saudi Arabia on the Red Sea. Pop. 1,300,000.

jiff (jĭf) *n. Informal* A jiffy.

jif•fy (jĭf′ē) *n., pl.* **jif•fies** *Informal* A short space of time; a moment. [?]

jig (jĭg) *n.* **1a.** Any of various lively dances in triple time. **b.** The music for such a dance. **2.** A joke or trick. Used chiefly in the phrase *The jig is up.* **3.** A typically metal fishing lure with one or more hooks, usu. deployed with a jiggling motion. **4.** An apparatus for cleaning or separating crushed ore by agitation in water. **5.** A device for guiding a tool or for holding machine work in place. ❖ *v.* **jigged, jig•ging, jigs** —*intr.* **1.** To dance or play a jig. **2.** To move or bob up and down jerkily and rapidly. **3.** To operate a jig. —*tr.* **1.** To bob or jerk (something) up and down or to and fro. **2.** To machine (an object) with the aid of a jig. **3.** To separate or clean (ore) by shaking a jig. [?]

jig•ger¹ (jĭg′ər) *n.* **1.** A person who jigs or operates a jig. **2a.** A small measure for liquor, usu. holding 1½ ounces. **b.** This amount of liquor. **3.** A device, such as a drill, that operates with a jerking or jolting motion. **4.** *Nautical* **a.** A light all-purpose tackle. **b.** A small sail set in the stern of a ketch or yawl. **c.** A boat having such a sail. **d.** A jigger mast. **5.** *Informal* An article or device, the name of which eludes one.

jig•ger² (jĭg′ər) *n.* **1.** See **chigger** 1. **2.** See **chigoe** 1. [Variant of CHIGGER.]

jigger mast *n. Nautical* **1.** The short after mast from which the jigger sail is set on a ketch or yawl. **2.** The fourth mast aft on a ship having five or more masts.

jig•ger•y-pok•er•y (jĭg′ə-rē-pō′kə-rē) *n.* Underhand scheming or behavior. [Alteration of *joukery-pawkery* : < Sc. *jouk,* to dodge (prob. < DUCK²) + Sc. *pawk,* trick.]

jig•gle (jĭg′əl) *v.* **-gled, -gling, -gles** —*intr.* To move or rock lightly up and down or to and fro in an unsteady jerky manner. —*tr.* To cause to jiggle. ❖ *n.* A jiggling motion. [Frequentative of JIG.] —**jig′gly** *adj.*

jig•saw (jĭg′sô′) *n.* A usu. power-driven saw with a narrow vertical blade, used to cut sharp curves.

jigsaw puzzle *n.* A puzzle consisting of irregularly shaped pieces that form a picture when fitted together.

ji•had also **je•had** (jĭ-häd′) *n.* **1.** *Islam* An individual's striving for spiritual self-perfection. **2.** *Islam* A Muslim holy war or spiritual struggle against infidels. **3.** A crusade or struggle. [Ar. *jihād* < *jahada,* to strive.]

Ji•lin also **Chi•lin** (jē′lĭn′) or **Ki•rin** (kē′rĭn′) **1.** A province of NE China bordering on North Korea. Cap. Changchun. Pop. 24,658,721. **2.** A city of NE China E of Changchun; founded 1673. Pop. 2,251,848.

jill (jĭl) *n.* Variant of **gill⁴.**

jil•lion (jĭl′yən) *n. Informal* An indeterminately huge number. [On the model of MILLION, BILLION, etc.]

jilt (jĭlt) *tr.v.* **jilt•ed, jilt•ing, jilts** To deceive or drop (a lover) suddenly or callously. ❖ *n.* One who discards a lover. [Poss. < obsolete *jilt,* harlot, alteration of *gillot,* dim. of *gille,* woman, girl < ME. See GILL⁴.]

Jim Crow or **jim crow** (jĭm) *n.* The systematic practice of discriminating against and segregating Black people, esp. as practiced in the American South from the end of Reconstruction to the mid-20th century. [< obsolete *Jim Crow,* derogatory name for a Black person, ult. < a 19th-cent. minstrel song title.] —**Jim Crow** *adj.* —**Jim′-Crow′ism** (jĭm′krō′ĭz′əm) *n.*

jim-dan•dy (jĭm′dăn′dē) *n., pl.* **-dies** *Informal* One that is very pleasing or excellent of its kind. [*Jim* (nickname for *James*) + DANDY.] —**jim′-dan′dy** *adj.*

Ji•mé•nez (hē-mē′nĕs, -nĕth), **Juan Ramón** 1881–1958. Spanish poet who won the 1956 Nobel Prize for literature.

jim-jams (jĭm′jămz′) *pl.n. Slang* **1.** The jitters. **2.** Delirium tremens. [Expressive of delirium tremens trembling.]

jim•mies (jĭm′ēz) *pl.n.* Small particles of chocolate or flavored candy sprinkled on ice cream as a topping.

jim•my *n., pl.* **-mies** A short crowbar with curved ends. ❖ *tr.v.* **-mied, -my•ing, -mies** To pry (something) open with or as if with a jimmy: *jimmy a door.* [Prob. < the name *Jimmy,* nickname for *James.*]

jim•son•weed (jĭm′sən-wēd′) *n.* A poisonous plant (*Datura stramonium*) with trumpet-shaped flowers and prickly capsules. [Alteration of *Jamestown weed,* after JAMESTOWN, VA.]

Jin also **Chin** (jĭn) Four Chinese dynasties, including **Western Jin** (A.D. 265–316), **Eastern Jin** (317–420), **Later Jin** (936–946), and **Jin** (1115–1234).

Ji•nan also **Tsi•nan** (jē′nän′) A city of E China on the Huang He (Yellow River) S of Tianjin; cap. of Shandong province. Pop. 2,403,946.

jin•gle (jĭng′gəl) *v.* **-gled, -gling, -gles** —*intr.* **1.** To make a tinkling or ringing metallic sound. **2.** To have the catchy sound of a simple repetitious rhyme or doggerel. —*tr.* To cause to make a jingle. ❖ *n.* **1.** The sound produced by or as if by bits of metal striking together. **2.** A piece of light singsong verse or rhyme. **3.** An often musical advertising slogan. [ME *ginglen,* of imit. orig.] —**jin′gly** *adj.*

jingle shell *n.* The translucent yellowish or grayish shell of any of several marine bivalve mollusks of the genus *Anomia.*

jin•go (jĭng′gō) *n., pl.* **-goes** One who vociferously supports one's country, esp. in a belligerent foreign policy; a chauvinistic patriot. ❖ *adj.* **1.** Of or relating to a chauvinistic patriot. **2.** Characterized by chauvinistic patriotism. ❖ *interj.* Used for emphasis or to express surprise: *by jingo!* [< the phrase *by jingo,* used in the refrain of a bellicose 19th-cent. English music-hall song < alteration of JESUS¹.] —**jin′go•ish** *adj.*

jin•go•ism (jĭng′gō-ĭz′əm) *n.* Extreme nationalism characterized esp. by a belligerent foreign policy; chauvinistic patriotism. —**jin′go•ist** *n.* —**jin′go•is′tic** *adj.*

jink (jĭngk) *v.* **jinked, jink•ing, jinks** —*intr.* To make a quick evasive turn. —*tr.* To cause (a vehicle or an aircraft, for example) to make a quick evasive turn. ❖ *n.* **1.** A quick evasive turn. **2.** **jinks** Rambunctious play; frolic. [?]

Jin•men (jĭn′mĕn′) See **Quemoy.**

Jin•nah (jĭn′ə), **Mohammed Ali** 1876–1948. Founder and first

Mohammed Ali Jinnah

governor-general (1947–48) of Pakistan.

jin·ni or **jin·nee** also **djin·ni** also **djin·ny** (jĭn′ē, jĭ-nē′) *n., pl.* **jinn** also **djinn** (jĭn) In Muslim legend, a spirit often capable of assuming human or animal form and exercising supernatural influence over people. [Ar. *jinnī*, demonic, demon < *jinn*, demons < *janna*, to cover, conceal.]

jin·rik·sha or **jin·rick·sha** also **jin·riki·sha** (jĭn-rĭk′shô′) *n.* A small two-wheeled carriage drawn by one or two persons. [J. *jinrikisha* : *jin*, person (< M Chin. n*r*in, rin) + *riki*, strength (< M Chin. lik) + *sha*, vehicle (< M Chin. chia,).]

jinx (jĭngks) *n.* 1. A person or thing that is believed to bring bad luck. 2. A condition or period of bad luck. ❖ *tr.v.* **jinxed, jinx·ing, jinx·es** To bring bad luck to. [Poss. < *jynx*, wryneck (< its use in witchcraft) < Lat. *iynx* < Gk. *iunx*, perh. < *iuzein*, to call, cry.]

Jin·zhou also **Chin·chow** (jĭn′jō′) A city of N China ENE of Beijing. Pop. 736,297.

ji·pi·ja·pa (hē′pē-hä′pə) *n.* A stemless palmlike plant (*Carludovica palmata*) of Central and South America having long-stalked fanlike leaves that are used to make Panama hats. [Am.Sp., after *Jipijapa*, a city of western Ecuador.]

jit·ney (jĭt′nē) *n., pl.* **-neys** 1. A small motor vehicle, such as a bus, that transports passengers on a route for a small fare. 2. *Archaic* A nickel. [?]

jit·ter (jĭt′ər) *intr.v.* **-tered, -ter·ing, -ters** 1. To be nervous or uneasy; fidget. 2. To make small quick jumpy movements. ❖ *n.* 1. A jittering movement; a tic. 2. **jitters** A fit of nervousness. [Perh. alteration of CHITTER.]

jit·ter·bug (jĭt′ər-bŭg′) *n.* 1. A strenuous dance performed to quick-tempo swing or jazz music and consisting of various two-step patterns embellished with twirls and sometimes acrobatic maneuvers. 2. One who performs this dance. ❖ *intr.v.* **-bugged, -bug·ging, -bugs** To perform this dance. [< *jitterbug*, heavy drinker who suffers from the jitters < JITTER.]

jit·ter·y (jĭt′ə-rē) *adj.* **-i·er, -i·est** 1. Having or feeling nervous unease. 2. Marked by jittering movements. —**jit′ter·i·ness** *n.*

jiu·jit·su (jōō-jĭt′sōō) *n.* Variant of jujitsu.

Ji·va·ro (hē′və-rō′) *n., pl.* **Jivaro** or **-ros** 1. A member of a South American Indian people of eastern Ecuador and northeast Peru. 2. The language of this people.

jive (jīv) *n.* 1a. Jazz or swing music. b. The jargon of jazz musicians and enthusiasts. 2. *Slang* Deceptive, nonsensical, or glib talk. ❖ *v.* **jived, jiv·ing, jives** —*intr.* 1. To play or dance to jive music. 2. *Slang* a. To talk nonsense; kid. b. To talk or chat. —*tr. Slang* To cajole or mislead. ❖ *adj. Slang* Misleading; phony. [?] —**jiv′er** *n.* —**jiv′ey, jiv′y** *adj.*

Ji·xi (jē′shē′) also **Ki·si** (kē′sē′, -shē′) A city of NE China near the Russian border E of Harbin. Pop. 835,496.

JJ *abbr. Law* 1. judges 2. justices

Jl *abbr. Bible* Joel

Jm *abbr. Bible* James

Jn *abbr. Bible* John

jnr. *abbr.* junior

jo (jō) *n., pl.* **joes** *Scots* Sweetheart; dear. [Alteration of JOY.]

Joan of Arc (jōn; ärk), Saint. Also **Jeanne d'Arc** (zhän därk′) 1412?–31. French heroine who organized the resistance that forced the English to end their siege of Orléans (1429), led an army of 12,000 to Rheims, and was tried for heresy and burned at the stake in Rouen.

João Pes·so·a (zhwouɴ′ pə-sō′ə) A city of NE Brazil near the Atlantic Ocean N of Recife; founded 1585. Pop. 497,306.

job[1] (jŏb) *n.* 1. A regular activity performed in exchange for payment, esp. as one's trade, occupation, or profession. 2. A position in which one is employed. 3a. A task that must be done. b. A specified duty or responsibility. See Syns at **task**. 4a. A specific piece of work to be done for a set fee. b. The object to be worked on. c. Something resulting from or produced by work. 5. *Computer Science* A program application that may consist of several steps but is performed as a single logical unit. 6. *Informal* A difficult or strenuous task. 7. *Informal* A bad or unsatisfactory piece of work. 8. *Informal* A state of affairs. 9. *Informal* A criminal act, esp. a robbery. ❖ *v.* **jobbed, job·bing, jobs** —*intr.* 1. To work at odd jobs. 2. To work by the piece. 3. To deal as a jobber. —*tr.* 1. To purchase (merchandise) from manufacturers and sell it to retailers. 2. To arrange for (contracted work) to be done in portions by others; subcontract. 3. To transact (official business) dishonestly for private profit. —**idiom: on the job 1.** At work. 2. Paying close attention; on the alert. [Perh. < obsolete *jobbe*, piece, alteration of ME *gobbe*, lump. See GOB[1].]

job[2] (jŏb) *Archaic tr. & intr.v.* **jobbed, job·bing, jobs** To jab or make a jab. ❖ *n.* A jab. [ME *jobben*, of imit. orig.]

Job[1] (jōb) In the Bible, an upright man whose faith in God survived the test of repeated calamities. [Heb. *'iyyŏb*, perh. "Where is the father?" (< Heb. dialectal *'ŏb*, father), or akin to Heb. *'ōyēb*, enemy.]

Job[2] (jōb) *n.* See table at **Bible**. [After JOB[1].]

job action (jŏb) *n.* A temporary action by workers to make demands or protest a company or managerial decision.

job·ber (jŏb′ər) *n.* 1. One that buys merchandise from manufacturers and sells it to retailers. 2. One that works by the piece or at odd jobs. 3. *Chiefly British* A middleman in the exchange of

stocks and securities among brokers.

job·ber·y (jŏb′ə-rē) *n.* Corruption among public officials.

job·hold·er (jŏb′hōl′dər) *n.* One who has a regular job.

job-hop (jŏb′hŏp′) *intr.v.* **-hopped, -hop·ping, -hops** *Informal* To change jobs frequently. —**job′-hop′per** *n.*

job-hunt (jŏb′hŭnt′) *intr.v.* **-hunt·ed, -hunt·ing, -hunts** To look actively for suitable employment. —**job hunter** *n.*

job·less (jŏb′lĭs) *adj.* 1. Having no job. 2. Of or relating to those who have no jobs. ❖ *n.* (*used with a pl. verb*) Unemployed people considered as a group. —**job′less·ness** *n.*

job lot (jŏb) *n.* 1. Miscellaneous merchandise sold in one lot. 2. A collection of cheap items.

Jobs (jŏbz), **Steven Paul** b. 1955. Amer. computer engineer who cofounded Apple Computers (1975).

Job's comforter (jōbz) *n.* One who is discouraging or saddening while seemingly offering sympathy or comfort. [After JOB[1], whose friends' comfort was actually criticism.]

job-share (jŏb′shâr′) *intr.v.* **-shared, -shar·ing, -shares** To share the responsibility for one job in alternation with one or more part-time workers. —**job′-shar′er** *n.*

Job's tears *pl.n.* 1. (*used with a sing. or pl. verb*) A tropical Asian grass (*Coix lacryma-jobi*) having white beadlike grains. 2. (*used with a pl. verb*) The grains of this plant.

Jo·cas·ta (jō-kăs′tə) *n. Greek Mythology* A queen of Thebes who unknowingly married her own son, Oedipus.

jock[1] (jŏk) *n.* 1. A jockey in horseracing. 2. A disc jockey.

jock[2] (jŏk) *n.* 1. An athletic supporter. 2. An athlete. 3. *Slang* One characterized by machismo.

jock·ey (jŏk′ē) *n., pl.* **-eys** 1. One who rides horses in races, esp. as a profession. 2. *Slang* One who operates a specified vehicle, machine, or device. ❖ *v.* **-eyed, -ey·ing, -eys** —*tr.* 1. To ride (a horse) as jockey. 2. To direct or maneuver by cleverness or skill. 3. To trick; cheat. —*intr.* 1. To ride a horse in a race. 2. To maneuver for a certain position or advantage. 3. To employ trickery. [Dim. of Sc. *Jock*, var. of *Jack*, nickname for John. See JACK.]

jock itch *n.* A fungal infection of the skin of the groin area, characterized by red ringlike areas and severe itching.

jock·strap also **jock strap** (jŏk′străp′) *n.* An athletic supporter. [*jock*, male genitals (of unknown orig.) + STRAP.]

jo·cose (jō-kōs′) *adj.* Given to joking; merry. 2. Characterized by joking; humorous. [Lat. *iocōsus* < *iocus*, joke.] —**jo·cose′ly** *adv.* —**jo·cose′ness, jo·cos′i·ty** (-kŏs′ĭ-tē) *n.*

joc·u·lar (jŏk′yə-lər) *adj.* 1. Marked by joking. 2. Given to joking. [Lat. *ioculāris*, droll < *ioculus*, dim. of *iocus*, joke.] —**joc′u·lar′i·ty** (-lăr′ĭ-tē) *n.* —**joc′u·lar·ly** *adv.*

joc·und (jŏk′ənd, jō′kənd) *adj.* Sprightly and lighthearted in disposition, character, or quality. [ME < OFr. *jocond* < Lat. *iūcundus, iōcundus* < *iuvāre*, to delight.] —**jo·cun′di·ty** (jō-kŭn′dĭ-tē) *n.* —**joc′und·ly** *adv.*

Jodh·pur (jŏd′pər, jōd′poŏr′) A city of W India SW of Delhi. Pop. 666,279.

jodh·purs (jŏd′pərz) *pl.n.* Wide-hipped riding pants of heavy cloth, fitting tightly from knee to ankle. [After JODHPUR.]

Jo·el[1] (jō′əl) A Hebrew prophet of the 6th cent. B.C. [Heb. *yô′ēl*, Yahweh is God : *yô*, Yahweh + *′ēl*, God.]

Jo·el[2] (jō′əl) *n.* See table at **Bible**. [After JOEL[1].]

joe-pye weed (jō′pī′) *n.* Any of several tall North American plants of the genus *Eupatorium*, having whorled leaves and small pinkish or purplish flower heads. [?]

jo·ey (jō′ē) *n., pl.* **-eys** *Australian* A young animal, esp. a baby kangaroo. [?]

Jof·fre (zhôf′rə), **Joseph Jacques Césaire** 1852–1931. French field marshal who commanded the World War I Allied armies in France.

Jof·frey (jŏf′rē, jôf′-), **Robert** Orig. Abdullah Jaffa Bey Khan. 1930–88. Amer. dancer and choreographer who founded the Robert Joffrey Ballet (1956).

jog[1] (jŏg) *v.* **jogged, jog·ging, jogs** —*tr.* 1. To move by shoving, bumping, or jerking; jar. 2. To give a push or shake to; nudge. 3. To rouse or stimulate as if by nudging. 4. To cause (a horse) to move at a leisurely pace. —*intr.* 1. To move with a jolting rhythm. 2a. To run or ride at a steady slow trot. b. *Sports* To run in such a way for sport or exercise. 3a. To go or travel at a slow or leisurely pace. b. To proceed in a leisurely manner. ❖ *n.* 1. A slight push or shake; a nudge. 2. A jogging movement or rhythm. 3. A slow steady trot. [Perh. alteration of ME *shoggen*, to shake, move with a jerk, perh. alteration of *shokken*, to move rapidly < MLGer. *schocken*, to shake.] —**jog′ger** *n.*

jog[2] (jŏg) *n.* 1. A protruding or receding part in a surface or line. 2. An abrupt change in direction. ❖ *intr.v.* **jogged, jog·ging, jogs** To turn sharply; veer. [Variant of JAG[1].]

jog·gle[1] (jŏg′əl) *v.* **-gled, -gling, -gles** —*tr.* To shake or jar slightly. —*intr.* To move with a joggle. ❖ *n.* A shaking or lightly jolting motion. [Perh. freq. of JOG[1].]

jog·gle[2] (jŏg′əl) *n.* 1. A joint between two pieces of building material formed by a notch and a fitted projection. 2. The notch or the projecting piece used in a joggle. ❖ *tr.v.* **-gled, -gling, -gles** To join or attach by means of a joggle. [Perh. < JOG[2].]

Jog·ja·kar·ta (jŏg′yə-kär′tə, jŏk′jä-) See **Yogyakarta**.

jog trot *n.* 1. A slow steady trot, as of a horse. 2. A regular, humdrum way of living or of doing something.

Joan of Arc
1854 portrait by Ingres

joey
kangaroo with joey

John Paul II

Jo·han·nes·burg (jō-hăn′ĭs-bûrg′, -hä′nĭs-) A city of NE South Africa NW of Durban; founded 1886. Pop. 1,609,000.

john (jŏn) n. Slang **1.** A toilet. **2.** A man who is a prostitute's customer. [< the name *John*.]

John[1] (jŏn) Known as John Lackland. 1167?–1216. King of England (1199–1216) who signed the Magna Carta (Jun. 15, 1215).

John[2] (jŏn) n. See table at **Bible.** [ME < OFr. *Jehan* < LLat. *Ioannes,* Iōannēs < Gk. *Iōannēs* < Heb. *yôhānān,* Yahweh has been gracious : *yô,* short form of *yahweh,* Yahweh + *hānan,* he has been gracious.]

John, Saint. Known as "the Evangelist" or "the Divine." fl. 1st cent. A.D. One of the 12 Apostles, traditionally considered the author of the fourth Gospel, three epistles, and the Book of Revelation.

John III So·bies·ki (sō-byĕs′kē) 1629–96. King of Poland (1674–96) who helped expel the Turks from Europe.

John XXIII Orig. Angelo Giuseppe Roncalli. 1881–1963. Pope (1958–63) who convoked Vatican II (1962).

John Barleycorn n. A personification of alcoholic liquor.

john·boat (jŏn′bōt′) n. A small flatbottom boat with square ends, paddled or poled on shallow waterways. [Prob. < the name *John*.]

John Bull n. **1.** A personification of England or the English. **2.** A typical Englishman. [After *John Bull,* a character in *Law Is a Bottomless Pit* by John Arbuthnot.]

John Day A river of N OR flowing c. 452 km (281 mi) to the Columbia R.

John Doe n. **1.** Used as a name in legal proceedings to designate an unknown or unidentified man or boy. **2.** An average or ordinary man.

John Dory n. Either of two North Atlantic fish (*Zeus faber* or *Z. ocellata*) having a laterally compressed body and long spines on the dorsal fin. [The name *John* + DORY[2].]

Joh·ne's disease (yō′nəz) n. A chronic diarrheal disease of domestic animals, esp. cattle and sheep, caused by the bacterium *Mycobacterium paratuberculosis.* [After Heinrich Albert *Johne* (1839–1910), German physician.]

John Hancock n. *Informal* A person's signature. [After John HANCOCK (< the prominence of his signature on the Declaration of Independence).]

john·ny (jŏn′ē) n., pl. **-nies** A short-sleeved gown opening in the back, worn by patients undergoing medical treatment or examination. [< the name *Johnny,* nickname for *John*.]

john·ny·cake also **jon·ny·cake** (jŏn′ē-kāk′) n. New England & Upper Midwest Cornmeal bread usu. shaped into a flat cake and baked or fried on a griddle. [Perh. by folk ety. < *jonakin*.]

REGIONAL NOTE When the Native Americans showed the Pilgrims how to cook with maize, they must have taught them to make *johnnycake,* a dense cornmeal bread whose thick batter is shaped into a flat cake and baked or fried on a griddle. *Johnnycake,* also spelled *jonnycake* and also called *journey cake* and *Shawnee cake,* is still considered a New England specialty. Outside New England the name *johnnycake* is best known in the Upper Midwest, but the food itself is most popular in the South and South Midland states, where it is known as *ashcake, batter bread, battercake, corn cake, cornpone,* or *hoe cake.* The color of the cornmeal, the consistency of the batter, the size of the cake, and the cooking method can vary from region to region.

John·ny-come-late·ly (jŏn′ē-kŭm-lāt′lē) n., pl. **John·ny-come-late·lies** or **John·nies-come-late·ly** (jŏn′ēz-) *Informal* A newcomer or latecomer.

John·ny-jump-up (jŏn′ē-jŭmp′ŭp′) n., pl. **Johnny-jump-ups** Any of various plants of the genus *Viola,* esp. a California violet (*V. pedunculata*) or a European pansy (*V. tricolor*), having variously colored flowers. [< its quick growth.]

John·ny-on-the-spot (jŏn′ē-ŏn′thə-spŏt′, -ŏn′-) n. *Informal* A person who is available and ready to act when needed.

Johnny Reb n. *Informal* A Confederate soldier in the American Civil War.

John of Gaunt (gônt, gänt) Duke of Lancaster. 1340–99. English soldier who ruled England during the last years of his father, Edward III, and in the beginning of Richard II's reign.

John of Lancaster Duke of Bedford. 1389–1435. English noble who was regent of England and France (1422–35) during the early reign of Henry VI.

John o'Groat's (ə-grōts′) A location on the NE coast of Scotland, considered the northernmost point of Great Britain.

John Paul I Orig. Albino Luciani. 1912–78. Pope (1978) who reigned for only 34 days.

John Paul II Orig. Karol Wojtyla. b. 1920. Pope (since 1978), the first non-Italian pope in 450 years.

John Q. Public n. Used as a name to designate a typical member of the general public.

Johns (jŏnz), **Jasper** b. 1930. Amer. artist and pioneer of pop art.

John·son (jŏn′sən), **Andrew** 1808–75. The 17th President of the US (1865–69), who was impeached on charges brought by Republican senators (1868) but acquitted by one vote.

Johnson, Claudia Alta Taylor Known as "Lady Bird." b. 1912. First Lady of the US (1963–69) who directed a nationwide beautification project.

John·son (yŏŏn′sôn), **Eyvind** 1900–76. Swedish writer who shared the 1974 Nobel Prize for literature.

John·son (jŏn′sən), **James Price** 1894–1955. Amer. pianist and composer noted for his ragtime compositions and show tunes, including "The Charleston" (1923).

John·son (jŏn′sən), **James Weldon** 1871–1938. Amer. writer whose works include *The Autobiography of an Ex-Colored Man* (1912).

Johnson, John Arthur Known as "Jack." 1878–1946. Amer. prizefighter who was world heavyweight champion (1908–15).

Johnson, Lyndon Baines 1908–73. The 36th President of the US (1963–69) who after 1964 faced increasing criticism over the mounting US involvement in Vietnam and did not stand for reelection in 1968.

Johnson, Philip Cortelyou b. 1906. Amer. architect who designed the New York State Theater in New York City (1964).

Johnson, Robert 1911–38. American singer, guitarist, and legendary representative of the Delta blues tradition.

Johnson, Samuel Known as "Dr. Johnson." 1709–84. British writer and lexicographer who wrote *Dictionary of the English Language* (1755) and *Lives of the Poets* (1779–81). —**John·so′ni·an** (jŏn-sō′nē-ən) adj. & n.

Johnson, Thomas 1732–1819. American jurist; associate justice of the US Supreme Court (1792–93).

Johnson, William 1771–1834. Amer. jurist; associate justice of the US Supreme Court (1804–34).

Johnson grass n. A coarse perennial Mediterranean forage grass (*Sorghum halepense*) that is often a troublesome weed. [After William *Johnson* (died 1859), American agriculturalist.]

Johnson noise n. See **thermal noise.** [After John Bertrand *Johnson* (1887–1970), Swedish-born American physicist.]

John·ston (jŏn′stən), **Albert Sidney** 1803–62. Amer. Confederate general who was defeated at Shiloh (1862).

Johnston, Joseph Eggleston 1807–91. Amer. Confederate general who surrendered to Sherman in 1865.

John the Baptist, Saint. 1st cent. B.C. Jewish prophet who baptized Jesus and was executed by Herod Antipas at Salome's behest.

Jo·hor Ba·ha·ru (jə-hôr′ bə-hä′rōō, jə-hôr′) also **Jo·hore Bah·ru** (bä′rōō) A city of Malaysia on the S tip of the Malay Peninsula opposite Singapore I.; connected with Singapore by a causeway across the narrow **Johore Strait.** Pop. 328,646.

joie de vi·vre (zhwä′ də vē′vrə) n. Hearty or carefree enjoyment of life. [Fr. : *joie,* joy + *de,* of + *vivre,* to live, living.]

join (join) v. **joined, join·ing, joins** —tr. **1.** To put or bring together so as to make continuous or form a unit. **2.** To put or bring into close association or relationship. **3.** To connect (points), as with a straight line. **4.** To meet and merge with: *where the creek joins the river.* **5.** To become a part or member of. **6.** To come into the company of. **7.** To participate with in an act or activity. **8.** To adjoin. **9.** To engage in; enter into. —intr. **1.** To come together so as to form a connection. **2.** To act together; form an alliance. **3.** To become a member of a group. **4.** To take part; participate. ❖ n. A joint; a junction. [ME *joinen* < OFr. *joindre, joign-, join-* < Lat. *iungere.* See **yeug-** in App.]

SYNONYMS join, combine, unite, link, connect These verbs mean to put or bring together. *Join* applies to the physical contact or union of at least two separate things and to the coming together of persons, as into a group: *The children joined hands. Combine* suggests the mixing or merging of components, often for a specific purpose: *The cook combined various ingredients. Unite* stresses the coherence or oneness of the persons or things joined: *The strike united the oppressed workers. Link* and *connect* imply a firm attachment in which individual components nevertheless retain their identities: *The study linked the high crime rate to unemployment. The reporter connected the police chief to the scandal.*

---

join·der (join′dər) n. **1.** The act of joining. **2.** *Law* **a.** A joining of causes of action or defense in a suit. **b.** A joining of parties in a suit. **c.** Formal acceptance of an issue offered. [< Fr. *joindre,* to join < OFr. See JOIN.]

join·er (joi′nər) n. **1.** A carpenter, esp. a cabinetmaker. **2.** *Informal* A person given to joining, as groups or causes.

join·er·y (joi′nə-rē) n. **1.** The art or craft of a joiner; cabinetmaking. **2.** Work done by a joiner; fine woodwork.

joint (joint) n. **1a.** A place or part at which two or more things are joined. **b.** A way in which two or more things are joined: *flexible joints.* **2.** *Anatomy* A point of articulation between two or more bones, esp. such a connection that allows motion. **b.** A point in the exoskeleton of an invertebrate at which movable parts join. **3.** *Botany* An articulation on a fruit or stem. **4.** *Geology* A fracture or crack in a rock mass along which no appreciable movement has occurred. **5.** A large cut of meat for roasting. **6.** *Slang* **a.** A cheap or disreputable gathering place. **b.** A building or dwelling. **c.** A prison. **7.** *Slang* A marijuana cigarette. **8.** *Vulgar Slang* A penis. ❖ adj. **1.** Shared by or common to two or more. **2.** Sharing with another or others. **3.** Formed or characterized by cooperation or united action. **4.** Involving both houses of a legislature. **5.** *Law* Regarded as one legal body; united in identity of interest or liability. **6.** *Mathematics* Involving two or more variables. ❖ tr.v. **joint·ed, joint·ing, joints 1.** To combine or attach with a joint

Andrew Johnson

Lady Bird Johnson
photographed in 1994

Lyndon B. Johnson

ă pat	oi boy
ā pay	ou out
âr care	ŏŏ took
ä father	ōō boot
ĕ pet	ŭ cut
ē be	ûr urge
ĭ pit	th thin
ī pie	th this
îr pier	hw which
ŏ pot	zh vision
ō toe	ə about,
ô paw	item

Stress marks:
′ (primary);
′ (secondary), as in
lexicon (lĕk′sĭ-kŏn′)

or joints. **2.** To provide or construct with joints. **3.** To separate (meat) at the joints. **—idiom: out of joint 1.** Dislocated, as a bone. **2.** *Informal* **a.** Not harmonious; inconsistent. **b.** Out of order; inauspicious or unsatisfactory. **c.** In bad spirits or humor; out of sorts. [ME < OFr. < p. part. of *joindre,* to join. See JOIN.]

Joint Chiefs of Staff *n.* The principal military advisory group to the US President, composed of the chiefs of the Army, Navy, and Air Force and the commandant of the Marine Corps.

joint compound *n.* A substance similar to plaster used to cover joints or the heads of screws or nails in plasterboard.

joint·er (join′tər) *n.* **1.** A machine or tool used in making joints. **2.** A tool used to cut grooves indicating the joints in cement. **3.** A triangular attachment to a plow used in covering trash or refuse.

joint·ly (joint′lē) *adv.* In common; together.

joint resolution *n.* A resolution passed by both houses of a bicameral legislature and eligible to become a law if signed by the chief executive or passed over the chief executive's veto.

joint stock *n.* Stock or capital funds of a company held jointly or in common by its owners.

joint-stock company (joint′stŏk′) *n.* A business whose capital is held in transferable shares of stock by its joint owners.

join·ture (join′chər) *n.* The act of joining or the state of being joined. [ME < AN < Lat. *iūnctūra,* joint. See JUNCTURE.]

joint venture *n.* A partnership or conglomerate, formed often to share risk or expertise.

joint·worm (joint′wûrm′) *n.* The larva of certain wasps of the family Eurytomidae, esp. of *Harmolita tritici,* that infests grains and causes hard swellings near the first joint of the stems.

Join·vi·le also **Join·vil·le** (zhoin-vē′lē) A city of S Brazil NNE of Pôrto Alegre; founded c. 1850. Pop. 346,332.

joist (joist) *n.* Any of the wood, steel, or concrete beams set parallel from wall to wall or across or abutting girders to support a floor or ceiling. ❖ *tr.v.* **joist·ed, joist·ing, joists** To construct with joists. [ME *giste, joiste* < OFr. *giste* < fem. p. part. of *gesir,* to lie, lie down < Lat. *iacēre.*]

jo·jo·ba (hə-hō′bə, hō-) *n.* A dioecious shrub (*Simmondsia chinensis*) of the southwest United States and northern Mexico having opposite leathery leaves and edible seeds that contain an oil used in cosmetics and as a lubricant. [Am.Sp.]

joke (jōk) *n.* **1.** Something said or done to evoke laughter or amusement, esp. an amusing story with a punch line. **2.** A mischievous trick; a prank. **3.** An amusing or ludicrous incident or situation. **4.** *Informal* **a.** Something not to be taken seriously; a triviality. **b.** An object of amusement or laughter; a laughingstock. ❖ *v.* **joked, jok·ing, jokes** —*intr.* **1.** To tell or play jokes; jest. **2.** To speak in fun; be facetious. —*tr.* To make fun of; tease. [Lat. *iocus.*] —**jok′ing·ly** *adv.*

jok·er (jō′kər) *n.* **1a.** One who tells or plays jokes. **b.** An insolent person who seeks to make a show of cleverness. **c.** *Informal* An annoying or inept person. **2.** *Games* A playing card, usu. printed with a picture of a jester, used in certain games as the highest-ranking card or as a wild card. **3.** A minor clause in a document such as a legislative bill that voids or changes its original purpose. **4.** An unforeseen but important difficulty, fact, or circumstance. **5.** A deceptive means of getting the better of someone.

jok·ey also **jok·y** (jō′kē) *adj.* **-i·er, -i·est** Characterized by joking or jokes, esp. stale or clumsy jokes. —**jok′i·ly** *adv.* —**jok′i·ness** *n.*

Jo·li·et (jō′lē-ĕt′, jō′lē-ĕt′) A city of NE IL SW of Chicago. Pop. 106,221.

Jo·liot-Cu·rie (zhô-lyō′kyōōr′ē, -kyŏō-rē′, -kü-), **Irène** 1897–1956. French physicist who shared a 1935 Nobel Prize with her husband, **Frédéric Joliot-Curie** (1900–58).

Jol·li·et also **Jo·li·et** (jō′lē-ĕt′, jō′lē-ĕt′, zhô-lyä′), **Louis** 1645–1700. French-Canadian explorer who with Jacques Marquette sighted the Mississippi R. (1673) and descended to the mouth of the Arkansas R.

jol·li·fi·ca·tion (jŏl′ə-fĭ-kā′shən) *n.* Festivity; revelry.

jol·li·ty (jŏl′ĭ-tē) *n., pl.* **-ties** Convivial merriment or celebration.

jol·ly (jŏl′ē) *adj.* **-li·er, -li·est 1.** Full of good humor and high spirits. **2.** Exhibiting or occasioning happiness or mirth; cheerful. **3.** Greatly pleasing; enjoyable. ❖ *adv. Chiefly British* To a great extent or degree; extremely. ❖ *v.* **-lied, -ly·ing, -lies** —*tr.* To keep amused or diverted for one's own purposes; humor. —*intr.* To amuse oneself with humorous banter. ❖ *n., pl.* **-lies 1.** *Chiefly British* A good or festive time. **2. jollies** *Slang* Amusement; kicks. [ME *joli* < OFr., perh. of Scand. orig.] —**jol′li·ly** *adv.* —**jol′li·ness** *n.*

jol·ly·boat (jŏl′ē-bōt′) *n.* A medium-sized ship's boat used for rough work and minor tasks.

Jolly Roger *n.* A black flag bearing the white skull and crossbones of a pirate ship. [?]

Jol·son (jōl′sən), **Al** 1886–1950. Amer. entertainer who starred in *The Jazz Singer* (1927), the first major film with synchronized sound.

jolt (jōlt) *v.* **jolt·ed, jolt·ing, jolts** —*tr.* **1.** To move or dislodge with a sudden hard blow; strike heavily or jarringly. **2.** To cause to move jerkily. **3.** To put into a specified condition by or as if by a blow. **4.** To make suddenly active or effective. **5.** To disturb suddenly and severely; stun. —*intr.* To proceed in an irregular, bumpy, or jerky fashion. ❖ *n.* **1.** A sudden jarring or jerking, as

from a heavy blow or an abrupt movement. **2a.** A sudden strong feeling of surprise or disappointment; a shock. **b.** The cause of such a feeling. **3.** A brief strong portion: *a jolt of electricity.* [?] —**jolt′er** *n.* —**jolt′i·ly** *adv.* —**jolt′y** *adj.*

Jo·ma·da (jə-mä′dä) *n.* Variant of **Jumada.**

Jo·nah¹ (jō′nə) In the Bible, a prophet who was swallowed by a great fish and disgorged unharmed three days later. [Heb. *yônâ,* dove.]

Jo·nah² (jō′nə) *n.* **1.** See table at **Bible. 2.** One thought to bring bad luck. [After JONAH¹.]

Jon·a·than¹ (jŏn′ə-thən) In the Bible, the eldest son of King Saul of Israel and friend of David.

Jon·a·than² (jŏn′ə-thən) *n.* A variety of red late-ripening apple. [After *Jonathan* Hasbrouck (died 1846), American jurist.]

jones (jōnz) *n. Slang* **1.** Heroin. **2.** An addiction, esp. to heroin. [Perh. < the name *Jones.*]

Jones (jōnz), **Charles Martin ("Chuck")** b. 1912. Amer. animator and animation director.

Jones, Inigo 1573–1652. English architect who brought the Palladian classical style to England.

Jones, John Paul 1747–92. Scottish-born Amer. Revolutionary naval officer who raided the British coast (1778–79).

Jones, LeRoi See Imamu Amiri **Baraka.**

Jones, Mary Harris Known as "Mother Jones." 1830–1930. Irish-born Amer. labor leader who helped found (1905) the Industrial Workers of the World.

Jones, Quincy Delight b. 1933. Amer. musician, composer, and record producer, known for his compositions for television and film.

jon·gleur (zhôn-glœr′) *n.* A wandering minstrel, poet, or entertainer in medieval England and France. [Fr. < OFr., var. of *jogleor* < Lat. *ioculător,* jester < *ioculārī,* to jest. See JUGGLE.]

jon·ny·cake (jŏn′ē-kāk′) *n. New England & Upper Midwest* Variant of **johnnycake.**

jon·quil (jŏng′kwəl, jŏn′-) *n.* A southern European ornamental plant (*Narcissus jonquilla*) having long narrow leaves and short-tubed yellow flowers. [Sp. *junquilla* < the name *Junquello,* dim. of *junco,* reed < Lat. *iuncus.*]

Jon·son (jŏn′sən), **Ben** 1572–1637. English poet and playwright whose plays include *Volpone* (1606).

Jop·lin (jŏp′lĭn) A city of SW MO near the KS border W of Springfield; founded 1839. Pop. 45,504.

Joplin, Scott 1868–1917. Amer. pianist and composer whose ragtime works include "Maple Leaf Rag" (1899).

Jor·dan (jôr′dn) Formerly **Trans·jor·dan** (trăns′-, trănz′-) A country of SW Asia in NW Arabia; a former British mandate (1923–46). Cap. Amman. Pop. 5,198,000. —**Jor·da′ni·an** (jôr-dā′nē-ən) *adj. & n.*

Jordan, Michael Jeffrey b. 1963. Amer. basketball player who set an NBA record for most seasons leading the league in scoring.

Jordan almond *n.* **1.** A large variety of almond from Málaga, Spain, used widely in confections. **2.** An almond with a hard, colored, flavored sugar coating. [By folk ety. < ME *jardin almaund* : OFr. *jardin,* garden; see JARDINIÈRE + *almande,* almond; see ALMOND.]

Jordan River A river of SW Asia rising in Syria and flowing c. 322 km (200 mi) through the Sea of Galilee to the Dead Sea.

jo·rum (jôr′əm, jōr′-) *n.* **1.** A large drinking bowl. **2.** The amount that such a bowl contains. [Perhaps after *Joram,* who brought vessels to King David (II Samuel 8:10).]

Jos *abbr. Bible* Joshua

jo·seph (jō′zəf, -səf) *n.* A long riding coat with a small cape, worn by women in the 18th century. [After JOSEPH¹, who left an outer garment when he fled Potiphar's wife (Genesis 39:12).]

Joseph¹ In the Bible, the older son of Jacob and Rachel and the forebear of one of the tribes of Israel.

Jo·seph² Known as "Chief Joseph." 1840?–1904. Nez Percé leader who conducted a skillful but unsuccessful retreat from US forces (1877).

Joseph, Saint. fl. 1st cent. A.D. The husband of Mary, mother of Jesus.

Joseph II 1741–90. Holy Roman emperor (1765–90) and king of Bohemia and Hungary (1780–90).

Jo·se·phine (jō′zə-fēn′, -sə-) See Josephine de **Beauharnais.**

Joseph of Ar·i·ma·the·a (ăr′ə-mə-thē′ə) fl. 1st cent. A.D. In the Bible, the disciple who buried the body of Jesus.

Jo·seph·son junction (jō′zəf-sən, -səf-) *n.* An insulating barrier separating two superconductors and exhibiting special electrical effects, such as supercurrent flow. [After Brian David *Josephson* (born 1940), British physicist.]

Jo·se·phus (jō-sē′fəs), **Flavius** A.D. 37–100? Jewish general whose *History of the Jewish War* is the major source of information about the siege of Masada (72–73).

josh (jŏsh) *v.* **joshed, josh·ing, josh·es** —*tr.* To tease (someone) good-humoredly. —*intr.* To make or exchange good-humored jokes; banter. ❖ *n.* A teasing or joking remark. [?] —**josh′er** *n.* —**josh′ing·ly** *adv.*

Josh·u·a¹ (jŏsh′ōō-ə) In the Bible, a Hebrew leader who succeeded Moses as leader of Israel. [Lat. *Ioshua* < Heb. *yəhôšûa',* Yahweh (is) salvation : *yahô,* short form of *yahweh,* Yahweh + **šûa',* salvation; akin to *yēša',* salvation.]

Mother Jones

Quincy Jones

Jordan

Michael Jordan

Josh·u·a² (jŏsh′ōō-ə) *n.* See table at **Bible.** [After JOSHUA¹.]

Joshua tree *n.* A treelike plant (*Yucca brevifolia*) of the southwest United States having sword-shaped leaves and greenish-white flowers. [Prob. after JOSHUA¹, comparing the tree's extended branches to Joshua's outstretched arm (Joshua 8:18).]

Jos·quin Des·prez (zhŏz′kăn dā-prā′) 1440?–1521. Flemish composer often considered the greatest of the Renaissance.

joss (jŏs) *n.* A Chinese image in a shrine. [Pidgin E. < Javanese *deyos* < Port. *deos*, god < Lat. *deus*. See dyeu- in App.]

joss house *n.* A Chinese temple or shrine.

joss stick *n.* A stick of incense of the kind burned before a Chinese image, idol, or shrine.

jos·tle (jŏs′əl) *v.* **-tled, -tling, -tles** —*intr.* **1.** To come in rough contact while moving; push and shove. **2.** To make one's way by pushing or elbowing. **3.** To vie for an advantage or position. —*tr.* **1.** To come into rough contact with while moving. **2.** To force by pushing or elbowing. **3.** To vie with for an advantage or position. ❖ *n.* **1.** A rough shove or push. **2.** The condition of being crowded together. [ME *justlen*, to have sexual relations with, freq. of *justen*, to joust < OFr. *juster.* See JOUST.] —**jos′tler** *n.*

jot (jŏt) *n.* The smallest bit; iota. ❖ *tr.v.* **jot·ted, jot·ting, jots** To write down briefly or hastily: *Jot down my name.* [ME *jote* < Lat. *iōta*, iota < Gk., iota. See IOTA.]

jot·ting (jŏt′ĭng) *n.* A brief note or memorandum.

jou·al (zhōō-äl′) *n. Chiefly Canadian* A dialect of Canadian French characterized by nonstandard pronunciations and grammar, and the presence of English loanwords and syntactic patterns. [Canadian Fr. dialectal, var. of Fr. *cheval.* See CHEVALET.]

joule (jōōl, joul) *n.* **1.** The International System unit of electrical, mechanical, and thermal energy. **2a.** A unit of electrical energy equal to the work done when a current of one ampere is passed through a resistance of one ohm for one second. **b.** A unit of energy equal to the work done when a force of one newton acts through a distance of one meter. [After James Prescott JOULE.]

Joule, James Prescott 1818–89. British physicist who discovered the first law of thermodynamics.

jounce (jouns) *intr. & tr.v.* **jounced, jounc·ing, jounc·es** To move or cause to move with bumps and jolts; bounce. ❖ *n.* A rough jolting movement; a jolt. [ME *jouncen.*]

jour·nal (jûr′nəl) *n.* **1a.** A personal record of occurrences, experiences, and reflections kept on a regular basis; a diary. **b.** An official record of daily proceedings, as of a legislative body. **c.** *Nautical* A ship's log. **2.** *Accounting* **a.** A daybook. **b.** A book of original entry in a double-entry system, listing all transactions and indicating the accounts to which they belong. **3.** A newspaper. **4.** A periodical presenting articles on a particular subject. **5.** The part of a machine shaft or axle supported by a bearing. [ME, breviary < OFr., daily, breviary < LLat. *diurnālis*, daily. See DIURNAL.]

journal box *n.* A housing in a machine enclosing a journal and its bearings.

jour·nal·ese (jûr′nə-lēz′, -lēs′) *n.* The style of writing often held to be characteristic of newspapers and magazines, distinguished by clichés, sensationalism, and triteness of thought.

jour·nal·ism (jûr′nə-lĭz′əm) *n.* **1.** The collecting, writing, editing, and presentation of news or news articles. **2.** Material written for publication in a newspaper or magazine or for broadcast. **3.** The style of writing characteristic of newspapers and magazines, marked by the direct presentation of facts. **4.** Newspapers and magazines. **5.** An academic course in journalism. **6.** Written material of current interest or popular appeal.

jour·nal·ist (jûr′nə-lĭst) *n.* **1.** One whose occupation is journalism. **2.** One who keeps a journal.

jour·nal·is·tic (jûr′nə-lĭs′tĭk) *adj.* Of or characteristic of journalism or journalists. —**jour′nal·is′ti·cal·ly** *adv.*

jour·nal·ize (jûr′nə-līz′) *v.* **-ized, -iz·ing, -iz·es** —*tr.* To record in a journal. —*intr.* To keep a personal or financial journal. —**jour′nal·iz′er** *n.*

jour·ney (jûr′nē) *n., pl.* **-neys** **1a.** The act of traveling from one place to another; a trip. **b.** A distance to be traveled or the time required for a trip. **2.** A process or course likened to traveling; a passage. ❖ *v.* **-neyed, -ney·ing, -neys** —*intr.* To make a journey; travel. —*tr.* To travel over or through. [ME *journei*, day, day's travel, journey < OFr. *jornee* < VLat. *diurnāta* < LLat. *diurnum*, day < neut. of Lat. *diurnus*, of a day < *diēs*, day. See DIARY.] —**jour′ney·er** *n.*

journey cake *n. New England & Upper Midwest* See **johnnycake.** See Regional Note at **johnnycake.** [Perh. by folk ety. < *jonakin.*]

jour·ney·man (jûr′nē-mən) *n.* **1.** One who has fully served an apprenticeship in a trade or craft and is a qualified worker in another's employ. **2.** An experienced and competent but undistinguished worker. [ME *journeiman* : *journei*, a day's work; see JOURNEY + *man*; see MAN.]

jour·ney·work (jûr′nē-wûrk′) *n.* The work of a journeyman.

joust (joust, jŭst, jōōst) also **just** (jŭst) *n.* **1a.** A combat between two mounted knights or men-at-arms using lances; a tilting match. **b.** **jousts** A series of tilting matches; a tournament. **2.** A personal competition or combat suggestive of combat with lances. ❖ *intr.v.* **joust·ed, joust·ing, jousts** also **just·ed, just·ing, justs 1.** To engage in mounted combat with lances; tilt. **2.** To engage in a personal combat or competition. [ME < OFr. *juste* < *juster*, to joust < VLat. *iūxtāre*, to be next to < Lat. *iūxtā*, close

by. See yeug- in App.] —**joust′er** *n.*

Jove (jōv) *n. Roman Mythology* See **Jupiter** 1. —*idiom:* **by Jove** Used as a mild oath to express surprise or emphasis. [ME < Archaic Lat. *Iovis* or < Lat. *Iov-*, stem of *Iuppiter.* See dyeu- in App.]

jo·vi·al (jō′vē-əl) *adj.* Marked by hearty conviviality and good cheer. [Fr., prob. < Ital. *giovale* < OItal., of Jupiter (the source of happiness) < LLat. *Ioviālis* < Lat. *Iuppiter, Iov-*, Jupiter. See dyeu- in App.] —**jo′vi·al′i·ty** (-ăl′ĭ-tē) *n.* —**jo′vi·al·ly** *adv.*

Jo·vi·an¹ (jō′vē-ən) Originally Flavius Jovianus A.D. 331?–364. Emperor of Rome (363–364) who made peace with the Persians by giving up all Roman territories beyond the Tigris R.

Jo·vi·an² (jō′vē-ən) *adj.* **1.** *Roman Mythology* Of, relating to, or resembling Jupiter. **2.** Of or resembling the planet Jupiter.

Jovian planet *n.* One of the four large, outer planets, Jupiter, Saturn, Uranus, and Neptune.

jowl¹ (joul) *n.* **1.** The jaw, esp. the lower jaw. **2.** The cheek. [ME *chavel, chaule, jaule* (influenced by *joue*, jaw, or *jol*, head) < OE *ceafl.*]

jowl² (joul) *n.* **1.** The flesh under the lower jaw, esp. when plump or flaccid. **2.** A fleshy part similar to a jowl, such as the wattle of a fowl. [Alteration of ME *cholle* (influenced by ME *joue*, jaw, or *jol*, head).]

jowl·y (jou′lē) *adj.* **-i·er, -i·est** Having heavy or sagging jowls. —**jowl′i·ness** *n.*

joy (joi) *n.* **1a.** Intense and ecstatic or exultant happiness. **b.** The expression or manifestation of such feeling. **2.** A source or object of pleasure or satisfaction. ❖ *v.* **joyed, joy·ing, joys** —*intr.* To take great pleasure; rejoice. —*tr. Archaic* **1.** To fill with ecstatic happiness, pleasure, or satisfaction. **2.** To enjoy. [ME *joie* < OFr. < Lat. *gaudia*, pl. of *gaudium*, joy < *gaudēre*, to rejoice.]

Joyce (jois), **James** 1882–1941. Irish writer whose works include *Ulysses* (1922) and *Finnegans Wake* (1939). —**Joyc′e·an** (joi′sē-ən) *adj.*

joy·ful (joi′fəl) *adj.* Feeling, causing, or indicating joy. See Syns at **glad¹.** —**joy′ful·ly** *adv.* —**joy′ful·ness** *n.*

joy·less (joi′lĭs) *adj.* Cheerless; dismal: *joyless drudgery.* —**joy′less·ly** *adv.* —**joy′less·ness** *n.*

joy·ous (joi′əs) *adj.* Feeling or causing joy; joyful. See Syns at **glad¹.** —**joy′ous·ly** *adv.* —**joy′ous·ness** *n.*

joy·pop (joi′pŏp′) *intr.v.* **-popped, -pop·ping, -pops** *Slang* To use narcotic drugs, esp. heroin, occasionally without becoming addicted. —**joy′pop′per** *n.*

joy ride *n. Slang* **1.** A ride taken for fun and often for the thrills provided by reckless driving. **2.** A hazardous, reckless, often costly venture. —**joy rider** *n.*

joy·stick (joi′stĭk′) *n. Slang* **1.** The control stick of an aircraft. **2.** A manual control or cursor device, as one attached to a computer or video game.

JP *abbr.* justice of the peace

J particle *n.* See **J/psi particle.**

JPEG (jā′pĕg′) *n. Computer Science* **1.** A standard algorithm for the compression of digital images. **2.** A digital image that has been compressed using this standard. [*J*(oint) *P*(hotographic) *E*(xperts) *G*(roup).]

J/psi particle (jā′sī′, -psī′) *n.* An electrically neutral meson having a mass 7,213 times that of the electron and a mean lifetime of approx. 1×10^{-20} seconds.

Jr *abbr. Bible* Jeremiah

jr. or **Jr.** *abbr.* junior

JRC *abbr.* Junior Red Cross

Js. *abbr. Bible* James

JSD *abbr. Latin* Juris Scientiae Doctor (Doctor of Juristic Science)

Jua·na I·nés de la Cruz (wä′nä ē-nĕs′ dĕ lä krōōs′, hwä′-) See Juana Inés de la **Cruz.**

Juan Car·los (wän kär′lōs, -lōs, hwän) b. 1938. Spanish king (since 1975) who acceded after the death of Francisco Franco.

Juan de Fu·ca (də fōō′kə, fyōō′-), **Strait of** A strait between NW WA and Vancouver I., British Columbia, Canada, linking Puget Sound and the Strait of Georgia with the Pacific Ocean.

Juan Fer·nán·dez Islands (fər-năn′dəs, fĕr-nän′dĕs) An island group of Chile, in the SE Pacific Ocean. Alexander Selkirk, a Scottish sailor and the inspiration for Defoe's *Robinson Crusoe*, lived on one of the islands from 1704 to 1709.

Juá·rez (wär′ĕz, hwä′rĕs) See Ciudad Juárez.

Juárez, Benito Pablo 1806–72. Mexican politician who served as president (1858–72).

ju·ba (jōō′bə) *n.* An 18th- and 19th-century group dance, probably of West African origin, characterized by complex body movements and practiced on southern US plantations. [?]

Ju·ba (jōō′bə, -bä) A river of S Ethiopia and S Somalia flowing c. 1,609 km (1,000 mi) to the Indian Ocean.

Ju·bal (jōō′bəl) In the Bible, a descendant of Cain who is said to have invented musical instruments.

Jub·bul·pore (jŭb′əl-pôr′, -pōr′) See Jabalpur.

ju·bi·lant (jōō′bə-lənt) *adj.* **1.** Exultingly joyful. **2.** Expressing joy. [Lat. *iūbilāns, iūbilant-*, pr. part. of *iūbilāre*, to raise a shout of joy.] —**ju′bi·lance** *n.* —**ju′bi·lant·ly** *adv.*

ju·bi·late (jōō′bə-lāt′) *intr.v.* **-lat·ed, -lat·ing, -lates** To rejoice; exult. [Lat. *iūbilāre, iūbilāt-*, to raise a shout of joy.]

Ju·bi·la·te (yōō′bə-lä′tā, -tē, jōō′-) *n.* **1a.** The 100th Psalm in

Joseph²
1878 portrait by
Cyrenius Hall (1830–?)

Joshua tree
Yucca brevifolia

Juan Carlos

the King James Bible and in most modern Catholic versions or the 99th in the Vulgate. **b.** A musical setting of the Jubilate. **2.** The third Sunday after Easter. **3.** A song or an outburst of joy and triumph. [ME < Lat. *iūbilātē*, second pers. pl. imper. of *iūbilāre*, to raise a shout of joy, the first word of the psalm.]

ju·bi·la·tion (jōō′bə-lā′shən) *n.* **1a.** The act of rejoicing. **b.** The condition or feeling of being jubilant. **2.** A celebration or other expression of joy.

ju·bi·lee (jōō′bə-lē′, jōō′bə-lē′) *n.* **1a.** A specially celebrated anniversary, esp. a 50th anniversary. **b.** The celebration of such an anniversary. **2.** A season or occasion of joyful celebration. **3.** Jubilation; rejoicing. **4.** often **Jubilee** *Bible* A year of rest in the historic land of Israel when land is to be left untilled, slaves are to be freed, and alienated property is to be restored. **5.** often **Jubilee** *Roman Catholic Church* A year during which plenary indulgence may be obtained by the performance of certain pious acts. [ME *jubile* < OFr. < LLat. *iūbilaeus*, the Jewish year of jubilee, alteration (influenced by *iūbilāre*, to raise a shout of joy) of Gk. *iōbē-laios* < *iōbēlos* < Heb. *yôbēl*, ram, ram's horn, jubilee.]

Ju·dah[1] (jōō′də) In the Bible, a son of Jacob and Leah and the forebear of one of the tribes of Israel.

Ju·dah[2] (jōō′də) An ancient kingdom (931–586 B.C.) of SW Asia between the Mediterranean and the Dead Sea.

Ju·da·ic (jōō-dā′ĭk) also **Ju·da·i·cal** (-ĭ-kəl) *adj.* Of or characteristic of Jews or Judaism. —**Ju·da′i·cal·ly** *adv.*

Ju·da·ism (jōō′dē-ĭz′əm) *n.* **1.** The monotheistic religion of the Jews, tracing its origins to Abraham and having its spiritual and ethical principles embodied chiefly in the Hebrew Scriptures and the Talmud. **2.** Conformity to the traditional ceremonies and rites of the Jewish religion. **3.** The cultural, religious, and social practices and beliefs of the Jews. **4.** The Jews considered as a people or community. [ME *Iudaisme* < OFr. *Judaisme* < LLat. *Iūdaismus* < Gk. *Ioudaismos* < *Ioudaios*, Jew. See JEW.]

Ju·da·ize (jōō′dē-īz′) *v.* **-ized, -iz·ing, -iz·es** —*tr.* To bring into conformity with Judaism. —*intr.* To adopt Jewish customs and beliefs. —**Ju′da·i·za′tion** (-ĭ-zā′shən) *n.* —**Ju′da·i′zer** *n.*

Ju·das (jōō′dəs) *n.* **1.** One who betrays another under the guise of friendship. **2. judas** A one-way peephole in a door. [ME < LLat. *Iūdas*, Judas Iscariot < Gk. *Ioudas* < Heb. *yəhûdâ*, Judah.]

Judas Is·car·i·ot (ĭ-skăr′ē-ət) d. c. A.D. 30. One of the 12 Apostles and the betrayer of Jesus.

Judas tree *n.* See **redbud.** [< the belief that Judas Iscariot hanged himself on such a tree.]

jud·der (jŭd′ər) *intr.v.* **-dered, -der·ing, -ders** To shake rapidly or spasmodically; vibrate conspicuously. ❖ *n.* A rapid or spasmodic shaking. [Perh. J(ERK)[1] + (SH)UDDER.]

Jude (jōōd) *n.* See table at **Bible.** [Gk. *Iouda* < Heb. *yəhûdâ*.]

Jude, Saint. fl. 1st cent. A.D. One of the 12 Apostles, traditionally invoked in prayer when a situation seems hopeless.

Ju·de·a also **Ju·dae·a** (jōō-dē′ə, -dā′ə) An ancient region and kingdom of SW Asia comprising present-day S Israel and SW Jordan. —**Ju·de′an** *adj. & n.*

Ju·de·o-Span·ish (jōō-dā′ō-spăn′ĭsh) *n.* See **Ladino 1.** [< Lat. *Iūdaeus*, Jewish < Gk. *Ioudaios*. See JEW.]

Judg. *abbr. Bible* Judges

judge (jŭj) *v.* **judged, judg·ing, judg·es** —*tr.* **1.** To form an opinion or estimation of after careful consideration. **2a.** *Law* To hear and decide on in a court of law; try. **b.** *Obsolete* To pass sentence on; condemn. **c.** To act as one appointed to decide the winners of. **3.** To determine or declare after consideration or deliberation. **4.** *Informal* To have an opinion or assumption; suppose. **5.** *Bible* To govern; rule. Used of an ancient Israelite leader. —*intr.* **1.** To form an opinion or evaluation. **2.** To act or decide as a judge. ❖ *n.* **1.** One who judges, esp.: **a.** One who makes estimates as to worth, quality, or fitness. **b.** *Law* A public official who hears and decides cases brought before a court of law. **c.** *Law* A bankruptcy referee. **d.** One appointed to decide the winners of a contest or competition. **2.** *Bible* **a.** A leader of the Israelites during a period of about 400 years between the death of Joshua and the accession of Saul. **b. Judges** (*used with a sing. verb*) See table at **Bible.** [ME *jugen* < AN *juger* < Lat. *iūdicāre* < *iūdex, iūdic-,* judge. See deik- in App.]

judge advocate *n., pl.* **judge advocates 1.** A commissioned officer in the US Army, Air Force, or Navy assigned to the Judge Advocate General's Corps. **2.** A staff officer serving as legal adviser to a commander. **3.** An officer acting as prosecutor at a court-martial.

judge advocate general *n., pl.* **judge advocates general** or **judge advocate generals** The chief legal officer of a branch of the US armed forces.

judge·ship (jŭj′shĭp′) *n.* The office or jurisdiction of a judge.

judg·mat·ic (jŭj-măt′ĭk) also **judg·mat·i·cal** (-ĭ-kəl) *adj.* Judicious. [Perh. JUDG(MENT) + (DOG)MATIC.]

judg·ment also **judge·ment** (jŭj′mənt) *n.* **1.** The act or process of judging; the formation of an opinion after consideration or deliberation. **2a.** The mental ability to perceive and distinguish relationships; discernment. **b.** The capacity to form an opinion by distinguishing and evaluating. **c.** The capacity to assess situations or circumstances and draw sound conclusions; good sense. **3.** An opinion or estimate formed after consideration or deliberation, esp. a formal or authoritative decision. **4.** *Law* **a.** A determi-

nation of a court of law; a judicial decision. **b.** A court act creating or affirming an obligation, such as a debt. **c.** A writ in witness of such an act. **5.** An assertion of something believed. **6.** A misfortune believed to be sent by God as punishment for sin. **7. Judgment** The Last Judgment. [ME *jugement* < OFr. < *jugier,* to judge < Lat. *iūdicāre.* See JUDGE.]

judg·men·tal (jŭj-měn′tl) *adj.* **1.** Of, relating to, or dependent on judgment. **2.** Inclined to make judgments, esp. moral or personal ones. —**judg·men′tal·ly** *adv.*

Judgment Day *n.* **1.** In Judeo-Christian and Muslim traditions, the day at the end of the world when God judges the moral worth of individual humans or the whole human race. **2. judgment day** A day of reckoning or final judgment.

ju·di·ca·to·ry (jōō′dĭ-kə-tôr′ē, -tōr′ē) *n., pl.* **-ries** A law court or system of law courts; a judiciary. ❖ *adj.* Of or relating to the administration of justice. [LLat. *iūdicātōrium* < neut. of *iūdicātōrius,* judicial < Lat. *iūdicāre,* to judge. See JUDGE.]

ju·di·ca·ture (jōō′dĭ-kə-chōōr′) *n.* **1.** Administration of justice. **2.** The position, function, or authority of a judge. **3.** The jurisdiction of a law court or judge. **4.** A court or system of courts of law. [Med.Lat. *iūdicātūra* < fem. fut. part. of Lat. *iūdicāre,* to judge. See JUDGE.]

ju·di·cial (jōō-dĭsh′əl) *adj.* **1.** *Law* **a.** Of, relating to, or proper to courts of law or to the administration of justice. **b.** Decreed by or proceeding from a court of justice. **c.** Belonging or appropriate to the office of a judge. **2.** Characterized by or expressing judgment. **3.** Proceeding from a divine judgment. [ME < AN < Lat. *iūdiciālis* < *iūdicium,* judgment < *iūdex, iūdic-,* judge. See deik- in App.] —**ju·di′cial·ly** *adv.*

ju·di·ci·ar·y (jōō-dĭsh′ē-ĕr′ē, -dĭsh′ə-rē) *n., pl.* **-ies 1.** The judicial branch of government. **2a.** A system of courts of law for the administration of justice. **b.** The judges of these courts. [Prob. < Lat. *iūdiciārius,* of the courts < *iūdicium,* judgment < *iūdex, iūdic-,* judge. See JUDGE.]

ju·di·cious (jōō-dĭsh′əs) *adj.* Having or exhibiting sound judgment; prudent. [< Fr. *judicieux* < Lat. *iūdicium,* judgment < *iūdex, iūdic-,* judge. See JUDGE.] —**ju·di′cious·ly** *adv.*

Ju·dith[1] (jōō′dĭth) In the Bible, a Jewish heroine who rescued her people by slaying an Assyrian general.

Ju·dith[2] (jōō′dĭth) *n.* See table at **Bible.**

ju·do (jōō′dō) *n.* A sport and method of physical training similar to wrestling, developed in Japan in the late 19th century and using principles of balance and leverage adapted from jujitsu. [J. *jūdō* < *jū,* soft (< M Chin. *nʸuw, riw*) + *dō,* way; see AIKIDO.] —**ju′do·ist** *n.*

Jud·son (jŭd′sən), **Edward Zane Carroll** Pen name **Ned Buntline.** 1823–86. Amer. writer best remembered for his dime novels.

jug (jŭg) *n.* **1a.** A large vessel of earthenware, glass, or metal with a small mouth, a handle, and usu. a stopper or cap. **b.** The amount a jug holds. **2.** A small pitcher. **3.** *Slang* A jail. ❖ *tr.v.* **jugged, jug·ging, jugs 1.** To stew (meat) in an earthenware jug or jar. **2.** *Slang* To jail. [ME *jugge.*]

ju·gate (jōō′gāt′, -gĭt) *adj.* Joined in or forming pairs or a pair. [Lat. *iugātus,* p. part. of *iugāre,* to join < *iugum,* yoke. See yeug- in App.]

jug band *n. Music* A group that uses unconventional or improvised instruments, such as jugs, kazoos, and washboards.

Ju·gend·stil (yōō′gənt-shtēl′) *n.* A style of architecture and decorative art similar to art nouveau, popular in German-speaking areas of Europe during the late 19th and early 20th centuries. [Ger. : *Jugend,* youth + *Stil,* style.]

jug·ger·naut (jŭg′ər-nôt′) *n.* **1.** Something, such as a belief or institution, that elicits blind devotion or sacrifice. **2.** An overwhelming, terrible, destructive force. **3. Juggernaut** Used as a title for the Hindu deity Krishna. [Hindi *jagannāth,* title of Krishna < Skt. *jagannāthaḥ,* lord of the world : *jagat,* moving, the world (< earlier pr. part. of *jigāti,* he goes; see gʷā- in App.) + *nāthaḥ,* lord (< *nāthate,* he helps, protects). Senses 1 and 2 < the fact that worshipers have thrown themselves under the wheels of a huge wagon which drew the idol of Krishna in an annual procession at Puri in east-central India.]

jug·gle (jŭg′əl) *v.* **-gled, -gling, -gles** —*tr.* **1.** To keep (two or more objects) in the air at one time by alternately tossing and catching them. **2.** To have difficulty holding; balance insecurely. **3.** To keep (more than two activities, for example) in motion or progress at one time. **4.** To manipulate in order to deceive. —*intr.* **1.** To juggle objects or perform other tricks of manual dexterity. **2.** To make rapid motions or manipulations. **3.** To use trickery; practice deception. ❖ *n.* **1.** The act of juggling. **2.** Trickery for a dishonest end. [ME *jogelen,* to entertain with tricks < OFr. *jogler* < Lat. *ioculārī,* to jest < *ioculus,* dim. of *iocus,* joke.] —**jug′gler** *n.*

jug·gler·y (jŭg′lə-rē) *n., pl.* **-ies 1.** The skill or performance of a juggler. **2.** Trickery; deception.

jug·u·lar (jŭg′yə-lər) *adj.* Of, relating to, or located in the region of the neck or throat. ❖ *n.* **1.** A jugular vein. **2.** The most vital part: *an attack on the enemy's jugular.* [LLat. *iugulāris,* jugular < Lat. *iugulum,* collarbone, dim. of *iugum,* yoke. See yeug- in App.]

jugular vein *n.* Any of several large veins of the neck that drain blood from the head.

ju·gum (jōō′gəm) *n., pl.* **-ga** (-gə) or **-gums** A yokelike structure

juggle

in certain insects that joins the forewings to the hind wings. [Lat. *iugum*, yoke. See **yeug-** in App.]

jug wine *n.* Inexpensive table wine sold in large bottles.

juice (jo͞os) *n.* **1a.** A fluid naturally contained in plant or animal tissue. **b.** A bodily secretion: *digestive juices.* **c.** The liquid contained in something that is chiefly solid. **2.** A substance or quality that imparts identity and vitality; essence. **3.** *Slang* Vigorous life; vitality. **4.** *Slang* Political power or influence; clout. **5.** *Slang* **a.** Electric current. **b.** Fuel for an engine. **6.** *Slang* Funds; money. **7.** *Slang* Alcoholic drink; liquor. **8.** *Slang* Racy or scandalous gossip. —*tr.* **juiced, juic•ing, juic•es** To extract the juice from. —*intr.* *Slang* To drink alcoholic beverages excessively. ***—phrasal verb:*** **juice up** *Slang* To give energy, spirit, or interest to. [ME *jus* < OFr. < Lat. *iūs.*]

juiced (jo͞ost) *adj. Slang* Intoxicated; drunk.

juice•head (jo͞os′hĕd′) *n. Slang* A heavy drinker; an alcoholic.

juic•er (jo͞o′sər) *n.* **1.** An appliance used to extract juice from fruits and vegetables. **2.** *Slang* One who drinks liquor or alcoholic beverages habitually or excessively.

juic•y (jo͞o′sē) *adj.* **-i•er, -i•est 1.** Full of juice; succulent. **2a.** Richly interesting. **b.** Racy; titillating: *a juicy bit of gossip.* **3.** Yielding profit; rewarding or gratifying. **—juic′i•ly** *adv.* **—juic′i•ness** *n.*

Juiz de Fo•ra (zhwēzh′ də fôr′ə) A city of SE Brazil N of Rio de Janeiro. Pop. 385,734.

ju•jit•su also **ju•jut•su** or **jiu•jit•su** or **jiu•jut•su** (jo͞o-jĭt′so͞o) *n.* An art of weaponless self-defense developed in Japan that uses throws, holds, and blows and derives added power from the attacker's own weight and strength. [J. *jūjitsu* : *jū*, soft; see JUDO + *jitsu*, arts (< M Chin. *zhwit*).]

ju•ju (jo͞o′jo͞o) *n.* **1.** An object used as a fetish, charm, or amulet in West Africa. **2.** The supernatural power ascribed to such an object. [Hausa *jūjū*, fetish, evil spirit.] **—ju′ju•ism** *n.*

ju•jube (jo͞o′jo͞ob′) *n.* **1a.** Any of several Old World trees of the genus *Ziziphus*, esp. *Z. jujuba*, having palmately veined leaves, spiny stipules, and dark red fruit. **b.** The fleshy edible drupe of this tree. **2.** (*also* jo͞o′jo͞o-bē′) A fruit-flavored, usu. chewy candy or lozenge. [ME, jujube fruit < OFr. < Med.Lat. *jujuba* < Lat. *zizyphum* < Gk. *zizuphon.*]

juke[1] (jo͞ok, jo͝ok) *Southeastern US n.* A roadside drinking establishment that offers inexpensive drinks, food, and music for dancing. ❖ *intr.v.* **juked, juk•ing, jukes** To dance, esp. in a roadside drinking establishment or to the music of a jukebox. [Prob. < Gullah *juke, joog*, disorderly, wicked, of W African orig.; akin to Wolof *dzug*, to live wickedly, and Bambara *dzugu*, wicked.]

REGIONAL NOTE Gullah, the English-based Creole language spoken by people of African ancestry off the coast of Georgia and South Carolina, retains a number of words from the West African languages brought over by slaves. One such word is *juke*, "bad, wicked, disorderly," the probable source of the English word *juke.* Used chiefly in the Southeastern states, *juke* (also appearing in the compound *juke joint*) means a roadside drinking establishment that offers cheap drinks, food, and music for dancing and often doubles as a brothel. "To juke" is to dance, particularly at a juke joint or to the music of a jukebox, whose name, no longer regional and having lost the connotation of sleaziness, contains the same word.

juke[2] (jo͞ok) *Football v.* **juked, juk•ing, jukes** —*tr.* To deceive or outmaneuver (a defender) by a feint; fake. —*intr.* To juke a defender. ❖ *n.* A feint or fake. [ME *jowken*, to bend supply.]

juke•box (jo͞ok′bŏks′) *n.* A money-operated phonograph or compact disk player, equipped with push buttons for the selection of particular recordings. See Regional Note at **juke**[1].

juke joint (jo͞ok, jo͝ok) *n. Informal* **1.** A bar, tavern, or roadhouse featuring music played on a jukebox. **2.** See **juke**[1]. See Regional Note at **juke**[1].

ju•ku (jo͞o′ko͞o′) *n.* A Japanese school that prepares students for entrance exams and is attended in addition to public school. [J. < M Chin. *dzhuwk.*]

Jul. *abbr.* July

ju•lep (jo͞o′lĭp) *n.* **1.** A mint julep. **2.** A sweet syrupy drink, esp. a medicinal one. [ME, a sugar syrup < OFr. < Med.Lat. < Ar. *julāb* < Pers. *gulāb*, rosewater : *gul*, rose (< MPers. *vardā*) + *āb*, water (< MPers. *āp* < OPers.).]

Jul•ian (jo͞ol′yən) A.D. 331?–363. Emperor of Rome (361–363) who attempted to restore the dominance of paganism.

Ju•li•an•a (jo͞o′lē-ăn′ə) b. 1909. Queen of the Netherlands (1948–80) who abdicated in favor of her daughter Beatrix.

Julian Alps A range of the E Alps in Slovenia and NE Italy rising to 2,864 m (9,390 ft).

Julian calendar *n.* The solar calendar introduced by Julius Caesar in Rome in 46 B.C., having a year of 12 months and 365 days and a leap year of 366 days every fourth year. See table at **calendar.**

ju•li•enne (jo͞o′lē-ĕn′, zhü-lyĕn′) *n.* Consommé or broth garnished with long thin strips of vegetables. ❖ *adj.* also **ju•li•enned** Cut into long thin strips. [Fr., prob. < the name *Julienne.*]

Ju•lius II (jo͞ol′yəs) Orig. Giuliano della Rovere. 1443–1513. Pope (1503–13) who enlarged the temporal power of the papacy and was active in military campaigns in Europe.

Ju•ly (jo͞o-lī′) *n.* The seventh month of the year in the Gregorian calendar. See table at **calendar.** [ME *Julie* < ONFr. < Lat. *Iūlius*, after *Iūlius* Caesar, Julius Caesar. See **dyeu-** in App.]

Ju•ma•da (jo͞o-mä′dä) also **Jo•ma•da** (jə-) *n.* Either the fifth or the sixth month of the year in the Islamic calendar. See table at **calendar.** [Ar. *jumādā* < *jamada*, to freeze.]

jum•ble (jŭm′bəl) *v.* **-bled, -bling, -bles** —*tr.* **1.** To mix in a confused way; throw together carelessly. **2.** To muddle; confuse. —*intr.* To be mixed in a confused way. ❖ *n.* **1.** A confused or disordered mass. **2.** A disordered state; a muddle. [?]

jum•bo (jŭm′bō) *n., pl.* **-bos** An unusually large person, animal, or thing. [After *Jumbo*, a large elephant exhibited by P.T. Barnum, prob. < slang, clumsy person.] **—jum′bo** *adj.*

Jum•na (jŭm′nə) See **Yamuna.**

jump (jŭmp) *v.* **jumped, jump•ing, jumps** —*intr.* **1a.** To spring off the ground or other base by a muscular effort of the legs and feet. **b.** To move suddenly and in one motion. **c.** To move involuntarily, as in surprise. **d.** To parachute from an aircraft. **2a.** *Informal* To move quickly; hustle. **b.** To take prompt advantage; respond quickly: *jump at a bargain.* **3a.** To enter eagerly into an activity; plunge. **b.** To begin or start. Often used with *off: The project jumped off with great enthusiasm.* **4.** To form an opinion or a judgment hastily: *jump to conclusions.* **5.** To make a sudden verbal attack; lash out: *jumped at me for being late.* **6a.** To undergo a sudden and pronounced increase. **b.** To rise suddenly in position or rank. **7.** To move discontinuously or change after a short period: *jumps from one subject to another.* **8.** To be displaced, as by a sudden jerk. **9.** *Computer Science* To move from one set of instructions in a program to another out of sequence. **10.** *Games* **a.** To move over an opponent's playing piece in a board game. **b.** To make a jump bid in bridge. **11.** *Slang* To be lively; bustle. —*tr.* **1.** To leap over or across. **2.** To leap onto. **3.** *Slang* To spring upon in sudden attack; assault or ambush. **4.** To move or start prematurely before. **5.** To cause to leap. **6.** To cause to increase suddenly. **7.** To pass over; skip. **8.** To raise in rank or position; promote. **9.** *Games* To move a piece over (an opponent's piece) in a board game, often thereby capturing the opponent's piece. **10.** To jump-start (a motor vehicle). **11.** To leave (a course), esp. through mishap: *The train jumped the rails.* **12.** *Slang* **a.** To leave hastily; skip. **b.** To leave (an organization, for example) suddenly or in violation of an agreement. **13.** To seize or occupy illegally. **14.** To forfeit (bail) by failing to appear in court. **15.** *Vulgar Slang* To have sexual intercourse with. ❖ *n.* **1a.** The act of jumping; a leap. **b.** The distance covered by a jump. **c.** An obstacle or a span to be jumped. **d.** A structure or course from which a jump is made. **2.** A descent from an aircraft by parachute. **3.** *Sports* Any of several track-and-field events in which contestants jump. **4.** *Informal* **a.** An initial competitive advantage; a head start. **b.** Energy or quickness. **5a.** A sudden pronounced rise, as in price or salary. **b.** An impressive promotion. **6.** A step or level. **7.** A sudden or major transition, as from one career or subject to another. **8a.** A short trip. **b.** One in a series of moves and stopovers, as with a circus or road show. **9.** *Games* A move in a board game over an opponent's piece. **10.** *Computer Science* A movement from one set of instructions to another. **11.** An involuntary nervous movement; a start. **12.** A jump-start of a motor vehicle. ***—idiom:*** **jump the gun** To start doing something too soon. [Perh. ME *jumpen*, to jump (sense uncertain).]

jump ball *n. Basketball* A method of starting play or determining possession in which the ball is tossed up between two opposing players who try to tap the ball to a teammate.

jump bid *n. Games* A bridge bid that skips at least one level of bidding.

jump cut *n.* A cut to later action from one filmed scene to the next, creating an effect of discontinuity or acceleration.

jump•er[1] (jŭm′pər) *n.* **1.** One that jumps. **2.** A type of coasting sled. **3.** *Electricity* A short length of wire used temporarily to complete a circuit or to bypass a break in a circuit. **4.** *Basketball* See **jump shot. 5.** A saddle horse that has been trained to jump over obstacles.

jump•er[2] (jŭm′pər) *n.* **1.** A sleeveless dress worn over a blouse or sweater. **2.** A loose protective garment worn over other clothes. **3.** A child's garment of straight-legged pants attached to a biblike bodice. Often used in the plural. **4.** *Chiefly British* A pullover sweater. [Prob. < *jump*, short coat, perh. < obsolete *jup*, bodice < obsolete Fr. *juppe*, ult. < Ar. *jubba*, long garment with wide open sleeves < *jabba*, to cut.]

jumper cable *n.* See **booster cable.**

jump•ing bean (jŭm′pĭng) *n.* A seed, as of certain Mexican plants of the genera *Sebastiana* and *Sapium*, containing the larva of the moth *Laspeyresia saltitans*, whose movements cause the seed to jerk or roll.

jumping jack *n.* **1.** A toy figure with jointed limbs that can be made to dance by pulling an attached string. **2.** *Sports* A physical exercise performed by jumping to a position with the legs spread wide and the hands touching overhead and then putting the feet together and the arms at the sides.

jumping mouse *n.* Any of various small Eurasian and North American rodents of the family Zapodidae, having a very long tail and long hind legs.

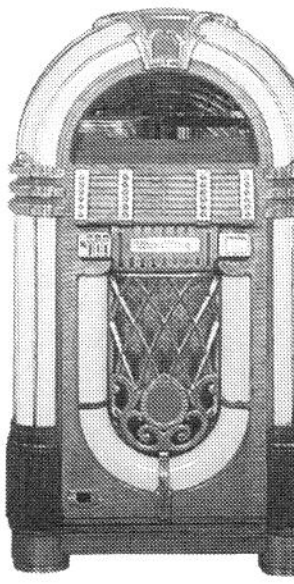

jukebox

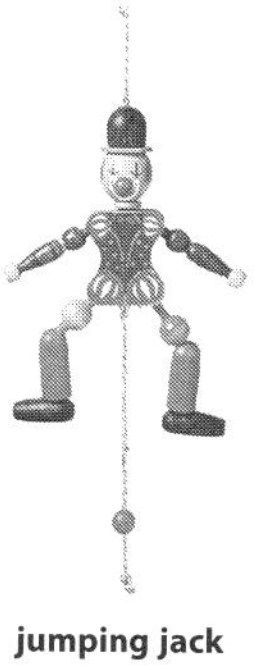

jumping jack

ă	pat	oi	**boy**
ā	pay	ou	**out**
âr	**care**	o͝o	took
ä	father	o͞o	boot
ĕ	pet	ŭ	cut
ē	be	ûr	urge
ĭ	pit	th	thin
ī	pie	*th*	this
îr	**pier**	hw	**which**
ŏ	pot	zh	vision
ō	toe	ə	about, item
ô	paw		

Stress marks:
′ (primary);
′ (secondary), as in
lexicon (lĕk′sĭ-kŏn′)

juniper
prickly juniper
Juniperus oxycedrus

jump·ing-off place (jŭm′pĭng-ôf′, -ŏf′) *n.* **1.** A beginning point for a journey or venture. **2.** A very remote spot.

jump jet *n.* A jet aircraft capable of vertical takeoffs and landings.

jump-off (jŭmp′ôf′, -ŏf′) *n.* The commencement of a race or of a planned military attack.

jump rope *n.* A rope that is twirled and jumped over in children's games or in conditioning exercises.

jump seat *n.* **1.** A small folding seat, as in an automobile between the front and rear seats. **2.** A small rear seat in a sports car.

jump shot *n. Basketball* A shot made by a player at the highest point of a jump.

jump-start (jŭmp′stärt′) *tr.v.* **-start·ed, -start·ing, -starts** **1.** To start (the engine of a motor vehicle) by using a booster cable connected to the battery of another vehicle or by engaging the drive train while the vehicle is rolling downhill or being pushed. **2.** *Informal* To start or set in motion (something stalled or sluggish). **—jump′-start′** *n.*

jump suit *n.* **1.** A parachutist's uniform. **2.** also **jump·suit** (jŭmp′sōot′) A one-piece garment consisting of a blouse or shirt with attached slacks or shorts.

jump·y (jŭm′pē) *adj.* **-i·er, -i·est** **1.** Characterized by fitful jerky movements. **2.** On edge; nervous. **—jump′i·ness** *n.*

jun. *abbr.* junior

Jun. *abbr.* June

jun·co (jŭng′kō) *n., pl.* **-cos** or **-coes** Any of various small North American birds of the genus *Junco*, having predominantly gray plumage, a gray or black head, and white outer tail feathers. [Sp., reed < Lat. *iuncus*.]

junc·tion (jŭngk′shən) *n.* **1.** The act or process of joining or the condition of being joined. **2.** A place where two things join or meet, esp. a place where two roads or railway routes come together and one terminates. **3.** A transition layer or boundary between two different materials or regions, esp.: **a.** A connection between conductors or sections of a transmission line. **b.** The interface between two different semiconductor regions in a semiconductor device. **c.** A contact between different metals or other conductors. [Lat. *iūnctiō, iūnction-* < *iūnctus,* p. part. of *iungere,* to join. See **yeug-** in App.] **—junc′tion·al** *adj.*

junction box *n.* An enclosure within which electric circuits are connected.

junc·ture (jŭngk′chər) *n.* **1.** The act of joining or the condition of being joined. **2.** A place where two things are joined; a junction or joint. **3.** A point in time, esp. a critical point. **4.** The transition or mode of transition from one sound to another in speech. [ME < Lat. *iūnctūra* < *iūnctus,* p. part. of *iungere,* to join. See **yeug-** in App.]

Jun·dia·í (zhōōn′dyə-ē′) A city of SE Brazil NNW of São Paulo; est. in the 17th cent. Pop. 288,644.

June (jōōn) *n.* The sixth month of the year in the Gregorian calendar. See table at **calendar.** [ME < OE *Junius* and < OFr. *juin,* both < Lat. *(mēnsis) Iūnius,* (month) of June < *Iūnō,* Juno. See JUNO.]

Ju·neau (jōō′nō′) The cap. of AK, in the Panhandle NE of Sitka; settled by gold miners in 1880. Pop. 30,711.

June beetle *n.* Any of various large North American scarabaeid beetles of the subfamily Melolonthinae, appearing in late spring and having larvae that are destructive to vegetation.

June·ber·ry (jōōn′bĕr′ē) *n.* See shadbush.

June bug *n.* See **June beetle.**

June·teenth (jōōn-tēnth′) *n.* June 19, an African-American holiday commemorating the date in 1865 when many slaves in Texas learned they had been freed by the Emancipation Proclamation (January 1, 1863).

Jung (yŏŏng), **Carl Gustav** 1875–1961. Swiss psychiatrist and founder of analytical psychology whose works include *The Psychology of the Unconscious* (1912). **—Jung′i·an** *adj.*

Jung·frau (yŏŏng′frou′) A mountain, 4,160.8 m (13,642 ft), in the Bernese Alps of S-central Switzerland.

jun·gle (jŭng′gəl) *n.* **1.** Land densely overgrown with tropical vegetation. **2.** A dense thicket or growth. **3.** A dense confused mass; a jumble. **4.** A bewildering complex or maze. **5.** A place or milieu characterized by ruthless competition or struggle for survival. **6.** *Slang* A place where hoboes camp. [Ult. < Skt. *jaṅgalam,* desert, wasteland, uncultivated area < *jaṅgala-,* desert, waste.] **—jun′gly** (-glē) *adj.*

jungle fever *n.* **1.** Malaria, esp. a severe form of the East Indies and other tropical regions. **2.** Any of various tropical diseases.

jungle fowl *n.* Any of several game birds of the genus *Gallus* of southeast Asia, esp. *G. gallus* considered to be the ancestor of the common domestic fowl.

jungle gym *n.* A structure of poles and bars for children to climb and play on. [Orig. a trademark.]

jun·ior (jōōn′yər) *adj.* **1.** Used to distinguish a son from his father when they have the same given name. **2.** Intended for or including youthful persons. **3.** Lower in rank or shorter in length of tenure. **4.** Of, for, or constituting students in the third year of a US high school or college. **5.** Lesser in scale than the usual. ❖ *n.* **1.** One who is younger than another: *a sister six years my junior.* **2.** A person lesser in rank or time of participation or service; subordinate. **3.** A student in the third year of a US high school or college. **4.** A class of clothing sizes for girls and slender women.

junk²
Hong Kong harbor

Jupiter

[ME < Lat. *iūnior,* comp. of *iuvenis,* young. See **yeu-** in App.]

junior college *n.* An educational institution offering a two-year course that is generally the equivalent of the first two years of a four-year undergraduate course.

junior high school *n.* A school in the US system generally including the seventh, eighth, and sometimes ninth grades.

junior varsity *n.* A high-school or college team that competes in interschool sports on the level below varsity.

ju·ni·per (jōō′nə-pər) *n.* Any of various evergreen trees or shrubs of the genus *Juniperus,* having needlelike or scalelike leaves and aromatic berrylike seed-bearing cones. [ME < Lat. *iūniperus.*]

junk¹ (jŭngk) *n.* **1.** Discarded material, such as glass, rags, paper, or metal, some of which may be reused in some form. **2.** *Informal* **a.** Articles that are worn-out or fit to be discarded. **b.** Cheap or shoddy material. **c.** Something meaningless, fatuous, or unbelievable. **3.** *Slang* Heroin. **4.** Hard salt beef for consumption on board a ship. ❖ *tr.v.* **junked, junk·ing, junks** To discard as useless or sell to be reused as parts; scrap. ❖ *adj.* **1.** Cheap, shoddy, or worthless. **2.** Having a superficial appeal or utility, but lacking substance. [ME *jonk,* an old cable or rope.]

WORD HISTORY The Middle English word *jonk,* ancestor of *junk,* originally had a very specific nautical meaning. First recorded in 1353, the word meant "an old cable or rope." On a sailing ship it made little sense to throw away useful material since new supplies might be distant. Old cable was used, for example, to make fenders, that is, material hung over the side of the ship to protect it from scraping other ships or wharves. *Junk* came to refer to this old cable as well. The big leap in meaning taken by the word seems to have occurred when *junk* was applied to discarded but useful material in general. This extension may also have taken place in a nautical context, for the earliest, more generalized use of *junk* is found in the compound *junk shop,* referring to a store where old materials from ships were sold. *Junk* has gone on to mean useless waste as well.

junk² (jŭngk) *n. Nautical* A Chinese flatbottom ship with a high stern and full-battened sails. [Port. *junco* or Du. *jonk,* both < Javanese *djong,* var. of *djung* < O Javanese *jong,* seagoing ship.]

junk art *n.* Three-dimensional art made from junked materials, such as metal, glass, or wood.

junk bond *n.* A corporate bond high in yield and in risk.

junk DNA *n.* DNA that does not code for proteins, is thought to be involved in the evolution of new genes, and constitutes approx. 95 percent of the human genome.

junker (jŭng′kər) *n. Slang* A car or truck that is old and in poor repair.

Jun·ker (yŏŏng′kər) *n.* A member of the Prussian landed aristocracy, a class formerly associated with political reaction and militarism. [Ger. < MHGer. *juncherre,* page, squire < OHGer. *juncherro : junc,* young; see **yeu-** in App. + *hērro,* lord; see HERR.] **—Jun′ker·dom** *n.*

jun·ket (jŭng′kĭt) *n.* **1.** A dessert made from flavored milk and rennet. **2.** A party, banquet, or outing. **3.** A trip or tour, esp.: **a.** One taken by an official at public expense. **b.** One taken by a person as the guest of a business or agency seeking favor or patronage. ❖ *v.* **-ket·ed, -ket·ing, -kets** *—intr.* **1.** To hold a party or banquet. **2.** To go on a junket. *—tr.* To fete at a party or banquet. [ME *jonket,* rush basket, a food served on rushes, feast < ONFr. *jonquette,* rush basket (prob. < *jonc,* rush), or < Med.Lat. *iuncāta,* rush basket, both < Lat. *iuncus,* rush.] **—jun′ket·er** *n.*

jun·ke·teer (jŭng′kĭ-tēr′) *n.* One who goes on a junket or junkets. ❖ *intr.v.* **-teered, -teer·ing, -teers** To go on a junket.

junk food *n.* A high-calorie food that is low in nutritional value.

junk·ie also **junk·y** (jŭng′kē) *n., pl.* **-ies** *Slang* **1.** A narcotics addict, esp. one using heroin. **2.** One who has an insatiable interest or devotion: *a sports junkie.*

junk mail *n.* Third-class mail, such as advertisements, mailed indiscriminately in large quantities.

junk·y¹ (jŭng′kē) *adj.* **-i·er, -i·est** **1.** Of or related to junk; worthy of being discarded. **2.** Meaningless, fatuous, or unbelievable: *a junky novel.*

junk·y² (jŭng′kē) *n.* Variant of **junkie.**

junk·yard (jŭngk′yärd′) *n.* A yard or lot that is used to store junk, such as scrap metal or resalable car parts.

Ju·no (jōō′nō) *n. Roman Mythology* The principal goddess of the Pantheon, the wife of Jupiter, worshiped as the goddess of women, marriage, childbirth and the moon, and as the protector of the state. [Lat. *Iūnō < iuvenis,* young (prob. < her association with the new moon). See **yeu-** in App.]

Ju·no·esque (jōō′nō-ĕsk′) *adj.* Having the stately bearing and imposing beauty of the goddess Juno.

jun·ta (hōōn′tə, jŭn′-) *n.* **1.** A group of military officers ruling a country after seizing power. **2.** A council or small legislative body in a government, esp. in Central or South America. **3.** A junta. [Sp. and Port., conference, prob. < VLat. **iūncta < fem. p. part.* of Lat. *iungere,* to join. See **yeug-** in App.]

jun·to (jŭn′tō) *n., pl.* **-tos** A small, usu. secret group united for a common interest. [Alteration of JUNTA.]

Ju·pi·ter (jōō′pĭ-tər) *n.* **1.** *Roman Mythology* The supreme god, patron of the Roman state and brother and husband of Juno. **2.**

Astronomy The fifth planet from the sun, the largest and most massive in the solar system. See table at **planet**. [Lat. *Iūpiter*. See **dyeu**- in App.]

ju•ral (jŏŏr′əl) *adj.* **1.** Of or relating to law. **2.** Of or relating to rights and obligations. [< Lat. *iūs, iūr-*, law.] —**ju′ral•ly** *adv.*

Ju•ra Mountains (jŏŏr′ə, zhü-rä′) A range extending c. 241 km (150 mi) along the French-Swiss border and rising to 1,723.9 m (5,652 ft).

Ju•ras•sic (jŏŏ-răs′ĭk) *adj.* Of or belonging to the geologic time of the second period of the Mesozoic Era, characterized by the existence of dinosaurs and the appearance of the earliest birds. See table at **geologic time**. ❖ *n.* The Jurassic Period or its deposits. [Fr. *jurassique*, after the JURA (MOUNTAINS).]

ju•rat (jŏŏr′ăt′) *n.* A certification on an affidavit declaring when, where, and before whom it was sworn. [ME, informant under oath < AN, member of a city ruling body < Med.Lat. *iūrātus*, juror < p. part. of Lat. *iūrāre*, to swear. See JURY[1].]

ju•rid•i•cal (jŏŏ-rĭd′ĭ-kəl) also **ju•rid•ic** (-ĭk) *adj.* Of or relating to the law and its administration. [< Lat. *iūridicus* : *iūs, iūr-*, law + *dīcere*, to say; see **deik**- in App.] —**ju•rid′i•cal•ly** *adv.*

ju•ris•con•sult (jŏŏr′ĭs-kŏn′sŭlt′) *n.* A person learned in law; a jurist. [Lat. *iūriscōnsultus* : *iūris*, genitive of *iūs*, law + *cōnsultus*, skilled, p. part. of *cōnsulere*, to take counsel.]

ju•ris•dic•tion (jŏŏr′ĭs-dĭk′shən) *n.* **1.** *Law* The right and power to interpret and apply the law. **2a.** Authority or control. **b.** The extent of authority or control. **3.** The territorial range of authority or control. [ME *jurisdiccioun* < OFr. *juridicion* < Lat. *iūrisdictiō, iūrisdictiōn-* : *iūris*, genitive of *iūs*, law + *dictiō, dictiōn-*, declaration (< *dictus*, p. part. of *dīcere*, to say; see **deik**- in App.).] —**ju′ris•dic′tion•al** *adj.* —**ju′ris•dic′tion•al•ly** *adv.*

ju•ris•pru•dence (jŏŏr′ĭs-prŏŏd′ns) *n.* **1.** The philosophy or science of law. **2.** A division or department of law. [LLat. *iūris-prūdentia* : Lat. *iūris*, genitive of *iūs*, law + Lat. *prūdentia*, knowledge (< *prūdēns, prūdent-*, knowing; see PRUDENT).] —**ju′ris•pru•den′tial** (-prŏŏ-dĕn′shəl) *adj.* —**ju′ris•pru•den′tial•ly** *adv.*

ju•ris•pru•dent (jŏŏr′ĭs-prŏŏd′nt) *adj.* Versed in jurisprudence. ❖ *n.* See **jurist**.

ju•rist (jŏŏr′ĭst) *n.* One who has thorough knowledge and experience of law, esp. an eminent judge, lawyer, or legal scholar. [ME < OFr. *juriste* < Med.Lat. *iūrista* < Lat. *iūs, iūr-*, law.]

ju•ris•tic (jŏŏ-rĭs′tĭk) also **ju•ris•ti•cal** (-tĭ-kəl) *adj.* **1.** Of or relating to a jurist or to jurisprudence. **2.** Of or relating to law or legality. —**ju•ris′ti•cal•ly** *adv.*

ju•ror (jŏŏr′ər, -ôr′) *n.* **1.** *Law* **a.** One who serves as a member of a jury. **b.** One who awaits or is called for service on a jury. **2.** One who serves on a deliberative body analogous to a jury. [ME *jurour* < AN < Lat. *iūrātor*, swearer < *iūrāre*, to swear. See JURY[1].]

Ju•ru•á (zhŏŏ′rŏŏ-ä′) A river of E Peru and NW Brazil flowing c. 1,931 km (1,200 mi) to the Amazon R.

ju•ry[1] (jŏŏr′ē) *n., pl.* **-ries 1.** *Law* A body of persons sworn to judge and give a verdict on a given matter, esp. a body of persons summoned by law and sworn to hand down a verdict upon a case presented in court. **2.** A committee, usu. of experts, that judges contestants or applicants. ❖ *tr.v.* **-ried, -ry•ing, -ries** To judge or evaluate by a jury. [ME *jure* < AN *juree* < fem. p. part. of *jurer*, to swear < Lat. *iūrāre* < *iūs, iūr-*, law.]

ju•ry[2] (jŏŏr′ē) *adj. Nautical* Intended or designed for temporary use; makeshift: *a jury sail.* [< JURY-RIG.]

ju•ry-rig (jŏŏr′ē-rĭg′) *tr.v.* **-rigged, -rig•ging, -rigs** To rig or assemble for temporary emergency use; improvise. [< *jury-rig, jury-rigging*, improvised rigging on a ship (modeled on *jury-mast*, temporary mast), perh. ult. < OFr. *ajurie*, help < *aider*, to help. See AID.]

jus gen•ti•um (yŏŏs gĕn′tē-əm, jŭs jĕn′shē-əm) *n.* The law of nations; international law. [Lat. *iūs gentium* : *iūs*, law + *gentium*, genitive pl. of *gēns*, nation.]

jus•sive (jŭs′ĭv) *n.* A word, mood, or form used to express a command. [< Lat. *iussus*, p. part. of *iubēre*, to command.] —**jus′sive** *adj.*

just[1] (jŭst) *adj.* **1.** Honorable and fair in one's dealings and actions. See Syns at **fair[1]**. **2.** Consistent with what is morally right; righteous: *a just cause.* **3.** Properly due or merited. **4.** *Law* Valid within the law; lawful. **5.** Suitable or proper in nature; fitting. **6.** Based on fact or sound reason; well-founded: *a just appraisal.* ❖ *adv.* (jəst, jĭst; jŭst *when stressed*) **1.** Precisely; exactly. **2.** Only a moment ago. **3.** By a narrow margin; barely. **4.** At a little distance. **5.** Merely; only. **6.** Simply; certainly: *It's just beautiful!* **7.** Perhaps; possibly. —**idioms: just about** Almost; very nearly. **just now** Only a moment ago. **just the same** Nevertheless. [ME *juste* < OFr. < Lat. *iūstus*.] —**just′ly** *adv.* —**just′ness** *n.*

just[2] (jŭst) *n. & v.* Variant of **joust**.

jus•tice (jŭs′tĭs) *n.* **1.** The quality of being just; fairness. **2a.** The principle of moral rightness; equity. **b.** Conformity to moral rightness in action or attitude; righteousness. **3a.** The upholding of what is just, esp. fair treatment and due reward in accordance with honor, standards, or law. **b.** *Law* The administration and procedure of law. **4.** Conformity to truth, fact, or sound reason. **5.** *Law* **a.** A judge. **b.** A justice of the peace. —**idiom: do justice to** To treat adequately, fairly, or with full appreciation. [ME < OFr. < Lat. *iūstitia < iūstus*, just. See JUST[1].]

justice of the peace *n., pl.* **justices of the peace** A magistrate of the lowest level of certain state court systems, having authority to act upon minor offenses, commit cases to a higher court for trial, perform marriages, and administer oaths.

jus•ti•ci•a•ble (jŭ-stĭsh′ə-bəl) *adj.* **1.** Appropriate for or subject to court trial: *a justiciable charge.* **2.** That can be settled by law or a court of law: *justiciable disputes.* [ME < OFr. < Med.Lat. *iūstiti-ābilis* < Lat. *iūstitiāre*, to try < Lat. *iūstitia*, justice. See JUS-TICE.] —**jus•ti′cia•bil′i•ty** *n.*

jus•ti•ci•ar•y (jŭ-stĭsh′ē-ĕr′ē) also **jus•ti•ci•ar** (-ē-ər) *n., pl.* **-ies** also **-ars** A high judicial officer in medieval England. [Med. Lat. *iūstitiāria* < fem. of *iūstitiārius*, of the administration of justice < Lat. *iūstitia*, justice. See JUSTICE.]

jus•ti•fi•a•ble (jŭs′tə-fī′ə-bəl, jŭs′tə-fī′-) *adj.* Having sufficient grounds for justification; possible to justify. —**jus′ti•fi′a•bil′i•ty** *n.* —**jus′ti•fi′a•bly** *adv.*

jus•ti•fi•ca•tion (jŭs′tə-fĭ-kā′shən) *n.* **1a.** The act of justifying. **b.** The condition or fact of being justified. **2.** Something, such as a fact or circumstance, that justifies.

jus•ti•fi•ca•tive (jŭs′tə-fĭ-kā′tĭv) also **jus•tif•i•ca•to•ry** (jŭ-stĭf′ĭ-kə-tôr′ē, -tōr′ē) *adj.* Serving as justification.

jus•ti•fy (jŭs′tə-fī′) *v.* **-fied, -fy•ing, -fies** —*tr.* **1.** To demonstrate or prove to be just, right, or valid: *justified each expense as necessary.* **2.** To declare free of blame; absolve. **3.** *Theology* To free (a human) of the guilt and penalty attached to grievous sin. Used only of God. **4.** *Law* **a.** To demonstrate sufficient legal reason for (an action taken). **b.** To prove to be qualified as a bondsman. **5.** *Printing* To adjust the spacing within (lines in a document, for example) so that the lines end evenly at a straight margin. —*intr.* **1.** *Printing* To be adjusted in spacing so as to end evenly at the margin. [ME *justifien* < OFr. *justifier* < LLat. *iūstificāre* < Lat., to act justly toward : *iūstus*, just + *-ficāre*, -fy.]

Jus•tin (jŭs′tĭn), Saint. A.D. 100?-165. Greek theologian who founded a school of Christian philosophy at Rome.

Jus•tin•i•an I (jŭ-stĭn′ē-ən) Orig. "Justinian the Great." A.D. 483–565. Byzantine emperor (527–565) who held the E frontier of his empire against the Persians.

jut (jŭt) *v.* **jut•ted, jut•ting, juts** —*intr.* To extend outward or upward beyond the limits of the main body; project. —*tr.* To cause to jut. ❖ *n.* Something that protrudes; a projection. [ME *jutten* < *gete, iutei*, jetty, projecting upper story < OFr. *jetee*. See JETTY[1].]

jute (jŏŏt) *n.* **1.** Either of two Asian plants (*Corchorus capsularis* or *C. olitorius*) yielding a fiber used for sacking and cordage. **2.** The fiber obtained from these plants. [Bengali *jhuṭo* < Skt. *jūṭaḥ*, twisted hair, prob. of Dravidian orig.]

Jute (jŏŏt) *n.* A member of a Germanic people who invaded Britain in the fifth and sixth centuries A.D. and settled in the south and southeast and on the Isle of Wight. [< ME *Jutes*, the Jutes < Med.Lat. *Iutae* < OE *Iotas, Iutan*; akin to OE *Gēat*, Geat.]

Jut•land (jŭt′lənd) A peninsula of N Europe comprising mainland Denmark and N Germany. The name is usu. applied only to the Danish section of the peninsula.

Ju•ve•nal (jŏŏ′və-nəl) A.D. 60?-140? Roman satirist whose works denounced the corruption of the privileged classes.

ju•ve•nes•cent (jŏŏ′və-nĕs′ənt) *adj.* Becoming young or youthful. [Lat. *iuvenēscēns, iuvenēscent-*, pr. part. of *iuvenēscere*, to reach the age of youth < *iuvenis*, young. See JUVENILE.] —**ju′ve•nes′cence** *n.*

ju•ve•nile (jŏŏ′və-nīl′, -nəl) *adj.* **1.** Not fully grown or developed; young. **2.** Of, relating to, characteristic of, intended for, or appropriate for children or young people. **3.** Marked by immaturity; childish. ❖ *n.* **1a.** A young person; a child. **b.** A young animal that has not reached sexual maturity. **2.** An actor who plays roles of children or young persons. **3.** A children's book. [Lat. *iuvenīlis < iuvenis*, young. See yeu- in App.] —**ju′ve•nile′ly** *adv.* —**ju′ve•nile′ness** *n.*

juvenile court *n. Law* A court with jurisdiction over all cases involving children under a specified age, usu. 18 years.

juvenile delinquency *n.* Antisocial or criminal behavior by children or adolescents.

juvenile delinquent *n.* A juvenile guilty of antisocial or criminal behavior.

juvenile hormone *n.* A hormone in arthropod larvae that inhibits ecdysone, thereby preventing molting and the development of larvae into adults until its level drops.

ju•ve•nil•i•a (jŏŏ′və-nĭl′ē-ə, -nĭl′yə) *pl.n.* Works produced in an author's or artist's youth. [Lat. *iuvenīlia* < neut. pl. of *iuvenīlis*, juvenile. See JUVENILE.]

ju•ve•nil•i•ty (jŏŏ′və-nĭl′ĭ-tē) *n., pl.* **-ties 1.** The quality or condition of being juvenile; youthfulness. **2a.** Foolishly juvenile behavior or character. **b.** An instance of juvenile behavior.

jux•ta•pose (jŭk′stə-pōz′) *tr.v.* **-posed, -pos•ing, -pos•es** To place side by side, esp. for comparison or contrast. [Fr. *juxta-poser* : Lat. *iūxtā*, close by; see yeug- in App. + Fr. *poser*, to place (< OFr. See POSE[1]).]

jux•ta•po•si•tion (jŭk′stə-pə-zĭsh′ən) *n.* The act or an instance of juxtaposing or the state of being juxtaposed. —**jux′ta•po•si′tion•al** *adj.*

JV *abbr.* junior varsity

ă	pat	oi	boy
ā	pay	ou	out
âr	care	ŏŏ	took
ä	father	ŏŏ	boot
ĕ	pet	ŭ	cut
ē	be	ûr	urge
ĭ	pit	th	thin
ī	pie	th	this
îr	pier	hw	which
ŏ	pot	zh	vision
ō	toe	ə	about,
ô	paw		item

Stress marks:
′ (primary);
″ (secondary), as in
lexicon (lĕk′sĭ-kŏn′)

Kk

k¹ or **K** (kā) *n., pl.* **k's** or **K's** also **ks** or **Ks 1.** The 11th letter of the modern English alphabet. **2.** Any of the speech sounds represented by the letter *k.* **3.** The 11th in a series. **4.** Something shaped like the letter K.

k² *abbr.* karat

K¹ *n. Slang* One thousand dollars. [K(ILO)–.]

K² The symbol for the element **potassium.** [< NLat. *kalium,* potassium. See HYPOKALEMIA.]

K³ *abbr.* **1.** kaon **2.** kelvin **3.** kilobyte **4.** kindergarten **5.** *Games* king **6.** *Bible* Kings **7.** strikeout

K. *abbr.* knight (title)

K2 (kā′tōō′) also **Mount God•win Aus•ten** (gŏd′wĭn ô′stən) A peak, 8,616.3 m (28,250 ft), in the Karakoram Range of N Kashmir; designated K2 in 1856 and later (1888) named for Henry Haversham Godwin-Austen (1834–1923), a British soldier and surveyor.

ka *abbr.* cathode

Kaa•ba (kä′bə) *n.* A Muslim shrine in Mecca toward which the faithful pray. [Ar. *ka'ba,* cube, cubic structure < *ka'aba,* to swell, be full (said of breasts).]

kab (kăb) *n.* Variant of **cab²**.

kab•ba•lah or **kab•ba•la** or **kab•a•la** also **cab•a•la** or **qab•a•lah** (kăb′ə-lə, kə-bä′lə) *n.* **1.** often **Kabbalah** A body of mystical teachings of rabbinical origin, often based on an esoteric interpretation of the Hebrew Scriptures. **2.** A secret doctrine resembling these teachings. [Med.Lat. *cabala* < Heb. *qabbālâ,* received doctrine, tradition < *qibbēl,* to receive.] —**kab′ba•lism** *n.* —**kab′ba•list** *n.*

> **USAGE NOTE** There are no less than two dozen variant spellings of *kabbalah,* the most common of which include *kabbalah, kabala, kabalah, qabalah, qabala, cabala, cabbala, kaballah, kabbala, kaballah,* and *qabbalah.* This sort of confusion is frequently seen with Hebrew and Arabic words borrowed into English because there exist several different systems for transliterating the Hebrew and Arabic alphabets into Roman letters. Often a more exact or scholarly transliteration, such as *Qur'an,* will coexist alongside a spelling that has been heavily Anglicized (*Koran*).

kab•ba•lis•tic or **kab•a•lis•tic** or **cab•a•lis•tic** or **qab•a•lis•tic** (kăb′ə-lĭs′tĭk) *adj.* Of or relating to the Kabbalah. —**kab′ba•lis′ti•cal•ly** *adv.*

ka•bob (kə-bŏb′) *n.* Variant of **kebab.**

Ka•bu•ki (kə-bōō′kē) *n.* A type of popular Japanese drama, evolved from No theater, in which elaborately costumed performers use stylized movements, dances, and songs to enact tragedies and comedies. [J., art of singing and dancing : *ka,* singing (< M Chin.) + *bu,* dancing (< M Chin. *muə, wuə*) + *ki,* art, artist (< M Chin. *giʔ, khi,*).]

Ka•bul (kä′bŏōl, kə-bōōl′) The cap. of Afghanistan, in the E part near the border with Pakistan on the **Kabul River,** c. 483 km (300 mi). Pop. 1,424,400.

Ka•byle (kə-bīl′) *n., pl.* **Kabyle** or **-byles 1.** A member of a Berber people of northeast Algeria. **2.** The Berber language of this people. [Ar. *qabā'ilu,* pl. of *qabīla,* tribe < *qabila,* to receive.]

ka•chi•na (kə-chē′nə) *n.* **1.** Any of numerous deified ancestral spirits of the Pueblo peoples. **2.** A masked dancer believed to embody a spirit during a religious ceremony. **3.** A carved doll in the costume of a particular spirit. [Hopi *katsina.*]

Ká•dar (kä′där), **János** 1912–89. Hungarian politician and first secretary-general of the Hungarian Communist Party (1956–88).

Kad•dish (kä′dĭsh) *n. Judaism* A prayer recited in daily services and by mourners after the death of a close relative. [< Aram. *qaddîš* < *qədaš,* to become holy, be sacred (after the first words of the prayer).]

kaf•fee•klatsch (kŏf′ē-klăch′, -kläch′, kô′fē-) *n.* Variant of **coffee klatch.**

kaf•fir also **kaf•ir** (kăf′ər) *n.* A tropical African variety of sorghum (*Sorghum bicolor*) grown in dry regions and in the Great Plains for grain and forage. [Short for *kaffir corn,* prob. transl. of Afr. *kafferkoring : kaffer,* Kaffir + *koring,* corn.]

Kaffir also **Kafir** *n., pl.* **Kaffir** or **-firs** also **Kafir** or **-irs 1.** *Offensive* **a.** A Xhosa. **b.** often **kaffir** Used esp. in southern Africa as a disparaging term for a Black person. **2. Kafir** A Nuristani. **3.** also **kaffir** *Islam* An infidel. [Ar. *kāfir,* infidel. See GIAOUR.]

kaffir lime *n.* An Asian tree (*Citrus hystrix*) having green fruit and dark leaves used in cooking.

kaf•fi•yeh (kä-fē′ə) *n.* A cloth headdress fastened by a band around the crown, usu. worn by Arab men. [Ar. *kaffīya,* colloquial var. of *kūfīya,* perh. < LLat. *cofea,* helmet. See COIF.]

Kaf•i•ri (kăf′ə-rē, kə-fîr′ē) *n.* The Dardic language of the Nuristani.

Kaf•ka (kăf′kə, -kä), **Franz** 1883–1924. Austrian writer whose novels include *The Trial* (1925).

Kaf•ka•esque (käf′kə-ĕsk′) *adj.* **1.** Of or relating to Franz Kafka or his writings. **2.** Marked by surreal distortion and often a sense of impending danger.

kaf•tan (kăf′tăn′, -tən, käf-tän′) *n.* Variant of **caftan.**

Ka•fu•e (kə-fōō′ä) A river rising along the border of Zambia and Congo (formerly Zaire) and meandering c. 965 km (600 mi) to the Zambezi R.

Ka•go•shi•ma (kä′gô-shē′mə) A city of S Kyushu, Japan, on **Kagoshima Bay,** an inlet of the East China Sea. Pop. 539,911.

Kah•lo (kä′lō), **Frida** 1907–54. Mexican artist known for her surrealist self-portraits.

Ka•ho•o•la•we (kä-hō′ō-lä′vä, -wä) An island of S-central HI SW of Maui.

kai•ak (kī′ăk′) *n. & v.* Variant of **kayak.**

Kai•e•teur Falls (kī′ĭ-tōōr′) A waterfall, 250.7 m (822 ft), in the Potaro R. of central Guyana.

Kai•feng (kī′fŭng′) A city of E-central China SSW of Beijing; founded in the 3rd cent. B.C. Pop. 693,148.

Kai•las (kī-läs′) A peak, 6,718.2 m (22,027 ft), in the **Kailas Range** of the Himalaya Mts. in SW China.

Kai•lu•a (kī-lōō′ə) A city of HI, a suburb of Honolulu on **Kailua Bay,** an inlet of the Pacific Ocean. Pop. 36,513.

Kail•yard School (kāl′yärd′) *n.* A group of Scottish writers, including J.M. Barrie, who used Scots dialect in their sentimental works about Scottish life. [Sc. *kailyard,* kitchen garden : *kail,* kale (< ME *kal;* see KALE) + YARD².]

kai•nite (kī′nīt′, kā′-) *n.* A white, gray, pink, or black mineral, MgSO₄·KCl·3H₂O, used as a fertilizer and a source of potassium compounds. [Gk. *kainos,* new + –ITE¹.]

Kai•ser (kī′zər) *n.* **1.** Any of the emperors of the Holy Roman Empire (962–1806), of Austria (1806–1918), or of Germany (1871–1918). **2.** Used as the title for such a man. [Ger. < MHGer. *keiser* < OHGer. *keisar* < Lat. *Caesar.* See CAESAR.]

Kai•ser•in (kī′zər-ĭn) *n.* **1.** The wife of a Kaiser. **2.** Used as the title for such a woman. [Ger., fem. of *Kaiser,* Kaiser. See KAISER.]

kaiser roll *n.* A large roll with a hard crust, often used for sandwiches. [Transl. of Ger. dialectal *Kaisersemmel : Ger. Kaiser,* Kaiser + Ger. dialectal *Semmel,* roll.]

ka•ka (kä′kə) *n.* A brownish-green New Zealand parrot (*Nestor meridionalis*). [Maori *kākā* < Proto-Polynesian **kākā* < redup. of **kā,* to screech.]

ka•ka•po (kä′kə-pō′) *n., pl.* **-pos** A New Zealand parrot (*Strigops habroptilus*) with greenish plumage. [Maori *kākāpō : kākā,* parrot; see KAKA + *pō,* night (perh. because it is active at night).]

ka•ke•mo•no (kä′kə-mō′nō) *n., pl.* **-nos** A vertical Japanese scroll painting. [J. : *kakeru,* to hang + *mono,* object.]

kak•is•toc•ra•cy (kăk′ī-stŏk′rə-sē, kä′kĭ-) *n., pl.* **-cies** Government by the least qualified or most unprincipled citizens. [Gk. *kakistos,* worst, superl. of *kakos,* bad; see CACO– + –CRACY.]

ka•la-a•zar (kä′lə-ə-zär′) *n.* A chronic, often fatal disease caused by the protozoan parasite *Leishmania donovani* and characterized by irregular fever, enlarged spleen and liver, and emaciation. [Urdu *kālā āzār : kālā,* black (< Skt. *kāla-;* see KALI) + *āzār,* disease (< Pers. < MPers., pain < *āzārdan, āzār-,* to torment : *ā-,* to + *-zār-,* to make angry).]

Ka•la•ha•ri (kä′lə-här′ē) A desert plateau region of S Botswana, E Namibia, and W South Africa.

Ka•lakh (kä′läkH) See Calah.

ka•la•ma•ta olive (kä′lə-mä′tə, käl′ə-) *n.* An edible variety of olive with a fruity flavor and meaty texture. [After *Kalamata,* Greece, city around which the olives are grown.]

Kal•a•ma•zoo (kăl′ə-mə-zōō′) A city of SW MI S of Grand Rapids; first settled in 1829. Pop. 77,145.

Ka•lash•ni•kov (kə-läsh′nə-kôf′, -kŏf′, -kôf′) *n.* Any of a series of assault rifles of Soviet design, esp. the AK-47. [After Mikhail Timofeevich *Kalashnikov* (born 1919), Soviet arms engineer.]

Kalb (kälb, kälp), **Johann** Known as "Baron de Kalb." 1721–80. German general in the American Revolution who was mortally wounded at the Battle of Camden.

kale (kāl) *n.* **1.** An edible plant (*Brassica oleracea* var. *acephala*) in the mustard family, having spreading crinkled leaves that do not form a compact head. **2.** *Slang* Money. [ME *col, kal.* See COLE.]

ka•lei•do•scope (kə-lī′də-skōp′) *n.* **1.** A tube-shaped optical instrument that is rotated to produce a succession of symmetrical

Kabuki
Kabuki performer

kaffiyeh

designs by means of mirrors reflecting the constantly changing patterns made by bits of colored glass at one end of the tube. **2.** A constantly changing set of colors. **3.** A series of changing phases or events. [Gk. *kalos*, beautiful + *eidos*, form; see **weid-** in App. + –SCOPE.] —**ka·lei'do·scop'ic** (-skŏp'ĭk), **ka·lei'do·scop'i·cal** *adj.* —**ka·lei'do·scop'i·cal·ly** *adv.*

kal·ends (kăl'əndz, kā'ləndz) *n.* Variant of **calends.**

Kal·gan (kăl'gän') See **Zhangjiakou.**

Ka·li (kä'lē) *n. Hinduism* One of the manifestations of the wife of Shiva and mother goddess Devi, esp. in her malevolent role as a goddess of death and destruction. [Skt. *Kālī* < *kālī*, fem. of *kāla-*, dark, of Dravidian orig.; akin to Kannada *kādu*, black, blackness.]

Ka·li·da·sa (kä'lē-dä'sə) A.D. 375?–415? Indian dramatist and lyric poet whose work includes the epic poem *Raghuvamsa.*

Ka·li·man·tan (kä'lə-män'tän', kä'lē-män'tän) The Indonesian part of Borneo.

ka·lim·ba (kə-lĭm'bə) *n.* An African musical instrument in the shape of a wooden box set with metal bars that are plucked with the fingers. [Bantu; akin to Bemba *ka-limba*, dim. of *ci-limba*, any musical instrument : *ci-*, n. classifier + *-limba*, musical instrument.]

Ka·li·nin (kə-lē'nĭn, kəl-yē'-) See **Tver'.**

Kalinin, Mikhail Ivanovich 1875–1946. Russian politician who was chairman of the All-Union Central Executive Committee (1919–38) and the Presidium of the Supreme Soviet (1938–46).

Ka·li·nin·grad (kə-lē'nĭn-grād', -grăd', -lyĭ-nĭn-grät') Formerly **Kö·nigs·berg** (kā'nĭgz-bûrg', kœ'nĭKHs-bĕrk') A city of extreme W Russia near the Polish border; founded by the Teutonic Knights in 1255. Pop. 413,491.

Ka·lisz (kä'lĭsh) A city of central Poland W of Łódź; an ancient settlement dating to c. 2nd cent. A.D. Pop. 106,359.

Kal·mar (kăl'mär', käl'-) A city of SE Sweden on **Kalmar Sound,** an arm of the Baltic Sea. The Union of Kalmar (1397) joined Sweden, Denmark, and Norway into a single monarchy that lasted until 1523. Pop. 30,300.

Kal·myk[1] (kăl'mĭk, käl-mĭk') also **Kal·muck** or **Kal·muk** (kăl'mŭk, käl-mŭk') *n., pl.* **Kalmyk** or **-myks** also **Kalmuck** or **-mucks** or **Kalmuk** or **-muks 1.** A member of a Buddhist Mongol people now located primarily in Kalmyk. **2.** The Mongolian language of this people. [Russ. < Kazan Tatar.]

Kal·myk[2] (kăl'mĭk, käl-mĭk') A region of SW Russia on the Caspian Sea; settled in the early 17th cent. by Kalmyk people from central China.

kal·pac (kăl'păk, käl-păk') *n.* Variant of **calpac.**

kal·so·mine (kăl'sə-mīn') *n. & v.* Variant of **calcimine.**

Ka·lu·ga (kə-lōō'gə) A city of W-central Russia SW of Moscow; founded in the 14th cent. Pop. 343,967.

Ka·ma[1] (kä'mə) *n. Hinduism* The god of love. [Skt. *kāmaḥ*, love, desire, Kama. See **kā-** in App.]

Ka·ma[2] (kä'mə) A river of W-central Russia rising in the central Ural Mts. and flowing c. 2,031 km (1,262 mi) to the Volga R.

ka·ma·la (kä'mə-lə, kăm'ə-) *n.* **1.** An Asian tree (*Mallotus philippinensis*) that bears a hairy capsular fruit. **2.** A vermifuge obtained from this fruit. [Skt. *kamalam*, lotus, pale red, prob. of Dravidian orig.]

Ka·ma·su·tra (kä'mə-sōō'trə) *n.* A Sanskrit treatise setting forth rules for sensuous and sensual pleasure, love, and marriage in accordance with Hindu law. [Skt. *kāmasūtram* : *kāmaḥ*, love; see **kā-** in App. + *sūtram*, string, manual; see **syū-** in App.]

Kam·chat·ka (kăm-chăt'kə, -chät'-, kəm-chyät'-) A peninsula of E Russia between the Sea of Okhotsk and the Bering Sea; first explored in the 18th cent.

kame (kām) *n.* A short ridge or mound of sand and gravel deposited during the melting of glacial ice. [Dialectal, a low ridge < ME *camb*, comb, comb < OE. See **gembh-** in App.]

Ka·me·ha·me·ha I (kə-mā'ə-mā'ə) Known as "Kamehameha the Great." 1758?–1819. King of the Hawaiian Is. (1795–1819) who united the islands under his rule.

Ka·me·nev (kä'mə-nĕf, -mĭ-nyĕf'), **Lev Borisovich** 1883–1936. Russian Communist leader who ruled with Stalin and Zinoviev (1924) but was expelled as a Trotskyite (1927).

Ka·met (kŭm'ĕt') A mountain, 7,761.3 m (25,447 ft), in the NW Himalaya Mts. on the India-China border.

ka·mi (kä'mĭ) *n., pl.* **kami** Any of the sacred beings worshiped in Shintoism, conceived as spirits abiding in natural phenomena. [J.]

ka·mi·ka·ze (kä'mĭ-kä'zē) *n.* **1.** A Japanese pilot in World War II trained to make a suicidal crash attack, esp. upon a ship. **2.** An airplane loaded with explosives to be piloted in a suicide attack. **3.** *Slang* An extremely reckless person who seems to court death. ❖ *adj.* **1.** Of or relating to a suicidal air attack. **2.** *Slang* So reckless in behavior as to be suicidal. [J., divine wind (< the legendary name of a typhoon tht destroyed the invading Mongol navy in 1201) : *kami*, divine wind + *kaze*, wind.]

Kam·pa·la (käm-pä'lə) The cap. of Uganda, in the S part on Lake Victoria. Pop. 458,503.

Kam·pu·che·a (kăm'pōō-chē'ə) See **Cambodia.**

ka·na (kä'nə) *n., pl.* **kana** or **-nas 1.** Japanese syllabic writing usu. used with kanji to write inflections, particles, and function words and show the pronunciations of some kanji and of all foreign

words. **2.** Any of the characters used in this system. [J., pseudo-characters, kana : *ka*, false (< M Chin. *kaiʔ*, *kja·*) + *na*, name.]

Ka·na·ka also **ka·na·ka** (kə-nä'kə, -näk'ə) *n.* **1.** A Hawaiian of Polynesian descent; a Native Hawaiian. **2.** *Australian & New Zealand* A South Sea Islander, esp. one brought to Australia as a laborer in the 19th and early 20th centuries. Often used disparagingly. [Hawaiian, human being, Kanaka.]

USAGE NOTE *Kanaka*, which simply means "human being" in Hawaiian, mostly occurs today in historical contexts and is not usually appropriate in ordinary discourse. As with many terms that refer to ethnic identity, *Kanaka* can suggest ethnic pride in some contexts while in others it may be taken as derogatory.

kan·a·my·cin (kăn'ə-mī'sĭn) *n.* A water-soluble broad-spectrum antibiotic, $C_{18}H_{36}O_{11}N_4$, obtained from the soil bacterium *Streptomyces kanamyceticus.* [NLat. *kanamyc(ēticus)*, specific epithet of a species of actinomycete (J. *kana*, golden (< the color of its colonies) + *mycēticus*, fungus < *-mycētēs*; see —MYCETE) + –IN.]

Ka·nan·ga (kə-näng'gə) A city of S-central Congo (formerly Zaire) ESE of Kinshasa; founded 1884. Pop. 298,693.

Kan·a·rese (kăn'ə-rēz', -rēs') *n., pl.* **Kanarese 1.** A member of a Kannada-speaking people of southwest India. **2.** See **Kannada.** [Alteration of Kannada *Kannaḍa* + –ESE.]

Ka·na·za·wa (kä'nä-zä'wə) A city of W Honshu, Japan, on the Sea of Japan N of Nagoya. Pop. 446,325.

Kan·chen·jun·ga (kŭn'chən-jŭng'gə, -jōōng'-, kän'-) A mountain, 8,603.4 m (28,208 ft), in the Himalaya Mts. on the India-Nepal border.

Kan·da·har (kŭn'də-här', kän'-) See **Qandahar.**

Kan·din·sky or **Kan·din·ski** (kăn-dĭn'skē, kən-dyĭn'-), **Wassily** 1866–1944. Russian painter who was a founder of the Blaue Reiter, a German group of abstract expressionists.

Kan·dy (kăn'dē) A city of central Sri Lanka ENE of Colombo; last cap. of the kings of Ceylon. Pop. 104,000.

Ka·ne·o·he (kä'nē-ō'ĕ, -nä-ō'hä) A city of HI in E Oahu on **Kaneohe Bay,** an inlet of the Pacific Ocean. Pop. 34,970.

kan·ga·roo (kăng'gə-rōō') *n., pl.* **kangaroo** or **-roos** Any of various herbivorous marsupials of the family Macropodidae of Australia and adjacent islands, having short forelimbs, large hind limbs adapted for leaping, and a long tapered tail. [Gugu Yimidhirr (Aboriginal language of NE Australia) *gaṉurru*.]

WORD HISTORY A widely held belief has it that the word *kangaroo* comes from an Australian aboriginal word meaning "I don't know." This is in fact untrue. The word was first recorded in 1770 by Captain James Cook. In 1820, one Captain Phillip K. King recorded a different word for the animal, written "mee-nuah." As a result, it was assumed that Captain Cook had been mistaken, and the myth grew up that what he had heard was a word meaning "I don't know" (presumably as the answer to a question in English that had not been understood). Recent research, however, has confirmed the existence of a word *ganguru* in the northeast Aboriginal language of Guugu Yimidhirr, referring to a species of kangaroo. What Captain King heard may have been the word *minha*, meaning "edible animal."

kangaroo court *n.* **1.** A mock court set up in violation of established legal procedure. **2.** A court characterized by dishonesty or incompetence.

kangaroo rat *n.* Any of various long-tailed rodents of the genus *Dipodomys* of arid areas of western North America, having long hind legs adapted for jumping.

kangaroo vine *n.* A climbing or trailing woody vine (*Cissus antarctica*) native to Australia, often grown as a houseplant.

Kan·i·a·pis·kau (kăn'ē-ə-pĭs'kō, -kou) See **Caniapiscau.**

kan·ji (kän'jē) *n., pl.* **kanji** or **-jis 1.** A Japanese system of writing based on Chinese characters. **2.** A character used in this system of writing. [J. : *kan*, Chinese (< M Chin. *xanh*) + *ji*, characters (< M Chin. *dzih*).]

Kan·ka·kee (kăng'kə-kē') A river rising in N Indiana and flowing 362 km (225 mi) SW to the Illinois River.

Kan·na·da (kä'nə-də) *n.* The principal Dravidian language of Mysore, a region of southern India. [Kannada *Kannaḍa.*]

Ka·no (kä'nō) A city of N-central Nigeria NE of Lagos; formerly a powerful Hausa city-state. Pop. 475,000.

Kan·pur (kän'pōōr') also **Cawn·pore** (kôn'pôr', -pōr') A city of N India on the Ganges R. SE of Delhi. Pop. 1,874,409.

Kan River (kän) See **Gan Jiang.**

Kans. *abbr.* Kansas

Kan·sa (kăn'zə, -sə) *n., pl.* **Kansa** or **-sas 1.** A member of a Native American people formerly inhabiting eastern and central Kansas, with a present-day population in eastern Oklahoma. **2.** The Siouan language of the Kansa.

Kan·san (kăn'zən) *adj.* **1.** Of or relating to Kansas or its residents. **2.** *Geology* Of or relating to the second glacial stage of the Pleistocene in North America. ❖ *n.* A native or resident of Kansas. [KANS(AS) + –AN[1].]

Kan·sas[1] (kăn'zəs, -səs) *n.* A plural of **Kansa.**

Kan·sas[2] (kăn'zəs, -səs) *n.* A state of the central US. It was admitted as the 34th state in 1861 after a conflict (1854–59) known as "Bleeding Kansas" between free and slave factions. Cap. Topeka. Pop. 2,688,418.

Frida Kahlo
Self-Portrait Dedicated to Leon Trotsky, 1937, oil on masonite

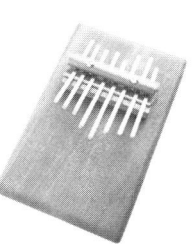

kalimba

ă	pat	oi	boy
ā	pay	ou	out
âr	care	ōō	took
ä	father	ōō	boot
ĕ	pet	ŭ	cut
ē	be	ûr	urge
ĭ	pit	th	thin
ī	pie	th	this
îr	pier	hw	which
ŏ	pot	zh	vision
ō	toe	ə	about,
ô	paw		item

Stress marks:
ʹ (primary);
ʹ (secondary), as in
lexicon (lĕk'sĭ-kŏn')

Kansas City 1. A city of NE KS on the Missouri R. adjacent to Kansas City MO. Pop. 146,866. **2.** A city of W MO on the Missouri R. WNW of St. Louis. Pop. 441,545.

Kansas River Locally known as **Kaw River** (kô) A river formed by the Republican and Smoky Hill rivers and flowing c. 272 km (169 mi) to the Missouri R. at Kansas City.

Kan·su (kän′sōō′, gän′-) See **Gansu.**

Kant (känt, känt), **Immanuel** 1724–1804. German philosopher who argued that reason is the means by which the phenomena of experience are translated into understanding, marking the beginning of idealism. —**Kant′i·an** *adj. & n.*

Ka·nu·ri (kə-nōōr′ē) *n., pl.* **Kanuri** or **-ris 1.** A member of a Muslim people in the Bornu region west of Lake Chad in northeast Nigeria. **2.** Their Nilo-Saharan language.

kan·zu (kän′zōō) *n.* A long, usu. white garment worn by men in Africa. [Swahili.]

Kao·hsiung (kou′shyōōng′, gou′-) A city of SW Taiwan on Taiwan Strait. Pop. 1,248,175.

ka·o·lin also **ka·o·line** (kā′ə-lĭn) *n.* A fine clay used in ceramics and refractories. [Fr. < Chin. (Mandarin) *Gāolíng,* an area of Jiangxi province.]

ka·o·lin·ite (kā′ə-lĭ-nīt′) *n.* A mineral, $Al_2Si_2O_5(OH)_4$, that is the main constituent of kaolin.

ka·on (kā′ŏn′) *n.* An unstable meson produced in a positive, negative, or neutral form as a result of high-energy particle collisions. [*ka,* pronunciation of the letter *K* + −ON[1].]

Ka·pell·meis·ter (kə-pĕl′mī′stər, kä-) *n.* The leader of a choir or orchestra. [Ger. : *Kapell,* choir (< Med.Lat. *capella;* see CHAPEL) + *Meister,* master; see MEISTERSINGER.]

kaph (käf, kôf) *n.* The 11th letter of the Hebrew alphabet. [Heb. *kap* < Phoenician **kapp,* palm of the hand, 11th letter of the Phoenician alphabet.]

Ka·pi·tsa (kä′pyĭ-tsə), **Pyotr Leonidovich** 1894–1984. Russian physicist who shared a 1978 Nobel Prize.

ka·pok (kā′pŏk′) *n.* A silky fiber from the fruit of the silk-cotton tree, used for insulation and padding. [Malay *kapuk.*]

Ka·po·si's sarcoma (kə-pō′sēz, kăp′ə-) *n.* A cancer characterized by bluish-red nodules on the skin, usu. on the lower extremities, that is endemic to equatorial Africa and often occurs in people with AIDS. [After Moritz *Kaposi* (1837–1902), Austrian dermatologist.]

kap·pa (kăp′ə) *n.* The tenth letter of the Greek alphabet. [Gk. < Phoenician **kapp,* palm of the hand, 11th letter of the Phoenician alphabet.]

Ka·pu·as (kä′pōō-äs′) A river of W Kalimantan, Borneo, flowing c. 1,142 km (710 mi) to the South China Sea.

ka·put also **ka·putt** (kä-pōōt′, -pŏŏt′, kə-) *adj. Informal* Incapacitated; destroyed. [Ger. *kaputt* < Fr. *capot,* not having won a single trick at piquet, poss. < Provençal.]

kar·a·bi·ner (kăr′ə-bē′nər) *n.* Variant of **carabiner.**

Ka·ra·chi (kə-rä′chē) A city of S Pakistan on the Arabian Sea; first cap. of Pakistan (1947–59). Pop. 5,180,562.

Ka·ra·gan·da (kär′ə-gən-dä′, kə-rə-) See **Qaraghandy.**

Ka·raj (kə-räj′) A city of N Iran NW of Tehran. Pop. 588,287.

Ka·ra·jan (kär′ə-yän′), **Herbert von** 1908–89. Austrian conductor. In 1955 he became conductor for life of the Berlin Philharmonic.

Ka·ra·ko·ram Range also **Ka·ra·ko·rum Range** (kăr′ə-kôr′əm, -kōr′-, kär′-) A mountain system of N Pakistan and India and SW China rising to 8,616.3 m (28,250 ft) at K2, the second-highest mountain in the world.

Ka·ra·ko·rum (kăr′ə-kôr′əm, -kōr′-, kär′-) A ruined ancient city in central Mongolia; cap. (1220–67) for Genghis Khan and Kublai Khan.

kar·a·kul also **car·a·cul** (kăr′ə-kəl) *n.* **1.** Any of a breed of Central Asian sheep having a wide tail and wool that is curled and glossy in the young but wiry and coarse in the adult. **2.** Fur made from the pelt of a karakul lamb. [After *Karakul,* a lake of eastern Tajikistan.]

Ka·ra Kum (kär′ə kōōm′) A desert region of Turkmenistan between the Caspian Sea and the Amu Darya.

kar·a·o·ke (kăr′ē-ō′kē) *n.* **1.** A music entertainment system providing prerecorded accompaniment to popular songs that a performer sings live, usu. by following the words on a video screen. **2.** The performance of such music. [J. *karaōke : kara,* void, empty + *ōke(sutora),* orchestra (< E. ORCHESTRA).]

Kara Sea A section of the Arctic Ocean between Novaya Zemlya and the Siberian mainland, connected with the Barents Sea by **Kara Strait.**

kar·at also **car·at** (kăr′ət) *n.* A unit of measure for the fineness of gold, equal to 1/24 part of pure gold. [Variant of CARAT.]

ka·ra·te (kə-rä′tē) *n.* A Japanese art of self-defense employing sharp blows and kicks. [J. : *kara,* empty + *te,* hand.]

Kar·ba·la (kär′bə-lə) also **Ker·be·la** (kûr′-) A city of central Iraq SSW of Baghdad. Pop. 296,705.

Ka·re·li·a (kə-rē′lē-ə, -rēl′yə, -ryē′lē-yə) A region and autonomous republic of NW Russia between the Gulf of Finland and the White Sea.

Ka·re·li·an (kə-rē′lē-ən, -rēl′yən) *adj.* Of or relating to Karelia or its people, language, or culture. ❖ *n.* **1.** A native or inhabitant of Karelia. **2.** The Finnic language spoken in Karelia.

Karelian Isthmus A land bridge of NW Russia between Lake Ladoga and the Gulf of Finland.

Ka·ren (kə-rĕn′) *n., pl.* **Karen** or **-rens 1.** A member of a Thai people inhabiting southern and eastern Myanmar (Burma). **2.** Any of the Tibeto-Burman languages of this people.

Ka·ri·ba (kə-rē′bə), **Lake** lake of S-central Africa on the Zambia-Zimbabwe border; formed by the Kariba Dam (completed 1958) on the Zambezi R.

Karl-Marx-Stadt (kärl-märks′shtät′) See **Chemnitz.**

Kar·loff (kär′lôf, -lŏf), **Boris** 1887–1969. British-born Amer. actor whose films include *Frankenstein* (1931).

Kar·lo·vy Va·ry (kär′lə-vē vär′ē) also **Karls·bad** (kärlz′băd′, kärls′bät′) A city of NW Czech Republic W of Prague; chartered in the 14th cent. Pop. 58,541.

Karls·ru·he also **Carls·ru·he** (kärlz′rōō′ə, kärls′-) A city of SW Germany on the Rhine R. WNW of Stuttgart; founded 1715. Pop. 277,998.

kar·ma (kär′mə) *n.* **1.** *Hinduism & Buddhism* The total effect of one's actions and conduct during the successive phases of one's existence, regarded as determining one's destiny. **2.** Fate; destiny. **3.** *Informal* A distinctive aura, atmosphere, or feeling. [Skt., deed, action that has consequences, karma.] —**kar′mic** (-mĭk) *adj.*

Kar·nak (kär′năk′) A village of E-central Egypt on the right bank of the Nile R. on the site of ancient Thebes. Its pharaonic remains include the Great Temple of Amen.

Kar·ok (kə-rŏk′) *n., pl.* **Karok** or **-oks 1.** A member of a Native American people inhabiting northwest California. **2.** The Hokan language of the Karok. [< Karok *káruk,* upstream.]

ka·roo also **kar·roo** (kə-rōō′) *n., pl.* **-roos** An arid plateau of southern Africa. [Afr. < Nama *!garo-b,* desert.]

Kar·rer (kär′ər), **Paul** 1889–1971. Russian-born Swiss chemist who shared a 1937 Nobel Prize.

Kar·roo also **Ka·roo** (kə-rōō′) A semiarid plateau region of SW South Africa divided into the **North Karroo,** along the Orange R.; the **Great,** or **Central, Karroo;** and the **Little Karroo,** near the coast.

Kars (kärs) A city of NE Turkey near the Armenian border; destroyed by Tamerlane c. 1386. Pop. 58,799.

Kar·sa·vi·na (kär-sä′və-nə), **Tamara** 1885–1978. Russian ballerina who was a founder of London's Royal Academy of Dancing (1920).

karst (kärst) *n.* An area of irregular limestone where erosion has produced sinkholes, fissures, underground streams, and caverns. [Ger., after the *Karst,* a limestone plateau near Trieste.] —**karst′ic** *adj.*

kart (kärt) *n.* A miniature car used in racing. [Prob. < GoKart, a trademark.] —**kart′ing** *n.*

Kart·ve·li·an (kärt-vē′lē-ən) *n.* A family of languages spoken in the Caucasus mountains that includes Georgian. [< Georgian *kartvel-,* Georgia, Georgian.] —**Kart·ve′li·an** *adj.*

Ka·run (kə-rōōn′, kä-) A river of W Iran flowing c. 724 km (450 mi) into the Shatt al Arab on the Iraq border.

karyo– or **caryo–** *pref.* **1.** Cell nucleus: *karyogamy.* **2.** Nut; kernel: *caryopsis.* [NLat. < Gk. *karuo–,* nut < *karuon.*]

kar·y·og·a·my (kär′ē-ŏg′ə-mē) *n.* The coming together and fusing of cell nuclei, as in fertilization.

kar·y·o·ki·ne·sis (kär′ē-ō-kə-nē′sĭs, -kī-) *n.* See **mitosis** 1.

kar·y·o·lymph (kär′ē-ə-lĭmf′) *n.* The colorless liquid component of the cell nucleus.

kar·y·o·plasm (kär′ē-ə-plăz′əm) *n.* See **nucleoplasm.**

kar·y·o·some (kär′ē-ə-sōm′) *n.* An irregular aggregation of chromatin in the nucleus of a cell not undergoing mitosis.

kar·y·o·type (kär′ē-ə-tīp′) *n.* **1.** The characterization of the chromosomal complement of an individual or a species, including number, form, and size of the chromosomes. **2.** A photomicrograph of chromosomes arranged according to a standard classification. ❖ *tr.v.* **-typed, -typ·ing, -types** To classify and array (the chromosome complement) by karyotype. —**kar′y·o·typ′ic** (-tīp′ĭk), **kar′y·o·typ′i·cal** *adj.*

Ka·sai (kə-sī′) A river of NE Angola and SW Congo (formerly Zaire) flowing c. 1,931 km (1,200 mi) to the Congo R.

Kas·bah (käz′bä′, käz′-) *n.* Variant of **Casbah.**

ka·sha (kä′shə) *n.* Buckwheat groats. [Russ. < ORuss.]

ka·sher (kä′shər) *adj. & v.* Variant of **kosher.**

Kash·mir also **Cash·mere** (kăzh′mîr′, kăsh′, kăzh-mîr′, kăsh-) **1.** A historical region of NW India and NE Pakistan; formerly part of the Mogul empire (after 1587) and an independent kingdom (1751–1816). **2.** See **Jammu and Kashmir.**

Kashmir goat *n.* Variant of **Cashmere goat.**

Kash·mir·i (kăsh-mîr′ē, kăzh-) *n., pl.* **Kashmiri** or **-is 1.** A native or inhabitant of Kashmir. **2.** A Dardic language of Jammu and Kashmir. —**Kash·mir′i** *adj.*

kash·rut also **kash·ruth** (käsh′rəth, -rəs, käsh-rōōt′) *n.* The body of Jewish dietary law. [Mishnaic Heb. *kašrût < kāšer,* fitting. See KOSHER.]

Kas·kas·ki·a (kəs-käs′kē-ə) *n., pl.* **Kaskaskia** or **-as** A member of a Native American people forming part of the Illinois confederacy.

Kaskaskia River A river rising in E-central IL and flowing c. 483 km (300 mi) to the Mississippi R.

Kas·sel also **Cas·sel** (käs′əl, kä′səl) A city of central Germany

SSW of Hanover; chartered 1198. Pop. 202,158.

ka·ta (kä′tä) *n., pl.* **kata** or **-tas** A system of basic body positioning and movement exercises, as in karate or judo. [J., style, traditional form.]

kat·a·bat·ic (kăt′ə-băt′ĭk) *adj.* Of or relating to a cold flow of air traveling downward. [Gk. *katabatikos*, pertaining to descent < *katabatos*, descending : *kata-*, *cata-* + *batos*, going; see **gʷā-** in App.]

Ka·tah·din (kə-täd′n), **Mount** A mountain, 1,606.7 m (5,268 ft), of N-central ME; N terminus of the Appalachian Trail.

ka·ta·ka·na (kä′tä-kä′nä) *n.* A relatively angular kana used for writing foreign words or official documents, such as telegrams. [J. : *kata*, one + *kana*, kana; see KANA.]

Ka·tan·ga (kə-täng′gə, -täng′-) See **Shaba.** —**Kat′an·gese′** (kät′äng-gēz′, -gēs′, -äng-) *adj. & n.*

Ka·tha·rev·u·sa (kä′thä-rĕv′ōō-sä′) *n.* The puristic, archaizing form of Modern Greek. [Mod.Gk. *katharevousa* < Gk., fem. pr. part. of *kathareuein*, to be pure < *katharos*, pure.]

Ka·thi·a·war (kä′tē-ə-wär′) A peninsula of W India on the Arabian Sea between the Gulfs of Kutch and Khambhat.

Kath·man·du also **Kat·man·du** (kăt′măn-dōō′, kät′män-) The cap. of Nepal, in the central part in the E Himalaya Mts.; founded c. 723. Pop. 235,160.

Kat·mai (kăt′mī′), **Mount** An active volcano, c. 2,048 m (6,715 ft), in the Aleutian Range of S AK.

Kat·o·wi·ce (kä′tə-vēt′sə, -tô-vē′tsĕ) A city of S Poland WNW of Kraków; chartered 1865. Pop. 366,465.

Kat·te·gat (kăt′ĭ-gät′) A strait of the North Sea between SW Sweden and E Jutland, Denmark, connecting with the North Sea through the Skagerrak.

ka·ty·did (kā′tē-dĭd′) *n.* Any of various green insects of the family Tettigoniidae related to the crickets, the male of which produces a shrill sound by rubbing together specialized organs on the forewings. [Imit. of its sound.]

katz·en·jam·mer (kăt′sən-jăm′ər) *n.* **1.** A loud discordant noise. **2.** A hangover. **3.** A state of depression or bewilderment. [Ger., hangover : *Katzen*, pl. of *Katze*, cat (< MHGer. *katze* < OHGer. *kazza*; akin to OE *catt*; see CAT) + *Jammer*, wailing (< MHGer. *jâmer* < OHGer. *jâmar*, misery).]

Kau·ai (kou′ī′, kou-ī′) An island of HI NW of Oahu.

Kauf·man (kôf′mən), **George Simon** 1889–1961. Amer. playwright noted for his many collaborations, including *You Can't Take It with You* (1936) with Moss Hart.

Kau·nas (kou′nəs, -näs) A city of central Lithuania on the Neman R. S of Riga; founded in the 11th cent. Pop. 421,600.

kau·ri (kou′rē) *n., pl.* **-ris 1.** Any of several coniferous evergreen trees of the genus *Agathis*, esp. *A. australis* of New Zealand, having broad leathery leaves. **2.** The white close-grained wood of one of these trees. **3.** A resinous copal or a fossilized resin of these trees. [Maori *kawri*.]

ka·va (kä′və) *n.* **1.** A dioecious shrub (*Piper methysticum*) native to the Pacific islands and having cordate leaves and minute flowers clustered in solitary spikes. **2.** The narcotic beverage made from the roots of this plant. [Tongan, acrid, kava.]

Kaw (kô) *n., pl.* **Kaw** or **Kaws** See **Kansa.**

Ka·wa·ba·ta (kä′wə-bä′tə), **Yasunari** 1899–1972. Japanese writer who won the 1968 Nobel Prize for literature.

Ka·wa·gu·chi (kä′wə-gōō′chē) A city of E-central Honshu, Japan, a suburb of Tokyo. Pop. 451,345.

Ka·wa·sa·ki (kä′wə-sä′kē) A city of E-central Honshu, Japan, a suburb of Tokyo on Tokyo Bay. Pop. 1,199,707.

Kaw River See **Kansas River.**

kay (kā) *n.* The letter *k*.

Kay (kā) *n.* The foster brother and steward of King Arthur.

kay·ak also **kai·ak** (kī′ăk′) *n.* **1.** An Inuit or Eskimo boat consisting of a light wooden frame covered with watertight skins except for a single or double opening in the center, and propelled by a double-bladed paddle. **2.** A lightweight canoe that is similar in design. ❖ *v.* **-aked, -ak·ing, -aks** —*intr.* To go, travel, or race in a kayak. —*tr.* To go or travel on (a body of water) by kayak. [Canadian Eskimo and Inuit *qajaq*.] —**kay′ak·er** *n.*

Kay·beck·er (kā-bĕk′ər) *n. Maine* A French-speaking Canadian lumberjack working in the United States. [< Fr. *québecois*, Québecois. See QUÉBECOIS.]

kay·o (kā-ō′, kā′ō′) *n., pl.* **-os** *Sports* A knockout in boxing. ❖ *tr.v.* **-oed, -o·ing, -os 1.** *Sports* To knock out. **2.** *Slang* To put out of commission. [Pronunciation of KO.]

Kay·se·ri (kī′zə-rē′, -sə-) A city of central Turkey SE of Ankara; founded in the 4th cent. A.D. Pop. 454,000.

Ka·zakh also **Ka·zak** (kä′zăk′, kə-zäk′) *n., pl.* **Kazakh** or **-zakhs** also **Kazak** or **-zaks 1.** A member of a pastoral Muslim people inhabiting Kazakhstan and parts of Xinjiang Uygur in China. **2.** The Turkic language of this people. [Russ. *kazakh* < Kazakh *qazaq* < O Turkic *qazhaq*, a profiteer < *qazghanmaq*, to acquire < *qazmaq*, to dig out.]

Ka·zakh·stan also **Ka·zak·stan** (kä′zăk-stän′, kə-zäk′-) A country S of Russia and NE of the Caspian Sea; ruled by Russia from 1730 to 1853 and a constituent republic of the USSR from 1936 to 1991. Cap. Astana. Pop. 17,027,000.

Ka·zan (kə-zăn′, -zän′) A city of W-central Russia on the Volga R. E of Moscow; founded 1401 and the cap. of a powerful Tartar

---

khanate (1455–1552). Pop. 1,085,944.

Ka·zan River (kə-zăn′) A river, c. 732 km (455 mi), of S Nunavut, Canada, flowing NNE to Baker Lake.

Ka·zan·tza·kis (kä′zăn-zä′kĭs, -zän-dzä′kēs), **Nikos** 1885–1957. Greek writer who wrote *Zorba the Greek* (1946).

Kaz·bek (kăz-bĕk′), **Mount** An extinct volcano, 5,042.3 m (16,532 ft), of N Georgia in the central Caucasus.

ka·zoo (kə-zōō′) *n., pl.* **-zoos** A toy musical instrument with a membrane that produces a buzzing sound when a player hums or sings into the mouthpiece. [Perh. imit. of its sound.]

Kaz·vin (kăz-vēn′) See **Qazvin.**

kb *abbr.* kilobar

Kb *abbr.* kilobit

KB *abbr.* kilobyte

Kbps *abbr.* kilobits per second

kc *abbr.* **1.** *also* **kC** kilocurie **2.** kilocycle

KC *abbr.* **1.** King's Counsel **2.** Knight of Columbus

kcal *abbr.* kilocalorie

KD *abbr.* **1.** kiln-dried **2.** knockdown

ke·a (kē′ə) *n.* A brownish-green mountain-dwelling New Zealand parrot (*Nestor notabilis*) that usu. eats insects. [Maori, perh. imit. of its call.]

Kean (kēn), **Edmund** 1789?–1833. British actor known for his portrayals of Shakespeare's tragic characters.

Kea·ton (kēt′n), **Joseph Francis** Known as "Buster." 1895–1966. Amer. actor who starred in silent film classics such as *The General* (1926).

Keats (kēts), **John** 1795–1821. British poet whose melodic works include "The Eve of St. Agnes" and "Ode on a Grecian Urn" (both 1819). —**Keats′i·an** *adj.*

keb·ab *also* **ke·bob** *also* **ka·bob** (kə-bŏb′) *n.* Shish kebab.

Ke·ble (kē′bəl), **John** 1792–1866. British cleric and poet known for his sermon "National Apostasy" (1833).

Kech·ua (kĕch′wə, -wä′) *n.* Variant of **Quechua.**

kedge (kĕj) *Nautical n.* A light anchor used to warp a vessel. ❖ *v.* **kedged, kedg·ing, kedg·es** —*tr.* To warp (a vessel) by using a light anchor. —*intr.* To move by using a light anchor. [< *kedge*, to warp a vessel, perh. < ME *caggen*, to tie, perh. of Scand. orig.]

kedg·er·ee (kĕj′ə-rē′, kĕj′ə-rē′) *n.* A dish of flaked fish, boiled rice, and eggs. [Urdu *khichrī*, perh. < Skt. *kṛsaraḥ, kṛsaraḥ*, dish containing sesame, peas, and lentils.]

keek (kēk) *Scots intr.v.* **keeked, keek·ing, keeks** To peek; peep. ❖ *n.* A look, esp. a quick one; a peek. [ME *kiken, keken*, perh. < MDu. *kiken*.]

keel¹ (kēl) *n.* **1.** *Nautical* **a.** The principal structural member of a ship, running lengthwise along the center line from bow to stern, to which the frames are attached. **b.** A ship. **2.** A structure that resembles a ship's keel in function or shape. **3.** The principal structural member of an aircraft, resembling a ship's keel. **4.** A pair of united petals in certain flowers. ❖ *intr. & tr.v.* **keeled, keel·ing, keels** *Nautical* To capsize or cause to capsize. —*phrasal verb:* **keel over** To collapse or fall into or as if into a faint. [ME *kele* < ON *kjölr*.]

keel² (kēl) *n.* **1.** *Nautical* **a.** A freight barge, esp. for carrying coal on the Tyne River in England. **b.** The load capacity of this barge. **2.** A British unit of weight formerly used for coal, equal to about 21.2 long tons. [ME *kele* < MDu. *kiel*.]

keel³ (kēl) *tr.v.* **keeled, keel·ing, keels** *Chiefly British* To make cool. [ME *kelen* < OE *cēlan*, to cool. See **gel-** in App.]

keel·boat (kēl′bōt′) *n.* A riverboat with a keel but without sails, used for carrying freight.

keel·haul (kēl′hôl′) *tr.v.* **-hauled, -haul·ing, -hauls 1.** *Nautical* To discipline by dragging under the keel of a ship. **2.** To rebuke harshly. [Alteration of Du. *kielhalen* : *kiel*, keel of a ship (< MDu.) + *halen*, to haul (< MDu.); see **kelə-** in App.]

Kee·ling Islands (kē′lĭng) See **Cocos Islands.**

keel·son (kĕl′sən, kēl′-) *also* **kel·son** (kĕl′-) *n.* A timber or girder fastened above and parallel to the keel of a ship or boat for additional strength. [Alteration (influenced by KEEL¹) of ME *kelswin*, prob. < ON **kjölsvín* : *kjölr*, keel + *svín*, swine, timber; see **sū-** in App.]

Kee·lung (kē′lōōng′) See **Chi-lung.**

keen¹ (kēn) *adj.* **keen·er, keen·est 1.** Having a fine sharp cutting edge or point. **2.** Having or marked by quick intelligence and acuity. See Syns at **sharp. 3.** Acutely sensitive: *a keen ear.* **4.** Sharp; vivid; strong. **5.** Intense; piercing: *a keen wind.* **6.** Pungent; acrid. **7a.** Ardent; enthusiastic. **b.** Eagerly desirous. **8.** *Slang* Great; splendid; fine. [ME *kene* < OE *cēne*, brave.] —**keen′ly** *adv.* —**keen′ness** *n.*

keen² (kēn) *n.* A loud wailing lament for the dead. ❖ *intr.v.* **keened, keen·ing, keens** To wail in lamentation, esp. for the dead. See Syns at **cry.** [< Ir.Gael. *caoineadh* < *caoinim*, I lament < OIr. *cainim, coínim*, perh. of Brittonic orig.] —**keen′er** *n.*

keep (kēp) *v.* **kept** (kĕpt), **keep·ing, keeps** —*tr.* **1.** To retain possession of: *kept my car for the weekend.* **2.** To have as a supply: *kept spare parts just in case.* **3a.** To support (a family, for example). **b.** To support (a mistress, for example) financially. **4.** To put customarily; store: *kept the ax in the shed.* **5a.** To supply with room and board for a charge: *keep boarders.* **b.** To raise: *keep chickens.* **6.** To maintain for use or service: *Who keeps your furnace?* **7.** To manage, tend, or have charge of: *keeps shop.* **8.** To pre-

---

katydid
true katydid
Pterophylla camellifolia

Kazakhstan

ă pat	oi boy
ā pay	ou out
âr care	ŏŏ took
ä father	ōō boot
ĕ pet	ŭ cut
ē be	ûr urge
ĭ pit	th thin
ī pie	th this
îr pier	hw which
ŏ pot	zh vision
ō toe	ə about,
ô paw	item

Stress marks:
′ (primary);
′ (secondary), as in
lexicon (lĕk′sĭ-kŏn′)

keeshond
adult dog with pup

Helen Keller
with Anne Sullivan

Kemal Atatürk

Jacqueline Kennedy
photographed in 1960

John F. Kennedy
detail from a 1966 portrait, from a 1962 life sketch, by William Franklin Draper (b. 1912)

serve (food). **9.** To cause to continue in a state or course of action: *kept the patient calm.* **10a.** To maintain records in: *keep a diary.* **b.** To enter (data) in a book. **11a.** To detain: *kept after school.* **b.** To restrain: *kept the crowd back.* **c.** To prevent or deter: *could not keep her from leaving.* **d.** To refrain from divulging: *keep a secret.* **e.** To save; reserve. **12.** To adhere or conform to; follow: *keep late hours.* **13.** To be faithful to; fulfill: *kept her word.* **14.** To celebrate; observe. *—intr.* **1.** To remain in a state or condition; stay. **2.** To continue to do: *keep guessing.* **3.** To remain fresh or unspoiled. **4.** To restrain oneself; hold oneself back: *keep from prying.* ❖ *n.* **1.** Care; charge. **2.** The means by which one is supported. **3a.** The stronghold of a castle. **b.** A jail. ***—phrasal verbs:*** **keep at** To persevere in an action. **keep down 1.** To prevent from growing, accomplishing, or succeeding. **2.** To hold under control or at a reduced level. **3.** To refrain from vomiting (the contents of the stomach). **keep off** To stay away from. **keep to** To adhere to. **keep up 1.** To maintain in good condition. **2a.** To persevere in; carry on. **b.** To preserve or sustain: *keep up appearances.* **3.** To continue at the same level or pace. **4.** To match one's fellows in success or lifestyle. **5.** To remain adequately informed. ***—idioms:*** **for keeps 1.** For an indefinitely long period. **2.** Seriously and permanently. **keep an eye on 1.** To watch over attentively; mind. **2.** To watch closely or carefully. **keep an eye out** To be watchful. **keep a stiff upper lip** To be courageous or stoic in the face of adversity. **keep company 1.** To carry on a courtship: *kept company but never married.* **2.** To socialize or associate. **keep (one's) chin up** To be courageous or optimistic in difficulties. **keep (one's) eyes open** (or **peeled**) To be on the lookout. **keep (one's) nose clean** *Informal* To stay out of trouble. **keep pace** To stay even with others, as in a contest. **keep the wolf from the door** To avoid the privation and suffering due to lack of money. **keep (someone) company** To accompany or remain with. **keep time 1.** To indicate the correct time. **2.** *Music* To maintain the tempo or rhythm. **keep to (oneself) 1.** To shun the company of others. **2.** To refrain from divulging. [ME *kepen* < OE *cēpan*, to observe, seize.]

SYNONYMS *keep, retain, withhold, reserve* These verbs mean to have and maintain in one's possession or control. *Keep* is the most general: *We received a few offers but decided to keep the house. Retain* means to continue to hold, especially in the face of possible loss: *Though unhappy, I retained my sense of humor. Withhold* implies reluctance or refusal to give, grant, or allow: *The tenants withheld their rent until the landlord repaired the boiler.* To *reserve* is to hold back for the future or for a special purpose: *The farmer reserved two acres for an orchard.*

keep•er (kē′pər) *n.* **1.** One that keeps, esp.: **a.** An attendant, a guard, or a warden. **b.** One in charge or care of something: *a lion keeper.* **c.** *Sports* A goalkeeper. **2.** *Football* A play made by the quarterback who keeps the ball after it is snapped and runs with it. **3.** *Informal* One worth keeping, esp. a fish large enough to be legally caught.

keep•ing (kē′pĭng) *n.* **1.** The act of holding, guarding, or supporting. **2.** Custody; care. See Syns at **care. 3.** Conformity; harmony: *"A facade had been added, in perfect keeping with* [the] *original architecture"* (Nancy Holmes).

keep•sake (kēp′sāk′) *n.* Something kept as a memento.

kees•hond (kās′hônt′, -hŏnd′) *n., pl.* **-hon•den** (-hôn′dən) or **-honds** Any of a breed of dog originating in the Netherlands and having a thick grayish-black coat. [Du. : prob. the name *Kees* (nickname for *Cornelis*, Cornelius) + *hond*, dog (< MDu.; see **kwon-** in App.).]

Kee•wa•tin (kē-wāt′n) A district and administrative region of S Nunavut, Canada, including islands in Hudson Bay.

kef (kĕf, kēf, kāf) *n.* Variant of **kif.**

Ke•fal•li•ní•a (kĕ′fä-lē-nē′ä) See **Cephalonia.**

ke•fir (kĕ-fîr′) *n.* A creamy drink made of fermented cow's milk. [Russ., prob. ult. < O Turkic *köpür*, (milk) froth, foam < *köpürmäk*, to froth, foam.]

keg (kĕg) *n.* **1a.** A small cask or barrel with a capacity of about 30 gallons (114 liters). **b.** Such a container and its contents. **2.** A unit of weight used for nails, equal to 100 pounds (45.5 kilograms). ❖ *tr.v.* **kegged, keg•ging, kegs** To put or store in a small cask or barrel. [ME *kag* < ON *kaggi.*]

Ke•gel exercise (kā′gəl) *n.* Any of various exercises involving controlled contraction and release of the muscles at the base of the pelvis, used esp. as a treatment for urinary incontinence. [After Arnold H. *Kegel* (died 1976), American gynecologist.]

keg•ler (kĕg′lər) *n.* A person who bowls; a bowler. [Ger. < *kegeln*, to bowl < *Kegel*, bowling pin < MHGer. *kegel* < OHGer. *kegil*, peg.]

kei•ret•su (kā-rĕt′so͞o) *n., pl.* **keiretsu** or **-sus** A network of businesses that own stakes in one another as a means of mutual security, esp. in Japan. [J., series, affiliation : *kei*, system + *retsu*, row, line.]

keis•ter (kē′stər) *n. Slang* **1.** The buttocks. **2.** The anus. [Earlier, satchel, suitcase.]

Kei•tel (kīt′l), **Wilhelm** 1882–1946. German general and chief of the supreme command of Nazi armed forces who signed an unconditional surrender (May 1945).

Kel•ler (kĕl′ər), **Helen Adams** 1880–1968. Amer. memoirist who lectured widely on behalf of sightless people.

Kel•logg (kĕl′ôg′, -ŏg′), **Frank Billings** 1856–1937. Amer. public official who cosponsored the Kellogg-Briand Pact (1928) and won the 1929 Nobel Peace Prize.

Kel•ly (kĕl′ē), **Emmett** 1898–1979. Amer. circus clown who was famous as "Weary Willie," a sad-faced hobo with the Ringling Brothers and Barnum & Bailey Circus (1942–56).

Kelly, Eugene Curran ("Gene") 1912–96. Amer. dancer, actor, choreographer, and director whose film credits include *An American in Paris* (1951).

Kelly, Grace Patricia. Princess Grace. 1929–82. Amer. actress who appeared in motion pictures such as *Country Girl* (1954) and married Prince Rainier III of Monaco (1956).

kelly green *n.* A strong yellowish green. [< the name *Kelly.*] **—kel′ly-green′** (kĕl′ē-grēn′) *adj.*

ke•loid also **che•loid** (kē′loid′) *n.* A red, raised formation of fibrous scar tissue caused by excessive tissue repair. [Fr. *kéloïde* : Gk. *khēlē*, claw + Fr. *-oïde*, resembling (< Gk. *-oeidēs*; see –OID).] **—ke•loid′al** (-loid′l) *adj.*

Ke•low•na (kə-lō′nə) A city of S British Columbia, Canada, on Okanagan Lake ENE of Vancouver. Pop. 89,442.

kelp (kĕlp) *n.* **1.** Any of various brown, often very large seaweeds of the order Laminariales. **2.** The ash of these seaweeds, used as a source of potash and iodine. [ME *culp.*]

kel•pie[1] also **kel•py** (kĕl′pē) *n., pl.* **-pies** A malevolent water spirit of Scottish legend, usu. having the shape of a horse and rejoicing in or causing drownings. [Prob. of Celt. orig.; akin to Sc. Gael. *colpach*, heifer.]

kel•pie[2] (kĕl′pē) *n.* Any of an Austrian breed of sheepdog. [< *Kelpie*, the name of an early specimen of the breed.]

kel•son (kĕl′sən) *n.* Variant of **keelson.**

Kelt (kĕlt) *n.* Variant of **Celt.**

Kelt•ic (kĕl′tĭk) *n. & adj.* Variant of **Celtic.**

kel•vin (kĕl′vĭn) *n.* **1.** A unit of absolute temperature equal to 1⁄273.16 of the absolute temperature of the triple point of water and equal in magnitude to one Celsius degree. See table at **measurement. 2. Kelvin** A temperature scale in which zero occurs at absolute zero and each degree equals one kelvin. Water freezes at 273.15 K and boils at 373.15 K. [After First Baron KELVIN.]

Kelvin, First Baron. Title of William Thomson. 1824–1907. British physicist who developed the Kelvin scale (1848).

Ke•mal At•a•türk (kə-mäl′ ăt′ə-tûrk′, kĕ-mäl′ ä-tä-türk′) 1881–1938. Turkish nationalist politician who served as president of the Turkish Republic (1923–38).

Ke•me•ro•vo (kĕm′ə-rō′və, kyĕ′mər-ə-və) A city of S-central Russia ENE of Novosibirsk. Pop. 512,778.

Ke•mi•jo•ki (kĕm′ē-yô′kē) A river of N Finland flowing c. 555 km (345 mi) to the Gulf of Bothnia.

Kem•pis (kĕm′pĭs), **Thomas à** See **Thomas à Kempis.**

kempt (kĕmpt) *adj.* Tidy; trim. [Back-formation < UNKEMPT.]

ken (kĕn) *n.* **1.** Perception; understanding. **2a.** Range of vision. **b.** View; sight. ❖ *v.* **kenned** or **kent** (kĕnt), **ken•ning, kens** *Scots —tr.* **1.** To know (a person or thing). **2.** To recognize. *—intr.* To have knowledge or an understanding. [< ME *kennen* < OE *cennan*, to declare. See **gnō-** in App.]

Ken. *abbr.* Kentucky

Ke•nai Peninsula (kē′nī′) A peninsula of S-central AK between Cook Inlet and the Gulf of Alaska.

Ken•dal green (kĕn′dl) *n.* **1.** A coarse green woolen fabric similar to tweed. **2.** The color of this fabric. [After *Kendal*, a municipal borough of northwest England.]

Ken•dall (kĕn′dl) A community of SE FL, a suburb of Miami. Pop. 75,226.

ken•do (kĕn′dō) *n.* The Japanese martial art of fencing with bamboo swords. [J. *kendō* : *ken*, sword (< M Chin. *kiamh, kiam*) + *dō*, way; see AIKIDO.]

Ken•drew (kĕn′dro͞o′), Sir **John Cowdery** b. 1917. British biologist who shared the 1962 Nobel Prize for chemistry.

Ken•il•worth (kĕn′əl-wûrth′) An urban district of central England SE of Birmingham; site of the ruins of Kenilworth Castle, built c. 1120 and celebrated in Sir Walter Scott's novel *Kenilworth* (1821). Pop. 19,315.

Kenilworth ivy *n.* A European creeping herb *(Cymbalaria muralis)* with palmately lobed leaves and solitary, pale purple flowers. [After *Kenilworth* Castle, Kenilworth.]

Ken•nan (kĕn′ən), **George Frost** b. 1904. Amer. diplomat and historian who served as US ambassador to the USSR (1952) and Yugoslavia (1961–63).

Ken•ne•bec (kĕn′ə-bĕk′) A river of W-central and S Maine flowing c. 257 km (160 mi) to the Atlantic Ocean.

Ken•ne•dy (kĕn′ĭ-dē), **Anthony M.** b. 1936. Amer. jurist; associate justice of the US Supreme Court (since 1988).

Kennedy, Cape See Cape **Canaveral.**

Kennedy, Jacqueline Lee Bouvier Former name of Jacqueline Kennedy Onassis. 1929–94. First Lady of the US (1961–63) who supervised the redecoration of the White House.

Kennedy, John Fitzgerald 1917–63. The 35th President of the US (1961–63), who approved the failed invasion of the Bay of Pigs (1961) and forced Khrushchev to remove Soviet missiles from Cuba (1962). He was assassinated in Dallas, Texas, on Nov. 22, 1963.

Kennedy, Joseph Patrick 1888–1969. Amer. financier who served as ambassador to Great Britain (1937–40).

Kennedy, Robert Francis 1925–68. Amer. politician who served as US attorney general (1961–64) and was assassinated in Los Angeles while campaigning for the presidency.

ken·nel[1] (kĕn′əl) *n.* **1.** A shelter for a dog. **2.** A pack of dogs, esp. hounds. **3.** An establishment where dogs are bred, trained, or boarded. **4.** The lair of a wild animal, such as a fox. ❖ *v.* **-neled, -nel·ing, -nels** or **-nelled, -nel·ling, -nels** —*tr.* To place or keep in or as if in a kennel. —*intr.* To take cover or lie in or as if in a kennel. [ME *kenel* < AN *kenil < Med.Lat. *canīle* < Lat. *canis,* dog. See **kwon-** in App.]

ken·nel[2] (kĕn′əl) *n.* A gutter along a street. [ME *cannel* < ONFr. *canel,* channel < Lat. *canālis.* See CANAL.]

Ken·nel·ly-Heav·i·side layer (kĕn′ə-lē-hĕv′ē-sīd′) *n.* See E layer. [After Edwin *Kennelly* (1861–1939), American physicist, and Oliver *Heaviside* (1850–1925), British physicist.]

Ken·ner (kĕn′ər) A city of SE LA, a suburb of New Orleans on the Mississippi R. Pop. 70,517.

ken·ning (kĕn′ĭng) *n.* A figurative, usu. compound expression used in place of a name or noun, esp. in Old English and Old Norse poetry. [ON < *kenna,* to know, to name with a kenning. See **gnō-** in App.]

Ken·ny (kĕn′ē), **Elizabeth** 1880?–1952. Australian nurse who developed a treatment for paralysis brought on by poliomyelitis.

ke·no (kē′nō) *n.* A game of chance, similar to lotto, that uses balls rather than counters. [Fr. *quine,* set of five winning numbers (< Lat. *quīnī,* five each; see **penk**ʷ**e** in App.) + *-o* (as in LOTTO).]

Ke·no·sha (kə-nō′shə) A city of extreme SE WI on Lake Michigan S of Milwaukee; founded 1835. Pop. 90,352.

ke·no·sis (kĭ-nō′sĭs) *n. Christianity* The relinquishment of the form of God by Jesus in becoming man and suffering death. [L.Gk. *kenōsis* < Gk., an emptying < *kenoun,* to empty < *kenos,* empty.] —**ke·not′ic** (-nŏt′ĭk) *adj.*

kent (kĕnt) *v. Scots* A past tense and a past participle of **ken.**

Kent 1. A region and former kingdom of SE England; settled by Jutes in the 5th cent. A.D. and one of the seven kingdoms of the Anglo-Saxon Heptarchy. **2.** A city of NE OH ENE of Akron; seat of Kent State University (founded 1910). Pop. 27,906.

Kent, Rockwell 1882–1971. Amer. artist best known for his stark woodcuts in special editions of classic literary works.

ken·te (kĕn′tā) *n.* **1.** A brightly patterned, handwoven ceremonial cloth of the Ashanti. **2.** A durable machine-woven fabric similar to this fabric, prominently featured in Afrocentric fashion. [Twi, cloth.]

Kent·ish (kĕn′tĭsh) *adj.* Of or relating to Kent, England, or its inhabitants. ❖ *n.* The dialect of English spoken in Kent.

kent·ledge (kĕnt′lĭj) *n. Nautical* Pig iron used as permanent ballast. [?]

Ken·tuck·y (kən-tŭk′ē) A state of the E-central US; admitted as the 15th state in 1792. Daniel Boone's Transylvania Co. settled the area in 1775. Cap. Frankfort. Pop. 4,041,769. —**Ken·tuck′i·an** *adj. & n.*

Kentucky bluegrass *n.* A perennial Eurasian and North African grass (*Poa pratensis*) that is commonly cultivated for pasture and lawns.

Kentucky coffee tree *n.* A deciduous North American tree (*Gymnocladus dioica*) having flat pulpy pods with large seeds formerly used as a coffee substitute.

Kentucky River A river, of N-central KY flowing c. 417 km (259 mi) to the Ohio R.

Ken·ya (kĕn′yə, kēn′-) A country of E-central Africa bordering on the Indian Ocean; gained independence from Great Britain in 1963. Cap. Nairobi. Pop. 29,292,000. —**Ken′yan** *adj. & n.*

Kenya, Mount An extinct volcano, 5,202.7 m (17,058 ft), in central Kenya.

Ken·yat·ta (kĕn-yä′tə), **Jomo** 1893?–1978. Kenyan nationalist and first president of independent Kenya (1964–78).

Ke·ogh plan (kē′ō) *n.* A retirement plan for the self-employed and their employees. [After Eugene James *Keogh* (1907–89), former US representative from New York.]

Ke·o·kuk (kē′ə-kŭk′) 1790?–1848? Amer. Sauk leader who negotiated peace between his people and the Sioux (1837).

keph·a·lin (kĕf′ə-lĭn) *n.* Variant of **cephalin.**

ke·pi (kā′pē, kĕp′ē) *n., pl.* **-pis** A French military cap with a flat circular top and a visor. [Fr. *képi* < Ger. dialectal *Käppi,* ult. prob. < LLat. *cappa,* head covering.]

Kep·ler (kĕp′lər), **Johannes** 1571–1630. German astronomer and mathematician who formulated three laws to describe how the planets revolve around the sun.

kept (kĕpt) *v.* Past tense and past participle of **keep.**

ker·a·tec·to·my (kĕr′ə-tĕk′tə-mē) *n., pl.* **-mies** Surgical removal of a part of the cornea.

ker·a·tin (kĕr′ə-tĭn) *n.* A tough insoluble protein and the chief constituent of hair, nails, horns, and hooves. [Gk. *keras, kerāt-,* horn; see **ker-**[1] in App. + -IN.] —**ke·rat′i·nous** (kə-răt′n-əs) *adj.*

ker·a·tin·ize (kĕr′ə-tə-nīz′) *v.* **-ized, -iz·ing, -iz·es** —*intr.* To produce or become like keratin. —*tr.* To convert (something) into keratin. —**ker′a·tin·i·za′tion** (-tə-nī-zā′shən) *n.*

ker·a·ti·tis (kĕr′ə-tī′tĭs) *n., pl.* **-tit·i·des** (-tĭt′ĭ-dēz′) In-

flammation of the cornea.

kerato– or **kerat–** also **cerato–** or **cerat–** *pref.* **1.** Horn; horny: *keratosis.* **2.** Cornea: *keratectomy.* [Gk. *kerāto-,* horn < *keras, kerāt-.* See **ker-**[1] in App.]

ker·a·to·sis (kĕr′ə-tō′sĭs) *n., pl.* **-ses** (-sēz) Excessive growth of horny tissue of the skin. —**ker′a·tot′ic** (-tŏt′ĭk) *adj.*

ker·a·tot·o·my (kĕr′ə-tŏt′ə-mē) *n., pl.* **-mies** Surgical incision of the cornea.

kerb (kûrb) *n. Chiefly British* Variant of **curb** 1.

Ker·be·la (kûr′bə-lə) See **Karbala.**

Kerch (kĕrch) A city of S Ukraine on **Kerch Strait,** a shallow waterway connecting the Black Sea with the Sea of Azov and bordered on the W by the **Kerch Peninsula;** founded by Greek colonists in the 6th cent. B.C. Pop. 180,500.

ker·chief (kûr′chĭf, -chēf′) *n., pl.* **-chiefs** also **-chieves** (-chĭvz, -chēvz) **1.** A woman's square scarf, often worn as a head covering. **2.** A handkerchief. [ME *coverchef, curchef* < AN *courchief* (var. of OFr. *couvrechef*) and < OFr. *couvrechef : covrir,* to cover (< Lat. *cooperīre*) + *chef,* head; see CHIEF.]

Ke·ren·sky (kə-rĕn′skē, kĕr′ən-, kyĕr′yĭn-), **Aleksandr Feodorovich** 1881–1970. Russian revolutionary who became head of government (Jul. 1917) after the abdication of Nicholas II but was overthrown by the Bolsheviks (Oct. 1917).

Ker·e·san (kĕr′ĭ-sən) *n.* Any of a group of languages spoken by certain Pueblo peoples. —**Ker′e·san** *adj.*

kerf (kûrf) *n.* **1.** A groove or notch made by a cutting tool, such as a saw or an ax. **2.** The width of a groove made by a cutting tool. [ME < OE *cyrf,* a cutting. See **gerbh-** in App.]

Ker·gue·len Islands (kûr′gə-lən, -lĕn′) A French-administered island group in the S Indian Ocean SE of South Africa.

Kér·ki·ra (kĕr′kē-rä′) See **Corfu.**

Ker·man (kər-män′, kĕr-) A city of E-central Iran SE of Tehran; long noted for its carpets. Pop. 349,626.

ker·mes (kûr′mēz) *n.* A red dyestuff once prepared from the dried bodies of various female scale insects of the genus *Kermes.* [Fr. *kermès,* short for *alkermès* < Ar. *al-qirmiz,* prob. < Skt. *kṛmija-,* (red dye) produced by worms. See **k**ʷ**rmi-** in App.]

ker·mis also **ker·mess** or **kir·mess** (kûr′mĭs) *n.* **1.** An outdoor fair in the Low Countries. **2.** A fundraising fair or carnival. [Du. < MDu. *kercmisse,* church dedication mass : *kerc,* church (ult. < L.Gk. *kūriakon, kūrikon (dōma),* (house) of the lord; see CHURCH) + *misse,* mass (< LLat. *missa;* see MASS).]

kern[1] also **kerne** (kûrn) *n.* **1.** A medieval Scottish or Irish foot soldier. **2.** A loutish person. [ME *kerne* < MIr. *ceithern,* band of soldiers < OIr.]

kern[2] (kûrn) *Printing n.* The portion of a typeface that projects beyond the body or shank of a character. ❖ *tr.v.* **kerned, kern·ing, kerns** **1.** To provide (type) with a kern. **2.** To adjust space between (characters) in typeset text. [Fr. *carne,* corner < ONFr. < Lat. *cardō, cardin-,* hinge.]

Kern, Jerome David 1885–1945. Amer. composer of numerous songs and musicals, including *Show Boat* (1927).

ker·nel (kûr′nəl) *n.* **1.** A grain or seed, as of a cereal grass, enclosed in a husk. **2.** The inner, usu. edible seed of a nut or fruit stone. **3.** The most material and central part; the core. [ME < OE *cyrnel.* See **grə-no-** in App.] —**ker′neled** *adj.*

kern·ite (kûr′nīt′) *n.* A colorless to white lustrous crystalline mineral, Na₂B₄O₇·4H₂O, that is a major source of boron ore. [After *Kern,* a county of southern California.]

ker·o·gen (kĕr′ə-jən) *n.* A fossilized material in shale and other sedimentary rock that yields oil upon heating. [Gk. *kēros,* wax + –GEN.]

ker·o·sene also **ker·o·sine** (kĕr′ə-sēn′, kăr′-, kĕr′ə-sēn′, kăr′-) *n.* A thin oil distilled from petroleum or shale oil, used as a fuel and a denaturant for alcohol. [< Gk. *kēros,* wax.]

Ker·ou·ac (kĕr′ōō-ăk′), **Jack** 1922–69. Amer. writer of the Beat Generation who wrote *On the Road* (1957).

ker·plunk (kər-plŭngk′) *n.* A sound like that of a heavy object falling rapidly into water. [*ker-,* intensive pref. (prob. < Sc.) + PLUNK.] —**ker·plunk′** *adv.*

Ker·ry (kĕr′ē) *n., pl.* **-ries** Any of an Irish breed of small black dairy cattle. [After *Kerry,* a county of southwest Ireland.]

Kerry blue terrier *n.* Any of an Irish breed of terriers having a bluish-gray coat. [After *Kerry,* a county of southwest Ireland.]

ker·sey (kûr′zē) *n., pl.* **-seys 1.** A twilled woolen fabric, sometimes with a cotton warp, used for coats. **2.** A garment made of this fabric. Often used in the plural. **3.** A woolen, often ribbed fabric formerly used for hose and trousers. [ME *kersei,* after *Kersey,* a village of southeast England.]

ker·sey·mere (kûr′zē-mîr′) *n.* A fine woolen cloth with a fancy twill weave. [KERSEY + (CASSI)MERE.]

Ker·u·len (kĕr′ōō-lĕn′) A river rising in NE Mongolia and flowing c. 1,263 km (785 mi) to a lake in NE China.

ke·ryg·ma (kə-rĭg′mə) *n. Christianity* The proclamation of religious truths, esp. as taught in the Gospels. [Gk. *kērugma,* preaching, proclamation < *kērux, kērug-,* herald.]

kes·trel (kĕs′trəl) *n.* Any of various small falcons belonging to the genus *Falco,* esp. the American kestrel and the European kestrel. [Prob. < obsolete Fr. *cresserelle* < OFr. *cresserele,* prob. < *cresselle,* clacker, kestrel.]

ke·ta·mine (kē′tə-mēn′) *n.* A general anesthetic used for minor

kente

Kenya

kestrel
American kestrel
Falco sparverius

ă pat	oi boy
ā pay	ou out
âr care	ŏŏ took
ä father	ōō boot
ĕ pet	ŭ cut
ē be	ûr urge
ĭ pit	th thin
ī pie	th this
îr pier	hw which
ŏ pot	zh vision
ō toe	ə about,
ô paw	item

Stress marks:
′ (primary);
′ (secondary); as in
lexicon (lĕk′sĭ-kŏn′)

surgical procedures and known for its use as an illegal drug. [KET(O)–]

ketch (kĕch) *n. Nautical* A two-masted fore-and-aft-rigged sailing vessel with a mizzenmast stepped aft of a taller mainmast but forward of the rudder. [ME *cache* < *cacchen*, to catch. See CATCH.]

Ketch·i·kan (kĕch′ĭ-kăn′) A city of SE AK on an island in the Alexander Archipelago; a supply point for miners during the gold rush of the 1890s. Pop. 7,922.

ketch·up (kĕch′əp, kăch′-) also **catch·up** (kăch′əp, kĕch′-) or **cat·sup** (kăt′səp, kăch′əp, kĕch′-) *n.* A condiment consisting of a thick, smooth-textured, spicy sauce usu. made from tomatoes. [Prob. Malay *kicap*, fish sauce, poss. < Chin. (Cantonese) *kē-chap*, equivalent to Chin. (Mandarin) *qié*, eggplant + Chin. (Mandarin) *zhī*, sap, gravy.]

REGIONAL NOTE The source of our word *ketchup* may be the Malay word *kēchap*, possibly taken into Malay from the Cantonese dialect of Chinese. *Kēchap*, like our word, referred to a kind of sauce but a sauce without tomatoes; rather, it contained fish brine, herbs, and spices. Sailors probably took the sauce to Europe, where it was made with local ingredients such as the juice of mushrooms or walnuts. When the juice of tomatoes was first used, ketchup as we know it was born. However, it is important to realize that in the 18th and 19th centuries *ketchup* was a generic term for sauces where only common ingredient was vinegar. The word is first recorded in English in 1690 in the form *catchup*, in 1711 in the form *ketchup*, and in 1730 in the form *catsup*. These three spelling variants of a foreign borrowing remain current.

ke·tene (kē′tēn′) *n.* A pungent, toxic, colorless gas, C_2H_2O, used chiefly as an acetylation agent.

keto– or **ket–** *pref.* Ketone; ketone group: *ketosis.* [< KETONE.]

ke·to·co·na·zole (kē′tō-kə-nā′zōl′) *n.* A broad-spectrum antifungal agent administered either orally or topically. [KETO(NE) + (MI)CONAZOLE.]

ke·to·gen·e·sis (kē′tō-jĕn′ĭ-sĭs) *n.* The formation of ketone bodies, as occurs in diabetes. —**ke′to·gen′ic** *adj.*

ke·tone (kē′tōn′) *n.* Any of a class of organic compounds having a carbonyl group linked to a carbon atom in each of two hydrocarbon radicals and the general formula R(CO)R′, where R may be the same as R′. [Ger. *Keton*, short for *Aketon*, acetone : Lat. *acētum*, vinegar; see ACETUM + Ger. *-on*, n. suff. (alteration of *-en* < Gk. *-ēnē*).] —**ke·ton′ic** (-tŏn′ĭk) *adj.*

ketone body *n.* A ketone-containing intermediate product of fatty acid metabolism produced excessively in individuals affected by starvation or uncontrolled diabetes mellitus.

ke·tose (kē′tōs′) *n.* Any of various carbohydrates containing a ketone group.

ke·to·sis (kē-tō′sĭs) *n., pl.* **-ses** (-sēz) A pathological increase in ketone bodies. —**ke·tot′ic** (-tŏt′ĭk) *adj.*

ke·to·ste·roid (kē′tō-stîr′oid′, -stĕr′-) *n.* A steroid containing a ketone group.

ket·tle (kĕt′l) *n.* **1.** A metal pot, usu. with a lid, for boiling or stewing. **2.** A teakettle. **3.** *Music* A kettledrum. **4.** *Geology* A depression left in a mass of glacial drift, formed by the melting of an isolated block of glacial ice. **5.** A pothole. [ME *ketel* < ON *ketill* and OE *cetel*, both < Lat. *catíllus*, dim. of *catínus*, large bowl.]

ket·tle·drum (kĕt′l-drŭm′) *n.* A large copper or brass hemispherical drum with a parchment head that can be tuned by adjusting the tension.

kettle of fish *n., pl.* **kettles of fish 1.** An awkward or embarrassing situation. **2.** A matter to be reckoned with.

Keu·ka Lake (kyōō′kə, kā-yōō′-) A lake of W-central New York, one of the Finger Lakes W of Seneca Lake.

keV *abbr.* kiloelectron volt

kev·el (kĕv′əl) *n.* A sturdy belaying pin for the heavier cables of a ship. [ME *kevil* < OFr. *keville*, wooden peg < Lat. *clāvicula*, dim. of *clāvis*, key.]

Kev·lar (kĕv′lär) A trademark used for a type of aramid fiber.

Kew (kyōō) A district of W Greater London in SE England; site of the Royal Botanic Gardens (est. 1759).

kew·pie (kyōō′pē) *n.* A small fat-cheeked wide-eyed doll with a curl of hair on top of the head. [Orig. a trademark.]

key¹ (kē) *n., pl.* **keys 1a.** A notched and grooved, usu. metal device that is turned to open or close a lock. **b.** A similar device for opening or winding: *the key of a clock.* **2.** A means of access, control, or possession. **3a.** A vital, crucial element. **b.** A set of answers to a test. **c.** A table, gloss, or cipher for decoding or interpreting. **4.** A device, such as a wedge, inserted to lock together mechanical or structural parts. **5.** *Architecture* The keystone in an arch. **6a.** A button or lever that is depressed to operate a machine. **b.** A button that is depressed to cause a corresponding character or function to be typed or executed by a typewriter or to be accepted as input by a computer. **c.** *Music* A button or lever that is depressed to produce or modulate the sound of an instrument, such as a clarinet. **7.** *Music* **a.** A tonal system consisting of seven tones in fixed relationship to a tonic; tonality. **b.** The principal tonality of a work: *an etude in the key of E.* **8.** The pitch of a voice or other sound. **9.** A characteristic tone or level of intensity, as of speech. Often used in combination: *high-key; low-key.* **10.** *Botany* A samara. **11.** An outline of the characteristics of a group of organisms,

used in taxonomic identification. **12.** *Basketball* An area at each end of the court between the base line and the foul line and including the jump-ball circle at the foul line. ❖ *adj.* Of crucial importance; significant: *key decisions.* ❖ *tr.v.* **keyed, key·ing, keys 1.** To lock with or as if with a key. **2.** *Architecture* To furnish (an arch) with a keystone. **3.** *Music* To regulate the pitch of. **4.** To bring into harmony; adjust or adapt. **5.** To supply an explanatory key for. **6a.** To operate (a key), as for typesetting, with a keyboard. **b.** To enter (data) into a computer with a keyboard. **7.** To identify (a biological specimen). **8.** To vandalize or mar by scratching with a key. —*phrasal verb:* **key up** To make intense, excited, or nervous. —*idioms:* **in key** In consonance with other factors. **out of key** Not in consonance with other factors. [ME *kai, kei* < OE *cǣg.*]

key² (kē) *n., pl.* **keys** A low offshore island or reef, esp. in the Gulf of Mexico; a cay. [Alteration of Sp. *cayo.* See CAY.]

key³ (kē) *n., pl.* **keys** *Slang* A kilogram of marijuana, cocaine, or heroin. [Shortening and alteration of KILOGRAM.]

Key, Francis Scott 1779–1843. Amer. lawyer and poet who wrote "Defense of Fort M'Henry" (1814), which was later set to music, renamed "The Star-Spangled Banner," and adopted in 1931 by Congress as the national anthem.

key·board (kē′bôrd′, -bōrd′) *n.* **1.** A set of keys, as on a computer terminal, typewriter, or piano. **2.** *Music* **a.** A piano. **b.** Any one of various instruments played by a set of pianolike keys, often connected to a synthesizer or amplifier. ❖ *tr.v.* **-board·ed, -board·ing, -boards 1a.** To set (copy) with a keyed typesetting machine. **b.** To enter (text or data) into a computer with a keyboard. **2.** *Music* To play (a composition) on a piano or keyboard. —**key′board′er, key′board′ist** *n.*

key·card (kē′kärd′) *n.* A usu. plastic card with a magnetically coded strip that is scanned to operate a mechanism.

key club *n.* A private club featuring liquor and entertainment.

Key deer *n.* A nearly extinct subspecies of white-tailed deer (*Odocoileus virginianus clavium*) native to the Florida Keys.

key fruit *n.* See samara. [< the shape of its bunches.]

key·hole (kē′hōl′) *n.* **1.** The hole in a lock into which a key fits. **2.** *Basketball* The key.

Key Largo An island in the Florida Keys off S FL.

Key lime *n.* **1.** A lime indigenous to the Florida Keys, having a yellow rind and yellowish-green fruit. **2.** A yellowish green.

key money *n.* Payment made to a landlord to assure a rental.

Keynes (kānz), **John Maynard.** 1st Baron of Tilton. 1883–1946. British economist who advocated government-sponsored fiscal programs and deficit spending to increase employment and stimulate business activity. —**Keynes′i·an** *adj. & n.* —**Keynes′i·an·ism** *n.*

key·note (kē′nōt′) *n.* **1.** The tonic of a musical key. **2.** A prime underlying element or theme. ❖ *tr.v.* **-not·ed, -not·ing, -notes 1.** To give or set the keynote of. **2.** *Informal* To give a keynote address at. —**key′not′er** *n.*

keynote address *n.* An opening address, as at a political convention, that outlines the issues to be considered.

keynote speech *n.* See keynote address.

key·pad (kē′păd′) *n.* An input device, sometimes part of a standard computer keyboard, consisting of a grid of numeric and function keys arranged for efficient data entry.

key·punch (kē′pŭnch′) *n.* A keyboard machine that is used to punch holes in cards or tapes for data-processing systems. —**key′punch** *v.* —**key′punch′er** *n.*

key signature *n. Music* The group of sharps or flats placed to the right of the clef on a staff to identify the key.

key·stone (kē′stōn′) *n.* **1.** *Architecture* The central wedge-shaped stone of an arch that locks its parts together. **2.** The central supporting element of a whole.

key·stroke (kē′strōk′) *n.* A stroke of a key, as on a computer keyboard. —**key′stroke′** *v.*

key·way (kē′wā′) *n.* **1.** A slot for a key in the hub or shaft of a wheel. **2.** The keyhole of a cylinder lock.

Key West A city of S FL on the island of **Key West,** the westernmost of the Florida Keys in the Gulf of Mexico. Pop. 25,478.

key·word also **key word** (kē′wûrd′) *n.* **1.** A word that serves as a key to a code or cipher. **2.** A significant or descriptive word. **3.** A word used as a reference point for finding other words or information.

kg *abbr.* kilogram

KGB (kā′jē-bē′) *n.* The intelligence and internal security agency of the former Soviet Union. [Russ. < *K(omitet)* *G(osudarstvennoĭ)* *B(ezopasnosti)* : *komitet*, committee + *gosudarstvennoĭ*, fem. genitive of *gosudarstvennyĭ*, of the state + *bezopasnosti*, genitive of *bezopasnost′*, security.]

kgf *abbr.* kilogram force

Kha·ba·rovsk (kə-bär′əfsk, кнə-) A city of SE Russia on the Amur R. near the Chinese border; built on the site of a fort est. in 1652. Pop. 607,669.

Kha·cha·tu·ri·an (kä′chä-tŏŏr′ē-ən, kăch′ə-, кнə-chə-tŏŏr-yän′), **Aram Ilich** 1903–78. Russian composer of Armenian parentage whose works include the ballet *Gayane* (1942).

Kha·da·fy (kə-dä′fē), **Muammar al-** See Muammar al-**Qad-dafi.**

khad·dar (kä′dər) *n.* A coarse homespun cloth made in India.

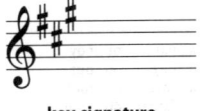

key signature
key signature for A major

[Hindi *khādar*, prob. ult. of Dravidian orig.; akin to Telugu *kaṇduvā*, upper garment.]

khak·i (kăk′ē, kä′kē) *n.* **1.** A light olive brown to moderate or light yellowish brown. **2a.** A sturdy cloth of this color. **b. khakis** A uniform made of this cloth. [Urdu *khākī*, dusty < Pers. < *khāk*, dust < MPers.] —**khak′i** *adj.*

Kha·lid (kä-lēd′, кнä-) 1913–82. King of Saudi Arabia (1975–82).

kha·lif (kā′lĭf, kăl′ĭf) *n.* Variant of **caliph.**

Khal·ki·dhi·kí (kăl-kē′thē-kē′, кнäl-) See **Chalcidice.**

Khal·kís (kăl-kēs′, кнäl-) See **Chalcis.**

Kham·bhat (kŭm′bət), **Gulf of** or **Gulf of Cam·bay** (kăm-bā′) An inlet of the Arabian Sea on the NW coast of India.

kham·sin (kăm-sēn′) *n.* A usu. southerly hot wind from the Sahara that blows across Egypt from late March to early May. [Ar. (*rīḥ al-)ḥamsīn*, (wind of the) 50 (days), khamsin < oblique case of *ḥamsūn*, fifty < *ḥams*, five.]

khan[1] (kän, kăn) *n.* **1.** A ruler, an official, or an important person in India and some central Asian countries. **2.** A medieval ruler of a Mongol, Tartar, or Turkish tribe. [ME *chan* < OFr. *can* < Turk. *khān* (< O Turkic *qaghan*) and < Mongolian *qā′ān*, ruler.]

khan[2] (kän, kăn) *n.* A caravansary in certain Asian countries. [Ar. *hān*, inn < Pers. *khān*, house < MPers.]

khan·ate (kä′nāt′, kăn′āt′) *n.* **1.** The realm of a khan. **2.** The position of a khan.

kha·pra beetle (kä′prə, kăp′rə) *n.* A beetle (*Trogoderma granarium*) accidentally brought into the United States that is a destructive grain pest. [Hindi *khaprā* < *khapnā*, to destroy, ult. < Skt. *kṣapayati*, he destroys.]

Khar·kiv (kär′kĭv′, кнär′kēw′) or **Khar·kov** (kär′kôf′, кнär′kəf) A city of NE Ukraine E of Kiev; founded 1656. Pop. 1,621,600.

Khar·toum also **Khar·tum** (kär-tōōm′) The cap. of Sudan, in the E-central part at the confluence of the Blue Nile and the White Nile; founded c. 1821. Pop. 924,505.

khat (kät) *n.* **1.** An evergreen shrub (*Catha edulis*) of tropical East Africa with leaves that are chewed as a stimulant. **2.** A tealike beverage prepared from its leaves. [Ar. *qatt*.]

Kha·tan·ga (kə-täng′gə, -täng′, кнä-tän′-) A river of N-central Russia flowing c. 1,150 km (715 mi) to **Khatanga Gulf,** an arm of the Laptev Sea.

Khay·yám (kī-yäm′, -äm′), **Omar** See **Omar Khayyám.**

khe·dive (kə-dēv′) *n.* One of several Turkish viceroys ruling Egypt from 1867 to 1914. [Fr. *khédive* < Turk. *hidiv* < Pers. *khidēw*, lord < MPers. *khwadāy* < OIran. *khvadāta*-. See **s(w)e-** in App.]

Kher·son (kĕr-sòn′, кнĕr-) A city of S-central Ukraine on the Dnieper R. near the Black Sea ENE of Odessa. Pop. 368,300.

khi (kī) *n.* Variant of **chi**[1].

Khí·os (kē′ôs, кнē′-) See **Chios.**

Khir·bet Qum·ran (kĭr′bĕt kōōm-rän′) See **Qumran.**

Khmer (kmâr) *n., pl.* **Khmer** or **Khmers** **1.** A member of a people of Cambodia whose civilization reached its height from the 9th to the 15th century. **2.** The Mon-Khmer language that is the official language of Cambodia.

Khmer Rouge *n.* A Cambodian Communist movement that was active as a guerrilla force from 1970 to the late 1990s and held power under the leadership of Pol Pot from 1975 to 1979. [Fr., Red Khmer : *khmer*, Khmer + *rouge*, red.]

Khoi·khoin (koi′koi′ĭn) or **Khoi·khoi** (koi′koi) *n., pl.* **Khoikhoin** or **-khoins** or **Khoikhoi** or **-khois** **1.** A member of a pastoral people of Namibia and South Africa. **2.** Any of the Khoisan languages of the Khoikhoin, including Nama. [Nama *khoi-khoi-n*, the Nama people : *khoi-khoi*, to speak Nama (< *khoi-*, human being) + *-n*, pl. common gender suff.]

Khoi·san (koi′sän′) *n.* A family of languages of southern Africa, including those of the Khoikhoin and the San. [Nama *khoi (-khoi-n)*, the Nama people; see KHOIKHOIN + Nama *san*, the San people; see SAN.]

Kho·mei·ni (kō-mā′nē, кнō-, kô′mä-nē′), Ayatollah **Ruholla** 1900–89. Iranian Shiite leader and head of state (1979–89) who enforced strict observance of the Islamic code.

Kho·per (kə-pyôr′, кнō-) A river, c. 1,006 km (625 mi), of SE Russia flowing S to the Don R.

Kho·ra·na (kō-rä′nə), **Har Gobind** b. 1922. Indian-born Amer. biochemist who shared a 1968 Nobel Prize.

Kho·ta·nese (kō′tə-nēz′, -nēs′) *n.* A Middle Iranian language preserved in Buddhist and secular documents from eastern Chinese Turkistan. [After *Khotan*, ancient kingdom where the language was spoken < Khotanese *Hvatana*-. See **swe-** in App.]

Khru·shchev (krōōsh′chĕf, -chôf, кнrōō-shchyôf′), **Nikita Sergeyevich** 1894–1971. Soviet politician who served as first secretary of the Communist Party (after 1953) and premier of the USSR (1958–64).

Khu·fu (kōō′fōō′) See **Cheops.**

Khul·na (kōōl′nə) A city of SW Bangladesh near the Ganges R. delta. Pop. 545,849.

Khwa·riz·mi (kwär′ĭz-mē, кнwär′-), **al-** Full name Muhammad ibn-Musa al-Khwarizmi. 780?–850? Arab mathematician whose works introduced Arabic numerals and algebraic concepts to Western mathematics.

Khy·ber Pass (kī′bər) A narrow pass, c. 53 km (33 mi) long and rising to c. 1,068 m (3,500 ft), through mountains on the border between W Afghanistan and N Pakistan.

kHz *abbr.* kilohertz

KIA (kā′ī-ā′) *n.* A member of the armed services who is reported killed during a combat mission. [*k(illed) i(n) a(ction)*.]

Kia·ling (kyä′lĭng′, jyä′-) See **Jialing.**

Kia·mu·sze (kyä′mōō′sōō′) See **Jiamusi.**

ki·ang (kē-äng′) *n.* A large wild ass (*Equus hemionus* subsp. *kiang*) of the mountains of Asia. [Tibetan *rkyan*.]

Kiang·si (kyäng′shē′) See **Jiangxi.**

Kiang·su (jyäng′sōō′) See **Jiangsu.**

kiaugh (kyäкн) *n. Scots* Trouble; anxiety. [Prob. < Sc. Gael. *cabhag*.]

kib·ble[1] (kĭb′əl) *n.* An iron bucket used in wells or mines for hoisting water, ore, or refuse to the surface. [Prob. < Ger. *Kübel*, pail < MHGer. < OHGer. *-chublī* (in *miluhchublī*, milk pail) < VLat. **cupia* < Lat. *cūpa*, vat.]

kib·ble[2] (kĭb′əl) *tr.v.* **-bled, -bling, -bles** To crush or grind (grain, for example) coarsely. ❖ *n.* Meal ground by this process and used in pellets esp. for pet food. [?]

kib·butz (kĭ-bŏŏts′, -bōōts′) *n., pl.* **kib·but·zim** (kĭb′ŏŏt-sēm′, -ōōt-) A collective farm or settlement in modern Israel. [Heb. *qibbúṣ*, gathering < *qibbēṣ*, derived stem of *qābaṣ*, to gather.]

kib·butz·nik (kĭ-bŏŏts′nĭk, -bōōts′-) *n.* A member of a kibbutz.

kibe (kīb) *n.* A chapped or inflamed area on the skin, esp. on the heel, resulting from exposure to cold; an ulcerated chillblain. [ME *kybe*.]

Ki·bei (kē-bā′) *n., pl.* **Kibei** or **-beis** A person born in the United States of Japanese immigrant parents and educated chiefly in Japan. [J., to go home, return to America, Kibei : *ki*, return (< M Chin. *kuj*) + *bei*, rice, America (< M Chin. *mej*, rice).]

kib·itz (kĭb′ĭts) *intr.v.* **-itzed, -itz·ing, -itz·es** *Informal* **1.** To look on and offer unwanted, usu. meddlesome advice to others. **2.** To chat; converse. [Yiddish *kibitsen* < Ger. *kiebitzen* < *Kiebitz*, pewit, kibitzer < MHGer. *gībitz*, pewit, of imit. orig.] —**kib′itz·er** *n.*

kib·lah (kĭb′lə) *n. Islam* The direction of the Kaaba, which Muslims face when praying. [Ar. *qibla*.]

ki·bosh (kī′bŏsh′, kĭ-bŏsh′) *n. Informal* A checking or restraining element: *put the kibosh on the plan.* [?]

kick (kĭk) *v.* **kicked, kick·ing, kicks** *—intr.* **1.** To strike out with the foot or feet. **2.** *Sports* **a.** To score or gain ground by kicking a ball. **b.** To punt in football. **c.** To propel the body in swimming by moving the legs. **3.** To recoil: *The rifle kicked hard.* **4.** *Informal* **a.** To express feelings vigorously; complain. **b.** To oppose by argument; protest. —*tr.* **1.** To strike with the foot. **2.** To propel by striking with the foot. **3.** To spring back against suddenly: *The rifle kicked my shoulder.* **4.** *Sports* To score (a goal or point) by kicking a ball. ❖ *n.* **1a.** A vigorous blow with the foot. **b.** *Sports* The motion of the legs that propels the body in swimming. **2.** A jolting recoil: *a rifle with a heavy kick.* **3.** A complaint; a protest. **4.** *Slang* Power; force: *an engine with a lot of kick.* **5.** *Slang* **a.** A feeling of pleasurable stimulation: *got a kick out of the show.* **b. kicks** Fun: *did it just for kicks.* **6.** *Slang* Temporary, often obsessive interest: *I'm on a science fiction kick.* **7.** *Slang* A sudden striking surprise; a twist. **8.** *Sports* **a.** The act or an instance of kicking a ball. **b.** A kicked ball. **c.** The distance spanned by a kicked ball. —*phrasal verbs:* **kick about** *Informal* To move from place to place. **kick around** *Informal* **1.** To treat badly; abuse. **2.** To move from place to place: *kicked around in town.* **3.** To give consideration or thought to (an idea). **kick back 1.** To recoil unexpectedly and violently. **2.** *Informal* To take it easy; relax: *kicked back at home and watched TV.* **3.** *Slang* To return (stolen items). **4.** *Slang* To pay a kickback. **kick in 1.** *Informal* To contribute (one's share): *kicked in ten dollars for the office party.* **2.** *Slang* To die. **kick off 1.** *Sports* To begin or resume play with a kickoff. **2.** *Informal* To begin; start. **3.** *Slang* To die. **kick out** *Slang* To throw out; dismiss. **kick over** To begin to fire: *The engine kicked over.* **kick up** *Informal* **1.** To increase in amount or force; intensify. **2.** To stir up (trouble): *kicked up a row.* **3.** To show signs of disorder: *His ulcer has kicked up again.* —**idioms:** **kick the bucket** *Slang* To die. **kick the habit** *Slang* To free oneself of an addiction, as to cigarettes. **kick up (one's) heels** *Informal* To cast off one's inhibitions and have a good time. **kick upstairs** *Slang* To promote to a higher yet less desirable position. [ME *kiken*, perh. of Scand. orig.]

Kick·a·poo (kĭk′ə-pōō′) *n., pl.* **Kickapoo** or **-poos** **1.** A member of a Native American people formerly inhabiting southern Wisconsin and northern Illinois, with small present-day populations in Kansas, Oklahoma, and northern Mexico. **2.** The Algonquian language of the Kickapoo.

kick·back (kĭk′băk′) *n.* **1.** A sharp reaction; a repercussion. **2.** *Slang* A return of a percentage of a sum of money already received, usu. as a result of coercion or a secret agreement.

kick·ball (kĭk′bôl′) *n.* A children's game having rules similar to baseball but played with a large ball that is rolled and kicked instead of being pitched and batted.

kick·board (kĭk′bôrd′, -bōrd′) *n.* A buoyant board used to keep the upper body of a swimmer afloat while allowing free movement of the legs.

ă	pat	oi	boy
ā	pay	ou	out
âr	care	ŏŏ	took
ä	father	ōō	boot
ĕ	pet	ŭ	cut
ē	be	ûr	urge
ĭ	pit	th	thin
ī	pie	*th*	this
îr	pier	hw	which
ŏ	pot	zh	vision
ō	toe	ə	about,
ô	paw		item

Stress marks:
′ (primary),
′ (secondary), as in
lexicon (lĕk′sĭ-kŏn′)

kick·box·ing (kĭk′bŏk′sĭng) *n.* A martial art and sport of attack and defense, in which competitors wear boxing gloves and throw punches as in boxing and kick with their bare feet as in karate. —**kick′box·er** *n.*

kick·er (kĭk′ər) *n.* **1.** One that kicks. **2.** *Informal* **a.** A sudden surprising turn of events or ending; a twist. **b.** A tricky or concealed condition; a pitfall. **3.** A condition that imposes an automatic increase, as in a pension plan.

kick·off (kĭk′ôf′, -ŏf′) *n.* **1.** *Sports* A place kick in football or soccer with which play is begun. **2.** *Informal* A beginning.

kick plate *n.* A protective sheet of metal at the bottom of a door.

kick·shaw (kĭk′shô′) *n.* **1.** A fancy food; a delicacy. **2.** A trinket; a gewgaw. [By folk ety. < Fr. *quelque chose,* something : *quelque,* some + *chose,* thing.]

kick·stand (kĭk′stănd′) *n.* A swiveling metal bar for holding a two-wheeled vehicle upright when it is not being ridden.

kick-start (kĭk′stärt′) *tr.v.* **-start·ed, -start·ing, -starts 1.** To start by using a kick starter: *kick-started the motorcycle.* **2.** *Informal* To start or reinvigorate (an activity, system, or process).

kick starter *n.* A starter that is operated by kicking downward on a pedal, as on a motorcycle.

kick·y (kĭk′ē) *adj.* **-i·er, -i·est** *Slang* So unusual or unconventional in character or nature as to provide a thrill.

kid (kĭd) *n.* **1a.** A young goat. **b.** The young of a similar animal, such as an antelope. **2a.** The flesh of a young goat. **b.** Leather made from the skin of a young goat; kidskin. **c.** An article made from this leather. **3.** *Informal* **a.** A child. **b.** A young person. **4.** *Slang* Pal. Used as a term of familiar address, esp. for a young person: *Hi, kid! What's up?* ❖ *adj.* **1.** Made of kid. **2.** *Informal* Younger than oneself: *my kid brother.* ❖ *v.* **kid·ded, kid·ding, kids** —*tr.* **1.** To mock playfully; tease. **2.** To deceive in fun; fool. —*intr.* **1.** *Informal* To engage in teasing or good-humored fooling. **2.** To bear young. Used of a goat or an antelope. —*idiom:* **no kidding 1.** Used to express surprise or disbelief. **2.** Used to express scornful acknowledgment of the obvious. [ME *kide* < ON *kidh.*] —**kid′der** *n.* —**kid′ding·ly** *adv.*

Kid, Thomas See **Kyd.**

Kidd (kĭd), **William** Known as "Captain Kidd." 1645?–1701. British sea captain who turned to piracy after being hired to protect British ships in the Indian Ocean (1696).

Kid·der·min·ster[1] (kĭd′ər-mĭn′stər) A municipal borough of W-central England WSW of Birmingham. Pop. 91,600.

Kid·der·min·ster[2] (kĭd′ər-mĭn′stər) *n.* An ingrain carpet originally made in Kidderminster.

kid·die or **kid·dy** (kĭd′ē) *n., pl.* **-dies** *Slang* A small child.

kid·do (kĭd′ō) *n., pl.* **-dos** *Slang* **1a.** A child. **b.** A young person. **2.** Pal. Used as a term of familiar address.

Kid·dush (kĭd′əsh, kē-dōōsh′) *n.* *Judaism* The traditional prayer recited over wine on the eve of the Sabbath or a festival. [Heb. *qiddûš,* sanctification < *qiddēš,* to sanctify, derived stem of *qādaš,* to be holy.]

kid glove *n.* A glove made of fine soft leather, esp. kidskin. —*idiom:* **with kid gloves** Tactfully and cautiously.

kid·nap (kĭd′năp′) *tr.v.* **-napped, -nap·ping, -naps** or **-naped, -nap·ing, -naps** To seize and detain unlawfully and usu. for ransom. [Prob. KID + *nap,* to snatch (perh. var. of NAB or, of Scand. orig.).] —**kid′nap·pee′, kid′nap·ee′** (-nă-pē′) *n.* —**kid′nap′per, kid′nap′er** *n.*

kid·ney (kĭd′nē) *n., pl.* **-neys 1.** *Anatomy* Either one of a pair of organs in the dorsal region of the vertebrate abdominal cavity, functioning to maintain water and electrolyte balance, regulate acid-base concentration, and filter the blood of metabolic wastes. **2.** The kidney of certain animals, eaten as food. **3.** An excretory organ of certain invertebrates. **4.** Temperament; kind: *a person of the same kidney.* [ME *kidenei.*]

kidney bean *n.* **1.** An annual plant (*Phaseolus vulgaris*) cultivated for its edible pods and seeds. **2.** Its pod or seed.

kidney stone *n.* A small hard mass in the kidney that forms from deposits chiefly of phosphates and urates.

kid·skin (kĭd′skĭn′) *n.* Soft leather made from the skin of a young goat.

kid stuff *n.* *Slang* **1.** Something suitable only for children. **2.** Something very easy or uncomplicated.

Kiel (kēl) A city of N Germany chartered in 1242. Pop. 248,931.

kiel·ba·sa (kĭl-bä′sə, kēl-) *n.* A spicy smoked Polish sausage. [Pol. *kiełbasa* < East and West Slav. **kŭlbasa* < East Turkic *kül bassï,* grilled cutlet < Turkic *kül bastï* : *kül,* coals, ashes + *bastï,* pressed (meat) < *basmaq,* to press).]

Kiel Canal also **Nord-Ost–see Ka·nal** (nôrt-ôst′zä kä-näl′) An artificial waterway, 98.1 km (61 mi), of N Germany connecting the North Sea with the Baltic Sea; built 1887–95.

Kiel·ce (kyĕl′tsĕ) A city of SE-central Poland S of Warsaw; founded 1173. Pop. 214,445.

Kier·ke·gaard (kîr′kĭ-gärd′, -gôr′), **Søren Aaby** 1813–55. Danish religious philosopher and precursor of modern existentialism whose works include *Either/Or* (1843).

kie·sel·guhr (kē′zəl-gŏŏr′) *n.* See **diatomite.** [Ger. *Kieselgur* : *Kiesel,* pebble (< MHGer. *kisel* < OHGer. *chisil*) + *Gur, Guhr,* ferment, earthy deposit from water (< *gären,* to ferment, blend of MHGer. *jĕsan* < OHGer., and MHGer. **jern,* to cause to ferment < OHGer. *jerian*).]

kie·ser·ite (kē′zə-rīt′) *n.* A whitish to yellowish hydrous magnesium sulfate mineral, MgSO₄·H₂O, found in salt residues. [After Dietrich Georg *Kieser* (1779–1862), German physician.]

Ki·ev (kē′ĕf, -ĕv) or **Ky·yiv** (-ēv) The cap. of Ukraine, in the N-central part on the Dnieper R.; center of the first Russian state. Pop. 2,642,700.

kif (kĭf, kēf) also **kef** (kĕf, kēf, kāf) *n.* **1.** Smoking material, such as Indian hemp, used esp. in the Maghreb. **2.** The euphoria caused by smoking kif. [Colloquial Ar. *kēf* < Ar. *kayf, kef,* condition, pleasure, opiate.]

Ki·ga·li (kĭ-gä′lē, kē-) The cap. of Rwanda, in the central part E of Lake Kivu. Pop. 156,700.

kike (kīk) *n. Offensive Slang* Used as a disparaging term for a Jew. [?]

Ki·klá·dhes (kē-klä′thĕs) See **Cyclades.**

Ki·kon·go (kē-kŏng′gŏ) *n.* See **Kongo** 2.

Ki·ku·yu (kĭ-kōō′yōō) also **Gi·ku·yu** (gĭ-kōō′yōō) *n., pl.* **Ki·kuyu** or **-yus** also **Gikuyu** or **-yus 1.** A member of a people of central and southern Kenya. **2.** Their Bantu language.

Ki·lau·e·a (kē′lou-ā′ə, kĭl′ə-wā′ə) An active volcanic crater on the SE slope of Mauna Loa in S-central Hawaii I.

kil·der·kin (kĭl′dər-kĭn) *n.* **1.** A cask. **2.** An obsolete English measure of capacity equal to about 18 gallons (68 liters). [ME, alteration of MFlem. *kinderkin* (var. of MDu. *kindekijn*) : *quintel, quintlein,* quintal (< Med.Lat. *quintāle;* see QUINTAL) + *-kijn,* diminutive suff.]

ki·lim (kē-lēm′, kĭl′ĭm) *n.* A tapestry-woven Turkish rug or other textile with geometric designs in rich brilliant colors. [Turk. < Pers. *gilīm,* perh. of Mongolian orig.]

Kil·i·man·ja·ro (kĭl′ə-mən-jär′ō), **Mount** A mountain of NE Tanzania near the Kenya border rising in two snow-capped peaks to 5,898.7 m (19,340 ft).

kill[1] (kĭl) *v.* **killed, kill·ing, kills** —*tr.* **1a.** To put to death. **b.** To deprive of life: *The Black Death killed millions.* **2.** To put an end to; extinguish: *The rain killed our plans for a picnic.* **3a.** To destroy a vitally essential quality in: *Too much garlic killed the taste of the meat.* **b.** To cause to cease operating; turn off: *killed the motor.* **c.** To tire out completely; exhaust. **4.** To pass (time) in aimless activity. **5.** To consume entirely; finish off: *kill a bottle of brandy.* **6.** *Sports* To prevent a hockey team on a power play from scoring during (a penalty). **7.** To cause extreme pain or discomfort to: *My shoes are killing me.* **8.** To mark for deletion; rule out: *killed the story.* **9.** To thwart passage of; veto. **10.** *Informal* To overwhelm with hilarity, pleasure, or admiration. **11.** *Sports* **a.** To hit (a ball) with great force. **b.** To hit (a ball) with such force as to make a return impossible, esp. in a racquet game. —*intr.* **1.** To cause death or extinction; be fatal. **2.** To commit murder. **3.** *Informal* To make such a strong impression as to overcome: *dress to kill.* ❖ *n.* **1.** The act of killing. **2a.** An animal killed, esp. in hunting. **b.** A person killed or to be killed. **c.** An enemy aircraft, vessel, or missile that has been attacked and destroyed. **3.** *Sports* A kill shot. ❖ *n.* —*phrasal verb:* **kill off** To destroy in such large numbers as to render extinct. —*idiom:* **in at (or on) the kill** Present at the moment of triumph. [ME *killen,* perh. < OE **cyllan.* See gʷelə- in App.]

kill[2] (kĭl) *n. New York State* See **creek** 1. See Regional Notes at **stoop**[2], **run.** [Du. *kil* < MDu. *kille.*]

Kil·lar·ney (kĭ-lär′nē), **Lakes of** Three small lakes of SW Ireland near the market town of Killarney (pop. 7,693).

kill·deer (kĭl′dîr′) *n., pl.* **killdeer** or **-deers** A New World plover (*Charadrius vociferus*) having a distinctive noisy cry and two black bands across its breast. [Prob. imit. of its call.]

killed (kĭld) *adj.* **1.** Put to death. Often used in combination: *fresh-killed meat.* **2.** Of or containing microorganisms or infectious agents that have been inactivated so as to be incapable of causing infection: *a killed virus; killed vaccines.*

kill·er (kĭl′ər) *n.* **1.** One that kills. **2.** *Slang* Something extremely difficult to deal with or withstand. ❖ *adj.* **1.** Causing death or destruction. **2.** Very impressive or effective; formidable: *made killer profits; a killer app.*

killer bee *n.* See **Africanized bee.**

killer cell *n.* Any of various large differentiated T cells that lyse target cells bearing a specific antigen and function in the body's defense against cancer cells.

killer T cell *n.* See **killer cell.**

killer whale *n.* A black and white predatory dolphin (*Orcinus orca*) that mostly feeds on fish and squid.

kil·lick also **kil·lock** (kĭl′ĭk) *n.* A small anchor, esp. one made of a stone in a wooden frame. [?]

kil·lie (kĭl′ē) *n.* A killifish.

kil·li·fish (kĭl′ĭ-fĭsh′) *n., pl.* **killifish** or **-fish·es** Any of numerous small fishes of the family Cyprinodontidae, including the guppy and mosquito fish, inhabiting chiefly fresh and brackish waters in warm regions. [Perh. KILL² + FISH.]

kill·ing (kĭl′ĭng) *n.* **1.** Murder; homicide. **2.** A kill; a quarry. **3.** A sudden large profit: *made a killing on the stock market.* ❖ *adj.* **1.** Intended or apt to kill; fatal. **2.** Thoroughly exhausting: *a killing pace.* **3.** *Informal* Hilarious. —**kill′ing·ly** *adv.*

kill·joy (kĭl′joi′) *n.* One who spoils the fun of others.

kill shot *n.* A shot in various games, esp. racquet games, so hit or placed that it cannot be returned.

Mount Kilimanjaro

killer whale
Orcinus orca

Kil·mer (kĭl′mər), **(Alfred) Joyce** 1886–1918. Amer. poet whose best-known work is "Trees" (1913).

kiln (kĭln, kĭl) *n.* Any of various ovens for hardening, burning, or drying substances such as grain, meal, or clay, esp. a brick-lined oven used to bake or fire ceramics. ❖ *tr.v.* **kilned, kiln·ing, kilns** To process in one of these ovens. [ME *kilne* < OE *cyln* < Lat. *culīna,* kitchen, stove. See **pek**ʷ- in App.]

ki·lo (kē′lō) *n., pl.* **-los 1.** A kilogram. **2.** A kilometer.

kilo– *pref.* **1.** One thousand (10³): *kilowatt.* **2.** 1,024 (2¹⁰): *kilobyte.* [Fr. < Gk. *khīlioi,* thousand. See **gheslo-** in App.]

kil·o·bar (kĭl′ə-bär′) *n.* A unit of pressure equal to 1,000 bars.

kil·o·bit (kĭl′ə-bĭt′) *n. Computer Science* **1.** One thousand bits. **2.** 1,024 (2¹⁰) bits. See Usage Note at **megabyte.**

kil·o·byte (kĭl′ə-bīt′) *n.* **1.** A unit of computer memory or data storage capacity equal to 1,024 (2¹⁰) bytes. **2.** One thousand bytes. See Usage Note at **megabyte.**

kil·o·cal·o·rie (kĭl′ə-kăl′ə-rē) *n.* See **calorie** 3a.

kil·o·cu·rie (kĭl′ə-kyoor-ē′, -kyoo′rē) *n.* One thousand curies.

kil·o·cy·cle (kĭl′ə-sī′kəl) *n.* Kilohertz.

kil·o·gram (kĭl′ə-grăm′) *n.* **1.** The base unit of mass in the International System, equal to 1,000 grams (2.2046 pounds). See table at **measurement.** **2.** Kilogram force.

kilogram calorie *n.* See **calorie** 3a.

kilogram force *n.* A force equal to a kilogram weight or a one-kilogram mass times the acceleration of gravity.

kil·o·gram-me·ter (kĭl′ə-grăm-mē′tər) *n.* A unit of work in a gravitational system, equal to the work performed by a one-kilogram force acting through a distance of one meter.

kil·o·hertz (kĭl′ə-hûrts′) *n.* A unit of frequency equal to 1,000 hertz.

kil·o·li·ter (kĭl′ə-lē′tər) *n.* A metric unit of volume equal to 1,000 liters (1,056 liquid quarts).

kil·o·me·ter (kĭ-lŏm′ĭ-tər, kĭl′ə-mē′tər) *n.* A metric unit of length equal to 1,000 meters (0.62 mile). See table at **measurement.** —**kil′o·met′ric** (kĭl′ə-mĕt′rĭk) *adj.*

kil·o·ton (kĭl′ə-tŭn′) *n.* **1.** A unit of weight or capacity equal to 1,000 metric tons. **2.** An explosive force equivalent to that of 1,000 metric tons of TNT.

kil·o·watt (kĭl′ə-wŏt′) *n.* A unit of power equal to 1,000 watts.

kil·o·watt-hour (kĭl′ə-wŏt-our′) *n.* A unit of electric energy equal to the work done by one kilowatt acting for one hour.

kilt (kĭlt) *n.* **1.** A knee-length skirt with deep pleats, usu. of a tartan wool, worn as part of the dress for men in the Scottish Highlands. **2.** A similar skirt worn by women, girls, and boys. ❖ *tr.v.* **kilt·ed, kilt·ing, kilts** To tuck up (something) around the body. [< *kilt,* to tuck up < ME *kilten,* of Scand. orig.]

kil·ter (kĭl′tər) *n.* Good condition; proper form. [?]

kil·tie (kĭl′tē) *n.* **1.** One who wears a kilt. **2.** A shoe having a fringed tongue that flaps over the instep. **3.** The tongue of such a shoe.

kim·ber·lite (kĭm′bər-līt′) *n.* A rock formation in South Africa containing peridotite, in which diamonds are formed. [After *Kimberley,* a city in central South Africa.] —**kim′ber·lit′ic** (-lĭt′ĭk) *adj.*

Kim·bun·du (kĭm-bōōn′dōō) *n.* See **Mbundu** 4.

kim·chi also **kim·chee** (kĭm′chē) *n., pl.* **-chis** also **-chees** A Korean dish made of seasoned vegetables, such as cabbage or radishes, that are stored in sealed containers to undergo lactic acid fermentation. [Korean *kimch'i* < O Korean *timchoi* : M Chin. *trhim,* to soak, steep + M Chin. *tshoj, tshaj,* vegetable, greens.]

Kim Dae Jung (kĭm′ dī′ jŏŏng′) b. 1925. Korean politician who has served as president of South Korea since 1997. He won the 2000 Nobel Peace Prize.

ki·mo·no (kə-mō′nə, -nō) *n., pl.* **-nos 1.** A long, wide-sleeved Japanese robe worn with an obi and often elaborately decorated. **2.** A loose, light robe worn chiefly by women. [J. : *kiru,* to wear + *mono,* object.]

kin (kĭn) *n.* **1.** (*used with a pl. verb*) One's relatives; family; kinfolk. **2.** A kinsman or kinswoman. ❖ *adj.* Related; akin. [ME < OE *cyn.* See **gen∂-** in App.]

–kin or **–kins** *suff.* Little one: *devilkin.* [ME, prob. < MDu. *-kijn, -kin.*]

ki·na (kē′nə) *n., pl.* **kina** See table at **currency.** [Indigenous word in Papua New Guinea.]

ki·nase (kī′nās′, -nāz′, kĭn′ās′, -āz′) *n.* Any of various enzymes that catalyze the transfer of a phosphate group from a donor, such as ADP, to an acceptor. [KIN(ETIC) + –ASE.]

kind¹ (kīnd) *adj.* **kind·er, kind·est 1.** Of a friendly, generous, or warm-hearted nature. **2.** Sympathetic or understanding; charitable: *a kind word.* **3.** Humane; considerate: *kind to animals.* **4.** Forbearing; tolerant. **5.** Generous; liberal. **6.** Agreeable; beneficial: *a dry climate kind to asthmatics.* [ME, natural, kind < OE *gecynde,* natural. See **gen∂-** in App.]

kind² (kīnd) *n.* **1.** A group of individuals linked by traits held in common. **2.** A particular variety; a sort. **3.** Fundamental underlying character as a determinant of the class to which a thing belongs; nature or essence. **4.** A doubtful or undesirable member of a given category: *built a kind of shelter.* **5.** *Archaic* Manner. —**idi·oms: all kinds of** *Informal* Plenty of; ample. **in kind 1.** With produce or commodities rather than with money. **2.** In the same manner or with an equivalent. **kind of** *Informal* Rather; some-

what. **of a kind** Of the same kind. [ME < OE *gecynd,* race, offspring, kind. See **gen∂-** in App.]

USAGE NOTE Even though writers from Pope to Churchill have used the singular form *kind* in plural constructions such as *These kind of errors,* this mixed singular and plural usage has long been condemned by usage commentators for being illogical. It is therefore prudent to use constructions that are either all singular or all plural: *This kind of film has never appealed to teenagers. These kinds of films have never been well received.*

kin·der·gar·ten (kĭn′dər-gär′tn, -dn) *n.* A program or class for four-year-old to six-year-old children that serves as an introduction to school. [Ger. : *Kinder,* genitive pl. of *Kind,* child (< MHGer. *kint* < OHGer. *kind*; see **gen∂-** in App.) + *Garten,* garden (< MHGer. *garte* < OHGer. *garto*; see **gher-** in App.).]

kin·der·gart·ner also **kin·der·gar·ten·er** (kĭn′dər-gärt′nər, -gärd′-) *n.* **1.** A child who attends kindergarten. **2.** A teacher in a kindergarten. [Ger. *Kindergärtner* < *Kindergarten,* kindergarten. See KINDERGARTEN.]

kind·heart·ed (kīnd′här′tĭd) *adj.* Having or proceeding from a kind heart. —**kind′heart′ed·ly** *adv.* —**kind′heart′ed·ness** *n.*

kin·dle¹ (kĭn′dl) *v.* **-dled, -dling, -dles** —*tr.* **1a.** To build or fuel (a fire). **b.** To set fire to; ignite. **2.** To cause to glow; light up: *The sunset kindled the skies.* **3.** To arouse (an emotion, for example): "*No spark had yet kindled in him an intellectual passion*" (George Eliot). —*intr.* **1.** To catch fire; burst into flame. **2.** To become bright; glow. **3.** To become inflamed. **4.** To be stirred up; rise. [ME *kindelen* (influenced by *kindelen,* to give birth to, cause), prob. < ON *kynda.*] —**kin′dler** *n.*

kin·dle² (kĭn′dl) *n.* A brood or litter, esp. of kittens. ❖ *intr.v.* **-dled, -dling, -dles** To give birth to young. Used esp. of rabbits. [ME *kindelen,* to give birth to < *kindel,* offspring < OE *gecynd.* See KIND².]

kind·less (kīnd′lĭs) *adj.* **1.** Exhibiting or feeling no kindness or compassion; heartless. **2.** *Obsolete* Inhuman. —**kind′less·ly** *adv.*

kind·li·ness (kīnd′lē-nĭs) *n.* **1.** The quality or state of being kindly. **2.** A kindly deed.

kin·dling (kĭnd′lĭng) *n.* Easily ignited material, such as dry sticks of wood, used to start a fire.

kindling point *n.* See **ignition point.**

kind·ly (kīnd′lē) *adj.* **-li·er, -li·est 1.** Of a sympathetic, helpful, or benevolent nature: *a kindly interest; a gentle, kindly soul.* **2.** Agreeable; pleasant: *a kindly breeze.* **3a.** *Archaic* Within the law; lawful. **b.** *Obsolete* Natural to its kind. ❖ *adv.* **1.** Out of kindness: *She kindly overlooked their mistake.* **2.** In a kind manner: *He spoke kindly to us.* **3.** Pleasantly; agreeably: *The sun shone kindly.* **4.** In an accommodating manner: *Would you kindly sign?* **5.** *Obsolete* In a way or course that is natural; fittingly.

kind·ness (kīnd′nĭs) *n.* **1.** The quality or state of being kind. **2.** An instance of kind behavior.

kin·dred (kĭn′drĭd) *n.* **1.** A group of related persons, as a clan or tribe. **2.** (*used with a pl. verb*) One's relatives; kinfolk. ❖ *adj.* **1.** Of the same ancestry or family. **2.** Having a similar or related origin, nature, or character. [ME *kinrede, kindrede* < Late OE *cynrēde* : *cyn,* kin; see **gen∂-** in App. + *-rēde,* condition (< OE *rǣden, -rǣden*; see **ar-** in App.).] —**kin′dred·ness** *n.*

kine (kīn) *n. Archaic* A plural of **cow¹.** [ME *kyn* < OE *cȳna,* genitive pl. of *cū,* cow. See COW¹.]

kin·e·mat·ics (kĭn′ə-măt′ĭks) *n.* (*used with a sing. verb*) The branch of mechanics that studies the motion of a body or a system without consideration given to mass or force. [< Gk. *kīnēma, kīnēmat-,* motion < *kīnein,* to move. See **kei-²** in App.] —**kin′e·mat′ic, kin′e·mat′i·cal** *adj.*

kin·e·scope (kĭn′ĭ-skōp′, kī′nĭ-) *n.* **1.** See **picture tube.** **2.** A film of a transmitted television program. ❖ *tr.v.* **-scoped, -scop·ing, -scopes** To make a film of (a transmitted television program). [KIN(ETIC) + -SCOPE. Orig. a trademark.]

ki·ne·sics (kə-nē′sĭks, -zĭks, kī-) *n.* (*used with a sing. verb*) The study of nonlinguistic bodily movements, such as gestures and facial expressions, as a systematic mode of communication. [< Gk. *kīnēsis,* movement. See KINESIS.] —**ki·ne′sic** (-sĭk, -zĭk) *adj.*

ki·ne·si·ol·o·gy (kə-nē′sē-ŏl′ə-jē, -zē-) *n.* The study of the anatomy, physiology, and mechanics of body movement, esp. in humans. [Gk. *kīnēsis,* movement; see KINESIS + -LOGY.] —**ki·ne′si·ol′o·gist** *n.*

ki·ne·sis (kə-nē′sĭs, kī-) *n., pl.* **-ses** (-sēz) Movement or activity of an organism in response to a stimulus such as light. [Gk. *kīnēsis,* movement < *kīnein,* to move. See **kei-²** in App.]

–kinesis *suff.* Motion: *photokinesis.* [< Gk. *kīnēsis,* movement. See KINESIS.]

kin·es·the·sia (kĭn′ĭs-thē′zhə, kī′nĭs-) *n.* The sense that detects bodily position, weight, or movement of the muscles, tendons,

kilt

kimono

ă	pat	oi	boy
ā	pay	ou	out
âr	care	ŏŏ	took
ä	father	ōō	boot
ĕ	pet	ŭ	cut
ē	be	ûr	urge
ĭ	pit	th	thin
ī	pie	th	this
îr	pier	hw	which
ŏ	pot	zh	vision
ō	toe	ə	about,
ô	paw		item

Stress marks:
′ (primary);
′ (secondary), as in
lexicon (lĕk′sĭ-kŏn′)

and joints. [Gk. *kīnein*, to move; see **kei-²** in App. + ESTHESIA.] —kin′es·thet′ic (-thĕt′ĭk) *adj.*

ki·net·ic (kə-nĕt′ĭk, kī-) *adj.* **1.** Of, relating to, or produced by motion. **2.** Relating to or exhibiting kinesis. [Gk. *kīnētikos* < *kīnētos*, moving < *kīnein*, to move. See **kei-²** in App.] —ki·net′i·cal·ly *adv.*

kinetic art *n.* An art form, such as a sculpture, made up of parts to be set in motion by an internal mechanism or an external stimulus, such as light or air. —**kinetic artist** *n.* —ki·net′i·cism (-ĭ-sĭz′əm) *n.* —ki·net′i·cist *n.*

kinetic energy *n.* The energy possessed by a body because of its motion, equal to one half the mass of the body times the square of its speed.

ki·net·ics (kə-nĕt′ĭks, kī-) *n.* (*used with a sing. verb*) **1.** See **dynamics** 1a. **2.** The branch of chemistry that is concerned with the rates of chemical reactions.

kinetic theory *n.* A statistical theory of the thermodynamic behavior of matter, esp. gases, that explains properties, such as temperature and pressure, in terms of the kinetic energies of the rapidly moving atoms and molecules composing a system.

ki·ne·tin (kī′nə-tĭn) *n.* A plant hormone that promotes cell division.

kineto– *pref.* Movement: kinetoplast. [Gk. *kīnēto–* < *kīnētos*, moving. See KINETIC.]

ki·net·o·chore (kə-nĕt′ə-kôr′, -kōr′, -nē′tə-, kī-) *n.* Either of two submicroscopic attachment points for chromosomal microtubules, present on each centromere during cell division. [KINETO– + Gk. *khōros*, place; see –CHORE.]

ki·net·o·plast (kə-nĕt′ə-plăst′, -nē′tə-, kī-) *n.* An independently replicating structure lying near the base of the flagellum in certain protozoans.

ki·net·o·some (kə-nĕt′ə-sōm′, -nē′tə-, kī-) *n.* See **basal body**.

kin·folk (kĭn′fōk′) also **kins·folk** (kĭnz′-) or **kin·folks** (kĭn′fōks′) *pl.n.* Relatives; kindred.

king (kĭng) *n.* **1.** A male sovereign. **2.** One that is supreme or preeminent in a particular group, category, or sphere. **3. King a.** The perfect, omniscient, omnipotent being; God. **b.** *Christianity* Jesus. **4.** *Games* **a.** A playing card bearing the figure of a king, ranking above a queen. **b.** The principal chess piece, which can move one square in any direction and must be protected against checkmate. **c.** A piece in checkers that has been moved to the last row on the opponent's side of the board and been crowned. **5. Kings** (*used with a sing. verb*) See table at **Bible.** ❖ *adj.* Principal or chief, as in size or importance. ❖ *tr.v.* **kinged, king·ing, kings** *Games* To make (a piece in checkers) into a king; crown. [ME < OE *cyning*. See **genə–** in App.]

King, Billie Jean Moffitt b. 1943. Amer. tennis player who won 20 titles at Wimbledon and 4 US Open championships (1967, 1971, 1972, and 1974).

King, Coretta Scott b. 1927. Amer. civil rights leader noted for her work for the Southern Christian Leadership Conference and the Martin Luther King, Jr., Memorial Foundation.

King, Martin Luther, Jr. 1929–68. Amer. cleric who led the civil rights movement in the 1950s and 1960s. He won the 1964 Nobel Peace Prize, four years before he was assassinated in Memphis TN.

King, William Lyon Mackenzie 1874–1950. Canadian prime minister (1921–26, 1926–30, and 1935–48).

king·bird (kĭng′bûrd′) *n.* Any of various American flycatchers of the genus *Tyrannus,* esp. *T. tyrannus.*

king·bolt (kĭng′bōlt′) *n.* A vertical bolt that joins the body of a vehicle to its front axle and usu. acts as a pivot.

King Charles spaniel *n.* Any of a variety of English toy spaniel with a curly black-and-tan coat and long ears. [After King CHARLES II.]

king cobra *n.* A large venomous snake (*Ophiophagus hannah*) of southeast Asia and the Philippines.

king crab *n.* **1.** A large edible crab (*Paralithodes camtschatica*) inhabiting the coastal waters of Alaska, Japan, and Siberia. **2.** See **horseshoe crab**.

king·craft (kĭng′krăft′) *n.* The artful exercise of power by a king.

king·cup (kĭng′kŭp′) *n. Chiefly British* **1.** Any of several plants with yellow flowers. **2.** The marsh marigold.

king·dom (kĭng′dəm) *n.* **1.** A political or territorial unit ruled by a sovereign. **2a.** The eternal spiritual sovereignty of God or Christ. **b.** The realm of this sovereignty. **3.** A realm or sphere in which one thing is dominant. **4.** One of the three main divisions (animal, vegetable, and mineral) into which natural organisms and objects are classified. **5.** In the Linnaean taxonomic system, the highest classification into which organisms are grouped, based on fundamental similarities and common ancestry. See table at **taxonomy**. [ME < OE *cyningdōm* : *cyning*, king; see KING + *-dōm*, -dom.]

kingdom come *n. Informal* **1.** The next world. **2.** The end of time. [< *thy kingdom come* in the Lord's Prayer.]

king·fish (kĭng′fĭsh′) *n., pl.* **kingfish** or **-fish·es 1a.** Any of several food and game fishes of the drum family, esp. of the genus *Menticirrhus,* indigenous to warm Atlantic waters. **b.** Any of several similar or related fishes, indigenous to the Pacific Ocean. **2.** *Informal* A person in a position of uncontested authority or influence.

Martin Luther King, Jr.
speaking to a crowd in
Jackson, Mississippi, 1966

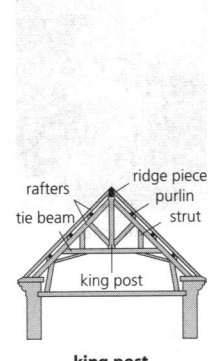

rafters ridge piece purlin
tie beam strut
king post

king post
king post roof

king·fish·er (kĭng′fĭsh′ər) *n.* Any of various birds of the family Alcedinidae, characteristically having a crested head, a long stout beak, a short tail, and brilliant coloration.

King James Bible *n.* An English translation of the Bible from Hebrew and Greek published in 1611 under the auspices of James I.

king·let (kĭng′lĭt) *n.* **1.** Any of several small grayish North American birds of the genus *Regulus,* having a yellowish or reddish patch on the crown of the head. **2.** A king ruling a kingdom considered small or unimportant.

king·ly (kĭng′lē) *adj.* **-li·er, -li·est 1.** Having the status or rank of king. **2.** Of, like, or befitting a king; majestic and regal. ❖ *adv.* In a royal way; royally. —**king′li·ness** *n.*

king mackerel *n.* A food and game fish (*Scomberomorus cavalla*) of warm Atlantic waters.

king·mak·er (kĭng′mā′kər) *n.* One who has the political power to influence the selection of a candidate for high public office. —**king′mak′ing** *adj. & n.*

king-of-arms (kĭng′əv-ärmz′) *n., pl.* **kings-of-arms** (kĭngz′-) A high-ranking heraldic officer in Great Britain.

king penguin *n.* A large penguin (*Aptenodytes patagonicus*) of Antarctic regions, having an orange oval on the side of the face and a yellow patch at the base of the throat.

king·pin (kĭng′pĭn′) *n.* **1.** See **headpin. 2.** One that is the most important in an enterprise or a system. **3.** See **kingbolt**.

king post *n. Architecture* A supporting post extending vertically from a crossbeam to the apex of a triangular truss.

king salmon *n.* See **Chinook salmon**.

King's Bench (kĭngz) *n.* A division of the British superior court system that hears criminal and civil cases. Used when the sovereign is a man.

King's Counsel *n.* A barrister appointed as counsel to the British crown. Used when the sovereign is a man.

King's English *n.* English speech or usage that is considered standard or accepted; Received Standard English.

king·ship (kĭng′shĭp′) *n.* **1.** The position, power, or province of a king. **2.** The domain ruled by a king; a kingdom. **3.** The period or tenure of a king; a reign. **4.** Used with *his* as a title for a king. **5.** A monarchy.

king-size (kĭng′sīz′) or **king-sized** (-sīzd′) *adj.* **1.** Larger than the usual or standard size: *a king-size desk.* **2a.** Measuring about 76 inches by 80 inches (1.9 meters by 2.0 meters). Used of a bed. **b.** Being of a size that will fit such a bed.

king snake *n.* Any of various nonvenomous constricting New World snakes of the genus *Lampropeltis,* having a black or brown body with white, yellow, or reddish markings.

Kings River A river, c. 201 km (125 mi), of central CA rising in Kings Canyon in the Sierra Nevada.

King·ston (kĭng′stən) The cap. of Jamaica, in the SE part on the Caribbean Sea; founded c. 1692. Pop. 586,930.

Kingston, Maxine Hong b. 1940. Amer. writer whose works include *The Woman Warrior* (1976).

King·ston-up·on-Hull (kĭng′stən-ə-pŏn-hŭl′, -pôn-) See **Hull**.

Kings·town (kĭngz′toun′) The cap. of St. Vincent and the Grenadines, on the SW coast of St. Vincent I. Pop. 18,378.

king·wood (kĭng′wŏod′) *n.* **1.** A South American tree (*Dalbergia cearensis*) with hard fine-textured purplish-brown wood used in cabinetmaking. **2.** The wood of this tree.

ki·nin (kī′nĭn) *n.* Any of various structurally related polypeptides, such as bradykinin, that act locally to induce vasodilation and contraction of smooth muscle. [Short for BRADYKININ.]

kink (kĭngk) *n.* **1.** A tight curl, twist, or bend in a length of thin material, as one caused by the tensing of a looped section of wire. **2.** A painful muscle spasm, as in the neck; a crick. **3.** A difficulty or flaw that is likely to impede operation, as in a plan. **4.** A mental peculiarity; a quirk. **5.** An unusual or eccentric idea. ❖ *intr. & tr.v.* **kinked, kink·ing, kinks** To form or cause to form a kink or kinks. [Du., twist in a rope.]

kink·a·jou (kĭng′kə-jōō′) *n.* An arboreal mammal (*Potos flavus*) of Central and South America having brownish fur and a long prehensile tail. [Fr. *quincajou,* wolverine, prob. blend of Ojibwa *gwiingwa'aage* and Montagnais *kuàkuàtsheu.*]

kink·y (kĭng′kē) *adj.* **-i·er, -i·est 1.** Tightly twisted or curled: *kinky hair.* **2.** *Slang* Showing or appealing to bizarre or deviant tastes, esp. of a sexual or erotic nature. —**kink′i·ly** *adv.* —**kink′i·ness** *n.*

kin·ni·kin·nick also **kin·ni·kin·nic** (kĭn′ĭ-kĭ-nĭk′) *n.* **1.** A preparation made from dried leaves, bark, and sometimes tobacco and smoked esp. by certain Native American peoples. **2.** See **bearberry**. [Unami *kələkkəníikkan,* item for mixing in, kinnikinnick.]

ki·no (kē′nō) *n., pl.* **-nos** A reddish resin obtained from several Old World trees of the genera *Eucalyptus, Pterocarpus,* and *Butea* and from tropical American trees of the genera *Coccoloba* and *Dipteryx.* [NLat., of West African orig.; akin to Mandingo keno.]

–kins *suff.* Variant of **–kin**.

Kin·sey (kĭn′zē), **Alfred Charles** 1894–1956. Amer. biologist whose works include *Sexual Behavior in the Human Male* (1948) and *Sexual Behavior in the Human Female* (1953).

Kinsey scale *n.* A classification system for gauging sexual orientation, ranging from 0 (exclusively heterosexual) to 6 (exclusively homosexual). [After Alfred Charles Kinsey.]

kins·folk (kĭnz′fōk′) *pl.n.* Variant of **kinfolk.**

Kin·sha·sa (kĭn-shä′sə) Formerly (before 1966) **Le·o·pold·ville** (lē′ə-pōld-vĭl′, lā′-) The cap. of Congo (formerly Zaire), in the W part on the Congo R.; founded 1881. Pop. 2,664,309.

kin·ship (kĭn′shĭp′) *n.* **1.** Connection by blood, marriage, or adoption. **2.** Relationship by nature or character; affinity.

kins·man (kĭnz′mən) *n.* **1.** A male relative. **2.** A man sharing the same racial, cultural, or national background as another.

kins·wom·an (kĭnz′wŏŏm′ən) *n.* **1.** A female relative. **2.** A woman sharing the same racial, cultural, or national background as another.

Kin·yar·wan·da (kĭn′yär-wän′də) *n.* A Bantu language of Rwanda, closely related to Kirundi and an official language of Rwanda.

Ki·o·ga or **Ky·o·ga** (kē-ō′gə), **Lake** An irregularly shaped lake of central Uganda; noted for its papyrus swamps.

ki·osk (kē′ŏsk, kē-ŏsk′) *n.* **1.** A small open gazebo or pavilion. **2.** A small structure, often open on one or more sides, used as a newsstand or booth. **3.** A cylindrical structure on which advertisements are posted. [Fr. *kiosque* < Turk. *köşk* < MPers. *gōshak,* corner < Avestan *gaoshaka-,* dim. of *gaosha-,* ear.]

WORD HISTORY The lowly kiosk where one buys a newspaper or on which one posts advertisements is like a child in a fairy tale who though raised by humble parents is really the descendant of kings. The word *kiosk* was originally taken into English from Turkish, in which its source *köşk* meant "pavilion." The open structures referred to by the Turkish word were used as pavilions and summerhouses in Turkey and Persia. The first recorded use of *kiosk* in English (1625) has reference to these Middle Eastern structures. In France and Belgium, where the Turkish word had also been borrowed, their word *kiosque* was applied to something lower on the scale, structures resembling these pavilions but used as places to sell newspapers or as bandstands. England borrowed this lowly structure from France and reborrowed the word, first recorded in 1865 with reference to a place to buy newspapers.

Ki·o·wa (kī′ə-wô′, -wä′, -wä′) *n.,* pl. **Kiowa** or **-was 1** A member of a Native American people formerly inhabiting the southern Great Plains, with a present-day population in southwest Oklahoma. **2.** The Tanoan language of the Kiowa.

Kiowa Apache *n., pl.* **Kiowa Apache** or **Kiowa Apaches 1.** A member of a Native American people of the southern Great Plains who formed part of the Kiowa tribe although speaking an unrelated Athabaskan language. **2.** The Athabaskan language of the Kiowa Apache.

kip[1] (kĭp) *n., pl.* **kip** See table at **currency.** [Thai.]

kip[2] (kĭp) *n.* **1.** The untanned hide of a small or young animal, such as a calf. **2.** A set or bundle of such hides. [ME, bundle of animal hides, perh. < MDu. or MLGer.]

kip[3] (kĭp) *Chiefly British Slang n.* **1.** A rooming house. **2.** A place to sleep; a bed. **3.** Sleep. ❖ *intr.v.* **kipped, kip·ping, kips** To sleep. [Perh. < Dan. *kippe,* cheap inn; akin to ON *-kippa* (as in *kornkippa,* seed-corn holder), and < LGer. *kiffe,* hovel.]

kip[4] (kĭp) *n.* A unit of weight equal to 1,000 pounds (455 kilograms). [KI(LO)- + P(OUND)[1].]

Kip·ling (kĭp′lĭng), **(Joseph) Rudyard** 1865–1936. British writer who wrote *The Jungle Book* (1894) and *Kim* (1901) and won the 1907 Nobel Prize for literature.

kip·per (kĭp′ər) *n.* **1.** A male salmon or seatrout during or shortly after the spawning season. **2.** A herring or salmon that has been split, salted, and smoked. ❖ *tr.v.* **-pered, -per·ing, -pers** To prepare (fish) by splitting, salting, and smoking. [ME *kipre* < OE *cypera,* spawning male salmon, prob. < *cyperen,* of copper < *coper,* copper (because of the fish's color during the spawning season). See COPPER[1].]

kir also **Kir** (kĭr) *n.* A drink consisting of dry white wine or champagne flavored with cassis. [After Canon Félix *Kir* (1876–1968), mayor of Dijon, France.]

Kirch·hoff (kĭr′kôf′, kĭrKH′hôf), **Gustav Robert** 1824–87. German physicist noted for his research in spectrum analysis, optics, and electricity.

Kirch·ner (kĭrk′nər, kĭrKH′-), **Ernst Ludwig** 1880–1938. German expressionist artist whose works include *The Street* (1913).

Kir·ghiz or **Kir·giz** (kĭr-gēz′) *n.* Variants of **Kyrgyz.**

Kir·ghi·zia (kĭr-gē′zhə, -zhē-ə, -zē-ə) See **Kyrgyzstan.**

Ki·ri·ba·ti (kĕr′ə-bä′tē, kĭr′ə-bäs′) An island country of the W-central Pacific including the former Gilbert Is. and the Phoenix and Line Islands; became independent from Great Britain in 1979. Cap. Tarawa. Pop. 56,213.

Ki·rin (kē′rĭn′) See **Jilin.**

Ki·riti·mati (kə-rĭs′məs) The largest of the Line Is. in the central Pacific Ocean near the equator.

kirk (kûrk) *n.* **1.** *Scots* A church. **2.** **Kirk** *Chiefly British* The Presbyterian Church of Scotland. Used with *the.* [ME < ON *kirkja* < OE *cirice,* church. See CHURCH.]

Kirk·pat·rick (kûrk-păt′rĭk), **Mount** A mountain, 4,531.1 m (14,856 ft), of Antarctica near the edge of the Ross Ice Shelf.

Kir·kuk (kĭr-kŏŏk′) A city of NE Iraq SE of Mosul; built on the site of a settlement dating to 3000 B.C. Pop. 418,624.

Kir·li·an photography (kĭr′lē-ən) *n.* The process of photographing an object by exposing film in a dark room to the ultraviolet light that is emitted after the object is placed in an intense electric field. [After Semyon Davidovich *Kirlian* (1900–80), Russian electrician, and his wife Valentina Khrisanovna *Kirlian* (died 1971), Russian journalist, codiscoverers of the static electric effect on which it is based.]

Kir·man (kĭr-män′, kər-) *n.* A Persian rug with a pastel background, a center medallion, and an ornately patterned border. [After KERMAN.]

kir·mess (kûr′mĭs) *n.* Variant of **kermis.**

Ki·rov (kē′rôf′, kyē′-rəf) A city of W-central Russia ENE of Moscow; founded c. 1174. Pop. 490,964.

Ki·ro·va·bad (kĭ-rō′və-bäd′, kyĭ′rə-və-bät′) See **Gäncä.**

Ki·ro·vo·hrad (kĭ-rō′və-hräd′, kē-rō′vō-hräd′) or **Ki·ro·vo·grad** (-gräd′, -gräd′) A city of central Ukraine SSE of Kiev. Pop. 280,300.

kirsch (kĭrsh) *n.* A colorless brandy made from the fermented juice of cherries. [Fr., short for Ger. *Kirschwasser.* See KIRSCHWASSER.]

kirsch·was·ser (kĭrsh′vä′sər) *n.* Kirsch. [Ger. : *Kirsche,* cherry (< MHGer. *kirse, kirsche* < OHGer. *kirsa* < VLat. *ceresia;* see CHERRY) + *Wasser,* water (< MHGer. *wasser* < OHGer. *wassar;* see wed- in App.).]

Kirt·land's warbler (kûrt′ləndz) *n.* A rare gray-backed warbler (*Dendroica kirtlandii*) that nests only in north-central Michigan. [After Jared Potter *Kirtland* (1793–1877), American naturalist and physician.]

kir·tle (kûr′tl) *n. Archaic* **1.** A man's knee-length tunic or coat. **2.** A woman's dress or skirt. [ME *kirtel* < OE *cyrtel,* prob. ult. < Lat. *curtus,* short. See **sker-**[1] in App.]

Ki·run·di (kē-rŏŏn′dē, -rōōn′-) *n.* A Bantu language, closely related to Kinyarwanda, that is an official language of Burundi.

Ki·san·ga·ni (kē′sän-gä′nē, kĭ-zäng′gä-nē) Formerly **Stan·ley·ville** (stăn′lē-vĭl′) A city of N Congo (formerly Zaire) on the Congo R. NE of Kinshasa; founded 1883. Pop. 317,581.

Kish (kĭsh) An ancient city of Mesopotamia in the Euphrates R. valley of present-day central Iraq. Its extensive ruins have yielded valuable archaeological evidence about Sumerian culture.

Ki·shi·nev (kĭsh′ə-nĕf′, -nôf′) See **Chişinău.**

kish·ke also **kish·ka** (kĭsh′kə) *n.* See **derma**[2]. [Yiddish < Russ. *kishka,* intestine. See **(s)keu-** in App.]

Ki·si (kē′sē′, -shē′) See **Jixi.**

Kis·lev (kĭs′ləv, kēs-lĕv′) *n.* The third month of the year in the Jewish calendar. See table at **calendar.** [Heb. *kislēw* < Akkadian *kislimu, kisliwu,* a month name (November/December).]

kis·met (kĭz′mĕt′, -mĭt) *n.* Fate; fortune. [Turk. < Pers. *qismat* < Ar. *qisma,* lot < *qasama,* to divide, allot.]

kiss (kĭs) *v.* **kissed, kiss·ing, kiss·es** —*tr.* **1.** To touch or caress with the lips as an expression of affection, greeting, respect, or amorousness. **2.** To touch lightly or gently: *leaves kissed by dew.* **3.** To strike lightly; brush against: *We barely kissed her car with our bumper.* —*intr.* **1.** To engage in mutual touching or caressing with the lips. **2.** To come into light contact. ❖ *n.* **1.** A caress or touch with the lips. **2.** A slight or gentle touch. **3.** A small piece of candy, esp. of chocolate. **4.** A drop cookie made of egg whites and sugar. —*phrasal verbs:* **kiss off** *Slang* **1.** To dismiss or reject. **2.** To give up or regard as lost: *He can kiss off that promotion.* **3.** To leave or disappear from notice. **kiss up** *Slang* To behave obsequiously; fawn. —*idioms:* **kiss ass** *Vulgar Slang* To act submissively or obsequiously to gain favor. **kiss goodbye** *Informal* To regard as lost, ruined, or hopeless. [ME *kissen* < OE *cyssan.*] —**kiss′a·ble** *adj.*

kiss-and-tell (kĭs′ən-tĕl′) *Informal adj.* Disclosing private or confidential information, esp. in a firsthand account.

kiss·er (kĭs′ər) *n.* **1.** One who kisses. **2.** *Slang* The mouth. **3.** *Slang* The face.

kiss·ing bug (kĭs′ĭng) *n.* See **conenose.**

kissing cousin *n.* **1.** A distant relative known well enough to be kissed when greeted. **2.** One of two or more things that are closely akin.

kissing disease *n. Informal* Infectious mononucleosis.

Kis·sin·ger (kĭs′ĭn-jər), **Henry Alfred** b. 1923. German-born Amer. diplomat who was US secretary of state (1973–77) and shared the 1973 Nobel Peace Prize.

kiss of death *n.* Something ultimately ruinous, destructive, or fatal: *"Divorce was once a political kiss of death"* (Ellen Goodman). [< Judas's kiss of betrayal (Mark 14:44–46).]

kiss-off (kĭs′ôf′, -ŏf′) *n. Slang* A dismissal, as from a job.

kiss of life *n.* Mouth-to-mouth resuscitation.

kiss of peace *n.* A ceremonial gesture, such as a kiss, used in some churches during the Eucharist.

kist (kĭst) *n.* Variant of **cist**[2].

Kist·na (kĭst′nə) See **Krishna**[2].

Ki·swa·hi·li (kē′swä-hē′lē) *n.* See **Swahili** 1.

kit[1] (kĭt) *n.* **1a.** A set of articles or implements used for a specific purpose: *a shaving kit.* **b.** A container for such a set. **2.** A set of parts or materials to be assembled: *a model airplane kit for children.* **3.** A packaged set of related materials: *a sales kit.* **4a.** A collection of personal effects used for travel. **b.** A container, such as a bag, for storing or holding such a collection. —*idiom:* **(whole) kit and caboodle** *Informal* The entire outfit or lot.

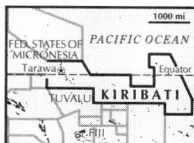

Kiribati

[ME *kitte*, wooden tub, prob. < MDu.]

kit² (kĭt) *n.* **1.** A kitten. **2.** A young, often undersized fur-bearing animal. [Short for KITTEN.]

kit³ (kĭt) *n.* A tiny narrow violin used by dancing masters in the 17th and 18th centuries. [?]

Ki·ta·kyu·shu (kē-tä′kyōō-shōō) A city of N Kyushu, Japan, NNE of Nagasaki. Pop. 1,019,996.

kit bag *n.* A traveling bag, such as a knapsack.

Kit Carson Mountain A peak, 4,320.3 m (14,165 ft), in the Sangre de Cristo Mts. of S-central CO.

kitch·en (kĭch′ən) *n.* **1.** A room or an area equipped for preparing and cooking food. **2.** A style of cooking; cuisine. **3.** A staff that prepares, cooks, and serves food. [ME *kichene* < OE *cycene*, prob. < VLat. **cocīna* < LLat. *coquīna* < fem. of Lat. *coquīnus*, of cooking < *coquus*, cook < *coquere*, to cook. See pekʷ- in App.]

kitchen cabinet *n.* A group of unofficial advisers to the head of a government. [< the story that Andrew Jackson met with his unofficial cabinet in the White House kitchen.]

Kitch·e·ner (kĭch′nər, kĭch′ə-nər) A city of S Ontario, Canada, WSW of Toronto; settled in 1806. Pop. 178,420.

Kitchener, Horatio Herbert. 1st Earl Kitchener of Khartoum and of Broome. 1850–1916. British soldier who led Egyptian troops in the retaking of the Sudan (1898) and brought the Boer War (1899–1902) to a conclusion.

kitch·en·ette (kĭch′ə-nĕt′) *n.* A small kitchen.

kitchen garden *n.* A garden in which vegetables, fruits, and herbs are grown for household consumption.

kitchen midden *n.* **1.** A mound of kitchen refuse. **2.** *Archaeology* See **midden** 2.

kitchen police *n.* **1.** Enlisted military personnel assigned to work in a kitchen. **2.** Military duty assisting cooks.

kitch·en·ware (kĭch′ən-wâr′) *n.* Utensils, such as pots and pans, for use in a kitchen.

kite (kīt) *n.* **1.** A light framework covered with cloth, plastic, or paper, designed to be flown in the wind at the end of a long string. **2.** Any of the light sails of a ship used in a light wind. **3.** Any of various predatory birds of the hawk family Accipitridae, having a long, often forked tail and long pointed wings. **4a.** A piece of negotiable paper representing a fictitious financial transaction and used temporarily to sustain credit or raise money. **b.** A bank check drawn on insufficient funds to take advantage of the time interval required for collection. **c.** A bank check altered to show a larger amount. ❖ *v.* **kit·ed, kit·ing, kites** —*intr.* **1.** To fly like a kite; soar or glide. **2.** To get money or credit with a kite. —*tr.* **1.** To use (a bad check) to sustain credit or raise money. **2.** To increase the amount of (a check) fraudulently. [ME, bird of prey < OE *cȳta*.]

kith and kin (kĭth′ ən kĭn′) *pl.n.* **1.** One's acquaintances and relatives. **2.** One's relatives. [ME *kith* < OE *cȳth*, kinsfolk, neighbors. See gnō- in App.]

kith·a·ra (kĭth′ər-ə) *n.* Variant of **cithara**.

Kí·thi·ra (kē′thē-rä′) See **Cythera**.

Ki·tik·me·ot (kī-tĭk′mē-ŏt′) A region of W Nunavut, Canada.

kitsch (kĭch) *n.* **1.** Sentimentality or vulgar, often pretentious bad taste, esp. in the arts. **2.** An example or examples of kitsch. ❖ *adj.* Of, being, or characterized by kitsch. [Ger., prob. of dialectal orig.] —**kitsch′i·fy** *v.* —**kitsch′y** *adj.*

kit·ten (kĭt′n) *n.* A young cat. ❖ *intr.v.* **-tened, -ten·ing, -tens** To bear kittens. [ME *kitoun*, prob. < ONFr. **caton*, dim. of *cat*, cat < LLat. *cattus*.]

kit·ten·ish (kĭt′n-ĭsh) *adj.* Playfully coy and frisky. —**kit′ten·ish·ly** *adv.* —**kit′ten·ish·ness** *n.*

kit·ti·wake (kĭt′ē-wāk′) *n.* Either of two gray gulls (*Rissa tridactyla* or *R. brevirostris*) of northern regions, that nest in colonies on sea cliffs. [Perh. imit. of its cry.]

kit·tle (kĭt′l) *Scots adj.* Touchy; unpredictable. ❖ *tr.v.* **-tled, -tling, -tles** **1.** To tickle; arouse. **2.** To puzzle; perplex. [< ME *kitillen*, to tickle, prob. < OE **citelian* or < ON *kitla*.]

Kit·tredge (kĭt′rĭj), **George Lyman** 1860–1941. Amer. scholar noted for his works on Chaucer and Shakespeare.

kit·ty¹ (kĭt′ē) *n., pl.* **-ties 1.** A fund made up of a portion of each pot in a poker game. **2.** A pool of money, esp. one to which people have contributed for a designated purpose. **3.** See **widow** 3. [Prob. < KIT¹.]

kit·ty² (kĭt′ē) *n., pl.* **-ties** A cat, esp. a kitten.

kit·ty-cor·nered (kĭt′ē-kôr′nərd) or **kit·ty-cor·ner** (-nər) *adj. & adv.* Variants of **cater-cornered**.

Kitty Hawk A village of NE NC on a sandy peninsula between Albemarle Sound and the Atlantic Ocean. Nearby Kill Devil Hill was the site of the Wright brothers' first two successful flights (Dec. 17, 1903).

ki·va (kē′və) *n.* An underground or partly underground chamber in a Pueblo village, used by men esp. for ceremonies or councils. [Hopi *kíva*.]

Ki·vu (kē′vōō), **Lake** A lake on the border of Congo (formerly Zaire) and Rwanda N of Lake Tanganyika at an altitude of 1,461 m (4,790 ft).

Ki·wa·ni·an (kĭ-wä′nē-ən) *n.* A member of Kiwanis International, a service organization made up of business and professional people, founded in 1915. [After *Kiwanis International*, a service organization.]

ki·wi (kē′wē) *n., pl.* **-wis 1.** Any of several flightless birds of the genus *Apteryx*, native to New Zealand and having vestigial wings and a long slender bill. **2a.** A woody Chinese vine (*Actinidia chinensis*) having brown edible fruit with a sweet green pulp. **b.** The fruit of this plant. **3.** *Informal* A New Zealander. [Maori, perh. of imit. orig.]

Ki·zil Ir·mak (kĭ-zĭl′ ĭr-mäk′) A river of N-central Turkey flowing c. 1,150 km (715 mi) to the Black Sea.

KJV *abbr.* King James Version

KKK *abbr.* Ku Klux Klan

kl *abbr.* kiloliter

Klai·pe·da (klī′pĭ-də, -pē-dä) Formerly **Me·mel** (mā′məl) A city of W Lithuania on the Baltic Sea; founded as a fortress in 1252. Pop. 204,300.

Klam·ath (klăm′əth) *n., pl.* **Klamath** or **-aths 1.** A member of a Native American people inhabiting an area of the Cascade Range in south-central Oregon and northern California. **2.** The Penutian language of the Klamath.

Klamath River A river flowing c. 423 km (263 mi) from SW OR through NW CA to the Pacific Ocean.

Klan (klăn) *n.* The Ku Klux Klan. —**Klans′man** (klănz′mən) *n.*

klatch or **klatsch** (klăch, klăch) *n.* A casual social gathering, usu. for conversation. [Ger. *Klatsch* < *klatschen*, to gossip, make a sharp noise, of imit. orig.]

klav·ern (klăv′ərn) *n.* A local organizational unit of the Ku Klux Klan. [KL(AN) + (C)AVERN.]

Klax·on (klăk′sən) A trademark used for a loud electric horn.

Klee (klā), **Paul** 1879–1940. Swiss artist noted for his expert use of line and color and his theories of abstract art.

Kleen·ex (klē′nĕks′) A trademark used for a soft facial tissue.

Klein (klīn), **Melanie** 1882–1960. Austrian-born British psychoanalyst who specialized in child development.

Klein bottle *n.* A one-sided topological surface having no inside or outside, depicted in ordinary space by inserting the small open end of a tapered tube through the side of the tube and making it contiguous with the larger open end, although a true Klein bottle would not intersect itself. [After Felix *Klein* (1849–1925), German mathematician.]

Kleist (klīst), **Heinrich von** 1777–1811. German writer whose works include the comedy *The Broken Pitcher* (1811).

Klem·per·er (klĕm′pər-ər), **Otto** 1885–1973. German conductor noted for his interpretations of Beethoven and Mahler.

klep·to·ma·ni·a (klĕp′tə-mā′nē-ə, -mān′yə) *n.* An obsessive impulse to steal regardless of economic need. [Gk. *kleptein*, to steal + -MANIA.] —**klep′to·ma·ni·ac′** (-nē-ăk′) *n.* —**klep′to·ma·ni′a·cal** (-mə-nī′ĭ-kəl) *adj.*

Kle·ve (klā′və) also **Cleves** (klēvz) A city of W-central Germany WSW of Münster. Pop. 44,223.

klez·mer (klĕz′mər) *n., pl.* **klez·mo·rim** (klĕz′mə-rēm′) **1.** A musician performing Jewish folk music of eastern Europe in a small band. **2.** The Jewish folk music played by small bands. [Yiddish < Mishnaic Heb. *kĕlê zemer*, musical instruments : *kĕlê*, pl. bound form of *kĕlî*, instrument + *zemer*, music, song.]

klick also **klik** (klĭk) *n. Slang* A kilometer. [Alteration of CLICK (prob. influenced by KILOMETER).]

klieg light (klēg) *n.* A powerful carbon-arc lamp producing an intense light and used esp. in making movies. [Alteration of *Klieglight*, trademark for such a lamp, after John H. *Kliegl* (1869–1959) and his brother Anton Tiberius *Kliegl* (1872–1927), German-born American lighting experts.]

Klimt (klĭmt), **Gustav** 1862–1918. Austrian painter whose richly decorative works include *The Kiss* (1908).

Kline (klīn), **Franz Joseph** 1910–62. Amer. painter known for his abstract expressionist works.

klip·spring·er (klĭp′sprĭng′ər) *n.* A small agile African antelope (*Oreotragus oreotragus*) having large ears. [Afr. : *klip*, cliff (< MDu. *klippe*) + *springer*, jumper (< *springen*, to leap < MDu.).]

Klon·dike (klŏn′dīk′) A region of Yukon Terr., Canada, just E of AK and traversed by the **Klondike River**, c. 145 km (90 mi). Gold was discovered here in Aug. 1896, leading to the gold rush of 1897–98.

kloof (klōōf) *n. South African* A deep ravine. [Afr. < MDu. *clove*, cleft.]

kludge or **kluge** (klōōj) *n. Slang* **1.** A system, esp. a computer system, constituted of poorly matched elements or of elements originally intended for other applications. **2.** A clumsy or inelegant solution to a problem. [< ironic use of earlier *kluge*, smart, clever < Ger. *kluge* < MHGer. *kluc* < MLGer. *klōk*.] —**kludge** *v.* —**kludg′y** *adj.*

klutz (klŭts) *n. Slang* **1.** A clumsy person. **2.** A stupid person; a dolt. [Yiddish *klots* < MHGer. *kloz*, block, lump < OHGer.] —**klutz′i·ness** *n.* —**klutz′y** *adj.*

kly·stron (klī′strŏn′) *n.* An electron tube used to amplify or generate ultrahigh frequency by means of velocity modulation. [Gk. *kluzein, klus-*, to wash, break over + -TRON.]

km *abbr.* kilometer

K-me·son (kā′mĕz′ŏn, -mē′zŏn, -mĕs′ŏn, -mē′sŏn) *n.* See **kaon**.

kn. *abbr. Nautical* knot

knack (năk) *n.* **1.** A clever, expedient way of doing something. **2.**

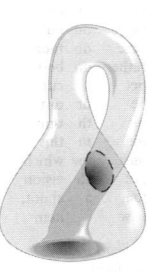

Klein bottle

A specific talent for something, esp. one difficult to explain or teach. **3.** *Archaic* **a.** A cleverly designed device. **b.** A knickknack. [ME *knakke* < MDu. *cnacken*, to strike, crack, prob. of imit. orig.]

knack•er (năk′ər) *n. Chiefly British* **1.** A person who buys worn-out or old livestock and slaughters them to sell the meat or hides. **2.** A person who buys discarded structures and dismantles them to sell the materials. [Prob. of Scand. orig.] —**knack′er•y** (-ə-rē) *n.*

knack•ered (năk′ərd) *adj. Chiefly British* Very tired; exhausted.

knack•wurst or **knock•wurst** (nŏk′wûrst′, -wŏŏrst′) *n.* A short, thick, highly seasoned sausage. [Ger. : *knacken*, to crack (< MHGer., of imit. orig.) + *Wurst*, sausage; see WURST.]

knap (năp) *tr.v.* **knapped, knap•ping, knaps 1.** To break or chip (stone) with sharp blows, as in shaping flint into tools. **2.** *Chiefly British* **a.** To strike sharply; rap. **b.** To snap at or bite. [ME *knappen*, prob. of imit. orig.] —**knap′per** *n.*

knap•sack (năp′săk′) *n.* A bag with shoulder straps, designed for carrying articles on the back. [Prob. LGer. *Knappsack* : *knappen*, to bite (prob. of imit. orig.) + *Sack*, bag (< MLGer. *sak* < OHGer. *sac* < LLat. *saccus*; see SACK¹).]

knap•weed (năp′wēd′) *n.* Any of various thistles of the genus *Centaurea*, having variously colored flowers grouped in a head with a spiny involucre. [ME *knopwed* : *knop*, knob; see KNOP + *wed*, weed; see WEED¹.]

knar also **knaur** (när) *n.* A knot or burl on a tree or in wood. [ME *knarre*, prob. < OE **cnear* or < MDu. and MLGer. *knorre*.]

knave (nāv) *n.* **1.** An unprincipled, crafty man. **2a.** A male servant. **b.** A man of humble birth. **3.** *Games* See **jack** 3. [ME < OE *cnafa*, boy, male servant.] —**knav′ish** *adj.* —**knav′ish•ly** *adv.* —**knav′ish•ness** *n.*

knav•er•y (nā′və-rē) *n., pl.* **-ies 1.** Dishonest or crafty dealing. **2.** An instance of trickery or mischief.

knawel (nôl) also **knawe** (nô) *n.* A low-growing weedy Eurasian annual (*Scleranthus annuus*) having narrow leaves and inconspicuous green flowers. [Ger. *Knäuel* < MHGer. *kliuwel, kniuwel*, dim. of *kliuwe*, ball of yarn < OHGer. *kliuwa*.]

knead (nēd) *tr.v.* **knead•ed, knead•ing, kneads 1.** To mix and work into a uniform mass, as with the hands: *kneads dough.* **2.** To make or shape by or as if by folding, pressing, and stretching with the hands. **3.** To squeeze, press, or roll with the hands, as in massaging: *kneaded a painful calf muscle.* [ME *kneden* < OE *cnedan*.] —**knead′er** *n.*

knee (nē) *n.* **1a.** The joint between the thigh and the lower leg, formed by the articulation of the femur and the tibia and covered anteriorly by the patella. **b.** The region of the leg that encloses and supports this joint. **2.** An analogous joint or part of a leg of a quadruped vertebrate. **3.** Something resembling the human knee, such as a bent piece of pipe. **4.** The part of a garment that covers the knee. **5.** An abrupt woody projection arising from the roots of some swamp-growing trees: *cypress knees.* ❖ *tr.v.* **kneed, knee•ing, knees** To strike with the knee. [ME < OE *cnēo*. See **genu-** in App.]

knee action *n.* An automotive front-wheel suspension that permits independent vertical motion of each wheel.

knee breeches *pl.n.* Trousers extending down to or just below the knee.

knee•cap (nē′kăp′) *n.* **1.** See **patella** 1a. **2.** See **kneepad**. ❖ *tr.v.* **-capped, -cap•ping, -caps** To cripple by shooting in the legs, esp. in the knees.

knee-deep (nē′dēp′) *adj.* **1.** Reaching as high as the knees: *knee-deep water.* **2.** Submerged to the knees: *knee-deep in mud.* **3.** Deeply occupied or involved: *knee-deep in work.*

knee-high (nē′hī′) *adj.* Reaching up to the knees. ❖ *n.* (nē′hī′) A sock or stocking that extends just below the knee.

knee jerk *n.* A sudden involuntary extension of the leg, produced by a sharp tap to the tendon below the patella; patellar reflex.

knee-jerk (nē′jûrk′) *adj. Slang* **1.** Easily predictable; automatic. **2.** Reacting spontaneously in the expected manner.

kneel (nēl) *intr.v.* **knelt** (nĕlt) or **kneeled, kneel•ing, kneels** To go down or rest on one or both knees. [ME *knelen* < OE *cnēowlian*. See **genu-** in App.]

kneel•er (nē′lər) *n.* **1.** One who kneels, as to pray. **2.** Something, such as a stool, cushion, or board, on which to kneel.

knee•pad (nē′păd′) *n.* A protective covering for the knee.

knee sock *n.* A sock that reaches just below the knee.

knell (nĕl) *v.* **knelled, knell•ing, knells** —*intr.* **1.** To ring slowly and solemnly, esp. for a funeral; toll. **2.** To give forth a mournful or ominous sound. —*tr.* To signal, summon, or proclaim by tolling. ❖ *n.* **1.** The sound of a bell knelling; a toll. **2.** A signal of disaster or destruction. [ME *knellen* < OE *cnyllan*.]

Knes•set (knĕs′ĕt′) *n.* The unicameral parliament of Israel. [Mod.Heb. *Kneset* < Mishnaic Heb. *kəneset*, assembly < Aram. *kəništā* < *knaš*, to assemble.]

knew (nōō, nyōō) *v.* Past tense of **know**.

Knick•er•bock•er (nĭk′ər-bŏk′ər) *n.* **1a.** A descendant of the Dutch settlers of New York. **b.** A native or inhabitant of New York. **2. knickerbockers** Full breeches gathered and banded just below the knee; knickers. [After Diedrich *Knickerbocker*, fictional name used by Washington Irving.]

knick•ers (nĭk′ərz) *pl.n.* **1a.** Long bloomers formerly worn as underwear by women and girls. **b.** *Chiefly British* Panties. **2.** Full breeches gathered and banded just below the knee. [Short for *knickerbockers.*]

knick•knack also **nick•nack** (nĭk′năk′) *n.* A small ornamental article; a trinket. [Reduplication of KNACK.]

knife (nīf) *n., pl.* **knives** (nīvz) **1.** A cutting instrument consisting of a sharp blade attached to a handle. **2.** A cutting edge; a blade. ❖ *v.* **knifed, knif•ing, knifes** —*tr.* **1.** To use a knife on, esp. to stab; wound with a knife. **2.** *Informal* To betray or attempt to defeat by underhand means. —*intr.* To cut or slash a way through something with or as if with a knife. —**idiom: under the knife** *Informal* Undergoing surgery. [ME *knif* < OE *cnīf* < ON *knīfr*.] —**knif′er** *n.*

knife-edge (nīf′ĕj′) *n.* **1.** A sharp cutting edge. **2.** A sharp narrow edge or border: *"saying lines that teeter on the knife-edge between literature and lunacy"* (Vincent Canby). **3.** A wedge of metal used as a low-friction fulcrum for a balancing beam or lever.

knight (nīt) *n.* **1a.** A medieval tenant serving a feudal landholder as a mounted man-at-arms. **b.** A medieval gentleman-soldier raised by a sovereign to privileged military status after training as a page and squire. **c.** A man holding a nonhereditary title conferred by a sovereign. **2.** A man belonging to an order or brotherhood. **3a.** A defender, champion, or zealous upholder of a cause or principle. **b.** The devoted champion of a lady. **4.** *Games* A chess piece, usu. in the shape of a horse's head, that can be moved two squares horizontally and one vertically or two squares vertically and one horizontally. ❖ *tr.v.* **knight•ed, knight•ing, knights** To raise (a person) to knighthood. [ME < OE *cniht*.] —**knight′ly** *adj. & adv.* —**knight′li•ness** *n.*

knight bachelor *n., pl.* **knights bachelors** or **knight bachelors** An English knight of the lowest rank; a bachelor.

knight-errant (nīt′ĕr′ənt) *n., pl.* **knights-errant** (nīts′-) **1.** A knight who wanders in search of adventures to prove his chivalry. **2.** One given to adventurous or quixotic conduct. —**knight′-er′rant•ry** (-ĕr′ən-trē) *n.*

knight•head (nīt′hĕd′) *n.* Either of two timbers rising from the keel of a sailing ship and supporting the inner end of the bowsprit. [< the fact that it was sometimes decorated with a carving of a man's head.]

knight•hood (nīt′hŏŏd′) *n.* **1.** The rank, dignity, or vocation of a knight. **2.** Behavior or qualities befitting a knight; chivalry. **3.** Knights considered as a group.

Knight of Columbus *n., pl.* **Knights of Columbus** A member of a society of Roman Catholic men founded in 1882.

Knight of Pythias *n., pl.* **Knights of Pythias** A member of a secret philanthropic fraternal order founded in 1864.

Knights of the Round Table *pl.n.* In Arthurian legend, the knights of King Arthur's court.

Knight Templar *n., pl.* **Knights Templars** or **Knights Templar** **1.** A member of an order of knights founded about 1118 to protect pilgrims in the Holy Land during the Second Crusade. **2.** A man belonging to a Masonic order in the United States.

knish (kə-nĭsh′) *n.* A piece of dough stuffed with potato, meat, or cheese and baked or fried. [Yiddish < Ukrainian *knysh*, prob. of Turkic orig.]

knit (nĭt) *v.* **knit** or **knit•ted, knit•ting, knits** —*tr.* **1.** To make (a fabric or garment) by intertwining yarn or thread in a series of connected loops with knitting needles or on a machine. **2.** To form (yarn or thread) into fabric by intertwining. **3.** To join closely; unite securely. **4.** To draw (the brows) together in wrinkles; furrow. —*intr.* **1.** To make a fabric or garment by knitting. **2.** To become securely joined or mended together closely, as a fractured bone. **3.** To come together in wrinkles or furrows, as the brows. ❖ *n.* **1.** A fabric or garment made by knitting. **2.** The way in which a fabric has been knit: *a loose knit.* [ME *knitten*, to tie in a knot < OE *cnyttan*.] —**knit′ter** *n.*

knit•ting (nĭt′ĭng) *n.* **1.** The act or process of producing something knitted. **2.** Material that has been knitted or is being knitted.

knitting needle *n.* A long thin pointed rod used in pairs to knit yarn into cloth.

knit•wear (nĭt′wâr′) *n.* Knitted garments.

knives (nīvz) *n.* Plural of **knife**.

knob (nŏb) *n.* **1.** A rounded protuberance. **2a.** A rounded handle, as on a drawer or door. **b.** A rounded control switch or dial. **3.** A prominent rounded hill or mountain. [ME *knobbe* < MLGer., knot in wood.] —**knobbed** (nŏbd) *adj.* —**knob′by** *adj.*

knob•ker•rie (nŏb′kĕr′ē) *n.* A short club with one knobbed end, used as a weapon by certain South African peoples. [Afr. *knopkierie* : *knop*, knob (< MDu. *cnoppe*) + *kieri*, club (< Khoikhoin *kirri*, stick).]

knock (nŏk) *v.* **knocked, knock•ing, knocks** —*tr.* **1.** To strike with a hard blow. **2.** To affect in a specified way by striking hard: *knocked the mugger senseless.* **3.** To cause to collide: *I knocked my head on a low beam.* **4.** To produce by hitting or striking: *knocked a hole in the wall.* **5.** To instill with or as if with blows: *We tried to knock some sense into his head.* **6.** *Slang* To find fault with; criticize: *Don't knock the food; it's free.* —*intr.* **1.** To strike a sharp audible blow or series of blows, as on a door. **2.** To collide with something: *knocked into the table.* **3.** To make a pounding or clanking noise. ❖ *n.* **1.** An instance of striking or colliding; a blow. **2.** The sound of a sharp tap on a hard surface; a rap. **3.** A

kneepad
in-line skater wearing
kneepads

ă	pat	oi	boy
ā	pay	ou	out
âr	care	ŏŏ	took
ä	father	ōō	boot
ĕ	be	ŭ	cut
ē	be	ûr	urge
ĭ	pit	th	thin
ī	pie	th	this
îr	pier	hw	which
ŏ	pot	zh	vision
ō	toe	ə	about,
ô	paw		item

Stress marks:
′ (primary);
′ (secondary), as in
lexicon (lĕk′sĭ-kŏn′)

pounding or clanking noise made by an engine, often as a result of faulty fuel combustion. **4.** *Slang* A cutting, often petty criticism. ***—phrasal verbs:* knock around** (or **about**) **1.** To be rough or brutal with; maltreat. **2.** To wander from place to place. **3.** *Informal* To discuss or consider. **knock back** *Informal* To gulp (an alcoholic drink). **knock down 1.** To bring to the ground with a blow; topple. **2.** To disassemble into parts, as for storage or shipping. **3.** To declare sold at an auction, as by striking a blow with a gavel. **4.** *Informal* To reduce, as in price. **5.** *Slang* To receive as wages; earn. **knock off 1.** *Informal* **a.** To take a break or rest from; stop. **b.** To cease work. **2.** *Informal* To complete, accomplish, or dispose of hastily or easily; finish. **3.** *Informal* To get rid of; eliminate. **4.** *Slang* To kill or overcome. **5.** *Slang* To hold up or rob. **6.** *Informal* To copy or imitate, esp. without permission. **knock out 1.** To render unconscious. **2.** *Sports* To defeat (a boxing opponent) by a knockout. **3.** To render useless or inoperative. **4.** *Informal* To exert or exhaust (oneself or another) to the utmost. **5.** *Informal* To produce in abundance. **6. knock together** To make or assemble quickly or carelessly. **knock up 1.** *Slang* To make pregnant. **2.** *Chiefly British* To wake up or summon, as by knocking at the door. **3.** *Chiefly British* To wear out; exhaust. ***—idioms:* knock cold** To render unconscious; knock out. **knock dead 1.** To kill with a blow. **2.** *Slang* To affect strongly and positively. **knock for a loop** *Slang* To surprise tremendously; astonish. **knock it off** *Slang* To stop doing something. Often used in the imperative. [ME *knokken* < OE *cnocian.*]

knock•a•bout (nŏk′ə-bout′) *adj.* **1.** Boisterous; rowdy. **2.** Appropriate for rough wear or use. ❖ *n.* A small sloop with a mainsail, jib, and keel but no bowsprit.

knock•down (nŏk′doun′) *n.* **1a.** The act or an instance of knocking down. **b.** The condition of being knocked down. **2.** An overwhelming blow or shock. **3.** Something designed to be easily assembled or disassembled. ❖ *adj.* **1.** Strong enough to knock down or overwhelm; powerful. **2.** Designed to be easily assembled or disassembled. **3.** Reduced: *knockdown prices.*

knock•down-drag•out (nŏk′doun′drăg′out′) *adj.* Marked by roughness, violence, and acrimony.

knock•er (nŏk′ər) *n.* **1.** A hinged fixture, such as a metal ring, used for knocking on a door. **2. knockers** *Vulgar Slang* A woman's breasts.

knock-knee (nŏk′nē′) *n.* A deformity of the legs in which the knees are abnormally close together and the ankles are spread widely apart. **—knock′-kneed′** *adj.*

knock•off (nŏk′ôf′, -ŏf′) *n. Informal* An unauthorized copy or imitation, as of designer clothing.

knock•out (nŏk′out′) *n.* **1a.** The act of knocking out. **b.** The state of being knocked out. **c.** A blow that knocks out an opponent. **2.** *Sports* **a.** A victory in boxing in which one's opponent is unable to rise from the canvas within a specified time after being knocked down or is judged too injured to continue. **b.** The act of winning a boxing match in this way: *won the fight by a knockout.* **3.** *Slang* A strikingly attractive or impressive person or thing. ❖ *adj.* also **knock-out** (nŏk′out′) **1.** Capable of knocking out: *a knockout punch.* **2.** Strikingly attractive or impressive. **3.** Having a specific single gene removed from the genome by genetic manipulation: *knockout mice used in an experiment.*

OUR LIVING LANGUAGE An attractive or exciting person or thing can colloquially be called a *knockout.* First used in the early 20th century, this expression comes from a metaphorical use of the boxing term *knock out.* The sport of boxing has produced many terms, such as *lightweight, heavyweight,* and *slaphappy,* that have entered our everyday language. Two political candidates will *square off* at the beginning of a debate, an expression with origins in the 18th- and 19th-century rules by which fighters began each round facing each other across a one-yard square in the center of the ring. One of our political candidates might anticipate a comment by the other and so *beat her to the punch.* If a candidate is clearly losing a debate, he may be said to be *on the ropes,* and he could even suffer a *knockout blow,* after which he might *throw in the sponge* or *towel* and quit his candidacy. Or, before any of that happens, perhaps time will run out on the other candidate, and he will be *saved by the bell.*

knockout drops *pl.n. Slang* A solution put into a drink surreptitiously in order to render the drinker unconscious.

knock•wurst (nŏk′wûrst′, -wo͝orst′) *n.* Variant of **knackwurst.**

knoll[1] (nōl) *n.* A small rounded hill or mound; a hillock. [ME *knol* < OE *cnoll.*]

knoll[2] (nōl) *Archaic v.* **knolled, knoll•ing, knolls** *—intr.* To ring mournfully; knell. *—tr.* To ring or sound (a bell, for example) mournfully; knell. ❖ *n.* A knell. [ME *knollen,* prob. alteration of *knellen,* to knell. See KNELL.]

knop (nŏp) *n.* A small decorative knob or boss. [ME *knop, knoppe* < OE *cnop.*]

Knos•sos also **Cnos•sos** or **Cnos•sus** (nŏs′əs) An ancient city of N Crete near present-day Iráklion; center of a Bronze Age culture that probably flourished c. 2000–1400 B.C.

knot[1] (nŏt) *n.* **1a.** A compact intersection of interlaced material, such as cord, ribbon, or rope. **b.** A fastening made by tying together lengths of material, such as rope, in a prescribed way. **2.** A decorative bow of ribbon, fabric, or braid. **3.** A unifying bond, esp. a marriage bond. **4.** A tight cluster of persons or things: *a knot of onlookers.* **5.** A feeling of tightness: *a knot in my stomach.* **6.** A complex problem. **7a.** A hard place or lump, esp. on a tree, at a point from which a stem or branch grows. **b.** The round cross section of such a lump on a piece of cut lumber. **8.** A protuberant growth or swelling in a tissue: *a knot in a gland.* **9a.** *Nautical* A division on a log line used to measure the speed of a ship. **b.** A unit of speed, one nautical mile per hour, approx. 1.85 kilometers (1.15 statute miles) per hour. **c.** A distance of one nautical mile. ❖ *v.* **knot•ted, knot•ting, knots** *—tr.* **1.** To tie in or fasten with a knot or knots. **2.** To snarl or entangle. **3.** To cause to form a knot or knots. *—intr.* **1.** To form a knot or knots. **2.** To become snarled or entangled. [ME < OE *cnotta.*]

USAGE NOTE In nautical usage *knot* is a unit of speed, not of distance, and has a built-in meaning of "per hour." Therefore, a ship would strictly be said to travel at ten knots (not ten knots per hour).

knot[2] (nŏt) *n.* Either of two migratory sandpipers *(Calidris canutus* or *C. tenuirostris)* that breed in Arctic regions. [ME, of Scand. orig.]

knot•grass (nŏt′grăs′) *n.* **1.** A low-growing weedy grass *(Paspalum distichum)* with spikelets arranged in two rows along the rachis. **2.** Any of several weedy plants of the genus *Polygonum* having stems with nodes.

knot•hole (nŏt′hōl′) *n.* A hole in a piece of lumber where a knot has dropped out or been removed.

knot•ty (nŏt′ē) *adj.* **-ti•er, -ti•est 1.** Tied or snarled in knots. **2.** Covered with knots or knobs; gnarled. **3.** Difficult to understand or solve. See Syns at **complex. —knot′ti•ness** *n.*

knot•weed (nŏt′wēd′) *n.* Any of several plants of the genus *Polygonum,* with jointed stems and inconspicuous flowers.

knout (nout) *n.* A leather scourge used for flogging. ❖ *tr.v.* **knout•ed, knout•ing, knouts** To flog with a knout. [Fr. < Russ. *knut* < ORuss. *knutŭ* < ON *knūtr,* knot in cord.]

know (nō) *v.* **knew** (no͞o, nyo͞o), **known** (nōn), **know•ing, knows** *—tr.* **1.** To perceive directly; grasp in the mind with clarity or certainty. **2.** To regard as true beyond doubt: *I know she won't fail.* **3.** To have a practical understanding of, as through experience; be skilled in: *knows how to cook.* **4.** To have fixed in the mind: *knows her Latin verbs.* **5.** To have experience of: *"a black stubble that had known no razor"* (William Faulkner). **6a.** To perceive as familiar; recognize: *I know that face.* **b.** To be acquainted with: *He doesn't know his neighbors.* **7.** To be able to distinguish; recognize as distinct: *knows right from wrong.* **8.** To discern the character or nature of: *knew him for a liar.* **9.** *Archaic* To have sexual intercourse with. *—intr.* **1.** To possess knowledge, understanding, or information. **2.** To be cognizant or aware. ***—idioms:* in the know** *Informal* Possessing special or secret information. **you know** *Informal* Used parenthetically in conversation, as to fill pauses or educe the listener's agreement or sympathy. [ME *knouen* < OE *cnāwan.* See **gnō-** in App.] **—know′a•ble** *adj.* **—know′er** *n.*

know-how (nō′hou′) *n.* The knowledge and skill required to do something correctly.

know•ing (nō′ĭng) *adj.* **1.** Possessing knowledge, information, or understanding. See Syns at **intelligent. 2.** Showing clever awareness and resourcefulness; shrewd. **3.** Suggestive of secret or private knowledge: *a knowing glance.* **4.** Deliberate; conscious. **—know′ing•ly** *adv.* **—know′ing•ness** *n.*

know-it-all (nō′ĭt-ôl′) *n. Informal* One who claims to know everything and rejects advice. **—know′-it-all′** *adj.*

knowl•edge (nŏl′ĭj) *n.* **1.** The state or fact of knowing. **2.** Familiarity, awareness, or understanding gained through experience or study. **3.** The sum or range of what has been perceived, discovered, or learned. **4.** Learning; erudition: *teachers of great knowledge.* **5.** Specific information about something. **6.** Carnal knowledge. [ME *knoulech* : *knouen,* to know; see KNOW + *-leche,* n. suff.]

knowl•edge•a•ble (nŏl′ĭ-jə-bəl) *adj.* Possessing or showing knowledge or intelligence; perceptive and well-informed. **—knowl′edge•a•bil′i•ty** *n.* **—knowl′edge•ably** *adv.*

known (nōn) *adj.* Proved or generally recognized: *a known authority.* ❖ *n.* Something that is known.

know-noth•ing (nō′nŭth′ĭng) *n.* **1.** A totally ignorant person; an ignoramus. **2.** An anti-intellectual. **3.** An agnostic. **4. Know-Nothing** A member of a political party in the United States during the 1850s that was antagonistic toward recent immigrants and Roman Catholics.

Knox (nŏks), **Henry** 1750–1806. Amer. Revolutionary soldier whose transport of 55 captured British cannon from Fort Ticonderoga helped force the British to evacuate Boston (1776).

Knox, John 1514?–72. Scottish religious reformer and founder of Scottish Presbyterianism.

Knox•ville (nŏks′vĭl′, -vəl) A city of E TN on the Tennessee R. NE of Chattanooga; settled c. 1785. Pop. 173,890.

Knt. *abbr.* knight

knuck•le (nŭk′əl) *n.* **1a.** The prominence of the dorsal aspect of a joint of a finger, esp. of one of the joints connecting the fingers to the hand. **b.** A rounded protuberance formed by the bones in a joint. **2.** A cut of meat centering on the carpal or tarsal joint, as of a pig. **3.** The part of a hinge through which the pin passes. **4.**

knot[1]
top: barrel and figure-eight knots
bottom: cross section of a piece of lumber

koala
Phascolarctos cinereus

Helmut Kohl

A sharp angle formed by the meeting of two surfaces, esp. two ship's timbers. **5. knuckles** Brass knuckles. ❖ *tr.v.* **-led, -ling, -les 1.** To press, rub, or hit with the knuckles. **2.** To shoot (a marble) with the thumb over the bent forefinger. **—phrasal verbs: knuckle down** To apply oneself earnestly to a task. **knuckle under** To yield to pressure; give in. [ME *knokel.*]

knuckle ball or **knuck·le·ball** (nŭk′əl-bôl′) *n. Baseball* A slow, randomly fluttering pitch thrown by gripping with the tips or nails of two or three fingers.

knuck·le·bone (nŭk′əl-bōn′) *n.* A knobbed bone, as of a knuckle or joint.

knuck·le·dust·er (nŭk′əl-dŭs′tər) *n. Slang* Brass knuckles.

knuck·le·head (nŭk′əl-hĕd′) *n. Informal* A stupid person; a blockhead.

knuckle joint *n.* A hinged joint in which a pin fastens the ends of two rods, one of which has an eye that fits between the two perforated projections of the other.

knur (nûr) *n.* A bump or knot, as on a tree trunk; a gnarl. [ME *knor.*]

knurl (nûrl) *n.* **1.** A knob, knot, or other small protuberance. **2.** One of a series of small ridges or grooves on the surface or edge of a metal object to aid in gripping. ❖ *tr.v.* **knurled, knurl·ing, knurls** To provide with knurls; mill. [Prob. dim. of KNUR.] **—knurled** (nûrld) *adj.* **—knurl′y** *adj.*

Knut (kə-nōōt′, -nyōōt′) See **Canute.**

KO (kā′ō′) *Slang tr.v.* **KO'd, KO'ing, KO's** To knock out, as in boxing. ❖ *n.* (kā-ō′, kā′ō′) A knockout, as in boxing.

ko·a (kō′ə) *n.* **1.** An acacia (*Acacia koa*) native to Hawaii having flowers arranged in axillary racemes and small sickle-shaped leaves. **2.** The brown or reddish wood of this tree, used esp. for cabinetry and musical instruments. [Hawaiian < Proto-Polynesian *to'a, ironwood tree.]

ko·a·la (kō-ä′lə) *n.* An arboreal Australian marsupial (*Phascolarctos cinereus*) that has grayish fur, large ears, and sharp claws. [Earlier *coola, koolah* < Dharuk (Aboriginal language of SE Australia) *gula, gulawan'.*]

ko·an (kō′än′) *n.* A puzzling, often paradoxical statement or story, used in Zen Buddhism as an aid to meditation and a means of gaining spiritual awakening. [J. *kōan* : *kō,* public (< M Chin. *kəwŋ*) + *an,* matter.]

kob (kŏb, kōb) *n.* An orange-brown African antelope (*Kobus kob*) whose habitat extends from Gambia eastward to Ethiopia. [Wolof.]

Ko·be (kō′bē′, -bā′) A city of S Honshu, Japan, on Osaka Bay SSW of Kyoto. Pop. 1,509,395.

Ko·blenz also **Co·blenz** (kō′blĕnts′) A city of W-central Germany at the confluence of the Rhine and Moselle rivers SE of Bonn; founded as a Roman frontier station. Pop. 109,907.

ko·bold (kō′bôld′) *n.* **1.** An often mischievous household elf in German folklore. **2.** A gnome that haunts underground places in German folklore. [Ger. < MHGer. *kobolt.* See COBALT.]

Koch (kôk, kōкн), **Robert** 1843–1910. German bacteriologist who won a 1905 Nobel Prize.

Ko·chi (kō′chē) A city of S Shikoku, Japan, on an inlet of the Pacific Ocean. Pop. 319,243.

Ko·dak (kō′dăk′) A trademark used for a hand-held camera and camera film.

Ko·dál·y (kō′dī′, kô′dä-yə), **Zoltán** 1882–1967. Hungarian composer whose works include the opera *Háry János* (1926).

Ko·di·ak bear (kō′dē-ăk′) *n.* A brown bear inhabiting islands and coastal areas of Alaska and sometimes considered a separate species (*Ursus middendorffi*). [After KODIAK (ISLAND).]

Kodiak Island An island of S AK in the Gulf of Alaska E of the Alaska Peninsula; site of the first permanent Russian settlement in the area (1784).

Koest·ler (kĕst′lər, kĕs′-), **Arthur** 1905–83. Hungarian-born British writer whose works include *Darkness at Noon* (1941).

kohl (kōl) *n.* A cosmetic preparation, such as powdered antimony sulfide, used esp. in the Middle East to darken the rims of the eyelids. [Ar. *kuḥl,* powder of antimony, kohl.]

Kohl, Helmut b. 1930. German politician elected chancellor of West Germany in 1982 and of Germany in 1990, serving until 1998.

Köh·ler (kœ′lər), **Wolfgang** 1887–1967. Estonian-born German psychologist and a founder of the Gestalt psychology movement.

kohl·ra·bi (kōl-rä′bē, -räb′ē) *n., pl.* **-bies** (*Brassica oleracea* var. *gongylodes*) in the mustard family, having a thick basal stem part that is eaten as a vegetable. [Ger., partial transl. of Ital. *cavoli rape* : *Kohl,* cabbage (ult. < Lat. *caulis*) + Ital. *rape,* pl. of *rapa,* turnip (< Lat. *rāpa*).]

Koi·ne (koi-nā′, koi′nā′) *n.* **1.** A dialect of Greek that became the common language of the Hellenistic world, from which later stages of Greek are descended. **2. koine** A lingua franca. **3.** A regional dialect or language that becomes the standard language over a wider area, losing its most extreme local features. [< Gk. (*hē*) *koinē* (*dialektos*), (the) common (language), fem. of *koinos.* See **kom** in App.]

Ko·kand (kō-känd′) See **Qūqon.**

Ko·ko·mo (kō′kə-mō′) A city of central IN N of Indianapolis; founded in the 1840s. Pop. 46,113.

Ko·ko Nor (kō′kō′ nôr′, nōr′) See **Qinghai Hu.**

Ko·kosch·ka (kə-kôsh′kə), **Oskar** 1886–1980. Austrian expressionist painter noted for his portraits and landscapes.

kok-sa·ghyz (kŏk′sə-gēz′) *n.* A central Asian dandelion (*Taraxacum koksaghyz*) having roots that yield a form of rubber. [NLat., specific epithet < Tatar *kök-sagyz* : *kök,* root + *sagyz,* rubber.]

ko·la (kō′lə) *n.* Variant of **cola⁴.**

Ko·la Peninsula (kō′lə) A peninsula of NW Russia between the White Sea and the Barents Sea.

Kol·ha·pur (kō′lə-pōōr′) A city of SW India SSE of Mumbai (Bombay); once the center of an important Deccan state. Pop. 406,370.

ko·lin·sky (kə-lĭn′skē) *n., pl.* **-skies 1.** A northern Eurasian mink (*Mustela siberica*) having a dark brown coat with tawny markings. **2.** The fur of this animal. [Russ. *kolinskiĭ,* of Kola < *Kola,* Kola Peninsula.]

kol·khoz (kŏl-kôz′, kŭl-кнôs′) *n.* A Soviet collective farm. [Russ. < *kol(lektivnoe) khoz(yaĭstvo)* : *kollektivnoe,* neut. of *kollektivnyĭ,* collective + *khozyaĭstvo,* economy, household farm.]

Koll·witz (kōl′wĭts′, kôl′vĭts′), **Käthe** or **Kaethe** 1867–1945. German artist noted for her sculptures and prints.

Köln (kœln) See **Cologne.**

Kol Nid·re (kōl nĭd′rā, -rə, kôl nē-drä′) *n. Judaism* The opening prayer recited on the eve of Yom Kippur. [Aram. *kol nidrê,* all vows (opening words of the prayer) : *kol,* all + *nidrê,* pl. bound form of *nidrā,* vow (< *nədar,* to vow).]

Ko·ly·ma (kə-lē′mä, kō-lē-mä′) A river of NE Russia rising in the Kolyma Mts. and flowing c. 2,148 km (1,335 mi) to the East Siberian Sea.

Kolyma Mountains A range of NE Russia extending c. 1,126 km (700 mi) roughly parallel to the coast of Siberia.

Ko·man·dor·ski Islands (kŏm′ən-dôr′skē) also **Ko·man·dor·ski·ye Islands** (-skē-yĕ′) An island group of NE Russia in the Bering Sea E of the Kamchatka Peninsula.

Ko·ma·ti (kə-mä′tē) A river of SE Africa flowing c. 805 km (500 mi) to an inlet of the Indian Ocean.

Ko·mo·do dragon (kə-mō′dō) *n.* An Indonesian monitor lizard (*Varanus komodoensis*) that is the largest living lizard. [After *Komodo,* an island of south-central Indonesia.]

Kom·so·molsk (kŏm′sə-môlsk′) A city of SE Russia N of Vladivostok; settled in 1932. Pop. 314,110.

Kon·go (kŏng′gō) *n., pl.* **Kongo** or **-gos 1.** A member of a people living in west-central Africa along the lower Congo River. **2.** A Bantu language of the Kongo, a lingua franca in southern Republic of the Congo, western Democratic Republic of the Congo (formerly Zaire), and northern Angola.

Kö·nigs·berg (kā′nĭgz-bûrg′, kœ′nĭкнs-bĕrk′) See **Kaliningrad.**

Ko·no·ye (kə-nô′ē, kô′nô-yĕ′), **Prince Fumimaro** 1891–1946. Japanese political leader who as premier (1937–39 and 1940–41) formed an alliance with Germany and Italy (1941).

Kon·stanz (kôn′stänts′) also **Con·stance** (kŏn′stəns) A city of SW Germany on the Lake of Constance S of Stuttgart; thought to have been founded c. A.D. 300. Pop. 68,605.

Kon·ya also **Kon·ia** (kôn-yä′) A city of SW-central Turkey S of Ankara; a powerful Seljuk sultanate from the 11th to the 13th cent. Pop. 576,000.

koo·doo (kōō′dōō) *n.* Variant of **kudu.**

kook (kōōk) *n. Slang* A person regarded as strange, eccentric, or crazy. [Poss. < CUCKOO.]

kook·a·bur·ra (kōōk′ə-bûr′ə, -bŭr′ə) *n.* A large kingfisher (*Dacelo novaeguineae*) of southern and eastern Australia and having a call that resembles raucous laughter. [Wiradhuri (Aboriginal language of SE Australia) *gugubarra.*]

kook·y also **kook·ie** (kōō′kē) *adj.* **-i·er, -i·est** *Slang* Characteristic of a kook; strange or crazy. **—kook′i·ness** *n.*

Koo·te·nay River also **Koo·te·nai River** (kōōt′n-ā′) A river, c. 655 km (407 mi), flowing from SE British Columbia, Canada, through NW MT to N ID and again into British Columbia, where it widens to form **Kootenay Lake** before joining the Columbia R.

ko·pek (kō′pĕk) *n.* A coin equal to ¹/₁₀₀ of the Russian ruble. [Russ. *kopeĭka* < M Russ. *kopeĭka* < *kopie,* spear.]

kor (kôr, kōr) *n.* See **homer².** [Heb. *kôr* < Akkadian *kurru* < Sumerian *gur,* a unit of measurement.]

Kor. *abbr.* **1.** Korea **2.** Korean

Ko·ran or **Qur·'an** (kə-rän′, -răn′, kô-, kō-) *n.* The sacred text of Islam, considered by Muslims to contain the revelations of God to Muhammad. [Ar. *(al-)qur'ān,* (the) reading, recitation, Koran < *qara'a,* to read, recite.] **—Ko·ran′ic** *adj.*

Kor·do·fan·i·an (kôr′də-făn′ē-ən) *n.* A small group of related languages spoken in Sudan and forming part of the Niger-Kordofanian language family.

ko·re (kôr′ē, kōr′ē, kôr′ā, kōr′ā) *n., pl.* **kor·ai** (kôr′ī, kōr′ī) A sculpture representing a standing young woman clothed in long robes. [Gk. *korē,* young girl, kore. See **ker-²** in App.]

Ko·re·a (kə-rē′ə, kô-, kō-) A peninsula and former country of E Asia between the Yellow Sea and the Sea of Japan; site of an ancient civilization dating to the 12th cent. B.C. The peninsula was divided into North Korea and South Korea after the Korean War (1950–53).

Korea Bay An inlet of the Yellow Sea between NE China and W North Korea.

kohlrabi
Brassica oleracea var.
gongylodes

Komodo dragon
Varanus komodoensis

kookaburra
Dacelo novaeguineae

ă	pat	oi	boy
ā	pay	ou	out
âr	care	ōō	took
ä	father	ōō	boot
ĕ	pet	ŭ	cut
ē	be	ûr	urge
ĭ	pit	th	thin
ī	pie	th	this
îr	pier	hw	which
ŏ	pot	zh	vision
ō	toe	ə	about,
ô	paw		item

Stress marks:
′ (primary);
′ (secondary), as in
lexicon (lĕk′sĭ-kŏn′)

Ko·re·an (kə-rē′ən, kô-, kō-) *n.* **1.** A native or inhabitant of Korea. **2.** The language of the Koreans. ❖ *adj.* Of or relating to Korea or its people, language, or culture.

Korean War *n.* A conflict that lasted from 1950 to 1953 between North Korea, aided by China, and South Korea, aided by United Nations forces consisting primarily of United States troops.

Korea Strait A channel between SE South Korea and SW Japan connecting the East China Sea with the Sea of Japan.

Kó·rin·thos (kô′rĭn-thôs′) See **Corinth.**

Ko·ri·ya·ma (kôr′ē-ä′mə, -yä′mä) A city of N-central Honshu, Japan, N of Tokyo. Pop. 322,255.

Korn·berg (kôrn′bûrg′), **Arthur** b. 1918. Amer. biochemist who shared a 1959 Nobel Prize.

Ko·ror (kôr′ôr) The cap. of Palau on Koror I. in the W Pacific Ocean. Pop. 10,500.

Kor·sa·koff's syndrome (kôr′sə-kôfs′, -kŏfs′) *n.* A syndrome of severe mental impairment characterized by confusion and amnesia in which memory of recent events is esp. impaired. [After Sergei Sergeevich *Korsakoff* (1854–1900), Russian neurologist.]

Kort·rijk (kôrt′rĭk′) also **Cour·trai** (koor-trā′, kōor-) A city of W Belgium W of Brussels. Pop. 76,081.

ko·ru·na¹ (kôr′ə-nä′) *n.* See table at **currency.** [Czech < Lat. *corōna,* crown. See CROWN.]

ko·ru·na² (kôr′ə-nä′) *n.* See table at **currency.** [Slovak < Lat. *corōna,* crown. See CROWN.]

Kos also **Cos** (kŏs, kôs) An island of SE Greece in the N Dodecanese Is. at the entrance to the **Gulf of Kos,** an inlet of the Aegean Sea on the SW coast of Turkey.

Kos·ci·us·ko (kŏs′ē-ŭs′kō, kŏs′kē-), **Mount** A mountain of SE Australia rising to 2,231.4 m (7,316 ft).

Kos·ci·us·ko (kŏs′ē-ŭs′kō, kŏs′kē-, kôsh-chōōsh′kō), **Thaddeus** 1746–1817. Polish general and patriot who fought with the colonists in the American Revolution.

ko·sher (kō′shər) also **ka·sher** (kä′-) *adj.* **1.** *Judaism* **a.** Conforming to dietary laws; ritually pure: *kosher meat.* **b.** Selling or serving food prepared in accordance with dietary laws. **2.** *Slang* **a.** Legitimate; permissible. **b.** Genuine; authentic. ❖ *tr.v.* **-shered, -sher·ing, -shers** To make proper or ritually pure. [Yiddish < Ashkenazi Heb. *kóšer* < Heb. *kāšēr,* fitting, proper < *kāšēr,* to be fitting, to succeed.]

Ko·ši·ce (kô′shĭ-tsĕ) A city of E Slovakia NE of Budapest, Hungary; chartered 1241. Pop. 236,984.

Ko·so·vo (kô′sə-vō′, kō′-) A province of S Yugoslavia in the Serbian republic; autonomous after World War II, it was stripped of autonomy in 1990 by Serbia, which led to armed conflict with the ethnic Albanian majority. —**Ko′so·var′** (-vär′) *adj. & n.*

Kos·suth (kŏs′ōōth′, kô-shōōt′), **Lajos** 1802–94. Hungarian revolutionary leader who sought Hungary's independence from Austria and briefly led a provisional government (1849).

Kos·tro·ma (kŏs′trə-mä′) A city of NW Russia on the Volga R. NE of Moscow; founded 1152. Pop. 281,497.

Ko·sy·gin (kə-sē′gən, -gyĭn) **Aleksei Nikolayevich** 1904–80. Soviet premier (1964–80) who was often overshadowed by party secretary Leonid Brezhnev.

Ko·ta (kō′tə) A city of NW India SSW of Delhi. Pop. 537,371.

ko·to (kō′tō) *n., pl.* **-tos** A Japanese musical instrument having usu. 13 silk strings stretched over an oblong box. [J.]

Kot·ze·bue Sound (kŏt′sə-byōō′) An inlet of the Chukchi Sea in NW AK N of Seward Peninsula.

Kou·fax (kō′făks′), **Sanford ("Sandy")** b. 1935. Amer. baseball pitcher for the Dodgers (1955–66) who struck out 2,396 batters.

kou·miss (kōō-mĭs′, kōō′mĭs) *n.* Variant of **kumiss.**

kou·ros (kōōr′ŏs) *n., pl.* **kou·roi** (kōōr′oi) A sculpture representing a standing nude young man. [Gk., boy. See ker-² in App.]

Kous·se·vitz·ky (kōō′sə-vĭt′skē), **Sergei Aleksandrovich** 1874–1951. Russian-born Amer. conductor of the Boston Symphony Orchestra (1924–49).

Kow·loon (kou′lōōn′) A city of SE China on **Kowloon Peninsula** opposite Hong Kong I.; ceded to the British in 1860 and transferred back to China in 1997. Pop. 799,123.

kow·tow (kou-tou′, kou′tou′) *intr.v.* **-towed, -tow·ing, -tows** **1.** To kneel and touch the forehead to the ground in expression of deep respect, worship, or submission, as formerly done in China. **2.** To show servile deference. ❖ *n.* **1.** The act of kneeling and touching the forehead to the ground. **2.** An obsequious act. [< Chin. (Mandarin) *kòu tóu,* a kowtow : *kòu,* to knock + *tóu,* head.]

Koy·u·kuk (kī′ə-kŭk′) A river of N AK flowing c. 805 km (500 mi) from the Brooks Range to the Yukon R.

Ko·zhi·kode (kō′zhĭ-kōd′) See **Calicut.**

KP *abbr.* kitchen police

kph *abbr.* kilometers per hour

Kr The symbol for the element **krypton.**

Kra (krä), **Isthmus of** A narrow strip of land linking the Malay Peninsula with the Asian mainland.

kraal (krôl, kräl) *n. South African* **1.** A rural village, typically consisting of huts surrounded by a stockade. **2.** An enclosure for livestock. [Afr. < Port. *curral,* pen, perh. < VLat. **currāle,* enclosure for carts. See CORRAL.]

Krafft-E·bing (kräft′ĕb′ĭng, kräft′ä′bĭng), Baron **Richard von** 1840–1902. German physician and neurologist particularly

krater
Hercules and the
Argonauts,
c. fourth century B.C.

Kufic
detail from an 11th-century
copy of the Koran

known for his studies of sexual deviance.

kraft (kräft) *n.* A tough, usu. brown paper made from wood pulp and used chiefly for bags and wrapping paper. [Short for Swed. *kraftpapper* : *kraft,* strength (< OSwed. *krapt*) + *papper,* paper.]

krait (krīt) *n.* Any of several highly venomous snakes of the genus *Bungarus* of southeast Asia and adjacent islands, having a generally black body with brightly colored bands. [Hindi *karait,* perh. ult. < Skt. *kāla-,* black. See KALI.]

Kra·ka·tau (kräk′ə-tou′, krä′kə-) or **Kra·ka·to·a** (-tō′ə) A volcanic island of Indonesia between Sumatra and Java; blown apart by a violent eruption in Aug. 1883.

kra·ken (krä′kən) *n.* A huge sea monster in Norwegian legend. [Norw. dialectal : *krake,* kraken + Norw. *-n,* the.]

Kra·ków also **Crac·ow** (krä′kou, krä′kou, -kōōf) A city of S Poland on the Vistula R. SSE of Warsaw; national cap. from 1305 to 1595. Pop. 750,588.

Kras·ner (kräz′nər), **Lee** 1908–84. Amer. artist who was a founder of the New York School of abstract expressionism.

Kras·no·dar (kräs′nə-där′, krə-snə-där′) A city of SW Russia S of Rostov; founded 1794. Pop. 635,856.

Kras·no·yarsk (kräs′nō-yärsk′, krə-snə-) A city of S-central Russia on the upper Yenisey R. E of Novosibirsk; founded as a Cossack fortress in 1628. Pop. 916,552.

kra·ter or **cra·ter** (krā′tər) *n.* A wide two-handled bowl used in ancient Greece and Rome. [Gk. *krātēr.*]

K ration *n.* An emergency field ration for US armed forces in World War II, consisting of a single packaged meal. [After Ancel Benjamin *Keys* (born 1904), American physiologist.]

kraut (krout) *n.* **1.** Sauerkraut. **2.** often **Kraut** *Offensive Slang* Used as a disparaging term for a German. [Ger. See SAUERKRAUT.]

Krebs (krĕbz, krĕps), Sir **Hans Adolf** 1900–81. German-born British biochemist who shared a 1953 Nobel Prize.

Krebs cycle (krĕbz) *n.* A series of enzymatic reactions in aerobic organisms involving oxidation of acetyl units and producing high-energy phosphate compounds, which are the main source of cellular energy. [After Sir Hans Adolf KREBS.]

Kre·feld (krā′fĕld′, -fĕlt′) A city of W-central Germany on the Rhine R. NNW of Cologne; chartered 1373. Pop. 249,565.

Krei·sler (krī′slər), **Fritz** 1875–1962. Austrian-born Amer. composer of the operetta *Apple Blossoms* (1919).

Kre·men·chuk (krĕm′ən-chōōk′) or **Kre·men·chug** (-chōōg′, -chōōk′) A city of E-central Ukraine on the Dnieper R. SE of Kiev; founded as a fortress in 1571. Pop. 244,500.

Krem·lin (krĕm′lĭn) *n.* **1.** The citadel of Moscow, housing government offices. **2.** The government of Russia and formerly that of the Soviet Union. **3. kremlin** The citadel of a Russian city. [Obsolete Ger. *Kremelin* < ORuss. **kremlĭnŭ,* separate < *kremlĭ,* a separate place, citadel.]

Krem·lin·ol·o·gy (krĕm′lə-nŏl′ə-jē) *n.* The study of the policies of the Soviet government. —**Krem′lin·ol·o·gist** *n.*

krep·lach (krĕp′läKH, -läKHn) *pl.n.* Small pockets of noodle dough filled with ground meat or cheese, usu. boiled and served in soups. [Yiddish *kreplech,* pl. of *krepel* < Ger. dialectal *Kräppel,* fried pastry, var. of Ger. *Krapfen* < MHGer. *krapfe* < OHGer. *krāpfo,* hook (< their hooklike shape).]

kreu·zer or **kreut·zer** (kroit′sər) *n.* Any of several coins of low value formerly used in Austria and Germany. [Ger. < MHGer. *kriuzer* < *kriuze,* cross (orig. stamped with a cross) < OHGer. *krūzi* < Lat. *crux, cruc-.*]

krewe (krōō) *n. New Orleans* Any of several groups whose members organize and participate in the annual Mardi Gras carnival. See Regional Note at **beignet.** [Alteration of CREW¹.]

REGIONAL NOTE In order to organize and stage the enormous Mardi Gras carnival every year, many New Orleans families have belonged for generations to *krewes,* groups that create elaborate costumes and floats for the many Mardi Gras parades in the two weeks leading up to "Fat Tuesday." Not only do the krewes participate in the parades, but, as leaders of New Orleans society, they also hold balls and other elaborate events during the carnival season, which lasts from Christmas up to Mardi Gras itself. *Krewe* is only an imitation of an old-fashioned spelling of *crew* in its standard meaning, but the word, thanks to its association with Mardi Gras and New Orleans high society, has taken on some of the mystique of the carnival.

Kriem·hild (krēm′hĭld′, -hĭlt′) also **Kriem·hil·de** (krēm-hĭl′də) *n.* The wife of Siegfried and sister of Gunther in the *Nibelungenlied.*

krill (krĭl) *n., pl.* **krill** The collection of small marine crustaceans of the order Euphausiacea that are the principal food of baleen whales. [Norw. *kril,* young fry of fish.]

krim·mer (krĭm′ər) *n.* Gray curly fur made from the pelts of lambs of the Crimean region. [Ger. < *Krim,* Crimea.]

kris also **creese** (krēs) *n.* A Malayan dagger with a wavy double-edged blade. [Malay *kris.*]

Krish·na¹ (krĭsh′nə) *n. Hinduism* The eighth and principal avatar of Vishnu, often depicted as a handsome young man playing a flute. [Skt. *Kṛṣṇaḥ* < *kṛṣṇa-,* black.] —**Krish′na·ism** *n.*

Krish·na² (krĭsh′nə) or **Kistna** (kĭst′nə) A river of S India rising in the Western Ghats and flowing c. 1,287 km (800 mi) to the Bay of Bengal.

Kriss Krin·gle (krĭs' krĭng'gəl) *n.* Santa Claus. [Alteration of Ger. dialectal *Christkindl*, Christ present : Ger. *Christ*, Christ (ult. < Lat. *Chrīstus*; see CHRIST) + Ger. dialectal *Kindl* (dim. of *Kind*, child, ult. < OHGer. *kind*; see **gena-** in App.).]

Kris·tall·nacht (krĭs'təl-näkt', -täl-näкнт') *n.* The night of November 9, 1938, on which the Nazis coordinated an attack on Jewish people and their property in Germany and German-controlled lands. [Ger., night of (broken) glass : *Kristall*, crystal (< MHGer. < OHGer. *cristalla* < Lat. *crystallus, crystallum*; see CRYSTAL) + *Nacht*, night (< MHGer. *naht* < OHGer.; see **nekʷ-t-** in App.).]

Kri·voi Rog (krĭ-voi' rôg', rôk') See **Kryvyy Rih**.

kro·na¹ (krō'nə) *n., pl.* **-nur** (-nər) See table at **currency**. [Icel. *króna* < ON *krūna* < MLGer. *krūne, krōne*, ult. < Lat. *corōna*, wreath, crown (< the crown printed on the coin). See CROWN.]

kro·na² (krō'nə) *n., pl.* **-nor** (-nôr', -nər) See table at **currency**. [Swed. < OSwed. *krūna* < MLGer. *krūne, krōne*.]

kro·ne¹ (krō'nə) *n., pl.* **-ner** (-nər) See table at **currency**. [Norw. < ON *krūna*. See KRONA¹.]

kro·ne² (krō'nə) *n., pl.* **-ner** (-nər) See table at **currency**. [Dan. *krone* < ON *krūna*. See KRONA¹.]

kroon (krōn) *n., pl.* **kroon·i** (krō'nē) See table at **currency**. [Estonian < Ger. *Krone* < MHGer. *krōn, krōne* < OHGer. *korōna* < Lat. *corōna*, crown (< the crown printed on the coin). See CROWN.]

Kro·pot·kin (krə-pŏt'kĭn, krō-), Prince **Pyotr Alekseyevich** 1842–1921. Russian anarchist and political philosopher who advocated cooperation as the means of bettering the human condition.

Kro·to (krō'tō'), Sir **Harold Walter** b. 1939. British chemist who shared a 1996 Nobel Prize for discovering fullerenes.

Kru (krōō) *n.* A group of Niger-Congo languages spoken primarily in Liberia and Côte d'Ivoire.

Kru·ger (krōō'gər, krü'-), **Stephanus Johannes Paulus** Known as "Oom Paul." 1825–1904. South African politician who was a founder (1852) and president (1883–1900) of Transvaal.

Kru·ger·rand (krōō'gə-rănd', -ränd') *n.* A one-ounce gold coin of South Africa. [Afr. : after Stephanus Johannes Paulus KRUGER + *rand*, rand; see RAND.]

krum·kake (krōōm'kä'kə, krŭm'kāk') *n. Upper Midwest* A large thin cookie made from batter poured into an embossed mold with hinged plates. [Norw. : *krum*, curved, crooked (< MLGer. < OHGer. *krump*) + *kake*, cake (< ON *kaka*).]

krumm·horn or **crum·horn** (krŭm'hôrn') *n.* A wind instrument of the Renaissance with a curving tube and a double reed. [Ger. : *krumm*, crooked (< MHGer. *krump, krum* < OHGer. *krump*) + *Horn*, horn; see ALPENHORN.]

Krung Thep (grōōng tĕp') See **Bangkok**.

Krupp (krōōp, krŭp) German family of steel and munitions manufacturers, including **Friedrich** (1787–1826), who founded the Krupp Works in Essen (1811). His great-granddaughter **Bertha** (1886–1957) and her husband **Gustav Krupp von Bohlen und Halbach** (1870–1950) were instrumental in the secret rearming of Germany after World War I.

Krup·ska·ya (krōōp'skə-yə), **Nadezhda Konstantinovna** 1869–1939. Russian revolutionary and wife of Vladimir Lenin who wrote *Memories of Lenin* (1930).

kryp·ton (krĭp'tŏn') *n. Symbol* **Kr** A largely inert gaseous element used in gas fluorescent lamps. Atomic number 36; atomic weight 83.80; melting point −156.6°C; boiling point −152.30°C; density 3.73 grams per liter (0°C). See table at **element**. [Gk. *krupton*, neut. of *kruptos*, hidden (< its rarity) < *kruptein*, to hide.]

Kry·vyy Rih (krĭ-vī' rīkн') or **Kri·voi Rog** (-voi' rōg', rôk') A city of S-central Ukraine NE of Odessa. Pop. 729,400.

KS *abbr.* **1.** Kansas **2.** Kaposi's sarcoma

Ksha·tri·ya (kə-shăt'rē-ə, -chät'-) *n.* A member of the second highest of the four castes of traditional Indian society, responsible for upholding justice and social harmony, and including people in governing and military positions. [Skt. *kṣatriyaḥ* < *kṣatram*, rule, power.]

kt *abbr.* kiloton

Kt *abbr.* knight (chess)

kt. *abbr.* **1.** karat **2.** *Nautical* knot

Kt. *abbr.* knight (title)

Kua·la Lum·pur (kwä'lə lōōm-pōōr') The cap. of Malaysia, on the SW Malay Peninsula NW of Singapore; founded by tin miners in 1857. Pop. 1,145,075.

Ku·ban (kōō-bän', -bän') A river of SW Russia flowing c. 917 km (570 mi) to the Sea of Azov.

Ku·blai Khan (kōō'blī kän') also **Ku·bla Khan** (-blə) 1215–94. Mongol emperor (1260–94) and founder of the Mongol dynasty in China.

ku·chen (kōō'kən, -кнən) *n.* A coffeecake leavened with yeast, often containing fruit and nuts. [Ger. < MHGer. *kuoche*, cake < OHGer. *kuocho*.]

ku·do (kōō'dō', kyōō'-) *n., pl.* **-dos** (-dōz') *Usage Problem* A praising remark; an accolade or compliment. See Usage Note at **kudos**. [Back-formation < KUDOS.]

ku·dos (kōō'dōz', -dōs', -dŏs', kyōō'-) *n.* Acclaim or praise for exceptional achievement. [Gk. *kūdos*, magical glory.]

ku·du also **koo·doo** (kōō'dōō) *n., pl.* **kudu** or **-dus** also **koodoo** or **-doos** Either of two large African antelopes (*Tragelaphus strepsiceros* or *T. imberbis*) having a brownish coat with narrow white vertical stripes and long, spirally curved horns in the male. [Afr. *koedoe* < Nguni (Xhosa) *i-quda, i-qudu*, perh. < Nama ≠*kudu*.]

kud·zu (kōōd'zōō) *n.* An eastern Asian vine (*Pueraria lobata*) having compound leaves and reddish-purple flowers. It is a widespread weed in the southeast US. [J. *kuzu*.]

Ku·fic also **Cu·fic** (kōō'fĭk, kyōō'-) *adj.* Relating to or being an angular form of the Arabic alphabet used in making fine copies of the Koran. [After Al-*Kūfa*, a town of south-central Iraq.]

ku·gel (kōō'gəl) *n.* A baked pudding of noodles or potatoes, eggs, and seasonings, traditionally eaten by Jews on the Sabbath. [Yiddish *kugel*, ball (< its puffed-up shape) < MHGer.]

Kuhn (kōōn), **Margaret ("Maggie")** 1905–95. Amer. activist who founded (1970) the Gray Panthers, an organization dedicated to ending age discrimination.

Kuhn, Richard 1900–67. Austrian chemist who won a 1938 Nobel Prize.

Kui·by·shev (kwē'bə-shĕf', -shĕv', kōō'ē-bə-shĭf') See **Samara**.

Ku Klux Klan (kōō' klŭks klăn', kyōō') *n.* **1.** A secret society organized in the South after the Civil War to reassert white supremacy by terrorism. **2.** A secret fraternal organization of similar intent founded in Georgia in 1915. [Perh. alteration of Gk. *kuklos*, circle; see CYCLE + alteration of CLAN.] —**Ku Klux'er** (kōō klŭk'sər, kyōō) *n.*

ku·lak (kōō-läk', kōō'läk', -lăk') *n.* A relatively prosperous landed peasant in czarist Russia, characterized by the Communists during the October Revolution as an exploiter. [Russ., fist, kulak, prob. of Turkic orig.]

Kul·tur (kōōl-tōōr') *n.* **1.** Culture; civilization. **2.** German culture and civilization as idealized during the Hohenzollern and Nazi regimes. [Ger. < Lat. *cultūra*, cultivation, care. See CULTURE.]

Kul·tur·kampf (kōōl-tōōr'kämpf') *n.* **1.** The struggle (1871–83) between the Roman Catholic Church and the German government under Bismarck for control over school and ecclesiastical appointments and civil marriage. **2.** A conflict between secular and religious authorities. [Ger. : *Kultur*, Kultur; see KULTUR + *Kampf*, struggle (< MHGer. < OHGer. *kamph*, prob. ult. < Lat. *campus*, field).]

Ku·ma·mo·to (kōō'mə-mō'tō) A city of W Kyushu, Japan, E of Nagasaki. Pop. 639,699.

Ku·ma·si (kōō-mä'sē) A city of S-central Ghana NW of Accra; founded c. 1700. Pop. 348,880.

ku·miss also **kou·miss** (kōō-mĭs', kōō'mĭs) *n.* The fermented milk of a mare or camel, used as a beverage. [Russ. *kumys* < ORuss. *komyzŭ* < O Turkic *qïmïz* < *qammaq*, to shake.]

küm·mel (kĭm'əl, kü'məl) *n.* A colorless liqueur flavored chiefly with caraway seeds. [Ger. < MHGer. *kümel*, cumin seed, ult. < Lat. *cumīnum*. See CUMIN.]

kum·quat also **cum·quat** (kŭm'kwŏt') *n.* **1.** Any of several trees or shrubs of the genus *Fortunella*, having small, edible orangelike fruit. **2.** The fruit of these plants. [Chin. (Cantonese) *kamkwat*, equivalent to Chin. (Mandarin) *xīn*, gold + Chin. (Mandarin) *jú*, orange, tangerine.]

Kun (kōōn), **Béla** 1886–1939? Hungarian politician who founded the Hungarian Communist Party (1918) and organized the revolution in Budapest (1919).

ku·na (kōō'nə) *n., pl.* **kuna** See table at **currency**. [Serbo-Croatian, marten, kuna (< the earlier use of marten skins for payment).]

Ku·na also **Cu·na** (kōō'nə) *n., pl.* **Kuna** or **Ku·nas** also **Cuna** or **Cu·nas 1.** A member of a Central American Indian people formerly inhabiting central Panama, now living primarily on islands in the Gulf of San Blas and adjacent coastal areas of northeast Panama. **2.** The Chibchan language of the Kuna.

Kun·der·a (kōōn-dĕr'ə, kōōn'dĕ-rä), **Milan** b. 1929. Czechborn writer best known for his novels, including *The Book of Laughter and Forgetting* (1979).

Ku·ne·ne (kōō-nā'nə) See **Cunene**.

!Kung (kōōng) *n.* **1.** A member of a San people of E Namibia and W Botswana. **2.** The Khoisan language of the !Kung.

kung fu (kŭng' fōō', kōōng', gōōng') *n.* Any of various Chinese martial arts, esp. those forms in which sharp blows and kicks are applied to pressure points. [Chin. (Mandarin) *gōngfu*, skill, art : *gōng*, work, merit + *fū*, man, laborer.]

Kun·lun (kōōn'lōōn') A mountain system of W China extending E from the Karakoram Range along the N edge of the Xizang (Tibet) plateau and rising to 7,729 m (25,341 ft).

Margaret Kuhn

kumquat
Fortunella margarita

ă pat	oi boy
ā pay	ou out
âr care	ōō took
ä father	ōō boot
ĕ pet	ŭ cut
ē be	ûr urge
ĭ pit	th thin
ī pie	th this
îr pier	hw which
ŏ pot	zh vision
ō toe	ə about,
ô paw	item

Stress marks:
' (primary);
' (secondary), as in
lexicon (lĕk'sĭ-kŏn')

Kuwait

kylix
c. sixth century B.C.

Kyrgyzstan

Kun·ming (kŏŏn'mĭng') A city of S China SW of Chongqing; cap. of Yunnan province. Pop. 1,611,969.

kunz·ite (kŏŏnt'sīt') *n.* A lilac-colored spodumene used as a gemstone. [After George Frederick *Kunz* (1856–1932), American gemologist.]

Kuo·yu (kwô'yōō') *n.* Variant of **Guoyu.**

Ku·ra (kŏŏ-rä') A river of NE Turkey and S Azerbaijan flowing c. 1,514 km (941 mi) to the Caspian Sea S of Baku.

Ku·ra·shi·ki (kŏŏ-rä'shē-kē) A city of W Honshu, Japan, a suburb of Okayama on the Inland Sea. Pop. 418,450.

Kurd (kûrd, kŏŏrd) *n.* A member of a pastoral and agricultural people inhabiting the transnational region of Kurdistan.

Kurd·ish (kûr'dĭsh, kŏŏr'-) *adj.* Of or relating to the Kurds or their language or culture. ❖ *n.* Their Iranian language.

Kurd·i·stan (kûr'dĭ-stăn', kŏŏr'dĭ-stän') An extensive plateau region of SW Asia divided among SE Turkey, NE Iraq, and NW Iran, with smaller sections in Syria and Armenia.

kur·gan (kŏŏr-gän', -gän') *n.* **1.** A type of tumulus or barrow characteristic of a culture located on the steppes of southern Russia about 5000 B.C. **2. Kurgan a.** The culture that produced these tumuli or barrows. **b.** A member of the people or peoples sharing this culture. [Russ., fortified place, grave mound < O Turkic *kurghan,* fortified place.]

Kur·gan (kŏŏr-gän') A city of W Russia ESE of Sverdlovsk; founded in the 17th cent. Pop. 360,205.

Ku·ril Islands also **Ku·rile Islands** (kŏŏr'ĭl, kŏŏ-rēl') An island chain of E Russia extending c. 1,207 km (750 mi) in the Pacific Ocean between Kamchatka Peninsula and N Hokkaido, Japan. —**Ku·ril'i·an** *adj. & n.*

Kur·land (kŏŏr'lənd) See **Courland.**

Ku·ro·sa·wa (kŏŏr'ə-sä'wə, kŏŏ'rô-sä'wä), **Akira** 1910–98. Japanese filmmaker whose works include *Rashomon* (1950) and *Ran* (1985).

Ku·ro·shi·o Current (kŏŏ-rō'shē-ō') *n.* See **Japan Current.**

kur·ra·jong (kûr'ə-jông', -jŏng', kŭr'-) *n.* An Australian evergreen tree (*Brachychiton populneus*) having palmately lobed leaves, yellowish or reddish flowers, and long-stalked follicles. [Dharuk (Aboriginal language of SE Australia) *garrajuŋ,* fishing line made from the tree's bark.]

Kursk (kŏŏrsk) A city of W Russia SSW of Moscow; destroyed by the Mongols in 1240 and rebuilt in 1586. Pop. 433,991.

kur·to·sis (kər-tō'sĭs) *n., pl.* **-ses** (-sēz') The general form or a quantity indicative of the general form of a statistical frequency curve near the mean of the distribution. [Gk. *kurtōsis,* curvature < *kurtos,* convex.]

ku·ru (kŏŏr'ōō) *n.* A transmissible spongiform encephalopathy found in certain peoples of New Guinea that is often attributed to prion infection and thought to be transmitted by cannibalistic ritual practices. [Fore (language of E Papua New Guinea).]

Kush (kŭsh, kŏŏsh) See **Cush²**.

Kush·ner (kŏŏsh'nər), **Tony** Born 1956. American playwright known esp. for his trilogy *Angels in America: A Gay Fantasia on National Themes* (1992).

Kus·ko·kwim (kŭs'kə-kwĭm') A river of SW AK flowing c. 965 km (600 mi) to **Kuskokwim Bay,** an inlet of the Bering Sea.

Ku·ta·i·si (kŏŏ-tī'sē, kŏŏ'tə-yĕf'syī) A city of W Georgia WNW of Tbilisi; cap. of ancient Colchis. Pop. 236,000.

Kutch (kŭch) See **Rann of Kutch.**

Kutch, Gulf of An inlet of the Arabian Sea in W India adjoining the Rann of Kutch.

Ku·te·nai (kŏŏt'n-ā', -n-ē') *n., pl.* **Kutenai** or **-nais 1.** A member of a Native American people inhabiting parts of southeast British Columbia, northeast Washington, and northern Idaho. **2.** The language of the Kutenai.

Ku·tu·zov (kŏŏ-tōō'zôf, -zəf), **Mikhail Ilarionovich.** Prince of Smolensk. 1745–1813. Russian field marshal who commanded (1805–12) the Russian opposition to Napoleon.

Ku·wait (kŏŏ-wāt') **1.** A country of the NE Arabian Peninsula at the head of the Persian Gulf; a British protectorate from 1897 to 1961 and briefly annexed by Iraq (1990–91). Cap. Kuwait. Pop. 1,620,000. **2.** The cap. of Kuwait, in the E-central part on the Persian Gulf. Pop. 151,060. —**Ku·wait'i** (-wä'tē) *adj. & n.*

Kuz·nets (kŏŏz'nĕts', kŏŏz'nĭts), **Simon** 1901–85. Russian-born Amer. economist who won a 1971 Nobel Prize.

Kuz·netsk Basin (kŏŏz-nĕtsk', -nyĕtsk') A coal-producing region of S-central Russia.

kV or **kv** *abbr.* kilovolt

kvass (kväs) *n.* A Russian fermented beverage similar to beer, made from rye or barley. [Russ. *kvas* < ORuss. *kvasŭ.*]

kvetch (kvĕch) *Slang intr.v.* **kvetched, kvetch·ing, kvetch·es** To complain persistently and whiningly. ❖ *n.* **1.** A chronic whining complainer. **2.** A nagging complaint. [Yiddish *kvetshn* < MHGer. *quetzen, quetschen,* to squeeze.]

kW *abbr.* kilowatt

Kwa (kwä) *n.* Any of several West African languages belonging to the South Central Niger-Congo language family, including Ewe. [< Kwa -*kwa,* people.]

kwa·cha (kwä'chə) *n., pl.* **kwacha** See table at **currency.** [Bemba and Chewa, dawn : *kw-,* infinitive pref. + *-acha,* to dawn.]

Kwa·ja·lein (kwä'jə-lən, -län') An atoll in the Marshall Is. of the W Pacific Ocean; used as a Japanese air and naval base during World War II.

Kwa·ki·u·tl (kwä'kē-ōōt'l) *n., pl.* **Kwakiutl** or **-tls 1.** A member of a Native American people inhabiting parts of coastal British Columbia and northern Vancouver Island. **2.** The Wakashan language of the Kwakiutl.

Kwan·do (kwän'dō) See **Cuando.**

Kwang·chow (kwäng'chō') See **Guangzhou.**

Kwang·ju (kwäng'jōō', gwäng'-) A city of SW South Korea SSE of Seoul. Pop. 1,214,347.

Kwang·si Chuang (kwäng'sē' chwäng') See **Guangxi Zhuangzu.**

Kwang·tung (kwäng'tōōng', gwäng'dōōng') See **Guangdong.**

kwan·za (kwän'zə) *n., pl.* **kwanza** or **-zas** See table at **currency.** [Of Bantu orig.]

Kwanza See **Cuanza.**

Kwan·zaa also **Kwan·za** (kwän'zə) *n.* An African-American cultural festival, celebrated from December 26 to January 1. [Poss. < Swahili *kwanzaa,* first fruit of the harvest < *kwanza,* first.]

kwa·shi·or·kor (kwä'shē-ôr'kôr') *n.* Severe protein malnutrition, esp. in children, marked by anemia, edema, potbelly, skin depigmentation, and hair loss or change in hair color. [Ga (Niger-Congo language of Ghana) *kwashiɔkɔ.*]

Kwaś·niew·ski (kväsh-nyĕf'skē), **Aleksander** b. 1954. Polish journalist and politician who was elected president in 1995.

Kwei·chow (kwā'chō') See **Guizhou.**

Kwei·lin (kwä'lĭn') See **Guilin.**

Kwei·yang (kwā'yäng') See **Guiyang.**

kWh or **kW-hr** *abbr.* kilowatt-hour

KY or **Ky.** *abbr.* Kentucky

ky·ack (kī'ăk') *n.* A packsack that hangs on either side of a packsaddle. [Prob. < KAYAK.]

ky·a·nite (kī'ə-nīt') also **cy·a·nite** (sī'ə-) *n.* A bluish-green to colorless mineral, Al_2SiO_5, used as a refractory. [Gk. *kuanos,* dark blue enamel + −ITE¹.]

kyat (chät) *n.* See table at **currency.** [Burmese *ca².*]

Kyd or **Kid** (kĭd), **Thomas** 1558–94. English dramatist who wrote *The Spanish Tragedy* (c. 1584).

ky·lix (kī'lĭks, kĭl'ĭks) *n., pl.* **ky·li·kes** (kī'lĭ-kēz', kĭl'ĭ-) A shallow stemmed two-handled drinking cup of ancient Greece. [Gk. *kulix.*]

ky·mo·gram (kī'mə-grăm') *n.* A graph or record made by a kymograph. [Gk. *kūma,* something swollen; see CYMA + −GRAM.]

ky·mo·graph (kī'mə-grăf') *n.* An instrument for recording variations in pressure or tension by means of a pen or stylus that marks a rotating drum. [Gk. *kūma,* something swollen; see CYMA + −GRAPH.] —**ky'mo·graph'ic** *adj.*

Kyo·ga (kī-ō'gə), **Lake** See Lake **Kioga.**

Kyo·to (kē-ō'tō, kyō'-) A city of W-central Honshu, Japan, NNE of Osaka; founded in the 8th cent. and former cap. of Japan (794–1869). Pop. 1,452,240.

ky·pho·sis (kī-fō'sĭs) *n.* Abnormal rearward curvature of the spine, resulting in protuberance of the upper back; hunchback. [Gk. *kūphōsis* < *kūphos,* bent.] —**ky·phot'ic** (-fŏt'ĭk) *adj.*

Kyr·gyz or **Kir·ghiz** or **Kir·giz** (kĭr-gēz') *n., pl.* **Kyrgyz** or **-gyz·es** or **Kirghiz** or **-ghiz·es** or **Kirgiz** or **-giz·es 1.** A member of a traditionally nomadic people living principally in Kyrgyzstan. **2.** The Turkic language of the Kyrgyz.

Kyr·gyz·stan (kĭr'gē-stän', kîr'gē-stän') Formerly **Kir·ghi·zia** (kĭr-gē'zhə, -zhē-ə, zē-ə) A region and republic of W-central Asia bordering on NW China. Probably inhabited before the 13th cent. by a Turkic-speaking Mongolian people, it was a constituent republic of the USSR from 1936–91. Cap. Bishkek. Pop. 3,967,000.

Kyr·i·e (kĭr'ē-ā') *n.* **1.** A brief petition and response used in various Christian liturgies, beginning with or composed of the words "Lord, have mercy." **2.** A musical setting for this prayer. [LLat. *Kyrie eleison* < Gk. *Kūrie eleēson,* Lord, have mercy : *Kūrie,* vocative of *kūrios,* lord, master + *eleēson,* aorist imper. of *elein,* to show mercy (< *eleos,* mercy).]

Kyrie e·le·i·son (ĭ-lā'ĭ-sŏn', -sən) *n.* The Kyrie. [LLat. *Kyrie eleison.* See KYRIE.]

Kyu·shu (kē-ōō'shōō, kyōō'-) An island of SW Japan on the East China Sea and the Pacific Ocean.

Ky·yiv (kē'ĕw) See **Kiev.**

Ky·zyl Kum (kĭ-zĭl' kōōm') A desert of N-central Uzbekistan and S-central Kazakhstan SE of the Aral Sea between the Amu Darya and the Syr Darya.

Ll

l¹ or **L** (ĕl) *n.*, *pl.* **l's** or **L's** also **ls** or **Ls** **1.** The 12th letter of the modern English alphabet. **2.** Any of the speech sounds represented by the letter *l.* **3.** The 12th in a series. **4.** Something shaped like the letter L.

l² *abbr.* **1.** length **2.** liter

L¹ also **l** The symbol for the Roman numeral 50.

L² *abbr.* **1.** lambert **2.** large **3.** left **4.** low

l. *abbr.* **1.** line **2.** lira

L. *abbr.* **1.** lake **2.** Latin

la¹ (lä) *n. Music* The sixth tone of the diatonic scale in solfeggio. [ME < Med.Lat. See GAMUT.]

la² (lä) *interj.* Used to express emphasis or indicate surprise.

La The symbol for the element **lanthanum.**

LA *abbr.* **1.** Latin America **2.** Legislative Assembly **3.** local agent **4.** Los Angeles **5.** also **La.** Louisiana

laa•ger (lä′gər) *n.* A defensive encampment encircled by armored vehicles or wagons. ❖ *intr.v.* **-gered, -ger•ing, -gers** To camp in a defensive encirclement. [Alteration of obsolete Afr. *lager*, prob. < Ger. *Lager*, camp, lair. See LAGER.]

lab (lăb) *n.* A laboratory.

Lab. *abbr.* Labrador

lab•a•rum (lăb′ər-əm) *n.*, *pl.* **-a•ra** (-ər-ə) **1.** An ecclesiastical banner, esp. one carried in processions. **2.** The banner adopted by Constantine I after his conversion to Christianity. [LLat., prob. < alteration of Gk. *labrāton*, laurel-leaf standard < Lat. *laureātum*, neut. of *laureātus*, adorned with laurel. See LAUREATE.]

lab•da•num (lăb′də-nəm) also **lad•a•num** (lăd′n-əm) *n.* A resin of certain Old World plants of the genus *Cistus*, yielding a fragrant essential oil used in flavorings and perfumes. [ME < Med.Lat. *lapdanum, labdanum*, alteration of Lat. *lādanum* < Gk. *lēdanon, lādanon* < *lēdon*, *lādon*, rockrose, of Semitic orig.; akin to Akkadian *ladinnu, laduru*, an aromatic.]

la•bel (lā′bəl) *n.* **1.** An item used to identify something or someone, as a small piece of paper or cloth attached to an article to designate its origin, owner, contents, use, or destination. **2.** A descriptive term; an epithet. **3.** A distinctive name or trademark identifying a product or manufacturer, esp. a recording company. **4.** *Architecture* A molding over a door or window; a dripstone. **5.** *Heraldry* A figure in a field consisting of a narrow horizontal bar with several pendants. **6.** *Chemistry* See **tracer** 4. ❖ *tr.v.* **-beled, -bel•ing, -bels** or **-belled, -bel′ling, -bels** **1.** To attach a label to. **2.** To identify or designate with a label; describe or classify. **3.** *Chemistry* To add a tracer to (a compound). [ME, ornamental strip of cloth < OFr., prob. of Gmc. orig.] **—la′bel•er, la′bel•ler** *n.*

la•bel•lum (lə-bĕl′əm) *n.*, *pl.* **-bel•la** (-bĕl′ə) **1.** The often enlarged petal of an orchid flower. **2.** A liplike part, as certain insect proboscis tips, used for lapping up liquids. [Lat., dim. of *labrum*, lip.] **—la•bel′late** (-īt) *adj.*

la•bi•a (lā′bē-ə) *n.* Plural of **labium.**

la•bi•al (lā′bē-əl) *adj.* **1.** Of or relating to the lips or labia. **2.** *Linguistics* Articulated mainly by closing or partly closing the lips, as the sounds (b), (m), or (w). ❖ *n.* **1.** *Linguistics* A labial consonant. **2.** *Music* See **flue¹** 2a. [Med.Lat. *labiālis* < Lat. *labium*, lip.] **—la′bi•al•ly** *adv.*

la•bi•al•ize (lā′bē-ə-līz′) *tr.v.* **-ized, -iz•ing, -iz•es** To round (a speech sound); make labial. **—la′bi•al•i•za′tion** (-lĭ-zā′shən) *n.*

labia ma•jo•ra (mə-jôr′ə, -jōr′ə) *pl.n.* The two outer rounded folds of adipose tissue on either side of the vaginal opening that form the external lateral boundaries of the vulva. [NLat. *labia mâiōra* : Lat. *labia*, pl. of *labium*, lip + Lat. *mâiōra*, neut. pl. of *mâior*, larger.]

labia mi•no•ra (mə-nôr′ə, -nōr′ə) *pl.n.* The two thin inner folds of skin within the vestibule of the vagina to either side of the cleft of the labia majora; nymphae. [NLat. *labia minōra* : Lat. *labia*, lips + Lat. *minōra*, smaller.]

la•bi•ate (lā′bē-ĭt, -āt′) *adj.* **1.** Having lips or liplike parts. **2.** *Botany* **a.** Having or being flowers with the corolla divided into two liplike parts, as in the snapdragon. **b.** Of or belonging to the mint family Labiatae. ❖ *n.* A plant belonging to the Labiatae. [Lat. *labium*, lip; see LABIUM + -ATE¹.]

la•bile (lā′bĭl′, -bəl) *adj.* **1.** Open to change; adaptable. **2.** *Chemistry* Constantly undergoing or likely to undergo change; unstable. [ME *labil*, wandering < OFr. *labile* < LLat. *lābilis*, apt to slip < Lat. *lābī*, to slip.] **—la•bil′i•ty** (-bĭl′ĭ-tē) *n.*

labio- *pref.* Lip; labial. [< Lat. *labium*, lip. See LABIUM.]

la•bi•o•den•tal (lā′bē-ō-dĕn′tl) *adj.* Articulated with the lower lip and upper teeth, as the sounds (f) and (v). ❖ *n.* A labiodental sound.

la•bi•o•ve•lar (lā′bē-ō-vē′lər) *adj.* Simultaneously labial and velar, as (kw) in *quick.* ❖ *n.* A labiovelar sound.

la•bi•um (lā′bē-əm) *n.*, *pl.* **-bi•a** (-bē-ə) **1.** *Anatomy* Any of four folds of tissue of the female external genitalia. **2.** *Zoology* **a.** A liplike structure, such as that forming the floor of the mouth of certain invertebrates, esp. insects. **b.** The inner margin of the opening of a gastropod shell. **3.** *Botany* One of the liplike divisions of a labiate corolla. [Lat., lip.]

la•bor (lā′bər) *n.* **1a.** Physical or mental exertion, esp. when difficult or exhausting; work. **b.** Something produced by work. **2.** A specific task. **3.** A particular form of work or method of working: *manual labor.* **4.** Work for wages. **5a.** Workers considered as a group. **b.** The trade union movement, esp. its officials. **6. Labor** A political party representing workers' interests, esp. in Great Britain. **7.** The process by which childbirth occurs, beginning with contractions of the uterus and ending with the expulsion of the fetus or infant and the placenta. ❖ *v.* **-bored, -bor•ing, -bors** *—intr.* **1.** To work; toil. **2.** To strive painstakingly. **3a.** To proceed with great effort; plod. **b.** *Nautical* To pitch and roll. **4.** To suffer from distress or a disadvantage. **5.** To undergo the efforts of childbirth. *—tr.* **1.** To deal with in exhaustive or excessive detail; belabor: *labor a point in the argument.* **2.** To distress; burden. ❖ *adj.* **1.** Of or relating to labor. **2. Labor** Of or relating to a Labor Party. [ME < OFr. *labour* < Lat. *labor.*] **—la′bor•er** *n.*

lab•o•ra•to•ry (lăb′rə-tôr′ē, -tōr′ē) *n.*, *pl.* **-ries 1a.** A room or building equipped for scientific experimentation or research. **b.** An academic period devoted to work or study in such a place. **2.** A place where drugs and chemicals are manufactured. **3.** A place for practice, observation, or testing. [Med.Lat. *labōrātōrium* < Lat. *labōrāre*, to labor < *labor*, labor.]

Labor Day *n.* The first Monday in September, observed as a holiday in some countries in honor of working people.

la•bored (lā′bərd) *adj.* **1.** Produced or done with effort: *labored breathing.* **2.** Lacking natural ease; strained.

la•bor•in•ten•sive (lā′bər-ĭn-tĕn′sĭv) *adj.* Requiring or having a large expenditure of labor in comparison to capital.

la•bo•ri•ous (lə-bôr′ē-əs, -bōr′-) *adj.* **1.** Marked by or requiring long, hard work. **2.** Hard-working; industrious. **—la•bo′ri•ous•ly** *adv.* **—la•bo′ri•ous•ness** *n.*

la•bor•ite (lā′bə-rīt′) *n.* **1.** A member or supporter of a labor movement or union. **2. Laborite** A member of a political party representing labor.

la•bor•sav•ing (lā′bər-sā′vĭng) *adj.* Designed to conserve human energy in performing work or decrease the amount of human labor needed.

labor union *n.* An organization of wage earners formed for the purpose of serving the members' interests with respect to wages and working conditions.

la•bour (lā′bər) *n.*, *v.*, *& adj. Chiefly British* Variant of **labor.**

La•bov (lə-bōv′), **William** b. 1927. Amer. linguist and author of *The Social Stratification of English in New York City* (1966).

Lab•ra•dor (lăb′rə-dôr′) The mainland territory of Newfoundland, Canada, on the NE portion of the Labrador Peninsula; visited by Norse seamen as early as the 10th cent. **—Lab′ra•dor′e•an, Lab′ra•dor′i•an** *adj. & n.*

Labrador Current *n.* A cold ocean current flowing southward along the coast of Labrador and turning east.

lab•ra•dor•ite (lăb′rə-dôr′īt′, -dô-rīt′) *n.* A variety of plagioclase feldspar found in igneous rocks and characterized by brilliant colors. [After the LABRADOR (PENINSULA).]

Labrador Peninsula A peninsula of E Canada between Hudson Bay and the Atlantic Ocean.

Labrador retriever *n.* Any of a breed of dog originating in Newfoundland, having a short yellow, black, or brown coat and a tapering tail and used in hunting. [After LABRADOR.]

la•bret (lā′brĭt) *n.* An ornament inserted into a perforation in the lip. [Lat. *labrum*, lip + -ET.]

la•brum (lā′brəm) *n.*, *pl.* **-bra** (-brə) **1.** A lip or liplike structure. **2.** The outer margin of the opening of a gastropod shell. [Lat., lip.]

La•bu•an (lə-bōō′ən, lä′bōō-än′) An island of Malaysia off the N coast of Borneo; became part of Malaysia in 1963.

la•bur•num (lə-bûr′nəm) *n.* Any of several trees or shrubs of the genus *Laburnum*, esp. *L. anagyroides*, having drooping clusters of yellow flowers. [NLat. *Laburnum*, genus name < Lat. *laburnum*, broad-leaved bean trefoil, perh. of Etruscan orig.]

lab•y•rinth (lăb′ə-rĭnth′) *n.* **1a.** An intricate structure of interconnecting passages through which it is difficult to find one's way; a maze. **b. Labyrinth** *Greek Mythology* The maze in which

lace

lacrosse

ladder-back

the Minotaur was confined. **2.** Something highly intricate or convoluted in character, composition, or construction: *a labyrinth of rules.* **3.** *Anatomy* **a.** A group of complex interconnecting anatomical cavities. **b.** See **inner ear.** [ME *laberinthe* < Lat. *labyrinthus* < Gk. *laburinthos.*] **lab•y•rin•thine** (-rĭn′thĭn, -thēn′), **lab′y•rin•thi•an** (-thē-ən) *adj.*

lac (lăk) *n.* A resinous secretion of various insects of the subfamily Lacciferinae, deposited on trees and used in making shellac. [Du. *lac* or Fr. *laque* (both < OFr. *lacce* < Med.Lat. *lacca* < Ar. *lakk* < Prakrit *lakkhā*) < Skt. *lākṣā,* red dye, resin.]

La•can (lä-kän′, lä-kän′), **Jacques** 1901–81. French psychiatrist whose collection of essays and lectures *Écrits* (1966) greatly influenced linguistics and literary theory.

Lac•ca•dive Islands (lăk′ə-dīv′, lä′kə-dēv′) A group of islands and coral reefs in the Arabian Sea off the SW coast of India; now part of the region of Lakshadweep.

lac•co•lith (lăk′ə-lĭth′) *n.* A mass of igneous rock intruded between layers of sedimentary rock, resulting in uplift. [Gk. *lakkos,* cistern + -LITH.]

lace (lās) *n.* **1.** A cord or ribbon used to draw and tie together two opposite edges, as of a shoe. **2.** A delicate fabric made of yarn or thread in an open weblike pattern. **3.** Gold or silver braid ornamenting an officer's uniform. ❖ *v.* **laced, lac•ing, lac•es** —*tr.* **1.** To thread a cord through the eyelets or around the hooks of. **2a.** To draw together and tie the laces of. **b.** To restrain or constrict by tightening laces, esp. of a corset. **3.** To pull or pass through; intertwine: *lace garlands through a trellis.* **4.** To trim or decorate with or as if with lace. **5a.** To add a touch of flavor or a dash of zest to. **b.** To add a substance, esp. an intoxicant or narcotic, to: *laced the eggnog with rum.* **6.** To streak with color. **7.** To give a beating to; thrash. —*intr.* To be fastened or tied with laces or a lace. —*phrasal verb:* **lace into** *Informal* To attack; assail: *laced into me.* [ME < OFr. *las,* noose, string < VLat. **laceum* < Lat. *laqueus,* noose; prob. akin to *lacere,* to entice, ensnare.] —**lace′less** *adj.* —**lac′er** *n.*

Lac•e•dae•mon (lăs′ĭ-dē′mən) See **Sparta.** —**Lac′e•dae•mo′ni•an** (-də-mō′nē-ən) *adj. & n.*

lac•er•ate (lăs′ə-rāt′) *tr.v.* **-at•ed, -at•ing, -ates** **1.** To rip, cut, or tear. **2.** To cause deep emotional pain to; distress. ❖ *adj.* (-rĭt, -rāt′) **1.** Torn; mangled. **2.** Wounded. **3.** Having jagged, deeply cut edges: *lacerate leaves.* [ME *laceraten* < Lat. *lacerāre, lacerāt-* < *lacer,* torn.]

lac•er•a•tion (lăs′ə-rā′shən) *n.* A jagged wound or cut.

La•cer•ta (lə-sûr′tə) *n.* A constellation in the Northern Hemisphere near Cygnus and Andromeda. [Lat. *lacerta,* lizard.]

lace•wing (lās′wĭng′) *n.* Any of various insects of the superfamily Hemerobioidea, having four gauzy wings, threadlike antennae, and larvae that feed on insect pests such as aphids.

lace•work (lās′wûrk′) *n.* See **lace** 2.

lach•es (lăch′ĭz) *n.* Negligence or undue delay in asserting a legal right or privilege. [ME, slackness, negligence < AN *lachesse, laches* < OFr. *laschesse* < *lasche,* loose, remiss. See LUSH[1].]

Lach•e•sis (lăk′ĭ-sĭs, lăch′-) *n. Greek Mythology* One of the three Fates, the measurer of the thread of destiny. [Ult. < Gk. *lankhanein, lakh-,* to obtain by lot.]

La•chish (lā′kĭsh) An ancient city of S Palestine SW of Jerusalem; probably inhabited as early as 3200 B.C.

Lach•lan (lăk′lən) A river of SE Australia flowing c. 1,483 km (922 mi) to the Murrumbidgee R.

lach•ry•mal (lăk′rə-məl) *adj.* Variant of **lacrimal.**

lach•ry•ma•tion (lăk′rə-mā′shən) *n.* Variant of **lacrimation.**

lach•ry•ma•tor also **lac•ri•ma•tor** (lăk′rə-mā′tər) *n.* Tear gas. [Lat. *lacrimāre,* to cry (< *lacrima,* tear; see LACHRYMAL) + -ATOR.]

lach•ry•mose (lăk′rə-mōs′) *adj.* **1.** Weeping or inclined to weep; tearful. **2.** Causing or tending to cause tears. [Lat. *lacrimōsus* < *lacrima,* tear. See LACHRYMAL.] —**lach′ry•mose′ly** *adv.* —**lach′ry•mos′i•ty** (-mŏs′ĭ-tē) *n.*

lac•ing (lā′sĭng) *n.* **1.** Something that laces; a lace. **2.** A touch of liquor added to a beverage or food. **3.** *Informal* A beating or thrashing.

la•cin•i•ate (lə-sĭn′ē-ĭt, -āt′) *adj.* **1.** Having a fringe; fringed. **2.** Shaped or formed like a fringe, as a ligament. **3.** Slashed into narrow pointed lobes: *a laciniate leaf.* [Lat. *lacinia,* fringe, hem + -ATE[1].] —**la•cin′i•a′tion** *n.*

lack (lăk) *n.* **1.** Deficiency or absence: *Lack of funding ended the project.* **2.** A particular deficiency or absence: *a lack of courtesy.* ❖ *v.* **lacked, lack•ing, lacks** —*tr.* To be without or in need of: *lacked the strength to lift the box.* —*intr.* **1.** To be wanting or deficient: *Proof of a crime was lacking.* **2.** To be in need of something: *She does not lack for friends.* [ME, perh. < MDu. *lac,* deficiency, fault.]

SYNONYMS *lack, want, need* These verbs mean to be without something, especially something that is necessary or desirable. *Lack* emphasizes the absence of something: *I lack the money to buy new shoes. Want* and *need* stress the urgent necessity for filling a void or remedying an inadequacy: *"Her pens were uniformly bad and wanted fixing"* (Bret Harte). *The garden needs care.*

lack•a•dai•si•cal (lăk′ə-dā′zĭ-kəl) *adj.* Lacking spirit, liveliness, or interest; languid. [< *lackadaisy,* alteration of LACKADAY.] —**lack′a•dai′si•cal•ness** *n.*

lack•a•day (lăk′ə-dā′) *interj. Archaic* Used to express regret or disapproval. [Alteration of *alack the day.*]

lack•ey (lăk′ē) *n., pl.* **-eys** **1.** A liveried male servant; a footman. **2.** A servile follower; a toady. ❖ *v.* **-eyed, -ey•ing, -eys** —*tr.* To wait on as a lackey; attend. —*intr.* To act in a servile manner; fawn. [Fr. *laquais* < OFr.]

lack•lus•ter (lăk′lŭs′tər) *adj.* Lacking brightness, luster, or vitality; dull.

La•co•ni•a (lə-kō′nē-ə) An ancient region in S Greece in the SE Peloponnesus; dominated by Sparta until the rise of the second Achaean League in the 3rd and 2nd cent. B.C.

la•con•ic (lə-kŏn′ĭk) *adj.* Using or marked by the use of few words; terse or concise. See Syns at **silent.** [Lat. *Lacōnicus,* Spartan < Gk. *Lakōnikos* < *Lakōn,* a Spartan (< the reputation of the Spartans for brevity of speech).] —**la•con′i•cal•ly** *adv.*

lac•o•nism (lăk′ə-nĭz′əm) *n.* Laconic style or expression.

La Co•ru•ña (lä′ kə-rōōn′yə, kō-rōō′nyä) A city of NW Spain on the Atlantic Ocean W of Oviedo; point of departure for the Spanish Armada (1588). Pop. 248,293.

lac•quer (lăk′ər) *n.* **1.** Any of various clear or colored synthetic coatings made by dissolving cellulose derivatives together with plasticizers in volatile solvents and used to impart a high gloss to surfaces. **2.** A glossy resinous material, such as the exudation of the lacquer tree, used as a surface coating. **3.** A finish baked onto the inside of food and beverage cans. ❖ *tr.v.* **-quered, -quer•ing, -quers** **1.** To coat with lacquer. **2.** To give a sleek glossy finish to. [Obsolete Fr. *lacre,* sealing wax < Port. < *lacca,* resin of the lac insect < Ar. *lakk.* See LAC.] —**lac′quer•er** *n.*

lacquer tree *n.* A poisonous eastern Asian tree (*Rhus verniciflua*) having pinnately compound leaves and a toxic exudation from which a black lacquer is obtained.

lac•ri•mal also **lach•ry•mal** (lăk′rə-məl) *adj.* **1.** Of or relating to tears. **2.** Of, relating to, or constituting the glands that produce tears. [ME *lacrimale* < OFr. *lacrymal* < Med.Lat. *lachrymālis* < Lat. *lacrima, lachryma,* tear. See **dakru-** in App.]

lac•ri•ma•tion also **lach•ry•ma•tion** (lăk′rə-mā′shən) *n.* Secretion of tears, esp. in excess.

lac•ri•ma•tor (lăk′rə-mā′tər) *n.* Variant of **lachrymator.**

la•crosse (lə-krôs′, -krŏs′) *n.* A game played on a rectangular field by two teams of ten players each, in which participants use a long-handled stick with a webbed pouch on one end to maneuver a ball into the opposing team's goal. [Canadian Fr. *la crosse* < Fr. *(jeu de) la crosse,* (game of) the hooked stick < OFr. *croce, crosse,* crosier, of Gmc. orig.]

lac•tal•bu•min (lăk′tăl-byōō′mĭn) *n.* The albumin contained in milk and obtained from whey.

lac•tase (lăk′tās′) *n.* An enzyme occurring in certain yeasts and in the intestinal juices of mammals and catalyzing the hydrolysis of lactose into glucose and galactose.

lac•tate[1] (lăk′tāt′) *intr.v.* **-tat•ed, -tat•ing, -tates** To secrete or produce milk. [Lat. *lactāre, lactāt-* < *lac, lact-,* milk. See LACTO–.]

lac•tate[2] (lăk′tāt′) *n.* A salt or ester of lactic acid. [LACT(O)- + -ATE[2].]

lac•ta•tion (lăk-tā′shən) *n.* **1.** Secretion or formation of milk by the mammary glands. **2.** The period during which the mammary glands secrete milk. —**lac•ta′tion•al** *adj.*

lac•te•al (lăk′tē-əl) *adj.* **1.** Of, relating to, or resembling milk. **2.** *Anatomy* Of or relating to any of numerous minute intestinal lymph-carrying vessels that convey chyle from the intestine. ❖ *n. Anatomy* A lacteal vessel. [< Lat. *lacteus* < *lac, lact-,* milk. See **melg-** in App.] —**lac′te•al•ly** *adv.*

lac•tes•cent (lăk-tĕs′ənt) *adj.* **1.** Becoming milky. **2.** Milky. **3.** *Biology* Secreting or yielding a milky juice, as certain plants and insects. [Lat. *lactēscēns, lactēscent-,* pr. part. of *lactēscere,* inchoative of *lactēre,* to be milky < *lac, lact-,* milk. See **melg-** in App.] —**lac•tes′cence** *n.*

lac•tic (lăk′tĭk) *adj.* Of, relating to, or derived from milk.

lactic acid *n.* A syrupy water-soluble liquid, $C_3H_6O_3$, produced as a result of anaerobic glucose metabolism, present in sour milk and wines, and used in prepared foods, pharmaceuticals, and industrial applications.

lac•tif•er•ous (lăk-tĭf′ər-əs) *adj.* **1.** Producing, secreting, or conveying milk. **2.** *Botany* Yielding latex.

lacto– or **lact–** *pref.* **1.** Milk: *lactoprotein.* **2.** Lactose: *lactase.* **3.** Lactic acid: *lactate.* [< Lat. *lac, lact-,* milk. See **melg-** in App.]

lac•to•ba•cil•lus (lăk′tō-bə-sĭl′əs) *n., pl.* **-cil•li** (-sĭl′ī′) Any of various rod-shaped nonmotile aerobic bacteria of the genus *Lactobacillus* that ferment lactic acid from sugars.

lac•to•gen•ic (lăk′tə-jĕn′ĭk) *adj.* Inducing lactation.

lac•tom•e•ter (lăk-tŏm′ĭ-tər) *n.* A device used to measure the specific gravity, and therefore the richness, of milk.

lac•tone (lăk′tōn′) *n.* An anhydride formed by the removal of a water molecule from the hydroxyl and carboxyl radicals of hydroxy acids. —**lac•ton′ic** (-tŏn′ĭk) *adj.*

lac•to•pro•tein (lăk′tō-prō′tēn′, -tē-ən) *n.* A protein normally present in milk.

lac•tose (lăk′tōs′) *n.* **1.** A disaccharide, $C_{12}H_{22}O_{11}$, found in milk, that may be hydrolyzed to yield glucose and galactose. **2.** A white crystalline substance obtained from whey and used as a diluent and excipient.

la·cu·na (lə-kyōō′nə) *n., pl.* **-nae** (-nē) or **-nas 1.** An empty space or a missing part; a gap. **2.** *Anatomy* A cavity, space, or depression, esp. in a bone, containing cartilage or bone cells. [Lat. *lacūna*. See LAGOON.] **—la·cu′nal** *adj.*

la·cu·nar (lə-kyōō′nər) *n.* **1.** A ceiling with recessed panels. **2.** *pl.* **lac·u·nar·i·a** (lăk′yə-nâr′ē-ə) A recessed panel in such a ceiling. [Lat. *lacūnar < lacūna*, hole. See LAGOON.]

la·cus·trine (lə-kŭs′trĭn) *adj.* **1.** Of or relating to lakes. **2.** Living or growing in or along the edges of lakes. [Fr. or Ital. *lacustre* (< Lat. *lacus*, lake) + -INE¹.]

lac·y (lā′sē) *adj.* **-i·er, -i·est** Of, relating to, or resembling lace. **—lac′i·ness** *n.*

lad (lăd) *n.* **1.** A young man; a youth. **2.** *Informal* A man of any age; a fellow. [ME *ladde*, perh. of Scand. orig.]

La·dakh (lə-däk′) A region of Jammu and Kashmir in India and Pakistan on the border of China.

lad·a·num (lăd′n-əm) *n.* Variant of **labdanum.**

lad·der (lăd′ər) *n.* **1a.** A structure consisting of two long sides crossed by parallel rungs, used to climb up and down. **b.** Something that resembles this device, esp. a run in a stocking. **2a.** A means of ascent and descent. **b.** A series of ranked stages or levels. ❖ *intr.v.* **-dered, -der·ing, -ders** To run, as a stocking does. [ME < OE *hlǣder* in App.]

lad·der·back (lăd′ər-băk′) *n.* **1.** A chair back consisting of two upright posts connected by horizontal slats. **2.** A chair with such a back. **—lad′der-back′** *adj.*

lad·die (lăd′ē) *n.* A boy or young man; a lad.

lade (lād) *v.* **lad·ed, lad·en** (lăd′n) or **lad·ed, lad·ing, lades** —*tr.* **1a.** To load with or as if with cargo. **b.** To place (something) as a load for or as if for shipment. **2.** To burden or oppress; weigh down. **3.** To take up or remove (water) with a ladle or dipper. —*intr.* **1.** To take on cargo. **2.** To ladle a liquid. [ME *laden* < OE *hladan*.]

lad·en (lăd′n) *adj.* **1.** Weighed down with a load; heavy. **2.** Oppressed; burdened: *laden with grief.*

la-di-da also **la-de-da** (lä′dē-dä′) *adj. Informal* Affectedly genteel; pretentious. ❖ *interj.* Used to express disdain for something viewed as pretentious. [Imit. of affected speech.]

la·dies′ man (lā′dēz) *n.* Variant of **lady's man.**

ladies′ room *n.* A restroom for women.

ladies′ tresses also **lady's tresses** *pl.n.* (*used with a sing. or pl. verb*) Any of various orchids of the genus *Spiranthes,* having a spike or raceme of small flowers usu. arranged in a spiral.

La·din (lə-dēn′) *n.* **1.** See **Romansh. 2.** A dialect of Romansh spoken in parts of Engadine. **3.** A person who is a native speaker of Ladin. [Romansh < Lat. *Latīnus,* Lat. See LATIN.]

lad·ing (lā′dĭng) *n.* **1.** The act of loading. **2.** Cargo; freight.

La·di·no (lə-dē′nō) *n., pl.* **-nos 1.** A nearly extinct Romance language, descended from medieval Spanish, spoken by Sephardic Jews esp. in the Balkans, Turkey, and the Near East. **2.** also **ladino** In Central America, a Spanish-speaking or acculturated Indian; a mestizo. [Sp. *ladino* < Lat. *Latīnus,* Latin. See LATIN.]

la·dle (lā′l) *n.* A long-handled spoon with a deep bowl for serving liquids. ❖ *tr.v.* **-dled, -dling, -dles** To lift out or serve with a long-handled spoon. [ME < OE *hlǣdel* < *hladan,* to draw out, lade.] **—la′dler** *n.*

La·do·ga (lä′də-gə), **Lake** A lake of NW Russia NE of St. Petersburg.

la·dy (lā′dē) *n., pl.* **-dies 1.** A well-mannered and considerate woman with high standards of proper behavior. **2a.** A woman regarded as proper and virtuous. **b.** A well-behaved girl. **3.** A woman who is the head of a household. **4.** A woman, esp. when spoken of or to in a polite way. **5a.** A woman to whom a man is romantically attached. **b.** *Informal* A wife. **6. Lady** *Chiefly British* A general feminine title of nobility and other rank, specifically: **a.** Used as the title for the wife or widow of a knight or baronet. **b.** Used as a form of address for a marchioness, countess, viscountess, baroness, or baronetess. **c.** Used as the title for the wife or widow of a baron. **d.** Used as a courtesy title for the daughter of a duke, marquis, or earl. **e.** Used as a courtesy title for the wife of a younger son of a duke or marquis. **7. Lady** The Virgin Mary. Often used with *Our.* **8.** *Slang* Cocaine. [ME, mistress of a household < OE *hlǣfdige.* See **dheigh-** in App.]

USAGE NOTE *Lady,* a social term, is properly used as a parallel to *gentleman* to emphasize norms expected in civil society or in situations requiring civil courtesies: *She is too much of a lady to tell your secrets to her friends.* The use of *lady* as an attributive with an occupational title, as in *lady doctor,* is widely regarded as condescending and inappropriate. When the sex of the person is relevant, both *woman* and *female* are acceptable: *the first woman vice-president; the female candidates.*

lady beetle also **la·dy·bee·tle** (lā′dē-bēt′l) *n.* See **ladybug.**

la·dy·bird (lā′dē-bûrd′) *n.* See **ladybug.**

la·dy·bug (lā′dē-bŭg′) *n.* Any of numerous small rounded beetles of the family Coccinellidae, often reddish with black spots and feeding primarily on insect pests, such as aphids. [Prob. < its seven spots being considered a symbol of the seven sorrows of the Virgin Mary.]

Lady Chapel also **lady chapel** *n.* A chapel within a church, usu. behind the sanctuary and dedicated to the Virgin Mary.

Lady Day *n. Chiefly British* Annunciation, March 25.

la·dy·fin·ger (lā′dē-fĭng′gər) also **la·dys·fin·ger** (lā′dĕz-) *n.* A small finger-shaped sponge cake.

la·dy·fish (lā′dē-fĭsh′) *n., pl.* **ladyfish** or **-fish·es** Any of several marine fishes, esp. the tarpon *Elops saurus.*

lady in waiting *n., pl.* **ladies in waiting** A lady of a court appointed to attend a queen, princess, or royal duchess.

la·dy-kill·er (lā′dē-kĭl′ər) *n. Slang* A man reputed to be exceptionally attractive to and often ruthless with women.

la·dy·like (lā′dē-līk′) *adj.* **1.** Characteristic of a lady; well-bred. **2.** Appropriate for or becoming to a lady. **—la′dy·like′ness** *n.*

la·dy·love (lā′dē-lŭv′) *n.* A woman or girl who is someone's sweetheart.

la·dy·ship also **La·dy·ship** (lā′dē-shĭp′) *n.* Used with *Your, Her,* or *Their* as a title and form of address for a woman or women holding the rank of lady.

la·dy′s man also **la·dies′ man** (lā′dĕz) *n.* A man who enjoys and attracts the company of women.

lady's slipper *n.* Any of various orchids of the genus *Cypripedium,* having variously colored flowers with an inflated pouchlike lip.

lady's smock *n.* See **cuckooflower** 1.

lady's thumb *n.* A European perennial weed (*Polygonum persicaria*) having very small pinkish flowers.

lady's tresses *pl.n.* (*used with a sing. or pl. verb*) Variant of **ladies′ tresses.**

lady tulip *n.* A central Asian tulip (*Tulipa clusiana*) having red outer perianth segments with white margins.

La·er·tes (lā-ûr′tēz, -âr′-) *n. Greek Mythology* The father of Odysseus.

la·e·trile (lā′ĭ-trĭl′, -trəl) *n.* A drug derived from amygdalin and purported to have antineoplastic properties. [*lae(vorotatory)* (var. of LEVOROTATORY) + (NI)TRILE.]

La·fa·yette (lăf′ē-ĕt′, lä′fē-, -fä-), Marquis **Marie Joseph Paul Yves Roch Gilbert du Motier de** 1757–1834. French soldier and politician who served in the American Revolution and in the 1789 and 1830 French revolutions.

Laf·fer curve or **Laf·fer Curve** (lăf′ər) *n.* A curved graph illustrating the theory that if tax rates pass a certain level, economic growth is discouraged and government revenues reduced. [After Arthur *Laffer* (born 1940), American economist.]

Laf·fite or **La·fitte** (lə-fēt′, lä-), **Jean** 1780?–1826? French pirate leader who aided US troops in the War of 1812.

La Fol·lette (lə fŏl′ət), **Robert Marion** 1855–1925. Amer. politician who served as a US senator from WI (1906–25).

La Fon·taine (lə fŏn-tān′, lä fôn-tĕn′), **Jean de** 1621–95. French writer known esp. for his collected *Fables* (1668–94).

lag¹ (lăg) *v.* **lagged, lag·ging, lags** —*intr.* **1.** To fail to keep up a pace; straggle. **2.** To proceed or develop with comparative slowness. **3.** To fail, weaken, or slacken gradually; flag. **4.** *Games* To determine the order of play in billiards by successively hitting the cue ball against the end rail, the ball rebounding closest to the head rail indicating the player to shoot first. —*tr.* **1.** To cause to hang back or fall behind. **2.** To shoot, throw, or pitch (a coin, for example) at a mark. ❖ *n.* **1.** The act, process, or condition of lagging. **2.** One that lags. **3.** A condition of slowness or retardation. **4a.** The extent or duration of lagging. **b.** An interval between events or phenomena considered together. [< earlier *lag,* last person < ME *lag-,* last (in *lagmon,* last man), perh. of Scand. orig.] **—lag′ger** *n.*

lag² (lăg) *n.* **1.** A barrel stave. **2.** A strip, as of wood, that forms a part of the covering for a cylindrical object. ❖ *tr.v.* **lagged, lag·ging, lags** To furnish or cover with lags. [Prob. of Scand. orig.; akin to Swed. *lagg.* See **leu-** in App.]

lag³ (lăg) *Chiefly British Slang tr.v.* **lagged, lag·ging, lags 1.** To arrest. **2.** To send to prison. ❖ *n.* **1.** A convict. **2.** An ex-convict. [?]

lag·an (lăg′ən) also **li·gan** (lī′gən) or **lag·end** (lăg′ənd) *n.* Cargo or equipment thrown into the sea but attached to a float or buoy so that it can be recovered. [Fr. < OFr., poss. < ON *lögn, lagn-.* See **legh-** in App.]

La·gash (lā′găsh) An ancient city of Sumer in S Mesopotamia; flourished c. 2400 B.C.

Lag b'O·mer (läg′ bō′mər, läg bə-ō′mĕr) *n.* A Jewish feast celebrated on the 33rd day of the Omer (the 18th day of Iyyar). [Mishnaic Heb. *lag bā 'ōmer* : *lag,* 33rd (< the numerical value of the letters *1,* 30 and *g,* 3) + *bā,* in the (*ba,* in + *hā,* the) + *'ōmer,* the Omer; see OMER.]

la·ger (lä′gər) *n.* A type of beer of German origin that contains a relatively small amount of hops and is aged from six weeks to six months to allow sedimentation. [Ger., short for *Lagerbier* : *Lager,* storehouse, cellar (< MHGer. *leger* < OHGer. *legar,* bed, lair; see **legh-** in App.) + *Bier,* beer.]

La·ger·kvist (lä′gər-kfĭst′), **Pär Fabian** 1891–1974. Swedish writer who won the 1951 Nobel Prize for literature.

La·ger·löf (lä′gər-lŏv, -lœf), **Selma Ottiliana Lovisa** 1858–1940. Swedish writer who was the first woman to win the Nobel Prize for literature (1909).

lag·gard (lăg′ərd) *n.* One that lags; a straggler. ❖ *adj.* Hanging back or falling behind; dilatory. **—lag′gard·ly** *adv.* **—lag′gard·ness** *n.*

ladybug

lady's slipper
pink lady's slipper
Cypripedium acaule

ă	pat	oi	boy
ā	pay	ou	out
âr	care	ŏŏ	took
ä	father	ōō	boot
ĕ	pet	ŭ	cut
ē	be	ûr	urge
ĭ	pit	th	thin
ī	pie	*th*	this
îr	pier	hw	which
ŏ	pot	zh	vision
ō	toe	ə	about,
ô	paw		item

Stress marks:
′ (primary);
′ (secondary); as in
lexicon (lĕk′sĭ-kŏn′)

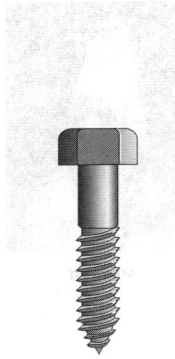

lag screw
hexagonal head lag screw

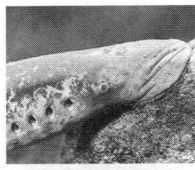

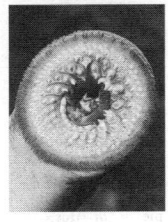

lamprey
top: attached to a rock
bottom: close-up of mouth

lag·ging (lăg′ĭng) n. 1. Insulation used to prevent heat diffusion, as from a steam pipe. 2. A wooden frame built esp. to support an arch until the keystone is positioned. [< LAG².]

la·gniappe (lăn′yəp, lăn-yăp′) n. Chiefly Southern Louisiana & Mississippi 1. A small gift presented by a storeowner to a customer with the customer's purchase. 2. An extra or unexpected gift or benefit. See Regional Note at **beignet**. [Louisiana Fr. < Am.Sp. la ñapa, the gift : la, the (< Lat. illa, fem. of ille, that, the; see **al-** in App.) + ñapa (var. of yapa, gift < Quechua < yapay, to give more).]

REGIONAL NOTE Lagniappe derives from New World Spanish la ñapa, "the gift," and ultimately from Quechua yapay, "to give more." The word came into the rich Creole dialect mixture of New Orleans and there acquired a French spelling. It is still used in the Gulf States, especially southern Louisiana, to denote a little bonus that a friendly shopkeeper might add to a purchase. It may also mean "an extra or unexpected gift or benefit."

lag·o·morph (lăg′ə-môrf′) n. Any of various plant-eating mammals having fully furred feet and two pairs of upper incisors and belonging to the order Lagomorpha, which includes the rabbits and hares. [< NLat. Lagomorpha, order name : Gk. lagōs, hare + Gk. morphē, shape.] —**lag′o·mor′phic** (-fĭk), **lag′o·mor′phous** (-fəs) adj.

la·goon (lə-gōōn′) n. 1. A shallow body of water, esp. one separated from a sea by sandbars or coral reefs. 2. A shallow body of liquid waste material, as in a dump. [Fr. lagune and Ital. laguna, both < Lat. lacūna, pool, hollow, gap < lacus, lake.]

La·gos (lā′gŏs′, lä′gōs) The largest city in Nigeria, in the SW part on the Gulf of Guinea. It was the capital from 1960 to 1991 when Abuja was designated the capital. Pop. 1,404,000.

La·grange (lə-grănj′, -gränj′, lä-gränzh′), Comte **Joseph Louis** 1736–1813. French mathematician and astronomer who developed the calculus of variations (1755).

La·gran·gi·an point (lə-grān′jē-ən) n. Astronomy Any of five points in the orbital plane of two bodies at which a third, smaller body will remain in equilibrium with respect to the other two bodies. [After Comte Joseph Louis LAGRANGE.]

lag screw n. A heavy wood screw having a square bolt head. [< LAG² (< its original use in securing barrel staves).]

La Guar·di·a (lə gwär′dē-ə), **Fiorello Henry** 1882–1947. Amer. politician who served as mayor of New York City (1934–45).

la·har (lä′här′) n. 1. A landslide or mudflow of volcanic fragments on the flanks of a volcano. 2. The deposit produced by such a landslide. [Javanese, lava.]

La·hore (lə-hôr′, -hōr′) A city of NE Pakistan SE of Rawalpindi; a Mogul cap. in the 16th cent. Pop. 2,952,689.

Lah·ti (lä′tē, läкн′-) A city of S Finland NNE of Helsinki. Pop. 94,347.

la·ic (lā′ĭk) also **la·i·cal** (-ĭ-kəl) adj. Of or relating to the laity; secular. ❖ n. A layperson. [LLat. lāicus. See LAY².] —**la′i·cal·ly** adv.

la·i·cize (lā′ĭ-sīz′) tr.v. -**cized**, -**ciz·ing**, -**ciz·es** 1. To free from ecclesiastical control; give over to laypeople. 2. To change to lay status; secularize. —**la′i·ci·za′tion** (-sĭ-zā′shən) n.

laid (lād) v. Past tense and past participle of **lay**¹.

laid-back (lād′băk′) adj. Informal Having a relaxed or casual atmosphere or character; easygoing.

laid paper n. A paper made on wire molds that give it a characteristic watermark of close thin lines.

lain (lān) v. Past participle of **lie**¹.

Laing (lăng), **R(onald) D(avid)** 1927–89. British writer and psychiatrist whose works include The Facts of Life (1976).

lair (lâr) n. 1. The den or dwelling of a wild animal. 2. A den or hideaway. 3. Obsolete A resting place; a couch. [ME < OE leger. See **legh-** in App.]

laird (lârd) n. Scots The owner of a landed estate. [Sc. < ME lard, var. of lord, owner, master. See LORD.]

lais·sez faire also **lais·ser faire** (lĕs′ā fâr′, lā′zā) n. 1. An economic doctrine that opposes governmental regulation of or interference in commerce. 2. Noninterference in the affairs of others. [Fr. : laissez, let + faire, to do.] —**lais′sez-faire′** adj.

lais·ser-pas·ser (lĕs′ā-pä-sā′) n. A pass, esp. one used in lieu of a passport. [Fr. : laissez, let + passer, to pass.]

la·i·ty (lā′ĭ-tē) n. 1. Laypeople considered as a group. 2. Those who are not members of a given profession or other specialized field. [ME laite < lay, of the laity. See LAY².]

La·ius (lā′əs) n. Greek Mythology A king of Thebes who was mistakenly killed by his son Oedipus.

lake¹ (lāk) n. 1. A large inland body of fresh water or salt water. 2. A scenic pond, as in a park. 3. A large pool of liquid. [ME < OFr. lac < OE lacu, both < Lat. lacus.]

lake² (lāk) n. 1. A pigment of organic coloring matter with an inorganic, usu. metallic base or carrier, used in dyes, inks, and paints. 2. A deep red. [< Fr. laque. See LAC.]

Lake or **Lake of** (lāk) or **Loch** (lŏk, lôкн) For the names of actual lakes, see the specific element of the name; for example, **Erie, Lake; Lucerne, Lake of; Lomond, Loch.**

lake·bed (lāk′bĕd′) n. The floor of a lake.

Lake Charles A city of SW LA E of Beaumont TX. Pop. 71,757.

Lake District A scenic area of NW England including the Cumbrian Mts. and some 15 lakes; associated with the 19th-cent. Lake Poets, notably Wordsworth and Coleridge.

lake dwelling n. A dwelling, esp. a prehistoric dwelling, built on piles in a shallow lake.

lake effect n. The effect of warm, usu. lacustrine water on the weather conditions of cooler, adjacent areas.

lake·front (lāk′frŭnt′) n. The land along the edge of a lake.

lake herring n. A food fish, esp. the trout Coregonus artedii of the Great Lakes region, related to the cisco and whitefishes.

Lake·land terrier (lāk′lənd) n. Any of a breed of small straight-legged slender dogs, originally bred in England for hunting foxes. [After Lakeland, a region of northwest England.]

lak·er (lā′kər) n. 1. A fish, such as the lake trout, that lives in a lake. 2. A ship used on lakes.

lake·shore (lāk′shôr′, -shōr′) n. Land by a lake.

lake·side (lāk′sīd′) n. See **lakeshore**.

lake trout n. A freshwater food and game fish (Salvelinus namaycush) of the Great Lakes.

Lake·wood (lāk′wŏŏd′) 1. A city of S CA, a suburb of Long Beach. Pop. 79,345. 2. A city of N-central CO, a suburb of Denver. Pop. 144,126.

La·ko·ta (lə-kō′tə) n., pl. **Lakota** or -**tas** 1. See **Teton**. 2. The dialect of Sioux spoken by the Teton.

Lak·shad·weep (lək-shäd′wēp′, lŭk′shə-dwēp′) A region of SW India comprising the Laccadive, Minicoy, and Amindivi islands.

la-la land (lä′lä) n. 1. A place renowned for its frivolous activity. 2. A state of mind characterized by unrealistic expectations or a lack of seriousness. [After L(OS) A(NGELES).]

La·lique (lə-lēk′, lä-), **René Jules** 1860–1945. French designer of art nouveau jewelry and glassware.

Lal·lan (lăl′ən) also **Lal·lans** (-ənz) n. Scots 1. The Lowlands of Scotland. 2. Scots as spoken in southern and eastern Scotland. [Sc., alteration of LOWLAND.] —**Lal′lan** adj.

lal·ly·gag (lăl′ē-găg′) v. Variant of **lollygag**.

lam¹ (lăm) v. **lammed**, **lam·ming**, **lams** Slang —tr. To give a thorough beating to; thrash. —intr. To strike; wallop. [Prob. of Scand. orig.; akin to ON lemja, to cripple by beating, flog.]

lam² (lăm) Slang intr.v. **lammed**, **lam·ming**, **lams** To escape, as from prison. ❖ n. Flight, esp. from the law. [?]

Lam. abbr. Bible Lamentations

la·ma (lä′mə) n. A Buddhist monk of Tibet or Mongolia. [Tibetan bla-ma, the upper one, lama < bla, superior.]

La·ma·ism (lä′mə-ĭz′əm) n. Tibetan Buddhism. —**La′ma·ist** n. —**La′ma·is′tic** adj.

La Man·cha (lä män′chə) A plateau region of S-central Spain; setting for Cervantes's Don Quixote.

La·marck (lə-märk′, lä-), Chevalier de **Jean Baptiste Pierre Antoine de Monet** 1744–1829. French naturalist whose ideas about evolution influenced Darwin's theory. —**La·marck′i·an** adj. & n.

La·marck·ism (lə-mär′kĭz′əm) also **La·marck·i·an·ism** (-kē-ə-nĭz′əm) n. A theory of biological evolution holding that acquired traits can be inherited. [After LAMARCK.]

La·mar·tine (lä-mär-tēn′), **Alphonse Marie Louis de Prat de** 1790–1869. French romantic poet who served briefly as minister of foreign affairs (1848).

la·ma·ser·y (lä′mə-sĕr′ē) n., pl. -**ies** A monastery of lamas. [Fr. lamaserie : lama, lama (< Tibetan bla-ma; see LAMA) + -serie, dwelling (prob. < Pers. sarāy, inn, palace; see **terə-²** in App.).]

La·maze (lə-mäz′) adj. Relating to or being a method of childbirth in which a woman is prepared psychologically and physically to give birth without the use of drugs. [After Fernand Lamaze (1890–1957), French physician.]

lamb (lăm) n. 1a. A young sheep, esp. one that is not yet weaned. b. The flesh of a young sheep used as meat. c. Lambskin. 2. A sweet, mild-mannered person; a dear. 3. One who can be duped or cheated esp. in financial matters. 4. **Lamb** Christianity Jesus. ❖ intr.v. **lambed**, **lamb·ing**, **lambs** To give birth to a young sheep. [ME < OE.]

Lamb, Charles Known as "Elia." 1775–1834. British critic and essayist who with his sister **Mary Ann** (1764–1847) wrote the children's book Tales from Shakespeare (1807).

Lamb, William. 2nd Viscount Melbourne. 1779–1848. British politician who served as prime minister (1834 and 1835–41).

lam·ba·da (ləm-bä′də, läm-bä′dä) n. 1. A Brazilian ballroom dance in which the partners press against each other tightly and gyrate sensually. 2. Music for this dance. [Port., beating, lashing < p. part. of lambar, to beat, var. of lombar, prob. < lombo, side, flank (of a horse) < Lat. lumbus, loin.]

lam·baste (lăm-bāst′) tr.v. -**bast·ed**, -**bast·ing**, -**bastes** Informal 1. To give a thrashing to; beat. 2. To scold sharply; berate. [Perh. LAM¹ + BASTE³.]

lamb·da (lăm′də) n. 1. The 11th letter of the Greek alphabet. 2. A lambda baryon. [Gk. < Phoenician *lamd, ox-goad (sense uncertain), 11th letter of the Phoenician alphabet.]

lambda baryon n. An unstable, electrically neutral baryon.

lamb·da-b baryon (lăm′də-bē′) n. An electrically neutral baryon having a mass 11,000 times that of the electron.

lamb·da-c baryon (lăm′də-sē′) n. A positively charged baryon having a mass 4,471 times that of the electron.

lamb•doid (lăm′doid′) *adj.* **1.** Having the shape of the Greek letter lambda. **2.** *Anatomy* Relating to the deeply serrated suture in the skull between the parietal bones and the occipital bone.

lam•bent (lăm′bənt) *adj.* **1.** Flickering lightly over or on a surface: *lambent moonlight.* **2.** Effortlessly light or brilliant: *lambent wit.* **3.** Having a gentle glow; luminous. See Syns at **bright.** [Lat. *lambēns, lambent-*, pr. part. of *lambere*, to lick.] —**lam′ben•cy** *n.* —**lam′bent•ly** *adv.*

lam•bert (lăm′bərt) *n.* A unit of brightness equivalent to the brightness of a perfectly diffusing surface that emits or reflects one lumen per square centimeter. [After Johann Heinrich *Lambert* (1728–77), German physicist and astronomer.]

lamb•kill (lăm′kĭl′) *n.* See **sheep laurel.**

Lamb of God *n.* Christianity Jesus.

lam•bre•quin (lăm′bər-kĭn, -brə-kĭn) *n.* **1.** A short ornamental drapery for the top of a window or door or the edge of a shelf. **2.** A cloth worn over a helmet in medieval times. [Fr., prob. < Du. *lamperkijn*, dim. of MDu. *lamper*, veil.]

lamb•skin (lăm′skĭn′) *n.* **1.** The hide of a lamb, esp. when dressed without removing the fleece, as for a garment. **2.** Leather made from the dressed hide of a lamb. **3.** Parchment made from such hide.

lamb's lettuce (lămz′) *n.* See **corn salad.**

lamb's quarters *pl.n.* (*used with a sing. or pl. verb*) A common weed (*Chenopodium album*) having lance-shaped leaves with a mealy surface and small green flowers.

lame[1] (lām) *adj.* **lam•er, lam•est 1.** Disabled so that movement, esp. walking, is difficult or impossible. **2.** Marked by pain or rigidness: *a lame back.* **3.** Weak and ineffectual; unsatisfactory: *a lame apology.* ❖ *tr.v.* **lamed, lam•ing, lames** To cause to become lame; cripple. [ME < OE *lama*.] —**lame′ly** *adv.* —**lame′ness** *n.*

lame[2] (lām) *n.* A thin metal plate, esp. one of the overlapping steel plates in medieval armor. [Fr. < OFr. < Lat. *lāmina*, thin plate.]

la•mé (lă-mā′) *n.* A brocaded fabric woven with metallic threads, often of gold or silver. [Fr., spangled, laminated, *lamé* < OFr. *lame*, thin metal plate. See LAME[2].]

lame•brain (lām′brān′) *n. Informal* A stupid person; a dolt. —**lame′brained′** (-brānd′) *adj.*

la•medh (lä′mĭd, -mĕd) *n.* The 12th letter of the Hebrew alphabet. [Heb. *lāmed* < Phoenician **lamd*, ox-goad (sense uncertain), 11th letter of the Phoenician alphabet.]

lame duck *n.* **1.** An elected officeholder continuing in office during the period before the inauguration of a successor. **2.** An ineffective person; a weakling. —**lame′-duck′** (lām′dŭk′) *adj.*

la•mel•la (lə-mĕl′ə) *n., pl.* **-mel•lae** (-mĕl′ē) or **-mel•las** A thin scale, plate, or layer of bone or tissue. [Lat. *lāmella*, dim. of *lāmina*, thin plate.] —**la•mel′lar** *adj.*

la•mel•late (lə-mĕl′āt′, lăm′ə-lāt′) *adj.* **1.** Having, composed of, or arranged in lamellae. **2.** Resembling a lamella. —**lam′el•lat′ed** *adj.* —**lam′el•la′tion** *n.*

lamelli– or **lamell–** *pref.* Lamella: *lamelliform.* [< LAMELLA.]

la•mel•li•branch (lə-mĕl′ə-brăngk′) *n.* Any of the bivalve mollusks belonging to the class Pelecypoda and the subclass Lamellibranchia. [< NLat. *Lāmellibranchia*, class name : LAMELLI– + Lat. *branchia*, gill; see BRANCHIA.] —**la•mel′li•branch′** *adj.*

la•mel•li•corn (lə-mĕl′ĭ-kôrn′) *adj.* Of or belonging to the superfamily Lamellicornia, which includes the scarabs and other beetles that have club-shaped lamellate antennae. [< NLat. *Lāmellicornia*, superfamily name : LAMELLI– + Lat. *cornū*, horn; see ker-[1] in App.] —**la•mel′li•corn** *n.*

la•mel•li•form (lə-mĕl′ə-fôrm′) *adj.* Having the form of a thin plate or lamella.

la•ment (lə-mĕnt′) *v.* **-ment•ed, -ment•ing, -ments** —*tr.* **1.** To express grief for or about; mourn: *lament a death.* **2.** To regret deeply; deplore. —*intr.* **1.** To grieve audibly; wail. **2.** To express sorrow or regret. See Syns at **grieve.** ❖ *n.* **1.** A feeling or expression of grief. **2.** A song or poem expressing deep grief or mourning. [ME *lementen* < OFr. *lamenter* < Lat. *lāmentārī* < *lāmentum*, lament.] —**la•ment′er** *n.*

la•men•ta•ble (lə-mĕn′tə-bəl, lăm′ən-) *adj.* Inspiring or deserving of lament or regret; deplorable or pitiable. —**lam′en•ta•bly** *adv.*

lam•en•ta•tion (lăm′ən-tā′shən) *n.* **1.** The act of lamenting. **2.** A lament. **3. Lamentations** (*used with a sing. verb*) See table at **Bible.**

la•ment•ed (lə-mĕn′tĭd) *adj.* Mourned for: *our late lamented president.* —**la•ment′ed•ly** *adv.*

lam•er (lā′mər) *n. Slang* A person regarded as inept or ineffectual.

la•mi•a (lā′mē-ə) *n., pl.* **-mi•as** or **-mi•ae** (-mē-ē′) **1.** also **Lamia** *Greek Mythology* A monster, represented as a serpent with the head and breasts of a woman, that ate children and sucked the blood from men. **2.** A female vampire. [ME < Lat. < Gk.]

lam•i•na (lăm′ə-nə) *n., pl.* **-nae** (-nē′) or **-nas 1.** A thin plate, sheet, or layer. **2.** *Botany* The expanded area of a leaf or petal; a blade. **3.** A thin layer of bone, membrane, or other tissue. **4.** *Zoology* A thin scalelike or platelike structure. **5.** *Geology* A narrow bed of rock. [Lat. *lāmina*.] —**lam′i•nar, lam′i•nal** *adj.*

laminar flow *n.* Nonturbulent flow of a viscous fluid in layers near a boundary, such as of lubricating oil in bearings.

lam•i•nate (lăm′ə-nāt′) *v.* **-nat•ed, -nat•ing, -nates** —*tr.* **1.** To beat or compress into a thin plate or sheet. **2.** To divide into thin layers. **3.** To make by uniting several layers. **4.** To cover with thin sheets. —*intr.* To split into thin layers or sheets. ❖ *adj.* (-nĭt, -nāt′) Consisting of, arranged in, or covered with laminae. ❖ *n.* (-nĭt, -nāt) A laminated product, such as plywood. —**lam′i•na′tor** *n.*

lam•i•nat•ed (lăm′ə-nā′tĭd) *adj.* **1.** Composed of layers bonded together. **2.** Arranged in laminae; laminate.

lam•i•na•tion (lăm′ə-nā′shən) *n.* **1a.** The act or process of laminating. **b.** The state of being laminated. **2.** Something laminated. **3.** A lamina.

lam•i•nec•to•my (lăm′ə-nĕk′tə-mē) *n., pl.* **-mies** Surgical removal of the posterior arch of a vertebra.

lam•i•ni•tis (lăm′ə-nī′tĭs) *n.* Inflammation of the sensitive vascular tissue laminae of the hoof, esp. in horses.

Lam•mas (lăm′əs) *n.* A feast formerly celebrated on August 1 in England, during which bread from the season's first wheat was consecrated at Mass. [ME *Lammasse* < OE *hlāfmæsse* : *hlāf*, loaf + *mæsse*, Mass; see MASS.]

lam•mer•gei•er also **lam•mer•gey•er** (lăm′ər-gī′ər) *n.* A large predatory bird (*Gypaetus barbatus*) of the vulture family, ranging from southern Europe to China and having a wide wingspan and black plumage. [Ger. *Lämmergeier* : *Lämmer*, genitive pl. of *Lamm*, lamb (< MHGer. *lamp* < OHGer. *lamb*) + *Geier*, vulture (< MHGer. *gīr* < OHGer.).]

lamp (lămp) *n.* **1a.** A device that generates light, heat, or therapeutic radiation. **b.** A vessel containing oil or alcohol burned through a wick for illumination. **2.** A celestial body that gives off or reflects light. **3.** Something that illumines the mind or soul. [ME *lampe* < OFr. < Lat. *lampas* < Gk. < *lampein*, to shine.]

lamp•black (lămp′blăk′) *n.* Fine soot collected from incompletely burned carbonaceous materials, used as a pigment and in matches, explosives, lubricants, and fertilizers.

lam•per eel (lăm′pər) *n.* See **lamprey.** [Alteration of LAMPREY.]

lam•pi•on (lăm′pē-ən) *n.* An oil-burning lamp, often of colored glass, for outdoor use. [Fr. < Ital. *lampione*, augmentative of *lampa*, lamp < OFr. *lampe*. See LAMP.]

lamp•light (lămp′līt′) *n.* The light shed by a lamp.

lamp•light•er (lămp′lī′tər) *n.* One that lights lamps, esp. gaslit lamps.

lamp oil *n.* See **kerosene.**

lam•poon (lăm-poōn′) *n.* **1.** A written attack ridiculing a person, group, or institution. **2.** A light good-humored satire. ❖ *tr.v.* **-pooned, -poon•ing, -poons** To ridicule or satirize in or as if in a lampoon. [Fr. *lampon*, perh. < *lampons*, let us drink (< drinking songs), first pers. pl. imper. of *lamper*, to gulp down, of Gmc. orig.] —**lam•poon′er, lam•poon′ist** *n.* —**lam•poon′er•y** *n.*

lamp•post (lămp′pōst′) *n.* A post supporting a street lamp.

lam•prey (lăm′prē) *n., pl.* **-preys** Any of various primitive elongated freshwater or anadromous fishes of the family Petromyzontidae, with a sucking mouth and rasping teeth. [ME *lamprei* < OFr. *lampreie* < Med.Lat. *lamprēda.*]

lamp•shade (lămp′shād′) *n.* Any of various protective or ornamental coverings used to screen a light bulb.

lamp•shell (lămp′shĕl′) *n.* See **brachiopod.**

lamp•work•ing (lămp′wûr′kĭng) *n.* The process of sculpting glass by twirling thin rods of glass over a gas-oxygen burner.

LAN (lăn) *n.* A system that links together electronic office equipment, such as computers, and forms a network within an office or building. [L(OCAL) A(REA) N(ETWORK).]

la•nai (lə-nī′) *n., pl.* **-nais** A veranda or roofed patio. [Hawaiian *lānai*.]

Lanai An island of central HI W of Maui; developed as a pineapple-growing area after 1922.

la•nate (lā′nāt′) *adj.* Having or consisting of woolly hairs. [Lat. *lānātus* < *lāna*, wool.]

Lan•ca•shire (lăng′kə-shĭr′, -shər) A historical region of NW England on the Irish Sea; part of the kingdom of Northumbria in Anglo-Saxon times.

Lan•cas•ter[1] (lăng′kə-stər, lăn′-) English royal house that from 1399 to 1461 produced three kings of England—Henry IV, Henry V, and Henry VI. During the Wars of the Roses its symbol was a red rose. —**Lan•cas′tri•an** (lăng-kăs′trē-ən) *adj. & n.*

Lan•cas•ter[2] (lăng′kə-stər, -kăs′tər, lăn′-) A municipal borough of NW England N of Liverpool; chartered 1193. Pop. 133,610.

lance (lăns) *n.* **1a.** A thrusting weapon with a long wooden shaft and a sharp metal head. **b.** A similar implement for spearing fish. **2.** A cavalry lancer. **3.** *Medicine* See **lancet** 1. ❖ *tr.v.* **lanced, lanc•ing, lanc•es 1.** To pierce with a lance. **2.** *Medicine* To make a surgical incision in; cut into. [ME < OFr. < Lat. *lancea*, prob. of Celt. orig.]

lance corporal *n.* A noncommissioned officer in the US Marine Corps, ranking above private first class and below corporal. [< *lancepesade* < obsolete Fr. *lancepessade* < Ital. *lancia spezzata*, superior soldier : *lancia*, lance (< Lat. *lancea*; see LANCE) + *spezzata*, fem. p. part. of *spezzare*, to break to pieces.]

lance•let (lăns′lĭt) *n.* Any of various small flattened marine organisms of the subphylum Cephalochordata.

Lan•ce•lot (lăn′sə-lət, -lŏt′, län′-) *n.* In Arthurian legend, a Knight of the Round Table whose love affair with Queen Guine-

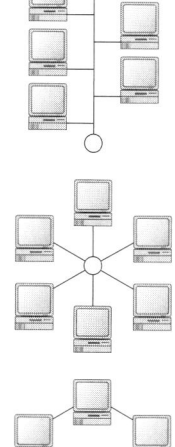

LAN
top to bottom: bus, star, and ring network configurations

vere resulted in a war with King Arthur.

lan·ce·o·late (lăn′sē-ə-lāt′) *adj.* Tapering from a rounded base toward an apex; lance-shaped: *lanceolate leaves.* [LLat. *lanceolātus* < Lat. *lanceola,* dim. of Lat. *lancea,* lance. See LANCE.]

lanc·er (lăn′sər) *n.* **1.** A cavalryman armed with a lance. **2.** A member of a regiment originally armed with lances. **3. lancers** (*used with a sing. verb*) **a.** A kind of quadrille. **b.** The music for this dance. [Fr. *lancier* < OFr., maker of lances < *lance,* lance. See LANCE.]

lan·cet (lăn′sĭt) *n.* **1.** *Medicine* A surgical knife with a short, wide, pointed double-edged blade. **2.** *Architecture* A lancet arch. **3.** A lancet window. [ME < OFr., dim. of *lance,* lance. See LANCE.]

lancet arch *n.* An arch that is narrow and pointed like the head of a spear.

lancet fish *n.* Either of two large elongated marine fishes (*Alepisaurus ferox* or *A. brevirostris*) having long sharp teeth, a large dorsal fin, and no scales.

lancet window *n.* A tall narrow window set in a lancet arch.

lance·wood (lăns′wŏŏd′) *n.* **1.** Any of several tropical American trees, esp. *Calycophyllum candidissimum,* having hard, durable, uniformly grained wood. **2.** The wood of this tree.

Lan·chow (lăn′jō′) See **Lanzhou.**

lan·ci·nat·ing (lăn′sə-nā′tĭng) *adj.* Characterized by a sensation of cutting, piercing, or stabbing. [< *lancinate,* to stab < Lat. *lancināre, lancināt-,* to lacerate.]

land (lănd) *n.* **1.** The solid ground of the earth. **2a.** Ground or soil: *tilled the land.* **b.** A topographically or functionally distinct tract: *desert land.* **3a.** A nation; a country. **b.** The people of a nation, district, or region. **c. lands** Territorial possessions or property. **4.** Public or private landed property; real estate. **5.** *Law* **a.** A tract that may be owned, together with everything growing or constructed on it. **b.** A landed estate. **6a.** An agricultural or farming area. **b.** Farming considered as a way of life. **7.** An area or realm: *the land of fantasy.* **8.** The raised portion of a grooved surface, as on a phonograph record. ❖ *v.* **land·ed, land·ing, lands** —*tr.* **1a.** To bring to and unload on land: *land cargo.* **b.** To set (a vehicle) down on land or another surface: *land an airplane smoothly.* **2.** *Informal* To cause to arrive in a place or condition: *Shoplifting landed him in jail.* **3a.** To catch and pull in (a fish). **b.** *Informal* To win; secure: *landed a big contract.* **4.** *Informal* To deliver: *landed a blow.* —*intr.* **1a.** To come to shore. **b.** To disembark. **2.** To descend toward and settle onto the ground or another surface: *The helicopter has landed.* **3.** *Informal* To arrive in a place or condition: *landed in trouble.* **4.** To come to rest in a certain way or place: *land on one's feet.* [ME < OE.]

Land, Edwin Herbert 1909–91. Amer. inventor who developed a light-polarizing plastic film (1932).

lan·dau (lăn′dô′, -dou′) *n.* **1.** A four-wheeled carriage with facing passenger seats and a roof in two sections that can be lowered or detached. **2.** A style of automobile with a similar roof. [After *Landau,* a city of southwest Germany.]

Lan·dau (län-dou′), **Lev Davidovich** 1908–68. Soviet physicist who won a 1962 Nobel Prize.

land bank *n.* A bank that issues long-term loans on real estate in return for mortgages.

land bridge *n.* An isthmus.

land·ed (lăn′dĭd) *adj.* **1.** Owning land: *the landed gentry.* **2.** Consisting of land or real estate: *landed property.*

land·er (lăn′dər) *n.* A space vehicle designed to land on a celestial body, such as the moon or a planet.

land·fall (lănd′fôl′) *n.* **1.** The act or an instance of sighting or reaching land after a voyage or flight. **2.** The land sighted or reached after a voyage or flight.

land·fill (lănd′fĭl′) *n.* **1.** A method of solid waste disposal in which refuse is buried between layers of dirt so as to fill in or reclaim low-lying ground. **2.** A site of such disposal. ❖ *v.* **-filled, -fill·ing, -fills** —*tr.* **1.** To dispose of (waste material) in a landfill. **2.** To fill in or reclaim (land) by this method. —*intr.* To dispose of refuse or reclaim land by filling in low-lying ground.

land·form (lănd′fôrm′) *n.* One of the features making up the earth's surface, such as a plain, mountain, or valley.

land grant *n.* A government grant of public land for a railroad, highway, or state college.

land·grave (lănd′grāv′) *n.* **1.** A man in medieval Germany who had jurisdiction over a particular territory. **2.** Used as the title for such a nobleman. [< MLGer. : *lant,* land + *grave,* count.]

land·gra·vi·ate (lănd-grā′vē-ĭt, -āt′) *n.* The rank and office of a landgrave or landgravine.

land·gra·vine (lănd′grə-vēn′) *n.* **1.** A woman holding the title to a landgraviate. **2.** The wife or widow of a landgrave. **3.** Used as the title for such a noblewoman. [< MLGer. *landgravin,* fem. of *landgrave,* landgrave. See LANDGRAVE.]

land·hold·er (lănd′hōl′dər) *n.* One that owns land. —**land′-hold′ing** *adj. & n.*

land·ing (lăn′dĭng) *n.* **1a.** The act or process of coming to land or rest, esp. after a voyage or flight. **b.** A termination, esp. of a voyage or flight. **2.** A site for loading and unloading passengers and cargo. **3a.** An intermediate platform on a flight of stairs. **b.** The area at the top or bottom of a staircase.

landing craft *n.* A naval craft designed to convey troops and equipment from ship to shore.

lanceolate
lanceolate leaf

lancet window

landing field *n.* A tract of land used by aircraft for landing and taking off.

landing gear *n.* The components of an aircraft or a spacecraft that support the weight of the craft and its load and give it mobility on ground or water.

landing strip *n.* An aircraft runway without airport facilities.

land·la·dy (lănd′lā′dē) *n.* **1.** A woman who owns and rents land, buildings, or dwelling units. **2.** A woman who runs a rooming house or an inn; an innkeeper.

land·less (lănd′lĭs) *adj.* Owning or having no land.

land·locked (lănd′lŏkt′) *adj.* **1.** Entirely or almost entirely surrounded by land: *a landlocked country.* **2.** Confined to inland waters, as certain salmon.

land·lord (lănd′lôrd′) *n.* **1.** One that owns and rents land, buildings, or dwelling units. **2.** A man who runs a rooming house or an inn; an innkeeper.

land·lub·ber (lănd′lŭb′ər) *n.* A person unfamiliar with the sea or seamanship. —**land′lub′ber·ly** *adj.*

land·mark (lănd′märk′) *n.* **1.** A prominent identifying feature of a landscape. **2.** A fixed marker, such as a concrete block, that indicates a boundary line. **3.** An event marking an important stage of development or a turning point in history. **4.** A building or site with historical significance, esp. one officially designated for preservation. ❖ *adj.* Having great import or significance: *a landmark ruling.*

land·mass (lănd′măs′) *n.* A large unbroken area of land.

land mine *n.* **1.** An explosive mine laid usu. just below the surface of the ground. **2.** *Informal* A concealed yet incipient crisis.

land office *n.* A government office that handles and keeps records of the sale or transfer of public land.

land-of·fice business (lănd′ô′fĭs, -ŏf′ĭs) *n.* A thriving, extensive, or rapidly moving volume of trade.

Lan·don (lăn′dən), **Alfred Mossman ("Alf")** 1887–1987. Amer. politician who served as governor of KS (1933–37) and ran unsuccessfully for President in 1936.

land·own·er (lănd′ō′nər) *n.* One that owns land. —**land′-own′er·ship′** *n.* —**land′own′ing** *adj. & n.*

Lan·dow·ska (lăn-dôf′skə, län-dôf′skä), **Wanda** 1879?–1959. Polish-born harpsichordist who was largely responsible for the modern revival of interest in the harpsichord.

land-poor (lănd′pŏŏr′) *adj.* Owning much unprofitable land but lacking the capital to improve or maintain it.

land reform *n.* Measures taken to bring about an equitable apportionment of agricultural land.

Land·sat (lănd′săt′) *n.* Any of various satellites used to gather data for images of the Earth's land surface and coastal regions. [LAND + SAT(ELLITE).]

land·scape (lănd′skāp′) *n.* **1.** An expanse of scenery that can be seen in a single view. **2.** A picture depicting an expanse of scenery. **3.** The branch of art dealing with the representation of natural scenery. **4.** The aspect of the land characteristic of a particular region. **5.** Grounds that have been landscaped. **6.** An extensive mental view; an interior prospect: *"They occupy the whole landscape of my thought"* (James Thurber). **7.** The orientation of a page such that the shorter side runs from top to bottom. ❖ *v.* **-scaped, -scap·ing, -scapes** —*tr.* To adorn or improve (a section of ground) by contouring and by planting flowers, shrubs, or trees. —*intr.* To arrange grounds artistically as a profession. [Du. *landschap* < MDu. *landscap,* region : *land,* land + *-scap,* state, condition (collective suff.).] —**land′scap′er** *n.*

landscape architect *n.* One whose profession is the decorative and functional alteration and planting of grounds, esp. at or around a building site. —**landscape architecture** *n.*

landscape gardener *n.* One whose occupation is the decoration of land by planting trees and shrubs and designing gardens. —**landscape gardening** *n.*

land·scap·ist (lănd′skā′pĭst) *n.* A painter of landscapes.

Land's End or **Lands End** (lăndz) A peninsula of SW England in Cornwall.

land·side (lănd′sīd′) *n.* The flat side of a plow opposite the furrow.

lands·leit (länts′līt′) *n.* Plural of **landsman**[2]. [Yiddish *landslayt* < MHGer. *lantsliute,* natives, compatriots : *lant,* land; see LANDSMAN[2] + *liute,* pl. of *liut,* person, people (< OHGer.; see *leudh-* in App.).]

land·slide (lănd′slīd′) *n.* **1a.** The downward sliding of a relatively dry mass of earth and rock. **b.** The mass that slides. **2a.** An overwhelming majority of votes for a political party or candidate. **b.** An election that sweeps a party or candidate into office. **3.** A great victory. —**land′slid′ing** *n.*

land·slip (lănd′slĭp′) *n.* See **landslide** 1.

Lands·mål (länts′môl′) *n.* See **New Norwegian.** [Norw. : *land,* country (< ON) + *mål,* speech (< ON Norw.).]

lands·man[1] (lăndz′mən) *n.* One who lives and works on land.

lands·man[2] (länts′mən) *n., pl.* **lands·leit** (-līt′) A Jew from one's place of origin, esp. in Eastern Europe. [Yiddish < MHGer. *lantsman,* countryman : *lant,* land (< OHGer.) + *man,* man (< OHGer.; see **man-**[1] in App.).]

Land·stei·ner (lănd′stī′nər, länt′shtī′-), **Karl** 1868–1943. Austrian-born pathologist who won a 1930 Nobel Prize.

Land·tag (länt′täk′) *n.* **1.** The legislative assembly of some German states. **2.** A diet or assembly in some German states in the 19th century. [Ger. : *Land,* country (< MHGer. *lant*; see LANDSMAN[2]) + *Tag,* day, diet, assembly (< MHGer. < OHGer., influenced by Med.Lat. *diēta,* diet; see **agh-** in App.).]

land·ward (lănd′wərd) *adv. & adj.* To or toward land: *sailing landward; the landward side.* **—land′wards** *adv.*

lane (lān) *n.* **1a.** A narrow country road. **b.** A narrow way or passage between walls, hedges, or fences. **2.** A narrow passage, course, or track, esp.: **a.** A prescribed course for ships or aircraft. **b.** A strip delineated on a street or highway for a single line of vehicles. **c.** *Sports* One of a set of parallel courses marking the bounds for contestants in a race, esp. in swimming or track. **d.** *Sports* A wood-surfaced passageway or alley along which a bowling ball is rolled. **e.** *Basketball* The rectangular area marked on a court from the end line to the foul line. [ME < OE.]

lang (lăng) *adj.* Scots Long.

Lang (lăng), **Andrew** 1844–1912. British writer and anthropologist best known for *The Blue Fairy Book* (1889).

Lang, Fritz 1890–1976. Austrian-born Amer. filmmaker whose films include *Metropolis* (1927) and *Fury* (1936).

lang·bein·ite (lăng′bī-nīt′, lăng′-) *n.* An evaporite mineral, $K_2Mg_2(SO_4)_3$, used as a source of potassium sulfate for fertilizer. [After A. *Langbein,* 19th-cent. German chemist.]

Lange (lăng), **Dorothea** 1895–1965. Amer. photographer noted for her portraits of rural workers during the Depression.

Lang·land (lăng′lənd), **William** 1332?–1400. English poet credited with the authorship of *Piers Plowman.*

lang·lauf (lăng′louf′) *n.* **1.** The sport of cross-country skiing. **2.** A cross-country ski run or race. [Ger. : *lang,* long (< MHGer. < OHGer.; see **del-** in App.) + *Lauf,* race (< MHGer. *louf* < OHGer. *hlouf*).] **—lang′lauf′er** *n.*

lang·ley (lăng′lē) *n., pl.* **-leys** A unit equal to one gram calorie per square centimeter of irradiated surface, used to measure solar radiation. [After Samuel Pierpoint LANGLEY.]

Langley, Mount A peak, 4,227.9 m (14,026 ft), in the Sierra Nevada of S CA.

Langley, Samuel Pierpoint 1834–1906. Amer. astronomer who built the first successful heavier-than-air flying machines.

Lang·muir (lăng′myŏŏr′), **Irving** 1881–1957. Amer. chemist who won a 1932 Nobel Prize.

Lan·go·bard (lăng′gə-bärd′) *n.* See **Lombard** 1. [Lat. *Lango-bardus.* See LOMBARD.] **—Lan′go·bar′dic** *adj.*

lan·gouste (län-gŏŏst′) *n.* The spiny lobster. [Fr. < OFr. < O Provençal *langosta* < VLat. **lacusta* < Lat. *locusta,* lobster, locust.]

lan·gous·tine (läng′gə-stēn′) *n.* A large edible prawn. [Fr., dim. of *langouste,* langouste.]

lan·grage (lăng′grĭj) *n.* A type of shot consisting of scrap iron loaded into a case and formerly used in naval warfare to damage sails and rigging. [?]

lang·syne also **lang syne** (lăng-zīn′) *Scots adv.* Long ago; long since. ❖ *n.* Time long past; times past. [Sc. *lang syne* < ME *lang sine* : *long, lang,* long; see LONG[1] + *sine,* since (contraction of *sithen, sithens;* see SINCE).]

Lang·try (lăng′trē), **Lillie** Known as "the Jersey Lily." 1853–1929. British actress famous for her love affair with Edward VII.

lan·guage (lăng′gwĭj) *n.* **1a.** Communication of thoughts and feelings through a system of arbitrary signals, such as voice sounds, gestures, or written symbols. **b.** Such a system including its rules for combining its components, such as words. **c.** Such a system as used by a nation, people, or other distinct community; often contrasted with *dialect.* **2a.** A system of signs, gestures, or rules used in communicating: *the language of algebra.* **b.** *Computer Science* A system of symbols and rules for communication with or between computers. **3.** Body language; kinesics. **4.** The special vocabulary and usages of a scientific, professional, or other group. **5.** A characteristic style of speech or writing. **6.** A particular manner of utterance: *persuasive language.* **7.** The manner or means of communication between living creatures other than humans. **8.** Verbal communication as a subject of study. **9.** The wording of a legal document or statute as distinct from the spirit. [ME < OFr. *langage < langue,* tongue, language < Lat. *lingua.* See **dnghū-** in App.]

language arts *pl.n.* The subjects, including reading, spelling, and composition, aimed at developing reading and writing skills, usu. taught in elementary and secondary school.

language isolate *n.* A language that has no known linguistic affiliation with any other language, such as Basque or Tarascan.

language laboratory *n.* A room for learning foreign languages, having equipment such as tape recorders connected to monitoring devices.

langue (läng, läNg) *n.* Language viewed as a system including the vocabulary, grammar, and pronunciation of a particular community. [Fr. < OFr. See LANGUAGE.]

Lan·gue·doc (läng-dôk′, läNg-) A historical region and former province of S-central France on the Gulf of Lions; included in the French royal domain in 1271.

langue d'oc (dôk′) *n.* The Romance language formerly spoken in and around Provence and Roussillon, developing into Provençal. [Fr. < OFr. : *langue,* language; see LANGUAGE + *de,* of (< Lat. *dē*); see DE–) + O Provençal *oc,* yes; see OCCITAN.]

langue d'o·ïl (doĭl′, doĭ′, dô-ēl′) *n.* The Romance language of

medieval France north of the Loire River, on which modern French is based. [Fr. < OFr. : *langue,* language; see LANGUAGE + *de,* of; see LANGUE D'OC + *oil,* yes (ult. < Lat. *hoc ille (fēcit),* he (did) this : *hoc,* this; see OCCITAN + *ille,* he; see **al-** in App.).]

lan·guet (lăng′gwĭt, läng-gwĕt′) *n.* One that functions or is shaped like a tongue. [ME < OFr. *languete,* dim. of *langue,* tongue < Lat. *lingua.* See **dnghū-** in App.]

lan·guid (lăng′gwĭd) *adj.* **1.** Lacking energy or vitality; weak: *a languid wave.* **2.** Showing little or no spirit or animation; listless. **3.** Lacking vigor or force; slow: *languid breezes.* [Fr. *languide* < Lat. *languidus < languēre,* to be languid.] **—lan′guid·ly** *adv.* **—lan′guid·ness** *n.*

lan·guish (lăng′gwĭsh) *intr.v.* **-guished, -guish·ing, -guish·es** **1.** To be or become weak or feeble; lose strength or vigor. **2.** To exist or continue in miserable or disheartening conditions: *languished away in prison.* **3.** To remain unattended or be neglected: *legislation that languished in committee.* **4.** To become downcast or pine away in longing. **5.** To affect a wistful or languid air, esp. to gain sympathy. [ME *languishen* < OFr. *languir, languiss-* < Lat. *languēre,* to be languid.]

lan·guor (lăng′gər, läng′ər) *n.* **1.** Lack of physical or mental energy; listlessness. **2.** A dreamy, lazy mood or quality. **3.** Oppressive quiet or stillness. [ME < OFr. < Lat. < *languēre,* to be languid. See LANGUISH.] **—lan′guor·ous** *adj.* **—lan′guor·ous·ly** *adv.* **—lan′guor·ous·ness** *n.*

lan·gur (läng-gŏŏr′) *n.* Any of various slender long-tailed Asian monkeys of the genus *Presbytis* and related genera that eat leaves, fruits, and seeds and have a chin tuft and bushy eyebrows. [Hindi *langūr,* perh. < Skt. *lāngūlam,* tail.]

lan·iard (lăn′yərd) *n.* Variant of **lanyard.**

La·nier (lə-nîr′), **Sidney** 1842–81. Amer. writer and musician noted for his melodic poems and *Tiger Lilies* (1867).

la·nif·er·ous (lə-nĭf′ər-əs) *adj.* Having wool or woollike hair. [Lat. *lānifer (lāna,* wool + *-fer, -fer)* + −OUS.]

La Ni·ña (lä nēn′yä) *n.* A cooling of the ocean surface off the western coast of South America, occurring periodically every 4 to 12 years and affecting Pacific and other weather patterns. [Am.Sp., the girl (to distinguish it from El Niño) : Sp. *la,* the (< Lat. *illa;* see **al-[1]** in App.) + *niña,* daughter (< OSpan. *ninna* < VLat. **ninna*).]

lank (lăngk) *adj.* **lank·er, lank·est** **1.** Long and lean. See Syns at **lean[2].** **2.** Long, straight, and limp: *lank hair.* [ME < OE *hlanc.*] **—lank′ly** *adv.* **—lank′ness** *n.*

lank·y (lăng′kē) *adj.* **-i·er, -i·est** Tall, thin, and ungainly. See Syns at **lean[2].** **—lank′i·ly** *adv.* **—lank′i·ness** *n.*

lan·ner (lăn′ər) *n.* **1.** A falcon (*Falco biarmicus*) of Africa, the Mediterranean, and southern Asia. **2.** A female of this species, used in falconry. [ME *laner* < OFr. *lanier,* woolweaver, coward < Lat. *lānārius,* woolworker < *lāna,* wool.]

lan·ner·et (lăn′ə-rĕt′) *n.* A male lanner, smaller than the female, used in falconry. [ME *laneret* < OFr., dim. of *lanier,* lanner. See LANNER.]

lan·o·lin (lăn′ə-lĭn) *n.* A fatty substance obtained from wool and used in soaps, cosmetics, and ointments. [Ger. : < Lat. *lāna,* wool + Lat. *oleum,* oil.]

la·nose (lā′nōs′) *adj.* Woolly. [Lat. *lānōsus < lāna,* wool.]

Lan·sing (lăn′sĭng) The cap. of MI, in the S-central part NW of Detroit. Pop. 119,128.

lan·ta·na (lăn-tä′nə, -tä′rə) *n.* Any of various aromatic, chiefly tropical shrubs of the genus *Lantana,* having dense spikes or heads and small colorful flowers. [NLat. *Lantana,* genus name < Ital. dialectal *lantana,* wayfaring tree, viburnum, perh. < VLat. **lentāgō, *lentāgin-* < Lat. *lentus,* light, flexible.]

lan·tern (lăn′tərn) *n.* **1a.** An often portable case with transparent or translucent sides for holding and protecting a light. **b.** A decorative casing for a light, often of paper. **c.** A light and its protective or decorative case. **2a.** The room at the top of a lighthouse where the light is located. **b.** *Obsolete* A lighthouse. **3.** A structure built on top of a roof or dome with open or windowed walls to admit light and air. [ME < OFr. *lanterne* < Lat. *lanterna* < Gk. *lamptēr < lampein,* to shine.]

lantern fish *n.* Any of numerous small deep-sea fishes of the family Myctophidae, having phosphorescent light organs along each body wall.

lantern fly *n.* Any of various chiefly tropical insects of the family Fulgoridae, having an enlarged elongated head, once thought to be luminescent.

lantern jaw *n.* **1.** A lower jaw that protrudes beyond the upper jaw. **2.** A long thin jaw that gives the face a gaunt appearance. **—lan′tern-jawed′** (lăn′tərn-jôd′) *adj.*

lantern wheel *n.* A small mechanical pinion consisting of circular disks connected by cylindrical bars that serve as teeth.

lan·tha·nide (lăn′thə-nīd′) *n.* See **rare-earth element.** [LANTHAN(UM) + −IDE.]

lanthanide series *n.* The set of chemically related elements with properties similar to those of lanthanum, with atomic numbers from 57 to 71; the rare-earth elements.

lan·tha·num (lăn′thə-nəm) *n. Symbol* **La** A soft malleable metallic rare-earth element, obtained chiefly from monazite and bastnaesite and used in glass manufacture. Atomic number 57; atomic weight 138.91; melting point 920°C; boiling point 3,469°

lane
swimming lanes

langur
Hanuman langur
Presbytis entellus

ă	pat	oi	boy
ā	pay	ou	out
âr	care	ŏŏ	took
ä	father	ōō	boot
ĕ	pet	ŭ	cut
ē	be	ûr	urge
ĭ	pit	th	thin
ī	pie	th	this
îr	pier	hw	which
ŏ	pot	zh	vision
ō	toe	ə	about,
ô	paw		item

Stress marks:
′ (primary);
′ (secondary), as in
lexicon (lĕk′sĭ-kŏn′)

C; specific gravity 5.98 to 6.186; valence 3. See table at **element**. [NLat. < Gk. *lanthanein*, to escape notice (< the finding of the element hidden in oxide of cerium).]

lant·horn (lănt′hôrn′, lăn′tərn) *n. Chiefly British* A lantern. [Alteration of LANTERN.]

la·nu·gi·nous (lə-nōō′jə-nəs, -nyōō′-) also **la·nu·gi·nose** (-nōs′) *adj.* Covered with soft short hair; downy. [< Lat. *lānūginōsus* < *lānūgō, lānūgin*-, lanugo. See LANUGO.]

la·nu·go (lə-nōō′gō, -nyōō′-) *n., pl.* **-gos** A covering of fine soft hair, as on a leaf or a newborn child. [ME, pith < Lat. *lānūgō*, down < *lāna*, wool.]

lan·yard also **lan·iard** (lăn′yərd) *n.* **1.** *Nautical* A short rope or gasket used for fastening something or securing rigging. **2.** A cord worn around the neck for carrying something, such as a knife. **3.** A cord with a hook at one end used to fire a cannon. [Perh. alteration of ME *lainere*, strap < OFr. *laniere* < *lasne*, perh. alteration of **nasle*, lace, of Gmc. orig.]

Lan·za (lăn′zə, län′-), **Mario** 1921–57. Amer. tenor and actor who recorded both popular music and opera.

Lan·zhou also **Lan·chow** (län′jō′) A city of central China on the Huang He (Yellow River) N of Chengdu; cap. of Gansu province. Pop. 1,617,761.

Lao (lou) *n., pl.* **Lao** or **Laos** (louz′) **1.** A member of a Buddhist people inhabiting the area bordering the Mekong River in Laos and Thailand. **2.** The Tai language of the Lao. ❖ *adj.* Of or relating to the Lao or their language or culture.

La·oc·o·on (lā-ŏk′ō-ŏn′) *n. Greek Mythology* A Trojan priest of Apollo who was killed along with his two sons by two sea serpents for having warned his people of the Trojan horse.

La·od·i·ce·a (lā-ŏd′ĭ-sē′ə, lā′ə-dī-) An ancient city of W Asia Minor in present-day W Turkey; built by the Seleucids in the 3rd cent. B.C.

La·od·i·ce·an (lā-ŏd′ĭ-sē′ən) *adj.* **1.** Of or relating to Laodicea. **2.** Indifferent or lukewarm esp. in matters of religion. ❖ *n.* A native or inhabitant of Laodicea. [Adj., sense 2, in reference to Revelation 3:14–16.]

La·om·e·don (lā-ŏm′ĭ-dŏn′) *n. Greek Mythology* The founder and first king of Troy and father of Priam.

La·os (lous, lā′ŏs′) A country of SE Asia; became part of French Indochina in 1893 and gained its independence in 1953. Cap. Vientiane. Pop. 4,742,000.

La·o·tian (lā-ō′shən, lou′shən) *adj.* **1.** Of or relating to Laos or its people, language, or culture. **2.** Of or relating to the Lao people. ❖ *n.* **1.** A native or inhabitant of Laos. **2.** A Lao.

Lao Tzu also **Lao-tse** or **Lao·zi** (lou′dzŭ′) fl. 6th cent. B.C. Chinese philosopher regarded as the founder of Taoism.

lap[1] (lăp) *n.* **1a.** The front area from the waist to the knees of a seated person. **b.** The portion of a garment that covers the lap. **2.** A hanging or flaplike part, esp. of a garment. **3.** An area of responsibility, interest, or control. *—idiom:* **the lap of luxury** Conditions of great affluence or material comfort. [ME *lappe*, lappet, lap < OE *læppa*, lappet.] **—lap′ful′** *n.*

lap[2] (lăp) *v.* **lapped, lap·ping, laps** *—tr.* **1a.** To place or lay (something) so as to overlap another. **b.** To lie partly over or on: *each shingle lapping the next.* **2.** To fold (something) over onto itself. **3.** To wrap or wind around (something); encircle. **4.** To envelop in something; swathe: *lapped in furs.* **5.** To join (pieces, as of wood) by means of a scarf or lap joint. **6.** To get ahead of (an opponent) in a race by one or more complete circuits of the course, as in running, or by two or more lengths of pool in swimming. **7.** To convert (cotton or other fibers) into a sheet or layer. **8a.** To polish (a surface) until smooth. **b.** To hone (two mating parts) against each other until closely fitted. *—intr.* **1.** To lie partly on or over something; overlap. **2.** To form a lap or fold. **3.** To wind around or enfold something. ❖ *n.* **1a.** A part that overlaps. **b.** The amount by which one part overlaps another. **2a.** One complete round or circuit, as of a racetrack. **b.** One complete length of a straight course, as of a swimming pool. **3.** A segment or stage, as of a trip. **4a.** A length, as of rope, required to make one complete turn around something. **b.** The act of lapping or encircling. **5.** A continuous band or layer of fiber. **6.** A wheel, disk, or slab of leather or metal, used for polishing and smoothing. [ME *lappen* < *lappe*, lap, lappet. See LAP[1].]

lap[3] (lăp) *v.* **lapped, lap·ping, laps** *—tr.* **1.** To take in (a liquid or food) by lifting it with the tongue. **2.** To wash or slap against with soft liquid sounds. *—intr.* **1.** To lap a liquid or food. **2.** To lap against something. ❖ *n.* **1a.** The act or an instance of lapping. **b.** The amount taken in by lapping. **2.** The sound of lapping. **3.** A watery food or drink. *—phrasal verb:* **lap up** To receive eagerly or greedily: *lapping up praise.* [ME *lapen* < OE *lapian*.]

lap·a·ro·scope (lăp′ər-ə-skōp′) *n.* A slender tubular endoscope inserted through an incision in the abdominal wall to view the abdominal or pelvic cavities. [Gk. *lapara*, flank (< fem. of *laparos*, soft) + –SCOPE.]

lap·a·ros·co·py (lăp′ə-rŏs′kə-pē) *n., pl.* **-pies** An operation in which a laparoscope is used, as in an examination of the liver. [Gk. *lapara*, flank; see LAPAROSCOPE + –SCOPY.] **—lap′a·ro·scop′ic** (-ə-skŏp′ĭk) *adj.* **—lap′a·ros′co·pist** *n.*

lap·a·rot·o·my (lăp′ə-rŏt′ə-mē) *n., pl.* **-mies** Surgical incision into the abdominal wall, esp. into the flank. [Gk. *lapara*, flank; see LAPAROSCOPE + –TOMY.]

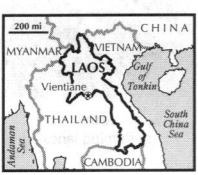

Laos

lap joint

La Paz (lə päz′, lä päs′) The administrative cap. of Bolivia, in the W part near Lake Titicaca. Pop. 784,976.

lap belt *n.* A seat belt that fastens across the lap.

lap·board (lăp′bôrd′, -bōrd′) *n.* A flat board held on the lap as a substitute for a table or desk.

lap dance *n.* An erotic dance that a stripper performs while straddling a customer's lap.

lap dissolve *n.* See **dissolve**.

lap dog *n.* **1.** A small pet dog. **2.** *Informal* One eager to do another's bidding, esp. in order to maintain a position of privilege or favor.

la·pel (lə-pĕl′) *n.* The part of a garment, such as a coat, that is an extension of the collar and folds back against the breast. [< LAP[1].] **—la·peled′, la·pelled′** *adj.*

lap·i·dar·i·an (lăp′ĭ-dâr′ē-ən) *adj.* Of or relating to the working of stone or gems; lapidary. [< Lat. *lapidārius*, stonecutter. See LAPIDARY.]

lap·i·dar·y (lăp′ĭ-dĕr′ē) *n., pl.* **-ies 1.** One who cuts, polishes, or engraves gems. **2.** A dealer in precious or semiprecious stones. ❖ *adj.* **1.** Of or relating to precious stones or the art of working with them. **2a.** Engraved in stone. **b.** Marked by conciseness, precision, or refinement of expression: *lapidary prose.* **c.** Sharply or finely delineated. [ME *lapidarie* < OFr. *lapidaire* < Lat. *lapidārius* < *lapis, lapid*-, stone.]

la·pil·lus (lə-pĭl′əs) *n., pl.* **-pil·li** (-pĭl′ī′) A small solidified fragment of lava. [Lat., dim. of *lapis*, stone.]

lap·in (lăp′ĭn, lä-păn′) *n.* Rabbit fur, esp. when dyed to imitate a more expensive fur. [Fr. < OFr. *lapriel* (prob. influenced by *connin*, rabbit).]

lap·is (lăp′ĭs) *n.* **1.** Lapis lazuli. **2.** A medium to dark blue. [Short for LAPIS LAZULI.]

lapis laz·u·li (lăz′ə-lē, -yə-, lăzh′ə-) *n.* An opaque to translucent blue, violet-blue, or greenish-blue semiprecious gemstone composed mainly of lazurite and calcite. [ME < OFr. < Med.Lat. *lapis lazulī* : Lat. *lapis*, stone + Med.Lat. *lazulī*, genitive of *lazulum*, lapis lazuli (< Ar. *lāzaward* < Pers. *lājward*).]

Lap·ith (lăp′ĭth) *n. Greek Mythology* One of a Thessalian tribe who at the wedding of their king defeated the drunken centaurs.

lap joint *n.* A joint, as between two boards or metal parts, in which the ends or edges are overlapped and fastened together.

La·place (lə-pläs′, lä-), Marquis **Pierre Simon de** 1749–1827. French mathematician and astronomer noted for his theory of a nebular origin of the solar system.

Lap·land (lăp′lănd′, -lənd) A region of extreme N Europe including N Norway, Sweden, and Finland and the Kola Peninsula of NW Russia. **—Lap′land·er** *n.*

La Pla·ta (lä plä′tä) A city of E-central Argentina SE of Buenos Aires; founded 1882. Pop. 520,647.

La Pla·ta Peak (lə plä′tə) A mountain, 4,380.1 m (14,361 ft), in the Sawatch Range of the Rocky Mts. in central CO.

Lapp (lăp) *n.* See **Sami**. [Swed. < OSwed. *lapper*, piece, perh. of Finn. orig.] **—Lapp′ish** *adj.*

lap·pet (lăp′ĭt) *n.* **1.** A decorative flap or loose fold on a garment or headdress. **2.** A flaplike structure, such as the earlobe.

lap robe *n.* A blanket or fur piece for the lap, legs, and feet.

lapse (lăps) *v.* **lapsed, laps·ing, laps·es** *—intr.* **1a.** To fall from a previous level or standard, as of accomplishment or conduct. **b.** To deviate from a prescribed or accepted way. **c.** To pass gradually or smoothly; slip. **2a.** To come to an end, esp. gradually or temporarily: *His attention had lapsed during the lecture.* **b.** To be no longer valid or active; expire. **3.** *Law* To pass to another through neglect or omission. Used of a right or privilege, a benefice, or an estate. **4.** To go by; elapse. *—tr.* To allow to lapse. ❖ *n.* **1.** The act or an instance of lapsing, as: **a.** A usu. minor or temporary failure; a slip. **b.** A deterioration or decline. **c.** A moral fall. **2.** A break in continuity; a pause. **3.** A period of time; an interval. **4.** *Law* The termination of a right or privilege through disuse, neglect, or death. [ME *lapsen*, to deviate from the normal < *laps*, lapse of time, sin (< OFr., lapse of time < Lat. *lāpsus* < p. part. of *lābī*, to lapse) and < Lat. *lāpsus*, freq. of *lābī*.] **—laps′er** *n.*

lapsed (lăpst) *adj.* No longer active or practicing.

lapse rate *n.* The rate of decrease of atmospheric temperature with increase in altitude.

lap·strake (lăp′strāk′) also **lap·streak** (-strēk′) *adj.* Clinker-built.

Lap·tev Sea (lăp′tĕf′, -tĕv′, läp′tyĭf) A section of the Arctic Ocean N of E Russia between the Taymyr Peninsula and the New Siberian Is.

lap·top (lăp′tŏp′) *n.* A portable computer small enough to use on one's lap.

La·pu·tan (lə-pyōōt′n) *adj.* Absurdly impractical or visionary. [After the flying island of *Laputa* in *Gulliver's Travels* by Jonathan Swift, where absurd projects are pursued and useful projects neglected.]

lap·wing (lăp′wĭng′) *n.* Any of several Old World birds of the genus *Vanellus*, esp. *V. vanellus*, related to the plovers and having a narrow crest. [By folk etym. < ME *lapwink*, hoopoe, lapwing < OE *hlēapewince* : *hlēapan*, to leap + **wincan*, to waver.]

Lar (lär) *n., pl.* **Lar·es** (lâr′ēz, lär′-) *Roman Mythology* A tutelary deity or spirit of an ancient Roman household. [Lat. *Lār*, prob. of Etruscan orig.]

Lar·a·mie (lăr′ə-mē) A city of SE WY WNW of Cheyenne; settled in 1868. Pop. 27,204.

La Ra·za (lärä′sä) n. Mexicans or Mexican Americans considered as a group, sometimes extending to all Spanish-speaking people of the Americas. [Am.Sp., the people.]

lar·board (lär′bərd) Nautical n. See port². ❖ adj. On the port side. [Alteration (influenced by STARBOARD) of ME laddebord : perh. laden, to load; see LOAD + borde, side of a ship; see STARBOARD.]

lar·ce·nist (lär′sə-nĭst) also **lar·ce·ner** (-nər) n. One who commits larceny.

lar·ce·nous (lär′sə-nəs) adj. 1. Of or involving larceny. 2. Guilty of or given to larceny. —**lar′ce·nous·ly** adv.

lar·ce·ny (lär′sə-nē) n., pl. -nies The unlawful taking and removing of another's personal property with the intent of permanently depriving the owner; theft. [ME < AN larcin, theft < Lat. latrōcinium, robbery < latrō, robber, mercenary, ultimately < Gk. latron, pay, hire.]

larch (lärch) n. 1. Any of several deciduous coniferous trees of the genus Larix, having needlelike leaves clustered on short shoots and heavy durable wood. 2. The wood of these trees. [Ger. Lärche < MHGer. larche < Lat. larix, laric-.]

Larch River A river of N Quebec, Canada, flowing c. 434 km (270 mi) NE to join the Caniapiscau R.

lard (lärd) n. The white solid or semisolid rendered fat of a hog. ❖ tr.v. **lard·ed, lard·ing, lards** 1. To cover or coat with lard or a similar fat. 2. To insert strips of fat or bacon in (meat) before cooking. 3. To enrich or lace heavily with extra material; embellish: larded the report with quotations. [ME < OFr. larde < Lat. lārdum.] —**lard′y** adj.

lar·der (lär′dər) n. 1. A place, such as a pantry or cellar, where food is stored. 2. A supply of food. [ME < AN < Med.Lat. lārdārium < Lat. lārdum, bacon.]

Lard·ner (lärd′nər), **Ringgold Wilmer ("Ring")** 1885–1933. Amer. humorist noted for his satirical short stories.

La·re·do (lə-rā′dō) A city of S TX on the Rio Grande SSW of San Antonio; settled in 1755. Pop. 176,576.

Lar·es (lâr′ēz) n. Plural of Lar.

lar·es and penates (lär′ēz, lär′-) pl.n. Treasured household possessions. [Partial transl. of Lat. Larēs et Penātēs : Larēs, pl. of Lār, Lar + et, and + Penātēs, Penates.]

large (lärj) adj. **larg·er, larg·est** 1. Of greater than average size, extent, quantity, or amount; big. 2. Of greater than average scope, breadth, or capacity; comprehensive. 3. Important; significant. 4a. Understanding and tolerant; liberal: a large and generous spirit. b. Of great magnitude or intensity; grand. 5a. Pretentious; boastful. Used of speech or manners. b. Obsolete Gross; coarse. Used of speech or language. 6. Nautical Favorable. Used of a wind. —**idiom: at large** 1. Not in confinement or captivity. 2. As a whole; in general. 3. Representing a nation, state, or district as a whole. Often used in combination: councilor-at-large. 4. Not assigned to a particular country. Often used in combination: ambassador-at-large. 5. At length; copiously. [ME < OFr. < Lat. largus, generous.] —**large′ness** n.

SYNONYMS large, big, great These adjectives mean being notably above the average in size or magnitude: a large sum of money; a big barn; a great old oak. **ANTONYM** small

large calorie n. See calorie 3a.

large cap adj. 1. Or or relating to corporations whose retained earnings are considerable and whose outstanding shares of common stock have a large market value. 2. Of or relating to mutual funds that invest in the stock of such corporations. [LARGE + CAP³.]

large-heart·ed (lärj′här′tĭd) adj. Having a generous disposition; sympathetic. —**large′-heart′ed·ness** n.

large intestine n. The portion of the intestine that extends from the ileum to the anus, arching around the small intestine and including the cecum, colon, rectum, and anal canal.

large·ly (lärj′lē) adv. 1. For the most part; mainly. 2. On a large scale; amply.

large-mind·ed (lärj′mīn′dĭd) adj. Marked by breadth or tolerance of views; broad-minded. —**large′-mind′ed·ly** adv.

large·mouth bass (lärj′mouth′) n. A North American freshwater food and game fish (Micropterus salmoides) with a large upper jaw extending past the eye.

larg·er than life (lär′jər) adj. Very impressive or imposing.

large-scale (lärj′skāl′) adj. 1. Large in scope or extent. 2. Drawn or made large to show detail.

lar·gess also **lar·gesse** (lär-zhĕs′, -jĕs′, lär′jĕs′) n. **1a.** Liberality in bestowing gifts. **b.** Money or gifts bestowed. **2.** Generosity of spirit or attitude. [ME largesse < OFr. < large, generous < Lat. largus.]

large-toothed aspen (lärj′tōotht′, -tōothd′) n. An eastern North American deciduous tree (Populus grandidentata) having ovate leaves with coarsely toothed margins.

lar·ghet·to (lär-gĕt′ō) Music adv. & adj. In a slow tempo, usu. slightly faster than largo but slower than adagio. ❖ n., pl. -tos A larghetto passage or movement. [Ital., dim. of largo, largo. See LARGO.]

larg·ish (lär′jĭsh) adj. Fairly large.

lar·go (lär′gō) Music adv. & adj. In a very slow tempo, usu. considered to be slower than adagio, and with great dignity. ❖ n., pl. -gos A largo passage or movement. [Ital. < Lat. largus, generous.]

la·ri (lä′rē) n. lari See table at currency. [Georgian.]

lar·i·at (lăr′ē-ət) n. 1. See lasso. 2. A rope for picketing grazing horses or mules. [Sp. la reata : la, the (< Lat. illa; see al- in App.) + reatar, to tie again (re-, again < Lat.; see RE- + atar, to tie < Lat. aptāre, to join < aptus, p. part. of apere, to tie).]

Lá·ri·sa (lä′rē-sä) or **La·ris·sa** (lə-rĭs′ə) A city of E Greece near the Aegean; chief city of ancient Thessaly. Pop. 102,048.

lark¹ (lärk) n. 1. Any of various chiefly Old World birds of the family Alaudidae, esp. the skylark, having a sustained melodious song. 2. Any of several similar birds, such as the meadowlark. [ME laveroc, larke < OE lāwerce.]

lark² (lärk) n. 1. A carefree or spirited adventure. 2. A harmless prank. ❖ intr.v. **larked, lark·ing, larks** To engage in spirited fun or merry pranks. [Short for SKYLARK, to frolic, or poss. alteration of dialectal lake, play (< ME leik, laik < ON leikr).] —**lark′er** n. —**lark′ish, lark′y** adj.

Lar·kin (lär′kĭn), **Philip** 1922–85. British poet whose works include The Whitsun Weddings (1964).

lark·spur (lärk′spûr′) n. See delphinium.

La Roche·fou·cauld (lä rōsh-fōō-kō′, -rōsh-), **Duc François de** 1613–80. French writer noted for his Maxims (1665).

La·rousse (lä-rōōs′), **Pierre Athanase** 1817–75. French lexicographer, grammarian, and encyclopedist who compiled the Grand Dictionnaire Universel du XIXe Siècle (1866–76).

lar·ri·gan also **Lar·ri·gan** (lär′ĭ-gən) n. A moccasin with knee-high leggings made of oiled leather. [?]

lar·ri·kin (lär′ĭ-kĭn) n. Australian A person given to comical or outlandish behavior. [?]

lar·rup (lär′əp) tr.v. **-ruped, -rup·ing, -rups** To beat, flog, or thrash. ❖ n. A blow. [Perh. < Du. larpen, to slap, thrash < larp, rod, whip.]

lar·um (lär′əm) n. An alarm. [ME larum-, as in larumbelle, short for alarum. See ALARUM.]

lar·va (lär′və) n., pl. -vae (-vē) or -vas 1. The newly hatched, wingless, often wormlike form of many insects before metamorphosis. 2. The earliest stage of any of various animals that undergo metamorphosis, differing markedly in form and appearance from the adult. 3. Roman Mythology A malevolent spirit of the dead; a lemur. [Lat. lārva, specter, mask (because it acts as a specter of or a mask for the adult form).] —**lar′val** adj.

lar·vi·cide (lär′vĭ-sīd′) n. An insecticide designed to kill larval pests. —**lar′vi·cid′al** (-sīd′l) adj.

la·ryn·ge·al (lə-rĭn′jē-əl, -jəl, lär′ən-jē′əl) also **la·ryn·gal** (lə-rĭng′gəl) adj. 1. Of, affecting, or near the larynx. 2. Produced in or with the larynx; glottal. ❖ n. 1. A laryngeal sound. 2. Any of a set of h-like sounds reconstructed for early Proto-Indo-European and partially preserved in Anatolian. [< NLat. laryngeus < Gk. larunx, larung-, larynx.]

lar·yn·gec·to·my (lăr′ən-jĕk′tə-mē) n., pl. -mies Surgical removal of part or all of the larynx.

lar·yn·gi·tis (lăr′ĭn-jī′tĭs) n. Inflammation of the larynx. —**lar′yn·git′ic** (-jĭt′ĭk) adj.

laryngo– or **laryng–** pref. Larynx: laryngoscope. [NLat. < Gk. larungo- < larunx, larung-, larynx.]

lar·yn·gol·o·gy (lăr′ən-gŏl′ə-jē) n. The branch of medicine that studies and treats the larynx, pharynx, and fauces.

la·ryn·go·phar·ynx (lə-rĭng′gō-făr′ĭngks) n. The portion of the pharynx just above the larynx.

la·ryn·go·scope (lə-rĭng′gə-skōp′, -rĭn′jə-) n. A tubular endoscope inserted into the larynx through the mouth and used for observing the interior of the larynx. —**la·ryn′go·scop′ic** (-skŏp′ĭk), **la·ryn′go·scop′i·cal** adj. —**la·ryn′go·scop′i·cal·ly** adv. —**lar′yn·gos′ka·pē**) n.

lar·ynx (lăr′ĭngks) n., pl. **la·ryn·ges** (lə-rĭn′jēz) or **lar·ynx·es** The part of the respiratory tract between the pharynx and the trachea, having walls of cartilage and muscle and containing the vocal cords. [NLat. < Gk. larunx.]

la·sa·gna also **la·sa·gne** (lə-zän′yə) n. 1. Pasta in flat, very wide strips. 2. A dish made by baking such pasta with layers of sauce and fillings such as cheese or meat. [Ital., poss. < VLat. *lasania < Lat. lasanum, cooking pot < Gk. lasanon.]

La Salle (lä salle′, lä), Sieur de. Title of Robert Cavelier. 1643–87. French explorer in North America who claimed Louisiana for France (1682).

las·car (lăs′kər) n. An East Indian sailor, army servant, or artillery trooper. [Urdu lashkar, army < Pers. < Ar. al-ʿaskar, the army : al-, the + ʿaskar, army.]

Las Ca·sas (läs kä′säs, -säs), **Bartolomé de** Known as "Apostle of the Indies." 1474–1566. Spanish missionary who sought to abolish the oppression of native peoples in the Americas.

Las·caux (lä-skō′) A cave of SW France in the Dordogne R. valley containing important Paleolithic paintings.

las·civ·i·ous (lə-sĭv′ē-əs) adj. 1. Given to or expressing lust; lecherous. 2. Exciting sexual desires; salacious. [ME < LLat. lascīviōsus < Lat. lascīvia, lewdness, playfulness < lascīvus, lustful, playful.] —**las·civ′i·ous·ly** adv. —**las·civ′i·ous·ness** n.

Las Cru·ces (läs krōō′sĭs) A city of S NM on the Rio Grande NNW of El Paso TX. Pop. 74,267.

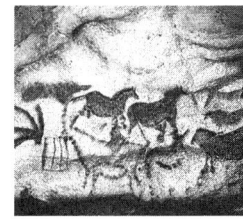

Lascaux
paintings on cave wall

lase (lāz) *intr.v.* **lased, las·ing, las·es** To function as a laser; emit coherent radiation by the action of a laser.

la·ser (lā′zər) *n.* Any of several devices that emit highly amplified and coherent radiation of one or more discrete frequencies by making use of a cascade of emitted radiation from the decay of atoms in a metastable energy state. [*l(ight) a(mplification by) s(timulated) e(mission of) r(adiation).*]

laser disk *n.* See **optical disk.**

laser printer *n.* A printer that uses a laser to make an image on a rotating drum and electrostatically transfers the image to paper.

laser radar *n.* See **lidar.**

laser trap *n.* A device made of magnetic coils and tuned lasers in which atoms or particles are slowed and then confined to a small region of space.

lash[1] (lăsh) *n.* **1a.** A stroke or blow with or as if with a whip. **b.** A whip. **c.** The flexible portion of a whip, such as a plait. **2.** Punishment administered with a whip. **3a.** A lacerating presence or power. **b.** A caustic verbal attack. **4.** An eyelash. ❖ *v.* **lashed, lash·ing, lash·es** —*tr.* **1.** To strike with or as if with a whip. **2.** To strike against with force or violence: *sleet lashing the roof.* **3.** To beat or swing rapidly. **4.** To make a scathing verbal attack against. **5.** To drive or goad; sting. —*intr.* **1.** To move swiftly or violently; thrash. **2a.** To aim a sudden blow; strike: *The mule lashed out with its hind legs.* **b.** To beat; flail. **3.** To make a scathing verbal or written attack. Often used with *out.* [ME, prob. < *lashen,* to deal a blow, perh. of imit. orig.] —**lash′er** *n.*

lash[2] (lăsh) *tr.v.* **lashed, lash·ing, lash·es** To secure or bind, as with a rope, cord, or chain. [ME *lashen, lasen,* to lace < OFr. *lachier, lacier* < VLat. **laceāre* < Lat. *laqueāre,* to ensnare < *laqueus,* snare. See LACE.]

lash·ing (lăsh′ĭng) *n.* Something used for securing or binding.

lash·ings (lăsh′ĭngz) *pl.n. Chiefly British* Lavish quantities. [< LASH[1], to lavish (obsolete).]

LA·SIK (lā′zĭk) *n.* Eye surgery in which the surface of the cornea is reshaped using a laser, performed to correct certain refractive disorders. [*la(ser in) si(tu) k(eratomileusis).*]

Las·ki (lăs′kē), **Harold Joseph** 1893–1950. British political scientist who led the British Labor Party (1945–46).

Las·ky (lăs′kē), **Jesse Louis** 1880–1958. Amer. motion-picture producer who helped found Paramount Studios (1933).

Las Pal·mas (läs päl′mäs) The chief city of the Canary Is. of Spain, on the NE coast of Grand Canary I. Pop. 359,611.

La Spe·zia (lä spĕt′sē-ə, spĕ′tsyä) A city of NW Italy ESE of Genoa on the **Gulf of La Spezia,** an arm of the Ligurian Sea. Pop. 101,701.

lass (lăs) *n.* **1.** A girl or young woman. **2.** A sweetheart. [ME *las,* prob. of Scand. orig.]

Las·sa fever (lä′sə, lăs′ə) *n.* An acute, often fatal viral disease endemic to West Africa and marked by high fever, headache, ulcers of the mucous membranes, and disturbances of the gastrointestinal tract. [After *Lassa,* a village of northeast Nigeria.]

Las·salle (lə-säl′, lä-säl′), **Ferdinand** 1825–64. German politician who was a founder (1863) of the predecessor of the Social Democratic Party.

Las·sen Peak (lăs′ən) An active volcano, 3,188.2 m (10,453 ft), in the Cascade Range of northern CA.

las·si (lä′sē) *n., pl.* **-sis** A beverage made of yogurt and water and flavored with spices, fruit, or other ingredients. [Hindi *lassī,* prob. ult. < Skt. *rasaḥ,* juice, liquid, milk.]

las·sie (lăs′ē) *n.* A lass.

las·si·tude (lăs′ĭ-tōōd′, -tyōōd′) *n.* A state or feeling of weariness, diminished energy, or listlessness. [ME < OFr. < Lat. *lassitūdō < lassus,* weary.]

las·so (lăs′ō, lă-sōō′) *n., pl.* **-sos** or **-soes** A long rope with a running noose at one end, used esp. to catch horses and cattle. ❖ *tr.v.* **-soed, -so·ing, -sos** or **-soes** To catch with or as if with a lasso. [Sp. *lazo* < VLat. **laceum,* noose. See LACE.] —**las′so·er** *n.*

Las·sus (lä′səs), **Roland de** or **Orlande de** 1532–94. Flemish composer whose works include masses, motets, and madrigals.

last[1] (lăst) *adj.* **1.** Being, coming, or placed after all others; final: *the last game of the season.* **2.** Being the only one left: *my last dollar.* **3.** Just past; most recent: *last year.* **4.** Most up-to-date; newest: *the last news.* **5.** Highest in extent or degree; utmost. **6.** Most valid, authoritative, or conclusive. **7a.** Least likely or expected. **b.** The least desirable or suitable. **8.** Being the latest possible. **9.** Lowest in rank or importance. **10.** Used as an intensive: *every last dollar.* **11.** Of or relating to a terminal period or stage, as of life. ❖ *adv.* **1.** After all others in chronology or sequence. **2.** Most recently: *last seen in 1986.* **3.** At the end; finally. ❖ *n.* **1.** One that is at the end or last. **2.** The end. **3.** The final mention or appearance. —*idioms:* **at last** After a considerable length of time; finally. **at long last** After a lengthy or troublesome wait or delay. [ME < OE *latost,* superl. of *læt,* late.] —**last′ly** *adv.*

SYNONYMS *last, final, terminal, ultimate* These adjectives mean coming after all others in chronology or sequence. *Last* applies to what comes at the end of a series: *the last day of the month.* *Final* stresses the definitiveness and decisiveness of the conclusion: *"I believe that unarmed truth and unconditional love will have the final word in reality"* (Martin Luther King, Jr.). *Terminal* applies to what marks or forms a limit or boundary, as in space, time, or development: *The railroad chose as its terminal city a town with a large harbor. Ultimate* applies to what concludes a series, process, or progression, to what constitutes a final result or objective, and to what is most distant or remote, as in time: *our ultimate goal.*

last[2] (lăst) *v.* **last·ed, last·ing, lasts** —*intr.* **1a.** To continue in time; go on. **b.** To continue; survive: *The regime couldn't last.* **2a.** To remain in good or usable condition. **b.** To continue in force or practice. **3.** To remain in adequate supply. —*tr.* **1.** To keep adequately supplied. **2.** To persist or endure for the entire length of; survive. [ME *lasten* < OE *lǣstan.*]

last[3] (lăst) *n.* A block or form shaped like a human foot and used in making or repairing shoes. ❖ *tr.v.* **last·ed, last·ing, lasts** To mold or shape on a last. [ME *leste, laste* < OE *lǣste < lǣst, lāst,* sole of the foot.]

last[4] (lăst) *n. Chiefly British* A unit of volume or weight varying for different commodities and in different districts, equal to about 80 bushels, 640 gallons, or 2 tons. [ME, load, a kind of measure < OE *hlæst,* load.]

last-ditch (lăst′dĭch′) *adj.* Done or made as a final recourse, esp. to prevent a crisis or disaster: *a last-ditch effort.*

last hurrah *n.* A final appearance or effort, esp. at the end of a career. [After *The Last Hurrah,* a novel by Edwin O'Connor (1918–68), American writer.]

last-in, first-out (lăst′ĭn′, fûrst′out′) *n.* A method of inventory accounting in which the most recently acquired items are assumed to have been the first sold.

last·ing (lăs′tĭng) *adj.* Continuing or remaining for a long time; enduring: *a lasting peace.* ❖ *n.* A sturdy twilled fabric. —**last′ing·ly** *adv.* —**last′ing·ness** *n.*

Last Judgment *n.* The final judgment by God of all humankind, esp. in Christian, Jewish, and Islamic scriptures.

last minute *n.* The period just before a significant or concluding moment such as a deadline. —**last′-min·ute** (lăst′mĭn′ĭt) *adj.*

last name *n.* See **surname** 1.

last rites *pl.n.* Rites performed for a person in danger of dying or in connection with burial, as the Anointing of the Sick in the Roman Catholic Church.

last straw *n.* The last of a series of troubles that leads one to a final loss of patience, trust, or hope. [< the proverb "It's the last straw that breaks the camel's back."]

Last Supper *n.* Jesus's supper with his disciples on the night before his crucifixion, at which he instituted the Eucharist.

last word *n.* **1.** The final statement in a verbal argument. **2a.** A conclusive or authoritative statement or treatment. **b.** Power or authority of ultimate decision. **3.** *Informal* The newest or most fashionable example of its kind; the latest thing.

Las Ve·gas (läs vā′gəs) A city of SE NV near the CA and AZ borders; known for its casinos. Pop. 478,434.

lat. *abbr.* latitude

Lat. *abbr.* **1.** Latin **2a.** Latvia **b.** Latvian

latch (lăch) *n.* **1.** A fastening, as for a door or gate, typically consisting of a bar that fits into a notch or slot and is lifted from either side by a lever or string. **2.** A spring lock, as for a door, that is opened from the outside by a key. ❖ *v.* **latched, latch·ing, latch·es** —*tr.* To close or lock with or as if with a latch. —*intr.* **1.** To have or be closed with a latch. **2.** To shut tightly so that the latch is engaged. —*idiom:* **latch on to** (or **onto**) To get hold of; obtain. [ME *latche < lacchen,* to seize < OE *læccan.*]

latch·et (lăch′ĭt) *n.* A leather thong or strap used to fasten a shoe or sandal on the foot. [ME *lachet* < OFr. *lacet, lachet* < *lace,* lace. See LACE.]

latch·key (lăch′kē′) *n.* A key for opening a latch or lock.

latchkey child *n.* A child who regularly spends time unsupervised at home while the parents are at work.

latch·string (lăch′strĭng′) *n.* A cord attached to a latch and often passed through a hole in the door to allow lifting of the latch from the outside.

late (lāt) *adj.* **lat·er, lat·est 1.** Coming, occurring, or remaining after the correct, usual, or expected time; delayed: *The bus is late.* **2a.** Beginning after or continuing past the usual or expected hour: *a late breakfast.* **b.** Occurring at an advanced hour, esp. well into the evening or night: *a late movie.* **3.** Of or toward the end or more advanced part, as of a period or stage. **4a.** Having begun or occurred just previous to the present time; recent. **b.** Contemporary; up-to-date: *the latest fashion.* **5a.** Having recently occupied a position or place: *The late president spoke.* **b.** Dead, esp. if recently deceased. ❖ *adv.* **later, latest 1.** After the expected, usual, or proper time. **2a.** At or until an advanced hour. **b.** At or into an advanced period or stage: *won late in her career.* **3.** Recently. —*idiom:* **of late** Recently; lately. [ME < OE *læt.*] —**late′ness** *n.*

USAGE NOTE It is technically correct to use a phrase such as *our late treasurer* to refer to a person who is still alive but who no longer holds the relevant post, but the use of *former* in this context will avoid any embarrassing misunderstanding.

late blight *n.* A disease of potato plants caused by the fungus *Phytophthora infestans* and marked by decaying foliage and tubers.

late·com·er (lāt′kŭm′ər) *n.* **1.** One that arrives late. **2.** A recent arrival, participant, or convert.

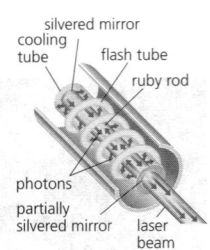

silvered mirror
cooling tube
flash tube
ruby rod
photons
partially silvered mirror
laser beam

laser
diagram showing the output stage of a ruby laser

lat·ed (lā′tĭd) *adj.* Belated. [< LATE.]

la·teen (lə-tēn′, lā-) *Nautical adj.* Being, relating to, or rigged with a triangular sail hung on a long yard that is attached at an angle to the top of a short mast. ❖ *n.* **1.** A lateen-rigged boat. **2.** A lateen sail. [Fr. *(voile) latine,* lateen (sail), fem. of *latin,* Lat. (< use in the Mediterranean) < OFr. See LATIN.]

Late Greek *n.* The Greek language as used in late antiquity and the early Byzantine period.

Late Hebrew *n.* The Hebrew language as used in the Mishnaic and medieval periods.

Late Latin *n.* The Latin language as used from the third to the seventh century A.D.

late·ly (lāt′lē) *adv.* Not long ago; recently.

lat·en (lāt′n) *tr. & intr.v.* **-ened, -en·ing, -ens** To make or grow late.

la·ten·cy (lāt′n-sē) *n., pl.* **-cies 1.** The state or quality of being latent. **2.** In psychoanalytic theory, of or relating to the fourth stage of psychosexual development during which a child apparently represses sexual urges and prefers to associate with members of the same sex.

La Tène (lä těn′) *adj.* Of or relating to a late Iron Age Celtic civilization dating from the fifth to the first century B.C., flourishing throughout most of northern Europe. [After *La Tène,* a district in Switzerland.]

la·tent (lāt′nt) *adj.* **1.** Present or potential but not evident or active. **2.** *Pathology* In a dormant or hidden stage. **3.** *Biology* Undeveloped but capable of normal growth under the proper conditions. **4.** *Psychology* Present and accessible in the unconscious mind but not consciously expressed. ❖ *n.* A fingerprint that is not apparent to the eye but can be made sufficiently visible, as by dusting, for use in identification. [ME < OFr. < Lat. *latēns, latent-,* pr. part. of *latēre,* to lie hidden.] —**la′tent·ly** *adv.*

latent heat *n.* The quantity of heat absorbed or released by a substance undergoing a change of state, such as ice changing to water, at constant temperature and pressure.

latent period *n.* **1.** The interval between exposure to an infectious organism or a carcinogen and the clinical appearance of disease. **2.** The interval between stimulus and response.

lat·er (lā′tər) *adj.* Comparative of **late.** ❖ *adv.* Comparative of **late. 1.** Subsequently; afterward. Often used with *on: She arrived on the ferry, and he came later. Later on, we watched a movie.* **2.** *Informal* Used to express goodbye.

lat·er·al (lāt′ər-əl) *adj.* **1.** Of, relating to, or situated at or on the side. **2.** Of or constituting a change within an organization or hierarchy to a position at a similar level, as in salary, to the one being left. **3.** *Linguistics* Of, relating to, or being a sound produced by breath passing along one or both sides of the tongue. ❖ *n.* A lateral part, projection, passage, or appendage. **2.** *Football* A lateral pass. **3.** *Linguistics* A lateral sound, such as (l). ❖ *v.* **-aled, -al·ing, -als** also **-alled, -al·ling, -als** *Football* —*intr.* To execute a lateral pass. —*tr.* To pass (the ball) sideways or backward. [ME < OFr. < Lat. *laterālis < latus, later-,* side.] —**lat′er·al·ly** *adv.*

lateral bud *n.* A bud located on the side of the stem, usu. in a leaf axil.

lat·er·al·i·ty (lăt′ə-răl′ĭ-tē) *n.* Preference in using one side of the body over the other.

lat·er·al·i·za·tion (lăt′ər-ə-lĭ-zā′shən) *n.* Localization of a function, such as speech, to the right or left side of the brain. —**lat′er·al·ize′** *v.*

lateral line *n.* A series of sensory pores along the head and sides of fish and some amphibians by which water currents, vibrations, and pressure changes are detected.

lateral pass *n. Football* A usu. underhand pass thrown sideways or somewhat backward with respect to downfield.

Lat·er·an Council (lăt′ər-ən) *n.* Any of a series of councils held in the Lateran Palace, a former papal residence, in Rome between the 7th and the 18th century, the fourth of which (in 1215) produced the doctrine of transubstantiation.

lat·er·ite (lăt′ə-rīt′) *n.* A red residual soil formed, esp. in humid climates, by the leaching of silica and enrichment of aluminum and iron hydroxides. [Lat. *later,* brick + –ITE[1].] —**lat′er·it′ic** (-rĭt′ĭk) *adj.*

lat·er·i·za·tion (lăt′ə-rĭ-zā′shən) *n.* **1.** The process by which soils and rocks are depleted of silica and bases and enriched with hydrated aluminum and iron oxides. **2.** The development of a laterite. [LATER(ITE) + –IZ(E) + –ATION.]

lat·est (lā′tĭst) *adj.* Superlative of **late.** ❖ *n.* Something that is the most recent or current of its kind. —**idiom: at the latest** No later than: *by Tuesday at the latest.*

late-term (lāt′tûrm′) *adj.* Occurring or performed after the 20th week of gestation in humans.

la·tex (lā′tĕks′) *n., pl.* **la·ti·ces** (lā′tĭ-sēz′, lăt′ĭ-) or **la·tex·es 1.** The colorless or milky sap of certain plants, such as the milkweed, that coagulates on exposure to air. **2.** An emulsion of rubber or plastic globules in water, used esp. in paints and synthetic rubber. **3.** Latex paint. [Lat., fluid.] —**la′tex′** *adj.*

latex paint *n.* A paint having a latex binder.

lath (lăth) *n., pl.* **laths** (lăthz, lăths) **1a.** A thin strip of wood or metal, usu. nailed in rows to framing supports as a substructure for plaster, shingles, slates, or tiles. **b.** A building material, such

as a sheet of metal mesh, used for similar purposes. **2a.** A quantity of laths; lathing. **b.** Work made with or from lath. ❖ *tr.v.* **lathed, lath·ing, laths** To build, cover, or line with laths. [ME *lathe,* prob. alteration (influenced by Welsh *llath,* rod) of OE *lætt.*]

lathe (lāth) *n.* A machine for shaping a piece of material, such as wood, by rotating it rapidly along its axis while pressing a fixed cutting or abrading tool against it. ❖ *tr.v.* **lathed, lath·ing, lathes** To cut or shape on a lathe. [ME, a device used by coopers, perh. a turning lathe, prob. of Scand. orig.]

lath·er (lăth′ər) *n.* **1.** A foam formed by soap or detergent agitated in water, as in washing. **2.** Froth formed by profuse sweating, as on a horse. **3.** *Informal* A condition of anxious or heated discomposure; agitation. ❖ *v.* **-ered, -er·ing, -ers** —*tr.* **1.** To spread with or as if with lather. **2.** *Informal* To give a beating to; whip. —*intr.* **1.** To produce lather; foam. **2.** To become coated with lather. [Prob. < ME *latheren,* to wash or soak clothes < OE *lēthran,* to cover with lather. See **leu(ə)-** in App.] —**lath′er·er** *n.* —**lath′er·y** *adj.*

lath·ing (lăth′ĭng, lăth′-) *n.* **1.** The act or process of building with laths. **2.** Work made of laths. **3.** A quantity of laths.

lath·y·rism (lăth′ə-rĭz′əm) *n.* A disease of humans and animals caused by eating legumes of the genus *Lathyrus,* and marked by spastic paralysis, hyperesthesia, and paresthesia. [< NLat. *Lathyrus,* genus name < Gk. *lathuros,* a type of pea < Akkadian *ladiru,* a type of plant.]

la·tic·i·fer (lā-tĭs′ə-fər) *n.* A plant duct containing latex. [Lat. *latex, latic-,* fluid; see LATEX + –FER.]

lat·i·cif·er·ous (lăt′ĭ-sĭf′ər-əs) *adj.* Producing or containing latex.

la·ti·fun·di·o (lä′tə-fōōn′dē-ō′) *n., pl.* **-os** A large landed estate in Spain or Latin America. [Sp. < Lat. *lātifundium,* latifundium. See LATIFUNDIUM.]

lat·i·fun·di·um (lăt′ə-fŭn′dē-əm) *n., pl.* **-di·a** (-dē-ə) A great landed estate, esp. of the ancient Romans. [Lat. *lātifundium : lātus,* broad + *fundus,* estate, base.]

la·til·la (lä-tē′yə) *n. Southwestern US* A usu. peeled limb or stick used as a ceiling material, as between beams or vigas. [Am.Sp., dim. of Sp. *lata,* small stick < VLat. **latta,* of Gmc. orig.]

Lat·i·mer (lăt′ə-mər), **Hugh** 1485?–1555. English prelate who refused to recant his Protestantism after the accession of Mary I and was executed for heresy.

Lat·in (lăt′n) *n.* **1a.** The Italic language of the ancient Latins and Romans. **b.** The Latin language and literature from the end of the third century B.C. to the end of the second century A.D. **2a.** A member of a Latin people, esp. a native or inhabitant of Latin America. **b.** A Latino or Latina. **3.** A native or resident of ancient Latium. ❖ *adj.* **1.** Of, relating to, or composed in Latin: *Latin verse.* **2a.** Of or relating to ancient Rome, its people, or its culture. **b.** Of or relating to Latium, its people, or its culture. **3.** Of or relating to the languages that developed from Latin, such as Spanish, or to the peoples that speak them. **4a.** Of or relating to the peoples, countries, or cultures of Latin America. **b.** Of or relating to Latinos or their culture. **5.** Of or relating to the Roman Catholic Church. [ME < OFr. and < OE *lēden,* both < Lat. *Latīnus < Latium,* Latium.]

La·ti·na (lə-tē′nə, lă-, lä-) *n.* **1.** A Latin-American woman or girl. **2.** A woman or girl of Spanish-speaking heritage, esp. in the United States. [Sp., fem. of *Latino,* Latino. See LATINO.] —**La·ti′na** *adj.*

USAGE NOTE The use of the feminine nouns *Latina* and *Chicana* is perfectly proper in American English, and failure to use the *-a* ending for women and girls (as in *She is a Latino*) may sometimes be resented. However, the use of these nouns as modifiers poses unfamiliar problems in English, since modifiers do not inflect for gender. Is it wrong to say *a Chicano woman,* or *She is a Latino novelist*? There is no one answer to these questions, though a few guidelines can be proposed. First, since English nouns do not have gender, the Spanish rules governing adjective-noun agreement cannot reasonably determine English usage; thus the choice between *She is the city's first Latino* or *Latina mayor* does not depend on the gender of the Spanish word for mayor. Second, the use of the more general masculine form as a modifier in referring to women—as in *"Bush Appoints Latino Woman to U.S. Court"* (headline in the *Sacramento Bee*)—is standard in American English. Finally, when the feminine form is in fact used to modify words like *woman* and *girl,* it is often, though not always, suggestive of a liberal or feminist viewpoint.

Latin alphabet *n.* The Roman alphabet adopted from the Greek by way of Etruscan, consisting of 23 letters upon which the modern western European alphabets and many others around the world are founded.

Latin America The countries of the Western Hemisphere S of the US, esp. those speaking Spanish, Portuguese, or French.

Latin American *n.* **1.** A native or inhabitant of Latin America. **2.** A person of Latin-American descent. —**Lat′in-A·mer′i·can** (lăt′n-ə-mĕr′ĭ-kən) *adj.*

Lat·in·ate (lăt′n-āt′) *adj.* Of, derived from, or suggestive of Latin: *a Latinate word.*

Latin Church *n.* The Roman Catholic Church.

lateen
in coastal waters, Kenya

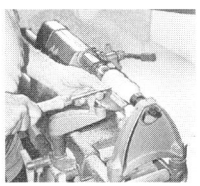

lathe

ă	pat	oi	boy
ā	pay	ou	out
âr	care	ŏŏ	took
ä	father	ōō	boot
ĕ	pet	ŭ	cut
ē	be	ûr	urge
ĭ	pit	th	thin
ī	pie	*th*	this
îr	pier	hw	which
ŏ	pot	zh	vision
ō	toe	ə	about,
ô	paw		item

Stress marks:
′ (primary)
′ (secondary), as in
lexicon (lĕk′sĭ-kŏn′)

Latin cross *n.* A cross with a shorter horizontal bar intersecting a longer vertical bar above the midpoint.

Lat•in•ism (lăt′n-ĭz′əm) *n.* An idiom, structure, or word derived from or suggestive of Latin.

Lat•in•ist (lăt′n-ĭst) *n.* A specialist in Latin.

La•tin•i•ty (lə-tĭn′ĭ-tē) *n.* **1.** The manner in which Latin is used in speaking or writing. **2.** Latin literature.

Lat•in•ize (lăt′n-īz′) *v.* **-ized, -iz•ing, -iz•es** —*tr.* **1a.** To translate into Latin. **b.** To transliterate into the letters of the Latin alphabet; Romanize. **c.** To make (a word) similar in appearance to Latin. **2.** To cause to adopt or acquire Latin characteristics or customs. **3.** To cause to follow or resemble the Roman Catholic Church in dogma or practices. **4.** To make Latino or Latin American, as in culture. —*intr.* To use Latinisms. —**Lat′in•i•za′tion** (-ĭ-zā′shən) *n.* —**Lat′in•iz′er** *n.*

La•ti•no (lə-tē′nō, lă-, lä-) *n., pl.* **-nos 1.** A Latin American. **2.** A person of Hispanic, esp. Latin-American, descent, often one living in the United States. See Usage Note at **Hispanic.** [Short for Sp. *latinoamericano,* Latin-American < *latino,* Latin < Lat. *Latīnus.* See LATIN.] —**La•ti′no** *adj.*

Latin Quarter A section of Paris on the S bank of the Seine R.

lat•ish (lā′tĭsh) *adv. & adj.* Fairly late.

la•tis•si•mus dor•si (lə-tĭs′ə-məs dôr′sī) *n., pl.* **la•tis•si•mi dorsi** (-mī′) Either of two broad flat triangular muscles running from the vertebral column to the humerus. [NLat. *(mūsculus) latissimus dorsī,* widest (muscle) of the back : Lat. *lātissimus,* superl. of *lātus,* wide + Lat. *dorsī,* genitive of *dorsum,* back.]

lat•i•tude (lăt′ĭ-tōōd′, -tyōōd′) *n.* **1a.** The angular distance north or south of the earth's equator, measured in degrees along a meridian, as on a map or globe. **b.** A region of the earth considered in relation to its distance from the equator. **2.** *Astronomy* The angular distance of a celestial body north or south of the ecliptic. **3.** Freedom from normal restraints, limitations, or regulations. **4.** A range of values or conditions, esp. the range of exposures over which a photographic film yields usable images. **5.** Extent; breadth. [ME < OFr., width < Lat. *lātitūdō,* width, geographic latitude < *lātus,* wide.] —**lat′i•tu′di•nal** (-tōōd′n-əl, -tyōōd′-) *adj.* —**lat′i•tu′di•nal•ly** *adv.*

lat•i•tu•di•nar•i•an (lăt′ĭ-tōōd′n-âr′ē-ən, -tyōōd′-) *adj.* Holding or expressing broad or tolerant views, esp. on religion. ❖ *n.* **Latitudinarian** Any of a group of Anglican Christians active from the 17th through the 19th century who were opposed to dogmatic positions of the Church of England. [Lat. *lātitūdō, lātitūdin-,* latitude; see LATITUDE + -ARIAN.] —**lat′i•tu′di•nar′i•an•ism** *n.*

La•ti•um (lā′shē-əm, -shəm) An ancient country of W-central Italy bordering on the Tyrrhenian Sea; dominated by Rome after the 3rd cent. B.C.

lat•ke (lät′kə) *n.* A pancake, esp. of grated potato. [Yiddish < Ukrainian *oladka* < ORuss., dim. of *olad′ya* < Gk. *eladia,* pl. of *eladion,* little oily thing, dim. of *elaion,* olive oil < *elaiā,* olive.]

lat•o•sol (lăt′ə-sôl′, -sŏl′) *n.* Soil that is rich in iron, alumina, or silica and formed in hot and humid tropical woodlands. [LAT(ERITE) + -*sol,* soil (< Lat. *solum*).]

la•trine (lə-trēn′) *n.* A communal toilet of a type often used in a camp or barracks. [< Fr. *latrines,* privies < OFr. < Lat. *lātrīna,* privy < *lavātrīna,* bath, privy. See **leu(ə)-** in App.]

La•trobe (lə-trōb′), **Benjamin Henry** 1764–1820. British-born Amer. architect whose works include the chambers of the US Congress and Supreme Court.

–latry *suff.* Worship: *bibliolatry.* [< Gk. *latreia,* service, worship.]

lats (läts) *n., pl.* **la•ti** (lä′tē′) See table at **currency.** [Latvian, prob. < shortening of *latvietis,* Latvian.]

lat•te (lät′tē) *n.* A caffe latte.

lat•ten (lăt′n) *n.* **1.** Brass or an alloy resembling brass, hammered thin and formerly used in the manufacture of church vessels. **2.** A thin sheet of metal, esp. of tin. [ME *laton* < OFr. < Ar. *lātūn,* prob. < O Turkic *altun,* gold.]

lat•ter (lăt′ər) *adj.* **1.** Being the second of two persons or things mentioned. See Usage Note at **former².** **2.** Near or nearer to the end: *the latter part of the book.* **3.** Further advanced in time or sequence; later: *popular in latter times.* [ME, later < OE *lætra.*] —**lat′ter•ly** *adv.*

lat•ter-day (lăt′ər-dā′) *adj.* Belonging to present or recent times; modern.

Latter-day Saint *n.* See **Mormon 2.**

lat•tice (lăt′ĭs) *n.* **1a.** An open framework made of strips of metal, wood, or similar material overlapped or overlaid in a regular, usu. crisscross pattern. **b.** A structure, such as a screen, made of or containing a lattice framework. **2.** Something, such as a heraldic bearing, that resembles an open, patterned framework. **3.** *Physics* **a.** A regular periodic configuration of points, particles, or objects throughout an area or space, esp. the arrangement of ions or molecules in a crystalline solid. **b.** The spatial arrangement of fissionable and nonfissionable materials in a nuclear reactor. ❖ *tr.v.* **-ticed, -tic•ing, -tic•es** To construct or furnish with a lattice or latticework. [ME *latis* < OFr. *lattis* < *latte,* lath, of Germanic orig.] —**lat′ticed** *adj.*

lat•tice•work (lăt′ĭs-wûrk′) *n.* **1.** A lattice or latticelike structure. **2.** An open crisscross pattern or weave.

Lat•vi•a (lăt′vē-ə) A country of N Europe on the Baltic Sea. Con-

Latvia

quered by the Livonian Brothers of the Sword in the 13th cent., Latvia passed under Russian control in the 18th cent. It officially became a constituent republic of the USSR in 1940. Latvia declared independence in 1990. Cap. Riga. Pop. 2,548,000.

Lat•vi•an (lăt′vē-ən) *adj.* Of or relating to Latvia or its people, language, or culture. ❖ *n.* **1a.** A native or inhabitant of Latvia. **b.** A person of Latvian descent. **2.** The Baltic language of the Latvians.

laud (lôd) *tr.v.* **laud•ed, laud•ing, lauds** To give praise to; glorify. See Syns at **praise.** ❖ *n.* **1.** Praise; glorification. **2.** A hymn or song of praise. **3. lauds** also **Lauds** (*used with a sing. or pl. verb*) *Ecclesiastical* The service of prayers following the matins. [ME *lauden* < OFr. *lauder* < Lat. *laudāre* < *laus, laud-,* praise.] —**laud′er** *n.*

Laud, William 1573–1645. English prelate who as archbishop of Canterbury (1633–45) was a strident supporter of Charles I and absolutism in church and state.

laud•a•ble (lô′də-bəl) *adj.* Commendable; praiseworthy. —**laud′a•bil′i•ty, laud′a•ble•ness** *n.* —**laud′a•bly** *adv.*

lau•da•num (lôd′n-əm) *n.* A tincture of opium, formerly used as a drug. [NLat., perh. alteration of Med.Lat. *labdanum,* labdanum. See LABDANUM.]

laud•a•tion (lô-dā′shən) *n.* The act of lauding; praise.

laud•a•tive (lô′də-tĭv) *adj.* Laudatory.

laud•a•to•ry (lô′də-tôr′ē, -tōr′ē) *adj.* Expressing or conferring praise: *a laudatory review of the new book.*

laugh (lăf, läf) *v.* **laughed, laugh•ing, laughs** —*intr.* **1.** To express certain emotions, esp. mirth or delight, by a series of spontaneous, usu. unarticulated sounds. **2.** To show or feel amusement or good humor. **3a.** To feel or express derision or contempt; mock. **b.** To feel a triumphant or exultant sense of well-being. **4.** To produce sounds resembling laughter: *laughing parrots.* —*tr.* **1.** To affect or influence by laughter: *laughed the proposal down.* **2.** To say with a laugh. ❖ *n.* **1.** The act of laughing. **b.** The sound of laughing; laughter. **2.** *Informal* Something amusing, absurd, or contemptible; a joke. **3.** *Informal* Fun; amusement. Often used in the plural: *just for laughs.* —**phrasal verbs: laugh at** To treat lightly; scoff at. **laugh off** (or **away**) To dismiss as laughably or ludicrously trivial. [ME *laughen* < OE *hlæhhan,* prob. ult. of imit. orig.] —**laugh′er** *n.* —**laugh′ing•ly** *adv.*

laugh•a•ble (lăf′ə-bəl, läf′ə-) *adj.* Causing or deserving laughter or derision. —**laugh′a•ble•ness** *n.* —**laugh′a•bly** *adv.*

laughing gas (lăf′ĭng, läf′ĭng) *n.* Nitrous oxide, esp. as used as an anesthetic.

laughing jackass *n.* See **kookaburra.**

laugh•ing•stock (lăf′ĭng-stŏk′, läf′ĭng-) *n.* An object of jokes or ridicule; a butt.

laugh•line (lăf′lĭn′, läf′-) *n.* **1.** A line of dialogue intended to cause laughter. **2.** A wrinkle formed at the outer corner of the eye, esp. noticeable when one laughs or smiles.

laugh•ter (lăf′tər, läf′-) *n.* **1.** The act of laughing. **2.** The sound produced by laughing. **3.** *Archaic* A cause or subject for laughter. [ME < OE *hleahtor.*]

laugh track *n.* Recorded laughter added to a soundtrack.

launce (läns, läns, lôns) *n.* See **sand lance.** [Perh. alteration of LANCE.]

launch¹ (lônch, länch) *v.* **launched, launch•ing, launch•es** —*tr.* **1a.** To throw or propel with force; hurl. **b.** To set or thrust (a self-propelled craft or projectile) in motion. **2.** *Nautical* To put (a boat) into the water in readiness for use. **3.** To set going; initiate. **4.** To introduce to the public or to a market. **5.** To give (someone) a start, as in a career or vocation. —*intr.* **1.** To begin a new venture or phase; embark: *launched out on her own.* **2.** To enter enthusiastically into something; plunge: *launched into a speech.* ❖ *n.* The act of launching. [ME *launchen* < ONFr. *lancher* < Lat. *lanceāre,* to wield a lance < *lancea,* lance. See LANCE.]

launch² (lônch, länch) *n.* **1.** A large ship's boat. **2.** A large open motorboat. [Prob. alteration of Malay *lancha.*]

launch•er (lôn′chər, län′-) *n.* One that launches, as: **a.** A rifle attachment for firing grenades. **b.** A device, such as an attached tube or a portable unit, for firing rockets.

launch•ing pad (lôn′chĭng, län′-) *n.* A launch pad.

launch pad *n.* **1.** The base or platform from which a rocket or space vehicle is launched. **2.** A foundation or starting point.

launch vehicle *n.* A rocket used to launch a spacecraft or satellite into an orbit or a trajectory.

launch window *n.* A brief period during which a spacecraft or a projectile must be launched to achieve its mission.

laun•der (lôn′dər, län′-) *v.* **-dered, -der•ing, -ders** —*tr.* **1a.** To wash (clothes, for example). **b.** To wash, fold, and iron. **2.** To disguise the source or nature of (illegal funds, for example) by channeling through an intermediate agent. **3.** To make more acceptable or presentable; sanitize. —*intr.* **1.** To undergo washing in a specified way: *This material launders well.* **2.** To wash or prepare laundry. ❖ *n.* A trough or flume used in washing ore. [< ME *launder,* lavender, launderer < OFr. *lavandier* < VLat. **lavandārius* < Lat. *lavandāria,* things to be washed < *lavanda,* neut. pl. gerundive of *lavāre,* to wash. See **leu(ə)-** in App.] —**laun′der•er** *n.*

laun•der•ette (lôn′də-rĕt′, län′-) *n.* A self-service laundry.

laun•dress (lôn′drĭs, län′-) *n.* A woman employed to launder clothes or linens. See Usage Note at **–ess.**

Laun•dro•mat (lôn′drə-măt′, län′-) A service mark used for a commercial establishment equipped with washing machines and dryers, usu. coin-operated and self-service.

laun•dry (lôn′drē, län′-) *n., pl.* **-dries 1.** Soiled or laundered clothes and linens; wash. **2a.** A commercial establishment for laundering clothes or linens. **b.** A room or area, as in a house, for doing the wash. [ME *lavendrye, laundry* < OFr. *lavanderie* < *lavandier.* See LAUNDER.]

laundry list *n. Informal* An item-by-item enumeration.

Laur•a•sia (lô-rā′zhə, -shə) *n.* The hypothetical supercontinent of the Northern Hemisphere, which according to the theory of plate tectonics broke up into North America, Europe, and Asia. [NLat. *Laur(entia),* geologic precursor of North America (after the ST. LAWRENCE RIVER) + (EUR)ASIA.]

lau•re•ate (lôr′ē-ĭt, lŏr′-) *adj.* **1.** Worthy of the greatest honor or distinction. **2.** Crowned or decked with laurel as a mark of honor. **3.** *Archaic* Made of laurel sprigs, as a wreath or crown. ❖ *n.* **1.** One honored or awarded a prize for great achievements esp. in the arts or sciences: *a Nobel laureate.* **2.** A poet laureate. [ME < Lat. *laureātus,* adorned with laurel < *laurea,* crown of laurel < fem. of *laureus,* of laurel < *laurus,* laurel.] —**lau′re•ate•ship′** *n.*

lau•rel (lôr′əl, lŏr′-) *n.* **1.** A Mediterranean evergreen tree *(Laurus nobilis)* having aromatic simple leaves and blackish berries. **2.** A shrub or tree having a similar aroma or leaf shape. **3a.** A wreath of laurel conferred as a mark of honor in ancient times upon poets, heroes, and athletes. Often used in the plural. **b.** Honor and glory won for great achievement. Often used in the plural. ❖ *tr.v.* **-reled, -rel•ing, -rels** also **-relled, -rel•ling, -rels 1.** To crown with laurel. **2.** To honor, esp. with an award or prize. —**idiom: rest on (one's) laurels** To be content with one's past achievements instead of working to bring about new ones. [ME < OFr. *laureole* < Lat. *laureola,* dim. of *laurea,* laurel.]

Laurel, Arthur Stanley Jefferson ("Stan") 1890–1965. British-born Amer. comedian who with Oliver Hardy formed the first great comedy team of talking films.

Lau•ren•cin (lô-rän-săn′), **Marie** 1885–1956. French artist noted for her soft pastel technique in portraiture.

Lau•rens (lôr′ənz, lŏr′-), **Henry** 1724–92. Amer. Revolutionary leader who was president (1777–78) of the Continental Congress.

Lau•ren•tian (lô-rĕn′shən) *adj.* **1.** Of, relating to, or being in the vicinity of the St. Lawrence River. **2.** *Geology* Of or relating to the Precambrian gneissic granite of the Lake Superior area. [< Lat. *Laurentius,* Lawrence.]

Laurentian Mountains A range of S Quebec, Canada, N of the St. Lawrence R. rising to 960.8 m (3,150 ft).

Laurentian Plateau or **Laurentian Highlands** also **Canadian Shield** A plateau region of E Canada extending from the Great Lakes and the St. Lawrence R. to the Arctic Ocean.

lau•ric acid (lôr′ĭk, lŏr′-) *n.* A fatty acid, $CH_3(CH_2)_{10}COOH$, obtained chiefly from coconut and laurel oils and used in making soaps and lauryl alcohol. [Lat. *laurus,* laurel + –IC.]

Lau•ri•er (lôr′ē-ā′, lŏr′-), Sir **Wilfrid** 1841–1919. Canadian politician who served as prime minister (1896–1911).

lau•ryl alcohol (lôr′əl, lŏr′-) *n.* A colorless solid alcohol, $CH_3(CH_2)_{11}OH$, used in synthetic detergents and pharmaceuticals. [LAUR(EL) + –YL.]

Lau•sanne (lō-zän′, -zän′) A city of W Switzerland on the N shore of Lake Geneva. Pop. 117,303.

la•va (lä′və, lăv′ə) *n.* **1.** Molten rock that reaches the earth's surface through a volcano or fissure. **2.** The rock formed by the cooling and solidifying of molten rock. [Ital., perh. < Lat. *lābēs,* fall < Lat. *lābī,* to fall.]

la•va•bo (lə-vä′bō, -vä′-) *n., pl.* **-boes 1.** often **Lavabo** In some Christian churches, the washing of the hands by the celebrant during the Eucharist. **2.** A washbowl attached to a wall and filled from a water tank fastened above. [< Lat. *lavābō,* I shall wash (opening word of the recited portion of Psalm 26), first pers. fut. t. of *lavāre,* to wash < Lat. *lavāre.* See LAVE.]

lav•age (lăv′ĭj, lə-väzh′) *n.* A washing, esp. of a hollow organ, such as the stomach, with repeated injections of water. [Fr. < OFr. < *laver,* to wash < Lat. *lavāre.* See leu(ə)- in App.]

La•val (lə-väl′, lä-väl′) A city of S Quebec, Canada, on an island opposite Montreal. Pop. 330,393.

Laval, Pierre 1883–1945. French politician who served as prime minister (1931–32 and 1935–36) and head of the Vichy government (1942) after the surrender of France.

la•va-la•va (lä′və-lä′və) *n.* A garment consisting of a rectangular piece of printed cloth tied loosely around the waist, worn by Polynesians, esp. by Samoans. [Samoan *lāvalava,* to put on clothes, clothes < redup. of Proto-Polynesian *lawa,* to bind.]

lav•a•liere (lăv′ə-lîr′) also **la•val•lière** (lä′vä-lyâr′) *n.* A pendant worn on a chain around the neck. [Fr. *lavallière,* type of necktie, after Duchesse de LA VALLIÈRE.]

La Val•lière (lä vəl-yĕr′, vä-lyâr′), Duchesse de. Title of Françoise Louise de la Baume Le Blanc. 1644–1710. French noblewoman and mistress of Louis XIV.

la•vash (lə-väsh′) *n.* A thin leavened flatbread of Armenian origin. [Armenian < Turk. *lavaş.*]

la•va•tion (lä-vä′shən, lă-) *n.* The process of washing; a cleans-

ing. [Lat. *lavātiō, lavātiōn-* < *lavātus,* p. part. of *lavāre,* to wash. See LAVE.]

lav•a•to•ry (lăv′ə-tôr′ē, -tōr′ē) *n., pl.* **-ries 1.** A room with washing and often toilet facilities; a bathroom. **2.** A washbowl or basin, esp. one permanently installed with running water. **3.** A flush toilet. [ME, piscina < LLat. *lavātōrium* < *lavātor,* launderer < Lat. *lavāre,* to wash. See leu(ə)- in App.]

lave (lāv) *v.* **laved, lav•ing, laves** —*tr.* **1.** To wash; bathe. **2.** To lap or wash against. **3.** To refresh or soothe as if by washing: *"The quiet and the cool laved her"* (Edna Ferber). —*intr. Archaic* To wash oneself. [ME *laven* < OE *gelafian* and < OFr. *laver,* both < Lat. *lavāre.* See leu(ə)- in App.]

lav•en•der (lăv′ən-dər) *n.* **1a.** Any of various aromatic Old World plants of the genus *Lavandula,* esp. *L. angustifolia,* having small purplish flower clusters that yield an oil used in perfumery. **b.** The fragrant dried leaves, stems, and flowers of this plant. **2.** A pale to light purple to very light or pale violet. [ME *lavendre* < AN < Med.Lat. *livendula, lavendula,* perh. < Lat. *līvidus,* bluish. See LIVID.] —**lav′en•der** *adj.*

la•ver[1] (lā′vər) *n.* **1.** A large basin used in the Temple in Jerusalem by a priest for ablutions before a sacrificial offering. **2.** *Archaic* A vessel, stone basin, or trough used for washing. [ME, water pitcher < OFr. *laveoir,* prob. < LLat. *lavātōrium.* See LAVATORY.]

la•ver[2] (lā′vər) *n.* Any of several dried edible seaweeds of the genera *Porphyra* (the red algae) and *Ulva* (the green algae). [ME, a water plant < OE *læfer* < Lat.]

Laver, Rod b. 1938. Australian tennis player who won the Grand Slam (Wimbledon, French, US, and Australian titles) twice (1962 and 1969).

La Vé•ren•drye (lä vä-rän-drē′), Sieur de. Title of Pierre Gaultier de Varennes. 1685–1749. French-Canadian explorer who established a chain of trading posts in New France.

lav•ish (lăv′ĭsh) *adj.* **1.** Marked by or produced with extravagance and profusion: *a lavish buffet.* **2.** Immoderate in giving or bestowing; unstinting. ❖ *tr.v.* **-ished, -ish•ing, -ish•es** To give or bestow in abundance; shower. [ME *laves,* prob. < OFr. *lavasse,* downpour < *laver,* to wash < Lat. *lavāre.* See LAVE.] —**lav′ish•er** *n.* —**lav′ish•ly** *adv.* —**lav′ish•ness** *n.*

La•voi•sier (lə-vwä′zē-ā′, lä-vwä-zyā′), **Antoine Laurent** 1743–94. French chemist regarded as the founder of modern chemistry.

law (lô) *n.* **1.** A rule of conduct or procedure established by custom, agreement, or authority. **2a.** The body of rules and principles governing the affairs of a community and enforced by a political authority; a legal system. **b.** The condition of social order and justice created by adherence to such a system: *a breakdown of law and order.* **3.** A set of rules or principles dealing with a specific area of a legal system: *tax law.* **4.** A piece of enacted legislation. **5a.** The system of judicial administration giving effect to the laws of a community. **b.** Legal action or proceedings; litigation. **c.** An impromptu or extralegal system of justice substituted for established judicial procedure. **6a.** An agency or agent responsible for enforcing the law: *The law caught up with them.* **b.** *Informal* A police officer. **7a.** The science and study of law; jurisprudence. **b.** Knowledge of law. **c.** The profession of an attorney. **8.** Something, such as an order or a dictum, having absolute or unquestioned authority. **9. Law a.** The body of principles or precepts held to express the divine will, esp. as set forth in the Bible. **b.** The first five books of the Bible; Torah. **10.** A code of principles based on morality, conscience, or nature. **11a.** A rule or custom generally established in a particular domain: *the laws of decency.* **b.** A way of life: *the law of the jungle.* **12a.** A statement describing a relationship observed to be invariable between or among phenomena for all cases in which the specified conditions are met: *the law of gravity.* **b.** A generalization based on consistent experience or results: *the law of supply and demand.* **13.** *Mathematics* A general principle or rule that is assumed or has been proven to hold between expressions. **14.** A principle of organization, procedure, or technique: *the laws of grammar.* ❖ *intr.v.* **lawed, law•ing, laws** To go to law; litigate. —*idioms:* **a law unto (oneself)** A totally independent operator. **lay down the law** To issue orders sharply or imperiously. **take the law into (one's) own hands** To mete out justice as one sees fit without recourse to law enforcement agencies or the courts. [ME < OE *lagu* < ON **lagu,* var. of *lag,* that which is laid down. See legh- in App.]

Law, (Andrew) Bonar 1858–1923. Canadian-born British politician who served as prime minister (1922–23).

Law, John 1671–1729. Scottish financier active in France who devised an ultimately disastrous speculation scheme for the development of Louisiana.

law-a•bid•ing (lô′ə-bī′dĭng) *adj.* Adhering to the law.

law•break•er (lô′brā′kər) *n.* One that breaks the law.

law clerk *n.* A person, typically an attorney, who assists a judge or another attorney, thereby gaining legal experience.

law•ful (lô′fəl) *adj.* **1.** Being within the law; allowed by law: *lawful dissent.* **2.** Established, sanctioned, or recognized by law: *the lawful heir.* **3.** Obeying the law; law-abiding. —**law′ful•ly** *adv.* —**law′ful•ness** *n.*

law•giv•er (lô′gĭv′ər) *n.* **1.** One who gives a code of laws to a people. **2.** See **lawmaker.**

law•less (lô′lĭs) *adj.* **1.** Unrestrained by law; unruly. **2.** Contrary

lava-lava

to the law; unlawful. **3.** Not governed by law. —**law′less•ly** *adv.* —**law′less•ness** *n.*

law•mak•er (lô′mā′kər) *n.* One who makes or enacts laws; a legislator. —**law′mak′ing** *n.*

law•man (lô′măn′, -mən) *n.* A law officer, such as a sheriff.

law merchant *n., pl.* **laws merchant** A body of principles and regulations applied to commercial transactions and deriving from the established customs of merchants and traders rather than the jurisprudence of a particular nation or state.

lawn¹ (lôn) *n.* A plot of grass, usu. tended or mowed, as one in a park. [Alteration of ME *launde*, glade < OFr., heath, pasture, wooded area, of Gmc. or Celt. orig.]

lawn² (lôn) *n.* A light cotton or linen fabric of very fine weave. [ME *laun*, after *Laon*, a city of northern France.]

lawn bowling *n.* A game played on a level lawn in which balls are rolled as close as possible to a smaller target ball.

lawn mower also **lawn•mow•er** (lôn′mō′ər) *n.* A machine with a rotating blade for cutting grass.

lawn tennis *n.* See **tennis** 1.

law of averages *n.* The principle holding that probability will influence all occurrences in the long term.

law of diminishing returns *n.* The tendency for continuing work toward a particular project or goal to decline in effectiveness after a certain level of result has been achieved.

law of independent assortment *n.* See **Mendel's law** 2.

law of large numbers *n.* The theorem that the average of a large number of independent measurements of a random quantity tends toward the theoretical average of that quantity.

Law of Moses *n.* See **Mosaic Law.**

law of nations *n.* See **international law.**

law of parsimony *n.* See **Ockham's razor.**

law of segregation *n.* See **Mendel's law** 1.

Law•rence (lôr′əns, lŏr′-) **1.** A city of NE KS on the Kansas R. ESE of Topeka; scene of a proslavery raid (1856) that sparked retaliatory killings by the abolitionist John Brown. Pop. 80,098. **2.** A city of NE MA on the Merrimack R. NNE of Lowell; laid out in 1845. Pop. 72,043.

Lawrence, D(avid) H(erbert) 1885–1930. British writer whose novels include *Lady Chatterley's Lover* (1928).

Lawrence, Ernest Orlando 1901–58. Amer. physicist who won a 1939 Nobel Prize.

Lawrence, Gertrude 1898–1952. British actress remembered for her performances in *Private Lives* (1930) and *The King and I* (1951).

Lawrence, T(homas) E(dward) Known as "Lawrence of Arabia." 1888–1935. Welsh-born British soldier, adventurer, and writer who led an Arab revolt against the Turks (1916–18) and wrote *The Seven Pillars of Wisdom* (1926).

law•ren•ci•um (lô-rĕn′sē-əm, lō-) *n.* **Symbol Lr** A radioactive synthetic element produced from californium and having isotopes with mass numbers 255 through 260 and half-lives of a few seconds to three minutes; atomic number 103. See table at **element.** [After Ernest Orlando LAWRENCE.]

law•suit (lô′sōōt′) *n.* An action or a suit brought before a court, as to recover a right or redress a grievance.

Law•ton (lôt′n) *n.* A city of SW OK SW of Oklahoma City. Pop. 92,757.

law•yer (lô′yər) *n.* One whose profession is to give legal advice and assistance to clients and represent them in legal matters. [ME *lauier* < *law*, law. See LAW.] —**law′yer•ly** *adv.*

law•yer•ing (lô′yər-ĭng) *n.* The profession or work of practicing law.

lax (lăks) *adj.* **lax•er, lax•est 1.** Lacking in rigor, strictness, or firmness. **2.** Not taut, firm, or compact. See Syns at **loose. 3.** Loose and not easily retained or controlled. Used of bowel movements. **4.** *Linguistics* Pronounced with the muscles of the tongue and jaw relatively relaxed, as the vowel (ĕ) in *let*. [ME < Lat. *laxus*, loose, lax.] —**lax•a′tion** *n.* —**lax′ly** *adv.* —**lax′ness** *n.*

lax•a•tive (lăk′sə-tĭv) *n.* A food or drug that stimulates evacuation of the bowels. ❖ *adj.* Of or being a laxative. [ME < OFr. *laxatif* < Med.Lat. *laxātīvus*, preventing constipation < LLat., assuaging < Lat. *laxātus*, p. part. of *laxāre*, to relax < *laxus*, loose. See LAX.]

lax•i•ty (lăk′sĭ-tē) *n.* The state or quality of being lax.

lay¹ (lā) *v.* **laid** (lād), **lay•ing, lays** —*tr.* **1.** To cause to lie down. **2a.** To place in or bring to a particular position. **b.** To bury. **3.** To cause to be in a particular condition: *laid him open to criticism.* **4.** To put or set down: *lay railroad track.* **5.** To produce and deposit: *lay eggs.* **6.** To cause to subside; calm or allay. **7.** To put up to or against something: *lay an ear to the door.* **8.** To put forward as a reproach or an accusation. **9.** To put or set in order or readiness for use: *lay the table.* **10.** To devise; contrive: *lay plans.* **11.** To spread over a surface. **12.** To place or give (importance). **13.** To impose as a burden or punishment. **14.** To present for examination: *lay a case before a committee.* **15.** To put forward as a demand or an assertion. **16.** *Games* To place (a bet); wager. **17.** To aim (a gun or cannon). **18a.** To place together (strands) to be twisted into rope. **b.** To make in this manner: *lay up cable.* **19.** *Vulgar Slang* To have sexual intercourse with. —*intr.* **1.** To produce and deposit eggs. **2.** To bet; wager. **3.** *Nonstandard* To lie. **4.** To engage energetically in an action. **5.** *Nautical* To put oneself

into the position indicated. ❖ *n.* **1a.** The direction the strands of a rope or cable are twisted in. **b.** The amount of such twist. **2.** The state of one that lays eggs. **3.** *Vulgar Slang* **a.** Sexual intercourse. **b.** A partner in sexual intercourse. —***phrasal verbs:*** **lay about** To strike blows on all sides. **lay down 1.** To give up; abandon. **2.** To save for the future. **lay away 1.** To reserve for the future; save. **2.** To put aside and hold for future delivery. **lay by** To save for future use. **lay down 1.** To give up and surrender. **2.** To specify: *laid down the rules.* **3.** To store for the future. **4.** *Nonstandard* To lie down. **lay for** *Informal* To be waiting to attack. **lay in** To store for future use. **lay into** *Slang* To scold sharply. **2.** To attack physically; beat up. **lay off 1.** To terminate the employment of (a worker), esp. temporarily. **2.** To mark off. **3.** *Slang* To stop doing something; quit. **4.** *Games* To place all or a part of (an accepted bet) with another bookie in order to reduce the risk. **lay on 1.** To apply (something) by or as if by spreading onto a flat surface. **2.** To prepare, usu. in an elaborate fashion; arrange. **3.** *Slang* To present or reveal to; confront with. **lay out 1.** To make a detailed plan for. **2.** To clothe and prepare (a corpse) for burial. **3.** To rebuke harshly. **4.** To knock to the ground or unconscious. **5.** To expend; spend. **6.** To display: *lay out merchandise; lay the merchandise out.* **lay over** To make a stopover in the course of a journey. **lay to** *Nautical* To bring (a ship) to a stop in open water. **lay up 1.** To stock for future use. **2.** *Informal* To confine with an illness or injury: *was laid up for a month.* **3.** *Nautical* To put (a ship) in dock, as for repairs. —***idioms:*** **lay it on thick** *Informal* **1.** To exaggerate; overstate. **2.** To flatter effusively. **lay of the land** The nature, arrangement, or disposition of something. **lay waste** To ravage: *Rebel troops laid waste the town.* [ME *leien* < OE *lecgan.* See **legh-** in App.]

lay² (lā) *adj.* **1.** Of, relating to, or involving the laity: *a lay preacher.* **2.** Not of or belonging to a particular profession; nonprofessional: *a lay opinion on the law.* [ME < OFr. *lai* < LLat. *lāicus* < Gk. *lāikos*, of the people < *lāos*, the people.]

lay³ (lā) *n.* **1.** A narrative poem, such as one sung by medieval minstrels; a ballad. **2.** A song; a tune. [ME < OFr. *lai.*]

lay⁴ (lā) *v.* Past tense of **lie**¹.

lay•a•bout (lā′ə-bout′) *n.* A lazy or idle person; a loafer.

Lay•a•mon (lā′ə-mən, lī′-) fl. 13th cent. English poet who wrote *The Brut* (c. 1205), the first English account of King Arthur.

lay•a•way (lā′ə-wā′) *n.* **1.** A payment plan in which a buyer reserves merchandise by placing a deposit until the balance is paid in full. **2.** An article reserved under such a plan.

lay•er (lā′ər) *n.* **1a.** One that lays: *a tile layer.* **b.** A hen kept for laying eggs. **2a.** A single thickness of a material covering a surface or forming an overlying part or segment: *a layer of dust.* **b.** A usu. horizontal deposit or expanse; a stratum. **c.** A depth or level: *several layers of meaning.* **3.** *Botany* A stem, branch, or twig that is covered with soil for rooting while still part of the living plant. **4.** An item of clothing worn over or under another. ❖ *v.* **-ered, -er•ing, -ers** —*tr.* **1.** To divide or form into layers. **2.** To cut (hair) into different, usu. overlapping lengths. **3.** *Botany* To propagate (a plant) by means of a layer. **4.** To wear (clothing) in layers. —*intr.* **1.** To form or come apart as layers. **2.** *Botany* To take root as a result of layering.

lay•ette (lā-ĕt′) *n.* A set of clothing and bedding for a newborn child. [Fr. < OFr., chest of drawers, dim. of *laie*, box < MDu. *laeye.*]

lay figure *n.* **1.** See **mannequin** 2. **2.** A subservient or insignificant person. [< obsolete *layman* < Du. *leeman*, var. of *ledenman* : obsolete Du. *led,* limb (< MDu. *lit*) + *man,* man (< MDu.; see MANIKIN).]

lay•man (lā′mən) *n.* **1.** A man who is not a cleric. **2.** A man who is a nonprofessional. See Usage Note at **man.**

lay•off (lā′ôf′, -ŏf′) *n.* **1.** The act of suspending or dismissing an employee, as for lack of work or because of corporate reorganization. **2.** A period of temporary inactivity or rest.

lay•out (lā′out′) *n.* **1.** The act or an instance of laying out. **2.** An arrangement or plan, esp. the schematic arrangement of parts or areas: *the layout of a factory.* **3.** *Printing* **a.** The art or process of arranging printed or graphic matter on a page. **b.** The overall design of a page, spread, or book, including elements such as page and type size. **c.** A page or set of pages marked to indicate this design. **4.** *Sports* The straight position, as in diving. **5.** *Informal* An establishment or property, esp. a large residence or estate. **6.** A midair position in sports such as gymnastics in which the body is kept straight and the arms are extended at the sides.

lay•o•ver (lā′ō′vər) *n.* A short stop or break in a journey, usu. imposed by scheduling requirements.

lay·peo·ple or **lay people** (lā′pē′pəl) *pl.n.* Laymen and lay-women.

lay·per·son (lā′pûr′sən) *n.* A layman or a laywoman.

lay reader *n.* A member of the laity in the Anglican or Roman Catholic church authorized by a bishop to read some parts of the service.

Lay·san Island (lī′sän′) An island of HI in the Leeward Is. NW of the main islands.

lay-up (lā′ŭp′) *n.* **1.** *Basketball* A usu. one-handed banked shot made close to the basket after driving in. **2.** The act or an instance of laying up.

lay·wom·an (lā′wŏom′ən) *n.* **1.** A woman who is not a cleric. **2.** A woman who is a nonprofessional.

la·zar (lā′zər, lăz′ər) *n. Archaic* A diseased person; a leper. [ME < OFr. *lazre* < LLat. *Lazarus*, the beggar full of sores in a New Testament parable (Luke 16:20).]

laz·a·ret·to (lăz′ə-rĕt′ō) also **laz·a·ret** or **laz·a·rette** (-rĕt′) *n., pl.* **-tos** also **-rets** or **-rettes 1.** A hospital treating contagious diseases. **2.** A building or ship used as a quarantine station. **3.** often **lazaret** A storage space between the decks of a ship. [Ital. *lazzaretto : lazzaro,* lazar (< LLat. *Lazarus*; see LAZAR) + dialectal *Nazareto,* popular name for a hospital maintained in Venice by the Church of Santa Maria di Nazaret.]

Laz·a·rus (lăz′ər-əs) In the New Testament, the brother of Mary and Martha.

Lazarus, Emma 1849–87. Amer. writer whose poem "The New Colossus" is inscribed on the Statue of Liberty.

laze (lāz) *v.* **lazed, laz·ing, laz·es** —*intr.* To be lazy; loaf. —*tr.* To spend (time) loafing. [Back-formation < LAZY.]

laz·u·lite (lăz′yŏo-līt′, lăz′ə-, lăzh′ə-) *n.* A relatively rare blue mineral, (Mg, Fe)Al₂(PO₄)₂(OH)₂, with a vitreous luster. [Med. Lat. *lazulum,* lapis lazuli; see LAPIS LAZULI + -ITE¹.]

laz·u·rite (lăz′yŏo-rīt′, lăz′ə-, lăzh′ə-) *n.* A relatively rare blue, violet-blue, or greenish-blue translucent mineral, Na₄₋₅Al₃Si₃O₁₂S, the chief component of lapis lazuli. [Med.Lat. *lāzūr,* lapis lazuli (< Ar. *lāzaward*); see LAPIS LAZULI) + -ITE¹.]

la·zy (lā′zē) *adj.* **-zi·er, -zi·est 1.** Resistant to work or exertion; disposed to idleness. **2.** Slow-moving; sluggish: *a lazy river.* **3.** Conducive to idleness or indolence. **4.** Depicted as reclining or lying on its side. Used of a brand on livestock. [Prob. of LGer. orig.] —**la′zi·ly** *adv.* —**la′zi·ness** *n.*

la·zy·bones (lā′zē-bōnz′) *pl.n. (used with a sing. verb) Informal* A lazy person.

lazy eye *n.* See **amblyopia.**

lazy Susan *n.* A revolving tray for food.

lazy tongs *pl.n. (used with a sing. or pl. verb)* Tongs having a jointed extensible framework operated by scissorslike handles, used for grasping an object at a distance.

LB *abbr.* linebacker

lb. *abbr.* **1.** libra (ancient Roman weight) **2.** pound (modern weight)

LBO *abbr.* leveraged buyout

lc *abbr.* lowercase

LC *abbr.* **1.** landing craft **2.** Library of Congress

L/C *abbr.* letter of credit

lcd *abbr.* least common denominator

LCD *abbr.* liquid-crystal display

lcm *abbr.* least common multiple

LD *abbr.* **1.** learning disability **2.** learning disabled

Ld. *abbr.* **1a.** limited company **b.** lord (title)

LDC *abbr.* less-developed country

LDL *abbr.* low-density lipoprotein

L-do·pa (ĕl-dō′pə) *n.* The levorotatory form of dopa, converted in the brain to dopamine and used in synthetic form chiefly to treat Parkinson's disease.

LDPE *abbr.* low-density polyethylene

lea (lē, lā) also **ley** (lā, lē) *n.* A grassland; a meadow. [ME *leie* < OE *lēah.* See **leuk-** in App.]

lea. *abbr.* league (measurement)

leach (lēch) *v.* **leached, leach·ing, leach·es** —*tr.* **1.** To remove soluble or other constituents from by the action of a percolating liquid. **2.** To empty; drain. —*intr.* To be dissolved or passed out by a percolating liquid. ❖ *n.* **1.** The act or process of leaching. **2.** A porous, perforated, or sievelike vessel that holds material that is to be leached. **3.** The substance through which a liquid is leached. [< ME *leche,* leachate < OE *lece,* muddy stream; akin to *leccan,* to moisten.] —**leach′a·bil′i·ty** *n.* —**leach′a·ble** *adj.* —**leach′er** *n.*

leach·ate (lē′chāt) *n.* A solution formed by leaching, esp. one containing contaminants leached from soil.

lead¹ (lēd) *v.* **led** (lĕd), **lead·ing, leads** —*tr.* **1.** To show the way to by going in advance. **2.** To guide or direct in a course: *lead a horse by the halter.* **3a.** To serve as a route for; take: *The path led them home.* **b.** To be a channel or conduit for (water or electricity, for example). **4.** To guide the behavior or opinion of; induce: *led us to believe otherwise.* **5a.** To direct the performance or activities of. **b.** To inspire the conduct of: *led the nation.* **6.** To play a principal or guiding role in: *lead a discussion.* **7a.** To go or be at the head of: *My name led the list.* **b.** To be ahead of: *led the runner-up by three strides.* **c.** To be foremost in or among. **8.** To pass or go through; live: *lead an independent life.* **9.** To begin or open

with, as in games: *led an ace.* **10.** To guide (a partner) in dancing. **11.** To aim in front of (a moving target). —*intr.* **1.** To be first; be ahead. **2.** To go first as a guide. **3.** To act as commander, director, or guide. **4.** To afford a passage, course, or route. **5.** To tend toward a certain goal or result. **6.** To make the initial play, as in a game or contest. **7.** To begin a presentation or account in a given way. **8a.** To go into a dance partner. **b.** To start a dance step on a specified foot. **9.** *Baseball* To advance a few paces toward the next base while the pitcher is in the delivery. Used of a base runner. **10.** *Sports* To begin an attack in boxing with a specified hand or punch. ❖ *n.* **1a.** The first or foremost position. **b.** One occupying such a position; a leader. **c.** The initiative. **2.** The margin by which one holds a position of advantage or superiority. **3a.** Information pointing toward a possible solution; a clue. **b.** An indication of potential opportunity; a tip. **4.** Command; leadership. **5.** An example; a precedent. **6a.** The principal role in a dramatic production. **b.** The person playing such a role. **7a.** The introductory portion of a news story. **b.** An important, usu. prominently displayed news story. **8.** *Games* **a.** The first play. **b.** The prerogative or turn to make the first play. **c.** A card played first in a round. **9.** *Baseball* A position taken by a base runner away from one base in the direction of the next. **10.** A leash. **11.** *Geology* **a.** A deposit of gold ore in an old riverbed. **b.** See **lode** 1. **12.** A channel of open water created by a break in a mass of ice. **13.** *Electronics* A conductor by which one circuit element is electrically connected to another. **14.** *Nautical* The direction in which a line runs. **15.** The distance aimed in front of a moving target. —*phrasal verbs:* **lead off 1.** To begin; start. **2.** *Baseball* To be the first batter in an inning. **lead on 1.** To keep in a state of expectation or hope; entice. **2.** To mislead; deceive. —*idiom:* **lead up to 1.** To result in by a series of steps. **2.** To proceed toward (a main topic) with preliminary remarks. [ME *leden* < OE *lǣdan.*]

Emma Lazarus

lead² (lĕd) *n.* **1.** *Symbol* **Pb** A soft ductile dense metallic element, extracted chiefly from galena and used in pipes, solder and type metal, bullets, radiation shielding, paints, and antiknock compounds. Atomic number 82; atomic weight 207.2; melting point 327.5°C; boiling point 1,744°C; specific gravity 11.35; valence 2, 4. See table at **element. 2.** A lead weight suspended by a line, used to make soundings. **3.** Bullets from or for firearms; shot. **4. leads** Strips of lead used to hold the panes of a window. **5.** *Printing* **a.** A thin strip of metal used to separate lines of type. **b.** A similar space between lines of photocomposed or computer-generated type. **6. leads** *Chiefly British* A flat roof covered with sheets of lead. **7a.** Any of various, often graphitic compositions used as the writing substance in pencils. **b.** A thin stick of such material. ❖ *tr.v.* **lead·ed, lead·ing, leads 1.** To cover, line, weight, or fill with lead. **2.** *Printing* To provide space between (lines of type) with leads. **3.** To secure (window glass) with leads. **4.** To treat with lead or a lead compound: *leaded paint.* —*idiom:* **get the lead out** *Informal* To start moving or move more rapidly. [ME *led* < OE *lēad,* prob. of Celt. orig.] —**lead** *adj.*

lead acetate (lĕd) *n.* A poisonous crystalline compound, Pb(C₂H₃O₂)₂·3H₂O, used in waterproofing and varnishes.

lead carbonate (lĕd) *n.* A poisonous white amorphous powder, PbCO₃, used as a paint pigment.

lead chromate (lĕd) *n.* A poisonous yellow crystalline compound, PbCrO₄, used as a paint pigment.

lead colic (lĕd) *n.* See **painter's colic.**

lead dioxide (lĕd) *n.* A poisonous brown crystalline compound, PbO₂, used as an oxidizing agent, as in batteries.

lead·en (lĕd′n) *adj.* **1.** Made of or containing lead. **2a.** Heavy and inert. **b.** Listless; sluggish. **3.** Lacking liveliness or sparkle; dull. **4.** Downcast; depressed. **5.** Dull dark gray in color: *a leaden sky.* —**lead′en·ly** *adv.* —**lead′en·ness** *n.*

lead·er (lē′dər) *n.* **1.** One that leads or guides. **2.** One who is in charge or in command of others. **3a.** One who heads a political party or organization. **b.** One who has influence or power, esp. politically. **4.** *Music* **a.** A conductor, esp. of an orchestra, band, or choral group. **b.** The principal performer in an orchestral section or a group. **5.** The foremost animal, such as a dog, in a harnessed team. **6.** A loss leader. **7.** *Chiefly British* The main editorial in a newspaper. **8. leaders** *Printing* Dots or dashes in a row leading the eye across a page, as in an index entry. **9.** A pipe for conducting liquid. **10.** A short length of gut, wire, or similar material by which a hook is attached to a fishing line. **11.** A blank strip at the end or beginning of a film or tape used in threading or winding. **12.** *Botany* The growing apex or main shoot of a shrub or tree. **13.** An economic indicator.

lead·er·board (lē′dər-bôrd′, -bōrd′) *n.* A board that displays the leaders in a competition.

lead·er·ship (lē′dər-shĭp′) *n.* **1.** The position or office of a leader. **2.** Capacity or ability to lead. **3.** A group of leaders. **4.** Guidance; direction: *the leadership of the new president.*

lead glass (lĕd) *n.* See **flint glass.**

lead-in (lĕd′ĭn′) *n.* **1.** Opening or introductory matter. **2.** A program, as for radio, scheduled to precede another. **3.** The wire between an outdoor antenna and an electronic transmitter or receiver.

lead·ing¹ (lē′dĭng) *adj.* **1.** Having a position in the lead; foremost. **2.** Chief; principal. **3.** Of or performing a lead in a theatrical production. **4.** Formulated so as to elicit a desired response: *a*

lead•ing² (lĕd′ĭng) n. 1. A border or rim of lead, as around a windowpane. 2. *Printing* The spacing between lines, usu. measured in points.

lead•ing economic indicator (lē′dĭng) n. An economic or financial variable that tends to move ahead of and in the same direction as general economic activity.

lead•ing edge (lē′dĭng) n. 1. *Nautical* The edge of a sail that faces the wind. 2. The front edge of an airplane propeller blade or wing. 3. The foremost position in a trend or movement; the vanguard. —**lead′ing-edge′** (lē′dĭng-ĕj′) adj.

lead•ing tone (lē′dĭng) n. *Music* The seventh tone or degree of a scale, a half tone below the tonic; a subtonic.

lead line (lĕd) n. See **sounding line.**

lead monoxide (lĕd) n. See **litharge.**

lead•off (lēd′ôf′, -ŏf′) n. 1. An opening play or move. 2. One that leads off. —**lead′off′** adj.

lead pencil (lĕd) n. A pencil that uses graphite as its marking substance.

lead•plant (lĕd′plănt′) n. A deciduous shrub (*Amorpha canescens*) of central North America having pinnately compound leaves covered with whitish hairs.

lead poisoning (lĕd) n. Acute or chronic poisoning by lead or any of its salts, causing anemia and damage to the gastrointestinal tract and nervous system.

leads•man (lĕdz′mən) n. *Nautical* The person using the lead line in taking soundings.

lead tetraethyl (lĕd) n. Tetraethyl lead.

lead-time (lĕd′tīm′) n. The time between the start of a project or policy and the results: *a long lead-time in oil production.*

lead•wort (lĕd′wûrt′, -wôrt′) n. 1. Any of various chiefly tropical plants of the genus *Plumbago*, having clusters of variously colored flowers. 2. Any of several similar plants.

leaf (lēf) n., pl. **leaves** (lēvz) 1. A usu. green, flattened lateral structure attached to a stem and functioning as a principal organ of photosynthesis and transpiration in most plants. 2. A leaflike organ or structure. 3a. Leaves considered as a group; foliage. b. The state or time of having or showing leaves: *trees in full leaf.* 4. The leaves of a plant used or processed for a specific purpose: *tobacco leaf.* 5. Any of the sheets of paper bound in a book, each side of which constitutes a page. 6a. A very thin sheet of material, esp. metal. b. Such leaves considered as a group. 7. A hinged or removable section for a table top. 8. A hinged or otherwise movable section of a folding door, shutter, or gate. 9. One of several metal strips forming a leaf spring. ❖ v. **leafed, leaf•ing, leafs** —*intr.* 1. To produce leaves; put forth foliage. 2. To turn pages, as in searching or browsing: *leafed through the catalog.* —*tr.* To turn through the pages of. [ME < OE *lēaf.*]

leaf•age (lē′fĭj) n. Foliage.

leaf butterfly n. Any of several butterflies of the genus *Kallima*, having wings that resemble leaves.

leaf fat n. Layered fat that encloses the kidneys of a hog, used in making lard.

leaf•hop•per (lēf′hŏp′ər) n. Any of numerous insects of the family Cicadellidae that suck juices from plants, often damaging crops.

leaf insect n. Any of various chiefly Asian insects of the family Phylliidae that resemble leaves in color and form.

leaf lard n. High-grade lard made from leaf fat.

leaf•let (lēf′lĭt) n. 1. One of the segments of a compound leaf. 2. A small leaf or leaflike part. 3. A printed, usu. folded handbill or flier intended for free distribution. ❖ v. **-let•ed, -let•ing, -lets** also **-let•ted, -let•ting, -lets** —*intr.* To hand out leaflets. —*tr.* To hand out leaflets to or in.

leaf miner n. Any of numerous small flies and moths that in the larval stage dig into and feed on leaf tissue.

leaf mold n. Humus or compost consisting of decomposed leaves and other organic material.

leaf spot n. Any of various plant diseases resulting in well-defined necrotic areas on the leaves.

leaf spring n. A composite spring, used esp. in automotive suspensions, consisting of several layers of flexible metallic strips joined to act as a single unit.

leaf•stalk or **leaf stalk** (lēf′stôk′) n. See **petiole** 1.

leaf•y (lē′fē) adj. **-i•er, -i•est** 1. Covered with or having leaves. 2. Consisting of leaves. 3. Similar to or resembling a leaf. —**leaf′i•ness** n.

league¹ (lēg) n. 1. An association of states, organizations, or individuals for common action; an alliance. 2. *Sports* An association of teams or clubs that compete chiefly among themselves. 3. A class or level of competition. ❖ v. **leagued, leagu•ing, leagues** —*intr.* To come together in or as if in a league. —*tr.* To bring together in or as if in a league. [Alteration of ME *liege* < OFr. *ligue* < Med.Lat. *liga* and < OItal. *lega, liga* (< *legare*, to bind), both < Lat. *ligāre*, to bind.]

league² (lēg) n. 1a. A unit of distance equal to 3.0 statute miles (4.8 kilometers). b. Any of various other units of about the same length. 2. A square league. [ME *lege* < OFr. *liue, leguee* < Lat. *leuga*, a measure of distance, of Gaulish orig.]

League of Arab States See **Arab League.**

League of Nations A world organization est. 1920 to promote cooperation and peace; officially dissolved 1946.

lea•guer¹ (lē′gər) n. 1. A siege. 2. The camp esp. of a besieging army. ❖ *tr.v.* **-guered, -guer•ing, -guers** *Archaic* To besiege; beleaguer. [Du. *leger,* lair, camp < MDu. *lēgher,* lair, camp, siege. See **legh-** in App.]

leagu•er² (lē′gər) n. One that belongs to a league.

Le•ah (lē′ə) In the Bible, the first wife of Jacob.

leak (lēk) v. **leaked, leak•ing, leaks** —*intr.* 1. To permit the escape, entry, or passage of something through a breach or flaw: *a boat leaking at the seams.* 2. To escape or pass through a breach or flaw. 3. *Informal* To become publicly known through a breach of secrecy. —*tr.* 1. To permit (a substance) to escape or pass through a breach or flaw. 2. *Informal* To disclose without authorization or official sanction. ❖ n. 1. A crack or flaw that permits something to escape or enter. 2a. The act or an instance of leaking. b. An amount leaked. 3. *Informal* An unauthorized or a deliberate disclosure of confidential information. 4a. Loss of electric current as a result of faulty insulation. b. The path or place at which this loss takes place. —*idiom:* **take a leak** *Vulgar Slang* To urinate. [ME *leken,* prob. < MDu. *lēken.*] —**leak′er** n.

leak•age (lē′kĭj) n. 1. The act or an instance of leaking. 2. Something that escapes by leaking. 3. An amount lost as the result of leaking.

Lea•key (lē′kē), **Louis Seymour Bazett** 1903–72. British anthropologist and archaeologist who influenced evolutionary theory with his analysis of the discovery, by his wife, **Mary** (1913–96), of early australopithecine and hominid skulls in Tanzania.

leak•proof (lēk′prōōf′) adj. So constructed or contrived as to prevent leaks or leakage.

leak•y (lē′kē) adj. **-i•er, -i•est** Permitting leaks or leakage.

lean¹ (lēn) v. **leaned, lean•ing, leans** —*intr.* 1. To bend or slant away from the vertical. 2. To incline the weight of the body so as to be supported. See Syns at **slant.** 3. To rely for assistance or support. 4. To have a tendency or preference. 5. *Informal* To exert pressure. —*tr.* 1. To set or place so as to be resting or supported. 2. To cause to incline. ❖ n. A tilt or an inclination away from the vertical. [ME *lenen* < OE *hleonian.* See **klei-** in App.]

lean² (lēn) adj. **lean•er, lean•est** 1. Not fleshy or fat; thin. 2. Containing little or no fat. 3a. Not productive or prosperous; meager. b. Containing little excess or waste; spare. c. Thrifty in management; economical. 4a. *Metallurgy* Low in ore mineral content. b. *Chemistry* Lacking in combustible material: *lean fuel.* ❖ n. Meat with little or no fat. [ME *lene* < OE *hlǣne.*] —**lean′ly** adv. —**lean′ness** n.

SYNONYMS lean, spare, skinny, scrawny, lank, lanky, rawboned, gaunt These adjectives mean lacking excess flesh. *Lean* emphasizes absence of fat: *fattened the lean cattle for market. Spare* sometimes suggests trimness and good muscle tone: "*an old man, very tall and spare, with an ascetic aspect*" (William H. Mallock). *Skinny* and *scrawny* imply unattractive thinness, as from undernourishment: *The child has skinny, freckled legs with prominent knees.* "*He* [had] *a long, scrawny neck that rose out of a very low collar*" (Winston Churchill). *Lank* describes one who is thin and tall, and *lanky*, one who is thin, tall, and ungraceful: "*He was . . . exceedingly lank, with narrow shoulders*" (Washington Irving); *a lanky adolescent. Rawboned* suggests a thin, bony, gangling build: *a rawboned cowhand. Gaunt* implies thinness and boniness and a haggard appearance; it may suggest illness or hardship: *her face gaunt from overwork.*

Lean, Sir David 1908–91. British filmmaker whose works include *Lawrence of Arabia* (1962).

Le•an•der (lē-ăn′dər) n. *Greek Mythology* A young man who loved Hero and drowned during one of his nightly swims across the Hellespont to be with her.

lean•ing (lē′nĭng) n. An inclination, tendency, or preference. See Syns at **predilection.**

leant (lĕnt) v. *Chiefly British* A past tense and a past participle of **lean¹.**

lean-to (lēn′tōō′) adj. Having or characterized by a single slope or pitch. ❖ n., pl. **-tos** 1. A structure with a lean-to roof attached to the side of a building as a wing or an extension. 2. A shelter or shed having a lean-to roof.

leap (lēp) v. **leaped** or **leapt** (lĕpt, lēpt), **leap•ing, leaps** —*intr.* 1. To spring or bound upward from or as if from the ground; jump. 2a. To move quickly or abruptly from one condition or subject to another. b. To act impulsively. —*tr.* 1. To jump over. 2. To cause to leap. ❖ n. 1a. The act of leaping; a jump. b. A place jumped over or from. c. The distance cleared in a leap. 2. An abrupt or precipitous passage, shift, or transition. —*idioms:* **by leaps and bounds** Very quickly. **leap in the dark** An act whose consequences cannot be predicted. **leap of faith** The act or an instance of believing or trusting in something intangible or incapable of being proved. [ME *lepen* < OE *hlēapan.*] —**leap′er** n.

leap•frog (lēp′frôg′, -frŏg′) n. A game in which one player kneels or bends over while the next in line leaps over him or her. ❖ v. **-frogged, -frog•ging, -frogs** —*tr.* 1. To jump over in or as if in leapfrog. 2. To advance (two military units) by engaging one with the enemy while moving the other to a position forward of the first unit. 3. To avoid by or as if by a roundabout route. —*intr.* To move forward or progress in or as if in leapfrog.

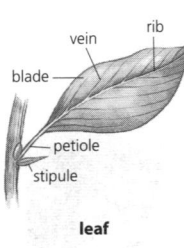

vein rib blade petiole stipule

leaf

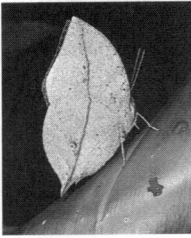

leaf butterfly
Indian leaf butterfly
Kallima paralekta

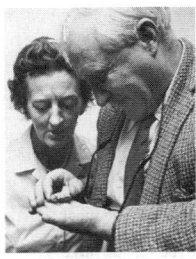

Louis and Mary Leakey
photographed in 1962

leap second *n.* A second of time, as measured by an atomic clock, added to or omitted from official timekeeping systems to compensate for changes in the rotation of the earth.

leap year *n.* **1.** A year in the Gregorian calendar having 366 days, with the extra day, February 29, intercalated to compensate for the quarter-day difference between an ordinary year and the astronomical year. **2.** An intercalary year in a calendar.

Lear (lîr) *n.* The protagonist in Shakespeare's tragedy *King Lear,* based on a legendary king of Britain.

Lear, Edward 1812–88. British artist and writer whose works include his first *Book of Nonsense* (1846).

learn (lûrn) *v.* **learned** also **learnt** (lûrnt), **learn•ing, learns** —*tr.* **1.** To gain knowledge, comprehension, or command of through experience or study. **2.** To fix in the mind or memory; memorize. **3a.** To acquire experience of or an ability or skill in: *learn tolerance.* **b.** To become aware. **4.** To become informed of; find out. See Syns at **discover. 5.** *Nonstandard* To cause to acquire knowledge; teach. **6.** *Obsolete* To give information to. —*intr.* To gain knowledge, information, comprehension, or skill. [ME *lernen* < OE *leornian.*] —**learn′a•ble** *adj.* —**learn′er** *n.*

learn•ed (lûr′nĭd) *adj.* **1.** Possessing or demonstrating profound, often systematic knowledge; erudite. **2.** Directed toward scholars: *a learned journal.* **3.** (lûrnd) Acquired by learning or experience. [ME *lerned,* educated, p. part. of *lernen,* to learn, teach. See LEARN.] —**learn′ed•ly** *adv.* —**learn′ed•ness** *n.*

SYNONYMS *learned, erudite, scholarly* These adjectives mean having or showing profound knowledge: *a learned jurist; an erudite professor; a scholarly treatise.*

learn•ing (lûr′nĭng) *n.* **1.** The act, process, or experience of gaining knowledge or skill. **2.** Knowledge or skill gained through schooling or study. **3.** *Psychology* Behavioral modification esp. through experience or conditioning.

learning disability *n.* Any of various cognitive, neurological, or psychological disorders that impede the ability to learn.

learn•ing-dis•a•bled (lûr′nĭng-dĭs-ā′bəld) *adj.* Having a learning disability.

learning disorder *n.* A learning disability.

lease (lēs) *n.* **1a.** A contract granting use or occupation of property during a specified period in exchange for rent. **b.** The term or duration of such a contract. **2.** Property used or occupied under the terms of a lease. ❖ *tr.v.* **leased, leas•ing, leas•es 1.** To grant a lease for. **2.** To get or hold by lease. —***idiom:* a new lease on life** An opportunity to improve one's circumstances or outlook. [ME *les* < AN < *lesser,* to lease, var. of OFr. *laissier,* to let go < Lat. *laxāre,* to loosen < *laxus,* loose.] —**leas′a•ble** *adj.* —**leas′er** *n.*

lease•back (lēs′băk′) *n.* A business arrangement whereby property is simultaneously sold and leased back to the seller for usu. long-term continued use.

lease•hold (lēs′hōld′) *n.* **1.** The fact or condition of holding property by lease. **2.** Property so held. —**lease′hold′er** *n.*

leash (lēsh) *n.* **1.** A chain, rope, or strap attached to the collar or harness of an animal, esp. a dog, and used to lead it or hold it in check. **2.** Control or restraint. **3a.** A set of three animals, such as hounds. **b.** A set of three. ❖ *tr.v.* **leashed, leash•ing, leash•es** To restrain with or as if with a leash. [ME *lees, lesh* < OFr. *laisse* < *laissier,* to let go. See LEASE.]

leas•ing (lē′sĭng) *n. Archaic* **1.** The act of lying. **2.** A lie; a falsehood. [ME *lesing* < OE *lēasung* < *lēasian,* to lie < *lēas,* untrue. See **leu-** in App.]

least (lēst) *adj.* A superlative of **little. 1.** Lowest in importance or rank. **2a.** Smallest in magnitude or degree. **b.** Slightest or tiniest: *the least bit.* ❖ *adv.* Superlative of **little.** To or in the lowest or smallest degree. ❖ *n.* One that is the lowest or smallest in importance, rank, magnitude, or degree. —***idioms:* at least 1.** According to the lowest possible assessment; not less than: *at least an hour.* **2.** In any event; anyway. **in the least** At all: *I don't mind in the least.* **least of all** Particularly not. [ME < OE *lǣst.*]

least common denominator *n.* The least common multiple of the denominators of a set of fractions.

least common multiple *n.* The smallest quantity divisible by two or more given quantities without a remainder.

least squares *pl.n. Statistics* A method of determining the curve that best describes the observed data by minimizing the sum of the squares of the deviations between observed values and the curve.

least•ways (lēst′wāz′) *adv. Chiefly Southern US* At least.

least•wise (lēst′wīz′) *adv. Informal* In any event; at least.

leath•er (lĕth′ər) *n.* **1.** The dressed or tanned hide of an animal, usu. with the hair removed. **2.** Any of various articles or parts made of leather, such as a boot or strap. **3.** The flap of a dog's ear. ❖ *tr.v.* **-ered, -er•ing, -ers 1.** To cover wholly or in part with leather. **2.** *Informal* To beat with a strap made of hide. ❖ *adj.* **1.** Made of, relating to, or resembling leather. **2.** *Slang* Of, relating to, or patronized by people who dress in leather clothing primarily to indicate a preference for sadomasochistic sex. [ME *lether* < OE *lether-* (as in *letherhose,* leather pants).]

leath•er•back (lĕth′ər-băk′) *n.* The largest living sea turtle *(Dermochelys coriacea),* found in tropical waters and having a tough leathery carapace with seven longitudinal ridges.

leath•er•ette (lĕth′ə-rĕt′) *n.* Imitation leather. [Orig. a trademark.]

leath•ern (lĕth′ərn) *adj.* Made of, covered with, or resembling leather. [ME *lethern* < OE.]

leath•er•neck (lĕth′ər-nĕk′) *n. Slang* A member of the US Marine Corps. [< the leather neckband once worn.]

leath•er•wood (lĕth′ər-wo͝od′) *n.* **1.** A deciduous shrub *(Dirca palustris)* of eastern North America having tough flexible branches and pliable bark. **2.** See **titi**[1] 1.

leath•er•work (lĕth′ər-wûrk′) *n.* **1.** Decorative work crafted in leather. **2.** Articles made of leather. —**leath′er•work′er** *n.* —**leath′er•work′ing** *n.*

leath•er•y (lĕth′ə-rē) *adj.* Having the texture or appearance of leather: *a leathery face.* —**leath′er•i•ness** *n.*

leave[1] (lēv) *v.* **left** (lĕft), **leav•ing, leaves** —*tr.* **1.** To go out of or away from. **2a.** To go without taking or removing: *left my book on the bus.* **b.** To omit or exclude: *left out the funniest part.* **3.** To have as a result, consequence, or remainder. **4.** To cause or allow to be or remain in a specified state. **5a.** To have remaining after death: *left a young son.* **b.** To bequeath. **6.** To give over to another to control or act on. **7a.** To abandon or forsake. **b.** To remove oneself from association with or participation in. **8a.** To give or deposit, as for use or information, upon one's departure or in one's absence: *left a note.* **b.** To cause or permit to be or remain: *left myself plenty of time.* **9.** *Nonstandard* To allow or permit; let. —*intr.* To set out or depart; go. —***phrasal verb:* leave off 1.** To stop; cease. **2.** To stop doing or using. —***idioms:* leave** (or **let**) **alone** To refrain from disturbing or interfering. **leave no stone unturned** To make every possible effort, esp. in a search. [ME *leaven* < OE *lǣfan.*] —**leav′er** *n.*

USAGE NOTE *Leave alone* is acceptable as a substitute for *let alone* in the sense "to refrain from disturbing or interfering." The following example was approved by a majority of the Usage Panel in an earlier survey: *Leave him alone and he will produce.* Those who did not accept this example generally felt that *leave alone* should mean simply "to depart from one who remains in solitude": *They were left alone in the wilderness.* • In formal writing *leave* is not an acceptable substitute for *let* in the sense "to allow or permit." Only *let* is acceptable in these examples: *Let me be. Let him go. Let it lie.*

leave[2] (lēv) *n.* **1.** Permission to do something. **2a.** Official permission to be absent from work or duty. **b.** The period of time granted by such permission. **3.** An act of departing; a farewell. [ME *leve* < OE *lēafe,* dative and accusative of *lēaf.*]

leave[3] (lēv) *intr.v.* **leaved, leav•ing, leaves** To put forth foliage; leaf. [ME *leaven* < *leaf,* leaf. See LEAF.]

leaved (lēvd) *adj.* **1.** Having or bearing a leaf or leaves. **2.** Having a specified number or kind of leaves. Often used in combination: *three-leaved; wide-leaved.*

leav•en (lĕv′ən) *n.* **1.** An agent, such as yeast, that causes batter or dough to rise, esp. by fermentation. **2.** An element, influence, or agent that works subtly to lighten, enliven, or modify a whole. ❖ *tr.v.* **-ened, -en•ing, -ens 1.** To add a rising agent to. **2.** To cause to rise, esp. by fermentation. **3.** To pervade with a lightening, enlivening, or modifying influence. [ME < OFr. *levain* < VLat. **levāmen* < Lat. *levāre,* to raise.]

leav•en•ing (lĕv′ə-nĭng) *n.* An agent that causes rising, fermentation, or ferment; leaven.

Leav•en•worth (lĕv′ən-wûrth′) A city of NE KS on the Missouri R. NW of Kansas City; settled in 1854. Pop. 35,420.

leave of absence *n., pl.* **leaves of absence** See **leave**[2] 2.

leaves (lēvz) *n.* Plural of **leaf.**

leave-tak•ing (lēv′tā′kĭng) *n.* A departure or farewell.

leav•ings (lē′vĭngz) *pl.n.* Scraps or remains; residue.

Leb•a•nese (lĕb′ə-nēz′, -nēs′) *adj.* Of or relating to Lebanon, its people, or their culture. ❖ *n., pl.* **Lebanese** A native or inhabitant of Lebanon. [Fr. *libanais* < *Liban,* Lebanon.]

Leb•a•non (lĕb′ə-nən, -nŏn′) A country of SW Asia on the Mediterranean Sea; proclaimed its independence in 1941 but did not achieve full self-government until 1945. Cap. Beirut. Pop. 2,915,000.

Lebanon Mountains A range of Lebanon parallel to the Mediterranean coast and rising to 3,090 m (10,131 ft).

le•bens•raum (lā′bəns-roum′) *n.* **1.** Additional territory deemed necessary to a nation, esp. Nazi Germany, for its continued existence or economic well-being. **2.** Adequate space in which to live, develop, or function. [Ger. : *Lebens,* genitive sing. of *Leben,* life (< MHGer. < OHGer. *lebēn*) + *Raum,* space (< MHGer. *roum* < OHGer. *rūm*).]

leb•ku•chen (lāb′ko͞o′kən, lāp′ko͞o′kʜən) *n., pl.* **lebkuchen** A chewy, usu. honey-flavored Christmas cookie containing nuts and candied fruits. [Ger. < MHGer. *lebekuoche* : *lebe-,* of unknown meaning + *kuoche,* cake; see KUCHEN.]

Le•brun (lə-brœɴ′), **Albert** 1871–1950. French politician who was the last president of the Third Republic (1932–40).

Lebrun, Charles 1619–90. French painter and designer who influenced the development of the Louis Quatorze style.

le Car•ré (lə kă-rā′), **John** Pen name David John Moore Cornwell. b. 1931. British writer of popular espionage novels, including *The Spy Who Came in from the Cold* (1963).

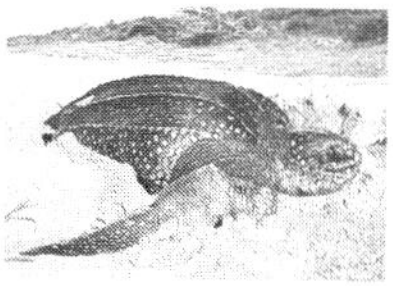

leatherback
Dermochelys coriacea

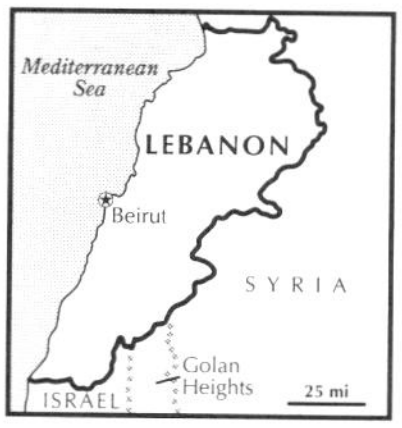

Lebanon

ă	pat	oi	boy
ā	pay	ou	out
âr	care	o͝o	took
ä	father	o͞o	boot
ĕ	pet	ŭ	cut
ē	be	ûr	urge
ĭ	pit	th	thin
ī	pie	*th*	this
îr	pier	hw	which
ŏ	pot	zh	vision
ō	toe	ə	about, item
ô	paw		

Stress marks:
′ (primary);
′ (secondary), as in
lexicon (lĕk′sĭ-kŏn′)

Lec•ce (lĕch′ā, lĕt′chĕ) A city of SE Italy E of Taranto; a semi-independent county from 1053 to 1463. Pop. 100,233.

lech[1] (lĕch) *Slang n.* **1.** A lecher. **2.** A lecherous desire. ❖ *intr.v.* **leched, lech•ing, lech•es** To behave lecherously.

lech[2] (lĕch) *n.* Variant of **letch.**

Lech (lĕk, lĕkн) A river rising in W Austria and flowing c. 249 km (155 mi) to the Danube R. in S Germany.

lech•er (lĕch′ər) *n.* A man given to lechery. [ME < OFr. *lecheor* < *lechier,* to lick, to live in debauchery, of Gmc. orig. See **leigh-** in App.]

lech•er•ous (lĕch′ər-əs) *adj.* Given to, marked by, or eliciting lechery. **—lech′er•ous•ly** *adv.* **—lech′er•ous•ness** *n.*

lech•er•y (lĕch′ə-rē) *n., pl.* **-ies 1.** Excessive indulgence in sexual activity; lewdness. **2.** A lecherous act.

lec•i•thin (lĕs′ə-thĭn) *n.* Any of a group of phospholipids found in egg yolks and the plasma membrane of plant and animal cells, used as an emulsifier in a wide range of commercial products. [Fr. *lécithine* : Gk. *lekithos,* egg yolk + Fr. *-ine,* -in.]

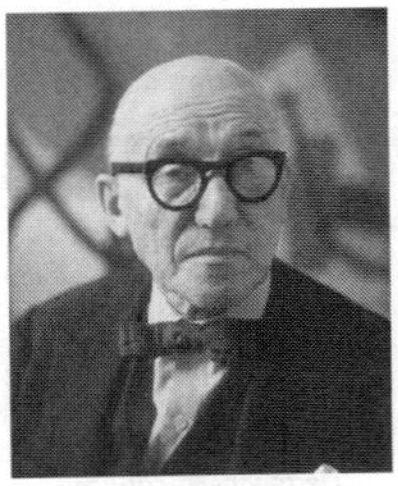

Le Corbusier

Le•conte de Lisle (lə-kôNt′ də lēl′), **Charles Marie** 1818–94. French poet noted for his *Poèmes Barbares* (1862).

Le Cor•bu•sier (lə kôr-bo͞o-zyā′, -bü-) Pseudonym of Charles Édouard Jeanneret. 1887–1965. Swiss-born French architect who was a powerful advocate of the modernist school.

lec•tern (lĕk′tərn) *n.* **1.** A desk with a slanted top holding the books read from during a church service. **2.** A stand that serves as a support for the notes or books of a speaker. [ME *lectorn* < OFr. *lettrun* < Med.Lat. *lēctrīnum* < LLat. *lēctrum* < Lat. *lēctus,* p. part. of *legere,* to read. See **leg-** in App.]

lec•tion (lĕk′shən) *n.* **1.** A variant reading or transcription of a text or copy. **2.** A reading from Scripture that forms a part of a church service. [Lat. *lēctiō, lēctiōn-,* a reading. See LESSON.]

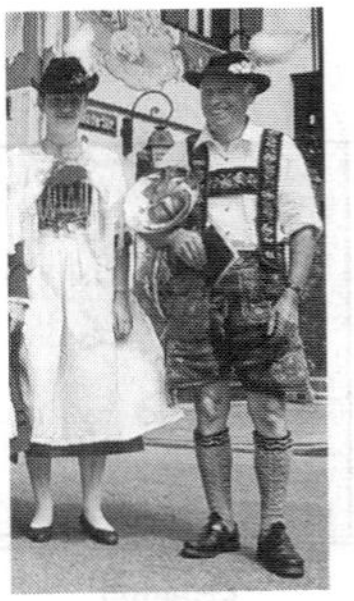

lederhosen

lec•tion•ar•y (lĕk′shə-nĕr′ē) *n., pl.* **-ies** A book or list of lections to be read at church services during the year. [Med.Lat. *lēctiōnārium* < Lat. *lēctiō, lēctiōn-,* a reading. See LESSON.]

lec•tor (lĕk′tər) *n.* **1.** One who reads aloud certain scriptural passages used in a church service. **2.** A public lecturer or reader in certain universities. [ME < LLat. *lēctor* < Lat., reader < *lēctus,* p. part. of *legere,* to read. See LECTURE.]

lec•to•type (lĕk′tə-tīp′) *n.* The specimen or element selected as the type of a species when a holotype has not been defined. [< Gk. *lektos,* chosen (< *legein,* to choose; see **leg-** in App.) + TYPE.] **—lec′to•typ′ic** (-tĭp′ĭk) *adj.*

lec•ture (lĕk′chər) *n.* **1.** An exposition of a given subject delivered before an audience or a class. **2.** An earnest admonition or reproof; a reprimand. ❖ *v.* **-tured, -tur•ing, -tures** *—intr.* To deliver a lecture or series of lectures. *—tr.* **1.** To deliver a lecture to (a class or an audience). **2.** To admonish or reprove earnestly, often at length. [ME, a reading < OFr. < Med.Lat. *lēctūra* < Lat. *lēctus,* p. part. of *legere,* to read. See **leg-** in App.]

lec•tur•er (lĕk′chər-ər) *n.* **1.** One who delivers lectures, esp. professionally. **2a.** A member of the faculty of a college or university usu. having qualified status without rank or tenure. **b.** A faculty member ranking below an assistant professor. **3.** *Chiefly British* A university teacher, esp. one ranking next below a reader.

lec•ture•ship (lĕk′chər-shĭp′) *n.* **1.** The status or position of a lecturer. **2.** An endowment or foundation supporting a series or course of lectures. [Alteration of *lecturership.*]

led (lĕd) *v.* Past tense and past participle of **lead**[1].

LED (ĕl′ē-dē′, lĕd) *n.* A semiconductor diode that converts applied voltage to light and is used in digital displays, as of a calculator. [*l(ight-)e(mitting) d(iode).*]

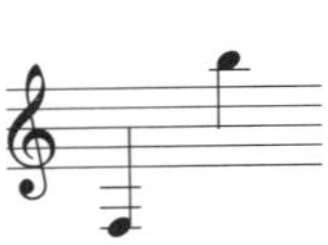

ledger line
Notes F (*left*) and B (*right*) are on ledger lines.

Le•da (lē′də) *n.* **1.** *Greek Mythology* A queen of Sparta and the mother, by Zeus in the form of a swan, of Helen and Pollux and, by her husband Tyndareus, of Castor and Clytemnestra. **2.** A satellite of Jupiter.

Led•bet•ter (lĕd′bĕt′ər), **Huddie** Known as "Leadbelly." 1885?–1949. Amer. folk and blues musician whose work was first brought to national attention in 1934.

Led•er•berg (lĕd′ər-bûrg′, lā′dər-), **Joshua** b. 1925. Amer. geneticist who shared a 1958 Nobel Prize.

le•der•ho•sen (lā′dər-hō′zən) *pl.n.* Leather shorts, often with suspenders, worn by men and boys, esp. in Bavaria. [Ger. < MHGer. *lederhose* : *leder,* leather (< OHGer. *ledar*) + *hose,* trousers (< OHGer. *hosa*; see **(s)keu-** in App.).]

ledge (lĕj) *n.* **1.** A horizontal projection forming a narrow shelf on a wall. **2.** A cut or projection forming a shelf on a cliff or rock wall. **3.** An underwater ridge or rock shelf. **4.** A level of rock-bearing ore; a vein. [ME, crossbar, prob. < *leggen,* to lay < OE *lecgan.* See **legh-** in App.] **—ledg′y** *adj.*

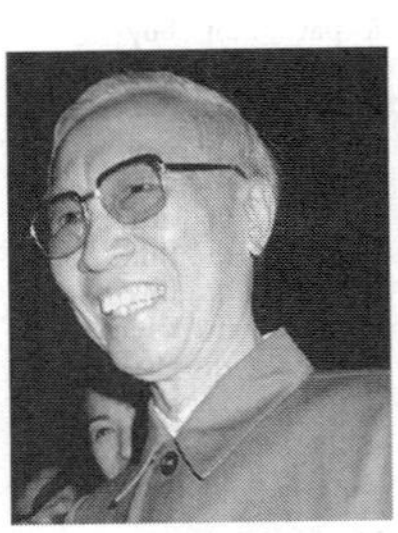

Le Duc Tho

ledg•er (lĕj′ər) *n.* **1a.** A book in which the monetary transactions of a business are posted in the form of debits and credits. **b.** A book to which the record of accounts is transferred as final entry from original postings. **2.** A slab of stone laid flat over a grave. **3.** A horizontal timber in a scaffold, attached to the uprights and supporting the putlogs. [ME *legger,* breviary, prob. < *leggen,* to lay. See LEDGE.]

ledger board *n.* **1.** The top railing of a fence or balustrade. **2.** A narrow horizontal board attached to a row of studs to support the ends of floor or ceiling joists.

ledger line *n. Music* A line placed above or below a staff to accommodate notes higher or lower than the staff range.

Le Duc Tho (lā′ dŭk′ tō′) 1911–90. Vietnamese political leader who helped negotiate the North Vietnamese–US cease-fire (1973) but refused the Nobel Peace Prize (1973).

lee (lē) *n.* **1.** *Nautical* The side away from the direction from which the wind blows; the side sheltered from the wind. **2.** An area sheltered from the wind. **3.** Cover; shelter. ❖ *adj.* **1.** *Nautical* Of or relating to the side sheltered from the wind. **2.** Located in or facing the path of an oncoming glacier. Used of a geologic formation. [ME *le* < OE *hlēo,* shelter, protection.]

Lee, Ann Known as "Mother Ann." 1736–84. British religious leader and founder (1776) of the Shakers in America.

Lee, Charles 1731–82. British-born Amer. general who was court-martialed after the Battle of Monmouth (1778).

Lee, Henry Known as "Lighthorse Harry." 1756–1818. Amer. politician and soldier who served as governor of VA (1792–95).

Lee, Kwan Yew b. 1923. Singaporean lawyer. He negotiated Singapore's independence from Great Britain and became the republic's first prime minister (1959–90).

Lee, (Nelle) Harper b. 1926. Amer. writer renowned for her novel *To Kill a Mockingbird* (1960).

Lee, Richard Henry 1732–94. Amer. Revolutionary leader who proposed the resolution calling for independence from England (1776).

Lee, Robert Edward 1807–70. Amer. Confederate general in the Civil War who won victories at Bull Run (1862), Fredericksburg (1862), and Chancellorsville (1863) before surrendering to Gen. Ulysses S. Grant at Appomattox (1865).

Lee, Shelton Jackson Known as "Spike." b. 1957. Amer. director, screenwriter, and actor whose films include *Do the Right Thing* (1989).

lee•board (lē′bôrd′, -bōrd′) *n.* One of a pair of movable boards or plates attached to the hull of a sailing vessel to reduce leeway.

leech[1] (lēch) *n.* **1.** Any of various chiefly aquatic bloodsucking or carnivorous annelid worms of the class Hirudinea, of which one species *(Hirudo medicinalis)* was formerly used by physicians to bleed patients. **2.** One that preys on or clings to another; a parasite. **3.** *Archaic* A physician. ❖ *v.* **leeched, leech•ing, leech•es** *—tr.* **1.** To bleed with leeches. **2.** To drain the essence or exhaust the resources of. *—intr.* To attach oneself to another in the manner of a leech. [ME *leche,* physician, leech < OE *lǣce.* See **leg-** in App.]

leech[2] (lēch) *n. Nautical* **1.** Either vertical edge of a square sail. **2.** The after edge of a fore-and-aft sail. [ME *leche,* prob. < MLGer. *līk,* leech line.]

Leeds (lēdz) A borough of N-central England NE of Manchester; incorp. 1626. Pop. 724,524.

leek (lēk) *n.* An edible plant *(Allium porrum)* related to the onion and having a white slender bulb and flat dark green leaves. [ME *lek* < OE *lēac.*]

leer (lîr) *intr.v.* **leered, leer•ing, leers** To look with a sidelong glance, indicative esp. of sexual desire or sly and malicious intent. ❖ *n.* A desirous, sly, or knowing look. [Prob. < obsolete *leer,* cheek < ME *ler* < OE *hlēor.* See **kleu-** in App.]

leer•y (lîr′ē) *adj.* **-i•er, -i•est** Suspicious or distrustful; wary. **—leer′i•ly** *adv.* **—leer′i•ness** *n.*

lees (lēz) *pl.n.* Sediment settling during fermentation, esp. in wine; dregs. [ME *lies,* pl. of *lie* < OFr. < Med.Lat. *lia,* prob. of Celt. orig. See **legh-** in App.]

lee shore *n.* A shore toward which the wind blows and toward which a ship is likely to be driven.

Leeu•wen•hoek or **Leu•wen•hoek** (lā′vən-ho͝ok′, lā′ü-wən-ho͝ok′), **Anton van** 1632–1723. Dutch naturalist who formulated early descriptions of bacteria and spermatozoa.

lee•ward (lo͞o′ərd, lē′wərd) *Nautical adj. & adv.* On or toward the side to which the wind is blowing. ❖ *n.* The lee side or quarter.

Lee•ward Islands (lē′wərd) **1.** The N group of the Lesser Antilles in the West Indies, extending from the Virgin Is. SE to Guadeloupe; hotly contested by the Spanish, French, and British in the 17th and 18th cent. **2.** A chain of small islets of HI in the central Pacific WNW of the main islands.

lee•way (lē′wā′) *n.* **1.** The drift of a ship or aircraft to leeward of the course being steered. **2.** A margin of freedom or variation, as of activity or time; latitude.

left[1] (lĕft) *adj.* **1a.** Of, belonging to, located on, or being the side of the body to the north when the subject is facing east. **b.** Of, relating to, directed toward, or located on the left side. **c.** Located on the left side of a person facing downstream: *the left bank of a river.* **2.** often **Left** Of or belonging to the political or intellectual left. ❖ *n.* **1a.** The direction or position on the left side. **b.** The left side. **c.** The left hand. **d.** A turn in the direction of the left hand or side. **2.** often **Left a.** The people and groups who advocate liberal, often radical measures to effect change. **b.** The opinion of those advocating such measures. **3.** *Sports* A blow delivered by a boxer's left hand. **4.** *Baseball* Left field. ❖ *adv.* Toward or on the left. [ME < OE *lyft-,* weak, useless (in *lyftādl,* paralysis).]

left[2] (lĕft) *v.* Past tense and past participle of **leave**[1].

Left Bank A district of Paris on the S bank of the Seine R.; long noted for its bohemian atmosphere.

left brain *n.* The left portion of the cerebral hemisphere, controlling activity on the right side of the body, and in humans, controlling speech and language functions.

left-brained (lĕft′brānd′) also **left-brain** (-brān′) *adj.* Of, relating to, or tending toward thought processes usu. associated with the left brain, esp. logical or analytical thinking.

left field *n.* **1.** *Baseball* **a.** The third of the outfield that is to the left, looking from home plate. **b.** The position played by the left fielder. **2.** *Informal* A position far from the center or mainstream, as of opinion or reason.

left fielder *n. Baseball* The player who defends left field.

left-hand (lĕft′hănd′) *adj.* **1.** Of, relating to, or located on the left. **2.** Relating to, designed for, or done with the left hand.

left-hand•ed (lĕft′hăn′dĭd) *adj.* **1a.** Using the left hand more skillfully or easily than the right. **b.** *Sports* Swinging from left to right. **2a.** Done with the left hand. **b.** Intended for wear on or use by the left hand. **3.** Awkward; maladroit. **4.** Of doubtful sincerity; dubious: *a left-handed compliment.* **5.** Of, relating to, or born of a morganatic marriage. **6a.** Turning or spiraling from right to left; counterclockwise. **b.** Rotating counterclockwise; levorotatory. ❖ *adv.* **1.** With the left hand. **2.** *Sports* From the left to the right. **—left′-hand′ed•ly** *adv.* **—left′-hand′ed•ness** *n.*

left-hand•er (lĕft′hăn′dər) *n.* One who is left-handed.

left•ism also **Left•ism** (lĕf′tĭz′əm) *n.* **1.** The ideology of the political left. **2.** Belief in or support of the tenets of the political left. **—left′ist** *adj. & n.*

left•o•ver (lĕft′ō′vər) *adj.* Remaining as an unused portion or amount. ❖ *n.* **1.** A remnant or an unused portion. **2. leftovers** Food remaining from a previous meal.

left•ward (lĕft′wərd) *adv. & adj.* To or on the left.

left wing also **Left Wing** *n.* **1.** The liberal or radical faction of a group. **2.** See **left**[1] 2a. **—left′-wing′** (lĕft′wĭng′) *adj.* **—left′-wing′er** *n.*

left•y (lĕf′tē) *Informal n., pl.* **-ies 1.** A left-handed person. **2.** An advocate or member of the political left. ❖ *adv.* With the left hand or in a left-handed manner.

leg (lĕg) *n.* **1a.** A limb or an appendage of an animal, used for locomotion or support. **b.** One of the lower or hind limbs in humans and primates. **c.** The part of the limb between the knee and foot in vertebrates. **d.** The back part of the hindquarter of a meat animal. **2.** A supporting part resembling a leg in shape or function. **3.** One of the branches of a forked or jointed object. **4.** The part of a garment, esp. of a pair of trousers, that covers the leg. **5.** *Mathematics* Either side of a right triangle that is not the hypotenuse. **6.** A stage of a journey or course, esp.: **a.** *Nautical* The distance traveled by a sailing vessel on a single tack. **b.** The part of an air route or a flight pattern between two successive stops, positions, or changes in direction. **c.** One of several contests that must be successfully completed in order to determine the winner of a competition. **d.** *Sports* One stretch of a relay race. **7. legs** The streams of swirled wine or spirits that run down along the inside of a glass. **8. legs** *Slang* The ability to sustain success: *a popular movie with legs.* ❖ *intr.v.* **legged, leg•ging, legs** *Informal* To go on foot; walk or run. Often used with the indefinite *it: We had to leg it across town.* ***—idioms:*** **a leg to stand on** *Slang* A justifiable or logical basis for defense; support. **a leg up** *Slang* **1.** The act or an instance of assisting; a boost. **2.** A position of advantage; an edge. **on (one's) last legs** At the end of one's strength or resources. [ME < ON *leggr.*]

leg. *abbr.* **1.** legate **2.** legato

leg•a•cy (lĕg′ə-sē) *n., pl.* **-cies 1.** Money or property bequeathed to another by will. **2.** Something handed down from an ancestor or a predecessor or from the past. [ME *legacie,* office of a deputy < OFr. < Med.Lat. *lēgātia* < Lat. *lēgātus,* p. part. of *lēgāre,* to depute, bequeath. See **leg-** in App.]

le•gal (lē′gəl) *adj.* **1.** Of, relating to, or concerned with law. **2a.** Authorized by or based on law: *a legal right.* **b.** Established by law; statutory: *the legal owner.* **3.** In conformity with or permitted by law. **4.** Recognized or enforced by law rather than by equity. **5.** In terms of or created by the law: *a legal offense.* **6.** Applicable to or characteristic of attorneys or their profession. ❖ *n.* One that is in accord with certain rules or laws. [ME < OFr. < Lat. *lēgālis* < *lēx, lēg-,* law. See **leg-** in App.] **—le′gal•ly** *adv.*

legal age *n.* The age at which a person may by law assume the rights and responsibilities of an adult.

legal aid *n.* Legal assistance provided, as by a specially established organization, for those unable to afford an attorney.

le•gal•ese (lē′gə-lēz′, -lēs′) *n.* The specialized vocabulary of the legal profession, esp. when considered to be abstruse.

legal holiday *n.* A holiday authorized by law and characterized by a limit or ban on work or official business.

le•gal•ism (lē′gə-lĭz′əm) *n.* **1.** Strict literal adherence to the law or to a particular code, as of religion or morality. **2.** A legal word, expression, or rule. **—le′gal•ist** *n.* **—le′gal•is′tic** *adj.* **—le′gal•is′ti•cal•ly** *adv.*

le•gal•i•ty (lē-găl′ĭ-tē) *n., pl.* **-ties 1.** The state or quality of being legal; lawfulness. **2.** Adherence to or observance of the law. **3.** A requirement enjoined by law. Often used in the plural.

le•gal•ize (lē′gə-līz′) *tr.v.* **-ized, -iz•ing, -iz•es** To make legal or lawful; authorize or sanction by law. **—le′gal•i•za′tion** (-gə-lĭ-zā′shən) *n.*

Le Gal•lienne (lə găl′yən, găl-yĕn′), **Eva** 1899–1991. British-born Amer. actress who founded (1926) and directed (1926–34) the Civic Repertory Theatre in New York City.

legal pad *n.* A pad of ruled, usu. yellow writing paper that measures 8½ by 14 inches.

legal reserve *n.* The sum of money that a bank or an insurance company is required by law to set aside as security.

legal separation *n.* A court decree recognizing that a married couple is living apart and regulating the couple's mutual rights and liabilities.

le•gal-size (lē′gəl-sīz′) *adj.* **1.** Being a sheet of paper that measures approx. 8½ by 14 inches. **2.** Designed to hold such sheets of paper.

legal tender *n.* Legally valid currency that may be offered in payment of a debt and that a creditor must accept.

Le•ga•nés (lĕ′gä-nĕs′) A city of central Spain, a suburb of Madrid. Pop. 171,589.

leg•ate (lĕg′ĭt) *n.* An official emissary, esp. an official representative of the pope. [ME < OFr. *legat* < Med.Lat. *lēgātus* < Lat., p. part. of *lēgāre,* to depute. See **leg-** in App.] **—leg′ate•ship′** *n.*

leg•a•tee (lĕg′ə-tē′) *n.* The inheritor of a legacy. [< *legate,* to bequeath < Lat. *lēgāre, lēgāt-.* See LEGACY.]

leg•a•tine (lĕg′ə-tĭn, -tīn′) *adj.* Of, directed by, or authorized by a legate.

le•ga•tion (lĭ-gā′shən) *n.* **1.** The act of sending a legate. **2a.** A diplomatic mission in a foreign country ranking below an embassy. **b.** The minister and staff of such a mission. **c.** The premises of such a mission. **—le•ga′tion•ar•y** *adj.*

le•ga•to (lĭ-gä′tō) *Music adv. & adj.* In a smooth, even style without any noticeable break between the notes. ❖ *n., pl.* **-tos** A legato passage or movement. [Ital., p. part. of *legare,* to bind, tie together < Lat. *ligāre.*]

le•ga•tor (lĭ-gā′tər) *n.* One that makes a will; a testator. [Lat. *lēgātor* < *lēgāre,* to bequeath. See LEGACY.]

leg•end (lĕj′ənd) *n.* **1a.** An unverified story handed down from earlier times, esp. one popularly believed to be historical. **b.** A body or collection of such stories. **c.** A romanticized or popularized myth of modern times. **2.** One that inspires legends or achieves legendary fame. **3a.** An inscription or title on an object, such as a coin. **b.** An explanatory caption accompanying an illustration. **c.** An explanatory table or list of the symbols appearing on a map or chart. [ME < OFr. *legende* < Med.Lat. *(lēctiō) legenda,* (lesson) to be read < Lat., fem. gerundive of *legere,* to read. See **leg-** in App.]

USAGE NOTE *Legend,* which historically has meant "traditional story," can also be a person or achievement worthy of inspiring such a story—anyone or anything whose fame promises to be enduring. Thus we speak of a contemporary famous person as *a legend in his own time,* or of the *legendary* voice of a famous opera singer. This usage is common in journalism, and 55 percent of the Usage Panel accepts it.

leg•en•dar•y (lĕj′ən-dĕr′ē) *adj.* **1.** Of, constituting, based on, or of the nature of a legend. **2a.** Celebrated in legend. **b.** Extremely well known; famous. See Usage Note at **legend.**

Le•gen•dre (lə-zhän′drə, -zhäN′-), **Adrien Marie** 1752–1833. French mathematician noted for his work on number theory.

leg•end•ry (lĕj′ən-drē) *n., pl.* **-ries** A collection or body of legends.

Lé•ger (lā-zhā′), **Alexis Saint-Léger** Pen name Saint-John Perse. (pĕrs, pûrs) 1887–1975. French poet who won the 1960 Nobel Prize for literature.

Léger, Fernand 1881–1955. French cubist artist who incorporated industrial and mechanical images into his work.

leg•er•de•main (lĕj′ər-də-mān′) *n.* **1.** Sleight of hand. **2.** A show of skill or deceitful cleverness. [ME *legerdemayn* < OFr. *leger de main* : *leger,* light (< VLat. **leviārius* < Lat. *levis*) + *de,* of (< Lat. *dē*; see DE–) + *main,* hand; see MORTMAIN.]

le•ger•i•ty (lə-jĕr′ĭ-tē) *n.* Quickness or agility of mind or body. [Fr. *légèreté* < OFr. *legerete* < *leger,* light. See LEGERDEMAIN.]

le•ges (lē′jēz′) *n.* Plural of **lex.**

leg•ged (lĕg′ĭd, lĕgd) *adj.* Having a specified kind or number of legs. Often used in combination: *long-legged; four-legged.*

leg•ging (lĕg′ĭng) *n.* **1.** A leg covering usu. extending from the ankle to the knee and often made of material such as leather or canvas, worn esp. by soldiers and workers. **2. leggings a.** Tight-fitting knit trousers, usu. worn by women and children. **b.** Warm outerwear trousers for children.

leg•gy (lĕg′ē) *adj.* **-gi•er, -gi•est 1.** Having disproportionately long legs. **2.** *Informal* Having long slender legs. **3.** Having long, spindly, often leafless stems. **—leg′gi•ness** *n.*

leg•horn (lĕg′hôrn′, -ərn) *n.* **1a.** The dried and bleached straw of an Italian variety of wheat. **b.** A plaited fabric made from this straw. **c.** A hat of this fabric. **2.** often **Leghorn** Any of a breed of small domestic fowl of Mediterranean origin, prolific in production of eggs. [After *Leghorn* (Livorno).]

Leghorn See **Livorno.**

leg•i•ble (lĕj′ə-bəl) *adj.* **1.** Possible to read or decipher: *legible handwriting.* **2.** Plainly discernible; apparent. [ME < LLat. *legibilis* < Lat. *legere,* to read. See **leg-** in App.] **—leg′i•bil′i•ty, leg′i•ble•ness** *n.* **—leg′i•bly** *adv.*

le•gion (lē′jən) *n.* **1.** The major unit of the Roman army consisting of 3,000 to 6,000 infantry troops and 100 to 200 cavalry

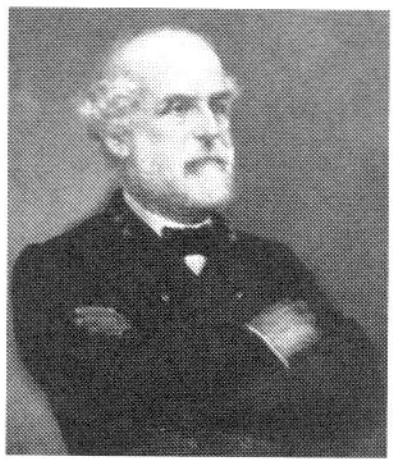

Robert E. Lee
detail from a portrait by
John Adams Elder
(1833–95)

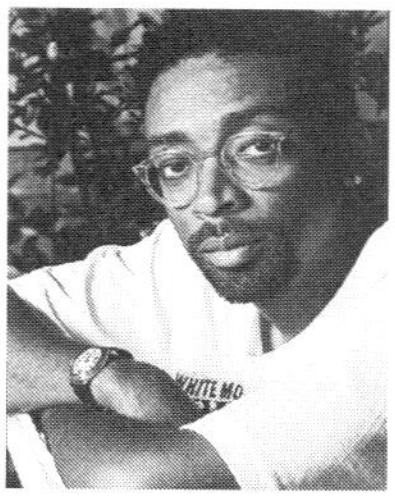

Spike Lee

ă pat	oi boy		
ā pay	ou out		
âr care	ŏŏ took		
ä father	ōō boot		
ĕ pet	ŭ cut		
ē be	ûr urge		
ĭ pit	th thin		
ī pie	*th* this		
îr pier	hw which		
ŏ pot	zh vision		
ō toe	ə about,		
ô paw	item		

Stress marks:
′ (primary);
′ (secondary), as in
lexicon (lĕk′sĭ-kŏn′)

lei¹

troops. **2.** A large military unit trained for combat; an army. **3.** A large number; a multitude. **4.** often **Legion** A national organization of former members of the armed forces. ❖ *adj.* Constituting a large number; multitudinous. [ME *legioun* < OFr. *legion* < Lat. *legiō, legiōn-* < *legere,* to gather. See **leg-** in App.]

le·gion·ar·y (lē′jə-nĕr′ē) *adj.* Of, relating to, or constituting a legion. ❖ *n., pl.* **-ies** A soldier of a legion.

le·gion·naire (lē′jə-nâr′) *n.* A member of a legion. [Fr. *légionnaire* < OFr. < *legion,* legion. See LEGION.]

Le·gion·naires′ disease (lē′jə-nârz′) *n.* An acute, sometimes fatal respiratory disease caused by a bacterium of the genus *Legionella,* esp. *L. pneumophila,* and characterized by severe pneumonia, headache, and a dry cough. [< its first recognized outbreak at an American Legion Convention in 1976.]

Legion of Honor *n.* A high French civilian or military decoration, instituted in 1802. [Transl. of Fr. *Légion d'honneur.*]

Legion of Merit *n.* A US military decoration for meritorious conduct in the performance of outstanding services.

leg·is·late (lĕj′ĭ-slāt′) *v.* **-lat·ed, -lat·ing, -lates** —*intr.* To create or pass laws. —*tr.* To create or bring about by or as if by legislation. [Back-formation < LEGISLATOR.]

leg·is·la·tion (lĕj′ĭ-slā′shən) *n.* **1.** The act or process of legislating. **2.** A proposed or enacted law or group of laws.

leg·is·la·tive (lĕj′ĭ-slā′tĭv) *adj.* **1.** Of or relating to the enactment of laws. **2.** Resulting from or decided by legislation. **3.** Having the power to create laws; intended to legislate. **4.** Of or relating to a legislature. ❖ *n.* The legislative body of a government; a legislature. —**leg′is·la′tive·ly** *adv.*

leg·is·la·tor (lĕj′ĭ-slā′tər) *n.* One that creates or enacts laws, esp. a member of a legislative body. [Fr. *législateur* < OFr. < Lat. *lēgis lātor : lēgis,* genitive of *lēx,* law; see **leg-** in App. + *lātor,* proposer, bearer (< *lātus,* p. part. of *ferre,* to propose, bear; see **telə-** in App.).] —**leg′is·la·to′ri·al** (-lə-tôr′ē-əl, -tōr′-) *adj.* —**leg′is·la′tor·ship′** *n.*

leg·is·la·ture (lĕj′ĭ-slā′chər) *n.* An officially elected or otherwise selected body of people vested with the responsibility and power to make laws for a political unit.

le·gist (lē′jĭst) *n.* A specialist in law. [ME *legiste* < OFr. < Med.Lat. *lēgista* < Lat. *lēx, lēg-,* law. See **leg-** in App.]

le·git (lə-jĭt′) *adj. Slang* Legitimate.

le·git·i·ma·cy (lə-jĭt′ə-mə-sē) *n.* The quality or fact of being legitimate.

le·git·i·mate (lə-jĭt′ə-mĭt) *adj.* **1.** Compliant with the law. **2.** Being in accordance with established or accepted patterns and standards. **3.** Based on logical reasoning; reasonable. **4.** Authentic; genuine. **5.** Born to legally married parents. **6.** Of, relating to, or ruling by hereditary right. **7.** Of or relating to drama of high professional quality that excludes burlesque, vaudeville, and some forms of musical comedy: *the legitimate theater.* ❖ *tr.v.* (-māt′) **-mat·ed, -mat·ing, -mates** To make legitimate, as: **a.** To give legal force or status to; make lawful. **b.** To establish (a child) as legitimate by legal means. **c.** To sanction formally or officially; authorize. **d.** To demonstrate or declare to be justified. [ME *legitimat,* born in wedlock < Med.Lat. *lēgitimātus,* p. part. of *lēgitimāre,* to make lawful < Lat. *lēgitimus,* legitimate < *lēx, lēg-,* law. See **leg-** in App.] —**le·git′i·mate·ly** *adv.* —**le·git′i·mate·ness** *n.* —**le·git′i·ma′tion** *n.* —**le·git′i·mat′or** (-māt′ər) *n.*

le·git·i·ma·tize (lə-jĭt′ə-mə-tīz′) *tr.v.* **-tized, -tiz·ing, -tiz·es** To legitimize.

le·git·i·mist (lə-jĭt′ə-mĭst) *n.* One that believes in or advocates rule by hereditary right. —**le·git′i·mism** *n.*

le·git·i·mize (lə-jĭt′ə-mīz′) *tr.v.* **-mized, -miz·ing, -miz·es** To legitimize. —**le·git′i·mi·za′tion** (-mĭ-zā′shən) *n.* —**le·git′i·miz′er** *n.*

lemming
Norway lemming
Lemmus lemmus

leg·man (lĕg′măn′, -mən) *n. Informal* **1.** A reporter whose job is to gather information at the scene of an event or by visiting various news sources. **2.** An assistant, as in an office, who performs tasks such as running errands.

leg-of-mut·ton (lĕg′ə-mŭt′n, lĕg′əv-) or **leg-o′-mut·ton** (lĕg′ə-) *adj.* Resembling a leg of mutton in shape; tapering sharply from one large end to a smaller end, as a sleeve or sail.

leg-pull (lĕg′pŏŏl′) *n.* A comical hoax or practical joke. —**leg′-pull′er** *n.*

leg·room (lĕg′rŏŏm′, -rŏŏm′) *n.* Room in which to stretch the legs while seated.

leg·ume (lĕg′yŏŏm′, lə-gyŏŏm′) *n.* **1a.** A pod, such as that of a pea or bean, that splits into two valves. **b.** Such a pod or seed used as food. **2.** A plant of the pea family. [Fr. *légume* < Lat. *legūmen,* bean.]

legume family *n.* The pea family.

le·gu·mi·nous (lə-gyŏŏ′mə-nəs) *adj.* **1.** Of, belonging to, or characteristic of the family Leguminosae, which includes peas, beans, clover, and other plants. **2.** Resembling a legume. [Ult. < Lat. *legūminōsus* < *legūmen, legūmin-,* bean.]

leg warmer also **leg·warm·er** (lĕg′wôr′mər) *n.* A knitted covering for the leg, resembling a stocking but without a foot.

leg·work (lĕg′wûrk′) *n. Informal* Work, such as collecting information, involving much walking or traveling about.

Le·hár (lā′här), **Franz** 1870–1948. Hungarian composer of light operas, most notably *The Merry Widow* (1905).

Le Ha·vre (lə hä′vrə, häv′) A city of N France on the English

lemur
ring-tailed lemur
Lemur catta

Vladimir Lenin

Channel WNW of Paris. Pop. 195,932.

Le·high River (lē′hī′) A river of E PA flowing c. 166 km (103 mi) to the Delaware R.

lei¹ (lā, lā′ē) *n., pl.* **leis** A garland of flowers, esp. one worn around the neck. [Hawaiian.]

lei² (lā) *n.* Plural of **leu.**

Leib·niz or **Leib·nitz** (līb′nĭts, līp′-), Baron **Gottfried Wilhelm von** 1646–1716. German philosopher and mathematician who proposed the metaphysical theory that we live in "the best of all possible worlds."

Leices·ter¹ (lĕs′tər) A borough of central England ENE of Birmingham; first settled in Roman times. Pop. 289,286.

Leices·ter² (lĕs′tər) *n.* **1.** Any of a breed of large white-faced sheep having long coarse wool, developed in Leicestershire, a county of England. **2.** A hard cheese similar to Cheddar.

Leicester, 1st Earl of. Title of Robert Dudley. 1532?–88. English courtier who was privy councilor to Elizabeth I.

Lei·den also **Ley·den** (līd′n) A city of SW Netherlands NE of The Hague; founded in Roman times. Pop. 114,365.

Leigh (lē), **Vivien** 1913–67. British actress whose films include *Gone With the Wind* (1939).

Lein·ster (lĕn′stər) A historical region of SE Ireland; often prey to Danish and Anglo-Saxon invasions.

Leip·zig (līp′sĭg, -sĭk, -tsĭk) A city of E-central Germany SSW of Berlin; orig. a Slavic settlement. Pop. 490,851.

leish·man·i·a·sis (lēsh′mə-nī′ə-sĭs) *n.* **1.** An infection caused by any of the flagellate protozoans of the genus *Leishmania,* transmitted by bloodsucking sand flies. **2.** A disease, such as kala-azar, caused by flagellate protozoans of the genus *Leishmania.* [< NLat. *Leishmania,* genus of protozoans, after Sir William Boog *Leishman* (1865–1926), British officer.]

leis·ter (lē′stər) *n.* A three-pronged spear used in fishing. [Prob. < ON *ljōstr* < *ljōsta,* to strike. See **leu-** in App.] —**leis′ter** *v.*

lei·sure (lē′zhər, lĕzh′ər) *n.* Freedom from time-consuming duties, responsibilities, or activities. —*idiom:* **at (one's) leisure** When one has free time; at one's convenience. [ME < Norman Fr. *leisour* < OFr. *leisir,* to be permitted < Lat. *licēre.*]

lei·sured (lē′zhərd, lĕzh′ərd) *adj.* Characterized by leisure.

lei·sure·ly (lē′zhər-lē, lĕzh′ər-) *adj.* Acting, proceeding, or done without haste; unhurried. ❖ *adv.* In an unhurried manner; slowly. —**lei′sure·li·ness** *n.*

leisure suit *n.* A man's suit for informal wear, consisting of a shirtlike jacket and matching slacks.

Leith (lēth) A district of Edinburgh, Scotland, on the S shore of the Firth of Forth.

leit·mo·tif also **leit·mo·tiv** (līt′mō-tēf′) *n.* **1.** A melodic passage or phrase, esp. in Wagnerian opera, associated with a specific character, situation, or element. **2.** A dominant and recurring theme, as in a work. [Ger. *Leitmotiv : leiten,* to lead (< MHGer. < OHGer. *leitan*) + *Motiv,* motif (< Fr. *motif*; see MOTIF).]

Lei·zhou Peninsula (lā′jō′) also **Lui·chow Peninsula** (lwē′jō′) A peninsula of S China between the Gulf of Tonkin and the South China Sea.

lek (lĕk) *n.* See table at **currency.** [Albanian, after *Lek* Dukagjini, 15th-cent. Albanian feudal lord and lawgiver.]

lek·var (lĕk′vär) *n.* A sweet spread or pastry filling made of prunes or apricots. [Hung. *lekvár,* jam < Slovak < Czech *lektvar,* electuary < MHGer. *lactwārje, latwērge* < OFr. *lettuaire* < LLat. *ēlēctuārium,* electuary. See ELECTUARY.]

LEM (lĕm) *n.* A lunar excursion module.

lem·an (lĕm′ən, lē′mən) *n. Archaic* **1.** A sweetheart; a lover. **2.** A mistress. [ME *leofman, lemman : leof,* dear (< OE *lēof*) + *man,* man; see MAN.]

Le·man (lē′mən, lə-măn′), **Lake** See Lake Geneva.

Le Mans (lə män′) A city of NW France WSW of Paris; famous for its annual sports car races. Population, 145,439.

lem·ma (lĕm′ə) *n., pl.* **lem·mas** or **lem·ma·ta** (lĕm′ə-tə) **1.** A subsidiary proposition assumed to be valid and used to demonstrate a principal proposition. **2.** A theme, argument, or subject indicated in a title. **3.** A word or phrase treated in a glossary or similar listing. [Lat. *lēmma* < Gk. < *lambanein,* to take.]

lem·ma² (lĕm′ə) *n.* The outer or lower of two bracts that enclose the flower in a grass spikelet. [Gk., husk < *lepein,* to peel.]

lem·ming (lĕm′ĭng) *n.* Any of various small thickset rodents, esp. of the genus *Lemmus,* of northern regions, known for mass migrations that sometimes end in drowning. [Norw. < ON *læmingi, læmingr.*]

lem·nis·cus (lĕm-nĭs′kəs) *n., pl.* **-nis·ci** (-nĭs′ī′, -nĭs′kī′, -nĭs′kē) *Anatomy* A bundle or band of sensory nerve fibers. [Lat. *lēmniscus,* ribbon < Gk. *lēmniskos,* perh. < *Lēmnos,* Lemnos.]

Lem·nos (lĕm′nŏs, -nōs, lĕm′nôs) also **Lím·nos** (lēm′nôs) An island of NE Greece in the Aegean Sea off the coast of Turkey NW of Lesbos.

lem·on (lĕm′ən) *n.* **1a.** A spiny Asian evergreen tree (*Citrus limon*) having yellow egg-shaped fruit. **b.** The fruit of this tree, having a yellow aromatic rind and juicy, acid pulp. **2.** Lemon yellow. **3.** *Informal* One that is unsatisfactory or defective: *That car I bought last year has turned out to be a real lemon.* ❖ *adj.* **1.** Lemon-yellow. **2a.** Made from lemons. **b.** Tasting or smelling like lemons. [ME *limon* < OFr. < OItal. *limone* < Ar. *laymūn, līmūn* < Pers. *līmūn.*] —**lem′on·y** *adj.*

lem·on·ade (lĕm′ə-nād′) *n.* A drink made of lemon juice, water, and sugar.
lemon balm *n.* See **balm** 1a.
lem·on·grass also **lemon grass** (lĕm′ən-grăs′) *n.* A tropical grass *(Cymbopogon citratus)* native to southern India and Sri Lanka and yielding an aromatic oil.
lemon stick *n. Baltimore* A lemon half garnished with a peppermint stick through which the lemon juice is sucked.
lemon verbena *n.* An aromatic shrub *(Aloysia triphylla)* native to Argentina and Chile having fragrant foliage and flowers.
lemon yellow *n.* A moderate to brilliant vivid yellow. **—lem′on-yel′low** (lĕm′ən-yĕl′ō) *adj.*
lem·pi·ra (lĕm-pîr′ə) *n.* See table at **currency.** [Am.Sp., after *Lempira* (1497–1537), Indian leader who resisted the Spanish conquistadors in Honduras.]
le·mur (lē′mər) *n.* Any of several small arboreal, mostly nocturnal primates chiefly of the family Lemuridae of Madagascar, having large eyes, a long slim muzzle, and a long tail. [NLat. *Lemur*, genus name, back-formation < Lat. *Lemurēs*, lemures (< their ghostly appearance and nocturnal habits).]
lem·u·res (lĕm′ə-rās′, lĕm′yə-rēz′) *pl.n.* The spirits of the dead considered in ancient Rome as frightening specters and often exorcised from the homes in rituals. [Lat. *Lemurēs*.]
Le·na (lē′nə, lyĕ′-) A river of E Russia rising near Lake Baikal and flowing c. 4,296 km (2,670 mi) to the Laptev Sea.
Len·a·pe (lĕn′ə-pē) *n., pl.* Lenape or **-pes** See **Delaware**¹ 1.
lend (lĕnd) *v.* **lent** (lĕnt), **lend·ing, lends** *—tr.* **1a.** To give or allow the use of temporarily on the condition that the same or its equivalent will be returned. **b.** To provide (money) temporarily on condition that the amount borrowed be returned, usu. with an interest fee. **2.** To contribute or impart. **3.** To accommodate or offer (itself) to; be suitable for. *—intr.* To make a loan. See Usage Note at **loan.** ***—idiom:*** **lend a hand** To be of assistance. [ME *lenen, lenden* < OE *lǣnan*. See **leik**ʷ- in App.] **—lend′er** *n.*
lend·a·ble (lĕn′də-bəl) *adj.* Available for lending.
lend·ing library (lĕn′dĭng) *n.* A library from which books may be borrowed or rented for a minimal fee.
L′En·fant (län-fänt′, läN-fäN′), **Pierre Charles** 1754–1825. French-born architect who designed the basic city plan for Washington DC.
length (lĕngkth, lĕngth, lĕnth) *n.* **1.** The state, quality, or fact of being long. **2.** The measurement of the extent of something along its greatest dimension. **3.** A piece, often of a standard size, normally measured along its greatest dimension. **4.** A measure used as a unit to estimate distances: *won by a length.* **5.** Extent or distance from beginning to end. **6.** The amount of time between specified moments; the duration. **7.** Extent or degree to which an action or policy is carried. Often used in the plural. **8.** *Linguistics* **a.** The duration of a vowel. **b.** The duration of a syllable. **9.** The vertical extent of a garment. Often used in combination: *knee-length; floor-length.* ***—idiom:*** **at length 1.** After some time; eventually. **2.** For a considerable time; fully. [ME < OE *lengthu.* See **del-** in App.]
length contraction *n.* See **Lorentz-FitzGerald contraction.**
length·en (lĕngk′thən, lĕng′-, lĕn′-) *tr. & intr.v.* **-ened, -en·ing, -ens** To make or become longer. **—length′en·er** *n.*
length·ways (lĕngkth′wāz′, lĕngth′-, lĕnth′-) *adv.* Lengthwise.
length·wise (lĕngkth′wīz′, lĕngth′-, lĕnth′-) *adv. & adj.* Of, along, or in reference to the direction of the length; longitudinally.
length·y (lĕngk′thē, lĕng′-, lĕn′-) *adj.* **-i·er, -i·est 1.** Of considerable length, esp. in time; extended. **2.** Tediously long; drawn-out. **—length′i·ly** *adv.* **—length′i·ness** *n.*
le·ni·ence (lē′nē-əns, lēn′yəns) *n.* Leniency.
le·ni·en·cy (lē′nē-ən-sē, lēn′yən-) *n., pl.* **-cies 1.** The condition or quality of being lenient. See Syns at **mercy. 2.** A lenient act.
le·ni·ent (lē′nē-ənt, lēn′yənt) *adj.* Inclined not to be harsh or strict; merciful, generous, or indulgent. [Obsolete Fr. < Lat. *lēniēns, lēnient-*, pr. part. of *lēnīre*, to pacify < *lēnis*, soft.] **—le′ni·ent·ly** *adv.*
Le·nin (lĕn′ĭn), **Vladimir Ilich** 1870–1924. Russian founder of the Bolsheviks, leader of the Russian Revolution (1917), and first head of the USSR (1917–24).
Len·in·grad (lĕn′ĭn-grăd′) See **Saint Petersburg.**
Len·in·ism (lĕn′ə-nĭz′əm) *n.* The theory and practice of proletarian revolution as developed by Lenin. **—Len′in·ist, Len′in·ite′** (lĕn′ə-nīt′) *adj. & n.*
Lenin Peak A mountain, 7,138.5 m (23,405 ft), in the Trans Alai on the Kyrgyzstan-Tajikistan border.
le·nis (lē′nĭs, lā′-) *adj.* Articulated with relatively low pressure of the airstream below the glottis, as English (b) and (d) compared with (p) and (t). [Lat. *lēnis*, soft.]
le·nite (lə-nīt′) *v.* **-nit·ed, -nit·ing, -nites** *—intr.* To undergo an increase in sonority or become lenis, as when (p) changes to (b), (b) to (v), or (v) to (w). *—tr.* To cause (a consonant sound) to lenite. **—le·ni′tion** (-nĭsh′ən) *n.*
len·i·tive (lĕn′ĭ-tĭv) *adj.* Capable of easing pain or discomfort. ❖ *n.* A lenitive medicine. [ME *lenitif* < OFr. < Med.Lat. *lēnītīvus* < Lat. *lēnītus*, p. part. of *lēnīre*, to soothe < *lēnis*, soft.] **—len′i·tive·ly** *adv.*
len·i·ty (lĕn′ĭ-tē) *n.* The condition or quality of being lenient. See Syns at **mercy.** [Lat. *lēnitās* < *lēnis*, soft.]
Len·ni Len·a·pe or **Len·i Len·a·pe** (lĕn′ē lĕn′ə-pē) *n.* See **Delaware**¹ 1.
Len·non (lĕn′ən), **John** 1940–80. British musician and composer who with Paul McCartney wrote many of the Beatles' songs, including "Yesterday."
le·no (lē′nō) *n., pl.* **-nos 1.** Weaving in which the warp yarns are paired and twisted. **2.** A fabric having such a weave. [Perh. < Fr. *linon*, linen fabric < *lin*, flax < OFr. < Lat. *līnum*.]
lens (lĕnz) *n., pl.* **lens·es 1.** A ground or molded piece of glass, plastic, or other transparent material with opposite surfaces either or both of which are curved, by means of which light rays are focused to form an image. **2.** A combination of two or more lenses, sometimes with other optical devices such as prisms, used to form an image for viewing or photographing. **3.** A device analogous to an optical lens that focuses radiation other than light. **4.** A transparent, biconvex body of the eye between the iris and the vitreous humor that focuses light rays entering through the pupil to form an image on the retina. ❖ *tr.v.* **lensed, lens·ing, lens·es** *Informal* To photograph or film. [NLat. *lēns* < Lat., lentil.] **—lensed** *adj.*
lent (lĕnt) *v.* Past tense and past participle of **lend.**
Lent *n.* The 40 weekdays from Ash Wednesday until Easter observed by Christians as a season of penitence. [ME *lente*, spring, Lent < OE *lencten*. See **del-** in App.]
len·ta·men·te (lĕn′tə-mĕn′tā) *adv. Music* In a very slow tempo. [Ital. < *lento*, slow. See LENTO.]
len·tan·do (lĕn-tän′dō) *adv. & adj. Music* With gradual slowness. [Ital., pr. part. of *lentare*, to make slow < *lento*, slow. See LENTO.]
Lent·en (lĕn′tən) *adj.* **1.** Of or relating to Lent. **2.** Characteristic of or appropriate to Lent; meager.
len·ti·cel (lĕn′tĭ-sĕl′) *n.* One of the small corky pores or narrow lines on the surface of the stems of woody plants that allow the interchange of gases between the interior tissue and the surrounding air. [NLat. *lenticella*, dim. of *lēns, lent-*, lens. See LENS.] **—len′ti·cel′late** (-sĕl′ĭt) *adj.*
len·tic·u·lar (lĕn-tĭk′yə-lər) *adj.* **1.** Shaped like a biconvex lens. **2.** Of or relating to a lens. [Lat. *lenticulāris*, lentil-shaped < *lenticula*, lentil. See LENTIL.]
len·ti·go (lĕn-tī′gō) *n., pl.* **-tig·i·nes** (-tĭj′ə-nēz′) A small flat pigmented spot on the skin. [Lat. *lentīgō, lentīgin-* < *lēns, lent-*, lentil.] **—len·tig′i·nous** (-tĭj′ə-nəs), **len·tig′i·nose′** (-nōs′) *adj.*
len·til (lĕn′təl) *n.* **1.** A leguminous plant *(Lens culinaris)* native to southwest Asia and having flat pods containing lens-shaped edible seeds. **2.** The round flattened seed of this plant. [ME < OFr. *lentille* < VLat. **lentīcula* < Lat. *lenticula*, dim. of *lēns, lent-*, lentil.]
len·tis·si·mo (lĕn-tĭs′ĭ-mō′, -tē′sē-) *adv. & adj. Music* Very slowly. [Ital., superl. of *lento*, slow. See LENTO.]
len·to (lĕn′tō) *Music adv. & adj.* In a slow tempo. ❖ *n., pl.* **-tos** A lento passage or movement. [Ital. < Lat. *lentus*, slow.]
Le·o (lē′ō) *n.* **1.** A constellation in the Northern Hemisphere near Cancer and Virgo. **2a.** The fifth sign of the zodiac in astrology. **b.** One born under Leo. [Lat. *Leō* < *leō*, lion. See LION.]
Leo I, Saint. Known as "Leo the Great." A.D. 400?–461. Pope (440–461) whose negotiations with Attila (452) and Genseric (455) saved Rome from barbarian invasion.
Leo III, Saint. d. 816. Pope (795–816) who crowned Charlemagne emperor (800).
Leo X Orig. Giovanni de Medici. 1475–1521. Pope (1513–21) who excommunicated Martin Luther (1521).
Leo Minor *n.* A constellation in the Northern Hemisphere near Leo and Ursa Major. [NLat. *Leō Minor*.]
Le·ón (lā-ōn′) **1.** A historical region and former kingdom of NW Spain; conquered by Castile in 1037, became independent in 1157, and was rejoined with Castile in 1230. **2.** A city of central Mexico ENE of Guadalajara; founded in the 1570s. Pop. 593,002. **3.** A city of NW Spain at the foot of the Cantabrian Mts. SSE of Oviedo; reconquered from the Moors in 882. Pop. 143,496.
Le·o·nar·do da Vin·ci (lē′ə-när′dō də vĭn′chē, dä, lā′-) 1452–1519. Italian painter, engineer, musician, and scientist whose works include *The Last Supper* (c. 1495).
Le·on·ca·val·lo (lā′ōn-kə-vä′lō, -kä-väl′-), **Ruggiero** 1858–1919. Italian composer who wrote *Pagliacci* (1892).
le·one (lē-ōn′) *n.* See table at **currency.** [After (SIERRA) LEONE.]
Le·o·nid (lē′ə-nĭd) *n., pl.* **Le·o·nids** or **Le·on·i·des** (lē-ŏn′ĭ-dēz′) One of the falling stars of the annual meteor shower in mid-November. [< Lat. *Leō, Leōn-*, Leo. See LEO.]
le·o·nine (lē′ə-nīn′) *adj.* Of, relating to, or characteristic of a lion. [ME < OFr. *leonin* < Lat. *leōnīnus* < *leō, leōn-*, lion. See LION.]
Le·on·tief (lē-ŏn′tyĕf, -ŏn′-), **Wassily** 1906–99. Russian-born Amer. economist who won a 1973 Nobel Prize.
leop·ard (lĕp′ərd) *n.* **1a.** A large, ferocious cat *(Panthera pardus)* of Africa and southern Asia, having spotted tawny or black fur. **b.** Any of several felines, such as the cheetah or the snow leopard. **c.** The pelt or fur of these animals. **2.** *Heraldry* A lion in side view, having one forepaw raised and the head facing the observer. [ME < OFr. *leupart* < LLat. *leopardus* < Gk. *leopardos* : Gk. *leōn*, lion;

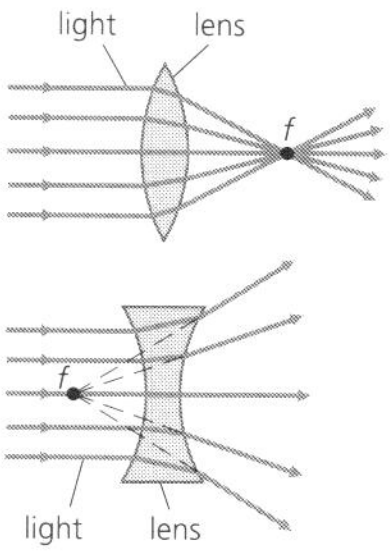

lens
Light rays converge, passing through a biconvex lens (*top*) and diverge, passing through a biconcave lens (*bottom*). The label *f* indicates the focal point.

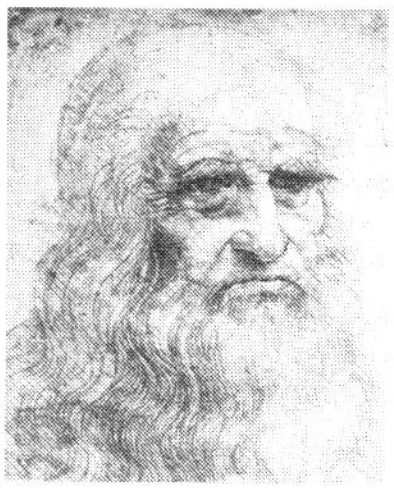

Leonardo da Vinci
1512 self-portrait

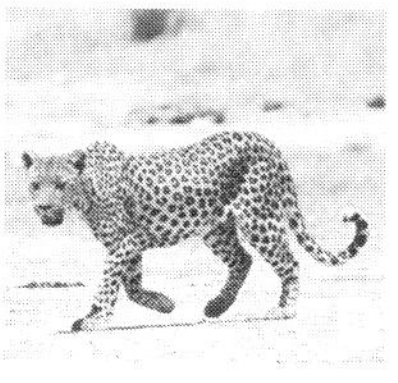

leopard
Panthera pardus

ă	pat	oi	boy
ā	pay	ou	out
âr	care	o͝o	took
ä	father	o͞o	boot
ĕ	pet	ŭ	cut
ē	be	ûr	urge
ĭ	pit	th	thin
ī	pie	*th*	this
îr	pier	hw	which
ŏ	pot	zh	vision
ō	toe	ə	about,
ô	paw		item

Stress marks:
′ (primary);
′ (secondary), as in
lexicon (lĕk′sĭ-kŏn′)

see LION + Gk. *pardos*, pard; see PARD.]

leop·ard·ess (lĕp′ər-dĭs) *n.* A female leopard.

Le·o·pold I (lē′ə-pōld′) 1640–1705. King of Hungary (1655–1705) and Bohemia (1656–1705) and Holy Roman emperor (1658–1705).

Leopold II 1835–1909. King of Belgium (1865–1909) who also reigned in the Congo Free State (later Zaire, now Congo) from 1876 to 1904, when he was forced to abdicate.

Le·o·pold·ville (lē′ə-pōld-vĭl′, lā′-) See **Kinshasa**.

le·o·tard (lē′ə-tärd′) *n.* **1.** A snugly fitting, stretchable one-piece garment with or without sleeves that covers the torso, worn esp. by dancers, gymnasts, acrobats, and those engaging in exercise workouts. **2. leotards** Tights. [After Jules *Léotard* (1830–70), French aerialist.] —**le′o·tard′ed** *adj.*

Le·pan·to (lĭ-păn′tō, lĕ′păn-), Gulf of See Gulf of **Corinth**.

Lep·cha (lĕp′chə) *n.*, *pl.* **Lepcha** or **-chas 1.** A member of a traditionally Buddhist people living in the Sikkim region of India and neighboring parts of Nepal and Bhutan. **2.** The Tibeto-Burman language of the Lepcha.

lep·er (lĕp′ər) *n.* **1.** A person affected by leprosy. **2.** One who is avoided by others. [ME *lepre*, leprosy < OFr. < LLat. *lepra* < Gk. *lepros*, scaly < *lepis*, scale.]

lepido– *pref.* Scale; flake: *lepidopteran.* [Gk. < *lepis*, *lepid-*.]

le·pid·o·lite (lĭ-pĭd′l-īt′) *n.* A lilac or pink to gray mineral of the mica group, K(Li,Al)₃(Si,Al)₄O₁₀(F,OH)₂, used as lithium ore and in ceramic production. [LEPIDO– + –LITE.]

lep·i·dop·ter·an (lĕp′ĭ-dŏp′tər-ən) *n.* An insect belonging to the large order Lepidoptera, which includes the butterflies and moths, characterized by four membranous wings covered with small scales. [< NLat. *Lepidoptera*, order name : LEPIDO– + Gk. *ptera*, pl. of *pteron*, wing, winged creature; see –PTER.] —**lep′i·dop′ter·an, lep′i·dop′ter·ous** *adj.*

lep·i·dop·ter·y (lĕp′ĭ-dŏp′tə-rē) also **lep·i·dop·ter·ol·o·gy** (-tə-rŏl′ə-jē) *n.* The branch of entomology that deals with lepidopterans. —**lep′i·dop′ter·ist** *n.*

lep·i·dote (lĕp′ĭ-dōt′) *adj.* Covered with small scurfy scales. [Gk. *lepidōtos*, scaly < *lepis*, *lepid-*, scale.]

Lep·i·dus (lĕp′ĭ-dəs), **Marcus Aemilius** d. 13 B.C. Roman leader and member of the triumvirate with Augustus and Mark Antony (43–36).

Le·pon·tic (lĭ-pŏn′tĭk) *n.* An ancient Celtic language of northeast Italy and southern Switzerland, perhaps a dialect of Gaulish. [< Lat. *Lēpontiī*, a people of Cisalpine Gaul.] —**Le·pon′tic** *adj.*

Le·pon·tine Alps (lĭ-pŏn′tīn′) A range of the central Alps in S Switzerland and along the Swiss-Italian border rising to 3,563.3 m (11,683 ft).

lep·o·rine (lĕp′ə-rīn′, -ər-īn) *adj.* Of or characteristic of rabbits or hares. [Lat. *leporīnus* < *lepus*, *lepor-*, hare.]

lep·re·chaun (lĕp′rĭ-kôn′, -kŏn′) *n.* An elf in Irish folklore who can reveal hidden treasure if caught. [Ir.Gael. *luprachán*, alteration of MIr. *luchrupán* < OIr. *luchorpán* : *luchorp* (*lū-*, small + *corp*, body < Lat. *corpus*; see kʷrep– in App.) + *-án*, diminutive suff.] —**lep′re·chaun′ish** *adj.*

WORD HISTORY Nothing seems more Irish than the leprechaun; yet, hiding within the word *leprechaun* is a word from another language entirely. If we look back beyond Modern Irish Gaelic *luprachán* and Middle Irish *luchrupán* to Old Irish *luchorpán*, we can see the connection. *Luchorpán* is a compound of Old Irish *lū*, meaning "small," and the Old Irish word *corp*, "body." *Corp* is borrowed from Latin *corpus*. Here is a piece of evidence attesting to the deep influence of Church Latin on the Irish language.

---

lep·ro·sar·i·um (lĕp′rə-sâr′ē-əm) *n.*, *pl.* **-i·ums** or **-i·a** (-ē-ə) A hospital for the treatment of leprosy. [Med.Lat. *leprōsārium* < LLat. *leprōsus*, leprous. See LEPROUS.]

lep·rose (lĕp′rōs′) *adj.* Scurfy or scaly; leprous. [LLat. *leprōsus*. See LEPROUS.]

lep·ro·sy (lĕp′rə-sē) *n.* A chronic, mildly contagious granulomatous disease, caused by the bacillus *Mycobacterium leprae* and characterized by ulceration of the skin, loss of sensation, paralysis, gangrene, and deformation. [ME *lepruse* < *leprus*, leprous. See LEPROUS.] —**lep·rot′ic** (lĕ-prŏt′ĭk) *adj.*

lep·rous (lĕp′rəs) *adj.* **1.** Having leprosy. **2.** Of, relating to, or resembling leprosy. **3.** *Biology* Having or consisting of loose scurfy scales. [ME *leprus* < OFr. *lepros* < LLat. *leprōsus* < *lepra*, leprosy. See LEPER.] —**lep′rous·ly** *adv.* —**lep′rous·ness** *n.*

–lepsy *suff.* Fit; seizure: *narcolepsy.* [NLat. *-lēpsia* < Gk. *-lēpsiā* < *lēpsis*, seizure < *lambanein*, *lēp-*, to take, seize.]

lep·tin (lĕp′tĭn′) *n.* A peptide hormone released by fat cells, under investigation for its role in appetite regulation. [LEPT(O)– + –IN.]

Lep·tis Mag·na (lĕp′tĭs măg′nə) An ancient city of N Africa in present-day Libya E of Tripoli; founded by Phoenicians.

lepto– or **lept–** *pref.* Slender; thin; fine: *leptocephalus.* [Gk. < *leptos*, fine, thin < *lepein*, to peel.]

lep·to·ceph·a·lus (lĕp′tə-sĕf′ə-ləs) *n.*, *pl.* **-li** (-lī′) One of the small flat larvae of eels and certain other fishes, characterized by a long narrow head. [NLat. : LEPTO– + *cephalus*, head (< Gk. *-kephalos*, -headed; see –CEPHALOUS).]

lep·ton (lĕp′tŏn′) *n.* Any of a family of elementary particles that participate in the weak interaction, including the electron, the

muon, and their associated neutrinos. [LEPTO– + –ON¹.] —**lep·ton′ic** (-tŏn′ĭk) *adj.*

lep·to·spi·ro·sis (lĕp′tō-spī-rō′sĭs) *n.* An infectious disease of domestic animals, esp. cattle, swine, and dogs, caused by spirochetes of the genus *Leptospira* and characterized by jaundice and fever. [NLat. *Leptospīra*, genus name (LEPTO– + Lat. *spīra*, coil; see SPIRAL) + –OSIS.]

Le·pus (lē′pəs) *n.* A constellation in the Southern Hemisphere near Orion and Columba. [Lat. < *lepus*, hare.]

Ler·mon·tov (lĕr′mən-tôf′, lyĕr′mən-təf), **Mikhail Yurievich** 1814–41. Russian writer best remembered for the novel *A Hero of Our Time* (1840).

Ler·ner (lûr′nər), **Alan Jay** 1918–86. Amer. lyricist who wrote a number of musicals with the composer Frederick Loewe, including *My Fair Lady* (1956).

Le·sage (lə-säzh′), **Alain René** 1668–1747. French writer best known for his novel *Gil Blas* (1715–35).

les·bi·an (lĕz′bē-ən) *n.* A woman whose sexual orientation is to women. ❖ *adj.* Of, relating to, or being a lesbian. [< the putative homosexuality of Sappho, lyric poet of Lesbos.]

Lesbian *n.* **1.** A native or inhabitant of Lesbos. **2.** The ancient Greek dialect of Lesbos. ❖ *adj.* Of or relating to Lesbos. [< Lat. *Lesbius* < Gk. *Lesbios* < LESBOS.]

les·bi·an·ism (lĕz′bē-ə-nĭz′əm) *n.* Sexual orientation of women to women.

Les·bos (lĕz′bŏs, -bōs) also **Lés·vos** (-vôs) An island of E Greece in the Aegean Sea near the NW coast of Turkey; noted for its lyric poets, including Sappho.

lese maj·es·ty also **lèse ma·jes·té** (lēz′ măj′ĭ-stē) *n.*, *pl.* **lese maj·es·ties** or **lèse ma·jes·tés 1.** An offense or crime committed against the ruler or supreme power of a state. **2.** An affront to another's dignity. [Partial transl. of Fr. *lèse-majesté* < Lat. (*crīmen*) *laesae māiestātis*, (the crime) of injured majesty : *laesae*, fem. genitive sing. of *laesus*, p. part. of *laedere*, to injure + *māiestātis*, genitive of *māiestās*, majesty.]

le·sion (lē′zhən) *n.* **1.** A wound or injury. **2.** A localized pathological change in a body organ or tissue. **3.** An infected or diseased patch of skin. ❖ *tr.v.* **-sioned, -sion·ing, -sions** To cause a lesion to form on or in. [ME *lesioun* < OFr. *lesion* < Lat. *laesiō*, *laesiōn-* < *laesus*, p. part. of *laedere*, to injure.]

Le·so·tho (lə-sō′tō, -sōō′tōō) Formerly **Ba·su·to·land** (bə-sōō′tō-lănd′) A country of S Africa forming an enclave within E-central South Africa; gained independence from Great Britain in 1966. Cap. Maseru. Pop. 1,996,000.

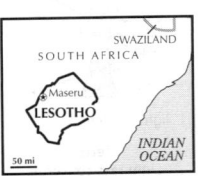

Lesotho

les·pe·de·za (lĕs′pĭ-dē′zə) *n.* See **bush clover**. [NLat. *Lespedeza*, genus name, after V.M. de *Céspedez* (misread as *Léspedez*; fl. 1785), Spanish governor of Florida.]

less (lĕs) *adj.* A comparative of **little. 1.** Not as great in amount or quantity. **2.** Lower in importance, esteem, or rank. **3.** Consisting of a smaller number. See Usage Note at **few.** ❖ *prep.* With the deduction of; minus: *Five less two is three.* ❖ *adv.* Comparative of **little.** To a smaller extent, degree, or frequency. ❖ *n.* **1.** A smaller amount: *received less than I wanted.* **2.** Something not as important as something else. —**idioms: less than** Not at all. **much (or still) less** Certainly not. [ME *lesse* < OE *lǣssa* (adj.) and *lǣs* (adv.).]

–less *suff.* **1.** Without; lacking: *blameless.* **2.** Unable to act or be acted on in a specified way: *dauntless.* [ME *-lesse* < OE *-lēas* < *lēas*, without. See leu– in App.]

les·see (lĕ-sē′) *n.* One that holds a lease. [ME < AN < p. part. of *lesser*, to let out, lease. See LEASE.]

less·en (lĕs′ən) *v.* **-ened, -en·ing, -ens** —*tr.* **1.** To make less; reduce. **2.** *Archaic* To make little of; belittle. —*intr.* To become less; decrease. See Syns at **decrease**. [ME *lessnen*, *lessenen* < *lesse*, less. See LESS.]

Les·seps (lĕs′əps, lĕ-sĕps′), Vicomte **Ferdinand Marie de** 1805–94. French diplomat and engineer who supervised the construction of the Suez Canal (1859–69).

less·er (lĕs′ər) *adj.* A comparative of **little. 1.** Smaller in amount, value, or importance, esp. in a comparison between two things. **2.** Of a smaller size than other similar forms. ❖ *adv.* A comparative of **little.** Less. Used before a participle: *a lesser-known writer.* ❖ *n.* One that is lower in importance, rank, magnitude, or degree: *the lesser of two evils.* [ME < *lesse*, less. See LESS.]

Lesser Antilles An island group of the E West Indies extending from Curaçao to the Virgin Is.

lesser celandine *n.* A Eurasian plant (*Ranunculus ficaria*) having heart-shaped leaves and solitary yellow flowers.

lesser omentum *n.* A fold of the peritoneum joining parts of the stomach and duodenum to the liver.

lesser panda *n.* See **panda** 2.

Les·sing (lĕs′ĭng), **Doris** b. 1919. British writer noted for works such as *The Golden Notebook* (1962).

Lessing, Gotthold Ephraim 1729–81. German playwright and critic whose works include *Nathan the Wise* (1779).

les·son (lĕs′ən) *n.* **1.** Something to be learned. **2a.** A period of instruction; a class. **b.** An assignment or exercise in which something is to be learned. **c.** The act or an instance of instructing; teaching. **3a.** An experience, example, or observation that imparts new knowledge or wisdom. **b.** The knowledge or wisdom so acquired. **4.** A rebuke or reprimand. **5.** often **Lesson** A reading from the Bible or other sacred text as part of a religious service. ❖ *tr.v.* **-soned, -son·ing, -sons** **1.** To teach a lesson to; instruct. **2.** To rebuke or reprimand. [ME *lessoun* < OFr. *leson* < Lat. *lēctiō, lēctiōn-,* a reading < *lēctus,* p. part. of *legere,* to read. See **leg-** in App.]

les·sor (lĕs′ôr′, lĕ-sôr′) *n.* One that lets property under a lease. [ME *lessour* < AN *lesser,* to let out, lease. See LEASE.]

lest (lĕst) *conj.* For fear that: *anxious lest he become ill.* [ME < OE (*thȳ) lǣs the,* (whereby) less that, so that not : *lǣs,* less; see LESS + *the,* relative conj.; see **to-** in App.]

Lés·vos (lĕz′vôs) See **Lesbos.**

let¹ (lĕt) *v.* **let, let·ting, lets** —*tr.* **1.** To give permission or opportunity to; allow: *I let them borrow the car. The inheritance let us finally buy a house.* See Usage Note at **leave¹. 2.** To cause to; make: *Let the news be known.* **3a.** Used as an auxiliary in the imperative to express a command, request, or proposal: *Let x equal y.* **b.** Used as an auxiliary in the imperative to express a warning or threat: *Just let her try!* **4.** To permit to enter, proceed, or depart: *let the dog in.* **5.** To release from or as if from confinement: *let the air out of the balloon.* **6.** To rent or lease: *let rooms.* **7.** To award, esp. after bids have been submitted. —*intr.* **1.** To become rented or leased. **2.** To be or become assigned, as to a contractor. —*phrasal verbs:* **let down 1.** To cause to come down gradually; lower. **2a.** To withdraw support from; forsake. **b.** To fail to meet the expectations of; disappoint. **let on 1.** To allow to be known; admit. **2.** To pretend. **let out 1.** To come to a close; end. **2.** To make known; reveal. **3.** To increase the size of (a garment, for example). **let up 1.** To slow down; diminish. **2.** To come to a stop; cease. —*idioms:* **let alone** Not to mention; much less. **let go** To cease to employ; dismiss. **let off on** *Informal* To cause to diminish, as in pressure; ease up on. **let (one's) hair down** To drop one's reserve or inhibitions. **let (someone) have it 1.** To beat, strike, or shoot at someone. **2.** To scold or punish. **let (someone) in on 1.** To reveal (a secret) to someone. **2.** To allow someone to participate in (something). **let up on** To be or become more lenient in (something). [ME *leten* < OE *lǣtan.*]

let² (lĕt) *n.* **1.** Something that hinders; an obstacle. **2.** *Sports* An invalid stroke in tennis and other net games that requires a replay. ❖ *tr.v.* **let·ted** or **let, let·ting, lets** *Archaic* To hinder or obstruct. [ME *lette* < *letten,* to hinder < OE *lettan.*]

–let *suff.* **1.** Small one: *ringlet.* **2.** Something worn on: *armlet.* [ME < OFr. *-elet,* diminutive suff. : *-el* (< Lat. *-ellus*) + *-et, -et.*]

letch also **lech** (lĕch) *n.* **1.** A strong, esp. sexual desire or craving. **2.** A lecher. [Perh. back-formation < obsolete *letcher,* var. of LECHER.]

let·down (lĕt′doun′) *n.* **1.** A decrease, decline, or relaxation, as of effort or energy. **2.** A disappointment. **3.** The descent made by an aircraft in order to land.

le·thal (lē′thəl) *adj.* **1.** Capable of causing death. **2.** Of, relating to, or causing death. **3.** Extremely harmful; devastating. [LLat. *lēthālis,* alteration (prob. influenced by *Lēthē,* Lethe) of Lat. *lētālis* < *lētum,* death.] —**le·thal′i·ty** (lē-thăl′ĭ-tē) *n.* —**le′thal·ly** *adv.*

lethal gene *n.* A gene whose expression results in the death of the organism.

le·thar·gic (lə-thär′jĭk) *adj.* Of, causing, or characterized by lethargy. —**le·thar′gi·cal·ly** *adv.*

leth·ar·gy (lĕth′ər-jē) *n., pl.* **-gies 1.** A state of sluggishness, inactivity, and apathy. **2.** A state of unconsciousness resembling deep sleep. [ME *letargie* < OFr. < LLat. *lēthargia* < Gk. *lēthargia* < *lēthargos,* forgetful : *lēthē,* forgetfulness + *argos,* idle (*a-,* without; see A-¹ + *ergon,* work; see **werg-** in App.).]

Leth·bridge (lĕth′brĭj′) A city of S Alberta, Canada, SSE of Calgary. Pop. 63,053.

le·the (lē′thē) *n.* **1. Lethe** *Greek Mythology* The river of forgetfulness, one of the five rivers in Hades. **2.** A condition of forgetfulness; oblivion. [Gk. *Lēthē* < *lēthē,* forgetfulness.] —**le′the·an** *adj.*

Le·to (lē′tō) *n. Greek Mythology* A lover of Zeus and the mother of Apollo and Artemis.

let's (lĕts) Contraction of *let us.*

Lett (lĕt) *n.* A member of a Baltic people constituting the main population of Latvia. [Ger. *Lette* < Latvian *Latvi.*]

let·ter (lĕt′ər) *n.* **1.** A symbol or character that is a component of an alphabet, is used in the writing of a word, and usu. indicates a speech sound. **2.** A written or printed communication directed to a person or organization. **3.** A certified document granting rights to its bearer. Often used in the plural. **4.** Literal meaning: *adhered to the letter of the law.* **5. letters** (*used with a sing. verb*) **a.** Literary culture; belles-lettres. **b.** Learning or knowledge, esp. of literature. **c.** Literature or writing as a profession. **6.** *Printing* **a.** A piece of type that prints a single character. **b.** A specific style of type. **c.** The characters in one style of type. **7.** An emblem in the shape of the initial of a school awarded for outstanding performance, esp. in varsity athletics. ❖ *v.* **-tered, -ter·ing, -ters** —*tr.* **1.** To write letters on. **2.** To write in letters. —*intr.* **1.** To write or form letters. **2.** To earn a school letter, as for outstanding athletic achievement: *She lettered in three collegiate sports.* —*idiom:* **to the letter** To the last detail; exactly: *followed instructions to the letter.* [ME < OFr. *lettre* < Lat. *littera,* perh. (via Etruscan) < Gk. *diphtherā,* hide, leather, writing surface.] —**let′ter·er** *n.*

let·ter·box (lĕt′ər-bŏks′) *n.* **1.** See **mailbox 2. 2.** A format for

presenting movies on television in the same proportions as the theater image, resulting in black space above and below the image. ❖ *tr.v.* **-boxed, -box·ing, -box·es** To produce or present (film) in a letterbox format.

letter carrier *n.* A person, esp. a postal worker, who delivers mail.

let·tered (lĕt′ərd) *adj.* **1a.** Educated to read and write; literate. **b.** Highly educated; learned. **2.** Of or relating to literacy or learning. **3.** Inscribed or marked with or as if with letters.

let·ter·form (lĕt′ər-fôrm′) *n.* The shape of an alphabet letter with regard to its development or design.

let·ter·head (lĕt′ər-hĕd′) *n.* **1.** The heading at the top of a sheet of letter paper, usu. consisting of a name and an address. **2.** Stationery imprinted with such a heading.

let·ter·ing (lĕt′ər-ĭng) *n.* **1.** The act, process, or art of forming letters. **2.** Letters inscribed, as on a sign.

let·ter·man (lĕt′ər-măn′, -mən) *n.* A student who has earned a letter in a particular activity, esp. a varsity sport.

letter of credence *n.* An official document conveying the credentials of a diplomatic envoy to a foreign government.

letter of credit *n., pl.* **letters of credit** A letter issued by a bank authorizing the bearer to draw a stated amount of money from the issuing bank or other associated banks or agencies.

letter of intent *n., pl.* **letters of intent** A written statement expressing the intention of the undersigned to enter into a formal agreement, esp. a business arrangement or transaction.

let·ter·per·fect (lĕt′ər-pûr′fĭkt) *adj.* Correct to the last detail, esp. being in or following the exact words.

let·ter·press (lĕt′ər-prĕs′) *n.* **1a.** The process of printing from a raised inked surface. **b.** Something printed in this fashion. **2.** *Chiefly British* The text, as of a book, distinct from illustrations or other ornamentation.

let·ter-qual·i·ty (lĕt′ər-kwŏl′ĭ-tē) *adj.* Of or producing printed characters similar in clarity to those produced by a conventional typewriter.

letters of administration *pl.n.* A legal document entrusting an individual with the administration of the estate of a deceased person.

letters of credence *pl.n.* See **letter of credence.**

letters of marque *pl.n.* **1.** A document issued by a nation allowing a private citizen to seize citizens or goods of another nation. **2.** A document issued by a nation allowing a private citizen to equip a ship with arms in order to attack enemy ships. [ME *letters of mark* < OFr. *marque,* mark, seizure, reprisal. See MARQUETRY.]

letters patent *pl.n.* A document issued by a government to a patentee granting an exclusive right to the enjoyment or possession of an invention.

letters testamentary *pl.n.* A document issued by a probate court or officer informing an executor of a will of his or her appointment and empowering the executor to discharge the appointed responsibilities.

Let·tish (lĕt′ĭsh) *adj.* Of or relating to the Letts or their language or culture. ❖ *n.* See **Latvian 1.**

let·tuce (lĕt′əs) *n.* **1a.** Any of various plants of the genus *Lactuca,* esp. *L. sativa,* having edible leaves. **b.** The leaves of *L. sativa,* used esp. in salads. **2.** *Slang* Paper money. [ME *lettuse* < OFr. *laitues,* pl. of *laitue* < Lat. *lactūca < lac, lact-,* milk (< its milky juice). See **melg-** in App.]

let·up (lĕt′ŭp′) *n.* **1.** A reduction in pace, force, or intensity; a slowdown. **2.** A temporary stop; a pause.

le·u (lē′ōō) *n., pl.* **lei** (lā) See table at **currency.** [Rom. < Lat. *leō,* lion. See LION.]

leu·cine (lōō′sēn′) *n.* An essential amino acid, $C_6H_{13}NO_2$, derived from the hydrolysis of protein during digestion. [LEUC(O)– + –INE².]

leu·cite (lōō′sīt′) *n.* A white or gray mineral of potassium aluminum silicate, $KAlSi_2O_6$. —**leu·cit′ic** (-sĭt′ĭk) *adj.*

leu·co·plast (lōō′kə-plăst′) also **leu·co·plas·tid** (lōō′kə-plăs′tĭd) *n.* A colorless plastid in the cytoplasm of plant cells around which starch collects.

Leuc·tra (lōōk′trə) A village of ancient Greece SW of Thebes; site of a major Theban defeat of the Spartans (371 B.C.).

leu·ke·mi·a (lōō-kē′mē-ə) *n.* Any of various acute or chronic neoplastic diseases of the bone marrow in which unrestrained proliferation of white blood cells occurs, accompanied by anemia and enlargement of the lymph nodes, liver, or spleen. —**leu·ke′mic** *adj. & n.*

leuko– or **leuk–** also **leuco–** or **leuc–** *pref.* **1.** White; colorless: *leukoderma.* **2.** Leukocyte: *leukopenia.* [Gk. < *leukos,* clear, white. See **leuk-** in App.]

leu·ko·cyte also **leu·co·cyte** (lōō′kə-sīt′) *n.* See **white blood cell.** —**leu′ko·cyt′ic** (-sĭt′ĭk) *adj.* —**leu′ko·cy′toid** *adj.*

leu·ko·cy·to·sis also **leu·co·cy·to·sis** (lōō′kə-sī-tō′sĭs) *n., pl.* **-ses** (-sēz) An abnormally large increase in the number of white blood cells in the blood, often occurring during an acute infection or inflammation. —**leu′ko·cy·tot′ic** (-tŏt′ĭk) *adj.*

leu·ko·der·ma also **leu·co·der·ma** (lōō′kə-dûr′mə) *n.* Partial or total loss of skin pigmentation, often occurring in patches. —**leu′ko·der′mal, leu′ko·der′mic** *adj.*

leu·ko·pe·ni·a also **leu·co·pe·ni·a** (lōō′kə-pē′nē-ə) *n.* An abnormally low number of leukocytes in the circulating blood. —**leu′ko·pe′nic** *adj.*

ă	pat	oi	boy
ā	pay	ou	out
âr	care	ŏŏ	took
ä	father	ōō	boot
ĕ	pet	ŭ	cut
ē	be	ûr	urge
ĭ	pit	th	thin
ī	pie	*th*	this
îr	pier	hw	which
ŏ	pot	zh	vision
ō	toe	ə	about,
ô	paw		item

Stress marks:
′ (primary);
′ (secondary), as in
lexicon (lĕk′sĭ-kŏn′)

leu·ko·pla·ki·a also **leu·co·pla·ki·a** (lōō'kə-plā'kē-ə) *n.* An abnormal condition characterized by white spots or patches on mucous membranes, esp. of the mouth and vulva. [NLat. : LEUKO- + Gk. *plax, plak-,* flat area.]

leu·kor·rhe·a also **leu·cor·rhe·a** (lōō'kə-rē'ə) *n.* A thick whitish discharge from the vagina or cervical canal.

Leu·wen·hoek (lā'vən-hōōk', lā'ü-wən-hōōk'), **Anton van** See Anton van **Leeuwenhoek.**

lev (lĕf) *n., pl.* **lev·a** (lĕv'ə) See table at **currency.** [Bulgarian < obs. var. of *lyv,* lion (ancient symbol of Bulgaria) < O Church Slavonic *lĭvŭ,* lion, prob. < OHGer. *lewo* < Lat. *leō.* See LION.]

lev– *pref.* Variant of **levo-.**

Lev. *abbr. Bible* Leviticus

Lev·al·loi·si·an (lĕv'ə-loi'zē-ən) *adj.* Of or relating to a western European stage in Lower Paleolithic culture, characterized by a distinctive method of striking off flake tools from pieces of stone. [After *Levallois*(-Perret), city in N-central France.]

le·vant (lə-vănt') *intr.v.* **-vant·ed, -vant·ing, -vants** *Chiefly British* To leave hurriedly or in secret to avoid unpaid debts. [Poss. < Sp. *levantar (el campo),* to lift or break (camp) < VLat. **levantāre* < Lat. *levāns, levant-,* pr. part. of *levāre,* to raise. See LEVER.]

Levant[1] The countries bordering on the E Mediterranean Sea from Turkey to Egypt. —**Le'van·tine** (lĕv'ən-tīn', -tēn', lə-văn'-) *adj. & n.*

Levant[2] *n.* A heavy coarse-grained morocco leather often used in bookbinding. [After LEVANT[1].]

le·vant·er (lə-văn'tər) *n.* **1.** A strong easterly wind of the Mediterranean area. **2. Levanter** A native or inhabitant of the Levant.

Levant morocco *n.* See **Levant**[2].

le·va·tor (lə-vā'tər) *n., pl.* **lev·a·to·res** (lĕv'ə-tôr'ēz, -tōr'-) **1.** A muscle that raises a bodily part. **2.** A surgical instrument for lifting the depressed fragments of a fractured skull. [NLat. < Med.Lat. *levātor,* one that raises < Lat. *levāre,* to raise. See LEVER.]

lev·ee[1] (lĕv'ē) *n.* **1.** An embankment raised to prevent a river from overflowing. **2.** A small ridge or raised area bordering an irrigated field. **3.** A landing place on a river; a pier. ❖ *tr.v.* **lev·eed, lev·ee·ing, lev·ees** To provide with a levee. [Fr. *levée* < OFr. *levee* < fem. p. part. of *lever,* to raise. See LEVER.]

lev·ee[2] (lĕv'ē, lə-vē', -vā') *n.* **1.** A reception held, as by royalty, upon arising from bed. **2.** A formal reception, as at a royal court. [< Fr. *lever,* a rising < OFr. < *lever,* to raise, rise. See LEVER.]

lev·el (lĕv'əl) *n.* **1a.** Relative position or rank on a scale. **b.** A relative degree, as of achievement, intensity, or concentration. **2.** A natural or proper position, place, or stage. **3.** Position along a vertical axis; height or depth. **4a.** A horizontal line or plane at right angles to the plumb. **b.** The position or height of such a line or plane. **5.** A flat horizontal surface. **6.** A land area of uniform elevation. **7a.** An instrument for ascertaining whether a surface is horizontal, vertical, or at a 45° angle, consisting essentially of an encased liquid-filled tube containing an air bubble that moves to a center window when the instrument is set on an even plane. **b.** A level combined with a telescope and used in surveying. **c.** A computation of the difference in elevation between two points by using a level. ❖ *adj.* **1.** Having a flat smooth surface. **2.** Being on a horizontal plane. **3a.** Being at the same height or position as another; even. **b.** Being at the same degree of rank, standing, or advantage as another; equal. **c.** Being or relating to a specified rank or standing. Often used in combination: *a lower-level administrator.* **4.** Exhibiting no abrupt variations; steady. **5.** Rational and balanced; sensible. **6.** Filled evenly to the top. ❖ *v.* **-eled, -el·ing, -els** or **-elled, -el·ling, -els** —*tr.* **1.** To make horizontal, flat, or even. **2.** To tear down; raze. **3.** To knock down with or as if with a blow. **4.** To place on the same level; equalize. **5.** To aim along a horizontal plane. **6.** To direct emphatically or forcefully toward someone. **7.** To measure the different elevations of (a tract of land) with a level. —*intr.* **1.** To bring persons or things to an equal level; equalize. **2.** To aim a weapon horizontally. **3.** *Informal* To be frank and open. ❖ *adv.* Along a flat or even line or plane. —*phrasal verb:* **level off 1.** To move toward stability or consistency. **2.** To maneuver an aircraft into a flight attitude parallel to the surface of the earth after gaining or losing altitude. —*idioms:* **(one's) level best** The best one can do in an earnest attempt. **on the level** *Informal* Without deception; honest. [ME, level (instrument) < OFr. *livel* < VLat. **lībellum* < Lat. *lībella,* dim. of *lībra,* balance.] —**lev'el·ly** *adv.* —**lev'el·ness** *n.*

level crossing *n. Chiefly British* A grade crossing.

lev·el·er also **lev·el·ler** (lĕv'ə-lər) *n.* **1.** One that levels. **2a.** One who advocates the abolition of social inequities. **b. Leveller** A member of an English radical political movement arising in the 1640s and advocating universal male suffrage, parliamentary democracy, and religious tolerance.

lev·el·head·ed (lĕv'əl-hĕd'ĭd) *adj.* Characteristically self-composed and sensible. —**lev'el·head'ed·ness** *n.*

lev·el·ing rod (lĕv'ə-lĭng) *n.* A graduated pole or stick with a movable marker, used by a surveyor's level to measure differences in elevation.

level of significance *n., pl.* **levels of significance** The probability of a false rejection of the null hypothesis in a statistical test.

lev·er (lĕv'ər, lē'vər) *n.* **1.** A simple machine consisting of a rigid bar pivoted on a fixed point and used to transmit force, as in moving a weight at one end by pushing down on the other. **2.** A projecting handle used to adjust or operate a mechanism. **3.** A means of accomplishing; a tool: *friendship as a lever to obtain a job.* ❖ *tr.v.* **-ered, -er·ing, -ers** To move or lift with or as if with a lever. [ME < OFr. *levier* < *lever,* to raise < Lat. *levāre* < *levis,* light.]

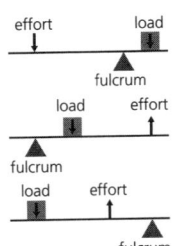

lever
top to bottom: first-class, second-class, and third-class levers

lev·er·age (lĕv'ər-ĭj, lēv'-) *n.* **1a.** The action of a lever. **b.** The mechanical advantage of a lever. **2.** Positional advantage; power to act effectively. **3.** The use of credit or borrowed funds to improve one's speculative capacity and increase the rate of return from an investment, as in buying securities on margin. ❖ *tr.v.* **-aged, -ag·ing, -ag·es 1a.** To provide (a company) with leverage. **b.** To supplement (money, for example) with leverage. **2.** To make effective or improved use of.

lev·er·aged buyout (lĕv'ər-ĭjd, lēv'ər-ĭjd) *n.* The use of a target company's asset value to finance the debt incurred in acquiring the company.

lev·er·et (lĕv'ər-ĭt) *n.* A young hare, esp. one less than a year old. [ME < AN, dim. of *levere,* hare < Lat. *lepus, lepor-.*]

Le·ver·ku·sen (lā'vər-kōō'zən) A city of W-central Germany on the Rhine R. N of Cologne. Pop. 161,761.

Lé·vesque (lə-věk'), **René** 1922–87. Canadian politician who cofounded (1967) the Parti Québécois.

Le·vi (lē'vī') In the Bible, a son of Jacob and Leah and the forebear of one of the tribes of Israel.

lev·i·a·ble (lĕv'ē-ə-bəl) *adj.* **1.** That can be levied: *leviable taxes.* **2.** Liable to be taxed: *leviable imports.*

le·vi·a·than (lə-vī'ə-thən) *n.* **1.** Something unusually large of its kind, esp. a ship. **2.** A very large animal, esp. a whale. **3.** A monstrous sea creature mentioned in the Bible. [ME, huge biblical sea creature < LLat. < Heb. *liwyātān;* akin to Ugaritic *ltn,* sea monster.]

lev·i·gate (lĕv'ĭ-gāt') *tr.v.* **-gat·ed, -gat·ing, -gates 1a.** To make into a smooth fine powder or paste, as by grinding when moist. **b.** To separate fine particles from coarse by grinding in water. **2.** To suspend in a liquid. **3.** To make smooth; polish. ❖ *adj.* (-gāt', -gĭt) Smooth. [Lat. *lēvigāre, lēvigāt-* : *lēvis,* smooth + *agere,* to make, do; see **ag-** in App.] —**lev'i·ga'tion** *n.*

lev·in (lĕv'ĭn) *n. Archaic* Lightning. [ME *levene, levin.* See leuk- in App.]

lev·i·rate (lĕv'ər-ĭt, -ə-rāt', lē'vər-ĭt, -və-rāt') *n.* The practice of marrying the widow of one's childless brother to maintain his line, as required by ancient Hebrew law. [< Lat. *lēvir,* husband's brother.]

Le·vi's (lē'vīz') A trademark used for denim trousers.

Lé·vi-Strauss (lā've-strous'), **Claude** b. 1908. French anthropologist who wrote *Structural Anthropology* (1958).

Levit. *abbr. Bible* Leviticus

lev·i·tate (lĕv'ĭ-tāt') *intr. & tr.v.* **-tat·ed, -tat·ing, -tates** To rise or cause to rise into the air and float in apparent defiance of gravity. [< Lat. *levis,* light. See LEVITY.] —**lev'i·ta'tion** *n.* —**lev'i·ta'tion·al** *adj.* —**lev'i·ta'tor** *n.*

Le·vite (lē'vīt') *n. Bible* A member of the tribe of Levi but not descended from Aaron and, if male, chosen to assist the Temple priests. [ME < LLat. *Lēvītēs, Lēvīta* < Gk. *Leuītēs < Leui,* Levi < Heb. *Lēwî.*]

Le·vit·i·cal (lə-vĭt'ĭ-kəl) also **Le·vit·ic** (-vĭt'ĭk) *adj. Bible* **1.** Of or relating to the Levites. **2.** Of or relating to Leviticus.

Le·vit·i·cus (lə-vĭt'ĭ-kəs) *n.* See table at **Bible.** [ME < LLat. *Levīticus* < Gk. *Leuītikos,* Levitical < *Leuītēs,* Levite. See LEVITE.]

lev·i·ty (lĕv'ĭ-tē) *n., pl.* **-ties 1.** Lightness of manner or speech, esp. when inappropriate; frivolity. **2.** Inconstancy; changeableness. **3.** The state or quality of being light; buoyancy. [Lat. *levitās* < *levis,* light.]

le·vo (lē'vō) *adj.* Levorotatory.

levo– or **lev–** *pref.* **1.** To the left: *levorotatory.* **2.** Levorotatory: *levulose.* [Fr. *lévo-* < Lat. *laevus,* left.]

le·vo·do·pa (lē'və-dō'pə) *n.* See **L-dopa.**

le·vo·ro·ta·tion (lē'və-rō-tā'shən) *n.* A counterclockwise rotation, esp. of the plane of polarized light.

le·vo·ro·ta·to·ry (lē'və-rō'tə-tôr'ē, -tōr'ē) also **le·vo·ro·ta·ry** (-tə-rē) *adj.* Of or relating to an optically active chemical that rotates the plane of polarized light to the left, or counterclockwise.

lev·u·lose (lĕv'yə-lōs', -lōz') *n.* See **fructose.** [LEV(O)- + -UL(E) + -OSE[2].]

lev·y (lĕv'ē) *v.* **-ied, -y·ing, -ies** —*tr.* **1.** To impose or collect (a tax, for example). **2.** To draft into military service. **3.** To declare and wage (a war). —*intr.* To confiscate property, esp. in accordance with a legal judgment. ❖ *n., pl.* **-ies 1.** The act or process of levying. **2.** Money, property, or troops levied. [ME *levien* < *leve, levy,* tax < OFr. *levee* < fem. p. part. of *lever,* to raise. See LEVER.] —**lev'i·er** *n.*

lewd (lōōd) *adj.* **lewd·er, lewd·est 1a.** Preoccupied with sex and sexual desire; lustful. **b.** Obscene; indecent. **2.** *Obsolete* Wicked. [ME *leued,* unlearned, lay, lascivious < OE *lǣwede,* ignorant, lay.] —**lewd'ly** *adv.* —**lewd'ness** *n.*

Lew·es River (lōō'ĭs) The upper course, c. 544 km (338 mi), of the Yukon R. above its junction with the Pelly R. in S Yukon Terr., Canada.

lew•is (lōō′ĭs) *n.* A dovetailed iron tenon designed to fit into a dovetail mortise in a large stone so that it can be lifted by a hoisting apparatus. [Perh. < the name *Lewis.*]

Lewis, Carl b. 1961. Amer. athlete who won four gold medals in track and field in the 1984 Olympics.

Lewis, Cecil Day See Cecil **Day** Lewis.

Lewis, C(live) S(taples) 1898–1963. British writer and critic whose works include *The Screwtape Letters* (1942).

Lewis, Edward b. 1918. Amer. biologist who shared a 1995 Nobel Prize in medicine.

Lewis, (Harry) Sinclair 1885–1951. Amer. novelist who was the first American to win a Nobel Prize for literature (1930).

Lewis, Henry 1932–96. Amer. conductor who became the first African American to conduct a major symphony orchestra (1961).

Lewis, Jerry Lee b. 1935. Amer. musician and singer whose hit songs include "Great Balls of Fire" (1957).

Lewis, John Llewellyn 1880–1969. Amer. labor leader who was president of the United Mine Workers of America (1920–60) and the Congress of Industrial Organizations (1935–40).

Lewis, Meriwether 1774–1809. Amer. soldier and explorer who led the Lewis and Clark expedition (1803–06) from St. Louis to the mouth of the Columbia R.

Lewis, (Percy) Wyndham 1884–1957. British writer and artist whose novels include *The Apes of God* (1930).

lew•is•ite (lōō′ĭ-sīt′) *n.* An oily colorless to violet or brown liquid, $C_2H_2AsCl_3$, used to make a highly toxic gas weapon. [After Winford Lee *Lewis* (1878–1943), American chemist.]

lew•is•son (lōō′ĭ-sən) *n.* See **lewis.** [< LEWIS.]

Lewis with Harris An island of NW Scotland, the largest and northernmost of the Outer Hebrides.

lex (lĕks) *n., pl.* **le•ges** (lē′jēz′) Law. [Lat. *lēx, lēg-.* See **leg-** in App.]

lex•eme (lĕk′sēm′) *n.* The fundamental unit of the lexicon of a language. *Find, finds, found,* and *finding* are forms of the English lexeme *find.* [LEX(ICON) + –EME.]

lex•i•cal (lĕk′sĭ-kəl) *adj.* 1. Of or relating to the vocabulary, words, or morphemes of a language. 2. Of or relating to lexicography or a lexicon. [LEXIC(ON) + –AL¹.] —**lex′i•cal′i•ty** (-kăl′ĭ-tē) *n.* —**lex′i•cal•ly** *adv.*

lex•i•cog•ra•phy (lĕk′sĭ-kŏg′rə-fē) *n.* The process or work of writing, editing, or compiling a dictionary. [LEXICO(N) + –GRAPHY.] —**lex′i•cog′ra•pher** *n.* —**lex′i•co•graph′ic** (-kə-grăf′ĭk), **lex′i•co•graph′i•cal** (-ĭ-kəl) *adj.*

lex•i•col•o•gy (lĕk′sĭ-kŏl′ə-jē) *n.* The branch of linguistics that deals with the lexical component of language. [LEXICO(N) + –LOGY.] —**lex′i•co•log′i•cal** (-kə-lŏj′ĭ-kəl) *adj.* —**lex′i•col′o•gist** *n.*

lex•i•con (lĕk′sĭ-kŏn′) *n., pl.* **-cons** or **-ca** (-kə) 1. A dictionary. 2. A stock of terms used in a particular profession, subject, or style; a vocabulary. 3. *Linguistics* The morphemes of a language considered as a group. [Med.Lat. < Gk. *lexikon (biblion),* word(book), neut. of *lexikos,* of words < *lexis,* word < *legein,* to speak. See **leg-** in App.]

Lex•ing•ton (lĕk′sĭng-tən) 1. A city of NE-central KY ESE of Louisville. Pop. 260,512. 2. A town of NE MA, a suburb of Boston; site of the battle (Apr. 19, 1775) that marked the start of the American Revolution. Pop. 30,355.

lex•is (lĕk′sĭs) *n.* The total set of words in a language as distinct from morphology; vocabulary. [Gk., speech, word. See LEXICON.]

ley (lā, lē) *n.* Variant of **lea.**

Ley•den (līd′n) See **Leiden.**

Leyden jar *n.* An early form of capacitor consisting of a glass jar lined inside and out with tinfoil and a conducting rod. [After *Leyden* (Leiden).]

Ley•te (lā′tē, -tĕ) An island of the E-central Philippines in the Visayan group N of Mindanao.

Leyte Gulf An inlet of the W Pacific in the Philippines S of Samar and E of Leyte. An invasion force led by Gen. Douglas MacArthur defeated the Japanese here on Oct. 25–26, 1944.

lf *abbr.* lightface

LF *abbr.* 1a. left field b. left fielder 2. low frequency

LG *abbr.* Low German

lg. *abbr.* 1. large 2. long

LH *abbr.* 1. left-hand 2. luteinizing hormone

Lha•sa (lä′sə, läs′ə) A city of SW China, the cap. of Xizang (Tibet); long known as "the Forbidden City." Pop. 139,822.

Lhasa ap•so (äp′sō) *n., pl.* **-sos** Any of a breed of small dog originating in Tibet and having a long straight coat. [LHASA + Tibetan *apso,* Lhasa apso.]

Lho•tse (lō′tsĕ′) A peak, 8,506.5 m (27,890 ft), of the central Himalaya Mts. on the Nepal-Xizang (Tibet) border.

li¹ (lē) *n., pl.* **li** A traditional Chinese measure of distance, today standardized at 500 meters (547 yards). [Chin. (Mandarin) *lǐ.*]

li² *abbr.* link (measurement)

Li The symbol for the element **lithium.**

L.I. *abbr.* Long Island

li•a•bil•i•ty (lī′ə-bĭl′ĭ-tē) *n., pl.* **-ties** 1. The state of being liable. 2a. Something for which one is liable; an obligation, responsibility, or debt. b. **liabilities** The financial obligations entered in the balance sheet of a business enterprise. 3. Something that holds

one back; a handicap. 4. Likelihood.

li•a•ble (lī′ə-bəl) *adj.* 1. Legally obligated; responsible. See Syns at **responsible.** 2. At risk of or subject to experiencing or suffering something unpleasant. Used with *to.* 3. Likely. Often used with reference to an unfavorable outcome. [ME, prob. < OFr. *lier,* to bind < Lat. *ligāre.*]

li•aise (lē-āz′) *intr.v.* **-aised, -ais•ing, -ais•es** 1. To effect or establish a liaison. 2. To act or serve as a liaison officer.

li•ai•son (lē′ā-zŏn′, lē-ā′-) *n.* 1a. An instance or a means of communication between different groups or units of an organization, esp. in the armed forces. b. One that maintains communication: *the President's liaison with Congress.* 2a. A close relationship, connection, or link. b. An adulterous relationship; an affair. 3. *Linguistics* Pronunciation of the usu. silent final consonant of a word when followed by a word beginning with a vowel, esp. in French. [Fr. < OFr. < Lat. *ligātiō, ligātiōn- < ligātus,* p. part. of *ligāre,* to bind.]

li•an•a (lē-ä′nə, -än′ə) also **li•ane** (-än′, -än′) *n.* Any of various climbing, woody, usu. tropical vines. [Alteration of Fr. *liane,* prob. < *lier,* to bind < OFr. See LIABLE.]

Liang (lyäng′) Two Chinese dynasties, the **Earlier Liang** (502–557) and the **Later Liang** (907–923).

Liao (lyou′) A Chinese dynasty that ruled from 916 to 1125.

Liao•dong (lyou′dŭng′) also **Liao•tung** (-tŏong′), **Gulf of** The N part of the Bo Hai in NE China bordering on the **Liaodong Peninsula,** projecting SW into the Yellow Sea.

Liao He (lyou′) A river of NE China flowing c. 1,448 km (900 mi) to the Gulf of Liaodong.

Liao•ning (lyou′nĭng′) A province of NE China on the Bo Hai and Korea Bay; under Japanese control from 1932 to 1945. Cap. Shenyang. Pop. 39,459,697.

Liao•yang (lyou′yäng′) A city of NE China SSW of Shenyang; one of the oldest cities in Manchuria. Pop. 639,553.

li•ar (lī′ər) *n.* One that tells lies.

Li•ard (lē′ərd, lē-ärd′) A river rising in SE Yukon Terr., Canada, and flowing c. 1,215 km (755 mi) to the Mackenzie R. in SW Northwest Terrs.

lib (lĭb) *n. Informal* A movement that seeks to achieve equal rights for a group; liberation.

li•ba•tion (lī-bā′shən) *n.* 1a. The pouring of a liquid offering as a religious ritual. b. The liquid so poured. 2. *Informal* a. A beverage, esp. an intoxicating beverage. b. The act of drinking an intoxicating beverage. [ME *libacioun* < Lat. *lībātiō, lībātiōn- < lībātus,* p. part. of *lībāre,* to pour out as an offering.] —**li•ba′tion•ar′y** (-shə-nĕr′ē) *adj.*

Lib•by (lĭb′ē), **Willard Frank** 1908–80. Amer. chemist who won a 1960 Nobel Prize.

li•bel (lī′bəl) *n.* 1a. A false publication in writing, print, signs, or pictures that damages a person's reputation. b. The act of presenting such material to the public. 2. The written claims presented by a plaintiff in an action at admiralty law or to an ecclesiastical court. ❖ *tr.v.* **-beled, -bel•ing, -bels** or **-belled, -bel•ling, -bels** To publish a libel about (a person). [ME, litigant's written complaint < OFr. < Lat. *libellus,* dim. of *liber,* book.] —**li′bel•er, li′bel•ist** *n.*

li•bel•ant also **li•bel•lant** (lī′bə-lənt) *n.* The plaintiff in a case of ecclesiastical or admiralty libel.

li•bel•ee also **li•bel•lee** (lī′bə-lē′) *n.* The defendant in a case of ecclesiastical or admiralty libel.

li•bel•ous also **li•bel•lous** (lī′bə-ləs) *adj.* Involving or constituting a libel; defamatory. —**li′bel•ous•ly** *adv.*

lib•er•al (lĭb′ər-əl, lĭb′rəl) *adj.* 1a. Not limited to or by traditional, orthodox, or authoritarian attitudes or dogmas; free from bigotry. b. Favoring proposals for reform, open to new ideas for progress, and tolerant of the ideas and behavior of others; broadminded. c. Of, relating to, or characteristic of liberalism. d. **Liberal** Of, being, or characteristic of a political party founded on or associated with principles of social and political liberalism, esp. in Great Britain and Canada. 2a. Tending to give freely; generous. b. Generous in amount; ample. 3. Not strict or literal; loose or approximate: *a liberal translation.* 4. Of, relating to, or based on the traditional arts and sciences of a college or university cur-

Carl Lewis
running a relay race at the 1987 World Championships

Lhasa apso

ă pat	oi boy
ā pay	ou out
âr care	ŏŏ took
ä father	ōō boot
ĕ pet	ŭ cut
ē be	ûr urge
ĭ pit	th thin
ī pie	*th* this
îr pier	hw which
ŏ pot	zh vision
ō toe	ə about,
ô paw	item

Stress marks:
′ (primary);
′ (secondary), as in
lexicon (lĕk′sĭ-kŏn′)

riculum. **5a.** *Archaic* Permissible or appropriate for a person of free birth; befitting a lady or gentleman. **b.** *Obsolete* Morally unrestrained; licentious. ❖ *n.* **1.** A person with liberal ideas or opinions. **2. Liberal** A member of a Liberal political party. [ME, generous < OFr. < Lat. *līberālis* < *līber*, free. See **leudh-** in App.] —**lib′er•al•ly** *adv.* —**lib′er•al•ness** *n.*

SYNONYMS *liberal, bounteous, bountiful, freehanded, generous, handsome, munificent, openhanded* These adjectives mean willing or marked by a willingness to give unstintingly: *a liberal donor; a bounteous feast; bountiful compliments; a freehanded host; a generous donation; a handsome offer; a munificent gift; openhanded grandparents.* See also Syns at **broad-minded. ANTONYM** *stingy*

liberal arts *pl.n.* **1.** Academic disciplines, such as languages, literature, history, philosophy, mathematics, and science, that provide information of general cultural concern. **2.** The disciplines comprising the trivium and quadrivium. [ME, transl. of Med.Lat. *artēs liberālēs*, the trivium and quadrivium : Lat. *artēs*, pl. of *ars*, subject of study + *liberālēs*, pl. of *liberālis*, proper to free persons.]

lib•er•al•ism (lĭb′ər-ə-lĭz′əm, lĭb′rə-) *n.* **1.** The state or quality of being liberal. **2a.** A political theory favoring civil and political liberties, government by law with the consent of the governed, and protection from arbitrary authority. **b.** often **Liberalism** The tenets or policies of a Liberal party. **3.** An economic theory in favor of laissez-faire, the free market, and the gold standard. **4. Liberalism a.** A 19th-century Protestant movement that favored free intellectual inquiry, stressed the ethical and humanitarian content of Christianity, and de-emphasized dogmatic theology. **b.** A 19th-century Roman Catholic movement that favored political democracy and ecclesiastical reform. —**lib′er•al•ist** *n.* —**lib′er•al•is′tic** (-lĭs′tĭk) *adj.*

lib•er•al•i•ty (lĭb′ə-răl′ĭ-tē) *n., pl.* **-ties 1.** The quality or state of being liberal or generous. **2.** An instance of being liberal.

lib•er•al•ize (lĭb′ər-ə-līz′, lĭb′rə-) *v.* **-ized, -iz•ing, -iz•es** —*tr.* To make liberal or more liberal. —*intr.* To become liberal or more liberal. —**lib′er•al•i•za′tion** (-lĭ-zā′shən) *n.* —**lib′er•al•iz′er** *n.*

lib•er•ate (lĭb′ə-rāt′) *tr.v.* **-at•ed, -at•ing, -ates 1.** To set free, as from oppression, confinement, or foreign control. **2.** *Chemistry* To release (a gas, for example) from combination. **3.** *Slang* To obtain by illegal or stealthy action. [Lat. *līberāre, līberāt-* < *līber*, free. See **leudh-** in App.] —**lib′er•a′tor** *n.*

lib•er•a•tion (lĭb′ə-rā′shən) *n.* **1.** The act of liberating or the state of being liberated. **2.** The act or process of trying to achieve equal rights and status. —**lib′er•a′tion•ist** *n.*

liberation theology *n.* A school of theology that finds in the Gospel a call to free people from political, social, and economic oppression. —**liberation theologian** *n.*

Li•be•ri•a (lī-bîr′ē-ə) A country of W Africa on the Atlantic Ocean; founded 1821 and gained independence in 1847. Cap. Monrovia. Pop. 2,700,000. —**Li•be′ri•an** *adj. & n.*

lib•er•tar•i•an (lĭb′ər-târ′ē-ən) *n.* **1.** One who advocates maximizing individual rights and minimizing the role of the state. **2.** One who believes in free will. [< LIBERTY.] —**lib′er•tar′i•an** *adj.* —**lib′er•tar′i•an•ism** *n.*

lib•er•tin•age (lĭb′ər-tē′nĭj) *n.* Libertinism.

lib•er•tine (lĭb′ər-tēn′) *n.* **1.** One who acts without moral restraint; a dissolute person. **2.** One who defies established religious precepts; a freethinker. ❖ *adj.* Morally unrestrained; dissolute. [ME, freedman < Lat. *lībertīnus* < *lībertus* < *līber*, free. See **leudh-** in App.]

lib•er•tin•ism (lĭb′ər-tē-nĭz′əm) *n.* **1.** The state or quality of being libertine. **2.** The behavior characteristic of a libertine.

lib•er•ty (lĭb′ər-tē) *n., pl.* **-ties 1a.** The condition of being free from restriction or control. **b.** The right and power to act, believe, or express oneself in a manner of one's own choosing. **c.** The condition of being physically and legally free from confinement, servitude, or forced labor. See Syns at **freedom. 2.** Freedom from unjust or undue governmental control. **3.** A right or immunity to engage in certain actions without control or interference. **4a.** A breach or overstepping of propriety or social convention. Often used in the plural. **b.** A statement, attitude, or action not warranted by conditions or actualities. Often used in the plural. **c.** An unwarranted risk; a chance. Often used in the plural. **5.** A period, usu. short, during which a sailor is authorized to go ashore. —**idiom: at liberty 1.** Not in confinement or under constraint; free. **2.** Not employed, occupied, or in use. [ME *liberte* < OFr. < Lat. *lībertās* < *līber*, free. See **leudh-** in App.]

liberty cap *n.* A conical cap fitting snugly around the head, given to a slave in ancient Rome upon manumission and used as a symbol of liberty by the French revolutionaries.

Liberty Island Formerly **Bed•loe's Island** (bĕd′lōz) An island of SE NY in Upper New York Bay SW of Manhattan; site of the Statue of Liberty.

li•bid•i•nous (lĭ-bĭd′n-əs) *adj.* Having or exhibiting lustful desires; lascivious. [ME, ult. < *libīdō, libīdin-*, lust. See LIBIDO.] —**li•bid′i•nous•ly** *adv.* —**li•bid′i•nous•ness** *n.*

li•bi•do (lĭ-bē′dō, -bī′-) *n., pl.* **-dos 1.** The energy associated with instinctual biological drives. **2a.** Sexual desire. **b.** Manifestation of the sexual drive. [Lat. *libīdō*, desire.] —**li•bid′i•nal** (-bĭd′n-

əl) *adj.* —**li•bid′i•nal•ly** *adv.*

Li Bo (lē′ bō′) See **Li Po.**

li•bra (lē′brə) *n., pl.* **-brae** (-brē′) A unit of weight in ancient Rome equivalent to about 12 ounces. [ME < Lat. *libra.*]

Libra *n.* **1.** A constellation in the Southern Hemisphere near Scorpius and Virgo. **2a.** The seventh sign of the zodiac in astrology. **b.** *pl.* **-bras** One born under this sign. [ME < Lat. *lībra*, balance, the constellation Libra.]

li•brar•i•an (lī-brâr′ē-ən) *n.* A specialist in library work. —**li•brar′i•an•ship′** *n.*

li•brar•y (lī′brĕr′ē) *n., pl.* **-ies 1a.** A place in which literary and artistic materials, such as books, newspapers, and tapes, are kept for reading, reference, or lending. **b.** A collection of such materials, esp. when systematically arranged. **c.** A room in a private home for such a collection. **d.** An institution or foundation maintaining such a collection. **2.** A commercial establishment that lends books for a fee. **3.** A series or set of books issued by a publisher. **4.** A collection of recorded data or tapes arranged for ease of use. **5.** A set of things similar to a library in appearance, function, or organization. **6.** *Genetics* A collection of cloned DNA sequences whose location and identity can be established by mapping the genome of a particular organism. [ME *librarie* < AN < Lat. *librārium*, bookcase < neut. of *librārius*, of books < *liber, libr-*, book.]

library science *n.* The principles, practice, or study of library administration.

li•bra•tion (lī-brā′shən) *n.* A very slow oscillation, real or apparent, of a satellite as viewed from the larger celestial body around which it revolves. [Lat. *lībrātiō, oscillation* < *lībrātus*, p. part. of *lībrāre*, to balance < *lībra*, balance.] —**li•bra′tion•al** *adj.* —**li′bra•to′ry** (-brə-tôr′ē, -tōr′ē) *adj.*

li•bret•tist (lĭ-brĕt′ĭst) *n.* The author of a libretto.

li•bret•to (lĭ-brĕt′ō) *n., pl.* **-bret•tos** or **-bret•ti** (-brĕt′ē) **1.** The text of a dramatic musical work, such as an opera. **2.** A book containing such a text. [Ital., dim. of *libro*, book < Lat. *liber*, book.]

Li•bre•ville (lē′brə-vĭl′, -vĕl′) The cap. of Gabon, in the NW part on the Gulf of Guinea; named after freed slaves who settled there in 1848. Pop. 235,700.

Lib•ri•um (lĭb′rē-əm) A trademark used for preparations of chlordiazepoxide hydrochloride.

Lib•y•a (lĭb′ē-ə) A country of N Africa on the Mediterranean Sea; achieved independence in 1951. Cap. Tripoli. Pop. 4,899,000.

Lib•y•an (lĭb′ē-ən) *adj.* Of or relating to Libya or its people, language, or culture. ❖ *n.* **1.** A native or inhabitant of Libya. **2.** A Berber language of ancient northern Africa.

Libyan Desert A desert of NE Africa in Egypt, Libya, and Sudan; a section of the Sahara Desert.

lice (līs) *n.* Plural of **louse** 1.

li•cence (lī′səns) *n. & v. Chiefly British* Variant of **license.**

li•cense (lī′səns) *n.* **1a.** Official or legal permission to do or own a specified thing. **b.** A document, card, plate, or tag issued as proof of official or legal permission: *a driver's license.* **2.** Deviation from normal rules, practices, or methods to achieve a certain end or effect. **3.** Latitude of action, esp. in behavior or speech. See Syns at **freedom. 4a.** Lack of due restraint; excessive freedom. **b.** Heedlessness for the precepts of proper behavior; licentiousness. ❖ *tr.v.* **-censed, -cens•ing, -cens•es 1.** To give or yield permission to or for. **2.** To grant a license to or for; authorize. [ME *licence* < OFr. < Med.Lat. *licentia*, authorization < Lat., freedom < *licēns, licent-*, pr. part. of *licēre*, to be permitted.] —**li′cens•a•ble** *adj.* —**li′cens•er, li′cen•sor′** (-sən-sôr′) *n.*

li•censed practical nurse (lī′sənst) *n.* A nurse who has completed a practical nursing program and is licensed by a state to provide routine patient care under the direction of a registered nurse or a physician.

licensed vocational nurse *n.* A licensed practical nurse in California or Texas.

li•cens•ee (lī′sən-sē′) *n.* One granted a license.

li•cen•sure (lī′sən-shər, -shŏŏr′) *n.* The act or an instance of granting a license, usu. to practice a profession.

li•cen•ti•ate (lī-sĕn′shē-ĭt) *n.* **1.** One granted a license by an authorized body to practice a specified profession. **2a.** A degree from certain European and Canadian universities ranking just below that of a doctor. **b.** One holding such a degree. [ME < Med.Lat. *licentiātus* < p. part. of *licentiāre*, to allow < *licentia*, authorization. See LICENSE.]

li•cen•tious (lī-sĕn′shəs) *adj.* **1.** Lacking moral discipline or ignoring legal restraint, esp. in sexual conduct. **2.** Having no regard for accepted rules or standards. [< Lat. *licentiōsus* < *licentia*, freedom, license. See LICENSE.] —**li•cen′tious•ly** *adv.* —**li•cen′tious•ness** *n.*

li•chee (lē′chē) *n.* Variant of **litchi.**

li•chen (lī′kən) *n.* **1.** A fungus, usu. of the class Ascomycetes, that grows symbiotically with algae, resulting in a composite organism that characteristically forms a crustlike or branching growth on rocks or tree trunks. **2.** *Pathology* Any of various skin diseases characterized by patchy eruptions of small firm papules. ❖ *tr.v.* **-chened, -chen•ing, -chens** To cover with lichens. [Lat. *līchēn*, a kind of plant < Gk. *leikhēn < leikhein*, to lick. See **leigh-** in App.] —**li′chen•ous** *adj.*

li•chen•ol•o•gy (lī′kə-nŏl′ə-jē) *n.* The branch of biology that

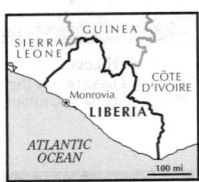

Liberia

Libya

deals with the study of lichens. —**li′chen•ol′o•gist** *n.*
lich gate (lĭch) *n.* Variant of **lych-gate.**
Lich•ten•stein (lĭk′tən-stīn′, -stēn′), **Roy** b. 1923. Amer. pop artist best known for his large-scale depictions of comic book panels.
lic•it (lĭs′ĭt) *adj.* Permitted by law; legal. [ME < OFr. *licite* < Lat. *licitus*, p. part. of *licēre*, to be permitted.] —**lic′it•ly** *adv.*
lick (lĭk) *v.* **licked, lick•ing, licks** —*tr.* **1.** To pass the tongue over or along. **2.** To lap up. **3.** To lap or flicker at like a tongue. **4.** *Slang* To punish with a beating; thrash. **5.** *Slang* To get the better of; defeat. —*intr.* To pass or lap quickly and rapidly. ❖ *n.* **1.** The act or process of licking. **2.** An amount obtained by licking. **3.** A small quantity; a bit: *a lick of sense.* **4.** A deposit of exposed natural salt that is licked by passing animals. **5.** A sudden hard stroke; a blow. **6.** An attempt; a try. **7.** *Informal* Speed; pace. **8.** *Music* A phrase improvised by a soloist, esp. on the guitar or banjo. ***—idioms:*** **lick and a promise** A superficial effort made without care or enthusiasm. **lick into shape** *Informal* To bring into satisfactory condition or appearance. **lick (one's) chops** To anticipate delightedly. **lick (one's) wounds** To recuperate after a defeat. **lick (someone's) boots** To behave servilely or obsequiously toward someone. [ME *licken* < OE *liccian*. See **leigh-** in App.] —**lick′er** *n.*
lick•er•ish (lĭk′ər-ĭsh) *adj.* **1.** Lascivious; lecherous. **2.** Greedy; desirous. **3a.** *Archaic* Relishing good food. **b.** *Obsolete* Arousing hunger; appetizing. [ME *likerous*, perh. < OFr. *lecheor*, *lekier*. See LECHER.]
lick•e•ty-split (lĭk′ĭ-tē-splĭt′) *adv. Informal* With great speed. [*lickety*, very fast, alteration of LICK, fast (dialectal) + SPLIT.]
lick•ing (lĭk′ĭng) *n. Slang* **1.** A beating, thrashing, or spanking. **2.** A severe loss or defeat.
Licking River A river of NE KY flowing c. 515 km (320 mi) to the Ohio R.
lick•spit•tle (lĭk′spĭt′l) *n.* A fawning underling; a toady.
lic•o•rice (lĭk′ər-ĭs, -ĭsh) *n.* **1a.** A Mediterranean perennial plant *(Glycyrrhiza glabra)* having blue flowers, pinnately compound leaves, and a sweet root. **b.** The root of this plant, used as a flavoring. **c.** A confection made from or flavored with the licorice root. **2.** Any of various similar plants. [ME < OFr. < LLat. *liquirītia*, alteration (influenced by Lat. *liquēre*, to flow) of Lat. *glycyrrhiza*, root of licorice < Gk. *glukurrhiza* : *glukus*, sweet + *rhiza*, root; see **wrād-** in App.]
lic•tor (lĭk′tər) *n.* A Roman functionary who carried fasces when attending a magistrate in public appearances. [< ME *littoures*, lictors < Lat. *lictōrēs*, pl. of *lictor*.]
lid (lĭd) *n.* **1.** A removable or hinged cover for a hollow receptacle or box. **2.** An eyelid. **3.** *Biology* A flaplike covering. **4.** A curb, restraint, or limit. **5.** *Informal* An act of concealment; a cover. **6.** *Slang* A hat. **7.** *Slang* An ounce of marijuana. ❖ *tr.v.* **lid•ded, lid•ding, lids** To cover with or as if with a lid. [ME < OE *hlid*. See **klei-** in App.]
li•dar (lī′där) *n.* **1.** A method of determining the position, velocity, or other characteristics of distant objects by analysis of pulsed laser light reflected from their surfaces. **2.** The equipment used in such detection. [LI(GHT)[1] + (RA)DAR.]
Li•di•ce (lĭd′ĭ-sē, lē′dē-tsĕ) A village of NW Czech Republic WNW of Prague. In reprisal for the murder of a Nazi official, German forces killed or deported its entire population to concentration camps (Jun. 9–10, 1942).
lid•less (lĭd′lĭs) *adj.* **1.** Having no lid or lids. **2.** *Archaic* Watchful; vigilant.
Li•do (lē′dō) An island reef of NE Italy separating the lagoon of Venice from the Adriatic Sea.
li•do•caine (lī′də-kān′) *n.* A synthetic amide, $C_{14}H_{22}N_2O$, used chiefly in the form of its hydrochloride as a local anesthetic and antiarrhythmic agent. [(ACETANI)LID(E) + -CAINE.]
lie[1] (lī) *intr.v.* **lay** (lā), **lain** (lān), **ly•ing** (lī′ĭng), **lies 1.** To be or place oneself at rest in a flat, horizontal, or recumbent position; recline: *She lay under a tree to sleep.* **2.** To be placed on or supported by a surface that is usu. horizontal: *Dirty dishes lay on the table.* See Usage Note at **lay**[1]. **3.** To be or remain in a specified condition: *He lay sick in bed.* **4a.** To exist; reside: *Our sympathies lie with the plaintiff.* **b.** To consist or have as a basis. Often used with *in: His strength lies in his training.* **5.** To occupy a position or place. **6.** To extend: *Our land lies along the river.* **7.** To be buried in a specific place. **8.** *Law* To be admissible or maintainable. **9.** *Archaic* To stay for a night or short while. ❖ *n.* **1.** The manner or position in which something is situated. **2.** A haunt or hiding place of an animal. **3.** *Sports* The position of a golf ball that has come to a stop. ***—phrasal verbs:*** **lie down** To do little or nothing. **lie in** To be in confinement for childbirth. **lie to** *Nautical* To remain stationary while facing the wind. **lie with 1.** To be decided by, dependent on, or up to. **2.** *Archaic* To have sexual intercourse with. ***—idiom:*** **lie (or lay) low 1.** To keep oneself or one's plans hidden. **2.** To bide one's time but remain ready for action. [ME *lien* < OE *licgan*. See **legh-** in App.]
lie[2] (lī) *n.* **1.** A false statement deliberately presented as being true; a falsehood. **2.** Something meant to deceive or give a wrong impression. ❖ *v.* **lied, ly•ing** (lī′ĭng), **lies** —*intr.* **1.** To present false information with the intention of deceiving. **2.** To convey a false image or impression. —*tr.* To cause to be in a specific condition or affect in a specific way by telling falsehoods. ***—idiom:*** **lie through (one's) teeth** To lie outrageously or brazenly. [ME < OE *lyge*.]
Lie (lē), **Trygve Halvden** 1896–1968. Norwegian politician and first secretary-general of the United Nations (1946–53).
Lie•big (lē′bĭg, -bĭKH), Baron **Justus von** 1803–73. German chemist who pioneered laboratory-based education (1826).
Liech•ten•stein (lĭk′tən-stīn′, lĭKH′tən-shtīn′) A small Alpine principality in central Europe between Austria and Switzerland; became independent in 1866. Cap. Vaduz. Pop. 27,076.
lied (lēt) *n., pl.* **lie•der** (lē′dər) A German art song for solo voice and piano. [Ger. *Lied*, ult. < OHGer. *liod*.]
lie detector (lī) *n.* A polygraph used to detect possible deception during an interrogation.
lief (lēf) *adv.* **lief•er, lief•est** Readily; willingly. ❖ *adj.* **liefer, liefest** *Archaic* **1.** Beloved; dear. **2.** Ready or willing. [ME *leve*, *lef*, dear, willingly < OE *lēof*, dear.]
liege (lēj) *n.* **1.** A lord or sovereign to whom allegiance and service are due according to feudal law. **2.** A vassal or subject owing allegiance and services to a lord or sovereign under feudal law. **3.** A loyal subject to a monarch. ❖ *adj.* **1a.** Entitled to the loyalty and services of vassals or subjects: *a liege lord.* **b.** Bound to give such allegiance and services to a lord or monarch. **2.** Loyal; faithful. [ME < OFr., entitled to feudal allegiance < LLat. *laeticus*, being a semifree colonist in Gaul < *laetus*, a semifree colonist, of Gmc. orig.]
Li•ège (lē-āzh′, lyĕzh) A city of E Belgium near the Dutch and German borders; first mentioned in 558. Pop. 195,201.
liege•man (lēj′mən) *n.* **1.** A feudal vassal or subject. **2.** A loyal supporter, follower, or subject.
lien (lēn, lē′ən) *n.* The right to take and hold or sell the property of a debtor as security or payment for a debt or duty. [Fr., tie, bond < OFr., constraint < Lat. *ligāmen*, bond < *ligāre*, to bind.]
li•erne (lē-ûrn′) *n.* A subordinate rib used in Gothic vaulting to connect the intersections and bosses of the primary ribs. [Fr. < *lier*, to bind < OFr. See LIABLE.]
lieu (lo͞o) *n. Archaic* Place; stead. ***—idiom:*** **in lieu of** In place of; instead of. [Fr. < OFr. < Lat. *locus*.]
lieu•ten•ant (lo͞o-tĕn′ənt) *n.* **1a.** A commissioned officer in the US Navy or Coast Guard ranking above lieutenant junior grade and below lieutenant commander. **b.** A first lieutenant. **c.** A second lieutenant. **2.** (lĕf-tĕn′ənt) A commissioned officer in the British and Canadian navies ranking just below a lieutenant commander. **3.** An officer in a police or fire department ranking below a captain. **4.** One who acts in place of or represents a superior; an assistant or deputy. [ME, deputy < OFr. : *lieu*, lieu; see LIEU + *tenant*, pr. part. of *tenir*, to hold (< Lat. *tenēre*; see **ten-** in App.).] —**lieu•ten′an•cy** *n.*
lieutenant colonel *n.* A commissioned officer in the US Army, Air Force, or Marine Corps ranking above major and below colonel.
lieutenant commander *n.* A commissioned officer in the US Navy or Coast Guard ranking above lieutenant and below commander.
lieutenant general *n.* A commissioned officer in the US Army, Air Force, or Marine Corps ranking above major general and below general.
lieutenant governor *n.* **1.** An elected official ranking just below the governor of a state in the United States. **2.** The nonelective chief of government of a Canadian province.
lieutenant junior grade *n., pl.* **lieutenants junior grade** A commissioned officer in the US Navy or Coast Guard ranking above ensign and below lieutenant.
life (līf) *n., pl.* **lives** (līvz) **1.** *Biology* **a.** The property or quality that distinguishes living organisms from dead organisms and inanimate matter, manifested in functions such as metabolism, growth, reproduction, and response to stimuli or adaptation to the environment originating from within the organism. **b.** The characteristic state or condition of a living organism. **2.** Living organisms considered as a group: *plant life.* **3.** A living being, esp. a person. **4.** The physical, mental, and spiritual experiences that constitute existence. **5a.** The interval of time between birth and death. **b.** The interval of time between one's birth and the present. **c.** A particular segment of one's life. **d.** The period from an occurrence until death: *barred for life.* **e.** *Slang* A sentence of imprisonment lasting till death. **6.** The time for which something exists or functions. **7.** A spiritual state regarded as a transcending of corporeal death. **8.** An account of a person's life; a biography. **9.** Human existence, relationships, or activity in general: *real life.* **10a.** A manner of living: *led a hard life.* **b.** A specific characteristic manner of existence. Used of inanimate objects. **c.** The activities and interests of a particular area or realm. **11a.** A source of vitality; an animating force. **b.** Liveliness or vitality; animation. **12a.** Something that actually exists regarded as a subject for an artist: *painted from life.* **b.** Actual environment or reality; nature. ❖ *adj.* **1.** Involved in or necessary for living: *life processes.* **2.** Continuing for a lifetime; lifelong: *a life partner.* **3.** Using a living model as a subject for an artist: *a life sculpture.* ***—idioms:*** **as big as life 1.** Life-size. **2.** Actually present. **bring to life 1.** To cause to regain consciousness. **2.** To put spirit into; to animate. **3.** To make lifelike. **come to life** To become animated; grow excited.

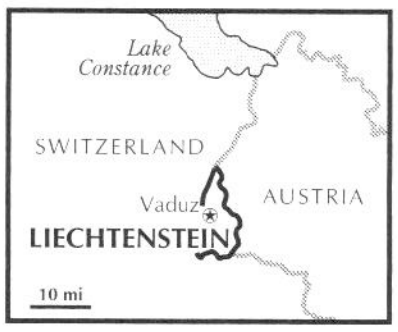

Liechtenstein

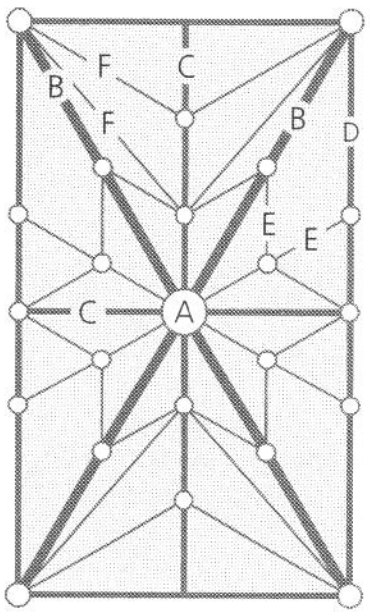

lierne
A. boss
B. diagonal ribs
C. ridge ribs
D. transverse rib
E. liernes
F. tiercerons

ă	pat	oi	boy
ā	pay	ou	out
âr	care	o͝o	took
ä	father	o͞o	boot
ĕ	pet	ŭ	cut
ē	be	ûr	urge
ĭ	pit	th	thin
ī	pie	*th*	this
îr	pier	hw	which
ŏ	pot	zh	vision
ō	toe	ə	about, item
ô	paw		

Stress marks:
′ (primary);
′ (secondary), as in
lexicon (lĕk′sĭ-kŏn′)

for dear life Desperately or urgently. **for life** Till the end of one's life. **for the life of (one)** Though trying hard. **not on your life** *Informal* Absolutely not; not for any reason whatsoever. **take (one's) life** To commit suicide. **take (someone's) life** To commit murder. **the good life** A wealthy, luxurious way of living. **the life of Riley** *Informal* An easy life. **to save (one's) life** No matter how hard one tries. **true to life** Conforming to reality. [ME < OE *līf.*]

life-and-death (līf′ən-dĕth′) or **life-or-death** (līf′ər-) *adj.* **1.** Involving or ending in life or death. **2.** Vitally important.

life belt *n.* A life preserver worn like a belt.

life·blood (līf′blŭd′) *n.* **1.** Blood regarded as essential for life. **2.** An indispensable or vital part.

life·boat (līf′bōt′) *n.* **1.** A boat carried on a ship for use if the ship has to be abandoned. **2.** A boat used for rescue.

life buoy *n.* A buoyant device, such as a cork or polystyrene ring, for keeping a person afloat in water.

life care also **life·care** (līf′kâr′) *n.* The provision of services, such as housing and health care, for elderly people. —**life care, life′-care′** *adj.*

life cycle *n.* **1.** The course of developmental changes through which an organism passes from its inception as a fertilized zygote to the mature state in which another zygote may be produced. **2.** A progression through a series of differing stages of development.

life expectancy *n.* The number of years that an individual is expected to live as determined by statistics.

life force *n.* See **élan vital.**

life form *n.* The characteristic morphology of a mature organism.

life·guard (līf′gärd′) *n.* An expert swimmer trained and employed to watch over other swimmers. —**life′guard′** *v.*

life history *n.* **1.** The history of changes undergone by an organism from inception or conception to death. **2.** The developmental history of an individual or a group in society.

life insurance *n.* Insurance that guarantees a sum of money to a beneficiary upon the death of the insured or to the insured if he or she lives beyond a certain age.

life jacket *n.* A life preserver in the form of a vest.

life·less (līf′lĭs) *adj.* **1.** Having no life; inanimate. **2.** Having lost life; dead. **3.** Not inhabited by living beings; not capable of sustaining life. **4.** Lacking vitality or animation; dull: *a lifeless party.* —**life′less·ly** *adv.* —**life′less·ness** *n.*

life·like (līf′līk′) *adj.* Accurately representing real life: *a lifelike statue.* See Syns at **graphic.** —**life′like′ness** *n.*

life·line (līf′līn′) *n.* **1.** An anchored line thrown as a support to someone falling or drowning. **2a.** A line used to secure a ship in distress. **b.** A rope or wire along the deck of a ship, used as a handhold. **c.** A line used to raise and lower deep-sea divers. **3a.** A means or route by which necessary supplies are transported. **b.** One regarded as a source of salvation in a crisis. **4.** A diagonal line crossing the palm of the hand and believed to indicate the major events and length of one's life.

life·long (līf′lông′, -lŏng′) *adj.* Continuing for a lifetime.

life-or-death (līf′ər-dĕth′) *adj.* Variant of **life-and-death.**

life preserver *n.* **1.** A buoyant device designed to keep a person afloat in the water. **2.** *Chiefly British* A weapon, such as a blackjack.

lif·er (līf′fər) *n.* **1.** *Slang* **a.** A prisoner serving a life sentence. **b.** One who makes a career in one of the armed forces. **2.** *Informal* A right-to-lifer.

life raft *n.* A raft usu. made of inflatable material or wood and used in an emergency on large bodies of water.

life·sav·er (līf′sā′vər) *n.* **1.** One that saves a life. **2.** See **lifeguard. 3.** One that provides help in a crisis or emergency. **4.** A life preserver shaped like a ring. —**life′sav′ing** *n.*

life science *n.* Any of several branches of science, such as biology, medicine, or ecology, studying living organisms and their organization, life processes, and relationships to each other and their environment.

life-size (līf′sīz′) also **life-sized** (-sīzd′) *adj.* Being of the same size as an original: *a life-size statue.*

life span or **life·span** (līf′spăn′) *n.* **1.** A lifetime. **2.** The average or maximum length of time an organism, material, or object can be expected to survive or last.

life·style also **life-style** or **life style** (līf′stīl′) *n.* A way of life or style of living that reflects the attitudes and values of a person or group.

life support *n.* A life-support system: *a patient on life support.*

ligature
opening notes of "The Star-Spangled Banner"

life-sup·port (līf′sə-pôrt′, -pōrt′) *adj.* Of or relating to the methods, equipment, or conditions needed to sustain life: *a life-support system.*

life·time (līf′tīm′) *n.* **1.** The period of time during which an individual is alive. **2.** The period of time during which property, an object, a process, or a phenomenon exists or functions. ❖ *adj.* **1.** Continuing for a lifetime; lifelong. **2.** Occurring or measured over a person's active career: *a lifetime batting average.*

life·way (līf′wā′) *n.* A customary manner of living; a way of life.

life·work (līf′wûrk′) *n.* The chief or entire work of a person's lifetime.

life zone *n.* A geographic region or area defined by its characteristic life forms.

LIFO (lī′fō) *abbr.* last-in, first-out

lift (lĭft) *v.* **lift·ed, lift·ing, lifts** —*tr.* **1a.** To direct or carry from a lower to a higher position; raise: *lift one's eyes; lifted the suitcase.* **b.** To transport by air: *Helicopters lifted supplies to the town.* **2a.** To revoke by taking back; rescind: *lifted the embargo.* **b.** To bring an end to (a blockade or siege) by removing forces. **3.** To cease (artillery fire) in an area. **4a.** To raise in condition, rank, or esteem. **b.** To uplift; elate. **5.** To remove (plants) from the ground for transplanting. **6.** To project or sound in loud, clear tones. **7.** *Informal* To steal; pilfer. **8.** *Informal* To copy from something already published; plagiarize. **9.** To pay off or clear (a debt or mortgage, for example). **10.** To perform cosmetic surgery on (the face, for example), esp. to remove wrinkles or sagging skin. **11a.** *Sports* To hit (a golf ball) very high into the air. **b.** To pick up (a golf ball) to place it in a better lie. **c.** To shoot or flip (a puck) so that it rises sharply off the ice. —*intr.* **1a.** To rise; ascend. **b.** To yield to upward pressure: *These windows lift easily.* **2a.** To disappear or disperse by or as if by rising: *The smog lifted.* **b.** To stop temporarily. **3.** To become elevated; soar: *Their spirits lifted.* ❖ *n.* **1.** The act or process of rising or raising to a higher position. **2.** Power or force available for raising: *the lift of a pump.* **3.** An amount or a weight raised or capable of being raised at one time; a load. **4a.** The extent or height to which something is raised or rises; the amount of elevation. **b.** The distance or space through which something is raised or rises. **5.** A rise or an elevation in the level of the ground. **6.** An elevation of one's spirits. **7.** A raised, high, or erect position, as of a part of the body: *the lift of his chin.* **8.** A machine or device designed to pick up, raise, or carry something. **9.** One of the layers making up the heel of a shoe. **10.** *Chiefly British* A passenger or cargo elevator. **11.** A ride in a vehicle given to help someone reach a destination. **12.** Assistance or help. **13.** A set of pumps used in a mine. **14.** The component of the total aerodynamic force acting on an airfoil or on an entire aircraft perpendicular to the relative wind and normally exerted in an upward direction. —*phrasal verb:* **lift off** To begin flight. [ME *liften* < ON *lypta.*] —**lift′a·ble** *adj.* —**lift′er** *n.*

SYNONYMS *lift, raise, elevate, hoist, heave, boost* These verbs mean to move something from a lower to a higher level or position. *Lift* sometimes stresses the expenditure of effort: *a trunk too heavy to lift.* *Raise* often implies movement to an approximately vertical position: *raised my hand.* *Elevate* is sometimes synonymous with the preceding terms (*elevated his ankle*), but it more often suggests exalting, ennobling, or raising morally or intellectually: "*A generous and elevated mind is distinguished by nothing more certainly than an eminent degree of curiosity*" (Samuel Johnson). *Hoist* is applied principally to the lifting of heavy objects, often by mechanical means: *hoist a sunken ship.* To *heave* is to lift or raise with great effort or force: *heaved the pack up.* *Boost* suggests upward movement effected by or as if by pushing from below: *boosted the child into the saddle.*

lift·gate (lĭft′gāt′) *n.* A closure at the rear of a vehicle that can be raised during loading and unloading.

lift·off (lĭft′ôf′, -ŏf′) *n.* The initial movement by which or the instant in which a rocket or other such craft commences flight.

lig·a·ment (lĭg′ə-mənt) *n.* **1.** *Anatomy* A sheet or band of tough fibrous tissue connecting bones or cartilages at a joint or supporting an organ. **2.** A unifying or connecting tie or bond. [ME < Med.Lat. *ligāmentum* < Lat., bandage < *ligāre,* to bind.] —**lig′a·men′tal** (-mĕn′tl), **lig′a·men′ta·ry** (-mĕn′tə-rē, -mĕn′trē), **lig′a·men′tous** *adj.*

li·gan (lī′gən) *n.* Variant of **lagan.**

li·gand (lī′gənd, lĭg′ənd) *n.* An ion, molecule, or molecular group that binds to another chemical entity to form a larger complex. [< Lat. *ligandus,* gerundive of *ligāre,* to bind.]

li·gase (lī′gās′, -gāz′) *n.* Any of a class of enzymes that catalyze the linkage of two molecules, generally utilizing ATP as the energy donor. [Lat. *ligāre,* to bind + -ASE.]

li·gate (lī′gāt′) *tr.v.* **-gat·ed, -gat·ing, -gates** To tie or bind with a ligature. [Lat. *ligāre, ligāt-.*]

li·ga·tion (lī-gā′shən) *n.* **1a.** The act of binding or of applying a ligature. **b.** The state of being bound. **2.** Something that binds; a ligature.

lig·a·ture (lĭg′ə-chŏŏr′, -chər) *n.* **1.** The act of tying or binding. **2a.** A cord, wire, or bandage used for tying or binding. **b.** A thread, wire, or cord used in surgery to close vessels or tie off ducts. **c.** Something that unites; a bond. **3.** A character, letter, or type, such as æ, combining two or more letters. **4.** *Music* **a.** A group of notes to be played or sung as one phrase. **b.** A curved line indicating such a phrase; a slur. **c.** A passage of notes sung by repeating the same syllable. **d.** A metal band that attaches the reed to the mouthpiece of some wind instruments. ❖ *tr.v.* **-tured, -tur·ing, -tures** To ligate. [Ult. < LLat. *ligātūra* < Lat. *ligātus*, p. part. of *ligāre*, to bind.]

li·ger (līʹgər) *n.* The offspring of a male lion and a female tiger, usu. larger than either. [LI(ON) + (TI)GER.]

Lig·e·ti (ligʹə-tē), **György Sándor** b. 1923. Hungarian-born Austrian composer whose experimental works include orchestral, chamber, and choral music.

light¹ (līt) *n.* **1.** *Physics* **a.** Electromagnetic radiation that has a wavelength in the range from about 4,000 (violet) to about 7,700 (red) angstroms and may be perceived by the normal unaided human eye. **b.** Electromagnetic radiation of any wavelength. **2.** The sensation of perceiving light; brightness. **3a.** A source of light, such as a lamp. **b.** The illumination derived from a source of light. **c.** The particular quantity or quality of such illumination: *better light near the lamp.* **d.** The pathway or route of such illumination to a person. **4.** A mechanical device that uses illumination as a signal or warning, esp. a traffic signal. **5a.** Daylight. **b.** Dawn; daybreak. **6.** Something, such as a window, that admits illumination. **7.** A source of fire, such as a match. **8.** Spiritual awareness; illumination. **9a.** Something that provides information or clarification. **b.** A state of awareness or understanding. **10.** Public attention; general knowledge: *brought the scandal to light.* **11.** A way of looking at or considering a matter; an aspect. **12.** *Archaic* Eyesight. **13. lights** One's individual opinions, choices, or standards. **14.** A person who inspires or is adored by another. **15.** A prominent or distinguished person; a luminary. **16.** An expression of the eyes. **17. Light** In Quaker doctrine, the guiding spirit or divine presence in each person. **18.** The representation of light in art. ❖ *v.* **light·ed** or **lit** (līt), **light·ing, lights** —*tr.* **1.** To set on fire; ignite or kindle. **2.** To cause to give out light; make luminous: *lit a lamp.* **3.** To provide, cover, or fill with light; illuminate. **4.** To signal, direct, or guide with or as if with illumination. **5.** To enliven or animate: *A smile lit her face.* —*intr.* **1.** To start to burn; be ignited or kindled. **2.** To emit light; be lighted: *The indicator lights up.* ❖ *adj.* **light·er, light·est 1a.** Having a greater rather than lesser degree of lightness. **b.** Of or being an additive primary color. **2.** Characterized by or filled with light; bright. **3.** Not dark in color; fair: *light hair.* **4.** Served with milk or cream. Used of coffee. —*phrasal verb:* **light up 1.** To become or cause to become animated or cheerful. **2.** To start smoking a cigarette, cigar, or pipe. —*idioms:* **in (the) light of** In consideration of; in relationship to. **light at the end of the tunnel** The prospect of success, relief, or escape after strenuous effort. [ME < OE *lēoht, līht.* See **leuk-** in App.]

light² (līt) *adj.* **light·er, light·est 1a.** Of relatively little weight; not heavy. **b.** Of relatively little weight for its size or bulk. **c.** Of less than the correct, standard, or legal weight: *a light pound.* **2.** Exerting little force or impact; gentle. **3.** Indistinct; faint: *The light print was hard to read.* **4a.** Of little quantity; scanty: *light snow.* **b.** Consuming or using relatively moderate amounts; abstemious. **c.** Not harsh or severe. **5.** Demanding little exertion or effort; not burdensome. **6.** Having little importance; insignificant. **7.** Intended primarily as entertainment; not serious or profound. **8.** Free from worries or troubles; blithe. **9.** Characterized by frivolity; silly or trivial. **10.** Liable to change; fickle. **11.** Mildly dizzy or faint. **12.** Lacking in ethical discrimination. **13.** Moving easily and quickly; nimble. **14.** Designed for ease and quickness of movement: *light aircraft.* **15.** Designed to carry relatively little weight: *a light truck.* **16.** Carrying little equipment or armament. **17.** Requiring relatively little equipment to produce consumer goods: *light industry.* **18.** Easily awakened or disturbed. **19a.** Easily digested: *a light supper.* **b.** Having a spongy or flaky texture; well-leavened. **20.** Having a loose, porous consistency: *light soil.* **21.** Containing a small amount of a potentially harmful ingredient, such as alcohol or fat. **22.** *Linguistics* **a.** Of, relating to, or being a syllable ending in a short vowel or a short vowel plus a consonant. **b.** Of, relating to, or being a vowel or syllable pronounced with little or no stress. ❖ *adv.* **lighter, lightest 1.** In a light manner; lightly. **2.** With little weight and few burdens. ❖ *intr.v.* **light·ed** or **lit** (līt), **light·ing, lights 1.** To get down, as from a vehicle or horse; dismount. **2.** To descend to the ground after flight; land. **3.** To come upon unexpectedly. **4.** To come upon by chance or accident. Used with *on* or *upon: lit on the solution.* —*phrasal verbs:* **light into** *Informal* To attack verbally or physically; assail. **light out** *Informal* To leave hastily; run off. —*idiom:* **go light on** To treat casually or gingerly. [ME < OE *lēoht, līht.*]

light adaptation *n.* The process, chiefly involving constriction of the pupil, by which the eye adapts to an increase in illumination. —**lightʹ-a·daptʹed** (-dăpʹtĭd) *adj.*

light bread *n. Chiefly Southern & Southwestern US* Leavened bread made with wheat flour.

light bulb *n.* An electric light in which a filament is heated to in-

light-e·mit·ting diode (lītʹĭ-mĭtʹĭng) *n.* LED.

light·en¹ (lītʹn) *v.* **-ened, -en·ing, -ens 1a.** To make light or lighter; illuminate or brighten. **b.** To make (a color) lighter. **2.** *Archaic* To enlighten. —*intr.* **1.** To become lighter; brighten. **2.** To be luminous; shine. **3.** To give off flashes of lightning.

light·en² (lītʹn) *v.* **-ened, -en·ing, -ens** —*tr.* **1.** To make less heavy. **2.** To lessen the oppressiveness, trouble, or severity of. See Syns at **relieve. 3.** To relieve of cares or worries; gladden. —*intr.* **1.** To become less in weight. **2.** To become less oppressive, troublesome, or severe. **3.** To become cheerful.

light·er¹ (līʹtər) *n.* **1.** One that ignites or kindles. **2.** A mechanical device for lighting a cigarette, cigar, or pipe.

light·er² (līʹtər) *n.* A large flatbottom barge, esp. one used to load and unload cargo ships. ❖ *tr.v.* **-ered, -er·ing, -ers** To convey (cargo) in a lighter. [ME, perh. < *lighten,* to make less heavy < OE *lihtan.*]

light·er·age (līʹtər-ĭj) *n. Nautical* **1.** Transportation of goods on a lighter. **2.** The fee charged for lightering.

light·er-than-air (līʹtər-thən-ârʹ) *adj.* Having a weight less than that of the air displaced. Used of certain aircraft.

light·face (lītʹfāsʹ) *n.* A typeface or font of characters having relatively thin light lines. —**lightʹfacedʹ** *adj.*

light-fin·gered (lītʹfĭngʹgərd) *adj.* **1.** Having quick and nimble fingers. **2.** Skilled at or given to petty thievery.

light-foot·ed (lītʹfŏotʹĭd) also **light·foot** (-fŏotʹ) *adj.* Treading with light and nimble ease. —**lightʹ-footʹed·ly** *adv.*

light-hand·ed (lītʹhănʹdĭd) *adj.* Having a light, delicate touch. —**lightʹ-handʹed·ly** *adv.*

light-head·ed (lītʹhĕdʹĭd) *adj.* **1.** Faint, giddy, or delirious: *lightheaded with wine.* **2.** Given to frivolity; silly. —**lightʹ-headʹed·ly** *adv.* —**lightʹheadʹed·ness** *n.*

light-heart·ed (lītʹhärʹtĭd) *adj.* Not being burdened by trouble, worry, or care; happy and carefree. See Syns at **glad¹.** —**lightʹheartʹed·ly** *adv.* —**lightʹheartʹed·ness** *n.*

light heavyweight *n.* **1.** A professional boxer weighing more than 160 and not more than 175 pounds (approx. 72.5–79.5 kilograms), heavier than a middleweight and lighter than a cruiserweight. **2.** A contestant in various other sports in a similar weight class.

light·house (lītʹhousʹ) *n.* A tall structure topped by a powerful light used to aid marine navigation.

light·ing (līʹtĭng) *n.* **1.** The state of being lighted; illumination. **2a.** The method or equipment used to provide artificial illumination. **b.** The illumination so provided. **3.** The act or process of igniting.

light·ly (lītʹlē) *adv.* **1.** With little weight or force; gently. **2.** To a slight extent or amount: *apply paint lightly.* **3a.** With little difficulty; easily. **b.** With agility and grace; nimbly. **4a.** In a carefree manner; cheerfully: *took the news lightly.* **b.** Without sufficient care or consideration; indifferently.

light machine gun *n.* An air-cooled machine gun not greater than .30 caliber.

light meter *n.* See **exposure meter.**

light-mind·ed (lītʹmīnʹdĭd) *adj.* Frivolous, silly, or inanely giddy. —**lightʹ-mindʹed·ly** *adv.* —**lightʹ-mindʹed·ness** *n.*

light·ness¹ (lītʹnĭs) *n.* **1.** The quality or condition of being illuminated. **2.** The dimension of the color of an object by which the object appears to reflect or transmit more or less of the incident light, varying from black to white for surface colors and from black to colorless for transparent volume colors.

light·ness² (lītʹnĭs) *n.* **1.** The state or quality of having little weight or force. **2.** Ease or quickness of movement; agility. **3.** Ease or cheerfulness in manner or style. **4.** Freedom from worry or trouble. **5.** Lack of appropriate seriousness; levity. **6.** Delicacy or subtlety in craft, performance, or effect.

light·ning (lītʹnĭng) *n.* **1a.** An abrupt discontinuous natural electric discharge in the atmosphere. **b.** The visible flash of light accompanying such a discharge. **2.** *Informal* A sudden, usu. improbable stroke of fortune. ❖ *intr.v.* **-ninged** (-nīngd), **-ning, -nings** To discharge a flash of lightning. ❖ *adj.* Moving or occurring with remarkable speed or suddenness. [ME, gerund of *lightnen,* to illuminate < *lighten* < OE *līhtan.* See **leuk-** in App.]

lightning arrester *n.* A protective device for electrical equipment that reduces excessive voltage resulting from lightning to a safe level by grounding the discharge.

lightning bug *n.* See **firefly.**

lightning rod *n.* **1.** A grounded metal rod placed high on a structure to prevent damage by conducting lightning to the ground. **2.** One that attracts and absorbs typically negative feelings and reactions, being a diversion from other issues.

light opera *n.* See **operetta.**

lighthouse
Yaquina Head lighthouse,
Newport, Oregon

ă	pat	oi	boy
ā	pay	ou	out
âr	care	ŏŏ	took
ä	father	ōō	boot
ĕ	pet	ŭ	cut
ē	be	ûr	urge
ĭ	pit	th	thin
ī	pie	*th*	this
îr	pier	hw	which
ŏ	pot	zh	vision
ō	toe	ə	about,
ô	paw		item

Stress marks:
ʹ (primary);
ʹ (secondary), as in
lexicon (lĕkʹsĭ-kŏnʹ)

light pen *n.* A small photosensitive device connected to a computer and moved by hand over an output display to manipulate information in the computer.

light·proof (līt′prōōf′) *adj.* Impenetrable by light.

lights (līts) *pl.n.* The lungs, esp. the lungs of an animal slaughtered for food. [ME *lightes* < *light*, light in weight (< the lightness of the lungs compared to other organs). See LIGHT².]

light·ship (līt′shǐp′) *n.* A ship with powerful lights or warning signals that is anchored in dangerous waters to alert other vessels.

light show *n.* A display of colored lights in shifting patterns, often accompanied by slides and film loops.

light·some¹ (līt′səm) *adj.* **1.** Providing light; luminous. **2.** Covered with or full of light; bright. —**light′some·ly** *adv.* —**light′some·ness** *n.*

light·some² (līt′səm) *adj.* **1.** Light, nimble, or graceful in movement. **2.** Free from worry or care; cheerful. **3.** Frivolous; silly. —**light′some·ly** *adv.* —**light′some·ness** *n.*

lights out *n.* **1.** A signal or command to extinguish lights for the night. **2.** Bedtime.

light-struck (līt′strŭk′) *adj.* Fogged by accidental exposure. Used of photosensitive materials.

light water *n.* Ordinary water, H_2O.

light·weight (līt′wāt′) *n.* **1.** One that weighs relatively little or less than average. **2.** *Sports* **a.** A professional boxer weighing more than 126 and not more than 135 pounds (approx. 57–61 kilograms), heavier than a featherweight and lighter than a welterweight. **b.** A contestant in various other sports in a similar weight class. **3.** A person of little ability, intelligence, influence, or importance. ❖ *adj.* **1.** Weighing relatively little; not heavy. **2.** *Sports* Of, relating to, or characteristic of a lightweight. **3.** Having no significance or influence.

light·wood (līt′wōōd′) *n. Chiefly Southern US* See **kindling.** See Regional Note at **kindling.**

light-year also **light year** (līt′yîr′) *n.* **1.** The distance that light travels in a vacuum in one year, approx. 9.46 trillion (9.46×10^{12}) kilometers or 5.88 trillion (5.88×10^{12}) miles. **2.** *Informal* A long way. Often used in the plural.

lig·ne·ous (lǐg′nē-əs) *adj.* Consisting of or having the texture or appearance of wood; woody. [< Lat. *ligneus* < *lignum*, wood. See **leg-** in App.]

ligni– or **ligno–** or **lign–** *pref.* Wood; lignocellulose. [< Lat. *lignum*, wood. See **leg-** in App.]

lig·ni·fy (lǐg′nə-fī′) *v.* **-fied, -fy·ing, -fies** —*intr.* To turn into wood or become woody through the formation and deposit of lignin in cell walls. —*tr.* To make woody or woodlike by the deposit of lignin. —**lig′ni·fi·ca′tion** (-fĭ-kā′shən) *n.*

lig·nin (lǐg′nǐn) *n.* A complex polymer, the chief noncarbohydrate constituent of wood, that binds to cellulose fibers and hardens and strengthens the cell walls of plants.

lig·nite (lǐg′nīt′) *n.* A soft brownish coal in which the alteration of vegetable matter is further along than in peat but not as far as in bituminous coal. —**lig·nit′ic** (-nǐt′ĭk) *adj.*

lig·no·cel·lu·lose (lǐg′nō-sĕl′yə-lōs′) *n.* A combination of lignin and cellulose that strengthens woody plant cells.

lig·num vi·tae (lǐg′nəm vī′tē) *n., pl.* **lignum vitaes 1.** Either of two tropical American trees (*Guaiacum officinale* or *G. sanctum*) having evergreen leaves and very heavy durable wood. **2.** The wood of either of these trees. [NLat. *lignum vitae* : Lat. *lignum*, wood + Lat. *vītae*, genitive of *vīta*, life.]

lig·ro·in (lǐg′rō-ĭn) *n.* A volatile flammable fraction of petroleum, distilled and used as a solvent. [Ger.]

lig·u·la (lǐg′yə-lə) *n., pl.* **-lae** (-lē′) or **-las** A strap-shaped or tonguelike structure, esp. a mouth part in certain insects. [Lat., dim. of *lingua*, tongue. See **dnghū-** in App.]

lig·u·late (lǐg′yə-lĭt, -lāt′) *adj.* **1.** Strap-shaped. **2.** Having a ligule.

lig·ule (lǐg′yōōl) *n.* A straplike structure, such as a membranous or hairy appendage between the sheaf and blade of a grass leaf. [Lat. *ligula*, dim. of *lingua*, tongue. See **dnghū-** in App.]

lig·ure (lǐg′yōōr′) *n.* A precious stone of ancient Israel. [ME *liguri* < LLat. *ligūrius* < Gk. *ligūrion*, dim. of *ligūros*, a precious stone < *ligus*.]

Li·gu·ri·a (lǐ-gyōōr′ē-ə) A region of NW Italy on the **Ligurian Sea,** an arm of the Mediterranean between NW Italy and Corsica; subdued by the Romans in the 2nd cent. B.C. and later (16th–19th cent. A.D.) controlled by Genoa. A small section of the coastline formed the **Ligurian Republic** (1797–1815). —**Li·gu′ri·an** *adj. & n.*

lik·a·ble also **like·a·ble** (lī′kə-bəl) *adj.* Pleasing; attractive. —**lik′a·ble·ness** *n.*

like¹ (līk) *v.* **liked, lik·ing, likes** —*tr.* **1.** To find pleasant or attractive; enjoy. **2.** To want to have: *would like some coffee.* **3.** To feel about; regard. **4.** *Archaic* To be pleasing to. —*intr.* **1.** To have an inclination or a preference: *If you like, we can go.* **2.** *Scots* To be pleased. ❖ *n.* Something that is liked; a preference. [ME *liken* < OE *līcian*, to please.]

like² (līk) *prep.* **1.** Possessing the characteristics of; resembling closely; similar to. **2a.** In the typical manner of: *It's not like you to take offense.* **b.** In the same way as: *lived like royalty.* **3.** Inclined or disposed to: *felt like running away.* **4.** As if the probability exists for: *looks like a bad year for farmers.* **5.** Such as; for example: saved things like old newspapers. ❖ *adj.* **1.** Possessing the same or almost the same characteristics; similar: *on this and like occasions.* **2.** Alike: *as like as two siblings.* **3.** Having equivalent value or quality. Usu. used in negative sentences: *There's nothing like a good night's sleep.* ❖ *adv.* **1.** In the manner of being; as if. Used as an intensifier of action: *ran like crazy.* **2.** *Informal* Probably; likely: *Like as not she'll change her mind.* **3.** Nearly; approximately: *a price more like 50 dollars.* **4.** *Nonstandard* Used to provide emphasis or a pause: *Like let's get going.* ❖ *n.* **1.** One similar to or like another. Used with *the*: *coughs and the like.* **2.** *Informal* An equivalent or similar person or thing. Often used in the plural: *never seen the likes of this before.* ❖ *conj. Usage Problem* **1.** In the same way that; as: *to dance like she does.* **2.** As if: *It looks like we'll finish.* [ME < *like*, similar (< OE *gelīc* and ON *līkr*) and < *like*, similarly (< OE *gelīce* < *gelīc*, similar).]

like³ (līk) also **liked** (līkt) *aux.v. Chiefly Southern US* Used with a past infinitive or with *to* and a simple past form to indicate being just on the point of or coming near to having done something in the past: *I like to died when I saw that.* [ME *liken*, to compare < *like*, similar. See LIKE².]

–like *suff.* Resembling or characteristic of: *ladylike.* [ME < *like*, similar. See LIKE².]

like·li·hood (līk′lē-hōōd′) *n.* **1.** The state of being probable; probability. **2.** Something probable.

like·ly (līk′lē) *adj.* **-li·er, -li·est 1.** Possessing or displaying the qualities or characteristics that make something probable: *likely to become angry.* See Usage Note at **liable. 2.** Within the realm of credibility; plausible: *not a likely excuse.* **3.** Apparently appropriate or suitable: *several likely candidates.* **4.** Apt to achieve success or yield a desired outcome; promising. **5.** Attractive; pleasant: *a likely spot for the picnic.* ❖ *adv.* Probably. [ME *likly* < OE *gelīclic* (< *gelīc*, similar), and < ON *līkligr* (< *līkr*, similar).]

like-mind·ed (līk′mīn′dĭd) *adj.* Of the same turn of mind.

lik·en (lī′kən) *tr.v.* **-ened, -en·ing, -ens** To see, mention, or show as similar. [ME *liknen* < *like*, similar. See LIKE².]

like·ness (līk′nĭs) *n.* **1.** The state, quality, or fact of being like; resemblance. **2.** An imitative appearance; a semblance. **3.** A pictorial, graphic, or sculptured representation of something.

like·wise (līk′wīz′) *adv.* **1.** In the same way; similarly. **2.** As well; also.

lik·ing (lī′kĭng) *n.* **1.** A feeling of attraction or love; fondness. **2.** Preference or taste.

li·lac (lī′lək, -lŏk, -lăk) *n.* **1.** Any of various shrubs of the genus *Syringa*, esp. *S. vulgaris*, having clusters of fragrant purplish or white flowers. **2.** A pale to light or moderate purple. [Obsolete Fr. < Ar. *līlak* < MPers. *nīlak* < *nīl*, indigo < Skt. *nīlī- < nīla-*, dark blue.] —**li′lac** *adj.*

li·lan·ge·ni (lǐ-läng′gĕ-nē) *n., pl.* **em·a·lan·ge·ni** (ĕm′ə-läng-gĕn′ē) [Swati (Nguni language of South Africa and Swaziland) : *li-*, sing. n. pref. + *-langeni*, money.]

Lil·ith (lĭl′ĭth) *n.* **1.** A female spirit in ancient Semitic legend, alleged to haunt deserted places and attack children. **2.** The first wife of Adam in Jewish folklore, believed to have been created before Eve. [Heb. *lîlît* < Akkadian *lilîtu* < Sumerian *lilla*, a demon.]

Li·li·u·o·ka·la·ni (lə-lē′ə-ō-kə-lä′nē, lē-lē′ō-ōō-kä-lä′nē) 1838–1917. Queen of the Hawaiian Is. (1891–93) who was the last Hawaiian ruler to govern the islands.

Lille (lēl) A city of N France NNE of Paris near the Belgian border; founded c. 1030. Pop. 172,149.

Lil·li·pu·tian also **Lil·li·pu·tian** (lĭl′ə-pyōō′shən) *n.* A very small person or being. ❖ *adj.* **1.** Very small; diminutive. **2.** Trivial; petty. [After *Lilliput*, a country in *Gulliver's Travels* by Jonathan Swift, where everything was diminutive.]

Liliuokalani
c. 1891 photograph by Menzies Dickson
(c. 1840–91)

Li·long·we (lĭ-lông′wā) The cap. of Malawi, in the S-central part; founded in the 1940s. Pop. 233,973.

lilt (lĭlt) *n.* **1.** A cheerful or lively manner of speaking, in which the pitch of the voice varies pleasantly. **2.** A light happy tune or song. **3.** A light or resilient manner of moving or walking. ❖ *v.* **lilt·ed, lilt·ing, lilts** —*tr.* To say, sing, or play (something) in a cheerful rhythmic manner. —*intr.* **1.** To speak, sing, or play with liveliness or rhythm. **2.** To move with lightness and buoyancy. [< ME *lulten, lilten,* to sound an alarm.]

lil·y (lĭl′ē) *n., pl.* **-ies 1.** Any of various plants of the genus *Lilium,* having variously colored, often trumpet-shaped flowers. **2.** Any of various similar or related plants, such as the day lily or the water lily. **3.** The flower of any of these plants. [ME *lilie* < OE < Lat. *līlium.*]

lily family *n.* A large family of plants, the Liliaceae, marked by showy flowers with six perianth segments, six stamens, and a superior ovary and usu. producing bulbs or rhizomes.

lil·y-liv·ered (lĭl′ē-lĭv′ərd) *adj.* Cowardly; timid. [< LILY, pale, bloodless.]

lily of the Nile *n., pl.* **lilies of the Nile** See **African lily.**

lily of the valley *n., pl.* **lilies of the valley** A widely cultivated ornamental European plant (*Convallaria majalis*) having one-sided racemes of fragrant bell-shaped white flowers.

lily pad *n.* One of the floating leaves of a water lily.

lil·y-trot·ter (lĭl′ē-trŏt′ər) *n.* See **jaçana.**

lil·y-white (lĭl′ē-hwīt′, -wīt′) *adj.* **1.** White as a lily. **2.** Beyond reproach; blameless. **3.** *Informal* Excluding or seeking to exclude Black people.

lim *abbr. Mathematics* limit

Li·ma (lē′mə) The cap. and largest city of Peru, in the W-central part near the Pacific Ocean; founded by Pizarro in 1535. Pop. 6,414,500.

li·ma bean (lī′mə) *n.* **1.** Any of several varieties of a tropical American plant (*Phaseolus limensis*) having flat pods containing large light green edible seeds. **2.** The seed of this plant. [After LIMA, Peru.]

lim·a·cine (lĭm′ə-sēn′, lī′mə-) *adj.* Of, relating to, or resembling a slug. [< Lat. *līmāx, līmāc-,* slug, snail; akin to *līmus,* slime.]

limb¹ (lĭm) *n.* **1.** One of the larger branches of a tree. **2.** One of the jointed appendages of an animal used for locomotion or grasping. **3.** An extension or projecting part, as of a building or mountain range. **4.** One regarded as an extension, member, or representative of a larger body or group. **5.** *Informal* An impish child. ❖ *tr.v.* **limbed, limb·ing, limbs** To dismember. —*idiom:* **(out) on a limb** *Informal* In a difficult, awkward, or vulnerable position. [Alteration (prob. influenced by LIMB²) of ME *lim* < OE.]

limb² (lĭm) *n.* **1.** *Astronomy* The circumferential edge of the apparent disk of a celestial body. **2.** *Mathematics* The edge of a graduated arc or circle used in an instrument to measure angles. **3.** *Botany* The expanded tip of a plant organ, such as a petal or corolla lobe. [ME, graduated edge of an astronomical instrument < OFr. *limbe* < Lat. *limbus,* border.]

lim·bate (lĭm′bāt′) *adj. Botany* Having an edge or margin of a different color. [LLat. *limbātus,* bordered < Lat. *limbus,* border.]

lim·ber¹ (lĭm′bər) *adj.* **1.** Bending or flexing readily; pliable. **2.** Capable of moving, bending, or contorting easily; supple. ❖ *v.* **-bered, -ber·ing, -bers** —*tr.* To make limber: *limbered up his legs.* —*intr.* To make oneself limber: *players limbering up before the game.* [?] —**lim′ber·ly** *adv.* —**lim′ber·ness** *n.*

lim·ber² (lĭm′bər) *n.* A two-wheeled horse-drawn vehicle used to tow a field gun or a caisson. [Alteration of ME *limour,* shaft of a cart, perh. < *limon* < OFr.]

lim·bers (lĭm′bərz) *pl.n.* Gutters or channels on each side of a ship's keelson that drain bilge water into the pump well. [Prob. alteration of Fr. *lumière,* one of the limbers < OFr. *lumiere,* opening, light < LLat. *lūmināria,* pl. of *lūmināre,* window < Lat., lamp. See LUMINARY.]

lim·bic (lĭm′bĭk) *adj.* **1.** Of, relating to, or characterized by a limbus. **2.** Of or relating to the limbic system. [Fr. *limbique* < *limbe,* edge < OFr., graduated edge. See LIMB².]

limbic system *n.* A group of interconnected deep brain structures, common to all mammals and involved in olfaction, emotion, motivation, behavior, and various autonomic functions.

lim·bo¹ (lĭm′bō) *n., pl.* **-bos 1.** often **Limbo** *Roman Catholic Church* The abode in the afterlife for souls excluded from full blessedness but not condemned to punishment, as for unbaptized but innocent or virtuous persons. **2.** A region or condition of oblivion or neglect: *My promotion was in limbo for months.* **3.** A state or place of confinement. **4.** An intermediate place or state. [ME < Med.Lat. *(in) limbō,* (in) Limbo, ablative of *limbus,* Limbo < Lat., border.]

lim·bo² (lĭm′bō) *n., pl.* **-bos** A West Indian dance in which the dancers keep bending over backward and passing under a pole that is lowered each time. [Prob. ult. of African orig.]

Lim·burg (lĭm′bûrg′, -bœrkʰ′) A former duchy of NW Europe; founded in the 11th cent. and divided into the Dutch and Belgian provinces of Limburg in 1839.

Lim·burg·er (lĭm′bûr′gər) *n.* A soft white cheese with a very strong odor and flavor. [Flem., one from Limburg, after *Limburg,* a province of northeast Belgium.]

lim·bus (lĭm′bəs) *n., pl.* **-bi** (-bī′) *Biology* A distinctive border or edge. [Lat., border.]

lime¹ (līm) *n.* **1.** A spiny Asian evergreen shrub or tree (*Citrus aurantifolia*) having leathery leaves, fragrant white flowers, and edible fruit. **2.** The fruit of this plant, having a green rind and acid juice used as flavoring. [Prob. French < Sp. *lima* < Ar. *līma, līm,* prob. < *līmūn,* lemon. See LEMON.]

lime² (līm) *n.* See **linden.** [Alteration of ME *line* < OE *lind.*]

lime³ (līm) *n.* **1a.** See **calcium oxide. b.** Any of various mineral and industrial forms of calcium oxide differing chiefly in water content and percentage of constituents such as silica, alumina, and iron. **2.** Birdlime. ❖ *tr.v.* **limed, lim·ing, limes 1.** To treat with lime. **2.** To smear with birdlime. **3.** To catch or snare with or as if with birdlime. [ME *lim* < OE *līm,* birdlime.] —**lim′y** *adj.*

lime·ade (lī-mād′) *n.* A sweetened beverage of lime juice and plain or carbonated water.

lime·kiln (līm′kĭl′, -kĭln′) *n.* A furnace used to reduce naturally occurring forms of calcium carbonate to lime.

lime·light (līm′līt′) *n.* **1.** A focus of public attention. **2a.** An early stage light in which lime was heated to incandescence. **b.** The brilliant white light so produced.

li·men (lī′mən) *n., pl.* **li·mens** or **lim·i·na** (lĭm′ə-nə) The threshold of a physiological or psychological response. [Lat. *līmen,* threshold.] —**lim′i·nal** (lĭm′ə-nəl) *adj.*

lim·er·ick (lĭm′ər-ĭk) *n.* A light humorous, nonsensical, or bawdy verse of five anapestic lines usu. with the rhyme scheme *aabba.* [After LIMERICK.]

Lim·er·ick (lĭm′ər-ĭk, lĭm′rĭk) A borough of SW Ireland on the Shannon R. estuary; an important Norse settlement in the 9th and 10th cent. Pop. 60,736.

lime·stone (līm′stōn′) *n.* A common sedimentary rock consisting mostly of calcium carbonate, $CaCO_3$, used as a building stone and in the manufacture of lime, carbon dioxide, and cement.

lime·wa·ter (līm′wô′tər, -wŏt′ər) *n.* A clear colorless alkaline aqueous solution of calcium hydroxide, used in calamine lotion and other skin preparations.

lim·ey (lī′mē) *n., pl.* **-eys** *Slang* **1.** A British sailor. **2.** An English person. [Short for *lime juicer* (< the use of lime juice on Brit. warships in order to prevent scurvy).]

li·mic·o·line (lī-mĭk′ə-lĭn′, -lĭn) *adj.* Of or relating to shore birds, esp. the plovers, sandpipers, and phalaropes. [< NLat. *Līmicolae,* former group name < pl. of LLat. *līmicola,* living in mud : Lat. *līmus,* slime + Lat. *-cola,* inhabitant; see —COLOUS.]

li·mic·o·lous (lī-mĭk′ə-ləs) *adj.* Living in mud. [< LLat. *līmicola.* See LIMICOLINE.]

lim·it (lĭm′ĭt) *n.* **1.** The point, edge, or line beyond which something cannot or may not proceed. **2. limits** The boundary surrounding a specific area; bounds. **3.** A confining or restricting object, agent, or influence. **4.** The greatest or least amount, number, or extent allowed or possible. **5.** *Games* The largest amount that may be bet at one time in games of chance. **6.** *Mathematics* A number or point k that is closely approximated by a function $f(x)$ when a suitable condition is placed on the independent variable $x,$ as when x increases beyond all bounds. **7.** *Informal* One that approaches or exceeds certain limits. ❖ *tr.v.* **-it·ed, -it·ing, -its 1.** To confine or restrict within a boundary or bounds. **2.** To fix definitely; to specify. [ME *limite* < OFr., border < Lat. *līmes, līmit-,* border, limit.] —**lim′it·a·ble** *adj.*

lim·i·tar·y (lĭm′ĭ-tĕr′ē) *adj. Archaic* **1a.** Of or relating to a limit or boundary. **b.** Limiting; restrictive. **2.** Limited.

lim·i·ta·tion (lĭm′ĭ-tā′shən) *n.* **1.** The act of limiting or the state of being limited. **2.** A restriction. **3.** A shortcoming or defect. **4.** *Law* A specified period during which, by statute, an action may be brought.

lim·it·ed (lĭm′ĭ-tĭd) *adj.* **1.** Confined or restricted within certain limits. **2a.** Not attaining the highest goals or level of achievement. **b.** Having only mediocre talent or range of ability. **3.** Having governmental or ruling powers restricted by enforceable limitations, as a constitution. **4.** Of, relating to, or being a limited company. **5.** Of, relating to, or being transportation facilities, such as trains or buses, that make few stops and carry relatively few passengers. ❖ *n.* A limited train or bus. —**lim′it·ed·ly** *adv.* —**lim′it·ed·ness** *n.*

limited company *n.* A firm, usu. British, organized in such a way as to give its owners limited liability.

limited edition *n.* An edition, as of a book or print, restricted to a specified number of copies.

limited liability *n.* The liability of a firm's owners for no more capital than they have invested in the business.

lim·it·er (lĭm′ĭ-tər) *n.* **1.** One that limits: *a limiter of choices.* **2.** *Electronics* A circuit that prevents the amplitude of a waveform from exceeding a specified value.

lim·it·ing (lĭm′ĭ-tĭng) *adj.* **1.** Acting as a limit. **2.** *Grammar* Restricting the range of application of the noun modified.

limit point *n.* See **limit 6.**

limn (lĭm) *tr.v.* **limned, limn·ing, limns 1.** To describe. **2.** To depict by painting or drawing. [ME *limnen,* to illuminate (a manuscript), prob. alteration of *luminen* < OFr. *luminer* < Lat. *lūmināre,* to illuminate, adorn < *lūmen, lūmin-,* light. See **leuk-** in App.] —**limn′er** (lĭm′nər) *n.*

lim·net·ic (lĭm-nĕt′ĭk) *adj.* Of or occurring in the deeper open

lily of the valley
Convallaria majalis

waters of lakes or ponds. [< Gk. *limnētēs*, marsh-dwelling < *limnē*, lake.]

lim•nol•o•gy (lĭm-nŏl′ə-jē) *n.* The scientific study of the life and phenomena of fresh water, esp. lakes and ponds. [Gk. *limnē*, lake + -LOGY.] **—lim′no•log′i•cal** (-nə-lŏj′ĭ-kəl) *adj.*

Lím•nos (lēm′nôs) See **Lemnos.**

lim•o (lĭm′ō) *n., pl.* **lim•os** *Informal* A limousine.

Li•moges (lē-mōzh′) A city of W-central France NE of Bordeaux; noted for its ceramic industry. Pop. 133,469.

lim•o•nene (lĭm′ə-nēn′) *n.* A liquid, $C_{10}H_{16}$, with a characteristic lemonlike fragrance, used as a solvent, wetting agent, and dispersing agent and in the manufacture of resins. [Fr. *limonène* < *limon*, lemon (obsolete) < OFr. See LEMON.]

li•mo•nite (lī′mə-nīt′) *n.* Any of a group of widely occurring iron oxide minerals, $Fe_2O_3{\cdot}nH_2O$, used as a minor ore of iron. [Ger. *Limonit* < Gk. *leimōn*, meadow.]

Li•mou•sin (lē-mōō-zăN′) A historical region and former province of central France W of the Auvergne Mts.; included in the dowry given by Eleanor of Aquitaine to Henry II of England in 1152 but reconquered by France (1370–74).

lim•ou•sine (lĭm′ə-zēn′, lĭm′ə-zēn′) *n.* **1.** Any of various large passenger vehicles, esp. a luxurious automobile usu. driven by a chauffeur. **2.** A van or small bus used to carry passengers esp. to airports and hotels. [Fr., perh. after LIMOUSIN.]

limp (lĭmp) *intr.v.* **limped, limp•ing, limps 1.** To walk lamely, esp. with irregularity, as if favoring one leg. **2.** To move or proceed haltingly or unsteadily: *The project limped along.* ❖ *n.* An irregular, jerky, or awkward gait. ❖ *adj.* **limp•er, limp•est 1.** Lacking or having lost rigidity, as of structure or substance. **2.** Lacking strength or firmness; weak or spiritless. [Prob. < obsolete *lymphault*, lame < OE *lemphealt* : *lemp-*, hanging loosely + *-healt*, lame, limping.] **—limp′ly** *adv.* **—limp′ness** *n.*

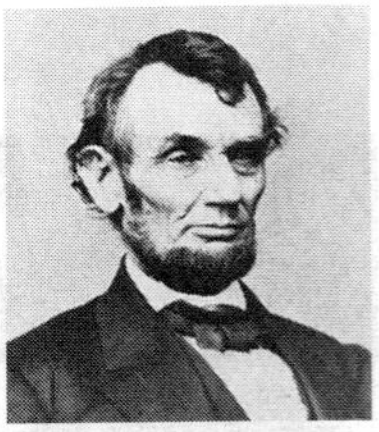

Abraham Lincoln
1864 photograph attributed to Mathew Brady

lim•pet (lĭm′pĭt) *n.* **1.** Any of numerous marine gastropod mollusks, as of the families Acmaeidae and Patellidae, having a conical shell and adhering to rocks of tidal areas. **2.** One that clings persistently. **3.** A type of explosive designed to cling to the hull of a ship and detonate on contact or signal. [Poss. ME *lempet*, European limpet (sense uncertain).]

lim•pid (lĭm′pĭd) *adj.* **1.** Transparent; clear: *a limpid pool.* **2.** Easily intelligible. **3.** Calm and untroubled. [Lat. *limpidus.*] **—lim•pid′i•ty, lim′pid•ness** *n.* **—lim′pid•ly** *adv.*

limp•kin (lĭmp′kĭn) *n.* A large brownish wading bird *(Aramus guarauna)* of warm swampy regions of the New World, having long legs and a drooping bill. [< its gait.]

Lim•po•po (lĭm-pō′pō) also **Crocodile River** A river of SE Africa rising in NE South Africa and flowing c. 1,770 km (1,100 mi) to the Indian Ocean in S Mozambique.

lim•u•lus (lĭm′yə-ləs) *n., pl.* **-li** (-lī, -lē) See **horseshoe crab.** [Lat. *līmulus*, sidelong (< its motion), dim. of *līmus.*]

Lin (lĭn), **Maya** b. 1959. Amer. sculptor and architect whose works include the Vietnam Veterans Memorial (1982).

lin. *abbr.* **1.** lineal **2.** linear

lin•ac (lĭn′ăk′) *n.* See **linear accelerator.** [LIN(EAR) AC(CELERATOR).]

lin•age also **line•age** (lī′nĭj) *n.* **1.** The number of lines of printed or written material. **2.** Payment for written work at a specified amount per line.

lin•al•o•ol (lĭ-năl′ō-ôl′, -ōl′, -ŏl′) *n.* A colorless fragrant liquid, $C_{10}H_{18}O$, distilled from essential oils, esp. rosewood and bergamot, and used in making perfume. [Sp. *lináloe*, aloe (< LLat. *lignum aloēs*, wood of the aloe : Lat. *lignum*, wood; see LIGNI- + Lat. *aloēs*, genitive of *aloē*, aloe; see ALOE) + -OL[1].]

Lin Biao (lĭn′ byou′) or **Lin Piao** (pyou′, byou′) 1907–71. Chinese political leader who fought to achieve a Communist takeover in China (1949).

linch•pin or **lynch•pin** (lĭnch′pĭn′) *n.* **1.** A locking pin inserted in the end of a shaft to prevent a wheel from slipping off. **2.** A central cohesive element. [ME *linspin* : *lins*, linchpin (< OE *lynis*) + *pin*, pin (< OE *pinn*; see PIN).]

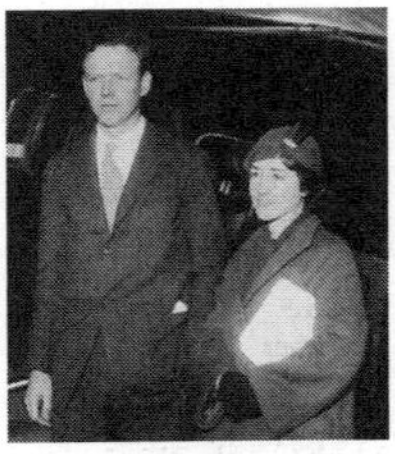

Charles and Anne Lindbergh

Lin•coln[1] (lĭng′kən) **1.** A borough of E England NE of Nottingham; first chartered 1157. Pop. 75,900. **2.** The cap. of NE, in the SE part SW of Omaha; founded 1864. Pop. 225,581.

Lin•coln[2] (lĭng′kən) *n.* Any of a breed of sheep with long wool, developed in Lincolnshire, a county of eastern England.

Lincoln, Abraham 1809–65. The 16th President of the US (1861–65), who led the Union during the Civil War and emancipated slaves in the South (1863); assassinated shortly after the end of the war by John Wilkes Booth. **—Lin′coln•esque′** *adj.*

Lincoln, Mary Todd 1818–82. First Lady of the US (1861–65); criticized for allegedly having Confederate sympathies.

Lincoln, Mount A peak, 4,357.2 m (14,286 ft), in the Park Range of the Rocky Mts. in central CO.

Lind (lĭnd), **Jenny** 1820–87. Swedish soprano who toured the US (1850–52).

lin•dane (lĭn′dān) *n.* A white crystalline powder, $C_6H_6Cl_6$, used chiefly as an agricultural pesticide but also used topically in the treatment of scabies and pediculosis. [After Teunis van der *Linden*, 20th-cent. Dutch chemist.]

Lind•bergh (lĭnd′bûrg′, lĭn′-), **Anne Spencer Morrow** 1906–2001. Amer. aviator and writer whose works include *Gift from the Sea* (1955).

Lindbergh, Charles Augustus Known as "Lucky Lindy." 1902–74. Amer. aviator who made the first solo transatlantic flight (May 20–21, 1927).

lin•den (lĭn′dən) *n.* Any of various deciduous shade trees of the genus *Tilia*, having heart-shaped leaves. [ME, made of linden wood < OE < *lind*, linden.]

Lin•dis•farne (lĭn′dĭs-färn′) See **Holy Island.**

Lind•say (lĭn′zē), **(Nicholas) Vachel** 1879–1931. Amer. poet who wrote *General William Booth Enters Heaven* (1913).

lin•dy or **Lin•dy** (lĭn′dē) *n., pl.* **-dies** A lively swing dance for couples. [After *Lindy*, nickname of Charles A. LINDBERGH.]

line[1] (līn) *n.* **1.** *Mathematics* A geometric figure formed by a point moving along a fixed direction and the reverse direction. **2a.** A thin continuous mark, as that made by a pen, pencil, or brush applied to a surface. **b.** A similar mark cut or scratched into a surface. **c.** A crease in the skin, esp. on the face; a wrinkle. **3a.** A real or imaginary mark positioned in relation to fixed points of reference. **b.** A degree or circle of longitude or latitude drawn on a map or globe. **c.** The equator. **4a.** A border or boundary. **b.** A demarcation. **c.** A contour or outline. **5a.** A mark used to define a shape or represent a contour. **b.** Any of the marks that make up the formal design of a picture. **6a.** A cable, rope, string, cord, or wire. **b.** *Nautical* A rope put to use aboard a ship. **c.** A fishing line. **d.** A clothesline. **e.** A cord or tape used for measuring, leveling, or straightening. **7.** A pipe or system of pipes for conveying a fluid: *gas lines.* **8.** An electric-power transmission cable. **9a.** A wire or system of wires connecting telephone or telegraph systems. **b.** An open or functioning telephone connection. **10a.** A passenger or cargo system of public or private transportation usu. over a definite route. **b.** A company owning or managing such a system. **11a.** A railway track or system of tracks. **b.** A particular section of a railway network. **12.** A course of progress or movement; a route. **13a.** A general method, manner, or course of procedure. **b.** A manner or course of procedure determined by a specified factor: *along socialist lines.* **c.** An official or prescribed policy. **14.** A general concept or model. Often used in the plural. **15.** A condition of agreement; alignment. **16a.** One's trade, occupation, or field of interest. **b.** Range of competence: *not in my line.* **17.** Merchandise or services of a similar or related nature: *a line of tools.* **18.** A group of persons or things arranged in a row or series. **19a.** Ancestry or lineage. **b.** A series of persons, esp. from one family, who succeed each other. **c.** A strain, as of livestock or plants, developed and maintained by selective breeding. **20a.** A sequence of related things that leads to a certain ending: *a line of argument.* **b.** An ordered system of operations that allows a sequential manufacture or assembly of goods. **c.** The personnel of an organization or business who actually make a product or perform a service. **21a.** A horizontal row of printed or written words or symbols. **b.** One of the horizontal scans forming a television image. **22.** A brief letter; a note. **23a.** A unit of verse ending in a visual or typographic break and generally characterized by its length and meter. **b.** The dialogue of a theatrical presentation. Often used in the plural. **24.** *Informal* Glib or insincere talk. **25. lines** *Chiefly British* **a.** A marriage certificate. **b.** A number of lines of prose or verse to be written out by a pupil as punishment. **26.** *Games* A horizontal demarcation on a scorecard in bridge dividing the bonus points from the points for making the contract. **27a.** A source of information. **b.** The information itself. **28a.** *Music* One of the five parallel marks constituting a staff. **b.** A sustained melodic or harmonic part in a piece. **29a.** A formation in which elements, such as troops, are arranged abreast of one another. **b.** The battle area closest to the enemy; the front. **c.** The combat troops or warships at the front. **d.** The regular forces of an army or a navy. **e.** The class of officers in direct command of warships or of army combat units. **f.** A bulwark or trench. **g.** An extended system of fortifications or defenses. **30.** *Sports* **a.** A foul line. **b.** A real or imaginary mark demarcating a specified section of a playing area or field. **c.** A real or imaginary mark or point at which a race begins or ends. **d.** The center and two wings making up a hockey team's offensive unit. **e.** *Football* A line of scrimmage. **f.** *Football* The linemen considered as a group. **31.** *Informal* The odds a bookmaker gives, esp. for sports events. **32.** The proportion of an insurance risk assumed by a particular underwriter or company. **33.** *Slang* A small amount of cocaine arranged in a thin strip for sniffing. **34.** *Archaic* One's lot or position in life. ❖ *v.* **lined, lin•ing, lines** *—tr.* **1.** To mark, incise, or cover with a line or lines. **2.** To represent with lines. **3.** To place in a series or row. **4.** To form a bordering line along. **5.** *Baseball* To hit (a ball) sharply so that it flies low and fast. *—intr. Baseball* To hit a line drive: *lined out to shortstop.* ***—phrasal verb:* line up 1.** To arrange in or form a line. **2.** *Football* To take one's position in a formation before a snap or kickoff. **3.** To organize and make ready. ***—idioms:* all along the line 1.** In every place. **2.** At every stage or moment. **down the line 1.** All the way; throughout. **2.** At a point or an end in the future. **in line for** Next in order for. **on the line 1.** Ready or available for immediate payment. **2.** So as to be risked; in jeopardy. **out of line 1.** Uncalled-for; improper. **2.** Unruly and out of control. [ME < OE *līne* and < OFr. *ligne*, both < Lat. *līnea*, string, cord < fem. of *līneus*, of linen < *līnum*, thread, linen.]

line[2] (līn) *tr.v.* **lined, lin•ing, lines 1.** To fit a covering to the inside surface of. **2.** To cover the inner surface of. **3.** To fill plentifully, as with money or food. **—idiom: line (one's) pockets** To make a profit, esp. by illegitimate means. [ME *linen < line*, flax, linen cloth < OE *līn < Lat. līnum.*]

lin·e·age¹ (lĭn′ē-ĭj) *n.* **1a.** Direct descent from a particular ancestor; ancestry. **b.** Derivation. **2.** The descendants of a common ancestor considered to be the founder of the line. [ME *linage, lineage < OFr. lignage < ligne*, line. See LINE¹.]

line·age² (lī′nĭj) *n.* Variant of **linage.**

lin·e·al (lĭn′ē-əl) *adj.* **1.** Belonging to or being in the direct line of descent from an ancestor. **2.** Derived from or relating to a particular line of descent; hereditary. **3.** Linear. [ME < OFr. < LLat. *lineālis*, consisting of lines < Lat. *līnea*, line. See LINE¹.] **—lin′e·al·ly** *adv.*

lin·e·a·ment (lĭn′ē-ə-mənt) *n.* **1.** A distinctive shape, contour, or line, esp. of the face. **2.** A definitive or characteristic feature. Often used in the plural. [ME *liniament* < Lat. *līneāmentum < līnea*, line. See LINE¹.]

lin·e·ar (lĭn′ē-ər) *adj.* **1.** Of, relating to, or resembling a line; straight. **2a.** In, of, describing, described by, or related to a straight line. **b.** Having only one dimension. **3.** Characterized by, composed of, or emphasizing drawn lines rather than painterly effects. **4.** *Botany* Narrow and elongated with nearly parallel margins: *a linear leaf.* [Lat. *līneāris < līnea*, line. See LINE¹.] **—lin′e·ar·ly** *adv.*

Linear A *n.* An undeciphered writing system used in Crete from the 18th to the 15th century B.C.

linear accelerator *n.* An electron, proton, or heavy-ion accelerator in which the paths of the particles accelerated are essentially straight lines rather than circles or spirals.

linear algebra *n.* **1.** The branch of mathematics that deals with systems of linear equations, matrices, vector spaces, determinants, and linear transformations. **2.** A ring that is also a vector space with scalars from an associated field, the multiplication of which is of the form (*aA*)(*bB*) = (*ab*)(**AB**), where *a* and *b* are scalars and **A** and **B** are vectors.

Linear B *n.* A syllabic script used in Mycenaean Greek documents chiefly from Crete and Pylos, mostly from the 14th to the 12th century B.C.

linear combination *n.* An expression of first order, composed of the sums and differences of elements with coefficients in a field, such as the field of real numbers.

linear dependence *n.* The property of a set of vectors having at least one linear combination equal to zero when at least one of the coefficients is not equal to zero.

linear equation *n.* An algebraic equation, such as $y = 2x + 7$, in which the highest degree term in the variable or variables is of the first degree.

linear independence *n.* The property of a set of vectors of having no linear combinations equal to zero unless all of the coefficients are equal to zero.

lin·e·ar·ize (lĭn′ē-ə-rīz′) *tr.v.* **-ized, -iz·ing, -iz·es** To put or project linearly. **—lin′e·ar·i·za′tion** (-ər-ĭ-zā′shən) *n.*

linear measure *n.* **1.** The measurement of length. **2.** A unit or system of units for measuring length.

linear momentum *n.* See **momentum** 1.

linear perspective *n.* A form of perspective in drawing and painting in which parallel lines are represented as converging so as to give the illusion of depth and distance.

lin·e·a·tion (lĭn′ē-ā′shən) *n.* **1.** The act of marking or outlining with lines. **2.** An outline. **3.** An arrangement of lines. [ME *lineacioun* < Lat. *līneātiō, līneātiōn- < līneātus*, p. part. of *līneāre*, to make straight < *līnea*, thread, line. See LINE¹.]

line·back·er (līn′băk′ər) *n. Football* Any of the defensive players forming a second line of defense behind the ends and tackles. **—line′back′ing** *n.*

line breeding *n.* Selective inbreeding to perpetuate certain desired qualities or characteristics in a strain of livestock.

line cut *n.* A letterpress printing plate made from a line drawing by a photoengraving process.

line dance *n.* A dance in which participants line up in rows and follow a choreographed pattern of steps to country music. **—line dance** *v.* **—line dancer** *n.*

line drawing *n.* A drawing made with lines only, esp. one used as copy for a line cut.

line drive *n. Baseball* A batted ball hit sharply so that it flies low and fast, usu. in a straight line.

line engraving *n.* **1a.** A metal plate, used in intaglio printing, on which design lines have been engraved by hand. **b.** The process of making such an engraving. **c.** A print made from such an engraving. **2.** See **line cut.**

Line Islands A group of islands in the central Pacific Ocean S of HI; now part of Kiribati.

line item *n.* A single item, esp. of a legislative appropriations bill.

line-i·tem veto (līn′ī′təm) *n.* Authority, as of a government executive, to reject provisions of a bill individually.

line·man (līn′mən) *n.* **1.** A person employed to install or repair telephone, telegraph, or electric power lines. **2.** *Football* A player positioned on the forward line.

lin·en (lĭn′ən) *n.* **1a.** Thread made from fibers of the flax plant. **b.** Cloth woven from this thread. **2.** Articles made from linen or

a similar cloth; bed sheets and tablecloths. Often used in the plural. **3.** Paper made from flax fibers or having a linenlike luster. ❖ *adj.* **1.** Made of flax or linen. **2.** Resembling linen. [ME < OE *līnen*, made of flax < Germanic *līnīn- < *līnam*, flax, prob. < Lat. *līnum.*]

line of credit *n., pl.* **lines of credit** See **credit line** 2.

line officer *n.* A commissioned officer in the armed forces who is assigned to the line for duty.

line of force *n., pl.* **lines of force** An imaginary line whose direction at any point is that of the field of force at that point.

line of scrimmage *n., pl.* **lines of scrimmage** *Football* Either of two imaginary lines parallel to the goal line at the ends of the ball as it rests prior to being snapped and at which each team lines up for a new play.

line of sight *n., pl.* **lines of sight** **1.** An imaginary line from the eye to a perceived object. **2.** An unobstructed path between sending and receiving antennas.

lin·e·o·late (lĭn′ē-ə-lāt′) *adj.* Marked with fine lines. [NLat. *līneolātus < Lat. līneola*, dim. of *līnea*, thread, line. See LINE¹.]

line printer *n.* A high-speed printing device, primarily used in data processing, that prints an entire line of type as a unit.

lin·er¹ (lī′nər) *n.* **1.** One that draws or makes lines. **2.** A large commercial ship or airplane, esp. one carrying passengers on a regular route. **3.** *Baseball* A line drive.

lin·er² (lī′nər) *n.* **1.** One that makes or puts in linings. **2a.** A lining. **b.** Material used as a lining. **3.** A woman's undergarment; a full-length slip. **4.** A jacket for a phonograph record.

lin·er·board (lī′nər-bôrd′, -bōrd′) *n.* A type of paperboard used in making corrugated cartons.

liner notes *pl.n.* Explanatory notes about a record album, cassette, or compact disk included on the jacket or in the packaging.

line score *n.* A summary of the scoring by period in a game displayed in a horizontal table, esp. an inning-by-inning record of the runs scored in a baseball game.

lines·man (līnz′mən) *n.* **1** *Football* An official who marks the downs and the position of the ball and watches for violations from the sidelines. **2.** *Sports* **a.** An official in various court games whose chief duty is to call shots that fall out of bounds. **b.** An official in soccer and other field games who indicates when the ball has gone out of bounds. **c.** An official in ice hockey whose chief duty is to call offsides and icing. **3.** See **lineman** 1.

line spectrum *n.* A spectrum appearing as distinct lines characteristic of the chemical elements in a luminous gas.

line squall *n.* A squall or a series of squalls occurring along a narrow band of thunderstorms.

lines·wom·an (līnz′wŏom′ən) *n.* **1.** A woman official in various court games who calls shots that are out of bounds. **2.** A woman official in soccer and other field games who indicates when the ball has gone out of bounds. **3.** A woman official in ice hockey whose chief duty is to call offsides and icing.

line·up (līn′ŭp′) *n.* **1.** A line of people that is formed for inspection or identification. **2.** *Sports* **a.** The members of a team chosen to start a game. **b.** A list of such players. **3.** A group of people, organizations, or things enlisted or arrayed for a purpose.

ling¹ (lĭng) *n., pl.* **ling** or **lings** Any of various marine food fishes related to or resembling the cod, esp. *Molva molva.* [ME, poss. of LGer. orig. See **del-** in App.]

ling² (lĭng) *n.* See **heather** 1. [ME < ON *lyng.*]

-ling¹ *suff.* **1.** One connected with: *worldling.* **2.** One having a specified quality: *underling.* **3.** One that is young, small, or inferior: *duckling.* [ME < OE.]

-ling² *suff.* In a specified direction, manner, way, or condition: *darkling.* [ME < OE.]

Lin·ga·la (lĭng-gä′lə) *n.* A creole based on Bantu, widely spoken as a lingua franca in Congo (formerly Zaire).

lin·gam (lĭng′gəm) also **lin·ga** (lĭng′gə) *n. Hinduism* A stylized phallus worshiped as a symbol of the god Shiva. [Skt. *liṅgam*, mark, penis.]

ling·ber·ry (lĭng′bĕr′ē) *n.* See **cowberry.** [Variant of LINGON-BERRY.]

ling·cod (lĭng′kŏd′) *n., pl.* **lingcod** or **-cods** A large northern Pacific food fish (*Ophiodon elongatus*).

lin·ger (lĭng′gər) *v.* **-gered, -ger·ing, -gers** *—intr.* **1.** To be slow in leaving, esp. out of reluctance. See Syns at **stay¹**. **2.** To remain feebly alive for some time before dying. **3.** To persist: *an odor that lingered.* **4.** To proceed slowly; saunter. **5.** To be tardy in acting; procrastinate. *—tr.* To pass (a period of time) slowly, leisurely, or aimlessly. [ME *lengeren*, freq. of *lengen*, to prolong < OE *lengan*. See **del-** in App.] **—lin′ger·er** *n.* **—lin′ger·ing·ly** *adv.*

lin·ge·rie (län′zhə-rā′, län′zhə-rē, län-zhə-rē′) *n.* **1.** Women's underwear. **2.** *Archaic* Linen articles, esp. garments. [Fr. < OFr. < *linge*, linen < Lat. *līneus*, made of linen < *līnum*, flax.]

lin·go (lĭng′gō) *n., pl.* **-goes** **1.** Language that is unintelligible or unfamiliar. **2.** The specialized vocabulary of a particular field or discipline. [Prob. < Port. *lingoa* < Lat. *lingua*, language. See **dṇghū-** in App.]

lin·gon·ber·ry (lĭng′gən-bĕr′ē) *n.* See **cowberry.** [Swed. *lingon*, a kind of berry + BERRY.]

lin·gua (lĭng′gwə) *n., pl.* **-guae** (-gwē′) A tongue or tonguelike organ. [Lat., tongue, language. See **dṇghū-** in App.]

lingua fran·ca (frăng′kə) *n., pl.* **lingua fran·cas** (-kəz) also **lin-**

linear perspective
The Marriage of the Virgin,
1504, by Raphael

guae fran·cae (fräng′kē, frän′sē) **1.** A medium of communication between peoples of different languages. **2.** A mixture of Italian with Provençal, French, Spanish, Arabic, Greek, and Turkish, formerly spoken on the eastern Mediterranean coast. [Ital. : *lingua*, language + *franca*, Frankish (that is, European).]

lin·gual (lĭng′gwəl) *adj.* **1.** Of, relating to, or situated near the tongue or a tonguelike organ. **2.** *Linguistics* Pronounced with the tongue and other organs of speech. **3.** Of languages; linguistic. ❖ *n. Linguistics* A sound, such as (t), (l), and (n), that is pronounced with the tongue and other organs of speech.

lin·gui·ça (lĭng-gwē′sə, -sä, lĭn-) *n.* A highly seasoned Portuguese pork sausage flavored with garlic, onions, and pepper. [Port., prob. ult. < LLat. *longao*, large intestine < Lat. *longus*, long. See **del-** in App.]

lin·gui·ne also **lin·gui·ni** (lĭng-gwē′nē) *n.* Pasta in long flat thin strands. [Ital., pl. of *linguina*, dim. of *lingua*, tongue < Lat. See LINGUA.]

lin·guist (lĭng′gwĭst) *n.* **1.** A person who speaks several languages fluently. **2.** A specialist in linguistics. [Lat. *lingua*, language; see **dnghū-** in App. + −IST.]

lin·guis·tic (lĭng-gwĭs′tĭk) *adj.* Of or relating to language or linguistics. —**lin·guis′ti·cal·ly** *adv.*

linguistic atlas *n.* A set of maps recording the geographic distribution of variations in speech.

linguistic form *n.* A meaningful unit of language, such as an affix, word, phrase, or sentence.

linguistic geography *n.* The branch of linguistics that studies regional variations of speech. —**linguistic geographer** *n.*

lin·guis·tics (lĭng-gwĭs′tĭks) *n. (used with a sing. verb)* The study of the nature, structure, and variation of language.

lin·gu·late (lĭng′gyə-lāt′) *adj.* Shaped like a tongue. [Lat. *lingulātus* < *lingula*, dim. of *lingua*, tongue. See LINGUA.]

lin·i·ment (lĭn′ə-mənt) *n.* A medicinal fluid rubbed into the skin to soothe pain or relieve stiffness. [ME < LLat. *linimentum* < Lat. *linere*, *linīre*, to rub over, anoint.]

lin·ing (lī′nĭng) *n.* **1.** A covering or coating for an inside surface. **2.** Material used for such covering or coating.

link[1] (lĭngk) *n.* **1.** One of the rings or loops forming a chain. **2a.** A unit in a connected series of units. **b.** A unit in a transportation or communications system. **c.** A connecting element; a tie or bond. **3a.** An association; a relationship. **b.** A causal, parallel, or reciprocal relationship; a correlation. **4.** A cuff link. **5.** A unit of length used in surveying, equal to 0.01 chain, 7.92 inches, or about 20.12 centimeters. **6.** A rod or lever transmitting motion in a machine. **7.** *Computer Science* A segment of text or a graphical item that serves as a cross-reference between parts of a hypertext document or between files or hypertext documents. ❖ *v.* **linked**, **link·ing**, **links** —*tr.* **1.** To connect with or as if with a link. See Syns at **join.** **2.** *Computer Science* To make a hypertext link in. —*intr.* **1.** To become connected with or as if with a link. **2.** *Computer Science* To follow a hypertext link. [ME *linke*, of Scand. orig.; akin to ON *hlenkr, hlekkr*.] —**link′er** *n.*

link[2] (lĭngk) *n.* A torch formerly used for lighting one's way in the streets. [Poss. < Med.Lat. *linchinus, lichnus*, candle < Lat. *lychnus* < Gk. *lukhnos*, lamp. See **leuk-** in App.]

link·age (lĭng′kĭj) *n.* **1a.** The act or process of linking. **b.** The condition of being linked. **2.** A connection or relation; an association. **3.** A negotiating policy of making agreement on one issue dependent on progress toward another objective. **4.** A system of interconnected machine elements used to transmit power or motion. **5.** A measure of the induced voltage in a circuit, equal to the magnetic flux times the number of turns in the coil that surrounds it. **6.** *Genetics* An association between two or more genes such that the traits they control tend to be inherited together.

linkage group *n.* A pair or set of genes on a chromosome that tend to be transmitted together.

linked (lĭngkt) *adj.* **1.** Connected, esp. by or as if by links. **2.** *Genetics* Exhibiting linkage.

link·ing verb (lĭng′kĭng) *n.* See **copula** 1.

Lin·kö·ping (lĭn′chœ′pĭng) A city of SE Sweden SW of Stockholm; a noted intellectual center during the Middle Ages. Pop. 126,377.

links (lĭngks) *pl.n.* **1.** A golf course. **2.** *Scots* Relatively flat or undulating sandy turf-covered ground usu. along a seashore. [< OE *link*, ridge of land, hill < OE *hlinc*, ridge.]

link·up (lĭngk′ŭp′) *n.* **1.** The act of linking or connecting. **2.** Something that serves to link or join; a connection. **3.** A set of linked elements that forms a functioning system.

linn (lĭn) *n. Scots* **1.** A waterfall. **2.** A steep ravine. [Sc. Gael. *linne*, pool, waterfall.]

Lin·nae·us (lĭ-nē′əs, -nā′-), **Carolus** 1707–78. Swedish botanist and founder of the modern classification system for plants and animals. —**Lin·nae′an, Lin·ne′an** *adj.*

lin·net (lĭn′ĭt) *n.* **1.** A small Old World finch (*Carduelis cannabina*) having brownish plumage. A similar bird (*Carpodacus mexicanus*) of Mexico and the western United States. [Obsolete Fr. *linette* < OFr. < *lin* (< its feeding on flax seed) < Lat. *līnum*.]

Linn·he (lĭn′ē), **Loch** An inlet of the Atlantic Ocean on the W coast of Scotland, part of the Caledonian Canal waterway.

lin·o·le·ic acid (lĭn′ə-lē′ĭk, -lĕ′ĭk) *n.* An unsaturated fatty acid, C₁₇H₃₁COOH, that is essential to the human diet and occurs widely in drying oils. [Gk. *linon*, flax + OLEIC ACID.]

lin·o·len·ic acid (lĭn′ə-lĕn′ĭk) *n.* An unsaturated fatty acid, C₁₇H₂₉COOH, that is essential to the human diet and occurs in natural drying oils. [Blend of LINOLEIC ACID and −ENE.]

li·no·le·um (lĭ-nō′lē-əm) *n.* A durable washable material made by pressing heated linseed oil, rosin, powdered cork, and pigments onto a burlap or canvas backing and used as a covering esp. for floors. [Orig. a trademark.]

Li·no·type (lī′nə-tīp′) A trademark used for a machine that sets type on a metal slug, operated by a keyboard.

Lin Piao (lĭn′ pyou′, byou′) See **Lin Biao.**

lin·sang (lĭn′săng′) *n.* Any of several Asian or African catlike carnivorous mammals of the genera *Poiana* or *Prionodon*, having a spotted coat and a long banded tail. [Malay.]

lin·seed (lĭn′sēd′) *n.* The seed of flax, esp. when used as the source of linseed oil; flaxseed. [ME *linsed* < OE *līnsǣd* : *līn*, flax (< Lat. *līnum*) + *sǣd*, seed; see SEED.]

linseed oil *n.* A drying oil extracted from flaxseed and used in paints, varnishes, printing inks, and synthetic resins.

lin·sey-wool·sey (lĭn′zē-wŏol′zē) *n., pl.* **-seys** A coarse woven fabric of wool and cotton or of wool and linen. [ME *linsiwolsie* : alteration of *linen*, linen; see LINEN + *wolle*, wool; see WOOL.]

lin·stock (lĭn′stŏk′) *n.* A long forked stick for holding a match. [Obsolete *lyntstock*, alteration of Du. *lontstok* : *lont*, match + *stok*, stick (< MDu. *stoc*).]

lint (lĭnt) *n.* **1.** Clinging bits of fiber and fluff; fuzz. **2.** Downy material obtained by scraping linen cloth and used for dressing wounds. **3.** The mass of soft fibers surrounding the seeds of unginned cotton. [ME, var. of *linet* (< OFr. *linette*, grain of flax, dim. of *lin*, flax) or < Med.Lat. *linteum*, lint (< Lat., linen cloth), both < Lat. *līnum*, flax.] —**lint′y** *adj.*

lin·tel (lĭn′tl) *n.* A horizontal structural member, such as a beam or stone, that spans an opening, as between the uprights of a door or window. [ME < OFr., prob. alteration of *lintier* < VLat. **līmitāris*, of a threshold < Lat., on a border < *līmes*, *līmit-*, boundary.]

lint·er (lĭn′tər) *n.* **1.** The short fibers that cling to cottonseeds after the first ginning. Often used in the plural. **2.** A machine that removes linters.

lint·white (lĭnt′hwīt′, -wīt′) *n.* A linnet. [By folk ety. < ME *linkwhitte*, alteration of OE *līnetwige* : *līn*, flax; see LINSEED + *-twige*, plucker, eater.]

Lin·ux (lĭn′ŭks) A trademark for an open-source version of the Unix operating system.

Linz (lĭnts) A city of N Austria on the Danube R. W of Vienna; orig. a Roman settlement. Pop. 203,044.

li·on (lī′ən) *n.* **1.** A large carnivorous feline mammal (*Panthera leo*) of Africa and northwest India having a short tawny coat and a long heavy mane in the male. **2.** Any of several large wildcats related to or resembling the lion. **3a.** A brave person. **b.** A person regarded as fierce or ferocious. **c.** An eminent person; a celebrity. **4.** Lion See **Leo.** —**idiom:** **lion's share** The greatest or best part. [ME < OFr. < Lat. *leō, leōn-* < Gk. *leōn*, of Semitic orig.; akin to Heb. *lābî′*.]

li·on·ess (lī′ə-nĭs) *n.* A female lion.

li·on·fish (lī′ən-fĭsh′) *n., pl.* **lionfish** or **-fish·es** Any of various brightly colored tropical Pacific scorpion fishes of the genus *Pterois*, having venomous spines in the dorsal fin.

li·on·heart·ed (lī′ən-här′tĭd) *adj.* Very courageous.

li·on·ize (lī′ə-nīz′) *tr.v.* **-ized, -iz·ing, -iz·es** To look on or treat (a person) as a celebrity. —**li′on·iz′er** *n.*

Li·ons (lī′ənz), **Gulf of** A wide inlet of the Mediterranean Sea on the S coast of France.

lip (lĭp) *n.* **1.** *Anatomy* Either of two fleshy folds that surround the opening of the mouth. **2.** A structure or part that encircles or bounds an orifice, as: **a.** *Anatomy* A labium. **b.** The margin of flesh around a wound. **c.** Either of the margins of the aperture of a gastropod shell. **d.** A rim, as of a vessel or bell. **3.** *Botany* One of the two divisions of a bilabiate corolla or calyx, as in the snapdragon. **4.** The tip of a pouring spout. **5.** *Slang* Insolent talk. ❖ *tr.v.* **lipped, lip·ping, lips 1.** To touch the lips to. **b.** To kiss. **2.** To utter. **3.** To lap or splash against. **4.** *Sports* To hit a golf ball so that it touches the edge of (the hole) without dropping in. [ME < OE *lippa*.]

lip– *pref.* Variant of **lipo–.**

Li·pan (lĭ-pän′) *n.* **1.** *pl.* **Lipan** or **-pans** A member of an Apache tribe formerly inhabiting western Texas, with a present-day population in southern New Mexico. **2.** The Apachean language of this tribe.

Lip·a·ri Islands (lĭp′ə-rē, lē′pä-) A group of volcanic islands of Italy off the NE coast of Sicily in the Tyrrhenian Sea.

lip·ase (lĭp′ās′, lī′pās′) *n.* Any of a group of enzymes that catalyze the hydrolysis of fats into glycerol and fatty acids.

Lip·chitz (lĭp′shĭts), **Jacques** 1891–1973. Russian-born French sculptor whose works include *Rape of Europa* (1941).

lip·ec·to·my (lĭ-pĕk′tə-mē, lī-) *n., pl.* **-mies** Surgical excision of subcutaneous fatty tissue.

Li·petsk (lē′pĕtsk′, lyĕ′pyĭtsk) A city of W-central Russia SSE of Moscow; orig. founded in the 13th cent. Pop. 465,753.

lip-gloss (lĭp′glôs′, -glŏs′) *n.* A cosmetic that gives shine or gloss to the lips.

lionfish

lip•id (lĭp′ĭd, lī′pĭd) also **lip•ide** (lĭp′īd′, lī′pīd′) *n.* Any of a group of organic compounds, including the fats, oils, waxes, sterols, and triglycerides, that are insoluble in water but soluble in organic solvents. [Fr. *lipide* : Gk. *lipos,* fat; see LIPO– + Fr. *-ide,* -ide.] —**lip•id′ic** *adj.*

Lip•iz•zan•er (lĭp′ĭt-sä′nər, -ə-zä′nər) or **Lip•iz•zan** (lĭp′ĭt-sän′, -ə-zən) *n.* Any of a breed of sturdy, compact horses developed from Spanish, Italian, Danish and Arab stock that are born black or dark brown and gradually turn white by the time they are five to eight years of age. [Ger. *Lippizaner,* after *Lippiza,* town near Trieste where the breed was developed.]

Lip•mann (lĭp′mən), **Fritz Albert** 1899–1986. German-born Amer. biochemist who shared a 1953 Nobel Prize.

Li Po (lē′ pō′, bō′) or **Li Bo** (bō′) d. c. 762. Chinese poet who composed romantic verse.

lipo– or **lip–** *pref.* **1.** Fat; fatty; fatty tissue: *lipolysis.* **2.** Lipid: *lipoprotein.* [< Gk. *lipos,* fat. Sense 2 < LIPID.]

lip•oid (lĭp′oid′, lī′poid′) *n.* **1.** A lipid. **2.** Any of various substances, such as lecithin, that resemble fat. ❖ *adj.* also **li•poi•dal** (lĭ-poid′l, lī-) Resembling fat; fatty.

li•pol•y•sis (lĭ-pŏl′ĭ-sĭs, lī-) *n., pl.* **-ses** (-sēz′) The hydrolysis of lipids. —**lip′o•lyt′ic** (lĭp′ə-lĭt′ĭk, lī′pə-) *adj.*

li•po•ma (lĭ-pō′mə, lī-) *n., pl.* **-ma•ta** (-mə-tə) or **-mas** A benign fatty tumor. —**li•pom′a•tous** (-pŏm′ə-təs) *adj.*

lip•o•phil•ic (lĭp′ə-fĭl′ĭk, lī′pə-) *adj.* Having an affinity for, tending to combine with, or capable of dissolving in lipids.

lip•o•pol•y•sac•cha•ride (lĭp′ō-pŏl′ē-săk′ə-rīd′, lī′pō-) *n.* A polysaccharide combined with a lipid.

lip•o•pro•tein (lĭp′ō-prō′tēn′, -tē-ĭn, lī′pō-) *n.* Any of a group of conjugated proteins, such as cholesterol, in which at least one of the components is a lipid.

lip•o•sculp•ture (lĭp′ō-skŭlp′chər, lī′pō-) *n.* Liposuction that uses ultrasound to break fat into small sections before removal.

lip•o•some (lĭp′ə-sōm′, lī′pə-) *n.* An artificial microscopic vesicle consisting of an aqueous core enclosed in one or more phospholipid layers, used to convey vaccines, drugs, enzymes, or other substances to target cells or organs.

lip•o•suc•tion (lĭp′ō-sŭk′shən, lī′pō-) *n.* A usu. cosmetic surgical procedure in which excess fatty tissue is removed from a specific area of the body by means of suction.

lip•o•trop•ic (lĭp′ō-trŏp′ĭk, -trō′pĭk, lī′pō-) *adj.* **1.** Preventing accumulation of fat in the liver. **2.** Having an affinity for lipids. —**li•pot′ro•py** (lĭ-pŏt′rə-pē, lī-), **li•pot′ro•pism** *n.*

lip•o•tro•pin (lĭp′ə-trō′pĭn, lī′pə-) *n.* A hormone produced by the anterior pituitary gland that promotes the utilization of fat and is a precursor to the endorphins. [LIPOTROP(IC) + –IN.]

Lip•pi (lĭp′ē), **Filippino** 1457?–1504? Italian painter who completed Masaccio's frescoes in the Brancacci Chapel in Florence.

Lippi, Fra **Filippo** 1406?–69? Italian Renaissance painter whose works include *Madonna Enthroned* (1437).

Lipp•mann (lēp-män′), **Gabriel** 1845–1921. French physicist who won a 1908 Nobel Prize.

Lipp•mann (lĭp′mən), **Walter** 1889–1974. Amer. journalist who cofounded (1914) the weekly *New Republic.*

lip-read (lĭp′rēd′) *v.* **-read** (-rĕd′), **-read•ing, -reads** —*tr.* To interpret (utterances) by lip reading. —*intr.* To interpret utterances by lip reading. —**lip′read′er** *n.*

lip reading *n.* A technique for understanding unheard speech by interpreting the lip and facial movements of the speaker.

Lip•scomb (lĭp′skəm), **William Nunn, Jr.** b. 1919. Amer. chemist who won a 1976 Nobel Prize.

lip service *n.* Verbal expression of agreement or allegiance, unsupported by real conviction or action; hypocritical respect.

lip•stick (lĭp′stĭk′) *n.* A small stick of waxy lip coloring enclosed in a cylindrical case.

lipstick tree *n.* See **annatto** 1.

lip-synch also **lip-sync** (lĭp′sĭngk′) *v.* **-synched, -synch•ing, -synchs** also **-synced, -sync•ing, -syncs** —*intr.* To move the lips in synchronization with recorded speech or song. —*tr.* To synchronize lip movement with (recorded speech or song).

Lip•tau•er (lĭp′tou′ər) *n.* **1.** A soft cheese originating in Hungary. **2.** A cheese spread made with Liptauer or a cream cheese substitute. [Ger., after *Liptau* (Liptó), Hungary.]

liq. *abbr.* **1.** liquid **2.** liquor

li•quate (lī′kwāt′) *tr.v.* **-quat•ed, -quat•ing, -quates** To separate (the metals in an alloy) by melting the more fusible constituents while leaving the less fusible ones solid. [Lat. *liquāre, liquāt-,* to melt.] —**li•qua′tion** *n.*

liq•ue•fac•tion (lĭk′wə-făk′shən) *n.* **1.** The process of liquefying. **2.** The state of being liquefied. [ME *liquefaccion* < OFr. *liquefacion* < LLat. *liquefactiō, liquefactiōn-* < Lat. *liquefactus,* p. part. of *liquefacere,* to make liquid. See LIQUEFY.]

liq•ue•fy also **liq•ui•fy** (lĭk′wə-fī′) *v.* **-fied, -fy•ing, -fies** —*tr.* To cause to become liquid, esp.: **a.** To melt (a solid) by heating. **b.** To condense (a gas) by cooling. —*intr.* To become liquid. [ME *liquefien* < OFr. *liquefier* < Lat. *liquefacere* : *liquēre,* to be liquid + *facere,* to make; see FACT.] —**liq′ue•fi′a•ble** *adj.* —**liq′ue•fi′er** *n.*

li•ques•cent (lĭ-kwĕs′ənt) *adj.* Becoming or tending to become liquid; melting. [Lat. *liquēscēns, liquēscent-,* pr. part. of *liquēscere,* to become liquid, inchoative of *liquēre,* to be liquid.] —**li•ques′cence, li•ques′cen•cy** *n.*

li•queur (lĭ-kûr′, -kyo͝or′) *n.* Any of various strongly flavored alcoholic beverages typically served in small quantities after dinner. [Fr. < OFr. *licour,* a liquid. See LIQUOR.]

liq•uid (lĭk′wĭd) *n.* **1a.** A state of matter characterized by a readiness to flow, little or no tendency to disperse, and relatively high incompressibility. **b.** Matter or a specific body of matter in this state. **2.** *Linguistics* A consonant articulated without friction and capable of being prolonged like a vowel, such as English *l* and *r.* ❖ *adj.* **1.** Of or being a liquid. **2.** Having been liquefied, esp.: **a.** Melted by heating. **b.** Condensed by cooling. **3.** Flowing readily; fluid. **4.** Having a flowing quality without harshness or abrupt breaks: *a liquid style of dancing.* **5.** *Linguistics* Articulated without friction and capable of being prolonged like a vowel. **6.** Clear and shining: *liquid eyes.* **7.** Existing as or readily convertible into cash: *liquid assets.* [< ME, of a liquid < OFr. *liquide* < Lat. *liquidus* < *liquēre,* to be liquid.] —**liq′uid•ly** *adv.* —**liq′uid•ness** *n.*

liq•uid•am•bar (lĭk′wĭd-ăm′bər) *n.* Any of several deciduous trees of the genus *Liquidambar,* such as the sweet gum. [NLat., genus name : Lat. *liquidus,* liquid; see LIQUID + Med.Lat. *ambar,* amber; see AMBER.]

liq•ui•date (lĭk′wĭ-dāt′) *v.* **-dat•ed, -dat•ing, -dates** —*tr.* **1a.** To pay off (a debt, for example); settle. **b.** To settle the affairs of (a business firm, for example) by determining the liabilities and applying the assets to their discharge. **2.** To convert (assets) into cash. **3.** To put an end to; abolish. **4.** To put to death; kill. —*intr.* **1.** To settle a debt, a claim, or an obligation. **2.** To liquidate a business or an estate. [LLat. *liquidāre, liquidāt-,* to melt < Lat. *liquidus,* liquid. See LIQUID.] —**liq′ui•da′tion** *n.* —**liq′ui•da′tor** *n.*

liquid crystal *n.* Any of various liquids in which the molecules are regularly arrayed in either one dimension or two dimensions, the order giving rise to characteristic optical properties.

liq•uid-crys•tal display (lĭk′wĭd-krĭs′təl) *n.* A low-power flat-panel display used in many digital devices, made up of a liquid crystal that is sandwiched between layers of glass or plastic and becomes opaque when electric current passes through it.

li•quid•i•ty (lĭ-kwĭd′ĭ-tē) *n.* **1.** The state of being liquid. **2.** The quality of being readily convertible into cash. **3.** Available cash or the capacity to obtain it on demand.

liq•ui•dize (lĭk′wĭ-dīz′) *tr.v.* **-dized, -diz•es, -diz•ing** To make liquid.

liquid measure *n.* **1.** The measurement of liquid capacity. **2.** A unit or system of units of liquid capacity.

liq•ui•fy (lĭk′wə-fī′) *v.* Variant of **liquefy.**

liq•uor (lĭk′ər) *n.* **1.** An alcoholic beverage made by distillation rather than by fermentation. **2.** A rich broth resulting from the prolonged cooking of meat or vegetables, esp. greens. **3.** An aqueous solution of a nonvolatile substance. **4.** A solution, emulsion, or suspension for industrial use. ❖ *tr.v.* **-uored, -uor•ing, -uors** **1.** To steep (malt, for example). **2.** *Slang* To make drunk with alcoholic liquor. Often used with *up: was all liquored up.* [ME *licour,* a liquid < OFr. < Lat. *liquor* < *liquēre,* to be liquid.]

li•quo•rice (lĭk′ər-ĭs, -ĭsh) *n.* *Chiefly British* Variant of **licorice.**

li•ra (lîr′ə, lē′rä) *n., pl.* **li•re** (lîr′ā, lē′rĕ) or **li•ras** See table at **currency.** [Ital. < OItal. < O Provençal *liura* < Lat. *lībra,* a unit of weight, pound.]

lir•i•pipe (lîr′ə-pīp′) *n.* A long scarf or cord attached to and hanging from a hood. [Med.Lat. *liripipium.*]

Lis•bon (lĭz′bən) The cap. of Portugal, in the W part on the Tagus R. estuary. An ancient Iberian settlement, it was devastated by a major earthquake in 1755. Pop. 663,315.

lisle (līl) *n.* **1.** A fine, smooth, tightly twisted thread spun from long-stapled cotton. **2.** Fabric knitted of this thread, used esp. for hosiery and underwear. [After *Lisle* (Lille), France.]

lisp (lĭsp) *n.* **1.** A speech defect or mannerism characterized by mispronunciation of the sounds (s) and (z) as (th) and (*th*). **2.** A sound of or like a lisp. ❖ *v.* **lisped, lisp•ing, lisps** —*intr.* **1.** To speak with a lisp. **2.** To speak imperfectly, as a child does. —*tr.* To pronounce with a lisp. [< ME *lispen,* to lisp < OE *-wlyspian* (in *āwlyspian,* to lisp) < *wlisp,* lisping.] —**lisp′er** *n.*

LISP *n.* A programming language designed to process lists of data and widely used in artificial intelligence research. [*lis(t) p(rocessing).*]

lis•some also **lis•som** (lĭs′əm) *adj.* **1.** Easily bent; supple. **2.** Having the ability to move with ease; limber. [Alteration of LITHESOME.] —**lis′some•ly** *adv.* —**lis′some•ness** *n.*

list[1] (lĭst) *n.* **1.** A series of names, words, or other items written, printed, or imagined one after the other: *guest list.* **2.** A considerable number; a long series. ❖ *v.* **list•ed, list•ing, lists** —*tr.* **1.** To make a list of; itemize. **2.** To enter in a list; register. **3.** To put (oneself) in a specific category. **4.** *Archaic* To recruit. —*intr.* **1.** To have a stated list price. **2.** *Archaic* To enlist in the armed forces. [Fr. *liste* < OFr. < OItal. *lista,* of Gmc. orig.] —**list′er** *n.*

list[2] (lĭst) *n.* **1a.** A narrow strip, esp. of wood. **b.** *Architecture* See **listel. c.** A border or selvage of cloth. **2.** A stripe or band of color. **3a.** An arena for jousting tournaments or other contests. Often used in the plural. **b.** A place of combat. Often used in the plural. **c.** An area of controversy. Often used in the plural. **4.** A ridge thrown up between two furrows by a lister in plowing. **5.** *Obsolete* A boundary; a border. ❖ *tr.v.* **list•ed, list•ing, lists 1.** To cover, line, or edge with list. **2.** To cut a thin strip from the edge of. **3.**

ă	pat	oi	boy
ā	pay	ou	out
âr	care	o͝o	took
ä	father	o͞o	boot
ĕ	pet	ŭ	cut
ē	be	ûr	urge
ĭ	pit	th	thin
ī	pie	*th*	this
îr	pier	hw	which
ŏ	pot	zh	vision
ō	toe	ə	about, item
ô	paw		

Stress marks:
′ (primary);
′ (secondary), as in
lexicon (lĕk′sĭ-kŏn′)

To furrow or plant (land) with a lister. [ME < OE *līste*.]

list³ (lĭst) *n.* An inclination to one side, as of a ship; a tilt. ❖ *intr. & tr.v.* **list•ed, list•ing, lists** To lean or cause to lean to the side: *The ship listed badly to starboard.* [?]

list⁴ (lĭst) *intr. & tr.v.* **list•ed, list•ing, lists** *Archaic* To listen or listen to. [ME < OE *hlystan*. See **kleu-** in App.]

list⁵ (lĭst) *Archaic v.* **list•ed, list•ing, lists** —*tr.* To be pleasing to; suit. —*intr.* To be disposed; choose. ❖ *n.* A desire or an inclination. [ME *listen*, to desire, please < OE *lystan*.]

lis•tel (lĭs'təl) *n. Architecture* A narrow border, molding, or fillet. [Fr. < Ital. *listello*, dim. of *lista*, border, of Gmc. orig.]

lis•ten (lĭs'ən) *intr.v.* **-tened, -ten•ing, -tens** 1. To make an effort to hear something: *listen to the radio.* 2. To pay attention; heed. ❖ *n.* An act of listening: *gave the CD a listen before buying it.* —*phrasal verb:* **listen in** 1. To listen to a conversation between others; eavesdrop. 2. To tune in and listen to a broadcast. [ME *listenen*, alteration (influenced by *listen*, to list, listen) of OE *hlysnan*; see **kleu-** in App.] —**lis'ten•er** *n.*

lis•ten•a•ble (lĭs'ə-nə-bəl) *adj.* Being such that listening is pleasurable: *a listenable soundtrack.* —**lis'ten•a•bil'i•ty** *n.*

lis•ten•er•ship (lĭs'ə-nər-shĭp', lĭs'nər-) *n.* The people who listen to a radio program or station.

list•er (lĭs'tər) *n.* A plow equipped with a double moldboard that turns up the soil on each side of the furrow. [< LIST².]

Lister, Joseph 1827–1912. British surgeon who demonstrated (1865) that carbolic acid was an effective antiseptic agent.

lis•te•ri•a (lĭ-stîr'ē-ə) *n.* Any of various rod-shaped, gram-positive bacteria of the genus *Listeria.* [NLat. *Listeria,* genus name, after Joseph LISTER.]

lis•te•ri•o•sis (lĭ-stîr'ē-ō'sĭs) *n.* A bacterial disease caused by *Listeria monocytogenes,* affecting animals and sometimes humans and marked by meningitis and encephalitis.

list•ing (lĭs'tĭng) *n.* 1. An entry in a list or directory. 2. A list or directory.

list•less (lĭst'lĭs) *adj.* Lacking energy or disinclined to exert effort; lethargic: *listless resignation.* [ME *listles* : prob. < *liste,* desire (< *listen,* to desire; see LIST⁵) + *-les, -lesse, -less.*] —**list'less•ly** *adv.* —**list'less•ness** *n.*

list price *n.* A basic published or advertised price, often subject to discount.

list•serv•er (lĭst'sûr'vər) *n.* A file server used in the management of e-mail for members of a discussion group.

Liszt (lĭst), **Franz** 1811–86. Hungarian composer whose works include the *Dante Symphony* (1856).

litchi
Litchi chinensis

lit¹ (lĭt) *v.* A past tense and a past participle of **light¹.** See Usage Note at **light¹.** ❖ *adj. Informal* Drunk or intoxicated. Often used with *up.*

lit² (lĭt) *v.* A past tense and a past participle of **light².**

lit³ (lĭt) *n. Informal* Literature: *enjoyed my course in French lit.*

lit. *abbr.* 1. liter 2a. literal b. literally 3. literary 4. literature

lit•a•ny (lĭt'n-ē) *n., pl.* **-nies** 1. A liturgical prayer consisting of a series of petitions recited by a leader alternating with fixed responses by the congregation. 2. A repetitive or incantatory recital. [ME *letanie* < OFr. < Med.Lat. *letania* < LLat. *litania* < L.Gk. *litaneia* < Gk., entreaty < *litaneuein,* to entreat < *litanos,* entreating < *litē,* supplication.]

lit•as (lĭt'äs) *n.* See table at **currency.** [Lith. *litas.*]

LitB *abbr.* Latin Litterarum Baccalaureus (Bachelor of Letters; Bachelor of Literature)

li•tchi also **li•chee** or **ly•chee** (lē'chē) *n., pl.* **-tchis** also **-chees** 1. A Chinese tree (*Litchi chinensis*) that bears bright red fruits, each of which has a large single seed with a white, fleshy, edible aril. 2. The nutlike fruit of this tree. [Chin. (Mandarin) *lì zhī* : *lì,* litchi + *zhī,* twig.]

lit crit (krĭt) *n. Informal* Literary criticism.

LitD *abbr.* Latin Litterarum Doctor (Doctor of Letters; Doctor of Literature)

lite (lĭt) *adj. Slang* Having less substance or weight or fewer calories than something else. [Alteration of LIGHT².]

–lite *suff.* Stone; mineral; fossil: *coprolite.* [Fr., alteration of *-lithe* < Gk. *lithos,* stone.]

li•ter (lē'tər) *n.* A metric unit of volume equal to approx. 1.056 liquid quarts, 0.908 dry quart, or 0.264 gallon. See table at **measurement.** [Fr. *litre* < obsolete *litron,* measure of capacity < Med.Lat. *litra* < Gk., unit of weight.]

lit•er•a•cy (lĭt'ər-ə-sē) *n.* 1. The condition or quality of being literate, esp. the ability to read and write. 2. The condition or quality of being knowledgeable in a particular subject or field: *cultural literacy.*

lit•er•al (lĭt'ər-əl) *adj.* 1. Conforming or limited to the simplest, nonfigurative, or most obvious meaning of a word or words. 2. Word for word; verbatim: *a literal translation.* 3. Avoiding exaggeration, metaphor, or embellishment; factual; prosaic: *a literal mind.* 4. Consisting of, using, or expressed by letters. ❖ *n. Computer Science* A letter or symbol that stands for itself as opposed to a feature, function, or entity associated with it in a programming language. [ME < OFr. < LLat. *litterālis,* of letters < Lat. *littera, lītera,* letter. See LETTER.] —**lit'er•al•ness** *n.*

lit•er•al•ism (lĭt'ər-ə-lĭz'əm) *n.* 1. Adherence to the explicit sense of a given text or doctrine. 2. Literal portrayal; realism. —**lit'er•al•ist** *n.* —**lit'er•al•is'tic** *adj.*

lit•er•al•ize (lĭt'ər-ə-līz') *tr.v.* **-ized, -iz•ing, -iz•es** To make literal.

lit•er•al•ly (lĭt'ər-ə-lē) *adv.* 1. In a literal manner; word for word. 2. In a literal or strict sense: *Don't take my remarks literally.* 3. *Usage Problem* a. Really; actually. b. Used as an intensive before a figurative expression.

lit•er•ar•y (lĭt'ə-rĕr'ē) *adj.* 1. Of, relating to, or dealing with literature: *literary criticism.* 2. Of or relating to writers or the profession of literature: *literary circles.* 3. Versed in or fond of literature or learning. 4a. Appropriate to literature rather than everyday speech or writing. b. Bookish; pedantic. [Lat. *litterārius,* of reading and writing < *littera, lītera,* letter. See LETTER.] —**lit'er•ar'i•ly** (-râr'ə-lē) *adv.* —**lit'er•ar'i•ness** *n.*

lit•er•ate (lĭt'ər-ĭt) *adj.* 1a. Able to read and write. b. Knowledgeable or educated in several fields or a particular field. 2. Familiar with literature; literary. 3. Well-written; polished: *a literate essay.* ❖ *n.* One who can read and write. [ME *litterate* < Lat. *litterātus* < *littera, lītera,* letter. See LETTER.] —**lit'er•ate•ly** *adv.* —**lit'er•ate•ness** *n.*

lit•er•a•ti (lĭt'ə-rä'tē) *pl.n.* The literary intelligentsia. [Lat. *litterātī, līterātī,* pl. of *litterātus,* literate. See LITERATE.]

lit•er•a•tim (lĭt'ə-rä'tĭm, -rä'-) *adv.* Letter for letter: *a word transcribed literatim.* [Med.Lat. *litterātim, līterātim* < Lat. *littera, lītera,* letter. See LETTER.]

lit•er•a•ture (lĭt'ər-ə-chŏŏr', -chər) *n.* 1. The body of written works of a language, period, or culture. 2. Imaginative or creative writing, esp. of recognized artistic value. 3. The art or occupation of a literary writer. 4. The body of written work produced by scholars or researchers in a given field. 5. Printed material. 6. *Music* All the compositions of a certain kind or for a specific instrument or ensemble: *the symphonic literature.* [ME, book learning < OFr. *litterature* < Lat. *litterātūra* < *litterātus,* lettered. See LITERATE.]

lith. *abbr.* 1. lithograph 2. lithography

Lith. *abbr.* 1. Lithuania 2. Lithuanian

lith– *pref.* Variant of **litho–.**

–lith *suff.* 1. Rock; stone: *xenolith.* 2. Stone implement or structure: *megalith.* 3. Mineral concretion; calculus: *cystolith.* [< Gk. *lithos,* stone.]

lith•arge (lĭth'ärj', lĭ-thärj') *n.* A lead oxide, PbO, used in storage batteries and glass. [ME *litarge* < OFr., alteration of *litargire* < Lat. *lithargyrus* < Gk. *litharguros* : *lithos,* stone + *arguros,* silver; see **arg–** in App.]

lithe (lĭth) *adj.* **lith•er, lith•est** 1. Readily bent; supple: *lithe birch branches.* 2. Marked by effortless grace: *a lithe ballet dancer.* [ME < OE *līthe,* flexible, mild.] —**lithe'ly** *adv.* —**lithe'ness** *n.*

lithe•some (lĭth'səm) *adj.* Lithe; lissome.

lith•i•a (lĭth'ē-ə) *n.* See **lithium oxide.** [NLat. < *lithion* < Gk., dim. of *lithos,* stone.]

li•thi•a•sis (lĭ-thī'ə-sĭs) *n., pl.* **-ses** (-sēz') Pathological formation of mineral concretions in the body.

lithia water *n.* Mineral water containing lithium salts.

lith•ic¹ (lĭth'ĭk) *adj.* Consisting of or relating to stone or rock.

lith•ic² (lĭth'ĭk) *adj.* Of or relating to lithium.

–lithic *suff.* Relating to or characteristic of a specified stage in the use of stone by humans: *Eolithic.* [< LITHIC¹.]

lith•i•um (lĭth'ē-əm) *n. Symbol* **Li** 1. A soft, highly reactive metallic element, used as a heat transfer medium and in various alloys, ceramics, and batteries. Atomic number 3; atomic weight 6.941; melting point 179°C; boiling point 1,317°C; specific gravity 0.534; valence 1. See table at **element.** 2. Any of several salts of lithium, esp. lithium carbonate. [< LITHIA.]

lithium carbonate *n.* A granular powder, Li_2CO_3, used in glass and ceramics and in the treatment of depression and bipolar disorder.

lithium oxide *n.* A strongly alkaline white powder, Li_2O, used in ceramics and glass.

lith•o (lĭth'ō) *n., pl.* **-os** A lithograph.

litho– or **lith–** *pref.* 1. Stone: *lithosphere.* 2. Lithium: *lithic.* 3. Mineral concretion; calculus: *lithotomy.* [Gk. < *lithos,* stone.]

lith•o•graph (lĭth'ə-grăf') *n.* A print produced by lithography. ❖ *tr.v.* **-graphed, -graph•ing, -graphs** To produce by lithography. —**li•thog'raph•er** (lĭ-thŏg'rə-fər) *n.* —**lith'o•graph'ic.** —**lith'o•graph'i•cal** *adj.* —**lith'o•graph'i•cal•ly** *adv.*

li•thog•ra•phy (lĭ-thŏg'rə-fē) *n.* A printing process in which the image to be printed is rendered on a flat surface, as on sheet zinc or aluminum, and treated to retain ink while the nonimage areas are treated to repel ink.

li•thol•o•gy (lĭ-thŏl'ə-jē) *n.* 1. The gross physical character of a rock or rock formation. **2.** The description of rock, esp. sedimentary rock. —**lith′o•log′ic** (lĭth′ə-lŏj′ĭk), **lith′o•log′i•cal** *adj.* —**li•thol′o•gist** *n.*

lith•o•phyte (lĭth′ə-fīt′) *n.* **1.** *Botany* A plant that grows on rock. **2.** *Zoology* An organism, such as coral, that has a stony structure. —**lith′o•phyt′ic** (-fĭt′ĭk) *adj.*

lith•o•pone (lĭth′ə-pōn′) *n.* A white pigment consisting of a mixture of zinc sulfide, zinc oxide, and barium sulfate. [LITHO- + Gk. *ponos,* toil, product.]

lith•o•sphere (lĭth′ə-sfîr′) *n.* The outer part of the earth, consisting of the crust and upper mantle, approx. 100 kilometers (62 miles) thick. —**lith′o•spher′ic** *adj.*

lith•o•stra•tig•ra•phy (lĭth′ō-strə-tĭg′rə-fē) *n.* **1.** Stratigraphy based on the physical and petrographic properties of rocks. **2.** Interpretation of the physical characters of sedimentary rocks. —**lith′o•strat′i•graph′ic** (-străt′ĭ-grăf′ĭk) *adj.*

li•thot•o•my (lĭ-thŏt′ə-mē) *n.,* *pl.* -**mies** Surgical removal of a stone or stones from the urinary tract.

lith•o•trip•sy (lĭth′ə-trĭp′sē) *n.,* *pl.* -**sies** Pulverization of kidney stones or gallstones by means of a lithotripter. [LITHO- + Gk. *tripsis,* a rubbing, pounding (< *tribein,* to rub, pound) + -Y².]

lith•o•trip•ter or **lith•o•trip•tor** (lĭth′ə-trĭp′tər) *n.* A device that uses shock waves to pulverize kidney stones or gallstones, which can then be expelled in the urine. [Ult. < Gk. *(pharmaka tōn en nephrōis) lithōn thruptika,* (drugs) crushing stones (in the kidneys) : *lithōn,* genitive pl. of *lithos,* stone + *thruptika,* neut. pl. of *thruptikos,* crushing (< *thruptein,* to crush).]

Lith•u•a•ni•a (lĭth′ōō-ā′nē-ə) *n.* A country of northern Europe on the Baltic Sea; perhaps settled as early as 1500 B.C. and a constituent republic of the USSR from 1940 to 1990. Cap. Vilnius. Pop. 3,721,000.

Lith•u•a•ni•an (lĭth′ōō-ā′nē-ən) *adj.* Of or relating to Lithuania or its people, language, or culture. ❖ *n.* **1a.** A native or inhabitant of Lithuania. **b.** A person of Lithuanian ancestry. **2.** The Baltic language of the Lithuanians.

lit•i•gant (lĭt′ĭ-gənt) *n.* A party engaged in a lawsuit. ❖ *adj.* Engaged in a lawsuit. [Fr. < OFr. < Lat. *lītigāns, lītigant-,* a disputant < pr. part. of *lītigāre,* to bring suit. See LITIGATE.]

lit•i•gate (lĭt′ĭ-gāt′) *v.* -**gat•ed, -gat•ing, -gates** —*tr.* To contest in legal proceedings. —*intr.* To engage in legal proceedings. [Lat. *lītigāre, lītigāt-* : *līs, līt-,* lawsuit + *agere,* to drive; see **ag-** in App.] —**lit′i•ga•ble** (-gə-bəl) *adj.* —**lit′i•ga′tion** *n.* —**lit′i•ga′tor** *n.*

li•ti•gious (lĭ-tĭj′əs) *adj.* **1.** Of, relating to, or characterized by litigation. **2.** Tending to engage in lawsuits. [ME < OFr. < Lat. *lītigiōsus < lītigium,* dispute < *lītigāre,* to quarrel. See LITIGATE.] —**li•ti′gious•ly** *adv.* —**li•ti′gious•ness** *n.*

lit•mus (lĭt′məs) *n.* A water-soluble blue powder derived from certain lichens that changes to red with increasing acidity and to blue with increasing basicity. [ME *litemose* (of Scand. orig.): akin to ON *litmosi,* dyer's herbs : *litr,* color, dye + *mosi,* bog, moss) and ME *lykemose* (< MDu. *lijkmoes,* var. of *lēcmoes* : *lēken,* to drip + *moes,* moss).]

litmus paper *n.* An unsized white paper impregnated with litmus and used as a pH or acid-base indicator.

litmus test *n.* **1.** A test for chemical acidity or basicity using litmus paper. **2.** A test that uses a single indicator to prompt a decision.

li•to•tes (lī′tə-tēz′, lĭt′ə-, lī-tō′tēz) *n.,* *pl.* **litotes** A figure of speech consisting of an understatement in which an affirmative is expressed by negating its opposite, as in *This is no small problem.* [Gk. *litotēs < lītos,* plain.]

li•tre (lē′tər) *n. Chiefly British* Variant of **liter.**

LittB *abbr. Latin* Litterarum Baccalaureus (Bachelor of Letters; Bachelor of Literature)

LittD *abbr. Latin* Litterarum Doctor (Doctor of Letters; Doctor of Literature)

lit•ter (lĭt′ər) *n.* **1a.** A disorderly accumulation of objects; a pile. **b.** Carelessly discarded refuse, such as wastepaper. **2.** The offspring produced at one birth by a multiparous mammal. **3a.** Material, such as straw, used as bedding for animals. **b.** An absorbent material for covering the floor of an animal's cage or excretory box. **4.** An enclosed or curtained couch mounted on shafts and used to carry a single passenger. **5.** A flat supporting framework for carrying a disabled or dead person; a stretcher. **6.** The uppermost layer of the forest floor consisting chiefly of fallen leaves and other decaying organic matter. ❖ *v.* -**tered, -ter•ing, -ters** —*tr.* **1.** To give birth to (a litter). **2.** To make untidy by discarding rubbish carelessly. **3.** To scatter about. **4.** To supply (animals) with litter for bedding or floor covering. —*intr.* **1.** To give birth to a litter. **2.** To scatter litter. [ME, a litter < AN *litere* < Med.Lat. *lectāria* (influenced by OFr. *lit,* bed) < Lat. *lectus,* bed. See **legh-** in App.] —**lit′ter•er** *n.*

lit•té•ra•teur also **lit•ter•a•teur** (lĭt′ər-ə-tûr′, lĭt′rə-) *n.* One who is devoted to the study or writing of literature. [Fr. < Lat. *litterātor,* critic, lettered person < *littera,* letter. See LETTER.]

lit•ter•bag (lĭt′ər-băg′) *n.* A bag used for disposal of trash.

lit•ter•bug (lĭt′ər-bŭg′) *n. Informal* A person who litters.

lit•ter•mate (lĭt′ər-māt′) *n.* One member of a given litter.

lit•tle (lĭt′l) *adj.* **lit•tler** or **less** (lĕs) also **less•er** (lĕs′ər), **lit•tlest** or **least** (lēst) **1.** Small in size. See Syns at **small. 2.** Short in extent

or duration; brief: *There is little time left.* **3.** Small in quantity or degree: *little money.* **4.** Unimportant; trivial: *a little matter.* **5.** Narrow; petty. **6.** Without much power or influence; of minor status. **7a.** Being at an early stage of growth; young. **b.** Younger or youngest. Used esp. of a sibling. ❖ *adv.* **less** or **lesser, least** **1.** Not much; scarcely. **2.** Not in the least; not at all. ❖ *n.* **1.** A small quantity or amount. **2.** Something much less than all: *I know little of their history.* **3.** A short distance or time. —*idioms:* **a little** Somewhat; a bit. **little by little** By small degrees or increments; gradually. [ME < OE *lȳtel.*] —**lit′tle•ness** *n.*

Little Alföld See **Alföld.**

Little America A US base for explorations in Antarctica on the Ross Ice Shelf.

little auk *n.* See **dovekie.**

Little Bear *n.* See **Ursa Minor.**

Little Bighorn River A river, c. 145 km (90 mi), rising in the Bighorn Mts. of N WY and flowing N to the Bighorn R. in S MT. Sioux and Cheyenne warriors defeated the forces of Gen. George A. Custer in the Little Bighorn valley on Jun. 25, 1876.

Little Cayman See **Cayman Islands.**

Little Colorado River A river of NE AZ flowing c. 507 km (315 mi) to the Colorado R.

Little Diomede Island See **Diomede Islands.**

Little Dipper *n.* The seven bright stars that form the constellation Ursa Minor.

little finger *n.* The smallest finger of the human hand.

little magazine *n.* A noncommercial, usu. literary magazine with a limited circulation.

Little Missouri River A river of the N US rising in NE WY and flowing c. 901 km (560 mi) to the Missouri R. in W ND.

lit•tle•neck (lĭt′l-nĕk′) *n.* The quahog clam when small and suitable for eating raw. [After *Little Neck* Bay, off W Long Island, NY.]

little owl *n.* A small European owl *(Athene noctua)* having streaked brownish plumage.

Little Rich•ard (rĭch′ərd) Pseudonym of Richard Wayne Penniman. b. 1932. Amer. rock 'n' roll singer noted for his flamboyant, influential style.

Little Rock The cap. of AR, in the central part on the Arkansas R. Pop. 183,133.

Little Saint Bernard Pass A mountain pass through the Savoy Alps between Italy and France.

little slam *n. Games* The winning of all but one of the tricks during the play of one hand of bridge.

little toe *n.* The smallest toe of the human foot.

lit•to•ral (lĭt′ər-əl) *adj.* Of or on a shore, esp. a seashore: *the littoral zone.* ❖ *n.* **1.** A coastal region; a shore. **2.** The zone between the limits of high and low tides. [Lat. *litorālis < litus, lītor-,* shore. N. < Ital. *littorale* < Lat. *lītorālis.*]

li•tur•gi•cal (lĭ-tûr′jĭ-kəl) also **li•tur•gic** (-tûr′jĭk) *adj.* **1.** Of, relating to, or in accordance with liturgy: *a book of liturgical forms.* **2.** Using or used in liturgy. —**li•tur′gi•cal•ly** *adv.*

li•tur•gics (lĭ-tûr′jĭks) *n.* (*used with a sing. verb*) The study of liturgies.

lit•ur•gi•ol•o•gy (lĭ-tûr′jē-ŏl′ə-jē) *n.* See **liturgics.** —**li•tur′gi•ol′o•gist** *n.*

lit•ur•gist (lĭt′ər-jĭst) *n.* **1.** One who uses or advocates the use of liturgical forms. **2.** A scholar in liturgics. **3.** A compiler of a liturgy or liturgies.

lit•ur•gy (lĭt′ər-jē) *n.,* *pl.* -**gies** **1.** A prescribed form or set of forms for public religious worship. **2.** often **Liturgy** *Christianity* The public celebration of the Eucharist. [LLat. *līturgia < Gk. leitourgiā,* public service < *leitourgos,* public servant < earlier *lēitourgos* : *lēiton,* town hall (< *lāos, lēos,* people) + *ergon,* work; see **werg-** in App.]

Liu•zhou (lyōō′jō′) also **Liu•chow** (-chō′) A city of S China NNE of Nanning. Pop. 751,311.

liv•a•ble also **live•a•ble** (lĭv′ə-bəl) *adj.* **1.** Suitable to live in; habitable. **2.** Possible to bear; endurable. —**liv′a•ble•ness** *n.*

live¹ (lĭv) *v.* **lived, liv•ing, lives** —*intr.* **1.** To be alive; exist. **2.** To continue to be alive. **3.** To support oneself; subsist. **4.** To reside; dwell. **5.** To conduct one's life in a particular manner: *lived frugally.* **6.** To pursue a positive, satisfying existence; enjoy life. **7.** To remain in human memory. —*tr.* **1.** To spend or pass (one's life). **2.** To go through; experience. **3.** To practice in one's life. —*phrasal verbs:* **live down** To overcome or reduce the shame of (a misdeed, for example) over a period of time. **live in** To reside in one's place of employment. **live out** To live outside one's place of domestic employment. **live with** To put up with; resign oneself to. —*idioms:* **live it up** *Slang* To engage in festive pleasures or extravagances. **live up to** **1.** To live or act in accordance with. **2.** To prove equal to. **3.** To carry out; fulfill. [ME *liven* < OE *libban, lifian.*]

live² (līv) *adj.* **1.** Having life; alive: *live animals.* **2.** Of, related to, or occurring during the life of one that is living: *the pig's live weight.* **3.** Of current interest or relevance: *a live topic.* **4.** Full of life, excitement, or activity: *a live crowd at the parade.* **5.** Glowing; burning: *live coals.* **6.** Not yet exploded but capable of being fired. **7.** *Electricity* Carrying an electric current or energized with electricity: *live cables.* **8.** Not mined or quarried; in the natural state: *live ore.* **9a.** Broadcast while actually being performed; not taped,

Lithuania

filmed, or recorded. **b.** Involving performers or spectators who are physically present. **10.** Of, relating to, or containing microorganisms or infectious agents that have not been rendered incapable of causing infection: *a live vaccine.* **11.** *Printing* Not yet set into type: *live copy.* **12.** *Sports* In play: *a live ball.* ❖ *adv.* At, during, or from the time of actual occurrence or performance. [Short for ALIVE.] —**live′ness** *n.*

live•bear•er (līv′bâr′ər) *n.* A fish, esp. of the family Poeciliidae, that bears live young. —**live′-bear′ing** *adj.*

live-for•ev•er (līv′fər-ĕv′ər) *n.* **1.** See **orpine. 2.** See **houseleek.**

live-in (līv′ĭn′) *adj.* **1.** Residing in one's place of employment. **2.** Residing together with another, esp. in a sexual relationship.

live•li•hood (līv′lē-hood′) *n.* Means of support; subsistence. [ME *livelyhed*, alteration of *livelode* < OE *līflād* : *līf*, life; see LIFE + *lād*, course.]

live load (līv) *n.* A moving, variable weight added to the dead load or intrinsic weight of a structure or vehicle.

live•long (līv′lông′, -lŏng′) *adj.* Complete; whole: *the livelong day.* [ME : *leve, lefe,* dear, used as an intensive (< OE *lēof,* dear) + *long,* long; see LONG[1].]

live•ly (līv′lē) *adj.* **-li•er, -li•est 1.** Full of life and energy; vigorous. **2.** Full of spirit; gay and animated. **3.** Marked by animated intelligence. **4.** Invigorating; refreshing. **5.** Effervescent; sparkling. **6.** Keen; brisk. **7.** Rebounding readily upon impact; resilient. ❖ *adv.* With energy or vigor; briskly. [ME *lifli* < OE *līflīc* < *līf,* life.] —**live′li•ly** *adv.* —**live′li•ness** *n.*

li•ven (lī′vən) *tr. & intr.v.* **-vened, -ven•ing, -vens** To make or become more lively: *liven up a party.*

live oak (līv) *n.* Any of several American evergreen oaks, such as *Quercus virginiana* of Mexico and the southeast United States or *Q. agrifolia* of California.

liv•er[1] (līv′ər) *n.* **1.** *Anatomy* A large reddish-brown glandular vertebrate organ located in the upper right portion of the abdominal cavity that secretes bile, makes certain blood proteins, and metabolizes carbohydrates, fats, and proteins. **2.** An organ in invertebrates that is similar to the vertebrate liver. **3.** The bile-secreting organ of an animal, used as food. **4.** A dark reddish brown. ❖ *adj.* **1.** Made of or flavored with liver: *liver pâté.* **2.** Of a dark reddish brown. [ME < OE *lifer.*]

liv•er[2] (līv′ər) *n.* One who lives in a specified manner.

liver fluke *n.* **1.** Any of several parasitic trematode worms, esp. *Clonorchis sinensis,* that infest the liver of various animals, including humans. **2.** Infestation with such worms.

liv•er•ied (līv′ə-rēd, līv′rēd) *adj.* Wearing livery.

liv•er•ish (līv′ər-īsh) *adj.* **1.** Resembling liver, esp. in color. **2.** Having a liver disorder; bilious. **3.** Having a disagreeable disposition; irritable. —**liv′er•ish•ness** *n.*

liv•er•leaf (līv′ər-lēf′) *n.* See **hepatica.**

Liv•er•pool (līv′ər-pool′) A borough of NW England on the Mersey R. near its mouth on the Irish Sea; chartered 1207. Pop. 476,969.

liver spot *n.* A benign, localized brownish patch on the skin, often occurring in old age and usu. in fair-skinned people with sun-damaged skin.

liv•er•wort (līv′ər-wûrt′, -wôrt′) *n.* Any of numerous small green nonvascular plants of the class Hepaticae. [< its use in treating diseases of the liver.]

liv•er•wurst (līv′ər-wûrst′, -woorst′) *n.* A sausage made of or containing ground liver. [Partial transl. of Ger. *Leberwurst* : *Leber,* liver + *Wurst,* sausage; see WURST.]

liv•er•y (līv′ə-rē, līv′rē) *n., pl.* **-ies 1.** A distinctive uniform worn by the male servants of a household. **2.** The distinctive dress worn by the members of a particular group; uniform. **3.** The costume or insignia worn by the retainers of a feudal lord. **4a.** The boarding and care of horses for a fee. **b.** The hiring out of horses and carriages. **c.** A livery stable. **5.** A business that offers vehicles for hire. **6.** *Law* Official delivery of property, esp. land, to a new owner. [ME *liveri* < OFr. *livree,* delivery < fem. p. part. of *livrer,* to deliver < Lat. *līberāre,* to free < *līber,* free. See **leudh-** in App.]

liv•er•y•man (līv′ə-rē-mən, līv′rē-) *n.* A man who is employed in or keeps a livery stable.

livery stable *n.* A stable that boards horses and keeps horses and carriages for hire.

lives (līvz) *n.* Plural of **life.**

live steam (līv) *n.* Steam coming from a boiler at full pressure.

live•stock (līv′stŏk′) *n.* Domestic animals, such as cattle or horses, raised for home use or for profit, esp. on a farm.

live wire (līv) *n.* **1.** A wire carrying electric current. **2.** *Informal* A vivacious, alert, or energetic person.

liv•id (līv′ĭd) *adj.* **1.** Discolored, as from a bruise; black-and-blue. **2.** Ashen or pallid. **3.** Extremely angry; furious. [ME *livide* < OFr. < Lat. *līvidus* < *līvēre,* to be bluish. See **sleia-** in App.] —**li•vid′i•ty, liv′id•ness** *n.* —**liv′id•ly** *adv.*

liv•ing (līv′ĭng) *adj.* **1.** Possessing life. **2.** In active function or use: *a living language.* **3.** Of persons who are alive: *within living memory.* **4.** Relating to the routine conduct or maintenance of life: *living conditions.* **5.** Full of life, interest, or vitality. **6.** True to life; realistic. **7.** *Informal* Used as an intensive. ❖ *n.* **1.** The condition or action of maintaining life. **2.** A manner or style of life. **3.** A means of maintaining life; livelihood. **4.** *Chiefly British* A church benefice, including the revenue attached to it.

llama
Lama glama

Andrew Lloyd Webber
photographed in 1997 at
the Academy Awards

living death *n.* A situation or period of time characterized by unremitting pain and suffering.

living fossil *n.* An organism, such as a coelacanth, that is the sole survivor of an otherwise extinct taxonomic group.

living room *n.* A room in a private residence intended for general social and leisure activities.

Liv•ing•ston (līv′ĭng-stən), **Robert R.** 1746–1813. Amer. Revolutionary leader who served in the Continental Congress (1775–81) and helped draft the Declaration of Independence.

Liv•ing•stone (līv′ĭng-stən), **David** 1813–73. Scottish missionary and explorer who attempted to find the source of the Nile with Henry M. Stanley.

living unit *n.* A dwelling for use by one family.

living wage *n.* A wage sufficient to provide minimally satisfactory living conditions.

living will *n.* A will in which the signer requests not to be kept alive by life-support systems in the event of a terminal illness.

Li•vo•ni•a (lĭ-vō′nē-ə, -vōn′yə) **1.** A region of S Estonia and N Latvia. **2.** A city of SE MI, a suburb of Detroit. Pop. 100,545.

Li•vo•ni•an (lĭ-vō′nē-ən) *adj.* Of or relating to the region of Livonia or its people or culture. ❖ *n.* A native or inhabitant of the region of Livonia.

Li•vor•no (lē-vôr′nō) or **Leghorn** (lĕg′hôrn′, -ərn) A city of NW Italy on the Ligurian Sea SE of Genoa. Pop. 167,445.

li•vre (lē′vər, lē′vrə) *n.* **1.** See table at **currency. 2.** A money of account formerly used in France and originally worth a pound of silver. [Fr. < OFr. < Lat. *lībra,* a unit of weight, pound.]

Liv•y (līv′ē) 59 B.C.–A.D. 17. Roman historian whose history of Rome consisted of 142 volumes.

lix•iv•i•ate (lĭk-sĭv′ē-āt′) *tr.v.* **-at•ed, -at•ing, -ates** To wash or percolate the soluble matter from. [LLat. *lixīvium,* lye (< Lat. *lixīvius,* of lye < *lix,* lye) + -ATE[1].] —**lix•iv′i•a′tion** *n.*

liz•ard (lĭz′ərd) *n.* **1.** Any of numerous reptiles of the suborder Sauria or Lacertilia, having a scaly elongated body, movable eyelids, four legs, and a tapering tail. **2.** Leather made from lizard skin. [ME < OFr. *lesarde* < Lat. *lacertus, lacerta.*]

liz•ard•fish (lĭz′ərd-fĭsh′) *n., pl.* **lizardfish** or **-fish•es** Any of various bottom-dwelling large-mouthed fishes of the family Synodontidae of warm seas, having a lizardlike head.

Lizard Point or **Lizard Head** A cape of SW England at the S tip of **The Lizard,** a peninsula extending S into the English Channel.

Lju•blja•na (loo′blē-ä′nə, lyoo′blyä-nä) The cap. of Slovenia, in the central part on the Sava R. WNW of Zagreb, Croatia; founded by Augustus in 34 B.C. Pop. 281,821.

Lk *abbr. Bible* Luke

ll. *abbr.* lines

′ll Contraction of *will: We'll arrive later.*

lla•ma (lä′mə) *n.* **1.** A domesticated South American ruminant mammal (*Lama glama*) related to the camel, raised for its wool and used as a beast of burden. **2.** Any of various other mammals of the genus *Lama.* [Sp. < Quechua.]

lla•no (lä′nō, yä′-) *n., pl.* **-nos** A large, grassy, almost treeless plain, esp. one in Latin America. [Sp., plain < Lat. *plānum* < neut. of *plānus,* level. See **pela-[2]** in App.]

Llano Es•ta•ca•do (ĕs′tə-kä′dō) An extensive semiarid plateau region of the S Great Plains in SE NM, W TX, and NW OK.

LLB *abbr. Latin* Legum Baccalaureus (Bachelor of Laws)

LLD *abbr. Latin* Legum Doctor (Master of Laws)

Llew•el•lyn (loo-ĕl′ĭn), **Richard** 1906–83. Welsh-born British writer best known for *How Green Was My Valley* (1940).

LLM *abbr. Latin* Legum Magister (Master of Laws)

Lloyd George (loid′ jôrj′), **David.** 1st Earl of Dwyfor. 1863–1945. British politician who served as prime minister (1916–22).

Lloyd Web•ber (wĕb′ər), Sir **Andrew** b. 1948. British composer whose many musicals include *Evita* (1976).

Llu•llai•lla•co (yoo′yī-yä′kō) A volcano, 6,727.4 m (22,057 ft), in the Andes of N Chile near the Argentine border.

lm *abbr. Physics* lumen

Lm *abbr. Bible* Lamentations

LM *abbr.* **1.** Legion of Merit **2.** lunar module

LMT *abbr.* local mean time

ln The symbol for **natural logarithm.**

LNG *abbr.* liquefied natural gas

lo (lō) *interj.* Used to attract attention or show surprise. [ME < OE *lā.*]

loach (lōch) *n.* Any of various Eurasian and African freshwater fishes of the family Cobitidae, having barbels around the mouth. [ME *loche* < OFr., perh. < VLat. **laukka,* fish, slug, poss. of Celt. orig.]

load (lōd) *n.* **1a.** A weight or mass that is supported. **b.** The overall force to which a structure is subjected in supporting a weight or mass or in resisting externally applied forces. **2a.** Something that is carried, as by a vehicle or person. **b.** The quantity that is or can be carried at one time. **3a.** The share of work allocated to or required of a person, machine, group, or organization. **b.** The demand for services or performance made on a machine or system. **4.** The amount of material that can be inserted into a device or machine at one time. **5.** A single charge of ammunition for a firearm. **6a.** A mental weight or burden. **b.** A responsibility regarded as oppressive. **7.** The external mechanical resistance against which a machine acts. **8.** *Electricity* **a.** The power output of a generator or power plant. **b.** A device or the resistance of a device to which power is delivered. **9.** A front-end load. **10.** *Informal* A great number or amount. Often used in the plural: *loads of fun.* **11.** *Slang* A heavy or overweight person. **12.** Genetic load. ❖ *v.* **load·ed, load·ing, loads** —*tr.* **1a.** To put (something) into or onto a structure or conveyance. **b.** To put something into or onto (a structure or conveyance). **2.** To provide or fill nearly to overflowing; heap. **3.** To weigh down; burden. **4.** To insert (a necessary material) into a device: *loaded bullets into the gun.* **5.** To insert a necessary material into: *loaded the camera.* **6.** *Games* To make (dice) heavier on one side by adding weight. **7.** To charge with additional meanings, implications, or emotional import: *loaded the question.* **8.** To dilute, adulterate, or doctor. **9.** To raise the power demand in (an electrical circuit), as by adding resistance. **10.** To increase (a mutual fund share price, for example) by adding expenses or sale costs. **11.** *Baseball* To have or put runners on (first, second, and third base). **12.** *Computer Science* **a.** To transfer (data) from a storage device into a computer's memory. **b.** To mount (an auxiliary storage device). —*intr.* **1.** To receive a load. **2.** To charge a firearm with ammunition. **3.** To put or place a load into or onto a structure, device, or conveyance. —*idioms:* **get a load of** *Slang* **1.** To look at; notice. **2.** To listen to. **take a load off** To sit or lie down. [ME *lode,* alteration (influenced by *laden,* to load) of *lade,* course, way < OE *lād.*]

load·ed (lō′dĭd) *adj.* **1.** Carrying a load. **2.** Equipped with many accessories or features. **3.** Heavy with meaning or emotional import. **4.** *Slang* Intoxicated; drunk. **5.** *Slang* Having a great deal of money.

load·er (lō′dər) *n.* A computer program that transfers data from offline memory into internal storage.

load·ing (lō′dĭng) *n.* **1.** A weight placed on something else; a burden. **2.** A substance added to something else; a filler. **3.** An addition to an insurance premium. **4.** *Electricity* The addition of inductance to a circuit to improve its transmission characteristics.

load line *n.* See **Plimsoll mark.**

load·mas·ter (lōd′măs′tər) *n.* An aircraft crew member in charge of loading and unloading cargo or heavy weapons.

load·star (lōd′stär′) *n.* Variant of **lodestar.**

load·stone (lōd′stōn′) *n.* Variant of **lodestone.**

loaf¹ (lōf) *n., pl.* **loaves** (lōvz) **1.** A shaped mass of bread baked in one piece. **2.** A shaped, usu. rounded or oblong mass of food: *veal loaf.* [ME *lof* < OE *hlāf.*]

WORD HISTORY *Loaf, lord,* and *lady* are closely related words that testify to bread's fundamental importance in the Middle Ages. *Loaf* derives from Old English *hlāf,* "bread, loaf of bread," related to Gothic *hlaifs,* Old Norse *hleifr,* and Modern German *Laib,* all of which mean "loaf of bread." A *lord,* Old English *hlāford,* was a compound meaning "loaf-ward, keeper of bread," because a lord maintains and feeds his household and offers hospitality. Similarly, *lady* derives from Old English *hlǣfdige,* which became *lady* by 1382. The *–dige* comes from *dæge,* "kneader," and is related to our *dough.* A lady, therefore, is "a kneader of bread, a breadmaker."

---

loaf² (lōf) *intr.v.* **loafed, loaf·ing, loafs** To pass time at leisure; idle. [Prob. back-formation < LOAFER.]

loaf·er (lō′fər) *n.* One who is habitually idle. [Short for obsolete *land-loafer,* vagabond, idler, poss. partial transl. of obsolete Ger. *Landläufer* < MHGer. *landloufer* : *land,* land + *löufer,* runner (< *loufen,* to run < OHGer. *hlouffan*).]

Loafer A trademark used for a low leather step-in shoe with an upper resembling a moccasin but with a broad flat heel.

loam (lōm) *n.* **1.** Soil composed of a mixture of sand, clay, silt, and organic matter. **2.** A mixture of moist clay and sand, and often straw, used esp. in making bricks and foundry molds. ❖ *tr.v.* **loamed, loam·ing, loams** To fill, cover, or coat with loam. [ME *lam, lom,* clay < OE *lām.*] —**loam′y** *adj.*

loan (lōn) *n.* **1a.** Something lent for temporary use. **b.** A sum of money lent at interest. **2.** An act of lending; a grant for temporary use. **3.** A temporary transfer to a duty or place away from a regular job: *an auditor on loan from the main office.* ❖ *tr.v.* **loaned, loan·ing, loans** *Usage Problem* To lend. [ME *lan, lon* < ON *lān.* See **leik-** in App.] —**loan′er** *n.*

USAGE NOTE The verb *loan* is well established in American usage and cannot be considered incorrect. But *loan* is used only to describe physical transactions, as of money or goods. For figurative transactions *lend* is the only possible form: *Distance lends enchantment. Lend* is also required in fixed expressions such as *lend-lease* and *moneylender.*

Lo·an·da (lō-än′də) See **Luanda.**

loan shark *n. Informal* One who lends money at exorbitant interest rates, esp. one connected with organized crime.

loan translation *n.* A form of borrowing from one language to another whereby the semantic components of a given term are literally translated into their equivalents in the borrowing language, as *superman* from German *Übermensch.*

loan·word (lōn′wûrd′) *n.* A word adopted from another language and completely or partially naturalized, as *very* and *hors d'oeuvre,* both from French.

loath also **loth** (lōth, lōth) *adj.* Unwilling or reluctant; disin-

---

clined. [ME *loth* < OE *lāth,* hateful, loathsome.]

loathe (lōth) *tr.v.* **loathed, loath·ing, loathes** To dislike (someone or something) greatly; abhor. [ME *lothen* < OE *lāthian.*] —**loath′er** *n.*

loath·ing (lō′thĭng) *n.* Great dislike; abhorrence.

loath·ly (lōth′lē, lōth′-) *adj.* Loathsome. [ME *lothly* < OE *lāthlīc* : *lāth,* hateful + *-līc,* like; see —LY¹.]

loath·some (lōth′səm, lōth′-) *adj.* Arousing loathing; abhorrent. [ME *lothsome* : *loth,* hateful; see LOATH + *-som,* adj. suff.; see —SOME¹.] —**loath′some·ly** *adv.* —**loath′some·ness** *n.*

loaves (lōvz) *n.* Plural of **loaf¹.**

lob (lŏb) *v.* **lobbed, lob·bing, lobs** —*tr.* To hit, throw, or propel in a high arc. —*intr.* **1.** To lob a ball. **2.** To move heavily or clumsily. ❖ *n.* **1.** A ball that is lobbed. **2.** *Slang* A clumsy dull person; a lout. [< ME, pollack, lout, prob. of LGer. orig.] —**lob′ber** *n.*

Lo·ba·chev·ski (lō′bə-chĕf′skē, lə-bə-chyĕf′-), Nikolai Ivanovich 1792–1856. Russian mathematician who developed (1826) a system of non-Euclidean geometry.

lo·bar (lō′bər, -bär′) *adj.* Of or relating to a lobe or lobes.

lo·bate (lō′bāt′) also **lo·bat·ed** (-bā′tĭd) *adj.* **1.** Having lobes; lobed. **2.** Shaped like a lobe. **3.** Having separate toes, each bordered by a weblike lobe. Used for the feet of certain birds. —**lo′bate·ly** *adv.*

lo·ba·tion (lō-bā′shən) *n.* **1.** The state of being lobed. **2.** A structure or part resembling a lobe. **3.** A lobe.

lob·by (lŏb′ē) *n., pl.* **-bies 1.** A hall, foyer, or waiting room at or near the entrance to a building, such as a hotel. **2.** A public room next to the assembly chamber of a legislative body. **3.** A group of persons engaged in trying to influence legislators or other public officials in favor of a specific cause: *the banking lobby.* ❖ *v.* **-bied, -by·ing, -bies** —*intr.* To try to influence the thinking of legislators or other public officials for or against a specific cause. —*tr.* **1.** To try to influence public officials on behalf of or against (proposed legislation, for example). **2.** To try to influence (an official) to take a desired action. [From LOBBY < Med.Lat. *lobia,* monastic cloister, of Gmc. orig.] —**lob′by·er, lob′by·ist** *n.* —**lob′by·ism** *n.*

lobe (lōb) *n.* **1.** A rounded projection, esp. a rounded, projecting anatomical part. **2.** A subdivision of a bodily organ or part bounded by fissures, connective tissue, or other structures. [ME < OFr. < LLat. *lobus,* hull, pod < Gk. *lobos,* lobe, pod.]

lo·bec·to·my (lō-bĕk′tə-mē) *n., pl.* **-mies** Surgical excision of a lobe, as of the lung.

lobed (lōbd) *adj.* Having a lobe or lobes: *lobed leaves.*

lobe-finned fish (lōb′fĭnd′) *n.* Any of various extinct bony fishes of the subclass Crossopterygii, regarded by some as ancestors of terrestrial vertebrates.

lo·be·li·a (lō-bē′lē-ə, -bēl′yə) *n.* Any of numerous plants of the genus Lobelia, having terminal racemes of variously colored flowers. [NLat. *Lobelia,* genus name, after Matthias de *Lobel* (1538–1616), Flemish botanist and physician.]

lob·lol·ly (lŏb′lŏl′ē) *n., pl.* **-lies 1.** *Chiefly Southern US* A mudhole; a mire. **2.** The loblolly pine. [Perh. dialectal *lob,* to bubble + *lolly,* broth.]

loblolly pine *n.* A pine (*Pinus taeda*) of the southeast United States having needles in fascicles of three, oblong cones, and strong wood used as lumber and for paper pulp.

lo·bo (lō′bō) *n., pl.* **-bos** *Chiefly Texas* The gray wolf. [Sp., wolf < Lat. *lupus.* See **wl̥kʷo-** in App.]

lo·bot·o·mize (lə-bŏt′ə-mīz′, lō-) *tr.v.* **-mized, -miz·ing, -miz·es 1.** To perform a lobotomy on (a patient). **2.** To deprive (a person) of energy or vitality.

lo·bot·o·my (lə-bŏt′ə-mē, lō-) *n., pl.* **-mies** Surgical incision into the frontal lobe of the brain, a technique used to treat certain mental disorders. [LOBE + —TOMY.]

lob·scouse (lŏb′skous′) *n.* A sailor's stew made of meat, vegetables, and hardtack. [Perh. dialectal *lob,* to bubble + *scouse,* of unknown orig.]

lob·ster (lŏb′stər) *n.* **1.** Any of several edible marine crustaceans of the family Homaridae, esp. of the genus *Homarus,* having long antennae and five pairs of legs, the first pair of which is modified into large pincers. **2.** Any of several crustaceans that are related to the lobsters. **3.** The flesh of a lobster used as food. ❖ *intr.v.* **-stered, -ster·ing, -sters** To search for and catch lobsters. [ME *lopster, lobstere* < OE *loppestre,* alteration (perh. influenced by *loppe, lobbe,* spider) of Lat. *locusta.*] —**lob′ster·er** *n.*

lob·ster·man (lŏb′stər-mən) *n.* **1.** A man whose occupation is catching lobsters. **2.** A boat used in locating and catching lobsters.

lobster pot *n.* A slatted cage with an opening covered by a funnel-shaped net, used for trapping lobsters.

lobster ther·mi·dor (thûr′mĭ-dôr′) *n.* A dish of cooked lobster meat mixed with a cream sauce, put into a lobster shell, sprinkled with cheese, and browned. [After Fr. *Thermidor,* the 11th calendar month during the Fr. Revolution : Gk. *thermē,* heat; see THERM + Gk. *dōron,* gift; see **dō-** in App.]

lob·u·late (lŏb′yə-lāt′) also **lob·u·lat·ed** (-lā′tĭd) *adj.* Having or consisting of lobules. —**lob′u·la′tion** *n.*

lob·ule (lŏb′yōōl) *n.* **1.** A small lobe. **2.** A section or subdivision of a lobe. —**lob′u·lar** (-yə-lər), **lob′u·lose′** (-yə-lōs′) *adj.* —**lob′u·lar·ly** *adv.*

lob·worm (lŏb′wûrm′) *n.* See **lugworm.** [Alteration (influenced by LOB, lump, something hanging) of LUGWORM.]

lobster pot

ă	pat	oi	boy
ā	pay	ou	out
âr	care	ŏŏ	took
ä	father	ōō	boot
ĕ	pet	ŭ	cut
ē	be	ûr	urge
ĭ	pit	th	thin
ī	pie	th	this
îr	pier	hw	which
ŏ	pot	zh	vision
ō	toe	ə	about,
ô	paw		item

Stress marks:
′ (primary);
′ (secondary); as in
lexicon (lĕk′sĭ-kŏn′)

lo·cal (lō′kəl) *adj.* **1a.** Of, relating to, or characteristic of a particular place. **b.** Of or relating to a city, town, or district rather than a larger area. **2.** Not broad or general; not widespread. **3.** Of or affecting a specific part of the body: *a local anesthetic.* **4.** Making all possible or scheduled stops on a route; not express: *a local train.* ❖ *n.* **1.** A public conveyance that makes intermediate stops before reaching the final destination. **2.** A local chapter or branch of an organization, esp. of a labor union. **3.** *Informal* A person from a particular locality. [ME < OFr. < LLat. *locālis* < Lat. *locus,* place.] —**lo′cal·ly** *adv.* —**lo′cal·ness** *n.*

local area network *n.* See **LAN.**

local color *n.* **1.** The interest or flavor of a locality imparted by the customs and sights peculiar to it. **2.** The use of regional detail in a literary or an artistic work.

lo·cale (lō-kǎl′) *n.* **1.** A place, esp. with reference to a particular event. **2.** The scene or setting, as of a novel. [< Fr. *local,* local, locale < OFr. See LOCAL.]

lo·cal·ism (lō′kə-lǐz′əm) *n.* **1a.** A local linguistic feature. **b.** A local custom or peculiarity. **2.** Devotion to local interests and customs. —**lo′cal·ist** *n.*

lo·cal·i·ty (lō-kǎl′ǐ-tē) *n., pl.* **-ties 1.** A particular neighborhood, place, or district. **2.** The fact or quality of having position in space.

lo·cal·ize (lō′kə-līz′) *v.* **-ized, -iz·ing, -iz·es** —*tr.* **1.** To make local. **2.** To confine or restrict to a particular place or locality. **3.** To attribute to a particular locality. —*intr.* To become local, esp. to become fixed in one area or part. —**lo′cal·i·za′tion** (-kə-lĭ-zā′shən) *n.*

local option *n.* The power granted to a local political subdivision to decide whether to apply a law within its jurisdiction.

Lo·car·no (lō-kär′nō) A town of S Switzerland at the N end of Lake Maggiore; first mentioned in historical records in 749. The Locarno Pact between Germany and various European powers was signed here on Dec. 1, 1925. Pop. 14,300.

lo·cate (lō′kāt′, lō-kāt′) *v.* **-cat·ed, -cat·ing, -cates** —*tr.* **1.** To determine or specify the position or limits of: *located Albany on the map.* **2.** To find by searching, examining, or experimenting: *locate the source of error.* **3.** To place at a certain location; station or situate. —*intr.* To become established; settle. [Lat. *locāre, locāt-,* to place < *locus,* place.] —**lo′cat′a·ble** *adj.* —**lo′cat′er** *n.*

lo·ca·tion (lō-kā′shən) *n.* **1.** The act or process of locating. **2.** A place where something is or could be located; a site. **3.** A site away from a studio at which part or all of a movie is shot. **4.** A tract of land that has been surveyed and marked off. —**lo′ca′tion·al** *adj.*

loc·a·tive (lŏk′ə-tĭv) *adj.* Of, relating to, or being a grammatical case in certain inflected languages that indicates place in or on which or time at which, as in Latin *domī,* "at home." ❖ *n.* **1.** The locative case. **2.** A form or construction in the locative case. [NLat. *locātīvus* < Lat. *locātus,* p. part. of *locāre,* to place. See LOCATE.]

lo·ca·tor (lō′kā′tər) *n.* One that locates, as a person who fixes the boundaries of mining claims.

loc. cit. *abbr. Latin* loco citato (in the place cited)

loch (lŏкн, lŏk) *n. Scots* **1.** A lake. **2.** An arm of the sea similar to a fjord. [ME *louch* < Sc. Gael. *loch* < OIr.]

Loch (lŏk, lŏкн) See **Lake.**

lo·chi·a (lō′kē-ə, lŏk′ē-ə) *pl.n. Medicine* The normal uterine discharge of blood, tissue, and mucus from the vagina after childbirth. [Gk. *lokhia* < neut. pl. of *lokhios,* of childbirth < *lokhos,* childbirth. See **legh-** in App.] —**lo′chi·al** *adj.*

lo·ci (lō′sī′, -kē, -kī′) *n.* Plural of **locus.**

lock¹ (lŏk) *n.* **1.** A device operated by a key, keycard, or combination and used for holding, closing, or securing. **2.** A section of a waterway closed off with gates, in which vessels in transit are raised or lowered by raising or lowering the water level. **3.** A mechanism in a firearm for exploding the charge. **4.** An interlocking or entanglement of elements or parts. **5a.** *Sports* A hold in wrestling or self-defense that is secured on a part of an opponent's body. **b.** A secure hold; control. **c.** A sure thing; a certainty. ❖ *v.* **locked, lock·ing, locks** —*tr.* **1a.** To fasten the lock of: *close and lock a drawer.* **b.** To shut or make secure with or as if with locks: *locked the house.* **2.** To confine or exclude by or as if by means of a lock: *locked the dog in.* **3.** To fix in place so that movement or escape is impossible; hold fast. **4a.** To sight and follow (a moving target) automatically. **b.** To aim (a weapon or other device) at a moving target so as to follow it automatically. **5.** To engage and interlock securely so as to be immobile. **6.** To clasp or link firmly; intertwine. **7.** To bind in close struggle or battle. **8a.** To equip (a waterway) with locks. **b.** To pass (a vessel) through a lock. **9.** *Printing* **a.** To secure (letterpress type) in a chase or press bed by tightening the quoins. **b.** To fasten (a curved plate) to the cylinder of a rotary press. **10.** To invest (funds) in such a way that they cannot easily be converted into cash. **11.** *Computer Science* **a.** To deny access to the contents of (a file or disk, for example). **b.** To protect (a file) from changes or deletion. —*intr.* **1.** To become fastened or as if by means of a lock. **2.** To become entangled; interlock. **3.** To become rigid or immobile. **4.** To pass through a lock or locks in a waterway. —*phrasal verb:* **lock out** To withhold work from (employees) during a labor dispute. —*idioms:* **lock horns** To become embroiled in conflict. **lock, stock, and barrel** To the greatest or most complete extent;

wholly. [ME < OE *loc,* bolt, bar.] —**lock′a·ble** *adj.*

lock² (lŏk) *n.* **1a.** A length or curl of hair; a tress. **b.** The hair of the head. Often used in the plural. **2.** A small wisp or tuft, as of wool or cotton. [ME < OE *locc.*]

lock·age (lŏk′ĭj) *n.* **1.** The passage of a ship through a lock. **2.** A toll paid for the use of a lock. **3.** A system of locks.

lock·down (lŏk′doun′) *n.* **1.** The confinement of prison inmates to their cells as a security measure following a disturbance in the prison. **2.** A prison, esp. a high-security one. **3.** A device that secures a piece of equipment so that it cannot be moved or stolen.

Locke (lŏk), **John** 1632–1704. English philosopher whose *Essay Concerning Human Understanding* (1690) set out the principles of empiricism.

lock·er (lŏk′ər) *n.* **1.** One that locks: *a locker of doors.* **2.** A small, usu. metal compartment that can be locked for the safekeeping of clothing and valuables. **3.** A flat trunk for storage. **4.** A heavily insulated refrigerated cabinet, compartment, or room for storing frozen foods.

locker room *n.* A room furnished with lockers, as in a gymnasium, where clothes are changed and equipment is stored.

lock·er-room (lŏk′ər-rōōm′, -rŏŏm′) *adj.* **1.** Relating to, found in, or appropriate for a locker room: *a locker-room interview.* **2.** Bawdy or crude: *locker-room language.* [Sense 2 < the kind of banter attributed to male athletes in a locker room.]

lock·et (lŏk′ĭt) *n.* A small ornamental case for a picture or keepsake, usu. worn as a pendant. [ME *loket,* crossbar < OFr. *loquet,* latch, dim. of *loc,* lock, of Gmc. orig.]

lock·jaw (lŏk′jô′) *n.* **1.** See **tetanus** 1. 2. An early sign of tetanus, in which the jaw is locked closed because of a tonic spasm of the muscles of mastication.

lock·keep·er (lŏk′kē′pər) *n.* One who is in charge of a lock on a waterway.

lock·mas·ter (lŏk′măs′tər) *n.* See **lockkeeper.**

lock·nut also **lock nut** (lŏk′nŭt′) *n.* **1.** A usu. thin nut screwed down on another nut to prevent it from loosening. **2.** A self-locking nut.

lock·out (lŏk′out′) *n.* The withholding of work and closing down of a workplace by an employer during a labor dispute.

lock·set (lŏk′sĕt′) *n.* A set of hardware for shutting or locking a door.

lock·smith (lŏk′smĭth′) *n.* One that makes or repairs locks.

lock·step (lŏk′stĕp′) *n.* **1.** A way of marching in which the marchers follow each other as closely as possible. **2.** A standardized procedure followed closely and often mindlessly.

lock stitch *n.* A stitch made on a sewing machine by the interlocking of the upper thread and the bobbin thread.

lock·up (lŏk′ŭp′) *n.* **1.** *Informal* A jail, esp. one in which offenders are held while awaiting a court hearing. **2a.** The act or an instance of locking. **b.** The state of being locked.

Lock·wood (lŏk′wŏŏd′), **Belva Ann Bennett** 1830–1917. Amer. lawyer who was the first woman admitted to practice before the US Supreme Court (1879).

Lock·yer (lŏk′yər), Sir **Joseph Norman** 1836–1920. British astronomer who edited (1869–1919) *Nature* magazine.

lo·co¹ (lō′kō) *adj. Slang* Mad; insane. ❖ *n., pl.* **-cos 1.** See **locoweed.** **2.** See **loco disease.** ❖ *tr.v.* **-coed, -co·ing, -cos 1.** To poison with locoweed. **2.** *Slang* To make insane; craze. [Sp., crazy, poss. < Ar. *lawqā′,* foolish, fem. sing. of *'alwaq* < *lāqa,* to soften.]

lo·co² (lō′kō) *adv. & adj. Music* At the pitch written. [< Ital. *loco* < Lat. *locō,* at the place, ablative of *locus,* place.]

loco disease *n.* A disease of livestock caused by locoweed poisoning and marked by trembling and partial paralysis.

lo·co·ism (lō′kō-ĭz′əm) *n.* See **loco disease.**

lo·co·mo·tion (lō′kə-mō′shən) *n.* **1.** The act of moving from place to place. **2.** The ability to move from place to place. [Lat. *locō,* from a place, ablative of *locus,* place + MOTION.]

lo·co·mo·tive (lō′kə-mō′tĭv) *n.* **1.** A self-propelled vehicle, usu. electric or diesel-powered, for pulling or pushing freight or passenger cars on railroad tracks. **2.** A driving or pulling force; an impetus. ❖ *adj.* **1a.** Of, relating to, or involved in locomotion. **b.** Serving to put into motion or propel forward. **2.** Able to move independently from place to place. **3.** Of or relating to a self-propelled locomotive. **4.** Of or relating to travel. [Lat. *locō,* from a place, ablative of *locus,* place + Med.Lat. *mōtīvus,* causing motion; see MOTIVE.]

lo·co·mo·tor (lō′kə-mō′tər) *adj.* Of or relating to locomotion; locomotive. [Lat. *locō,* from a place, ablative of *locus,* place + MOTOR.]

locomotor ataxia *n.* See **tabes dorsalis.**

lo·co·weed (lō′kō-wēd′) *n.* Any of several plants of the genera *Oxytropis* and *Astragalus* in the pea family, found in western North America and poisonous to livestock.

loc·u·lar (lŏk′yə-lər) also **loc·u·late** (-lāt′, -lĭt) or **loc·u·lat·ed** (-lā′tĭd) *adj.* Having, made of, or divided into small cavities or compartments. [LOCUL(US) + -AR.] —**loc′u·la′tion** *n.*

loc·ule (lŏk′yōōl) or **loc·u·lus** (-yə-ləs) *n., pl.* **-ules** or **-li** (-lī′) A small cavity or compartment within an animal or plant part, as in a plant ovary. [Lat. *loculus,* little place, dim. of *locus,* place.]

loc·u·li·cid·al (lŏk′yə-lə-sīd′l) *adj. Botany* Longitudinally dehiscent along the capsule wall between the partitions of the locule, as in the fruits of irises and lilies. [LOCUL(US) + Lat. *-cīda,*

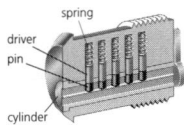

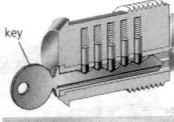

lock¹
top: pin-tumbler cylinder lock
bottom: ships in the Miraflores Locks, Panama Canal

locket

one who cuts; see –CIDE + –AL[1].]

lo•cum te•nens (lō′kəm tē′nĕnz′, tĕn′ənz) *n., pl.* **locum te•nen•tes** (tə-nĕn′tēz) A person, esp. a physician or cleric, who substitutes temporarily for another. [Med.Lat. *locum tenēns* : Lat. *locum*, place + Lat. *tenēns*, holding.]

lo•cus (lō′kəs) *n., pl.* **-ci** (-sī′, -kē, -kī′) **1.** A locality; a place. **2.** A center or focus of great activity or intense concentration: *the locus of power.* **3.** *Mathematics* The set or configuration of all points whose coordinates satisfy a single equation or one or more algebraic conditions. **4.** The position of a given gene on a chromosome. [Lat.]

locus clas•si•cus (klăs′ĭ-kəs) *n., pl.* **loci clas•si•ci** (klăs′ĭ-sī′, -kī′) A passage from a classic or standard work that is cited as an illustration or instance. [NLat. : Lat. *locus*, place + Lat. *classicus*, belonging to the highest class.]

lo•cust (lō′kəst) *n.* **1.** Any of numerous grasshoppers of the family Acrididae, often migrating in immense swarms that devour vegetation and crops. **2.** The seventeen-year locust. **3a.** Any of several North American deciduous trees of the genus *Robinia*, esp. *R. pseudoacacia,* having compound leaves, fragrant white flowers, and durable hard wood. **b.** Any of several similar or related trees, such as the carob. **c.** The wood of one of these trees. [ME < OFr. *locuste* < Lat. *locusta*.]

lo•cu•tion (lō-kyo͞o′shən) *n.* **1.** A particular word, phrase, or expression, esp. one used by a particular person or group. **2.** Style of speaking; phraseology. [ME *locucion* < OFr. *locution* < Lat. *locūtiō, locūtiōn-* < *locūtus*, p. part. of *loquī*, to speak.]

lode (lōd) *n.* **1a.** The metalliferous ore that fills a fissure in a rock formation. **b.** A vein of mineral ore deposited between clearly demarcated layers of rock. **2.** A rich source or supply. [ME, way, load < OE *lād*, way.]

lo•den (lōd′n) *n.* **1.** A durable, water-repellent, coarse woolen fabric used chiefly for coats and jackets. **2.** A deep olive green. [Ger., coarse fabric < MHGer. *lode* < OHGer. *lodo*.]

lode•star also **load•star** (lōd′stär′) *n.* **1.** A star, esp. Polaris, used as a point of reference. **2.** A guiding principle, interest, or ambition. [ME *lodesterre* : *lode*, way; see LODE + *sterre*, star; see STAR.]

lode•stone also **load•stone** (lōd′stōn′) *n.* **1.** A piece of magnetite that has magnetic properties and attracts iron or steel. **2.** One that attracts strongly. [ME *lode*, way; see LODE + STONE (< its use by sailors to show the way).]

lodge (lŏj) *n.* **1a.** A cottage or cabin used as a temporary abode or shelter: *a ski lodge.* **b.** A small house on the grounds of an estate or a park, used by a caretaker or gatekeeper. **c.** An inn. **2a.** Any of various Native American dwellings, such as a hogan or wigwam. **b.** The group living in such a dwelling. **3a.** A local chapter of certain fraternal organizations. **b.** The meeting hall of such a chapter. **c.** The members of such a chapter. **4.** The den of certain animals, such as the dome-shaped structure built by beavers. ❖ *v.* **lodged, lodg•ing, lodg•es** —*tr.* **1a.** To provide with temporary quarters, esp. for sleeping. **b.** To rent a room to. **c.** To place or establish in quarters. **2.** To serve as a depository for; contain. **3.** To place, leave, or deposit, as for safety. **4.** To fix, force, or implant: *lodge a bullet in a wall.* **5.** To register (a charge or complaint, for example) before an authority, such as a court; file. **6.** To vest (authority, for example). **7.** To beat (crops) down flat: *rye lodged by the cyclone.* —*intr.* **1a.** To live in a place temporarily. **b.** To rent accommodations, esp. for sleeping. **2.** To be or become embedded. [ME < OFr. *loge*, of Gmc. orig.]

Lodge, Henry Cabot 1850–1924. Amer. politician who as Senate majority leader (1918–24) successfully opposed US membership in the League of Nations.

Lodge, Henry Cabot, Jr. 1902–85. Amer. politician who served as ambassador to South Vietnam (1963–67).

lodge•pole pine (lŏj′pōl′) *n.* A pine *(Pinus contorta* subsp. *latifolia)* of western North America having light wood used in construction.

lodg•er (lŏj′ər) *n.* One that lodges, esp. one who rents and lives in a furnished room.

lodg•ing (lŏj′ĭng) *n.* **1.** A place to live. **2.** Sleeping accommodations. Often used in the plural. **3. lodgings** Furnished rooms in another's house rented for accommodation.

lodg•ment also **lodge•ment** (lŏj′mənt) *n.* **1a.** The act of lodging. **b.** The state of being lodged. **2.** A place for lodging. **3.** An accumulation or a deposit. **4.** A foothold or beachhead gained by troops in enemy or neutral territory.

lod•i•cule (lŏd′ĭ-kyo͞ol′) *n.* One of two or three small scales at the base of the ovary in a grass flower. [Lat. *lōdīcula*, small blanket, dim. of *lōdīx, lōdīc-*, blanket.]

Łódź (lŏdz, wo͞och) A city of central Poland WSW of Warsaw; chartered 1423. Pop. 846,514.

lo•ess (lō′əs, lĕs, lŭs) *n.* A buff to gray windblown deposit of fine-grained calcareous silt or clay. [Ger. *Löss* < Ger. dialectal *Lösch* < *lösch*, loose. See **leu-** in App.] —**lo•es′si•al** (lō-ĕs′ē-əl, lĕs′ē-əl, lŭs′-) *adj.*

Loew (lō), **Marcus** 1870–1927. Amer. motion-picture producer who founded a national chain of movie theaters (1912) and helped to form Metro-Goldwyn-Mayer (1924).

Loewe (lō), **Frederick** 1901–87. Austrian-born Amer. composer who collaborated with Alan Jay Lerner on a number of musicals, including *My Fair Lady* (1956).

loft (lôft, lŏft) *n.* **1a.** A large, usu. unpartitioned floor over a factory, warehouse, or other commercial or industrial space. **b.** Such a floor converted into an apartment or artist's studio. **2.** An open space under a roof; an attic or garret. **3.** A gallery or balcony. **4.** A hayloft. **5.** *Sports* **a.** The backward slant of the face of a golf club head, designed to drive the ball in a high arc. **b.** A golf stroke that drives the ball in a high arc. **c.** The upward course of a ball driven in a high arc. **6a.** The thickness of a fabric or yarn. **b.** The thickness of an item, such as a down coat, that is filled with compressible insulating material. ❖ *v.* **loft•ed, loft•ing, lofts** —*tr.* **1.** To put, store, or keep in a loft. **2.** To propel in a high arc. **3.** *Nautical* To lay out a full-size drawing of (the parts of a ship's hull, for example). —*intr.* **1.** To propel something, esp. a ball, in a high arc. **2.** To rise high into the air. [ME, sky, upstairs room < OE, air < ON *lopt*, upstairs room, sky, air.]

loft•y (lôf′tē, lŏf′-) *adj.* **-i•er, -i•est 1.** Of imposing height. **2.** Elevated in character; exalted. **3.** Affecting grandness; pompous. **4.** Arrogant; haughty. [ME, noble < *loft*, upstairs room, sky. See LOFT.] —**loft′i•ly** *adv.* —**loft′i•ness** *n.*

log[1] (lôg, lŏg) *n.* **1a.** A usu. large section of a trunk or limb of a fallen or felled tree. **b.** A long thick section of trimmed unhewn timber. **2a.** A device trailed from a ship to determine its speed through the water. **b.** A record of a ship's speed, its progress, and any shipboard events of navigational importance. **c.** The book in which this record is kept. **3.** A record of a vehicle's performance, as an aircraft's flight record. **4.** A record, as of the performance of a machine. ❖ *v.* **logged, log•ging, logs** —*tr.* **1a.** To cut down, trim, and haul the timber of (a piece of land). **b.** To cut (timber) into unhewn sections. **2.** To enter in a record, as of a ship. **3.** To travel (a specified distance, time, or speed). **4.** To spend or accumulate (time). —*intr.* To cut down, trim, and haul timber. ***—phrasal verbs:*** **log in** (or **on**) To enter into a computer the information required to begin a session. **log out** (or **off**) To enter into a computer the command to end a session. [ME *logge*.]

log[2] (lôg, lŏg) *n.* A logarithm.

log– *pref.* Variant of **logo–.**

–log *suff.* Variant of **–logue.**

Lo•gan (lō′gən), **Mount** A peak, 5,954.8 m (19,524 ft), of the St. Elias Mts. in SW Yukon Terr., Canada, near the AK border.

lo•gan•ber•ry (lō′gən-bĕr′ē) *n.* A trailing plant *(Rubus ursinus* var. *loganobaccus)* native to Oregon and south to Baja California and cultivated for its edible red fruit. [After James Harvey *Logan* (1841–1928), American jurist.]

log•a•rithm (lô′gə-rĭth′əm, lŏg′ə-) *n.* The power to which a base, such as 10, must be raised to produce a given number. If $n^x = a$, the logarithm of *a*, with *n* as the base, is *x;* symbolically, $\log_n a = x$. For example, $10^3 = 1{,}000$; therefore, $\log_{10} 1{,}000 = 3$. [NLat. *logarithmus* : Gk. *logos*, reason, proportion; see **leg-** in App. + Gk. *arithmos*, number.] —**log′a•rith′mic** (-rĭth′mĭk), **log′a•rith′mi•cal** (-mĭ-kəl) *adj.* —**log′a•rith′mi•cal•ly** *adv.*

log•book (lôg′bo͝ok′, lŏg′-) *n.* **1.** The official record book of a ship or an aircraft. **2.** A record book with periodic entries.

loge (lōzh) *n.* **1.** A small compartment, esp. a box in a theater. **2.** The front rows of the mezzanine in a theater. [Fr. < OFr., covered walk, lodge. See LODGE.]

log•ger (lô′gər, lŏg′ər) *n.* **1a.** One who logs trees. **b.** One engaged in the logging business. **2.** A machine, such as a crane or tractor, that is used for hauling or loading logs.

log•ger•head (lô′gər-hĕd′, lŏg′ər-) *n.* **1.** A loggerhead turtle. **2.** An iron tool consisting of a long handle with a bulbous end heated to melt tar or to warm liquids. **3.** *Nautical* A post on a whaleboat used to secure the harpoon rope. **4.** *Informal* **a.** A blockhead; a dolt. **b.** A disproportionately large head. ***—idiom:*** **at loggerheads** Engaged in a dispute. [Prob. dialectal *logger*, wooden block (prob. < LOG[1]) + HEAD.]

loggerhead shrike *n.* A common North American bird *(Lanius ludovicianus)* having gray, black, and white plumage, a black facial mask, and a hooked beak. [< its large head.]

loggerhead turtle *n.* A large marine turtle *(Caretta caretta)* inhabiting warm ocean waters and having a large head.

log•gi•a (lô′jē-ə, lŏj′ē-ə) *n.* **1.** An open-sided, roofed or vaulted gallery, either free-standing or along the front or side of a building, often at an upper level. **2.** An open balcony in a theater. [Ital. < OItal. < OFr. *loge*. See LOGE.]

log•ging (lô′gĭng, lŏg′ĭng) *n.* The work or business of felling and trimming trees and transporting the logs to a mill.

log•ic (lŏj′ĭk) *n.* **1.** The study of the principles of reasoning, esp. of the structure of propositions as distinguished from their content and of method and validity in deductive reasoning. **2a.** A system of reasoning: *Aristotle's logic.* **b.** A mode of reasoning. **c.** The formal guiding principles of a discipline, school, or science. **3.** Valid reasoning. **4.** The relationship between elements and between an element and the whole in a set of objects, individuals, principles, or events: *There's a certain logic to gridlock.* **5.** *Computer Science* **a.** The nonarithmetic operations performed by a computer, such as sorting, that involve yes-no decisions. **b.** Computer circuitry. **c.** Graphic representation of computer circuitry. [ME < OFr. *logique* < Lat. *logica* < Gk. *logikē (tekhnē)*, (art) of reasoning, logic, fem. of *logikos*, of reasoning < *logos*, reason. See **leg-** in App.]

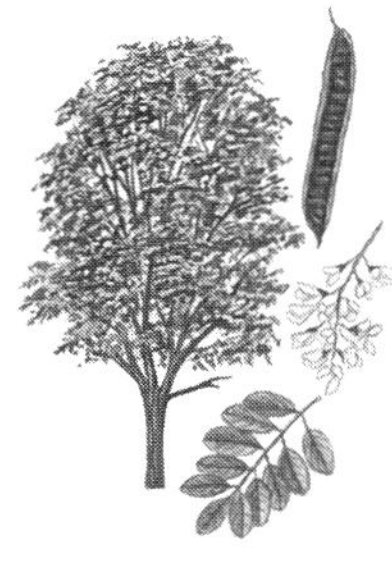

locust
black locust
Robinia pseudoacacia

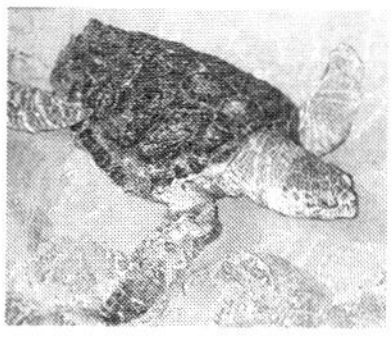

loggerhead turtle
Caretta caretta

ă	pat	oi	boy
ā	pay	ou	out
âr	care	o͝o	took
ä	father	o͞o	boot
ĕ	pet	ŭ	cut
ē	be	ûr	urge
ĭ	pit	th	thin
ī	pie	*th*	this
îr	pier	hw	which
ŏ	pot	zh	vision
ō	toe	ə	about, item
ô	paw		

Stress marks:
′ (primary);
′ (secondary), as in
lexicon (lĕk′sĭ-kŏn′)

log·i·cal (lŏj′ĭ-kəl) *adj.* **1.** Of, relating to, in accordance with, or of the nature of logic. **2.** Based on earlier or otherwise known statements, events, or conditions; reasonable: *Rain was a logical expectation in April.* **3.** Reasoning or capable of reasoning in a clear and consistent manner. —**log′i·cal·i·ty** (-kăl′ĭ-tē), **log′i·cal·ness** *n.* —**log′i·cal·ly** *adv.*

logical empiricism *n.* See **logical positivism**.

logical operation also **logic operation** *n.* An instruction (such as AND, OR, or NAND) in which the quantity being operated on and the results of the operation can each have two values.

logical operator also **logic operator** *n.* **1.** A symbol, as in a programming language, or a function that denotes a logical operation. **2.** An electronic device that performs logical operations on incoming signals.

logical positivism *n.* A philosophy asserting that in assessing truth observation has primacy and that metaphysical and subjective arguments not based on it are meaningless.

logic bomb *n.* A computer virus that remains hidden until it is triggered when certain specific conditions are met.

logic circuit *n.* A computer switching circuit that consists of logic gates and performs logical operations on data.

logic gate *n.* A mechanical, optical, or electronic system that performs a logical operation on an input signal.

lo·gi·cian (lō-jĭsh′ən) *n.* **1.** A practitioner of a system of logic. **2.** A student or scholar of logic.

log·in (lôg′ĭn′, lŏg′-) also **log·on** (-ŏn′, -ôn′) *n.* The process of identifying oneself to a computer, usu. by entering one's username and password.

lo·gi·on (lō′gē-ŏn′) *n., pl.* **-gi·a** (-gē-ə) A saying attributed to Jesus in the Gospels or in other ancient sources. [Gk., oracle < *legein*, to speak. See **leg-** in App.]

lo·gis·tic (lō-jĭs′tĭk) also **lo·gis·ti·cal** (-tĭ-kəl) *adj.* **1.** Of or relating to symbolic logic. **2.** Of or relating to logistics. [Med.Lat. *logisticus*, of calculation < Gk. *logistikos*, skilled in calculating < *logistēs*, calculator < *logizesthai*, to calculate < *logos*, reckoning, reason. See **leg-** in App.] —**lo·gis′ti·cal·ly** *adv.* —**lo′gis·ti′cian** (-jĭ-stĭsh′ən) *n.*

lo·gis·tics (lō-jĭs′tĭks, lə-) *n.* (*used with a sing. or pl. verb*) **1.** The aspect of military operations that deals with the procurement, distribution, maintenance, and replacement of materiel and personnel. **2.** The management of the details of an operation. [Fr. *logistiques* < *logistique*, logic < Med.Lat. *logisticus*, of calculation. See LOGISTIC.]

log·jam (lôg′jăm′, lŏg′-) *n.* **1.** An immovable mass of floating logs crowded together. **2.** A deadlock, as in talks; an impasse.

lo·go (lō′gō′) *n., pl.* **-gos** A name, symbol, or trademark designed for easy recognition, esp. one borne on a single printing plate or piece of type. [Short for LOGOGRAM and LOGOTYPE.]

logo– or **log–** *pref.* Word; speech: *logogram.* [Gk. < *logos*, word, speech. See **leg-** in App.]

log·o·gram (lô′gə-grăm′, lŏg′ə-) *n.* A written symbol representing a word without expressing its pronunciation; for example, for 4 read "four" in English, "quattro" in Italian. —**log′o·gram·mat′ic** (-grə-măt′ĭk) *adj.* —**log′o·gram·mat′i·cal·ly** *adv.*

log·o·graph (lô′gə-grăf′, lŏg′ə-) *n.* See **logogram**. —**log′o·graph′i·cal·ly** *adv.*

lo·gog·ra·phy (lō-gŏg′rə-fē) *n.* The use of logotypes in design and printing.

log·o·griph (lô′gə-grĭf′, lŏg′ə-) *n.* A word puzzle, such as an anagram or one in which clues are given in a set of verses. [LOGO– + Gk. *gríphos*, fishing basket, riddle.]

log·o·mach·y (lō-gŏm′ə-kē) *n., pl.* **-chies 1.** A dispute about words. **2.** A dispute carried on in words only; a battle of words. [Gk. *logomakhía* < *logomakhein*, to fight about words : *logo-*, logo- + *makhē*, battle.]

log·or·rhe·a (lô′gə-rē′ə, lŏg′ə-) *n.* Excessive use of words.

Lo·gos (lō′gŏs′, lŏg′ŏs′) *n.* **1.** *Philosophy* **a.** In pre-Socratic philosophy, the principle governing the cosmos, the source of this principle, or reasoning about the cosmos. **b.** Among the Sophists, the topics of rational argument or the arguments themselves. **c.** In Stoicism, the active, material, rational principle of the cosmos, identified with God and constituting the power of reason in the human soul. **2.** *Judaism* **a.** In biblical Judaism, the creative word of God, which is God's medium of communication with the human race. **b.** In Hellenistic Judaism, a hypostasis associated with divine wisdom. **3.** *Christianity* In Saint John's Gospel, the creative word of God, which is itself God and incarnate in Jesus. [Gk. See **leg-** in App.]

lo·go·type (lô′gə-tīp′, lŏg′ə-) *n.* **1.** *Printing* A single piece of type bearing two or more elements. **2.** A logo.

log·roll (lôg′rōl′, lŏg′-) *v.* **-rolled, -roll·ing, -rolls** —*tr.* To work toward the passage of (legislation) by logrolling. —*intr.* **1.** To engage in political logrolling. **2.** To birl. —**log′roll′er** *n.*

log·roll·ing (lôg′rō′lĭng, lŏg′-) *n.* **1.** The exchanging of political favors, esp. the trading of influence or votes among legislators to achieve passage of projects that are of interest to one another. **2.** The exchanging of favors or praise, as among artists. **3.** See **birling**. [< the early American practice of neighbors gathering to help clear land by rolling off and burning felled timber.]

–logue or **–log** *suff.* Speech; discourse: *travelogue.* [Fr. < Gk. *-logos* < *legein*, to speak. See **leg-** in App.]

log·wood (lôg′wo͝od′, lŏg′-) *n.* **1.** A spiny tropical American tree (*Haematoxylon campechianum*) in the pea family, having dark heartwood. **2.** The heartwood of this tree. **3.** The purplish-red dye obtained from the heartwood of this tree.

lo·gy (lō′gē) *adj.* **-gi·er, -gi·est** Sluggish; lethargic. [Perh. < Du. *log*, heavy, heavy or var. of E. *loggy*, heavy, sluggish (< LOG[1]).]

–logy or **–ology** *suff.* **1.** Discourse; expression: *phraseology.* **2.** Science; theory; study: *dermatology.* [ME *-logie* < Lat. *-logia* < Gk. *-logiā* (< *logos*, word, speech), and < *-logos*, one who deals with (< *legein*, to speak.)]

loin (loin) *n.* **1.** The part of the body of a human or quadruped on either side of the backbone and between the ribs and hips. **2.** One of several cuts of meat, such as tenderloin, taken from this part of an animal's body, usu. including the vertebrae. **3. loins a.** The region of the hips, groin, and lower abdomen. **b.** The reproductive organs. [ME *loine* < OFr. *loigne* < VLat. **lumbea (carō)*, loin (meat), fem. of **lumbeus* < Lat. *lumbus*, loin.]

loin·cloth (loin′klôth′, -klŏth′) *n.* A strip of cloth worn around the loins.

Loir (lwär) A river, c. 311 km (193 mi), of NW France flowing generally W to the Sarthe R.

Loire (lwär) The longest river of France, rising in the Cévennes and flowing c. 1,014 km (630 mi) to the Bay of Biscay.

loi·ter (loi′tər) *intr.v.* **-tered, -ter·ing, -ters 1.** To stand idly about; linger aimlessly. **2.** To proceed slowly or with many stops. **3.** To delay or dawdle: *loiter over a task.* [ME *loitren*, prob. < MDu. *loteren*, to totter, be loose.] —**loi′ter·er** *n.*

Lo·ki (lō′kē) *n. Mythology* A Norse god who created discord, esp. among other gods.

Lo·li·ta (lō-lē′tə) *n.* An adolescent girl regarded as seductive. [After *Lolita*, heroine of *Lolita* by Vladimir Nabokov.]

loll (lŏl) *v.* **lolled, loll·ing, lolls** —*intr.* **1.** To move, stand, or recline in an indolent or relaxed manner. **2.** To hang or droop laxly. —*tr.* To permit to hang or droop laxly. ❖ *n. Archaic* An act or attitude of lolling. [ME *lollen*, prob. < MDu., to doze.] —**loll′er** *n.* —**loll′ing·ly** *adv.*

Lol·land (lŏl′ənd, lô′län) An island of SE Denmark in the Baltic Sea S of Sjaelland.

lol·la·pa·loo·za (lŏl′ə-pə-lōō′zə) *n. Slang* Something outstanding of its kind. [?]

Lol·lard (lŏl′ərd) *n.* A member of a sect of religious reformers in England who were followers of John Wycliffe in the 14th and 15th centuries. [ME < MDu. *Lollaerd*, mumbler, mutterer, heretic < *lollen*, doze, to mumble.]

lol·li·pop also **lol·ly·pop** (lŏl′ē-pŏp′) *n.* A confection consisting of hard candy on the end of a small stick. [Perh. dialectal *lolly*, tongue (< LOLL, to dangle the tongue) + POP[1].]

lol·lop (lŏl′əp) *intr.v.* **-loped, -lop·ing, -lops 1.** To move with a bobbing motion. **2.** *Chiefly British* To lounge about; loll. [Alteration of LOLL.] —**lol′lop·y** *adj.*

lol·ly (lŏl′ē) *n., pl.* **-lies** *Chiefly British* **1a.** A piece of candy, esp. hard candy. **b.** A lollipop. **2.** Money. [Short for LOLLIPOP.]

lol·ly·gag (lŏl′ē-găg′) also **lal·ly·gag** (lăl′ē-) *intr.v.* **-gagged, -gag·ging, -gags** To waste time by puttering aimlessly; dawdle. [?]

Lo·ma·mi (lō-mä′mē) A river of Congo (formerly Zaire) flowing c. 1,448 km (900 mi) to the Congo R.

Lo·mas de Za·mo·ra (lō′mäs də zä-môr′ə, sä-mō′rä) A city of E Argentina, a suburb of Buenos Aires. Pop. 572,769.

Lo·max (lō′mäks′), **John Avery** 1867–1948. Amer. folklorist who with his son **Alan Lomax** (b. 1915) toured the country recording blues and folk musicians for the Library of Congress.

Lom·bard (lŏm′bərd, -bärd′, lŭm′-) *n.* **1.** A member of a Germanic people that invaded northern Italy in the sixth century A.D. **2.** A native or inhabitant of Lombardy. **3.** A banker or moneylender. [ME *Lumbarde* < OFr. *lombard* < OItal. *lombardo* < Med.Lat. *lombardus* < Lat. *Langobardus, Longobardus*. See **del-** in App.]

Lom·bard (lŏm′bärd′, lŭm′-), **Peter** 1100?–60? Italian theologian noted for his *Sententiarum Libri IV* (1148–51).

Lom·bar·dy (lŏm′bər-dē, lŭm′-) A region of N Italy bordering on Switzerland; center of the kingdom of the Lombards in the 6th cent. A.D.

Lombardy poplar *n.* A deciduous tree (*Populus nigra* var. *italica*) having upward-pointing branches that form a slender columnar outline. [After LOMBARDY.]

Lom·bok (lŏm-bŏk′) An island of S-central Indonesia in the Lesser Sundas E of Bali, from which it is separated by the **Lombok Strait**.

Lo·mé (lō-mā′) The cap. of Togo, in the S part on the Gulf of Guinea. Pop. 369,926.

lo mein (lō′ mān′) *n.* A Chinese dish of boiled wheat noodles stir-fried with vegetables, seasonings, and other ingredients, such as chicken. [Cantonese.]

lo·ment (lō′mĕnt′) *n.* An indehiscent legume, as of the tick trefoil, usu. constricted between the seeds and separating at maturity into one-seeded segments. [Lat. *lōmentum*, skin conditioner made of bean meal < *lavere*, to wash. See **leu(ə)-** in App.]

Lo·mond (lō′mənd), **Loch** A lake in S-central Scotland; noted for its associations with the 18th-cent. outlaw Rob Roy.

Lon·don (lŭn′dən) **1.** The cap. of the United Kingdom, on the

Thames R. in SE England; built on the site of a Roman outpost named Londinium. Pop. 6,904,600. **2.** A city of SE Ontario, Canada, SW of Toronto; settled in 1826. Pop. 325,646.

London, John ("Jack") Griffith 1876–1916. Amer. writer whose adventure novels include *The Call of the Wild* (1903).

London broil *n.* Broiled flank steak cut into thin slices. [After LONDON, England.]

Lon·don·der·ry (lŭn′dən-dĕr′ē, lŭn′dən-dĕr′ē) See **Derry.**

lone (lōn) *adj.* **1a.** Without accompaniment; solitary. **b.** Without companionship; isolated or lonely. **2.** Being the only one; sole. **3.** Situated by itself. [ME, short for ALONE. See ALONE.]

lone·ly (lōn′lē) *adj.* **-li·er, -li·est 1a.** Without companions; lone. **b.** Characterized by aloneness; solitary. **2.** Unfrequented by people; desolate. **3a.** Dejected by the awareness of being alone. See Syns at **alone. b.** Producing such dejection: *a lonely night of the week.* —**lone′li·ly** *adv.* —**lone′li·ness** *n.*

lone·ly-hearts or **lone·ly·hearts** (lōn′lē-härts′) *adj.* Of or relating to people who are looking for dates or partners.

lon·er (lō′nər) *n.* One who avoids company.

lone·some (lōn′səm) *adj.* **1a.** Dejected because of a lack of companionship. See Syns at **alone. b.** Producing such dejection: *a lonesome hour.* **2.** Deserted; unfrequented: *a lonesome valley.* **3.** Solitary; lone. ❖ *n. Informal* Self: *He ate by his lonesome.* —**lone′some·ly** *adv.* —**lone′some·ness** *n.*

lone wolf *n.* One who prefers no company or help.

long[1] (lông, lŏng) *adj.* **long·er, long·est 1a.** Extending a relatively great distance. **b.** Having relatively great height; tall. **c.** Having the greater length of two or the greatest length of several. **2.** Of relatively great duration. **3.** Of a specified linear extent or duration: *a mile long.* **4.** Made up of many members or items: *a long list.* **5a.** Extending beyond an average or a standard: *a long game.* **b.** Extending or landing beyond a given boundary, limit, or goal: *Her serve was long.* **6.** Tediously protracted; lengthy: *a long speech.* **7.** Concerned with distant issues; far-reaching: *a long view.* **8.** Involving substantial chance; risky: *long odds.* **9.** Having an abundance or excess: *a story that is long on local detail.* **10.** Holding a commodity or security in expectation of a rise in price. **11.** *Linguistics* **a.** Having a comparatively great duration. Used of a vowel or consonant. **b.** *Grammar* Relating to or being English speech sounds (ā, ē, ī, ō, ōō) that are tense vowels or diphthongs. **12a.** Stressed or accented. Used of a syllable in accentual prosody. **b.** Being of relatively great duration. Used of a syllable in quantitative prosody. ❖ *adv.* **longer, longest 1.** During or for an extended period of time. **2.** At or to a considerable distance; far. **3.** Beyond a given boundary, limit, or goal. **4.** For or throughout a specified period: *all night long.* **5.** At a point of time distant from that referred to. **6.** Into or in a long position, as of a commodity market. ❖ *n.* **1.** A long time: *It took long.* **2.** A long syllable, vowel, or consonant. **3.** One who acquires holdings in a security or commodity in expectation of a rise in price. **4a.** A garment size for a tall person. **b. longs** Trousers extending to the feet or ankles. —*idioms:* **any longer** For more time. **before long** Soon. **long ago 1.** At a time or during a period well before the present. **2.** A time well before the present. **long in the tooth** Growing old. **no longer** Not now as formerly. **not long for** Unlikely to remain for much more time in. **the long and the short of it** The substance or gist. [ME < OE *lang.* See **del-** in App.]

long[2] (lông, lŏng) *intr.v.* **longed, long·ing, longs** To have an earnest, heartfelt desire, esp. for something beyond reach. [ME *longen* < OE *langian.* See **del-** in App.]

Long, Huey Pierce Called "the Kingfish." 1893–1935. Amer. politician who served as governor of LA (1928–31) and US senator (1932–35).

long. *abbr.* longitude

lon·gan (lông′gən, lŏng′-) *n.* **1.** An Asian evergreen tree (*Euphoria longan*) having yellowish-brown drupes with edible flesh. **2.** Its fruit. [NLat. *longan,* specific epithet < Chin. (Mandarin) *lóng yǎn* : *lóng,* dragon + *yǎn,* eye.]

lon·ga·nim·i·ty (lông′gə-nĭm′ĭ-tē, lŏng′-) *n.* Calmness in the face of suffering and adversity; forbearance. [ME *longanimite* < OFr. < LLat. *longanimitās* < *longanimis,* patient : Lat. *longus,* long; see LONGITUDE + Lat. *animus,* mind, reason; see **anə-** in App.]

Long Beach A city of S CA on an arm of the Pacific Ocean SE of Los Angeles. Pop. 461,522.

long·boat (lông′bōt′, lŏng′-) *n.* The longest boat carried by a sailing ship, esp. by a merchant ship.

long·bow (lông′bō′, lŏng′-) *n.* A long hand-drawn bow, such as that used in medieval England, which sometimes exceeded 6 feet (1.8 meters) in length.

long distance *n.* **1.** An operator or a system that places long-distance telephone calls. **2.** A long-distance telephone call.

long-dis·tance (lông′dĭs′təns, lŏng′-) *adj.* **1.** Covering a long distance. **2.** Of, relating to, or being telephone communication to a distant station. —**long′-dis′tance** *adv.*

long division *n.* A process of division in arithmetic, usu. used with a large divisor, in which each step of the division is written out.

long dozen *n.* A baker's dozen; thirteen.

long-drawn-out (lông′drôn′out′, lŏng′-) *adj.* Greatly extended or protracted; prolonged: *a long-drawn-out speech.*

lon·ge·ron (lŏn′jər-ən) *n.* A major structural member of an aircraft fuselage, running from front to rear. [Fr. < OFr., beam < *long,* long < Lat. *longus.* See **del-** in App.]

lon·gev·i·ty (lŏn-jĕv′ĭ-tē, lôn-) *n., pl.* **-ties 1a.** Long life; great duration of life. **b.** Length or duration of life. **2.** Long duration or continuance, as in an occupation. [LLat. *longaevitās* < Lat. *longaevus,* ancient : *longus,* long; see **del-** in App. + *aevum,* age; see **aiw-** in App.] —**lon·ge′vous** (-jē′vəs) *adj.*

long face *n.* A discontented or sullen facial expression.

Long·fel·low (lông′fĕl′ō, lŏng′-), **Henry Wadsworth** 1807–82. Amer. writer whose works include *The Song of Hiawatha* (1855).

long green *n. Slang* Paper money.

long·hair (lông′hâr′, lŏng′-) *n. Informal* **1.** One dedicated to the arts and esp. to classical music. **2.** One whose taste in the arts is considered overrefined. **3.** A person with long hair, esp. a hippie. —**long′hair′, long′haired′** *adj.*

long·hand (lông′hănd′, lŏng′-) *n.* Cursive writing.

long haul *n.* **1.** A long distance. **2.** A long period of time. —**long′-haul′** (lông′hôl′, lŏng′-) *adj.*

long·head (lông′hĕd′, lŏng′-) *n. Anthropology* **1.** A head having a cephalic index less than 76. **2.** A person having such a head.

long·head·ed also **long-head·ed** (lông′hĕd′ĭd, lŏng′-) *adj.* **1.** *Anthropology* Dolichocephalic. **2.** Foresighted; wise.

long·horn (lông′hôrn′, lŏng′-) *n.* **1.** Any of a breed of cattle with long horns. **2.** A kind of Cheddar cheese made in long cylinders.

long-horned beetle (lông′hôrnd′, lŏng′-) *n.* Any of numerous beetles of the family Cerambycidae, having long antennae.

long-horned grasshopper *n.* Any of various large insects of the family Tettigoniidae, having long slender antennae.

long·house or **long house** (lông′hous′, lŏng′-) *n.* A long communal dwelling, esp. of certain Native American, Polynesian, and Indonesian peoples.

lon·gi·corn (lŏn′jĭ-kôrn′) *n.* See **long-horned beetle.** ❖ *adj.* **1.** Having long antennae. **2.** Of or belonging to the family Cerambycidae, which includes the long-horned beetles. [< NLat. *Longicornia,* former genus name : Lat. *longus,* long; see LONGITUDE + Lat. *cornū,* horn; see **ker-**[1] in App.]

long·ing (lông′ĭng, lŏng′-) *n.* A strong persistent yearning or desire, esp. one that cannot be fulfilled. —**long′ing·ly** *adv.*

Lon·gi·nus (lŏn-jī′nəs), **Dionysius Cassius** A.D. 210?–273. Greek philosopher. The volume of literary criticism *On The Sublime* is attributed to him.

Long Island A long narrow island of SE NY bordered on the S by the Atlantic Ocean and separated from CT on the N by **Long Island Sound,** an arm of the Atlantic. The W part of Long I. includes two boroughs of New York City.

lon·gi·tude (lŏn′jĭ-tōōd′, -tyōōd′, lôn′-) *n.* **1.** Angular distance on the earth's surface, measured east or west from the prime meridian at Greenwich, England, to the meridian passing through a position, expressed in degrees (or hours), minutes, and seconds. **2.** Celestial length, a measured length < OFr. < Lat. *longitūdō, longitūdin-* < *longus,* long. See **del-** in App.]

lon·gi·tu·di·nal (lŏn′jĭ-tōōd′n-əl, -tyōōd′-, lôn′-) *adj.* **1a.** Of or relating to longitude or length. **b.** Concerned with the development of persons or groups over time. **2.** Placed or running lengthwise. —**lon′gi·tu′di·nal·ly** *adv.*

long johns *pl.n. Informal* Long warm underwear. [< the name *John.*]

long jump *n.* A jump in track and field that is made for distance rather than height.

long·leaf pine (lông′lēf′, lŏng′-) *n.* An evergreen tree (*Pinus palustris*) of the southeast United States with long needles and resinous wood.

long·line (lông′līn′, lŏng′-) *n.* A heavy fishing line usu. several miles long and having a series of baited hooks. —**long′-lin′ing** *n.*

long-lived (lông′līvd′, -lĭvd′, lŏng′-) *adj.* **1.** Having a long life. **2.** Lasting a long time; persistent: *a long-lived rumor.* **3.** Functioning a long time; durable. [ME *long-lifed* : *long,* long; see LONG[1] + *life,* life; see LIFE + *-ed,* having; see **-ed**[3].] —**long′-lived′ness** *n.*

long measure *n.* **1.** See **linear measure. 2.** See **long meter.**

long meter *n.* A quatrain in iambic tetrameter, rhyming in the second and fourth lines and often in the first and third.

long·neck (lông′nĕk′, lŏng′-) *n.* A glass beer bottle with an elongated neck.

long-play·ing (lông′plā′ĭng, lŏng′-) *adj.* Relating to or being a phonograph record that turns at 33⅓ revolutions per minute.

long-range (lông′rānj′, lŏng′-) *adj.* **1.** Of, suitable for, or reaching long distances: *long-range missiles.* **2.** Requiring or involving an extended span of time: *long-range planning.*

long run *n.* A long period of time: *It worked in the long run.*

long·shore (lông′shôr′, -shōr′, lŏng′-) *adj.* Occurring, living, or working along a seacoast. [Short for ALONGSHORE.]

long·shore·man (lông′shôr′mən, -shōr′-, lŏng′-) *n.* A dock worker who loads and unloads ships.

long shot *n.* **1.** An entry, as in a horserace, that has only a slight chance of winning. **2a.** A bet that is made at great odds. **b.** A venture that offers a great reward but has little chance of success. **3.** A photograph or a film or television shot in which the subject appears small or distant in relation to the rest of the image. —*idiom:* **by a long shot** *Informal* To any extent; at all.

longhorn
Texas longhorn

Usu. used in negative sentences.

long-sight·ed (lông′sī′tĭd, lŏng′-) *adj.* Farsighted. **—long′-sight′ed·ly** *adv.* **—long′-sight′ed·ness** *n.*

long·some (lông′səm, lŏng′-) *adj.* Tiresomely long.

Longs Peak (lôngz) A mountain, 4,347.8 m (14,255 ft), in the Front Range of the Rocky Mts. in N-central CO.

long·spur (lông′spûr′, lŏng′-) *n.* Any of several birds, esp. of the genus *Calcarius* of northern regions, having brownish plumage and long-clawed hind toes.

long-stand·ing (lông′stăn′dĭng, lŏng′-) *adj.* Of long duration or existence: *a long-standing friendship.*

Long·street (lông′strēt′, lŏng′-), **James** 1821–1904. Amer. Confederate general whose delay in carrying out orders contributed to the Confederate defeat at Gettysburg (1863).

long-suf·fer·ing (lông′sŭf′ər-ĭng, lŏng′-) *adj.* Patiently enduring wrongs or difficulties. ❖ *n.* Patient endurance. See Syns at **patience.** **—long′-suf′fer·ing·ly** *adv.*

long suit *n.* **1.** *Games* The suit in which a given hand has the most cards. **2.** One's strongest asset in quality or talent.

long-tailed duck (lông′tāld′, lŏng′-) *n.* See **oldsquaw.**

long-term (lông′tûrm′, lŏng′-) *adj.* Involving, maturing after, or being in effect for a long time: *a long-term investment.*

long·time (lông′tīm′, lŏng′-) *adj.* Having existed or persisted for a long time.

long ton *n.* See **ton** 2.

Lon·gueuil (lông-gāl′) A city of S Quebec, Canada, on the St. Lawrence R. opposite Montreal. Pop. 127,977.

lon·gueur (lông-gûr′, lŏng′-) *n.* A long, tedious passage in a work of literature or performing art. [Fr. < OFr. *longor*, a protracted discussion < *long*, long < Lat. *longus*. See LONGITUDE.]

long-waist·ed (lông′wā′stĭd, lŏng′-) *adj.* Having a distance between shoulders and waist that is longer than average.

long wave *n.* A radio wave with a wavelength in excess of 1000 meters.

long-wind·ed (lông′wĭn′dĭd, lŏng′-) *adj.* **1.** Wearisomely verbose. **2.** Able to maintain breathing power during exertion. **—long′-wind′ed·ly** *adv.* **—long′-wind′ed·ness** *n.*

long·wise (lông′wīz′, lŏng′-) *adv.* & *adj.* Lengthwise.

loo¹ (lo͞o) *n.*, *pl.* **loos** A card game in which each player contributes stakes to a pool. [Short for obsolete *lanterloo* < Fr. *lanturlu*, a meaningless refrain, loo.]

loo² (lo͞o) *n.*, *pl.* **loos** *Chiefly British* A toilet. [?]

loo·fa or **loo·fah** (lo͞o′fə) also **luf·fa** (lo͞o′fə, lŭf′ə) *n.* **1.** Any of several Old World tropical vines of the genus *Luffa*, having cylindrical fruit with a fibrous spongelike interior. **2.** The interior, used as a washing sponge or filter. [Ar. *lūfa* < *lūf*, loofas.]

look (lo͝ok) *v.* **looked, look·ing, looks** —*intr.* **1a.** To employ one's sight, esp. in a given direction or on a given object: *looked at the wall.* **b.** To search. **2a.** To turn one's glance or gaze: *looked to the right.* **b.** To turn one's attention; attend. **c.** To turn one's expectations: *looked to us for help.* **3.** To seem or appear to be: *looks morose.* **4.** To face in a specified direction: *The cottage looks on the river.* —*tr.* **1.** To turn one's eyes on: *looked him in the eye.* **2.** To convey by one's expression. **3a.** To have an appearance of conformity with: *He looks his age.* **b.** To appear to be. ❖ *n.* **1a.** The act or instance of looking. **b.** A gaze or glance expressive of something: *a mournful look.* **2a.** Appearance or aspect: *a look of great age.* **b. looks** Physical appearance, esp. when pleasing. **c.** A distinctive, unified manner of dress or fashion. **—phrasal verbs: look after** To take care of. **look for 1.** To search for; seek. **2.** To expect. **look into** To inquire into; investigate. **look on** (or **upon**) To regard in a certain way. **look out** To be watchful or careful; take care. **look over** To examine or inspect, often hastily. **look to 1.** *Usage Problem* To expect or hope to. **2.** To see about or promise to: *a policy that looked to reduce taxes.* **look up 1.** To search for and find, as in a reference book. **2.** To visit. **3.** To become better; improve. **—idioms: look a gift horse in the mouth** To be critical or suspicious of something one has received without expense. **look alive** (or **sharp**) *Informal* To act or respond quickly. **look down on** (or **upon**) To regard with contempt or condescension. **look down (one's) nose at** (or **on**) To regard with contempt or condescension. **look forward to** To think of (a future event) with pleasurable anticipation. **look in on** To visit. **look the other way** To deliberately overlook something. **look up to** To admire. [ME *loken* < OE *lōcian*.]

USAGE NOTE The phrasal verb *look to* has recently developed the meaning "expect to, hope to," as in *I'm looking to sell my car.* Probably because of its informal nature, this usage is not acceptable in writing for 52 percent of the Usage Panel.

look-a·like also **look·a·like** (lo͝ok′ə-līk′) *n.* One that closely resembles another; a double.

look·er (lo͝ok′ər) *n.* **1.** One that looks, esp. a spectator or an onlooker. **2.** *Slang* A very attractive person.

look·er-on (lo͝ok′ər-ŏn′, -ôn′) *n.*, *pl.* **look·ers-on** (lo͝ok′ərz-ŏn′) A spectator; an onlooker.

look-in (lo͝ok′ĭn′) *n.* **1.** A short visit. **2.** A quick glance.

look·ing glass (lo͝ok′ĭng) *n.* See **mirror** 1.

look·ism (lo͝ok′ĭz′əm) *n.* Discrimination or prejudice against people based on their appearance. **—look′ist** *adj.* & *n.*

look·out (lo͝ok′out′) *n.* **1.** The act of observing or keeping watch.

2. A high place or structure commanding a wide view, used for observation. **3.** One who keeps watch. **4.** *South Atlantic US* Outlook; view. **5.** An object of concern or worry.

look-see (lo͝ok′sē′) *n. Informal* A quick survey or glance.

look·up (lo͝ok′ŭp′) *n.* A procedure in which a table of values stored in a computer is searched until a specified value is found.

loom¹ (lo͞om) *intr.v.* **loomed, loom·ing, looms 1.** To come into view as a massive, distorted, or indistinct image. **2.** To appear to the mind in a magnified and threatening form. **3.** To seem imminent; impend: *Revolution loomed.* ❖ *n.* A distorted, threatening appearance of something, as through fog or darkness. [Perh. of Scand. orig.]

loom² (lo͞om) *n.* An apparatus for making thread or yarn into cloth by weaving strands together at right angles. ❖ *tr.v.* **loomed, loom·ing, looms** To weave (cloth) on a loom. [ME *lome* < OE *gelōma*, tool : *ge-*, collective pref.; see YCLEPT + *-lōma*, tool (as in *handlōman*, tools).]

loon¹ (lo͞on) *n.* Any of several fish-eating diving birds of the genus *Gavia* of northern regions, having a short tail, webbed feet, and a laughlike cry. [Perh. alteration of dialectal *loom*, guillemot, diver < ON *lōmr*.]

loon² (lo͞on) *n. Informal* One who is crazy or deranged. [Prob. < LOON¹ (< its loud cry) and influenced by LUNATIC.]

loon·ie (lo͞o′nē) *n. Informal* **1.** A Canadian coin worth one dollar. **2.** The Canadian dollar. [< the image of a loon on one side of the coin.]

loon·y or **loon·ey** also **lun·y** (lo͞o′nē) *Informal adj.* **-i·er, -i·est 1.** Extremely foolish or silly. **2.** Crazy; insane. ❖ *n.*, *pl.* **-ies** also **-eys** A foolish or crazy person. [Shortening and alteration of LUNATIC or < LOON².] **—loon′i·ly** *adv.* **—loon′i·ness** *n.*

loony bin *n. Offensive Slang* An institution for the mentally ill.

loop¹ (lo͞op) *n.* **1a.** A length of line, thread, or other thin material that is curved or doubled over making an opening. **b.** The opening formed by such a doubled line. **2.** Something having a shape, order, or path of motion that is circular or curved over on itself. **3.** *Electricity* A closed circuit. **4.** *Computer Science* A sequence of instructions that repeats either a specified number of times or until a particular condition is met. **5.** A type of loop-shaped intrauterine device. **6.** A flight maneuver in which an aircraft flies a circular path in a vertical plane with the lateral axis of the aircraft remaining horizontal. **7.** A segment of film or magnetic tape whose ends are joined, making a strip that can be continuously replayed. **8.** *Sports* See **league¹** 2. ❖ *v.* **looped, loop·ing, loops** —*tr.* **1.** To form into a loop. **2.** To fasten, join, or encircle with loops or a loop. **3.** To fly (an aircraft) in a loop. **4.** To move in a loop or an arc. **5.** *Electricity* To join (conductors) so as to complete a circuit. **6.** To add or substitute (words) in a film by altering the sound track. —*intr.* **1.** To form a loop. **2.** To move in a loop. **3.** To make a loop in an aircraft. **—idioms: in the loop** Part of a group that is kept informed about something. **knock (or throw) for a loop** *Slang* To surprise tremendously; astonish. **out of the loop** Not part of a group that is kept informed about something. [ME *loupe*, prob. < MIr. *lúb* (perh. influenced by ME *lep*, basket).]

loop² (lo͞op) *n. Archaic* A loophole through which small arms may be fired. [ME *loupe*; akin to MDu. *lūpen*, to lie in wait, peer.]

looped (lo͞opt) *adj.* **1.** Formed into or having a loop or loops. **2.** *Slang* Intoxicated; drunk.

loop·er (lo͞o′pər) *n.* **1.** One that makes loops. **2.** See **measuring worm.**

loop·hole (lo͞op′hōl′) *n.* **1.** A way of escaping a difficulty, esp. an omission or ambiguity in the wording of a contract or law that allows one to evade compliance. **2.** A small hole or slit in a wall, esp. one through which small arms may be fired. [LOOP² + HOLE.]

loop of Hen·le (hĕn′lē) *n.* The segment of the nephron of a vertebrate kidney between the proximal and distal convoluted tubules that helps transport ions and water and concentrate urine. [After Friedrich Gustav Jacob *Henle* (1809–85), German pathologist.]

loop·y (lo͞o′pē) *adj.* **-i·er, -i·est 1.** Consisting of or covered with loops. **2.** Offbeat; crazy.

Loos (lo͞os), **Anita** 1893?–1981. Amer. writer best known for *Gentlemen Prefer Blondes* (1925).

loose (lo͞os) *adj.* **loos·er, loos·est 1.** Not fastened, restrained, or contained: *loose bricks.* **2.** Not taut, fixed, or rigid: *a loose chair leg.* **3.** Free from confinement or imprisonment; unfettered: *dogs that are loose on the streets.* **4.** Not tight-fitting or tightly fitted: *loose shoes.* **5.** Not bound, bundled, or gathered together: *loose papers.* **6.** Not compact or dense in arrangement or structure: *loose gravel.* **7.** Lacking a sense of restraint or responsibility; idle: *loose talk.* **8.** Not formal; relaxed. **9.** Lacking conventional moral restraint in sexual behavior. **10.** Not literal or exact: *a loose translation.* **11.** Characterized by a free movement of fluids in the body. ❖ *adv.* In a loose manner. ❖ *v.* **loosed, loos·ing, loos·es** —*tr.* **1.** To let loose; release. **2.** To make loose; undo. **3.** To cast loose; detach. **4.** To let fly; discharge. **5.** To release pressure or obligation from; absolve. **6.** To make less strict; relax. —*intr.* **1.** To become loose. **2.** To discharge a missile; fire. **—idiom: on the loose 1.** At large; free. **2.** Acting in an uninhibited fashion. [ME *louse, los* < ON *lauss*. See **leu-** in App.] **—loose′ly** *adv.* **—loose′ness** *n.*

loom²

loon¹
common loon
Gavia immer

SYNONYMS *loose, lax, slack* These adjectives mean not tautly bound, held, or fastened: *loose reins; a lax rope; slack sails.*

loose cannon *n. Slang* One that is uncontrolled and therefore poses danger. [< the threat posed by loose cannon rolling about a warship under sail.]

loose end *n.* A minor unresolved problem or difficulty. Often used in the plural.

loose-joint·ed (lōōs′join′tĭd) *adj.* **1.** Having freely articulated, highly mobile joints. **2.** Limber or agile in movement.

loose-leaf (lōōs′lēf′) *adj.* Relating to, having, or being leaves that are easy to remove, rearrange, or replace.

loose-lipped (lōōs′lĭpt′) *adj.* Given to indiscreet or incessant talk.

loos·en (lōō′sən) *v.* **-ened, -en·ing, -ens** —*tr.* **1.** To untie or make looser. **2.** To free from restraint, pressure, or strictness. **3.** To free (the bowels) from constipation. —*intr.* To become loose or looser. [ME *lousnen, losnen < losen < los,* loose. See LOOSE.]

loose·strife (lōōs′strīf′) *n.* **1.** Any of various plants of the genus *Lysimachia,* having usu. yellow flowers. **2.** Any of various plants of the genus *Lythrum,* having purple or white flowers. [Mistranslation of Lat. *lysimachia* (as if < Gk. *lusis,* loosening + Gk. *makhē,* battle) < Gk. *lūsimakheios,* perhaps after *Lūsimakhos,* Lysimachos, Greek physician of the fifth or fourth cent. B.C.]

loot (lōōt) *n.* **1.** Valuables pillaged in time of war; spoils. **2.** Stolen goods. **3.** *Informal* Goods illicitly obtained, as by bribery. **4.** *Informal* Things of value, such as gifts, received on one occasion. **5.** *Slang* Money. ❖ *v.* **loot·ed, loot·ing, loots** —*tr.* **1.** To pillage; spoil. **2.** To take as spoils; steal. —*intr.* To engage in pillaging. [Hindi *lūṭ* < Skt. *loptram, lotram,* plunder. See reup- in App.] —**loot′er** *n.*

lop¹ (lŏp) *tr.v.* **lopped, lop·ping, lops 1.** To cut off (a part), esp. from a tree or shrub. **2.** To cut off a part or parts from; trim: *lopped her curls shorter.* **3.** To eliminate or excise as superfluous. [Perh. < ME *loppe,* small branches and twigs.] —**lop′per** *n.*

lop² (lŏp) *intr. & tr.v.* **lopped, lop·ping, lops** To hang or let hang loosely; droop. [?]

lope (lōp) *intr.v.* **loped, lop·ing, lopes** To run or ride with a steady easy gait. ❖ *n.* A steady easy gait. [ME *lopen,* to leap < ON *hlaupa.*] —**lop′er** *n.*

lop-eared (lŏp′îrd′) *adj.* Having bent or drooping ears.

loph·o·phore (lŏf′ə-fôr′, -fōr′) *n.* A horseshoe-shaped ciliated organ located near the mouth of brachiopods, bryozoans, and phoronids that is used to gather food. [Gk. *lophos,* crest of a helmet + –PHORE.] —**lo·phoph′o·rate′** (lə-fŏf′ə-rāt′) *adj.*

Lop Nur (lŏp′ nōōr′) also **Lop Nor** (nôr′) A marshy depression of NW China, once a large salt lake.

lop·py (lŏp′ē) *adj.* Hanging limp; pendulous.

lop·sid·ed (lŏp′sī′dĭd) *adj.* **1.** Heavier, larger, or higher on one side than on the other. **2.** Sagging or leaning to one side. **3.** Characterized by a large margin of victory. —**lop′sid′ed·ly** *adv.* —**lop′sid′ed·ness** *n.*

loq. *abbr. Latin* loquitur (speaks)

lo·qua·cious (lō-kwā′shəs) *adj.* Very talkative; garrulous. [< Lat. *loquāx, loquāc- < loquī,* to speak.] —**lo·qua′cious·ly** *adv.* —**lo·qua′cious·ness, lo·quac′i·ty** (-kwăs′ĭ-tē) *n.*

lo·quat (lō′kwŏt′, -kwăt′) *n.* **1.** A small evergreen tree (*Eriobotrya japonica*) native to China and Japan and having fragrant white flowers and yellow fruit. **2.** The edible fruit of this plant. [Chin. (Cantonese) *lo kwat : lo,* kind of tree + *kwêt,* an orange (corresponding to Chin. (Mandarin) *jú*).]

Lo·rain (lə-rān′, lō-) A city of N OH on Lake Erie W of Cleveland; settled in 1807. Pop. 68,652.

lo·ran (lôr′ăn′, lōr′-) *n.* A long-range navigational system in which position is determined by an analysis involving the time intervals between pulsed radio signals from two or more pairs of ground stations of known position. [*lo*(*ng-*)*ra*(*nge*) *n*(*avigation*).]

Lor·ca (lôr′kə, -kä) **Federico García** See Federico **García Lorca.**

lord (lôrd) *n.* **1.** A man of high rank in a feudal society or in one that retains feudal forms and institutions, esp.: **a.** A king. **b.** A territorial magnate. **c.** The proprietor of a manor. **2. Lords** The House of Lords. **3. Lord** *Chiefly British* The general masculine title of nobility and other rank: **a.** Used as a form of address for a marquis, earl, or viscount. **b.** Used as the usual style for a baron. **c.** Used as a courtesy title for a younger son of a duke or marquis. **d.** Used as a title for certain high officials and dignitaries: *Lord Chamberlain.* **e.** Used as a title for a bishop. **4. Lord a.** God. **b.** Jesus. **5a.** A man of renowned power or authority. **b.** A man with mastery in a given field or activity. **c.** *Archaic* The male head of a household. **d.** *Archaic* A husband. ❖ *intr.v.* **lord·ed, lord·ing, lords** To act like a lord; domineer. Often used with the indefinite *it: lorded it over their subordinates.* [ME < OE *hlāford : hlāf,* bread + *weard,* guardian.]

Lord Chancellor *n., pl.* **Lords Chancellor** The presiding officer of the House of Lords.

lord·ing (lôr′dĭng) *n.* **1.** *Archaic* Used as a form of address for a lord. **2.** Obsolete A lordling.

lord·ling (lôrd′lĭng) *n.* A lord regarded as immature or insignificant.

lord·ly (lôrd′lē) *adj.* **-li·er, -li·est 1.** Of, relating to, or characteristic of a lord. **2.** Very dignified and noble: *lordly manners.* **3.** Pre-

tentiously arrogant and overbearing. ❖ *adv.* **1.** In a lordly manner. **2.** In a pretentiously arrogant and overbearing manner. —**lord′li·ness** *n.*

Lord of Misrule *n., pl.* **Lords of Misrule** One who presided at English Christmas revelry during the 15th and 16th centuries.

lor·do·sis (lôr-dō′sĭs) *n., pl.* **-ses** (-sēz) An abnormal forward curvature of the spine in the lumbar region. [Gk. *lordōsis < lordos,* bent backward.] —**lor·dot′ic** (-dŏt′ĭk) *adj.*

Lord's Day or **Lord's day** (lôrdz) *n.* The Christian Sabbath, observed on Sunday.

lord·ship (lôrd′shĭp′) *n.* **1.** often **Lordship** Used with *Your, His,* or *Their* as a title and form of address for a man or men holding the rank of lord. **2.** The position or authority of a lord. **3.** The territory belonging to a feudal lord.

Lord's Prayer (prâr′) *n. Christianity* The prayer taught by Jesus to his disciples.

Lord's Supper *n.* **1.** See Last Supper. **2.** The sacrament of the Eucharist.

lore¹ (lôr, lōr) *n.* **1.** Accumulated facts, traditions, or beliefs about a particular subject. **2.** Knowledge acquired through education or experience. **3.** *Archaic* Material taught or learned. [ME < OE *lār.*]

lore² (lôr, lōr) *n.* The space between the eye and the base of the bill of a bird or between the eye and nostril of a snake. [Lat. *lōrum,* thong.]

Lo·re·lei (lôr′ə-lī′, lō′rə-) *n.* A siren of Germanic legend whose singing lures sailors to shipwreck.

Lo·rentz (lôr′ənts, lōr′-, lō′rĕnts), **Hendrik** 1853–1928. Dutch physicist who shared a 1902 Nobel Prize.

Lo·rentz-Fitz·Ger·ald contraction (lôr′ənts-fĭts-jĕr′ld, lōr′-) *n.* The shortening of an object along its direction of motion as its speed approaches the speed of light, as measured by an observer at rest with respect to the body. [After Hendrik LORENTZ and George Francis FitzGerald (1851–1901), Irish physicist.]

Lorentz force *n.* The orthogonal force on a charged particle traveling in a magnetic field. [After Hendrik LORENTZ.]

Lo·renz (lō′rĕnts′), **Konrad Zacharias** 1903–89. Austrian psychologist who shared a 1973 Nobel Prize.

lor·gnette (lôrn-yĕt′) *n.* A pair of eyeglasses or opera glasses with a short handle. [Fr. < *lorgner,* to peer at < OFr. < *lorgne,* squinting, of Gmc. orig.]

lo·ri·ca (lə-rī′kə, lō-) *n., pl.* **-cae** (-sē) **1.** *Zoology* A protective external shell or case, as of a rotifer or certain other microscopic animals. **2.** A cuirass or corselet worn by Roman soldiers. [Lat. *lōrīca,* leather cuirass, perh. < *lōrum,* thong.] —**lor′i·cate′** (lôr′ĭ-kāt′, lŏr′-) **lor′i·ca′ted** (-kā′tĭd) *adj.*

lor·i·keet (lôr′ĭ-kēt′, lŏr′-) *n.* Any of several small, often brilliantly colored Australasian parrots that feed primarily on fruits or nectar and pollen. [LOR(Y) + (PARA)KEET.]

lo·ris (lôr′ĭs, lōr′-) *n.* Any of several slow-moving nocturnal prosimian primates of the genera *Loris* and *Nycticebus* of tropical Asia, having woolly fur and a vestigial tail. [Fr., poss. < obsolete Du. *loeris,* simpleton < *loer* < OFr. *lourt* < Lat. *lūridus,* pale. See LURID.]

lorn (lôrn) *adj.* Bereft; forlorn. [ME < OE *-loren,* p. part. of *-lēosan,* to lose (as in *forlēosan,* to lose). See leu- in App.]

Lorne also **Lorn** (lôrn), **Firth of** An inlet of the Atlantic Ocean on the W coast of Scotland between Mull I. and the mainland.

Lor·rain (lō-răn′, lô-răn′), **Claude** 1600–82. French painter known esp. for his landscapes.

Lor·raine (lō-răn′, lô-, lô-rĕn′) A historical region and former province of NE France; ceded with Alsace to Germany after the Franco-Prussian War (1871) and returned to France by the Treaty of Versailles (1919).

Lor·re (lôr′ē), **Peter** 1904–64. Hungarian-born Amer. actor whose films include *The Maltese Falcon* (1941).

lor·ry (lôr′ē, lŏr′ē) *n., pl.* **-ries** *Chiefly British* A motor truck. [Perh. akin to dialectal *lurry,* to lug, haul.]

lo·ry (lôr′ē, lōr′ē) *n., pl.* **-ries** Any of various brightly colored Australasian parrots having a tongue with a brushlike tip that is used to feed on nectar and pollen. [Malay *luri.*]

LOS *abbr.* **1.** length of stay **2.** line of scrimmage **3.** line of sight

Los Al·a·mos (lôs ăl′ə-mōs′, lŏs) An unincorporated community of N-central NM NW of Santa Fe; chosen in 1942 as a research site to produce the first atomic bombs. Pop. 11,909.

Los An·ge·les (ăn′jə-ləs, -lēz′, ăng′gə-ləs) A city of S CA on the Pacific Ocean in a widespread metropolitan area; founded by the Spanish in 1781. Pop. 3,694,820.

lose (lōōz) *v.* **lost** (lôst, lŏst), **los·ing, los·es** —*tr.* **1.** To be unsuccessful in retaining possession of; mislay. **2a.** To be deprived of (something one has had). **b.** To be left alone or desolate because of the death of: *lost his wife.* **c.** To be unable to keep alive: *a surgeon who lost few patients.* **3.** To be unable to keep control or allegiance of: *lost his temper; lost supporters.* **4.** To fail to win; fail in **5.** To fail to use or take advantage of: *lost the chance for victory.* **6.** To fail to hear, see, or understand. **7a.** To let (oneself) become unable to find the way. **b.** To remove (oneself), as from everyday reality into a fantasy world. **8.** To rid oneself of: *lost five pounds.* **9.** To consume aimlessly; waste: *lost a week to bad weather.* **10.** To wander from or become ignorant of: *lose one's way.* **11a.** To elude or outdistance. **b.** To be outdistanced by: *chased them but lost them.* **12.** To become slow by (a specified amount of time). Used

lorgnette

loris
slender loris
Loris tardigradus

of a timepiece. **13.** To cause or result in the loss of: *That remark lost us the job.* **14.** To cause to be destroyed. Usu. used in the passive: *Both planes were lost in the crash.* **15.** To cause to be damned. —*intr.v.* **1.** To suffer loss. **2.** To be defeated. **3.** To operate or run slow. Used of a timepiece. —*phrasal verb:* **lose out** To fail to achieve or receive an expected gain. —*idioms:* **lose it** Slang **1.** To lose control; blow up. **2.** To become deranged or mentally disturbed. **3.** To become less capable or proficient; decline. **lose out on** To miss (an opportunity, for example). **lose time 1.** To operate too slowly. Used of a timepiece. **2.** To delay advancement. [ME *losen* < OE *losian,* to perish < *los,* loss. See **leu-** in App.]

lo•sel (lō′zəl, loō′-, lōz′əl) *n.* One that is worthless. [ME < *lōsen,* p. part. of *lēsen,* to lose < OE -*lēosan.* See LORN.]

los•er (loō′zər) *n.* **1a.** One that fails to win: *the losers of the game.* **b.** One who takes loss in a given way: *a graceful loser.* **2a.** One that fails consistently, esp. a person with bad luck or poor skills. **b.** One that is bad in quality.

los•ing (loō′zĭng) *adj.* **1.** Failing to win, as in a sport or game. **2.** Of or relating to one that fails to win: *a losing season.* ❖ *n.* **1.** The act of one that loses; loss. **2.** Something lost, such as money at gambling. Often used in the plural.

loss (lôs, lŏs) *n.* **1.** The act or an instance of losing. **2a.** One that is lost: *wrote their flooded house off as a loss.* **b.** The condition of being deprived or bereaved of something or someone. **c.** The amount of something lost. **3.** The harm or suffering caused by losing or being lost. **4.** **losses** People lost in wartime; casualties. **5.** Destruction. **6.** *Electricity* The power decrease caused by resistance in a circuit, circuit element, or device. **7.** The amount of a claim on an insurer by an insured. —*idiom:* **at a loss 1.** Below cost. **2.** Perplexed; puzzled. [ME *los* < OE. See LOSE.]

loss leader *n.* A commodity offered esp. by a retail store at cost or below cost to attract customers.

loss ratio *n.* The ratio between the premiums paid to an insurance company and the claims settled by the company.

lost (lôst, lŏst) *adj.* **1.** Unable to find one's way: *a lost child.* **2a.** No longer in one's possession, care, or control: *a lost pen.* **b.** No longer in existence; vanished or spent: *lost youth.* **c.** No longer known or practiced: *a lost art.* **d.** Beyond reach, communication, or influence: *lost to the world.* **3.** Not used to one's benefit or advantage: *a lost opportunity.* **4.** Not won or unlikely to be won; unsuccessful: *a lost cause.* **5.** Beyond recovery or redemption; fallen or destroyed: *a lost soul.* **6a.** Completely involved or absorbed; rapt. **b.** Bewildered or confused: *I'm lost—can you start over?* —*idiom:* **be lost on** To fail to influence or be understood by.

lost and found or **lost-and-found** (lôst′ən-found′, lŏst′-) *n.* A repository in a public place, as in a school, where found items are kept for reclaiming by their owners.

Lost River Range A chain of mountains in E-central ID rising to 3,861.9 m (12,662 ft).

lot (lŏt) *n.* **1.** An object used in making a determination or choice at random. **2a.** The use of objects in making a determination or choice at random: *chosen by lot.* **b.** The determination or choice so made. **3.** Something that befalls one because of or as if because of determination by lot. **4.** One's fortune in life; fate. **5.** A number of associated people or things. **6.** Kind; type: *That dog is a contented lot.* **7.** Miscellaneous articles sold as one unit. **8.** *Informal* A large extent, amount, or number: *a lot of trouble; made lots of new friends.* Often used adverbially with *a* or in the plural: *felt a lot better; ran lots faster.* **9a.** A piece of land having specific boundaries, esp. one constituting a part of a city, town, or block. **b.** A piece of land used for a given purpose. **10a.** The complete grounds of a film studio. **b.** The outdoor area of a film studio. ❖ *tr.v.* **lot•ted, lot•ting, lots 1.** To apportion by lots; allot. **2.** To divide (land) into lots. [ME < OE *hlot.*]

Lot[1] (lŏt) In the Bible, Abraham's nephew, whose wife was turned into a pillar of salt when she looked back as they fled Sodom.

Lot[2] (lŏt, lôt) A river of S France rising in the Cévennes and flowing c. 483 km (300 mi) to the Garonne R.

loth (lōth, lôth) *adj.* Variant of **loath.**

Lo•thair I (lō-thâr′, -târ′) 795?–855. Holy Roman emperor (840–855) who received the Middle Kingdom in 843.

Lothair II 1070?–1137. King of Germany (1125–37) and Holy Roman emperor (1133–37) who invaded Italy in 1136.

Lo•thar•i•o also **lo•thar•i•o** (lō-thâr′ē-ō) *n., pl.* -**os** A man who seduces women. [After *Lothario,* a character in *The Fair Penitent,* a play by Nicholas Rowe (1674–1718).]

lo•ti (lō′tē) *n., pl.* **ma•lo•ti** (mä-) See table at **currency.** [Sotho, from *Maloti,* a range of mountains in Lesotho.]

lo•tic (lō′tĭk) *adj.* Of, relating to, or living in moving water. [< Lat. *lōtus,* p. part. of *lavere,* to wash. See LOTION.]

lo•tion (lō′shən) *n.* **1.** A medicated liquid for external application. **2.** Any of various externally applied cosmetic liquids. [ME *locion* < OFr. *lotion* < Lat. *lōtiō, lōtiōn-,* a washing < *lōtus,* p. part. of *lavere,* to wash. See **leu(ə)-** in App.]

lot•ter•y (lŏt′ə-rē) *n., pl.* -**ies 1.** A contest in which tokens are distributed or sold, the winning token or tokens being secretly predetermined or ultimately selected in a random drawing. **2.** A selection made by lot from a number of applicants or competitors. **3.** An event or activity regarded as having an outcome depending on fate: *Success seemed a lottery.* [Fr. *loterie,* prob. < Du. *loterije* < MDu. < *lot,* lot.]

lotus
Nelumbo nucifera

Joe Louis

lot•to (lŏt′ō) *n., pl.* -**tos 1.** A game of chance similar to bingo. **2.** A lottery in which participants choose and play numbers in a random drawing. [Ital. and Fr. *loto,* both < Fr. *lot,* lot < OFr. < Frankish **lot.*]

lo•tus also **lo•tos** (lō′təs) *n.* **1a.** An aquatic plant (*Nelumbo nucifera*) native to southern Asia and Australia and having large leaves, pinkish flowers, a perforated seedpod, and fleshy rhizomes. **b.** The edible seed, leaf, or rhizome of this plant. **c.** Any of several similar or related plants. **2.** A representation of any of various lotuses or similar plants in Egyptian or classical sculpture, architecture, or art. **3.** Any of several leguminous plants of the genus *Lotus.* **4.** *Greek Mythology* **a.** A small Mediterranean tree or shrub whose fruit was eaten by the lotus-eaters. **b.** The fruit of this plant. [Lat. *lōtus,* name of several plants < Gk. *lōtos.*]

lo•tus-eat•er (lō′təs-ē′tər) *n.* **1.** **Lotus-eater** or **Lotus Eater** *Greek Mythology* One of a people described in the *Odyssey* who lived in a drugged, indolent state from feeding on the lotus. **2.** A lazy person devoted to pleasure and luxury.

lotus land *n.* *Informal* A place or state of languid contentment. [After the *Land of the Lotus-eaters* in the *Odyssey.*]

lotus position *n.* A cross-legged sitting position used in yoga. [Transl. of Skt. *padmāsanam* : *padmaḥ,* lotus + *āsanam,* sitting posture (< its resemblance to a lotus).]

louche (loōsh) *adj.* Of questionable taste or morality; decadent: *a louche disco.* [Fr. < OFr. *losche,* squint-eyed, fem. of *lois* < Lat. *luscus,* blind in one eye.]

loud (loud) *adj.* **loud•er, loud•est 1.** Characterized by high volume and intensity. Used of sound. **2.** Producing sound of high volume and intensity. **3.** Clamorous and insistent: *loud denials.* **4a.** Having offensively bright colors: *a loud necktie.* **b.** Having an offensively strong odor. **c.** Offensive in manner. ❖ *adv.* **louder, loudest** In a loud manner. [ME < OE *hlūd.* See **kleu-** in App.] —**loud′ly** *adv.* —**loud′ness** *n.*

loud•en (loud′n) *tr. & intr.v.* -**ened, -en•ing, -ens** To make or become louder.

loud•mouth (loud′mouth′) *n. Informal* One given to loud, irritating, or indiscreet talk. —**loud′mouthed′** (-mouth d′, -moutht′) *adj.*

loud pedal *n.* See **sustaining pedal.**

loud•speak•er (loud′spē′kər) *n.* A device that converts electric signals to audible sound.

Lou Geh•rig's disease (loō gĕr′ĭgz) *n.* See **amyotrophic lateral sclerosis.** [After Henry Louis ("Lou") GEHRIG.]

lough (lŏкн, lŏk) *n. Irish* **1.** A lake. **2.** A bay or an inlet of the sea. [ME < OE *luh,* ult. < OIr. *loch.*]

Lou•is VII (loō′ē, loō-ē′) 1120?–80. King of France (1137–80) who led the unsuccessful Second Crusade (1147–49).

Louis IX Known as "Saint Louis." 1214–70. King of France (1226–70) who led the Seventh Crusade (1248–54).

Louis XIII 1601–43. King of France (1610–43) who relied heavily on his political adviser Cardinal Richelieu.

Louis XIV Known as "the Sun King." 1638–1715. King of France (1643–1715) whose reign was characterized by the expansion of French influence in Europe.

Louis XV 1710–74. King of France (1715–74) who led France into the War of the Austrian Succession (1740–48) and the Seven Years' War (1756–63).

Louis XVI 1754–93. King of France (1774–92) who summoned the Estates-General (1789) but did not grant the reforms demanded. Louis and his queen, Marie Antoinette, were guillotined in 1793.

Louis XVIII 1755–1824. King of France (1814–24) whose reign was interrupted by Napoleon's return to power (1815).

Lou•is (loō′ĭs), Joe 1914–81. Amer. prizefighter who held the heavyweight title for nearly 12 years (1937–49).

Lou•is•bourg or **Lou•is•burg** (loō′ĭs-bûrg′) A town of Nova Scotia, Canada, on E Cape Breton I. near the site of the fortress of Louisbourg, built c. 1712–40 by the French. Pop. 1,261.

Lou•ise (loō-ēz′), Lake A lake of SW Alberta, Canada, in the Rocky Mts. near Banff.

Lou•i•si•an•a (loō-ē′zē-ăn′ə, loō′ē-zē-) A state of the S US on the Gulf of Mexico; admitted as the 18th state in 1812. Cap. Baton Rouge. Pop. 4,468,976.

Louisiana French *n.* French as spoken by the descendants of the original French settlers of Louisiana.

Louisiana Purchase A territory of the W US extending from the Mississippi R. to the Rocky Mts. between the Gulf of Mexico and the Canadian border; purchased from France on Apr. 30, 1803, for $15 million.

Lou•is Napoleon (loō′ē, loō-ē′) See **Napoleon III.**

Lou•is Phi•lippe (loō′ē fĭ-lēp′, loō-ē′ fē-lēp′) Known as "the Citizen King." 1773–1850. King of France (1830–48) who ruled after the overthrow of the Bourbons in the July Revolution (1830) and abdicated during the Revolution of 1848.

Louis Qua•torze (kä-tôrz′) *adj.* Of, relating to, or characteristic of the baroque style in architecture, furniture, and decoration of the reign of Louis XIV. [Fr.]

Louis Quinze (kănz′) *adj.* Of, relating to, or characteristic of the rococo style in architecture, furniture, and decoration of the reign of Louis XV. [Fr.]

Louis Seize (sĕz′) *adj.* Of, relating to, or characteristic of the neoclassic style in architecture, furniture, and decoration of the reign of Louis XVI. [Fr.]

Louis Treize (trĕz′) *adj.* Of, relating to, or characteristic of the heavy late-Renaissance style in architecture, furniture, and decoration of the reign of Louis XIII. [Fr.]

Lou·is·ville (loō′ē-vĭl′, -ə-vəl) A city of N-central KY on the Ohio R. W of Lexington. Pop. 256,231.

lounge (lounj) *v.* **lounged, loung·ing, loung·es** *—intr.* **1.** To move or act in a lazy, relaxed way; loll. **2.** To pass time idly. *—tr.* To pass (time) in a lazy, relaxed, or idle way: *lounged the day away.* ❖ *n.* **1.** A public waiting room often having smoking or lavatory facilities. **2.** An establishment or a room in an establishment, as in a restaurant, where cocktails are served. **3a.** A living room. **b.** A lobby. **4.** A long couch, esp. one having no back and a headrest at one end. [Poss. < Fr. *s'allonger*, to stretch out < OFr. *alonger*, to lengthen < Med.Lat. *allongāre* : Lat. *ad-*, ad- + Lat. *longus*, long; see LONG¹.] *—loung′er n.*

lounge car *n.* See **club car.**

lounge lizard *n. Slang* **1.** A generally idle man who haunts establishments or gatherings frequented by the rich or fashionable; a social parasite. **2.** A habitué of cocktail lounges.

loupe (loōp) *n.* A small magnifying glass usu. set in an eyepiece and used chiefly by watchmakers and jewelers. [Fr. < OFr., flawed gem, prob. of Gmc. orig.]

loup-ga·rou (loō′gə-roō′, -gä-) *n., pl.* **loups-ga·rous** (loō′gə-roōz′, -gä-roō′) A werewolf. [Fr. < OFr. *leu garoul* : *leu*, wolf (< Lat. *lupus*; see **w|k**ʷ**o-** in App.) + *garoul*, werewolf (of Gmc. orig.; see **wi-ro-** in App.).]

loup·ing ill (lou′pĭng, lō′-) *n.* See **tremble** 3a. [< Sc. *loup*, to leap < ME *lopen.* See LOPE.]

Loup River (loōp) A river of E-central NE flowing a total length of c. 451 km (280 mi) to the Platte R.

lour (lour) *v. & n.* Variant of **lower¹.**

Lourdes (loōrd, loōrdz) A town of SW France at the foot of the Pyrenees; noted for its shrine marking the site where the Virgin Mary is said to have appeared to Saint Bernadette in 1858. Pop. 16,581.

Lou·ren·ço Mar·ques (lə-rĕn′sō mär′kĕs, lô-rĕn′soō mär′kĕsh) See **Maputo.**

lou·ry (lour′ē) *adj.* Variant of **lowery.**

louse (lous) *n.* **1.** *pl.* **lice** (līs) Any of numerous small wingless insects of the orders Mallophaga or Anoplura, many of which are external parasites on various animals, including humans. **2.** *pl.* **lous·es** (lou′zĭz) *Slang* A mean or despicable person. ❖ *tr.v.* **loused, lous·ing, lous·es** *Slang* To bungle: *loused up the project.* [ME < OE *lūs.* See App.]

louse·wort (lous′wûrt′, -wôrt′) *n.* Any of numerous plants of the genus *Pedicularis*, having clusters of irregular, variously colored flowers.

lous·y (lou′zē) *adj.* **-i·er, -i·est** **1.** Infested with lice. **2.** Extremely contemptible; nasty. **3.** Very painful or unpleasant. **4.** Inferior or worthless. **5.** *Slang* Abundantly supplied: *lousy with money.* *—lous′i·ly adv. —lous′i·ness n.*

lout¹ (lout) *n.* An awkward and stupid person; an oaf. [Poss. < LOUT².]

lout² (lout) *intr.v.* **lout·ed, lout·ing, louts** **1.** To bow or curtsy. **2.** To bend or stoop. [ME *louten* < OE *lūtan.*]

lout·ish (lou′tĭsh) *adj.* Having the characteristics of a lout; awkward and stupid. *—lout′ish·ly adv. —lout′ish·ness n.*

lou·ver also **lou·vre** (loō′vər) *n.* **1a.** A framed opening, as in a door or window, fitted with horizontal slats for admitting air and light and shedding rain. **b.** One of the slats used in such an opening. **c.** One of the narrow openings formed by such slats. **2.** A slatted ventilating opening, as on the hood of a motor vehicle. **3.** A lantern-shaped cupola on the roof of a medieval building for admitting air and providing for the escape of smoke. [ME *lover*, skylight, chimney < OFr. < MDu. *love*, gallery < MHGer. *lauble.*] *—lou′vered adj.*

lov·a·ble also **love·a·ble** (lŭv′ə-bəl) *adj.* Having characteristics that attract love or affection. *—lov′a·bil′i·ty, lov′a·ble·ness n. —lov′a·bly adv.*

lov·age (lŭv′ĭj) *n.* A Mediterranean perennial plant (*Levisticum officinale*), having edible leaves and umbels of small, aromatic seedlike fruit used as seasoning. [ME < AN *luvesche* < OE *lufestice* < Med.Lat. *levistica* < LLat. *levisticum*, alteration of Lat. *ligusticum* < neut. of *ligusticus*, Ligurian < *Ligurēs*, the Ligurians.]

love (lŭv) *n.* **1.** A deep, tender feeling of affection and solicitude toward a person, such as that arising from kinship or a sense of oneness. **2.** A feeling of intense desire and attraction toward a person with whom one is disposed to make a pair; the emotion of sex and romance. **3a.** Sexual passion. **b.** Sexual intercourse. **c.** A love affair. **4.** An intense emotional attachment, as for a pet or treasured object. **5.** A person who is the object of deep or intense affection or attraction; beloved. Often used as a term of endearment. **6.** An expression of one's affection: *Send him my love.* **7a.** A strong predilection or enthusiasm. **b.** The object of such an enthusiasm. **8.** Love *Mythology* Eros or Cupid. **9.** often **Love** *Christianity* Charity. **10.** *Sports* A zero score in tennis. ❖ *v.* **loved, lov·ing, loves** *—tr.* **1.** To feel deep, tender affection and solicitude toward (a person). **2.** To feel intense desire and attraction toward (a person). **3.** To be emotionally attached to. **4a.** To embrace or

caress. **b.** To have sexual intercourse with. **5.** To like or desire enthusiastically. **6.** *Christianity* To have charity for. **7.** To thrive on; need. *—intr.* To experience deep affection or intense desire for another. *—idioms:* **for love** Out of compassion; with no thought for a reward. **for love or money** Under any circumstances. Usu. used in negative sentences. **for the love of** For the sake of; in consideration for. **in love 1.** Deeply or passionately enamored. **2.** Highly or immoderately fond: *in love with Japanese cuisine.* **no love lost** No affection; animosity. [ME < OE *lufu.*]

love affair *n.* **1.** An intimate sexual relationship or episode between lovers. **2.** A strong enthusiasm.

love apple *n.* A tomato. [Prob. transl. of Fr. *pomme d'amour* (< the former belief in the tomato's aphrodisiacal powers) : *pomme*, apple + *de*, of + *amour*, love.]

love beads *pl.n.* Small beads on a necklace, esp. ones worn by hippies as a symbol of love and peace.

love·bird (lŭv′bûrd′) *n.* **1.** Any of various small Old World parrots, esp. of the genus *Agapornis*, often kept as cage birds and noted for the apparent affection between mates. **2.** lovebirds *Informal* An affectionate or demonstrative couple.

love child *n.* A child born of parents not legally married.

Love·craft (lŭv′krăft′), **H**(oward) **P**(hillips) 1890–1937. Amer. writer of *The Outsider and Others* (1939).

love feast *n.* **1a.** A meal shared among early Christians as a symbol of love. **b.** A similar meal among modern Christians. **2.** A gathering meant to promote goodwill.

love handle *n. Slang* A deposit of fat at the waistline.

love-in (lŭv′ĭn′) *n. Slang* A gathering to engender and promote love.

love-in-a-mist (lŭv′ĭn-ə-mĭst′) *n.* A Mediterranean plant (*Nigella damascena*) having blue or whitish flowers surrounded by threadlike bracts.

love knot *n.* A knot symbolizing the constancy of two lovers.

Love·lace (lŭv′lās′), **Richard** 1618–57? English Cavalier poet who is noted esp. for the lyrics "To Althea, from Prison" and "To Lucasta, Going to the Wars."

love·less (lŭv′lĭs) *adj.* **1.** Characterized by an absence of love: *a loveless marriage.* **2.** Feeling or receiving no love; unloving: *a loveless glance.* **3.** Receiving no love; unloved.

love-lies-bleed·ing (lŭv′līz-blē′dĭng) *n.* A tropical Indian plant (*Amaranthus caudatus*) having clusters of small red flowers.

love life *n.* The amatory or sexual aspect of one's life.

love·lock (lŭv′lŏk′) *n.* A lock of hair hanging separately from the rest of the hair, as one tied with ribbon and worn by courtiers during the 17th and 18th centuries.

love·lorn (lŭv′lôrn′) *adj.* Bereft of love or one's lover.

love·ly (lŭv′lē) *adj.* **-li·er, -li·est** **1.** Full of love; loving. **2.** Inspiring love or affection. **3.** Having beauty that appeals to the emotions as well as to the eye. **4.** Enjoyable; delightful: *spent a lovely evening with friends.* ❖ *n., pl.* **-lies** **1.** A beautiful person, esp. a woman. **2.** A lovely object. *—love′li·ness n. —love′ly adv.*

love·mak·ing (lŭv′mā′kĭng) *n.* **1.** Sexual activity, esp. sexual intercourse. **2.** Courtship; wooing.

lov·er (lŭv′ər) *n.* **1.** One who loves another, esp. one who feels sexual love. **2.** lovers A couple in love with each other. **3a.** A paramour. **b.** A sexual partner. **4.** One who is fond of or devoted to something. *—lov′er·ly adv. & adj.*

lov·ers' knot (lŭv′ərz) *n.* See **love knot.**

love seat or **love·seat** (lŭv′sēt′) *n.* A small sofa or double chair that seats two people.

love·sick (lŭv′sĭk′) *adj.* **1.** So affected by love as to be unable to act normally. **2.** Exhibiting a lover's yearning.

lov·ey-dov·ey (lŭv′ē-dŭv′ē) *adj. Informal* Expressing affection in an extravagantly sentimental way; mushy.

lov·ing (lŭv′ĭng) *adj.* **1.** Feeling love; affectionate. **2.** Indicative of or exhibiting love.

loving cup *n.* **1.** A large ornamental wine vessel, usu. made of silver and having two or more handles. **2.** A large ornamental vessel awarded in modern sporting contests, for example.

low¹ (lō) *adj.* **low·er, low·est** **1a.** Having little relative height; not high or tall. **b.** Rising only slightly above surrounding surfaces. **c.** Situated below normal height: *a low lighting fixture.* **d.** Situated below the surrounding surfaces: *water standing in low spots.* **e.** Cut to show the neck and chest; décolleté: *a low neckline.* **2.** Near or at the horizon. **3.** Close or closer to a reference point: *was low in the offensive zone.* **4.** *Linguistics* Produced with part or all of the tongue depressed, as *a*, pronounced (ä), in *father.* Used of vowels. **5.** Of less than usual or average depth; shallow: *The river is low.* **6.** Humble in status or character: *of low birth.* **7.** *Biology* Of relatively simple structure in the scale of living organisms. **8.** Unrefined; coarse: *low humor.* **9.** Violating standards of decency; base. **10a.** Lacking strength or vigor; weak. **b.** Lacking liveliness or good spirits; discouraged or

louver

loving cup

Juliette Gordon Low

lowboy
Queen Anne walnut lowboy

low relief
detail from an Assyrian relief depicting the capture of Lachish, c. 701 B.C.

dejected. **11a.** Below average in degree, intensity, or amount. **b.** Below an average or a standard: *a low level of understanding.* **c.** Ranked near the beginning of an ascending series or scale. **d.** Relating to or being latitudes nearest to the equator. **e.** Relatively small. Used of a cost, price, or other value. **12.** Having a pitch corresponding to a relatively small number of sound-wave cycles per second. **13.** Not loud; soft. **14.** Being near total depletion. **15.** Not adequately provided or equipped; short. **16.** Depreciatory; disparaging: *has a low opinion of himself.* **17.** Brought down or reduced in health or wealth. **18.** Of, relating to, or being the gear configuration or setting, as in a car transmission, that produces the least vehicular speed with respect to engine speed. ❖ *adv.* **lower, lowest 1a.** In or to a low position, level, or space. **b.** In or to a low condition or rank; humbly. **2.** In or to a reduced, humbled, or degraded condition: *brought low by failure.* **3.** Softly; quietly. **4.** With a deep pitch. **5.** At a small price. ❖ *n.* **1.** A low level, position, or degree. **2.** *Meteorology* A region of atmospheric pressure that is below normal. **3.** The low gear configuration of a transmission. [ME *loue* < ON *lāgr.* See **legh-** in App.] —**low′ness** *n.*

low² (lō) *n.* The characteristic sound uttered by cattle; a moo. ❖ *intr.v.* **lowed, low·ing, lows** To utter the sound made by cattle; moo. [< ME *lowen,* to moo < OE *hlōwan.* See **kelə-** in App.]

Low, Juliette Magill Kinzie Gordon 1860–1927. Amer. founder of the Girl Scouts (1912).

low-ball (lō′bôl′) *tr.v.* **-balled, -bal·ling, -balls** *Slang* To underestimate or understate (a cost) deliberately. [< the card game of the same name.] —**low′-ball** *adj.*

low beam *n.* The beam of a vehicle's headlight that provides short-range illumination.

low blood pressure *n.* Hypotension.

low blow *n.* **1.** *Sports* An illegal blow in boxing that lands below the opponent's waist. **2.** An unscrupulous attack; an insult.

low·born (lō′bôrn′) *adj.* Of humble birth.

low·boy (lō′boi′) *n.* A low tablelike chest of drawers.

low·bred (lō′brĕd′) *adj.* Coarse; vulgar.

low·brow (lō′brou′) *adj.* also **low·browed** (-broud′) Uncultivated; vulgar. ❖ *n.* One with lowbrow tastes and preferences. [LOW¹ + (HIGH)BROW.]

low-cal (lō′kăl′) *adj.* Having comparatively fewer calories than what is standard or typical.

Low Church *n.* The evangelical branch of the Anglican Church. —**Low′-Church′** (-chûrch′) *adj.*

low-class (lō′klăs′) *adj.* **1.** Of or relating to the lower socioeconomic classes. **2.** Vulgar or crude; common.

low comedy *n.* Comedy characterized by slapstick, burlesque, and horseplay.

Low Countries A region of NW Europe comprising Belgium, the Netherlands, and Luxembourg.

low-den·si·ty (lō′dĕn′sĭ-tē) *adj.* Having a low concentration.

low-density lipoprotein *n.* A complex of lipids and proteins that functions as a transporter of cholesterol in the blood, high levels of which are associated with increased risk of cardiovascular disease.

low·down (lō′doun′) *n. Slang* The whole truth.

low-down or **low·down** (lō′doun′) *adj.* **1.** Despicable; base. **2a.** Gloomy; depressed. **b.** Earthy; funky: *low-down blues.*

Low·ell (lō′əl) A city of NE MA on the Merrimack R. NW of Boston; settled in 1653. Pop. 105,167.

Lowell, Amy 1874–1925. Amer. poet whose works include *Sword Blades and Poppy Seed* (1914).

Lowell, James Russell 1819–91. Amer. poet and diplomat who edited the *Atlantic Monthly* (1857–61).

Lowell, Percival 1855–1916. Amer. astronomer who founded the Lowell Observatory in AZ (1894).

Lowell, Robert Traill Spence, Jr. 1917–77. Amer. poet whose works include *The Dolphin* (1973).

low-end (lō′ĕnd′) *adj.* **1.** Cheapest in a line of merchandise. **2.** *Informal* Of, relating to, or intended for low-income consumers; downscale.

low·er¹ (lou′ər, lour) also **lour** (lour) *intr.v.* **low·ered, low·er·ing, low·ers** also **loured, lour·ing, lours 1.** To look angry, sullen, or threatening. **2.** To appear dark or threatening, as the sky. ❖ *n.* **1.** A threatening, sullen, or angry look. **2.** A dark and ominous look: *the lower of thunderheads.* [ME *louren.*] —**low′er·ing·ly** *adv.*

low·er² (lō′ər) *adj.* Comparative of **low¹. 1.** Below another in position or authority. **2.** Physically situated below a similar or comparable thing: *a lower shelf.* **3. Lower** *Geology & Archaeology* Relating to or being an earlier or older division of the period named. **4.** *Biology* Less advanced in organization or evolutionary development. **5.** Denoting the larger and usu. more representative of two houses of a legislature. ❖ *v.* **-ered, -er·ing, -ers** —*tr.* **1.** To let, bring, or move down to a lower level. **2.** To reduce in value, degree, or quality. **3.** To weaken; undermine. **4.** To reduce in standing or respect. —*intr.* **1.** To move down. **2.** To become less; diminish.

lower bound (lō′ər) *n.* A number less than or equal to any number in a set.

Low·er California (lō′ər) See **Baja California.**

Lower Canada The mainly French-speaking portion of S Que-
bec, Canada, from 1791 until 1841, when it was reunited with Upper Quebec to form the province of Quebec.

Lower Carboniferous *n.* See **Mississippian** 2.

low·er·case or **low·er-case** (lō′ər-kās′) *adj.* Of, printed, written, or formatted in lowercase letters. ❖ *tr.v.* **-cased, -cas·ing, -cas·es** To put (type or text) in lowercase letters. —**low′er·case′** *n.*

lowercase letter *n.* A written or printed letter smaller than and often different from its corresponding capital. [< their storage in the lower of two trays used by compositors.]

low·er class (lō′ər) *n.* The lower socioeconomic class or classes in a society. —**low′er-class′** (lō′ər-klăs′) *adj.*

low·er·class·man (lō′ər-klăs′mən) *n.* See **underclassman.**

low·er criticism (lō′ər) *n.* Critical study, esp. of the Bible, that explores the meaning of the words of the work being examined in order to establish an accurate text. [As against HIGHER CRITICISM.]

Lower Egypt The part of ancient Egypt comprising the Nile R. delta; united with Upper Egypt c. 3100 B.C.

low·er·most (lō′ər-mōst′) *adj.* Lowest.

Lower Palatinate See **Palatinate.**

Lower Peninsula also **Lower Michigan** The section of MI between Lakes Michigan and Huron and S of the Straits of Mackinac.

Lower Tunguska See **Tunguska.**

low·er world (lō′ər) *n. Mythology* The abode of the dead, considered to be beneath the surface of the earth.

low·er·y (lou′ə-rē) also **lour·y** (lour′ē) *adj.* Overcast; threatening.

low·est common denominator (lō′ĭst) *n.* **1.** *Mathematics* See **least common denominator. 2a.** The most basic, least sophisticated level of taste, sensibility, or opinion among a group of people. **b.** The group having such taste, sensibility, or opinion.

lowest common multiple *n.* See **least common multiple.**

lowest terms *pl.n.* The numerator and denominator of a fraction that have no common factors except 1.

low frequency *n.* A radio frequency in the range from 30 to 300 kilohertz.

Low German *n.* **1.** The German dialects of northern Germany. **2.** The continental West Germanic languages except High German. [Transl. of Ger. *Niederdeutsch : nieder,* low (< the lowland terrain of N Germany) + *Deutsch,* German.]

low-grade (lō′grād′) *adj.* **1.** Of inferior grade or quality. **2.** Reduced in degree or intensity: *a low-grade fever.*

low-key (lō′kē′) also **low-keyed** (-kēd′) *adj.* **1.** Having low intensity; restrained, as in style; subdued. **2.** Having or producing uniformly dark tones with few areas of contrast, as in a photograph or film.

low·land (lō′lənd) *n.* An area of land that is low in relation to the surrounding country. ❖ *adj.* Relating to or characteristic of low, usu. level land.

low·land·er (lō′lən-dər) *n.* A native or inhabitant of a lowland.

Low·lands (lō′ləndz) A region of Scotland S of the Highlands. —**Low′land** *adj.* —**Low′land·er** *n.*

low-lev·el (lō′lĕv′əl) *adj.* **1.** Situated or occurring near the ground or other reference point. **2.** Being low on a scale or in relation to a standard: *a low-level job.* **3.** Of or relating to a computer language, such as an assembly language, in which each instruction corresponds to an instruction in machine language.

low·life (lō′līf′) *n., pl.* **-lifes** also **-lives** (-līvz′) A person of low social status or morals. —**low′-life** *adj.*

low·ly (lō′lē) *adj.* **-li·er, -li·est 1.** Having or suited for a low rank or position. **2.** Humble or meek in manner. **3.** Plain or prosaic in nature. ❖ *adv.* **1.** In a low manner, condition, or position. **2.** In a meek or humble manner. **3.** Low in sound. —**low′li·ness** *n.*

low-ly·ing (lō′lī′ĭng) *adj.* **1.** Lying close to water or ground level. **2.** Situated below the normal height or altitude.

Low Mass *n.* A Mass of simple ceremony that was recited rather than sung by the priest. No longer in official use.

low-mind·ed (lō′mīn′dĭd) *adj.* Exhibiting a coarse, vulgar character. —**low′-mind′ed·ness** *n.*

low-necked (lō′nĕkt′) also **low-neck** (-nĕk′) *adj.* Having a low-cut neckline; décolleté.

low-pass filter (lō′păs′) *n.* A filter designed to transmit only those electromagnetic frequencies below a certain value.

low-pitched (lō′pĭcht′) *adj.* **1.** Low in tone or tonal range. **2.** Having a moderate slope: *a low-pitched roof.*

low-pres·sure (lō′prĕsh′ər) *adj.* **1.** Having, working under, or exerting little pressure. **2.** Relaxed in attitude, nature, or style; easygoing: *a low-pressure lifestyle.*

low profile *n.* Behavior or activity carried out with deliberate restraint or modesty so as not to attract attention: *keep a low profile.* —**low′-pro′file′** (lō′prō′fīl′) *adj.*

low relief *n.* Sculptural relief that projects very little from the background.

low-rent (lō′rĕnt′) *adj. Informal* **1.** Having inexpensive rent. **2.** Of low social status or moral character. **3.** Lacking taste or refinement: *a low-rent television drama.*

low·rid·er or **low rider** (lō′rī′dər) *n. Chiefly Southwestern US* **1.** A customized car whose springs have been shortened so that the chassis rides close to the ground. **2.** A person who drives such a car. —**low rid′er** *adj.*

low-rise (lō′rīz′) *adj.* Of or relating to a building having few stories and often no elevators. [LOW¹ + (HIGH)-RISE.]

Low·ry (lou′rē), **(Clarence) Malcolm** 1909–57. British writer whose works include *Under the Volcano* (1947).

low-spir·it·ed (lō′spĭr′ĭ-tĭd) *adj.* Being in low spirits; depressed. —**low′-spir′it·ed·ness** *n.*

Low Sunday *n.* The first Sunday after Easter.

low-tech (lō′tĕk′) *adj.* Of or relating to low technology.

low technology *n.* Technology that does not involve highly advanced or specialized systems or devices. —**low′-tech·nol′o·gy** (lō′tĕk-nŏl′ə-jē) *adj.*

low-ten·sion (lō′tĕn′shən) *adj.* **1.** Of or at low potential or voltage. **2.** Operating at low voltage.

low-test (lō′tĕst′) *adj.* Having low volatility and a high boiling point. Used of gasoline. [LOW¹ + (HIGH)-TEST.]

low tide *n.* **1.** The lowest level of the tide. **2.** The time at which the tide is lowest.

low water *n.* **1.** The lowest level of water in a body of water, such as a river, lake, or reservoir. **2.** See **low tide.** —**low′-wa′ter** (lō′wô′tər, -wŏt′ər) *adj.*

lox¹ (lŏks) *n., pl.* **lox** or **lox·es** Smoked salmon. [Yiddish *laks* < MHGer. *lahs*, salmon < OHGer. See **laks-** in App.]

lox² (lŏks) *n.* Liquid oxygen, esp. when used as a rocket fuel oxidizer. [L(IQUID) + OX(YGEN).]

lox·o·drome (lŏk′sə-drōm′) *n.* See **rhumb line.** [Gk. *loxos*, slanting + Gk. *dromos*, course.] —**lox′o·drom′ic** (-drŏm′ĭk), **lox′o·drom′i·cal** (-ĭ-kəl) *adj.*

loy·al (loi′əl) *adj.* **1.** Steadfast in allegiance to one's homeland, government, or sovereign. **2.** Faithful to a person, ideal, custom, or duty. **3.** Of, relating to, or marked by loyalty. See Syns at **faithful.** [Fr. < OFr. *leial, loial* < Lat. *lēgālis,* legal < *lēx, lēg-,* law. See **leg-** in App.] —**loy′al·ly** *adv.*

loy·al·ist (loi′ə-lĭst) *n.* **1.** One who maintains loyalty to an established government, political party, or sovereign, esp. during war or revolutionary change. **2.** **Loyalist** See **Tory** 2. **3.** **Loyalist** One who supported the established government of Spain during the Spanish Civil War. —**loy′al·ism** *n.*

loy·al·ty (loi′əl-tē) *n., pl.* **-ties 1.** The state or quality of being loyal. **2.** A feeling or attitude of devoted attachment and affection. Often used in the plural: *My loyalties lie with my family.*

Lo·yang (lō′yäng′) See **Luoyang.**

Loy·o·la (loi-ō′lə), **Saint Ignatius of** See **Saint Ignatius of Loyola.**

loz·enge (lŏz′ĭnj) *n.* **1.** A small medicated candy intended to be dissolved slowly in the mouth to lubricate and soothe irritated tissues of the throat. **2a.** A four-sided planar figure with a diamondlike shape; a rhombus that is not a square. **b.** Something having this shape, esp. a heraldic device. [ME, rhombus < OFr. *losenge,* perh. of Celt. orig.]

LP (ĕl′pē′) *n.* A long-playing phonograph record. [Orig. a trademark.]

LPG *abbr.* liquefied petroleum gas

LPGA *abbr.* Ladies Professional Golf Association

lpm *abbr.* lines per minute

LPN *abbr.* licensed practical nurse

Lr The symbol for the element **lawrencium.**

LR *abbr.* living room

L.S. *abbr.* Latin *locus sigilli* (the place of the seal)

LSAT *abbr.* Law School Admissions Test

LSD¹ (ĕl′ĕs-dē′) *n.* A crystalline compound, C₂₀H₂₅N₃O, derived from lysergic acid and used as a powerful hallucinogenic drug. [L(Y)S(ERGIC ACID) D(IETHYLAMIDE).]

LSD² *abbr.* least significant digit

LST (ĕl′ĕs-tē′) *n.* A flatbottom vessel developed during World War II to land troops and cargo on open beaches. [*l(anding) s(hip) t(ank).*]

LT *abbr.* **1.** or **Lt.** lieutenant **2.** long ton

lt. *abbr.* light

Lt Col or **LTC** *abbr.* lieutenant colonel

Ltd. *abbr.* **1.** or **ltd.** limited **2.** limited company

Lt Gen or **LTG** *abbr.* lieutenant general

Lt. Gov. *abbr.* lieutenant governor

LTJG *abbr.* lieutenant junior grade

L-tryp·to·phan (ĕl′trĭp′tə-făn′) *n.* The biologically active form of tryptophan, used as an ingredient in dietary supplements and under investigation in the United States for its potentially adverse health effects. [L(EVOROTATORY) + TRYPTOPHAN.]

Lu The symbol for the element **lutetium.**

Lu·an·da (lōō-än′də) also **Lo·an·da** (lō-än′də) The cap. of Angola, in the NW part on the Atlantic Ocean; founded by the Portuguese in 1575. Pop. 1,200,000.

Lu·ang·wa (lōō-äng′wä) A river of E Zambia flowing c. 805 km (500 mi) to the Zambezi R.

lu·au (lōō′ou′, lōō′ou′) *n.* An elaborate Hawaiian feast featuring traditional foods and entertainment. [Hawaiian *lū′au,* young taro tops, feast (at which taro tops are served).]

Lu·ba (lōō′bə) *n., pl.* **Luba** or **-bas 1.** A member of a Bantu people inhabiting southeast Congo (formerly Zaire). **2.** Their Bantu language.

Lu·ba·vitch·er (lōō-bä′vĭ-chər, lōō′bə-vĭch′ər) *n. Judaism* A member of a Hasidic community founded in the late

18th century that stresses religious study. [Yiddish *Libavitsher* < *Libavitsh,* Jewish town in Russia where the movement originated.] —**Lu·ba′vitch·er** *adj.*

lub·ber (lŭb′ər) *n.* **1.** A clumsy person. **2.** An inexperienced sailor; a landlubber. [ME *lobur,* lazy lout; akin to *lob,* lout. See LOB.] —**lub′ber·ly** *adv. & adj.*

lubber line also **lub·ber's line** (lŭb′ərz) *n.* A line or mark on a mariner's compass or cathode-ray indicator that represents the heading of a ship or an aircraft.

Lub·bock (lŭb′ək) A city of NW TX S of Amarillo; settled in 1879. Pop. 199,564.

lube (lōōb) *Informal tr.v.* **lubed, lub·ing, lubes** To lubricate (a car's joints, for example). ❖ *n.* A lubricant. [Shortening and alteration of LUBRICANT and LUBRICATE.]

Lü·beck (lōō′bĕk′, lü′-) A city of N-central Germany NE of Hamburg; a free city from 1226 to 1937. Pop. 217,269.

Lu·bitsch (lōō′bĭch), **Ernst** 1892–1947. German filmmaker whose sophisticated comedies include *Ninotchka* (1939).

Lu·blin (lōō′blən, -blĕn′) A city of E Poland SE of Warsaw; chartered 1317. Pop. 352,163.

lu·bri·cant (lōō′brĭ-kənt) *n.* **1.** A substance, such as grease or oil, that reduces friction when applied as a surface coating to moving parts. **2.** One that helps reduce difficulty or conflict. —**lu′bri·cant** *adj.*

lu·bri·cate (lōō′brĭ-kāt′) *v.* **-cat·ed, -cat·ing, -cates** —*tr.* **1.** To apply a lubricant to. **2.** To make slippery or smooth. —*intr.* To act as a lubricant. [Lat. *lūbricāre, lūbricāt-* < *lūbricus,* slippery.] —**lu′bri·ca′tive** *adj.*

lu·bri·ca·tor (lōō′brĭ-kā′tər) *n.* **1.** One that lubricates, esp. a lubricant. **2.** A device for applying a lubricant.

lu·bri·cious (lōō-brĭsh′əs) also **lu·bri·cous** (lōō′brĭ-kəs) *adj.* **1.** Having a slippery or smooth quality. **2.** Shifty or tricky. **3a.** Lewd; wanton. **b.** Sexually stimulating; salacious. [Alteration of *lubricous* < Lat. *lūbricus,* slippery.] —**lu·bri′cious·ly** *adv.* —**lu·bri′cious·ness** *n.*

lu·bric·i·ty (lōō-brĭs′ĭ-tē) *n.* The quality or condition of being lubricious. [LLat. *lūbricitās,* slipperiness < Lat. *lūbricus,* slippery.]

Lu·bum·ba·shi (lōō′bŏŏm-bä′shē) Formerly **E·lis·a·beth·ville** (ĭ-lĭz′ə-bəth-vĭl′) A city of SE Congo (formerly Zaire) near the Zambia border; founded 1910. Pop. 564,830.

Lu·can (lōō′kən) A.D. 39–65. Roman poet who wrote the epic *Pharsalia.*

Lu·ca·ni·a (lōō-kā′nē-ə, -kān′yə), **Mount** A peak, 5,229.8 m (17,147 ft), of the St. Elias Mts. in SW Yukon Terr., Canada.

lu·carne (lōō-kärn′) *n.* A dormer window. [Fr. < OFr., alteration of O Provençal *lucana,* poss. of Germanic orig.]

Lu·cas (lōō′kəs), **George** b. 1944. Amer. film director, producer, and screenwriter whose movies include the *Star Wars* motion-picture series.

Luc·ca (lōō′kə) A city of NW Italy W of Florence; a free commune in the 12th cent. and later an independent republic. Pop. 91,097.

Luce (lōōs), **Clare Boothe** 1902–87. Amer. writer who wrote several plays, including *The Women* (1936), and served as ambassador to Italy (1953–56).

Luce, Henry Robinson 1898–1967. Amer. editor and publisher who cofounded *Time* (1923) and founded *Fortune* (1930), *Life* (1936), and *Sports Illustrated* (1954).

lu·cent (lōō′sənt) *adj.* **1.** Giving off light; luminous. **2.** Translucent; clear. [Lat. *lūcēns, lūcent-,* pr. part. of *lūcēre,* to shine. See **leuk-** in App.] —**lu′cen·cy** *n.* —**lu′cent·ly** *adv.*

lu·cerne (lōō-sûrn′) *n. Chiefly British* Alfalfa. [Fr. *luzerne* < Provençal *luzerno,* glowworm (perh. < its shiny seeds) < Lat. *lūcerna,* lamp < *lūcēre,* to shine. See LUCID.]

Lu·cerne (lōō-sûrn′, lü-sĕrn′) A city of central Switzerland on the N shore of the **Lake of Lucerne,** an irregularly shaped lake surrounded by mountains. Pop. 59,724.

lu·ces (lōō′sēz) *n.* A plural of **lux.**

Lu·cian (lōō′shən) fl. 2nd cent. A.D. Greek satirist whose works include *Dialogues of the Gods.*

lu·cid (lōō′sĭd) *adj.* **1.** Easily understood; intelligible. **2.** Mentally sound; sane or rational. **3.** Translucent or transparent. [Lat. *lūcidus* < *lūcēre,* to shine. See **leuk-** in App.] —**lu·cid′i·ty, lu′cid·ness** *n.* —**lu′cid·ly** *adv.*

Lu·ci·fer (lōō′sə-fər) *n.* **1.** The archangel cast from heaven for leading the revolt of the angels; Satan. **2.** The planet Venus in its appearance as the morning star. **3.** **lucifer** A friction match. [ME < OE, morning star, Lucifer < Lat. *Lūcifer* < *lūcifer,* lightbringer : *lūx, lūc-,* light; see **leuk-** in App. + *-fer,* -fer.]

lu·cif·er·ase (lōō-sĭf′ə-rās′, -rāz′) *n.* An enzyme that catalyzes the oxidation of luciferin.

lu·cif·er·in (lōō-sĭf′ər-ĭn) *n.* A chemical substance present in the cells of bioluminescent organisms, such as fireflies, that produces a bluish-green light when oxidized. [Lat. *lūcifer,* lightbringing; see LUCIFER + –IN.]

Lu·ci·na (lōō-sī′nə) *n. Archaic* A midwife. [Lat. *Lūcīna,* goddess of childbirth < fem. of *lūcīnus,* light-bringing < *lūx, lūc-,* light. See **leuk-** in App.]

Lu·cite (lōō′sīt′) A trademark used for a transparent thermoplastic acrylic resin employed in paints, enamels, and primers.

luck (lŭk) *n.* **1.** The chance happening of fortunate or adverse events; fortune. **2.** Good fortune or prosperity; success. **3.** One's personal fate or lot. ❖ *intr.v.* **lucked, luck·ing, lucks** *Informal* To gain success or something desirable by chance: *lucked into a good apartment.* —**idioms: in luck** Enjoying success; fortunate. **out of luck** Lacking good fortune. **press** (or **push**) (**one's**) **luck** To risk one's good fortune, often by acting overconfidently. **try** (**one's**) **luck** To attempt something without knowing if one will be successful. [ME *lucke* < MDu. *luc*, short for *gheluc*.]

luck·i·ly (lŭk′ə-lē) *adv.* With or by favorable chance.

luck·less (lŭk′lĭs) *adj.* Marked by, suffering, or promising lack of luck; unlucky.

Luck·now (lŭk′nou) A city of N-central India ESE of Delhi; besieged for five months during the Indian Mutiny of 1857. Pop. 1,619,115.

luck·y (lŭk′ē) *adj.* **-i·er, -i·est 1.** Having or attended by good luck. **2.** Occurring by chance; fortuitous. **3.** Believed to bring good luck. —**luck′i·ness** *n.*

lu·cra·tive (lōo′krə-tĭv) *adj.* Producing wealth; profitable. [ME *lucratif* < OFr. < Lat. *lucrātīvus* < *lucrātus*, p. part. of *lucrārī*, to profit < *lucrum*, profit.]

lu·cre (lōo′kər) *n.* Money or profits. [ME < Lat. *lucrum*.]

Lu·cre·tius (lōo-krē′shəs, -shē-əs) 96?–55? B.C. Roman philosopher famous for *De Rerum Natura.* —**Lu·cre′tian** (-shən) *adj.*

lu·cu·brate (lōo′kyōo-brāt′) *intr.v.* **-brat·ed, -brat·ing, -brates** To write in a scholarly fashion; produce scholarship. [Lat. *lūcubrāre, lūcubrāt-*, to work at night by lamplight. See **leuk-** in App.]

lu·cu·bra·tion (lōo′kyōo-brā′shən) *n.* **1.** Laborious study or meditation. **2.** Writing produced by laborious study, esp. pedantic or pretentious writing. Often used in the plural.

lu·cu·lent (lōo′kyōo-lənt) *adj.* Easily understood; clear or lucid. [ME, shiny < Lat. *lūculentus* < *lūx, lūc-*, light. See **leuk-** in App.]

Lu·cul·lan (lōo-kŭl′ən) *adj.* **1.** Lavish; luxurious. **2.** Of or relating to Lucullus or his luxurious banquets. [After Lucius Licinius LUCULLUS.]

Lu·cul·lus (lōo-kŭl′əs), **Lucius Licinius** 110?–57? B.C. Roman general and consul noted for his self-indulgence.

Lu·cy (lōo′sē) *n.* The skeletal remains of a female hominid, *Australopithecus afarensis,* found in Tanzania in 1974 and dated at about 3 million years old.

Lü·da also **Lü·ta** (lōo′dä′, lü′-) An industrial conurbation of NE China at the S end of the Liaodong Peninsula including the cities of Lüshun and Dalian. Pop. 3,473,832.

Lud·dite (lŭd′īt) *n.* **1.** Any of a group of British workers who between 1811 and 1816 rioted and destroyed laborsaving textile machinery that they thought would diminish employment. **2.** One who opposes technical or technological change. [After Ned *Ludd,* English laborer supposed to have destroyed weaving machinery around 1779.] —**Lud′dism** *n.*

lude (lōod) *n. Slang* A pill or tablet containing methaqualone. [Short for QUAALUDE.]

Lu·den·dorff (lōo′dn-dôrf′), **Erich Friedrich Wilhelm von** 1865–1937. German chief of staff during World War I.

Lu·dhi·a·na (lōo′dē-ä′nə) A city of NW India NNW of Delhi. Pop. 1,042,740.

lu·dic (lōo′dĭk) *adj.* Of or relating to play or playfulness. [Fr. *ludique* < Lat. *lūdus,* play.]

lu·di·crous (lōo′dĭ-krəs) *adj.* Laughable or hilarious because of obvious absurdity or incongruity. [< Lat. *lūdicrus,* sportive < *lūdus,* game.] —**lu′di·crous·ly** *adv.* —**lu′di·crous·ness** *n.*

Lud·wigs·ha·fen (lōod′vĭgz-hä′fən, lōot′vĭKHs-) A city of SW Germany on the Rhine R. opposite Mannheim; founded as a fortress in the early 17th cent. Pop. 168,130.

lu·es (lōo′ēz) *n., pl.* **lues** Syphilis. [NLat. *luēs* < Lat., plague. See **leu-** in App.] —**lu·et′ic** (-ĕt′ĭk) —**lu·et′i·cal·ly** *adv.*

luff (lŭf) *n.* **1a.** The act of sailing closer into the wind. **b.** The forward side of a fore-and-aft sail. **2.** *Archaic* The fullest part of the bow of a ship. ❖ *v.* **luffed, luff·ing, luffs** —*intr.* **1.** To steer a sailing vessel closer into the wind, esp. with the sails flapping. **2.** To flap while losing wind. Used of a sail. —*tr.* **1.** To sail (a vessel) closer into the wind. **2.** To raise or lower (the boom of a crane or derrick). [ME *lof,* spar holding out the windward tack of a square sail < OFr., prob. of Gmc. orig.]

luf·fa (lōo′fə, lŭf′ə) *n.* Variant of **loofa.**

Luft·waf·fe (lōoft′väf′ə) *n.* The German air force before and during World War II. [Ger. : *Luft,* air (< MHGer. < OHGer.) + *Waffe,* weapon (< MHGer. *wāfen* < OHGer. *waffan*).]

lug[1] (lŭg) *n.* **1.** A handle or projection used as a hold or support. **2.** A lug nut. **3.** *Nautical* A lugsail. **4.** A projection that helps to provide traction, as on a tire or the sole of a boot. **5.** A copper or brass fitting to which electrical wires can be soldered or otherwise connected. **6.** *Slang* A clumsy fool; a blockhead. [ME *lugge,* earflap, prob. of Scand. orig.]

lug[2] (lŭg) *v.* **lugged, lug·ging, lugs** —*tr.* **1.** To drag or haul (an object) laboriously. **2.** To pull or drag with short jerks. —*intr.* **1.** To pull something with difficulty; tug. **2.** To move along by jerks or as if under a heavy burden. **3.** To run poorly or hesitate because of strain. Used of an engine. ❖ *n.* **1.** *Archaic* **a.** The act of lugging. **b.** Something lugged. **2.** A box for shipping fruit or vegetables. [ME *luggen,* of Scand. orig.]

Lug (lōo, lōog) or **Lugh** (lōo) *n. Mythology* The ancient Celtic god

lug sole

luna moth
Actias luna

of artisanship and warriors, said to be the father of Cuchulain. [OIr.]

luge (lōozh) *n.* **1.** A racing sled for one or two riders lying supine. **2.** A competition involving these sleds. [Fr. dialectal < Med.Lat. *sludia,* perh. of Celt. orig.] —**luge** *v.* —**lug′er** *n.*

Lu·ger (lōo′gər) *n.* A German semiautomatic pistol widely used by German troops in World War II. [Orig. a trademark.]

lug·gage (lŭg′ĭj) *n.* **1.** Containers for a traveler's belongings. **2.** The cases and belongings of a traveler. [Prob. LUG[2] + (BAG)GAGE.]

lug·ger (lŭg′ər) *n.* A small boat used for fishing, sailing, or coasting and having two or three masts, each with a lugsail, and two or three jibs set on the bowsprit. [< LUGSAIL.]

lug nut (lŭg) *n.* A heavy nut that fits over a bolt, used esp. to attach an automotive vehicle's wheel to its axle.

Lu·go·si (lōo-gō′sē, lə-), **Bela** 1884–1956. Hungarian-born Amer. actor known for horror films such as *Dracula* (1931).

lug·sail (lŭg′səl) *n.* A quadrilateral sail that lacks a boom, has the foot larger than the head, and is bent to a yard hanging obliquely on the mast. [Poss. < LUG[1].]

lug sole (lŭg) *n.* A thick rubber sole having deep indentations for enhanced stability and traction.

lu·gu·bri·ous (lōo-gōo′brē-əs, -gyōo′-) *adj.* Mournful, dismal, or gloomy, esp. to an exaggerated or ludicrous degree. [< Lat. *lūgubris* < *lūgēre,* to mourn.] —**lu·gu′bri·ous·ly** *adv.* —**lu·gu′bri·ous·ness** *n.*

lug·worm (lŭg′wûrm′) *n.* Any of various segmented, burrowing marine worms of the genus *Arenicola,* esp. *A. marina,* often used as fishing bait. [?]

Lu·hans′k (lōo-hänsk′) A city of E Ukraine in the Donets Basin SE of Kharkiv. Pop. 505,000.

Lui·chow Peninsula (lwē′jō′) See **Leizhou Peninsula.**

Lui·se·ño (lwē-sān′yō) *n., pl.* **Luiseño** or **-ños 1.** A member of a Native American people inhabiting the coastal area of California south of Los Angeles. **2.** The Uto-Aztecan language of the Luiseño. [Am.Sp., after San *Luis* Rey de Francia, a mission in southern California.]

Lu·kács (lōo′käch), **György** 1885–1971. Hungarian philosopher, literary critic, and politician whose Marxist writings include *History and Class Consciousness* (1923).

Luke (lōok) *n.* See table at **Bible.**

Luke, Saint. 1st cent. A.D. Companion of Saint Paul and author of the third Gospel of the New Testament.

luke·warm (lōok′wôrm′) *adj.* **1.** Mildly warm; tepid. **2.** Lacking conviction or enthusiasm; indifferent. [ME *leukwarm : leuk, luke* (poss. var. of *leu* (< OE *hlēow) + warm,* warm; see WARM.] —**luke′warm′ly** *adv.* —**luke′warm′ness** *n.*

Luks (lŭks), **George** 1867–1933. Amer. painter known for his studies of urban life, including *The Spielers* (1905).

Lu·le·älv (lōo′lĕ-ĕlv′, lōo′lə-ĕlv′) A river of N Sweden flowing c. 443 km (275 mi) to the Gulf of Bothnia.

lull (lŭl) *v.* **lulled, lull·ing, lulls** —*tr.* **1.** To cause to sleep or rest; soothe or calm. **2.** To deceive into trustfulness. —*intr.* To become calm. ❖ *n.* **1.** A relatively calm interval, as in a storm. **2.** An interval of lessened activity. [ME *lullen,* poss. of LGer. orig.]

lull·a·by (lŭl′ə-bī′) *n., pl.* **-bies** A soothing song with which to lull a child to sleep. ❖ *tr.v.* **-bied, -by·ing, -bies** To quiet with or as if with a lullaby. [Obsolete *lulla,* word used in lullabies (< ME *lullai* < *lullen,* to lull; see LULL) + BYE[2].]

Lul·ly (lōo-lē′, lü-), **Jean Baptiste** 1632–87. Italian-born French composer who founded the national French opera.

lu·lu (lōo′lōo) *n. Slang* A remarkable person, object, or idea. [Alteration of obsolete *looly.*]

lum·ba·go (lŭm-bā′gō) *n.* A painful condition of the lower back, as one resulting from muscle strain or a slipped disk. [LLat. *lumbāgō* < Lat. *lumbus,* loin.]

lum·bar (lŭm′bər, -bär′) *adj.* Of, near, or situated in the part of the back and sides between the lowest ribs and the pelvis. ❖ *n.* A lumbar artery, nerve, vertebra, or part. [NLat. *lumbāris* < Lat. *lumbus,* loin.]

Lum·bee (lŭm′bē) *n., pl.* **Lumbee** or **-bees** A member of a Native American people of southeast North Carolina.

lum·ber[1] (lŭm′bər) *n.* **1.** Timber sawed into boards, planks, or other structural members of standard or specified length. **2.** Something useless or cumbersome. **3.** *Chiefly British* Miscellaneous stored articles. ❖ *v.* **-bered, -ber·ing, -bers** —*tr.* **1a.** To cut down (trees) and prepare as marketable timber. **b.** To cut down the timber of. **2.** *Chiefly British* To clutter with or as if with unused articles. —*intr.* To cut and prepare timber for marketing. [Perh. < LUMBER[2].] —**lum′ber** *adj.* —**lum′ber·er** *n.*

lum·ber[2] (lŭm′bər) *intr.v.* **-bered, -ber·ing, -bers 1.** To walk or move with heavy clumsiness. See Syns at **blunder.** **2.** To move with a rumbling noise. [ME *lomeren,* poss. of Scand. orig.; akin to Swed. dialectal *loma,* to move heavily.] —**lum′ber·ing·ly** *adv.*

lum·ber·jack (lŭm′bər-jăk′) *n.* **1.** One who fells trees and transports the timber to a mill; a logger. **2.** A short warm outer jacket.

lum·ber·man (lŭm′bər-mən) *n.* **1.** A person who trades in lumber. **2.** A lumberjack or logger.

lum·ber·yard (lŭm′bər-yärd′) *n.* An establishment that sells lumber and other building materials from a yard.

lu·men (lōo′mən) *n., pl.* **-mens** or **-mi·na** (-mə-nə) **1.** *Anatomy* The inner open space or cavity of a tubular organ, as of a blood vessel. **2.** *Physics* The unit of luminous flux in the International System, equal to the amount of light given out through a solid angle by a source of one candela intensity radiating equally in all directions. **3.** *Botany* The cavity bounded by a plant cell wall. [Lat. *lūmen,* an opening, light. See **leuk-** in App.] —**lu′men·al, lu′min·al** *adj.*

lu·mi·nance (lōō′mə-nəns) *n.* **1.** The condition or quality of being luminous. **2.** *Physics* The intensity of light per unit area of its source.

lu·mi·nar·i·a (lōō′mə-när′ē-ə) *n.* **1.** A votive candle in a small decorative paper bag weighted with sand and lined up with others as a holiday decoration. **2.** *New Mexico* A bonfire built in front of each house in a pueblo to celebrate Christmas Eve. [Sp. < Lat. *lūmināria,* pl. of *lūmināre,* lamp. See LUMINARY.]

lu·mi·nar·y (lōō′mə-nĕr′ē) *n., pl.* **-ies 1.** An object, such as a celestial body, that gives light. **2.** A person who is an inspiration to others. **3.** A person who has achieved eminence in a field. [ME < OFr. *luminarie* < Lat. *lūmināre,* to shine < *lūmen, lūmin-,* light. See **leuk-** in App.] —**lu′mi·nar′y** *adj.*

lu·mi·nesce (lōō′mə-nĕs′) *intr.v.* **-nesced, -nesc·ing, -nesc·es** To be or become luminescent.

lu·mi·nes·cence (lōō′mə-nĕs′əns) *n.* **1.** The emission of light that does not derive energy from the temperature of the emitting body, as in fluorescence, and is caused, for example, by radiation-induced excitation of atoms. **2.** The light so emitted.

lu·mi·nes·cent (lōō′mə-nĕs′ənt) *adj.* Capable of, suitable for, or exhibiting luminescence. [Lat. *lūmen, lūmin-,* light; see LUMEN + −ESCENT.]

lu·mi·nif·er·ous (lōō′mə-nĭf′ər-əs) *adj.* Generating, yielding, or transmitting light.

lu·mi·nos·i·ty (lōō′mə-nŏs′ĭ-tē) *n., pl.* **-ties 1.** The condition or quality of being luminous. **2.** Something luminous. **3.** The ratio of luminous flux at a specific wavelength to the radiant flux at the same wavelength.

lu·mi·nous (lōō′mə-nəs) *adj.* **1.** Emitting light, esp. emitting self-generated light. **2.** Full of light; illuminated. See Syns at **bright. 3a.** Easily comprehended; clear: *luminous prose.* **b.** Enlightened and intelligent; inspiring: *luminous ideas.* [ME < OFr. *lumineux* < Lat. *lūminōsus* < *lūmen, lūmin-,* light. See **leuk-** in App.] —**lu′mi·nous·ly** *adv.* —**lu′mi·nous·ness** *n.*

luminous energy *n.* The total radiant energy of light emitted by a source.

luminous flux *n.* The rate of flow of light per unit time, esp. the flux of visible light expressed in lumens.

luminous intensity *n.* The luminous flux per solid angle as measured in a given direction relative to the emitting source.

lum·mox (lŭm′əks) *n. Informal* A clumsy or stupid person. [?]

lump¹ (lŭmp) *n.* **1.** An irregularly shaped mass or piece. **2.** A small cube of sugar. **3.** *Pathology* A swelling or small palpable mass. **4.** A collection or totality; an aggregate. **5.** A person regarded as ungainly or dull-witted. **6. lumps** *Informal* **a.** Severe punishment or treatment, as an unsparing criticism. **b.** One's just deserts; comeuppance. ❖ *adj.* **1.** Formed into lumps: *lump sugar.* **2.** Not broken or divided into parts: *a lump payment.* ❖ *v.* **lumped, lump·ing, lumps** —*tr.* **1.** To put together in a single group without discrimination. **2.** To move with heavy clumsiness. **3.** To make into lumps. —*intr.* **1.** To become lumpy. **2.** To move heavily. —*idiom:* **lump in (one's) throat** A feeling of constriction in the throat caused by emotion. [ME *lumpe,* of LGer. orig.; akin to obsolete Du. *lompe.*]

lump² (lŭmp) *tr.v.* **lumped, lump·ing, lumps** *Informal* To tolerate (what must be endured): *like it or lump it.* [Perh. < dialectal *lump,* to look sullen.]

lump·ec·to·my (lŭm-pĕk′tə-mē) *n., pl.* **-mies** Surgical excision of a tumor from the breast along with a minimal amount of surrounding tissue.

lum·pen (lŭm′pən, lōōm′-) *adj.* **1.** Of or relating to dispossessed, often displaced people who have been cut off from the socioeconomic class with which they would ordinarily be identified. **2.** Of or relating to the lumpenproletariat. **3.** Vulgar or common; plebeian. ❖ *pl.n.* The lumpenproletariat. [< Ger. *Lumpenproletariat,* the lowest section of the proletariat. See LUMPENPROLETARIAT.]

lum·pen·pro·le·tar·i·at (lŭm′pən-prō′lĭ-târ′ē-ət, lōōm′-) *n.* **1.** The lowest, most degraded stratum of the proletariat; originally in Marxist theory, those members of the proletariat who lacked class consciousness. **2.** The underclass of a human population. [Ger. : *Lumpen,* pl. of *Lump,* ragamuffin (< MHGer. *lumpe,* rag) + *Proletariat,* proletariat (< Fr. *prolétariat;* see PROLETARIAT).]

lump·fish (lŭmp′fĭsh′) *n., pl.* **lumpfish** or **-fish·es** Any of various fishes of the family Cyclopteridae, esp. *Cyclopterus lumpus,* having prominent tubercles and pelvic fins united to form a suction disk. [Obsolete *lump* (perh. < Du. *lomp,* blenny, loach < MDu. *lompe,* cod) + FISH.]

lump·ish (lŭm′pĭsh) *adj.* **1.** Stupid or dull. **2.** Clumsy or cumbersome. —**lump′ish·ly** *adv.* —**lump′ish·ness** *n.*

lump sum *n.* A single sum of money that serves as complete payment. —**lump′-sum′** (lŭmp′sŭm′) *adj.*

lump·y (lŭm′pē) *adj.* **-i·er, -i·est 1.** Covered or filled with lumps. **2.** Thickset or cumbersome. **3.** Exhibiting short jumbled waves; choppy: *lumpy seas.* —**lump′i·ly** *adv.* —**lump′i·ness** *n.*

lumpy jaw *n.* See **actinomycosis.**

Lu·mum·ba (lōō-mōōm′bə), **Patrice Emery** 1925–61. First prime minister (1960–61) of the Congo (later Zaire).

Lu·na (lōō′nə) *n. Roman Mythology* The goddess of the moon. [Lat. *Lūna* < *lūna,* moon. See LUNAR.]

lu·na·cy (lōō′nə-sē) *n., pl.* **-cies 1.** Insanity, esp. insanity relieved intermittently by periods of clear-mindedness. **2a.** Great or wild foolishness. **b.** A wildly foolish act. **3.** *Archaic* Intermittent mental derangement associated with the changing phases of the moon. [< LUNATIC.]

luna moth *n.* A large pale-green North American moth *(Actias luna)* having elongated taillike hind wings. [NLat. *lūna,* species name < Lat., moon. See LUNAR.]

lu·nar (lōō′nər) *adj.* **1.** Of, involving, caused by, or affecting the moon. **2.** Measured by the revolution of the moon. **3.** Of or relating to silver. [ME, crescent-shaped < OFr. *lunaire* < Lat. *lūnāris,* of the moon < *lūna,* moon. See **leuk-** in App.]

lunar caustic *n.* Silver nitrate in the form of sticks used in cauterization.

lunar month *n.* The average time between successive new or full moons, equal to 29 days, 12 hours, 44 minutes.

lunar year *n.* An interval of 12 lunar months.

lu·nate (lōō′nāt′) *also* **lu·nat·ed** (-nā′tĭd) *adj.* Shaped like a crescent. [Lat. *lūnātus,* p. part. of *lūnāre,* to bend like a crescent < *lūna,* moon. See **leuk-** in App.]

lu·na·tic (lōō′nə-tĭk) *adj.* **1.** Suffering from lunacy; insane. **2.** Of or for the insane. **3.** Wildly or giddily foolish. **4.** Characterized by lunacy or eccentricity. [ME *lunatik* < OFr. *lunatique* < Lat. *lūnāticus* < *lūna,* moon. See **leuk-** in App.] —**lu′na·tic** *n.*

lunatic fringe *n.* The fanatical, extremist, or irrational members of a society or group.

lu·na·tion (lōō-nā′shən) *n.* The time that elapses between successive new moons, averaging 29 days, 12 hours, 44 minutes; a lunar month. [ME *lunacioun* < Med.Lat. *lūnātiō, lūnātiōn-* < Lat. *lūna.* See LUNAR.]

lunch (lŭnch) *n.* **1.** A meal eaten at midday. **2.** The food provided for a midday meal. ❖ *intr.v.* **lunched, lunch·ing, lunch·es** To eat a midday meal. —*idiom:* **out to lunch** *Slang* Not in touch with the real world; crazy. [Short for LUNCHEON.] —**lunch′er** *n.*

lunch·eon (lŭn′chən) *n.* **1.** A lunch, esp. a formal one. **2.** An afternoon party at which a light meal is served. [Prob. alteration of obsolete *nuncheon,* light snack < ME *nonschench : none,* noon; see NOON + *schench,* drink (< OE *scenc* < *scencan,* to pour out).]

lunch·eon·ette (lŭn′chə-nĕt′) *n.* A small restaurant that serves simple, easily prepared meals.

luncheon meat *n.* Prepackaged processed meat, often molded into a loaf and served sliced for use in sandwiches or salads.

lunch·room (lŭnch′rōōm′, -rōōm′) *n.* **1.** A luncheonette. **2.** A room in a facility where lunches are purchased or eaten.

lune (lōōn) *n.* A crescent-shaped portion of a plane or sphere bounded by two arcs of circles. [Lat. *lūna,* moon. See **leuk-** in App.]

lu·nette (lōō-nĕt′) *n.* **1.** *Architecture* **a.** A small circular or crescent-shaped opening in a vaulted roof. **b.** A crescent-shaped or semicircular space, as over a door, that may contain another window, a sculpture, or a mural. **2.** A fortification with two projecting faces and two parallel flanks. **3.** A broad, typically crescent-shaped mound of sandy or loamy matter formed by the wind. [Fr. < OFr. *lunete,* moon-shaped object, dim. of *lune,* moon < Lat. *lūna.* See LUNE.]

lung (lŭng) *n.* **1.** Either of two spongy saclike respiratory organs in the thorax of most vertebrates, removing carbon dioxide from the blood and providing it with oxygen. **2.** A similar organ in some invertebrates, including spiders. —*idiom:* **at the top of (one's) lungs** As loudly as one's voice will allow. [ME *lunge* < OE *lungen,* lungs.]

lunge (lŭnj) *n.* **1.** A sudden thrust or pass, as with a sword. **2.** A sudden forward movement or plunge. ❖ *v.* **lunged, lung·ing, lung·es** —*intr.* **1.** To make a sudden thrust or pass. **2.** To move with a sudden thrust. —*tr.* To cause (someone) to lunge. [< alteration of obsolete *allonge,* to thrust < Fr. *allonger* < OFr. *alongier,* to lengthen : *a-,* to (< Lat. *ad-;* see AD−) + *long,* long (< Lat. *longus;* see **del-** in App.).]

lung·fish (lŭng′fĭsh′) *n., pl.* **lungfish** or **-fish·es** Any of several elongated tropical freshwater fishes that have lunglike organs as well as gills and are able to breathe air.

lung·worm (lŭng′wûrm′) *n.* Any of various nematode worms, esp. of the family Metastrongylidae, that are parasitic in the lungs of mammals.

lung·wort (lŭng′wûrt′, -wôrt′) *n.* **1.** Any of various plants of the genus *Mertensia,* such as the Virginia cowslip, having drooping clusters of tubular, usu. blue flowers. **2.** Any of several European plants of the genus *Pulmonaria,* having long-stalked leaves and coiled clusters of blue or purple flowers and formerly used in treating respiratory disorders.

lu·ni·so·lar (lōō′nĭ-sō′lər) *adj.* Of or caused by both the sun and the moon. [Lat. *lūna,* moon; see LUNAR + SOLAR.]

lu·ni·ti·dal (lōō′nĭ-tīd′l) *adj.* Of or relating to tidal phenomena caused by the moon. [Lat. *lūna,* moon; see LUNAR + TIDAL.]

lunk·er (lŭng′kər) *n. Informal* Something, esp. a game fish, that is large for its kind. [?]

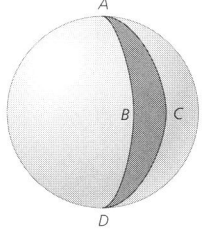

lune
a lune bounded by the arcs *ABD* and *ACD*

lunette
St. Mark's Basilica,
Venice, Italy

ă pat	oi boy
ā pay	ou out
âr care	ōō took
ä father	ōō boot
ĕ pet	ŭ cut
ē be	ûr urge
ĭ pit	th thin
ī pie	th this
îr pier	hw which
ŏ pot	zh vision
ō toe	ə about,
ô paw	item

Stress marks:
′ (primary);
′ (secondary), as in
lexicon (lĕk′sĭ-kŏn′)

lute¹

Martin Luther
1529 portrait by Lucas
Cranach the Elder

Luxembourg

lunk·head (lŭngk′hĕd′) n. Slang A stupid person; a dolt. [Prob. alteration of LUMP¹ + HEAD.] —**lunk′head′ed** adj.

Lunt (lŭnt), **Alfred** 1893–1977. Amer. actor who performed with his wife Lynn Fontanne in productions such as Pygmalion (1926).

lu·nu·la (lōō′nyə-lə) n., pl. **-lae** (-lē′) A small crescent-shaped structure or marking, esp. the white area at the base of a fingernail that resembles a half-moon. [NLat. lūnula < Lat., crescent-shaped ornament, dim. of lūna, moon. See leuk- in App.]

lu·nu·lar (lōōn′yə-lər) adj. Shaped like a crescent.

lu·nu·late (lōōn′yə-lāt′, -lĭt) also **lu·nu·lat·ed** (-lā′tĭd) adj. **1.** Small and lunular. **2.** Having crescent-shaped markings.

lu·nule (lōōn′yōōl) n. A lunula.

lun·y (lōō′nē) adj. Informal Variant of **loony**.

Luo·yang (lwō′yäng′) also **Lo·yang** (lō′-) A city of E-central China ENE of Xi'an; cap. of several ancient dynasties, including the Han and Tang. Pop. 1,202,192.

Lu·per·ca·li·a (lōō′pər-kā′lē-ə, -kăl′yə) n. A fertility festival in ancient Rome, celebrated on February 15 in honor of the pastoral god Lupercus. [Lat. Lupercālia < Lupercus, Roman god of flocks.] —**Lu′per·ca′li·an** adj.

lu·pine¹ also **lu·pin** (lōō′pən) n. Any of numerous plants of the genus Lupinus in the pea family, having compound leaves and flowers grouped in spikes or racemes. [ME < OFr. lupin < Lat. lupīnum < neut. of lupīnus, wolflike. See LUPINE².]

lu·pine² (lōō′pīn′) adj. **1.** Resembling a wolf. **2.** Rapacious; ravenous. [Fr. < Lat. lupīnus < lupus, wolf. See w⌊k⌋o- in App.]

Lu·pi·no (lōō-pē′nō), **Ida** 1918–95. British-born Amer. actress and director whose films include The Hitch-Hiker (1953).

lu·pus (lōō′pəs) n. Systemic lupus erythematosis. [Med.Lat. < Lat., wolf. See w⌊k⌋o- in App.]

Lupus n. A constellation of stars in the Southern Hemisphere near Centaurus and Scorpius. [Lat. < lupus, wolf. See LUPUS.]

lupus er·y·the·ma·to·sus (ĕr′ə-thē′mə-tō′səs, -thĕm′ə-) n. Any of various disorders of connective tissue, esp. systemic lupus erythematosus, that primarily affect women of childbearing age. [NLat. lupus erythēmatōsus : LUPUS + erythēmatōsus, erythematous.]

lurch¹ (lûrch) intr.v. **lurched, lurch·ing, lurch·es** **1.** To stagger. See Syns at **blunder**. **2.** To roll or pitch suddenly or erratically. ❖ n. **1.** A staggering or tottering movement or gait. **2.** An abrupt rolling or pitching. [?] —**lurch′ing·ly** adv.

lurch² (lûrch) n. The losing position of a cribbage player who scores 30 points or less to the winner's 61. —**idiom: in the lurch** In a difficult or embarrassing position. [Perh. back-formation < ME lurching, a total victory at lorche, a kind of game; perh. akin to lurken, to lurk. See LURK.]

lurch·er (lûr′chər) n. **1.** Chiefly British A crossbred dog used by poachers. **2.** Archaic A sneak thief. [ME < lorchen, to lurk, perh. < lurken. See LURK.]

lure (lōōr) n. **1a.** Something that tempts or attracts with the promise of pleasure or reward. **b.** An attraction or appeal. **2.** A decoy used in catching animals, esp. an artificial bait used in catching fish. **3.** A bunch of feathers attached to a long cord, used in falconry to recall the hawk. ❖ tr.v. **lured, lur·ing, lures** **1.** To attract by wiles or temptation; entice. **2.** To recall (a falcon) with a lure. [ME < AN, < Gmc. orig.] —**lur′er** n. —**lur′ing·ly** adv.

lu·rid (lōōr′ĭd) adj. **1.** Causing shock or horror; gruesome. **2.** Marked by sensationalism: a lurid account of the crime. **3.** Glowing or shining with the glare of fire through a haze: lurid flames. **4.** Sallow or pallid in color. [Lat. lūridus, pale < lūror, paleness.] —**lu′rid·ly** adv. —**lu′rid·ness** n.

lurk (lûrk) intr.v. **lurked, lurk·ing, lurks** **1.** To lie in wait, as in ambush. **2.** To move furtively; sneak. **3.** To exist unobserved or unsuspected: danger lurking around every bend. **4.** To read but not contribute to the discussion in a newsgroup or chatroom. [ME lurken, poss. of Scand. orig.] —**lurk′ing·ly** adv.

Lu·sa·ka (lōō-sä′kə) The cap. of Zambia, in the S-central part; founded 1905. Pop. 982,362.

Lu·sa·ti·a (lōō-sā′shē-ə, -shə) A region of central Europe in E Germany and SW Poland; settled by descendants of the Wends, a Slavic people. —**Lu·sa′tian** adj. & n.

lus·cious (lŭsh′əs) adj. **1.** Sweet and pleasant to taste or smell. **2.** Having strong sensual or sexual appeal; seductive. **3.** Richly appealing to the senses or the mind. **4.** Archaic Excessively sweet; cloying. [ME lucius, alteration of licious, perh. short for delicious, delicious. See DELICIOUS.] —**lus′cious·ly** adv. —**lus′cious·ness** n.

lush¹ (lŭsh) adj. **lush·er, lush·est** **1a.** Having or characterized by luxuriant vegetation. **b.** Abundant; plentiful. **c.** Extremely productive; thriving. **2a.** Luxurious; opulent. **b.** Extremely pleasing to the senses: a lush scent. **c.** Voluptuous or sensual. **3.** Overelaborate or extravagant: lush rhetoric. [ME, relaxed, soft, prob. alteration of lache, loose, weak < OFr., soft, succulent < laschier, to loosen < LLat. laxicāre, to become shaky, freq. of Lat. laxāre, to open, relax < laxus, loose.] —**lush′ly** adv. —**lush′ness** n.

lush² (lŭsh) Slang n. A drunkard. ❖ intr.v. **lushed, lush·ing, lush·es** To drink liquor to excess. [?]

Lü·shun (lōō′shōōn′, lü′-) A city of NE China at the tip of the Liaodong Peninsula, part of Lüda. Pop. 40,752.

Lu·si·ta·ni·a (lōō′sĭ-tā′nē-ə) An ancient region and Roman province of the Iberian Peninsula, corresponding roughly to modern-day Portugal. —**Lu′si·ta′ni·an** adj. & n.

lust (lŭst) n. **1.** Intense or unrestrained sexual craving. **2a.** An overwhelming desire or craving. **b.** Intense eagerness or enthusiasm. **3.** Obsolete Pleasure; relish. ❖ intr.v. **lust·ed, lust·ing, lusts** To have an intense or obsessive desire. esp. one that is sexual. [ME < OE, desire.] —**lust′ful·ly** adv. —**lust′ful·ness** n.

lus·ter (lŭs′tər) n. **1.** Soft reflected light; sheen. **2.** Brilliance or radiance of light; brightness. **3.** Glory, distinction, or splendor, as of beauty. **4.** A glass pendant, esp. on a chandelier. **5.** A decorative object that gives off light. **6.** Any of various substances, such as wax, used to give an object a gloss or polish. **7.** The surface glossiness of ceramic ware after glazing, esp. the metallic sheen of lusterware. **8.** A fabric, such as alpaca, having a glossy surface. **9.** The appearance of a mineral surface judged by its brilliance and ability to reflect light. ❖ v. **-tered, -ter·ing, -ters** —tr. **1.** To give a gloss, glaze, or sheen to. **2.** To give or add glory, distinction, or splendor to. —intr. To be or become lustrous. [Fr. lustre < OFr. < OItal. lustro < lustrare, to make bright < Lat. lūstrāre < lūstrum, purification. See leuk- in App.]

lus·ter·ware (lŭs′tər-wâr′) n. Pottery or porcelain having a metallic sheen produced by metallic oxides in the glaze.

lust·ful (lŭst′fəl) adj. Excited or driven by lust.

lus·tral (lŭs′trəl) adj. Of, relating to, or used in a rite of purification. [Lat. lūstrālis < lūstrum, purification. See LUSTER.]

lus·trate (lŭs′trāt′) tr.v. **lus·trat·ed, lus·trat·ing, lus·trates** To purify by means of ceremony. [Lat. lūstrāre, lūstrāt-, to purify, make bright. See LUSTER.] —**lus′tra′tion** n.

lus·tre (lŭs′tər) n. & v. Chiefly British Variant of **luster**.

lus·trous (lŭs′trəs) adj. **1.** Having a sheen or glow; gleaming: lustrous pearls. See Syns at **bright**. **2.** Well-known or distinguished; illustrious. —**lus′trous·ly** adv. —**lus′trous·ness** n.

lus·trum (lŭs′trəm) n., pl. **-trums** (-trəmz) or **-tra** (-trə) **1.** A ceremonial purification of the entire ancient Roman population after the census every five years. **2.** A period of five years. [Lat. lūstrum. See LUSTER.]

lust·y (lŭs′tē) adj. **-i·er, -i·est** **1.** Full of vigor or vitality; robust. **2.** Powerful; strong: a lusty cry. **3.** Lustful. **4.** Merry; joyous. —**lust′i·ly** adv. —**lust′i·ness** n.

Lü·ta (lōō′dä′, lü′-) See **Lüda**.

lute¹ (lōōt) n. A stringed instrument having a body shaped like a pear sliced lengthwise and a neck with a fretted fingerboard that is usu. bent just below the tuning pegs. [ME < OFr. lut < O Provençal laut < Ar. al-'ūd : al-, the + 'ūd, wood, stem, lute.]

lute² (lōōt) n. A substance, such as dried clay or cement, used to pack and seal pipe joints and other connections or coat a porous surface. ❖ tr.v. **lut·ed, lut·ing, lutes** To coat, pack, or seal with lute. [ME < OFr. lut < Lat. lutum, potter's clay.]

lu·te·al (lōō′tē-əl) adj. Of, relating to, or involving the corpus luteum.

lu·te·fisk (lōō′tə-fĭsk′) also **lut·fisk** (lōōt′fĭsk′) n. A traditional Scandinavian dish prepared by soaking air-dried cod in a lye solution for several weeks before skinning, boning, and boiling it. [Norw. : lut, lye (< Swed. < ON laudhr, soap, foam; see leu(ə)- in App.) + fisk, fish (< ON fiskr).]

lu·te·in (lōō′tē-ĭn, -tēn′) n. **1.** A yellow carotenoid pigment, $C_{40}H_{56}O_2$, found widely in nature, as in corpus luteum, body fats, egg yolk, and green plants; xanthophyll. **2.** A dried preparation of corpus luteum. [Lat. lūteum, yellow, egg yolk < neut. of lūteus, yellow (< lūtum, yellowweed) + -IN.]

lu·te·in·ize (lōō′tē-ə-nīz′) v. **-ized, -iz·ing, -iz·es** —tr. To cause the production of a corpus luteum in. —intr. To develop into or become part of the corpus luteum. —**lu′te·in·i·za′tion** (-ə-nĭ-zā′shən) n.

lu·te·in·iz·ing hormone (lōō′tē-ə-nī′zĭng) n. A hormone produced by the anterior lobe of the pituitary gland that stimulates ovulation and the development of the corpus luteum in the female and the production of testosterone in the male.

lu·te·nist also **lu·ta·nist** (lōōt′n-ĭst) n. A lute player. [Med.Lat. lūtānista < lūtāna, lute, poss. < OFr. lut. See LUTE¹.]

lu·te·ous (lōō′tē-əs) adj. Of a light or moderate greenish yellow. [< Lat. lūteus, yellow. See LUTEIN.]

lu·te·ti·um also **lu·te·ci·um** (lōō-tē′shē-əm) n. Symbol **Lu** A rare-earth element that is difficult to separate from other rare-earth elements, used in nuclear research. Atomic number 71; atomic weight 174.97; melting point 1,663°C; boiling point 3,395°C; specific gravity 9.840 (at 25°C); valence 3. See table at **element**. [Lat. Lutetia, ancient name of Paris, France (where it was discovered) + -IUM.]

Lu·ther (lōō′thər), **Martin** 1483–1546. German theologian and leader of the Reformation.

Lu·ther·an (lōō′thər-ən) adj. **1.** Of or relating to Luther or his religious teachings and esp. to the doctrine of justification by faith alone. **2.** Of or relating to the branch of the Protestant Church adhering to the views of Luther. ❖ n. A member of the Lutheran Church. —**Lu′ther·an·ism, Lu′ther·ism** n.

lu·thi·er (lōō′tē-ər) n. One that makes or repairs stringed instruments, such as violins. [Fr. < luth, lute < OFr. lut. See LUTE¹.]

Lu·thu·li (lōō-tōō′lē, -tyōō′-), **Albert John** 1898–1967. Zulu leader who won the 1960 Nobel Peace Prize.

lut·ing (lōō′tĭng) n. See **lute²**.

lut·ist (lōō′tĭst) n. Music **1.** A maker of lutes. **2.** See **lutenist**.

Lu·ton (lōōt′n) A borough of SE England NNW of London. Pop. 178,642.

Luts′k (lōōtsk) A city of W-central Ukraine NE of L'viv; first mentioned in 1085. Pop. 214,500.

Lutz also **lutz** (lŭts) *n.* A jump in figure skating in which the skater takes off from the back outer edge of one skate and makes one full rotation before landing on the back outer edge of the other skate. [Perhaps after Alois *Lutz* (1898–1918), Austrian figure skater.]

Lu·vi·an (lōō′vē-ən) also **Lu·wi·an** (-wē-ən) *n.* **1.** An Indo-European language of the Anatolian family, attested in documents from the second and first millennia B.C. and now extinct. **2.** A speaker of Luvian. [< Hittite *Lūiya*, ancient region in Anatolia.] —**Lu′vi·an** *adj.*

lux (lŭks) *n., pl.* **lux·es** or **lu·ces** (lōō′sēz) The International System unit of illumination, equal to one lumen per square meter. [Lat. *lūx*, light. See **leuk-** in App.]

Lux. *abbr.* Luxembourg

lux·ate (lŭk′sāt′) *tr.v.* **-at·ed, -at·ing, -ates** To put out of joint; dislocate. [Lat. *luxāre, luxāt-* < *luxus*, dislocated.] —**lux·a′tion** *n.*

luxe (lōōks, lŭks) *n.* **1.** The condition of being elegantly sumptuous. **2.** Something luxurious; a luxury. [Fr., luxury < Lat. *luxus*.] —**luxe** *adj.*

Lux·em·bourg also **Lux·em·burg** (lŭk′səm-bûrg′) **1.** A country of NW Europe; created as a duchy in 1354 and declared a neutral territory in 1867. Cap. Luxembourg. Pop. 401,000. **2.** also **Luxembourg City** The cap. of Luxembourg, in the S part. Pop. 75,833. —**Lux′em·bourg′er, Lux′em·burg′er** *n.*

Lux·em·burg (lŭk′səm-bûrg′, lōōk′səm-bŏŏrk′), **Rosa** 1870–1919. German socialist leader who cofounded (1918) the Spartacus Party.

Lux·or (lŭk′sôr, lōōk′-) A city of central Egypt on the E bank of the Nile R.; built partially on the site of ancient Thebes. Pop. 146,000.

lux·u·ri·ant (lŭg-zhŏŏr′ē-ənt, lŭk-shŏŏr′-) *adj.* **1a.** Marked by rich or profuse growth. **b.** Producing or yielding in abundance. **2.** Excessively florid or elaborate. **3.** Marked by or displaying luxury; luxurious. [Lat. *luxuriāns, luxuriant-*, pr. part. of *luxuriāre*, to be luxuriant. See LUXURIATE.] —**lux·u′ri·ance** *n.* —**lux·u′ri·ant·ly** *adv.*

lux·u·ri·ate (lŭg-zhŏŏr′ē-āt′, lŭk-shŏŏr′-) *intr.v.* **-at·ed, -at·ing, -ates 1.** To take luxurious pleasure; indulge oneself. **2.** To proliferate. **3.** To grow profusely; thrive. [Lat. *luxuriāre, luxuriāt-*, to be luxuriant < *luxuria*, luxury. See LUXURY.]

lux·u·ri·ous (lŭg-zhŏŏr′ē-əs, lŭk-shŏŏr′-) *adj.* **1.** Fond of or given to luxury. **2.** Marked by or contributing to luxury. **3.** Of a sumptuous, costly, or rich variety. —**lux·u′ri·ous·ly** *adv.* —**lux·u′ri·ous·ness** *n.*

lux·u·ry (lŭg′zhə-rē, lŭk′shə-) *n., pl.* **-ries 1.** Something inessential but conducive to pleasure and comfort. **2.** Something expensive or hard to obtain. **3.** Sumptuous living or surroundings. ❖ *adj.* Providing luxury: *a luxury car.* [ME *luxurie*, lust < OFr. < Lat. *luxuria*, excess, luxury < *luxus*.]

Lu·zon (lōō-zŏn′) An island of the NW Philippines; the largest and most populous island in the archipelago.

Lv *abbr.* Bible Leviticus

L′viv or **Lviv** (lə-vĭv′, lə-vēw′) or **L′vov** or **Lvov** (lə-vôv′, -vôf′) A city of W-central Ukraine near the Polish border; founded 1256. Pop. 742,000.

LVN *abbr.* licensed vocational nurse

LW *abbr.* low water

LWM *abbr.* low-water mark

Lwoff (lwôf), **André Michel** 1902–94. French microbiologist who shared a 1965 Nobel Prize.

LWV *abbr.* League of Women Voters

lx *abbr.* lux

–ly[1] *suff.* **1.** Like; resembling; having the characteristics of: *sisterly.* **2.** Recurring at a specified interval of time: *hourly.* [ME *-li* < OE *-līc* (influenced by ON *-ligr*).]

–ly[2] *suff.* **1.** In a specified manner; in the manner of: *gradually.* **2.** At a specified interval of time: *weekly.* **3.** With respect to: *partly.* [ME *-li* < OE *-līce* (influenced by ON *-liga*) < *-līc*, adj. suff.]

Ly·all·pur (lī′əl-pŏŏr′) See Faisalabad.

ly·ase (lī′ās′) *n.* Any of a group of enzymes that catalyze the formation of double bonds without hydrolysis. [Gk. *lūein*, to loosen; see **leu-** in App. + –ASE.]

ly·can·thrope (lī′kən-thrōp′, lī-kăn′-) *n.* A werewolf. [Gk. *lukanthrōpos* : *lukos*, wolf; see **wl̥kwo-** in App. + *anthrōpos*, man.]

ly·can·thro·py (lī-kăn′thrə-pē) *n.* **1.** In folklore, the magical ability to assume the form and characteristics of a wolf. **2.** A delusion that one has become a wolf.

ly·cée (lē-sā′) *n.* A French public secondary school. [Fr. < OFr., lyceum < Lat. *Lycēum*. See LYCEUM.]

ly·ce·um (lī-sē′əm) *n.* **1.** A hall in which public lectures, concerts, and similar programs are presented. **2.** An organization sponsoring public programs and entertainment. **3.** A lycée. [Lat. *Lycēum* < Gk. *Lukeion*, the school outside Athens where Aristotle taught (335–323 B.C.).]

ly·chee (lē′chē) *n.* Variant of **litchi.**

lych-gate or **lych gate** also **lich gate** (lĭch′gāt′) *n.* A roofed gateway to a churchyard used originally as a resting place for a bier

before burial. [ME *lycheyate* : *lyche*, corpse, body (< OE *līc*) + *gate, yate*, gate; see GATE[1].]

lych·nis (lĭk′nĭs) *n.* Any of various plants of the genus *Lychnis*, which includes the campions. [NLat. *Lychnis*, genus name < Lat. *lychnis*, a red flower < Gk. *lukhnis*; akin to *lukhnos*, lamp. See **leuk-** in App.]

Ly·ci·a (lĭsh′ē-ə, lĭsh′ə) An ancient country and Roman province of SW Asia Minor on the Aegean Sea; annexed by Rome in the 1st cent. A.D.

Ly·ci·an (lĭsh′ē-ən, lĭsh′ən) *adj.* Of or relating to Lycia or its people, language, or culture. ❖ *n.* **1.** A native or inhabitant of Lycia. **2.** The extinct Anatolian language of the Lycians.

ly·co·pene (lī′kə-pēn′) *n.* A red carotenoid pigment, $C_{40}H_{56}$, found chiefly in blood, the reproductive organs, tomatoes, and palm oils. [Alteration of earlier *lycopin* : NLat. *Lycop(ersicon)*, tomato genus < Gk. *lukos*, wolf + Gk. *persikon*, peach < *persikē*, peach tree; see PEACH[1]) + –IN.]

ly·co·po·di·um (lī′kə-pō′dē-əm) *n.* **1.** A plant of the genus *Lycopodium*, which includes the club mosses. **2.** The yellowish powdery spores of certain club mosses, esp. *Lycopodium clavatum*, used in fireworks and explosives and as a covering for pills. [NLat. *Lycopodium*, genus name : Gk. *lukos*, wolf; see **wl̥kwo-** in App. + Gk. *podion*, dim. of *pous*, foot; see **ped-** in App.]

Ly·cra (lī′krə) A trademark used for a brand of spandex.

Ly·cur·gus (lī-kûr′gəs) fl. 9th cent. B.C. Spartan lawmaker who is considered the founder of the Spartan constitution.

lyd·dite (lĭd′īt′) *n.* An explosive consisting chiefly of picric acid. [After *Lydd*, a municipal borough of SE England.]

Lyd·gate (lĭd′gāt′, -gət), **John** 1370?–1451? English poet who is best known for his long narrative works.

Lyd·i·a (lĭd′ē-ə) An ancient country of W-central Asia Minor on the Aegean Sea in present-day NW Turkey.

Lyd·i·an (lĭd′ē-ən) *adj.* Of or relating to Lydia or its people, language, or culture. ❖ *n.* **1.** A native or inhabitant of Lydia. **2.** The extinct Anatolian language of the Lydians.

lye (lī) *n.* **1.** The liquid obtained by leaching wood ashes. **2.** See **potassium hydroxide. 3.** See **sodium hydroxide.** [ME *lie* < OE *lēag*. See **leu(ə)-** in App.]

Ly·ell (lī′əl), **Sir Charles** 1797–1875. British geologist whose *Principles of Geology* (1830–33) opposed the catastrophic theory of geologic change.

ly·gus bug (lī′gəs) *n.* Any of various North American bugs of the genus *Lygus*, including certain species that are destructive to plants. [NLat. *Lȳgus*, genus name < Gk. *lūgaios*, murky < *lūgē*, twilight.]

ly·ing[1] (lī′ĭng) *v.* Present participle of **lie**[1].

ly·ing[2] (lī′ĭng) *v.* Present participle of **lie**[2]. ❖ *adj.* Disposed to or characterized by untruth: *a lying witness.*

ly·ing-in (lī′ĭng-ĭn′) *n., pl.* **ly·ings-in** (lī′ĭngz-) or **ly·ing-ins** The condition of a woman in the process of giving birth. ❖ *adj.* Of or intended for use during childbirth: *a lying-in hospital.*

Lyl·y (lĭl′ē), **John** 1554?–1606. English playwright who wrote a number of comedies that influenced English drama.

Lyme disease (līm) *n.* An inflammatory disease caused by a spirochete (*Borrelia burgdorferi*) that is transmitted by ticks, usu. characterized by a rash followed by flulike symptoms including fever, joint pain, and headache. [After *Lyme*, a town of SE Connecticut.]

lymph (lĭmf) *n.* **1.** A clear watery fluid that contains white blood cells and circulates throughout the lymphatic system, removing bacteria and certain proteins from body tissues, transporting fat from the small intestine, and supplying mature lymphocytes to the blood. **2.** *Archaic* A spring or stream of pure clear water. [Lat. *lympha*, water nymph < Gk. *numphē*, young bride, water nymph.]

lym·phad·e·ni·tis (lĭm-făd′n-ī′tĭs, lĭm′fə-də-nī′-) *n.* Inflammation of one or more lymph nodes.

lym·phad·e·nop·a·thy (lĭm-făd′n-ŏp′ə-thē, lĭm′fə-dn-) *n., pl.* **-thies** A chronic, abnormal enlargement of the lymph nodes. [LYMPH + ADENO- + –PATHY.]

lym·phan·gi·og·ra·phy (lĭm-făn′jē-ŏg′rə-fē) *n., pl.* **-phies** Examination of the lymph nodes and lymphatic vessels following the injection of a radiopaque substance. —**lym·phan′gi·o·gram′** (-ə-grăm′) *n.*

lym·phat·ic (lĭm-făt′ĭk) *adj.* **1.** Of or relating to lymph, a lymph vessel, or a lymph node. **2.** Lacking energy or vitality; sluggish. ❖ *n.* A vessel that conveys lymph. [NLat. *lymphaticus* < Lat. *lympha*, lymph. See LYMPH.] —**lym·phat′i·cal·ly** *adv.*

lymphatic system *n.* The interconnected system of spaces and vessels between body tissues and organs by which lymph circulates throughout the body.

lymph gland *n.* See **lymph node.**

lymph node *n.* Any of the small bodies located along the lymphatic vessels, esp. at the neck, armpit, and groin, that filter bacteria and foreign particles from the lymph.

lympho– or **lymph–** *pref.* Lymphatic system; lymph: *lymphocyte.* [< LYMPH.]

lym·pho·blast (lĭm′fə-blăst′) *n.* A cell that gives rise to a mature lymphocyte. —**lym′pho·blas′tic** *adj.*

lym·pho·cyte (lĭm′fə-sīt′) *n.* Any of the nearly colorless cells found in the blood, lymph, and lymphoid tissues that function in the development of immunity and include B cells and T cells.

lych-gate

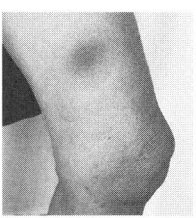

Lyme disease
rash caused by Lyme disease

—**lym•pho•cyt′ic** (-sĭt′ĭk) *adj.*

lym•pho•cy•to•sis (lĭm′fō-sī-tō′sĭs) *n.* A condition marked by an abnormal increase in the number of lymphocytes in the bloodstream. —**lym′pho•cy•tot′ic** (-tŏt′ĭk) *adj.*

lym•pho•gran•u•lo•ma ve•ne•re•um (lĭm′fə-grăn′yə-lō′mə və-nîr′ē-əm) *n.* A sexually transmitted disease caused by a bacterium (*Chlamydia trachomatis*) and characterized initially by a genital lesion followed by enlargement of the lymph nodes in the groin area. [NLat. : LYMPHO– + GRANULOMA + Lat. *venereum*, neut. of *venereus*, venereal.]

lym•phog•ra•phy (lĭm-fŏg′rə-fē) *n.* See **lymphangiography.**

lym•phoid (lĭm′foid) *adj.* Of or relating to lymph or the lymphatic tissue where lymphocytes are formed.

lym•pho•kine (lĭm′fə-kīn′) *n.* Any of various substances released by T cells that function in the immune response through a variety of actions, including stimulating the production of nonsensitized lymphocytes and activating macrophages. [LYMPHO– + Gk. *kīnein*, to move; see KININ.]

lym•pho•ma (lĭm-fō′mə) *n., pl.* -**ma•ta** (-mə-tə) or -**mas** Any of various usu. malignant tumors that arise in the lymph nodes or in other lymphoid tissue. —**lym•pho′ma•toid′, lym•pho′ma•tous** (-təs) *adj.*

lym•pho•poi•e•sis (lĭm′fō-poi-ē′sĭs) *n., pl.* -**ses** (-sēz′) The formation of lymphocytes. —**lym′pho•poi•et′ic** (-ĕt′ĭk) *adj.*

lynch (lĭnch) *tr.v.* **lynched, lynch•ing, lynch•es** To execute without due process of law, esp. to hang, as by a mob. [Short for LYNCH LAW.] —**lynch′er** *n.* —**lynch′ing** *n.*

Lynch•burg (lĭnch′bûrg′) An independent city of SW-central VA ENE of Roanoke. Pop. 65,269.

lynch law *n.* The punishment of persons suspected of crime without due process of law. [After William *Lynch* (1742–1820).]

lynch•pin (lĭnch′pĭn′) *n.* Variant of **linchpin.**

Lynd (lĭnd), **Robert Staughton** 1892–1970. Amer. sociologist who wrote *Middletown: A Study in Contemporary American Culture* (1929) with his wife, **Helen Merrell Lynd** (1896–1982).

Lynn (lĭn) A city of NE MA, a suburb of Boston; formerly an important shoe-making center. Pop. 89,050.

Lynn Canal An inlet of the Pacific Ocean in SE AK connecting Skagway with Juneau; a major route to the goldfields during the Alaskan gold rush (1896–98).

lynx (lĭngks) *n., pl.* **lynx** or **lynx•es** Any of several wildcats of the genus *Lynx*, esp. *L. canadensis* of northern North America or *L. lynx* of Eurasia, having a black-tipped short tail and tufted ears. [ME < Lat. < Gk. *lunx*. See **leuk-** in App.]

lynx-eyed (lĭngks′īd′) *adj.* Keen of vision.

lyo– *pref.* Dispersion; dissolution: *lyophilic.* [< Gk. *lūein*, to loosen, dissolve. See **leu-** in App.]

Ly•on or **Lyons** (lē-ōN′, lyôN′) A city of E-central France at the confluence of the Rhone and Saône rivers S of Mâcon; founded 43 B.C. as a Roman colony. Pop. 415,479.

Ly•on (lī′ən), **Mary Mason** 1797–1849. Amer. educator who founded (1837) Mount Holyoke College.

Ly•on•nais (lē-ô-nĕ′) A historical region and former province of E-central France; became part of the French royal domain in the 14th cent.

ly•on•naise (lī′ə-nāz′, lē′ə-nĕz′) *adj.* Cooked with onions: *lyonnaise potatoes.* [< Fr. *(à la) Lyonnaise*, (in the manner) of Lyon < LYON.]

ly•o•phil•ic (lī′ə-fĭl′ĭk) *adj.* Characterized by strong attraction between the colloid medium and the dispersion medium of a colloidal system.

ly•oph•i•lize (lī-ŏf′ə-līz′) *tr.v.* -**lized, -liz•ing, -liz•es** To freeze-dry (blood plasma or other biological substances).

ly•o•pho•bic (lī′ə-fō′bĭk) *adj.* Characterized by a lack of attraction between the colloid medium and the dispersion medium of a colloidal system.

Ly•ra (lī′rə) *n.* A constellation in the Northern Hemisphere near Cygnus and Hercules. [Lat. < *lyra*, lyre. See LYRE.]

ly•rate (lī′rāt′, -rĭt) *adj.* Having a form or curvature suggestive of a lyre.

lyre (līr) *n.* A stringed instrument of the harp family having two curved arms connected at the upper end by a crossbar, used to accompany a singer or reciter of poetry, esp. in ancient Greece. [ME *lire* < OFr. < Lat. *lyra* < Gk. *lura*.]

lyre•bird (līr′bûrd′) *n.* Either of two Australian birds of the genus *Menura*, the male of which has long tail feathers that are spread in a lyre-shaped display during courtship.

lyr•ic (lĭr′ĭk) *adj.* **1a.** Of or relating to a category of poetry that expresses subjective thoughts and feelings, often in a songlike style or form. **b.** Relating to or constituting a poem in this category, such as a sonnet or ode. **c.** Of or relating to a writer of poems in this category. **2.** Lyrical. **3.** *Music* **a.** Having a singing voice of light volume and modest range. **b.** Of, relating to, or being musical drama, esp. opera. **c.** Having a pleasing succession of sounds; melodious. **d.** Of or relating to the lyre or harp. **e.** Appropriate for accompaniment by the lyre. ❖ *n.* **1.** A lyric poem. **2.** *Music* The words of a song. Often used in the plural. [Fr. *ly-*

rique, of a lyre < OFr. < Lat. *lyricus* < Gk. *lurikos* < *lura*, lyre.]

lyr•i•cal (lĭr′ĭ-kəl) *adj.* **1a.** Expressing deep personal emotion or observations. **b.** Highly enthusiastic; rhapsodic: *a lyrical description.* **2.** Lyric. —**lyr′i•cal•ly** *adv.* —**lyr′i•cal•ness** *n.*

lyr•i•cism (lĭr′ĭ-sĭz′əm) *n.* **1a.** The character or quality of subjectivity and sensuality of expression, esp. in the arts. **b.** The quality or state of being melodious; melodiousness. **2.** An intense outpouring of exuberant emotion.

lyr•i•cist (lĭr′ĭ-sĭst) *n.* A writer of song lyrics.

lyr•i•cize (lĭr′ĭ-sīz′) *v.* -**cized, -ciz•ing, -ciz•es** —*intr.* **1.** *Music* To write or sing lyrics. **2.** To write lyrically or in a lyric style. —*tr.* To treat (something) lyrically; put into lyric style.

lyr•ism (lĭr′ĭz′əm) *n.* Lyricism. [Fr. *lyrisme* < Gk. *lurismos*, act of playing on the lyre < *lura*, lyre.]

lyr•ist (lĭr′ĭst) *n.* **1.** *Music* See **lyricist. 2.** (lī′rĭst) *Music* One who plays a lyre. **3.** A lyric poet. [Lat. *lyristēs*, lyre player < Gk. *luristēs* < *lura*, lyre.]

Lys (lēs) A river rising in N France and flowing c. 217 km (135 mi) NE to the Scheldt R.

lys– *pref.* Variant of **lyso–.**

Ly•san•der (lī-săn′dər) d. 395 B.C. Spartan military leader who defeated Athens (404) in the Peloponnesian War.

lyse (līs, līz) *intr. & tr.v.* **lysed, lys•ing, lys•es** To undergo or cause to undergo lysis. [Back-formation < LYSIS.]

—**lyse** *suff.* Chiefly British Variant of **–lyze.**

Ly•sen•ko (lī-sĕng′kō, -syĕn′kə), **Trofim Denisovich** 1898–1976. Soviet biologist and director of the Institute of Genetics of the Soviet Academy of Sciences (1940–64).

Ly•sen•ko•ism (lī-sĕng′kō-ĭz′əm) *n.* A biological doctrine developed by Trofim Lysenko that maintains the possibility of inheriting environmentally acquired characteristics.

ly•ser•gic acid (lī-sûr′jĭk, lĭ-) *n.* A crystalline alkaloid, $C_{16}H_{16}N_2O_2$, derived from ergot and used in medical research as a psychotomimetic agent. [LYS(O)– + ERG(OT) + –IC.]

lysergic acid di•eth•yl•am•ide (dī′ĕth-əl-ăm′īd′) *n.* LSD.

ly•sin (lī′sĭn) *n.* A substance, esp. an antibody, that causes lysis of cells.

ly•sine (lī′sēn′, -sĭn) *n.* An essential amino acid, $C_6H_{14}N_2O_2$, obtained by the hydrolysis of proteins.

Ly•sip•pus (lī-sĭp′əs) fl. 4th cent. B.C. Greek sculptor who created figures that were more lifelike than traditional forms.

ly•sis (lī′sĭs) *n., pl.* -**ses** (-sēz′) **1.** *Biochemistry* The dissolution or destruction of cells, such as blood cells or bacteria, as by the action of a specific lysin. **2.** *Medicine* The gradual subsiding of the symptoms of an acute disease. [NLat. < Lat., a loosening < Gk. *lusis* < *lūein*, to loosen. See **leu-** in App.]

—**lysis** *suff.* Decomposition; dissolving; disintegration: *hydrolysis.* [NLat. < Gk. *lusis*, a loosening. See LYSIS.]

Ly•sith•e•a (lī-sĭth′ē-ə) *n.* A satellite of Jupiter. [Prob. < Gk. *Lūsithoē*, daughter of Oceanus and mother of Herakles.]

lyso– or **lysi–** or **lys–** *pref.* Lysis: *lysin.* [< Gk. *lusis*, a loosening < *lūein*, to loosen. See **leu-** in App.]

ly•so•gen (lī′sə-jən) *n.* **1.** An agent capable of inducing lysis of cells. **2.** A bacterium in a state of lysogeny.

ly•so•gen•ic (lī′sə-jĕn′ĭk) *adj.* **1.** Capable of causing or undergoing lysis. **2.** Of or relating to lysogeny.

ly•sog•e•nize (lī-sŏj′ĭ-nīz′) *tr.v.* -**nized, -niz•ing, -niz•es** To make lysogenic. —**ly•sog′e•ni•za′tion** (-nī-zā′shən) *n.*

ly•sog•e•ny (lī-sŏj′ə-nē) *n.* The fusion of the nucleic acid of a bacteriophage with that of a host bacterium so that the potential exists for the newly integrated genetic material to be transmitted to daughter cells at each subsequent cell division.

Ly•sol (lī′sôl′, -sōl′, -sŏl′) A trademark used for a liquid antiseptic and disinfectant.

ly•so•some (lī′sə-sōm′) *n.* A membrane-bound organelle in the cytoplasm of most cells containing various hydrolytic enzymes that function in intracellular digestion.

ly•so•zyme (lī′sə-zīm′) *n.* An enzyme occurring naturally in egg white, human tears, saliva, and other body fluids, capable of destroying the cell walls of certain bacteria and thereby acting as a mild antiseptic.

—**lyte** *suff.* A substance that can be decomposed by a specified process: *electrolyte.* [< Gk. *lutos*, soluble < *lūein*, to loosen. See **leu-** in App.]

lyt•ic (lĭt′ĭk) *adj.* **1.** Of, relating to, or causing lysis: *a lytic enzyme.* **2.** Of or relating to a lysin. [Gk. *lutikos*, able to loosen. See –LYTIC.]

—**lytic** *suff.* Of, relating to, or causing a specified kind of decomposition: *cellulolytic.* [< Gk. *lutikos*, able to loosen < *lūein*, to loosen. See **leu-** in App.]

Lyt•ton (lĭt′n), First Baron. See Edward George Earle Lytton **Bulwer-Lytton.**

Lytton, First Earl of. Title of Edward Robert Bulwer-Lytton. 1831–91. British politician who served as viceroy of India (1875–80) and ambassador to Paris (1887–91).

—**lyze** *suff.* To cause or undergo lysis: *pyrolyze.* [< –LYSIS.]

LZ *abbr.* landing zone

Mm

m¹ or **M** (ĕm) *n.*, *pl.* **m's** or **M's** also **ms** or **Ms 1.** The 13th letter of the modern English alphabet. **2.** Any of the speech sounds represented by the letter *m.* **3.** The 13th in a series. **4.** Something shaped like the letter M.

m² *abbr.* **1.** *Grammar* masculine **2.** *Physics* mass **3.** meter (measurement) **4.** minute **5.** also **M** *Physics* modulus

M¹ also **m** The symbol for the Roman numeral 1,000.

M² *abbr.* **1.** *Printing* em **2.** *Bible* Maccabees **3.** Mach number **4.** male **5.** medium **6.** metal **7.** middle term **8.** million **9.** *Chemistry* molar **10.** *Physics* moment **11.** Monday **12.** month **13.** *Physics* mutual inductance

m. *abbr.* **1.** married **2.** or **M.** *Latin* merides (noon) **3.** meridian **4.** mile

M. *abbr.* **1.** master **2.** mill (currency) **3.** minim **4.** Monsieur

'm Contraction of *am: I'm feeling fine.*

M-1 (ĕm′wŭn′) *n.* A .30-caliber, gas-operated semiautomatic rifle capable of firing eight rounds before reloading, used by US forces during World War II and the Korean War. [*M*, military classification.]

M-16 (ĕm′sĭk-stēn′) *n.* A .223-caliber, gas-operated, clip-fed assault rifle, first used by US troops during the Vietnam War. [*M*, military classification.]

M-80 (ĕm′ā′tē) *n.* A powerful cylindrical firecracker. [*M*, military classification.]

ma (mä, mô) *n. Informal* Mother. [Short for MAMA.]

mA *abbr.* milliampere

Ma (mä), **Yo-Yo** b. 1955. Amer. cellist known for his performances and recordings of orchestral, recital, and chamber music.

MA *abbr.* **1.** *Latin* Magister Artium (Master of Arts) **2.** Maritime Administration **3.** Massachusetts **4.** mental age

ma'am (măm) *n.* Used as a form of polite address for a woman.

maar (mär) *n.* A circular volcanic crater of explosive origin that is often filled with water. [Ger. < VLat. *mara, standing water, lake < Lat. *mare*, sea. See MARE².]

Maas (mäs) Variant of **Meuse.**

Maa·sai (mä-sī′, mä′sī) *n.* Variant of **Masai** 2.

Maas·tricht (mäs′trĭkt′, mäs-trĭкнт′) A city of extreme SE Netherlands near the Belgian border; founded on the site of a Roman settlement. Pop. 118,194.

mac (măk) *n. Chiefly British* A mackintosh.

Mac *n. Slang* Used as a form of address for a man whose name is unknown. [< *Mac-*, Sc. and Ir. surname pref.]

Mac. *abbr.* **1.** *Bible* Maccabees **2a.** Macedonia **b.** Macedonian

ma·ca·bre (mə-kä′brə, mə-käb′, -käb′ər) *adj.* **1.** Suggesting the horror of death and decay; gruesome: *macabre tales of war.* **2.** Constituting or including a representation of death. [Ult. < OFr. *(Danse) Macabre*, (dance) of death, perh. alteration of *Macabe*, one of the Maccabees < Lat. *Maccabaeus* < Gk. *Makkabios*.] —**ma·ca′bre·ly** *adv.*

ma·ca·co (mə-kä′kō) *n., pl.* **-cos** Any of various lemurs, esp. the species *Lemur macaco.* [Port., of Bantu orig.; akin to Kongo *makako*, monkeys : *ma-*, pl. n. pref. + *kako*, monkey.]

mac·ad·am (mə-kăd′əm) *n.* Pavement of layers of compacted broken stone, now usu. bound with tar or asphalt. [After John L. *McAdam* (1756–1836), Scottish engineer.]

mac·a·da·mi·a nut (măk′ə-dā′mē-ə) *n.* The round hard-shelled nut or the edible seed of the Australian tree *Macadamia ternifolia.* [NLat. *Macadamia*, genus name, after John *Macadam* (1827–65), Scottish-born Australian chemist.]

mac·ad·am·ize (mə-kăd′ə-mīz′) *tr.v.* **-ized, -iz·ing, -iz·es** To construct or pave (a road) with macadam. —**mac·ad′am·i·za′tion** (-ə-mĭ-zā′shən) *n.* —**mac·ad′am·iz′er** *n.*

Ma·cao also **Ma·cau** (mə-kou′) An administrative region of SE China comprising **Macao Peninsula** and two offshore islands in the South China Sea W of Hong Kong; a Portuguese overseas province until 1999, when it reverted to Chinese sovereignty. The city of **Macao,** coextensive with the peninsula, is the capital. Pop. 398,000.

ma·caque (mə-kăk′, -käk′) *n.* Any of several short-tailed monkeys of the genus *Macaca* of southeast Asia, Japan, and northern Africa. [Fr. < Port. < MACACO.]

mac·a·ro·ni (măk′ə-rō′nē) *n.*, *pl.* **macaroni** Pasta in any of various hollow shapes, esp. short curved tubes. **2.** *pl.* **macaroni** or **-nies a.** A well-traveled young Englishman of the 18th and 19th centuries with foreign affectations. **b.** A fop. [Ital. dialectal *maccaroni*, pl. of *maccarone*, dumpling, macaroni.]

mac·a·ron·ic (măk′ə-rŏn′ĭk) *adj.* **1.** Of or containing a mixture of vernacular words with Latin words or with vernacular words given Latinate endings: *macaronic verse.* **2.** Of or involving a mix-

ture of two or more languages. [NLat. *macaronicus* < Ital. *maccheronea*, macaronic verse, after *Maccharonea*, title of a work containing such verse by Tifi Odasi, 15th-cent. Italian author < *maccherone*, maccaroni, course food.] —**mac′a·ron′ic** *n.*

mac·a·roon (măk′ə-rōon′) *n.* A chewy cookie made with sugar, egg whites, and almond paste or coconut. [Fr. *macaron* < Ital. dialectal *maccarone*, dumpling, macaroni.]

Mac·Ar·thur (mĭk-är′thər), **Douglas** 1880–1964. Amer. general who served as US chief of staff (1930–35), commanded Allied forces in the South Pacific during World War II, and led United Nations forces in Korea (1950–51).

Ma·cau·lay (mə-kô′lē), **Dame Rose** 1881–1958. British writer whose witty, urbane novels include *Potterism* (1920).

Macaulay, Thomas Babington. 1st Baron Macaulay. 1800–59. British historian noted for his *History of England* (1849–61).

ma·caw (mə-kô′) *n.* Any of various parrots of the genera *Ara* and *Anodorhynchus* of Central and South America, characterized by long tails, curved bills, and usu. brilliant plumage. [Port. *macaú* < *macaúba*, kind of palm tree < Tupi *macahuba*, palm tree : *maca*, palm + *ybá*, tree.]

Mac·beth (mək-běth′) d. 1057. King of Scotland (1040–57) who ascended the throne after killing King Duncan in battle.

Mac·Bride (mĭk-brīd′), **Sean** 1904–88. Irish politician who shared the 1974 Nobel Peace Prize.

Macc. *abbr. Bible* Maccabees

Mac·ca·bees¹ (măk′ə-bēz′) A family of Jewish patriots of the 2nd and 1st cent. B.C., active in the liberation of Judea from Syrian rule.

Mac·ca·bees² (măk′ə-bēz′) *pl.n.* See table at **Bible.** —**Mac′ca·be′an** *adj.*

Mac·ca·be·us also **Mac·ca·bae·us** (măk′ə-bē′əs), **Judas** or **Judah** d. 160 B.C. Jewish patriot of the Maccabees family who rededicated the Temple at Jerusalem (164 B.C.).

Mac·don·ald (mĭk-dŏn′əld), Sir **John Alexander** 1815–91. Canadian politician and first prime minister of the Dominion of Canada (1867–73 and 1878–91).

Mac·Don·ald (mĭk-dŏn′əld), **(James) Ramsay** 1866–1937. British prime minister (1924 and 1929–35).

Mac·Dow·ell (mĭk-dou′əl), **Edward Alexander** 1861–1908. Amer. composer whose works include *Sea Pieces* (1898).

mace¹ (mās) *n.* **1.** A ceremonial staff borne or displayed as the symbol of authority of a legislative body. **2.** A macebearer. **3.** A heavy medieval war club with a spiked or flanged metal head, used to crush armor. [ME < OFr. *masse* < VLat. *mattea.*]

mace² (mās) *n.* An aromatic spice made from the dried waxy covering that partly encloses the kernel of the nutmeg. [ME < OFr. < Med.Lat. *macis*, alteration of Lat. *macir*, fragrant ailanthus resin < Gk. *makir.*]

Mace A trademark used for an aerosol used to immobilize an attacker temporarily.

mace·bear·er (mās′bâr′ər) *n.* One who bears an official mace.

mace·é·doine (măs′ə-dwän′) *n.* **1.** A mixture of finely cut vegetables or fruits. **2.** A mixture; a medley. [Fr. < *Macédoine*, Macedonia (perh. < its ethnic variety).]

Mac·e·do·ni·a (măs′ĭ-dō′nē-ə, -dōn′yə) **1.** also **Mac·e·don** (-dən, -dŏn′) An ancient kingdom of N Greece; a powerful empire under Philip II and his son Alexander the Great (4th cent. B.C.). **2.** A historical region of SE Europe on the Balkan Peninsula, including modern Macedonia, N Greece, and SW Bulgaria. **3.** A country of the S-central Balkan Peninsula S of Serbia; a constituent republic of Yugoslavia from 1946 to 1991. Cap. Skopje. Pop. 2,142,000.

Mac·e·do·ni·an (măs′ĭ-dō′nē-ən) *n.* **1.** A native or inhabitant of ancient or modern Macedonia. **2.** The language of ancient Macedonia, of uncertain affiliation within Indo-European. **3.** The Slavic language of modern Macedonia, closely related to Bulgarian. —**Mac′e·do′ni·an** *adj.*

Ma·cei·ó (măs′ā-ō′, mä′sä-) A city of NE Brazil on the Atlantic Ocean SSW of Recife. Pop. 628,241.

mac·er (mā′sər) *n.* A macebearer.

mac·er·ate (măs′ə-rāt′) *v.* **-at·ed, -at·ing, -ates** —*tr.* **1.** To make soft by soaking or steeping in a liquid. **2.** To separate into constituents by soaking. **3.** To cause to become lean, usu. by starvation; emaciate. —*intr.* To become soft or separated into constituents by soaking. ❖ *n.* (-ĭt) A substance produced by macerating. [Lat. *mācerāre, mācerāt-.*] —**mac′er·a′tion** *n.* —**mac′er·a′tor, mac′er·at′er** *n.*

Mach also **mach** (mäk) *n.* Mach number.

Mach (mäk, mäкн), **Ernst** 1838–1916. Austrian physicist and phi-

losopher who maintained that knowledge is the organization of sensory experience.

Ma·chaut (mä-shō′), **Guillaume de** 1300?–77. French poet and composer influential in establishing polyphonic song in France.

mache also **mâche** (mäsh) *n.* See **corn salad.** [Fr. *mâche* < dialectal *pomache* < VLat. *pōmasca* < Lat. *pōmum,* fruit.]

ma·chet·e (mə-shĕt′ē, -chĕt′ē) *n.* A large knife with a broad blade, used as a weapon and for cutting vegetation. [Sp., dim. of *macho,* sledge hammer, alteration of *mazo,* club, prob. < *maza,* mallet < VLat. **mattea,* mace. See MACE[1].]

Ma·chi·a·vel·li (mäk′ē-ə-vĕl′ē, mä′kyä-), **Niccolò** 1469–1527. Italian philosopher known for his treatise on political expediency, *The Prince* (1513).

Ma·chi·a·vel·li·an (mäk′ē-ə-vĕl′ē-ən) *adj.* **1.** Of or relating to Machiavelli or Machiavellianism. **2.** Suggestive of or characterized by expediency, deceit, and cunning. —**Ma′chi·a·vel′li·an,** Ma′chi·a·vel′list *n.*

Ma·chi·a·vel·li·an·ism (mäk′ē-ə-vĕl′ē-ə-nĭz′əm) also **Ma·chi·a·vel·lism** (-vĕl′ĭz′əm) *n.* The political doctrine of Machiavelli, which denies the relevance of morality in politics and justifies craft and deceit.

ma·chic·o·late (mə-chĭk′ə-lāt′) *tr.v.* **-lat·ed, -lat·ing, -lates** To provide or furnish with machicolations. [Med.Lat. *machicolāre, machicolāt-* < OFr. *machicoller* < *machicoleis,* machicolation < O Provençal *machacol* < *macar,* to crush (< VLat. **maccāre*) + *col,* neck (< Lat. *collum;* see k**ʷel-** in App.).].

ma·chic·o·la·tion (mə-chĭk′ə-lā′shən) *n.* **1a.** A projecting gallery at the top of a castle wall, supported by corbeled arches and having openings through which stones and boiling liquids could be dropped on attackers. **b.** Such an opening. **2.** A row of corbeled arches used ornamentally.

Ma·chi·da (mə-chē′də, mä-chē′dä) A city of E-central Honshu, Japan, a suburb of Tokyo. Pop. 358,891.

mach·i·nate (mäk′ə-nāt′, mäsh′-) *v.* **-nat·ed, -nat·ing, -nates** —*tr.* To devise (a plot). —*intr.* To engage in plotting. [Lat. *māchinārī, māchināt-,* to design, contrive < *māchina,* device. See MACHINE.] —**mach′i·na′tor** *n.*

mach·i·na·tion (mäk′ə-nā′shən, mäsh′-) *n.* **1.** The act of plotting. **2.** A crafty scheme or cunning design for the accomplishment of a sinister end.

ma·chine (mə-shēn′) *n.* **1a.** A device consisting of fixed and moving parts that modifies mechanical energy and transmits it in a more useful form. **b.** A simple device, such as a lever, that alters the magnitude or direction, or both, of an applied force; a simple machine. **2.** A system or device for doing work, such as a jackhammer, together with its power source and auxiliary equipment. **3.** A system or device, such as a computer, that performs or helps perform a human task. **4.** An intricate natural system or organism, such as the human body. **5.** A person who acts in a rigid, mechanical, or unconscious manner. **6.** An organized group of people whose members are or appear to be under the control of one or more leaders. **7a.** A device used to produce a stage effect, esp. a mechanical means of lowering an actor onto the stage. **b.** A literary device used to produce an effect, esp. to resolve a plot. **8.** An answering machine. ❖ *adj.* Of, relating to, or felt to resemble a machine. ❖ *v.* **-chined, -chin·ing, -chines** —*tr.* To cut, shape, or finish by machine. —*intr.* To be cut, shaped, or finished by machine. [Fr. < OFr. < Lat. *māchina* < Gk. *mēkhanē, mākhanā.*] —**ma·chin′a·ble** *adj.*

machine bolt *n.* A bolt with a square or hexagonal head.

machine code *n.* See **machine language.**

machine gun *n.* A gun that fires rapidly and repeatedly.

ma·chine-gun (mə-shēn′gŭn′) *tr.v.* **-gunned, -gun·ning, -guns** To fire at or kill with a machine gun. ❖ *adj.* Fast and staccato: *machine-gun speech.* —**machine gunner** *n.*

machine language *n.* A set of instructions for a specific central processing unit, designed to be usable by a computer without being translated.

machine pistol *n.* A lightweight automatic submachine gun designed to be fired when held by one or two hands.

ma·chine-read·a·ble (mə-shēn′rē′də-bəl) *adj.* Capable of being read by a computer.

ma·chin·er·y (mə-shē′nə-rē, -shēn′rē) *n., pl.* **-ies 1.** Machines or machine parts considered as a group. **2.** The working parts of a particular machine. **3.** A system of related elements that operate in a definable manner. **4a.** A device or means of achieving or effecting a result. **b.** A literary device for bringing about an effect.

machine screw *n.* A screw with a thread along the entire length of the shaft.

machine shop *n.* A workshop where power-driven tools are used to make, finish, or repair machines or machine parts.

machine tool *n.* A power-driven tool, such as a lathe, used for machining. —**ma·chine′-tooled′** (mə-shēn′tōōld′) *adj.*

machine translation *n.* Automatic translation, as by computer, from one natural language to another.

ma·chine-wash (mə-shēn′wŏsh′, -wôsh′) *tr. & intr.v.* **-washed, -wash·ing, -wash·es** To wash or undergo washing in a washing machine.

ma·chin·ist (mə-shē′nĭst) *n.* **1.** One who is skilled in operating machine tools. **2.** One who makes, operates, or repairs machines. **3.** A warrant officer who assists the engineering officer in the en-

gine room of a naval vessel. **4.** *Archaic* A person in charge of stage machinery.

ma·chis·mo (mä-chēz′mō) *n.* A strong sense of masculinity usu. entailing aggressiveness, domination of women, virility, and physical courage. [Sp. < *macho,* male. See MACHO.]

Mach·me·ter (mäk′mē′tər) *n.* An aircraft instrument that indicates speed in Mach numbers.

Mach number also **mach number** (mäk) *n.* The ratio of the speed of an object to the speed of sound in the surrounding medium. [After Ernst MACH.]

ma·cho (mä′chō) *adj.* Characterized or motivated by machismo. ❖ *n., pl.* **-chos 1.** Machismo. **2.** A person characterized by or exhibiting machismo. [Sp., male < Lat. *masculus.* See MASCULINE.] —**ma′cho·ism** *n.*

MA·CHO (mä′chō) *n., pl.* **-CHOs** Any of various massive dark objects, such as a large planet, in the outermost regions of galaxies, that may explain why most galaxies have anomalous rotations. [*m*(*assive*) *a*(*strophysical*) *c*(*ompact*) *h*(*alo*) *o*(*bject*).]

Ma·chu Pic·chu (mä′chōō pēk′chōō, pē′-) An ancient Inca fortress city in the Andes NW of Cuzco, Peru.

mach·zor (mäкн′zôr′, -zər, mäкн-zôr′) *n.* Variant of **mahzor.**

mac·in·tosh (mäk′ĭn-tŏsh′) *n.* Variant of **mackintosh.**

Ma·cke (mär′kə), **August** 1887–1914. German painter whose works include *Lady in a Green Jacket* (1913).

Mac·ken·zie (mə-kĕn′zē), **Alexander** 1822–92. British-born Canadian politician who served as prime minister (1873–78).

Mackenzie, William Lyon 1795–1861. British-born Canadian politician who led an armed insurrection in Toronto (1837) to protest colonial rule.

Mackenzie Mountains A range of the N Rocky Mts. in E Yukon Terr. and W Northwest Terrs., Canada, rising to 2,973.8 m (9,750 ft).

Mackenzie River A river of NW Canada rising in Great Slave Lake in S Northwest Terrs. and flowing c. 1,802 km (1,120 mi) to **Mackenzie Bay,** an arm of the Beaufort Sea.

mack·er·el (mäk′ər-əl, mäk′rəl) *n., pl.* **mackerel** or **-els 1.** Any of several marine fishes of the family Scombridae, esp. the Atlantic mackerel (*Scomber scombrus*), an important food fish. **2.** Any of the smaller fishes of the suborder Scombroidea, such as the Spanish mackerel. **3.** Any of various similar fishes. [ME *makerel* < OFr. *maquerel.*]

mackerel shark *n.* Any of various sharks of the family Lamnidae, including the great white shark, having a nearly symmetrical tail and a reputation for aggressiveness.

mackerel sky *n. Chiefly Northeastern US* A sky covered with many small cirrocumulus or altocumulus clouds, resembling the markings found on a mackerel.

Mack·i·nac Island (mäk′ə-nô′) An island of N MI in the **Straits of Mackinac,** a passage connecting Lakes Huron and Michigan between the Upper and Lower peninsulas.

mack·i·naw (mäk′ə-nô′) *n.* **1.** A short double-breasted coat of heavy, usu. plaid material. **2.** The cloth from which such a coat is made, usu. of wool, often with a heavy nap. **3.** A flatbottom boat with a pointed bow and square stern, once used on the upper Great Lakes. [After Old *Mackinac,* a fort on the site of *Mackinaw City* in N Michigan.]

Mackinaw blanket *n.* A thick woolen blanket in solid colors or stripes.

Mackinaw trout *n.* See **lake trout.**

mack·in·tosh also **mac·in·tosh** (mäk′ĭn-tŏsh′) *n. Chiefly British* **1.** A raincoat. **2.** A lightweight waterproof fabric that was originally of rubberized cotton. [After Charles *Macintosh* (1766–1843), Scottish inventor.]

Mackintosh, Charles Rennie 1868–1928. Scottish architect whose art nouveau designs emphasized elegant, rational forms.

mack·le (mäk′əl) also **mac·ule** (mäk′yōōl′) *n.* A blurred or double impression in printing. ❖ *v.* **-led, -ling, -les** also **-uled, -ul·ing, -ules** —*tr.* To blur or double (a printed impression). —*intr.* To become blurred. [ME *macule,* spot < OFr. < Lat. *macula.*]

mac·le (mäk′əl) *n.* **1.** Chiastolite. **2.** A twinned crystal. **3.** A dark spot or discoloration in a mineral. [Fr. < OFr., lozenge < Lat. *macula,* mesh.]

Mac·Leish (mĭk-lēsh′), **Archibald** 1892–1982. Amer. poet who served as Librarian of Congress (1939–44).

Mac·Len·nan (mə-klĕn′ən), **Hugh** 1907–90. Canadian writer whose novels include *Two Solitudes* (1945).

Mac·leod (mə-kloud′), **John James Rickard** 1876–1935. British physiologist who shared a 1923 Nobel Prize.

Mac·mil·lan (mĭk-mĭl′ən), **(Maurice) Harold** 1894–1986. British politician who served as prime minister (1957–63).

Mac·Neice (mĭk-nēs′), **(Frederick) Louis** 1907–63. Irish-born British poet whose works include *Blind Fireworks* (1929).

Ma·con (mā′kən) A city of central GA SE of Atlanta; settled in the early 1820s. Pop. 97,255.

Mâ·con (mä-kôn′) A city of E-central France on the Saône R. N of Lyon; noted for its Burgundy wines. Pop. 38,404.

Ma·coun (mə-koun′, -kōōn′) *n.* A variety of apple having red skin and white, crisp flesh. [After William Tyrrell *Macoun* (1869–1933), Canadian farmer.]

Mac·pher·son (mək-fûr′sən), **James** 1736–96. Scottish poet

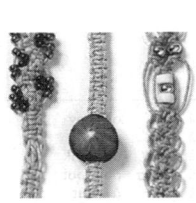
machicolation

macramé
variety of macramé knotting

who claimed to have translated the works of Ossian, a 3rd-cent. A.D. Gaelic poet and warrior.

Mac·quar·ie (mə-kwär′ē, -kwôr′ē) A river of SE Australia flowing c. 949 km (590 mi) to the Darling R.

mac·ra·mé (măk′rə-mā′) n. Coarse lace work made by weaving and knotting cords into a pattern. [Fr. < Ital. *macramè* < Turk. *makrama*, towel < Ar. *miqrama*, embroidered veil < *qarama*, to gnaw, nibble.]

mac·ro (măk′rō) adj. 1. Of great size; large. 2. Large in scope or extent; large-scale. ❖ n., pl. **-ros** *Computer Science* 1. A single, user-defined command that is part of an application and executes a series of commands. 2. A shorthand representation for a number of lines of code. [Short for MACROINSTRUCTION.]

macro- or **macr-** pref. 1. Large: *macronucleus*. 2. Long: *macrobiotics*. 3. Inclusive: *macroinstruction*. [Gk. *makro-* < *makros*, large.]

mac·ro·bi·ot·ics (măk′rō-bī-ŏt′ĭks) n. (*used with a sing. verb*) The theory or practice of promoting well-being and longevity, principally by means of a diet consisting chiefly of whole grains and beans. —**mac′ro·bi·ot′ic** adj.

mac·ro·ceph·a·ly (măk′rō-sĕf′ə-lē) also **mac·ro·ce·pha·li·a** (-sə-fā′lē-ə, -fāl′yə) n. Abnormal largeness of the head. —**mac′ro·ce·phal′ic** (-sə-făl′ĭk), **mac′ro·ceph′a·lous** adj.

mac·ro·cli·mate (măk′rō-klī′mĭt) n. The climate of a large geographic area. —**mac′ro·cli·mat′ic** (-măt′ĭk) adj.

mac·ro·cosm (măk′rə-kŏz′əm) n. 1. The entire world; the universe. 2. A system reflecting on a large scale one of its component systems or parts. [Med.Lat. *macrocosmus* : Gk. *makro-*, macro- + Gk. *kosmos*, world.] —**mac′ro·cos′mic** adj. —**mac′ro·cos′mic·al·ly** adv.

mac·ro·cyte (măk′rō-sīt′) n. An abnormally large red blood cell, esp. one associated with pernicious anemia.

mac·ro·ec·o·nom·ics (măk′rō-ĕk′ə-nŏm′ĭks, -ē′kə-) n. (*used with a sing. verb*) The study of the overall aspects and workings of a national economy. —**mac′ro·ec′o·nom′ic** adj. —**mac′ro·e·con′o·mist** (-ĭ-kŏn′ə-mĭst) n.

mac·ro·ev·o·lu·tion (măk′rō-ĕv′ə-lōō′shən, -ē′və-) n. Large-scale evolution occurring over geologic time that results in the formation of new taxonomic groups.

mac·ro·gam·ete (măk′rō-găm′ēt, -gə-mēt′) n. The larger, usu. female of two conjugating gametes in a heterogamous organism.

ma·crog·ra·phy (mə-krŏg′rə-fē) n. 1. Photographic imaging using magnification up to ten times the size of the object being photographed. 2. Abnormally large handwriting.

mac·ro·in·struc·tion (măk′rō-ĭn-strŭk′shən) n. A macro.

mac·ro·mere (măk′rə-mîr′) n. A large blastomere.

mac·ro·mol·e·cule (măk′rō-mŏl′ĭ-kyōōl′) n. A large molecule, such as a protein, consisting of many smaller units linked together. —**mac′ro·mo·lec′u·lar** (-mə-lĕk′yə-lər) adj.

ma·cron (mā′krŏn′, -krən, măk′rŏn′) n. 1. A diacritical mark placed above a vowel to indicate a long sound or phonetic value in pronunciation, such as (ā) in the word *make*. 2. The horizontal mark (¯) used to indicate a stressed or long syllable in a foot of verse. [Gk. *makron* < neut. of *makros*, long.]

mac·ro·nu·cle·us (măk′rō-nōō′klē-əs, -nyōō′-) n., pl. **-cle·i** (-klē-ī′) The larger of two nuclei present in ciliate protozoans, which controls nonreproductive functions of the cell, such as metabolism. —**mac′ro·nu′cle·ar** adj.

mac·ro·nu·tri·ent (măk′rō-nōō′trē-ənt, -nyōō′-) n. An element, such as carbon, required in large proportion for the normal growth and development of a plant.

mac·ro·phage (măk′rə-fāj′) n. Any of the large phagocytic cells of the reticuloendothelial system. —**mac′ro·phag′ic** (-făj′ĭk) adj.

mac·ro·phyte (măk′rə-fīt′) n. A macroscopic plant.

ma·crop·ter·ous (mə-krŏp′tər-əs) adj. Having very large fins or wings.

mac·ro·scop·ic (măk′rə-skŏp′ĭk) also **mac·ro·scop·i·cal** (-ĭ-kəl) adj. 1. Large enough to be perceived or examined by the unaided eye. 2. Relating to observations made by the unaided eye. —**mac′ro·scop′i·cal·ly** adv.

macroscopic anatomy n. See gross anatomy.

mac·ro·spo·ran·gi·um (măk′rō-spə-răn′jē-əm) n., pl. **-gi·a** (-jē-ə) See megasporangium.

mac·ro·spore (măk′rə-spôr′, -spōr′) n. See megaspore.

mac·u·la (măk′yə-lə) n., pl. **-lae** (-lē′) or **-las** 1. The macula lutea. 2. also **mac·ule** (-yōōl) A discolored spot or area on the skin that is not elevated above the surface. [ME < Lat.] —**mac′u·lar** adj.

macula lu·te·a (lōō′tē-ə) n., pl. **maculae lu·te·ae** (lōō′tē-ē′) A minute yellowish area containing the fovea centralis located near the center of the retina where visual perception is most acute. [NLat. *macula lūtea* : Lat. *macula*, spot + Lat. *lūtea*, yellow.]

macular degeneration n. A condition in which the cells of the macula lutea degenerate, resulting in visual impairment.

mac·u·late (măk′yə-lāt′) tr.v. **-lat·ed, -lat·ing, -lates** To spot, blemish, or pollute. ❖ adj. (-lĭt) 1. Spotted or blotched. 2. Stained; impure. [ME *maculaten* < Lat. *maculāre*, *maculāt-* < *macula*, spot.]

mac·u·la·tion (măk′yə-lā′shən) n. 1. The act of spotting or staining or the condition of being spotted or stained. 2. The spotted markings of a plant or animal.

mac·ule¹ (măk′yōōl′) n. & v. Variant of **mackle**.

mac·ule² (măk′yōōl′) n. Variant of **macula** 2.

mad (măd) adj. **mad·der, mad·dest** 1. Angry; resentful. 2. Suffering from a disorder of the mind; insane. 3. Temporarily or apparently deranged, as by violent emotions: *mad with jealousy*. 4. Lacking restraint or reason; foolish. 5. Feeling or showing strong liking or enthusiasm: *mad about sports*. 6. Marked by extreme excitement, confusion, or agitation; frantic: *a mad scramble for the bus*. 7. Boisterously merry; hilarious: *had a mad time*. 8. Affected by rabies; rabid. ❖ tr. & intr.v. **mad·ded, mad·ding, mads** To make or become mad; madden. —*idiom:* **like mad** *Informal* 1. Wildly; impetuously: *drove like mad*. 2. To an intense degree or great extent: *snowed like mad*. [ME < OE *gemædde*, p. part. of *gemǣdan*, to madden < *gemād*, insane.] —**mad′dish** adj.

Mad·a·gas·car (măd′ə-găs′kər) Formerly **Mal·a·gas·y Republic** (măl′ə-găs′ē) A country in the Indian Ocean off SE Africa comprising the island of Madagascar and several small islands; gained independence from France in 1960. Cap. Antananarivo. Pop. 14,303,000. —**Mad′a·gas′can** (-kən) adj. & n.

Madagascar periwinkle n. A perennial plant (*Catharanthus roseus*) native to Madagascar and India that has flowers with a salverform corolla and is poisonous to domestic animals.

Mad·am (măd′əm) n. 1. pl. **Mes·dames** (mā-däm′, -dăm′) Used formerly as a courtesy title before a woman's given name but now used only before a surname or title indicating rank or office: *Madam Ambassador*. 2. Used as a salutation in a letter: *Dear Madam or Sir*. 3. **madam** Used as a form of polite address for a woman. 4. **madam** The mistress of a household. 5. **madam** A woman who manages a brothel. [ME *madame* < OFr. *ma dame*. See MADAME.]

Ma·dame (mə-dăm′, măd′əm) n., pl. **Mes·dames** (mā-däm′, -dăm′) 1. Used as a courtesy title before the surname or full name of a married woman in a French-speaking area. 2. **madame** Used as a form of polite address for a woman in a French-speaking area. [Fr. < OFr. *ma dame* : *ma*, my (< Lat. *mea*, fem. of *meus*; see **me-¹** in App.) + *dame*, lady (< Lat. *domina*, fem. of *dominus*, lord, master of a household; see **dem-** in App.).]

mad·cap (măd′kăp′) adj. Behaving or acting impulsively or rashly; wild. [MAD + CAP¹, head.] —**mad′cap′** n.

mad cow disease n. See bovine spongiform encephalopathy.

mad·den (măd′n) v. **-dened, -den·ing, -dens** —tr. 1. To make angry; irritate. 2. To drive insane. —intr. To become infuriated.

mad·den·ing (măd′n-ĭng) adj. 1. Tending to anger or irritate. 2. Tending to drive insane. —**mad′den·ing·ly** adv.

mad·der (măd′ər) n. **1a.** A southwest Asian perennial plant (*Rubia tinctorum*) having small yellow flowers, whorled leaves, and a red root. **b.** The root of this plant, formerly a source of the dye alizarin. **c.** A red dye obtained from the roots of this plant. **2.** A medium to strong red or reddish orange. [ME < OE *mædere*.]

mad·ding (măd′ĭng) adj. *Archaic* In a state of frenzy.

made (măd) v. Past tense and past participle of **make**. ❖ adj. **1.** Produced or manufactured by constructing, shaping, or forming. Often used in combination: *handmade lace*. **2.** Produced or created artificially: *bought some made goods*. **3.** Having been invented; contrived. **4.** Assured of success: *a made man*. —*idiom:* **made for** Perfectly suited for: *made for each other*.

Ma·dei·ra¹ (mə-dîr′ə, -dĕr′ə) A river of NW Brazil rising on the Bolivian border and flowing c. 3,315 km (2,060 mi) to the Amazon R. near Manaus.

Ma·dei·ra² (mə-dîr′ə, -dĕr′ə) n. A fortified dessert wine, esp. from the island of Madeira.

Madeira Islands An archipelago of Portugal in the NE Atlantic Ocean W of Morocco. —**Ma·dei′ran** adj. & n.

mad·e·leine (măd′ə-lĕn′) n. A small rich cake, baked in a shell-shaped mold. [After *Madeleine* Paulmier, 19th-cent. French pastry cook.]

Mad·e·moi·selle (măd′ə-mə-zĕl′, măd-mwä-zĕl′) n., pl. **Mad·e·moi·selles** (-zĕlz) or **Mes·de·moi·selles** (mād′mwä-zĕl′) 1. Used as a courtesy title before the surname or full name of a girl or an unmarried woman in a French-speaking area. 2. **mademoiselle** Used as a form of polite address for a girl or young woman in a French-speaking area. 3. **mademoiselle** pl. **mademoiselles** A French governess. 4. **mademoiselle**, pl. **mademoiselles** or **-selles** See silver perch. [Fr. < OFr. *ma demoiselle* : *ma*, my; see MADAME + *demoiselle*, young lady (< *damisele* < VLat. **dominicella*, dim. of Lat. *domina*, lady; see MADAME).]

Ma·de·ro (mə-dĕr′ō, mä-dĕr′ō), **Francisco Indalecio** 1873–1913. Mexican revolutionary who forced the resignation of Porfirio Díaz and assumed the presidency (1911).

made-to-or·der (măd′tōō-ôr′dər) adj. 1. Made to fit instructions or requirements; custom-made. 2. Very suitable.

made-up (măd′ŭp′) adj. 1. Having been fabricated; invented. 2. Changed or adorned by the application of cosmetics or makeup. **3a.** Complete; finished. **b.** Put together; arranged.

mad·house (măd′hous′) n. 1. *Offensive* An institution for the mentally ill. 2. *Informal* A place of great disorder and confusion.

Mad·i·son (măd′ĭ-sən) The cap. of WI, in the S-central part W of Milwaukee. Pop. 208,054.

Madison, Dolley Payne Todd 1768–1849. First Lady of the US (1809–17). She earlier served as the White House hostess for the widowed Thomas Jefferson.

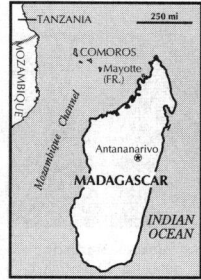

Madagascar

Dolley Madison
1804 portrait after Gilbert Stuart

ă pat	oi boy	
ā pay	ou out	
âr care	ŏŏ took	
ä father	ōō boot	
ĕ pet	ŭ cut	
ē be	ûr urge	
ĭ pit	th thin	
ī pie	th this	
îr pier	hw which	
ŏ pot	zh vision	
ō toe	ə about,	
ô paw	item	

Stress marks:
′ (primary);
′ (secondary), as in
lexicon (lĕk′sĭ-kŏn′)

James Madison
detail from a portrait, c.
1830, by Chester Harding
(1792–1866)

Madonna
image from the Rila
Monastery, Bulgaria

Magen David

Madison, James 1751–1836. The fourth President of the US (1809–17). A member of the Constitutional Convention (1787) and a contributor to *The Federalist Papers* (1787–88). —**Mad′i•so′ni•an** (-sō′nē-ən) *adj.*

Madison Avenue *n.* The American advertising industry. [After *Madison Avenue* in New York City.] —**Madison Avenue** *adj.*

mad•ly (măd′lē) *adv.* **1.** In a crazy way; insanely. **2.** In a wild manner; frantically. **3.** In a foolish manner; rashly.

mad•man (măd′măn′, -mən) *n.* A man who is or seems to be mentally ill.

mad money *n. Slang* A small sum of money kept for unlikely contingencies.

mad•ness (măd′nĭs) *n.* **1.** The quality or condition of being insane. **2.** Great folly. **3.** Fury; rage. **4.** Enthusiasm; excitement.

Ma•don•na (mə-dŏn′ə) *n.* **1.** The Virgin Mary. **2.** *Obsolete* Used as a form of polite address for a married woman in an Italian-speaking area. [Ital. < OItal. : *mia, ma-*, my (< Lat. *mea*; see MADAME) + *donna*, lady (< Lat. *domina*; see MADAME).]

Madonna lily *n.* An eastern Mediterranean plant *(Lilium candidum)* having white bell-shaped flowers.

mad•ras (măd′rəs, mə-drăs′, -dräs′) *n.* **1.** A cotton cloth of fine texture, usu. with a plaid, striped, or checked pattern. **2.** A silk, generally striped cloth. **3.** A light cotton or rayon cloth used for drapery. **4.** A large handkerchief of brightly colored silk or cotton, often worn as a turban. [After *Madras* (Chennai), India.]

Ma•dras (mə-drăs′, -dräs′) See **Chennai.**

ma•dra•sah also **ma•dra•sa** or **ma•dras′sah** (mə-drä′sə) *n.* A building or group of buildings used for teaching Islamic theology and religious law, typically including a mosque. [Ar. *madrasa* < *darasa*, to study.]

Ma•dre de Di•os (mä′drā dä dē-ōs′, mä′drĕ dĕ dyōs′) A river of SE Peru and NW Bolivia flowing c. 1,126 km (700 mi) from the Andes to the Beni R.

mad•re•pore (măd′rə-pôr′, -pōr′) *n.* Any of various stony corals of the order Madreporaria, which includes the reef builders of tropical seas. [Ital. *madrepora* : *madre*, mother (< Lat. *māter, mātr-*; see **mater-** in App.) + *-pora* (alteration of *poro*, tufa, pore < LLat. *porus*, passageway; see PORE², or < Lat. *pōrus*, calcareous stone, stalactite < Gk. *pōros*).] —**mad′re•po′ri•an, mad′re•por′ic** *adj.*

mad•re•por•ite (măd′rə-pôr′īt, -pōr′-) *n.* A perforated platelike structure in most echinoderms that forms the intake for their water-vascular systems. [So called because the perforations resemble those of a madrepore.]

Ma•drid (mə-drĭd′) The cap. of Spain, on the central plateau NNE of Toledo; became cap. in 1561. Pop. 2,976,064.

mad•ri•gal (măd′rĭ-gəl) *n.* **1a.** A song for two or three unaccompanied voices, developed in Italy in the late 13th and early 14th centuries. **b.** A short poem, often about love, suitable for being set to music. **2a.** A polyphonic song using a vernacular text and written for four to six voices, developed in Italy in the 16th century. **b.** A part song. [Ital. *madrigale*, prob. < dialectal *madregal*, simple < LLat. *mātrīcālis*, invented, original < Lat., of the womb < *mātrīx, mātrīc-*, womb < *māter, mātr-*, mother. See MATER.] —**mad′ri•gal•ist** *n.*

ma•dri•lène also **ma•dri•lene** (măd′rĭ-lĕn′) *n.* A consommé flavored with tomato, often served jellied and chilled. [Fr. *(consommé) madrilène*, Madrid (consommé) < Sp. *madrileño*, of Madrid < *Madrid*, Madrid.]

ma•dro•ña (mə-drō′nyə) also **ma•dro•ño** (-drō′nyō) or **ma•dro•ne** (-drō′nə) *n., pl.* **-ñas** also **-ños** or **-nes** An evergreen tree *(Arbutus menziesii)* native to Pacific North America and having leathery glossy leaves and orange or red edible berries. [Am.Sp. < Sp. *madroño*, strawberry tree.]

mad tom *n.* Any of several small freshwater North American catfishes of the genus *Noturus*, having poisonous spines.

Ma•du•rai (mä′də-rī′, măd′ŏŏ-rī′) A city of S India SSW of Chennai (Madras); a Hindu pilgrimage site. Pop. 940,989.

mad•wom•an (măd′wŏŏm′ən) *n.* A woman who is or seems to be mentally ill.

mad•wort (măd′wûrt′, -wôrt′) *n.* **1.** A low-growing Eurasian plant *(Asperugo procumbens)* having rough stems and small blue flowers. **2.** See **alyssum** 2. [Because it was supposedly able to cure rabies.]

MAE *abbr.* **1.** Master of Aeronautical Engineering **2.** Master of Art Education **3.** Master of Arts in Education

Mae•an•der (mē-ăn′dər) The Menderes R. of W Turkey.

Mae•ce•nas (mē-sē′nəs, mī-), **Gaius** 70?–8 B.C. Roman politician and patron of Horace and Virgil.

MAEd *abbr.* Master of Arts in Education

mael•strom (māl′strəm) *n.* **1.** A violent or turbulent situation. **2.** A whirlpool of extraordinary size or violence. [Obsolete Du. : Du. *malen*, to grind, whirl (< MDu.; see **melə-** in App.) + Du. *stroom*, stream (< MDu.; see **sreu-** in App.).]

mae•nad (mē′năd′) *n.* **1.** *Greek Mythology* A woman in the orgiastic cult of Dionysus. **2.** A frenzied woman. [Lat. *Maenas, Maenad-* < Gk. *mainas*, raving, madwoman, Maenad < *mainesthai*, to be mad. See **men-¹** in App.]

ma•es•to•so (mä′ĕs-tō′sō, -zō) *adv. & adj. Music* In a majestic and stately manner. [Ital. < *maestà*, majesty, greatness < Lat. *māiestās*. See **meg-** in App.]

maes•tro (mīs′trō) *n., pl.* **-tros** or **-tri** (-trē) A master in an art, esp. a composer, conductor, or music teacher. [Ital. < Lat. *magister, magistr-*, master. See **meg-** in App.]

Mae•ter•linck (mā′tər-lĭngk′, mĕt′ər-, mä-tĕr-lăn′), **Count Maurice** 1862–1949. Belgian writer who won the 1911 Nobel Prize for literature.

Mae West (mā′ wĕst′) *n.* An inflatable vestlike life preserver. [After Mae WEST.]

maf•fick (măf′ĭk) *intr.v.* **-ficked, -fick•ing, -ficks** *Chiefly British* To rejoice or celebrate with boisterous public demonstrations. [After *Mafeking*, South Africa, town with a British garrison besieged for 217 days during the Boer War whose relief (May 17, 1900) was celebrated in London.]

Ma•fi•a (mä′fē-ə) *n.* **1.** A secret terrorist organization in Sicily, operating since the early 19th century in opposition to legal authority. **2.** A secret criminal organization of Italian origin operating in the United States. **3.** Any of various similar criminal organizations, esp. when dominated by members of the same nationality. **4.** often *mafia Informal* A tightly knit group of trusted associates, as of a political leader. [Ital., perh. < dialectal *mafia*, bluster, boldness.]

maf•ic (măf′ĭk) *adj.* Containing or relating to a group of dark-colored minerals, composed chiefly of magnesium and iron, in igneous rocks. [MA(GNESIUM) + Lat. *f(errum)*, iron + -IC.]

Ma•fi•o•so (mä′fē-ō′sō) *n., pl.* **-si** (-sē) or **-sos** A member of the Mafia. [Ital. < *mafia*, mafia. See MAFIA.]

mag (măg) *n. Slang* A magazine: *surfing mags.*

mag. *abbr.* magnitude

Ma•ga•dha (mä′gə-də) An ancient kingdom of NE India; esp. powerful from the 4th cent. B.C. to the 5th cent. A.D.

mag•a•zine (măg′ə-zēn′, măg′ə-zēn′) *n.* **1.** A periodical containing articles, stories, pictures, or other features. **2.** A television program that presents a variety of topics, usu. on current events. **3a.** A place where goods, esp. ammunition and explosives, are stored. **b.** The contents of a storehouse, esp. a stock of ammunition. **4a.** A compartment in some types of firearms, often detachable, from which cartridges are fed into the firing chamber. **b.** A compartment in a camera from which rolls or cartridges of film are fed through the exposure mechanism. **c.** Any of various compartments attached to machines, used for storing or supplying necessary material. ❖ *adj.* Of or relating to periodicals. [Fr. *magasin*, storehouse < OFr. *magazin* (poss. via OItal. *magazzino*) < Ar. *maḫāzin*, pl. of *maḫzan < ḫazana*, to store < Aram. *ḫassen*, to possess, hoard, derived stem of *ḥasan*, to be strong.]

Mag•da•le•na (măg′də-lā′nə, mäg′dä-lĕ′nä) A river rising in the Andes of SW Colombia and flowing c. 1,601 km (1,000 mi) to the Caribbean Sea.

Mag•da•le•ni•an (măg′də-lē′nē-ən) *adj.* Of or relating to the last Upper Paleolithic culture of Europe, succeeding the Aurignacian. [Fr. *magdalénien*, after La *Madeleine*, a prehistoric site of SW France.]

Mag•de•burg (măg′də-bûrg′, mäg′də-bŏŏrk′) A city of central Germany on the Elbe R. WSW of Berlin. Pop. 270,546.

mage (māj) *n.* A magician or sorcerer. [< ME *mages*, magicians, var. of *magi*. See MAGUS.]

Ma•gel•lan (mə-jĕl′ən), **Ferdinand** 1480?–1521. Portuguese navigator who first sailed through the strait that now bears his name in 1520.

Magellan, Strait of A channel between South America and Tierra del Fuego connecting the S Atlantic and Pacific oceans.

Mag•el•lan•ic Clouds (măg′ə-lăn′ĭk) *pl.n.* Two small, irregularly shaped galaxies that are the galaxies closest to the Milky Way. [After Ferdinand MAGELLAN.]

Ma•gen Da•vid also **Mo•gen Da•vid** (mŏ′gən dô′vĭd, dä′vĭd, mä-gĕn′ dä-vēd′) *n.* A six-pointed star, a symbol of Judaism, formed by placing two triangles together, one inverted over the other or interlaced. [Heb. *māgēn dāwīd*, shield of David : *māgēn*, shield (< *gānan*, to cover) + *dāwīd*, David; see DAVID.]

ma•gen•ta (mə-jĕn′tə) *n.* **1.** See **fuchsin. 2.** A purplish red, one of the subtractive primary colors. [After *Magenta* in NW Italy.]

Mag•gio•re (mə-jôr′ē, mäd′jô′rĕ), **Lake** An alpine lake of N Italy and S Switzerland.

mag•got (măg′ət) *n.* **1.** The legless, soft-bodied, wormlike larva of any of various flies of the order Diptera, often found in decaying matter. **2.** *Slang* A despicable person. **3.** An extravagant notion; a whim. [ME *magot*, perh. alteration of *mathek, maddokk*, perh. < OE *matha*.] —**mag′got•y** *adj.*

Ma•ghreb or **Ma•ghrib** (mŭg′rəb) A region of NW Africa in Morocco, Algeria, and Tunisia.

ma•gi (mā′jī′) *n.* Plural of **magus.**

mag•ic (măj′ĭk) *n.* **1.** The art that purports to control or forecast natural events, effects, or forces by invoking the supernatural. **2a.** The practice of using charms, spells, or rituals to attempt to produce supernatural effects or control events in nature. **b.** The charms, spells, and rituals so used. **3.** The exercise of sleight of hand or conjuring for entertainment. **4.** A mysterious quality of enchantment. ❖ *adj.* **1.** Of, relating to, or invoking the supernatural. **2.** Possessing distinctive qualities that produce unaccountable or baffling effects. **3.** Required or requested, esp. as an answer or social duty: *I'll give it to you if you say the magic word.* ❖ *tr.v.* **-icked, -ick•ing, -ics** To produce or make by or as if by magic.

[ME *magik* < OFr. *magique* < LLat. *magica* < Lat. *magicē* < Gk. *magikē* < fem. of *magikos*, of the Magi, magical < *magos*, magician, magus. See MAGUS.]

mag·i·cal (măj′ĭ-kəl) *adj.* **1.** Of, relating to, or produced by magic. **2.** Enchanting; bewitching. **—mag′i·cal·ly** *adv.*

magical realism *n.* A chiefly literary style or genre originating in Latin America that combines realistic and fantastic elements.

ma·gi·cian (mə-jĭsh′ən) *n.* **1.** A sorcerer; a wizard. **2.** One who performs magic for entertainment or diversion. **3.** One whose skill or art seems to be magical.

magic lantern *n.* An optical device formerly used to project an enlarged image of a picture.

magic number *n.* Any of the numbers, 2, 8, 20, 28, 50, 82, or 126, that represent the number of neutrons or protons in strongly bound and exceptionally stable atomic nuclei.

magic square *n.* **1.** A square that contains numbers arranged in equal rows and columns such that the sum of each row, column, and sometimes diagonal is the same. **2.** A similar square containing letters in particular arrangements that spell out the same word or words.

Ma·gi·not (măzh′ə-nō′, măj′-, mä-zhē-nō′), André 1877–1932. French politician who proposed the Maginot Line of fortifications along France's border with Germany. The line was bypassed and captured by the Germans in 1940.

mag·is·te·ri·al (măj′ĭ-stîr′ē-əl) *adj.* **1a.** Of, relating to, or characteristic of a master or teacher; authoritative. **b.** Sedately dignified in appearance or manner: "*She would appear on the porch and reign over the street in magisterial beauty*" (Harper Lee). **2.** Dogmatic; overbearing. **3.** Of or relating to a magistrate or a magistrate's official functions. [LLat. *magisteriālis* < *magisterius* < Lat. *magister*, master, teacher. See **meg-** in App.] **—mag′is·te′ri·al·ly** *adv.*

mag·is·te·ri·um (măj′ĭ-stîr′ē-əm) *n. Roman Catholic Church* The authority to teach religious doctrine. [Lat., office of a teacher < *magister*, master. See MAGISTERIAL.]

mag·is·tra·cy (măj′ĭs-trə-sē) *n., pl.* **-cies 1.** The position, function, or term of office of a magistrate. **2.** A body of magistrates. **3.** The district under jurisdiction of a magistrate.

mag·is·tral (măj′ĭ-strəl) *adj.* **1.** Of or relating to a magistrate; magisterial. **2.** Prepared as specified by a physician's prescription. **3.** Principal; main. [LLat. *magistrālis*, belonging to a master < Lat. *magister*, *magistr-*, former chief officer of a college. See **meg-** in App.]

mag·is·trate (măj′ĭ-strāt′, -strĭt) *n.* A civil officer with power to administer and enforce law, as: **a.** A local member of the judiciary having limited jurisdiction, esp. in criminal cases. **b.** A minor official, such as a justice of the peace, having administrative and limited judicial authority. [ME *magistrat* < OFr. < Lat. *magistrātus* < *magister*, *magistr-*, master. See **meg-** in App.]

mag·is·tra·ture (măj′ĭ-strā′chər, -strə-choŏr′) *n.* Magistracy.

Ma·gle·mo·si·an (mä′glə-mō′zē-ən) *adj. Archaeology* Of or relating to a Mesolithic forest culture of northern Europe. [After *Maglemose*, a Mesolithic site of western Sjaelland, Denmark.]

mag·lev or **Mag·lev** (măg′lĕv′) *n.* Magnetic levitation.

mag·ma (măg′mə) *n., pl.* **-ma·ta** (-mä′tə) or **-mas 1.** A mixture of finely divided solids with enough liquid to produce a pasty mass. **2.** *Geology* The molten rock material under the earth's crust, from which igneous rock is formed by cooling. **3.** *Pharmacology* A suspension of particles in a liquid, such as milk of magnesia. **4.** The residue of fruits after the juice has been expressed; pomace. [ME, sediment, dregs < Lat. < Gk., unguent < *massein*, *mag-*, to knead.] **—mag·mat′ic** (-măt′ĭk) *adj.*

Mag·na Car·ta or **Mag·na Char·ta** (măg′nə kär′tə) *n.* **1.** The charter of English political and civil liberties granted by King John at Runnymede in June 1215. **2.** A document or piece of legislation guaranteeing basic rights. [ME < Med.Lat. : Lat. *magna*, great + Med.Lat. *charta*, charter.]

magna cum lau·de (koŏm lou′də) *adv. & adj.* With high honors. Used to express high academic distinction. [Lat. *magnā cum laude* : *magnā*, fem. ablative sing. of *magnus*, great + *cum*, with + *laude*, ablative sing. of *laus*, praise.]

Magna Grae·cia (grē′shə) The ancient Greek seaport colonies of S Italy and Sicily from the 8th to the 4th cent. B.C.

mag·na·nim·i·ty (măg′nə-nĭm′ĭ-tē) *n., pl.* **-ties 1.** The quality of being magnanimous. **2.** A magnanimous act.

mag·nan·i·mous (măg-năn′ə-məs) *adj.* **1.** Courageously noble in mind and heart. **2.** Generous in forgiving; eschewing resentment or revenge; unselfish. [< Lat. *magnanimus* : *magnus*, great; see **meg-** in App. + *animus*, soul, mind; see **anə-** in App.] **—mag·nan′i·mous·ly** *adv.* **—mag·nan′i·mous·ness** *n.*

mag·nate (măg′nāt′, -nĭt) *n.* A powerful or influential person, esp. in business or industry: *an oil magnate.* [< ME *magnates*, magnates < LLat. *magnātēs*, pl. of *magnās*, magnate < Lat. *magnus*, great. See **meg-** in App.]

mag·ne·sia (măg-nē′zhə, -shə) *n.* Magnesium oxide. [ME, mineral ingredient of the philosophers' stone < Med.Lat. *magnēsia* < Gk. *magnēsiā*, a kind of ore < *Magnēsia*, Magnesia, an ancient city of Asia Minor.] **—mag·ne′sian** *adj.*

mag·ne·site (măg′nə-sīt′) *n.* A white, yellowish, or brown mineral, magnesium carbonate, $MgCO_3$, used in the manufacture of magnesium oxide and carbon dioxide.

mag·ne·si·um (măg-nē′zē-əm, -zhəm) *n. Symbol* **Mg** A light metallic element that burns with a brilliant white flame and is used in structural alloys, pyrotechnics, flash photography, and incendiary bombs. Atomic number 12; atomic weight 24.305; melting point 649°C; boiling point 1,090°C; specific gravity 1.74 (at 20°C); valence 2. See table at **element.** [< MAGNESIA.]

magnesium carbonate *n.* A light odorless powdery compound, $MgCO_3$, used as a drying agent in a variety of manufactured products.

magnesium hydroxide *n.* A white powder, $Mg(OH)_2$, used as an antacid and a laxative.

magnesium oxide *n.* A white powdery compound, MgO, having a high melting point (2,800°C), used in high-temperature refractories, electrical insulation, and cosmetics.

magnesium sulfate *n.* A crystalline compound, $MgSO_4$, used in fireproofing, ceramics, matches, explosives, and fertilizers.

mag·net (măg′nĭt) *n.* **1.** An object that is surrounded by a magnetic field and has the property, either natural or induced, of attracting iron or steel. **2.** An electromagnet. **3.** A person, place, object, or situation that exerts attraction. [ME < OFr. *magnete* < Lat. *magnēs*, *magnēt-* < Gk. *Magnēs* (lithos), Magnesian (stone), magnet < *Magnēsiā*, Magnesia, an ancient city of Asia Minor.]

mag·net·ic (măg-nĕt′ĭk) *adj.* **1a.** Of or relating to magnetism or magnets. **b.** Having the properties of a magnet. **c.** Operating by means of magnetism. **d.** Capable of being magnetized or attracted by a magnet. **2.** Relating to the magnetic poles of the earth: *a magnetic compass.* **3.** Unusually attractive. **—mag·net′i·cal·ly** *adv.*

magnetic bottle *n.* A magnetic field used to confine plasma, as during controlled nuclear fusion.

magnetic bubble memory *n.* A memory that stores data in the form of bubbles, or circular areas, on a thin film of magnetic silicate.

magnetic card *n.* A card, such as a bankcard, that has a magnetizable strip or surface on which data can be recorded.

magnetic compass *n.* An instrument that uses a magnetized steel bar to indicate direction relative to the earth's magnetic poles.

magnetic core *n.* See **core** 6b.

magnetic declination *n.* The angle between magnetic north and true north at a particular location.

magnetic dip *n.* See **magnetic inclination.**

magnetic disk *n.* A memory device, such as a floppy disk, a hard disk, or a removable cartridge, that is covered with a magnetic coating on which digital information is stored in the form of microscopically small, magnetized needles.

magnetic equator *n.* A line connecting all points on the earth's surface at which a magnetic needle balances horizontally without dipping.

magnetic field *n.* A condition found in the region around a magnet or an electric current, characterized by the existence of a detectable magnetic force at every point in the region and by the existence of magnetic poles.

magnetic field strength *n.* Magnetic intensity.

magnetic flux *n.* A measure of the quantity of magnetism, being the total number of magnetic lines of force passing through a specified area in a magnetic field.

magnetic flux density *n. Symbol* **B** The amount of magnetic flux through a unit area taken perpendicular to the direction of the magnetic flux.

magnetic force *n.* **1.** The force exerted between magnetic poles, producing magnetization. **2.** A force that exists between two electrically charged moving particles.

magnetic head *n.* An electromagnet, as in a tape recorder, that converts electrical impulses into variations in the magnetism of a surface for storage and retrieval.

magnetic inclination *n.* The angle that a magnetic needle makes with the horizontal plane at any specific location.

magnetic induction *n.* **1.** The process by which a substance, such as iron, becomes magnetized by a magnetic field. **2.** See **magnetic flux density.**

magnetic intensity *n.* A quantity used in describing magnetic phenomena in terms of their magnetic fields and magnetization.

magnetic levitation *n.* A high-speed rail technology by which a train can travel free of friction while suspended on a magnetic cushion about half an inch above an elevated magnetic track.

magnetic meridian *n.* A line passing through both magnetic poles of the earth.

magnetic mine *n.* A marine mine detonated by a mechanism that responds to a mass of magnetic material.

magnetic moment *n.* The product of the pole strength of a magnet and the distance between the poles.

magnetic monopole *n.* A hypothetical particle that has only one pole of magnetic charge instead of the usual two.

magnetic needle *n.* A slender bar of magnetized steel usu. suspended on a low-friction mounting and used in various instruments, esp. in a magnetic compass, to indicate the direction of the earth's magnetic poles.

magnetic north *n.* The direction of the earth's magnetic pole, to which the north-seeking pole of a magnetic needle points when free from local magnetic influence.

S	A	T	O	R
A	R	E	P	O
T	E	N	E	T
O	P	E	R	A
R	O	T	A	S

16	3	2	13
5	10	11	8
9	6	7	12
4	15	14	1

magic square
top: the SATOR letter square
bottom: the number square from Albrecht Dürer's engraving *Melencolia I*

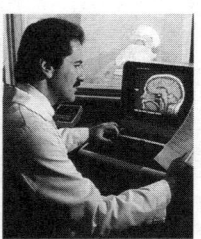

magnetic resonance imaging

magnetic permeability The ability of a substance to acquire magnetization in a given magnetic field.

magnetic pole *n.* **1.** Either of two limited regions in a magnet at which the magnet's field is most intense, each of which is designated by the approximate geographic direction to which it is attracted. **2.** Either of two variable points on the earth, close to but not coinciding with the geographic poles, where the earth's magnetic field is most intense and toward which a compass needle points.

magnetic pyrites *n.* See **pyrrhotite.**

magnetic recording *n.* **1.** The recording of a signal, such as sound, in a magnetic pattern on a magnetizable surface for storage and retrieval. **2.** A surface storing such a recording.

magnetic resonance *n.* The absorption of specific frequencies of radio and microwave radiation by atoms placed in a magnetic field, revealing molecular structure.

magnetic resonance imaging *n.* The use of a nuclear magnetic resonance spectrometer to produce electronic images of specific molecular structures in solids, esp. human tissues.

magnetic storm *n.* A disturbance or fluctuation in the earth's magnetic field, associated with solar flares.

magnetic tape *n.* A plastic tape coated with iron oxide for use in magnetic recording.

magnetic variation *n.* **1.** Differences in the earth's magnetic field in time and location. **2.** See **magnetic declination.**

mag·net·ism (măg′nĭ-tĭz′əm) *n.* **1.** The class of phenomena exhibited by a magnetic field. **2.** The study of magnets and their effects. **3.** The force exerted by a magnetic field. **4.** Unusual power to attract or influence. **5.** Animal magnetism.

mag·net·ite (măg′nĭ-tīt′) *n.* The mineral form of black iron oxide, Fe_3O_4, that often occurs with magnesium, zinc, and manganese and is an important ore of iron.

mag·net·i·za·tion (măg′nĭ-tĭ-zā′shən) *n.* **1a.** The process of making a substance temporarily or permanently magnetic, as by insertion in a magnetic field. **b.** The extent to which an object is magnetized. **2.** The property of being magnetic.

mag·net·ize (măg′nĭ-tīz′) *tr.v.* **-ized, -iz·ing, -iz·es 1.** To make magnetic. **2.** To attract, charm, or influence. **—mag′net·iz′a·ble** *adj.* **—mag′net·iz′er** *n.*

mag·ne·to (măg-nē′tō) *n., pl.* **-tos** A device that produces alternating current for distribution to the spark plugs, used in the ignition systems of some internal-combustion engines. [Short for *magnetoelectric machine.*]

magneto– or **magnet–** *pref.* **1.** Magnetism; magnetic: *magnetoelectric.* **2.** Magnetic field: *magnetometer.* [< MAGNET.]

mag·ne·to·e·lec·tric (măg-nē′tō-ĭ-lĕk′trĭk) *adj.* Of or relating to electricity produced by magnetic means. **—mag′ne·to·e·lec′tric·i·ty** (-ĭ-lĕk-trĭs′ĭ-tē, -tē̆, -ĕk-) *n.*

mag·ne·to·hy·dro·dy·nam·ics (măg-nē′tō-hī′drō-dī-năm′ĭks) *n.* (*used with a sing. verb*) The study of the interaction of magnetic fields and electrically conducting liquids or gases, such as molten metal. **—mag′ne·to·hy′dro·dy·nam′ic** *adj.*

mag·ne·tom·e·ter (măg′nĭ-tŏm′ĭ-tər) *n.* An instrument for measuring the magnitude and direction of a magnetic field. **—mag′ne·to·met′ric** (-tə-mĕt′rĭk) *adj.* **—mag′ne·tom′e·try** *n.*

mag·ne·to·mo·tive force (măg-nē′tō-mō′tĭv) *n.* The work required to carry a hypothetical isolated magnetic pole of unit strength completely around a magnetic circuit.

mag·ne·ton (măg′nĭ-tŏn′) *n.* A unit of the magnetic moment of a molecular, atomic, or subatomic particle, esp.: **a.** The Bohr magneton, calculated using the mass and charge of the electron. **b.** The nuclear magneton, calculated using the mass of the nucleon.

mag·ne·to·pause (măg-nē′tə-pôz′) *n.* The outer boundary of the magnetosphere.

mag·ne·to·re·sis·tance (măg-nē′tō-rĭ-zĭs′təns) *n.* A change in electrical resistance of a conductor or semiconductor when a magnetic field is applied.

mag·ne·to·rhe·ol·o·gy (măg-nē′tō-rē-ŏl′ə-jē) *n.* The study of the changes in flow properties of certain fluids exposed to magnetic field.

mag·ne·to·sphere (măg-nē′tō-sfîr′) *n.* An asymmetrical region surrounding the earth, extending from about one hundred to several thousand kilometers above the surface, in which the earth's magnetic field controls charged particles. **—mag·ne′to·spher′ic** (-sfîr′ĭk, -sfĕr′-) *adj.*

mag·ne·to·stric·tion (măg-nē′tō-strĭk′shən) *n.* Deformation of a ferromagnetic material subjected to a magnetic field. [MAGNETO– + (CON)STRICTION.] **—mag′ne·to·stric′tive** *adj.*

mag·ne·to·tail (măg-nē′tō-tāl′) *n.* The long, trailing part of the earth's magnetosphere on the side facing away from the sun. [MAGNETO(SPHERE) + TAIL[1].]

mag·ne·tron (măg′nĭ-trŏn′) *n.* A microwave tube in which electrons generated from a heated cathode are affected by magnetic and electric fields in such a way as to produce microwave radiation used in radar, for example.

magnet school *n.* A public school offering a specialized curriculum, often with high academic standards, to a student body representing a cross section of the community.

mag·nif·ic (măg-nĭf′ĭk) also **mag·nif·i·cal** (-ĭ-kəl) *adj.* **1.** Mag-

magnolia
saucer magnolia
Magnolia soulangiana

nificent. **2.** Imposingly large. **3.** Exalted. **4.** Pompous; grandiloquent. [ME *magnifique* < OFr. < Lat. *magnificus* : *magnus*, great; see **meg-** in App. + *-ficus*, *-fic.*] **—mag·nif′i·cal·ly** *adv.*

Mag·nif·i·cat (măg-nĭf′ĭ-kăt′) *n.* **1a.** The canticle beginning *Magnificat anima mea Dominum* ("My soul doth magnify the Lord"; Luke 1:46). **b.** A musical setting of this canticle. **2. magnificat** A song of praise. [ME < Med.Lat. < Lat. *magnificat*, it magnifies, third pers. sing. pr. t. of *magnificāre*, to magnify, extol. See MAGNIFY.]

mag·ni·fi·ca·tion (măg′nə-fĭ-kā′shən) *n.* **1.** The act of magnifying or the state of being magnified. **2a.** The process of enlarging the size of something, as an optical image. **b.** Something that has been magnified; an enlargement. **3.** The ratio of the size of an image to the size of an object.

mag·nif·i·cence (măg-nĭf′ĭ-səns) *n.* **1.** Greatness or lavishness of surroundings; splendor. **2.** Grand or imposing beauty.

mag·nif·i·cent (măg-nĭf′ĭ-sənt) *adj.* **1.** Splendid in appearance; grand: *a magnificent palace.* **2.** Grand or noble in thought or deed; exalted. **3.** Outstanding of its kind; superlative: *a magnificent view.* See Syns at **grand.** [ME < OFr. < *magnificence*, splendor < Lat. *magnificentia* < *magnificent-*, comp. and superl. stem of *magnificus*, magnificent. See MAGNIFIC.] **—mag·nif′i·cent·ly** *adv.*

mag·nif·i·co (măg-nĭf′ĭ-kō′) *n., pl.* **-coes 1.** A person of distinguished rank, importance, or appearance. **2.** A nobleman of the Venetian Republic. [Ital., magnificent, magnifico < Lat. *magnificus.* See MAGNIFIC.]

mag·ni·fi·er (măg′nə-fī′ər) *n.* **1.** One that magnifies, esp. a magnifying glass. **2.** A system of optical components that magnifies.

mag·ni·fy (măg′nə-fī′) *v.* **-fied, -fy·ing, -fies** *—tr.* **1.** To make greater in size; enlarge. **2.** To cause to appear greater or seem more important than is in fact the case; exaggerate. See Syns at **exaggerate. 3.** To increase the apparent size of, esp. by means of a lens. **4.** To glorify or praise. *—intr.* To increase or have the power to increase the size or volume of an image or a sound. [ME *magnifien*, to extol < OFr. *magnifier* < Lat. *magnificāre* < *magnificus*, magnificent. See MAGNIFY.]

mag·ni·fy·ing glass (măg′nə-fī′ĭng) *n.* A lens or combination of lenses that enlarges the image of an object.

mag·nil·o·quent (măg-nĭl′ə-kwənt) *adj.* Lofty and extravagant in speech; grandiloquent. [Back-formation < *magniloquence*, grandiloquence < Lat. *magniloquentia* : *magnus*, great; see **meg-** in App. + *loquēns, loquent-*, pr. part. of *loquī*, to speak.] **—mag·nil′o·quence** *n.* **—mag·nil′o·quent·ly** *adv.*

Mag·ni·to·gorsk (măg-nē′tə-gôrsk′, məg-nyē-tə-gôrsk′) A city of SW Russia SSW of Chelyabinsk. Pop. 438,808.

mag·ni·tude (măg′nĭ-tōōd′, -tyōōd′) *n.* **1a.** Greatness of rank or position. **b.** Greatness in size or extent. **c.** Greatness in significance or influence. **2.** *Astronomy* The degree of brightness of a celestial body according to a logarithmic scale, on which the brightest star has magnitude −1.4 and the faintest visible star has magnitude 6. **3.** *Mathematics* **a.** A number assigned to a quantity so that it may be compared with other quantities. **b.** A property that can be described by a real number, such as the length of a vector. **4.** *Geology* A measure of the amount of energy released by an earthquake, as indicated on the Richter scale. [ME < OFr., size < Lat. *magnitūdō*, greatness, size < *magnus*, great. See **meg-** in App.]

mag·no·lia (măg-nōl′yə) *n.* Any of numerous evergreen or deciduous trees and shrubs of the genus *Magnolia* of the Western Hemisphere and Asia, having aromatic twigs and showy flowers. [NLat. *Magnolia*, genus name, after Pierre *Magnol* (1638–1715), French botanist.]

magnolia warbler *n.* A black-and-yellow songbird (*Dendroica magnolia*) of northern North America.

mag·num (măg′nəm) *adj.* **1.** Of or relating to a cartridge that has more explosive charge than others of the same size. **2.** Designed to shoot magnum cartridges. ❖ *n.* **1.** A magnum cartridge or firearm. **2a.** A bottle, holding about two fifths of a gallon (1.5 liters), for wine or liquor. **b.** The amount of liquid that this bottle can hold. [< Lat., neut. of *magnus*, great. See **meg-** in App.]

magnum opus *n.* **1.** A great work, esp. a literary or artistic masterpiece. **2.** The greatest single work of an artist, writer, or composer. [Lat. : *magnum*, great + *opus*, work.]

mag·nus hitch (măg′nəs) *n.* A clove hitch with one extra turn. [?]

ma·got (mă-gō′, măg′ət) *n.* **1.** See **Barbary ape. 2.** A fanciful, often grotesque figurine in the Japanese or Chinese style rendered in a crouching position. [Fr. < OFr. *magos*, a kind of monkey < *Magog, Magos*, Magog, name of biblical land (Ezekiel 38–39) and tribe (Revelation 20:8–9).]

mag·pie (măg′pī′) *n.* **1.** Any of various birds of the family Corvidae found worldwide, having a long tail and black, blue, or green plumage with white markings and noted for their chattering call. **2.** Any of various birds resembling the magpie. **3.** A person who chatters. [*Mag*, a name used in proverbs about chatterers (a nickname for *Margaret*) + PIE[2].]

MAgr *abbr.* Master of Agriculture

Ma·gritte (mä-grēt′), René 1898–1967. Belgian painter whose surreal works include *Steps of Summer* (1938).

ma·guey (mə-gā′, măg′wā) *n., pl.* **-gueys 1.** Any of various American plants of the genus *Agave*, esp. the century plant. **2.** Any of various plants of the related genus *Furcraea*. **3.** The fiber obtained from any of these plants. [Sp., of Cariban orig.]

ma·gus (mā′gəs) *n., pl.* **ma·gi** (mā′jī′) **1.** A member of the Zoroastrian priestly caste of the Medes and Persians. **2.** *Magus* In the New Testament, one of the wise men from the East who traveled to Bethlehem to pay homage to the infant Jesus. **3.** A sorcerer; a magician. [< ME *magi*, magi < Lat. *magī*, pl. of *magus*, sorcerer, magus < Gk. *magos* < OPers. *maguš*.] **—ma′gi·an** (mā′jē-ən) *adj.*

Mag·yar (măg′yär′, măg′-, mä′dyär′) *n.* **1.** A member of the principal ethnic group of Hungary. **2.** See **Hungarian** 2. [Hung.] **—Mag′yar** *adj.*

Ma·ha·bha·ra·ta (mä′hə-bä′rə-tə) *n.* A Sanskrit epic set in about the 9th century B.C. that contains the text of the *Bhagavad-Gita*. [Skt. *Mahābhāratam*, great (telling) of the Bharatas (a family) : *mahā-*, great; see **meg-** in App. + *Bhāratam*, of the Bharatas, descendants of the legendary Indian king Bharata.]

Ma·hal·la el Ku·bra (mə-häl′ə el kōō′brə) A city of N Egypt in the Nile R. delta N of Cairo. Pop. 408,000.

Ma·han (mə-hăn′), **Alfred Thayer** 1840–1914. Amer. naval officer and historian noted for *The Influence of Sea Power upon History, 1660–1783* (1890).

Ma·ha·na·di (mə-hä′nə-dē) A river of central India flowing c. 885 km (550 mi) to the Bay of Bengal.

ma·ha·ra·jah or **ma·ha·ra·ja** (mä′hə-rä′jə, -zhə) *n.* **1.** A king or prince in India ranking above a rajah, esp. the sovereign of one of the former native states. **2.** Used as a title for such a king or prince. [Skt. *mahārājaḥ* : *mahā-*, great; see **meg-** in App. + *rājā*, *rājaḥ*, king; see **reg-** in App.]

> **WORD HISTORY** Countless Indian restaurants are named *Maharajah*, from the Sanskrit word *mahārājaḥ*, meaning "great king." The element *mahā–* is related to Greek *mega–* and Latin *magnus*, both meaning the same thing as the Sanskrit, "great." All three forms derive from an Indo-European root that also has descendants in Germanic, in particular, the Old English word *micel*, pronounced (mĭ′chəl). This survives today in *much* (shortened from Middle English *muchel*) and in the family name *Mitchell*.

ma·ha·ra·ni or **ma·ha·ra·nee** (mä′hə-rä′nē) *n., pl.* **-nis** or **-nees 1.** The wife of a maharajah. **2.** A princess in India ranking above a rani, esp. the sovereign ruler of one of the former native states. **3.** Used as a title for such a woman. [Hindi *mahārānī* < Skt. *mahārājñī* : *mahā-*, great; see **meg-** in App. + *rājñī*, queen; see **reg-** in App.]

Ma·ha·rash·tra (mä′hə-räsh′trə) A historical region of W-central India; controlled by the Muslim rulers of India from the early 14th to the mid-17th cent.

ma·ha·ri·shi (mä′hə-rē′shē, mə-här′ə-shē) *n., pl.* **-shis** *Hinduism* **1.** A teacher of mysticism and spiritual knowledge. **2.** Used as a title for such a person. [Skt. *mahārṣiḥ* : *mahā-*, great; see **meg-** in App. + *ṛṣih*, seer, sage, saint.]

ma·hat·ma (mə-hät′mə, -hăt′-) *n.* **1.** In India and Tibet, one of a class of persons venerated for great knowledge and love of humanity. **2.** *Mahatma Hinduism* Used as a title of respect for a person renowned for spirituality and high-mindedness. [Skt. *mahātmā* : *mahā-*, great; see **meg-** in App. + *ātmā*, life, spirit.]

Ma·ha·ya·na (mä′hə-yä′nə) *n.* One of the major schools of Buddhism, which teaches social concern and universal salvation. [Skt. *Mahāyānam*, greater vehicle (as contrasted with *Hīnayānam*, lesser vehicle; see HINAYANA) : *mahā-*, great; see **meg-** in App. + *yānam*, vehicle; see **ei-** in App.] **—Ma′ha·ya′nist** *n.*

Mah·di (mä′dē) *n., pl.* **-dis** *Islam* **1.** The messiah who, it is believed, will appear at the world's end and establish a reign of peace and righteousness. **2.** A leader who assumes the role of a messiah. [Ar. *mahdī*, rightly guided one, Mahdi, passive part. of *hadā*, to lead.] **—Mah′dism** *n.* **—Mah′dist** *n.*

Mah·fouz (mä-fōōz′), **Naguib** b. 1911. Egyptian writer who won the 1988 Nobel Prize for literature.

Ma·hi·can (mə-hē′kən) also **Mo·hi·can** (mō-, mə-) *n., pl.* **Mahican** or **-cans** also **Mohican** or **-cans 1.** A member of a Native American confederacy of subtribes formerly inhabiting the upper Hudson River valley from Albany south to the Catskill Mountains and north to Lake Champlain. **2.** The Algonquian language of the Mahican.

Ma·hi·lyow (mä-hē-lou′, mä-hē-lyou′) or **Mo·gi·lev** (mŏg′ə-lĕf′, mə-gĭ-lyôf′) A city of E-central Belarus on the Dnieper R. E of Minsk; founded around a castle built in 1267. Pop. 363,600.

ma·hi·ma·hi also **ma·hi·ma·hi** (mä′hē-mä′hē) *n., pl.* **-his** See **dolphin** 2a. [Hawaiian *mahimahi*.]

mah·jong also **mah·jongg** (mä′zhŏng′, -zhông′) *n.* A game of Chinese origin usu. played by four persons with tiles resembling dominoes and bearing various designs. [Chin. (Mandarin) *májiàng* : *má*, spotted + *jiàng*, main piece in Chinese chess.]

Mah·ler (mä′lər), **Gustav** 1860–1911. Austrian composer and conductor whose works include *Das Lied von der Erde* (1908) and Symphony Number 9 (1909).

mahl·stick (môl′stĭk′) *n.* Variant of **maulstick**.

ma·hog·a·ny (mə-hŏg′ə-nē) *n., pl.* **-nies 1a.** Any of various tropical American evergreen trees of the genus *Swietenia*, valued for their hard reddish-brown wood. **b.** The wood of any of these trees, used in making furniture. **2a.** Any of several trees having wood resembling true mahogany. **b.** The wood of any of these trees. **3.** A moderate reddish brown. [Obsolete Sp. *mahogani*, perh. of Mayan orig.]

ma·hout (mə-hout′) *n.* The keeper and driver of an elephant. [Hindi *mahāvat, mahāut* < Skt. *mahāmātraḥ*, one having great measure, mahout : *mahā-*, great; see **meg-** in App. + *mātram*, measure (< *mimīte, mā-*, he measures; see **mē-¹** in App.).]

Mah·ra·ti (mə-rä′tē, -răt′ē) *n.* Variant of **Marathi**.

Mah·rat·ta (mə-rä′tə, -răt′ə) *n.* Variant of **Maratha**.

Mah·rat·ti (mə-rä′tē, -răt′ē) *n.* Variant of **Marathi**.

ma huang also **ma·huang** (mä-hwäng′) *n.* Any of various Asian shrubs of the genus *Ephedra*, esp. *E. sinica*, from which the drug ephedrine is obtained. [Chin. (Mandarin) *máhuáng* : *má*, hemp + *huáng*, yellow.]

mah·zor also **mach·zor** (mäкн′zôr′, -zôr, mäкн-zôr′) *n., pl.* **-zor·im** (-zôr′ĭm, -zô-rēm′) or **-zors** The Jewish prayer book containing rituals prescribed for holidays. [Mishnaic Heb. *maḥzor*, cycle, mahzor < *ḥāzar*, to go around, return.]

mai·a·saur (mī′ə-sôr′) or **mai·a·sau·ra** (mī′ə-sôr′ə) *n.* An ornithischian herbivorous dinosaur of the genus *Maiasaura* of the late Cretaceous Period of North America, noted for remains suggesting that the adults cared for their young. [NLat. *Māiasaura*, genus name : Gk. *maia*, good mother + NLat. *saura*, fem. of *saurus*, lizard (< Gk. *sauros*).]

maid (mād) *n.* **1a.** An unmarried girl or woman. **b.** A virgin. **2.** A woman servant. **3.** A housemaid or chambermaid. [ME *maide* < OE *mægden*.]

maid·en (mād′n) *n.* **1a.** An unmarried girl or woman. **b.** A virgin. **2.** A machine resembling the guillotine, used in Scotland in the 16th and 17th centuries to behead criminals. **3.** *Sports* A racehorse that has never won a race. ❖ *adj.* **1.** Of, relating to, or befitting a maiden: *a maiden blush*. **2.** Being an unmarried girl or woman: *a maiden aunt*. **3.** Being a racehorse that has never won a race. **4.** First or earliest: *a maiden voyage*. [ME < OE *mægden*.]

maid·en·hair fern (mād′n-hâr′) *n.* Any of various ferns of the genus *Adiantum*, having purplish to black stalks, usu. feathery fronds, and delicate fan-shaped leaflets with marginal sori. [< fineness of its stems.]

maidenhair tree *n.* See **ginkgo**.

maid·en·head (mād′n-hĕd′) *n.* **1.** The condition or quality of being a maiden; virginity. **2.** The hymen. [ME *maidenhed* : *maiden*, MAIDEN + *-hed*, -hood.]

maid·en·hood (mād′n-hōōd′) *n.* The condition or time of being a maiden.

maid·en·ly (mād′n-lē) *adj.* Of, relating to, or suitable for a maiden. **—maid′en·li·ness** *n.*

maiden name *n.* The family name of a woman before changing her surname when marrying.

maid·hood (mād′hōōd′) *n.* Maidenhood.

maid in waiting *n., pl.* **maids in waiting** An unmarried woman attending a queen or princess.

Maid Marian *n.* Robin Hood's sweetheart.

maid of honor *n., pl.* **maids of honor 1.** The chief unmarried woman attendant of a bride. **2.** An unmarried noblewoman attendant upon a queen or princess.

maid·ser·vant (mād′sûr′vənt) *n.* A woman servant.

Maid·stone (mād′stən, -stōn′) A municipal borough of SE England ESE of London; first chartered 1549. Pop. 72,500.

Mai·du (mī′dōō) *n., pl.* **Maidu** or **-dus 1.** A member of a Native American people inhabiting northeast California south of Lassen Peak. **2.** The Penutian language of the Maidu.

ma·ieu·tic (mā-yōō′tĭk, mī-) also **ma·ieu·ti·cal** (-tĭ-kəl) *adj.* Of or relating to the aspect of the Socratic method that induces a person to bring forth latent concepts through a logical sequence of questions. [Gk. *maieutikos* < *maieuesthai*, to act as midwife < *maia*, midwife, nurse.]

mail¹ (māl) *n.* **1a.** Materials, such as letters, handled in a postal system. **b.** Postal material for a specific person or organization. **c.** Material processed for distribution from a post office at a specified time: *the morning mail*. **2.** A system by which letters and other postal materials are transported. Often used in the plural. **3.** A vehicle by which mail is transported. **4.** Mail or messages sent electronically; e-mail. ❖ *v.* **mailed**, **mail·ing**, **mails** **—*tr.*** To send by mail. **—*intr.*** To send postal material by mail. [ME *male, maile* < OFr., of Gmc. orig.] **—mail′a·ble** *adj.* **—mail′a·bil′i·ty** *n.*

mail² (māl) *n.* **1.** Flexible armor composed of small overlapping metal rings, loops of chain, or scales. **2.** The protective covering of certain animals, as the shell of a turtle. ❖ *tr.v.* **mailed**, **mail·ing**, **mails** To cover with or armor with mail. [ME < OFr. *maile* < Lat. *macula*, blemish, mesh.]

mail²
replica of Norman armor

mail³ (māl) *n. Scots* Rent, payment, or tribute. [ME *mol, maile* < ON *māl*, lawsuit.]

mail·bag (māl′băg′) *n.* **1.** A large canvas sack used for transporting mail. **2.** A bag suspended from the shoulder, used by letter carriers for carrying mail.

mail·box (māl′bŏks′) *n.* **1.** A public container for deposit of outgoing mail. **2.** A private box for incoming mail. **3.** A computer file or set of files for e-mail.

mail carrier *n.* See **letter carrier**.

mail drop *n.* **1.** A receptacle or slot for the delivery of mail. **2.** An address or place at which a nonresident person receives mail, often of a secret nature.

mailed (māld) *adj.* **1.** Covered with or made of plates of mail: *a mailed sleeve.* **2.** Having a hard covering of scales, spines, or horny plate, as an armadillo or a lobster.

mailed fist *n.* The threat of military force.

mail·er (mā′lər) *n.* **1.** One that uses the mails: *commercial mailers.* **2.** One who addresses or otherwise prepares mail. **3.** A container used to hold material to be mailed: *a book mailer.* **4.** An advertising leaflet included with a letter.

Mailer, Norman b. 1923. Amer. writer whose works include *The Armies of the Night* (1968).

Mail·gram (māl′grăm′) A trademark used for a telegram to a post office and delivered by the postal service.

mail·ing (mā′lĭng) *n.* **1.** Something sent by mail. **2.** A batch of mail dispatched at one time by a sender.

Mail·lol (mä-yôl′), **Aristide** 1861–1944. French sculptor noted for his classically influenced statues of female nudes.

mail·lot (mä-yō′) *n.* **1.** A coarsely knitted stretchable jersey fabric. **2.** A pair of tights or a leotard of such fabric. **3.** A woman's one-piece swimsuit cut. cut high on the leg. [Fr. < OFr., swaddling clothes < *maille*, mesh < Lat. *macula*.]

mail·man (māl′măn′, -mən) *n.* A man who delivers mail.

mail order *n.* An order for goods to be shipped by mail. **—mail′or′der** (māl′ôr′dər) *adj.*

mail·room (māl′rōōm′, -rōōm′) *n.* A room in which ingoing and outgoing mail is handled for an organization.

maim (mām) *tr.v.* **maimed, maim·ing, maims** **1.** To disable or disfigure, usu. by depriving of the use of a body part. **2.** To make imperfect or defective; impair. [ME *maimen* < OFr. *mahaignier.* See MAYHEM.] **—maim′er** *n.*

Mai·mon·i·des (mī-mŏn′ĭ-dēz′), **Moses** Orig. Moses Ben Maimon. 1135–1204. Spanish-born Jewish philosopher and physician who codified the Talmud.

main (mān) *adj.* **1.** Most important; principal. **2.** Exerted to the utmost; sheer: *by main strength.* **3.** *Nautical* Connected to or associated with the mainmast: *a main skysail.* **4.** *Grammar* Of, relating to, or being the principal clause or verb of a complex sentence. **5.** *Obsolete* Of a continuous area or stretch. ❖ *n.* **1.** The chief or largest part: *Your ideas are, in the main, impractical.* **2.** The principal pipe or conduit in a system for conveying gas or other utility. **3.** Physical strength: *fought with might and main.* **4.** A mainland. **5.** The open ocean. **6.** *Nautical* **a.** A mainsail. **b.** A mainmast. [ME < OE *mægen*, strength.]

Main (mān, mīn) A river rising in E Germany and flowing c. 499 km (310 mi) to the Rhine R. at Mainz.

main clause *n.* A clause in a complex sentence that contains at least a subject and a verb and can stand alone syntactically as a complete sentence.

main deck *n.* The principal deck of a large ship or vessel.

main drag *n. Slang* The principal street of a city or town.

Maine (mān) **1.** (*also* mĕn) A historical region and former province of NW France S of Normandy; passed to England in 1154 but reverted to the French crown in 1481. **2.** A state of the NE US; admitted as the 23rd state in 1820. Cap. Augusta. Pop. 1,274,923.

Maj. or **Maj** or **MAJ** *abbr.* major

main·frame (mān′frām′) *n.* A large powerful computer, often serving many terminals and usu. used by large complex organizations.

main·land (mān′lănd′, -lənd) *n.* The principal landmass of a continent. **—main′land′er** *n.*

main·line (mān′līn′) *v.* **-lined, -lin·ing, -lines** *Slang —tr.* To inject (a drug) directly into a major vein. *—intr.* To inject a drug intravenously. ❖ *adj.* Being in a principal or well-established position: *the mainline churches.* **—main′lin′er** *n.*

main line *n.* **1.** A principal section of a railroad line. **2.** *Slang* A principal vein into which a drug can be injected.

main·ly (mān′lē) *adv.* For the most part; chiefly.

main·mast (mān′məst, -măst′) *n.* **1.** The principal mast of a sailing vessel. **2.** The taller mast, whether forward or aft, of a two-masted sailing vessel. **3.** The second mast aft of a sailing ship with three or more masts.

main royalmast *n.* The section of the mainmast of a square-rigged vessel above the main topgallantmast.

main·sail (mān′səl, -sāl′) *n.* **1.** The principal sail of a vessel. **2.** A quadrilateral or triangular sail set from the after part of the mainmast on a fore-and-aft rigged vessel. **3.** A square sail set from the main yard on a square-rigged vessel.

main sequence *n.* The largest grouping of stars plotted on the Hertzsprung-Russell diagram.

main·sheet (mān′shēt′) *n.* The sheet that controls the angle at which a mainsail is trimmed and set.

main·spring (mān′sprĭng′) *n.* **1.** The principal spring in a mechanical device, esp. a watch or clock, that drives the mechanism by uncoiling. **2.** The chief motivating force.

main·stay (mān′stā′) *n.* **1.** A chief support. **2.** *Nautical* A stay leading forward from the mainmast of a sailing vessel.

main·stream (mān′strēm′) *n.* The prevailing current of thought, influence, or activity. ❖ *adj.* Representing the prevalent attitudes, values, and practices of a society or group: *mainstream*

morality. ❖ *tr.v.* **-streamed, -stream·ing, -streams** **1.** To integrate (a student with special needs) into regular school classes. **2.** To incorporate into a prevailing group. **—main′stream′er** *n.*

main street *n.* **1.** The principal street of a small town. **2. Main Street a.** The inhabitants of small towns considered as a group. **b.** A place that represents narrowmindedness and smug complacency. [Sense 2, after *Main Street*, a novel by Sinclair Lewis.]

main·tain (mān-tān′) *tr.v.* **-tained, -tain·ing, -tains** **1.** To keep up or carry on; continue: *maintain good relations.* **2.** To keep in an existing state; preserve or retain: *maintain one's composure.* **3.** To keep in a condition of good repair or efficiency. **4a.** To provide for; support: *maintain a family.* **b.** To keep in existence; sustain. **5.** To defend or hold against criticism or attack. **6.** To declare to be true; affirm: *maintained her innocence.* **7.** To adhere to or conform to; keep: *maintain a busy schedule.* [ME *maintainen* < OFr. *maintenir* < Med.Lat. *manutenēre* < Lat. *manū tenēre*, to hold in the hand : *manū*, ablative of *manus*, hand; see **man-²** in App. + *tenēre*, to hold; see **ten-** in App.] **—main·tain′a·bil′i·ty** *n.* **—main·tain′a·ble** *adj.* **—main·tain′er** *n.*

main·te·nance (mān′tə-nəns) *n.* **1.** The act of maintaining or the state of being maintained. **2.** The work of keeping something in proper condition; upkeep. **3a.** Provision of support or livelihood. **b.** Means of support or livelihood. **4.** *Law* The unlawful meddling in a suit by providing either party with the means to carry it on. [ME *maintenaunce* < OFr. *maintenance* < *maintenir*, to maintain. See MAINTAIN.]

Main·te·non (măn′tə-nôn′, mănt-nôN′), **Marquise de** Françoise d'Aubigné. Title of "Madame de Maintenon." 1635–1719. French consort of Louis XIV who secretly married the king (c. 1685) after the death of his first wife.

main·top (mān′tŏp′) *n.* A platform at the head of the mainmast on a square-rigged vessel.

main topgallant *n.* A sail or yard set from the topgallant section of a mainmast.

main top·gal·lant·mast (tə-găl′ənt-məst, tŏp-) *n.* The section of the mainmast next above the main topmast on a square-rigged sailing vessel.

main topmast *n.* The section of the mainmast on a square-rigged sailing vessel between the lower mast and the main topgallantmast.

main topsail *n.* The sail that is set above the mainsail.

main yard *n.* The lowest yard on a mainmast.

Mainz (mīnts) A city of W-central Germany at the confluence of the Rhine and Main rivers WSW of Frankfurt; built on the site of a Roman camp. Pop. 185,487.

mai tai (mī′ tī′) *n., pl.* **mai tais** A cocktail made with rum, curaçao, and fruit juices. [Tahitian *maitai*, good.]

maî·tre d' (mā′trə dē′, mā′tər) *n., pl.* **maî·tre d's** (dēz′) *Informal* A maitre d'hôtel.

maître d'hôtel (mā′trə dō-tĕl′) *n., pl.* **maî·tres d'hô·tel** (mā′trə dō-tĕl′) **1.** A headwaiter. **2.** A major-domo. **3.** A sauce of melted butter, chopped parsley, lemon juice, salt, and pepper. [Fr. *maître d'hôtel* : *maître*, master + *de*, of + *hôtel*, house.]

maize (māz) *n.* **1.** See **corn¹** 1. **2.** A light yellow to moderate orange yellow. [Sp. *maíz* < Arawakan *mahiz, mahís*.]

ma·jes·tic (mə-jĕs′tĭk) *also* **ma·jes·ti·cal** (-tĭ-kəl) *adj.* Having or showing lofty dignity or nobility; stately. See Syns at **grand**. **—ma·jes′ti·cal·ly** *adv.*

maj·es·ty (măj′ĭ-stē) *n., pl.* **-ties 1a.** The greatness and dignity of a sovereign. **b.** The sovereignty and power of God. **2.** Supreme authority or power. **3a.** A royal personage. **b. Majesty** Used with *His, Her,* or *Your* as a title and form of address for a sovereign. **4a.** Royal dignity of bearing or aspect; grandeur. **b.** Stately splendor; magnificence, as of style or character. [ME *mageste, maieste* < OFr. *majeste* < Lat. *māiestās*. See **meg-** in App.]

Maj Gen or **MajGen** *abbr.* major general

ma·jol·i·ca (mə-jŏl′ĭ-kə, -yŏl′-) *n.* **1.** Tin-glazed earthenware, often richly colored and decorated, esp. an earthenware of this type made in Italy. **2.** Pottery made in imitation of this earthenware. [Ital. *maiolica* < Med.Lat. *Māiōlica*, Majorca (where it was made), alteration of LLat. *Māiōrica*.]

ma·jor (mā′jər) *adj.* **1.** Greater than others in importance or rank: *a major artist.* **2.** Great in scope or effect: *a major improvement.* **3.** Great in number, size, or extent: *the major portion of the population.* **4.** Requiring great attention or concern; very serious: *a major illness.* **5.** Of or relating to the field of academic study in which a student specializes. **6.** *Music* **a.** Designating a scale or mode having half steps between the third and fourth and the seventh and eighth degrees. **b.** Equivalent to the distance between the tonic note and the second or third or sixth or seventh degrees of a major scale or mode. **c.** Based on a major scale: *a major key.* ❖ *n.* **1.** An officer in the US Army, Air Force, or Marine Corps ranking above captain and below lieutenant colonel. **2.** One that is superior in rank, importance, or ability. **3a.** A field of study chosen as an academic specialty. **b.** A student specializing in such studies: *a linguistics major.* **4.** *Logic* **a.** A major premise. **b.** A major term. **5.** *Music* **a.** A major scale, key, interval, or mode. **b.** A chord containing a major third between the first and second notes and a minor third between the second and third notes. **6.**

majors *Sports* The major leagues. ❖ *intr.v.* **-jored, -jor·ing, -jors**

majolica
c. 1530 plate from Deruta,
Italy

To pursue academic studies in a major: *majoring in mathematics.* [ME *majour* < Lat. *māior*. See **meg-** in App.]

Major, John b. 1943. British politician and prime minister (1990–97).

major axis *n.* The longer of the two lines about which an ellipse is symmetrical.

Ma•jor•ca (mə-jôr′kə, -yôr′-) also **Mal•lor•ca** (mä-yôr′kä, -lyôr′-) An island of Spain in the W Mediterranean Sea off the E-central coast of the mainland; center of an independent kingdom (1276–1343). —**Ma•jor′can** *adj. & n.*

ma•jor-do•mo (mā′jər-dō′mō) *n., pl.* **-mos 1.** The head steward or butler in the household of a sovereign or great noble. **2.** A steward or butler. **3.** One who makes arrangements or directs affairs for another. [Ital. *maggiordomo* or Sp. *mayordomo,* both < Med.Lat. *māior domūs* : Lat. *māior,* chief; see **meg-** in App. + Lat. *domūs,* genitive of *domus,* house; see **dem-** in App.]

ma•jor•ette (mā′jə-rĕt′) *n.* A drum majorette.

major general *n.* A commissioned officer in the US Army, Air Force, or Marine Corps ranking above brigadier general and below lieutenant general.

major histocompatibility complex *n.* A group of genes that code for cell-surface histocompatibility antigens and are the principle determinants of tissue type.

ma•jor•i•tar•i•an•ism (mə-jôr′ĭ-târ′ē-ə-nĭz′əm, -jŏr′-) *n.* Rule by simple numerical majority in an organized group. —**ma•jor′i•tar′i•an** *adj. & n.*

ma•jor•i•ty (mə-jôr′ĭ-tē, -jŏr′-) *n., pl.* **-ties 1.** The greater number or part; a number more than half of the total. **2.** The amount by which the greater number of votes cast, as in an election, exceeds the total number of remaining votes. **3.** The political party, group, or faction having the larger representation or electoral strength. **4.** *Law* The status of having reached full legal age. **5.** The military rank, commission, or office of a major. **6.** *Obsolete* The fact or state of being greater; superiority. [Fr. *majorité* < Med.Lat. *māiōritās* < Lat. *māior,* greater. See **meg-** in App.]

USAGE NOTE When *majority* refers to a particular number of votes, it takes a singular verb: *Her majority was five votes.* When it refers to a group in the majority, it may take either a singular or plural verb, depending on whether the group is considered as a whole or individually. So we say *The majority elects the candidate it wants,* since the election is accomplished by the group as a whole, but *The majority of the voters live in the city,* since living in the city is something that each voter does individually.

majority leader *n.* The leader of the majority party in a legislature, as in the US Senate or House of Representatives.

majority rule *n.* A doctrine by which a numerical majority of an organized group holds the power to make decisions binding on all in the group.

major league *n.* **1.** Either of the two principal groups of professional baseball teams in the United States. **2.** A league of principal importance in other professional sports. —**ma′jor-lea′guer** (mā′jər-lē′gər) *n.*

major-league (mā′jər-lēg′) *n.* **1.** *Sports* Of or relating to a major league. **2.** *Informal* Prominent or important: *a major-league decision.* **3.** *Informal* Thoroughgoing, extreme, or extensive.

ma•jor•ly (mā′jər-lē) *adv. Slang* To a great or an intense degree; extremely.

major medical *n.* Insurance that covers all or most of the medical bills of major illnesses above a set amount.

major order *n. Ecclesiastical* A principal order of clergy, esp. the rank of bishop, priest, and deacon, in the Roman Catholic, Eastern Orthodox, and Anglican churches.

major premise *n.* The premise containing the major term in a syllogism.

Major Prophets *pl.n. Bible* The Hebrew prophets Isaiah, Jeremiah, and Ezekiel.

major scale *n. Music* A diatonic scale having half steps between the third and fourth and the seventh and eighth degrees.

major suit *n. Games* A suit of superior scoring value, either spades or hearts in bridge.

major term *n.* The term of a syllogism that forms the predicate of the conclusion.

ma•jus•cule (mə-jŭs′kyo͞ol, măj′ə-skyo͞ol′) *n.* A large letter, either capital or uncial, used in writing or printing. [Fr. < Lat. *māiusculus,* somewhat larger, dim. of *māior,* greater. See **meg-** in App.] —**ma•jus′cule, ma•jus′cu•lar** (-kyə-lər) *adj.*

Mak•a•lu (mŭk′ə-lo͞o′) A mountain, 8,476 m (27,790 ft), in the Himalaya Mts. of NE Nepal.

mak•ar (mä′kər, mā′-) *n. Chiefly Scots* A poet. [ME, var. of *maker,* maker, poet.]

Ma•kar•i•os III (mə-kăr′ē-əs, -ōs′, mä-kä′rē-ôs) 1913–77. Cypriot prelate and first president of Cyprus (1959–77).

Ma•kas•sar or **Ma•ka•sar** (mə-kăs′ər) See **Ujung Pandang.**

Makassar Strait A strait between Borneo and Sulawesi connecting the Java Sea with the Celebes Sea.

make (māk) *v.* **made** (mād), **mak•ing, makes** —*tr.* **1.** To cause to exist or happen; bring about; create: *made problems for us; making a commotion.* **2.** To bring into existence by shaping, modifying, or putting together material; construct: *made a dress; made a stone wall.* **3.** To form by assembling individuals or constituents: *make a quorum.* **4.** To change from one form or function to another: *make clay into bricks.* **5a.** To cause to be or become: *made her position clear.* **b.** To cause to assume a specified function or role: *made Chicago his home.* **6a.** To cause to act in a specified manner: *Heat makes gases expand.* **b.** To compel: *made him quit.* **7a.** To form in the mind: *make an estimate.* **b.** To compose: *make verses.* **8a.** To prepare; fix: *make dinner.* **b.** To get ready or set in order for use: *made the bed.* **c.** To gather and light the materials for (a fire). **9a.** To engage in: *make war.* **b.** To carry out; perform: *make an incision.* **10.** To achieve, produce, or attain: *made the quota.* **11a.** To institute or establish; enact: *make laws.* **b.** To draw up and execute in a suitable form: *make a will.* **c.** To arrange or agree to: *make a date.* **12a.** To arrive at; reach: *made Seattle in two hours.* **b.** To reach in time: *just made the plane.* **13a.** To attain the rank or position of: *made lieutenant.* **b.** To acquire a place in or on: *made the team.* **14a.** To gain or earn: *make money.* **b.** To behave so as to acquire: *make friends.* **c.** To score or achieve: *made a field goal.* **15a.** To assure the success of: *a good review that made the play.* **b.** To favor the development of: *Practice makes a winning team.* **16.** To be suited for: *Oak makes strong furniture.* **17.** To develop into: *She will make a fine doctor.* **18a.** To draw a conclusion as to the significance or nature of: *don't know what to make of the decision.* **b.** To calculate as being; estimate: *I make the height 20 feet.* **c.** To consider as being: *wasn't the problem some people made it.* **19a.** To constitute: *Ten members make a quorum.* **b.** To add up to: *Two and two make four.* **c.** To amount to: *makes no difference.* **20.** To cover (a distance): *made 200 miles before sunset.* **21.** To constitute the essence or nature of: *Clothes make the man.* **22.** To cause to be very enjoyable or rewarding: *You made my day.* **23.** To appear to begin (an action): *She made to leave.* **24.** *Slang* To persuade to have sexual intercourse. —*intr.* **1.** To act or behave in a specified manner: *make merry.* **2.** To begin or appear to begin an action: *made as if to shake my hand.* **3.** To cause something to be as specified: *make ready.* **4.** To proceed in a certain direction. **5.** *Slang* To pretend to be; imitate. Used with *like.* **6.** To undergo fabrication or manufacture: *Wool makes up into a warm shawl.* **7.** To rise or accumulate: *The tide is making.* ❖ *n.* **1.** The act or process of making; manufacturing. **2.** The style or manner in which a thing is made. **3.** The amount produced, esp. the output of a factory. **4.** A specific line of manufactured goods, identified by the manufacturer's name or trademark. **5.** The physical or moral nature of a person; character or disposition. **6.** *Slang* Identification of a person or thing, often from police records: *Did you get a make on the thief?* ***—phrasal verbs:*** **make for 1.** To have or produce (a particular effect or result): *details that make for comfort.* **2.** To help promote; further: *Respect makes for better communication.* **make off** To depart in haste; run away. **make out 1.** To discern or see, esp. with difficulty. **2.** To understand: *couldn't make out what she said.* **3.** To write out; draw up. **4.** To fill in (a form, for example). **5.** *Informal* To represent as being: *made me out to be a liar.* **6.** *Informal* To try to establish or prove. **7.** To get along in a given way; fare: *made out well in business.* **8.** *Slang* **a.** To neck; pet. **b.** To have sexual intercourse. **make over 1.** To redo; renovate. **2.** To change or transfer the ownership of, usu. by means of a legal document. **make up 1.** To put together; construct or compose: *make up a prescription.* **2.** To constitute; form: *Ten years make up a decade.* **3a.** To alter one's appearance for a role on the stage, as with a costume and cosmetics. **b.** To apply cosmetics. **4.** To devise as a fiction or falsehood; invent. **5a.** To make good (a deficit or lack). **b.** To compensate for: *make up for lost time.* **6.** To resolve a quarrel: *kissed and made up.* **7.** To make ingratiating or fawning overtures. Used with *to: made up to his boss.* **8.** To take (an examination or a course) again or at a later time because of previous absence or failure. **9.** To set in order: *make up a room.* **10.** *Printing* To select and arrange material for: *made up the front page.* **make with** *Slang* **1.** To bring into use: *a flirt making with the eyes.* **2.** To put forth; produce: *always making with the jokes.* ***—idioms:*** **make a clean breast of** To confess fully. **make a face** To distort the features of the face; grimace. **make a go of** To achieve success in. **make away with 1.** To carry off; steal. **2.** To use up or consume. **3.** To kill or destroy. **make believe** To pretend. **make bold** To venture. **make book** To accept bets on a race, game, or contest. **make do** To manage to get along with the means available: *had to make do on less income.* **make ends meet** To manage so that one's means are sufficient for one's needs. **make eyes** To ogle. **make fun of** To mock; ridicule. **make good 1.** To carry out successfully: *made good his escape.* **2.** To fulfill: *made good her promise.* **3.** To make compensation for; make up for: *made good the loss.* **4.** To succeed: *made good as a writer.* **make hay** To turn to one's advantage. **make it 1.** *Informal* To achieve a goal; be successful. **2.** *Slang* To have sexual intercourse. **make light of** To treat as unimportant. **make love 1.** To engage in amorous caressing. **2.** To engage in sexual intercourse. **make much of** To treat as of great importance. **make no bones about** To be forthright and candid about; acknowledge freely. **make off with** To snatch or steal. **make sail 1.** To begin a voyage. **2.** To set sails. **make sense 1.** To be coherent or intelligible: *an explanation that made sense.* **2.** To be practical or advisable: *It makes sense to go now.* **make something of** To start a fight or quarrel over. **make the best of** To accept (a bad situation) in as good a light as possible. **make the grade** To

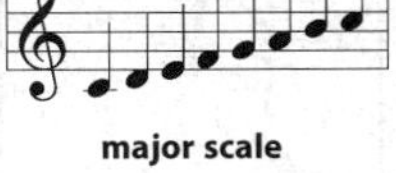

major scale

ă	pat	oi	boy
ā	pay	ou	out
âr	care	o͝o	took
ä	father	o͞o	boot
ĕ	pet	ŭ	cut
ē	be	ûr	urge
ĭ	pit	th	thin
ī	pie	*th*	this
îr	pier	hw	which
ŏ	pot	zh	vision
ō	toe	ə	about, item
ô	paw		

Stress marks:
′ (primary);
′ (secondary), as in
lexicon (lĕk′sĭ-kŏn′)

malamute

Malawi

measure up to a given standard. **make the most of** To use to the greatest advantage. **make the scene** *Slang* **1.** To put in an appearance. **2.** To participate in a specified activity. **make time 1.** To travel speedily. **2.** To travel at a specified rate: *made good time getting to town.* **3.** *Slang* To make progress toward attracting someone. **make tracks** *Slang* To move or leave in a hurry. **make up (one's) mind** To decide between alternatives; come to a definite decision or opinion. **make waves** *Slang* To cause a disturbance or controversy. **make way 1.** To give room for passage; move aside. **2.** To make progress. **on the make** *Slang* **1.** Aggressively striving for financial or social improvement. **2.** Eagerly seeking a sexual partner. [ME *maken* < OE *macian.*] —**mak′a·ble, make′a·ble** *adj.*

make-be·lieve (māk′bĭ-lēv′) *n.* Playful or fanciful pretense. —**make′-be·lieve** *adj.*

make·fast (māk′făst′) *n. Nautical* An object, such as a buoy, post, or pile, to which a boat is moored.

make-or-break (māk′ər-brāk′) *adj.* Resulting in great success or utter failure: *a make-or-break investment plan.*

mak·er (mā′kər) *n.* **1.** One that makes or manufactures. Often used in combination: *a policymaker.* **2.** *Law* A party that signs a promissory note. **3. Maker** God. Often used with a possessive adjective: *prayed to her Maker.* **4.** *Archaic* A poet.

make-read·y (māk′rĕd′ē) *n. Printing* The preparation of a form by adjusting and leveling the plates to get a clear impression.

make·shift (māk′shĭft′) *n.* A temporary or expedient substitute. —**make′shift′** *adj.*

make·up or **make-up** (māk′ŭp′) *n.* **1.** The way in which something is composed or arranged; composition or construction. **2.** *Printing* The arrangement or composition, as of type, on a page or in a book. **3.** The qualities or temperament that constitute a personality; disposition. **4.** Cosmetics applied esp. to the face. **5.** Materials, such as cosmetics, that an actor uses in portraying a role. **6.** A special examination for a student who has missed or failed a previous examination.

make·weight (māk′wāt′) *n.* **1.** Something added on a scale in order to meet a required weight. **2.** Something added only to fill a lack. **3.** A counterweight; a counterbalance.

make-work (māk′wûrk′) *n.* Work of little value assigned or taken on only to keep someone from being idle.

Ma·khach·ka·la (mə-käch′kə-lä′, -кнәch-) A city of SW Russia on the W coast of the Caspian Sea; founded 1844. Pop. 325,140.

ma·ki·mo·no (mä′kĭ-mō′nō) *n., pl.* **-nos** A horizontal Japanese decorative scroll featuring pictures or calligraphy. [J., scroll : *maki,* rolled + *mono,* thing.]

mak·ing (mā′kĭng) *n.* **1a.** The act of one that makes. **b.** The process of coming into being. **2.** The means of gaining success or realizing potential. **3a.** Something made. **b.** The quantity made at one time. **4a.** The abilities or qualities needed for development. Often used in the plural. **b.** The material or ingredients needed for making or doing something. Often used in the plural. **5. makings** *Informal* The paper and tobacco for rolling a cigarette.

Ma·ki·yiv·ka or **Ma·ke·yev·ka** (mə-kē′əv-kə, mä-kē′yēw-kä) A city of E Ukraine NE of Donetsk. Pop. 425,600.

ma·ko (mä′kō) *n., pl.* **-kos** Either of two large mackerel sharks of the genus *Isurus.* [Maori.]

Mal. *abbr.* **1.** *Bible* Malachi **2.** Malawi **3.** Malaysia

mal– *pref.* **1.** Bad; badly: *maladminister.* **2.** Abnormal; abnormally: *malformation.* [ME < OFr. < Lat. < *male,* badly, and *malus,* bad. See **mel-** in App.]

Mal·a·bar Coast (măl′ə-bär′) A region of SW India between the Arabian Sea and the Western Ghats.

Mal·a·bo (măl′ə-bō′, mä-lä′bō) Formerly **San·ta Is·a·bel** (săn′tə ĭz′ə-bĕl′, sän′tä ē-sä-bĕl′) The cap. of Equatorial Guinea, on Bioko in the Gulf of Guinea. Pop. 30,710.

mal·ab·sorp·tion (măl′əb-sôrp′shən, -zôrp′-) *n.* Defective or inadequate absorption of nutrients from the intestinal tract.

Ma·lac·ca (mə-läk′ə, -lä′kə) *n.* The stem of the rattan palm, used for making canes and umbrella handles. [After *Malacca* (now Melaka), a town of western Malaysia.]

Malacca, Strait of A channel between Sumatra and the Malay Peninsula connecting the Andaman and South China seas.

Mal·a·chi[1] (măl′ə-kī′) A Hebrew prophet of the 6th cent. B.C. [Heb. *Mal'ākî,* my messenger : *mal'āk,* messenger + -*î,* my.]

Mal·a·chi[2] (măl′ə-kī′) *n.* See table at **Bible.** [After MALACHI[1].]

mal·a·chite (măl′ə-kīt′) *n.* A light to dark green carbonate mineral, $Cu_2CO_3(OH)_2$, used as a source of copper and for ornamental stoneware. [ME *melochite* < Lat. *molochītes* < Gk. *molokhītis* < *malakhē, molokhē,* mallow.]

mal·a·col·o·gy (măl′ə-kŏl′ə-jē) *n.* The branch of zoology that deals with mollusks. [Fr. *malacologie,* contraction of *malacozoologie* < NLat. *Malacozōa,* former classification that includes mollusks : Gk. *malakos,* soft + NLat. *-zōa,* pl. of *-zōon,* -zoon.] —**mal′a·col′o·gist** *n.*

mal·ad·ap·ta·tion (măl′ăd-ăp-tā′shən) *n.* Faulty or inadequate adaptation.

mal·a·dap·ted (măl′ə-dăp′tĭd) *adj.* Poorly suited to a particular function or situation.

mal·a·dap·tive (măl′ə-dăp′tĭv) *adj.* **1.** Marked by faulty or inadequate adaptation. **2.** Not promoting adaptation.

mal·ad·just·ed (măl′ə-jŭs′tĭd) *adj.* **1.** Poorly adjusted: *a mal-*

adjusted carburetor. **2.** Inadequately adjusted to the demands or stresses of daily living.

mal·ad·just·ment (măl′ə-jŭst′mənt) *n.* **1.** Faulty or inadequate adjustment. **2.** Inability to adjust to the stresses of daily living or of interpersonal relationships.

mal·ad·min·is·ter (măl′əd-mĭn′ĭ-stər) *tr.v.* **-tered, -ter·ing, -ters** To administer or manage inefficiently or dishonestly. —**mal′ad·min′is·tra′tion** *n.*

mal·a·droit (măl′ə-droit′) *adj.* Marked by a lack of adroitness; inept. ❖ *n.* An inept person. [Fr. : *mal-,* mal- + *adroit,* adroit; see ADROIT.] —**mal′a·droit′ly** *adv.* —**mal′a·droit′ness** *n.*

mal·a·dy (măl′ə-dē) *n., pl.* **-dies 1.** A disease, disorder, or ailment. **2.** An unwholesome condition: *the malady of discontent.* [ME *maladie* < OFr. < *malade,* sick < Lat. *male habitus,* in poor condition : *male,* badly; see **mel-** in App. + *habitus,* p. part. of *habēre,* to hold; see **ghabh-** in App.]

Mal·a·ga (măl′ə-gə) *n.* A sweet fortified wine originally from Málaga, Spain.

Má·la·ga (măl′ə-gə, mä′lä-gä′) A city of S Spain NE of Gibraltar; founded in the 12th cent. B.C. Pop. 523,450.

Mal·a·gas·y (măl′ə-găs′ē) *n., pl.* **Malagasy** or **-gas·ies 1.** A native or inhabitant of Madagascar. **2.** The Austronesian language of the Malagasy. ❖ *adj.* Of or relating to Madagascar, the Malagasy, or their language or culture.

Malagasy Republic See **Madagascar.**

ma·la·gue·ña (mä′lə-gā′nyə) *n.* **1.** A dance native to Málaga, Spain, that is a variety of the fandango. **2.** Any of several Spanish folk tunes, esp. one native to Málaga that is similar to the fandango. [Sp., fem. of *malagueño,* of Málaga < MÁLAGA.]

mal·aise (mă-lāz′, -lēz′) *n.* **1.** A vague feeling of bodily discomfort. **2.** A general sense of depression or unease. [Fr. < OFr. : *mal-,* mal- + *aise,* ease; see EASE.]

Mal·a·mud (măl′ə-məd), **Bernard** 1914–86. Amer. writer whose works include *The Fixer* (1966).

mal·a·mute or **mal·e·mute** (măl′ə-myōōt′) *n.* Any of a breed of powerful dog developed in Alaska as a sled dog. [Short for *malamute dog* < Inupiaq *Malimiut,* a subgroup of the Inupiaq.]

Ma·lang (mə-läng′) A city of E Java, Indonesia, S of Surabaya. Pop. 511,780.

mal·a·pert (măl′ə-pûrt′) *adj.* Impudently bold in speech or manner; saucy. [ME < OFr. : *mal-,* mal- + *apert,* clever, alteration of Lat. *expertus.* See EXPERT.] —**mal′a·pert′** *n.* —**mal′a·pert′ly** *adv.* —**mal′a·pert′ness** *n.*

mal·ap·por·tioned (măl′ə-pôr′shənd, -pōr′-) *adj.* Marked by inappropriate or unfair proportioning of representatives to a legislative body. —**mal′ap·por′tion·ment** *n.*

mal·a·prop (măl′ə-prŏp′) *n.* A malapropism. [After Mrs. *Malaprop,* a character in *The Rivals,* a play by Richard Brinsley Sheridan < MALAPROPOS.]

mal·a·prop·ism (măl′ə-prŏp-ĭz′əm) *n.* **1.** Ludicrous misuse of a word, esp. by confusion with one of similar sound. **2.** An example of such misuse. [< MALAPROP.] —**mal′a·prop′i·an** (-prŏp′ē-ən) *adj.*

mal·a·pro·pos (măl′ăp-rə-pō′) *adj.* Out of place; inappropriate. ❖ *adv.* In an inappropriate or inopportune manner. [Fr. *mal à propos : mal,* badly + *à propos,* to the purpose.]

ma·lar (mā′lər, -lär′) *adj.* Of or relating to the zygomatic bone or the cheek. ❖ *n.* The zygomatic bone. [NLat. *mālāris* < Lat. *māla,* cheekbone.]

Mä·lar·en (mä′lär′ən) A lake of SE Sweden connected by waterway with the Baltic Sea.

ma·lar·i·a (mə-lâr′ē-ə) *n.* **1.** An infectious disease characterized by cycles of chills, fever, and sweating, caused by a protozoan of the genus *Plasmodium* transmitted by the bite of an infected female anopheles mosquito. **2.** *Archaic* Bad or foul air; miasma. [Ital. < *mala aria,* bad air : *mala,* fem. of *malo,* bad (< Lat. *malus;* see **mel-** in App.) + *aria,* air; see ARIA.] —**ma·lar′i·al, ma·lar′i·an, ma·lar′i·ous** *adj.*

ma·lar·key also **ma·lar·ky** (mə-lär′kē) *n. Slang* Exaggerated or foolish talk, usu. intended to deceive. [?]

mal·as·sim·i·la·tion (măl′ə-sĭm′ə-lā′shən) *n.* Incomplete or imperfect assimilation of nutrients by the body.

mal·ate (măl′āt′, mā′lāt′) *n.* A salt or ester of malic acid. [MAL(IC ACID) + -ATE[2].]

Mal·a·thi·on (măl′ə-thī′ŏn′) A trademark used for an organic compound, $C_{10}H_{19}O_6PS_2$, used as an insecticide.

Ma·la·tya (mä′lə-tyä′) A city of E-central Turkey in the Taurus Mts.; cap. of a Hittite kingdom c. 1100 B.C. Pop. 319,700.

Ma·la·wi (mə-lä′wē) Formerly **Ny·as·a·land** (nī-ăs′ə-lănd′, nyä′sä-) A country of SE Africa; achieved independence from Great Britain in 1964. Cap. Lilongwe. Pop. 9,461,000. —**Ma·la′wi·an** *adj. & n.*

Malawi, Lake See **Lake Nyasa.**

Ma·lay (mə-lā′, mā′lā′) *n.* **1.** A member of a people inhabiting Malaysia, the northern Malay Peninsula, and parts of the western Malay Archipelago. **2.** The Austronesian language of the Malays. ❖ *adj.* **1.** Of, relating to, or characteristic of the Malays or their language. **2.** Of or relating to Malaysia, the Malay Peninsula, or the Malay Archipelago. [Obsolete Du. *Malayo* < Malay *Melayu.*] —**Ma·lay′an** *adj. & n.*

Mal·a·ya·lam (măl′ə-yä′ləm) *n.* A Dravidian language spoken

Malaysia

Malcolm X
photographed c. 1964

in the state of Kerala in southwest India.

Malay Archipelago An island group of SE Asia between Australia and the Asian mainland separating the Indian and Pacific oceans.

Ma·lay·o-Pol·y·ne·sian (mə-lā′ō-pŏl′ə-nē′zhən, -shən) *n.* A subgroup of the Austronesian language family. —**Ma·lay′o-Pol′y·ne′sian** *adj.*

Malay Peninsula also **Ma·la·ya** (mə-lā′ə, mā-) A peninsula of SE Asia comprising SW Thailand, W Malaysia, and the island of Singapore.

Ma·lay·sia (mə-lā′zhə, -shə) A country of SE Asia consisting of the S Malay Peninsula and the N part of Borneo; under British rule from 1946 to 1963. Cap. Kuala Lumpur. Pop. 19,489,000. —**Ma·lay′sian** *adj.* & *n.*

Mal·colm X (măl′kəm ĕks′) Orig. Malcolm Little. 1925–65. Amer. activist who as a member of the Black Muslims (1952–63) advocated separatism and Black pride.

mal·con·tent (măl′kən-tĕnt′) *adj.* Dissatisfied with existing conditions. ❖ *n.* **1.** A chronically dissatisfied person. **2.** One who rebels against the established system.

mal de mer (măl′ də mâr′) *n.* Seasickness. [Fr. : *mal*, sickness + *de*, of + *mer*, sea.]

mal·dis·tri·bu·tion (măl′dĭs-trə-byōō′shən) *n.* Faulty distribution or apportionment over an area or among a group.

Mal·dives (môl′dīvz, -dēvz, măl′-) Formerly **Mal·dive Islands** (-dīv, -dēv) An island country in the Indian Ocean SW of Sri Lanka; achieved independence from Great Britain in 1965. Cap. Male. Pop. 246,000. —**Mal·div′i·an** (-dīv′ē-ən), **Mal·di′van** *adj.* & *n.*

male (māl) *adj.* **1a.** Of, relating to, or being the sex that has organs to produce spermatozoa for fertilizing ova. **b.** Characteristic of or appropriate to this sex; masculine. **2.** Virile; manly. **3.** *Botany* **a.** Of, relating to, or being organs that produce gametes capable of fertilizing those produced by female organs. **b.** Bearing stamens but not pistils; staminate. **4.** Designed to be inserted into a recessed part or socket, as an electric plug. ❖ *n.* **1.** One who belongs to the sex that begets young by fertilizing ova. **2.** A man or boy. **3.** *Botany* A plant having only staminate flowers. [ME < OFr. < Lat. *masculus*, dim. of *mās*, male.] —**male′ness** *n.*

Ma·le (mä′lē) The cap. of the Maldives, on **Male,** the chief atoll of the island country. Pop. 46,334.

ma·le·ate (mā′lē-āt′, mə-lē′ət) *n.* A salt or ester of maleic acid. [MALE(IC ACID) + -ATE².]

male chauvinist *n.* A sexist man. —**male chauvinism** *n.*

Mal·e·cite (măl′ə-sīt′) *n.* Variant of Maliseet.

mal·e·dict (măl′ĭ-dĭkt′) *Archaic adj.* Accursed. ❖ *tr.v.* **-dict·ed, -dict·ing, -dicts** To pronounce a curse against. [ME *maledicte* < Lat. *maledictus,* p. part. of *maledīcere,* to curse : *male,* ill; see **mel-** in App. + *dīcere,* to speak; see **deik-** in App.]

mal·e·dic·tion (măl′ĭ-dĭk′shən) *n.* **1a.** The calling down of a curse. **b.** A curse. 2. Slander. —**mal′e·dic′to·ry** (-dĭk′tə-rē) *adj.*

mal·e·fac·tor (măl′ə-făk′tər) *n.* **1.** One that has committed a crime; a criminal. **2.** An evildoer. [ME *malefactour* < Lat. *malefactor* < *malefacere,* to do wrong : *male,* ill; see **mel-** in App. + *facere,* to do; see **dhē-** in App.] —**mal′e·fac′tion** (-făk′shən) *n.*

male fern *n.* A fern (*Dryopteris filix-mas*) having rhizomes and stalks that yield an oleoresin used to expel tapeworms.

ma·lef·ic (mə-lĕf′ĭk) *adj.* **1.** Having or exerting a malignant influence. **2.** Evil; malicious. [Lat. *maleficus* : *male,* ill; see **mel-** in App. + *-ficus,* -fic.]

ma·lef·i·cence (mə-lĕf′ĭ-səns) *n.* **1.** The doing of evil or harm; mischief. **2.** Harmful or evil nature or quality. [Lat. *maleficentia* < *maleficus,* malefic. See MALEFIC.]

ma·lef·i·cent (mə-lĕf′ĭ-sənt) *adj.* Harmful or evil.

ma·le·ic acid (mə-lē′ĭk) *n.* A crystalline acid, $C_4H_4O_4$, used as an oil and fat preservative. [< Fr. *acide maléique,* alteration of *acide malique,* malic acid. See MALIC ACID.]

mal·e·mute (măl′ə-myōōt′) *n.* Variant of malamute.

Ma·len·kov (mə-lĕn′kôf, -lyĭn-kôf′), **Georgi Maximilianovich** 1902–88. Soviet premier (1953–55).

mal·en·ten·du (măl′ŏn-tŏn-dōō′) *n.* A misunderstanding. [Fr. < *mal entendu,* misunderstood : *mal,* badly (< Lat. *male;* see **mel-** in App.) + *entendu,* p. part. of *entendre,* to understand (< OFr.; see INTEND).]

male pattern baldness *n.* A progressive, diffuse loss of scalp hair in men related to the increased levels of androgens that occur after puberty.

ma·lev·o·lence (mə-lĕv′ə-ləns) *n.* **1.** The quality or state of being malevolent. **2.** Malicious behavior. [ME < OFr. *malivolence* < Lat. *malevolentia* < *malevolēns, malevolent-,* malevolent : *male,* badly; see **mel-** in App. + *volēns,* pr. part. of *velle,* to want.]

ma·lev·o·lent (mə-lĕv′ə-lənt) *adj.* **1.** Having or exhibiting ill will; wishing harm to others; malicious. **2.** Having an evil or harmful influence. —**ma·lev′o·lent·ly** *adv.*

mal·fea·sance (măl-fē′zəns) *n.* Misconduct or wrongdoing, esp. by a public official. [AN *malfaisance* < OFr. *malfaisant,* malfeasant, pr. part. of *malfaire,* to do evil < Lat. *malefacere.* See MALEFACTOR.] —**mal·fea′sant** *adj.* & *n.*

mal·for·ma·tion (măl′fôr-mā′shən) *n.* Abnormal or anomalous formation or structure; deformity.

mal·formed (măl-fôrmd′) *adj.* Abnormally or faultily formed.

mal·func·tion (măl-fŭngk′shən) *intr.v.* **-tioned, -tion·ing, -tions** **1.** To fail to function. **2.** To function improperly. ❖ *n.* **1.** Failure to function. **2.** Faulty or abnormal functioning.

Ma·li (mä′lē) A country of W Africa; achieved independence from France in 1960. Cap. Bamako. Pop. 10,462,000. —**Ma′li·an** *adj.* & *n.*

mal·ic acid (măl′ĭk, mā′lĭk) *n.* A crystalline compound, $C_4H_6O_5$, that occurs naturally in many fruits, including apples and cherries, and is used in the aging of wine. [Fr. *(acide) malique* < Lat. *mālum,* apple < Gk. *mēlon, malon.*]

mal·ice (măl′ĭs) *n.* **1.** A desire to harm others or see others suffer. **2.** *Law* The intent, without just cause or reason, to commit a wrongful act that will result in harm to another. [ME < OFr. < Lat. *malitia* < *malus,* bad. See **mel-** in App.]

ma·li·cious (mə-lĭsh′əs) *adj.* Having the nature of or resulting from malice; deliberately harmful; spiteful: *malicious gossip.* —**ma·li′cious·ly** *adv.* —**ma·li′cious·ness** *n.*

malicious mischief *n.* Willful or wanton destruction of another's property.

ma·lign (mə-līn′) *tr.v.* **-ligned, -lign·ing, -ligns** To make evil, harmful, and often untrue statements about; speak evil of. ❖ *adj.* **1.** Evil in disposition, nature, or intent. **2.** Evil in influence; injurious. **3.** Having or showing malice or ill will; malevolent. [ME *malignen,* to attack < OFr. *malignier* < LLat. *malignārī* < Lat. *malignus,* malign. See **genə-** in App.] —**ma·lign′er** *n.* —**ma·lign′ly** *adv.*

ma·lig·nan·cy (mə-lĭg′nən-sē) *n., pl.* **-cies** **1.** also **ma·lig·nance** (-nəns) The state or quality of being malignant. **2.** *Pathology* A malignant tumor.

ma·lig·nant (mə-lĭg′nənt) *adj.* **1.** Showing great malevolence; disposed to do evil. **2.** Highly injurious; pernicious. **3.** *Pathology* **a.** Threatening to life; virulent. **b.** Tending to metastasize; cancerous. Used of a tumor. —**ma·lig′nant·ly** *adv.*

ma·lig·ni·ty (mə-lĭg′nĭ-tē) *n., pl.* **-ties** **1a.** Intense ill will or hatred; great malice. **b.** An act or a feeling of great malice. **2.** The condition or quality of being highly dangerous or injurious.

ma·li·hi·ni (mä′lĭ-hē′nē) *n., pl.* **-nis** *Hawaii* A newcomer to Hawaii. [Hawaiian, stranger; akin to Tahitian *manihini,* visitor, guest, and Maori *manuhiri,* all perh. ult. < Proto-Polynesian **manu,* bird (figuratively applied to humans).]

ma·lines (mə-lēn′) *n.* **1.** also **ma·line** (-lēn′) A thin stiff net woven in a hexagonal pattern and used in dressmaking. **2.** See Mechlin². [Fr., after *Malines* (Mechlin), Belgium.]

Ma·lines (mə-lēnz′, mä-lēn′) See Mechlin¹.

ma·lin·ger (mə-lĭng′gər) *intr.v.* **-gered, -ger·ing, -gers** To feign illness or other incapacity in order to avoid duty or work. [< Fr. *malingre,* sickly.] —**ma·lin′ger·er** *n.*

Ma·lin·ke (mə-lĭng′kē) *n., pl.* **Malinke** or **-kes** **1.** A member of a Mandingo people of Senegal and Gambia. **2.** The Mandingo language of this people.

Mal·i·now·ski (măl′ə-nôf′skē, mä′lĭ-), **Bronislaw Kasper** 1884–1942. Polish-born British anthropologist who maintained that customs and beliefs have specific social functions.

Mal·i·seet (măl′ə-sēt′) or **Mal·e·cite** (-sīt′), *n., pl.* **Maliseet** or **-seets** or **Malecite** or **-cites** **1.** A member of a Native American people inhabiting New Brunswick and northeast Maine. **2.** The Algonquian language of the Maliseet. [Micmac *malisiit,* one who speaks an incomprehensible language.]

mal·i·son (măl′ĭ-sən, -zən) *n. Archaic* A curse. [ME *malisoun* < OFr. *maleiçon* < Lat. *maledictiō* < *maledictiōn-* < *maledictus,* p. part. of *maledīcere,* to speak ill, curse. See MALEDICT.]

mall¹ (môl, măl) *n.* **1.** A large, often enclosed shopping complex with stores and restaurants. **2.** A street lined with shops and closed to vehicles. **3.** A shady public walk or promenade. **4.** *Chiefly Upstate New York* See **median strip.** See Regional Note at **neutral ground.** [After *The Mall* in London, England, originally a pall-mall alley.]

mall² (môl) *n.* Variant of **maul** 1. ❖ *v.* Variant of **maul.**

mal·lard (măl′ərd) *n., pl.* **mallard** or **-lards** A wild duck (*Anas platyrhynchos*) of which the male has a green head and neck. [ME *malarde* < OFr. *mallart* : perh. < *male,* male; see MALE + *-ard,* -ard, or poss. of Gmc. orig.]

Mal·lar·mé (măl′är-mā′), **Stéphane** 1842–98. French poet whose works include *The Afternoon of a Faun* (1876).

Malle (mäl), **Louis** 1932–95. French film director whose works include *Au Revoir les Enfants* (1987).

mal·le·a·ble (măl′ē-ə-bəl) *adj.* **1.** Capable of being shaped, as by hammering. **2.** Easily controlled or influenced; tractable. **3.** Able to adjust to changing circumstances; adaptable. [ME < OFr. < Med.Lat. *malleābilis* < *malleāre,* to hammer < Lat. *malleus,* hammer. See **melə-** in App.] —**mal′le·a·bil′i·ty** *n.* —**mal′le·a·bly** *adv.*

mal·lee (măl′ē) *n.* **1.** Any of several west Australian evergreen shrubs or trees of the genus *Eucalyptus.* **2.** A thicket or growth of these plants. [Wemba-wemba (Aboriginal language of SE Australia) *mali.*]

mal·le·muck (măl′ə-mŭk′) *n.* Any of several sea birds, such as the fulmar, albatross, or shearwater. [Du. *mallemok,* fulmar : *mal,* silly (< MDu.) + *mok,* gull.]

mal·le·o·lus (mə-lē′ə-ləs) *n., pl.* **-li** (-lī′) Either of the two

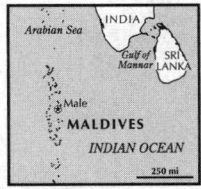

Maldives

Mali

ă	pat	oi	boy
ā	pay	ou	out
âr	care	ŏŏ	took
ä	father	ŏŏ	boot
ĕ	pet	ŭ	cut
ē	be	ûr	urge
ĭ	pit	th	thin
ī	pie	th	this
îr	pier	hw	which
ŏ	pot	zh	vision
ō	toe	ə	about,
ô	paw		item

Stress marks:
′ (primary);
′ (secondary), as in
lexicon (lĕk′sĭ-kŏn′)

rounded protuberances on each side of the ankle. [NLat. < Lat., dim. of *malleus*, hammer. See **melə-** in App.] —**mal·le·o·lar** (-ə-lər) *adj.*

mal·let (măl′ĭt) *n.* **1a.** A short-handled hammer, usu. with a cylindrical head of wood, used chiefly to drive a chisel or wedge. **b.** A tool with a large head, used to strike a surface without damaging it. **2.** *Sports* A long-handled implement used to strike a ball, as in polo. **3.** *Music* A light hammer with a rounded head for striking a percussion instrument. [ME < OFr. *maillet*, dim. of *mail*, maul. See MAUL.]

mal·le·us (măl′ē-əs) *n., pl.* **mal·le·i** (măl′ē-ī′) The hammer-shaped bone that is the outermost of the three bones in the mammalian middle ear. [Lat., hammer. See **melə-** in App.]

Mal·lor·ca (mä-yôr′kä, -lyôr′-) See **Majorca.**

mal·low (măl′ō) *n.* **1.** Any of various plants of the genus *Malva*, having pink or white flowers, palmate leaves, and disklike fruits. **2.** Any of various related plants, such as the rose mallow. [ME *malwe* < OE *mealwe* and < OFr. *malve*, both < Lat. *malva*.]

mall rat *n. Slang* A person, esp. a teenager or young adult, who frequently passes time wandering through shopping malls.

Mal·mö (măl′mō, măl′mœ) A city of S Sweden on the Oresund opposite Copenhagen; passed from Denmark to Sweden in 1658. Pop. 236,684.

malm·sey (mäm′zē) *n., pl.* **-seys** A sweet fortified wine now produced mainly in Madeira. [ME, ult. < Med.Lat. *malvasia, malmasia*, alteration of Med.Gk. *Monemvasia* (Malvasia), a village of S Greece.]

mal·nour·ished (măl-nûr′ĭsht, -nŭr′-) *adj.* Affected by improper nutrition or an insufficient diet.

mal·nour·ish·ment (măl′nûr′ĭsh-mənt, -nŭr′-) *n.* Malnutrition.

mal·nu·tri·tion (măl′nōō-trĭsh′ən, -nyōō-) *n.* Poor nutrition because of an insufficient or poorly balanced diet or faulty digestion or utilization of foods.

mal·oc·clu·sion (măl′ə-klōō′zhən) *n.* **1.** Faulty contact between the upper and lower teeth when the jaw is closed. **2.** An instance of this.

mal·o·dor (măl-ō′dər) *n.* A bad odor; a stench.

mal·o·dor·ous (măl-ō′dər-əs) *adj.* Having a bad odor; foul. —**mal·o′dor·ous·ly** *adv.* —**mal·o′dor·ous·ness** *n.*

ma·lon·ic acid (mə-lō′nĭk, -lŏn′ĭk) *n.* A crystalline acid, CH₂(COOH)₂, used in making barbiturates. [Fr. *(acide) malonique*, alteration of *malique*, malic (acid). See MALIC ACID.]

Mal·o·ry (măl′ə-rē), Sir **Thomas** fl. 1470. English writer of *Le Morte d'Arthur* (1485).

ma·lo·ti (mä-lō′tē) *n.* Plural of **loti.**

Mal·pi·ghi (măl-pē′gē, mäl-), **Marcello** 1628–94. Italian anatomist who discovered the capillary system.

Mal·pigh·i·an corpuscle (măl-pĭg′ē-ən) *n.* **1.** A mass of arterial capillaries enveloped in a capsule and attached to a tubule in the kidney. **2.** A nodule of lymphatic tissue in the spleen. [After Marcello MALPIGHI.]

Malpighian layer *n.* The deepest layer of the epidermis.

Malpighian tube *n.* Any of the excretory tubules leading from the posterior portion of the alimentary canal of insects and other arthropods. [After Marcello MALPIGHI.]

mal·po·si·tion (măl′pə-zĭsh′ən) *n.* An abnormal position.

mal·prac·tice (măl-prăk′tĭs) *n.* **1.** Improper or negligent treatment of a patient, as by a physician, resulting in injury, damage, or loss. **2.** Improper or unethical conduct by the holder of a professional or official position. **3.** The act or an instance of improper practice. —**mal′prac·ti′tion·er** (-tĭsh′ə-nər) *n.*

Mal·raux (măl-rō′, mäl-), **André** 1901–76. French writer and politician who served as minister of culture (1959–69).

malt (môlt) *n.* **1.** Grain, usu. barley, that has been allowed to sprout, used chiefly in brewing and distilling. **2.** An alcoholic beverage brewed from malt. **3.** See **malted milk 2.** ❖ *v.* **malt·ed, malt·ing, malts** —*tr.* **1.** To process (grain) into malt. **2.** To treat or mix with malt or a malt extract. —*intr.* To become malt. [ME < OE *mealt*.]

Mal·ta (môl′tə) An island country in the Mediterranean Sea S of Sicily, comprising the island of **Malta** and two smaller islands; granted to the Knights Hospitalers in 1530, passed to France in 1798 and Great Britain in 1800, and gained independence in 1964. Cap. Valletta. Pop. 364,000.

Malta fever *n.* See **brucellosis 1.**

mal·tase (môl′tās′, -tāz′) *n.* An enzyme that catalyzes the hydrolysis of maltose to glucose.

malt·ed milk (môl′tĭd) *n.* **1.** A soluble powder of dried milk, malted barley, and wheat flour. **2.** A beverage made with this powder by adding milk, ice cream, and flavoring.

Mal·tese (môl-tēz′, -tēs′) *adj.* Of or relating to Malta or its people, language, or culture. ❖ *n., pl.* **Maltese 1.** A native or inhabitant of Malta. **2.** The Semitic language of the people of Malta. **3.** Any of a breed of toy dogs having a long silky white coat. **4.** A Maltese cat.

Maltese cat *n.* A short-haired domestic cat having a silky bluish-gray coat.

Maltese cross *n.* A cross having four equal arms resembling arrowheads joined at the points.

mal·tha (măl′thə) *n.* A black, viscous natural bitumen. [Ult.

< Gk., a mixture of wax and pitch.]

Mal·thus (măl′thəs), **Thomas Robert** 1766–1834. British economist who wrote *An Essay on the Principle of Population* (1798), arguing that population tends to increase faster than food supply, with inevitably disastrous results. —**Mal·thu′sian** (-thōō′zhən, -zē-ən) *adj. & n.* —**Mal·thu′sian·ism** *n.*

malt liquor *n.* A fermented liquor made with malt.

mal·tose (môl′tōs′, -tōz′) *n.* A sugar, C₁₂H₂₂O₁₁·H₂O, formed by the digestion of starch. [Fr. < E. MALT.]

mal·treat (măl-trēt′) *tr.v.* **-treat·ed, -treat·ing, -treats** To treat in a rough or cruel way; abuse. —**mal·treat′ment** *n.*

malt sugar *n.* See **maltose.**

Mal·vern Hills (môl′vərn, mô′) A range of hills of W-central England rising to 425.5 m (1,395 ft).

mal·ver·sa·tion (măl′vər-sā′shən) *n.* Misconduct in public office. [Fr. < *malverser*, to misbehave < OFr. < Lat. *male versārī* : *male*, badly; see **mel-** in App. + *versārī*, to behave; see **wer-²** in App.]

ma·ma or **mam·ma** also **mom·ma** (mä′mə) *n.* **1.** (*also* mə-mä′) *Informal* Mother. **2.** *Slang* **a.** A woman. **b.** A wife. [Of baby-talk orig.]

ma·ma's boy (mä′məz) *n.* A boy or man characterized by unusual closeness to his mother and often by timidity and overly refined manners.

mam·ba (mäm′bə) *n.* Any of several venomous tree snakes of the genus *Dendroaspis* of tropical Africa, esp. *D. angusticeps*, whose bite is often fatal. [Zulu *-mâmbà*.]

Mam·be·ra·mo (mäm′bə-rä′mō) A river of W New Guinea flowing c. 805 km (500 mi) to the Pacific Ocean.

mam·bo (mäm′bō) *n., pl.* **-bos 1.** A dance of Latin American origin, resembling the rumba. **2.** The music for this dance. ❖ *intr.v.* **-boed, -bo·ing, -bos** To perform this dance. [Am.Sp. < *mamboo*, wooden cane, percussion instrument.]

Mam·e·luke (mäm′ə-lōōk′) *n.* A member of a military caste, originally composed of Turkish slaves, that held the Egyptian throne from about 1250 until 1517 and remained powerful until 1811. [Fr. *mameluk* < Ar. *mamlūk*, slave, Mameluke, passive part. of *malaka*, to possess.]

ma·mey (mä-mā′, -mē′) *n., pl.* **-meys 1.** A West Indian tree (*Mammea americana*) having glossy leaves and large edible drupes with toxic seeds. **2.** Its fruit. [Sp. < Arawak or Taino.]

mam·ma¹ (mä′mə) *n.* Variant of **mama.**

mam·ma² (măm′ə) *n., pl.* **mam·mae** (măm′ē) An organ of female mammals that contains milk-producing glands; a mammary gland. [Lat.] —**mam′mate′** (măm′āt′) *adj.*

mam·mal (măm′əl) *n.* Any of various warm-blooded vertebrate animals of the class Mammalia, including humans, characterized by a covering of hair on the skin and, in the female, mammary glands for nourishing the young. [< LLat. *mammālis*, of the breast < Lat. *mamma*, breast.] —**mam·ma′li·an** (mă-mā′lē-ən) *adj. & n.*

mam·mal·o·gy (mă-măl′ə-jē, -mŏl′-) *n.* The branch of zoology that deals with mammals. —**mam′ma·log′i·cal** (măm′ə-lŏj′ĭ-kəl) *adj.* —**mam·mal′o·gist** *n.*

mam·ma·plas·ty or **mam·mo·plas·ty** (măm′ə-plăs′tē) *n., pl.* **-ties** Reconstructive or cosmetic plastic surgery to alter the size or shape of the breast.

mam·ma·ry (măm′ə-rē) *adj.* Of or relating to a breast or mamma.

mammary gland *n.* Any of the milk-producing, typically paired glands in female mammals, consisting of lobes containing alveoli with ducts to convey the milk to an external nipple or teat.

mam·mee apple (mă-mā′, -mē′) *n.* See **mamey.**

mam·mif·er·ous (mă-mĭf′ər-əs) *adj.* Having mammary glands.

mam·mil·la (mă-mĭl′ə) *n., pl.* **-mil·lae** (-mĭl′ē) **1.** A nipple or teat. **2.** A nipple-shaped protuberance. [Lat. *mamilla, mammilla*, dim. of *mamma*, breast.] —**mam′mil·lar′y** (măm′ə-lĕr′ē) *adj.*

mam·mil·late (măm′ə-lāt′) also **mam·mil·lat·ed** (-lā′tĭd) *adj.* **1.** Having nipples or mammillae. **2.** Shaped like a nipple or mammilla. —**mam′mil·la′tion** *n.*

mam·mo·gram (măm′ə-grăm′) *n.* An x-ray image of the breast produced by mammography.

mam·mog·ra·phy (mă-mŏg′rə-fē) *n., pl.* **-phies** X-ray examination of the breasts for early detection of tumors.

Mam·mon (măm′ən) *n.* **1.** *Bible* Riches, avarice, and worldly gain personified as a false god in the Bible. **2.** often **mammon** Material wealth regarded as evil. [ME < LLat. *mammon* < Gk. *mamōnās* < Aram. *māmonā*, riches, prob. < Mishnaic Heb. *māmôn*.]

mam·moth (măm′əth) *n.* **1.** Any of various large hairy extinct elephants of the genus *Mammuthus*, esp. the woolly mammoth. **2.** Something of great size. ❖ *adj.* Of enormous size; huge. [Obsolete Russ. *mamut, mamot*.]

mam·my (măm′ē) *n., pl.* **-mies 1.** Mother. **2.** *Offensive* A Black nursemaid, esp. one formerly in the southern United States. [< dialectal *mam*, var. of MAMA.]

Ma·mo·ré (mä-mə-rā′) A river, c. 965 km (600 mi), of N Bolivia that joins the Beni R. to form the Madeira R.

man (măn) *n., pl.* **men** (měn) **1.** An adult male human. **2.** A human regardless of sex or age; a person. **3.** A human or an adult male human belonging to a specific occupation, nationality, or other category. Often used in combination: *a milkman; a free-*

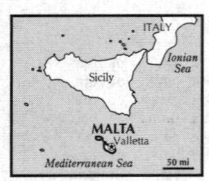

ITALY

Sicily

Ionian Sea

MALTA
Valletta

Mediterranean Sea   50 mi

Malta

man. 4. The human race; humankind. **5.** *Zoology* A member of the genus *Homo,* family Hominidae, order Primates, class Mammalia, characterized by erect posture and an opposable thumb, esp. a member of the species *Homo sapiens,* distinguished by a highly developed brain, the capacity for abstract reasoning, and the ability to communicate by means of organized speech and a variety of symbolic systems. **6.** A male human endowed with qualities considered characteristic of manhood. **7.** *Informal* **a.** A husband. **b.** A male lover or sweetheart. **8. men a.** Workers. **b.** Enlisted personnel of the armed forces. **9.** A male representative, as of a company. **10.** A male servant or subordinate. **11.** *Informal* Used as a familiar form of address for a man. **12.** One who swore allegiance to a lord in the Middle Ages; a vassal. **13.** *Games* Any of the pieces used in a board game, such as chess. **14.** *Nautical* A ship. Often used in combination: *a man-of-war.* **15.** often **Man** *Slang* A person or group felt to be in a position of power or authority. ❖ *tr.v.* **manned, man·ning, mans 1.** To supply with men. **2.** To take stations at. **3.** To fortify or brace. ❖ *interj.* Used as an expletive to indicate intense feeling: *Man! What fun!* —**idioms: as one man 1.** In complete agreement; unanimously. **2.** With no exception. **(one's) own man** Independent in judgment and action. **to a man** Without exception. [ME < OE *mann.* See **man-¹** in App.]

USAGE NOTE Traditionally, *man* and words derived from it have been used to designate any or all of the human race regardless of sex, as in *A man is known by the company he keeps.* Since *woman* cannot be used in this way to refer to any human being, the generic use of *man* has been criticized as sexist. Although a majority of the Usage Panel still finds such usages acceptable, a large percentage of women panelists do not, suggesting that use of such words will likely cause irritation among many of one's readers. • For example, the use of *man* to mean "humankind" in the sentence *If early man suffered from a lack of information, modern man is tyrannized by an excess of it* is acceptable to 81 percent of the Panel; however, a breakdown by sex shows that only 58 percent of the women Panelists accept it, while 92 percent of the men do. A majority of the Panel also accepts compound words derived from generic *man,* such as *man-made,* acceptable to 86 percent (76 percent of the women and 91 percent of the men), and *mankind,* acceptable to 76 percent (63 percent of the women and 82 percent of the men). The Panel finds such compounds less acceptable when applied to women, however; only 66 percent of the Panel members (57 percent of the women and 71 percent of the men) accept the use of the word *manpower* in the sentence *Countries that do not permit women to participate in the work force are at a disadvantage in competing with those that do avail themselves of that extra source of manpower.* • Similar controversy surrounds the generic use of *–man* compounds to indicate occupational and social roles. Thus the use of *chairman* in the sentence *The chairman will be appointed by the Faculty Senate* is acceptable to 67 percent of the Panel (52 percent of the women and 76 percent of the men). Approval rates fall much lower, however, for *–man* compounds applied to women. Only 48 percent (43 percent of the women and 50 percent of the men) accept the phrase *Emily Owen, chairman of the Mayor's Task Force.* Similarly, a majority of the Panel also rejects the verb *man* when used to refer to an activity performed by women. Fifty-six percent of the Panel (61 percent of the women and 54 percent of the men) disapprove of the sentence *Members of the League of Women Voters will be manning the registration desk.* See Usage Notes at **–ess, people.**

Man, Isle of An island of Great Britain in the Irish Sea off the NW coast of England; purchased by Parliament in 1765 and still an autonomous possession of the British crown.

Man. *abbr.* Manitoba

ma·na (mä′nə) *n.* **1.** A supernatural force believed to dwell in a person or sacred object. **2.** Power; authority. [Maori, integrity, charisma, prestige.]

man about town *n., pl.* **men about town** A sophisticated, socially active man who frequents fashionable places.

man·a·cle (măn′ə-kəl) *n.* **1.** A device for confining the hands, usu. consisting of two metal rings that are fastened about the wrists and joined by a metal chain. **2.** Something that confines or restrains. ❖ *tr.v.* **-cled, -cling, -cles** To confine or restrain with or as if with manacles; fetter. [ME < OFr. *manicle* < Lat. *mānicula,* dim. of *manus,* hand. See **man-²** in App.]

man·age (măn′ĭj) *v.* **-aged, -ag·ing, -ag·es** —*tr.* **1.** To direct or control the use of; handle: *manage a complex machine tool.* **2a.** To exert control over. **b.** To make submissive to one's authority, discipline, or persuasion. **3.** To direct the affairs or interests of: *manage a company.* **4.** To succeed in accomplishing or achieving, esp. with difficulty; contrive or arrange: *managed to get a promotion.* —*intr.* **1.** To direct or conduct business affairs. **2.** To continue to get along; carry on. [Ital. *maneggiare* < VLat. **manidiāre* < Lat. *manus,* hand. See **man-²** in App.]

man·age·a·ble (măn′ĭ-jə-bəl) *adj.* That can be managed or controlled: *manageable problems.* —**man′age·a·bil′i·ty, man′age·a·ble·ness** *n.* —**man′age·a·bly** *adv.*

managed care (măn′ĭjd) *n.* A health-care system or plan in which medical costs are controlled by limiting services to a spe-

cific network of medical personnel and requiring authorization by a primary-care physician for most services.

managed competition *n.* A system for determining the best value for delivery of a public service in which public service providers compete with private companies for government contracts.

man·age·ment (măn′ĭj-mənt) *n.* **1.** The act, manner, or practice of managing; handling, supervision, or control. **2.** The person or persons who control or direct a business or other enterprise. **3.** Skill in managing; executive ability.

man·ag·er (măn′ĭ-jər) *n.* **1.** One who handles, controls, or directs, esp.: **a.** One who directs a business or other enterprise. **b.** One who controls resources and expenditures. **2.** One who is in charge of an entertainer's business affairs. **3.** *Sports* **a.** One who is in charge of the training and performance of an athlete or team. **b.** A student who is in charge of the equipment and records of a school or college team. —**man′ag·er·ship′** *n.*

man·a·ge·ri·al (măn′ĭ-jîr′ē-əl) *adj.* Of or relating to a manager or management. —**man′a·ge′ri·al·ly** *adv.*

man·ag·ing editor (măn′ĭ-jĭng) *n.* An editor who supervises and coordinates the editorial activities of a publishing house or publication, such as a newspaper.

Ma·na·gua (mə-näg′wə, mä-nä′gwä) The cap. of Nicaragua, in the W part on the S shore of **Lake Managua;** designated cap. in the 1850s. Pop. 644,588. —**Ma·na′guan** *adj. & n.*

man·a·kin (măn′ə-kĭn) *n.* Any of various small colorful birds of the family Pipridae, found in forests of Central and South America. [Alteration of MANIKIN.]

Ma·na·ma (mə-näm′ə, -nä′mə) or **Al Ma·na·mah** (ăl mə-näm′ə, äl mə-nä′mə) The cap. of Bahrain, on the Persian Gulf; became cap. in 1971. Pop. 136,999.

ma·ña·na (mä-nyä′nə) *adv.* **1.** Tomorrow. **2.** At an unspecified future time. ❖ *n.* An indefinite time in the future. [Sp. < VLat. **(crās) māneāna,* early (tomorrow) < Lat. *māne,* morning.]

Ma·nas·sas (mə-năs′əs) An independent city of NE VA W of Alexandria. The Civil War Battles of Bull Run (called the Battles of Manassas by the Confederates) were fought nearby in Jul. 1861 and Aug. 1862. Pop. 35,135.

Ma·nas·seh (mə-năs′ə) In the Bible, the eldest son of Joseph and the forebear of one of the tribes of Israel.

ma·nat (mä-nät′) *n., pl.* **manat** See table at **currency.** [Azerbaijani and Turkmen < Russ. *moneta,* coin < Lat. *monēta,* coinage. See MONEY.]

man-at-arms (măn′ət-ärmz′) *n., pl.* **men-at-arms** (mĕn′-) A soldier, esp. a medieval cavalryman supplied with heavy arms.

man·a·tee (măn′ə-tē′) *n.* Any of various herbivorous aquatic mammals of the genus *Trichechus,* found in warm coastal waters and having paddlelike front flippers. [Sp. *manatí* < Cariban *manati-.*]

Ma·naus (mə-nous′, mä-) A city of NW Brazil on the Río Negro; founded in the 1660s. Pop. 1,010,544.

Man·ches·ter (măn′chĕs′tər, -chĭ-stər) **1.** A borough of NW England ENE of Liverpool; chartered 1301. The **Manchester Ship Canal** (completed in 1894) affords access for oceangoing vessels. Pop. 432,038. **2.** A city of SE NH on the Merrimack R. N of Nashua; incorp. in 1751. Pop. 107,006.

Manchester terrier *n.* Any of various shorthaired, black-and-tan dogs of a breed that originated in Manchester, England.

man-child (măn′chīld′) *n., pl.* **men-chil·dren** (mĕn′chĭl′drən) A male child; a boy; a son.

man·chi·neel (măn′chĭ-nēl′) *n.* A tropical American tree (*Hippomane mancinella*) having poisonous fruit and a milky vesicant sap. [Fr. *mancenille* < Sp. *manzanilla,* dim. of *manzana,* apple < OSpan. < Lat. *(māla) Matiāna,* (apples) of Matius, possibly after Caius *Matius* Calvena (fl. 1st cent. B.C.), Roman cookbook author.]

Man·chu (măn′chōō, măn-chōō′) *n., pl.* **Manchu** or **-chus 1.** A member of a people native to Manchuria who ruled China during the Qing dynasty. **2.** The Tungusic language of the Manchu. ❖ *adj.* Of or relating to the Manchu or their language or culture.

Man·chu·kuo (măn′chōō′kwō′) also **Man·chu·guo** (măn′chōō′kwō′) A former state of E Asia in Manchuria and E Nei Monggol (Inner Mongolia); est. as a puppet state (1932) by the Japanese and returned to Chinese sovereignty in 1945.

Man·chu·ri·a (măn-chŏŏr′ē-ə) A region of NE China comprising the modern-day provinces of Heilongjiang, Jilin, and Liaoning; homeland of the Manchu people who conquered China in the 17th cent. —**Man·chu′ri·an** *adj. & n.*

Man·chu-Tun·gus (măn′chōō-tŏŏng-gōōz′, -tŭn-, măn-chōō′-) *n.* See **Tungusic.** —**Man′chu-Tun′gus′ic** *adj.*

man·ci·ple (măn′sə-pəl) *n.* A steward or purchaser of provisions, as for a monastery or college. [ME *maunciple* < OFr. *manciple,* bondsman, var. of *mancipe* < Lat. *mancipium,* servant, ownership by acquisition < *manceps, mancip-,* contractor, dealer : *manus,* hand; see **man-²** in App. + *capere,* to take; see **kap-** in App.]

Man·co Ca·pac¹ (mäng′kō kä-päk′) fl. 12th cent. Legendary founder of the Inca dynasty who established Cuzco as the center of what would later become the Inca empire.

Man·co Ca·pac² (mäng′kō kä-päk′) also **Manco In·ca Yu·pan·qui** (ĭng′kə yōō-päng′kē) d. 1544. Last Incan emperor who

manatee
Florida manatee
*Trichechus manatus
latirostris*

mandarin collar

mandarin duck
Aix galericulata

Nelson Mandela
photographed in the early 1990s

mandolin

was crowned (1534) as a puppet ruler by Francisco Pizarro and later mounted an unsuccessful rebellion against Spanish rule.

–mancy *suff.* Divination: *bibliomancy.* [ME < OFr. *-mancie* < LLat. *-mantīa* < Gk. *manteia, -manteia < manteuesthai,* to prophesy < *mantis,* prophet. See **men-**[1] in App.]

Man·dae·an (măn-dē′ən) *n.* Variant of **Mandean.**

man·da·la (mŭn′də-lə) *n.* Any of various geometric designs symbolic of the universe and its powers, used in Hinduism and Buddhism to transform the adept through meditation. [Skt. *maṇḍalam,* circle, perh. < Tamil *muṭalai,* ball.] —**man·dal′ic** (mŭn-dăl′ĭk) *adj.*

Man·da·lay (măn′dl-ā′, măn′dl-ā′) A city of central Myanmar (Burma) on the Irrawaddy R. N of Yangon; cap. of the kingdom of Burma (1860–85). Pop. 532,949.

man·da·mus (măn-dā′məs) *Law n.* A writ issued by a superior court ordering a public official or body or a lower court to perform a specified duty. ❖ *tr.v.* **-mused, -mus·ing, -mus·es** To serve or compel with such a writ. [Lat. *mandāmus,* we order (used in such a writ), first pers. pl. pr. t. of *mandāre,* to order. See **man-**[2] in App.]

Man·dan (măn′dăn) *n., pl.* **Mandan** or **-dans 1.** A member of a Native American people formerly living in south-central North Dakota, with present-day descendants in west-central North Dakota. **2.** The Siouan language of the Mandan. [Fr. *Mandane,* prob. < Dakota *mawátaɴna.*]

man·da·rin (măn′də-rĭn) *n.* **1.** A high public official in the Chinese Empire. **2.** A high government official or bureaucrat. **3.** A member of an elite group, esp. a person having influence or high status in intellectual or cultural circles. **4. Mandarin** The official standard spoken language of China, based on the principal dialect spoken in and around Beijing. **5.** A mandarin orange. ❖ *adj.* **1.** Of, relating to, or resembling a mandarin. **2.** Marked by elaborate and refined language or literary style. [< Sp. *mandarín,* ult. < Skt. *mantrī, mantrin-,* counselor < *mantraḥ,* counsel. See **men-**[1] in App.]

mandarin collar *n.* A narrow upright collar usu. divided in front.

mandarin duck *n.* An Asian duck *(Aix galericulata)* having brightly colored plumage and a crested head.

mandarin orange *n.* **1.** A small spiny evergreen tree *(Citrus reticulata)* native to southeast Asia, having sweet edible fruit. **2.** The small, loose-skinned, orange fruit of this tree.

man·da·tar·y (măn′də-tĕr′ē) *n., pl.* **-ies** A person or nation receiving a mandate.

man·date (măn′dāt′) *n.* **1.** An authoritative command or instruction. **2.** A command or an authorization given by a political electorate to its representative. **3a.** A commission from the League of Nations authorizing a member nation to administer a territory. **b.** A region under such administration. **4.** *Law* **a.** An order issued by a superior court or an official to a lower court. **b.** A contract by which one party agrees to perform services for another without payment. ❖ *tr.v.* **-dat·ed, -dat·ing, -dates 1.** To assign (a colony or territory) to a specified nation under a mandate. **2.** To make mandatory, as by law; decree or require. [Lat. *mandātum* < neut. p. part. of *mandāre,* to order. See **man-**[2] in App.] —**man′da·tor** *n.*

man·da·to·ry (măn′də-tôr′ē, -tōr′ē) *adj.* **1.** Required or commanded by authority; obligatory. **2.** Of, having the nature of, or containing a mandate. **3.** Holding a League of Nations mandate over a territory. ❖ *n., pl.* **-ries** A mandatary.

man-day (măn′dā′) *n.* An industrial unit of production equal to the work one person can produce in a day.

Man·de (măn′dā′) *n., pl.* **Mande** or **-des 1.** A branch of the Niger-Congo language family, spoken in the upper Niger River valley. **2.** A member of a Mande-speaking people. [Mandingo *mandi, mande,* dim. of *ma,* mother.]

Man·de·an also **Man·dae·an** (măn-dē′ən) *n.* **1.** A member of a Gnostic sect in Iraq. **2.** A form of Aramaic used by the Mandeans. [Mandean *mandaya,* having knowledge < *manda,* knowledge < earlier Aram. *manda', madda',* infinitive of *yəda',* to know.] —**Man·de′an** *adj.*

Man·de·kan (măn-dē′kən, măn-dā′-) *n.* See **Mandingo 2.**

Man·de·la (măn-dĕl′ə), **Nelson Rolihlahla** b. 1918. South African president (1994–99) and Black political leader imprisoned for nearly 30 years for his antiapartheid activities. He shared the 1993 Nobel Peace Prize.

Man·del·brot set (măn′dəl-brŏt′) *n.* The set of complex numbers C for which the iteration $z_{n+1} = z_n^2 + C$ produces finite z_n for all n when started at $z_0 = 0$. The boundary of the Mandelbrot set is a fractal. [After Benoit B. *Mandelbrot* (born 1924), Polish-born American mathematician.]

Man·del·stam (măn′dəl-stəm, mən-dyĭl-shtâm′), **Osip Emilyevich** 1892–1938? Russian poet. His early works were highly regarded, but he went unpublished in the Soviet Union after 1933, when he denounced Stalin. He endured years of internal exile and eventually died in a concentration camp.

Man·de·ville (măn′də-vĭl′), **Sir John** Pen name of the unknown compiler of *The Voyage and Travels of Sir John Mandeville, Knight* (c. 1371).

man·di·ble (măn′də-bəl) *n.* **1.** The lower jaw of a vertebrate animal. **2.** Either the upper or lower part of the beak in birds. **3.** Any

of various mouth organs of invertebrates used for seizing and biting food, esp. either of a pair of such organs in arthropods. [ME < OFr. < LLat. *mandibula* < Lat. *mandere,* to chew.] —**man·dib′u·lar** (-dĭb′yə-lər) *adj.*

man·dib·u·late (măn-dĭb′yə-lĭt, -lāt′) *adj.* Having a mandible or mandibles. ❖ *n.* An insect having mandibles.

Man·din·go (măn-dĭng′gō) *n., pl.* **Mandingo** or **-gos** also **-goes 1.** A member of any of various peoples inhabiting a large area of the upper Niger River valley. **2.** A group of related Mande languages including Bambara, Malinke, and Maninka, widely spoken in western Africa. [Mandingo *mandeŋga < mandi,* Mande. See **MANDE.**]

man·do·lin (măn′də-lĭn′, măn′dl-ĭn) *n.* A small lutelike instrument with a typically pear-shaped body and a straight fretted neck. [Fr. *mandoline* < Ital. *mandolino,* dim. of *mandola,* lute < Fr. *mandore* < LLat. *pandūra,* three-string lute < Gk. *pandoura.*] —**man′do·lin′ist** *n.*

man·do·line (măn′də-lĭn′, măn′dl-ĭn′) *n.* **1.** A utensil consisting of a base into which adjustable blades are set, used to slice or cut fruits and vegetables. **2.** A mandolin. [Variant of MANDOLIN.]

man·drag·o·ra (măn-drăg′ər-ə) *n.* See **mandrake 1.** [ME. See MANDRAKE.]

man·drake (măn′drāk′) *n.* **1a.** A southern European plant *(Mandragora officinarum)* once believed to have magical powers because its root resembles the human body. **b.** The root of this plant, containing the poisonous alkaloid hyoscyamine. **2.** See **May apple.** [ME, alteration of *mandragora* < OE < Lat. *mandragorās* < Gk.]

man·drel or **man·dril** (măn′drəl) *n.* **1.** A spindle or an axle used to secure or support material being machined or milled. **2.** A metal rod or bar around which material, such as metal or glass, may be shaped. **3.** A shaft on which a working tool is mounted, as in a dental drill. [Poss. alteration of Fr. *mandrin,* lathe < Provençal *mandre,* axle, crank < O Provençal, beam of a balance < Lat. *mamphur,* bow drill, perh. < Oscan.]

man·drill (măn′drəl) *n.* A large fierce baboon *(Papio sphinx* syn. *Mandrillus sphinx)* of western Africa, having brilliant blue, purple, and scarlet facial markings in the adult male. [MAN + DRILL[4].]

mane (mān) *n.* **1.** The long hair along the top and sides of the neck of certain mammals, such as the horse. **2.** A long thick growth of hair on a person's head. [ME < OE *manu.*]

man-eat·er (măn′ē′tər) *n.* **1.** An animal that eats or is reputed to eat human flesh. **2.** A cannibal. —**man′-eat′ing** *adj.*

ma·nège also **ma·nege** (mă-nĕzh′) *n.* **1.** The art of training and riding horses. **2.** The movements and paces of a trained horse. **3.** A school for teaching equestrianship and training horses. [Fr. < Ital. *maneggio < maneggiare,* to manage. See MANAGE.]

ma·nes or **Ma·nes** (mā′nēz′, mä′nās′) *pl.n.* **1.** The spirits of the dead, regarded as minor supernatural powers in ancient Roman religion. **2.** *(used with a sing. verb)* The revered spirit of one who has died. [ME < Lat. *mānēs,* perh. < *mānis,* good.]

Ma·ni (mä′nēz) also **Ma·ni** (mä′nē) A.D. 216?–276? Persian prophet and founder of Manichaeism.

Ma·net (mə-nā′, mä-), **Edouard** 1832–83. French painter whose works include *Déjeuner sur l'herbe* (1862).

ma·neu·ver (mə-nōō′vər, -nyōō′-) *n.* **1a.** A strategic or tactical military or naval movement. **b.** A large-scale tactical exercise carried out under simulated war conditions. Often used in the plural. **2.** A controlled change in movement or direction of a moving vehicle or vessel. **3.** A movement or procedure involving skill and dexterity. **4a.** A strategic action intended to gain an end. **b.** Artful handling of affairs that is often marked by scheming and deceit. ❖ *v.* **-vered, -ver·ing, -vers** —*intr.* **1.** To carry out a military or naval maneuver. **2.** To make a controlled series of changes in movement or direction toward an objective. **3.** To shift ground; change tactics. **4.** To use stratagems in gaining an end. —*tr.* **1.** To alter the tactical placement of (troops or warships). **2.** To direct through a series of movements or changes in course: *maneuvered the car through traffic.* **3.** To manipulate into a desired position or toward a predetermined goal: *maneuvered him into signing the contract.* See Syns at **manipulate.** [Fr. *manœuvre* < OFr. *maneuvre,* manual work < Med.Lat. *manuopera* < Lat. *manū operārī,* to work by hand : *manū,* ablative of *manus,* hand; see **man-**[2] in App. + *operārī,* to work.] —**ma·neu′ver·a·bil′i·ty** *n.* —**ma·neu′ver·a·ble** *adj.* —**ma·neu′ver·er** *n.*

man Friday *n., pl.* **men Friday** or **men Fridays** An efficient, faithful male aide or employee. [After *Friday,* a character in *Robinson Crusoe,* a novel by Daniel Defoe.]

man·ful (măn′fəl) *adj.* Having or showing the bravery and resoluteness considered characteristic of a man. —**man′ful·ly** *adv.* —**man′ful·ness** *n.*

man·ga·bey (măng′gə-bā′, -bē′) *n., pl.* **-beys** Any of various forest-dwelling monkeys of the genus *Cercocebus* of central Africa. [After *Mangabey,* a region of Madagascar.]

man·ga·nate (măng′gə-nāt′) *n.* A salt containing manganese in its anion, esp. a salt containing the MnO_4 radical.

man·ga·nese (măng′gə-nēz′, -nēs′) *n. Symbol* **Mn** A brittle metallic element, having several allotropes and found in the ores pyrolusite and rhodochrosite and in nodules on the ocean floor. It is alloyed with steel to increase strength and with other metals to form ferromagnetic materials. Atomic number 25; atomic weight

54.9380; melting point 1,244°C; boiling point 1,962°C; specific gravity 7.21 to 7.44; valence 1, 2, 3, 4, 6, 7. See table at **element.** [Fr. *manganèse* < Ital. *manganese* < Med.Lat. *magnēsia*, mineral ingredient of the philosophers' stone. See MAGNESIA.] —**man′ga•ne′sian** (-nē′zhən, -shən) *adj.*

manganese dioxide *n.* A crystalline compound, MnO_2, used as a depolarizer in dry cell batteries.

man•gan•ic (măn-găn′ĭk, măng-) *adj.* Containing manganese, esp. with valence of 3 or 6.

man•ga•nite (măng′gə-nīt′) *n.* A gray to black mineral, $MnO(OH)$, a manganese ore found in North America and Europe.

mangano– or **mangan–** *pref.* Manganese: *manganite.*

man•ga•nous (măng′gə-nəs) *adj.* Relating to bivalent manganese or a compound containing bivalent manganese.

mange (mānj) *n.* Any of several chronic skin diseases of mammals caused by parasitic mites and characterized by skin lesions, itching, and loss of hair. [ME *manjeue* < OFr. *manjue* < *mangier*, to eat. See MANGER.]

man•gel-wur•zel (măng′gəl-wûr′zəl) *n.* A variety of the common beet having a large yellow root and used chiefly as cattle feed. [Ger. *Mangelwurzel*, alteration of *Mangoldwurzel* : *Mangold*, beet (< MHGer. *mānegolt*) + *Wurzel*, root; see **wrād-** in App.]

man•ger (mān′jər) *n.* A trough or an open box holding feed for livestock. [ME < OFr. *mangeoire* < *mangier*, to eat < Lat. *mandūcāre* < *mandūcō*, glutton < *mandere*, to chew.]

man•gle[1] (măng′gəl) *tr.v.* **-gled, -gling, -gles 1.** To mutilate or disfigure by battering, hacking, cutting, or tearing. **2.** To ruin or spoil through ineptitude or ignorance. [ME *manglen* < AN *mangler*, freq. of OFr. *mangoner*, to cut to bits; poss. akin to *mahaignier*, to maim. See MAYHEM.] —**man′gler** *n.*

man•gle[2] (măng′gəl) *n.* **1.** A machine for pressing fabrics by means of heated rollers. **2.** *Chiefly British* A clothes wringer. ❖ *tr.v.* **-gled, -gling, -gles** To press with a mangle. [Du. *mangel* < Ger. < MHGer., dim. of *mange*, mangonel < LLat. *manganum*, catapult. See MANGONEL.]

man•go (măng′gō) *n., pl.* **-goes** or **-gos 1a.** A tropical Asian evergreen tree *(Mangifera indica).* **b.** The edible fruit of this tree, having a smooth rind and sweet juicy flesh. **2.** Any of various pickles, esp. a pickled stuffed sweet pepper. [< Port. *manga*, fruit of the mango tree < Malay *manga* < Tamil *mānkāy* : *mān*, mango tree + *kāy*, fruit.]

man•go•nel (măng′gə-nĕl′) *n.* A military engine used during the Middle Ages for hurling stones and other missiles. [ME < OFr. < Med.Lat. *mangonellus*, dim. of LLat. *manganum*, catapult < Gk. *manganon*, war machine.]

man•go•steen (măng′gə-stēn′) *n.* **1.** A Malaysian evergreen tree *(Garcinia mangostana)* having thick leathery leaves. **2.** The edible berry of this tree. [Malay *manggista*, *mangustan*, var. of *manggis.*]

man•grove (măn′grōv′, măng′-) *n.* **1.** Any of several tropical evergreen trees or shrubs of the genus *Rhizophora*, having stiltlike roots and stems and forming dense thickets along tidal shores. **2.** Any of various similar shrubs or trees, esp. of the genus *Avicennia.* [Prob. Port. *mangue* (< Taino) + GROVE.]

mang•y (mān′jē) *adj.* **-i•er, -i•est 1.** Affected with, caused by, or resembling mange. **2.** Having many worn spots; shabby: *a mangy old fur coat.* **3.** Rundown and filthy; squalid: *mangy tenements.* **4.** Mean; contemptible. —**mang′i•ly** *adv.* —**mang′i•ness** *n.*

man•han•dle (măn′hăn′dəl) *tr.v.* **-dled, -dling, -dles 1.** To handle roughly. **2.** To move or handle by manpower alone.

Man•hat•tan[1] (măn-hăt′n, mən-) A borough of New York City in SE NY, mainly on **Manhattan Island** at the N end of New York Bay; bought from the Manhattan Indians in 1626, supposedly for some $24 worth of merchandise. Pop. 1,537,195. —**Man•hat′tan•ite′** (-ĭt′) *n.*

Man•hat•tan[2] also **man•hat•tan** (măn-hăt′n, mən-) *n.* A cocktail made of sweet vermouth, whiskey, and a dash of bitters. [After MANHATTAN[1], a borough of New York City.]

Manhattan clam chowder *n.* A tomato clam chowder.

man•hole (măn′hōl′) *n.* A hole, usu. with a cover, through which a person may enter a sewer, boiler, or similar structure.

man•hood (măn′ho͝od′) *n.* **1.** The state or time of being an adult male human. **2.** The composite of qualities, such as courage and vigor, often thought to be appropriate to a man. **3.** Adult males considered as a group; men. **4.** The state of being human.

man-hour (măn′our′) *n.* An industrial unit of production equal to the work one person can produce in an hour.

man•hunt (măn′hŭnt′) *n.* An extensive organized search for a person, usu. a fugitive criminal.

Ma•ni (mä′nē) See **Manes.**

ma•ni•a (mā′nē-ə, mān′yə) *n.* **1.** An excessively intense enthusiasm, interest, or desire; a craze. **2.** *Psychology* A manifestation of bipolar disorder, characterized by profuse and rapidly changing ideas, exaggerated gaiety, and decreased sleep. [ME, madness < LLat. < Gk. *maniā*. See **men-**[1] in App.]

–mania *suff.* An exaggerated desire or enthusiasm for: *balletomania.* [< MANIA.]

ma•ni•ac (mā′nē-ăk′) *n.* **1.** An insane person. **2.** A person who has an excessive enthusiasm or desire for something: *a sports maniac.* **3.** A person who acts in a wildly irresponsible way: *maniacs on the highway.* [< LLat. *maniacus*, maniacal < Gk. *maniakos* < *maniā*, madness. See **men-**[1] in App.]

ma•ni•a•cal (mə-nī′ə-kəl) also **ma•ni•ac** (mā′nē-ăk′) *adj.* **1.** Characterized by excessive enthusiasm or excitement. **2.** Marked by insanity, esp. in behavior; insane. —**ma•ni′a•cal•ly** *adv.*

man•ic (măn′ĭk) *adj. Psychology* Relating to, affected by, or resembling mania. [Gk. *manikos*, mad < *maniā*, madness. See MANIA.]

man•ic-de•pres•sive (măn′ĭk-dĭ-prĕs′ĭv) *adj.* Of, relating to, or having bipolar disorder. ❖ *n.* A person with bipolar disorder.

manic-depressive illness *n.* See **bipolar disorder.**

Man•i•chae•an or **Man•i•che•an** (măn′ĭ-kē′ən) also **Man•i•chee** (măn′ĭ-kē′) *n.* A believer in Manichaeism. ❖ *adj.* Of or relating to Manichaeism; dualistic. [< ME *Maniche* < LLat. *Manichaeus* < L.Gk. *Manikhaios* < *Manikhaios*, Manes, the founder of the philosophy.]

Man•i•chae•ism (măn′ĭ-kē′ĭz′əm) also **Man•i•chae•an•ism** (-kē′ə-nĭz′əm) *n.* **1.** The syncretic, dualistic religious philosophy taught by the Persian prophet Manes, combining elements of Zoroastrian, Christian, and Gnostic thought. **2.** A dualistic philosophy dividing the world between good and evil principles or regarding matter as intrinsically evil and mind as intrinsically good.

man•i•cot•ti (măn′ĭ-kŏt′ē) *n.* **1.** Pasta in large-sized tubes. **2.** A dish consisting of such tubes stuffed with meat or cheese, usu. served with a tomato sauce. [Ital., pl. of *manicotto*, muff < *manica*, sleeve < Lat. *manicae*, sleeves < *manus*, hand. See **man-**[2] in App.]

man•i•cure (măn′ĭ-kyo͝or′) *n.* A cosmetic treatment of the fingernails, including shaping and polishing. ❖ *tr.v.* **-cured, -cur•ing, -cures 1.** To trim, clean, and polish (the fingernails). **2.** To clip or trim evenly and closely. [Fr. : Lat. *manus*, hand; see **man-**[2] in App. + Lat. *cūra*, care; see CURE.]

man•i•cur•ist (măn′ĭ-kyo͝or′ĭst) *n.* One who gives manicures.

man•i•fest (măn′ə-fĕst′) *adj.* Clearly apparent to the sight or understanding; obvious. See Syns at **apparent.** ❖ *tr.v.* **-fest•ed, -fest•ing, -fests 1.** To show or demonstrate plainly; reveal. **2.** To be evidence of; prove. **3a.** To record in a ship's manifest. **b.** To display or present a manifest of (cargo). ❖ *n.* **1.** A list of cargo or passengers carried on a ship or plane. **2.** An invoice of goods carried on a truck or train. **3.** A list of railroad cars according to owner and location. [ME *manifeste* < OFr. < Lat. *manufestus*, *manifestus*, caught in the act, blatant, obvious.] —**man′i•fest′ly** *adv.*

man•i•fes•tant (măn′ə-fĕs′tənt) *n.* A participant in a public demonstration.

man•i•fes•ta•tion (măn′ə-fĕ-stā′shən) *n.* **1a.** The act of manifesting. **b.** The state of being manifested. **2.** An indication of the existence, reality, or presence of something. **3a.** One of the forms in which someone or something, as a god or an idea, is revealed. **b.** The materialized form of a spirit. **4.** A public, usu. political demonstration.

manifest destiny *n.* **1.** A policy of imperialistic expansion defended as necessary or benevolent. **2.** often **Manifest Destiny** The 19th-century doctrine that the United States had the right and duty to expand throughout North America.

man•i•fes•to (măn′ə-fĕs′tō) *n., pl.* **-toes** or **-tos** A public declaration of principles, policies, or intentions, esp. of a political nature. ❖ *intr.v.* **-toed, -to•ing, -toes** To issue a manifesto. [Ital. < Lat. *manifestus*, clear, evident. See MANIFEST.]

man•i•fold (măn′ə-fōld′) *adj.* **1.** Many and varied; of many kinds; multiple. **2.** Having many features or forms: *manifold intelligence.* **3.** Being such for a variety of reasons: *a manifold traitor.* **4.** Consisting of or operating several devices of one kind at the same time. ❖ *n.* **1.** A whole composed of diverse elements. **2.** One of several copies. **3.** A pipe or chamber having multiple apertures for making connections. **4.** *Mathematics* A topological space or surface. ❖ *tr.v.* **-fold•ed, -fold•ing, -folds 1.** To make several copies of. **2.** To make manifold; multiply. [ME < OE *manigfeald* : *manig*, many; see MANY + *-feald*, *-fald*, -fold.] —**man′i•fold′ly** *adv.* —**man′i•fold′ness** *n.*

man•i•kin or **man•ni•kin** (măn′ĭ-kĭn) *n.* **1.** A short man. **2.** A mannequin. **3.** An anatomical model of the human body for use in teaching. [Du. *mannekijn* < MDu., dim. of *man*, man. See **man-**[1] in App.]

ma•nil•a or **ma•nil•la** (mə-nĭl′ə) *n.* **1.** often **Manila** A cheroot made in Manila. **2.** See **abaca** 2. **3.** Manila paper. **4.** A light yellow brown.

Manila The cap. of the Philippines, on SW Luzon I. and **Manila Bay,** an inlet of the South China Sea; founded 1571 and seized by US troops in 1898. Pop. 1,728,441.

Manila hemp *n.* See **abaca** 2.

Manila paper *n.* A strong thick paper with a smooth finish, usu. buff in color, made from Manila hemp or similar fibers.

Ma•nin•ka (mə-nĭng′kä, -kē) *n., pl.* **Maninka** or **-kas 1.** A member of a Mandingo people inhabiting Senegal and Mali. **2.** The Mandingo language of this people.

man in the street *n., pl.* **men in the street** The ordinary citizen.

man•i•oc (măn′ē-ŏk′) also **man•i•o•ca** (măn′ē-ō′kə) *n.* See **cassava.** [Fr. < Tupi *mandioca*, *manioca.*]

man•i•ple (măn′ə-pəl) *n.* **1.** An ornamental silk band hung as an ecclesiastical vestment on the left arm. **2.** A subdivision of an ancient Roman legion, containing 60 or 120 men. [ME < OFr. < Lat.

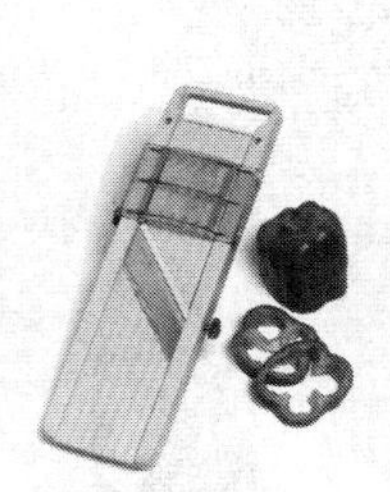

mandoline

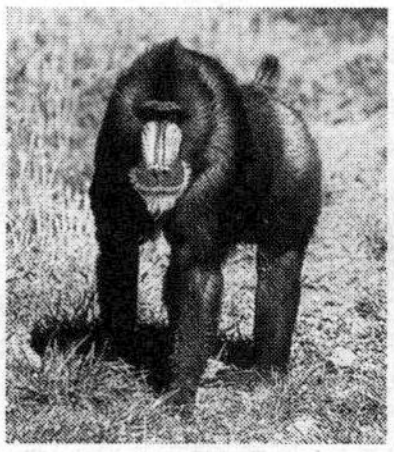

mandrill
male mandrill
Papio sphinx syn. *Mandrillus sphinx*

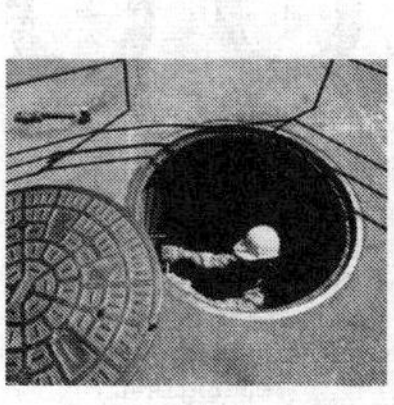

manhole

ă	pat	oi	boy
ā	pay	ou	out
âr	care	o͝o	took
ä	father	o͞o	boot
ĕ	pet	ŭ	cut
ē	be	ûr	urge
ĭ	pit	th	thin
ī	pie	*th*	this
îr	pier	hw	which
ŏ	pot	zh	vision
ō	toe	ə	about, item
ô	paw		

Stress marks:
′ (primary);
′ (secondary), as in
lexicon (lĕk′sĭ-kŏn′)

mannequin
modeling an American
ready-to-wear dress,
c. 1924–28

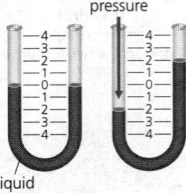

manometer
To calculate pressure in a
U-tube manometer, add
the sum of the readings
above and below zero.
This diagram shows a
reading of 4.

manipulus, handful : *manus*, hand; see **man-²** in App. + *-pulus*, perh. -ful; see **pelə-¹** in App.]

ma·nip·u·la·ble (mə-nĭp′lə-bəl) *adj.* Possible to manipulate: *a manipulable populace.* —**ma·nip′u·la·bil′i·ty** *n.*

ma·nip·u·lar (mə-nĭp′yə-lər) *adj.* **1.** Of or relating to an ancient Roman maniple. **2.** Of or relating to manipulation. ❖ *n.* A soldier in a Roman maniple.

ma·nip·u·late (mə-nĭp′yə-lāt′) *tr.v.* **-lat·ed, -lat·ing, -lates 1.** To arrange, operate, or control by the hands or by mechanical means. **2.** To influence or manage shrewdly or deviously. **3.** To tamper with or falsify for personal gain. **4.** *Medicine* To handle and move in an examination or for therapeutic purposes. —**ma·nip′u·la·bil′i·ty** *n.* —**ma·nip′u·lat′a·ble** *adj.* —**ma·nip′u·la′tive** *adj.* —**ma·nip′u·la′tive·ly** *adv.* —**ma·nip′u·la′tive·ness** *n.* —**ma·nip′u·la′tor** *n.* —**ma·nip′u·la·to′ry** (-lə-tôr′ē, -tōr′ē) *adj.*

SYNONYMS *manipulate, exploit, maneuver* These verbs mean to influence, manage, use, or control to one's advantage by artful or indirect means: *manipulated me into helping him; exploits natural resources; maneuvered me out of one job and into another.*

ma·nip·u·la·tion (mə-nĭp′yə-lā′shən) *n.* **1a.** The act or practice of manipulating. **b.** The state of being manipulated. **2.** Shrewd or devious management, esp. for one's own advantage. [Fr. < *manipule,* handful (as of grain) < Lat. *manipulus,* sheaf, handful. See MANIPLE.]

Man·i·to·ba (măn′ĭ-tō′bə) A province of S-central Canada; admitted to the confederation in 1870. Cap. Winnipeg. Pop. 1,113,898. —**Man′i·to′ban** *adj. & n.*

Manitoba, Lake A lake of S Manitoba, Canada, a remnant of the glacial age Lake Agassiz.

man·i·tou (măn′ĭ-tōo′) also **man·i·tu** (măn′ĭ-tōo′) also **man·i·to** (-tō′) *n., pl.* **-tous** or **-tus** also **-tos 1.** In Algonquian religion, a supernatural power that permeates the world, possessed in varying degrees by both spiritual and human beings. **2.** A deity or spirit. [Fr. < Ojibwa *manitoo.*]

Man·i·tou·lin Islands (măn′ĭ-tōo′lĭn) A group of islands of S Ontario, Canada, in N Lake Huron.

Ma·ni·za·les (măn′ĭ-zä′lĭs, -zäl′ĭs, mä′nē-sä′lĕs) A city of W-central Colombia W of Bogotá. Pop. 283,365.

man·kind (măn′kīnd′) *n.* **1.** The human race; humankind. See Usage Note at **man. 2.** Men as opposed to women.

Man·ley (măn′lē), **Michael** 1924–97. Jamaican politician who served as prime minister (1972–80 and 1989).

man·like (măn′līk′) *adj.* **1.** Resembling a human. **2.** Belonging to or befitting a man.

man·ly (măn′lē) *adj.* **-li·er, -li·est 1.** Having qualities traditionally attributed to a man. **2.** Belonging to or befitting a man. ❖ *adv.* In a manly manner. —**man′li·ness** *n.*

man-made or **man·made** (măn′mād′) *adj.* Made by humans rather than occurring in nature; synthetic: *man-made fibers; a manmade lake.* See Usage Note at **man.**

Mann (măn), **Horace** 1796–1859. Amer. educator who introduced reforms that greatly influenced public education.

Mann (măn, män), **Thomas** 1875–1955. German writer who won the 1929 Nobel Prize for literature.

man·na (măn′ə) *n.* **1.** In the Bible, the food miraculously provided for the Israelites in the wilderness after their flight from Egypt. **2.** Spiritual nourishment of divine origin. **3.** Something of value that a person receives unexpectedly: *viewed the bonus as manna from heaven.* **4.** The dried exudate of certain plants, as that of the Mediterranean ash tree, formerly used as a laxative. **5.** A sweet granular substance excreted on the leaves of plants by certain insects, esp. aphids, and often harvested by ants. [ME < OE < LLat. < Gk. < Aram. *mannā* < Heb. *mān*; akin to Ar. *manna,* to be kind.]

man·nan (măn′ăn′, -ən) *n.* Any of a group of plant polysaccharides that are polymers of mannose. [MANN(OSE) + -AN².]

Man·nar (mə-när′), **Gulf of** An inlet of the Indian Ocean between S India and Sri Lanka.

manned (mănd) *adj.* Transporting, operated by, or performed by a human: *a manned spacecraft.*

man·ne·quin (măn′ĭ-kĭn) *n.* **1.** A life-size full or partial representation of the human body, as for the displaying of clothes; a dummy. **2.** A jointed model of the human body used by artists, esp. to demonstrate the arrangement of drapery. **3.** One who models clothes; a model. [Fr. < OFr., little man, figurine < MDu. *mannekijn.* See MANIKIN.]

man·ner (măn′ər) *n.* **1.** A way of doing something or the way in which a thing is done or happens. See Syns at **method. 2.** A way of acting; bearing or behavior. **3. manners a.** The socially correct way of acting; etiquette. **b.** The prevailing customs, social conduct, and norms of a specific society, period, or group, esp. as the subject of a literary work. **4.** Practice, style, execution, or method in the arts. **5a.** Kind; sort. **b.** Kinds; sorts. —*idioms:* **in a manner of speaking** In a way; so to speak. **to the manner born** Accustomed to a position, custom, or lifestyle from or as if from birth. [ME *manere* < OFr. *maniere* < fem. of *manier,* handmade, skillful < VLat. **manuārius,* convenient, handy < Lat., of the hand < *manus,* hand. See **man-²** in App.]

man·nered (măn′ərd) *adj.* **1.** Having manners of a specific kind:

ill-mannered children. **2a.** Having or showing a certain manner: *a mild-mannered supervisor.* **b.** Artificial or affected. **3.** Of, relating to, or exhibiting mannerisms.

man·ner·ism (măn′ə-rĭz′əm) *n.* **1.** A distinctive behavioral trait; an idiosyncrasy. **2.** Exaggerated or affected style or habit, as in dress. **3. Mannerism** An artistic style of the late 16th century marked by distortion of elements such as scale and perspective. —**man′ner·ist** *n.* —**man′ner·is′tic** *adj.*

man·ner·ly (măn′ər-lē) *adj.* Having or showing good manners. See Syns at **polite.** ❖ *adv.* With good manners; politely. —**man′ner·li·ness** *n.*

Mann·heim (măn′hīm′, män′-) A city of SW Germany at the confluence of the Rhine and Neckar rivers NNW of Stuttgart; chartered 1607. Pop. 318,025.

man·ni·kin (măn′ĭ-kĭn) *n.* Variant of **manikin.**

man·nish (măn′ĭsh) *adj.* **1.** Of, characteristic of, or natural to a man. **2.** Resembling or imitative of a man rather than a woman. —**man′nish·ly** *adv.* —**man′nish·ness** *n.*

man·nite (măn′īt′) *n.* Mannitol. [MANN(A) + -ITE¹.]

man·ni·tol (măn′ĭ-tôl′, -tōl′, -tŏl′) *n.* A crystalline, water-soluble, slightly sweet alcohol, $C_6H_8(OH)_6$, used as a dietary supplement and in tests of renal function. [MANNIT(E) + -OL¹.]

man·nose (măn′ōs′) *n.* A monosaccharide, $C_6H_{12}O_6$, obtained from mannan or by the oxidation of mannitol. [MANN(A) + -OSE².]

ma·no (mä′nō) *n., pl.* **-nos** A hand-held stone or roller for grinding corn or other grains on a metate. [Sp., hand, mano < Lat. *manus,* hand. See MANNER.]

ma·no a ma·no (mä′nō ä mä′nō) *n., pl.* **ma·nos a ma·nos** (mä′nōs ä mä′nōs) **1.** A bullfight in which two rival matadors take turns fighting several bulls each. **2.** A face-to-face confrontation or competitive struggle. [Sp. : *mano,* hand + *a,* to.] —**ma′no a ma′no** *adj. & adv.*

ma·noeu·vre (mə-nōo′vər, -nyōo′-) *n. & v.* Chiefly British Variant of **maneuver.**

man of God *n., pl.* **men of God** A clergyman.

man of letters *n., pl.* **men of letters** A man who is devoted to literary or scholarly pursuits.

man of the cloth *n., pl.* **men of the cloth** A clergyman.

man of the house *n., pl.* **men of the house** The primary male in a household.

man of the world *n., pl.* **men of the world** A sophisticated, worldly man.

man-of-war (măn′ə-wôr′) *n., pl.* **men-of-war** (mĕn′-) **1.** See **warship. 2.** A Portuguese man-of-war.

ma·nom·e·ter (mă-nŏm′ĭ-tər) *n.* **1.** An instrument used for measuring the pressure of liquids and gases. **2.** A sphygmomanometer. [Gk. *manos,* sparse; see **men-²** in App. + -METER.] —**man′o·met′ric** (măn′ə-mĕt′rĭk), **man′o·met′ri·cal** *adj.* —**man′o·met′ri·cal·ly** *adv.* —**ma·nom′e·try** *n.*

man on horseback *n., pl.* **men on horseback 1.** A man, usu. a military leader, whose popularity and power may make him a dictator, as in a crisis. **2.** A dictator.

man·or (măn′ər) *n.* **1a.** A landed estate. **b.** The main house on an estate. **2.** A tract of land in certain North American colonies with hereditary rights granted to the proprietor by royal charter. **3a.** The district over which a lord had domain in medieval western Europe. **b.** The lord's residence in such a district. [ME < OFr. *maneir,* manoir, manor < Lat. *manēre,* to remain.] —**ma·no′ri·al** (mə-nôr′ē-əl, -nōr′-) *adj.*

manor house *n.* **1.** The main house on an estate. **2.** The house of the lord of a manor.

man-o′-war bird (măn′ə-wôr′) *n.* See **frigate bird.**

man·pow·er (măn′pou′ər) *n.* **1.** The power of human physical strength. **2.** Power in terms of the workers available to a particular group or required for a particular task. See Usage Note at **man.**

man·qué (män-kā′) *adj.* Unfulfilled or frustrated in the realization of one's ambitions or capabilities. [Fr. < p. part. of *manquer,* to fail < OFr. < OItal. *mancare* < *manco,* lacking < Lat. *mancus,* maimed, infirm. See **man-²** in App.]

man·rope (măn′rōp′) *n. Nautical* A rope rigged as a handrail on a gangplank or ladder.

man·sard (măn′särd′) *n.* The upper story formed by the lower slope of a mansard roof. [Fr. *mansarde,* after François *Mansart* (1598–1666), French architect.] —**man′sard′ed** *adj.*

mansard roof *n.* A four-sided roof having a double slope on all sides, with the lower slope much steeper than the upper.

manse (măns) *n.* **1.** A Protestant cleric's house and land, esp. of a Presbyterian minister's residence. **2.** A large stately residence. **3.** *Archaic* The dwellings belonging to a householder. [ME *manss,* a manor house < Med.Lat. *mānsa,* a dwelling < Lat., fem. p. part. of *manēre,* to dwell, remain.]

man·ser·vant (măn′sûr′vənt) *n., pl.* **men·ser·vants** (mĕn′sûr′vənts) A male servant, esp. a valet.

Mans·field (mănz′fēld′), **Katherine** 1888–1923. New Zealand-born British writer known for her short stories.

man·sion (măn′shən) *n.* **1.** A large stately house. **2.** A manor house. **3.** *Archaic* **a.** A dwelling; an abode. **b.** *mansions* A separate dwelling in a large house or structure. **4a.** See **house** 10. **b.** Any one of the 28 divisions of the moon's monthly path. [ME, *a* dwelling < OFr. < Lat. *mānsiō, mānsiōn-* < *mānsus,* p. part. of *manēre,* to dwell, remain.]

man·sized (măn′sīzd′) also **man-size** (-sīz′) *adj.* **1.** *Informal* Very large: *a man-sized piece of pie.* **2.** Calling for the strength traditionally attributed to a man: *a man-sized job.*

man·slaugh·ter (măn′slô′tər) *n.* The unlawful killing of one human by another without intent to do injury.

man·slay·er (măn′slā′ər) *n.* One that kills a human.

man·sue·tude (măn′swĭ-tōōd′, -tyōōd′) *n.* Gentleness of manner; mildness. [ME < OFr. < Lat. *mānsuētūdō* < *mānsuētus,* p. part. of *mānsuēscere,* to tame : *manus,* hand; see **man-²** in App. + *suēscere,* to accustom; see **s(w)e-** in App.]

Man·sur (măn-sōōr′), **al-** 712?–775. Arab caliph (754–775) who founded Baghdad in 764.

man·ta (măn′tə) *n.* **1.** A rough-textured cotton fabric or blanket made and used in Spanish America and the southwest United States. **2.** Any of several rays of the family Mobulidae, having a large flattened body and winglike pectoral fins. [Sp., blanket, manta (< its blanketlike shape), alteration of *manto,* cloak, perh. < Lat. *mantēlum,* *mantēlum.*]

man·tai·lored (măn′tā′lərd) *adj.* Of or being a style of women's clothing tailored after the simple unadorned style of men's suits.

manta ray *n.* See **manta** 2.

man·teau (măn-tō′) *n., pl.* **-teaus** (-tōz′) or **-teaux** (-tō′) A loose cloak or mantle. [Fr. < OFr. *mantel.* See MANTLE.]

Man·te·gna (măn-tān′yə, -tē′nyä), **Andrea** 1431–1506. Italian artist noted for his works in the Renaissance style.

man·tel also **man·tle** (măn′tl) *n.* **1.** An ornamental facing around a fireplace. **2.** The protruding shelf over a fireplace. [ME *mantel,* as in *mantiltre,* beam over fireplace opening. See MANTLE.]

man·tel·et (măn′tl-ĭt, măn′lĭt) *n.* **1.** A short cape. **2.** also **mant·let** (măn′lĭt) A mobile screen or shield formerly used to protect besieging soldiers. [ME < OFr., dim. of *mantel,* mantle. See MANTLE.]

man·tel·let·ta (măn′tə-lĕt′ə) *n.* A knee-length sleeveless vestment worn by Roman Catholic prelates. [Ital., prob. < Med.Lat. *mantellētum,* dim. of Lat. *mantellum,* mantle.]

man·tel·piece (măn′tl-pēs′) *n. Chiefly Eastern & Southern US* See **mantel** 1, 2.

man·tel·shelf (măn′tl-shĕlf′) *n., pl.* **-shelves** *Chiefly Southern US* See **mantel** 2.

man·tel·tree (măn′tl-trē′) *n.* A beam, a stone, or an arch that supports the masonry above a fireplace.

man·tic (măn′tĭk) *adj.* Of, relating to, or having the power of divination; prophetic. [Gk. *mantikos* < *mantis,* seer. See **men-¹** in App.] —**man′tic·al·ly** *adv.*

man·ti·core (măn′tĭ-kôr′, -kōr′) *n.* A legendary monster having the head of a man, the body of a lion, and the tail of a dragon or scorpion. [ME *manticores* < Lat. *mantichōra* < Gk. *mantikhōras,* var. of *martiokhōras* < OIran. **martiya-khvāra-,* man-eater : **martiya-,* man; see **mer-** in App. + *-*khvāra-,* eater; akin to Avestan *khuuar-,* to eat.]

man·tid (măn′tĭd) *n.* See **mantis.** [< NLat. *Mantidae,* family name < *Mantis,* type genus < Gk. *mantis,* seer. See MANTIS.]

man·til·la (măn-tē′yə, -tĭl′ə) *n.* **1.** A lightweight lace or silk scarf worn over the head and shoulders, often over a high comb, by women in Spain and Latin America. **2.** A short cloak or cape. [Sp., dim. of *manta,* cape. See MANTA.]

Man·ti·ne·a (măn′tə-nē′ə) An ancient city of S Greece in the E Peloponnesus; site of a Theban defeat of Sparta (362 B.C.).

man·tis (măn′tĭs) *n., pl.* **-tis·es** or **-tes** (-tēz) Any of various predatory insects of the family Mantidae, usu. pale green and having two pairs of walking legs and grasping forelimbs. [Gk., seer. See **men-¹** in App.]

mantis crab *n.* See **squilla.**

man·tis·sa (măn-tĭs′ə) *n.* The decimal part of a logarithm; for example, in the logarithm 2.95424, the mantissa is 0.95424. [Lat., makeweight, perhaps of Etruscan orig.]

mantis shrimp *n.* See **squilla.**

man·tle (măn′tl) *n.* **1.** A loose sleeveless coat worn over outer garments; a cloak. **2.** Something that covers, envelops, or conceals. **3.** Variant of **mantel.** **4.** The outer covering of a wall. **5.** A zone of hot gases around a flame. **6.** A sheath of threads in gas lamps that gives off brilliant illumination when heated by the flame. **7.** *Anatomy* The cerebral cortex. **8.** *Geology* The zone of the earth between the crust and the core. **9.** The outer wall and casing of a blast furnace above the hearth. **10.** The wings, shoulder feathers, and back of a bird when differently colored from the rest of the body. **11.** *Zoology* **a.** A fold or pair of folds of the body wall that lines the shell and secretes the substance that forms the shell in mollusks and brachiopods. **b.** The soft outer wall lining the shell of a tunicate or barnacle. ❖ *v.* **-tled, -tling, -tles** —*tr.* To cover with or as if with a mantle; conceal. —*intr.* **1.** To spread or become extended over a surface. **2.** To become covered with a coating, as froth on a liquid. **3.** To be overspread by blushes or colors. [ME < OE *mentel* and < OFr. *mantel,* both < Lat. *mantellum.*]

Mantle, Mickey Charles 1931–95. Amer. baseball player (1951–68) who hit 536 home runs.

mantle rock *n.* See **regolith.**

mant·let (mănt′lĭt) *n.* Variant of **mantelet** 2.

man-to-man (măn′tə-măn′) *adj.* **1.** Marked by forthrightness and honesty; heart-to-heart. **2.** *Sports* Of, relating to, or being a system of defense in which a defensive player guards a specific offensive player.

Man·toux test (măn-tōō′, măn-) *n.* A tuberculin test in which a small amount of tuberculin is injected under the skin. [After Charles *Mantoux* (1877–1947), French physician.]

man·tra (măn′trə, mŭn′-) *n.* **1.** *Hinduism* A sacred verbal formula repeated in prayer, meditation, or incantation. **2.** A commonly repeated word or phrase. [Skt. *mantraḥ.* See **men-¹** in App.] —**man′tric** *adj.*

man·tu·a (măn′chōō-ə, -tōō-ə) *n.* A gown worn by European women in the 17th and 18th centuries, consisting of a bodice and full skirt cut from a single length of fabric that opens in front to reveal a contrasting underskirt. [Alteration of MANTEAU.]

Man·tu·a (măn′chōō-ə, -tōō-ə) A city of N Italy SSW of Verona; orig. an Etruscan settlement. Pop. 60,932. —**Man′tu·an** *adj.* & *n.*

Ma·nu (mä′nōō, mŭ′-) *n. Hinduism* The primordial father of the human race and sovereign of the earth. [Skt. *Manuḥ* < *manuḥ,* man. See **man-¹** in App.]

man·u·al (măn′yōō-əl) *adj.* **1a.** Of or relating to the hands: *manual skill.* **b.** Done by, used by, or operated with the hands. **c.** Employing human rather than mechanical energy: *manual labor.* **2.** Of, relating to, or resembling a small reference book. ❖ *n.* **1.** A small reference book, esp. one giving instructions. **2.** *Music* A keyboard, as of an organ, played with the hands. **3.** A machine operated by hand. **4.** Prescribed movements in the handling of a weapon, esp. a rifle: *the manual of arms.* [ME < OFr. *manuel* < Lat. *manuālis* < *manus,* hand. See MANUS.] —**man′u·al·ly** *adv.*

manual alphabet *n.* An alphabet used esp. by hearing-impaired people in which finger positions represent the letters.

manual training *n.* A course of training to develop manual dexterity in practical arts, such as woodworking.

ma·nu·bri·um (mə-nōō′brē-əm, -nyōō′-) *n., pl.* **-bri·a** (-brē-ə) **1.** A body part or process shaped like a handle. **2a.** The broad upper division of the sternum with which the clavicle and first two ribs articulate. **b.** The long tapering process of the malleus attached to the central portion of the eardrum. [Lat., handle < *manus,* hand. See **man-²** in App.]

man·u·fac·to·ry (măn′yə-făk′tə-rē) *n., pl.* **-ries** A factory or manufacturing plant. [Prob. MANUFACT(URE) + −ORY.]

man·u·fac·ture (măn′yə-făk′chər) *v.* **-tured, -tur·ing, -tures** —*tr.* **1a.** To make or process (a raw material) into a finished product, esp. by a large-scale industrial operation. **b.** To make or process (a product), esp. with industrial machines. **2.** To create, produce, or turn out in a mechanical manner. **3.** To concoct or invent; fabricate. —*intr.* To make or process goods, esp. in large quantities and by means of industrial machines. ❖ *n.* **1a.** The act, craft, or process of manufacturing products, esp. on a large scale. **b.** An industry in which mechanical power and machinery are employed. **2.** A product that is manufactured. **3.** The making or producing of something. [< Fr., manufacture < OFr. < Med.Lat. *manūfactūra : Lat. *manū,* ablative of *manus,* hand; see **man-²** in App. + Lat. *factūra,* working of a metal < *factus,* p. part. of *facere,* to make. See **dhē-** in App.] —**man′u·fac′tur·a·ble** *adj.* —**man′u·fac′tur·al** *adj.* —**man′u·fac′tur·ing** *n.*

man·u·fac·tured gas (măn′yə-făk′chərd) *n.* A gaseous fuel made from soft coal or various petroleum products.

man·u·fac·tur·er (măn′yə-făk′chər-ər) *n.* A person, an enterprise, or an entity that manufactures something.

man·u·mit (măn′yə-mĭt′) *tr.v.* **-mit·ted, -mit·ting, -mits** To free from slavery or bondage; emancipate. [ME *manumitten* < OFr. *manumitter* < Lat. *manūmittere : manū,* ablative of *manus,* hand; see **man-²** in App. + *mittere,* to send from.] —**man′u·mis′sion** (-mĭsh′ən) *n.* —**man′u·mit′ter** *n.*

ma·nure (mə-nōōr′, -nyōōr′) *n.* Material, esp. dung, often with discarded animal bedding, used to fertilize soil. ❖ *tr.v.* **-nured, -nur·ing, -nures** To fertilize (soil) by applying manure. [< ME *manuren,* to cultivate land < AN *mainouver* < VLat. **manuoperāre,* to work with the hands < Lat. *manus,* hand; see **man-²** in App. + Lat. *operārī,* to work.] —**ma·nur′er** *n.* —**ma·nu′ri·al** *adj.*

ma·nus (mä′nŭs, mä′-) *n., pl.* **manus** The distal part of the forelimb of a vertebrate, including the wrist and hand or the carpus and forefoot. [Lat., hand. See **man-²** in App.]

man·u·script (măn′yə-skrĭpt′) *n.* **1.** A book, document, or other composition written by hand. **2.** A typewritten or handwritten version of a book or other work, esp. the author's own copy, submitted for publication in print. **3.** Handwriting. [< Med.Lat. *manūscrīptum* < neut. of *manūscrīptus,* handwritten : Lat. *manū,* ablative of *manus,* hand; see **man-²** in App. + Lat. *scrīptus,* p. part. of *scrībere,* to write; see **skrībh-** in App.]

Ma·nu·tius (mə-nōō′shəs, -shē-əs, -nyōō′-), **Aldus** 1450–1515. Italian scholar and printer who established (c. 1498) the Aldine Press to publish Greek and Latin classics.

man·ward (măn′wərd) *adv. & adj.* Of, at, or toward humankind. —**man′wards** *adv.*

man·wise (măn′wīz′) *adv.* In a manner characteristic of humans.

Manx (măngks) *adj.* Of or relating to the Isle of Man or its people,

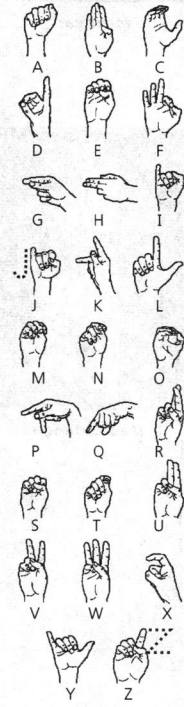

manual alphabet

ă	pat	oi	boy
ā	pay	ou	out
âr	care	ŏŏ	took
ä	father	ōō	boot
ĕ	pet	ŭ	cut
ē	be	ûr	urge
ĭ	pit	th	thin
ī	pie	th	this
îr	pier	hw	which
ŏ	pot	zh	vision
ō	toe	ə	about,
ô	paw		item

Stress marks:
′ (primary);
′ (secondary), as in
lexicon (lĕk′sĭ-kŏn′)

Manx cat

Mao Zedong

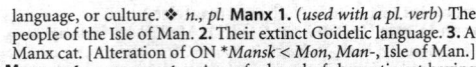

language, or culture. ❖ *n., pl.* **Manx 1.** (*used with a pl. verb*) The people of the Isle of Man. **2.** Their extinct Goidelic language. **3.** A Manx cat. [Alteration of ON *Mansk < *Mon, Man-*, Isle of Man.]

Manx cat or **manx cat** *n.* Any of a breed of domestic cat having short hair and lacking an external tail.

Manx·man (măngks′mən) *n.* A man who is a native or inhabitant of the Isle of Man.

Manx·wom·an (măngks′wŏŏm′ən) *n.* A woman who is a native or inhabitant of the Isle of Man.

man·y (měn′ē) *adj.* **more** (môr, mōr), **most** (mōst) **1.** Being one of a large indefinite number; numerous: *many a child.* **2.** Amounting to or consisting of a large indefinite number: *many friends.* ❖ *n.* (*used with a pl. verb*) **1.** A large indefinite number: *A good many of us.* **2.** The majority of the people; the masses: *"The many fail, the one succeeds"* (Tennyson). ❖ *pron.* (*used with a pl. verb*) A large number of persons or things: *Many came.* —**idiom: as many** The same number of: *moved three times in as many years.* [ME < OE *manig.*]

man-year (măn′yîr′) *n.* A unit measuring the work of one person in a year, based on a standard number of man-days.

man·y·fold (měn′ē-fōld′) *adv.* By many times.

man·y·plies (měn′ĭ-plīz′) *n.* See **omasum.**

man·y-sid·ed (měn′ē-sī′dĭd) *adj.* **1.** Having many sides. **2.** Having many aspects, talents, or interests. —**man′y-sid′ed·ness** *n.*

Man·za·nil·la (măn′zə-nē′yə, -nĭl′ə) *n.* A pale dry sherry from Spain. [Sp., dim. of *manzana,* apple. See MANCHINEEL.]

man·za·ni·ta (măn′zə-nē′tə) *n.* Any of several evergreen shrubs or small trees of the genus *Arctostaphylos* of the Pacific coast of North America, esp. *A. manzanita,* bearing white or pink flowers and producing red berrylike drupes. [Sp., dim. of *manzana,* apple. See MANCHINEEL.]

Man·zo·ni (män-zō′nē, -dzō′-), **Alessandro** 1785–1873. Italian writer best known for *The Betrothed* (1825–27).

MAO *abbr.* monoamine oxidase

MAOI *abbr.* monoamine oxidase inhibitor

Mao·ism (mou′ĭz′əm) *n.* Marxism-Leninism developed in China esp. by Mao Zedong. —**Mao′ist** *adj. & n.*

Mao·ri (mou′rē) *n., pl.* **Maori** or **-ris 1.** A member of a people of New Zealand, of Polynesian-Melanesian descent. **2.** The Austronesian language of the Maori. ❖ *adj.* Of or relating to the Maori or their language or culture.

mao-tai (mou′tī′) *n.* A clear, very strong Chinese liquor distilled from sorghum. [After *Mao-Tai,* a town of Guizhou province, China.]

Mao Ze·dong (mou′ dzŭ′dŏng′) also **Mao Tse-tung** (tsŭ′tŏŏng′) 1893–1976. Chinese political leader who was a founder of the Chinese Communist Party (1921) and proclaimed the People's Republic of China in 1949.

map (măp) *n.* **1a.** A representation, usu. on a plane surface, of a region of the earth or heavens. **b.** Something that suggests such a representation, as in clarity. **2.** *Mathematics* The correspondence of elements in one set to elements in the same set or another set. **3.** *Slang* The human face. **4.** *Genetics* A genetic map. ❖ *tr.v.* **mapped, map·ping, maps 1a.** To make a map of. **b.** To depict as if on a map. **2.** To explore or make a survey of (a region) for the purpose of making a map. **3.** To plan or delineate, esp. in detail; arrange: *mapping out her future.* **4.** *Genetics* To locate (a gene or DNA sequence) in a specific region of a chromosome in relation to known genes or DNA sequences. **5.** *Mathematics* To establish a mapping of (an element or set). —**idioms: put on the map** To make well-known or famous. **wipe off the map** To destroy completely; annihilate. [< ME *mapemounde* < OFr. *mapemond* < Med.Lat. *mappa (mundi),* map (of the world) < Lat., napkin, cloth (on which maps were drawn), perh. of Punic orig.] —**map′pa·ble** *adj.* —**map′per** *n.*

ma·ple (mā′pəl) *n.* **1.** Any of numerous deciduous trees or shrubs of the genus *Acer* of the North Temperate Zone, having opposite, usu. palmate leaves and long-winged fruits. **2.** The wood of any of these trees, esp. that of the sugar maple. **3.** The flavor of the concentrated sap of the sugar maple. [ME < OE *mapul-* (as in *mapultrēo,* maple tree).]

maple sugar *n.* A sugar made by boiling down maple syrup.

maple syrup *n.* **1.** A sweet syrup made from the sap of the sugar maple. **2.** Syrup made from various sugars and flavored with maple syrup or artificial maple flavoring.

map·mak·er (măp′mā′kər) *n.* A person who makes maps; a cartographer. —**map′mak·ing** (-mā′kĭng) *n.*

map·ping (măp′ĭng) *n.* **1.** The act or process of making a map. **2.** *Mathematics* A function.

Ma·pu·che (mä-pŏŏ′chä, -chĕ) *n., pl.* **Mapuche** or **-ches 1.** A member of a South American Indian people inhabiting south-central Chile. **2.** The Araucanian language of the Mapuche. [Mapuche : *mapu,* earth + *che,* people.]

Ma·pu·to (mə-pŏŏ′tō) Formerly **Lou·ren·ço Mar·ques** (lə-rĕn′sō mär′kĕs, lô-rĕn′sŏŏ mär′kĕsh) The cap. of Mozambique, in the S part on the Indian Ocean; founded in the late 18th cent. Pop. 882,601.

ma·quette (mä-kĕt′) *n.* A usu. small model of an intended work, such as a sculpture. [Fr. < Ital. *macchietta,* sketch, dim. of *macchia,* spot < Lat. *macula.*]

ma·qui (mä′kē) *n., pl.* **-quis 1.** A Chilean evergreen shrub (*Aris-*

maraca
pair of maracas

totelia chilensis) bearing edible purple berries. **2.** A Chilean wine made from maqui fruit. [Sp., of Araucanian orig.]

ma·qui·la (mə-kē′lə, mä-kē′lä) *n.* A maquiladora.

ma·qui·la·do·ra (mä-kē′lä-dô′rä) *n.* An assembly plant in Mexico, esp. one along the US border, that finishes products for another company. [Am.Sp., place to pay miller's fee, maquiladora < Sp. *maquila,* miller's portion for milling one's grain < OSpan. < Ar. *makīla,* measured, measure of capacity, fem. passive part. of *kāla,* to measure.]

ma·quil·lage (mä′kē-äzh′) *n.* Cosmetic or theatrical makeup. [Fr. < *maquiller,* to apply makeup < OFr. *macquiller,* to work < ONFr. *maquier* < MDu. *maken,* to make.]

ma·quis (mä-kē′) *n., pl.* **maquis 1.** A dense growth of small trees and shrubs in the Mediterranean area. **2. Maquis a.** A member of the French Resistance that fought against the German occupation forces during World War II. **b.** The French Resistance. [Fr. < Ital. *macchie,* pl. of *macchia,* thicket, spot. See MAQUETTE.]

Ma·qui·sard (mäk′ē-zärd′, -zär′) *n.* See **maquis** 2a. [Fr. < *maquis,* the French underground. See MAQUIS.]

mar (mär) *tr.v.* **marred, mar·ring, mars 1.** To inflict damage, esp. disfiguring damage, on. **2.** To impair the soundness, perfection, or integrity of; spoil. ❖ *n.* A disfiguring mark; a blemish. [ME *merren* < OE *mierran, merran,* to impede.]

mar. *abbr.* **1.** maritime **2.** married

Mar. *abbr.* March

ma·ra (mə-rä′) *n.* Any of various long-eared and long-legged cavies of the genus *Dolichotis,* inhabiting central and southern Argentina. [Am.Sp. *mará,* perh. of Araucanian orig.]

mar·a·bou also **mar·a·bout** (mär′ə-bōō′) *n.* **1.** Any of several large African storks of the genus *Leptoptilos* that have a soft white down on the underside. **2a.** The down of one of these storks or an imitation of it. **b.** A hat or garment trimmed with marabou. **3a.** A raw silk that can be dyed without being separated from its coating of sericin. **b.** A fabric or an article of apparel made from such silk. [Fr. *marabout,* Muslim hermit, marabout. See MARABOUT[1].]

mar·a·bout[1] (mär′ə-bōō′, -bōŏt′) *n.* **1.** A Muslim hermit or saint, esp. in northern Africa. **2.** The tomb of such a hermit or saint. [Fr. < Port. *marabuto* < Ar. *murābiṭ,* posted, stationed, marabout, part. of *rābaṭa,* to be posted, derived stem of *rabaṭa,* to bind, tie.]

mar·a·bout[2] (mär′ə-bōō′) *n.* Variant of **marabou.**

ma·ra·ca (mə-rä′kə) *n.* A Latin-American percussion instrument consisting of a hollow gourd rattle containing pebbles or beans and often played in pairs. [Port. *maracá,* prob. < Tupi.]

Ma·ra·cai·bo (mär′ə-kī′bō, mä′rä-kī′vō) A city of NW Venezuela S of the Gulf of Venezuela at the outlet of **Lake Maracaibo;** founded 1571. Pop. 1,207,513.

Ma·ra·cay (mär′ə-kī′) A city of N Venezuela WSW of Caracas. Pop. 384,782.

Ma·ra·ñón (mär′ən-yōn′, mä′rä-nyōn′) A river flowing c. 1,609 km (1,000 mi) from W-central to NE Peru, where it joins the Ucayali R. to form the Amazon R.

ma·ras·ca (mə-răs′kə) *n.* A European cultivar of the sour cherry tree (*Prunus cerasus*) bearing bitter red fruit from which maraschino is made. [Ital. See MARASCHINO.]

mar·a·schi·no (mär′ə-skē′nō, -shē′-) *n., pl.* **-nos** A cordial made from the fermented juice and crushed pits of the marasca cherry. [Ital. < *marasca,* marasca < *amarasca* < *amaro,* bitter < Lat. *amārus.*]

maraschino cherry *n.* A cherry preserved in a syrup flavored with real or imitation maraschino.

ma·ras·mus (mə-răz′məs) *n.* A progressive wasting of the body, occurring chiefly in young children and associated with insufficient intake or malabsorption of food. [NLat. < Gk. *marasmos* < *marainein,* to waste away. See **mer-** in App.] —**ma·ras′mic** *adj.*

Ma·rat (mə-rä′, mä-), **Jean Paul** 1743–93. Swiss-born French revolutionary who founded (1789) *L'Ami du peuple.*

Ma·ra·tha also **Mah·rat·ta** (mə-rä′tə, -răt′ə) *n., pl.* **Maratha -thas** also **Mahratta** or **-tas** A member of a Hindu people inhabiting Maharashtra in west-central India. [Marathi *Marāṭhā* < Skt. *Mahārāṣṭraḥ,* Maharashtra.]

Ma·ra·thi also **Mah·ra·ti** or **Mah·rat·ti** (mə-rä′tē, -răt′ē) *n.* The principal Indic language of Maharashtra. [Marathi *Marāṭhī* < Skt. *Mahārāṣṭrī* < *Mahārāṣṭraḥ,* Maharashtra.]

mar·a·thon (mär′ə-thŏn′) *n.* **1.** *Sports* **a.** A cross-country footrace of 26 miles, 385 yards (42.195 kilometers). **b.** A long-distance race other than a footrace. **2a.** A contest of endurance. **b.** An event or activity that requires prolonged effort or endurance. [After MARATHON (a messenger having run from there to Athens to announce victory).]

Marathon A plain of ancient Greece NE of Athens; site of a major victory over the Persians (490 B.C.).

mar·a·thon·er (mär′ə-thŏn′ər) *n.* One that participates in a marathon, esp. a marathon runner. —**mar′a·thon′ing** *n.*

ma·raud (mə-rôd′) *v.* **-raud·ed, -raud·ing, -rauds** —*intr.* To rove and raid in search of plunder. —*tr.* To raid or pillage for spoils. [Fr. < *marauder* < *maraud,* tomcat, vagabond.] —**ma·raud′er** *n.*

mar·ble (mär′bəl) *n.* **1a.** A metamorphic rock formed from limestone or dolomite, often irregularly colored by impurities and used esp. in architecture and sculpture. **b.** A piece of this rock. **c.** A sculpture made from this rock. **2.** Something resembling marble, as in hardness. **3.** *Games* **a.** A small hard ball, usu. of glass, used in children's games. **b.** **marbles** (*used with a sing. verb*) Any of various games played with marbles. **4.** **marbles** (*used with a sing. verb*) *Slang* Common sense; sanity. **5.** Marbling. ❖ *tr.v.* **-bled, -bling, -bles** To mottle and streak (paper, for example) with colors and veins in imitation of marble. ❖ *adj.* **1.** Composed of marble. **2.** Resembling marble. [ME < OFr. *marbre* < Lat. *marmor* < Gk. *marmaros*.] —**mar′bly** *adj.*

marble cake *n.* A cake with a streaked or mottled appearance achieved by mixing light and dark batter.

mar•bled (mär′bəld) *adj.* **1.** Made of or covered with marble. **2.** Having a mix of fat and lean, as a cut of meat.

mar•ble•ize (mär′bə-līz′) *tr.v.* **-ized, -iz•ing, -iz•es** To marble.

mar•ble•wood (mär′bəl-wŏod′) *n.* An Asian tree (*Diospyros kurzii*) having mottled gray wood used in cabinetwork.

mar•bling (mär′blĭng) *n.* **1.** A mottling or streaking that resembles marble. **2.** The process or operation of giving something the surface appearance of marble. **3.** The decorative marble patterns printed on page edges and endpapers of books. **4.** Flecks or thin strips of fat, esp. in a cut of meat.

Mar•burg (mär′bûrg′, -bŏork′) A city of W-central Germany N of Frankfurt; site of Europe's first Protestant university (founded 1527). Pop. 76,260.

marc (märk) *n.* **1.** The pulpy residue left after the juice has been pressed from fruits. **2.** Brandy distilled from grape or apple residue. [Fr. < OFr. *march* < *marchier*, to trample. See MARCH¹.]

Marc, Franz 1880–1928. German painter whose expressionist works include *Blue Horses* (1911).

mar•ca•site (mär′kə-sīt′, -zīt′) *n.* **1.** A mineral with the same composition as pyrite, FeS₂, but differing in crystal structure. **2.** An ornament of pyrite, polished steel, or white metal. [ME < Med.Lat. *marcasīta* < Ar. *marqašīṭā* < Aram. *marqašīṯā* < Akkadian *marḥašu* < *marḥašu*, ancient region in the E Iran. plateau.]

mar•ca•to (mär-kä′tō) *Music adv. & adj.* With strong accentuation. ❖ *n., pl.* **-tos** A marcato passage or movement. [Ital., p. part. of *marcare*, to mark, accent < OItal. See DEMARCATION.]

Mar•ceau (mär-sō′), **Marcel** b. 1923. French mime whose most famous character is Bip, a sad-faced clown.

mar•cel (mär-sĕl′) *n.* A hairstyle with deep regular waves made by a curling iron. ❖ *v.* **-celled, -cell•ing, -cels** —*tr.* To style (the hair) in a marcel. —*intr.* To make a marcel. [After *Marcel Grateau* (1852–1936), French hairdresser.]

Mar•cel•lus (mär-sĕl′əs), **Marcus Claudius** 268?–208 B.C. Roman general in the Second Punic War.

mar•ces•cent (mär-sĕs′ənt) *adj. Botany* Withering but not falling off, as a blossom. [Lat. *marcēscēns, marcēscent-*, p. part. of *marcēscere*, inchoative of *marcēre*, to wither.]

march¹ (märch) *v.* **marched, march•ing, march•es** —*intr.* **1.** To walk steadily and rhythmically forward in step with others. **2a.** To proceed directly and purposefully: *marched in and demanded to see the manager.* **b.** To progress steadily onward; advance: *Time marches on.* **3.** To be arranged in an orderly fashion that suggests steady rhythmical progression. **4.** To participate in an organized walk, as for a public cause. —*tr.* **1.** To cause to move or otherwise progress in a steady rhythmical manner: *march soldiers into battle.* **2.** To traverse by progressing steadily and rhythmically: *They marched the route in a day.* ❖ *n.* **1.** The act of marching, esp.: **a.** The steady forward movement of troops. **b.** A long tiring journey on foot. **2.** Steady forward movement or progression: *the march of time.* **3.** A regulated pace: *quick march.* **4.** The distance covered within a certain period of time by marching: *a week's march away.* **5.** *Music* A composition in regularly accented, usu. duple meter that can accompany marching. **6.** An organized walk or procession by a group of people for a specific cause or issue. —*idioms:* **on the march** Advancing steadily; progressing. **steal a march on** To get ahead of, esp. by quiet enterprise. [ME *marchen* < OFr. *marchier*, of Gmc. orig. See **merg-** in App.]

march² (märch) *n.* **1.** The border or boundary of a country or an area of land; a frontier. **2.** A tract of land bordering on two countries and claimed by both. ❖ *intr.v.* **marched, march•ing, march•es** To have a common boundary. [ME < OFr. *marche*, of Gmc. orig. See **merg-** in App.]

March *n.* The third month of the year in the Gregorian calendar. See table at **calendar.** [ME < AN < Lat. *Mārtius (mēnsis)*, (month) of Mars < *Mārs, Mārt-*, Mars.]

March. *abbr.* marchioness

Marche¹ (märsh) A historical region and former province of central France; part of the crown lands after 1531.

Mar•che² (mär′kā) or **Mar•ches** (-chĭz) A region of E-central Italy extending from the E slopes of the Apennines to the Adriatic Sea; colonized by Rome in the 3rd cent. B.C.

Mär•chen (mâr′ḵHən) *n., pl.* **Märchen** A folktale or fairy story. [Ger. < MHGer. *merechyn*, short verse narrative, dim. of *mære*, narrative < OHGer. *märi*, famous, narrative.]

march•er¹ (mär′chər) *n.* One that marches, esp. for a cause.

march•er² (mär′chər) *n.* One who lives in a border district.

---

mar•che•sa (mär-kā′zə, -kĕ′zä) *n., pl.* **-se** (-zā, -zĕ) **1.** The wife or widow of a marchese. **2.** An Italian noblewoman ranking above a countess and below a princess. **3.** Used as the title for such a noblewoman. [Ital., fem. of *marchese*, marchese. See MARCHESE.]

mar•che•se (mär-kā′zā, -kĕ′zĕ) *n., pl.* **-si** (-zē) **1.** An Italian nobleman ranking above a count and below a prince. **2.** Used as the title for such a nobleman. [Ital. < Med.Lat. *(comes) marcēnsis*, (count) of the border < *marca*, border region, of Gmc. orig. See **merg-** in App.]

march•ing orders *pl.n.* Orders to move on or depart.

mar•chio•ness (mär′shə-nĭs, mär′shə-nĕs′) *n.* **1.** The wife or widow of a marquis. **2.** A noblewoman ranking above a countess and below a duchess. **3.** Used as a title for such a noblewoman. [Med.Lat. *marchiōnissa*, fem. of *marchiō, marchiōn-*, marquis < *marca*, boundary, of Gmc. orig. See **merg-** in App.]

march•land (märch′lănd′) *n.* A borderland.

march•pane (märch′pān′) *n. Archaic* Marzipan. [Perh. obsolete Fr. *marcepain* < Ital. *marzapane*, marzipan. See MARZIPAN.]

Mar•cion•ism (mär′shə-nĭz′əm) *n.* A Christian heresy of the second and third centuries A.D. that rejected the Old Testament and denied the incarnation of God in Jesus as a human. [After *Marcion* (died c. A.D. 160), Pontic merchant and heretic in Rome.] —**Mar′cion•ite′** (-shə-nīt′) *n.*

Mar•co•ni (mär-kō′nē), **Guglielmo** 1874–1937. Italian engineer and inventor who shared a 1909 Nobel Prize.

Marconi rig *n.* See Bermuda rig. [After Guglielmo MARCONI (< its resemblance to early aerials used by him).]

Mar•cos (mär′kōs), **Ferdinand Edralin** 1917–89. Philippine president and prime minister (1965–86).

Mar•cus Au•re•li•us An•to•ni•nus (mär′kəs ô-rē′lē-əs ăn′tə-nī′nəs) A.D. 121–180. Philosopher and emperor of Rome (161–180) noted for his *Meditations.*

Mar•cu•se (mär-kŏo′zə), **Herbert** 1898–1979. German-born Amer. philosopher who wrote *Eros and Civilization* (1955).

Mar del Pla•ta (mär′ dĕl plä′tə, -tä) A city of E-central Argentina on the Atlantic Ocean SSE of Buenos Aires. Pop. 519,707.

Mar•di Gras (mär′dē grä′) *n.* **1a.** Shrove Tuesday, celebrated in many places with carnivals, masquerades, and parades. **b.** A carnival period coming to a climax on this day. **2.** An occasion of great festivity and merrymaking. [Fr. : *mardi*, Tuesday + *gras*, fat (< the feasting on Mardi Gras before Lenten fasting).]

Mar•duk (mär′dook) *n. Mythology* The chief Babylonian god.

mare¹ (mâr) *n.* A female horse or the female of other equine species. [ME, alteration of OE *mȳre* (influenced by forms of *mearh*, horse).]

ma•re² (mä′rā) *n., pl.* **-ri•a** (-rē-ə) *Astronomy* Any of the large dark areas on the moon, Mars, or other planets. [Lat., sea. See **mori-** in App.]

ma•re clau•sum (mä′rā klou′səm, klô′-) *n.* A navigable body of water under the jurisdiction of one nation and closed to all others. [NLat. : Lat. *mare*, sea + Lat. *clausum*, closed.]

ma•re li•be•rum (mä′rā lē′bə-room′) *n.* A navigable body of water open to navigation by vessels of all nations. [NLat. *mare līberum* : Lat. *mare*, sea + Lat. *līberum*, free.]

Ma•ren•go (mä-rĕng′gō) *adj.* Prepared with tomatoes, mushrooms, garlic, onion, and white wine: *veal Marengo.* [After *Marengo*, a village of NW Italy.]

ma•re nos•trum (mä′rā nō′strəm) *n.* A navigable body of water under the jurisdiction of one nation or shared by two or more nations. [Lat., the Mediterranean : *mare*, sea + *nostrum*, our.]

mare's nest (mârz) *n., pl.* **mare's nests** or **mares' nests 1.** A hoax or fraud. **2.** An extraordinarily complicated situation.

mare's-tail (mârz′tāl′) *n., pl.* **mare's-tails** or **mares'-tails** (mârz′tālz′) **1.** A cosmopolitan aquatic herb (*Hippuris vulgaris*) having minute flowers and linear whorled leaves. **2.** A long narrow cirrus cloud with a flowing appearance.

Mar•fan syndrome (mär′făn) *n.* A hereditary disorder principally affecting connective tissue, manifested by excessive bone elongation and joint flexibility. [After Antonin Bernard Jean *Marfan* (1858–1942), French pediatrician.]

Mar•gar•et of An•jou (mär′gə-rət, -grət; ăn-jŏo′, äN-zhŏo′) 1430–82. Queen of Henry VI of England who led the Lancastrians in the Wars of the Roses.

Margaret of Na•varre (nə-vär′, nä-) 1492–1549. Queen of Navarre (1527–49) who wrote the *Heptameron.*

Margaret of Val•ois (văl-wä′) 1553–1615. Queen consort whose marriage (1572) to Henry of Navarre, later Henry IV of France, was dissolved in 1599.

mar•gar•ic (mä-gär′ĭk) *adj.* Resembling pearl; pearly. [< Gk. *margaron*, pearl. See MARGARINE.]

margaric acid *n.* A synthetic crystalline fatty acid, C₁₇H₃₄O₂.

mar•ga•rine also **mar•ga•rin** (mär′jər-ĭn) *n.* A fatty solid butter substitute of hydrogenated vegetable oils, emulsifiers, and other ingredients. [Fr. < Gk. *margaron*, pearl, prob. back-formation < *margaritēs*. See MARGARITE.]

mar•ga•ri•ta (mär′gə-rē′tə) *n.* A cocktail made with tequila, an orange-flavored liqueur, and lime or lemon juice. [Sp. < the name *Margarita*, Margaret.]

mar•ga•rite (mär′gə-rīt′) *n.* **1.** A rock formation that resembles

Guglielmo Marconi

ă	pat	oi	boy
ā	pay	ou	out
âr	care	ŏŏ	took
ä	father	ōō	boot
ĕ	pet	ŭ	cut
ē	be	ûr	urge
ĭ	pit	th	thin
ī	pie	*th*	this
îr	pier	hw	which
ŏ	pot	zh	vision
ō	toe	ə	about,
ô	paw		item

Stress marks:
′ (primary);
′ (secondary), as in
lexicon (lĕk′sĭ-kŏn′)

Marie Antoinette
detail from a 1786 portrait
attributed to Élisabeth
Vigée-Lebrun

beads, found in glassy igneous rocks. **2.** *Archaic* A pearl. [Ult. < Gk. *margarītēs*, pearl, prob. of Iran. orig.]

mar•gay (mär′gā, mär-gā′) *n., pl.* **-gays** A spotted Central and South American wildcat (*Felis wiedi*) resembling a small long-tailed ocelot. [Fr. < Port. *maracajá* < Tupi.]

mar•gin (mär′jĭn) *n.* **1.** An edge and the area immediately adjacent to it; a border. See Syns at **border. 2.** The blank space bordering the written or printed area on a page. **3.** A limit in a condition or process, beyond or below which something is no longer possible or acceptable. **4.** An amount allowed beyond what is needed. **5.** A measure, quantity, or degree of difference. **6.** *Economics* **a.** The minimum return that an enterprise may earn and still pay for itself. **b.** The difference between the cost and the selling price of securities or commodities. **c.** The difference between the market value of collateral and the face value of a loan. **7.** An amount in money, or represented by securities, deposited by a customer with a broker as a provision against loss on transactions made on account. **8.** *Botany* The border of a leaf. ❖ *tr.v.* **-gined, -gin•ing, -gins 1.** To provide with a margin. **2.** To be a margin to; border. **3.** To inscribe or enter in the margin of a page. **4.** *Economics* **a.** To add margin to: *margin up a brokerage account.* **b.** To deposit margin for. **c.** To buy or hold (securities) by depositing or adding to a margin. [ME < OFr. < Lat. *margō, margin-.* See **merg-** in App.] —**mar′gined** *adj.*

mar•gin•al (mär′jə-nəl) *adj.* **1.** Of, relating to, located at, or constituting a margin, border, or edge. **2.** Being adjacent geographically: *states marginal to Canada.* **3.** Written or printed in the margin of a book: *marginal notes.* **4.** Barely within a lower standard or limit of quality. **5.** *Economics* **a.** Having to do with enterprises that produce goods or are capable of producing goods at a rate that barely covers production costs. **b.** Relating to commodities thus manufactured and sold. **6.** *Psychology* Relating to or located at the fringe of consciousness. ❖ *n.* One that is considered to be at a lower or outer limit, as of social acceptability. —**mar′gin•al′i•ty** (-jə-năl′ĭ-tē) *n.* —**mar′gin•al•ly** *adv.*

mar•gi•na•li•a (mär′jə-nā′lē-ə) *pl.n.* Notes in the margin or margins of a book. [NLat., neut. pl. of Med.Lat. *marginālis,* marginal < Lat. *margō, margin-,* margin. See MARGIN.]

mar•gin•al•ize (mär′jə-nə-līz′) *tr.v.* **-ized, -iz•ing, -iz•es** To relegate or confine to a lower or outer limit or edge, as in society. —**mar′gin•al•i•za′tion** (-lĭ-zā′shən) *n.*

mar•gin•ate (mär′jə-nāt′) *tr.v.* **-at•ed, -at•ing, -ates 1.** To provide with or be a margin to; border. **2.** To add margin to (a stock portfolio). ❖ *adj.* **marginate** (-nĭt, -nāt) also **mar•gin•at•ed** (-nā′tĭd) *Biology* Having a border or an edge of distinctive color or pattern. —**mar′gin•a′tion** *n.*

mar•grave (mär′grāv′) *n.* **1.** The lord or military governor of a medieval German border province. **2.** Used as a hereditary title for certain princes in the Holy Roman Empire. [Prob. MDu. *marcgrāve* : *marc,* march, border; see **merg-** in App. + *grāve,* count (perh. ult. < Gk. *grapheus,* scribe; see **gerbh-** in App.).] —**mar′gra•vi•al** (-grā′vē-əl) *adj.*

mar•gra•vi•ate (mär-grā′vē-ĭt, -āt′) also **mar•gra•vate** (mär′grə-vāt′) *n.* The territory governed by a margrave.

mar•gra•vine (mär′grə-vēn′) *n.* **1.** The wife or widow of a margrave. **2.** Used as a title for such a woman. [Prob. MDu. *marcgravinne,* fem. of *marcgrāve,* margrave. See MARGRAVE.]

Mar•gue•the II (mär-grā′tə) b. 1940. Queen of Denmark who inherited the throne (1972) after the Danish constitution was amended to permit the accession of a woman.

mar•gue•rite (mär′gə-rēt′, -gyə-) *n.* **1.** Either of two plants, *Chrysanthemum frutescens* of the Canary Islands or *C. leucanthemum* of Eurasia, having white or pale yellow daisylike flowers. **2.** Any of several similar or related plants. [Fr. < OFr. *margarite,* daisy, pearl < Lat. *margarīta,* pearl < Gk. *margarītēs.* See MARGARITE.]

ma•ri•a (mä′rē-ə) *n. Astronomy* Plural of **mare**[2].

ma•ri•a•chi (mä′rē-ä′chē) *n., pl.* **-chis 1.** A street band in Mexico. **2a.** The music performed by such a band. **b.** A musician belonging to such a band. [Am.Sp., perh. < Fr. *mariage,* marriage (so called because the music may have originated at weddings in Jalisco, a state of W-central Mexico). See MARRIAGE.]

Mar•i•an[1] (mâr′ē-ən, mär′-) *adj.* **1.** Of or relating to the Virgin Mary, her cult, or her theology. **2.** Of or relating to Mary I of England or Mary Queen of Scots.

Mar•i•an[2] (mâr′ē-ən, mär′-) *adj.* Of Gaius Marius.

Mar•i•an•a Islands (mâr′ē-ăn′ə, mär′-, mä′rē-ä′nə) An island group and US commonwealth in the W Pacific Ocean E of the Philippines. Guam, the largest island of the group, is independent of the commonwealth, known as the **Northern Mariana Islands.** Pop. 43,345.

Ma•ri•a The•re•sa (mə-rē′ə tə-rā′sə, -zə) 1717–80. Queen of Hungary and Bohemia (1740–80).

Mar•i•co•pa (mär′ĭ-kō′pə) *n., pl.* **Maricopa** or **-pas 1.** A member of a Native American people sharing reservation lands with the Pima in south-central Arizona. **2.** The Yuman language of the Maricopa.

mar•i•cul•ture (mär′ĭ-kŭl′chər) *n.* Cultivation of marine organisms in their natural habitats, usu. for commercial purposes. [Lat. *mare, mari-,* sea; see **mori-** in App. + CULTURE.] —**mar′i•cul′tur•al** *adj.*

marigold

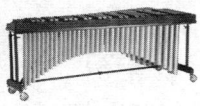

marimba

marionette

Ma•rie An•toi•nette (mə-rē′ ăn′twə-nĕt′) 1755–93. Queen of France (1774–93) as the wife of Louis XVI; she was executed by the Revolutionary Tribunal.

Marie Byrd Land A region of W Antarctica E of the Amundsen Sea; claimed for the US in 1929.

Marie de Mé•di•cis (də mā′dē-sēs′) 1573–1642. Queen of France as the wife (1600–10) of Henry IV and regent (1610–17) for her son Louis XIII.

Marie Louise 1791–1847. Austrian archduchess and empress of the French as the second wife of Napoleon.

mar•i•gold (mär′ĭ-gōld′, mâr′-) *n.* **1.** Any of various American plants of the genus *Tagetes,* widely cultivated for their showy yellow or orange flowers. **2.** Any of several plants related to the marigold or having similar flowers. [ME : *Mari,* Mary (< LLat. *Maria;* see MARY[1]) + *golde,* marigold (< OE *golde;* prob. akin to GOLD).]

mar•i•jua•na also **mar•i•hua•na** (mär′ə-wä′nə) *n.* **1.** The cannabis plant. **2.** A preparation made from the dried flower clusters and leaves of the cannibis plant, usu. smoked or eaten to induce euphoria. [Sp. *marijuana.*]

ma•rim•ba (mə-rĭm′bə) *n.* A large wooden percussion instrument with resonators, resembling a xylophone. [Port., of Bantu orig.; akin to Kimbundu *ma-rimba* : *ma-,* pl. n. pref. + *-rimba,* xylophone, hand piano.]

Mar•in (mär′ĭn), **John** 1870–1953. Amer. painter noted for his expressionist watercolors.

ma•ri•na (mə-rē′nə) *n.* A boat basin that has docks, moorings, and other facilities for small boats. [Ital. and Sp., seashore < fem. of *marino* < Lat. *marīnus.* See MARINE.]

mar•i•nade (mär′ə-nād′) *n.* A liquid mixture, usu. of vinegar or wine and oil with various spices and herbs, in which meat, fowl, fish, or vegetables are soaked before cooking. ❖ *tr.v.* (mär′ə-nād′) **-nad•ed, -nad•ing, -nades** To soak (food) in such a mixture; marinate. [Fr., prob. < Ital. *marinare,* to marinate < Lat. *(aqua) marīna,* sea(water), brine, pickle < fem. of *marīnus,* of the sea. See MARINE.]

ma•ri•na•ra (mär′ə-när′ə, mär′ə-när′ə) *adj.* Being or served with a sauce of tomatoes, onions, garlic, and spices: *spaghetti marinara.* ❖ *n.* Marinara sauce. [Ital. *(alla) marinara,* in sailor style, fem. of *marinaro,* sailor < *marino,* marine. See MARINA.]

mar•i•nate (mär′ə-nāt′) *v.* **-nat•ed, -nat•ing, -nates** —*tr.* To soak (food) in a marinade. —*intr.* To become marinated. [Prob. < Ital. *marinato,* p. part. of *marinare,* to marinate. See MARINADE.] —**mar′i•na′tion** *n.*

ma•rine (mə-rēn′) *adj.* **1a.** Of or relating to the sea. **b.** Native to, inhabiting, or formed by the sea: *marine animals.* **2.** Of or relating to shipping or maritime affairs. **3.** Of or relating to sea navigation; nautical. See Syns at **nautical. 4.** Of or relating to the Marine Corps. ❖ *n.* **1a.** A soldier serving on a ship or at a naval installation. **b. Marine** A member of the Marine Corps. **2.** The mercantile or naval ships or shipping fleet of a country. **3.** The governmental department in charge of naval affairs in some nations. **4.** A painting or photograph of the sea. [ME *marin, marine* < OFr. < Lat. *marīnus* < *mare,* sea. See **mori-** in App.]

Marine Corps *n.* A branch of the US armed forces composed chiefly of amphibious troops under the authority of the Secretary of the Navy.

mar•i•ner (mär′ə-nər) *n.* One who operates or helps operate a ship. [ME < OFr. *marinier* < *marin,* marine. See MARINE.]

mar•i•ner's compass (mär′ə-nərz) *n.* A large magnetic compass used aboard ships, consisting of a compass card suspended in a gimbal-mounted bowl.

Ma•ri•net•ti (mär′ə-nĕt′ē, mä′rē-nĕt′tē), **Emilio Filippo Tommaso** 1876–1944. Italian writer who founded futurism with the publication of his 1909 manifesto.

Mar•i•ol•a•try (mär′ē-ŏl′ə-trē) *n.* Excessive veneration or worship of the Virgin Mary. —**Mar′i•ol′a•ter** *n.* —**Mar′i•ol′a•trous** *adj.*

Mar•i•ol•o•gy also **Mar•y•ol•o•gy** (mär′ē-ŏl′ə-jē) *n.* The theological study of the Virgin Mary and her role in the Incarnation. —**Mar′i•o•log′i•cal** *adj.*

Mar•i•on (mär′ē-ən, mâr′-), **Frances** 1887–1973. Amer. screenwriter whose screenplays include *The Big House* (1930).

Marion, Francis Called "the Swamp Fox." 1732?–95. Amer. Revolutionary noted for his guerrilla tactics against the British.

mar•i•o•nette (mär′ē-ə-nĕt′) *n.* A jointed puppet manipulated from above by strings or wires attached to its limbs. [Fr. *marionnette* < OFr., musical instrument, dim. of *mariole,* the Virgin Mary < dim. of *Marie,* Mary (influenced by the name *Marion*) < LLat. *Maria.* See MARY[1].]

mar•i•po•sa lily (mär′ə-pō′zə, -sə) *n.* Any of several bulbous plants of the genus *Calochortus* of western North America, having variously colored tuliplike flowers. [Prob. < Am.Sp. *mariposa* < Sp., butterfly < *María pósate,* Mary alight! : *María,* Mary + *pósate,* second pers. sing. reflexive imper. of *posar,* to perch (< LLat. *pausāre,* to pause < Lat. *pausa,* pause).]

Mar•ist (mär′ĭst, mâr′-) *n.* **1.** A member of the Society of Mary, a congregation of Roman Catholic missionary priests founded in 1824. **2.** A member of the Little Brothers of Mary, a Roman Catholic teaching congregation founded in 1817. [Fr. *Mariste* < *Marie,* the Virgin Mary < LLat. *Maria.* See MARIONETTE.]

mar•i•tal (mär′ĭ-tl) *adj.* **1.** Of or relating to marriage: *marital* *problems.* **2.** Of or relating to a husband. [Lat. *marītālis* < *marītus,* married.] —**mar′i•tal•ly** *adv.*

mar•i•time (măr′ĭ-tīm′) *adj.* **1.** Of, relating to, or adjacent to the sea. **2.** Of or relating to marine shipping or navigation. See Syns at **nautical. 3.** Of or resembling a mariner. [Lat. *maritimus* < *mare, mari-,* sea. See **mori-** in App.]

Maritime Alps A range of the SW Alps on the French-Italian border rising to 3,299.2 m (10,817 ft).

Maritime Provinces Nova Scotia, New Brunswick, and Prince Edward Island. —**Mar′i•tim′er** *n.*

Ma•ri•tsa (mə-rēt′sə) A river of W Bulgaria and W Turkey flowing c. 483 km (300 mi) to the Aegean Sea.

Ma•ri•u•pol′ (mä′rē-o͞o′pôl′) Formerly **Zhdanov** (zhdä′nəf) A city of SE Ukraine on the Sea of Azov; founded 1779. Pop. 522,900.

Mar•i•us (mâr′ē-əs, măr′-), **Gaius** 155?–86 B.C. Roman general and politician who lost a civil war (88) to Sulla.

mar•jo•ram (mär′jər-əm) *n.* Any of several aromatic Eurasian or Mediterranean plants of the genus *Origanum,* esp. *O. majorana* or *O. vulgare,* having opposite leaves used as seasoning. [ME *majorane* < OFr. < Med.Lat. *maiorana.*]

mark[1] (märk) *n.* **1.** A visible trace or impression, such as a line or spot. **2.** A sign made in lieu of a signature. **3.** A written or printed symbol used for punctuation; a punctuation mark. **4a.** A number, letter, or symbol used to indicate various grades of academic achievement: *got a mark of 95.* **b.** An appraisal; a rating. Often used in the plural: *earned high marks.* **5a.** An inscription, name, stamp, label, or seal placed on an article to signify ownership, quality, manufacture, or origin. **b.** A notch in an animal's ear or hide indicating ownership. **6.** *Nautical* **a.** A knot or piece of material placed at various measured lengths on a sounding line to indicate the depth of the water. **b.** A Plimsoll mark. **7a.** A distinctive trait or property: *Trust is the mark of friendship.* **b.** A lasting effect: *The experience had left its mark.* **c. Mark** A particular mode, brand, size, or quality of a product. **8.** A recognized standard of quality: *schoolwork that is not up to the mark.* **9a.** Importance; prominence: *"a fellow of no mark nor likelihood"* (Shakespeare). **b.** Notice; attention: *a matter unworthy of mark.* **10.** A target: *"A mounted officer would be a conspicuous mark"* (Ambrose Bierce). **11.** Something that one wishes to achieve; a goal. **12.** An object or point that serves as a guide. **13.** *Slang* The intended victim of a swindler; a dupe. **14a.** *Sports* The place from which racers begin and sometimes end their contest. **b.** A point reached or gained: *the halfway mark of the race.* **c.** An unsurpassed achievement; a record. **15.** *Sports* **a.** A strike or spare in bowling. **b.** A stationary ball in lawn bowling; a jack. **16.** A boundary between countries. **17.** A tract of land in medieval England and Germany held in common by a community. **18.** *Computer Science* A character or feature in a file, record, or data stream used to locate a specific point or condition. ❖ *v.* **marked, mark•ing, marks** —*tr.* **1a.** To make a visible trace or impression on, as with a spot, line, or dent: *marked a square on the board.* **b.** To form, make, or depict by making a mark. **c.** To supply with natural markings: *gray fur that is marked with stripes.* **2a.** To single out or indicate by or as if by a mark. **b.** To distinguish or characterize: *marked the occasion with celebrations.* **c.** To make conspicuous: *a concert marking the composer's birthday.* **3.** To set off or separate by or as if by a line or boundary: *marked off our property.* **4.** To attach or affix identification, such as a price tag, to. **5.** To evaluate (academic work) according to a scale of letters or numbers; grade. **6a.** To give attention to; notice: *Mark my words: they are asking for trouble.* **b.** To take note of in writing; write down: *marked the appointment on my calendar.* **c.** *Sports & Games* To record (the score) in various games. **7.** *Sports* To guard (an opponent), as in soccer. —*intr.* **1.** To make a visible impression: *This pen will mark under water.* **2.** To receive a visible impression: *The floor marks easily.* **3.** *Sports & Games* To keep score. **4.** To determine academic grades. **5.** *Archaic* To pay attention; notice. ***—phrasal verbs:*** **mark down** To mark for sale at a lower price. **mark up 1.** To deface by covering with marks. **2.** To mark for sale at a higher price. ***—idioms:*** **beside the mark** Beside the point; irrelevant. **mark time 1.** To move the feet alternately in the rhythm of a marching step without advancing. **2.** To suspend progress for the time being; wait in readiness. **3.** To function in an apathetic or ineffective manner. [ME < OE *mearc.* See **merg-** in App.]

mark[2] (märk) *n.* **1.** An English and Scottish monetary unit that was equal to 13 shillings and 4 pence. **2.** Any of several European units of weight that were equal to about 8 ounces (227 grams), used esp. for weighing gold and silver. **3.** A deutsche mark. **4.** A markka. [ME < OE *marc.* See **merg-** in App. Sense 3, transl. of Ger. *Mark.* Sense 4, transl. of Finn. *markka,* markka.]

Mark[1] *n.* See table at **Bible.**

Mark[2] *n.* In Arthurian legend, a king of Cornwall who was the husband of Iseult and the uncle of her lover Tristan.

Mark, Saint. Disciple of Saint Peter and author of the second Gospel in the New Testament.

mar•ka (mär′kä) *n.* See table at **currency.** [Serbo-Croatian < Ger. *Mark,* mark < MHGer. *marc, marke,* stamped precious metal bar, half-pound of silver or gold. See **merg-** in App.]

Mark An•to•ny (ăn′tə-nē) or **Mark An•tho•ny** (ăn′thə-nē) Orig. Marcus Antonius. 83?–30 B.C. Roman politician and soldier whose love affair with Cleopatra split the triumvirate he had formed with Octavian and Lepidus and led to war. Antony and Cleopatra were defeated in 31 B.C.

mark•down (märk′doun′) *n.* **1.** A reduction in price. **2.** The amount by which a price is reduced.

marked (märkt) *adj.* **1.** Having one or more distinguishing marks. **2.** Clearly defined and evident; noticeable: *a marked limp.* **3.** Singled out, esp. for a dire fate. **4.** *Linguistics* Explicitly characterized by a particular linguistic feature, esp. by contrast with another word or form not so characterized. For example, *lioness* is marked for gender, whereas *lion* is not. —**mark′ed•ly** (mär′kĭd-lē) *adv.* —**mark′ed•ness** *n.*

mark•er (mär′kər) *n.* **1.** One that marks or serves as a mark, as: **a.** A bookmark. **b.** A tombstone. **c.** A milestone. **2.** An implement, esp. a felt-tipped pen, used for marking or writing. **3.** One who marks objects, esp. for industrial purposes. **4.** One who grades student papers. **5.** *Sports* **a.** A device, such as a line, set on a playing field and showing the playing or scoring position. **b.** A player who guards an opponent, as in soccer. **6.** *Games* **a.** One that keeps score in various games. **b.** A score in a game. **7.** *Slang* A written, signed promissory note. **8.** A genetic marker. **9.** *Medicine* A physiological substance, such as human chorionic gonadotropin, that when present in abnormal amounts in the serum may indicate disease, as that caused by a malignancy. **10.** *Linguistics* An element that indicates grammatical class or function; a derivational or inflectional morpheme.

mar•ket (mär′kĭt) *n.* **1.** A public gathering held for buying and selling merchandise. **2.** A place where goods are offered for sale. **3.** A store or shop that sells a particular type of merchandise: *a vegetable market.* **4a.** The business of buying and selling a specified commodity: *the soybean market.* **b.** A market price. **c.** A geographic region considered as a place for sales. **d.** A subdivision of a population considered as buyers. **5.** The opportunity to buy or sell; extent of demand for merchandise. **6a.** An exchange for buying and selling stocks or commodities. **b.** The entire enterprise of buying and selling commodities and securities. ❖ *v.* **-ket•ed, -ket•ing, -kets** —*tr.* **1.** To offer for sale. **2.** To sell. —*intr.* **1.** To deal in a market. **2.** To buy household supplies: *marketed for dinner.* ***—idioms:*** **in the market** Interested in buying. **on the market 1.** Available for buying. **2.** Up for sale. [ME < ONFr. < VLat. **marcātus* < Lat. *mercātus* < p. part. of *mercārī,* to buy < *merx, merc-,* merchandise.]

mar•ket•a•ble (mär′kĭ-tə-bəl) *adj.* **1.** Fit to be offered for sale, as in a market: *marketable produce.* **2.** In demand by buyers or employers; salable: *marketable skills.* —**mar′ket•a•bil′i•ty** *n.*

market basket *n.* **1.** A grocery cart. **2.** A group of products or services in a specific market, esp. when considered in terms of its fluctuating cost in determining a consumer price index.

market economy *n.* An economy that operates by voluntary exchange in a free market and is not planned or controlled by a central authority; a capitalistic economy.

mar•ket•er (mär′kĭ-tər) also **mar•ket•eer** (-kĭ-tîr′) *n.* One that sells goods or services in or to a market, esp. one that markets a specified commodity: *a major wine marketer.*

market fund *n.* See **index fund.**

mar•ket•ing (mär′kĭ-tĭng) *n.* **1.** The act or process of buying and selling in a market. **2.** The commercial functions involved in transferring goods from producer to consumer. **3.** The act or business of promoting sales of a product, as by advertising and packaging.

market order *n.* An order to buy or sell stocks or commodities at the prevailing market price.

mar•ket•place (mär′kĭt-plās′) *n.* **1.** An open area or square in a town where a public market or sale is set up. **2.** The world of business and commerce. **3.** A situation or place in which values, opinions, and ideas are put forward.

market price *n.* The prevailing price at which merchandise, securities, or commodities are sold.

market research *n.* The gathering and evaluation of data regarding consumers' preferences for products and services.

market value *n.* The amount that a seller may expect to obtain for merchandise, services, or securities in the open market.

Mark•ham (mär′kəm) A town of S Ontario, Canada, NNE of Toronto. Pop. 173,383.

Markham, Beryl 1903–86. British aviator who was the first to fly solo across the Atlantic Ocean from E to W (1936).

Markham, (Charles) Edwin 1852–1940. Amer. poet best known for "The Man with the Hoe" (1899).

Markham, Mount A peak, 4,353 m (14,272 ft), of Victoria Land, Antarctica; discovered in 1902.

mar•khor (mär′kôr) *n.* A large wild Himalayan goat *(Capra falconeri)* having spirally curved horns and a long mane in the male. [Pers. *mārkhōr* : *mār,* snake (< Avestan *mairiia-,* treacherous; see **mel-** in App.) + *-khōr,* eater (< OIran. **-khvāra-*; see MANTICORE).]

mark•ing (mär′kĭng) *n.* **1a.** A making or giving of a mark. **b.** A mark or marks made. **2.** The characteristic pattern of coloration of a plant or animal.

mark•ka (mär′kä′) *n.* See table at **currency.** [Finn. < Swed. *mark,* a mark of money. See **merg-** in App.]

markhor
male markhor
Capra falconeri

ă pat	oi boy
ā pay	ou out
âr care	o͝o took
ä father	o͞o boot
ĕ pet	ŭ cut
ē be	ûr urge
ĭ pit	th thin
ī pie	*th* this
îr pier	hw which
ŏ pot	zh vision
ō toe	ə about, item
ô paw	

Stress marks:
′ (primary);
′ (secondary), as in
lexicon (lĕk′sĭ-kŏn′)

Mar·ko·va (mär-kō′və, mär′kə-və), Dame **Alicia** b. 1910. British ballerina known esp. for her performance in *Giselle.*

marks·man (märks′mən) *n.* A man skilled in shooting at a target. —**marks′man·ship′** *n.*

marks·wom·an (märks′wŏŏm′ən) *n.* A woman skilled in shooting at a target.

mark·up (märk′ŭp′) *n.* **1.** A raise in the price of an item for sale. **2.** An amount added to a cost price in calculating a selling price, esp. one taking into account overhead and profit. **3.** A session of a US congressional committee at which a legislative bill is put into final form. **4a.** The collection of stylistic instructions written on a manuscript that is to be typeset. **b.** *Computer Science* The collection of tags describing the specifications of an electronic document, as for formatting.

markup language *n. Computer Science* A coding system, such as HTML, used to structure, index, and link text files.

marl (märl) *n.* A loose deposit consisting of a mixture of clays and calcium carbonate, and used to fertilize acidic soils. ❖ *tr.v.* **marled, marl·ing, marls** To fertilize with marl. [ME *marle* < OFr. < Med.Lat. *margila, marla,* dim. of Lat. *marga,* marl, of Celt. orig.] —**marl′y** *adj.*

Marl·bor·ough (märl′bər-ə, -brə, môl′-), 1st Duke of. See John **Churchill.**

Mar·ley (mär′lē), **Robert Nesta ("Bob")** 1945–81. Jamaican musician and songwriter who, with his group the Wailers, made reggae popular internationally.

Bob Marley

mar·lin[1] (mär′lĭn) *n.* Any of several large marine game fishes of the genera *Makaira* and *Tetrapturus,* having an elongated spearlike upper jaw. [Short for MARLINESPIKE.]

mar·lin[2] (mär′lĭn) *n.* Variant of **marline.**

mar·line also **mar·lin** (mär′lĭn) *n. Nautical* A light rope made of two loosely twisted strands. [ME < MDu. *marlijn,* alteration (influenced by *lijn,* line) of *marling* < *marren,* to tie.]

mar·line·spike also **mar·lin·spike** (mär′lĭn-spīk′) or **mar·ling·spike** (-lĭng-spīk′) *n. Nautical* A pointed metal spike, used to separate strands of rope or wire in splicing.

mar·lite (mär′līt′) *n.* Marlstone. —**mar·lit′ic** (-lĭt′ĭk) *adj.*

Mar·lowe (mär′lō), **Christopher** 1564–93. English playwright and poet whose works include *Tamburlaine* (c. 1587).

marl·stone (märl′stōn′) *n.* A rock containing clay materials and calcium and magnesium carbonates, with approximately the same composition as marl.

mar·ma·lade (mär′mə-lād′) *n.* A clear jellylike preserve made from the pulp and rind of fruits, esp. citrus fruits. [Fr. *marmelade* < Port. *marmelada* < *marmelo,* quince, alteration of Lat. *melimēlum,* a kind of sweet apple < Gk. *melimēlon : meli,* honey; see **melit-** in App. + *mēlon,* apple.]

marmalade box *n.* See **genipap.**

marmalade plum *n.* See **sapote.**

Mar·ma·ra (mär′mər-ə), **Sea of** A sea of NW Turkey between Europe and Asia connected to the Black Sea through the Bosporus and to the Aegean through the Dardanelles.

mar·mite (mär′mīt, mär-mēt′) *n.* **1a.** A large covered earthenware or metal cooking pot. **b.** A small covered earthenware casserole that holds an individual serving. **2.** A petite marmite. [Fr. < OFr., hypocritical, marmite (poss. because the food is hidden inside) : *marm-;* akin to *marmouser,* to murmur + *mite,* cat (of imit. orig.).]

Mar·mo·la·da (mär′mō-lä′də, -dä) A peak, 3,344.3 m (10,965 ft), in the Dolomite Alps of NE Italy.

mar·mo·re·al (mär-môr′ē-əl, -mōr′-) also **mar·mo·re·an** (-ē-ən) *adj.* Resembling marble, as in hardness. [< Lat. *marmoreus < marmor,* marble.] —**mar·mo′re·al·ly** *adv.*

mar·mo·set (mär′mə-sĕt′, -zĕt′) *n.* Any of various small, clawed monkeys of the genera *Callithrix* and *Cebuella* of the American tropics, having tufted ears and long tails. [ME *marmusette,* a small monkey < OFr. *marmouset,* grotesque figurine, alteration of *marmotte,* marmot. See MARMOT.]

mar·mot (mär′mət) *n.* Any of various burrowing rodents of the genus *Marmota,* having short legs and ears and short bushy tails. [Fr. *marmotte* < OFr., perh. < *marmotter,* to mumble, prob. of imit. orig.]

marmot
Alpine marmot
Marmota marmota

Marne (märn) A river of NE France flowing c. 523 km (325 mi) to the Seine R. near Paris; scene of heavy fighting in World War I and World War II.

Mar·o·nite (mär′ə-nīt′) *n.* A member of a Christian Uniat church, chiefly of Lebanon, the liturgy of which is in Syriac. [Med.Lat. *marōnīta,* after *Maro,* 4th-cent. A.D. Syrian religious leader.] —**Mar′o·nite′** *adj.*

ma·roon[1] (mə-rōōn′) *tr.v.* **-rooned, -roon·ing, -roons** **1.** To put ashore on a deserted island or coast and intentionally abandon. **2.** To abandon or isolate with little hope of ready rescue or escape: *marooned by the blizzard.* ❖ *n.* **1.** often **Maroon** a. A fugitive Black slave in the West Indies in the 17th and 18th centuries. **b.** A descendant of such a slave. **2.** A person who is marooned, as on an island. [< Fr. *marron,* fugitive slave < Am.Sp. *cimarrón,* wild, runaway, perh. < *cima,* summit (< runaways' fleeing to the mountains) < Lat. *cȳma,* sprout. See CYMA.]

ma·roon[2] (mə-rōōn′) *n.* A dark reddish brown to dark purplish red. [Fr. *marron,* chestnut < Ital. *marrone.*]

Maroon Peak A mountain, 4,317.6 m (14,156 ft) high, in the Elk

Thurgood Marshall

Mountains of W-central CO.

mar·plot (mär′plŏt′) *n.* An officious meddler whose interference compromises an undertaking. [After *Marplot,* in a play by Susannah Centlivre (1669–1723).]

Mar·quand (mär-kwŏnd′), **John Phillips** 1893–1960. Amer. writer whose works include *The Late George Apley* (1937).

marque (märk) *n.* A model or brand of a manufactured product, esp. an automobile. [Fr. < OFr. See MARQUETRY.]

mar·quee (mär-kē′) *n.* **1.** A large tent, often with open sides, used chiefly for outdoor entertainment. **2.** A rooflike structure, often bearing a signboard, projecting over an entrance, as to a theater. ❖ *adj.* Being an athlete of exceptional skill and popularity: *a marquee point guard.* [Fr. *marquise,* marquise, marquee. See MARQUISE.]

Mar·que·san (mär-kā′zən, -sən) *n.* **1.** A native or inhabitant of the Marquesas Islands. **2.** The Austronesian language of the Marquesans. —**Mar·que′san** *adj.*

Mar·que·sas Islands (mär-kā′zəz, -səz, -səs) A volcanic archipelago in the S Pacific, part of French Polynesia since 1842.

mar·que·try also **mar·que·terie** (mär′kĭ-trē) *n., pl.* **-tries** also **-teries** Material, such as ivory, inlaid piece by piece into a wood surface in an intricate design and veneered to another surface, esp. of furniture, for decoration. [Fr. *marqueterie* < OFr. < *marqueter,* to checker < *marque,* mark, ult. < ON *merki,* mark. See **merg-** in App.]

Mar·quette (mär-kĕt′), **Père Jacques** 1637–75. French missionary who accompanied Louis Jolliet on his 1673 exploration of the Wisconsin, Mississippi, and Illinois rivers.

mar·quis (mär′kwĭs, mär-kē′) or **mar·quess** (mär′kwĭs) *n., pl.* **-quis·es** (-kwĭ-sĭz) or **mar·quis** (-kēz′) or **-quess·es** (-kwĭ-sĭz) **1.** A nobleman ranking below a duke and above an earl or a count. **2.** Used as a title for such a nobleman. [ME *marques* < OFr. *marchis, marquis < marche,* border country, of Gmc. orig. See **merg-** in App.]

Mar·quis (mär′kwĭs), **Donald Robert Perry** 1878–1937. Amer. humorist whose work includes *archy and mehitabel* (1927).

mar·quis·ate (mär′kwĭ-zĭt, -sĭt) *n.* The rank or territory of a marquis.

mar·quise (mär-kēz′) *n.* **1.** See **marchioness** 2. **2.** See **marquee** 2. **3a.** A finger ring set with a pointed oval stone or cluster of pointed oval stones. **b.** A pointed oval shape of a gem. [Fr., fem. of *marquis,* marquis. See MARQUIS.]

mar·qui·sette (mär′kĭ-zĕt′, -kwĭ-) *n.* A sheer fabric of cotton, rayon, silk, or nylon, used for clothing and curtains.

Mar·quis of Queens·ber·ry rules (mär′kwĭs, mär-kē′) *pl.n.* A set of rules in modern boxing calling for the use of gloves, the division of matches into rounds, and the ten-second count for a knockout, among other provisions. [After the 8th Marquis of QUEENSBERRY.]

Mar·ra·kesh or **Mar·ra·kech** (mär′ə-kĕsh′, mə-rä′kĕsh) A city of W-central Morocco in the foothills of the Atlas Mts.; founded 1062. Pop. 602,000.

mar·ram (mär′əm) *n.* See **beach grass.** [Of Scand. orig. See **mori-** in App.]

Mar·ra·no (mə-rä′nō) *n., pl.* **-nos** *Offensive* Used as a disparaging term for a Converso. [Sp., pig, Marrano (< the Jewish prohibition against eating pork), prob. < Ar. *maḥram,* something forbidden < *ḥarama,* to forbid.]

mar·riage (mär′ĭj) *n.* **1a.** The legal union of a man and woman as husband and wife. **b.** The state of being married; wedlock. **c.** A common-law marriage. **d.** A union between two persons having the customary but usu. not the legal force of marriage: *a same-sex marriage.* **2.** A wedding. **3.** A close union. **4.** *Games* The combination of the king and queen of the same suit, as in pinochle. [ME *mariage* < OFr. < *marier,* to marry. See MARRY[1].]

mar·riage·a·ble (mär′ĭ-jə-bəl) *adj.* Suitable for marriage. —**mar′riage·a·bil′i·ty, mar′riage·a·ble·ness** *n.*

marriage of convenience *n., pl.* **marriages of convenience** A marriage or joint undertaking arranged for political, economic, or social benefit rather than from personal attachment.

mar·ried (mär′ēd) *adj.* **1a.** Having a spouse. **b.** United in matrimony. **2a.** Of or relating to the state of marriage. **b.** Acquired through marriage. **3.** Closely connected; united. ❖ *n., pl.* **marrieds** or **married** A married person.

mar·ron (mär′ən, mă-rôn′) *n.* See **Spanish chestnut.** [Fr. See MAROON[2].]

mar·rons gla·cés (mă-rōn′ glă-sā′) *pl.n.* Chestnuts glazed with sugar or preserved in vanilla-flavored syrup. [Fr. : *marrons,* marrons + *glacés,* pl. of *glacé,* glazed.]

mar·row (mär′ō) *n.* **1.** Bone marrow. **2.** The spinal cord. **3a.** The inmost, choicest, or essential part; the pith. **b.** Strength or vigor; vitality. [ME *marow* < OE *mearg.*] —**mar′row·y** *adj.*

mar·row·bone (mär′ō-bōn′) *n.* **1.** A bone for flavoring soup. **2.** **marrowbones** *Informal* The knees.

mar·row·fat (mär′ō-făt′) *n.* One of several varieties of pea that produces large seeds.

marrow squash *n.* An edible squash having very large, elongated, greenish fruit.

mar·ry[1] (mär′ē) *v.* **-ried, -ry·ing, -ries** —*tr.* **1a.** To join as spouses by exchanging vows. **b.** To take as a spouse. **c.** To give in marriage. **2.** To perform a marriage ceremony for. **3.** To obtain by marriage. **4.** *Nautical* To join (two ropes) end to end by interweaving their strands. **5.** To unite in a close, usu. permanent way. —*intr.* **1.** To take a spouse; wed. **2.** To combine or blend agreeably. [ME *marien* < OFr. *marier* < Lat. *marītāre* < *marītus*, married.]

mar·ry² (mărʹē) *interj. Archaic* Used as an exclamation of surprise or emphasis. [ME *Marie*, the Virgin Mary < LLat. *Maria.* See MARY¹.]

Mars (märz) *n.* **1.** *Roman Mythology* The god of war. **2.** The fourth planet from the sun. See table at **planet.** [ME < Lat. *Mārs.*]

Mar·sa·la¹ (mär-säʹlə) A city of W Sicily on the Mediterranean Sea; founded c. 397 B.C. Pop. 46,300.

Mar·sa·la² (mär-säʹlə) *n.* A sweet or dry fortified wine of Sicilian origin. ❖ *adj.* Cooked or flavored with Marsala: *veal Marsala.* [Ital., after MARSALA¹.]

Mar·sal·is (mär-sălʹĭs), **Wynton** b. 1961. Amer. trumpeter who has won acclaim as both a jazz and classical soloist.

mar·seille (mär-sālʹ) also **mar·seilles** (-sālzʹ) *n.* A heavy cotton fabric with a raised pattern of stripes or figures. [After MARSEILLE.]

Mar·seille also **Mar·seilles** (mär-sāʹ) A city of SE France on an arm of the Mediterranean Sea WNW of Toulon; founded c. 600 B.C. Pop. 800,309.

marsh (märsh) *n.* An area of soft, wet, low-lying land, marked by grassy vegetation and often being a transition between water and land. [ME < OE *mersc.* See **mori-** in App.]

Marsh, Ngaio 1899–1982. New Zealand writer whose detective novels include *A Man Lay Dead* (1934).

Marsh, Reginald 1898–1954. Amer. painter whose works, such as *The Bowery* (1930), depict life in New York City.

mar·shal (märʹshəl) *n.* **1a.** A military officer of the highest rank in some countries. **b.** A field marshal. **2a.** A US federal officer of a judicial district who carries out court orders and discharges duties similar to those of a sheriff. **b.** A city law enforcement officer in the United States who carries out court orders. **c.** The head of a police or fire department in the United States. **3.** A person in charge of a parade or ceremony. **4.** A high official in a royal court, esp. one aiding the sovereign in military affairs. ❖ *v.* **-shaled, -shal·ing, -shals** also **-shalled, -shal·ling, -shals** —*tr.* **1.** To arrange or place (troops, for example) in line for a parade, maneuver, or review. **2.** To arrange, place, or set in methodical order. See Syns at **arrange. 3.** To enlist and organize. **4.** To guide ceremoniously; conduct or usher. —*intr.* **1.** To take up positions in or as if in a military formation. **2.** To take form or order. [ME < OFr. *mareschal*, of Gmc. orig.] —**marʹshal·cy, marʹshal·ship**ʹ *n.*

Mar·shall (märʹshəl), **George Catlett** 1880–1959. Amer. soldier and diplomat who organized the European Recovery Program, or Marshall Plan, and received the 1953 Nobel Peace Prize.

Marshall, John 1755–1835. Amer. jurist; chief justice of the US Supreme Court (1801–35) who helped establish the practice of judicial review.

Marshall, Thurgood 1908–93. Amer. jurist; associate justice of the US Supreme Court (1967–91).

Marshall Islands A self-governing island group in the central Pacific Ocean; became a republic in 1986. Pop. 58,363. —**Marʹshall·ese**ʹ (-shə-lēzʹ, -lēsʹ) *adj. & n.*

marsh elder *n.* Any of several herbs or shrubs of the genus *Iva* of North America, found in salt marshes and having greenish flower heads.

marsh gas *n.* Methane.

marsh hawk *n.* See **northern harrier.**

marsh hen *n.* Any of various marsh birds of the family Rallidae, which includes the gallinules, coots, and rails.

marsh·land (märshʹlănd)ʹ *n.* A marshy tract of land.

marsh·mal·low (märshʹmĕlʹō, -mălʹō) *n.* **1a.** A light spongy confection made of corn syrup, gelatin, sugar, and starch. **b.** A confection of sweetened paste, once made from the marshmallow root. **2.** often **marsh mallow** *Botany* A perennial plant (*Althaea officinalis*) native to Europe and having pink flowers and a mucilaginous root. **3.** *Slang* A timid, cowardly, or ineffective person. —**marshʹmalʹlow·y** *adj.*

marsh marigold *n.* Any of several plants of the genus *Caltha*, esp. *C. palustris*, growing in swampy places and having bright yellow flowers.

marsh·y (märʹshē) *adj.* **-i·er, -i·est 1.** Of, resembling, or characterized by a marsh or marshes; boggy. **2.** Growing in marshes. —**marshʹi·ness** *n.*

Mar·ston (märʹstən), **John** 1575?–1634. English playwright whose works include *The Malcontent* (1604).

Marston Moor An area in N England W of York; site of the first Parliamentary victory of the English Civil War (1644).

mar·su·pi·al (mär-sooʹpē-əl) *n.* Any of various nonplacental mammals of the order Marsupialia, including kangaroos and wombats, found principally in Australia and the Americas. ❖ *adj.* **1.** Of or belonging to the order Marsupialia. **2.** Of or relating to a marsupium. [< MARSUPIUM.]

mar·su·pi·um (mär-sooʹpē-əm) *n., pl.* **-pi·a** (-pē-ə) **1.** A pouch or fold on the abdomen of most female marsupials, containing the mammary glands and in which the young develop after leaving the uterus. **2.** A temporary egg pouch in various fishes and crustaceans. [LLat. *marsūpium*, pouch < Lat. *marsuppium* < Gk. *marsuppion*, dim. of *marsuppos*, purse, perh. of Iran. orig.; akin to Avestan *marsū-*, belly, paunch.]

mart (märt) *n.* **1.** A trading center; a market. **2.** A place where goods are sold; a store. **3.** *Archaic* A fair. [ME, prob. < MFlem. < VLat. *marcātus.* See MARKET.]

Mart. *abbr.* Martinique

Mar·ta·ban (märʹtə-bănʹ, -bänʹ), **Gulf of** An arm of the Andaman Sea off S Myanmar (Burma).

mar·ta·gon (märʹtə-gən) *n.* A Eurasian lily (*Lilium martagon*) usu. having spotted pinkish-purple flowers. [ME < OFr. < OSpan. < Ottoman Turk. *mārtağān*, a kind of turban.]

Mar·tel (mär-tĕlʹ), **Charles** See **Charles Martel.**

Mar·tel·lo tower (mär-tĕlʹō) *n.* A short, circular tower, usu. made of stone and located near a shoreline as a defensive fortification. [After Cape *Martello*, Corsica, where such a tower was taken by British forces in 1794.]

mar·ten (märʹtn) *n., pl.* **marten** or **-tens 1.** Any of several principally arboreal carnivorous mammals of the genus *Martes*, mainly inhabiting northern forests and having a slender body, bushy tail, and soft fur. **2.** The fur of the marten. [ME *martrin*, *marten* < OFr. *martrine* < fem. of *martrin*, of the marten (< *martre*, marten), and < Med.Lat. *martrīna*, both of Gmc. orig.]

mar·ten·site (märʹtn-zītʹ) *n.* A solid solution of iron and up to one percent of carbon, the chief constituent of hardened carbon tool steels. [After Adolf *Martens* (1850–1914), German metallurgist.] —**marʹten·sitʹic** (-zĭtʹĭk) *adj.*

Mar·tha (märʹthə) In the Bible, the sister of Lazarus and Mary and a friend of Jesus.

Mar·tha's Vineyard (märʹthəz) An island of SE MA off the SW coast of Cape Cod; settled in 1642.

Mar·tí (mär-tēʹ), **José Julian** 1853–95. Cuban revolutionary killed while fighting for Cuban independence from Spain.

mar·tial (märʹshəl) *adj.* **1.** Of, relating to, or suggestive of war. **2.** Relating to or connected with the armed forces or the military profession: *martial training.* **3.** Characteristic of or befitting a warrior. [ME < Lat. *Mārtiālis* < *Mārs*, *Mārt-*, Mars.] —**marʹtial·ism** *n.* —**marʹtial·ist** *n.* —**marʹtial·ly** *adv.*

Martial fl. 1st cent. B.C. Roman poet known for his epigrams.

martial art *n.* Any of several Asian arts of combat or self-defense, such as aikido, karate, judo, or tae kwon do, usu. practiced as sport. Often used in the plural.

martial law *n.* **1.** Temporary rule by military authorities imposed on a civilian population esp. in time of war or when civil authority has broken down. **2.** The law imposed on an occupied territory by occupying military forces.

Mar·tian (märʹshən) *adj.* Of or relating to the planet Mars or its hypothetical inhabitants. ❖ *n.* A hypothetical inhabitant of the planet Mars. [ME *marcien* < Lat. *Mārtius* < *Mārs*, *Mārt-*, Mars.]

mar·tin (märʹtn) *n.* Any of various swallows, such as the house martin or the purple martin. [ME *martoune*, prob. < the name *Martin*, Martin.]

Martin I, Saint. d. 655. Pope (649–655) who was banished by Emperor Constans II (630–668).

Martin V 1366–1431. Pope (1417–31) who restored the authority of the Church in the Papal States.

Martin, Homer Dodge 1836–97. Amer. painter whose landscapes include *Lake Sanford* (1870).

Martin, Mary 1913–90. Amer. actress who appeared in numerous Broadway hits, including *Peter Pan* (1954).

Mar·tin Du Gard (mär-tănʹ dü gärʹ), **Roger** 1881–1958. French writer who won the 1937 Nobel Prize for literature.

Mar·ti·neau (märʹtn-ō), **Harriet** 1802–76. British writer known for *Illustrations of Political Economy* (1832–34).

mar·ti·net (märʹtn-ĕtʹ) *n.* **1.** A rigid military disciplinarian. **2.** One who demands absolute adherence to forms and rules. [After Jean *Martinet* (died 1672), French army officer.]

mar·tin·gale (märʹtn-gālʹ) also **mar·tin·gal** (-gălʹ) *n.* **1.** The strap of a horse's harness that connects the girth to the noseband and prevents the horse from throwing back its head. **2.** *Nautical* Any of several parts of standing rigging strengthening the bowsprit and jib boom against the force of the head stays. **3.** *Games* A method of gambling in which one doubles the stakes after each loss. **4.** A loose half belt or strap placed on the back of a garment, such as a coat. [Fr., perh. alteration of Sp. *almártaga*, *almártiga*, rein, harness, perh. < Ar. orig.]

mar·ti·ni (mär-tēʹnē) *n., pl.* **-nis** A cocktail made of gin or vodka and dry vermouth. [?]

Mar·ti·nique (märʹtĭ-nēkʹ, -tn-ēkʹ) An island and overseas department of France in the Windward Is. of the West Indies; colonized by French settlers after 1635. Cap. Fort-de-France. Pop. 375,000. —**Marʹti·niʹcan** *adj. & n.*

Mar·tin Luther King Day (märʹtn) *n.* The third Monday in January, observed in honor of the birthday of Martin Luther King, Jr.

Mar·tin·mas (märʹtn-məs) *n.* A Christian feast commemorating the death and burial of Saint Martin of Tours, traditionally observed on November 11. [ME *martinmesse* : *Martin*, Saint Martin of Tours + *messe*, *masse*, Mass; see MASS.]

Mar·ti·nů (märʹtyĭ-nōō), **Bohuslav Jan** 1890–1959. Czech com-

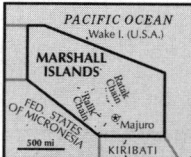

Marshall Islands

martagon
Lilium martagon

marten
American marten
Martes americana

ă pat	oi boy
ā pay	ou out
âr care	oo took
ä father	oo boot
ĕ pet	ŭ cut
ē be	ûr urge
ĭ pit	th thin
ī pie	th this
îr pier	hw which
ŏ pot	zh vision
ō toe	ə about,
ô paw	item

Stress marks:
ʹ (primary);
ʹ (secondary), as in
lexicon (lĕkʹsĭ-kŏnʹ)

poser and violinist whose works combine Czech folk music with the formal principles of ragtime, jazz, and Baroque music styles.

Mar•tin of Tours (mär′tn, mär-tăn′; tŏŏr, tōor), Saint. A.D. 316?–397? French prelate and patron saint of France.

Mar•tin•son (mär′tn-sôn′, -tēn-), **Harry Edmund** 1904–78. Swedish writer who shared the 1974 Nobel Prize for literature.

mart•let (märt′lĭt) n. 1. See **house martin**. 2. Heraldry An image of a bird without feet, used as a crest or bearing to indicate a fourth son. [Fr. martelet < Martin, Saint Martin of Tours.]

mar•tyr (mär′tər) n. 1. One who chooses to suffer death rather than renounce religious principles. 2. One who makes great sacrifices or suffers much for a belief, cause, or principle. 3a. One who suffers greatly. b. One who makes a great show of suffering to arouse sympathy. ❖ tr.v. **-tyred, -tyr•ing, -tyrs 1.** To make a martyr of, esp. to put to death for religious beliefs. 2. To inflict great pain on; torment. [ME, ult. < L.Gk. martur < Gk. martus, martur-, witness.]

mar•tyr•dom (mär′tər-dəm) n. 1a. The state of being a martyr. b. The suffering of death by a martyr. 2. Extreme suffering of any kind.

mar•tyr•ize (mär′tə-rīz′) tr.v. **-ized, -iz•ing, -iz•es** To martyr. —**mar′tyr•i•za′tion** (-tər-ĭ-zā′shən) n.

mar•tyr•ol•o•gy (mär′tə-rŏl′ə-jē) n., pl. **-gies 1.** An official list or catalog of religious martyrs, esp. of Christian martyrs. 2a. An account of the life and manner of death of a martyr. b. The branch of ecclesiastical history or hagiography that deals with martyrs. —**mar′tyr•ol′o•gist** n.

mar•vel (mär′vəl) n. 1. One that evokes surprise, admiration, or wonder. See Syns at **wonder.** 2. Strong surprise; astonishment. ❖ v. **-veled, -vel•ing, -vels** also **-velled, -vel•ling, -vels** —intr. To become filled with wonder or astonishment. —tr. To feel amazement or bewilderment at or about: We marveled that they walked away unhurt from the car accident. [ME marvail < OFr. merveille < VLat. *miribilia, alteration of Lat. mīrābilia, wonderful things < neut. pl. of mīrābilis, wonderful < mīrārī, to wonder < mīrus, wonderful.]

Mar•vell (mär′vəl), **Andrew** 1621–78. English metaphysical poet whose works include "To His Coy Mistress" (1650).

mar•vel•ous also **mar•vel•lous** (mär′və-ləs) adj. 1. Causing wonder or astonishment. 2. Miraculous; supernatural. 3. Of the highest or best kind or quality; first-rate: a marvelous library. —**mar′vel•ous•ly** adv. —**mar′vel•ous•ness** n.

Marx (märks) Family of Amer. comedians, including the brothers **Julius** (1890–1977), "Groucho"; **Leonard** (1891–1961), "Chico"; **Arthur** (1893–1964), "Harpo"; **Milton** (1894–1977), "Gummo"; and **Herbert** (1901–79), "Zeppo."

Marx, Karl 1818–83. German philosopher, economist, and revolutionary who with Friedrich Engels wrote The Communist Manifesto (1848) and Das Kapital (1867–94).

Marx•i•an (märk′sē-ən) n. One that studies, advocates, or uses Marxism. —**Marx′i•an** adj. —**Marx′i•an•ism** n.

Marx•ism (märk′sĭz′əm) n. The political and economic philosophy of Karl Marx and Friedrich Engels in which the concept of class struggle plays a central role in understanding society's allegedly inevitable development from bourgeois oppression under capitalism to a socialist and ultimately classless society. —**Marx′ist** n. & adj.

Marx•ism-Len•in•ism (märk′sĭz′əm-lĕn′ĭ-nĭz′əm) n. The ideology derived from the expansion of Marxism to include both Lenin's concept of imperialism as the final form of capitalism and a focus on underdeveloped countries. —**Marx′ist-Len′in•ist** adj. & n.

Mar•y[1] (mâr′ē) In the New Testament, the mother of Jesus and the principal saint of many Christian churches. [LLat. Maria < Gk. Mariā, Mariam < Heb. miryām, .]

Mar•y[2] In the New Testament, a sister of Lazarus and Martha and a friend of Jesus.

Mar•y[3] also **Mary of Teck** (těk) 1867–1953. Queen of George V of Great Britain.

Mary I or **Mary Tu•dor** (tōō′dər, tyōō′-) 1516–58. Queen of England and Ireland (1553–58) who reestablished Roman Catholicism (1555).

Mary II 1662–94. Queen of England, Scotland, and Ireland (1689–94) who ruled jointly with her husband, William III.

Mary Jane n. Slang Marijuana. [Alteration of MARIJUANA.]

Mar•y•land (mĕr′ə-lənd) A state of the E-central US; admitted as one of the original Thirteen Colonies in 1788. Cap. Annapolis. Pop. 5,296,486. —**Mar′y•land•er** n.

Mary Mag•da•lene (măg′də-lən, -lēn′) In the New Testament, a woman whom Jesus cured of evil spirits. She is also identified with the repentant prostitute who washed the feet of Jesus.

Mar•y•ol•o•gy (mâr′ē-ŏl′ə-jē) n. Variant of **Mariology.**

Mary Queen of Scots also **Mary Stuart** 1542–87. Queen of Scotland (1542–67) who was forced to abdicate in favor of her son, the future James I of England.

mar•zi•pan (mär′zə-păn′, märt′sə-pän′) n. A confection made of ground almonds or almond paste, egg whites, and sugar. [Ger. < Ital. marzapane, standard container, marzipan < obsolete Ital., fine coin or comfit box, perh. < Ar. mawṭabān, throned king, Byzantine coin with throned Christ, perh. < Aram. mawtabā, mawtabānā, seat, throne < yateb, to sit.]

mascot
St. Louis Cardinals' mascot

masher

ma•sa (mä′sə) n. Dough made of dried corn that has been soaked in limewater then rinsed and ground, used esp. in tortillas and tamales. [Am.Sp. < Sp., dough < OSpan. < Lat. massa, mass, dough. See MASS.]

Ma•sac•cio (mə-sä′chē-ō, mä-sät′chō) 1401–28. Italian painter noted for his revolutionary use of linear perspective.

Ma•sa•da (mə-sä′də, -tsä-dä′) An ancient mountaintop fortress in SE Israel on the SW shore of the Dead Sea. In A.D. 73, after a two-year siege, members of the Zealot Jewish movement committed mass suicide rather than surrender to the Romans.

Ma•sai (mä-sī′, mä′sī) n., pl. **Masai** or **-sais 1.** A member of a chiefly pastoral people of Kenya and parts of Tanzania. 2. also **Maa•sai** The Nilotic language of this people.

Ma•san (mä′sän′) A city of SE South Korea W of Pusan. Pop. 493,731.

Mas•a•ryk (măs′ə-rĭk, mä′sä-), **Tomáš Garrigue** 1850–1937. Czechoslovakian politician who served as the first president of independent Czechoslovakia (1918–35). His son **Jan Garrigue Masaryk** (1886–1948) was also a politician.

Mas•ba•te (mäs-bä′tĕ, -tĕ) An island of the central Philippines S of Luzon.

masc. abbr. masculine

mas•car•a (mă-skăr′ə) n. A cosmetic applied to darken the eyelashes. ❖ tr.v. **-car•aed, -car•a•ing, -car•as** To apply mascara to. [Prob. Sp. máscara, mask; akin to Ital. maschera. See MASK.]

Mas•ca•rene Islands (măs′kə-rēn′) An island group including Mauritius and Réunion.

mas•car•po•ne (măs′kär-pō′nĕ, -pōn′) n. A soft Italian cheese with a high butterfat content, made from cow's milk and cream. [Ital., augmentative of dialectal mascarpa, whey cheese.]

mas•con (măs′kŏn′) n. A mare on the moon having rock of greater density than that of the surrounding area, thus exerting a slightly higher gravitational force. [MAS(S) + CON(CENTRATION).]

mas•cot (măs′kŏt′, -kət) n. A person, animal, or object believed to bring good luck, as the symbol of a sports team. [Fr. mascotte, sorcerer's charm, mascot < Provençal mascoto, sorcery, fetish < masco, witch, ult. < Med.Lat. masca, mask, specter, witch.]

mas•cu•line (măs′kyə-lĭn) adj. 1. Of or relating to men or boys; male. 2. Suggestive or characteristic of a man; mannish. 3. Grammar Relating or belonging to the gender of words or forms that refer chiefly to males or to things grammatically classified as male. 4. Music Ending on an accented beat: a masculine cadence. ❖ n. 1. Grammar a. The masculine gender. b. A masculine word or word form. 2. A male person. [ME masculin < OFr. < Lat. masculīnus < masculus, male, dim. of mās.] —**mas′cu•line•ly** adv. —**mas′cu•line•ness** n.

masculine ending n. 1. A stressed syllable that ends a line of verse. 2. Grammar A final syllable or termination that marks or forms words in the masculine gender.

masculine rhyme n. A rhyme made on a masculine ending.

mas•cu•lin•i•ty (măs′kyə-lĭn′ĭ-tē) n., pl. **-ties 1.** The quality or condition of being masculine. 2. Something traditionally considered to be characteristic of a male.

mas•cu•lin•ize (măs′kyə-lə-nīz′) tr.v. **-ized, -iz•ing, -iz•es 1.** To give a masculine appearance or character to. 2. To cause (a female) to assume masculine characteristics, as by hormone therapy. —**mas′cu•lin•i•za′tion** (-lə-nĭ-zā′shən) n.

Mase•field (mās′fēld′), **John** 1878–1967. British writer who became poet laureate in 1930.

ma•ser (mā′zər) n. Any of several devices that amplify or generate electromagnetic waves, esp. microwaves. [m(icrowave) a(mplification by) s(timulated) e(mission of) r(adiation).]

Mas•er•u (măz′ə-rōō′, mä′sə-rōō′) The cap. of Lesotho, in the W part; founded 1869. Pop. 14,686.

mash (măsh) n. 1. A fermentable starchy mixture from which alcohol or spirits can be distilled. 2. A mixture of ground grain and nutrients fed to livestock and fowl. 3. A soft pulpy mixture or mass. 4. A crushing or grinding. ❖ tr.v. **mashed, mash•ing, mash•es 1.** To convert (malt or grain) into mash. 2. To convert into a soft pulpy mixture: mash potatoes. 3. To crush or grind. 4. Chiefly Southern & South Midland US To apply pressure to; press. 5. Slang To flirt with or make sexual advances to. [ME mash- (as in mashfat, mash tub) < OE *māsc, māx- (in māxwyrt, wort). V., sense 5, perh. < Romany mash, to entice.]

MASH abbr. Mobile Army Surgical Hospital

mash•er (măsh′ər) n. 1. A kitchen utensil for mashing vegetables or fruit. 2. Slang A man who attempts to force his attentions on a woman.

Ma•sher•brum (mŭsh′ər-brŏŏm′) A peak, 7,826.3 m (25,660 ft), in the Himalaya Mts. of Kashmir.

mash•gi•ah or **mash•gi•ach** (mäsh-gē′äкн), n., pl. **-gi•him** or **-gi•chim** (-gē′кнĭm, -gē-кнĕм) Judaism One trained to inspect kosher establishments to ensure that kashrut is observed. [Heb. mašgîaḥ < hišgîaḥ, to look, inspect.]

Mash•had (mə-shäd′, mäsh-häd′) or **Me•shed** (mĕ-shĕd′) A city of NE Iran near the Turkmenistan and Afghanistan borders; long an important caravan center. Pop. 1,964,489.

mash•ie (măsh′ē) n. A five iron used in golf. [Perh. < Fr. massue, club < OFr. < VLat. *matteūca < *mattea, mace. See MACE[1].]

mashie niblick n. A seven iron used in golf.

mas•jid (mŭs′jĭd) n. A mosque. [Ar. < Aram. *masgid, place of worship < *səged*, to worship.]

mask (măsk) *n.* **1.** A covering worn on the face to conceal one's identity, as: **a.** A covering that has openings for the eyes and is worn esp. at a masquerade ball. **b.** A grotesque or comical representation of a face, worn esp. to frighten or amuse. **c.** A facial covering worn for ritual. **d.** A figure of a head worn by actors in Greek and Roman drama to identify a character or trait and to amplify the voice. **2a.** A protective covering for the face or head. **b.** A gas mask. **c.** A usu. rubber frame forming a watertight seal around the eyes and nose and containing a transparent covering for use in seeing underwater. **d.** A covering for the nose and mouth that is used for inhaling oxygen or an anesthetic. **e.** A covering worn over the nose and mouth, as by a dentist, to prevent infection. **3.** A representation of a face or head. **4.** The face or facial markings of certain animals, such as dogs. **5.** A face having a blank, fixed, or enigmatic expression. **6.** Something, often a trait, that disguises or conceals. **7.** A feature of terrain that conceals and protects military forces or installations. **8a.** An opaque border or pattern placed between a source of light and a photosensitive surface to prevent exposure of specified portions of the surface. **b.** The translucent border framing a television picture tube and screen. **9.** *Computer Science* A bit pattern used to eliminate or retain another pattern of characters, bits, or bytes. **10.** A cosmetic preparation that is applied to the face and allowed to dry before removal, used esp. for cleansing and tightening the skin. **11.** Variant of **masque. 12.** A person wearing a mask. ❖ *v.* **masked, mask•ing, masks** —*tr.* **1.** To cover with a decorative or protective mask. **2.** To make indistinct or blurred to the senses. **3.** To cover in order to conceal, protect, or disguise. **4.** To block the view of. **5.** To cover (a part of a photographic film) by the application of a mask. **6.** *Chemistry* To prevent (an atom or atoms) from taking part in a normal reaction. —*intr.* **1.** To put on a mask, esp. for a masquerade ball. **2.** To conceal one's real personality, character, or intentions. [Fr. *masque* < Ital. *maschera* < Med.Lat. *masca*, specter, witch, mask.] —**mask′a•ble** *adj.*

masked (măskt) *adj.* **1.** Wearing a mask. **2.** Disguised or concealed as if by a mask: *masked emotions.* **3.** Latent or hidden, as a symptom. **4.** *Botany* Personate. **5.** *Zoology* **a.** Having masklike markings on the head or face. **b.** Having the anatomy of the next developmental form outlined beneath the integument.

masked ball *n.* A ball at which masks are worn.

mas•keg (măs′kĕg′) *n.* Variant of **muskeg.**

mask•er also **mas•quer** (măs′kər) *n.* One who wears a mask, esp. a participant in a masquerade or masque.

mask•ing (măs′kĭng) *n.* **1.** *Physiology* The concealment or screening of one sensory process or sensation by another. **2.** A piece of theatrical scenery that hides part of the stage.

masking tape *n.* An adhesive tape used for a variety of purposes, as to protect a surface that is not to be painted.

mas•och•ism (măs′ə-kĭz′əm) *n.* **1.** The deriving of pleasure or gratification, esp. of a sexual nature, from physical pain or abuse or from being humiliated or otherwise mistreated. **2.** The turning of destructive tendencies upon oneself. **3.** The willingness to subject oneself to unpleasant or trying experiences. [After Leopold von Sacher-*Masoch* (1836–95), Austrian novelist.] —**mas′och•ist** *n.* —**mas′och•is′tic** *adj.* —**mas′och•is′ti•cal•ly** *adv.*

ma•son (mā′sən) *n.* **1.** One who builds or works with stone or brick. **2. Mason** A Freemason. ❖ *tr.v.* **-soned, -son•ing, -sons** To build or strengthen with masonry. [ME < OFr. *maçon, masson*, of Gmc. orig.]

Mason, George 1725–92. Amer. Revolutionary politician who was instrumental in ensuring inclusion of the Bill of Rights in the US Constitution.

mason bee *n.* Any of various solitary bees of the family Megachilidae, found worldwide, that build clay nests.

Ma•son-Dix•on Line (mā′sən-dĭk′sən) The boundary between PA and MD, regarded as the division between free and slave states before the Civil War.

Ma•son•ic (mə-sŏn′ĭk) *adj.* Of or relating to Freemasons or Freemasonry.

Ma•son•ite (mā′sə-nīt′) A trademark used for a type of fiberboard employed for insulation, paneling, or partitions.

Mason jar *n.* A wide-mouthed glass jar with a screw top, used for canning and preserving food. [After John L. *Mason* (1832–1902), American inventor.]

ma•son•ry (mā′sən-rē) *n., pl.* **-ries 1a.** The trade of a mason. **b.** Work done by a mason. **c.** Stonework or brickwork. **2. Masonry** Freemasonry.

mason wasp *n.* Any of various solitary wasps, esp. of the subfamily Eumeninae, that build nests of mud.

Ma•so•ra also **Ma•so•rah** (mə-sôr′ə, -sōr′ə) *Judaism n.* **1.** Jewish traditional vocalization and reading of the Bible. **2.** The pretenth-century critical notes that embody this tradition. [Heb. *māsôrâ* < *māsar*, to hand over.] —**Mas′o•ret′ic** (măs′ə-rĕt′ĭk) *adj.*

masque also **mask** (măsk) *n.* **1.** A dramatic entertainment, usu. performed by masked players representing mythological or allegorical figures, popular in England in the 16th and early 17th centuries. **2.** A dramatic verse composition written for such an entertainment. **3.** See **masquerade** 1a. [Fr. See MASK.]

mas•quer (măs′kər) *n.* Variant of **masker.**

mas•quer•ade (măs′kə-rād′) *n.* **1a.** A costume party at which masks are worn; a masked ball. **b.** A costume for such a party or ball. **2a.** A disguise or false outward show; a pretense. **b.** An involved scheme; a charade. ❖ *intr.v.* **-ad•ed, -ad•ing, -ades 1.** To wear a mask or disguise, as at a masquerade: *masqueraded as a shepherd.* **2.** To go about as if in disguise; have or put on a deceptive appearance. [Fr. *mascarade* < Ital. *mascarata*, var. of *mascherata* < OItal. *maschera*, mask. See MASK.] —**mas′quer•ad′er** *n.*

mass (măs) *n.* **1.** A unified body of matter with no specific shape. **2.** A grouping of individual parts or elements that compose a unified body of unspecified size or quantity: *the mass of students.* **3.** A large but nonspecific amount or number: *a mass of bruises.* **4.** A lump or aggregate of coherent material: *a cancerous mass.* **5.** The principal part; the majority. **6.** The physical volume or bulk of a solid body. **7.** *Physics* The quantity of matter constituting an object, equal to the measure of the object's resistance to changes in either the speed or direction of its motion. It is proportional to the object's weight. **8.** An area of unified light, shade, or color in a painting. **9.** *Pharmacology* A thick pasty mixture containing drugs from which pills are formed. **10. masses** The body of common people or people of low socioeconomic status. ❖ *tr. & intr.v.* **massed, mass•ing, mass•es** To gather or be gathered into a mass. ❖ *adj.* **1.** Of, relating to, characteristic of, directed at, or attended by a large number of people. **2.** Done or carried out on a large scale. **3.** Total; complete. [ME *masse* < OFr. < Lat. *massa* < Gk. *māza, maza.*]

Mass also **mass** *n.* **1a.** The liturgy of the Eucharist, esp. in the Roman Catholic Church. **b.** The sacrament of the Eucharist. **2.** A musical setting of certain parts of the Mass. [ME *masse* < OE *mæsse* < VLat. **messa* < LLat. *missa* < Lat., fem. p. part. of *mittere*, to send away, dismiss.]

Mass. *abbr.* Massachusetts

Mas•sa•chu•sett also **Mas•sa•chu•set** (măs′ə-cho͞o′sĭt, -zĭt) *n., pl.* **Massachusett** or **-setts** also **Massachuset** or **-sets 1.** A member of an extinct Native American people located along Massachusetts Bay from Plymouth north to Salem. **2.** Their extinct Algonquian language. [< the Massachusett name of Great Blue Hill south of Boston.]

Mas•sa•chu•setts (măs′ə-cho͞o′sĭts) A state of the NE US; admitted as one of the original Thirteen Colonies in 1788. The first European settlement was made by the Pilgrims of the *Mayflower* in 1620. Cap. Boston. Pop. 6,349,097.

Massachusetts Bay An inlet of the Atlantic Ocean off E MA extending from Cape Ann to Cape Cod.

mas•sa•cre (măs′ə-kər) *n.* **1.** The act or an instance of cruel, indiscriminate killing of a large number of people. **2.** The slaughter of a large number of animals. **3.** *Informal* A severe defeat. ❖ *tr.v.* **-cred** (-kərd), **-cring** (-krĭng, -kər-ĭng), **-cres 1.** To kill indiscriminately and wantonly. **2.** *Informal* To defeat decisively. **3.** *Informal* To botch; to bungle. [Fr. < OFr. *macecle, macecre*, butchery, shambles.] —**mas′sa•crer** (-kər-ər, -krər) *n.*

mas•sage (mə-säzh′, -säj′) *n.* **1.** The rubbing or kneading of parts of the body esp. to aid circulation or relax the muscles. **2.** An act or instance of such rubbing or kneading. ❖ *tr.v.* **-saged, -sag•ing, -sag•es 1.** To give a massage to. **2.** To treat by means of a massage. **3.** To coddle or cajole. **4.** To manipulate (data, for example): *Pollsters massaged the numbers.* [Fr. < *masser*, to massage < Ar. *masaḥa*, to stroke, anoint, or *massa*, to touch.] —**mas•sag′er** *n.*

massage parlor *n.* **1.** An establishment that offers therapeutic massage. **2.** An establishment that offers illicit sexual services under the guise of therapeutic massage.

mas•sa•sau•ga (măs′ə-sô′gə) *n.* A small, variably colored rattlesnake *(Sistrurus catenatus)* found in parts of the United States, Canada, and Mexico. [After the *Mississagi*, a river of SE Ontario, Canada.]

Mas•sa•soit (măs′ə-soit′) 1580?–1661. Wampanoag leader who aided the Pilgrim colonists.

mass defect *n.* The amount by which the mass of an atomic nucleus is less than the sum of the masses of its nucleons.

mas•sé (mă-sā′) *n.* A stroke in billiards made by striking the cue ball off center with the cue held nearly vertically. [Fr. < p. part. of *masser*, to make a massé shot < *masse*, mace (an early form of billiard cue) < OFr., club. See MACE[1].]

mass-en•er•gy equivalence (măs′ĕn′ər-jē) *n.* The physical principle that a measure of the energy of a system is its mass, as expressed by Einstein's equation, $E = mc^2$, where E is energy, m the equivalent mass, and c the speed of light.

Mas•se•net (măs′ə-nā′, mäs-nā′), **Jules Émile Frédéric** 1842–1912. French composer of the opera *Thaïs* (1894).

mas•se•ter (mə-sē′tər, mă-) *n.* A muscle in the cheek that closes the jaws during chewing. [NLat. *massētēr* < Gk. *masētēr, massētēr* < *masāsthai*, to chew.] —**mas′se•ter′ic** (măs′ĭ-tĕr′ĭk) *adj.*

mas•seur (mă-sûr′, mə-) *n.* A man who gives massages professionally. [Fr. < *masser*, to massage. See MASSAGE.]

mas•seuse (mă-sœz′) *n.* A woman who gives massages professionally. [Fr., fem. of *masseur*, masseur. See MASSEUR.]

mas•si•cot (măs′ĭ-kŏt′, -kō′) *n.* **1.** The mineral form of lead monoxide, PbO. **2.** A yellow powder, PbO, used as a pigment. [ME *masticot* < OFr., perh. < OItal. *marzacotto*, potter's glaze (perh. < Sp. *mazacote*, mortar), poss. < Ar. *mashaqūnīyā*, perh. of Gk. orig.]

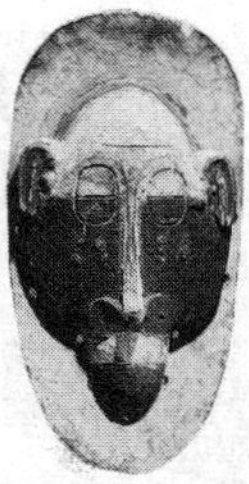

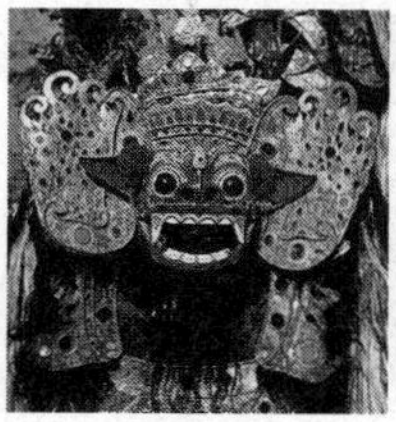

mask
top: African
bottom: Indonesian

ă	pat	oi	boy
ā	pay	ou	out
âr	care	o͝o	took
ä	father	o͞o	boot
ĕ	pet	ŭ	cut
ē	be	ûr	urge
ĭ	pit	th	thin
ī	pie	*th*	this
îr	pier	hw	which
ŏ	pot	zh	vision
ō	toe	ə	about, item
ô	paw		

Stress marks:
′ (primary);
′ (secondary), as in
lexicon (lĕk′sĭ-kŏn′)

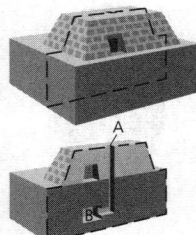

mastaba
top: exterior view
bottom: cross section
revealing the shaft (*A*) and
the burial chamber (*B*)

mas•sif (mă-sēf′) *n.* **1.** A mountain or compact group of connected mountains forming an independent portion of a range. **2.** A large section of the earth's crust that is more rigid than the surrounding rock and has been moved or displaced as a unit. [Fr., massive, massif < OFr. See MASSIVE.]

Massif Cen•tral (sĕn-träl′, sän-) A mountainous plateau of S-central France rising to 1,887.3 m (6,188 ft).

Mas•sine (mä-sēn′), **Léonide** 1896–1979. Russian-born Amer. choreographer whose ballets include *Parade* (1917).

Mas•sin•ger (măs′ĭn-jər), **Philip** 1583–1640. English playwright best known for *A New Way to Pay Old Debts* (c. 1625).

mas•sive (măs′ĭv) *adj.* **1.** Consisting of or making up a large mass; bulky, heavy, and solid: *a massive piece of furniture.* **2.** Large or imposing, as in quantity, scope, or degree. **3.** Large in comparison with the usual amount: *a massive dose of a drug.* **4.** *Pathology* Affecting a large area of bodily tissue; widespread and severe: *massive gangrene.* **5.** *Mineralogy* Lacking internal crystalline structure; amorphous. **6.** *Geology* Without internal structure or layers and homogeneous in composition. Used of a rock. [ME *massif* < OFr. < *masse,* mass. See MASS.] —**mas′sive•ly** *adv.* —**mas′sive•ness** *n.*

Massive, Mount A peak, 4,398.4 m (14,421 ft), in the Sawatch Range of the Rocky Mts. in central CO.

mass•less (măs′lĭs) *adj.* Having a mass of zero.

mass medium *n., pl.* **mass media** A means of public communication to a large audience.

mass noun *n.* A noun, such as *sand, oil,* or *honesty,* that denotes a substance or concept indivisible into countable units and is preceded in English indefinite constructions by modifiers such as *some* or *much* rather than *a* or *one.*

mass number *n.* The sum of the number of neutrons and protons in an atomic nucleus.

mass production *n.* The manufacture of goods in large quantities, often using standardized designs and assembly-line techniques. —**mass′-pro•duce′** (măs′prə-dōōs′) *v.*

mass spectrograph *n.* An instrument used to determine the masses of atoms or molecules, in which an electromagnetic field separates ions according to their masses and the resulting spectrum is recorded on a photographic plate. —**mass spectrography** *n.*

mass spectrometer *n.* A mass spectroscope that records its data electronically. —**mass spectrometry** *n.*

mass spectroscope *n.* Any of various devices that use magnetic fields, electric fields, or both to determine the masses of isotopes in a sample by producing a mass spectrum. —**mass spectroscopy** *n.*

mass•y (măs′ē) *adj.* **-i•er, -i•est** Having great mass or bulk.

mast[1] (măst) *n.* **1.** *Nautical* A tall vertical spar that rises from the keel or deck of a sailing vessel to support the sails and the standing and running rigging. **2a.** A vertical pole. **b.** A tall vertical antenna, as for a radio. **3.** A captain's mast. [ME < OE *mæst.*]

mast[2] (măst) *n.* The nuts of forest trees accumulated on the ground, used esp. as food for swine. [ME < OE *mæst.*]

mast– *pref.* Variant of **masto–.**

mas•ta•ba also **mas•ta•bah** (măs′tə-bə) *n.* An ancient Egyptian tomb with a rectangular base, sloping sides, and a flat roof. [Ar. *maṣṭabba,* stone bench < Aram. *miṣṭubbā,* perh. of Pers. or Gk. orig.]

mast cell *n.* A cell found in connective tissue that releases substances such as histamine in response to injury or inflammation of bodily tissues. [Partial transl. of Ger. *Mastzelle,* well-fed cell (because the granules were thought to be from phagocytosis) : *Mast,* food, mast (< MHGer. < OHGer.) + *Zelle,* cell.]

mas•tec•to•my (mă-stĕk′tə-mē) *n., pl.* **-mies** Surgical removal of all or part of a breast, sometimes including excision of the underlying pectoral muscles and regional lymph nodes, usu. performed as a treatment for cancer.

mas•ter (măs′tər) *n.* **1.** One that has control over another or others. **2a.** The owner or keeper of an animal. **b.** The owner of a slave. **3.** One who has control over or ownership of something. **4.** The captain of a merchant ship. **5.** An employer. **6.** A man who is the head of a household. **7.** One who defeats another; a victor. **8a.** One whose teachings or doctrines are accepted by followers. **b. Master** *Christianity* Jesus. **9.** A male teacher, schoolmaster, or tutor. **10.** One who holds a master's degree. **11a.** An artist or performer of great and exemplary skill. **b.** An old master. **12.** A worker qualified to teach apprentices and carry on the craft independently. **13.** An expert. **14a.** Used formerly as a title for a man holding a naval office ranking next below a lieutenant on a warship. **b.** Used as a title for a man who serves as the head or presiding officer of certain societies, clubs, orders, or institutions. **c.** *Chiefly British* Used as a title for any of various male law court officers. **d. Master** Used as a title for any of various male officers having specified duties concerning the management of the British royal household. **e. Master** Used as a courtesy title before the given or full name of a boy. **f.** *Archaic* Used as a form of address for a man; mister. **15. Master** A man who owns a pack of hounds or is the chief officer or master of a hunt. **16.** An original from which copies can be made. ❖ *adj.* **1.** Of, relating to, or characteristic of a master. **2.** Principal or predominant. **3.** Controlling all other parts of a mechanism. **4.** Highly skilled or proficient. **5.** Being an

original from which copies are made. ❖ *tr.v.* **-tered, -ter•ing, -ters 1.** To act as or be the master of. **2.** To make oneself a master of: *mastered the language.* **3.** To overcome or defeat: *mastered his addiction.* **4.** To reduce to subjugation; break or tame (an animal, for example). **5.** To produce a master audio recording for. **6.** To season or age (dyed goods). [ME < OE *mægister, mægister* < OFr. *maistre,* both < Lat. *magister.* See **meg-** in App.] —**mas′ter•dom** *n.*

mas•ter-at-arms (măs′tər-ət-ärmz′) *n., pl.* **mas•ters-at-arms** (măs′tərz-) A petty officer assigned to maintain order.

master chief petty officer *n.* An officer of the highest noncommissioned rank in the US Navy or Coast Guard.

master class *n.* An advanced music class taught by an eminent musician.

mas•ter•ful (măs′tər-fəl) *adj.* **1.** Given to playing the master; imperious or domineering. **2.** Fit to command. **3.** Revealing mastery or skill; expert: *a masterful technique.* —**mas′ter•ful•ly** *adv.* —**mas′ter•ful•ness** *n.*

master gunnery sergeant *n.* A noncommissioned officer in the US Marine Corps ranking above master sergeant and equivalent to a sergeant major.

master key *n.* A key that opens each of a given set of locks.

mas•ter•ly (măs′tər-lē) *adj.* Having or showing the knowledge or skill of a master. ❖ *adv.* With the skill of a master. —**mas′ter•li•ness** *n.*

master mariner *n.* See **master** 4.

mas•ter•mind (măs′tər-mīnd′) *n.* A highly intelligent person, esp. one who plans and directs a complex or difficult project. ❖ *tr.v.* **-mind•ed, -mind•ing, -minds** To direct, plan, or supervise (a project or activity).

master of ceremonies *n., pl.* **masters of ceremonies 1.** One who acts as host at a formal event, making the welcoming speech and introducing other speakers. **2.** One who conducts a program of entertainment by introducing other performers.

mas•ter•piece (măs′tər-pēs′) *n.* **1.** An outstanding work of art or craft. **2.** The greatest work, as of an artist. **3.** Something superlative of its kind. [Prob. transl. of Du. *meesterstuk* or Ger. *Meisterstück* : Du. *meester* and Ger. *Meister,* master + Du. *stuk* and Ger. *Stück,* piece of work.]

master race *n.* A people who consider themselves to be superior to other races and therefore suited to rule over them.

Mas•ters (măs′tərz), **Edgar Lee** 1869–1950. Amer. poet known for his *Spoon River Anthology* (1915).

mas•ter's degree (măs′tərz) *n.* An academic degree conferred by a college or university upon those who complete at least one year of prescribed study beyond the bachelor's degree.

master sergeant *n.* **1.** A noncommissioned officer in the US Army ranking above sergeant first class and below sergeant major. **2.** A noncommissioned officer in the US Air Force ranking above technical sergeant and below senior master sergeant. **3.** A noncommissioned officer in the US Marine Corps ranking above gunnery sergeant and below sergeant major.

mas•ter•ship (măs′tər-shĭp′) *n.* **1.** The office, function, or authority of a master. **2.** The skill or dexterity of a master.

mas•ter•sing•er (măs′tər-sĭng′ər) *n.* See **Meistersinger.**

Mas•ter•son (măs′tər-sən), **William Barclay ("Bat")** 1853–1921. Amer. frontier marshal famed for his exploits as an army scout, gambler, and law enforcer.

mas•ter•stroke (măs′tər-strōk′) *n.* An achievement or action revealing consummate skill.

mas•ter•work (măs′tər-wûrk′) *n.* See **masterpiece** 2.

mas•ter•y (măs′tə-rē) *n., pl.* **-ies 1.** Possession of consummate skill. **2.** The status of master or ruler; control: *mastery of the seas.* **3.** Full command of a subject of study.

mast•head (măst′hĕd′) *n.* **1.** *Nautical* The top of a mast. **2.** The listing in a newspaper or periodical of information about its staff, operation, and circulation. **3.** The title of a newspaper or periodical on the first page, front cover, or title page.

mas•tic (măs′tĭk) *n.* **1.** The mastic tree. **2.** The aromatic resin of the mastic tree, used esp. in varnishes, lacquers, adhesives, and condiments and as an astringent. **3.** A pastelike cement used in highway construction, esp. one made with powdered lime or brick and tar. [ME, mastic resin < OFr. *mastich* < Lat. *mastichum, mastichē* < Gk. *mastikhē,* chewing gum, mastic < *mastikhān,* to grind the teeth.]

mas•ti•cate (măs′tĭ-kāt′) *v.* **-cat•ed, -cat•ing, -cates** —*tr.* **1.** To chew (food). **2.** To grind and knead (rubber, for example) into a pulp. —*intr.* To chew food. [LLat. *masticāre, masticāt-,* to masticate < Gk. *mastikhān,* to grind the teeth.] —**mas′ti•ca′tion** *n.* —**mas′ti•ca′tor** *n.*

mas•ti•ca•to•ry (măs′tĭ-kə-tôr′ē, -tōr′ē) *adj.* **1.** Of, relating to, or used in mastication. **2.** Adapted for chewing. ❖ *n., pl.* **-ries** A medicinal substance chewed to increase salivation.

mastic tree *n.* A small evergreen shrub (*Pistacia lentiscus*) of the Mediterranean region, cultivated for its resin.

mas•tiff (măs′tĭf) *n.* Any of an ancient breed of large strong dogs, probably originating in Asia and having a short, often fawn-colored coat. [ME *mastif,* alteration of OFr. *mastin* < VLat. **(canis) mānsuētīnus,* tame (dog) < Lat. *mānsuētus,* p. part. of *mānsuēscere,* to tame : *manus,* hand; see **man-**[2] in App. + *suēscere,* to accustom; see **s(w)e-** in App.]

mastiff

mastiff bat *n.* Any of various snub-nosed bats of the family Molossidae, found in warm regions of most parts of the world and having narrow wings and brown, gray, or black fur.

mas·ti·goph·o·ran (măs′tĭ-gŏf′ər-ən) *n.* Any of various protozoans of the class Mastigophora, having one or more flagella. [< NLat. *Mastigophora*, class name : Gk. *mastīx, mastīg-*, whip + NLat. *-phora* (< Gk., neut. pl. of *-phoros, -phore*.] —**mas′ti·goph′o·ran** *adj.*

mas·ti·tis (mă-stī′tĭs) *n.* Inflammation of the breast or udder.

masto– or **mast–** *pref.* Breast; mammary gland; nipple: *mastectomy.* [< Gk. *mastos*, breast.]

mas·to·don (măs′tə-dŏn′) *n.* Any of several very large extinct proboscidian mammals of the genus *Mammut* (sometimes *Mastodon*), resembling the elephant but having molar teeth of a different structure. [NLat. *Mastodōn*, genus name : Gk. *mastos*, nipple + Gk. *odōn, odont-*, tooth (< the nipple-shaped protrusions on the crowns of its molars); see **dent-** in App.]

mas·to·dont (măs′tə-dŏnt′) *adj.* Of, relating to, or characteristic of a mastodon. [< NLat. *Mastodōn*, genus name. See MASTODON.]

mas·toid (măs′toid′) *n.* The mastoid process. ❖ *adj.* **1.** Of or relating to the mastoid process. **2.** Shaped like a breast or nipple. [NLat. *mastoīdēs*, nipplelike, mastoid (< its shape) < Gk. *mastoeidēs* : *mastos*, breast + *-oeidēs*, -oid.]

mastoid bone *n.* See **mastoid process.**

mastoid cell *n.* Any of numerous air-filled spaces of various sizes in the mastoid process.

mas·toid·ec·to·my (măs′toi-děk′tə-mē) *n., pl.* **-mies** Surgical removal of mastoid cells or part or all of the mastoid process.

mas·toid·i·tis (măs′toid-ī′tĭs) *n.* Inflammation of the mastoid process and mastoid cells.

mastoid process *n.* A conical protuberance of the temporal bone that is situated behind the ear in many vertebrates and serves as a site of muscle attachment.

mas·to·pex·y (măs′tə-pěk′sē) *n., pl.* **-ies** Plastic surgery in which the breasts are lifted or reshaped. [MASTO- + Gk. *-pēxiā*, fixing (< *pēgnunai*, to fix in place).]

Ma·stro·ian·ni (mä′stroi-ä′nē, -strō-yän′nē), Marcello 1924–96. Italian actor whose films include *La Dolce Vita* (1960).

mas·tur·bate (măs′tər-bāt′) *v.* **-bat·ed, -bat·ing, -bates** —*intr.* To perform an act of masturbation. —*tr.* To perform an act of masturbation on. [Lat. *masturbārī, masturbāt-*.]

mas·tur·ba·tion (măs′tər-bā′shən) *n.* Excitation of one's own or another's genital organs, usu. to orgasm, by manual contact or means other than sexual intercourse. —**mas′tur·ba′tor** *n.*

mas·tur·ba·to·ry (măs′tər-bə-tôr′ē, -tōr′ē) *adj.* **1.** Of or relating to masturbation. **2.** Excessively self-indulgent or self-involved.

Ma·su·ri·a (mə-zŏŏr′ē-ə) A historical region of NE Poland. —**Ma·su′ri·an** *adj.*

mat¹ (măt) *n.* **1.** A flat piece of coarse fabric or other material, used for wiping one's shoes or feet or in various other forms as a floor covering. **2.** A small flat piece of decorated material placed under a lamp, dish of food, or other object. **3.** *Sports* A floor pad to protect athletes. **4.** A densely woven or thickly tangled mass: *a mat of hair.* **5.** The solid part of a lace design. **6.** A heavy woven net of rope or wire cable placed over a blasting site to keep debris from scattering. ❖ *v.* **mat·ted, mat·ting, mats** —*tr.* **1.** To cover, protect, or decorate with mats or a mat. **2.** To pack or interweave into a thick mass. —*intr.* To be packed or interwoven into a thick mass; become entangled. [ME < OE *matte* < LLat. *matta*, poss. < Phoenician (Punic) *maṭṭe*; akin to Heb. *miṭṭâ*, bed, couch.]

mat² (măt) *n.* **1.** A decorative border around a picture to serve as a frame or provide contrast between the picture and the frame. **2.** also **matte** *a.* A dull, often rough finish, as of paint, glass, metal, or paper. *b.* A special tool for producing such a surface or finish. **3.** *Printing* See **matrix** 10a. ❖ *tr.v.* **mat·ted, mat·ting, mats** **1.** To put a mat around (a picture). **2.** To produce a dull finish on. ❖ *adj.* also **matte** Having a dull finish. [< Fr., dull < OFr., defeated, withered, perh. < Lat. *mattus*, stupefied, senseless, poss. < **maditus*, p. part. of *madēre*, to be wet.]

MAT *abbr.* Master of Arts in Teaching

mat. *abbr.* matinee

Ma·ta·be·le (mä′tə-bĕl′ā, -tä-) *n., pl.* **Matabele** or **-les** See **Ndebele.**

Ma·ta·be·le·land (mä′tə-bĕl′ā-lănd′) A former province of Rhodesia, now divided into the two provinces of Matabeleland North and Matabeleland South, in S Zimbabwe.

mat·a·dor (măt′ə-dôr′) *n.* **1.** A bullfighter who performs the final passes and kills the bull. **2.** *Games* One of the highest trumps in certain card games. [Sp. < *matar*, to kill, poss. < VLat. **mattāre*, to beat senseless, perh. < Lat. *mattus*, stupefied. See MAT².]

Ma·ta Ha·ri (mä′tə här′ē, măt′ə här′ē) 1876–1917. Dutch dancer who apparently spied for Germany in World War I.

Ma·ta·mo·ros (măt′ə-môr′əs, mä′tä-mō′rōs) A city of NE Mexico near the mouth of the Rio Grande opposite Brownsville, TX. Pop. 188,745.

Ma·tan·zas (mə-tăn′zəs, mä-tän′säs) A city of NW-central Cuba E of Havana; founded 1693. Pop. 120,988.

Mat·a·pan (măt′ə-păn′), **Cape** See Cape **Taínaron.**

match¹ (măch) *n.* **1a.** One that is exactly like another; a counterpart. **b.** One that is like another in one or more specified qualities. **2.** One that is able to compete equally with another. **3a.** One that closely resembles or harmonizes with another. **b.** A pair, each one of which resembles or harmonizes with the other. **4.** *Sports* **a.** A game or contest in which two or more persons, animals, or teams oppose and compete with each other. **b.** A tennis contest won by the player or side that wins a specified number of sets. **5.** A marriage or an arrangement of marriage. **6.** A person viewed as a prospective marriage partner. ❖ *v.* **matched, match·ing, match·es** —*tr.* **1a.** To be exactly like; correspond exactly to. **b.** To be like with respect to specified qualities. **2.** To resemble or harmonize with: *The coat matches the dress.* **3.** To adapt or suit so that a balanced or harmonious result is achieved; cause to correspond: *You should match your deeds to your beliefs.* **4.** To find or produce a counterpart to: *It's difficult to match the color of old paint.* **5.** To fit together or cause to fit together. **6.** To join or give in marriage. **7.** To place in opposition or competition; pit: *She matched her skill against all comers.* **8.** To provide with an adversary or competitor. **9.** To do as well as or better than in competition; equal. **10.** To set in comparison; compare: *beauty that could never be matched.* **11.** To provide funds so as to equal or complement: *The government matched all private donations to the museum.* **12.** To flip or toss (coins) and compare the sides that land face up. **13.** To couple (electric circuits) by means of a transformer. —*intr.* To be a close counterpart; correspond. [ME *macche* < OE *gemæcca*, companion, mate.] —**match′er** *n.*

match² (măch) *n.* **1.** A narrow piece of material, usu. wood or cardboard, coated on one end with a compound that ignites when scratched against a rough or chemically treated surface. **2.** An easily ignited cord or wick, formerly used to detonate powder charges or to fire cannons and muzzleloading firearms. [ME *matche*, lamp wick < OFr. *mesche* < VLat. **micca* < Lat. *myxa*, a lamp's nozzle < Gk. *muxa*, mucus, lamp wick.]

match·a·ble (măch′ə-bəl) *adj.* That can be matched.

match·board (măch′bôrd′, -bōrd′) *n.* A board cut with a tongue on one side and a matching groove on the other to fit with other boards of similar cut.

match·book (măch′bŏŏk′) *n.* A small folder containing safety matches and having a striking surface along the bottom.

match·box (măch′bŏks′) *n.* A box for matches.

match·less (măch′lĭs) *adj.* Having no match or equal; unsurpassed. —**match′less·ly** *adv.*

match·lock (măch′lŏk′) *n.* **1.** A gunlock in which powder is ignited by a match. **2.** A musket having such a gunlock.

match·mak·er (măch′mā′kər) *n.* **1.** One who arranges or tries to arrange marriages. **2.** One who arranges athletic competitions, esp. in professional boxing. —**match′mak′ing** *n.*

match play *n.* A method of scoring golf games by counting only the number of holes won by each side.

match point *n.* The final point needed to win a sports match.

match·stick (măch′stĭk′) *n.* **1.** A short slender piece of wood from which a match is made. **2.** Something similar to a matchstick, as in slenderness. ❖ *adj.* Short and slender.

match·up (măch′ŭp′) *n.* The pairing of two people or things, as for athletic competition or for comparison.

match·wood (măch′wŏŏd′) *n.* **1.** Wood in small pieces or splinters suitable esp. for making matches. **2.** Splinters.

mate¹ (māt) *n.* **1.** One of a matched pair: *the mate to this glove.* **2.** A spouse. **3a.** Either of a pair of animals or birds that associate in order to propagate. **b.** Either of a pair of animals brought together for breeding. **4a.** A person with whom one is in close association; an associate. **b.** *Chiefly British* A good friend or companion. **c.** A person with whom one shares living quarters. Often used in combination: *chose a new flatmate.* **5.** A deck officer on a merchant ship ranking next below the master. **6.** A US Navy petty officer who is an assistant to a warrant officer. ❖ *v.* **mat·ed, mat·ing, mates** —*tr.* **1.** To join closely; pair. **2.** To unite in marriage. **3.** To pair (animals) for breeding. —*intr.* **1.** To become joined in marriage; breed. **2a.** To be paired for reproducing; breed. **b.** To copulate. [ME < MLGer. *gemate, mate*, messmate.]

mate² (māt) *Games n.* A checkmate. ❖ *tr. & intr.v.* **mat·ed, mat·ing, mates** To checkmate or achieve a checkmate. [ME < OFr. *mat*, checkmated < Ar. *māt*, he has died. See CHECKMATE.]

ma·té (mä′tā, mä-tě′) *n.* **1.** A South American evergreen tree (*Ilex paraguariensis*), the dried leaves of which are used to prepare a tealike beverage. **2.** This tealike beverage, popular in South America. [Fr. < Am.Sp. *mate* < Quechua, hollow gourd used to brew yerba maté.]

mat·e·lote (măt′l-ōt′, mä-tə-lōt′) *n.* A fish stew cooked in a wine sauce. [Fr. < *matelot*, sailor < OFr. *matenot*, bunkmate, sailor, poss. < MDu. *mattenoot* (perh. < mate bed < LLat. *matta*; see MAT¹ + *noot*, fellow) or < ON *mǫtunautr*, messmate (*mata*, food, mess + *nautr*, companion).]

ma·ter (mā′tər) *n. Chiefly British* Mother. [Lat. *māter*. See **māter-** in App.]

ma·ter·fa·mil·i·as (mā′tər-fə-mĭl′ē-əs) *n.* A woman who is the head of a household or the mother of a family. [Lat. *māterfamiliās* : *māter*, mother; see MATER + *familiās*, archaic genitive of *familia*, household; see FAMILY.]

ma·te·ri·al (mə-tîr′ē-əl) *n.* **1.** The substance or substances out of which a thing is or can be made. **2.** Something, such as an idea, that is to be refined and made or incorporated into a finished effort. **3. materials** Tools or apparatus for the performance of a given task. **4.** Yard goods or cloth. **5.** A person qualified or suited for a position or activity. ❖ *adj.* **1.** Of, relating to, or composed of matter. **2.** Of, relating to, or affecting material well-being; bodily. **3.** Of or concerned with the physical as distinct from the intellectual or spiritual. **4.** Being both relevant and consequential; crucial. **5.** *Philosophy* Of or relating to the matter of reasoning, rather than the form. [ME, consisting of matter, material < OFr. < LLat. *materiālis* < Lat. *materia*, matter. See **māter-** in App.] —**ma•te′ri•al•ness** *n.*

ma•te•ri•al•ism (mə-tîr′ē-ə-lĭz′əm) *n.* **1.** *Philosophy* The theory that physical matter is the only reality and that everything can be explained in terms of matter and physical phenomena. **2.** The theory or attitude that physical well-being and worldly possessions constitute the greatest good and highest value in life. **3.** A great or excessive regard for worldly concerns. —**ma•te′ri•al•ist** *n.* —**ma•te′ri•al•is′tic** *adj.*

ma•te•ri•al•i•ty (mə-tîr′ē-ăl′ĭ-tē) *n., pl.* **-ties 1.** The state or quality of being material. **2.** Physical substance; matter.

ma•te•ri•al•ize (mə-tîr′ē-ə-līz′) *v.* **-ized, -iz•ing, -iz•es** —*tr.* **1.** To cause to become real or actual. **2.** To cause to become materialistic. —*intr.* **1.** To assume material or effective form. **2.** To take physical form or shape. **3.** To appear, esp. suddenly. —**ma•te′ri•al•i•za′tion** (-ə-lĭ-zā′shən) *n.* —**ma•te′ri•al•iz′er** *n.*

ma•te•ri•al•ly (mə-tîr′ē-ə-lē) *adv.* **1.** With regard to the physical world. **2.** With regard to matter as distinguished from form. **3.** To a significant extent or degree; substantially.

materials science *n.* The study of the characteristics and uses of the various materials, such as ceramics and plastics, employed in science and technology.

matilija poppy
Romneya coulteri

ma•te•ri•a med•i•ca (mə-tîr′ē-ə měd′ĭ-kə) *n.* **1.** (*used with a sing. verb*) The scientific study of medicinal drugs and their sources, preparation, and use. **2.** (*used with a pl. verb*) Substances used in the preparation of medicinal drugs. [NLat. *materia medica* (transl. of Gk. *hulē iatrikē*) : Lat. *materia*, material + Lat. *medica*, fem. of *medicus*, medical.]

ma•te•ri•el or **ma•té•ri•el** (mə-tîr′ē-ĕl′) *n.* The equipment, apparatus, and supplies of a military force or other organization. [Fr. *matériel*, consisting of matter, materiel < OFr. *material*. See MATERIAL.]

ma•ter•nal (mə-tûr′nəl) *adj.* **1.** Relating to or characteristic of a mother or motherhood; motherly: *maternal instinct.* **2.** Inherited from one's mother. **3.** Related through one's mother. [ME < OFr. *maternel* < Med.Lat. *māternālis* < Lat. *māternus*. See **māter-** in App.] —**ma•ter′nal•ism** *n.* —**ma•ter′nal•ly** *adv.*

ma•ter•ni•ty (mə-tûr′nĭ-tē) *n., pl.* **-ties 1.** The state of being a mother; motherhood. **2.** The feelings or characteristics associated with being a mother; motherliness. **3.** A maternity ward. ❖ *adj.* Relating to or effective during pregnancy, childbirth, or the first months of motherhood: *maternity leave.* [Fr. *maternité* < Med.Lat. *māternitās* < Lat. *māternus*, maternal. See MATERNAL.]

maternity ward *n.* The part of a hospital that provides care for women before and during childbirth and for their infants.

mat•ey (mā′tē) *adj. Chiefly British* Sociable; friendly.

math (măth) *n.* Mathematics.

math•e•mat•i•cal (măth′ə-măt′ĭ-kəl) also **math•e•mat•ic** (-ĭk) *adj.* **1.** Of or relating to mathematics. **2a.** Precise; exact. **b.** Absolute; certain. **3.** Possible according to mathematics but highly improbable. [ME < Med.Lat. *mathēmaticālis* < Lat. *mathēmaticus* < Gk. *mathēmatikos* < *mathēma, mathēmat-*, science, learning < *manthanein, math-*, to learn.] —**math′e•mat′i•cal•ly** *adv.*

mathematical induction *n.* Induction.

mathematical logic *n.* See **symbolic logic.**

math•e•ma•ti•cian (măth′ə-mə-tĭsh′ən) *n.* A person skilled or learned in mathematics.

math•e•mat•ics (măth′ə-măt′ĭks) *n.* (*used with a sing. verb*) The study of the measurement, properties, and relationships of quantities and sets, using numbers and symbols. [< ME *mathematik* < OFr. *mathematique* < Lat. *mathēmatica* < Gk. *mathēmatikē (tekhnē)*, mathematical (science), fem. of *mathēmatikos*. See MATHEMATICAL.]

math•e•ma•tize (măth′ə-mə-tīz′) *tr.v.* **-tized, -tiz•ing, -tiz•es** To reduce to or as if to mathematical formulas. —**math′e•ma•ti•za′tion** (-tĭ-zā′shən) *n.*

Math•er (măth′ər), **Increase** 1639–1723. Amer. clergyman and writer who with his son **Cotton** (1663–1728) exerted great influence on the colony of Massachusetts.

Ma•thu•ra (mŭt′ər-ə) also **Mut•tra** (mŭt′rə) A city of N-central India NW of Agra; a Hindu pilgrimage site revered as the reputed birthplace of Krishna. Pop. 226,691.

ma•ti•li•ja poppy (mə-tĭl′ē-hä′) *n.* A subshrub (*Romneya coulteri*) of California and Baja California having very large white flowers with yellow centers. [After *Matilija* Canyon in SW CA.]

mat•in (măt′n) also **mat•in•al** (-əl) *adj.* Of or relating to matins or to the early part of the day. [ME < OFr., sing. of *matines, matins*. See MATINS.]

mat•i•nee or **mat•i•née** (măt′n-ā′) *n.* An entertainment, such as a movie or musical performance, given in the daytime, usu. in

the afternoon. [Fr. *matinée* < *matin*, morning < OFr. *matines, matins*. See MATINS.]

mat•ins (măt′nz) *n.* (*used with a sing. or pl. verb*) **1.** *Ecclesiastical* The office that formerly constituted together with lauds the first of the seven canonical hours. **2.** often **Matins** See **Morning Prayer.** [ME *matines* < OFr. < Med.Lat. (*vigiliae*) *mātūtīnae*, morning (vigils), fem. pl. of Lat. *mātūtīnus*, of the morning < *Mātūta*, goddess of dawn.]

Ma•tisse (mə-tēs′, mä-), **Henri** 1869–1954. French artist whose works include *The Dance* (1930–32).

mat•jes herring (măt′yĭs) *n.* Unspawned herring that are filleted and pickled. [Partial transl. of Du. *maatjesharing* : *maatjes* (alteration of *maeghdekins*, genitive of *maeghdekin*, maiden, dim. of *maagd*, maid) + *haring*, herring.]

matri- or **matro-** or **matr-** *pref.* Mother; maternal: *matrilineal.* [Lat. *mātri-* < *māter, mātr-*, mother. See MATER.]

ma•tri•arch (mā′trē-ärk′) *n.* **1.** A woman who rules a family, clan, or tribe. **2.** A woman who dominates a group or an activity. **3.** A highly respected mother. —**ma′tri•ar′chal** (-är′kəl), **ma′tri•ar′chic** *adj.* —**ma′tri•ar′chal•ism** *n.*

ma•tri•ar•chate (mā′trē-är′kĭt, -kāt′) *n.* **1.** See **matriarchy. 2.** A hypothetical stage in the evolution of a society in which authority is held by women.

ma•tri•ar•chy (mā′trē-är′kē) *n., pl.* **-chies 1.** A social system in which the mother is head of the family. **2.** A family, community, or society based on this system or governed by women.

mat•ri•cide (măt′rĭ-sīd′) *n.* **1.** The act of killing one's mother. **2.** One who kills one's mother. —**mat′ri•cid′al** (-sīd′l) *adj.*

ma•tric•u•late (mə-trĭk′yə-lāt′) *tr. & intr.v.* **-lat•ed, -lat•ing, -lates** To admit or be admitted into a group, esp. a college or university. ❖ *n.* (-lĭt, -lāt′) One who is admitted as a student to a college or university. [< Med.Lat. *mātrīculāre, mātrīculāt-* < LLat. *mātrīcula*, list, dim. of *mātrīx, mātrīc-.* See MATRIX.] —**ma•tric′u•lant** (mə-trĭk′yə-lənt) *n.* —**ma•tric′u•la′tion** *n.*

mat•ri•lin•e•age (măt′rə-lĭn′ē-ĭj) *n.* Line of descent as traced through women on the maternal side of a family.

mat•ri•lin•e•al (măt′rə-lĭn′ē-əl) *adj.* Relating to, based on, or tracing ancestral descent through the maternal line. —**mat′ri•lin′e•al•ly** *adv.*

mat•ri•lo•cal (măt′rə-lō′kəl) *adj. Anthropology* Of or relating to residence with a wife's kin group or clan.

mat•ri•mo•ny (măt′rə-mō′nē) *n., pl.* **-nies** The act or state of being married; marriage. [ME < OFr. *matrimoine* < Lat. *mātrimōnium* < *māter, mātr-*, mother. See **māter-** in App.] —**mat′ri•mo′ni•al** *adj.* —**mat′ri•mo′ni•al•ly** *adv.*

matrimony vine *n.* Any of various often thorny shrubs of the genus *Lycium*, some species of which are cultivated for their purplish flowers and brightly colored berries.

ma•trix (mā′trĭks) *n., pl.* **ma•tri•ces** (mā′trĭ-sēz′, măt′rĭ-) or **ma•trix•es 1.** A situation or surrounding substance within which something else originates, develops, or is contained. **2.** The womb. **3.** *Anatomy* **a.** The formative cells or tissue of a fingernail, toenail, or tooth. **b.** See **ground substance** 1. **4.** *Geology* **a.** The solid matter in which a fossil or crystal is embedded. **b.** Groundmass. **5.** A mold or die. **6.** The principal metal in an alloy, as the iron in steel. **7.** A binding substance, as cement in concrete. **8a.** *Mathematics* A rectangular array of numeric or algebraic quantities subject to mathematical operations. **b.** Something resembling such an array, as in the regular formation of elements into columns and rows. **9.** *Computer Science* The network of intersections between input and output leads in a computer, functioning as an encoder or a decoder. **10.** *Printing* **a.** A mold used in stereotyping and designed to receive positive impressions of type or illustrations from which metal plates can be cast. **b.** A metal plate used for casting typefaces. [ME *matrice* < OFr. < LLat. *mātrīx, mātrīc-* < Lat., breeding-animal < *māter, mātr-*, mother. See **māter-** in App.]

matro- *pref.* Variant of **matri-.**

ma•tron (mā′trən) *n.* **1.** A married woman or a widow, esp. a mother of dignity, mature age, and established social position. **2.** A woman who acts as a supervisor or monitor in a public institution. [ME *matrone* < OFr. < Lat. *mātrōna* < *māter, mātr-*, mother. See **māter-** in App.] —**ma′tron•al** *adj.* —**ma′tron•li•ness** *n.* —**ma′tron•ly** *adv. & adj.*

matron of honor *n., pl.* **matrons of honor** A married woman serving as chief attendant of the bride at a wedding.

mat•ro•nym•ic (măt′rə-nĭm′ĭk) also **me•tro•nym•ic** (mē′trə-, mĕt′rə-) *adj.* Of, relating to, or derived from the name of one's mother or maternal ancestor. ❖ *n.* A name so derived. [Gk. *mātronumikos*, dialectal var. of *mētronumikos* : *mētēr, mētr-*, mother; see METRO- + *onuma*, name; see **nō-men-** in App.]

Mat•su (măt′sōō′) An island administered by Taiwan in the East China Sea off the SE coast of mainland China.

Ma•tsu•do (mä-tsōō′dō) A city of E-central Honshu, Japan, a suburb of Tokyo. Pop. 463,517.

Ma•tsu•ya•ma (mä′tsōō-yä′mä) A city of W Shikoku, Japan, on the Inland Sea. Pop. 454,374.

Matt. *abbr. Bible* Matthew

Mat•tag•a•mi (mə-tăg′ə-mē) A river of E Ontario, Canada, rising in **Mattagami Lake** and flowing c. 443 km (275 mi) N to the Moose R.

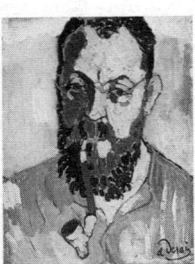
Henri Matisse
1905 portrait by
André Derain

matte¹ (măt) *n.* Variant of **mat²** 2. ❖ *adj.* Variant of **mat²**.

matte² (măt) *n.* A mixture of a metal and its sulfides, made by smelting the sulfide ores of copper, lead, or nickel. [Fr., curdled milk, matte < fem. of obsolete *mat*, compact < OFr., dull < Lat. *mattus*, stupefied. See MAT².]

mat·ted (măt′ĭd) *adj.* **1.** Covered with or made from mats. **2.** Tangled in a dense mass: *matted undergrowth.*

mat·ter (măt′ər) *n.* **1a.** Something that occupies space and can be perceived by one or more senses; a physical body, a physical substance, or the universe as a whole. **b.** *Physics* Something that has mass and exists as a solid, liquid, gas, or plasma. **2.** A specific type of substance: *inorganic matter.* **3.** Discharge or waste, such as pus or feces, from a living organism. **4.** *Philosophy* In Aristotelian and Scholastic use, that which is in itself undifferentiated and formless and which, as the subject of change and development, receives form and becomes substance and experience. **5.** The substance of thought or expression as opposed to the manner in which it is stated or conveyed. **6.** A subject of concern, feeling, or action. See Syns at **subject**. **7.** Trouble or difficulty. **8.** An approximated quantity, amount, or extent: *a matter of years.* **9.** Something printed or otherwise set down in writing: *reading matter.* **10.** Something sent by mail. **11.** *Printing* **a.** Composed type. **b.** Material to be set in type. ❖ *intr.v.* **-tered, -ter·ing, -ters** To be of importance. See Syns at **count¹**. *—idioms:* **as a matter of fact** In fact; actually. **for that matter** So far as that is concerned; as for that. **no matter** Regardless of. [ME < OFr. *matere* < Lat. *māteria*, wood, timber, matter < *māter*, mother (because the woody part was seen as the source of growth). See **māter-** in App.]

Mat·ter·horn (măt′ər-hôrn′, mä′tər-) A mountain, 4,481.1 m (14,692 ft), in the Pennine Alps on the Italian-Swiss border.

matter of course *n.* A natural or logical outcome.

mat·ter-of-fact (măt′ər-əv-făkt′) *adj.* **1.** Relating or adhering to facts; literal. **2.** Straightforward or unemotional. **—mat′ter-of-fact′ly** *adv.* **—mat′ter-of-fact′ness** *n.*

Mat·thew (măth′yōō) *n.* See table at Bible. [LLat. *Matthaeus* < Gk. *Matthaios* < Heb. *Mattayyāh*, gift of Yahweh : *mattān*, gift (< *nātan*, to give) + *yāh*, Yahweh.]

Matthew, Saint. 1st cent. A.D. One of the 12 Apostles and the author of the first Gospel of the New Testament.

mat·ting¹ (măt′ĭng) *n.* **1a.** Material formed into or considered a mat. **b.** A coarsely woven fabric used to cover floors, for example. **2.** The activity of making mats.

mat·ting² (măt′ĭng) *n.* **1.** A dull surface or finish. **2.** The process of dulling a surface, as of metal.

mat·tins (măt′nz) *n.* (*used with a sing. or pl. verb*) *Chiefly British* Variant of **matins**.

mat·tock (măt′ək) *n.* A digging tool with a flat blade set at right angles to the handle. [ME < OE *mattuc*, perh. < VLat. **matteūca*, club; akin to **mattea*. See MACE¹.]

mat·tress (măt′rĭs) *n.* **1a.** A usu. rectangular pad of heavy cloth filled with soft material or an arrangement of coiled springs, used as or on a bed. **b.** An airtight inflatable pad used as or on a bed or as a cushion. **2.** A closely woven mat of brush and poles used to protect an embankment, a dike, or a dam from erosion. [ME *mattresse* < OFr. *materas* < OItal. *materasso* and < Med.Lat. *matracium*, both < Ar. *maṭraḥ*, place where something is thrown, mat, cushion < *ṭaraḥa*, to throw.]

WORD HISTORY The history of the word *mattress* is a small lesson in the way amenities have come to Europe from the Middle East. During the earlier part of the Middle Ages, Arabic culture was more advanced than that of Europe. One of the amenities of life enjoyed by the Arabs was sleeping on cushions thrown on the floor. Derived from the Arabic word *ṭaraḥa*, "to throw," the word *maṭraḥ* meant "place where something is thrown" and "mat, cushion." This kind of sleeping surface was adopted by the Europeans during the Crusades, and the Arabic word was taken into Old Italian (*materasso*), Old French (*materas*), and Medieval Latin (*matracium*). English borrowed the word from Old French and Medieval Latin, *materas* being first recorded around 1300.

mat·u·rate (măch′ə-rāt′) *v.* **-rat·ed, -rat·ing, -rates** *—intr.* **1.** To mature, ripen, or develop. **2.** To suppurate. *—tr.* To cause to suppurate. [Lat. *mātūrāre, mātūrāt-* < *mātūrus*, mature. See MATURE.] **—mat′u·ra′tive** *adj.*

mat·u·ra·tion (măch′ə-rā′shən) *n.* **1.** The process of becoming mature. **2.** *Biology* **a.** The processes by which gametes are formed. **b.** The final differentiation processes in biological systems, such as those of a mature cell. **—mat′u·ra′tion·al** *adj.*

maturation division *n.* Either of the two successive cell divisions of meiosis, with only one duplication of the chromosomes, that results in the formation of haploid gametes.

ma·ture (mə-tyŏŏr′, -tŏŏr′, -chŏŏr′) *adj.* **-tur·er, -tur·est 1a.** Having reached full natural growth or development: *a mature cell.* **b.** Having reached a desired or final condition; ripe: *a mature cheese.* **2.** Of, relating to, or characteristic of full development, either mental or physical: *mature for her age.* **3a.** Suitable or intended for adults: *mature subject matter.* **b.** Composed of adults: *a mature audience.* **4.** Worked out fully by the mind; considered: *a mature plan of action.* **5.** Having reached the limit of its time; due: *a mature bond.* **6.** No longer subject to great expansion or

development. Used of an industry, market, or product. **7.** *Geology* Having reached maximum development of form. Used of streams and landforms. ❖ *v.* **-tured, -tur·ing, -tures** *—tr.* **1.** To bring to full development; ripen. **2.** To work out fully in the mind. *—intr.* **1.** To evolve toward or reach full maturity. **2.** To become due. Used of notes and bonds. [ME < OFr. < Lat. *mātūrus*.] **—ma·ture′ly** *adv.* **—ma·ture′ness** *n.*

SYNONYMS *mature, age, develop, ripen* These verbs mean to bring or come to full development or maximum excellence: *maturing wines in vats; aged the cheese; developed the flavor; fruits ripened on the vine.*

ma·ture-on·set diabetes (mə-tyŏŏr′ŏn′sĕt′, -ŏn′, -tŏŏr′-, -chŏŏr′-) *n.* Diabetes mellitus.

ma·tur·i·ty (mə-tyŏŏr′ĭ-tē, -tŏŏr′-, -chŏŏr′-) *n., pl.* **-ties 1a.** The state or quality of being fully grown or developed. **b.** The state or quality of being mature. **2a.** The time at which a note or bond is due. **b.** The state of a note or bond being due. **3.** *Geology* A stage in the evolution of streams or landscapes at which maximum development has been reached or erosion is going on with maximum vigor. [ME *maturite* < OFr. < Lat. *mātūritās* < *mātūrus*, mature. See MATURE.]

ma·tu·ti·nal (mə-tōōt′n-əl, -tyōōt′-, măch′ŏŏ-tī′nəl) *adj.* Of, relating to, or occurring in the morning; early. [LLat. *mātūtīnalis* < Lat. *mātūtīnus*. See MATINS.]

mat·zo or **mat·zah** (măt′sə, -sō′, -sô′, mät-sä′) *n., pl.* **-zos** or **-zahs** (măt′səz, -sōs′) or **-zot** or **-zoth** (mät-sôt′) Flat unleavened bread, eaten esp. during Passover. [Yiddish *matse* < Heb. *maṣṣā*.]

matzo ball *n.* A small dumpling made of crushed matzo.

maud·lin (môd′lĭn) *adj.* Effusively or tearfully sentimental. [Alteration of (MARY) MAGDALENE, frequently depicted as a tearful penitent.] **—maud′lin·ly** *adv.* **—maud′lin·ness** *n.*

Maugham (môm), **W(illiam) Somerset** 1874–1965. British writer whose works include *Of Human Bondage* (1915).

mau·gre (mô′gər) *prep. Archaic* Notwithstanding. [ME < OFr. : *mal-, mau-*, bad; see MAL- + *gre*, pleasure (< Lat. *grātum* < neut. of *grātus*, pleasing).]

Mau·i (mou′ē) An island of HI NW of Hawaii I.

maul (môl) *n.* **1.** also **mall** (môl) **a.** A heavy long-handled hammer used esp. to drive stakes, piles, or wedges. **b.** A heavy hammer with a wedge-shaped head used for splitting logs. **2.** *Sports* **a.** A play in Rugby in which a mass of players gathers around a ball carrier being tackled in order to gain possession of the ball when it is released. **b.** The mass of players during such a play. ❖ *tr.v.* **mauled, maul·ing, mauls** also **mall·ing, malls 1.** To injure by or as if by beating. **2.** To handle roughly: *The package was mauled by the careless messenger.* **3.** To split (wood) with a maul and wedge. [ME *malle* < OFr. *mail* < Lat. *malleus*. See **melə-** in App.] **—maul′er** *n.*

Maul·din (môl′dĭn), **William Henry ("Bill")** b. 1921. Amer. editorial cartoonist noted for his realistic, bitterly comic drawings of frontline soldiers.

maul·stick also **mahl·stick** (môl′stĭk′) *n.* A long wooden stick used by painters as a support for the hand that holds the brush. [Partial transl. of obsolete Du. *maalstok* : *malen*, to paint (< MDu. *mal*, a spot, mark) + *stok*, stick.]

Mau·na Ke·a (mô′nə kā′ə, kē′ə) An active volcano, c. 4,208 m (13,796 ft), of N-central Hawaii I.

Mauna Lo·a (lō′ə) An active volcano, 4,172.4 m (13,680 ft), of S-central Hawaii I.

maund (mônd) *n.* A unit of weight varying in different countries of Asia from 11.2 to 37.4 kilograms (24.8 to 82.6 pounds) avoirdupois, the latter being the official maund in India. [Hindi *mān* < Skt. *mānam*, measure < *mimīte, mā-*, he measures. See **mē-¹** in App.]

maun·der (môn′dər, män′-) *intr.v.* **-dered, -der·ing, -ders 1.** To talk incoherently or aimlessly. **2.** To move or act aimlessly or vaguely; wander. [Poss. dialectal var. of MEANDER (prob. influenced by WANDER).]

Maun·dy Thursday (môn′dē, män′-) *n.* The Thursday before Easter, commemorating the Last Supper. [< ME *maunde*, foot-washing ceremony on this day < OFr. *mande* < Lat. (*novum*) *mandātum*, (new) commandment (< Jesus's words in John 13:34). See MANDATE.]

Mau·pas·sant (mō′pə-sänt′, mō-pä-sän′), **(Henri René Albert) Guy de** 1850–93. French writer known esp. for his realistic short stories.

Mau·re·ta·ni·a (môr′ĭ-tā′nē-ə, -tän′yə, mär′-) An ancient district of the Roman Empire in present-day Morocco and Algeria; ruled by Rome from c. 100 B.C. to the 5th cent. A.D. **—Mau·re·ta′ni·an** *adj.* & *n.*

Mau·ri·ac (môr′ē-äk′, môr-yäk′), **François** 1885–1970. French writer who won the 1952 Nobel Prize for literature.

Mau·rice of Nassau (môr′ĭs, mŏr′-) Prince of Orange. 1567–1625. Dutch general who drove Spanish forces from Dutch territory (1590–1609).

Mau·ri·ta·ni·a (môr′ĭ-tā′nē-ə, -tän′yə, mär′-) A country of NW Africa bordering on the Atlantic Ocean; achieved independence from France in 1960. Cap. Nouakchott. Pop. 2,211,000. **—Mau′ri·ta′ni·an** *adj.* & *n.*

Matterhorn

mattock

Mauritania

ă pat	oi boy
ā pay	ou out
âr care	ŏŏ took
ä father	ōō boot
ĕ pet	ŭ cut
ē be	ûr urge
ĭ pit	th thin
ī pie	th this
îr pier	hw which
ŏ pot	zh vision
ō toe	ə about,
ô paw	item

Stress marks:
′ (primary);
′ (secondary), as in
lexicon (lĕk′sĭ-kŏn′)

Mau·ri·tius (mô-rĭsh′əs, -ē-əs) An island country in the SW Indian Ocean comprising the island of **Mauritius** and small dependencies in the Mascarene Is.; achieved independence from Great Britain in 1968. Cap. Port Louis. Pop. 1,104,000. —**Mau·ri′tian** adj. & n.

Mau·rois (môr-wä′), **André** Pen name of Émile Herzog. 1885–1967. French writer noted for his essays, biographies, and novels.

Mau·ry (môr′ē), **Matthew Fontaine** 1806–73. Amer. naval officer who charted the currents and winds of the Atlantic, Pacific, and Indian oceans.

mau·so·le·um (mô′sə-lē′əm, -zə-) n., pl. **-le·ums** or **-le·a** (-lē′ə) 1. A large stately tomb or a building housing such a tomb or several tombs. 2. A gloomy, usu. large room or building. [ME < Lat. Mausōlēum < Gk. Mausōleion < Mausōlos, Mausolus (died c. 353 B.C.), Persian satrap whose tomb was considered one of the Seven Wonders of the World.] —**mau′so·le′an** adj.

mauve (mōv) n. A grayish violet to reddish purple. [Fr. < OFr. mallow < Lat. malva. See MALLOW.] —**mauve** adj.

ma·ven also **ma·vin** (mā′vən) n. A person who has special knowledge or experience; an expert. [Yiddish meyvn < Heb. mēbîn, active part. of hēbîn, to understand, derived stem of bîn, to discern.]

mav·er·ick (măv′ər-ĭk, măv′rĭk) n. 1. An unbranded range animal, esp. a calf separated from its mother. 2. One that rejects the dictates of or resists adherence to a group; a dissenter. 3. Independent in thought and action or exhibiting such independence. [Possibly after Samuel Augustus Maverick (1803–70), American cattleman who left his calves unbranded.]

ma·vis (mā′vĭs) n. See **song thrush**. [ME < OFr. mauvis, prob. < mauve, seagull, mew.]

ma·vour·nin also **ma·vour·neen** (mə-vŏŏr′nēn′) n. Irish My darling. [Ir.Gael. mo mhuirnín : mo, my (< OIr.; see me-¹ in App.) + muirnín, darling, dim. of muirn, delight (< OIr., tumult, revels).]

maw (mô) n. 1. The mouth, stomach, jaws, or gullet of a voracious animal, esp. a carnivore. 2. The opening into something felt to be insatiable. [ME mawe < OE maga.]

mawk·ish (mô′kĭsh) adj. 1. Excessively and objectionably sentimental. 2. Sickening or insipid in taste. [< ME mawke, maggot, var. of magot. See MAGGOT.] —**mawk′ish·ly** adv.

max (măks) n. Slang The maximum. ❖ v. **maxed, max·ing, max·es** —tr. To reach the upper limit of: maxed out his credit. —intr. To reach an upper limit, as of endurance. —**max** adj. & adv.

max. abbr. maximum

max·i (măk′sē) n., pl. **max·is** A long skirt, coat, or dress that usu. extends to or just past the ankles. [< MAXIMUM.]

max·il·la (măk-sĭl′ə) n., pl. **max·il·lae** (măk-sĭl′ē) or **max·il·las** 1. Anatomy Either of a pair of bones of the human skull fusing in the midline and forming the upper jaw. 2. A homologous bone of the skull in other vertebrates. 3. Either of two laterally moving appendages situated behind the mandibles in insects and most other arthropods. [Lat., jawbone.]

max·il·lar·y (măk′sə-lĕr′ē) adj. Of or relating to a jaw or jawbone, esp. the upper one. ❖ n., pl. **-ies** A maxillary bone.

max·il·li·ped (măk-sĭl′ə-pĕd′) n. One of the three pairs of crustacean head appendages located just posterior to the maxillae and used in feeding. [MAXILL(A) + -PED.]

max·il·lo·fa·cial (măk-sĭl′ō-fā′shəl) adj. Relating to or involving the maxilla and the face.

max·im (măk′sĭm) n. A succinct formulation of a fundamental principle, general truth, or rule of conduct. [ME maxime < OFr. < Med.Lat. maxima < maxima (prōpositiō), greatest (premise), fem. of Lat. maximus, greatest. See **meg-** in App.]

Maxim, Sir Hiram Stevens 1840–1916. Amer.-born British inventor of an automatic recoil-operated machine gun (1884). His brother **Hudson** (1853–1927) invented smokeless gun powder, and his son **Hiram Percy** (1896–1936) developed a silencer for firearms.

max·i·mal (măk′sə-məl) adj. 1. Of, relating to, or consisting of a maximum. 2. Being the greatest or highest possible. ❖ n. Mathematics An element in an ordered set that is followed by no other. —**max′i·mal·ly** adv.

max·i·mal·ist (măk′sə-mə-lĭst) n. One who advocates direct or radical action to secure a social or political goal in its entirety. [Russ. maksimalist, name of a splinter group of the Russian Socialist Revolutionary Party, ult. < Lat. maximum, maximum. See MAXIMUM.] —**max′i·mal·ist** adj.

Max·i·mil·ian (măk′sə-mĭl′yən) 1832–67. Austrian archduke and emperor of Mexico (1864–67) who was appointed emperor by the French and executed by Mexican republicans.

Maximilian I 1459–1519. King of Germany (1486–1519) and Holy Roman emperor (1493–1519) who added greatly to the territory and power of the Hapsburgs.

Maximilian II 1527–76. Holy Roman emperor (1564–76) who was tolerant of Lutheranism.

max·i·mize (măk′sə-mīz′) tr.v. **-mized, -miz·ing, -miz·es** 1. To increase or make as great as possible. 2. To assign the greatest possible importance to. 3. Mathematics To find the largest value of (a function). —**max′i·mi·za′tion** (-mĭ-zā′shən) n. —**max′i·miz′er** n.

max·i·mum (măk′sə-məm) n., pl. **-mums** or **-ma** (-mə) 1a. The greatest possible quantity or degree. b. The greatest quantity or degree reached or recorded; the upper limit of variation. c. The time or period during which the highest point or degree is attained. 2. An upper limit permitted by law or other authority. 3. Astronomy a. The moment when a variable star is most brilliant. b. The magnitude of the star at such a moment. 4. Mathematics a. The greatest value assumed by a function over a given interval. b. The largest number in a set. ❖ adj. 1. Having or being the greatest possible or attainable: maximum temperature. 2. Of, relating to, or making up a maximum: the maximum number in a series. [Lat. < neut. of maximus, greatest. See **meg-** in App.]

max·well (măks′wĕl′, -wəl) n. The unit of magnetic flux in the centimeter-gram-second system, equal to 10⁻⁸ weber. [After James Clerk MAXWELL.]

Maxwell, James Clerk 1831–79. British physicist who made fundamental contributions to electromagnetic theory and the kinetic theory of gases.

Max·well's demon (măks′wĕlz′, -wəlz) n. An imaginary creature who is able to sort hot molecules from cold molecules without expending energy, thus violating the second law of thermodynamics. [After James Clerk MAXWELL.]

may¹ (mā) aux.v. Past tense **might** (mīt) 1. To be allowed or permitted to: May I go? 2. Used to indicate a certain measure of likelihood or possibility: It may rain. 3. Used to express a desire or fervent wish: Long may he live! 4. Used to express contingency, purpose, or result in clauses introduced by that or so that: so that you may understand. 5. To be obliged; must. Used in deeds and other legal documents. See Usage Note at **can¹**. [ME, to be able < OE mæg, first and third pers. sing. of magan, to be strong, be able.]

may² (mā) n. Chiefly British The blossoms of the hawthorn. [Fr. mai, hawthorn < Mai, May (when it blooms). See MAY.]

May n. 1. The fifth month of the year in the Gregorian calendar. See table at **calendar**. 2. The springtime of life; youth. 3. The celebration of May Day. [ME < OFr. Mai < Lat. Māius (mēnsis), (the month) of Maia < Māia, an Italic goddess. See **meg-** in App.]

May, Cape A peninsula of S NJ between the Atlantic Ocean and Delaware Bay. The S tip forms **Cape May Point**.

ma·ya (mä′yə) n. Hinduism 1. The power of a god or demon to transform a concept into an element of the sensible world. 2. The transitory manifold appearance of the sensible world, which obscures the undifferentiated spiritual reality from which it originates. [Skt. māyā.]

Ma·ya (mä′yə) n., pl. **Maya** or **-yas** 1a. A member of a Mesoamerican Indian people inhabiting southeast Mexico, Guatemala, and Belize, whose civilization reached its height around A.D. 300–900. b. A modern-day descendant of these people. 2. Any of the Mayan languages, esp. Quiché and Yucatec. [Sp.] —**Ma′ya** adj.

Ma·ya·güez (mī′ə-gwĕz′, mä′yä-gwĕs′) A city of W Puerto Rico WSW of San Juan. Pop. 78,647.

Ma·ya·kov·ski (mä′yə-kôf′skē, mə-), **Vladimir Vladimirovich** 1893–1930. Soviet poet who was a leader of Russian futurism.

Ma·yan (mä′yən) n. 1. A Maya. 2. A linguistic stock of Central America that includes Quiché and Yucatec. ❖ adj. Of or relating to the Mayas, their culture, or the Mayan linguistic stock.

May apple n. 1. A rhizomatous plant (Podophyllum peltatum) of eastern North America having a single nodding white flower and oval yellow fruit. 2. The fruit of this plant.

may·be (mā′bē) adv. Perhaps; possibly. ❖ n. Informal 1. An uncertainty. 2. An uncertain reply.

Maybeck (mā′bĕk′), **Bernard Ralph** 1882–1957. Amer. architect whose designs include the Palace of Fine Arts in San Francisco (1915).

May beetle n. See **June beetle**.

may·bird (mā′bûrd′) n. Chiefly Southeastern US See **bobolink**. [< its seasonal arrival in May.]

may·day (mā′dā′) n. An international radiotelephone signal word used by aircraft and ships in distress. [< Fr. (venez) m'aider, (come) help me!]

May Day n. 1. May 1, observed in some countries in celebration of spring. 2. May 1, observed as a holiday in some countries in honor of labor and labor organizations.

May·er (mā′ər), **Louis Burt** 1885–1957. Russian-born Amer. motion-picture producer whose films include Ben Hur (1926).

may·est (mā′ĭst) or **mayst** (māst) aux.v. Archaic Second person singular present tense of **may¹**.

May·fair (mā′fâr′) A fashionable district in the West End of London, England.

may·flow·er (mā′flou′ər) n. 1. Any of various plants that bloom in May. 2. See **trailing arbutus**.

may·fly (mā′flī′) n. Any of various fragile winged insects of the order Ephemeroptera that develop from aquatic nymphs and live in the adult stage no longer than a few days.

may·hap (mā′hăp′, mā-hăp′) adv. Perhaps; perchance. [< the phrase it may hap.]

may·hem (mā′hĕm′, mā′əm) n. 1. Law The offense of willfully maiming or crippling a person. 2. Infliction of violent injury on a person or thing; wanton destruction. 3. A state of violent disorder or riotous confusion; havoc. [ME maim, mayhem < AN maihem < OFr. mahaigne, injury < mahaignier, to maim < VLat.

MADAGASCAR
INDIAN OCEAN
MAURITIUS
Réunion (FR.)
Port Louis
200 mi

Mauritius

Mayan
detail from a Mayan codex

mahanāre, prob. of Gmc. orig.]

may·ing or **May·ing** (mā′ĭng) *n.* The celebration of May Day, esp. by the gathering of spring flowers.

may·n't (mā′ənt, mānt) Contraction of *may not.*

may·o (mā′ō) *n. Informal* Mayonnaise.

Ma·yo (mā′ō), **William James** 1861–1939. Amer. surgeon who with his brother **Charles Horace Mayo** (1865–1939) founded the Mayo Clinic in Rochester MN.

Ma·yon (mä-yōn′), **Mount** An active volcano, 2,461.4 m (8,070 ft), of SE Luzon, Philippines.

may·on·naise (mā′ə-nāz′, mā′ə-nāz′) *n.* A dressing made of beaten raw egg yolk, oil, lemon juice or vinegar, and seasonings. [Fr. *mahonnaise, mayonnaise,* possibly from *Mahón,* Spanish city captured by the French in 1756 (mayonnaise being made in honor of the victory).]

may·or (mā′ər, mâr) *n.* The head of government of a city, town, borough, or municipal corporation. [ME *maire* < OFr. < Med.Lat. *māior* < Lat., greater, superior. See **meg-** in App.] —**may′or·al** (mā′ər-əl, mā-ôr′əl, -ōr′-) *adj.* —**may′or·ship′** *n.*

may·or·al·ty (mā′ər-əl-tē, mâr′əl-) *n., pl.* **-ties 1.** The office of a mayor. **2.** The term of office of a mayor. [ME *mairalte* < AN < OFr. *maire,* mayor. See MAYOR.]

may·or·ess (mā′ər-ĭs, mâr′ĭs) *n.* **1.** A woman serving as the head of government of a city, town, borough, or municipal corporation. See Usage Note at **-ess. 2.** The wife of a mayor.

Ma·yotte (mä-yôt′) A French island territory of the E Comoros in the Mozambique Channel of the Indian Ocean.

May·pole also **may·pole** (mā′pōl′) *n.* A pole decorated with streamers that those celebrating May Day hold while dancing.

may·pop (mā′pŏp′) *n.* **1.** A vine (*Passiflora incarnata*) of the southeast United States having purple and white flowers, three-lobed leaves, and edible yellow fruit. **2.** The fruit of this plant. [Alteration of *maycock* < earlier *maracock,* perh. of Virginia Algonquian orig.]

Mayr (mīr′ər), **Ernst** b. 1904. German-born Amer. biologist known for his research into genetic variation in new populations.

Mays (māz), **Willie Howard, Jr.** b. 1931. Amer. baseball player (1951–72) who hit 660 home runs.

mayst (māst) *aux.v.* Variant of **mayest.**

may tree *n. Chiefly British* The hawthorn.

may·weed (mā′wēd′) *n.* A weed (*Anthemis cotula*) with rank-smelling leaves and white-rayed flower heads. [ME *maythe weed, mayyen wed,* alteration of *maithe* < OE *mægtha.*]

May wine *n.* **1.** A still white wine with woodruff flavoring. **2.** A punch of champagne, claret, and Moselle or Rhine wine, flavored with woodruff. [Transl. of Ger. *Maiwein.*]

Maz·a·rin (măz′ə-răn′), **Jules** 1602–61. Italian-born French cardinal who served as chief minister to Louis XIV.

Ma·za·tlán (mä′sət-län′) A city of W Mexico on the Pacific Ocean NW of Guadalajara. Pop. 199,830.

Maz·da·ism also **Maz·de·ism** (măz′də-ĭz′əm) *n.* Zoroastrianism. [< Avestan *mazdå,* the good principle < *mazda-,* wise. See AHURA MAZDA.]

maze (māz) *n.* **1a.** An intricate, usu. confusing network of interconnecting pathways; a labyrinth. **b.** A situation in which it is easy to get lost. **2.** A graphic puzzle, the solution of which is an uninterrupted path through an intricate pattern of line segments from a starting point to a goal. **3.** Something made up of many confused or conflicting elements; a tangle: *a maze of government regulations.* ❖ *tr.v.* **mazed, maz·ing, maz·es** *Chiefly Southern US* **1.** To bewilder or astonish. **2.** To stupefy; daze. See Regional Note at **possum.** [ME *mase,* confusion, maze < *masen,* to confuse, daze < OE *āmasian,* to confound. See AMAZE.]

ma·zel tov also **ma·zal tov** (mä′zəl tôf′, tôv′, tōv′) *interj.* Used to express congratulations or best wishes. [Mishnaic Heb. *mazzāl ṭôb* : *mazzāl,* constellation, destiny (ult. < Akkadian *manzaltu, mazzaztum,* position of a star < *izuzzu,* to stand) + *ṭôb,* good.]

ma·zer (mā′zər) *n.* A large drinking bowl or goblet made of metal or hard wood. [ME < OFr. *masere,* kind of wood, maple burl, of Gmc. orig.]

ma·zu·ma (mə-zōō′mə) *n. Slang* Money; cash. [Yiddish *mazume, mezumen,* cash < Med. Heb. *məzummān,* fixed currency < Mishnaic Heb., fixed, passive part. of *zimmēn,* to arrange, invite < Heb. *zəmān,* appointed time < Aram. *zəmān, zaman* < Akkadian *simānu,* season, time < *wasāmu,* to be fitting.]

ma·zur·ka (mə-zûr′kə, -zōōr′-) *n.* **1.** A Polish dance resembling the polka. **2.** A piece of music for such a dance, written in 3/4 or 3/8 time. [Russ., poss. < Pol. (*tańczyć*) *mazurka,* (to dance) the mazurka, accusative of *mazurek,* Mazovian dance < dim. of *Mazur,* person from Mazovia, historical region of E Poland.]

maz·y (mā′zē) *adj.* **-i·er, -i·est** Mazelike, as in design; labyrinthine. —**maz′i·ly** *adv.* —**maz′i·ness** *n.*

maz·zard (măz′ərd) *n.* A wild sweet cherry (*Prunus avium*) often used as grafting stock. [Perh. alteration of ME *mazer,* goblet, hard wood. See MAZER.]

Maz·zi·ni (mät-sē′nē), **Giuseppe** 1805–72. Italian patriot who spurred the movement for an independent unified Italy.

mb *abbr.* millibar

Mb *abbr.* megabit

MB *abbr.* **1.** *Latin* Medicinae Baccalaureus (Bachelor of Medicine) **2.** Manitoba **3.** megabyte

MBA *abbr.* Master of Business Administration

Mba·bane (əm-bä-bän′, -bä-bä′nē) The cap. of Swaziland, in the NW part. Pop. 38,290.

Mbe·ki (əm-bä′kē), **Thabo** b. 1942. South African economist and politician who was elected president of South Africa in 1999.

mbi·ra (ĕm-bîr′ə, əm-) *n.* An African musical instrument consisting of a hollow gourd or wooden resonator and a number of usu. metal strips that vibrate when plucked. [Of Bantu orig.; akin to Shona *m-birà.*]

Mbu·ji Ma·yi (əm-bōō′jē mä′yē) A city of S-central Congo (formerly Zaire) E of Kinshasa. Pop. 486,235.

Mbun·du (əm-bōōn′dōō) *n., pl.* **Mbundu** or **-dus 1.** A member of a Bantu people inhabiting southern and central Angola. **2.** Their Bantu language. **3.** A member of a Bantu people inhabiting northern Angola. **4.** Their Bantu language.

mc *abbr.* millicurie

Mc *abbr.* **1.** *Bible* Maccabees **2.** megacycle

MC[1] (ĕm′sē′) *n.* A master of ceremonies.

MC[2] *abbr.* **1.** Marine Corps **2.** Medical Corps **3.** member of Congress

Mc·Al·len (mĭ-kăl′ən) A city of S TX on the Rio Grande WNW of Brownsville. Pop. 106,414.

MCAT *abbr.* Medical College Admissions Test

Mc·Car·thy (mə-kär′thē), **Joseph Raymond** 1908–57. Amer. politician who as a US senator from WI (1947–57) publicly accused many citizens of being Communists. His charges were never proved and he was censured by the Senate in 1954.

McCarthy, Mary Therese 1912–89. Amer. writer noted esp. for her novel *The Group* (1963).

Mc·Car·thy·ism (mə-kär′thē-ĭz′əm) *n.* **1.** The practice of publicizing accusations of political disloyalty or subversion with insufficient regard to evidence. **2.** The use of unfair investigatory or accusatory methods in order to suppress opposition. [After Joseph MCCARTHY.] —**Mc·Car′thy·ist** *n.*

Mc·Cart·ney (mə-kärt′nē), **Sir (James) Paul** b. 1942. British musician and composer who as a member of the Beatles wrote many notable songs with John Lennon.

Mc·Cau·ley (mə-kô′lē), **Mary Ludwig Hays** Known as "Molly Pitcher." 1754–1832. Amer. Revolutionary heroine of the Battle of Monmouth (Jun. 28, 1778).

Mc·Cay (mə-kā′), **Winsor** 1871–1934. Amer. cartoonist credited with creating the first Amer. animated film, *The Sinking of the Lusitania* (1918).

Mc·Clel·lan (mə-klĕl′ən), **George Brinton** 1826–85. Amer. commander of the Union Army (1861–62) whose overcautious tactics prompted Lincoln to relieve him of duty.

Mc·Clin·tock (mə-klĭn′tək, -tŏk′), **Barbara** 1902–92. Amer. genetic botanist who won a 1983 Nobel Prize.

Mc·Cor·mack (mə-kôr′mək, -mĭk), **John** 1884–1945. Irish-born Amer. operatic tenor whose notable roles included Rodolpho in *La Boheme* and Pinkerton in *Madame Butterfly.*

Mc·Cor·mick (mə-kôr′mĭk), **Anne Elizabeth O'Hare** 1882–1954. British-born Amer. journalist who was the first woman to receive a Pulitzer Prize for journalism (1937).

McCormick, Cyrus Hall 1809–84. Amer. inventor and manufacturer who developed a mechanical harvester (1831).

Mc·Coy (mə-koi′) *n. Informal* The authentic thing or quality; something that is not an imitation or substitute. [Alteration of earlier *McKay,* prob. < Sc., good unadulterated whiskey.]

Mc·Cul·lers (mə-kŭl′ərz), **Carson Smith** 1917–67. Amer. writer noted for *The Heart is a Lonely Hunter* (1940).

Mc·En·roe (măk′ən-rō), **John Patrick, Jr.** b. 1959. Amer. tennis player who won the US Open four times (1979–81 and 1984) and Wimbledon three times (1981, 1983, and 1984).

mcf *abbr.* thousand cubic feet

Mc·Gov·ern (mə-gŭv′ərn), **George Stanley** b. 1922. Amer. politician who ran unsuccessfully for President in 1972.

Mc·Guf·fey (mə-gŭf′ē), **William Holmes** 1800–73. Amer. educator known for the *McGuffey Eclectic Readers* (1836–57).

mCi *abbr.* millicurie

Mc·In·tosh (măk′ĭn-tŏsh′) *n.* A variety of red eating apple. [After John *McIntosh* (fl. 1796), Canadian farmer.]

Mc·Job (mĭk-jŏb′) *n. Slang* A job, usu. in the retail or service sector, that is low paying and offers few or no benefits and little or no chance for promotion. [*Mc(Donald's),* trademark of a fast-food restaurant chain (< its mass-produced nature) + JOB[1].]

Mc·Kay (mə-kā′), **Claude** 1890–1948. Jamaican-born Amer. writer whose novels include *Home to Harlem* (1928).

Mc·Kim (mə-kĭm′), **Charles Follen** 1847–1909. Amer. architect whose designs include the Boston Public Library (1887).

Mc·Kin·ley (mə-kĭn′lē), **Mount** or **De·na·li** (də-nä′lē) A peak, 6,197.6 m (20,320 ft), in the Alaska Range of S-central AK.

McKinley, William 1843–1901. The 25th President of the US (1897–1901), whose presidency was marked by the Spanish-American War (1898).

MCL *abbr.* **1.** Master of Civil Law **2.** Master of Comparative Law

Mc·Lu·han (mə-klōō′ən), **(Herbert) Marshall** 1911–80. Canadian critic who wrote *The Medium is the Message* (1967).

Mc·Mil·lan (mĭk-mĭl′ən), **Edwin Mattison** 1907–91. Amer. physicist and chemist who shared a 1951 Nobel Prize.

Mc·Mur·do Sound (mĭk-mûr′dō) An inlet of the Ross Sea in

Willie Mays

William McKinley
detail from an 1892 pastel
on paper

ă	pat	oi	boy
ā	pay	ou	out
âr	care	ŏŏ	took
ä	father	ōō	boot
ĕ	pet	ŭ	cut
ē	be	ûr	urge
ĭ	pit	th	thin
ī	pie	th	this
îr	pier	hw	which
ŏ	pot	zh	vision
ō	toe	ə	about,
ô	paw		item

Stress marks:

′ (primary);

′ (secondary), as in

lexicon (lĕk′sĭ-kŏn′)

Antarctica off the coast of Victoria Land; site of a US research and exploration base.

Mc·Nal·ly (mĭk-năl′ē), **Terence** b. 1939. Amer. playwright whose works include *Kiss of the Spider Woman* (1990).

Mc·Pher·son (mĭk-fûr′sən), **Aimee Semple** 1890–1944. Canadian-born Amer. evangelist who founded the International Church of the Foursquare Gospel (1927).

Mc·Rae (mə-krā′), **Carmen** 1920–94. Amer. jazz singer, songwriter, and pianist whose performing style is distinguished by its wit and rigor.

MCS *abbr.* multiple chemical sensitivity

Md The symbol for the element **mendelevium.**

MD *abbr.* **1.** also **Md.** Maryland **2.** medical department **3.** *Latin* Medicinae Doctor (Doctor of Medicine) **4.** muscular dystrophy

M-day (ĕm′dā′) *n.* The day on which national mobilization for war is ordered; mobilization day.

Mde·wa·kan·ton (əm-dē-wô′kən-tōn′, mĕd′ē-wô′-) *n., pl.* **Mdewakanton** or **-tons** A member of a Native American people of the Santee branch of the Sioux.

MDiv *abbr.* Master of Divinity

Mdm. *abbr.* Madam

MDMA (ĕm′dē-ĕm-ā′) *n.* A drug, $C_{11}H_{15}NO_2$, related to amphetamine and mescaline and used illicitly for its euphoric and hallucinogenic effects. [*m(ethylene)d(ioxy)m(eth)a(mphetamine).*]

MDS *abbr.* Master of Dental Surgery

mdse. *abbr.* merchandise

MDT *abbr.* Mountain Daylight Time

me (mē) *pron.* The objective case of **I**[1]. **1.** Used as the direct object of a verb: *He assisted me.* **2.** Used as the indirect object of a verb: *They offered me a ride.* **3.** Used as the object of a preposition: *This letter is addressed to me.* **4.** *Informal* Used as a predicate nominative: *It's me.* See Usage Notes at **be, but, I**[1]. **5.** *Nonstandard* Used reflexively as the indirect object of a verb: *I bought me a new car.* [ME < OE *mē.* See **me-**[1] in App.]

OUR LIVING LANGUAGE Speakers of vernacular varieties of English, especially in the South, will commonly utter sentences like *I bought me some new clothes* or *She got her a good job,* in which the objective form of the pronoun (*me, her*) rather than the reflexive pronoun (*myself, herself*) is used to refer back to the subject of the sentence (*I, her*). However, the reflexive pronoun of Standard English cannot always be replaced by the vernacular objective pronoun. For example, *Jane baked her and John some cookies* doesn't mean "Jane baked herself and John some cookies." In this sentence, *her* must refer to someone other than Jane, just as it does in Standard English. In addition, forms like *me* and *her* cannot be used in place of *myself* or *herself* unless the noun in the phrase following the pronoun is preceded by a modifier such as *some, a,* or *a bunch of.* Thus, sentences such as *I cooked me some dinner* and *We bought us a bunch of candy* are commonplace; sentences such as *I cooked me dinner* and *We bought us candy* do not occur at all. Sometimes objective pronouns can occur where reflexive pronouns cannot. For example, some Southerners might say *I'm gonna write me a letter to the President;* nobody, no matter what variety he or she speaks, would say *I'm gonna write myself a letter to the President.*

ME *abbr.* **1.** also **Me.** Maine **2a.** mechanical engineer **b.** mechanical engineering **3.** medical examiner **4.** Middle English

me·a cul·pa (mā′ə kŭl′pə, mē′ə) *n.* An acknowledgment of a personal error or fault. [Lat. *meā culpa,* through my fault : *meā,* fem. ablative sing. of *meus,* my + *culpā,* ablative of *culpa,* fault.]

mead[1] (mēd) *n.* An alcoholic beverage made from fermented honey and water. [ME < OE *meodu.* See **medhu-** in App.]

mead[2] (mēd) *n. Archaic* A meadow. [ME *mede* < OE *mǣd.* See **mē-**[2] in App.]

Mead, George Herbert 1863–1931. Amer. philosopher who was a leader in the development of social psychology.

Mead, Lake A reservoir of SE NV and NW AZ formed by Hoover Dam on the Colorado R.

Mead, Margaret 1901–78. Amer. anthropologist whose landmark studies include *Coming of Age in Samoa* (1928).

Meade (mēd), **George Gordon** 1815–72. Amer. Union general who commanded the costly victory at Gettysburg (1863).

Meade, James Edward 1907–95. British economist who shared a 1977 Nobel Prize.

mead·ow (mĕd′ō) *n.* A tract of grassland, in its natural state, as pasture, or for growing hay. [ME *medoue* < OE *mǣdwe,* oblique case of *mǣd.* See **mē-**[2] in App.] —**mead′ow·y** *adj.*

meadow beauty *n.* Any of several North American plants of the genus *Rhexia,* growing in wet ground and having opposite leaves and showy purple flowers.

meadow fern *n.* See **sweet gale.**

meadow fescue *n.* A grass (*Festuca eliator*) grown for hay.

mead·ow·land (mĕd′ō-lănd′) *n.* A tract of land having the characteristics of or used for a meadow.

mead·ow·lark (mĕd′ō-lärk′) *n.* Any of various songbirds of the genus *Sturnella* of North America, esp. *S. magna,* the eastern meadowlark, and *S. neglecta,* the western meadowlark, having brownish plumage and a yellow breast.

meadow mouse *n.* See **field mouse.**

meadow mushroom *n.* A widely cultivated edible mushroom

Margaret Mead

(*Agaricus campestris*) that thrives in moist soil.

meadow nematode *n.* Any of various nematodes of the genus *Pratylenchus* that are parasitic on the roots of plants.

meadow rue *n.* Any of various plants of the genus *Thalictrum,* having compound leaves and clusters of small white, yellowish, or purplish apetalous flowers.

meadow saffron *n.* See **autumn crocus.**

mead·ow·sweet (mĕd′ō-swēt′) *n.* **1.** Either of two North American shrubs (*Spiraea alba* or *S. latifolia*) having umbel-shaped clusters of white flowers. **2.** Any of various perennial herbs of the genus *Filipendula* in the rose family.

mea·ger also **mea·gre** (mē′gər) *adj.* **1.** Deficient in quantity, fullness, or extent; scanty. **2.** Deficient in richness, fertility, or vigor; feeble: *the meager soil of an eroded plain.* **3.** Having little flesh; lean. [ME *megre,* thin < OFr. < Lat. *macer.*] —**mea′ger·ly** *adv.* —**mea′ger·ness** *n.*

meal[1] (mēl) *n.* **1.** The edible whole or coarsely ground grains of a cereal grass. **2.** A granular substance produced by grinding. [ME *mele* < OE *melu.* See **melə-** in App.]

meal[2] (mēl) *n.* **1.** The food served and eaten in one sitting. **2.** A customary time or occasion of eating food. [ME *mele* < OE *mǣl.* See **mē-**[1] in App.]

mea·lie (mē′lē) *n. South African* **1.** An ear of corn. **2. mealies** Corn; maize. [Afr. *mielie,* ult. < Lat. *milium,* millet. See **melə-** in App.]

meal ticket *n.* **1.** A card or ticket entitling the holder to a meal or meals. **2.** *Informal* A person or thing depended on financially.

meal·time (mēl′tīm′) *n.* The usual time for eating a meal.

meal·worm (mēl′wûrm′) *n.* The larvae of various beetles of the genus *Tenebrio* that infest grain products such as flour.

meal·y (mē′lē) *adj.* **-i·er, -i·est 1.** Resembling meal in texture or consistency; granular. **2a.** Made of or containing meal. **b.** Sprinkled or covered with meal or a similar substance. **3.** Flecked with spots; mottled. **4.** Lacking healthy coloring; pale. **5.** Mealymouthed. —**meal′i·ness** *n.*

meal·y·bug (mē′lē-bŭg′) *n.* Any of various homopterous insects, esp. of the family Pseudococcidae, some of which are destructive to plants. [< its powdery covering.]

meal·y-mouthed (mē′lē-mouthd′, -moutht′) *adj.* Unwilling to state facts or opinions simply and directly.

mean[1] (mēn) *v.* **meant** (mĕnt), **mean·ing, means** —*tr.* **1a.** To be used to convey; denote: "'The question is,' said Alice, 'whether you can make words mean so many different things'" (Lewis Carroll). **b.** To act as a symbol of; signify or represent: *In this poem, the budding flower means youth.* **2.** To intend to convey or indicate. **3.** To have as a purpose or intention; intend: *I meant to go running this morning, but I overslept.* **4.** To design, intend, or destine for a certain purpose or end: *a building that was meant for storage.* **5.** To have as a consequence; bring about: *Friction means heat.* **6.** To have the importance or value of: *Their opinions meant nothing.* —*intr.* To have intentions of a specified kind; be disposed: *They mean well but lack tact.* —**idiom:** **mean business** *Informal* To be in earnest. [ME *menen* < OE *mǣnan,* to tell of.]

mean[2] (mēn) *adj.* **mean·er, mean·est 1a.** Selfish in a petty way; unkind. **b.** Cruel, spiteful, or malicious. **2.** Ignoble; base: *a mean motive.* **3.** Miserly; stingy. **4a.** Low in quality or grade; inferior. **b.** Low in value or amount; paltry. **5.** Common or poor in appearance; shabby. **6.** Low in social status; of humble origins. **7.** Humiliated or ashamed. **8.** In poor physical condition; sick or debilitated. **9.** Extremely unpleasant or disagreeable: *a mean storm.* **10.** *Informal* Ill-tempered. **11.** *Slang* **a.** Hard to cope with; difficult or troublesome. **b.** Excellent; skillful: *a mean game of bridge.* [ME < OE *gemǣne,* common.]

mean[3] (mēn) *n.* **1.** Something having a position, quality, or condition midway between extremes; a medium. **2.** *Mathematics* **a.** A number that typifies a set of numbers, such as a geometric mean or an arithmetic mean. **b.** The average value of a set of numbers. **3.** *Logic* The middle term in a syllogism. **4. means** (used with a *sing.* or *pl. verb*) A method, course of action, or instrument by which an act can be accomplished or an end achieved. **5. means** (used with a *pl. verb*) **a.** Money, property, or other wealth. **b.** Great wealth: *a woman of means.* ❖ *adj.* **1.** Occupying a middle or intermediate position between two extremes. **2.** Intermediate in size, extent, quality, time, or degree; medium. —**idioms:** **by all means** Without fail; certainly. **by any means** In any way possible; to any extent. **by means of** With the use of; owing to. **by no means** In no sense; certainly not. [ME *mene,* middle < OFr. *meien* < Lat. *mediānus* < *medius.* See **medhyo-** in App.]

USAGE NOTE In the sense of "financial resources" *means* takes a plural verb: *His means are more than adequate.* In the sense of "a way to an end" *means* is singular when referring to a particular strategy or method: *The best means of traveling there is by plane.* It is plural when it refers to a group of strategies or methods: *What are the most effective means for dealing with the drug problem?* • *Means* is most often followed by *of: a means of noise reduction.* But *for, to,* and *toward* are also used: *a means for transmitting signals; a means to an end; a means toward achieving social equality.*

mean calorie *n.* See **calorie** 2.

me·an·der (mē-ăn′dər) *intr.v.* **-dered, -der·ing, -ders 1.** To follow a winding and turning course. **2.** To move aimlessly and idly without fixed direction. See Syns at **wander.** ❖ *n.* **1. mean-ders** Circuitous windings or sinuosities, as of a stream or path. **2.** A circuitous journey or excursion; ramble. Often used in the plural. **3.** An ornamental pattern of winding or intertwining lines, used in art and architecture. [< Lat. *maeander,* circuitous windings < Gk. *maiandros,* after *Maiandros,* the Maeander River in Phrygia, noted for its windings.] —**me•an′der•er** *n.* —**me•an′drous** (-drəs) *adj.*

mean deviation *n.* In a statistical distribution, the average of the absolute values of the differences between individual numbers and their mean.

mean•ie (mē′nē) *n. Informal* A malicious or petty person.

mean•ing (mē′nĭng) *n.* **1.** Something conveyed or signified; sense or significance. **2.** Something one wishes to convey, esp. by language. **3.** An interpreted goal, intent, or end. **4.** Inner significance. ❖ *adj.* **1.** Full of meaning; expressive. **2.** Disposed or intended in a specified manner. Often used in combination: *a well-meaning cousin.*

SYNONYMS *meaning, acceptation, import, sense, significance, signification* These nouns refer to the idea conveyed by something, such as a word, action, gesture, or situation: *Synonyms are words with the same or nearly the same meaning. In one of its acceptations* value *is a technical term in music. The import of his statement is ambiguous. The term* anthropometry *has only one sense. The significance of a green traffic light is widely understood. Linguists have determined the hieroglyphs' signification.*

mean•ing•ful (mē′nĭng-fəl) *adj.* **1.** Having meaning, function, or purpose. **2.** Fraught with meaning; significant. See Syns at **expressive.** —**mean′ing•ful•ness** *n.*

mean•ing•less (mē′nĭng-lĭs) *adj.* Having no meaning or significance.

mean•ly (mēn′lē) *adv.* In a poor, lowly, or base manner.

mean•ness (mēn′nĭs) *n.* **1.** The state of being inferior in quality, character, or value; commonness. **2.** The quality or state of being selfish or stingy. **3.** A spiteful or malicious act.

mean solar day *n.* The period of time between two successive transits of the mean sun; the standard for the 24-hour day.

mean-spir•it•ed *or* **mean•spir•it•ed** (mēn′spĭr′ĭ-tĭd) *adj.* Having or characterized by a malicious or petty spirit. —**mean′-spir′it•ed•ly** *adv.* —**mean′-spir′it•ed•ness** *n.*

mean square *n.* The average of the squares of a set of numbers.

means test (mēnz) *n.* An investigation into a person's finances to determine eligibility for financial assistance. —**means′-test′** (mēnz′tĕst′) *v.*

mean sun *n.* A hypothetical sun conceived as moving at a uniform rate along the celestial equator at the mean speed with which the real sun apparently moves along the ecliptic.

meant (mĕnt) *v.* Past tense and past participle of **mean¹**.

mean•time (mēn′tīm′) *n.* The time between one occurrence and another; an interval. ❖ *adv.* During a period of intervening time; meanwhile.

mean time *n.* Time measured with reference to the mean sun, giving equal 24-hour days throughout the year.

mean•while (mēn′hwīl′, -wīl′) *n.* The intervening time. ❖ *adv.* **1.** During or in the intervening time: *Meanwhile, life goes on.* **2.** At the same time.

Mea•ny (mē′nē), **George** 1894–1980. Amer. labor leader who was the first president of the AFL-CIO (1955–79).

mea•sles (mē′zəlz) *n. (used with a sing. or pl. verb)* **1a.** An acute contagious viral disease, usu. occurring in childhood and characterized by eruption of red spots on the skin, fever, and catarrh. **b.** Black measles. **c.** Any of several other diseases, esp. German measles, that cause similar but milder symptoms. **2.** A disease of cattle and swine caused by tapeworm larvae. **3.** A plant disease, usu. caused by fungi, that produces minute spots on leaves and stems. [ME *maseles, mesels,* pl. of *masel,* measles spot, of MLGer. orig.]

mea•sly (mēz′lē) *adj.* **-sli•er, -sli•est 1.** *Slang* Contemptibly small; meager: *a measly tip.* **2.** Infected with measles.

meas•ur•a•ble (mĕzh′ər-ə-bəl) *adj.* **1.** That can be measured: *measurable depths.* **2.** Of distinguished importance; significant. —**meas′ur•a•bil′i•ty** *n.* —**meas′ur•a•bly** *adv.*

meas•ure (mĕzh′ər) *n.* **1.** Dimensions, quantity, or capacity as ascertained by comparison with a standard. **2.** A reference standard or sample used for the quantitative comparison of properties. **3.** A unit specified by a scale, such as an inch, or by variable conditions, such as a day's march. **4.** A system of measurement, such as the metric system. **5.** A device used for measuring. **6.** The act of measuring. **7.** An evaluation or a basis of comparison. **8.** Extent or degree. **9.** A definite quantity that has been measured out: *a measure of wine.* **10.** A fitting amount: *a measure of recognition.* **11.** A limited amount or degree: *a measure of goodwill.* **12.** Limit; bounds: *generosity knows no measure.* **13.** Appropriate restraint; moderation. **14.** An action taken as a means to an end; an expedient. Often used in the plural: *desperate measures.* **15.** A legislative bill or enactment. **16.** Poetic meter. **17.** *Music* The metric unit between two bars on the staff; a bar. ❖ *v.* **-ured, -ur•ing, -ures** —*tr.* **1.** To ascertain the dimensions, quantity, or capacity of: *measured the height of the ceiling.* **2.** To mark, lay out, or estab-

lish dimensions for by measuring: *measure off an area.* **3.** To estimate by evaluation or comparison. **4.** To bring into comparison. **5a.** To mark off or apportion, usu. with reference to a given unit of measurement: *measure out a pint of milk.* **b.** To allot or distribute as if by measuring; mete: *measured out harsh justice.* **6.** To serve as a measure of: *The inch measures length.* **7.** To consider or choose with care; weigh: *He measures his words with caution.* **8.** *Archaic* To travel over. —*intr.* **1.** To have a measurement of a certain amount: *The room measures 12 by 20 feet.* **2.** To take a measurement. **3.** To allow of measurement: *White sugar measures more easily than brown.* —**phrasal verb: measure up 1.** To be the equal of something; have similar quality. **2.** To have the necessary qualifications. —**idioms: beyond measure 1.** In excess. **2.** Without limit. **for good measure** In addition to the required amount. **in a (or some) measure** To a degree. [ME *OFr. mesure* < Lat. *mēnsūra* < *mēnsus,* p. part. of *mētīrī,* to measure. See **mē-¹** in App.] —**meas′ur•er** *n.*

meas•ured (mĕzh′ərd) *adj.* **1.** Determined by measurement. **2.** Careful; restrained: *spoke in measured words.* **3.** Calculated; deliberate: *with measured irony.* **4.** Regular in rhythm and number. **5.** Slow and stately. **6.** Written in meter. **7.** *Music* Mensural. —**meas′ured•ly** *adv.* —**meas′ured•ness** *n.*

meas•ure•less (mĕzh′ər-lĭs) *adj.* Too great to be measured; immeasurable: *measureless happiness.* See Syns at **incalculable.** —**meas′ure•less•ly** *adv.* —**meas′ure•less•ness** *n.*

meas•ure•ment (mĕzh′ər-mənt) *n.* **1.** The act of measuring or the process of being measured. **2.** A system of measuring: *measurement in miles.* See table on page 860. **3.** The dimension, quantity, or capacity determined by measuring: *the measurements of a room.*

meas•ur•ing worm (mĕzh′ə-rĭng) *n.* A geometrid caterpillar that moves in alternate contractions and expansions.

meat (mēt) *n.* **1.** The edible flesh of animals, esp. that of mammals as opposed to that of fish or poultry. **2.** The edible part, as of fruit. **3.** The essence, substance, or gist: *the meat of the editorial.* **4.** *Slang* Something that one enjoys or excels in; a forte: *Tennis is her meat.* **5.** Nourishment; food: *"Love is not all: it is not meat nor drink"* (Edna St. Vincent Millay). **6.** *Vulgar Slang* The human body regarded as an object of sexual desire. [ME *mete* < OE, food.]

meat and potatoes *pl.n. (used with a sing. or pl. verb) Informal* The fundamental parts or part; the basis.

meat-and-po•ta•toes (mēt′n-pə-tā′tōz, -təz) *adj. Informal* Fundamental; basic.

meat•ball (mēt′bôl′) *n.* **1.** A small ball of ground meat seasoned and cooked. **2.** *Slang* A stupid, clumsy, or dull person.

meat•head (mēt′hĕd′) *n. Slang* A stupid or dull person.

meat hook *n.* **1.** A hook used to hang the carcasses of slaughtered animals or large pieces of meat. **2. meat hooks** *Slang* The hands or fists.

meat•less (mēt′lĭs) *adj.* **1.** Lacking meat. **2.** Being or relating to a time when meat is not to be eaten: *meatless days.*

meat loaf *or* **meat•loaf** (mēt′lōf′) *n.* A usu. baked dish of molded ground meat and other ingredients.

meat market *n.* **1.** A market where meat is sold. **2.** *Slang* An establishment, such as a nightclub, where one looks for a sexual partner. **3.** *Slang* A situation, such as an audition, in which people are viewed as commodities.

meat•pack•ing (mēt′păk′ĭng) *n.* The business activity of slaughtering animals and preparing the meat for sale. —**meat′-pack•er** *n.*

me•a•tus (mē-ā′təs) *n., pl.* **-tus•es** *or* **meatus** A body opening or passage, such as the opening of the ear. [Lat. *meātus,* passage < p. part. of *meāre,* to pass.]

meat•y (mē′tē) *adj.* **-i•er, -i•est 1a.** Of or relating to meat. **b.** Having the flavor or smell of meat. **c.** Full of or containing meat. **2.** Heavily fleshed. **3.** Prompting considerable thought: *a meaty theme for study and debate.* —**meat′i•ness** *n.*

mec•ca (mĕk′ə) *n.* **1a.** A place regarded as the center of an activity or interest. **b.** A goal to which adherents of a religion aspire. **2.** A place visited by many people. [After MECCA.]

Mecca A city of W Saudi Arabia near the Red Sea; birthplace of Muhammad and pilgrimage site as the holiest city of Islam. Pop. 689,010. —**Mec′can** *adj. & n.*

mech. *abbr.* **1.** mechanical **2.** mechanics

mechan– *pref.* Variant of **mechano–**.

me•chan•ic (mĭ-kăn′ĭk) *n.* A worker skilled in making, using, or repairing machines, vehicles, and tools. [< ME, mechanical < OFr. *mecanique* < Lat. *mēchanicus* < Gk. *mēkhanikos* < *mēkhanē,* machine, device.] —**me•chan′ic** *adj.*

me•chan•i•cal (mĭ-kăn′ĭ-kəl) *adj.* **1.** Of or relating to machines or tools. **2.** Operated or produced by a mechanism or machine. **3.** Of, relating to, or governed by mechanics. **4.** Performed or performing in an impersonal or machinelike manner; automatic. **5.** Relating to, produced by, or dominated by physical forces. **6.** *Philosophy* Interpreting and explaining the phenomena of the universe by referring to causally determined material forces; mechanistic. **7.** Of or relating to manual labor. ❖ *n. Printing* A layout consisting of type proofs, artwork, or both, exactly positioned and prepared for making an offset or other printing plate. —**me•chan′i•cal•ly** *adv.* —**me•chan′i•cal•ness** *n.*

measure
from "Roses of the South," a waltz by Johann Strauss the Younger

ă pat	oi boy
ā pay	ou out
âr care	ōō took
ä father	ōō boot
ĕ pet	ŭ cut
ē be	ûr urge
ĭ pit	th thin
ī pie	th this
îr pier	hw which
ŏ pot	zh vision
ō toe	ə about,
ô paw	item

Stress marks:
′ (primary);
′ (secondary); as in
lexicon (lĕk′sĭ-kŏn′)

CONVERSION BETWEEN METRIC AND US CUSTOMARY UNITS

When you know	multiply by	to find	When you know	multiply by	to find
inches	25.4	millimeters	millimeters	0.04	inches
	2.54	centimeters	centimeters	0.39	inches
feet	30.48	centimeters	meters	3.28	feet
yards	0.91	meters		1.09	yards
miles	1.61	kilometers	kilometers	0.62	miles
teaspoons	4.93	milliliters	milliliters	0.20	teaspoons
tablespoons	14.79	milliliters		0.07	tablespoons
fluid ounces	29.57	milliliters		0.03	fluid ounces
cups	0.24	liters	liters	1.06	quarts
pints	0.47	liters		0.26	gallons
quarts	0.95	liters		4.23	cups
gallons	3.79	liters		2.12	pints
cubic feet	0.028	cubic meters	cubic meters	35.31	cubic feet
cubic yards	0.76	cubic meters		1.35	cubic yards
ounces	28.35	grams	grams	0.035	ounces
pounds	0.45	kilograms	kilograms	2.20	pounds
short tons (2,000 lbs)	0.91	metric tons	metric tons (1,000 kg)	1.10	short tons
square inches	6.45	square centimeters	square centimeters	0.155	square inches
square feet	0.09	square meters	square meters	1.20	square yards
square yards	0.84	square meters	square kilometers	0.39	square miles
square miles	2.59	square kilometers	hectares	2.47	acres

TEMPERATURE CONVERSION BETWEEN CELSIUS AND FAHRENHEIT

$$°C = (°F - 32) \div 1.8 \qquad °F = (°C \times 1.8) + 32$$

US CUSTOMARY SYSTEM (COMPARISON OF UNITS)

Unit	US	Metric	Unit	US	Metric
LENGTH			**VOLUME OR CAPACITY (LIQUID MEASURE)**		
inch	$1/12$ foot	2.54 centimeters	ounce	$1/16$ pint	29.574 milliliters
foot	12 inches or $1/3$ yard	0.3048 meter	gill	4 ounces	0.1183 liter
yard	36 inches or 3 feet	0.9144 meter	pint	16 ounces	0.4732 liter
rod	$16 1/2$ feet or $5 1/2$ yards	5.0292 meters	quart	2 pints or $1/4$ gallon	0.9463 liter
furlong	220 yards or $1/8$ mile	0.2012 kilometer	gallon	128 ounces or 8 pints	3.7854 liters
mile (statute)	5,280 feet (1,760 yards)	1.6093 kilometers	oil barrel	42 gallons	158.99 liters
mile (nautical)	6,076 feet (2,025 yards)	1.852 kilometers			
WEIGHT			**VOLUME OR CAPACITY (DRY MEASURE)**		
grain	$1/7000$ pound	64.799 milligrams	pint	$1/2$ quart	0.5506 liter
dram	$1/16$ ounce	1.7718 grams	quart	2 pints	1.1012 liters
ounce	16 drams	28.350 grams	peck	8 quarts or $1/4$ bushel	8.8098 liters
pound	16 ounces	453.6 grams	bucket	2 pecks	17.620 liters
ton (short)	2,000 pounds	907.18 kilograms	bushel	2 buckets or 4 pecks	35.239 liters
ton (long)	2,240 pounds	1,016.0 kilograms			

UNITS OF THE INTERNATIONAL SYSTEM

The **International System** (abbreviated **SI**, for Système International, the French name for the system) was adopted in 1960 by the 11th General Conference on Weights and Measures. An expanded and modified version of the metric system, the International System addresses the needs of modern science for additional and more accurate units of measurement. The key features of the International System are decimalization, a system of prefixes, and a standard defined in terms of an invariable physical measure.

BASE UNITS

Unit	Quantity	Symbol
meter	length	m
kilogram	mass	kg
second	time	s
ampere	electric current	A
kelvin	temperature	K
mole	amount of matter	mol
candela	luminous intensity	cd

SUPPLEMENTARY UNITS

Two units are based on abstract geometry, not physical standards.

Unit	Quantity	Symbol
radian	plane angles	rad
steradian	solid angles	sr

PREFIXES

A multiple of a unit in the International System is formed by adding a prefix to the name of that unit. (**MF** = Multiplying Factor)

Prefix	Symbol	MF	Prefix	Symbol	MF
yotta-	Y	10^{24}	deci-	d	10^{-1}
zetta-	Z	10^{21}	centi-	c	10^{-2}
exa-	E	10^{18}	milli-	m	10^{-3}
peta-	P	10^{15}	micro-	μ	10^{-6}
tera-	T	10^{12}	nano-	n	10^{-9}
giga-	G	10^{9}	pico-	p	10^{-12}
mega-	M	10^{6}	femto-	f	10^{-15}
kilo-	k	10^{3}	atto-	a	10^{-18}
hecto-	h	10^{2}	zepto-	z	10^{-21}
deca-	da	10	yocto-	y	10^{-24}

BRITISH IMPERIAL SYSTEM (COMPARISON OF UNITS)

VOLUME OR CAPACITY (LIQUID MEASURE)				**VOLUME OR CAPACITY (DRY MEASURE)**			
Unit	Other British	US	Metric	Unit	Other British	US	Metric
pint	$1/2$ quart	1.201 pints	0.5683 liter	peck	$1/4$ bushel	1.0314 pecks	9.087 liters
quart	2 pints ($1/4$ gallon)	1.201 quarts	1.137 liters	bushel	4 pecks	1.0320 bushels	36.369 liters
gallon	8 pints (4 quarts)	1.201 gallons	4.546 liters				

mechanical advantage *n.* The ratio of the output force produced by a machine to the applied input force.

mechanical drawing *n.* **1.** Drafting. **2.** A drawing, such as an architect's plans, that enables measurements to be interpreted.

mechanical engineering *n.* The branch of engineering that encompasses the generation and application of heat and mechanical power and the design, production, and use of machines and tools. —**mechanical engineer** *n.*

me·chan·ics (mĭ-kăn′ĭks) *n.* **1.** (*used with a sing. verb*) The branch of physics that is concerned with the analysis of the action of forces on matter or material systems. **2.** (*used with a sing. or pl. verb*) Design, construction, and use of machinery, tools, or mechanical devices. **3.** (*used with a pl. verb*) The functional and technical aspects of an activity.

mech·a·nism (mĕk′ə-nĭz′əm) *n.* **1a.** A machine or mechanical appliance. **b.** The arrangement of connected parts in a machine. **2.** A system of parts that operate or interact like those of a machine: *the mechanism of the solar system.* **3.** An instrument or a process, physical or mental, by which something is done or comes into being. **4.** A habitual manner of acting to achieve an end. **5.** *Biology* The involuntary and consistent response of an organism to a stimulus. **6.** *Psychology* A usu. unconscious mental and emotional pattern that shapes behavior in a given situation or environment. **7.** The sequence of steps in a chemical reaction. **8.** *Philosophy* The doctrine that all natural phenomena are explicable by material causes and mechanical principles. [NLat. *mĕchanismus* < LLat. *mĕchanisma* < Gk. *mĕkhanē*, machine.]

mech·a·nist (mĕk′ə-nĭst) *n. Philosophy* One who believes in the doctrine of mechanism.

mech·a·nis·tic (mĕk′ə-nĭs′tĭk) *adj.* **1.** Mechanically determined. **2.** *Philosophy* Of or relating to mechanism. **3.** Automatic and impersonal. —**mech′a·nis′ti·cal·ly** *adv.*

mech·a·nize (mĕk′ə-nīz′) *tr.v.* **-nized, -niz·ing, -niz·es 1.** To equip with machinery. **2.** To equip (a military unit) with motor vehicles, such as tanks and trucks. **3.** To make automatic; render routine or monotonous. **4.** To produce by or as if by machines. —**mech′a·ni·za′tion** (-nĭ-zā′shən) *n.* —**mech′a·niz′er** *n.*

mechano– or **mechan–** *pref.* **1.** Machine; machinery: *mechanize.* **2.** Mechanical: *mechanotherapy.* [Gk. *mĕkhano–* < *mĕkhanē*, machine.]

mech·a·no·chem·i·cal (mĕk′ə-nō-kĕm′ĭ-kəl) *adj.* Of or relating to conversion of chemical energy into mechanical work.

mech·a·no·re·cep·tor (mĕk′ə-nō-rĭ-sĕp′tər) *n.* A specialized sensory organ that responds to mechanical stimuli such as tension, pressure, or displacement. —**mech′a·no·re·cep′tion** *n.* —**mech′a·no·re·cep′tive** *adj.*

mech·a·no·ther·a·py (mĕk′ə-nō-thĕr′ə-pē) *n., pl.* **-pies** Medical treatment by mechanical methods, such as massage. —**mech′a·no·ther′a·pist** *n.*

me·chi·tza (mə-кнē′tsə, -кнē-tsä′) *n., pl.* **-tzas** or **-tzot** (-tsôt) *Judaism* A partition erected in the seating section of an Orthodox synagogue to prevent the mixing of men and women. [Mishnaic Heb. *mǝḥiṣṣâ*, partition < Heb. *ḥāṣaṣ*, to divide.]

Mech·lin¹ (mĕk′lĭn) also **Mech·e·len** (mĕk′ə-lən, mĕкн′-) or **Ma·lines** (mə-lēnz′, mä-lēn′) A city of N-central Belgium NNE of Brussels. Pop. 77,010.

Mech·lin² (mĕk′lĭn) *n.* A lace in which the pattern details are defined by a flat thread. [After MECHLIN¹.]

Meck·len·burg (mĕk′lən-bûrg′, -bŏŏrk′) A historical region of NE Germany on the Baltic Sea; orig. occupied c. 6th cent. A.D. by Slavic peoples.

mec·li·zine (mĕk′lĭ-zēn′) *n.* A whitish crystalline powder, $C_{25}H_{27}ClN_2$, used to treat nausea and motion sickness. [ME(THYLBENZENE) + C(H)L(ORO–) + alteration of (PIPERA)ZINE.]

me·co·ni·um (mĭ-kō′nē-əm) *n.* A dark green fecal material that accumulates in fetal intestines and is excreted at or near birth. [Lat. *mēcōnium*, poppy juice < Gk. *mēkōnion* < *mēkōn*, poppy.]

me·cop·ter·an (mĭ-kŏp′tər-ən) *n.* Any of various carnivorous insects of the order Mecoptera, including the scorpion flies, characterized by membranous wings and a beaklike head having chewing mouthparts at the tip. [< NLat. *Mĕcoptera*, order name : Gk. *mĕkos*, length; see **māk-** in App. + Gk. *ptera*, pl. of *pteron*, wing.] —**me·cop′ter·ous** *adj.*

med (mĕd) *adj. Informal* Medical: *med students.*

med. *abbr.* **1.** medicine **2.** medieval **3.** medium

MEd *abbr.* Master of Education

mé·dail·lon (mā-dä-yôn′, mə-däl′yən) *n., pl.* **-lons** (-yôn′, -yənz) A circular portion of food; a medallion. [Fr. See MEDALLION.]

me·da·ka (mĭ-dä′kə) *n.* A small Japanese fish (*Oryzias latipes*) often used in biological research or in stocking aquariums. [J., killifish : *me*, eye + *daka*, high.]

med·al (mĕd′l) *n.* **1.** A flat piece of metal stamped with a commemorative design or inscription, often given as an award. **2.** A piece of metal stamped with a religious device, used as an object of veneration or commemoration. [Fr. *médaille* < OFr. < Ital. *medaglia*, coin worth half a denarius, medal < VLat. **medalia*, coins worth half a denarius < LLat. *mediālia*, little halves < neut. pl. of *mediālis*, of the middle, medial. See MEDIAL.] —**med′al** *v.* —**me·dal′lic** (mə-dăl′ĭk) *adj.*

Medal for Merit *n.* A decoration awarded by the United States to

civilians for outstanding service.

med·al·ist (mĕd′l-ĭst) *n.* **1.** One who has received a medal. **2.** *Sports* The winner at medal play in a golf tournament. **3.** One who designs, makes, or collects medals.

me·dal·lion (mĭ-dăl′yən) *n.* **1.** A large medal. **2.** An emblem of registration for a taxicab. **3.** Any of various large ancient Greek coins. **4.** Something resembling a large medal, as: **a.** An oval or circular design used as decoration. **b.** A painting or an engraving set in an oval or circular frame. **c.** A circular portion of food, esp. a boneless cut of meat. [Fr. *médaillon* < Ital. *medaglione*, augmentative of *medaglia*, medal < OItal. See MEDAL.]

Medal of Freedom *n.* A decoration awarded by the United States to civilians for outstanding achievement.

Medal of Honor *n.* The Congressional Medal of Honor.

medal play *n.* Golf competition in which the total number of strokes taken is the basis of the score.

Me·dan (mā-dän′) A city of Indonesia on N Sumatra NNW of Padang. Pop. 1,378,955.

Med·a·war (mĕd′ə-wər), Sir **Peter Brian** 1915–87. British biologist who shared a 1960 Nobel Prize.

med·dle (mĕd′l) *intr.v.* **-dled, -dling, -dles 1.** To intrude into other people's affairs or business; interfere. See Syns at **interfere.** **2.** To handle something idly or ignorantly; tamper. [ME *medlen* < AN *medler*, var. of OFr. *mesler* < VLat. **misculāre*, to mix thoroughly < Lat. *miscēre*, to mix. See **meik-** in App.] —**med′dler** (mĕd′lər, mĕd′l-ər) *n.*

med·dle·some (mĕd′l-səm) *adj.* Inclined to meddle or interfere. —**med′dle·some·ly** *adv.* —**med′dle·some·ness** *n.*

Mede (mēd) *n.* A member of an Iranian people, closely related to the Persians, inhabiting ancient Media. [Ult. < Gk. *Mēdos* < OPers. *Māda.*]

Me·de·a (mĭ-dē′ə) *n. Greek Mythology* A princess and sorceress of Colchis who helped Jason obtain the Golden Fleece.

Me·del·lín (mĕd′l-ēn′, mĕ′dĕ-yēn′) A city of NW Colombia NW of Bogotá; founded 1675. Pop. 1,473,351.

med·e·vac (mĕd′ĭ-văk′) *n.* **1.** Air transport of persons to a place where they can receive medical or surgical care; medical evacuation. **2.** A helicopter or other aircraft used for such transport. [MED(ICAL) + EVAC(UATION).] —**med′e·vac′** *v.*

Med·fly also **med·fly** (mĕd′flī′) *n. Informal* The Mediterranean fruit fly.

Med. Gr. *abbr.* Medieval Greek

me·di·a¹ (mē′dē-ə) *n.* A plural of **medium.** See Usage Note at **medium.**

me·di·a² (mē′dē-ə) *n.* **1.** *Linguistics* See **medial** 1. **2.** The middle, often muscular layer of the wall of a blood vessel. [LLat. < Lat., fem. of Latin *medius*, middle. See MEDIUM.]

Media An ancient country of SW Asia in present-day NW Iran; orig. settled by an Indo-European people and conquered c. 550 B.C. by Cyrus. —**Me′di·an** *adj. & n.*

me·di·a·cy (mē′dē-ə-sē) *n.* The state or quality of being mediate.

me·di·ae·val (mē′dē-ē′vəl, mĕd′ē-, mĭ-dē′vəl) *adj.* Variant of **medieval.**

me·di·ae·val·ism (mē′dē-ē′və-lĭz′əm, mĕd′ē-) *n.* Variant of **medievalism.**

me·di·ae·val·ist (mē′dē-ē′və-lĭst, mĕd′ē-) *n.* Variant of **medievalist.**

media event *n.* **1.** An occasion that attracts prominent coverage by news organizations. **2.** *Informal* Its central figure.

me·di·a·gen·ic (mē′dē-ə-jĕn′ĭk) *adj.* Attractive as a subject for reporting by news media.

me·di·al (mē′dē-əl) *adj.* **1.** Relating to, situated in, or extending toward the middle; median. **2.** *Linguistics* Being a sound, syllable, or letter occurring between the initial and final positions in a word or morpheme. **3.** *Mathematics* Being or relating to an average or a mean. **4.** Average; ordinary. ❖ *n. Linguistics* **1.** A voiced stop, such as (b), (d), or (g). **2.** A sound, letter, or form of a letter that is neither initial nor final. [LLat. *mediālis* < Lat. *medius*, middle. See **medhyo-** in App.] —**me′di·al·ly** *adv.*

medial strip *n. Pennsylvania* See **median strip.** See Regional Note at **neutral ground.**

me·di·an (mē′dē-ən) *adj.* **1.** Relating to, located in, or extending toward the middle. **2.** *Anatomy* Of, relating to, or situated in or near the plane that divides a bilaterally symmetrical animal into right and left halves; mesial. **3.** *Statistics* Relating to or being the middle value in a series of values arranged in order of size. ❖ *n.* **1a.** A median point, plane, line, or part. **b.** See **median strip.** See Regional Note at **neutral ground.** **2.** *Statistics* A median value. **3.** *Mathematics* **a.** A line that joins a vertex of a triangle to the midpoint of the opposite side. **b.** The line that joins the midpoints of the nonparallel sides of a trapezoid. [Lat. *mediānus* < *medius*, middle. See **medhyo-** in App.] —**me′di·an·ly** *adv.*

median plane *n.* A plane dividing a bilaterally symmetrical animal into right and left halves.

median point *n.* The intersection of the medians of a triangle.

median strip *n. Eastern, Midwestern, & Southern US* The dividing area between opposing lanes of traffic on some highways. See Regional Note at **neutral ground.**

me·di·ant (mē′dē-ənt) *n.* The third tone in a diatonic musical scale, determining the major or minor quality of the tonic chord.

me·di·as·ti·num (mē′dē-ə-stī′nəm) *n.*, *pl.* **-na** (-nə) The region in mammals between the pleural sacs, containing the heart and all of the thoracic viscera except the lungs. [NLat. *mediastīnum* < neut. of Med.Lat. *mediastīnus*, medial < Lat., inferior servant, drudge (anatomical sense prob. influenced by Lat. *intestīnum*, intestine) < *medius*, middle. See **medhyo-** in App.] —**me′di·as·ti′nal** (-nəl) *adj.*

me·di·ate (mē′dē-āt′) *v.* **-at·ed, -at·ing, -ates** —*tr.* 1. To settle (differences) by working with conflicting parties: *mediate a labor-management dispute.* 2. To bring about (a settlement, for example) by working with conflicting parties. 3. To effect or convey as an intermediate agent. —*intr.* 1. To intervene between disputants to bring about an agreement or a compromise. 2. To mediate differences. 3. To have a relation to two differing persons or things. ❖ *adj.* (-ĭt) 1. Acting through, involving, or dependent on an intervening agency. 2. Being in a middle position. [LLat. *mediāre, mediāt-*, to be in the middle < Lat. *medius*, middle. See **medhyo-** in App.] —**me′di·ate·ly** (-ĭt-lē) *adv.*

me·di·a·tion (mē′dē-ā′shən) *n.* 1. The act of mediating; intervention. 2. The state of being mediated. 3. *Law* An attempt to bring about a peaceful settlement between disputants through the intervention of a neutral party. —**me′di·a′tive, me′di·a·to′ry** (mē′dē-ə-tôr′ē, -tōr′ē) *adj.*

me·di·a·tize (mē′dē-ə-tīz′) *tr.v.* **-tized, -tiz·ing, -tiz·es** To annex (a lesser state) to a greater state as a means of permitting the ruler of the lesser state to retain title and partial authority. [Prob. Fr. *médiatiser* < *médiat*, dependent < OFr., back-formation < *immediat*, independent < LLat. *immediātus*. See IMMEDIATE.] —**me′di·a·ti·za′tion** (-tĭ-zā′shən) *n.*

me·di·a·tor (mē′dē-ā′tər) *n.* 1. One that mediates, esp. differences between disputants. 2. *Physiology* A substance or structure that mediates a specific response in a body tissue.

med·ic¹ or **med·ick** (mĕd′ĭk) *n.* Any of several Old World herbs of the genus *Medicago* in the pea family, having clusters of small, usu. yellow flowers and compound leaves with three leaflets. [ME *medike* < Lat. *Mēdica* < Gk. *Mēdikē* < fem. of *Mēdikos*, of Media < *Mēdos*, a Mede. See MEDE.]

med·ic² (mĕd′ĭk) *n.* 1. A member of a military medical corps. 2. A physician or surgeon. 3. A medical student or intern. [Lat. *medicus*, physician. See MEDICAL.]

Lorenzo de Medici
portrait by Agnolo Bronzino
(1503–72)

med·i·ca·ble (mĕd′ĭ-kə-bəl) *adj.* Potentially responsive to treatment with medicine; curable.

Med·i·caid also **med·i·caid** (mĕd′ĭ-kād′) *n.* A US health care program reimbursing hospitals and physicians for care of those needing financial assistance. [MEDIC(AL) + AID.]

med·i·cal (mĕd′ĭ-kəl) *adj.* 1. Of or relating to the study or practice of medicine. 2. Requiring treatment by medicine. [Med.Lat. *medicālis* < Lat. *medicus*, physician < *medērī*, to heal. See **med-** in App.] —**med′i·cal·ly** *adv.*

medical examiner *n.* 1. A physician authorized by a government to ascertain causes of deaths, esp. those not occurring under natural circumstances. 2. A physician who examines employees of a firm or applicants for life insurance.

med·i·ca·lize (mĕd′ĭ-kə-līz′) *tr.v.* **-lized, -liz·ing, -liz·es** To identify or categorize (a condition or behavior) as a medical disorder requiring treatment. —**med′i·ca·li·za′tion** (-lĭ-zā′shən) *n.*

medical jurisprudence *n.* See **forensic medicine.**

medical law *n.* The branch of law that deals with the application of medical knowledge to legal problems.

me·dic·a·ment (mĭ-dĭk′ə-mənt, mĕd′ĭ-kə-) *n.* An agent that promotes recovery from injury or ailment; a medicine. [Lat. *medicāmentum* < *medicāre*, to cure. See MEDICATE.]

Med·i·care also **med·i·care** (mĕd′ĭ-kâr′) *n.* A program under the US Social Security Administration that reimburses hospitals and physicians for medical care provided to qualifying people over 65 years old. [MEDI(CAL) + CARE.]

med·i·cate (mĕd′ĭ-kāt′) *tr.v.* **-cat·ed, -cat·ing, -cates** 1. To treat with medicine. 2. To tincture or permeate with a medicinal substance. [Lat. *medicāre, medicāt-* < *medicus*, doctor < *medērī*, to heal. See **med-** in App.] —**med′i·ca′tive** *adj.*

med·i·ca·tion (mĕd′ĭ-kā′shən) *n.* 1. A medicine; a medicament. 2. The act or process of treating with medicine. 3. Administration of medicine.

Med·i·ci (mĕd′ĭ-chē′, mā′dē-) Italian noble family, including **Cosimo** "the Elder" (1389–1464), the first of the family to rule Florence, and **Lorenzo** "the Magnificent" (1449–92), an outstanding patron of learning and the arts. —**Med′i·ce′an** (-chē′ən, -sē′-) *adj.*

me·dic·i·nal (mĭ-dĭs′ə-nəl) *adj.* 1. Of, relating to, or having the properties of medicine. 2. Having an unappealing bitter flavor. ❖ *n.* A medicinal preparation or product. —**me·dic′i·nal·ly** *adv.*

med·i·cine (mĕd′ĭ-sĭn) *n.* 1a. The science of diagnosing, treating, or preventing disease and injury to the body or mind. b. The branch of this science encompassing treatment by drugs, diet, exercise, and other nonsurgical means. 2. The practice of medicine. 3. An agent, such as a drug, used to treat disease or injury. 4. Something that serves as a remedy or corrective. 5a. Shamanistic practices or beliefs, esp. among Native Americans. b. Something, such as a rite, believed to control natural or supernatural powers. [ME < OFr. < Lat. *medicīna* < fem. of *medicīnus*, of a doctor < *medicus*, physician. See MEDICAL.]

medicine ball *n.* A large heavy stuffed ball used in conditioning exercises.

Medicine Bow Mountains (bō′) A range of the E Rocky Mts. in SE WY and N CO rising to 3,664 m (12,013 ft) at **Medicine Bow Peak** in S-central WY.

medicine bundle *n.* A parcel containing items of religious significance, used by certain Native American peoples.

medicine dance *n.* A ritual dance performed by some Native American peoples for supernatural assistance, as in healing.

Medicine Hat A city of SE Alberta, Canada, SE of Calgary; founded 1883. Pop. 46,783.

medicine lodge *n.* A building or structure used by certain Native American peoples for ceremonies.

medicine man *n.* 1. A male shaman or shamanistic healer, esp. among Native American peoples. 2. A hawker of brews and potions in a medicine show.

medicine show *n.* A traveling show, popular esp. in the 19th century, that offered varied entertainment, between the acts of which medicines were peddled.

medicine woman *n.* A female shaman or shamanistic healer, esp. among Native American peoples.

med·ick (mĕd′ĭk) *n.* Variant of **medic¹.**

med·i·co (mĕd′ĭ-kō′) *n., pl.* **-cos** *Informal* 1. A physician. 2. A medical student. [Ital. *medico* or Sp. *médico*, both < Lat. *medicus.* See MEDICAL.]

med·i·co·le·gal (mĕd′ĭ-kō-lē′gəl) *adj.* Of, relating to, or concerned with medicine and law.

me·di·e·val also **me·di·ae·val** (mē′dē-ē′vəl, mĕd′ē-, mĭ-dē′vəl) *adj.* 1. also **Medieval** Relating or belonging to the Middle Ages. 2. *Informal* Old-fashioned; unenlightened. [< NLat. *medium aevum*, the middle age : Lat., neut. of *medius*, middle; see **medhyo-** in App. + Lat. *aevum*, age; see **aiw-** in App.] —**me′di·e′val·ly** *adv.*

Medieval Greek *n.* The Greek language as used from about 800 to about 1500.

me·di·e·val·ism also **me·di·ae·val·ism** (mē′dē-ē′və-lĭz′əm, mĕd′ē-) *n.* 1. The spirit or the body of beliefs or practices of the Middle Ages. 2. Devotion to or acceptance of the ideas of the Middle Ages. 3. Scholarly study of the Middle Ages.

me·di·e·val·ist also **me·di·ae·val·ist** (mē′dē-ē′və-lĭst, mĕd′ē-) *n.* 1. A specialist in the study of the Middle Ages. 2. A connoisseur of medieval culture.

Medieval Latin *n.* The Latin language as used from about 700 to about 1500.

Medieval Welsh *n.* Welsh from the 12th through the 15th century.

Med·i·gap (mĕd′ĭ-găp′) *n.* Private health insurance designed to supplement the coverage provided under governmental programs such as Medicare. [MEDI(CARE) or MEDI(CAID) + GAP.]

me·di·na (mĭ-dē′nə) *n.* The old section of an Arab city in North Africa. [Ar. *madīna*, city < Aram. *madintā, madinā*, jurisdiction, district < *dān*, to judge, administer.]

Medina A city of W Saudi Arabia N of Mecca; a pilgrimage site for Muslims. Pop. 290,000.

me·di·o·cre (mē′dē-ō′kər) *adj.* Moderate to inferior in quality; ordinary. See Syns at **average.** [Fr. *médiocre* < Lat. *mediocris* : *medius*, middle; see **medhyo-** in App. + *ocris*, a rugged mountain; see **ak-** in App.]

me·di·oc·ri·ty (mē′dē-ŏk′rĭ-tē) *n., pl.* **-ties** 1. The state or quality of being mediocre. 2. Mediocre ability, achievement, or performance. 3. One that displays mediocre qualities. —**me·di·oc′ri·tize′** (-tīz′) *v.* —**me·di·oc′ri·ti·za′tion** *n.*

med·i·tate (mĕd′ĭ-tāt′) *v.* **-tat·ed, -tat·ing, -tates** —*tr.* 1. To reflect on; contemplate. 2. To plan in the mind; intend. —*intr.* 1a. *Buddhism & Hinduism* To train, calm, or empty the mind, often by achieving an altered state, as by focusing on a single object. b. To engage in devotional contemplation, esp. prayer. 2. To think or reflect, esp. in a deliberate manner. [Lat. *meditārī, meditāt-.* See **med-** in App.] —**med′i·ta′tor** *n.*

med·i·ta·tion (mĕd′ĭ-tā′shən) *n.* 1a. The act or process of meditating. b. A devotional exercise of or leading to contemplation. 2. A contemplative discourse, usu. on a religious or philosophical subject. —**med′i·ta′tion·al** *adj.*

med·i·ta·tive (mĕd′ĭ-tā′tĭv) *adj.* Characterized by or prone to meditation. See Syns at **pensive.** —**med′i·ta′tive·ly** *adv.* —**med′i·ta′tive·ness** *n.*

med·i·ter·ra·ne·an (mĕd′ĭ-tə-rā′nē-ən, -rān′yən) *adj.* Surrounded nearly or completely by dry land. Used of large bodies of water. [Lat. *mediterrāneus*, inland : *medius*, middle; see **medhyo-** in App. + *terra*, land; see **ters-** in App.]

Mediterranean The region surrounding the Mediterranean Sea; dominated in ancient times by Phoenicia, Carthage, Greece, Sicily, and Rome. —**Med′i·ter·ra′ne·an** *adj. & n.*

Mediterranean fever *n.* See **brucellosis** 1.

Mediterranean flour moth *n.* A small gray moth (*Anagasta kuehniella*), whose larvae destroy stored grain products.

Mediterranean fruit fly *n.* A black and white, two-winged fly

(*Ceratitis capitata*), whose larvae destroy fruit crops.

Mediterranean Sea An inland sea surrounded by Europe, Asia, Asia Minor, the Near East, and Africa and connecting with the Atlantic Ocean through the Strait of Gibraltar; with the Black Sea through the Dardanelles, the Sea of Marmara, and the Bosporus; and with the Red Sea through the Suez Canal.

me·di·um (mē′dē-əm) *n., pl.* **-di·a** (-dē-ə) or **-di·ums 1.** Something, such as an intermediate course of action, that occupies a position or represents a condition midway between extremes. **2.** An intervening substance through which something else is transmitted or carried on. **3.** An agency by which something is accomplished, conveyed, or transferred. **4.** *pl.* **media** Usage Problem **a.** A means of mass communication, such as newspapers or television. **b. media** (*used with a sing. or pl. verb*) The group of journalists and others in the communications industry. **5.** *pl.* **media** *Computer Science* An object or device, such as a disk, on which data is stored. **6.** *pl.* **mediums** A person thought to have the power to communicate with the spirits of the dead or with agents of another world or dimension. **7.** *pl.* **media a.** A surrounding environment in which something functions and thrives. **b.** The substance in which a specific organism lives and thrives. **c.** A culture medium. **8a.** A specific kind of artistic technique or means of expression as determined by the materials used or the creative methods involved. **b.** The materials used in a specific artistic technique. **9.** A solvent for thinning paint. **10.** *Chemistry* A filtering substance, such as filter paper. **11.** A size of paper, usu. 18 × 23 inches or 17½ × 22 inches. ❖ *adj.* Occurring or being between two degrees, amounts, or quantities; intermediate. See Syns at **average.** [Lat. < neut. of *medius*, middle. See medhyo- in App.]

> **USAGE NOTE** The etymologically plural form *media* is often used as a singular to refer to a particular means of communication, as in *The most exciting new media since television is the Internet.* Many people regard this usage as incorrect, preferring *medium* in such contexts. • People also use *media* with the definite article as a collective term, roughly equivalent to "the press." Like other collective nouns, it may take a singular or plural verb depending on the intended meaning. In *The media have covered the trial in a variety of formats,* the multifaceted nature of the press is emphasized, while in *The media has not shown much interest in covering the trial,* the journalists and broadcasters are treated as an aggregate.

medium frequency *n.* A radio frequency or radio-frequency band in the range 300 to 3,000 kilohertz.

medium of exchange *n., pl.* **media of exchange** or **mediums of exchange** Something, such as a precious metal, commonly used in a specific area or among a certain group as money.

med·lar (mĕd′lər) *n.* **1.** A deciduous European tree (*Mespilus germanica*) having white flowers and edible apple-shaped fruit. **2.** Its fruit. [ME *medler* < OFr. < *mesle, medle,* fruit of the medlar < LLat. *mespila* < Gk. *mespilē*.]

Med. Lat. *abbr.* Medieval Latin

med·ley (mĕd′lē) *n., pl.* **-leys 1.** An often jumbled assortment; a mixture. **2.** *Music* An arrangement made from a series of melodies, often from various sources. **3.** *Sports* A swimming race in which backstroke, breaststroke, butterfly, and freestyle are swum in equal distances by an individual or as parts of a relay. [ME *medlee* < AN, meddling < p. part. of *medler,* to meddle. See MED-DLE.]

Mé·doc[1] (mā-dŏk′, -dôk′) A region of SW France N of Bordeaux between the Bay of Biscay and the Gironde R. estuary.

Mé·doc[2] (mā-dŏk′, -dôk′) *n.* A red Bordeaux wine.

me·dul·la (mĭ-dŭl′ə, -doo′lə) *n., pl.* **-dul·las** or **-dul·lae** (-dŭl′ē, -doo′lē) **1.** The inner core of certain organs or body structures, such as the marrow of bone. **2.** The medulla oblongata. **3.** See **myelin. 4.** *Botany* **a.** The pith in the stems or roots of certain plants. **b.** The central portion of a thallus in certain lichens and red or brown algae. [ME < Lat., perh. alteration (influenced by *medius,* middle) of **merulla.*] —**me·dul′lar, med·ul′lar′y** (mĕd′l-ĕr′ē, mə-dŭl′ə-rē, mĭ-doo′lə-) *adj.*

medulla ob·lon·ga·ta (ŏb′lông-gä′tə) *n., pl.* **-tas** or **medullae ob·lon·ga·tae** (-tē) The lowermost portion of the vertebrate brain, continuous with the spinal cord and controlling respiration, circulation, and certain other bodily functions. [NLat. *medulla oblongāta* : Lat. *medulla,* medulla + NLat. *oblongāta,* fem. of *oblongātus,* oblong.]

medullary sheath *n.* See **myelin sheath.**

med·ul·lat·ed (mĕd′l-ā′tĭd) *adj.* **1.** Myelinated. **2.** *Anatomy* Having a medulla.

med·ul·li·za·tion (mĕd′l-ĭ-zā′shən) *n.* Replacement of bone tissue by marrow, as in inflammatory bone disease.

me·du·sa (mĭ-doo′sə, -doo′zə, -dyoo′-) *n., pl.* **-sas** or **-sae** (-sē, -zē) The tentacular, usu. bell-shaped, free-swimming sexual stage in the life cycle of a cnidarian. [Lat. *Medūsa,* Medusa (< the Medusa's snaky locks). See MEDUSA.]

Medusa *n. Greek Mythology* The Gorgon who was killed by Perseus. [ME *Meduse* < Lat. *Medūsa* < Gk. *Medousa* < fem. pr. part. of *medein,* to protect, rule over. See med- in App.]

me·du·soid (mĭ-doo′soid′, -zoid′, -dyoo′-) *n.* **1.** A shape resembling a jellyfish. **2.** A jellyfish. —**me·du′soid′** *adj.*

meed (mēd) *n.* **1.** A fitting recompense. **2.** *Archaic* A merited gift

or wage. [ME *mede* < OE *mēd.*]

meek (mēk) *adj.* **meek·er, meek·est 1.** Showing patience and humility; gentle. **2.** Easily imposed on; submissive. [ME *meke,* of Scand. orig.; akin to ON *mjūkr,* soft.] —**meek′ly** *adv.*

meer·kat (mîr′kăt′) *n.* See **suricate.** [Afr. < MDu. *meercatte,* monkey : *meer,* sea (because monkeys came from overseas); see **mori-** in App. + *catte,* cat (< Gmc. **kattuz;* see CAT).]

meer·schaum (mîr′shəm, -shôm′) *n.* **1.** A fine, compact, usu. white claylike mineral of hydrous magnesium silicate, $H_4Mg_2Si_3O_{10}$, found in the Mediterranean area and used in fashioning tobacco pipes and as a building stone. **2.** A tobacco pipe with a bowl made of this mineral. [Ger. : *Meer,* sea (< MHGer. *mer* < OHGer. *mari;* see **mori-** in App.) + *Schaum,* foam (< MHGer. *schūm* < OHGer. *scūm;* see **(s)keu-** in App.).]

Mee·rut (mā′rət, mîr′ət) A city of N-central India NE of Delhi; site of the first uprising (May 1857) against the British in the Indian Mutiny. Pop. 753,778.

meet[1] (mēt) *v.* **met** (mĕt), **meet·ing, meets** —*tr.* **1.** To come upon by chance or arrangement. **2.** To be present at the arrival of: *met the train.* **3.** To be introduced to. **4.** To come into conjunction with; join: *where the river meets the sea.* **5.** To come into the company or presence of, as for a conference. **6.** To come to the notice of (the senses): *more here than meets the eye.* **7.** To experience; undergo: *met a grim fate.* **8.** To deal with; oppose: *met the enemy.* **9.** To cope or contend effectively with: *met each problem as it arose.* **10.** To come into conformity with the views, wishes, or opinions of: *They met us on each point.* **11.** To satisfy (a need, for example); fulfill. See Syns at **satisfy. 12.** To pay; settle: *money to meet expenses.* —*intr.* **1.** To come together: *Let's meet tonight.* **2.** To come into conjunction; be joined. **3.** To come together as opponents; contend. **4.** To become introduced. **5.** To assemble. **6.** To experience or undergo. Used with *with: The housing bill met with approval.* **7.** To occur together, esp. in one person or entity. ❖ *n.* A meeting or contest, esp. an athletic competition. —*phrasal verb:* **meet with 1.** To experience or undergo. **2.** To receive: *meet with approval.* —*idioms:* **meet (one's) Maker** To die. **meet (someone) halfway** To make a compromise with. [ME *meten* < OE *mētan.*]

meet[2] (mēt) *adj.* Fitting; proper. [ME *mete* < OE *gemǣte.* See med- in App.] —**meet′ly** *adv.*

meet·ing (mē′tĭng) *n.* **1.** The act or process or an instance of coming together; an encounter. **2.** An assembly or gathering of people. —*idiom:* **meeting of the minds** Agreement.

meet·ing·house (mē′tĭng-hous′) *n.* A building for public meetings, esp. for Protestant or Quaker religious services.

mef·e·nam·ic acid (mĕf′ə-năm′ĭk) *n.* A crystalline compound, $C_{15}H_{15}NO_2$, used as an anti-inflammatory drug and analgesic. [(DI)ME(THYL) + alteration of PHEN(YL) + AM(INOBENZO)IC ACID.]

meg (mĕg) *n. Informal* A megabyte.

mega- *pref.* **1.** Large: *megadose.* **2.** Surpassing other examples of its kind: *megahit.* **3.** One million (10^6): *megahertz.* **4.** 1,048,576 (2^{20}): *megabyte.* See **meg-** in App.]

meg·a·bit (mĕg′ə-bĭt′) *n. Computer Science* **1.** One million bits. **2.** 1,048,576 (2^{20}) bits. See Usage Note at **megabyte.**

meg·a·buck (mĕg′ə-bŭk′) *n. Slang* **1.** One million dollars. **2. megabucks** A large but unspecified amount of money.

meg·a·byte (mĕg′ə-bīt′) *n.* **1.** A unit of computer memory or data storage capacity equal to 1,048,576 (2^{20}) bytes. **2.** One million

> **USAGE NOTE** The calculation of data storage capacity (measured in bytes) is based on powers of two because of the binary nature of bits (1 byte is 8, or 2^3, bits). Here, the prefix *mega*– refers to the power of two closest to 1,000,000, which is 2^{20}, or 1,048,576. Thus, a megabyte is 1,048,576 bytes, although it is also used less technically to refer to a million bytes. With data transmission rates (measured in bits per second), a bit is considered as a signal pulse, and calculations are generally based on powers of ten. Thus, a rate of one megabit per second is equal to one million bits per second. However, in certain technical contexts, megabit can also refer to 1,048,576 bits. Similarly, the prefix *kilo*– refers to 1,000 or 2^{10} (1,024); *giga*– to 1,000,000,000 (one billion) or 2^{30} (1,073,741,824); and *tera*– to 1,000,000,000,000 (one trillion) or 2^{40} (1,099,511,627,776).

meg·a·church (mĕg′ə-chûrch′) *n.* A large, independent, usu. nondenominational worship group, esp. one formed as an offshoot of a Protestant church.

meg·a·cy·cle (mĕg′ə-sī′kəl) *n.* See **megahertz.**

meg·a·death (mĕg′ə-dĕth′) *n.* One million deaths. Used as a unit in reference to nuclear warfare.

meg·a·dose (mĕg′ə-dōs′) *n.* An exceptionally large dose, as of a drug or vitamin.

Me·gae·ra (mə-jîr′ə) *n. Greek Mythology* One of the Furies.

meg·a·fau·na (mĕg′ə-fô′nə) *n.* (*used with a sing. or pl. verb*) Large animals, as of a particular region or period, considered as a group. —**meg·a·fau′nal** *adj.*

meg·a·flop (mĕg′ə-flŏp′) *n.* A measure of computing speed equal to one million floating-point operations per second. [MEGA- + FLOP.]

meg·a·gam·ete (mĕg′ə-găm′ēt′, -gə-mēt′) *n.* See **macrogamete.**

863

Mediterranean Sea

——

megagamete

Medusa
c. 1590–1600
shield painting by
Caravaggio

ă	pat	oi	boy
ā	pay	ou	out
âr	care	oŏ	took
ä	father	oō	boot
ĕ	pet	ŭ	cut
ē	be	ûr	urge
ĭ	pit	th	thin
ī	pie	th	this
îr	pier	hw	which
ŏ	pot	zh	vision
ō	toe	ə	about,
ô	paw		item

Stress marks:
′ (primary);
′ (secondary), as in
lexicon (lĕk′sĭ-kŏn′)

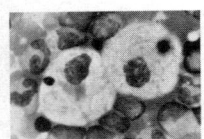

megakaryocyte
photomicrograph of two
megakaryocyte cells

megalith
c. 1800 B.C. standing stones
at Callanish, Isle of Lewis,
Scotland

megaphone

meg·a·ga·me·to·phyte (mĕg′ə-gə-mē′tə-fīt′) n. The female gametophyte that arises from a megaspore.

meg·a·hertz (mĕg′ə-hûrts′) n. One million hertz. Used esp. as a radio-frequency unit.

meg·a·hit (mĕg′ə-hĭt′) n. A product or event that is exceedingly successful.

meg·a·kar·y·o·cyte (mĕg′ə-kăr′ē-ō-sīt′, -ə-sīt′) n. A large bone marrow cell with a lobulate nucleus that gives rise to blood platelets.

meg·a·lith (mĕg′ə-lĭth′) n. A very large stone used in various prehistoric architectures or monumental styles. —**meg′a·lith′ic** adj.

megalo- or **megal-** pref. Large; of exaggerated size or greatness: *megalocephaly.* [Gk. < *megas, megal-*, great. See **meg-** in App.]

meg·a·lo·blast (mĕg′ə-lō-blăst′) n. An abnormally large nucleated red blood cell found esp. in people having pernicious anemia or vitamin deficiencies. —**meg′a·lo·blas′tic** adj.

meg·a·lo·ceph·a·ly (mĕg′ə-lō-sĕf′ə-lē) n., pl. **-lies** See **macrocephaly.** —**meg′a·lo·ce·phal′ic** (-sə-făl′ĭk), **meg′a·lo·ceph′a·lous** (-ə-ləs) adj.

meg·a·lo·ma·ni·a (mĕg′ə-lō-mā′nē-ə, -mān′yə) n. **1.** A psychopathological condition characterized by delusional fantasies of wealth, power, or omnipotence. **2.** An obsession with grandiose or extravagant things or actions. —**meg′a·lo·ma′ni·ac′** n. —**meg′a·lo·ma·ni′a·cal** (-mə-nī′ə-kəl), **meg′a·lo·man′ic** (-măn′ĭk) adj.

meg·a·lop·o·lis (mĕg′ə-lŏp′ə-lĭs) also **me·gap·o·lis** (mĭ-găp′ə-lĭs, mĕ-) n. A region made up of several large cities and their surrounding areas in sufficient proximity to be considered a single urban complex. [MEGALO- + Gk. *polis*, city.] —**meg′a·lop·o·lis′tic** adj. —**meg′a·lo·pol′i·tan** (-lō-pŏl′ĭ-tən) adj.

meg·a·lo·saur (mĕg′ə-lə-sôr′) n. A large carnivorous dinosaur of the genus *Megalosaurus* of the Jurassic Period. [NLat. *Megalosaurus*, genus name : MEGALO- + Gk. *sauros*, lizard.] —**meg′a·lo·sau′ri·an** adj. & n.

meg·a·par·sec (mĕg′ə-pär′sĕk) n. One million parsecs.

meg·a·phone (mĕg′ə-fōn′) n. A funnel-shaped device used to direct and amplify the voice. —**meg′a·phone′** v. —**meg′a·phon′ic** (-fŏn′ĭk) adj. —**meg′a·phon′i·cal·ly** adv.

meg·a·pode (mĕg′ə-pōd′) n. Any of various large-footed ground-dwelling birds of the family Megapodiidae, found in Australia and many South Pacific islands, that build mounds or burrows for their eggs. [< *Megapodius*, type genus : MEGA- + NLat. *-podius*, masc. of *-podium*, -pod.]

Meg·a·ra (mĕg′ər-ə) An ancient city of E-central Greece; cap. of Megaris, a Dorian state between the Saronic Gulf and the Gulf of Corinth.

meg·a·ron (mĕg′ə-rŏn′) n., pl. **-ara** (-ər-ə) The main hall or central room of a palace or house, esp. of Mycenaean Greece, having a pillared porch and a central hearth. [Gk.]

meg·a·scop·ic (mĕg′ə-skŏp′ĭk) adj. Macroscopic. —**meg′a·scop′i·cal·ly** adv.

meg·a·spo·ran·gi·um (mĕg′ə-spə-răn′jē-əm) n., pl. **-gi·a** (-jē-ə) A structure that produces one or more megaspores.

meg·a·spore (mĕg′ə-spôr′, -spōr′) n. Botany The larger of two types of spores, giving rise to a female gametophyte. —**meg′a·spor′ic** adj.

meg·a·spo·ro·phyll (mĕg′ə-spôr′ə-fĭl′, -spōr′-) n. A leaflike structure that bears megasporangia.

meg·a·struc·ture (mĕg′ə-strŭk′chər) n. An extremely large tall building.

meg·a·there (mĕg′ə-thîr′) n. A large extinct ground sloth of the family Megatheriidae of the Miocene Epoch through the Pleistocene Epoch. [< NLat. *Megatherium*, type genus : MEGA- + Gk. *thērion*, wild beast; see TREACLE.] —**meg′a·the′ri·an** adj.

meg·a·ton (mĕg′ə-tŭn′) n. A unit of explosive force equal to that of one million metric tons of TNT. —**meg′a·ton′nage** (-tŭn′ĭj) n.

meg·a·vi·ta·min (mĕg′ə-vī′tə-mĭn) n. A dose of a vitamin greatly exceeding the amount required to maintain health.

meg·a·volt (mĕg′ə-vōlt′) n. One million volts.

meg·a·watt (mĕg′ə-wŏt′) n. One million watts.

Me·gid·do (mĭ-gĭd′ō) An ancient city of NW Palestine on the S edge of the Plain of Esdraelon.

Me·gil·lah (mə-gĭl′ə) n. **1.** Judaism The scroll containing the biblical narrative of the Book of Esther, read in synagogues at Purim. **2.** **megillah** Slang A tediously detailed or embroidered account. [Heb. *măgillā*, scroll < *gălal*, to roll.]

Me·grez (mē′grĕz′) n. A star in the Big Dipper. [Short for Ar. *maģriz aḍ-ḍanab aḍ-dubb al-akbar*, the root of the tail of the greater bear < *maģriz*, root < *ģaraza*, to prick, insert.]

me·grim (mē′grĭm) n. **1.** A migraine. **2.** A caprice or fancy. Often used in the plural. **3.** **megrims** Depression or unhappiness. [ME *migrem*, var. of *migraine*. See MIGRAINE.]

Meigh·en (mē′ən), **Arthur** 1874–1960. Canadian politician who served as prime minister (1920–21 and 1926).

Mei·ji (mā′jē′) See **Mutsuhito.**

Meil·let (mā-yā′), **Antoine** 1866–1936. French linguist and Indo-Europeanist whose works include *The Comparative Method in Historical Linguistics* (1925).

mei·o·sis (mī-ō′sĭs) n., pl. **-ses** (-sēz′) **1.** Genetics Cell division in sexually reproducing organisms that reduces the number of chromosomes in reproductive cells from diploid to haploid, leading to the formation of gametes in animals and spores in plants. **2.** Rhetorical understatement. [Gk. *meiōsis*, diminution < *meioun*, to diminish < *meiōn*, less.] —**mei·ot′ic** (-ŏt′ĭk) adj. —**mei·ot′i·cal·ly** adv.

Me·ir (mī′ər, mä-ēr′), **Golda** 1898–1978. Russian-born Israeli politician who served as prime minister (1969–74).

Meis·sen¹ (mī′sən) A city of E-central Germany on the Elbe R. NW of Dresden. Pop. 38,710.

Meis·sen² (mī′sən) n. A delicate porcelain ware originally made in Meissen, Germany.

-meister suff. One who is renowned for, has expertise in, or is a connoisseur of: *spinmeister.* [Ger. < *Meister*, master. See MEISTERSINGER.]

Meis·ter·sing·er (mīs′tər-sĭng′ər) n., pl. **Meistersinger** or **-ers** A member of one of the guilds in German cities in the 14th, 15th, and 16th centuries that composed and performed music and poetry. [Ger. < MHGer. : *meister*, master (< OHGer. *meistar* < Lat. *magister*; see MASTER) + *singer*, singer (< *singen*, to sing < OHGer. *singan*; see **seng**ʷ**h-** in App.).]

Meit·ner (mīt′nər), **Lise** 1878–1968. Austrian-born Swedish physicist and pioneer in the study of nuclear fission.

meit·ner·i·um (mīt-nûr′ē-əm) n. Symbol **Mt** An artificially produced radioactive element with atomic number 109 whose most long-lived isotopes have mass numbers of 266 and 268 with half-lives of 3.4 milliseconds and 70 milliseconds, respectively. See table at **element.** [After Lise MEITNER.]

Mek·nes (mĕk-nĕs′) A city of N Morocco WSW of Fez; cap. of Moroccan sultans after c. 1672. Pop. 401,000.

Me·kong (mā′kŏng′, -kŏng′) A river of SE Asia flowing c. 4,183 km (2,600 mi) from SE China to the South China Sea through the vast **Mekong Delta** in S Vietnam.

mel·a·mine (mĕl′ə-mēn′) n. **1.** A white crystalline compound, $C_3H_6N_6$, used in making melamine resins and for tanning leather. **2.** A plastic made from such resin. [Ger. *Melamin* : *Melam*, distillate of ammonium thiocyanate (*mel-*, arbitrary pref. + *Am(monium)*, ammonium) + *Amin*, amine.]

melamine resin n. A thermosetting resin used for molded products, adhesives, and surface coatings.

melan- pref. Variant of **melano-**.

mel·an·cho·li·a (mĕl′ən-kō′lē-ə) n. A psychological disorder characterized by severe depression, hopelessness, and withdrawal. [LLat., melancholy. See MELANCHOLY.] —**mel′an·cho′li·ac** (-lē-ăk′) adj. & n.

mel·an·chol·ic (mĕl′ən-kŏl′ĭk) adj. **1.** Affected with or subject to melancholy. **2.** Of or relating to melancholia. —**mel′an·chol′ic** n. —**mel′an·chol′i·cal·ly** adv.

mel·an·chol·y (mĕl′ən-kŏl′ē) n. **1.** Sadness or depression of the spirits; gloom. **2.** Pensive reflection or contemplation. **3.** *Archaic* **a.** Black bile. **b.** An emotional state characterized by sullenness and outbreaks of violent anger, believed to arise from black bile. ❖ adj. **1.** Affected with or marked by depression of the spirits; sad. See Syns at **sad. 2.** Tending to promote sadness or gloom. **3.** Pensive; thoughtful. [ME *melancolie* < OFr. < LLat. *melancholia* < Gk. *melankholiā* : *melas, melan-*, black + *kholē*, bile; see **ghel-** in App.] —**mel′an·chol′i·ly** adv. —**mel′an·chol′i·ness** n.

Me·lanch·thon (mə-lăngk′thən, mä-läNKH′tôn), **Philipp** 1497–1560. German theologian and Reformation leader who wrote *Loci Communes* (1521).

Mel·a·ne·sia (mĕl′ə-nē′zhə, -shə) A division of Oceania in the SW Pacific Ocean NE of Australia and S of the equator.

Mel·a·ne·sian (mĕl′ə-nē′zhən, -shən) adj. Of or relating to Melanesia or its peoples, languages, or cultures. ❖ n. **1.** A member of any of the indigenous peoples of Melanesia. **2.** A subfamily of the Austronesian languages that includes the languages of Melanesia.

mé·lange also **me·lange** (mā-länzh′) n. A mixture. [Fr. < OFr. *meslance* < *mesler*, to mix. See MEDDLE.]

mel·an·ic (mə-lăn′ĭk) adj. **1.** Of, relating to, or exhibiting melanism. **2.** Of, relating to, or affected with melanosis.

mel·a·nin (mĕl′ə-nĭn) n. Any of a group of naturally occurring dark pigments, esp. one in skin, hair, fur, and feathers.

mel·a·nism (mĕl′ə-nĭz′əm) n. **1.** See **melanosis. 2.** Dark coloration of the skin, hair, fur, or feathers because of a high concentration of melanin. —**mel′a·nis′tic** adj.

melano- or **melan-** pref. Black; dark: *melanin.* [Gk. < *melas, melan-*, black.]

mel·a·no·blast (mĕl′ə-nō-blăst′, mə-lăn′ə-) n. A precursor cell of a melanocyte or melanophore.

mel·a·no·cyte (mĕl′ə-nō-sīt′) n. An epidermal cell capable of synthesizing melanin.

mel·a·no·cyte-stim·u·lat·ing hormone (mĕl′ə-nō-sīt′stĭm′yə-lā′tĭng, mə-lăn′ə-) n. A hormone secreted by the pituitary gland that regulates skin color in humans and other vertebrates by stimulating melanin dispersal.

mel·a·noid (mĕl′ə-noid′) adj. **1.** Of or related to melanin; black-pigmented. **2.** Of or affected with melanosis.

mel·a·no·ma (mĕl′ə-nō′mə) n., pl. **-mas** or **-ma·ta** (-ə-tə) A dark-pigmented, usu. malignant tumor arising from a melanocyte and occurring most commonly in the skin.

mel·a·no·phore (mĕl′ə-nə-fôr′, -fōr′, mə-lăn′ə-) *n.* A pigment cell that contains melanin, esp. as found in the skin of amphibians and reptiles.

mel·a·no·sis (mĕl′ə-nō′sĭs) *n., pl.* **-ses** (-sēz) Abnormally dark pigmentation of the skin or other tissues, due to a disorder of pigment metabolism. —**mel′a·not′ic** (-nŏt′ĭk) *adj.*

mel·a·nous (mĕl′ə-nəs) *adj.* Having a swarthy or black complexion and black hair. —**mel′a·nos′i·ty** (-nŏs′ĭ-tē) *n.*

mel·a·phyre (mĕl′ə-fīr′) *n.* A dark igneous porphyry embedded with feldspar crystals. [Fr. *mélaphyre* < Gk. *melās*, black + Fr. *porphyre*, porphyry < Med.Lat. *porphyrium*; see PORPHYRY.]

mel·a·to·nin (mĕl′ə-tō′nĭn) *n.* A hormone produced by the pineal gland that stimulates color change in the epidermis of amphibians and reptiles and plays a role in sleep, aging, and reproduction in mammals. [Gk. *melās*, black + TON(E) + –IN.]

Mel·ba (mĕl′bə), Dame **Nellie** 1861–1931. Australian soprano associated primarily with London's Covent Garden (1889–1926).

Melba toast *n.* Very thinly sliced crisp toast. [After Dame Nellie MELBA.]

Mel·bourne (mĕl′bərn) A city of SE Australia SW of Canberra; settled in 1835. Pop. 3,189,200.

Melbourne, 2nd Viscount. Title of William Lamb. 1779–1848. British politician who served as prime minister (1834 and 1835–41).

Mel·chi·or (mĕl′kē-ôr′) One of the three Magi.

Melchior, Lauritz Lebrecht Hommel 1890–1973. Danish-born Amer. operatic tenor noted for his Wagnerian roles.

Mel·chite (mĕl′kīt) *n.* Variant of Melkite.

Mel·chiz·e·dek[1] (mĕl-kĭz′ĭ-dĕk′) In the Bible, the high priest and king of Salem who blessed Abraham. [Heb. *malkî-ṣedeq*, my king (is) righteousness : *melek*, king + *-î*, my + *ṣedeq*, righteousness.]

Mel·chiz·e·dek[2] (mĕl-kĭz′ĭ-dĕk′) *n. Mormon Church* The higher order of priesthood. [After MELCHIZEDEK[1].]

meld[1] (mĕld) *v.* **meld·ed, meld·ing, melds** —*tr.* To declare or display (a card or combination of cards in a hand) for inclusion in one's score in various card games, such as pinochle. —*intr.* To present a meld. ❖ *n.* A combination of cards of value in scoring. [Prob. Ger. *melden*, to announce < MHGer. < OHGer. *meldōn*.]

meld[2] (mĕld) *v.* **meld·ed, meld·ing, melds** —*tr.* To cause to merge. —*intr.* To become merged. ❖ *n.* A blend or merger. [Perh. blend of MELT and WELD[1].]

me·lee (mā′lā′, mā-lā′) also **mê·lée** (mĕ-lā′) *n.* **1a.** Confused hand-to-hand fighting in a pitched battle. **b.** A violent free-for-all. **2.** A confused tumultuous mingling, as of a crowd: *the rush-hour melee.* [Fr. *mêlée* < OFr. *meslee*, p. part. of *mesler*, to mix. See MEDDLE.]

me·le·na (mə-lē′nə) *n.* A condition marked by black tarry stool or vomit composed largely of blood that has been acted on by gastric juices, due to hemorrhage along the digestive tract. [NLat. *melēna* < Gk. *melaina*, fem. of *melās*, black.]

mel·ic (mĕl′ĭk) *adj.* Of or relating to verse intended to be sung, esp. Greek lyric verse of the seventh to the fifth century B.C. [Gk. *melikos* < *melos*, song.]

Mé·liès (māl-yĕs′), **Georges** 1861–1938. French film director who was the first to film fictional narratives and created the earliest special effects.

Me·lil·la (mā-lēl′yä) A Spanish city on the Mediterranean coast of NE Morocco; site of the army revolt that triggered the Spanish Civil War in 1936. Pop. 56,247.

mel·i·lot (mĕl′ə-lŏt′) *n.* Any of several Old World plants of the genus *Melilotus* in the pea family, having compound leaves with three leaflets and narrow racemes of small white or yellow flowers. [ME *melilote* < OFr. < Lat. *melilōtos* < Gk. : *meli*, honey; see *melit-* in App. + *lōtos*, lotus; see LOTUS.]

mel·io·rate (mĕl′yə-rāt′, mē′lē-ə-) *v.* **-rat·ed, -rat·ing, -rates** —*tr.* To make better; improve. —*intr.* To grow better. [Lat. *meliōrāre, meliōrāt-* < *melior*, better.] —**mel′io·ra·ble** (-rə-bəl) *adj.* —**mel′io·ra′tive** *adj. & n.* —**mel′io·ra′tor** *n.*

mel·io·ra·tion (mĕl′yə-rā′shən, mē′lē-ə-) *n.* **1a.** The act or process of improving something or the state of being improved. **b.** An improvement. **2.** The linguistic process by which a word becomes loftier in meaning or more positive in connotation.

mel·io·rism (mĕl′yə-rĭz′əm, mē′lē-ə-) *n.* The belief that improvement of society depends on human effort. [Lat. *melior*, better + –ISM.] —**mel′io·rist** *n.* —**mel′io·ris′tic** *adj.*

me·lis·ma (mə-lĭz′mə) *n., pl.* **-ma·ta** (-mə-tə) or **-mas** A passage of several notes sung to one syllable of text, as in Gregorian chant. [Gk., melody < *melizein*, to sing < *melos*, song.] —**mel′is·mat′ic** (mĕl′ĭz-măt′ĭk) *adj.*

Mel·kite or **Mel·chite** (mĕl′kīt) *n.* **1.** A member of the Christian churches in Egypt and Syria that accepted the Council of Chalcedon. **2.** A member of any eastern Christian church of the patriarchates of Alexandria, Antioch, or Jerusalem, esp. a Uniat Christian. [NLat. *Melchītae*, Melkites < Med.Gk. *Melkhītai* < Aram. *malkāye*, pl. of *malkāy*, royalist < *malkā*, king.]

mel·lif·er·ous (mə-lĭf′ər-əs) also **mel·lif·ic** (-lĭf′ĭk) *adj.* Forming or bearing honey. [< Lat. *mellifer* : *mel, mell-*, honey; see *melit-* in App. + *-fer, -*fer.]

mel·lif·lu·ent (mə-lĭf′lōō-ənt) *adj.* Mellifluous.

mel·lif·lu·ous (mə-lĭf′lōō-əs) *adj.* **1.** Flowing with sweetness or honey. **2.** Smooth and sweet: *a mellifluous voice.* [ME < LLat. *mellifluus* : Lat. *mel, mell-*, honey; see *melit-* in App. + Lat. *-fluus, fluous,* flowing.] —**mel·lif′lu·ous·ly** *adv.* —**mel·lif′lu·ous·ness** *n.*

Mel·lon (mĕl′ən), **Andrew William** 1855–1937. Amer. financier and patron of the arts.

mel·lo·phone (mĕl′ō-fōn′) *n.* A brass wind instrument, similar to the French horn. [MELLO(W) + –PHONE.]

mel·low (mĕl′ō) *adj.* **-er, -est 1a.** Soft, sweet, juicy, and full-flavored because of ripeness: *a mellow fruit.* **b.** Suggesting softness or sweetness: "*The mellow air brought in the feel of imminent autumn*" (Thomas Hardy). **2.** Rich and soft in quality: *a mellow sound.* **3.** Having the gentleness, wisdom, or tolerance often characteristic of maturity. **4.** Relaxed and unhurried; easygoing. **5.** *Slang* **a.** Slightly and pleasantly intoxicated. **b.** Pleasantly high from a drug, esp. from smoking marijuana. **6.** Moist, rich, soft, and loamy. Used of soil. ❖ *tr. & intr.v.* **-lowed, -low·ing, -lows** To make or become mellow. —*phrasal verb:* **mellow out** *Slang* To become genial and pleasant; relax. [ME *melwe*, perh. < *melowe*, oblique case of *mele*, ground grain, meal. See MEAL[1].] —**mel′low·ly** *adv.* —**mel′low·ness** *n.*

me·lo·de·on (mə-lō′dē-ən) *n.* A small harmonium. [Prob. alteration of *melodium* < MELODY.]

me·lod·ic (mə-lŏd′ĭk) *adj.* Of, relating to, or containing melody. —**me·lod′i·cal·ly** *adv.*

me·lo·di·ous (mə-lō′dē-əs) *adj.* **1.** Of, relating to, or containing a pleasing tune or melody. **2.** Agreeable to hear. —**me·lo′di·ous·ly** *adv.* —**me·lo′di·ous·ness** *n.*

mel·o·dize (mĕl′ə-dīz′) *v.* **-dized, -diz·ing, -diz·es** —*tr.* **1.** To write a melody for (a lyric). **2.** To make melodious. —*intr.* To write a melody. —**mel′o·diz′er, mel′o·dist** *n.*

mel·o·dra·ma (mĕl′ə-drä′mə, -drăm′ə) *n.* **1a.** A drama marked by exaggerated emotions, stereotypical characters, and interpersonal conflicts. **b.** The dramatic genre marked by this treatment. **2.** Behavior or occurrences having such characteristics. [Alteration of *melodrame* < Fr. *mélodrame*, spoken drama with some music, melodrama : Gk. *melos*, song + Fr. *drame*, drama (< LLat. *drāma*; see DRAMA).]

mel·o·dra·mat·ic (mĕl′ə-drə-măt′ĭk) *adj.* **1.** Having the excitement and emotional appeal of melodrama. **2.** Exaggeratedly emotional or sentimental; histrionic. **3.** Marked by false pathos and sentiment. —**mel′o·dra·mat′i·cal·ly** *adv.*

mel·o·dra·mat·ics (mĕl′ə-drə-măt′ĭks) *n.* **1.** (*used with a sing. verb*) Melodramatic theatrical performance. **2.** (*used with a pl. verb*) Exaggeratedly emotional behavior; histrionics.

mel·o·dy (mĕl′ə-dē) *n., pl.* **-dies 1.** A pleasing succession or arrangement of sounds. **2.** Musical quality: *the melody of verse.* **3.** *Music* **a.** A rhythmic sequence of single related tones that make up a particular phrase or idea. **b.** Structure with respect to the arrangement of such tones. **c.** The leading part or the air in a composition with accompaniment. **4.** A poem suitable for setting to music or singing. [ME *melodie* < OFr. < LLat. *melōdia* < Gk. *melōidiā*, singing choral song : *melos*, tune + *aoidē*, song.]

mel·oid (mĕl′oid′, mĕl′ō-ĭd) *n.* See **blister beetle**. [< NLat. *Meloidae*, family name < *Meloē*, type genus.] —**mel′oid′** *adj.*

mel·on (mĕl′ən) *n.* **1.** Any of several varieties of two related vines (*Cucumis melo* or *Citrullus lanatus*) widely cultivated for their edible fruit. **2.** Their fruit, having a hard rind and juicy flesh. [Ult. < Lat. *mēlō, mēlōn-*, short for Lat. *mēlopepō* < Gk. *mēlopepōn* : *mēlon*, apple + *pepōn*, gourd.]

mel·on·gene (mĕl′ən-jēn′) *n.* See **eggplant** 1. [Fr. *mélongène* < OFr. *melanjan, melonge* < Med.Lat. *melongēna* < OItal. *melanzana, melongiane* < Med.Gk. *melintzana, melanzana,* alteration (influenced by Gk. *melās*, dark) of Ar. *bāḏinjān* < Pers. *bādin-gān.*]

Me·los (mē′lŏs) See **Milos.**

Mel·pom·e·ne (mĕl-pŏm′ə-nē′) *n. Greek Mythology* The Muse of tragedy. [Gk. *Melpomenē* < fem. pr. middle part. of *melpein,* to sing.]

melt (mĕlt) *v.* **melt·ed, melt·ing, melts** —*intr.* **1.** To be changed from a solid to a liquid esp. by the application of heat. **2.** To dissolve: *Sugar melts in water.* **3.** To disappear or vanish gradually as if by dissolving: *The crowd melted away after the rally.* **4.** To pass or merge imperceptibly into something else: *Sea melted into sky along the horizon.* **5.** To become softened in feeling: *Our hearts melted at the child's tears.* **6.** *Obsolete* To be overcome or crushed, as by grief, dismay, or fear. —*tr.* **1.** To change (a solid) to a liquid esp. by the application of heat. **2.** To dissolve: *The tide melted our sand castle away.* **3.** To cause to disappear gradually; disperse. **4.** To cause (units) to blend. **5.** To soften (someone's feelings); make gentle or tender. ❖ *n.* **1.** A melted solid; a fused mass. **2.** The state of being melted. **3a.** The act or operation of melting. **b.** The quantity melted at a single operation or in one period. **4.** A usu. open sandwich topped with melted cheese: *a tuna melt.* [ME *melten* < OE *meltan.*] —**melt′a·bil′i·ty** *n.* —**melt′a·ble** *adj.* —**melt′er** *n.* —**melt′ing·ly** *adv.* —**melt′y** *adj.*

melt·age (mĕl′tĭj) *n.* **1.** The substance or quantity of a substance produced by melting. **2.** The act or process of melting.

melt·down (mĕlt′doun′) *n.* **1.** Severe overheating of a nuclear reactor core, resulting in its melting and the escape of radiation. **2.** *Informal* A disastrous or rapidly developing situation likened to a meltdown: "*After several corporate meltdowns, only two re-*

ă pat | oi boy
ā pay | ou out
âr care | ŏŏ took
ä father | ōō boot
ĕ pet | ŭ cut
ē be | ûr urge
ĭ pit | th thin
ī pie | th this
îr pier | hw which
ŏ pot | zh vision
ō toe | ə about,
ô paw | item

Stress marks:
′ (primary);
′ (secondary), as in
lexicon (lĕk′sĭ-kŏn′)

porters remain in the *bureau*" (David Fitzpatrick). **3.** *Informal* An emotional breakdown.

melt·ing point (měl′tǐng) *n.* **1.** The temperature at which a solid becomes a liquid at standard atmospheric pressure. **2.** The temperature at which a solid and its liquid are in equilibrium, at any fixed pressure.

melting pot *n.* **1.** A container in which a substance is melted. **2.** A place where immigrants of different cultures or races form an integrated society.

mel·ton (měl′tən) *n.* A heavy woolen cloth used chiefly for making overcoats and hunting jackets. [After *Melton* Mowbray, an urban district of central England.]

melt·wa·ter (mělt′wô′tər, -wŏt′ər) *n.* Water that comes from melting snow or ice.

Mel·ville (měl′vǐl), **Herman** 1819–91. Amer. writer whose works include the novel *Moby Dick* (1851). —**Mel·vil′le·an** (-vǐl′ē-ən) *adj.*

Melville, Lake A saltwater lake of Newfoundland, Canada, in SE Labrador.

Melville Island 1. An island of N Australia in the Timor Sea. **2.** An island of N Canada, in the Queen Elizabeth Is. N of Victoria I.

Melville Peninsula A peninsula of central Nunavut, Canada, separated from Baffin I. by a narrow strait.

mem (měm) *n.* The 13th letter of the Hebrew alphabet. [Heb. *mēm* < Phoenician **mēm*, water, 13th letter of the Phoenician alphabet.]

mem·ber (měm′bər) *n.* **1.** A distinct part of a whole, esp.: **a.** *Linguistics* A syntactic unit of a sentence; a clause. **b.** *Logic* A proposition of a syllogism. **c.** *Mathematics* An element in a set. **2.** A part or an organ of a human or animal body, as: **a.** A limb, such as an arm or a leg. **b.** The penis. **3.** A part of a plant. **4.** One that belongs to a group or organization: *a bank that is a member of the FDIC.* **5.** *Mathematics* The expression on either side of an equality sign. **6.** A structural unit, such as a beam or wall. [ME *membre* < OFr. < Lat. *membrum*.]

mem·ber·ship (měm′bər-shǐp′) *n.* **1.** The state of being a member. **2.** The total number of members in a group.

mem·brane (měm′brān′) *n.* **1.** *Biology* **a.** A thin pliable layer of tissue covering, lining, or connecting surfaces or parts of an animal or a plant. **b.** Cell membrane. **2.** A piece of parchment. **3.** *Chemistry* A thin sheet of natural or synthetic material that is permeable to substances in solution. [Lat. *membrāna*, skin < *membrum*, body member.] —**mem′bra·nal** (-brə-nəl) *adj.*

membrane bone *n.* A bone that forms directly in membranous connective tissue rather than in cartilage.

mem·bra·nous (měm′brə-nəs) *adj.* **1.** Relating to, made of, or similar to a membrane. **2.** *Pathology* Characterized by the formation of a membrane or a layer similar to a membrane.

membranous labyrinth *n.* The fluid-filled membranous sacs of the inner ear that are associated with hearing and balance.

meme (mēm) *n.* A unit of cultural information, such as a cultural practice or idea, that is transmitted verbally or by repeated action from one mind to another. [Shortening (modeled on GENE) of *mimeme* < Gk. *mimēma*, something imitated < *mimeisthai*, to imitate. See MIMESIS.]

Me·mel (mā′məl) See **Klaipeda.**

me·men·to (mə-měn′tō) *n., pl.* **-tos** or **-toes** A reminder of the past; a keepsake. [ME, commemoration of the living or the dead in the Canon of the Mass < Lat. *mementō*, imper. of *meminisse*, to remember. See **men-¹** in App.]

memento mo·ri (môr′ē) *n., pl.* **memento mori 1.** A reminder of death or mortality, esp. a death's-head. **2.** A reminder of human failures or errors. [NLat. *mementō morī*, be mindful of dying : Lat. *mementō*, sing. imper. of *meminisse*, to remember + Lat. *morī*, to die.]

me·met·ics (mē-mět′ĭks) *n.* (*used with a sing. verb*) The study of memes and their social and cultural effects. [MEME + -ETICS (as in AESTHETICS).]

Mem·ling (měm′lĭng) also **Mem·linc** (-lĭngk), **Hans** 1430?–94. Flemish painter of portraits and religious works.

Mem·non (měm′nŏn′) *n. Greek Mythology* An Ethiopian king killed by Achilles and made immortal by Zeus.

mem·o (měm′ō) *n., pl.* **-os** A memorandum.

mem·oir (měm′wär′, -wôr′) *n.* **1.** An account of an author's personal experiences. **2.** An autobiography. Often used in the plural. **3.** A biography or biographical sketch. **4.** A report, esp. on a scientific or scholarly topic. **5. memoirs** The report of the proceedings of a learned society. [Fr. *mémoire* < OFr. *memoire*, memory < Lat. *memoria*. See MEMORY.] —**mem′oir·ist** *n.*

mem·o·ra·bil·i·a (měm′ər-ə-bǐl′ē-ə, -bǐl′yə) *pl.n.* **1.** Objects valued for their connection with historical events, culture, or entertainment. **2.** Events or experiences worthy of remembrance. [Lat. *memorābilia*, neut. pl. of *memorābilis*, memorable. See MEMORABLE.]

mem·o·ra·ble (měm′ər-ə-bəl) *adj.* Worth being remembered or noted; remarkable. [ME < OFr. < Lat. *memorābilis* < *memorāre*, to bring to remembrance < *memor*, mindful. See **(s)mer-** in App.] —**mem′o·ra·bil′i·ty, mem′o·ra·ble·ness** *n.* —**mem′o·ra·bly** *adv.*

mem·o·ran·dum (měm′ə-răn′dəm) *n., pl.* **-dums** or **-da** (-də) **1.** A short note written as a reminder. **2.** A written record or com-

munication, as in business. **3.** *Law* A short written statement of the terms of an agreement, transaction, or contract. **4.** A business statement made by a consignor about a shipment of goods that may be returned. **5.** A brief, unsigned diplomatic communication. [ME, to be remembered (a manuscript notation) < Lat., neut. sing. gerundive of *memorāre*, to bring to remembrance. See MEMORABLE.]

me·mo·ri·al (mə-môr′ē-əl, -mōr′-) *n.* **1.** Something, as a holiday, intended to celebrate or honor the memory of a person or event. **2.** A written statement of facts or a petition presented to a legislature or executive. ❖ *adj.* **1.** Serving as a remembrance of a person or event; commemorative. **2.** Of, relating to, or being in memory. [ME < OFr. < LLat. *memoriāle* < neut. of Lat. *memoriālis*, of memory < *memoria*, memory. See MEMORY.] —**me·mo′ri·al·ly** *adv.*

Memorial Day *n.* May 30, observed in the United States to commemorate members of the armed forces killed in war, officially observed on the last Monday in May.

me·mo·ri·al·ist (mə-môr′ē-ə-lǐst, -mōr′-) *n.* **1.** A person who writes memoirs. **2.** A person who writes or signs a memorial.

me·mo·ri·al·ize (mə-môr′ē-ə-līz′, mə-mōr′-) *tr.v.* **-ized, -iz·ing, -iz·es 1.** To provide a memorial for; commemorate. **2.** To present a memorial to; petition. —**me·mo′ri·al·i·za′tion** (-ə-lǐ-zā′shən) *n.* —**me·mo′ri·al·iz′er** *n.*

memorial park *n.* A cemetery.

mem·o·rize (měm′ə-rīz′) *tr.v.* **-rized, -riz·ing, -riz·es 1.** To commit to memory; learn by heart. **2.** *Computer Science* To store in memory. —**mem′o·riz′a·ble** *adj.* —**mem′o·ri·za′tion** (-rǐ-zā′shən) *n.* —**mem′o·riz′er** *n.*

mem·o·ry (měm′ə-rē) *n., pl.* **-ries 1.** The mental faculty of retaining and recalling past experience. **2.** The act or an instance of remembering; recollection: *spent the morning lost in memory.* **3.** All that a person can remember. **4.** Something remembered: *pleasant childhood memories.* **5.** The fact of being remembered; remembrance: *dedicated to their memory.* **6.** The period of time covered by the remembrance or recollection of a person or group of persons. **7.** *Biology* Persistent modification of behavior resulting from an animal's experience. **8.** *Computer Science* **a.** A unit of a computer that preserves data for retrieval. **b.** Capacity for storing information: *two gigabytes of memory.* **9.** *Statistics* The set of past events affecting a given event in a stochastic process. **10.** The capacity of a material, such as plastic or metal, to return to a previous shape after deformation. **11.** *Immunology* The ability of the immune system to respond to an antigen to which it has previously been exposed. [ME *memorie* < Anglo-Fr. < Lat. *memoria* < *memor*, mindful. See **(s)mer-** in App.]

memory engram *n.* An engram.

memory trace *n.* An engram.

Mem·phis (měm′fǐs) **1.** An ancient city of Egypt S of Cairo; reputedly founded by Menes, the first king of united Egypt. **2.** A city of SW TN on the Mississippi R. near the MS border; est. and named (1819) by Andrew Jackson on the site of a fort built in 1797. Pop. 650,100.

mem·sa·hib (měm′sä′ĭb) *n.* Used formerly as a form of respectful address for a European woman in colonial India. [MA'AM + SAHIB.]

men (měn) *n.* Plural of **man.**

men- *pref.* Variant of **meno-.**

men·ace (měn′ĭs) *n.* **1a.** A possible danger; a threat: *the menace of war.* **b.** The act of threatening. **2.** A troublesome or annoying person. ❖ *v.* **-aced, -ac·ing, -ac·es** —*tr.* **1.** To utter threats against. **2.** To constitute a threat to; endanger. —*intr.* To make threats. [ME < OFr. < VLat. **minācia*, sing. of Lat. *mināciae*, threats, menaces < *mināx, mināc-*, threatening < *minārī*, to threaten < *minae*, threats.] —**men′ac·er** *n.* —**men′ac·ing·ly** *adv.*

men·a·di·one (měn′ə-dī′ōn′) *n.* A yellow crystalline powder, $C_{11}H_8O_2$, used in medicine as a vitamin K supplement. [ME(THYL) + NA(PHTHALENE) + DI-¹ + -ONE.]

mé·nage (mā-näzh′) *n.* **1.** People living together as a unit; a household. **2.** The management of a household. [Fr. < OFr. *manage, mesnage* < *maneir*, to stay < Lat. *manēre*, to remain.]

ménage à trois (ä trwä′) *n.* A relationship in which three people, such as a married couple and a lover, live together and have sexual relations. [Fr. : *ménage*, household + *à*, for + *trois*, three.]

me·nag·er·ie (mə-năj′ə-rē, -năzh′-) *n.* **1a.** A collection of live wild animals on exhibition. **b.** An enclosure in which wild animals are kept. **2.** A diverse or miscellaneous group. [Fr. *ménagerie* < OFr. *mesnage*, ménage. See MÉNAGE.]

Me·nan·der (mə-năn′dər) 342–292 B.C. Greek dramatist whose works were influential in the development of comedy.

me·nar·che (mə-när′kē) *n.* The first menstrual period, usu. occurring during puberty. [MEN(O)– + Gk. *arkhē*, beginning (< *arkhein*, to begin).] —**me·nar′che·al** *adj.*

men-at-arms (měn′ət-ärmz′) *n.* Plural of **man-at-arms.**

men-chil·dren (měn′chǐl′drən) *n.* Plural of **man-child.**

Men·chú (měn′chōō), **Rigoberta** b. 1959. Guatemalan human rights activist who won the 1992 Nobel Peace Prize.

Men·ci·us (měn′shē-əs) Orig. Mengzi. 4th cent. B.C. Chinese Confucian philosopher who taught that people are innately good.

Menck·en (měng′kən), **H(enry) L(ouis)** 1880–1956. Amer. edi-

tor and critic who founded and edited (1924–33) the *American Mercury.* —**Menck•e′ni•an** (mĕng-kē′nē-ən) *adj.*

mend (mĕnd) *v.* **mend•ed, mend•ing, mends** —*tr.* **1.** To make repairs or restoration to; fix. **2.** To reform or correct: *mend one's ways.* —*intr.* **1a.** To improve in health or condition: *The patient is mending well.* **b.** To heal: *The bone mended in a month.* **2.** To make repairs or corrections. ❖ *n.* **1.** The act of mending. **2.** A mended place. —*idioms:* **mend fences** To improve poor relations, esp. in politics. **on the mend** Improving, esp. in health. [ME *menden,* short for *amenden,* to amend. See AMEND.] —**mend′a•ble** *adj.* —**mend′er** *n.*

men•da•cious (mĕn-dā′shəs) *adj.* **1.** Lying; untruthful. **2.** False; untrue. [< Lat. *mendācium,* lie < *mendāx, mendāc-,* mendacious.] —**men•da′cious•ly** *adv.*

men•dac•i•ty (mĕn-dăs′ĭ-tē) *n., pl.* **-ties 1.** The condition of being mendacious; untruthfulness. **2.** A lie; a falsehood.

Men•de (mĕn′dē, -dā) *n., pl.* **Mende** or **-des 1.** A language of the Mande branch of the Niger-Congo language family spoken in southern Sierra Leone and eastern Liberia. **2.** A member of a Mende-speaking people.

Men•del (mĕn′dl), **Gregor Johann** 1822–84. Austrian botanist and founder of the science of genetics. —**Men•de′li•an** (mĕn-dē′lē-ən, -dēl′yən) *adj.*

Men•de•le•ev (mĕn′də-lā′əf, myĭn-dĭ-lā′yĕf), **Dmitri Ivanovich** 1834–1907. Russian chemist who first devised and published the periodic table of the elements (1869).

men•de•le•vi•um (mĕn′də-lē′vē-əm) *n. Symbol* **Md** A synthetic radioactive element; its most stable isotope is Md 258 with a half-life of approx. 51.5 days. Atomic number 101. See table at **element.** [After Dmitri Ivanovich MENDELEEV.]

Men•del•ism (mĕn′dl-ĭz′əm) also **Men•de•li•an•ism** (mĕn-dē′lē-ə-nĭz′əm) *n.* The theoretical principles of heredity formulated by Gregor Mendel; Mendel's laws.

Men•del's law (mĕn′dlz) *n.* **1.** The principle stating that the members of a pair of homologous chromosomes segregate during meiosis and are distributed to different gametes. **2.** The principle stating that each member of a pair of homologous chromosomes segregates during meiosis independently of the members of other pairs, so that alleles on different chromosomes are distributed randomly to the gametes.

Men•dels•sohn (mĕn′dl-sən, -zōn′), **Felix** 1809–47. German conductor, pianist, and composer.

Mendelssohn, Moses 1729–86. German philosopher noted for his writings on the inborn ability of humans to recognize beauty, truth, and goodness.

Men•de•res (mĕn′də-rĕs′) A river of W Turkey flowing c. 402 km (250 mi) to the Aegean Sea.

Men•dès-France (mĕn′dĭs-fräns′, män-dĕs-fräɴs′), **Pierre** 1907–82. French prime minister (1954–55).

men•di•cant (mĕn′dĭ-kənt) *adj.* Depending on alms for a living; practicing begging. ❖ *n.* **1.** A beggar. **2.** A member of an order of friars forbidden to own property in common who work or beg for their living. [ME < OFr. < Lat. *mendīcāns, mendīcant-,* pr. part. of *mendīcāre,* to beg < *mendīcus,* needy, beggar < *mendum,* physical defect.] —**men′di•can•cy, men•dic′i•ty** (-dĭs′ĭ-tē) *n.*

mend•ing (mĕn′dĭng) *n.* Articles, as clothes, needing repair.

Men•do•ci•no (mĕn′də-sē′nō), **Cape** A promontory of NW CA SSW of Eureka.

Men•do•za (mĕn-dō′zə, -sä) A city of W Argentina ENE of Santiago, Chile; founded c. 1560. Pop. 121,739.

Men•e•la•us (mĕn′ə-lā′əs) *n. Greek Mythology* The king of Sparta who was husband of Helen and brother of Agamemnon.

Men•e•lik II (mĕn′ə-lĭk) 1844–1913. Ethiopian emperor (1889–1913) who established independence from Italy.

Me•nén•dez de A•vi•lés (mə-nĕn′dəs dā ä′və-lās′, mĕ-nĕn′dĕth thĕ ä′vē-lĕs′), **Pedro** 1519–74. Spanish colonizer who founded the city of St. Augustine in Florida (1565).

Me•nes (mē′nēz) fl. 3000 B.C. King of Egypt who founded the first dynasty uniting Upper and Lower Egypt.

men•folk (mĕn′fōk′) or **men•folks** (-fōks′) *pl.n.* **1.** Men considered as a group. **2.** The males of a community or family.

Meng•zi (mŭng′dzŭ′) See **Mencius.**

men•ha•den (mĕn-hād′n) *n., pl.* **menhaden** or **-dens** Any of several species of fish of the genus *Brevoortia,* esp. *B. tyrannus* of American Atlantic and Gulf waters. [Prob. blend of Narragansett *munnahhatteaûg,* a herringlike fish (akin to *munnohquohteau,* he enriches the land < its use as a fertilizer) and S. dialectal *poghaden* (prob. of Algonquian orig.).]

men•hir (mĕn′hîr′) *n.* Any of a type of prehistoric monument, chiefly of the British Isles and northern France, consisting of a tall upright megalith. [Fr. < Breton : *men,* stone (< M Breton) + *hir,* long (< M Breton).]

me•ni•al (mē′nē-əl, mēn′yəl) *adj.* **1.** Of or relating to work regarded as servile. **2.** Of, relating to, or appropriate for a servant. ❖ *n.* **1.** A servant, esp. a domestic servant. **2.** A person of a servile or low nature. [ME *meinial,* belonging to a household < AN *meignial* < *meignee,* household < VLat. **mānsiōnāta* < Lat. *mānsiō, mānsiōn-,* house. See MANSION.] —**me′ni•al•ly** *adv.*

Mé•nière's disease (mān-yârz′) *n.* A disease of the inner ear marked by dizziness, ringing in the ears, and progressive loss of hearing. [After Prosper *Ménière* (1799–1862), French physician.]

me•nin•ge•al (mə-nĭn′jē-əl) *adj.* Of or affecting the meninges.

me•nin•gi•o•ma (mə-nĭn′jē-ō′mə) *n., pl.* **-mas** or **-ma•ta** (-mə-tə) A slow-growing tumor of the meninges, occurring usu. in adults. [Short for *meningothelioma* : MENINGO- + (ENDO)THELIOMA.]

men•in•gi•tis (mĕn′ĭn-jī′tĭs) *n.* Inflammation of the meninges usu. caused by a bacterium or virus and characterized by fever, vomiting, intense headache, and stiff neck. —**men′in•git′ic** (-jĭt′ĭk) *adj.*

meningo– or **meningi–** or **mening–** *pref.* Meninges: *meningococcus.* [< Gk. *mēninx, mēning-,* meninx.]

me•nin•go•coc•cus (mə-nĭng′gə-kŏk′əs, -nĭn′jə-) *n., pl.* **-coc•ci** (-kŏk′sī, -kī) A bacterium (*Neisseria meningitidis*) that causes cerebrospinal meningitis. —**me•nin′go•coc′cal** (-kŏk′əl), **me•nin′go•coc′cic** (-kŏk′sĭk) *adj.*

me•nin•go•en•ceph•a•li•tis (mə-nĭng′gō-ĕn-sĕf′ə-lī′tĭs) *n.* Inflammation of the brain and meninges. —**me•nin′go•en•ceph′a•lit′ic** (-lĭt′ĭk) *adj.*

me•ninx (mē′nĭngks) *n., pl.* **me•nin•ges** (mə-nĭn′jēz) A membrane, esp. one of the three membranes enclosing the brain and spinal cord in vertebrates. [Gk. *mēninx.*]

me•nis•cus (mə-nĭs′kəs) *n., pl.* **-nis•ci** (-nĭs′ī, -kī, -kē) or **-nis•cus•es 1.** A crescent-shaped body. **2.** A concavo-convex lens. **3.** The concave or convex upper surface of a nonturbulent liquid in a container. **4.** A cartilage disk that acts as a cushion between the ends of bones that meet in a joint. [NLat. < Gk. *mēniskos,* dim. of *mēnē,* moon, month. See mē-[1] in App.] —**me•nis′cal** (-kəl), **me•nis′cate** (-kāt′), **me•nis′coid** (-koid′), **men′is•coi′dal** (mĕn′ĭs-koid′l) *adj.*

Men•lo Park (mĕn′lō) An unincorporated community of central NJ N of New Brunswick. Thomas Edison perfected the incandescent light bulb here (1879).

Men•ning•er (mĕn′ĭng-jər) Family of American psychiatrists, including **Charles Frederick** (1862–1953) and his sons **Karl Augustus** (1893–1990) and **William Claire** (1899–1966).

Men•non•ite (mĕn′ə-nīt′) *n.* A member of an Anabaptist church characterized particularly by simplicity of life, pacifism, and nonresistance. [Ger. *Mennonit,* after *Menno* Simons (1492–1559), Frisian religious leader.]

meno– or **men–** *pref.* **1.** Menstruation: *menarche.* **2.** Menses: *menorrhagia.* [Gk. < *mēn,* month. See mē-[1] in App.]

men-of-war (mĕn′ə-wôr′) *n.* Plural of **man-of-war.**

Me•nom•i•nee (mə-nŏm′ə-nē) *n., pl.* **Menominee** or **-nees 1.** A member of a Native American people formerly inhabiting an area along the Menominee River, with a present-day population in northeast Wisconsin. **2.** The Algonquian language of the Menominee.

Menominee River A river rising in the Upper Peninsula of NW MI and flowing c. 190 km (118 mi) to Green Bay.

me•no mos•so (mā′nō môs′sō, mĕ′nō) *adv. & adj. Music* At a lower speed. [Ital. : *meno,* less + *mosso,* agitated.]

men•o•pause (mĕn′ə-pôz′) *n.* The period marked by the natural and permanent cessation of menstruation, occurring usu. between the ages of 45 and 55. [NLat. *mēnopausis* : MENO- + Gk. *pausis,* pause; see PAUSE.] —**men′o•paus′al** *adj.*

me•no•rah (mə-nôr′ə, -nōr′ə) *n. Judaism* **1.** A nine-branched candelabrum used in celebration of Hanukkah. **2.** often **Menorah** A seven-branched candelabrum of the Jewish Temple symbolizing the seven days of the Creation. [Heb. *mᵉnôrâ.*]

Me•nor•ca (mə-nôr′kə, mĕ-nôr′kä) See **Minorca[1].**

men•or•rha•gi•a (mĕn′ə-rā′jē-ə) *n.* Abnormally heavy or extended menstrual flow. —**men′or•rhag′ic** (-jĭk) *adj.*

Me•not•ti (mə-nŏt′ē), **Gian Carlo** b. 1911. Italian-born Amer. composer whose operas include *The Consul* (1950).

Men•sa (mĕn′sə) *n.* A southern constellation between Hydrus and Volans. [Lat. *mēnsa,* table.]

men•sal (mĕn′səl) *adj.* Belonging to or used at the table. [ME < LLat. *mēnsālis* < Lat. *mēnsa,* table.]

mensch or **mensh** (mĕnsh) *n., pl.* **mensch•es** or **mensch•en** (mĕn′shən) *Informal* A person having admirable characteristics, such as firmness of purpose. [Yiddish < MHGer., human being < OHGer. *mennisco.* See man-[1] in App.]

men•ses (mĕn′sēz) *pl.n.* (*used with a sing. or pl. verb*) The monthly flow of blood and cellular debris from the uterus that begins at puberty in women and the females of other primates. [Lat. *mēnsēs,* pl. of *mēnsis,* month. See mē-[1] in App.]

Men•she•vik (mĕn′shə-vĭk′) *n., pl.* **-viks** or **-vi•ki** (-vē′kē) A member of the liberal minority faction of the Social Democratic Party that struggled against the Bolsheviks before and during the Russian Revolution. [Russ. *men'shevik,* minority, less (< their relegation by Lenin to minority status).] —**Men′she•vism** *n.* —**Men′she•vist** *n.*

men's room (mĕnz) *n.* A restroom for men.

men•stru•al (mĕn′strōō-əl) also **men•stru•ous** (-əs) *adj.* **1.** Of or relating to menstruation. **2a.** Taking place on a monthly basis. **b.** Lasting for one month. [ME < OFr. *menstruel* < Lat. *mēnstruālis* < *mēnstruus,* menstrual < *mēnsis,* month. See mē-[1] in App.]

men•stru•ate (mĕn′strōō-āt′) *intr.v.* **-at•ed, -at•ing, -ates** To undergo menstruation. [LLat. *mēnstruāre, mēnstruāt-* < Lat. *mēnstrua,* menses < neut. pl. of *mēnstruus,* menstrual. See MENSTRUAL.]

menorah

ă pat   oi boy
ā pay   ou out
âr care   ŏŏ took
ä father   ōō boot
ĕ pet   ŭ cut
ē be   ûr urge
ĭ pit   th thin
ī pie   *th* this
îr pier   hw which
ŏ pot   zh vision
ō toe   ə about,
ô paw   item

Stress marks:
′ (primary);
′ (secondary), as in
lexicon (lĕk′sĭ-kŏn′)

men·stru·a·tion (mĕn′strōō-ā′shən) *n.* The process or an instance of discharging the menses.

men·stru·um (mĕn′strōō-əm) *n., pl.* **-stru·ums** or **-stru·a** (-strōō-ə) A solvent, esp. one used in extracting compounds from plant and animal tissues and preparing drugs. [ME, menstruation < Med.Lat. mēnstruum, sing. of Lat. mēnstrua, menses. See MENSTRUATE.]

men·su·ra·ble (mĕn′sər-ə-bəl, -shər-) *adj.* **1.** That can be measured: *a mensurable increase in the cost of oil.* **2.** Having fixed rhythm and measure; mensural. —**men′su·ra·bil′i·ty, men′su·ra·ble·ness** *n.*

men·su·ral (mĕn′sər-əl, -shər-) *adj.* **1.** Of or relating to measure. **2.** *Music* Having notes of fixed rhythmic value. [LLat. mēnsūrālis < Lat. mēnsūra, measure. See MEASURE.]

men·su·ra·tion (mĕn′sə-rā′shən, -shə-) *n.* **1.** The act, process, or art of measuring. **2.** Measurement of geometric quantities. [LLat. mēnsūrātiō, mēnsūrātiōn- < mēnsūrātus, p. part. of mēnsūrāre, to measure < Lat. mēnsūra, measure. See MEASURE.] —**men′su·ra′tive** *adj.*

mens·wear also **men's wear** (mĕnz′wâr′) *n.* Clothing for men.

-ment *suff.* **1.** Action; process: *appeasement.* **2.** Result of an action or process: *advancement.* **3.** Means, instrument, or agent of an action or process: *adornment.* [ME < OFr. < Lat. -mentum, n. suff.]

men·tal[1] (mĕn′tl) *adj.* **1.** Of or relating to the mind; intellectual: *mental powers.* **2.** Executed or performed by the mind; existing in the mind: *mental images of happy times.* **3.** Of, relating to, or affected by a disorder of the mind. **4.** Intended for treatment of people affected with disorders of the mind. **5.** Of or relating to telepathy or mind reading. **6.** *Slang* **a.** Emotionally upset; crazed. **b.** *Offensive Slang* Mentally or psychologically disturbed. [ME < OFr. < LLat. mentālis < Lat. mēns, ment-, mind. See men-[1] in App.] —**men′tal·ly** *adv.*

men·tal[2] (mĕn′tl) *adj.* Of or relating to the chin. [< Lat. mentum, chin.]

mental age *n.* A measure of mental development as determined by intelligence tests, expressed as the age at which that level is typically attained.

mental block *n.* *Psychology* A sudden cessation of speech or thought without an immediate observable cause, sometimes considered a consequence of repression.

mental deficiency *n.* Mental retardation.

men·tal·ese (mĕn′tl-ēz′, -lēs′) *n.* A hypothetical language in which concepts and propositions are represented in the mind without words.

mental health *n.* **1.** A state of emotional and psychological well-being in which an individual's cognitive, emotional, and behioral functioning is intact. **2.** A branch of health care that deals with the achievement and maintenance of psychological well-being. **3.** A person's overall emotional and psychological condition: *poor mental health.*

mental hospital *n.* See **psychiatric hospital.**

mental illness *n.* Any of various conditions characterized by impairment of an individual's normal cognitive, emotional, or behavioral functioning.

men·tal·ism (mĕn′tl-ĭz′əm) *n.* **1.** Parapsychological activities. **2.** The belief that some mental phenomena are inexplicable by physical laws. —**men′tal·ist** *n.* —**men′tal·is′tic** *adj.*

men·tal·i·ty (mĕn-tăl′ĭ-tē) *n., pl.* **-ties 1.** Cast or turn of mind: *a vindictive mentality.* **2.** The sum of a person's intellectual capabilities or endowment.

mentally ill *adj.* Suffering from a mental illness. ❖ *n.* (*used with a pl. verb*) People who are mentally ill considered as a group. Often used with *the.*

mental retardation *n.* Subnormal intellectual development as a result of congenital abnormality or brain injury or disease and marked by varying degrees of cognitive impairment.

mental telepathy *n.* Telepathy.

men·ta·tion (mĕn-tā′shən) *n.* Mental activity; thinking. [< Lat. mēns, ment-, mind. See MENTAL[1].]

men·thol (mĕn′thôl′) *n.* A white crystalline organic compound, $CH_3C_6H_9(C_3H_7)OH$, found in peppermint oil and used in perfumes, in cigarettes, and as a mint flavoring. [Ger. < Lat. menta, mentha, mint. See MINT[2].] —**men′tho·lat′ed** *adj.*

men·tion (mĕn′shən) *tr.v.* **-tioned, -tion·ing, -tions** To refer to, esp. incidentally. ❖ *n.* **1a.** The act of referring to something briefly or casually. **b.** An incidental reference or allusion. **2.** Honorable mention. —*idiom:* **not to mention** In addition to; as well as. [< ME mencioun, reference < OFr. < Lat. mentiō, mentiōn-. See men-[1] in App.] —**men′tion·a·ble** *adj.*

men·tor (mĕn′tôr′, -tər) *n.* **1.** A wise and trusted counselor or teacher. **2. Mentor** *Greek Mythology* Odysseus's trusted counselor, in whose guise Athena became the guardian and teacher of Telemachus. [Fr. *Mentor,* Mentor < Lat. *Mentōr* < Gk. See men-[1] in App.] —**men′tor** *v.*

men·u (mĕn′yōō) *n.* **1.** A list of the dishes served or available for a meal. **2.** The dishes served or available at a meal. **3.** A list of available options, esp. as displayed on a screen. [Fr., small, minute, menu < OFr. menut, small < Lat. minūtus, p. part. of minuere, to diminish.]

men·u-driv·en (mĕn′yōō-drĭv′ən) *adj.* Of or relating to a type

of GUI in which commands are issued by making selections from onscreen menus.

Men·u·hin (mĕn′yŏō-ĭn), **Yehudi** 1916–99. Amer. violinist considered among the great virtuosos of his time.

Men·zies (mĕn′zēz), Sir **Robert Gordon** 1894–1978. Australian prime minister (1939–41 and 1949–66).

Me·o (mē-ou′) *n.* Variant of **Miao.**

me·ow (mē-ou′) *n.* **1.** The cry of a cat. **2.** *Informal* A malicious, spiteful comment. ❖ *intr.v.* **-owed, -ow·ing, -ows** To make the crying sound of a cat. [Imit.]

MEP *abbr.* member of the European Parliament

me·per·i·dine (mə-pĕr′ĭ-dēn) *n.* A synthetic narcotic compound, $C_{15}H_{21}NO_2$, used in its hydrochloride form as an analgesic and sedative. [ME(THYL) + (PI)PERIDINE.]

Meph·i·stoph·e·les (mĕf′ĭ-stŏf′ə-lēz′) also **Me·phis·to** (mə-fĭs′tō) *n.* The devil in the Faust legend to whom Faust sold his soul. —**Me·phis′to·phe′le·an, Me·phis′to·phe′li·an** (mə-fĭs′tō-fē′lē-ən, -fĕl′yən, mĕf′ĭ-stō-) *adj.*

me·phit·ic (mə-fĭt′ĭk) also **me·phit·i·cal** (-ĭ-kəl) *adj.* Of, relating to, or resembling mephitis; poisonous or foul-smelling.

me·phi·tis (mə-fī′tĭs) *n.* **1.** A foul smell. **2.** A poisonous or foul-smelling gas emitted from the earth. [Lat. mefītis, mephītis.]

mep·ro·bam·ate (mĕp′rō-băm′āt′, mě-prō′bə-) *n.* A bitter white powder, $C_9H_{18}N_2O_4$, used as a tranquilizer and anticonvulsant. [ME(THYL) + PRO(PYL) + (CAR)BAMATE.]

mer. *abbr.* meridian

mer– *pref.* Variant of **mero-.**

-mer *suff.* Variant of **-mere.**

mer·bro·min (mər-brō′mĭn) *n.* A green crystalline organic compound, $C_{20}H_8Br_2HgNa_2O_6$, that forms a red aqueous solution, used as a germicide and antiseptic. [mer(curic acetate) + (DI)BROM(IDE) + (FLUORESCE)IN.]

Mer·cal·li scale (mər-kä′lē, mĕr-) *n.* A scale of earthquake intensity based on observed effects and ranging from I (detectable only with instruments) to XII (causing almost total destruction). [After Giuseppi *Mercalli* (1850–1914), Italian seismologist.]

mer·can·tile (mûr′kən-tēl′, -tīl′, -tĭl) *adj.* **1.** Of or relating to merchants or trade. **2.** Of or relating to mercantilism. [Fr. < Ital. < mercante, merchant < Lat. mercāns, mercant- < pr. part. of mercārī, to trade < merx, merc-, merchandise, goods.]

mer·can·til·ism (mûr′kən-tē-lĭz′əm, -tī-) *n.* **1.** The theory and system of political economy prevailing in Europe after feudalism, based on national policies of accumulating bullion, establishing colonies and a merchant marine, and developing industry and a favorable balance of trade. **2.** The practice, methods, or spirit of merchants; commercialism. —**mer′can·til·ist** *adj. & n.* —**mer′can·til·is′tic** *adj.*

mer·cap·tan (mər-kăp′tăn′) *n.* A sulfur-containing organic compound, RSH, where R is any radical, esp. ethyl mercaptan, C_2H_5SH. [Ger. < Dan. < Med.Lat. (*corpus*) mercurium captāns, (substance) seizing mercury : mercurium, accusative of mercurius, mercury; see MERCURY + Lat. captāns, pr. part. of captāre, freq. of capere, to seize; see CAPTURE.]

mercapto– *pref.* Containing the univalent radical –SH: *mercaptopurine.* [< MERCAPTAN.]

mer·cap·to·pu·rine (mər-kăp′tō-pyŏor′ēn) *n.* A purine analogue, $C_5H_4N_4S$, that acts as an antimetabolite by interfering with purine synthesis, used in the treatment of acute leukemia.

Mer·ca·tor (mər-kā′tər, mĕr-kä′tôr), **Gerhardus** 1512–94. Flemish cartographer who developed the Mercator projection (1568).

Mercator projection *n.* A cylindrical map projection in which the meridians and parallels of latitude appear as lines crossing at right angles and in which areas appear greater farther from the equator. [After Gerhardus MERCATOR.]

Mer·ce·da·rio (mĕr′sə-dä′rē-ō, -sĕ-dä′ryō) A mountain, 6,774.4 m (22,211 ft), in the Andes of W Argentina.

mer·ce·nar·y (mûr′sə-nĕr′ē) *adj.* **1.** Motivated solely by a desire for monetary or material gain. **2.** Hired for service in a foreign army. ❖ *n., pl.* **-ies 1.** One who serves or works merely for monetary gain; a hireling. **2.** A professional soldier hired for service in a foreign army. [ME mercenarie, a mercenary < OFr. mercenaire < Lat. mercēnnārius < mercēs, wages, price.] —**mer′ce·nar′i·ly** *adv.* —**mer′ce·nar′i·ness** *n.*

mer·cer (mûr′sər) *n.* *Chiefly British* A dealer in textiles, esp. silks. [ME < OFr. mercier, trader < merz, merchandise < Lat. merx, merc-, merchandise.]

Mercer Island A city of W-central WA, coextensive with **Mercer Island** in Lake Washington near Seattle. Pop. 22,036.

mer·cer·ize (mûr′sə-rīz′) *tr.v.* **-ized, -iz·ing, -iz·es** To treat (cotton thread) with sodium hydroxide so as to shrink the fiber and increase its luster and affinity for dye. [After John *Mercer* (1791–1866), British calico printer.]

mer·chan·dise (mûr′chən-dīz′, -dīs′) *n.* Goods bought and sold in business; commercial wares. ❖ **merchandise** (-dīz′) also **mer·chan·dize** (-dīz′) *v.* **-dised, -dis·ing, -dis·es** also **-dized, -diz·ing, -diz·es** —*tr.* **1.** To buy and sell (goods). **2.** To promote the sale of, as by advertising. —*intr.* To buy and sell goods; trade commercially. [ME merchaundise < OFr. marchandise, trade < marcheant, marchand, merchant. See MERCHANT.] —**mer′chan·dis′a·ble** *adj.* —**mer′chan·dis′er** *n.*

Yehudi Menuhin

mer·chan·dis·ing also **mer·chan·diz·ing** (mûr′chən-dī′-zĭng) *n.* The promotion of merchandise sales, as by coordinating production and marketing.

mer·chant (mûr′chənt) *n.* **1.** One who buys goods wholesale and sells them retail for profit. **2.** One who runs a retail business; a shopkeeper. ❖ *adj.* **1.** Of or relating to merchants, merchandise, or commercial trade. **2.** Of or relating to the merchant marine. [ME *merchaunt* < OFr. *marchaunt* < VLat. **mercātāns,* pr. part. of **mercātāre,* freq. of Lat. *mercārī,* to trade < *merx, merc-,* merchandise.]

mer·chant·a·ble (mûr′chənt-ə-bəl) *adj.* Suitable for buying and selling; marketable. —**mer′chant·a·bil′i·ty** *n.*

mer·chant·man (mûr′chənt-mən) *n.* **1.** *Nautical* A ship used in commerce. **2.** *Archaic* A merchant.

merchant marine *n.* **1.** A nation's commercial ships. **2.** The personnel of a nation's commercial ships.

Mer·ci·a (mûr′shē-ə, -shə) An Anglo-Saxon kingdom of central England; settled by Angles c. A.D. 500.

Mer·ci·an (mûr′shē-ən, -shən) *adj.* Of or relating to Mercia or its people, dialect, or culture. ❖ *n.* **1.** A native or inhabitant of Mercia. **2.** The Old English dialect of Mercia.

mer·ci·ful (mûr′sĭ-fəl) *adj.* Full of mercy; compassionate: *merciful treatment of captives.* See Syns at **humane.** —**mer′ci·ful·ly** *adv.* —**mer′ci·ful·ness** *n.*

mer·ci·less (mûr′sĭ-lĭs) *adj.* Having no mercy; cruel. —**mer′ci·less·ly** *adv.* —**mer′ci·less·ness** *n.*

mer·cu·rate (mûr′kyə-rāt′) *tr.v.* **-rat·ed, -rat·ing, -rates** To treat or combine with mercury or a mercury compound. —**mer′cu·ra′tion** *n.*

mer·cu·ri·al (mər-kyŏŏr′ē-əl) *adj.* **1.** often **Mercurial a.** *Roman Mythology* Of or relating to the god Mercury. **b.** *Astronomy* Of or relating to the planet Mercury. **2.** Having the characteristics of eloquence, shrewdness, swiftness, and thievishness attributed to the god Mercury. **3.** Containing or caused by the action of the element mercury. **4.** Quick and changeable in temperament; volatile: *a mercurial nature.* ❖ *n.* A pharmacological or chemical preparation containing mercury. [ME, of the planet Mercury < Lat. *mercuriālis,* of the god or planet Mercury < *Mercurius,* Mercury.] —**mer′cu′ri·al·ly** *adv.*

mer·cu·ri·al·ism (mər-kyŏŏr′ē-ə-lĭz′əm) *n.* Poisoning caused by mercury or a compound containing mercury.

mer·cu·ric (mər-kyŏŏr′ĭk) *adj.* Relating to or containing mercury, esp. with valence 2.

mercuric chloride *n.* A poisonous white crystalline compound, $HgCl_2$, used as an antiseptic and a disinfectant, in insecticides, preservatives, and batteries, and in photography.

mercuric sulfide *n.* A poisonous compound, HgS, having two forms, both used as pigments: **a.** Black mercuric sulfide, a black powder obtained from mercury salts or by the reaction of mercury with sulfur. **b.** Red mercuric sulfide, a bright scarlet powder derived from heating mercury with sulfur.

mercuro– or **mercur–** *pref.* Mercury: *mercurous.* [< MERCURY.]

Mer·cu·ro·chrome (mər-kyŏŏr′ə-krōm′) A trademark used for a solution of merbromin.

mer·cu·rous (mər-kyŏŏr′əs, mûr′kyər-əs) *adj.* Relating to or containing mercury, esp. with valence 1.

mercurous chloride *n.* See **calomel.**

mer·cu·ry (mûr′kyə-rē) *n.* **1.** *Symbol* **Hg** A silvery-white poisonous metallic element, liquid at room temperature and used in thermometers, barometers, and batteries. Atomic number 80; atomic weight 200.59; melting point −38.87°C; boiling point 356.58°C; specific gravity 13.546 (at 20°C); valence 1, 2. See table at **element.** **2.** Temperature. **3.** A weedy plant of the genus *Mercurialis* or *Acalypha.* [ME *mercurie* < Med.Lat. *mercurius* < Lat. *Mercurius,* Mercury.]

Mercury *n.* **1.** *Roman Mythology* The messenger of the gods, himself the god of commerce, travel, and thievery. **2.** The planet closest to the sun and smallest in the solar system. See table at **planet.** [ME *Mercurie* < OFr. < Lat. *Mercurius.*]

mer·cu·ry-va·por lamp (mûr′kyə-rē-vā′pər) *n.* A lamp in which ultraviolet and yellowish-green to blue visible light is produced by an electric discharge through mercury vapor.

mer·cy (mûr′sē) *n., pl.* **-cies 1.** Compassionate treatment, esp. of those under one's power; clemency. **2.** A disposition to be kind and forgiving. **3.** Something for which to be thankful; a blessing. **4.** Alleviation of distress; relief. **—idiom: at the mercy of** Without any protection against; helpless before. [ME < OFr. *merci* < Med.Lat. *mercēs* < Lat. *mercēs,* reward.]

SYNONYMS *mercy, leniency, lenity, clemency, charity* These nouns mean humane and kind, forgiving, or sympathetic treatment of or disposition toward others. *Mercy* is compassionate forbearance: *"We hand folks over to God's mercy, and show none ourselves"* (George Eliot). *Leniency* and *lenity* imply mildness, gentleness, and often a tendency to reduce punishment: *"When you have gone too far to recede, do not sue* [appeal] *me for leniency"* (Charles Dickens). *"His Majesty gave many marks of his great lenity, often . . . endeavoring to extenuate your crimes"* (Jonathan Swift). *Clemency* is mercy shown by someone with judicial authority: *The judge believed in clemency for youthful offenders. Charity* is goodwill and benevolence in judging others: *"But how*

shall we expect charity towards others, when we are uncharitable to ourselves?" (Thomas Browne).

mercy killing *n.* Euthanasia.

mercy seat *n.* **1.** The golden covering of the Ark of the Covenant, regarded as the resting place of God. **2.** The throne of God.

mere[1] (mîr) *adj.* Superlative **mer·est 1.** Being nothing more than what is specified: *a mere child; a mere 50 cents an hour.* **2.** Considered apart from anything else: *shocked by the mere idea.* **3.** Small; slight: *could detect only the merest whisper.* **4.** *Obsolete* Pure; unadulterated. [ME, absolute, pure < OFr. *mier,* pure < Lat. *merus.*]

mere[2] (mîr) *n.* A small lake, pond, or marsh. [ME < OE. See **mori–** in App.]

mere[3] (mîr) *n. Archaic* A boundary. [ME < OE *mǣre.*]

–mere or **–mer** *suff.* Part; segment: *blastomere.* [Fr. < Gk. *meros,* part.]

Mer·e·dith (mĕr′ĭ-dĭth), **George** 1828–1909. British writer whose works include *The Ordeal of Richard Feverel* (1859).

Meredith, James Howard b. 1933. Amer. civil rights advocate who was the first Black student to register (1963) at the traditionally segregated University of Mississippi.

mere·ly (mîr′lē) *adv.* And nothing else or more; only.

me·ren·gue (mə-rĕng′gā) *n.* **1.** A ballroom dance of Dominican and Haitian folk origin, characterized by a sliding step. **2.** Music for this dance, in rapid 2/4 time. [Am.Sp. < Sp., meringue < Fr. *méringue.*]

mer·e·tri·cious (mĕr′ĭ-trĭsh′əs) *adj.* **1a.** Attracting attention in a vulgar manner. **b.** Plausible but false or insincere; specious. **2.** Of or relating to prostitutes or prostitution. [Lat. *meretrīcius,* of prostitutes < *meretrīx, meretrīc-,* prostitute < *merēre,* to earn money.] —**mer′e·tri′cious·ly** *adv.* —**mer′e·tri′cious·ness** *n.*

mer·gan·ser (mər-găn′sər) *n.* Any of various fish-eating diving ducks of the genus *Mergus* or related genera, having a slim hooked bill. [NLat. : Lat. *mergus,* diver (< *mergere,* to plunge) + Lat. *ānser,* goose; see **ghans–** in App.]

merge (mûrj) *v.* **merged, merg·ing, merg·es** —*tr.* **1.** To cause to be absorbed, esp. in gradual stages. **2.** To combine or unite: *merging two sets of data.* —*intr.* **1.** To blend together, esp. in gradual stages. **2.** To become combined or united. [Lat. *mergere,* to plunge.] —**mer′gence** *n.*

Mer·gen·thal·er (mûr′gən-thô′lər, mĕr′gən-tä′-), **Ottmar** 1854–99. German-born Amer. inventor of the Linotype typesetting machine (patented 1884).

merg·er (mûr′jər) *n.* **1.** The act or an instance of merging; union. **2.** The union of two or more commercial interests or corporations. **3.** *Law* The absorption of a lesser estate, liability, right, action, or offense into a greater one.

Mé·ri·da (mĕr′ĭ-də, mĕ′rē-dä) A city of SE Mexico on the Yucatán Peninsula; founded 1542. Pop. 400,142.

me·rid·i·an (mə-rĭd′ē-ən) *n.* **1a.** An imaginary great circle on the earth's surface passing through the North and South geographic poles. **b.** Either half of such a great circle from pole to pole. **2.** *Astronomy* A great circle passing through the two poles of the celestial sphere and the zenith of an observer. **3.** *Mathematics* **a.** A curve on a surface of revolution, formed by the intersection of the surface with a plane containing the axis of revolution. **b.** A plane section of a surface of revolution containing the axis of revolution. **4.** Any of the longitudinal lines or pathways on the body along which the acupuncture points are distributed. **5.** *Archaic* **a.** The highest point in the sky reached by the sun or another celestial body; a zenith. **b.** Noon. **6.** The highest point or stage of development; peak. **7.** *Midwestern US* See **median strip.** See Regional Note at **neutral ground.** ❖ *adj.* **1.** Of or relating to a meridian; meridional. **2.** Of or at midday: *the meridian hour.* **3.** Of, relating to, or constituting the highest point, as of development or power. [ME < OFr., midday < Lat. *merīdiānus,* of midday < *merīdiēs,* midday < *merīdiē,* at midday, alteration of earlier **mediei diē : *mediei,* dative (locative) of *medius,* middle; see **medhyo–** in App. + *diē,* dative of *diēs,* day; see **dyeu–** in App.]

Meridian A city of E MS near the AL border E of Jackson. Pop. 39,968.

me·rid·i·o·nal (mə-rĭd′ē-ə-nəl) *adj.* **1.** Of or relating to meridians or a meridian. **2.** Located in the south; southern. **3.** Of or characteristic of southern areas or people. ❖ *n.* An inhabitant of a southern region, esp. the south of France. [ME, pertaining to the sun's position at noon < OFr. *meridionel,* southern < LLat. *merīdiōnālis* < Lat. *merīdiānus,* of midday, southern. See MERIDIAN.]

Mé·ri·mée (mĕr′ə-mā′, mā-rē-mā′), **Prosper** 1803–70. French writer of romantic works such as *Carmen* (1846).

me·ringue (mə-răng′) *n.* **1.** A topping for pastry or pies made of stiffly beaten baked egg whites and sugar. **2.** A small pastry shell or cake made of meringue. [Fr. *méringue.*]

me·ri·no (mə-rē′nō) *n., pl.* **-nos 1a.** Any of a breed of sheep, originally from Spain, having long fine wool. **b.** The wool of this sheep. **2.** A soft lightweight fabric that was made originally of merino wool but is now made of any fine wool. **3a.** A fine wool and cotton yarn that is used esp. for knitting underwear and hosiery. **b.** A knitted fabric that is made from this yarn. [Sp., perh. < Berber *Benī Merīn,* name of the tribe that developed the breed, or < Sp. *merino,* local magistrate (< Lat. *māiōrīnus,* larger

Mercury
top: bronze sculpture by
Giambologna (1529–1608)
bottom: the planet Mercury

ă	pat	oi	boy
ā	pay	ou	out
âr	care	ŏŏ	took
ä	father	ōō	boot
ĕ	pet	ŭ	cut
ē	be	ûr	urge
ĭ	pit	th	thin
ī	pie	*th*	this
îr	pier	hw	which
ŏ	pot	zh	vision
ō	toe	ə	about,
ô	paw		item

Stress marks:
′ (primary);
′ (secondary), as in
lexicon (lĕk′sĭ-kŏn′)

< *māior*; see MAJOR.).] —**me•ri′no** *adj.*

mer•i•stem (mĕr′ĭ-stĕm′) *n.* The undifferentiated plant tissue from which new cells are formed, as that at the tip of a stem or root. [Gk. *meristos*, divided (< *merizein*, to divide < *meris*, division) + *-em* (as in *xylem* and *phloem*).] —**mer′i•ste•mat′ic** (-stə-măt′ĭk) *adj.*

me•ris•tic (mə-rĭs′tĭk) *adj. Biology* **1.** Having or composed of segments; segmented. **2.** Relating to a change in the number or placement of body parts or segments: *meristic variation.* [< Gk. *meristos*, divided. See MERISTEM.] —**me•ris′ti•cal•ly** *adv.*

mer•it (mĕr′ĭt) *n.* **1a.** Superior quality or worth; excellence: *a superb plan with great merit.* **b.** A quality deserving praise or approval; virtue. **2.** Demonstrated ability or achievement. **3.** An aspect of character or behavior deserving approval or disapproval. Often used in the plural: *judging people according to their merits.* **4.** *Christianity* Spiritual credit granted for good works. **5. merits a.** *Law* A party's strict legal rights, excluding jurisdictional, personal, or technical aspects. **b.** The factual content of a matter, apart from emotional, contextual, or formal considerations. ❖ *v.* **-it•ed, -it•ing, -its** —*tr.* To earn; deserve. See Syns at **earn**[1]. —*intr.* To be worthy or deserving. [ME < OFr. *merite*, reward or punishment < Lat. *meritum* < neut. p. part. of *merēre*, to deserve.]

mer•i•toc•ra•cy (mĕr′ĭ-tŏk′rə-sē) *n., pl.* **-cies** **1.** A system in which advancement is based on ability or achievement. **2a.** A group of leaders or officeholders selected for individual ability or achievement. **b.** Leadership by such a group. —**mer′it•o•crat′** (-ĭ-tə-krăt′) *n.* —**mer′it•o•crat′ic** *adj.*

mer•i•to•ri•ous (mĕr′ĭ-tôr′ē-əs, -tōr′-) *adj.* Deserving reward or praise; having merit. [ME < Lat. *meritōrius*, earning money < *meritus*, p. part. of *merēre*, to earn. See MERIT.] —**mer′i•to′ri•ous•ly** *adv.* —**mer′i•to′ri•ous•ness** *n.*

merit system *n.* The system of appointing and promoting civil service personnel on the basis of merit rather than political affiliation or loyalty.

merle[1] also **merl** (mûrl) *n.* See **blackbird** 2. [ME < OFr. < Lat. *merulus, merula*.]

merle[2] (mûrl) *adj.* Having a reddish or bluish gray coat streaked or speckled with black. Used of certain dogs. ❖ *n.* A dog with a merle coat. [Perh. < MERLE[1].]

mer•lin (mûr′lĭn) *n.* A small falcon (*Falco columbarius*) of northern regions having dark plumage and a black-striped tail. [ME < AN *merilun* < OFr. *esmerillon*, dim. of *esmeril*, of Gmc. orig.]

Merlin *n.* In Arthurian legend, a magician and prophet who served as counselor to King Arthur.

Mer•lo (mĕr′lō) A city of E Argentina, a suburb of Buenos Aires. Pop. 293,059.

mer•lon (mûr′lən) *n.* A solid portion of a crenelated wall between two open spaces. [Fr. < Ital. *merlone*, augmentative of *merlo*, battlement, perh. < Med.Lat. *merulus* < Lat., merle (< their imagined similarity to blackbirds sitting on a wall).]

Mer•lot or **mer•lot** (mər-lō′, mĕr-) *n.* **1.** A variety of grape originating in southern France and Italy. **2.** A dry red wine made from this grape. [Fr., young blackbird, Merlot, dim. of *merle*, blackbird (prob. < the grape's color) < OFr. See MERLE[1].]

mer•maid (mûr′mād′) *n.* A legendary sea creature having the head and upper body of a woman and the tail of a fish. [ME : *mere*, sea, lake; see MERE[2] + *maid*, maid; see MAID.]

mer•man (mûr′măn′, -mən) *n.* A legendary sea creature having the head and upper body of a man and the tail of a fish.

mero– or **mer–** *pref.* **1.** Part; segment: *merozoite.* **2.** Partial; partially: *meropia.* [< Gk. *meros*, part.]

mer•o•blas•tic (mĕr′ə-blăs′tĭk) *adj. Embryology* Undergoing partial cleavage. Used of a fertilized egg.

mer•o•crine (mĕr′ə-krĭn, -krīn′, -krēn′) *adj.* Of or relating to a gland whose secretory cells remain undamaged during secretion. [MERO– + Gk. *krīnein*, to separate; see ENDOCRINE.]

Mer•o•ë also **Mer•o•we** (mĕr′ō-ē′) An ancient city of N Sudan on the Nile R. N of Khartoum; cap. of a Cush dynasty from 530 B.C. to A.D. 350.

mer•o•my•o•sin (mĕr′ō-mī′ə-sĭn) *n.* Either of two protein subunits of a myosin molecule, obtained esp. through the digestive action of trypsin.

me•ro•pi•a (mə-rō′pē-ə) *n.* Partial blindness. —**me•ro′pic** (-rō′pĭk, -rŏp′ĭk) *adj.*

mer•o•plank•ton (mĕr′ə-plăngk′tən) *n.* Any of various organisms that spend part of their life cycle, usu. the larval or egg stages, as plankton.

–merous *suff.* Having a specified kind or number of parts: *isomerous.* [< NLat. *-merus* < Gk. *-meros* < *meros*, part.]

Mer•o•vin•gi•an (mĕr′ə-vĭn′jē-ən, -jən) A Frankish ruling dynasty (c. A.D. 450–751). —**Mer′o•vin′gi•an** *adj.*

mer•o•zo•ite (mĕr′ə-zō′īt) *n.* A protozoan cell that arises from the schizogony of a parent sporozoan and may enter either the asexual or sexual phase of the life cycle.

Mer•rill (mĕr′əl) James 1926–95. American poet whose works include *Divine Comedies* (1976).

Mer•ri•mack River (mĕr′ə-măk′) A river rising in S-central NH and flowing c. 177 km (110 mi) to the Atlantic Ocean.

mer•ri•ment (mĕr′ĭ-mənt) *n.* High-spirited fun and enjoyment; hilarity.

mesa
Arizona desert landscape

Mer•ritt Island (mĕr′ĭt) A city of E-central FL on **Merritt Island** between the mainland and Cape Canaveral. Pop. 36,090.

mer•ry (mĕr′ē) *adj.* **-ri•er, -ri•est** **1.** Full of high-spirited gaiety; jolly. **2.** Marked by or offering fun and gaiety; festive. **3.** Brisk: *a merry pace.* **4.** *Archaic* Delightful; entertaining. [ME *merri* < OE *mirige*, pleasant.] —**mer′ri•ly** *adv.* —**mer′ri•ness** *n.*

mer•ry-an•drew (mĕr′ē-ăn′drōō) *n.* A clown; a buffoon. [MERRY + the name *Andrew.*]

mer•ry-bells (mĕr′ē-bĕlz′) *pl.n.* (*used with a sing. or pl. verb*) See **bellwort.**

mer•ry-go-round (mĕr′ē-gō-round′) *n.* **1.** A revolving circular platform with seats, ridden for amusement. **2.** A toy consisting of a small circular platform that revolves when pushed or pedaled. **3.** A busy round; a whirl.

mer•ry•mak•ing (mĕr′ē-mā′kĭng) *n.* **1.** Participation in festive activities. **2a.** A festivity; a revelry. **b.** Festive activities. —**mer′ry•mak′er** *n.*

mer•ry•thought (mĕr′ē-thôt′) *n. Chiefly British* A wishbone.

merry widow *n.* A short strapless corset with half cups for the breasts and long garters. [Orig. a trademark.]

Mer•sey (mûr′zē) A river of NW England flowing c. 113 km (70 mi) to the Irish Sea at Liverpool.

Mer•sin (mĕr-sēn′) A city of S Turkey on the Mediterranean Sea WSW of Adana. Pop. 523,000.

Mer•thi•o•late (mər-thī′ə-lāt′) A trademark used for thimerosal.

Mer•ton (mûr′tn) Thomas 1915–68. Amer. Trappist monk and author whose works include *The Seven Story Mountain* (1948).

mes– *pref.* Variant of **meso–.**

me•sa (mā′sə) *n.* A broad flat-topped elevation with one or more clifflike sides, common in the southwest United States. [Sp., table, mesa < OSpan., table < Lat. *mēnsa.*]

Mesa A city of S-central AZ E of Phoenix. Pop. 396,375.

Me•sa•bi Range (mə-sä′bē) A series of low hills in NE MN where extensive iron ore deposits were discovered in 1887.

mé•sal•li•ance (mā-zăl′ē-əns, mā′ză-lyäns′) *n.* A marriage with a person of inferior social position. [Fr. < *més-*, bad (< OFr. *mes-*; see MIS–[1]) + *alliance*, alliance (< OFr. *aliance*; see ALLIANCE.)]

mes•arch (mĕz′ärk′, mĕs′-, mē′zärk′, -särk′) *adj. Ecology* Originating in a moderately moist habitat. Used of a sere. [MES(O)– + Gk. *arkhē*, beginning.]

mes•cal (mĕs-kăl′) also **mez•cal** (mĕz-) *n.* **1.** See **peyote** 1. **2a.** A Mexican liquor distilled from fermented agave juice. **b.** A food prepared by cooking the fleshy leaf base and trunk of certain agaves. **3.** See **maguey** 1. [Am.Sp. < Nahuatl *mexcalli*, mescal liquor : *metl*, maguey plant + perh. *ixca, xca*, to bake.]

mescal button *n.* The fresh or dried buttonlike tubercles of peyote, chewed as a drug by certain Native American peoples.

Mes•ca•le•ro (mĕs′kə-lâr′ō) *n., pl.* **Mescalero** or **-ros** A member of an Apache tribe formerly inhabiting southern New Mexico, western Texas, and north-central Mexico, with a present-day population in southern New Mexico.

mes•ca•line (mĕs′kə-lēn′, -lĭn) *n.* An alkaloid drug, $C_{11}H_{17}NO_3$, obtained from mescal buttons and producing hallucinations.

mes•clun (mĕs′klən) *n.* A mixture of young leafy greens, often including young lettuces, used as salad. [Provençal *mesclom, mesclumo*, mixture < VLat. **misculāre*, to mix thoroughly. See MEDDLE.]

Mes•dames (mā-däm′, -dăm′) *n.* **1.** Plural of **Madam** 1. **2.** Plural of **Madame.**

Mes•de•moi•selles also **mes•de•moi•selles** (mād′mwä-zĕl′) *n.* Plural of **Mademoiselle.**

me•seems (mē-sēmz′) *intr.v.* Past tense **-seemed** *Archaic* It seems to me. [ME *me semeth* : *me*, to me; see ME + *semeth*, third pers. sing. pr. t. of *semen*, to seem; see SEEM.]

mes•en•ceph•a•lon (mĕz′ĕn-sĕf′ə-lŏn′, mĕs′-) *n.* The midbrain. —**mes′en•ce•phal′ic** (-sə-făl′ĭk) *adj.*

mes•en•chyme (mĕz′ən-kīm′, mĕs′-) *n.* The part of the embryonic mesoderm from which connective tissue and the circulatory and lymphatic systems develop. [MES(O)– + –ENCHYMA.] —**mes′en•chy′mal, mes′en•chym′a•tous** (-kī′mə-təs, -kĭm′ə-) *adj.*

mes•en•ter•on (mĕz-ĕn′tə-rŏn′, mĕs′-) *n.* See **midgut** 1.

mes•en•ter•y (mĕz′ən-tĕr′ē, mĕs′-) *n., pl.* **-ies** Any of several folds of the peritoneum connecting the intestines to the dorsal abdominal wall, esp. one enveloping the jejunum and ileum. [ME *mesenterie* < Med.Lat. *mesenterium* < Gk. *mesenterion* : *meso-*, meso- + *enterion*, dim. of *enteron*, entrails; see **en** in App.] —**mes′en•ter′ic** *adj.*

mesh (mĕsh) *n.* **1a.** Any of the open spaces in a net or network; an interstice. **b.** The cords, threads, or wires surrounding these spaces. Often used in the plural. **2.** An openwork fabric or structure; a net or network: *a screen made of wire mesh.* **3.** Something that snares or entraps. Often used in the plural. **4a.** The engagement of gear teeth. **b.** The state of being so engaged: *gear teeth in mesh.* ❖ *v.* **meshed, mesh•ing, mesh•es** —*tr.* **1.** To catch in or as if in a net; ensnare. **2.** To cause (gear teeth) to become engaged. **3.** To cause to work closely together; coordinate. —*intr.* **1.** To become entangled. **2.** To become interlocked: *gears that are not meshing properly.* **3a.** To fit together effectively; be coordinated. **b.** To accord with another or each other; harmonize. [ME *mesch*, prob. < MDu. *maesche.*] —**mesh′y** *adj.*

Me·shach (mē′shăch) In the Bible, a young man who with Abednego and Shadrach emerged unharmed from the fiery furnace of Babylon.

Me·shed (mĕ-shĕd′) See **Mashhad.**

me·shu·ga also **me·shug·ga** (mə-shŏŏg′ə) *adj. Slang* Crazy; senseless. [Yiddish *meshuge* < Heb. *məšuggāʻ*, part. of *šuggaʻ*, to be mad.]

me·shu·gaas or **mish·e·gaas** or **mish·e·goss** (mĭsh′ə-gäs′) *n. Slang* Crazy or senseless activity or behavior; craziness. [Yiddish *meshegas* < Heb. *məšuggāʻ*. See MESHUGA.]

me·shug·ge·neh (mə-shŏŏg′ə-nə) or **me·shug·ge·ner** (-nər) *adj.* Crazy; senseless. ❖ *n.* One who is crazy. [Yiddish *meshugene, meshugene,* masc. and fem. sing. of *meshuge.* See MESHUGA.]

mesh·work (mĕsh′wûrk′) *n.* Meshed material; network.

me·si·al (mē′zē-əl, -zhəl) *adj.* 1. Of, in, near, or toward the middle. 2. Situated toward the middle of the front of the jaw along the curve of the dental arch. —**me′si·al·ly** *adv.*

mes·ic (mĕz′ĭk, mĕs′-, mē′zĭk, -sĭk) *adj. Ecology* Of, characterized by, or adapted to a moderately moist habitat.

me·sit·y·lene (mə-sĭt′l-ēn′) *n.* A hydrocarbon, $C_6H_3(CH_3)_3$, occurring in petroleum and coal tar or synthesized from acetone and used as a solvent. [MESITYL (OXIDE) + -ENE.]

mes·i·tyl oxide (mĕs′ĭ-tĭl) *n.* An oily liquid, $(CH_3)_2C:CHCOCH_3$, obtained from acetones and used as a solvent and in lacquers, paints, and varnishes. [Gk. *mesītēs,* mediator (< its use as an intermediate in organic synthesis) (< *mesos,* middle; see **medhyo-** in App.]

Mes·mer (mĕz′mər, mĕs′-), **Franz** or **Friedrich Anton** 1734-1815. Austrian physician who sought to treat disease through animal magnetism, an early application of hypnotism.

mes·mer·ism (mĕz′mə-rĭz′əm, mĕs′-) *n.* 1. A strong or spellbinding appeal; fascination. 2. Hypnosis believed to be induced by animal magnetism. 3. Hypnotism. [After Franz MESMER.] —**mes·mer′ic** (-mĕr′ĭk) *adj.* —**mes·mer′i·cal·ly** *adv.* —**mes′mer·ist** *n.*

mes·mer·ize (mĕz′mə-rīz′, mĕs′-) *tr.v.* **-ized, -iz·ing, -iz·es** 1. To spellbind; enthrall. 2. To hypnotize. —**mes′mer·i·za′tion** (-mər-ĭ-zā′shən) *n.* —**mes′mer·iz′er** *n.*

meso– or **mes–** *pref.* 1. In the middle; middle: *mesoderm.* 2. Intermediate: *mesophyte.* [Gk. < *mesos,* middle. See **medhyo-** in App.]

Mes·o·a·mer·i·ca (mĕz′ō-ə-mĕr′ĭ-kə, mĕs′-) A region extending S and E from central Mexico to include parts of Guatemala, Belize, Honduras, and Nicaragua. —**Mes′o·a·mer′i·can** *adj. & n.*

mes·o·blast (mĕz′ə-blăst′, mĕs′-) *n.* The middle germinal layer of an early embryo, consisting of undifferentiated cells destined to become the mesoderm. —**mes′o·blas′tic** *adj.*

mes·o·carp (mĕz′ə-kärp′, mĕs′-) *n.* The middle, usu. fleshy layer of a fruit wall.

mes·o·ceph·al·ic (mĕz′ō-sə-făl′ĭk, mĕs′-) *adj.* Having a head of medium breadth, with a cephalic index between 76 and 80. —**mes′o·ceph′al·ly** (-ə-sĕf′ə-lē) *n.*

mes·o·derm (mĕz′ə-dûrm′, mĕs′-) *n.* The embryonic germ layer that lies between the ectoderm and the endoderm, from which connective tissue, muscle, and the urogenital and circulatory systems develop. —**mes′o·der′mal, mes′o·der′mic** *adj.*

mes·o·gas·tri·um (mĕz′ə-găs′trē-əm, mĕs′-) *n., pl.* **-tri·a** (-trē-ə) 1. The portion of the embryonic mesentery that is attached to the early stomach. 2. The region of the abdomen surrounding the navel. —**mes′o·gas′tric** *adj.*

mes·o·gle·a also **mes·o·gloe·a** (mĕz′ə-glē′ə, mĕs′-, mē′zə-, -sə-) *n.* The layer of gelatinous material that separates the inner and outer cell layers of a cnidarian. [NLat. *mesogloea* : MESO- + Med.Gk. *gloia, glia,* glue; see ZOOGLEA.]

Mes·o·lith·ic (mĕz′ə-lĭth′ĭk, mĕs′-) *adj.* Of or being the cultural period of the Stone Age between the Paleolithic and Neolithic periods, marked by the appearance of microlithic tools and weapons and by changes in the nature of settlements. ❖ *n.* The Mesolithic Period.

mes·o·mere (mĕz′ə-mîr′, mĕs′-) *n.* 1. A blastomere of intermediate size, larger than a micromere but smaller than a macromere. 2. The middle zone of the mesoderm of a chordate vertebrate embryo, from which excretory tissue develops.

mes·o·morph (mĕz′ə-môrf′, mĕs′-) *n.* An individual with a robust, muscular build caused by the predominance of structures developed from the mesodermal embryonic layer. [MESO(DERM) + -MORPH.]

mes·o·mor·phic (mĕz′ə-môr′fĭk, mĕs′-) *adj.* 1. also **mes·o·mor·phous** (-môr′fəs) Of, relating to, or existing in a state of matter intermediate between liquid and crystal. 2. Of or relating to a mesomorph. —**mes′o·mor′phism** *n.*

mes·on (mĕz′ŏn′, mĕs′-, mē′zŏn′, -sŏn′) *n.* Any of a family of subatomic particles that participate in strong interactions, composed of a quark and an antiquark.

mes·o·neph·ros (mĕz′ə-nĕf′rəs, -rŏs′, mĕs′-) *n.* The second of the three excretory organs that develop in a vertebrate embryo, becoming the functioning kidney in fish and amphibians but replaced by the metanephros in higher vertebrates. [MESO- + Gk. *nephros,* kidney.]

mes·o·pause (mĕz′ə-pôz′, mĕs′-) *n.* An atmospheric area about 80 kilometers (50 miles) above the earth's surface, forming the upper boundary of the mesosphere.

mes·o·pe·lag·ic (mĕz′ə-pə-lăj′ĭk, mĕs′-) *adj.* Of, relating to, or living at ocean depths between about 180 and 900 meters (600 and 3,000 feet): *mesopelagic organisms.*

mes·o·phyll (mĕz′ə-fĭl′, mĕs′-) *n.* The photosynthetic tissue of a leaf. —**mes′o·phyl′lic, mes′o·phyl′lous** *adj.*

mes·o·phyte (mĕz′ə-fīt′, mĕs′-) *n.* A land plant that grows in an environment having a moderate amount of moisture.

Mes·o·po·ta·mi·a (mĕz′ə-pə-tā′mē-ə, mĕs′-) An ancient region of SW Asia between the Tigris and Euphrates rivers in modern-day Iraq; probably settled before 5000 B.C. —**Mes′o·po·ta′mi·an** *adj. & n.*

mes·o·some (mĕz′ə-sōm′, mĕs′-, mē′zə-, -sə-) *n.* An invagination of the cytoplasmic membrane in some bacterial cells.

mes·o·sphere (mĕz′ə-sfîr′, mĕs′-) *n.* The portion of the atmosphere from about 50 to 80 kilometers (31 to 50 miles) above the earth's surface, characterized by decreasing temperatures with increasing altitude. —**mes′o·spher′ic** (-sfîr′ĭk, -sfĕr′-) *adj.*

mes·o·the·li·o·ma (mĕz′ə-thē′lē-ō′mə, mĕs′-, mē′zə-, -sə-) *n., pl.* **-ma·ta** (-mə-tə) or **-mas** A usu. malignant tumor of mesothelial tissue, esp. that of the pleura or peritoneum.

mes·o·the·li·um (mĕz′ə-thē′lē-əm, mĕs′-) *n., pl.* **-li·a** (-lē-ə) The layer of flat cells of mesodermal origin that gives rise to the squamous cells of the peritoneum, pericardium, and pleura. [MESO- + (EPI)THELIUM.] —**mes′o·the′li·al** *adj.*

mes·o·tho·rax (mĕz′ə-thôr′ăks′, -thōr′-, mĕs′-) *n., pl.* **-tho·rax·es** or **-tho·ra·ces** (-thôr′ə-sēz′, -thōr′-) The middle of the three divisions of the thorax of an insect, bearing the middle pair of legs and the first pair of wings. —**mes′o·tho·rac′ic** (-thôrăs′ĭk, -thō-) *adj.*

mes·o·tho·ri·um (mĕz′ə-thôr′ē-əm, -thōr′-, mĕs′-) *n.* Either of two decay products of thorium, mesothorium I, an isotope of radium, or mesothorium II, an isotope of actinium.

Mes·o·zo·ic (mĕz′ə-zō′ĭk, mĕs′-) *adj.* Of or belonging to the second era of geologic time, between approx. 245 and 65 million years ago, characterized by the development of flowering plants and by the appearance and extinction of dinosaurs. See table at **geologic time.** ❖ *n.* The Mesozoic Era or its deposits.

mes·quite (mĕ-skēt′, mə-) *n.* Any of several small spiny trees or shrubs of the genus *Prosopis* in the pea family, native to hot dry regions of the New World and important as cattle forage, esp.: **a.** *P. glandulosa,* of the southwest United States and northern Mexico. **b.** *P. juliflora,* of the Gulf Coast and Caribbean islands. [Sp. *mezquite* < Nahuatl *mizquitl.*]

Mes·quite (mĕ-skēt′, mē-) A city of NE TX, a suburb of Dallas. Pop. 124,523.

mess (mĕs) *n.* 1. A disorderly or dirty accumulation, heap, or jumble. **2a.** A cluttered, untidy, usu. dirty condition. **b.** A confused, troubling, or embarrassing condition; a muddle. **c.** One that is in such a condition. **3a.** An amount of food, as for a meal, course, or dish. **b.** A serving of soft, semiliquid food. **4a.** A group of people, usu. soldiers or sailors, who regularly eat meals together. **b.** Food or a meal served to such a group. **c.** A mess hall. ❖ *v.* **messed, mess·ing, mess·es** —*tr.* 1. To make disorderly or soiled; clutter or foul. 2. To botch; bungle. —*intr.* 1. To cause or make a mess. 2. To use or handle something carelessly; fiddle. 3. To intrude; interfere. 4. To take a meal in a military mess. —*phrasal verbs:* **mess around** *Informal* 1. To pass time in aimless puttering. 2. To associate casually or playfully. 3. To be sexually unfaithful. **mess up** 1. *Informal* To make a mistake, esp. from nervousness or confusion. 2. *Slang* To beat up; manhandle. [ME *mes,* meal course, food, group eating together < OFr. < LLat. *missus* < Lat., p. part. of *mittere,* to place.]

mes·sage (mĕs′ĭj) *n.* **1a.** A usu. short communication transmitted by words, signals, or other means from one person, station, or group to another. **b.** The substance of such a communication; the point or points conveyed. 2. A statement made or read before a gathering. 3. A basic thesis or lesson; a moral. —*tr.* **-saged, -sag·ing, -sag·es** To send a message to. 2. To send as a message. —*intr.* To send a message; communicate. [ME < OFr. < Med.Lat. *missāticum* < Lat. *missus,* p. part. of *mittere,* to send.]

Mes·sa·li·na (mĕs′ə-lī′nə), **Valeria** d. A.D. 48. Roman empress as the third wife of Claudius I who was executed after she married a lover in Claudius's absence.

mes·sa·line (mĕs′ə-lēn′) *n.* A lightweight soft shiny silk cloth with a twilled or satin weave. [Fr. < *Messaline,* Messalina.]

Mes·sa·pic (mĕ-să′pĭk) *n.* An extinct Indo-European language spoken in southern Italy. [< Lat. *Messāpia,* ancient name for the region of Italy containing Apulia and Calabria.] —**Mes·sa′pic** *adj.*

Mes·sei·gneurs (mā-sĕ-nyœr′) *n.* Plural of **Monseigneur.**

Mes·se·ne (mĭ-sē′nē) An ancient Greek city in the SW Peloponnesus; founded c. 369 B.C.

mes·sen·ger (mĕs′ən-jər) *n.* 1. One that carries messages or performs errands, as: **a.** A person employed to carry telegrams, letters, or parcels. **b.** A military or official courier. **c.** An envoy to another person, party, or government. 2. A bearer of news. 3. A forerunner; a harbinger. 4. A prophet. 5. *Nautical* A light, easily heaved line used to haul in a heavier line. ❖ *tr.v.* **-gered, -ger·**

ă pat — oi boy
ā pay — ou out
âr care — ŏŏ took
ä father — ōō boot
ĕ pet — ŭ cut
ē be — ûr urge
ĭ pit — th thin
ī pie — *th* this
îr pier — hw which
ŏ pot — zh vision
ō toe — ə about,
ô paw — item

Stress marks:
′ (primary);
′ (secondary), as in
lexicon (lĕk′sĭ-kŏn′)

ing, -gers To send by messenger. [ME *messenger* < OFr. *messagier* < *message*, message. See MESSAGE.]

messenger RNA *n.* The form of RNA that mediates the transfer of genetic information from the cell nucleus to ribosomes in the cytoplasm, where it serves as a template for protein synthesis.

Mes·se·ni·a (mĭ-sē′nē-ə, -sēn′yə) An ancient region of SW Greece in the Peloponnesus on the Ionian Sea; conquered by Romans in 146 B.C. —**Mes·sen′i·an** *adj. & n.*

mess hall *n.* A building or room for serving meals.

Mes·siaen (mě-syän′, -syän′), **Olivier Eugène Prosper Charles** 1908–92. French composer and organist who was a noted teacher and theorist.

Mes·si·ah (mĭ-sī′ə) *n.* **1.** also **Mes·si·as** (mĭ-sī′əs) The anticipated savior of the Jews. **2.** also **Messias** *Christianity* Jesus. **3. messiah** One who is anticipated as, regarded as, or professes to be a savior or liberator. [ME *Messias* < OFr. *Messie* < LLat. *Messīās* < Gk. < Aram. *mašîaḥ*, the anointed one (< *mašah*, to anoint), or Heb. *māšîaḥ*, anointed (< *māšaḥ*, to anoint).]

mes·si·an·ic also **Mes·si·an·ic** (měs′ē-ăn′ĭk) *adj.* **1.** Of or relating to a messiah: *messianic hopes.* **2.** Of or characterized by messianism: *messianic nationalism.* [NLat. *messiānicus* < LLat. *Messīās*, Messiah. See MESSIAH.]

mes·si·a·nism (měs′ē-ə-nĭz′əm, mĭ-sī′-) *n.* **1.** Belief in a messiah. **2.** Belief that a particular cause or movement is destined to triumph or save the world. **3.** Zealous devotion to a leader, cause, or movement. —**mes′si·a·nist** *n.*

Mes·sieurs (mā-syœ′, měs′ərz) *n.* Plural of **Monsieur.**

Mes·si·na (mĭ-sē′nə, mě-) A city of NE Sicily, Italy, on the **Strait of Messina,** a channel separating Sicily from mainland Italy; founded in the 8th cent. B.C. Pop. 255,890.

mess jacket *n.* A waist-length fitted jacket, worn chiefly as part of a uniform on formal occasions.

mess kit *n.* A set of cooking and eating utensils compactly arranged in a kit, used by soldiers and campers.

mess·mate (měs′māt′) *n.* A person with whom one eats regularly, as in a military mess.

Messrs.[1] (měs′ərz) *n.* Plural of **Mr.**

Messrs.[2] *abbr.* Messieurs

mess·y (měs′ē) *adj.* **-i·er, -i·est 1.** Disorderly and dirty: *a messy bedroom.* **2.** Exhibiting carelessness: *messy reasoning.* **3.** Unpleasantly difficult to settle or resolve: *a messy court case.* —**mess′i·ly** *adv.* —**mess′i·ness** *n.*

mes·ti·za (měs-tē′zə) *n.* A woman or a girl who is a mestizo. [Sp., fem. of *mestizo.* See MESTIZO.]

mes·ti·zo (měs-tē′zō) *n., pl.* **-zos** or **-zoes** A person, esp. a man or a boy, of mixed racial ancestry, in particular of mixed European and Native American ancestry. [Sp., mixed, mestizo < OSpan., mixed < LLat. *mixtīcius* < Lat. *mixtus*, p. part. of *miscēre*, to mix. See **meik-** in App.]

met (mět) *v.* Past tense and past participle of **meet**[1].

Me·ta (mā′tə, mě′tä) A river, c. 1,102 km (685 mi), of NE Colombia flowing partially along the border with Venezuela.

meta– or **met–** *pref.* **1a.** Later in time: *metestrus.* **b.** At a later stage of development: *metanephros.* **2.** Situated behind: *metacarpus.* **3a.** Change; transformation: *metachromatism.* **b.** Alternation: *metagenesis.* **4a.** Beyond; more comprehensive: *metalinguistics.* **b.** More highly developed: *metazoan.* **5.** Having undergone metamorphosis: *metasomatic.* **6a.** Derivative or related chemical substance: *metaprotein.* **b.** Of or relating to a benzene ring with two attached chemical groups, in which the carbon atoms with attached groups are separated by one unsubstituted carbon atom: *meta-dibromobenzene.* [Gk. < *meta*, beside, after. See **me-²** in App.]

met·a·a·nal·y·sis (mět′ə-ə-năl′ĭ-sĭs) *n.* The process or technique of synthesizing research results by using various statistical methods to retrieve, select, and combine results from previous separate but related studies.

met·a·bol·ic (mět′ə-bŏl′ĭk) *adj.* Of, relating to, or resulting from metabolism. [Gk. *metabolikos*, changeable < *metabolē*, change. See METABOLISM.] —**met′a·bol′i·cal·ly** *adv.*

me·tab·o·lism (mĭ-tăb′ə-lĭz′əm) *n.* **1.** The complex of chemical processes occurring within a living cell or organism that are necessary for the maintenance of life. **2.** The processing of a specific substance within the living body. [< Gk. *metabolē*, change < *metaballein*, to change : *meta-*, meta- + *ballein*, to throw; see **gʷelə-** in App.]

me·tab·o·lite (mĭ-tăb′ə-līt′) *n.* **1.** A substance produced by metabolism. **2.** A substance necessary for or taking part in a particular metabolic process. [METABOL(ISM) + –ITE[1].]

me·tab·o·lize (mĭ-tăb′ə-līz′) *v.* **-lized, -liz·ing, -liz·es** —*tr.* **1.** To subject (a substance) to metabolism. **2.** To produce (a substance) by metabolism. —*intr.* To undergo change by metabolism. —**me·tab′o·liz′a·ble** *adj.*

met·a·car·pal (mět′ə-kär′pəl) *adj.* Relating to the metacarpus. ❖ *n.* Any of the bones of the metacarpus.

met·a·car·pus (mět′ə-kär′pəs) *n., pl.* **-pi** (-pī) **1.** The part of the human hand that includes the five bones between the fingers and the wrist. **2.** The corresponding part of the forefoot of a quadruped.

met·a·cen·ter (mět′ə-sěn′tər) *n.* The intersection of vertical lines through the center of buoyancy of a floating body when it is at equilibrium and when it is floating at an angle.

met·a·cen·tric (mět′ə-sěn′trĭk) *adj.* **1.** Of or relating to a metacenter. **2.** *Genetics* Having the centromere in the median position. Used of a chromosome. ❖ *n.* A metacentric chromosome. —**met′a·cen·tric′i·ty** (-sěn-trĭs′ĭ-tē) *n.*

met·a·chro·ma·tism (mět′ə-krō′mə-tĭz′əm) *n.* A change in color caused by variation of the physical conditions to which a body is subjected, esp. such a change caused by variation in temperature. —**met′a·chro·mat′ic** (-măt′ĭk) *adj.*

Met·a·com (mět′ə-kŏm′) Also called **Phil·ip** (fĭl′ĭp) d. 1676. Wampanoag leader who waged King Philip's War (1675–76) with New England colonists who had encroached on Native American territory.

met·a·eth·ics (mět′ə-ĕth′ĭks) *n.* (*used with a sing. verb*) The study of the meaning and nature of ethical terms, judgments, and arguments. —**met′a·eth′i·cal** *adj.*

met·a·fic·tion (mět′ə-fĭk′shən) *n.* Fiction that deals, often playfully and self-referentially, with the writing of fiction or its conventions. —**met′a·fic′tion·al** *adj.*

met·a·gal·ax·y (mět′ə-găl′ək-sē) *n., pl.* **-ies** The assemblage of all galaxies; the entire physical universe.

met·a·gen·e·sis (mět′ə-jěn′ĭ-sĭs) *n.* See **alternation of generations.** —**met′a·ge·net′ic** (-jə-nět′ĭk) *adj.*

me·tag·na·thous (mĭ-tăg′nə-thəs) *adj.* Having a bill in which the tips of the mandibles cross. Used of a bird.

Met·ai·rie (mět′ə-rē) A community of SE LA, a suburb of New Orleans. Pop. 141,136.

met·al (mět′l) *n.* **1.** Any of a category of electropositive elements that usu. have a shiny surface, are generally good conductors of heat and electricity, and can be melted or fused, hammered into thin sheets, or drawn into wires. **2.** An alloy of two or more metallic elements. **3.** An object made of metal. **4.** Basic character; mettle. **5.** Broken stones used for road surfaces or railroad beds. **6.** Molten glass, esp. when used in glassmaking. **7.** Molten cast iron. **8.** *Printing* Type made of metal. **9.** *Music* Heavy metal. ❖ *tr.v.* **-aled, -al·ing, -als** also **-alled, -al·ling, -als** To cover or surface with broken stones. [ME < OFr. < Lat. *metallum* < Gk. *metallon*, mine, mineral, metal.]

WORD HISTORY In modern English, *metal* and *mettle* are pronounced the same, and they are in fact both related. Middle English borrowed *metal* from Old French in the 14th century; Old French *metal, metail,* came from Latin *metallum,* from Greek *metallon,* "mine, quarry, ore, metal." By the 16th century, *metal* had also come to mean "the stuff one is made of, one's character," but there was no difference in spelling between the literal and figurative senses until about 1700, when the spelling *mettle,* originally just a variant of *metal,* was fixed for the sense "fortitude." The history of English has numerous examples of pairs of words, like *metal* and *mettle,* that are (historically speaking) spelling variants of the same word; two other such pairs are *trump/triumph* and *through/thorough.*

met·a·lan·guage (mět′ə-lăng′gwĭj) *n.* **1.** A language or vocabulary used to describe or analyze language. **2.** *Computer Science* A language used to define another language.

met·al·head (mět′l-hěd′) *n. Slang* A fan of heavy metal music.

met·a·lin·guis·tics (mět′ə-lĭng-gwĭs′tĭks) *n.* (*used with a sing. verb*) The study of the interrelationship between language and other cultural behavior. —**met′a·lin·guis′tic** *adj.*

me·tal·lic (mĭ-tăl′ĭk) *adj.* **1.** Of, relating to, or having the characteristics of a metal. **2.** Containing a metal. **3.** Having a quality suggesting or associated with metal, esp.: **a.** Lustrous; sparkling: *metallic colors.* **b.** Sharp-tasting. **4.** Harshly resonant. ❖ *n.* **1.** A yarn or fiber made of or containing metal. **2.** A fabric, typically shiny or iridescent, made of such yarn or fiber. —**me·tal′li·cal·ly** *adv.*

metallic bond *n.* The chemical bond characteristic of metals, in which mobile valence electrons are shared among atoms in a usu. stable crystalline structure.

met·al·lif·er·ous (mět′l-lĭf′ər-əs) *adj.* Containing metal. Used of a mineral deposit or an ore. [< Lat. *metallifer* : *metallum,* metal; see METAL + *-fer,* -fer.]

met·al·line (mět′l-īn, -ĭn′) *adj.* **1.** Of, resembling, or having the properties of a metal. **2.** Containing metal ions.

metallo– or **metall–** or **metalli–** *pref.* Metal: *metallography.* [< Lat. *metallum,* metal. See METAL.]

met·al·log·ra·phy (mět′l-ŏg′rə-fē) *n.* The study of the structure of metals and alloys, esp. by optical and electron microscopy and x-ray diffraction. —**met′al·log′ra·pher** *n.* —**me·tal′lo·graph′ic** (mə-tăl′ə-grăf′ĭk) *adj.*

met·al·loid (mět′l-oid′) *n.* **1.** A nonmetallic element, such as arsenic, that has some of the chemical properties of a metal. **2.** A nonmetallic element, such as carbon, that can form an alloy with metals. ❖ *adj.* also **met·al·loi·dal** (mět′l-oid′l) **1.** Relating to or having the properties of a metalloid. **2.** Having the appearance of a metal.

met·al·lur·gy (mět′l-ûr′jē) *n.* The science and technology that studies metals, esp. the processes used in extracting metals from their ores. [NLat. *metallūrgia* < Gk. *metallourgos,* miner, worker in metals : *metallon,* a mine, metal + *-ourgos,* -worker (< *ergon,* work; see **werg-** in App.).] —**met′al·lur′gic, met′al·lur′gi·cal**

adj. —**met·al·lur·gi·cal·ly** adv. —**met·al·lur·gist** n.

met·al·mark (mĕt′l-märk′) n. Any of several small, darkly colored butterflies of the family Riodinidae of mainly tropical regions, having iridescent lines or spots on the wings.

met·al·work (mĕt′l-wûrk′) n. Articles, esp. decorative objects, made of metal.

met·al·work·ing (mĕt′l-wûr′kĭng) n. The process or art of shaping things out of metal. —**met′al·work′er** n.

met·a·math·e·mat·ics (mĕt′ə-măth′ə-măt′ĭks) n. (used with a sing. verb) The branch of mathematics that deals with the logic and consistency of mathematical proofs, formulas, and equations. —**met′a·math′e·mat′i·cal** adj.

met·a·mere (mĕt′ə-mîr′) n. Any of the homologous segments, lying in a longitudinal series, that compose the body of certain animals, such as earthworms. —**met·a·mer′ic** (-mĕr′ĭk, -mîr′-) adj. —**met·a·mer′i·cal·ly** adv.

me·tam·er·ism (mĭ-tăm′ə-rĭz′əm) n. The condition of having the body divided into metameres, exhibited in most animals only in the early embryonic stages of development.

met·a·mor·phic (mĕt′ə-môr′fĭk) adj. 1. also **met·a·mor·phous** (-fəs) Of, relating to, or characterized by metamorphosis. 2. Geology Changed in structure or composition as a result of metamorphism. Used of rock.

met·a·mor·phism (mĕt′ə-môr′fĭz′əm) n. The process by which rocks are altered in composition, texture, or internal structure by extreme heat, pressure, and the introduction of new chemical substances. [METAMORPH(IC) + -ISM.]

met·a·mor·phose (mĕt′ə-môr′fōz′, -fōs′) v. **-phosed, -phos·ing, -phos·es** —tr. 1. To change into a wholly different form or appearance; transform. 2. To subject to metamorphosis or metamorphism. —intr. To be changed or transformed by or as if by metamorphosis or metamorphism. [Fr. métamorphoser < OFr. < metamorphose, metamorphosis < Lat. metamorphōsis. See METAMORPHOSIS.]

met·a·mor·pho·sis (mĕt′ə-môr′fə-sĭs) n., pl. **-ses** (-sēz′) 1. A transformation, as by magic or sorcery. 2. A marked change in appearance, character, condition, or function. 3. Biology Change in the form and often habits of an animal during normal development after the embryonic stage. 4. Pathology A usu. degenerative change in the structure of a particular body tissue. [Lat. metamorphōsis < Gk. < metamorphoun, to transform : meta-, meta- + morphē, form.]

met·a·neph·ros (mĕt′ə-nĕf′rŏs′) n. The third and final excretory organ that develops in a vertebrate embryo, replacing the mesonephros as the excretory organ and developing into the adult kidney. [META- + Gk. nephros, kidney.]

met·a·phase (mĕt′ə-fāz′) n. The stage of mitosis and meiosis, following prophase and preceding anaphase, during which the chromosomes are aligned along the metaphase plate.

metaphase plate n. An imaginary plane perpendicular to the spindle fibers of a dividing cell, along which chromosomes align during metaphase.

met·a·phor (mĕt′ə-fôr′, -fər) n. 1. A figure of speech in which a word or phrase that designates one thing is applied to another in an implicit comparison, as in "All the world's a stage" (Shakespeare). 2. One thing conceived as representing another; a symbol. [ME methaphor < OFr. metaphore < Lat. metaphora < Gk., transference, metaphor < metapherein, to transfer : meta-, meta- + pherein, to carry; see bher-¹ in App.] —**met·a·phor′ic** (-fôr′ĭk, -fŏr′-), **met′a·phor′i·cal** adj. —**met′a·phor′i·cal·ly** adv.

met·a·phos·phate (mĕt′ə-fŏs′fāt′) n. A salt or ester of metaphosphoric acid.

met·a·phos·phor·ic acid (mĕt′ə-fŏs-fôr′ĭk, -fŏr′-) n. An inorganic compound, HPO₃, used as a dehydrating agent.

met·a·phrase (mĕt′ə-frāz′) n. A word-for-word translation. ❖ tr.v. **-phrased, -phras·ing, -phras·es** 1. To translate, esp. literally. 2. To alter the wording of (a text), esp. subtly. [NLat. metaphrasis < Gk., transl., paraphrase < metaphrazein, to translate : meta-, meta- + phrazein, to tell, show.] —**met′a·phras′tic** (-frăs′tĭk) adj.

met·a·phrast (mĕt′ə-frăst′) n. One who changes the form of a text, as by recasting prose in verse. [Med.Gk. metaphrastēs < Gk. metaphrazein, to translate. See METAPHRASE.]

met·a·phys·ic (mĕt′ə-fĭz′ĭk) n. 1a. Metaphysics. b. A system of metaphysics. 2. An underlying philosophical or theoretical principle: luck, the metaphysic of the gambler. [ME methaphisik, metaphisik. See METAPHYSICS.]

met·a·phys·i·cal (mĕt′ə-fĭz′ĭ-kəl) adj. 1. Of or relating to metaphysics. 2. Based on speculative or abstract reasoning. 3. Highly abstract or theoretical; abstruse. 4a. Immaterial; incorporeal. b. Supernatural. 5. often **Metaphysical** Of or relating to the poetry of certain 17th-century English poets whose verse is marked by conceits. [ME metaphisicalle < Med.Lat. metaphysicālis, of metaphysics, metaphysica. See METAPHYSICS.] —**met′a·phys′i·cal·ly** adv.

met·a·phy·si·cian (mĕt′ə-fĭ-zĭsh′ən) n. One who specializes or is skilled in metaphysics.

met·a·phys·ics (mĕt′ə-fĭz′ĭks) n. 1. (used with a sing. verb) Philosophy The branch of philosophy that addresses questions about the ultimate composition of reality, including the relationships

between mind and matter, substance and attribute, and fact and value. 2. (used with a pl. verb) The theoretical or first principles of a particular discipline. 3. (used with a sing. verb) A priori speculation upon questions that are unanswerable to scientific observation, analysis, or experiment. 4. (used with a sing. verb) Excessively subtle or recondite reasoning. [< pl. of ME methaphisik < Med.Lat. metaphysica < Med.Gk. (ta) metaphusika < Gk. (Ta) meta (ta) phusika, (the works) after the physics, the title of Aristotle's treatise on first principles (following his work on physics) : meta, after; see META- + phusika, physics; see PHYSICS.]

met·a·pla·sia (mĕt′ə-plā′zhə, -zhē-ə) n. 1. Normal transformation of tissue from one type to another. 2. Transformation of cells from a normal to an abnormal state. —**met·a·plas′tic** (-plăs′tĭk) adj.

met·a·plasm¹ (mĕt′ə-plăz′əm) n. Alteration of a word by the addition, omission, or transposition of sounds or syllables or the letters that represent them. [Ult. < Gk. metaplasmos, remodeling < metaplassein, to remold : meta-, meta- + plassein, to mold; see pelə-² in App.] —**met·a·plas′tic** (-plăs′tĭk), **met′a·plas′mic** (-plăz′mĭk) adj.

met·a·plasm² (mĕt′ə-plăz′əm) n. Nonliving material in the protoplasm of a cell, such as pigment granules or nutritive substances. [META- + -PLASM.] —**met′a·plas′mic** (-plăz′mĭk) adj.

Met·a·pon·tum (mĕt′ə-pŏn′təm) An ancient city of SE Italy on the Gulf of Taranto; settled by Greeks c. 700 B.C.

met·a·pro·tein (mĕt′ə-prō′tēn′, -prō′tē-ĭn) n. Any of various protein derivatives that result from the action of an acid or alkali and are soluble in weak acids or alkalis.

met·a·psy·chol·o·gy (mĕt′ə-sī-kŏl′ə-jē) n. Philosophical inquiry or theory supplementing the empirical science of psychology.

met·a·so·ma·tism (mĕt′ə-sō′mə-tĭz′əm) also **met·a·so·ma·to·sis** (-sō′mə-tō′sĭs) n. The process by which the chemical composition of a rock is changed by interaction with fluids; replacement of one mineral by another without melting. —**met′a·so·mat′ic** (-măt′ĭk) adj.

met·a·sta·ble (mĕt′ə-stā′bəl) adj. Of, relating to, or being a relatively stable but transient state of a chemical or physical system, as of an excited atom. —**met′a·sta·bil′i·ty** (-stə-bĭl′ĭ-tē) n.

me·tas·ta·sis (mĭ-tăs′tə-sĭs) n., pl. **-ses** (-sēz′) 1. Transmission of pathogenic microorganisms or cancerous cells from an original site to one or more sites elsewhere in the body. 2. A secondary cancerous growth formed by transmission of cancerous cells from a primary growth located elsewhere in the body. [Gk. < methistanai, to change : meta-, meta- + histanai, to cause to stand, place; see stā- in App.] —**met′a·stat′ic** (mĕt′ə-stăt′ĭk) adj. —**met′a·stat′i·cal·ly** adv.

me·tas·ta·size (mə-tăs′tə-sīz′) intr.v. **-sized, -siz·ing, -siz·es** To be transmitted or transferred by or as if by metastasis.

met·a·tag (mĕt′ə-tăg′) n. An HTML tag that contains descriptive information about a webpage and does not appear when the webpage is displayed in a browser.

met·a·tar·sal (mĕt′ə-tär′səl) adj. Of or relating to the metatarsus. ❖ n. Any of the bones of the metatarsus.

met·a·tar·sus (mĕt′ə-tär′səs) n., pl. **-si** (-sī, -sē) 1. The middle part of the human foot that forms the instep and includes the five bones between the toes and the ankle. 2. The corresponding part of the quadruped hind foot or the bird foot.

me·ta·te (mĭ-tä′tē, mĕ-tä′tĕ) n. A stone block with a shallow concave surface, used with a mano for grinding corn or other grains. [Am.Sp. < Nahuatl metlatl.]

me·tath·e·sis (mĭ-tăth′ĭ-sĭs) n., pl. **-ses** (-sēz′) 1. Linguistics Transposition within a word of letters, sounds, or syllables, as in the change from Old English brid to modern English bird. 2. Chemistry Double decomposition. [LLat. < Gk. < metatithenai, to transpose : meta-, meta- + tithenai, to place; see dhē- in App.] —**met′a·thet′ic** (mĕt′ə-thĕt′ĭk), **met′a·thet′i·cal** adj. —**met′a·thet′i·cal·ly** adv.

me·tath·e·size (mĭ-tăth′ĭ-sīz′) tr. & intr.v. **-sized, -siz·ing, -siz·es** To subject to or undergo metathesis.

met·a·tho·rax (mĕt′ə-thôr′ăks′, -thōr′-) n., pl. **-tho·rax·es** or **-tho·ra·ces** (-thə-sēz′, -thôr′-) The hindmost of the three divisions of the thorax of an insect, bearing the third pair of legs and the second pair of wings. —**met′a·tho·rac′ic** (-thō-răs′ĭk, -thō-) adj.

met·a·zo·an (mĕt′ə-zō′ən) n. A multicellular animal of the subkingdom Metazoa. [< NLat. Metazōa, a subdivision of the animal kingdom : META- + -zōa, pl. of -zōon, animal; see -ZOON.] —**met′a·zo′al, met′a·zo′an, met′a·zo′ic** adj.

Metch·ni·koff also **Metch·ni·kov** (mĕch′nĭ-kôf′, myĕch′nĭ-kəf), **Elie** 1845–1916. Russian zoologist who shared a 1908 Nobel Prize.

mete¹ (mēt) tr.v. **met·ed, met·ing, metes** 1. To distribute by or as if by measure; allot: mete out punishment. 2. Archaic To measure. [ME meten < OE metan. See med- in App.]

mete² (mēt) n. A boundary line; a limit: metes and bounds. [ME < AN < Lat. mēta, turning post, boundary.]

me·tem·psy·cho·sis (mə-tĕm′sī-kō′sĭs, mĕt′əm-sī-) n., pl. **-ses** (-sēz) Reincarnation. [LLat. metempsychōsis < Gk. metempsukhōsis < metempsukhousthai, to transmigrate : meta-, meta- +

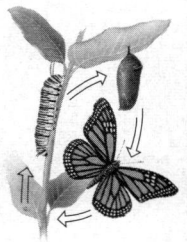

metamorphosis
development of a monarch butterfly

empsūkhos, animate (*en,* in; see EN-² + *psūkhē,* soul; see **bhes-** in App.).]

met·en·ceph·a·lon (mĕt′ĕn-sĕf′ə-lŏn′) *n., pl.* **-la** (-lə) The anterior part of the embryonic hindbrain, giving rise to the cerebellum and pons. —**met′en·ce·phal′ic** (-sə-făl′ĭk) *adj.*

me·te·or (mē′tē-ər, -ôr′) *n.* A bright trail or streak that appears in the sky when a meteoroid is heated to incandescence by friction with the earth's atmosphere. [ME *meteour,* atmospheric phenomenon < OFr. *meteore* < Med.Lat. *meteōrum* < Gk. *meteōron,* astronomical phenomenon < neut. of *meteōros,* high in the air : *meta-, meta-* + *-āoros,* lifted; akin to *āeirein,* to lift up.]

me·te·or·ic (mē′tē-ôr′ĭk, -ŏr′-) *adj.* **1.** Of, relating to, or formed by a meteoroid. **2.** Of or relating to the earth's atmosphere. **3.** Similar to a meteor in speed, brilliance, or brevity: *a meteoric rise to fame.* —**me′te·or′i·cal·ly** *adv.*

me·te·or·ite (mē′tē-ə-rīt′) *n.* A stony or metallic mass of matter that has fallen to the earth's surface from outer space. —**me′te·or·it′ic** (-ə-rĭt′ĭk), **me′te·or·it′i·cal** *adj.*

me·te·or·it·ics (mē′tē-ə-rĭt′ĭks) *n.* (*used with a sing. verb*) The branch of astronomy that deals with meteors. [METEORIT(E) + -ICS.]

me·te·or·oid (mē′tē-ə-roid′) *n.* A solid body, moving in space, that is smaller than an asteroid and at least as large as a speck of dust.

me·te·or·ol·o·gist (mē′tē-ə-rŏl′ə-jĭst) *n.* **1.** One who studies meteorology. **2.** One who reports and forecasts weather conditions.

me·te·or·ol·o·gy (mē′tē-ə-rŏl′ə-jē) *n.* The science that deals with the phenomena of the atmosphere, esp. weather. [Ult. < Gk. *meteōrologiā,* discussion of astronomical phenomena : *meteōron,* astronomical phenomenon; see METEOR + *-logiā,* -logy.] —**me′te·or·o·log′i·cal** (-ər-ə-lŏj′ĭ-kəl), **me′te·or·o·log′ic** *adj.* —**me′te·or·o·log′i·cal·ly** *adv.*

meteor shower *n.* A large number of meteors that appear together and seem to come from the same area in the sky.

me·ter¹ (mē′tər) *n.* **1a.** The measured arrangement of words in poetry, as by accentual rhythm. **b.** A particular arrangement of words in poetry, such as iambic pentameter, determined by the kind and number of metrical units in a line. **c.** The rhythmic pattern of a stanza, determined by the kind and number of lines. **2.** *Music* **a.** Division into measures or bars. **b.** A specific rhythm determined by the number of beats and the time value assigned to each note in a measure. [ME < OE *meter* and < OFr. *metre,* both < Lat. *metrum* < Gk. *metron,* measure, poetic meter. See **mē-**¹ in App.]

me·ter² (mē′tər) *n.* The International System unit of length that is equal to the distance traveled by light in a vacuum in 1/299,792,458 of a second and is approx. equal to 39.37 inches. See table at **measurement.** [Fr. *mètre* < Gk. *metron,* measure. See **mē-**¹ in App.]

me·ter³ (mē′tər) *n.* **1.** Any of various devices designed to measure time, distance, speed, or intensity or indicate and record or regulate the amount or volume, as of an electric current. **2.** A postage meter. **3.** A parking meter. ❖ *tr.v.* **-tered, -ter·ing, -ters** **1.** To measure with a meter. **2.** To supply in a measured or regulated amount. **3.** To imprint with revenue stamps by means of a postage meter or similar device. **4.** To provide with a parking meter or parking meters. [< –METER.]

–meter *suff.* Measuring device: *anemometer.* [Fr. *-mètre* < Gk. *metron,* measure. See **mē-**¹ in App.]

me·ter-kil·o·gram-sec·ond (mē′tər-kĭl′ə-grăm-sĕk′ənd) *adj.* Of or being a system of units for mechanics, using the meter, the kilogram, and the second as basic units of length, mass, and time.

meter maid *n.* A woman member of a police traffic control department who issues tickets for parking violations.

me·tes·trus (mē-tĕs′trəs) *n.* The period of sexual inactivity that follows estrus. —**me·tes′trous** (-trəs) *adj.*

meth (mĕth) *n. Slang* Methamphetamine.

meth– *pref.* Methyl: *methane.* [< METHYL.]

meth·ac·ry·late (mĕth-ăk′rə-lāt′) *n.* **1.** An ester of methacrylic acid, CH₂:C(CH₃)COOR, R being an organic radical. **2.** A resin derived from methacrylic acid.

meth·a·cryl·ic acid (mĕth′ə-krĭl′ĭk) *n.* A colorless liquid, CH₂:C(CH₃)COOH, used in the manufacture of resins and plastics.

meth·a·done (mĕth′ə-dōn) *n.* A potent synthetic narcotic drug, C₂₁H₂₇NO, that is less addictive than morphine or heroin and is used as a substitute for these drugs in addiction treatment programs. [Short for *methadone hydrochloride* : (DI)METH(YL) + A(MINO) + D(IPHENYL) + (heptan)one, a ketone.]

meth·am·phet·a·mine (mĕth′ăm-fĕt′ə-mēn′, -mĭn) *n.* An amine derivative of amphetamine, C₁₀H₁₅N, used in the form of its crystalline hydrochloride as a stimulant.

meth·ane (mĕth′ān′) *n.* An odorless colorless flammable gas, CH₄, the major constituent of natural gas, that is used as a fuel and as a source of hydrogen and organic compounds.

methane series *n.* See **alkane series.**

me·than·o·gen (mə-thăn′ə-jən) *n.* Any of various archaea capable of producing methane from the decomposition of organic material.

meth·a·nol (mĕth′ə-nôl′, -nōl′, -nŏl′) *n.* A colorless toxic flam-

mable liquid, CH₃OH, used as an antifreeze, a solvent, a fuel, and a denaturant for ethyl alcohol. [METHAN(E) + -OL¹.]

meth·a·qua·lone (mĕth′ə-kwā′lōn′) *n.* A potentially habit-forming drug, C₁₆H₁₄N₂O, formerly used as a sedative and hypnotic. [METH(YL) + *qu(in)a(zo)l(inon),* a derivative of quinoline + -ONE.]

Meth·e·drine (mĕth′ĭ-drĕn′, -drĭn) A trademark used for methamphetamine.

me·theg·lin (mə-thĕg′lĭn) *n.* A beverage typically made of fermented honey and water; mead. [Welsh *meddyglyn* : *meddyg,* medicinal (< Lat. *medicus* < *mederī,* to heal; see **med–** in App.) + *llyn,* liquor.]

met·he·mo·glo·bin (mĕt-hē′mə-glō′bĭn) *n.* A brownish-red crystalline compound formed in the blood when hemoglobin is oxidized. [MET(A)– + HEMOGLOBIN.]

me·the·na·mine (mə-thē′nə-mēn′, -mĭn) *n.* An organic compound, (CH₂)₆N₄, used as a urinary tract antiseptic and in rubber vulcanizing. [METH- + -EN(E) + AMINE.]

meth·i·cil·lin (mĕth′ĭ-sĭl′ĭn) *n.* A synthetic antibiotic, C₁₇H₁₉N₂O₆NaS, related to penicillin. [METH- + (PEN)ICILLIN.]

me·thinks (mĭ-thĭngks′) *intr.v.* Past tense **me·thought** (-thôt′) *Archaic* It seems to me. [ME *me thinkes* < OE *mēthyncth* : *mē,* to me; see ME + *thyncth,* it seems.]

me·thi·o·nine (mə-thī′ə-nēn′) *n.* A sulfur-containing essential amino acid, C₅H₁₁NO₂S, obtained from various proteins or prepared synthetically and used as a dietary supplement and in pharmaceuticals. [ME(TH)– + THION– + -INE².]

meth·od (mĕth′əd) *n.* **1.** A means or manner of procedure, esp. a regular and systematic way of accomplishing something. See Usage Note at **methodology.** **2.** Orderly arrangement of parts or steps to accomplish an end. **3.** The procedures and techniques characteristic of a particular discipline or field of knowledge: *archaeological method.* **4. Method** A technique of acting in which the actor recalls emotions and reactions from past experience and uses them in portraying a character. [ME, medical procedure < Lat. *methodus,* method < Gk. *methodos,* pursuit, method : *meta-,* beyond, after; see META– + *hodos,* way, journey.]

SYNONYMS *method, system, routine, manner, mode, fashion, way* These nouns refer to the plans or procedures followed to accomplish a task or attain a goal. *Method* implies a detailed, logically ordered plan: "*I do not know of a better method for choosing a presidential nominee*" (Harry S. Truman). *System* suggests order, regularity, and coordination of methods: "*Of generalship, of strategic system . . . there was little or none*" (John Morley). A *routine* is a habitual, often tiresome method: "*The common business of the nation . . . is carried on in a constant routine by the clerks of the different offices*" (Tobias Smollett). *Manner* and *fashion* emphasize a personal or distinctive behavior: *a clearly articulated manner of speaking; issuing orders in an arbitrary and abrasive fashion.* *Mode* often denotes a manner influenced by or arising from tradition or custom: *a nomadic mode of life.* *Way* is the least specific of these terms: "*It is absurd to think that the only way to tell if a poem is lasting is to wait and see if it lasts*" (Robert Frost).

me·thod·i·cal (mə-thŏd′ĭ-kəl) also **me·thod·ic** (-ĭk) *adj.* **1.** Arranged or proceeding in regular, systematic order. **2.** Marked by ordered and systematic habits or behavior. —**me·thod′i·cal·ly** *adv.* —**me·thod′i·cal·ness** *n.*

Meth·od·ism (mĕth′ə-dĭz′əm) *n.* **1.** The beliefs, worship, and system of organization of the Methodists. **2. methodism** Emphasis on systematic procedure.

Meth·od·ist (mĕth′ə-dĭst) *n.* **1.** A member of an evangelical Protestant church founded on the principles of John and Charles Wesley in 18th-century England and concerned with social welfare and public morals. **2. methodist** One who emphasizes or insists on systematic procedure.

Me·tho·di·us (mĭ-thō′dē-əs), Saint. See Saint **Cyril.**

meth·od·ize (mĕth′ə-dīz′) *tr.v.* **-ized, -iz·ing, -iz·es** To reduce to or organize by a method; systematize. —**meth′od·i·za′tion** (-dĭ-zā′shən) *n.* —**meth′od·iz′er** *n.*

meth·od·ol·o·gist (mĕth′ə-dŏl′ə-jĭst) *n.* One who studies methodology.

meth·od·ol·o·gy (mĕth′ə-dŏl′ə-jē) *n., pl.* **-gies 1a.** A body of practices, procedures, and rules used in a discipline or an inquiry; a set of working methods: *the methodology of genetic studies.* **b.** The study or theoretical analysis of such working methods. **2.** The branch of logic that deals with the principles of the formation of knowledge. **3.** *Usage Problem* Means, technique, or procedure; method. —**meth′od·o·log′i·cal** (mĕth′ə-də-lŏj′ĭ-kəl) *adj.* —**meth′od·o·log′i·cal·ly** *adv.*

USAGE NOTE In recent years *methodology* has been increasingly used as a pretentious substitute for *method* in scientific and technical contexts, as in *The oil company has not yet decided on a methodology for restoring the beaches.* The misuse of *methodology* obscures an important conceptual distinction between the tools of scientific investigation (properly *methods*) and the principles that determine how such tools are deployed and interpreted (properly *methodology*).

meth·o·trex·ate (mĕth′ə-trĕk′sāt) *n.* A toxic antimetabolite, C₂₀H₂₂N₈O₅, that acts as a folic acid antagonist to interfere with cellular reproduction and is used esp. to treat psoriasis and certain cancers. [*methotre-* (prob. shortening and alteration of *methylaminopterin,* one of its chemical names : METHYL + *aminopterin,* a folic acid antagonist, ult. < Gk. *pteron,* wing; see **pet-** in App.) + perh. (O)X(Y)− + −ATE².]

me·thought (mĭ-thôt′) *v. Archaic* Past tense of **methinks.**

me·thox·y·chlor (mə-thŏk′sĭ-klôr′, -klōr′) *n.* A white crystalline compound, Cl₃CCH(C₆H₄OCH₃)₂, used as an insecticide. [METH− + OXY− + (*tri*)*chlor*(*oethane*), a chemical compound used in pesticides.]

Me·thu·se·lah¹ (mə-thōo′zə-lə) A biblical patriarch said to have lived 969 years.

Me·thu·se·lah² (mə-thōo′zə-lə) *n.* An extremely old man.

meth·yl (mĕth′əl) *n.* The univalent hydrocarbon radical, CH₃−, derived from methane and occurring in many important organic compounds. See METHYLENE.] [Fr. *méthyle,* back-formation < *méthylène,* methylene. See METHYLENE.] —**me·thyl·ic** (mə-thĭl′ĭk) *adj.*

methyl acetate *n.* An organic compound, CH₃COOCH₃, used as a paint remover and solvent.

meth·yl·al (mĕth′ə-lăl′) *n.* A colorless flammable liquid, CH₃OCH₂OCH₃, used as an industrial solvent.

methyl alcohol *n.* See **methanol.**

meth·yl·a·mine (mĕth′ə-lə-mēn′, -lăm′ēn, mə-thĭl′ə-mēn′) *n.* A toxic flammable gas, CH₃NH₂, used in the manufacture of other organic chemicals.

meth·yl·ate (mĕth′ə-lāt′) *n.* An organic compound in which the hydrogen of the hydroxyl group of methyl alcohol is replaced by a metal. ❖ *tr.v.* **-at·ed, -at·ing, -ates 1.** To mix or combine with methyl alcohol. **2.** To combine with the methyl radical. —**meth′yl·a′tion** *n.* —**meth′yl·a′tor** *n.*

meth·yl·at·ed spirit (mĕth′ə-lā′tĭd) *n.* A denatured alcohol consisting of a mixture of ethyl alcohol and methyl alcohol. Often used in the plural.

meth·yl·ben·zene (mĕth′əl-bĕn′zēn, -bĕn-zēn′) *n.* See **toluene.**

methyl bromide *n.* A toxic gas, CH₃Br, used as a fumigant.

meth·yl·cel·lu·lose (mĕth′əl-sĕl′yə-lōs′, -lōz′) *n.* A powder prepared synthetically by the methylation of natural cellulose and used as a food additive and a bulk-forming laxative.

methyl chloride *n.* An explosive gas, CH₃Cl, used in organic synthesis and polymerization and as a refrigerant.

meth·yl·do·pa (mĕth′əl-dō′pə) *n.* A drug, C₁₀H₁₃NO₄, used in the treatment of high blood pressure.

meth·yl·ene (mĕth′ə-lēn′) *n.* A bivalent hydrocarbon radical, CH₂−, a component of unsaturated hydrocarbons. [Fr. *méthylène* : Gk. *methu,* wine; see **medhu-** in App. + Gk. *hūlē,* wood, substance.]

methylene blue *n.* A basic aniline dye, C₁₆H₁₈N₃SCl·3H₂O, that forms a deep blue solution when dissolved in water and is used as an antidote for cyanide poisoning and a bacteriological stain.

methyl ethyl ketone *n.* See **butanone.**

methyl methacrylate *n.* A volatile colorless liquid, CH₂C(CH₃)COOCH₃, used as a monomer in plastics.

meth·yl·phen·i·date (mĕth′əl-fĕn′ĭ-dāt′, -fē′nĭ-) *n.* A drug, C₁₄H₁₉NO₂, chemically related to amphetamine, that acts as a mild stimulant of the central nervous system and is used to treat narcoleptic adults and hyperkinetic children. [METHYL + PHEN(YL) + (PIPER)ID(INE) + (ACET)ATE.]

met·i·cal (mĕt′ĭ-käl′, mĕt′ĭ-käl′) *n., pl.* **met·i·cais** (-kīsh′) See table at **currency.** [Port. < Ar. *miṭqāl, mitqāl,* a unit of weight < *taqula,* to be heavy.]

me·tic·u·lous (mĭ-tĭk′yə-ləs) *adj.* **1.** Extremely careful and precise. **2.** Extremely or excessively concerned with details. [< Lat. *metīculōsus,* timid < *metus,* fear.] —**me·tic′u·los′i·ty** (-lŏs′ĭ-tē), **me·tic′u·lous·ness** *n.* —**me·tic′u·lous·ly** *adv.*

mé·tier (mĕ-tyā′, mā-) *n.* **1.** An occupation, trade, or profession. **2.** Work or activity for which a person is particularly suited; one's specialty. [Fr. < OFr. *mestier* < VLat. **misterium* < Lat. *ministerium.* See MINISTRY.]

mé·tis (mā-tēs′, -tē′) *n., pl.* **métis** (-tēs′, -tēz′) **1.** A person of mixed racial ancestry. **2.** often **Métis** A person of mixed Native American and French-Canadian ancestry. **3.** A crossbred animal. [Canadian Fr. < OFr. *metis,* of mixed race < LLat. *mīxtīcius,* mixed. See MESTIZO.]

Me·tis (mē′tĭs) *n.* A satellite of Jupiter. [After *Mētis,* Titaness who was a consort of Zeus (Jupiter) < Gk. *mētis,* wisdom. See **mē-¹** in App.]

Me·ton·ic cycle (mĭ-tŏn′ĭk) *n.* A period of 235 lunar months, or about 19 years, at the end of which the phases of the moon recur in the same order and on the same days as in the preceding cycle. [After *Meton* (fl. 5th cent. B.C.), Athenian astronomer.]

met·o·nym (mĕt′ə-nĭm′) *n.* A word used in metonymy.

me·ton·y·my (mə-tŏn′ə-mē) *n., pl.* **-mies** A figure of speech in which one word or phrase is substituted for another with which it is closely associated, as in the use of *the sword* for *military power.* [LLat. *metōnymia* < Gk. *metōnumiā* : *meta-,* meta- + *onuma,* name; see **nŏ-men-** in App.] —**met′o·nym′ic** (mĕt′ə-nĭm′ĭk), **met′o·nym′i·cal** *adj.* —**met′o·nym′i·cal·ly** *adv.*

met·o·pe (mĕt′ə-pē) *n. Architecture* Any of the spaces between two triglyphs on a Doric frieze. [Gk. *metopē* : *meta,* between; see META- + *opē,* opening; see **ok^w-** in App.]

me·top·ic (mə-tŏp′ĭk) *adj.* Of or relating to the forehead. [Gk. *metōpikos* < *metōpon,* forehead : *meta,* between; see META- + *ōp-,* eye; see **ok^w-** in App.]

metr- *pref.* Variant of **metro-.**

me·tral·gi·a (mĭ-trăl′jē-ə) *n.* Pain in the uterus.

me·tre¹ (mē′tər) *n. Chiefly British* Variant of **meter¹.**

me·tre² (mē′tər) *n. Chiefly British* Variant of **meter².**

met·ric¹ (mĕt′rĭk) *adj.* Of or relating to the meter or the metric system. [Fr. *métrique* < *mètre,* meter. See METER².]

met·ric² (mĕt′rĭk) *n.* **1.** A standard of measurement. **2.** *Mathematics* A geometric function that describes the distances between pairs of points in a space. ❖ *adj.* Of or relating to distance. [< Lat. *metricus,* of measurement. See METRICAL.]

met·ric³ (mĕt′rĭk) *n. Poetic* meter. [Gk. (*hē*) *metrikē* (*tekhnē*), (the art) of meter, fem. of *metrikos,* of measurement. See METRICAL.]

-metric *suff.* Of or relating to measurement: *volumetric.* [Lat. *metricus.* See METRICAL.]

met·ri·cal (mĕt′rĭ-kəl) *adj.* **1.** Of, relating to, or composed in poetic meter: *metrical verse.* **2.** Of or relating to measurement. [ME < Lat. *metricus* < Gk. *metrikos* < *metron,* measure, poetic meter. See **mē-¹** in App.] —**met′ri·cal·ly** *adv.*

met·ri·ca·tion (mĕt′rĭ-kā′shən) *n.* Conversion to the metric system of weights and measures; metrification.

met·rics (mĕt′rĭks) *n.* (*used with a sing. verb*) The use or study of metrical structures in verse; prosody.

-metrics *suff.* The application of statistics and mathematical analysis to a field of study: *econometrics.* [< METRIC².]

metric system *n.* A decimal system of units based on the meter as a unit length, the kilogram as a unit mass, and the second as a unit time. See table at **measurement.**

metric ton *n.* A unit of mass equal to 1,000 kilograms (2,205 pounds).

met·ri·fy¹ (mĕt′rə-fī′) *tr.v.* **-fied, -fy·ing, -fies** To put into or compose in poetic meter; versify. [Fr. *métrifier* < OFr. < Med.Lat. *metrificāre* : Lat. *metrum,* measure; see METER¹ + Lat. *-ficāre,* -fy.] —**met′ri·fi·ca′tion** (-fĭ-kā′shən) *n.*

met·ri·fy² (mĕt′rə-fī′) *tr. & intr.v.* **-fied, -fy·ing, -fies** To convert into or adopt the metric system.

me·tri·tis (mĭ-trī′tĭs) *n.* Inflammation of the uterus.

met·ro¹ (mĕt′rō) *n., pl.* **-ros** A subway system. [Fr. *métro,* short for (*chemin de fer*) *métropolitain,* metropolitan (railway) < LLat. *mētropolītānus.* See METROPOLITAN.]

met·ro² (mĕt′rō) *Informal adj.* Metropolitan: *metro Los Angeles.* ❖ *n., pl.* **-ros** A metropolitan area.

metro- or **metr-** *pref.* Uterus: *metritis.* [< Gk. *mētrā,* uterus < *mētēr, mētr-,* mother. See **māter-** in App.]

me·trol·o·gy (mĕ-trŏl′ə-jē) *n., pl.* **-gies 1.** The science that deals with measurement. **2.** A system of measurement. [Fr. *métrologie* < Gk. *metrologiā,* theory of ratios : *metron,* measure; see **mē-¹** in App. + *-logiā,* -logy.] —**met′ro·log′i·cal** (mĕt′rə-lŏj′ĭ-kəl) *adj.* —**me·trol′o·gist** *n.*

me·tro·ni·da·zole (mĕt′rō-nī′də-zōl′) *n.* A synthetic antimicrobial drug, C₆H₉N₃O₃, used in the treatment of vaginal trichomoniasis and intestinal amebiasis. [ME(THYL) + *-tron-* (alteration of NITRO−) + (IM)IDAZOLE.]

met·ro·nome (mĕt′rə-nōm′) *n. Music* A device that marks time with ticks or flashes at regular, adjustable intervals. [Gk. *metron,* measure; see **mē-¹** in App. + Gk. *nomos,* rule, division; see **nem-** in App.]

met·ro·nom·ic (mĕt′rə-nŏm′ĭk) also **met·ro·nom·i·cal** (-ĭ-kəl) *adj.* **1.** Of or relating to a metronome. **2.** Mechanically or unvaryingly regular in rhythm: *a metronomic rendition of the piece.* —**met′ro·nom′i·cal·ly** *adv.*

me·tro·nym·ic (mē′trə-nĭm′ĭk, mĕt′rə-) *adj. & n.* Variant of **matronymic.**

me·trop·o·lis (mĭ-trŏp′ə-lĭs) *n.* **1.** A major city, esp. the chief city of a country or region. **2.** A city or an urban area regarded as the center of a specific activity. **3.** *Ecclesiastical* The chief see of a metropolitan bishop. **4.** The mother city or country of an overseas colony, esp. in ancient Greece. [ME *metropol* < LLat. *mētropolis,* mother city < Gk. : *mētēr, mētr-,* mother; see **māter-** in App. + *polis,* city.]

met·ro·pol·i·tan (mĕt′rə-pŏl′ĭ-tən) *adj.* **1a.** Of, relating to, or characteristic of a major city. **b.** Of or constituting a large city or urbanized area, including adjacent suburbs and towns. **2.** Of, relating to, or constituting the home territory of an imperial or colonial state. **3.** Of or relating to an ecclesiastical metropolitan. ❖ *n.* **1.** A citizen of a metropolis, esp. one who is urbane. **2a.** In the Western Christian churches, a bishop who has provincial powers, with some authority over suffragan bishops. **b.** *Eastern Orthodox Church* A bishop who is head of an ecclesiastical province and ranks next below the patriarch. [ME, of a metropolitan bishop < LLat. *mētropolītānus,* metropolitan < Gk. *mētropolītēs,* citizen of a metropolis < *mētropolis,* mother city. See METROPOLIS.]

me·tror·rha·gi·a (mē′trə-rā′jē-ə, -jə) *n.* Bleeding from the uterus that is not associated with menstruation. —**me′tror·rha′gic** (-rā′jĭk) *adj.*

-metry *suff.* Process or science of measuring: *isometry.* [Gk. *-metriā* < *metron,* measure. See **mē-¹** in App.]

Met·ter·nich (mĕt′ər-nĭk′, -nĭкн), Prince **Klemens Wenzel**

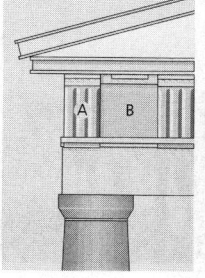

metope
entablature of a
Doric order building
A. triglyph
B. metope

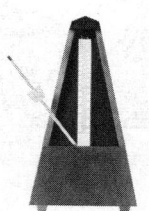

metronome

ă	pat	oi	boy
ā	pay	ou	out
âr	care	ŏŏ	took
ä	father	ōō	boot
ĕ	pet	ŭ	cut
ē	be	ûr	urge
ĭ	pit	th	thin
ī	pie	th	this
îr	pier	hw	which
ŏ	pot	zh	vision
ō	toe	ə	about,
ô	paw		item

Stress marks:
′ (primary);
′ (secondary), as in
lexicon (lĕk′sĭ-kŏn′)

Nepomuk Lothar von 1773–1859. Austrian politician who helped form the Quadruple Alliance to defeat Napoleon I.

met·tle (mĕt′l) *n.* **1.** Courage and fortitude; spirit. **2.** Inherent quality of character and temperament. **—idiom:** on (one's) mettle Prepared to accept a challenge and do one's best. [Variant of METAL.]

met·tle·some (mĕt′l-səm) *adj.* Full of mettle; plucky.

Metz (mĕts, mĕs) A city of NE France on the Moselle R. N of Nancy; ruled by Germany from 1871 to 1918. Pop. 114,232.

meu·nière (mən-yâr′) *adj.* Rolled in flour and fried in butter, usu. with lemon juice and chopped parsley to garnish. Used of fish. [Fr. < *(à la) meunière,* (in the style of) a miller's wife < OFr. *munoiere,* fem. of *mounier,* miller < LLat. *molīnārius* < *molīna,* mill. See MILL¹.]

Meuse (myōōz, mœz) also **Maas** (mäs) A river of W Europe flowing c. 901 km (560 mi) from NE France to the North Sea.

MeV *abbr.* **1.** mega-electron volt **2.** or **mev** million electron volts

mew¹ (myōō) *n.* **1.** A cage for hawks, esp. when molting. **2.** A secret place; a hideaway. **3.** mews *(used with a sing. or pl. verb)* **a.** A group of buildings originally containing private stables, often converted into residential apartments. **b.** A small street, alley, or courtyard on which such buildings stand. ❖ *v.* **mewed, mew·ing, mews** *—tr.* To confine in or as if in a cage. *—intr.* To molt. Used of a hawk. [ME *meue* < OFr. *mue* < *muer,* to molt < Lat. *mūtāre,* to change.]

mew² (myōō) *intr.v.* **mewed, mew·ing, mews** To make the high-pitched, crying sound of a cat; meow. ❖ *n.* The crying sound of a cat; a meow. [ME *meuen,* of imit. orig.]

mew³ (myōō) *n.* A seagull *(Larus canus)* of northern Eurasia and northwest North America. [ME *meue* < OE *mǣw, mēu.*]

mewl (myōōl) *intr.v.* **mewled, mewl·ing, mewls** To cry weakly; whimper. [Perh. of imit. orig.]

Mex. *abbr.* **1.** Mexican **2.** Mexico

Mex·i·cal·i (mĕk′sĭ-kăl′ē, mĕ′hē-kä′lē) A city of NW Mexico near the CA border E of Tijuana. Pop. 341,559.

Mex·i·can (mĕk′sĭ-kən) *n.* A native or inhabitant of Mexico. ❖ *adj.* Of or relating to Mexico or its people, language, or culture.

Mexican American *n.* A US citizen or resident of Mexican descent. **—Mex′i·can-A·mer′i·can** (mĕk′sĭ-kən-ə-mĕr′ĭ-kən) *adj.*

Mexican bean beetle *n.* A spotted ladybug *(Epilachna varivestis)* of the southern United States and Mexico that feeds on the leaves of the bean plant.

Mexican hairless *n.* Any of a breed of small dog of unknown origin, found in Mexico and having a smooth hairless body except for tufts on the head and tail.

Mexican Spanish *n.* The Spanish language as used in Mexico.

Mexican War *n.* A war (1846–48) between the United States and Mexico, resulting in the cession by Mexico of lands now constituting all or most of the states of California, Arizona, New Mexico, Nevada, Utah, and Colorado.

Mex·i·co (mĕk′sĭ-kō′) A country of S-central North America; inhabited in pre-Columbian times by the Aztecs and Maya among others and held by the Spanish from 1521 to 1821. Cap. Mexico City. Pop. 93,008,000.

Mexico, Gulf of An arm of the Atlantic Ocean bordering on E Mexico, the SE US, and Cuba.

Mexico City The cap. of Mexico, at the S end of the central plateau; founded on the site of an ancient Aztec capital destroyed by Cortés in 1521. Pop. 8,235,744.

Mey·er (mī′ər), Annie Florance Nathan 1867–1951. Amer. writer and a founder of Barnard College (1889).

Mey·er·beer (mī′ər-bîr′), Giacomo 1791–1864. German composer of French operas, notably *Les Huguenots* (1836).

mez·cal (mĕz-kăl′) *n.* Variant of **mescal.**

me·ze·re·on (mə-zîr′ē-ən) or **me·ze·re·um** (-əm) *n.* **1.** A poisonous Eurasian ornamental shrub *(Daphne mezereum)* having fragrant lilac-purple flowers and small scarlet fruit. **2.** The dried bark of this plant, formerly used externally as a vesicant and internally for arthritis. [ME *mizerion* < Med.Lat. *mezereon* < Ar. *māzaryūn,* of Pers. orig.]

me·zu·zah also **me·zu·za** (mə-zŏŏz′ə, -zŏŏ-zä′) *n., pl.* **-zu·zahs** also **-zu·zas** (-zŏŏz′əz) or **-zu·zot** (-zŏŏ-zôt′) A small copy of the Hebrew text of Deuteronomy 6:4–9 and 11:13–21 in a container marked with the word *Shaddai,* a name of God, and affixed by Jews to their door frames in conformity with Jewish law and as a sign of their faith. [Heb. *məzûzâ,* doorpost, mezuzah; akin to Mishnaic Heb. *zāz,* to move.]

mez·za·lu·na (mĕt′sə-lōō′nə) *n.* A curved steel blade, often with a vertical handle at each end, used to chop food. [Ital., crescent, mezzaluna : *mezza,* fem. of *mezzo,* half (< Lat. *medius*; see medhyo- in App.) + *luna,* moon (< Lat. *lūna*; see leuk- in App.).]

mez·za·nine (mĕz′ə-nēn′, mĕz′ə-nēn′) *n.* **1.** A partial story between two main stories of a building. **2.** The lowest balcony in a theater or the first few rows of that balcony. [Fr. < Ital. *mezzanino,* dim. of *mezzano,* middle < Lat. *mediānus,* in the middle. See MEDIAN.]

mez·za vo·ce (mĕt′sə vō′chä, mĕd′zə, mĕd′zə) *adv. & adj. Music* With moderate volume or in a subdued tone. [Ital. : *mezza,* half + *voce,* voice.]

mez·zo (mĕt′sō, mĕd′zō, mĕz′ō) *n., pl.* **-zos** A mezzo-soprano.

mezzo for·te (fôr′tä) *adv. & adj. Music* Moderately loud.

[Ital. : *mezzo,* half + *forte,* loud.]

mezzo pi·a·no (pē-ä′nō) *adv. & adj. Music* Moderately soft. [Ital. : *mezzo,* half + *piano,* soft.]

mez·zo-re·lie·vo (mĕt′sō-rĭ-lē′vō, -rēl-yā′vō, mĕd′zō-, mĕz′ō-) *n., pl.* **-vos** See half relief. [Ital. *mezzorilievo* : *mezzo,* half (< Lat. *medius*; see MEDIUM) + *rilievo,* relief; see RELIEVO.]

mez·zo-so·pran·o (mĕt′sō-sə-prăn′ō, -prä′nō, mĕd′zō-, mĕz′ō-) *n., pl.* **-nos** *Music* **1a.** A voice having a range between soprano and contralto. **b.** A vocal part calling for a mezzo-soprano range. **2.** A woman having such a voice. [Ital. : *mezzo,* half + *soprano,* soprano.]

mez·zo·tint (mĕt′sō-tĭnt′, mĕd′zō-, mĕz′ō-) *n.* **1.** A method of engraving a copper or steel plate by scraping and burnishing areas to produce effects of light and shadow. **2.** A print made from a plate engraved by mezzotint. [Alteration of Ital. *mezzotinta,* halftone : *mezza,* fem. of *mezzo,* half (< Lat. *medius*; see MEDIUM) + *tinta,* tint < fem. p. part. of *tingere,* to dye (< Lat.).]

mf *abbr.* **1.** mezzo forte **2.** also **mF** millifarad

MF *abbr.* **1.** medium frequency **2.** multiplying factor

MFA *abbr.* Master of Fine Arts

mg *abbr.* milligram

Mg The symbol for the element **magnesium.**

MG *abbr.* **1.** machine gun **2.** major general **3.** military government

mgmt. *abbr.* management

mgr. *abbr.* manager

Mgr. *abbr.* **1.** Monseigneur **2.** Monsignor

mgt. *abbr.* management

MGySgt *abbr.* master gunnery sergeant

mh also **mH** *abbr.* millihenry

MH *abbr.* **1.** Medal of Honor **2.** mental health

MHC *abbr.* major histocompatibility complex

MHD *abbr.* magnetohydrodynamics

mho (mō) *n., pl.* **mhos** A siemens. [Backward spelling of OHM.]

MHW *abbr.* mean high water

MHz *abbr.* megahertz

mi (mē) *n. Music* The third tone of the diatonic scale in solfeggio. [ME < Med.Lat. See GAMUT.]

Mi *abbr. Bible* Micah

MI *abbr.* **1.** Michigan **2.** military intelligence **3.** myocardial infarction

mi. *abbr.* **1.** or **mi** mile **2.** mill (currency)

MIA (ĕm′ī-ā′) *n.* A member of the armed services reported missing after a combat mission whose status is unknown. [*m(issing) i(n) a(ction).*]

Mi·am·i¹ (mī-ăm′ē, -ăm′ə) *n., pl.* **Miami** or **-is** **1.** A member of a Native American people originally of the Green Bay area of Wisconsin, with present-day populations inhabiting parts of northern Indiana and northeast Oklahoma. **2.** The variety of Illinois spoken by the Miami.

Mi·am·i² (mī-ăm′ē, -ăm′ə) A city of SE FL on Biscayne Bay S of Fort Lauderdale. Pop. 362,470. **—Mi·am′i·an** *adj. & n.*

Miami Beach A city of SE FL across from Miami on an island between Biscayne Bay and the Atlantic Ocean. Pop. 87,933.

Miami River or **Great Miami River** A river rising in W OH and flowing c. 257 km (160 mi) to the Ohio R. at the IN border.

Miao (myou′) also **Me·o** (mē-ou′) *n., pl.* **Miao** or **Miaos** also **Meo** or **Me·os** See **Hmong.**

Miao-Yao (myou′you′) *n.* A small group of languages of uncertain affinity, including Hmong and Yao, spoken in southern China, northern Laos, Thailand, and Vietnam.

mi·as·ma (mī-ăz′mə, mē-) *n., pl.* **-mas** or **-ma·ta** (-mə-tə) **1.** A noxious atmosphere or influence. **2a.** A poisonous atmosphere once thought to rise from swamps and putrid matter and cause disease. **b.** A vaporous atmosphere or emanation. [Gk., pollution, stain < *miainein,* to pollute.] **—mi·as′mal, mi·as·mat′ic** (mī′əz-măt′ĭk), **mi·as′mic** (-mĭk) *adj.*

mic (mīk) *n. Informal* Variant of **mike.**

Mic. *abbr. Bible* Micah

mi·ca (mī′kə) *n.* Any of a group of chemically and physically related aluminum silicate minerals, characteristically splitting into flexible sheets used in insulation and electrical equipment. [Lat. *mīca,* grain (sense perh. influenced by *micāre,* to flash).] **—mi·ca′ceous** (-kā′shəs) *adj.*

Mi·cah¹ (mī′kə) also **Mi·che·as** (mī-kē′əs) A Hebrew prophet of the 8th cent. B.C. [Heb. *Mîkâ,* short for *Mîkâ'ēl,* Michael. See MICHAEL.]

Mi·cah² (mī′kə) also **Mi·che·as** (mī-kē′əs) *n.* See table at **Bible.** [After MICAH¹.]

Mic·co·su·kee (mĭk′ə-sōō′kē) *n.* Variant of **Mikasuki.**

mice (mīs) *n.* Plural of **mouse.**

mi·celle (mī-sĕl′) *n.* **1.** A submicroscopic aggregation of molecules, as a droplet in a colloidal system. **2.** A coherent strand or structure in fibers. **3.** A submicroscopic structural unit of protoplasm, composed of a cluster of molecules. [NLat. *mīcella* < Lat. *mīca,* grain.] **—mi·cel′lar** (-sĕl′ər) *adj.*

Mich. *abbr.* Michigan

Mi·chael (mī′kəl) *n.* The guardian archangel of the Jews in the Hebrew Scriptures. [Heb. *mîkā'ēl,* who (is) like God? : *mî,* who + *kā,* like + *'ēl,* God.]

Mich·ael·mas (mĭk′əl-məs) *n.* A Christian feast observed on September 29 in honor of the archangel Michael. [ME *mychel-*

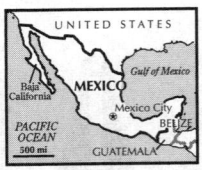
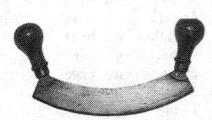

messe < OE *(Sanct) Michaeles mæsse,* (Saint) Michael's mass.]

Michaelmas daisy *n.* Any of several North American species of asters that have leafy stems and flower in the fall.

Mi·che·as (mī-kē′əs) *n. Bible* Variant of **Micah.**

Mi·chel·an·ge·lo Buo·nar·ro·ti (mī′kəl-ăn′jə-lō′ bwōn′ə-rô′tē, mĭk′-, mē′kĕl-än′jĕ-lō bwōn′är-rō′tē) 1475–1564. Italian sculptor, painter, architect, and poet whose works include the marble sculpture *David* (1501), the paintings on the ceiling of the Sistine Chapel (1508–12), and the plans for Saint Peter's Church in Rome.

Mi·che·let (mēsh-ə-lā′, mēsh-lā′), **Jules** 1798–1874. French historian noted for his *Histoire de France* (1833–67).

Mi·chel·son (mī′kəl-sən), **Albert Abraham** 1852–1931. German-born Amer. physicist who won a 1907 Nobel Prize.

Mich·i·gan (mĭsh′ĭ-gən) A state of the N-central US; admitted as the 26th state in 1837. Cap. Lansing. Pop. 9,938,444. —**Mich′i·gan′der** (-găn′dər) *adj. & n.*

Michigan, Lake The third largest of the Great Lakes, between WI and MI, linked with the Atlantic Ocean by the St. Lawrence Seaway.

mick (mĭk) *n. Offensive Slang* Used as a disparaging term for a person of Irish birth or descent. [Prob. < the name *Mick,* nickname for *Michael.*]

mick·ey (mĭk′ē) *n., pl.* **-eys 1.** *Informal* A roasted potato. **2.** *Canadian Slang* A small bottle of liquor, shaped to fit in a pocket. **3.** also **Mickey** *Slang* A Mickey Finn. —*idiom:* **take the mickey out of** *Chiefly British* To tease or mock (someone). [Perh. < MICK.]

Mickey Finn *n. Slang* An alcoholic beverage surreptitiously altered to be incapacitating. [Prob. after a notorious Chicago bar shut down in 1903, allegedly because its customers were served spiked drinks and then robbed.]

Mickey Mouse *adj. Slang* **1a.** Unimportant; trivial. **b.** Irritatingly petty. **2.** Intellectually unchallenging; simple. [After *Mickey Mouse,* created by Walt Disney.]

mick·le (mĭk′əl) *Scots adj.* Great. ❖ *adv.* Greatly. [ME *mikel* < OE *micel* and < ON *mikill;* see **meg-** in App.]

Mic·mac or **Mi'k·maq** (mĭk′măk′) *n., pl.* **Micmac** or **-macs** or **Mi'kmaq** or **-maqs 1.** A member of a Native American people inhabiting Nova Scotia, New Brunswick, Prince Edward Island, and the Gaspé Peninsula of Quebec. **2.** The Algonquian language of the Micmac.

mi·con·a·zole (mĭ-kŏn′ə-zōl′) *n.* An antifungal used topically or parenterally. [Alteration of MYCO– + (BE)N(ZIMID)AZOLE.]

MICR *abbr.* magnetic ink character recognition

mi·cra (mī′krə) *n.* A plural of **micron.**

mi·cro (mī′krō) *adj.* **1.** Very small or microscopic. **2.** Basic or small-scale: *the economy at the micro level.* ❖ *n., pl.* **-cros 1.** A microcomputer. **2.** A microprocessor. [< MICRO–.]

micro– or **micr–** *pref.* **1a.** Small: *microcircuit.* **b.** Abnormally small: *microcephaly.* **c.** Requiring or involving microscopy: *microsurgery.* **2.** One millionth (10⁻⁶): *microampere.* [Gk. *mīkro–* < *mīkros,* small.]

mi·cro·am·pere (mī′krō-ăm′pîr) *n.* A unit of electric current equal to one millionth of an ampere.

mi·cro·a·nal·y·sis (mī′krō-ə-năl′ĭ-sĭs) *n., pl.* **-ses** (-sēz′) The chemical identification and analysis of extremely small quantities of matter. —**mi′cro·an′a·lyst** (-ăn′ə-lĭst) *n.* —**mi′cro·an′a·lyt′ic** (-ăn′ə-lĭt′ĭk), **mi′cro·an′a·lyt′i·cal** *adj.*

mi·cro·a·nat·o·my (mī′krō-ə-năt′ə-mē) *n.* Histology. —**mi′cro·an′a·tom′i·cal** (-ən′ə-tŏm′ĭ-kəl) *adj.*

mi·cro·bal·ance (mī′krō-băl′əns) *n.* A balance designed to weigh very small loads, up to 0.1 gram.

mic·ro·bar·o·graph (mī′krō-băr′ə-grăf′) *n.* An instrument used to record very small changes in atmospheric pressure.

mi·crobe (mī′krōb′) *n.* A minute life form; a microorganism, esp. a bacterium that causes disease. Not in technical use. [Fr. : Gk. *mīkro–,* micro- + Gk. *bios,* life; see **g***ʷ***eiə-** in App.] —**mi·cro′bi·al** (mī-krō′bē-al), **mi·cro′bic** (-krō′bĭk) *adj.*

mi·cro·bi·ol·o·gy (mī′krō-bī-ŏl′ə-jē) *n.* The branch of biology that deals with microorganisms and their effects on other living organisms. —**mi′cro·bi′o·log′i·cal** (-bī′ə-lŏj′ĭ-kəl), **mi′cro·bi′o·log′ic** *adj.* —**mi′cro·bi·ol′o·gist** *n.*

mi·cro·brew (mī′krō-brōō′) *n.* A beer or ale brewed in a microbrewery.

mi·cro·brew·er·y (mī′krō-brōō′ə-rē, -brōōr′ē) *n., pl.* **-ies** A small, usu. local brewery that often sells its products on the premises.

mi·cro·burst (mī′krō-bûrst′) *n.* A sudden violent downdraft of air over a small area that is hazardous to airplanes during landing or takeoff.

mi·cro·bus (mī′krō-bŭs′) *n., pl.* **-bus·es** or **-bus·ses** A station wagon in the shape of a small bus.

mi·cro·cap (mī′krō-kăp′) *adj.* **1.** Or or relating to companies whose retained earnings are very small and whose outstanding shares of common stock have a very small market value. **2.** Of or relating to mutual funds that invest in the stock of such companies. [MICRO– + CAP³.]

mi·cro·cap·sule (mī′krō-kăp′səl, -sōōl) *n.* A small, sometimes microscopic capsule designed to release its contents when broken by pressure, dissolved, or melted.

mi·cro·ceph·a·ly (mī′krō-sĕf′ə-lē) *n., pl.* **-lies** Abnormal smallness of the head. —**mi′cro·ce·phal′ic** (-sə-făl′ĭk) *adj. & n.* —**mi′cro·ceph′a·lous** (-sĕf′ə-ləs) *adj.*

mi·cro·chem·is·try (mī′krō-kĕm′ĭ-strē) *n.* Chemistry that deals with minute quantities of materials, frequently less than one milligram in mass or one milliliter in volume. —**mi′cro·chem′i·cal** (-ĭ-kəl) *adj.* —**mi′cro·chem′ist** *n.*

mi·cro·chip (mī′krə-chĭp′) *n.* An integrated circuit.

mi·cro·cir·cuit (mī′krō-sûr′kĭt) *n.* An electric circuit of miniaturized components. —**mi′cro·cir′cuit·ry** (-kĭ-trē) *n.*

mi·cro·cli·mate (mī′krō-klī′mĭt) *n.* The climate of a small specific place within an area. —**mi′cro·cli·mat′ic** (-măt′ĭk) *adj.* —**mi′cro·cli·ma·to·log′ic** (-mə-tə-lŏj′ĭk), **mi′cro·cli·ma·to·log′i·cal** *adj.* —**mi′cro·cli′ma·tol′o·gy** (-tŏl′ə-jē) *n.*

mi·cro·cline (mī′krō-klīn′) *n.* A mineral of the feldspar group, chiefly KAlSi₃O₈, used in making glass and porcelain. [MICRO– (because its cleavage angle is not exactly equal to 90°) + Gk. *klīnein,* to lean; see CLINE.]

mi·cro·coc·cus (mī′krō-kŏk′əs) *n., pl.* **-coc·ci** (-kŏk′sī′, -kŏk′ī′) A spherical aerobic gram-positive bacterium of the genus *Micrococcus,* usu. occurring in irregular clusters. —**mi′cro·coc′cal** (-kŏk′əl) *adj.*

mi·cro·com·put·er (mī′krō-kəm-pyōō′tər) *n.* A personal computer.

mi·cro·cop·y (mī′krō-kŏp′ē) *n., pl.* **-ies** A greatly reduced photographic copy, usu. reproduced by projection.

mi·cro·cosm (mī′krə-kŏz′əm) *n.* A small representative system having analogies to a larger system in constitution, configuration, or development. [ME *microcosme,* man as a little world < OFr. < LLat. *mīcrocosmus* < Gk. *mīkros kosmos* : *mīkros,* small + *kosmos,* world, order.] —**mi′cro·cos′mic** (-kŏz′mĭk), **mi′cro·cos′mi·cal** (-mĭ-kəl) *adj.* —**mi′cro·cos′mi·cal·ly** *adv.*

microcosmic salt *n.* A white crystalline salt of phosphorus, HNaNH₄PO₄·4H₂O, used in blowpipe analysis of minerals to test for the presence of certain metals.

mi·cro·cred·it (mī′krō-krĕd′ĭt) *n.* The business or policy of making microloans to impoverished entrepreneurs.

mi·cro·crys·tal·line (mī′krō-krĭs′tə-lĭn) *adj.* Having a crystalline structure visible only under a microscope. —**mi′cro·crys′tal** *n.*

mi·cro·cyte (mī′krə-sīt′) *n.* An abnormally small red blood cell that may occur in certain forms of anemia. [MICRO– + (ERYTHRO)CYTE.] —**mi′cro·cyt′ic** (-sĭt′ĭk) *adj.*

mi·cro·dot (mī′krə-dŏt′) *n.* A copy or photograph that has been reduced to an extremely small size.

mi·cro·ec·o·nom·ics (mī′krō-ĕk′ə-nŏm′ĭks, -ēk′ə-) *n.* (*used with a sing. verb*) The study of the operations of the components of a national economy, such as individual firms, households, and consumers. —**mi′cro·ec′o·nom′ic** *adj.*

mi·cro·e·lec·tron·ics (mī′krō-ĭ-lĕk-trŏn′ĭks) *n.* (*used with a sing. verb*) The branch of electronics that deals with miniature components. —**mi′cro·e·lec·tron′ic** *adj.*

mi·cro·en·cap·su·late (mī′krō-ĕn-kăp′sə-lāt′) *tr.v.* **-lat·ed, -lat·ing, -lates** To enclose in microcapsules.

mi·cro·en·vi·ron·ment (mī′krō-ĕn-vī′rən-mənt, -vī′ərn-) *n.* The environment of a very small specific area.

mi·cro·ev·o·lu·tion (mī′krō-ĕv′ə-lōō′shən, -ē′və-) *n.* Evolution resulting from a succession of relatively small genetic variations that often cause the formation of new subspecies. —**mi′cro·ev′o·lu′tion·ar′y** *adj.*

mi·cro·far·ad (mī′krō-făr′əd, -ăd) *n.* A unit of capacitance equal to one millionth (10⁻⁶) of a farad.

mi·cro·fi·ber (mī′krō-fī′bər) *n.* An extremely fine synthetic fiber woven into textiles to make them more washable, breathable, and water repellant than natural-fiber cloth.

mi·cro·fiche (mī′krō-fēsh′) *n., pl.* **microfiche** or **-fich·es** A card or sheet of microfilm capable of preserving printed text in reduced form. [Fr. : Gk. *mīkro–,* micro– + Fr. *fiche,* peg, slip of paper, index card (< OFr., peg < *fichier,* to drive in, fasten < VLat. **fīgicāre* < Lat. *fīgere.*)]

mi·cro·fil·a·ment (mī′krō-fĭl′ə-mənt) *n.* Any of the minute fibers throughout the cytoplasm of a cell, functioning primarily in maintaining its structural integrity.

mi·cro·fi·lar·i·a (mī′krō-fə-lâr′ē-ə) *n., pl.* **-i·ae** (-ē-ē′) The minute larval form of a filarial worm.

mi·cro·film (mī′krə-fĭlm′) *n.* **1.** A film on which printed materials are photographed at greatly reduced size for ease of storage. **2.** A reproduction on this kind of film. ❖ *tr.v.* **-filmed, -film·ing, -films** To reproduce (documents, for example) on microfilm.

mi·cro·form (mī′krə-fôrm′) *n.* An arrangement of images reduced in size, as on microfilm or microfiche.

mi·cro·fos·sil (mī′krō-fŏs′əl) *n.* A microscopic fossil, as of a pollen grain or unicellular organism.

mi·cro·gam·ete (mī′krō-găm′ēt′, -gə-mēt′) *n.* The smaller of a pair of conjugating gametes, usu. the male, in an organism that reproduces by heterogamy.

mi·cro·gli·a (mī′krō-glē′ə, -glī′ə) *n.* (*used with a pl. verb*) Neuroglia consisting of phagocytic cells active in immune reactions of the central nervous system.

mi·cro·gram (mī′krō-grăm′) *n.* A unit of mass that is equal to one millionth (10^{-6}) of a gram.

mi·cro·graph (mī′krə-grăf′) *n.* **1.** A drawing or photograph of an object as viewed through a microscope. **2.** An instrument used to make tiny writing or engraving. —**mi′cro·graph′ic** *adj.* —**mi·crog′ra·phy** (mī-krŏg′rə-fē)

mi·cro·grav·i·ty (mī′krō-grăv′ĭ-tē) *n.* **1.** A condition in which the effects of gravity are greatly reduced, as in free fall through the atmosphere. **2.** A minute shift in gravity that can occur through geologic factors in a region, such as the movement of the earth's crust along fault lines.

mi·cro·hab·i·tat (mī′krō-hăb′ĭ-tăt′) *n.* A very small specialized habitat, such as a clump of grass.

mi·cro·in·jec·tion (mī′krō-ĭn-jĕk′shən) *n.* Injection of minute amounts of a substance into a microscopic structure.

mi·cro·in·struc·tion (mī′krō-ĭn-strŭk′shən) *n.* A small specific instruction, used in microprogramming.

mi·cro·lend·ing (mī′krō-lĕn′dĭng) *n.* See **microcredit.**

mi·cro·lith (mī′krō-lĭth′) *n. Archaeology* A very small blade made of flaked stone and used as a tool, esp. in the European Mesolithic Period. —**mi′cro·lith′ic** (-lĭth′ĭk) *adj.*

mi·cro·loan (mī′krō-lōn′) *n.* A very small, often short-term loan made to an impoverished entrepreneur, as in an underdeveloped country.

mi·cro·man·age (mī′krō-măn′ĭj) *tr.v.* **-aged, -ag·ing, -ag·es** To direct or control in a detailed, often meddlesome manner.

mi·cro·mere (mī′krō-mîr′) *n.* A very small blastomere.

mi·cro·me·te·or·ite (mī′krō-mē′tē-ə-rīt′) *n.* A tiny particle of meteoric dust.

mi·cro·me·te·or·oid (mī′krō-mē′tē-ə-roid′) *n.* A very small meteoroid, often the size of a particle of dust.

mi·cro·me·te·or·ol·o·gy (mī′krō-mē′tē-ə-rŏl′ə-jē) *n.* The study of weather conditions on a small scale, such as the area immediately around a smokestack or mountain. —**mi′cro·me′te·or′o·log′i·cal** (-ôr′ə-lŏj′ĭ-kəl, -ər-ə-) *adj.* —**mi′cro·me′te·or·ol′o·gist** *n.*

mi·crom·e·ter¹ (mī-krŏm′ĭ-tər) *n.* A device for measuring very small distances, objects, or angles, esp. one based on the rotation of a finely threaded screw.

mi·cro·me·ter² (mī′krō-mē′tər) *n.* A unit of length equal to one thousandth (10^{-3}) of a millimeter or one millionth (10^{-6}) of a meter.

mi·crom·e·try (mī-krŏm′ĭ-trē) *n.* Measurement of minute objects with a micrometer. —**mi′cro·met′ric** (mī′krō-mĕt′rĭk), **mi′cro·met′ri·cal** (-rĭ-kəl) *adj.*

mi·cro·min·i·a·tur·ize (mī′krō-mĭn′ē-chə-rīz′, -mĭn′ə-) *tr.v.* **-ized, -iz·ing, -iz·es** To construct (devices) on an extremely small scale. Used esp. of electronic circuitry.

mi·cron (mī′krŏn) *n., pl.* **-crons** or **-cra** (-krə) A micrometer (unit of length). No longer in technical use. [< Gk. *mīkron,* neut. of *mīkros,* small.]

Mi·cro·ne·si·a (mī′krō-nē′zhə, -shə) A division of Oceania in the W Pacific Ocean E of the Philippines and N of the equator.

Micronesia, Federated States of A group of associated islands in the Caroline Is. of the western Pacific Ocean; self-governing under a compact of free association with the US. Cap. Palikir. Pop. 104,937.

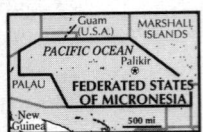

Micronesia

Mi·cro·ne·sian (mī′krə-nē′zhən, -shən) *adj.* Of or relating to Micronesia or its peoples, languages, or cultures. ❖ *n.* **1.** A member of any of the peoples inhabiting Micronesia. **2.** A subfamily of the Austronesian language family that includes the languages of Micronesia.

mi·cron·ize (mī′krə-nīz′) *tr.v.* **-ized, -iz·ing, -iz·es** To reduce to particles that are only a few micrometers in diameter.

mi·cro·nu·cle·us (mī′krō-nōō′klē-əs, -nyōō′-) *n., pl.* **-cle·i** (-klē-ī′) or **-cle·us·es** The smaller of two nuclei in ciliate protozoans that contains genetic material and functions in reproduction. —**mi′cro·nu′cle·ar** *adj.*

mi·cro·nu·tri·ent (mī′krō-nōō′trē-ənt, -nyōō′-) *n.* A substance, such as a vitamin or mineral, that is essential in minute amounts for the proper growth of a living organism.

mi·cro·or·gan·ism (mī′krō-ôr′gə-nĭz′əm) *n.* A microscopic or submicroscopic organism, esp. a bacterium or protozoan.

mi·cro·pa·le·on·tol·o·gy (mī′krō-pā′lē-ŏn-tŏl′ə-jē, -ən-) *n.* The branch of paleontology that deals with microfossils. —**mi′cro·pa′le·on′to·log′ic** (-ŏn′tl-ŏj′ĭk), **mi′cro·pa′le·on′to·log′i·cal** *adj.* —**mi′cro·pa′le·on·tol′o·gist** *n.*

mi·cro·phage (mī′krə-fāj′) *n.* A small phagocyte.

mi·cro·phone (mī′krə-fōn′) *n.* An instrument that converts sound waves into an electric current, usu. fed into an amplifier, recorder, or transmitter. —**mi′cro·phon′ic** (-fŏn′ĭk) *adj.*

mi·cro·pho·to·graph (mī′krō-fō′tə-grăf′) *n.* **1.** A photograph requiring magnification for viewing. **2.** A photograph on microfilm. **3.** See **photomicrograph.** —**mi′cro·pho′to·graph′ic** *adj.* —**mi′cro·pho·tog′ra·pher** (-fə-tŏg′rə-fər) *n.* —**mi′cro·pho·tog′ra·phy** (-rə-fē) *n.*

mi·cro·phyte (mī′krə-fīt′) *n.* A plant of microscopic size.

mi·cro·pi·pette (mī′krō-pī-pĕt′) *n.* **1.** A very small pipette used in microinjection. **2.** A pipette used to measure very small volumes of liquids.

mi·cro·print (mī′krə-prĭnt′) *n.* The printed or positive reproduction of a microphotograph.

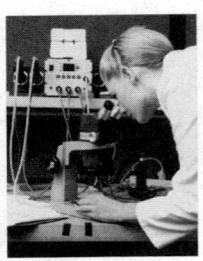

microscope

mi·cro·proc·es·sor (mī′krō-prŏs′ĕs-ər) *n.* An integrated circuit that contains the entire central processing unit of a computer on a single chip.

mi·cro·pro·gram·ming (mī′krō-prō′grăm-ĭng, -grə-mĭng) *n.* A method of operating the control unit of a computer by breaking down the control instructions into a sequence of small steps.

mi·cro·pyle (mī′krə-pīl′) *n.* **1.** *Botany* A minute opening in the ovule of a seed plant through which the pollen tube usu. enters. **2.** *Zoology* A pore in the membrane covering the ovum of some animals through which a spermatozoon can enter. [MICRO- + Gk. *pulē,* gate.] —**mi′cro·py′lar** *adj.*

mi·cro·ra·di·o·graph (mī′krō-rā′dē-ō-grăf′) *n.* An enlarged x-ray photograph, used to study small details. —**mi′cro·ra′di·og′ra·phy** (-ŏg′rə-fē) *n.*

mi·cro·read·er (mī′krō-rē′dər) *n.* A device for reading materials in microform, such as microfilm and microfiche.

mi·cro·scope (mī′krə-skōp′) *n.* **1.** An optical instrument that uses a lens or a combination of lenses to produce magnified images of objects too small to be seen by the unaided eye. **2.** An instrument that uses electronic or other processes to magnify objects.

mi·cro·scop·ic (mī′krə-skŏp′ĭk) also **mi·cro·scop·i·cal** (-ĭ-kəl) *adj.* **1a.** Too small to be seen by the unaided eye but large enough to be studied under a microscope. **b.** Of, relating to, or concerned with a microscope. **2.** Exceedingly small; minute. **3.** Characterized by or done with extreme attention to detail. —**mi′cro·scop′i·cal·ly** *adv.*

Mi·cro·sco·pi·um (mī′krə-skō′pē-əm) *n.* A constellation in the Southern Hemisphere. [NLat. *Microscopium,* microscope, Microscopium : MICRO- + -*scopium,* -scope.]

mi·cros·co·py (mī-krŏs′kə-pē) *n., pl.* **-pies 1a.** The study of microscopes. **b.** The use of microscopes. **2.** Investigation employing a microscope. —**mi·cros′co·pist** *n.*

mi·cro·sec·ond (mī′krō-sĕk′ənd) *n.* One millionth (10^{-6}) of a second.

mi·cro·seism (mī′krə-sī′zəm) *n.* A faint earth tremor caused by natural phenomena, such as winds and strong ocean waves. —**mi′cro·seis′mic** (-sīz′mĭk, -sīs′-) *adj.*

mi·cro·sleep (mī′krə-slēp′) *n.* A period of sleep lasting for a few seconds, usu. seen in people with narcolepsy.

mi·cro·some (mī′krə-sōm′) *n.* A small particle in the cytoplasm of a cell, typically consisting of fragmented endoplasmic reticulum to which ribosomes are attached. —**mi′cro·so′mal** (-sō′məl), **mi′cro·so′mic** (-sō′mĭk) *adj.*

mi·cro·spo·ran·gi·um (mī′krō-spə-răn′jē-əm) *n., pl.* **-gi·a** (-jē-ə) A structure in which microspores are formed. —**mi′cro·spo·ran′gi·ate** (-jē-ĭt) *adj.*

mi·cro·spore (mī′krə-spôr′, -spōr′) *n. Botany* The smaller of two types of spores, giving rise to a male gametophyte. —**mi′cro·spo′ric, mi′cro·spo′rous** (mī′krə-spôr′əs, -spōr′-, mī-krŏs′pər-əs) *adj.*

mi·cro·spo·ro·cyte (mī′krə-spôr′ə-sīt′, -spōr′-) *n.* A cell that undergoes meiosis to produce four microspores.

mi·cro·spo·ro·phyll (mī′krə-spôr′ə-fĭl′, -spōr′-) *n.* A leaflike structure that bears microsporangia.

mi·cro·state (mī′krə-stāt′) *n.* An independent country that is very small in area and population.

mi·cro·struc·ture (mī′krō-strŭk′chər) *n.* The structure of an organism or object as revealed through microscopy.

mi·cro·sur·ger·y (mī′krō-sûr′jə-rē) *n., pl.* **-ies** Surgery on minute body structures or cells performed with the aid of a microscope and other specialized instruments. —**mi′cro·sur′gi·cal** (-jĭ-kəl) *adj.*

mi·cro·tome (mī′krə-tōm′) *n.* An instrument used to cut a specimen into thin sections for microscopic examination.

mi·crot·o·my (mī-krŏt′ə-mē) *n., pl.* **-mies** The preparation of specimens with a microtome. —**mi′cro·tom′ic** (mī′krə-tŏm′ĭk) *adj.*

mi·cro·tone (mī′krə-tōn′) *n. Music* An interval smaller than a semitone. —**mi′cro·ton′al** (-tō′nəl) *adj.* —**mi′cro·to·nal′i·ty** (-tō-năl′ĭ-tē) *n.* —**mi′cro·ton′al·ly** *adv.*

mi·cro·tu·bule (mī′krō-tōō′byōōl, -tyōō-) *n.* Any of the proteinaceous cylindrical structures found throughout the cytoplasm of eukaryotic cells, providing structural support and assisting in cellular locomotion and transport.

mi·cro·vil·lus (mī′krō-vĭl′əs) *n., pl.* **-vil·li** (-vĭl′ī′) Any of the minute hairlike structures projecting from the surface of certain types of epithelial cells, esp. of the small intestine.

mi·cro·volt (mī′krə-vōlt′) *n.* A unit of electric potential equal to one millionth (10^{-6}) of a volt.

mi·cro·watt (mī′krō-wŏt′) *n.* A unit of power equal to one millionth (10^{-6}) of a watt.

mi·cro·wave (mī′krə-wāv′, -krō-) *n.* **1.** An electromagnetic wave having a wavelength of 0.3 to 30 centimeters, intermediate between infrared and short-wave radio wavelengths. **2.** *Informal* A microwave oven. ❖ *tr.v.* **-waved, -wav·ing, -waves** To cook or heat (food) in a microwave oven. —**mi′cro·wav′a·ble, mi′cro·wave′a·ble** *adj.*

microwave oven *n.* An oven using microwaves as energy for cooking.

mic·tu·rate (mĭk′chə-rāt′, mĭk′tə-) *intr.v.* **-rat·ed, -rat·ing,**

-rates To urinate. [< Lat. *micturīre*, to want to urinate, desiderative of *meiere*, to urinate.] —**mic′tu·ri′tion** (-rĭsh′ən) *n.*

mid¹ (mĭd) *adj.* **1.** Middle; central. **2.** Being the part in the middle or center: *in the mid Pacific.* **3.** *Linguistics* Of, relating to, or being a vowel produced with the tongue in a position approximately intermediate between high and low, as the vowel in *but.* [ME < OE *midd.* See **medhyo-** in App.]

mid² (mĭd) *prep.* Surrounded by; amid. [Alteration of AMID.]

mid. *abbr.* middle

mid– *pref.* Middle: *midsummer.* [ME < *mid*, middle. See MID¹.]

> **USAGE NOTE** In forming compounds, *mid–* is normally joined to the following word or element without a space or hyphen: *midpoint.* However, if the second element begins with a capital letter, it is always separated with a hyphen: *mid-May.* It is always acceptable to use a hyphen to prevent possible confusion with another form, as to distinguish *mid-den* (the middle of a den) from the word *midden.* Note that the adjective *mid¹* is a separate word. It can take a hyphen, however, as can any adjective, when joined to another word to form a modifier: *in the mid Pacific* but *a mid-Pacific island.*

mid·air (mĭd′âr′) *n.* **1.** A point or region in the air. **2.** *Informal* A collision of two or more airborne aircraft.

Mi·das (mī′dəs) *n.* The fabled king of Phrygia to whom Dionysus gave the power of turning to gold all that he touched. [Lat. *Midās* < Gk.]

Midas touch *n.* The ability to make, manage, and keep huge amounts of money. [After MIDAS.]

mid·brain (mĭd′brān′) *n.* The portion of the vertebrate brain that develops from the middle section of the embryonic brain.

mid·cap (mĭd′kăp′) *adj.* **1.** Or or relating to corporations whose retained earnings and outstanding shares of common stock have a value between those of small cap companies and large cap corporations. **2.** Of or relating to mutual funds that invest in the stock of such corporations. [MID– + CAP³.]

mid·day (mĭd′dā′) *n.* The middle of the day; noon.

mid·den (mĭd′n) *n.* **1.** A dunghill or refuse heap. **2.** A mound or deposit containing shells, animal bones, and other refuse that indicates the site of a human settlement. [ME *midding*, of Scand. orig.]

mid·dle (mĭd′l) *adj.* **1.** Equally distant from extremes or limits; central. **2.** Being at neither one extreme nor the other; intermediate. **3a.** Intervening between an earlier and a later period of time; being an intermediate part of a sequence or series. **b. Middle** *Geology* Of or relating to a division of geologic time between an earlier and a later division. **4. Middle** Of or relating to a stage in the development of a language or literature between earlier and later stages. **5.** *Grammar* Of a verb form or voice in which the subject both performs and is affected by the action specified. ❖ *n.* **1.** An area or point equidistant between extremes; a center. **2.** Something intermediate between extremes; a mean. **3.** The interior portion. **4.** The middle part of the human body; the waist. **5.** *Logic* A middle term. **6.** *Grammar* **a.** The middle voice. **b.** A verb form in the middle voice. ❖ *tr.v.* **-dled, -dling, -dles** **1.** To place in the middle. **2.** *Nautical* To fold in the middle: *middle the line.* [ME *middel* < OE. See **medhyo-** in App.]

middle age *n.* The time of human life between youth and old age, usu. reckoned as the years between 40 and 60.

mid·dle-aged (mĭd′l-ājd′) *adj.* Of or relating to middle age.

Middle Ages *pl.n.* The period in European history between antiquity and the Renaissance, often dated from A.D. 476 to 1453.

Middle America¹ A region of S North America comprising Mexico, Central America, and sometimes the West Indies. —**Middle American** *adj. & n.*

Middle America² *n.* **1.** That part of the US middle class thought of as being average in income and education and moderately conservative in values and attitudes. **2.** The American heartland thought of as being made up of small towns, small cities, and suburbs.

Middle Atlantic States also **Mid-At·lan·tic States** (mĭd′ăt-lăn′tĭk) The US states of NY, PA, NJ, and usu. DE and MD.

mid·dle·brow (mĭd′l-brou′) *adj.* Being somewhat cultured; neither highbrow nor lowbrow. ❖ *n.* One with middlebrow tastes or preferences.

middle C *n. Music* The tone represented by a note on the first ledger line below a treble clef or the first ledger line above a bass clef. It is the first C below international pitch.

Middle Chinese *n.* The Chinese language during the Sui and Tang dynasties (581–907).

middle class *n.* The socioeconomic class between the working class and the upper class, usu. including professionals, highly skilled laborers, and lower and middle management.

middle distance *n.* **1.** The area between the foreground and background in a painting, drawing, or photograph. **2.** *Sports* A division of competition in racing with events usu. ranging from 400 meters to 1 mile.

Middle Dutch *n.* The Dutch language from the middle of the 12th through the 15th century.

middle ear *n.* The space between the eardrum and the inner ear containing the three auditory ossicles that convey vibrations through the oval window to the cochlea.

Middle East also **Mid·east** (mĭd-ēst′) An area comprising the countries of SW Asia and NE Africa. —**Middle Eastern** *adj.* —**Middle Easterner** *n.*

Middle English *n.* The English language from about 1100 to 1500.

middle ground *n.* **1.** See **middle distance** 1. **2.** A point of view midway between extremes.

Middle High German *n.* High German from the 11th through the 15th century.

Middle Irish *n.* Irish from the 10th through the 13th century.

middle lamella *n.* The pectin-rich material cementing together the primary walls of adjacent plant cells.

Middle Low German *n.* Low German from the middle of the 13th through the 15th century.

mid·dle·man (mĭd′l-măn′) *n.* **1.** A trader who buys from producers and sells to retailers or consumers. **2.** An intermediary; a go-between.

middle management *n.* The middle tier of management, usu. including lower executives and employees who manage supervisors overseeing day-to-day operations. —**middle manager** *n.*

middle name *n.* A name that occurs between a person's first name and surname.

mid·dle·most (mĭd′l-mōst′) *adj.* Midmost.

mid·dle-of-the-road (mĭd′l-əv-thə-rōd′) *adj.* **1.** Pursuing a course of action midway between extremes, esp. following a course in politics that is neither liberal nor conservative. **2.** Of, relating to, or being a type of entertainment that appeals to a wide audience. —**mid′dle-of-the-road′er** *n.*

Middle Palisade A mountain, 4,273.7 m (14,012 ft), of the Sierra Nevada in E-central CA.

Mid·dles·brough (mĭd′lz-brə) A borough of NE England at the mouth of the Tees R. Pop. 150,600.

middle school *n.* A school at a level between elementary and high school, typically including grades five through eight.

Middle Stone Age *n.* See **Mesolithic**.

middle term *n. Logic* The term in a syllogism presented in both premises but not appearing in the conclusion.

Mid·dle·ton (mĭd′l-tən), **Thomas** 1570?–1627. English playwright noted for his comedies.

mid·dle·ware (mĭd′l-wâr′) *n.* Software that serves as an intermediary between systems software and an application.

mid·dle·weight (mĭd′l-wāt′) *n.* **1.** A professional boxer weighing more than 147 and not more than 160 pounds (approx. 66.5–72.5 kilograms), heavier than a welterweight and lighter than a light heavyweight. **2.** A contestant in various other sports in a similar weight class.

Middle Welsh *n.* See **Medieval Welsh**.

Middle West See **Midwest**. —**Middle Western** *adj.* —**Middle Westerner** *n.*

mid·dling (mĭd′lĭng, -lĭn) *adj.* **1.** Of medium size, position, or quality. **2.** Mediocre. See Syns at **average**. ❖ *n.* **1.** *Chiefly Southern US* **a.** Pork or bacon cut from between the ham and shoulder of a pig. Often used in the plural. **b.** Salt pork. Often used in the plural. **2. middlings** Any of various products that are intermediate in quality, size, price, or grade. **3. middlings** (*used with a sing. or pl. verb*) Coarsely ground wheat mixed with bran. ❖ *adv. Informal* Fairly; moderately. [Prob. ME *midlin* : *mid*, mid; see MID¹ + *-ling*, having a quality; see -LING¹.] —**mid′dling·ly** *adv.*

mid·dy (mĭd′ē) *n., pl.* **-dies** **1.** *Informal* A midshipman. **2.** A middy blouse.

middy blouse *n.* A woman's or child's loose blouse with a sailor collar.

Mid·east (mĭd-ēst′) See **Middle East**. —**Mid·east′ern** *adj.* —**Mid·east′ern·er** *n.*

Mid·gard (mĭd′gärd′) *Mythology n.* The middle region of the world, inhabited by people and imagined as a fortress encircled by a huge serpent. [ON *Midhgardhr*. See **medhyo-** in App.]

midge (mĭj) *n.* **1.** Any of various gnatlike flies of the family Chironomidae, frequently occurring in swarms near ponds and lakes. **2.** Any of various similar dipteran insects. **3.** A little person. [ME < OE *mycg.*]

midg·et (mĭj′ĭt) *n.* **1.** *Offensive* An extremely small person who is otherwise normally proportioned. **2.** A small or miniature version of something. ❖ *adj.* **1.** Miniature; diminutive. **2.** Belonging to a type or class much smaller than what is considered standard. [Dim. of MIDGE.]

mid·gut (mĭd′gŭt′) *n.* **1.** The middle section of the digestive tract in a vertebrate embryo from which the ileum, jejunum, and portions of the duodenum and colon develop. **2.** The middle portion of the digestive tract of certain invertebrates, such as arthropods, lined with an enzyme-secreting tissue and serving as the main site of digestion and absorption.

mid·i (mĭd′ē) *n., pl.* **mid·is** A skirt or coat of midcalf length. [Short for *midiskirt*, blend of MID¹ and MINISKIRT.]

Mi·di (mē-dē′) *n.* The S of France.

MID·I (mĭd′ē) *n., pl.* **MID·Is** **1.** A standard for representing musical information in a digital format. **2.** Software that conforms to this standard, used for composing and editing electronic music. [M(usical) I(nstrument) D(igital) I(nterface).]

Mid·i·an (mĭd′ē-ən) *n.* An ancient tribe in northwest Arabia, said in the Hebrew Scriptures to be descendants of Abraham.

ă	pat	oi	boy
ā	pay	ou	out
âr	care	ŏŏ	took
ä	father	ōō	boot
ĕ	pet	ŭ	cut
ē	be	ûr	urge
ĭ	pit	th	thin
ī	pie	*th*	this
îr	pier	hw	which
ŏ	pot	zh	vision
ō	toe	ə	about,
ô	paw		item

Stress marks:
′ (primary);
′ (secondary), as in
lexicon (lĕk′sĭ-kŏn′)

[Heb. *midyān*, place of judgment (sense uncertain) < *dān*, to judge.] —**Mid'i·an·ite'** *adj. & n.*

mid·i·ron (mĭd'ī'ərn) *n.* **1.** An iron golf club for middle-distance shots, esp. a four, five, or six iron. **2.** A number two golf iron.

mid·land (mĭd'lənd) *n.* The middle or interior part of a country or region. —**mid'land** *adj.*

Midland A city of W-central TX WSW of Abilene. Pop. 94,996.

Mid·lands (mĭd'ləndz) A region of central England roughly corresponding to the Anglo-Saxon kingdom of Mercia.

mid·life (mĭd'līf') *n., pl.* **-lives** (-līvz') See **middle age.** —**mid'life'** *adj.* —**mid'lif'er** *n.*

midlife crisis *n.* A period of psychological doubt and anxiety that some people experience in middle age.

mid·line (mĭd'līn') *n.* A medial line, esp. the medial line or plane of the body.

mid·list (mĭd'lĭst') *n.* The portion of a publisher's list of new or current titles made up of books expected to have less popular appeal than the frontlist.

Mid·lo·thi·an (mĭd-lō'thē-ən) A region of SE Scotland on the Firth of Forth surrounding Edinburgh.

mid·most (mĭd'mōst') *adj.* **1.** Situated in the very middle; middlemost. **2.** Situated nearest the middle. **3.** Most private; innermost. ❖ *adv.* In the middle.

Midn. *abbr.* midshipman

mid·night (mĭd'nīt') *n.* **1.** The middle of the night, specifically 12 o'clock at night. **2a.** Intense darkness or gloom. **b.** A period of darkness and gloom.

midnight sun *n.* The sun as seen at midnight during the summer within the Arctic and Antarctic regions.

mid-o·cean ridge (mĭd'ō'shən) *n.* Any of a series of long mountain ranges on the ocean floor extending through the Atlantic Ocean, the Indian Ocean, and the South Pacific Ocean, and located on either side of rift valleys from which magma extrudes and forms new oceanic crust.

mid·point (mĭd'point') *n.* **1.** *Mathematics* The point of a line segment or curvilinear arc that divides it into two parts of the same length. **2.** A position midway between two extremes.

Mid·rash (mĭd'räsh') *n., pl.* **Mid·rash·im** (mĭd-rô'shĭm, mĭd'rä-shēm') Any of a group of Jewish commentaries on the Bible compiled between A.D. 400 and 1200 and based on exegesis, parable, and haggadic legend. [Heb. *midrāš*, commentary, explanation, Midrash < *dāraš*, to seek, study.]

mid·rib (mĭd'rĭb') *n.* The central or principal vein of a leaf.

mid·riff (mĭd'rĭf') *n.* **1.** See **diaphragm** 1. **2.** The middle portion of the front of the human body, from just below the breast to the waistline. [ME *midrif* < OE *midhrif* : *midd*, mid; see MID¹ + *hrif*, belly; see k^wrep- in App.] —**mid'riff** *adj.*

mid-rise (mĭd'rīz') *adj.* Moderately tall: *a mid-rise office building.* ❖ *n.* A moderately tall building.

mid·sec·tion (mĭd'sĕk'shən) *n.* A middle section, esp. the midriff of the human body.

mid·ship (mĭd'shĭp') *adj.* Of or located in the middle of a ship.

mid·ship·man (mĭd'shĭp'mən, mĭd-shĭp'mən) *n.* A student training to be a commissioned naval officer, esp. a student at a naval academy.

mid·ships (mĭd'shĭps') *adv.* **1.** Amidships. **2.** In the center position. Used of the helm. [Prob. short for AMIDSHIPS.]

mid·size or **mid-size** (mĭd'sīz') or **mid·sized** (sīzd') *adj.* Of intermediate size. Used esp. of motor vehicles, such as cars.

mid·sole (mĭd'sōl') *n.* The middle layer of a sole, as of an athletic shoe, often designed to disperse weight or provide stability to the foot.

midst (mĭdst, mĭtst) *n.* **1.** The middle position or part; the center: *in the midst of the desert.* **2.** A position of proximity to others: *a stranger in our midst.* **3.** The condition of being surrounded or beset by something: *in the midst of all of our problems.* **4.** A period of time in the middle of a continuing condition or act: *in the midst of the war.* ❖ *prep.* Among; amid. [ME *middes, middest*, alteration of OE *midde*, middle. See medhyo- in App.]

mid·stream (mĭd'strēm') *n.* **1.** The middle part of a stream. **2.** The part of a course in the middle.

mid·sum·mer (mĭd'sŭm'ər) *n.* **1.** The middle of the summer. **2.** The summer solstice, about June 21.

Midsummer Day *n.* **1.** June 24, observed in many countries in commemoration of the summer solstice. **2.** June 24, observed in many Christian churches in commemoration of the birth of Saint John the Baptist.

mid·term (mĭd'tûrm') *n.* **1.** The middle of an academic term or a political term of office. **2.** An examination given at the middle of a school or college term.

mid·town (mĭd'toun') *n.* A central portion of a city, between uptown and downtown.

mid-Vic·to·ri·an (mĭd'vĭk-tôr'ē-ən, -tōr'-) *adj.* Relating to, occurring in, or characteristic of the middle period of the reign of Queen Victoria in Great Britain (1837–1901), a period known for rigid social standards. ❖ *n.* **1.** A person living in this period. **2.** A person having rigid social standards.

mid·way (mĭd'wā') *n.* **1.** The area, as of a carnival, where sideshows are located. **2.** *Obsolete* **a.** The middle of a way or distance. **b.** A middle course of action or thought. ❖ *adv.* In the middle of

a way or distance; halfway. —**mid'way'** *adj.*

Midway Islands A US territory comprising two small islands and a surrounding coral atoll in the central Pacific NW of Honolulu; site of a decisive World War II Allied victory (Jun. 3–6, 1942).

mid·week (mĭd'wēk') *n.* **1.** The middle of the week. **2.** Midweek Wednesday. —**mid'week'ly** *adj. & adv.*

Mid·west (mĭd'wĕst') or **Middle West** A region of the N-central US generally considered to include OH, IN, IL, MI, WI, MN, IA, MO, KS, and NE. —**Mid·west'ern** *adj.* —**Mid·west'ern·er** *n.*

mid·wife (mĭd'wīf') *n., pl.* **-wives** (-wīvz') **1.** A person, usu. a woman, who is trained to assist women in childbirth. **2.** One who assists in or takes a part in bringing about a result. ❖ *tr.v.* **-wifed** or **-wived** (-wīvd'), **-wif·ing** or **-wiv·ing** (-wī'vĭng), **-wives** (-wīvz') **1.** To assist in the birth of (a baby). **2.** To assist in bringing forth or about. [ME *midwif* : prob. *mid*, with (< OE; see me-² in App.) + *wif*, woman; see WIFE.]

WORD HISTORY When the compound *midwife* was formed in Middle English (first recorded around 1300), *wife* meant "woman," not just "a married woman." *Mid* is probably a preposition, meaning "together with." Thus a *midwife* was literally a "with woman" or "a woman who assists other women in childbirth." The etymology of *midwife* is thus rather similar to the etymology of the Latin word for this professional, *obstetrīx*, literally "woman who stands in front (of the baby)"—the source of English *obstetric.*

mid·wife·ry (mĭd-wīf'ə-rē, mĭd'wīf'rē, -wī'fə-rē) *n.* The techniques and practice of a midwife.

mid·win·ter (mĭd'wĭn'tər) *n.* **1.** The middle of the winter. **2.** The period of the winter solstice, about December 22.

mid·year (mĭd'yîr') *n.* **1.** The middle of the calendar or academic year. **2.** An examination in the middle of a school year.

mien (mēn) *n.* **1.** Bearing or manner, esp. as it reveals an inner state of mind. **2.** An appearance or aspect. [Alteration (influenced by Fr. *mine*, appearance) of ME *demeine*, demeanor < OFr. < *demener*, to behave. See DEMEAN¹.]

Mies Van Der Ro·he (mēz' vän dər rō'ə, rō', fän, mēs'), **Ludwig** 1886–1969. German-born Amer. architect; a founder of the International Style. —**Mies'i·an** (mē'sē-ən) *adj.*

mi·fep·ri·stone (mĭ-fĕp'rĭ-stōn') *n.* RU 486. [(A)MI(NO) + alteration of PHE(NYL) + PR(OPYL) + alteration of EST(RADIOL) + -ONE.]

miff (mĭf) *n.* **1.** A petulant, bad-tempered mood; a huff. **2.** A petty quarrel or argument; a tiff. ❖ *tr.v.* **miffed, miff·ing, miffs** To cause to become offended or annoyed. [Poss. expressive of disgust.]

miff·y (mĭf'ē) *adj.* **-fi·er, -fi·est** *Informal* Easily offended; oversensitive. —**miff'i·ness** *n.*

MiG (mĭg) *n.* Any of a series of Russian fighter aircraft using piston and later jet engines. [After Artem Ivanovich *Mi(koyan)* (1905–70) and Mikhail Iosifovich *G(urevich)* (1892–1976), Russian aircraft designers.]

might¹ (mīt) *n.* **1.** The power, force, or influence held by a person or group. **2.** Physical strength. **3.** Strength or ability to do something. See Syns at **strength.** [ME < OE *meaht, miht.*]

might² (mīt) *aux.v.* Past tense of **may¹.** **1a.** Used to indicate a condition or state contrary to fact: *She might help if she knew the truth.* **b.** Used to indicate a possibility or probability that is weaker than *may: We might discover gold.* **2.** Used to express possibility or probability or permission in the past: *She told him he might not go.* **3.** Used to indicate a higher degree of deference or politeness than *may, ought,* or *should: Might I speak?* [ME < OE *meahte, mihte,* first and third pers. sing. p. t. of *magan,* to be able. See MAY¹.]

OUR LIVING LANGUAGE In many Southern US varieties of English, *might* can be paired with other auxiliary verbs such as *could,* as in *We might could park over there.* Words like *might* and *could* are known as *modals,* since they express certain "moods" (for example, *I might go* indicates an uncertain mood on the part of the speaker). Combinations such as *might could, might would,* and *might can* are known as *double modals.* Other less common combinations include *may can, may will,* and *might should.* Since double modals typically begin with *may* or *might,* they lessen the degree of conviction or certainty (much like the word *possibly*) more than a single modal does. Double modals are used, for example, to minimize the force of what one is saying, as when asking someone for a favor or when indicating displeasure. • Although double modals may sound odd outside of the South, they carry little if any social stigma in the South and are used by speakers of all social classes and educational levels—even in formal instances like political addresses.

might·i·ly (mīt'l-ē) *adv.* **1.** In a mighty manner; powerfully. **2.** To a great degree; greatly.

might·n't (mīt'nt) Contraction of might not.

might·y (mī'tē) *adj.* **-i·er, -i·est** **1.** Having or showing great power, skill, strength, or force. **2.** Imposing or awesome in size, degree, or extent. ❖ *adv. Informal* To a great degree; extremely. Used as an intensive: *mighty fine.* —**might'i·ness** *n.*

mi·gnon·ette (mĭn'yə-nĕt') *n.* Any of several Mediterranean plants of the genus *Reseda,* esp. *R. odorata,* having spikelike clusters of very fragrant but inconspicuous greenish flowers. [Fr. < fem. of *mignonnet*, dainty, pretty < OFr., dim. of *mignon*, lover, dainty.]

mi·graine (mī′grān′) *n.* A severe recurring headache, usu. affecting only one side of the head, characterized by sharp pain and often accompanied by nausea and visual disturbances. [ME < OFr. < LLat. *hēmicrānia* < Gk. *hēmikrānia* : *hēmi*-, hemi- + *krānion*, head; see ker-¹ in App.] —**mi·grain′ous** *adj.*

mi·grant (mī′grənt) *n.* 1. One that moves from one region to another by chance, instinct, or plan. 2. An itinerant worker who travels from one area to another in search of work. ❖ *adj.* Migratory.

mi·grate (mī′grāt′) *intr.v.* -**grat·ed**, -**grat·ing**, -**grates** 1. To move from one country or region and settle in another. 2. To change location periodically, esp. by moving seasonally from one region to another. [Lat. *migrāre, migrāt*-.] —**mi′gra′tor** *n.*

USAGE NOTE *Migrate*, which is used of people and animals, sometimes implies a lack of permanent settlement, especially as a result of seasonal or periodic movement. *Emigrate* and *immigrate* are used only of people and imply a permanent move, generally across a political boundary. *Emigrate* describes the move relative to the point of departure: *After the Nazis came to power in Germany, many scientists emigrated.* By contrast, *immigrate* describes the move relative to the destination: *The promise of prosperity in the United States encouraged many people to immigrate.*

mi·gra·tion (mī-grā′shən) *n.* 1. The act or an instance of migrating. 2. A group migrating together. 3. *Chemistry & Physics* **a.** The movement of one atom or more from one position to another within a molecule. **b.** The movement of ions between electrodes during electrolysis. —**mi·gra′tion·al** *adj.*

mi·gra·to·ry (mī′grə-tôr′ē, -tōr′ē) *adj.* 1. Characterized by migration; undergoing periodic migration: *migratory birds.* 2. Of or relating to a migration. 3. Roving; nomadic.

mih·rab (mir′əb) *n. Islam* 1. A niche in the wall of a mosque or a mosque room that indicates the direction of Mecca. 2. A niche design in the middle of a Muslim prayer rug, pointed toward Mecca during worship. [Ar. *miḥrāb*, prob. < O South Arabian *mhrb*, part of a temple < *ḥrb*, to fight, perform a certain ritual in a temple.]

mi·ka·do (mī-kä′dō) *n., pl.* -**dos** An emperor of Japan. [J. : *mi*, honorific pref. + *kado*, gate.]

Mik·a·su·ki also **Mic·co·su·kee** (mĭk′ə-sōō′kē) *n., pl.* **Mikasuki** or -**kis** also **Miccosukee** or -**kees** 1. A member of a Native American people formerly inhabiting northwest Florida, now forming part of the Seminole people of southern Florida. 2. The Muskogean language of the Mikasuki.

mike (mīk) *Informal n.* also **mic** (mīk) A microphone. ❖ *tr.v.* **miked, mik·ing, mikes** To supply with or transmit through a microphone.

Mi′k′maq (mĭk′măk′) *n.* Variant of **Micmac.**

Mí·ko·nos (mē′kô-nôs′) See **Mykonos.**

mik·vah (mĭk′və, mēk-vä′) *n., pl.* -**voth** or -**vot** (-vōt′) or -**vos** (-vōs) 1. A ritual bath taken by Jews for purification on certain occasions, as before the Sabbath or after menstruation. 2. A building, room, or fixture in which this bath takes place. [Heb. *miqwâ*, reservoir, or *miqwe*, collection (of water), immersion pool, both < *qāwâ*, to collect.]

mil¹ (mĭl) *n.* 1. A unit of length equal to one thousandth (10⁻³) of an inch (0.0254 millimeter), used, for example, to specify the diameter of wire. 2. A milliliter; one cubic centimeter. 3. A unit of angular measurement used in artillery and equal to 1/6400 of a complete revolution. [Short for Lat. *millēsimus*, thousandth < *mille*, thousand.]

mil² (mĭl) *n. Slang* A million dollars.

mil. *abbr.* 1. military 2. militia

mi·la·dy (mī-lā′dē) *n., pl.* -**dies** 1. An English noblewoman or gentlewoman. 2. Used as a form of address for such a woman. 3. A chic or fashionable woman. [Fr. < E., my lady.]

Mi·lan (mī-lăn′, -län′) A city of N Italy NE of Genoa; probably of Celtic origin. Pop. 1,371,008. —**Mil′a·nese** (mĭl′ə-nēz′, -nēs′) *adj. & n.*

milch (mĭlch) *adj.* Giving milk. [ME *milche* < OE *-milce* (in *thrīmilce*, May, month when cows can be milked thrice a day). See melg- in App.]

mil·chig (mĭl′KHĭk) *adj.* Derived from or made of milk or dairy products. [Yiddish *milkhik* < *milkh*, milk < MHGer. *milch* < OHGer. *miluh*. See melg- in App.]

mild (mīld) *adj.* **mild·er, mild·est** 1. Gentle or kind in disposition or behavior. **2a.** Moderate in type, degree, effect, or force: *a mild pipe tobacco; a mild sedative.* **b.** Not extreme: *a mild winter storm.* **c.** Warm and full of sunshine; pleasant: *a mild spring day.* 3. Not severe or acute: *a mild fever.* 4. Easily molded, shaped, or worked; malleable: *mild steel.* ❖ *intr.v.* **mild·ed, mild·ing, milds** *Texas & Virginia* To diminish or decrease. Used of the wind or a storm. [ME < OE *milde.*] —**mild′ly** *adv.* —**mild′ness** *n.*

mil·dew (mĭl′dōō′, -dyōō′) *n.* 1. Any of various fungi that form a superficial, usu. whitish growth on plants and various organic materials. 2. A superficial coating or discoloration, as of paper or leather, caused by fungi. 3. A plant disease caused by such fungi. ❖ *tr. & intr.v.* -**dewed**, -**dew·ing**, -**dews** To affect or become

affected with mildew. [ME < OE *mildēaw*, honeydew, nectar. See melit- in App.] —**mil′dew′y** *adj.*

mile (mīl) *n.* 1. A unit of length equal to 5,280 feet or 1,760 yards (1,609 meters), used in the United States and other English-speaking countries. See table at **measurement.** 2. A nautical mile. 3. An air mile. 4. *Sports* A race that is one mile long. 5. A relatively great distance. [ME < OE *mīl* < Lat. *mīlia* (*passuum*), a thousand (double paces), a Roman mile, pl. of *mīlle*, thousand.]

mile·age also **mil·age** (mī′lĭj) *n.* 1. Total length, extent, or distance measured or expressed in miles. 2. Total miles covered or traveled in a given time. 3. The amount of service, use, or wear estimated by miles used or traveled. 4. The number of miles traveled by a motor vehicle on a given quantity of fuel. **5a.** An allowance for travel expenses established at a specified rate per mile. **b.** Expense per mile, as for the use of a car. 6. *Informal* The amount of service something has yielded or may yield in the future; usefulness.

mile·post (mīl′pōst′) *n.* A post set up to indicate distance in miles, as along a highway.

mil·er (mī′lər) *n. Sports* One that competes in races one mile long.

mi·les glo·ri·o·sus (mē′lăs glôr′ē-ō′səs, glôr′-) *n., pl.* **mi·li·tes glo·ri·o·si** (mē′lĭ-tās glôr′ē-ō′sē, glôr′-) A bragging and often cowardly soldier, esp. as a stock character in comedy. [Lat. *miles glōriōsus*, after *Miles Glōriōsus* by Plautus.]

Mi·le·sian¹ (mī-lē′zhən, -shən) *adj.* Of or relating to Miletus or its inhabitants. ❖ *n.* A native or inhabitant of Miletus. [< Lat. *Milēsius* < Gk. *Milēsios* < *Milētos*, Miletus.]

Mi·le·sian² (mī-lē′zhən, -shən) *n.* 1. *Mythology* A member of a people who invaded Ireland and became the ancestors of the Irish. 2. A native or inhabitant of Ireland. [After *Milesius*, legendary ancestor of the Irish people.] —**mi·le′sian** *adj.*

mile·stone (mīl′stōn′) *n.* 1. A stone marker set up on a roadside to indicate the distance in miles from a given point. 2. An important event, as in the history of a nation; a turning point.

Mi·le·tus (mī-lē′təs) An ancient Ionian city of W Asia Minor in present-day Turkey; occupied by Greeks c. 1000 B.C.

mil·foil (mĭl′foil′) *n.* 1. See **yarrow.** 2. Water milfoil. [ME < OFr. < Lat. *mīlifolium* : *mīlle*, thousand + *folium*, leaf; see bhel- in App.]

Mil·haud (mē-yō′), **Darius** 1892–1974. French composer who experimented with polytonality and jazz styles.

mil·i·a (mĭl′ē-ə) *n.* Plural of **milium.**

mil·i·ar·i·a (mĭl′ē-âr′ē-ə) *n.* See **heat rash.** [NLat. (*febris*) *miliāria*, miliary (fever), fem. of Lat. *miliārius*, of millet. See MILIARY.] —**mil′i·ar′i·al** *adj.*

mil·i·ar·y (mĭl′ē-ĕr′ē) *adj.* 1. Having the appearance of millet seeds. 2. *Pathology* Characterized by the presence of small miliary skin lesions. [< ME *miliaris, miliari*, miliary skin disease < Med.Lat. *miliāris* < Lat. *miliārius*, of millet < *milium*, millet. See MILLET.]

mi·lieu (mĭl-yōō′, mē-lyœ′) *n., pl.* -**lieus** or -**lieux** (-lyœ′) An environment or a setting. [Fr. < OFr., center : *mi*, middle (< Lat. *medius*; see medhyo- in App.) + *lieu*, place (< Lat. *locus*).]

mil·i·tant (mĭl′ĭ-tənt) *adj.* 1. Fighting or warring. 2. Having a combative character; aggressive, esp. on behalf of a cause. ❖ *n.* A militant person or party. [ME < OFr. < Lat. *mīlitāns, mīlitant*-, pr. part. of *mīlitāre*, to serve as a soldier. See MILITATE.] —**mil′i·tance, mil′i·tan·cy** *n.* —**mil′i·tant·ly** *adv.*

mil·i·tar·i·a (mĭl′ĭ-târ′ē-ə) *pl.n.* Objects of historical interest related to warfare or military service that are collected. [MILITARY + -IA².]

mil·i·ta·rism (mĭl′ĭ-tə-rĭz′əm) *n.* 1. Glorification of the ideals of a professional military class. 2. Predominance of the armed forces in the administration or policy of the state. 3. A policy in which military preparedness is of primary importance to a state. —**mil′i·ta·rist** *n.* —**mil′i·ta·ris′tic** (-rĭs′tĭk) *adj.* —**mil′i·ta·ris′ti·cal·ly** *adv.*

mil·i·ta·rize (mĭl′ĭ-tə-rīz′) *tr.v.* -**rized**, -**riz·ing**, -**riz·es** 1. To equip or train for war. 2. To imbue with militarism. 3. To adopt for use by or in the military. —**mil′i·ta·ri·za′tion** (-tər-ĭ-zā′shən) *n.*

mil·i·tar·y (mĭl′ĭ-tĕr′ē) *adj.* 1. Of, relating to, or characteristic of members of the armed forces. 2. Performed or supported by the armed forces: *military service.* 3. Of or relating to war: *military operations.* 4. Of or relating to land forces. ❖ *n., pl.* **military** also -**ies** 1. Armed forces. 2. Members, esp. officers, of an armed force. [ME < Lat. *mīlitāris* < *mīles, mīlit*-, soldier.] —**mil′i·tar′i·ly** (-târ′ə-lē) *adv.*

mil·i·tar·y-in·dus·tri·al complex (mĭl′ĭ-tĕr′ē-ĭn-dŭs′trē-əl) *n.* The aggregate of a nation's armed forces and the industries that supply their equipment, materials, and armaments.

military law *n.* The statutes, codes, and traditions concerned with the discipline and trial of military personnel.

military police *n.* The branch of an armed force assigned to perform law enforcement duties, as on a military installation.

military science *n.* The principles of military conflict and of warfare.

mil·i·tate (mĭl′ĭ-tāt′) *intr.v.* -**tat·ed**, -**tat·ing**, -**tates** To have force or influence; bring about an effect or a change. [Lat. *mīlitāre, mīlitāt*-, to be a soldier < *mīles, mīlit*-.]

mihrab
18th-century Turkish
prayer rug

ă pat	oi boy
ā pay	ou out
âr care	ŏŏ took
ä father	ōō boot
ĕ pet	ŭ cut
ē be	ûr urge
ĭ pit	th thin
ī pie	th this
îr pier	hw which
ŏ pot	zh vision
ō toe	ə about,
ô paw	item

Stress marks:
′ (primary);
′ (secondary), as in
lexicon (lĕk′sĭ-kŏn′)

mi·li·tes glo·ri·o·si (mē′lĭ-tās glôr′ē-ō′sē, glōr′-) *n.* Plural of miles gloriosus.

mi·li·tia (mə-lĭsh′ə) *n.* **1.** An army of ordinary citizens. **2.** A military force that is not part of a regular army, subject to call for emergency service. **3.** The body of physically fit civilians legally eligible for military service. [Lat. *mīlitia*, warfare, military service < *mīles, mīlit-*, soldier.]

mi·li·tia·man (mə-lĭsh′ə-mən) *n.* A male militia member.

mil·i·um (mĭl′ē-əm) *n.*, *pl.* **-i·a** (-ē-ə) A small white or yellowish cyst on the skin, caused by retention of sebaceous gland secretions. [ME, millet < Lat. See **melə-** in App.]

milk (mĭlk) *n.* **1.** A whitish liquid containing proteins, fats, lactose, vitamins, and minerals produced by the mammary glands of female mammals to nourish their young. **2.** The milk of cows, goats, or other animals, used as food by humans. **3.** A liquid, such as coconut milk, or various medical emulsions, with a milklike appearance. ❖ *v.* **milked, milk·ing, milks** —*tr.* **1a.** To draw milk from the teat or udder of (a female mammal). **b.** To draw or extract a liquid from. **2.** To press out, drain off, or remove by or as if by milking: *milk venom from a snake.* **3.** *Informal* **a.** To draw out or extract something from, as if by milking: *milked the witness for information.* **b.** To obtain money or benefits from, in order to achieve personal gain; exploit. —*intr.* **1.** To yield or supply milk. **2.** To draw milk from a female mammal. [ME < OE *milc.* See **melg-** in App.] —**milk′er** *n.*

milk chocolate *n.* Sweetened chocolate made with milk.

milk fever *n.* **1.** A mild fever, usu. occurring at the beginning of lactation, associated with infection. **2.** A disease affecting dairy cows, esp. soon after giving birth.

milk·fish (mĭlk′fĭsh′) *n.*, *pl.* **milkfish** or **-fish·es** A large silvery fish (*Chanos chanos*) of the South Pacific and Indian oceans, widely used for food. [< its color.]

milk glass *n.* An opaque or translucent whitish glass.

milk leg *n.* A painful swelling of the leg occurring in women after childbirth as a result of clotting of the femoral veins.

milk·maid (mĭlk′mād′) *n.* A girl or woman who milks cows.

milk·man (mĭlk′măn′) *n.* A man who sells or delivers milk.

milk of magnesia *n.* A white aqueous suspension of magnesium hydroxide, Mg(OH)$_2$, used as an antacid and a laxative.

Milk River A river rising in the Rocky Mts. of NW MT and flowing c. 1,006 km (625 mi) to S Alberta then back to N MT, where it joins the Missouri R.

milk run *n.* *Slang* A routine trip with stops at many places.

milk shake *n.* **1.** A beverage made of milk, flavoring, and ice cream, shaken or whipped until foamy. **2.** *New England* A beverage made of milk and flavored syrup, whipped until foamy.

REGIONAL NOTE To most Americans, a milk shake naturally includes ice cream. To a person living in Rhode Island or the adjoining part of Massachussetts, a milk shake consists of milk shaken up with flavored syrup; if ice cream is included, the drink is called a *cabinet,* possibly, says food writer John F. Mariani in *The Dictionary of American Food and Drink,* named after the square wooden cabinet in which the mixer was encased. Farther north in New England the same drink is called a *velvet* or a *frappe* (from French *frapper,* "to ice").

milk sickness *n.* **1.** A disease characterized by vomiting and intestinal pain caused by eating dairy products or meat from a cow that has fed on white snakeroot. **2.** See **tremble** 3b.

milk snake *n.* Any of various nonvenomous king snakes of the species *Lampropeltis triangulum* ranging from the United States south to Ecuador, often having red, black, and yellow bands. [< the claim that it sucks milk from cows.]

milk·sop (mĭlk′sŏp′) *n.* A man lacking courage and other qualities deemed manly. —**milk′sop′py** *adj.*

milk sugar *n.* See **lactose.**

milk toast *n.* Toast, usu. buttered, served in warm milk, often with sugar or seasonings.

milk tooth *n.* Any of the deciduous teeth of a young mammal.

milk vetch *n.* Any of various plants of the genus *Astragalus,* having compound leaves and purple, white, or yellowish flowers. [< the belief that it increases the milk yield of goats.]

milk·weed (mĭlk′wēd′) *n.* Any of numerous plants of the genus *Asclepias,* having milky juice, usu. opposite leaves, and pods that split open to release seeds with downy tufts.

milk·wort (mĭlk′wûrt′, -wôrt′) *n.* Any of various plants of the genus *Polygala,* having variously colored flowers with two petaloid sepals. [Thought to increase human lactation.]

milk·y (mĭl′kē) *adj.* **-i·er, -i·est 1.** Resembling milk in color or consistency. **2.** Filled with, consisting of, or yielding milk or a fluid resembling milk. **3.** Meek; timid. —**milk′i·ness** *n.*

milky disease *n.* A bacterial disease of scarabaeid grubs that eventually turns them a milky white color.

Milky Way *n.* The galaxy containing our solar system, visible as a broad band of faint light in the night sky. [ME, transl. of Lat. *via lactea* : *via,* way + *lactea,* fem. of *lacteus,* milky.]

mill¹ (mĭl) *n.* **1a.** A building equipped with machinery for grinding grain into flour or meal. **b.** A device or mechanism that grinds grain. **2.** A machine or device that reduces a solid or coarse substance into pulp or minute grains by crushing, grinding, or pressing: *a pepper mill.* **3.** A machine that releases the juice of fruits

milk snake
Honduran milk snake
Lampropeltis triangulum
hondurensis

Edna St. Vincent Millay

and vegetables by pressing or grinding: *a cider mill.* **4a.** A machine, such as one for stamping coins, that produces something by the repetition of a simple process. **b.** A steel roller bearing a raised design, used for making a die or a printing plate by pressure. **c.** Any of various machines for shaping, cutting, polishing, or dressing metal surfaces. **5a.** A building or group of buildings equipped with machinery for processing raw materials into finished or industrial products: *a textile mill.* **b.** A building or collection of buildings that has machinery for manufacture; a factory. **6.** A process, agency, or institution that operates in a routine way or turns out products in the manner of a factory: *a diploma mill.* **7.** A slow or laborious process. ❖ *v.* **milled, mill·ing, mills** —*tr.* **1.** To grind, pulverize, or break down into smaller particles in a mill. **2.** To transform or process mechanically in a mill. **3.** To shape, polish, dress, or finish in or with a milling tool. **4a.** To produce a ridge around the edge of (a coin). **b.** To groove or flute the rim of (a coin or other metal object). **5.** To agitate or stir until foamy. **6.** *Western US* To cause (cattle) to move in a circle or tightening spiral in order to stop a stampede. —*intr.* **1.** To move around in churning confusion. **2.** *Slang* To fight with the fists; box. **3.** To undergo milling. [ME *milne, mille* < OE *mylen* < LLat. *molīna, molīnum* < fem. and neut. of *molīnus,* of a mill < Lat. *mola,* millstone < *molere,* to grind. See **melə-** in App.]

mill² (mĭl) *n.* A monetary unit equal to ¹⁄₁₀₀₀ of a US dollar or ¹⁄₁₀ of a cent. [Short for Lat. *millēsimus,* thousandth. See **MIL¹**.]

Mill, James 1773–1836. Scottish philosopher and economist who was a founder of utilitarianism.

Mill, John Stuart 1806–73. British philosopher known esp. for his interpretations of empiricism and utilitarianism in works such as *Principles of Political Economy* (1848).

mill·age (mĭl′ĭj) *n.* A tax rate on property, expressed in mills per dollar of value of the property.

Mil·lais (mĭ-lā′), Sir **John Everett** 1829–96. British painter and a founder of the Pre-Raphaelite Brotherhood (1848).

Mil·lay (mĭ-lā′), **Edna Saint Vincent** 1892–1950. Amer. poet who wrote *The Harp Weaver and Other Poems* (1923).

mill·board (mĭl′bôrd′, -bōrd′) *n.* A stiff heavy paperboard used primarily for book covers. [Alteration of *milled board.*]

mill·dam (mĭl′dăm′) *n.* A dam constructed across a stream to raise the water level so that the overflow will have sufficient power to turn a mill wheel.

mille·fleur (mēl-flûr′, -floor′) *adj.* Having a background with a pattern of flowers and plants. [< Fr. *(de) mille fleurs, (de) millefleurs,* (of) a thousand flowers : *mille,* thousand (< OFr. *milie,* thousands < Lat. *mīlia,* pl. of *mīlle,* thousand) + *fleurs,* pl. of *fleur,* flower; see ENFLEURAGE.]

mil·le·nar·i·an (mĭl′ə-nâr′ē-ən) *adj.* **1.** Of or relating to a thousand, esp. to a thousand years. **2.** Of, relating to, or believing in the doctrine of the millennium. ❖ *n.* One who believes the millennium will occur. —**mil′le·nar′i·an·ism** *n.*

mil·le·nar·y (mĭl′ə-nĕr′ē, mə-lĕn′ə-rē) *adj.* **1.** Of or relating to a thousand, esp. to a thousand years; millenarian. **2a.** Of or relating to the doctrine of the millennium; millenarian. **b.** Of or relating to millenarians. ❖ *n.*, *pl.* **-ies 1.** A sum or total of one thousand, esp. a thousand years. **2.** A millenarian. [Lat. *millēnārius* < *millēnī,* a thousand each < *mīlle,* thousand.]

mil·len·ni·um (mə-lĕn′ē-əm) *n.*, *pl.* **-len·ni·a** (-lĕn′ē-ə) or **-len·ni·ums 1.** A span of one thousand years. **2.** A thousand-year period of holiness mentioned in Revelation 20, during which Jesus and his followers are to rule on earth. **3.** A hoped-for period of joy, prosperity, and justice. **4.** A thousandth anniversary. [NLat. : Lat. *mille,* thousand + Lat. *annus,* year.] —**mil·len′ni·al** (-əl) *adj.* —**mil·len′ni·al·ism** *n.* —**mil·len′ni·al·ist** *n.*

millennium bug *n.* See **Y2K bug.**

mil·le·pede (mĭl′ə-pēd′) *n.* Variant of **millipede.**

mil·le·pore (mĭl′ə-pôr′, -pōr′) *n.* Any of various reef-building organisms of the order Milleporina of tropical marine waters, forming white or yellowish calcareous structures and resembling the true corals of the class Anthozoa. [Ital. *millepora* : *mille,* thousand (< Lat. *mīlle*) + *-pora* (alteration of *poro,* tufa, pore; see MADREPORE).]

mill·er (mĭl′ər) *n.* **1.** One who works in, operates, or owns a mill, esp. a grain mill. **2.** A milling machine. **3.** Any of various moths whose wings and bodies have a powdery appearance.

Miller, Arthur b. 1915. Amer. playwright whose works include *Death of a Salesman* (1949).

Miller, Glenn 1909–44. Amer. bandleader and composer from the Big Band era.

Miller, Henry Valentine 1891–1980. Amer. writer noted for *Tropic of Cancer* (1934) and *Tropic of Capricorn* (1939).

Miller, Joaquin Pseudonym of Cincinnatus Hiner Miller. 1837–1913. Amer. poet whose work is based on his adventures in the West.

mil·ler·ite (mĭl′ə-rīt′) *n.* A nickel sulfide mineral, NiS, usu. occurring in long hairlike crystals and used as a nickel ore. [After William H. *Miller* (1801–80), British mineralogist.]

miller's thumb (mĭl′ərz) *n.* Any of several small freshwater sculpins of the genus *Cottus,* esp. *C. gobio,* having a large spiny head and spiny fins. [< its thumblike shape.]

mil·les·i·mal (mə-lĕs′ə-məl) *adj.* **1.** Thousandth. **2.** Consisting of a thousandth. **3.** Relating to thousandths. ❖ *n.* A thousandth.

[< Lat. *millēsimus* < *mīlle*, thousand.]

mil·let (mĭl′ĭt) *n.* **1a.** An annual grass (*Panicum miliaceum*) cultivated in Eurasia for its grains and in North America for hay. **b.** The grains of this plant. **2.** Any of several similar or related grasses. [ME *milet* < OFr., dim. of *mil*, millet < Lat. *milium*. See **melə-** in App.]

Mil·let (mĭ-lā′, mē-), **Jean François** 1814–75. French painter whose works include *The Gleaners* (1857).

Mil·lett (mĭl′ĭt), **Kate** b. 1934. Amer. feminist leader who wrote *Sexual Politics* (1970).

milli– *pref.* One thousandth (10⁻³): *millisecond*. [Lat. *milli–* < *mīlle*, thousand.]

mil·li·am·pere (mĭl′ē-ăm′pîr′) *n.* A unit of current equal to one thousandth (10⁻³) of an ampere.

mil·liard (mĭl′yərd, -yärd′, mĭl′ē-ärd′) *n. Chiefly British* The cardinal number equal to 10⁹. [Fr. < OFr. *milliart* < *milion*, million. See **MILLION**.]

mil·li·ar·y (mĭl′ē-ĕr′ē) *adj.* Relating to or marking the distance of an ancient Roman mile, equal to 1,000 paces. [Lat. *milliārius*, of a thousand, one mile long < *mīlle (passuum)*, a thousand (double paces), a Roman mile.]

mil·li·bar (mĭl′ə-bär′) *n.* A unit of atmospheric pressure equal to one thousandth (10⁻³) of a bar.

mil·li·cu·rie (mĭl′ĭ-kyŏŏr′ē, -kyŏŏ-rē′) *n.* A unit of radioactivity equal to one thousandth (10⁻³) of a curie.

mil·li·gram (mĭl′ĭ-grăm′) *n.* A unit of mass equal to one thousandth (10⁻³) of a gram. See table at **measurement**.

mil·li·hen·ry (mĭl′ə-hĕn′rē) *n., pl.* **-rys** or **-ries** A unit of inductance equal to one thousandth (10⁻³) of a henry.

Mil·li·kan (mĭl′ĭ-kən), **Robert Andrews** 1868–1953. Amer. physicist who won a 1923 Nobel Prize.

mil·li·li·ter (mĭl′ə-lē′tər) *n.* A unit of volume equal to one thousandth (10⁻³) of a liter. See table at **measurement**.

mil·li·me·ter (mĭl′ə-mē′tər) *n.* A unit of length equal to one thousandth (10⁻³) of a meter, or 0.0394 inch. See table at **measurement**.

mil·li·mi·cron (mĭl′ə-mī′krŏn) *n.* A unit of length equal to one thousandth (10⁻³) of a micrometer or one billionth (10⁻⁹) of a meter.

mil·line (mĭl′lĭn) *n.* **1.** A unit of advertising copy equal to one agate line one column wide printed in one million copies of a publication. **2.** The cost of a unit of advertising copy.

mil·li·ner (mĭl′ə-nər) *n.* One that makes, trims, designs, or sells hats. [Prob. alteration of ME *Milener*, native of Milan < **MILAN**, the source of goods such as bonnets and lace.]

mil·li·ner·y (mĭl′ə-nĕr′ē) *n., pl.* **-ies** **1.** Articles, esp. women's hats, sold by a milliner. **2.** The profession or business of a milliner.

mill·ing (mĭl′ĭng) *n.* **1.** The act or process of grinding, esp. grinding grain into flour or meal. **2.** The operation of cutting, shaping, finishing, or working products manufactured in a mill. **3.** The ridges cut on the edges of coins.

mil·lion (mĭl′yən) *n., pl.* **million** or **-lions** **1.** The cardinal number equal to 10⁶. **2.** A million monetary units, such as dollars. **3.** An indefinitely large number. Often used in the plural. **4.** The common people; the masses. Often used in the plural. [ME < OFr. *milion*, prob. < OItal. *milione*, augmentative of *mille*, thousand < Lat. *mīlle*. See **gheslo-** in App.] —**mil′lion** *adj.*

mil·lion·aire (mĭl′yə-nâr′) *n.* A person whose wealth amounts to at least a million dollars, pounds, or the equivalent in other currency. [Fr. *millionnaire* < *million*, million < OFr. *milion*. See **MILLION**.]

mil·lionth (mĭl′yənth) *n.* **1.** The ordinal number matching the number million in a series. **2.** One of a million equal parts. —**mil′lionth** *adv. & adj.*

mil·li·pede or **mil·le·pede** (mĭl′ə-pēd′) *n.* Any of various crawling myriapods of the class Diplopoda, having a cylindrical segmented body with two pairs of legs attached to all segments except for the first four in the thoracic region. [Lat. *milipeda*, a kind of insect : *mīlle*, thousand + *pēs, ped-*, foot; see **ped–** in App.]

mil·li·rem (mĭl′ə-rĕm′) *n.* One thousandth (10⁻³) of a rem.

mil·li·sec·ond (mĭl′ĭ-sĕk′ənd) *n.* One thousandth (10⁻³) of a second.

mil·li·volt (mĭl′ə-vōlt′) *n.* A unit of potential difference equal to one thousandth (10⁻³) of a volt.

mil·li·watt (mĭl′ə-wŏt′) *n.* A unit of power equal to one thousandth (10⁻³) of a watt.

mill·pond (mĭl′pŏnd′) *n.* A pond formed by a milldam.

mill·race (mĭl′rās′) *n.* **1.** The fast-moving stream of water that drives a mill wheel. **2.** The channel for the water that drives a mill wheel.

mill·run (mĭl′rŭn′) *n.* **1.** See **millrace. 2.** The output of a sawmill. **3a.** A test of the mineral quality or content of an ore by milling. **b.** The mineral yielded by this test.

mill-run (mĭl′rŭn′) *adj.* Being in the state in which a product leaves a mill; unsorted and uninspected: *mill-run fabric*.

mill·stone (mĭl′stōn′) *n.* **1.** One of a pair of cylindrical stones used in a mill for grinding grain. **2.** A heavy weight; a burden.

mill·stream (mĭl′strēm′) *n.* The rapid stream of water flowing in a millrace.

mill wheel *n.* A wheel, usu. driven by water, that powers a mill.

mill·work (mĭl′wûrk′) *n.* Woodwork, such as doors, window casings, and baseboards, ready-made by a lumber mill.

mill·wright (mĭl′rīt′) *n.* One that designs, builds, or repairs mills or mill machinery.

Milne (mĭln), **A(lan) A(lexander)** 1882–1956. British writer best known for *Winnie-the-Pooh* (1926).

mi·lo (mī′lō) *n., pl.* **-los** An early-growing, usu. drought-resistant grain sorghum, esp. *Sorghum bicolor*, resembling millet. [Poss. < Afr. *mealie*, corn, prob. < Port. *milho* < Lat. *milium*, millet. See **MILLET**.]

mi·lord (mĭ-lôrd′) *n.* **1.** An English nobleman or gentleman. **2.** Used as a form of address for such a man. [Fr. < E. *my lord*.]

Mi·los also **Me·los** (mē′lŏs) or **Mi·lo** (mē′lō, mī′-) An island of SE Greece in the Cyclades Is. of the Aegean Sea. The *Venus de Milo* was found here in 1820.

Mi·lo·se·vić (mĭ-lō′sə-vĭch′), **Slobodan** b. 1941. Serbian politician; served as president of the Yugoslav federation of Serbia and Montenegro from 1997–2000. In 2001 he was indicted on war crimes charges by the International War Crimes Tribunal.

Mi·losz (mē′lŏsh′, -wŏsh′), **Czeslaw** b. 1911. Polish-born writer who won the 1980 Nobel Prize for literature.

milque·toast (mĭlk′tōst′) *n.* One who has a meek timid nature. [After Caspar *Milquetoast*, comic-strip character by H.T. Webster (1885–1952).] —**milque′toast′y** *adj.*

milt (mĭlt) *n.* **1a.** Fish sperm, including the seminal fluid. **b.** The reproductive glands of male fishes when filled with this fluid. **2.** The spleen of certain vertebrate animals, such as cows or pigs. ✣ *tr.v.* **milt·ed, milt·ing, milts** To fertilize (fish roe) with milt. [ME, roe, spleen, partly < MDu. *milte* and partly < OE *milte*, spleen.]

milt·er (mĭl′tər) *n.* A male fish that is ready to breed.

Mil·ti·a·des (mĭl-tī′ə-dēz′) 540?–489? B.C. Athenian general who defeated the Persians at Marathon (490 B.C.).

Mil·ton (mĭl′tən), **John** 1608–74. English poet and scholar who is best known for the epic poem *Paradise Lost* (1667).

Milton Keynes (kēnz) A town of S-central England NE of Oxford; designated as a new town in 1967. Pop. 184,440.

Mil·wau·kee (mĭl-wô′kē) A city of SE WI on Lake Michigan; est. as a fur-trading post in 1795. Pop. 596,974.

Mi·mas (mī′măs, mē′-) *n.* A satellite of Saturn. [After *Mimas*, one of the Giants slain by Hercules.]

mime (mīm) *n.* **1a.** A form of ancient Greek and Roman theater in which the familiar was farcically portrayed on stage. **b.** A performance of or dialogue for such an entertainment. **c.** A performer in a mime. **2.** A modern performer who specializes in comic mimicry. **3a.** The art of portraying characters and acting out situations or a narrative by gestures and body movement without the use of words; pantomime. **b.** A performance of pantomime. **c.** An actor skilled in pantomime. ✣ *v.* **mimed, mim·ing, mimes** —*tr.* **1.** To ridicule by imitation; mimic. **2.** To act out with gestures and body movement. —*intr.* **1.** To act as a mimic. **2.** To portray characters and situations by gesture and body movement. [Lat. *mīmus* < Gk. *mīmos*.] —**mim′er** *n.*

MIME *n. Computer Science* A communications protocol that allows for the transmission of data in many forms, such as audio, binary, or video. [M(ultipurpose) I(nternet) M(ail) E(xtensions).]

mim·e·o (mĭm′ē-ō′) *Informal n., pl.* **-os** A mimeograph. ✣ *tr.v.* **-oed, -o·ing, -os** To mimeograph.

mim·e·o·graph (mĭm′ē-ə-grăf′) *n.* **1.** A duplicator that makes copies of written, drawn, or typed material from a stencil fitted around an inked drum. **2.** A copy made by this method of duplication. [Orig. a trademark.] —**mim′e·o·graph′** *v.*

mi·me·sis (mĭ-mē′sĭs, mī-) *n.* **1.** The imitation or representation of aspects of the sensible world, esp. human actions, in literature and art. **2.** *Biology* Mimicry. **3.** *Medicine* The appearance of symptoms of a disease not actually present. [Gk. *mīmēsis* < *mīmeisthai*, to imitate < *mīmos*, imitator, mime.]

mi·met·ic (mĭ-mĕt′ĭk, mī-) *adj.* **1.** Relating to, characteristic of, or exhibiting mimicry. **2a.** Of or relating to an imitation; imitative. **b.** Using imitative means of representation: *a mimetic dance.* [Gk. *mīmētikos* < *mīmēsis*, mimicry. See **MIMESIS**.] —**mi·met′i·cal·ly** *adv.*

mim·ic (mĭm′ĭk) *tr.v.* **-icked, -ick·ing, -ics** **1.** To copy or imitate closely, esp. in speech, expression, and gesture; ape. **2.** To copy or imitate so as to ridicule; mock. See Syns at **imitate**. **3.** To resemble closely; simulate. **4.** To take on the appearance of. ✣ *n.* **1.** One who imitates, esp.: **a.** An actor in a mime. **b.** One who practices the art of mime. **c.** One who copies or mimics others. **2.** A copy or an imitation. ✣ *adj.* **1.** Relating to, acting as, resembling, or characteristic of a mimic or mimicry. **2a.** Tending to imitate; imitative. **b.** Make-believe; mock. [< Lat. *mīmicus*, mimic < Gk. *mīmikos* < *mīmos*, imitator, mime.] —**mim′ick·er** *n.*

mim·ic·ry (mĭm′ĭ-krē) *n., pl.* **-ries** **1a.** The act, practice, or art of mimicking. **b.** An instance of mimicking. **2.** *Biology* The resemblance of one organism to another or to an object in its surroundings for concealment and protection from predators.

Mi·mir (mē′mĭr′) *n. Mythology* A Norse giant who lived by the roots of Yggdrasil, where he guarded the well of wisdom. [ON. See **(s)mer–** in App.]

mi·mo·sa (mĭ-mō′sə, -zə) *n.* **1.** Any of various mostly tropical herbs, shrubs, and trees of the genus *Mimosa*, having globular

mill wheel
Mabry Mill, Blue Ridge
Parkway, Virginia

Slobodan Milosević
photographed in 1995

ă pat	oi boy
ā pay	ou out
âr care	ŏŏ took
ä father	ōō boot
ĕ pet	ŭ cut
ē be	ûr urge
ĭ pie	th thin
ī pie	*th* this
îr pier	hw which
ŏ pot	zh vision
ō toe	ə about,
ô paw	item

Stress marks:
′ (primary);
′ (secondary), as in
lexicon (lĕk′sĭ-kŏn′)

minaret
Selimiye Mosque in
Edirne, Turkey

heads of small flowers and usu. bipinnate leaves that are often sensitive to touch or light. **2.** See **silk tree. 3.** A drink consisting of champagne and orange juice. [NLat. *Mīmosa*, genus name < Lat. *mīmus*, mime < Gk. *mīmos*.]

min. *abbr.* **1.** minim **2.** minimum **3. Min.** minister **4.** minor **5.** minute

mi·na[1] (mī′nə) *n., pl.* **-nas** or **-nae** (-nē) A varying unit of weight or money used in ancient Greece and Asia. [Lat. < Gk. *mnā* < Akkadian *manû*, a unit of weight < *manû*, to count.]

mi·na[2] (mī′nə) *n.* Variant of **myna.**

min·a·ble or **mine·a·ble** (mī′nə-bəl) *adj.* That can be mined.

mi·na·cious (mī-nā′shəs) *adj.* Of a menacing or threatening nature; minatory. [Lat. *mināx, mināc-* (< *minārī,* to threaten < *minae,* threats) + -IOUS.] —**mi·na′cious·ly** *adv.* —**mi·na′-cious·ness, mi·nac′i·ty** (mī-năs′ĭ-tē) *n.*

Min·a·ma·ta disease (mĭn′ə-mä′tə) *n.* A degenerative neurological disorder caused by poisoning with a mercury compound found in seafood from contaminated waters. [After *Minamata,* a town of western Kyushu, Japan.]

min·a·ret (mĭn′ə-rĕt′) *n.* A tower attached to a mosque, from which a muezzin summons the people to prayer. [Fr. < Turk. *mināret* < Ar. *manāra,* lamp.]

Mi·nas Basin (mī′nəs) An arm of the Bay of Fundy extending into W-central Nova Scotia, Canada; connected with the bay by **Minas Channel.**

min·a·to·ry (mĭn′ə-tôr′ē, -tōr′ē) also **min·a·to·ri·al** (mĭn′ə-tôr′ē-əl, -tōr′-) *adj.* Of a menacing or threatening nature; minacious. [Fr. *minatoire* < LLat. *minātōrius* < Lat. *minātus,* p. part. of *minārī,* to threaten. See MINACIOUS.] —**min′a·to′ri·ly** *adv.*

min·au·dière (mē′nō-dyâr′) *n., pl.* **-dières** (-dyâr′, -dyâr′) A small ornamental case for a woman's cosmetics, jewelry, or personal items. [Fr. < fem. of *minaudier,* affected, smirking < *minauder,* to simper, smirk < *mine,* appearance, countenance < OFr., prob. < Breton *min,* muzzle.]

mince (mĭns) *v.* **minced, minc·ing, minc·es** —*tr.* **1a.** To cut or chop into very small pieces. **b.** To subdivide (land, for example) into minute parts. **2.** To pronounce in an affected way, as with refinement. **3.** To moderate or restrain (words) for the sake of politeness; euphemize. —*intr.* **1.** To walk with very short steps or with exaggerated primness. **2.** To speak in an affected way. **n.** Finely chopped food, esp. mincemeat. [ME *mincen* < OFr. *mincier* < VLat. *minūtiāre < Lat. *minūtia,* smallness. See MINUTIA.] —**minc′er** *n.*

mince·meat (mĭns′mēt′) *n.* **1.** A mixture, as of finely chopped apples, raisins, spices, meat, and sometimes rum or brandy, used esp. as a pie filling. **2.** Finely chopped meat. —***idiom:* make mincemeat of** *Slang* To destroy utterly.

minc·ing (mĭn′sĭng) *adj.* Affectedly refined or dainty. —**minc′-ing·ly** *adv.*

mind (mīnd) *n.* **1.** The human consciousness that originates in the brain and is manifested esp. in thought, perception, emotion, will, memory, and imagination. **2.** The collective conscious and unconscious processes in a sentient organism that direct and influence mental and physical behavior. **3a.** In some philosophies, a principle of intelligence or consciousness pervading reality; the spirit of consciousness regarded as an aspect of reality. **b.** Intelligence or the nonmaterial aspect of being in contrast to the material. **4.** The faculty of thinking, reasoning, and applying knowledge. **5.** A person of great mental ability. **6a.** Individual consciousness, memory, or recollection: *I'll bear the problem in mind.* **b.** A person or group that embodies certain mental qualities: *the public mind.* **c.** The thought processes characteristic of a person or group; psychological makeup: *the criminal mind.* **7.** Opinion or sentiment: *changed his mind.* **8.** Desire or inclination. **9.** Focus of thought; attention: *I can't keep my mind on work.* **10.** A healthy mental state; sanity: *losing one's mind.* **v. mind·ed, mind·ing, minds** —*tr.* **1.** To bring (an object or idea to mind); remember. **2a.** To become aware of; notice. **b.** *Upper Southern US* To have in mind as a goal or purpose; intend. **3.** To heed in order to obey: *The children minded their babysitter.* **4.** To attend to: *Mind closely what I tell you.* **5.** To be careful about: *Mind the icy sidewalk!* **6a.** To care about; be concerned about. **b.** To object to; dislike: *doesn't mind doing the chores.* **7.** To take care or charge of; look after. See Syns at **tend**[2]. —*intr.* **1.** To take notice; give heed. **2.** To behave obediently. **3.** To be concerned or troubled; care. **4.** To be cautious or careful. [ME *minde* < OE *gemynd.* See **men-**[1] in App.] —**mind′er** *n.*

mind-al·ter·ing (mīnd′ôl′tər-ĭng) *adj.* Producing mood changes or distorted perceptions; hallucinogenic.

Min·da·na·o (mĭn′də-nä′ō, -nou′) An island of the S Philippines NE of Borneo bordering on the **Mindanao Sea.**

mind-bend·ing (mīnd′bĕn′dĭng) *adj. Informal* Intensely affecting the mind, esp. to the extent of producing hallucinations. —**mind′-bend′er** *n.* —**mind′-bend′ing·ly** *adv.*

mind-blow·ing (mīnd′blō′ĭng) *adj. Informal* **1.** Producing hallucinatory effects: *mind-blowing drugs.* **2.** Intensely affecting the mind or emotions. —**mind′blow′er** *n.*

mind-bod·y (mīnd′bŏd′y) *adj.* Of, involving, or resulting from the connection between one's physical health and the state of one's mind or spirit.

mind-bog·gling (mīnd′bŏg′lĭng) *adj. Informal* Intellectually or

emotionally overwhelming. —**mind′-bog′gler** *n.*

mind·ed (mīn′dĭd) *adj.* **1.** Disposed; inclined. **2.** Having a specified kind of mind. Often used in combination: *fair-minded; evil-minded.* **3.** Directed or oriented toward something specified. Often used in combination: *civic-minded; career-minded.* —**mind′ed·ness** *n.*

Min·den (mĭn′dən) A city of NW Germany on the Weser R. S of Bremen; founded c. 800 by Charlemagne. Pop. 75,419.

mind-ex·pand·ing (mīnd′ĭk-spăn′dĭng) *adj.* **1.** Producing intensified or distorted perceptions; psychedelic. **2.** Producing an increased perceptive awareness.

mind·ful (mīnd′fəl) *adj.* Attentive; heedful. See Syns at **careful.** —**mind′ful·ly** *adv.* —**mind′ful·ness** *n.*

mind game *n.* An act or series of acts of calculated psychological manipulation. Often used in the plural.

mind·less (mīnd′lĭs) *adj.* **1a.** Lacking intelligence or good sense; foolish. **b.** Having no intelligent purpose, meaning, or direction. **2.** Giving or showing little attention or care; heedless. —**mind′-less·ly** *adv.* —**mind′less·ness** *n.*

Min·do·ro (mĭn-dôr′ō, -dōr′ō) An island of the W-central Philippines S of Luzon; first visited by Spaniards in 1570.

mind reading *n.* The faculty of discerning another's thoughts through extrasensory means of communication; telepathy. —**mind reader** *n.*

mind·set or **mind-set** (mīnd′sĕt′) *n.* **1.** A fixed mental attitude or disposition that predetermines a person's responses to and interpretations of situations. **2.** An inclination or a habit.

mind's eye (mīndz) *n.* **1.** The inherent mental ability to imagine or remember scenes. **2.** The imagination.

mine[1] (mīn) *n.* **1a.** An excavation in the earth from which ore or minerals can be extracted. **b.** The site of such an excavation, with its surface buildings, elevator shafts, and equipment. **2.** A deposit of ore or minerals in the earth or on its surface. **3.** An abundant supply or source of something valuable. **4a.** A tunnel dug under an enemy emplacement to cause it to collapse, lay explosives, or gain an avenue of attack. **b.** An explosive device used to destroy enemy personnel, shipping, fortifications, or equipment, often designed to be detonated by contact, proximity, or a time fuse. **5.** A burrow or tunnel made by an insect, esp. a corridor on a leaf made by a leaf miner. **v. mined, min·ing, mines** —*tr.* **1a.** To extract (ore or minerals) from the earth. **b.** To dig a mine in (the earth) to obtain ore or minerals. **2a.** To tunnel under (the earth or a surface feature). **b.** To make (a tunnel) by digging. **3.** To lay explosive mines in or under. **4.** To attack, damage, or destroy by underhand means; subvert. **5.** To delve into and make use of; exploit. —*intr.* **1a.** To excavate the earth for the purpose of extracting ore or minerals. **b.** To work in a mine. **2.** To dig a tunnel under the earth, esp. under an enemy emplacement or fortification. **3.** To lay explosive mines. [ME < OFr. < VLat. **mīna,* prob. of Celt. orig.]

mine[2] (mīn) *pron. (used with a sing. or pl. verb)* Used to indicate the one or ones belonging to me: *The green gloves are mine. If you can't find your hat, take mine.* **adj.** *Archaic* A possessive form of I[1]. Used instead of *my* before an initial vowel or the letter *h.* [ME < OE *mīn.* See **me-**[1] in App.]

mine·a·ble (mī′nə-bəl) *adj.* Variant of **minable.**

mine·field (mīn′fēld′) *n.* **1.** An area in which explosive mines have been placed. **2.** A situation that has many potential hazards or dangers.

mine·lay·er (mīn′lā′ər) *n.* A ship equipped for laying explosive underwater mines.

min·er (mī′nər) *n.* **1.** One whose work or business it is to extract ore or minerals from the earth. **2.** A machine for the extraction of minerals, esp. of coal. **3.** A soldier, often a specialist, engaged in mining operations. **4.** *Zoology* A leaf miner.

min·er·al (mĭn′ər-əl) *n.* **1.** A naturally occurring, homogeneous inorganic solid substance having a definite chemical composition and characteristic crystalline structure, color, and hardness. **2.** Any of various natural substances, as: **a.** An element, such as gold. **b.** An organic derivative, such as coal. **c.** A substance, such as stone or coal, extracted or obtained from the ground or water and used in economic activities. **3.** A substance that is neither animal nor vegetable; inorganic matter. **4.** An inorganic element, such as calcium, essential to the nutrition of humans, animals, and plants. **5.** An ore. **6. minerals** *Chiefly British* Mineral water. **adj.** **1.** Of or relating to minerals. **2.** Impregnated with minerals. [ME < Med.Lat. *minerāle* < neut. of *minerālis,* of mines < OFr. *miniere,* mine < *mine.* See MINE[1].]

min·er·al·ize (mĭn′ər-ə-līz′) *v.* **-ized, -iz·ing, -iz·es** —*tr.* **1.** To convert to a mineral substance. **2.** To transform a metal into a mineral by oxidation. **3.** To impregnate with minerals. —*intr.* **1.** To develop or hasten mineral formation. **2.** To collect or study minerals. —**min′er·al·iz′a·ble** *adj.* —**min′er·al·i·za′tion** (-ə-lĭ-zā′shən) *n.* —**min′er·al·iz′er** *n.*

mineral kingdom *n.* The group of natural objects and substances that are composed only of inorganic matter.

min·er·al·o·cor·ti·coid (mĭn′ər-ə-lō-kôr′tĭ-koid′) *n.* Any of a group of corticoid hormones, such as aldosterone, that regulate the balance of water and electrolytes in the body.

min·er·al·o·gy (mĭn′ə-rŏl′ə-jē, -răl′-) *n., pl.* **-gies 1.** The study of minerals, including their distribution, identification, and properties. **2.** A book or treatise on mineralogy. —**min′er•a•log′i•cal** (-ər-ə-lŏj′ĭ-kəl) *adj.* —**min′er•a•log′i•cal•ly** *adv.* —**min′er•al′o•gist** *n.*

mineral oil *n.* **1.** Any of various light hydrocarbon oils, esp. a distillate of petroleum. **2.** A refined distillate of petroleum, used as a laxative.

mineral tar *n.* Maltha.

mineral water *n.* Naturally occurring or prepared water that contains dissolved mineral salts, elements, or gases.

mineral wax *n.* Ozocerite.

mineral wool *n.* An inorganic fibrous substance produced by steam blasting and cooling molten glass or a similar substance and used as an insulator and a filtering material.

Mi•ner•va (mĭ-nûr′və) *n. Roman Mythology* The goddess of wisdom, invention, the arts, and martial prowess. [Lat. See **men-**[1] in App.]

mine•shaft (mīn′shăft′) *n.* A vertical or sloping passageway made in the earth for finding or mining ore and ventilating underground excavations.

mine•stro•ne (mĭn′ĭ-strō′nē -strōn′) *n.* A thick soup of Italian origin containing assorted vegetables, beans, pasta, and herbs in a broth. [Ital., augmentative of *minestra*, dish of pasta, rice, vegetables or beans < OItal. < *minestrare*, to dish up < Lat. *ministrāre*, to serve food < *minister*, servant.]

mine•sweep•er (mīn′swēp′ər) *n.* A ship equipped for detecting, destroying, removing, or neutralizing explosive marine mines. —**mine′sweep′ing** *n.*

Ming (mĭng) A Chinese dynasty (1368–1644) noted esp. for its development of the arts. —**Ming** *adj.*

min•gle (mĭng′gəl) *v.* **-gled, -gling, -gles** —*tr.* **1.** To mix or bring together in combination, usu. without loss of individual characteristics. **2.** To mix so that the components become united; merge. —*intr.* **1.** To be or become mixed or united. **2.** To join or take part with others: *The faculty mingled with the trustees.* [ME *menglen*, freq. of *mengen*, to mix < OE *mengan*.] —**min′gler** *n.*

Min•gus (mĭng′gəs), **Charles** 1922–79. Amer. jazz bassist and composer of complex works incorporating elements of jazz, classical, and gospel.

min•gy (mĭn′jē) *adj.* **-gi•er, -gi•est** *Informal* **1.** Small in quantity; meager: *mingy wages.* **2.** Mean and stingy. [Perh. < M(EAN)[2] + (ST)INGY.]

Mi•nho (mē′nyōō) or **Mi•ño** (-nyō) A river flowing c. 338 km (210 mi) from NW Spain to the Atlantic Ocean.

min•i (mĭn′ē) *n., pl.* **min•is 1.** Something distinctively smaller than others of its type. **2.** A miniskirt. [< MINI-. Sense 2 < MINISKIRT.] —**min′i** *adj.*

mini- *pref.* Small; miniature: *minibike.* [< MINIATURE and MINIMUM.]

min•i•a•ture (mĭn′ē-ə-choŏr′, -chər, mĭn′ə-) *n.* **1a.** A copy or model that represents or reproduces something in a greatly reduced size. **b.** Something small of its class. **2a.** A small painting executed with great detail. **b.** A small portrait, picture, or decorative letter on an illuminated manuscript. **c.** The art of painting miniatures. ❖ *adj.* Being on a small or greatly reduced scale. See Syns at **small.** [Ital. *miniatura*, illumination of manuscripts < *miniare*, to illuminate < Lat. *miniāre*, to color red < *minium*, red lead.] —**min′i•a•tur′ist** *n.*

miniature golf *n.* A version of golf played with a putter on a miniature course having obstacles.

min•i•a•tur•ize (mĭn′ē-ə-chə-rīz′, mĭn′ə-) *tr.v.* **-ized, -iz•ing, -iz•es** To plan or make on a greatly reduced scale. —**min′i•a•tur′i•za′tion** (-chər-ĭ-zā′shən) *n.*

min•i•bike (mĭn′ē-bīk′) *n.* A small motorbike having a low frame, small wheels, and elevated handlebars. [Orig. a trademark.] —**min′i•bik′er** *n.*

min•i•bus (mĭn′ē-bŭs′) *n., pl.* **-bus•es** or **-bus•ses** A small bus typically used for short trips.

min•i•cam (mĭn′ē-kăm′) *n.* A small portable television camera used esp. for on-the-scene videotaping. [MINI- + CAM(ERA).]

min•i•car (mĭn′ē-kär′) *n.* A very small car, esp. a subcompact.

min•i•com•put•er (mĭn′ē-kəm-pyoŏ′tər) *n.* A mid-sized computer, usu. fitting within a single cabinet about the size of a refrigerator, that has less memory than a mainframe.

Min•i•con•jou also **Min•ne•con•jou** (mĭn′ĭ-kŏn′jōō) *n., pl.* **Miniconjou** or **-jous** also **Minneconjou** or **-jous** A member of a Native American people constituting a subdivision of the Teton Sioux, once inhabiting an area from the Black Hills to the Platte River and presently in South Dakota.

Mi•ni•coy Island (mĭn′ĭ-koi′) An island in the Arabian Sea off the SW coast of India.

min•ié ball (mĭn′ē, mĭn′ē-ā′) *n.* A conical rifle bullet used in the 19th century, having a hollow base that expanded when fired. [After Claude Étienne *Minié* (1814?–79), French army officer.]

min•i•fy (mĭn′ə-fī′) *tr.v.* **-fied, -fy•ing, -fies** To make smaller or less significant; reduce. [MIN(IMUM) + (MAGN)IFY.]

min•i•kin (mĭn′ĭ-kĭn) *n. Archaic* A very small delicate creature. [Obsolete Du. *minneken*, darling < MDu., dim. of *minne*, love. See **men-**[1] in App.]

min•im (mĭn′əm) *n.* **1.** A unit of fluid measure, as: **a.** In the United States, ¹⁄₆₀ of a fluid dram (0.0616 milliliter). **b.** In Great Britain, ¹⁄₂₀ of a scruple (0.0592 milliliter). **2.** *Music* A half note.

3. An insignificantly small portion or thing. **4.** A downward vertical stroke in handwriting. [ME, half note < Med.Lat. *minimus*, least < Lat.]

min•i•mal (mĭn′ə-məl) *adj.* **1a.** Smallest in amount or degree. **b.** Small in amount or degree. **c.** Only barely adequate. **2.** often **Minimal** Of, relating to, or being minimalism. —**min′i•mal′i•ty** (-măl′ĭ-tē) *n.* —**min′i•mal•ly** *adv.*

minimal art *n.* See **minimalism 1.** —**minimal artist** *n.*

min•i•mal•ism (mĭn′ə-mə-lĭz′əm) *n.* **1.** A school of abstract art that emphasizes simplification of form, as by the use of basic shapes. **2.** Use of the fewest and barest essentials or elements, as in literature or design. **3.** *Music* A school or mode of contemporary music marked by simplified rhythms, patterns, and harmonies and prolonged chordal or melodic repetitions.

min•i•mal•ist (mĭn′ə-mə-lĭst) *n.* **1.** One who advocates a moderate or conservative approach, action, or policy, as in a political organization. **2.** A practitioner of minimalism. ❖ *adj.* **1.** Of, relating to, characteristic of, or in the style of minimalism. **2.** Being or providing the bare minimum.

min•i•mal•ize (mĭn′ə-mə-līz′) *tr.v.* **-ized, -iz•ing, -iz•es** To make minimal. —**min′i•mal•i•za′tion** (-mə-lĭ-zā′shən) *n.*

min•i•mize (mĭn′ə-mīz′) *tr.v.* **-mized, -miz•ing, -miz•es 1a.** To reduce to the smallest possible amount, extent, size, or degree. **b.** To reduce. **2.** To represent as having the least degree of importance, value, or size. [< MINIMUM.] —**min′i•mi•za′tion** (-mī-zā′shən) *n.* —**min′i•miz′er** *n.*

min•i•mum (mĭn′ə-məm) *n., pl.* **-mums** or **-ma** (-mə) **1a.** The least possible quantity or degree. **b.** The lowest degree or amount reached or recorded; the lower limit of variation. **2.** A lower limit permitted by law or other authority. **3.** A sum of money set by a nightclub or restaurant as the least amount each patron must spend. **4.** *Mathematics* **a.** The smallest number in a finite set of numbers. **b.** A value of a function that is less than any other value of the function over a specific interval. ❖ *adj.* Of, consisting of, or representing the lowest possible amount or degree permissible or attainable. [Lat. < neut. of *minimus*, least.]

minimum wage *n.* **1.** The lowest wage, determined by law or contract, that an employer may pay an employee for a specified job. **2.** See **living wage.**

min•ing (mī′nĭng) *n.* **1.** The process or business of extracting ore or minerals from the ground. **2a.** The process of digging under an enemy emplacement to cause it to collapse, lay explosives, or gain access for an attack. **b.** The process of laying explosive mines.

min•ion (mĭn′yən) *n.* **1.** An obsequious follower or dependent; a sycophant. **2.** A subordinate official. **3.** One highly esteemed or favored; a darling. [Fr. *mignon*, darling < OFr.]

min•is•cule (mĭn′ĭ-skyoŏl′) *adj.* Variant of **minuscule.**

min•i•se•ries (mĭn′ē-sîr′ēz) *n., pl.* **miniseries** A televised production of a novel, shown in a number of episodes.

min•i•skirt (mĭn′ē-skûrt′) *n.* A short skirt with a hemline that falls several inches above the knee. —**min′i•skirt′ed** *adj.*

min•i•state (mĭn′ē-stāt′) *n.* See **microstate.**

min•is•ter (mĭn′ĭ-stər) *n.* **1a.** One who is authorized to perform religious functions in a Christian church, esp. a Protestant church. **b.** *Roman Catholic Church* The superior in certain orders. **2.** A high officer of state appointed to head an executive or administrative department of government. **3.** An authorized diplomatic representative of a government, usu. ranking next below an ambassador. **4.** A person serving as an agent for another by carrying out specified orders or functions. ❖ *v.* **-tered, -ter•ing, -ters** —*intr.* **1.** To attend to others' wants and needs. See Syns at **tend**[2]. **2.** To perform the functions of a cleric. —*tr.* To administer or dispense (a sacrament, for example). [ME < OFr. *ministre* < Lat. *minister*, servant.]

min•is•te•ri•al (mĭn′ĭ-stîr′ē-əl) *adj.* **1.** Of, relating to, or characteristic of a minister of religion or of the ministry. **2.** Of or relating to administrative and executive duties and functions of government. **3.** *Law* Of, relating to, or being a mandatory act or duty admitting of no personal discretion or judgment in its performance. **4.** Acting or serving as an agent; instrumental. —**min′is•te′ri•al•ly** *adv.*

minister plenipotentiary *n., pl.* **ministers plenipotentiary** A diplomatic representative ranking below an ambassador but having full governmental power and authority.

minister resident *n., pl.* **ministers resident** A diplomatic agent ranking below a minister plenipotentiary.

min•is•trant (mĭn′ĭ-strənt) *n.* One who ministers. ❖ *adj.* Serving attendance on someone.

min•is•tra•tion (mĭn′ĭ-strā′shən) *n.* **1.** The act or process of serving or aiding. **2.** The act of performing the duties of a cleric. [ME < OFr. < Lat. *ministrātiō*, *ministrātiōn-* < *ministrātus*, p. part. of *ministrāre*, to serve < *minister*, servant. See MINISTER.] —**min′is•tra′tive** *adj.*

min•is•try (mĭn′ĭ-strē) *n., pl.* **-tries 1a.** The act of serving; ministration. **b.** One that serves as a means; an instrumentality. **2a.** The profession, duties, and services of a minister. **b.** The Christian clergy. **c.** The period of service of a minister. **3a.** A governmental department presided over by a minister. **b.** The building in which such a department is housed. **c.** The duties, functions, or term of a governmental minister. **d.** often **Ministry** Govern-

minitower

mink
American mink
Mustela vison

minor scale

mental ministers considered as a group. [ME *ministerie* < OFr. *ministere* < Lat. *ministerium* < *minister*, servant.]

min·i·tow·er (mĭn′ē-tou′ər) *n.* A computer cabinet that is about half the height of a cabinet that houses a tower computer.

min·i·track (mĭn′ĭ-trăk′) *n.* An electronic system designed to follow the course of satellites and rockets and to correlate radio signals received by a network of ground stations.

min·i·um (mĭn′ē-əm) *n.* Red lead. [Lat.]

min·i·van (mĭn′ē-văn′) *n.* A small passenger van having a box-like shape and typically removable rear seats for cargo.

min·i·ver (mĭn′ə-vər) *n.* A white or light gray fur used as a trim on medieval robes and on ceremonial robes of state. [ME *meniver* < OFr. *menu vair*, small vair : *menu*, small; see MINUET + *vair*, vair; see VAIR.]

mink (mĭngk) *n., pl.* **mink** or **minks 1.** Any of various semi-aquatic carnivores of the genus *Mustela*, esp. *M. vison* of North America, having short ears, a pointed snout, and short legs. **2a.** The fur of the mink. **b.** A coat, stole, or hat made of mink. [ME, mink fur, poss. of Scand. orig.]

mink·e whale (mĭng′kē) *n.* See **piked whale**. [Partial transl. of Norw. *minkehval* : *minke* (perhaps after *Meincke*, member of a 19th-cent. Norwegian whaling crew) + *hval*, whale.]

Minn. *abbr.* Minnesota

Min·ne·ap·o·lis (mĭn′ē-ăp′ə-lĭs) A city of SE MN on the Mississippi R. adjacent to St. Paul. Pop. 382,618.

Min·ne·con·jou (mĭn′ĭ-kŏn′jōō) *n.* Variant of **Miniconjou.**

min·ne·sing·er (mĭn′ĭ-sĭng′ər, -zĭng′-) *n.* One of the German lyric poets and singers in the troubadour tradition who flourished from the 12th to the 14th century. [Ger. < MHGer. : *minne*, love (< OHGer. *minna*; see **men-**[1] in App.) + *singer*, singer; see MEISTERSINGER.]

Min·ne·so·ta (mĭn′ĭ-sō′tə) A state of the N US bordering on Lake Superior and on Manitoba and Ontario, Canada; admitted as the 32nd state in 1858. Cap. St. Paul. Pop. 4,919,479. —**Min′ne·so′tan** *adj. & n.*

Minnesota River A river of S MN flowing c. 534 km (332 mi) to the Mississippi R. near St. Paul.

Min·ne·wit (mĭn′ə-wĭt), **Peter** See Peter Minuit.

min·now (mĭn′ō) *n., pl.* **minnow** or **-nows 1.** Any of a large group of small freshwater fishes of the family Cyprinidae, widely used as live bait. **2.** Any of various other small, often silver-colored fishes. [ME *meneu.* See **men-**[2] in App.]

Mi·ño (mē′nyō) See **Minho.**

Mi·no·an (mĭ-nō′ən) *adj.* Of or relating to the advanced Bronze Age culture that flourished in Crete from about 3000 to 1100 B.C. ✦ *n.* A native or inhabitant of ancient Crete. [< Lat. *Mīnōus*, of Minos < Gk. *Mīnōios* < *Mīnōs*, Minos.]

mi·nor (mī′nər) *adj.* **1.** Lesser or smaller in amount, extent, or size. **2.** Lesser in importance, rank, or stature: *a minor politician.* **3.** Lesser in seriousness or danger: *a minor injury.* **4.** *Law* Being under legal age; not yet a legal adult. **5.** *Chiefly British* Relating to or being the younger or junior of two pupils with the same surname. **6.** Of or relating to a secondary area of academic specialization. **7.** *Logic* Dealing with a more restricted category. **8.** *Music* **a.** Relating to or being a minor scale. **b.** Less in distance by a half step than the corresponding major interval. **c.** Based on a minor scale: *a minor key.* ✦ *n.* **1.** One that is lesser in comparison with others of the same class. **2.** *Law* One who has not reached full legal age. **3a.** A minor area of academic study. **b.** One studying a minor field: *She is a physics minor.* **4.** *Logic* **a.** A minor premise. **b.** A minor term. **5.** *Music* A minor key, scale, or interval. **6.** **minors** *Sports* The minor leagues of a sport, esp. baseball. ✦ *intr.v.* **-nored, -nor·ing, -nors** To pursue academic studies in a minor field: *minored in music.* [ME < Lat.]

Mi·nor·ca[1] (mĭ-nôr′kə) also **Me·nor·ca** (mə-nôr′kə, mĕ-nôr′kä) A Spanish island in the Balearics of the W Mediterranean Sea. —**Mi·nor′can** *adj. & n.*

Mi·nor·ca[2] (mĭ-nôr′kə) *n.* A domestic fowl of a breed originating in the Mediterranean region and having white or black plumage. [After MINORCA[1].]

Mi·nor·ite (mī′nə-rīt′) *n.* A Franciscan friar. [< Med.Lat. (*Frātrēs*) *Minōrēs*, minor (friars) < Lat. *minōrēs*, pl. of *minor*, lesser. See MINOR.]

mi·nor·i·ty (mə-nôr′ĭ-tē, -nŏr′-, mī-) *n., pl.* **-ties 1a.** The smaller in number of two groups forming a whole. **b.** A group or party having fewer than a controlling number of votes. **2a.** An ethnic, racial, religious, or other group having a distinctive presence within a society. **b.** A group having little power or representation relative to other groups within a society. **c.** A member of one of these groups. See Usage Note at **color. 3.** *Law* The state or period of being under legal age: *still in her minority.*

minority leader *n.* The head of the minority party in a legislative body.

minor league *n.* A league of professional sports clubs that are not in the major leagues but are usu. owned by or affiliated with major-league teams. —**mi′nor-league′** (mī′nər-lēg′) *adj.* —**mi′nor-leagu′er** *n.*

minor order *n. Ecclesiastical* One of the lower grades of the priesthood or ministry in some Christian churches. Often used in the plural.

minor planet *n.* See **asteroid** 1.

minor premise *n.* The premise in a syllogism containing the minor term, which will form the subject of the conclusion.

Minor Prophets *pl.n.* The Hebrew prophets Hosea, Joel, Amos, Obadiah, Jonah, Micah, Nahum, Habakkuk, Zephaniah, Haggai, Zechariah, and Malachi.

minor scale *n. Music* A diatonic scale having a half step between the second and third degrees and any of several intervalic arrangements above the fifth.

minor suit *n. Games* A suit of inferior scoring value, either clubs or diamonds in bridge.

minor term *n.* The term in a syllogism that is stated in the minor premise and forms the subject of the conclusion.

Mi·nos (mī′nəs, -nŏs′) *n. Greek Mythology* A king of Crete who was made one of the three judges in the underworld.

Mi·not (mī′nŏt′) A city of NW-central ND NNW of Bismarck. Pop. 36,567.

Min·o·taur (mĭn′ə-tôr′, mī′nə-) *n. Greek Mythology* A monster who was half man and half bull, to whom young Athenian men and women were sacrificed in the Cretan labyrinth.

mi·nox·i·dil (mə-nŏk′sĭ-dĭl′) *n.* A vasodilator, C₉H₁₅N₅O, administered orally to treat hypertension and used topically to promote hair growth in male pattern baldness. [(A)MIN(O)– + OXID(E) + *-il* (alteration of –YL).]

Minsk (mĭnsk, myĕnsk) The cap. of Belarus, in the central part; ruled since the 13th cent. by various powers, including Lithuania, Russia, Poland, and Sweden. Pop. 1,654,800.

min·ster (mĭn′stər) *n. Chiefly British* A monastery church. [ME < OE *mynster* < VLat. **monistērium* < LLat. *monastērium*, monastery. See MONASTERY.]

min·strel (mĭn′strəl) *n.* **1.** A medieval entertainer who traveled from place to place, esp. to sing and recite poetry. **2a.** A lyric poet. **b.** A musician. **3.** A performer in a minstrel show. [ME *minstral* < OFr. *menestrel*, servant, entertainer < LLat. *ministeriālis*, imperial household official < Lat. *ministerium*, ministry. See MINISTRY.]

minstrel show *n.* A comic variety show of the 19th and early 20th centuries, usu. featuring white performers in blackface.

min·strel·sy (mĭn′strəl-sē) *n., pl.* **-sies 1.** The art or profession of a minstrel. **2.** A troupe of minstrels. **3.** Ballads and lyrics sung by minstrels. [ME *minstralsie* < AN *menestralsie* < OFr. *menestrel*, entertainer. See MINSTREL.]

mint[1] (mĭnt) *n.* **1.** A place where the coins of a country are manufactured by authority of the government. **2.** A place or source of manufacture or invention. **3.** An abundant amount, esp. of money. ✦ *tr.v.* **mint·ed, mint·ing, mints 1.** To produce (money) by stamping metal; coin. **2.** To invent or fabricate. ✦ *adj.* Undamaged as if freshly minted. [ME < OE *mynet*, coin < Lat. *monēta*. See MONEY.] —**mint′er** *n.*

mint[2] (mĭnt) *n.* **1.** A member of the mint family. **2a.** Any of various plants of the genus *Mentha*, some of which are cultivated for their aromatic oil and used for flavoring. **b.** The aromatic foliage of some of these plants. **3.** Any of various similar or related plants. **4.** A candy flavored with mint. [ME *minte* < OE < Gmc. **minta* < Lat. *menta*, poss. < Gk. *minthē*.] —**mint′y** *adj.*

mint·age (mĭn′tĭj) *n.* **1.** The act or process of minting coins. **2.** Coins manufactured in a mint. **3.** The fee paid to a mint by a government. **4.** The impression stamped on a coin.

mint family *n.* A large family of aromatic herbs, the Labiatae (or Lamiaceae), characterized by opposite leaves, square stems, and bilaterally symmetrical flowers.

mint julep *n.* A drink of bourbon, sugar, and mint leaves.

min·u·end (mĭn′yōō-ĕnd′) *n.* The quantity from which another quantity, the subtrahend, is to be subtracted. [Lat. *minuendum*, thing to be diminished < neut. gerundive of *minuere*, to lessen.]

min·u·et (mĭn′yōō-ĕt′) *n.* **1.** A slow stately pattern dance in 3/4 time for groups of couples, originating in 17th-century France. **2.** The music for or in the rhythm of the minuet. **3.** A movement in 3/4 time that is usu. the third of four movements in a symphony or string quartet. [Fr. *menuet* < OFr., small, dainty (< its small steps), dim. of *menu*, small < Lat. *minūtus*. See MINUTE[2].]

Min·u·it (mĭn′yōō-ĭt) also **Min·ne·wit** (-ə-wĭt), **Peter** 1580–1638. Dutch colonial administrator who purchased Manhattan from the Wappinger for trade goods legendarily valued at $24.

mi·nus (mī′nəs) *prep.* **1.** *Mathematics* Reduced by the subtraction of; less: *Nine minus three is six.* **2.** *Informal* Without: *I went to work minus my ID.* ✦ *adj.* **1.** *Mathematics* Negative or on the negative part of a scale. **2.** Ranking on the lower end of a designated scale. ✦ *n.* **1.** *Mathematics* **a.** The minus sign (–). **b.** A negative quantity. **2.** A deficiency or defect. [ME < Lat. *minus*, neut. of *minor*, less.]

mi·nus·cule (mĭn′ə-skyōōl′, mĭ-nŭs′kyōōl′) also **min·is·cule** (mĭn′ĭ-skyōōl′) *adj.* **1.** Very small; tiny. See Syns at **small. 2.** Of, relating to, or written in minuscule. ✦ *n.* **1.** A small cursive script developed from uncial and used in medieval manuscripts. **2.** Letter written in minuscule. **3.** A lowercase letter. [Fr. < Lat. *minusculus*, rather small, dim. of *minus*, neut. of *minor*, smaller.] —**mi·nus′cu·lar** (mĭ-nŭs′kyə-lər) *adj.*

minus sign *n.* The symbol –, as in 4 – 2 = 2, that is used to indicate subtraction or a negative quantity.

min·ute[1] (mĭn′ĭt) *n.* **1.** A unit of time equal to one sixtieth of an hour, or 60 seconds. **2.** A unit of angular measurement equal to one sixtieth of a degree, or 60 seconds. **3.** A measure of the distance one can cover in a minute. **4.** A short interval of time; moment. **5.** A specific point in time. **6.** A note or summary covering points to be remembered; a memorandum. **7. minutes** An official record of the proceedings at a meeting. ❖ *tr.v.* **-ut•ed, -ut•ing, -utes** To record in a memorandum or the minutes of a meeting. [ME < OFr. < Med.Lat. *(pars) minūta (prīma)*, (first) minute (part) < Lat. *minūta*, fem. of *minūtus*, small. See MINUTE².]

mi•nute² (mī-nōōt′, -nyōōt′, mī-) *adj.* **1.** Exceptionally small; tiny. See Syns at **small. 2.** Beneath notice; insignificant. **3.** Characterized by careful scrutiny and close examination. [ME < Lat. *minūtus*, p. part. of *minuere*, to lessen.] **—mi•nute′ness** *n.*

min•ute hand (mĭn′ĭt) *n.* The long hand on a clock or watch that indicates minutes.

mi•nute•ly¹ (mī-nōōt′lē, -nyōōt′-, mī-) *adv.* **1.** With attention to small details. **2.** On a very small scale. **3.** Into tiny pieces.

min•ute•ly² (mĭn′ĭt-lē) *adj.* *Archaic* On a minute-by-minute basis.

min•ute•man (mĭn′ĭt-măn′) *n.* An armed man pledged to be ready to fight on a minute's notice just before and during the Revolutionary War in the United States.

min•ute of arc (mĭn′ĭt) *n.* See minute¹ 2.

min•ute steak (mĭn′ĭt) *n.* A small thin steak, often scored or cubed, that can be cooked quickly.

mi•nu•ti•a (mĭ-nōō′shē-ə, -shə, -nyōō′-) *n.*, *pl.* **-ti•ae** (-shē-ē′) A small or trivial detail. [< LLat. *minūtiae*, petty details < Lat. *minūtia*, smallness < *minūtus*, small. See MINUTE².]

minx (mĭngks) *n.* **1.** A girl or young woman considered pert, flirtatious, or impudent. **2.** *Obsolete* A promiscuous woman. [Prob. < obsolete *mynx*, playful little dog, perh. < alteration of obsolete Du. *minneken*, darling, dear.] **—minx′ish** *adj.*

min•yan (mĭn′yən, mēn-yän′) *n.*, *pl.* **min•ya•nim** (mēn-yä-nēm′, mĭn-yô′nĭm) or **min•yans** (mĭn′yənz) The minimum number of ten adult Jews or, among the Orthodox, Jewish men required for a communal religious service. [Heb. *minyān*, number, minyan < Aram. *minyānā* < *mənā*, to count.]

Mi•o•cene (mī′ə-sēn′) *adj.* Of or belonging to the geologic time of the fourth epoch of the Tertiary Period, characterized by the development of grasses and grazing mammals. See table at **geologic time.** ❖ *n.* The Miocene Epoch or its deposits. [Gk. *meiōn*, less + -CENE.]

mi•o•sis also **my•o•sis** (mī-ō′sĭs) *n.*, *pl.* **-ses** (-sēz) Constriction of the pupil of the eye, resulting from a normal response to an increase in light or caused by certain drugs or pathological conditions. [Gk. *mūein*, to close the eyes + -OSIS.]

mi•ot•ic (mī-ŏt′ĭk) *n.* A substance that causes miosis. ❖ *adj.* Characterized by, involving, or causing miosis. [< MIOSIS.]

MIPS *abbr.* million instructions per second

Mi•que•lon (mĭk′ə-lŏn′, mēk-lôn′) A French island in the Atlantic Ocean off the S coast of Newfoundland, Canada.

mir (mĭr) *n.* A village community of peasant farmers in prerevolutionary Russia. [Russ., commune, peace < O Church Slavonic *mirŭ*, peace, poss. of Iran. orig.]

Mi•ra•beau (mĭr′ə-bō′, mē-rä-bō′), Comte de. 1749–91. French revolutionist who advocated a constitutional monarchy.

mi•ra•bi•le dic•tu (mĭ-rä′bĭ-lē dĭk′tōō) *interj.* Wonderful to relate. [Lat. *mīrābile dictū* : *mīrābile*, neut. sing. of *mīrābilis*, wonderful + *dictū*, ablative sing. supine of *dīcere*, to say.]

mir•a•cle (mĭr′ə-kəl) *n.* **1.** An event that appears inexplicable by the laws of nature, held to be supernatural in origin or an act of God: *"Miracles are spontaneous, they cannot be summoned, but come of themselves"* (Katherine Anne Porter). **2.** One that excites admiring awe. See Syns at **wonder. 3.** A miracle play. [ME < OFr. < Lat. *mīrāculum* < *mīrārī*, to wonder at < *mīrus*, wonderful.]

miracle drug *n.* A usu. new, extremely effective drug.

miracle play *n.* A medieval drama portraying events in the lives of saints and martyrs.

mi•rac•u•lous (mĭ-răk′yə-ləs) *adj.* **1.** Of the nature of a miracle; preternatural. **2.** So astounding as to suggest a miracle; phenomenal: *a miraculous recovery.* **3.** Able to work miracles. [Ult. < Lat. *mīrāculum*, miracle. See MIRACLE.] **—mi•rac′u•lous•ly** *adv.* **—mi•rac′u•lous•ness** *n.*

mir•a•dor (mĭr′ə-dôr′, -dôr′) *n.* A window, balcony, or small tower affording an extensive view. [Catalan < *mirar*, to view < Lat. *mīrārī*, to wonder at. See MIRAGE.]

mi•rage (mĭ-räzh′) *n.* **1.** An optical phenomenon that creates the illusion of water and results from distortion of light by alternate layers of hot and cool air. **2.** Something illusory or insubstantial. [Fr. < *mirer*, to look at < Lat. *mīrārī*, to wonder at < *mīrus*, wonderful.]

Mi•ran•da¹ (mə-răn′də) *n.* A satellite of Uranus. [After *Miranda*, daughter of the magician Prospero in *The Tempest* by William Shakespeare.]

Mi•ran•da² (mə-răn′də) *adj.* Of or relating to a warning given by police to a criminal suspect advising of the constitutional right against self-incrimination and of the right to have a lawyer present during any interrogation. [After Ernesto A. *Miranda* (1940?–76), plaintiff in *Miranda v. Arizona* (1966).]

mire (mīr) *n.* **1.** An area of wet, soggy, muddy ground; a bog. **2.** Deep slimy soil or mud. **3.** A disadvantageous or difficult condition or situation. ❖ *v.* **mired, mir•ing, mires** *—tr.* **1a.** To cause

---

to sink or become stuck in or as if in mire. **b.** To hinder, entrap, or entangle as if in mire. **2.** To soil with mud or mire. *—intr.* To sink or become stuck in mire. [ME < ON *mȳrr*, bog.]

mi•rex (mī′rĕks) *n.* An insecticide, C₁₀Cl₁₂, used esp. against ants. [Perh. (PIS)MIR(E) + EX(TERMINATE).]

mir•in (mĭr′ĭn) *n.* A sweet Japanese rice wine used esp. in cooking. [J. : M Chin. *mei*, flavor + M Chin. *lan*, remove the astringency of persimmons by soaking in rice wine (misread as *lin*, grove).]

mirk (mûrk) *n. & adj.* Variant of **murk.**

mirk•y (mûr′kē) *adj.* Variant of **murky.**

mir•li•ton (mĭr′lĭ-tŏn, mĭr-lē-tôn′) *n. Southern Louisiana* See **chayote.** [Louisiana Fr. < Fr., toy reed flute, tube-shaped pastry, perh. of imit. orig.]

Mi•ró (mē-rō′), Joan 1893–1983. Spanish artist whose paintings are characterized by bright colors and simple bold forms.

mir•ror (mĭr′ər) *n.* **1.** A surface capable of reflecting sufficient undiffused light to form an image of an object placed in front of it. **2.** Something that faithfully reflects or gives a true picture of something else. **3.** Something worthy of imitation. ❖ *tr.v.* **-rored, -ror•ing, -rors** To reflect in or as if in a mirror. [ME *mirour* < OFr. *mireor* < *mirer*, to look at < Lat. *mīrārī*, to wonder at < *mīrus*, wonderful.]

mirror image *n.* An image that has its parts arranged with a reversal of right and left, as it would appear in a mirror.

mirth (mûrth) *n.* Gladness and gaiety, esp. when expressed by laughter. [ME < OE *myrgth.*]

mirth•ful (mûrth′fəl) *adj.* **1.** Full of gladness and gaiety. **2.** Characterized by or expressing gladness and gaiety. **—mirth′ful•ly** *adv.* **—mirth′ful•ness** *n.*

mirth•less (mûrth′lĭs) *adj.* Devoid of gladness and gaiety. **—mirth′less•ly** *adv.* **—mirth′less•ness** *n.*

MIRV (mûrv) *n.* **1.** An offensive ballistic missile system having warheads aimed at independent targets that can be launched by a single booster rocket. **2.** Such a warhead. [*m(ultiple) i(ndependently-targeted) r(eentry) v(ehicles).*]

mir•y (mīr′ē) *adj.* **-i•er, -i•est 1.** Full of or resembling mire; swampy. **2.** Smeared with mire; muddy. **—mir′i•ness** *n.*

mis-¹ *pref.* **1.** Bad; badly; wrong; wrongly: *misconduct.* **2.** Failure; lack: *misfire.* **3.** Used as an intensive: *misdoubt.* [Partly < ME *mis-* (< OE) and partly < ME *mes-, mis-* (< OFr.).]

mis-² *pref.* Variant of **miso-.**

mis•ad•ven•ture (mĭs′əd-vĕn′chər) *n.* An instance of misfortune; a mishap. [ME *misaventure* < OFr. *mesaventure* < *mesavenir*, to result in misfortune : *mes-*, badly; see MIS-¹ + *avenir*, to turn out (< Lat. *advenīre*, to come to; see ADVENT).]

mis•al•li•ance (mĭs′ə-lī′əns) *n.* **1.** An unsuitable alliance, esp. in marriage. **2.** A mésalliance.

mis•an•thrope (mĭs′ən-thrōp′, mĭz′-) also **mis•an•thro•pist** (mĭs-ăn′thrə-pĭst, mĭz′-) *n.* One who hates or mistrusts humankind. [Fr. < Gk. *mīsanthrōpos*, hating mankind : *mīso-*, miso- + *anthrōpos*, man.]

mis•an•throp•ic (mĭs′ən-thrŏp′ĭk, mĭz′-) *adj.* **1.** Of, relating to, or characteristic of a misanthrope. **2.** Characterized by a hatred or mistrustful scorn for humankind. **—mis′an•throp′i•cal•ly** *adv.*

mis•an•thro•py (mĭs-ăn′thrə-pē, mĭz-) *n.* Hatred or mistrust of humankind.

mis•ap•pro•pri•ate (mĭs′ə-prō′prē-āt′) *tr.v.* **-at•ed, -at•ing, -ates 1a.** To appropriate wrongly. **b.** To appropriate dishonestly for one's own use; embezzle. **2.** To use illegally. **—mis′ap•pro′pri•a′tion** *n.*

mis•be•got•ten (mĭs′bĭ-gŏt′n) *adj.* **1a.** Of, relating to, or being a child or children born to parents not married to each other. **b.** Not lawfully obtained. **2.** Having an improper basis or origin: *misbegotten ideas about education.*

mis•be•have (mĭs′bĭ-hāv′) *v.* **-haved, -hav•ing, -haves** *—intr.* To behave badly. *—tr.* To behave (oneself) in an inappropriate way. **—mis′be•hav′er** *n.* **—mis′be•hav′ior** (-hāv′yər) *n.*

mis•be•lief (mĭs′bĭ-lēf′) *n.* **1.** A wrong or faulty belief. **2.** A heretical or unorthodox religious belief.

mis•be•lieve (mĭs′bĭ-lēv′) *intr.v.* **-lieved, -liev•ing, -lieves** *Obsolete* To hold a false or erroneous belief or opinion, esp. in religious matters. **—mis′be•liev′er** *n.*

mis•brand (mĭs-brănd′) *tr.v.* **-brand•ed, -brand•ing, -brands** To brand or label misleadingly or fraudulently.

misc. *abbr.* miscellaneous

mis•call (mĭs-kôl′) *tr.v.* **-called, -call•ing, -calls** To call by a wrong name.

mis•car•riage (mĭs′kăr′ĭj, mĭs-kăr′-) *n.* **1.** The premature expulsion of a nonviable fetus from the uterus. **2a.** Bad administration; mismanagement. **b.** A failure of administration or management: *a miscarriage of justice.*

mis•car•ry (mĭs′kăr′ē, mĭs-kăr′ē) *intr.v.* **-ried, -ry•ing, -ries 1.** To have a miscarriage; abort. **2.** To go astray or be lost in transit, as mail or cargo. **3.** To fail to attain an intended goal.

mis•cast (mĭs-kăst′) *tr.v.* **-cast, -cast•ing, -casts 1.** To cast in an unsuitable role. **2.** To cast (a role, play, or film) inappropriately.

mis•ceg•e•na•tion (mĭ-sĕj′ə-nā′shən, mĭs′ĭ-jə-) *n.* **1.** The interbreeding of different races or of persons of different racial backgrounds. **2.** Cohabitation, sexual relations, or marriage in-

---

Minotaur
detail from a 6th-century
B.C. amphora showing
Theseus killing the Minotaur

Joan Miró

ă	pat	oi	boy
ā	pay	ou	out
âr	care	ŏŏ	took
ä	father	ōō	boot
ĕ	pet	ŭ	cut
ē	be	ûr	urge
ĭ	pit	th	thin
ī	pie	th	this
îr	pier	hw	which
ŏ	pot	zh	vision
ō	toe	ə	about,
ô	paw		item

Stress marks:
′ (primary);
′ (secondary), as in
lexicon (lĕk′sĭ-kŏn′)

volving persons of different races. **3.** A mixture or hybridization. [Lat. *miscēre*, to mix; see **meik-** in App. + *genus*, race; see **genə-** in App. + –ATION.] —**mis·ceg'e·na'tion·al** *adj.*

mis·cel·la·ne·a (mĭs'ə-lā'nē-ə) *pl.n.* Miscellaneous items or written works collected together. [Lat. *miscellānea* < neut. pl. of *miscellāneus*, miscellaneous. See MISCELLANEOUS.]

mis·cel·la·ne·ous (mĭs'ə-lā'nē-əs) *adj.* **1.** Made up of a variety of parts or ingredients. **2.** Having a variety of characteristics, abilities, or appearances. **3.** Concerned with diverse subjects or aspects. [< Lat. *miscellāneus* < *miscellus*, mixed < *miscēre*, to mix. See **meik-** in App.] —**mis'cel·la'ne·ous·ly** *adv.* —**mis'cel·la'ne·ous·ness** *n.*

SYNONYMS *miscellaneous, heterogeneous, mixed, varied, assorted* These adjectives mean consisting of a number of different kinds. *Miscellaneous* implies a varied, often haphazard combination: *sold postcards, magazines, and miscellaneous novelties. Heterogeneous* emphasizes diversity and dissimilarity: *a heterogenous urban population. Mixed* suggests a combination of differing but not necessarily conflicting elements: *a mixed program of baroque and contemporary music. Varied* stresses absence of uniformity: *"The assembly was large and varied, containing clergy and laity, men and women"* (Nicholas P.S. Wisemen). *Assorted* often suggests the purposeful arrangement of different but complementary elements: *an arrangement of assorted flowers.*

mis·cel·la·nist (mĭs'ə-lā'nĭst, mĭ-sĕl'ə-) *n. Chiefly British* One who compiles, writes, or edits miscellanies.

mis·cel·la·ny (mĭs'ə-lā'nē) *n., pl.* **-nies 1.** A collection of various items, parts, or ingredients, esp. of diverse literary works. **2.** **miscellanies** A publication containing various literary works. [Lat. *miscellānea*, miscellanea. See MISCELLANEA.]

mis·chance (mĭs-chăns') *n.* **1.** An unfortunate occurrence; a mishap. **2.** Bad luck.

mis·chief (mĭs'chĭf) *n.* **1.** Behavior that causes discomfiture or annoyance in another. **2.** An inclination or tendency to play pranks or cause embarrassment. **3.** One that causes minor trouble or disturbance. **4.** Damage, destruction, or injury caused by a specific person or thing. **5.** The state or quality of being mischievous. [ME *mischef* < OFr. *meschief*, misfortune < *meschever*, to end badly : *mes-*, badly; see MIS-¹ + *chever*, to happen, come to an end (< VLat. **capāre*, to come to a head < **capum*, head < Lat. *caput*; see **kaput-** in App.).]

mis·chief-mak·er (mĭs'chĭf-mā'kər) *n.* One who causes mischief, esp. one who makes trouble by spreading gossip. —**mis'chief-mak'ing** *n.*

mis·chie·vous (mĭs'chə-vəs) *adj.* **1.** Causing mischief. **2.** Playful in a naughty or teasing way. **3.** Troublesome; irritating: *a mischievous prank.* **4.** Causing harm, injury, or damage. [ME *chevous < mischef*, mischief. See MISCHIEF.] —**mis'chie·vous·ly** *adv.* —**mis'chie·vous·ness** *n.*

mis·ci·ble (mĭs'ə-bəl) *adj. Chemistry* That can be mixed in all proportions. Used of liquids. [Med.Lat. *miscibilis* < Lat. *miscēre*, to mix. See **meik-** in App.] —**mis'ci·bil'i·ty** *n.*

mis·com·mu·ni·ca·tion (mĭs'kə-myoō'nĭ-kā'shən) *n.* **1.** Lack of clear or adequate communication. **2.** An unclear or inadequate communication.

mis·con·ceive (mĭs'kən-sēv') *tr.v.* **-ceived, -ceiv·ing, -ceives** To interpret incorrectly; misunderstand.

mis·con·cep·tion (mĭs'kən-sĕp'shən) *n.* A mistaken thought, idea, or notion; a misunderstanding.

mis·con·duct (mĭs-kŏn'dŭkt) *n.* **1a.** Behavior not conforming to prevailing standards or laws; impropriety. **b.** The act or an instance of adultery. **2.** Dishonest or bad management, esp. by persons entrusted or engaged to act on another's behalf. **3.** Deliberate wrongdoing, esp. by government officials. ❖ *v.* (mĭs'kən-dŭct') *tr.v.* **-duct·ed, -duct·ing, -ducts 1.** To mismanage. **2.** To behave (oneself) improperly.

mis·con·struc·tion (mĭs'kən-strŭk'shən) *n.* **1.** An inaccurate explanation, interpretation, or report; a misunderstanding. **2.** *Grammar* A faulty construction, esp. of a sentence or clause.

mis·count (mĭs-kount') *v.* **-count·ed, -count·ing, -counts** —*tr.* To count (something) incorrectly; miscalculate. —*intr.* To

make a miscount. ❖ *n.* (mĭs'kount') An inaccurate count.

mis·cre·ant (mĭs'krē-ənt) *n.* **1.** An evildoer; a villain. **2.** An infidel; a heretic. [ME *miscreaunt*, heretic < OFr. *mescreant*, pr. part. of *mescroire*, to disbelieve : *mes-*, wrongly, not; see MIS-¹ + *croire*, to believe (< Lat. *crēdere*; see **kerd-** in App.).] —**mis'cre·ant** *adj.*

mis·cre·ate (mĭs'krē-āt') *tr.v.* **-at·ed, -at·ing, -ates** To make or shape badly. ❖ *adj.* (mĭs'krē-ĭt, -āt') Formed unnaturally; misshapen or deformed. —**mis'cre·a'tion** *n.*

mis·cue (mĭs-kyoō') *n.* **1.** *Games* A stroke in billiards that misses or just brushes the ball because of a slip of the cue. **2.** A mistake. ❖ *intr.v.* **-cued, -cu·ing, -cues 1.** To make a miscue. **2.** To miss a stage cue.

mis·date (mĭs-dāt') *tr.v.* **-dat·ed, -dat·ing, -dates** To date (a document or event, for example) inaccurately. ❖ *n.* An inaccurate date.

mis·deal (mĭs-dēl') *v.* **-dealt** (-dĕlt') **, -deal·ing, -deals** —*tr.* To deal (cards) incorrectly. —*intr.* To deal cards incorrectly. —**mis'deal'** *n.* —**mis'deal'er** *n.*

mis·de·mean·ant (mĭs'dĭ-mē'nənt) *n. Law* One who has been convicted of a misdemeanor.

mis·de·mean·or (mĭs'dĭ-mē'nər) *n.* **1.** A misdeed. **2.** *Law* An offense less serious than a felony.

mis·di·al (mĭs-dī'əl) *tr. & intr.v.* **-aled, -al·ing, -als** or **-alled, -al·ling, -als** To dial or be dialed incorrectly. —**mis'di·al** *n.*

mis·di·rect (mĭs'dĭ-rĕkt', -dī-) *tr.v.* **-rect·ed, -rect·ing, -rects 1.** To aim (a blow or projectile, for example) badly. **2.** To give wrong instructions or directions to. **3.** To put a wrong address on (a piece of mail).

mis·di·rec·tion (mĭs'dĭ-rĕk'shən, -dī-) *n.* **1.** Inaccurate aim. **2.** Incorrect instructions or directions.

mis·doubt (mĭs-dout') *tr.v.* **-doubt·ed, -doubt·ing, -doubts** To feel doubt or distrust about.

mise en scène (mēz' än sĕn') *n., pl.* **mise en scènes** (sĕn') **1a.** The arrangement of performers and properties on a stage for a theatrical production or before the camera in a film. **b.** Such an arrangement within a motion picture frame. **c.** A stage setting. **2.** Physical environment; surroundings. [Fr., putting on stage.]

mi·ser (mī'zər) *n.* **1.** One who lives very meagerly in order to hoard money. **2.** A greedy or avaricious person. [< Lat., wretched.]

mis·er·a·ble (mĭz'ər-ə-bəl, mĭz'rə-) *adj.* **1.** Very uncomfortable or unhappy; wretched. **2.** Causing or accompanied by great discomfort or distress: *a miserable climate.* **3.** Mean or shameful; contemptible. **4.** Wretchedly inadequate: *lived in a miserable shack.* **5.** Of poor quality; inferior. [ME < OFr. < Lat. *miserābilis*, pitiable < *miserārī*, to pity < *miser*, wretched.] —**mis'er·a·ble** *n.* —**mis'er·a·ble·ness** *n.* —**mis'er·a·bly** *adv.*

mis·e·re·re (mĭz'ə-râr'ē, -rĭr'ē) *n.* **1.** Miserere **a.** The 51st Psalm. **b.** A musical setting of this psalm. **2a.** A prayer for mercy. **b.** An expression of lamentation or complaint. **3.** See misericord **2.** [Lat. *miserēre*, have mercy, the first word of the psalm, imper. sing. of *miserērī*, to feel pity < *miser*, wretched.]

mis·er·i·cord or **mis·er·i·corde** (mĭz'ər-ĭ-kôrd', mĭ-zĕr'-) *n.* **1a.** Relaxation of monastic rules, as a dispensation from fasting. **b.** The room in a monastery used by monks granted such a dispensation. **2.** A bracket attached to the underside of a hinged seat in a church stall against which a standing person may lean. **3.** A narrow dagger used in medieval times to deliver the death stroke to a seriously wounded knight. [ME, pity < OFr. < Lat. *misericordia* < *misericors, misericord-*, merciful : *miserērī*, to feel pity; see MISERERE + *cor, cord-*, heart; see **kerd-** in App.]

mi·ser·ly (mī'zər-lē) *adj.* Of, relating to, or characteristic of a miser; avaricious or penurious. —**mi'ser·li·ness** *n.*

mis·er·y (mĭz'ə-rē) *n., pl.* **-ies 1a.** The state of suffering and want as a result of physical circumstances or extreme poverty. **b.** Mental or emotional unhappiness or distress. **2.** A cause or source of suffering. **3.** *Informal* A physical ache or ailment. [Ult. < Lat. *miseria* < *miser*, wretched.]

misery index *n.* The sum of national unemployment and inflation rates, used unofficially to assess a nation's economic health.

mis·es·teem (mĭs'ə-stēm') *tr.v.* **-teemed, -teem·ing, -teems** To fail to regard with deserved esteem.

mis·ad·dress' *tr.v.*	**mis·clas·si·fi·ca'tion** *n.*	**mis·i·den'ti·fi·ca'tion** *n.*	**mis·pro·nun'ci·a'tion** *n.*
mis·ad·vise' *tr.v.*	**mis·clas'si·fy** *tr.v.*	**mis·i·den'ti·fy** *tr.v.*	**mis·quo·ta'tion** *n.*
mis·a·ligned' *adj.*	**mis'con·strue'** *tr.v.*	**mis·im·pres'sion** *n.*	**mis·quote'** *tr.v.*
mis·a·lign'ment *n.*	**mis·deed'** *n.*	**mis·in·form'** *tr.v.*	**mis·quot'er** *n.*
mis·al'lo·cate' *tr.v.*	**mis·de·scribe'** *tr.v.*	**mis·in·form'ant** *n.*	**mis·reck'on** *tr. & intr.v.*
mis·al'lo·ca'tion *n.*	**mis·di·ag·nose'** *tr.v.*	**mis·in·for·ma'tion** *n.*	**mis·re·mem'ber** *tr.v.*
mis·al'ly *tr.v.*	**mis·di·ag·no'sis** *n.*	**mis·in·form'er** *n.*	**mis·re·port'** *tr.v.*
mis·ap·pli·ca'tion *n.*	**mis·do'** *tr.v.*	**mis·judge'** *tr. & intr.v.*	**mis·re·port'er** *n.*
mis·ap·ply' *tr.v.*	**mis·do'er** *n.*	**mis·judg'ment** *n.*	**mis·spend'** *tr.v.*
mis·ap·pre·hend' *tr.v.*	**mis·do'ing** *n.*	**mis·la'bel** *tr.v.*	**mis·state'** *tr.v.*
mis·ap·pre·hen'sion *n.*	**mis·ed'u·cate'** *tr.v.*	**mis·man·age** *tr.v.*	**mis·state'ment** *n.*
mis·at·trib'ute *tr.v.*	**mis·ed'u·ca'tion** *n.*	**mis·man'age·ment** *n.*	**mis·time'** *tr.v.*
mis·at·tri·bu'tion *n.*	**mis·file'** *tr.v.*	**mis·name'** *tr.v.*	**mis·trans·late'** *tr.v.*
mis·cal'cu·late' *tr. & intr.v.*	**mis·gov'ern** *tr.v.*	**mis·name'** *n.*	**mis·trans·la'tion** *n.*
mis·cal'cu·la'tion *n.*	**mis·gov'ern·ment** *n.*	**mis·per·ceive'** *tr.v.*	**mis·val'ue** *tr.v.*
mis·char'ac·ter·i·za'tion *n.*	**mis·gov'er·nor** *n.*	**mis·per·cep'tion** *n.*	**mis·word'** *tr.v.*
mis·char'ac·ter·ize' *tr.v.*	**mis·hear'** *tr. & intr.v.*	**mis·pro·nounce'** *tr. & intr.v.*	**mis·write'** *tr.v.*

mis·fea·sance (mĭs-fē′zəns) *n.* Improper and unlawful execution of an act that in itself is lawful and proper. [AN *mesfesance* < *mesfere,* to do wrong : *mes-,* wrongly (< OFr.; see MIS-[1]) + *fere,* to do (< Lat. *facere*; see **dhē-** in App.).]

mis·fea·sor (mĭs-fē′zər) *n.* One guilty of misfeasance.

mis·fire (mĭs-fīr′) *intr.v.* **-fired, -fir·ing, -fires 1.** To fail to ignite when expected. Used of an internal-combustion engine. **2.** To fail to discharge. Used of a firearm. **3.** To fail to achieve an anticipated result. —**mis′fire′** (mĭs′fīr′, mĭs-fīr′) *n.*

mis·fit (mĭs′fĭt′, mĭs-fĭt′) *n.* **1.** Something of the wrong size or shape for its purpose. **2.** One unable to adjust to one's circumstances or considered disturbingly different.

mis·for·tune (mĭs-fôr′chən) *n.* **1a.** Bad fortune or ill luck. **b.** The condition resulting from bad fortune or ill luck: *wanted to help those in misfortune.* **2.** A distressing occurrence.

mis·give (mĭs-gĭv′) *v.* **-gave** (-gāv′), **-giv·en** (-gĭv′ən), **-giv·ing, -gives** —*tr.* To arouse suspicion or apprehension in (one's mind, for example). —*intr.* To be suspicious, apprehensive, or doubtful. [MIS-[1] + GIVE, to suggest (obsolete).]

mis·giv·ing (mĭs-gĭv′ĭng) *n.* A feeling of doubt, distrust, or apprehension.

mis·guide (mĭs-gīd′) *tr.v.* **-guid·ed, -guid·ing, -guides** To lead or guide in the wrong direction; lead astray. —**mis·guid′ance** (-gīd′ns) *n.* —**mis·guid′er** *n.*

mis·guid·ed (mĭs-gī′dĭd) *adj.* Based or acting on error; misled. —**mis·guid′ed·ly** *adv.*

mis·han·dle (mĭs-hăn′dl) *tr.v.* **-dled, -dling, -dles 1.** To deal with clumsily or inefficiently; mismanage. **2.** To treat roughly; maltreat.

mis·hap (mĭs′hăp′, mĭs-hăp′) *n.* **1.** Bad luck. **2.** An unfortunate accident.

mish·e·gaas or **mish·e·goss** (mĭsh′ə-gäs′) *n. Slang* Variants of **meshugaas.**

Mi·shi·ma (mē-shē′mä, mē′shē-mä′), **Yukio** Orig. Kimitake Hiraoka. 1925–70. Japanese author best known for the tetralogy *The Sea of Fertility* (1970).

mis·hit (mĭs-hĭt′) *tr.v.* **-hit, -hit·ting, -hits** To hit (a tennis or cricket ball, for example) incorrectly or badly. —**mis′hit′** *n.*

mish·mash (mĭsh′mäsh′, -măsh′) *n.* A collection or mixture of unrelated things; a hodgepodge. [ME *misse-masche,* prob. redup. of *mash,* soft mixture. See MASH.]

Mish·nah also **Mish·na** (mĭsh′nə) *n. Judaism* **1.** The first section of the Talmud, being a collection of early oral interpretations of the scriptures as compiled about A.D. 200. **2.** A paragraph from this section of the Talmud. **3.** The teaching of a rabbi or other authority on Jewish laws. [Mishnaic Heb. *mišnâ,* repetition, instruction < *šānâ,* to repeat.] —**Mish·na′ic** (mĭsh-nā′ĭk) *adj.*

Mishnaic Hebrew *n.* The Hebrew language as used from the second to the tenth century A.D.

mis·in·ter·pret (mĭs′ĭn-tûr′prĭt) *tr.v.* **-pret·ed, -pret·ing, -prets 1.** To interpret inaccurately. **2.** To explain inaccurately. —**mis′in·ter′pre·ta′tion** *n.* —**mis′in·ter′pret·er** *n.*

mis·join·der (mĭs-join′dər) *n.* Improper joining of different causes of action or of different parties to a lawsuit.

Mis·ki·to (mĭ-skē′tō) *n., pl.* **Miskito** or **-tos 1.** A member of an American Indian people inhabiting the Caribbean coast of northeast Nicaragua and southeast Honduras. **2.** The language of the Miskito.

mis·know (mĭs-nō′) *tr.v.* **-knew** (-nōō′, -nyōō′), **-known** (-nōn′), **-know·ing, -knows** To misunderstand. —**mis·knowl′edge** (-nŏl′ĭj) *n.*

Mis·kolc (mĭsh′kôlts′) A city of NE Hungary NE of Budapest. Pop. 190,330.

mis·lay (mĭs-lā′) *tr.v.* **-laid** (-lād′), **-lay·ing, -lays 1.** To put in a place that is afterward forgotten. **2.** To place or put down incorrectly: *They mislaid the linoleum.* —**mis·lay′er** *n.*

mis·lead (mĭs-lēd′) *tr.v.* **-led** (-lĕd′), **-lead·ing, -leads 1.** To lead in the wrong direction. **2.** To lead into error of thought or action, esp. by intentionally deceiving. See Syns at **deceive.** —**mis·lead′er** *n.*

mis·lead·ing (mĭs-lē′dĭng) *adj.* Tending to mislead.

mis·like (mĭs-līk′) *tr.v.* **-liked, -lik·ing, -likes 1.** To disapprove of; dislike. **2.** *Archaic* To displease. ❖ *n.* Disapproval; dislike. [ME *misliken* < OE *mislīcian* : *mis-,* ill; see MIS-[1] + *līcian,* to please; see LIKE[1].]

mis·no·mer (mĭs-nō′mər) *n.* **1.** An error in naming a person or place. **2a.** Application of a wrong name. **b.** A name wrongly or unsuitably applied to a person or object. [ME *misnoumer* < OFr. *mesnomer,* to misname : *mes-,* wrongly; see MIS-[1] + *nommer,* to name (< Lat. *nōmināre* < *nōmen,* name; see **nŏ-men-** in App.).] —**mis·no′mered** *adj.*

mi·so (mē′sō) *n., pl.* **-sos** A thick fermented paste made of cooked soybeans, salt, and often rice or barley, and used esp. in making soups and sauces. [J.]

miso– *pref.* Hatred: *misogamy.* [Gk. *mīso-* < *mīsein,* to hate, and *mīsos,* hatred.]

mi·sog·a·my (mĭ-sŏg′ə-mē) *n.* Hatred of marriage. —**mis′o·gam′ic** (mĭs′ə-găm′ĭk) *adj.* —**mi·sog′a·mist** *n.*

mi·sog·y·nist (mĭ-sŏj′ə-nĭst) *n.* One who hates women. ❖ *adj.* Of or characterized by a hatred of women. —**mi·sog′y·nis′tic, mi·sog′y·nous** *adj.*

mi·sog·y·ny (mĭ-sŏj′ə-nē) *n.* Hatred of women. [Gk. *mīsogunīā* : *mīso-,* miso- + *gunē,* woman; see -GYNY.] —**mis′o·gyn′ic** (mĭs′ə-jĭn′ĭk, -gĭn′ĭk) *adj.*

mi·sol·o·gy (mĭ-sŏl′ə-jē) *n.* Hatred of reason, argument, or enlightenment. —**mi·sol′o·gist** *n.*

mis·o·ne·ism (mĭs′ə-nē′ĭz′əm) *n.* Hatred or fear of change or innovation. [Ital. *misoneismo* : Gk. *mīso-,* miso- + Gk. *neos,* new; see **newo-** in App.] —**mis′o·ne′ist** *n.*

mis·o·ri·ent (mĭs-ôr′ē-ənt, -ĕnt′, -ōr′-) *tr.v.* **-ent·ed, -ent·ing, -ents** To orient incorrectly or inappropriately. —**mis·o′ri·en·ta′tion** *n.*

mis·pick·el (mĭs′pĭk′əl) *n.* See **arsenopyrite.** [Obsolete Ger. *Misspickel* < earlier *Misspult, Misspückel,* .]

mis·place (mĭs-plās′) *tr.v.* **-placed, -plac·ing, -plac·es 1a.** To put into a wrong place. **b.** To mislay: *I misplaced my wallet.* **2.** To bestow (confidence, for example) on an improper, unsuitable, or unworthy person or idea. —**mis·place′ment** *n.*

misplaced modifier (mĭs′plāst′) *n.* A modifying clause or phrase placed so awkwardly as to create ambiguity or misunderstanding, as in *Streaking through the sky, we watched the rocket re-enter the atmosphere.*

mis·play (mĭs-plā′, mĭs′plā′) *Sports & Games n.* A mistaken or unskillful play. ❖ *tr.v.* (mĭs-plā′) **-played, -play·ing, -plays** To make a misplay of.

mis·print (mĭs-prĭnt′) *tr.v.* **-print·ed, -print·ing, -prints** To print incorrectly. ❖ *n.* (mĭs′prĭnt′, mĭs-prĭnt′) An error in printing.

mis·pri·sion[1] (mĭs-prĭzh′ən) *n.* **1.** Maladministration of public office. **2.** Neglect in preventing or reporting a felony or treason by one not an accessory. **3.** An act of sedition against a government or the courts. [ME < AN, var. of OFr. *mesprison* < *mespris,* p. part. of *mesprendre,* to make a mistake : *mes-,* wrongly; see MIS-[1] + *prendre,* to take, seize (< Lat. *prehendere, prĕndere*; see **ghend-** in App.).]

mis·pri·sion[2] (mĭs-prĭzh′ən) *n.* Contempt; disdain. [*mispris(e)* (var. of MISPRIZE) + –ION.]

mis·prize (mĭs-prīz′) *tr.v.* **-prized, -priz·ing, -priz·es 1.** To despise. **2.** To undervalue. —**mis·priz′er** *n.*

mis·read (mĭs-rēd′) *tr.v.* **-read** (-rĕd′), **-read·ing, -reads 1.** To read inaccurately. **2.** To misinterpret or misunderstand.

mis·rep·re·sent (mĭs-rĕp′rĭ-zĕnt′) *tr.v.* **-sent·ed, -sent·ing, -sents 1.** To give an incorrect or misleading representation of. **2.** To serve incorrectly or dishonestly as an official representative of. —**mis′rep′re·sen·ta′tion** *n.* —**mis′rep′re·sen′ta·tive** (-zĕn′tə-tĭv) *adj.* —**mis′rep′re·sent′er** *n.*

mis·rule (mĭs-rōōl′) *n.* **1.** Disorder or lawless confusion. **2.** Inept or unwise rule; misgovernment. ❖ *tr.v.* **-ruled, -rul·ing, -rules** To rule ineptly, unjustly, or unwisely; misgovern.

miss[1] (mĭs) *v.* **missed, miss·ing, miss·es** —*tr.* **1.** To fail to hit, reach, catch, meet, or otherwise make contact with. **2.** To fail to perceive, understand, or experience: *missed the point of the film.* **3.** To fail to accomplish, achieve, or attain (a goal). **4.** To fail to attend or perform: *missed a day of work.* **5a.** To leave out; omit. **b.** To let go by; let slip: *miss a chance.* **6.** To escape or avoid: *narrowly missed crashing into the tree.* **7.** To discover the absence or loss of: *I missed my book after getting off the bus.* **8.** To feel the lack or loss of. —*intr.* **1.** To fail to hit or otherwise make contact with something. **2a.** To be unsuccessful; fail. **b.** To misfire, as an internal-combustion engine. ❖ *n.* **1.** A failure to hit, succeed, or find. **2.** The misfiring of an engine. —*idioms:* **miss fire 1.** To fail to discharge. Used of a firearm. **2.** To fail to achieve the anticipated result. **miss out on** To lose a chance for. **miss the boat** *Informal* **1.** To fail to avail oneself of an opportunity. **2.** To fail to understand. [ME *missen* < OE *missan.*]

miss[2] (mĭs) *n.* **1. Miss** Used as a courtesy title before the surname or full name of a girl or an unmarried woman. See Usage Note at **Ms. 2.** Used as a form of polite address for a girl or young woman: *Thanks, miss.* **3.** A young unmarried woman. **4. mis·ses** A series of clothing sizes for women and girls of average height and proportions. [Short for MISTRESS.]

Miss. *abbr.* Mississippi

mis·sa cantata (mĭs′ə) *n.* A Mass in which the liturgical parts are sung but which is less elaborate than a High Mass. [NLat. *missa cantāta* < LLat. *missa,* Mass + Lat. *cantāta,* sung, fem. p. part. of *canere,* to sing.]

mis·sal (mĭs′əl) *n.* **1.** *Roman Catholic Church* A book containing all the prayers and responses necessary for celebrating the Mass throughout the year. **2.** A prayer book. [ME *messel* < OFr. < Med.Lat. *missāle* < neut. of *missālis,* of the Mass < LLat. *missa,* Mass. See MASS.]

mis·sel thrush (mĭs′əl) *n.* Variant of **mistle thrush.**

mis·sense (mĭs′sĕns′) *adj. Genetics* Of or relating to a mutation that changes a codon for one amino acid into a codon for a different amino acid. [MIS-[1] + (NON)SENSE.]

mis·shape (mĭs-shāp′) *tr.v.* **-shaped, -shaped** or **-shap·en** (-shā′pən), **-shap·ing, -shapes** To shape badly; deform. —**mis·shap′en·ly** *adv.* —**mis·shap′er** *n.*

mis·sile (mĭs′əl, -īl′) *n.* **1.** An object or weapon that is fired, thrown, dropped, or otherwise projected at a target; a projectile. **2.** A guided missile. **3.** A ballistic missile. [Lat. < neut. of *missilis,* able to be thrown < *missus,* p. part. of *mittere,* to let go, throw.]

ă	pat	oi	boy
ā	pay	ou	out
âr	care	ōō	took
ä	father	ōō	boot
ĕ	pet	ŭ	cut
ē	be	ûr	urge
ĭ	pit	th	thin
ī	pie	th	this
îr	pier	hw	which
ŏ	pot	zh	vision
ō	toe	ə	about,
ô	paw		item

Stress marks:
′ (primary);
′ (secondary), as in
lexicon (lĕk′sĭ-kŏn′)

mis·sile·ry also **mis·sil·ry** (mĭs′əl-rē) *n.* **1.** The science and technology of making and using guided or ballistic missiles. **2.** Missiles considered as a group.

miss·ing (mĭs′ĭng) *adj.* **1a.** Not present; absent. **b.** Lost: *a missing person.* **2.** Lacking; wanting.

missing link *n.* **1.** A theoretical primate postulated to bridge the evolutionary gap between the anthropoid apes and humans. Not in scientific use. **2.** Something lacking that is needed to complete a series.

missing mass *n.* **1.** The mass needed to account for the difference between the observed mass of the universe and the mass required to halt the expansion of the universe. **2.** The unobserved mass required by theoretical explanations to account for the observed rotation of most galaxies.

mis·sion (mĭsh′ən) *n.* **1a.** A body of persons sent to conduct negotiations or establish relations with a foreign country. **b.** The business with which such a body of persons is charged. **c.** A permanent diplomatic office abroad. **d.** A body of experts or dignitaries sent to a foreign country. **2a.** A body of persons sent to a foreign land by a religious organization, to spread its faith and provide assistance. **b.** A mission established abroad. **c.** The district assigned to a mission worker. **d.** A building or compound housing a mission. **e.** An organization for carrying on missionary work in a territory. **f. missions** Missionary duty or work. **3.** A Christian church or congregation with no cleric of its own that depends for support on a larger religious organization. **4.** A series of special Christian services for purposes of proselytizing. **5.** A welfare or educational organization established for the needy people of a district. **6a.** A special assignment given to a person or group. **b.** A combat operation assigned to a person or military unit. **c.** An aerospace operation intended to carry out specific program objectives. **7.** An inner calling to pursue an activity or perform a service; a vocation. ❖ *tr.v.* **-sioned, -sion·ing, -sions** **1.** To send on a mission. **2.** To organize or establish a religious mission among or in. ❖ *adj.* **1.** Of or relating to a mission. **2.** Of or relating to a style of architecture or furniture used in the early Spanish missions of California. **3.** often **Mission** Of, relating to, or having the distinctive qualities of an early-20th-century style of plain heavy dark-stained wood furniture. [Fr. < OFr. < Lat. *missiō, missiōn-* < *missus,* p. part. of *mittere,* to send off.] —**mis′sion·al** *adj.*

mis·sion·ar·y (mĭsh′ə-nĕr′ē) *n., pl.* **-ies** **1.** One sent on a mission, esp. to do religious or charitable work in a territory or foreign country. **2.** One who attempts to persuade or convert others, as to a doctrine; a propagandist. ❖ *adj.* **1.** Of or relating to missions or missionaries. **2.** Engaged in the activities of a mission or missionary. **3.** Tending to propagandize or persuade insistently.

missionary position *n.* A position for sexual intercourse in which a woman and man lie facing each other, with the woman on the bottom and the man on the top. [< Christian missionaries′ supposed advocacy of this position over other copulatory positions.]

Missionary Ridge A range of hills in SE TN and NW GA; site of an important Union victory (Nov. 25, 1863) in the Civil War.

mis·sion·er (mĭsh′ə-nər) *n.* A missionary.

mis·sion·ize (mĭsh′ə-nīz′) *v.* **-ized, -iz·ing, -iz·es** —*intr.* To do missionary work. —*tr.* **1.** To perform missionary work in or among. **2.** To bring under the influence or control of a mission.

Mission Vie·jo (vē-ā′hō) A community of S CA SE of Irvine. Pop. 93,102.

mis·sis or **mis·sus** (mĭs′ĭz, -ĭs) *n. Informal* **1.** The mistress of a household. **2.** Used as a term of reference by a man of his wife. [Alteration of MISTRESS.]

Mis·sis·sau·ga (mĭs′ĭ-sô′gə) A town of S Ontario, Canada, a suburb of Toronto on Lake Ontario. Pop. 544,382.

Mis·sis·sip·pi (mĭs′ĭ-sĭp′ē) A state of the SE US; admitted as the 20th state in 1817. The **Mississippi Territory,** organized in 1798 and enlarged in 1804 and 1813, also included the present state of AL. Cap. Jackson. Pop. 2,844,658.

Mis·sis·sip·pi·an (mĭs′ĭ-sĭp′ē-ən) *adj.* **1.** Of or relating to the state or residents of Mississippi or the Mississippi River. **2.** Of or belonging to the geologic time of the fifth period of the Paleozoic Era, characterized by the submergence of extensive land areas under shallow seas. See table at **geologic time.** ❖ *n.* **1.** A native or resident of Mississippi. **2.** The Mississippian Period or its deposits.

Mississippi River The chief river of the US, rising in the lake region of N MN and flowing c. 3,781 km (2,350 mi) to enter the Gulf of Mexico through a huge delta in SE LA. La Salle claimed the entire region for France after he descended the river's mouth in 1682.

mis·sive (mĭs′ĭv) *n.* A written message; a letter. [< ME *(letter) missive,* (letter) sent (by superior authority) < Med.Lat. *(litterae) missīvae,* fem. pl. of *missīvus,* sent < Lat. *missus,* p. part. of *mittere,* to send.]

Mis·sou·la (mĭ-zoo′lə) A city of W MT WNW of Helena. Pop. 57,053.

Mis·sou·ri[1] (mĭ-zoor′ē) *n., pl.* **Missouri** or **-ris 1.** A member of a Native American people formerly inhabiting north-central Missouri, with present-day descendants in north-central Oklahoma. **2.** The Siouan language of the Missouri. [Fr. < Illinois *ouemessourita,* those who have dugout canoes.]

Mis·sou·ri[2] (mĭ-zoor′ē, -zoor′ə) A state of the central US; admitted as the 24th state in 1821. Its application for admission as a slaveholding state in 1817 sparked a bitter controversy over the question of allowing slavery in new territories. By the Missouri Compromise (1820) ME was admitted as a free state and MO as a slave state. Cap. Jefferson City. Pop. 5,595,211. —**Mis·sou′ri·an** *adj. & n.*

Missouri River A river of the US rising in the Rocky Mts. as various headstreams that join to form the Missouri proper in SW MT. The longest river in the US, it flows c. 4,127 km (2,565 mi) to the Mississippi R. N of St. Louis MO.

mis·speak (mĭs-spēk′) *v.* **-spoke** (-spōk′), **-spo·ken** (-spō′kən), **-speak·ing, -speaks** —*tr.* To speak or pronounce incorrectly. —*intr.* To speak mistakenly or inappropriately.

mis·spell (mĭs-spĕl′) *tr.v.* **-spelled** or **-spelt** (-spĕlt′), **-spell·ing, -spells** To spell incorrectly.

mis·spell·ing (mĭs-spĕl′ĭng) *n.* **1.** The act or an instance of spelling incorrectly. **2.** A word spelled incorrectly.

mis·step (mĭs-stĕp′) *n.* **1.** A misplaced or awkward step. **2.** An instance of wrong or improper conduct; a blunder. ❖ *intr.v.* **-stepped, -step·ping, -steps** To make a mistake.

mis·sus (mĭs′ĭz, -ĭs) *n.* Variant of **missis.**

miss·y (mĭs′ē) *n., pl.* **-ies** *Informal* Used as a familiar term of address for a young woman or girl.

mist (mĭst) *n.* **1.** A mass of fine droplets of water in the atmosphere near or in contact with the earth. **2.** Water vapor condensed on and clouding the appearance of a surface. **3.** Fine drops of a liquid, such as water, perfume, or medication, sprayed into the air. **4.** A suspension of fine drops of a liquid in a gas. **5.** Something that dims or conceals. **6.** A haze before the eyes that blurs the vision. **7.** Something that produces or gives the impression of dimness or obscurity. **8.** A drink of liquor over cracked ice. ❖ *v.* **mist·ed, mist·ing, mists** —*intr.* **1.** To be or become obscured by or as if by mist. **2.** To rain in a fine shower. —*tr.* **1.** To conceal or veil with or as if with mist. **2.** To moisturize (plants, for example) with a fine spray of water. [ME < OE.]

mis·tak·a·ble (mĭ-stā′kə-bəl) *adj.* Capable of being mistaken or misunderstood: *mistakable signals.* —**mis·tak′a·bly** *adv.*

mis·take (mĭ-stāk′) *n.* **1.** An error or fault resulting from defective judgment, deficient knowledge, or carelessness. **2.** A misconception or misunderstanding. ❖ *v.* **mis·took** (mĭ-stook′), **mis·tak·en** (mĭ-stā′kən), **mis·tak·ing, mis·takes** —*tr.* **1.** To understand wrongly; misinterpret: *mistook my politeness for friendliness.* **2.** To recognize or identify incorrectly: *He mistook her for her sister.* —*intr.* To make a mistake; err. [< ME *mistaken,* to misunderstand < ON *mistaka,* to take in error : *mis-,* wrongly + *taka,* to take.] —**mis·tak′er** *n.*

mis·tak·en (mĭ-stā′kən) *adj.* **1.** Wrong or incorrect in opinion, understanding, or perception. **2.** Based on error; wrong: *a mistaken view of the situation.* —**mis·tak′en·ly** *adv.*

Mis·tas·si·ni (mĭs′tə-sē′nē), **Lake** A lake of S-central Quebec, Canada, draining into James Bay via the Rupert R.

Mis·ter (mĭs′tər) *n.* **1.** Used as a courtesy title before the surname, full name, or professional title of a man, usu. written in its abbreviated form: *Mr. Jones.* **2.** Used as the official term of address for certain US military personnel, such as warrant officers. **3. mister** *Informal* Used as a term of address for a man: *Thanks, mister.* **4.** *Informal* Used by a woman to refer to her husband. [Alteration of MASTER.]

mist·flow·er (mĭst′flou′ər) *n.* A perennial plant (*Eupatorium coelestinum*) of the southeast and central United States having corymbs of small blue flowers.

Mis·ti (mē′stē), **El** See **El Misti.**

mis·tle thrush also **mis·sel thrush** (mĭs′əl) *n.* A European thrush (*Turdus viscivorus*) that feeds on berries, esp. those of mistletoe. [< obsolete *missel,* mistletoe < *missel* < ME < OE.]

mis·tle·toe (mĭs′əl-tō′) *n.* **1.** A Eurasian parasitic shrub (*Viscum album*) having leathery evergreen leaves and waxy white berries. **2.** Any of several American parasitic shrubs, such as *Phoradendron flavescens* of eastern North America. **3.** A sprig of mistletoe, often used as a Christmas decoration. [ME *mistelto,* back-formation < OE *misteltān* (*tān,* taken for pl. of *tā,* toe) : *mistel,* mistletoe + *tān,* twig.]

mis·tral (mĭs′trəl, mĭ-sträl′) *n.* A dry cold northerly wind that blows in squalls toward the Mediterranean coast of southern France. [Fr. < Provençal *maestral* < O Provençal < LLat. *magistrālis,* of a master < Lat. *magister, magistr-,* master. See **meg-** in App.]

Mis·tral (mĭ-sträl′, mē-), **Frédéric** 1830–1914. French Provençal writer who shared the 1904 Nobel Prize for literature.

Mistral, Gabriela 1889–1957. Chilean poet who won the 1945 Nobel Prize for literature.

mis·treat (mĭs-trēt′) *tr.v.* **-treat·ed, -treat·ing, -treats** To treat roughly or wrongly; abuse. —**mis·treat′ment** *n.*

mis·tress (mĭs′trĭs) *n.* **1.** A woman who has a continuing sexual relationship with and receives financial support from a usu. married man. **2.** A woman in a position of authority, control, or ownership, as the head of a household: *"Thirteen years had seen her mistress of Kellynch Hall"* (Jane Austen). **3a.** A woman who owns or keeps an animal: *a cat sitting in its mistress's lap.* **b.** A woman

mission
San Xavier del Bac
Mission, Tucson, Arizona;
completed 1797

mistletoe
Viscum album

who owns a slave. **4.** A woman with ultimate control over something. **5a.** A nation or country that has supremacy over others. **b.** Something personified as female that directs or reigns. **6.** A woman who has expertise in a skill or a branch of learning. **7. Mistress** Used formerly as a courtesy title when speaking to or of a woman. **8.** *Chiefly British* A woman schoolteacher. [ME *maistresse* < OFr., fem. of *maistre*, master < Lat. *magister*. See MASTER.]

mis•tri•al (mĭs′trī′əl, -trīl′, mĭs-trī′əl, -trīl′) *n.* **1.** A trial that becomes invalid because of basic prejudicial error in procedure. **2.** An inconclusive trial, as one in which the jurors fail to agree.

mis•trust (mĭs-trŭst′) *n.* Lack of trust or confidence arising from suspicion. See Syns at **uncertainty.** ❖ *v.* **-trust•ed, -trust•ing, -trusts** —*tr.* To regard with mistrust. —*intr.* To be wary, suspicious, or doubtful. **—mis•trust′ful** *adj.* **—mis•trust′ful•ly** *adv.* **—mis•trust′ful•ness** *n.*

mist•y (mĭs′tē) *adj.* **-i•er, -i•est 1.** Consisting of or marked by mist: *a misty rain.* **2.** Obscured or clouded by or as if by mist. **3a.** Vague; hazy: *a misty recollection.* **b.** Full of tender emotion; sentimental. **—mist′i•ly** *adv.* **—mist′i•ness** *n.*

mist•y-eyed (mĭs′tē-īd′) *adj.* **1.** Having the eyes blurred, as with tears. **2.** Having a sentimental or dreamy quality.

mis•un•der•stand (mĭs′ŭn-dər-stănd′) *tr.v.* **-stood** (-sto͝od′), **-stand•ing, -stands** To understand incorrectly.

mis•un•der•stand•ing (mĭs′ŭn-dər-stăn′dĭng) *n.* **1.** A failure to understand or interpret correctly. **2.** A disagreement or quarrel.

mis•un•der•stood (mĭs′ŭn-dər-sto͝od′) *adj.* **1.** Incorrectly understood or interpreted. **2.** Not appreciated or given sympathetic understanding: *a sorely misunderstood child.*

mis•us•age (mĭs-yo͞o′sĭj, -zĭj) *n.* **1.** Abusive treatment. **2.** Improper application, as of words.

mis•use (mĭs-yo͞os′) *n.* Improper, unlawful, or incorrect use; misapplication. ❖ *tr.v.* (-yo͞oz′) **-used, -us•ing, -us•es 1.** To use incorrectly. **2.** To mistreat or abuse.

mis•us•er (mĭs-yo͞o′zər) *n.* **1.** One that misuses. **2.** *Law* Unlawful use of an authorized privilege, right, or form of empowerment, as that of a franchise by a corporation.

Mitch•ell (mĭch′əl), **Margaret Munnerlyn** 1900–49. Amer. writer known for her novel *Gone With the Wind* (1936).

Mitchell, Maria 1818–89. Amer. astronomer who discovered a comet (1847) and was the first woman elected to the Academy of Arts and Sciences (1848).

Mitchell, Mount A peak, 2,038.6 m (6,684 ft), in the Appalachian Mts. of W NC.

Mitchell, William ("Billy") 1879–1936. Amer. soldier who was one of the first advocates of military air power.

mite[1] (mīt) *n.* Any of various small or minute arachnids of the order Acarina that are often parasitic on animals and plants, infest stored food products, and in some species transmit disease. [ME < OE *mīte.*]

mite[2] (mīt) *n.* **1a.** A very small contribution or amount of money. **b.** A widow's mite. **2.** A very small object, creature, or particle. **3.** A coin of very small value, esp. an obsolete British coin worth half a farthing. ***—idiom:* a mite** To a small degree; somewhat: *a mite sore.* [ME < MDu. and MLGer. *mīte*, a small Flemish coin, tiny animal.]

mi•ter (mī′tər) *n.* **1.** The liturgical headdress and part of the insignia of a Christian bishop. **2a.** A thong for binding the hair, worn by women in ancient Greece. **b.** The ceremonial headdress worn by ancient Jewish high priests. **3a.** A miter joint. **b.** The edge of a piece of material that has been beveled preparatory to making a miter joint. **c.** A miter square. ❖ *v.* **-tered, -ter•ing, -ters** —*tr.* **1.** To bestow a miter upon. **2a.** To make (two pieces or surfaces) join with a miter joint. **b.** To bevel the edges of for joining with a miter joint. —*intr.* To meet in a miter joint. [ME *mitre* < OFr. < Med.Lat. < Lat. *mitra*, headdress of the Jewish high priest < Gk.] **—mi′ter•er** *n.*

miter box *n.* A fixed or adjustable device for guiding handsaws in cutting miter joints or in making crosscuts.

miter joint *n.* A joint made with two surfaces each beveled usu. at a 45° angle, to form a corner, usu. a 90° angle.

miter square *n.* An instrument with straight edges that are set at a 45° angle or are adjustable, used for marking the angles of a miter joint.

mi•ter•wort (mī′tər-wûrt′, -wôrt′) *n.* Any of several North American plants of the genus *Mitella*, having heart-shaped leaves and clusters of small white flowers with pinnately divided petals. [< the shape of its capsule.]

Mith•ra•ism (mĭth′rə-ĭz′əm, -rā-) *n.* A religious cult that worshiped Mithras, esp. popular among the Roman military and a strong rival to Christianity during the late Roman Empire. **—Mith•ra′ic** (mĭ-thrā′ĭk) *adj.* **—Mith•ra′ist** *n.*

Mith•ras (mĭth′rəs) *n.* *Mythology* The ancient Persian god of light and guardian against evil, often identified with the sun. [Gk. *Mithrās* < Avestan *Mithrō* and OPers. *Mithra.*]

mith•ri•date (mĭth′rĭ-dāt′) *n.* An antidote against poison, esp. a confection formerly held to be an antidote to all poisons. [Ult. < Gk. *mithridāteios*, of Mithridates, after MITHRIDATES VI, who is said to have acquired tolerance for poison.]

Mith•ri•da•tes VI (mĭth′rĭ-dā′tēz) Known as "Mithridates the Great." 132?–63 B.C. King of Pontus (120–63) who expanded the kingdom through victories over the Romans but was later driven from Pontus by Pompey (66).

mith•ri•da•tism (mĭth′rĭ-dā′tĭz′əm) *n.* Tolerance or immunity to a poison acquired by taking gradually larger doses of it. **—mith′ri•dat′ic** (-dăt′ĭk) *adj.*

mi•ti•cide (mī′tĭ-sīd′) *n.* An agent that kills mites. **—mi′ti•cid′al** (-sīd′l) *adj.*

mit•i•gate (mĭt′ĭ-gāt′) *v.* **-gat•ed, -gat•ing, -gates** —*tr.* To moderate (a quality or condition) in force or intensity; alleviate. See Syns at **relieve.** —*intr.* To become milder. [ME *mitigaten* < Lat. *mītigāre, mītigāt-* : *mītis*, soft + *agere*, to drive, do; see ACT.] **—mit′i•ga•ble** (-gə-bəl) *adj.* **—mit′i•ga′tion** *n.* **—mit′i•ga′tive, mit′i•ga•to′ry** (-gə-tôr′ē, -tōr′ē) *adj.* **—mit′i•ga′tor** *n.*

mi•to•chon•dri•on (mī′tə-kŏn′drē-ən) *n., pl.* **-dri•a** (-drē-ə) A spherical or elongated organelle in the cytoplasm of nearly all eukaryotic cells, containing genetic material and many enzymes important for cell metabolism, including those responsible for the conversion of food to usable energy. [NLat. : Gk. *mitos*, warp thread + Gk. *khondrion*, dim. of *khondros*, grain, granule; see **ghrendh-** in App.] **—mi′to•chon′dri•al** *adj.*

mi•to•gen (mī′tə-jən) *n.* An agent that induces mitosis. [MITO(SIS) + –GEN.] **—mi′to•gen′ic** (mī′tə-jĕn′ĭk, mĭt′ə-) *adj.* **—mi′to•ge•nic′i•ty** (-jə-nĭs′ĭ-tē) *n.*

mi•to•my•cin (mī′tə-mī′sĭn) *n.* Any of a group of antibiotics produced by the soil actinomycete *Streptomyces caespitosus* that inhibit DNA synthesis and are used against bacteria and cancerous tumor cells. [Prob. MITO(SIS) + –MYCIN.]

mi•to•sis (mī-tō′sĭs) *n., pl.* **-ses** (-sēz) *Biology* **1.** The process in cell division by which the nucleus divides, normally resulting in two new nuclei, each of which contains a complete copy of the parental chromosomes. **2.** The entire process of cell division including division of the nucleus and the cytoplasm. [Gk. *mitos*, warp thread + –OSIS.] **—mi•tot′ic** (-tŏt′ĭk) *adj.* **—mi•tot′i•cal•ly** *adv.*

Mit•ra (mĭt′rə) *n.* The Hindu god of friendship and alliances. [Skt. *Mitraḥ* < *mitraḥ*, friend.]

mi•tral (mī′trəl) *adj.* **1.** Relating to or resembling a miter worn by certain ecclesiastics. **2.** Relating to a mitral valve.

mitral stenosis *n.* A narrowing of the mitral valve, usu. caused by rheumatic fever, resulting in an obstruction to the flow of blood from the left atrium to the left ventricle.

mitral valve *n.* A valve of the heart that regulates blood flow between the left atrium and left ventricle.

mi•tre (mī′tər) *n. & v.* *Chiefly British* Variant of **miter.**

mitt (mĭt) *n.* **1.** A glove that extends over the hand but only partially covers the fingers. **2.** A mitten. **3.** *Baseball* A large padded protective leather glove used by catchers and first basemen. **4.** *Slang* A hand or fist. [Short for MITTEN.]

mit•ten (mĭt′n) *n.* A covering for the hand that encases the thumb separately and the four fingers together. [ME < OFr. *mitaine* (< *mite*, cat's caress, mitten < *mit*, cat) and < Med.Lat. *mitta*, mitten (poss. < OFr. *mite*).]

Mit•ter•rand (mē′tə-rănd′, -räN′), **François Maurice** 1916–96. French politician and president (1981–95).

mitz•vah (mĭts′və) *n., pl.* **-voth** (-vōt′, -vōs′) or **-vahs 1a.** A commandment of the Jewish law. **b.** The fulfillment of such a commandment. **2.** A worthy deed. [Heb. *miṣwâ* < *ṣiwwâ*, to command.]

Mi•wok (mē′wŏk) *n., pl.* **Miwok** or **-woks 1.** A member of a Native American people formerly inhabiting central California from the Sierra Nevada foothills to the San Francisco Bay area, with present-day descendants in the same region. **2.** Any of the Penutian languages of this people.

mix (mĭks) *v.* **mixed, mix•ing, mix•es** —*tr.* **1a.** To combine or blend into one mass or mixture. **b.** To create or form by combining ingredients: *mix a drink; mix cement.* **c.** To add (an ingredient or element) to another: *mix an egg into batter.* **2.** To combine or join: *mix joy with sorrow.* **3.** To bring into social contact: *mix boys and girls in the classroom.* **4.** To produce (an organism) by crossbreeding. **5.** *Electronics* **a.** To combine (two or more audio tracks or channels) to produce a composite audio recording. **b.** To produce (a soundtrack or recording) in this manner. —*intr.* **1a.** To become mixed or blended together. **b.** To be capable of being blended together: *Oil does not mix with water.* **2.** To associate socially or get along with others: *He does not mix well at parties.* **3.** To mate so as to produce a hybrid; crossbreed. **4.** To become involved. ❖ *n.* **1.** An act of mixing. **2a.** A mixture, esp. of ingredients packaged and sold commercially: *a cake mix.* **b.** A blend of diverse elements; an amalgamation. **3.** *Electronics* A recording that is produced by combining and adjusting two or more audio tracks or channels. ***—phrasal verbs:* mix down** *Electronics* To combine all of the audio components of a recording into a final soundtrack or mix. **mix up 1.** To confuse; confound: *His explanation just mixed me up more.* **2.** To involve or implicate: *He got himself mixed up with the wrong people.* ***—idiom:* mix it up** *Slang* To fight. [Back-formation < ME *mixt, mixed*, mixed < AN *mixte* < Lat. *mixtus*, p. part. of *miscēre*, to mix. See **meik-** in App.] **—mix′a•ble** *adj.*

mixed (mĭkst) *adj.* **1.** Blended together into one unit or mass; intermingled. **2.** Composed of a variety of differing, sometimes conflicting entities. See Syns at **miscellaneous. 3.** Made up of

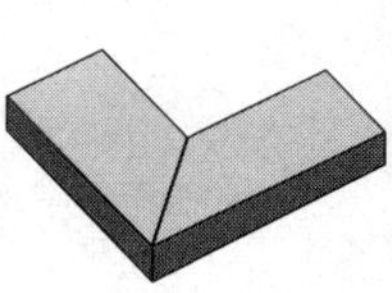

miter joint

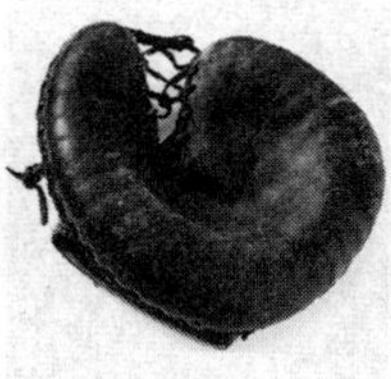

mitt
baseball catcher's mitt

ă pat	oi boy
ā pay	ou out
âr care	o͝o took
ä father	o͞o boot
ĕ pet	ŭ cut
ē be	ûr urge
ĭ pit	th thin
ī pie	*th* this
îr pier	hw which
ŏ pot	zh vision
ō toe	ə about, item
ô paw	

Stress marks:
′ (primary);
′ (secondary), as in
lexicon (lĕk′sĭ-kŏn′)

moat
Caerphilly Castle, Wales

people of different sex, race, or social class. **4a.** Descended from two or more races or breeds. **b.** Crossbred.

mixed bag *n.* A collection of dissimilar things; an assortment.

mixed doubles *pl.n.* (*used with a sing. verb*) A game of doubles played with one man and one woman on each term.

mixed drink *n.* A drink made of liquor combined with other ingredients, usu. shaken or stirred before serving.

mixed grill *n.* A dish consisting of a variety of broiled meats and vegetables.

mixed marriage *n.* Marriage between persons of different races or religions.

mixed media *pl.n.* (*used with a sing. verb*) **1.** A technique involving the use of two or more artistic media, such as painting and collage, combined in a single composition. **2.** The combined use of media, such as television, radio, print, and the Internet, as for advertising or publicity. —**mixed′-me′di·a** (mĭkst′mē′dē-ə) *adj.*

mixed metaphor *n.* A succession of incongruous metaphors, as in *The negotiator played his cards to the hilt.*

mixed nerve *n.* A nerve that contains both sensory and motor fibers.

mixed number *n.* A number, such as 7¼, consisting of an integer and a fraction or decimal.

mixed-up (mĭkst′ŭp′) *adj. Informal* In a state of confusion.

mix·er (mĭk′sər) *n.* **1.** One that mixes: *a mixer of cement.* **2.** A sociable person. **3.** An informal party where people can get acquainted. **4.** A device that blends or mixes substances or ingredients, esp. by mechanical agitation. **5.** A nonalcoholic beverage, such as soda water, used in mixed drinks. **6.** *Electronics* **a.** One who mixes the audio components of a recording. **b.** A device used in mixing.

mix·ol·o·gy (mĭk-sŏl′ə-jē) *n.* The study or skill of preparing mixed drinks. —**mix·ol′o·gist** *n.*

mixt (mĭkst) *v. Archaic* A past tense and a past participle of **mix.**

Mix·tec (mēs′tĕk) *n., pl.* **Mixtec** or **-tecs 1a.** A member of a Mesoamerican Indian people of southern Mexico whose civilization was overthrown by the Aztecs in the 16th century. **b.** A modern-day descendant of this people. **2.** The language of this people. [Sp. < Nahuatl *mixtecatl,* inhabitant of Mixtecapán, a province of the Mexican empire.]

mix·ture (mĭks′chər) *n.* **1a.** The act or process of mixing. **b.** The condition of being mixed. **2.** Something produced by mixing. **3.** One that consists of diverse elements: *a mixture of sun and clouds.* **4.** A fabric made of different kinds of thread or yarn. **5.** *Chemistry* A composition of two or more substances that are not chemically combined with each other and are capable of being separated. [ME < OFr. < Lat. *mixtūra* < *mixtus,* p. part. of *miscēre,* to mix. See **meik-** in App.]

SYNONYMS *mixture, blend, admixture, compound, composite, amalgam* These nouns refer to a combination produced by mixing. *Mixture* has the widest application: *"He showed a curious mixture of eagerness and terror"* (Francis Parkman). *Blend* and *amalgam* imply that the original components have lost their distinctness: *The novel is a fascinating blend of romance and realism. The comedian's act was an amalgam of incisive wit and unceasing good humor. Admixture* suggests that one of the components is dissimilar to the others: *The essential oil in the perfume contains a large admixture of alcohol.* A *compound* constitutes a new and independent entity: *The school's program is a compound of scholarship and athleticism.* A *composite* has components that may retain part of their identities: *The suite is a composite of themes for various parts of the opera.*

mix-up also **mix′up** (mĭks′ŭp′) *n.* **1.** A state or an instance of confusion; a muddle. **2.** *Informal* A fight or melee.

Mi·ya·za·ki (mē-yä′zä-kē, mē′yä-zä′kē) A city of SE Kyushu, Japan, SE of Kumamoto. Pop. 293,590.

Mi·zar (mī′zär) *n.* The double star in the middle of the handle of the Big Dipper. [Ar. *mi'zar,* cloak, girdle < *azara,* to surround.]

miz·zen or **miz·en** (mĭz′ən) *Nautical* **1.** A fore-and-aft sail set on the mizzenmast. **2.** A mizzenmast. [ME *mesan* < OFr. *misaine,* OSpan. *mezana* or OItal. *mezzana,* all ult. < Lat. *mediānus,* of the middle < *medius,* middle. See **medhyo-** in App.] —**miz′zen** *adj.*

miz·zen·mast or **miz·en·mast** (mĭz′ən-məst, -măst′) *n.* The third mast or the mast aft of a mainmast on a ship having three or more masts.

miz·zle¹ (mĭz′əl) *intr.v.* **-zled, -zling, -zles** To rain in fine mistlike droplets; drizzle. ✦ *n.* A mistlike rain; a drizzle. [ME *misellen;* prob. akin to Du. dialectal *mieselen.*] —**miz′zly** *adv.*

miz·zle² (mĭz′əl) *intr.v.* **-zled, -zling, -zles** *Chiefly British Slang* To make a sudden departure. [?]

Mk *abbr. Bible* Mark

mks *abbr.* meter-kilogram-second

mL also **ml** *abbr.* milliliter

Ml *abbr. Bible* Malachi

MLA *abbr.* Modern Language Association

MLD *abbr.* **1.** median lethal dose **2.** minimum lethal dose

Mlle. *abbr.* Mademoiselle

Mlles. *abbr.* Mesdemoiselles

MLS *abbr.* Master of Library Science

MLW *abbr.* mean low water

mobcap
detail of a portrait of
Hannah Bull Thompson,
1824, by Ammi Phillips
(1788?–1865)

Möbius strip

mm *abbr.* millimeter

M.M. *abbr.* Messieurs

Mme. *abbr.* Madame

Mmes. *abbr.* Mesdames

mmf *abbr.* magnetomotive force

Mn The symbol for the element **manganese.**

MN *abbr.* **1.** magnetic north **2.** Minnesota

mne·mon·ic (nĭ-mŏn′ĭk) *adj.* Relating to, assisting, or intended to assist the memory. ✦ *n.* A device, such as a rhyme, used to aid memory. [Gk. *mnēmonikos* < *mnēmōn, mnēmon-,* mindful. See **men-¹** in App.] —**mne·mon′i·cal·ly** *adv.*

mne·mon·ics (nĭ-mŏn′ĭks) *n.* (*used with a sing. verb*) A system to develop or improve the memory.

Mne·mos·y·ne (nĭ-mŏs′ə-nē, -mŏz′-) *n. Greek Mythology* The goddess of memory and mother of the Muses. [Gk. *Mnēmosunē* < *mnēmosunē,* memory < *mnēmē.* See **men-¹** in App.]

Mo The symbol for the element **molybdenum.**

MO *abbr.* **1.** mail order **2.** medical officer **3.** also **Mo.** Missouri **4.** modus operandi **5.** money order

mo. *abbr.* month

-mo *suff.* Used after numerals to indicate the number of leaves a sheet of paper is folded into: *twelvemo.* [< (DUODECI)MO.]

mo·a (mō′ə) *n.* Any of various extinct flightless ostrichlike birds of the family Dinornithidae of New Zealand. [Maori.]

Mo·ab (mō′ăb) An ancient kingdom E of the Dead Sea in present-day SW Jordan; first settled c. 13th cent. B.C.

Mo·ab·ite (mō′ə-bīt′) *n.* **1.** A native or inhabitant of Moab. **2.** The Semitic language of Moab. —**Mo′a·bite′, Mo′a·bit′ish** *adj.*

moan (mōn) *n.* **1a.** A low, sustained mournful cry, usu. indicative of sorrow or pain. **b.** A similar sound. **2.** Lamentation. ✦ *v.* **moaned, moan·ing, moans** —*intr.* **1a.** To utter a moan or moans. **b.** To make a sound resembling a moan. **2.** To complain, lament, or grieve: *moans about his youth.* —*tr.* **1.** To bewail or bemoan. **2.** To utter with moans or a moan. [ME *mone* < OE **mān.*]

moat (mōt) *n.* **1.** A deep wide ditch, usu. filled with water, typically surrounding a fortification as a protection against assault. **2.** A ditch similar to one surrounding a fortification. ✦ *tr.v.* **moat·ed, moat·ing, moats** To surround with or as if with a moat. [ME *mote,* mound, moat < OFr., mound, or Med.Lat. *mota.*]

mob (mŏb) *n.* **1.** A large disorderly crowd or throng. **2.** The mass of common people; the populace. **3.** *Informal* An organized gang of criminals; a crime syndicate. **b.** often **Mob** Organized crime: *has links to the Mob.* **4.** An indiscriminate or loosely associated group of persons or things. **5.** *Australian* A flock or herd of animals. ✦ *tr.v.* **mobbed, mob·bing, mobs 1.** To crowd around and jostle or annoy, esp. in anger or excessive enthusiasm. **2.** To crowd into. **3.** To attack in large numbers; overwhelm. [Short for *mobile* < Lat. *mōbile (vulgus),* fickle (crowd), neut. of *mōbilis.* See MOBILE.] —**mob′bish** *adj.* —**mob′bish·ly** *adv.*

mob·cap (mŏb′kăp′) *n.* A large high frilly cap with a full crown, worn indoors by women in the 18th and early 19th centuries. [Prob. *mob,* mobcap (poss. < Du. *mopmuts,* cap : obsolete Du. *mop-,* to cover up + *muts,* cap) + CAP¹.]

mo·bile (mō′bəl, -bēl′, -bīl′) *adj.* **1.** Capable of moving or of being moved readily from place to place. **2.** Capable of moving or changing quickly from one state or condition to another. **b.** Fluid; unstable. **3a.** Marked by the easy intermixing of different social groups. **b.** Moving relatively easily from one social class or level to another. **c.** Tending to travel and relocate frequently. **4.** Flowing freely; fluid: *a mobile liquid.* ✦ *n.* (mō′bēl′) A sculpture of carefully equilibrated parts that move, esp. in air currents. [ME < OFr. < Lat. *mōbilis* < **movibilis* < *movēre,* to move.]

Mo·bile (mō-bēl′, mō′bēl′) A city of SW AL at the mouth of the **Mobile River,** c. 61 km (38 mi), the N shore of **Mobile Bay,** an arm of the Gulf of Mexico; founded c. 1710. Pop. 198,915.

mo·bile home (mō′bəl, -bēl′, -bīl′) *n.* A large trailer fitted with parts for connection to utilities and used as a residence.

mobile telephone also **mobile phone** *n.* See **cellular telephone.**

mo·bil·i·ty (mō-bĭl′ĭ-tē) *n.* **1.** The quality or state of being mobile. **2.** The movement of people, as from one social group, class, or level to another.

mo·bi·lize (mō′bə-līz′) *v.* **-lized, -liz·ing, -liz·es** —*tr.* **1.** To make mobile or capable of movement. **2a.** To assemble, prepare, or put into operation for or as if for war: *mobilize the snowplows.* **b.** To assemble, marshal, or coordinate for a purpose. —*intr.* To become prepared for or as if for war. —**mo′bi·li·za′tion** (-lĭ-zā′shən) *n.*

Mö·bi·us strip (mœ′bē-əs, mä′-, mō′-) *n.* A continuous one-sided surface formed from a rectangular strip by rotating one end 180° and attaching it to the other end. [After August Ferdinand *Möbius* (1790–1868), German mathematician.]

mob·oc·ra·cy (mŏb-ŏk′rə-sē) *n., pl.* **-cies 1.** Political control by a mob. **2.** The mass of common people as the source of political control. —**mob′o·crat** (mŏb′ə-krăt′) *n.* —**mob′o·crat′ic, mob′o·crat′i·cal** *adj.*

mob·ster (mŏb′stər) *n. Informal* A member of a criminal gang or crime syndicate.

Mo·bu·to Lake (mə-bōō′tō, mō-) See Lake **Albert.**

Mobutu Se·se Se·ko (sā′sā sā′kō) Orig. Joseph Désiré Mobutu.

1930–97. Zairean president (1967–97). A general in the army, Mobutu overthrew the existing government of the Congo (1965) and renamed the country Zaire (1971).

moc·ca·sin (mŏkʹə-sĭn) *n.* **1.** A soft leather slipper traditionally worn by certain Native American peoples. **2.** Footwear resembling such a slipper. **3.** A water moccasin. [Of Virginia Algonquian orig.; akin to Powhatan *mäkäsĭn*, shoe, and Ojibwa *makisin.*]

moccasin flower *n.* See **lady's slipper.**

mo·cha (mōʹkə) *n.* **1.** A pungent rich Arabian coffee. **2.** Coffee of high quality. **3.** A coffee beverage flavored with milk, sugar, and cocoa. **4.** A flavoring made of coffee mixed with chocolate. **5.** A soft thin suede-finished glove leather usu. made from sheepskin. **6.** A dark olive brown. [After *Mocha*, a town of SW Yemen.] —**moʹcha** *adj.*

Mo·chi·ca (mō-chēʹkə) or **Mo·che** (mōʹchä, -chĕ) *n., pl.* **Mochica** or **-cas** or **Moche** or **-ches 1.** A pre-Incan civilization that flourished on the northern coast of Peru from about 200 B.C. to A.D. 600. **2.** A member of a people sharing the Mochica culture.

mock (mŏk) *v.* **mocked, mock·ing, mocks** —*tr.* **1.** To treat with ridicule or contempt; deride. **2a.** To mimic, as in sport or derision. See Syns at **ridicule. b.** To imitate; counterfeit. **3.** To frustrate the hopes of; disappoint. —*intr.* To express scorn or ridicule; jeer. ❖ *n.* **1a.** The act of mocking. **b.** Mockery; derision. **2.** An object of scorn or derision. **3.** An imitation or counterfeit. ❖ *adj.* Simulated; false; sham: *a mock battle.* ❖ *adv.* In an insincere or pretending manner. [ME *mokken* < OFr. *mocquer.*] —**mockʹer** *n.* —**mockʹing·ly** *adv.*

mock·er·y (mŏkʹə-rē) *n., pl.* **-ies 1.** Scornfully contemptuous ridicule; derision. **2.** An act of ridicule or derision. **3.** An object of scorn or ridicule. **4.** A false, derisive, or impudent imitation. **5.** Something ludicrously futile or unsuitable.

mock-he·ro·ic (mŏkʹhĭ-rōʹĭk) *n.* A satirical imitation or burlesque of the heroic manner or style. —**mockʹ-he·roʹic** *adj.* —**mockʹ-he·roʹi·cal·ly** *adv.*

mock·ing·bird (mŏkʹĭng-bûrdʹ) *n.* Any of several species of New World birds of the family Mimidae, esp. *Mimus polyglottos,* a gray and white bird of the southern and eastern United States, noted for the ability to mimic other birds.

mock moon *n.* A paraselene.

mock orange *n.* **1.** Any of numerous deciduous shrubs of the genus *Philadelphus,* having opposite simple leaves and white, usu. fragrant flowers with four petals and numerous stamens. **2.** Any of various similar or related shrubs or trees.

mock sun *n.* A parhelion.

mock·tail (mŏkʹtālʹ) *n.* A cocktail containing no alcohol. [Blend of MOCK and COCKTAIL.]

mock turtle soup *n.* Soup made from calf's head, veal, or other meat and spiced to taste like green turtle soup.

mock-up also **mock-up** (mŏkʹŭpʹ) *n.* **1.** A usu. full-sized scale model of a structure. **2.** A layout of printed matter.

Moc·te·zu·ma (mŏkʹtĭ-zōōʹmə) See **Montezuma II.**

mod¹ (mŏd) *n.* An unconventionally modern style of fashionable dress originating in England in the 1960s. ❖ *adj.* **1.** In or characteristic of this style. **2.** Fashionably up-to-date, esp. in style, design, or dress. [After *the Mods*, name of several gangs of English youths in the 1960s, short for MODERN.]

mod² *abbr. Mathematics* modulus

mod. *abbr.* **1.** moderate **2.** moderato **3.** modern

mod·a·cryl·ic (mŏdʹə-krĭlʹĭk) *n.* One of several synthetic, long-chain polymer textile fibers containing 35–85 percent acrylonitrile. [*mod*(ified) *acrylic.*]

mod·al (mōdʹl) *adj.* **1.** Of, relating to, or characteristic of a mode. **2.** *Grammar* Of, relating to, or expressing the mood of a verb. **3.** *Music* Of, relating to, characteristic of, or composed in any of the modes typical of medieval church music. **4.** *Philosophy* Of or relating to mode without referring to substance. **5.** *Logic* Expressing or characterized by modality. **6.** *Statistics* Of or relating to a statistical mode or modes. ❖ *n.* See **modal auxiliary.** [Med.Lat. *modālis* < Lat. *modus,* measure. See **med-** in App.] —**modʹal·ly** *adv.*

modal auxiliary *n.* A verb characteristically used with other verbs to express mood or tense. In English, the modal auxiliaries are *can, may, must, ought, shall, should, will,* and *would.*

mo·dal·i·ty (mō-dălʹĭ-tē) *n., pl.* **-ties 1.** The fact, state, or quality of being modal. **2.** A tendency to conform to a pattern or belong to a group or category. **3.** *Logic* The classification of propositions based on whether they assert or deny the possibility, impossibility, contingency, or necessity of their content. **4. modalities** The ceremonial forms, protocols, or conditions that surround formal agreements or negotiations. **5.** *Medicine* A therapeutic method or agent, such as surgery, that involves the physical treatment of a disorder. **6.** *Physiology* Any of the various types of sensation, such as vision.

mode (mōd) *n.* **1a.** A manner, way, or method of doing or acting. See Syns at **method. b.** A particular form, variety, or manner: *a mode of expression.* **c.** A given condition of functioning; a status. **2.** The current or customary fashion or style. **3.** *Music* **a.** Any of certain fixed arrangements of the diatonic tones of an octave. **b.** A patterned arrangement, as the one characteristic of the music of classical Greece. **4.** *Philosophy* The particular appearance,

form, or manner in which an underlying substance or a permanent aspect or attribute of it is manifested. **5.** *Logic* **a.** See **modality** 3. **b.** The arrangement or order of the propositions in a syllogism according to both quality and quantity. **6.** *Statistics* The value or item occurring most frequently in a series of observations or statistical data. **7.** *Mathematics* The number or range of numbers in a set that occurs most frequently. **8.** *Geology* The mineral composition of an igneous rock expressed in terms of percentage of the total sample weight or volume. **9.** *Physics* Any of numerous patterns of wave motion or vibration. **10.** *Grammar* Mood. [ME, tune < Lat. *modus,* measure, tune; see **med-** in App. Sense 2, Fr. < OFr., fashion, manner < Lat. *modus.*]

mod·el (mŏdʹl) *n.* **1.** A small object, usu. built to scale, that represents in detail another, often larger object. **2a.** A preliminary work or construction that serves as a plan from which to make a final product: *a clay model ready for casting.* **b.** Such a work or construction used in testing or perfecting a final product: *a test model of a solar-powered vehicle.* **3.** A schematic description of a system, theory, or phenomenon that accounts for its properties and may be used for further study of its characteristics: *a model of an atom.* **4.** A style or design of an item: *My car is last year's model.* **5.** One serving as an example to be imitated or compared: *a model of decorum.* **6.** One that serves as the subject for an artist, esp. a person employed to pose. **7.** A person employed to display merchandise, such as clothing. **8.** *Zoology* An animal whose appearance is copied by a mimic. ❖ *v.* **-eled, -el·ing, -els** also **-elled, -el·ling, -els** —*tr.* **1.** To make or construct a model of. **2.** To plan, construct, or fashion according to a model. **3.** To make conform to a standard. **4a.** To make by shaping a plastic substance: *modeled a bust from clay.* **b.** To form (clay, for example) into a shape. **5.** To display by wearing or posing. **6.** In painting, drawing, and photography, to give a three-dimensional appearance to, as by shading or highlighting. —*intr.* **1.** To make a model. **2.** To serve or work as a model. ❖ *adj.* **1.** Being, serving as, or used as a model. **2.** Worthy of imitation. [Fr. *modèle* < Ital. *modello,* dim. of *modo,* form < Lat. *modus,* measure, standard. See **med-** in App.] —**modʹel·er** *n.*

mod·el·ing (mŏdʹl-ĭng) *n.* **1.** The act or art of sculpturing or forming in a pliable material, such as clay. **2a.** Representation of depth and solidity in painting, drawing, or photography. **b.** Visual shape and texture of something regarded aesthetically. **3.** The act or profession of being a model.

mo·dem (mōʹdəm) *n.* A device for transmitting usu. digital data over telephone wires by modulating the data into an audio signal to send it and demodulating an audio signal into data to receive it. ❖ *tr. & intr.v.* **-demed, -dem·ing, -dems** To transmit or be transmitted by modem. [MO(DULATOR) + DEM(ODULATOR).]

Mo·de·na (môdʹn-ə, mōʹdĕ-nä) A city of N Italy WNW of Bologna; orig. settled by Etruscans. Pop. 176,148.

mod·er·ate (mŏdʹər-ĭt) *adj.* **1.** Being within reasonable limits; not excessive or extreme: *a moderate price.* **2.** Not violent or subject to extremes; mild or calm; temperate: *a moderate climate.* **3a.** Of medium or average quantity or extent. **b.** Of limited or average quality; mediocre. **4.** Opposed to radical or extreme views or measures, esp. in politics or religion. ❖ *n.* One who holds or champions moderate views or opinions. ❖ *v.* (mŏdʹə-rātʹ) **-at·ed, -at·ing, -ates** —*tr.* **1.** To lessen the violence, severity, or extremeness of. **2.** To preside over. —*intr.* **1.** To become less violent, severe, or extreme; abate. **2.** To act as a moderator. [ME *moderat* < Lat. *moderātus,* p. part. of *moderārī,* to moderate. See **med-** in App.] —**modʹer·ate·ly** *adv.* —**modʹer·ate·ness** *n.* —**modʹer·aʹtion** *n.*

mod·e·ra·to (mŏdʹə-räʹtō) *adv. & adj. Music* In moderate tempo that is slower than allegretto but faster than andante. [Ital. < Lat. *moderātus,* moderate. See MODERATE.]

mod·er·a·tor (mŏdʹə-rāʹtər) *n.* **1.** One that moderates, as: **a.** One that arbitrates or mediates. **b.** One who presides over a meeting, forum, or debate. **2.** The officer who presides over a synod or general assembly of the Presbyterian Church. **3.** *Physics* A substance used in a nuclear reactor to slow down fast neutrons and increase the likelihood of fission.

mod·ern (mŏdʹərn) *adj.* **1a.** Of or relating to recent times or the present: *modern history.* **b.** Characteristic or expressive of recent times or the present; contemporary or up-to-date. **2a.** Of or relating to a recently developed or advanced style, technique, or technology: *modern art.* **b.** Avant-garde; experimental. **3.** often **Modern** *Linguistics* Of, relating to, or being a living language or group of languages: *Modern Italian.* ❖ *n.* **1.** One who lives in modern times. **2.** One who has modern ideas, standards, or beliefs. **3.** *Printing* Any of a variety of typefaces characterized by strongly contrasted heavy and thin parts. [Fr. *moderne* < OFr. < LLat. *modernus* < Lat. *modo,* in a certain manner, just now < *modō,* ablative of *modus,* manner. See **med-** in App.] —**modʹern·ly** *adv.* —**modʹern·ness** *n.*

modern dance *n.* Theatrical dance that emphasizes expressive movement over the formalism of ballet.

mo·derne (mō-dârnʹ) *adj.* Striving to be modern in appearance or style but lacking taste or refinement; pretentious. [Fr., modern < OFr. See MODERN.]

Modern English *n.* English since about 1500.

Modern Greek *n.* Greek since the early 16th century.

ă	pat	oi	boy
ā	pay	ou	out
âr	care	ŏŏ	took
ä	father	ōō	boot
ĕ	pet	ŭ	cut
ē	be	ûr	urge
ĭ	pit	th	thin
ī	pie	*th*	this
îr	pier	hw	which
ŏ	pot	zh	vision
ō	toe	ə	about,
ô	paw		item

Stress marks:
ʹ (primary);
ʹ (secondary); as in
lexicon (lĕkʹsĭ-kŏnʹ)

Modern Hebrew *n.* The Hebrew language as used from the 18th century to the present, and an official language of Israel.

mod·ern·ism (mŏd′ər-nĭz′əm) *n.* **1a.** Modern thought, character, or practice. **b.** Sympathy with or conformity to modern ideas, practices, or standards. **2.** A usage or style, as of a word, peculiar to modern times. **3.** often **Modernism** The use of nontraditional innovative forms of expression characteristic of many styles in the arts and literature of the 20th century. **4.** often **Modernism** A Roman Catholic movement that examined traditional belief according to contemporary philosophy, criticism, and historiography. —**mod′ern·ist** *n.* —**mod′ern·is′tic** *adj.*

mo·der·ni·ty (mŏ-dûr′nĭ-tē, mō-) *n., pl.* -**ties** The state or quality of being modern.

mod·ern·ize (mŏd′ər-nīz′) *v.* -**ized**, -**iz·ing**, -**iz·es** —*tr.* To make modern in appearance, style, or character; update. —*intr.* To accept or adopt modern ways, ideas, or style. —**mod′ern·i·za′tion** (-nĭ-zā′shən) *n.* —**mod′ern·iz′er** *n.*

modern pentathlon *n.* An athletic contest in which each participant competes in five events: running, swimming, horseback riding, fencing, and pistol shooting.

mod·est (mŏd′ĭst) *adj.* **1.** Having or showing a moderate estimation of one's talents, abilities, and value. **2.** Having or proceeding from a disinclination to call attention to oneself; retiring or diffident. See Syns at **shy**[1]. **3.** Observing conventional proprieties in speech, behavior, or dress. **4.** Free from showiness or ostentation; unpretentious. **5.** Moderate or limited in size, quantity, or range; not extreme: *a newspaper with a modest circulation.* [Lat. *modestus.* See **med-** in App.] —**mod′est·ly** *adv.*

Mo·des·to (mə-dĕs′tō) A city of central CA SE of Stockton; founded 1870. Pop. 188,856.

mod·es·ty (mŏd′ĭ-stē) *n.* **1.** The state or quality of being modest. **2.** Reserve or propriety in speech, dress, or behavior. **3.** Lack of pretentiousness; simplicity.

mod·i·cum (mŏd′ĭ-kəm) *n., pl.* -**cums** or -**ca** (-kə) A small, moderate, or token amount. [ME < Lat. < neut. of *modicus*, moderate < *modus*, measure. See **med-** in App.]

mod·i·fi·ca·tion (mŏd′ə-fĭ-kā′shən) *n.* **1.** The act of modifying or the condition of being modified. **2.** A result of modifying. **3.** A small alteration, adjustment, or limitation. **4.** *Biology* Any of the changes in an organism caused by environment or activity and not genetically transmissable to offspring. **5.** *Linguistics* **a.** A change undergone by a word borrowed from another language. **b.** A phonological change undergone by a word or morpheme when used in a construction, as the change of *will* to *'ll* in *they'll.* —**mod′i·fi·ca′tor** *n.* —**mod′i·fi·ca′to·ry** (-kā′tə-rē), **mod′i·fi·ca′tive** *adj.*

mod·i·fi·er (mŏd′ə-fī′ər) *n.* A word, phrase, or clause that modifies another word or word group.

mod·i·fy (mŏd′ə-fī′) *v.* -**fied**, -**fy·ing**, -**fies** —*tr.* **1.** To change in form or character; alter. **2.** To make less extreme, severe, or strong. **3.** *Grammar* To qualify or limit the meaning of. **4.** *Linguistics* To change (a vowel) by umlaut. —*intr.* To be or become modified; change. [ME *modifien* < OFr. *modifier* < Lat. *modificāre*, to measure, limit : *modus*, measure; see **med-** in App. + -*ficāre*, -fy.] —**mod′i·fi·a·bil′i·ty** *n.* —**mod′i·fi·a·ble** *adj.*

Mo·di·glia·ni (mō-dē′lē-ä′nē, mō′dē-glyä′nē), **Amedeo** 1884–1920. Italian painter and sculptor noted for graceful elongated lines in works such as *Reclining Nude* (1917).

mo·dil·lion (mō-dĭl′yən) *n.* An ornamental bracket used in series under a cornice, esp. a cornice of the Corinthian, Composite, or Ionic orders. [Ital. *modiglione* < VLat. **mutiliō*, **mutiliōn-* < Lat. *mūtulus*, perh. of Etruscan orig.]

mo·di·o·lus (mō-dī′ə-ləs) *n., pl.* -**li** (-lī′) The central conical bony core of the cochlea. [Lat., socket, hub, dim. of *modius*, a measure of grain, measuring vessel. See **med-** in App.]

mod·ish (mŏd′ĭsh) *adj.* Being in or conforming to the prevailing or current fashion; stylish. —**mod′ish·ly** *adv.* —**mod′ish·ness** *n.*

mo·diste (mō-dēst′) *n.* One that produces, designs, or deals in women's fashions. [Fr. < *mode*, fashion. See **MODE**.]

Mo·doc (mō′dŏk) *n., pl.* **Modoc** or -**docs 1.** A member of a Native American people inhabiting an area of the Cascade Range in south-central Oregon and northern California. **2.** The dialect of Klamath spoken by the Modoc.

mod·u·lar (mŏj′ə-lər) *adj.* **1.** Of, relating to, or based on a module or modulus. **2.** Designed with standardized units or dimensions, as for easy assembly and repair. —**mod′u·lar** *n.* —**mod′u·lar′i·ty** (-lär′ĭ-tē) *n.* —**mod′u·lar·ly** *adv.*

mod·u·lar·ized (mŏj′ə-lə-rīzd′) *adj.* Having or made up of modules: *modularized housing.*

mod·u·late (mŏj′ə-lāt′) *v.* -**lat·ed**, -**lat·ing**, -**lates** —*tr.* **1.** To adjust or adapt to a certain proportion; regulate or temper. **2.** To change the pitch, intensity, or tone of (one's voice, for example). **3.** *Electronics* **a.** To vary the frequency, amplitude, phase, or other characteristic of (electromagnetic waves). **b.** To vary (electron velocity) in an electron beam. —*intr. Music* To move from one key or tonality to another by means of a melody or chord progression. [Lat. *modulārī*, *modulāt-*, to measure off, to regulate < *modulus*, dim. of *modus*, measure. See **med-** in App.] —**mod′u·la·bil′i·ty** *n.* —**mod′u·la′tive**, **mod′u·la′to·ry** (-lə-tôr′ē, -tōr′ē) *adj.*

modular
Habitat housing complex in Montreal, Canada, designed by Moshe Safdie (b. 1938)

mogul
mogul course for an Olympic race

mod·u·la·tion (mŏj′ə-lā′shən) *n.* **1.** The act or process of modulating. **2.** The state of being modulated. **3.** *Music* **a.** A passing or transition from one key or tonality to another. **b.** The result of such a transition. **4a.** A change in stress, pitch, loudness, or tone of the voice. **b.** An instance of such a change. **5.** The harmonious use of language, as in poetry or prose. **6.** *Electronics* The variation of a property of an electromagnetic wave or signal, such as its frequency or phase.

mod·u·la·tor (mŏj′ə-lā′tər) *n.* A device used to modulate an electromagnetic wave.

mod·ule (mŏj′ool) *n.* **1.** A standard or unit of measurement. **2.** *Architecture* The dimensions of a structural component, such as the base of a column, used in determining the proportions of the rest of the construction. **3.** A standardized, often interchangeable component of a system or construction designed for easy assembly or flexible use. **4.** *Electronics* A self-contained assembly of electronic components and circuitry installed as a unit. **5.** *Computer Science* A portion of a program that carries out a specific function and may be used alone or combined with other modules of the same program. **6.** A self-contained unit of a spacecraft that performs a specific task or class of tasks in support of the major function of the craft. **7.** A unit of education or instruction with a relatively low student-to-teacher ratio in which a single topic is studied. [Lat. *modulus*, dim. of *modus*, measure. See **med-** in App.]

mod·u·lo (mŏj′ə-lō) *prep.* **1.** *Mathematics* With respect to a specified modulus. **2.** Correcting or adjusting for something, as by leaving something out of account: *This proposal is the best so far, modulo the fact that parts of it need modification.* [Lat. *modulō*, ablative of *modulus*, dim. of *modus*, measure. See **MODE**.]

mod·u·lus (mŏj′ə-ləs) *n., pl.* -**li** (-lī′) **1.** *Physics* A quantity that expresses the degree to which a substance possesses a property, such as elasticity. **2a.** *Mathematics* The absolute value of a complex number. **b.** A number by which two given numbers can be divided and produce the same remainder; for example, 18 and 42 leave 6 as a remainder when divided by 12. **c.** The number by which a logarithm in one system must be multiplied to obtain the corresponding logarithm in another system. [Lat., dim. of *modus*, measure. See **med-** in App.]

mo·dus op·er·an·di (mō′dəs ŏp′ə-răn′dē, -dī′) *n., pl.* **mo·di operandi** (mō′dē, -dī) **1.** A method of operating or functioning. **2.** A person's manner of working. [NLat. *modus operandī* : Lat. *modus*, mode + Lat. *operandī*, genitive sing. gerund of *operārī*, to work.]

modus vi·ven·di (vĭ-vĕn′dē, -dī′) *n., pl.* **modi vivendi 1.** A manner of living; a way of life. **2.** A temporary agreement between contending parties pending a final settlement. [NLat. *modus vīvendī* : Lat. *modus*, mode + Lat. *vīvendī*, genitive sing. gerund of *vīvere*, to live.]

Moe·sia (mē′shə, -shē-ə) An ancient region of SE Europe S of the Danube R. in what is now Serbia and N Bulgaria; orig. inhabited by Thracians.

mo·fette also **mof·fette** (mō-fĕt′) *n.* **1.** An opening in the earth from which carbon dioxide and other gases escape, usu. marking the last stage of volcanic activity. **2.** The gases escaping from such an opening. [Fr., gaseous exhalation < Ital. *moffetta*, dim. of *muffa*, mold, moldy smell, prob. of Gmc. orig.]

Mo·ga·di·shu (mō′gə-dē′shoo, -dĭsh′oo, mô′-) The cap. of Somalia, on the Indian Ocean; settled by Arab colonists in the 9th or 10th century. Pop. 400,000.

Mo·gen Da·vid (mō′gən dô′vĭd, dä′vĭd, mä-gĕn′ dä-vēd′) *n.* Variant of **Magen David.**

Mo·gi·lev (mŏg′ə-lĕf′, mə-gĭ-lyôf′) See **Mahilyow.**

Mo·gol·lon (mō′gə-yōn′) *n.* A Native American culture flourishing from the 2nd century B.C. to the 13th century A.D. in southeast Arizona and southwest New Mexico, esp. noted for its development of pottery. [After the MOGOLLON (PLATEAU).]

Mogollon Plateau A tableland, 2,135–2,440 m (7,000–8,000 ft), of E-central AZ. Its S edge is the rugged escarpment **Mogollon Rim.**

mo·gul (mō′gəl) *n.* A small hard mound or bump on a ski slope. [Prob. of Scand. orig.; akin to ON *mūgi*, heap.]

Mo·gul (mō′gəl, mō-gŭl′) *n.* **1.** also **Mo·ghul** (mōō-gŭl′) or **Mu·ghal** (mōō-gŭl′) **a.** A member of the force that under Baber conquered India in 1526. **b.** A member of the Muslim dynasty founded by Baber that ruled India until 1857. **2.** A Mongol or Mongolian. **3. mogul** A very rich or powerful person; a magnate. [Pers. and Ar. *mugul* < Mongolian *Mongul*.]

mo·hair (mō′hâr′) *n.* **1.** The long silky hair of the Angora goat. **2.** Fabric made with yarn from this hair. [Alteration of obsolete Ital. *mocaiaro* < Ar. *muḥayyar*, choice, select, mohair, passive part. of *ḥayyara*, to prefer, derived stem of *ḥāra*, to choose.]

Mo·ham·med (mō-hăm′ĭd, -hä′mĭd, mō-) See **Muhammad.**

Mohammed II 1429?–81. See **Muhammad II.**

Mohammed Ali See **Muhammad Ali.**

Mo·ham·med·an (mō-hăm′ĭ-dən) *adj. & n.* Variant of **Muhammadan.**

Mo·ham·med·an·ism (mō-hăm′ĭ-də-nĭz′əm) *n.* Variant of **Muhammadanism.**

Mo·har·ram (mō-hăr′əm) *n.* Variant of **Muharram.**

Mo·ha·ve also **Mo·ja·ve** (mō-hä′vē) *n., pl.* **Mohave** or -**ves**

also Mojave or **-ves** **1.** A member of a Native American people inhabiting lands along the lower Colorado River on the Arizona-California border. **2.** The Yuman language of the Mohave. [Mohave *hàmakháav.*]

Mohave Desert *See* **Mojave Desert.**

Mo·hawk[1] (mō′hôk′) *n., pl.* **Mohawk** or **-hawks** **1.** A member of a Native American people formerly inhabiting northeast New York, with present-day populations chiefly in southern Ontario and extreme northern New York. **2.** The Iroquoian language of the Mohawk. [Narragansett *Mohowaúg.*]

Mo·hawk[2] (mō′hôk′) *n., pl.* **-hawks** A hairstyle in which the scalp is shaved except for a strip of hair that runs from the forehead to the nape of the neck. [After MOHAWK[1].]

Mohawk River A river of E-central NY flowing c. 225 km (140 mi) to the Hudson R.

Mo·he·gan (mō-hē′gən) *n., pl.* **Mohegan** or **-gans** **1.** A member of a Native American people formerly inhabiting eastern Connecticut, with present-day descendants in southeast Connecticut and Wisconsin. **2.** Their Algonquian language.

Mo·hen·jo-Da·ro (mō-hĕn′jō-där′ō) A ruined prehistoric city of Pakistan in the Indus R. valley NE of Karachi.

Mo·hi·can (mō-hē′kən, mə-) *n.* Variant of **Mahican.**

Mo·ho (mō′hō′) *n.* The Mohorovičić discontinuity.

Mo·ho·ro·vi·čić discontinuity (mō′hə-rō′və-chĭch) *n.* The boundary between the earth's crust and the underlying mantle, averaging 8 kilometers (5 miles) in depth under the oceans and 32 kilometers (20 miles) in depth under the continents. [After Andrija *Mohorovičić* (1857–1936), Croatian geophysicist.]

Mohs scale (mōz) *n.* A scale for classifying minerals based on relative hardness and including, in order from softest to hardest: 1. talc; 2. gypsum; 3. calcite; 4. fluorite; 5. apatite; 6. orthoclase; 7. quartz; 8. topaz; 9. corundum; 10. diamond. [After Friedrich *Mohs* (1773–1839), German mineralogist.]

mo·hur (mō′ər, mə-hoor′) *n.* A gold coin, equal to 15 rupees, used in British India. [Hindi *muhr,* gold coin, seal < Pers.; akin to Skt. *mudrā,* seal. See MUDRA.]

moi·dore (moi′dôr′, -dōr′, moi-dôr′, -dōr′) *n.* A former Portuguese or Brazilian gold coin. [Alteration of Port. *moeda d'ouro* : *moeda* (< Lat. *monēta,* coin; see MONEY) + *de,* of (< Lat. *dē*; see DE-) + *ouro,* gold (< Lat. *aurum*).]

moi·e·ty (moi′ĭ-tē) *n., pl.* **-ties** **1.** A half. **2.** A part, portion, or share. **3.** Either of two kinship groups based on unilateral descent that together make up a tribe or society. [ME *moite* < OFr. *meitiet, moitie* < LLat. *medietās* < Lat., middle < *medius,* middle. See **medhyo-** in App.]

moil (moil) *intr.v.* **moiled, moil·ing, moils** **1.** To toil; slave. **2.** To churn about continuously. ❖ *n.* **1.** Toil; drudgery. **2.** Confusion; turmoil. [ME *moillen,* to soften by wetting < OFr. *moillier* < VLat. **molliāre* < Lat. *mollia (pānis),* the soft part (of bread) < neut. pl. of *mollis,* soft.] —**moil′er** *n.* —**moil′ing·ly** *adv.*

moire (mwär, mwä-rä′, môr, mô-rä′) *n.* A watered or moiré fabric. [Fr., prob. < E. MOHAIR.]

moi·ré (mwä-rä′, mô-) *adj.* Having a wavy or rippled surface pattern. Used of fabric. ❖ *n.* **1.** Fabric, such as silk or rayon, finished so as to have a wavy or rippled surface pattern. **2.** A similar pattern produced on cloth by engraved rollers. [Fr. < p. part. of *moirer,* to water < *moire,* moiré fabric. See MOIRE.]

moiré effect *n.* **1.** The effect of superimposing a repetitive design on the same or another design to produce a distinct pattern. **2.** *Computer Science* The perceived flickering or distortion of printed or displayed high-contrast images.

moist (moist) *adj.* **1.** Slightly wet; damp or humid. *See Syns at* **wet. 2.** Filled with or characterized by moisture. **3.** Tearful. [ME *moiste* < OFr., alteration of VLat. **muscidus,* alteration of Lat. *mūcidus,* moldy < *mūcus,* mucus.] —**moist′ly** *adv.* —**moist′ness** *n.*

mois·ten (moi′sən) *tr. & intr.v.* **-tened, -ten·ing, -tens** To make or become moist. —**moist′en·er** *n.*

mois·ture (mois′chər) *n.* **1.** Diffuse wetness that can be felt as vapor in the atmosphere or condensed liquid on the surfaces of objects; dampness. **2.** The state or quality of being damp. [ME < OFr. *moiste,* moist. See MOIST.]

mois·tur·ize (mois′chə-rīz′) *tr.v.* **-ized, -iz·ing, -iz·es** To add or restore moisture to: *lotion that moisturizes the face.*

mois·tur·iz·er (mois′chə-rī′zər) *n.* A cosmetic lotion or cream applied to the skin to counter dryness.

mo·jar·ra (mō-här′ə) *n., pl.* **mojarra** or **-ras** Any of several species of small, silvery, mainly tropical American marine fishes of the family Gerridae, having extremely protrusile mouths. [Sp., knife, a fish < Ar. *muḥarrab,* pointed < *harraba,* to sharpen, point < *ḥarba,* lance, spear.]

Mo·ja·ve (mō-hä′vē) *n.* Variant of **Mohave.**

Mojave Desert *also* **Mo·ha·ve Desert** (mō-hä′vē) An arid region of S CA SE of the Sierra Nevada.

mo·jo (mō′jō′) *n., pl.* **-jos** or **-joes** **1.** A magic charm or spell. **2.** An amulet, often a small bag containing one or more magic items, worn by adherents of hoodoo or voodoo. **3.** Personal magnetism; charm. [Perh. ult. < Fula *moco'o,* medicine man.]

moke (mōk) *n.* **1.** *Slang* A dull person. **2.** *Chiefly British* A donkey. **3.** *Australian* An old broken-down horse. [?]

mol (mōl) *n.* Variant of **mole**[5].

mol. *abbr.* **1.** molecular **2.** molecule

mo·la[1] (mō′lä, -lä) *n., pl.* **-las** A colorful fabric panel of Central American origin, used for decorative purposes. [Kuna, clothing, blouse, mola.]

mo·la[2] (mō′lä) *n., pl.* **mola** or **-las** *See* **ocean sunfish.** [Lat., millstone (< its shape and rough skin). See **mela-** in App.]

mo·lal (mō′läl) *adj.* Of or being a solution that contains one mole of solute in 1,000 grams of solvent.

mo·lal·i·ty (mō-läl′ĭ-tē) *n., pl.* **-ties** The molal concentration of a solute, usu. expressed as the number of moles of solute per 1,000 grams of solvent.

mo·lar[1] (mō′lər) *adj.* **1.** *Chemistry* **a.** Relating to or being a solution that contains one mole of solute per liter of solution. **b.** Containing one mole of a substance. **2.** *Physics* Of or relating to a body of matter as a whole, perceived apart from molecular or atomic properties. [< MOLE[5].]

mo·lar[2] (mō′lər) *n.* A tooth with a broad crown used to grind food, located behind the premolars. ❖ *adj.* **1.** Of or relating to the molars. **2.** Capable of grinding. [< ME *molares,* molars < Lat. *molāris,* of a mill, grinder, molar < *mola,* millstone. See **mela-** in App.]

mo·lar·i·ty (mō-lăr′ĭ-tē) *n., pl.* **-ties** *Chemistry* The molar concentration of a solution, usu. expressed as the number of moles of solute per liter of solution.

mo·las·ses (mə-läs′ĭz) *n., pl.* **molasses** A thick syrup produced in refining raw sugar and ranging from light to dark brown in color. [Port. *melaços,* pl. of *melaço* < LLat. *mellāceum,* must < Lat. *mel, mell-,* honey. See **melit-** in App.]

mold[1] (mōld) *n.* **1.** A hollow form or matrix for shaping a fluid or plastic substance. **2.** A frame or model around or on which something is formed or shaped. **3.** Something that is made in or shaped on a mold. **4.** The shape or pattern of a mold. **5.** General shape or form. **6.** Distinctive character or type. **7.** A fixed or restrictive pattern or form. **8.** *Architecture See* **molding** 3. ❖ *v.* **mold·ed, mold·ing, molds** —*tr.* **1.** To shape in or on a mold. **2a.** To form into a particular shape; give shape to. **b.** To guide or determine the growth or development of; influence: *a teacher who helps to mold the mind of her students.* **3.** To fit closely by following the contours of. **4.** To make a mold of or from (molten metal, for example) before casting. **5.** To ornament with moldings. —*intr.* To be shaped in or as if in a mold: *The shoes gradually molded to my feet.* [ME *molde* < OFr. *molle, molde* < Lat. *modulus,* dim. of *modus,* measure. See **med-** in App.] —**mold′a·ble** *adj.* —**mold′er** *n.*

mold[2] (mōld) *n.* **1.** Any of various fungi that often cause disintegration of organic matter. **2.** The growth of such fungi. ❖ *intr.v.* **mold·ed, mold·ing, molds** To become moldy. [ME *moulde,* prob. < p. part. of *moulen,* to grow moldy < ON *mygla.*]

mold[3] (mōld) *n.* **1.** Loose friable soil, rich in humus and fit for planting. **2.** *Chiefly British* **a.** The earth; the ground. **b.** The earth of the grave. **3.** *Archaic* Earth as the substance of the human body. [ME < OE *molde.* See **mela-** in App.]

Mol·da·vi·a (mŏl-dā′vē-ə, -dāv′yə, mŏl-) **1.** A historical region of E Romania E of Transylvania; united with Walachia in 1859 to form the nucleus of modern Romania. **2.** *See* **Moldova.** —**Mol·da·vi·an** *adj. & n.*

mold·board (mōld′bôrd′, -bōrd′) *n.* The curved plate of a plow that turns over the soil. [MOLD[3] + BOARD.]

mold·er (mōl′dər) *v.* **-ered, -er·ing, -ers** —*intr.* To crumble to dust; disintegrate. —*tr.* To cause to crumble. [Prob. freq. of MOLD[3].]

mold·ing (mōl′dĭng) *n.* **1.** The act or process of molding. **2.** Something that is molded. **3.** An embellishment in strip form made of wood or other structural material and used to decorate or finish a surface, such as the surface of a door.

Mol·do·va (mŏl-dō′və, mōl-) Formerly **Mol·da·vi·a** (-dā′vē-ə, -dāv′yə) A country of E Europe bordering on Romania. Acquired by Russia from the Romanian region of Moldavia in the late 18th and early 19th cent., it was a constituent republic of the USSR from 1940 until 1991. Cap. Chişinău. Pop. 4,111,000.

mold·y (mōl′dē) *adj.* **-i·er, -i·est 1.** Covered with or containing mold: *moldy bread.* **2.** Musty or stale, as from age or decay. —**mold′i·ness** *n.*

mole[1] (mōl) *n.* A small congenital growth on the human skin, usu. slightly raised and dark and sometimes hairy, esp. a pigmented nevus. [ME < OE *māl.*]

mole[2] (mōl) *n.* **1.** Any of various small insectivorous mammals of the family Talpidae, usu. living underground and having light brown to dark gray silky fur, rudimentary eyes, and strong forefeet for burrowing. **2.** A machine that bores through hard surfaces, used esp. for tunneling through rock. **3.** A spy within an organization, esp. a double agent. [ME *molle;* poss. akin to MOLD[3].]

mole[3] (mōl) *n.* **1.** A massive, usu. stone wall constructed in the sea, used to enclose or protect an anchorage or harbor. **2.** The anchorage or harbor enclosed by a mole. [Fr. *môle* < Ital. *molo* < L.Gk. *mōlos* < Lat. *mōlēs,* mass, mole.]

mole[4] (mōl) *n.* An abnormal fleshy mass formed in the uterus by the degeneration or abortive development of an ovum. [Fr. *môle* < Lat. *mola,* millstone, mole. See **mela-** in App.]

mole[5] or **mol** (mōl) *n.* **1.** The amount of a substance that contains

Moldova

ă pat	oi boy
ā pay	ou out
âr care	ŏŏ took
ä father	ōō boot
ĕ pet	ŭ cut
ē be	ûr urge
ĭ pit	th thin
ī pie	*th* this
îr pier	hw which
ŏ pot	zh vision
ō toe	ə about,
ô paw	item

Stress marks:
′ (primary);
′ (secondary), as in
lexicon (lĕk′sĭ-kŏn′)

as many elementary units as the number of atoms in 0.012 kilogram of carbon 12. The number is 6.0225×10^{23}, or Avogadro's number. **2.** The mass in grams of this amount of a substance, numerically equal to the molecular weight of the substance. See table at **measurement.** [Ger. *Mol*, short for *Molekulargewicht*, molecular weight < *molekular*, molecular < Fr. *moléculaire* < *molécule*, molecule. See MOLECULE.]

mo·le[6] (mō′lā′) *n.* Any of various sauces of Mexican origin made with chocolate and a variety of chilies and spices and usu. served with meat or poultry. [Am.Sp. < Nahuatl *mōlli*.]

mole cricket (mōl) *n.* Any of various burrowing crickets of the family Gryllotalpidae, having short wings and front legs well adapted for digging and feeding mainly on the roots of plants.

mo·lec·u·lar (mə-lĕk′yə-lər) *adj.* **1.** Of, relating to, or consisting of molecules. **2.** Of or relating to simple or basic structure or form. —**mo·lec′u·lar′i·ty** (-lăr′ĭ-tē) *n.* —**mo·lec′u·lar·ly** *adv.*

molecular biology *n.* The branch of biology that deals with the formation, structure, and activity of macromolecules essential to life and esp. with their role in cell replication and the transmission of genetic information. —**molecular biologist** *n.*

molecular formula *n.* A chemical formula that shows the number and kinds of atoms in a molecule.

molecular genetics *n. (used with a sing. verb)* The branch of genetics that deals with sequencing the DNA that codes for specific genes and manipulating DNA sequences to study gene functions.

molecular medicine *n.* The branch of medicine that deals with the influence of gene expression on disease processes and with genetically based treatments, such as gene therapy.

molecular weight *n.* The sum of the atomic weights of all the atoms in a molecule.

mol·e·cule (mŏl′ĭ-kyōōl′) *n.* **1.** The smallest particle of a substance that retains its chemical and physical properties and is composed of two or more atoms; a group of like or different atoms held together by chemical forces. **2.** A small particle; a tiny bit. [Fr. *molécule* < NLat. *mōlēcula*, dim. of Lat. *mōlēs*, mass.]

mole·hill (mōl′hĭl′) *n.* A small mound of loose earth raised by a burrowing mole. —**idiom: make a mountain out of a molehill** To exaggerate a minor problem.

mole·skin (mōl′skĭn′) *n.* **1.** The silky fur of a mole. **2a.** A heavy-napped cotton twill fabric. **b. moleskins** Clothing, esp. trousers, of this fabric. **3.** A soft material, often with an adhesive backing, used esp. to prevent the feet from chafing.

mo·lest (mə-lĕst′) *tr.v.* **-lest·ed, -lest·ing, -lests** **1.** To disturb, interfere with, or annoy. **2.** To subject to unwanted or improper sexual activity. [ME *molesten* < OFr. *molester* < Lat. *molestāre* < *molestus*, troublesome.] —**mo′les·ta′tion** (mō′lĕ-stā′shən) *n.* —**mo·lest′er** *n.*

Mo·lière (mōl-yâr′), **Jean Baptiste Poquelin** 1622–73. French playwright whose works include *Tartuffe* (1664).

Mo·li·na (mə-lē′nə, mō-), **Mario José** b. 1943. Mexican-born Amer. chemist who shared a 1995 Nobel Prize for his work on the formation and decomposition of ozone.

Mo·li·se (mō′lĭ-zā′) A region of S-central Italy bordering the Adriatic Sea; ruled by a Lombard duchy from the 6th to the 11th cent. A.D.

moll (mŏl) *n. Slang* **1.** A woman companion of a gunman or gangster. **2.** A woman prostitute. [Prob. < the name *Moll*, nickname for *Mary*.]

mol·li·fy (mŏl′ə-fī′) *tr.v.* **-fied, -fy·ing, -fies** **1.** To calm in temper or feeling; soothe. See Syns at **pacify.** **2.** To lessen in intensity; temper. **3.** To reduce the rigidity of; soften. [ME *mollifien* < OFr. *mollifier* < LLat. *mollificāre* : Lat. *mollis*, soft + Lat. *-ficāre*, -fy.] —**mol′li·fi·a·ble** *adj.* —**mol′li·fi·ca′tion** (-fi-kā′shən) *n.* —**mol′li·fi′er** *n.*

mol·lus·can also **mol·lus·kan** (mə-lŭs′kən) *adj.* Of or relating to the mollusks. ❖ *n.* A mollusk.

mol·lus·ci·cide (mə-lŭs′kĭ-sīd′) *n.* An agent that kills mollusks. —**mol·lus′ci·cid′al** (-sīd′l) *adj.*

mol·lus·coid (mə-lŭs′koid) *adj.* Of, belonging to, or resembling the mollusks.

mol·lus·cum (mə-lŭs′kəm) *n., pl.* **-ca** (-kə) Any of various skin diseases in which soft spherical tumors form on the face or other part of the body. [Lat., a kind of fungus < neut. of *molluscus*, soft. See MOLLUSK.]

mol·lusk also **mol·lusc** (mŏl′əsk) *n.* Any of numerous chiefly marine invertebrates of the phylum Mollusca, typically having a soft unsegmented body, a mantle, and a protective calcareous shell. [Fr. *mollusque* < NLat. *Mollusca*, phylum name < neut. pl. of Lat. *molluscus*, thin-shelled < *mollis*, soft.] —**mol·lus′cous** (mə-lŭs′kəs) *adj.*

mol·ly also **mol·lie** (mŏl′ē) *n., pl.* **-lies** Any of several tropical and subtropical live-bearing fishes of the genus *Poecilia* or *Mollienesia*, commonly kept in aquariums. [< NLat. *Mollienesia*, former genus name, after Comte François Nicolas Mollien (1758–1850), French politician.]

mol·ly·cod·dle (mŏl′ē-kŏd′l) —*tr.* **-dled, -dling, -dles** To be overprotective and indulgent toward. ❖ *n.* A person, esp. a man or boy, who is pampered and overprotected. [*molly*, milksop (< the name *Molly*) + CODDLE.] —**mol′ly·cod′dler** *n.*

Mol·nár (mōl′när′, mŏl′-), **Ferenc** 1878–1952. Hungarian

writer whose comedies include *Liliom* (1909).

mo·loch (mō′lŏk′, mŏl′ək) *n.* A lizard (*Moloch horridus*) of central and southern Australia having large spiny scales. [LLat. *Moloch*, Semitic deity. See MOLOCH.]

Moloch *n.* **1.** In the Bible, the god of the Canaanites and Phoenicians to whom children were sacrificed. **2.** Something possessing the power to exact severe sacrifice. [LLat. *Moloch* < Gk. *Molokh* < Heb. *Mōlek* < Canaanite **mulk*, perh. var. of **malk, *milk*, king.]

Mo·lo·kai (mŏl′ə-kī′, mō′lə-) An island of central HI between Oahu and Maui.

Mo·lo·po (mə-lō′pō) An intermittent river of South Africa flowing c. 965 km (600 mi) to the Orange R.

Mo·lo·tov (mŏl′ə-tôf′, mŏl′-, mō′lə-), **Vyacheslav Mikhailovich** 1890–1986. Soviet politician who served as foreign minister (1939–49 and 1953–56).

Molotov cocktail *n.* A makeshift bomb made of a breakable container filled with flammable liquid and provided with a usu. rag wick. [After Vyacheslav Mikhailovich MOLOTOV.]

molt (mōlt) *v.* **molt·ed, molt·ing, molts** —*intr.* To shed periodically part or all of an outer covering, which is then replaced by a new growth. —*tr.* To shed or cast off (a bodily covering). ❖ *n.* **1.** The act or process of molting. **2.** The material cast off during molting. [Alteration of ME *mouten* < OE *-mūtian* (in *bemūtian*, to exchange for) < Lat. *mūtāre*, to change.] —**molt′er** *n.*

mol·ten (mōl′tən) *v. Archaic* A past participle of **melt.** ❖ *adj.* **1.** Made liquid by heat; melted: *molten lead.* **2.** Made by melting and casting in a mold. **3.** Brilliantly glowing from or as if from intense heat.

mol·to (mōl′tō) *adv. Music* Very; much. [Ital. < Lat. *multum* < neut. sing. of *multus*, many, much.]

Mo·luc·cas (mə-lŭk′əz) Formerly **Spice Islands.** A group of islands of E Indonesia between Sulawesi and New Guinea; settled by the Portuguese but taken in the 17th cent. by the Dutch. —**Mo·luc′can** *adj. & n.*

mol. wt. *abbr.* molecular weight

mo·ly (mō′lē) *n., pl.* **-lies** *Greek Mythology* A magic herb with black roots and white flowers given to Odysseus by Hermes to ward off the spells of Circe. [Lat. *mōly* < Gk. *mōlu*.]

mo·lyb·de·nite (mə-lĭb′də-nīt′) *n.* A mineral form of molybdenum sulfide, MoS_2, the principal ore of molybdenum.

mo·lyb·de·num (mə-lĭb′də-nəm) *n. Symbol* **Mo** A hard metallic element that is a necessary trace element in plant and animal nutrition and is used to toughen alloy steels. Atomic number 42; atomic weight 95.94; melting point 2,617°C; boiling point 4,612°C; specific gravity 10.22 (at 20°C); valence 2, 3, 4, 5, 6. See table at **element.** [NLat. < earlier *molybdena*, lead ore < Lat. *molybdaena*, galena < Gk. *molubdaina* < *molubdos*, lead.]

mo·lyb·dic (mə-lĭb′dĭk) *adj.* Of, relating to, or being molybdenum or a compound containing molybdenum, esp. with valence 6.

mo·lyb·dous (mə-lĭb′dəs) *adj.* Of, relating to, or being molybdenum or a compound containing molybdenum, esp. with a valence less than 6.

mom (mŏm) *n. Informal* Mother. [Alteration of MAMA.]

MOM *abbr.* middle of month

Mom·a·day (mŏm′ə-dā′), **N(avarro) Scott** b. 1934. Native American writer whose works include the novel *House Made of Dawn* (1968).

mom-and-pop (mŏm′ən-pŏp′) *adj.* Of or being a small business typically owned and run by a family.

Mom·ba·sa (mŏm-băs′ə, -bä′sä) A city of SE Kenya mainly on **Mombasa Island,** in the Indian Ocean N of Zanzibar; ruled successively by Portugal, Oman, Zanzibar, and Great Britain until the early 20th cent. Pop. 425,600.

mo·ment (mō′mənt) *n.* **1.** A brief indefinite interval of time. **2.** A specific point in time, esp. the present time. **3.** A particular period of importance, influence, or significance in a series of events or developments. **4.** Outstanding significance or value; importance. **5.** A brief period of time that is characterized by a quality, such as excellence. **6.** *Philosophy* **a.** An essential or constituent element, as of a complex idea. **b.** A phase or aspect of a logically developing process. **7.** *Physics* **a.** The product of a quantity and its perpendicular distance from a reference point. **b.** The tendency to cause rotation about a point or axis. **8.** *Statistics* The expected value of a positive integral power of a random variable, the first moment being the mean of the distribution. [ME < OFr. < Lat. *mōmentum*. See MOMENT.]

mo·men·tar·i·ly (mō′mən-târ′ə-lē) *adv.* **1.** For a moment or an instant. **2.** *Usage Problem* In a moment; very soon. **3.** Moment by moment; progressively.

USAGE NOTE Some critics maintain that *momentarily* should be used only in the sense "for a moment," as in *The network is momentarily unavailable.* However, the widespread use of *momentarily* to mean "in a moment," as in *The doctor will be with you momentarily,* appears to be gaining acceptability. In 1988, 41 percent of the Usage Panel found the "in a moment" usage unacceptable; in 1999, 68 percent accepted it.

mo·men·tar·y (mō′mən-tĕr′ē) *adj.* **1.** Lasting for only a moment. **2.** Occurring or present at every moment: *in momentary fear.* **3.** Short-lived or ephemeral, as a life. [ME *momentare* < Lat.

mō·men·tar·ius < *mōmentum*, moment. See MOMENTUM.]
—**mo′men·tar′i·ness** *n.*

mo·ment·ly (mō′mənt-lē) *adv.* **1.** From moment to moment. **2.** At any moment. **3.** For a moment.

moment of inertia *n., pl.* **moments of inertia** A measure of a body's resistance to angular acceleration, equal to the sum of the products of each mass element of a body multiplied by the square of its distance from an axis.

moment of truth *n., pl.* **moments of truth** **1.** A critical or decisive time on which much depends. **2.** *Sports* The point in a bullfight at which the matador makes the kill.

mo·men·tous (mō-měn′təs) *adj.* Of utmost importance; of outstanding significance or consequence: *a momentous decision.* —**mo·men′tous·ly** *adv.* —**mo·men′tous·ness** *n.*

mo·men·tum (mō-měn′təm) *n., pl.* **-ta** (-tə) or **-tums** **1.** *Symbol* **p** *Physics* A measure of the motion of a body equal to the product of its mass and velocity. **2a.** Impetus of a physical object in motion. **b.** Impetus of a nonphysical process, such as an idea. **3.** *Philosophy* See **moment** 6a. [Lat. *mōmentum,* movement, movement < **movimentum* < *movēre,* to move.]

mom·ma (mä′mə) *n.* Variant of **mama.**

Momm·sen (mŏm′zən), **Theodor** 1817–1903. German historian who won the 1902 Nobel Prize for literature.

mom·my (mŏm′ē) *n., pl.* **-mies** *Informal* A mother. [Alteration of MAMMY.]

mommy track *n.* A career path determined by work arrangements offering mothers certain benefits, such as flexible hours, but usu. providing fewer opportunities for advancement.

Mo·mus (mō′məs) *n. Greek Mythology.* The god of blame and ridicule.

mon (mŏn) *n. Scots* Man.

Mon (mŏn) *n., pl.* **Mon** or **Mons** **1.** A member of a Buddhist people inhabiting an area of eastern Myanmar (Burma) and adjacent parts of Thailand. **2.** The Mon-Khmer language of the Mon.

Mon. *abbr.* Monday

mon– *pref.* Variant of **mono–.**

mon·a·chism (mŏn′ə-kĭz′əm) *n.* Monasticism. [Ult. < L.Gk. *monakhismos* < *monakhos,* monk. See MONK.]

Mon·a·co (mŏn′ə-kō′, mə-nä′kō) A principality on the Mediterranean Sea consisting of an enclave in SE France; ruled by the Grimaldi family since the 13th cent. Cap. **Monaco,** or **Monaco-Ville.** Pop. 27,063. —**Mon′a·can** *adj. & n.*

mo·nad (mō′năd′) *n.* **1.** *Philosophy* An indivisible impenetrable unit of substance viewed as the basic constituent element of physical reality in the metaphysics of Leibnitz. **2.** *Biology* A single-celled microorganism, esp. a flagellate protozoan of the genus *Monas.* **3.** *Chemistry* An atom or radical with valence 1. [Lat. *monas, monad–,* unit < Gk. *monos,* single. See **men–²** in App.] —**mo·nad′ic** (mə-năd′ĭk), **mo·nad′i·cal** *adj.* —**mo·nad′i·cal·ly** *adv.*

mon·a·del·phous (mŏn′ə-děl′fəs, mō′nə-) *adj.* Related to or being stamens with all the filaments united into a single tubelike group. [MON– + Gk. *adelphos,* brother; see **sem–¹** in App.]

mo·nad·nock (mə-năd′nŏk′) *n.* A mountain or rocky mass that has resisted erosion and stands isolated in an essentially level area. [After Mount *Monadnock,* a peak of SW New Hampshire.]

mo·nan·drous (mə-năn′drəs) *adj.* **1.** *Botany* Having flowers bearing a single stamen, as in the poinsettia. **2.** Of, relating to, or characterized by monandry.

mo·nan·dry (mə-năn′drē) *n.* **1.** The state or practice of having one husband at a time. **2.** *Botany* The condition of being monandrous.

mo·nan·thous (mə-năn′thəs) *adj. Botany* Bearing one flower.

Mo·na Passage (mō′nə) A strait between Puerto Rico and the Dominican Republic connecting the N Atlantic Ocean with the Caribbean Sea.

mon·arch (mŏn′ərk, -ärk′) *n.* **1.** One who reigns over a state or territory, usu. for life and by hereditary right, esp.: **a.** A sole and absolute ruler. **b.** A sovereign, such as a king or empress, often with constitutionally limited authority. **2.** One that commands or rules. **3.** One that surpasses others in power or preeminence. **4.** A monarch butterfly. [ME *monarke* < OFr. *monarque* < LLat. *monarcha* < Gk. *monarkhos : mono-, mono-* + *arkhein,* to rule.] —**mo·nar′chal** (mə-när′kəl), **mo·nar′chic** (-kĭk), **mo·nar′chi·cal** (-kĭ-kəl) —**mo·nar′chal·ly, mo·nar′chi·cal·ly** *adv.*

monarch butterfly *n.* A large migratory American butterfly (*Danaus plexippus*) having light orange-brown wings with black veins and noted for its brightly striped caterpillars.

Mon·ar·chi·an·ism (mŏn-är′kē-ə-nĭz′əm) *n.* Any of several Christological heresies of the second and third centuries A.D. that denied the independent hypostasis of God the Son. [< Lat. *Monarchiāni,* the Monarchians < *monarchia,* monarchy. See MONARCHY.] —**Mo·nar′chi·an** *n.*

mon·ar·chism (mŏn′ər-kĭz′əm, -är′-) *n.* **1.** The system or principles of monarchy. **2.** Belief in or advocacy of monarchy. —**mon′ar·chist** (-kĭst) *n.* —**mon′ar·chis′tic** *adj.*

mon·ar·chy (mŏn′ər-kē, -är′-) *n., pl.* **-chies** **1.** Government by a monarch. **2.** A state ruled or headed by a monarch. [ME *monarchie* < OFr. < Lat. *monarchia* < Gk. *monarkhiā* < *monarkhos,* monarch. See MONARCH.] —**mo·nar′chi·al** (mə-när′kē-əl) *adj.*

mo·nar·da (mə-när′də) *n.* Any of various aromatic plants of the genus *Monarda* in the mint family, such as the bee balm. [NLat. *Monarda,* genus name, after Nicolas *Monardes* (1493–1588), Spanish botanist.]

mon·as·ter·y (mŏn′ə-stĕr′ē) *n., pl.* **-ies** **1.** A community, esp. of monks, bound by vows to an often secluded religious life. **2.** The dwelling place of such a community. [ME *monasterie* < OFr. *monastere* < LLat. *monastērium* < L.Gk. *monastērion* < Gk. *monazein,* to live alone < *monos,* alone. See **men–²** in App.] —**mon′as·te′ri·al** (-stîr′ē-əl, -stĕr′-) *adj.*

mo·nas·tic (mə-năs′tĭk) *adj.* also **mo·nas·ti·cal** (-tĭ-kəl) **1.** Of, relating to, or characteristic of a monastery. **2.** Resembling life in a monastery, esp.: **a.** Secluded and contemplative. **b.** Strictly disciplined or regimented. **c.** Self-abnegating; austere. ❖ *n.* A monk. [Ult. < LLat. *monasticus* < Gk. *monazein,* to live alone. See MONASTERY.] —**mo·nas′ti·cal·ly** *adv.*

mo·nas·ti·cism (mə-năs′tĭ-sĭz′əm) *n.* The monastic life or system, esp. as practiced in a monastery.

mon·a·tom·ic (mŏn′ə-tŏm′ĭk) *adj.* **1.** Occurring as single atoms: *Helium is a monatomic gas.* **2.** Having one replaceable atom or radical. **3.** Univalent. —**mon′a·tom′ic·al·ly** *adv.*

mon·au·ral (mŏn-ôr′əl) *adj.* **1.** Of, relating to, or being sound reception by one ear. **2.** *Electronics* Monophonic. —**mon·au′ral·ly** *adv.*

mon·ax·i·al (mŏn-ăk′sē-əl) *adj.* Uniaxial.

mon·a·zite (mŏn′ə-zīt′) *n.* A reddish-brown phosphate mineral containing rare-earth metals, (Ce, La, Y, Th)PO_4, important as a source of cerium and thorium. [Gk. *monazein,* to live alone; see MONASTERY + **-ite¹**.]

Mön·chen·glad·bach (mün′kən-glät′bäk, mœn′кнən-glät′bäкн) A city of W-central Germany WSW of Düsseldorf; chartered 1336. Pop. 265,312.

Monck or **Monk** (mŭngk), **George.** 1st Duke of Albemarle. 1608–70. English general who was instrumental in the restoration of Charles II (1660).

Monc·ton (mŭngk′tən) A city of SE New Brunswick, Canada, NE of Saint John. Pop. 59,313.

Mon·dale (mŏn′dāl′), **Walter Frederick** b. 1928. Vice President of the US (1977–81) who ran unsuccessfully for President in 1984.

Mon·day (mŭn′dē, -dā′) *n.* The second day of the week. [ME < OE *Mōnandæg* (transl. of Lat. *lūnae diēs,* day of the moon) : *mōnan,* genitive of *mōna,* moon; see MOON + *dæg,* day.] —**Mon′days** *adv.*

Monday morning quarterback *n. Informal* One who criticizes or passes judgment from a position of hindsight.

mon·de·green (mŏn′də-grēn′, mŏn′-) *n.* A series of words that result from the mishearing or misinterpretation of a statement or song lyric. For example, *I led the pigeons to the flag* for *I pledge allegiance to the flag.* [After *(Lady) Mondegreen,* a misinterpretation of the line *(hae laid) him on the green* in the song "The Bonny Earl of Murray."]

mon·do (mŏn′dō′) *Slang adj.* Enormous; huge: *a mondo list of pizza toppings.* ❖ *adv.* Extremely; very: *a mondo big mistake.* [< *mondo (bizarro),* very bizarre < Ital. *Mondo (Cane),* (A Dog's) *World,* name of movie with bizarre scenes that was a cult favorite in the 1960s.]

Mon·dri·an (môn′drē-än′, mŏn′-), **Piet** 1872–1944. Dutch painter whose artworks and writings, notably *Neoplasticism* (1920), profoundly influenced abstract art.

mo·ne·cious (mə-nē′shəs) *adj.* Variant of **monoecious.**

Mo·né·gasque (mō-nā-gäsk′) *n.* A native or inhabitant of Monaco; a Monacan. [Fr. < Provençal *mounegasc* < *Mounegue,* Monaco.] —**Mo·né·gasque′** *adj.*

Mo·nel (mō-něl′) A trademark used for an alloy of nickel, copper, iron, and manganese.

mo·ne·ran (mə-nîr′ən) *n.* See **prokaryote.** [< NLat. *Monēra,* kingdom name < Gk. *monērēs,* solitary < *monos,* single, alone. See MONAD.] —**mo·ne′ran** *adj.*

mon·es·trous (mŏn-ěs′trəs) *adj.* Having one estrous cycle per year. Used of certain mammals.

Mo·net (mō-nā′, mô-), **Claude** 1840–1926. French painter whose works include *Water Lilies* (1899–1925).

mon·e·ta·rism (mŏn′ĭ-tə-rĭz′əm, mŭn′-) *n.* **1.** A theory holding that economic variations within a given system are usu. caused by fluctuations in the money supply. **2.** A policy that seeks to regulate an economy by altering the domestic money supply, esp. by increasing it in a moderate but steady manner. —**mon′e·ta·rist** *adj. & n.*

mon·e·tar·y (mŏn′ĭ-tĕr′ē, mŭn′-) *adj.* **1.** Of or relating to money. **2.** Of or relating to a nation's currency or coinage. [LLat. *monētārius* < Lat. *monēta,* money, mint. See MONEY.] —**mon′e·tar′i·ly** *adv.*

mon·e·tize (mŏn′ĭ-tīz′, mŭn′-) *tr.v.* **-tized, -tiz·ing, -tiz·es** **1.** To establish as legal tender. **2.** To coin (money). **3.** To convert (government debt) from securities into currency that can be used to purchase goods and services. [< Lat. *monēta,* money. See MONEY.] —**mon′e·ti·za′tion** (-tĭ-zā′shən) *n.*

mon·ey (mŭn′ē) *n., pl.* **-eys** or **-ies** **1.** A medium that can be exchanged for goods and services and is used as a measure of their values on the market, including among its forms a commodity

Monaco

monarch butterfly
Danaus plexippus

ă pat oi boy
ā pay ou out
âr care ŏŏ took
ä father ōō boot
ĕ pet ŭ cut
ē be ûr urge
ĭ pit th thin
ī pie *th* this
îr pier hw which
ŏ pot zh vision
ō toe ə about,
ô paw item

Stress marks:
′ (primary);
′ (secondary), as in
lexicon (lĕk′sĭ-kŏn′)

such as gold, an officially issued coin or note, or a deposit in a checking account or other readily liquefiable account. **2.** The official currency, coins, and negotiable paper notes issued by a government. **3.** Assets and property considered in terms of monetary value; wealth. **4a.** Pecuniary profit or loss. **b.** One's salary; pay. **5.** An amount of cash or credit. **6.** A sum of money, esp. of a specified nature. Often used in the plural: *state tax moneys.* **7.** A wealthy person, family, or group. **—idioms: for (one's) money** According to one's opinion, choice, or preference. **in the money 1.** *Slang* Rich; affluent. **2.** *Sports & Games* Taking first, second, or third place in a contest on which a bet has been placed, such as a horserace. **on the money** Exact; precise. **put money on** *Sports & Games* To place a bet on. **put (one's) money where (one's) mouth is** *Slang* To live up to one's words; act according to one's own advice. [ME *moneie* < OFr. < Lat. *monēta,* mint, coinage < *Monēta,* epithet of Juno, temple of Juno at Rome where money was coined.]

mon•ey•bag (mŭn′ē-băg′) *n.* **1.** A bag for holding money. **2. moneybags** (*used with a sing. or pl. verb*) Wealth. **3. moneybags** (*used with a sing. verb*) A rich, often extravagant person.

money belt *n.* A belt having a usu. concealed pocket for holding money.

mon•ey•chang•er (mŭn′ē-chān′jər) *n.* **1.** One that exchanges money, as from one currency to another. **2.** A machine that holds and dispenses coins.

mon•eyed also **mon•ied** (mŭn′ēd) *adj.* **1.** Having a great deal of money: *the moneyed classes.* **2.** Representing or arising from the possession of money or wealth.

mon•ey•grub•ber (mŭn′ē-grŭb′ər) *n.* One intent on accumulating money. **—mon′ey•grub′bing** *adj. & n.*

mon•ey•lend•er (mŭn′ē-lĕn′dər) *n.* One that lends money at an interest rate.

mon•ey•mak•ing (mŭn′ē-mā′kĭng) *n.* Acquisition of wealth. ❖ *adj.* **1.** Engaged or successful in acquiring wealth. **2.** Actually or potentially profitable. **—mon′ey•mak′er** *n.*

money market *n.* **1.** The trade in short-term low-risk securities, such as US Treasury notes. **2.** A mutual fund that sells shares to purchase short-term securities.

money of account *n.* A monetary unit in which accounts are kept and that may or may not correspond to actual current denominations.

money order *n.* An order for the payment of an amount of money, usu. issued and payable at a bank or post office.

money plant *n.* See **honesty** 4.

money shell *n.* See **butter clam.**

money supply *n.* The amount of money in the economy, measured according to varying methods or principles.

mon•ey•wort (mŭn′ē-wûrt′, -wôrt′) *n.* A European creeping plant (*Lysimachia nummularia*) having rounded opposite leaves and single, axillary yellow flowers.

mon•ger (mŭng′gər, mŏng′-) *n.* **1.** A dealer in a specific commodity. Often used in combination: *an ironmonger.* **2.** A person promoting something undesirable or discreditable. Often used in combination: *a warmonger.* ❖ *tr.v.* **-gered, -ger•ing, -gers** To peddle. [ME *mongere* < OE *mangere* < Lat. *mangō,* dealer in slaves, prob. of Gk. orig.]

Mon•gol (mŏng′gəl, -gōl, mŏn′-) *n.* **1.** A member of any of the traditionally nomadic peoples of Mongolia. **2.** See **Mongolian** 4. **3.** *Anthropology* A member of the Mongoloid racial division. Not in scientific use. ❖ *adj.* **1.** Of or relating to Mongolia, the Mongols, or their language or culture. **2.** *Anthropology* Of or relating to the Mongoloid racial division. Not in scientific use. [Mongolian *Mongol.*]

Mon•go•li•a (mŏng-gō′lē-ə, -gōl′yə, mŏn-) **1.** An ancient region of E-central Asia comprising modern-day Nei Monggol (Inner Mongolia) and the country of Mongolia; center of a great empire forged by Genghis Khan in the 13th cent. **2.** Formerly **Outer Mongolia.** A country of N-central Asia between Russia and China; under Chinese control (1691–1911 and 1919–21) until it formed a separate state under the protection of the USSR. Cap. Ulaanbaatar. Pop. 2,363,000.

Mongolia

Mon•go•li•an (mŏng-gō′lē-ən, -gōl′yən, mŏn-) *adj.* **1.** Of or relating to Mongolia, the Mongols, or their language or culture. **2.** also **mongolian** *Offensive* Of or relating to Down syndrome. ❖ *n.* **1.** A native or inhabitant of Mongolia. **2.** A member of the Mongol people. **3.** *Anthropology* A member of the Mongoloid racial division. Not in scientific use. **4a.** A subfamily of the Altaic language family, including Mongolian and Kalmyk. **b.** Any of the various dialects and languages of the Mongols living in Mongolia and China.

Mon•gol•ic (mŏng-gŏl′ĭk, mŏn-) *adj. Anthropology* Of or relating to the Mongoloid racial division. Not in scientific use.

mon•gol•ism also **Mon•gol•ism** (mŏng′gə-lĭz′əm, mŏn′-) *n. Offensive* Down syndrome. [< MONGOLIAN, term used in a system of classification for mentally retarded people devised by John Langdon Haydon Down (1828–96), Brit. physician.]

Mon•gol•oid (mŏng′gə-loid′, mŏn′-) *adj.* **1.** *Anthropology* Of or being a human racial classification distinguished esp. by yellowish-brown skin and straight black hair and including peoples indigenous to central and eastern Asia. **2.** Characteristic of or resembling a Mongol. **3.** also **mongoloid** *Offensive* Of or relating

to Down syndrome. ❖ *n.* **1.** *Anthropology* A member of the Mongoloid racial classification. **2.** also **mongoloid** *Offensive* A person affected with Down syndrome.

mon•goose (mŏng′gōōs′, mŏn′-) *n., pl.* **-goos•es** Any of various Old World carnivorous mammals of the genus *Herpestes* and related genera, having a slender agile body and a long tail and noted for the ability to seize and kill venomous snakes. [Marathi *mangūs,* of Dravidian orig.]

mon•grel (mŭng′grəl, mŏng′-) *n.* **1.** An animal or plant resulting from various interbreedings, esp. a dog of mixed or undetermined breed. **2.** A cross between different breeds, groups, or varieties, esp. a mixture that is or appears to be incongruous. ❖ *adj.* Of mixed origin or character. [ME, prob. < *mong,* mixture < OE *gemang.*] **—mon′grel•ism** *n.* **—mon′grel•ly** *adv.*

mon•grel•ize (mŭng′grə-līz′, mŏng′-) *tr.v.* **-ized, -iz•ing, -iz•es** To make mongrel in race, nature, or character. **—mon′grel•i•za′tion** (-grə-lĭ-zā′shən) *n.*

mon•ied (mŭn′ēd) *adj.* Variant of **moneyed.**

mon•ies (mŭn′ēz) *n.* A plural of **money.**

mon•i•ker or **mon•ick•er** (mŏn′ĭ-kər) *n. Slang* A personal name or nickname. [Prob. < Shelta *munik,* name, poss. alteration of Ir.Gael. *ainm* < OIr. See **nō-men-** in App.]

mo•ni•li•a•sis (mō′nə-lī′ə-sĭs, mŏn′ə-) *n.* See **candidiasis.** [NLat. *Monīlia,* type genus (< Lat. *monīle,* necklace) + –IASIS.]

mo•nil•i•form (mō-nĭl′ə-fôrm′) *adj.* Resembling a string of beads, as the antennae of certain insects. [Lat. *monīle,* necklace + –FORM.] **—mo•nil′i•form′ly** *adv.*

mon•ish (mŏn′ĭsh) *tr.v.* **-ished, -ish•ing, -ish•es** To admonish; warn. [ME *monesten, monishe* < OFr. *monester* < VLat. **monestāre,* alteration of Lat. *monēre,* to warn. See **men-¹** in App.]

mo•nism (mō′nĭz′əm, mŏn′ĭz′əm) *n. Philosophy* **1.** The view in metaphysics that reality is a whole and that all existing things can be ascribed to or described by a single concept or system. **2.** The doctrine that mind and matter are formed from or reducible to the same substance or principle of being. **—mo′nist** *n.* **—mo•nis′tic** (mō-nĭs′tĭk, mŏ-) *adj.* **—mo•nis′ti•cal•ly** *adv.*

mo•ni•tion (mō-nĭsh′ən, mə-) *n.* **1.** A warning or intimation of something imminent, esp. danger. **2.** Cautionary advice or counsel; an admonition. **3.** A formal order from a bishop or ecclesiastical court to stop a specified offense. **4.** A summons or citation in civil or admiralty law. [ME *monicioun* < OFr. *monicion* < Lat. *monitiō, monitiōn-* < *monitus,* p. part. of *monēre,* to warn. See **men-¹** in App.]

mon•i•tor (mŏn′ĭ-tər) *n.* **1.** One that admonishes, cautions, or reminds, esp. with respect to matters of conduct. **2.** A pupil who assists a teacher in routine duties. **3a.** A usu. electronic device used to record, regulate, or control a process or system. **b.** A receiver, such as a screen, used to check the quality or content of an electronic transmission. **c.** *Computer Science* A device that accepts video signals from a computer and displays information on a screen; a video display. **4.** An articulated device with a rotating nozzle that regulates a jet of water, used in mining and firefighting. **5.** A heavily ironclad warship of the 19th century with a low flat deck and one or more gun turrets. **6.** *Biology* Any of various tropical carnivorous lizards of the family *Varanidae,* ranging in length from several centimeters to 3 meters (10 feet). ❖ *v.* **-tored, -tor•ing, -tors** *—tr.* **1.** To check the quality or content of (an electronic audio or visual signal) by means of a receiver. **2.** To check by means of an electronic receiver for significant content, such as illegal activity. **3.** To keep track of systematically with a view to collecting information. **4a.** To test or sample on a regular or ongoing basis. **b.** To test (air or an object's surface, for example) for radiation intensity. **5.** To keep close watch over; supervise. **6.** To direct. *—intr.* To act as a monitor. [Lat. < *monēre,* to warn. See **men-¹** in App.] **—mon′i•tor•ship′** *n.*

mon•i•to•ri•al (mŏn′ĭ-tôr′ē-əl, -tōr′-) *adj.* **1.** Of or relating to monitors. **2.** Monitory. **—mon′i•to•ri•al•ly** *adv.*

mon•i•to•ry (mŏn′ĭ-tôr′ē, -tōr′ē) *adj.* Conveying an admonition or warning. ❖ *n., pl.* **-ries** A letter of admonition, such as one from a bishop or ecclesiastical court. [Ult. < Med.Lat. *monitōria,* admonition < fem. of Lat. *monitōrius,* monitory < *monitor.* See MONITOR.]

monk (mŭngk) *n.* A member of a brotherhood living in a monastery and devoted to a discipline prescribed by his order. [ME *munk* < OE *munuc* < LLat. *monachus* < L.Gk. *monakhos* < Gk., single < *monos.* See **men-²** in App.]

Monk, George See George **Monck.**

Monk, Thelonious Sphere 1917–82. Amer. jazz pianist and composer noted for his unusual harmonic style.

monk•er•y (mŭng′kə-rē) *n., pl.* **-ies 1.** Monastic life or practices. **2.** Monks considered as a group. **3.** A monastery.

mon•key (mŭng′kē) *n., pl.* **-keys 1.** Any of various long-tailed medium-sized members of the order Primates, including the macaques and baboons. **2.** One who behaves in a way suggestive of a monkey, as a mischievous child. **3.** The iron block of a pile driver. **4.** *Slang* One who is mocked, duped, or made to appear a fool: *They made a monkey out of him.* **5.** *Slang* Drug addiction. ❖ *v.* **-keyed, -key•ing, -keys** *—intr. Informal* **1.** To play, trifle, or tamper with something. **2.** To behave in a mischievous or apish manner: *Stop monkeying around!* *—tr.* To imitate or mimic; ape. [?]

monkey bars *pl.n.* A jungle gym.

monkey bread *n.* The hanging, edible gourdlike fruit of the baobab.

monkey business *n. Slang* Silly, mischievous, or deceitful acts or behavior.

mon·key-faced owl (mŭng′kē-fāst′) *n.* See **barn owl.**

monkey flower *n.* Any of various herbs or shrubs of the genus *Mimulus,* having variously colored, two-lipped flowers.

monkey jacket *n.* **1.** A short tight-fitting jacket traditionally worn by sailors. **2.** See **mess jacket.**

monkey pot *n.* **1a.** Any of various tropical American trees of the genus *Lecythis,* having a large woody urn-shaped pod that dehisces by a lid. **b.** The fruit of this tree. **2.** A cylindrical or barrel-shaped melting pot used in making flint glass.

mon·key-puz·zle (mŭng′kē-pŭz′əl) *n.* A coniferous evergreen tree *(Araucaria araucana)* native to Chile and having intricately ramifying branches covered with overlapping, leathery, lanceolate prickle-tipped leaves.

mon·key·shine (mŭng′kē-shīn′) *n. Slang* A mischievous or playful trick; a prank. Often used in the plural.

monkey wrench *n.* **1.** A hand tool with adjustable jaws for turning nuts of varying sizes. **2.** *Informal* Something that disrupts. [?]

monk·fish (mŭngk′fĭsh′) *n., pl.* **monkfish** or **-fish·es** See **goosefish.** [Perh. < cowled appearance of its head.]

Mon-Khmer (mŏn′kmĕr′) *n.* A subfamily of the Austro-Asiatic language family that includes Mon and Khmer.

monk·hood (mŭngk′hŏŏd′) *n.* **1.** The character, condition, or profession of a monk. **2.** Monks considered as a group.

monk·ish (mŭng′kĭsh) *adj.* **1.** Of, relating to, or characteristic of monks or monasticism. **2.** Inclined to self-denial; ascetic. **—monk′ish·ly** *adv.* **—monk′ish·ness** *n.*

monk's cloth (mŭngks) *n.* A heavy cotton cloth in a coarse basket weave, now used chiefly for draperies.

monk seal *n.* Any of several small subtropical seals of the genus *Monachus* found in the Hawaiian, Mediterranean, and Caribbean regions and characterized by a dark brown coat and by folds of skin on the neck. [< the resemblance of the skin folds to a monk's cowl.]

monks·hood (mŭngks′hŏŏd′) *n.* **1.** See **aconite. 2.** A poisonous perennial herb *(Aconitum napellus)* native to northern Europe, whose dried leaves and roots yield aconite.

Mon·mouth (mŏn′məth), Duke of. Title of James Scott. 1649–85. English pretender to the throne who led a rebellion after the succession of the Catholic James II.

mon·o[1] (mŏn′ō) *n. Informal* Infectious mononucleosis.

mon·o[2] (mŏn′ō) *adj. Informal* Monaural; monophonic.

mono– or **mon–** *pref.* **1.** One; single; alone: *monomorphic.* **2.** Containing a single atom, radical, or group: *monobasic.* **3.** Monomolecular; monatomic: *monolayer.* [ME < OFr. < Lat. < Gk. < *monos,* single, alone. See **men-**[2] in App.]

mon·o·ac·id (mŏn′ō-ăs′ĭd) *n.* An acid having one replaceable hydrogen atom. ❖ *adj.* also **mon·o·a·cid·ic** (-ə-sĭd′ĭk) Having only one hydroxyl group to react with acids.

mon·o·am·ine (mŏn′ō-ăm′ēn, -ə-mēn′) *n.* An amine compound containing one amino group, esp. a compound that functions as a neurotransmitter.

monoamine oxidase *n.* An enzyme in the cells of most tissues that catalyzes the oxidation of monoamines such as norepinephrine and serotonin.

monoamine oxidase inhibitor *n.* Any of a class of antidepressant drugs that block the action of monoamine oxidase in the brain, thereby allowing the accumulation of monoamines such as norepinephrine.

mon·o·ba·sic (mŏn′ə-bā′sĭk) *adj.* **1.** Having only one hydrogen ion to donate to a base in an acid-base reaction; monoprotic. **2.** Having only one metal ion or positive radical.

mon·o·carp (mŏn′ə-kärp′) *n.* A monocarpic plant.

mon·o·car·pel·lar·y (mŏn′ə-kär′pə-lĕr′ē) *adj.* Consisting of only one carpel.

mon·o·car·pic (mŏn′ə-kär′pĭk) also **mon·o·car·pous** (-kär′pəs) *adj.* Flowering and bearing fruit only once.

mon·o·ce·phal·ic (mŏn′ō-sə-făl′ĭk) *adj.* Bearing one flower head, as in the scape of a dandelion.

Mo·noc·er·os (mə-nŏs′ər-əs) *n.* A constellation near Canis Major and Canis Minor. [Ult. < Gk. *monokerōs,* having one horn : *mono-,* mono- + *keras,* horn; see **ker-**[1] in App.]

mon·o·chas·i·um (mŏn′ə-kā′zē-əm, -zhē-) *n., pl.* **-si·a** (-zē-ə, -zhē-ə, -zhə) A cyme having a single flower on each axis. [MONO- + (DI)CHASIUM.] **—mon′o·cha′si·al** *adj.*

mon·o·chord (mŏn′ə-kôrd′) *n.* An acoustic instrument consisting of a sounding box with one string and a movable bridge, used to study musical tones. [Ult. < Gk. *monokhordon* : *mono-,* mono- + *khordē,* string; see CORD.]

mon·o·chro·mat (mŏn′ə-krō′măt′) *n.* A person with monochromatism.

mon·o·chro·mat·ic (mŏn′ə-krō-măt′ĭk) *adj.* **1.** Having or appearing to have only one color. **2.** Of or composed of radiation of only one wavelength: *monochromatic light.* **3.** Done in monochrome: *monochromatic prints.* **4.** Of or exhibiting monochromatism. **—mon′o·chro·mat′i·cal·ly** *adv.* **—mon′o·chro·mat·ic′i·ty** (-mə-tĭs′ĭ-tē) *n.*

mon·o·chro·ma·tism (mŏn′ə-krō′mə-tĭz′əm) *n.* The condition of being completely colorblind.

mon·o·chrome (mŏn′ə-krōm′) *n.* **1a.** A picture, esp. a painting, done in different shades of a single color. **b.** The art or technique of executing such a picture. **2.** The state of being in a single color. **3.** A black-and-white image, as in photography or on television. [Med.Lat. *monochrōma* < fem. of Gk. *monokhrōmos* : one color : *mono-,* mono- + *khrōma,* color.] **—mon′o·chrome′, mon′o·chro′mic** (-krō′mĭk) *adj.*

mon·o·cle (mŏn′ə-kəl) *n.* An eyeglass for one eye. [Fr. < LLat. *monoculus,* having one eye : Gk. *mono-,* mono- + Lat. *oculus,* eye; see **ok**ʷ- in App.] **—mon′o·cled** (-kəld) *adj.*

mon·o·cline (mŏn′ə-klīn′) *n.* A geologic structure having all layers inclined in the same direction. **—mon′o·cli′nal** *adj.*

mon·o·clin·ic (mŏn′ə-klĭn′ĭk) *adj.* Of or relating to three unequal crystal axes, two of which intersect obliquely and are perpendicular to the third.

mon·o·cli·nous (mŏn′ə-klī′nəs) *adj.* Having pistils and stamens in the same flower. [NLat. *monoclīnus* : MONO- + Gk. *klīnē,* bed; see **klei-** in App.]

mon·o·clo·nal (mŏn′ə-klō′nəl) *adj.* Of, forming, or derived from a single clone. ❖ *n.* A monoclonal product, esp. a monoclonal antibody.

monoclonal antibody *n.* Any of a class of highly specific antibodies produced by the clones of a single hybrid cell formed by the fusion of a B cell with a tumor cell.

mon·o·coque (mŏn′ə-kōk′, -kŏk′) *n.* A metal structure, such as an aircraft, in which the skin absorbs all or most of the stresses to which the body is subjected. [Fr. : *mono-,* mono- + *coque,* shell (< OFr. < Lat. *coccum,* berry < Gk. *kokkos*).]

mon·o·cot·y·le·don (mŏn′ə-kŏt′l-ēd′n) also **mon·o·cot** (mŏn′ə-kŏt′) *n.* Any of various flowering plants, such as grasses and lilies, having a single cotyledon in the seed. **—mon′o·cot′y·le′don·ous** *adj.*

mo·noc·ra·cy (mə-nŏk′rə-sē, mŏ-) *n., pl.* **-cies** Government or rule by a single person; autocracy. **—mon′o·crat** (mŏn′ə-krăt′) *n.* **—mon′o·crat′ic** *adj.*

mo·noc·u·lar (mə-nŏk′yə-lər, mŏ-) *adj.* **1.** Having or relating to one eye. **2.** Of, relating to, or intended for use by only one eye: *a monocular microscope.* [< LLat. *monoculus,* having one eye. See MONOCLE.] **—mo·noc′u·lar·ly** *adv.*

mon·o·cul·ture (mŏn′ə-kŭl′chər) *n.* **1.** The cultivation of a single crop on a farm or in a region or country. **2.** A single homogeneous culture without diversity or dissension. **—mon′o·cul′tur·al** *adj.* **—mon′o·cul′tur·al·ism** *n.*

mon·o·cy·cle (mŏn′ə-sī′kəl) *n.* A unicycle.

mon·o·cy·clic (mŏn′ə-sī′klĭk, -sĭk′lĭk) *adj.* **1.** Having a single cycle, as of development. **2.** *Biology* Having a single whorl. **3.** *Chemistry* Having a molecular structure with only one ring.

mon·o·cyte (mŏn′ə-sīt′) *n.* A large circulating phagocytic white blood cell having a single well-defined nucleus and very fine granulation in the cytoplasm.

mon·o·cy·to·sis (mŏn′ə-sī-tō′sĭs) *n., pl.* **-ses** (-sēz) An abnormal increase of monocytes in the blood.

Mo·nod (mô-nō′), Jacques Lucien 1910–76. French biochemist who shared a 1965 Nobel Prize.

mon·o·dac·tyl (mŏn′ə-dăk′təl) *n.* An animal having one digit or claw on each extremity. **—mon′o·dac′ty·lous** *adj.*

mon·o·dra·ma (mŏn′ə-drä′mə, -drăm′ə) *n.* A dramatic composition written for one performer. **—mon′o·dra·mat′ic** (-drə-măt′ĭk) *adj.*

mon·o·dy (mŏn′ə-dē) *n., pl.* **-dies 1.** An ode for one voice or actor, as in Greek drama. **2.** A poem in which the poet or speaker mourns another's death. **3.** *Music* **a.** A style of composition dominated by a single melodic line. **b.** A style of composition having a single melodic line; monophony. **c.** A composition in either of these styles. [LLat. *monōdia* < Gk. *monōidiā* : *mono-,* mono- + *aoidē, ōidē,* song.] **—mo·nod′ic** (mə-nŏd′ĭk), **mo·nod′i·cal** (-ĭ-kəl) **—mo·nod′i·cal·ly** *adv.* **—mon′o·dist** (mŏn′ə-dĭst′) *n.*

mon·oe·cious also **mon·e·cious** (mə-nē′shəs) *adj.* **1.** *Botany* Having unisexual reproductive organs or flowers, with the organs or flowers of both sexes on a single plant, as in corn. **2.** *Biology* Relating to or exhibiting hermaphroditism; hermaphroditic. [NLat. *Monoecia,* class name : MONO- + Gk. *oikiā,* dwelling; see **weik-** in App.] **—mo·noe′cious·ly** *adv.* **—mo·noe′cism** (mə-nē′sĭz′əm) *n.*

mon·o·es·ter (mŏn′ō-ĕs′tər) *n.* An ester having only one ester group.

mon·o·fil·a·ment (mŏn′ə-fĭl′ə-mənt) *n.* A strand of untwisted synthetic fiber used esp. for fishing line.

mo·nog·a·my (mə-nŏg′ə-mē) *n.* **1.** The practice or condition of having a single sexual partner during a period of time. **2a.** The practice or condition of being married to only one person at a time. **b.** The practice of marrying only once in a lifetime. **3.** *Zoology* The condition of having only one mate. **—mo·nog′a·mist** *n.* **—mo·nog′a·mous** *adj.* **—mo·nog′a·mous·ly** *adv.*

mon·o·gen·e·sis (mŏn′ə-jĕn′ĭ-sĭs) *n.* **1.** The theory that all living organisms are descended from a single cell or organism. **2.** Asexual reproduction, as by sporulation. **—mo·nog′e·nous** (mə-nŏj′ə-nəs) *adj.*

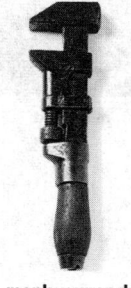

monkey wrench

monopod

mon·o·ge·net·ic (mŏn′ə-jə-nĕt′ĭk) *adj.* **1.** Relating to or exhibiting monogenesis. **2.** Having a single host through the course of the life cycle. **3.** Produced under a single set of continuing conditions. Used of soil.

mon·o·gen·ic (mŏn′ə-jĕn′ĭk) *adj.* **1a.** Of or relating to monogenesis; monogenetic. **b.** Relating to monogenism. **2.** Of or regulated by one gene or one of a pair of allelic genes. **3.** Producing offspring of only one sex, as some species of aphids. —**mon′o·gen′i·cal·ly** *adv.*

mo·nog·e·nism (mə-nŏj′ə-nĭz′əm) *n.* The theory that all humans are descended from a single pair of ancestors.

mon·o·glot (mŏn′ə-glŏt′) *n.* A person who knows only one language. [MONO– + (POLY)GLOT.] —**mon′o·glot′** *adj.*

mon·o·gram (mŏn′ə-grăm′) *n.* A design composed of one or more letters, typically the initials of a name, used as an identifying mark. ❖ *tr.v.* **-grammed, -gram·ming, -grams** also **-gramed, -gram·ing, -grams** To mark with a monogram. [LLat. *monogramma* < L.Gk. *monogrammon* < neut. of *monogrammos*, consisting of a single letter : Gk. *mono-*, mono– + Gk. *gramma*, letter; see –GRAM.] —**mon′o·gram·mat′ic** (-grə-măt′ĭk) *adj.*

mon·o·graph (mŏn′ə-grăf′) *n.* A piece of scholarly writing of essay or book length on a specific, often limited subject. —**mon′o·graph** *v.* —**mo·nog′ra·pher** (mə-nŏg′rə-fər) *n.* —**mon′o·graph′ic** *adj.* —**mon′o·graph′i·cal·ly** *adv.*

mo·nog·y·ny (mə-nŏj′ə-nē) *n.* The practice or condition of having only one wife at a time. —**mo·nog′y·nist** *n.* —**mo·nog′y·nous** *adj.*

mon·o·hy·drate (mŏn′ō-hī′drāt′) *n.* A crystalline compound that contains one molecule of water.

mo·noi·cous (mə-noi′kəs) *adj. Botany* Having archegonia and antheridia on the same plant; bisexual. [Alteration of MONOECIOUS.]

mon·o·lay·er (mŏn′ō-lā′ər) *n.* **1.** A film or layer of a compound one molecule thick. **2.** A layer of cells one cell thick, grown in a culture.

mon·o·lin·gual (mŏn′ə-lĭng′gwəl) *adj.* Using only one language. —**mon′o·lin′gual** *n.* —**mon′o·lin′gual·ism** *n.*

mon·o·lith (mŏn′ə-lĭth′) *n.* **1.** A large block of stone, esp. one used in architecture or sculpture. **2.** Something, such as a column or monument, made from a large block of stone. **3.** Something suggestive of a large block of stone, as in massiveness or uniformity.

mon·o·lith·ic (mŏn′ə-lĭth′ĭk) *adj.* **1.** Constituting a monolith. **2.** Massive, solid, and uniform. **3.** Constituting or acting as a single, often rigid uniform whole. —**mon′o·lith′i·cal·ly** *adv.*

mon·o·logue also **mon·o·log** (mŏn′ə-lôg′, -lŏg′) *n.* **1a.** A dramatic soliloquy. **b.** A literary composition in such form. **2.** A series of jokes delivered by one comedian. **3.** A long speech made by one person, often monopolizing a conversation. ❖ *v.* **-logued, -logu·ing, -logues** also **-logged, -log·ging, -logs** —*intr.* To give or perform a monologue. —*tr.* To address a monologue to. [Fr. : Gk. *mono-*, mono– + Gk. *-logos*, -logue.] —**mon′o·log′ic** (-lŏj′ĭk), **mon′o·log′i·cal** (-ĭ-kəl) —**mon′o·logu′ist** (mŏn′ə-lôg′ĭst, -lŏg′-), **mo·nol′o·gist** (mə-nŏl′ə-jĭst, mŏn′ə-lôg′ĭst, -lŏg′-) *n.*

mon·o·ma·ni·a (mŏn′ə-mā′nē-ə, -mān′yə) *n.* **1.** Pathological obsession with one idea or subject. **2.** Intent concentration on or exaggerated enthusiasm for one subject or idea. —**mon′o·ma′ni·ac′** —**mon′o·ma·ni′a·cal** (-mə-nī′ə-kəl) *adj.* —**mon′o·ma·ni′a·cal·ly** *adv.*

mon·o·mer (mŏn′ə-mər) *n.* A molecule that can combine with others to form a polymer. [MONO– + (POLY)MER.] —**mon′o·mer′ic** (-mĕr′ĭk) *adj.*

mon·o·me·tal·lic (mŏn′ō-mə-tăl′ĭk) *adj.* **1.** Consisting of or containing one metal. **2.** Of, advocating, or practicing monometallism.

mon·o·met·al·lism (mŏn′ō-mĕt′l-ĭz′əm) *n.* The economic theory or practice of using only one metal as a monetary standard. —**mon′o·met′al·list** *n.*

mo·nom·e·ter (mə-nŏm′ĭ-tər) *n.* A verse consisting of a single metrical foot or one dipody.

mo·no·mi·al (mō-nō′mē-əl, mə-) *n.* **1.** *Mathematics* An algebraic expression consisting of only one term. **2.** *Biology* A taxonomic name consisting of a single word. [MON(O)– + (BIN)OMIAL.] —**mo·no′mi·al** *adj.*

mon·o·mo·lec·u·lar (mŏn′ō-mə-lĕk′yə-lər) *adj.* **1.** Of or relating to a single molecule. **2.** Of or consisting of a layer one molecule thick. —**mon′o·mo·lec′u·lar·ly** *adv.*

mon·o·mor·phic (mŏn′ō-môr′fĭk) also **mon·o·mor·phous** (-fəs) *adj.* **1.** *Chemistry* Having only one form, such as one crystal form. **2.** *Zoology* Having one or the same genotype, form, or structure through a series of developmental changes. —**mon′o·mor′phism** *n.*

Mo·non·ga·he·la River (mə-nŏng′gə-hē′lə, -hā′-) A river rising in N WV and flowing c. 206 km (128 mi) into SW PA, where it joins the Allegheny R. to form the Ohio R.

mon·o·nu·cle·ar (mŏn′ō-nōō′klē-ər, -nyōō′-) *adj.* **1.** Having only one nucleus. **2.** *Chemistry* Monocyclic.

mon·o·nu·cle·o·sis (mŏn′ō-nōō′klē-ō′sĭs, -nyōō′-) *n.* **1.** The presence of an abnormally large number of white blood cells with single nuclei in the bloodstream. **2.** Infectious mononucleosis.

[MONO– + NUCLE(US) + –OSIS.]

mon·o·nu·cle·o·tide (mŏn′ō-nōō′klē-ə-tīd′, -nyōō′-) *n.* A nucleotide.

mo·noph·a·gous (mə-nŏf′ə-gəs) *adj.* Eating only one kind of food. —**mon′o·phag′y** (-ə-jē) *n.*

mon·o·pho·bi·a (mŏn′ō-fō′bē-ə) *n.* An abnormal fear of being alone. —**mon′o·pho′bic** *adj.*

mon·o·phon·ic (mŏn′ə-fŏn′ĭk) *adj.* **1.** *Music* Having a single melodic line. **2.** *Electronics* Relating to a system of transmitting, recording, or reproducing sound in which one or more sources are connected to a single channel; monaural. —**mon′o·phon′i·cal·ly** *adv.*

mo·noph·o·ny (mə-nŏf′ə-nē) *n., pl.* **-nies** *Music* A style of composition having a single melodic line. [MONO– + (POLY)PHONY.]

mon·oph·thong (mŏn′əf-thông′, -thŏng′) *n.* **1.** A single vowel articulated without change in quality throughout the course of a syllable, as the vowel of English *bed*. **2.** Two written vowels representing a single sound, as *oa* in *boat*. [L.Gk. *monophthongos* : Gk. *mono-*, mono– + Gk. *phthongos*, sound.] —**mon′oph·thon′gal** *adj.*

mon·o·phy·let·ic (mŏn′ō-fī-lĕt′ĭk) *adj.* **1.** Of or concerning a single taxon of animals. **2.** Relating to or derived from one stock or source. —**mon′o·phy·let′i·cal·ly** *adv.*

Mo·noph·y·site (mə-nŏf′ə-sīt′) *n. Christianity* An adherent of the doctrine that in the person of Jesus there was but a single divine nature. Coptic and Syrian Christians profess this doctrine. [LLat. *monophysita* < L.Gk. *monophusitēs* : Gk. *mono-*, mono– + Gk. *phusis*, nature; see **bheuə-** in App.] —**Mo·noph′y·site,** **Mo·noph′y·sit′ic** (-sĭt′ĭk) *adj.* —**Mo·noph′y·sit′ism** *n.*

mon·o·plane (mŏn′ə-plān′) *n.* An airplane with only one pair of wings.

mon·o·ple·gi·a (mŏn′ə-plē′jē-ə, -plē′jə) *n.* Complete paralysis of a single limb, muscle, or muscle group. —**mon′o·ple′gic** (-plē′jĭk) *adj.*

mon·o·ploid (mŏn′ə-ploid′) *adj.* Having a single set of chromosomes; haploid. ❖ *n.* A monoploid cell or organism.

mon·o·pod (mŏn′ə-pŏd′) *n.* A single-legged support for a camera or other hand-held device.

mon·o·pode (mŏn′ə-pōd′) *n.* **1.** A creature having only one foot. **2.** *Botany* A monopodium. [LLat. *monopodius*, one-footed. See MONOPODIUM.]

mon·o·po·di·um (mŏn′ə-pō′dē-əm) *n., pl.* **-di·a** (-dē-ə) A main axis of a plant that maintains a single line of growth, giving off lateral branches. [NLat. < LLat. *monopodius*, one-footed < Gk. *monopous* : mono-, mono– + *pous*, pod-, foot; see **ped-** in App.] —**mon′o·po′di·al** (-dē-əl) *adj.*

mon·o·pole (mŏn′ə-pōl′) *n.* A magnetic monopole.

mo·nop·o·lize (mə-nŏp′ə-līz′) *tr.v.* **-lized, -liz·ing, -liz·es** **1.** To acquire or maintain a monopoly of. **2.** To dominate by excluding others: *monopolized the conversation.* —**mo·nop′o·li·za′tion** (-lĭ-zā′shən) *n.* —**mo·nop′o·liz′er** *n.*

mo·nop·o·ly (mə-nŏp′ə-lē) *n., pl.* **-lies** **1.** Exclusive control by one group of the means of producing or selling a commodity or service. **2.** *Law* A right granted by a government giving exclusive control over a specified commercial activity to a single party. **3a.** A company or group having exclusive control over a commercial activity. **b.** A commodity or service so controlled. **4a.** Exclusive possession or control. **b.** Something that is exclusively possessed or controlled. [Lat. *monopolium* < Gk. *monopolion* : mono-, mono– + *pōlein*, to sell.] —**mo·nop′o·lism** *n.* —**mo·nop′o·list** *n.* —**mo·nop′o·lis′tic** *adj.* —**mo·nop′o·lis′ti·cal·ly** *adv.*

mon·o·pro·pel·lant (mŏn′ō-prə-pĕl′ənt) *n.* A rocket propellant containing both fuel and oxidizer in a single substance.

mon·o·pro·tic (mŏn′ə-prō′tĭk) *adj.* Monobasic. [MONO– + PROT(ON) + –IC.]

mo·nop·so·ny (mə-nŏp′sə-nē) *n., pl.* **-nies** A market in which the product or service of several sellers is sought by only one buyer. [MON(O)– + Gk. *opsōnia*, purchase of food (< *opsōnein*, to buy food : *opson*, cooked food + *ōnē*, buying < *ōneisthai*, to buy; see **wes-³** in App.).] —**mo·nop′so·nist** *n.* —**mo·nop′so·nis′tic** *adj.*

mon·o·rail (mŏn′ə-rāl′) *n.* **1.** A single rail serving as a track for wheeled vehicles traveling on it or suspended from it. **2.** A railway system using a single rail.

mon·o·sac·cha·ride (mŏn′ə-săk′ə-rīd′, -rĭd) *n.* Any of several carbohydrates, such as hexoses, that cannot be broken down to simpler sugars by hydrolysis.

mon·o·so·di·um glu·ta·mate (mŏn′ə-sō′dē-əm glōō′tə-māt′) *n.* A white, water-soluble, crystalline compound, $COOH(CH_2)_2CH(NH_2)COONa$, that is used as a flavor enhancer in foods.

mon·o·some (mŏn′ə-sōm′) *n.* **1.** A chromosome with no homologue, esp. an unpaired X-chromosome. **2.** A single ribosome. —**mon′o·so′mic** *adj.* —**mon′o·so′my** *n.*

mon·o·stich (mŏn′ə-stĭk′) *n.* **1.** A poem consisting of a single line. **2.** A single line of poetry.

mon·o·syl·lab·ic (mŏn′ə-sĭ-lăb′ĭk) *adj.* **1.** Having only one syllable. **2.** Characterized by or consisting of monosyllables. —**mon′o·syl·lab′i·cal·ly** *adv.*

mon·o·syl·la·ble (mŏn′ə-sĭl′ə-bəl) *n.* A word or utterance of one syllable. [< Lat. *monosyllabum* < Gk. *monosyllabon* : mono-, mono- + *syllabē*, syllable; see SYLLABLE.]

mon·o·the·ism (mŏn′ə-thē-ĭz′əm) *n.* The doctrine or belief that there is only one God. —**mon′o·the′ist** *n.* —**mon′o·the·is′tic** *adj.* —**mon′o·the·is′ti·cal·ly** *adv.*

mon·o·the·mat·ic (mŏn′ə-thē-măt′ĭk) *adj.* Having only one theme.

mon·o·tint (mŏn′ə-tĭnt′) *n.* A monochrome painting or print.

mon·o·tone (mŏn′ə-tōn′) *n.* **1.** A succession of sounds or words uttered in a single tone of voice. **2.** *Music* **a.** A single tone repeated with different words or time values, esp. in a rendering of a liturgical text. **b.** A chant in a single tone. **3.** Sameness or dull repetition in sound, style, manner, or color. ❖ *adj.* **1.** Characterized by or uttered in a monotone. **2.** Of or having a single color. **3.** *Mathematics* Of or being a sequence, the successive members of which either consistently increase or decrease but do not oscillate in relative value. —**mon′o·ton′ic** (-tŏn′ĭk) *adj.* —**mon′o·ton′i·cal·ly** *adv.*

mo·not·o·nous (mə-nŏt′n-əs) *adj.* **1.** Sounded or spoken in an unvarying tone. **2.** Tediously repetitious or lacking in variety. See Syns at **boring.** [< Gk. *monotonos* : mono-, mono- + *tonos*, tone; see TONE.] —**mo·not′o·nous·ly** *adv.* —**mo·not′o·nous·ness** *n.*

mo·not·o·ny (mə-nŏt′n-ē) *n., pl.* **-nies** **1.** Uniformity or lack of variation in pitch, intonation, or inflection. **2.** Tedious sameness or repetitiousness. [Gk. *monotoniā* < *monotonos*, monotonous. See MONOTONOUS.]

mon·o·treme (mŏn′ə-trēm′) *n.* A member of the Monotremata, an order of primitive egg-laying mammals restricted to Australia and New Guinea and consisting of only the platypus and the echidna. [< NLat. *Monotrēmata*, order name : MONO- + Gk. *trēma*, *trēmat-*, perforation; see **terə-**[1] in App.] —**mon′o·trem′a·tous** (-trĕm′ə-təs) *adj.*

mo·not·ri·chous (mə-nŏt′rĭ-kəs) also **mon·o·trich·ic** (mŏn′ə-trĭk′ĭk) or **mon·o·tri·chate** (mə-nŏt′rĭ-kĭt) *adj.* Having one flagellum at only one pole or end.

mon·o·type (mŏn′ə-tīp′) *n.* **1.** *Biology* The sole member of its group, such as a single species that constitutes a genus. **2.** A unique print made by pressing paper against a painted or inked surface. —**mon′o·typ′ic** (-tĭp′ĭk) *adj.*

mon·o·un·sat·u·rat·ed (mŏn′ō-ŭn-săch′ə-rā′tĭd) *adj.* Of or relating to an organic compound, esp. an oil or fatty acid, having only one double or triple bond per molecule.

mon·o·va·lent (mŏn′ə-vā′lənt) *adj.* **1.** *Chemistry* Having a valence of 1; univalent. **2.** *Immunology* **a.** Containing antigens from a single strain of a microorganism: *a monovalent serum.* **b.** Having only one site of attachment. Used of an antibody or antigen. —**mon′o·va′lence**, **mon′o·va′len·cy** *n.*

mon·ox·ide (mə-nŏk′sīd′) *n.* An oxide with each molecule containing one oxygen atom.

mon·o·zy·got·ic (mŏn′ō-zī-gŏt′ĭk) *adj.* Derived from a single fertilized ovum or embryonic cell mass. Used esp. of identical twins.

Mon·roe (mən-rō′), **James** 1758–1831. The fifth President of the US (1817–25), whose administration was marked by the Monroe Doctrine (1823), which declared US opposition to European interference in the Americas.

Monroe, Marilyn Orig. *Norma Jean Baker.* 1926–62. Amer. actress whose films include *Some Like It Hot* (1959).

Monroe, William Smith ("Bill") 1911–96. Amer. guitarist, singer, and songwriter widely regarded as the father of bluegrass.

Mon·ro·vi·a (mən-rō′vē-ə) The cap. of Liberia, in the NW part on the Atlantic Ocean; founded 1822 as a haven for freed slaves. Pop. 421,053.

mons (mŏnz) *n., pl.* **mon·tes** (mŏn′tēz) A protuberance of the human body, esp. that formed by the pubic bones. [Lat. *mōns*, mountain.]

Mon·sei·gneur (môN-sĕ-nyœr′) *n., pl.* **Mes·sei·gneurs** (mā-sĕ-nyœr′) Used as an honorific in French-speaking areas, esp. for princes and prelates. [Fr. < OFr. : *mon*, my; see MONSIEUR + *seignor*, lord, sir; see SEIGNIOR.]

Mon·sieur (mə-syœr′) *n., pl.* **Mes·sieurs** (mā-syœr′, mĕs′ərz) **1.** Used as a courtesy title before the surname, full name, or professional title of a man in a French-speaking area: *Monsieur Cartier; Monsieur Jacques Cartier.* **2. monsieur** Used as a form of polite address for a man in a French-speaking area. [Fr. < OFr. : *mon*, my (< Lat. *meum*, accusative of *meus*; see **me-**[1] in App.) + *sieur*, lord, sir (< VLat. *seiorem*, accusative of *seior*; see SIRE).]

Mon·si·gnor also **mon·si·gnor** (mŏn-sēn′yər) *n. Roman Catholic Church* **1.** A title conferred on a cleric by a pope. **2.** Used as a form of address prefixed to the name of such a cleric. [Ital. < Fr. *Monseigneur.* See MONSEIGNEUR.] —**Mon′si·gnor′i·al** (mŏn′-sēn-yôr′ē-əl, -yōr′-) *adj.*

mon·soon (mŏn-sōōn′) *n.* **1.** A wind system that influences large climatic regions and reverses direction seasonally. **2a.** A wind from the southwest or south that brings heavy rainfall to southern Asia in the summer. **b.** The rain that accompanies this wind. [Obsolete Du. *monssoen* < Port. *monção* < Ar. *mawsim*, season < *wasama*, to mark.] —**mon·soon′al** *adj.*

mons pubis *n., pl.* **montes pubis** A rounded fleshy protuberance situated over the pubic bones in female humans that becomes covered with hair during puberty. [NLat. *mōns pūbis* : Lat. *mōns*, mount + Lat. *pūbis*, genitive of *pūbēs*, pubis.]

mon·ster (mŏn′stər) *n.* **1a.** An imaginary or legendary creature, such as a centaur, that combines parts from various animal or human forms. **b.** A creature having a strange or frightening appearance. **2.** An animal, plant, or other organism having structural defects or deformities. **3.** *Pathology* A fetus or infant that is grotesquely abnormal and usu. not viable. **4.** A very large animal, plant, or object. **5.** One who inspires horror or disgust. [ME *monstre* < OFr. < Lat. *mōnstrum*, portent, monster < *monēre*, to warn. See **men-**[1] in App.]

mon·strance (mŏn′strəns) *n. Roman Catholic Church* A receptacle in which the host is held. [ME < OFr. < Med.Lat. *mōnstrantia* < Lat. *mōnstrāns, mōnstrant-*, pr. part. of *mōnstrāre*, to show < *mōnstrum*, portent, monster. See MONSTER.]

mon·stros·i·ty (mŏn-strŏs′ĭ-tē) *n., pl.* **-ties** **1.** One that is monstrous. **2.** The quality or character of being monstrous. [ME *monstruosite* < OFr. < LLat. *mōnstrōsitās* < Lat. *mōnstruōsus*, monstrous. See MONSTROUS.]

mon·strous (mŏn′strəs) *adj.* **1.** Shockingly hideous or frightful. **2.** Exceptionally large; enormous: *a monstrous tidal wave.* **3.** Deviating greatly from the norm in appearance or structure; abnormal. **4.** Of or resembling a fabulous monster. [ME < OFr. *monstruos* < Lat. *mōnstruōsus* < *mōnstrum*, portent, monster. See MONSTER.] —**mon′strous·ly** *adv.* —**mon′strous·ness** *n.*

mons ve·ne·ris (vĕn′ər-ĭs) *n., pl.* **montes veneris** The mons pubis. [NLat. *mōns veneris* : Lat. *mōns*, mount + Lat. *Veneris*, genitive of *Venus*, Venus.]

Mont. *abbr.* Montana

mon·tage (mŏn-täzh′, môN-) *n.* **1a.** A single pictorial composition made by juxtaposing or superimposing many pictures or designs. **b.** The art or process of making such a composition. **2a.** A rapid succession of different shots in a movie. **b.** The juxtaposition of such successive shots as a cinematic technique. **c.** Film editing. **3.** A composite of closely juxtaposed elements: *a montage of voices on an audiotape.* ❖ *tr.v.* **-taged, -tag·ing, -tag·es** To use or incorporate in a montage. [Fr. < *monter*, to mount < OFr. See MOUNT[1].]

Mon·tag·nais (mŏn′tən-yā′) *n., pl.* **Montagnais** **1.** A member of a Native American people inhabiting an extensive area in Quebec and Labrador. **2.** The Algonquian language of the Montagnais and Naskapi. [Canadian Fr. < Fr. *montagne*, mountain. See MONTAGNARD.]

Mon·ta·gnard also **mon·ta·gnard** (mŏn′tən-yärd′) *n.* A member of a people inhabiting the highlands of southern Vietnam near the Cambodian border. [Fr., mountaineer < *montagne*, mountain < OFr. *montaigne*. See MOUNTAIN.]

Mon·ta·gu (mŏn′tə-gyōō′), **Ashley** 1905–99. British-born Amer. anthropologist whose books include *The Natural Superiority of Women* (1953).

Montagu, Lady Mary Wortley 1689–1762. English writer noted for her letters, travel writing, and social commentary.

Mon·taigne (mŏn-tān′, môN-tĕn′yə), **Michel Eyquem de** 1533–92. French writer known for his essays.

Mon·ta·le (mŏn-tä′lā, -lē), **Eugenio** 1896–1981. Italian poet who won the 1975 Nobel Prize for literature.

Mon·tan·a (mŏn-tăn′ə) A state of the NW US bordering on Canada; admitted as the 41st state in 1889. Cap. Helena. Pop. 902,195. —**Mon·tan′an** *adj. & n.*

mon·tane (mŏn-tān′, mŏn′tān′) *adj.* Of, growing in, or inhabiting mountain areas. [Lat. *montānus* < *mōns, mont-*, mountain.]

mon·tan wax (mŏn′tən, -tän′) *n.* A hard white wax obtained from lignite and used in the manufacture of polishes, paints, and phonograph records. [< Lat. *montānus*, montane. See MONTANE.]

Mon·tauk (mŏn′tôk′) *n., pl.* **Montauk** or **-tauks** **1.** A member of a Native American people formerly inhabiting the eastern end of Long Island in New York. **2.** The Algonquian language of the Montauk. **3.** A member of any of various Algonquian peoples of eastern and central Long Island connected with the Montauk. [< a place name of Montauk orig.]

Montauk Point The eastern extremity of Long I., in SE NY.

Mont Blanc (mônt blängk, môN blän′) See Mont **Blanc.**

Mont·calm de Saint-Ve·ran (mŏnt-käm′ də săn′vä-rän′, môN-kälm′), Marquis **Louis Joseph de** 1712–59. French commander in Canada during the French and Indian War who repelled a British attack on Fort Ticonderoga (1758).

mon·te (mŏn′tē) *n.* A card game in which two cards are chosen from four laid out face-up and a player bets that one of the two will be matched in suit by the dealer before the other one. [Sp., mountain, pile, monte < Lat. *mōns, mont-*, mountain.]

Mon·te Al·bán (mŏn′tě äl-bän′) A ruined Zapotec city of S Mexico near Oaxaca; site of an advanced culture that flourished c. 200 B.C.

Mon·te Car·lo[1] (mŏn′tē kär′lō) A resort town of Monaco on the French Riviera. Pop. 11,599.

Mon·te Car·lo[2] (mŏn′tē kär′lō) *adj.* Of a problem-solving technique using statistical methods to solve mathematical or physical problems. [After MONTE CARLO[1].]

Mon·te·go Bay (mŏn-tē′gō) A town of NW Jamaica on the Caribbean Sea; visited by Columbus in 1494. Pop. 70,285.

Mon·te·ne·gro (mŏn′tə-nĕg′rō, -nē′grō) A constituent repub-

James Monroe
detail from a c. 1820
portrait by Rembrandt
Peale

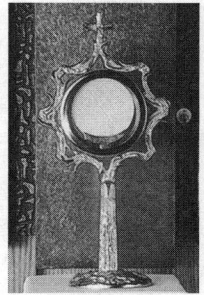

monstrance

ă	pat	oi	boy
ā	pay	ou	out
âr	care	ōō	took
ä	father	ōō	boot
ĕ	pet	ŭ	cut
ē	be	ûr	urge
ĭ	pit	th	thin
ī	pie	*th*	this
îr	pier	hw	which
ŏ	pot	zh	vision
ō	toe	ə	about,
ô	paw		item

Stress marks:
′ (primary);
′ (secondary), as in
lexicon (lĕk′sĭ-kŏn′)

Maria Montessori

Monticello

monument
Washington Monument,
Washington, DC

lic of Yugoslavia; joined (1918) the Kingdom of the Serbs, Croats, and Slovenes, which became Yugoslavia after 1929 and with Serbia formed present-day Yugoslavia in 1992. Cap. Podgorica. Pop. 502,207. —**Mon·te·neg·rin** (-rĭn) adj. & n.

Mon·te·rey (mŏn′tə-rā′) A city of W CA S of San Francisco on **Monterey Bay**, an inlet of the Pacific Ocean; a Spanish colonial cap. for much of the time from 1774 to 1846. Pop. 29,674.

Monterey jack n. A pale semisoft cheese with a high moisture content and a mild flavor. [After MONTEREY + JACK (CHEESE).]

mon·te·ro (mŏn-târ′ō) n., pl. -**ros** A hunter's cap with side flaps. [Sp., hunter < monte, mountain < Lat. mōns, mont-. See MOUNTAIN.]

Mon·ter·rey (mŏn′tə-rā′, mŏn′tĕ-) A city of NE Mexico E of Matamoros; founded 1579. Pop. 1,090,099.

mon·tes (mŏn′tēz) n. Plural of **mons.**

Mon·tes·quieu (mŏn′tə-skyōō′, môn′tĕ-skyœ′) Baron de la Brede et de Montesquieu. Title of Charles de Secondat. 1689–1755. French philosopher and jurist whose works include The Spirit of the Laws (1748).

Mon·tes·so·ri (mŏn′tĭ-sôr′ē, -sōr′ē), **Maria** 1870–1952. Italian physician and educator known for her reforms of methods for teaching young children.

Montessori method n. A method of educating young children that stresses development of a child's own initiative and natural abilities, esp. through practical play.

Mon·teux (mŏn-tœ′, môn-tœ′), **Pierre** 1875–1964. French-born Amer. conductor noted as an interpreter of 20th-cent. music.

Mon·te·ver·di (mŏn′tə-vâr′dē, môn′tĕ-), **Claudio** 1567–1643. Italian composer who wrote the opera Orfeo (1607).

Mon·te·vi·de·o (mŏn′tə-vĭ-dā′ō, -vĭd′ē-ō′, môn′tĕ-vē-dĕ′ō) The cap. of Uruguay, in the S part on the Río de la Plata estuary; founded by the Spanish c. 1726 on the site of a captured Portuguese fort. Pop. 1,360,258.

Mon·te·zu·ma II (mŏn′tĭ-zōō′mə) or **Moc·te·zu·ma** (mŏk′-) 1466?–1520. Last Aztec emperor in Mexico (1502–20); overthrown by Cortés.

Mont·fer·rat (mŏnt-fə-rät′) A historical region of NW Italy S of the Po R.; awarded to Savoy in 1713.

Mont·fort (mŏnt′fərt, môn-fôr′), **Simon de.** Earl of Leicester. 1208?–65. French-born English nobleman who defeated Henry III at Lewes in SE England (1264) and became the virtual ruler of England.

Mont·gom·er·y (mŏnt-gŭm′ə-rē, -gŭm′rē) The cap. of AL, in the SE-central part SSE of Birmingham; first cap. (Feb.–May 1861) of the Confederacy. Pop. 201,568.

Montgomery, Sir Bernard Law. 1st Viscount Montgomery of Alamein. 1887–1976. British army officer who commanded the British victories over German forces in North Africa (1942) and the Allied advance through Normandy (1944).

Montgomery, Lucy Maud 1874–1942. Canadian writer best known for her novel Anne of Green Gables (1908).

Montgomery, John Leslie Known as "Wes." 1923–68. Amer. jazz guitarist noted for the unique, mellow tones he produced by playing without a pick.

month (mŭnth) n. 1. A unit of time corresponding approx. to one cycle of the moon's phases, or about 30 days or 4 weeks. 2. One of the 12 divisions of a year as determined by a calendar, esp. the Gregorian calendar. 3. A period extending from a date in one calendar month to the corresponding date in the following month. 4. A sidereal month. 5. A lunar month. 6. A solar month. —**idiom: month of Sundays** Informal An indefinitely long period of time. [ME moneth < OE mōnath. See mē-¹ in App.]

USAGE NOTE The singular month, preceded by a number and a hyphen, is used as a compound attributive: a three-month vacation. The plural possessive form without a hyphen is also possible: a three months' vacation.

month·ly (mŭnth′lē) adj. 1. Occurring, appearing, or coming due every month: a monthly meeting. 2. Continuing or lasting for a month. ❖ adv. Once a month; every month. ❖ n., pl. -**lies** 1. A periodical publication appearing once each month. 2. **monthlies** Informal The menses.

Mon·ti·cel·lo (mŏn′tĭ-chĕl′ō, -sĕl′ō) An estate of central VA SE of Charlottesville; designed by Thomas Jefferson.

mon·ti·cule (mŏn′tĭ-kyōōl′) n. A minor cone of a volcano. [Fr. < LLat. monticulus, dim. of Lat. mōns, mont-, mountain.]

Mont·mar·tre (môN-mär′trə) A hill and district of N Paris, France, on the Right Bank; noted for its nightlife and its associations with artists.

Mont·par·nasse (môN-pär-näs′) A district of S-central Paris, France, on the Left Bank; long famous for its cafés patronized by artists, writers, and intellectuals.

Mont·pel·ier (mŏnt-pēl′yər) The cap. of VT, in the N-central part; founded 1780. Pop. 8,035.

Mont·pel·lier (môN-pĕl-yā′) A city of S France near the Mediterranean Sea WNW of Marseille; founded in the 8th cent. and later an important Huguenot center. Pop. 208,103.

Mon·tre·al (mŏn′trē-ôl′) or **Mont·ré·al** (môN-rā-äl′) A city of S Quebec, Canada, on **Montreal Island** in the St. Lawrence R. Montreal was founded by the French in 1642 and captured by the

English in 1760. Pop. 1,016,376.

Montreal North or **Mont·ré·al-Nord** (môN′rā-äl-nôr′) A town of S Quebec, Canada, on Montreal I. Pop. 81,581.

Mont-Saint-Mi·chel (môN-săN-mē-shĕl′) A small island off the coast of NW France in an arm of the English Channel; crowned by an abbey founded c. 708.

Mont·ser·rat (mŏnt′sə-rät′) An island in the Leeward Is. of the British West Indies NW of Guadaloupe; colonized by the English after 1632 but held by the French at various periods before 1783.

mon·u·ment (mŏn′yə-mənt) n. 1. A structure, such as a sculpture, erected as a memorial. 2. An inscribed marker placed at a grave; a tombstone. 3. Something venerated for its enduring historic significance or association with a notable past person or thing. 4a. An outstanding enduring achievement: a monument of scholarship. b. An exceptional example. 5. An object, such as a post or stone, fixed in the ground to mark a boundary or position. 6. A written document; a legal one. [ME < Lat. monumentum, memorial < monēre, to remind. See men-¹ in App.]

mon·u·men·tal (mŏn′yə-mĕn′tl) adj. 1. Of, resembling, or serving as a monument. 2. Impressively large, sturdy, and enduring. 3. Of outstanding significance: Einstein's monumental contributions to physics. 4. Astounding: monumental talent. —**mon′u·men·tal′i·ty** (-mĕn-tăl′ĭ-tē) n. —**mon′u·men′tal·ly** adv.

mon·u·men·tal·ize (mŏn′yə-mĕn′tl-īz′) tr.v. -**ized, -iz·ing, -iz·es** To memorialize with a monument.

mon·u·ron (mŏn′yə-rŏn′) n. A crystalline compound, $C_9H_{11}ClN_2O$, used as a herbicide for grasses and broad-leaved weeds. [MON(O)– + UR(EA) + –ON³.]

Mon·za (mŏn′zə, -tsä) A city of N Italy NNE of Milan; an ancient cap. of Lombardy. Pop. 122,151.

mon·zo·nite (mŏn-zō′nīt′, mŏn′zə-nīt′) n. An igneous rock composed chiefly of plagioclase and orthoclase, with small amounts of other minerals. [Fr., after Mount Monzoni in NE Italy.] —**mon′zo·nit′ic** (mŏn′zə-nĭt′ĭk) adj.

moo (mōō) intr.v. **mooed, moo·ing, moos** To emit the deep bellowing sound made by a cow; low. ❖ n., pl. **moos** The lowing of a cow or a similar sound. [Imit.]

mooch (mōōch) Slang v. **mooched, mooch·ing, mooch·es** —tr. 1. To obtain or try to obtain by begging; cadge. 2. To steal; filch. —intr. 1. To get or try to get something free of charge; sponge. 2. To wander about aimlessly. 3. To skulk around; sneak. ❖ n. 1. One who begs or cadges; a sponge. 2. A dupe, as in a confidence game. [ME mowchen, prob. < OFr. muchier, to hide, skulk.] —**mooch′er** n.

mood¹ (mōōd) n. 1. A state of mind or emotion. 2. A pervading impression of an observer. 3. An incidence of sulking or angry behavior. 4. Inclination; disposition. [ME mod < OE mōd, disposition.]

SYNONYMS mood, humor, temper These nouns refer to a temporary state of mind and feeling. Mood is the most inclusive term: "I was in no mood to laugh" (Mary Shelley). Humor often implies a state of mind resulting from one's characteristic disposition or temperament: "All which had been done . . . was the effect not of humor, but of system" (Edmund Burke). Temper most often refers to irritability or intense anger: "The nation was in such a temper that the smallest spark might raise a flame" (Thomas Macaulay).

mood² (mōōd) n. 1. Grammar A set of verb forms used to indicate the speaker's attitude toward the factuality or likelihood of the action or condition expressed. In English the indicative mood is used to state facts, the subjunctive mood to indicate doubt or unlikelihood, and the imperative mood to express a command. 2. Logic The arrangement or form of a syllogism. [Alteration of MODE.]

mood·y (mōō′dē) adj. -**i·er, -i·est** 1. Given to frequent changes of mood; temperamental. 2. Subject to periods of depression; sulky. 3. Expressive of a mood, esp. a sullen or gloomy mood. —**mood′i·ly** adv. —**mood′i·ness** n.

moo goo gai pan (mōō′ gōō′ gī′ pän′) n. A Cantonese dish of chicken, mushrooms, vegetables, and spices sautéed together. [Cantonese mōhkoo kai paân, equivalent to Chin. (Mandarin) mógu jī piàn : mógu, mushroom (mó, mushroom + gū, mushroom) + jī, chicken + piàn, slice.]

moo·la or **moo·lah** (mōō′lə) n. Slang Money. [?]

moon (mōōn) n. 1. often Moon The natural satellite of Earth, visible by reflection of sunlight and having a slightly elliptical orbit, approx. 356,000 kilometers (221,600 miles) distant at perigee and 406,997 kilometers (252,950 miles) at apogee; its mean diameter is 3,475 kilometers (2,160 miles), and its average period of revolution around Earth 29 days, 12 hours, 44 minutes. 2. A natural satellite revolving around a planet. 3. The moon as it appears at a particular time in its cycle of phases. 4. A month, esp. a lunar month. 5. A disk, globe, or crescent resembling the natural satellite of Earth. 6. Moonlight. 7. Something unreasonable or unattainable: He acted as if I had asked for the moon. 8. Slang The bared buttocks. ❖ v. **mooned, moon·ing, moons** —intr. 1. To wander about or pass time languidly and aimlessly. 2. To yearn or pine as if infatuated. 3. Slang To expose one's buttocks in public as a prank or disrespectful gesture. —tr. Slang To expose one's buttocks to (others) as a prank or disrespectful gesture. [ME *moone* < OE *mōna.* See **mē-¹** in App.]

Moon, Sun Myung b. 1920. Korean-born Amer. religious leader and founder of the Unification Church (1954).

moon•beam (mōōn′bēm′) *n.* A ray of moonlight.

moon•blind (mōōn′blīnd′) *adj.* Affected with moon blindness.

moon blindness *n.* Recurrent inflammation of a horse's eyes, often ending in blindness.

moon•calf (mōōn′kăf′, -käf′) *n.* **1.** A fool. **2.** A freak. [Earlier, unformed embryo (< the supposed influence of the moon).]

moon•child (mōōn′chīld′) *n.* One born under the sign of Cancer. [< Cancer's astrological tie with the moon.]

moon dog *n.* A paraselene.

moon•eye (mōōn′ī′) *n.* **1.** A silvery freshwater fish of the family Hiodontidae, esp. *Hiodon tergisus* of eastern North America. **2.** See **moon blindness.**

moon-eyed (mōōn′īd′) *adj.* **1.** Having the eyes wide-open, as in wonder or grief. **2.** Able to see well at night. **3.** Moonblind.

moon-faced (mōōn′fāst′) *adj.* Having a round face.

moon•fish (mōōn′fīsh′) *n., pl.* **moonfish** or **-fish•es** **1.** Any of several marine fishes of the family Carangidae, found in warm American coastal waters and having short compressed bodies and a silvery color. **2.** See **opah.**

moon•flow•er (mōōn′flou′ər) *n.* Any of several night-blooming vines related to the morning glories.

Moon•ie (mōō′nē) *n. Often Offensive* A member of the Unification Church. [After Sun Myung **Moon.**]

moon•let (mōōn′lĭt) *n.* A small natural or artificial satellite.

moon•light (mōōn′līt′) *n.* The light reflected from the surface of the moon. ❖ *intr.v.* **-light•ed, -light•ing, -lights** *Informal* To work at another job, often at night, in addition to one's full-time job. —**moon′light′er** *n.*

moon•lit (mōōn′lĭt′) *adj.* Lighted by moonlight.

moon•quake (mōōn′kwāk′) *n.* A quake on the moon similar to an earthquake but usu. of very low magnitude.

moon•rise (mōōn′rīz′) *n.* The event or time of the appearance of the moon above the eastern horizon.

moon•scape (mōōn′skāp′) *n.* **1.** A view or picture of the surface of the moon. **2.** A desolate landscape. [MOON + (LAND)SCAPE.]

moon•seed (mōōn′sēd′) *n.* Any of several dioecious vines of the closely related genera *Cocculus* and *Menispermum,* having inconspicuous flowers and red or blackish fruit. [< its lunate seeds.]

moon•set (mōōn′sĕt′) *n.* The event or time of the disappearance of the moon below the western horizon.

moon shell *n.* Any of various marine gastropod mollusks of the family Naticidae, having a smooth rounded shell.

moon•shine (mōōn′shīn′) *n.* **1.** Moonlight. **2.** *Informal* Foolish talk or thought; nonsense. **3.** Illegally distilled whiskey. ❖ *intr.v.* **-shined, -shin•ing, -shines** To distill and sell liquor illegally. —**moon′shin′er** *n.*

moon•stone (mōōn′stōn′) *n.* A variety of feldspar valued as a gem for its pearly translucence.

moon•struck (mōōn′strŭk′) also **moon•strick•en** (-strĭk′ən) *adj.* **1.** Romantically dazed or distracted. **2.** Affected by insanity; crazed. [< the belief that the moon caused lunacy.]

moon•walk (mōōn′wôk′) *n.* A walk on the moon's surface by an astronaut. —**moon′walk′** *v.* —**moon′walk′er** *n.*

moon•ward (mōōn′wərd) *adv. & adj.* Toward the moon.

moon•wort (mōōn′wûrt′, -wôrt′) *n.* See **grape fern.**

moon•y (mōō′nē) *adj.* **-i•er, -i•est** **1.** Of or suggestive of the moon or moonlight. **2.** Moonlit. **3.** Dreamy in mood or nature; absent-minded.

moor¹ (mōōr) *v.* **moored, moor•ing, moors** —*tr.* **1.** To make fast (a vessel, for example) by means of cables, anchors, or lines. **2.** To fix in place; secure. —*intr.* **1.** To secure a vessel or aircraft with lines or anchors. **2.** To be secured with lines or anchors. [ME *mōre.*]

moor² (mōōr) *n.* A broad area of open land, often high but poorly drained, with patches of heath and peat bogs. [ME *mor* < OE *mōr.*]

Moor (mōōr) *n.* **1.** A member of a Muslim people of mixed Berber and Arab descent, now living chiefly in northwest Africa. **2.** One of the Muslims who invaded Spain in the eighth century and established a civilization in Andalusia that lasted until 1492. [ME *More* < OFr. < Med.Lat. *Mōrus* < Lat. *Maurus,* Mauritanian < Gk. *Mauros.*]

moor•age (mōōr′ĭj) *n.* **1.** The act or an instance of mooring. **2.** A place where a ship or an aircraft may be moored. **3.** A charge for mooring.

moor cock *n.* The male red grouse.

Moore, Clement Clarke 1779–1863. Amer. scholar and poet who wrote "A Visit from St. Nicholas" (1823).

Moore, George 1852–1933. Irish writer whose works include poetry, drama, criticism, and novels.

Moore, George Edward 1873–1958. British philosopher who wrote *Principia Ethica* (1903).

Moore, Henry 1898–1986. British sculptor noted for his human figures, characterized by smooth organic forms.

Moore, Marianne Craig 1887–1972. Amer. poet whose descriptive works are marked by unconventional meter.

moor•fowl (mōōr′foul′) *n.* See **red grouse.** [MOOR² + FOWL.]

moor•hen (mōōr′hĕn′) *n. Chiefly British* **1.** A common, widely distributed species of gallinule, *Gallinula chloropus.* **2.** The female red grouse. [MOOR² + HEN.]

moor•ing (mōōr′ĭng) *n.* **1.** The act or an instance of making fast an aircraft or a vessel, as by a cable or anchor. **2.** A place or structure to which a vessel or aircraft can be moored. **3.** Equipment, such as anchors, for holding fast a vessel or aircraft. **4.** An element providing stability or security. Often used in the plural.

Moor•ish (mōōr′ĭsh) *adj.* **1.** Of or relating to the Moors or their culture. **2.** Of, relating to, or being a style of Spanish architecture of the 8th to the 16th century, characterized by the horseshoe arch and ornate decoration.

moor•land (mōōr′lănd′) *n.* Land consisting of moors.

moose (mōōs) *n., pl.* **moose** A hoofed mammal *(Alces alces)* found in forests of northern North America and in Eurasia and having a broad pendulous muzzle and large palmate antlers in the male. [Eastern Abenaki *mos.*]

moose•bird (mōōs′bûrd′) *n.* See **gray jay.**

Moose•head Lake (mōōs′hĕd′) A lake of W-central ME N of Augusta.

Moose River A river of NE Ontario, Canada, flowing c. 547 km (340 mi) to James Bay.

moose•wood (mōōs′wŏŏd′) *n.* See **leatherwood.**

moot (mōōt) *adj.* **1a.** Of no practical importance; irrelevant. **b.** Subject to debate; arguable: *a moot question.* **2.** *Law* Without legal significance through having been previously decided or settled. ❖ *n.* **1.** *Law* A hypothetical case argued by law students as an exercise. **2.** A medieval English meeting, esp. a representative meeting of the freemen of a shire. ❖ *tr.v.* **moot•ed, moot•ing, moots** **1a.** To bring up as a subject for discussion or debate. **b.** To discuss or debate. **2.** *Law* To plead or argue (a case) in a moot court. [ME, meeting < OE *mōt, gemōt.*] —**moot′ness** *n.*

> **USAGE NOTE** As an adjective *moot* originally had the legal sense "arguable, open to debate," but it is now widely used to mean "no longer important, irrelevant." A number of critics have objected to this use, but it was accepted by 59 percent of the Usage Panel.

mop (mŏp) *n.* **1.** A household implement made of absorbent material attached to a handle and used for washing, dusting, or drying floors. **2.** A loosely tangled bunch or mass. ❖ *v.* **mopped, mop•ping, mops** —*tr.* To wash or wipe with or as if with a mop. —*intr.* To use a mop to wash or dry surfaces. —*phrasal verb:* **mop up** **1.** To clear (an area) of remaining enemy troops after a victory. **2.** *Informal* To perform the minor tasks that end an activity. [ME *mappe,* perh. < OFr. dialectal, napkin < Lat. *mappa,* towel, cloth. See MAP.] —**mop′per** *n.*

mop•board (mŏp′bôrd′, -bōrd′) *n.* See **baseboard.**

mope (mŏp) *intr.v.* **moped, mop•ing, mopes** **1a.** To be gloomy or dejected. **b.** To brood or sulk. See Syns at **brood. 2.** To move in a leisurely or aimless manner; dawdle. ❖ *n.* **1.** A person given to gloomy or dejected moods. **2. mopes** Low spirits; the blues. Often used with *the.* [?] —**mop′er** *n.* —**mop′ish, mop′ey** *adj.* —**mop′ish•ly** *adv.*

mo•ped (mō′pĕd′) *n.* A lightweight motorized bicycle that can be pedaled as well as driven by a low-powered gasoline engine. [< MO(TOR) + PED(AL).]

mop•pet (mŏp′ĭt) *n.* A young child. [< obsolete *mop,* fool, child < ME *moppe.*]

mop-up (mŏp′ŭp′) *n.* The act or an instance of mopping up; a concluding operation.

mo•quette (mō-kĕt′) *n.* **1.** A heavy fabric with a thick nap, used for upholstery. **2.** A carpet with a deep tufted pile. [Fr., alteration of obsolete *moucade.*]

MOR *abbr.* middle-of-the-road

Mor. *abbr.* **1.** Morocco **2.** Moroccan

mo•ra (môr′ə, mōr′ə) *n., pl.* **mo•rae** (môr′ē, mōr′ē) or **mo•ras** The minimal unit of metrical time in quantitative verse, equal to the short syllable. [Lat., pause.]

Mo•rad•a•bad (mə-rä′də-bäd′, môr′ə-də-băd′) A city of N-central India ENE of Delhi; founded 1625. Pop. 429,214.

mo•raine (mə-rān′) *n.* An accumulation of boulders, stones, or other debris carried and deposited by a glacier. [Fr. < Fr. dialectal *morena,* mound of earth < Provençal *morre,* muzzle < VLat. *murrum.*] —**mo•rain′al, mo•rain′ic** *adj.*

mor•al (môr′əl, mŏr′-) *adj.* **1.** Of or concerned with the judgment of the goodness or badness of human action and character; ethical: *moral scrutiny.* **2.** Teaching or exhibiting goodness or correctness of character and behavior: *a moral lesson.* **3.** Conforming to standards of what is right or just in behavior; virtuous: *a moral life.* **4.** Arising from conscience or the sense of right and wrong: *a moral obligation.* **5.** Having psychological rather than physical or tangible effects: *moral support.* **6.** Based on strong likelihood or firm conviction, rather than on the actual evidence: *a moral certainty.* ❖ *n.* **1.** The lesson or principle in a fable, story, or event. **2.** A concisely expressed precept or general truth; a maxim. **3. morals** Rules or habits of conduct, esp. of sexual conduct, in regard to standards of right and wrong: *a decline in the public morals.* [ME < OFr. < Lat. *mōrālis* < *mōs, mōr-,* custom.] —**mor′al•ly** *adv.*

SYNONYMS *moral, ethical, virtuous, righteous* These adjectives

moon
top: first quarter moon, 7 days old
center: full moon, 14 days old
bottom: waning crescent moon, 23 days old

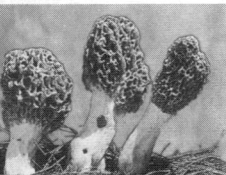

morel
black morels
Morchella conica

morion

morning glory

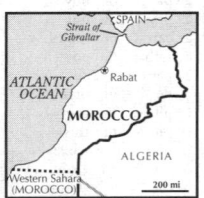

Morocco

---

mean in accord with right or good conduct. *Moral* applies to personal character and behavior, especially sexual conduct: "*Our moral sense dictates a clearcut preference for these societies which share with us an abiding respect for individual human rights*" (Jimmy Carter). *Ethical* stresses idealistic standards of right and wrong: "*Ours is a world of nuclear giants and ethical infants*" (Omar N. Bradley). *Virtuous* implies moral excellence and loftiness of character: "*The life of the nation is secure only while the nation is honest, truthful, and virtuous*" (Frederick Douglass). *Righteous* emphasizes moral uprightness; when it is applied to actions, reactions, or impulses, it often implies justifiable outrage: "*He was . . . stirred by righteous wrath*" (John Galsworthy).

mo·rale (mə-răl′) *n.* The state of the spirits of a person or group as exhibited by confidence, cheerfulness, discipline, and willingness to perform assigned tasks. [Fr., morality, good conduct < fem. of *moral*, moral < OFr. See MORAL.]

moral hazard *n.* A risk to an insurance company resulting from uncertainty about the honesty of the insured.

mor·al·ism (môr′ə-lĭz′əm, mŏr′-) *n.* **1.** A conventional moral maxim or attitude. **2.** The act or practice of moralizing. **3.** Often undue concern for morality.

mor·al·ist (môr′ə-lĭst, mŏr′-) *n.* **1.** A teacher or student of moral philosophy. **2.** One who follows a system of moral principles. **3.** One unduly concerned with others' morals.

mor·al·is·tic (môr′ə-lĭs′tĭk, mŏr′-) *adj.* **1.** Characterized by or displaying a concern with morality. **2.** Marked by a narrow-minded morality. —**mor′al·is′ti·cal·ly** *adv.*

mo·ral·i·ty (mə-răl′ĭ-tē, mô-) *n., pl.* **-ties 1.** The quality of being in accord with standards of right or good conduct. **2.** A system of ideas of right and wrong conduct. **3.** Virtuous conduct. **4.** A rule or lesson in moral conduct.

morality play *n.* **1.** A medieval drama using allegorical characters to portray the soul's struggle to achieve salvation. **2.** Something viewed as exhibiting a struggle between good and evil and offering a moral lesson.

mor·al·ize (môr′ə-līz′, mŏr′-) *v.* **-ized, -iz·ing, -iz·es** —*intr.* To think about or express moral judgments or reflections. —*tr.* **1.** To interpret or explain the moral meaning of. **2.** To improve the morals of; reform. —**mor′al·i·za′tion** (-ə-lĭ-zā′shən) *n.* —**mor′al·iz′er** *n.*

moral philosophy *n.* Ethics.

mo·rass (mə-răs′, mô-) *n.* **1.** An area of low-lying soggy ground. **2.** Something that hinders, engulfs, or overwhelms: *a morass of details.* [Du. *moeras* < MDu. *maras* < OFr. *mareis*, prob. of Gmc. orig. See mori- in App.]

mor·a·to·ri·um (môr′ə-tôr′ē-əm, -tōr′-, mŏr′-) *n., pl.* **-to·ri·ums** or **-to·ri·a** (-tôr′ē-ə, -tōr′-) **1.** *Law* **a.** An authorization to a debtor, such as a bank, permitting temporary suspension of payments. **b.** An authorized period of delay in the performance of an obligation. **2.** A suspension of an activity. [< LLat. *morātōrium*, neut. of *morātōrius*, delaying. See MORATORY.]

mor·a·to·ry (môr′ə-tôr′ē, -tōr′ē, mŏr′-) *adj.* Authorizing delay in payment. [Fr. *moratoire* < LLat. *morātōrius*, delaying. See MORATORIUM.]

Mo·ra·va (môr′ə-və, mō′rä-vä) **1.** A river of E Czech Republic flowing c. 386 km (240 mi) to the Danube R. near Bratislava. **2.** A river of E Yugoslavia flowing c. 209 km (130 mi) NNW to the Danube R. E of Belgrade.

Mo·ra·vi·a (mə-rā′vē-ə, mō-) A region of central and E Czech Republic; settled by a Slavic people at the end of the 6th cent. A.D.

Mo·ra·vi·a (mō-rä′vē-ə, -vyä), **Alberto** 1907–90. Italian writer whose novels include *Time of Desecration* (1978).

Mo·ra·vi·an (mə-rā′vē-ən) *n.* **1.** A native or inhabitant of Moravia. **2.** The Czech dialects spoken in Moravia. **3.** A member of a Protestant church founded in Saxony in 1722 by Hussites from Moravia. —**Mo·ra′vi·an** *adj.*

Moravian Gate or **Moravian Gap** A mountain pass of central Europe between the Sudetes and the W Carpathian Mts.

mo·ray (môr′ā, mə-rā′) *n.* Any of numerous chiefly tropical, brightly colored marine eels of the family Muraenidae that are ferocious fighters and commonly inhabit coral reefs. [Port. *moréia* < Lat. *mūrēna* < Gk. *mūraina* < *mūros*, a kind of eel.]

Mor·ay Firth (mûr′ē) An inlet of the North Sea on the NE coast of Scotland; N outlet of the Caledonian Canal system.

mor·bid (môr′bĭd) *adj.* **1a.** Of, relating to, or caused by disease; pathological or diseased. **b.** Psychologically unhealthy or unwholesome: "*He suffered much from a morbid acuteness of the senses*" (Edgar Allan Poe). **2.** Characterized by preoccupation with unwholesome thoughts or feelings. **3.** Gruesome; grisly. [Lat. *morbidus*, diseased < *morbus*, disease. See mer- in App.] —**mor′bid·ly** *adv.* —**mor′bid·ness** *n.*

mor·bid·i·ty (môr-bĭd′ĭ-tē) *n., pl.* **-ties 1.** The quality of being morbid; morbidness. **2.** The rate of incidence of a disease.

mor·da·cious (môr-dā′shəs) *adj.* **1.** Given to biting; biting. **2.** Caustic; sarcastic. [Lat. *mordāx, mordāc-* (< *mordēre*, to bite; see mer- in App.) + -IOUS.] —**mor·da′cious·ly** *adv.* —**mor·dac′i·ty** (-dăs′ĭ-tē) *n.*

mor·dant (môr′dnt) *adj.* **1a.** Bitingly sarcastic: *mordant satire.* **b.** Incisive and trenchant: *an inquisitor's mordant questioning.* **2.** Bitingly painful. **3.** Serving to fix colors in dyeing. ❖ *n.* **1.** A reagent,

such as tannic acid, that fixes dyes to cells, textiles, or other materials. **2.** A corrosive substance, such as an acid, used in etching. ❖ *tr.v.* **-dant·ed, -dant·ing, -dants** To treat with a mordant. [Fr. < OFr., pr. part. of *mordre*, to bite < VLat. **mordere* < Lat. *mordēre*. See mer- in App.] —**mor′dan·cy** *n.* —**mor′dant·ly** *adv.*

mor·dent (môr′dnt, môr-dĕnt′) *n.* A melodic ornament in which a principal tone is rapidly alternated with the tone a half or full step below. [Ger. < Ital. *mordente* < *mordere*, to bite < VLat. **mordere* < Lat. *mordēre*. See mer- in App.]

Mord·vin·i·a (môrd-vĭn′ē-ə) also **Mor·do·vi·a** (môr-dō′vē-ə) A region of W-central Russia; settled by a Finno-Ugric people and annexed by Russia in 1552.

more (môr, mōr) *adj.* Comparative of **many, much. 1a.** Greater in number: *a hall with more seats.* **b.** Greater in size, amount, extent, or degree: *more support.* **2.** Additional; extra: *needs more time.* ❖ *n.* A greater or additional quantity, number, degree, or amount: *The more I see of you the more I like you.* ❖ *pron.* (used with a *pl. verb*) A greater or additional number of persons or things: *Here's one bottle, and more are in the kitchen.* ❖ *adv.* Comparative of **much. 1a.** To or in a greater extent or degree: *loved him even more.* **b.** Used to form the comparative of many adjectives and adverbs: *more softly.* **2.** In addition: *phoned twice more.* **3.** Moreover; furthermore. —*idioms:* **more and more** To a steadily increasing extent or degree: *getting more and more worried.* **more or less 1.** About; approximately: *holds a ton, more or less.* **2.** To an undetermined degree: *more or less happy.* [ME < OE *māra* and *mǣre*.]

More, Sir Thomas 1478–1535. English politician and humanist scholar noted for his political essay *Utopia* (1516) who refused to recognize Henry VIII's authority over the pope and was beheaded for treason.

Mo·reau River (môr′ō, mōr′ō) A river of NW SD flowing c. 402 km (250 mi) to the Missouri R.

mo·reen (mə-rēn′, mô-) *n.* A sturdy ribbed fabric of wool, cotton, or wool and cotton, often with an embossed finish, used for clothing and upholstery. [Poss. < MOIRÉ.]

mo·rel (mə-rĕl′, mô-) *n.* Any of various edible mushrooms of the genus *Morchella* and related genera, characterized by a brownish spongelike cap. [Fr. *morille* < OFr., perh. < VLat. **maurīcula*, fem. dim. of Lat. *Maurus*, Mauritanian, Moor. See MOOR.]

Mo·re·lia (mə-rāl′yə, mō-rē′lyä) A city of SW Mexico WNW of Mexico City; founded 1541 as Valladolid. Pop. 297,544.

mo·rel·lo (mə-rĕl′ō) *n., pl.* **-los** A variety of the sour cherry (*Prunus cerasus* var. *austera*) having double flowers and fruit with dark red skin. [Perh. < Ital. *amarello* < Med.Lat. *amārellum*, dim. of Lat. *amārus*, bitter.]

more·o·ver (môr-ō′vər, mōr-, môr′ō′vər, mōr′-) *adv.* Beyond what has been stated; besides.

mo·res (môr′āz′, -ēz, mōr′-) *pl.n.* **1.** The accepted customs and usages of a social group. **2.** Moral attitudes. **3.** Manners; ways. [Lat. *mōrēs*, pl. of *mōs*, custom.]

Mo·resque (mô-rĕsk′, mə-) *adj.* Characteristic of Moorish art or architecture. ❖ *n.* An ornament or a decoration in Moorish style. [Fr. < OFr. < Sp. *Morisco*, Morisco. See MORISCO.]

Mor·gan (môr′gən) *n.* Any of a breed of American saddle and trotting horses noted for strength, speed, and endurance. [After Justin *Morgan* (1747–98), American schoolteacher.]

Morgan, Sir Henry 1635?–88. Welsh buccaneer who was acting governor of Jamaica (1680–82).

Morgan, John Hunt 1825–64. Amer. Confederate soldier who led cavalry raids behind Union lines.

Morgan, John Pierpont 1837–1913. Amer. financier and philanthropist noted for his consolidation of the US Steel Corporation (1901) and the establishment of the Morgan Library in New York City, which was donated to the public (1924) by his son **John Pierpont, Jr.** (1867–1943).

Morgan, Julia 1872–1957. Amer. architect who designed over 700 buildings in California and Hawaii.

Morgan, Lewis Henry 1818–81. Amer. anthropologist whose works on Native Americans include *Ancient Society* (1877).

Morgan, Thomas Hunt 1866–1945. Amer. biologist who won a 1933 Nobel Prize.

mor·ga·nat·ic (môr′gə-năt′ĭk) *adj.* Of or being a marriage between a person of noble birth and a partner of a lower rank in which it is agreed that the partner and any offspring share no titles or estates of the noble partner. [NLat. *morganāticus* < Med.Lat. (*mātrimōnium ad*) *morganāticam*, (marriage for the) morning-gift, of Gmc. orig.]

mor·gan·ite (môr′gə-nīt′) *n.* A rose-pink variety of beryl, valued as a semiprecious gem. [After John Pierpont MORGAN.]

Morgan le Fay (lə fā′) *n.* In Arthurian legend, the sorceress sister and enemy of King Arthur.

Mor·gan·town (môr′gən-toun′) A city of N WV on the Monongahela R. near the PA border. Pop. 26,809.

mor·gen (môr′gən) *n., pl.* **morgen** or **-gens** A Dutch and South African unit of land area equal to 2.1 acres. [Du., morning (amount plowable in a morning) < MDu. *morghen.*]

morgue (môrg) *n.* **1.** A place in which the bodies of persons found dead are kept until identified and claimed or until arrangements for burial have been made. **2.** A reference file in a

mor·i·bund (môr′ə-bŭnd′, mŏr′-) adj. **1.** Approaching death; about to die. **2.** On the verge of becoming obsolete: *moribund customs.* [Lat. *moribundus* < *morī,* to die. See **mer-** in App.] —**mor′i·bun′di·ty** (-bŭn′dĭ-tē) n. —**mor′i·bund′ly** adv.

mo·ri·on (môr′ē-ŏn′, mŏr′-) n. **1.** A crested metal helmet with a curved peak in front and back, worn by soldiers in the 16th and 17th centuries. **2.** A black or blackish-brown form of smoky quartz. [Fr. < Sp. *morrión* < *morro,* round object, prob. < VLat. **murrum,* muzzle.]

Mo·ris·co (mə-rĭs′kō) n., pl. **-cos** or **-coes** A Moor, esp. a Spanish Moor. [Sp. < *Moro,* Moor < Lat. *Maurus.* See MOOR.] —**Mo·ris′co** adj.

Mor·i·son (môr′ĭ-sən, mŏr′-), **Samuel Eliot** 1887–1976. Amer. historian noted for his works on maritime history.

Mo·ri·sot (mô-rē-zô′), **Berthe** 1841–95. French impressionist painter of domestic subjects and portraits.

Mor·ley (môr′lē), **Edward Williams** 1838–1923. Amer. chemist and physicist who disproved the existence of ether, the hypothetical medium of electromagnetic waves.

Mor·mon (môr′mən) *Mormon Church* n. **1.** An ancient prophet believed to have compiled a sacred history of the Americas, which were translated and published by Joseph Smith as the Book of Mormon in 1830. **2.** A member of the Mormon Church. —**Mor′mon** adj. —**Mor′mon·ism** n.

Mormon Church n. A church founded by Joseph Smith at Palmyra, New York, in 1830 and having its headquarters since 1847 in Salt Lake City, Utah.

Mormon cricket n. A large wingless long-horned grasshopper (*Anabrus simplex*) of the western United States that is often destructive to crops.

morn (môrn) n. **1.** The morning. **2.** The dawn. [ME < OE *morgen.*]

Mor·nay sauce (môr-nā′) n. A béchamel sauce flavored with grated cheese and seasonings. [Perh. after Philippe de MORNAY.]

Mornay, Philippe de 1549–1623. French Huguenot leader during the reigns of Henry III and Henry IV.

morn·ing (môr′nĭng) n. **1.** The first or early part of the day, from midnight to noon or from sunrise to noon. **2.** The dawn. **3.** The first or early part. [ME < *morn,* morn. See MORN.]

morn·ing-af·ter pill (môr′nĭng-ăf′tər) n. A pill containing a drug, esp. an estrogen, that prevents implantation of a fertilized ovum after sexual intercourse.

morning glory n. Any of numerous vines of the genera *Argyreia, Calystegia, Convolvulus, Merremia,* and *Ipomoea,* with funnel-shaped flowers that close late in the day.

Morning Prayer (prâr) n. The liturgical service used for morning worship in the Anglican Church.

morning sickness n. Nausea and vomiting upon rising in the morning, esp. during early pregnancy.

morning star n. A planet, esp. Venus, visible in the east just before or at sunrise.

Mo·ro (môr′ō, mōr′ō) n., pl. **Moro** or **-ros 1.** A member of any of the predominantly Muslim Malay tribes of the southern Philippines. **2.** Any of the Austronesian languages of the Moro. [Sp., Moor, Moro < Lat. *Maurus,* Moor. See MOOR.]

mo·roc·co (mə-rŏk′ō) n., pl. **-cos** A soft fine leather of goatskin tanned with sumac, used for book bindings and shoes.

Morocco A country of NW Africa on the Mediterranean Sea and the Atlantic Ocean; achieved independence from France in 1956. Cap. Rabat. Pop. 26,590,000. —**Mo·roc′can** adj. & n.

Moro Gulf An inlet of the Celebes Sea SW of Mindanao, Philippines.

mo·ron (môr′ŏn′, mōr′-) n. **1.** A stupid person; a dolt. **2.** A person of mild mental retardation having a mental age of from 7 to 12 years. Not in scientific use. [< Gk. *mōron,* neut. of *mōros,* stupid, foolish.] —**mo·ron′ic** (mə-rŏn′ĭk, mô-) adj. —**mo·ron′i·cal·ly** adv. —**mo·ron′ism, mo·ron′i·ty** (mə-rŏn′ĭ-tē, mô-) n.

Mo·ro·ni[1] (mə-rō′nē) n. *Mormon Church* An ancient prophet believed to have buried the sacred history of the Americas compiled by his father, Mormon, near Palmyra, New York, in the early fifth century A.D.

Mo·ro·ni[2] (mə-rō′nē, mô-) The cap. of the Comoros, on Grand Comoro I. and the Mozambique Channel. Pop. 20,112.

mo·rose (mə-rōs′, mô-) adj. Sullenly melancholy; gloomy. [Lat. *mōrōsus,* peevish < *mōs, mōr-,* self-will, manner.] —**mo·rose′ly** adv. —**mo·rose′ness** n.

morph[1] (môrf) n. An allomorph. [< MORPHEME.]

morph[2] (môrf) n. One of various distinct forms of an organism or species. [< Gk. *morphē,* form, shape.]

morph[3] (môrf) v. **morphed, morph·ing, morphs** —tr. To transform (an image) by computer. —intr. To be transformed. [Shortening of METAMORPHOSE.]

morph- pref. Variant of **morpho-.**

-morph suff. **1.** Form; shape; structure: *endomorph.* **2.** Morpheme. [Gk. *-morphos < morphē,* shape.]

mor·phal·lax·is (môr′fə-lăk′sĭs) n., pl. **-lax·es** (-lăk′sēz) The regeneration of a body part by means of structural or cellular re-

organization with only limited production of new cells, observed primarily in invertebrate organisms, such as certain lobsters. [NLat. : MORPH(O)– + Gk. *allaxis,* exchange (< *allassein,* to exchange < *allos,* other; see **al-** in App.).]

mor·pheme (môr′fēm′) n. A meaningful linguistic unit consisting of a word, such as *man,* or a word element, such as *-ed* in *walked,* that cannot be divided into smaller meaningful parts. [Fr. *morphème,* blend of Gk. *morphē,* form, and Fr. *phonème,* phoneme; see PHONEME.] —**mor·phem′ic** adj. —**mor·phem′i·cal·ly** adv.

mor·phem·ics (môr-fē′mĭks) n. (used with a sing. verb) **1.** The study, description, and classification of morphemes. **2.** The morphemic structure of a language.

Mor·phe·us (môr′fē-əs, -fyōos′) n. The god of dreams in Ovid's *Metamorphoses.* —**Mor′phe·an** (-fē-ən) adj.

mor·phi·a (môr′fē-ə) n. See **morphine.** [NLat. < Lat. *Morpheus,* Morpheus.]

-morphic suff. Having a specified shape or form: *geomorphic.*

mor·phine (môr′fēn′) n. A bitter crystalline alkaloid, $C_{17}H_{19}NO_3 \cdot H_2O$, extracted from opium and used in medicine as an analgesic, anesthetic, or sedative. [Fr. < *Morphée,* Morpheus < Lat. *Morpheus.*]

mor·phin·ism (môr′fē-nĭz′əm, môr′fə-) n. **1.** Addiction to morphine. **2.** A diseased condition caused by habitual or addictive use of morphine. —**mor′phin·ist** n.

-morphism suff. The condition or quality of having a specified form: *homomorphism.*

mor·pho (môr′fō) n., pl. **-phos** Any of various large, brightly colored butterflies of the genus *Morpho,* found in Central and South America. [NLat. *Morphō,* genus name < Gk., epithet of Aphrodite, perh. < *morphē,* shape.]

morpho- or **morph-** pref. **1.** Form; shape; structure: *morphogenesis.* **2.** Morpheme: *morphophonemics.* [Gk. < *morphē,* shape.]

mor·pho·gen·e·sis (môr′fō-jĕn′ĭ-sĭs) n. Differentiation and growth of tissues and organs during development. —**mor′pho·ge·net′ic** (-jə-nĕt′ĭk), **mor′pho·gen′ic** adj.

mor·phol·o·gy (môr-fŏl′ə-jē) n., pl. **-gies 1a.** The branch of biology that deals with the form and structure of organisms apart from function. **b.** The form and structure of an organism or one of its parts. **2.** *Linguistics* The study of the structure and form of words in language or a language, including inflection, derivation, and the formation of compounds. —**mor′pho·log′i·cal** (-fə-lŏj′ĭ-kəl), **mor′pho·log′ic** adj. —**mor·phol′o·gist** n.

mor·pho·pho·ne·mics (môr′fō-fə-nē′mĭks) n. **1.** (used with a pl. verb) The changes in pronunciation undergone by allomorphs of morphemes as they are modified by neighboring sounds or for grammatical reasons in the course of inflection or derivation. **2.** (used with a sing. verb) The study of the morphophonemics of a language. —**mor′pho·pho·ne′mic** adj.

mor·pho·sis (môr-fō′sĭs) n., pl. **-ses** (-sēz) The manner in which an organism or any of its parts changes form or undergoes development. [Gk. *morphōsis,* process of forming < *morphoun,* to form < *morphē,* form.]

mor·pho·syn·tax (môr′fō-sĭn′tăks′) n. **1.** The study of grammatical categories or linguistic units that have both morphological and syntactic properties. **2.** The set of rules that govern such linguistic units. [MORPHO(LOGY) + SYNTAX.]

-morphous suff. Having a specified shape or form: *polymorphous.* [Gk. *-morphos < morphē,* shape.]

mor·ris (môr′ĭs, mŏr′-) n. An English folk dance in which a story is enacted by costumed dancers. [ME *moreys (daunce),* morris (dance) < *moreys,* Moorish < OFr. *morois < More,* Moor. See MOOR.] —**mor′ris** adj.

Morris, Esther Hobart McQuigg Slack 1814–1902. Amer. suffragist who was the first woman justice of the peace in the US (1870).

Morris, Gouverneur 1752–1816. Amer. political leader who helped draft the US Constitution (1787).

Morris, Robert 1734–1806. Amer. Revolutionary politician and financier who signed the Declaration of Independence and raised money for the Continental Army.

Morris, William 1834–96. British poet, painter, craftsman, and social reformer best remembered for his wallpaper and furniture designs.

Morris chair n. A large easy chair with arms, an adjustable back, and removable cushions. [After William MORRIS.]

Morris Jes·up (jĕs′əp), **Cape** A cape of N Greenland on the Arctic Ocean; the northernmost point of land in the world.

Mor·ris·on (môr′ĭ-sən, mŏr′-), **Toni** b. 1931. Amer. writer who won the 1993 Nobel Prize for literature. Her novels include *Beloved* (1987).

Mor·ris·town (môr′ĭs-toun′, mŏr′-) A town of N NJ WNW of Newark; site of the Continental Army encampment during the winters of 1776–77 and 1779–80. Pop. 18,544.

mor·row (môr′ō, mŏr′ō) n. **1.** The following day. **2.** The time immediately after an event. **3.** *Archaic* The morning. [ME *morwe, morow,* var. of *morwen* < OE *morgen,* morning.]

Morse (môrs), **Samuel Finley Breese** 1791–1872. Amer. painter and inventor who refined (1838) and patented (1854) the telegraph and developed a telegraphic code.

Morse code n. Either of two codes used for transmitting mes-

Toni Morrison

Morse code
international Morse code

A	B	C	D
·–	–···	–·–·	–··
E	F	G	H
·	··–·	––·	····
I	J	K	L
··	·–––	–·–	·–··
M	N	O	P
––	–·	–––	·––·
Q	R	S	T
––·–	·–·	···	–
U	V	W	X
··–	···–	·––	–··–
	Y	Z	
	–·––	––··	

ă	pat	oi	boy
ā	pay	ou	out
âr	care	ōō	took
ä	father	ōō	boot
ĕ	pet	ŭ	cut
ē	be	ûr	urge
ĭ	pit	th	thin
ī	pie	*th*	this
îr	pier	hw	which
ŏ	pot	zh	vision
ō	toe	ə	about,
ô	paw		item

Stress marks:
′ (primary);
′ (secondary); as in
lexicon (lĕk′sĭ-kŏn′)

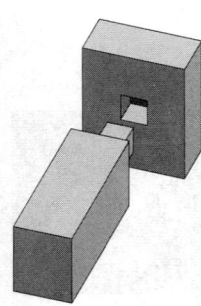

mortise
mortise-and-tenon joint

mosaic
detail from a third-century
A.D. Roman mosaic at
Paphos, Cyprus

sages in which letters of the alphabet and numbers are represented by various sequences of dots and dashes or short and long signals. [After Samuel Finley Breese MORSE.]

mor•sel (môr′səl) n. 1. A small piece of food. 2. A tasty delicacy; a tidbit. 3. A small amount; a piece. 4. One that is delightful and pleasing. [ME < OFr., dim. of mors, bite < Lat. morsum < neut. p. part. of mordēre, to bite. See mer- in App.]

mort¹ (môrt) n. The note sounded on a hunting horn to announce the death of a deer. [ME, death < OFr. < Lat. mors, mort-. See mer- in App.]

mort² (môrt) n. A great number or quantity. [Perh. < MORTAL.]

mor•ta•del•la (môr′tə-dĕl′ə) n. A smoked Italian sausage made of ground pork and beef and cubes of pork fat, flavored with wine and spices. [Ital., fem. dim. of murtato, seasoned with myrtle berries < Lat. myrtātus, murtātus < myrtus, myrta, myrtle. See MYRTLE.]

mor•tal (môr′tl) adj. 1. Liable or subject to death. 2. Of or relating to humankind; human: the mortal limits of understanding. 3. Of, relating to, or accompanying death: mortal throes. 4. Causing death; fatal: a mortal wound. 5. Fighting or fought to the death; unrelenting: a mortal attack. 6. Of great intensity or severity; dire: mortal terror. 7. Conceivable: no mortal reason to go. 8. Used as an intensive: a mortal fool. ❖ n. A human. [ME < OFr. < Lat. mortālis < mors, mort-, death. See mer- in App.] —mor′tal•ly adv.

mor•tal•i•ty (môr-tăl′ĭ-tē) n., pl. -ties 1. The quality or condition of being mortal. 2. Mortals considered as a group; the human race. 3. Death, esp. of large numbers; heavy loss of life. 4. Death rate. 5. The rate of failure or loss.

mortal sin n. Christianity A sin, such as murder, that is so heinous it deprives the soul of sanctifying grace and causes damnation if unpardoned at the time of death.

mor•tar (môr′tər) n. 1. A vessel in which substances are crushed or ground with a pestle. 2. A machine in which materials are ground and blended or crushed. 3a. A portable muzzleloading cannon that fires shells at low velocities, short ranges, and high trajectories. b. Any of several similar devices, such as one that shoots lifelines across water. 4. Any of various bonding materials used in masonry, surfacing, and plastering, esp. a mixture of cement or lime, sand, and water used to bind together bricks or stones. ❖ tr.v. -tared, -tar•ing, -tars 1. To bombard with mortar shells. 2. To plaster or join with mortar. [ME morter < OE mortere and < OFr. mortier, both < Lat. mortārium. See mer- in App.]

mor•tar•board (môr′tər-bôrd′, -bōrd′) n. 1. A square board with a handle used for holding and carrying masonry mortar. 2. An academic cap topped by a flat square.

mort•gage (môr′gĭj) n. 1. A temporary conditional pledge of property to a creditor as security for performance of an obligation or repayment of a debt. 2. A contract or deed specifying the terms of a mortgage. 3. The claim of a mortgagee upon mortgaged property. ❖ tr.v. -gaged, -gag•ing, -gag•es 1. To pledge or convey (property) by means of a mortgage. 2. To make subject to a claim or risk. [ME morgage < OFr. : mort, dead (< VLat. *mortus < Lat. mortuus, p. part. of morī, to die; see mer- in App.) + gage, pledge (of Gmc. orig.).]

mort•ga•gee (môr′gĭ-jē′) n. One that holds a mortgage.

mort•ga•gor (môr′gĭ-jôr′, môr′gĭ-jər) also **mort•gag•er** (môr′gĭ-jər) n. One that mortgages property.

mor•ti•cian (môr-tĭsh′ən) n. See funeral director. [Lat. mors, mort-, death; see MORTAL + -ICIAN.]

mor•ti•fi•ca•tion (môr′tə-fĭ-kā′shən) n. 1. A feeling of shame, humiliation, or wounded pride. 2. Discipline of the body and the appetites by self-denial. 3. Pathology Death or decay of one part of a living body; gangrene or necrosis.

mor•ti•fy (môr′tə-fī′) v. -fied, -fy•ing, -fies —tr. 1. To cause to experience shame, humiliation, or wounded pride. 2. To discipline (one's body and physical appetites) by self-denial. —intr. 1. To practice ascetic discipline or self-denial. 2. Pathology To undergo mortification. [ME mortifien, to deaden, subdue < OFr. mortifier < Lat. mortificāre, to kill : mors, mort-, death; see mer- in App. + -ficāre, -fy.]

Mor•ti•mer (môr′tə-mər), Roger de 1287–1330. Welsh rebel who invaded England from France (1326), deposed Edward II (1327), and ruled until 1330, when Edward III seized power.

mor•tise also **mor•tice** (môr′tĭs) n. 1. A usu. rectangular cavity in a piece of wood, stone, or other material, prepared to receive a tenon and thus form a joint. 2. Printing A hole cut in a plate for insertion of type. ❖ tr.v. -tised, -tis•ing, -tis•es also -ticed, -tic•ing, -tic•es 1. To join or fasten securely, as with a mortise and tenon. 2. To make a mortise in. 3. Printing a. To cut a hole in (a plate) for the insertion of type. b. To cut such a hole and insert (type). [ME mortaise < OFr., perh. < Ar. murtazz, fastened < irtazza, to be fixed (in place), derived stem of razza, to fix, insert.]

mort•main (môrt′mān′) n. 1. Law Perpetual ownership of real estate by institutions such as churches that cannot transfer or sell it. 2. The often oppressive influence of the past on the present. [ME mortemayne < OFr. mortemain : morte, fem. of mort, dead; see MORTGAGE + main, hand (< Lat. manus; see man-² in App.).]

Mor•ton (môr′tn), **Ferdinand Joseph La Menthe** Known as "Jelly Roll." 1885–1941. Amer. musician and composer who recorded seminal jazz works during the 1920s.

Morton, William Thomas Green 1819–68. Amer. dentist who demonstrated the use of ether as an anesthetic (1846).

mor•tu•ar•y (môr′chōō-ĕr′ē) n., pl. -ies A place, esp. a funeral home, where dead bodies are kept before burial or cremation. ❖ adj. 1. Of or relating to burial practices. 2. Relating to or characteristic of death. [Ult. < Lat. mortuārium, receptacle for dead things, neut. of mortuārius, of the dead < mortuus, dead, p. part. of morī, to die. See mer- in App.]

mor•u•la (môr′yə-lə, môr′ə-) n., pl. -lae (-lē′) The spherical embryonic mass of blastomeres formed before the blastula and resulting from cleavage of the fertilized ovum. [NLat. mōrula, fem. dim. of Lat. mōrum, mulberry.] —mor′u•lar adj. —mor′u•la′tion n.

MOS abbr. metal oxide semiconductor

mos. abbr. months

mo•sa•ic (mō-zā′ĭk) n. 1a. A picture or decorative design made by setting small colored pieces, as of stone or tile, into a surface. b. The process or art of making such pictures or designs. 2. A composite picture made of overlapping, usu. aerial photographs. 3. Something that resembles a mosaic. 4. Botany A virus disease of plants, resulting in mottled leaves. 5. A photosensitive surface, as in the iconoscope of a television camera. 6. Biology An individual exhibiting mosaicism. ❖ tr.v. -icked, -ick•ing, -ics 1. To make by mosaic. 2. To adorn with or as if with mosaic. [ME musycke < OFr. mosaique < OItal. mosaico < Med.Lat. mūsāicum, neut. of mūsāicus, of the Muses < Lat. Mūsa, Muse < Gk. Mousa. See men-¹ in App.] —mo•sa′i•cist (mō-zā′ĭ-sĭst) n.

Mo•sa•ic (mō-zā′ĭk) adj. Of or relating to Moses or the laws and writings attributed to him.

mosaic gold n. Ormolu. [< its use in making mosaics.]

mo•sa•i•cism (mō-zā′ĭ-sĭz′əm) n. A condition in which tissues of genetically different types occur in the same organism.

Mosaic Law n. The ancient law of the Hebrews, attributed to Moses and contained in the Pentateuch.

mo•sa•saur (mō′sə-sôr′) n. Any of various very large extinct aquatic lizards of the genus Mosasaurus, having modified limbs that served as paddles for swimming. [NLat. Mosasaurus, genus name : Lat. Mosa, the Meuse River (where fossils of the genus were first discovered) + Gk. sauros, lizard.]

mos•cha•tel (mŏs′kə-tĕl′, mŏs′kə-tĕl′) n. A perennial herb (Adoxa moschatellina) native to northern Eurasia and North America and having greenish-white, musk-scented flowers. [Fr. moscatelle < Ital. moscatella, fem. dim. of moscato, musk < LLat. muscus. See MUSK.]

Mos•cow (mŏs′kou, -kō) The cap. of Russia, in the W-central part on the **Moscow River**, flowing c. 499 km (310 mi) E to the Oka R. Inhabited since Neolithic times, it became the cap. of the Russian state by the 15th cent. The cap. was transferred to St. Petersburg in 1712 but returned to Moscow by the Soviets in 1918. Pop. 8,526,750.

Mo•selle¹ (mō-zĕl′) also **Mo•sel** (mō′zəl) A river rising in the Vosges Mts. of NE France and flowing c. 547 km (340 mi) to the Rhine R. in W Germany.

Mo•selle² (mō-zĕl′) n. A light dry white wine made from the Riesling grape, produced in the German valley of the Moselle River.

Mos•es (mō′zĭz, -zĭs) In the Bible, the Hebrew prophet and lawgiver who led the Israelites out of Egypt. [LLat. Mōsēs < Gk. < Heb. mōše < Egypt. ms, child.]

Moses, Anna Mary Robertson Known as "Grandma Moses." 1860–1961. Amer. painter noted for her primitive paintings.

mo•sey (mō′zē) intr.v. -seyed, -sey•ing, -seys Informal 1. To move leisurely; saunter. 2. To get going; move along. [?]

mosh (mŏsh) v. moshed, mosh•ing, mosh•es —intr. To knock against others intentionally while dancing at a rock concert. —tr. To knock against (someone) intentionally while dancing at a rock concert. [Perh. alteration of MASH.] —mosh′er n.

mo•shav (mō-shäv′) n., pl. mo•sha•vim (mō′shä-vēm′) An Israeli cooperative settlement consisting of small separate farms. [Mod.Heb. môšāb < Heb., dwelling < yāšab, to sit, dwell.]

mosh pit n. An area in front of a concert stage in which audience members mosh.

Mos•lem (mŏz′ləm, mŏs′-) n. Variant of **Muslim** 1. —Mos′lem adj.

mosque (mŏsk) n. A Muslim house of worship. [Fr. mosquée < OFr. mousquaie < OItal. moschea < moscheta < OSpan. mezquita < Ar. masjid. See MASJID.]

mos•qui•to (mə-skē′tō) n., pl. -toes or -tos Any of various two-winged insects of the family Culicidae, in which the female of most species has a long proboscis for sucking blood. See Regional Note at possum. [Sp. and Port. < dim. of mosca, fly < Lat. musca.]

WORD HISTORY If one were to try to shoot a mosquito with a musket, one would be using a small fly to kill a small fly—etymologically speaking, at least. Mosquito and musket both ultimately derive from Latin musca, "fly." In two of the Romance languages descended from Latin, namely Spanish and Portuguese, this word became mosca, from which a diminutive was formed, mosquito, "little fly, mosquito," the source of our word mosquito.

Italian also inherited the Latin word for "fly" as *mosca*, and its diminutive was *moschetta*. This word for "little fly" developed by extension to mean "bolt for a crossbow or catapult" (since a launched bolt buzzes like a fly). It also came to mean "small artillery piece," and in this sense was used to form the word *moschetto*, "musket." This was borrowed into French as *mousquet*, which wound up in English as *musket*.

Mosquito *n., pl.* **Mosquito** or **-tos** See **Miskito**.

mosquito boat *n. Chiefly British* A PT boat.

Mosquito Coast A region of E Nicaragua and NE Honduras.

mosquito fern *n.* Any of several free-floating ferns of the genus *Azolla* of warm regions, having two-lobed minute leaves.

mosquito fish *n.* Any of various fishes that feed on the larvae of mosquitoes, esp. a small gambusia (*Gambusia affinis*).

mosquito fly *n. Lower Southern US* See **dragonfly**. See Regional Note at **dragonfly**.

mosquito hawk *n.* **1.** See **nighthawk** 1a. **2.** *Lower Southern US* See **dragonfly**. See Regional Note at **dragonfly**.

mosquito net *n.* A fine net or screen used to keep out mosquitoes.

moss (môs, mŏs) *n.* **1a.** Any of various green, usu. small nonvascular plants of the class Musci of the division Bryophyta. **b.** A patch or covering of such plants. **2.** Any of various unrelated plants having a similar appearance or manner of growth, such as the club moss. ❖ *tr.v.* **mossed, moss·ing, moss·es** To cover with moss. [ME < OE *mos*, bog, and < Med.Lat. *mossa*, moss (of Gmc. orig.).]

moss animal *n.* See **bryozoan**.

moss·back (môs′băk′, mŏs′-) *n.* **1.** An old shellfish or turtle with a growth of algae on its back. **2.** An old, large, or sluggish fish. **3.** One who is extremely conservative or old-fashioned. —**moss′backed′** *adj.*

Möss·bau·er effect (mœs′bou′ər, môs′-, mŏs′-) *n.* The recoilless emission of gamma rays by radioactive nuclei of crystalline solids and the subsequent absorption of the emitted rays by other nuclei. [After Rudolf Ludwig *Mössbauer* (born 1929), German physicist.]

moss·bunk·er (môs′bŭng′kər, mŏs′-) *n.* See **menhaden**. [Du. *marsbanker*.]

moss campion *n.* A low-growing plant (*Silene acaulis*) having purplish-red flowers and forming dense cushionlike mats.

moss green *n.* A moderate to dark yellow, olive, or grayish green.

moss·grown (môs′grōn′, mŏs′-) *adj.* **1.** Overgrown with moss. **2.** Old-fashioned; antiquated.

mos·so (môs′sō) *adv. Music* With motion or animation. [Ital., p. part. of *muovere*, to move < Lat. *movēre*.]

moss pink *n.* A low-growing eastern North American plant (*Phlox subulata*) forming dense mosslike mats and widely cultivated for its profuse pink or white flowers.

moss rose *n.* A variety of rose (*Rosa centifolia*) native to the Caucasus and having a mossy flower stalk and calyx and fragrant pink flowers used as a source of attar.

moss-troop·er (môs′trōo′pər, mŏs′-) *n.* **1.** One of a band of raiders operating in the bogs on the borders of England and Scotland during the 17th century. **2.** A plunderer; a marauder.

moss·y (mô′sē, mŏs′ē) *adj.* **-i·er, -i·est** **1.** Covered with moss or something like moss: *mossy banks.* **2.** Resembling moss. **3.** Old-fashioned; antiquated. —**moss′i·ness** *n.*

most (mōst) *adj.* Superlative of **many, much. 1a.** Greatest in number. **b.** Greatest in amount, extent, or degree: *the most compassion.* **2.** In the greatest number of instances: *Most fish have fins.* ❖ *n.* **1.** The greatest amount or degree: *the most to gain.* **2.** *Slang* The greatest, best, or most exciting: *That party was the most!* ❖ *pron.* (*used with a sing. or pl. verb*) The greatest part or number: *Most of the town left.* ❖ *adv.* Superlative of **much. 1.** In or to the highest degree or extent. Used with many adjectives and adverbs to form the superlative degree: *most honest.* **2.** Very: *most impressive.* **3.** *Informal* Almost: *Most everyone agrees.* —**idiom: at (the) most** At the maximum. [ME < OE *mæst, māst.* Adv., sense 3, short for ALMOST.]

-most *suff.* **1.** Most: *innermost.* **2.** Nearest to: *aftmost.* [ME, alteration (influenced by *most, most*) of *-mest* < OE : *-mo, -ma,* superl. suff. + *-est,* superl. suff.]

mos·tac·cio·li (mô-stä′chə-lē′, -stät′chō-) Pasta in short tubes with slanted ends. [Ital., pl. of *mostaccioli,* cake, bun < Lat. *mustaceum,* must cake < *mustum,* must. See MUST³.]

most-fav·ored-na·tion (mōst′fā′vərd-nā′shən) *adj.* Of or relating to a commercial treaty in which the signatories agree to accord each other the same favorable terms that are offered in agreements with any other nation.

most·ly (mōst′lē) *adv.* **1.** For the greatest part; mainly. **2.** Generally; usually.

Mó·sto·les (mō′stō-lĕs′) A city of central Spain, a suburb of Madrid. Pop. 192,018.

Mo·sul (mō-sōōl′, mō′səl) A city of N Iraq on the Tigris R. NNW of Baghdad. Pop. 664,221.

mot (mō) *n.* A witty or incisive remark. [Fr. < OFr., word, saying, prob. < VLat. **mŏttum* < LLat. *muttum,* grunt, mutter, of imit. orig.]

mote¹ (mōt) *n.* A very small particle; a speck. [ME *mot* < OE.]

mote² (mōt) *aux.v. Archaic* May; might. [ME *moten* < OE *mōtan.* See **med-** in App.]

mo·tel (mō-tĕl′) *n.* An establishment that provides lodging for motorists in rooms usu. having direct access to a parking area. [Blend of MOTOR and HOTEL.]

mo·tet (mō-tĕt′) *n.* A polyphonic composition based on a sacred text and usu. sung without accompaniment. [ME < OFr., dim. of *mot,* word. See MOT.]

moth (môth, mŏth) *n., pl.* **moths** (môthz, mŏthz, môths, mŏths) **1.** Any of numerous insects of the order Lepidoptera, generally distinguished from butterflies by their nocturnal activity, hairlike or feathery antennae, stout bodies, and frenula. **2.** A clothes moth. [ME *motthe* < OE *moththe.*]

moth·ball (môth′bôl′, mŏth′-) *n.* **1.** A marble-sized ball, originally of camphor but now of naphthalene, stored with clothes to repel moths. **2. mothballs a.** A condition of long storage for possible future use. **b.** A condition of being set aside or discarded. ❖ *tr.v.* **-balled, -ball·ing, -balls** **1.** To remove (a ship, for example) from active use and put into protective storage. **2.** To defer indefinitely; shelve: *mothballed the plan.*

moth·eat·en (môth′ĕt′n, mŏth′-) *adj.* **1.** Eaten away by moth larvae. **2.** Old and timeworn: *a moth-eaten phrase.* **3.** Shabby; decrepit.

moth·er¹ (mŭth′ər) *n.* **1.** A woman who conceives, gives birth to, or raises and nurtures a child. **2.** A female parent of an animal. **3.** A female ancestor. **4.** A woman who holds a position of authority or responsibility similar to that of a mother: *a den mother.* **5.** *Roman Catholic Church* **a.** A mother superior. **b.** Used as a form of address for a mother superior. **6.** A woman who creates, originates, or founds something. **7.** A creative source; an origin. **8.** Used as a title for a woman respected for her wisdom and age. **9.** Maternal love and tenderness. **10.** The biggest or most significant example of its kind: *the mother of all battles.* **11.** *Vulgar Slang* Something extraordinary, as in disagreeableness or size. ❖ *adj.* **1.** Relating to or being a mother. **2.** Characteristic of a mother. **3.** Being the source or origin. **4.** Derived from or as if from one's mother; native. ❖ *v.* **-ered, -er·ing, -ers** —*tr.* **1.** To give birth to; create and produce. **2.** To watch over, nourish, and protect maternally. —*intr.* To act or serve as a mother. [ME *moder, mother* < OE *mōdor.* See **māter-** in App. N., sense 10, transl. of Iraqi Ar. *'umm.* N., sense 11, short for MOTHERFUCKER.]

moth·er² (mŭth′ər) *n.* A stringy slime composed of yeast cells and bacteria that forms on the surface of fermenting liquids and is added to wine or cider to start the production of vinegar. [Prob. alteration of obsolete Du. *moeder* < MDu., prob. < *moeder,* mother of children. See **māter-** in App.]

moth·er·board (mŭth′ər-bôrd′, -bōrd′) *n.* The main board of a computer, usu. containing the circuitry for the central processing unit, keyboard, and monitor.

Mother Car·ey's chicken (kâr′ēz) *n.* A petrel, esp. a storm petrel. [Poss. transl. and alteration of Med.Lat. *māter cāra,* Virgin Mary : Lat. *māter,* mother + Lat. *cāra,* fem. of *cārus,* dear; see **kā-** in App.]

mother cell *n.* A cell that divides to produce two or more daughter cells.

mother country *n.* **1.** The country of one's birth or one's ancestors. **2.** The country from which the settlers of a territory originally came.

moth·er·fuck·er (mŭth′ər-fŭk′ər) *n. Vulgar Slang* **1.** A person regarded as thoroughly despicable. **2.** Something regarded as thoroughly unpleasant, frustrating, or despicable. —**moth′er·fuck′ing** *adj.*

Mother Goose *n.* The imaginary author of *Mother Goose's Tales,* a collection of nursery rhymes first published in London in the 18th century.

mother hen *n.* One who fusses over others overprotectively.

moth·er·hood (mŭth′ər-hōŏd′) *n.* **1.** The state of being a mother. **2.** The qualities of a mother. **3.** Mothers considered as a group.

moth·er·house (mŭth′ər-hous′) *n.* **1.** The convent in which the mother superior of a religious community lives. **2.** The original convent of a religious community.

Mother Hub·bard (hŭb′ərd) *n.* A woman's loose unbelted dress. [Probably from illustrations of *Mother Hubbard,* character in a nursery rhyme by Sarah C. Martin (1768–1826).]

moth·er-in-law (mŭth′ər-ĭn-lô′) *n., pl.* **moth·ers-in-law** (mŭth′ərz-) **1.** The mother of one's wife or husband. **2.** *Archaic* A stepmother.

moth·er·land (mŭth′ər-lănd′) *n.* **1.** One's native land. **2.** The land of one's ancestors. **3.** A country considered as the origin of something.

moth·er·less (mŭth′ər-ləs′) *adj.* **1.** Having no living mother. **2.** Having no known mother. —**moth′er·less·ness** *n.*

mother lode *n.* **1.** The main vein of ore in a region. **2.** An abundant or rich source.

moth·er·ly (mŭth′ər-lē) *adj.* **1.** Of, like, or appropriate to a mother. **2.** Showing the affection of a mother. ❖ *adv.* In a manner befitting a mother. —**moth′er·li·ness** *n.*

Mother Nature *n.* The personification of nature as a powerful and nurturing woman.

moth·er-of-pearl (mŭth′ər-əv-pûrl′) *n.* The pearly internal

Grandma Moses

mosque
Sultanahmet Mosque, also known as the Blue Mosque; constructed 1609–16, Istanbul, Turkey

ă	pat	oi	boy
ā	pay	ou	out
âr	care	ŏŏ	took
ä	father	ōō	boot
ĕ	pet	ŭ	cut
ē	be	ûr	urge
ĭ	pit	th	thin
ī	pie	*th*	this
îr	pier	hw	which
ŏ	pot	zh	vision
ō	toe	ə	about,
ô	paw		item

Stress marks:
′ (primary);
′ (secondary), as in
lexicon (lĕk′sĭ-kŏn′)

layer of certain mollusk shells, used to make decorative objects. —**moth′er-of-pearl′** *adj.*

Moth·er's Day (mŭth′ərz) *n.* The second Sunday in May, observed in the United States in honor of mothers.

mother superior *n., pl.* **mothers superior** or **mother superiors** A woman in charge of a religious community of women.

mother tongue *n.* **1.** One's native language. **2.** A parent language.

Moth·er·well (mŭth′ər-wĕl′), **Robert** 1915–91. Amer. artist noted for his abstract expressionist paintings.

mother wit *n.* Innate intelligence or common sense.

moth·er·wort (mŭth′ər-wûrt′, -wôrt′) *n.* Any of several Eurasian plants of the genus *Leonurus,* esp. *L. cardiaca,* a weed with small purple or pink flowers. [ME *moderwort* : *moder,* mother, womb (< its use in treating diseases of the uterus); see MOTHER[1] + *wort,* wort; see WORT[1].]

moth·proof (môth′proof′, mŏth′-) *adj.* Resistant to damage by moths. ❖ *tr.v.* **-proofed, -proof·ing, -proofs** To make resistant to damage by moths.

moth·y (mô′thē, mŏth′ē) *adj.* **-i·er, -i·est** **1.** Infested by moths. **2.** Moth-eaten.

mo·tif (mō-tēf′) *n.* **1a.** A recurrent thematic element in an artistic or literary work. **b.** A dominant theme or central idea. **2.** *Music* A short passage that is repeated or evoked in a composition. **3.** A repeated figure or design in architecture or decoration. [Fr. < OFr., motive. See MOTIVE.]

motor scooter

mo·tile (mōt′l, mō′tīl′) *adj.* **1.** *Biology* Moving or having the power to move spontaneously. **2.** *Psychology* Of mental imagery that arises primarily from sensations of bodily movement and position. [Lat. *mōtus,* motion < p. part. of *movēre,* to move; see MOTION + –ILE[1].] —**mo·til′i·ty** (mō-tĭl′ĭ-tē) *n.*

mo·tion (mō′shən) *n.* **1.** The act or process of changing position or place. **2.** A meaningful or expressive change in the position of the body or a part of the body; a gesture. **3.** Active operation: *set the plan in motion.* **4.** The ability or power to move. **5.** The manner in which the body moves, as in walking. **6.** A prompting from within; an impulse or inclination. **7.** *Music* Melodic ascent and descent of pitch. **8.** *Law* An application made to a court for an order or ruling. **9.** A formal proposal put to the vote under parliamentary procedures. **10a.** A mechanical device or piece of machinery that moves or causes motion; a mechanism. **b.** The movement or action of such a device. ❖ *v.* **-tioned, -tion·ing, -tions** —*tr.* To direct by making a gesture. —*intr.* To signal by making a gesture. —*idiom:* **go through the motions** To do something without interest or involvement. [ME *mocioun* < OFr. *motion* < Lat. *mōtiō, mōtiōn-* < *mōtus,* p. part. of *movēre,* to move.]

mo·tion·less (mō′shən-lĭs) *adj.* Having or making no motion. —**mo′tion·less·ly** *adv.* —**mo′tion·less·ness** *n.*

motion picture *n.* **1.** A movie. **2.** **motion pictures** The movie industry. —**mo′tion-pic′ture** (mō′shən-pĭk′chər) *adj.*

motion sickness *n.* Nausea and dizziness induced by motion, as in travel by aircraft, car, or ship.

motion study *n.* See **time and motion study.**

mo·ti·vate (mō′tə-vāt′) *tr.v.* **-vat·ed, -vat·ing, -vates** To provide with an incentive; move to action; impel. —**mo′ti·va′tor** *n.*

mo·ti·va·tion (mō′tə-vā′shən) *n.* **1a.** The act or process of motivating. **b.** The state of being motivated. **2.** Something that motivates; an inducement. —**mo′ti·va′tion·al** *adj.*

mo·tive (mō′tĭv) *n.* **1.** An emotion, desire, physiological need, or similar impulse that acts as an incitement to action. **2.** (mō′tĭv, mō-tēv′) A motif in art, literature, or music. ❖ *adj.* **1.** Causing or able to cause motion: *motive power.* **2.** Impelling to action. **3.** Of or constituting an incitement to action. ❖ *tr.v.* **-tived, -tiv·ing, -tives** To motivate. [ME *motif, motive* < OFr. *motif* < LLat. *mōtīvus,* of motion < Lat. *mōtus,* p. part. of *movēre,* to move.]

mo·tiv·ic (mō-tĭv′ĭk′) *adj. Music* Of or relating to a motif.

mo·ti·vi·ty (mō-tĭv′ĭ-tē) *n., pl.* **-ties** The power of moving or causing motion.

mot juste (mō zhüst′) *n., pl.* **mots justes** (mō zhüst′) Exactly the right word or expression. [Fr. : *mot,* word + *juste,* right.]

mot·ley (mŏt′lē) *adj.* **1.** Having elements of great variety or incongruity; heterogeneous. **2.** Having many colors; parti-colored. ❖ *n., pl.* **-leys** **1.** The parti-colored attire of a court jester. **2.** A heterogeneous, often incongruous mixture of elements. [ME *motlei,* variegated cloth, variegated, prob. < AN, prob. < ME *mot,* speck. See MOTE[1].]

mot·mot (mŏt′mŏt′) *n.* Any of several tropical American birds of the family Momotidae, usu. having green and blue plumage. [NLat. *motmot,* prob. of imit. orig.]

mo·to·cross (mō′tō-krôs′, -krŏs′) *n.* A cross-country motorcycle race over rough terrain. [Fr. *moto-cross* : *moto,* motorcycle (short for *motocyclette* < *moto-,* motor < *moteur* < Lat. *mōtor,* mover; see MOTOR) + E. CROSS(-COUNTRY).]

mo·to·neu·ron (mō′tə-nŏŏr′ŏn′, -nyŏŏr′-) *n.* A motor neuron. [MOTO(R) + NEURON.]

mouflon

male mouflon
Ovis musimon

mo·tor (mō′tər) *n.* **1.** Something, such as an engine, that produces or imparts motion. **2.** A device that converts any form of energy into mechanical energy, as an internal-combustion engine. **3.** A motor vehicle, esp. an automobile. ❖ *adj.* **1.** Causing or producing motion. **2.** Driven by or having a motor. **3.** Of or for motors or motor vehicles: *motor oil.* **4.** Of, relating to, or being nerves that carry impulses to the muscles. **5.** Involving or relating to movements of the muscles: *motor coordination.* ❖ *v.* **-tored, -tor·ing, -tors** —*intr.* To drive or travel in a motor vehicle. —*tr.* To carry by motor vehicle. [ME *motour,* prime mover < Lat. *mōtor* < *mōtus,* p. part. of *movēre,* to move.]

mo·tor·bike (mō′tər-bīk′) *n.* **1.** A lightweight motorcycle. **2.** A pedal bicycle that has an attached motor.

mo·tor·boat (mō′tər-bōt′) *n.* A boat propelled by an internal-combustion engine or other motor.

mo·tor·bus (mō′tər-bŭs′) *n., pl.* **-bus·es** or **-bus·ses** A passenger bus powered by a motor.

mo·tor·cade (mō′tər-kād′) *n.* A procession of motor vehicles, as in a parade. —**mo′tor·cade′** *v.*

mo·tor·car (mō′tər-kär′) *n.* See **automobile.**

motor court *n.* See **motel.**

mo·tor·cy·cle (mō′tər-sī′kəl) *n.* A two-wheeled motor vehicle resembling a heavy bicycle. [MOTOR + (BI)CYCLE.] —**mo′tor·cy′cle** *v.* —**mo′tor·cy′clist** *n.*

motor drive *n.* A system consisting of an electric motor and accessory parts, used to power machinery.

motor home *n.* A motor vehicle built on a truck or bus chassis and designed to serve as living quarters for recreational travel.

motor inn *n.* An urban motel usu. having several stories.

mo·tor·ist (mō′tər-ĭst) *n.* One who drives or travels in an automotive vehicle.

mo·tor·ize (mō′tə-rīz′) *tr.v.* **-ized, -iz·ing, -iz·es** **1.** To equip with a motor. **2.** To supply with motor-driven vehicles. **3.** To provide with automobiles. —**mo′tor·i·za′tion** (-tər-ĭ-zā′shən) *n.*

motor lodge *n.* See **motel.**

mo·tor·man (mō′tər-mən) *n.* One who drives an electrically powered streetcar, locomotive, or subway train.

motor mouth *n. Slang* An incessant talker.

motor neuron *n.* A neuron that conveys impulses from the central nervous system to muscular or other effector tissue.

motor pool *n.* A centrally managed group of motor vehicles for the use of personnel, as of a governmental agency.

motor scooter *n.* A usu. two-wheeled vehicle with small wheels and a low-powered gasoline engine geared to the rear wheel.

motor vehicle *n.* A self-propelled wheeled conveyance, such as a car or truck, that does not run on rails.

mo·tor·way (mō′tər-wā′) *n. Chiefly British* A superhighway.

Mott (mŏt), **John Raleigh** 1865–1955. Amer. religious leader who shared the 1946 Nobel Peace Prize.

Mott, Lucretia Coffin 1793–1880. Amer. feminist and abolitionist who with Elizabeth Cady Stanton called the first convention for women's rights, held at Seneca Falls NY (1848).

motte[1] also **mott** (mŏt) *n. Texas* A copse or small stand of trees on a prairie. [Am.Sp. *mata* < Sp., shrub, prob. < LLat. *matta,* mat. See MAT[1].]

motte[2] also **mott** (mŏt) *n. Upper Southern US* A tuft of human or animal hair standing up on the head or body. [< Fr. < OFr. *mote,* mound.]

mot·tle (mŏt′l) *tr.v.* **-tled, -tling, -tles** To mark with spots or blotches of different shades or colors. ❖ *n.* **1.** A spot or blotch of color. **2.** A variegated pattern, as on marble. [Prob. back-formation < MOTLEY.] —**mot′tled** *adj.* —**mot′tler** *n.*

mot·to (mŏt′ō) *n., pl.* **-toes** or **-tos** **1.** A brief statement used to express a principle, goal, or ideal. **2.** An appropriate sentence, phrase, or word inscribed on or attached to an object. **3.** A maxim that guides one's conduct. [Ital., word, motto, prob. < VLat. *mōttum,* word. See MOT.]

mouch (mooch) *v. Chiefly British* Variant of **mooch.**

moue (moo) *n.* A small grimace; a pout. [Fr. < OFr. *moe,* of Gmc. orig.]

mou·flon also **mouf·lon** (moof′lŏn′) *n., pl.* **mouflon** or **-flons** also **moufflon** or **-flons** A small wild European sheep (*Ovis musimon*) native to Sardinia and Corsica and having large curving horns in the male. [Fr., alteration of Ital. dialectal *muvrone* < LLat. *mufrō, mufrōn-.*]

mouil·lé (moo-yā′) *adj.* Pronounced as a palatal sound, as the *ll* in French *fille.* [Fr., p. part. of *mouiller,* to moisten, palatalize < OFr. *moillier,* to soften by soaking. See MOIL.]

mou·jik (moo-zhēk′, -zhĭk′) *n.* Variant of **muzhik.**

mou·lage (moo-läzh′) *n.* **1.** A mold, as of a footprint, for use in a criminal investigation. **2.** The making of a moulage. [Fr. < earlier *mollage,* wood inspection fee < OFr. *molle,* mold. See MOLD[1].]

mould[1] (mōld) *n. & v. Chiefly British* Variant of **mold**[1].

mould[2] (mōld) *n. & v. Chiefly British* Variant of **mold**[2].

mould[3] (mōld) *n. Chiefly British* Variant of **mold**[3].

moul·der (mōl′dər) *v. Chiefly British* Variant of **molder.**

mould·ing (mōl′dĭng) *n. Chiefly British* Variant of **molding.**

mould·y (mōl′dē) *adj. Chiefly British* Variant of **moldy.**

mou·lin (moo-lăn′) *n.* A nearly vertical cavity worn in a glacier by surface or rock debris falling through a crack. [Fr. < OFr. *molin,* mill < LLat. *molīnum.* See MILL[1].]

Moul·mein (mool-mān′, mōl-) A city of S Myanmar (Burma) on the Gulf of Martaban E of Yangon. Pop. 219,991.

moult (mōlt) *v. & n. Chiefly British* Variant of **molt.**

mound (mound) *n.* **1.** A pile of earth, gravel, sand, rocks, or debris heaped for protection or concealment. **2.** A natural elevation, such as a small hill. **3.** A raised mass; a heap. **4.** *Archaeology* A large artificial pile of earth or stones often marking a burial site. **5.** *Baseball* The slightly elevated pitcher's area in the center of the diamond. ❖ *tr.v.* **mound·ed, mound·ing, mounds 1.** To fortify or conceal with a mound. **2.** To heap into a raised mass. [?]

mound·bird (mound′bûrd′) *n.* See **megapode**.

mound builder *n.* See **megapode**.

Mound Builder *n.* A member of any of various Native American peoples flourishing from around the 5th century B.C. to the 16th century A.D. esp. in the Ohio and Mississippi valleys, known for their often large burial and effigy mounds.

mount[1] (mount) *v.* **mount·ed, mount·ing, mounts** —*tr.* **1.** To climb or ascend: *mount stairs.* **2.** To place oneself upon; get up on: *mount a horse.* **3.** To climb onto (a female) for copulation. Used of male animals. **4a.** To furnish with a horse for riding. **b.** To set on a horse. **5.** To set in a raised position. **6a.** To fix securely to a support: *mount an engine in a car.* **b.** To place or fix on or in a support or setting for display or study: *mount stamps in an album.* **7.** To provide with scenery and other equipment necessary for production. **8.** To organize and equip: *mount an army.* **9.** To prepare and set in motion: *mount an attack.* **10a.** To set in position for use. **b.** To carry as equipment. **11.** To post (a guard). —*intr.* **1.** To go upward; rise. **2.** To get up on something, such as a horse. **3.** To increase in amount, extent, or intensity. ❖ *n.* **1.** The act or manner of mounting. **2.** A means of conveyance, such as a horse, on which to ride. **3.** An opportunity to ride a horse in a race. **4.** An object to which another is affixed or on which another is placed for accessibility, display, or use, esp.: **a.** A glass slide for use with a microscope. **b.** A hinge used to fasten stamps in an album. **c.** A setting for a jewel. **d.** An undercarriage or stand on which a device rests while in service. [ME *mounten* < OFr. *monter* < VLat. *montāre* < Lat. *mōns, mont-,* mountain.] —**mount′a·ble** *adj.* —**mount′er** *n.*

mount[2] (mount) *n.* **1.** A mountain or hill. Used esp. as part of a proper name. **2.** Any of the seven fleshy cushions around the edges of the palm of the hand in palmistry. [ME *mont* < OE *munt* and < OFr. *mont, munt,* both < Lat. *mōns, mont-.*]

moun·tain (moun′tən) *n.* **1.** A natural elevation of the earth's surface having considerable mass, generally steep sides, and a height greater than that of a hill. **2a.** A large heap. **b.** A huge quantity. [ME *mountaine* < OFr. *montaigne, muntaigne,* ult. < Lat. *montānus* < *mōns, mont-,* mountain.] —**moun′tain·y** *adj.*

mountain ash *n.* Any of various deciduous trees of the genus *Sorbus,* having small white flowers and orange-red berries.

mountain avens *n.* A creeping evergreen plant (*Dryas octopetala*) in the rose family, having flowers with white petals.

mountain bike *n.* A sturdy bicycle distinguished by wide tires and horizontal handlebars, often used for off-road cycling. —**mountain biking** *n.*

mountain bluebird *n.* A bluebird (*Sialia currucoides*) of the western United States having a light blue breast.

mountain cat *n.* See **mountain lion**.

mountain cranberry *n.* See **cowberry**.

mountain dew *n.* Illegally distilled corn liquor.

moun·tain·eer (moun′tə-nîr′) *n.* **1.** A native or inhabitant of a mountainous area. **2.** One who climbs mountains for sport. ❖ *intr.v.* **-eered, -eer·ing, -eers** To climb mountains for sport. —**moun′tain·eer′ing** *n.*

mountain goat *n.* A goat antelope (*Oreamnos americanus*) of the northwest North American mountains having curved black horns and shaggy yellowish-white hair.

mountain laurel *n.* An evergreen shrub (*Kalmia latifolia*) of eastern North America having leathery poisonous leaves and clusters of pink or white flowers.

mountain lion *n. Chiefly Western US* A large powerful wild cat (*Felis concolor*) of mountainous regions of the Western Hemisphere having an unmarked tawny body.

moun·tain·ous (moun′tə-nəs) *adj.* **1.** Having many mountains. **2.** Resembling a mountain in size; huge.

mountain range *n.* A series of mountain ridges alike in form, direction, and origin.

mountain sheep *n.* **1.** See **bighorn**. **2.** A wild sheep inhabiting a mountainous area.

mountain sickness *n.* Altitude sickness brought on by the diminished oxygen pressure at mountain elevations.

moun·tain·side (moun′tən-sīd′) *n.* The side of a mountain.

Mountain Standard Time *n.* Standard time in the seventh time zone west of Greenwich, England, reckoned at 105° west and used in the Rocky Mountain states of the United States.

moun·tain·top (moun′tən-tŏp′) *n.* A mountain summit.

Mount Ath·os (ăth′ŏs, ā′thŏs, ā′thôs) See **Athos**.

Mount·bat·ten (mount-băt′n), Louis. 1st Earl Mountbatten of Burma. 1900–79. British naval officer who was Allied commander in SE Asia (1943–46) and the last viceroy and governor-general of India (1947).

Mount Des·ert Island (dĕz′ərt) A resort island in the Atlantic Ocean off the S coast of ME.

moun·te·bank (moun′tə-băngk′) *n.* **1.** A hawker of quack medicines who attracts customers with stories, jokes, or tricks. **2.** A flamboyant charlatan. ❖ *v.* **-banked, -bank·ing, -banks**

—*intr.* To act as a mountebank. —*tr. Archaic* To ensnare or prevail over with trickery. [Ital. *montambanco* < the phrase *monta im banco,* one gets up onto the bench : *monta,* third pers. sing. pr. t. of *montare,* to get up (< VLat. **montāre;* see MOUNT[1]) + *in,* on, onto (< Lat.; see IN–[2]) + *banco,* bench (var. of *banca* < OItal., bench, table < OHGer. *bank*).]

Mount·ie also **Mount·y** (moun′tē) *n., pl.* **-ies** *Informal* A member of the Royal Canadian Mounted Police.

mount·ing (moun′tĭng) *n.* Something that serves as a support, backing, or backing.

Mount Ver·non (vûr′nən) An estate of NE VA on the Potomac R. near Washington DC; built in 1743 and the home of George Washington from 1752 until his death in 1799.

mourn (môrn, mōrn) *v.* **mourned, mourn·ing, mourns** —*intr.* **1.** To feel or express grief or sorrow. See Syns at **grieve. 2.** To show grief for a death by conventional signs, as by wearing black. **3.** To make a low, indistinct mournful sound. Used esp. of a dove. —*tr.* **1.** To feel or express deep regret for. **2.** To grieve over (the dead). **3.** To utter sorrowfully. [ME *mournen* < OE *murnan.* See **(s)mer-** in App.] —**mourn′er** *n.* —**mourn′ing·ly** *adv.*

mourn·ful (môrn′fəl, mōrn′-) *adj.* **1.** Feeling or expressing sorrow or grief; sorrowful. **2.** Expressing or suggesting sadness or melancholy. —**mourn′ful·ly** *adv.* —**mourn′ful·ness** *n.*

mourn·ing (môr′nĭng, mōr′-) *n.* **1.** The actions or expressions of one who has suffered a bereavement. **2.** Conventional outward signs of grief for the dead, such as a black armband. **3.** The period during which a death is mourned.

mourning cloak *n.* A large butterfly (*Nymphalis antiopa*) of Europe and North America having purplish-brown wings with a broad yellow border.

mourning dove *n.* A grayish-brown wild dove (*Zenaidura macroura*) of North America noted for its mournful call.

mourning warbler *n.* A yellow and olive warbler (*Oporornis philadelphia*) of eastern North America having a bluish-gray hood set off by a black band on its breast.

mouse (mous) *n., pl.* **mice** (mīs) **1a.** Any of numerous small rodents of the families Muridae and Cricetidae, such as the common house mouse (*Mus musculus*), characteristically having a pointed snout, small rounded ears, and a long tail. **b.** Any of various similar or related animals, such as the jumping mouse or the vole. **2.** A cowardly or timid person. **3.** *Informal* A discolored swelling under the eye caused by a blow; a black eye. **4.** *pl.* **mice** or **mous·es** (mous′ĭz) *Computer Science* A hand-held, button-activated input device that when rolled along a flat surface directs an indicator to move correspondingly about a computer screen. ❖ *intr.v.* (mouz) **moused, mous·ing, mous·es 1.** To hunt mice. **2.** To search furtively for something; prowl. [ME *mous* < OE *mūs.* See **mūs-** in App.]

mouse deer *n.* See **chevrotain**. [Prob. alteration of MUSK DEER (influenced by MOUSE, from its small size).]

mouse-ear chickweed (mous′îr′) *n.* Any of numerous herbs of the genus *Cerastium,* having opposite leaves and cylindrical capsules with ten toothlike projections.

mouse·pad or **mouse pad** (mous′păd′) *n. Computer Science* A flat pad, as of coated foam rubber, on which a mouse is used.

mous·er (mou′zər, -sər) *n.* An animal, esp. a cat, that catches mice.

mouse-tail (mous′tāl′) *n.* A plant of the genus *Myosurus,* esp. *M. minimus,* having a taillike flower spike.

mouse·trap (mous′trăp′) *n.* A trap for catching mice. ❖ *tr.v.* **-trapped, -trap·ping, -traps** To trap or ensnare.

mous·ing (mou′zĭng) *n. Nautical* A binding or metal shackle around the point and shank of a hook to prevent it from slipping from an eye. [< MOUSE, mouselike rope knot.]

mous·sa·ka (moo-sä′kə, moo′sä-kä′) *n.* A Greek dish consisting of layers of ground lamb or beef and sliced eggplant topped with a cheese sauce and baked. [Serbo-Croatian < Turk. *mus-sakka* < colloquial Egypt. Ar. *musaqqa'a,* to chill, moussaka, fem. passive part. of *saqqa'a,* to chill, var. of *saqqa'a < saq'a,* cold, frost < *saqi'a,* to be white.]

mousse (moos) *n.* **1.** A chilled dessert made with flavored whipped cream, gelatin, and eggs. **2.** A molded dish containing meat, fish, or shellfish combined with whipped cream and gelatin. **3.** An aerosol foam used to style the hair. ❖ *tr.v.* **moussed, mouss·ing, mouss·es** To apply a mousse to (the hair). [Fr., foam, mousse < OFr., foam, mousse, partly of Gmc. orig. and partly < Lat. *mulsa,* hydromel < fem. of *mulsus,* honey-sweet; see **melit-** in App.]

mousse·line (moos-lēn′) *n.* **1.** A fine sheer fabric resembling muslin, originally made in Mosul, Iraq. **2.** A hollandaise sauce or an aspic containing whipped cream. [Fr. See MUSLIN.]

mousseline de soie (də swä′) *n., pl.* **mousse·lines de soie** (moos-lēn′) A fine crisp fabric made of silk or rayon. [Fr. : *mousseline,* muslin + *de,* of + *soie,* silk.]

mous·tache (mŭs′tăsh′, mə-stăsh′) *n.* Variant of **mustache**.

Mous·te·ri·an (moo-stîr′ē-ən) *adj.* Of or being a Middle Paleolithic culture associated with Neanderthals and marked by the use of flake tools. [Fr. *moustérien,* after *Le Moustier,* cave in southwest France.]

mous·y also **mous·ey** (mou′sē, -zē) *adj.* **-i·er, -i·est 1.** Resembling a mouse, esp.: **a.** Having a drab pale brown color: *mousy*

mountain ash
European mountain ash
Sorbus aucuparia

mountain goat
Oreamnos americanus

ă	pat	oi	boy
ā	pay	ou	out
âr	care	oŏ	took
ä	father	oō	boot
ĕ	pet	ŭ	cut
ē	be	ûr	urge
ĭ	pit	th	thin
ī	pie	*th*	this
îr	pier	hw	which
ŏ	pot	zh	vision
ō	toe	ə	about,
ô	paw		item

Stress marks:
′ (primary);
′ (secondary); as in
lexicon (lĕk′sĭ-kŏn′)

hair. **b.** Having small sharp features: *a mousy face.* **c.** Quiet; timid; shy. **2.** Infested with mice.

mouth (mouth) *n., pl.* **mouths** (mouth*z*) **1a.** The body opening through which an animal takes in food. **b.** The cavity lying at the upper end of the alimentary canal, bounded on the outside by the lips and inside by the oropharynx and containing in higher vertebrates the tongue, gums, and teeth. **c.** This cavity regarded as the source of sounds and speech. **d.** The opening to any cavity or canal in an organ or a body part. **2.** The part of the lips visible on the human face. **3.** A person viewed as a consumer of food: *has three mouths to feed at home.* **4.** A pout, grimace, or similar expression. **5a.** Utterance; voice: *gave mouth to her doubts.* **b.** A tendency to talk excessively or unwisely. **c.** Impudent or vulgar talk: *Watch your mouth.* **6.** A spokesperson; a mouthpiece. **7.** A natural opening, as the entrance to a harbor or canyon. **8.** The opening through which a container is filled or emptied. **9.** The opening between the jaws of a vise or other holding or gripping tool. **10.** *Music* **a.** An opening in the pipe of an organ. **b.** The opening in the mouthpiece of a flute across which the player blows. ❖ *v.* (mou*th*) **mouthed, mouth•ing, mouths** —*tr.* **1.** To speak or pronounce, esp.: **a.** To declare in a pompous manner; declaim. **b.** To utter without conviction or understanding: *mouthing empty compliments.* **c.** To form soundlessly: *I mouthed the words as the others sang.* **d.** To utter indistinctly; mumble. **2.** To take or move around in the mouth. —*intr.* **1.** To orate affectedly; declaim. **2.** To grimace. ***—phrasal verb:*** **mouth off** *Slang* **1.** To express one's opinions or complaints in a loud, indiscreet manner. **2.** To speak impudently; talk back. ***—idiom:*** **down in** (or **at**) **the mouth** Discouraged; sad; dejected. [ME < OE *mūth.*]

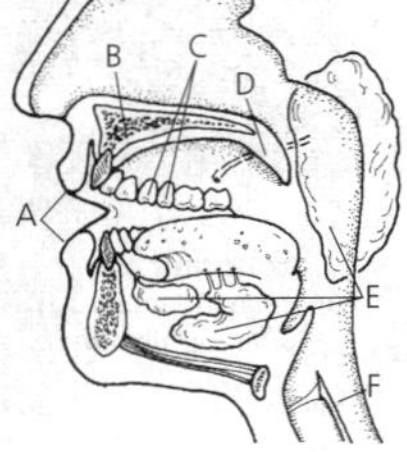

mouth
A. lips
B. hard palate
C. teeth
D. soft palate
E. salivary glands
F. esophagus

mouth•breed•er (mouth′brē′dər) *n.* Any of various fishes, esp. of the genera *Haplochromis* and *Tilapia,* that carry their eggs and young in the mouth.

mouth•ful (mouth′fo͝ol′) *n.* **1.** The amount of food or other material that can be held in the mouth at one time. **2.** A small amount to be tasted or eaten. **3.** A long word, name, or phrase that is difficult to pronounce. **4.** An important or perceptive remark.

mouth harp *n.* See **harmonica** 1.

mouth organ *n.* **1.** See **harmonica** 1. **2.** See **panpipe.**

mouth•part (mouth′pärt′) *n.* Any of the parts of the mouth of an insect or other arthropod, esp. a part for feeding.

mouth•piece (mouth′pēs′) *n.* **1.** A part, as of a musical instrument or a telephone, that functions in or near the mouth. **2.** *Sports* A protective rubber device worn over the teeth, as by boxers. **3.** *Informal* One through which views are expressed. **4.** *Slang* A defense lawyer.

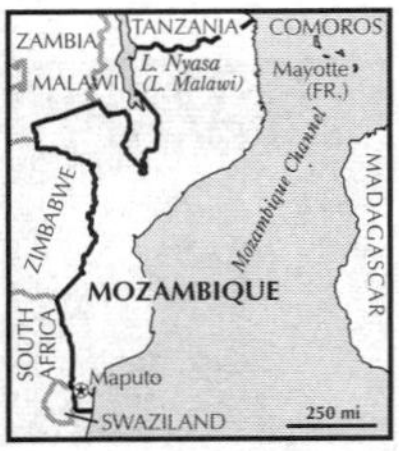

Mozambique

mouth-to-mouth resuscitation (mouth′tə-mouth′) *n.* A technique used to resuscitate a person who has stopped breathing, in which the rescuer forces air into the lungs at intervals of several seconds.

mouth•wash (mouth′wŏsh′, -wôsh′) *n.* A flavored, usu. antiseptic solution for cleaning the mouth and freshening the breath.

mouth•wa•ter•ing or **mouth-wa•ter•ing** (mouth′wô′tər-ĭng) *adj.* Appealing to the sense of taste; appetizing.

mouth•y (mou′*th*ē, -thē) *adj.* **-i•er, -i•est 1.** Annoyingly talkative. **2.** Given to ranting or bombast. **—mouth′i•ness** *n.*

mou•ton (mo͞o′tŏn′) *n.* Sheepskin that has been sheared and processed to resemble beaver or seal. [Fr., sheep < OFr. See MUTTON.]

mou•ton•née (mo͞o′tə-nā′) also **mou•ton•néed** (-nād′) *adj. Geology* Rounded by glacial action into a shape likened to a sheep's back. Used of a rock formation. [Short for Fr. *roche moutonnée* : *roche,* rock + *moutonnée,* fleecy, p. part. of *moutonner,* to make fleecy (< *mouton,* sheep; see MOUTON).]

mov•a•ble also **move•a•ble** (mo͞o′və-bəl) *adj.* **1.** Possible to move. **2.** Varying in date from year to year. ❖ *n.* Something, esp. a piece of furniture, that can be moved. **—mov′a•bil′i•ty, mov′a•ble•ness** *n.* **—mov′a•bly** *adv.*

movable feast *n.* A religious holiday, such as Easter, that changes in date from year to year.

movable type *n. Printing* Type in which each character is cast on a separate piece of metal.

move (mo͞ov) *v.* **moved, mov•ing, moves** —*intr.* **1.** To change in position from one point to another: *moved away from the window.* **2.** To progress in sequence; go forward: *a novel that moves slowly.* **3.** To follow a specified course: *The earth moves around the sun.* **4.** To progress toward a particular state or condition: *moving up in the company.* **5.** To go from one residence or location to another; relocate. **6.** To start off; depart. **7.** To be disposed of by sale: *Woolens move slowly in the summer.* **8.** To change posture or position; stir: *was afraid to move.* **9.** *Games* To change the position of a piece in a board game. **10.** To be put in motion or to turn according to a prescribed motion. Used of machinery. **11.** To exhibit great activity or energy. **12.** To initiate an action; act. **13.** To be active in a particular environment: *moves in diplomatic circles.* **14.** To stir the emotions: *words that have the power to move.* **15.** To make a formal motion in parliamentary procedure: *move for an adjournment.* **16.** To evacuate. Used of the bowels. —*tr.* **1.** To change the place or position of: *moved her office; could not move his arm.* **2.** To cause to go from one place to another: *moved the crowd away.* **3.** *Games* To change (a piece) from one position to another in a board game: *moved a pawn.* **4.** To change the course of: *moved the discussion to other matters.* **5.** To dislodge from a fixed point of view, as by persuasion: *"Speak to him, ladies, see if you can move him"* (Shakespeare). **6.** To prompt to an action; rouse: *Anger moved her to speak out.* **7a.** To set or keep in motion. **b.** To cause to function. **c.** To cause to progress or advance. **8a.** To arouse the emotions of; affect. **b.** To excite or provoke to the expression of an emotion: *The film moved me to tears.* **9a.** To propose or request in formal parliamentary procedure. **b.** To make formal application to (a court, for example). **10.** To dispose of by sale. **11.** To cause (the bowels) to evacuate. ❖ *n.* **1a.** The act or an instance of moving. **b.** A particular manner of moving. **2.** A change of residence or location. **3.** *Games* **a.** An act of transferring a piece from one position to another in board games. **b.** The prescribed manner in which a piece may be played. **c.** A participant's turn to make a play. **4.** An action taken to achieve an objective; a maneuver. ***—phrasal verb:*** **move in** To begin to occupy a residence or place of business. ***—idioms:*** **get a move on** *Informal* To get started; get going. **move in on 1.** To make intrusive advances toward; intrude on. **2.** To attempt to seize control of. **on the move 1.** Busily moving about; active. **2.** Going from one place to another. **3.** Making progress; advancing. [ME *moven* < OFr. *movoir* < Lat. *movēre.*]

move•ment (mo͞ov′mənt) *n.* **1a.** The act or an instance of moving; a change in place or position. **b.** A particular manner of moving. **2.** A change in the location of troops, ships, or aircraft for tactical or strategic purposes. **3a.** A series of actions and events that foster a principle or policy. **b.** An organized effort by supporters of a common goal. **4.** A tendency or trend. **5.** A change in the market price of a security or commodity. **6a.** An evacuation of the bowels. **b.** The matter so evacuated. **7.** The suggestion or illusion of motion in a painting, sculpture, or design. **8.** The progression of events in the development of a literary plot. **9.** The rhythmic or metrical structure of a poetic composition. **10.** *Music* A self-contained section of an extended composition. **11.** A mechanism, such as the works of a watch, that produces or transmits motion.

mov•er (mo͞o′vər) *n.* **1.** One that moves. **2.** One that transports household or office goods as an occupation. Often used in the plural.

mover and shaker *n., pl.* **movers and shakers** One who wields power and influence in a sphere of activity.

mov•ie (mo͞o′vē) *n.* **1a.** A sequence of images projected onto a screen with sufficient rapidity to create the illusion of motion and continuity. **b.** A cinematic narrative represented in this form. **2.** A showing of a movie. Often used in the plural: *laughed during the movie; went to the movies last night.* **3. movies** The movie industry. [Shortening and alteration of MOVING PICTURE.]

mov•ie•dom (mo͞o′vē-dəm) *n.* See **filmdom.**

mov•ie•go•er (mo͞o′vē-gō′ər) *n.* One who goes to see movies. **—mov′ie•go′ing** *adj. & n.*

mov•ie•mak•er (mo͞o′vē-mā′kər) *n.* One that makes movies, esp. professionally. **—mov′ie•mak′ing** *adj. & n.*

mov•ing (mo͞o′vĭng) *adj.* **1.** Changing or capable of changing position. **2.** Of or involved in a transfer of furnishings from one location to another. **3.** Causing or producing motion. **4.** Involving a motor vehicle in motion. **5.** Arousing or capable of arousing deep emotion. **—mov′ing•ly** *adv.*

moving picture *n.* A movie.

mow[1] (mou) *n.* **1.** The place in a barn where hay, grain, or other feed is stored. **2.** A stack of hay or other feed stored in a barn. [ME, stack of hay < OE *mūga.*]

mow[2] (mō) *v.* **mowed, mowed** or **mown** (mōn), **mow•ing, mows** —*tr.* **1.** To cut down (grass or grain) with a scythe or a mechanical device. **2.** To cut (grass or grain) from: *mow the lawn.* —*intr.* To cut down grass or other growth. ***—phrasal verb:*** **mow down 1.** To destroy in great numbers as if cutting down, as in battle. **2.** To overwhelm. [ME *mowen* < OE *māwan.* See **mē-**[2] in App.] **—mow′er** (mō′ər) *n.*

mox•a (mŏk′sə) *n.* A herbal preparation that is heated for use on acupuncture needles prior to insertion in order to enhance the effects of the treatment. [J. *mogusa* : *moeru,* to burn + *kusa,* herb.]

mox•ie (mŏk′sē) *n. Slang* **1.** The ability to face difficulty with spirit and courage. **2.** Aggressive energy; initiative. **3.** Skill; know-how. [< *Moxie,* trademark for a soft drink.]

Mo•zam•bique (mō′zəm-bēk′, -zăm-) A country of SE Africa; colonized by the Portuguese after 1505 and an overseas province from 1951 to 1975. Cap. Maputo. Pop. 16,614,000. **—Mo′zam•bi′can** (-bē′kən) *adj. & n.*

Mozambique Channel An arm of the Indian Ocean between Madagascar and the mainland of SE Africa.

Moz•ar•ab (mō-zăr′əb) *n.* One of a group of Spanish Christians who adopted certain aspects of Arab culture under Muslim rule but practiced a modified form of Christian worship. [Sp. *Mozárabe* < Ar. *musta'rib,* would-be Arab, active part. of *ista'raba,* to become an Arab, adopt Ar. customs < *'arab,* Arab.]

Moz•ar•a•bic (mō-zăr′ə-bĭk) *adj.* Of or relating to the Mozarabs, their language, or their culture. ❖ *n.* Any of the early Romance dialects spoken in the parts of the Iberian Peninsula under Moorish power and heavily influenced by Arabic.

Mo•zart (mōt′särt), **Wolfgang Amadeus** 1756–91. Austrian

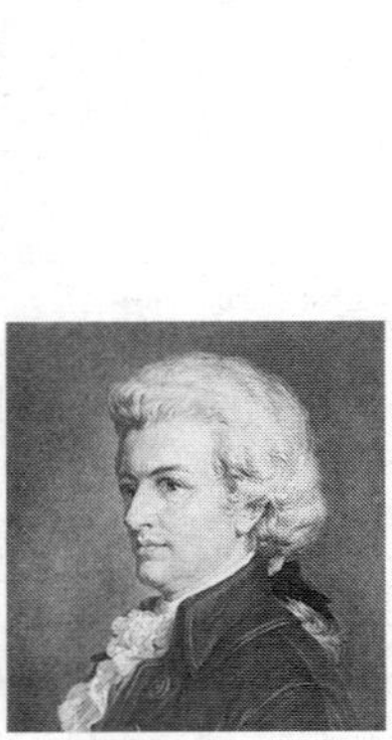

Wolfgang Amadeus Mozart
detail from an 1870 portrait by Carl Jager (1833–87)

composer whose works include *Don Giovanni* (1787).

mo·zo (mō′zō) *n., pl.* **-zos** *Southwestern US* **1.** A man who helps with a pack train or serves as a porter. **2.** An assistant. [Sp., boy, servant, mozo < OSpan. *moço*.]

moz·za·rel·la (mŏt′sə-rĕl′ə, mōt′-) *n.* A mild white Italian cheese with a rubbery texture, often eaten melted, as on pizza. [Ital., dim. of mozza < *mozzare*, to cut off < *mozzo*, mutilated < VLat. **mutius* < Lat. *mutilus.*]

moz·zet·ta or **mo·zet·ta** (mō-zĕt′ə, mōt-sĕt′tä) *n. Roman Catholic Church* A short hooded cape worn over the rochet, as by the pope. [Ital. < Med.Lat. *almutia.*]

mp *abbr.* **1.** melting point **2.** mezzo piano

MP[1] (ĕm′pē′) *n.* A military police officer. [< *m(ilitary) p(olice).*]

MP[2] *abbr.* **1.** member of Parliament **2.** military police **3.** mounted police

MP3 (ĕm′pē-thrē′) *n.* **1.** An MPEG standard used esp. for digitally transmitting music over the Internet. **2.** A digital recording stored as a file using this standard. [< *MP(EG-1 layer)* 3.]

MPA *abbr.* **1.** Master of Public Administration **2.** Master of Public Accounting

MPAA *abbr.* Motion Picture Association of America

MPE *abbr.* Master of Public Education

MPEG (ĕm′pĕg′) *n.* **1.** Any of a set of standards established for the compression of digital video and audio data. **2.** A digital recording that has been compressed using one of these standards. [*m(oving) p(ictures) e(xperts) g(roup).*]

mpg *abbr.* miles per gallon

mph *abbr.* miles per hour

MPH *abbr.* Master of Public Health

Mr. (mĭs′tər) *n., pl.* **Messrs.** (mĕs′ərz) Mister. Used as a courtesy title before the surname or full name of a man. See Usage Note at **Ms.** [ME, abbr. of *maister*, master. See MASTER.]

Mr. Char·lie (chär′lē) *n. Offensive Slang* A white person or white people considered as a group. [< the name *Charlie*, nickname for *Charles.*]

MRI *abbr.* **1.** machine-readable information **2.** magnetic resonance imaging

mRNA *abbr.* messenger RNA

Mrs. (mĭs′ĭz) *n., pl.* **Mmes.** (mā-däm′, -dăm′) **1.** Used as a courtesy title for a married or widowed woman before the surname or her husband: *Mrs. Doe; Mrs. John Doe.* **2.** Used as a courtesy title for a married, widowed, or divorced woman before her own surname or full name: *Mrs. Doe; Mrs. Jane Doe.* See Usage Note at **Ms.** [Abbreviation of MISTRESS.]

Mrs. Grun·dy (grŭn′dē) *n.* A very conventional or priggish person. [After *Mrs. Grundy*, character alluded to in the play *Speed the Plough* by Thomas Morton (1764–1838).]

ms *abbr.* **1.** or **ms.** manuscript **2.** millisecond

MS *abbr.* **1.** *Latin* Magister Scientiae (Master of Science) **2.** Mississippi **3.** multiple sclerosis

Ms. also **Ms** (mĭz) *n., pl.* **Mses.** also **Mses** also **Mss.** or **Mss** (mĭz′ĭz) Used as a courtesy title before the surname or full name of a woman or girl: *Ms. Doe; Ms. Jane Doe.* [Blend of MISS and MRS.]

USAGE NOTE Many of us think of *Ms.* or *Ms* as a fairly recent invention of the women's movement, but in fact the term was first suggested as a convenience to writers of business letters by such publications as the *Bulletin of the American Business Writing Association* (1951) and *The Simplified Letter*, issued by the National Office Management Association (1952). *Ms.* is now widely used in both professional and social contexts. As a courtesy title *Ms.* serves exactly the same function that *Mr.* does for men, and like *Mr.* it may be used with a last name alone or with a full name. Furthermore, *Ms.* is correct regardless of a woman's marital status, thus relegating that information to the realm of private life, where many feel it belongs anyway. Some women prefer *Miss* or *Mrs.*, however, and courtesy requires that their wishes be respected.

MSA *abbr.* **1.** medical savings account **2.** Metropolitan Statistical Area

MSc *abbr. Latin* Magister Scientiae (Master of Science)

MS-DOS (ĕm′ĕs-dôs′, -dŏs′) A trademark for a computer operating system.

msec *abbr.* millisecond

MSG *abbr.* monosodium glutamate

Msgr. *abbr.* **1.** Monseigneur **2.** Monsignor

MSGT or **MSgt** *abbr.* master sergeant

MSH *abbr.* melanocyte-stimulating hormone

MS in LS *abbr.* Master of Science in Library Science

MSL *abbr.* mean sea level

MSN *abbr.* Master of Science in Nursing

mss or **mss.** *abbr.* manuscripts

MST *abbr.* Mountain Standard Time

MSW *abbr.* **1.** Master of Social Welfare **2.** Master of Social Work

Mt[1] The symbol for the element **meitnerium.**

Mt[2] *abbr. Bible* Matthew

MT *abbr.* **1.** machine translation **2.** megaton **3.** metric ton **4.** Montana **5.** Mountain Time

Mt. *abbr.* **1.** mount **2.** mountain

mtg. *abbr.* **1.** meeting **2.** or **mtge.** mortgage

Mtn. *abbr.* mountain

Mts. *abbr.* mountains

mu (myōō, mōō) *n.* The 12th letter of the Greek alphabet. [Gk. *mū* < Phoenician **mēm*, water, 13th letter of the Phoenician alphabet (influenced by *nū*, nu).]

Mu·bar·ak (mōō-bär′ək), **Hosni** b. 1929. Egyptian politician who was appointed president after the assassination of Anwar el-Sadat (1981).

muc– *pref.* Variant of **muco–.**

much (mŭch) *adj.* **more** (môr, mōr), **most** (mōst) Great in quantity, degree, or extent: *not much rain; much affection.* ❖ *n.* **1.** A large quantity or amount: *Much has been written.* **2.** Something great or remarkable: *The campus wasn't much to look at.* ❖ *adv.* **more, most 1.** To a great degree or extent: *much smarter.* **2.** Just about; almost: *much the same.* **3.** Frequently; often: *doesn't get out much.* **—idiom:** as much Almost the same: *She said as much.* [ME *muche*, short for *muchel* < OE *mycel.* See **meg-** in App.]

much as *conj.* However much.

much less *conj.* And certainly not: *"Happiness is an emotion not often spoken of at the magazine, much less experienced"* (Brendan Gill).

much·ness (mŭch′nĭs) *n.* Greatness of quantity, degree, or extent.

mu·cic acid (myōō′sĭk) *n.* An organic acid, $C_6H_{10}O_8$, often derived from milk sugar.

mu·cif·er·ous (myōō-sĭf′ər-əs) *adj.* Secreting, producing, or containing mucus.

mu·ci·lage (myōō′sə-lĭj) *n.* **1.** A sticky substance used as an adhesive. **2.** A gummy substance obtained from certain plants. [ME *muscilage*, gelatinous plant substance < OFr. *mucilage* < LLat. *mūcilāgō, mūcilāgin-* < Lat. *mūcēre*, to be musty < *mūcus*, mucus.]

mu·ci·lag·i·nous (myōō′sə-lăj′ə-nəs) *adj.* **1.** Resembling mucilage; moist and sticky. **2.** Of or secreting mucilage.

mu·cin (myōō′sĭn) *n.* Any of a group of glycoproteins produced esp. by mucous membranes. —**mu′cin·ous** *adj.*

muck (mŭk) *n.* **1.** A moist sticky mixture, esp. of mud and filth. **2.** Moist farmyard dung; manure. **3.** Dark fertile soil containing decaying vegetable matter. **4.** Something filthy or disgusting. **5.** Earth, rocks, or clay excavated in mining. ❖ *tr.v.* **mucked, muck·ing, mucks 1.** To fertilize with manure or compost. **2.** To make dirty with or as if with muck. **3.** To remove muck or dirt from (a mine, for example). —**phrasal verbs: muck about** *Chiefly British* To spend time idly; putter. **muck up** *Informal* To bungle, damage, or ruin. [ME *muk*, of Scand. orig.] —**muck′i·ly** *adv.* —**muck′y** *adj.*

muck·a·muck (mŭk′ə-mŭk′) also **muck·e·ty-muck** (mŭk′ə-tē-) *n. Slang* A high muckamuck.

muck·rake (mŭk′rāk′) *intr.v.* **-raked, -rak·ing, -rakes** To search for and expose misconduct in public life. [< the man with the *muckrake*, tool for raking muck, who cannot look up to heaven because of his obsession with the muck of worldly profit, in *Pilgrim's Progress* by John Bunyan.] —**muck′rak′er** *n.*

muck·worm (mŭk′wûrm′) *n.* Any wormlike insect larva, as of certain beetles, that lives and grows in manure.

muco– or **muci–** or **muc–** *pref.* **1.** Mucus: mucoprotein. **2.** Mucosa: mucin. [< Lat. *mūcus*, mucus.]

mu·coid (myōō′koid′) *n.* Any of various glycoproteins similar to the mucins. ❖ *adj.* Of, relating to, or resembling mucus.

mu·co·lyt·ic (myōō′kə-lĭt′ĭk) *adj.* Breaking down or hydrolyzing mucus or glycosaminoglycans.

mu·co·pol·y·sac·cha·ride (myōō′kō-pŏl′ē-săk′ə-rīd′) *n.* See glycosaminoglycan.

mu·co·pro·tein (myōō′kō-prō′tēn′, -prō′tē-ĭn) *n.* Any of a group of organic compounds, such as the mucins, that consist of a complex of proteins and glycosaminoglycans.

mu·co·pu·ru·lent (myōō′kō-pyōōr′ə-lənt, -yə-lənt) *adj.* Containing mucus and pus.

mu·co·sa (myōō-kō′sə) *n., pl.* **-sae** (-sē) or **-sas** See **mucous membrane.** [< Lat. *mūcōsa*, fem. of *mūcōsus*, mucous. See MUCOUS.] —**mu·co′sal** *adj.*

mu·cous (myōō′kəs) *adj.* **1.** Containing, producing, or secreting mucus. **2.** Relating to, consisting of, or resembling mucus. [Lat. *mūcōsus* < *mūcus*, mucus.]

mucous membrane *n.* A mucus-secreting membrane lining all body passages that communicate with the air.

mu·cro (myōō′krō) *n., pl.* **mu·cro·nes** (myōō-krō′nēz) A sharp, pointed part or organ, esp. a sharp terminal point, as of a leaf or shell. [Lat. *mūcrō, mūcrōn-*, sharp point.]

mu·cro·nate (myōō′krə-nāt′) *adj.* Of or having a mucro; ending abruptly in a sharp point. —**mu′cro·na′tion** *n.*

mu·cus (myōō′kəs) *n.* The viscous slippery substance that consists chiefly of mucin, water, cells, and inorganic salts and is secreted as a protective lubricant coating by cells and glands of the mucous membranes. [Lat. *mūcus.*]

mud (mŭd) *n.* **1.** Wet sticky soft earth. **2.** *Slang* Wet plaster, mortar, or cement. **3.** Slanderous or defamatory charges or comments. ❖ *tr.v.* **mud·ded, mud·ding, muds** To cover or spatter with or as if with mud. [ME *mudde*, prob. < MLGer. and MDu. *modde.*]

MUD (mŭd) *n.* A computer program, usu. running over the Internet, that allows multiple users to participate in virtual-reality

---

Hosni Mubarak

Mudéjar
tower of the Church of Our
Savior, Teruel, Spain

mule[1]

mule[2]
pair of mules

role-playing games. [*m(ulti-)u(ser) d(ungeon), m(ulti-)u(ser) d(i-mension),* and *m(ulti-)u(ser) d(omain).*] —**MUD′der** *n.* —**MUD′-ding** *n.*

mud·bug (mŭd′bŭg′) *n.* See **crayfish** 1.

mud cat *n. Chiefly Southern US* See **catfish**.

mud dauber *n. Midland & Western US* Any of various wasps that build nests of mud with cellular compartments for eggs and paralyzed prey.

> **REGIONAL NOTE** There is no nationwide name for the wasp that makes itself a nest of mud. In the South, it is known as a *dirt dauber.* In the Northeast, and also scattered throughout the Midwest, it is a *mud wasp.* In between, in the Midlands, and also in the West, it has an in-between name, combining the first word of the Northern name and the last word of the Southern one to make *mud dauber.* One kind of mud-nesting wasp is also known as a *potter wasp.*

mud·der (mŭd′ər) *n.* A racehorse that runs well on a wet or muddy track.

mud·dle (mŭd′l) *v.* **-dled, -dling, -dles** —*tr.* **1.** To make turbid or muddy. **2.** To mix confusedly; jumble. **3.** To confuse or befuddle (the mind). See Syns at **confuse. 4.** To mismanage or bungle. **5.** To stir or mix (a drink) gently. —*intr.* To think, act, or proceed in a confused or aimless manner. ❖ *n.* **1.** A disordered condition; a mess or jumble. **2.** Mental confusion. —*phrasal verb:* **muddle through** To push on to a favorable outcome in a disorganized way. [Poss. < obsolete Du. *moddelen,* to make water muddy < MDu., freq. of **modden,* to make muddy < *modde,* mud.] —**mud′dler** *n.*

mud·dle·head·ed (mŭd′l-hĕd′ĭd) *adj.* **1.** Mentally confused. **2.** Inept; blundering. —**mud′dle·head′ed·ness** *n.*

mud·dy (mŭd′ē) *adj.* **-di·er, -di·est 1.** Full of or covered with mud. **2a.** Not bright or pure: *a muddy color.* **b.** Not clear; cloudy, as with sediment. **3.** Lacking luster; dull. **4.** Confused or vague. ❖ *tr.v.* **-died, -dy·ing, -dies 1.** To make dirty or muddy. **2.** To make dull or cloudy. **3.** To make obscure or confused. —**mud′di·ly** *adv.* —**mud′di·ness** *n.*

mud eel *n.* A small eellike amphibian *(Siren lacertina)* of the southeast United States having only front legs that are partially concealed by external gills.

Mu·dé·jar (moo-thē′här) *n., pl.* **-ja·res** (-hä-rĕs′) A Muslim who remained in Spain after its Christian reconquest in the Middle Ages. ❖ *adj.* Of or relating to a style of Spanish architecture of the 13th to the 16th century, combining Moorish and Gothic forms. [Sp. < Ar. *mudajjan,* permitted to remain, Mudéjar, passive part. of *dajjana,* to allow to remain < *dajana,* to remain, stay.]

mud·fish (mŭd′fĭsh′) *n., pl.* **mudfish** or **-fish·es** See **bowfin.**

mud flat *n.* Low-lying muddy land that is covered at high tide and exposed at low tide.

mud·flow (mŭd′flō′) *n.* A downhill movement of soft wet earth and debris, made fluid by rain or melted snow and often building up great speed.

mud·guard (mŭd′gärd′) *n.* A shield over or behind a vehicle's wheel to limit splashing of mud or water.

mud hen *n.* Any of various birds, such as the coot or rail, inhabiting marshy or coastal regions.

mud minnow *n.* Any of various very small fishes of the family Umbridae, esp. of the genus *Umbra,* living in the muddy areas of North American lakes and ponds and often used as bait.

mud·pup·py or **mud puppy** (mŭd′pŭp′ē) *n., pl.* **-pies 1.** Any of several large North American salamanders of the genus *Necturus,* esp. *N. maculosus,* living in lakes and streams and having conspicuous clusters of dark red external gills. **2.** See **hellbender.**

mu·dra (mə-drä′) *n.* A series of symbolic body postures and hand movements used in East Indian classical dancing. [Skt. *mudrā,* seal, mystery, mudra < Iran. **mudrā,* perh. ult. < Akkadian *musarû, mušarû,* object bearing a royal inscription < Sumerian *mu-sar : mu,* name, fame + *sar,* to write.]

mud·room (mŭd′room′, -room′) *n.* A small room or entryway in a house where wet or muddy clothing can be removed.

mud·sill (mŭd′sĭl′) *n.* The lowest sill, block, or timber supporting a building, located at or below ground level.

mud·skip·per (mŭd′skĭp′ər) *n.* Any of several tropical African and Indo-Pacific fishes of the family Gobiidae, esp. of the genus *Periophthalmus,* able to survive on land.

mud·slide (mŭd′slīd′) *n.* A mudflow, esp. a slow-moving one.

mud·sling·er (mŭd′slĭng′ər) *n.* One who makes malicious charges and otherwise attempts to discredit an opponent, as in a political campaign. —**mud′sling′ing** *n.*

mud snake *n.* A burrowing snake *(Farancia abacura)* of swamps and lowlands of the southeast United States, having black scales with reddish markings.

mud·stone (mŭd′stōn′) *n.* A fine-grained, dark gray sedimentary rock, similar to shale but without laminations.

mud turtle *n.* Any of various small turtles of the genus *Kinosternon,* having hinged lobes on the ventral part of the shell and found in fresh waters of the Western Hemisphere.

mud wasp *n. Chiefly Northeastern US* See **mud dauber.** See Regional Note at **mud dauber.**

Muen·ster or **Mun·ster** (mŭn′stər, moŏn′-) *n.* A semisoft creamy cheese of mild flavor. [After *Munster* in NE France.]

mues·li (myoōz′lē) *n.* A mixture of usu. untoasted rolled oats and dried fruit, often used as a breakfast cereal. [Ger. dialectal, dim. of Ger. *Mus,* mash < MHGer. *muos,* a meal, mushlike food < OHGer.]

mu·ez·zin (myoō-ĕz′ĭn, moō-) *n. Islam* The crier who calls the faithful to prayer five times a day. [Ottoman Turk. *müezzin* or Pers. *muazzin* < Ar. *mu'aḏḏin,* active part. of *'aḏḏana,* to call to prayer. See AZAN.]

muff[1] (mŭf) *v.* **muffed, muff·ing, muffs** —*tr.* **1.** To perform or handle clumsily; bungle. See Syns at **botch. 2.** *Sports* To fail to make (a catch). —*intr.* To perform an act clumsily. ❖ *n.* **1.** A clumsy or bungled action. **2.** *Sports* A failure to make a catch. [?]

muff[2] (mŭf) *n.* **1.** A small cylindrical fur or cloth cover, open at both ends, in which the hands are placed for warmth. **2.** A cluster of feathers on the face of certain breeds of fowl. **3.** *Vulgar Slang* The vulva. [Du. *mof* < MDu. *moffel* < OFr. *mofle,* mitten < Med.Lat. *muffula,* perh. of Gmc. orig.]

muf·fin (mŭf′ĭn) *n.* **1.** A small cup-shaped quick bread, often sweetened. **2.** An English muffin. [Poss. < LGer. *Muffen,* pl. of *Muffe,* small cake < MLGer.]

muf·fle (mŭf′əl) *tr.v.* **-fled, -fling, -fles 1.** To wrap up, as in a blanket or shawl, for warmth, protection, or secrecy. **2a.** To wrap or pad in order to deaden the sound. **b.** To deaden (a sound). **3.** To make vague or obscure. **4.** To repress; stifle. ❖ *n.* **1.** Something that muffles. **2.** A kiln or part of a kiln in which pottery can be fired without being exposed to direct flame. [ME *muflen,* poss. < OFr. *mofler,* to stuff < *moufle, mofle,* glove. See MUFF[2].]

muf·fle[2] (mŭf′əl) *n.* The fleshy hairless snout of certain mammals, such as ruminants. [Fr. *mufle,* perh. blend of *moufle,* mitten, chubby face (< OFr.; see MUFF[2]) and *museau,* muzzle (< OFr. *musel;* see MUZZLE).]

muf·fler (mŭf′lər) *n.* **1.** A heavy scarf worn around the neck for warmth. **2.** A device that absorbs noise, esp. one used with an internal-combustion engine.

muf·fu·let·ta (moō′fə-lŏt′ə, -lĕt′-) *n. New Orleans* A sandwich made with a round loaf of Italian bread filled with layers of hard salami, ham, provolone, and olive salad. [Ital. dialectal, bread with a filling < Ital. *muffa,* mold, prob. of Gmc. orig.]

muf·ti[1] (mŭf′tē, moōf′-) *n., pl.* **-tis** A Muslim scholar who interprets the shari'a. [Ar. *muftī,* one who gives legal opinions < *'aftā,* to decide by legal opinion.]

muf·ti[2] (mŭf′tē) *n., pl.* **-tis** Civilian dress, esp. when worn by one who normally wears a uniform. [Prob. < MUFTI[1].]

mug[1] (mŭg) *n.* **1.** A cylindrical drinking cup usu. having a handle. **2.** The amount that a mug can hold. [Perh. of Scand. orig.]

mug[2] (mŭg) *n.* **1.** *Informal* **a.** The human face. **b.** The area of the human mouth, chin, and jaw. **c.** A grimace. **d.** A mug shot. **2.** A thug; a hoodlum. **3.** *Chiefly British Slang* A victim or dupe. ❖ *v.* **mugged, mug·ging, mugs** —*tr.* **1.** *Informal* To photograph (a person's face) for police files. **2.** To threaten or assault (a person) with the intent to rob. —*intr.* To make exaggerated facial expressions, esp. for humorous effect: *The partygoers mugged for the camera.* [Prob. < MUG[1] (poss. in allusion to mugs decorated with grotesque faces).]

Mu·ga·be (moō-gä′bē), **Robert Gabriel** b. 1924. Zimbabwean politician who led the Black nationalists in Rhodesia.

mug·ger[1] (mŭg′ər) *n.* **1.** One who commits a mugging. **2.** One who makes exaggerated faces, as in performing.

mug·ger[2] (mŭg′ər) *n.* A large crocodile *(Crocodilus palustris)* of southwest Asia having a very broad wrinkled snout. [Hindi *magar* < Skt. *makaraḥ,* crocodile, of Dravidian orig.]

mug·ging (mŭg′ĭng) *n.* An assault upon a person esp. with the intent to rob.

mug·gy (mŭg′ē) *adj.* **-gi·er, -gi·est** Warm and extremely humid. [Prob. < ME *mugen,* to drizzle; akin to ON *mugga,* a drizzle.] —**mug′gi·ness** *n.*

Mu·ghal (moō-gŭl′) *n.* Variant of **Mogul** 1.

mu·gho pine or **mu·go pine** (myoō′gō, moō′-) *n.* A shrubby European pine *(Pinus mugo).* [Fr. < Ital. *mugo.*]

mug shot *n. Informal* A photograph of a person's face, esp. one made for police files.

mug·wort (mŭg′wûrt′, -wôrt′) *n.* Any of several aromatic plants of the genus *Artemisia,* esp. *A. vulgaris,* native to Eurasia. [ME *mugwort, mugwyrt* < OE *mucgwyrt : mucg-,* var. of *mycg,* midge + *wyrt,* plant; see WORT[1].]

mug·wump (mŭg′wŭmp′) *n.* **1.** A person who acts independently or remains neutral, esp. in politics. **2.** often **Mugwump** A Republican who bolted the party in 1884, refusing to support presidential candidate James G. Blaine. [Massachusett *muggu-omp, mummugguomp,* war leader.]

Mu·ham·mad (moō-hăm′ĭd, -hä′mĭd) also **Mo·ham·med** (mō-, -hăm′-) 570?-632 A.D. Arab prophet of Islam who began to preach as God's prophet of the true religion at the age of 40. [Ar. *muḥammad,* praised, commendable, passive part. of *ḥammada,* to praise highly < *ḥamida,* to extol.]

Muhammad II also **Mohammed II** 1429?-81. Sultan of Turkey (1451–81) and founder of the Ottoman Empire who conquered Constantinople in 1453.

Muhammad, Elijah Orig. Elijah Poole. 1897–1975. Amer. activist and leader of the Black Muslims (1934–75).

Muhammad Ali also **Mohammed Ali** 1769–1849. Turkish soldier and viceroy of Egypt (1805–48) who wrested control of Egypt from the Ottoman Empire (1811) and established a modern state.

Mu·ham·mad·an (mōō-hăm′ĭ-dən) also **Mo·ham·med·an** (mō-) *adj.* **1.** Of or relating to Muhammad. **2.** *Offensive* Of or relating to Islam; Muslim. ❖ *n. Offensive* A Muslim.

Mu·ham·mad·an·ism (mōō-hăm′ĭ-də-nĭz′əm) also **Mo·ham·med·an·ism** (mō-) *n. Offensive* The religion of Muslims; Islam.

Mu·har·ram (mōō-hăr′əm) also **Mo·har·ram** (mō-) or **Mu·har·rum** (mōō-) *n.* **1.** The first month of the Islamic calendar. See table at **calendar. 2.** A Shiite festival held during the first ten days of this month. [Ar. *muḥarram*, passive part. of *ḥarrama*, to forbid < *ḥarama*.]

Muir (myōor), **John** 1838–1914. British-born Amer. naturalist who promoted the creation of national parks.

mu·ja·hi·deen also **mu·ja·he·deen** or **mu·ja·hi·din** (mōō-jä′hĕ-dēn′) *pl.n.* Muslim guerrilla warriors engaged in a jihad. [Ar. or Pers. *mujāhidīn*, pl. of Ar. *mujāhid*, one who fights in a jihad, active part. of *jāhada*, to fight.]

mu·jik (mōō-zhēk′, -zhĭk′) *n.* Variant of **muzhik.**

Muk·den (mōōk′dən, -dĕn′, mōōk′-) See **Shenyang.**

muk·luk (mŭk′lŭk′) *n.* **1.** A soft boot made of reindeer skin or sealskin and worn by Eskimos. **2.** A slipper with a soft sole resembling this boot. [Yupik *maklak*, bearded seal.]

muk·tuk (mŭk′tŭk′) *n.* Whale blubber and skin, eaten as food. [Inuit *maktak*.]

mu·lat·to (mōō-lăt′ō, -lä′tō, myōō-) *n., pl.* **-tos** or **-toes 1.** A person having one white and one Black parent. **2.** A person of mixed white and Black ancestry. [Sp. *mulato*, small mule, person of mixed race, mulatto < *mulo*, mule < OSpan. < Lat. *mūlus*.]

mul·ber·ry (mŭl′bĕr′ē, -bə-rē) *n.* **1a.** Any of several deciduous trees of the genus *Morus*, having unisexual flowers in drooping catkins and edible multiple fruit. **b.** The sweet fruit of any of these trees. **2.** Any of several similar or related trees. **3.** A grayish to dark purple. [ME *mulberrie* < OE *mōrberie* and MLGer. *mūlberi*, *mūrberi* : both < Lat. *mōrum* < OE *berie*, berry, or OHGer. *beri*, berry.]

mulch (mŭlch) *n.* A protective covering, usu. of organic matter such as leaves, placed around plants to prevent the evaporation of moisture, the freezing of roots, and the growth of weeds. ❖ *tr.v.* **mulched, mulch·ing, mulch·es** To cover or surround with mulch. [Prob. < ME *melsche*, *molsh*, soft < OE *melsc*, mellow, mild.]

mulct (mŭlkt) *n.* A penalty such as a fine. ❖ *tr.v.* **mulct·ed, mulct·ing, mulcts 1.** To penalize by fining or demanding forfeiture. **2.** To acquire by trickery or deception. **3.** To defraud or swindle. [< ME *multen*, to fine < Lat. *multāre*, *mulctāre* < *mulcta*, fine.]

mule¹ (myōol) *n.* **1.** The sterile hybrid offspring of a male donkey and a female horse, having long ears and a short mane. **2.** A sterile hybrid, as between birds or plants. **3.** *Informal* A stubborn person. **4.** A spinning machine that makes thread or yarn from fibers. **5.** A small, usu. electric tractor or locomotive used for hauling over short distances. **6.** *Slang* A person who serves as a courier of illegal drugs. [ME < OFr. *mul* and < OE *mūl*, both < Lat. *mūlus*.]

mule² (myōol) *n.* A slipper or shoe that has no counter or strap to fit around the heel. [Prob. Fr., slipper, poss. < MDu. *muil*, ult. < Lat. *mulleus (calceus)*, reddish-purple (ceremonial shoe).]

mule deer *n.* A brownish-gray deer (*Odocoileus hemionus*) of western North America having long mulelike ears, large branching antlers in the male, and a black-tipped tail.

mule·skin·ner (myōol′skĭn′ər) *n. Informal* A driver of mules.

mu·le·ta (mōō-lā′tə, -lĕt′ə) *n.* A short red cape used by a matador during the final passes before a kill. [Sp., dim. of *mula*, she-mule < Lat. *mūla*, fem. of *mūlus*, mule.]

mu·le·teer (myōo′lə-tîr′) *n.* A driver of mules. [Fr. *muletier* < OFr. < *mulet*, dim. of *mul*, mule. See MULE¹.]

mu·ley (myōo′lē, mōol′ē, mōo′lē) *adj.* Having no horns. ❖ *n., pl.* **-leys** An animal without horns, esp. a cow. [< Ir.Gael. *maol* (< OIr. *mael*) or < Welsh *moel*, bald, hornless.]

mul·ish (myōo′lĭsh) *adj.* Stubborn and intractable; recalcitrant. See Syns at **obstinate. —mul′ish·ly** *adv.* **—mul′ish·ness** *n.*

mull¹ (mŭl) *tr.v.* **mulled, mull·ing, mulls** To heat and spice (wine, for example). [?]

mull² (mŭl) *v.* **mulled, mull·ing, mulls** *—tr.* To go over extensively in the mind; ponder. *—intr.* To ruminate; ponder. [Prob. ME *mollen*, *mullen*, to moisten, crumble. See MOIL.]

mull³ (mŭl) *n.* A soft thin muslin used in dresses and for

trimmings. [Short for *mulmull* < Hindi *malmal*.]

Mull An island of W Scotland in the Inner Hebrides, separated from the mainland on the NE by the **Sound of Mull.**

mul·lah also **mul·la** (mŭl′ə, mŏŏl′ə) *n. Islam* **1.** A religious teacher or leader, usu. male. **2.** Used as a form of address for such a person. [Urdu *mullā* < Pers. < Ar. *mawlā*, master, friend < *waliya*, to become near, be in charge.]

mul·lein (mŭl′ən) *n.* Any of various Eurasian plants of the genus *Verbascum*, esp. *V. thapsus*, a tall plant having leaves covered with dense woolly down. [ME *moleine* < AN, prob. < *mol*, soft < Lat. *mollis*. See MOIL.]

mullein pink *n.* See **rose campion.**

mul·ler (mŭl′ər) *n.* An implement of stone or other hard substance used as a pestle to grind paints or drugs. [ME *molour*, prob. < *mullen*, to grind. See MULL².]

Muller, Hermann Joseph 1890–1967. Amer. geneticist who won a 1946 Nobel Prize.

Mül·ler (mŭl′ər, myōol′lər, mü′-), **(Friedrich) Max** 1823–1900. German-born British philologist and Orientalist noted for his studies of Sanskrit language and literature.

Müller, Johann Known as Regiomontanus. 1436–76. German mathematician and astronomer who contributed to the revival of astronomy during the Renaissance.

Mül·le·ri·an mimicry (myōo-lîr′ē-ən, mə-, mĭ-) *n.* A form of protective mimicry in which two or more distasteful or harmful species, esp. of insects, closely resemble each other and are therefore avoided equally by all their natural predators. [After Johann Friedrich Theodor (Fritz) *Müller* (1821–97), German-born Brazilian zoologist.]

mul·let (mŭl′ĭt) *n., pl.* **mullet** or **-lets 1.** Any of various stout-bodied edible fishes of the family Mugilidae. **2.** The red mullet. [ME *molet* < Med.Lat. *mulettus*, prob. < OFr. *mulet* < *mul* < Lat. *mullus* < Gk. *mullos*.]

mul·li·gan stew (mŭl′ĭ-gən) *n.* A stew made of bits of various meats and vegetables. [Prob. < the name *Mulligan*.]

mul·li·ga·taw·ny (mŭl′ĭ-gə-tô′nē) *n., pl.* **-nies** An East Indian soup having a meat or chicken base and curry seasoning. [Tamil *milagutaṇṇi* : *miḷagu*, pepper + *taṇṇīr*, cool water (*taṇ*, cool + *nīr*, water).]

Mul·li·ken (mŭl′ĭ-kən), **Robert Sanderson** 1896–1986. Amer. chemist and physicist who won a 1966 Nobel Prize.

mul·lion (mŭl′yən) *n.* A vertical member, as of stone or wood, dividing a window or other opening. [Alteration of ME *moniel* < AN *moynel*, perh. < *moienel*, middle < *moien* < Lat. *mediānus* < *medius*. See medhyo- in App.] **—mul′lioned** *adj.*

Mul·lis (mŭl′ĭs), **Kary Banks** b. 1944. Amer. biochemist who shared a 1993 Nobel Prize in chemistry.

Mul·ro·ney (mŭl-rō′nē, -rōo′-), **(Martin) Brian** b. 1939. Canadian politician who served as prime minister (1984–93).

Mul·tan (mōol-tän′) A city of E-central Pakistan SW of Lahore. Pop. 732,070.

multi– *pref.* **1.** Many; much; multiple: *multicolored.* **2a.** More than one: *multiparous.* **b.** More than two: *multilateral.* [ME < OFr. < Lat. < *multus*, much, many.]

mul·ti·cel·lu·lar (mŭl′tĭ-sĕl′yə-lər, -tī-) *adj.* Having or consisting of many cells. **—mul′ti·cel′lu·lar′i·ty** (-lăr′ĭ-tē) *n.*

mul·ti·col·ored (mŭl′tī-kŭl′ərd) also **mul·ti·col·or** (-kŭl′ər) *adj.* **1.** Having many colors. **2.** *Printing* Capable of printing in two or more colors simultaneously.

mul·ti·cul·tur·al (mŭl′tē-kŭl′chər-əl, -tī-) *adj.* **1.** Of, relating to, or including several cultures. **2.** Of or relating to a social or educational theory that encourages interests in many cultures within a society rather than in only a mainstream culture. **—mul′ti·cul′tur·al·ism** *n.* **—mul′ti·cul′tur·al·ist** *n.*

mul·ti·di·men·sion·al (mŭl′tī-dī-mĕn′shə-nəl) *adj.* Of, relating to, or having several dimensions. **—mul′ti·di·men′sion·al′i·ty** (-shə-năl′ĭ-tē) *n.*

mul·ti·di·rec·tion·al (mŭl′tē-dī-rĕk′shə-nəl, -dī-, -tī-) *adj.* **1.** Reaching out in several directions. **2.** Operating or functioning in more than one direction.

mul·ti·dis·ci·pli·nar·y (mŭl′tē-dĭs′ə-plə-nĕr′ē, -tī-) *adj.* Of, relating to, or making use of several disciplines at once.

mul·ti·eth·nic (mŭl′tē-ĕth′nĭk, -tī-) *adj.* Of, relating to, or including several ethnic groups.

mul·ti·fac·et·ed (mŭl′tē-făs′ĭ-tĭd, -tī-) *adj.* Having many facets or aspects.

mul·ti·fac·to·ri·al (mŭl′tī-făk-tôr′ē-əl, -tōr′-) *adj.* **1.** Involving, dependent on, or controlled by several factors. **2.** Of or relating to a pattern of familial inheritance resulting from multiple genetic or environmental factors or from a combination of both.

mul·ti·far·i·ous (mŭl′tə-fâr′ē-əs) *adj.* Having great variety; diverse. [< Lat. *multifāriam*, in many places : *multi-*, multi- + *-fāriam*, adv. suff.; see dhē- in App.] **—mul′ti·far′i·ous·ly** *adv.*

mul·ti·fid (mŭl′tə-fĭd′) *adj. Biology* Having many clefts forming lobes.

mul·ti·flo·ra rose (mŭl′tə-flôr′ə, -flōr′ə) *n.* A climbing or sprawling shrub (*Rosa multiflora*) of eastern Asia having clusters of small fragrant flowers. [Partial transl. of NLat. *Rosa multiflora*, species name : Lat. *rosa*, rose + LLat. *multiflōra*, fem. of *multiflōrus*, multiflorous (Lat. *multi-*, multi- + Lat. *flōs, flōr-*, flower; see FLORA).]

Müllerian mimicry
viceroy butterfly (*top*) mimicking the foul-tasting monarch butterfly

multiflora rose
Rosa multiflora

ă pat	oi boy
ā pay	ou out
âr care	ōō took
ä father	ōō boot
ĕ pet	ŭ cut
ē be	ûr urge
ĭ pit	th thin
ī pie	th this
îr pier	hw which
ŏ pot	zh vision
ō toe	ə about,
ô paw	item

Stress marks:
′ (primary);
′ (secondary), as in
lexicon (lĕk′sĭ-kŏn′)

mul·ti·foil (mŭl′tə-foil′) *n. Architecture* A flat object or opening with scalloped edges or ornaments.

mul·ti·fold (mŭl′tə-fōld′) *adj.* Numerous and varied; manifold.

mul·ti·form (mŭl′tə-fôrm′) *adj.* Occurring in or having many forms or shapes. —**mul′ti·for′mi·ty** (-fôr′mĭ-tē) *n.*

mul·ti·lat·er·al (mŭl′tĭ-lăt′ər-əl) *adj.* **1.** Having many sides. **2.** Involving more than two nations or parties: *multilateral trade agreements.* —**mul′ti·lat′er·al·ism** *n.* —**mul′ti·lat′er·al·ist** *n.* —**mul′ti·lat′er·al·ly** *adv.*

mul·ti·lin·gual (mŭl′tē-lĭng′gwəl, -tĭ-) *adj.* **1.** Of, including, or expressed in several languages. **2.** Using or having the ability to use several languages. —**mul′ti·lin′gual·ism** *n.*

mul·ti·loc·u·lar (mŭl′tĭ-lŏk′yə-lər) *adj.* Having or consisting of many small compartments or cavities.

mul·ti·me·di·a (mŭl′tē-mē′dē-ə, -tĭ-) *pl.n.* (*used with a sing. verb*) **1.** The combined use of media, such as movies, music, lighting, CD-ROMs, and the Internet, as for education or entertainment. **2.** The combined use of media, such as television, radio, print, and the Internet, as for advertising or publicity. ❖ *adj.* **1.** Of or relating to the combined use of several media. **2.** *Computer Science* Of or relating to an application that integrates text, graphics, full-motion video, and sound.

mul·ti·mil·lion·aire (mŭl′tē-mĭl′yə-nâr′, -tĭ-) *n.* One whose financial assets equal at least two million dollars.

mul·ti·na·tion·al (mŭl′tē-năsh′ə-nəl, -năsh′nəl, -tĭ-) *adj.* **1.** Having operations, subsidiaries, or investments in more than two countries. **2.** Of or involving more than two countries. ❖ *n.* A multinational company or corporation. —**mul′ti·na′tion·al·ism** *n.*

mul·ti·no·mi·al (mŭl′tĭ-nō′mē-əl) *n.* See **polynomial** 2. [MULTI– + (BI)NOMIAL.] —**mul′ti·no′mi·al** *adj.*

multinomial theorem *n.* The theorem that establishes the rule for forming the terms of the *n*th power of a sum of numbers in terms of products of powers of those numbers.

mul·ti·nu·cle·ar (mŭl′tē-nōō′klē-ər, -nyōō′-, -tĭ-) *adj.* Multinucleate.

mul·ti·nu·cle·ate (mŭl′tē-nōō′klē-ət, -nyōō′-, -tĭ-) *also* **mul·ti·nu·cle·at·ed** (-ā′tĭd) *adj.* Having two or more nuclei.

mul·tip·a·ra (mŭl-tĭp′ər-ə) *n., pl.* **-ras** *also* **-rae** (-rē) A woman who has given birth two or more times. [NLat. : MULTI– + Lat. *-para*, fem. of *-parus*, having given birth (< *parere*, to give birth).]

mul·tip·a·rous (mŭl-tĭp′ər-əs) *adj.* **1.** Having given birth two or more times. **2.** Giving birth to more than one offspring at a time. —**mul′ti·par′i·ty** (mŭl′tĭ-păr′ĭ-tē) *n.*

mul·ti·par·tite (mŭl′tĭ-pär′tīt′) *adj.* **1.** Divided into many parts. **2.** Involving more than two nations or parties.

mul·ti·par·ty (mŭl′tə-pär′tē) *adj.* Of, relating to, or involving more than two political parties.

mul·ti·ped (mŭl′tə-pĕd′) *also* **mul·ti·pede** (-pēd′) *adj.* Having many feet. ❖ *n.* An animal with many feet.

mul·ti·ple (mŭl′tə-pəl) *adj.* Of, having, or consisting of more than one individual, part, or other component; manifold. ❖ *n.* A number that is divisible by another number with no remainder. [Fr. < OFr. < LLat. *multiplum*, a multiple : Lat. *multi-*, multi- + Lat. *-plus*, -fold.]

multiple allele *n.* Any of a set of three or more alleles, only two of which can be present in a diploid organism.

multiple chemical sensitivity *n.* A group of symptoms typified by chronic allergy that have been attributed to extreme sensitivity to various environmental or industrial chemicals.

mul·ti·ple-choice (mŭl′tə-pəl-chois′) *adj.* **1.** Offering several answers from which the correct one is to be chosen. **2.** Consisting of questions of this type.

multiple factor *n.* See **polygene.**

multiple fruit *n.* A fruit, such as a fig, derived from several flowers that are combined into a single structure.

multiple myeloma *n.* A malignant proliferation of plasma cells in bone marrow causing numerous tumors and characterized by the presence of abnormal proteins in the blood.

multiple personality *n.* A disputed psychological disorder in which a person exhibits two or more disassociated personalities, each functioning as a distinct entity.

multiple sclerosis *n.* A chronic autoimmune disease marked by the gradual destruction of myelin in the brain and spinal cord and resulting in varying degrees of muscular weakness and disability.

multiple star *n.* A group of three or more stars, usu. with a common gravitational center, that appear as one to the unaided eye.

multiple store *n. Chiefly British* A chain store.

mul·ti·plet (mŭl′tə-plĕt′, -plĭt) *n.* **1.** A spectral line split into more than one component, representing the energy states characteristic of an atom. **2.** Any of several groupings of subatomic particles, each of whose members have the same quantum numbers except for electric charge. [MULTIPL(E) + (DOUBL)ET.]

mul·ti·plex (mŭl′tə-plĕks′) *adj.* **1.** Relating to, having, or consisting of multiple elements or parts. **2.** Relating to or being a system of simultaneous communication of two or more messages on the same wire or radio channel. ❖ *n.* A building, esp. a movie theater or dwelling, with multiple separate units. [ME, a multiple < Lat., various, complicated : *multi-*, multi- + *-plex*, -fold; see **plek-** in App.]

mul·ti·pli·a·ble (mŭl′tə-plī′ə-bəl) *also* **mul·ti·plic·a·ble**

(-plĭk′ə-bəl) *adj.* That can be multiplied.

mul·ti·pli·cand (mŭl′tə-plĭ-kănd′) *n.* The number that is or is to be multiplied by another, such as 32 in 8 × 32. [Lat. *multiplicandum*, neut. gerundive of *multiplicāre*, to multiply. See MULTIPLY¹.]

mul·ti·pli·cate (mŭl-tĭp′lĭ-kĭt) *adj.* **1.** Having more than one layer or fold, as some shells. **2.** Multiple. [ME < Lat. *multiplicātus*, p. part. of *multiplicāre*, to multiply. See MULTIPLY¹.]

mul·ti·pli·ca·tion (mŭl′tə-plĭ-kā′shən) *n.* **1.** The act or process of multiplying or the condition of being multiplied. **2.** Propagation of plants and animals; procreation. **3.** *Mathematics* **a.** The operation that for positive integers consists of adding a number (the multiplicand) to itself a certain number of times and is extended to other real numbers according to the rules governing the multiplication of positive integers. **b.** Any of certain analogous algebraic operations involving expressions other than real numbers. —**mul′ti·pli·ca′tion·al** *adj.*

multiplication sign *n.* The sign used to indicate multiplication, either a times sign (×) or a centered dot (·).

multiplication table *n.* A table, used as an aid in memorization, that lists the products of certain numbers multiplied together, typically the numbers 1 to 12.

mul·ti·pli·ca·tive (mŭl′tə-plĭ-kā′tĭv, mŭl′tə-plĭk′ə-tĭv) *adj.* **1.** Tending to multiply or capable of multiplying or increasing. **2.** Having to do with multiplication.

multiplicative inverse *n.* See **inverse** 2a.

mul·ti·plic·i·ty (mŭl′tə-plĭs′ĭ-tē) *n., pl.* **-ties** **1.** The state of being various or manifold. **2.** A large number: *a multiplicity of ideas.* [ME < OFr. *multiplicite* < LLat. *multiplicitās* < *multiplex, multiplic-*, various. See MULTIPLEX.]

mul·ti·pli·er (mŭl′tə-plī′ər) *n.* **1.** One that multiplies. **2.** *Mathematics* The number by which another number is multiplied, such as 8 in 8 × 32. **3.** *Physics* A device, such as a phototube, used to enhance or increase an effect.

mul·ti·ply¹ (mŭl′tə-plī′) *v.* **-plied, -ply·ing, -plies** —*tr.* **1.** To increase the amount, number, or degree of. **2.** *Mathematics* To perform multiplication on. —*intr.* **1.** To grow in amount, number, or degree. See Syns at **increase.** **2.** To breed or propagate. **3.** *Mathematics* To perform multiplication. [ME *multiplien* < OFr. *multiplier* < Lat. *multiplicāre* < *multiplex*, multiplex. See MULTIPLEX.]

mul·ti·ply² (mŭl′tə-plē′) *adv.* In many or multiple ways.

mul·ti·po·lar (mŭl′tə-pō′lər) *adj.* Having or conceiving multiple centers of power or influence: *a multipolar world.* —**mul′ti·po·lar′i·ty** (-pō-lăr′ĭ-tē, -pə-) *n.*

mul·ti·port (mŭl′tə-pôrt′, -pōrt′) *adj.* Having, relating to, or being a system of multiple ports for injecting fuel separately into each cylinder of an engine.

mul·ti·proc·ess·ing (mŭl′tē-prŏs′ĕs′ĭng, -prō′sĕs′ĭng, -ə-sĭng, -tĭ-) *n.* A method of computing in which different parts of a task are distributed between two or more similar central processing units.

mul·ti·pronged (mŭl′tə-prôngd′, -prŏngd′) *adj.* **1.** Having many prongs. **2.** Involving several different directions, aspects, or elements: *a multipronged attack.*

mul·ti·ra·cial (mŭl′tē-rā′shəl, -tĭ-) *adj.* **1.** Made up of, involving, or acting on behalf of various races: *a multiracial society.* **2.** Having ancestors of several or various races.

mul·ti·stage (mŭl′tĭ-stāj′) *adj.* **1.** Functioning in more than one stage: *a multistage design project.* **2.** Relating to or composed of two or more propulsion units.

mul·ti·task·ing (mŭl′tē-tăs′kĭng, -tĭ-) *n.* The concurrent operation by one central processing unit of two or more processes. —**mul′ti·task′** *v.*

mul·ti·thread·ed (mŭl′tē-thrĕd′ĭd, -tĭ-) *adj. Computer Science* **1.** Having more than one thread of execution. Used of applications. **2.** Supporting multithreaded applications. Used of programming languages.

mul·ti·tude (mŭl′tĭ-tōōd′, -tyōōd′) *n.* **1.** The condition or quality of being numerous. **2.** A very great number. **3.** The masses; the populace: *the concerns of the multitude.* [ME < OFr. < Lat. *multitūdō < multus*, many.]

mul·ti·tu·di·nous (mŭl′tĭ-tōōd′n-əs, -tyōōd′-) *adj.* **1.** Very numerous; existing in great numbers. **2.** Consisting of many parts. **3.** Populous; crowded. [< Lat. *multitūdō, multitūdin-*, multitude. See MULTITUDE.] —**mul′ti·tu′di·nous·ly** *adv.*

mul·ti·us·er (mŭl′tē-yōō′zər, -tĭ-) *adj.* Of or relating to a device or product, such as a computer system, that two or more people can use at the same time.

mul·ti·va·lent (mŭl′tĭ-vā′lənt, mŭl-tĭv′ə-lənt) *adj.* **1.** *Chemistry* Polyvalent. **2.** *Genetics* Of or relating to the association of three or more homologous chromosomes during the first division of meiosis. **3.** *Immunology* Having several sites of attachment for an antibody or antigen. **4.** Having various meanings or values: *multivalent allegory.* —**mul′ti·va′lence** *n.*

mul·ti·ver·si·ty (mŭl′tĭ-vûr′sĭ-tē) *n., pl.* **-ties** A university that has numerous constituent and affiliated institutions, such as separate colleges, campuses, and research centers.

mul·ti·vi·ta·min (mŭl′tə-vī′tə-mĭn) *adj.* Containing many vitamins. ❖ *n.* A preparation containing many vitamins.

mum¹ (mŭm) *adj.* Not verbalizing; silent. ❖ *interj.* Used as a command to stop speaking. **—idiom: mum's the word** Say nothing of the secret you know. [ME, perh. imit. of closing one's lips.]

mum² (mŭm) *intr.v.* **mummed, mum·ming, mums 1.** To act or play in a pantomime. **2.** To go merrymaking in a mask or disguise esp. during a festival. [ME *mummen* < OFr. *momer,* to wear a mask.]

mum³ (mŭm) *n. Chiefly British* Mother. [Short for MUMMY².]

mum⁴ (mŭm) *n.* A chrysanthemum.

mum⁵ (mŭm) *n.* A strong beer originally brewed in Brunswick, Germany. [Ger. *Mumme.*]

Mum·bai (mŭm′bī′) Formerly **Bom·bay** (bŏm-bā′) A city of W-central India on coastal **Mumbai Island** and adjacent Salsette I. Pop. 9,925,891.

mum·ble (mŭm′bəl) *v.* **-bled, -bling, -bles** *—tr.* **1.** To utter indistinctly by lowering the voice or partially closing the mouth. **2.** To chew slowly or ineffectively, as from being without teeth. *—intr.* **1.** To mumble words. **2.** To mumble food. ❖ *n.* A low indistinct sound or utterance. [ME *momelen* < MDu. *mommelen.*] **—mum′bler** *n.* **—mum′bly** *adj.*

mum·ble·ty-peg (mŭm′bəl-tē-pĕg′, mŭm′blē-pĕg′) also **mum·ble-the-peg** (-bəl-*tho*-) *n.* A game in which players toss a jackknife in prescribed ways in order to make it stick into the ground. [< the phrase *mumble the peg,* the loser originally having to pull up with the teeth a peg driven into the ground.]

mum·bo jum·bo or **mum·bo-jum·bo** (mŭm′bō-jŭm′bō) *n., pl.* **-bos 1.** Unintelligible language; gibberish. **2.** Language or ritualistic activity intended to confuse. **3.** A complicated or obscure ritual. **4.** An object believed to have supernatural powers; a fetish. [Perh. of Mandingo orig.]

Mum·ford (mŭm′fərd), **Lewis** 1895–1990. Amer. social critic whose works include *The Culture of Cities* (1938).

mum·mer (mŭm′ər) *n.* **1.** A masked or costumed merrymaker. **2a.** One who mums in a pantomime. **b.** An actor. [ME < OFr. *momeur* < *momer,* to wear a mask, pantomime.]

mum·mer·y (mŭm′ə-rē) *n., pl.* **-ies 1.** A performance by mummers. **2.** A pretentious or hypocritical show or ceremony.

mum·mi·chog (mŭm′ĭ-chŏg′) *n.* A stout-bodied killifish (*Fundulus heteroclitus*) of the Atlantic coast south of the Gulf of St. Lawrence, valued as bait. [Narragansett *moamitteaûg.*]

mum·mi·fy (mŭm′ə-fī′) *v.* **-fied, -fy·ing, -fies** *—tr.* **1.** To make into a mummy by embalming and drying. **2.** To cause to shrivel and dry up. *—intr.* To shrivel or dry up like a mummy. **—mum′mi·fi·ca′tion** (-fĭ-kā′shən) *n.*

mum·my¹ (mŭm′ē) *n., pl.* **-mies 1.** The dead body of a human or animal that has been embalmed and prepared for burial, as according to ancient Egyptian practice. **2.** A withered, shrunken, or well-preserved body that resembles a mummy. [ME *mummie,* medicinal material from embalmed corpses < OFr. *momie* < Med.Lat. *mumia* < Ar. *mūmīya* < *mūm,* wax < Pers.]

mum·my² (mŭm′ē) *n., pl.* **-mies** *Informal* Mother. [Alteration of MOMMY or MUM³.]

mumps (mŭmps) *pl.n.* (*used with a sing. or pl. verb*) An acute, inflammatory contagious disease caused by a paramyxovirus and marked by swollen salivary glands and sometimes pancreas, ovaries, or testes. [Perh. < pl. of dialectal *mump,* grimace.]

munch (mŭnch) *v.* **munched, munch·ing, munch·es** *—intr.* **1.** To chew food audibly or with a steady working of the jaws. **2.** To eat with pleasure. *—tr.* To chew or eat (food) audibly or with pleasure. [ME *monchen.*] **—munch′er** *n.*

Munch (mo͝ongk), **Edvard** 1863–1944. Norwegian artist whose works include *The Scream* (1893).

Mun·chau·sen syndrome (mŭn′chou′zən, mŭnch′hou′-) *n.* A psychological disorder characterized by the repeated fabrication or causation of disease symptoms or trauma for the purpose of gaining medical attention or treatment. [After Baron Karl Friedrich Hieronymus von MÜNCHHAUSEN (because the fabricated diseases recalled his fictionalized accounts of his life).]

Munchausen syndrome by proxy *n.* A psychological disorder in which a parent or other caregiver gains attention from medical professionals by repeatedly causing or fabricating disease symptoms in a child.

Münch·hau·sen (mŭnкн′hou′zən) also **Mun·chau·sen** (mŭn′chou′-, mŭnch′hou′-), Baron **Karl Friedrich Hieronymus von** 1720–97. German soldier and raconteur known for his fantastic stories about his adventures.

munch·ies (mŭn′chēz) *pl.n. Slang* **1.** Food for snacking. **2.** A craving for snack food.

munch·kin (mŭnch′kĭn) *n.* **1.** A very small person. **2.** *Informal* A child. **3.** *Informal* A minor official. [After the *Munchkins,* characters in *The Wonderful Wizard of Oz* by L. Frank Baum.]

Mun·cie (mŭn′sē) A city of E-central IN NE of Indianapolis; the setting for Robert and Helen Lynd's pioneering sociological study *Middletown* (1929). Pop. 67,430.

Mun·da (mo͝on′də) *n.* An Austro-Asiatic language family spoken in northeast India and adjacent regions and including Santali.

mun·dane (mŭn-dān′, mŭn′dān′) *adj.* **1.** Of, relating to, or typical of this world; secular. **2.** Relating to, concerned with, or concerned with commonplaces; ordinary. [ME *mondeine* < OFr. *mondain* < Lat. *mundānus* < *mundus,* world.] **—mun·dane′ly** *adv.* **—mun·dane′ness** *n.*

---

mung bean (mŭng) *n.* **1.** An Asian plant (*Vigna radiata*) in the pea family, cultivated for its edible seeds, pods, and sprouts. **2.** The seeds or pods of this plant. [Hindi *mūng* < Skt. *mudgaḥ.*]

Mu·nich (myo͞o′nĭk) A city of SE Germany near the Bavarian Alps SE of Augsburg; founded 1158. Pop. 1,255,623.

mu·nic·i·pal (myo͞o-nĭs′ə-pəl) *adj.* **1a.** Of, relating to, or typical of a municipality. **b.** Having self-government. **c.** Issued on the authority of a state government. **2.** Of or relating to the internal affairs of a nation. ❖ *n.* A municipal bond. [Lat. *mūnicipālis* < *mūnicipium,* town < *mūniceps,* citizen : *mūnus,* public office, duty + *capere,* to take; see kap- in App.] **—mu·nic′i·pal·ly** *adv.*

municipal bond *n.* An often tax-exempt bond issued by a city, county, state, or other government to finance public projects.

mu·nic·i·pal·i·ty (myo͞o-nĭs′ə-păl′ĭ-tē) *n., pl.* **-ties 1.** A political unit, such as a city, town, or village, incorporated for local self-government. **2.** A body of officials appointed to manage the affairs of a local political unit.

mu·nic·i·pal·ize (myo͞o-nĭs′ə-pə-līz′) *tr.v.* **-ized, -iz·ing, -iz·es 1.** To place under municipal ownership. **2.** To make into a municipality. **—mu·nic′i·pal·i·za′tion** (-pə-lĭ-zā′shən) *n.*

mu·nif·i·cent (myo͞o-nĭf′ĭ-sənt) *adj.* **1.** Very liberal in giving; generous. **2.** Showing great generosity: *a munificent gift.* See Syns at **liberal.** [Lat. *mūnificēns, mūnificent-* < *mūnificus* : *mūnus,* gift + *facere,* to make; see FACT.] **—mu·nif′i·cence** *n.* **—mu·nif′i·cent·ly** *adv.*

mu·ni·ment (myo͞o′nə-mənt) *n.* **1. muniments** *Law* Documentary evidence by which one can defend a title to property or a claim to rights. **2.** *Archaic* A means of defense or protection. [ME < OFr. < Med.Lat. *mūnīmentum* < Lat., defense, protection < *mūnīre,* to fortify. See MUNITION.]

mu·ni·tion (myo͞o-nĭsh′ən) *n.* War materiel, esp. weapons and ammunition. Often used in the plural. ❖ *tr.v.* **-tioned, -tion·ing, -tions** To supply with munitions. [ME *municion,* privilege supported by a document < OFr., fortification < Lat. *mūnītiō, mūnītiōn-* < *mūnītus,* p. part. of *mūnīre,* to defend < *moenia,* defensive walls of a town.]

Mu·ñoz Ma·rín (mo͞o-nyôs′ mä-rēn′), **Luis** 1898–1980. Puerto Rican journalist and politician who served as the first elected governor of Puerto Rico (1948–64).

Mun·ro (mən-rō′), **Alice** b. 1931. Canadian writer noted for vivid novels and short stories of life in rural Ontario.

Munro, Hector Hugh Pen name **Sa·ki** (sä′kē) 1870–1916. British writer known for his witty and sometimes bitter short stories.

Mun·see (mŭn′sē) *n., pl.* **Munsee** or **-sees 1.** One of the two Algonquian languages of the Delaware peoples, spoken in New Jersey and New York State. **2.** A member of the Munsee-speaking branch of the Delaware peoples.

Mun·ster¹ (mŭn′stər) A historical region and province of SW Ireland; one of the kingdoms of ancient Ireland.

Mun·ster² (mŭn′stər, mo͝on′-) *n.* Variant of **Muenster.**

Mün·ster (mo͝on′stər, mŭn′-, myo͝on′-) A city of W-central Germany NNE of Cologne; founded c. 800 as a Carolingian episcopal see. Pop. 267,367.

mun·tin (mŭn′tən) *n.* **1.** A strip of wood or metal separating and holding panes of glass in a window. **2.** A vertical framing member set between two rails in a door or in paneling. [ME *mountaunt,* upright post or stud < OFr. *montant* < pr. part. of *monter,* to mount. See MOUNT¹.]

munt·jac also **munt·jak** (mŭnt′jăk′) *n.* Any of several small deer of the genus *Muntiacus* of southeast Asia and the East Indies. [Malay *menjangan,* deer.]

mu·on (myo͞o′ŏn′) *n.* An elementary particle in the lepton family, having a mass 209 times that of the electron, a negative electric charge, and a mean lifetime of 2.2 ×10⁻⁶ second. [Short for *mu meson.*]

muon neutrino *n.* *Physics* A stable elementary particle in the lepton family having a mass less than 0.49 times that of the electron and no charge.

Mur (mo͝or) also **Mu·ra** (mo͝or′ə) A river of S-central Austria, E Slovenia, and N Croatia flowing c. 483 km (300 mi) to the Drava R.

mu·ral (myo͝or′əl) *n.* A very large image, such as a painting, applied directly to a wall or ceiling. ❖ *adj.* **1.** Of or resembling a wall. **2.** Painted on or applied to a wall. [ME, of a wall < OFr. < Lat. *mūrālis* < *mūrus,* wall.] **—mu′ral·ist** *n.*

mu·raled also **mu·ralled** (myo͝or′əld) *adj.* Decorated with murals or a mural: *muraled halls.*

mu·ram·ic acid (myo͞o-răm′ĭk) *n.* An amino sugar, C₉H₁₇NO₇, found in the cell walls of many bacteria. [Lat. *mūrus,* wall + AM(IDE) + -IC.]

Mu·ra·sa·ki Shi·ki·bu (mo͞o′rä-sä′kē shē′kē-bo͞o′), Baroness. 978?–1031? Japanese writer noted for *The Tale of Genji.*

Mu·rat (myo͞o-rä′, mü-), **Joachim** 1767?–1815. French marshal who aided Napoleon's coup d'état (1799) and was appointed king of Naples (1808).

Mur·chi·son River (mûr′chĭ-sən) An intermittent river of W Australia flowing c. 708 km (440 mi) to the Indian Ocean.

Mur·cia (mûr′shə, -shē-ə, mo͝or′thyä) **1.** A region and former kingdom of SE Spain on the Mediterranean Sea; an independent Moorish kingdom from the 11th to the 13th cent. **2.** A city of SE

Luis Muñoz Marín
photographed in 1961

mural
Beale Street, Memphis, Tennessee

ă	pat	oi	boy
ā	pay	ou	out
âr	care	o͝o	took
ä	father	o͞o	boot
ĕ	pet	ŭ	cut
ē	be	ûr	urge
ĭ	pit	th	thin
ī	pie	th	this
îr	pier	hw	which
ŏ	pot	zh	vision
ō	toe	ə	about,
ô	paw		item

Stress marks:
′ (primary);
′ (secondary), as in
lexicon (lĕk′sĭ-kŏn′)

Spain NNW of Cartagena; cap. of the ancient kingdom of Murcia. Pop. 331,898.

mur·der (mûr′dər) n. **1.** The unlawful killing of one human being by another, esp. when premeditated. **2.** Slang Something that is very uncomfortable, difficult, or hazardous. **3.** A flock of crows. ❖ v. **-dered, -der·ing, -ders** —tr. **1.** To kill (another human being) unlawfully. **2.** To kill brutally or inhumanly. **3.** To put an end to; destroy. **4.** To spoil by ineptness; mutilate. **5.** Slang To defeat decisively; trounce. —intr. To commit murder. —**idioms: get away with murder** Informal To escape punishment for or detection of an egregiously blameworthy act. **murder will out** Secrets or misdeeds will eventually be disclosed. [ME murther < OE morthor. See mer- in App.]

mur·der·er (mûr′dər-ər) n. One who commits murder.

mur·der·ess (mûr′dər-ĭs) n. A woman who commits murder. See Usage Note at **-ess.** [MURDER(ER) + -ESS.]

mur·der·ous (mûr′dər-əs) adj. **1.** Capable of, guilty of, or intending murder: murderous thugs. **2.** Characteristic of or giving rise to murder or bloodshed: murderous mistrust. **3.** Informal Capable of devastating or overwhelming. —**mur′der·ous·ly** adv. —**mur′der·ous·ness** n.

Mur·doch (mûr′dŏk′), Dame **(Jean) Iris** 1919–99. Irish-born writer whose intricate novels include Under the Net (1954).

Murdoch, (Keith) Rupert b. 1931. Australian-born Amer. communications magnate with worldwide multimedia holdings.

Rupert Murdoch

Mu·re·şul (mŏŏ′ə-sŏŏl′, mŏŏ′ə-shŏŏl′) or **Mu·reş** (mŏŏ′rĕsh) A river rising in the Carpathian Mts. of N-central Romania and flowing c. 756 km (470 mi) into S Hungary.

mu·rex (myŏŏr′ĕks) n., pl. **mu·ri·ces** (myŏŏr′ĭ-sēz′) or **mu·rex·es** Any of various marine gastropods of the genus Murex, common in tropical seas and having rough spiny shells, esp. M. trunculus, the source of Tyrian purple. [NLat. Mūrex, genus name < Lat. mūrex, purple-fish.]

Mur·ghob also **Mur·ghab** (mŏŏr-gäb′) A river rising in NE Afghanistan and flowing c. 853 km (530 mi) to the Kara Kum Desert.

mu·ri·at·ic acid (myŏŏr′ē-ăt′ĭk) n. Hydrochloric acid. [Lat. muriāticus, pickled < muria, brine.]

mu·ri·cate (myŏŏr′ĭ-kāt′) also **mu·ri·cat·ed** (-kā′tĭd) adj. Covered with many short spines. [Lat. mūricātus, shaped like a murex, pointed < mūrex, murex.]

mu·rine (myŏŏr′ĭn′) adj. **1.** Of or relating to a rodent of the family Muridae or subfamily Murinae, including mice. **2.** Caused, transmitted, or affected by such a rodent. ❖ n. A murine rodent. [Lat. mūrīnus, of mice < mūs, mūr-, mouse. See mūs- in App.]

murk also **mirk** (mûrk) n. Partial or total darkness; gloom. ❖ adj. Archaic Partially or totally dark; gloomy. [ME mirke < ON myrkr or OE mirce.]

murk·y also **mirk·y** (mûr′kē) adj. **-i·er, -i·est 1.** Dark, dim, or gloomy: a murky dungeon. See Syns at **dark. 2a.** Heavy and thick with smoke, mist, or fog; hazy. **b.** Darkened or clouded with sediment: murky waters. **3.** Lacking clarity or distinctness; cloudy or obscure. —**murk′i·ly** adv. —**murk′i·ness** n.

Mur·mansk (mŏŏr-mänsk′, mŏŏr′mənsk) A city of NW Russia on the N Kola Peninsula. Pop. 453,590.

mur·mur (mûr′mər) n. **1.** A low indistinct continuous sound. **2.** An indistinct, whispered, or confidential complaint; a mutter. **3.** Medicine An abnormal sound, usu. emanating from the heart, that sometimes indicates a diseased condition. ❖ v. **-mured, -mur·ing, -murs** —intr. **1.** To make a murmur or succession of murmurs. **2.** To complain in low mumbling tones; grumble. —tr. To say in a low indistinct voice; utter indistinctly: murmured his approval. [ME murmure < OFr. < Lat. murmur, a humming, roaring, of imit. orig.] —**mur′mur·er** n. —**mur′mur·ing·ly** adv. —**mur′mur·ous** adj. —**mur′mur·ous·ly** adv.

Mur·phy bed (mûr′fē) n. A bed that folds or swings into a closet for concealment. [After William Lawrence Murphy (1876–1959), American inventor.]

Mur·phy's Law (mûr′fēz) n. Any of certain humorous axioms stating that anything that can possibly go wrong will go wrong. [< the name Murphy.]

mur·rain (mûr′ĭn) n. **1.** Any of various highly infectious diseases of cattle, as anthrax. **2.** Obsolete A pestilence or dire disease. [ME moreine < OFr. morine < Med.Lat. morina < Lat. morī, to die. See mer- in App.]

Mur·ray (mûr′ē), Sir **James Augustus Henry** 1837–1915. British philologist and the original lexicographer (1879–1915) of the Oxford English Dictionary.

Murray River A river of SE Australia flowing c. 2,589 km (1,609 mi) to an arm of the Indian Ocean S of Adelaide.

murre (mûr) n., pl. **murre** or **murres** Any of several large auks of the genus Uria, with black plumage and white markings. [?]

mur·rey (mûr′ē) n. See **mulberry** 3. [ME murrei < OFr. more < Lat. mōrum, mulberry, blackberry.]

Mur·row (mûr′ō, mŭr′ō), **Edward R(oscoe)** 1908–65. Amer. broadcast journalist noted for his reports from London during World War II.

Mur·rum·bidg·ee (mûr′əm-bĭj′ē) A river of SE Australia flowing c. 1,689 km (1,050 mi) to the Murray R.

mur·ther (mûr′thər) n. & v. Obsolete Variant of **murder.**

mus. abbr. **1.** museum **2.** music

MusB abbr. Latin Musicae Baccalaureus (Bachelor of Music)

Mus·ca (mŭs′kə) n. A constellation in the polar region of the Southern Hemisphere near Apus and Carina. [< Lat. musca, fly.]

Mus·ca·det (mŭs′kə-dā′) n. A dry white wine made from grapes originating in the Loire River valley. [Fr. < OFr. < musc, musky odor. See MUSK.]

mus·ca·dine (mŭs′kə-dīn′, -dĭn) n. A woody vine (Vitis rotundifolia) of the southeast United States bearing a musky grape used to make wine. [Alteration of MUSCATEL.]

mus·ca·rine (mŭs′kə-rēn′) n. A highly toxic alkaloid, $C_9H_{20}NO_2$, related to the cholines, derived from the mushroom Amanita muscaria and found in decaying animal tissue. [NLat. muscāria, specific epithet (< fem. of Lat. muscārius, of flies < musca, fly) + -INE[2].] —**mus′ca·rin′ic** (-rĭn′ĭk) adj.

mus·cat (mŭs′kăt, -kət) n. **1.** Any of various sweet white grapes used for making wine or raisins. **2.** Muscatel wine. [Fr. < OFr. < O Provençal *muscat < musc, musk < LLat. muscus. See MUSK.]

Mus·cat (mŭs′kăt, -kət, məs-kät′) The cap. of Oman, in the N part on the Gulf of Oman. Pop. 30,000.

Muscat and Oman See **Oman.**

mus·ca·tel (mŭs′kə-tĕl′) n. **1.** A rich sweet wine made from muscat grapes. **2.** A muscat grape or raisin. [ME muscadelle, partly < Med.Lat. muscātellum (< muscātus, nutmeg, musky < LLat. muscus, musk; see MUSK) and partly < OFr. muscadel (< O Provençal, dim. of *muscat, muscat; see MUSCAT).]

mus·cid (mŭs′ĭd) n. A fly of the family Muscidae, including the housefly. [< NLat. Muscidae, family name < Musca, type genus < Lat. musca, fly.] —**mus′cid** adj.

mus·cle (mŭs′əl) n. **1.** A tissue composed of fibers capable of contracting to effect bodily movement. **2.** A contractile organ consisting of a special bundle of muscle tissue, which moves a particular bone, part, or substance of the body. **3.** Muscular strength. **4.** Informal Power or authority. ❖ v. **-cled, -cling, -cles** Informal —intr. To make one's way by or as if by force: muscled into the conversation. —tr. To move or force with strength: muscled legislation through Congress. [ME < OFr. < Lat. mūsculus, dim. of mūs, mouse. See mūs- in App.] —**mus′cly** adj.

mus·cle-bound also **mus·cle-bound** (mŭs′əl-bound′) adj. **1.** Having inelastic overdeveloped muscles, usu. as the result of excessive exercise. **2a.** Hindered by or as if by overdeveloped muscles. **b.** Characterized by inflexibility; rigid.

muscle fiber n. A cylindrical multinucleate cell composed of numerous myofibrils that contracts when stimulated.

mus·cle·man also **muscle man** (mŭs′əl-măn′) n. Informal **1.** A physically powerful man, esp. with well-developed muscles. **2.** A strong man hired as a bodyguard or thug.

mus·co·vite (mŭs′kə-vīt′) n. A potassium aluminum silicate mineral, $KAl_2(AlSi_3O_{10})(OH)_2$, the most common form of mica, which has a pearly luster and is used as an insulator. [Muscovy glass, its former name + -ITE[1].]

Muscovite n. A native or resident of Moscow or Muscovy. ❖ adj. Of or relating to Moscow, Muscovy, or the Muscovites.

Mus·co·vy (mŭs′kə-vē) A former principality in W-central Russia; founded c. 1280 and nucleus of the Russian empire.

Muscovy duck n. A gooselike duck (Cairina moschata) found wild from Mexico to northern Argentina and widely domesticated for food. [Alteration of musk duck.]

mus·cu·lar (mŭs′kyə-lər) adj. **1.** Of, relating to, or consisting of muscle: muscular contraction. **2.** Having well-developed muscles. **3.** Having or suggesting great forcefulness, esp. at the expense of subtlety. [< Lat. mūsculus, muscle. See MUSCLE.] —**mus′cu·lar′i·ty** (-lăr′ĭ-tē) n. —**mus′cu·lar·ly** adv.

SYNONYMS muscular, athletic, brawny, burly, sinewy These adjectives mean strong and powerfully built: a muscular skater; an athletic swimmer; brawny arms; a burly stevedore; a lean and sinewy frame.

muscular dystrophy n. **1.** Any of a group of progressive muscle disorders caused by a defect in one or more genes that control muscle function and marked by gradual irreversible wasting of skeletal muscle. **2.** Duchenne's muscular dystrophy.

mus·cu·la·ture (mŭs′kyə-lə-chŏŏr′) n. The system or arrangement of muscles in a body or a body part. [Fr. < Lat. mūsculus, muscle. See MUSCLE.]

mus·cu·lo·skel·e·tal (mŭs′kyə-lō-skĕl′ĭ-tl) adj. Relating to or involving the muscles and the skeleton. [Lat. mūsculus, muscle; see MUSCLE + SKELETAL.]

MusD abbr. Latin Musicae Doctor (Doctor of Music)

MusDr abbr. Latin Musicae Doctor (Doctor of Music)

muse (myŏŏz) v. **mused, mus·ing, mus·es** —intr. To be absorbed in one's thoughts; engage in meditation. —tr. To consider or say thoughtfully. ❖ n. A state of meditation. [ME musen < OFr. muser (poss. < mus, snout < Med.Lat. mūsum) or of Germanic orig.] —**mus′er** n.

Muse n. **1.** Greek Mythology Any of the nine daughters of Mnemosyne and Zeus, each of whom presided over a different art or science. **2. muse a.** A guiding spirit. **b.** A source of inspiration. **3. muse** A poet. [ME < OFr. < Lat. Mūsa < Gk. Mousa. See men-[1] in App.]

mu·se·ol·o·gy (myŏŏ′zē-ŏl′ə-jē) n. The discipline of museum

Muscovy duck
Cairina moschata

design, organization, and management. —**mu•se•o•log•i•cal** (-ə-lŏj′ĭ-kəl) *adj.* —**mu′se•ol′o•gist** *n.*

mu•sette (myōō-zĕt′) *n.* **1a.** A small French bagpipe operated with a bellows and having a soft sound. **b.** A soft pastoral air that imitates bagpipe music. **2.** A musette bag. [ME < OFr., dim. of *muse* < *muser*, to play the musette, muse. See MUSE.]

musette bag *n.* A small canvas or leather bag with a shoulder strap, as one used by soldiers or travelers.

mu•se•um (myōō-zē′əm) *n.* A building, place, or institution devoted to the acquisition, conservation, study, and exhibition of objects having scientific, historical, or artistic value. [Lat. *Mūsēum* < Gk. *Mouseion*, shrine of the Muses < *Mouseios*, of the Muses < *Mousa*, Muse. See **men-**[1] in App.]

Mu•se•ve•ni (mōō-sĕv′ə-nē), **Yoweri Kaguta** b. 1944. Ugandan president (since 1986) who worked to overthrow the dictatorship of Idi Amin.

mush[1] (mŭsh) *n.* **1.** A thick porridge or pudding of cornmeal boiled in water or milk. **2.** Something thick, soft, and pulpy. **3.** *Informal* Mawkish sentimentality, affection, or amorousness. ❖ *tr.v.* **mushed, mush•ing, mush•es** To reduce to mush; mash or crush. [Prob. alteration of MASH.]

mush[2] (mŭsh) *v.* **mushed, mush•ing, mush•es** —*intr.* To travel, esp. over snow with a dogsled. —*tr.* To drive (a dogsled or team of dogs). ❖ *n.* A journey, esp. by dogsled. ❖ *interj.* Used to order a dog team to begin or speed up. [Poss. alteration of Fr. *marchons*, first pers. pl. imper. of *marchier*, to walk, go < OFr. See MARCH[1].] —**mush′er** *n.*

mush•room (mŭsh′rōōm′, -rŏŏm′) *n.* **1.** Any of various fleshy fungi of the class Basidiomycota, having an umbrella-shaped cap borne on a stalk, esp. any of the edible kinds. **2.** Something shaped like one of these fungi. ❖ *intr.v.* **-roomed, -room•ing, -rooms** **1.** To multiply, grow, or expand rapidly. **2.** To swell or spread out into a shape similar to a mushroom. ❖ *adj.* **1.** Relating to, consisting of, or containing mushrooms. **2.** Resembling mushrooms in rapidity of growth or evanescence. [ME *musheron* < AN *musherum* < OFr. *mousseron* < Med.Lat. *musariō, musariōn-*.]

mushroom cloud *n.* A mushroom-shaped cloud of smoke and debris, esp. one created by the detonation of a nuclear bomb.

mu shu or **mu-shu** (mōō′shōō′) *n.* A Chinese dish of stir-fried vegetables, egg, and often meat or fish served wrapped in a thin pancake. [Chin. (Mandarin) *mùxū* : *mù*, wood, wood ear + *xū*, day lily (whose petals are used as an herb).]

mush•y (mŭsh′ē, mŏŏsh′ē) *adj.* **-i•er, -i•est** **1.** Resembling mush in consistency; soft. **2.** *Informal* **a.** Excessively sentimental. **b.** Given to or displaying mawkish affection. —**mush′i•ly** *adv.* —**mush′i•ness** *n.*

mu•sic (myōō′zĭk) *n.* **1.** The art of arranging sounds in time so as to produce a continuous, unified, and evocative composition, as through melody, rhythm, and timbre. **2.** Vocal or instrumental sounds possessing a degree of melody, harmony, or rhythm. **3a.** A musical composition. **b.** The written or printed score for such a composition. **c.** Such scores considered as a group. **4.** A musical accompaniment. **5.** A particular category or kind of music. **6.** An aesthetically pleasing or harmonious sound or combination of sounds: *the music of the wind*. [ME < OFr. *musique* < Lat. *mūsica* < Gk. *mousikē (tekhnē)*, (art) of the Muses, fem. of *mousikos* < *Mousa*, Muse. See **men-**[1] in App.]

mu•si•cal (myōō′zĭ-kəl) *adj.* **1.** Of, relating to, or capable of producing *musical instruments*. **2.** Characteristic of or resembling music; melodious: *a musical voice*. **3.** Set to or accompanied by music. **4.** Devoted to or skilled in music. ❖ *n.* **1a.** A play or movie that contains musical numbers. **b.** A musical comedy. **2.** *Archaic* A musicale. —**mu′si•cal•ly** *adv.*

musical chairs *pl.n.* (*used with a sing. verb*) **1.** A game in which players walk to music around a group of chairs containing one chair fewer than the number of players and vie for seats when the music stops. **2.** *Informal* A rearrangement having little practical influence or significance.

musical comedy *n.* A comedic play or movie in which dialogue is interspersed with songs, esp. one with a focus on musical numbers and a simple plot.

mu•si•cale (myōō′zĭ-kăl′) *n.* A program of music performed at a party or social gathering. [Fr. < (*soirée*) *musicale*, musical (evening), fem. of *musical* < musique, music. See MUSIC.]

mu•si•cal•i•ty (myōō′zĭ-kăl′ĭ-tē) *n.* **1.** The quality or condition of being musical. **2.** Musical sensitivity or talent.

mu•si•cal•ize (myōō′zĭ-kə-līz′) *tr.v.* **-ized, -iz•ing, -iz•es** To adapt for performance with singing and musical accompaniment; set to music. —**mu′si•cal•i•za′tion** (-lĭ-zā′shən) *n.*

musical saw *n.* A handsaw on which varying musical tones are produced by flexing the blade and stroking it with a violin bow or striking it with a hammer.

music box *n.* A music-making device consisting of a housing or box enclosing a sounding mechanism, esp. one in which pins set in a revolving cylinder pluck tuned steel teeth.

music drama *n.* An opera that avoids discrete numbers such as arias, recitatives, or ensembles, and in which the music reflects or embodies the action of the drama.

music hall *n.* **1.** An auditorium for musical performances. **2.** *Chiefly British* **a.** A vaudeville theater. **b.** Vaudeville.

mu•si•cian (myōō-zĭsh′ən) *n.* One who composes, conducts, or performs music, esp. instrumental music. [ME *musicien* < OFr. < Lat. *mūsica*, music. See MUSIC.] —**mu•si′cian•ly** *adj.* —**mu•si′cian•ship** *n.*

music of the spheres *n.* A perfectly harmonious music, inaudible on the earth, thought by Pythagoras and certain later philosophers to be produced by the movement of celestial bodies.

mu•si•col•o•gy (myōō′zĭ-kŏl′ə-jē) *n.* The historical and scientific study of music. —**mu′si•co•log′i•cal** (-kə-lŏj′ĭ-kəl) *adj.* —**mu′si•co•log′i•cal•ly** *adv.* —**mu′si•col′o•gist** *n.*

music video *n.* A filmed or videotaped rendition of a song.

mus•ing (myōō′zĭng) *adj.* Deep in thought; contemplative. ❖ *n.* **1.** Contemplation; meditation. **2.** A product of contemplation; a thought. —**mus′ing•ly** *adv.*

mu•sique con•crète (mōō-zēk′ kôn-krĕt′, mü-zĕk′ kôn-krĕt′) *n.* Electronic music composed of instrumental and natural sounds often altered or distorted in recording. [Fr.]

musk (mŭsk) *n.* **1a.** A greasy secretion with a powerful odor, produced in a glandular sac beneath the skin of the abdomen of the male musk deer and used in making perfumes. **b.** A similar secretion of other animals, such as the otter. **c.** A synthetic chemical like natural musk in odor or use. **2.** The odor of musk. **3.** A musk deer. [ME < OFr. *musc* < LLat. *muscus* < Gk. *moskhos* < Pers. *mušk*, prob. < Skt. *muṣkaḥ*, testicle. See **mūs-** in App.]

musk deer *n.* An antlerless deer (*Moschus moschiferus*) of central and northeast Asia, the male of which secretes musk.

musk duck *n.* **1.** See Muscovy duck. **2.** A waterfowl (*Biziura lobata*) of Australia, the male of which has a leathery chin lobe and emits a musky odor during the breeding season.

mus•keg (mŭs′kĕg′) also **mas•keg** (măs′-) *n.* A swamp or bog formed by an accumulation of sphagnum moss, leaves, and decayed matter resembling peat. [Cree *maskek*.]

Mus•ke•gon (mŭ-skē′gən) A city of SW MI WNW of Grand Rapids at the mouth of the **Muskegon River**, flowing c. 365 km (227 mi) to Lake Michigan. Pop. 40,105.

mus•kel•lunge or **mus•ke•lunge** (mŭs′kə-lŭnj′) *n., pl.* **muskellunge** or **-lung•es** or **muskelunge** or **-lung•es** A large food and game fish (*Esox masquinongy*) of the pike family, found in lakes and rivers of North America. [Canadian Fr. *maskinongé* < Ojibwa *maashkinoozhe*.]

mus•ket (mŭs′kĭt) *n.* A smoothbore shoulder gun used from the late 16th through the 18th century. [Fr. *mousquet* < Ital. *moschetto*, a type of crossbow, musket < *moschetta*, little fly, bolt of a crossbow, dim. of *mosca*, fly < Lat. *musca*.]

mus•ket•eer (mŭs′kĭ-tîr′) *n.* **1.** A soldier armed with a musket. **2.** A member of the French royal household bodyguard in the 17th and 18th centuries. [Fr. *mousquetaire* < *mousquet*, musket. See MUSKET.]

mus•ket•ry (mŭs′kĭ-trē) *n.* **1.** The technique of using small arms. **2.** Muskets considered as a group. **3.** Musketeers considered as a group.

mus•kie or **mus•ky** (mŭs′kē) *n., pl.* **-kies** The muskellunge.

musk mallow *n.* **1.** See abelmosk. **2.** A European and North African herb (*Malva moschata*).

musk•mel•on (mŭsk′mĕl′ən) *n.* **1.** Any of several varieties of the melon *Cucumis melo*, such as the cantaloupe, having fruit characterized by a netted rind and edible flesh with a musky aroma. **2.** The fruit of any of these plants.

Mus•ko•ge•an also **Mus•kho•ge•an** (mŭs-kō′gē-ən) *n.* A family of Native American languages of the southeast United States that includes Choctaw, Chickasaw, and Creek.

Mus•ko•gee[1] (mŭs-kō′gē) *n.* See Creek. [Creek *maaskóoki*.]

Mus•ko•gee[2] (mə-skō′gē) A city of E OK on the Arkansas R. SE of Tulsa; founded 1872. Pop. 38,310.

musk•ox or **musk ox** (mŭsk′ŏks′) *n., pl.* **-ox•en** (-ŏk′sən) A large stocky oxlike bovid (*Ovibos moschatus*) of northern Canada and Greenland, having broad flat horns with curved tips, a shaggy dark coat, and a musky odor.

musk•rat (mŭs′krăt′) *n., pl.* **muskrat** or **-rats** **1.** A large aquatic rodent (*Ondatra zibethica*) of North America related to the lemming and having a dense brown coat and musk glands under a broad flat tail. **2.** The fur of this rodent.

musk•root (mŭsk′rōōt′, -rŏŏt′) *n.* See moschatel.

musk rose *n.* A prickly Mediterranean shrub (*Rosa moschata*) cultivated for its clustered musk-scented white flowers.

musk turtle *n.* Any of several small freshwater turtles of the genus *Sternotherus* of the eastern United States and Canada that emit a musky odor when disturbed.

musk•y[1] (mŭs′kē) *adj.* **-i•er, -i•est** Of, relating to, or having the odor of musk. —**musk′i•ness** *n.*

mus•ky[2] (mŭs′kē) *n.* Variant of **muskie**.

Mus•lim (mŭz′ləm, mŏŏz′-, mŭs′-, mŏŏs′-) *n.* **1.** also **Moslem** (mŏz′ləm, mŏs-) A believer in or adherent of Islam. **2.** A member of the Nation of Islam; a Black Muslim. [Ar. *muslim*, one who surrenders, active part. of *'aslama*, to surrender. See ISLAM.] —**Mus′lim** *adj.*

Mus•lin (mŭz′lĭn) *n.* Any of various sturdy cotton fabrics of plain weave, used esp. for sheets. [Fr. *mousseline* < Ital. *mussolina* < *Mussolo*, Mosul, Iraq < Ar. (*al-*)*Mawṣil* < *mawṣil*, place of joining < *waṣala*, to join.]

muskox
Ovibos moschatus

ă pat	oi boy
ā pay	ou out
âr care	ōō took
ä father	ōō boot
ĕ pet	ŭ cut
ē be	ûr urge
ĭ pit	th thin
ī pie	th this
îr pier	hw which
ŏ pot	zh vision
ō toe	ə about,
ô paw	item

Stress marks:
′ (primary);
′ (secondary), as in
lexicon (lĕk′sĭ-kŏn′)

MusM *abbr. Latin* Musicae Magister (Master of Music)

mus·quash (mŭs′kwŏsh′, -kwôsh′) *n.* See **muskrat** 1. [Perh. of Massachusett orig.; akin to Western Abenaki *mòskwas.*]

muss (mŭs) *tr.v.* **mussed, muss·ing, muss·es** To make messy or untidy; rumple. ❖ *n.* A state of disorder; a mess. [Prob. alteration of MESS.] —**muss′i·ly** *adv.* —**muss′i·ness** *n.* —**muss′y** *adj.*

mus·sel (mŭs′əl) *n.* **1.** Any of several marine bivalve mollusks, esp. the edible members of the family Mytilidae and in particular *Mytilus edulis,* a species raised commercially in Europe. **2.** Any of several freshwater bivalve mollusks of the genera *Anodonta* and *Unio,* found in the central United States, that burrow in the sand or mud of lakes and streams. [Alteration of ME *muscle* < OE *muscelle* < Med.Lat. *mūscula* < Lat. *mūsculus,* sea mussel. See MUSCLE.]

Mus·sel·shell (mŭs′əl-shĕl′) A river of central MT flowing c. 483 km (300 mi) to the Missouri R.

Mus·set (mōō-sā′, mü-), **(Louis Charles) Alfred de** 1810–57. French writer whose comedies include *Lorenzaccio* (1834).

Mus·so·li·ni (mōō′sə-lē′nē, mōōs′ə-, mōōs′ō-), **Benito** Known as "Il Duce." 1883–1945. Italian Fascist dictator and prime minister (1922–43) who brought Italy into World War II (1940).

Mus·sorg·sky (mə-zôrg′skē, -sôrg′-, mōō′sərg-), **Modest Petrovich** 1839–81. Russian composer whose works include the piano suite *Pictures at an Exhibition* (1874).

Mus·sul·man (mŭs′əl-mən) *n., pl.* **-men** or **-mans** *Archaic* A Muslim. [Turk. *musulmān,* prob. alteration of Ar. *muslim,* Muslim. See MUSLIM.]

must¹ (mŭst) *v.* —*aux.* **1.** To be obliged or required by morality, law, or custom: *I must register my car.* **2.** To be compelled, as by a physical necessity or requirement: *Plants must have oxygen.* **3.** Used to express a command or admonition: *You must be careful.* **4.** To be determined to; have as a fixed resolve: *If you must leave, do it quietly.* **5a.** Used to indicate inevitability or certainty: *We all must die.* **b.** Used to indicate logical probability or presumptive certainty: *If the lights were on, they must have been at home.* —*intr. Archaic* To be required or obliged to go: "*I must from hence*" (Shakespeare). ❖ *n.* Something that is absolutely required or indispensable: *Promptness on the job is a must.* [ME *moste* < OE *mōste,* p. t. of *mōtan,* to be allowed. See med- in App.]

must² (mŭst) *n.* The quality or condition of being stale or musty. [Prob. back-formation < MUSTY.]

must³ (mŭst) *n.* The juice expressed from fruit, esp. grapes. [ME < OE < Lat. *mustum* < neut. of *mustus,* new, fresh.]

must⁴ (mŭst) *n.* Variant of **musth.**

must⁵ (mŭst) *n.* Musk. [Sc. < OFr., var. of *musc.* See MUSK.]

mus·tache also **mous·tache** (mŭs′tăsh′, mə-stăsh′) *n.* **1.** The hair on the human upper lip, esp. when groomed on a man. **2.** Something like a groomed mustache, as: **a.** A group of bristles or hairs about the mouth of an animal. **b.** Distinctive coloring or feathers near the beak of a bird. **c.** Food or drink sticking conspicuously to the upper lip. [Fr. *moustache* < Ital. dialectal *mustaccio* < Med.Gk. *moustakion* < Gk. *mustax.*] —**mus′tached** (mŭs′tăsht, mə-stăsht′) *adj.*

mus·ta·chio (mə-stăsh′ō, -stăsh′ē-ō′, -stä′shō, -shē-ō′) *n., pl.* **-chios** A mustache, esp. a luxuriant one. [Ult. < Ital. dialectal *mustaccio,* mustache. See MUSTACHE.] —**mus·ta′chioed** (-stăsh′ōd, -stăsh′shōd, -shē-ōd′) *adj.*

mus·tang (mŭs′tăng′) *n.* A small wild horse of the North American plains, descended from horses brought to the New World by Spanish explorers. [Am.Sp. *mesteño, mestengo,* stray animal < OSpan. < *mesta,* association of livestock owners < Med.Lat. *(animālia) mixta,* assorted (animals) < Lat., neut. pl. p. part. of *miscēre,* to mix. See meik- in App.]

mus·tard (mŭs′tərd) *n.* **1a.** Any of various Eurasian plants of the genus *Brassica,* esp. *B. nigra* and *B. juncea,* cultivated for their pungent seeds and edible leaves. **b.** A condiment made from these seeds. **2.** A member of the mustard family. **3.** A dark yellow to light olive brown. [ME < OFr. *mustarde* < Lat. *mustum,* must, unfermented wine. See MUST³.] —**mus′tard·y** *adj.*

mustard family *n.* A large family of herbs, the Cruciferae (Brassicaceae), characterized by pungent juice and four-petaled flowers in a cross and including broccoli and kale.

mustard gas *n.* An oily volatile liquid, (ClCH₂CH₂)₂S, corrosive to the skin and mucous membranes and causing severe respiratory damage, introduced in World War I as a chemical weapon. [< its smell.]

mustard oil *n.* An oil obtained from mustard seeds that is used in making soap.

mustard plaster *n.* A medicinal plaster made with a pastelike mixture of powdered black mustard, flour, and water, used esp. as a counterirritant.

mus·te·line (mŭs′tə-līn′, -lĭn) *adj.* Of, relating to, or belonging to the Mustelidae, the family of fur-bearing mammals that includes the badger and weasel. [Lat. *mūstēlīnus,* of a weasel < *mūstēla,* weasel, prob. < *mūs,* mouse. See mūs- in App.]

mus·ter (mŭs′tər) *v.* **-tered, -ter·ing, -ters** —*tr.* **1.** To call (troops) together, as for inspection. **2.** To cause to come together; gather. **3.** To call forth; summon up: *mustering up her strength.* —*intr.* To assemble or gather. ❖ *n.* **1a.** A gathering, esp. of troops, as for service or inspection. **b.** The persons assembled for such a gathering. **2.** A muster roll. **3.** A gathering or collection. **4.** A flock of peacocks. —*phrasal verbs:* **muster in** To enlist or be enlisted in military service. **muster out** To discharge or be discharged from military service. —*idiom:* **pass muster** To be judged as acceptable. [ME *mustren* < OFr. *moustrer* < Lat. *mōnstrāre,* to show < *mōnstrum,* sign < *monēre,* to warn. See men-¹ in App.]

muster roll *n.* **1.** The official roll of persons in a military or naval unit. **2.** An inventory; a roster.

musth also **must** (mŭst) *n.* An annual period of heightened aggressiveness and sexual activity in male elephants, during which violent frenzies occur. [Urdu *mast* < Pers., drunk < MPers.]

must·n't (mŭs′ənt) Contraction of *must not.*

must·y (mŭs′tē) *adj.* **-i·er, -i·est** **1.** Stale or moldy in odor or taste. **2a.** Hackneyed or trite; dull. **b.** Out of date; antiquated. **c.** Out of use or practice; rusty. [Alteration of obsolete *moisty* < MOIST.] —**must′i·ly** *adv.* —**must′i·ness** *n.*

mu·ta·ble (myōō′tə-bəl) *adj.* **1a.** Capable of or subject to change or alteration. **b.** Prone to frequent change; inconstant: *mutable weather.* **2.** Tending to undergo genetic mutation. —**mu′ta·bil′i·ty** *n.* —**mu′ta·bly** *adv.*

mu·ta·gen (myōō′tə-jən, -jĕn′) *n.* An agent, such as a chemical, that can induce or increase the frequency of mutation in an organism. —**mu′ta·gen′ic** *adj.* —**mu′ta·gen′i·cal·ly** *adv.*

mu·ta·gen·e·sis (myōō′tə-jĕn′ĭ-sĭs) *n.* Formation or development of a mutation.

mu·ta·gen·ize (myōō′tə-jĕn′īz, -jə-nīz′) *tr.v.* **-ized, -iz·ing, -iz·es** To cause or induce mutation in (a cell or organism).

mu·tant (myōōt′nt) *n.* An individual, organism, or new genetic character arising or resulting from mutation. ❖ *adj.* Resulting from or undergoing mutation.

mu·tase (myōō′tās, -tāz) *n.* An enzyme that catalyzes the shifting of a chemical group from one position to another within the same molecule. [Lat. *mūtāre,* to change, move; see MUTATE + -ASE.]

mu·tate (myōō′tāt, myōō-tāt′) *intr. & tr.v.* **-tat·ed, -tat·ing, -tates** To undergo or cause to undergo mutation. [Lat. *mūtāre, mūtāt-,* to change.] —**mu′ta·tive** (-tā′tĭv, -tə-tĭv) *adj.*

mu·ta·tion (myōō-tā′shən) *n.* **1.** The act or process of being altered or changed. **2.** An alteration or change, as in nature, form, or quality. **3.** *Genetics* **a.** A change of the DNA sequence within a gene or chromosome of an organism resulting in the creation of a new character or trait not found in the parental type. **b.** The process by which such a change occurs, either through an alteration in the nucleotide sequence of the DNA coding for a gene or through a change in the physical arrangement of a chromosome. **c.** A mutant. **4.** *Linguistics* The change that is caused in a sound by its assimilation to another sound, such as umlaut. [ME *mutacioun* < OFr. *mutacion* < Lat. *mūtātiō, mūtātiōn-* < p. part. of *mūtāre,* to change. See MUTATE.] —**mu·ta′tion·al** *adj.* —**mu·ta′tion·al·ly** *adv.*

mu·ta·tis mu·tan·dis (mōō-tä′tĭs mōō-tän′dĭs) *adv.* The necessary changes having been made; having substituted new terms; with respective differences taken into consideration. [Lat. *mūtātīs mūtandīs* : *mūtātīs,* ablative pl. p. part. of *mūtāre,* to change + *mūtandīs,* ablative pl. gerundive of *mūtāre.*]

mutch·kin (mŭch′kĭn) *n.* Scots A unit of liquid measure equal to 0.9 US pint (0.42 liter). [ME *muchekyn* < MDu. *mudseken,* dim. of *mutse,* a kind of measure < Lat. *modius,* grain measure. See med- in App.]

mute (myōōt) *adj.* **mut·er, mut·est** **1.** Refraining from producing speech or vocal sound. **2a.** Unable to speak. **b.** Unable to vocalize, as in certain animals. **3.** Expressed without speech; unspoken: *a mute appeal.* **4.** *Linguistics* **a.** Not pronounced; silent, as the *e* in the word *house.* **b.** Pronounced with a temporary stoppage of breath, as the sounds (p) and (b); plosive. ❖ *n.* **1.** *Offensive* One who is incapable of speech. **2.** *Music* Any of various devices used to muffle or soften the tone of an instrument. **3.** *Linguistics* **a.** A silent letter. **b.** A plosive; a stop. ❖ *tr.v.* **mut·ed, mut·ing, mutes** **1.** To soften or muffle the sound of. **2.** To soften the tone, color, shade, or hue of. [ME *muet* < OFr. < dim. of *mu* < Lat. *mūtus.*] —**mute′ly** *adv.* —**mute′ness** *n.*

mut·ed (myōō′tĭd) *adj.* **1a.** Muffled; indistinct: *a muted voice.* **b.** Subdued; softened: *muted colors.* **2.** *Music* Produced by or provided with a mute. —**mut′ed·ly** *adv.*

mute swan *n.* A white swan (*Cygnus olor*) of Europe and Asia having an orange bill with a black knob and being much less vocal than most swans.

mu·ti·late (myōōt′l-āt′) *tr.v.* **-lat·ed, -lat·ing, -lates** **1.** To deprive of a limb or an essential part; cripple. **2.** To disfigure by damaging irreparably: *mutilate a statue.* **3.** To make imperfect by excising or altering parts. [Lat. *mutilāre, mutilāt-* < *mutilus,* maimed.] —**mu′ti·la′tion** *n.* —**mu′ti·la′tive** *adj.* —**mu′ti·la′tor** *n.*

mu·ti·neer (myōōt′n-îr′) *n.* One who takes part in a mutiny. [Obsolete Fr. *mutinier* < OFr. *mutin,* rebellious. See MUTINY.]

mu·ti·nous (myōōt′n-əs) *adj.* **1.** Of, relating to, engaged in, disposed to, or being mutiny. **2.** Unruly; disaffected. **3.** Turbulent and uncontrollable. [< obsolete *mutine,* mutiny. See MUTINY.] —**mu′ti·nous·ly** *adv.* —**mu′ti·nous·ness** *n.*

mu·ti·ny (myōōt'n-ē) *n.*, *pl.* **-nies** Open rebellion against authority, esp. rebellion of sailors against superior officers. ❖ *intr.v.* **-nied, -ny·ing, -nies** To engage in mutiny. [Obsolete *mutine* < OFr. *mutin*, rebellious < *muete*, revolt < VLat. *movita* < Lat. *movēre*, to move. See MOVE.]

mut·ism (myōō'tĭz'əm) *n.* The condition of being unable or unwilling to speak as a result of a physical or psychological disorder.

mu·ton (myōō'tŏn') *n.* The smallest unit of DNA at which a mutation can occur; a nucleotide. [MUT(ATION) + –ON¹.]

Mu·tsu·hi·to (mōō'tsōō-hē'tō) Imperial name Meiji. 1852–1912. Emperor of Japan (1867–1912) who helped transform feudal Japan into a modern state.

mutt (mŭt) *n. Informal* **1.** A mongrel dog. **2.** A stupid person; a dolt. [Short for MUTTONHEAD.]

mut·ter (mŭt'ər) *v.* **-tered, -ter·ing, -ters** —*intr.* **1.** To speak indistinctly in low tones. **2.** To complain or grumble morosely. —*tr.* To utter or say in low indistinct tones. ❖ *n.* A low grumble or indistinct utterance. [ME *muttren*, poss. < Lat. *muttīre*.] —**mut'ter·er** *n.*

mut·ton (mŭt'n) *n.* The flesh of fully grown sheep. [ME < OFr. *mouton, moton* < Med.Lat. *multō, multōn-*, of Celt. orig.]

mut·ton·chops (mŭt'n-chŏps') *pl.n.* Side whiskers that are narrow at the temple, broad along the lower cheek or jawline, and separated by a shaven chin.

mut·ton·fish (mŭt'n-fĭsh') *n.*, *pl.* **muttonfish** or **-fish·es 1.** An eelpout (*Macrozoarces americanus*) of the coastal waters of northeast North America. **2.** Mutton snapper.

mut·ton·head (mŭt'n-hĕd') *n. Informal* A stupid person; a fool. —**mut'ton·head'ed** *adj.*

mutton snapper *n.* A usu. olive-green snapper (*Lutjanus analis*) of warm western Atlantic waters valued as a game fish.

Mut·tra (mŭt'rə) See **Mathura.**

mu·tu·al (myōō'chōō-əl) *adj.* **1.** Having the same relationship each to the other: *mutual predators.* **2.** Directed and received by each toward the other; reciprocal: *mutual respect.* **3.** Possessed in common: *mutual interests.* **4.** Of, relating to, or in the form of mutual insurance. ❖ *n.* A mutual fund. [French *mutuel* < OFr. < Lat. *mūtuus*, borrowed.] —**mu'tu·al'i·ty** (-ăl'ĭ-tē) *n.* —**mu'tu·al·ly** *adv.*

USAGE NOTE *Mutual* is used to describe a reciprocal relationship between two or more people or things. Thus, *their mutual animosity* means "their animosity for each other." But many people also use *mutual* to mean "shared in common," as in *the mutual interests of management and labor.* This usage is perhaps most familiar in the expression *our mutual friend,* which was widespread even before Charles Dickens used it as the title of a novel. While some language critics have objected to this usage because it does not include the notion of reciprocity, it has appeared in the writings of respected authors since Shakespeare's day.

mutual fund *n.* An investment company that continually offers new shares, buys existing shares back at the request of the shareholder, and invests in diversified securities.

mutual inductance *n.* The ratio of the electromotive force in a circuit to the corresponding change of current in a neighboring circuit.

mutual induction *n.* The production of an electromotive force in a circuit resulting from a change of current in a neighboring circuit.

mutual insurance *n.* An insurance system in which the insured persons become company members, each paying specified amounts into a common fund from which members are entitled to indemnification in case of loss.

mu·tu·al·ism (myōō'chōō-ə-lĭz'əm) *n.* An association between organisms of two different species in which each member benefits. —**mu'tu·al·is'tic** *adj.*

mu·tu·al·ize (myōō'chōō-ə-līz') *v.* **-ized, -iz·ing, -iz·es** —*tr.* **1.** To make mutual. **2.** To set up or reorganize (a corporation) so that the majority of common stock is owned by customers or employees. —*intr.* To become mutual. —**mu'tu·al·i·za'tion** (-ə-lĭ-zā'shən) *n.*

mu·tule (myōō'chōōl) *n.* A projecting rectangular block or bracket situated above the triglyph and beneath the corona of a Doric cornice. [Lat. *mutulus.*]

muu·muu (mōō'mōō') *n.* A long loose dress that hangs free from the shoulders. [Hawaiian *mu'umu'u*, cut off, muumuu < redup. of *muku*, to cut off.]

Muy·bridge (mī'brĭj'), **Eadweard** 1830–1904. British-born motion-picture pioneer noted for his motion studies.

Mu·zak (myōō'zăk') A trademark used for recorded background music transmitted by wire or radio, as to places of business, on a subscription basis.

mu·zhik also **mou·jik** or **mu·jik** (mōō-zhēk', -zhĭk') *n.* A Russian peasant. [Russ. < *muzh*, man. See **man-**¹ in App.]

Muz·tag or **Muz·tagh** (mōōs-tä', -täg') A mountain, 7,286.8 m (23,891 ft), in the Kunlun Range of W China.

Muz·tag·a·ta also **Muz·tagh A·ta** (mōōs-tä'-tä', mōōs-täg'-) A mountain, 7,550.9 m (24,757 ft), of the **Muztagata Range** in W China near Tajikistan.

muz·zle (mŭz'əl) *n.* **1.** The forward projecting part of the head

---

of certain animals, such as dogs, including the mouth, nose, and jaws; the snout. **2.** A leather or wire restraining appliance fitted over an animal's snout to prevent biting. **3.** The forward discharging end of the barrel of a firearm. **4.** A restraint on free movement or expression. ❖ *tr.v.* **-zled, -zling, -zles 1.** To put a muzzle on (an animal). **2.** To restrain from expression: *tried to muzzle the opposition.* [ME *mosel* < OFr. *musel* < Med.Lat. *mūsellum*, dim. of *mūsus*, snout < Lat. *mūsum.*] —**muz'zler** *n.*

muz·zle·load·er (mŭz'əl-lō'dər) *n.* A firearm loaded at the muzzle. —**muz'zle·load'ing** *adj.*

muz·zy (mŭz'ē) *adj.* **-zi·er, -zi·est 1.** Mentally confused; muddled. **2.** Blurred; indistinct. [?] —**muz'zi·ly** *adv.* —**muz'zi·ness** *n.*

mV *abbr.* millivolt

MV *abbr.* **1.** mean variation **2.** megavolt

MVP *abbr. Sports* most valuable player

mW *abbr.* milliwatt

MW *abbr.* megawatt

Mwe·ru (mwā'rōō), **Lake** A lake of central Africa on the Zambia-Congo (formerly Zaire) border W of the S end of Lake Tanganyika.

Mx *abbr.* maxwell

my (mī) *adj.* The possessive form of I¹. **1.** Used as a modifier before a noun: *my boots.* **2.** Used preceding various forms of polite, affectionate, or familiar address: *Yes, my friend.* **3.** Used in various interjectional phrases: *My word!* ❖ *interj.* Used as an exclamation of surprise, pleasure, or dismay: *Oh, my! What a joke.* [ME *mi* < OE *mīn.* See **me-**¹ in App. Interj., short for *My God!*]

my- *pref.* Variant of **myo-.**

my·al·gi·a (mī-ăl'jē-ə, -jə) *n.* Muscular pain or tenderness, esp. when diffuse and nonspecific. —**my·al'gic** (-jĭk) *adj.*

Myan·mar (myän-mär') Formerly **Bur·ma** (bûr'mə) A country of SE Asia on the Bay of Bengal and the Andaman Sea; gained independence from Great Britain in 1948. Cap. Rangoon. Pop. 45,555,000.

my·as·the·ni·a (mī'əs-thē'nē-ə) *n.* **1.** Abnormal muscular weakness or fatigue. **2.** Myasthenia gravis. —**my'as·then'ic** (-thĕn'ĭk) *adj.*

myasthenia grav·is (grăv'ĭs) *n.* A disease characterized by progressive fatigue and generalized weakness of the skeletal muscles, caused by impaired transmission of nerve impulses following an autoimmune attack on acetylcholine receptors. [NLat. : MYASTHENIA + Lat. *gravis*, heavy, severe.]

myc (mĭk) *n.* Any of a group of vertebrate oncogenes whose product, a DNA binding protein, is thought to promote the growth of tumor cells. [Poss. < *my(elo)c(ytomatosis virus).*]

my·ce·li·um (mī-sē'lē-əm) *n.*, *pl.* **-li·a** (-lē-ə) **1.** The vegetative part of a fungus, consisting of a mass of branching threadlike hyphae. **2.** A similar mass of fibers formed by certain bacteria. [NLat. : MYC(O)- + Gk. *hēlos*, wart.] —**my·ce'li·al** (-lē-əl) *adj.*

My·ce·nae (mī-sē'nē) An ancient Greek city in the NE Peloponnesus; center of an early Bronze Age civilization.

My·ce·nae·an also **My·ce·ne·an** (mī'sə-nē'ən) *adj.* **1.** Of or relating to Mycenae or its inhabitants. **2.** Of, relating to, or being the Aegean civilization that spread its influence from Mycenae to many parts of the Mediterranean region from about 1580 to 1120 B.C. **3.** Of, relating to, or being the archaic dialect of Greek written in the Linear B script. ❖ *n.* **1.** A native or inhabitant of Mycenae. **2.** Mycenaean Greek.

-mycete *suff.* Fungus: *basidiomycete.* [NLat. *-mycētes* < Gk. *mukēs, mukēt-*, fungus.]

my·ce·to·ma (mī'sĭ-tō'mə) *n.*, *pl.* **-mas** or **-ma·ta** (-mə-tə) A chronic, slowly progressing bacterial or fungal infection usu. of the foot or leg, characterized by nodules that discharge an oily pus. [Gk. *mukēs, mukēt-*, fungus + -OMA.] —**my'ce·to'ma·tous** (-tō'mə-təs, -tōm'ə-) *adj.*

-mycin *suff.* A substance derived from a bacterium in the order Actinomycetales: *neomycin.* [MYC(O)- (the original bacterial source having been mistaken for fungi) + -IN.]

myco- or **myc-** *pref.* Fungus: *mycology.* [< Gk. *mukēs*, fungus.]

my·co·bac·te·ri·um (mī'kō-băk-tîr'ē-əm) *n.*, *pl.* **-te·ri·a** (-tîr'ē-ə) Any of various slender rod-shaped aerobic bacteria of the genus *Mycobacterium*, which includes the bacteria that cause tuberculosis and leprosy. —**my'co·bac·te'ri·al** *adj.*

my·col·o·gy (mī-kŏl'ə-jē) *n.*, *pl.* **-gies 1.** The branch of botany that deals with fungi. **2.** The fungi native to a region. **3.** The composition or characteristics of a particular fungus. —**my'co·log'i·cal** (-kə-lŏj'ĭ-kəl), **my'co·log'ic** *adj.* —**my'col·og'i·cal·ly** *adv.* —**my·col'o·gist** *n.*

my·coph·a·gous (mī-kŏf'ə-gəs) *adj.* Fungivorous.

my·co·plas·ma (mī'kō-plăz'mə) *n.* Any of numerous parasitic pathogenic microorganisms of the genus *Mycoplasma*, lacking a true cell wall, gram-negative, and needing sterols such as cholesterol for growth. —**my'co·plas'mal** *adj.*

my·cor·rhi·za or **my·co·rhi·za** (mī'kô-rī'zə) *n.*, *pl.* **-zae** (-zē) The symbiotic association of the mycelium of a fungus with the roots of certain plants. [MYCO- + Gk. *rhiza*, root; see **wrād-** in App.] —**my'cor·rhi'zal** *adj.*

my·co·sis (mī-kō'sĭs) *n.*, *pl.* **-ses** (-sēz) **1.** A fungal infection in or on a part of the body. **2.** A disease caused by a fungus.

my·co·tox·i·co·sis (mī'kō-tŏk'sĭ-kō'sĭs) *n.* Poisoning that is

---

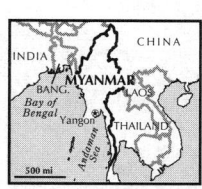

Myanmar

ă	pat	oi	boy
ā	pay	ou	out
âr	care	ŏŏ	took
ä	father	ōō	boot
ĕ	pet	ŭ	cut
ē	be	ûr	urge
ĭ	pit	th	thin
ī	pie	th	this
îr	pier	hw	which
ŏ	pot	zh	vision
ō	toe	ə	about,
ô	paw		item

Stress marks:
' (primary);
' (secondary); as in
lexicon (lĕk'sĭ-kŏn')

caused by ingestion of a mycotoxin.

my·co·tox·in (mī′kō-tŏk′sĭn) *n.* A toxin produced by a fungus.

my·dri·a·sis (mĭ-drī′ə-sĭs) *n.* Prolonged abnormal dilatation of the pupil of the eye caused by disease or a drug. [Lat. *mydriāsis* < Gk. *mudriāsis*.]

myd·ri·at·ic (mĭd′rē-ăt′ĭk) *adj.* Causing dilatation of the pupils. ❖ *n.* A mydriatic drug. [< MYDRIASIS.]

my·el·en·ceph·a·lon (mī′ə-lĕn-sĕf′ə-lŏn′) *n.* The posterior portion of the embryonic hindbrain, from which the medulla oblongata develops. —**my′e·len·ce·phal′ic** (-sə-făl′ĭk) *adj.*

my·e·lin (mī′ə-lĭn) also **my·e·line** (-lĭn, -lēn′) *n.* A white fatty material, composed chiefly of lipids and lipoproteins, that encloses certain axons and nerve fibers. —**my′e·lin′ic** *adj.*

my·e·li·nat·ed (mī′ə-lə-nā′tĭd) *adj.* Having a myelin sheath.

my·e·li·na·tion (mī′ə-lə-nā′shən) also **my·e·li·ni·za·tion** (-nĭ-zā′shən) *n.* The process of forming a myelin sheath.

myelin sheath *n.* The insulating envelope of myelin that surrounds the core of a nerve fiber or axon and facilitates the transmission of nerve impulses.

my·e·li·tis (mī′ə-lī′tĭs) *n.* **1.** Inflammation of the spinal column. **2.** Osteomyelitis.

myelo– or **myel–** *pref.* **1.** Spinal cord: *myelitis.* **2.** Bone marrow: *myeloma.* [NLat. < Gk. *muelos,* marrow, prob. < *mūs,* muscle. See **mūs–** in App.]

my·e·lo·blast (mī′ə-lə-blăst′) *n.* An immature cell of the bone marrow that is the precursor of a myelocyte.

my·e·lo·cyte (mī′ə-lə-sīt′) *n.* A large cell of the bone marrow that is a precursor of the mature granulocyte of the blood. —**my′e·lo·cyt′ic** (-sĭt′ĭk) *adj.*

my·e·lo·fi·bro·sis (mī′ə-lō-fī-brō′sĭs) *n.* Proliferation of fibroblastic cells in bone marrow, causing anemia and sometimes enlargement of the spleen and liver.

my·e·log·e·nous (mī′ə-lŏj′ə-nəs) also **my·e·lo·gen·ic** (-lə-jĕn′ĭk) *adj.* Originating in or produced by the bone marrow.

my·e·lo·gram (mī′ə-lə-grăm′) *n.* An x-ray of the spinal cord after injection of air or a radiopaque substance into the subarachnoid space. —**my′e·log′ra·phy** (-lŏg′rə-fē) *n.*

my·e·loid (mī′ə-loid′) *adj.* **1.** Of, relating to, or derived from the bone marrow. **2.** Of or relating to the spinal cord.

my·e·lo·ma (mī′ə-lō′mə) *n., pl.* **-mas** or **-ma·ta** (-mə-tə) A malignant tumor formed by the cells of the bone marrow. —**my′e·lo′ma·toid′** (-toid′) *adj.*

my·ia·sis (mī′ə-sĭs, mī-ī′ə-sĭs) *n., pl.* **my·ia·ses** (mī′ə-sēz′) Infestation of tissue by fly larvae. **2.** A disease resulting from such infestation. [Gk. *muia, mūa,* fly + –IASIS.]

My·ko·la·yiv (mī′kə-lä′yĭv, -yēw) or **Ni·ko·la·yev** (nĭk′ə-lä′yəf, nyĭ′kə-) A city of S Ukraine at the mouth of the Western Bug R. NE of Odessa; founded c. 1784 as a fortress. Pop. 515,400.

My·ko·nos (mĭk′ə-nŏs′, -nōs′, mē′kô-nôs′) also **Mí·ko·nos** (mē′kô-nôs′) An island of SE Greece in the Cyclades Is.

My Lai (mē′ lī′) A village of S Vietnam where more than 300 unarmed civilians were massacred by US troops (1968) during the Vietnam War.

My·lar (mī′lär′) A trademark used for a thin strong polyester film.

my·lo·nite (mī′lə-nīt′) *n.* A fine-grained laminated rock formed by the shifting of rock layers along faults. [Gk. *mulōn,* mill (< *mulē,* handmill; see **mela–** in App.) + –ITE¹.]

my·na or **my·nah** also **mi·na** (mī′nə) *n.* Any of various starlings of southeast Asia having bluish-black or dark brown coloration and yellow bills. [Hindi *mainā,* perh. < Skt. *madanaḥ* < *madana-,* delightful, joyful < *madati,* it bubbles.]

Myn·heer (mə-nîr′) *n.* **1a.** Used as a courtesy title before the name of a man in a Dutch-speaking area. **b.** Used as a form of polite address for a man in a Dutch-speaking area. **2. mynheer** *Informal* A Dutchman. [Du. *mijnheer : mijn,* my (< MDu.; see **me-¹** in App.) + *heer,* lord (< MDu. *here.*).]

myo– or **my–** *pref.* Muscle: *myograph.* [NLat. < Gk. *mūs,* muscle. See **mūs–** in App.]

myocardial infarction *n.* See **heart attack.**

my·o·car·di·tis (mī′ō-kär-dī′tĭs) *n.* Inflammation of the myocardium.

my·o·car·di·um (mī′ō-kär′dē-əm) *n., pl.* **-di·a** (-dē-ə) The muscular tissue of the heart. [NLat. : MYO– + Gk. *kardiā,* heart; see **kerd–** in App.] —**my′o·car′di·al** *adj.*

my·o·clo·nus (mī-ŏk′lə-nəs) *n.* A sudden twitching of muscles or parts of muscles, without any rhythm or pattern, occurring in various brain disorders.

my·o·e·lec·tric (mī′ō-ĭ-lĕk′trĭk) *adj.* Of or relating to the electrical properties of muscle tissue from which impulses may be amplified, used in the operation of prostheses.

my·o·fi·bril (mī′ə-fī′brəl, -fĭb′rəl) *n.* Any of the threadlike fibrils of the contractile part of a striated muscle fiber.

my·o·gen·ic (mī′ə-jĕn′ĭk) also **my·o·ge·net·ic** (mī′ō-jə-nĕt′ĭk) *adj.* **1.** Giving rise to or forming muscular tissue. **2.** Of muscular origin; arising from the muscles.

my·o·glo·bin (mī′ə-glō′bĭn) *n.* An iron-containing protein found in muscle fibers, having a higher affinity for oxygen than hemoglobin of the blood.

my·o·graph (mī′ə-grăf′) *n.* An instrument for recording muscular contractions.

Alva Myrdal

my·ol·o·gy (mī-ŏl′ə-jē) *n.* The scientific study of muscles. —**my′o·log′ic** (mī′ə-lŏj′ĭk) *adj.* —**my·ol′o·gist** *n.*

my·o·ma (mī-ō′mə) *n., pl.* **-mas** or **-ma·ta** (-mə-tə) A tumor composed of muscle tissue. —**my·o′ma·tous** (-ō′mə-təs, -ŏm′ə-) *adj.*

my·o·neu·ral (mī′ō-nŏor′əl, -nyŏor′-) *adj.* Of or relating to both muscles and nerves, esp. to nerve endings in muscle.

my·op·a·thy (mī-ŏp′ə-thē) *n., pl.* **-thies** A disease of muscle or muscle tissue. —**my′o·path′ic** (mī′ə-păth′ĭk) *adj.*

my·ope (mī′ōp′) *n.* One who is affected by myopia. [Fr. < LLat. *myōps,* near-sighted < Gk. *muōps.* See MYOPIA.]

my·o·pi·a (mī-ō′pē-ə) *n.* **1.** A visual defect in which distant objects appear blurred because their images are focused in front of the retina rather than on it; nearsightedness. **2.** Lack of discernment or long-range perspective in thinking or planning. [Gk. *muōpiā* < *muōps,* nearsighted : *mūein,* to close the eyes + *ōps, ōp-,* eye; see **ok**ʷ– in App.] —**my·op′ic** (-ŏp′ĭk, -ō′pĭk) *adj.* —**my·op′i·cal·ly** *adv.*

my·o·sin (mī′ə-sĭn) *n.* The commonest protein in muscle cells, responsible for the elastic and contractile properties of muscle. [Gk. *muos,* genitive of *mūs,* muscle; see MYO– + *–in.*]

my·o·sis (mī-ō′sĭs) *n.* Variant of **miosis.**

my·o·si·tis (mī′ə-sī′tĭs) *n.* Inflammation of a muscle, esp. a voluntary muscle, characterized by pain, tenderness, and sometimes spasm in the affected area.

my·o·so·tis (mī′ə-sō′tĭs) *n.* Any of various plants of the genus *Myosotis,* such as the forget-me-not. [NLat. *Myosōtis,* genus name < Lat. *myosōtis,* mouse-ear, a kind of plant < Gk. *muosōtis : muos,* genitive of *mūs,* mouse; see **mūs–** in App. + *ous, ōt-,* ear; see **ous–** in App.]

my·o·tome (mī′ə-tōm′) *n.* **1.** The segment of a somite in a vertebrate embryo that differentiates into skeletal muscle. **2.** A muscle or group of muscles derived from one somite and innervated by a single segment of a spinal nerve.

my·o·to·ni·a (mī′ə-tō′nē-ə) *n.* Tonic spasm or temporary rigidity of one or more muscles, often characteristic of various muscular disorders. —**my′o·ton′ic** (-tŏn′ĭk) *adj.*

My·ra (mī′rə) An ancient Lycian city of S Asia Minor.

Myr·dal (mür′däl′, mîr′-), **Alva** 1902–86. Swedish sociologist and diplomat who shared the 1982 Nobel Peace Prize.

Myrdal, (Karl) Gunnar 1898–1987. Swedish economist who shared a 1974 Nobel Prize.

myr·i·ad (mîr′ē-əd) *adj.* **1.** Constituting a myriad; innumerable. **2.** Composed of numerous diverse elements or facets. ❖ *n.* **1.** A vast number. **2.** *Archaic* Ten thousand. [Gk. *mūrias, mūriad-,* ten thousand < *mūrios,* countless.]

myr·i·a·pod also **myr·i·o·pod** (mîr′ē-ə-pŏd′) *n.* Any of several arthropods, such as the centipede, having segmented bodies, one pair of antennae, and at least nine pairs of legs. [< NLat. *Mȳriapoda,* class name : Gk. *mūrias,* ten thousand; see MYRIAD + NLat. *-poda,* -pod.] —**myr′i·ap′o·dous** (-ăp′ə-dəs) *adj.*

my·ris·tic acid (mə-rĭs′tĭk, mī-) *n.* A fatty acid, $CH_3(CH_2)_{12}COOH$, occurring in animal and vegetable fats and used in the manufacture of cosmetics, soaps, perfumes, and flavorings. [Lat. *muristikos,* fragrant < *muron,* perfume.]

myrmeco– *pref.* Ant: *myrmecology.* [Lat. *myrmēco-* < Gk. *murmēko-* < *murmēx, murmēk-,* ant.]

myr·me·col·o·gy (mûr′mĭ-kŏl′ə-jē) *n.* The branch of entomology that deals with ants. —**myr′me·col′o·gist** *n.*

myr·me·co·phile (mûr′mĭ-kə-fīl′) *n.* An organism, such as a beetle, that habitually shares the nest of an ant colony. —**myr′me·coph′i·lous** (-kŏf′ə-ləs) *adj.*

Myr·mi·don (mûr′mə-dŏn′, -dn) *n.* **1.** *Greek Mythology* A member of a warlike Thessalian people who were ruled by Achilles and followed him on the expedition against Troy. **2. myrmidon** A follower who carries out orders without question. [< ME *Mirmidones,* Myrmidons < Lat. *Myrmidones* < Gk. *Murmidones.*]

myr·rob·a·lan (mĭ-rŏb′ə-lən, mə-) *n.* **1.** See **cherry plum. 2.** The fruit of this plant. [Obsolete Fr. *mirobolan* < Lat. *myrobalanum,* a fragrant oil < Gk. *murobalanos : muron,* perfume + *balanos,* acorn.]

myrobalan plum *n.* See **cherry plum.**

My·ron (mī′rən) 5th cent. B.C. Greek sculptor of the *Discus Thrower.*

myrrh (mûr) *n.* **1.** An aromatic gum resin obtained from several trees and shrubs of the genus *Commiphora* of India, Arabia, and eastern Africa, used in perfume and incense. **2.** See **sweet cicely** 2. [ME *mirre* < OE *myrrha* < Lat. < Gk. *murrha,* of Semitic orig.; akin to Akkadian *murru.*]

myr·tle (mûr′tl) *n.* **1.** Any of several evergreen shrubs or trees of the genus *Myrtus,* esp. *M. communis,* an aromatic shrub of the Mediterranean region and western Asia having blue-black berries and cultivated as a hedge plant. **2.** See **periwinkle²** 1. [ME *mirtille* < OFr. < Med.Lat. *myrtillus,* dim. of Lat. *myrtus* < Gk. *murtos.*]

my·self (mī-sĕlf′) *pron.* **1.** That one identical with me. **a.** Used reflexively as the direct or indirect object of a verb or as the object of a preposition: *I bought myself a new car.* **b.** Used for emphasis: *I myself was certain of the facts.* **c.** Used in an absolute construction: *In office myself, I helped her get a job.* **2.** My normal or healthy condition or state: *I'm feeling myself again.* [ME *mi-self* < OE *mē selfum, mē selfne : mē,* me; see **me-¹** in App. + *selfum,* selfne, dative and accusative of *self* SELF.]

My•si•a (mĭsh′ē-ə) An ancient region of NW Asia Minor. —**My′si•an** *adj. & n.*

My•sore (mī-sôr′, -sōr′) A city of S India SW of Bangalore; inhabited before the 3rd cent. B.C. Pop. 480,692.

mys•ta•gogue (mĭs′tə-gŏg′, -gôg′) *n.* **1.** One who prepares candidates for initiation into a mystery cult. **2.** One who holds or spreads mystical doctrines. [< Lat. *mystagōgus* < Gk. *mustagōgos* : *mustēs,* an initiate; see MYSTERY[1] + *agōgos,* guide, leader (< *agein,* to lead; see **ag-** in App.).] —**mys′ta•gog′ic** (-gŏj′ĭk) *adj.* —**mys′ta•go′gy** (-gō′jē) *n.*

mys•te•ri•ous (mĭ-stîr′ē-əs) *adj.* **1.** Of, relating to, or being a mystery: *mysterious and infinite truths.* **2.** Simultaneously arousing wonder and inquisitiveness and eluding explanation or comprehension: *a mysterious visitor; mysterious conduct.* [Fr. *mystérieux* < *mystère,* secret < Lat. *mystērium.* See MYSTERY[1].] —**mys•te′ri•ous•ly** *adv.* —**mys•te′ri•ous•ness** *n.*

SYNONYMS *mysterious, esoteric, arcane, occult, inscrutable* These adjectives mean beyond human power to explain or understand. Something *mysterious* arouses wonder and inquisitiveness and also eludes comprehension: *"The sea lies all about us. . . . In its mysterious past it encompasses all the dim origins of life"* (Rachel Carson). What is *esoteric* is mysterious because only a small select group knows and understands it: *a compilation of esoteric philosophical essays. Arcane* applies to what is hidden from the knowledge of all but those having the key to a secret: *arcane economic theories. Occult* suggests knowledge reputedly gained only by secret, magical, or supernatural means: *an occult rite.* Something that is *inscrutable* cannot be fathomed by means of investigation or scrutiny: *"It is not for me to attempt to fathom the inscrutable workings of Providence"* (Earl of Birkenhead).

mys•ter•y[1] (mĭs′tə-rē) *n., pl.* **-ies 1.** Something not fully understood or eluding the understanding; an enigma. **2.** One whose identity is unknown. **3.** A mysterious character or quality. **4.** A work of fiction, drama, or film dealing with a puzzling crime. **5.** The skills, lore, or practices that are peculiar to a particular activity or group and are regarded as the special province of initiates. Often used in the plural. **6.** *Theology* A religious truth that is incomprehensible to the reason and knowable only through divine revelation. **7.** An incident in the life of Jesus or Mary serving as a subject of meditation. **8a.** also **Mystery** One of the Christian sacraments, esp. the Eucharist. **b. mysteries** The consecrated elements of the Eucharist. **9a.** A religious cult having secret rites. **b.** A secret rite of such a cult. [ME *misterie* < Lat. *mystērium* < Gk. *mustērion,* secret rite < *mustēs,* an initiate < *muein,* to close the eyes, initiate.]

mys•ter•y[2] (mĭs′tə-rē) *n., pl.* **-ies 1.** *Archaic* A trade or occupation. **2.** *Archaic* A guild, as of artisans. **3.** A mystery play. [ME *misterie,* service, craft < Med.Lat. *misterium,* craft-guild < LLat. alteration of Lat. *ministerium,* occupation < *minister,* assistant, servant.]

mystery play *n.* A medieval drama based on scriptural events esp. in the life of Jesus. [< MYSTERY[1].]

mys•tic (mĭs′tĭk) *adj.* **1.** Of or relating to religious mysteries or occult rites and practices. **2.** Of or relating to mysticism or mystics. **3.** Inspiring a sense of mystery and wonder. **4a.** Mysterious; strange. **b.** Enigmatic; obscure. **5.** Magical. ❖ *n.* One who practices or believes in mysticism or a given form of mysticism: *Muslim mystics.* [ME *mystik* < Lat. *mysticus* < Gk. *mustikos* < *mustēs,* initiate. See MYSTERY[1].]

mys•ti•cal (mĭs′tĭ-kəl) *adj.* **1a.** Of or relating to mystics or mysticism. **b.** Of or relating to mystic rites or practices. **2a.** Strange; mysterious. **b.** Enigmatic; obscure. —**mys′ti•cal•ly** *adv.* —**mys′ti•cal•ness** *n.*

mys•ti•cete (mĭs′tĭ-sēt′) *n.* See **baleen whale.** [NLat. *mysticētus* < Gk. *mustikētos,* alteration of (*ho*) *mūs to kētos,* (the) whale (called) the mouse : *mūs,* mouse; see **mūs-** in App. + *to,* neut. of *ho,* the; see **to-** in App. + *kētos,* whale.] —**mys′ti•ce′tous** (-sē′təs) *adj.*

mys•ti•cism (mĭs′tĭ-sĭz′əm) *n.* **1a.** Immediate consciousness of the transcendent or ultimate reality or God. **b.** The experience of

mystical communion. **2.** A belief in the existence of essential realities beyond perceptual or intellectual apprehension that are accessible by subjective experience. **3.** Vague, groundless speculation.

mys•ti•fi•ca•tion (mĭs′tə-fĭ-kā′shən) *n.* **1.** The act or an instance of mystifying. **2.** The fact or condition of being mystified. **3.** Something intended to mystify.

mys•ti•fy (mĭs′tə-fī′) *tr.v.* **-fied, -fy•ing, -fies 1.** To confuse or puzzle mentally; bewilder. **2.** To make obscure or mysterious. [Fr. *mystifier* : *mystère,* mystery (< Lat. *mystērium;* see MYSTERY[1]) + *-fier,* -fy.] —**mys′ti•fi′er** *n.* —**mys′ti•fy′ing•ly** *adv.*

mys•tique (mĭ-stēk′) *n.* An aura of heightened value, interest, or meaning surrounding something to which special power or mystery is imputed: *the cowboy mystique.* [Fr., mystical, mystique < Lat. *mysticus.* See MYSTIC.]

myth (mĭth) *n.* **1a.** A traditional story dealing with supernatural beings, ancestors, or heroes that informs or shapes the worldview of a people, as by explaining aspects of the natural world or delineating the customs or ideals of society. **b.** Such stories considered as a group. **2.** A popular belief or story associated with a person, institution, or occurrence, esp. one considered to illustrate a cultural ideal: *the pioneer myth.* **3.** A fiction or half-truth, esp. one that forms part of an ideology. **4.** A fictitious story, person, or thing. [NLat. *mȳthus* < LLat. *mȳthos* < Gk. *mūthos.*]

myth•i•cal (mĭth′ĭ-kəl) also **myth•ic** (-ĭk) *adj.* **1.** Of or existing in myth: *the mythical unicorn.* **2.** Imaginary; fictitious. **3.** often **mythic** Of, relating to, or having the nature of a myth. —**myth′i•cal•ly** *adv.*

myth•i•cize (mĭth′ĭ-sīz′) *tr.v.* **-cized, -ciz•ing, -ciz•es 1.** To turn (a person or an event) into myth. **2.** To interpret as a myth or in terms of mythology.

myth•mak•er (mĭth′mā′kər) *n.* One that creates myths or mythical situations. —**myth′mak′ing** *n.*

my•thog•ra•pher (mĭ-thŏg′rə-fər) *n.* One who records, narrates, or comments on myths. [< Gk. *mūthographos,* writer of legends : *mūthos,* word, story + *-graphos,* -grapher.]

my•thog•ra•phy (mĭ-thŏg′rə-fē) *n., pl.* **-phies 1.** The artistic representation of mythical subjects. **2.** A collection of myths, often with critical commentary.

myth•o•log•i•cal (mĭth′ə-lŏj′ĭ-kəl) also **myth•o•log•ic** (-ĭk) *adj.* **1.** Of, relating to, or recorded in myths or mythology. **2.** Fabulous; imaginary. —**myth′o•log′i•cal•ly** *adv.*

my•thol•o•gize (mĭ-thŏl′ə-jīz′) *v.* **-gized, -giz•ing, -giz•es** —*tr.* To convert into myth; mythicize. —*intr.* **1.** To construct or relate a myth. **2.** To interpret or write about myths or mythology. —**my•thol′o•giz′er** *n.*

my•thol•o•gy (mĭ-thŏl′ə-jē) *n., pl.* **-gies 1a.** A body or collection of myths belonging to a people and addressing their history, deities, ancestors, and heroes. **b.** A body of myths associated with an individual, event, or institution. **2.** The field of scholarship dealing with the systematic collection and study of myths. [Fr. *mythologie* < LLat. *mȳthologia* < Gk. *mūthologia,* story-telling : *mūthos,* story + *logos,* saying; see –LOGY.] —**my•thol′o•gist** *n.*

myth•o•ma•ni•a (mĭth′ə-mā′nē-ə, -mān′yə) *n.* A compulsion to embroider the truth, engage in exaggeration, or tell lies. —**myth′o•ma′ni•ac′** (-ăk′) *n.*

myth•o•poe•ic or **myth•o•pe•ic** (mĭth′ə-pē′ĭk) also **myth•o•po•et•ic** (-pō-ĕt′ĭk) *adj.* **1.** Of or relating to the making of myths. **2.** Serving to create myths; productive in mythmaking. [< Gk. *mūthopoios,* composer of fiction < *mūthopoiein,* to create a story : *mūthos,* story + *poiein,* to make.] —**myth′o•poe′ia** (-pē′ə), **myth′o•po•e′sis** (-pō-e′sĭs) *n.*

my•thos (mī′thŏs, mĭth′ŏs) *n., pl.* **my•thoi** (mī′thoi, mĭth′oi) **1.** Myth. **2.** Mythology. **3.** The pattern of basic values and attitudes of a people. [Gk. *mūthos.*]

myx•a•moe•ba also **myx•a•me•ba** (mĭk′sə-mē′bə) *n., pl.* **-bas** also **-bae** (-bē) A slime mold when it is an amoebalike free-swimming cell and before it forms a plasmodium.

myx•e•de•ma or **myx•oe•de•ma** (mĭk′sĭ-dē′mə) *n.* A disease caused by decreased activity of the thyroid gland in adults and characterized by dry skin, swellings around the lips and nose, and mental deterioration. —**myx′e•dem′a•tous** (-dĕm′ə-təs, -dē′mə-), **myx′e•dem′ic** (-dĕm′ĭk) *adj.*

myxo– or **myx–** *pref.* Mucus: *myxoma.* [NLat. < Gk. *muxa,* mucus, slime.]

myx•o•ma (mĭk-sō′mə) *n., pl.* **-mas** or **-ma•ta** (-mə-tə) A benign tumor that is composed of connective tissue embedded in mucus. —**myx•o′ma•tous** (-sō′mə-təs, -sŏm′ə-) *adj.*

myx•o•ma•to•sis (mĭk-sō′mə-tō′sĭs) *n., pl.* **-ses** (-sēz) **1.** A highly infectious, usu. fatal disease of rabbits, characterized by many skin tumors similar to myxomas. **2.** A condition characterized by the growth of many myxomas.

myx•o•my•cete (mĭk′sō-mī′sēt) *n.* See **slime mold** 2.

myx•o•vi•rus (mĭk′sə-vī′rəs) *n., pl.* **-rus•es** Any of a group of RNA-containing viruses, including those that cause influenza, typically having an affinity for certain mucins.

ă	pat	oi	boy
ā	pay	ou	out
âr	care	ŏŏ	took
ä	father	ōō	boot
ĕ	pet	ŭ	cut
ē	be	ûr	urge
ĭ	pit	th	thin
ī	pie	*th*	this
îr	pier	hw	which
ŏ	pot	zh	vision
ō	toe	ə	about,
ô	paw		item

Stress marks:
′ (primary);
′ (secondary), as in
lexicon (lĕk′sĭ-kŏn′)

n¹ or **N** (ĕn) *n.*, *pl.* **n's** or **N's** also **ns** or **Ns** **1.** The 14th letter of the modern English alphabet. **2.** Any of the speech sounds represented by the letter *n*. **3.** The 14th in a series. **4.** Something shaped like the letter N.

n² *abbr.* **1.** *Grammar* neuter **2.** neutron **3.** also **N** *Chemistry* normal

N¹ The symbol for the element **nitrogen**.

N² *abbr.* **1.** *Printing* en **2.** knight (chess) **3.** needs improvement **4.** newton **5.** nominative **6a.** north **b.** northern

n. *abbr.* **1.** *Latin* natus (born) **2.** noun

N. *abbr.* Norse

'n' or **'n** *conj. Informal* Contraction of *and*: *scratch 'n' sniff*.

Na¹ The symbol for the element **sodium**. [< NLat. *natrium* < Fr. *natron*, natron. See NATRON.]

Na² *abbr.* Nahum

NA *abbr.* **1.** North America **2.** also **n/a** not applicable

NAACP *abbr.* National Association for the Advancement of Colored People

naan or **nan** (nän, năn) *n.* A flat, leavened bread of northwest India, made of white flour and baked in a tandoor. [Hindi *nān*, bread < Pers., ult. < OPers. *nagna*, naked, bare (prob. < being baked uncovered in an oven rather than covered in ash).]

nab (năb) *tr.v.* **nabbed, nab•bing, nabs** *Informal* **1.** To seize (a fugitive or wrongdoer); arrest. **2.** To grab; snatch. [Perh. var. of dialectal *nap*, to seize, prob. of Scand. orig.] —**nab'ber** *n.*

NAB *abbr.* New American Bible

Nab•a•tae•a (năb'ə-tē'ə) An ancient kingdom of N Arabia; flourished from the 4th cent. B.C. to A.D. 106.

Nab•a•tae•an also **Nab•a•te•an** (năb'ə-tē'ən) *n.* **1.** A subject of the kingdom of Nabataea. **2.** The Aramaic dialect of the Nabataeans.

Na•blus (näb'ləs, nä'bləs) also **Nab•u•lus** (näb'ə-lōos') A city in the West Bank N of Jerusalem; biblical home of Jacob and the chief city of Samaria. Pop. 64,000.

na•bob (nā'bŏb') *n.* **1.** A governor in India under the Mogul Empire. **2.** A person of wealth and prominence. [Hindi *nawāb*, *nabāb* < Ar. *nuwwāb*, pl. of *nā'ib*, deputy, active part. of *nāba*, to represent.]

Na•bo•kov (nə-bô'kəf, nä'bə-kôf', näb'ə-), **Vladimir Vladimirovich** 1899–1977. Russian-born Amer. writer whose works include *Lolita* (1955) and *Ada* (1969).

na•celle (nə-sĕl') *n.* A separate streamlined enclosure on an aircraft for housing the crew, the cargo, or an engine. [Fr., dinghy, gondola < OFr. *nacele*, small boat < LLat. *nāvicella*, dim. of Lat. *nāvis*, ship.]

na•cho (nä'chō) *n.*, *pl.* **-chos** A small piece of tortilla topped with cheese or chili-pepper sauce and broiled. [Am.Sp., poss. dim. of the name *Ignacio* or alteration of *ñato*, pug-nosed, ugly, poor < alteration of Sp. *chato*, flat, snub-nosed < VLat. *plattus*, flat; see PLATE.]

na•cre (nā'kər) *n.* See **mother-of-pearl**. [Fr. < OFr. *nacle* < OItal. *naccaro*, drum, nacre < Ar. *naqqāra* < *naqara*, to bore, pierce.] —**na'cred** (-kərd), **na'cre•ous** (-krē-əs) *adj.*

nacreous cloud *n.* A cloud resembling a cirrus, appearing iridescent when the sun is several degrees below the horizon.

NAD (ĕn'ā-dē') *n.* A coenzyme, $C_{21}H_{27}N_7O_{14}P_2$, occurring in most living cells and utilized alternately with NADH as an oxidizing or reducing agent in various metabolic processes. [N(ICOTINAMIDE) A(DENINE) D(INUCLEOTIDE).]

Na-De•ne also **Na•Dé•né** (nä'dā'nē, -dā-nā') *n.* A proposed phylum of North American Indian languages including Athabaskan, Tlingit, and possibly Haida. [Haida *náa-*, house, to live, and Tlingit *naa*, tribe + Proto-Athabaskan **dənæ*, person.]

Na•der (nā'dər), **Ralph** b. 1934. Amer. lawyer and pioneer in the field of consumer protectionism.

NADH (ĕn'ā-dē-āch') *n.* The reduced form of NAD. [NAD + H¹.]

na•dir (nā'dər, -dîr') *n.* **1.** *Astronomy* A point on the celestial sphere directly below the observer, diametrically opposite the zenith. **2.** The lowest point: *the nadir of their fortunes.* [ME < Med.Lat. < Ar. *nazīr (as-samt)*, opposite (the zenith) < *nazara*, to see, watch.]

NADP (ĕn'ā-dē-pē') *n.* A coenzyme, $C_{21}H_{28}N_7O_{17}P_3$, occurring in most living cells and utilized similarly to NAD but interacting with different metabolites. [< *n(icotinamide) a(denine) d(inucleotide) p(hosphate)*, its chemical name.]

NADPH (ĕn'ā-dē'pē-āch') *n.* The reduced form of NADP. [NADP + H¹.]

nae (nā) *adv. Scots* **1.** No. **2.** Not.

naff¹ (năf) *adj. Chiefly British Slang* Unstylish, clichéd, or outmoded. [Poss. of dialectal orig.]

naff² (năf) *intr.v.* **naff•ed, naff•ing, naffs** *Chiefly British Slang* To fool around or go about. —**phrasal verb: naff off** Used in the imperative as a signal of angry dismissal. [?]

NAFTA (năf'tə) *abbr.* North American Free Trade Agreement

Na•fud (nä-fōod') See **Nefud**.

nag¹ (năg) *v.* **nagged, nag•ging, nags** —*tr.* **1.** To annoy by constant scolding, complaining, or urging. **2.** To torment persistently, as with pain. —*intr.* **1.** To scold, complain, or find fault constantly. **2.** To be a constant source of anxiety or annoyance. ❖ *n.* One who nags. [Prob. of Scand. orig.; akin to ON *gnaga*, to bite, gnaw.] —**nag'ger** *n.*

nag² (năg) *n.* **1.** A horse, esp.: **a.** An old or worn-out horse. **b.** *Slang* A racehorse. **2.** *Archaic* A small saddle horse or pony. [ME *nagge*, poss. of LGer. orig.]

na•ga•na also **n'ga•na** (nə-gä'nə) *n.* An often fatal disease of African ungulates caused by various species of trypanosomes and transmitted by the tsetse fly. [Zulu *-nakane*.]

Na•ga•no (nä-gä'nō, nä'gä-nō') A city of central Honshu, Japan, NW of Tokyo. Pop. 352,378.

Na•ga•sa•ki (nä'gə-sä'kē, näg'ə-säk'ē) A city of W Kyushu, Japan, on **Nagasaki Bay**, an inlet of the East China Sea; devastated by the second US atomic bomb used in World War II (Aug. 9, 1945). Pop. 441,308.

Na•go•ya (nə-goi'ə, nä'gô-yä') A city of central Honshu, Japan, at the head of Ise Bay E of Kyoto. Pop. 2,158,713.

Nag•pur (näg'pŏor') A city of central India NE of Mumbai (Bombay); founded in the 18th cent. Pop. 1,624,752.

nah (nä, nă) *interj. Informal* No. [Variant of NO¹.]

Nah. *abbr. Bible* Nahum.

Na•ha (nä'hä) A city of SW Okinawa, Japan, in the Ryukyu Is. on the East China Sea. Pop. 301,679.

Na•hua•tl (nä'wät'l) *n.*, *pl.* **Nahuatl** or **-tls** **1.** A member of any of various Indian peoples of central Mexico, including the Aztecs. **2.** The Uto-Aztecan language of the Nahuatl. [Sp. *náhuatl* < Nahuatl, that which pleases the ear < *nahua-*, audible, intelligent, clear.]

Na•hum¹ (nä'həm, nā'əm) A Hebrew prophet of the 7th cent. B.C. who predicted the fall of Nineveh. [Heb. *naḥûm*, comfort < *niḥam*, to console.]

Na•hum² (nä'həm, nā'əm) *n.* See table at **Bible**. [After NAHUM¹.]

NAIA *abbr.* National Association of Intercollegiate Athletes

nai•ad (nā'əd, -ăd', nī'-) *n.*, *pl.* **-a•des** (-ə-dēz') or **-ads** **1.** *Greek Mythology* One of the nymphs who lived in and presided over brooks, springs, and fountains. **2.** Naiad A satellite of Neptune. **3.** The aquatic nymph of certain insects, such as the dragonfly. **4.** An aquatic plant of the genus *Naias*. [ME < Lat. *nāias*, *nāiad-* < Gk. < *nān*, to flow. See **(s)nāu-** in App.]

na•if or **na•ïf** (nä-ēf') *adj. & n.* Variants of **naive**.

nail (nāl) *n.* **1.** A slim pointed piece of metal hammered into material as a fastener. **2a.** The thin horny transparent plate covering the upper surface of each finger and toe. **b.** A claw or talon. **3.** Something resembling a nail in shape, sharpness, or use. **4.** A measure of length formerly used for cloth, equal to 1/16 yard (5.7 centimeters). —*tr.* **nailed, nail•ing, nails** **1.** To fasten, join, or attach with or as if with a nail. **2.** To cover, enclose, or shut by fastening with nails: *nail up a window.* **3.** To keep fixed, motionless, or intent. **4.** *Slang* **a.** To stop and seize; catch. **b.** To detect and expose. **5.** *Slang* **a.** To strike or bring down. **b.** To perform successfully or have noteworthy success in: *nailed the exam.* —**phrasal verb: nail down 1.** To discover or establish conclusively. **2.** To win. **3.** To specify or fix: *nailed down a meeting time.* [ME < OE *nægl*, fingernail, toenail.] —**nail'er** *n.* —**nailed** *adj.*

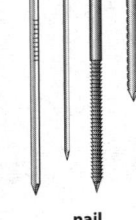

nail
left to right: common, finishing, ring, and roofing nails

nail bed *n.* The formative layer of cells at the base of the fingernail or toenail; the matrix.

nail biter also **nail•bit•er** (nāl'bī'tər) *n.* **1.** One who bites one's fingernails as a nervous habit. **2.** A situation marked by tense nervousness, esp. an athletic contest whose outcome is uncertain. —**nail biting** *n.*

nail•brush (nāl'brŭsh') *n.* A small brush with firm bristles used for scrubbing the hands and cleaning the fingernails and toenails.

nail file *n.* A small flat file used to shape the fingernails and toenails.

nail polish *n.* A cosmetic lacquer for fingernails or toenails.

nail punch *n.* See **nail set**.

nail scissors *pl.n.* (*used with a sing. or pl. verb*) Small scissors with curved blades for cutting fingernails or toenails.

nail set *n.* A tool used for driving a nail so that its head is below or flush with a surface.

nain·sook (nān′sŏok′) *n.* A soft light cotton material, often with a woven stripe. [< Hindi *nainsukh*, pleasant : *nain*, eye (< Skt. *nayanam* < *nayati*, he leads) + *sukh*, pleasure (< Skt. *sukha*-, running easily (of chariots) : *su*-, good + *kham*, axle-hole).]

Nai·paul (nī′pôl), **V(idiadhar) S(urajprasad)** b. 1932. Trinidadian-born British writer who won the 2001 Nobel Prize for literature.

nai·ra (nī′rə) *n., pl.* **naira** See table at **currency**. [Alteration of NIGERIA.]

Nai·ro·bi (nī-rō′bē) The cap. of Kenya, in the S-central part; founded 1899. Pop. 1,162,189.

nai·ru (nā′rōo) *n.* The lowest unemployment rate that an economy can accommodate without causing inflation. [*n(on)a(ccelerating)* *i(nflation)* *r(ate of)* *u(nemployment)*.]

na·ive or **na·ïve** (nī-ēv′, nä-) also **na·if** or **na·ïf** (nī-ēf′, nä-) *adj.* **1.** Lacking worldly experience and understanding, esp.: **a.** Simple and guileless; artless. **b.** Unsuspecting or credulous. **2.** Showing or characterized by a lack of sophistication and critical judgment. **3a.** Not previously subjected to experiments: *testing naive mice.* **b.** Not having previously taken or received a particular drug. ❖ *n.* One who is artless, credulous, or uncritical. [Fr. *naïve*, fem. of *naïf* < OFr. *naif*, natural, native < Lat. *nātīvus*, native, native : *nātus*, p. part. of *nāscī*, to be born. See **genə**- in App.] —**na·ive′ly** *adv.* —**na·ive′ness** *n.*

SYNONYMS *naive, simple, ingenuous, unsophisticated, unaffected, guileless, artless* These adjectives mean free from guile, cunning, or sham. *Naive* sometimes connotes a credulity that impedes effective functioning in a practical world: "*this naive simple creature, with his straightforward and friendly eyes so eager to believe appearances*" (Arnold Bennett). *Simple* stresses absence of complexity, artifice, pretentiousness, or dissimulation: "*Among simple people she had the reputation of being a prodigy of information*" (Harriet Beecher Stowe). *Ingenuous* denotes childlike directness, simplicity, and innocence; it connotes an inability to mask one's feelings: *an ingenuous admission.* *Unsophisticated* indicates absence of worldliness: *unsophisticated tourists.* *Unaffected* implies sincerity and lack of affectation: "*With men he can be rational and unaffected*" (Jane Austen). *Guileless* signifies absence of insidious or treacherous cunning: *a guileless, disarming look.* *Artless* stresses absence of plan or purpose and suggests unconcern for or unawareness of the reaction produced in others: *artless grace and simple goodness.*

na·ive·té or **na·ïve·té** (nī′ēv-tā′, nä′-, nī-ē′vĭ-tā′, nä-) *n.* **1.** The state or quality of being inexperienced or unsophisticated, esp. in being artless, credulous, or uncritical. **2.** A naive statement or act. [Fr. *naïveté* < OFr. *naiveté*, native disposition < *naif*, artless. See NAIVE.]

na·ive·ty or **na·ïve·ty** (nī-ēv′tē, nä-, nī-ē′vĭ-tē, nä-) *n.* Naiveté.

Najd (nä́jd) See **Nejd**.

na·ked (nā′kĭd) *adj.* **1.** Having no clothing on the body; nude. **2.** Having no covering, esp. the usual one: *a naked sword.* **3.** Devoid of vegetation, trees, or foliage. **4.** Being without addition, concealment, disguise, or embellishment: *the naked facts.* **5.** Devoid of a specified quality, characteristic, or element. **6.** Exposed to harm; vulnerable. **7.** *Botany* **a.** Not encased in ovaries. **b.** Unprotected by scales. **c.** Lacking a perianth. **d.** Without leaves or pubescence. **8.** *Zoology* Lacking outer covering such as scales or fur. [ME < OE *nacod*.] —**na′ked·ly** *adv.* —**na′ked·ness** *n.*

nak·fa (näk′fä′) *n.* See table at **currency**. [Tigré *naqfa*, after *Naqfa*, town in Eritrea that became a symbol of Eritrean resistance.]

na·led (nā′lĕd′) *n.* A nonpersistent insecticide, $C_4H_7O_4PBr_2Cl_2$, used against mosquitoes and crop pests. [?]

nal·ox·one (năl′ək-sōn′, nə-lŏk′sōn) *n.* A drug, $C_{19}H_{21}NO_4$, used as an antagonist to narcotic drugs, such as morphine. [N(ORMAL) + AL(LYL) + (HYDR)OX(Y) + (*morphin*)one, compound related to morphine.]

nal·trex·one (năl-trĕk′sōn) *n.* A drug, $C_{20}H_{23}NO_4$, used as an antagonist to narcotic drugs. [Blend of NALOXONE and *tre*- (prob. alteration of TRI-, from the three carbon atoms of the propyl group distinguishing it from naloxone).]

Nam (năm) *Slang* Vietnam.

Na·ma (nä′mä, -mə) *n., pl.* **Nama** or **-mas** **1.** A member of a people of southwest Africa. **2.** The Khoikhoin language of the Nama.

Na·man·gan (nä′män-gän′, nə-mən-) A city of E Uzbekistan E of Tashkent. Pop. 312,000.

Na·ma·qua·land (nə-mä′kwə-länd′) or **Na·ma·land** (nä′mə-) A mostly arid region of SW Africa divided by the Orange R. into **Great Namaqualand** in Namibia and **Little Namaqualand** in South Africa.

nam·ay·cush (năm′ī-kŭsh′, năm′ā-) *n.* See **lake trout**. [Cree *namekos*.]

nam·by-pam·by (năm′bē-păm′bē) *adj.* **1.** Insipid and sentimental. **2.** Lacking vigor or decisiveness; spineless. ❖ *n., pl.* **-bies** One that is insipid, sentimental, or weak. [After *Namby-Pamby*, a satire on the poetry of Ambrose Philips (1674–1749) by Henry Carey (1687?–1743).]

name (nām) *n.* **1.** A word or words by which an entity is designated and distinguished from others. **2.** A word or group of words to describe or evaluate, often disparagingly. **3.** Repre-

sentation or repute, as opposed to reality: *a democracy in name, a police state in fact.* **4a.** A reputation: *has a bad name.* **b.** A distinguished reputation; renown: *made a name for himself as a drummer.* **5.** An illustrious or outstanding person. ❖ *tr.v.* **named, nam·ing, names** **1.** To give a name to. **2.** To mention, specify, or cite by name. **3.** To call by an epithet. **4.** To nominate for or appoint to a duty, office, or honor. **5.** To specify or fix. ❖ *adj.* *Informal* Well known by a name. —*idioms:* **in the name of** **1.** By the authority of. **2.** For the reason of. **to (one's) name** Belonging to one. [ME < OE *nama*. See **nō-men**- in App.] —**nam′a·ble,** **name′a·ble** *adj.* —**nam′er** *n.*

name brand *n.* **1.** A trademark or distinctive name identifying a product or manufacturer. **2.** A product or manufacturer having a name brand. —**name′-brand′** *adj.*

name day *n.* The feast day of the saint after whom one is named.

name-drop (nām′drŏp′) *intr.v.* **-dropped, -drop·ping, -drops** To mention the names of well-known people so as to imply acquaintance, intended as a means of self-promotion. —**name′-drop′per** *n.*

name·less (nām′lĭs) *adj.* **1.** Having or bearing no name. **2.** Unknown by name; obscure. **3.** Not designated by name; anonymous. **4.** Defying description; inexpressible. —**name′less·ly** *adv.* —**name′less·ness** *n.*

name·ly (nām′lē) *adv.* That is to say; specifically.

name of the game *n. Slang* The essential or indispensable part or quality necessary for success.

name·plate (nām′plāt′) *n.* **1.** A plate or plaque, as on an office door, inscribed with a name. **2.** See **masthead** 3.

name·sake (nām′sāk′) *n.* One that is named after another. [< the phrase *for the name's sake*.]

Na·mib Desert (nä′mĭb) A dry region of SW Africa extending along the coast of Namibia.

Na·mib·i·a (nə-mĭb′ē-ə) Formerly **South-West Africa.** A country of SW Africa on the Atlantic Ocean; occupied in 1915 by South Africa and finally achieved full independence in 1990. Cap. Windhoek. Pop. 1,500,000. —**Na·mib′i·an** *adj. & n.*

Nam·oi (năm′oi′) A river of SE Australia flowing c. 846 km (526 mi) to a tributary of the Darling R.

Nam·pa (năm′pə) A city of SW ID W of Boise. Pop. 51,867.

nan (nän, năn) *n.* Variant of **naan**.

Nan (nän) A river of W Thailand flowing c. 563 km (350 mi) to join the Ping R. and form the Chao Phraya.

nan·a (năn′ə, nän′nə) *n.* **1.** A grandmother. **2.** A nanny. [Of baby-talk orig.]

Na·nai·mo (nə-nī′mō) A city of SW British Columbia, Canada, on Vancouver I. and the Strait of Georgia. Pop. 70,130.

Na·nak (nä′nək) 1469–1538? Indian religious leader who broke from orthodox Hinduism to found Sikhism.

Nan·chang (nän′chäng′) A city of SE China on the Gan Jiang SE of Wuhan; dating from the 12th cent. and cap. of Jiangxi province. Pop. 1,262,031.

nan·cy (năn′sē) also **nance** (năns) *n., pl.* **nan·cies** also **nanc·es** *Offensive Slang* Used as a disparaging term for an effeminate man, esp. a homosexual man. [< the name *Nancy*.]

Nan·cy (năn′sē, nän-sē′) A city of NE France E of Paris; passed to France in 1766. Pop. 96,317.

NAND (nănd) *n.* A logical operator that consists of a logical AND followed by a logical NOT and returns a false value only if both operands are true. [N(OT) + AND.]

Nan·da De·vi (nŭn′də dā′vē) A peak, 7,821.7 m (25,645 ft), of the Himalaya Mts. in N India.

na·nism (nā′nĭz′əm, năn′ĭz′-) *n.* **1.** *Ecology* The condition of being stunted or dwarfed, as in certain climates. **2.** See **dwarfism**. [Fr. *nanisme* < Lat. *nānus*, dwarf < Gk. *nānos*. See NANO-.]

Nan·ga Par·bat (nŭng′gə pŭr′bət) A peak, 8,131.3 m (26,660 ft), of the Himalaya Mts. in NW Kashmir.

Nan·jing (nän′jĭng′) also **Nan·king** (năn′kĭng′, nän′-) A city of E-central China on the Chang Jiang (Yangtze R.); NW of Shanghai; a former cap. of China and now the cap. of Jiangsu province. Pop. 2,610,594.

nan·keen (năn-kēn′) also **nan·kin** (-kēn′, -kĭn′) *n.* **1a.** A sturdy yellow or buff cotton cloth. **b.** **nankeens** Trousers made of this cloth. **2. Nankeen** A Chinese porcelain with a blue and white pattern. [After NANJING.]

Nan Ling (nän′ lĭng′) A mountain range of SE China running along the N border of Guangdong province.

Nan·ning (nän′nĭng′) A city of extreme S China W of Guangzhou; cap. of Guangxi Zhuangzu province. Pop. 1,159,099.

nan·no·fos·sil also **nan·o·fos·sil** (năn′ə-fŏs′əl) *n.* A very small fossil organism, esp. one of the nannoplankton.

nan·no·plank·ton also **nan·o·plank·ton** (năn′ə-plăngk′tən) *n.* Plankton of minute size, esp. plankton composed of organisms measuring from 2 to 20 micrometers.

nan·ny also **nan·nie** (năn′ē) *n., pl.* **-nies** A children's nurse. [Alteration of NANA.] —**nan′ny·ish** *adj.*

nan·ny·ber·ry (năn′ē-bĕr′ē) *n.* See **sheepberry**.

nanny goat *n.* A female goat. [< *Nanny*, nickname for Anne.]

nanny state *n. Informal* A government perceived as excessively involved in protecting the welfare of its citizens, as in the implementation of extensive public health regulations.

nano– *pref.* **1.** often **nanno–** **a.** Extremely small: *nannoplankton.*

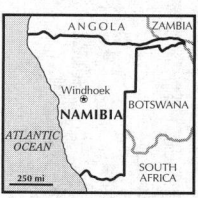

Namibia

ă	pat	oi	boy
ā	pay	ou	out
âr	care	ŏŏ	took
ä	father	ōō	boot
ĕ	pet	ŭ	cut
ē	be	ûr	urge
ĭ	pit	th	thin
ī	pie	th	this
îr	pier	hw	which
ŏ	pot	zh	vision
ō	toe	ə	about,
ô	paw		item

Stress marks:
′ (primary);
′ (secondary); as in
lexicon (lĕk′sĭ-kŏn′)

b. At the molecular level: *nanotechnology.* **2.** One billionth (10⁻⁹): *nanosecond.* [Gk. *nānos, nannos,* little old man, dwarf < *nannās,* uncle.]

nan·o·fab·ri·ca·tion (năn′ə-făb′rĭ-kā′shən) *n.* Any technique used to create objects or mechanisms on the scale of nanotechnology.

nan·o·me·ter (năn′ə-mē′tər) *n.* One billionth (10⁻⁹) of a meter.

nan·o·scale (năn′ə-skāl′) *adj.* Relating to or occurring on a scale of nanometers.

nan·o·sec·ond (năn′ə-sĕk′ənd) *n.* One billionth (10⁻⁹) of a second.

nan·o·tech·nol·o·gy (năn′ə-tĕk-nŏl′ə-jē) *n.* The science and technology of building electronic circuits and devices from individual atoms and molecules. —**nan′o·tech·nol′o·gist** *n.*

nan·o·tes·la (năn′ə-tĕs′lə) *n.* One billionth (10⁻⁹) of a tesla.

nan·o·tube (năn′ə-tōōb′, -tyōōb′) *n.* A carbon nanotube.

Nan·sen (năn′sən, nän′-), **Fridtjof** 1861–1930. Norwegian Arctic explorer who won the 1922 Nobel Peace Prize.

Nansen bottle *n.* An ocean-water sampling bottle with spring-loaded valves at both ends. [After Fridtjof NANSEN.]

Nan Shan (năn′ shän′) See Qilian Shan.

Nantes (nănts, nÄNt) A city of W France on the Loire R. W of Tours. The Edict of Nantes, granting limited religious and civil liberties to the Huguenots, was issued in 1598 by Henry IV of France and revoked in 1685 by Louis XIV. Pop. 244,514.

Nan·ti·coke (năn′tĭ-kōk′) *n., pl.* **Nanticoke** or **-cokes 1.** A member of a Native American people formerly inhabiting Delaware and eastern Maryland between Chesapeake Bay and the Atlantic coast. **2.** Their Algonquian language.

Nan·tong also **Nan·tung** (năn′tŏŏng′) A city of E-central China on the N bank of the Chang Jiang (Yangtze R.) estuary E of Nanjing. Pop. 1,602,029.

Nan·tuck·et (năn-tŭk′ĭt) An island of SE MA S of Cape Cod, from which it is separated by **Nantucket Sound,** an arm of the Atlantic Ocean. —**Nan·tuck′et·er** *n.*

Naoi·se (nē′sĕ, nä′-) *n.* The husband of Deidre in Irish legend.

Na·o·mi (nā-ō′mē) In the Bible, the mother-in-law of Ruth.

nap¹ (năp) *n.* A brief sleep, often during the day. ❖ *intr.v.* **napped, nap·ping, naps 1.** To take a nap, often during the day; doze. **2.** To be unaware of imminent danger or trouble; be off guard. [ME < *nappen,* to doze < OE *hnappian.*] —**nap′per** *n.*

nap² (năp) *n.* A soft or fuzzy surface on fabric or leather. ❖ *tr.v.* **napped, nap·ping, naps** To form or raise a nap on (fabric or leather). [Alteration of ME *noppe* < MDu.]

nap³ (năp) *n.* **1a.** A card game that resembles whist. **b.** The highest bid in this game, announcing the intention to win five tricks, the maximum number in a hand. **2.** See **napoleon** 2. [Short for NAPOLEON.]

na·pa or **nap·pa** (năp′ə, nä′pə) *n.* See **Chinese cabbage** 1. [Prob. J. *nappa,* greens.]

Nap·a (năp′ə) A city of W CA N of Oakland; center of the **Napa Valley,** a region famous for its vineyards. Pop. 72,585.

na·palm (nā′päm′) *n.* **1.** An aluminum soap of various fatty acids that when mixed with gasoline makes a firm jelly used in some bombs and in flamethrowers. **2.** Jelly made from napalm. [*na(phthenate),* salt of naphthenic acid (< NAPHTHENE) + PALM(ITATE).] —**na′palm′** *v.*

nape (nāp) *n.* The back of the neck. [ME.]

na·per·y (nā′pə-rē) *n., pl.* **-ies** Household linen, esp. table linen. [ME *naperie* < OFr. < *nape, nappe,* tablecloth. See NAPPE.]

Naph·ta·li (năf′tə-lī′) In the Bible, a son of Jacob and the forebear of one of the tribes of Israel.

naph·tha (năf′thə, năp′-) *n.* **1.** Any of several highly volatile flammable liquid mixtures of hydrocarbons distilled from petroleum, coal tar, and natural gas and used as fuel and solvents. **2.** *Obsolete* Petroleum. [Lat. < Gk., liquid bitumen, of Semitic orig.; akin to Akkadian *naptu,* naphtha.] —**naph′thous** *adj.*

naph·tha·lene also **naph·tha·line** (năf′thə-lēn′, năp′-) or **naph·tha·lin** (-lĭn) *n.* A white crystalline compound, $C_{10}H_8$, derived from coal tar or petroleum and used in manufacturing dyes and moth repellents and as a solvent. [NAPHTH(A) + AL(COHOL) + -ENE.] —**naph′tha·len′ic** (-lĕn′ĭk) *adj.*

naph·thene (năf′thēn′, năp′-) *n.* Any of several cycloalkanes having the general formula C_nH_{2n} and found in various petroleums. [NAPHTH(A) + -ENE.]

naph·thol (năf′thôl′, -thōl′, -thŏl′, năp′-) also **naph·tol** (-tôl, -tōl, -tŏl) *n.* An organic compound, $C_{10}H_7OH$, occurring in two isomeric forms, occurring in two isomeric forms, and used in organic synthesis and in making antioxidants, dyes, and perfumes. [NAPHTH(ALENE) + -OL².]

Na·pi·er (nā′pē-ər, nə-pîr′), **John.** Laird of Merchiston. 1550–1617. Scottish mathematician who introduced the use of the decimal point in writing numbers.

Na·pi·er·i·an logarithm (nə-pîr′ē-ən, nā-) *n.* See **natural logarithm.** [After John NAPIER.]

Na·pi·er's bones (nā′pē-ərz, nə-pîrz′) *pl.n.* (*used with a sing. verb*) A set of graduated rods used to perform multiplication quickly. [After John NAPIER.]

na·pi·form (nā′pə-fôrm′) *adj.* Shaped like a turnip: *napiform roots.* [Lat. *nāpus,* turnip + -FORM.]

Napoleon I
Napoleon I at Malmaison in 1804, by François Gerard (1770–1837)

nap·kin (năp′kĭn) *n.* **1.** A piece of cloth or absorbent paper used to protect the clothes or wipe the lips and fingers while eating. **2.** A cloth or towel. **3.** A sanitary napkin. **4.** *Chiefly British* A diaper. [ME : OFr. *nape, nappe,* tablecloth; see NAPPE + *-kin,* -kin.]

Na·ples (nā′pəlz) A city of S-central Italy on the **Bay of Naples,** an arm of the Tyrrhenian Sea; formerly an independent duchy (8th cent. A.D.) and cap. of the kingdom of Naples (1282–1860). Pop. 1,054,601.

Na·po (nä′pō) A river of NE Ecuador and N Peru flowing c. 1,126 km (700 mi) to the Amazon R.

na·po·le·on (nə-pō′lē-ən, -pōl′yən) *n.* **1.** A rectangular piece of pastry made with crisp flaky layers filled with custard cream. **2.** A 20-franc gold coin formerly used in France. **3.** *Games* See **nap³** 1. [After NAPOLEON I.]

Napoleon I Orig. Napoleon Bonaparte. 1769–1821. Emperor of the French (1804–14) who conquered much of Continental Europe but was forced to abdicate (1814) following a disastrous winter campaign in Russia. He escaped from exile on the island of Elba, briefly regained power, and was ultimately defeated at Waterloo (1815) and exiled to St. Helena. —**Na·po′le·on′ic** (-ŏn′ĭk) *adj.*

Napoleon II Orig. François Charles Joseph Bonaparte. 1811–32. Titular king of Rome who succeeded his father, Napoleon I, as emperor of the French (1814).

Napoleon III Orig. Charles Louis Napoleon Bonaparte. Known as "Louis Napoleon." 1808–73. Emperor of the French (1852–71) who became president of the Second Republic (1848) and proclaimed himself emperor (1852).

nap·pa (năp′ə, nä′pə) *n.* Variant of **napa.**

nappe (năp) *n.* **1.** A sheet of water flowing over a dam or similar structure. **2.** *Geology* A large sheetlike body of rock that has been moved far from its original position. **3.** *Mathematics* Either of the two parts into which a cone is divided by the vertex. [Fr., tablecloth, nappe < OFr., tablecloth < Lat. *mappa,* napkin. See MAP.]

nap·py¹ (năp′ē) *adj.* **-pi·er, -pi·est 1.** Having a nap; fuzzy. **2.** Kinky; frizzy.

nap·py² (năp′ē) *n., pl.* **-pies** A shallow round cooking or serving dish with a flat bottom and sloping sides. [Prob. < dialectal *nap,* bowl < ME < OE *hnæp.*]

nap·py³ (năp′ē) *n., pl.* **-pies** *Chiefly British* A diaper. [Alteration of NAPKIN.]

na·prox·en (nə-prŏk′sən) *n.* A drug, $C_{14}H_{14}O_3$, used to reduce inflammation and pain, esp. in the treatment of arthritis. [Shortening and alteration of *methoxynaphthylpropionic acid,* one of its chemical names.]

Na·ra (när′ə) A city of S-central Honshu, Japan, E of Osaka; first permanent cap. of Japan (710–784). Pop. 355,869.

Nar·ba·da (nər-bŭd′ə) See Narmada.

Nar·bonne (när-bŏn′, -bôn′) A city of S France near the Mediterranean Sea SW of Montpellier; perhaps the first Roman colony in Transalpine Gaul (118 B.C.). Pop. 41,565.

narc or **nark** (närk) *n.* *Slang* A law enforcement officer who deals with narcotics violations. [Short for *narcotics agent.*]

nar·cis·sism (när′sĭ-sĭz′əm) also **nar·cism** (-sĭz′əm) *n.* **1.** Excessive self-love, together with a lack of empathy for others. **2.** In psychoanalysis, erotic pleasure derived from the contemplation or admiration of one's own body or self, esp. as a fixation on an infantile stage of development. [After NARCISSUS.] —**nar′cis·sist** *n.* —**nar′cis·sis′tic** *adj.* —**nar′cis·sis′ti·cal·ly** *adv.*

nar·cis·sus (när-sĭs′əs) *n., pl.* **-cis·sus·es** or **-cis·si** (-sĭs′ī′, -sĭs′ē) Any of several bulbous plants of the genus *Narcissus,* having long narrow leaves and flowers with a cup-shaped or trumpet-shaped central crown. [Lat. < Gk. *narkissos.*]

Narcissus *n. Greek Mythology* A young man who pined away in love for his own image in a pool of water and was transformed into a narcissus.

narco– *pref.* **1.** Numbness; stupor; lethargy: *narcolepsy.* **2.** Narcotic drug: *narcoanalysis.* [Gk. *narko-* < *narkoun,* to numb < *narkē,* numbness.]

nar·co·lep·sy (när′kə-lĕp′sē) *n., pl.* **-sies** A disorder characterized by sudden and uncontrollable, though often brief attacks of deep sleep, sometimes accompanied by paralysis and hallucinations. —**nar′co·lep′tic** (-lĕp′tĭk) *adj.*

nar·co·ma (när-kō′mə) *n., pl.* **-mas** also **-ma·ta** (-mə-tə) Stupor induced by a narcotic. [NLat. *narcōma* < Gk. *narkoun,* to benumb. See NARCOSIS.]

nar·co·sis (när-kō′sĭs) *n., pl.* **-ses** (-sēz) A condition of deep stupor or unconsciousness produced by a drug or other chemical substance. [NLat. *narcōsis* < Gk. *narkōsis,* a numbing < *narkoun,* to benumb < *narkē,* numbness.]

nar·co·syn·the·sis (när′kō-sĭn′thĭ-sĭs) *n., pl.* **-ses** (-sēz′) Narcoanalysis directed toward making the patient recall repressed memories and emotional traumas.

nar·cot·ic (när-kŏt′ĭk) *n.* **1.** An addictive drug, such as opium, heroin, or morphine, that reduces pain, alters mood and behavior, and usu. induces sleep or stupor. **2.** A soothing, numbing agent or thing. ❖ *adj.* **1.** Inducing sleep or stupor; causing narcosis. **2.** Of or relating to narcotics, their effects, or their use. **3.** Of, relating to, or intended for one who is addicted to a narcotic. [ME *narcotik* < OFr. *narcotique* < Med.Lat. *narcōticum* < Gk. *narkōtikon,* neut. of *narkōtikos,* numbing < *narkōsis,* a numbing. See

nar•co•tism (när′kə-tĭz′əm) *n.* **1.** Addiction to narcotics such as opium, heroin, or morphine. **2.** Narcosis.

nar•co•tize (när′kə-tīz′) *tr.v.* **-tized, -tiz•ing, -tiz•es 1.** To place under the influence of a narcotic. **2.** To put to sleep; lull. **3.** To dull; deaden. —nar′co•ti•za′tion (-tĭ-zā′shən) *n.*

nar•co•traf•fick•ing (när′kō-trăf′ĭ-kĭng) or **nar•co•traf•fic** (-trăf′ĭk) *n.* The smuggling and distribution of illegal drugs. —nar′co•traf′fick•er *n.*

nard (närd) *n.* See **spikenard 1.** [ME *narde* < OFr. < Lat. *nardus* < Gk. *nardos,* prob. ult. < Skt. *naladam,* Indian spikenard.]

Na•rew also **Na•rev** (när′əf) A river rising in W Belarus and flowing c. 442 km (275 mi) to the Western Bug R.

nar•ghi•le also **nar•gi•leh** (när′gə-lē′) *n.* See **hookah.** [Fr. *narghilé,* obs. var. of *narguilé* < Pers. *nārgīleh* < *nārgīl,* coconut (from which the receptacle was made) < Skt. *nārikelah.*]

nar•is (nâr′ĭs) *n., pl.* **-es** (-ēz) An external opening in the nasal cavity of a vertebrate; a nostril. [Lat. *nāris.* See **nas-** in App.] —nar′i•al (-ē-əl) *adj.*

nark[1] (närk) *n. Slang* Variant of **narc.**

nark[2] (närk) *Chiefly British Slang n.* An informer, esp. a police informer. ❖ *intr.v.* **narked, nark•ing, narks** To be an informer. [Perh. < Romany *nāk,* nose. See **nas-** in App.]

Nar•ma•da (nər-mŭd′ə) also **Nar•ba•da** (-bŭd′ə) A river of central India flowing c. 1,247 km (775 mi) to the Gulf of Khambhat.

Nar•ra•gan•sett also **Nar•ra•gan•set** (năr′ə-găn′sĭt) *n., pl.* **Narragansett** or **-setts** also **Narraganset** or **-sets 1a.** A member of a Native American people formerly inhabiting Rhode Island west of Narragansett Bay, with present-day descendants in the same area. **b.** The Algonquian language of the Narragansett. **2.** Any of a breed of small sturdy saddle horse developed in Rhode Island. [< a Narragansett place name.] —Nar′ra•gan′sett *adj.*

Narragansett Bay A deep inlet of the Atlantic Ocean in E RI.

nar•rate (năr′āt′, nă-rāt′) *v.* **-rat•ed, -rat•ing, -rates** —*tr.* **1.** To tell (a story, for example) in speech or writing or by means of images. **2.** To give an account of (events, for example). —*intr.* **1.** To give an account or description. **2.** To supply a running commentary for a movie or performance. [Lat. *narrāre, narrāt-* < *gnārus,* knowing. See **gnō-** in App.] —nar′rat•a•bil′i•ty *n.* —nar′rat•a•ble *adj.* —nar′ra′tor, nar′rat′er *n.*

nar•ra•tion (nă-rā′shən) *n.* **1.** The act, process, or an instance of narrating. **2.** Narrated material. —nar•ra′tion•al *adj.*

nar•ra•tive (năr′ə-tĭv) *n.* **1.** A narrated account; a story. **2.** The art, technique, or process of narrating. ❖ *adj.* **1.** Consisting of or characterized by the telling of a story: *narrative poetry.* **2.** Of or relating to narration: *narrative skill.* —nar′ra•tive•ly *adv.*

nar•row (năr′ō) *adj.* **-row•er, -row•est 1.** Of small or limited width, esp. in comparison with length. **2.** Limited in area or scope; cramped. **3.** Lacking flexibility; rigid: *narrow opinions.* **4.** Barely sufficient; close: *a narrow margin of victory.* **5.** Painstakingly thorough or attentive; meticulous: *narrow scrutiny.* **6.** *Linguistics* Tense. ❖ *v.* **-rowed, -row•ing, -rows** —*tr.* **1.** To reduce in width or extent; make narrower. **2.** To limit or restrict: *narrowed the possibilities down to three.* —*intr.* To become narrower; contract. ❖ *n.* **1.** A part of little width, such as a pass through mountains. **2. narrows** (*used with a sing. or pl. verb*) **a.** A body of water with little width that connects two larger bodies of water. **b.** A part of a river or an ocean current that is not wide. [ME *narwe* < OE *nearu.*] —nar′row•ish *adj.* —nar′row•ly *adv.* —nar′row•ness *n.*

nar•row-bod•ied (năr′ō-bŏd′ēd) *adj.* Being a jet aircraft with seats for passengers on either side of a single aisle running the length of the fuselage.

nar•row•cast (năr′ō-kăst′) *intr.v.* **-cast, -cast•ing, -casts** To transmit, as by cable, programs confined to the interests of a specific group of viewers, subscribers, or listeners.

narrow gauge *n.* A distance between the rails of a railroad track that is less than the standard width of 56½ inches (143.5 centimeters). **2.** A locomotive, car, or railway line of this gauge.

nar•row-mind•ed (năr′ō-mīn′dĭd) *adj.* Lacking tolerance, breadth of view, or sympathy; petty. —nar′row-mind′ed•ly *adv.* —nar′row-mind′ed•ness *n.*

Nar•rows (năr′ōz) A strait of SE NY between Brooklyn and Staten I. in New York City.

nar•thex (när′thĕks) *n.* **1.** A narrow portico or lobby of a basilica. **2.** An entrance hall leading to the nave of a Byzantine church. [L.Gk. *narthēx* < Gk., box, giant fennel, perh. of Indic orig.]

nar•whal also **nar•wal** (när′wəl) or **nar•whale** (-hwāl′, -wāl′) *n.* An Arctic whale (*Monodon monoceros*) that has a spotted whitish pelt and is characterized in the male by a long, spirally twisted ivory tusk. [Norw. or Dan. *narhval* < ON *nāhvalr* : *nār,* corpse (being whitish) + *hvalr,* whale.]

nar•y (nâr′ē) *adj.* Not one. [Alteration of *ne'er a.*]

NASA (năs′ə) *abbr.* National Aeronautics and Space Administration.

na•sal (nā′zəl) *adj.* **1.** Of, in, or relating to the nose. **2.** *Linguistics* Articulated by lowering the soft palate so that air resonates in the nasal cavities and passes out the nose, as in the pronunciation of (m), (n), and (ng). **3.** Characterized by or resembling a resonant sound produced through the nose: *a nasal whine.* ❖ *n.* **1.** *Linguis-*

tics A nasal consonant. **2.** A nasal part or bone forming part of the bridge of the nose. **3.** The nosepiece of a helmet. [Poss. < ME *nasale* < Med.Lat. *nāsālis* < Lat. *nāsus,* nose. See **nas-** in App.] —na•sal′i•ty (nā-zăl′ĭ-tē) *n.* —na′sal•ly *adv.*

na•sal•ize (nā′zə-līz′) *tr. & intr.v.* **-ized, -iz•ing, -iz•es** To make nasal or produce nasal sounds. —na′sal•i•za′tion (nā′zə-lĭ-zā′shən) *n.*

NASCAR (năs′kär′) *abbr.* National Association for Stock Car Auto Racing.

nas•cence (năs′əns, nā′səns) *n.* A coming into being; birth. See Syns at **beginning.**

nas•cent (năs′ənt, nā′sənt) *adj.* Coming into existence; emerging. [Lat. *nāscēns, nascent-,* pr. part. of *nāscī,* to be born. See **gena-** in App.] —nas′cen•cy *n.*

NASDAQ (năz′dăk′) *abbr.* National Association of Securities Dealers Automated Quotation System

nase•ber•ry (nāz′bĕr′ē) *n.* See **sapodilla.** [Alteration of Sp. *néspera* < Lat. *mespila,* medlar. See MEDLAR.]

Nase•by (nāz′bē) A village of central England near Northampton where Cromwell defeated Royalist troops in Jun. 1645.

Nash (năsh), **Ogden** 1902–71. Amer. writer known for his droll epigrammatic verse.

Nash or **Nashe** (năsh), **Thomas** 1567–1601. English writer noted for his witty literary criticism.

Nash•u•a (năsh′ōō-ə) A city of S NH on the Merrimack R. S of Manchester; settled c. 1655. Pop. 86,605.

Nash•ville[1] (năsh′vĭl′) The cap. of TN, in the N-central part NE of Memphis; founded 1779. Pop. 569,891.

Nash•ville[2] (năsh′vĭl′) *n.* **1.** Country music. **2.** The country music industry. [After NASHVILLE[1].]

na•si•on (nā′zē-ŏn′) *n.* The point in the skull where the nasal and frontal bones unite. [NLat. *nāsion* : NAS(O)- + Gk. -*ion,* diminutive suff.]

Nas•ka•pi (năs′kə-pē) *n., pl.* **Naskapi** or **-pis 1.** A member of a Native American people inhabiting northern Quebec and Labrador. **2.** The variety of Montagnais spoken by the Naskapi. [Fr., of Montagnais orig.]

naso- *pref.* Nose: *nasopharynx.* [NLat. < Lat. *nāsus,* nose. See **nas-** in App.]

na•so•fron•tal (nā′zō-frŭn′təl) *adj.* Of or relating to the nasal and frontal bones.

na•so•phar•ynx (nā′zō-făr′ĭngks) *n., pl.* **-pha•ryn•ges** (-fə-rĭn′jēz) or **-phar•ynx•es** The part of the pharynx above the soft palate that is continuous with the nasal passages. —na′so•pha•ryn′ge•al (-fə-rĭn′jē-əl, -jəl, -făr′ən-jē′əl) *adj.*

Nas•sau (năs′ô′) **1.** (*also* nä′sou′) A region and former duchy of central Germany N and E of the Main and Rhine rivers; became a duchy in 1806 and was absorbed by Prussia in 1866. **2.** The cap. of the Bahamas, on the NE coast of New Providence I. in the Atlantic Ocean E of Miami FL; settled in the 17th cent. Pop. 172,196.

Nas•ser (năs′ər, nä′sər), **Gamal Abdel** 1918–70. Egyptian army officer and politician who served as prime minister (1954–56) and president (1956–58) of Egypt and as president of the United Arab Republic (1958–70).

Nast (năst), **Thomas** 1840–1902. German-born Amer. editorial cartoonist who established the donkey and the elephant as symbols of the Democratic and Republican parties.

nas•tic (năs′tĭk) *adj.* Of, relating to, or characterized by the tendency in plant parts to move in a direction determined by an internal stimulus, as an increased rate of cellular growth on one side of the plant part. [Gk. *nastos,* pressed close (< *nassein,* to press) + -IC.]

nas•tur•tium (nə-stûr′shəm, nă-) *n.* **1.** Any of various New World plants of the genus *Tropaeolum,* having pungent juice and long-spurred, usu. yellow, orange, or red irregular flowers. **2.** A brilliant orange yellow. [ME *nasturcium,* a kind of cress < Lat. *nasturtium* : perh. *nāsus,* nose; see **nas-** in App. + **tortāre,* freq. of *torquēre,* to twist.]

nas•ty (năs′tē) *adj.* **-ti•er, -ti•est 1a.** Disgustingly dirty. **b.** Physically repellent. **2.** Morally offensive; indecent. **3.** Malicious; spiteful. **4.** Very unpleasant or annoying. **5.** Painful or dangerous; grave. **6.** Exasperatingly difficult to solve or handle. ❖ *n., pl.* **-ties** One that is nasty. [ME *nasti,* poss. alteration of OFr. *nastre,* bad, short for *villenastre* : *vilein,* bad; see VILLAIN + *-astre,* pejorative suff. (< Lat. *-aster*).] —nas′ti•ly *adv.* —nas′ti•ness *n.*

–nasty *suff.* Nastic response or change: *epinasty.* [Gk. *nastos,* pressed down; see NASTIC + -Y[2].]

na•tal (nāt′l) *adj.* **1.** Of, relating to, or accompanying birth. **2.** Of or relating to the time or place of one's birth. [ME < Lat. *nātālis* < *nātus,* p. part. of *nāscī,* to be born. See **gena-** in App.]

Na•tal (nə-tăl′, -täl′) **1.** A region of SE Africa on the Indian Ocean; a founding province of the country of South Africa (1910). **2.** A city of NE Brazil on the Atlantic Ocean N of Recife; founded in the late 1500s. Pop. 606,681.

na•tal•i•ty (nā-tăl′ĭ-tē, nə-) *n., pl.* **-ties** See **birthrate.** [NATAL + (MORTAL)ITY.]

Natal plum (nə-tăl′, -täl′) *n.* A South African evergreen shrub (*Carissa grandiflora*) often cultivated as a hedge plant and having forked spines and an edible scarlet berry.

na•tant (nāt′nt) *adj.* Floating or swimming in water. [Lat. *na-*

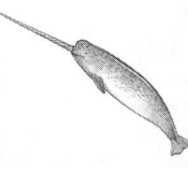

narwhal
male narwhal
Monodon monoceros

ă pat	oi boy	
ā pay	ou out	
âr care	ŏŏ took	
ä father	ōō boot	
ĕ pet	ŭ cut	
ē be	ûr urge	
ĭ pit	th thin	
ī pie	th this	
îr pier	hw which	
ŏ pot	zh vision	
ō toe	ə about,	
ô paw	item	

Stress marks:
′ (primary);
′ (secondary), as in
lexicon (lĕk′sĭ-kŏn′)

tāns, natant-, pr. part. of *natāre*, freq. of *nāre*, to swim. See **snā-** in App.]

na·ta·tion (nā-tā'shən, nă-) *n.* The act or skill of swimming. [Lat. *natātiō, natātiōn-* < *natātus*, freq. of *nāre*, to swim. See **snā-** in App.]

na·ta·to·ri·al (nā'tə-tôr'ē-əl, -tōr'-, năt'ə-) also **na·ta·to·ry** (nā'tə-tôr'ē, -tōr'ē, năt'ə-) *adj.* Of, relating to, adapted for, or characterized by swimming: *natatorial birds.* [< LLat. *natātōrius* < Lat. *natātor*, swimmer < *natātus*, p. part. of *natāre*, to swim, freq. of *nāre*, to swim. See **snā-** in App.]

na·ta·to·ri·um (nā'tə-tôr'ē-əm, -tōr'-, năt'ə-) *n.* An indoor swimming pool. [LLat. *natātōrium*, place for swimming < neut. of Lat. *natātōrius*, of swimming < *natātus*, act of swimming < p. part. of *natāre*, freq. of *nāre*, to swim. See NATATORIAL.]

natch (năch) *adv. Slang* Of course; naturally. [Shortening and alteration of NATURALLY.]

Natch·ez¹ (năch'ĭz) *n., pl.* **Natchez 1.** A member of a Native American people formerly located near present-day Natchez. **2.** Their language. [Fr. < Natchez.]

Natch·ez² (năch'ĭz) A city of SW MS on the Mississippi R. SSW of Vicksburg; founded as a fortified settlement in 1716 and the S terminus of the **Natchez Trace**, an old road connecting the city with Nashville TN. Pop. 18,464.

na·tes (nā'tēz) *pl.n.* The buttocks. [Lat. *natēs*, pl. of *natis*, buttock.]

Na·than (nā'thən) In the Bible, a prophet during the reigns of David and Solomon.

Nathan, George Jean 1882–1958. Amer. critic who cofounded and edited (1924–30) the *American Mercury.*

Na·than·ael (nə-thăn'yəl) See Saint **Bartholomew.**

nathe·less (năth'lĭs) also **nath·less** (năth'-) *adv. Archaic* Nevertheless; notwithstanding. [ME < OE *nā thē lǣs*, not less by that : *nā*, no; see NO¹ + *thē, thȳ*, instrumental case of *se*, this, that; see **to-** in App. + *lǣs*, less; see LESS.]

Na·tick (nā'tĭk) *n.* The variety of Massachusett presumed to have been spoken in the mission town of Natick, Massachusetts, and used in the Massachusett Bible.

na·tion (nā'shən) *n.* **1a.** A relatively large group of people organized under a single, usu. independent government; a country. **b.** The territory occupied by such a group of people. **2.** The government of a sovereign state. **3.** A people who share common customs, origins, history, and frequently language; a nationality. **4a.** A federation or a tribe, esp. one composed of Native Americans. **b.** The territory occupied by such a federation or tribe. [ME *nacioun* < OFr. *nation* < Lat. *nātiō, nātiōn-* < *nātus*, p. part. of *nāscī*, to be born. See **genə-** in App.] —**na'tion·hood'** *n.* —**na'tion·less** *adj.*

Nation, Carry Amelia Moore 1846–1911. Amer. temperance crusader known for her raids on saloons.

na·tion·al (năsh'ə-nəl, năsh'nəl) *adj.* **1.** Of, relating to, or belonging to a nation as an organized whole. **2.** Of or relating to nationality. **3.** Characteristic of or peculiar to the people of a nation. **4.** Of or maintained by the government of a nation. **5.** Being in the interest of one's own nation. **6.** Devoted to one's own nation or its interests; patriotic. ❖ *n.* **1.** A citizen of a particular nation. **2.** A contest or tournament involving participants from all parts of a nation. Often used in the plural. —**na'tion·al·ly** *adv.*

national bank *n.* **1.** A bank in a system of federally chartered privately owned banks in the United States, required by law to belong to the Federal Reserve Bank and be insured by the Federal Deposit Insurance Corporation. **2.** A bank associated with national finances and usu. owned or controlled by a government.

national forest *n.* A large expanse of forest in which a government limits harvesting and hunting.

National Guard *n.* The military reserve units controlled by each state of the United States, equipped federally and subject to the call of both the federal and the state governments.

na·tion·al·ism (năsh'ə-nə-lĭz'əm, năsh'nə-) *n.* **1.** Devotion to the interests or culture of one's nation. **2.** The belief that nations will benefit from acting independently rather than collectively, emphasizing national rather than international goals. **3.** Aspirations for national independence in a country under foreign domination. —**na'tion·al·ist** *adj. & n.* —**na'tion·al·is'tic** *adj.* —**na'tion·al·is'ti·cal·ly** *adv.*

na·tion·al·i·ty (năsh'ə-năl'ĭ-tē, năsh-năl'-) *n., pl.* **-ties 1.** The status of belonging to a particular nation by origin, birth, or naturalization. **2.** A people having common origins or traditions and often constituting a nation. **3.** Existence as a politically autonomous entity; national independence. **4.** National character. **5.** Nationalism.

na·tion·al·ize (năsh'ə-nə-līz', năsh'nə-) *tr.v.* **-ized, -iz·ing, -iz·es 1.** To convert from private to governmental ownership and control. **2a.** To make national in character, scope, or notoriety. **b.** To render distinctively national. —**na'tion·al·i·za'tion** (-lĭ-zā'shən) *n.* —**na'tion·al·iz'er** *n.*

national monument *n.* A natural landmark or a structure or site of historic interest set aside by a national government and maintained for public enjoyment or study.

national park *n.* A tract of land protected and maintained by a national government for public enjoyment or study.

national seashore *n.* A seacoast recreational area protected and

Nativity
c. 1435–45 fresco in the church of San Marco, Florence, Italy; attributed to a follower of Fra Angelico

maintained by a national government for public use.

National Socialism *n.* Nazism.

Nation of Islam *n.* A religious organization founded in 1931 in the United States, espousing Islamic principles and favoring political and economic independence for African Americans.

na·tion-state (nā'shən-stāt') *n.* A political unit consisting of an autonomous state inhabited predominantly by a people sharing a common culture, history, and language.

na·tion·wide (nā'shən-wīd') *adv. & adj.* Throughout a whole nation: *a speech broadcast nationwide.*

na·tive (nā'tĭv) *adj.* **1.** Existing in or belonging to one by nature; innate: *native ability.* **2.** Being such by birth or origin: *a native Scot.* **3.** Being one's own because of the place or circumstances of one's birth: *our native land.* **4.** Originating, growing, or produced in a certain place or region; indigenous: *a plant native to Asia.* **5a.** Being a member of the original inhabitants of a particular place. **b.** Of, belonging to, or characteristic of such inhabitants. **6.** Occurring in nature pure or uncombined with other substances: *native copper.* **7.** Natural; unaffected. **8.** Of or relating to the naturally occurring conformation of a macromolecule, such as a protein. **9.** *Archaic* Closely related, as by birth or race. ❖ *n.* **1a.** One born in or connected with a place by birth. **b.** One of the original inhabitants or lifelong residents of a place. **2.** An animal or plant that originated in a particular place or region. [ME < OFr. *natif* < Lat. *nātīvus* < *nātus*, p. part. of *nāscī*, to be born. See **genə-** in App.] —**na'tive·ly** *adv.* —**na'tive·ness** *n.*

Native Alaskan *n.* See Alaska Native.

Native American *n.* A member of any of the aboriginal peoples of the Western Hemisphere. —**Native American** *adj.*

USAGE NOTE Many Americans have come to prefer *Native American* over *Indian* both as a term of respect and as a corrective to the famous misnomer bestowed on the peoples of the Americas by a geographically befuddled Columbus. There are solid arguments for this preference. *Native American* eliminates any confusion between indigenous American peoples and the inhabitants of India. It is also historically accurate, since one sense of *native* is "being a member of the original inhabitants of a particular place," and Native Americans' claim to being the original inhabitants of the Americas is unchallenged. • For some, *Indian* is seen as wrong and offensive, while for others, it smacks of bureaucracy and the manipulation of language for political purposes. This controversy appears to have subsided somewhat, and the two terms are now commonly used interchangeably in the same piece of writing. While generally welcoming the respectful tone of *Native American*, most Indian writers have continued to use *Indian* at least as often. • *Native American* and *Indian* are not exact equivalents when referring to the aboriginal peoples of Canada and Alaska. *Native American* is properly used of all such peoples, whereas *Indian* is customarily used of the northern Athabaskan and Algonquian peoples in contrast to the Eskimos, Inuit, and Aleuts. *Alaska Native* (or less commonly *Native Alaskan*) is also properly used of all indigenous peoples residing in Alaska.

na·tive-born (nā'tĭv-bôrn') *adj.* Belonging to a place by birth.

Native Hawaiian *n.* A member or descendant of the indigenous Polynesian people of the Hawaiian Islands.

na·tiv·ism (nā'tĭ-vĭz'əm) *n.* **1.** A sociopolitical policy, esp. in the United States in the 19th century, favoring the interests of established inhabitants over those of immigrants. **2.** The reestablishment or perpetuation of native cultural traits, esp. in opposition to acculturation. **3.** *Philosophy* The doctrine that the mind produces ideas that are not derived from external sources. —**na'tiv·ist** *n.* —**na'tiv·is'tic** *adj.*

na·tiv·i·ty (nə-tĭv'ĭ-tē, nā-) *n., pl.* **-ties 1.** Birth, esp. the place, conditions, or circumstances of being born. **2. Nativity a.** The birth of Jesus. **b.** A representation, such as a painting, of the birth of Jesus just after birth. **c.** Christmas. **3.** A horoscope for the time of one's birth. [ME *nativite* < OFr. < Lat. *nātīvitās* < *nātīvus*, born. See NATIVE.]

natl. *abbr.* national

NATO (nā'tō) *abbr.* North Atlantic Treaty Organization

na·tri·u·re·sis (nā'trə-yoo-rē'sĭs) *n.* Excretion of excessive amounts of sodium in the urine. [NLat. *natriūrēsis* : *natrium*, sodium (< Fr. *natron*, natron; see NATRON) + *ūrēsis*, urination (< Gk. *ourēsis* < *ourein*, to urinate; see URETIC).] —**na'tri·u·ret'ic** (-rĕt'ĭk) *adj.*

na·tro·lite (nā'trə-līt') *n.* A mineral in the zeolite family, $Na_2Al_2Si_3O_{10} \cdot 2H_2O$. [NATRO(N) + -LITE.]

na·tron (nā'trŏn', -trən) *n.* A mineral of hydrous sodium carbonate, $Na_2CO_3 \cdot 10H_2O$, often found crystallized with other salts. [Fr. < Sp. *natrón*, natron, niter < Gk. *nitron*. See NITER.]

Nat·ta (nä'tä), **Giulio** 1903–79. Italian chemist who shared a 1963 Nobel Prize.

nat·ter (năt'ər) *intr.v.* **-tered, -ter·ing, -ters** To talk idly; chatter. [Variant of dialectal *gnatter*, to nibble, natter.]

nat·ty (năt'ē) *adj.* **-ti·er, -ti·est** Neat, trim, and smart; dapper. [Perh. var. of obsolete *netty* < elegant < ME < OFr. See NEAT¹.] —**nat'ti·ly** *adv.* —**nat'ti·ness** *n.*

nat·u·ral (năch'ər-əl, năch'rəl) *adj.* **1.** Present in or produced by nature. **2.** Of, relating to, or concerning nature. **3.** Conforming to the usual or ordinary course of nature. **4a.** Not acquired; inherent. **b.** Having a particular character by nature. **c.** *Biology* Not produced or changed artificially; not conditioned. **5.** Characterized by spontaneity and freedom from artificiality, affectation, or inhibitions. **6.** Not altered, treated, or disguised. **7.** Faithfully representing nature or life. **8.** Expected and accepted. **9.** Established by moral certainty or conviction: *natural rights.* **10.** Being in a state regarded as primitive, uncivilized, or unregenerate. **11a.** Related by blood. **b.** Born of unwed parents. **12.** *Mathematics* Of or relating to positive integers, sometimes including zero. **13.** *Music* As sharped or flatted. **b.** Having no sharps or flats. ❖ *n.* **1a.** One having all the qualifications necessary for success. **b.** One suited by nature for a certain purpose or function. **2.** *Music* **a.** The sign (♮) placed before a note to cancel a preceding sharp or flat. **b.** A note so affected. **3.** A yellowish gray to pale orange yellow. **4.** *Games* A combination in certain card and dice games that wins immediately. **5.** An Afro hairstyle. [ME < OFr. < Lat. *nātūrālis* < *nātūra*, nature. See NATURE.] —**nat′u·ral·ness** *n.*

natural childbirth *n.* A method of childbirth with minimal medical intervention in which the mother often practices relaxation and breathing techniques to control pain and ease delivery.

natural food *n.* Food that does not contain any additives.

natural gas *n.* A mixture of hydrocarbon gases that occurs with petroleum deposits, chiefly methane with some ethane, propane, and butane, used widely as a fuel.

natural history *n.* **1.** The study and description of organisms and natural objects, esp. their origins, evolution, and interrelationships. **2a.** A collection of facts about the development of a natural process or entity: *the natural history of early hominids.* **b.** A work or treatise containing such facts.

nat·u·ral·ism (năch′ər-ə-lĭz′əm, năch′rə-) *n.* **1.** Factual or realistic representation, esp.: **a.** The practice of describing precisely the actual circumstances of human life in literature. **b.** The practice of reproducing subjects as precisely as possible in the visual arts. **2a.** A movement or school advocating such representation. **b.** The principles and methods of such a movement or of its adherents. **3.** *Philosophy* The system of thought holding that all phenomena can be explained in terms of natural causes and laws. **4.** *Theology* The doctrine that all religious truths are derived from nature and natural causes and not from revelation. **5.** Conduct or thought prompted by natural desires or instincts.

nat·u·ral·ist (năch′ər-ə-lĭst, năch′rə-) *n.* **1.** One versed in natural history, esp. in zoology or botany. **2.** One who believes in and follows the tenets of naturalism.

nat·u·ral·is·tic (năch′ər-ə-lĭs′tĭk, năch′rə-) *adj.* **1.** Imitating or producing the effect or appearance of nature. **2.** Of or in accordance with the doctrines of naturalism. —**nat′u·ral·is′ti·cal·ly** *adv.*

nat·u·ral·ize (năch′ər-ə-līz′, năch′rə-) *v.* **-ized, -iz·ing, -iz·es** —*tr.* **1.** To grant full citizenship to (one of foreign birth). **2.** To adopt (something foreign) into general use. **3.** To adapt or acclimate (a plant or animal) to a new environment; introduce and establish as if native. **4.** To cause to conform to nature. —*intr.* To become naturalized or acclimated; undergo adaptation. —**nat′u·ral·iz′a·ble** *adj.* —**nat′u·ral·i·za′tion** (-lĭ-zā′shən) *n.*

natural killer cell *n.* A lymphocyte that is activated by double-stranded RNA or lymphokines and fights off viral infections and tumors.

natural language *n.* A human written or spoken language as opposed to a computer language or an invented language.

natural law *n.* A law or body of laws that derives from nature and is believed to be binding upon human actions apart from or in conjunction with laws established by human authority.

natural logarithm *n.* *Symbol* **ln** A logarithm in which the base is the irrational number e (= 2.71828 . . .).

nat·u·ral·ly (năch′ər-ə-lē, năch′rə-) *adv.* **1.** In a natural manner. **2.** By nature; inherently. **3.** Without a doubt; surely.

natural number *n.* One of the set of positive whole numbers; a positive integer.

natural philosophy *n.* The study of nature and the physical universe before the advent of modern science. —**natural philosopher** *n.*

natural resource *n.* A material source of wealth, such as timber, that occurs in a natural state and has economic value.

natural science *n.* A science, such as biology, chemistry, or physics, that deals with the objects, phenomena, or laws of nature and the physical world. —**natural scientist** *n.*

natural selection *n.* The process in nature by which, according to Darwin, the organisms best adapted to their environment tend to survive and transmit their genetic characteristics in increasing numbers to succeeding generations while those less adapted tend to be eliminated.

natural theology *n.* A theology holding that knowledge of God may be acquired by human reason alone without the aid of revealed knowledge.

natural virtue *n.* Cardinal virtue.

na·ture (nā′chər) *n.* **1.** The material world and its phenomena. **2.** The forces and processes that produce and control all the phenomena of the material world. **3.** The world of living things and the outdoors. **4.** A primitive state of existence, untouched and uninfluenced by civilization or artificiality. **5.** *Theology* Humankind's natural state as distinguished from the state of grace. **6.** A

kind or sort. **7.** The essential characteristics and qualities of a person or thing. **8.** The fundamental character or disposition of a person; temperament. **9.** The natural or real aspect of a person, place, or thing. **10.** The processes and functions of the body. [ME, essential properties of a thing < OFr. < Lat. *nātūra* < *nātus*, p. part. of *nāscī*, to be born. See **gena-** in App.]

na·tured (nā′chərd) *adj.* Having a nature or temperament of a specified kind. Often used in combination: *mean-natured.*

nature trail *n.* A trail, as through woods or by a seashore, usu. with natural features labeled esp. for study.

na·tur·ism (nā′chə-rĭz′əm) *n.* Nudism. —**na′tur·ist** *n.*

na·tur·op·a·thy (nā′chə-rŏp′ə-thē) *n., pl.* **-thies** A system of therapy that relies on natural remedies, such as sunlight supplemented with diet and massage, to treat illness.

Nau·cra·tis (nô′krə-tĭs) An ancient city of Egypt in the Nile R. delta SE of Alexandria; probably settled by Greek colonists in the 7th cent. B.C.

Nau·ga·hyde (nô′gə-hīd′) A trademark used for an artificial leather made of vinyl-coated fabric.

Nau·ga·tuck (nô′gə-tŭk′) A town of W-central CT S of Waterbury on the **Naugatuck River.** Pop. 30,989.

naught also **nought** (nôt) *n.* **1.** Nonexistence; nothingness. **2.** The figure 0; a cipher; a zero. ❖ *pron.* Nothing: *All their work was for naught.* ❖ *adj.* **1.** Nonexistent. **2.** Insignificant. [ME < OE *nāwiht* : *nā*, no; see **ne** in App. + *wiht*, thing.]

naugh·ty (nô′tē) *adj.* **-ti·er, -ti·est 1.** Behaving disobediently or mischievously. **2.** Indecent; improper: *a naughty wink.* **3.** *Archaic* Wicked; immoral. ❖ *n., pl.* **-ties** One that is naughty. [ME *noughti*, wicked < *nought*, nothing, evil < OE *nāwiht*, nothing. See NAUGHT.] —**naugh′ti·ly** *adv.* —**naugh′ti·ness** *n.*

nau·pli·us (nô′plē-əs) *n., pl.* **-pli·i** (-plē-ī′) The free-swimming first stage of the larva of certain crustaceans, having an unsegmented body with three pairs of appendages and a single median eye. [Lat., a kind of shellfish < Gk. *nauplios.*]

Na·u·ru (nä-ōō′rōō) Formerly **Pleasant Island.** An island country of the central Pacific S of the equator and W of Kiribati; administered by Australia from 1914 until it became independent in 1968. Cap. Yaren. Pop. 11,000. —**Na·u′ru·an** *adj. & n.*

nau·se·a (nô′zē-ə, -zhə, -sē-ə, -shə) *n.* **1.** A feeling of sickness in the stomach characterized by an urge to vomit. See Usage Note at **nauseous. 2.** Strong aversion; disgust. [ME < Lat. < Gk. *nautiā, nausiē,* seasickness < *nautēs,* sailor < *naus,* ship.]

nau·se·ant (nô′zē-ənt, -zhē-, -sē-, -shē-) *adj.* Inducing nausea or vomiting. —**nau′se·ant** *n.*

nau·se·ate (nô′zē-āt′, -zhē-, -sē-, -shē-) *intr. & tr.v.* **-at·ed, -at·ing, -ates 1.** To feel or cause to feel nausea. **2.** To feel or cause to feel loathing or disgust. See Syns at **disgust.** —**nau′se·a′tion** *n.*

nau·se·at·ing (nô′zē-ā′tĭng, -zhē-, -sē-, -shē-) *adj.* **1.** Causing nausea; nauseous. **2.** Causing disgust, loathing, or revulsion. See Usage Note at **nauseous.** —**nau′se·at′ing·ly** *adv.*

nau·seous (nô′shəs, -zē-əs) *adj.* **1.** Causing nausea; sickening. **2.** *Usage Problem* Affected with nausea. —**nau′seous·ly** *adv.*

USAGE NOTE Traditional critics have insisted that *nauseous* is appropriately used only to mean "causing nausea" and that it is incorrect to use it to mean "affected with nausea," as in *Roller coasters make me nauseous.* In this example *nauseated* was preferred by 61 percent of the Usage Panel in the 1999 survey. Curiously, though, only 24 percent of the Panelists preferred using *nauseous* in the sentence *The children looked a little green from too many candy apples and nauseous rides.* Since there is a lot of evidence to show that *nauseous* is widely used to mean "feeling sick," it appears that people use *nauseous* mainly in the sense in which it is considered incorrect. In its "correct" sense it is being supplanted by *nauseating.*

Nau·sic·a·a (nô-sĭk′ē-ə, -ā-ə, nou-) *n. Greek Mythology* In the *Odyssey,* a young woman who befriended the stranded Odysseus.

nau·ti·cal (nô′tĭ-kəl) *adj.* Of, relating to, or characteristic of ships, shipping, sailors, or navigation on a body of water. [< Lat. *nauticus* < Gk. *nautikos* < *nautēs,* sailor < *naus,* ship.] —**nau′ti·cal·ly** *adv.*

SYNONYMS nautical, marine, maritime, naval These adjectives mean of or relating to the sea, ships, shipping, sailors, or navigation: *nautical charts; marine insurance; maritime law; a naval officer.*

nautical mile *n.* A unit of length used in navigation, based on the length of one minute of arc of a great circle, esp. an international and US unit equal to 1,852 meters (about 6,076 feet).

nau·ti·loid (nôt′l-oid′) *n.* A mollusk of the subclass Nautiloidea, which includes the nautiluses and numerous extinct species known only from fossils. [< NLat. Nautiloidea, subclass name : Lat. *nautilus,* nautilus; see NAUTILUS + Gk. *-oeidēs,* -oid.] —**nau′ti·loid** *adj.*

nau·ti·lus (nôt′l-əs) *n., pl.* **nau·ti·lus·es** or **nau·ti·li** (nôt′l-ī′) **1.** A cephalopod mollusk of the genus *Nautilus,* esp. *N. pompilius,* found in the Indian and Pacific oceans and having a spiral pearly-lined shell with a series of air-filled chambers. **2.** The paper nautilus. [Lat. < Gk. *nautilos,* sailor, nautilus < *nautēs,* mariner < *naus,* ship.]

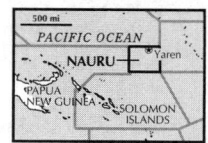

Nauru

nautilus
Nautilus pompilius

ă	pat	oi	boy
ā	pay	ou	out
âr	care	ŏŏ	took
ä	father	ōō	boot
ĕ	pet	ŭ	cut
ē	be	ûr	urge
ĭ	pit	th	thin
ī	pie	*th*	this
îr	pier	hw	which
ŏ	pot	zh	vision
ō	toe	ə	about,
ô	paw		item

Stress marks:
′ (primary);
′ (secondary); as in
lexicon (lĕk′sĭ-kŏn′)

Nav·a·jo also **Nav·a·ho** (năv'ə-hō', nä'və-) *n., pl.* **Navajo** or **-jos** also **Navaho** or **-hos 1.** A member of a Native American people inhabiting extensive reservation lands in Arizona, New Mexico, and southeast Utah. **2.** The Apachean language of the Navajo. [Am.Sp. *Navajó*, orig. a place name < Tewa *navahū*, large arroyo with cultivated fields.] **—Nav'a·jo'** *adj.*

na·val (nā'vəl) *adj.* **1.** Of or relating to ships or shipping. See Syns at **nautical. 2.** Of or relating to a navy. **3.** Having a navy: *a great naval power.* [ME < OFr. < Lat. *nāvālis* < *nāvis*, ship.]

naval architect *n.* One who designs ships.

naval stores *pl.n.* Products, such as turpentine or pitch, originally used to caulk the seams of wooden ships.

Na·varre (nə-vär', nä-) A historical region and former kingdom of SW Europe in the Pyrenees of N Spain and SW France. The S part was annexed to Spain (1512–15), and the N part became part of the French crown lands (1589).

nave[1] *n.* The central part of a church, extending from the narthex to the chancel and flanked by aisles. [Med.Lat. *nāvis* < Lat., ship (< its shape).]

nave[2] (nāv) *n.* The hub of a wheel. [ME < OE *nafu.* See **nobh-** in App.]

na·vel (nā'vəl) *n.* **1.** The mark on the surface of the abdomen of mammals where the umbilical cord was attached during gestation. **2.** A central point; a middle. [ME < OE *nafela.* See **nobh-** in App.]

navel orange *n.* A sweet, usu. seedless orange having at its apex a navellike formation enclosing an underdeveloped fruit.

na·vel·wort (nā'vəl-wûrt', -wôrt') *n.* **1.** See **pennywort** a. **2.** Any of various Eurasian plants of the genus *Omphalodes,* having one-sided cymes of usu. blue flowers.

na·vic·u·lar (nə-vĭk'yə-lər) *n.* **1.** A comma-shaped bone of the human wrist, located in the first row of carpals. **2.** A concave bone of the human foot, located between the talus and the metatarsals. ❖ *adj.* Shaped like a boat; scaphoid. [< Lat. *nāvicula,* boat, dim. of *nāvis,* ship.]

nav·i·ga·ble (năv'ĭ-gə-bəl) *adj.* Sufficiently deep and wide to provide passage for vessels: *navigable waters.* **—nav'i·ga·bil'i·ty, nav'i·ga·ble·ness** *n.* **—nav'i·ga·bly** *adv.*

nav·i·gate (năv'ĭ-gāt') *v.* **-gat·ed, -gat·ing, -gates** *—tr.* **1.** To plan, record, and control the course and position of (a ship or aircraft). **2.** To follow a planned course on, across, or through: *navigate a stream.* *—intr.* **1.** To control the course of a ship or aircraft. **2.** To voyage over water in a boat or ship; sail. **3a.** To make one's way. *b. Informal* To walk. [Lat. *nāvigāre, nāvigāt-* : *nāvis,* ship + *agere,* to drive, lead; see **ag-** in App.]

nav·i·ga·tion (năv'ĭ-gā'shən) *n.* **1.** The theory and practice of navigating, esp. the charting of a course for a ship or aircraft. **2.** Travel or traffic by vessels, esp. commercial shipping. **—nav'i·ga'tion·al** *adj.* **—nav'i·ga'tion·al·ly** *adv.*

nav·i·ga·tor (năv'ĭ-gā'tər) *n.* **1.** One who navigates. **2.** A device that directs the course of an aircraft or missile.

Nav·ra·ti·lo·va (năv'rə-tĭ-lō'və, nä'vrə-), **Martina** b. 1956. Czechoslovakian-born Amer. tennis player who won nine Wimbledon singles championships between 1978 and 1990.

nav·vy (năv'ē) *n., pl.* **-vies** *Chiefly British* A laborer, esp. one employed in construction or excavation projects. [Short for NAVIGA-TOR, canal laborer (obsolete).]

na·vy (nā'vē) *n., pl.* **-vies 1.** All of a nation's warships. **2.** often **Navy** A nation's entire military organization for sea warfare and defense, including vessels, personnel, and shore establishments. **3.** A group of ships; a fleet. **4.** Navy blue. [ME < OFr. *navie* < Lat. *nāvigia,* pl. of *nāvigium,* ship < *nāvigāre,* to sail. See NAVIGATE.]

navy bean *n.* Any of several varieties of the kidney bean, cultivated for their edible white seeds. [< its former use as a standard provision of the US Navy.]

navy blue *n.* A dark grayish blue. [< the color of the Brit. naval uniform.]

Navy Cross *n.* A US Navy decoration awarded for exceptional heroism.

navy gray *n.* A dark gray.

navy yard *n.* A dockyard for the construction, repair, equipping, or docking of naval vessels.

na·wab (nə-wŏb') *n.* See **nabob** 1.

Nax·os or **Náx·os** (năk'sŏs, -sōs, -səs, näk'sôs) An island in the Cyclades in SE Greece in the Aegean Sea; famous in ancient times as a center of Dionysian worship.

nay (nā) *adv.* **1.** No. **2.** And moreover: *He was ill-favored, nay, hideous.* ❖ *n.* **1.** A denial or refusal. **2.** A negative vote or voter. [ME < ON *nei* : *ne,* not; see **ne** in App. + *ei,* ever; see **aiw-** in App.]

nay·say (nā'sā') *tr.v.* **-said** (-sĕd'), **-say·ing, -says** (-sĕz') To oppose, deny, or take a pessimistic or negative view of. **—nay'say'er** *n.*

Naz·a·rene (năz'ə-rēn', năz'ə-rēn') *n.* **1a.** A native or inhabitant of Nazareth. **b.** Jesus. **2.** A member of a sect of early Christians of Jewish origin who retained many of the prescribed Jewish observances. **3.** A member of an American Protestant denomination, the Church of the Nazarene, that follows many of the doctrines of early Methodism. ❖ *adj.* Of or relating to Nazareth or its inhabitants. [ME < LLat. *Nazarēnus* < Gk. *Nazarēnos* < *Nazaret,* Nazareth.]

Naz·a·reth (năz'ər-əth) A town of N Israel SE of Haifa; the boy-

hood home of Jesus. Pop. 46,300.

Naz·ca (näz'kə, näs'kä) A pre-Incan civilization that flourished on the southern coast of Peru from about 200 B.C. to about A.D. 600, known esp. for the drawings of geometric and zoomorphic forms etched in the desert floor 200 miles south of Lima. [After *Nazca,* city in southern Peru.]

Na·zi (nät'sē, năt'-) *n., pl.* **-zis 1.** A member of the National Socialist German Workers' Party, brought to power in Germany in 1933 under Adolf Hitler. **2.** often **nazi** An adherent or advocate of Nazi policies; a fascist. ❖ *adj.* Of, relating to, controlled by, or typical of the National Socialist German Workers' Party. [Ger., short for *Nationalsozialistische deutsche Arbeiter-Partei,* National Socialist German Workers' Party.] **—Na'zi·fi·ca'tion** (-sə-fĭ-kā'shən) *n.* **—Na'zi·fy'** (-fī') *v.*

Na·zism (nät'sĭz'əm, năt'-) also **Na·zi·ism** (-sē-ĭz'əm) *n.* The ideology and practice of the Nazis, esp. the policy of racist nationalism, expansionism, and state control of the economy.

Nb[1] The symbol for the element **niobium.**

Nb[2] *abbr. Bible* Numbers

NB *abbr.* **1.** also **N.B.** New Brunswick **2.** nota bene

NBA *abbr.* **1.** National Basketball Association **2.** National Boxing Association

NbE *abbr.* north by east

NbW *abbr.* north by west

NC *abbr.* **1.** no charge **2.** no credit **3.** or **N.C.** North Carolina

NC-17 (ĕn'sē-sĕv'ən-tēn') A trademark used for a movie rating indicating that admission will not be granted to anyone under the age of 17.

NCAA *abbr.* National Collegiate Athletic Association

NCC *abbr.* National Council of Churches

NCO *abbr.* noncommissioned officer

Nd The symbol for the element **neodymium.**

ND or **N.D.** *abbr.* North Dakota

n.d. *abbr.* no date

N.Dak. *abbr.* North Dakota

Nde·be·le (ən'də-bĕl'ā) *n., pl.* **Ndebele** or **-les 1.** A member of a Zulu people of southwest Zimbabwe. **2.** The Nguni language of the Ndebele.

N'Dja·me·na (ən-jä'mə-nə) Formerly **Fort-La·my** (fôr-lä-mē') The cap. of Chad, in the SW part on the Shari R.; founded by the French in 1900. Pop. 303,000.

Ndong·o (ən-dông'gō) *n., pl.* **Ndongo** or **-os** See **Mbundu** 3.

Ne[1] The symbol for the element **neon** 1.

Ne[2] *abbr. Bible* Nehemiah

NE *abbr.* **1.** Nebraska **2.** New England **3a.** northeast **b.** northeastern **4.** not equal to

NEA *abbr.* **1.** National Education Association **2.** National Endowment for the Arts

Ne·an·der·thal (nē-ăn'dər-thôl', -tôl', nā-än'dər-täl') also **Ne·an·der·tal** (-tôl', -täl') *n.* **1.** A member of an extinct human species (*Homo neanderthalensis*) or subspecies (*Homo sapiens neanderthalensis*) living during the late Pleistocene Epoch in the Old World and associated with Middle Paleolithic tools. **2.** *Slang* A crude, boorish, or slow-witted person. ❖ *adj.* **1.** Of, having to do with, or resembling Neanderthals. **2.** *Slang* Crude, boorish, or slow-witted. [After *Neanderthal* (Neandertal), a valley of western Germany near Düsseldorf.] **—Ne·an'der·thal'oid'** (-thô'loid', -tô'-, -tä'-) *adj.*

Neanderthal man *n.* The Neanderthal human species or subspecies. Not in scientific use.

ne·an·throp·ic (nē'ən-thrŏp'ĭk) *adj.* Of or relating to members of the extant species *Homo sapiens* as compared with other, now extinct species of *Homo.*

Ne·a·pol·i·tan (nē'ə-pŏl'ĭ-tən) *adj.* Of, belonging to, or characteristic of Naples, Italy. ❖ *n.* A native or resident of Naples, Italy. [ME < Lat. *Neāpolītānus* < Gk. *neāpolītēs* < *Neāpolis,* Naples, Italy.]

Neapolitan ice cream *n.* Ice cream in brick form with layers of different colors and flavors.

neap tide (nēp) *n.* A tide that occurs during the first and third quarters of the moon when the difference between high and low tide is least; the lowest level of high tide. [ME *neep* < OE *nēp(flōd),* neap (tide).]

near (nîr) *adv.* **near·er, near·est 1.** To, at, or within a short distance or interval in space or time. **2.** Just about; almost; nearly. **3.** With or in a close relationship. ❖ *adj.* **nearer, nearest 1.** Close in time, space, position, or degree. **2.** Closely related by kinship or association; intimate. See Syns at **close. 3a.** Nearly occurring but not actually happening. **b.** Just barely avoided. **4a.** Closely corresponding to or resembling an original. **b.** Closely resembling the genuine article. **5a.** Closer of two or more: *on the near side.* **b.** Being on the left side of an animal or vehicle. **c.** Being the animal or vehicle on the left. **6.** Short and direct. **7.** Stingy; parsimonious. ❖ *prep.* Close to. ❖ *v.* **neared, near·ing, nears** *—tr.* To come close or closer to. *—intr.* To draw near or nearer; approach. [ME *ner* < OE *nēar* < comp. of *nēah,* nigh, near.] **—near'ness** *n.*

near beer *n.* A malt liquor that does not contain enough alcohol to be considered an alcoholic beverage.

near·by (nîr'bī') *adj.* Located a short distance away; close at hand. See Syns at **close.** ❖ *adv.* Not far away.

Ne·arc·tic (nē-ärk'tĭk, -är'tĭk) *adj.* Of or being the biogeo-

nave[1]
St. Patrick's Cathedral,
Dublin, Ireland

Martina Navratilova

graphic region that includes the Arctic and Temperate areas of North America and Greenland. [NE(O)- + ARCTIC.]

Near East A region of SW Asia generally thought to include Turkey, Lebanon, Israel, Iraq, Jordan, Saudi Arabia, and the other countries of the Arabian Peninsula. —**Near Eastern** *adj.* —**Near Easterner** *n.*

near-in·fra·red radiation (nîr′ĭn′frə-rĕd′) *n.* See **near-red radiation.**

Near Islands An island group of SW AK in the W Aleutians.

near·ly (nîr′lē) *adv.* **1.** Almost but not quite: *I nearly failed.* **2.** In a close manner; intimately.

near miss *n.* **1.** A narrowly avoided collision. **2.** A missile strike that is extremely close to but not directly on target. [Blend of *near thing,* something that nearly ends in disaster, and MISS[1].]

near point *n.* The nearest point at which an object can be seen distinctly by the eye.

near-red radiation (nîr′rĕd′) *n.* Electromagnetic radiation having the shortest wavelengths in the infrared region, between approx. 0.75 and 2.5 micrometers.

near rhyme *n.* See **off rhyme.**

near·sight·ed (nîr′sī′tĭd) *adj.* Unable to see distant objects clearly. —**near′sight′ed·ly** *adv.*

near·sight·ed·ness (nîr′sī′tĭd-nĭs) *n.* See **myopia.**

neat[1] (nēt) *adj.* **neat·er, neat·est** **1.** Orderly and clean; tidy. **2.** Orderly and precise in procedure; systematic. **3.** Marked by ingenuity and skill; adroit: *a neat turn of phrase.* **4.** Not diluted or mixed with other substances: *neat whiskey.* **5.** Left after all deductions; net: *neat profit.* **6.** *Slang* Wonderful; terrific. [AN *neit,* clear, pure, var. of OFr. *net* < Lat. *nitidus,* elegant, gleaming < *nitēre,* to shine.] —**neat′ly** *adv.* —**neat′ness** *n.*

SYNONYMS neat, tidy, trim, shipshape These adjectives mean clean and in good order. *Neat* is the most general: *a neat room; neat hair. Tidy* emphasizes precise arrangement and order: *"When she saw me come in tidy and well dressed, she even smiled"* (Charlotte Brontë). *Trim* stresses especially smart appearance: *"A trim little sailboat was dancing out at her moorings"* (Herman Melville). *Shipshape* evokes meticulous order: *"We'll try to make this barn a little more shipshape"* (Rudyard Kipling).

neat[2] (nēt) *n., pl.* **neat** *Archaic* A cow or other domestic bovine animal. [ME *net* < OE *nēat.*]

neat·en (nēt′n) *tr.v.* **-ened, -en·ing, -ens** To put into order; make neat.

neath or **'neath** (nēth) *prep.* Beneath.

neat·herd (nēt′hûrd′) *n. Archaic* A cowherd.

neat·nik (nēt′nĭk) *n.* One who is habitually neat and orderly.

neat's-foot oil (nēts′fŏŏt′) *n.* A light yellow oil obtained from the feet and shinbones of cattle, used chiefly to dress leather.

neb (nĕb) *n.* **1a.** A beak of a bird. **b.** A nose; a snout. **2.** A projecting part, esp. a nib. [ME < OE.]

NEB *abbr.* New English Bible

neb·bish (nĕb′ĭsh) *n.* A person regarded as weak-willed or timid. [Yiddish *nebekh,* poor, unfortunate, of Slav. orig. See **bhag-** in App.] —**neb′bish·y** *adj.*

NEbE *abbr.* northeast by east

NEbN *abbr.* northeast by north

Nebr. *abbr.* Nebraska

Ne·bras·ka (nə-brăs′kə) A state of the central US in the Great Plains; admitted as the 37th state in 1867. Cap. Lincoln. Pop. 1,711,263.

Ne·bras·kan (nə-brăs′kən) *adj.* **1.** Of or relating to Nebraska. **2.** *Geology* Of or relating to the first glacial stage of the Pleistocene in North America. ❖ *n.* A Nebraska native or resident.

Neb·u·chad·nez·zar II (nĕb′ə-kəd-nĕz′ər, nĕb′yə-) 630?–562 B.C. King of Babylonia (605–562) who captured (597) and destroyed (586) Jerusalem.

neb·u·la (nĕb′yə-lə) *n., pl.* **-lae** (-lē′) or **-las** **1.** *Astronomy* **a.** A diffuse mass of interstellar dust or gas or both, visible as luminous patches or areas of darkness depending on the way the mass absorbs or reflects incident radiation. **b.** See **galaxy** 1a. **2.** *Pathology* **a.** A cloudy spot on the cornea. **b.** Cloudiness in the urine. **3.** A liquid medication that is sprayed. [ME *nebule,* mist < Lat. *nebula.* See **nebh-** in App.] —**neb′u·lar** *adj.*

nebular hypothesis *n.* An explanation of the origin of the solar system according to which a rotating nebula cooled and contracted into the planets and the sun.

neb·u·lize (nĕb′yə-līz′) *tr.v.* **-lized, -liz·ing, -liz·es** **1.** To convert (a liquid) to a fine spray; atomize. **2.** To treat with a medicated spray. —**neb′u·li·za′tion** (-lĭ-zā′shən) *n.* —**neb′u·liz′er** *n.*

neb·u·los·i·ty (nĕb′yə-lŏs′ĭ-tē) *n., pl.* **-ties** **1.** The quality or condition of being nebulous. **2.** *Astronomy* **a.** A nebula or a nebulalike object. **b.** A mass of material constituting a nebula.

neb·u·lous (nĕb′yə-ləs) *adj.* **1.** Cloudy, misty, or hazy. **2.** Lacking definite form or limits; vague: *nebulous promises.* **3.** Of, relating to, or characteristic of a nebula. [ME < Lat. *nebulōsus* < *nebula,* cloud. See **nebh-** in App.] —**neb′u·lous·ly** *adv.* —**neb′u·lous·ness** *n.*

nec·es·sar·i·ly (nĕs′ĭ-sâr′ə-lē, -sĕr′-) *adv.* Of necessity; inevitably.

nec·es·sar·y (nĕs′ĭ-sĕr′ē) *adj.* **1.** Absolutely essential. See Syns at **indispensable. 2.** Needed to achieve a certain result or effect; requisite. **3a.** Unavoidably determined by conditions or circumstances; inevitable. **b.** Logically inevitable. **4.** Required by obligation, compulsion, or convention. ❖ *n., pl.* **-ies** Something indispensable. [ME *necessarie* < OFr. *necessaire* < Lat. *necessārius* < *necesse.*]

ne·ces·si·tar·i·an·ism (nə-sĕs′ĭ-târ′ē-ə-nĭz′əm) *n. Philosophy* The doctrine holding that events are inevitably determined by preceding causes. —**ne·ces′si·tar′i·an** *adj. & n.*

ne·ces·si·tate (nə-sĕs′ĭ-tāt′) *tr.v.* **-tat·ed, -tat·ing, -tates** **1.** To make necessary or unavoidable. **2.** To require or compel. [Med.Lat. *necessitāre, necessitāt-* < Lat. *necessitās,* necessity. See NECESSITY.] —**ne·ces′si·ta′tion** *n.* —**ne·ces′si·ta′tive** *adj.*

ne·ces·si·tous (nə-sĕs′ĭ-təs) *adj.* **1.** Needy; indigent. **2.** Compelling; urgent. [Fr. *nécessiteux* < OFr., necessary < *necessite,* necessity. See NECESSITY.] —**ne·ces′si·tous·ly** *adv.*

ne·ces·si·ty (nə-sĕs′ĭ-tē) *n., pl.* **-ties 1a.** The condition or quality of being necessary. **b.** Something necessary. **2a.** Something dictated by invariable physical laws. **b.** The force exerted by circumstance. **3.** The state or fact of being in need. **4.** Pressing or urgent need, esp. that arising from poverty. —*idiom:* **of necessity** As an inevitable consequence; necessarily. [ME *necessite* < OFr. < Lat. *necessitās* < *necesse,* necessary. See NECESSARY.]

Ne·chak·o (nə-chăk′ō) A river of central British Columbia, Canada, flowing c. 462 km (287 mi) to the Fraser R.

Nech·es (nĕch′ĭz) A river of E TX flowing c. 669 km (416 mi) to Sabine Lake.

neck (nĕk) *n.* **1.** The part of the body joining the head to the shoulders or trunk. **2.** The part of a garment around or near the neck. **3.** *Anatomy* **a.** A narrow or constricted part of a structure, as of a bone, that joins its parts; a cervix. **b.** The part of a tooth between the crown and the root. **4.** A relatively narrow elongation, projection, or connecting part. **5.** *Music* The narrow part along which the strings of an instrument extend to the pegs. **6.** *Printing* See **beard** 5. **7.** *Geology* Solidified lava filling the vent of an extinct volcano. **8.** The siphon of a bivalve mollusk, such as a clam. **9.** A narrow margin. ❖ *v.* **necked, neck·ing, necks** —*intr. Informal* To kiss and caress amorously. —*tr.* To strangle or decapitate (a fowl). —*idioms:* **neck and neck** So close that the lead between competitors is virtually indeterminable. **up to (one's) neck** Deeply involved or occupied fully: *I'm up to my neck in paperwork.* [ME *nekke* < OE *hnecca.*]

Neck·ar (nĕk′ər, -är) A river of SW Germany rising in the Black Forest and flowing c. 337 km (228 mi) to the Rhine R.

neck·band (nĕk′bănd′) *n.* The band around the collar of a garment.

necked (nĕkt) *adj.* Having a neck or neckline of a specified kind. Often used in combination: *a long-necked bird.*

neck·er·chief (nĕk′ər-chĭf, -chēf′) *n.* A kerchief worn around the neck.

neck·ing (nĕk′ĭng) *n.* **1.** *Architecture* A molding between the upper part of a column and the projecting part of the capital. **2.** *Informal* The act of amorously kissing and caressing.

neck·lace (nĕk′lĭs) *n.* An ornament worn around the neck.

neck·line (nĕk′līn′) *n.* The line formed by the edge of a garment at or near the neck.

neck of the woods *n., pl.* **necks of the woods** *Informal* A region; a neighborhood. [< NECK, narrow stretch of forest.]

neck·piece (nĕk′pēs′) *n.* A scarf, often of fur.

neck·tie (nĕk′tī′) *n.* A narrow fabric band of varying length worn around the neck and tied in a knot or bow close to the throat.

neck·wear (nĕk′wâr′) *n.* Articles, such as neckties, worn around the neck.

necro- or **necr-** *pref.* **1.** Dead body; corpse: *necrophilia.* **2.** Death: *necrobiosis.* [Gk. *nekro-* < *nekros,* corpse. See **nek-** in App.]

nec·ro·bi·o·sis (nĕk′rō-bī-ō′sĭs) *n.* The natural death of cells or tissues through aging, as distinguished from necrosis or pathological death. —**nec′ro·bi·ot′ic** (-ŏt′ĭk) *adj.*

ne·crol·o·gy (nə-krŏl′ə-jē, nĕ-) *n., pl.* **-gies** **1.** A list of people who have died, esp. in the recent past or during a specific period. **2.** An obituary. —**nec′ro·log′ic** (nĕk′rə-lŏj′ĭk), **nec′ro·log′i·cal** *adj.* —**ne·crol′o·gist** *n.*

nec·ro·man·cy (nĕk′rə-măn′sē) *n.* **1.** The practice of supposedly communicating with the spirits of the dead in order to predict the future. **2.** Black magic; sorcery. **3.** Magic qualities. [Ult. < LLat. *necromantīa* < Gk. *nekromanteia* : *nekros,* corpse; see **nek-** in App. + *manteia,* divination; see -MANCY.] —**nec′ro·man′cer** *n.* —**nec′ro·man′tic** (-măn′tĭk) *adj.*

nec·ro·pha·gia (nĕk′rə-fā′jə) *n.* The act or practice of feeding on dead bodies or carrion.

nec·roph·a·gous (nĕ-krŏf′ə-gəs, nĕ-) *adj.* Feeding on carrion or corpses: *necrophagous organisms.*

nec·ro·phil·i·a (nĕk′rə-fĭl′ē-ə) also **nec·roph′i·lism** (nĭ-krŏf′ə-lĭz′əm, nĕ-) *n.* **1.** Obsessive fascination with death and corpses. **2.** Erotic attraction to or sexual contact with corpses. —**nec′ro·phil′i·ac** (-ē-ăk′) *adj. & n.* —**nec′ro·phile** (-fīl′) *n.* —**nec′ro·phil′ic** (-fĭl′ĭk) *adj.*

nec·ro·pho·bi·a (nĕk′rə-fō′bē-ə) *n.* An abnormal fear of death or corpses. —**nec′ro·pho′bic** *adj.*

ne·crop·o·lis (nə-krŏp′ə-lĭs, nĕ-) *n., pl.* **-lis·es** or **-leis** (-lās′) A

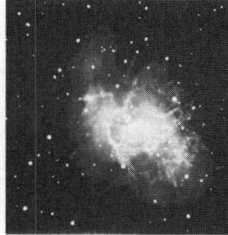

nebula
Crab Nebula

neck
Devils Tower, Wyoming

ă pat	oi boy
ā pay	ou out
âr care	ŏŏ took
ä father	ōō boot
ĕ pet	ŭ cut
ē be	ûr urge
ĭ pit	th thin
ī pie	th this
îr pier	hw which
ŏ pot	zh vision
ō toe	ə about,
ô paw	item

Stress marks:
′ (primary),
′ (secondary), as in
lexicon (lĕk′sĭ-kŏn′)

cemetery, esp. a large and elaborate one belonging to an ancient city. [Gk. *nekropolis* : *nekro-*, necro- + *polis*, city.]

nec•rop•sy (nĕk′rŏp′sē) *n., pl.* **-sies** See **autopsy** 1. —**nec′rop′sy** *v.*

ne•crose (nĕ-krōs′, -krōz′, nĕk′rōs′, -rōz′) *intr. & tr.v.* **-crosed, -cros•ing, -cros•es** To undergo or cause to undergo necrosis. [Back-formation < NECROSIS.]

ne•cro•sis (nə-krō′sĭs, nĕ-) *n., pl.* **-ses** (-sēz′) Death of cells or tissues through injury or disease, esp. in a localized area of the body. [LLat. *necrōsis*, a causing to die, killing < Gk. *nekrōsis*, death < *nekroun*, to make dead < *nekros*, corpse. See **nek-** in App.] —**ne•crot′ic** (-krŏt′ĭk) *adj.*

nec•ro•tize (nĕk′rə-tīz′) *intr. & tr.v.* **-tized, -tiz•ing, -tiz•es** To undergo necrosis or cause to necrose.

nec•rot•o•my (nĭ-krŏt′ə-mē, nĕ-) *n., pl.* **-mies** 1. Surgical excision of dead tissue. 2. Dissection of a dead body.

nec•tar (nĕk′tər) *n.* 1. A sweet liquid secreted by flowers of various plants, consumed by pollinators, such as hummingbirds, and gathered by bees for making honey. 2. *Greek & Roman Mythology* The drink of the gods. 3. A delicious or invigorating drink. [Lat. < Gk. *nektar*, drink of the gods. See **nek-** in App.] —**nec′tar•ous** *adj.*

nec•tar•ine (nĕk′tə-rēn′) *n.* A variety of aromatic peach of ancient origin, having a smooth waxy skin. [< obsolete *nectarine*, sweet as nectar < NECTAR.]

nec•ta•ry (nĕk′tə-rē) *n., pl.* **-ries** A glandlike organ, located outside or within a flower, that secretes nectar. [NLat. *nectārium* < NECTAR.] —**nec•tar′i•al** (-tär′ē-əl) *adj.*

née also **nee** (nā) *adj.* 1. Born. Used to indicate the maiden name of a married woman. 2. Formerly known as. [Fr., fem. p. part. of *naître*, to be born < OFr. *naistre* < Lat. *nāscī*. See **gena-** in App.]

need (nēd) *n.* 1. A condition or situation in which something is required or wanted: *crops in need of water; a need for affection.* See Syns at **lack.** 2. Something required or wanted; a requisite. 3. Necessity; obligation: *There is no need for you to go.* 4. A condition of poverty or misfortune: *The family is in dire need.* ❖ *v.* **need•ed, need•ing, needs** —*aux.* To be under the necessity of or the obligation to: *They need not come.* —*tr.* To have need of; require: *They need money.* —*intr.* 1. To be in need or want. 2. To be necessary. [ME *nede* < OE *nēod, nēd*, distress, necessity.]

need•ful (nēd′fəl) *adj.* Necessary; required. See Syns at **indispensable.** —**need′ful•ly** *adv.* —**need′ful•ness** *n.*

nee•dle (nēd′l) *n.* 1a. A small slender implement used for sewing or surgical suturing, made usu. of polished steel and having an eye at one end through which thread is passed and held. b. Any one of various other implements, such as one used in knitting or crocheting. 2. A slender piece of jewel or steel used to transmit vibrations from the grooves of a phonograph record. 3a. A slender pointer or indicator on a dial, scale, or similar part of a mechanical device. b. A magnetic needle. 4a. A hypodermic needle. b. *Informal* A hypodermic injection; a shot. 5. *Chiefly Upper Northern US* See **dragonfly.** See Regional Note at **dragonfly.** 6. A narrow stiff leaf, as those of conifers. 7. A fine sharp projection, as a spine of a sea urchin. 8. A sharp-pointed instrument used in engraving. 9. *Informal* A goading, provoking, or teasing remark or act. ❖ *v.* **-dled, -dling, -dles** —*tr.* 1. To prick, pierce, or stitch with a needle. 2. *Informal* To goad, provoke, or tease. 3. *Slang* To increase the alcoholic content of (a beverage). —*intr.* To sew or do similar work with a needle. [ME *nedle* < OE *nǣdl*. See **(s)nē-** in App.] —**nee′dler** *n.*

nee•dle•craft (nēd′l-krăft′) *n.* The art or process of needlework.

nee•dle•fish (nēd′l-fĭsh′) *n., pl.* **needlefish** or **-fish•es** 1. Any of several marine fishes of the family Belonidae, having slender bodies, needlelike teeth, and narrow jaws. 2. Any of various other fishes, such as the pipefish, having projecting jaws.

nee•dle•point (nēd′l-point′) *n.* 1. Decorative needlework on canvas, usu. in a diagonal stitch covering the entire surface of the material. 2. A type of lace worked on paper patterns with a needle. —**nee′dle•point′** *v.*

need•less (nēd′lĭs) *adj.* Not needed or wished for; unnecessary. —**need′less•ly** *adv.* —**need′less•ness** *n.*

needle valve *n.* A valve having a slender point fitting into a conical seat, used to regulate fluid flow accurately.

nee•dle•wom•an (nēd′l-wŏŏm′ən) *n.* A woman who does needlework, esp. a seamstress.

nee•dle•work (nēd′l-wûrk′) *n.* Work, such as sewing or embroidery, done with a needle.

need•n′t (nēd′nt) Contraction of *need not.*

needs (nēdz) *adv.* Of necessity; necessarily: *We must needs go.* [ME *nedes < nede* < OE *nēde*, genitive of *nēd*, necessity. See NEED.]

need•y (nē′dē) *adj.* **-i•er, -i•est.** 1. Being in want; impoverished. See Syns at **poor.** 2. Wanting or needing attention or reassurance, esp. to an excessive degree. —**need′i•ly** *adv.* —**need′i•ness** *n.*

neem (nēm) *n.* A tall, usu. evergreen East Indian tree (*Azadirachta indica*) widely cultivated for its timber, resin, bitter bark, and aromatic seed oil. [Hindi *nīm* < Skt. *nimbaḥ*.]

ne′er (nâr) *adv.* Never.

ne′er-do-well (nâr′dōō-wĕl′) *n.* An idle irresponsible person. —**ne′er′-do-well′** *adj.*

ne•far•i•ous (nə-fâr′ē-əs) *adj.* Infamous by way of being ex-

tremely wicked. [< Lat. *nefarius* < *nefās*, crime, transgression : *ne-*, not; see **ne** in App. + *fās*, divine law; see **dhē-** in App.] —**ne•far′i•ous•ly** *adv.* —**ne•far′i•ous•ness** *n.*

Nef•er•tar•i (nĕf′ər-tär′ē) 14th–13th century B.C. Queen of Egypt as the wife of Rameses II.

Nef•er•ti•ti (nĕf′ər-tē′tē) 14th cent. B.C. Queen of Egypt as the wife of Akhenaton.

Ne•fud (nĕ-fōōd′) also **Na•fud** (nä-) A desert region of N Saudi Arabia; noted for its red sand and violent winds.

ne•gate (nĭ-gāt′) *tr.v.* **-gat•ed, -gat•ing, -gates** 1. To make ineffective or invalid; nullify. 2. To rule out; deny. [Lat. *negāre*, *negāt-*, to deny. See **ne** in App.] —**ne•ga′tor, ne•gat′er** *n.*

ne•ga•tion (nĭ-gā′shən) *n.* 1. The act or process of negating. 2. A denial, contradiction, or negative statement. 3. The opposite or absence of something regarded as actual, positive, or affirmative. —**ne•ga′tion•al** *adj.*

neg•a•tive (nĕg′ə-tĭv) *adj.* 1a. Expressing, containing, or consisting of a negation, refusal, or denial. b. Indicating opposition or resistance. 2. Lacking positive or constructive features, esp.: a. Unpleasant; disagreeable: *a negative experience.* b. Gloomy; pessimistic: *a negative outlook.* c. Unfavorable or detrimental: *a negative review.* d. Hostile or disparaging; malicious: *a negative campaign.* 3. *Medicine* Not indicating the presence of a particular disease, condition, or organism. 4. *Logic* Being a proposition that denies agreement between a subject and its predicate. 5. *Mathematics* a. Relating to or being a quantity less than zero. b. Relating to or being the sign (–). c. Relating to or being a quantity to be subtracted. d. Relating to or being a quantity, number, angle, velocity, or direction in a sense opposite to another indicated or understood to be positive. 6. *Physics* a. Relating to or being an electric charge of the same sign as that of an electron, symbolized by (–). b. Relating to or being a body having an excess of electrons. 7. *Chemistry* Of or being an ion that is attracted to a positive electrode. 8. *Biology* Moving or turning away from a stimulus, such as light. ❖ *n.* 1. A statement or act indicating or expressing a contradiction, denial, or refusal. 2a. A statement or act that is highly critical of another or of others. b. Something that lacks all positive, affirmative, or encouraging features. c. A feature or characteristic that is not deemed positive, affirmative, or desirable. 3. *Grammar* A word or part of a word, such as *no, not,* or *non-*, that indicates negation. See Usage Note at **double negative.** 4. The side in a debate that contradicts or opposes the question being debated. 5a. An image in which the light areas of the object rendered appear dark and the dark areas appear light. b. A film, plate, or other photographic material containing such an image. 6. *Mathematics* A negative quantity. ❖ *tr.v.* **-tived, -tiv•ing, -tives** 1. To refuse to approve; veto. 2. To deny; contradict. 3. To demonstrate to be false; disprove. 4. To counteract or neutralize. [ME < OFr. *negatif* < Lat. *negātīvus* < *negātus*, p. part. of *negāre*, to deny. See NEGATE.] —**neg′a•tive•ly** *adv.* —**neg′a•tive•ness, neg′a•tiv′i•ty** (-tĭv′ĭ-tē) *n.*

negative feedback *n.* Feedback that reduces the output of a system, as the action of heat on a thermostat to limit the output of a furnace.

negative transfer *n.* The interference of previous learning in the process of learning something new.

neg•a•tiv•ism (nĕg′ə-tĭ-vĭz′əm) *n.* 1. A habitual attitude of skepticism or resistance to the suggestions, orders, or instructions of others. 2. Behavior characterized by persistent refusal, without apparent or logical reasons, to act on or carry out suggestions, orders, or instructions of others. —**neg′a•tiv•ist** *n.* —**neg′a•tiv•is′tic** *adj.*

neg•a•tron (nĕg′ə-trŏn′) *n.* An electron with a negative charge, as contrasted with a positron.

Ne•gev (nĕg′ĕv) also **Ne•geb** (-ĕb) A desert region of S Israel; assigned to Israel after the partition of Palestine in 1948.

ne•glect (nĭ-glĕkt′) *tr.v.* **-glect•ed, -glect•ing, -glects** 1. To pay little or no attention to; fail to heed; disregard: *neglected their warnings.* 2. To fail to care for or attend to properly. 3. To fail to do or carry out, as through carelessness or oversight: *neglected to return the call.* ❖ *n.* 1. The act or an instance of neglecting something. 2. The state of being neglected. 3. Habitual lack of care. [Lat. *neglegere, neglēct-* : *neg-*, not; see **ne** in App. + *legere*, to choose, pick up; see **leg-** in App.] —**ne•glect′er** *n.*

ne•glect•ful (nĭ-glĕkt′fəl) *adj.* Characterized by neglect; heedless. —**ne•glect′ful•ly** *adv.* —**ne•glect′ful•ness** *n.*

neg•li•gee also **neg•li•gée** or **neg•li•gé** (nĕg′lĭ-zhā′, nĕg′lĭ-zhā′) *n.* 1. A woman's loose dressing gown, often of soft delicate fabric. 2. Informal or incomplete attire. [Fr. *négligée* < fem. p. part. of *négliger*, to neglect < Lat. *neglegere.* See NEGLECT.]

neg•li•gence (nĕg′lĭ-jəns) *n.* 1. The state or quality of being negligent. 2. A negligent act or a failure to act. 3. *Law* Failure to exercise the degree of care considered reasonable under the circumstances, resulting in an unintended injury to another party.

neg•li•gent (nĕg′lĭ-jənt) *adj.* 1. Characterized by or inclined to neglect, esp. habitually. 2. Characterized by careless ease or informality; casual. 3. *Law* Guilty of negligence. [ME < OFr. < Lat. *neglegēns, neglegent-*, pr. part. of *neglegere*, to neglect. See NEGLECT.] —**neg′li•gent•ly** *adv.*

neg•li•gi•ble (nĕg′lĭ-jə-bəl) *adj.* Not significant or important enough to be worth considering; trifling. [Lat. *neglegere, negligere*,

Nefertiti
painted limestone bust,
14th century B.C.

[left margin:]

needle
left to right: sailmaking,
sewing machine, and
tapestry needles
bottom right: spring needle

to neglect; see NEGLECT + –IBLE.] —**neg′li·gi·bil′i·ty, neg′li·gi·ble·ness** *n.* —**neg′li·gi·bly** *adv.*

ne·go·tia·ble (nĭ-gō′shə-bəl, -shē-ə-) *adj.* **1.** Easy or possible to negotiate or be negotiated. **2.** Transferable from one person to another by delivery or by delivery and endorsement. —**ne·go′tia·bil′i·ty** *n.* —**ne·go′tia·bly** *adv.*

ne·go·ti·ate (nĭ-gō′shē-āt′) *v.* **-at·ed, -at·ing, -ates** —*intr.* To confer with another or others in order to come to terms or reach an agreement. —*tr.* **1.** To arrange or settle by discussion and mutual agreement. **2a.** To transfer title to or ownership of (a promissory note, for example) to another party by delivery or by delivery and endorsement in return for value received. **b.** To sell or discount (securities, for example). **3a.** To succeed in going over or coping with: *negotiate a sharp curve.* **b.** To succeed in accomplishing or managing. [Lat. *negōtiārī, negōtiāt-*, to transact business < *negōtium*, business : *neg-*, not; see **ne** in App. + *ōtium*, leisure.] —**ne·go′ti·a′tor** *n.* —**ne·go′tia·to′ry** (-shə-tôr′ē, -tôr′-, -shē-ə-) *adj.*

ne·go·ti·a·tion (nĭ-gō′shē-ā′shən) *n.* The act or process of negotiating: *successful negotiation of a contract.*

Ne·gress (nē′grĭs) *n. Offensive* A Black woman or girl.

Ne·gri·to (nĭ-grē′tō) *n., pl.* **-tos** or **-toes** A member of any of various peoples of short stature inhabiting parts of Malaysia, the Philippines, and southeast Asia. Not in scientific use. [Sp., dim. of *negro*, Black person. See NEGRO.]

ne·gri·tude or **Ne·gri·tude** (nē′grĭ-tōōd′, -tyōōd′, nĕg′rĭ-) *n.* An aesthetic and ideological concept affirming the independent nature, quality, and validity of Black culture. [Fr. *négritude* < *nègre*, Black person < Sp. *negro*. See NEGRO.]

Ne·gro (nē′grō) *n., pl.* **-groes** *Often Offensive* **1.** A Black person. See Usage Note at **black**. **2.** A member of the Negroid race. Not in scientific use. [Sp. and Port. *negro*, black, Black person < Lat. *niger, nigr-*, black. See **nekʷ-t-** in App.] —**Ne′gro** *adj.*

Ne·gro (nā′grō, nĕ′grō, -grōō), **Río 1.** A river rising in central Argentina and flowing c. 644 km (400 mi) to the Atlantic. **2.** A river rising in S Brazil and flowing c. 805 km (500 mi) to the Uruguay R. in central Uruguay. **3.** A river of NW South America flowing c. 2,253 km (1,400 mi) from E Colombia to the Amazon R. near Manaus, Brazil.

Ne·groid (nē′groid′) *Anthropology adj.* Of or being a human racial classification distinguished esp. by brown to black pigmentation and often tightly curled hair and including peoples indigenous to sub-Saharan Africa. [NEGR(O) + –OID.] —**Ne′groid′** *n.*

Ne·gro·phile (nē′grə-fīl′) *n.* One who admires and supports Black people and their culture. —**ne′gro·phil′ism** (nē′grə-fī′lĭz′əm, nĭ-grŏf′ə-) *n.*

Ne·gro·pho·bi·a (nē′grə-fō′bē-ə) *n.* **1.** Fear of or contempt for Black people and their culture. **2.** Behavior based on such an attitude or feeling. —**Ne′gro·phobe′** *n.* —**Ne′gro·pho′bic** *adj.*

Ne·gros (nā′grōs, nĕ′-) An island of the central Philippines in the Visayan Is. between Panay and Cebu.

ne·gus (nē′gəs) *n.* A beverage of wine, hot water, lemon juice, sugar, and nutmeg. [After Francis *Negus* (died 1732), English army officer.]

Ne·gus (nē′gəs, nĭ-gōōs′) *n.* Used formerly as a title for emperors of Ethiopia. [Amharic *nagus* < Classical Ethiopic *naguś*, king, ruler, verbal adj. of *nagśa*, to rule, become king < Ethiopic *nĕgūśā*, king of kings.]

NEH *abbr.* National Endowment for the Humanities

Neh. *abbr. Bible* Nehemiah

Ne·he·mi·ah¹ (nē′hə-mī′ə, nē′ə-) A Jewish leader and governor of Judea in the 5th century B.C. [Heb. *nĕḥemyāh*, Yahweh comforted : *niḥam, naḥem*, he comforted + *yāh*, Yahweh.]

Ne·he·mi·ah² (nē′hə-mī′ə, nē′ə-) *n.* See table at **Bible.** [After NEHEMIAH¹.]

Neh·er (nā′ər), **Erwin** b. 1944. German physicist who shared a 1991 Nobel Prize in medicine.

Neh·ru (nā′rōō), **Pandit Motilal** 1861–1931. Indian nationalist politician who was an influential leader in the years leading to India's independence. His son **Jawaharlal Nehru** (1889–1964) was the first prime minister of independent India (1947–64).

neigh (nā) *n.* The long high-pitched sound made by a horse. ❖ *intr.v.* **neighed, neigh·ing, neighs** To utter a neigh; whinny. [< ME *neighen*, to neigh < OE *hnǣgan*, prob. of imit. orig.]

neigh·bor (nā′bər) *n.* **1.** One who lives near or next to another. **2.** A person, place, or thing adjacent to or located near another. **3.** A fellow human. **4.** Used as a form of familiar address. ❖ *v.* **-bored, -bor·ing, -bors** —*tr.* To lie close to or border directly on. —*intr.* To live near or be situated close by. ❖ *adj.* Situated or living near another: *a neighbor state.* [ME *neighebor* < OE *nēahgebūr* : *nēah*, near + *gebūr*, dweller; see **bheua-** in App.]

neigh·bor·hood (nā′bər-hōōd′) *n.* **1.** A district or area with distinctive characteristics. **2.** The people who live near one another or in a particular district or area. **3.** The surrounding area; vicinity. **4.** *Informal* Approximate amount or range: *in the neighborhood of five million dollars.* **5.** Friendliness appropriate to a neighbor. **6.** *Mathematics* The set of points surrounding a specified point, each of which is within a certain, usu. small distance from the specified point.

neigh·bor·ly (nā′bər-lē) *adj.* Having or exhibiting the qualities of a friendly neighbor. —**neigh′bor·li·ness** *n.*

---

neigh·bour (nā′bər) *n., v.,* & *adj. Chiefly British* Variant of **neighbor.**

Nei Mong·gol (nā′ mŏn′gŏl′, mŏng′-) also **Inner Mongolia** An autonomous region of NE China; became an integral part of China in 1911. Cap. Hohhot. Pop. 21,456,798.

Neis·se (nī′sə) A river rising in N Czech Republic and flowing c. 225 km (140 mi) to the Oder R.

nei·ther (nē′thər, nī′-) *adj.* Not one or the other; not either: *Neither shoe feels comfortable.* ❖ *pron.* Not either one; not the one or the other: *Neither of the twins is here.* ❖ *conj.* **1.** Not either; not in either case. Used with the correlative conjunction *nor: I got neither the gift nor the card.* **2.** Also not: *If he won't go, neither will she.* ❖ *adv.* Similarly not; also not: *Just as you would not, so neither would they.* [ME < OE *nāwther, nāhwæther* (influenced by *ǣghwæther, ǣgther*, either) : *nā*, not; see **ne** in App. + *hwæther*, which of two; see **kʷo-** in App.]

> **USAGE NOTE** According to the traditional rule, *neither* is used only to mean "not one or the other of two." To refer to "none of several," *none* is preferred: *None* (not *neither*) *of the three opposition candidates would make a better president than the incumbent.* • The traditional rule also holds that *neither* is grammatically singular: *Neither candidate is having an easy time with the press.* However, it is often used with a plural verb, especially when followed by *of* and a plural: *Neither of the candidates are really expressing their own views.* • As a conjunction *neither* is properly followed by *nor,* not *or,* in formal style: *Neither prayers nor curses* (not *or curses*) *did any good.* See Usage Notes at **either, every, he, none, nor¹, or¹.**

Nejd (nĕjd) also **Najd** (nājd) A vast plateau region of the central Arabian Peninsula; nucleus of modern Saudi Arabia.

nek·ton (nĕk′tən, -tŏn′) *n.* The collection of marine and freshwater organisms that can swim freely, ranging in size from microscopic organisms to whales. [Gk. *nēkton*, neut. of *nēktos*, swimming < *nēkhein*, to swim. See **snā-** in App.]

nel·son (nĕl′sən) *n.* Any of several wrestling holds in which the user places an arm under the opponent's upper arm or armpit and presses the wrist or the palm of the hand against the back of the opponent's neck. [Perh. < name *Nelson.*]

Nelson, Horatio. Viscount Nelson. 1758–1805. British admiral who defeated French and Spanish naval forces at Trafalgar (1805).

Nelson River A river of Manitoba, Canada, flowing c. 644 km (400 mi) from Lake Winnipeg to Hudson Bay.

Nem·an (nĕm′ən, nyĕm′mən) also **Nie·men** (nē′mən, nyĕ′-) A river of W Belarus flowing c. 933 km (580 mi) through Lithuania to the Baltic Sea.

ne·mat·ic (nə-măt′ĭk) *adj.* Of or relating to the mesomorphic phase of a liquid crystal in which the molecules are oriented in loose parallel lines. [< Gk. *nēma, nēmat-*, thread. See **(s)nē-** in App.]

nemato– or **nemat–** *pref.* Thread; threadlike: *nematocyst.* [NLat. *nēmato–* < Gk. *nēma, nēmat-*, thread. See **(s)nē-** in App.]

nem·a·to·cide also **nem·a·ti·cide** (nĕm′ə-tĭ-sīd′, nə-măt′ĭ-) *n.* A substance used to kill nematodes. —**nem′a·to·cid·al, nem′a·ti·cid′al** (-sīd′l) *adj.*

nem·a·to·cyst (nĕm′ə-tə-sĭst′, nĭ-măt′ə-) *n.* A capsule within certain cnidarians, such as jellyfish, containing a barbed threadlike tube that delivers a paralyzing sting.

nem·a·tode (nĕm′ə-tōd′) *n.* Any of several worms of the phylum Nematoda, having unsegmented cylindrical bodies and including parasitic forms such as the hookworm. [< NLat. *Nēmatōda*, phylum name : NEMATO– + NLat. *-ōda* (alteration of *-oīdea* < neut. pl. of Gk. *-oeidēs*, -oid).] —**nem′a·tode′** *adj.*

nem·a·tol·o·gy (nĕm′ə-tŏl′ə-jē) *n.* The branch of zoology that deals with nematodes. —**nem′a·tol′o·gist** *n.*

Nem·bu·tal (nĕm′byə-tôl′) A trademark used for the drug pentobarbital sodium.

Ne·me·a (nē′mē-ə) A valley of N Argolis in ancient Greece; site of Nemean games after 573 B.C. —**Ne′me·an** *adj.* & *n.*

ne·mer·te·an (nĭ-mûr′tē-ən) also **nem·er·tine** (nĕm′ər-tīn′) *n.* Any of several velvety, usu. brightly colored worms of the phylum Nemertina (or Nemertea) that have a flat unsegmented body with an extensible proboscis and live in the sea or in the mud of the intertidal zone. [< NLat. *Nēmertēs*, type genus < Gk., name of a Nereid.] —**ne·mer′te·an** *adj.*

nem·e·sis (nĕm′ĭ-sĭs) *n., pl.* **-ses** (-sēz′) **1.** A source of harm or ruin. **2.** Retributive justice in its execution or outcome. **3.** An opponent that cannot be beaten or overcome. **4.** One that inflicts retribution or vengeance. **5. Nemesis** *Greek Mythology* The goddess of retributive justice or vengeance. [Gk., retribution, the goddess Nemesis < *nemein*, to allot. See **nem-** in App.]

ne·ne (nā′nā) *n.* A rare wild goose (*Branta sandvicensis*) of the Hawaiian Islands having a grayish-brown body with a black face. [Hawaiian *nēnē*, imit. of its cry.]

Nen·ets (nĕn′ĕts) *n., pl.* **Nenets 1.** A member of a reindeer-herding people of extreme northwest Russia. **2.** The Uralic language of this people. [Nenets, human being, Nenets.]

Nen Jiang (nŭn′ jyäng′) also **Nen Chiang** (chyäng′) A river of NE China flowing c. 1,191 km (740 mi) to the Songhua Jiang.

neo– *pref.* **1.** New; recent: *Neolithic.* **2a.** New and different: *neo-impressionism.* **b.** New and abnormal: *neoplasm.* **3.** New World:

Jawaharlal Nehru

nene
Branta sandvicensis

ă	pat	oi	boy
ā	pay	ou	out
âr	care	ōō	took
ä	father	ōō	boot
ĕ	pet	ŭ	cut
ē	be	ûr	urge
ĭ	pit	th	thin
ī	pie	*th*	this
îr	pier	hw	which
ŏ	pot	zh	vision
ō	toe	ə	about,
ô	paw		item

Stress marks:
′ (primary);
′ (secondary), as in
lexicon (lĕk′sĭ-kŏn′)

Neotropical. [Gk. < *neos*, new. See **newo-** in App.]

ne·o·clas·si·cism also **Ne·o·clas·si·cism** (nē′ō-klăs′ĭ-sĭz′əm) *n.* **a.** A revival of classical aesthetics and forms, esp.: **a.** A revival in literature in the late 17th and 18th centuries marked by a regard for the classical ideas of reason, form, and restraint. **b.** A revival in the 18th and 19th centuries in architecture and art, esp. in the decorative arts, marked by order, symmetry, and simplicity of style. **c.** A movement in music lasting roughly from 1915 to 1940 that sought to avoid subjective emotionalism and to return to the style of the pre-Romantic composers. —**ne′o·clas′sic, ne′o·clas′si·cal** *adj.* —**ne′o·clas′si·cist** *n.*

ne·o·co·lo·ni·al·ism (nē′ō-kə-lō′nē-ə-lĭz′əm) *n.* A policy whereby a major power uses economic and political means to perpetuate or extend its influence over underdeveloped nations or areas. —**ne′o·co·lo′ni·al** *adj.* —**ne′o·co·lo′ni·al·ist** *n.*

ne·o·con·ser·va·tism also **ne·o-con·ser·va·tism** (nē′ō-kən-sûr′və-tĭz′əm) *n.* An intellectual and political movement in favor of political, economic, and social conservatism that arose in opposition to the perceived liberalism of the 1960s. —**ne′o·con·ser′va·tive** *adj. & n.*

ne·o·cor·tex (nē′ō-kôr′tĕks) *n., pl.* **-ti·ces** (-tĭ-sēz′) or **-tex·es** The dorsal region of the cerebral cortex, esp. large in higher mammals and the most recently evolved part of the brain. —**ne′o·cor′ti·cal** (-tĭ-kəl) *adj.*

Ne·o-Dar·win·ism (nē′ō-där′wə-nĭz′əm) *n.* Darwinism as modified by the findings of modern genetics. —**Ne′o-Dar′win·i·an** (-där-wĭn′ē-ən) *adj.* —**Ne′o-Dar′win·ist** *n.*

ne·o·dym·i·um (nē′ō-dĭm′ē-əm) *n.* *Symbol* **Nd** A rare-earth element found in monazite and bastnaesite and used for coloring glass and doping some glass lasers. Atomic number 60; atomic weight 144.24; melting point 1,024°C; boiling point 3,027°C; specific gravity 6.80 or 7.004 (depending on allotropic form); valence 3. See table at **element.** [NEO– + (DI)DYMIUM.]

ne·o·fas·cism (nē′ō-făsh′ĭz′əm) *n.* A movement inspired by the tenets and methods of fascism or Nazism. —**ne′o·fas′cist** *adj. & n.*

Ne·o-Freud·i·an (nē′ō-froi′dē-ən) *adj.* Of, relating to, or characterizing any psychoanalytic system based on but modifying Freudian doctrine by emphasizing social factors, interpersonal relations, or other cultural influences in personality development or in causation of mental symptoms and illnesses. —**Ne′o-Freud′i·an** *n.*

Ne·o·gae·a also **Ne·o·ge·a** (nē′ə-jē′ə) *n.* A region that is coextensive with the Neotropical region and is considered one of the primary biogeographic realms. [NLat. : NEO– + Gk. *gaia,* earth.] —**Ne′o·gae′an** *adj.*

ne·o·gen·e·sis (nē′ō-jĕn′ĭ-sĭs) *n.* **1.** Regeneration of biological tissue. **2.** The formation of new minerals. —**ne′o·ge·net′ic** (-jə-nĕt′ĭk) *adj.*

ne·o·im·pres·sion·ism or **ne·o-im·pres·sion·ism** (nē′ō-ĭm-prĕsh′ə-nĭz′əm) *n.* A movement in late 19th-century painting led by Georges Seurat that was stricter and more formal than impressionism in composition and employed pointillism. —**ne′o·im·pres′sion·ist** *n. & n.*

ne·o·lib·er·al·ism (nē′ō-lĭb′ər-ə-lĭz′əm, -lĭb′rə-) *n.* A political movement beginning in the 1960s that blends traditional liberal concerns for social justice with an emphasis on economic growth. —**ne′o·lib′er·al** *adj. & n.*

ne·o·lith (nē′ə-lĭth′) *n.* A stone implement of the Neolithic Period. [Back-formation < NEOLITHIC.]

Ne·o·lith·ic (nē′ə-lĭth′ĭk) *adj.* Of or relating to the cultural period of the Stone Age beginning around 10,000 B.C. in the Middle East and later elsewhere and marked by the development of agriculture and the making of polished stone implements. ❖ *n.* The Neolithic Period.

ne·ol·o·gism (nē-ŏl′ə-jĭz′əm) *n.* **1.** A new word, expression, or usage. **2.** The creation or use of new words or senses. **3.** *Psychology* **a.** The invention of new words regarded as a symptom of certain psychotic disorders, such as schizophrenia. **b.** A word so invented. **4.** *Theology* A new doctrine or interpretation of scripture. —**ne·ol′o·gist** *n.* —**ne·ol′o·gis′tic, ne·ol′o·gis′ti·cal** *adj.*

ne·ol·o·gize (nē-ŏl′ə-jīz′) *intr.v.* **-gized, -giz·ing, -giz·es** To coin or use neologisms.

ne·ol·o·gy (nē-ŏl′ə-jē) *n., pl.* **-gies** Neologism. —**ne·ol′o·gi·cal** (nē′ə-lŏj′ĭ-kəl) *adj.* —**ne·o·log′i·cal·ly** *adv.*

Ne·o·Mal·thu·sian·ism (nē′ō-măl-thōō′zhə-nĭz′əm, -mŏl-) *n.* A doctrine advocating control of population growth. —**Ne′o·Mal·thu′sian** *adj. & n.*

ne·o·my·cin (nē′ə-mī′sĭn) *n.* A broad-spectrum antibiotic produced from strains of the actinomycete *Streptomyces fradiae* and used esp. in the form of its sulfate against gastrointestinal bacteria.

ne·on (nē′ŏn′) *n.* **1.** *Symbol* **Ne** A rare inert colorless gaseous element that occurs in air, glows reddish orange in an electric discharge, and is used in display and television tubes. Atomic number 10; atomic weight 20.180; melting point –248.67°C; boiling point –245.95°C. See table at **element.** **2.** A neon tetra. **3.** An extremely bright color. ❖ *adj.* Extremely bright or vivid; fluorescent. [Gk., neut. of *neos,* new. See **newo-** in App.]

ne·o·na·tal (nē′ō-nāt′l) *adj.* Of or relating to newborn infants or an infant. —**ne′o·na′tal·ly** *adv.*

ne·o·nate (nē′ə-nāt′) *n.* A newborn infant, esp. one less than four weeks old. [NEO– + Lat. *nātus,* p. part. of *nāscī,* to be born; see **genə–** in App.]

ne·o·na·tol·o·gy (nē′ō-nā-tŏl′ə-jē) *n.* The branch of pediatrics that deals with the diseases and care of newborn infants. —**ne′o·na·tol′o·gist** *n.*

ne·o-Na·zi (nē′ō-nät′sē, -nät′-) *n., pl.* **-zis** A member of a fringe group inspired by Adolf Hitler's Nazis. —**ne′o-Na′zism** *n.*

neon tetra *n.* A small tropical freshwater fish (*Hyphessobrycon innesi*) of the Amazon River having blue and red markings.

ne·o-or·tho·dox·y (nē′ō-ôr′thə-dŏk′sē) *n.* A Protestant movement arising during World War I that opposes liberalism and favors Calvinism. —**ne′o-or′tho·dox′** *adj.*

Ne·o-Pa·gan·ism (nē′ō-pā′gə-nĭz′əm) *n.* Any of various religious movements that arose in the late 20th century that combine worship of pagan nature deities with benign witchcraft. —**Ne′o-Pa′gan** *adj. & n.*

ne·o·phyte (nē′ə-fīt′) *n.* **1.** A recent convert to a belief; a proselyte. **2.** A beginner or novice. **3a.** *Roman Catholic Church* A newly ordained priest. **b.** A novice of a religious order or congregation. [ME < LLat. *neophytus* < Gk. *neophutos* : *neo-,* neo- + *-phutos,* planted (< *phuein,* to bring forth; see **bheuə–** in App.).]

ne·o·pla·sia (nē′ō-plā′zhə, -zhē-ə) *n.* **1.** Formation of new tissue. **2.** Formation of a neoplasm or neoplasms.

ne·o·plasm (nē′ə-plăz′əm) *n.* An abnormal new growth of tissue; a tumor. —**ne′o·plas′tic** (-plăs′tĭk) *adj.*

Ne·o·Pla·to·nism also **Ne·o·pla·to·nism** (nē′ō-plāt′n-ĭz′əm) *n.* **1.** A philosophical system developed in the third century A.D. that is based on Platonism with elements of mysticism and some Judaic and Christian concepts and posits a single source from which all existence emanates and with which an individual soul can be mystically united. **2.** A revival of Neo-Platonism or a system derived from it, as in the Middle Ages. —**Ne′o·Pla·ton′ic** (-plə-tŏn′ĭk) *adj.* —**Ne′o·Pla′to·nist** *n.*

ne·o·prene (nē′ə-prēn′) *n.* A synthetic rubber produced by polymerization of chloroprene and used in weather-resistant products, adhesives, shoe soles, paints, and rocket fuels. [NEO– + (CHLORO)PRENE.]

Ne·o-Scho·las·ti·cism (nē′ō-skə-lăs′tĭ-sĭz′əm) *n.* A chiefly Roman Catholic intellectual movement arising in the late 19th century that seeks to revive medieval Scholasticism by infusing it with modern concepts. —**Ne′o-Scho·las′tic** (-lăs′tĭk) *n.*

Ne·o·sho (nē-ō′shō, -shə) A river rising in E-central KS and flowing c. 740 km (460 mi) to the Arkansas R. in E OK.

ne·o·stig·mine (nē′ō-stĭg′mēn, -mĭn) *n.* Either of two related white, crystalline cholinergic compounds, $C_{12}H_{19}BrN_2O_2$ or $C_{13}H_{22}N_2O_6S$, used in the treatment of glaucoma and myasthenia gravis. [NEO– + (PHYSO)STIGMINE.]

ne·o·tec·ton·ics (nē′ō-tĕk-tŏn′ĭks) *n.* (used with a sing. verb) The study of geologic structures formed between the end of the Miocene and the present.

ne·ot·e·ny (nē-ŏt′n-ē) *n.* **1.** Retention of juvenile characteristics in the adults of a species. **2.** The attainment of sexual maturity by an organism still in its larval stage. [NLat. *neotenia* : NEO– + Gk. *teinein,* ten-, to extend; see TENESMUS.] —**ne′o·ten′ic** (nē′ə-tĕn′ĭk, -tē′nĭk), **ne·ot′e·nous** (-ŏt′n-əs) *adj.*

ne·o·ter·ic (nē′ə-tĕr′ĭk) *adj.* Of recent origin; modern. [LLat. *neōtericus* < Gk. *neōterikos* < *neōteros,* younger, comp. of *neos,* new. See **newo-** in App.]

Ne·o·trop·i·cs (nē′ō-trŏp′ĭks) *n.* The biogeographic region of the New World that stretches southward from the Tropic of Cancer and includes southern Mexico, Central and South America, and the West Indies. —**Ne′o·trop′i·cal** (-ĭ-kəl) *adj.*

ne·o·type (nē′ə-tīp′) *n.* A new specimen selected to replace a holotype that has been lost or destroyed.

Ne·pal (nə-pôl′, -päl′, -păl′, nā-) A country of central Asia in the Himalaya Mts. between India and SE China. Cap. Kathmandu. Pop. 21,360,000.

Nep·al·ese (nĕp′ə-lēz′, -lēs′) *n., pl.* **Nepalese 1.** A native or inhabitant of Nepal. **2.** The Nepali language. ❖ *adj.* Of or relating to Nepal or its people, language, or culture.

Ne·pal·i (nə-pô′lē, -pä′-, -păl′ē) *n., pl.* **-is 1.** A native or inhabitant of Nepal. **2.** The Indic language of Nepal, closely related to Hindi. —**Ne·pal′i** *adj.*

Ne·pe·an (nə-pē′ən) A city of SE Ontario, Canada, a suburb of Ottawa. Pop. 115,100.

ne·pen·the (nĭ-pĕn′thē) *n.* **1.** A drug mentioned in the *Odyssey* as a remedy for grief. **2.** Something that induces forgetfulness of sorrow or eases pain. [Alteration of Lat. *nēpenthes* < Gk. *nēpenthes (pharmakon),* grief-banishing (drug), nepenthe, neut. of *nēpenthēs* : *nē-,* not; see **ne** in App. + *penthos,* grief.] —**ne·pen′the·an** (-thē-ən) *adj.*

neph·e·line (nĕf′ə-lēn′, -lĭn) also **neph·e·lite** (-līt′) *n.* A mineral of sodium-potassium aluminum silicate, occurring in igneous rocks and used in the manufacture of glass. [< Greek *nephelē,* cloud (its fragments become cloudy when in nitric acid). See **nebh-** in App.] —**neph′e·lin′ic** (-lĭn′ĭk) *adj.*

neph·e·lin·ite (nĕf′ə-lĭ-nīt′) *n.* An igneous rock consisting chiefly of pyroxene and nepheline.

neph·e·lom·e·ter (nĕf′ə-lŏm′ĭ-tər) *n.* An apparatus used to measure the size and concentration of particles in a liquid by

neoclassicism
La Marseillaise by François Rude (1784–1855), on the Arc de Triomphe, Paris

CHINA

NEPAL
Kathmandu

INDIA

100 mi

Nepal

analysis of light scattered by the liquid. [Gk. *nephelē*, cloud; see **nebh-** in App. + −METER.] —**neph′e·lo·met′ric** (-lō-mĕt′rĭk) *adj.* —**neph′e·lom′e·try** *n.*

neph·ew (nĕf′yōō) *n.* **1.** A son of one's brother or sister or of one's spouse's brother or sister. **2.** The illegitimate son of an ecclesiastic who has taken a vow of celibacy. [ME *neveu, nephew* < OFr. *nevo, neveu* < Lat. *nepōs*. See **nepōt-** in App.]

ne·phrec·to·my (nə-frĕk′tə-mē) *n., pl.* **-mies** Surgical removal of a kidney.

neph·ric (nĕf′rĭk) *adj.* Relating to or connected with a kidney.

ne·phrid·i·um (nə-frĭd′ē-əm) *n., pl.* **-i·a** (-ē-ə) **1.** A tubular excretory organ in many invertebrates, such as mollusks and earthworms. **2.** The excretory organ of a vertebrate embryo from which the kidney develops. [NEPHR(O)- + NLat. *-idium*, diminutive suff. (< Gk. *-idion*).] —**ne·phrid′i·al** *adj.*

neph·rite (nĕf′rīt′) *n.* A white to dark green variety of jade, chiefly a metasilicate of iron, calcium, and magnesium. [Greek *nephros*, kidney (believed to cure kidney diseases) + *-ITE*¹.]

ne·phrit·ic (nə-frĭt′ĭk) *adj.* **1.** Of or relating to the kidneys; renal. **2.** Of, relating to, or affected with nephritis.

ne·phri·tis (nə-frī′tĭs) *n., pl.* **-phrit·i·des** (-frĭt′ĭ-dēz′) or **-phri·tis·es** Any of various acute or chronic inflammations of the kidneys, such as Bright's disease.

nephro- or **nephr-** *pref.* Kidney; kidneylike structure: *nephrotomy.* [< Gk. *nephros*, kidney.]

ne·phrog·e·nous (nə-frŏj′ə-nəs) or **neph·ro·gen·ic** (nĕf′rə-jĕn′ĭk) *adj.* **1.** Originating in the kidney. **2.** Able to develop into kidney tissue.

ne·phrol·o·gy (nə-frŏl′ə-jē) *n.* The science that deals with the function and diseases of the kidneys. —**ne·phrol′o·gist** *n.*

neph·ron (nĕf′rŏn) *n.* Any of the numerous filtering units of the vertebrate kidney that remove waste matter from the blood. [Ger. < Gk. *nephros*, kidney.]

ne·phrop·a·thy (nə-frŏp′ə-thē) *n., pl.* **-thies** A disease or abnormality of the kidney. —**neph′ro·path′ic** (nĕf′rə-păth′ĭk) *adj.*

ne·phro·sis (nə-frō′sĭs) *n., pl.* **-ses** (-sēz) A disease of the kidneys marked by degenerative lesions. —**ne·phrot′ic** (-frŏt′ĭk) *adj.*

neph·ro·stome (nĕf′rə-stōm′) *n.* The ciliated funnel-shaped inner opening of a nephridium in some invertebrates and lower vertebrates. [NEPHRO- + Gk. *stoma*, mouth.]

ne·phrot·o·my (nə-frŏt′ə-mē) *n., pl.* **-mies** Surgical incision into the kidney.

ne plus ul·tra (nē′ plŭs ŭl′trə, nā′ plŏŏs ōōl′trä) *n.* **1.** The highest point, as of excellence or achievement; the ultimate. **2.** The most profound degree, as of a condition or quality. [Lat. *nē plūs ultrā*, (go) no more beyond (this point) : *nē*, no + *plūs*, more + *ultrā*, beyond.]

nep·o·tism (nĕp′ə-tĭz′əm) *n.* Favoritism shown or patronage granted to relatives. [Fr. *népotisme* < Ital. *nepotismo* < *nepote*, nephew < Lat. *nepōs, nepōt-*. See **nepōt-** in App.] —**nep′o·tist** *n.* —**nep′o·tis′tic,** **nep′o·tis′ti·cal** *adj.*

Nep·tune (nĕp′tōōn′, -tyōōn′) *n.* **1a.** *Roman Mythology* The god of water, later identified with the Greek Poseidon. **b.** The sea. **2.** The eighth planet from the sun. See table at **planet.** [Lat. *Neptūnus.*] —**Nep·tu′ni·an** (-tōō′nē-ən, -tyōō′-) *adj.*

nep·tu·ni·um (nĕp-tōō′nē-əm, -tyōō′-) *n. Symbol* **Np** A metallic radioactive element found in trace quantities in uranium ores or synthesized; its longest-lived isotope is Np 237 with a half-life of 2.1 million years. Atomic number 93. See table at **element.** [After the planet NEPTUNE (< the fact that it follows uranium in the periodic table).]

nerd also **nurd** (nûrd) *n. Slang* A foolish, socially inept, or unattractive person. [Perhaps after *Nerd,* a character in *If I Ran the Zoo,* by Theodor Seuss Geisel.] —**nerd′y** *adj.*

WORD HISTORY The word *nerd* first appears in 1950 in Dr. Seuss's *If I Ran the Zoo:* "And then, just to show them, I'll sail to Ka-Troo And Bring Back an It-Kutch a Preep and a Proo a Nerkle a Nerd and a Seersucker, too!" (The nerd itself is a small humanoid creature looking comically angry, like a thin, cross Chester A. Arthur.) *Nerd* next appears, with a gloss, in the February 10, 1957, issue of the Glasgow, Scotland, *Sunday Mail* in a column entitled "ABC for SQUARES": "Nerd—a square, any explanation needed?" Authorities disagree whether Dr. Seuss's *nerd* and the Glaswegian *nerd* are the same word. Some claim there is no semantic connection and the identity of the words is fortuitous. Others maintain that Dr. Seuss is the true originator of *nerd* and that the word was picked up by the five- and six-year-olds of 1950 and passed on to their older siblings, who by 1957, as teenagers, had applied *nerd* to the most comically obnoxious creature of their own class, a "square."

Ne·re·id (nîr′ē-ĭd) *n.* **1.** *Greek Mythology* Any of the sea nymphs, the 50 daughters of Nereus. **2.** A satellite of Neptune. [Lat. *Nērēis, Nērēid-* < Gk. < *Nēreus,* Nereus.]

ne·re·is (nîr′ē-ĭs) *n., pl.* **ne·re·i·des** (nə-rē′ĭ-dēz′) See **clamworm.** [Lat. *Nērēis,* Nereid. See NEREID.]

Ne·re·us (nîr′ē-əs, nîr′yōōs) *n. Greek Mythology* A sea god, son of Oceanus and Gaea and father of the Nereids.

Ne·ri (nā′rē), Saint **Philip** 1515–95. Italian ecclesiastic who

---

founded (1564) the Fathers of the Oratory.

ne·rit·ic (nə-rĭt′ĭk) *adj.* Of, relating to, or inhabiting the ocean waters between the low tide mark and a depth of about a hundred fathoms (200 meters). [Ger. *neritisch,* perh. ult. < *Nereus,* Nereus.]

Nernst (nĕrnst), **Walther Hermann** 1864–1941. German physicist and chemist who won a 1920 Nobel Prize.

Ne·ro (nîr′ō, nē′rō) In full Nero Claudius Caesar. A.D. 37–68. Emperor of Rome (54–68) noted for his cruelty who may have set the Great Fire of Rome (64). —**Ne·ro′ni·an** (nĭ-rō′nē-ən) *adj.*

ne·rol (nîr′ôl, -ōl, -ōl, nĕr′-) *n.* A colorless liquid, C₉H₁₇COH, derived from orange blossoms and used in perfumery. [NER(OLI OIL) + -OL¹.]

ner·o·li oil (nĕr′ə-lē) *n.* An essential oil distilled from orange flowers and used in perfumery. [Fr. *néroli* < Ital. *neroli,* after Anna Maria de la Trémoille, 17th-cent. princess of *Nerola.*]

nerts (nûrts) *interj. Slang* Used to express disgust, contempt, or refusal. [Alteration of NUTS.]

Ne·ru·da (nĕ-rōō′də, -dä), **Pablo** 1904–73. Chilean poet and diplomat who won the 1971 Nobel Prize for literature.

ner·vate (nûr′vāt′) *adj. Botany* Having veins. Used of leaves.

ner·va·tion (nûr-vā′shən) *n.* A pattern of veins or nerves; venation.

nerve (nûrv) *n.* **1.** Any of the cordlike bundles of fibers made up of neurons through which sensory stimuli and motor impulses pass between the brain or other parts of the central nervous system and the eyes, glands, muscles, and other parts of the body. **2.** The sensitive tissue in the pulp of a tooth. **3.** A sore point or sensitive subject. **4a.** Courage and control under pressure. **b.** Fortitude; stamina. **c.** Forceful quality. **d.** Brazen boldness; effrontery: *had the nerve to deny it.* **5. nerves** Nervous agitation caused by fear, anxiety, or stress. **6.** A vein or rib in the wing of an insect. **7.** The midrib and larger veins in a leaf. ❖ *tr.v.* **nerved, nerv·ing, nerves** To give strength or courage to. ◆ *idioms:* **get on (someone's) nerves** To irritate or exasperate. **strain every nerve** To make every effort. [ME, sinew, nerve < OFr. *nerf* < Med.Lat. *nervus* < Lat.]

nerve cell *n.* **1.** See **neuron. 2.** The body of a neuron without its axon and dendrites.

nerve center *n.* **1.** A group of closely connected nerve cells that perform a specific function. **2.** A source of power or control.

nerve fiber *n.* A threadlike process of a neuron, esp. the prolonged axon that conducts nerve impulses.

nerve gas *n.* Any of various poisonous gases that interfere with the functioning of nerves by inhibiting cholinesterase.

nerve growth factor *n.* A protein that stimulates the growth of sympathetic and sensory nerve cells.

nerve impulse *n.* A wave of physical and chemical excitation along a nerve fiber in response to a stimulus.

nerve·less (nûrv′lĭs) *adj.* **1.** Lacking strength or energy; spiritless; weak. **2.** Lacking courage; spineless or cowardly. **3.** Calm and controlled in trying circumstances; cool. —**nerve′less·ly** *adv.* —**nerve′less·ness** *n.*

nerve net *n.* A diffuse network of cells that conducts impulses in all directions, forming a primitive nervous system in ctenophores, cnidarians, and certain other organisms.

nerve-rack·ing or **nerve-wrack·ing** (nûrv′răk′ĭng) *adj.* Intensely distressing or irritating to the nerves.

nerve trunk *n.* The main stem of a nerve, consisting of a bundle of nerve fibers bound together by connective tissue.

ner·vos·i·ty (nûr-vŏs′ĭ-tē) *n.* The quality or state of being nervous. [Lat. *nervōsitās,* sinewy strength < *nervōsus,* sinewy. See NERVOUS.]

nerv·ous (nûr′vəs) *adj.* **1a.** Of or relating to the nerves or nervous system. **b.** Stemming from or affecting the nerves or nervous system: *a nervous disorder.* **2.** Easily agitated or distressed; highstrung or jumpy. **3.** Marked by or having a feeling of unease or apprehension: *nervous moments before takeoff.* **4.** Vigorous in style or feeling; spirited. **5.** *Archaic* Strong; sinewy. [ME, sinewy, containing nerves < Lat. *nervōsus,* sinewy < *nervus,* sinew. See NERVE.] —**nerv′ous·ly** *adv.* —**nerv′ous·ness** *n.*

nervous breakdown *n.* A severe or incapacitating emotional disorder marked by depression. Not in scientific use.

nervous Nel·lie or **nervous Nel·ly** (nĕl′ē) *n., pl.* **-lies** *Informal* An unduly timid or anxious person.

nervous system *n.* The system of cells, tissues, and organs that in vertebrates consists of the brain, spinal cord, nerves, ganglia, and parts of the receptor and effector organs and regulates the body's responses to stimuli.

ner·vure (nûr′vyər) *n.* **1.** *Botany* See **vein** 2. **2.** *Zoology* See **vein** 3. [Fr. < OFr. *nerveure,* strap < *nerf,* sinew < Lat. *nervus.* See NERVE.]

nerv·y (nûr′vē) *adj.* **-i·er, -i·est 1.** Arrogantly impudent; brazen. **2.** Showing or requiring courage and fortitude; bold. **3.** *Chiefly British* Jumpy; nervous. **4.** *Archaic* Full of muscular force; sinewy. —**nerv′i·ness** *n.*

n.e.s. *abbr.* not elsewhere specified

Nes·bit (nĕz′bĭt′), **E(dith)** 1858–1924. British writer of children's books, including *Five Children and It* (1902).

nes·cience (nĕsh′əns, nĕsh′ē-əns, nĕsh′-, nĕs′ē-əns, nĕ′sē-) *n.* **1.** Absence of knowledge or awareness; ignorance. **2.** Agnosticism.

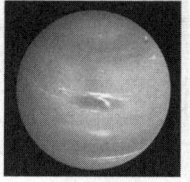

Neptune
top: *Triumph of Neptune,*
third-century A.D. Tunisian
mosaic
bottom: the planet
Neptune

Pablo Neruda

ă	pat	oi	boy
ā	pay	ou	out
âr	care	ŏŏ	took
ä	father	ōō	boot
ĕ	pet	ŭ	cut
ē	be	ûr	urge
ĭ	pit	th	thin
ī	pie	*th*	this
îr	pier	hw	which
ŏ	pot	zh	vision
ō	toe	ə	about,
ô	paw		item

Stress marks:
′ (primary);
′ (secondary), as in
lexicon (lĕk′sĭ-kŏn′)

[LLat. *nescientia* < Lat. *nesciēns, nescient-*, pr. part. of *nescīre*, to be ignorant : *ne-*, not; see **ne** in App. + *scīre*, to know.] —**nes′-cient** *adj. & n.*

ness (nĕs) *n.* A cape or headland. [ME *ness* < OE *næss*. See **nas-** in App.]

Ness, Loch A lake of N-central Scotland draining through the **Ness River** into the Moray Firth; reputed location of the Loch Ness Monster.

–ness *suff.* State; quality; condition; degree: *brightness.* [ME *-nes* < OE.]

Nes·sel·rode (nĕs′əl-rōd′) *n.* A mixture of chopped and boiled chestnuts, maraschino cherries, candied fruits, and liqueur or rum, used in deserts. [After Count Karl Robert von *Nesselrode* (1780–1862), Russian politician.]

nest (nĕst) *n.* **1a.** A container or shelter made by a bird out of twigs, grass, or other material to hold its eggs and young. **b.** A similar structure made by fish, insects, or other animals. **c.** A place in which young are reared; a lair. **d.** A number of insects, birds, or other animals occupying such a place: *a nest of hornets.* **2.** A place affording snug refuge or lodging; a home. **3a.** A place or environment that fosters rapid growth or development, esp. of something undesirable; a hotbed. **b.** Those who occupy or frequent such a place or environment. **4a.** A set of objects of graduated size that can be stacked together, each fitting within the one immediately larger. **b.** A cluster of similar things. **5.** *Computer Science* A set of data contained sequentially within another. **6.** A group of weapons in a prepared position. ❖ *v.* **nest·ed, nest·ing, nests** —*intr.* **1.** To build or occupy a nest. **2.** To create and settle into a warm and secure refuge. **3.** To hunt for birds' nests, esp. in order to collect the eggs. **4.** To fit together in a stack. —*tr.* **1.** To place in or as if in a nest. **2.** To put snugly together or inside one another. [ME < OE. See **sed-** in App.]

nest egg *n.* **1.** An artificial or natural egg placed in a nest to induce a bird to continue to lay eggs in that place. **2.** A sum of money put by as a reserve.

nest·er (nĕs′tər) *n.* **1.** One, such as a bird, that nests. **2.** *Western US* A squatter, homesteader, or farmer who settles in cattle-grazing territory.

nes·tle (nĕs′əl) *v.* **-tled, -tling, -tles** —*intr.* **1.** To settle snugly and comfortably. **2.** To lie in a sheltered position. **3.** To draw or press close, as in affection; snuggle. **4.** *Archaic* To nest. —*tr.* **1.** To snuggle or press contentedly. **2.** To place or settle as if in a nest: *I nestled the puppy in my arms.* [ME *nestlen*, to make a nest < OE *nestlian* < *nest*, nest.] —**nes′tler** *n.*

nest·ling (nĕst′lĭng, nĕs′-) *n.* **1.** A bird too young to leave its nest. **2.** A young child.

Nes·tor (nĕs′tər, -tôr′) *n.* *Greek Mythology* **1.** An elderly and wise counselor to the Greeks at Troy. **2.** often **nestor** A venerable and wise old man. [Gk. *Nestōr*.]

Nes·to·ri·an (nĕ-stôr′ē-ən, -stōr′-) *adj.* **1.** Of or relating to the theological doctrine, declared heretical in 431, that within Jesus are two distinct persons, divine and human, rather than a single divine person. **2.** Of or relating to an Eastern church. Not in scholarly use. ❖ *n.* **1.** An adherent of Nestorian doctrine. **2.** A member of an Eastern church. Not in scholarly use. [After **Nestorius**, accused of propounding this doctrine.] —**Nes·to′ri·an·ism** *n.*

Nes·to·ri·us (nĕ-stôr′ē-əs, -stōr′-) d. A.D. 451. Syrian-born patriarch of Constantinople whose beliefs were declared heretical in 431.

net[1] (nĕt) *n.* **1.** An openwork fabric made of threads or cords that are woven or knotted together at regular intervals. **2.** Something made of openwork fabric, esp.: **a.** A device for capturing birds, fish, or insects. **b.** A barrier against flying insects. **c.** A mesh for holding the hair in place. **d.** Something that entraps; a snare. **e.** A fine mesh fabric used as curtain or dress material or as the foundation for various laces. **3.** *Sports* **a.** A barrier of meshwork cord or rope strung to divide a court in half, as in tennis. **b.** A ball that is hit into this meshwork barrier. **c.** The goal in soccer, hockey, and lacrosse. **d.** The cord meshwork attached to the hoop of a basket in basketball. **4.** A meshed network of lines, figures, or fibers. **5.** A radio, television, or telephone network. **6.** *Computer Science* See **network** 4b. ❖ *tr.v.* **net·ted, net·ting, nets** **1.** To catch or ensnare in or as if in a net. **2.** To cover, protect, or surround with or as if with a net. **3.** *Sports* To hit (a ball) into the net. **4.** To make into a net. [ME < OE.] —**net′ter** *n.*

net[2] (nĕt) *adj.* **1.** *Business* **a.** Remaining after all deductions have been made, as for expenses: *net profit.* **b.** Remaining after tare is deducted: *net weight.* **2.** Ultimate; final: *the net result.* ❖ *n.* **1.** *Business* A net amount, as of profit or weight. **2.** The main point; the essence. ❖ *tr.v.* **net·ted, net·ting, nets** **1.** To bring in or yield as profit. **2.** To clear as profit. [ME, elegant, remaining after deductions < OFr., and < OItal. *netto*, remaining after deductions, both < Lat. *nitidus*, clean, elegant. See **NEAT**[1].]

Net *n.* The Internet.

Ne·tan·ya·hu (nĕt′n-yä′hoo, nĕ′tän-), **Benjamin** or **Binyamin** b. 1949. Israeli prime minister (1996–99). He became the leader of the conservative Likud party in 1993.

Neth. *abbr.* Netherlands

neth·er (nĕth′ər) *adj.* Located beneath or below; lower or under. [ME < OE *neothera* < *neother*, down.]

Neth·er·lands (nĕth′ər-ləndz) Often called **Hol·land** (hŏl′ənd) A country of NW Europe on the North Sea. The kingdom of the Netherlands, proclaimed at the Congress of Vienna (1814–15), included Belgium until 1830. Constitutional cap. Amsterdam; seat of government, The Hague. Pop. 15,380,000. —**Neth′er·land′ish** (-lăn′dĭsh) *adj.*

Netherlands Antilles Formerly **Dutch West Indies.** An autonomous island territory of the Netherlands off the coast of Venezuela and in the S Windward Is. Cap. Willemstad, on Curaçao. Pop. 192,056.

neth·er·most (nĕth′ər-mōst′) *adj.* Farthest down; lowest.

neth·er·world also **nether world** (nĕth′ər-wûrld′) *n.* **1.** The world of the dead. **2.** The part of society engaged in crime and vice.

net·i·quette (nĕt′ĭ-kĕt′, -kĭt) *n.* Etiquette practiced or advocated in electronic communication over a computer network. [Blend of (INTER)NET and ETIQUETTE.]

net·i·zen (nĕt′ĭ-zən) *n.* A person who is a frequent or habitual user of the Internet. [Blend of NET and CITIZEN.]

net·su·ke (nĕt′sə-kē′) *n., pl.* **netsuke** or **-kes** A small toggle, often in the form of a carved ivory or wood figure, used to secure a purse or container suspended on a cord from the sash of a kimono. [J.]

net·ting (nĕt′ĭng) *n.* **1.** An openwork fabric; a net. **2.** The act or process of making a net. **3.** The act or process of fishing with a net.

net·tle (nĕt′l) *n.* **1.** Any of numerous plants of the genus *Urtica,* having toothed leaves and stinging hairs that cause skin irritation. **2.** Any of various hairy, stinging, or prickly plants. ❖ *tr.v.* **-tled, -tling, -tles** **1.** To sting with or as if with a nettle. **2.** To irritate; vex. [ME < OE *netele.*]

nettle rash *n.* See **hives.**

net·tle·some (nĕt′l-səm) *adj.* Causing irritation or distress; vexatious.

net ton *n.* See **ton** 1.

net·work (nĕt′wûrk′) *n.* **1.** An openwork fabric or structure in which cords, threads, or wires cross at regular intervals. **2.** Something resembling an openwork fabric or structure in form or concept, esp.: **a.** A system of lines or channels that cross or interconnect: *a network of railroads.* **b.** A complex interconnected group or system: *an espionage network.* **c.** An extended group of people with similar interests or concerns who interact for mutual assistance or support. **3a.** A chain of radio or television broadcasting stations linked by wire or microwave relay. **b.** A company that produces the programs for these stations. **4a.** A group or system of electric components and connecting circuitry. **b.** *Computer Science* A system of computers interconnected by telephone wires or other means in order to share information. ❖ *v.* **-worked, -work·ing, -works** —*tr.* **1.** To cover with or as if with an openwork fabric or structure. **2.** To broadcast over a radio or television network. **3.** *Computer Science* To connect (computers) into a network. —*intr.* To interact or engage in informal communication with others for mutual assistance.

Ne·tza·hual·có·yotl (nĕ-tsä′wäl-kō′yōt′l) A city of S-central Mexico, a suburb of Mexico City. Pop. 1,341,230.

Neu·châ·tel (nōō′shə-tĕl′, nyōō′-, nœ-shä-), **Lake of** A narrow lake of NW Switzerland near the French border.

Neuf·châ·tel (nōō′shə-tĕl′, nyōō′-, nœ′shä-) *n.* A soft white cheese made from cow's milk. [After *Neufchâtel,* a town of northeast France.]

Neu·mann (noi′män′), **John von** 1903–57. Hungarian-born Amer. mathematician who contributed to game theory, quantum mechanics, and functional analysis.

neume or **neum** (nōōm, nyōōm) *n.* A sign used in the notation of plainsong during the Middle Ages, used today in transcriptions of Gregorian chants. [ME, series of notes sung on one syllable < Med.Lat. *pneuma* < Gk., breath. See PNEUMA.] —**neu·mat′ic** (nōō-măt′ĭk, nyōō-) *adj.*

neur– *pref.* Variant of **neuro–**.

neu·ral (nōōr′əl, nyōōr′-) *adj.* **1.** Of or relating to a nerve or the nervous system. **2.** Of, relating to, or located on the same side of the body as the spinal cord; dorsal. —**neu′ral·ly** *adv.*

neural arch *n.* A bony or cartilaginous arch that arises from the dorsal side of a vertebra to enclose the spinal cord.

neural crest *n.* The part of the ectoderm in a vertebrate embryo that lies on either side of the neural tube and develops into the cranial, spinal, and autonomic ganglia.

neu·ral·gia (nōō-răl′jə, nyōō-) *n.* Sharp paroxysmal pain extending along a nerve or group of nerves. —**neu·ral′gic** *adj.*

neural network also **neural net** *n.* A real or virtual device, modeled after the human brain, in which several interconnected elements process information simultaneously, adapting and learning from past patterns.

neural tube *n.* A dorsal tubular structure in the vertebrate embryo formed by longitudinal folding of the neural plate and differentiating into the brain and spinal cord.

neu·ras·the·ni·a (nōōr′əs-thē′nē-ə, nyōōr′-) *n.* A psychological disorder characterized by chronic fatigue and weakness, loss of memory, and generalized aches and pains. Not in scientific use. —**neu′ras·then′ic** (-thĕn′ĭk) *adj. & n.* —**neu′ras·then′i·cal·ly** *adv.*

nest
wasp nest

Benjamin Netanyahu

Netherlands

neu•rec•to•my (nŏŏ-rĕk′tə-mē, nyŏŏ-) *n., pl.* **-mies** Surgical removal of a nerve or part of a nerve.

neu•ri•lem•ma (nŏŏr′ə-lĕm′ə, nyŏŏr′-) *n.* The membranous covering of a nerve fiber. [Alteration of Fr. *névrilème* : *névr-*, nerve (< Gk. *neuro-*, neuro-) + Gk. *eilēma*, veil (< *eilein*, to wind, turn; see **wel-** in App.).] —**neu′ri•lem′mal** *adj.*

neu•ri•tis (nŏŏ-rī′tĭs, nyŏŏ-) *n.* Inflammation of a nerve or group of nerves, characterized by pain, loss of reflexes, and atrophy of the affected muscles. —**neu•rit′ic** (-rĭt′ĭk) *adj.*

neuro- or **neur-** *pref.* **1.** Nerve: *neuroblast.* **2.** Neural: *neuropathology.* [Greek, sinew, string < *neuron.*]

neu•ro•a•nat•o•my (nŏŏr′ō-ə-nät′ə-mē, nyŏŏr′-) *n., pl.* **-mies 1.** The branch of anatomy that deals with the nervous system. **2.** The neural structure of an organ or part. —**neu′ro•an′a•tom′i•cal** (-ăn′ə-tŏm′ĭ-kəl) *adj.* —**neu′ro•a•nat′o•mist** *n.*

neu•ro•bi•ol•o•gy (nŏŏr′ō-bī-ŏl′ə-jē, nyŏŏr′-) *n.* The biological study of the nervous system or a part of it. —**neu′ro•bi′o•log′i•cal** (-bī-ə-lŏj′ĭ-kəl) *adj.* —**neu′ro•bi•ol′o•gist** *n.*

neu•ro•blast (nŏŏr′ə-blăst′, nyŏŏr′-) *n.* An embryonic cell from which a nerve cell develops.

neu•ro•blas•to•ma (nŏŏr′ō-blă-stō′mə, nyŏŏr′-) *n., pl.* **-mas** or **-ma•ta** (-mə-tə) A malignant tumor composed of neuroblasts, occurring chiefly in infants and young children.

neu•ro•chem•is•try (nŏŏr′ō-kĕm′ĭ-strē, nyŏŏr′-) *n.* The study of the chemical composition and processes of the nervous system and the effects of chemicals on it. —**neu′ro•chem′i•cal** (-kəl) *adj.* —**neu′ro•chem′ist** *n.*

neu•ro•en•do•crine (nŏŏr′ō-ĕn′də-krĭn, -krēn′, -krīn′, nyŏŏr′-) *adj.* Of or involving the interaction between the nervous system and the hormones of the endocrine glands.

neu•ro•en•do•cri•nol•o•gy (nŏŏr′ō-ĕn′də-krə-nŏl′ə-jē, nyŏŏr′-) *n.* The study of the interaction between the nervous system and the endocrine glands and their secretions. —**neu′ro•en′do•cri′no•log′i•cal** (-krĭn′ə-lŏj′ĭ-kəl) *adj.* —**neu′ro•en′do•cri•nol′o•gist** *n.*

neu•ro•fi•bril (nŏŏr′ō-fī′brəl, -fĭb′rəl, nyŏŏr′-) *n.* Any of the long thin microscopic fibrils of a neuron.

neu•ro•fi•bro•ma (nŏŏr′ō-fī-brō′mə, nyŏŏr′-) *n., pl.* **-mas** or **-ma•ta** (-mə-tə) A usu. benign tumor originating in peripheral nerve fibers and composed chiefly of Schwann cells.

neu•ro•fi•bro•ma•to•sis (nŏŏr′ō-fī′brō-mə-tō′sĭs, nyŏŏr′-) *n.* A genetic disease characterized by the formation of neurofibromas, sometimes accompanied by physical deformation and a predisposition to various forms of cancer.

neu•ro•gen•ic (nŏŏr′ə-jĕn′ĭk, nyŏŏr′-) *adj.* **1.** Originating in the nerves or nervous tissue. **2.** Caused or affected by the nerves or nervous system. —**neu′ro•gen′i•cal•ly** *adv.*

neu•rog•li•a (nŏŏ-rŏg′lē-ə, nyŏŏ-, nŏŏr′ə-glē′ə, -glī′, nyŏŏr′-) *n.* **1.** The delicate network of branched cells and fibers that supports the tissue of the central nervous system. **2.** (*used with a pl. verb*) Any of the groups of cells or cell types making up this network. [NEURO– + Med.Gk. *glia*, glue; see ZOOGLEA.] —**neu•rog′li•al** *adj.*

neu•ro•hor•mone (nŏŏr′ō-hôr′mōn, nyŏŏr′-) *n.* A hormone secreted by or acting on a part of the nervous system. —**neu′ro•hor•mo′nal** *adj.*

neu•ro•hy•poph•y•sis (nŏŏr′ō-hī-pŏf′ĭ-sĭs, -hī-, nyŏŏr′-) *n., pl.* **-ses** (-sēz′) The posterior portion of the pituitary gland, having a rich supply of nerve fibers and releasing oxytocin and vasopressin. —**neu′ro•hy′po•phys′e•al, neu′ro•hy′po•phys′i•al** (-hī′pə-fĭz′ē-əl, -hīp′ə-, -hī-pŏf′ĭ-sē′əl) *adj.*

neu•ro•lep•tic (nŏŏr′ə-lĕp′tĭk, nyŏŏr′-) *n.* See anti. ❖ *adj.* Antipsychotic. ❖ *n.* See **antipsychotic.** [Fr. *neuroleptique* : *neuro-*, nerve (< Gk.; see NEURO–) + *-leptique*, affecting (< Gk. *lēptikos*, seizing < *lēptos*, seized < *lambanein*, *lēp-*, to seize, take).]

neu•rol•o•gy (nŏŏ-rŏl′ə-jē, nyŏŏ-) *n.* The medical science that deals with the nervous system and disorders affecting it. —**neu′ro•log′ic** (nŏŏr′ə-lŏj′ĭk, nyŏŏr′-), **neu′ro•log′i•cal** (-ĭ-kəl) *adj.* —**neu′ro•log′i•cal•ly** *adv.* —**neu•rol′o•gist** *n.*

neu•ro•ma (nŏŏ-rō′mə, nyŏŏ-) *n., pl.* **-mas** or **-ma•ta** (-mə-tə) A tumor composed of nerve tissue.

neu•ro•mus•cu•lar (nŏŏr′ō-mŭs′kyə-lər, nyŏŏr′-) *adj.* **1.** Of or affecting both nerves and muscles. **2.** Having the characteristics of both nervous and muscular tissue.

neu•ron (nŏŏr′ŏn′, nyŏŏr′-) *n.* Any of the impulse-conducting cells that constitute the brain, spinal column, and nerves, consisting of a nucleated cell body with one or more dendrites and a single axon. [Gk., sinew, string, nerve.] —**neu′ro•nal** (nŏŏ-rōn′l, nyŏŏ-, nŏŏr′ə-nəl, nyŏŏr′-), **neu•ron′ic** *adj.*

neu•rone (nŏŏr′ōn′, nyŏŏr′-) *n.* Chiefly British Variant of **neuron.**

neu•ro•pa•thol•o•gy (nŏŏr′ō-pə-thŏl′ə-jē, nyŏŏr′-) *n.* The scientific study of diseases of the nervous system. —**neu′ro•path′o•log′ic** (-păth′ə-lŏj′ĭk), **neu′ro•path′o•log′i•cal** (-ĭ-kəl) *adj.* —**neu′ro•pa•thol′o•gist** *n.*

neu•rop•a•thy (nŏŏ-rŏp′ə-thē, nyŏŏ-) *n., pl.* **-thies** A disease or abnormality of the nervous system.

neu•ro•pep•tide (nŏŏr′ō-pĕp′tĭd, nyŏŏr′-) *n.* Any of various peptides, such as endorphins, that are secreted by the brain and function as neurotransmitters.

neu•ro•phar•ma•col•o•gy (nŏŏr′ō-fär′mə-kŏl′ə-jē, nyŏŏr′-) *n.* The study of the action of drugs on the nervous system. —**neu′ro•phar′ma•co•log′i•cal** (-kə-lŏj′ĭ-kəl) *adj.* —**neu′ro•phar′ma•col′o•gist** *n.*

neu•ro•phys•i•ol•o•gy (nŏŏr′ō-fĭz′ē-ŏl′ə-jē, nyŏŏr′-) *n.* The branch of physiology that deals with the functions of the nervous system. —**neu′ro•phys′i•o•log′ic** (-ə-lŏj′ĭk), **neu′ro•phys′i•o•log′i•cal** *adj.* —**neu′ro•phys′i•ol′o•gist** *n.*

neu•ro•psy•chi•a•try (nŏŏr′ō-sĭ-kī′ə-trē, -sī-, nyŏŏr′-) *n.* The study of disorders with both neurological and psychiatric features. —**neu′ro•psy′chi•at′ric** (-sī′kē-ăt′rĭk) *adj.* —**neu′ro•psy•chi′a•trist** *n.*

neu•ro•psy•chol•o•gy (nŏŏr′ō-sī-kŏl′ə-jē, nyŏŏr′-) *n.* The branch of psychology that deals with the relationship between the nervous system and cerebral or mental functions such as language, memory, and perception. —**neu′ro•psy′cho•log′i•cal** (-sī′kə-lŏj′ĭ-kəl) *adj.* —**neu′ro•psy•chol′o•gist** *n.*

neu•rop•ter•an (nŏŏ-rŏp′tər-ən, nyŏŏ-) *n.* A carnivorous insect of the order Neuroptera, such as the ant lion, having four net-veined wings and mouthparts adapted for chewing. [< NLat. *Neuroptera*, order name : Gk. *neuron*, vein, tendon; see NEURON + Gk. *ptera*, pl. of *pteron*, wing; see –PTER.] —**neu•rop′ter•an, neu•rop′ter•ous** *adj.*

neu•ro•sci•ence (nŏŏr′ō-sī′əns, nyŏŏr′-) *n.* Any of the sciences, such as neuroanatomy and neurobiology, that deal with the nervous system. —**neu′ro•sci′en•tif′ic** (-sī′ən-tĭf′ĭk) *adj.* —**neu′ro•sci′en•tist** (-sī′ən-tĭst) *n.*

neu•ro•sen•so•ry (nŏŏr′ō-sĕn′sə-rē, nyŏŏr′-) *adj.* Relating to the sensory activity or functions of the nervous system.

neu•ro•sis (nŏŏ-rō′sĭs, nyŏŏ-) *n., pl.* **-ses** (-sēz) Any of various mental or emotional disorders, such as hypochondria, arising without evidence of organic disease and involving symptoms such as anxiety and depression. Not in scientific use.

neu•ro•sur•ger•y (nŏŏr′ō-sûr′jə-rē, nyŏŏr′-) *n., pl.* **-ies** Surgery on any part of the nervous system. —**neu′ro•sur′geon** (-jən) *n.* —**neu′ro•sur′gi•cal** (-jĭ-kəl) *adj.*

neu•rot•ic (nŏŏ-rŏt′ĭk, nyŏŏ-) *adj.* **1.** Of, relating to, or affected with a neurosis. Not in scientific use. **2.** Overanxious. ❖ *n.* **1.** A person suffering from a neurosis. Not in scientific use. **2.** An overly anxious person. —**neu•rot′i•cal•ly** *adv.*

neu•rot•o•my (nŏŏ-rŏt′ə-mē, nyŏŏ-) *n., pl.* **-mies** The surgical cutting or stretching of a nerve, usu. to relieve pain.

neu•ro•tox•in (nŏŏr′ō-tŏk′sĭn, nyŏŏr′-) *n.* A toxin that damages or destroys nerve tissue. —**neu′ro•tox′ic** (-tŏk′sĭk) *adj.* —**neu′ro•tox•ic′i•ty** (-tŏk-sĭs′ĭ-tē) *n.*

neu•ro•trans•mit•ter (nŏŏr′ō-trăns′mĭt-ər, -trănz′-, nyŏŏr′-) *n.* A chemical substance, such as acetylcholine, that transmits nerve impulses across a synapse.

neu•ro•trop•ic (nŏŏr′ō-trŏp′ĭk, -trō′pĭk, nyŏŏr′-) *adj.* Tending to affect or attack nervous tissue. —**neu•rot′ro•pism** (nŏŏ-rŏt′rə-pĭz′əm, nyŏŏ-) *n.*

Neuse (nŏŏs, nyŏŏs) A river of E-central NC flowing c. 442 km (275 mi) to Pamlico Sound.

Neuss (nois) A city of W-central Germany across the Rhine R. from Düsseldorf; chartered in the 12th cent. Pop. 148,560.

neus•ton (nŏŏ′stŏn, nyŏŏ′-) *n.* The collection of minute or microscopic organisms that inhabit the surface layer of a body of water. [Gk. *neuston*, neut. of *neustos*, swimming < *nein*, to swim. See **(s)nāu-** in App.]

Neus•tri•a (nŏŏ′strē-ə, nyŏŏ′-) The W part of the kingdom of the Merovingian Franks from the 6th to the 8th cent., in present-day NW France. —**Neu′stri•an** *adj. & n.*

neut. *abbr.* **1.** neuter **2.** neutral

neu•ter (nŏŏ′tər, nyŏŏ′-) *adj.* **1.** *Grammar* **a.** Neither masculine nor feminine in gender. **b.** Neither active nor passive; intransitive. Used of verbs. **2a.** *Biology* Having undeveloped or imperfectly developed sexual organs. **b.** *Botany* Having no pistils or stamens; asexual. **c.** *Zoology* Lacking reproductive organs. **3.** Taking no side; neutral. ❖ *n.* **1.** *Grammar* **a.** The neuter gender. **b.** A neuter word. **c.** A neuter noun. **2.** A castrated animal. **3.** A sexually undeveloped or imperfectly developed insect, such as a worker bee. **4.** A plant without stamens or pistils. **5.** One that is neutral. ❖ *tr.v.* **-tered, -ter•ing, -ters** To castrate or spay. [ME *neutre* < OFr. < Lat. *neuter*, neither, neuter : *ne-*, not; see **ne** in App. + *uter*, either; see **kʷo-** in App.]

neu•tral (nŏŏ′trəl, nyŏŏ′-) *adj.* **1.** Not aligned with, supporting, or favoring either side in a war, dispute, or contest. **2.** Belonging to neither side in a controversy: *on neutral ground.* **3.** Belonging to neither kind; one thing nor the other. **4.** Sexless; neuter. **5.** *Chemistry* **a.** Of or relating to a solution or compound that is neither acidic nor alkaline. **b.** Of or relating to a compound that does not ionize in solution. **6.** *Physics* **a.** Of or relating to a particle, object, or system that has no electric charge. **b.** Of or relating to a particle, object, or system that has a net electric charge of zero. **7.** Of or being a color, such as gray, black, or white, that lacks hue; achromatic. **8.** *Linguistics* Pronounced with the tongue in a middle position, neither high nor low. ❖ *n.* **1a.** A nation nonaligned with either side in a war. **b.** A citizen of such a nation. **2.** One who takes no side in a controversy. **3.** A neutral hue. **4.** A position in which a set of gears is disengaged so that power cannot be transmitted. [ME *neutral* < OFr. *neutral* < Lat. *neutrālis*,

netsuke
carved wooden horse

nettle
stinging nettle
Urtica dioica

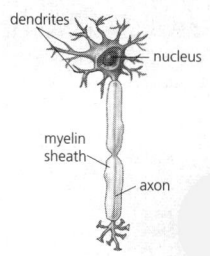

dendrites
nucleus
myelin
sheath
axon

neuron
multipolar neuron

ă	pat	oi	boy
ā	pay	ou	out
âr	care	ŏŏ	took
ä	father	ŏŏ	boot
ĕ	pet	ŭ	cut
ē	be	ûr	urge
ĭ	pit	th	thin
ī	pie	th	this
îr	pier	hw	which
ŏ	pot	zh	vision
ō	toe	ə	about,
ô	paw		item

Stress marks:
′ (primary);
′ (secondary), as in
lexicon (lĕk′sĭ-kŏn′)

grammatically neuter < *neuter, neutr-*. See NEUT.] —**neu′tral•ly** *adv.*

Neutral *n., pl.* **Neutral** or **-trals** A member of a confederacy of Iroquoian-speaking Native American peoples formerly inhabiting the northern shore of Lake Erie.

neutral ground *n. Louisiana & Southern Mississippi* **1.** See **median strip**. **2.** See **parking** 3.

REGIONAL NOTE The strip of grass dividing the opposing lanes of an avenue or a highway is known by many terms in the United States. The most common term is *median strip* or *median*. The strip is known regionally as a *mall* (Upstate New York), a *medial strip* (Pennsylvania), a *meridian* or *boulevard* (Midwest), and *neutral ground* (Louisiana and southern Mississippi). See Regional Note at **parking**.

neu•tral•ism (nōō′trə-lĭz′əm, nyōō′-) *n.* **1.** The state of being neutral; neutrality. **2.** A political policy or advocacy of nonalignment or noninvolvement in conflicting alliances and of attempting to mediate or conciliate in conflicts between states. —**neu′tral•ist** *adj. & n.* —**neu′tral•is′tic** *adj.*

neu•tral•i•ty (nōō-trăl′ĭ-tē, nyōō-) *n.* The state or policy of being neutral, esp. nonparticipation in war.

neu•tral•i•za•tion (nōō′trə-lĭ-zā′shən, nyōō′-) *n.* **1a.** The act or process of neutralizing. **b.** The state or quality of being neutralized. **2.** *Chemistry* A reaction between an acid and a base that yields a salt and water.

neu•tral•ize (nōō′trə-līz′, nyōō′-) *tr.v.* **-ized, -iz•ing, -iz•es 1.** To make neutral. **2.** To counterbalance or counteract the effect of; render ineffective. **3.** To declare neutral and therefore inviolable during a war. **4.** *Chemistry* **a.** To make (a solution) neutral. **b.** To cause (an acid or base) to undergo neutralization. **5.** *Medicine* To counteract the effect of (a drug or toxin). **6.** *Slang* To remove as a threat, esp. by killing. —**neu′tral•iz′er** *n.*

neutral spirits *pl.n.* (*used with a sing. or pl. verb*) Ethyl alcohol distilled at or above 190 proof, often used in blended alcoholic beverages.

neutral zone *n.* **1.** *Football* An imaginary area as wide as the length of the football extending across the field between the lines of scrimmage. **2.** *Sports* The area of an ice hockey rink between the two bluelines that is neither an offensive nor a defensive zone.

neu•tri•no (nōō-trē′nō, nyōō-) *n., pl.* **-nos** Any of three electrically neutral subatomic particles in the lepton family. [Ital. < *neutro*, neuter < Lat. *neuter, neutr-*. See NEUTER.]

neu•tron (nōō′trŏn′, nyōō′-) *n.* An electrically neutral subatomic particle in the baryon family, having a mass 1,839 times that of the electron, stable when bound in an atomic nucleus, and having a mean lifetime of approx. 1.0×10^3 seconds as a free particle. [NEUTR(AL) + -ON^1.]

neutron bomb *n.* A nuclear bomb that would produce great numbers of neutrons but little blast and thus destroy life but spare property.

neutron star *n.* A celestial body consisting of a superdense mass of neutrons from a collapsed massive star, and having a powerful gravitational attraction from which only neutrinos and high-energy photons can escape.

neu•tro•pe•ni•a (nōō′trə-pē′nē-ə, nyōō′-) *n.* An abnormal decrease in the number of neutrophils in the blood. [NEUTRO(PHIL) + -PENIA.] —**neu′tro•pen′ic** (-pĕn′ĭk) *adj.*

neu•tro•phil (nōō′trə-fĭl′, nyōō′-) *adj.* Stained readily by neutral dyes. Used esp. of white blood cells. ❖ *n.* A neutrophil cell, esp. a type of granular white blood cell that is highly destructive of microorganisms. [NEUTR(AL) + -PHIL(E).] —**neu′tro•phile′** (-fĭl′), **neu′tro•phil′ic** (-fĭl′ĭk) *adj.*

Nev. *abbr.* Nevada

Ne•va (nē′və, nyĭ-vä′) A river of NW Russia flowing c. 74 km (46 mi) from Lake Ladoga to the Gulf of Finland.

Ne•vad•a (nə-văd′ə, -vä′də) A state of the W US; admitted as the 36th state in 1864. It became a territory in 1861 after the discovery (1859) of the Comstock Lode. Cap. Carson City. Pop. 1,998,257. —**Ne•vad′an, Ne•vad′i•an** *adj. & n.*

né•vé (nā-vā′) *n.* **1.** The upper part of a glacier where the snow turns into ice. **2a.** A snow field at the head of a glacier. **b.** The granular snow typically found in such a field. [Fr. < Fr. dialectal *névi* < VLat. **nivātum* < neut. of Lat. *nivātus*, cooled by snow < *nix, niv-*, snow.]

Nev•el•son (nĕv′əl-sən), **Louise** 1899–1988. Russian-born Amer. sculptor known for her massive abstract works.

nev•er (nĕv′ər) *adv.* **1.** Not ever; on no occasion; at no time: *had never been there before.* **2.** Not at all; in no way; absolutely not: *That will never do.* —**idiom: never mind 1.** Don't bother: *I had wanted help, but never mind, I'll do it myself.* **2.** Not to mention; and certainly not: *I can't tread water, never mind swim.* [ME < OE *nǣfre*: *ne*, not; see **ne** in App. + *ǣfre*, ever; see **aiw-** in App.]

nev•er-end•ing (nĕv′ər-ĕn′dĭng) *adj.* Having no foreseeable end.

nev•er•more (nĕv′ər-môr′, -mōr′) *adv.* Never again.

nev•er-nev•er land (nĕv′ər-nĕv′ər) *n.* An imaginary and wonderful place; a fantasy land. [After *Never-Never Land*, fictional setting used in the play *Peter Pan* by J.M. Barrie.]

nev•er•the•less (nĕv′ər-thə-lĕs′) *adv.* In spite of that; nonetheless; however: *a small, nevertheless fatal error.*

Ne•vis (nē′vĭs, nĕv′ĭs) One of the Leeward Is. of the E West Indies in the Caribbean Sea; colonized by the English after 1628 and now part of St. Kitts and Nevis.

ne•vus (nē′vəs) *n., pl.* **-vi** (-vī′) A congenital growth or mark on the skin, such as a birthmark. [Lat. *naevus*.] —**ne′void′** (-void′) *adj.*

new (nōō, nyōō) *adj.* **new•er, new•est 1.** Having been made or come into being only a short time ago; recent: *a new law.* **2a.** Still fresh: *a new coat of paint.* **b.** Never used or worn before now: *a new car; a new hat.* **3.** Just found, discovered, or learned: *new information.* **4.** Not previously experienced or encountered; novel or unfamiliar: *ideas new to me.* **5.** Different from the former or the old. **6.** Recently obtained or acquired. **7.** Additional; further. **8.** Recently arrived or established in a place, position, or relationship. **9.** Changed for the better; rejuvenated: *The nap has made a new person of me.* **10.** Being the later or latest in a sequence: *a new edition.* **11.** Currently fashionable. **12. New** In the most recent form, period, or development. **13.** Inexperienced or unaccustomed: *new at the job.* ❖ *adv.* Freshly; recently. Often used in combination: *new-mown.* [ME *newe* < OE *nīwe, nēowe*. See **newo-** in App.] —**new′ness** *n.*

SYNONYMS *new, fresh, novel, original* These adjectives describe what has existed for only a short time, has only lately come into use, or has only recently arrived at a state or position, as of prominence. *New* is the most general: *"It is time for a new generation of leadership"* (John F. Kennedy). Something *fresh* has qualities of newness such as briskness, brightness, or purity: *fresh footprints; fresh hope. Novel* applies to the new and strikingly unusual: *"His sermons were considered bold in thought and novel in language"* (Edith Wharton). Something *original* is novel and the first of its kind: *"The science of pure mathematics, in its modern development, may claim to be the most original creation of the human spirit"* (Alfred North Whitehead).

New Age *adj.* **1.** Of or relating to a complex of spiritual and consciousness-raising movements of the 1980s, including belief in spiritualism and reincarnation and holistic approaches to health and ecology. **2.** Of, relating to, or resembling New Age music. ❖ *n.* Modern music that is marked by drones, quiet harmonies, and soft rhythms, often using synthesizers. —**New Ager** *n.*

New Amsterdam A settlement est. in 1624 by the Dutch at the mouth of the Hudson R. on the S end of Manhattan I.; cap. of New Netherland (1626–64).

New•ark (nōō′ərk, nyōō′-) A city of NE NJ on **Newark Bay,** an inlet of the Atlantic Ocean; settled in 1666. Pop. 273,546.

New Bedford A city of SE MA on Buzzards Bay ESE of Fall River; settled in the mid-1600s. Pop. 93,768.

new•bie (nōō′bē, nyōō′-) *n. Slang* One that is new to something, esp. a novice at using computer technology or the Internet. [< NEW (with *b* as in FREEBIE).]

new blood *n.* New people considered as a revitalizing force, as in an organization.

new•born (nōō′bôrn′, nyōō′-) *adj.* **1.** Very recently born. **2.** Born anew: *newborn courage.* ❖ *n.* A neonate.

New Britain[1] A volcanic island of Papua New Guinea in the SW Pacific Ocean.

New Britain[2] A city of central CT SSW of Hartford. Pop. 71,538.

New Brunswick A province of E Canada on the Gulf of St. Lawrence; joined Nova Scotia, Quebec, and Ontario to form the confederated Dominion of Canada in 1867. Cap. Fredericton. Pop. 738,133.

New•burg also **New•burgh** (nōō′bûrg′, nyōō′-) *adj.* Served in a sauce made of cream, egg yolks, butter, and sherry. [?]

New Caledonia A French overseas territory in the SW Pacific consisting of the island of **New Caledonia** and several smaller islands; annexed by France in 1853. Cap. Nouméa. Pop. 145,368.

New Castile A historical region of central Spain that combined with the N region of Old Castile to form the kingdom of Castile; united with Aragon after the marriage of Ferdinand and Isabella (1469).

New•cas•tle (nōō′kăs′əl, nyōō′-) or **Newcastle upon Tyne** (tīn) A borough of NE England on the Tyne R. N of Leeds. Pop. 285,310.

new•com•er (nōō′kŭm′ər, nyōō′-) *n.* One who has only recently arrived.

New Criticism *n.* A method of close textual literary criticism chiefly of the mid-20th century that pays little regard to biographical or historical information. —**New Critic** *n.*

New Deal *n.* **1.** The programs and policies of economic recovery and social reform introduced in the 1930s by Franklin D. Roosevelt. **2.** The period of development of the New Deal. —**New Dealer** *n.*

New Delhi The cap. of India, in the N-central part S of Delhi; constructed between 1912 and 1929 and officially inaugurated in 1931. Pop. 301,297.

new•el (nōō′əl, nyōō′-) *n.* **1.** A vertical support at the center of a circular staircase. **2.** A post that supports a handrail at the bottom or at the landing of a staircase. [ME *nouel, niewel* < OFr. *noiel* < VLat. **nōdellus*, little knot, dim. of Lat. *nōdulus*, dim. of *nōdus*, knot. See NODE.]

newel

New England A region of the NE US comprising the modern-day states of ME, NH, VT, MA, CT, and RI. —**New Eng′land•er** n.

New England boiled dinner n. A dish consisting of meat simmered with carrots, potatoes, and cabbage.

New England clam chowder n. A thick soup made with clams, onions, potatoes, milk, and sometimes salt pork.

New English n. See Modern English.

New English Bible n. A modern translation of the Bible by a British interdenominational team published in 1970.

Newf. abbr. Newfoundland

new•fan•gled (nōō′făng′gəld, nyōō′-) adj. **1.** New and often needlessly novel. **2.** Fond of novelty. [ME newfanglyd, fond of novelty, alteration of neufangel : new, new; see NEW + *-fangel, taken.] —**new′fan′gled•ness** n.

new-fash•ioned (nōō′făsh′ənd, nyōō′-) adj. **1.** Up-to-date; current. **2.** Created in a new form or fashion.

New Forest A region of S England set aside as a hunting ground by William the Conqueror in 1079.

new•found (nōō′found′, nyōō′-) adj. Recently discovered.

New•found•land¹ (nōō′fən-lənd, -lănd′, -fənd-, nyōō′-) A province of E Canada including the island of **Newfoundland** and nearby islands and the mainland area of Labrador with its adjacent islands; joined the confederation in 1949. The province of Quebec claimed Labrador until 1927. Cap. St. John's. Pop. 551,792. —**New′found•land•er** n.

New•found•land² (nōō′fən-lənd, nyōō′-) n. Any of a breed of large strong dog developed in Newfoundland and having a thick, usu. black coat.

New France The possessions of France in North America from the 16th cent. until the Treaty of Paris (1763), when the French holdings were awarded to Great Britain and Spain.

New Georgia Island An island of the Solomon Is. in the SW Pacific Ocean.

New Gra•na•da (grə-nä′də) A former Spanish colony (c. 1530–1819) of N South America including present-day Colombia, Ecuador, Panama, and Venezuela.

New Greek n. See Modern Greek.

New Guinea An island in the SW Pacific N of Australia; divided between Indonesia and Papua New Guinea. —**New Guinean** adj. & n.

New Guinea, Trust Territory of A former trust territory of Australia consisting of NE New Guinea, the Bismarck Archipelago, and Bougainville in the Solomon Is.

New Hampshire A state of the NE US between VT and ME; admitted as one of the original Thirteen Colonies in 1788. Cap. Concord. Pop. 1,235,786. —**New Hamp′shir•ite′** n.

New Harmony A village of SW IN on the Wabash R. WNW of Evansville; founded in 1814 by the Harmony Society led by George Rapp and the site (1825–28) of a utopian community est. by Robert Owen.

New Haven A city of S CT on Long Island Sound NE of Bridgeport; settled 1637–38. Pop. 123,626.

New Hebrew n. See Modern Hebrew.

New Hebrides See Vanuatu.

New Ireland A volcanic island of Papua New Guinea in the Bismarck Archipelago in the SW Pacific Ocean.

new•ish (nōō′ish, nyōō′-) adj. Fairly new.

New Jersey A state of the E-central US on the Atlantic Ocean; admitted as one of the original Thirteen Colonies in 1787. Cap. Trenton. Pop. 8,414,350. —**New Jer′sey•ite′** n.

New Jerusalem n. **1.** Christianity The final resting place of souls redeemed by Jesus. **2.** An ideal community on earth.

New Journalism n. Journalism that is characterized by the reporter's subjective interpretations and often features fictional dramatized elements. —**New Journalist** n.

New Kingdom Ancient Egypt during the XVIII–XX Dynasties, from c. 1580 to 1090 B.C.; noted as a period of territorial expansion and flourishing art and architecture.

New Latin n. Latin as used since about 1500.

New Left n. A political movement originating in the United States in the 1960s, marked by active advocacy of radical changes in government, politics, and society. —**New Leftist** n.

new•ly (nōō′lē, nyōō′-) adv. **1.** Not long ago; recently: newly baked bread. **2.** Once more; anew: a newly painted room. **3.** In a new or different way; freshly.

new•ly•wed (nōō′lē-wĕd′, nyōō′-) n. A person recently married.

New•man (nōō′mən, nyōō′-), John Henry 1801–90. British prelate who converted to Roman Catholicism (1845) and was made a cardinal (1879).

new math n. Mathematics taught in elementary and secondary schools that uses set theory.

New Mexico A state of the SW US on the Mexican border; admitted as the 47th state in 1912. The region was ceded to the US by the Treaty of Guadalupe Hidalgo (1848). Cap. Sante Fe. Pop. 1,819,046. —**New Mexican** adj. & n.

new moon n. **1.** The phase of the moon occurring when it passes between the earth and the sun and is invisible or visible only as a narrow crescent at sunset. **2.** The crescent moon.

New Neth•er•land (nĕth′ər-lənd) A Dutch colony (after 1624) in North America along the Hudson and lower Delaware rivers; renamed New York by the English in 1664.

New Norwegian n. A Norwegian national standard language based on the spoken, esp. rural dialects, devised in 1853 and recognized as a second national language in 1885.

New Or•leans (nōō ôr′lē-ənz, ôr′lənz, ôr-lēnz′, ô′lənz, nyōō, nô′lənz) A city of SE LA between the Mississippi R. and Lake Pontchartrain; founded 1718. Pop. 484,674. —**New Or•lea′ni•an** (ôr-lē′nē-ən, -lēn′yən) n.

New•port (nōō′pôrt′, -pōrt′, nyōō′-) **1.** A city of SE RI SSE of Providence; settled 1639. Pop. 26,475. **2.** A borough of SE Wales NE of Cardiff. Pop. 137,037.

Newport News An independent city of SE VA at the mouth of the James R. off Hampton Roads NNW of Norfolk; settled c. 1620. Pop. 180,150.

New Providence An island of the Bahamas in the West Indies.

New River A river of the SE US flowing c. 515 km (320 mi) from the Blue Ridge in NW NC to the Allegheny Plateau in S-central WV.

New Ro•chelle (rə-shĕl′, rō-) A city of SE NY on Long Island Sound E of Mount Vernon; settled in 1688. Pop. 72,182.

news (nōōz, nyōōz) pl.n. (used with a sing. verb) **1a.** Information about recent events or happenings, esp. as reported by the newspapers, periodicals, radio, or television. **b.** A presentation of such information, as in a newspaper. **2.** New information of any kind. **3.** Newsworthy material. [ME newes, new things, tidings, pl. of newe, new thing, new. See NEW.]

news agency n. An organization that provides news coverage to subscribers, as to newspapers or periodicals.

news•boy (nōōz′boi′, nyōōz′-) n. A boy who sells or delivers newspapers.

news•break (nōōz′brāk′, nyōōz′-) n. **1.** An urgent or immediate item of news. **2.** The act or an instance of interrupting a broadcast in order to report a newsworthy event or story.

news•cast (nōōz′kăst′, nyōōz′-) n. A radio or television news broadcast. [NEWS + (BROAD)CAST.] —**news′cast′er** n.

news conference n. See press conference.

news flash n. See newsbreak.

news•girl (nōōz′gûrl′, nyōōz′-) n. A girl who sells or delivers newspapers.

news•group (nōōz′grōōp′, nyōōz′-) n. An area on a computer network, esp. the Internet, devoted to the discussion of a specified topic.

New Siberian Islands An archipelago of NE Russia in the Arctic Ocean between the Laptev and East Siberian seas; discovered in the 1770s.

news•let•ter (nōōz′lĕt′ər, nyōōz′-) n. A printed report giving news or information of interest to a special group.

news•mag•a•zine (nōōz′măg′ə-zēn′, nyōōz′-) n. **1.** A magazine that contains reports and analyses of current events. **2.** A television program that presents a variety of topics, usu. on current events.

news•mak•er (nōōz′mā′kər, nyōōz′-) n. One that is newsworthy.

news•man (nōōz′măn′, -mən, nyōōz′-) n. A man who gathers, reports, or edits news.

news•mon•ger (nōōz′mŭng′gər, -mŏng′-, nyōōz′-) n. One who spreads news, esp. a gossip.

New Spain **1.** A former Spanish viceroyalty (1521–1821) in North America, including the SW US, Mexico, Central America N of Panama, and some West Indian islands. It also included the Philippines. **2.** The former Spanish possessions in the New World, including South America (except Brazil), Central America, Mexico, the West Indies, Florida, and much of the land W of the Mississippi R.

news•pa•per (nōōz′pā′pər, nyōōz′-) n. **1.** A publication, usu. issued daily or weekly, containing current news, editorials, feature articles, and usu. advertising. **2.** See newsprint.

news•pa•per•ing (nōōz′pā′pər-ĭng, nyōōz′-) n. Journalism.

news•pa•per•man (nōōz′pā′pər-măn′, nyōōz′-) n. **1.** A man who owns or publishes a newspaper. **2.** A man who is a newspaper reporter, writer, or editor.

news•pa•per•wom•an (nōōz′pā′pər-wōōm′ən, nyōōz′-) n. **1.** A woman who owns or publishes a newspaper. **2.** A woman who is a newspaper reporter, writer, or editor.

new•speak (nōō′spēk, nyōō′-) n. Deliberately ambiguous and contradictory language used to mislead and manipulate the public. [< Newspeak, a language invented by George Orwell in the novel 1984.]

news•per•son (nōōz′pûr′sən, nyōōz′-) n. A newsman or a newswoman.

news•print (nōōz′prĭnt′, nyōōz′-) n. Inexpensive paper made from wood pulp and used chiefly for printing newspapers.

news•reel (nōōz′rēl′, nyōōz′-) n. A short film dealing with recent or current events.

news release n. A prepared publicity or news announcement.

news•room (nōōz′rōōm′, -rŏŏm′, nyōōz′-) n. A room, as in a newspaper office, where news stories are written and edited.

news•stand (nōōz′stănd′, nyōōz′-) n. An open booth or stand at which newspapers and periodicals are sold.

New Stone Age n. See Neolithic.

ă	pat	oi	boy
ā	pay	ou	out
âr	care	ŏŏ	took
ä	father	ōō	boot
ĕ	pet	ŭ	cut
ē	be	ûr	urge
ĭ	pit	th	thin
ī	pie	th	this
îr	pier	hw	which
ŏ	pot	zh	vision
ō	toe	ə	about,
ô	paw		item

Stress marks:
′ (primary);
′ (secondary); as in
lexicon (lĕk′sĭ-kŏn′)

newt
red-spotted newts
Notophthalmus viridescens
in eft stage

Isaac Newton
detail of a portrait
attributed to Godfrey
Kneller (1646–1723)

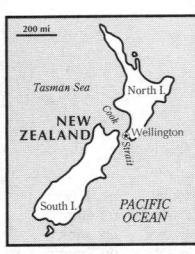

New Zealand

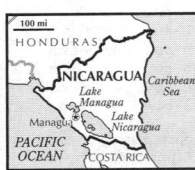

Nicaragua

New Style *n.* The current method of reckoning the months and days of the year according to the Gregorian calendar.

New Sweden A Swedish colony (1638–55) in North America along the Delaware R.

news•week•ly (nōōz′wĕk′lē, nyōōz′-) *n., pl.* **-lies** A weekly newsmagazine or newspaper that reports current events.

news•wom•an (nōōz′wōōm′ən, nyōōz′-) *n.* A woman who gathers, reports, or edits news.

news•wor•thy (nōōz′wûr′thē, nyōōz′-) *adj.* **-thi•er, -thi•est** Of sufficient interest or importance to the public to warrant reporting in the media. —**news′wor′thi•ness** *n.*

news•y (nōō′zē, nyōō′-) *adj.* **-i•er, -i•est** *Informal* Full of news; informative. —**news′i•ness** *n.*

newt (nōōt, nyōōt) *n.* Any of several small, often brightly colored semiaquatic salamanders of the genus *Triturus* and related genera. [ME *neute* < *a neute*, alteration of *an eute*, var. of *evete* < OE *efete.*]

New Testament *n. Bible* The second of the two main divisions of the Christian Bible, consisting of the Gospels, Acts, Pauline and other Epistles, and the Book of Revelation. See table at **Bible.**

new•ton (nōōt′n, nyōōt′n) *n.* In the meter-kilogram-second system, the unit of force required to accelerate a mass of one kilogram one meter per second per second, equal to 100,000 dynes. [After Sir Isaac NEWTON.]

Newton A city of E MA, a suburb of Boston. Pop. 83,829.

Newton, Sir Isaac 1642–1727. English mathematician and scientist who invented differential calculus and formulated the theory of universal gravitation, a theory about the nature of light, and three laws of motion. —**New•to′ni•an** *adj.*

New•ton's laws of motion (nōōt′nz, nyōōt′-) *pl.n.* The three laws proposed by Sir Isaac Newton to define the concept of a force and describe motion, used as the basis of classical mechanics. [After Isaac NEWTON.]

new town *n.* A planned urban community designed for self-sufficiency.

new wave *n.* **1.** often **New Wave** *a.* A movement in French cinema in the 1960s that abandoned traditional narrative techniques in favor of greater use of discontinuity and abstraction. **b.** Any of various new movements in cinema, esp. one led by a group of experimental filmmakers. **2.** An avant-garde or experimental movement, as in the arts. **3.** A style of rock music popularized in the early 1980s, marked by the use of synthesizers. [Transl. of Fr. *nouvelle vague : nouvelle,* new + *vague,* wave.]

New World The Western Hemisphere. The term was first used by the Italian historian Peter Martyr (1457–1526), whose *De Rebus Oceanicis et Novo Orbe* (1516) chronicled the discovery of America.

New Year *n.* The first day or days of the calendar year.

New Year's Day *n.* January 1, the first day of the year, celebrated as a holiday in many countries.

New Year's Eve *n.* The eve of New Year's Day.

New York 1. A state of the NE US; admitted as one of the original Thirteen Colonies in 1788. Cap. Albany. Pop. 18,976,457. **2.** or **New York City** A city of S NY on New York Bay at the mouth of the Hudson R. Founded by the Dutch as New Amsterdam, it includes the boroughs of Manhattan, the Bronx, Brooklyn, Queens, and Staten I. Pop. 8,008,278. —**New York′er** *n.*

New York aster *n.* A wild aster (*Aster novi-belgi*) of eastern North America with pointed leaves and bluish-violet flowers.

New York Bay An arm of the Atlantic Ocean at the mouth of the Hudson R. between W Long I. and NE NJ divided into Upper New York Bay and Lower New York Bay by the Narrows.

New York State Barge Canal A system of inland waterways, c. 845 km (525 mi), traversing NY and connecting the Great Lakes with the Hudson R. and Lake Champlain.

New Zealand An island country in the S Pacific SE of Australia; set off from Australia in 1841, received dominion status in 1907, and achieved full independence from Great Britain in 1931. Cap. Wellington. Pop. 3,493,000. —**New Zea′land•er** *n.*

NEX *abbr.* Navy exchange

next (nĕkst) *adj.* **1.** Nearest in space or position; adjacent: *the next room.* **2.** Immediately following, as in time, order, or sequence: *next week.* ❖ *adv.* **1.** In the time, order, or place nearest or immediately following: *our next oldest child.* **2.** On the first subsequent occasion: *when I write next.* ❖ *n.* The next person or thing: *The next will be better.* —**idiom: next to 1.** Following in order or degree. **3.** Almost; practically. [ME *nexte* < OE *nīehsta, nēhst,* superl. of *nēah,* near.]

next door *adv.* To or in the adjacent house, building, apartment, or room. —**next′-door′** (nĕkst′dôr′, -dōr′) *adj.*

next friend *n.* A person appointed by or admitted to a court to act in behalf of a minor or other party under legal disability.

next of kin *n., pl.* **next of kin 1.** The person or persons most closely related by blood to another person. **2.** *Law* **a.** The closest relative of a deceased person. **b.** (*used with a pl. verb*) The relative or relatives entitled to share in the personal property of one who dies intestate.

nex•us (nĕk′səs) *n., pl.* **nexus** or **-us•es 1.** A means of connection; a link or tie. **2.** A connected series or group. **3.** The core or center. [Lat., p. part. of *nectere,* to bind.]

Ney (nā), **Michel** 1769–1815. French commander of the rear

guard in Napoleon I's retreat from Moscow (1812).

Nez Perce (nĕz′ pûrs′, nĕs′) also **Nez Per•cé** (pər-sā′) *n., pl.* **Nez Perce** or **Nez Per•ces** (pûr′sĭz) also **Nez Percé** or **Nez Per•cés** (-sāz′) **1.** A member of a Native American people formerly inhabiting the lower Snake River and its tributaries, with present-day populations in western Idaho and northeast Washington. **2.** The Sahaptian language of the Nez Perce. [Fr. *Nez-Percé : nez,* nose + *percé,* pierced.]

NF *abbr.* **1.** National Formulary **2.** neurofibromatosis **3.** Newfoundland **4.** or **n/f** no funds

NFC *abbr.* National Football Conference

NFL *abbr.* National Football League

Nfld. *abbr.* Newfoundland

NG *abbr.* **1.** National Guard **2.** natural gas **3.** no good

Nga•mi (əng-gä′mē), **Lake** A marshy lake of N Botswana N of the Kalahari Desert.

n′ga•na (ə-gä′nə) *n.* Variant of **nagana.**

NGF *abbr.* nerve growth factor

NGO *abbr.* nongovernmental organization

ngul•trum (əng-gŭl′trəm) *n.* See table at **currency.** [Bhutanese.]

Ngu•ni (əng-gōō′nē) *n., pl.* **Nguni** or **-nis 1.** A member of a group of peoples of southern and southeast Africa, including the Swazi, Ndebele, Xhosa, and Zulu. **2.** Any of the Bantu languages of the Nguni.

NH or **N.H.** *abbr.* New Hampshire

NHI *abbr.* National Health Insurance

NHL *abbr.* National Hockey League

NHS *abbr.* National Health Service

Ni The symbol for the element **nickel** 1.

ni•a•cin (nī′ə-sĭn) *n.* A white crystalline acid, C_5H_4NCOOH, that is a component of the vitamin B complex, found in meat, wheat germ, dairy products, and yeast and used to treat and prevent pellagra. [NI(COTINIC) AC(ID) + -IN.]

Ni•ag•a•ra (nī-ăg′rə, -ər-ə) *n.* A torrent or flood. [After NIAGARA (FALLS)[1].]

Niagara Falls[1] Falls in the Niagara R. between the cities of Niagara Falls NY and Niagara Falls, Ontario, Canada; divided by Goat I. into the American Falls, 50.9 m (167 ft), and the Canadian, or Horseshoe, Falls, 48.2 m (158 ft).

Niagara Falls[2] **1.** A city of SE Ontario, Canada, on the Niagara R. opposite Niagara Falls NY. Pop. 76,917. **2.** A city of W NY on the Niagara R. NNW of Buffalo. Pop. 55,593.

Niagara River A river flowing c. 55 km (34 mi) from Lake Erie to Lake Ontario.

Nia•mey (nē-ä′mā, nyä-mā′) The cap. of Niger, in the SW part on the Niger R. Pop. 399,100.

nib (nĭb) *n.* **1a.** The sharpened point of a quill pen. **b.** A tapered point of a pen, for insertion into a penholder or a fountain pen. **2.** A sharp point or tip. **3.** A bird's beak or bill. [Alteration of NEB.]

nib•ble (nĭb′əl) *v.* **-bled, -bling, -bles** —*tr.* **1.** To bite at gently and repeatedly. **2.** To eat with small quick bites or in small morsels: *nibble a cracker.* **3.** To wear away or diminish bit by bit. —*intr.* To take small or hesitant bites. ❖ *n.* **1.** A very small quantity, esp. of food; a morsel. **2.** The act or an instance of nibbling. [ME *nebyllen;* akin to LGer. *nibbelen.*] —**nib′bler** *n.*

Ni•be•lung (nē′bə-lōōng′) *n. Mythology* **1.** Any of a race of dwarfs whose hoard of riches and magic ring were taken from them by Siegfried. **2.** A follower of Siegfried. **3.** One of the Burgundian kings in the *Nibelungenlied.* [Ger. < MHGer. *Nibelunc* < OHGer. *Nibulunc, Nibilung.*]

Ni•be•lung•en•lied (nē′bə-lōōng′ən-lēd′) *n.* A Middle High German epic poem written in the early 13th century and based on the legends of Siegfried and of the Burgundian kings.

nib•lick (nĭb′lĭk) *n.* A nine iron in golf. [?]

nibs (nĭbz) *n. Informal* A person in authority, esp. one who is self-important. Used with *his* or *her.* [Perh. alteration of NOB[2].]

Ni•cae•a (nī-sē′ə) An ancient city of Bithynia in NW Asia Minor; dating from the 4th cent. B.C. —**Ni•cae′an** *adj.*

Nic•a•ra•gua (nĭk′ə-rä′gwə) A country of Central America on the Caribbean Sea and the Pacific Ocean; declared its independence in 1821 and became a republic in 1838. Cap. Managua. Pop. 4,401,000. —**Ni′ca•ra′guan** *adj. & n.*

Nicaragua, Lake The largest lake of Central America, in SW Nicaragua; part of the Caribbean Sea until landmasses rose around it in prehistoric times.

nic•co•lite (nĭk′ə-līt′) *n.* A nickel ore, essentially nickel arsenide, NiAs, found in America and Europe. [NLat. *niccolum,* nickel (perh. < Swed. *nickel;* see NICKEL) + -ITE[1].]

nice (nīs) *adj.* **nic•er, nic•est 1.** Pleasing and agreeable in nature: *had a nice time.* **2.** Having a pleasant or attractive appearance. **3.** Exhibiting courtesy and politeness: *a nice gesture.* **4.** Of good character and reputation; respectable. **5.** Overdelicate or fastidious; fussy. **6.** Showing or requiring great precision or sensitive discernment; subtle: *a nice distinction.* **7.** Done with delicacy and skill. **8.** Used as an intensive with *and:* nice *and warm.* **9.** *Obsolete* **a.** Wanton; profligate. **b.** Affectedly modest; coy. [ME, foolish < OFr. < Lat. *nescius,* ignorant < *nescīre,* to be ignorant. See NESCIENCE.] —**nice′ly** *adv.* —**nice′ness** *n.*

Nice (nēs) A resort city of SE France on the Mediterranean Sea NE of Cannes; ceded to France in 1860. Pop. 342,903.

Ni•cene Creed (nī′sēn′, nī-sēn′) *n. Christianity* A formal statement of doctrine of the Christian faith adopted at the Council of Nicaea in A.D. 325 to defend orthodoxy from Arianism and expanded in later councils.

nice-nel•ly (nīs′nĕl′ē) *adj.* **1.** Priggish. **2.** Marked by the use of euphemism: *nice-nelly language.* [< the name *Nelly,* nickname for *Helen.*] **—nice′-nel′ly•ism** *n.*

ni•ce•ty (nī′sĭ-tē) *n., pl.* **-ties 1.** The quality of showing or requiring careful, precise treatment. **2.** Delicacy of character or feeling; fastidiousness; scrupulousness. **3.** A fine point, small detail, or subtle distinction: *the niceties of etiquette.* **4.** An elegant or refined feature; an amenity. [ME *nicete,* silliness, exactitude < OFr., silliness < *nice,* silly. See NICE.]

niche (nĭch, nēsh) *n.* **1.** A recess in a wall, as for holding a statue or urn. **2.** A cranny, hollow, or crevice. **3a.** A situation or activity specially suited to a person's interests, abilities, or nature. **b.** A special area of demand for a product or service. **4.** *Ecology* **a.** The function or position of an organism or population within an ecological community. **b.** The particular area within a habitat occupied by an organism. ❖ *tr.v.* **niched, nich•ing, nich•es** To place in a niche. [Fr. < OFr. < *nichier,* to nest (< VLat. **nīdicāre* < Lat. *nīdus,* nest; see **sed-** in App.), or < OItal. *nicchio,* seashell (perh. < Lat. *mītulus,* mussel).]

Ni•chi•ren (nē′chē-rĕn′) Orig. Zennichimaro. 1222–82. Japanese Buddhist monk and founder of a sect of Buddhism that bears his name.

Nich•o•las (nĭk′ə-ləs), Saint. 4th cent. A.D. Bishop of Myra in Asia Minor who is often associated with Santa Claus.

Nicholas I 1796–1855. Czar of Russia (1825–55) who suppressed the Decembrist movement and led Russia into the Crimean War (1853–56).

Nicholas II 1868–1918. The last czar of Russia (1894–1917), who was forced to abdicate and was executed by the Bolsheviks after the Revolution of 1917.

Nicholas of Cu•sa (kyo͞o′zə, -sə) 1401–64. German prelate, scientist, and philosopher who emphasized the incompleteness of the human knowledge of God and nature.

Nich•ols (nĭk′əlz), **Mike** b. 1931. German-born Amer. stage and film director whose credits include *The Odd Couple* (1965) and the film *The Graduate* (1967).

nick (nĭk) *n.* **1.** A shallow notch, cut, or indentation on an edge or surface. **2.** *Chiefly British Slang* A prison or police station. **3.** *Printing* A groove down the side of a piece of type used to ensure that it is correctly placed. ❖ *tr.v.* **nicked, nick•ing, nicks 1a.** To cut a nick or notch in. **b.** To cut into and wound slightly. **2.** To cut short; check. **3.** *Slang* To cheat, esp. by overcharging. **4.** *Chiefly British Slang* **a.** To steal. **b.** To arrest. ***—idiom:* in the nick of time** Just in time. [ME *nik,* poss. alteration of *niche.* See NICHE.]

nick•el (nĭk′əl) *n.* **1.** *Symbol* **Ni** A silvery hard ductile ferromagnetic metallic element used in alloys and in corrosion-resistant surfaces and batteries and for electroplating. Atomic number 28; atomic weight 58.69; melting point 1,453°C; boiling point 2,732° C; specific gravity 8.902; valence 0, 1, 2, 3. See table at **element. 2.** A US coin worth five cents, made of a nickel and copper alloy. **3.** *Slang* A nickel bag. ❖ *tr.v.* **-eled, -el•ing, -els** or **-elled, -el•ling, -els** To coat with nickel. [Swed., short for *kopparnickel,* niccolite, partial transl. of Ger. *Kupfernickel* : *Kupfer,* copper + *Nickel,* demon, rascal < the deceptive copper color of the ore (< the name *Nikolaus,* Nicholas).]

nick•el-and-dime (nĭk′əl-ən-dīm′) *Informal adj.* **1.** Involving or paying only a small amount of money. **2.** Minor; small-time. ❖ *v.* **nick•el-and-dimed, nick•el-and-dim•ing, nick•el-and-dimes** or **nick•eled-and-dimed, nick•el•ing-and-dim•ing, nick•els-and-dimes** *—intr.* To spend very little money. *—tr.* **1.** To drain or destroy bit by bit, esp. financially. **2.** To accumulate in small amounts.

nick•el•ic (nĭ-kĕl′ĭk) *adj.* Of or containing trivalent nickel, Ni^{3+}.

nick•el•if•er•ous (nĭk′ə-lĭf′ər-əs) *adj.* Bearing or containing nickel. Used of ores.

nick•el•o•de•on (nĭk′ə-lō′dē-ən) *n.* **1.** An early movie theater charging an admission price of five cents. **2.** A player piano. **3.** A jukebox. [NICKEL + *(Mel)odeon,* music hall; see MELODEON.]

nick•el•ous (nĭk′ə-ləs) *adj.* Of or containing bivalent nickel, Ni^{2+}.

nickel silver *n.* A silvery hard corrosion-resistant ductile malleable alloy of copper, zinc, and nickel, used in tableware.

nick•er (nĭk′ər) *intr.v.* **-ered, -er•ing, -ers** To neigh softly. [Perh. alteration of *nicher,* freq. of NEIGH.] **—nick′er** *n.*

Nick•laus (nĭk′ləs), **Jack William** b. 1940. Amer. golfer who won 17 major international tournaments.

nick•nack (nĭk′năk′) *n.* Variant of **knickknack.**

nick•name (nĭk′nām′) *n.* **1.** A descriptive name added to or replacing the actual name of a person, place, or thing. **2.** A familiar or shortened form of a proper name. ❖ *tr.v.* **-named, -nam•ing, -names 1.** To give a nickname to. **2.** *Archaic* To call by an incorrect name; misname. [ME *neke name* < *a neke name,* alteration of *an eke name* : *eke,* addition (< OE *ēaca*; see **aug-** in App.) + *name,* name; see NAME.] **—nick′nam′er** *n.*

Nic•o•bar Islands (nĭk′ə-bär′) An island group in the Bay of Bengal NW of Sumatra, part of the Andaman and Nicobar Is. belonging to India.

ni•çoise olive (nē-swäz′) *n.* A small edible variety of olive with a rich flavor. [Fr. *niçoise,* fem. of *niçois,* of Nice.]

Nic•o•let (nĭk′ə-lā′, nē-kô-lĕ′), **Jean** 1598–1642. French explorer of the Great Lakes region (1634).

Nic•ol•son (nĭk′əl-sən), Sir **Harold George** 1886–1968. British diplomat noted for his biographies and literary criticism.

Nic•o•me•di•a (nĭk′ə-mē′dē-ə) An ancient city of NW Asia Minor near the Bosporus in present-day Turkey.

Nic•o•si•a (nĭk′ə-sē′ə) The cap. of Cyprus, in the N-central part; probably founded before the 7th cent. B.C. Pop. 186,400.

ni•co•ti•an•a (nĭ-kō′shē-ăn′ə, -ä′nə, -ā′nə) *n.* Any of various flowering annual or perennial herbs of the genus *Nicotiana,* native to the Americas and including the tobacco plant. [NLat. *(herba) nicotiāna,* (herb of) Nicot, nicotiana, after Jean *Nicot* (1530?–1600), French diplomat.]

nicotin– *pref.* **1.** Nicotine: *nicotinic.* **2.** Nicotinic acid: *nicotinamide.* [< NICOTINE.]

nic•o•tin•a•mide adenine dinucleotide (nĭk′ə-tĭn′ə-mīd′, -tē′nə-) *n.* NAD.

nic•o•tine (nĭk′ə-tēn′) *n.* A poisonous alkaloid, $C_{10}H_{14}N_2$, derived from the tobacco plant and the substance to which cigarette smokers become addicted. [Fr. < NLat. *nicotiāna.* See NICOTIANA.]

nic•o•tin•ic (nĭk′ə-tĭn′ĭk, -tē′nĭk) *adj.* **1.** Of or relating to nicotine. **2.** Of or relating to niacin.

nicotinic acid *n.* See **niacin.** [So called because it is often obtained by oxidizing nicotine.]

nic•o•tin•ism (nĭk′ə-tē-nĭz′əm) *n.* Nicotine poisoning, caused by excessive use of tobacco.

nic•ti•tate (nĭk′tĭ-tāt′) also **nic•tate** (nĭk′tāt′) *intr.v.* **-tat•ed, -tat•ing, -tates** To wink. [Med.Lat. *nictitāre, nictitāt-,* freq. of Lat. *nictāre.*] **—nic′ti•ta′tion** *n.*

nic•ti•tat•ing membrane (nĭk′tĭ-tā′tĭng) also **nic•tat•ing membrane** (nĭk′tā′tĭng) *n.* A transparent inner eyelid in birds, reptiles, and some mammals that protects and moistens the eye.

ni•date (nī′dāt) *tr.v.* **-dat•ed, -dat•ing, -dates** To become implanted in the uterus. Used of a fertilized cell. [NID(US) + –ATE[1].] **—ni•da′tion** *n.*

nid•der•ing (nĭd′ər-ĭng) *n. Archaic* A cowardly person; a wretch. [Misreading of ME *nithing* < OE *nīthing* < ON *nīdhingr* < *nīdh,* scorn.]

nide (nīd) *n.* A nest or brood of pheasants. [Lat. *nīdus,* nest. See **sed-** in App.]

ni•dic•o•lous (nī-dĭk′ə-ləs) *adj.* **1.** Remaining in the nest after hatching until grown or nearly grown. Used of birds. **2.** Sharing the nest of of another animal species. Used of insects. [Lat. *nīdus,* nest; see **sed-** in App. + –COLOUS.]

ni•dif•u•gous (nī-dĭf′yə-gəs) *adj.* Leaving the nest a short time after hatching. [Lat. *nīdus,* nest; see **sed-** in App. + Lat. *-fugus,* fleeing (< *fugere,* to flee; see FUGITIVE).]

nid•i•fy (nĭd′ə-fī′) *intr.v.* **-fied, -fy•ing, -fies** To build a nest. [Lat. *nīdificāre* : *nīdus,* nest; see **sed-** in App. + *-ficāre,* -fy.] **—nid′i•fi•ca′tion** (-fĭ-kā′shən) *n.*

ni•dus (nī′dəs) *n., pl.* **-dus•es** or **-di** (-dī) **1.** A nest, esp. one for the eggs of insects, spiders, or small animals. **2.** A cavity where spores develop. **3.** *Pathology* A central point or focus of bacterial growth in an organism. **4.** A point or place at which something originates, accumulates, or develops. [Lat. *nīdus.* See **sed-** in App.]

Nie•buhr (nē′bo͝or′, -bər), **Barthold George** 1776–1831. German historian who developed the scientific study of history.

Niebuhr, Reinhold 1892–1971. Amer. theologian who argued that Christianity is obligated to confront ethical, social, and moral problems.

niece (nēs) *n.* **1.** The daughter of one's brother or sister or of the brother or sister of one's spouse. **2.** The illegitimate daughter of an ecclesiastic who has taken a vow of celibacy. [ME *nece* < OFr. < VLat. **neptia* < Lat. *neptis.* See **nepōt-** in App.]

ni•el•lo (nē-ĕl′ō) *n., pl.* **-el•li** (-ĕl′ē) or **-el•los 1.** Any of several black metallic alloys of sulfur with copper, silver, or lead, used to fill an incised design on the surface of another metal. **2.** A surface or object decorated with niello. **3.** The art or process of ornamenting metal surfaces with niello. ❖ *tr.v.* **-loed, -lo•ing, -los** To decorate or inlay with niello. [Ital. < Med.Lat. *nigellum* < neut. of Lat. *nigellus,* dim. of *niger,* black. See **nekʷ-t-** in App.] **—ni•el′list** *n.*

Nie•men (nē′mən, nyĕ′-) See **Neman.**

Nie•mey•er (nē′mī′ər), **Oscar** b. 1907. Brazilian architect who directed the creation of Brazil's capital, Brasília (1950–60).

Nie•tzsche (nē′chə, -chē), **Friedrich Wilhelm** 1844–1900. German philosopher whose works include *Thus Spake Zarathustra* (1883–92). **—Nie′tzsche•an** *adj. & n.*

Nif•l•heim (nĭv′əl-hām′) *n. Mythology* The realm of the dead in Norse myth. [ON *niflheimr* : *nifl-,* mist, dark; see **nebh-** in App. + *heimr,* home; see **tkei-** in App.]

nif•ty (nĭf′tē) *Slang adj.* **-ti•er, -ti•est** First-rate; great: *a nifty idea.* ❖ *n., pl.* **-ties** A nifty person or thing, esp. a clever joke. [?] **—nif′ti•ly** *adv.* **—nif′ti•ness** *n.*

Nig. *abbr.* Nigeria

Ni•ger (nī′jər, nē-zhâr′) A country of W-central Africa; achieved independence from France in 1960. Cap. Niamey. Pop. 8,846,000.

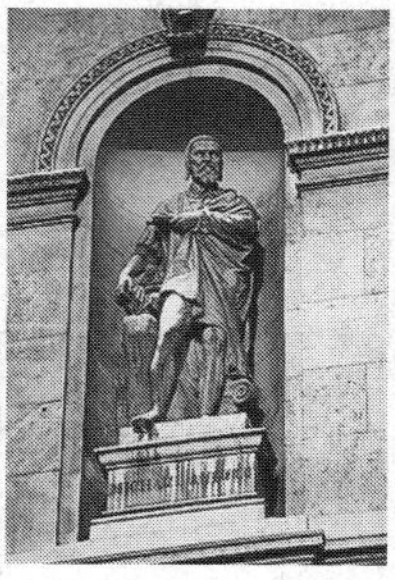

niche
statue of Michelangelo, Royal Academy of Arts, London

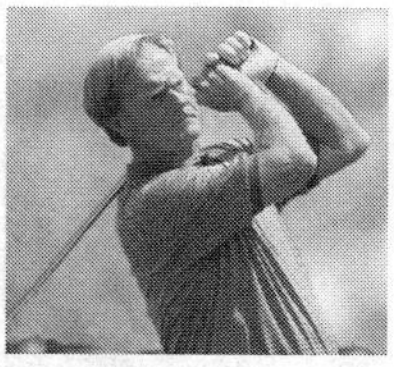

Jack Nicklaus

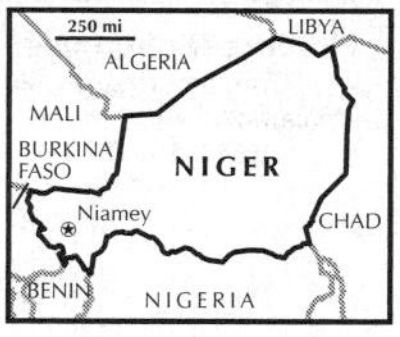

Niger

ă	pat	oi	boy
ā	pay	ou	out
âr	care	o͝o	took
ä	father	o͞o	boot
ĕ	pet	ŭ	cut
ē	be	ûr	urge
ĭ	pit	th	thin
ī	pie	*th*	this
îr	pier	hw	which
ŏ	pot	zh	vision
ō	toe	ə	about, item
ô	paw		

Stress marks:
′ (primary);
′ (secondary), as in
lexicon (lĕk′sĭ-kŏn′)

Ni·ger-Con·go (nī'jər-kŏng'gō) *n.* A large, widely dispersed language family of sub-Saharan Africa including the Mande, West Atlantic, and Central Niger-Congo branches.

Ni·ge·ri·a (nī-jîr'ē-ə) A country of W Africa on the Gulf of Guinea; gained independence from Great Britain in 1960. Cap. Abuja. Pop. 108,467,000. —**Ni·ge'ri·an** *adj. & n.*

Ni·ger-Kor·do·fan·i·an (nī'jər-kôr'də-făn'ē-ən, -făn'yən) *n.* The largest language family of sub-Saharan Africa, consisting of the Niger-Congo and Kordofanian branches.

Niger River A river of W Africa rising in Guinea and flowing c. 4,183 km (2,600 mi) to the Gulf of Guinea.

nig·gard (nĭg'ərd) *n.* A stingy, grasping person; a miser. ❖ *adj.* Stingy; miserly. [ME *nigard,* perh. < *nig,* stingy person, of Scand. orig.]

nig·gard·ly (nĭg'ərd-lē) *adj.* **1.** Grudging and petty in giving or spending. **2.** Meanly small; scanty or meager. —**nig'gard·li·ness** *n.* —**nig'gard·ly** *adv.*

nig·ger (nĭg'ər) *n. Offensive Slang* **1a.** Used as a disparaging term for a Black person. **b.** Used as a disparaging term for a member of any dark-skinned people. **2.** Used as a disparaging term for a member of any socially, economically, or politically deprived group of people. [Alteration of dialectal *neger,* black person < Fr. *nègre* < Sp. *negro.* See NEGRO.]

nig·gle (nĭg'əl) *intr.v.* **-gled, -gling, -gles** **1.** To be preoccupied with trifles or petty details. **2.** To find fault constantly and trivially; carp. [Perh. of Scand. orig.] —**nig'gler** *n.*

nig·gling (nĭg'lĭng) *adj.* **1.** Petty, esp. in a nagging or annoying way; trifling. **2.** Overconcerned with details; exacting and fussy. —**nig'gling** *n.* —**nig'gling·ly** *adv.*

nigh (nī) *adv.* **nigh·er, nigh·est** **1.** Near in time, place, or relationship. **2.** Nearly; almost. ❖ *adj.* **nigher, nighest** **1.** Being near in time, place, or relationship; close. See Syns at **close.** **2a.** Being on the left side of an animal or vehicle. **b.** Being the animal or vehicle on the left. ❖ *prep.* Not far from; near. ❖ *tr. & intr.v.* **nighed, nigh·ing, nighs** To come near to or draw near. [ME *neigh* < OE *nēah, nēh.*]

night (nīt) *n.* **1a.** The period between sunset and sunrise, esp. the hours of darkness. **b.** This period considered as a unit of time: *for two nights running.* **c.** This period considered in terms of its conditions: *a rainy night.* **2.** The period between dusk and midnight of a given day. **3a.** The period between evening and bedtime. **b.** This period considered in terms of its activities: *a night at the opera.* **c.** This period set aside for a specific purpose: *Parents' Night at school.* **4a.** The period between bedtime and morning. **b.** One's sleep during this period: *a restless night.* **5.** Nightfall. **6.** Darkness: *vanished into the night.* **7a.** A time or condition of gloom, obscurity, ignorance, or despair. **b.** A time or condition marked by absence of moral or ethical values. ❖ *adj.* **1.** Of or relating to the night. **2.** Intended for use at night. **3.** Working during the night. **4.** Active chiefly at night. **5.** Occurring after dark. [ME < OE *niht.* See nek*ʷ*-t- in App.]

night-blind (nīt'blīnd') *adj.* Affected with night blindness.

night blindness *n.* A condition of the eyes in which vision is normal in daylight or other strong light but is abnormally weak or completely lost at night or in dim light.

night-bloom·ing cereus (nīt'bloo'mĭng) *n.* Any of various night-blooming cacti of the genera *Hylocereus, Nyctocereus, Peniocereus,* and *Selenicereus,* having large fragrant flowers.

night·cap (nīt'kăp') *n.* **1.** A usu. alcoholic drink taken just before bedtime. **2.** *Sports & Games* The last event in a day's competition, esp. the final game in a baseball double-header. **3.** A cloth cap worn esp. in bed.

night·clothes (nīt'klōz', -klōthz') *pl.n.* Clothes, such as pajamas or a nightgown, worn in bed.

night·club (nīt'klŭb') *n.* An establishment that stays open late at night and provides food, drink, entertainment, and music for dancing. —**night'club'ber** *n.* —**night'club'by** *adj.*

night court *n.* A criminal court holding sessions at night for routine disposition of charges and granting of bail.

night crawler *n.* Any of various large earthworms that crawl out from the ground at night and are often used as fish bait.

night·dress (nīt'drĕs') *n.* **1.** See **nightgown. 2.** See **nightclothes.**

night·fall (nīt'fôl') *n.* The approach of darkness; dusk.

night·glow (nīt'glō') *n.* Airglow occurring at night.

night·gown (nīt'goun') *n.* A loose garment worn in bed by women and girls.

night·hawk (nīt'hôk') *n.* **1a.** Any of several chiefly nocturnal birds of the genus *Chordeiles,* esp. *C. minor,* having mottled grayish-brown plumage. **b.** The European nightjar. **2.** *Informal* A night owl.

night heron *n.* Any of several nocturnal or crepuscular herons of the genus *Nycticorax,* esp. the black-crowned heron (*N. nycticorax*).

night·ie or **night·y** (nī'tē) *n., pl.* **-ies** *Informal* A nightgown.

night·in·gale (nīt'n-gāl', nī'tĭng-) *n.* **1.** A European songbird (*Luscinia megarhynchos*) with reddish-brown plumage, noted for the melodious song of the male at night during the breeding season. **2.** Any of various other nocturnal songbirds of the genus *Luscinia.* [ME < OE *nihtegale* : *niht,* night; see NIGHT + *galan,* to sing.]

Nightingale, Florence 1820–1910. British nurse who is considered the founder of modern nursing.

night·jar (nīt'jär') *n.* A goatsucker, esp. *Caprimulgus europaeus* of Europe, having gray and brown mottled plumage. [NIGHT + JAR[2] (< its harsh call).]

night latch *n.* A spring lock that can be opened from the inside by turning a knob but from the outside only with a key.

night letter *n.* A telegram sent at night at a reduced rate for delivery the next morning.

night·life (nīt'līf') *n.* Social activities or entertainment available or pursued in the evening.

night-light (nīt'līt') *n.* A small dim light left on all night.

night·long (nīt'lông', -lŏng') *adj.* Lasting through the night. ❖ *adv.* Through the night; all night.

night·ly (nīt'lē) *adj.* **1.** Of or occurring during the night; nocturnal. **2.** Happening or done every night: *the physician's nightly rounds.* —**night'ly** *adv.*

night·mare (nīt'mâr') *n.* **1.** A dream arousing feelings of intense fear, horror, and distress. **2.** An event or experience that is intensely distressing. **3.** A demon or spirit once thought to plague people who are asleep. [ME, a female demon that afflicts sleeping people : *night,* night; see NIGHT + *mare,* goblin (< OE; see mer- in App.).] —**night'mar'ish** *adj.* —**night'mar'ish·ly** *adv.* —**night'mar'ish·ness** *n.*

night owl *n. Informal* A person who habitually stays up and is active late into the night.

night·rid·er (nīt'rī'dər) *n.* One of a secret band of mounted, usu. masked white men who engaged in nocturnal terrorism in the southern United States esp. during Reconstruction.

nights (nīts) *adv.* During the nighttime on every day or most days: *works nights at the restaurant.*

night school *n.* A school that holds classes in the evening.

night·shade (nīt'shād') *n.* **1.** Any of several plants of the genus *Solanum,* most of which have a poisonous juice. **2.** Any of various similar or related plants, such as belladonna.

night shift or **night·shift** (nīt'shĭft') *n.* **1.** A group of employees working during the night in a factory or business. **2.** The period of time for such work.

night·shirt (nīt'shûrt') *n.* A long, loose shirt worn in bed.

night soil *n.* Human excrement collected for use as fertilizer.

night·spot (nīt'spŏt') *n.* See **nightclub.**

night·stand (nīt'stănd') *n.* See **night table.**

night·stick (nīt'stĭk') *n.* A club carried by a police officer.

night table *n.* A small table or stand placed at a bedside.

night terror *n.* A state of intense fear and agitation sometimes experienced, esp. by children, on awakening from a stage of sleep characterized by extremely vivid hallucinations.

night·time (nīt'tīm') *n.* The time between sunset and sunrise. ❖ *adj.* Occurring in or appropriate for use during the night.

night vision *n.* Vision in dim light.

Night Vision A trademark used for a technology that enables vision at night, as by amplification of low light to create visible images or by detection of infrared wavelengths.

night·walk·er (nīt'wô'kər) *n.* **1.** One, esp. a robber or prostitute, who walks the streets at night. **2.** See **night crawler.**

night watch *n.* **1.** A watch or guard kept during the night. **2.** The person or persons on such a watch.

night watchman *n.* A man who serves as a guard at night.

night·wear (nīt'wâr') *n.* See **nightclothes.**

night·y (nī'tē) *n.* Variant of **nightie.**

ni·gres·cence (nī-grĕs'əns) *n.* **1.** The process of becoming black or dark. **2.** Blackness or darkness, as of complexion. [< *nigrescent,* blackish < Lat. *nigrēscēns, nigrēscent-,* pr. part. of *nigrēscere,* to become black < *niger, nigr-,* black. See nek*ʷ*-t- in App.] —**ni·gres'cent** *adj.*

ni·gro·sine (nī'grə-sēn', -sĭn) *n.* Any of a class of dyes, varying from blue to black, used in the manufacture of inks and for dyeing wood. [Lat. *niger, nigr-,* black; see nek*ʷ*-t- in App. + -OS(E)[2] + -INE[2].]

NIH *abbr.* National Institutes of Health

ni·hil·ism (nī'ə-lĭz'əm, nē'-) *n.* **1.** *Philosophy* **a.** An extreme form of skepticism that denies all existence. **b.** A doctrine holding that all values are baseless and that nothing can be known or communicated. **2.** Rejection of all distinctions in moral or religious value and a willingness to repudiate all previous theories of morality or religious belief. **3.** The belief that destruction of existing political or social institutions is necessary for future improvement. **4.** also **Nihilism** A movement of mid 19th-century Russia that believed in radical societal and governmental change through terrorism and assassination. **5.** *Psychology* A delusion that the world or one's mind, body, or self does not exist. [Lat. *nihil,* nothing; see ne in App. + -ISM.] —**ni'hil·ist** *n.* —**ni'hil·is'tic** *adj.* —**ni'hil·is'ti·cal·ly** *adv.*

ni·hil·i·ty (nī-hĭl'ĭ-tē, nē-) *n.* Nonexistence; nothingness. [Fr. *nihilité* < OFr. < Med.Lat. *nihilitās* < Lat. *nihil,* nothing. See NIHILISM.]

ni·hil ob·stat (nī'hĭl ŏb'stăt', -stăt', nē'-) *n.* **1.** *Roman Catholic Church* An attestation by a church censor that a book contains nothing damaging to faith or morals. **2.** Official approval, as of an artistic work. [Lat., nothing hinders : *nihil,* nothing + *obstat,* third pers. sing. pr. t. of *obstāre,* to hinder.]

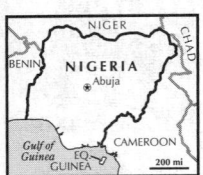

Nigeria

Florence Nightingale
detail from a portrait by Sir
William Blake Richmond
(1842–1921)

Ni·i·ga·ta (nē′ē-gä′tə, -tä) A city of NW Honshu, Japan, on the Sea of Japan NNW of Tokyo. Pop. 490,237.

Ni·i·ha·u (nē′ē-hou′, nē′hou′) An island of NW HI W of Kauai I.

Ni·jin·sky (nĭ-zhĭn′skē, -jĭn′-), Vaslav or Waslaw 1890–1950. Russian-born dancer and choreographer noted for his leading roles with Diaghilev's Ballets Russes in Paris.

Nij·me·gen (nī′mā′gən, -кнэн) A city of E Netherlands on the Waal R. near the German border. Pop. 147,102.

-nik *suff.* One associated with or characterized by: *beatnik; peacenik.* [Yiddish and Russ. [Yiddish < Russ.).]

Ni·ke (nī′kē) *n. Greek Mythology* The goddess of victory.

Nik·kei (nē′kā) A trademark used for an index of the relative price of selected stocks listed on the Tokyo Stock Exchange.

Ni·ko·la·yev (nĭk′ə-lä′yəf, nyĭ′kə-) See **Mykolayiv**.

nil (nĭl) *n.* Nothing; zero. [Lat. *nīl*, contraction of *nihil*. See **ne** in App.] —**nil** *adj.*

Nile (nīl) A river of NE Africa flowing c. 6,677 km (4,150 mi) from its sources in Burundi to a delta on the Mediterranean Sea in NE Egypt. The main headstreams, the **Blue Nile** and the **White Nile**, join at Khartoum to form the Nile proper.

Nile blue *n.* A light greenish blue.

Nile crocodile *n.* A large crocodile (*Crocodylus niloticus*) common in most parts of Africa.

Nile green *n.* A moderate yellow green to vivid light green.

nil·gai (nĭl′gī) *n., pl.* **-gais** A large long-legged antelope (*Boselaphus tragocamelus*) of India, the male of which has short sturdy horns and a tuft of long hair under the chin. [Hindi *nīlgāī*, fem. of *nīlgāw* : *nīla-*, dark blue (< Skt. *nīla-*) + *gāw*, ox, cow (< Skt. *gauh*; see **g"ou-** in App.).]

nill (nĭl) *v.* **nilled, nill·ing, nills** *Obsolete* —*tr.* Not to will; not to wish. —*intr.* To be unwilling; will not. [ME *nilen* < OE *nyllan* : *ne*, not; see **ne** in App. + *willan*, to desire.]

Ni·lo-Sa·har·an (nī′lō-sə-hăr′ən, -hä′rən) *n.* A language family of sub-Saharan Africa spoken from Nigeria to Kenya and including Kanuri, Nubian, and the Nilotic languages.

Ni·lot·ic (nī-lŏt′ĭk) *adj.* **1.** Of the Nile or the Nile Valley. **2.** Of or relating to the peoples who speak Nilotic languages. ❖ *n.* A large group of Nilo-Saharan languages, spoken in southern Sudan, Uganda, Kenya, and northern Tanzania. [Lat. *Nīlōticus* < *Nīlōtis* < Gk. *Neilōtis* < *Neilos*, Nile.]

nil·po·tent (nĭl-pōt′nt, nĭl′pōt′nt) *n.* An algebraic quantity that when raised to a certain power equals zero. [NIL + Lat. *potēns*, *potent-*, having power; see POTENT.] —**nil·po′ten·cy** *n.*

nim[1] (nĭm) *tr. & intr.v.* **nimmed, nim·ming, nims** *Archaic* To steal; pilfer. [ME *nimen*, to take < OE *niman*. See **nem-** in App.]

nim[2] (nĭm) *n.* A game in which players in turn remove small objects from a collection, such as matchsticks arranged in rows, and attempt to take, or avoid taking, the last one. [Perh. < Ger. *nimm*, second pers. sing. imper. of *nehmen*, to take < MHGer. *nemen* < OHGer. *neman*. See **nem-** in App.]

nim·ble (nĭm′bəl) *adj.* **-bler, -blest 1.** Quick, light, or agile in movement or action; deft: *nimble fingers.* **2.** Quick, clever, and acute in devising or understanding. See Syns at **dexterous**. [ME *nemel* < OE *nǣmel*, quick to seize, and *numol*, quick at learning; see **nem-** in App.] —**nim′ble·ness** *n.* —**nim′bly** *adv.*

nim·bo·strat·us (nĭm′bō-străt′əs, -strä′təs) *n., pl.* **-strat·i** (-străt′ī, -strä′tī) A low, gray, often dark cloud that precipitates rain, snow, or sleet. [NIMB(US) + STRATUS.]

nim·bus (nĭm′bəs) *n., pl.* **-bi** (-bī′) or **-bus·es 1.** A cloudy radiance said to surround a classical deity when on earth. **2.** A radiant light that appears usu. in the form of a circle or halo about or over the head in the representation of a god, saint, or sacred person. **3.** A splendid atmosphere or aura, as of glamour, that surrounds a person or thing. **4.** A rain cloud, esp. a nimbostratus. [Lat., cloud. See **nebh-** in App.]

NIM·BY (nĭm′bē) *n., pl.* **-BYs** *Slang* One who objects to having institutions or projects, such as prisons or incinerators, in close proximity. [*n(ot) i(n) m(y) b(ack) y(ard)*.] —**nim′by·ness** *n.*

Nîmes (nēm) A city of S France NE of Montpellier; a leading city of Roman Gaul. Pop. 128,549.

ni·mi·e·ty (nĭ-mī′ĭ-tē) *n.* Superfluity; excess. [LLat. *nimietās* < Lat. *nimius*, excessive < *nimis*, excessively. See **ne** in App.]

Nim·itz (nĭm′ĭts), Chester William 1885–1966. Amer. admiral of the Pacific fleet during World War II.

nim·rod also **Nim·rod** (nĭm′rŏd′) *n.* **1.** A hunter. **2.** *Informal* A silly, foolish, or stupid person. [After NIMROD. Sense 2, prob. < the phrase "Poor little Nimrod," used by the cartoon character Bugs Bunny to mock the hapless hunter Elmer Fudd.]

Nimrod In the Bible, a hunter and king of Shinar who was a grandson of Ham and a great-grandson of Noah.

Nin (nēn, nĭn), Anaïs 1903–77. French-born Amer. writer best known for her diaries (published 1966–80).

nin·com·poop (nĭn′kəm-pōōp′, nĭng′-) *n.* A silly, foolish, or stupid person. [?] —**nin′com·poop′er·y** *n.*

nine (nīn) *n.* **1.** The cardinal number equal to 8 + 1. **2.** The ninth in a set or sequence. **3.** Something having nine parts, units, or members. **4.** *Games* A playing card marked with nine pips. **5.** A set of nine persons or things, esp.: **a.** *Baseball* The nine players on a team. **b.** **Nine** *Greek Mythology* The nine Muses. **6.** A size, as in clothing or shoes, designated as nine. **7.** *Sports* The first or second

9 holes of an 18-hole golf course. —*idiom:* **to the nines** *Informal* To the highest degree. [ME < OE *nigon*. See **newn** in App.] —**nine** *adj. & pron.*

nine-band·ed armadillo (nīn′băn′dĭd) *n.* The most common species of armadillo, *Dasypus novemcinctus*, usu. having nine jointed bands of bony plates.

nine days′ wonder *n.* A thing or event that creates a brief sensation.

9-11 or **9/11** (nīn′ĭ-lĕv′ən) *n.* September 11, 2001, the date on which two hijacked airliners were flown into the World Trade Center in New York City and another into the Pentagon. A fourth hijacked airliner crashed in open land in Pennsylvania.

nine·pin (nīn′pĭn′) *n.* **1. ninepins** (*used with a sing. or pl. verb*) A bowling game in which nine wooden pins are the target. **2.** A wooden pin used in the game of ninepins.

nine·teen (nīn-tēn′) *n.* **1.** The cardinal number equal to 18 + 1. **2.** The 19th in a set or sequence. [ME *nintene* < OE *nigontēne*. See **newn** in App.] —**nine′teen′** *adj. & pron.*

nine·teenth (nīn-tēnth′) *n.* **1.** The ordinal number matching the number 19 in a series. **2.** One of 19 equal parts. —**nine′teenth′** *adv. & adj.*

nine·ti·eth (nīn′tē-ĭth) *n.* **1.** The ordinal number matching the number 90 in a series. **2.** One of 90 equal parts. —**nine′ti·eth** *adv. & adj.*

nine-to-fiv·er (nīn′tə-fī′vər) *n.* One who works regular daytime hours, as in an office.

nine·ty (nīn′tē) *n., pl.* **-ties 1.** The cardinal number equal to 9 × 10. **2. nineties a.** A decade or the numbers from 90 to 99: *The temperature stayed in the nineties.* **b.** often **Nineties** The decade from 90 to 99 in a century. [ME *ninti* < OE *nigontig*. See **newn** in App.] —**nine′ty** *adj. & pron.*

Nin·e·veh (nĭn′ə-və) An ancient city of Assyria on the Tigris R. opposite the site of present-day Mosul, Iraq; captured and destroyed by Babylonia and its allies in 612 B.C.

Ning·bo (nĭng′bō′) also **Ning·po** (-pō′) A city of E China ESE of Hangzhou on Hangzhou Bay. Pop. 3,350,851.

Ning·xia Hui·zu (nĭng′shyä′ hwē′dzōō′) also **Ning·sia Hui** (hwē′) An autonomous region of N China. Cap. Yinchuan. Pop. 4,655,451.

nin·ja (nĭn′jə) *n., pl.* **ninja** or **-jas** A member of a class of 14th-century Japanese mercenary agents who were trained in the martial arts and hired for covert operations such as assassination and sabotage. [J. : *nin*, to endure + *ja*, person (< M Chin. *tšia?*).]

nin·ny (nĭn′ē) *n., pl.* **-nies** A fool; a simpleton. [Perh. < alteration of *an inno(cent)*.]

ni·non (nē′nŏn′) *n.* A sheer fabric of silk, rayon, or nylon made in a variety of tight smooth weaves or open lacy patterns. [Prob. < Fr. *Ninon*, nickname for *Anne*.]

ninth (nīnth) *n.* **1.** The ordinal number matching the number nine in a series. **2.** One of nine equal parts. **3.** *Music* **a.** A harmonic or melodic interval of an octave and a second. **b.** The tone at the upper limit of such an interval. **c.** A chord consisting of a root with its third, seventh, and ninth. [ME *ninthe* < OE *nigonthe* < *nigon*, nine. See **newn** in App.] —**ninth** *adv. & adj.*

Ni·o·be (nī′ə-bē) *n. Greek Mythology* The daughter of Tantalus who turned to stone while bewailing the loss of her children.

ni·o·bite (nī′ə-bīt′) *n.* Columbite. [NIOB(IUM) + -ITE[1].]

ni·o·bi·um (nī-ō′bē-əm) *n. Symbol* **Nb** A soft ductile metallic element that occurs chiefly in columbite-tantalite and is used in steel alloys and superconductors. Atomic number 41; atomic weight 92.906; melting point 2,468°C; boiling point 4,927°C; specific gravity 8.57; valence 2, 3, 5. See table at **element**. [After NIOBE (because extracted from tantalite).]

Ni·o·brar·a (nī′ə-brâr′ə) A river rising in E WY and flowing c. 692 km (430 mi) to the Missouri R. in NE NE.

nip[1] (nĭp) *v.* **nipped, nip·ping, nips** —*tr.* **1.** To seize and pinch or bite. **2.** To remove or sever by pinching or snipping: *nipped off the plant leaf.* **3.** To bite or sting with the cold; chill. **4.** To check or cut off the growth or development of. **5.** *Slang* **a.** To snatch up hastily. **b.** To take (the property of another) unlawfully; steal. —*intr.* *Chiefly British* To move quickly; dart. ❖ *n.* **1.** The act or an instance of seizing, pinching, or biting. **2a.** A pinch or snip that cuts off or removes a small part. **b.** The small bit or portion so removed. **3a.** A sharp stinging quality, as of frosty air. **b.** Severely stinging cold or frost. **4.** A cutting remark. **5.** A sharp biting flavor; a tang. [ME *nippen*, perh. < MDu. *nipen*.]

nip[2] (nĭp) *n.* A small amount of liquor. ❖ *v.* **nipped, nip·ping, nips** —*tr.* To sip (alcoholic liquor) in small amounts. —*intr.* To take a sip or sips of alcoholic liquor. [Prob. short for *nipperkin*, of Du. or LGer. orig.]

ni·pa (nē′pə) *n.* **1.** A large palm (*Nipa frutescens*) of the Philippines and Australia having long leaves often used for thatching. **2.** An alcoholic beverage made from the sap of this plant. [NLat. < Malay *nipah*.]

nip and tuck *adv. & adj.* So close that the advantage or lead shifts from one to another and is virtually indeterminable.

Nip·i·gon (nĭp′ĭ-gŏn′), **Lake** A lake of SW-central Ontario, Canada, N of Lake Superior.

Nip·is·sing (nĭp′ĭ-sĭng), **Lake** A lake of SE Ontario, Canada, between the Ottawa R. and Georgian Bay.

nip·per (nĭp′ər) *n.* **1.** A tool, such as pliers, used for squeezing or

nimbostratus

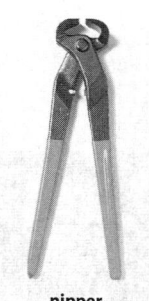

nipper

ă pat	oi boy
ā pay	ou out
âr care	ŏŏ took
ä father	ōō boot
ĕ pet	ŭ cut
ē be	ûr urge
ĭ pit	th thin
ī pie	th this
îr pier	hw which
ŏ pot	zh vision
ō toe	ə about,
ô paw	item

Stress marks:
′ (primary);
′ (secondary), as in
lexicon (lĕk′sĭ-kŏn′)

nipping. Often used in the plural. **2.** A pincerlike part, such as a large crustacean claw. **3.** *Chiefly British* A small boy.

nip•ping (nĭp′ĭng) *adj.* **1.** Sharp and biting, as the cold. **2.** Bitingly sarcastic. —**nip′ping•ly** *adv.*

nip•ple (nĭp′əl) *n.* **1a.** The small projection near the center of the mammary gland containing the outlets of the milk ducts through which young mammals obtain milk from the adult female; a teat. **b.** A corresponding projection of the male breast. **2a.** The rubber cap on a bottle from which a baby nurses. **b.** A pacifier for an infant. **3.** Any of various devices functioning like or resembling a nipple, esp.: **a.** A regulated opening for discharging a liquid, as in a small stopcock. **b.** A pipe coupling threaded on both ends. **c.** A small projection through which grease can be forced into a bearing. **4.** A natural or geographic projection resembling a nipple, as a mountain crest. [< obsolete *neble*, dim. of NEB.]

Nip•pon (nĭ-pŏn′, nĭp′ŏn, nē-pŏn′) Japan.

Nip•pon•ese (nĭp′ə-nēz′, -nēs′) *adj. & n.* Japanese.

Nip•pur (nĭ-poor′) An ancient city of Babylonia on the Euphrates R. SE of Babylon; an important religious center in Sumerian times.

nip•py (nĭp′ē) *adj.* -**pi•er**, -**pi•est** **1.** Tending to nip: *an exuberant, nippy puppy.* **2.** Sharp or biting: *nippy cheese.* **3.** Bitingly cold: *a nippy day.* —**nip′pi•ly** *adv.* —**nip′pi•ness** *n.*

nip-up (nĭp′ŭp′) *n. Sports* An acrobatic spring from a supine to an upright position.

N.Ire. *abbr.* Northern Ireland

nir•va•na (nîr-vä′nə, nər-) *n.* **1.** often **Nirvana a.** *Buddhism* The state in which one has attained disinterested wisdom and compassion. **b.** *Hinduism* Emancipation from ignorance and the extinction of all attachment. **2.** An ideal condition of rest, harmony, or joy. [Skt. *nirvāṇam*, a blowing out, extinction, nirvana : *nis-, nir-*, out, away + *vāti*, it blows; see **wē-** in App.]

Niš also **Nish** (nĭsh) A city of SE Yugoslavia near the Bulgarian border; birthplace of Constantine the Great. Pop. 175,555.

Nis•san (nĭs′ən, nē-sän′) *n.* The seventh month of the year in the Jewish calendar. See table at **calendar.** [Heb. *nîsân* < Akkadian *nisānu*, the first month in the Babylonian calendar (corresponding to parts of March and April) < Sumerian *nisag*, first fruits : *nig, ni*, thing, nominalizing pref. + *sag*, head, top, first.]

Ni•sei (nē-sā′, nē′sā′) *n., pl.* **Nisei** or **-seis** A person born to parents who emigrated from Japan. [J. : *ni*, second (< M Chin. *n'ih*) + *sei*, generation; see ISSEI.]

Ni•shi•no•mi•ya (nĭsh′ə-nō′mē-ä, nē′shē-nô′mē-yä′) A city of S Honshu, Japan, on Osaka Bay E of Kobe. Pop. 424,719.

ni•si (nī′sī′) *adj. Law* Taking effect at a specified date unless cause is shown for modification or nullification: *a decree nisi.* [Lat., unless. See **ne** in App.]

Nis•sen hut (nĭs′ən) *n.* A prefabricated building of corrugated steel in the shape of a half cylinder. [After Peter Norman *Nissen* (1871–1930), British mining engineer.]

NIST *abbr.* National Institute of Standards and Technology

ni•sus (nī′səs) *n., pl.* **nisus** An effort or endeavor to realize an aim. [Lat. *nisus* < p. part. of *nītī*, to strive.]

nit[1] (nĭt) *n.* The egg or young of a parasitic insect, such as a louse. [ME < OE *hnitu.*] —**nit′ty** *adj.*

nit[2] (nĭt) *n.* A unit of illuminative brightness equal to one candela per square meter, measured perpendicular to the rays of the source. [< Lat. *nitor*, brightness < *nitēre*, to shine.]

nite (nīt) *n. Informal* Night.

ni•ter (nī′tər) *n.* A white, gray, or colorless mineral of potassium nitrate, KNO₃, used in making gunpowder. [ME *nitre*, sodium carbonate, natron < OFr. < Lat. *nitrum* < Gk. *nitron* < Egypt. *ntr.*]

Ni•te•rói (nē′tə-roi′) A city of SE Brazil on Guanabara Bay opposite Rio de Janeiro; founded 1671. Pop. 435,658.

nit•pick (nĭt′pĭk′) *intr.v.* -**picked**, -**pick•ing**, -**picks** To be concerned with or find fault with insignificant details. —**nit′pick′er** *n.*

nit•pick•ing (nĭt′pĭk′ĭng) *n.* Minute, trivial, unnecessary, and unjustified criticism or faultfinding.

nitr– *pref.* Variant of **nitro–.**

Ni•tra (nē′trə) A city of W Slovakia on the **Nitra River,** a tributary of the Danube. Pop. 83,338.

ni•trate (nī′trāt′, -trĭt) *n.* **1.** The univalent radical NO₃ or a compound containing it, as a salt or ester of nitric acid. **2.** Fertilizer consisting of sodium nitrate or potassium nitrate. ❖ *tr.v.* -**trat•ed**, -**trat•ing**, -**trates** To treat or combine with nitric acid or a nitrate, usu. to change into a nitrate. —**ni•tra′tion** *n.* —**ni′tra•tor** *n.*

ni•tre (nī′tər) *n. Chiefly British* Variant of **niter.**

ni•tric (nī′trĭk) *adj.* Of, derived from, or containing nitrogen, esp. in a valence state higher than that in a comparable nitrous compound.

nitric acid *n.* A fuming corrosive liquid, HNO₃, a highly reactive oxidizing agent used in the production of fertilizers and explosives and in a wide variety of metallurgical processes.

nitric oxide *n.* A colorless poisonous gas, NO, produced as an intermediate during the manufacture of nitric acid from ammonia or atmospheric nitrogen and as a product of cellular metabolism.

ni•tride (nī′trīd′) *n.* A compound containing nitrogen with another more electropositive element, such as phosphorus.

ni•tri•fy (nī′trə-fī′) *tr.v.* -**fied**, -**fy•ing**, -**fies** **1.** To oxidize (an ammonia compound) into nitric acid, nitrous acid, or any nitrate or nitrite, esp. by the action of nitrobacteria. **2.** To treat or combine with nitrogen or compounds containing nitrogen. —**ni′tri•fi•ca′tion** (-fĭ-kā′shən) *n.* —**ni′tri•fi′er** *n.*

ni•trile also **ni•tril** (nī′trəl) *n.* An organic cyanide containing a CN group. [NITR(O)- + -*ile*, chemical suff. (prob. var. of –YL).]

ni•trite (nī′trīt′) *n.* The univalent radical NO₂ or a compound containing it, such as a salt or ester of nitrous acid.

nitro– or **nitr–** *pref.* **1.** Nitrate; niter: *nitrobacterium.* **2a.** Nitrogen: *nitrile.* **b.** Containing the univalent group NO₂: *nitromethane.* [NLat. < Lat. *nitrum*, natron. See NITER.]

ni•tro•bac•te•ri•um (nī′trō-băk-tîr′ē-əm) *n., pl.* -**te•ri•a** (-tîr′ē-ə) Any of various soil bacteria that take part in the nitrogen cycle, oxidizing ammonium compounds into nitrites or nitrites into nitrates.

ni•tro•ben•zene (nī′trō-běn′zēn′, -běn-zēn′) *n.* A poisonous organic compound, C₆H₅NO₂, an oily liquid having the odor of almonds and used in the manufacture of aniline.

ni•tro•cel•lu•lose (nī′trō-sěl′yə-lōs′, -lōz′) *n.* A pulpy or cottonlike polymer derived from cellulose treated with sulfuric and nitric acids and used in the manufacture of explosives, collodion, plastics, and solid monopropellants.

ni•tro•fu•ran (nī′trō-fyŏor′ăn′, -fyŏo-răn′) *n.* Any of several drugs derived from furan that are used to inhibit bacterial growth.

ni•tro•gen (nī′trə-jən) *n. Symbol* **N** A nonmetallic element that constitutes nearly four-fifths of the air by volume, occurring as a colorless, odorless, almost inert diatomic gas, N₂, in various minerals and in all proteins and used in a wide variety of important manufactures, including ammonia, nitric acid, TNT, and fertilizers. Atomic number 7; atomic weight 14.0067; melting point –209.86°C; boiling point –195.8°C; valence 3, 5. See table at **element.** [Fr. *nitrogène* : *nitro-*, nitric acid (< NLat.; see NITRO–) + -*gène*, -gen.] —**ni•trog′e•nous** (nī-trŏj′ə-nəs) *adj.*

ni•trog•e•nase (nī-trŏj′ə-nās′, -nāz′, nī′trə-jə-) *n.* An enzyme of nitrogen-fixing bacteria that catalyzes the conversion of nitrogen to ammonia.

nitrogen balance *n.* The difference between the amount of nitrogen taken into the body or the soil and the amount excreted or lost.

nitrogen cycle *n.* **1.** *Ecology* The circulation of nitrogen in nature, consisting of a cycle in which atmospheric nitrogen is compounded, dissolved in rain, and deposited in the soil, where it is assimilated by bacteria and plants, eventually returning to the atmosphere by bacterial decomposition of organic matter. **2.** *Physics* See **carbon-nitrogen cycle.**

nitrogen dioxide *n.* A poisonous brown gas, NO₂, often found in smog and automobile exhaust fumes and synthesized for use as a nitrating agent, a catalyst, and an oxidizing agent.

nitrogen fixation *n.* **1.** The conversion of atmospheric nitrogen into compounds, such as ammonia, by natural agencies or industrial processes. **2.** The conversion by certain soil microorganisms, such as rhizobia, of atmospheric nitrogen into compounds that plants and other organisms can assimilate. —**ni′tro•gen-fix′er** (nī′trə-jən-fĭk′sər) *n.* —**ni′tro•gen-fix′ing** *adj.*

ni•trog•en•ize (nī-trŏj′ə-nīz′, nī′trə-jə-) *tr.v.* -**ized**, -**iz•ing**, -**iz•es** To combine or treat with nitrogen or a nitrogen compound.

nitrogen narcosis *n.* A condition of confusion or stupor resulting from increased levels of dissolved nitrogen in the blood.

ni•tro•glyc•er•in also **ni•tro•glyc•er•ine** (nī′trō-glĭs′ər-ĭn, -trə-) *n.* An explosive liquid, CH₂NO₃CHNO₃CH₂NO₃, that is used in the production of dynamite and blasting gelatin and as a vasodilator in medicine.

ni•tro•hy•dro•chlo•ric acid (nī′trō-hī′drə-klôr′ĭk, -klōr′-) *n.* See **aqua regia.**

ni•tro•meth•ane (nī′trō-měth′ān′) *n.* A colorless, oily liquid, CH₃NO₂, used in making dyes and resins, in organic synthesis, as a fuel in race car engines, and as a rocket propellant.

ni•tro•par•af•fin (nī′trō-păr′ə-fĭn) *n.* Any of a group of compounds formed by replacing one or more of the hydrogen atoms of a paraffin hydrocarbon with the nitrogen group, NO₂.

ni•tros•a•mine (nī-trō′sə-mēn′, nī′trōs-ăm′ēn) *n.* Any of a class of compounds with the general formula R₂NNO, present in various cooked foods and carcinogenic in laboratory animals. [Lat. *nitrōsus*, full of natron (< *nitrum*, natron; see NITER) + AMINE.]

ni•tro•starch (nī′trə-stärch′) *n.* An explosive powder, C₁₂H₁₂(NO₂)₈O₁₀, derived from starch and used for demolition.

ni•trous (nī′trəs) *adj.* Of, derived from, or containing nitrogen, esp. in a valence state lower than that in a comparable nitric compound.

nitrous acid *n.* A weak inorganic acid, HNO₂, existing only in solution or in the form of its salts.

nitrous oxide *n.* A colorless sweet-tasting gas, N₂O, used as a mild anesthetic in dentistry and surgery.

nit•ty-grit•ty (nĭt′ē-grĭt′ē) *n. Informal* The specific or practical details; the heart of a matter. [?]

nit•wit (nĭt′wĭt′) *n.* A stupid or silly person. [Prob. obsolete *nit*, nothing (< Ger. dialectal < MHGer. *niht, nit*; see NIX[2]) + WIT[1].]

Richard M. Nixon

Pat Nixon

Niu·e (nyōō'ā) An island dependency of New Zealand in the S-central Pacific E of Tonga; became internally self-governing in 1974. Cap. Alofi. Pop. 3,578.

ni·val (nī'vəl) *adj.* Of, relating to, or growing in or under snow: *nival species of plants.* [Lat. *nivālis < nix, niv-,* snow.]

niv·e·ous (nĭv'ē-əs) *adj.* Resembling snow; snowy. [< Lat. *niveus < nix, niv-,* snow.]

Ni·ver·nais (nĭv'ər-nā', nē-vĕr-nĕ') A historical region and former province of central France; became part of the royal domain in 1669.

nix¹ (nĭks) *n. Mythology* A water sprite of German mythology, usu. in human form or half-human and half-fish. [Ger. < MHGer. *nickes* < OHGer. *nihhus.*]

nix² (nĭks) *Slang n.* Nothing. ❖ *adv.* Not so; no. ❖ *tr.v.* **nixed, nix·ing, nix·es** To forbid, refuse, or veto: *Congress nixed the tax hike.* [Ger. dialectal < MHGer. *nihtes,* genitive of *niht* < OHGer. *niwiht : ni,* not, no; see **ne** in App. + *wiht,* thing.]

nix·ie also **nix·y** (nĭk'sē) *n., pl.* **-ies** *Slang* A misaddressed or illegible piece of mail, therefore undeliverable. [< NIX².]

Nix·on (nĭk'sən), **Richard Milhous** 1913–94. The 37th President of the US (1969–74). When Congress recommended three articles of impeachment for Nixon's involvement in the Watergate scandal, he resigned from office (Aug. 9, 1974).

Nixon, Thelma Catherine Ryan ("Pat") 1912–93. First Lady of the US (1969–74) who worked to make the White House more accessible for disabled and visually impaired people.

Ni·zam (nī-zăm', -zäm', nĭ-) *n.* **1.** Used formerly as a title for rulers of Hyderabad, India. **2.** The Turkish army, esp. in the 19th century. [Urdu *nizām(-almulk),* governor (of the empire) < Ar. *nizām,* order, arrangement < *nazama,* to arrange.]

Nizh·ne·var·tovsk (nĭzh'nə-vär-tôfsk', nyĭzh-) A city of central Russia on the Ob R. Pop. 244,519.

Nizh·niy Nov·go·rod (nĭzh'nē nôv'gə-rŏd', nyĕ'zhnē nôv'gə-rət) A city of W Russia on the Volga R. W of Kazan; founded 1221 and renamed Gorky from 1932 until 1990. Pop. 1,399,000.

Nizhniy Ta·gil (tə-gēl', -gyēl') A city of central Russia in the E-central Ural Mts.; founded 1725. Pop. 419,000.

NJ or **N.J.** *abbr.* New Jersey

Nkru·mah (ən-krōō'mə, əng-), **Kwame** 1909–72. Ghanaian politician who served as president (1960–66).

NKVD *abbr. Russian* Narodnyĭ Kommissariat Vnutrennikh Del (People's Commissariat of Internal Affairs)

NL *abbr.* **1.** *Baseball* National League **2.** New Latin **3.** *Latin* non licet (not permitted) **4.** *Latin* non liquet (not clear)

NLRB *abbr.* National Labor Relations Board

nm *abbr.* **1.** nanometer **2.** nuclear magneton **3.** nautical mile

NM or **N.M.** also **N.Mex.** *abbr.* New Mexico

NMR *abbr.* nuclear magnetic resonance

NNE *abbr.* north-northeast

NNW *abbr.* north-northwest

no¹ (nō) *adv.* **1.** Used to express refusal, denial, disbelief, emphasis, or disagreement: *No, I'm not going. No, you're wrong.* **2.** Not at all; not by any degree. Often used with the comparative: *no better; no more.* **3.** Not: *whether or no.* ❖ *n., pl.* **noes** (nōz) **1.** A negative response; a denial or refusal: *The proposal produced only noes.* **2.** A negative vote or voter. ❖ *interj.* Used to express strong refusal, doubt, or disbelief. [ME < OE *nā : ne,* not; see **ne** in App. + *ā,* ever; see *aiw-* in App.]

no² (nō) *adj.* **1.** Not any; not one; not a: *No cookies are left.* **2.** Not at all; not close to being: *He is no child.* **3.** Hardly any: *got there in no time.* See Usage Note at **nor¹.** [ME, var. of *non* < OE *nān, none : ne,* not; see **ne** in App. + *ān,* one; see ONE.]

Nō¹ also **Noh** (nō) *n.* The classical drama of Japan, with music and dance performed in a highly stylized manner by elaborately dressed performers on an almost bare stage. [J. *nō,* talent, ability, Nō < M Chin. *nəŋ.*]

No² The symbol for the element **nobelium.**

No (nō), **Lake** A lake of S-central Sudan formed by the flood waters of the White Nile.

no. or **No.** *abbr.* **1a.** north **b.** northern **2.** number

NOAA *abbr.* National Oceanic and Atmospheric Administration

no-ac·count (nō'ə-kount') *adj. Informal* Worthless.

No·a·chi·an (nō-ā'kē-ən) also **No·ach·ic** (-ăk'ĭk) or **No·ach·i·cal** (-ĭ-kəl) *adj.* **1.** *Bible* Of or relating to Noah or his time. **2.** Antiquated; ancient; long obsolete.

No·ah (nō'ə) In the Bible, the patriarch who was chosen by God to build an ark, in which he, his family, and a pair of every animal were saved from the Flood.

No·a·tak (nō-ä'tăk, -täk) A river of NW AK flowing c. 644 km (400 mi) to Kotzebue Sound.

nob¹ (nŏb) *n. Slang* The human head. **2.** The jack of the same suit as the card turned up by the dealer in cribbage, scoring one point for the holder. [Perh. var. of KNOB.]

nob² (nŏb) *n. Chiefly British Slang* A person of wealth or social standing. [Poss. < NOB¹ or KNOB.]

nob·ble (nŏb'əl) *tr.v.* **-bled, -bling, -bles** *Chiefly British* **1.** To disable (a racehorse), esp. by drugging. **2.** To win (a person) over. **3.** To outdo or get the better of by devious means. **4.** To filch or steal. **5.** To kidnap. [?] —**nob'bler** *n.*

nob·by (nŏb'ē) *adj.* **-bi·er, -bi·est** Fashionable; stylish.

No·bel (nō-bĕl'), **Alfred Bernhard** 1833–96. Swedish chemist

and engineer who invented dynamite (1866) and bequeathed his fortune to institute the Nobel Prizes.

No·bel·ist (nō-bĕl'ĭst) *n.* A recipient of a Nobel prize.

no·bel·i·um (nō-bĕl'ē-əm) *n. Symbol* **No** A radioactive synthetic element in the actinide series; its longest-lived isotope is No 259 with a half-life of 58 minutes. Atomic number 102. See table at **element.** [After Alfred Bernhard NOBEL.]

Nobel Prize *n.* Any of the six international prizes awarded annually by the Nobel Foundation for outstanding achievements in the fields of physics, chemistry, physiology or medicine, literature, and economics and for the promotion of world peace. [After Alfred Bernhard NOBEL.]

no·bil·i·ar·y (nō-bĭl'ē-ĕr'ē, -bĭl'yə-rē) *adj.* Of or relating to the nobility. [Fr. *nobiliaire* < Lat. *nōbilis,* noble. See NOBLE.]

no·bil·i·ty (nō-bĭl'ĭ-tē) *n., pl.* **-ties 1.** A class of persons distinguished by high birth or rank. **2.** Noble rank or status: *titles of nobility.* **3.** The state or quality of being exalted in character. [ME *nobilite,* the quality of being noble < OFr. < Lat. *nōbilitās < nōbilis,* noble. See NOBLE.]

no·ble (nō'bəl) *adj.* **-bler, -blest 1.** Possessing high rank, often hereditary, in a political system or social class derived from a feudalistic stage of a country's development. **2a.** Having or showing qualities of high moral character, such as courage, generosity, or honor: *a noble spirit.* **b.** Proceeding from or indicative of such a character; showing magnanimity. **3.** Grand and stately in appearance; majestic. **4.** *Chemistry* Inactive or inert. ❖ *n.* **1.** A member of the nobility. **2.** A gold coin formerly used in England, worth half of a mark. [ME < OFr. < Lat. *nōbilis.* See **gnō-** in App.] —**no'ble·ness** *n.* —**no'bly** *adv.*

noble gas *n.* Any of the elements in Group O of the periodic table, including helium, neon, argon, krypton, xenon, and radon, that are monatomic and largely chemically inert.

no·ble·man (nō'bəl-mən) *n.* A man of noble rank.

noble metal *n.* A metal or alloy, such as gold, that is highly resistant to oxidation and corrosion.

no·blesse (nō-blĕs') *n.* **1.** Noble birth or condition. **2.** The members of the nobility, esp. the French nobility. [ME < OFr. < *noble,* noble < Lat. *nōbilis.* See NOBLE.]

noblesse o·blige (ō-blēzh') *n.* Benevolent honorable behavior considered to be the responsibility of persons of high birth or rank. [Fr., nobility is an obligation : *noblesse,* nobility + *oblige,* third pers. sing. pr. t. of *obliger,* to obligate.]

no·ble·wom·an (nō'bəl-wŏŏm'ən) *n.* A woman of noble rank.

no·bod·y (nō'bŏd'ē, -bŭd'ē, -bə-dē) *pron.* No person; not anyone. ❖ *n., pl.* **-ies** An unimportant or uninfluential person.

no-brain·er (nō'brā'nər) *n. Informal* Something so simple or easy as to require no thought.

no·cent (nō'sənt) *adj.* Causing injury; harmful. [ME *nocent,* guilty < Lat. *nocēns, nocent-,* pr. part. of *nocēre,* to harm. See **nek-** in App.]

no·ci·cep·tive (nō'sĭ-sĕp'tĭv) *adj.* **1.** Causing pain. Used of a stimulus. **2.** Caused by or responding to a painful stimulus: *a nociceptive spinal reflex.* [< NOCICEPTOR.]

no·ci·cep·tor (nō'sĭ-sĕp'tər) *n.* A sensory receptor that responds to pain. [Lat. *nocēre,* to hurt; see NOCENT + (RE)CEPTOR.]

nock (nŏk) *n.* **1.** The groove at either end of a bow for holding the bowstring. **2.** The notch in the end of an arrow that fits on the bowstring. ❖ *tr.v.* **nocked, nock·ing, nocks 1.** To put a nock in (a bow or arrow). **2.** To fit (an arrow) to a bowstring. [ME *nokke.*]

noc·tam·bu·lism (nŏk-tăm'byə-lĭz'əm) also **noc·tam·bu·la·tion** (-tăm'byə-lā'shən) *n.* See **sleepwalking.** [NOCT(I)– + Lat. *ambulāre,* to walk + –ISM.] —**noc·tam'bu·list** *n.*

nocti– or **noct–** *pref.* Night: *noctilucent.* [NLat. < Lat. *nox, noct-,* night. See **nekʷ-t-** in App.]

noc·ti·lu·ca (nŏk'tə-lōō'kə) *n.* Any of various bioluminescent dinoflagellates of the genus *Noctiluca* that when grouped in large numbers make the sea phosphorescent. [NLat. *Noctilūca,* genus name < Lat. *noctilūca,* lantern, moon : *nocti-,* nocti- + *lūcēre,* to shine; see **leuk-** in App.]

noc·ti·lu·cent (nŏk'tə-lōō'sənt) *adj.* Luminous at night. Used esp. of certain high clouds.

noc·tu·id (nŏk'chōō-ĭd) *n.* Any of numerous night-flying moths of the family Noctuidae, having a proboscis for sucking nectar and larvae that are destructive, as to young trees. [< NLat. Noctuidae, family name < *Noctua,* type genus < Lat. *noctua,* night owl. See **nekʷ-t-** in App.] —**noc'tu·id** *adj.*

noc·tule (nŏk'chōōl') *n.* A large insectivorous bat of the genus Nyctalus, found in Eurasia, Indonesia, and the Philippines. [Fr. < Ital. *nottola,* bat, owl < LLat. *noctula* < Lat., dim. of *noctua,* night owl. See **nekʷ-t-** in App.]

noc·turn (nŏk'tûrn') *n.* Any of the three canonical divisions of the office of matins. [ME *nocturne* < Med.Lat. *nocturna* < Lat., fem. of *nocturnus,* of the night. See NOCTURNAL.]

noc·tur·nal (nŏk-tûr'nəl) *adj.* **1.** Of, relating to, or occurring in the night: *nocturnal stillness.* **2.** *Botany* Having flowers that open during the night. **3.** *Zoology* Most active at night. [ME < OFr. < LLat. *nocturnālis* < Lat. *nocturnus < nox, noct-,* night. See **nekʷ-t-** in App.] —**noc·tur'nal·ly** *adv.*

noc·turne (nŏk'tûrn') *n.* **1.** A painting of a night scene. **2.** A pensive, dreamy instrumental composition. [Fr. < OFr., noctur-

Nō¹

ă	pat	oi	boy
ā	pay	ou	out
âr	care	ŏŏ	took
ä	father	ōō	boot
ĕ	pet	ŭ	cut
ē	be	ûr	urge
ĭ	pit	th	thin
ī	pie	th	this
îr	pier	hw	which
ŏ	pot	zh	vision
ō	toe	ə	about,
ô	paw		item

Stress marks:
ʹ (primary);
ʹ (secondary), as in
lexicon (lĕkʹsĭ-kŏnʹ)

nal < Lat. *nocturnus.* See NOCTURNAL.]

noc·u·ous (nŏk′yōō-əs) *adj.* Harmful; noxious. [< Lat. *nocuus* < *nocēre,* to harm. See **nek-** in App.] —**noc′u·ous·ly** *adv.*

nod (nŏd) *v.* **nod·ded, nod·ding, nods** —*intr.* **1.** To lower and raise the head quickly, as in agreement. **2.** To let the head fall forward when sleepy. **3.** To be careless or momentarily inattentive as if sleepy; lapse. **4.** To sway, move up and down, or droop, as flowers in the wind. —*tr.* **1.** To lower and raise (the head) quickly in agreement or acknowledgment. **2.** To express by lowering and raising the head: *She nodded her agreement.* **3.** To summon, guide, or send by nodding the head. ❖ *n.* **1.** A forward or up-and-down movement of the head, usu. expressive of drowsiness or agreement. **2.** An indication of approval or assent. —*phrasal verb:* **nod off** To doze momentarily: *nodded off during the lecture.* [ME *nodden;* perh. akin to MHGer. *notten.*] —**nod′der** *n.*

nod·al (nŏd′l) *adj.* Of, relating to, resembling, being, or situated near or at a node. —**nod′al·ly** *adv.*

nod·dle (nŏd′l) *n.* The head. [ME *noddel,* back of the head, perh. < Lat. *nōdulus,* lump, knob. See NODULE.]

nod·dy (nŏd′ē) *n., pl.* **-dies 1.** A dunce or fool; a simpleton. **2.** Any of several terns of the genera *Anous* and *Micranous,* found in tropical waters and having a dark brown or black color with a white or gray head. [Perh. < obsolete *noddy,* foolish, poss. < NOD.]

node (nŏd) *n.* **1.** A knob, knot, protuberance, or swelling. **2a.** *Botany* The point on a stem where a leaf is attached or has been attached; a joint. **b.** See knot¹ 7. **3.** *Physics* A point or region of virtually zero amplitude in a periodic system. **4.** *Mathematics* The point at which a continuous curve crosses itself. **5.** *Computer Science* A terminal in a computer network. **6.** *Astronomy* **a.** Either of two points at which the orbit of a planet intersects the ecliptic. **b.** Either of two points at which the orbit of a satellite intersects the orbital plane of a planet. [ME, lump in the flesh < Lat. *nōdus,* knot.]

node of Ran·vier (răn′vyā, rän-vyā′, rän-) *n., pl.* **nodes of Ranvier** A constriction in the myelin sheath, occurring at varying intervals along the length of a nerve fiber. [After Louis Antoine Ranvier (1835–1922), French histologist.]

no·dose (nō′dōs′) *adj.* Characterized by or having many nodes or protuberances; jointed or knobby at intervals. —**no·dos′i·ty** (-dŏs′ĭ-tē) *n.*

nod·ule (nŏj′ōōl) *n.* **1.** A small knotlike protuberance. **2.** *Anatomy* A small mass of tissue or aggregation of cells. **3.** *Botany* A small knoblike outgrowth, as those found on the roots of many leguminous plants. **4.** *Mineralogy* A small rounded lump of a mineral or mixture of minerals, usu. harder than the surrounding rock or sediment. [ME < Lat. *nōdulus,* dim. of *nōdus,* knot.] —**nod′u·lar** (nŏj′ə-lər), **nod′u·lose′** (-lōs′), **nod′u·lous** (-ləs) *adj.*

no·dus (nō′dəs) *n., pl.* **-di** (-dī) A difficult situation or problem; a complication. [Lat. *nōdus,* knot.]

No·ël also **No·el** (nō-ĕl′) *n.* **1.** Christmas. **2. noël** A Christmas carol. [ME *noel* < OFr., var. of *nael* < Lat. *nātālis* (*diēs*), (day) of birth < *nātus,* p. part. of *nāscī,* to be born. See genə- in App.]

No·el-Ba·ker (nō′əl-bā′kər), **Philip John** 1889–1982. British politician who helped draft the United Nations Charter (1945) and won the 1959 Nobel Peace Prize.

noes (nōz) *v.* Plural of no¹.

no·e·sis (nō-ē′sĭs) *n.* The cognitive process; cognition. [Gk. *noēsis,* understanding < *noein,* to perceive < *nous,* mind.]

no·et·ic (nō-ĕt′ĭk) *adj.* Of, relating to, originating in, or apprehended by the intellect.

no-fault (nō′fôlt′) *adj.* **1.** Of, indicating, or being a system of motor vehicle insurance in which accident victims are compensated by their insurance companies without assignment of blame. **2.** *Law* Of, indicating, or being a type of divorce in which blame is assigned to neither party.

no-frills (nō′frĭlz′) *adj. Informal* Marked by the absence of extra or special features; basic: *no-frills airline service.*

nog¹ (nŏg) *n.* **1.** A wooden block built into a masonry wall to hold nails that support joinery structures. **2.** A wooden peg or pin. [?]

nog² (nŏg) *n.* Eggnog.

nog·gin (nŏg′ĭn) *n.* **1.** A small mug or cup. **2.** A unit of liquid measure equal to one quarter of a pint. **3.** *Slang* The human head. [?]

no-go (nō′gō′) *adj.* Not proceeding or functioning properly.

no-good (nō′gŏŏd′) *adj.* Having no value, use, merit, or virtue. ❖ *n.* One that is worthless.

No·gu·chi (nō-gōō′chē), **Hideyo** 1876–1928. Japanese-born Amer. bacteriologist who discovered the cause of syphilis and yellow fever.

Noguchi, Isamu 1925–88. Amer. sculptor noted for his abstract works of bronze, stone, and terra cotta.

Noh (nō) *n.* Variant of No¹.

no-hit (nō′hĭt′) *adj. Baseball* Of, relating to, or being a no-hitter.

no-hit·ter (nō′hĭt′ər) *n. Baseball* A game in which one pitcher allows the opposing team no hits.

no-holds-barred (nō′hōldz′bärd′) *adj. Informal* Open and unrestrained.

no·how (nō′hou′) *adv. Nonstandard* In no way; not at all.

noil (noil) *n.* A short fiber combed from long fibers during the

preparation of textile yarns. [Perh. < ME **noil* < OFr. *noel* < Med.Lat. *nōdellus* < Lat., dim. of *nōdus,* knot.]

noir (nwär) *adj.* **1.** Of or relating to film noir. **2.** Of or relating to a genre of crime literature featuring tough, cynical characters and bleak settings. [Short for FILM NOIR. Sense 2, short for Fr. *roman noir,* black novel.] —**noir′ish** *adj.*

noise (noiz) *n.* **1a.** Sound or a sound that is loud, unpleasant, unexpected, or undesired. **b.** Sound or a sound of any kind. **2.** A loud outcry or commotion. **3.** *Physics* A disturbance, esp. a random and persistent disturbance, that obscures or reduces the clarity of a signal. **4.** *Computer Science* Irrelevant or meaningless data. **5.** *Informal* **a.** A complaint or protest. **b.** Rumor; talk. **c. noises** Remarks or actions intended to convey a specific impression or to attract attention. ❖ *v.* **noised, nois·ing, nois·es** —*tr.* To spread the rumor or report of. —*intr.* **1.** To talk much or volubly. **2.** To be noisy; make noise. [ME < OFr., perh. < VLat. **nausea,* discomfort < Lat. *nausea,* seasickness. See NAUSEA.]

SYNONYMS noise, din, racket, hubbub, clamor These nouns refer to loud, confused, or disagreeable sound or sounds. *Noise* is the least specific: *the noise of cannon fire.* A *din* is a jumble of loud, usually discordant sounds: *the din in the factory.* *Racket* is loud, distressing noise: *the racket of trucks rolling along cobblestone streets.* *Hubbub* emphasizes turbulent activity and concomitant din: *the hubbub of bettors.* *Clamor* is loud, usually sustained noise, as of a public outcry of dissatisfaction: *"not in the clamor of the crowded street"* (Henry Wadsworth Longfellow).

noise·mak·er (noiz′mā′kər) *n.* One that makes noise, esp. a horn or rattle used to make noise at a party. —**noise′mak′ing** *n.*

noise pollution *n.* Environmental noise that is annoying, distracting, or physically harmful.

noi·sette (nwä-zĕt′) *n.* A small round piece of meat. ❖ *adj.* Made or flavored with hazelnuts. [Fr. < OFr., dim. of *nois,* nut < Lat. *nux.*]

noi·some (noi′səm) *adj.* **1.** Offensive to the point of arousing disgust; foul: *a noisome odor.* **2.** Harmful or dangerous: *noisome fumes.* [ME *noiesom* : *noie,* harm (short for *anoi,* annoyance < OFr. < *anoier,* to annoy; see ANNOY) + *-som,* adj. suff.; see –SOME¹.] —**noi′some·ly** *adv.* —**noi′some·ness** *n.*

nois·y (noi′zē) *adj.* **-i·er, -i·est 1.** Making noise: *a small, noisy dog.* **2.** Full of, characterized by, or accompanied by noise: *a noisy cafeteria.* —**nois′i·ly** *adv.* —**nois′i·ness** *n.*

Nol·de (nôl′də), **Emile** 1867–1956. German painter whose expressionist works include landscapes and religious paintings.

no·lens vo·lens (nō′lĕnz vō′lĕnz, nō′lĕns wō′lĕns) *adv.* Whether willing or unwilling. [Lat. *nōlēns volēns* : *nōlēns,* pr. part. of *nōlle,* to be unwilling + *volēns,* pr. part. of *velle,* to wish, be willing.]

no·li-me-tan·ge·re (nō′lē-mē-tăn′jə-rē, nō′lī-) *n.* **1.** A warning or prohibition against touching or interfering. **2.** A representation of Jesus appearing to Mary Magdalen after his resurrection. [LLat. *nōlī mē tangere,* do not touch me (Jesus's words to Mary Magdalene, John 20:17) : Lat. *nōlī,* do not, sing. imper. of *nōlle,* to be unwilling + Lat. *mē,* me + Lat. *tangere,* to touch.]

nol·le pros·e·qui (nŏl′ē prŏs′ĭ-kwī′, -kwē′) *n.* A declaration that the plaintiff in a civil case or the prosecutor in a criminal case will drop prosecution of all or part of a suit or indictment. [Lat. *nōlle prōsequī,* to be unwilling to pursue : *nōlle,* to be unwilling + *prōsequī,* to pursue.]

no·lo (nō′lō) *n., pl.* **-los** Nolo contendere.

no-load (nō′lōd′) *adj. Business* Sold directly to customers at net asset value without a sales commission.

no·lo con·ten·de·re (nō′lō kən-tĕn′də-rē) *n.* A plea made by the defendant in a criminal action that is substantially but not technically an admission of guilt and subjects the defendant to punishment but permits denial of the alleged facts in other proceedings. [Lat. *nōlō contendere,* I do not wish to contend : *nōlō,* first pers. sing. pr. t. of *nōlle,* to be unwilling + *contendere,* to contend.]

no-lose (nō′lōōz′) *adj. Slang* Certain to end happily or successfully.

nol-pros (nŏl′prŏs′) *tr.v.* **-prossed, -pros·sing, -pros·ses** To drop prosecution by entering a nolle prosequi in court records. [Short for NOLLE PROSEQUI.]

nol. pros. *abbr.* nolle prosequi

nom. *abbr.* nominative

no·ma (nō′mə) *n.* A severe, often gangrenous inflammation of the mouth or genitals, occurring usu. after an infectious disease and found most often in children in poor hygienic or malnourished condition. [Lat. *nomē,* ulcer < Gk., feeding, spreading (of a sore). See nem- in App.]

no·mad (nō′măd) *n.* **1.** A member of a group of people who have no fixed home and move according to the seasons from place to place in search of food, water, and grazing land. **2.** A person with no fixed residence who roams about; a wanderer. [Fr. *nomade* < Lat. *nomas, nomad-* < Gk. *nomas,* wandering in search of pasture. See nem- in App.] —**no·mad′ic** *adj.* —**no·mad′i·cal·ly** *adv.* —**no′mad′ism** *n.*

no man's land *n.* **1.** Land disputed by two parties, esp. between two armies. **2.** An area of uncertainty or ambiguity. **3.** An unclaimed or unowned piece of land.

nom·ar·chy (nŏm′är′kē) *n., pl.* **-chies** Any of the administrative provinces of the modern Greek state. [Mod.Gk. *nomarkhia* < Gk. *nomarkhiā*, district : *nomos*, district; see NOME + *-arkhiā*, -archy.]

nom·bril (nŏm′brəl) *n. Heraldry* The point on an escutcheon between the fess point and the base point; the midpoint in the lower half of the escutcheon. [Fr. < OFr. < (*u*)*n ombril*, (a) navel < VLat. **umbilīculus* < Lat., dim. of *umbilīcus*. See **nobh-** in App.]

nom de guerre (nŏm′ də gâr′) *n., pl.* **noms de guerre** (nŏm′) A fictitious name; a pseudonym. [Fr. : *nom*, name + *de*, of + *guerre*, war.]

nom de plume (nŏm′ də ploōm′) *n., pl.* **noms de plume** (nŏm′) See **pen name.** [Fr. : *nom*, name + *de*, of + *plume*, pen.]

nome (nōm) *n.* **1.** A province of Pharaonic, Hellenistic, and Roman Egypt. **2.** A nomarchy. [Gk. *nomos*, district, custom. See **nem-** in App.]

Nome A city of W AK on the S coast of Seward Peninsula; founded as a gold-mining camp in 1896. Pop. 3,505.

no·men·cla·tor (nō′mən-klā′tər) *n.* One who assigns names, as in scientific classification. [Lat. *nōmenclātor*, a slave who accompanied his master to tell him the names of people he met, var. of *nōmenculātor* : *nōmen*, name; see **nō-men-** in App. + *calātor*, servant, crier (< *calāre*, to call; see **kelə-** in App.).]

no·men·cla·to·ri·al (nō′mən-klə-tôr′ē-əl, -tōr′-) *adj.* Of or relating to nomenclature.

no·men·cla·ture (nō′mən-klā′chər, nō-mĕn′klə-) *n.* **1.** A system of names used in an art or science. **2.** The procedure of assigning names to organisms listed in a taxonomic classification. [Lat. *nōmenclātūra* < *nōmenclātor*, nomenclator. See NOMENCLATOR.]

no·men·kla·tu·ra (nō′mən-klä-toor′ə, nō′myĕn-klä-toor′ä) *n.* (*used with a sing. or pl. verb*) The privileged class of bureaucrats appointed by the government in the former Soviet Union and certain other countries. [Russ. < Lat. *nōmenclātūra*, list of names. See NOMENCLATURE.]

nom·i·nal (nŏm′ə-nəl) *adj.* **1a.** Of, resembling, relating to, or consisting of a name or names. **b.** Assigned to or bearing a person's name: *nominal shares.* **2.** Existing in name only. **3.** *Philosophy* Of or relating to nominalism. **4.** Insignificantly small; trifling: *a nominal sum.* **5.** *Business* **a.** Of, relating to, or being the amount or face value of a sum of money or a stock certificate, for example, and not the purchasing power or market value. **b.** Of, relating to, or being the rate of interest or return without adjustment for compounding or inflation. **6.** *Grammar* Of or relating to a noun or word group that functions as a noun. **7.** *Aerospace & Engineering* According to plan or design: *a nominal flight check.* ❖ *n. Grammar* A word or group of words functioning as a noun. [ME *nominalle*, of nouns < Lat. *nōminālis*, of names < *nōmen, nōmin-*, name. See **nō-men-** in App.] **—nom′i·nal·ly** *adv.*

nom·i·nal·ism (nŏm′ə-nə-lĭz′əm) *n. Philosophy* The doctrine holding that abstract concepts, general terms, or universals have no independent existence but exist only as names. **—nom′i·nal·ist** *n.* **—nom′i·nal·is′tic** *adj.*

nominal value *n.* See **par value.**

nominal wages *pl.n.* Wages measured in terms of money paid, not in terms of purchasing power.

nom·i·nate (nŏm′ə-nāt′) *tr.v.* **-nat·ed, -nat·ing, -nates** **1.** To propose by name as a candidate, esp. for election. **2.** To designate or appoint to an office, responsibility, or honor. [Lat. *nōmināre, nōmināt-*, to name < *nōmen, nōmin-*, name. See **nō-men-** in App.] **—nom′i·na′tor** *n.*

nom·i·na·tion (nŏm′ə-nā′shən) *n.* **1.** The act or an instance of appointing a person to office. **2.** The act or an instance of submitting a name for candidacy or appointment. **3.** The state of being nominated.

nom·i·na·tive (nŏm′ə-nā′tĭv) *adj.* **1a.** Appointed to office. **b.** Nominated as a candidate for office. **2.** Having or bearing a person's name. **3.** (-nə-tĭv) *Grammar* Of, relating to, or being the case of the subject of a finite verb and of words identified with the subject of a copula, such as a predicate nominative. ❖ *n.* (-nə-tĭv) *Grammar* **1.** The nominative case. **2.** A word or form in the nominative case.

nom·i·nee (nŏm′ə-nē′) *n.* **1.** One who has been nominated to an office or for a candidacy. **2.** A person or organization in whose name a security is registered through true ownership is held by another party. [NOMIN(ATE) + -EE¹.]

nom·o·graph (nŏm′ə-grăf′, nō′mə-) or **nom·o·gram** (-grăm′) *n.* **1.** A graph consisting of three coplanar curves, each graduated for a different variable so that a straight line cutting all three curves intersects the related values of each variable. **2.** A chart representing numerical relationships. [Gk. *nomos*, law; see **nem-** in App. + -GRAPH.] **—nom′o·graph′ic** *adj.* **—no·mog′ra·phy** (nō-mŏg′rə-fē) *n.*

no·mol·o·gy (nō-mŏl′ə-jē) *n.* The study and discovery of general physical and logical laws. [Gk. *nomos*, law; see **nem-** in App. + -LOGY.] **—nom′o·log′ic** (nŏm′ə-lŏj′ĭk, nō′mə-), **nom′o·log′i·cal** (-ĭ-kəl) *adj.* **—nom′o·log′i·cal·ly** *adv.* **—no·mol′o·gist** *n.*

nom·o·thet·ic (nŏm′ə-thĕt′ĭk) or **nom·o·thet·i·cal** (-ĭk-əl) *adj.* **1.** Of or relating to lawmaking; legislative. **2.** Based on a sys-

tem of law. **3.** Of or relating to the philosophy of law. **4.** Of or relating to the study or discovery of general scientific laws. [Gk. *nomothetikos* : *nomos*, law; see **nem-** in App. + *thetikos*, thetic; see THETIC.] **—nom·o·thet′i·cal·ly** *adv.*

-nomy *suff.* A system of laws governing or a body of knowledge about a specified field: *aeronomy.* [Gk. *-nomiā* < *nomos*, law. See **nem-** in App.]

non– *pref.* Not: *noncombatant.* [ME < OFr. < Lat. *nōn*, not. See **ne** in App.]

nona– *pref.* Ninth; nine: *nonagon.* [< Lat. *nōnus*, ninth. See **newn** in App.]

non·age (nŏn′ĭj, nō′nĭj) *n.* **1.** The period during which one is legally underage. **2.** A period of immaturity. [ME *nounage* < AN, var. of OFr. *nonaage* : *non-*, non- + *aage*, age; see AGE.]

non·a·ge·nar·i·an (nŏn′ə-jə-nâr′ē-ən, nō′nə-) *n.* A person 90 years old or between 90 and 100 years old. [< Lat. *nōnāgēnārius* < *nōnāgēnī*, ninety each < *nōnāgintā*, ninety : *nōnus*, ninth; see NONA– + *-gintā*, ten times; see **dekm** in App.] **—non′a·ge·nar′i·an** *adj.*

non·a·gon (nŏn′ə-gŏn′, nō′nə-) *n.* A polygon with nine sides.

non·al·co·hol·ic (nŏn′ăl-kə-hô′lĭk, -hŏl′ĭk) *n.* A beverage usu. containing less than 0.5 percent alcohol by volume. ❖ *adj.* **1.** Of, relating to, or being a beverage whose alcohol content is very low or negligible. **2.** Containing no alcohol: *nonalcoholic medication.* **3.** Dealcoholized.

non·a·ligned (nŏn′ə-līnd′) *adj.* Not allied with any other nation or bloc; neutral. **—non′a·lign′ment** *n.*

non-A, non-B hepatitis (nŏn-ā′ nŏn-bē′) *n.* Any of various forms of hepatitis, esp. hepatitis C, caused by a virus that is antigenically different from hepatitis viruses A and B.

non·ap·pear·ance (nŏn′ə-pîr′əns) *n. Law* Failure of a witness or party to appear in response to a subpoena or notice.

non·as·sess·a·ble (nŏn′ə-sĕs′ə-bəl) *adj.* **1.** Impossible to estimate, set, or determine: *nonassessable damages.* **2.** Of or relating to capital stock for which owners cannot be assessed additional funds to cover liabilities of the firm and therefore cannot lose more than their original investments.

non·black or **non-Black** or **non-black** (nŏn-blăk′) *n.* A person who is not Black. **—non·black′** *adj.*

non·book (nŏn′boŏk′) *n.* A book having little or no literary merit. ❖ *adj.* Of, relating to, or being something other than a book, such as microfilm or microfiche in a library.

non·can·di·date (nŏn-kăn′dĭ-dāt′, -dĭt) *n. Informal* A person who has announced that he or she is not a candidate.

nonce (nŏns) *n.* The present or particular occasion. [< ME *for the nones*, for the occasion, alteration of *for then anes* : *for*, for; see FOR + *then*, neut. dative sing. of *the*; see THE¹ + *ones, anes*, once; see ONCE.]

nonce word *n.* A word occurring, invented, or used just for a particular occasion.

non·cha·lance (nŏn′shə-läns′) *n.* Casual lack of concern.

non·cha·lant (nŏn′shə-länt′) *adj.* Seeming to be coolly unconcerned or indifferent. [Fr. < OFr., pr. part. of *nonchaloir*, to be unconcerned : *non-*, non- + *chaloir*, to cause concern to (< Lat. *calēre*, to be warm; see CELESTIAL).] **—non′cha·lant′ly** *adv.*

non·chro·mo·som·al (nŏn′krō-mə-sō′məl) *adj.* Not situated on or involving a chromosome: *nonchromosomal DNA.*

non·cit·i·zen (nŏn-sĭt′ĭ-zən) *n.* See **alien** 1.

non·com (nŏn′kŏm′) *n. Informal* A noncommissioned officer.

non·com·bat·ant (nŏn′kəm-băt′nt, -kŏm′bə-tnt) *n.* **1.** A member of the armed forces whose duties lie outside combat. **2.** A civilian in wartime, esp. one in a war zone.

non·com·mis·sioned officer (nŏn′kə-mĭsh′ənd) *n.* An enlisted member of the armed forces appointed to a rank conferring leadership over other enlisted personnel.

non·com·mit·tal (nŏn′kə-mĭt′l) *adj.* Refusing commitment to a particular opinion or course of action; not revealing what one feels or thinks. **—non′com·mit′tal·ly** *adv.*

non com·pos men·tis (nŏn kŏm′pəs mĕn′tĭs) *adj.* Not of sound mind and hence not legally responsible; mentally incompetent. [Lat. *nōn compos mentis* : *nōn*, not + *compos*, in control + *mentis*, genitive sing. of *mēns*, mind.]

non·con·duc·tor (nŏn′kən-dŭk′tər) *n.* A material that conducts little or no electricity, heat, or sound.

non·con·form·ist (nŏn′kən-fôr′mĭst) *n.* **1.** One who does not conform to or refuses to be bound by accepted beliefs, customs, or practices. **2.** often **Nonconformist** A member of a Protestant church not observing the doctrines, usage, or polity of a national or established church, esp. the Church of England. **—non′con·form′ist** *adj.* **—non′con·form′ism** *n.*

non·con·form·i·ty (nŏn′kən-fôr′mĭ-tē) *n.* **1a.** Refusal or failure to conform to accepted standards, conventions, rules, or laws. **b.** An instance of this: *a measure aimed at reducing nonconformities to the housing code.* **2.** often **Nonconformity** Refusal to accept or conform to the doctrines, usage, or polity of the Church of England.

non·co·op·er·a·tion (nŏn′kō-ŏp′ə-rā′shən) *n.* Failure or refusal to cooperate, esp. nonviolent civil disobedience against a government or an occupying power. **—non′co·op′er·a′tion·ist, non′co·op′er·a′tor** *n.* **—non′co·op′er·a·tive** (-ŏp′ər-ə-tĭv, -ŏp′ə-rā′-) *adj.*

non·de·nom·i·na·tion·al (nŏn′dĭ-nŏm′ə-nā′shə-nəl) *adj.* Not restricted to or associated with a religious denomination.

non·de·script (nŏn′dĭ-skrĭpt′) *adj.* Lacking distinctive qualities; having no individual character or form. [NON– + Lat. *dēscrīptus,* p. part. of *dēscrībere,* to describe; see DESCRIBE.] —**non′de·script′** *n.*

non·dis·junc·tion (nŏn′dĭs-jŭngk′shən) *n.* The failure of paired chromosomes or sister chromatids to separate and go to different cells during meiosis.

non·dis·tinc·tive (nŏn′dĭ-stĭngk′tĭv) *adj.* Not phonemically distinctive; not serving to distinguish meaning.

non·drink·er (nŏn-drĭng′kər) *n.* One who does not drink alcoholic beverages.

non·du·ra·ble (nŏn-dŏor′ə-bəl, -dyŏor′-) *adj.* Not enduring; being in a state of constant consumption: *nondurable items such as paper products.* ❖ *n.* A consumable item.

none (nŭn) *pron.* **1.** No one; not one; nobody. **2.** Not any: *None of them went.* **3.** No part; not any: *none of your business.* ❖ *adv.* **1.** Not at all: *He is none too ill.* **2.** In no way: *none the worse for wear.* [ME < OE *nān* : *ne,* no, not; see **ne** in App. + *ān,* one; see **oi-no-** in App.]

> **USAGE NOTE** It is widely asserted that *none* is equivalent to *no one* and hence requires a singular verb and singular pronoun: *None of the prisoners was given his soup.* But the word has been used as both a singular and a plural from Old English onward, and the choice between a singular or plural verb depends on the desired effect. Either a singular or a plural verb is acceptably used in a sentence such as *None of the conspirators has* (or *have*) *been brought to trial.* When *none* is modified by *almost,* it is difficult to avoid treating the word as a plural: *Almost none of the officials were interviewed by the committee.* And in sentences such as *None but his most loyal supporters believe his story,* none can only be plural. See Usage Notes at **every, neither, nothing.**

non·e·go (nŏn-ē′gō, -ĕg′ō) *n.* All of the psyche that is not part of the ego or the conscious self.

non·en·ti·ty (nŏn-ĕn′tĭ-tē) *n., pl.* **-ties 1.** A person regarded as being of no importance. **2.** Nonexistence. **3.** Something that does not exist or that exists only in the imagination.

nones (nōnz) *pl.n.* **1.** The ninth day before the ides of a month. **2.** *Ecclesiastical* The fifth of the seven canonical hours. No longer in liturgical use. [ME < OFr. < Lat. *nōnae,* fem. pl. of *nōnus,* ninth. See **newn** in App.]

non·es·sen·tial (nŏn′ĭ-sĕn′shəl) *adj.* **1.** Having little or no importance; not essential. **2.** *Biochemistry* Being a substance required for normal functioning but not needed in the diet because the body synthesizes it from other nutrients.

none·such also **non·such** (nŭn′sŭch′) *n.* **1.** A person or thing without equal. **2.** See **black medic.** —**none′such′** *adj.*

no·net (nō-nĕt′) *n.* **1.** A combination of nine instruments or voices. **2.** A composition written for a nonet. [Ital. *nonetto* < dim. of *nono,* ninth < Lat. *nōnus.* See NONES.]

none·the·less (nŭn′thə-lĕs′) *adv.* Nevertheless; however.

non-Eu·clid·e·an (nŏn′yōō-klĭd′ē-ən) *adj.* Of, relating to, or being any of several modern geometries that are not based on the postulates of Euclid.

non·e·vent (nŏn′ĭ-vĕnt′) *n.* *Informal* A highly anticipated event that fails to occur or live up to its promise.

non·ex·is·tence (nŏn′ĭg-zĭs′təns) *n.* **1.** The state of not existing. **2.** Something not in existence. —**non′ex·is′tent** *adj.*

non·fat (nŏn′făt′) *adj.* Lacking fat solids or having the fat content removed: *nonfat milk.*

non·fea·sance (nŏn-fē′zəns) *n.* Failure to perform an act that is either an official duty or a legal requirement. [NON– + (MIS)FEASANCE.]

non·fer·rous (nŏn-fĕr′əs) *adj.* **1.** Not composed of or containing iron. **2.** Of or relating to metals other than iron.

non·fic·tion (nŏn-fĭk′shən) *n.* **1.** Prose works other than fiction. **2.** The category of literature comprising works of this kind. —**non·fic′tion·al** *adj.*

non gra·ta (nŏn grä′tə, grăt′ə, nōn) *adj.* Not welcome; not approved. [< PERSONA NON GRATA.]

non-Hodg·kin's lymphoma (nŏn′hŏj′kĭnz) *n.* Any of various malignant lymphomas producing symptoms similar to those of Hodgkin's disease but distinguished from it by the type of lymphocyte from which the lymphoma cells originated.

no·nil·lion (nō-nĭl′yən) *n.* **1.** The cardinal number equal to 10^{30}. **2.** *Chiefly British* The cardinal number equal to 10^{54}. [Fr. : Lat. *nōnus,* ninth; see NONA– + Fr. *million,* million (< OFr. *milion;* see MILLION).] —**no·nil′lion** *adj.*

no·nil·lionth (nō-nĭl′yənth) *n.* **1.** The ordinal number matching the number nonillion in a series. **2.** One of nonillion equal parts. —**no·nil′lionth** *adv. & adj.*

non·in·duc·tive (nŏn′ĭn-dŭk′tĭv) *adj.* *Electricity* Having low or zero inductance.

non·in·er·tial frame (nŏn′ĭ-nûr′shəl) *n.* An accelerating reference frame for which Newton's laws of motion do not apply.

non·in·ter·ven·tion (nŏn′ĭn-tər-vĕn′shən) *n.* Failure or refusal to intervene, esp. in the affairs of another nation. —**non′in·ter·ven′tion·ist** *n.*

non·in·va·sive (nŏn′ĭn-vā′sĭv) *adj.* **1.** Not penetrating the body, as by incision or injection: *noninvasive surgery.* **2.** Not invading healthy tissue: *noninvasive cancer.*

non·is·sue (nŏn′ĭsh′ōō) *n.* A matter of so little import that it does not merit controversy and comment.

non·join·der (nŏn-join′dər) *n.* Omission of a party, plaintiff, defendant, or cause of action that should have been included as a part of an action or suit.

non·ju·ror (nŏn-jŏor′ər, -ôr′) *n.* **1.** One who refuses to take an oath, as of allegiance. **2. Nonjuror** A beneficed Anglican clergyman who refused to take the Oaths of Allegiance and Supremacy to William and Mary and their successors after the Glorious Revolution of 1688. [NON– + JUROR, one who takes an oath (obsolete).] —**non·jur′ing** *adj.*

non·lin·e·ar (nŏn-lĭn′ē-ər) *adj.* **1.** Not in a straight line. **2.** *Mathematics* Containing a variable with an exponent other than one. Used of an equation. **3a.** Of or relating to a system of equations whose effects are not proportional to their causes. **b.** Of or relating to a device whose behavior is described by such a system of equations. **c.** Of or relating to the output of such a device.

non·lit·er·ate (nŏn-lĭt′ər-ĭt) *adj.* Having no written language; preliterate. —**non·lit′er·ate** *n.*

non·met·al (nŏn-mĕt′l) *n.* Any of a number of elements, such as sulfur, that lack the physical and chemical properties of metals.

non·me·tal·lic (nŏn′mə-tăl′ĭk) *adj.* **1.** Not metallic. **2.** *Chemistry* Of, relating to, or being a nonmetal.

non·mor·al (nŏn-môr′əl, -mŏr′-) *adj.* **1.** Unrelated to moral or ethical considerations. **2.** Having no moral or ethical standards; lacking a moral sense.

no-no (nō′nō′) *n., pl.* **-noes** *Informal* **1.** Something unacceptable or impermissible. **2.** A social blunder; a faux pas.

non·ob·jec·tive (nŏn′əb-jĕk′tĭv) *adj.* Of, relating to, or being a style of art in which natural objects are not represented realistically; abstract.

non ob·stan·te (nŏn′ əb-stän′tē, -stän′-, nōn′) *prep.* Notwithstanding. [ME < Med.Lat. *nōn obstante (aliquō statūtō in contrārium),* notwithstanding (any statute to the contrary) : Lat. *nōn,* not + Lat. *obstante,* ablative pr. part. of *obstāre,* to withstand.]

no·non·sense (nō-nŏn′sĕns′, -səns) *adj.* Not tolerating irrelevancies; direct, efficient, and practical: *no-nonsense talk.*

non·ox·y·nol-9 (nŏn-ŏk′sə-nôl′nīn′, -nŏl′-, -nōl′-) *n.* A spermicide widely used in contraceptive creams, foams, and lubricants. [*non(ane),* alkane having nine carbons (< Lat. *nōnus,* ninth; see NOON) + OXY– + (ETHA)NOL.]

non·pa·reil (nŏn′pə-rĕl′) *adj.* Having no equal; peerless: *a nonpareil artist.* ❖ *n.* **1.** A person or thing that has no equal; a paragon. **2.** See **painted bunting. 3.** A small flat chocolate drop covered with white pellets of sugar. [ME *nounparalle* < OFr. *nonpareil* : *non-,* non- + *pareil,* equal (< VLat. **pariculus,* dim. of Lat. *pār,* equal; see **perə-** in App.).]

non·par·ti·san (nŏn-pär′tĭ-zən, -sən) *adj.* Based on, influenced by, affiliated with, or supporting no single political party. —**non·par′ti·san** *n.* —**non·par′ti·san·ship′** *n.*

non·per·sis·tent (nŏn′pər-sĭs′tənt) *adj.* Having a short life or existence under natural conditions.

non·per·son (nŏn-pûr′sən) *n.* A person whose existence is systematically ignored or concealed, esp. for political reasons.

non·plus (nŏn-plŭs′) *tr.v.* **-plused, -plus·ing, -plus·es** also **-plussed, -plus·sing, -plus·ses** To put at a loss as to what to think, say, or do; bewilder. ❖ *n.* A state of perplexity, confusion, or bewilderment. [< Lat. *nōn plūs,* no more : *nōn,* not; see NON– + *plūs,* more; see **pelə-¹** in App.]

non·point (nŏn′point′) *adj.* Of or relating to pollution lacking a specific identifiable source, as after being diffused by the movement of rainfall or snowmelt over or through contaminated ground.

non·pre·scrip·tion (nŏn′prĭ-skrĭp′shən) *adj.* Sold legally without a physician's prescription; over-the-counter.

non·pro·duc·tive (nŏn′prə-dŭk′tĭv) *adj.* **1.** Not yielding or

---

non′ag·gres′sion *n.*	**non′dair′y** *adj.*	**non·mar′ket·a·ble** *adj.*	**non′read′er** *n.*
non′be·liev′er *n.*	**non′de·duct′i·ble** *adj.*	**non′neg′a·tive** *adj.*	**non′re·cov′er·a·ble** *adj.*
non′busi′ness *adj.*	**non·e·las′tic** *adj.*	**non′nu′cle·ar** *adj.*	**non′smok′er** *n.*
non′ca·lor′ic *adj.*	**non′ex·plo′sive** *adj. & n.*	**non′ob·serv′ance** *n.*	**non′ste·roi′dal** *adj. & n.*
non·can′di·date′ *n.*	**non·flam′ma·ble** *adj.*	**non′ob·serv′ant** *adj.*	**non′tar′get** *adj.*
non′com·pli′ance *n.*	**non′food′** *adj.*	**non′ob·serv′ant·ly** *adv.*	**non′ten′ured** *adj.*
non′com·pli′ant *adj. & n.*	**non′i·den′ti·cal** *adj.*	**non′po′lar** *adj.*	**non·us′er** *n.*
non′con·trib′u·to′ry *adj.*	**non′judg·men′tal** *adj.*	**non′pro·fes′sion·al** *n. & adj.*	**non′vot′er** *n.*
non′cred′it *adj.*	**non·lead′ed** *adj.*	**non′pro·fes′sion·al·ly** *adv.*	

producing: *nonproductive land.* **2.** Not engaged in the direct production of goods. ❖ *n.* A person who produces no useful work. —**non′pro·duc′tive·ly** *adv.*

non·prof·it (nŏn-prŏf′ĭt) *adj.* Not seeking or producing a profit or profits: *a nonprofit organization.*

non·pro·lif·er·a·tion (nŏn′prə-lĭf′ə-rā′shən) *adj.* Of, relating to, or calling for an end to the acquisition of nuclear weapons by additional nations: *a nonproliferation treaty.*

non pro·se·qui·tur (nŏn′ rə-sĕk′wĭ-tər, nŏn′) *n.* The judgment entered against a plaintiff who fails to appear in court to prosecute a suit. [LLat. *nōn prosequitur,* he does not prosecute.]

non·re·com·bi·nant (nŏn′rē-kŏm′bə-nənt) *adj.* Not resulting from or involved in genetic recombination.

non·re·new·a·ble (nŏn′rĭ-nōō′ə-bəl, -nyōō′-) *adj.* **1.** That cannot be renewed: *a nonrenewable license.* **2.** Of or relating to an energy source, such as oil, or a natural resource, such as a metallic ore, that cannot be replenished.

non·rep·re·sen·ta·tion·al (nŏn′rĕp′rĭ-zĕn-tā′shə-nəl) *adj.* Of, relating to, or being a style of art in which natural objects are not represented realistically; nonobjective.

non·res·i·dent (nŏn-rĕz′ĭ-dənt, -dĕnt′) *adj.* **1.** Not living in a particular place: *nonresident students.* **2.** *Chiefly New England* Of or relating to real estate owned by persons who are resident only in the summer. —**non·res′i·dence, non·res′i·den·cy** *n.* —**non·res′i·dent** *n.*

non·re·sis·tance (nŏn′rĭ-zĭs′təns) *n.* **1.** The practice or principle of complete obedience to authority even if unjust or arbitrary. **2.** The practice or principle of refusing to resort to force even in defense against violence.

non·re·sis·tant (nŏn′rĭ-zĭs′tənt) *adj.* **1.** Not resistant, esp. to a disease or an environmental factor, such as heat or moisture. **2.** Submissively obedient. —**non′re·sis′tant** *n.*

non·re·stric·tive (nŏn′rĭ-strĭk′tĭv) *adj.* **1.** Not restrictive: *nonrestrictive zoning.* **2.** *Grammar* Of, relating to, or being a subordinate clause or phrase that describes but does not identify or restrict what it modifies, as the clause *who live in a small house* in the sentence *The Smiths, who live in a small house, have 11 cats.*

non·re·turn·a·ble (nŏn′rĭ-tûr′nə-bəl) *adj.* **1.** That cannot be returned. **2.** Not exchangeable for a deposit.

non·rig·id (nŏn-rĭj′ĭd) *adj.* **1.** Not rigid: *a nonrigid frame.* **2.** Of, relating to, or being a lighter-than-air aircraft that holds its shape by gas pressure.

non·sched·uled (nŏn-skĕj′ōōld) *adj.* Operating without a regular schedule of flights: *a nonscheduled airline.*

non·sec·tar·i·an (nŏn′sĕk-târ′ē-ən) *adj.* Not limited to or associated with a particular religious denomination. —**non′sec·tar′i·an·ism** *n.*

non·self (nŏn-sĕlf′) *n.* That which the immune system identifies as foreign to the body.

non·sense (nŏn′sĕns′, -səns) *n.* **1.** Words or signs having no intelligible meaning. **2.** Foolish or absurd subject matter, behavior, or language. **3.** Extravagant foolishness or frivolity. **4.** Matter of little or no importance or usefulness. **5.** Insolent talk or behavior; impudence. ❖ *adj. Genetics* Of or relating to a mutation in a structural gene that alters a nucleotide triplet so that it cannot code for an amino acid, thus prematurely terminating synthesis of a protein. ❖ *interj.* Used to express disagreement or exasperation.

nonsense verse *n.* Verse characterized by humor or whimsy and often featuring nonsense words.

non·sen·si·cal (nŏn-sĕn′sĭ-kəl) *adj.* **1.** Lacking intelligible meaning: *a nonsensical jumble of words.* **2.** Foolish; absurd: *nonsensical ideas.* —**non·sen′si·cal′i·ty** (-kăl′ĭ-tē), **non·sen′si·cal·ness** (-kəl-nĭs) *n.* —**non·sen′si·cal·ly** *adv.*

non se·qui·tur (nŏn sĕk′wĭ-tər, -tōōr′) *n.* **1.** An inference or conclusion that does not follow from the premises or evidence. **2.** A statement that does not follow logically from what preceded it. [Lat. *nōn sequitur,* it does not follow.]

non·sex·ist (nŏn-sĕk′sĭst) *adj.* **1.** Not discriminating on the basis of gender. **2.** Not promoting sexual stereotypes.

non·sig·nif·i·cant (nŏn′sĭg-nĭf′ĭ-kənt) *adj.* **1.** Not significant. **2.** *Statistics* Having, producing, or being a value that lies within the limits for random occurrence. —**non′sig·nif′i·cance** *n.* —**non′sig·nif′i·cant·ly** *adv.*

non·skid (nŏn′skĭd′) *adj.* Designed to prevent or inhibit skidding: *nonskid tires.*

non·smok·ing (nŏn′smō′kĭng) *adj.* **1.** Not engaging in the smoking of tobacco. **2.** Designated or reserved for nonsmokers.

non·stan·dard also **non-stan·dard** (nŏn-stăn′dərd) *adj.* **1.** Varying from or not adhering to the standard: *nonstandard lengths of board.* **2.** *Linguistics* Associated with a language variety used by uneducated speakers or socially disfavored groups.

> **USAGE NOTE** The term *nonstandard* was introduced by linguists and lexicographers to describe usages and language varieties that had previously been labeled with terms such as *vulgar* and *illiterate. Nonstandard* reflects the empirical discovery that the varieties used by low-prestige groups have rich and systematic grammatical structures.

non·start·er (nŏn-stär′tər) *n.* **1.** One that fails to start. **2.** An idea, proposal, or candidate with no chance of being accepted or

successful: *eliminated nonstarters from the discussion.*

non·stick (nŏn′stĭk′) *adj.* Permitting easy removal of adherent food particles: *a frying pan with a nonstick surface.*

non·stop (nŏn′stŏp′) *adj.* **1.** Made or done without stops: *a nonstop flight.* **2.** Unceasing; unremitting. —**non′stop′** *adv.*

non·such (nŭn′sŭch′) *n.* Variant of **nonesuch.**

non·suit (nŏn-sōōt′) *n.* A judgment against a plaintiff for failure to prosecute the case or to introduce sufficient evidence. ❖ *tr.v.* **-suit·ed, -suit·ing, -suits** To render a judgment of nonsuit against (a plaintiff). [ME, failure of a plaintiff to prosecute < AN *nounsuite : noun-,* no (< Lat. *nōn;* see NON–) + *suite,* suit; see SUIT.]

non·sup·port (nŏn′sə-pôrt′, -pōrt′) *n.* Failure to provide for the maintenance of one's legal dependents.

non·triv·i·al (nŏn-trĭv′ē-əl) *adj.* **1.** Not trivial; of some importance. **2.** *Mathematics* Of, relating to, or being an expression in which at least one variable is not equal to zero.

non trop·po (nŏn trô′pō, nŏn trŏp′pō) *adv. & adj. Music* In moderation. [Ital. : *non,* not + *troppo,* too much.]

non-U (nŏn-yōō′) *adj. Chiefly British* Not characteristic of the upper class, esp. in language usage. [NON– + U².]

non·un·ion (nŏn-yōōn′yən) *adj.* **1.** Not belonging to a labor union: *nonunion plumbers.* **2.** Not recognizing or dealing with a labor union or employing union members.

non·u·ple (nŏn′yə-pəl) *adj.* **1.** Consisting of nine parts or members. **2.** Nine times as much in size, strength, number, or amount. ❖ *n.* A number nine times larger than another. [Fr. *nonuple* (on the model of QUADRUPLE) < Lat. *nōnus,* nine. See NONA–.]

non·ver·bal (nŏn-vûr′bəl) *adj.* Not involving little or no use of words: *nonverbal communication; nonverbal tasks.*

non·vi·a·ble (nŏn-vī′ə-bəl) *adj.* **1.** Not capable of living or developing: *a nonviable fetus.* **2.** Not workable or practicable.

non·vi·o·lence (nŏn-vī′ə-ləns) *n.* **1.** Lack of violence. **2.** The doctrine, policy, or practice of rejecting violence in favor of peaceful tactics as a means of gaining political objectives. —**non·vi′o·lent** *adj.* —**non·vi′o·lent·ly** *adv.*

non·white (nŏn-hwīt′, -wīt′) *n.* A person who is not white. —**non′white′** *adj.*

non·wo·ven (nŏn-wō′vən) *adj.* Made by a process not involving weaving. Used of textiles. ❖ *n.* Material or a fabric made by a process not involving weaving.

non·ze·ro (nŏn-zîr′ō, -zē′rō) *adj.* Not equal to zero.

noo·dle¹ (nōōd′l) *n.* A narrow ribbonlike strip of dried dough, usu. made of flour, eggs, and water. [Ger. *Nudel.*]

noo·dle² (nōōd′l) *n. Slang* **1.** The human head. **2.** A weak, foolish, or stupid person. [Prob. alteration of NODDLE.]

noo·dle³ (nōōd′l) *intr.v.* **-dled, -dling, -dles** *Slang* To improvise music on an instrument idly and haphazardly. [Imit.]

nook (nōōk) *n.* **1.** A small corner, alcove, or recess, esp. one in a large room. **2.** A hidden or secluded spot. [ME *nok,* prob. of Scand. orig.; akin to Norw. dialectal *nōk,* hook.]

nook·y or **nook·ie** (nōōk′ē) *n. Vulgar Slang* Sexual intercourse. [?]

noon (nōōn) *n.* **1a.** Twelve o'clock in the daytime; midday. **b.** The time or point in the sun's path at which the sun is on the local meridian. **2.** The highest point; the zenith. **3.** *Archaic* Midnight. [ME *non* < OE *nōn,* canonical hour of nones (3 P.M. in early Middle Ages) < LLat. *nōna (hōra),* ninth (hour after sunrise), nones, fem. sing. of Lat. *nōnus,* ninth. See **newn** in App.]

noon·day (nōōn′dā′) *n.* Midday; noon.

no one *pron.* No person; nobody.

noon·tide (nōōn′tīd′) *n.* See **noon** 1.

noon·time (nōōn′tīm′) *n.* See **noon** 1.

noose (nōōs) *n.* **1.** A loop formed in a rope by a slipknot so that it binds tighter as the rope is pulled. **2.** A snare or trap. ❖ *tr.v.* **noosed, noos·ing, noos·es** **1.** To capture or hold by or as if by a noose. **2.** To make a noose of or in. [ME *nose,* prob. < OFr. *nos, nous,* knot < Lat. *nōdus.*]

Noot·ka (nōōt′kə, nōōt′-) *n., pl.* **Nootka** or **-kas** **1.** A member of a Native American people inhabiting Vancouver Island in British Columbia and Cape Flattery in northwest Washington. **2.** The Wakashan language of the Nootka.

Nootka Sound An inlet of the Pacific Ocean on the W coast of Vancouver I. in SW British Columbia, Canada.

no·pal (nō′pəl, nō-päl′, -päl′) *n.* **1.** Any of various cacti of the genera *Nopalea* and *Opuntia,* including the prickly pear and similar species. **2.** The fleshy, edible pad of such a cactus. [Am.Sp. < Nahuatl *nopalli.*]

no-par (nō′pär′) *adj.* Being without face value; having no par value: *a no-par stock certificate.*

nope (nōp) *adv. Informal* No. [Alteration of NO¹.]

nor¹ (nôr; nər *when unstressed*) *conj.* Not or; and not; not either: *neither plants nor animals.* [ME : *ne,* no; see NO¹ + *or,* or; see OR¹.]

> **USAGE NOTE** When using *neither* in a balanced construction that negates two parts of a sentence, *nor* (not *or*) must be used in the second clause: *She is neither able nor (not or) willing to go.* Similarly, when negating the second of two negative independent clauses, *nor* (not *or*) must be used: *He cannot find anyone now, nor does he expect to find anyone in the future.* Note that in such constructions, *nor* causes an inversion of the auxiliary verb and

ă	pat	oi	boy
ā	pay	ou	out
âr	care	ōō	took
ä	father	ōō	boot
ĕ	pet	ŭ	cut
ē	be	ûr	urge
ĭ	pit	th	thin
ī	pie	th	this
îr	pier	hw	which
ŏ	pot	zh	vision
ō	toe	ə	about,
ô	paw		item

Stress marks:
′ (primary);
′ (secondary), as in
lexicon (lĕk′sĭ-kŏn′)

the subject (*does he* . . .). However, when a verb is negated by *not* or *never*, and is followed by a verb phrase (but not an entire clause) that is also to be negated, either *or* or *nor* can be used: *He will not permit the change, or* (or *nor*) *even consider it.* In noun phrases of the type *no this or that, or* is actually more common than *nor: He has no experience or interest* (less frequently *nor interest*) *in chemistry. Or* is also more common than *nor* when such a noun phrase, adjective phrase, or adverb phrase is introduced by *not: They were not rich or happy.* See Usage Notes at **neither, or¹.**

nor² (nôr, nər *when unstressed*) *conj. Chiefly Southern & Midland US* Than. [ME, perh. ult. < *nor*, no. See NOR¹.]

NOR (nôr) *n.* A logical operator that consists of a logical OR followed by a logical NOT and returns a true value only if both operands are false.

Nor. *abbr.* **1.** Norman **2.** or **nor. a.** north **b.** northern **3a.** Norway **b.** Norwegian

nor– *pref.* An unaltered parent compound: *norepinephrine.* [Short for NORMAL.]

NORAD *abbr.* North American Aerospace (formerly Air) Defense Command

nor·a·dren·a·line (nôr′ə-drĕn′ə-lĭn) *n.* See **norepinephrine.**

nor·ad·re·ner·gic (nôr′ăd-rə-nûr′jĭk) *adj.* Stimulated by or releasing norepinephrine. —**nor′ad·re·ner′gi·cal·ly** *adv.*

Nor·den·skjöld (nôr′dn-shōld′, -shəld, nōōr′dən-shœld′), Baron **Nils Adolf Erik** 1832–1901. Finnish-born Swedish explorer and geologist who was the first to navigate the Northeast Passage (1878–80).

Nor·dic (nôr′dĭk) *adj.* **1.** Of, relating to, or characteristic of Scandinavia or its peoples, languages, or cultures. **2.** Of or relating to a human physical type exemplified esp. by the tall, narrow-headed, light-skinned blond-haired peoples of Scandinavia. Not in scientific use. **3.** *Sports* Of or relating to ski competition featuring ski jumping and cross-country racing. ❖ *n.* A person of the Nordic physical type. [Fr. *nordique* < *nord*, north < OFr. *nort* < OE *north.*]

Nord·kyn (nôr′kən, -kün) **Cape** The northernmost point of the European mainland, in N Norway.

Nord·mann fir (nôrd′mən) *n.* A widely planted evergreen tree (*Abies nordmanniana*) native to Greece, Turkey, and the Caucasus and having erect reddish-brown cones. [After Alexander von Nordmann (1803–66), Finnish naturalist.]

Nord-Ost·see Ka·nal (nôrt-ôst′zä kä-näl′) See **Kiel Canal.**

nor·east·er (nôr-ē′stər) *n.* A northeaster.

nor·ep·i·neph·rine (nôr′ĕp-ə-nĕf′rĭn) *n.* A substance, $C_8H_{11}NO_3$, both a hormone and neurotransmitter, secreted by the adrenal medulla and the nerve endings of the sympathetic nervous system and used medically to cause vasoconstriction.

Nor·folk (nôr′fək, -fôk) **1.** A historical region of E England bordering on the North Sea; settled in prehistoric times and part of the Anglo-Saxon kingdom of East Anglia. **2.** An independent city of SE VA on Hampton Roads SE of Richmond; founded 1682. Pop. 234,403.

Norfolk Island An island territory of Australia in the S Pacific NE of Sydney; formerly a British penal colony.

Norfolk Island pine *n.* An evergreen tree (*Araucaria heterophylla*) with incurved decurrent needles, native to Norfolk Island and grown as an indoor plant.

Norfolk jacket *n.* A belted jacket with two box pleats in front and back. [After NORFOLK, England.]

Nor·gay (nôr′gā), **Tenzing** 1914–86. Sherpa guide who with Sir Edmund Hillary first climbed Mt. Everest (1953).

no·ri (nôr′ē) *n.*, *pl.* **-ris** An edible dried preparation of red algae of the genus *Porphyra.* [J.]

no·ri·a (nôr′ē-ə, nōr′-) *n.* A water wheel with buckets attached to its rim, used to raise water from a stream, esp. for transfer to an irrigation channel. [Sp. < Ar. *nāʿūra* < Aram. *nāʿurā* < *naʿar*, to shake, roar.]

Nor·i·cum (nôr′ĭ-kəm, nŏr′-) An ancient country and province of the Roman Empire S of the Danube R. in present-day Austria W of Vienna.

No·ri·e·ga (nôr′ē-ā′gə, nōr′-), **Manuel Antonio** b. 1936. Panamanian general. As commander in chief of the Panamanian National Guard, he assumed the role of head of state (1985) despite having never been formally elected.

nor·ite (nôr′īt) *n.* See **gabbro.** [Norw. *Norge*, Norway + –ITE¹.] —**nor·it′ic** (nô-rĭt′ĭk) *adj.*

norm (nôrm) *n.* **1.** A standard, model, or pattern regarded as typical: *social norms.* **2.** *Mathematics* **a.** A mode. **b.** An average. **c.** The length of a vector. [Fr. *norme* < OFr. < Lat. *norma*, carpenter's square, norm. See gnō- in App.]

Norm. *abbr.* Norman

Nor·ma (nôr′mə) *n.* A constellation in the Southern Hemisphere within the Milky Way near Lupus and Ara. [Lat. *norma*, carpenter's square. See gnō- in App.]

nor·mal (nôr′məl) *adj.* **1.** Conforming with, adhering to, or constituting a norm, standard, pattern, level, or type; typical: *normal room temperature.* **2.** *Biology* Functioning or occurring in a natural way; lacking observable abnormalities or deficiencies. **3.** *Chemistry* **a.** Having one gram equivalent weight of solute per

liter. Used of a solution. **b.** Having a straight unbranched chain of carbon atoms. Used of an aliphatic hydrocarbon. **4.** *Mathematics* **a.** Being at right angles; perpendicular. **b.** Perpendicular to the direction of a tangent line to a curve or a tangent plane to a surface. **5a.** Relating to or characterized by average intelligence or development. **b.** Free from mental illness; sane. ❖ *n.* **1.** Something normal; the standard: *scored close to the normal.* **2.** The usual or expected state, form, amount, or degree. **3a.** Correspondence to a norm. **b.** An average. **4.** *Mathematics* A perpendicular, esp. a perpendicular to a line tangent to a plane curve or a plane tangent to a space curve. [ME < LLat. *normālis* < Lat., made according to the square < *norma*, carpenter's square. See gnō- in App.] —**nor′mal·ly** *adv.*

normal curve *n.* See **bell curve.**

nor·mal·cy (nôr′məl-sē) *n.* Normality.

normal distribution *n.* A theoretical frequency distribution for a set of variable data, usu. represented by a bell-shaped curve symmetrical about the mean.

normal fault *n.* A geologic fault in which the hanging wall has moved downward relative to the footwall.

nor·mal·i·ty (nôr-măl′ĭ-tē) *n.* **1.** The state or fact of being normal. **2.** *Chemistry* The concentration of a solution, expressed in gram equivalent weights of solute per liter.

nor·mal·ize (nôr′mə-līz′) *v.* **-ized, -iz·ing, -iz·es** —*tr.* **1.** To make normal, esp. to cause to conform to a standard or norm: *normalizing relations with a former enemy.* **2.** To make (a text or language) regular and consistent, esp. in spelling or style. **3.** To remove strains and reduce coarse crystalline structures in (metal), esp. by heating and cooling. —*intr.* To become or return to normal. —**nor′mal·i·za′tion** (-mə-lĭ-zā′shən) *n.* —**nor′mal·iz′er** *n.*

normal mode *n.* The vibrational state of a mechanical system in which the frequency of vibration is the same in all directions.

normal school *n.* A school that trains teachers, chiefly for the elementary grades. [Transl. of Fr. *école normale* (so called because the first school so named was intended as a model).]

Nor·man¹ (nôr′mən) *n.* **1a.** A member of a Scandinavian people who settled in northern France in the tenth century. **b.** A descendant of this people, esp. one ruling or inhabiting England from the time of the Norman Conquest. **2.** A native or inhabitant of Normandy. ❖ *adj.* **1.** Of or relating to Normandy, the Normans, their culture, or their language. **2.** Of or being a style of Romanesque architecture that was introduced from Normandy into England before 1066 and flourished until about 1200. [ME < OFr. *Normant* < ON *Nordhmadhr* (*nordhr*, north + *madhr*, man) and < OE *Norman* (var. of *Northman* : *north*, north + *man*, man; see man-¹ in App.).]

Nor·man² (nôr′mən) A city of central OK S of Oklahoma City. Pop. 95,694.

Norman, Jessye b. 1945. Amer. operatic soprano acclaimed for her versatility and diverse repertoire.

Norman Conquest *n.* The conquest of England by the Normans under William the Conqueror, esp. the Battle of Hastings in 1066.

Nor·man·dy (nôr′mən-dē) A historical region and former province of NW France on the English Channel. Its beaches were the focal point of Allied landings on D-day (Jun. 6, 1944) in World War II.

Norman French *n.* The dialect of Old French used in medieval Normandy.

nor·ma·tive (nôr′mə-tĭv) *adj.* Of, relating to, or prescribing a norm or standard: *normative grammar.* —**nor′ma·tive·ly** *adv.* —**nor′ma·tive·ness** *n.*

nor·mo·ten·sive (nôr′mō-tĕn′sĭv) *adj.* Having normal blood pressure; not hypertensive or hypotensive. [Lat. *norma*, norm; see NORM + (HYPER)TENSIVE.] —**nor′mo·ten′sive** *n.*

nor·mo·ther·mi·a (nôr′mō-thûr′mē-ə) *n.* A condition of normal body temperature. [Lat. *norma*, norm; see NORM + THERM(O)- + –IA¹.] —**nor′mo·ther′mic** *adj.*

Norn (nôrn) *n. Mythology* Any of the three goddesses of fate in Norse myth.

Nor·ris (nôr′ĭs, nŏr′-), **Benjamin Franklin Jr.** ("**Frank**") 1870–1902. Amer. writer noted for *McTeague* (1899).

Norris, George William 1861–1944. Amer. politician from NE who drafted the 20th Amendment to the US Constitution, which limits the President to two full terms.

Norr·kö·ping (nôr′chœ′pĭng) A city of SE Sweden on **Norrköping Bay,** an inlet of the Baltic Sea SW of Stockholm; chartered 1384. Pop. 120,798.

Norse (nôrs) *adj.* **1.** Of or relating to medieval Scandinavia or its peoples, languages, or cultures. **2.** Of or relating to Norway or its people, language, or cultures. **3.** Of, relating to, or being the branch of the North Germanic languages that includes Norwegian, Icelandic, and Faroese. ❖ *n.* **1a.** The people of Scandinavia. **b.** The people of Norway; the Norwegians. **c.** Speakers of Norwegian, Icelandic, and Faroese. **2a.** See **North Germanic. b.** Any of the West Scandinavian languages, esp. Norwegian. [Prob. Du. *Noorsch*, Scand. < MDu. *Noortsch* < *nort*, north.]

Norse·man (nôrs′mən) *n.* A member of any of the peoples of medieval Scandinavia.

north (nôrth) *n.* **1a.** The direction along a meridian 90° counterclockwise from east; the direction to the left of sunrise. **b.** The

Norman¹
St. Mary's Parish Church,
Iffley, England

Jessye Norman

cardinal point on the compass located at 0°. **2.** An area or region lying in the north. **3.** often **North a.** The northern part of the earth. **b.** The northern part of a region or country. **4. North** The northern part of the United States, esp. the states that fought for the Union in the Civil War. ❖ *adj.* **1.** To, toward, of, facing, or in the north. **2.** Originating in or coming from the north: *a cold north wind.* ❖ *adv.* In, from, or toward the north. [ME < OE.]

North, Frederick. 2nd Earl of Guilford. Known as "Lord North." 1732–92. British politician who served as prime minister (1770–82) under George III.

North Africa A region of N Africa generally considered to include the modern-day countries of Morocco, Algeria, Tunisia, and Libya. —**North African** *adj. & n.*

North America The N continent of the Western Hemisphere, extending N from the Colombia-Panama border and including Central America, Mexico, the islands of the Caribbean Sea, the US, Canada, the Arctic Archipelago, and Greenland. —**North American** *adj. & n.*

North•amp•ton (nôr-thămp′tən, nôrth-hămp′-) A borough of central England NNW of London. Pop. 158,900.

North Atlantic Ocean The N part of the Atlantic, extending N from the equator to the Arctic Ocean.

north•bound (nôrth′bound′) *adj.* Going toward the north.

north by east *n.* The direction or compass point halfway between due north and north-northeast, or 11°15′ east of due north. ❖ *adv. & adj.* Toward or from north by east.

north by west *n.* The direction or compass point halfway between due north and north-northwest, or 11°15′ west of due north. ❖ *adv. & adj.* Toward or from north by west.

North Canadian River A river rising in NE NM and flowing c. 1,223 km (760 mi) to the Canadian R.

North Car•o•li•na (kăr′ə-lī′nə) A state of the SE US bordering on the Atlantic Ocean; admitted as one of the original Thirteen Colonies in 1789. It was part of the province of Carolina until 1691. Cap. Raleigh. Pop. 8,049,313. —**North Car•o•lin′i•an** (-lĭn′ē-ən) *adj. & n.*

North Channel A strait between Scotland and Northern Ireland connecting the Atlantic Ocean with the Irish Sea.

North•cliffe (nôrth′klĭf′), Viscount. See **Alfred Charles William Harmsworth.**

North Dakota A state of the N-central US bordering on Canada; admitted as the 39th state in 1889. Cap. Bismarck. Pop. 642,200. —**North Dakotan** *adj. & n.*

North Downs See **Downs.**

north•east (nôrth-ēst′, nôr-ēst′) *n.* **1.** The direction or compass point halfway between due north and due east, or 45° east of due north. **2.** An area or region lying in the northeast. **3. Northeast** A region of the northeast United States, generally including the New England states, New York, and sometimes Pennsylvania and New Jersey. ❖ *adj.* **1.** To, toward, of, facing, or in the northeast. **2.** Originating in or coming from the northeast: *a northeast wind.* ❖ *adv.* In, from, or toward the northeast. —**north′east′ern** *adj.*

northeast by east *n.* The direction or compass point halfway between northeast and east-northeast, or 56°15′ east of due north. ❖ *adv. & adj.* Toward or from northeast by east.

northeast by north *n.* The direction or compass point halfway between northeast and north-northeast, or 33°45′ east of due north. ❖ *adv. & adj.* Toward or from northeast by north.

north•east•er (nôrth-ē′stər, nôr-ē′-) *n.* A storm or gale blowing from the northeast.

north•east•er•ly (nôrth-ē′stər-lē, nôr-ē′-) *adj.* **1.** Situated toward the northeast. **2.** Coming or being from the northeast. —**north•east′er•ly** *adv.*

Northeast Passage A water route along the N coast of Europe and Asia between the Atlantic and Pacific oceans.

north•east•ward (nôrth-ēst′wərd, nôr-ēst′-) *adv. & adj.* Toward, to, or in the northeast. ❖ *n.* A northeastward direction, point, or region. —**north•east′ward•ly** *adv. & adj.* —**north•east′wards** *adv.*

north•er (nôr′thər) *n.* A sudden cold gale coming from the north.

north•er•ly (nôr′thər-lē) *adj.* **1.** Situated toward the north. **2.** Coming or being from the north. ❖ *n., pl.* **-lies** A storm or wind coming from the north. —**north′er•ly** *adv.*

north•ern (nôr′thərn) *adj.* **1.** Situated in, toward, or facing the north. **2.** Coming from the north: *northern breezes.* **3.** Native to or growing in the north. **4.** often **Northern** Of, relating to, or characteristic of northern regions or the North. **5.** Being north of the equator. [ME *northerne* < OE.] —**north′ern•ness′** *n.*

Northern Cross *n.* See **Cygnus.**

Northern Crown *n.* See **Corona Borealis.**

Northern Dvina See **Dvina** 1.

north•ern•er also **North•ern•er** (nôr′thər-nər) *n.* A native or inhabitant of the north, esp. the northern United States.

northern harrier *n.* A slim-bodied marsh hawk (*Circus cyaneus*) found in marshy areas of northern North America and Eurasia and having an owllike face and a white patch on the tail.

Northern Hemisphere *n.* **1.** The half of the earth north of the equator. **2.** *Astronomy* The half of the celestial sphere north of the celestial equator.

Northern Ireland A division of the United Kingdom in the NE section of the island of Ireland occupying much of the ancient Irish kingdom of Ulster and often known by that name; colonized by the British in the 17th cent. and a part of the United Kingdom since 1920. Cap. Belfast. Pop. 1,488,077.

Northern Kingdom See **Israel²**.

northern lights *pl.n.* See **aurora borealis.**

Northern Mariana Islands A commonwealth in political union with the US comprising most of the Mariana Islands (except Guam) in the W Pacific Ocean. Cap. Saipan. Pop. 52,284.

north•ern•most (nôr′thərn-mōst′) *adj.* Farthest north.

northern oriole *n.* A species of American songbird (*Icterus galbula*) composed of two subspecies, the Baltimore and Bullock's orioles.

Northern Paiute *n.* **1.** See **Paiute** 1. **2.** The Uto-Aztecan language of the Northern Paiute.

northern pike *n.* See **pike²** 1.

Northern Shoshone *n.* See **Shoshone** 1a.

Northern Spy *n.* A large yellowish-red late-ripening apple. [?]

North Frigid Zone See **Frigid Zone.**

North Frisian Islands See **Frisian Islands.**

North Germanic *n.* A subdivision of the Germanic languages including Norwegian, Icelandic, Swedish, Danish, and Faroese.

north•ing (nôr′thĭng, -thĭng) *n.* **1.** The difference in latitude between two positions as a result of a movement to the north. **2.** Progress toward the north.

North Island An island of New Zealand separated from South I. by Cook Strait.

North Korea A country of NE Asia on the Korean Peninsula; present boundaries est. after the cease-fire ending the Korean War (1950–53). Cap. Pyongyang. Pop. 23,904,000. —**North Korean** *adj. & n.*

north•land also **North•land** (nôrth′lănd′, -lənd) *n.* A region in the north of a country or an area. —**north′land′er** *n.*

North•man (nôrth′mən) *n.* A Norseman.

north-north•east (nôrth′nôrth-ēst′, nôr′nôr-ēst′) *n.* The direction or compass point halfway between due north and northeast, or 22°30′ east of due north. ❖ *adj.* To, toward, of, facing, or in the north-northeast. ❖ *adv.* In, from, or toward the north-northeast.

north-north•west (nôrth′nôrth-wĕst′, nôr′nôr-wĕst′) *n.* The direction or compass point halfway between due north and northwest, or 22°30′ west of due north. ❖ *adj.* To, toward, of, facing, or in the north-northwest. ❖ *adv.* In, from, or toward the north-northwest.

North Pacific Ocean The N part of the Pacific Ocean, extending from the equator to the Arctic Ocean.

North Platte River A river rising in N CO and flowing c. 1,094 km (680 mi) into SE WY then through W-central NE, where it joins the South Platte R. to form the Platte R.

North Polar Region See **Polar Regions.**

North Pole *n.* **1a.** The northern end of the earth's axis of rotation, a point in the Arctic Ocean. **b.** The celestial zenith of this terrestrial point. **c. north pole** The northern end of the axis of rotation of a planet or other celestial body. **2. north pole** The north-seeking magnetic pole of a straight magnet.

North River An estuary of the Hudson R. between NJ and New York City flowing into Upper New York Bay.

North Saskatchewan A river of S-central Canada flowing c. 1,223 km (760 mi) from the Rocky Mts. in W Alberta to central Saskatchewan, where it joins the South Saskatchewan R. to form the Saskatchewan R.

North Sea An arm of the Atlantic Ocean between Great Britain and NW Europe connected with the English Channel by the Strait of Dover.

North Slope A region of N AK between the Brooks Range and the Arctic Ocean.

North Star *n.* See **Polaris.**

North Temperate Zone See **Temperate Zone.**

North•um•ber•land Strait (nôr-thŭm′bər-lənd) An arm of the Gulf of St. Lawrence separating Prince Edward I. from New Brunswick and Nova Scotia in SE Canada.

North•um•bri•a (nôr-thŭm′brē-ə) An Anglo-Saxon kingdom of N England formed in the 7th cent. Much of it fell to Danes in the 9th cent. and was annexed to Wessex in 954.

North•um•bri•an (nôr-thŭm′brē-ən) *adj.* **1.** Of or relating to Northumbria or its Old English dialect. **2.** Of or relating to the former or present-day county of Northumberland in northeast England. ❖ *n.* **1.** A native or inhabitant of Northumbria. **2.** A native or inhabitant of Northumberland. **3.** The Old English dialect of Northumbria.

North Vietnam A former country of SE Asia (1954–75); now part of Vietnam. —**North Vietnamese** *adj. & n.*

north•ward (nôrth′wərd) *adv. & adj.* Toward, to, or in the north. ❖ *n.* A northern direction, point, or region. —**north′ward•ly** *adv. & adj.* —**north′wards** *adv.*

north•west (nôrth-wĕst′, nôr-wĕst′) *n.* **1.** The direction or compass point halfway between due north and due west, or 45° west of due north. **2.** An area or region lying in the northwest. **3. Northwest a.** A historical region of the north-central United States west of the Mississippi River and north of the Missouri River. **b.** A region of the northwest United States, generally in-

North Korea

cluding Washington, Oregon, and Idaho. ❖ *adj.* **1.** To, toward, of, facing, or in the northwest. **2.** Originating in or coming from the northwest. ❖ *adv.* In, from, or toward the northwest. —**north•west′ern** *adj.*

northwest by north *n.* The direction or compass point halfway between northwest and north-northwest, or 33°45′ west of due north. ❖ *adv. & adj.* Toward or from northwest by north.

northwest by west *n.* The direction or compass point halfway between northwest and west-northwest, or 56°15′ west of due north. ❖ *adv. & adj.* Toward or from northwest by west.

north•west•er (nôrth-wĕs′tər, nôr-wĕs′-) *n.* A storm or gale blowing from the northwest.

north•west•er•ly (nôrth-wĕs′tər-lē, nôr-wĕs′-) *adj.* **1.** Situated toward the northwest. **2.** Coming or being from the northwest. —**north•west′er•ly** *adv.*

North-West Frontier Province A historical region of NW Pakistan on the Afghanistan border; traditional home of the Pathans, an Indo-Iranian people.

Northwest Passage A water route from the Atlantic to the Pacific through the Arctic Archipelago of N Canada and along the N coast of AK.

Northwest Territories A territory of N Canada between Yukon Territory and Nunavut and including islands of the W Arctic Archipelago. Original territory formed 1870; Alberta and Saskatchewan were carved out in 1905 and in 1999 it was divided again, with the E portion becoming the new territory of Nunavut. Cap. Yellowknife. Pop. 64,402.

Northwest Territory Formerly **Old Northwest**. A historical region of the N-central US extending from the Ohio and Mississippi rivers to the Great Lakes; officially designated a territory in 1787.

north•west•ward (nôrth-wĕst′wərd) *adv. & adj.* Toward, to, or in the northwest. ❖ *n.* A northwestward direction, point, or region. —**north•west′ward•ly** *adv. & adj.* —**north•west′wards** *adv.*

North Yemen The former country of Yemen (1962–90).

Nor•ton (nôr′tn), **Charles Eliot** 1827–1908. Amer. educator who founded *The Nation* (1865).

Norton Sound An inlet of the Bering Sea in W AK S of Seward Peninsula.

Norw. *abbr.* **1.** Norway **2.** Norwegian

Nor•walk (nôr′wôk′) **1.** A city of S CA NNE of Long Beach; settled in the 1850s. Pop. 103,298. **2.** A city of SW CT on Long Island Sound NE of Stamford. Pop. 82,951.

Nor•way (nôr′wā′) A country of N Europe in the W part of the Scandinavian Peninsula; unified in the 12th cent. and achieved independence from Sweden in 1905. Cap. Oslo. Pop. 4,325,000.

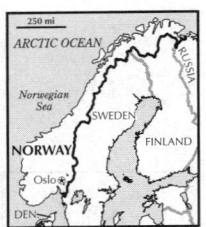

Norway

Norway maple *n.* A tall Eurasian tree (*Acer platanoides*) having greenish-yellow flowers and drooping fruits with horizontally spreading wings.

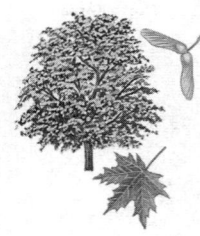

Norway maple
Acer platanoides

Norway pine *n.* See **red pine.** [After *Norway* in southwest Maine.]

Norway rat *n.* The common domestic rat (*Rattus norvegicus*), highly destructive and found worldwide.

Norway spruce *n.* A tall evergreen tree (*Picea abies*) native to Europe and having long dark green needles.

Nor•we•gian (nôr-wē′jən) *adj.* Of or relating to Norway or its people, language, or culture. ❖ *n.* **1a.** A native or inhabitant of Norway. **b.** A person of Norwegian descent. **2a.** Dano-Norwegian. **b.** New Norwegian. [< Med.Lat. *Norvegia,* Norway (influenced by NORWAY) < ON *Norvegr* : perh. *nordhr,* north + *vegr,* region; see **wegh-** in App.]

Norwegian elkhound *n.* Any of a Scandinavian breed of hunting dog, having a compact body, heavy grayish coat, and a tail that curls over the back.

Norwegian Sea A section of the Atlantic Ocean off the coast of Norway N of the North Sea.

Nor•wich (nôr′ĭch) A borough of E England NE of London; sacked by Danes in the 11th cent. and devastated by the Black Death in 1348. Pop. 128,050.

nos. or **Nos.** *abbr.* numbers

n.o.s. *abbr.* not otherwise specified

nose (nōz) *n.* **1.** The part of the human face or the forward part of the head of other vertebrates that contains the nostrils and organs of smell and forms the beginning of the respiratory tract. **2.** The sense of smell: *a dog with a good nose.* **3.** The ability to detect, sense, or discover as if by smell: *has a nose for gossip.* **4.** The characteristic smell of a wine or liqueur; bouquet. **5.** *Informal* The nose considered as a symbol of prying. **6.** Something, such as the forward end of an aircraft, that resembles a nose. **7.** A very short distance or narrow margin: *won the race by a nose.* ❖ *v.* **nosed, nos•ing, nos•es** —*tr.* **1.** To find out by or as if by smell: *nosed out the hiding place.* **2.** To touch with the nose; nuzzle. **3.** To move, push, or make with or as if with the nose. **4.** To advance the forward part of cautiously. —*intr.* **1.** To smell or sniff. **2.** *Informal* To search or inquire meddlesomely; snoop or pry: *nosing around for opportunities.* **3.** To advance with caution. —*phrasal verb:* **nose out** To defeat by a narrow margin. —*idioms:* **down (one's) nose** *Informal* With disapproval, contempt, or arrogance. **on the nose** Exactly; precisely. **under (someone's) nose** In plain view. [ME < OE *nosu.* See **nas-** in App.]

Norwegian elkhound

nose•bag (nōz′băg′) *n.* See **feedbag.**

nose•band (nōz′bănd′) *n.* The part of a bridle or halter that passes over an animal's nose.

nose•bleed (nōz′blēd′) *n.* A nasal hemorrhage; bleeding from the nose.

nose cone *n.* The forwardmost, usu. separable section of a rocket or guided missile that is shaped to offer minimum aerodynamic resistance and often bears protective cladding against heat.

nose•dive (nōz′dīv′) *n.* **1.** A very steep dive of an aircraft. **2.** A sudden swift drop or plunge.

nose-dive (nōz′dīv′) *intr.v.* **-dived** or **-dove** (-dōv′), **-div•ing, -dives** To perform a nosedive. —**nose′div•er** *n.*

no-see-um (nō-sē′əm) *n.* See **punkie.** [Alteration of *no see them.*]

nose•gay (nōz′gā′) *n.* A small bunch of flowers; a bouquet. [ME : *nose,* nose; see NOSE + *gai,* joyous, ornament; see GAY.]

nose job *n. Informal* Plastic surgery on the nose, esp. to improve its appearance; rhinoplasty.

nose•piece (nōz′pēs′) *n.* **1.** A piece of armor that forms part of a helmet and protects the nose. **2.** The part of a pair of eyeglasses that fits across the nose. **3.** See **noseband.** **4.** The part of a microscope, often rotatable, to which one or more objective lenses are attached.

nose ring *n.* **1.** A ring inserted in an animal's nose. **2.** A ring worn as an ornament in the nose.

nos•ey (nō′zē) *adj.* Variant of **nosy.**

nosh (nŏsh) *Informal n.* A snack or light meal. ❖ *intr.v.* **noshed, nosh•ing, nosh•es** To eat a snack or light meal. [Yiddish *nash* < *nashn,* to eat sweets, nibble on < MHGer. *naschen,* to nibble < OHGer. *hnascōn.*] —**nosh′er** *n.*

no-show (nō′shō′) *Informal n.* One that is expected but does not appear, esp.: **a.** One who reserves a place, as on an airplane, but neither uses nor cancels the reservation. **b.** One who buys a ticket for an event but does not attend. **c.** One who unexplainedly fails to keep an appointment. ❖ *adj.* Requiring little or no actual attendance or work: *a no-show job.*

nos•ing (nō′zĭng) *n.* **1a.** The horizontally projecting edge of a stair tread. **b.** A shield covering this edge. **2.** A projecting edge of a molding.

noso– *pref.* Disease: *nosography.* [Gk. < *nosos,* a disease.]

no•sog•ra•phy (nō-sŏg′rə-fē, -zŏg′-) *n.* The systematic description of diseases. —**no•sog′ra•pher** *n.* —**no′so•graph′ic** (nō′sə-grăf′ĭk), **no′so•graph′i•cal** (-ĭ-kəl) *adj.*

no•sol•o•gy (nō-sŏl′ə-jē, -zŏl′-) *n., pl.* **-gies 1.** The branch of medicine that deals with the classification of diseases. **2.** A classification of diseases. —**no′so•log′i•cal** (-sə-lŏj′ĭ-kəl), **no′so•log′ic** (-ĭk) *adj.* —**no′so•log′i•cal•ly** *adv.* —**no•sol′o•gist** *n.*

nos•tal•gi•a (nō-stăl′jə, nə-) *n.* **1.** A bittersweet longing for things, persons, or situations of the past. **2.** The condition of being homesick; homesickness. [Gk. *nostos,* a return home; see **nes-¹** in App. + -ALGIA.] —**nos•tal′gic** (-jĭk) *adj.* —**nos•tal′gi•cal•ly** *adv.* —**nos•tal′gist** *n.*

nos•toc (nŏs′tŏk′) *n.* A freshwater blue-green alga of the genus *Nostoc,* forming spherical colonies of filaments embedded in a gelatinous substance. [NLat., coined by Paracelsus.]

Nos•tra•da•mus (nŏs′trə-dā′məs, -dä′-, nō′strə-) Orig. Michel de Notredame. 1503–66. French physician and astrologer who wrote *Centuries* (1555), a book of prophecies.

Nos•trat•ic (nə-străt′ĭk) *n.* A hypothetical language proposed as the parent language of Afro-Asiatic, Altaic, Dravidian, Indo-European, Kartvelian, Uralic-Yukaghir, and perhaps other language families. [Dan. *nostratisk* < Lat. *nostrās, nostrāt-,* belonging to our country or people < *noster,* our, ours. See **nes-²** in App.]

nos•tril (nŏs′trəl) *n.* Either of the external openings of the nose; a naris. [ME *nostrille* < OE *nosthyrl* : *nosu,* nose; see **nas-** in App. + *thyrl,* hole; see **terə-²** in App.]

nos•trum (nŏs′trəm) *n.* **1.** A medicine whose effectiveness is unproved and whose ingredients are usu. secret; a quack remedy. **2.** A favorite but untested remedy for problems or evils. [< Lat. *nostrum (remedium),* our (remedy), neut. of *noster.* See **nes-²** in App.]

nos•y or **nos•ey** (nō′zē) *adj.* **-i•er, -i•est** *Informal* **1.** Given to prying into the affairs of others. See Syns at **curious. 2.** Prying; inquisitive. —**nos′i•ly** *adv.* —**nos′i•ness** *n.*

not (nŏt) *adv.* In no way; to no degree. Used to express negation, denial, refusal, or prohibition: *I will not go.* [ME, alteration of *naught, nought.* See NAUGHT.]

USAGE NOTE In formal writing the *not only . . . but also* construction should be used so that each of its elements is followed by a construction of the same grammatical type. Instead of *She not only bought a car but also a truck,* one should write *She bought not only a car but also a truck.* • Omitting the *also* tends to intensify the second part of the construction but then it no longer functions merely as a supplement to the first part: *She is not only smart but brilliant.* See Usage Note at **only.**

NOT *n.* A logical operator that returns a false value if the operand is true and a true value if the operand is false.

no•ta (nō′tə) *n.* Plural of **notum.**

no•ta be•ne (nō′tə bĕn′ē, bĕ′nē) Used to direct attention to something esp. important. [Lat. *notā bene,* note well.]

no·ta·bil·i·ty (nō′tə-bĭl′ĭ-tē) *n., pl.* **-ties 1.** The state or quality of being eminent or worthy of notice. **2.** A prominent or notable person.

no·ta·ble (nō′tə-bəl) *adj.* **1.** Worthy of note or notice; remarkable. **2.** Characterized by excellence or distinction; eminent. See Syns at **noted**. ❖ *n.* **1.** A person of distinction or great reputation. **2.** often **Notable** One of a council of prominent persons in pre-Revolutionary France called into assembly to deliberate at times of emergency. —**no′ta·ble·ness** *n.* —**no′ta·bly** *adv.*

no·tar·i·al (nō-târ′ē-əl) *adj.* **1.** Of or relating to a notary public. **2.** Executed or drawn up by a notary public. —**no·tar′i·al·ly** *adv.*

no·ta·rize (nō′tə-rīz′) *tr.v.* **-rized, -riz·ing, -riz·es** To certify or attest to (the validity of a signature on a document, for example) as a notary public. —**no′ta·ri·za′tion** (-rĭ-zā′shən) *n.*

no·ta·ry (nō′tə-rē) *n., pl.* **-ries** A notary public. [ME *notarie* < OFr. *notaire, notarie* < Lat. *notārius,* relating to shorthand, shorthand writer < *nota,* mark. See NOTE.]

notary public *n., pl.* **notaries public** A person legally empowered to witness and certify the validity of documents and take affidavits and depositions.

no·tate (nō′tāt′) *tr.v.* **-tat·ed, -tat·ing, -tates** To put into notation. [Back-formation < NOTATION.]

no·ta·tion (nō-tā′shən) *n.* **1a.** A system of figures or symbols used in a specialized field to represent numbers, quantities, tones, or values: *musical notation.* **b.** The act or process of using such a system. **2.** A brief note; an annotation: *marginal notations.* [Lat. *notātiō, notātiōn-* < *notātus,* p. part. of *notāre,* to note < *nota,* note. See NOTE.] —**no·ta′tion·al** *adj.*

notch (nŏch) *n.* **1a.** A V-shaped cut. **b.** Such a cut used for keeping a record. **2.** A narrow pass between mountains. **3.** *Informal* A level or degree: *a notch higher.* ❖ *tr.v.* **notched, notch·ing, notch·es 1.** To cut a notch in. **2.** To record by or as if by making notches: *notched the score on a stick.* **3.** *Informal* To achieve; score. [Prob. < *a notch,* alteration of *an otch* < Fr. *oche* < OFr. < *ochier,* to notch.]

note (nōt) *n.* **1.** A brief record, esp. one written down to aid the memory. **2.** A brief informal letter. **3.** A formal written diplomatic or official communication. **4.** A comment or explanation, as on a passage in a text. **5a.** A piece of paper currency. **b.** A certificate issued by a government or a bank and sometimes negotiable as money. **c.** A promissory note. **6.** *Music* **a.** A tone of definite pitch. **b.** A symbol for such a tone, indicating pitch by its position on the staff and duration by its shape. **c.** A key of an instrument, such as a piano. **7.** The characteristic vocal sound made by a songbird or other animal. **8.** The sign of a particular quality or emotion. **9.** Importance; consequence. **10.** Notice; observation. **11.** *Obsolete* A song, melody, or tune. ❖ *tr.v.* **not·ed, not·ing, notes 1.** To observe carefully; notice. See Syns at **see**[1]. **2.** To make a note of; write down: *noted the time of each arrival.* **3.** To show; indicate. **4.** To make mention of; remark. [ME < OFr. < Lat. *nota,* annotation. See *gnō-* in App.] —**not′er** *n.*

note·book (nōt′bŏŏk′) *n.* **1.** A book of blank pages for notes. **2.** A light portable computer, usu. thinner than a laptop.

not·ed (nō′tĭd) *adj.* Distinguished by reputation; famous: *a noted physician.* —**not′ed·ly** *adv.*

> **SYNONYMS** noted, celebrated, eminent, famed, famous, illustrious, notable, preeminent, renowned These adjectives mean widely known and esteemed: *a noted author; a celebrated musician; an eminent scholar; a famed scientist; a famous actor; an illustrious judge; a notable historian; a preeminent archaeologist; a renowned painter.* **ANTONYM** obscure

note of hand *n., pl.* **notes of hand** See **promissory note**.

note·pad (nōt′păd′) *n.* A pad or tablet of usu. lined paper.

note·pa·per (nōt′pā′pər) *n.* Writing paper used esp. for brief letters or notes.

note·wor·thy (nōt′wûr′thē) *adj.* **-thi·er, -thi·est** Deserving notice or attention; notable: *a noteworthy advance in cancer research.* —**note′wor′thi·ly** *adv.* —**note′wor′thi·ness** *n.*

noth·er (nŭth′ər) *adj. Informal* Other. Usu. used in the phrase *a whole nother,* as in *That's a whole nother story.* [< alteration of ANOTHER (interpreted as *a nother*).]

noth·ing (nŭth′ĭng) *pron.* **1.** No thing; not anything: *The box held nothing.* **2.** No part; no portion: *Nothing remains of the old house.* **3.** One of no consequence, significance, or interest: *He is nothing to me.* ❖ *n.* **1.** Something that has no existence. **2.** Something that has no quantitative value; zero: *a score of two to nothing.* **3.** One that has no substance or importance; a nonentity. ❖ *adj.* Insignificant or worthless. ❖ *adv.* In no way or degree; not at all: *She looks nothing like you.* —**idioms: for nothing 1.** Free of charge. **2.** To no avail. **3.** For no reason. **nothing doing** *Informal* Certainly not. [ME < OE *nāthing : nā,* no; see NO[2] + *thing,* thing; see THING.]

> **USAGE NOTE** According to the traditional rule, *nothing* is invariably treated as a singular, even when followed by an exception phrase containing a plural noun: *Nothing except your fears stands* (not *stand*) *in your way.*

noth·ing·ness (nŭth′ĭng-nĭs) *n.* **1.** The condition or quality of being nothing; nonexistence. **2.** Empty space; a void. **3.** Lack of

consequence; insignificance. **4.** Something inconsequential or insignificant.

no·tice (nō′tĭs) *n.* **1.** The act of noting or observing; perception or attention: *That detail escaped my notice.* **2.** Respectful attention or consideration. **3.** A written or printed announcement. **4a.** A formal announcement, notification, or warning, esp. an announcement of one's intention to withdraw from an agreement or leave a job. **b.** The condition of being formally warned or notified. **5.** A printed critical review, as of a play or book. ❖ *tr.v.* **-ticed, -tic·ing, -tic·es 1.** To take notice of; observe. See Syns at **see**[1]. **2.** To perceive with the mind; detect. **3.** To comment on; mention. **4.** To treat with courteous attention. **5.** To give or file a notice of. [ME, knowledge < OFr. < Lat. *nōtitia* < *nōtus,* known, p. part. of *nōscere,* to get to know. See *gnō-* in App.]

no·tice·a·ble (nō′tĭ-sə-bəl) *adj.* **1.** Evident; observable. See Syns at **perceptible**. **2.** Worthy of notice; significant. —**no′tice·a·bil′i·ty** *n.* —**no′tice·a·bly** *adv.*

no·ti·fi·ca·tion (nō′tə-fĭ-kā′shən) *n.* **1.** The act or an instance of notifying. **2.** Something, such as a letter, by which notice is given.

no·ti·fy (nō′tə-fī′) *tr.v.* **-fied, -fy·ing, -fies 1.** To give notice to; inform: *notified them of the curfew.* **2.** *Chiefly British* To give notice of; make known. [ME *notifien* < OFr. *notifier* < Lat. *nōtificāre : nōtus,* known, p. part. of *nōscere,* to get to know; see *gnō-* in App. + *-ficāre,* -fy.] —**no′ti·fi′er** *n.*

no-till (nō′tĭl′) *n.* A cultivation system that reduces soil erosion and preserves soil nutrients by the avoidance of plowing and the reliance on herbicides.

no·tion (nō′shən) *n.* **1.** A belief or opinion. **2.** A mental image or representation; an idea or conception. **3.** A fanciful impulse; a whim. See Syns at **idea**. **4. notions** Small lightweight items for household use, such as needles and buttons. [ME *nocioun,* concept < Lat. *nōtiō, nōtiōn-* < *nōtus,* known, p. part. of *nōscere,* to get to know. See *gnō-* in App.]

no·tion·al (nō′shə-nəl) *adj.* **1.** Of, containing, or being a notion; mental or imaginary. **2.** Speculative or theoretical. **3.** *Linguistics* Conveying an idea of a thing or action; having full lexical meaning as distinguished from relational meaning. The word *did* is notional in *We did the work* and relational in *We did not agree.* —**no′tion·al·ly** *adv.*

no·to·chord (nō′tə-kôrd′) *n.* **1.** A flexible rodlike structure that forms the main support of the body in the lowest chordates; a primitive backbone. **2.** A similar structure in embryos of higher vertebrates, from which the spinal column develops. [Gk. *nōton,* back + CHORD[2].] —**no′to·chord′al** *adj.*

No·to·gae·a or **No·to·ge·a** (nō′tə-jē′ə) *n.* A zoogeographic region including Australia, New Zealand, and the islands of the SW Pacific Ocean.

no·to·ri·e·ty (nō′tə-rī′ĭ-tē) *n.* The quality or condition of being notorious; ill fame.

no·to·ri·ous (nō-tôr′ē-əs, -tōr′-) *adj.* Known widely and usu. unfavorably; infamous: *a notorious gangster.* [< Med.Lat. *nōtōrius,* well-known < Lat. *nōtus,* known, p. part. of *nōscere,* to get to know. See *gnō-* in App.] —**no·to′ri·ous·ly** *adv.* —**no·to′ri·ous·ness** *n.*

no·tor·nis (nō-tôr′nĭs) *n., pl.* **notornis** Any of several flightless New Zealand birds, now rare, of the genus *Notornis.* [NLat. *Notornis,* genus name : Gk. *notos,* south + Gk. *ornis,* bird.]

no-trump (nō′trŭmp′) *n.* **1.** A declaration to play a hand without a trump suit in bridge and other card games. **2.** A hand played without a trump suit. —**no′-trump′** *adj.*

Not·ta·way (nŏt′ə-wā′) A river of SW Quebec, Canada, flowing c. 644 km (400 mi) into James Bay.

Not·ting·ham (nŏt′ĭng-əm) A borough of central England N of Leicester. Charles I raised his standard here in 1642, marking the beginning of the English Civil War. Pop. 282,590.

no·tum (nō′təm) *n., pl.* **-ta** (-tə) The dorsal part of the thoracic segment of an insect. [NLat. *nōtum* < Gk. *nōton,* back.]

not·with·stand·ing (nŏt′wĭth-stăn′dĭng, -wĭth-) *prep.* In spite of: *We walked, notwithstanding the rain.* ❖ *adv.* All the same; nevertheless: *We proceeded, notwithstanding.* ❖ *conj.* In spite of the fact that; although. [ME *notwithstanding* (transl. of Lat. *nōn obstante*) : *not,* not; see NOT + *withstanding,* pr. part. of *withstanden,* to resist; see WITHSTAND.]

Nouak·chott (nwäk-shŏt′) The cap. of Mauritania, in the W part on the Atlantic Ocean. Pop. 150,000.

nou·gat (nōō′gət) *n.* A confection made from a sugar or honey paste into which nuts are mixed. [Fr. < Provençal < *nougo,* nut < O Provençal *noga* < VLat. **nuca* < Lat. *nux, nuc-,* nut.]

nought (nôt) *n., pron.,* & *adj.* Variant of **naught**.

Nou·mé·a (nōō-mā′ə) The cap. of New Caledonia, on the SW coast of the island of New Caledonia in the SW Pacific Ocean. Pop. 65,110.

nou·me·non (nōō′mə-nŏn′) *n., pl.* **-na** (-nə) In the philosophy of Kant, an object as it is in itself independent of the mind, as opposed to a phenomenon. [Ger. < Gk. < neut. pr. passive part. of *noein,* to perceive by thought < *nous,* mind.] —**nou′men·al** (-mə-nəl) *adj.*

noun (noun) *n.* **1.** The part of speech that is used to name a person, place, thing, quality, or action and can function as the subject or object of a verb, the object of a preposition, or an appositi-

nose ring

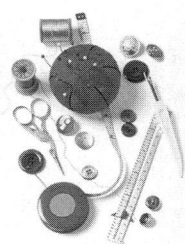

notions
sewing notions

tive. **2.** A word belonging to this part of speech. [ME, name, noun < AN < Lat. *nōmen*. See **nō‑men‑** in App.]

noun phrase *n.* A phrase whose head is a noun, as *my red car.*

nour•ish (nûr**′**ĭsh, nŭr**′**‑) *tr.v.* **-ished, -ish•ing, -ish•es 1.** To provide with food or other substances necessary for life and growth; feed. **2.** To foster the development of; promote. **3.** To keep alive; maintain: *nourish a hope.* [ME *norishen* < OFr. *norrir, norriss‑* < VLat. **nutrīre* < Lat. *nūtrīre*. See **(s)nāu‑** in App.] **—nour′ish•er** *n.*

nour•ish•ment (nûr**′**ĭsh‑mənt, nŭr**′**‑) *n.* **1a.** The act of nourishing. **b.** The state of being nourished. **2.** Something that nourishes; food.

nous (nōōs, nous) *n.* **1.** *Philosophy* **a.** Reason and knowledge as opposed to sense perception. **b.** The rational part of the individual human soul. **c.** The principle of the cosmic mind or soul responsible for the rational order of the cosmos. **d.** In Stoicism, the equivalent of Logos. **e.** In Neo‑Platonism, the image of the absolute good, containing the cosmos of intelligible beings. **2.** *Chiefly British* Good sense; shrewdness. [Gk.]

nou•veau (nōō**′**vō, nōō‑vō**′**) *adj.* New and different, often fashionably so. [< phrases such as ART NOUVEAU.]

nou•veau riche (nōō**′**vō rēsh**′**) *n., pl.* **nou•veaux riches** (nōō**′**vō rēsh**′**) One who has recently become rich, esp. one who flaunts newly acquired wealth. [Fr.]

nou•velle cuisine (nōō‑vĕl**′**) *n.* A school of French cooking that uses light low‑calorie sauces and stocks. [Fr. : *nouvelle,* new + *cuisine,* cuisine.]

nouvelle vague (väg**′**) *n.* See **new wave** 1a. [Fr.]

Nov. *abbr.* November

no•va (nō**′**və) *n., pl.* **-vae** (‑vē) or **-vas** A star that suddenly becomes much brighter and then gradually returns to its original brightness over a period of weeks to years. [NLat. *(stella) nova,* new (star), nova, fem. of Lat. *novus,* new. See **newo‑** in App.]

no•vac•u•lite (nō‑văk**′**yə‑līt**′**) *n.* A very hard, dense, even‑textured, silica‑bearing sedimentary rock used in whetstones. [Lat. *novācula,* razor + –ITE[1].]

No•va I•gua•çu (nō**′**vä ē**′**gwä‑sōō**′**) A city of SE Brazil, a suburb of Rio de Janeiro. Pop. 1,293,611.

No•va Sco•tia (nō**′**və skō**′**shə) A province of E Canada comprising a mainland peninsula and the adjacent Cape Breton I.; joined the confederation in 1867. France and Great Britain contested the area, part of Acadia, until 1763. Cap. Halifax. Pop. 909,282. **—No′va Sco′tian** *adj. & n.*

no•va•tion (nō‑vā**′**shən) *n. Law* Substitution of a new obligation for an old one. [LLat. *novātiō, novātiōn‑* < Lat., a renewing < *novātus,* p. part. of *novāre,* to make new < *novus,* new. See **newo‑** in App.]

No•va•ya Zem•lya (nō**′**və‑yə zĕm**′**lē‑ä**′**, zĭm‑lyä**′**) An archipelago of N‑central Russia in the Arctic Ocean between the Barents and Kara seas.

nov•el[1] (nŏv**′**əl) *n.* **1.** A fictional prose narrative of considerable length, typically having a plot that is unfolded by the actions, speech, and thoughts of the characters. The literary genre represented by novels. [Ult. < Ital. *novella* < OItal., piece of news, chit‑chat, tale < VLat. **novella* < neut. pl. of Lat. *novellus,* dim. of *novus,* new. See **newo‑** in App.]

nov•el[2] (nŏv**′**əl) *adj.* Strikingly new, unusual, or different. See Syns at **new.** [ME < OFr. < Lat. *novellus,* dim. of *novus.* See **newo‑** in App.] **—nov′el•ly** *adv.*

nov•el•ette (nŏv**′**ə‑lĕt**′**) *n.* A short novel.

nov•el•ist (nŏv**′**ə‑lĭst) *n.* A writer of novels.

nov•el•is•tic (nŏv**′**ə‑lĭs**′**tĭk) *adj.* Of, relating to, or characteristic of novels. **—nov′el•is′ti•cal•ly** *adv.*

nov•el•ize (nŏv**′**ə‑līz**′**) *tr.v.* **-ized, -iz•ing, -iz•es 1.** To write a novel based on. **2.** To turn into fiction; fictionalize. **—nov′el•i•za′tion** (‑ə‑lĭ‑zā**′**shən) *n.* **—nov′el•iz′er** *n.*

nov•el•la (nō‑vĕl**′**ə) *n., pl.* **-vel•las** or **-vel•le** (‑vĕl**′**ē, ‑vĕl**′**ä) **1.** A short prose tale often characterized by moral teaching or satire. **2.** A short novel. [Ital. See NOVEL[1].]

nov•el•ty (nŏv**′**əl‑tē) *n., pl.* **-ties 1.** The quality of being novel; newness. **2.** Something new and unusual; an innovation. **3.** A small mass‑produced article, such as a toy or trinket.

No•vem•ber (nō‑vĕm**′**bər) *n.* The 11th month of the year in the Gregorian calendar. See table at **calendar.** [ME *Novembre* < OFr. < Lat. *November,* ninth month < *novem,* nine. See **newn** in App.]

no•vem•de•cil•lion (nō**′**vəm‑dĭ‑sĭl**′**yən) *n.* **1.** The cardinal number equal to 10[60]. **2.** *Chiefly British* The cardinal number equal to 10[114]. [Lat. *novemdecim,* nineteen (*novem,* nine; see **newn** in App. + *decem,* ten; see DECI–) + (M)ILLION.] **—no′vem•de•cil′lion** *adj.* **—no′vem•de•cil′lionth** *adj., adv. & n.*

no•ve•na (nō‑vē**′**nə) *n., pl.* **-nas** or **-nae** (‑nē) In some western Christian churches, a nine‑day period of prayer and devotion. [Med.Lat. *novēna* < fem. of Lat. *novēnus,* nine each < *novem,* nine. See **newn** in App.]

no•ver•cal (nō‑vûr**′**kəl) *adj.* Of, relating to, or characteristic of a stepmother. [Lat. *novercālis* < *noverca,* stepmother. See **newo‑** in App.]

Nov•go•rod (nŏv**′**gə‑rŏd**′**, nôv**′**gə‑rət) A city of NW Russia SSE of St. Petersburg. Pop. 232,534.

nov•ice (nŏv**′**ĭs) *n.* **1.** A person new to a field or activity; a beginner. **2.** A person who has entered a religious order but has not yet

taken vows. [ME < OFr. < Med.Lat. *novīcius* < Lat., recently entered into a condition < Lat. *novus,* new. See **newo‑** in App.]

No•vi Sad (nō**′**vē säd**′**) A city of N Serbia on the Danube R. NW of Belgrade. Pop. 178,896.

no•vi•ti•ate also **no•vi•ci•ate** (nō‑vĭsh**′**ē‑ĭt, ‑āt**′**) *n.* **1.** The period of being a novice. **2.** A place where novices live. **3.** See **novice.** [Med.Lat. *novīciātus* < *novīcius,* novice. See NOVICE.]

no•vo•bi•o•cin (nō**′**vō‑bī**′**ə‑sĭn) *n.* An antibiotic, $C_{31}H_{36}N_2O_{11}$, produced by the actinomycete *Streptomyces nivens* and used to treat infections by gram‑positive bacteria. [Prob. Lat. *novus,* new; see NOVICE + (ANTI)BIO(TIC) + –IN.]

No•vo•cain (nō**′**və‑kān**′**) A trademark used for an anesthetic preparation of the drug procaine.

No•vo•kuz•netsk (nō**′**və‑kōōz‑nĕtsk**′**, nə‑və‑kōōz‑nyĕtsk**′**) A city of S‑central Russia SE of Novosibirsk; founded by Cossacks in 1617. Pop. 577,000.

No•vo•si•birsk (nō**′**və‑sə‑bîrsk**′**, nə‑) A city of S‑central Russia on the Ob R. E of Omsk. Pop. 1,423,860.

now (nou) *adv.* **1.** At the present time: *goods now on sale.* **2.** At once; immediately: *Stop now.* **3.** In the immediate past; very recently: *left the room just now.* **4.** At this point in the series of events; then: *The ship was now listing to port.* **5.** At times; sometimes: *now hot, now cold.* **6.** Nowadays. **7.** In these circumstances; as things are: *Now we won't be able to stay.* **8a.** Used to introduce a command, reproof, or request: *Now pay attention.* **b.** Used to indicate a change of subject or to preface a remark: *Now, let's get down to work.* ❖ *conj.* Seeing that; since: *Now that it's spring, we can travel.* ❖ *n.* The present time or moment: *wouldn't work up to now.* ❖ *adj.* **1.** Of the present time; current: *our now governor.* **2.** *Slang* Currently fashionable; trendy: *the now sound.* **—idiom: now and again** (or **then**) Occasionally. [ME < OE *nū.* See **nu‑** in App.] **—now′ness** *n.*

NOW *abbr.* National Organization for Women

NOW account (nou) *n.* An interest‑bearing savings account against which drafts may be written. [*n(egotiable) o(rder of) w(ithdrawal).*]

now•a•days (nou**′**ə‑dāz**′**) *adv.* During the present time; now. [ME *nouadaies* : *nou,* now; see NOW + *a* (var. of *on,* on; see ON) + *daies,* genitive of *dai,* day; see DAY.]

no•way (nō**′**wā**′**) *Informal adv.* also **no•ways** (‑wāz**′**) In no way or degree; nowise. ❖ *interj.* also **no way** Used to express emphatic negation.

no•where (nō**′**hwâr**′**, ‑wâr**′**) *adv.* **1.** Not anywhere. **2.** To no place or result. ❖ *n.* **1.** A remote or unknown place. **2.** A state of nonexistence: *an idea that came out of nowhere.* **—idiom: nowhere near** Not nearly: *has nowhere near enough money to buy a car.*

no•wheres (nō**′**hwârz**′**, ‑wârz**′**) *adv. Nonstandard* Nowhere.

no•whith•er (nō**′**hwĭth**′**ər, ‑wĭth**′**‑) *adv.* In no definite direction.

no‑win (nō**′**wĭn**′**) *adj. Informal* Certain to end in failure or disappointment.

no•wise (nō**′**wīz**′**) *adv.* In no way or degree; not at all.

nox•ious (nŏk**′**shəs) *adj.* **1.** Harmful to living things; injurious to health. **2.** Harmful to the mind or morals; corrupting: *noxious ideas.* [ME *noxius* < Lat. < *noxa,* damage. See **nek‑** in App.] **—nox′ious•ly** *adv.* **—nox′ious•ness** *n.*

Noyes (noiz), **John Humphrey** 1811–86. Amer. religious leader who founded (1848) an experimental community at Oneida NY.

noz•zle (nŏz**′**əl) *n.* **1.** A projecting part with an opening, as at the end of a hose, for regulating and directing a flow of fluid. **2.** *Slang* The human nose. [ME *noselle,* socket on a candlestick, dim. of *nose.* See NOSE.]

Np The symbol for the element **neptunium.**

NP *abbr.* **1.** neuropsychiatry **2.** notary public **3.** noun phrase **4.** nurse practitioner

NPR *abbr.* National Public Radio

NRA *abbr.* **1.** National Recovery Administration **2.** National Rifle Association **3.** Naval Reserve Association

NRC *abbr.* **1.** National Research Council **2.** Nuclear Regulatory Commission

ns *abbr.* nanosecond

NS *abbr.* **1.** or **N/S** New Style **2.** not specified **3.** also **N.S.** Nova Scotia **4.** nuclear ship

n/s *abbr.* not sufficient

NSA *abbr.* National Security Agency

NSAID also **Nsaid** (ĕn**′**sād**′**, ‑sĕd**′**) *n.* A nonsteroidal anti‑inflammatory drug, such as ibuprofen. [*n(on)s(teroidal) a(nti‑)i(nflammatory) d(rug).*]

NSC *abbr.* National Security Council

nsec *abbr.* nanosecond

NSF *abbr.* **1.** National Science Foundation **2.** not sufficient funds

NSPCA *abbr.* National Society for the Prevention of Cruelty to Animals

NT *abbr.* **1.** New Testament **2.** Northwest Territories

–n't Contraction of *not.*

nth (ĕnth) *adj.* **1.** Relating to an unspecified ordinal number: *ten to the nth power.* **2.** Highest; utmost: *delighted to the nth degree.* [N[2], indefinite number + –TH[3].]

nth root *n.* See **root**[1] 9a.

NTP *abbr.* normal temperature and pressure

nt. wt. *abbr.* net weight

nu (nōō, nyōō) *n.* The 13th letter of the Greek alphabet. [Gk. *nū* < Phoenician **nūn*, fish, 14th letter of the Phoenician alphabet.]

nu·ance (nōō′äns′, nyōō′-, nōō-äns′, nyōō′-) *n.* **1.** A subtle or slight degree of difference, as in meaning; a gradation. **2.** Expression or appreciation of nuances: *a performance full of nuance.* [Fr. < OFr. < *nuer*, to shade, cloud < *nue*, cloud < VLat. **nūba* < Lat. *nūbēs.*] —**nu′anced** *adj.*

nub (nŭb) *n.* **1.** A protuberance or knob. **2.** A small lump. **3.** The essence; the core. [Variant of *knub*, prob. < LGer. *knubbe* < MLGer., var. of *knobbe.*] —**nub′by** *adj.*

Nu·ba (nōō′bə, nyōō′-) *n., pl.* **Nuba 1.** A member of any of several peoples inhabiting the hills of south-central Sudan. **2.** See **Nubian 2.**

nub·bin (nŭb′ĭn) *n.* **1.** A small stunted ear of corn. **2.** A small stunted or projecting part. [< NUB.]

Nu·bi·a (nōō′bē-ə, nyōō′-) A desert region and ancient kingdom in the Nile R. valley of S Egypt and N Sudan.

Nu·bi·an (nōō′bē-ən, nyōō′-) *adj.* Of or relating to Nubia or its peoples, languages, or cultures. ❖ *n.* **1.** A native or inhabitant of Nubia. **2.** Any of a group of closely related Nilo-Saharan languages spoken in the Sudan.

Nubian Desert A desert region of NE Sudan extending E of the Nile R. to the Red Sea.

nu·bile (nōō′bĭl, -bīl′, nyōō′-) *adj.* **1.** Ready for marriage; of a marriageable age or condition. Used of young women. **2.** Sexually mature and attractive. Used of young women. [Lat. *nūbilis* < *nūbere*, to take a husband.] —**nu·bil′i·ty** (nōō-bĭl′ĭ-tē, nyōō-) *n.*

nu·cel·lus (nōō-sĕl′əs, nyōō′-) *n., pl.* **-cel·li** (-sĕl′ī) *Botany* The central portion of an ovule containing the embryo. [NLat. < *nux, nuc-*, nut.] —**nu·cel′lar** *adj.*

nu·cha (nōō′kə, nyōō′-) *n.* The nape of the neck. [ME, spinal cord < Med.Lat. < Ar. *nuḥā′*, marrow, spinal cord.] —**nu′chal** *adj.*

nucle– *pref.* Variant of **nucleo–.**

nu·cle·ar (nōō′klē-ər, nyōō′-) *adj.* **1.** *Biology* Of, relating to, or forming a nucleus: *a nuclear membrane.* **2.** *Physics* Of or relating to atomic nuclei. **3.** Using or derived from the energy of atomic nuclei: *nuclear power.* **4.** Of, using, or possessing atomic or hydrogen bombs: *nuclear war.* [< NUCLEUS.]

> **USAGE NOTE** The pronunciation (nōō′kyə-lər), which is generally considered incorrect, is an example of how a familiar phonological pattern can influence an unfamiliar one. The usual pronunciation of the final two syllables of this word is (-klē-ər), but this sequence of sounds is rare in English. Much more common is the similar sequence (-kyə-lər), which occurs in words like *particular, circular, spectacular,* and in many scientific words like *molecular, ocular,* and *vascular.*

nuclear age *n.* The atomic age.

nuclear emulsion *n.* Any of several photographic emulsions used to detect and visually display the paths of charged subatomic particles, esp. of charged cosmic ray particles.

nuclear energy *n.* **1.** The energy released by a nuclear reaction, esp. by fission or fusion. **2.** Nuclear energy regarded as a source of power.

nuclear family *n.* A family unit consisting of a mother and father and their children. [< NUCLEAR, basic, central.]

nuclear force *n.* *Physics* The strong interaction.

nu·cle·ar-free zone (nōō′klē-ər-frē′) *n.* An area in which the siting of nuclear weapons or reactors is banned.

nu·cle·ar·ize (nōō′klē-ə-rīz′, nyōō′-) *tr.v.* **-ized, -iz·ing, -iz·es** To supply with nuclear weapons or deploy nuclear weapons in: *nuclearize outer space.* —**nu′cle·ar·i·za′tion** (-ə-rī-zā′shən) *n.*

nuclear magnetic resonance *n.* The absorption of electromagnetic radiation of a specific frequency by an atomic nucleus in a strong magnetic field, used esp. in spectroscopy and in medicine to measure rates of metabolism.

nuclear magneton *n.* A unit of the magnetic moment of a nucleon.

nuclear medicine *n.* The branch of medicine that deals with the use of radionuclides in the diagnosis and treatment of disease.

nuclear membrane *n.* The double-layered membrane enclosing the nucleus of a cell.

nuclear physics *n.* (*used with a sing. verb*) The study of the forces, reactions, and internal structures of atomic nuclei.

nuclear power *n.* **1.** Power, esp. electricity, the source of which is nuclear fission or fusion. **2.** A nation or group possessing nuclear weapons.

nuclear reaction *n.* A reaction, as in fission, that alters the energy, composition, or structure of an atomic nucleus.

nuclear reactor *n.* Any of several devices in which a chain reaction is initiated and controlled, with the resulting heat typically used for power generation.

nuclear weapon *n.* A device, such as a bomb, whose great explosive power derives from the release of nuclear energy.

nuclear winter *n.* A darkening and cooling of the atmosphere with consequent devastation of surviving life, considered to be a possible outcome of large-scale nuclear war.

nu·cle·ase (nōō′klē-ās′, -āz′, nyōō′-) *n.* Any of several en-

zymes, such as endonucleases, that hydrolize nucleic acids.

nu·cle·ate (nōō′klē-ĭt) *adj.* Nucleated. ❖ *v.* (-āt′) **-at·ed, -at·ing, -ates** —*tr.* **1.** To bring together into a nucleus. **2.** To act as a nucleus for. **3.** To provide a nucleus for. —*intr.* To form a nucleus. —**nu′cle·a′tor** *n.*

nu·cle·at·ed (nōō′klē-ā′tĭd, nyōō′-) *adj.* Having a nucleus or nuclei: *the nucleated cell of a spermatozoon.*

nu·cle·i (nōō′klē-ī′, nyōō′-) *n.* A plural of **nucleus.**

nu·cle·ic acid (nōō-klē′ĭk, -klā′-, nyōō′-) *n.* Any of a group of complex compounds found in all living cells and viruses, composed of purines, pyrimidines, carbohydrates, and phosphoric acid.

nu·cle·in (nōō′klē-ĭn, nyōō′-) *n.* Any of the substances present in the nucleus of a cell, consisting chiefly of proteins, phosphoric acid, and nucleic acids. —**nu′cle·in′ic** *adj.*

nucleo– or **nucle–** *pref.* **1.** Nucleus: *nucleon; nucleoplasm.* **2.** Nucleic acid: *nucleoprotein.* [< NUCLEUS.]

nu·cle·o·cap·sid (nōō′klē-ō-kăp′sĭd, nyōō′-) *n.* The basic structure of a virus, consisting of a core of nucleic acid enclosed in a protein coat.

nu·cle·oid (nōō′klē-oid′, nyōō′-) *n.* The part of a bacterium or virus that contains nucleic acid and is analogous in function to the nucleus of a eukaryotic cell.

nu·cle·o·late (nōō′klē-ə-lāt′, nyōō′-) also **nu·cle·o·lat·ed** (-lā′tĭd) *adj.* Having a nucleolus or nucleoli. [NUCLEOL(US) + –ATE[1].]

nu·cle·o·lus (nōō-klē′ə-ləs, nyōō′-) *n., pl.* **-li** (-lī′) A small, typically round granular body composed of protein and RNA in the nucleus of a cell, usu. associated with a specific chromosomal site and involved in ribosomal RNA synthesis and the formation of ribosomes. [NLat. < Lat., dim. of *nucleus*, kernel. See NUCLEUS.] —**nu·cle′o·lar** (-lər) *adj.*

nu·cle·on (nōō′klē-ŏn′, nyōō′-) *n.* A proton or a neutron, esp. as part of an atomic nucleus. —**nu′cle·on′ic** *adj.*

nu·cle·on·ics (nōō′klē-ŏn′ĭks, nyōō′-) *n.* (*used with a sing. verb*) **1.** The study of atomic nuclei, esp. the application of nuclear research. **2.** Development of instruments for use in nuclear research. [< NUCLEON.]

nucleon number *n.* See **mass number.**

nu·cle·o·phile (nōō′klē-ə-fīl′, nyōō′-) *n.* A chemical compound or group that tends to donate or share electrons.

nu·cle·o·plasm (nōō′klē-ə-plăz′əm, nyōō′-) *n.* The protoplasm of a cell nucleus. —**nu′cle·o·plas′mic, nu′cle·o·plas·mat′ic** (-ō-plăz-măt′ĭk) *adj.*

nu·cle·o·pro·tein (nōō′klē-ō-prō′tēn′, -prō′tē-ĭn, nyōō′-) *n.* Any of a group of substances composed of protein and nucleic acid that are found in the nuclei and cytoplasm of all living cells and in viruses.

nu·cle·o·side (nōō′klē-ə-sīd′, nyōō′-) *n.* Any of various compounds consisting of a sugar, usu. ribose or deoxyribose, and a purine or pyrimidine base, esp. a compound obtained by hydrolysis of a nucleic acid, such as adenosine or guanine.

nucleoside analogue *n.* Any of a group of antiviral drugs, including AZT, DDC, and DDI, that inhibit replication of retroviruses and are used in the treatment of HIV.

nu·cle·o·some (nōō′klē-ə-sōm′, nyōō′-) *n.* Any of the repeating subunits of chromatin, consisting of a DNA chain coiled around a core of histones. —**nu′cle·o·som′al** (-sō′məl) *adj.*

nu·cle·o·syn·the·sis (nōō′klē-ō-sĭn′thĭ-sĭs, nyōō′-) *n.* The process by which heavier chemical elements are synthesized from hydrogen nuclei in the interiors of stars. —**nu′cle·o·syn·thet′ic** (-sĭn-thĕt′ĭk) *adj.*

nu·cle·o·tide (nōō′klē-ə-tīd′, nyōō′-) *n.* Any of various compounds consisting of a nucleoside combined with a phosphate group and forming the basic constituent of DNA and RNA. [Alteration of NUCLEOSIDE.]

nu·cle·us (nōō′klē-əs, nyōō′-) *n., pl.* **-cle·i** (-klē-ī′) or **-cle·us·es 1.** A central or essential part around which other parts are gathered or grouped; a core. **2.** Something regarded as a basis for future development and growth; a kernel. **3.** *Biology* A large, membrane-bound, usu. spherical protoplasmic structure within a living cell, containing the cell's hereditary material and controlling its metabolism, growth, and reproduction. **4.** *Botany* **a.** The central kernel of a nut or seed. **b.** The center of a starch granule. **5.** *Anatomy* A group of specialized nerve cells or a localized mass of gray matter in the brain or spinal cord. **6.** *Physics* The positively charged central region of an atom, composed of protons and neutrons and containing almost all of the atomic mass. **7.** *Chemistry* A group of atoms bound in a stable structure, such as a benzene ring. **8.** *Astronomy* **a.** The central portion of the head of a comet. **b.** The central or brightest part of a nebula or galaxy. **9.** *Meteorology* A small particle on which water vapor molecules accumulate in free air to form a droplet or ice crystal. **10.** *Linguistics* The part of a syllable having the greatest sonority. [Lat. *nucleus*, *nucleus*, kernel < *nucula*, little nut, dim. of *nux, nuc-*, nut.]

nu·clide (nōō′klīd′, nyōō′-) *n.* A type of atom specified by its atomic number, atomic mass, and energy state, such as carbon 14. —**nu·clid′ic** (nōō-klĭd′ĭk, nyōō′-) *adj.*

nude (nōōd, nyōōd) *adj.* **nud·er, nud·est 1.** Having no clothing; naked. **2.** Permitting or featuring full exposure of the body: *a nude beach.* ❖ *n.* **1.** An unclothed human figure, esp. an artistic

ă pat   oi boy
ā pay   ou out
âr care   ōō took
ä father   ōō boot
ĕ pet   ŭ cut
ē be   ûr urge
ĭ pit   th thin
ī pie   th this
îr pier   hw which
ŏ pot   zh vision
ô toe   ə about,
ô paw   item

Stress marks:
′ (primary);
′ (secondary); as in
lexicon (lĕk′sĭ-kŏn′)

representation. **2.** The condition of being unclothed. [Lat. *nūdus.*] —**nude′ly** *adv.* —**nu′di•ty** (nōō′dĭ-tē, nyōō′-), **nude′ness** *n.*

nudge¹ (nŭj) *tr.v.* **nudged, nudg•ing, nudg•es 1.** To push against gently, esp. in order to gain attention or give a signal. **2.** To come close to; near. ❖ *n.* A gentle push. [Prob. of Scand. orig.] —**nudg′er** *n.*

nudge² or **nudzh** (nōōj) *Slang* One who persistently pesters, annoys, or complains. ❖ *v.* **nudged, nudg•ing, nudg•es** or **nudzhed, nudzh•ing, nudzh•es** —*tr.* To annoy persistently; pester. —*intr.* To complain or carp persistently. [< Yiddish *nudyen,* to pester, bore < Pol. *nudzić.*]

nudi– *pref.* Naked; bare: *nudibranch.* [Lat. *nūdi–* < *nūdus,* naked.]

nu•di•branch (nōō′də-brăngk′, nyōō′-) *n.* See **sea slug.** [< NLat. *Nūdibranchia,* order name : NUDI– + BRANCHIA.] —**nu′di•bran′chi•ate** (-brăng′kē-ĭt), **nu′di•bran′chi•an** (-kē-ən) *adj. & n.*

nud•ism (nōō′dĭz′əm, nyōō′-) *n.* The belief in or practice of going nude, esp. in secluded, sexually mixed groups for reasons of health. —**nud′ist** *adj. & n.*

nud•nik also **nud•nick** (nōōd′nĭk) *n. Slang* An obtuse, boring, or bothersome person; a pest. [Yiddish, *nudne,* boring (< *nudyen,* to bore; see NUDGE²) + *-nik,* -nik.]

Nu•e•ces (nōō-ā′sĭs, nyōō-) A river of S TX flowing c. 507 km (315 mi) to **Nueces Bay,** an inlet of the Gulf of Mexico.

Nue•vo La•re•do (nōō-ā′vō lə-rā′dō, nwĕ′vō lä-rĕ′dō) A city of NE Mexico across the Rio Grande from Laredo TX; founded 1755. Pop. 201,731.

nu•ga•to•ry (nōō′gə-tôr′ē, -tōr′ē, nyōō′-) *adj.* **1.** Of little or no importance; trifling. **2.** Having no force; invalid. [Lat. *nūgātōrius* < *nūgātor,* trifler < *nūgārī,* to trifle < *nūgae,* jokes.]

nug•get (nŭg′ĭt) *n.* **1.** A small, solid lump, esp. of gold. **2.** A small compact portion or unit: *nuggets of information.* [Perh. dim. of E. dialectal *nug,* lump.]

nui•sance (nōō′səns, nyōō′-) *n.* **1.** One that is inconvenient, annoying, or vexatious; a bother: *The long line was a nuisance.* **2.** *Law* A use of property or course of conduct that interferes with the legal rights of others by causing damage, annoyance, or inconvenience. [ME < OFr. < *nuire, nuis-,* to harm < VLat. **nocere* < Lat. *nocēre.* See **nek–** in App.]

nuisance tax *n.* A small excise tax levied on separate purchases and collected directly from the purchaser.

nuke (nōōk, nyōōk) *Slang n.* **1.** A nuclear device or weapon. **2.** A nuclear-powered electric generating plant. ❖ *tr.v.* **nuked, nuk•ing, nukes 1.** To attack with nuclear weapons. **2.** To heat in a microwave oven.

Nu•ku•'a•lo•fa (nōō′kōō-ə-lô′fə) The cap. of Tonga, in the SW Pacific Ocean. Pop. 21,745.

null (nŭl) *adj.* **1.** Having no legal force; invalid. **2.** Of no consequence, effect, or value; insignificant. **3.** Amounting to nothing; absent or nonexistent: *a null result.* **4.** *Mathematics* Of or relating to a set having no members or to zero magnitude. ❖ *tr.v.* **nulled, null•ing, nulls** To make null. ❖ *n.* **1.** Zero; nothing. **2.** An instrument reading of zero. [Fr. *nul* < OFr. < Lat. *nūllus.* See **ne** in App.]

nul•lah (nŭl′ə) *n.* A ravine or gully, esp. in southern Asia. [Hindi *nālā,* rivulet, prob. of Dravidian orig.]

nul•li•fi•ca•tion (nŭl′ə-fĭ-kā′shən) *n.* **1a.** The act of nullifying. **b.** The state of being nullified. **2.** Refusal or failure of a US state to recognize or enforce a federal law within its boundaries. —**nul′li•fi•ca′tion•ist** *n.*

nul•li•fi•er (nŭl′ə-fī′ər) *n.* **1.** One that nullifies. **2.** One who believes in nullification by US states.

nul•li•fy (nŭl′ə-fī′) *tr.v.* **-fied, -fy•ing, -fies 1.** To make null; invalidate. **2.** To counteract the force or effectiveness of. [Lat. *nūllificāre,* to despise : *nūllus,* none; see **ne** in App. + *-ficāre,* -fy.]

nul•lip•a•ra (nŭl′ə-lĭp′ər-ə) *n.* A woman who has never given birth. [Lat., none; see **ne** in App. + –PARA.] —**nul′lip′a•rous** *adj.*

nul•li•ty (nŭl′ĭ-tē) *n., pl.* **-ties 1.** The state or quality of being null. **2.** Something that is null, esp. legally.

Num. *abbr. Bible* Numbers

numb (nŭm) *adj.* **numb•er, numb•est 1.** Deprived of the power to feel or move normally; benumbed: *numb with cold.* **2.** Emotionally unresponsive; indifferent. ❖ *tr. & intr.v.* **numbed, numb•ing, numbs** To make or become numb. [ME *nome,* var. of *nomin,* p. part. of *nimen,* to seize < OE *niman.* See **nem–** in App.] —**numb′ly** *adv.* —**numb′ness** *n.*

WORD HISTORY Old English had a number of strong verbs (often loosely called "irregular" verbs) that did not survive into Modern English. One such was the verb *niman,* "to take," later replaced by *take,* a borrowing from Old Norse. The verb had a past tense *nam* and a past participle *numen;* if the verb had survived, it would likely have become *nim, nam, num,* like *swim, swam, swum.* Although we do not have the verb as such anymore, its past participle is alive and well, now spelled *numb,* literally "taken, seized," as by cold or grief. (The *b* was added in the 17th century by analogy to words like *limb* and *dumb;* the older spelling without the *b* is still seen in the compound *numskull.*) The verb also lives on indirectly in the word *nimble,* which used to mean "quick to take," and then later "light, quick on one's feet."

num•ber (nŭm′bər) *n.* **1.** *Mathematics* **a.** A member of the set of positive integers; one of a series of symbols of unique meaning in a fixed order that can be derived by counting. **b.** A member of any of the further sets of mathematical objects, such as negative integers and real numbers. **2. numbers** *Arithmetic.* **3a.** A symbol or word used to represent a number. **b.** A numeral or a series of numerals used for reference or identification: *telephone numbers.* **4a.** A position in an ordered sequence that corresponds to one of the positive integers: *house number three.* **b.** One item in a group or series considered to be in numerical order: *an old number of a magazine.* **5.** A total; a sum: *the number of feet in a mile.* **6.** An indefinite quantity of units or individuals: *a number of people.* **7. numbers a.** A large quantity; a multitude: *numbers of people.* **b.** Numerical superiority: *Numbers were on our side.* **8.** *Grammar* The indication, as by inflection, of the singularity, duality, or plurality of a linguistic form. **9. numbers a.** Metrical feet or lines; verses. **b.** *Obsolete* Poetic meter. **10. numbers** *Archaic* Musical periods or measures. **11. numbers** (*used with a sing. or pl. verb*) *Games* A numbers game. **12. Numbers** (*used with a sing. verb*) See table at **Bible. 13.** One of the separate offerings in a program of music or other entertainment. **14.** *Slang* A frequently repeated, characteristic speech, argument, or performance: *doing her usual number.* **15.** *Slang* A person or thing singled out for a particular characteristic: *a crafty number.* ❖ *v.* **-bered, -ber•ing, -bers** —*tr.* **1.** To assign a number to. **2.** To determine the number or amount of; count. **3.** To total in number or amount; add up to. **4.** To include in a group or category. **5.** To mention one by one; enumerate. **6.** To limit or restrict in number: *Our days are numbered.* —*intr.* **1.** To call off numbers; count. **2.** To constitute a group or number. —*idioms:* **by the numbers 1.** In unison as numbers are called out by a leader. **2.** In a strict step-by-step or mechanical way. **do a number on** *Slang* To defeat, abuse, or humiliate in a calculated and thorough way. **get** (or **have**) (**someone's**) **number** To determine or know someone's real character or motives. **without** (or **beyond**) **number** Too many to be counted; countless. [ME *nombre* < OFr. < Lat. *numerus.* See **nem–** in App.] —**num′ber•er** *n.*

number cruncher *n. Slang* **1.** A computer that is able to perform complex, lengthy calculations. **2.** A person who performs numerous calculations, esp. an accountant. —**number crunching** *n.*

num•ber•less (nŭm′bər-lĭs) *adj.* Innumerable; countless.

number line *n.* A graph that represents the real numbers as ordered points on a line and their magnitudes as distances from an arbitrary zero point.

number one *n.* **1.** One that is first in rank, order, or importance. **2.** *Slang* One's own interests; oneself. **3.** *Informal* **a.** The act of urinating. **b.** Urine. ❖ *adj.* **1.** First in rank, order, or importance: *our number one problem.* **2.** Foremost in quality; first-rate.

numbers game *n.* A lottery in which bets are made on an unpredictable number, such as a daily stock quotation.

number sign *n.* The symbol (#), used to represent the word *number.*

number system *n.* Any system of naming or representing numbers, as the decimal system or the binary system.

number two *n. Informal* **1.** The act of defecating. **2.** Feces.

numb•fish (nŭm′fĭsh′) *n., pl.* **numbfish** or **-fish•es** See **electric ray.**

numb•skull (nŭm′skŭl′) *n.* Variant of **numskull.**

num•chuck (nŭm′chŭk′) *n.* Variant of **nunchaku.**

nu•men (nōō′mən, nyōō′-) *n., pl.* **-mi•na** (-mə-nə) **1.** A presiding deity or spirit of a place. **2.** A spirit believed by animists to inhabit natural phenomena or objects. **3.** Creative energy; genius. [Lat. *nūmen,* nod of the head, divine power, numen.]

nu•mer•a•ble (nōō′mər-ə-bəl, nyōō′-) *adj.* That can be counted; countable: *numerable assets.*

nu•mer•al (nōō′mər-əl, nyōō′-) *n.* **1.** A symbol or mark used to represent a number. **2. numerals** The numbers, usu. the last two digits, indicating by year a graduating class in a school or college. ❖ *adj.* Of, relating to, or representing numbers. [< ME, of number < LLat. *numerālis* < Lat. *numerus,* number. See NUMBER.] —**nu′mer•al•ly** *adv.*

numeral system *n.* See **number system.**

nu•mer•ar•y (nōō′mə-rĕr′ē, nyōō′-) *adj.* Of or relating to a number or numbers. [Med.Lat. *numerārius* < LLat., an accountant < Lat. *numerus,* number. See NUMBER.]

nu•mer•ate (nōō′mə-rāt′, nyōō′-) *tr.v.* **-at•ed, -at•ing, -ates** To enumerate; count. ❖ *adj.* (-mər-ĭt) Able to think and express oneself effectively in quantitative terms. [Lat. *numerāre, numerāt–* < *numerus,* number. See NUMBER.] —**nu′mer•a•cy** (-mər-ə-sē) *n.*

nu•mer•a•tion (nōō′mə-rā′shən, nyōō′-) *n.* **1.** The act or process of counting or numbering; enumeration. **2.** A system of numbering.

nu•mer•a•tor (nōō′mə-rā′tər, nyōō′-) *n.* **1.** *Mathematics* **a.** The expression written above the line in a common fraction to indicate the number of parts of the whole. **b.** An expression to be divided by another; a dividend. **2.** One that numbers; an enumerator.

nu·mer·ic (nōō-mĕr′ĭk, nyōō-) *n.* A number or numeral.

nu·mer·i·cal (nōō-mĕr′ĭ-kəl, nyōō-) *also* **nu·mer·ic** (-mĕr′ĭk) *adj.* **1.** Of or relating to a number or series of numbers: *numerical order.* **2.** Designating number or a number: *a numerical symbol.* **3.** Expressed in or counted by numbers: *numerical strength.* [< Lat. *numerus*, number. See NUMBER.] —**nu·mer′i·cal·ly** *adv.*

numerical analysis *n.* The study of approximation techniques for solving mathematical problems.

numerical taxonomy *n.* The branch of taxonomy that uses mathematical methods to evaluate observable differences and similarities between taxonomic groups.

numerical value *n.* See **absolute value** 1.

nu·mer·ol·o·gy (nōō′mə-rŏl′ə-jē, nyōō′-) *n.* The study of the occult meanings and influence on human life of numbers. [Lat. *numerus*, number; see NUMBER + -LOGY.] —**nu′mer·o·log′i·cal** (-mûr-ə-lŏj′ĭ-kəl) *adj.* —**nu′mer·ol′o·gist** *n.*

nu·me·ro u·no (nōō′mə-rō ōō′nō, nyōō′-) *n. Slang* **1.** One that is first in rank, order, or importance. **2.** One's own interests; oneself. ❖ *adj.* Number one. [Sp. *número uno* or Ital. *numero uno*, number one.]

nu·mer·ous (nōō′mər-əs, nyōō′-) *adj.* Amounting to a large number; many. [ME < Lat. *numerōsus* < *numerus*. See NUMBER.] —**nu′mer·ous·ly** *adv.* —**nu′mer·ous·ness** *n.*

Nu·mid·i·a (nōō-mĭd′ē-ə, nyōō-) An ancient country of NW Africa corresponding roughly to present-day Algeria; part of the Carthaginian empire before the Punic Wars and a separate kingdom after 201 B.C. —**Nu·mid′i·an** *adj. & n.*

nu·mi·na (nōō′mə-nə, nyōō′-) *n.* Plural of **numen**.

nu·mi·nous (nōō′mə-nəs, nyōō′-) *adj.* **1.** Of or relating to a numen; supernatural. **2.** Filled with or characterized by a sense of a supernatural presence: *a numinous place.* **3.** Spiritually elevated; sublime. [< Lat. *nūmen*, *nūmin*-, numen.]

nu·mis·mat·ic (nōō′mĭz-măt′ĭk, -mĭs-, nyōō′-) *adj.* **1.** Of or relating to coins or currency. **2.** Of or relating to numismatics. [Fr. *numismatique* < LLat. *numisma*, *numismat*-, coin, var. of Lat. *nomisma* < Gk., custom, current coin < *nomizein*, to have in use < *nomos*, custom. See **nem-** in App.] —**nu′mis·mat′i·cal·ly** *adv.*

nu·mis·mat·ics (nōō′mĭz-măt′ĭks, -mĭs-, nyōō′-) *n.* (*used with a sing. verb*) The study or collection of money, coins, and often medals. —**nu·mis′ma·tist** (nōō-mĭz′mə-tĭst, -mĭs′-, nyōō′-) *n.*

num·mu·lar (nŭm′yə-lər) *adj.* Shaped like a coin; oval or circular. [< Lat. *nummulus*, dim. of *nummus*, coin, prob. < Gk. *nomimos*, customary, legal. See **nem-** in App.]

num·mu·lite (nŭm′yə-līt′) *n.* A large coin-shaped fossil foraminifer of the genus *Nummulites*. [< NLat. *Nummulītēs* < genus < Lat. *nummulus*, dim. of *nummus*, coin, prob. < Gk. *nomimos*, customary, legal. See **nem-** in App.] —**num′mu·lit′ic** (-lĭt′ĭk) *adj.*

num·skull *also* **numb·skull** (nŭm′skŭl′) *n.* A stupid person; a nitwit. [*num* (var. of NUMB) + SKULL.]

nun¹ (nŭn) *n.* A woman who belongs to a religious community, living under vows of poverty, chastity, and obedience. [ME < OE *nunne* and < OFr. *nonne*, both < LLat. *nonna*, fem. of *nonnus*, tutor, monk.]

nun² (nōōn) *n.* The 14th letter of the Hebrew alphabet. [Mishnaic Heb. *nûn* < Phoenician *nūn*, fish, 14th letter of the Phoenician alphabet.]

Nu·na·vut (nōō′nə-vōōt′) A territory of N Canada including part of the mainland W of Hudson Bay and N of latitude 60° N, islands in the Hudson Bay, and most of the Arctic Archipelago. It comprises the former E portion of the Northwest Territories; became a new territory of Canada on April 1, 1999. Cap. Iqaluit.

Nunc Di·mit·tis (nŭngk′ dĭ-mĭt′ĭs, nōōngk′) *n.* A Christian canticle or hymn using the words of Simeon in Luke 2:29–32, beginning *"Nunc dimittis servum tuum"* ("Now lettest thou thy servant depart"). [LLat. *Nunc Dīmittis* : Lat. *nunc*, now + Lat. *dīmittis*, second pers. sing. pr. t. of *dīmittere*, to send away.]

nun·cha·ku (nŭn-chä′kōō) *or* **num·chuck** (nŭm′chŭk′) *n.* A pair of hardwood sticks joined by a chain or cord and used as a weapon. [Okinawan J., prob. < Chin. (Taiwanese) *neng-cak*, type of farming implement, equivalent to Chin. (Mandarin) *liǎng*, two, paired + Chin. (Mandarin) *záo*, to dig, digger.]

nun·ci·a·ture (nŭn′sē-ə-chōōr′, -chər, nōōn′-) *n.* The office or term of office of a nuncio. [Ital. *nunciatura* < *nuncio*, nuncio. See NUNCIO.]

nun·ci·o (nŭn′sē-ō′, nōōn′-) *n., pl.* **-os** A papal ambassador or representative. [Ital. < Lat. *nūntius*, messenger.]

nun·cle (nŭng′kəl) *n. Chiefly British* An uncle. [< the phrases *an uncle*, *mine uncle*.]

nun·cu·pa·tive (nŭn′kyə-pā′tĭv, nŭng′-, nŭn-kyōō′pə-tĭv) *adj. Law* Delivered orally to witnesses rather than written: *a nuncupative will.* [Med.Lat. *nūncupātīvus* < LLat., so-called < Lat. *nūncupātus*, p. part. of *nūncupāre*, to name : *nōmen*, name; see **nō-men-** in App. + *capere*, to take; see **kap-** in App.]

nun·ner·y (nŭn′ə-rē) *n., pl.* **-ies** A convent of nuns.

nuoc mam (nwôk′ mäm′) *n.* A pungent salty liquid made from fermented anchovies or other fish, used as a seasoning and condi-

---

ment in Southeast Asian cuisine. [Vietnamese *nuóc mám*, pickling brine, fish sauce : *nuóc*, water + *mám*, salted fish.]

nup·tial (nŭp′shəl, -chəl) *adj.* **1.** Of or relating to marriage or the wedding ceremony. **2.** Of, relating to, or occurring during the mating season: *the nuptial plumage of male birds.* ❖ *n.* A wedding ceremony. Often used in the plural. [ME *nupcialle* < OFr. *nuptial* < Lat. *nūptiālis* < *nū*, wedding < *nū*, fem. p. part. of *nūbere*, to take a husband.] —**nup′tial·ly** *adv.*

nurd (nûrd) *n. Slang* Variant of **nerd**.

Nu·rem·berg (nōōr′əm-bûrg′, nyōōr′-) *also* **Nürn·berg** (nōōrn′bĕrk′, nürn′-) A city of SE Germany NNW of Munich; became a free imperial city in the 13th cent. and a center of the German cultural renaissance in the 15th and 16th cent. The city served as the venue for the Allied trials of war criminals (1945–46). Pop. 498,945.

Nu·re·yev (nōōr′ī-yĕf, nōō-rā′-), **Rudolf** 1938–93. Russian-born ballet dancer and choreographer.

Nu·ri·stan (nōōr′ĭ-stän′, -stän′) A region of NE Afghanistan on the S slopes of the Hindu Kush.

Nu·ri·sta·ni (nōōr′ĭ-stä′nē) *n., pl.* **Nuristani** *or* **-nis** A member of a Dardic-speaking people inhabiting parts of the Hindu Kush in northeast Afghanistan.

nurse (nûrs) *n.* **1.** A person educated and trained to care for the sick or disabled. **2a.** A woman employed to take care of a child; a nursemaid. **b.** A woman employed to suckle children other than her own; a wet nurse. **3.** One that nurtures or fosters. **4.** *Zoology* A worker ant or bee that feeds and cares for the colony's young. ❖ *v.* **nursed, nurs·ing, nurs·es** —*tr.* **1.** To serve as a nurse for. **2a.** To cause or allow to take milk from the breast. **b.** To feed at the breast of; suckle. **3.** To try to cure by special care or treatment. **4.** To treat carefully, esp. in order to prevent pain. **5.** To manage or guide carefully; look after with care; foster. See Syns at **nurture**. **6.** To bear privately in the mind. **7.** To consume slowly, esp. in order to conserve. —*intr.* **1.** To serve as a nurse. **2.** To take nourishment from the breast; suckle. [ME *norice*, *nurse*, wet nurse < OFr. *norrice* < VLat. **nutricia* < LLat. *nūtrīcia* < fem. of Lat. *nūtrīcius*, that suckles < *nūtrīx*, *nūtrīc*-, wet nurse. See **(s)nāu-** in App.] —**nurs′er** *n.*

nurse·maid (nûrs′mād′) *n.* A woman employed to take care of children.

nurse practitioner *n.* A registered nurse with special training for providing primary health care, including many tasks customarily performed by a physician.

nurs·er·y (nûr′sə-rē, nûrs′rē) *n., pl.* **-ies** **1.** A room or area in a household set apart for children. **2a.** A place for the temporary care of children in the absence of their parents. **b.** A nursery school. **3.** A place where plants are grown for sale, transplanting, or experimentation. **4.** A place in which something is produced, fostered, or developed. [ME *noricerie*, prob. < OFr. *norricerie* < *norrice*, nursemaid. See NURSE.]

nursery rhyme *n.* A short rhymed poem or tale for children.

nursery school *n.* A school for children, usu. between the ages of three and five, who are not old enough to attend kindergarten. —**nursery schooler** *n.*

nurse's aide (nûr′sĭz) *n., pl.* **nurses' aides** A person who assists nurses at a hospital or other medical facility.

nurs·ing (nûr′sĭng) *n.* **1.** The profession of a nurse. **2.** The tasks or care of a nurse.

nursing home *n.* A private establishment that provides living quarters and care for the elderly or the chronically ill.

nurs·ling (nûrs′lĭng) *n.* **1.** A nursing infant or young animal. **2.** A carefully nurtured person or thing.

nur·tur·ance (nûr′chər-əns) *n.* The providing of loving care and attention. —**nur′tur·ant** *adj.*

nur·ture (nûr′chər) *n.* **1.** Something that nourishes; sustenance. **2.** The act of bringing up. **3.** *Biology* The sum of environmental influences and conditions acting on an organism. ❖ *tr.v.* **-tured, -tur·ing, -tures** **1.** To nourish; feed. **2.** To educate; train. **3.** To help grow or develop; cultivate: *nurture talent.* [ME < OFr. < LLat. *nūtrītūra*, act of suckling < Lat. *nūtrītus*, p. part. of *nūtrīre*, to suckle. See **(s)nāu-** in App.] —**nur′tur·er** *n.*

Nüss·lein-Vol·hard (nüs′līn′fôl′härt′), **Christiane** b. 1942. German biologist who shared a 1995 Nobel Prize in medicine for her work with fruit flies.

nut (nŭt) *n.* **1a.** An indehiscent hard-shelled one-seeded fruit, such as an acorn. **b.** A seed borne within a fruit having a hard shell, as in the almond. **c.** The kernel of any of these. **2.** *Slang* **a.** A crazy or eccentric person. **b.** An enthusiast; a buff: *a movie nut.* **3.** *Informal* A difficult endeavor or problem. **4.** *Slang* The human head. **5.** *Music* **a.** A ridge of wood at the top of the fingerboard or neck of a stringed instrument, over which the strings pass. **b.** A device on the bow of a stringed instrument for tightening the hairs. **6.** A small block of metal or wood with a central threaded hole that is designed to fit around and secure a bolt or screw. **7.** *Slang* **a.** The cost of launching a business venture. **b.** The operating expenses of a theater, theatrical production, or similar enter-

---

Rudolf Nureyev

nut
clockwise from top: T-nut, hex cap, wing, and hex nuts

ă	pat	oi	boy
ā	pay	ou	out
âr	care	ōō	took
ä	father	ōō	boot
ĕ	pet	ŭ	cut
ē	be	ûr	urge
ĭ	pit	th	thin
ī	pie	th	this
îr	pier	hw	which
ŏ	pot	zh	vision
ō	toe	ə	about,
ô	paw		item

Stress marks:
′ (primary);
′ (secondary), as in
lexicon (lĕk′sĭ-kŏn′)

prise. **8. nut** *Vulgar Slang* A testicle. ❖ *intr.v.* **nut•ted, nut•ting, nuts** To gather or hunt for nuts. [ME *nute* < OE *hnutu*.] —**nut′ter** *n.*

nu•ta•tion (no͞o-tā′shən, nyo͞o-) *n.* **1.** The act or an instance of nodding the head. **2.** A wobble in a spinning gyroscope or other rotating body. **3.** *Astronomy* A small periodic motion of the celestial pole of the earth with respect to the pole of the ecliptic. **4.** *Botany* A slight curving or circular growth in a stem, as of a twining plant. [Lat. *nūtātiō, nūtātiōn-* < *nūtātus*, p. part. of *nūtāre*, freq. of *-nuere*, to nod.] —**nu•ta′tion•al** *adj.*

nut case *n. Slang* A person regarded as eccentric or crazy.

nut•crack•er (nŭt′krăk′ər) *n.* **1.** An implement used to crack nuts, typically consisting of two hinged metal levers between which the nut is squeezed. **2a.** Any of various birds of the genus *Nucifraga* that are related to the crow and feed chiefly on the seeds of pine cones. **b.** See **nuthatch.**

nut•gall (nŭt′gôl′) *n.* A nutlike swelling produced on an oak or other tree by certain parasitic wasps.

nut•hatch (nŭt′hăch′) *n.* Any of several small short-tailed birds of the family Sittidae, having a long sharp bill and known for climbing down trees headfirst. [ME *notehache* : *note*, nut; see NUT + *hache*, hatchet < OFr., perh. of Gmc. orig. (< its wedging nuts in bark and hacking them open).]

nut house *n. Offensive Slang* An institution for the mentally ill.

nut•let (nŭt′lĭt) *n.* **1.** A small nut. **2.** The stone or pit of certain fruits such as the peach or cherry.

nut•meat (nŭt′mēt′) *n.* The edible kernel of a nut.

nut•meg (nŭt′mĕg′) *n.* **1.** An evergreen tree (*Myristica fragrans*) native to the East Indies and cultivated for its spicy seeds. **2.** The hard aromatic seed of this tree, used as a spice when grated or ground. **3.** A grayish to moderate brown. [ME *notemuge*, prob. ult. < OFr. *nois mugede*, alteration of *nois muscade*, nut smelling like musk < O Provençal *notz muscada* : *notz*, nut (< Lat. *nux, nuc-*, nut) + *muscada*, smelling like musk (< *musc*, musk < LLat. *muscus*; see MUSK).]

nut pick also **nut•pick** (nŭt′pĭk′) *n.* A small sharp-pointed tool used for digging the meat from nuts.

nut pine *n.* See **piñon.**

nu•tra•ceu•ti•cal (no͞o′trə-so͞o′tĭ-kəl) *n.* A food or naturally occurring food supplement thought to have a beneficial effect on human health. [NUTR(ITIOUS) + (PHARM)ACEUTICAL.]

Nu•tra•Sweet (no͞o′trə-swēt′) A trademark for aspartame.

nu•tri•a (no͞o′trē-ə, nyo͞o′-) *n.* **1.** See **coypu. 2.** The light brown fur of the coypu. [Sp. < VLat. **nutria*, var. of Lat. *lutra.* See **wed-** in App.]

nu•tri•ent (no͞o′trē-ənt, nyo͞o′-) *n.* A source of nourishment, esp. a nourishing ingredient in a food. ❖ *adj.* Providing nourishment. [Lat. *nūtriēns, nūtrient-*, pr. part. of *nūtrīre*, to suckle. See **(s)nāu-** in App.]

nu•tri•ment (no͞o′trə-mənt, nyo͞o′-) *n.* **1.** A source of nourishment; food. **2.** An agent that promotes growth or development. [ME < Lat. *nūtrīmentum* < *nūtrīre*, to suckle. See **(s)nāu-** in App.] —**nu′tri•men′tal** (-mĕn′tl) *adj.*

nu•tri•tion (no͞o-trĭsh′ən, nyo͞o-) *n.* **1.** The process of nourishing or being nourished, esp. the process by which a living organism assimilates food and uses it for growth and for maintenance of tissues. **2.** The science or study that deals with food and nourishment, esp. in humans. **3.** A source of nourishment; food. [ME *nutricion* < OFr. *nutrition* < LLat. *nūtrītiō, nūtrītiōn-* < Lat. *nūtrītus*, p. part. of *nūtrīre*, to suckle. See **(s)nāu-** in App.] —**nu•tri′tion•al** *adj.* —**nu•tri′tion•al•ly** *adv.*

nu•tri•tion•ist (no͞o-trĭsh′ə-nĭst, nyo͞o-) *n.* One who is trained or an expert in the field of nutrition.

nu•tri•tion•ist's calorie (no͞o-trĭsh′ə-nĭsts, nyo͞o-) *n.* See **calorie** 3b.

nu•tri•tious (no͞o-trĭsh′əs, nyo͞o-) *adj.* Providing nourishment; nourishing. [< Lat. *nūtrītius < nūtrīx, nūtrīc-*, nurse. See NURSE.] —**nu•tri′tious•ly** *adv.* —**nu•tri′tious•ness** *n.*

nu•tri•tive (no͞o′trĭ-tĭv, nyo͞o′-) *adj.* **1.** Nutritious; nourishing. **2.** Of or relating to nutrition. [ME *nutritif* < OFr. < LLat. *nūtrītīvus < Lat. nūtrītus*, p. part. of *nūtrīre*, to suckle. See **(s)nāu-** in App.] —**nu′tri•tive•ly** *adv.*

nuts (nŭts) *Slang adj.* **1.** Crazy; insane. **2.** Extremely enthusiastic: *I'm nuts about opera.* ❖ *interj.* Used to express contempt, disappointment, or refusal. [< NUT.]

nuts and bolts *pl.n. Slang* The basic working components or practical aspects. —**nuts′-and-bolts′** (nŭts′ən-bŏlts′) *adj.*

nut sedge *n.* Either of two Old World sedges (*Cyperus esculentus* or *C. rotundus*) having aromatic tubers.

nut•shell (nŭt′shĕl′) *n.* The shell enclosing the meat of a nut. —*idiom:* **in a nutshell** In a few words; concisely.

nut•ty (nŭt′ē) *adj.* **-ti•er, -ti•est 1.** Containing or producing nuts: *nutty trees.* **2.** Having a flavor like that of nuts. **3.** *Slang* Crazy; idiotic. —**nut′ti•ly** *adv.* —**nut′ti•ness** *n.*

Nuuk (no͞ok) See **Godthåb.**

nux vom•i•ca (nŭks vŏm′ĭ-kə) *n.* A tree (*Strychnos nux-vomica*) native to southeast Asia and having poisonous seeds that are the source of the medicinal alkaloids strychnine and brucine.

nyala
Tragelaphus angasi

Julius Nyerere
photographed in 1971

[Med.Lat. : Lat. *nux*, nut + Med.Lat. *vomica*, fem. of *vomicus*, emetic (< Lat. *vomere*, to vomit; see **wemə-** in App.).]

Nu•yo•ri•can (no͞o′yə-rē′kən) *n. Informal* A person of Puerto Rican birth or descent living primarily in New York City. [Blend of NEW YORK and (PUERTO) RICAN.] —**Nu′yo•ri′can** *adj.*

nuz•zle (nŭz′əl) *v.* **-zled, -zling, -zles** —*tr.* **1.** To rub or push against gently with or as if with the nose or snout: *nuzzled the kitten.* **2.** To root or move with the snout. —*intr.* **1.** To make rubbing or pressing motions with or as if with the nose or snout. **2.** To nestle together. [ME *noselen*, to bend down, perh. back-formation < *noselyng*, on the face, prostrate < *nose*, nose. See NOSE.] —**nuz′zler** *n.*

NV *abbr.* **1.** Nevada **2.** not voting

NW *abbr.* **1.** northwest **2.** northwestern

NWbN *abbr.* northwest by north

NWbW *abbr.* northwest by west

NWT or **N.W.T.** *abbr.* Northwest Territories

n. wt. *abbr.* net weight

NY or **N.Y.** *abbr.* New York

nya•la (nyä′lə) *n., pl.* **nyala** or **-las** Any of several African antelopes of the genus *Tragelaphus*, having vertical stripes on the sides of the body. [Prob. of Bantu orig.]

Nyan•ja (nyän′jə) *n.* A Bantu language closely related to Chewa and spoken in Malawi.

Ny•as•a (nī-ăs′ə, nyä′sä), **Lake** also **Lake Malawi** A lake of southeast-central Africa between Tanzania, Mozambique, and Malawi.

Ny•as•a•land (nī-ăs′ə-lănd′, nyä′sä-) See **Malawi.**

NYC *abbr.* New York City

nyc•ta•lo•pi•a (nĭk′tə-lō′pē-ə) *n.* See **night blindness.** [LLat. *nyctalōpia* < Gk. *nuktalōps*, night-blind : *nux, nukt-*, night; see **nek**ʷ**-t-** in App. + *alaos*, blind + *ōps, ōp-*, eye; see **okʷ-** in App.] —**nyc′ta•lo′pic** (-lō′pĭk, -lŏp′ĭk) *adj.*

nyc•tit•ro•pism (nĭk-tĭt′rə-pĭz′əm) *n.* The tendency of the leaves of some plants to change their position at nightfall. [Gk. *nux, nukt-*, night; see **nek**ʷ**-t-** in App. + –TROPISM.] —**nyc′ti•tro′pic** (-tĭ-trō′pĭk, -trŏp′ĭk) *adj.*

nyc•to•pho•bi•a (nĭk′tə-fō′bē-ə) *n.* An abnormal fear of the night or darkness. [Gk. *nux, nukt-*, night; see NYCTALOPIA + –PHOBIA.]

Nye•re•re (nyĕ-rĕ′rĕ), **Julius Kambarage** 1921–99. Tanzanian politician who led his country to independence from Britain and served as its first president (1962–85).

ny•lon (nī′lŏn′) *n.* **1a.** Any of a family of high-strength, resilient synthetic polymers containing recurring amide groups. **b.** Cloth or yarn made from one of these synthetic materials. **2. nylons** Stockings made of one of these synthetic materials. [Coined by E.I. Du Pont de Nemours and Co.]

nymph (nĭmf) *n.* **1.** *Greek & Roman Mythology* Any of numerous minor deities represented as beautiful young women inhabiting and sometimes personifying features of nature such as trees. **2.** A girl, esp. a beautiful one. **3.** The immature form of an insect, such as a tick, that does not pass through a pupal stage. Nymphs usually resemble the adult form, but are smaller and lack fully developed wings. [ME *nimphe* < OFr. < Lat. *nympha* < Gk. *numphē*.] —**nymph′al** (nĭm′fəl) *adj.*

nym•pha (nĭm′fə) *n., pl.* **-phae** (-fē) **1.** See **nymph** 3. **2. nymphae** The labia minora. [Lat. < Gk. *numphē*.]

nym•pha•lid (nĭm′fə-lĭd) *n.* Any of various cosmopolitan butterflies of the family Nymphalidae, characterized by vestigial forelegs and often brilliant coloring. [< NLat. *Nymphālidae*, family name < *Nymphālis*, type genus, ult. < Lat. *nympha*, nymph. See NYMPH.]

nym•phet (nĭm-fĕt′, nĭm′fĭt) *n.* A pubescent girl regarded as sexually desirable.

nym•pho (nĭm′fō) *n. Informal* A female with nymphomania; a nymphomaniac.

nym•pho•lep•sy (nĭm′fə-lĕp′sē) *n., pl.* **-sies 1.** A frenzy supposed by ancient peoples to have been induced by nymphs. **2.** An emotional frenzy. [< NYMPHOLEPT.]

nym•pho•lept (nĭm′fə-lĕpt′) *n.* One who is in a state of nympholepsy. [Gk. *numpholēptos*, caught by nymphs, frenzied : *numphē*, nymph + *lēptos*, seized (< *lambanein, lēp-*, to seize).] —**nym′pho•lep′tic** *adj.*

nym•pho•ma•ni•a (nĭm′fə-mā′nē-ə, -mān′yə) *n.* Excessive sexual desire in and behavior by a female. [NLat. : Gk. *numphē*, nymph + –MANIA.] —**nym′pho•ma′ni•ac′** (-nē-ăk′) *adj. & n.*

Ny•norsk (no͞o-nôrsk′, nü′nôshk′) *n.* See **New Norwegian.** [Norw. : *ny*, new (< ON *nȳr*; see SPAN-NEW) + *norsk*, Norw. (< **noregsk* < ON *Nōregr*, Norway).]

NYSE *abbr.* New York Stock Exchange

nys•tag•mus (nĭ-stăg′məs) *n.* A rapid, involuntary oscillatory motion of the eyeball. [NLat. < Gk. *nustagmos*, drowsiness.] —**nys•tag′mic** (-mĭk) *adj.*

nys•ta•tin (nĭs′tə-tĭn) *n.* An antibiotic, $C_{46}H_{77}NO_{19}$, produced by the actinomycete *Streptomyces noursei* and used esp. in the treatment of fungal infections. [N(ew) Y(ork) Stat(e) + –IN.]

NZ *abbr.* New Zealand

Oo

o or **O** (ō) *n., pl.* **o's** or **O's** also **os** or **Os 1.** The 15th letter of the modern English alphabet. **2.** Any of the speech sounds represented by the letter *o*. **3.** The 15th in a series. **4.** Something shaped like the letter O. **5. O** One of the four major blood groups in the ABO system. **6.** A zero.

O¹ (ō) *interj.* **1.** Used before the name of or a pronoun referring to a person or thing being formally addressed. **2.** Used to express surprise or strong emotion.

O² The symbol for the element **oxygen.**

O³ *abbr.* **1.** *Baseball* out **2.** outstanding

o. *abbr.* **1.** *Latin* octarius (pint) **2.** also **O.** octavo

O. *abbr.* **1.** ocean **2.** Ohio

-o *suff.* Used to form an informal, abbreviated, or slang word or variant: *ammo.* [Perh. < OH¹ and < shortenings such as HIPPO.]

-o- Used as a connective to join word elements: *acidophilic.* [ME < OFr. < Lat. < Gk., thematic vowel of nouns and adjectives used in compounds.]

o' (ə) *prep. Informal* Of: *lots o' luck.* [ME *o, a,* shortening of *of.* See OF.]

o/a *abbr.* on or about

oaf (ōf) *n.* A stupid or clumsy person. [ON *alfr,* elf, silly person. See albho- in App.] —**oaf′ish** *adj.* —**oaf′ish·ly** *adv.* —**oaf′ish·ness** *n.*

O·a·hu (ō-ä′hōō) An island of central HI between Molokai and Kauai; the chief island of the state.

oak (ōk) *n.* **1a.** Any of numerous monoecious deciduous or evergreen trees or shrubs of the genus *Quercus,* bearing acorns as fruit. **b.** The durable wood of an oak. **c.** Something made of oak. **2.** Any of various similar trees or shrubs. [ME *ok* < OE *āc.*] —**oak′en** (ō′kən) *adj.*

oak apple *n.* An insect gall on oak trees.

Oak·land (ōk′lənd) A city of W CA on San Francisco Bay opposite San Francisco. Pop. 399,484.

oak leaf cluster *n.* A decoration of bronze or silver oak leaves and acorns given to holders of various US military medals who earn another award of the same medal.

Oak·ley (ōk′lē), **Annie** 1860–1926. Amer. sharpshooter who was the star of Buffalo Bill's Wild West Show.

Oak Park A village of NE IL, a suburb of Chicago. Pop. 52,524.

oa·kum (ō′kəm) *n.* Loose hemp or jute fiber, sometimes treated with tar, creosote, or asphalt, used for caulking seams in wooden ships and packing pipe joints. [ME *okom* < OE *ācumba.* See gembh- in App.]

Oak·ville (ōk′vĭl′) A town of SE Ontario, Canada, on Lake Ontario SW of Toronto. Pop. 128,405.

oak wilt *n.* A disease of oak trees caused by the fungus *Chalara quercina* and often resulting in wilting and dropping of leaves.

oar (ôr, ōr) *n.* **1.** A long, usu. wooden pole with a blade at one end, used to row or steer a boat. **2.** A person who rows, esp. in a race. ❖ *v.* **oared, oar·ing, oars** —*tr.* **1.** To propel with or as if with oars or an oar. **2.** To traverse with or as if with oars or an oar. —*intr.* To move forward by or as if by rowing. [ME *or* < OE *ār.*] —**oared** *adj.* —**oar′less** *adj.*

oar·fish (ôr′fĭsh′, ōr′-) *n., pl.* **oarfish** or **-fish·es** A widespread marine fish (*Regalecus glesne*) having a slender body, a red dorsal fin, and an undulating motion.

oar·lock (ôr′lŏk′, ōr′-) *n.* A device, usu. a U-shaped metal hoop on a swivel in the gunwale, used to hold an oar in place and as a fulcrum in rowing.

oars·man (ôrz′mən, ōrz′-) *n.* A man who rows.

oars·wom·an (ôrz′wŏŏm′ən) *n.* A woman who rows.

OAS *abbr.* Organization of American States

o·a·sis (ō-ā′sĭs) *n., pl.* **-ses** (-sēz) **1.** A fertile or green spot in a desert or wasteland, made so by the presence of water. **2.** A situation or place preserved from surrounding unpleasantness; a refuge. [< LLat. *Oasis,* an oasis in the Libyan desert < Gk. < Coptic *ouahe* < Egypt. *wḥ′t.*]

oast (ōst) *n.* A kiln for drying hops or malt or drying and curing tobacco. [ME *ost* < OE *āst.*]

oat (ōt) *n.* **1.** often **oats** (*used with a sing. or pl. verb*) **a.** Any of various grasses of the genus *Avena,* esp. *A. sativa.* **b.** The grain of any of these plants, used as food and fodder. **2.** *Archaic* A musical pipe made of an oat straw. [ME *ote* < OE *āte.*]

oat·cake (ōt′kāk′) *n.* A flattened cake of baked oatmeal.

oat·en (ōt′n) *adj.* Of, made of, or containing oats, oatmeal, or oat straw: *oaten fodder.*

oat·er (ō′tər) *n. Slang* A western movie. [< the prominence of horses in such films.]

Oates (ōts), **Joyce Carol** b. 1938. Amer. writer whose novels in-

clude *Bellefleur* (1980) and *American Appetites* (1989).

Oates, Titus 1649–1705. English conspirator who forged evidence of a Jesuit plot to assassinate Charles II (1678).

oat grass *n.* **1.** Any of various grasses of the genera *Arrhenatherum* and *Danthonia.* **2.** Any of several oatlike grasses.

oath (ōth) *n., pl.* **oaths** (ōthz, ōths) **1a.** A solemn formal declaration or promise, often calling on God, a god, or a sacred object as witness. **b.** The words or formula of an oath. **c.** Something declared or promised. **2.** An irreverent or blasphemous use of the name of God or something held sacred. **3.** An imprecation; a curse. [ME *oth* < OE *āth.*]

oat·meal (ōt′mēl′) *n.* **1.** Meal made from oats; rolled or ground oats. **2.** A porridge made from rolled or ground oats.

OAU *abbr.* Organization of African Unity

Oa·xa·ca (wə-hä′kə) A city of SE Mexico S of Orizaba; probably founded in 1486 by the Aztecs. Pop. 154,223.

Ob (ŏb, ôb, ôp) A river of central Russia flowing c. 3,700 km (2,300 mi) to the **Gulf of Ob,** an arm of the Arctic Ocean.

OB or **Ob.** also **ob.** *abbr.* **1a.** obstetric **b.** obstetrics **2.** obstetrician

ob. *abbr.* **1.** *Latin* obiit (he died; she died) **2.** *Latin* obiter (incidentally)

Ob. *abbr. Bible* Obadiah

ob- *pref.* Inverse; inversely: *obcordate.* [NLat., short for *obversē, obversely* < Lat. *obversus,* p. part. of *obvertere,* to turn toward : *ob-,* toward, against (< *ob;* see **epi** in App.) + *vertere,* to turn; see VERSUS.]

o·ba (ō′bə) *n.* A hereditary chief or king among various peoples of Benin and Nigeria. [Of African orig.]

O·ba·di·ah¹ (ō′bə-dī′ə) also **Ab·di·as** (ăb-dī′əs) A Hebrew prophet of the 6th cent. B.C. [Heb. *'ōbadyāh,* servant of Yahweh : *'ebed, 'ōbad,* servant + *yāh,* Yahweh.]

O·ba·di·ah² (ō′bə-dī′ə) *n.* See table at **Bible.** [< OBADIAH¹.]

ob·bli·ga·to also **ob·li·ga·to** (ŏb′lĭ-gä′tō) *Music adj.* Not to be left out. Used of an accompaniment. ❖ *n., pl.* **-tos** or **-ti** (-tē) An obbligato accompaniment. [Ital., p. part. of *obbligare,* to obligate < Lat. *obligāre,* to oblige. See OBLIGE.]

ob·com·pressed (ŏb′kəm-prĕst′) *adj.* Flattened from back to front instead of side to side, as in the fruit of pennycress.

ob·cor·date (ŏb-kôr′dāt′) *adj. Botany* Heart-shaped, with the point of attachment at the narrow end: *an obcordate leaf.*

ob·du·ra·cy (ŏb′dŏŏr-ə-sē, -dyŏŏr-) *n.* The state or quality of being intractable or hardened.

ob·du·rate (ŏb′dŏŏr-ĭt, -dyŏŏr-) *adj.* **1a.** Hardened in wrongdoing or wickedness; stubbornly impenitent. **b.** Hardened against feeling; hardhearted: *an obdurate miser.* **2.** Not giving in to persuasion; intractable. [ME *obdurat* < LLat. *obdūrātus,* p. part. of *obdūrāre,* to harden < Lat., to be hard, endure : *ob-,* intensive pref.; see OB- + *dūrus,* hard; see deru- in App.] —**ob′du·rate·ly** *adv.* —**ob′du·rate·ness** *n.*

OBE *abbr.* Order of the British Empire

o·be·ah (ō′bē-ə) also **o·bi** (ō′bē) *n., pl.* **o·be·ahs** also **o·bis 1.** A form of religious belief of African origin, practiced in some parts of the West Indies, Jamaica, and nearby tropical America, involving sorcery. **2.** An object, charm, or fetish used in the practice of this religion. [Black and West Indian E., of West African orig.; akin to Efik *ubio,* anything noxious, bad omen.]

o·be·di·ence (ō-bē′dē-əns) *n.* **1a.** The quality or condition of being obedient. **b.** The act of obeying. **2a.** A sphere of ecclesiastical authority. **b.** A group of people under it.

o·be·di·ent (ō-bē′dē-ənt) *adj.* Dutifully complying with the commands, orders, or instructions of one in authority. [ME < OFr. < Lat. *oboediēns, oboedient-,* pr. part. of *oboedīre,* to obey. See OBEY.] —**o·be′di·ent·ly** *adv.*

o·bei·sance (ō-bā′səns, ō-bē′-) *n.* **1.** A gesture or movement of the body that expresses deference or homage. **2.** An attitude of deference or homage. [ME *obeisaunce* < OFr. *obeissance* < *obeissant,* pr. part. of *obeir,* to obey. See OBEY.] —**o·bei′sant** *adj.*

o·be·lia (ō-bēl′yə) *n.* Any of various colonial marine hydroids of the genus *Obelia,* growing in a branchlike form and found on wooden piles. [NLat. *Obelia,* genus name, prob. < Gk. *obeliās,* a loaf baked on a spit < *obelos,* a spit.]

ob·e·lisk (ŏb′ə-lĭsk) *n.* **1.** A tall four-sided shaft of stone, usu. tapered and monolithic, that rises to a pointed pyramidal top. **2.** *Printing* The dagger sign (†), used esp. as a reference mark. [Lat. *obeliscus* < Gk. *obeliskos,* dim. of *obelos,* a spit, obelisk.] —**ob′e·lis′cal** (-lĭs′kəl). —**ob′e·lis′koid** (-koid′) *adj.*

ob·e·lize (ŏb′ə-līz′) *tr.v.* **-lized, -liz·ing, -liz·es** To mark or annotate with an obelus. [Gk. *obelizein* < *obelos,* obelus.]

oak apple
gall on a red oak tree

Annie Oakley

obelisk
Obelisk of Thutmose I,
Karnak Temple, Luxor,
Egypt

ob·e·lus (ŏb′ə-ləs) *n.*, *pl.* **-li** (-lī′) **1.** A mark (— or ÷) used in ancient manuscripts to indicate a doubtful or spurious passage. **2.** *Printing* See **obelisk** 2. [ME < LLat. *obelus* < Gk. *obelos*, a spit, obelus.]

o·ben·to (ō-bĕn′tō) or **ben·to** (bĕn′-) *n.*, *pl.* **-tos** A Japanese meal that is packed in a partitioned lacquered box. [J. *obentō* : *o-*, politeness pref. + *bentō*, box lunch.]

O·ber·am·mer·gau (ō′bər-äm′ər-gou′) A town of S Germany in the Bavarian Alps SSW of Munich; famed for its Passion plays, held every ten years since 1634.

O·ber·hau·sen (ō′bər-hou′zən) A city of W-central Germany in the Ruhr Valley WNW of Essen. Pop. 226,254.

O·ber·on (ō′bə-rŏn′, -rən) *n.* **1.** The king of the fairies and husband of Titania in medieval folklore. **2.** A satellite of Uranus. [Fr. < OFr. *Auberon*, of Gmc. orig. See **albho-** in App.]

o·bese (ō-bēs′) *adj.* Extremely fat; grossly overweight. See Syns at **fat**. [Lat. *obēsus* < p. part. of **obedere*, to eat away : *ob-*, away; see OB– + *edere*, to eat; see **ed-** in App.] —**o·bese′ly** *adv.* —**o·bese′ness** *n.*

o·be·si·ty (ō-bē′sĭ-tē) *n.* The condition of being obese; increased body weight caused by excessive fat.

o·bey (ō-bā′) *v.* **o·beyed, o·bey·ing, o·beys** —*tr.* **1.** To carry out or fulfill the command, order, or instruction of. **2.** To carry out or comply with (a command, for example). —*intr.* **3.** To behave obediently. [ME *obeien* < OFr. *obeir* < Lat. *oboedīre*, to listen to : *ob-*, to; see OB– + *audīre*, to hear.] —**o·bey′er** *n.*

ob·fus·cate (ŏb′fə-skāt′, ŏb-fŭs′kāt′) *tr.v.* **-cat·ed, -cat·ing, -cates 1.** To make so confused or opaque as to be difficult to perceive or understand. **2.** To render indistinct or dim; darken. [Lat. *obfuscāre, obfuscāt-*, to darken : *ob-*, over; see OB– + *fuscāre*, to darken (< *fuscus*, dark).] —**ob′fus·ca′tion** *n.* —**ob·fus′ca·to′ry** (ŏb-fŭs′kə-tôr′ē, -tōr′ē, ŏb-) *adj.*

ob-gyn (ō′bē-jē′-wī-ĕn′) *n. Informal* **1.** The practice or field of obstetrics and gynecology. **2.** A specialist in this field.

o·bi¹ (ō′bē) *n.*, *pl.* **o·bis** A wide sash fastened in the back with a flat bow, traditionally worn by Japanese women. [J.]

o·bi² (ō′bē) *n.* Variant of **obeah.**

O·bie (ō′bē) *n.* An award for excellence in the creation and production of off-Broadway theater. [< *O.B.*, abbr. for OFF-BROADWAY.]

o·bit (ō′bĭt, ō-bĭt′) *n. Informal* An obituary. [ME, record of death date < OFr., death < Lat. *obitus*. See OBITUARY.]

o·bi·ter dictum (ō′bĭ-tər) *n.*, *pl.* **obiter dicta 1.** *Law* An opinion voiced by a judge that has only incidental bearing on the case in question and is therefore not binding. **2.** An incidental remark or observation; a passing comment. [Lat., something said in passing : *obiter*, in passing + *dictum*, something said < neut. p. part. of *dīcere*, to say.]

o·bit·u·ar·y (ō-bĭch′ōō-ĕr′ē) *n.*, *pl.* **-ies** A published notice of a death. [Med.Lat. *obituārius*, (report) of death < Lat. *obitus*, death < p. part. of *obīre*, meet one's death : *ob-*, toward; see OB– + *īre*, to go; see **ei-** in App.] —**o·bit′u·ar′y** *adj.*

obj. *abbr.* **1.** object **2.** objective

ob·ject (ŏb′jĭkt, -jĕkt′) *n.* **1.** Something perceptible by one or more of the senses, esp. by vision or touch; a material thing. **2.** A focus of attention, feeling, thought, or action. **3.** The purpose, aim, or goal of a specific action or effort. **4.** *Grammar* **a.** A noun, pronoun, or noun phrase that receives or is affected by the action of a verb within a sentence. **b.** A noun or substantive governed by a preposition and typically following it. **5.** *Philosophy* Something intelligible or perceptible by the mind. **6.** *Computer Science* A discrete item that can be selected and maneuvered, such as an on-screen graphic. In object-oriented programming, objects include data and the procedures necessary to operate on that data. ❖ *v.* (əb-jĕkt′) **-ject·ed, -ject·ing, -jects** —*intr.* **1.** To present a dissenting or opposing argument; raise an objection. **2.** To be averse to or express disapproval of something. —*tr.* To put forward in or as a reason for opposition; offer as criticism. [ME < OFr. < Med.Lat. *obiectum*, thing put before the mind < neut. p. part. of Lat. *obicere*, to put before : *ob-*, before, toward; see OB– + *iacere*, to throw. V. < ME *obiecten* < OFr. *objecter* < Lat. *obiectāre*, freq. of *obicere*.] —**ob·jec′tor** *n.*

SYNONYMS *object, protest, demur, remonstrate, expostulate* These verbs mean to express opposition to something, usually by presenting arguments against it. *Object* implies the expression of disapproval or distaste: *"Freedom of the press in Britain is freedom to print such of the proprietor's prejudices as the advertisers don't object to"* (Hannen Swaffer). *Protest* suggests strong opposition, usually forthrightly expressed: *The citizens protested against the tax hike.* To *demur* is to raise an objection that may delay decision or action: *We proposed a revote, but the president demurred.* *Remonstrate* implies the presentation of objections, complaints, or reproof in the form of argument or pleading: *"The people of Connecticut . . . remonstrated against the bill"* (George Bancroft). To *expostulate* is to express objection through earnest reasoning: *expostulated with them on the foolhardiness of their behavior.* See also Syns at **intention.**

oboe

object ball *n.* The ball in billiards or pool that a player hits or intends to hit first with the cue ball.

object code *n.* The code produced by a compiler from the source

---

code, usu. in the form of machine language that a computer can execute directly.

object glass *n.* See **objective** 4.

ob·jec·ti·fy (əb-jĕk′tə-fī′) *tr.v.* **-fied, -fy·ing, -fies 1.** To present or regard as an object: *"Because we have objectified animals, we are able to treat them impersonally"* (Barry Lopez). **2.** To make objective, external, or concrete: *thoughts objectified in art.* —**ob·jec′ti·fi·ca′tion** (-fĭ-kā′shən) *n.* —**ob·jec′ti·fi′er** *n.*

ob·jec·tion (əb-jĕk′shən) *n.* **1.** The act of objecting. **2.** A statement presented in opposition. **3.** A ground, reason, or cause for expressing opposition.

ob·jec·tion·a·ble (əb-jĕk′shə-nə-bəl) *adj.* Arousing disapproval; offensive. —**ob·jec′tion·a·bil′i·ty, ob·jec′tion·a·ble·ness** *n.* —**ob·jec′tion·a·bly** *adv.*

ob·jec·tive (əb-jĕk′tĭv) *adj.* **1.** Of or having to do with a material object. **2.** Having actual existence or reality. **3a.** Uninfluenced by emotions or personal prejudices. See Syns at **fair¹**. **b.** Based on observable phenomena; presented factually: *an objective appraisal.* **4.** *Medicine* Indicating a symptom perceived as a sign of disease by someone other than the person affected. **5.** *Grammar* **a.** Of, relating to, or being the case of a noun or pronoun that serves as the object of a verb or a preposition. **b.** Of or relating to a noun or pronoun used in this case. ❖ *n.* **1.** Something that actually exists. **2.** Something worked or striven for; a goal. See Syns at **intention**. **3.** *Grammar* **a.** The objective case. **b.** A noun or pronoun in the objective case. **4.** The lens or lens system in a microscope or other optical instrument that first receives light from the object. —**ob·jec′tive·ly** *adv.* —**ob·jec′tive·ness** *n.*

objective complement *n.* A noun, adjective, or pronoun serving as a complement to a verb and qualifying its direct object, as *governor* in *They elected him governor.*

objective correlative *n.* A situation or a series of events or objects that evokes an emotion in a reader or audience.

objective lens *n.* See **objective** 4.

ob·jec·tiv·ism (ŏb-jĕk′tə-vĭz′əm) *n.* **1.** *Philosophy* One of several doctrines holding that all reality is objective and that knowledge is reliably based on observed objects and events. **2.** An emphasis on objects rather than feelings or thoughts in literature or art. —**ob·jec′tiv·ist** *n.* —**ob·jec′tiv·is′tic** *adj.*

ob·jec·tiv·i·ty (ŏb′jĕk-tĭv′ĭ-tē) *n.* **1.** The state or quality of being objective. **2.** External or material reality.

ob·jec·ti·vize (əb-jĕk′tə-vīz′) *tr.v.* **-vized, -viz·ing, -viz·es** To make objective or impersonal; objectify. —**ob·jec′ti·vi·za′tion** (-vĭ-zā′shən) *n.*

object language *n.* See **target language.**

object lens *n.* See **objective** 4.

object lesson *n.* **1.** A concrete illustration of a moral or principle. **2.** A lesson taught by using a material object.

ob·ject-o·ri·ent·ed (ŏb′jĭkt-ôr′ē-ən-tĭd, -ĕn′-, -ôr′-, -jĕkt′-) *adj. Computer Science* Of, related to, or being a language or system that can use and support objects: *an object-oriented interface.*

ob·jet d'art (ŏb′zhĕ där′) *n.*, *pl.* **ob·jets d'art** (ŏb′zhĕ där′) An object of artistic merit. [Fr. : *objet*, object + *de*, of + *art*, art.]

ob·jet trou·vé (ô-bzhā′ trōō-vā′) *n.*, *pl.* **ob·jets trou·vés** (ŏb-zhā′ trōō-vā′) See **found object**. [Fr. : *objet*, object + *trouvé*, p. part. of *trouver*, to find.]

ob·jur·gate (ŏb′jər-gāt′, ŏb-jûr′gāt′) *tr.v.* **-gat·ed, -gat·ing, -gates** To scold or rebuke sharply; berate. [Lat. *obiūrgāre, obiūrgāt-*, against; see OB– + *iūrgāre*, to scold, sue at law (prob. *iūs, iūr-*, law + *agere*, to do, proceed; see **ag-** in App.).] —**ob′jur·ga′tion** *n.* —**ob·jur′ga·to′ri·ly** (ŏb-jûr′gə-tôr′ə-lē, -tōr′-) *adv.* —**ob·jur′ga·to′ry** (-tôr′ē, -tōr′ē) *adj.*

obl. *abbr.* **1.** oblique **2.** oblong

ob·lan·ce·o·late (ŏb-lăn′sē-ə-lāt′) *adj. Botany* Lance-shaped but broadest above the middle: *an oblanceolate leaf.*

o·blast (ô′blăst, ô′bläst′) *n.* An administrative territorial division within Russia and other former Soviet republics. [Russ. *oblast'* < O Church Slavonic *oblastĭ* : *ob*, on; see **epi** in App. + *vlastĭ*, power.]

ob·late¹ (ŏb′lāt′, ŏ-blāt′) *adj.* **1.** Having the shape of a spheroid generated by rotating an ellipse about its shorter axis. **2.** Having an equatorial diameter greater than the distance between poles; flattened at the poles. [Prob. NLat. *oblātus* : Lat. *ob-*, toward; see OB– + *lātus* (*prō*)*lātus*; see PROLATE.] —**ob′late′ly** *adv.* —**ob′late′ness** *n.*

ob·late² (ŏb′lāt′) *n.* **1.** A layperson dedicated to religious life. **2.** **Oblate** *Roman Catholic Church* A member of one of various religious communities for men or women. [Med.Lat. *oblātus* < Lat., p. part. of *offerre*, to offer. See OFFER.]

ob·la·tion (ə-blā′shən, ŏ-blā′-) *n.* **1.** The act of offering something to a deity. **2.** **Oblation a.** The act of offering the bread and wine of the Eucharist. **b.** Something offered, esp. the bread and wine of the Eucharist. **3.** A charitable offering or gift. [ME *oblacioun* < OFr. *oblacion* < LLat. *oblātiō, oblātiōn-* < Lat. *oblātus*, p. part. of *offerre*, to offer : *ob-, ob-* + *lātus*, brought; see **telə-** in App.] —**ob·la′tion·al, ob·la′to·ry** (ŏb′lə-tôr′ē, -tōr′ē) *adj.*

ob·li·gate (ŏb′lĭ-gāt′) *tr.v.* **-gat·ed, -gat·ing, -gates 1.** To bind, compel, or constrain by a social, legal, or moral tie. **2.** To cause to be grateful or indebted; oblige. **3.** To commit (money, for example) in order to fulfill an obligation. ❖ *adj.* (-gĭt, -gāt′) **1.** *Biology* Able to survive only in a particular environment or by assuming a particular role. **2.** Absolutely indispensable. [Lat. *obligāre, obligāt-*. See OBLIGE.] **—ob′li•ga•ble** (-gə-bəl) *adj.* **—ob′li•gate•ly** *adv.* **—ob′li•ga′tor** *n.*

ob•li•ga•tion (ŏb′lĭ-gā′shən) *n.* **1.** The act of binding oneself by a social, legal, or moral tie. **2a.** A social, legal, or moral requirement that compels one to follow or avoid a particular course of action. **b.** A course of action imposed by society, law, or conscience by which one is bound or restricted. **3.** The constraining power of a promise, contract, law, or sense of duty. **4.** *Law* **a.** A legal agreement stipulating a specified payment or action, esp. if the agreement also specifies a penalty for failure to comply. **b.** The document detailing such an agreement. **5a.** Something owed as payment or in return for a special service or favor. **b.** This service or favor. **6.** The state, fact, or feeling of being indebted to another for this service or favor. **—ob′li•ga′tion•al** *adj.*

ob•li•ga•to (ŏb′lĭ-gä′tō) *adj. & n.* Variant of **obbligato.**

o•blig•a•to•ry (ə-blĭg′ə-tôr′ē, -tōr′ē, ŏb′lĭ-gə-) *adj.* **1.** Morally or legally constraining; binding. **2.** Imposing or recording an obligation. **3.** Of the nature of an obligation; compulsory. **4.** *Biology* Obligate. **—o•blig′a•to′ri•ly** *adv.*

o•blige (ə-blīj′) *v.* **o•bliged, o•blig•ing, o•blig•es** *—tr.* **1.** To constrain by physical, legal, social, or moral means. **2.** To make indebted or grateful. **3.** To do a service or favor for. *—intr.* To do a service or favor. [ME *obligen* < OFr. *obligier* < Lat. *obligāre* : *ob-*, to; see OB– + *ligāre*, to bind.] **—o•blig′er** *n.*

ob•li•gee (ŏb′lə-jē′) *n.* One to whom another is bound by contract or legal agreement.

o•blig•ing (ə-blī′jĭng) *adj.* Ready to do favors for others; accommodating. **—o•blig′ing•ly** *adv.* **—o•blig′ing•ness** *n.*

ob•li•gor (ŏb′lĭ-gôr′, -jôr′) *n.* One who binds oneself to another by contract or legal agreement.

o•blique (ō-blēk′, ə-blēk′) *adj.* **1a.** Having a slanting or sloping direction, course, or position. **b.** *Mathematics* Being lines or planes that are neither parallel nor perpendicular. **2.** *Botany* Having sides of unequal length or form. **3.** *Anatomy* Situated in a slanting position; not transverse or longitudinal. **4a.** Indirect or evasive. **b.** Devious, misleading, or dishonest. **5.** Not direct in descent; collateral. **6.** *Grammar* Being any case except nominative or vocative. ❖ *n.* An oblique thing, such as a line or muscle. ❖ *adv.* (ō-blīk′, ə-blīk′) At an angle of 45°. [ME < OFr. < Lat. *oblīquus*.] **—o•blique′ly** *adv.* **—o•blique′ness** *n.*

oblique angle *n.* An angle that is not a right angle or a multiple of a right angle.

oblique rhyme *n.* See **off rhyme.**

oblique triangle *n.* A triangle having no right angle.

o•bliq•ui•ty (ō-blĭk′wĭ-tē, ə-blĭk′-) *n., pl.* **-ties 1.** The quality or condition of being oblique. **2a.** A deviation from the vertical or the horizontal. **b.** The angle or extent of such a deviation. **3a.** A mental deviation or aberration. **b.** Immoral conduct. **4a.** Obscurity in conduct or verbal expression. **b.** An obscure statement. **—o•bliq′ui•tous** *adj.*

o•blit•er•ate (ə-blĭt′ə-rāt′, ō-blĭt′-) *tr.v.* **-at•ed, -at•ing, -ates 1.** To do away with completely so as to leave no trace. **2.** To wipe out, rub off, or erase (writing or other markings). **3.** *Medicine* To remove completely (a body organ or part), as by surgery or disease. [Lat. *oblitterāre, oblitterāt-*, to erase < *ob litterās (scrībere)*, (to write) over letters (*ob*, over; see OB– + *litterās*, accusative pl. of *littera*, letter) and < *oblītus*, p. part. of *oblīvīscī*, to forget; see OBLIVION.] **—o•blit′er•a′tion** *n.* **—o•blit′er•a′tive** (-ə-rā′tĭv, -ər-ə-tĭv) *adj.* **—o•blit′er•a′tor** *n.*

o•bliv•i•on (ə-blĭv′ē-ən) *n.* **1.** The condition or quality of being completely forgotten. **2.** The act or an instance of forgetting; total forgetfulness. **3.** Official overlooking of offenses; amnesty. [ME < OFr. < Lat. *oblīviō, oblīviōn-* < *oblīvīscī*, to forget.]

o•bliv•i•ous (ə-blĭv′ē-əs) *adj.* **1.** Lacking all memory; forgetful. **2.** Lacking conscious awareness; unmindful. **—o•bliv′i•ous•ly** *adv.* **—o•bliv′i•ous•ness** *n.*

USAGE NOTE While either *of* or *to* can be used acceptably with *oblivious, to* is more common: *He was oblivious to my presence.*

ob•long (ŏb′lông′, -lŏng′) *adj.* **1.** Deviating from a square, circular, or spherical form by being elongated in one direction. **2.** Having the shape of or resembling a rectangle or ellipse. **3.** *Botany* Having a somewhat elongated form with approximately parallel sides: *an oblong leaf.* ❖ *n.* An oblong object or figure. [ME < Lat. *oblongus* : *ob-*, intensive pref. (sense uncertain); see OB– + *longus*, long; see **del-** in App.]

ob•lo•quy (ŏb′lə-kwē) *n., pl.* **-quies 1.** Abusively detractive language or utterance; calumny. **2.** The condition of disgrace suffered as a result of abuse or vilification; ill repute. [ME *obloqui* < LLat. *obloquium*, abusive contradiction < Lat. *obloquī*, to interrupt : *ob-*, against; see OB– + *loquī*, to speak.]

ob•nox•ious (ŏb-nŏk′shəs, əb-) *adj.* **1.** Very annoying or objectionable; offensive or odious. **2.** *Archaic* Exposed to harm or evil. **3.** *Archaic* Deserving of or liable to censure. [Lat. *obnoxiōsus*, subordinate < *obnoxius*, liable : *ob-*, to; see OB– + *noxa*, injury; see **nek-** in App.] **—ob•nox′ious•ly** *adv.* **—ob•nox′ious•ness** *n.*

o•boe (ō′bō) *n.* A slender double-reed woodwind instrument with a conical bore and a penetrating, poignant sound. [Ital. < Fr. *hautbois*. See HAUTBOY.] **—o′bo•ist** *n.*

ob•ol (ŏb′əl) also **ob•o•lus** (ŏb′ə-ləs) *n., pl.* **-ols** also **-o•li** (-ə-lī′) A silver coin or unit of weight equal to one sixth of a drachma, used in ancient Greece. [Lat. *obolus* < Gk. *obolos*, var. of *obelos*, spit, obol.]

ob•o•vate (ŏb-ō′vāt′) *adj. Botany* Egg-shaped and flat, with the narrow end attached to the stalk: *an obovate leaf.*

ob•o•void (ŏb-ō′void′) *adj. Botany* Egg-shaped and solid, with the narrow end attached to the stem: *an obovoid fruit.*

O•bre•no•vić (ō-brĕn′ə-vĭch′), **Alexander** See **Alexander I**[2].

O'Bri•en (ō-brī′ən), **Edna** b. 1932. Irish writer whose works include *Johnny I Hardly Knew You* (1977).

Edna O'Brien

obs. *abbr.* **1.** observation **2.** observatory **3.** obsolete

ob•scene (ŏb-sēn′, əb-) *adj.* **1.** Offensive to accepted standards of decency or modesty. **2.** Inciting lustful feelings; lewd. **3.** Repulsive; disgusting. **4.** So large in amount as to be objectionable or outrageous: *an obscene increase in rent.* [Lat. *obscēnus*.] **—ob•scene′ly** *adv.*

ob•scen•i•ty (ŏb-sĕn′ĭ-tē, əb-) *n., pl.* **-ties 1.** The state or quality of being obscene. **2.** Indecency, lewdness, or offensiveness in behavior, expression, or appearance. **3.** Something, such as a word, act, or expression, that is indecent or lewd. **4.** Something that is offensive or repulsive to the senses.

ob•scur•ant (ŏb-skyo͝or′ənt, əb-) *n.* One who opposes intellectual advancement and political reform. ❖ *adj.* **1.** Characterized by opposition to intellectual advancement and political reform. **2.** Tending to make obscure.

ob•scur•ant•ism (ŏb-skyo͝or′ən-tĭz′əm, əb-, ŏb′skyo͝o-răn′-) *n.* **1.** The principles or practice of obscurants. **2.** A policy of withholding information from the public. **3a.** A style in art and literature of deliberate vagueness or obliqueness. **b.** An instance of this style. **—ob•scur′ant•ist** *n.*

ob•scure (ŏb-skyo͝or′, əb-) *adj.* **-scur•er, -scur•est 1.** Deficient in light; dark. **2a.** So faintly perceptible as to lack clear delineation; indistinct. See Syns at **dark. b.** Indistinctly heard; faint. **c.** *Linguistics* Having the reduced, neutral sound represented by schwa (ə). **3a.** Far from centers of human population. **b.** Out of sight; hidden: *an obscure retreat.* **4.** Not readily noticed or seen; inconspicuous: *an obscure flaw.* **5.** Of undistinguished or humble station or reputation: *an obscure poet.* **6.** Not clearly understood or expressed; ambiguous or vague. ❖ *tr.v.* **-scured, -scur•ing, -scures 1.** To make dim or indistinct. See Syns at **block. 2.** To conceal in obscurity; hide. **3.** *Linguistics* To reduce (a vowel) to the neutral sound represented by schwa (ə). ❖ *n.* Something obscure or unknown. [ME < OFr. *obscur* < Lat. *obscūrus*. See **(s)keu-** in App.] **—ob•scure′ly** *adv.* **—ob•scure′ness** *n.*

observatory
Big Bear Solar Observatory, California

ob•scu•ri•ty (ŏb-skyo͝or′ĭ-tē, əb-) *n., pl.* **-ties 1.** Deficiency or absence of light; darkness. **2a.** The quality or state of being unknown. **b.** One that is unknown. **3a.** The quality or state of being imperfectly known or difficult to understand. **b.** An instance of such obscurity.

ob•se•qui•ous (ŏb-sē′kwē-əs, əb-) *adj.* Full of or exhibiting servile compliance; fawning. [ME < Lat. *obsequiōsus* < *obsequium*, compliance < *obsequī*, to comply : *ob-*, to; see OB– + *sequī*, to follow; see **sekʷ-**[1] in App.] **—ob•se′qui•ous•ly** *adv.* **—ob•se′qui•ous•ness** *n.*

ob•se•quy (ŏb′sĭ-kwē) *n., pl.* **-quies** A funeral rite or ceremony. Often used in the plural. [ME *obsequi* < OFr. *obseque* < Med.Lat. *obsequiae*, alteration of Lat. *obsequia*, pl. of *obsequium*, dutiful service. See OBSEQUIOUS.]

ob•serv•a•ble (əb-zûr′və-bəl) *adj.* **1.** Possible to observe. **2.** Deserving or worthy of note; noteworthy. ❖ *n.* A physical property, such as weight, that can be observed or measured directly. **—ob•serv′a•bly** *adv.*

ob•ser•vance (əb-zûr′vəns) *n.* **1.** The act or practice of observing or complying with a law, custom, command, or rule. **2.** The act or custom of keeping or celebrating a holiday or other ritual occasion. **3.** A customary rite or ceremony. **4.** The act of watching; observation. **5.** *Roman Catholic Church* The rule governing a religious order.

ob•ser•vant (əb-zûr′vənt) *adj.* **1.** Quick to perceive or apprehend; alert. See Syns at **careful. 2.** Diligent in observing a law, custom, duty, or principle. **—ob•ser′vant•ly** *adv.*

ob•ser•va•tion (ŏb′zər-vā′shən) *n.* **1a.** The act or faculty of observing. **b.** The fact of being observed. **2a.** The act of noting and recording something with instruments. **b.** The result or record of such notation. **3.** A comment or remark. See Syns at **comment. 4.** An inference or a judgment that is acquired from or based on observing. **—ob′ser•va′tion•al** *adj.*

ob•ser•va•to•ry (əb-zûr′və-tôr′ē, -tōr′ē) *n., pl.* **-ries 1.** A building, place, or institution designed and equipped for making observations of astronomical, meteorological, or other natural phenomena. **2.** A structure overlooking an extensive view. [Fr. *observatoire* (influenced by CONSERVATORY) < *observer*, to observe < OFr. See OBSERVE.]

ob•serve (əb-zûrv′) *v.* **-served, -serv•ing, -serves** *—tr.* **1.** To be or become aware of, esp. through careful and directed attention; notice. See Syns at **see**[1]. **2.** To watch attentively. **3.** To make a systematic or scientific observation of. **4.** To say casually; remark. **5.** To adhere to or abide by: *observe the terms of a contract.* **6.** To keep or celebrate (a holiday, for example). *—intr.* **1.** To take notice. **2.** To say something; make a comment or remark. **3.** To watch or be present without participating actively. [ME *observen*,

ă	pat	oi	boy
ā	pay	ou	**out**
âr	**care**	o͝o	took
ä	father	o͞o	boot
ĕ	pet	ŭ	cut
ē	be	ûr	**urge**
ĭ	pit	th	**thin**
ī	pie	*th*	this
îr	**pier**	hw	**which**
ŏ	pot	zh	vision
ō	**toe**	ə	about,
ô	paw		item

Stress marks:
′ (primary);
′ (secondary), as in
lexicon (lĕk′sĭ-kŏn′)

to conform to < OFr. *observer* < Lat. *observāre*, to abide by, watch : *ob-*, over; see OB– + *servāre*, to keep, watch.]

ob·serv·er (əb-zûr′vər) *n.* **1.** One that observes. **2.** A delegate sent to observe and report on the proceedings of an assembly or meeting. **3a.** A crew member on a military aircraft who makes observations. **b.** A member of an armed force who watches and reports from an observation post.

ob·sess (əb-sĕs′, ŏb-) *v.* **-sessed, -sess·ing, -sess·es** —*tr.* To preoccupy the mind of excessively. —*intr.* To have the mind excessively preoccupied with a single emotion or topic. [Lat. *obsidēre, obsess-,* to beset, occupy : *ob-,* on; see OB– + *sedēre,* to sit; see **sed-** in App.] —**ob·ses′sor** *n.*

ob·ses·sion (əb-sĕsh′ən, ŏb-) *n.* **1.** Compulsive preoccupation with a fixed idea or an unwanted feeling or emotion, often accompanied by symptoms of anxiety. **2.** A compulsive, often unreasonable idea or emotion. —**ob·ses′sion·al** *adj.*

ob·ses·sive (əb-sĕs′ĭv, ŏb-) *adj.* **1.** Of, relating to, characteristic of, or causing an obsession. **2.** Excessive in degree or nature. —**ob·ses′sive** *n.* —**ob·ses′sive·ly** *adv.* —**ob·ses′sive·ness** *n.*

ob·ses·sive-com·pul·sive (əb-sĕs′ĭv-kəm-pŭl′sĭv, ŏb-) *adj.* Relating to or characterized by a tendency to dwell on unwanted thoughts or ideas or perform certain repetitive rituals, esp. as a defense against anxiety from unconscious conflicts. ❖ *n.* An obsessive-compulsive person.

ob·sid·i·an (əb-sĭd′ē-ən) *n.* A usu. black or banded, hard volcanic glass that is formed by rapid cooling of lava. [Lat. *obsidiānus,* misreading of *obsiānus (lapis),* Obsian (stone), obsidian, after *Obsius,* Roman who may have discovered it.]

ob·so·lesce (ŏb′sə-lĕs′) *intr.v.* **-lesced, -lesc·ing, -lesc·es** To undergo the process of becoming obsolete. [Lat. *obsolēscere.* See OBSOLESCENT.]

ob·so·les·cent (ŏb′sə-lĕs′ənt) *adj.* **1.** Being in the process of passing out of use or usefulness; becoming obsolete. **2.** *Biology* Gradually disappearing; imperfectly or only slightly developed. Used of a part of an organism. [Lat. *obsolēscēns, obsolēscent-,* pr. part. of *obsolēscere,* to fall into disuse : *ob-,* away; see OB– + *solēre,* to be accustomed to.] —**ob′so·les′cence** *n.* —**ob′so·les′cent·ly** *adv.*

ob·so·lete (ŏb′sə-lēt′, ŏb′sə-lēt′) *adj.* **1.** No longer in use. **2.** Outmoded in design, style, or construction. **3.** *Biology* Vestigial or imperfectly developed, esp. in comparison with other individuals or related species. Used of a part of an organism. ❖ *tr.v.* **-let·ed, -let·ing, -letes** To cause to become obsolete. [Lat. *obsolētus,* p. part. of *obsolēscere,* to fall into disuse. See OBSOLESCENT.] —**ob′so·lete′ly** *adv.* —**ob′so·lete′ness** *n.* —**ob′so·let′ism** *n.*

ob·sta·cle (ŏb′stə-kəl) *n.* One that opposes, stands in the way of, or holds up progress. [ME < OFr. < Lat. *obstāculum* < *obstāre,* to hinder : *ob-,* against; see OB– + *stāre,* to stand; see **stā-** in App.]

obstacle course *n.* **1.** A training course with obstacles that must be negotiated speedily, as by troops in training. **2.** A situation full of obstacles that must be overcome.

ob·stet·ric (ŏb-stĕt′rĭk, əb-) also **ob·stet·ri·cal** (-rĭ-kəl) *adj.* Of or relating to the profession of obstetrics or the care of women during and after pregnancy. [Lat. *obstetrīcius,* pertaining to a midwife < *obstetrīx, obstetrīc-,* midwife < *obstitus,* p. part. of *obstāre,* to stand opposite to : *ob-,* opposite to; see OB– + *stāre,* to stand; see **stā-** in App.] —**ob·stet′ri·cal·ly** *adv.*

ob·ste·tri·cian (ŏb′stĭ-trĭsh′ən) *n.* A physician who specializes in obstetrics.

ob·stet·rics (ŏb-stĕt′rĭks, əb-) *n.* (*used with a sing. or pl. verb*) The branch of medicine that deals with the care of women during pregnancy and during and following childbirth.

ob·sti·na·cy (ŏb′stə-nə-sē) *n., pl.* **-cies 1.** The state or quality of being stubborn or refractory. **2.** The act or an instance of being stubborn or refractory.

ob·sti·nate (ŏb′stə-nĭt) *adj.* **1.** Stubbornly adhering to an attitude, opinion, or course of action; obdurate. **2.** Difficult to manage, control, or subdue. **3.** Difficult to alleviate or cure. [ME *obstinat* < Lat. *obstinātus,* p. part. of *obstināre,* to persist. See **stā-** in App.] —**ob′sti·nate·ly** *adv.* —**ob′sti·nate·ness** *n.*

SYNONYMS *obstinate, stubborn, headstrong, stiff-necked, bull-headed, pigheaded, mulish, dogged, pertinacious* These adjectives mean tenaciously unwilling to yield. *Obstinate* implies unreasonable rigidity: "*Mr. Quincy labored hard with the governor to obtain his assent, but he was obstinate*" (Benjamin Franklin). *Stubborn* pertains to innate, often perverse resoluteness or unyieldingness: "*She was very stubborn when her mind was made up*" (Samuel Butler). One who is *headstrong* is stubbornly, often recklessly willful: *The headstrong teenager ignored school policy. Stiff-necked* implies stubbornness combined with arrogance or aloofness: *the stiff-necked family patriarch. Bullheaded* suggests foolish or irrational obstinacy, and *pigheaded,* stupid obstinacy: *Don't be bullheaded; see a doctor.* "*It's a pity pious folks are so apt to be pigheaded*" (Harriet Beecher Stowe). *Mulish* implies obstinacy and intractability: "*Obstinate is no word for it, for she is mulish*" (Ouida). *Dogged* emphasizes stubborn perseverance: "*two warring ideals in one dark body, whose dogged strength alone keeps it from being torn asunder*" (W.E.B. Du Bois). *Pertinacious* stresses a tenacity, as of purpose, that is sometimes vexatious: *a tax bill led to defeat by pertinacious critics.* See also Syns at **unruly.**

obtuse angle
Angle *AOB* is
an obtuse angle.

ob·strep·er·ous (ŏb-strĕp′ər-əs, əb-) *adj.* **1.** Noisily and stubbornly defiant. **2.** Aggressively boisterous. [< Lat. *obstreperus,* noisy < *obstrepere,* to make a noise against : *ob-,* against; see OB– + *strepere,* to make a noise (of imit. orig.).] —**ob·strep′er·ous·ly** *adv.* —**ob·strep′er·ous·ness** *n.*

ob·struct (əb-strŭkt′, ŏb-) *tr.v.* **-struct·ed, -struct·ing, -structs 1.** To block or fill (a passage) with obstacles or an obstacle. See Syns at **block. 2.** To impede, retard, or interfere with; hinder: *obstructed my progress.* **3.** To get in the way of so as to hide from sight. [Lat. *obstruere, obstrūct-* : *ob-,* against; see OB– + *struere,* to pile up.] —**ob·struct′er, ob·struc′tor** *n.* —**ob·struc′tive** *adj.* —**ob·struc′tive·ly** *adv.* —**ob·struc′tive·ness** *n.*

ob·struc·tion (əb-strŭk′shən, ŏb-) *n.* **1.** One that obstructs; an obstacle. **2a.** The act or an instance of obstructing. **b.** The condition of being obstructed. **3.** The act of causing a delay or an attempt to cause a delay in the conduct of business, esp. in a legislative body. **4.** *Sports* The act of impeding another player in a match or race.

ob·struc·tion·ist (əb-strŭk′shə-nĭst, ŏb-) *n.* One who systematically blocks or interrupts a process, esp. one who attempts to impede passage of legislation by the use of delaying tactics. —**ob·struc′tion·ism** *n.* —**ob·struc′tion·is′tic** *adj.*

obstruction of justice *n.* The criminal offense, under common law and according to the statutes of many jurisdictions, of obstructing the administration and due process of law.

ob·stru·ent (ŏb′strŏŏ-ənt) *adj.* Obstructing or closing natural openings or passages of the body. ❖ *n.* **1.** An obstruent medicine or agent. **2.** *Linguistics* A sound, such as an affricate, produced with complete blockage or at least partial constriction of the airflow through the nose or mouth. [Lat. *obstruēns, obstruent-,* pr. part. of *obstruere,* to obstruct. See OBSTRUCT.]

ob·tain (əb-tān′, ŏb-) *v.* **-tained, -tain·ing, -tains** —*tr.* To succeed in gaining possession of as the result of planning or endeavor; acquire. —*intr.* **1.** To be established, accepted, or customary. **2.** *Archaic* To succeed. [ME *obteinen* < OFr. *obtenir* < Lat. *obtinēre* : *ob-,* intensive pref.; see OB– + *tenēre,* to hold; see **ten-** in App.] —**ob·tain′a·ble** *adj.* —**ob·tain′er** *n.*

ob·tect (ŏb-tĕkt′) also **ob·tect·ed** (-tĕk′tĭd) *adj.* Having the wings and appendages enclosed or covered by a secretion that forms a hard shell or horny case, as the pupae of most butterflies and moths. [Lat. *obtēctus,* p. part. of *obtegere,* to cover over : *ob-,* over; see OB– + *tegere,* to cover; see **(s)teg-** in App.]

ob·test (ŏb-tĕst′) *tr.v.* **-test·ed, -test·ing, -tests** To supplicate; entreat. [Lat. *obtestārī* : *ob-,* to; see OB– + *testārī,* to call as a witness (< *testis,* witness; see **trei-** in App.] —**ob′tes·ta′tion** *n.*

ob·trude (ŏb-trŏŏd′, əb-) *v.* **-trud·ed, -trud·ing, -trudes** —*tr.* **1.** To impose (oneself or one's ideas) on others with undue insistence or without invitation. **2.** To thrust out; push forward. —*intr.* To impose oneself on others. [Lat. *obtrūdere* : *ob-,* against; see OB– + *trūdere,* to thrust.] —**ob·trud′er** *n.* —**ob·tru′sion** (-trŏŏ′zhən) *n.*

ob·tru·sive (ŏb-trŏŏ′sĭv, -zĭv, əb-) *adj.* **1.** Thrusting out; protruding. **2.** Tending to push self-assertively forward; brash: *obtrusive behavior.* **3.** Undesirably noticeable: *an obtrusive scar.* [< Lat. *obtrūsus,* p. part. of *obtrūdere,* to obtrude. See OBTRUDE.] —**ob·tru′sive·ly** *adv.* —**ob·tru′sive·ness** *n.*

ob·tund (ŏb-tŭnd′) *tr.v.* **-tund·ed, -tund·ing, -tunds** To make less intense; dull or deaden. [ME *obtunden* < Lat. *obtundere* : *ob-,* against; see OB– + *tundere,* to beat.] —**ob·tund′ent** *adj.* —**ob·tun′di·ty** *n.*

ob·tu·rate (ŏb′tə-rāt′, -tyə-) *tr.v.* **-rat·ed, -rat·ing, -rates** To close or obstruct. [Lat. *obtūrāre, obtūrāt-* : *ob-, ob-* + *tūrāre,* to stop up.] —**ob′tu·ra′tion** *n.*

ob·tu·ra·tor (ŏb′tə-rā′tər, -tyə-) *n.* **1.** An organic structure, such as the soft palate, that closes an opening in the body. **2.** A prosthetic device serving to close an opening in the body.

ob·tuse (ŏb-tŏŏs′, -tyŏŏs′, əb-) *adj.* **-tus·er, -tus·est 1a.** Lacking quickness of perception or intellect. **b.** Characterized by a lack of intelligence or sensitivity: *an obtuse remark.* **2a.** Not sharp, pointed, or acute in form; blunt. **b.** Having an obtuse angle: *an obtuse triangle.* **c.** *Botany* Having a blunt or rounded tip. [ME < OFr. < Lat. *obtūsus,* p. part. of *obtundere,* to blunt. See OBTUND.] —**ob·tuse′ly** *adv.* —**ob·tuse′ness** *n.*

obtuse angle *n.* An angle between 90° and 180°.

ob·verse (ŏb-vûrs′, əb-, ŏb′vûrs′) *adj.* **1.** Facing or turned toward the observer. **2.** Serving as a counterpart or complement. ❖ *n.* (ŏb′vûrs′, ŏb-vûrs′, əb-) **1.** The side of a coin, medal, or badge that bears the principal stamp or design. **2.** The more conspicuous of two possible alternatives, cases, or sides. **3.** *Logic* The counterpart of a proposition obtained by exchanging the affirmative for the negative quality of the whole proposition and then negating the predicate: *The obverse of "Every act is predictable" is "No act is unpredictable."* [Lat. *obversus,* p. part. of *obvertere,* to turn toward. See OBVERT.] —**ob·verse′ly** *adv.*

ob·ver·sion (ŏb-vûr′zhən, -shən, əb-) *n.* **1.** The process of obverting or the condition so resulting. **2.** *Logic* Inference of the obverse of a proposition.

ob·vert (ŏb-vûrt′, əb-) *tr.v.* **-vert·ed, -vert·ing, -verts 1.** To turn (something) so as to present another side or aspect to view. **2.** To alter the appearance of. **3.** *Logic* To subject (a proposition) to obversion. [Lat. *obvertere*, to turn toward : *ob-*, toward; see OB– + *vertere*, to turn; see **wer-²** in App.]

ob·vi·ate (ŏb′vē-āt′) *tr.v.* **-at·ed, -at·ing, -ates** To anticipate and dispose of effectively; render unnecessary. [Lat. *obviāre, obviāt-*, to hinder < *obvius*, in the way. See OBVIOUS.] —**ob′vi·a′tion** *n.* —**ob′vi·a′tor** *n.*

ob·vi·ous (ŏb′vē-əs) *adj.* **1.** Easily perceived or understood. See Syns at **apparent. 2.** Easily seen through because of a lack of subtlety: *an obvious political ploy.* **3.** *Archaic* Standing in the way or in front. [< Lat. *obvius* < *obviam*, in the way, within reach : *ob-*, against; see OB– + *viam*, accusative sing. of *via*, way; see **wegh-** in App.] —**ob′vi·ous·ly** *adv.* —**ob′vi·ous·ness** *n.*

Oc. *abbr.* ocean

OC *abbr.* **1.** Officer Commanding **2.** Old Catholic

o.c. *abbr.* Latin *opere citato* (in the work cited)

o/c *abbr.* overcharge

o·ca (ō′kə) *n.* **1.** A perennial plant (*Oxalis tuberosa*) of the high Andes. **2.** The edible tuber of this plant. [Sp., poss. < Quechua *oqa*.]

oc·a·ri·na (ŏk′ə-rē′nə) *n.* A small wind instrument with finger holes, a mouthpiece, and an elongated ovoid shape. [Ital. < dialectal *ucarenna*, dim. of Ital. *oca*, goose < VLat. *auca* < *avica* < Lat. *avis*, bird. See **awi-** in App.]

OCAS *abbr.* Organization of Central American States

O'Ca·sey (ō-kā′sē), **Sean** 1880–1964. Irish playwright whose dramas include *Juno and the Paycock* (1924).

Oc·cam (ŏk′əm), **William of** See William of Ockham.

Oc·cam's razor (ŏk′əmz) *n.* Variant of Ockham's razor.

oc·ca·sion (ə-kā′zhən) *n.* **1a.** An event or happening; an incident. **b.** The time at which an event occurs. **2.** A significant event. **3.** A favorable or appropriate time or juncture; an opportunity. **4.** Something that brings on or precipitates an action, condition, or event, esp. the immediate cause. **5.** Something that provides a reason or justification; a ground. **6.** A need created by a particular circumstance. **7.** A large or important social gathering. **8. occasions** *Archaic* Personal requirements or necessities. ❖ *tr.v.* **-sioned, -sion·ing, -sions** To provide occasion for; cause. —*idiom:* **on occasion** From time to time; now and then. [ME < OFr. *occāsio, occāsiōn-* < *occāsus*, p. part. of *occidere*, to fall : *ob-*, down; see OB– + *cadere*, to fall.]

oc·ca·sion·al (ə-kā′zhə-nəl) *adj.* **1a.** Occurring from time to time. See Syns at **periodic. b.** Not habitual; infrequent. **2.** Created for a special occasion. **3.** Intended for use as the occasion requires. **4.** Acting as a cause. **5.** Acting in a specified capacity from time to time.

oc·ca·sion·al·ly (ə-kā′zhə-nə-lē) *adv.* Now and then; from time to time.

oc·ci·dent (ŏk′sĭ-dənt, -dĕnt′) *n.* **1.** Western lands or regions; the west. **2. Occident** The countries of Europe and the Western Hemisphere. [ME < OFr. < Lat. *occidēns, occident-* < pr. part. of *occidere*, to set (used of the sun). See OCCASION.]

oc·ci·den·tal or **Oc·ci·den·tal** (ŏk′sĭ-dĕn′tl) *adj.* Of or relating to the Occident or its peoples or cultures; western. ❖ *n.* A native or inhabitant of an Occidental country.

Oc·ci·den·tal·ism (ŏk′sĭ-dĕn′tl-ĭz′əm) *n.* **1.** A quality, mannerism, or custom specific to or characteristic of the Occident. **2.** Scholarly knowledge of Occidental cultures, languages, and peoples.

oc·ci·den·tal·ize or **Oc·ci·den·tal·ize** (ŏk′sĭ-dĕn′tl-īz′) *tr.v.* **-ized, -iz·ing, -iz·es** To make Occidental, as in character or way of life. —**oc′ci·den′tal·i·za′tion** (-ĭ-zā′shən) *n.*

oc·cip·i·tal (ŏk-sĭp′ĭ-tl) *adj.* Of or relating to the occiput or to the occipital bone: *an occipital fracture.* ❖ *n.* The occipital bone. —**oc′cip′i·tal·ly** *adv.*

occipital bone *n.* A curved trapezoid compound bone that forms the lower posterior part of the skull.

occipital lobe *n.* The posterior lobe of each cerebral hemisphere, having the shape of a three-sided pyramid.

oc·ci·put (ŏk′sə-pŭt′, -pət) *n., pl.* **oc·cip·i·ta** (ŏk-sĭp′ĭ-tə) or **oc·ci·puts** The back part of the head or skull. [ME < Lat. *occiput, occipit-* : *ob-*, against; see OB– + *caput*, head; see **kaput-** in App.]

Oc·ci·tan (ŏk′sĭ-tăn′) *n.* **1.** Langue d'oc. **2.** The modern Provençal language. [Med.Lat. *Occitānus* : O Provençal *oc*, yes (< Lat. *hoc*, neut. sing. of *hic*, this) + *-itānus*, adj. suff. (prob. < (*Aqu*)*itānus*, of Aquitaine, Occitan-speaking region of France).]

oc·clude (ə-klōōd′) *v.* **-clud·ed, -clud·ing, -cludes** —*tr.* **1.** To cause to become closed; obstruct. **2.** To prevent the passage of. **3.** *Chemistry* To absorb or adsorb and retain (a substance). **4.** *Meteorology* To force (air) upward, as when a cold front overtakes and undercuts a warm front. **5.** *Dentistry* To bring together (the upper and lower teeth) in proper alignment. —*intr. Dentistry* To close so that the cusps fit together. [Lat. *occlūdere* : *ob-*, intensive pref.; see OB– + *claudere*, to close.] —**oc·clud′ent** *adj.*

oc·clud·ed front (ə-klōō′dĭd) *n. Meteorology* The front formed when a cold front occludes a warm front.

oc·clu·sal (ə-klōō′zəl, -səl) *adj.* Of or relating to occlusions of the teeth, esp. the chewing or biting surfaces: *occlusal wear.*

oc·clu·sion (ə-klōō′zhən) *n.* **1a.** The process of occluding. **b.** Something that occludes. **2.** *Medicine* An obstruction or a closure of a passageway or vessel. **3.** *Dentistry* The alignment of the upper and lower teeth when brought together. **4.** *Meteorology* An occluded front. **5.** *Linguistics* Closure at some point in the vocal tract that blocks the flow of air in the production of an oral or nasal stop. [< Lat. *occlūsus*, p. part. of *occlūdere*, to occlude. See OCCLUDE.]

oc·clu·sive (ə-klōō′sĭv, -zĭv) *adj.* Occluding or tending to occlude. ❖ *n. Linguistics* An oral or nasal stop.

oc·cult (ə-kŭlt′, ŏk′ŭlt′) *adj.* **1.** Of, relating to, or dealing with supernatural influences, agencies, or phenomena. **2.** Beyond the realm of human comprehension. **3.** Available only to the initiate; secret. See Syns at **mysterious. 4.** Hidden from view; concealed. **5a.** *Medicine* Detectable only by microscopic examination or chemical analysis. **b.** Not accompanied by readily detectable signs or symptoms: *occult carcinoma.* ❖ *n.* Occult practices or techniques. ❖ *v.* (ə-kŭlt′) **-cult·ed, -cult·ing, -cults** —*tr.* **1.** To conceal or cause to disappear from view. **2.** *Astronomy* To conceal by occultation. —*intr.* To become concealed or extinguished at regular intervals. [Lat. *occultus*, secret, p. part. of *occulere*, to cover over. See **kel-** in App.] —**oc·cult′ly** *adv.* —**oc·cult′ness** *n.*

oc·cul·ta·tion (ŏk′ŭl-tā′shən) *n.* **1.** The act of occulting or the state of being occulted. **2.** *Astronomy* **a.** The passage of a celestial body across a line between an observer and another celestial object. **b.** The progressive blocking of light or other radiation from a celestial source during such a passage. **c.** An observational technique for determining the position or radiant structure of a celestial source so occulted. [ME *occultacion* < Lat. *occultātiō, occultātiōn-* < *occultātus*, p. part. of *occultāre*, freq. of *occulere*, to conceal. See OCCULT.]

oc·cult·ism (ə-kŭl′tĭz′əm, ŏk′ŭl-) *n.* **1.** The study of the supernatural. **2.** A belief in occult powers and the possibility of bringing them under human control. —**oc·cult′ist** *n.*

oc·cu·pan·cy (ŏk′yə-pən-sē) *n., pl.* **-cies 1a.** The act of occupying or the state of being occupied. **b.** The state of being an occupant or tenant. **2a.** The period during which one owns, rents, or uses certain premises or land. **b.** The use to which something occupied is put.

oc·cu·pant (ŏk′yə-pənt) *n.* **1.** One that occupies a position or place. **2.** One who has certain legal rights to or control over the premises occupied; a tenant or owner.

oc·cu·pa·tion (ŏk′yə-pā′shən) *n.* **1a.** An activity that is one's regular source of livelihood; a vocation. **b.** An activity engaged in esp. as a pastime; an avocation. **2a.** The act or process of holding or possessing a place. **b.** The state of being held or possessed. **3a.** Conquest and control of a nation or territory by foreign armed forces. **b.** The military government controlling an occupied nation or territory. [ME *occupacioun* < OFr. *occupacion* < Lat. *occupātiō, occupātiōn-* < *occupātus*, p. part. of *occupāre*, to occupy. See OCCUPY.]

oc·cu·pa·tion·al (ŏk′yə-pā′shə-nəl) *adj.* Of, relating to, or caused by engagement in a particular occupation: *occupational hazards.* —**oc′cu·pa′tion·al·ly** *adv.*

occupational disease *n.* A disease resulting from the conditions of a person's work, trade, or occupation.

occupational medicine *n.* The branch of medicine that deals with the prevention and treatment of diseases and injuries occurring at work or in specific occupations.

occupational therapy *n.* The use of productive or creative activity in the treatment or rehabilitation of physically or emotionally disabled people. —**occupational therapist** *n.*

oc·cu·py (ŏk′yə-pī′) *tr.v.* **-pied, -py·ing, -pies 1.** To fill up (time or space). **2.** To dwell or reside in. **3.** To hold or fill (an office or position). **4.** To seize possession of and maintain control over by or as if by conquest. **5.** To engage or employ the attention or concentration of. [ME *occupien*, alteration of OFr. *occuper* < Lat. *occupāre*, to seize : *ob-*, intensive pref.; see OB– + *capere*, to take; see **kap-** in App.] —**oc′cu·pi′er** *n.*

oc·cur (ə-kûr′) *intr.v.* **-curred, -cur·ring, -curs 1.** To take place; come about. **2.** To be found to exist or appear: *Copper deposits occur in the region.* **3.** To come to mind: *The idea occurred to me.* [Lat. *occurrere* : *ob-*, toward; see OB– + *currere*, to run.]

oc·cur·rence (ə-kûr′əns) *n.* **1.** The action, fact, or instance of occurring. **2.** Something that takes place. —**oc·cur′rent** *adj.*

SYNONYMS *occurrence, happening, event, incident, episode, circumstance* These nouns refer to something that takes place or comes to pass. *Occurrence* and *happening* are the most general: *an everyday occurrence; a happening of no great importance. Event* usually signifies a notable occurrence: "Great *events* make me quiet and calm" (Victoria). *Incident* may apply to a minor occurrence: *exciting incidents.* An *episode* is an incident in the course of a progression or within a larger sequence: "Happiness was but the occasional *episode* in a genera! drama of pain" (Thomas Hardy). *Circumstance* denotes a particular incident or occurrence: "Billy had found Alice, thus bringing about the odd *circumstance* of their renewing their acquaintanceship" (Eleanor H. Porter).

OCD *abbr.* obsessive-compulsive disorder

o·cean (ō′shən) *n.* **1.** The entire body of salt water that covers more than 70 percent of the earth's surface. **2.** Any of the principal divisions of the ocean, including the Atlantic, Pacific, Indian, and Arctic oceans. **3.** A great expanse or amount. [ME *ocean*

ocarina

< OFr. < Lat. *ōceanus* < Gk. *Ōkeanos*, the god Oceanus, a great river encircling the earth.]

o•cean•ar•i•um (ō′shə-nâr′ē-əm) *n., pl.* **-i•ums** or **-i•a** (-ē-ə) A large aquarium for the study or display of marine life.

o•cean•aut (ō′shə-nôt′, -nŏt′) *n.* See **aquanaut.**

o•cean•front (ō′shən-frŭnt′) *n.* Land bordering an ocean.

o•cean•go•ing (ō′shən-gō′ĭng) *adj.* Made or used for ocean voyages.

O•ce•an•i•a (ō′shē-ăn′ē-ə, -ā′nē-ə, -ă′nē-ə) The islands of the S, W, and central Pacific Ocean, including Melanesia, Micronesia, and Polynesia and sometimes also Australia, New Zealand, and the Malay Archipelago. —**O′ce•an′i•an** *adj. & n.*

o•ce•an•ic (ō′shē-ăn′ĭk) *adj.* **1.** Of or relating to the ocean. **2.** Produced by or living in an ocean, esp. in the open sea. **3.** Resembling an ocean in expanse; vast.

O•ce•an•i•des (ō′sē-ăn′ĭ-dēz′) *n., pl.* **O•ce•an•i•des** (ō′sē-ăn′ĭ-dēz′) *Greek Mythology* Any of the ocean nymphs believed to be the daughters of Oceanus and Tethys. [Gk. *ōkeanis, ōkeanid-* < *Ōkeanos,* Oceanus.]

o•cean•og•ra•phy (ō′shə-nŏg′rə-fē) *n.* The exploration and scientific study of the ocean and its phenomena. —**o′cean•og′ra•pher** *n.* —**o′cean•o•graph′ic** (ō′shə-nə-grăf′ĭk), **o′cean•o•graph′i•cal** *adj.* —**o′cean•o•graph′i•cal•ly** *adv.*

o•cean•ol•o•gy (ō′shə-nŏl′ə-jē) *n.* See **oceanography.** —**o′cean•o•log′ic** (ō′shə-nə-lŏj′ĭk), **o′cean•o•log′i•cal** (-ĭ-kəl) *adj.* —**o′cean•o•log′i•cal•ly** *adv.* —**o′cean•ol′o•gist** *n.*

ocean perch *n.* See **rosefish.**

ocean sunfish *n.* A marine fish (*Mola mola*) with a large globular body, found in warm and temperate seas.

O•ce•a•nus (ō-sē′ə-nəs) *n. Greek Mythology* A Titan who rules over the outer sea encircling the earth.

oc•el•lat•ed (ŏs′ə-lā′tĭd, ō′sə-, ō-sĕl′ā′-) also **oc•el•late** (-lāt′) *adj.* **1.** Having an ocellus or ocelli. **2.** Resembling an ocellus. **3.** Having spots. [Lat. *ocellātus,* having little eyes < *ocellus,* dim. of *oculus,* eye. See OCELLUS.] —**oc′el•la′tion** *n.*

o•cel•lus (ō-sĕl′əs) *n., pl.* **o•cel•li** (ō-sĕl′ī′) **1.** A small, simple invertebrate eye, usu. consisting of a few sensory cells and a single lens. **2.** A marking like an eye; an eyespot. [Lat., dim. of *oculus,* eye. See **ok⁻** in App.] —**o•cel′lar** (ō-sĕl′ər) *adj.*

oc•e•lot (ŏs′ə-lŏt′, ō′sə-) *n.* A nocturnal wildcat (*Felis pardalis* or *Leopardus pardalis*) of the southwest United States and Central and South America, having a grayish or yellow coat with black spots. [Fr. < Nahuatl *ocelotl.*]

o•cher or **o•chre** (ō′kər) *n.* **1.** Any of several yellow, brown, or red earthy iron oxides used as pigments. **2.** A moderate orange yellow. [ME *oker* < OFr. *ocre* < LLat. *ōcra* < Lat. *ōchra* < Gk. *ōkhra* < *ōkhros,* pale yellow.] —**o′cher•ous, o′cher•y** (ō′krē) *adj.*

och•loc•ra•cy (ŏk-lŏk′rə-sē) *n., pl.* **-cies** Government by the masses; mob rule. [Fr. *ochlocratie* < Gk. *okhlokratiā* < *okhlos,* mob; see **wegh-** in App. + *-kratiā,* -cracy.] —**och′lo•crat′** (ŏk′lə-krăt′) *n.* —**och′lo•crat′ic, och′lo•crat′i•cal** *adj.*

och•lo•pho•bi•a (ŏk′lə-fō′bē-ə) *n.* An abnormal fear of crowds. [Gk. *okhlos,* crowd. See **wegh-** in App. + -PHOBIA.]

O•cho•a (ō-chō′ə), **Severo** 1905–93. Spanish-born Amer. biochemist who shared a 1959 Nobel Prize.

Ochs (ŏks), **Adolph Simon** 1858–1935. Amer. newspaper publisher who published the *New York Times* (1896–1935).

Ock•ham also **Oc•cam** (ŏk′əm), **William of** 1285?–1349? English scholastic philosopher who rejected the reality of universal concepts.

Ock•ham's razor also **Oc•cam's razor** (ŏk′əmz) *n.* A rule stating that entities should not be multiplied needlessly, meaning that the simplest of two or more competing theories is preferable and that the unknown should first be explained in terms of the known. [After William of OCKHAM.]

o′clock (ə-klŏk′) *adv.* **1.** Of or according to the clock: *three o'clock.* **2.** According to an imaginary clock dial with the observer at the center and 12 o'clock considered as straight ahead or straight up. Used to indicate relative position: *enemy planes at 10 o'clock.* [Short for *of the clock.*]

Oc•mul•gee (ŏk-mŭl′gē) A river, c. 410 km (255 mi), of central GA joining the Oconee R. to form the Altahama R.

O•co•nee (ə-kō′nē) A river rising in N GA and flowing c. 454 km (282 mi) to the Ocmulgee R. to form the Altamaha R.

O′Con•nell (ō-kŏn′əl), **Daniel** Known as "the Liberator." 1775–1847. Irish political leader who founded the Catholic Association (1823).

O′Con•nor (ō-kŏn′ər), **Flannery** 1925–64. Amer. writer renowned for her novels and short stories.

O′Connor, Sandra Day b. 1930. Amer. jurist; appointed (1981) the first woman associate justice of the US Supreme Court.

o•co•til•lo (ō′kə-tē′yō) *n., pl.* **-los** A cactuslike tree (*Fouquieria splendens*) of Mexico and the southwest United States having clusters of scarlet tubular flowers. [Am.Sp., dim. of *ocote,* a Mexican pine < Nahuatl *ocotl,* pitch pine.]

OCR *abbr.* **1.** optical character reader **2.** optical character recognition

oc•re•a (ŏk′rē-ə) *n., pl.* **-re•ae** (-rē-ē′) A sheath that is formed at the node of a stem by the fusion of two stipules, as in the

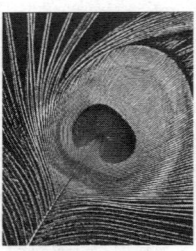
ocellus
close-up of a peacock
feather

ocelot
Felis pardalis

Sandra Day O'Connor

rhubarb plant. [Lat., greave.]

OCS *abbr.* Officer Candidate School

oct. *abbr.* octavo

Oct. *abbr.* October

oct– or **octa–** *pref.* Variants of **octo–.**

oc•tad (ŏk′tăd′) *n.* A group or sequence of eight. [Gk. *oktas, oktad-* < *oktō,* eight. See **oktō(u)** in App.] —**oc•tad′ic** *adj.*

oc•ta•gon (ŏk′tə-gŏn′) *n.* A polygon with eight sides and eight angles. —**oc•tag′o•nal** (ŏk-tăg′ə-nəl) *adj.* —**oc•tag′o•nal•ly** *adv.*

oc•ta•he•dron (ŏk′tə-hē′drən) *n., pl.* **-drons** or **-dra** (-drə) A polyhedron with eight plane surfaces. —**oc′ta•he′dral** *adj.* —**oc′ta•he′dral•ly** *adv.*

oc•tal (ŏk′təl) *adj.* Of, relating to, or based on the number eight.

oc•tam•e•ter (ŏk-tăm′ĭ-tər) *n.* A line of verse consisting of eight metrical feet.

oc•tane (ŏk′tān′) *n.* **1.** Any of various isomeric paraffin hydrocarbons with the formula C_8H_{18}, found in petroleum and used as a fuel and solvent. **2.**

octane number *n.* A numerical representation of the antiknock properties of motor fuel, compared with a standard reference fuel, such as isooctane, which has an octane number of 100.

Oc•tans (ŏk′tănz′) *n.* The constellation that includes the southern celestial pole. [Lat. *Octāns,* half quadrant < *octō,* eight. See **oktō(u)** in App.]

oc•tant (ŏk′tənt) *n.* **1.** One eighth of a circle. **2a.** A 45° arc. **b.** The area enclosed by two radii at a 45° angle and the intersected arc. **3.** An instrument resembling the sextant but employing a 45° angle, used in navigation. **4.** *Astronomy* The position of a celestial body when it is separated from another by a 45° angle. **5.** One of eight parts into which space is divided by three usu. perpendicular coordinate planes. [Lat. *octāns, octant-* < *octō,* eight. See **oktō(u)** in App.]

oc•tave (ŏk′tĭv, -tāv′) *n.* **1.** *Music* **a.** The interval of eight diatonic degrees between two tones of the same name, the higher of which has twice as many vibrations per second as the lower. **b.** A tone that is eight diatonic degrees above or below another tone. **c.** Two tones eight diatonic degrees apart that are sounded together. **d.** The consonance that results when two such tones are sounded. **e.** A series of tones included within this interval or the keys of an instrument that produce such a series. **f.** An organ stop that produces tones an octave above those usu. produced by the keys played. **g.** The interval between any two frequencies having a ratio of 2 to 1. **2.** *Ecclesiastical* **a.** The eighth day after a feast day, counting the feast day as one. **b.** The entire period between a feast day and the eighth day following it. **3.** A group or series of eight. **4a.** A group of eight lines of poetry, esp. the first eight lines of a Petrarchan sonnet. **b.** A poem or stanza containing eight lines. [ME, eighth day after a feast day < OFr. < Med.Lat. *octāva (diēs)* < Lat., fem. of *octāvus,* eighth < *octō,* eight. See **oktō(u)** in App.] —**oc•ta′val** (ŏk-tā′vəl, ŏk′tə-vəl) *adj.*

Oc•ta•vi•an (ŏk-tā′vē-ən) See **Augustus.**

oc•ta•vo (ŏk-tā′vō, -tä′-) *n., pl.* **-vos 1.** The page size, from 5 by 8 inches to 6 by 9½ inches, of a book composed of printer's sheets folded into eight leaves. **2.** A book composed of octavo pages. [Med.Lat. *(in) octāvō, (in)* an eighth < Lat., ablative sing. of *octāvus,* eighth < *octō,* eight. See **oktō(u)** in App.]

oc•tet (ŏk-tĕt′) *n.* *Music* **a.** A composition for eight voices or eight instruments. **b.** A group of eight singers or eight instrumentalists. **2.** A group of eight. **3.** see **octave** 4a. **4.** A set of eight valence electrons forming a stable configuration. [Alteration (influenced by OCTO– and DUET) of Ital. *ottetto* < *otto,* eight < Lat. *octō.* See **oktō(u)** in App.]

oc•til•lion (ŏk-tĭl′yən) *n.* **1.** The cardinal number equal to 10²⁷. **2.** *Chiefly British* The cardinal number equal to 10⁴⁸. [OCT(O)– + (M)ILLION.] —**oc•til′lion** *adj.*

oc•til•lionth (ŏk-tĭl′yənth) *n.* **1.** The ordinal number that matches the number octillion in a series. **2.** One of an octillion equal parts. —**oc•til′lionth** *adj. & n.*

octo– or **octa–** or **oct–** *pref.* Eight: *octane.* [Gk. *okta-, oktō-* (< *oktō*) and Lat. *octo-* (< *octō*); see **oktō(u)** in App.]

Oc•to•ber (ŏk-tō′bər) *n.* **1.** The tenth month of the year in the Gregorian calendar. See table at **calendar. 2.** *Chiefly British* Ale brewed in October. [ME *Octobre* < OFr. and < OE *October,* both < Lat. *Octōber,* eighth month < *octō,* eight. See **oktō(u)** in App.]

oc•to•de•cil•lion (ŏk′tō-dĭ-sĭl′yən) *n.* **1.** The cardinal number equal to 10⁵⁷. **2.** *Chiefly British* The cardinal number equal to 10¹⁰⁸. [Lat. *octōdecim,* eighteen: see OCTODECIMO + (M)ILLION.] —**oc′to•de•cil′lion** *adj.* —**oc′to•de•cil′lionth** *adj., adv. & n.*

oc•to•dec•i•mo (ŏk′tə-dĕs′ə-mō′) *n., pl.* **-mos 1.** The page size, 4 by 6½ inches, of a book composed of printer's sheets folded into 18 leaves. **2.** A book composed of octodecimo pages. [LLat. *(in) octōdecimō, (in)* an eighteenth, ablative sing. of *octōdecimus,* eighteenth < Lat. *octōdecim,* eighteen : *octō,* eight; see **oktō(u)** in App. + *decem,* ten; see **dekm̥** in App.]

oc•to•ge•nar•i•an (ŏk′tə-jə-nâr′ē-ən) *adj.* Being between 80 and 90 years of age. ❖ *n.* A person between 80 and 90 years of age. [< Fr. *octogénaire* < Lat. *octōgēnārius,* containing eighty < *octōgēnī,* eighty each < *octōgintā,* eighty : *octō,* eight; see **oktō(u)** in App. + *-gintā,* ten times; see **dekm̥** in App.]

oc•to•nar•y (ŏk′tə-nĕr′ē) *adj.* **1.** Of or relating to the number

eight. 2. Consisting of eight members or of groups containing eight. ❖ *n.,* pl. **-ies** A group of eight. [Lat. *octōnārius,* containing eight < *octōnī,* eight each < *octō,* eight. See **oktō(u)** in App.]

oc·to·pod (ŏk′tə-pŏd′) *n.* Any of various cephalopod mollusks of the order Octopoda, such as an octopus, having eight tentacles. [< NLat. *Octopoda,* order name < Gk. *oktōpoda,* neut. pl. of *oktō-pous,* octopus. See OCTOPUS.] —**oc′to·pod′, oc′to·pod′ous** *adj.*

oc·to·pus (ŏk′tə-pəs) *n.,* pl. **-pus·es** or **-pi** (-pī′) **1.** Any of numerous carnivorous marine mollusks of the genus *Octopus* or related genera, found worldwide and having a rounded soft body, eight tentacles with each bearing two rows of suckers, and a large distinct head. **2.** Something, such as a corporation, that has many powerful, centrally controlled branches. [NLat. *Octŏpūs,* genus name < Gk. *oktōpous,* eight-footed : *oktō,* eight; see **oktō(u)** in App. + *pous,* foot; see **ped-** in App.]

oc·to·roon (ŏk′tə-ro͞on′) *n.* A person whose ancestry is one-eighth Black. [OCTO– + (QUAD)ROON.]

oc·to·syl·la·ble (ŏk′tə-sĭl′ə-bəl) *n.* **1.** also **oc·to·syl·lab·ic** (ŏk′tō-sĭ-lăb′ĭk) **a.** A line of verse containing eight syllables. **b.** A poem having eight syllables in each line. **2.** A word of eight syllables. —**oc′to·syl·lab′ic** *adj.*

oc·tu·ple (ŏk′tə-pəl, -to͞o′pəl, -tyo͞o′-) *adj.* **1.** Consisting of eight parts or members. **2.** Eight times as much in size, strength, number, or amount. ❖ *n.* A number eight times larger than another. ❖ *tr.v.* **-pled, -pling, -ples** To multiply by eight. [Lat. *octuplus* : *octō-,* eight < *octō,* eight + *-plus,* fold.]

oc·tu·plet (ŏk′-tŭp′lĭt, -to͞o′plĭt, -tyo͞o′-) *n.* **1.** One of eight offspring delivered at a single birth. **2.** A group or combination of eight associated by common properties or behavior. [< OCTUPLE (modeled on TRIPLET).]

oc·u·lar (ŏk′yə-lər) *adj.* **1a.** Of or relating to the eye. **b.** Resembling the eye in form or function: *ocular spots.* **2.** Of or relating to the sense of sight. **3.** Seen by the eye; visual: *ocular proof.* ❖ *n.* The eyepiece of an optical instrument. [LLat. *oculāris* < Lat. *oculus,* eye. See **okw-** in App.]

oc·u·list (ŏk′yə-lĭst) *n.* **1.** A physician who treats diseases of the eyes; an ophthalmologist. **2.** An optometrist. [< Lat. *oculus,* eye. See **okw-** in App.]

oc·u·lo·gy·ric (ŏk′yə-lō-jī′rĭk) *adj.* Of or relating to the turning of the eyeballs in the sockets.

oc·u·lo·mo·tor (ŏk′yə-lō-mō′tər) *adj.* **1.** Of or relating to movements of the eyeball. **2.** Of or relating to the oculomotor nerve. [Lat. *oculus,* eye; see **okw-** in App. + MOTOR.]

oculomotor nerve *n.* Either of the third pair of cranial nerves controlling most of the muscles that move the eyeballs.

oc·u·lus (ŏk′yə-ləs) *n.,* pl. **-li** (-lī′) *Architecture* An eyelike opening or ornament, esp.: **a.** A round window. **b.** A circular opening at the apex of a dome. [Med.Lat. < Lat. *oculus,* eye. See **okw-** in App.]

Od or **Odd** (ŏd) *interj. Archaic* Used as a mild oath. [Alteration of GOD.]

OD¹ (ō′dē′) *Slang v.* **1a.** An overdose of a drug. **b.** An overdose of something. **2.** One who has taken an overdose. ❖ *intr.v.* **OD′ed, OD′·ing, OD's** To overdose. [O(VER)D(OSE).]

OD² *abbr.* **1.** Doctor of Optometry **2.** *Latin* oculus dexter (right eye) **3.** officer of the day **4.** also **O/D** overdraft **5.** overdrawn

o·da·lisque also **o·da·lisk** (ō′də-lĭsk′) *n.* A concubine or woman slave in a harem. [Fr. < Turk. *ōdalik,* chambermaid : *ōdah,* room + *-lik,* suff. expressing function.]

O'Day (ō-dā′), **Anita** b. 1919. Amer. jazz singer noted for her scat singing.

odd (ŏd) *adj.* **odd·er, odd·est 1.** Deviating from what is ordinary, usual, or expected; strange or peculiar. See Syns at **strange. 2.** Being in excess of the indicated or approximate number, extent, or degree. Often used in combination: *30-odd guests.* **3a.** Constituting a remainder. **b.** Small in amount. **4a.** Being one of an incomplete pair or set: *an odd shoe.* **b.** Remaining after others have been paired or grouped. **5.** *Mathematics* Designating an integer not divisible by two, such as 1, 3, and 5. **6.** Not expected, regular, or planned: *called at odd intervals.* **7.** Remote; out-of-the-way. ❖ *n.* Something odd. [ME *odde* < ON *oddi,* point of land, triangle, odd number.] —**odd′ly** *adv.* —**odd′ness** *n.*

odd·ball (ŏd′bôl′) *n. Informal* A person regarded as eccentric.

Odd Fellow *n.* A member of the Independent Order of Odd Fellows, a fraternal and benevolent secret society.

odd·ish (ŏd′ĭsh) *adj.* Somewhat odd.

odd·i·ty (ŏd′ĭ-tē) *n.,* pl. **-ties 1.** One that is odd. **2.** The state or quality of being odd; strangeness.

odd job *n.* Any of various nonspecialized unrelated jobs. —**odd′-job′ber** (ŏd′jŏb′ər) *n.*

odd lot *n.* A quantity other than a standard trading unit, esp. of fewer than 100 shares of stock. —**odd′-lot′** (ŏd′lŏt′) *adj.*

odd man out *n.,* pl. **odd men out** One who, because of behavior or belief, stands alone in or out from a group.

odd·ment (ŏd′mənt) *n.* **1a.** Something left over. **b. oddments** Odds and ends. **2.** An oddity.

odd-pin·nate (ŏd′pĭn′āt′) *adj.* Pinnately compound with a single terminal leaflet. —**odd′-pin′nate·ly** *adv.*

odds (ŏdz) *pl.n.* **1.** A certain number of points given beforehand to a weaker side in a contest to equalize the chances of all participants. **2a.** The ratio of the probability of an event's occurring to the probability of its not occurring. **b.** The likelihood of the oc-

currence of one thing rather than the occurrence of another thing, as in a contest. **3.** *Games* A ratio expressing the amount by which the stake of one bettor differs from that of an opposing bettor. **4.** An amount or degree by which one thing exceeds or falls short of another. —*idioms:* **at odds** In disagreement; in conflict. **by all odds** In every possible way; unquestionably. [Pl. of ODD.]

odds and ends *pl.n.* Miscellaneous items or remnants.

odds·mak·er (ŏdz′mā′kər) *n.* One who calculates and sets betting odds based on the prediction of the result of a contest such as a horserace or an election.

odds-on (ŏdz′ŏn′, -ôn′) *adj. Informal* Having a better chance than others to win or succeed: *the odds-on favorite.*

ode (ōd) *n.* **1.** A lyric poem, usu. of a serious or meditative nature and having a formal stanzaic structure. **2a.** A choric song of classical Greece, often accompanied by a dance and performed at a public festival or as part of a drama. **b.** A classical Greek poem modeled on the choric ode and usu. consisting of a strophe, an antistrophe, and an epode. [Fr., choric song < OFr. < LLat. *ōdē,* *ōda* < Gk. *aoidē, ōidē,* song.] —**od′ic** (ō′dĭk) *adj.*

–ode *suff.* **1.** Way; path: *electrode.* **2.** Electrode: *dynode.* [Gk. *-odos* < *hodos.*]

O·den·se (ō′dn-sə, ōōd′-) A city of S Denmark on Fyn I. near the **Odense Fjord,** an arm of the Kattegat. Pop. 180,799.

O·der (ō′dər) A river of central Europe flowing c. 904 km (562 mi) from NE Czech Republic to the Baltic Sea.

O·des·sa (ō-dĕs′ə) **1.** (*also* ə-dyĕ′sə) A city of S Ukraine on **Odessa Bay,** an arm of the Black Sea; est. as a Tartar fortress in the 14th cent. Pop. 1,095,800. **2.** A city of W TX SSW of Lubbock. Pop. 90,943.

O·dets (ō-dĕts′), **Clifford** 1906–63. Amer. playwright whose works include *Waiting for Lefty* (1935).

o·de·um (ō-dē′əm, ō′dē-) *n.,* pl. **o·de·a** (ō-dē′ə, ō′dē-ə) **1.** A small building of ancient Greece and Rome used for public performances. **2.** A contemporary theater or concert hall. [Lat. *ōdēum* < Gk. *ōideion* < *aoidē, ōidē,* song. See ODE.]

O·din (ō′dĭn) *n. Mythology* The Norse god of wisdom and war, who created the cosmos. [ON *Ōdhinn.* See **wet-¹** in App.]

o·di·ous (ō′dē-əs) *adj.* Arousing or meriting strong dislike, aversion, or intense displeasure. [ME < OFr. *odieus* < Lat. *odiōsus* < *odium,* hatred. See ODIUM.] —**o′di·ous·ly** *adv.* —**o′di·ous·ness** *n.*

o·di·um (ō′dē-əm) *n.* **1.** The state or quality of being odious. **2.** Strong dislike, contempt, or aversion. **3.** A state of disgrace resulting from detestable conduct. [Lat., hatred.]

O·do·a·cer (ō′dō-ā′sər) also **O·do·va·car** or **O·do·va·kar** (-vä′kər) A.D. 434?–493. Germanic tribal leader who deposed Romulus Augustulus (reigned 475–476), bringing the Western Roman Empire to an end.

o·do·graph (ō′də-grăf′) *n.* An instrument for recording the distance and course traveled by a vehicle. [Gk. *hodos,* journey + –GRAPH.]

o·dom·e·ter (ō-dŏm′ĭ-tər) *n.* An instrument that indicates distance traveled by a vehicle. [Fr. *odomètre* < Gk. *hodometron* : *hodos,* journey + *metron,* measure; see –METER.] —**o·dom′e·try** *n.*

–odon *suff.* An animal having a specified kind of teeth: *sphenodon.* [NLat. < Gk. *odōn,* tooth. See **dent-** in App.]

o·do·nate (ō′də-nāt′, ō-dŏn′-) *n.* Any of the insects of the order Odonata, including the dragonflies, having two pairs of wings and compound eyes. [< NLat. *Odōnāta,* order name < Gk. *odōn,* tooth. See –ODON.] —**o′do·nate′** *adj.*

–odont *suff.* Having teeth of a specified kind: *pleurodont.* [Gk. *-odōn, -odont-* < *odous, odont-.* See **dent-** in App.]

o·don·tal·gia (ō′dŏn-tăl′jə, -jē-ə) *n.* A toothache.

–odontia *suff.* The form of, manner of treating, or condition of the teeth: *orthodontia.*

odonto– or **odont–** *pref.* Tooth: *odontophore.* [Gk. < *odous, odont-,* tooth. See **dent-** in App.]

o·don·to·blast (ō-dŏn′tə-blăst′) *n.* One of the dentin-forming cells of the outer surface of dental pulp.

o·don·toid (ō-dŏn′toid′) *adj.* **1.** Resembling a tooth. **2.** Of or relating to the odontoid process: *the odontoid ligaments.*

odontoid process *n.* A small projection from the second vertebra of the neck around which the first vertebra rotates.

o·don·tol·o·gy (ō′dŏn-tŏl′ə-jē) *n.* The study of the structure, development, and abnormalities of the teeth. —**o·don′to·log′i·cal** (-tə-lŏj′ĭ-kəl) *adj.* —**o′don·tol′o·gist** *n.*

o·don·to·phore (ō-dŏn′tə-fôr′, -fōr′) *n.* A structure at the base of the mouth of most mollusks over which the radula is drawn back and forth in breaking up food.

o·dor (ō′dər) *n.* **1.** The property or quality of a thing that affects, stimulates, or is perceived by the sense of smell. See Syns at **smell. 2.** A sensation, stimulation, or perception of the sense of smell. **3.** A strong, pervasive quality. **4.** Esteem; repute. [ME *odour* < OFr. < Lat. *odor.*]

o·dor·if·er·ous (ō′də-rĭf′ər-əs) *adj.* Having or giving off an odor. —**o′dor·if′er·ous·ness** *n.*

o·dor·ous (ō′dər-əs) *adj.* Having a distinctive odor: *odorous jasmine flowers.* —**o′dor·ous·ly** *adv.* —**o′dor·ous·ness** *n.*

o·dour (ō′dər) *n. Chiefly British* Variant of **odor.**

ocotillo
Fouquieria splendens

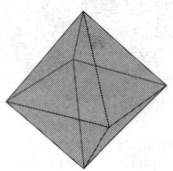

octahedron

ă	pat	oi	boy
ā	pay	ou	out
âr	care	o͝o	took
ä	father	o͞o	boot
ĕ	pet	ŭ	cut
ē	be	ûr	urge
ĭ	pit	th	thin
ī	pie	th	this
îr	pier	hw	which
ŏ	pot	zh	vision
ō	toe	ə	about,
ô	paw		item

Stress marks:
′ (primary);
′ (secondary), as in
lexicon (lĕk′sĭ-kŏn′)

Kenzaburo Oe

Oedipus
detail of Oedipus and the Sphinx on an Attic red-figure kylix, c. 470 B.C.

O•do•va•car or **O•do•va•kar** (ō′dō-vā′kər) See **Odoacer.**

O•dys•seus (ō-dĭs′yo͞os′, ō-dĭs′ē-əs) *n. Greek Mythology* The king of Ithaca, a leader of the Greeks in the Trojan War, who reached home after ten years of wandering.

od•ys•sey (ŏd′ĭ-sē) *n., pl.* **-seys 1.** A long adventurous voyage or trip. **2.** An intellectual or spiritual quest. [After the ODYSSEY.]

Odyssey *n.* The younger of the two surviving ancient Greek epic poems, traditionally ascribed to Homer, that concerns the ordeals of Odysseus after the fall of Troy as he struggles to return home to Ithaca.

Oe *abbr.* oersted

O•e (ō′ā), **Kenzaburo** b. 1935. Japanese writer who won the 1994 Nobel Prize for literature.

OE *abbr.* Old English

OECD *abbr.* Organization for Economic Cooperation and Development

OED *abbr. Oxford English Dictionary*

oe•de•ma (ĭ-dē′mə) *n.* Variant of **edema.**

oed•i•pal also **Oed•i•pal** (ĕd′ə-pəl, ē′də-) *adj.* Of or relating to the Oedipus complex. **—oed′i•pal•ly** *adv.*

Oed•i•pus (ĕd′ə-pəs, ē′də-) *n. Greek Mythology* A son of Laius and Jocasta, who unwittingly killed his father and then married his mother. [Lat. < Gk. *Oidipous* : *oidein,* to swell + *pous,* foot; see OCTOPUS.]

Oedipus complex *n.* In psychoanalysis, a subconscious sexual desire in a child, esp. a male child, for the parent of the opposite sex, usu. accompanied by hostility to the parent of the same sex.

OEM *abbr.* original equipment manufacturer

oe•nol•o•gy (ē-nŏl′ə-jē) *n.* Variant of **enology.**

oe•no•mel (ē′nə-mĕl′) *n.* An ancient Greek beverage of wine and honey. [LLat. *oenomeli* < Gk. *oinomeli* : *oinos,* wine + *meli,* honey; see **melit-** in App.]

oe•no•phile also **e•no•phile** (ē′nə-fīl′) *n.* **1.** One who appreciates and enjoys wine. **2.** A collector of wine. [Gk. *oinos,* wine + -PHILE.] **—oe′no•phil′i•a** (ē′nə-fĭl′ē-ə) *n.* **—oe′no•phil′ic** (-fĭl′ĭk) *adj.*

OEO *abbr.* Office of Economic Opportunity

o'er (ôr, ōr) *prep. & adv.* Over.

oer•sted (ûr′stĕd′) *n.* The centimeter-gram-second electromagnetic unit of magnetic field strength. [After Hans Christian *Oersted* (1777–1851), Danish physicist.]

oe•soph•a•gus (ĭ-sŏf′ə-gəs) *n.* Variant of **esophagus.**

oes•tro•gen (ĕs′trə-jən) *n.* Variant of **estrogen.**

oes•trus (ĕs′trəs) *n.* Variant of **estrus.**

oeu•vre (œ′vrə) *n., pl.* **oeu•vres** (œ′vrə) **1.** A work of art. **2.** The sum of the lifework of an artist, writer, or composer. [Fr. *œuvre* < OFr. *uevre,* work < Lat. *opera* < pl. of *opus,* work. See OPUS.]

of (ŭv, ŏv; əv *when unstressed*) *prep.* **1.** Derived or coming from; originating at or from: *customs of the South.* **2.** Caused by; resulting from: *a death of flu.* **3.** Away from; at a distance from: *a mile east of here.* **4.** So as to be separated or relieved from: *cured of distemper.* **5.** From the total or group comprising: *most of the cases.* **6.** Composed or made from: *a dress of silk.* **7.** Associated with or adhering to: *people of your religion.* **8.** Belonging or connected to: *the rungs of a ladder.* **9a.** Possessing; having: *a person of honor.* **b.** On one's part: *nice of you.* **10.** Containing or carrying: *a bag of food.* **11.** Specified as; named or called: *the Garden of Eden.* **12.** Centering on; directed toward: *a love of horses.* **13.** Produced by; issuing from: *products of the vine.* **14.** Characterized or identified by: *a year of famine.* **15a.** With reference to; about: *will speak of it later.* **b.** In respect to: *slow of speech.* **16.** Set aside for; taken up by: *a day of rest.* **17.** Before; until: *five minutes of two.* **18.** During or on a specified time: *of recent years.* **19.** By: *beloved of the family.* **20.** Used to indicate an appositive: *that idiot of a driver.* **21.** *Archaic* On. [ME < OE. See **apo-** in App.]

USAGE NOTE Grammarians have sometimes objected to the so-called double genitive construction, as in *a friend of my father's; a book of mine.* But the construction has been used in English since the 14th century and serves a useful purpose. It can help sort out ambiguous phrases like *Bob's photograph,* which could refer either to a photograph revealing Bob's image or to one in Bob's possession. *A photograph of Bob's* can only be a photo belonging to Bob. Moreover, in some sentences the double genitive offers the only way to express what is meant. There is no substitute for it in a sentence such as *That's the only friend of yours that I've ever met,* since alternative wordings are awkward or inaccurate.

OF *abbr.* **1.** outfield **2.** outfielder

O'Fao•lain (ō-făl′ən, ō-fā′lən), **Sean** 1900–91. Irish writer best known for his short stories.

o•fay (ō′fā′) *n. Offensive Slang* Used as a disparaging term for a white person. [Poss. of West African orig.]

off (ôf, ŏf) *adv.* **1.** From a place or position: *drove off.* **2a.** At a certain distance in space or time: *a week off.* **b.** From a given course or route; aside: *off the road.* **c.** Into a state of unconsciousness: *dozed off.* **3a.** So as to be no longer on, attached, or connected: *shaved off his beard.* **b.** So as to be divided: *marked off the field.* **4.** So as to be no longer continuing, operating, or functioning: *switched off the TV.* **5.** So as to be completely removed, finished, or eliminated: *kill off the mice.* **6.** So as to be smaller, fewer, or less: *Sales dropped off.* **7.** So as to be away from work or duty: *a day off.* **8.** Offstage. ❖ *adj.* **1a.** Distant or removed; farther: *the off side.* **b.** Remote; slim: *The sun was shining, but I brought an umbrella on the off chance that it might rain.* **2.** Not on, attached, or connected: *with my shoes off.* **3.** Not operating or operational: *The oven is off.* **4.** No longer taking place; canceled: *The trip is off.* **5.** Slack: *Sales are off.* **6a.** Not up to standard; below a normal or satisfactory level. **b.** Not accurate; incorrect: *Your results are off.* **c.** Somewhat crazy; eccentric. **7.** Started on the way; going: *I'm off to school.* **8a.** Away from or not engaged in work or duty. **b.** Spent away from work or duty: *My off day is Saturday.* **9a.** Being on the right side of an animal or vehicle. **b.** Being the animal or vehicle on the right. **10.** *Sports* Toward or being the side of the field facing the batsman in cricket. **11.** Off-color. ❖ *prep.* **1.** So as to be removed or distant from: *off the branch.* **2.** Away or relieved from: *off duty.* **3a.** By consuming: *living off milk.* **b.** With the means provided by: *living off my pension.* **c.** *Informal* From. **4.** Extending or branching out from: *an artery off the heart.* **5.** Not up to the usual standard of: *off his game.* **6.** So as to abstain from: *off narcotics.* **7.** *Nautical* To seaward of. ❖ *v.* **offed, off•ing, offs** *—intr.* To go away; leave. *—tr. Slang* To murder. ***—idiom:* off and on** In an intermittent manner. [Variant of ME *of* < OE. See **apo-** in App.]

USAGE NOTE In Modern English the compound preposition *off of* is best avoided in formal speech and writing: *He stepped off* (not *off of*) *the platform. Off* is informal as well when used to indicate a source; formal style requires *I borrowed it from* (not *off*) *my brother.*

Of•fa (ô′fə) d. 796. King of Mercia (757–796) who signed the first recorded English commercial treaty (796).

off-air (ôf′âr′, ŏf′-) *adj.* Spoken, occurring, or used not during broadcasting or not while being recorded for broadcasting.

of•fal (ô′fəl, ŏf′əl) *n.* **1.** Waste parts, esp. of a butchered animal. **2.** Refuse; rubbish. [ME : *of-,* off (< OE < *of;* see **apo-** in App.) + *fal,* fall.]

off•beat (ôf′bēt′, ŏf′-) *n. Music* An unaccented beat in a measure. ❖ *adj.* (ôf′bēt′, ŏf′-) *Slang* Not conforming to an ordinary type or pattern; unconventional: *offbeat humor.*

off-brand (ôf′brănd′, ŏf′-) *adj.* Of or being an product sold inexpensively under an unfamiliar brand name. **—off′-brand′** *n.*

off-Broad•way (ôf′brôd′wā′, ŏf′-) *n.* Theatrical work, often experimental, presented in New York City outside the Broadway entertainment district. ❖ *adj.* **1.** Of or being such a theatrical work. **2.** Located outside the Broadway entertainment district. **—off′-Broad′way′** *adv.*

off-col•or (ôf′kŭl′ər, ŏf′-) *adj.* **1.** Exhibiting bad taste: *an off-color joke.* **2.** Varying from the usual, expected, or required color. **3.** Not in good health or spirits.

Of•fen•bach (ô′fən-bäk′, ŏf′ən-, ô-fĕn-bäk′), **Jacques** 1819–80. French composer noted for the opera *Tales of Hoffman.*

of•fence (ə-fĕns′) *n. Chiefly British* Variant of **offense.**

of•fend (ə-fĕnd′) *v.* **-fend•ed, -fend•ing, -fends** *—tr.* **1.** To cause displeasure, anger, resentment, or wounded feelings in. **2.** To be displeasing or disagreeable to. **3a.** To transgress; violate: *offend all laws of humanity.* **b.** To cause to sin. *—intr.* **1.** To result in displeasure. **2a.** To violate a moral or divine law; sin. **b.** To violate a rule or law. [ME *offenden* < OFr. *offendre* < Lat. *offendere.* See **gʷhen-** in App.]

of•fend•er (ə-fĕn′dər) *n.* One that offends, esp. one that breaks a public law: *youthful offenders.*

of•fense (ə-fĕns′) *n.* **1a.** The act of causing anger, resentment, displeasure, or affront. **b.** The state of being offended. **2a.** A violation or infraction of a moral or social code; a transgression or sin. **b.** A transgression of law; a crime. **3.** Something that outrages moral sensibilities. **4.** (ŏf′ĕns′) The act of attacking or assaulting. **5.** (ŏf′ĕns′) *Sports* **a.** The means or tactics used in attempting to score. **b.** The team in possession of the ball or puck, or those players whose primary duty is to attempt to score. [ME < OFr. *ofense* < Lat. *offēnsa* < fem. p. part. of *offendere,* to offend. See OFFEND.]

of•fen•sive (ə-fĕn′sĭv) *adj.* **1.** Disagreeable to the senses. **2.** Causing anger, displeasure, resentment, or affront. **3a.** Making an attack: *offensive troops.* **b.** Of, relating to, or designed for attack. **4.** (ŏf′ĕn-) *Sports* Of or relating to a team having possession of a ball or puck. ❖ *n.* **1.** An attitude or position of attack. **2.** An attack or assault. **—of•fen′sive•ly** *adv.* **—of•fen′sive•ness** *n.*

of•fer (ô′fər, ŏf′ər) *v.* **-fered, -fer•ing, -fers** *—tr.* **1.** To present for acceptance or rejection; proffer. **2a.** To put forward for consideration; propose. **b.** To present in order to meet a need or satisfy a requirement. **3a.** To make available; afford: *Her staying late offered us the chance to talk.* **b.** To present for sale. **c.** To provide; furnish: *The hotel offers free parking.* **4.** To propose as payment; bid. **5.** To present as an act of worship. **6.** To exhibit readiness or desire (to do something); volunteer. **7.** To put up; mount: *offer resistance.* **8.** To threaten: *offered to leave if they didn't get ready.* **9.** To produce or introduce on the stage. *—intr.* **1.** To present an offering in worship or devotion. **2.** To make an offer or proposal, esp. of marriage. **3.** To present itself. ❖ *n.* **1.** The act of offering. **2.** Something, such as a suggestion, proposal, or bid, that is offered. **3.** *Law* A proposal that if accepted constitutes a legally binding contract. **4.** The condition of being offered, esp. for sale.

5a. An attempt; a try. **b.** A show of intention. [ME *offren* < OE *offrian*, to offer in worship, and < OFr. *offrir*, to propose, present, both < Lat. *offerre*, to offer < *ob-*, to; see OB– + *ferre*, to bring; see **bher-**[1] in App.] —**of′fer·er, of′fer·or** *n.*

SYNONYMS *offer, proffer, tender, present* These verbs mean to put before another for acceptance or rejection. *Offer* is the most general: *offered us some tea.* *Proffer* implies voluntary action motivated especially by courtesy or generosity: *"Mr. van der Luyden . . . proffered to Newland low-voiced congratulations"* (Edith Wharton). To *tender* is to offer formally: *tendered her respects.* *Present* suggests formality and often ceremony: *"A footman entered, and presented . . . some mail on a silver tray"* (Winston Churchill).

of·fer·ing (ô′fər-ĭng, ŏf′ər-) *n.* **1.** The act of making an offer. **2.** Something that is offered. **3.** A presentation made to a deity as an act of religious worship or sacrifice; an oblation. **4.** A contribution or gift, esp. one made at a religious service.

of·fer·to·ry (ô′fər-tôr′ē, -tōr′ē, ŏf′ər-) *n., pl.* **-ries 1.** often **Offertory a.** One of the principal parts of the Eucharistic liturgy at which the celebrant offers bread and wine to God. **b.** A musical setting for this part of the liturgy. **2.** A collection of offerings at a religious service. [ME *offertori* < LLat. *offertōrium* < Lat. *offerre*, to offer. See OFFER.]

off-guard (ôf′gärd′, ŏf′-) *adj.* Off one's guard; unprepared: *Her reply caught me off-guard.*

off·hand (ôf′hănd′, ŏf′-) *adv.* Without preparation or forethought. ❖ *adj.* also **off·hand·ed** (-hăn′dĭd) Extemporaneous. —**off′hand′ed·ly** *adv.* —**off′hand′ed·ness** *n.*

off-hour (ôf′our′, ŏf′-) *n.* A period of time during which motor vehicular and pedestrian traffic is light.

of·fice (ô′fĭs, ŏf′ĭs) *n.* **1a.** A place in which business, clerical, or professional activities are conducted. **b.** The administrative personnel, executives, or staff working in such a place. **2.** A duty or function assigned to or assumed by someone. See Syns at **function. 3.** A position of authority, duty, or trust given to a person, as in a government or corporation. **4a.** A subdivision of a governmental department. **b.** A major executive division of a government. **5.** A public position. **6. offices** *Chiefly British* The parts of a house, such as the kitchen, in which servants carry out household work. **7.** A usu. beneficial act performed for another. Often used in the plural. **8.** *Ecclesiastical* A ceremony, rite, or service, usu. prescribed by liturgy, esp.: **a.** The canonical hours. **b.** A prayer service in the Anglican Church, such as Evening Prayer. **c.** A ceremony, rite, or service for a special purpose, esp. the Office of the Dead. [ME < OFr., duty < Lat. *officium*. See **dhē-** in App.]

office boy *n.* A boy or young man employed in a business office to do odd jobs and errands.

office girl *n.* A girl or young woman employed in a business office to do odd jobs and errands.

of·fice·hold·er (ô′fĭs-hōl′dər, ŏf′ĭs-) *n.* One who holds public office.

Office of the Dead *n. Ecclesiastical* An office traditionally sung or said before a burial mass in the Roman Catholic Church, now obligatory only on All Souls' Day.

of·fi·cer (ô′fĭ-sər, ŏf′ĭ-) *n.* **1.** One who holds an office of authority or trust in an organization. **2.** One who holds a commission in the armed forces. **3.** A person licensed in the merchant marine as master, mate, chief engineer, or assistant engineer. **4.** A police officer. ❖ *tr.v.* **-cered, -cer·ing, -cers 1.** To furnish with officers. **2.** To command or manage as an officer. [ME < OFr. *officier* < Med.Lat. *officiārius* < Lat. *officium*, service, duty. See OFFICE.]

officer of the day *n., pl.* **officers of the day** A military officer who, for a given day, assumes responsibility for security, order, and supervision of the guard.

officer of the deck *n., pl.* **officers of the deck** A naval officer assigned to represent the commanding officer of a vessel or installation for a specified period.

of·fi·cial (ə-fĭsh′əl) *adj.* **1.** Of or relating to an office or a post of authority. **2.** Authorized by a proper authority; authoritative. **3.** Holding office or serving in a public capacity. **4.** Characteristic of or befitting a person of authority; formal. **5.** Authorized by or contained in the US Pharmacopoeia or National Formulary. Used of drugs. ❖ *n.* **1.** One who holds an office or position, esp. one who acts in a subordinate capacity for an institution. **2.** *Sports* A referee or umpire. [< ME, ecclesiastical officer < OFr. < Lat. *officiālis*, an attendant of an office < *officium*, duty, service. See OFFICE.] —**of·fi′cial·dom** *n.* —**of·fi′cial·ly** *adv.*

of·fi·cial·ese (ə-fĭsh′ə-lēz′, -lēs′) *n.* Language characteristic of official documents or statements, esp. when obscure, pretentiously wordy, or excessively formal.

of·fi·cial·ism (ə-fĭsh′ə-lĭz′əm) *n.* Rigid adherence to official regulations, forms, and procedures.

of·fi·ci·ant (ə-fĭsh′ē-ənt) *n.* One who performs a religious rite or presides over a religious service or ceremony.

of·fi·ci·ar·y (ə-fĭsh′ē-ĕr′ē) *n., pl.* **-ies 1.** A body of officials or officers. **2.** An official or officer. ❖ *adj.* **1.** Attached to or resulting from an office held. Used of a title. **2.** Having a title resulting from the holding of an office. Used of a dignitary.

of·fi·ci·ate (ə-fĭsh′ē-āt′) *v.* **-at·ed, -at·ing, -ates** —*tr.* **1.** To perform the duties and functions of an office or a position of authority. **2.** To serve as an officiant. **3.** *Sports* To serve as a referee or an umpire. —*tr. Usage Problem* **1.** To perform from a position of authority (an official duty or function). **2.** To serve as an officiant at (a ceremony). **3.** To serve as a referee or umpire at (a game). [Med.Lat. *officiāre, officiāt-*, to conduct < Lat. *officium*, service, duty. See OFFICE.] —**of·fi′ci·a′tion** *n.* —**of·fi′ci·a′tor** *n.*

USAGE NOTE *Officiate* has long seen use as an intransitive verb, but it has recently developed a transitive use. The Usage Panel views this use unfavorably. In sporting contexts, as in the sentence *He officiated National Hockey League games for 15 years,* transitive *officiate* is approved by only 38 percent of the Panel. Support for this usage in more traditional contexts, such as weddings, goes down further. Only 22 percent of the Panel approves of the sentence *A minister officiated the wedding.*

of·fic·i·nal (ə-fĭs′ə-nəl, ô′fĭ-sī′nəl, ŏf′ĭ-) *adj.* **1.** Readily available in pharmacies; not requiring special preparation. **2.** Recognized by a pharmacopoeia: *an officinal herb.* ❖ *n.* An officinal drug. [Fr. < Med.Lat. *officīnālis*, of a storeroom or workshop < Lat. *officīna*, workshop, alteration of *opificīna* < *opifex, opific-*, workman : *opus*, work + *facere*, to do; see **dhē-** in App.] —**of·fic′i·nal·ly** *adv.*

of·fi·cious (ə-fĭsh′əs) *adj.* **1.** Marked by excessive eagerness in offering unwanted services or advice to others. **2.** Informal; unofficial. **3.** *Archaic* Eager to render services or help others. [Lat. *officiōsus*, obliging, dutiful < *officium*, duty. See OFFICE.] —**of·fi′cious·ly** *adv.* —**of·fi′cious·ness** *n.*

off·ing (ô′fĭng, ŏf′ĭng) *n.* The part of the sea visible from shore that is very distant or beyond anchoring ground. —*idiom:* **in the offing 1.** In the near or immediate future; soon to come. **2.** Nearby; at hand.

off·ish (ô′fĭsh, ŏf′ĭsh) *adj.* Inclined to be distant and reserved; aloof. —**off′ish·ly** *adv.* —**off′ish·ness** *n.*

off-key (ôf′kē′, ŏf′-) *adj.* **1.** *Music* Pitched higher or lower than the correct notes of a melody. **2.** Being out of accord with what is considered normal or appropriate. —**off′key′** *adv.*

off-la·bel (ôf′lā′bəl, ŏf′-) *adj.* Of or relating to a drug prescribed to treat a condition for which it has not been officially approved.

off-li·cence (ôf′lī′səns, ŏf′-) *n. Chiefly British* A store that sells alcoholic beverages for consumption off the premises.

off-lim·its (ôf-lĭm′ĭts, ŏf-) *adj.* Not to be entered or frequented by a designated group.

off·line or **off-line** (ôf′lĭn′, ŏf′-) *adj.* **1.** Not under the control of a central computer, as in a manufacturing process. **2.** Not connected to a computer or computer network.

off·load or **off-load** (ôf′lōd′, ŏf′-) *v.* **-load·ed, -load·ing, -loads** —*tr.* **1.** To unload (a vehicle or container). **2.** *Computer Science* To transfer (data) to a peripheral device. —*intr.* To unload a vehicle or container.

off of *prep. Informal* Off. See Usage Note at **off.**

off-off-Broad·way (ôf′ôf-brôd′wā′, ŏf′ôf-) *n.* The avant-garde or experimental theatrical productions of New York City, typically performed in small or multipurpose venues. —**off′-off-Broad′way** *adv. & adj.*

off-peak (ôf′pēk′, ŏf′-) *adj.* Not in the period of most frequent or heaviest use: *off-peak airfares.*

off-price (ôf′prīs′, ŏf′-) *adj.* **1.** Of, relating to, or being a retail store that sells merchandise at prices lower than usual. **2.** For sale at prices lower than usual.

off·print (ôf′prĭnt′, ŏf′-) *n.* A reproduction of or an excerpt from an article originally contained in a larger publication. ❖ *tr.v.* **-print·ed, -print·ing, -prints** To reproduce or reprint (an article or excerpt).

off-put·ting (ôf′pŏŏt′ĭng, ŏf′-) *adj.* Tending to disconcert or repel.

off rhyme *n.* A partial or imperfect rhyme, often using assonance or consonance only, as in *dry* and *died.*

off-road (ôf′rōd′, ŏf′-) *adj.* Existing, occurring, or made for use off paved roads or in rugged areas. —**off′-road′** *adv.*

off-scour·ing (ôf′skour′ĭng, ŏf′-) *n.* **1.** Something scoured off or disposed of; refuse. Often used in the plural. **2.** A person fallen from society; an outcast. Often used in the plural.

offscreen (ôf′skrēn′, ŏf′-) *adj.* **1.** Existing or occurring outside the frame of a movie or television screen: *sounds of offscreen mayhem.* **2.** Existing or occurring out of public view or knowledge; private. —**off′screen′** *adv.*

off-sea·son (ôf′sē′zən, ŏf′-) *n.* A part of the year marked by a cessation or lessening of normal activity, as of a business. —**off′-sea′son** *adv. & adj.*

off·set (ôf′sĕt′, ŏf′-) *n.* **1.** An agent, element, or thing that balances, counteracts, or compensates for something else. **2.** One thing set off or developed from something else. **3.** The start or initial stage; the outset. **4.** *Architecture* A ledge or recess in a wall formed by a reduction in thickness above; a setoff. **5.** *Botany* A shoot that develops laterally at the base of a plant, often rooting to form a new plant. **6.** *Geology* A spur of a mountain range or hills. **7.** A bend in a pipe, bar, or other straight continuous piece made to allow it to pass around an obstruction. **8.** A short distance measured perpendicularly from the main line in surveying,

ă pat   oi boy
ā pay   ou out
âr care ŏŏ took
ä father ōō boot
ĕ pet   ŭ cut
ē be   ûr urge
ĭ pit   th thin
ī pie   th this
îr pier hw which
ŏ pot   zh vision
ō toe   ə about,
ô paw   item

Stress marks:
′ (primary);
′ (secondary), as in
lexicon (lĕk′sĭ-kŏn′)

used to help in calculating the area of an irregular plot. **9.** A descendant of a race or family; an offshoot. **10.** *Printing* **a.** An unintentional or faulty transfer of wet ink from a printed sheet to another surface in contact with it. **b.** Offset printing. ❖ *v.* (ôf′sĕt′, ŏf′-, ôf-sĕt′, ŏf-) **-set, -set·ting, -sets** —*tr.* **1.** To counterbalance, counteract, or compensate for. **2.** *Printing* **a.** To cause (printed matter) to transfer or smear onto another surface. **b.** To produce by offset printing. **3.** To make or form an offset in (a wall, bar, or pipe). —*intr.* **1.** To develop, project, or be situated as an offset. **2.** *Printing* To become marked by or cause an unintentional transfer of ink. —**off′set′** *adv. & adj.*

offset printing *n.* The process of printing by indirect image transfer, esp. by using a metal or paper plate to ink a smooth rubber cylinder that transfers the ink to the paper.

off·shoot (ôf′sho͞ot′, ŏf′-) *n.* **1.** Something that branches out or derives its origin from a particular source. **2.** A branch, descendant, or member of a family or social group. **3.** *Botany* A lateral shoot from the main stem of a plant.

off·shore (ôf′shôr′, -shōr′, ŏf′-) *adj.* **1.** Moving or directed away from the shore. **2a.** Located at a distance from the shore. **b.** Located or based in a foreign country and not subject to tax laws: *offshore bank accounts.* ❖ *adv.* **1.** Away from the shore. **2.** At a distance from the shore. ❖ *n.* The flat region of submerged land between the breaker zone and the edge of the continental shelf.

off·side (ôf′sīd′, ŏf′-) also **off·sides** (-sīdz′) *adv. & adj. Sports* Illegally ahead of the ball or puck in the attacking zone. **2.** *Football* Illegally beyond the line of scrimmage when the ball is snapped or ahead of the ball when the ball is kicked on a kickoff. ❖ *n. Sports* An offside motion or play.

off-site (ôf′sīt′, ŏf′-) *adj.* Taking place or located away from the site, as of a particular activity. —**off′-site′** *adv.*

off-speed (ôf′spēd′, ŏf′-) *adj. Sports* Slower than expected.

off·spring (ôf′sprĭng′, ŏf′-) *n., pl.* **offspring 1.** The progeny of a person, animal, or plant considered as a group. **2.** A child of particular parentage. **3.** A result; a product. [ME *ofspring* < OE : *of*, off; see OFF + *springan*, to rise.]

off·stage (ôf′stāj′, ŏf′-) *adj.* **1.** Situated or taking place in the area of a stage invisible to the audience. **2.** Of, relating to, or taking place in private life. ❖ *adv.* **1.** Away from the area of a stage visible to the audience. **2a.** In private life. **b.** Behind the scenes.

off-the-cuff (ôf′thə-kŭf′, ŏf′-) *adj.* Not prepared in advance; impromptu: *an off-the-cuff remark.*

off-the-rack (ôf′thə-răk′, ŏf′-) *adj.* Of or being merchandise, esp. clothing, made in standard sizes; ready-made.

off-the-rec·ord (ôf′thə-rĕk′ərd, ŏf′-) *adj.* Not for publication or attribution: *off-the-record comments.*

off-the-shelf (ôf′thə-shĕlf′, ŏf′-) *adj.* Available from merchandise in stock; not custom-made.

off-the-wall (ôf′thə-wôl′, ŏf′-) *adj. Informal* **1.** Very unconventional or unusual: *off-the-wall humor.* **2.** Exhibiting bizarre behavior; crazy: *their off-the-wall friends.*

off-track (ôf′trăk′, ŏf′-) *adj.* Of or relating to gambling on races that is conducted away from a racetrack.

off-track betting *n.* A system of placing bets away from a racetrack.

off-white (ôf′hwīt′, -wīt′, ŏf′-) *n.* A grayish or yellowish white. —**off′-white′** *adj.*

off year *n.* **1.** A year in which no major political elections occur. **2.** A year of reduced activity or production.

O′Fla·her·ty (ō-flă′hər-tē) **Liam** 1896–1984. Irish writer whose collected works include *Two Lovely Beasts* (1948).

OFM *abbr.* Order of Friars Minor

oft (ôft, ŏft) *adv.* Often. Often used in combination: *his oft-expressed philosophy.* [ME < OE. See **upo** in App.]

of·ten (ôf′ən, ŏf′ən, ôf′tən, ŏf′-) *adv.* **-er, -est** Many times; frequently. [ME, alteration of *oft* < OE. See **upo** in App.]

of·ten·times (ôf′ən-tīmz′, ôf′tən-, ŏf′ən-, ŏf′tən-) also **oft·times** (ôf′tīmz′, ŏf′-) *adv.* Frequently; repeatedly.

OG *abbr.* officer of the guard

Og·bo·mo·sho (ŏg′bə-mō′shō) A city of SW Nigeria NNE of Ibadan. Pop. 514,400.

Og·den (ôg′dən, ŏg′-) A city of N-central UT N of Salt Lake City; settled by Mormons in the 1840s. Pop. 77,226.

o·gee (ō′jē′) *n. Architecture* **1.** A double curve with the shape of an elongated S. **2.** A molding having the profile of an S-shaped curve. **3.** An arch formed by two S-shaped curves meeting at a point. [ME *oggifs, ogeus,* pl. of *ogif,* ogive. See OGIVE.]

O·gee·chee (ō-gē′chē) A river of E GA flowing c. 402 km (250 mi) generally SE to the Atlantic Ocean.

og·ham or **og·am** (ŏg′əm, ŏ′əm) *n.* **1a.** An alphabetic system of inscribed notches for vowels and lines for consonants used to write Old Irish, chiefly on the edges of memorial stones, from the fifth to the early seventh century. **b.** A character used in this alphabet. **2a.** An inscription in the ogham alphabet. **b.** A stone inscribed in the ogham alphabet. [Ir.Gael. < OIr. *ogom,* after *Ogma,* name of a Celtic god. See **ag-** in App.]

o·give (ō′jīv′) *n.* **1.** *Statistics* **a.** A distribution curve in which the frequencies are cumulative. **b.** A frequency distribution. **2.** *Architecture* **a.** A diagonal rib of a Gothic vault. **b.** A pointed arch. [ME *ogif* and Fr. *ogive,* diagonal rib of a vault, both < OFr. *augive,* prob. < VLat. **obviātīva* < LLat. *obviāta,* fem. p. part. of *obviāre,*

ogee
Lotus Mahal in the Hampi palace complex, India

ohia lehua
Metrosideros polymorpha

Georg Simon Ohm

to resist. See OBVIATE.] —**o·gi′val** *adj.*

O·gla·la (ō-glä′lə) *n., pl.* **Oglala** or **-las** A member of a Native American people constituting a subdivision of the Teton Sioux, formerly inhabiting the Black Hills region of western South Dakota, with a present-day population mainly in southwest South Dakota.

o·gle (ō′gəl, ŏ′gəl) *v.* **o·gled, o·gling, o·gles** —*tr.* **1.** To stare at. **2.** To stare at in an ogling way. —*intr.* To stare in an impertinent, flirtatious, or amorous manner. ❖ *n.* An ogling stare. [Perh. < LGer. *oghelen,* freq. of *oegen,* to eye < *oghe, oge,* eye. See **okʷ-** in App.] —**o′gler** *n.*

O·gle·thorpe (ō′gəl-thôrp′) **James Edward** 1696–1785. English soldier and philanthropist who secured a charter for the colony of Georgia (1732).

o·gre (ō′gər) *n.* **1.** A giant or monster in legends and fairy tales that eats humans. **2.** A person who is felt to be particularly cruel, brutish, or hideous. [Fr., prob. ult. < Lat. *Orcus,* god of the underworld.] —**o′gre·ish** or **o′gr·ish** *adj.*

o·gress (ō′grĭs) *n.* **1.** A female giant or monster in legends and fairy tales that eats humans. **2.** A woman who is felt to be particularly cruel, brutish, or hideous.

oh[1] (ō) *interj.* **1.** Used to express strong emotion, such as surprise, fear, anger, or pain. **2.** Used in direct address: *Oh, sir! You forgot your keys.* **3.** Used to indicate understanding or acknowledgment of a statement.

oh[2] (ō) *n.* Zero. [< the number zero's resemblance to the letter O.]

OH *abbr.* **1.** Ohio **2.** open house

O′Ha·ra (ō-hâr′ə, ō-hăr′ə) **Frank** 1926–66. Amer. poet whose collections include *Lunch Poems* (1964).

O′Hara, John Henry 1905–70. Amer. writer whose novels include *Butterfield 8* (1935).

O. Henry See William Sydney **Porter.**

o·hi·a le·hu·a (ō-hē′ə lā-ho͞o′ə) *n.* Any of several evergreen shrubs or trees of the genus *Metrosideros* of Hawaii and other Pacific islands, having showy red flowers. [Hawaiian *′ōhi′a lehua* : *′ōhi′a,* ohia lehua + *lehua,* flower of the ohia lehua.]

O′Hig·gins (ō-hĭg′ĭnz) **Bernardo** 1778–1842. Chilean general and politician who led the revolt against the Spanish and ruled Chile (1817–23).

O·hi·o (ō-hī′ō) A state of the N-central US in the Great Lakes region; admitted as the 17th state in 1803. Cap. Columbus. Pop. 11,353,140. —**O·hi′o·an** *adj. & n.*

Ohio buckeye *n.* A large shrub or tree (*Aesculus glabra*) of the central United States having compound leaves and yellowish-green flowers.

Ohio River A river formed by the confluence of the Allegheny and Monongahela rivers in W PA and flowing c. 1,578 km (981 mi) to the Mississippi R. in S IL.

ohm (ōm) *n. Symbol* Ω A unit of electrical resistance equal to that of a conductor in which a current of one ampere is produced by a potential of one volt across its terminals. [After Georg Simon OHM.] —**ohm′ic** *adj.*

Ohm, Georg Simon 1789–1854. German physicist noted for contributions to the study of electrical resistance.

ohm·age (ō′mĭj) *n.* Electrical resistance expressed in ohms.

ohm·me·ter (ōm′mē′tər) *n.* An instrument for direct measurement of the resistance of a conductor in ohms.

OHMS *abbr.* On Her (or His) Majesty's Service

Ohm's law (ōmz) *n.* The law stating that the direct current flowing in a conductor is directly proportional to the potential difference between its ends. It is usu. formulated as $V = IR$, where V is the potential difference, or voltage, I is the current, and R is the resistance of the conductor. [After Georg Simon OHM.]

o·ho (ō-hō′) *interj.* Used to express surprise, comprehension, or mock astonishment.

–oholic *suff.* Variant of **–aholic.**

Ohr·mazd also **Or·mazd** or **Or·muzd** (ôr′məzd, ôr-mŭzd′) *n.* See Ahura Mazda. [MPers. < OPers. *Ahuramazdā* : *ahura,* lord + *mazdā-,* wise; see **men-**[1] in App.]

–oic *suff.* Containing a carboxyl group or one of its derivatives: *decanoic acid.* [**–O–** + **–IC.**]

–oid *suff.* **1.** Resembling; having the appearance of; related to: *acanthoid.* **2.** One that resembles something specified or has a specified quality: *humanoid.* [Gk. *-oeidēs* < *eidos,* shape, form. See **weid-** in App.]

o·id·i·um (ō-ĭd′ē-əm) *n., pl.* **-i·a** (-ē-ə) A thin-walled spore produced by fragmentation in certain filamentous fungi. [NLat. *Oidium,* fungus genus < Gk. *ōion,* egg. See OO–.]

oil (oil) *n.* **1.** Any of numerous mineral, vegetable, and synthetic liquids and animal or plant fats that are generally combustible, viscous, soluble in various organic solvents such as ether but not in water, and used in a great variety of products, esp. lubricants, fuels, and foods. **2a.** Petroleum. **b.** A petroleum derivative, such as a lubricant. **3.** A substance with an oily consistency. **4.** Oil paint. **5.** A painting done in oil paint. **6.** Insincere flattery. ❖ *tr.v.* **oiled, oil·ing, oils** To lubricate, supply, cover, or polish with oil. —*idiom:* **oil (someone's) hand** (or **palm**) *Informal* **1.** To bribe. **2.** To give a tip to. [ME < OFr. *oile* < Lat. *oleum,* olive oil < Gk. **elaiwon, elaion* < **elaiwā, elaiā,* olive.]

oil beetle *n.* Any of various blister beetles of the genus *Meloe* that exude an oily substance when disturbed.

oil·bird (oil′bûrd′) *n.* See **guacharo.**

oil cake *n.* The solid residue that is left after certain oily seeds, such as cottonseed, have been pressed free of their oil.

oil·can (oil′kăn′) *n.* A can for oil, esp. having a spout to release oil drop by drop, as for lubricating machinery.

oil·cloth (oil′klôth′, -klŏth′) *n.* Fabric treated with clay, oil, and pigments to make it waterproof.

oil color *n.* See **oil paint.**

oiled (oild) *adj.* **1.** Treated or covered with oil. **2.** *Slang* Intoxicated; drunk.

oil·er (oi′lər) *n.* **1.** One that oils engines or machinery. **2.** *Nautical* **a.** An oil tanker. **b.** A ship that burns oil as fuel. **3.** See **oilcan.** **4.** See **oil well.** **5.** *Informal* An oilskin garment.

oil field *n.* An area with reserves of recoverable petroleum.

oil gland *n.* **1.** A gland that secretes an oily substance. **2.** See **uropygial gland.**

oil of turpentine *n.* See **turpentine** 1.

oil of vitriol *n.* See **sulfuric acid.**

oil paint *n.* A paint in which the vehicle is a drying oil.

oil painting *n.* **1.** A painting done in oil paints. **2.** The art or practice of painting with oils.

oil palm *n.* **1.** A tall palm tree (*Elaeis guineensis*) native to tropical Africa and having nutlike fruits that yield a commercially valuable oil. **2.** Any of several palms that yield oil.

oil pan *n.* The bottom of the crankcase in an internal-combustion engine, serving as an oil reservoir.

oil·pa·per (oil′pā′pər) *n.* Paper that is soaked in oil to make it transparent and water-resistant.

oil patch *n. Informal* **1.** The petroleum and natural gas industry. **2.** An oil-producing region.

oil sand *n.* A stratum of sand or sandstone containing petroleum.

oil-seed rape (oil′sēd′) *n.* See **rape²**.

oil shale *n.* A black or dark brown shale containing hydrocarbons that yield petroleum by distillation.

oil·skin (oil′skĭn′) *n.* **1.** Cloth treated with oil to make it waterproof. **2.** A garment made of oilskin.

oil slick *n.* A layer of oil floating on the surface of water.

oil·stone (oil′stōn′) *n.* A fine-grained whetstone lubricated with oil, used for fine sharpening.

oil well *n.* A hole drilled or dug in the earth from which petroleum flows or is pumped.

oil·y (oi′lē) *adj.* **-i·er, -i·est** **1.** Of or relating to oil. **2.** Impregnated, smeared with, or containing oil; greasy. **3.** Excessively suave; unctuous. —**oil′i·ly** *adv.* —**oil′i·ness** *n.*

oink (oingk) *n.* The characteristic grunting noise of a hog. [Imit.] —**oink** *v.*

oint·ment (oint′mənt) *n.* A viscous or semisolid substance used on the skin as a cosmetic, emollient, or medicament; a salve. [ME *oinement* < OFr. *oignement* < VLat. **unguimentum* < Lat. *unguentum.* See **UNGUENT.**]

Oise (wäz) A river rising in the Ardennes Mts. of S Belgium and flowing c. 299 km (186 mi) to the Seine R. in N France.

O·i·ta (ō-ē′tä′) A city of NE Kyushu, Japan, ENE of Nagasaki; a castle town in the 16th cent. Pop. 420,361.

OJ *abbr.* orange juice

O·jib·wa (ō-jĭb′wä′, -wə) also **O·jib·way** (-wā′) or **O·jib·we** (-wĕ) *n., pl.* **Ojibwa** or **-was** also **Ojibway** or **-ways** or **Ojibwe** or **-wes** **1.** A member of a Native American people originally located north of Lake Huron before moving westward in the 17th and 18th centuries into the upper Midwest, with later migrations onto the northern Great Plains. **2.** Their Algonquian language. [Ojibwa *ojibwe.*]

O·jos del Sa·la·do (ō′hōz dĕl′ sə-lä′dō, sä-, ō′hōs) A peak, 6,874.3 m (22,539 ft), in the Andes on the border between Argentina and Chile.

OK¹ or **o·kay** (ō-kā′) *Informal adj.* **1.** Acceptable or satisfactory: *Is your hotel room OK?* **2.** Mediocre: *The food was only OK.* **3.** In proper working order: *The battery is OK.* **4.** Correct: *The answer is OK.* **5.** Healthy or uninjured: *fell but was OK.* ❖ *adv.* **1.** Used to express approval or agreement. **2.** Well enough; adequately: *an oven that works OK despite its age.* ❖ *n.* Approval; agreement. ❖ *tr.v.* **OK'ed** or **OK'd** or **o·kayed, OK'ing** or **o·kay·ing, OK's** or **o·kays** To approve of or agree to; authorize. [Abbreviation of *oll korrect,* slang respelling of *all correct.*]

OK² *abbr.* Oklahoma

O·ka (ō-kä′) **1.** A river, c. 1,488 km (925 mi), of W Russia that joins the Volga R. near Nizhny Novgorod. **2.** A river of S-central Russia flowing c. 965 km (600 mi) to the Angara R.

O·ka·nog·an also **O·ka·na·gan** (ō′kə-nŏg′ən) A river, c. 483 km (300 mi), flowing from **Lake Okanagan** in S British Columbia, Canada, to the Columbia R. in N-central WA.

o·ka·pi (ō-kä′pē) *n., pl.* **okapi** or **-pis** A ruminant (*Okapia johnstoni*) of the Congo River basin related to the giraffe but having a short neck. [Perh. of Mbuba (Nilo-Saharan language of Congo) orig.]

O·ka·van·go (ō′kə-văng′gō) A river of SW-central Africa flowing c. 1,609 km (1,000 mi) from central Angola to N Botswana.

O·ka·ya·ma (ō′kä-yä′mä) A city of W Honshu, Japan, on an inlet of the Inland Sea W of Kobe. Pop. 604,513.

O·ka·za·ki (ō-kä′zä-kē, ō-kä′zä′kē) A city of S Honshu, Japan, SE of Nagoya. Pop. 318,983.

O·kee·cho·bee (ō′kĭ-chō′bē), **Lake** A lake of SE FL N of the Everglades; part of the **Okeechobee Waterway,** or **Cross-Florida Waterway,** from the Atlantic Ocean to the Gulf of Mexico.

O'Keeffe (ō-kēf′), **Georgia** 1887–1986. Amer. painter known esp. for her sensuous close-up paintings of flowers.

O·ke·fe·no·kee Swamp (ō′kə-fə-nō′kē, -kē-) A large swampy area of SE GA and NE FL.

O'Kel·ly (ō-kĕl′ē), **Seán Thomas** 1883–1966. Irish political leader who served as president of Ireland (1945–59).

O·khotsk (ō-kŏtsk′, ə-кнôtsk′), **Sea of** An arm of the NW Pacific Ocean W of the Kamchatka Peninsula and Kuril Is.

O·kie (ō′kē) *n.* **1.** *Offensive Slang* A migrant farm worker from the south-central United States, esp. one seeking work in the West or Southwest during the 1930s and 1940s. **2.** *Slang* A native or inhabitant of Oklahoma. [OK(LAHOMA) + -IE.]

O·ki·na·wa (ō′kĭ-nä′wə, -nou′-) An island group of the central Ryukyu Is. in the W Pacific Ocean SW of Japan; scene of fierce combat between Japanese and US forces in World War II.

Okla. *abbr.* Oklahoma

O·kla·ho·ma (ō′klə-hō′mə) A state of the S-central US; admitted as the 46th state in 1907. The W part was organized in 1890 as the **Oklahoma Territory,** which was later merged with the adjoining Indian Terr. Cap. Oklahoma City. Pop. 3,450,654. —**O′kla·ho′man** *adj. & n.*

Oklahoma City The cap. of OK, in the central part; settled in 1889. Pop. 506,132.

o·kra (ō′krə) *n.* **1a.** A tall tropical Asian annual plant (*Abelmoschus esculentus*) widely cultivated for its edible mucilaginous pods. **b.** The edible pods of this plant. **2.** See **gumbo** 2. [Of West African orig.; akin to Akan (Twi) *nkruma.*]

Ok·to·ber·fest (ŏk-tō′bər-fĕst′) *n.* A carousing beer festival held in early autumn. [Ger. : *Oktober,* October (< Lat. *Octōber;* see OCTOBER) + *Fest,* festival (< MHGer. *vëst* < Lat. *fëstum* < neut. of *fëstus,* festive; see **dhēs-** in App.).]

–ol¹ *suff.* An alcohol or a phenol: *glycerol.* [< (ALCOH)OL.]

–ol² *suff.* Variant of **–ole.**

O·laf II (ō′läf, ō′lăf, ōō′läf) or **O·lav II** (ō′läv) Known as Saint Olaf. 995?–1030. Patron saint and king of Norway (1016–28).

Ö·land (œ′länd′) A narrow island of SE Sweden in the Baltic Sea; site of numerous Stone Age monuments.

O·la·the (ō-lā′thə) A city of E KS SW of Kansas City. Pop. 92,962.

old (ōld) *adj.* **old·er, old·est 1a.** Having lived or existed for a relatively long time; far advanced in years or life. **b.** Relatively advanced in age: *our oldest child.* **2.** Made long ago; in existence for many years. **3.** Of or relating to a long life or to people who have had long lives. **4.** Having or exhibiting the physical characteristics of age. **5.** Having or exhibiting the wisdom of age; mature. **6.** Having lived or existed for a specified length of time. **7a.** Belonging to a remote or former period in history; ancient. **b.** Belonging to or being of an earlier time. **8.** often **Old** Being the earlier or earliest of two or more related objects, stages, versions, or periods. **9.** *Geology* **a.** Having become slower in flow and less vigorous in action. Used of a river. **b.** Having become simpler in form and of lower relief. Used of a landform. **10.** Exhibiting the effects of time or long use; worn. **11.** Known through long acquaintance; long familiar. **12.** Skilled or able through long experience; practiced. **13.** often **ol'** (ōl) **a.** Used as an intensive: *Come back any old time.* **b.** Used to express affection or familiarity: *Good ol' Sam.* ❖ *n.* **1.** An individual of a specified age: *a five-year-old.* **2.** Old people considered as a group. Used with *the: caring for the old.* **3.** Former times; yore: *In days of old.* [ME < OE *eald.*] —**old′ness** *n.*

USAGE NOTE *Old* is the bluntest of the adjectives most commonly used in referring to persons of advanced or advancing age. It generally suggests at least a degree of age-related infirmity, and for that reason it is often avoided in formal or polite speech. Many prefer *elderly* as a more neutral and respectful term, but it too can suggest frailty. And while *senior* enjoys wide usage as both a noun and adjective in many civic or social contexts, it is often considered unpleasantly euphemistic in a phrase such as *the senior couple living next door.* • As a comparative form, *older* would logically seem to indicate greater age than *old.* Except when a direct comparison is being made, however, the opposite is generally true. *The older man in the tweed jacket* suggests a somewhat younger or more vigorous man than if one substitutes *old* or *elderly.* Where *old* expresses an absolute, an arrival at old age, *older* takes a more relative view of aging as a continuum— older, but not yet old. As such, *older* is more than just a euphemism for the blunter *old,* offering as it does a more precise term

okra
Abelmoschus esculentus

ă	pat	oi	boy
ā	pay	ou	out
âr	care	ŏŏ	took
ä	father	ōō	boot
ĕ	pet	ŭ	cut
ē	be	ûr	urge
ĭ	pit	th	thin
ī	pie	th	this
îr	pier	hw	which
ŏ	pot	zh	vision
ō	toe	ə	about,
ô	paw		item

Stress marks:
′ (primary);
′ (secondary), as in
lexicon (lĕk′sĭ-kŏn′)

for someone between middle and advanced age. And unlike *elderly, older* does not particularly suggest frailness or infirmity, making it the natural choice in many situations. See Usage Note at elder[1].

old-boy network (ōld′boi′) *n.* An informal system of mutual assistance through which men of a particular group exchange favors and connections, as in politics or business.

Old Bulgarian *n.* See **Old Church Slavonic.**

Old Castile A historical region of N-central Spain that combined with the S region of New Castile to form the kingdom of Castile; united with Aragon after the marriage of Ferdinand and Isabella (1469).

Old Catholic *n.* A member of a group of German Roman Catholics who refused to accept papal infallibility.

Old Church Slavonic *n.* The medieval Slavic language used by Cyril and Methodius in their translation of the Bible and still used as a liturgical language in several Eastern churches.

old country *n.* The native country of an immigrant.

Old Danish *n.* The Danish language from the beginning of the 12th to the end of the 14th century.

Old Dutch *n.* Old Low Franconian.

old·en (ōl′dən) *adj.* Of, relating to, or belonging to time long past; old or ancient: *olden days.*

Old·en·burg (ōl′dən-bûrg′, -bŏŏrk′), **Claes Thure** b. 1929. Swedish-born Amer. sculptor known esp. for his large-scale outdoor works representing everyday objects.

Old English *n.* **1.** The English language from the middle of the 5th to the beginning of the 12th century. **2.** *Printing* See **black letter.**

Old English sheepdog *n.* Any of an English breed of sturdy dog having a docked tail and a thick, shaggy, bluish-gray and white coat with fur that hangs over the eyes.

Old Faithful A geyser in Yellowstone National Park in NW WY known for its eruptions lasting about 4 minutes.

old·fan·gled or **old-fan·gled** (ōld′făng′gəld) *adj. Informal* Old-fashioned. [OLD + (NEW)FANGLED.]

old-fash·ioned (ōld′făsh′ənd) *adj.* **1.** Of a style or method formerly in vogue; outdated. **2.** Attached to or favoring methods, ideas, or customs of an earlier time. ❖ *n.* A cocktail made of whiskey, bitters, sugar, and fruit.

old-field (ōld′fēld′) *n. Southern US* An overcultivated field allowed to lie fallow.

old-field colt *n. Virginia* A child born out of wedlock.

Old French *n.* The French language from the 9th to the early 16th century.

Old Frisian *n.* The Frisian language until about 1575.

old-girl network (ōld′gûrl′) *n.* An informal system of mutual assistance through which women of a particular group exchange favors and connections, as in politics or business.

Old Glory *n.* The flag of the United States.

old gold *n.* A dark yellow, from light olive or olive brown to deep or strong yellow.

old growth *n.* Forest or woodland having a mature ecosystem characterized by old woody plants and the wildlife and plants associated with them. —**old′-growth′** (ōld′grōth′) *adj.*

old guard also **Old Guard** *n.* A conservative, often reactionary element of a class, society, or political group.

Old·ham (ōl′dəm) A borough of NW England NE of Manchester. Pop. 220,520.

old hand *n.* One who is experienced; a veteran.

old hat *adj.* **1.** Old-fashioned. **2.** Overused; trite.

Old High German *n.* High German from the middle of the 9th to the end of the 11th century.

Old Icelandic *n.* Icelandic from the middle of the 12th to the middle of the 16th century.

old·ie (ōl′dē) *n.* Something old, esp. a once popular song.

Old Iranian *n.* Any of the Iranian languages in use before the beginning of the Christian era.

Old Irish *n.* The Irish language from 725 to about 950.

Old Italian *n.* The Italian language until the middle of the 16th century.

Old Kingdom Ancient Egypt during the III–VI Dynasties, from c. 2980 to 2475 B.C.; noted as the "Age of the Pyramids," with monuments built by rulers such as Cheops.

old lady *n. Slang* **1.** One's mother. **2a.** One's wife. **b.** One's girlfriend, esp. a lover with whom one lives.

Old Latin *n.* See **Archaic Latin.**

old-line (ōld′līn′) *adj.* **1.** Adhering to conservative or reactionary principles. **2.** Long established: *an old-line family.*

Old Low Franconian *n.* The Frankish dialects spoken in the lower Rhine valley in the 10th and 11th centuries that are ancestral to Dutch.

old maid *n.* **1.** *Offensive* A woman who has remained single beyond the conventional age for marrying. **2.** *Informal* A person regarded as being primly fastidious. **3.** *Games* **a.** A card game in which the player who holds a designated card at the end is the loser. **b.** The loser of this game. **4.** *Chiefly Southern US* See **zinnia.** —**old′-maid′ish** (ōld′mā′dĭsh) *adj.*

old maid flower *n. Chiefly Southern US* See **zinnia.**

old man *n.* **1.** *Slang* One's father. **2.** *Slang* **a.** One's husband. **b.**

Old Faithful

One's boyfriend, esp. a lover with whom one lives. **3.** *Informal* **a.** A man in authority; a boss. **b.** often **Old Man** The commanding officer, esp. of a US naval vessel. **4.** See **southernwood.**

old-man-and-wom·an (ōld′măn′-and-wŏŏm′ən) *n., pl.* **old-man-and-wom·ans** (-wŏŏm′ənz) See **houseleek.**

old-man cactus (ōld′măn′) *n.* A treelike central Mexican cactus (*Cephalocereus senilis*) having rose-colored flowers and tufts of long white hair on the tips of its branches.

old-man's-beard (ōld′mănz-bîrd′) *n.* **1.** Any of various plants having parts suggestive of a beard, as Spanish moss. **2.** See **fringe tree. 3.** See **virgin's bower.**

old master *n.* **1.** A distinguished European artist of the period from about 1500 to the early 1700s, esp. one of the great painters of this period. **2.** A work created by one of these artists.

old money *n.* **1.** The inherited wealth of established upper-class families. **2.** A person, family, or lineage with old money.

old moon *n.* The waning moon.

Old Nick *n.* The Devil; Satan.

Old Norse *n.* **1.** The North Germanic languages until the middle of the 14th century. **2a.** Old Icelandic. **b.** Old Norwegian.

Old North French *n.* The dialects of Old French spoken in northern France, esp. in Normandy and Picardy.

Old Northwest See **Northwest Territory.**

Old Norwegian *n.* The Norwegian language from the middle of the 12th to the end of the 14th century.

Ol·do·wan (ōl′də-wən, ôl′-) *adj.* Of or relating to an early stage of African Paleolithic tool culture characterized by choppers and bifacial chopping tools. [After the *Oldoway* (Olduvai) Gorge.]

Old Persian *n.* An Old Iranian language attested in cuneiform inscriptions dating from the sixth to the fifth century B.C.

Old Portuguese *n.* The Portuguese language until the middle of the 16th century.

Old Provençal *n.* The Provençal language before the middle of the 16th century.

Old Prussian *n.* The Baltic language of eastern Prussia that became extinct in the 18th century.

old rose *n.* A dark pink to grayish or moderate red.

Old Russian *n.* The Russian language as used in documents from the middle of the 11th to the end of the 16th century.

Old Saxon *n.* The Low German language of the continental Saxons until the 12th century.

old school *n.* A group committed to traditional ideas or practices: *a diplomat of the old school.*

old school tie *n.* **1.** A necktie that has the colors of a British public school. **2.** The upper-middle-class exclusive solidarity attributed to alumni of such schools. **3.** The narrow clannish attitudes of the members of a clique.

Old Scratch *n. Chiefly Southern US* The Devil; Satan. [Prob. alteration of *scrat* < ME, hermaphrodite goblin < ON *skratte*, wizard, goblin.]

old snow *n.* See **firn.**

Old Spanish *n.* Spanish before the middle of the 16th century.

old·squaw (ōld′skwô′) *n.* A marine duck (*Clangula hyemalis*) that is black with a white breast and found in Arctic and North Temperate regions.

old·ster (ōld′stər) *n. Informal* An elderly person.

Old Stone Age *n.* See **Paleolithic.**

old style *n.* **1.** *Printing* A style of type originating in the 18th century and characterized by slight contrast between light and heavy strokes and slanting serifs. **2. Old Style** The method of reckoning dates according to the Julian calendar.

Old Swedish *n.* Swedish from the early 13th to the late 14th century.

Old Testament *n. Bible* The first of the two main divisions of the Christian Bible, corresponding to the Hebrew Scriptures. See table at **Bible.**

old-time (ōld′tīm′) *adj.* Of, relating to, or characteristic of a time in the past.

old-tim·er (ōld′tī′mər) *n. Informal* **1a.** An elderly person. **b.** A person with considerable tenure or experience in a given place or activity. **2.** Something very old or antiquated.

Old Turkic *n.* The language of the oldest texts of the Turkic dialects, dating from the 7th to the 12th century.

Ol·du·vai Gorge (ōl′də-vī′, ôl′dōō-) A ravine in N Tanzania W of Mt. Kilimanjaro containing archaeological sites rich in fossils and Paleolithic implements.

Old Welsh *n.* The Welsh language before the 12th century.

old·wife (ōld′wīf′) *n., pl.* **-wives** (-wīvz′) **1.** See **oldsquaw. 2.** Any of various fishes such as the alewife and the menhaden.

old wives' tale *n.* A superstitious belief or story belonging to traditional folklore.

old-world (ōld′wûrld′) *adj.* Of, relating to, or characteristic of the ancient world or a past era.

Old World The Eastern Hemisphere. The term is often used to refer specifically to Europe. —**Old′-World′** (ōld′wûrld′) *adj.*

olé– *pref.* Variant of **oleo–.**

–ole or **–ol** *suff.* **1.** A usu. heterocyclic chemical compound containing a five-membered ring: *pyrrole.* **2.** A chemical compound, esp. an ether, that does not contain hydroxyl: *eucalyptol.* [Partly < Fr. (< Lat. *oleum*, oil; see OIL) and partly var. of –OL[1].]

o·lé (ō-lā′) *interj.* Used to express excited approval. ❖ *n.* A cry of

"olé." [Sp., perh. < Ar. *wa-llāh*, by God! (used to express admiration) : *wa-*, and + *allāh*, God.]

o·le·a (ō′lē-ə) *n.* A plural of **oleum.**

o·le·ag·i·nous (ō′lē-ăj′ə-nəs) *adj.* **1.** Of or relating to oil. **2.** Falsely or smugly earnest; unctuous. [< ME *oliaginose* and < Fr. *oléagineux* (< OFr.), both < Lat. *oleāginus,* of the olive tree < *olea,* olive tree, alteration of *olīva.* See OLIVE.] **—o′le·ag′i·nous·ly** *adv.* **—o′le·ag′i·nous·ness** *n.*

o·le·an·der (ō′lē-ăn′dər, ō′lē-ăn′dər) *n.* A poisonous Eurasian evergreen shrub (*Nerium oleander*) having fragrant white, rose, or purple flowers and whorled leaves. [Med.Lat., prob. alteration of LLat. *lorandrum,* rhododendron, ult. < Lat. *rhododendron.* See RHODODENDRON.]

o·le·as·ter (ō′lē-ăs′tər) *n.* **1.** A small Eurasian tree (*Elaeagnus angustifolia*) having oblong silvery leaves, fragrant greenish flowers, and olivelike fruit. **2.** The fruit of this tree. [ME < Lat. < *olea,* olive tree. See OLEAGINOUS.]

o·le·ate (ō′lē-āt′) *n.* A salt or ester of oleic acid.

o·lec·ra·non (ō-lĕk′rə-nŏn′) *n.* The large process on the upper end of the ulna that projects behind the elbow joint and forms the point of the elbow. [Gk. *ōlekrānon* : *ōlenē,* elbow + *krānion,* skull, head; see ker-¹ in App.] **—o·lec′ra·nal** (-nəl), **o′le·cra′ni·al** (ō′lĭ-krā′nē-əl) *adj.*

o·le·fin (ō′lə-fĭn) *n.* Any of a class of unsaturated open-chain hydrocarbons, such as ethylene, having the general formula C_nH_{2n}; an alkene with only one carbon-carbon double bond. [Fr. (*gaz*) *oléfiant,* oil-forming (gas), ethylene : Lat. *oleum,* oil; see OIL + Fr. *-fiant,* pr. part. of *-fier, -fy.*] **—o′le·fin′ic** *adj.*

o·le·ic (ō-lē′ĭk) *adj.* **1.** Of, relating to, or derived from oil. **2.** Of or relating to oleic acid.

oleic acid *n.* An oily liquid, $C_{17}H_{33}COOH$, occurring in animal and vegetable oils and used in making soap.

o·le·in (ō′lē-ĭn) also **o·le·ine** (-ĭn, -ēn′) *n.* An oily yellow liquid, $(C_{17}H_{33}COO)_3C_3H_5$, occurring naturally in most fats and oils and used as a textile lubricant.

O·lek·ma (ō-lĕk′mə) A river of E Russia flowing c. 1,319 km (820 mi) to the Lena R.

O·le·nek (ō′lə-nyŏk′, ə-lə-nyŏk′) A river of NE Russia flowing c. 2,172 km (1,350 mi) to the Laptev Sea.

o·le·o (ō′lē-ō′) *n., pl.* **-os** Margarine.

oleo- or **ole-** *pref.* Oil: *oleoresin.* [Fr. *oléo-* < *oléine,* olein < Lat. *oleum,* oil. See OIL.]

o·le·o·graph (ō′lē-ə-grăf′) *n.* A chromolithograph printed with oil paint on canvas in imitation of an oil painting. **—o′le·og′ra·pher** (-ŏg′rə-fər) *n.* **—o′le·og′ra·phy** *n.*

o·le·o·mar·ga·rine (ō′lē-ō-mär′jə-rĭn, -rēn′) *n.* Margarine.

o·le·o·res·in (ō′lē-ō-rĕz′ĭn) *n.* A naturally occurring mixture of an oil and a resin extracted from various plants, such as pine or balsam fir. **—o′le·o·res′in·ous** *adj.*

o·les·tra (ō-lĕs′trə) *n.* A calorie-free fat substitute synthesized from sucrose and vegetable oil that is capable of passing through the body without being digested. [OL(EO)– + alteration of (POLY)ESTER.]

o·le·um (ō′lē-əm) *n., pl.* **o·le·a** (ō′lē-ə) or **o·le·ums** A corrosive solution of sulfur trioxide in sulfuric acid. [Lat., olive oil. See OIL.]

O level *n. Chiefly British* **1.** The earlier of two standardized tests in a secondary school subject. **2.** The educational background and skills required to pass this test. [*O(rdinary) level.*]

ol·fac·tion (ŏl-făk′shən, ōl-) *n.* **1.** The sense of smell. **2.** The act or process of smelling. [Lat. *olfactus,* p. part. of *olfacere,* to smell; see OLFACTORY + –ION.]

ol·fac·tom·e·ter (ŏl′făk-tŏm′ĭ-tər, ōl′-) *n.* An apparatus for measuring the acuity of the sense of smell. **—ol·fac′to·met′ric** (-tə-mĕt′rĭk) *adj.* **—ol′fac·tom′e·try** *n.*

ol·fac·to·ry (ŏl-făk′tə-rē, -trē, ōl-) *adj.* Of, relating to, or contributing to the sense of smell. [Lat. *olfactōrius,* used to sniff at < *olfacere,* to smell : *olēre,* to smell + *facere,* to do; see FACT.]

olfactory bulb *n.* The bulblike distal end of the olfactory lobe, where the olfactory nerves terminate.

olfactory lobe *n.* A projection of the lower anterior portion of each cerebral hemisphere, functioning in the sense of smell.

olfactory nerve *n.* Either of the first pair of cranial nerves that conduct impulses from the nose to the olfactory bulb.

ol·i·cook (ō′lĭ-koŏk′, ŏl′ĭ-) *n. Hudson Valley* See **doughnut** 1. See Regional Note at **stoop²**. [Du. *oliekoek* : *olie,* oil (< MDu. < Lat. *oleum, olium* < OIL) + *koeke,* cake.]

ol·i·garch (ŏl′ĭ-gärk′, ō′lĭ-) *n.* A member of a small governing faction. [Gk. *oligarkhēs* : *oligos,* few + *-arkhēs,* -arch.]

ol·i·gar·chy (ŏl′ĭ-gär′kē, ō′lĭ-) *n., pl.* **-chies 1a.** Government by a few, esp. by a small faction of persons or families. **b.** Those making up such a government. **2.** A state governed by an oligarchy. **—ol′i·gar′chic, ol′i·gar′chi·cal** *adj.*

oligo- or **olig-** *pref.* Few: *oligosaccharide.* [Gk. < *oligos,* little, few.]

Ol·i·go·cene (ŏl′ĭ-gō-sēn′, ō′lĭ-) *adj.* Of or belonging to the geologic time of the third epoch of the Tertiary Period, characterized by further development of modern mammalian fauna, including the rise of the true carnivores and their gradual replacement of the creodonts. See table at **geologic time.** ❖ *n.* The

---

Oligocene Epoch or its deposits.

ol·i·go·chaete or **ol·i·go·chete** (ŏl′ĭ-gō-kēt′, ō′lĭ-) *n.* Any of various annelid worms of the class Oligochaeta, including the earthworms and a few small freshwater forms. [< NLat. *Oligochaeta,* class name : OLIGO– + CHAETA.] **—ol′i·go·chae′tous** (-kē′təs) *adj.*

ol·i·go·clase (ŏl′ĭ-gō-klās′, -klāz′, ō′lĭ-) *n.* See plagioclase. [OLIGO– + Gk. *klasis,* cleavage (< *klān,* to break; see PLAGIOCLASE).]

ol·i·go·den·dro·cyte (ŏl′ĭ-gō-dĕn′drə-sīt′, ō′lĭ-) *n.* One of the cells comprising the oligodendroglia.

ol·i·go·den·drog·li·a (ŏl′ĭ-gō-dĕn-drŏg′lē-ə, ō′lĭ-) *n. (used with a pl. verb)* Neuroglia consisting of cells found in the central nervous system and associated with the formation of myelin. [OLIGO– + DENDRO– + (NEURO)GLIA.]

o·li·go·mer (ō-lĭg′ə-mər) *n.* A polymer that consists of two, three, or four monomers. **—o·lig′o·mer′ic** (-mĕr′ĭk) *adj.* **—o·lig′o·mer′i·za′tion** *n.*

ol·i·go·nu·cle·o·tide (ŏl′ĭ-gō-noō′klē-ə-tīd′, -nyoō′-, ō′lĭ-) *n.* A short polymer of two to ten nucleotides.

ol·i·goph·a·gous (ŏl′ĭ-gŏf′ə-gəs, ō′lĭ-) *adj.* Feeding on a restricted range of food substances, esp. a limited number of plants. Used chiefly of insects. **—ol′i·goph′a·gy** (-jē) *n.*

ol·i·gop·o·ly (ŏl′ĭ-gŏp′ə-lē, ō′lĭ-) *n., pl.* **-lies** A market in which sellers are so few that the actions of any one of them will affect price and their competitors. [OLIGO– + (MONO)POLY.] **—ol′i·gop′o·lis′tic** (-lĭs′tĭk) *adj.*

ol·i·gop·so·ny (ŏl′ĭ-gŏp′sə-nē, ō′lĭ-) *n., pl.* **-nies** A market in which purchasers are so few that the actions of one can affect price and the costs that competitors must pay. [OLIG(O)– + (MONO)PSONY.] **—ol′i·gop′so·nis′tic** (-nĭs′tĭk) *adj.*

ol·i·go·sac·cha·ride (ŏl′ĭ-gō-săk′ə-rīd′, ō′lĭ-) *n.* A carbohydrate that consists of a relatively small number of monosaccharides.

ol·i·go·tro·phic (ŏl′ĭ-gō-trō′fĭk, -trŏf′ĭk, ō′lĭ-) *adj.* Lacking in plant nutrients and having a large amount of dissolved oxygen throughout. Used of a pond or lake. **—ol′i·got′ro·phy** (-gŏt′rə-fē) *n.*

O·lin·da (ō-lĭn′də, ōō-lēn′dä) A city of NE Brazil, a suburb of Recife; founded 1537. Pop. 341,059.

o·lin·go (ō-lĭng′gō) *n., pl.* **-gos** A small nocturnal, chiefly arboreal mammal of the genus *Bassaricyon,* native to Central and South America and resembling the kinkajou but having a nonprehensile tail. [Am.Sp., howler monkey.]

o·li·o (ō′lē-ō′) *n., pl.* **-os 1.** A spicy stew of meat, vegetables, and chickpeas. **2a.** A mixture or medley; a hodgepodge. **b.** A collection of various artistic or literary works or musical pieces; a miscellany. **3.** Vaudeville or musical entertainment presented between the acts of a burlesque or minstrel show. [Alteration of Sp. *olla,* pot. See OLLA.]

ol·i·va·ceous (ŏl′ə-vā′shəs) *adj.* Olive-green.

ol·ive (ŏl′ĭv) *n.* **1.** A Mediterranean evergreen tree (*Olea europaea*) having fragrant white flowers, usu. lance-shaped leathery leaves, and edible drupes. **2.** The small ovoid fruit of this tree, an important food and source of oil. **3.** Olive green. [ME < Lat. *olīva* < Gk. **elaiwā, elaiā.*] **—ol′ive** *adj.*

olive-backed thrush *n.* A North American thrush (*Hylocichla ustulata*) having a dark olive-brown back and common in spruce and fir forests.

olive branch *n.* **1.** A branch of an olive tree regarded as an emblem of peace. **2.** An offer of peace.

olive drab *n.* **1.** A grayish olive to dark olive brown or olive gray. **2a.** Cloth of this color, often used in military uniforms. **b.** A uniform made from cloth of this color. Also used in the plural.

olive green *n.* A green-yellow hue of low to medium lightness and low to moderate saturation.

olive oil *n.* Oil pressed from olives, used in salad dressings, for cooking, as an ingredient in soaps, and as an emollient.

Ol·ives (ŏl′ĭvz), **Mount of** also **Ol·i·vet** (ŏl′ə-vĕt′) A ridge of hills in the West Bank E of Jerusalem. At its W foot is the biblical site of the Garden of Gethsemane.

O·liv·i·er (ō-lĭv′ē-ā′), Sir **Laurence Kerr.** Baron Olivier of Brighton. 1907–89. British actor and director best known for his interpretations of Shakespeare's *Othello* and *Richard III.*

ol·i·vine (ŏl′ə-vēn′) *n.* A mineral silicate of iron and magnesium, $(Mg, Fe)_2SiO_4$, found in igneous and metamorphic rocks and used in refractories. [OLIVE (< its color) + –INE¹.]

ol·la (ŏl′ə, ō′yə) *n.* **1.** *Southwestern US* A rounded earthenware pot or jar. **2.** An olla podrida. [Sp. < OSpan. < Lat., var. of *aula, aulla,* pot, jar.]

REGIONAL NOTE The unglazed earthenware *olla,* a large crock or jar, was used for generations in southwestern parts of the United States where Spanish culture predominates, particularly in south Texas and California. Usually used to store water on a patio, it was wrapped in burlap to keep the water cool.

olla po·dri·da (pə-drē′də) *n., pl.* **olla po·dri·das** also **ol·las po·dri·das 1.** A spicy stew of meat and vegetables. **2.** An assorted mixture; a miscellany. [Sp. : *olla,* olla; see OLLA + *podrida,* fem. of *podrido,* rotten (< Lat. *putridus;* see PUTRID).]

Ol·mec (ŏl′mĕk, ōl′-) *n., pl.* **Olmec** or **-mecs 1.** An early Mesoamerican Indian civilization centered in the Veracruz region of

---

oleander
Nerium oleander

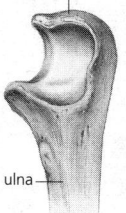

olecranon

ulna

olecranon

olla
Cíbola pottery,
Chaco Canyon, Arizona

ă	pat	oi	boy
ā	pay	ou	out
âr	care	oŏ	took
ä	father	oō	boot
ĕ	pet	ŭ	cut
ē	be	ûr	urge
ĭ	pit	th	thin
ī	pie	th	this
îr	pier	hw	which
ŏ	pot	zh	vision
ō	toe	ə	about,
ô	paw		item

Stress marks:
′ (primary);
′ (secondary), as in
lexicon (lĕk′sĭ-kŏn′)

Frederick Law Olmsted

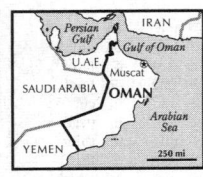

Oman

southeast Mexico that flourished between 1300 and 400 B.C. and had a widespread cultural influence. **2.** A member of any of various peoples sharing the Olmec culture.

Olm·sted (ōm'stěd', -stĭd), **Frederick Law** 1822–1903. Amer. landscape architect who was the chief designer of Central Park in New York City (1858–61).

ol·o·gy (ŏl'ə-jē) n., pl. **-gies** Informal A branch of learning. [< –OLOGY.]

–ology suff. Variant of **–logy.**

O·lo·mouc (ō'lō-mōts') A city of NE Czech Republic on the Morava R. NE of Brno; it was the cap. of Moravia until c. 1640. Pop. 105,516.

Olsz·tyn (ôl'shtĭn) A city of N Poland SE of Gdańsk; founded by the Teutonic Knights in 1348. Pop. 163,905.

O·lym·pi·a[1] (ō-lĭm'pē-ə, ə-lĭm'-) A plain of S Greece in the NW Peleponnesus; a religious center devoted to the worship of Zeus and the site of the ancient Olympic Games.

O·lym·pi·a[2] (ō-lĭm'pē-ə, ə-lĭm'-) The cap. of WA, in the W part on S Puget Sound; settled in 1845. Pop. 42,514.

O·lym·pi·ad (ō-lĭm'pē-ăd') n. **1.** An interval of four years between celebrations of the Olympic Games, by which the ancient Greeks reckoned dates. **2.** Sports A celebration of the modern Olympic Games. [Ult. < Gk. Olumpias, Olumpiad-, Olympiad < Olumpiā, Olympia, Greece, site of the Olympic games.]

O·lym·pi·an (ō-lĭm'pē-ən) adj. **1.** Greek Mythology Of or relating to the 12 greater deities of the ancient Greek pantheon, whose abode was Mount Olympus. **2a.** Majestic in manner. **b.** Superior to mundane affairs. **c.** Surpassing all others in scope and effect: Olympian efforts. **3.** Of or relating to the Olympic Games. **4.** Of or relating to the region of Olympia in Greece or its inhabitants. ❖ n. **1.** Greek Mythology One of the 12 major deities. **2.** One who is superior to all others. **3.** A contestant in the ancient or the modern Olympic Games. **4.** A native or inhabitant of the region of Olympia in Greece.

Olympian Games pl.n. See **Olympic Games** 2.

O·lym·pic (ō-lĭm'pĭk) adj. Of or relating to the Olympic Games.

Olympic Games pl.n. **1.** A group of modern international athletic contests held every four years in a different city. **2.** A Pan-Hellenic festival in ancient Greece consisting of athletic games and contests of choral poetry and dance, first celebrated in 776 B.C. and held periodically until A.D. 393 on the plain of Olympia in honor of the Olympian Zeus.

Olympic Mountains A section of the Coast Ranges on the **Olympic Peninsula** of NW WA, bounded by the Pacific Ocean, the Strait of Juan de Fuca, and Puget Sound. Mount Olympus, the highest peak, rises to 2,429.3 m (7,965 ft).

O·lym·pics (ō-lĭm'pĭks) pl.n. See **Olympic Games** 1.

O·lym·pus (ə-lĭm'pəs, ō-lĭm'-) A mountain range of N Greece near the Aegean coast rising to 2,918.9 m (9,570 ft) at **Mount Olympus,** home of the mythical Greek gods.

O·lyn·thus (ō-lĭn'thəs) An ancient city of NE Greece on the Chalcidice Peninsula; head of the Chalcidian League after the late 5th cent. B.C.

Om[1] (ŏm) A river, c. 724 km (450 mi), of S-central Russia that joins the Irtysh R. at Omsk.

Om[2] also **Aum** (ŏm) n. Hinduism & Buddhism A sacred syllable uttered as a mantra and in affirmations and blessings. [Skt. om, aum.]

–oma suff. Tumor: lipoma. [NLat. -ōma < Gk. -ōma, -ōmat-, n. suff.]

O·ma·ha[1] (ō'mə-hô', -hä') n., pl. **Omaha** or **-has 1.** A member of a Native American people inhabiting northeast Nebraska from the late 17th century. **2.** The Siouan language of the Omaha. [Omaha umóNhoN.] **—O'ma·ha'** adj.

O·ma·ha[2] (ō'mə-hô', -hä') A city of E NE on the Missouri R. and the IA border; founded 1854. Pop. 390,007.

O·man (ō-män') Formerly **Mus·cat and Oman** (mŭs'kăt', -kət, mŭs-kăt') A sultanate on the SE Arabian Peninsula on the **Gulf of Oman,** an arm of the Arabian Sea; mainly controlled by the Portuguese from 1508 to 1659 and the Turks until 1741. Cap. Muscat. Pop. 2,077,000. **—O·man'i** (ō-mä'nē) adj. & n.

O·mar Khay·yám (ō'mär kī-yäm', -ăm') 1050?–1123. Persian poet, mathematician, and astronomer remembered for his collection of quatrains The Rubáiyat of Omar Khayyám.

o·ma·sum (ō-mā'səm) n., pl. **-sa** (-sə) The third division of a ruminant's stomach, between the abomasum and the reticulum. [Lat. omāsum, bullock's tripe, prob. of Celt. orig.]

O·may·yad (ō-mī'ăd) See **Umayyad.**

OMB abbr. Office of Management and Budget

om·bre also **om·ber** (ŏm'bər) or **hom·bre** (hŏm'bər, ŏm'-) n. A card game, played by three players with 40 cards, popular in Europe during the 17th and 18th centuries. [Sp. hombre, man, ombre < Lat. homō, homin-, man. See **dhghem-** in App.]

om·buds·man (ŏm'bŭdz'mən, -bədz-, -bōōdz'-) n. **1.** A man who investigates complaints and mediates fair settlements, esp. between aggrieved parties. **2.** A government official, esp. in Scandinavian countries, who investigates citizens' complaints against the government. [Swed. < ON umbodhsmadhr, deputy, plenipotentiary : umbodh, commission (um, about; see **ambhi** in App. + bodh, command; see **bheudh-** in App.) + madhr, man; see **man-**[1] in App.]

om·buds·per·son (ŏm'bŭdz-pûr'sən, -bədz-, -bōōdz-) n. An ombudsman or ombudswoman.

om·buds·wom·an (ŏm'bŭdz-wōōm'ən, -bədz-, -bōōdz-) n. A woman who investigates complaints and mediates fair settlements, esp. between aggrieved parties.

Om·dur·man (ŏm'dōōr-män') A city of NE-central Sudan on the White Nile opposite Khartoum. Pop. 526,287.

–ome suff. Mass: biome. [NLat. -ōma, -ōmat- < Gk., n. suff.]

o·me·ga (ō-měg'ə, ō-mē'gə, ō-mā'-) n. **1.** The 24th letter of the Greek alphabet. **2.** The end. **3.** See omega baryon. **4.** See omega meson. [ME < Gk. ō mega, large o (< its being a long vowel in Greek) : ō, the letter o + mega, neut. of megas, large, great; see **meg-** in App.]

o·me·ga-3 fatty acid (ō-měg'ə-thrē', -mē'gə-, -mā'-) n. Any of several polyunsaturated fatty acids that are found esp. in certain fish oils and are capable of reducing serum cholesterol levels.

omega baryon n. A negatively charged baryon having a mass 3,272 times that of the electron.

o·me·ga-c baryon (ō-měg'ə-sē', -mē'gə, -mā'-) n. An electrically neutral baryon having a mass 5,292 times that of the electron.

omega meson n. A neutral meson having a mass 1,532 times that of the electron.

om·e·let also **om·e·lette** (ŏm'ə-lĭt, ŏm'lĭt) n. A dish consisting of beaten eggs cooked until set and folded over, often around a filling. [Fr. omelette < OFr. amlette, alteration of alumette, var. of alumelle, < (la) lemelle, (the) knife blade < Lat. lāmella, dim. of lāmina, thin plate.]

o·men (ō'mən) n. **1.** A phenomenon portending good or evil; a prophetic sign. **2.** Prognostication; portent: birds of ill omen. ❖ tr.v. **o·mened, o·men·ing, o·mens** To be a prophetic sign of; portend. [Lat. ōmen.]

o·men·tum (ō-měn'təm) n., pl. **-ta** (-tə) or **-tums** One of the peritoneal folds connecting the stomach and other abdominal organs, esp.: **a.** The greater omentum. **b.** The lesser omentum. [Lat. omentum.] **—o·men'tal** (-təl) adj.

o·mer (ō'mər, ō'měr) n. Judaism **1.** An ancient Hebrew unit of dry measure equal to ¹⁄₁₀ ephah, about 3.5 liters (3.7 quarts). **2a.** An offering of a sheaf or an omer of the first harvest of barley to a priest in the Temple on the second day of Passover. **b. Omer** A 49-day liturgical season, originally a harvest festival, from the second day of Passover to the first day of Shavuot, during which marriages are prohibited and signs of mourning are observed, except during Passover and on Lag b'Omer. [Heb. 'ōmer. Sense 2b < the offering of a sheaf of barley on the second day of Passover.]

om·i·cron (ŏm'ĭ-krŏn', ō'mĭ-) n. The 15th letter of the Greek alphabet. [Gk. o mikron : o, the letter o + mikron, neut. of mīkros, small.]

om·i·nous (ŏm'ə-nəs) adj. **1.** Menacing; threatening: ominous rumblings of discontent. **2.** Of or being an omen, esp. an evil one. [Lat. ōminōsus < ōmen, ōmin-, omen.] **—om'i·nous·ly** adv. **—om'i·nous·ness** n.

o·mis·si·ble (ō-mĭs'ə-bəl) adj. Possible to omit. [< Lat. omissus, p. part. of omittere, to disregard. See OMIT.]

o·mis·sion (ō-mĭsh'ən) n. **1.** The act or an instance of omitting. **2.** The state of having been omitted. **3.** Something omitted or neglected. [ME < OFr. < LLat. omissiō, omissiōn- < Lat. omissus, p. part. of omittere, to disregard. See OMIT.]

o·mis·sive (ō-mĭs'ĭv) adj. Characterized by omission or omitting.

o·mit (ō-mĭt') tr.v. **o·mit·ted, o·mit·ting, o·mits 1.** To fail to include or mention; leave out. **2a.** To pass over; neglect. **b.** To desist or fail in doing; forbear. [ME omitten < Lat. omittere : ob-, against, away; see OB- + mittere, to send.]

O·mi·ya (ō-mē'ə, ō'mē-yä') A city of E-central Honshu, Japan, a suburb of Tokyo. Pop. 422,023.

om·ma·tid·i·um (ŏm'ə-tĭd'ē-əm) n., pl. **-i·a** (-ē-ə) One of the structural elements, resembling a single simplified eye, that make up the compound eye of arthropods. [NLat., dim. of Gk. omma, ommat-, eye. See ok**ʷ**- in App.]

Om·mi·ad (ŏm'ē-ăd') See **Umayyad.**

omni– pref. All: omnidirectional. [Lat. < omnis, all.]

om·ni·bus (ŏm'nĭ-bŭs', -bəs) n. **1.** A long motor vehicle for passengers; a bus. **2.** A printed anthology of the works of one author or of writings on related subjects. ❖ adj. Including or covering many things or classes: an omnibus trade bill. [Fr. < Lat., for all, dative pl. of omnis, all.]

om·ni·di·rec·tion·al (ŏm'nē-dĭ-rĕk'shə-nəl, -dī-) adj. Capable of transmitting or receiving signals in all directions, as an antenna.

omnidirectional radio range n. See **omnirange.**

om·ni·far·i·ous (ŏm'nĭ-fâr'ē-əs) adj. Of all kinds: omnifarious knowledge; a bus. [< Lat. omnifāriam, on every side : omni-, -fāriam, adv. suff.; see **dhē-** in App.] **—om'ni·far'i·ous·ly** adv. **—om'ni·far'i·ous·ness** n.

om·nip·o·tent (ŏm-nĭp'ə-tənt) adj. Having unlimited or universal power, authority, or force. See Usage Note at **infinite.** ❖ n. **1.** One who is omnipotent. **2. Omnipotent** God. Used with the. [ME < OFr. < Lat. omnipotēns, omnipotent- : omni-, + potēns, pr. part. of posse, to be able; see **poti-** in App.] **—om·nip'o·tence, om·nip'o·ten·cy** n. **—om·nip'o·tent·ly** adv.

om·ni·pres·ent (ŏm′nĭ-prĕz′ənt) *adj.* Present everywhere simultaneously. —**om′ni·pres′ence** *n.*

om·ni·range (ŏm′nĭ-rānj′, -nē-) *n.* A radio network that provides aircraft with complete information on bearings.

om·nis·cient (ŏm-nĭsh′ənt) *adj.* Having total knowledge; knowing everything. ❖ *n.* One having total knowledge. [Med.Lat. *omnisciēns, omniscient-* : Lat. *omni-,* omni- + Lat. *sciēns,* pr. part. of *scīre,* to know.] —**om·nis′cience, om·nis′cien·cy** *n.* —**om·nis′cient·ly** *adv.*

om·ni·sex·u·al (ŏm′nē-sĕk′shōō-əl) *adj.* Pansexual. ❖ *n.* A pansexual person. —**om′ni·sex′u·al′i·ty** *n.*

om·ni·um-gath·er·um (ŏm′nē-əm-găth′ər-əm) *n.* A miscellaneous collection; a hodgepodge. [Lat. *omnium,* genitive pl. of *omnis,* all + *gatherum* (mock-Latinate alteration of GATHER).]

om·ni·vore (ŏm′nə-vôr′, -vōr′) *n.* **1.** An omnivorous person or animal. **2.** One that takes in everything available, as with the mind. [< NLat. *Omnivora,* omnivores < neut. pl. of Lat. *omnivorus,* omnivorous. See OMNIVOROUS.]

om·niv·o·rous (ŏm-nĭv′ər-əs) *adj.* **1.** Eating both animal and vegetable foods. **2.** Taking in everything available, as with the mind: *an omnivorous reader.* —**om·niv′o·rous·ly** *adv.*

Om·o·lon (ŏm′ə-lôn′) A river of NE Russia flowing c. 965 km (600 mi) to the Kolyma R.

O·mot·ic (ō-mŏt′ĭk) *n.* A branch of the Afro-Asiatic language family, spoken in Ethiopia. [After the *Omo* River in W Ethiopia.]

om·pha·los (ŏm′fə-lŏs′, -ləs) *n.,* pl. **-li** (-lī) **1.** The navel. **2.** A central part; a focal point. [Gk. See **nobh-** in App.]

Omsk (ômsk) A city of S-central Russia at the confluence of the Irtysh and Om rivers; founded 1716. Pop. 1,163,885.

on (ŏn, ôn) *prep.* **1a.** Used to indicate position above and supported by or in contact with: *The vase is on the table.* **b.** Used to indicate contact with or extent over (a surface) regardless of position: *a picture on the wall.* **c.** Used to indicate location at or along: *a house on the highway.* **d.** Used to indicate proximity: *a town on the border.* **e.** Used to indicate attachment to or suspension from: *beads on a string.* **f.** Used to indicate figurative or abstract position: *stopped on Chapter 2.* **2a.** Used to indicate actual motion toward, against, or onto: *the march on Washington.* **b.** Used to indicate figurative or abstract motion toward, against, or onto: *going on six o'clock.* **3a.** Used to indicate occurrence at a given time: *on July third.* **b.** Used to indicate the particular occasion or circumstance: *on arrival.* **4a.** Used to indicate the object affected by actual, perceptible action: *knocked on the door.* **b.** Used to indicate the object affected by a figurative action: *Have pity on them.* **c.** Used to indicate the object of an action directed, tending, or moving against it: *an attack on the fortress.* **d.** Used to indicate the object of perception or thought: *meditated on his actions.* **5.** Used to indicate the agent or agency of a specified action: *talked on the telephone.* **6a.** Used to indicate a medicine or other corrective taken or undertaken routinely: *went on a diet.* **b.** Used to indicate a substance that is the cause of an addiction, a habit, or an altered state of consciousness: *high on dope.* **7a.** Used to indicate a source or basis: *"We will reach our judgments not on intentions or on promises but on deeds and on results"* (Margaret Thatcher). **b.** Used to indicate a source of power or energy: *The car runs on methane.* **8a.** Used to indicate the state or process of: *on the way.* **b.** Used to indicate the purpose of: *travel on business.* **c.** Used to indicate a means of conveyance: *ride on a train.* **9.** Used to indicate availability by means of: *beer on tap.* **9.** Used to indicate belonging to: *a nurse on the staff.* **10.** Used to indicate addition or repetition: *error on error.* **11a.** Concerning; about: *a book on astronomy.* **b.** Concerning to the disadvantage of: *some evidence on him.* **12.** *Informal* In one's possession; with: *not a cent on me.* **13.** At the expense of; compliments of: *drinks on the house.* ❖ *adv.* **1.** In or into a position or condition of being supported by or in contact with something: *Put the coffee on.* **2.** In or into a position of being attached to or covering something: *Put your clothes on.* **3.** In the direction of something: *He looked on while the ship docked.* **4a.** Toward or at a point lying ahead in space or time; forward: *moved on to the next city.* **b.** At or to a more distant point in time or space: *later on.* **5.** In a continuous course: *He worked on.* **6a.** In or into performance or operation: *Turn on the radio.* **b.** In progress or action; in a state of activity: *The show must go on.* **7.** In or at the present position or condition: *hang on.* **8.** In a condition of being scheduled for or decided upon: *a party on tonight.* ❖ *adj.* **1.** Being in operation: *The television is on.* **2.** Engaged in a given function or activity, such as a vocal or dramatic role: *You're on in five minutes!* **b.** Under or behaving as if under observation: *A minister is always on.* **3.** *Slang* Functioning or performing at a high degree of competence or energy: *The goalie is really on.* **4a.** Planned; intended: *nothing on for tonight.* **b.** Happening; taking place: *The parade is on.* **5.** *Baseball* Having reached base safely; on base. —**idioms: be on to** *Informal* To be aware of or have information about. **on and off** Intermittently. **on and on** Without stopping; continuously. [ME < OE *an, on.*]

USAGE NOTE To indicate motion toward a position, both *on* and *onto* can be used, but *onto* indicates clearly motion initiated from an outside point, as in *He ran onto the field. He ran on the field* may mean that his running began on the field. • In constructions where *on* is an adverb attached to a verb, it should not be joined

with *to* to form the single word *onto: move on to* (not *onto*) *new subjects.* • In their uses to indicate spatial relations, *on* and *upon* are often interchangeable: *It rests on* (or *upon*) *a table.* To indicate a relation between two things, however, instead of between an action and an end point, *upon* cannot always be used: *Hand me the book on* (not *upon*) *the table.* Similarly, *upon* cannot always be used in place of *on* when the relation is not spatial: *a book on* (not *upon*) *birds.*

ON *abbr.* **1.** Old Norse **2.** Ontario

–on[1] *suff.* **1a.** Subatomic particle: *baryon.* **b.** Unit; quantum: *photon.* **2.** Basic hereditary unit: *codon.* [< ION.]

–on[2] *suff.* Inert gas: *radon.* [NLat. < (ARG)ON.]

–on[3] *suff.* A chemical compound that is not a ketone, or a compound that contains oxygen in a carbonyl group: *parathion.* [Alteration of –ONE.]

on·a·ger (ŏn′ə-jər) *n.* **1.** A wild ass *(Equus hemionus* subsp. *onager)* of central Asia having an erect mane and a broad black stripe along its back. **2.** An ancient and medieval stone-propelling siege engine. [ME < LLat. < Lat. < Gk. *onagros* : *onos,* ass + *agrios,* wild; see **agro-** in App.]

on-air (ŏn′âr′, ôn′-) *adj.* Spoken, occurring, or used during broadcasting: *an on-air gaffe.*

o·nan·ism (ō′nə-nĭz′əm) *n.* **1.** Masturbation. **2.** Coitus interruptus. [After *Onan,* son of Judah (Genesis 38:9).] —**o′nan·ist** *n.* —**o′nan·is′tic** *adj.*

O·nas·sis (ō-năs′ĭs, ō-nä′sĭs), **Jacqueline Lee Bouvier** Kennedy See Jacqueline Lee Bouvier **Kennedy.**

on·board or **on-board** (ŏn-bôrd′, -bōrd′, ôn-) *adj.* Carried or used aboard a vehicle or vessel. —**on·board′** *adv.*

once (wŭns) *adv.* **1.** One time only: *once a day.* **2.** At one time in the past; formerly. **3.** At any time; ever: *Once known, never forgotten.* **4.** By one degree of relationship: *my first cousin once removed.* ❖ *n.* A single occurrence; one time: *Once will have to do.* ❖ *conj.* As soon as; if ever; when: *Once he goes, we can clean up.* ❖ *adj.* Having been formerly; former: *the once capital.* —**idiom: at once 1.** All at one time; simultaneously. **2.** Immediately; instantly: *Leave the room at once.* [ME *ones* < *on,* one < OE *ān.* See **oi-no-** in App.]

once-o·ver (wŭns′ō′vər) *n. Informal* A quick but comprehensive survey or performance.

oncet (wŭnst) *adv. Southern & South Midland US* Once. [Variant of ONCE.]

on·cho·cer·ci·a·sis (ŏng′kō-sər-kī′ə-sĭs) *n.* A tropical disease caused by infestation with filarial worms of the genus *Onchocerca* and characterized by nodular swellings on the skin and lesions of the eyes. [NLat. : *Onchocerca,* genus name (Gk. *onkos,* barb + Gk. *kerkos,* tail) + –IASIS.]

on·ci·di·um (ŏn-sĭd′ē-əm, ŏng-kĭd′-) *n.* Any of numerous epiphytic tropical American orchids of the genus *Oncidium,* having clusters of showy flowers. [NLat. *Oncidium,* genus name : Gk. *onkos,* barb, hook (< the shape of its labellum) + NLat. -idium, diminutive suff. (< Gk. -idion).]

on·co·gene (ŏn′kə-jēn, ŏng′-) *n.* A gene that causes the transformation of normal cells into cancerous tumor cells, esp. a viral gene that transforms a host cell into a tumor cell. [Gk. *onkos,* mass, tumor; see ONCOLOGY + GENE.]

on·co·gen·e·sis (ŏn′kō-jĕn′ĭ-sĭs, ŏng′-) *n.* The formation and development of tumors. [Gk. *onkos,* mass, tumor + –GENESIS.] —**on′co·gen′ic** *adj.* —**on′co·ge·nic′i·ty** (-jə-nĭs′ĭ-tē) *n.*

on·col·o·gy (ŏn-kŏl′ə-jē, ŏng-) *n.* The branch of medicine that deals with tumors. [Gk. *onkos,* mass, tumor + –LOGY.] —**on′co·log′i·cal** (-kə-lŏj′ĭ-kəl), **on′co·log′ic** (-lŏj′ĭk) *adj.* —**on·col′o·gist** *n.*

on·com·ing (ŏn′kŭm′ĭng, ôn′-) *adj.* Coming nearer; approaching. ❖ *n.* An approach; an advance.

on·cor·na·vi·rus (ŏn-kôr′nə-vī′rəs, ŏng-) *n.* Any of a group of viruses that contain single-stranded RNA and produce tumors in birds and mammals. [Gk. *onkos,* mass, tumor; see ONCOLOGY + RNA + VIRUS.]

one (wŭn) *adj.* **1.** Being a single entity, unit, object, or living being. **2.** Characterized by unity; undivided: *They spoke with one voice.* **3a.** Of the same kind or quality: *animals of one species.* **b.** Forming a single entity of two or more components: *three chemicals combining into one solution.* **4.** Being a single member or element of a group, category, or kind: *I'm just one player on the team.* **5.** Being a single thing in contrast with or relation to another or others of its kind: *One day is just like the next.* **6.** Occurring or existing as something indefinite, as in time or position: *He will come one day.* **7.** Occurring or existing as something particular but unspecified, as in time past: *late one evening.* **8.** *Informal* Used as an intensive: *That is one fine dog.* **9.** Being the only individual of a specified or implied kind: *the one horse that can win this race.* ❖ *n.* **1.** The cardinal number, represented by the symbol 1, designating the first unit in a series. **2.** A single person or thing; a unit: *This is the one I like best.* **3.** A one-dollar bill. ❖ *pron.* **1.** An indefinitely specified individual: *one of her cousins.* **2.** An unspecified individual; anyone: *"The older one grows the more one likes indecency"* (Virginia Woolf). —**idioms: at one** In accord or unity. **one and all** Everyone. **one by one** Individually in succession. [ME *on* < OE *ān.* See **oi-no-** in App.]

ă	pat	oi	boy
â	pay	ou	out
âr	care	ōō	took
ä	father	ōō	boot
ĕ	pet	ŭ	cut
ē	be	ûr	urge
ĭ	pit	th	thin
ī	pie	th	this
îr	pier	hw	which
ŏ	pot	zh	vision
ō	toe	ə	about,
ô	paw		item

Stress marks:
′ (primary);
′ (secondary), as in
lexicon (lĕk′sĭ-kŏn′)

USAGE NOTE When constructions headed by *one* appear as the subject of a sentence or relative clause, there may be a question whether the verb should be singular or plural, as in *One of every ten rotors was/were defective.* Although the plural *were* is sometimes used in such sentences, an earlier survey found that the singular was preferred by a large majority of the Usage Panel. • In the sentence *The defeat turned out to be one of the most costly blows that were ever inflicted on our forces,* most grammarians would hold that the plural *were* is correct, inasmuch as the subject of the verb is the plural noun *blows.* However, constructions of this sort are often used with a singular verb even by the best writers, and use of a singular verb was accepted by 42 percent of the Usage Panel in an earlier survey. Note also that when the phrase containing *one* is introduced by the definite article, the verb in the relative clause must be singular: *He is the only one of us who has* (not *have*) *already taken Latin.* See Usage Note at **he**[1].

–one *suff.* **1.** A ketone: *acetone.* **2.** A chemical compound containing oxygen, esp. in a carbonyl group: *lactone.* [Prob. < Gk. *-ōnē,* fem. patronymic suff.]

one another *pron.* Used to indicate a reciprocal relationship or reciprocal actions among the members of the set referred to by the antecedent, often with the implication that the actions are temporally ordered: *The students help one another.*

one-armed bandit (wŭn′ärmd′) *n.* A slot machine for gambling operated by pulling a lever on the side.

one-base hit (wŭn′bās′) *n. Baseball* A base hit by which a batter can reach first base safely.

one-di·men·sion·al (wŭn′dĭ-mĕn′shə-nəl, -dī-) *adj.* **1.** Having or existing in one dimension only. **2.** Lacking depth; superficial.

O·ne·ga (ō-nē′gə, ə-nyĕ′-), **Lake** A lake of NW Russia between Lake Ladoga and the White Sea.

Onega Bay An arm of the White Sea in NW Russia that receives the **Onega River,** c. 418 km (260 mi) long.

one-hand·ed (wŭn′hăn′dĭd) *adj.* **1.** Having or making use of only one hand. **2.** Calling for or brought about by the use of only one hand. **—one′-hand′ed** *adv.*

one-horse (wŭn′hôrs′) *adj.* **1.** Drawn by or using only one horse. **2.** Very small or insignificant: *a one-horse town.*

O·nei·da[1] (ō-nī′də) *n., pl.* **Oneida** or **-das 1.** A member of a Native American people formerly inhabiting central New York, with present-day populations in Wisconsin, New York, and Ontario. **2.** The Iroquoian language of the Oneida. [Oneida *oneʔyóteʔ,* erected stone, a village name.]

O·nei·da[2] (ō-nī′də) A city of central NY ENE of Syracuse; site of the Oneida Community, a Utopian society est. in 1848 by John Humphrey Noyes. Pop. 10,987.

Oneida Lake A lake of central NY NE of Syracuse.

O'Neill (ō-nēl′), **Eugene Gladstone** 1888–1953. Amer. playwright whose works include *Long Day's Journey into Night* (produced 1956). He won the 1936 Nobel Prize for literature.

o·nei·ric (ō-nī′rĭk) *adj.* Of, relating to, or suggestive of dreams. [Gk. *oneiros,* dream + –IC.]

o·nei·ro·man·cy (ō-nī′rə-măn′sē) *n.* The art of predicting the future through interpretation of dreams. [Gk. *oneiros,* dream + –MANCY.] **—o·nei′ro·man′cer** *n.*

one-lin·er (wŭn′lī′nər) *n.* A short joke or witticism.

one-man (wŭn′măn′) *adj.* **1.** Consisting of, featuring, or controlled by one man: *a one-man business.* **2.** Designed for or restricted to one person. **3.** Emotionally attached to or romantically involved with one man only.

one·ness (wŭn′nĭs) *n.* **1.** The quality or state of being one; singleness or wholeness. **2.** Singularity; uniqueness. **3.** A state or condition of perfect harmony or accord. **4.** Sameness of character: *the oneness of roadside landscapes.* **5.** Unison; agreement.

one-night stand (wŭn′nīt′) *n.* **1a.** A performance by a musical or dramatic performer or group in one place on one night only. **b.** The place at which such a performance is given. **2.** *Slang* A sexual encounter limited to only one occasion.

one-note (wŭn′nōt′) *adj.* Unvarying, as in quality or character; monotonous.

one-on-one (wŭn′ŏn-wŭn′, -ŏn-) *adj.* **1.** Relating to or being direct exchange between two people: *one-on-one instruction.* **2.** *Sports* Playing directly or exclusively against a single opponent. **—one′-on-one′** *adv.*

one-per·son (wŭn′pûr′sən) *adj.* **1.** Consisting of a single person. **2.** Designed for or restricted to one person.

one-piece (wŭn′pēs′) *adj.* Consisting of or fashioned in a single whole piece: *a one-piece wetsuit.* ❖ *n.* A one-piece garment, such as a swimsuit.

on·er·ous (ŏn′ər-əs, ō′nər-) *adj.* **1.** Troublesome or oppressive; burdensome. **2.** *Law* Entailing obligations that exceed advantages. [ME < OFr. *onereus* < Lat. *onerōsus* < *onus, oner-,* burden.] **—on′er·ous·ly** *adv.* **—on′er·ous·ness** *n.*

one·self (wŭn-sĕlf′) also **one's self** (wŭn sĕlf′, wŭnz sĕlf′) *pron.* **1.** One's own self: **a.** Used reflexively as the direct or indirect object of a verb or the object of a preposition: *congratulate oneself on one's victories.* **b.** Used in an absolute construction: *When in charge oneself, one may make decisions.* **2.** One's normal or healthy condition or state.

one-shot (wŭn′shŏt′) *adj. Informal* **1.** Becoming effective after

onion dome
atop the Bell Tower of Ivan the Great, the Kremlin, Moscow

only one attempt: *a one-shot solution.* **2.** Being the only one and unlikely to be repeated.

one-sid·ed (wŭn′sī′dĭd) *adj.* **1.** Favoring one side or group; partial or biased. **2.** Characterized by the domination of one competitor over another. **3.** Larger or more developed on one side. **4.** Existing or occurring on one side only. **—one′-sid′ed·ly** *adv.* **—one′-sid′ed·ness** *n.*

one-step (wŭn′stĕp′) *n.* **1.** A ballroom dance consisting of a series of unbroken rapid steps in 2/4 time. **2.** A piece of music for this dance. **—one′-step′** *v.*

one-time (wŭn′tīm′) *adj.* **1.** or **one-time** (wŭn′tīm′) **a.** Occurring or undertaken only once: *a one-time winner in 2001.* **b.** Having been in the past; former: *his one-time associate.* **2.** *Sports* Relating to or being a shot made from a pass that is not stopped prior to shooting. ❖ *v.* **-timed, -tim·ing, -times** *Sports* To shoot (a ball or puck) directly from a pass. **—one′-tim′er** *n.*

one-to-one (wŭn′tə-wŭn′) *adj.* **1.** Allowing the pairing of each member of a class uniquely with a member of another class. **2.** *Mathematics* Relating to or being a correspondence that assigns to different members of one set different members of another set.

one-track (wŭn′trăk′) *adj.* Obsessively limited to a single idea or purpose: *a one-track mind.*

one-two (wŭn′tōō′) *n.* A one-two punch.

one-two punch *n.* **1.** A combination of two blows delivered in rapid succession in boxing, esp. a left lead followed by a right cross. **2.** *Informal* An esp. forceful or effective combination or sequence of two things.

one-up (wŭn′ŭp′) *tr.v.* **-upped, -up·ping, -ups** *Informal* To keep one step ahead of (a competitor, for example).

one-up·man·ship (wŭn-ŭp′mən-shĭp′) also **one-ups·man·ship** (-ŭps′-) *n. Informal* The art of outdoing or showing up a rival or competitor.

one-way (wŭn′wā′) *adj.* **1.** Moving or permitting movement in one direction only. **2.** Providing for travel in one direction only: *a one-way ticket.*

one-way mirror *n.* A mirror that is reflective on one side and transparent on the other, often used in surveillance.

one-wom·an (wŭn′wŏom′ən) *adj.* **1.** Consisting of, featuring, or controlled by one woman: *a one-woman dramatic performance.* **2.** Emotionally attached to or romantically involved with one woman only.

on·go·ing (ŏn′gō′ĭng, ôn′-) *adj.* **1.** Currently taking place: *an ongoing festival.* **2.** In progress or evolving.

on·ion (ŭn′yən) *n.* **1.** A bulbous plant (*Allium cepa*) cultivated worldwide as a vegetable. **2.** The rounded edible bulb of this plant, composed of fleshy tight concentric leaf bases having a pungent odor and taste. [ME *oinyon* < OFr. *oignon* < Lat. *uniō, uniōn-.*]

onion dome *n.* A pointed bulbous domelike roof, used esp. in parts of Russia and eastern Europe.

On·ions (ŭn′yənz), **Charles Talbut** 1873–1965. British lexicographer who was coeditor (1914–33) of the *Oxford English Dictionary.*

on·ion·skin (ŭn′yən-skĭn′) *n.* A thin strong translucent paper.

on·lay (ŏn′lā′, ôn′-) *n.* **1.** Something laid or applied over something else, as to add relief to a surface. **2.** *Medicine* A graft applied to the surface of the recipient organ or structure. **3.** *Dentistry* A cast, usu. of gold, attached to the occlusal surface of a tooth.

on·line also **on-line** (ŏn′līn′, ôn′-) *adj.* **1a.** Under the control of a central computer, as in a manufacturing process. **b.** Connected to a computer or computer network. **c.** Accessible via a computer or computer network. **2.** In progress; ongoing. **—on′line′** *adv.*

on·load (ŏn′lōd′, ôn′-) *v.* **-load·ed, -load·ing, -loads** *—tr.* To load (a vehicle or container). *—intr.* To load a vehicle or container.

on·look·er (ŏn′lŏok′ər, ôn′-) *n.* One that looks on; a spectator.

on·ly (ōn′lē) *adj.* **1.** Alone in kind or class; sole: *an only child.* **2.** Standing alone by reason of superiority or excellence. ❖ *adv.* **1.** Without anyone or anything else; alone: *room for only one passenger.* **2a.** At the very least: *If you would only come home.* **b.** And nothing else or more: *I only work here.* **3.** Exclusively; solely: *known only to us.* **4a.** In the last analysis or final outcome: *will only make things worse.* **b.** With the final result; nevertheless: *hired only to be laid off.* **5a.** As recently as: *only last month.* **b.** In the immediate past: *only just saw her.* ❖ *conj.* **1.** Were it not that; except. **2a.** With the restriction that; but: *You may go, only be careful.* **b.** However; and yet: *It's good, only we can't use it.* [ME < OE *ānlīc : ān,* one; see ONE + *-līc,* having the form of; see -LY[1].]

USAGE NOTE When used as an adverb, *only* should be placed with care to avoid ambiguity. Generally this means having *only* adjoin the word or words that it limits. Variation in the placement of *only* can change the meaning of the sentence, as the following example shows: *Dictators respect only force; they are not moved by words. Dictators only respect force; they do not worship it.* See Usage Note at **not.**

on·o·mas·tic (ŏn′ə-măs′tĭk) *adj.* **1.** Of, relating to, or explaining a name or names. **2.** Of or relating to onomastics. [Fr. *onomastique* < Gk. *onomastikos* < *onomazein,* to name < *onoma,* name. See **nŏ-men-** in App.]

on·o·mas·tics (ŏn′ə-măs′tĭks) n. (used with a sing. or pl. verb) **1a.** The study of the origins and forms of proper names. **b.** The study of the origins and forms of terms used in specialized fields. **2.** The system that underlies the formation and use of proper names or terms used in specialized fields.

on·o·mat·o·poe·ia (ŏn′ə-mǎt′ə-pē′ə, -mä′tə-) n. The formation or use of words such as buzz that imitate the sounds associated with the objects or actions they refer to. [LLat. < Gk. onomatopoiiā < onomatopoios, coiner of names : onoma, onomat-, name; see nŏ-men- in App. + poiein, to make.] —**on′o·mat′o·poe′ic,** **on′o·mat′o·po·et′ic** (-pō-ĕt′ĭk) adj. —**on′o·mat′o·poe′i·cal·ly,** **on′o·mat′o·po·et′i·cal·ly** adv.

On·on·da·ga (ŏn′ən-dô′gə, -dä′-) n., pl. **Onondaga** or **-gas** **1.** A member of a Native American people formerly inhabiting the eastern Finger Lakes region of west-central New York, with present-day populations in this same area and in southeast Ontario. **2.** Their Iroquoian language. [Onondaga onó·ntà′ke, on the hill, a village name.] —**On′on·da′gan** adj.

on·rush (ŏn′rŭsh′, ôn′-) n. **1.** A forward rush or flow. **2.** A violent physical or verbal attack. —**on′rush′ing** adj.

On·sa·ger (ŏn′sä′gər), Lars 1903–76. Norwegian-born Amer. chemist who won a 1968 Nobel Prize.

on·screen or **on-screen** (ŏn′skrēn′, ôn′-) adj. **1.** As shown on a movie, television, or display screen. **2.** Within public view; in public. —**on′screen′** adv.

on·set (ŏn′sĕt′, ôn′-) n. **1.** An onslaught; an assault. **2.** A beginning; a start: the onset of a cold. **3.** Linguistics The part of a syllable preceding the nucleus.

on·shore (ŏn′shôr′, -shōr′, ôn′-) adj. **1.** Moving or directed toward the shore: an onshore wind. **2.** Located on the shore: an onshore beacon. ❖ adv. Toward the shore.

on·side (ŏn′sīd′, ôn′-) adv. & adj. Sports In such a position as to be able to play or receive a ball or puck legally.

onside kick n. Football A kickoff in which the ball carries far enough, at least ten yards, to be recovered by the kicking team.

on·site (ŏn′sīt′, ôn′-) adj. Done or located at the site, as of a particular activity: an on-site film shoot. —**on′-site′** adv.

on·slaught (ŏn′slôt′, ôn′-) n. **1.** A violent attack. **2.** An overwhelming outpouring. [Alteration (influenced by obsolete slaughte, slaughter) of Du. aanslag, a striking at < MDu. aenslach : aen-, on + slach, a striking.]

on·stage (ŏn-stāj′, ôn-) adj. Situated or taking place in the area of a stage visible to the audience. ❖ adv. In or into the area of a stage visible to the audience.

Ont. abbr. Ontario

–ont suff. Cell; organism: -biont. [< Gk. ōn, ont-, pr. part. of einai, to be. See es- in App.]

On·tar·i·o (ŏn-târ′ē-ō′) **1.** A province of E-central Canada; joined the confederation in 1867. First visited by French explorers in the early 1600s, it passed to the British in 1763. Cap. Toronto. Pop. 10,753,573. **2.** A city of S CA E of Los Angeles. Pop. 158,007.

Ontario, Lake The smallest of the Great Lakes, between SE Ontario, Canada, and NW NY.

on-the-job (ŏn′thə-jŏb′, ôn′-) adj. Acquired or learned while working at a job: on-the-job training.

on·tic (ŏn′tĭk) adj. Ontological.

on·to (ŏn′tōō′, -tə, ôn′-) prep. **1.** On top of; to a position on; upon. See Usage Note at **on. 2.** Informal Fully aware of; informed about. ❖ adj. Mathematics Of, relating to, or being a mapping such that every element of the target set referred to is the image of an element in the domain.

onto– or **ont–** pref. **1.** Existence; being: ontology. **2.** Organism: ontogeny. [L.Gk. < Gk. ōn, ont-, pr. part. of einai, to be. See es- in App.]

on·to·gen·e·sis (ŏn′tō-jĕn′ĭ-sĭs) n., pl. **-ses** (-sēz′) See **ontogeny.**

on·tog·e·ny (ŏn-tŏj′ə-nē) n., pl. **-nies** The development of an individual organism from embryo to adult. —**on′to·ge·net′ic** (ŏn′tō-jə-nĕt′ĭk) adj. —**on′to·ge·net′i·cal·ly** adv.

on·to·log·i·cal (ŏn′tə-lŏj′ĭ-kəl) adj. **1.** Of or relating to ontology. **2.** Of or relating to essence or the nature of being. **3.** Of or relating to the argument for the existence of God holding that the existence of the concept of God entails the existence of God. —**on′to·log′i·cal·ly** adv.

on·tol·o·gy (ŏn-tŏl′ə-jē) n. The branch of metaphysics that deals with the nature of being. —**on·tol′o·gist** n.

o·nus (ō′nəs) n. **1.** A difficult or disagreeable responsibility or necessity; a burden or obligation. **2a.** A stigma. **b.** Blame. **3.** The burden of proof. [Lat.]

on·ward (ŏn′wərd, ôn′-) adj. Moving or tending forward. ❖ adv. also **on·wards** (-wərdz) In a direction or toward a position that is ahead in space or time; forward.

–onym suff. Word; name: acronym. [Gk. -ōnumon, neut. of -ōnumos, having a specified kind of name < onuma, name. See nŏ-men- in App.]

–onymy suff. A set of names; the study of a kind of names: toponymy. [Gk. -ōnumiā < -ōnumos, having a specified kind of name < onuma, name. See nŏ-men- in App.]

on·yx (ŏn′ĭks) n. A chalcedony that occurs in bands of different colors and is used as a gemstone, esp. in cameos and intaglios.

[ME onix < OFr. < Lat. onyx < Gk. onux, nail, onyx.]

oo– pref. Egg; ovum: oogenesis. [Gk. ōio- < ōion, egg. See awi- in App.]

o·o·cyst (ō′ə-sĭst′) n. A thick-walled structure in which sporozoan zygotes develop.

o·o·cyte (ō′ə-sīt′) n. A cell from which an egg or ovum develops by meiosis; a female gametocyte.

OOD abbr. officer of the deck

O′o·dham (ō′ə-däm) n., pl. **O′odham** or **-dhams** See **Papago.**

oo·dles (ōōd′lz) pl.n. Informal A great amount or number: oodles of fun. [?]

o·o·gam·ete (ō′ə-găm′ēt′, -gə-mēt′) n. A female gamete, esp. the larger of two gametes produced by an oogamous species.

o·og·a·mous (ō-ŏg′ə-məs) adj. Characterized by or having small motile male gametes and large nonmotile female gametes. —**o·og′a·my** n.

o·o·gen·e·sis (ō′ə-jĕn′ĭ-sĭs) n. The formation, development, and maturation of an ovum. —**o′o·ge·net′ic** (-jə-nĕt′ĭk) adj.

o·o·go·ni·um (ō′ə-gō′nē-əm) n., pl. **-ni·a** (-nē-ə) or **-ni·ums** **1.** A descendant of a primordial germ cell that differentiates into an oocyte. **2.** A female reproductive structure in certain thallophytes, usu. a rounded cell or sac containing one or more oospheres. [OO– + NLat. gonium, cell (< Gk. gonos, seed; see GONO–).] —**o′o·go′ni·al** (-nē-əl) adj.

ooh (ōō) interj. Used to express pleasure, satisfaction, surprise, or great joy. ❖ intr.v. **oohed, ooh·ing, oohs** To exclaim in pleasure, satisfaction, surprise, or great joy. —**ooh** n.

o·o·lite (ō′ə-līt′) also **o·o·lith** (-lĭth′) n. **1.** A small round calcareous grain found in sedimentary rock. **2.** Rock, usu. limestone, composed of oolites. —**o′o·lit′ic** (-lĭt′ĭk) adj.

o·ol·o·gy (ō-ŏl′ə-jē) n. The branch of zoology that deals with the study of eggs. —**o′o·log′ic** (ō′ə-lŏj′ĭk), **o′o·log′i·cal** (-ĭ-kəl) adj. —**o′o·log′i·cal·ly** adv. —**o·ol′o·gist** n.

oo·long (ōō′lông′, -lŏng′) n. A dark Chinese tea that has been partially fermented before drying. [Chin. (Mandarin) wūlóng(chá), black dragon (tea) : wū, dark, black + lóng, dragon.]

oo·mi·ak (ōō′mē-ăk′) n. Variant of **umiak.**

oom·pah (ōōm′pä, ōōm′-) also **oom·pah-pah** (ōōm′pä′pä′, ōōm′-) n. A rhythmic sound made by a tuba or other brass instrument. [Imit.]

oomph (ōōmf) n. Slang **1.** Spirited vigor. **2.** Physical or sexual attractiveness. [Expressive of exertion.]

o·o·pho·rec·to·my (ō′ə-fə-rĕk′tə-mē) n., pl. **-mies** Surgical removal of one or both ovaries.

o·o·pho·ri·tis (ō′ə-fə-rī′tĭs) n. Inflammation of an ovary.

oops (ōōps) interj. Used to express acknowledgement of a minor accident, blunder, or mistake.

Oort cloud (ôrt, ōrt) n. A swarm of comets orbiting the sun at a distance of one to two light-years. [After Jan Hendrix Oort (1900–92), Dutch astronomer.]

o·o·sphere (ō′ə-sfîr′) n. A large nonmotile female gamete or egg cell, formed in an oogonium and ready for fertilization.

o·o·spore (ō′ə-spôr′, -spōr′) n. A fertilized female cell or zygote, esp. one with thick chitinous walls, developed from a fertilized oosphere.

Oost·en·de (ō-stĕn′də) See **Ostend.**

o·o·the·ca (ō′ə-thē′kə) n., pl. **-cae** (-sē) The egg case of certain insects and mollusks. —**o′o·the′cal** adj.

o·o·tid (ō′ə-tĭd′) n. A haploid cell that results from the meiotic division of an oocyte and becomes a female gamete or an ovum. [OO– + (SPERMA)TID.]

ooze¹ (ōōz) v. **oozed, ooz·ing, ooz·es** —intr. **1.** To flow or leak out slowly, as through small openings. **2.** To disappear or ebb slowly: His courage oozed away. **3.** To progress slowly but steadily. **4.** To exude moisture. **5.** To emit a particular essence or quality. —tr. **1.** To give off; exude. **2.** To emit or radiate in abundance: She oozes confidence. ❖ n. **1.** The act of oozing. **2.** Something that oozes. **3.** An infusion of vegetable matter, as from oak bark, used in tanning. [ME wosen < wose, juice < OE wōs.]

ooze² (ōōz) n. **1.** Soft mud or slime. **2.** A layer of mudlike sediment on the floor of oceans and lakes, composed chiefly of remains of microscopic sea animals. **3.** Muddy ground. [ME wose < OE wāse.]

ooz·y¹ (ōō′zē) adj. **-i·er, -i·est** Exuding moisture. —**ooz′i·ly** adv. —**ooz′i·ness** n.

ooz·y² (ōō′zē) adj. **-i·er, -i·est** Of, resembling, or containing soft mud or slime: soft oozy ground. —**ooz′i·ly** adv. —**ooz′i·ness** n.

OP abbr. **1.** observation post **2.** Roman Catholic Church Order of Preachers (Dominican) **3.** out of print

op. or **Op.** abbr. opus

o·pac·i·fi·er (ō-păs′ə-fī′ər) n. A chemical agent added to a material to make it opaque.

o·pac·i·ty (ō-păs′ĭ-tē) n., pl. **-ties** **1.** The quality or state of being opaque. **2.** Something opaque. **3a.** Obscurity; impenetrability. **b.** Dullness of mind. [Fr. opacité < OFr. < Lat. opācitās < opācus, dark.]

o·pah (ō′pə) n. A large, oval-shaped, vividly colored marine fish (Lampris regius) having edible red flesh. [Of West African orig.; akin to Igbo uba.]

o·pal (ō′pəl) n. **1.** A translucent mineral of hydrated silica, often

ă pat	oi	boy
ā pay	ou	out
âr care	ōō	took
ä father	ōō	boot
ĕ pet	ŭ	cut
ē be	ûr	urge
ĭ pit	th	thin
ī pie	th	this
îr pier	hw	which
ō toe	ə	about,
ô paw		item

Stress marks:
′ (primary);
′ (secondary), as in
lexicon (lĕk′sĭ-kŏn′)

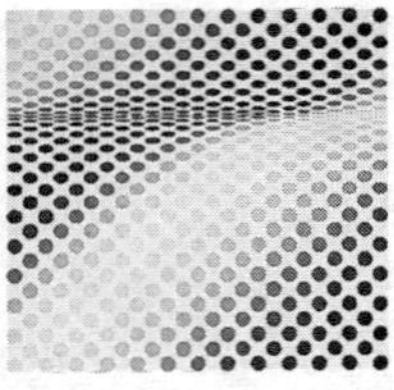

op art
Hesitate, 1964, by Bridget Riley (b. 1931)

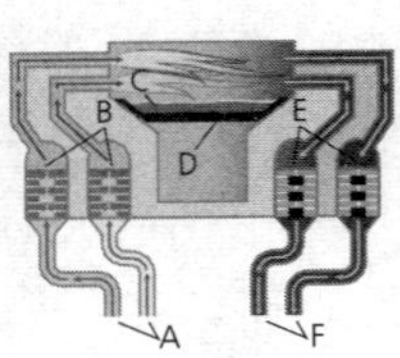

open-hearth
A. gas and air enter
B. pre-heated chamber
C. molten pig iron
D. hearth
E. heating chamber (cold)
F. gas and air exit

used as a gem. **2.** A gemstone made of this mineral, noted for its rich iridescence. [ME *opalus* < Lat., alteration of Gk. *opallios,* prob. < Skt. *upalaḥ* < var. of *upara-*, lower < *upa,* below. See **upo** in App.] —**o′pal•ine′** (ō′pə-līn′, -lēn′) *adj.*

o•pal•esce (ō′pə-lĕs′) *intr.v.* **-esced, -esc•ing, -esc•es** To exhibit an iridescent shimmer of colors.

o•pal•es•cent (ō′pə-lĕs′ənt) *adj.* Exhibiting a milky iridescence like that of an opal. —**o′pal•es′cence** *n.*

o•paque (ō-pāk′) *adj.* **1a.** Impenetrable by light; neither transparent nor translucent. **b.** Not reflecting light; having no luster. **2.** Impenetrable by a form of radiant energy other than visible light. **3a.** So obscure as to be unintelligible. **b.** Obtuse of mind; dense. ❖ *n.* Something that is opaque, esp. an opaque pigment used to darken parts of a photographic print or negative. [ME *opake,* shady, and Fr. *opaque,* opaque (< OFr., shady), both < Lat. *opācus.*] —**o•paque′ly** *adv.* —**o•paque′ness** *n.*

op art also **Op Art** (ŏp) *n.* A school of abstract art characterized by the use of geometric shapes and brilliant colors to create optical illusions, as of motion, and free the art of all but visual associations. [OP(TICAL) ART.]

op. cit. *abbr. Latin* opere citato (in the work cited)

OPEC (ō′pĕk′) *abbr.* Organization of Petroleum Exporting Countries

op-ed or **Op-Ed** (ŏp′ĕd′) *adj.* Of or being a newspaper page, usu. opposite the editorial page, that features articles expressing personal viewpoints. [OP(POSITE) + ED(ITORIAL).]

o•pen (ō′pən) *adj.* **1a.** Affording unobstructed entrance and exit; not shut or closed. **b.** Affording unobstructed passage or view: *open waters.* **2a.** Having no protecting or concealing cover: *an open wound.* **b.** Completely obvious; blatant. **c.** Carried on in full view: *open warfare.* **d.** *Sports* Not closely defended by an opponent: *an open receiver.* **3a.** Not sealed or tied. **b.** Spread out; unfolded: *an open book.* **4.** Having interspersed gaps, spaces, or intervals: *an open weave.* **5a.** Accessible to all; unrestricted as to participants. **b.** Free from limitations, boundaries, or restrictions. **c.** Enterable by registered voters regardless of political affiliation. **d.** *Computer Science* Of or relating to a file that can be accessed. **6a.** Lacking effective regulation. **b.** Not legally repressed: *open drug trafficking.* **7a.** Susceptible; vulnerable: *open to interpretation.* **b.** Willing to consider or deal with something: *open to suggestions.* **8a.** Available; obtainable: *The job is still open.* **b.** Available for use: *an open account.* **9.** Ready to transact business. **10.** Not engaged or filled: *an open hour for the meeting.* **11.** Not yet decided; subject to further thought. **12a.** Characterized by lack of pretense or reserve; candid. See Syns at **frank**[1]. **b.** Free of prejudice; receptive to new ideas and arguments. **c.** Generous. **13.** *Printing* **a.** Widely spaced or leaded. Used of typeset or other printed matter. **b.** Having constituent elements separated by a space in writing or printing: *The word* sea horse *is an open compound.* **14.** *Music* **a.** Not stopped by a finger. Used of a string or hole of an instrument. **b.** Produced by an unstopped string or hole or without the use of slides, valves, or keys. **c.** Played without a mute. **15a.** Articulated with the tongue in a low position, as the vowel in *far.* **b.** Ending in a vowel or diphthong. **16.** Being a method of punctuation in which commas and other marks are used sparingly. **17.** Being in operation; live: *an open microphone.* **18.** *New England* Clear. Used of weather. **19.** Containing a gap across which electricity cannot pass: *an open switch.* **20.** *Mathematics* **a.** Of, relating to, or being a set such that at least one neighborhood of every point in the set is within the set. **b.** Of, relating to, or being a set that is the complement of a closed set. **21.** *Sports* Having the forward foot farther than the rear foot from the intended point of impact with the ball: *an open stance.* **22.** *Physics* Of or relating to a model of the universe in which there is not sufficient matter to halt its expansion. ❖ *v.* **o•pened, o•pen•ing, o•pens** —*tr.* **1.** To release from a closed or fastened position. **2.** To remove obstructions from; clear. **3.** To make or force an opening in. **4a.** To form spaces or gaps between: *soldiers opening ranks.* **b.** To break the continuity of; make a gap in: *open a circuit.* **5a.** To remove the cover, cork, or lid from. **b.** To remove the wrapping from; undo. **6.** To unfold so that the inner parts are displayed; spread out. **7a.** To get (something) going; initiate. **b.** To commence the operation of: *open a new business.* **8.** *Games* To begin (the action in a game of cards) by making the first bid, placing the first bet, or playing the first lead. **9.** To make available for use. **10.** To make more responsive or understanding. **11.** To reveal the secrets of; bare. —*intr.* **1.** To become open: *The door opened.* **2.** To draw apart; separate: *The wound opened.* **3.** To spread apart; unfold. **4.** To come into view; become revealed. **5.** To become receptive or understanding. **6a.** To begin; commence. **b.** To begin business or operation. **7.** To be performed, shown, or made available to the public for the first time: *When does the play open?* **8.** To be priced or listed at a specified amount when trading begins. **9.** *Games* To make a bid, bet, or lead in starting a game of cards. **10.** To give access: *The room opens onto a terrace.* ❖ *n.* **1.** An unobstructed area of land or water. **2.** The outdoors. **3.** An undisguised or unconcealed state. **4.** A tournament or contest in which both professional and amateur players may participate. ***—phrasal verb:*** **open up 1.** To spread out; unfold. **2a.** To begin operation. **b.** To begin firing. **3.** *Informal* To speak freely and candidly. **4.** To make an opening in by cutting. **5.** To make available or accessible. **6.** *Informal* To accelerate. Used of a motor vehicle. ***—idioms:*** **open fire** To begin firing on. **open (one's) eyes** To become aware of the truth of a situation. [ME < OE. See **upo** in App.] —**o′pen•ly** *adv.* —**o′pen•ness** *n.*

open admissions *pl.n.* (*used with a sing. or pl. verb*) A policy that permits enrollment of a student in a college or university regardless of academic qualifications or financial situation.

o•pen-air (ō′pən-âr′) *adj.* Outdoor: *an open-air concert.*

o•pen-and-shut (ō′pən-ən-shŭt′) *adj.* So obvious as to present no difficulties; easily settled or determined.

open chain *n.* An arrangement of atoms, as in aliphatic hydrocarbons, that does not form a ring. —**o′pen-chain′** (ō′pən-chān′) *adj.*

open city *n.* A city that is declared demilitarized during a war, thus gaining immunity from attack under international law.

open door *n.* **1.** Unhindered opportunity; free access. **2.** Admission to all on equal terms. **3.** A policy whereby a nation trades with all other nations on equal terms. —**o′pen-door′** (ō′pən-dôr′, -dōr′) *adj.*

o•pen-end (ō′pən-ĕnd′) *adj.* **1.** Having no definite limit of duration or amount. **2.** Continually issuing new shares or buying back existing shares from shareholders: *an open-end mutual fund.* **3.** Permitting the borrowing of additional funds under existing terms: *an open-end mortgage.*

o•pen-end•ed (ō′pən-ĕn′dĭd) *adj.* **1.** Not restrained by definite limits, restrictions, or structure. **2.** Allowing for or adaptable to change. **3.** Inconclusive or indefinite. **4.** Allowing for a spontaneous unstructured response. —**o′pen-end′ed•ly** *adv.*

open enrollment *n.* See **open admissions.**

o•pen•er (ō′pə-nər) *n.* **1.** One that opens, esp. a device to open cans or bottles. **2.** *Games* **a.** The player who opens in a game of cards. **b. openers** Cards of sufficient value to enable the holder to open the betting. **3.** The first act in a theatrical variety show. **4.** *Sports* The first game in a series. ***—idiom:*** **for openers** *Informal* To begin with.

o•pen-eyed (ō′pən-īd′) *adj.* **1.** Having the eyes wide open, as in surprise. **2.** Watchful and alert.

o•pen-faced (ō′pən-fāst′) *adj.* **1.** Having a face that seems to exhibit honesty and sincerity. **2.** Having a side uncovered.

o•pen•hand•ed (ō′pən-hăn′dĭd) *adj.* Giving freely; generous. See Syns at **liberal.** —**o′pen•hand′ed•ly** *adv.* —**o′pen•hand′ed•ness** *n.*

o•pen•heart•ed (ō′pən-här′tĭd) *adj.* **1.** Frank. **2.** Kindly. —**o′pen•heart′ed•ly** *adv.* —**o′pen•heart′ed•ness** *n.*

o•pen-hearth (ō′pən-härth′) *adj.* **1.** Of or being a reverberatory furnace used in the production of high-quality steel. **2.** Of or relating to the steel produced in such a furnace.

o•pen-heart surgery (ō′pən-härt′) *n.* Surgery in which the thoracic cavity is opened to expose the heart and the blood is recirculated and oxygenated by a heart-lung machine.

open house *n.* **1.** A social event in which hospitality is extended to all. **2.** An occasion when a school or institution is open for visiting by the public. **3a.** A period of time during which a house or apartment for sale or rent is open for public viewing. **b.** A house or apartment open for such viewing.

o•pen•ing (ō′pə-nĭng) *n.* **1.** The act or an instance of becoming open or being made to open. **2.** An open space serving as a passage or gap. **3.** A breach or aperture. **4.** A clearing in the woods. **5.** The first part or stage, as of a book. **6.** The first performance: *the opening of a play.* **7.** A formal commencement of operation. **8.** *Games* A specific pattern or series of beginning moves in certain games, esp. chess. **9.** An opportunity affording a chance of success. **10.** An unfilled job or position; a vacancy.

open interval *n.* A set of numbers consisting of all the numbers between a pair of given numbers but not including the endpoints.

open letter *n.* A letter of general interest, addressed to a person but published for general readership.

open market *n.* A freely competitive market operating without restrictions.

open marriage *n.* A marriage in which the partners agree that each is free to engage in extramarital relationships.

o•pen-mind•ed (ō′pən-mīn′dĭd) *adj.* Receptive to new and different ideas or the opinions of others. See Syns at **broad-minded.** —**o′pen-mind′ed•ly** *adv.* —**o′pen-mind′ed•ness** *n.*

o•pen-mouthed (ō′pən-mouthd′, -moutht′) *adj.* **1.** Having the mouth open. **2.** Gaping in astonishment or wonder. **3.** Loudly insistent. —**o′pen-mouth′ed•ly** *adv.*

o•pen-pol•li•nat•ed (ō′pən-pŏl′ə-nā′tĭd) *adj.* Pollinated without human intervention, as by the wind or insects.

open season *n.* **1.** The period during which it is legal to hunt or catch game or fish. **2.** *Informal* A time of unrestrained harassment, criticism, or attack.

open secret *n.* Something supposedly secret but in fact generally known.

open sesame *n.* A simple, trusty means of attaining a goal. [< *Open Sesame,* magical formula used by Ali Baba in the *Arabian Nights* to open the robbers' cave door.]

open shop *n.* A business or factory in which workers are employed without regard to union membership.

o•pen-source (ō′pən-sôrs′, -sōrs′) *adj. Computer Science* Of or relating to source code that is available to the public.

open stock *n.* Merchandise kept in stock so as to enable customers to replace or supplement articles purchased in sets.

open universe *n.* A model of the universe in which there is insufficient matter, and thus insufficient gravitational force, to halt the expansion initiated by the big bang.

o·pen·work (ō′pən-wûrk′) *n.* Ornamental or structural work, as of embroidery or metal, containing numerous openings, usu. in set patterns.

op·er·a¹ (ŏp′ər-ə, ŏp′rə) *n.* **1.** A theatrical presentation in which a dramatic performance is set to music. **2.** The score of such a work. **3.** A theater designed primarily for operas. [Ital., work, opera < Lat., work, service.]

o·pe·ra² (ō′pər-ə, ō′prə-ə) *n.* A plural of **opus.**

op·er·a·ble (ŏp′ər-ə-bəl, ŏp′rə-) *adj.* **1.** Being such that use or operation is possible. **2.** Possible to put into practice; practicable. **3.** Treatable by surgery with a reasonable chance of success. —**op′er·a·bil′i·ty** *n.* —**op′er·a·bly** *adv.*

o·pé·ra bouffe (ŏp′ər-ə boo̅f′ə, ŏp′rə, ō′pĕ-rä boof′fä) *n.* A comic, often farcical opera. [Fr. < Ital. *opera buffa.* See OPERA BUFFA.]

o·pe·ra buf·fa (ŏp′ər-ə boo̅f′ə, ŏp′rə, ō′pĕ-rä boof′fä) *n.* An Italian comic opera of the 18th century. [Ital. : *opera,* opera + *buffa,* fem. of *buffo,* comic.]

o·pé·ra co·mique (ŏp′ər-ə kŏ-mēk′, ŏp′rə, ô-pā-rä kô-mĕk′) *n.* A French comic opera. [Fr.]

op·er·a glass (ŏp′ər-ə, ŏp′rə) *n.* A pair of small low-powered binoculars for use esp. at a theatrical performance. Often used in the plural.

opera house *n.* A theater designed chiefly for the performance of operas.

op·er·and (ŏp′ər-ənd) *n.* A quantity on which a mathematical or logical operation is performed. [< Lat. *operandum,* neut. gerundive of *operāri,* to operate. See OPERATE.]

op·er·ant (ŏp′ər-ənt) *adj.* **1.** Operating to produce effects; effective. **2.** *Psychology* Of, relating to, or being a response that occurs spontaneously and is identified by its reinforcing or inhibiting effects. ❖ *n.* **1.** One that operates. **2.** *Psychology* An element of operant behavior. —**op′er·ant·ly** *adv.*

operant conditioning *n. Psychology* A process of behavior modification in which a subject is encouraged to behave in a desired manner through positive or negative reinforcement.

op·er·ate (ŏp′ə-rāt′) *v.* **-at·ed, -at·ing, -ates** —*intr.* **1.** To perform a function; work. **2.** To perform surgery. **3a.** To exert an influence: *forces operating on the economy.* **b.** To produce a desired or proper effect. **4.** To carry on a military or naval action or campaign. **5.** *Informal* To conduct business in an irregular or devious manner. —*tr.* **1.** To control the functioning of; run. **2.** To conduct the affairs of; manage. [Lat. *operārī, operāt-* < *opera,* work.]

op·er·at·ic (ŏp′ə-răt′ĭk) *adj.* Of, relating to, or typical of the opera. [< OPERA¹.] —**op′er·at′i·cal·ly** *adv.*

op·er·at·ics (ŏp′ə-răt′ĭks) *n.* (*used with a sing. or pl. verb*) Exaggerated behavior of a type associated with grand opera.

op·er·at·ing room (ŏp′ə-rā′tĭng) *n.* A room equipped for performing surgical operations.

operating system *n.* Software designed to control the hardware of a specific data-processing system in order to allow users and application programs to make use of it.

op·er·a·tion (ŏp′ə-rā′shən) *n.* **1.** The act or process of operating or functioning. **2.** The state of being operative or functional. **3.** A process or series of acts involved in a particular form of work. **4.** An instance or method of efficient, productive activity. **5.** An unethical or illegal business. **6.** *Medicine* A surgical procedure for remedying an injury, ailment, defect, or dysfunction. **7.** *Mathematics* A process or action, such as addition or differentiation, performed according to specific rules. **8.** *Computer Science* An action resulting from a single instruction. **9.** A logical operation. **10a.** A military or naval action, campaign, or mission. **b.** **operations** The headquarters or center from which a military action or other activities are controlled. **11. operations** The division of an organization that carries out the major planning and operating functions.

op·er·a·tion·al (ŏp′ə-rā′shə-nəl) *adj.* **1.** Of or relating to an operation or a series of operations. **2.** Of, intended for, or involved in military operations. **3.** Fit for proper functioning; ready for use. **4.** Being in effect or operation. —**op′er·a′tion·al·ly** *adv.*

op·er·a·tion·al·ism (ŏp′ə-rā′shə-nə-lĭz′əm) *n. Philosophy* The view that all theoretical terms in science are to be defined in terms of experimental procedures or operations with no reference to unobservable entities or processes. —**op′er·a′tion·al·ist** *n.*

operations research *n.* Mathematical analysis of a process or an operation, used in making decisions.

op·er·a·tive (ŏp′ər-ə-tĭv, -ə-rā′tĭv, ŏp′rə-tĭv, ŏp′rə-) *adj.* **1.** Being in effect; having force; operating. **2.** Functioning effectively; efficient. **3.** Engaged in or concerned with physical or mechanical activity. **4.** Of or relating to a surgical operation. **5.** Most important; key: *The operative word is "low-fat."* ❖ *n.* **1.** A skilled worker, esp. in industry. **2a.** A secret agent; a spy. **b.** A private investigator. **3.** One who works for a political organization, often wielding influence out of public view. —**op′er·a·tive·ly** *adv.*

op·er·a·tor (ŏp′ə-rā′tər) *n.* **1.** One who operates a machine or device. **2.** The owner or manager of a business or an industrial enterprise. **3.** One who deals aggressively in stocks or commodities. **4.** *Informal* A person who accomplishes goals through shrewd or unscrupulous maneuvers. **5.** *Mathematics* A function, esp. one from a set to itself, such as differentiation of a differentiable function. **6.** A logical operator. **7.** *Genetics* A chromosomal segment of DNA that regulates the activity of the structural genes of an operon by interacting with a specific repressor.

o·per·cu·late (ō-pûr′kyə-lĭt) also **o·per·cu·lat·ed** (-lā′tĭd) *adj.* Having an operculum.

o·per·cu·lum (ō-pûr′kyə-ləm) *n., pl.* **-la** (-lə) or **-lums** A lid or flap covering an aperture, such as the gill cover in some fishes. [Lat., lid < *operīre,* to cover.] —**o·per′cu·lar** (-lər) *adj.* —**o·per′cu·lar·ly** *adv.*

op·er·et·ta (ŏp′ə-rĕt′ə) *n.* A theatrical production that has many of the musical elements of opera but is lighter and more popular in subject and style and contains spoken dialogue. [Ital., dim. of *opera,* opera. See OPERA¹.]

op·er·on (ŏp′ə-rŏn′) *n.* A unit of genetic material that functions in a coordinated manner by means of an operator, a promoter, and one or more structural genes that are transcribed together. [OPER(ATOR) + -ON¹.]

op·er·ose (ŏp′ə-rōs′) *adj.* **1.** Involving great labor; laborious. **2.** Industrious; diligent. [Lat. *operōsus* < *opus, oper-,* work.] —**op′er·ose′ly** *adv.* —**op′er·ose′ness** *n.*

oph·i·cleide (ŏf′ĭ-klīd′) *n.* A keyed brass instrument of the bugle family with a baritone range that was the structural precursor of the bass saxophone. [Fr. : Gk. *ophis,* snake (< its resemblance to the serpent, a musical instrument) + Gk. *kleis, kleid-,* key.]

o·phid·i·an (ō-fĭd′ē-ən) *adj.* Of, relating to, or resembling snakes. ❖ *n.* A member of the suborder Ophidia or Serpentes; a snake. [< NLat. *Ophidia,* suborder name < Gk. *ophis,* snake.]

oph·i·ol·o·gy (ŏf′ē-ŏl′ə-jē, ō′fē-) *n.* The branch of herpetology that deals with snakes. [Gk. *ophis,* snake + -LOGY.] —**oph′i·o·log′i·cal** (-ə-lŏj′ĭ-kəl) *adj.* —**oph′i·ol′o·gist** *n.*

oph·ite (ŏf′īt′, ō′fīt′) *n.* **1.** A mottled green rock composed of diabase. **2.** Any of various green rocks, such as serpentine. [ME *ophites* < Lat. *ophītēs* < Gk. *ophītēs (lithos),* serpentlike (stone) < *ophis,* serpent.]

o·phit·ic (ō-fĭt′ĭk, ō-fīt′-) *adj.* **1.** Of or relating to ophite. **2.** Having a texture composed of lath-shaped plagioclase crystals in a matrix of pyroxene crystals.

Oph·i·u·chus (ŏf′ē-yoo̅′kəs, ō′fē-) *n.* A constellation in the equatorial region near Scorpius. [Lat. *Ophiūchus* < Gk. *ophioukhos : ophis,* serpent + *okhos,* holder (< *ekhein,* to hold; see segh- in App.).]

oph·thal·mi·a (ŏf-thăl′mē-ə, ŏp-) *n.* Inflammation of the eye, esp. of the conjunctiva. [Ult. < Gk. *ophthalmiā < ophthalmos,* eye. See OPHTHALMO-.]

oph·thal·mic (ŏf-thăl′mĭk, ŏp-) *adj.* Of or relating to the eye.

ophthalmo- or **ophthalm-** *pref.* Eye; eyeball: *ophthalmoscope.* [Gk. < *ophthalmos,* eye. See ok"- in App.]

oph·thal·mol·o·gist (ŏf′thəl-mŏl′ə-jĭst, -thăl-, ŏp′-) *n.* A physician who specializes in ophthalmology.

oph·thal·mol·o·gy (ŏf′thəl-mŏl′ə-jē, -thăl-, ŏp′-) *n.* The branch of medicine that deals with the anatomy, functions, pathology, and treatment of the eye. —**oph·thal′mo·log′ic** (-thăl′mə-lŏj′ĭk), **oph·thal′mo·log′i·cal** (-ĭ-kəl) *adj.* —**oph·thal′mo·log′i·cal·ly** *adv.*

oph·thal·mo·scope (ŏf-thăl′mə-skōp′, ŏp-) *n.* An instrument for examining the interior structures of the eye, esp. the retina, consisting of a mirror that reflects light into the eye and a central hole through which the eye is examined. —**oph·thal′mo·scop′ic** (-skŏp′ĭk), **oph·thal′mo·scop′i·cal** *adj.* —**oph′thal·mos′co·py** (ŏf′thăl-mŏs′kə-pē, ŏp′-) *n.*

-opia *suff.* A visual condition or defect of a specified kind: *anisometropia.* [Gk. *-ōpiā < ōps,* eye. See PELOPS.]

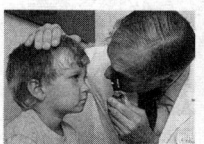
o·pi·ate (ō′pē-ĭt, -āt′) *n.* **1.** Any of various sedative narcotics containing opium or one or more of its derivatives. **2.** A drug or other substance having effects similar to those containing opium or its derivatives. **3.** Something that dulls the senses and induces relaxation or torpor. ❖ *adj.* **1a.** Containing opium or any of its derivatives. **b.** Resembling opium or its derivatives in activity. **2.** Inducing sleep or sedation. **3.** Causing dullness or apathy; deadening. ❖ *tr.v.* (-āt′) **-at·ed, -at·ing, -ates 1.** To subject to the action of an opiate. **2.** To dull or deaden as if with a narcotic drug. [ME < Med.Lat. *opiātum* < Lat. *opium,* opium. See OPIUM.]

o·pine (ō-pīn′) *tr. & intr.v.* **o·pined, o·pin·ing, o·pines** To state as or express an opinion. [ME *opinen* < OFr. *opiner* < Lat. *opīnārī,* to suppose.]

o·pin·ion (ə-pĭn′yən) *n.* **1.** A belief or conclusion held with confidence but not substantiated by positive knowledge or proof. **2.** A judgment based on special knowledge and given by an expert. **3.** A judgment or estimation of the merit of a person or thing. **4.** The prevailing view. **5.** *Law* A formal statement by a court or other adjudicative body of the legal reasons and principles for the conclusions of the court. [ME < OFr. < Lat. *opīniō, opīniōn-* < *opīnārī,* to think.]

ă	pat	oi	boy
ā	pay	ou	out
âr	care	oo	took
ä	father	oo	boot
ĕ	pet	ŭ	cut
ē	be	ûr	urge
ĭ	pit	th	thin
ī	pie	th	this
îr	pier	hw	which
ŏ	pot	zh	vision
ō	toe	ə	about,
ô	paw		item

Stress marks:
′ (primary);
′ (secondary), as in
lexicon (lĕk′sĭ-kŏn′)

o·pin·ion·at·ed (ə-pĭn′yə-nā′tĭd) *adj.* Holding stubbornly and often unreasonably to one's own opinions. [Prob. < obsolete *opinionate* : OPINION + –ATE[1].] —**o·pin′ion·at′ed·ly** *adv.*

o·pin·ion·a·tive (ə-pĭn′yə-nā′tĭv) *adj.* **1.** Of, based on, or of the nature of an opinion. **2.** Opinionated. —**o·pin′ion·a′tive·ly** *adv.*

o·pi·oid (ō′pē-oid′) *n.* See **opiate** 2. ❖ *adj.* Opiate.

o·pis·tho·branch (ə-pĭs′thə-brăngk′) *n., pl.* **-branchs** Any of various marine gastropod mollusks of the subclass Opisthobranchia, characterized by gills, a reduced or absent shell, and two pairs of tentacles. [< NLat. Opisthobranchia, subclass name : Gk. *opistho-*, behind; see OPISTHOGNATHOUS + Gk. *brankhia*, gills.]

op·is·thog·na·thous (ŏp′ĭs-thŏg′nə-thəs) *adj.* Having receding jaws. [Gk. *opistho-*, behind (< *opisthen*; see **epi** in App.) + –GNATHOUS.] —**op′is·thog′na·thism** *n.*

o·pi·um (ō′pē-əm) *n.* **1.** A bitter, strongly addictive narcotic drug prepared from the dried juice of unripe pods of the opium poppy. **2.** Something that numbs or stupefies. [ME < Lat. < Gk. *opion*, dim. of *opos*, vegetable juice.]

opium poppy *n.* An annual plant (*Papaver somniferum*) native to Turkey and adjacent areas and having grayish-green leaves and variously colored flowers.

O·por·to (ō-pôr′tō, ō-pōr′-) also **Por·to** or **Pôr·to** (pôr′tōō) A city of NW Portugal near the mouth of the Douro R. N of Lisbon; probably of pre-Roman origin. Pop. 302,467.

o·pos·sum (ə-pŏs′əm, pŏs′əm) *n., pl.* **opossum** or **-sums** **1.** Any of various nocturnal, usu. arboreal marsupials of the family Didelphidae, esp. *Didelphis marsupialis* of the Western Hemisphere, having a thick coat of hair, a long snout, and a long prehensile tail. See Regional Note at **possum**. **2.** Any of several similar marsupials of Australia belonging to the family Phalangeridae. [Virginia Algonquian.]

Op·pen·hei·mer (ŏp′ən-hī′mər), **J(ulius) Robert** 1902–67. Amer. physicist who directed the Los Alamos NM laboratory during the development of the first atomic bomb (1942–45).

op·po·nent (ə-pō′nənt) *n.* One that opposes another or others, as in a battle, contest, or debate. See Syns at **enemy**. ❖ *adj.* **1.** Acting against an antagonist or opposing force. **2.** Located in front. [Lat. *opponens, opponent-*, pr. part. of *opponere*, to oppose. See OPPOSE.] —**op·po′nen·cy** *n.*

op·por·tune (ŏp′ər-toōn′, -tyoōn′) *adj.* **1.** Suited or right for a particular purpose. **2.** Occurring at a fitting or advantageous time. [ME < OFr. *opportun* < Lat. *opportunus* < *ob portum* (*veniēns*), (coming) toward port : *ob*, to; see OB– + *portum*, accusative of *portus*, harbor; see **per-**[2] in App.] —**op′por·tune′ly** *adv.* —**op′por·tune′ness** *n.*

op·por·tun·ist (ŏp′ər-toō′nĭst, -tyoō′-) *n.* One who takes advantage of any opportunity to achieve an end, often regardless of principles or consequences. —**op′por·tun′ism** *n.*

op·por·tun·is·tic (ŏp′ər-toō-nĭs′tĭk, -tyoō-) *adj.* Taking immediate advantage, often unethically, of any circumstance of possible benefit.

opportunistic infection *n.* An infection by a microorganism that normally does not cause disease but becomes pathogenic when the body's immune system is impaired.

op·por·tu·ni·ty (ŏp′ər-toō′nĭ-tē, -tyoō′-) *n., pl.* **-ties** **1a.** A favorable or advantageous circumstance or combination of circumstances. **b.** A favorable or suitable occasion or time. **2.** A chance for progress or advancement.

op·pos·a·ble (ə-pō′zə-bəl) *adj.* **1.** Possible to oppose or resist. **2.** That can be placed opposite something else: *The thumb is an opposable digit.* —**op·pos′a·bil′i·ty** *n.*

op·pose (ə-pōz′) *v.* **-posed, -pos·ing, -pos·es** —*tr.* **1.** To be in contention or conflict with. **2.** To be resistant to: *opposes new ideas.* **3.** To place opposite in contrast or counterbalance. **4.** To place so as to be opposite something else. —*intr.* To act or be in opposition. —*idiom:* **as opposed to** In contrast to. [ME *posen*, to question, interrogate < OFr. *opposer*, alteration (influenced by *poser*, to place) of Lat. *opponere*, to oppose (*ob-*, against; see OB– + *pōnere*, to put; see **apo-** in App.).] —**op·pos′er** *n.*

SYNONYMS *oppose, fight, combat, resist, contest* These verbs mean to set someone or something in opposition to another. *Oppose* has the widest application: *"The idea is inconsistent with our constitutional theory and has been stubbornly opposed . . . since the early days of the Republic"* (E.B. White). *Fight* and *combat* suggest vigor and aggressiveness: *"All my life I have fought against prejudice and intolerance"* (Harry S. Truman). *"We are not afraid . . . to tolerate any error so long as reason is left free to combat it"* (Thomas Jefferson). To *resist* is to strive to fend off or offset the actions, effects, or force of: *"Pardon was freely extended to all who had resisted the invasion"* (John R. Green). To *contest* is to call something into question and take an active stand against it: *contested her neighbor's claims to her property in court.*

op·po·site (ŏp′ə-zĭt) *adj.* **1.** Placed or located directly across from something else or from each other. **2.** Facing the other way; moving or tending away from each other: *opposite directions.* **3.** Being the other of two complementary or mutually exclusive things: *the opposite sex.* **4a.** Altogether different, as in nature, quality, or significance. **b.** Sharply contrasting; antithetical: *opposite views on the subject.* **5.** *Botany* Growing in pairs on either side

J. Robert Oppenheimer

of a stem. ❖ *n.* **1.** One that is opposite or contrary to another. **2.** An opponent or antagonist. **3.** An antonym. ❖ *adv.* In an opposite position. ❖ *prep.* **1.** Across from or facing. **2.** In a complementary dramatic role to. [ME < OFr. < Lat. *oppositus*, p. part. of *opponere*, oppose. See OPPOSE.] —**op′po·site·ly** *adv.* —**op′po·site·ness** *n.*

opposite field *n. Baseball* The part of the field that is across from or opposite the side of home plate at which the batter stands, as right field for a left-handed batter.

opposite number *n.* A person who holds a position in an organization or system that corresponds to that of a person in another organization or system; a counterpart.

op·po·si·tion (ŏp′ə-zĭsh′ən) *n.* **1a.** The act of opposing or resisting. **b.** The condition of being in conflict; antagonism. **2.** Placement opposite to or in contrast with another. **3.** Something that serves as an obstacle. **4.** often **Opposition** A political party or an organized group opposed to the group, party, or government in power. **5.** *Astronomy* **a.** A configuration in which the earth lies on a straight line between the sun and a superior planet or the moon. **b.** The position of the superior planet or the moon in this configuration. **6.** *Logic* The relation existing between two propositions having an identical subject and predicate but differing in quantity, quality, or both. **7.** *Linguistics* Contrast in a language between two phonemes or other linguistically important elements. —**op′po·si′tion·al** *adj.*

op·po·si·tion·ist (ŏp′ə-zĭsh′ə-nĭst) *n.* A member of an opposition. —**op′po·si′tion·ist** *adj.*

op·press (ə-prĕs′) *tr.v.* **-pressed, -press·ing, -press·es** **1.** To keep down by severe and unjust use of force or authority. **2.** To weigh heavily on: *Poverty oppresses the spirit.* **3.** *Obsolete* To overwhelm or crush. [Ult. < Lat. *oppressus*, p. part. of *opprimere*, to press against : *ob-*, against; see OB– + *premere*, to press.] —**op·pres′sor** *n.*

op·pres·sion (ə-prĕsh′ən) *n.* **1a.** The act of oppressing; arbitrary and cruel exercise of power. **b.** The state of being oppressed. **2.** Something that oppresses. **3.** A feeling of being heavily weighed down in mind or body.

op·pres·sive (ə-prĕs′ĭv) *adj.* **1.** Difficult to bear; burdensome: *oppressive laws.* **2.** Exercising power arbitrarily and often unjustly; tyrannical. **3.** Weighing heavily on the senses or spirit. —**op·pres′sive·ly** *adv.* —**op·pres′sive·ness** *n.*

op·pro·bri·ous (ə-prō′brē-əs) *adj.* **1.** Expressing contemptuous reproach; scornful or abusive. **2.** Bringing disgrace; shameful or infamous. —**op·pro′bri·ous·ly** *adv.*

op·pro·bri·um (ə-prō′brē-əm) *n.* **1.** Disgrace arising from exceedingly shameful conduct; ignominy. **2.** Scornful reproach or contempt. **3.** A cause of shame or disgrace. [Lat. < *opprobrāre*, to reproach : *ob-*, against; see OB– + *probrum*, reproach; see **bher-**[1] in App.]

op·pugn (ə-pyoōn′) *tr.v.* **-pugned, -pugn·ing, -pugns** To oppose, contradict, or call into question. [ME *oppugnen* < Lat. *oppugnāre*, to attack : *ob-*, against; see OB– + *pugnāre*, to fight with the fist.] —**op·pugn′er** *n.*

op·sin (ŏp′sĭn) *n.* A protein of the retina, esp. the protein constituent of rhodopsin, that makes up one of the visual pigments. [Prob. back-formation < RHODOPSIN.]

–opsis *suff.* Something resembling a specified thing: *caryopsis.* [Gk., sight, seeing, like < *opsis*, sight, appearance. See **okʷ-** in App.]

op·so·nin (ŏp′sə-nĭn) *n.* An antibody or other protein in blood serum that causes bacteria or other foreign cells to become more susceptible to the action of phagocytes. [Lat. *opsōnāre*, to buy provisions (< Gk. *opsōnein* < *opson*, condiment, delicacy; see **epi** in App.) + –IN.] —**op·son′ic** (ŏp-sŏn′ĭk) *adj.*

op·so·nize (ŏp′sə-nīz′) *tr.v.* **-nized, -niz·ing, -niz·es** To make (bacteria or other cells) more susceptible to the action of phagocytes. [< OPSONIN.] —**op′so·ni·za′tion** (-nĭ-zā′shən) *n.*

–opsy *suff.* Examination: *biopsy.* [Gk. *–opsiā*, sight, seeing < *opsis.* See **okʷ-** in App.]

opt (ŏpt) *intr.v.* **opt·ed, opt·ing, opts** To make a choice or decision. —*phrasal verb:* **opt out** *Slang* To choose not to participate in something. [Fr. *opter* < OFr. < Lat. *optāre*.]

opt. *abbr.* **1.** optative **2.** optical **3.** optional

op·ta·tive (ŏp′tə-tĭv) *adj.* **1.** Expressing a wish or choice. **2.** *Grammar* **a.** Of, relating to, or being a mood of verbs in some languages, such as Greek, used to express a wish. **b.** Of, relating to, or being a statement using a verb in the subjunctive mood to indicate a wish or desire, as in *Were it possible, I would do it.* ❖ *n. Grammar* **1.** The optative mood. **2.** A verb or an expression in the optative mood. [ME *optatif* < OFr. < LLat. *optātīvus* < Lat. *optātus*, p. part. of *optāre*, to wish.] —**op′ta·tive·ly** *adv.*

op·tic (ŏp′tĭk) *adj.* **1.** Of or relating to the eye or vision. **2.** Of or relating to the science of optics or optical equipment. ❖ *n.* **1.** An eye. **2.** Any of the lenses, prisms, or mirrors of an optical instrument. [ME *optik* < OFr. < Med.Lat. *opticus* < Gk. *optikos* < *optos*, visible. See **okʷ-** in App.]

op·ti·cal (ŏp′tĭ-kəl) *adj.* **1.** Of or relating to sight; visual. **2.** Designed to assist sight. **3.** Of or relating to optics. **4.** Relating to or using visible light: *optical astronomy.* **5.** Using light-sensitive devices. —**op′ti·cal·ly** *adv.*

optical activity *n. Chemistry* A property caused by asymmetrical molecular structure that enables a substance to rotate the plane of incident polarized light.

optical art *n.* Op art.

optical character recognition *n.* The electronic identification and digital encoding of printed or handwritten characters by means of an optical scanner and specialized software.

optical disk or **optical disc** *n.* A plastic-coated disk that stores digital data, such as music or text, as tiny pits etched into the surface and is read with a laser. See Usage Note at **compact disk.**

optical fiber *n.* A flexible, optically transparent fiber, usu. glass or plastic, through which light can be transmitted by successive internal reflections.

optical illusion *n.* A visually perceived image that is deceptive or misleading.

optical isomer *n.* See **enantiomorph.**

optical scanner *n.* A device that converts printed images and text into digital information that can be stored as a computer file.

optic axis *n.* An optical path through a crystal along which a ray of light can pass without undergoing double refraction.

optic chiasma *n.* The partial intersection or crossing of the optic nerve fibers on the underside of the hypothalamus.

optic disk *n. Anatomy* See **blind spot** 1.

op·ti·cian (ŏp-tĭsh′ən) *n.* **1.** One that makes lenses and eyeglasses. **2.** One that sells lenses, eyeglasses, and other optical instruments.

optic nerve *n.* Either of the second pair of cranial nerves that carry visual information from the retina to the brain.

op·tics (ŏp′tĭks) *n. (used with a sing. verb)* The branch of physics that deals with visible light, vision, and usu. ultraviolet and infrared electromagnetic radiation.

op·ti·mal (ŏp′tə-məl) *adj.* Most favorable or desirable; optimum. —**op′ti·mal·ly** *adv.*

op·ti·mism (ŏp′tə-mĭz′əm) *n.* **1.** A tendency to expect the best possible outcome or dwell on the most hopeful aspects of a situation. **2.** *Philosophy* **a.** The doctrine, asserted by Leibnitz, that this world is the best of all possible worlds. **b.** The belief that the universe is improving and that good will ultimately triumph over evil. [Fr. *optimisme* < NLat. *optimum,* the greatest good. See OPTIMUM.]

op·ti·mist (ŏp′tə-mĭst) *n.* **1.** One who usu. expects a favorable outcome. **2.** A believer in philosophical optimism. —**op′ti·mis′tic** *adj.* —**op′ti·mis′ti·cal·ly** *adv.*

op·ti·mi·za·tion (ŏp′tə-mĭ-zā′shən) *n.* The procedure or procedures used to make a system or design most effective or functional, esp. the mathematical techniques involved.

op·ti·mize (ŏp′tə-mīz′) *tr.v.* **-mized, -miz·ing, -miz·es 1.** To make most perfect or effective. **2.** *Computer Science* To increase the computing speed and efficiency of (a program), as by rewriting instructions. **3.** To make the most of.

op·ti·mum (ŏp′tə-məm) *n., pl.* **-ma** (-mə) or **-mums 1.** The point at which the condition, degree, or amount of something is the most favorable. **2.** *Biology* The most favorable condition for growth and reproduction. ❖ *adj.* Most favorable or advantageous; best. [Lat., neut. sing. of *optimus,* best.]

op·tion (ŏp′shən) *n.* **1.** The act of choosing; choice. See Syns at **choice. 2.** The power or freedom to choose. **3a.** The exclusive right, usu. obtained for a fee, to buy or sell something within a specified time at a set price. **b.** The privilege of demanding fulfillment of a contract at a specified time. **c.** A stock option. **d.** The right of the holder of an insurance policy to specify how payments are to be made or credited to the policyholder. **e.** *Baseball* The right of a major-league team to transfer a player to a minor-league team while being able to recall the player within a specified period. **4.** Something chosen or available as a choice. **5.** An item or feature that may be chosen to replace or enhance standard equipment, as in a car. **6.** *Football* An offensive play in which a back can run with the ball or pass. ❖ *tr.v.* **-tioned, -tion·ing, -tions 1.** To acquire or grant an option on. **2.** *Baseball* To transfer (a major-league player) to a minor-league club on option. [Lat. *optiō, optiōn-.*]

op·tion·al (ŏp′shə-nəl) *adj.* Left to choice; not compulsory or automatic. —**op′tion·al·ly** *adv.*

op·to·e·lec·tron·ics (ŏp′tō-ĭ-lĕk′trŏn′ĭks, -ē′lĕk-) *n. (used with a sing. verb)* The branch of physics that deals with the interconversion of electricity and light. [Gk. *optos,* visible; see **ok**ʷ- in App. + ELECTRONICS.]

op·tom·e·trist (ŏp-tŏm′ĭ-trĭst) *n.* A person who is professionally trained and licensed to examine the eyes for visual defects, diagnose problems or impairments, and prescribe corrective lenses or provide other types of treatment.

op·tom·e·try (ŏp-tŏm′ĭ-trē) *n.* The practice or profession of an optometrist. [Gk. *optos,* visible; see **ok**ʷ- in App. + -METRY.] —**op′to·met′ric** (ŏp′tə-mĕt′rĭk), **op′to·met′ri·cal** *adj.*

op·u·lence (ŏp′yə-ləns) also **op·u·len·cy** (-lən-sē) *n.* **1.** Wealth; affluence. **2.** Great abundance; profusion.

op·u·lent (ŏp′yə-lənt) *adj.* **1.** Possessing or exhibiting great wealth; affluent. **2.** Characterized by rich abundance; luxuriant. [Lat. *opulentus.*] —**op′u·lent·ly** *adv.*

o·pun·ti·a (ō-pŭn′shē-ə, -shə) *n.* Any of various cacti of the genus *Opuntia,* esp. the prickly pear. [Lat. *(herba) Opūntia,* Opuntian (herb), after *Opūs, Opūnt-,* Opus, ancient town of E-

central Greece < Gk. *Opous, Opount-.*]

o·pus (ō′pəs) *n., pl.* **o·pe·ra** (ō′pər-ə, ŏp′ər-ə) or **o·pus·es** A creative work, esp. a musical piece numbered by its place in the order of a composer's works. [Lat.]

o·pus·cule (ō-pŭs′kyōōl) *n.* A small minor work. [Lat. *opusculum,* dim. of *opus,* work. See OPUS.]

O·pus De·i (ō′pəs dā′ē, dā′) *n.* A Roman Catholic organization composed of both clergy and lay members and dedicated to fostering Christian principles at all levels of society. [NLat. *Opus Deī,* work of God : Lat. *opus,* work + Lat. *Deī,* genitive of *Deus,* God.]

or[1] (ôr; ər *when unstressed*) *conj.* **1a.** Used to indicate an alternative, usu. only before the last term of a series: *this, that, or the other.* **b.** Used to indicate the second of two alternatives, the first being preceded by *either* or *whether: I didn't know whether to laugh or cry.* **c.** *Archaic* Used to indicate the first of two alternatives, with the force of *either* or *whether.* **2.** Used to indicate a synonymous or equivalent expression: *acrophobia, or fear of great heights.* **3.** Used to indicate uncertainty or indefiniteness: *two or three.* [ME < *other,* or (< OE < *oththe)* and < *outher* (< OE *āhwæther, āther;* see EITHER).]

USAGE NOTE When all the elements in a series connected by *or* are singular, the verb they govern is singular: *Beer, ale, or wine is included in the charge.* When all the elements are plural, the verb is plural. When the elements do not agree in number, some grammarians suggest that the verb should agree in number with the nearest element: *The girls or their brother is coming.* Other grammarians, however, argue that such constructions must be avoided and that substitutes be found in which the problem of agreement does not arise: *Either the girls are coming or their brother is.* See Usage Notes at **and/or, either, neither, nor**[1].

or[2] (ôr) *Archaic conj.* Before. Followed by *ever* or *ere: "I doubt he will be dead or ere I come"* (Shakespeare). ❖ *prep.* Before. [ME, var. of *er* < OE *ǣr,* soon, early, and < ON *ār.*]

or[3] (ôr) *n. Heraldry* Gold, represented in heraldic engraving by a white field with small dots. [ME < OFr. < Lat. *aurum.*]

OR[1] (ôr) *n.* A logical operator that returns a true value if one or both operators are true.

OR[2] *abbr.* **1.** operating room **2.** operations research **3.** Oregon **4.** owner's risk

-or[1] *suff.* One that performs a specified action: *accelerator.* [ME *-or, -our* < OFr. *-eor, -eur* and AN *-our, -ur,* all < Lat. *-or.*]

-or[2] *suff.* State; quality; activity: *valor.* [ME *-our* < OFr. *-eur* < Lat. *-or.*]

o·ra (ôr′ə, ōr′ə) *n.* Plural of **os**[1].

or·ach also **or·ache** (ôr′ĭch, -ĭj) *n.* Any of various plants of the genus *Atriplex,* esp. *A. hortensis,* having edible spinachlike leaves. [ME *orage, arage* < OFr. *arrache* < VLat. **ātripica* < Lat. *atriplex, ātriplic-* < Gk. *atraphaxus.*]

or·a·cle (ôr′ə-kəl, ŏr′-) *n.* **1a.** A shrine consecrated to the worship and consultation of a prophetic deity, as that of Apollo at Delphi. **b.** A person, such as a priestess, through whom a deity is held to respond when consulted. **c.** The response given through such a medium, often an enigmatic statement or allegory. **2a.** A person considered a source of wise counsel or prophetic opinions. **b.** An authoritative or wise statement or prediction. **3.** A command or revelation from God. **4.** In the Bible, the sanctuary of the Temple. [ME < OFr. < Lat. *ōrāculum* < *ōrāre,* to speak.]

o·rac·u·lar (ô-răk′yə-lər, ō-răk′-) *adj.* **1.** Of, relating to, or being an oracle. **2a.** Solemnly prophetic. **b.** Enigmatic; obscure. [< Lat. *ōrāculum,* oracle < *ōrāre,* to speak.] —**o·rac′u·lar′i·ty** (-lăr′ĭ-tē) *n.* —**o·rac′u·lar·ly** *adv.*

O·ra·dea (ô-räd′yä) A city of NW Romania near the Hungarian border; ceded to Romania by Hungary in 1919 and again after World War II. Pop. 221,559.

o·ral (ôr′əl, ōr′-) *adj.* **1.** Spoken rather than written. See Usage Note at **verbal. 2.** Of or relating to the mouth: *oral surgery.* **3.** Used in or taken through the mouth: *an oral vaccine.* **4.** Consisting of or using speech: *oral instruction.* **5.** *Linguistics* Articulated through the mouth only, with the nasal passages closed. **6.** *Psychology* In psychoanalytic theory, of or relating to the first stage of psychosexual development, during which the mouth is the chief focus of exploration and pleasure. ❖ *n.* An academic examination in which questions and answers are spoken rather than written. Often used in the plural. [LLat. *ōrālis* < Lat. *ōs, ōr-,* mouth. See **ōs-** in App.] —**o′ral·ly** *adv.*

O·ral (ôr′əl) or **U·ralsk** (yōō-rälsk′, ōō-rälsk′) A city of NW Kazakhstan on the Ural R.; founded c. 1622. Pop. 220,000.

oral contraceptive *n.* A pill, usu. containing estrogen or progesterone, that inhibits ovulation and prevents conception.

o·ral-for·mu·la·ic (ôr′əl-fôr′myə-lā′ĭk, ōr′-) *adj.* Of or relating to poetry in which traditional material is improvised at each performance by using verbal formulas to aid memory.

oral history *n.* **1.** Historical information, usu. tape-recorded or videotaped, obtained in interviews with persons having firsthand knowledge. **2.** An audiotape, videotape, or written account of such an interview or interviews.

oral sex *n.* Sexual activity involving oral stimulation of one's partner's sex organs.

O·ran (ō-rän′, ô-rän′) A city of NW Algeria on the **Gulf of Oran,**

opuntia
beavertail cactus
Opuntia basilaris

ă	pat	oi	boy
ā	pay	ou	out
âr	care	ōō	took
ä	father	ōō	boot
ĕ	pet	ŭ	cut
ē	be	ûr	urge
ĭ	pit	th	thin
ī	pie	th	this
îr	pier	hw	which
ŏ	pot	zh	vision
ō	toe	ə	about,
ô	paw		item

Stress marks:
′ (primary);
′ (secondary), as in
lexicon (lĕk′sĭ-kŏn′)

an inlet of the Mediterranean Sea WSW of Algiers; held by Vichy France during World War II. Pop. 490,788.

o·rang (ō-răng′, ô′răng) *n. Informal* An orangutan.

or·ange (ôr′ĭnj, ŏr′-) *n.* **1a.** Any of several southeast Asian evergreen trees of the genus *Citrus*, having fragrant white flowers and round fruit with a yellowish or reddish rind and a sectioned pulpy interior. **b.** The fruit of any of these trees, having a sweetish acidic juice. **2.** Any of several similar plants, such as the mock orange. **3.** The hue of that portion of the visible spectrum lying between red and yellow, with wavelengths of approx. 590 to 630 nanometers; any of a group of colors between red and yellow in hue, of medium lightness and moderate saturation. ❖ *adj.* **1.** Of the color orange. **2.** Made from oranges. **3.** Tasting or smelling like oranges. [ME < OFr. *pume orenge*, transl. and alteration (influenced by *Orenge*, Orange, a town in France) of OItal. *melarancio* : *mela*, fruit + *arancio*, orange tree (alteration of Ar. *nāranj* < Pers. *nārang* < Skt. *nāraṅgaḥ*, poss. of Dravidian orig.).] —**or′ang·y**, **or′ang·ey** (-ĭn-jē) *adj.*

orangutan
Pongo pygmaeus

WORD HISTORY Oranges originated in China, then were introduced to India, and traveled on to the Middle East, into Europe, and finally to the New World. The history of the word *orange* keeps step with this journey only part of the way. The word is possibly from Dravidian, a family of languages spoken in southern India and northern Sri Lanka. The Dravidian word or words were adopted into Sanskrit with the form *nāraṅgaḥ*. As the fruit passed westward, so did the word, as evidenced by Persian *nārang* and Arabic *nāranj*. The important word for the development of our term is Old Italian *melarancio*, derived from *mela*, "fruit," and *arancio*, "orange tree," from Arabic *nāranj*. Old Italian *melarancio* was translated into Old French as *pume orenge*, the *o* replacing the *a* because of the influence of the name of the town of Orange, from which oranges reached northern France. The final stage of the odyssey of the word was its borrowing into English from the Old French form *orenge*. Our word is first recorded in Middle English in a text probably composed around 1380.

Orange[1] Princely family of Europe ruling continuously in the Netherlands since 1815.

Orange[2] A city of S CA NNE of Santa Ana. Pop. 128,821.

or·ange·ade (ôr′ĭn-jād′, ŏr′-) *n.* A beverage of orange juice, sugar, and water.

Orange Free State A province and historical region of E-central South Africa, a Boer republic (1854–1900) later controlled by Great Britain as the **Orange River Colony** (1900–07). The renamed Orange Free State became a founding province of South Africa in 1910.

orange hawkweed *n.* A European perennial weed (*Hieracium aurantiacum*) with hairy leaves and orange-red flower heads.

Or·ange·man (ôr′ĭnj-mən, ŏr′-) *n.* **1.** A member of a secret society founded in Northern Ireland in 1795 to maintain the political and religious ascendancy of Protestantism. **2.** An Irish Protestant. [After William, Prince of ORANGE[1].]

orange pekoe *n.* A grade of black tea consisting of the end buds of the shoot or their surrounding two full leaves. [< the orange color of its infusion.]

Orange River A river of Lesotho, South Africa, and Namibia flowing c. 2,092 km (1,300 mi) to the Atlantic Ocean.

or·ange·ry (ôr′ĭnj-rē, ŏr′-) *n., pl.* **-ries** A sheltered place, esp. a greenhouse, used for growing orange trees in cool climates.

orange stick *n.* A stick of orangewood with tapered ends, used in manicuring.

or·ange·wood (ôr′ĭnj-wŏŏd′, ŏr′-) *n.* The fine-grained wood of the orange tree, used in fine woodwork.

o·rang·u·tan (ô-răng′ə-tăn′, ō-răng′-, ə-răng′-) *also* **o·rang·ou·tang** (-ə-tăng′) *n.* An arboreal anthropoid ape (*Pongo pygmaeus*) of Borneo and Sumatra having a shaggy reddish-brown coat, very long arms, and no tail. [Malay *orang hutan* : *orang*, man + *hutan*, wilderness, jungle.]

o·rate (ô-rāt′, ō-rāt′, ôr′āt′, ōr′-) *intr.v.* **o·rat·ed**, **o·rat·ing**, **o·rates** To speak in a formal, often pompous manner. [Lat. *ōrāre*, *ōrāt-*, to pray, speak publicly.]

o·ra·tion (ô-rā′shən, ō-rā′-) *n.* **1.** A formal speech, esp. one given on a ceremonial occasion. **2.** A speech delivered in a high-flown or pompous manner. [ME *oracion*, prayer < LLat. *ōrātiō*, *ōrātiōn-* < Lat., discourse < *ōrātus*, p. part. of *ōrāre*, to speak.]

o·ra·tor (ôr′ə-tər, ŏr′-) *n.* **1.** One who gives an oration. **2.** An eloquent and skilled public speaker. —**or′a·tor·ship′** *n.*

Or·a·to·ri·an (ôr′ə-tôr′ē-ən, -tōr′-, ŏr′-) *n. Roman Catholic Church* A member of an Oratory.

or·a·tor·i·cal (ôr′ə-tôr′ĭ-kəl, -tōr′-, ŏr′-) *adj.* Of or relating to oratory or an orator. —**or′a·tor′i·cal·ly** *adv.*

or·a·to·ri·o (ôr′ə-tôr′ē-ō′, -tōr′-, ŏr′-) *n., pl.* **-os** A musical composition for voices and orchestra, telling a sacred story without costumes, scenery, or dramatic action. [Ital., after *Oratorio*, the Oratory of St. Philip Neri at Rome, where famous musical services were held in the 16th cent.]

orchid
moth orchid

or·a·to·ry[1] (ôr′ə-tôr′ē, -tōr′-, ŏr′-) *n.* **1.** The art of public speaking. **2.** Eloquence or skill in making speeches to the public. **3.** Public speaking marked by the use of overblown rhetoric. [Lat. *(ars) ōrātōria*, (art) of speaking, fem. of *ōrātōrius*, oratorical < *ōrātor*, speaker < *ōrātus*, p. part. of *ōrāre*, to speak.]

or·a·to·ry[2] (ôr′ə-tôr′ē, -tōr′-, ŏr′-) *n., pl.* **-ries** **1.** A place for prayer, such as a chapel. **2.** *also* **Oratory a.** A Roman Catholic religious society of secular priests founded in 1575 by Saint Philip Neri. **b.** A branch or church of this society. [ME *oratorie* < OFr. < LLat. *ōrātōrium*, place of prayer < Lat., neut. of *ōrātōrius*, for praying < *ōrāre*, to pray.]

orb (ôrb) *n.* **1.** A sphere or spherical object. **2a.** A celestial body, such as the sun or moon. **b.** *Archaic* The earth. **3.** One of a series of concentric transparent spheres thought by ancient and medieval astronomers to revolve about the earth and carry the celestial bodies. **4.** A globe surmounted by a cross, used as a symbol of monarchial power and justice. **5.** An eye or eyeball. **6.** *Archaic* Something of circular form; a circle or orbit. **7.** *Archaic* A range of endeavor or activity; a province. ❖ *v.* **orbed**, **orb·ing**, **orbs** —*tr.* **1.** To shape into a circle or sphere. **2.** *Archaic* To encircle; enclose. —*intr. Archaic* To move in an orbit. [ME *orbe*, orbit < OFr. < Lat. *orbis*, circle, disk, orbit.]

or·bic·u·lar (ôr-bĭk′yə-lər) *adj.* Circular or spherical. [ME *orbiculer* < LLat. *orbiculāris* < Lat. *orbiculus*, dim. of *orbis*, circle, disk.] —**or·bic′u·lar′i·ty** (-lăr′ĭ-tē) *n.* —**or·bic′u·lar·ly** *adv.*

or·bic·u·late (ôr-bĭk′yə-lĭt, -lāt′) *also* **or·bic·u·lat·ed** (-lā′tĭd) *adj.* Orbicular. [Lat. *orbiculātus* < *orbiculus*, dim. of *orbis*, circle, disk.] —**or·bic′u·late·ly** *adv.*

Or·bi·son (ôr′bĭ-sən), Roy 1936–88. Amer. singer and songwriter noted for his smooth tenor voice and haunting ballads.

or·bit (ôr′bĭt) *n.* **1a.** The path of a celestial body or an artificial satellite as it revolves around another body. **b.** One complete revolution of such a body. **2.** The path of a body in a field of force surrounding another body; for example, the movement of an atomic electron in relation to a nucleus. **3a.** A range of activity, experience, or knowledge. **b.** A range of control or influence. **4.** Either of two bony cavities in the skull containing an eye and its external structures; an eye socket. ❖ *v.* **-bit·ed**, **-bit·ing**, **-bits** —*tr.* **1.** To put into an orbit. **2.** To revolve around (a center of attraction). —*intr.* To move in an orbit. [ME *orbite*, eye socket < OFr. < Lat. *orbita*, orbit, prob. < *orbis*.]

or·bi·tal (ôr′bĭ-tl) *adj.* Of or relating to an orbit. ❖ *n.* The wave function of an electron in an atom or molecule, indicating the electron's probable location.

or·bit·er (ôr′bĭ-tər) *n.* Something that orbits, esp. a spacecraft that orbits a planet or moon without landing on it.

or·ca (ôr′kə) *n.* See killer whale. [Lat. *ōrca*, whale, prob. alteration of Gk. *orux*, *orug-*, pickax, a kind of large fish or whale, perh. < *orussein*, to dig.]

orch. *abbr.* orchestra

or·chard (ôr′chərd) *n.* **1.** An area of land devoted to the cultivation of fruit or nut trees. **2.** The trees cultivated in such an area. [ME < OE *orceard*, alteration of *ortgeard* : perh. *wyrt*, *wort*, plant; see WORT[1] + *geard*, yard; see **gher-** in App.]

orchard grass *n.* A Eurasian grass (*Dactylis glomerata*) widely planted in pastures.

or·char·dist (ôr′chər-dĭst) *n.* One who owns or cultivates an orchard.

or·ches·tra (ôr′kĭ-strə, -kĕs′trə) *n.* **1.** *Music* **a.** A large group of musicians who play together on various instruments, usu. including strings, woodwinds, and brass and percussion instruments. **b.** The instruments played by such a group. **2.** The area in a theater or concert hall where the musicians sit, immediately in front of and below the stage. **3a.** The front section of seats nearest the stage in a theater. **b.** The entire main floor of a theater. **4.** A semicircular space in front of the stage used by the chorus in ancient Greek theaters. [Lat. *orchēstra*, space in front of the stage in Greek theaters where the chorus performed < Gk. *orkhēstra* < *orkheisthai*, to dance.] —**or·ches′tral** (ôr-kĕs′trəl) *adj.* —**or·ches′tral·ly** *adv.*

or·ches·trate (ôr′kĭ-strāt′) *tr.v.* **-trat·ed**, **-trat·ing**, **-trates** **1.** To compose or arrange (music) for performance by an orchestra. **2.** To arrange or control the elements of, as to achieve a desired overall effect. —**or′ches·tra′tor** *n.*

or·ches·tra·tion (ôr′kĭ-strā′shən) *n.* **1a.** A musical composition that has been orchestrated. **b.** Arrangement of music for performance by an orchestra. **2.** Arrangement or control.

or·chid (ôr′kĭd) *n.* **1a.** A member of the orchid family. **b.** The flower of any of these plants, esp. one cultivated for ornament. **2.** A pale to light purple, from grayish to purplish pink to strong reddish purple. [< NLat. *Orchideae*, former family name < NLat. *orchis*, *orchid-*, orchid < Lat. *orchis*, a kind of orchid < Gk. *orkhis*, testicle, orchid (< the shape of its tubers).] —**or′chid** *adj.*

or·chi·da·ceous (ôr′kĭ-dā′shəs) *adj.* **1.** Of, relating to, or characteristic of the orchid family. **2.** Suggesting ostentatious luxury; showy. [< NLat. *Orchidaceae*, family name < Lat. *orchis*, orchid. See ORCHID.]

orchid family *n.* A large family of epiphytic or terrestrial perennial herbs, the Orchidaceae, found chiefly in the tropics and subtropics and characterized by bilaterally symmetrical, showy flowers with an inferior ovary and dustlike seeds.

or·chi·ec·to·my (ôr′kē-ĕk′tə-mē) *or* **or·chi·dec·to·my** (-kĭ-dĕk′-) *n., pl.* **-mies** Surgical removal of one or both testes. [Gk. *orkhis*, *orkhi-*, testicle + -ECTOMY.]

or·chil (ôr′kĭl, -chĭl) *also* **ar·chil** (är′-) *n.* **1.** Any of several lichens, chiefly of the genera *Roccella* and *Lecanora,* from which a dye is obtained. **2.** The violet dyestuff obtained from any of these organisms. [ME *orchell,* ult. < O Catalan *orxella,* perh. of Mozarabic orig.]

or·chis (ôr′kĭs) *n.* Any of numerous orchids of the genus *Orchis,* having magenta, white, or magenta-spotted flowers. [Lat., orchid. See ORCHID.]

Or·cus (ôr′kəs) *n. Roman Mythology* **1.** The world of the dead; Hades. **2.** Pluto, the god of the underworld.

ord. *abbr.* **1.** order **2.** ordinal **3.** ordinance **4.** ordnance

or·dain (ôr-dān′) *tr.v.* **-dained, -dain·ing, -dains 1a.** To invest with ministerial or priestly authority; confer holy orders on. **b.** To authorize as a rabbi. **2.** To order by virtue of superior authority; decree or enact. **3.** To prearrange unalterably; predestine: *by fate ordained.* See Syns at **dictate.** [ME *ordeinen* < OFr. *ordener, ordein-* < Lat. *ōrdināre,* to organize, appoint to office < *ōrdō, ōrdin-,* order.] —**or·dain′er** *n.* —**or·dain′ment** *n.*

or·deal (ôr-dēl′) *n.* **1.** A difficult or painful experience, esp. one that severely tests character or endurance. **2.** A method of trial in which the accused is subjected to physically painful or dangerous tests, the result being regarded as a divine judgment of guilt or innocence. [Alteration (influenced by DEAL¹) of ME *ordal,* trial by ordeal < OE *ordāl.*]

or·der (ôr′dər) *n.* **1.** A condition of logical or comprehensible arrangement among the separate elements of a group. **2a.** A condition of methodical or prescribed arrangement among component parts such that proper functioning or appearance is achieved. **b.** Condition or state in general: *in good working order.* **3a.** The established system of social organization. **b.** A condition in which freedom from disorder or disruption is maintained through respect for established authority. **4.** A sequence or arrangement of successive things: *changed the order of the files.* **5.** The prescribed form or customary procedure: *the order of worship.* **6.** An authoritative indication to be obeyed; a command or direction. **7a.** A command given by a superior military officer requiring obedience, as in the execution of a task. **b. orders** Formal written instructions to report for military duty at a specified time and place. **8a.** A commission or instruction to buy, sell, or supply something. **b.** That which is supplied, bought, or sold. **9a.** A request made by a customer at a restaurant for a portion of food. **b.** The food requested. **10.** *Law* A direction or command delivered by a court or other adjudicative body and entered into the record but not necessarily included in the final judgment or verdict. **11.** *Ecclesiastical* **a.** Any of several grades of the Christian ministry: *the order of priesthood.* **b.** The rank of an ordained Christian minister or priest. Often used in the plural. **c.** The sacrament or rite of ordination. Often used in the plural. **12.** Any of the nine grades or choirs of angels. **13.** A group of persons living under a religious rule: *Order of Saint Benedict.* **14.** An organization of people united by a common fraternal bond or social aim. **15a.** A group of people upon whom a government or sovereign has formally conferred honor for unusual service or merit, entitling them to wear a special insignia: *the Order of the Garter.* **b.** The insignia worn by such people. **16.** A social class. Often used in the plural: *the lower orders.* **17.** A class defined by the common attributes of its members; a kind. **18.** Degree of quality or importance; rank: *poetry of a high order.* **19.** *Architecture* **a.** Any of several styles of classical architecture characterized by type of column and entablature employed. **b.** A style of building: *a cathedral of the Gothic order.* **20.** *Biology* A taxonomic category of organisms ranking above a family and below a class. See table at **taxonomy. 21.** *Mathematics* **a.** The sum of the exponents to which the variables in a term are raised; degree. **b.** The number of successive differentiations to be performed. **c.** The number of elements in a finite group. **d.** The number of rows or columns in a determinant or matrix. ❖ *v.* **-dered, -der·ing, -ders** —*tr.* **1.** To issue a command or instruction to. **2.** To give a command or instruction for: *ordered a recount of the ballots.* **3.** To direct to proceed as specified: *ordered them off the property.* **4.** To give an order for; request to be supplied with. **5.** To put into a methodical, systematic arrangement. See Syns at **arrange. 6.** To predestine; ordain. —*intr.* To give an order or orders; request that something be done or supplied. —*idioms:* **in order that** So that. **in order to** For the purpose of. **in short order** With no delay; quickly. **on order** Requested but not yet delivered. **on the order of 1.** Of a kind or fashion similar to; like. **2.** Approximately; about. **to order** According to the buyer's specifications. [ME *ordre* < OFr., var. of *ordene* < Lat. *ōrdō, ōrdin-.*] —**or′der·er** *n.*

order arms *n.* **1.** A position in the military manual of arms in which the rifle is held vertically by the right leg, its butt resting on the ground. **2.** A command to assume order arms.

or·der·ly (ôr′dər-lē) *adj.* **1a.** Free from disorder; neat. **b.** Having a systematic arrangement. **2.** Marked by or adhering to method or system. **3.** Devoid of violence or disruption; peaceful. ❖ *n., pl.* **-lies 1.** An attendant who does routine nonmedical work in a hospital. **2.** A soldier assigned to attend a superior officer. ❖ *adv.* Systematically; regularly. —**or′der·li·ness** *n.*

order of battle *n., pl.* **orders of battle** The identification, command structure, strength, and disposition of personnel, equipment, and units of an armed force.

order of business *n., pl.* **orders of business** A matter, such as

a task, that must be addressed.

order of magnitude *n., pl.* **orders of magnitude 1.** An estimate of size or magnitude expressed as a power of ten. **2.** A range of values between a designated lower value and an upper value ten times as large.

order of the day *n., pl.* **orders of the day 1.** The business to be considered or done by a legislature or other body on a particular day. Often used in the plural. **2.** The characteristic or most significant aspect or activity.

or·di·nal (ôr′dn-əl) *adj.* **1.** Being of a specified position in a numbered series: *an ordinal rank of seventh.* **2.** Of or relating to a taxonomic order. ❖ *n.* **1.** An ordinal number. **2.** *Ecclesiastical* **a.** A book of instructions for daily services. **b.** A book of forms for ordination. [ME *ordinel,* orderly, regular < LLat. *ōrdinālis,* ordinal < Lat. *ōrdō, ōrdin-,* order.]

ordinal number *n.* A number indicating position in a series or order, such as first (1st), second (2nd), and third (3rd).

or·di·nance (ôr′dn-əns) *n.* **1.** An authoritative command or order. **2.** A custom or practice established by long usage. **3.** A Christian rite, esp. the Eucharist. **4.** A statute or regulation, esp. one enacted by a city government. [ME *ordinaunce* < OFr. *ordenance* < Med.Lat. *ōrdinantia* < Lat. *ōrdināns, ōrdinant-,* pr. part. of *ōrdināre,* to ordain < *ōrdō, ōrdin-,* order.]

or·di·nand (ôr′dn-ănd) *n. Ecclesiastical* A person who is a candidate for ordination. [< Lat. *ōrdinandus,* gerundive of *ōrdināre,* to set in place, appoint. See ORDINATE.]

or·di·nar·i·ly (ôr′dn-âr′ə-lē, ôr′dn-ĕr′-) *adv.* **1.** As a general rule; usually. **2.** In the common or usual manner. **3.** To the usual extent or degree: *an ordinarily small profit.*

or·di·nar·y (ôr′dn-ĕr′ē) *adj.* **1.** Commonly encountered; usual. **2a.** Of no exceptional ability, degree, or quality; average. **b.** Of inferior quality; second-rate. **3.** Having immediate rather than delegated jurisdiction, as a judge. **4.** *Mathematics* Designating a differential equation containing no more than one independent variable. ❖ *n., pl.* **-ies 1.** The usual or normal condition or course of events. **2.** *Law* The judge of a probate court in some states of the United States. **3.** often **Ordinary** *Ecclesiastical* **a.** The part of the Mass that remains unchanged from day to day. **b.** A division of the Roman Breviary containing the unchangeable parts of the office other than the Psalms. **c.** A cleric, such as the residential bishop of a diocese, with ordinary jurisdiction over a specified territory. **4.** *Heraldry* One of the simplest and commonest charges, such as the bend and the cross. **5.** *Chiefly British* **a.** A complete meal provided at a fixed price. **b.** A tavern or an inn providing such a meal. [ME *ordinarie* < OFr. < Lat. *ōrdinārius* < *ōrdō, ōrdin-,* order.] —**or′di·nar′i·ness** *n.*

ordinary seaman *n.* A seaman of the lowest grade in the merchant marine.

or·di·nate (ôr′dn-ĭt, -āt′) *adj.* Arranged in regular rows, as the spots on the wings of an insect. ❖ *n. Symbol* **y** The plane Cartesian coordinate representing the distance from a specified point to the *x*-axis, measured parallel to the *y*-axis. [ME, properly ordered < Lat. *ōrdinātus,* p. part. of *ōrdināre,* to set in order < *ōrdō, ōrdin-,* order.]

or·di·na·tion (ôr′dn-ā′shən) *n.* **1.** The act of ordaining or the state of being ordained. **2.** *Ecclesiastical* The ceremony of consecration to the ministry. **3.** An arrangement or ordering.

ordn. *abbr.* ordnance

ord·nance (ôrd′nəns) *n.* **1.** Military materiel, such as weapons, ammunition, combat vehicles, and equipment. **2.** The branch of an armed force that procures, maintains, and issues such materiel. **3.** Cannon; artillery. [ME *ordnaunce,* var. of *ordinaunce,* order, military provision. See ORDINANCE.]

or·do (ôr′dō) *n., pl.* **-di·nes** (-də-nēz′) or **-dos** *Roman Catholic Church* An annual calendar containing instructions for the Mass and office to be celebrated on each day of the year. [Med.Lat. *ōrdō* < Lat., order.]

or·don·nance (ôr′dn-əns, ôr′dô-näns′) *n.* The arrangement of elements in a literary or artistic work or an architectural plan. [Fr., var. of OFr. *ordenance,* an arranging. See ORDINANCE.]

Or·do·vi·cian (ôr′də-vĭsh′ən) *adj.* Of or belonging to the geologic time of the second period of the Paleozoic Era, marked by the appearance of primitive fishes. See table at **geologic time.** ❖ *n.* The Ordovician Period or its deposits. [< Lat. *Ordovicēs,* an ancient Celtic tribe of Wales < Celt. *Ordovices.*]

or·dure (ôr′jər) *n.* **1.** Excrement; dung. **2.** Something morally offensive; filth. [ME < OFr. < *ord,* filthy < Lat. *horridus,* frightful < *horrēre,* to shudder.]

Or·dzho·ni·kid·ze (ôr′jŏn-ĭ-kĭd′zə, ər-jə-nyĭ-kyē′dzĭ) See **Vladikavkaz.**

ore (ôr, ōr) *n.* A mineral or an aggregate of minerals from which a valuable constituent, esp. a metal, can be profitably mined or extracted. [ME < OE *ōra* and < OE *ār,* brass, copper, bronze.]

Ore. *abbr.* Oregon

o·re·ad (ôr′ē-ăd′, ōr′-) *n. Greek Mythology* Any of a group of mountain nymphs. [Lat. *Orēas, Orēad-* < Gk. *Oreias* < *oreios,* of mountains < *oros,* mountain.]

Ör·e·bro (œ′rə-brŏŏ′) A city of S-central Sweden W of Stockholm. Pop. 123,188.

o·reg·a·no (ə-rĕg′ə-nō′, ô-rĕg′-) *n.* A perennial Eurasian herb (*Origanum vulgare*) of the mint family, having aromatic leaves used as a seasoning. [Sp. *orégano*, wild marjoram < Lat. *orīganum* < Gk. *orīganon*, prob. of N African orig.]

Or•e•gon (ôr′ĭ-gən, -gŏn′, ôr′-) A state of the NW US in the Pacific Northwest; admitted as the 33rd state in 1859. The **Oregon Country**, a region stretching from AK to CA and the Pacific Ocean to the Rocky Mts., was held jointly by Great Britain and the US from 1818 until 1846. In 1848 the **Oregon Territory** was created, including present-day WA and ID. Cap. Salem. Pop. 3,421,399. —**Or′e•go′ni•an** (-gō′nē-ən) *adj. & n.*

Oregon grape *n.* Any of various evergreen shrubs of the genus *Mahonia,* esp. *M. aquifolium* of northwest North America, having compound leaves and black berries with blue bloom.

Oregon Trail A historical overland route to the W US extending from various cities on the Missouri R. to the Pacific Northwest; opened in 1842 and abandoned in the 1870s.

O•rel (ô-rěl′, ō-rěl′, ôr-yôl′) A city of W Russia on the Oka R. S of Moscow; founded 1564. Pop. 342,846.

O•rem (ôr′əm, ōr′-) A city of N-central UT NNW of Provo. Pop. 84,324.

O•ren•burg (ôr′ən-bûrg′, ōr′-, ə-rĭn-bōōrk′) Formerly (1938–57) **Chka•lov** (chə-kä′ləf, chkä′-) A city of W Russia on the Ural R.; founded as a fortress in 1735. Pop. 554,144.

or•e•o•dont (ôr′ē-ə-dŏnt′) *n.* Any of various extinct sheep-sized ruminant artiodactyls of the family Merycoidodontidae, widespread during part of the Tertiary in North America. [< NLat. *Oreodōn,* type genus : Gk. *oros, ore-,* mountain + Gk. *-odōn, -odont-,* -odont.]

O•res•tes (ô-rěs′tēz) *n. Greek Mythology* The son of Agamemnon and Clytemnestra, who with his sister Electra avenged the murder of his father by killing his mother and her lover.

O•re•sund or **Ø•re•sund** (œ′rə-sŭn′, -sōōnd′) A narrow strait between S Sweden and E Denmark connecting the Baltic Sea with the Kattegat.

Orff (ôrf), **Carl** 1895–1982. German composer and educator who developed a system of music instruction for children.

or•fray (ôr′frā′) *n.* Variant of **orphrey.**

org. *abbr.* **1.** organic **2a.** organization **b.** organized

or•gan (ôr′gən) *n.* **1.** *Music* **a.** An instrument consisting of a number of pipes that sound tones when supplied with air and a keyboard that operates a mechanism controlling the flow of air to the pipes. **b.** Any of various other instruments that resemble a pipe organ in mechanism or sound. **2.** *Biology* A differentiated part of an organism, such as an eye or leaf, with a specific function. **3.** An instrument or agency dedicated to the performance of specified functions. **4.** An instrument or means of communication, esp. a periodical issued by a political party, business firm, or other group. [ME < OFr. *organe* and < OE *organe,* both < Lat. *organum,* tool, instrument < Gk. *organon.* See **werg-** in App.]

organ– *pref.* Variant of **organo–.**

or•ga•na[1] (ôr′gə-nə) *n.* A plural of **organon.**

or•ga•na[2] (ôr′gə-nə) *n.* A plural of **organum**[1].

or•gan•dy also **or•gan•die** (ôr′gən-dē) *n., pl.* **-dies** A stiff transparent fabric of cotton or silk, used for trim, curtains, and light apparel. [Fr. *organdi,* perh. after OFr. *Organzi* (Urganch), a city of W Uzbekistan.]

or•gan•elle (ôr′gə-něl′) *n.* A differentiated structure within a cell, such as a mitochondrion, that performs a specific function. [NLat. *organella,* dim. of Med.Lat. *organum,* organ of the body < Lat., implement, tool. See ORGAN.]

organ

organ grinder *n.* A musician who plays a hurdy-gurdy and usu. performs on the street.

or•gan•ic (ôr-găn′ĭk) *adj.* **1.** Of, relating to, or derived from living organisms. **2.** Of, relating to, or affecting a bodily organ. **3a.** Of, marked by, or involving the use of fertilizers or pesticides that are strictly of animal or vegetable origin: *organic gardening.* **b.** Raised or conducted without the use of drugs, hormones, or synthetic chemicals: *organic chicken.* **c.** Serving organic food: *an organic restaurant.* **d.** Simple, healthful, and close to nature: *an organic lifestyle.* **4a.** Having properties associated with living organisms. **b.** Resembling a living organism in organization or development; interconnected. **5.** Constituting an integral part of a whole; fundamental. **6.** *Law* Relating to or being the fundamental or constitutional laws and precepts of a government or organization. **7.** *Chemistry* Of or being carbon compounds. ❖ *n.* **1.** A substance, esp. a fertilizer, of animal or vegetable origin. **2.** *Chemistry* An organic compound. —**or•gan′i•cal•ly** *adv.* —**or′gan•ic′i•ty** (ôr′gə-nĭs′ĭ-tē) *n.*

organic chemistry *n.* The chemistry of carbon compounds.

or•gan•i•cism (ôr-găn′ĭ-sĭz′əm) *n.* **1.** The concept that society is analogous to a biological organism. **2.** The doctrine that the total organization of an organism, rather than the functioning of individual organs, is the principal or exclusive determinant of every life process. **3.** The theory that all disease is associated with structural alterations of organs. —**or•gan′i•cist** *n.*

or•gan•ism (ôr′gə-nĭz′əm) *n.* **1.** A body made up of organs, organelles, or other parts that work together to carry on the various processes of life; an individual form of life. **2.** A system regarded as analogous in its structure or functions to a living body: *the social organism.* —**or′gan•is′mal** (-nĭz′məl), **or′gan•is′mic** (-mĭk) *adj.* —**or′gan•is′mi•cal•ly** *adv.*

or•gan•ist (ôr′gə-nĭst) *n.* A musician who plays the organ.

organ-pipe cactus
Lemaireocereus marginatus

or•gan•i•za•tion (ôr′gə-nĭ-zā′shən) *n.* **1a.** The act or process of organizing. **b.** The state or manner of being organized. **2.** Something that has been organized or made into an ordered whole. **3.** Something made up of elements with varied functions that contribute to the whole and to collective functions; an organism. **4.** A group of persons organized for a particular purpose; an association. **5a.** A structure through which individuals cooperate systematically to conduct business. **b.** The administrative personnel of such a structure. —**or′gan•i•za′tion•al** *adj.* —**or′gan•i•za′tion•al•ly** *adv.*

or•gan•ize (ôr′gə-nīz′) *v.* **-ized, -iz•ing, -iz•es** —*tr.* **1.** To put together into an orderly, functional, structured whole. **2a.** To arrange in a coherent form; systematize: *organized her thoughts.* **b.** To arrange in a desired pattern or structure. **3.** To arrange systematically for harmonious or united action: *organize a strike.* See Syns at **arrange.** **4a.** To establish as an organization. See Syns at **found**[1]. **b.** To induce (employees) to form or join a labor union. **c.** To induce the employees of (a business or industry) to form or join a union. —*intr.* **1.** To develop into or assume an organic structure. **2.** To form or join an activist group, esp. a labor union. [ME *organisen* < OFr. *organiser* < Med.Lat. *organizāre* < Lat. *organum,* tool, instrument. See ORGAN.] —**or′gan•iz′er** *n.*

or•gan•ized (ôr′gə-nīzd′) *adj.* **1.** Functioning within a formal structure, as in the coordination of activities. **2.** Affiliated in an organization, esp. a union. **3.** Efficient and methodical.

organized crime *n.* **1.** Widespread criminal activities that occur within a centrally controlled structure. **2.** The people and the groups involved in such criminal activities.

organo– or **organ–** *pref.* **1.** Organ: *organogenesis.* **2.** Organic: *organometallic.* [Gk. < *organon.* See ORGAN.]

or•gan•o•chlo•rine (ôr-găn′ə-klôr′ēn′, -ĭn, -klōr′-) *n.* Any of various hydrocarbon pesticides, such as DDT, that contain chlorine. —**or•gan•o•chlo′rine** *adj.*

organ of Cor•ti (kôr′tē) *n.* A structure in the cochlea containing hair cells that transmit sound vibrations to the nerve fibers. [After Alfonso *Corti* (1822–88), Italian anatomist.]

or•gan•o•gen•e•sis (ôr′gə-nō-jěn′ĭ-sĭs, ôr-găn′ə-) *n., pl.* **-ses** (-sēz′) The formation and development of the organs of living things. —**or′gan•o•ge•net′ic** (-jə-nět′ĭk) *adj.* —**or′gan•o•ge•net′i•cal•ly** *adv.*

or•gan•o•lep•tic (ôr′gə-nō-lěp′tĭk, ôr-găn′ə-) *adj.* **1.** Relating to perception by a sensory organ. **2.** Involving the use of sense organs. [Fr. *organoleptique* : Gk. *organo-,* organo- + Gk. *lēptikos,* receptive (< *lēptos,* taken, seized < *lambanein, lēp-,* to take).] —**or′gan•o•lep′ti•cal•ly** *adv.*

or•gan•ol•o•gy (ôr′gə-nŏl′ə-jē) *n.* The branch of biology that deals with the structure and function of organs. —**or′gan•o•log′ic** (ôr′gə-nə-lŏj′ĭk, ôr-găn′ə-), **or′gan•o•log′i•cal** (-ĭ-kəl) *adj.*

or•gan•o•me•tal•lic (ôr′gə-nō-mə-tăl′ĭk, ôr-găn′ō-) *adj.* Of, relating to, or being an organic compound containing a metal, esp. one in which a metal atom is bonded to a carbon atom.

or•ga•non (ôr′gə-nŏn′) also **or•ga•num** (-nəm) *n., pl.* **-na** (-nə) or **-nons** also **-na** or **-nums** A set of principles for use in scientific or philosophical investigation. [Gk., tool, organ of the body, instrument. See **werg-** in App.]

or•gan•o•phos•phate (ôr′gə-nō-fŏs′fāt, ôr-găn′ə-) *n.* Any of several organic compounds containing phosphorus, some of which are used as fertilizers and pesticides.

or•gan•o•phos•pho•rus (ôr′gə-nō-fŏs′fər-əs, -fŏs-fôr′əs, -fōr′-, ôr-găn′ə-) *n.* An organophosphate.

or•gan•ot•ro•pism (ôr′gə-nŏt′rə-pĭz′əm) also **or•gan•ot•ro•py** (-pē) *n.* The attraction of certain chemical compounds or microorganisms to specific tissues or organs of the body. —**or′gan•o•trop′ic** (ôr′gə-nō-trŏp′ĭk, -trō′pĭk, ôr-găn′ō-) *adj.* —**or′gan•o•trop′i•cal•ly** *adv.*

or•gan-pipe cactus (ôr′gən-pīp′) *n.* A tall treelike cactus (*Lemaireocereus marginatus*) native to central Mexico and the southwest United States.

organ point *n.* See **pedal point.**

or•ga•num[1] (ôr′gə-nəm) *n., pl.* **-na** (-nə) or **-nums** Any of several types of medieval vocal polyphony, usu. based on Gregorian chant. [Med.Lat. < LLat., church organ < Lat., instrument. See ORGAN.]

or•ga•num[2] (ôr′gə-nəm) *n., pl.* **-nums** Variant of **organon.**

or•gan•za (ôr-găn′zə) *n.* A sheer stiff fabric of silk or synthetic material used for trimming, neckwear, or evening dresses. [Probably after *Organzi* (Urganch), a city of W Uzbekistan.]

or•gan•zine (ôr′gən-zēn′) *n.* A raw-silk thread, usu. used as a warp thread. [Fr. *organsin* < Ital. *organzino,* probably after *Organzi* (Urgench), a city of W Uzbekistan.]

or•gasm (ôr′găz′əm) *n.* **1.** The peak of sexual excitement, characterized by involuntary contractions of the genital muscles and usu. accompanied by ejaculation of semen by the male. **2.** A similar point of intense emotional excitement. ❖ *intr.v.* **or•gasmed** (-găz′əmd), **or•gasm•ing** (-găz′ə-mĭng), **or•gasms** (-găz′əmz) To experience an orgasm. [Fr. *orgasme* or NLat. *orgasmus,* both < Gk. *orgasmos,* swelling, excitement < *organ,* to swell up, be excited.] —**or•gas′mic** (ôr-găz′mĭk), **or•gas′tic** (-tĭk) *adj.* —**or•gas′mi•cal•ly, or•gas′ti•cal•ly** *adv.*

or•geat (ôr′zhä′) *n.* A sweet flavoring of orange and almond used in cocktails and food. [Fr. < OFr. < O Provençal *orjat* < *ordj, orge*, barley < Lat. *hordeum*.]

or•gi•as•tic (ôr′jē-ăs′tĭk) *adj.* **1.** Of, relating to, or characteristic of an orgy. **2.** Arousing or causing unrestrained emotion; frenzied. [Gk. *orgiastikos* < *orgiastēs*, celebrant of orgies < *orgiazein*, to celebrate orgies < *orgia*, orgies. See ORGY.] **—or′gi•ast′** *n.* **—or′gi•as′ti•cal•ly** *adv.*

or•gone (ôr′gōn) *n.* A theoretical universal life force emanating from all organic material that purportedly can be used to restore psychological well-being. [Prob. ORG(ANISM) + –ONE.]

or•gy (ôr′jē) *n., pl.* **-gies 1.** A revel involving unrestrained indulgence, esp. in sexual activity. **2.** Uncontrolled or immoderate indulgence in an activity. See Syns at **binge. 3.** A secret rite in the cults of ancient Greek or Roman deities, typically involving frenzied singing, dancing, drinking, and sexual activity. [< *orgies*, secret rites < OFr. < Lat. *orgia* < Gk. See **werg-** in App.]

or•i•bi (ôr′ə-bē, ŏr′-) *n., pl.* **oribi** or **-bis** A small brownish African antelope *(Ourebia ourebia)* having long legs, short horns, and a short tail. [Afr. < Khoikhoin *arab* : *ara*, to provide with stripes + *-b*, masc. n. suff.]

o•ri•el (ôr′ē-əl, ōr′-) *n.* A bay window projecting from an upper floor, supported from below with a corbel or bracket. [ME < OFr. *oriol*, porch < Med.Lat. *oriolum*.]

o•ri•ent (ôr′ē-ənt, -ĕnt′, ōr′-) *n.* **1. Orient** The countries of Asia, esp. of eastern Asia. **2a.** The luster characteristic of a pearl of high quality. **b.** A pearl having exceptional luster. **3.** *Archaic* The place on the horizon where the sun rises; the east. ❖ *adj.* **1.** Having exceptional luster: *orient gemstones.* **2.** *Archaic* Eastern; oriental. **3.** *Archaic* Rising in the sky; ascending. ❖ *v.* (ôr′ē-ĕnt′, ōr′-) **-ent•ed, -ent•ing, -ents** *—tr.* **1.** To locate or place in a particular relation to the points of the compass: *orient the swimming pool north and south.* **2a.** To locate or position so as to face the east. **b.** To build (a church) with the nave laid out in an east-west direction and the main altar usu. at the eastern end. **3.** To align or position with respect to a point or system of reference: *oriented the telescope toward the moon; oriented her interests toward health care.* **4.** To determine the bearings of. **5.** To make familiar with or adjusted to facts, principles, or a situation. **6.** To focus (a story or film, for example) toward the interests of a specific group. *—intr.* **1.** To turn toward the east. **2.** To become adjusted or aligned. [ME < OFr. < Lat. *oriēns, orient-*, rising sun, east < pr. part. of *orīrī*, to arise, be born. See **er-** in App.]

o•ri•en•tal (ôr′ē-ĕn′tl, ōr′-) *adj.* **1.** often **Oriental** Of or relating to the countries of the Orient or their peoples or cultures; eastern. **2. Oriental** Of, relating to or being the biogeographic region that includes Asia south of the Himalaya Mountains and the islands of the Malay Archipelago. **3.** Lustrous and valuable: *oriental pearls.* **4a.** Of or relating to a genuine or superior gem: *an oriental ruby.* **b.** Relating to or being corundum that resembles another stone in color. ❖ *n.* often **Oriental** *Often Offensive* An Asian. **—o′ri•en′tal•ly** *adv.*

USAGE NOTE *Asian* is now strongly preferred in place of *Oriental* for persons native to Asia or descended from an Asian people. *Oriental*, when used as a noun in contemporary contexts (as in *the first Oriental to be elected from the district*), is now widely taken to be offensive. However, it should not be thought of as an ethnic slur to be avoided in all situations. As with *Asiatic*, its use other than as an ethnonym, in phrases such as *Oriental cuisine* or *Oriental medicine*, is not usually considered objectionable.

Oriental black mushroom *n.* See **shiitake.**

Oriental garlic *n.* See **Chinese chive.**

O•ri•en•tal•ism also **o•ri•en•tal•ism** (ôr′ē-ĕn′tl-ĭz′əm, ōr′-) *n.* **1.** A quality, mannerism, or custom specific to or characteristic of the Orient. **2.** Scholarly knowledge of Asian cultures, languages, and peoples. **—O′ri•en′tal•ist** *adj. & n.*

o•ri•en•tal•ize also **O•ri•en•tal•ize** (ôr′ē-ĕn′tl-īz′, ōr′-) *v.* **-ized, -iz•ing, -iz•es** *—tr.* To give an oriental character or appearance to. *—intr.* To become oriental in character.

Oriental poppy *n.* A southwest Asian plant *(Papaver orientale)* widely cultivated for its brilliant scarlet and black flowers.

Oriental radish *n.* See **daikon.**

Oriental rug *n.* A rug made of wool that is knotted or woven by hand, produced in the Middle East and in many other parts of Asia.

o•ri•en•tate (ôr′ē-ĕn-tāt′, -ən-, ōr′-) *v.* **-tat•ed, -tat•ing, -tates** *—tr.* To orient. *—intr.* To face or turn to the east.

o•ri•en•ta•tion (ôr′ē-ĕn-tā′shən, -ən-, ōr′-) *n.* **1.** The act of orienting or the state of being oriented. **2.** Location or position relative to the compass points. **3.** The orienting of a church. **4.** The direction followed in the course of a trend, movement, or development. **5.** A tendency of thought; a general inclination. **6.** Sexual orientation. **7a.** An adjustment or adaptation to a new situation or set of ideas. **b.** Introductory instruction concerning a new situation. **8.** *Psychology* Awareness of the objective world in relation to one's self.

o•ri•en•teer•ing (ôr′ē-ĕn-tîr′ĭng, -ən-, ōr′-) *n. Sports* A cross-country contest in which competitors use a map and compass to find their way through unfamiliar territory. [Alteration of Swed. *orientering* < *orientera*, to orient < Fr. *orienter* < *orient*, east. See ORIENT.] **—o′ri•en•teer′** *n.*

or•i•fice (ôr′ə-fĭs, ŏr′-) *n.* An opening, esp. to a body cavity; a mouth or vent. [ME < OFr. < LLat. *ōrificium* : Lat. *ōs, ōr-*, mouth; see **ōs-** in App. + Lat. *-ficium*, a making, doing (< *facere*, to make; see **dhē-** in App.).] **—or′i•fi′cial** (-fĭsh′əl) *adj.*

or•i•flamme (ôr′ə-flăm′, ŏr′-) *n.* **1.** An inspiring standard or symbol. **2.** The red or orange-red flag of the Abbey of Saint Denis in France, used as a standard by the early French kings. [ME *oriflamble*, banner of St. Denis < OFr., var. of *oriflambe*, poss. < Med.Lat. *aurea flamma, auriflamma* (Lat. *aurea*, fem. of *aureus*, golden < *aurum*, gold + Lat. *flamma*; see FLAME) or alteration of OFr. **lorie flambe* (< LLat. *laurea flammula*, laureled standard : Lat. *laurea*, fem. of *laureus*, of laurel; see LAUREATE + Lat. *flammula*, banner, dim. of *flamma*, flame).]

o•ri•ga•mi (ôr′ĭ-gä′mē) *n., pl.* **-mis 1.** The Japanese art of folding paper into shapes representing animals, for example. **2.** A decorative object made by folding paper. [J. : *ori*, to fold + *kami*, paper.]

Or•i•gen (ôr′ĭ-jĕn′, -jən, ŏr′-) A.D. 185?–254? Greek philosopher and theologian who reinterpreted Christian doctrine through Neo-Platonist philosophy.

or•i•gin (ôr′ə-jĭn, ŏr′-) *n.* **1.** The point at which something comes into existence or from which it derives or is derived. **2.** Ancestry; national, ethnic, racial, religious, or class background. **3.** The fact of originating; rise or derivation: *The rumor had its origin in an impulsive remark.* **4.** *Anatomy* The point of attachment of a muscle that remains relatively fixed during contraction. **5.** *Mathematics* The point of intersection of axes in a coordinate system. [ME *origine*, ancestry < Lat. *orīgō, orīgin-* < *orīrī*, to arise, be born. See **er-** in App.]

SYNONYMS *origin, source, root* These nouns signify the point at which something originates. *Origin* is the point at which something comes into existence: *The origins of some words are unknown. Source* signifies the point at which something springs into being or from which it derives or is obtained: *"The mysterious . . . is the source of all true art and science"* (Albert Einstein). *Root* often denotes what is considered the fundamental cause of or basic reason for something: *"Lack of money is the root of all evil"* (George Bernard Shaw).

o•rig•i•nal (ə-rĭj′ə-nəl) *adj.* **1.** Preceding all others in time; first. **2a.** Not derived from something else; fresh and unusual: *an original play, not an adaptation.* **b.** Showing a marked departure from previous practice; new. See Syns at **new. 3.** Productive of new things or ideas; inventive. **4.** Being the source from which a copy, reproduction, or translation is made. ❖ *n.* **1.** A first form from which other forms are made or developed. **2a.** An authentic work of art. **b.** Work that has been composed firsthand. **3.** A person who is appealingly odd or curious; a character. **4.** *Archaic* The source from which something arises; an originator. [ME < OFr. < Lat. *orīginālis* < *orīgō, orīgin-*, source. See ORIGIN.]

o•rig•i•nal•ism (ə-rĭj′ə-nə-lĭz′əm) *n.* The belief that the US Constitution should be interpreted as intended by those who composed and adopted it. **—o•rig′i•nal•ist** *adj. & n.*

o•rig•i•nal•i•ty (ə-rĭj′ə-năl′ĭ-tē) *n., pl.* **-ties 1.** The quality of being original. **2.** The capacity to act or think independently. **3.** Something original.

o•rig•i•nal•ly (ə-rĭj′ə-nə-lē) *adv.* **1.** With reference to origin: *originally named Johnston.* **2.** At first: *not what I had originally expected.* **3.** In a highly distinctive manner.

original sin *n. Christianity* The condition of sin that marks people as a result of Adam's first act of disobedience.

o•rig•i•nate (ə-rĭj′ə-nāt′) *v.* **-nat•ed, -nat•ing, -nates** *—tr.* To bring into being; create. *—intr.* To come into being; start. See Syns at **stem**[1]. **—o•rig′i•na′tion** *n.* **—o•rig′i•na′tive** *adj.* **—o•rig′i•na′tive•ly** *adv.* **—o•rig′i•na′tor** *n.*

origination fee *n.* A fee charged by a lender to a borrower on initiation of the loan.

o•ri•na•sal (ôr′ə-nā′zəl, ōr′-) *adj.* Pronounced with both nasal and oral passages open. ❖ *n.* An orinasal speech sound, such as a French nasal vowel. [Lat. *ōs, ōr-*, mouth; see **ōs-** in App. + NASAL.]

O-ring (ō′rĭng′) *n.* A flat ring made of rubber or plastic, used as a gasket.

O•ri•no•co (ôr′ə-nō′kō, ōr′-) A river of Venezuela flowing more than 2,414 km (1,500 mi) to the Atlantic Ocean.

o•ri•ole (ôr′ē-ōl′, ōr′-) *n.* **1.** Any of various Old World passerine birds of the family Oriolidae, of which the males are characteristically black and bright yellow or orange. **2.** Any of various similar New World birds of the family Icteridae. [Obsolete Fr. *oriol* < OFr. < Lat. *aureolus*, dim. of *aureus*, golden < *aurum*, gold.]

O•ri•on (ō-rī′ən, ə-rī′-) *n.* **1.** *Greek Mythology* A giant hunter, pursuer of the Pleiades and lover of Eos, who was killed by Artemis. **2.** A constellation in the region of the celestial equator near Gemini and Taurus. [ME *Orioun* < Lat. *Ōrīōn* < Gk.]

or•i•son (ôr′ĭ-sən, -zən, ŏr′-) *n.* A prayer. [ME *orisoun* < OFr. *orison* < LLat. *ōrātiō, ōrātiōn-*. See ORATION.]

O•ri•ya (ô-rē′yə) *n.* The Indic language of Orissa, a state in eastern India.

O•ri•za•ba (ôr′ĭ-zä′bə, ō′rē-sä′vä), **Mount** See **Citlaltépetl.**

Ork•ney Islands (ôrk′nē) An archipelago comprising c. 70 islands in the Atlantic Ocean and the North Sea off the NE coast of Scotland; orig. settled by Picts.

oriel

origami
origami cranes

ă	pat	oi	boy
ā	pay	ou	out
âr	care	o͝o	took
ä	father	o͞o	boot
ĕ	pet	ŭ	cut
ē	be	ûr	urge
ĭ	pit	th	thin
ī	pie	*th*	this
îr	pier	hw	which
ŏ	pot	zh	vision
ō	toe	ə	about, item
ô	paw		

Stress marks:
′ (primary);
′ (secondary), as in
lexicon (lĕk′sĭ-kŏn′)

Or·lan·do (ôr-lăn′dō) A city of central FL ENE of Tampa. Pop. 185,951.

Or·lan·do (ôr-lăn′dō, -län′-), **Vittorio Emanuele** 1860–1952. Italian prime minister (1917–19).

Or·lé·a·nais (ôr′lē-ə-nā′, ôr-lā-ä-nĕ′) A historical region and former province of N-central France; part of the royal domain since the 10th cent.

Or·le·an·ist (ôr′lē-ə-nĭst) n. A supporter of the Orléans branch of the French royal family, descended from a younger brother of Louis XIV.

Or·lé·ans (ôr-lā-än′) A city of N-central France on the Loire R. SSW of Paris; center of the Frankish kingdom of **Orléans**. The siege of Orléans by the English (1428–29) was lifted by troops led by Joan of Arc. Pop. 105,099.

Or·lon (ôr′lŏn′) A trademark used for an acrylic fiber or yarns made from this fiber.

or·lop (ôr′lŏp′) n. The lowest deck of a ship, esp. a warship, having at least four decks. [ME overlop, floor covering a ship's hold < MLGer. overlop : over, over; see **uper** in App. + lōp, a running.]

Or·mazd also **Or·muzd** (ôr′məzd, ôr-mŭzd′) n. Variants of **Ohrmazd**. [Pers. Hormazd < MPers. Ohrmazd. See OHRMAZD.]

or·mer (ôr′mər) n. Chiefly British An abalone, esp. of the species Haliotis tuberculata, found chiefly in the Channel Islands. [Fr. dialectal < Fr. ormier, short for oreille-de-mer, transl. of Lat. auris maris, sea ear : auris, ear; see **ous–** in App. + maris, genitive of mare, sea; see **mori–** in App.]

or·mo·lu (ôr′mə-lōō′) n. **1.** Any of several copper and zinc or tin alloys resembling gold in appearance and used to ornament furniture and jewelry, for example. **2.** An imitation of gold. [Fr. or moulu : or, gold (< OFr.; see OR³) + obsolete Fr. molu, p. part. of moudre, to grind up (< OFr. < Lat. molere; see **melə–** in App.).]

Or·muz (ôr′mŭz′, ôr-mōōz′), **Strait of** See Strait of **Hormuz**.

or·na·ment (ôr′nə-mənt) n. **1.** Something that decorates or adorns; an ornamentation. **2.** A person considered as a source of pride, honor, or credit. **3.** Music A note or group of notes that embellishes a melody. ❖ tr.v. (-mĕnt′) -ment·ed, -ment·ing, -ments **1.** To furnish with ornaments. **2.** To be an ornament to. [ME ournement < OFr. ornement < Lat. ōrnāmentum < ōrnāre, to adorn.] —**or′na·ment′er** n.

or·na·men·tal (ôr′nə-mĕn′tl) adj. Of, relating to, or serving as an ornament or decoration. ❖ n. Something that serves as ornamentation, esp. a plant grown for its beauty. —**or′na·men′tal·ly** adv.

or·na·men·ta·tion (ôr′nə-mĕn-tā′shən) n. **1a.** The act or process of decorating, adorning, or embellishing. **b.** The state of being ornamented. **2.** An ornament.

or·nate (ôr-nāt′) adj. **1.** Elaborately, heavily, and often excessively ornamented. **2.** Flashy, showy, or florid in style or manner; flowery. [ME < Lat. ōrnātus, p. part. of ōrnāre, to embellish.] —**or·nate′ly** adv. —**or·nate′ness** n.

or·ner·y (ôr′nə-rē) adj. -i·er, -i·est Mean-spirited and disagreeable; cantankerous. [Alteration of ORDINARY.] —**or′ner·i·ness′** n.

or·nith·ic (ôr-nĭth′ĭk) adj. Of or relating to birds.

or·ni·thine (ôr′nə-thēn′) n. An amino acid, $C_5H_{12}N_2O_2$, formed by hydrolyzing arginine and important in the formation of urea. [ornith(uric acid), an acid found in birds' urine (ORNITH(O)– + URIC ACID) + –INE².]

or·nith·is·chi·an (ôr′nə-thĭs′kē-ən) n. A dinosaur of the order Ornithischia, having a pelvic structure like that of a bird. [< NLat. Ornithischia, order name : ORNITH(O)– + Gk. iskhion, hip joint.] —**or′nith·is′chi·an** adj.

ornitho– or **ornith–** pref. Bird: ornithosis. [NLat. ornitho– < Gk. < ornis, ornith-, bird.]

or·ni·thol·o·gy (ôr′nə-thŏl′ə-jē) n. The branch of zoology that deals with the study of birds. —**or′ni·tho·log′ic** (-thə-lŏj′ĭk), **or′ni·tho·log′i·cal** (-ĭ-kəl) adj. —**or′ni·tho·log′i·cal·ly** adv. —**or′ni·thol′o·gist** n.

or·nith·o·pod (ôr-nĭth′ə-pŏd′) n. Any of various large ornithischian dinosaurs of the suborder Ornithopoda, including the hadrosaurs. ❖ adj. Of or relating to the suborder Ornithopoda. [NLat. Ornithopoda, suborder name : ORNITHO– + NLat. -poda, -pod.]

or·ni·thop·ter (ôr′nə-thŏp′tər) n. A machine shaped like an aircraft that is held aloft and propelled by wing movements.

or·ni·tho·sis (ôr′nə-thō′sĭs) n. Psittacosis, esp. as contracted from birds by humans.

oro– pref. Mountain: orogeny. [Gk. < oros, mountain.]

o·rog·e·ny (ô-rŏj′ə-nē) also **or·o·gen·e·sis** (ôr′ə-jĕn′ĭ-sĭs, ôr′-) n. The process of mountain formation by crustal folding and faulting. —**or′o·gen′ic** (ôr′ə-jĕn′ĭk, ôr′-) adj.

o·rog·ra·phy (ô-rŏg′rə-fē) n. The study of the physical geography of mountains. —**or′o·graph′ic** (ôr′ə-grăf′ĭk, ôr′-), **or′o·graph′i·cal** (-ĭ-kəl) adj. —**or′o·graph′i·cal·ly** adv.

o·ro·ide (ôr′ō-īd′, ôr′-) n. An alloy of copper, zinc, and tin, used in imitation gold jewelry. [Alteration of Fr. oréide : or, gold; see OR³ + -éide, resembling (< Gk. -oeidēs, -oid).]

o·rol·o·gy (ô-rŏl′ə-jē) n. The study of mountains. —**o′ro·log′i·cal** (ôr′ə-lŏj′ĭ-kəl, ôr′-) adj. —**o′ro·log′i·cal·ly** adv. —**o·rol′o·gist** n.

O·ro·mo (ô-rō′mō) n., pl. Oromo or -mos **1.** A member of a widely acculturated people of southern and central Ethiopia and northern Kenya. **2.** The Cushitic language of the Oromo.

O·ron·tes (ô-rŏn′tēz) A river, c. 402 km (250 mi), flowing through Lebanon, Syria, and S Turkey to the Mediterranean Sea.

o·ro·phar·ynx (ôr′ō-făr′ĭngks, ōr′-) n., pl. -**pha·ryn·ges** (-fə-rĭn′jēz) or -**phar·ynx·es** The part of the pharynx between the soft palate and the epiglottis. [Lat. ōs, ōr-, mouth; see OS¹ + PHARYNX.] —**o′ro·pha·ryn′ge·al** (-fə-rĭn′jē-əl, -făr′ən-jē′əl) adj.

o·ro·tund (ôr′ə-tŭnd′, ōr′-) adj. **1.** Pompous and bombastic: orotund talk. **2.** Full in sound; sonorous: orotund tones. [< alteration of Lat. ōre rotundō, with a round mouth : ōre, ablative of ōs, mouth; see **ōs–** in App. + rotundō, ablative of rotundus, round; see ROTUND.] —**o′ro·tun′di·ty** (-tŭn′dĭ-tē) n.

O·roz·co (ō-rōz′kō, -rōs′-), **José Clemente** 1883–1949. Mexican painter best known for his murals.

or·phan (ôr′fən) n. **1a.** A child whose parents are dead. **b.** A child who has been deprived of parental care and has not been adopted. **2.** A young animal without a mother. **3.** One that lacks support, supervision, or care. **4a.** A line of type beginning a new paragraph at the bottom of a column or page. **b.** A short line of type at the bottom of a paragraph, column, or page; a widow. ❖ adj. **1.** Deprived of parents. **2.** Intended for orphans: an orphan home. **3.** Lacking support or supervision; abandoned. **4.** Not developed, researched, or marketed for being commercially unprofitable: an orphan drug. ❖ tr.v. -**phaned**, -**phan·ing**, -**phans** To deprive (a child or young animal) of one parent or both parents. [ME < LLat. orphanus < Gk. orphanos, orphaned. See **orbh–** in App.] —**or′phan·hood′** n.

or·phan·age (ôr′fə-nĭj) n. **1.** A public institution for the care and protection of children without parents. **2.** The condition of being a child without parents.

Or·phe·us (ôr′fē-əs, -fyōōs′) n. Greek Mythology A legendary Thracian poet and musician who almost succeeded in rescuing his wife Eurydice from Hades. —**Or·phe′an** (ôr-fē′ən, ôr′fē-ən) adj.

Or·phic (ôr′fĭk) adj. **1.** Greek Mythology Of or ascribed to Orpheus: the Orphic poems. **2.** Of, relating to, or characteristic of the dogmas, mysteries, and philosophies in the poems ascribed to Orpheus. **3.** Capable of casting a charm or spell; entrancing. **4.** often **orphic** Mystic or occult. [Gk. Orphikos < Orpheus, Orpheus.] —**Or′phi·cal·ly** adv.

Or·phism (ôr′fĭz′əm) n. **1.** An ancient Greek mystery religion, a synthesis of pre-Hellenic beliefs, the Thracian cult of Zagreus, the Eleusinian mysteries, and Pythagoreanism. **2.** often **orphism** A movement in early 20th-century painting, derived from cubism but marked by a lyrical style and bold color. [Fr. orphisme < Orphée, Orpheus < Gk. Orpheus.] —**Or′phist** n.

or·phrey (ôr′frē) also **or·fray** (-frā′) n., pl. -**phreys** also -**frays** **1.** A band of elaborate embroidery on certain ecclesiastical vestments. **2.** Elaborate embroidery, esp. when made of gold. [ME orfrey, alteration of orfreis < OFr. < Med.Lat. aurifrigium : Lat. aurum, gold + Lat. Phrygius, Phrygian.]

or·pi·ment (ôr′pə-mənt) n. Arsenic trisulfide, As_2S_3, a yellow mineral used as a pigment. [ME < OFr. < Lat. auripigmentum : aurum, gold + pigmentum, pigment; see PIGMENT.]

or·pine (ôr′pĭn) n. Any of several succulent plants of the genus Sedum, esp. the Eurasian species S. telephium, having clusters of reddish-purple flowers. [ME orpin < OFr. < orpiment, orpiment. See ORPIMENT.]

Or·ping·ton (ôr′pĭng-tən) n. Any of a breed of large whiteskinned fowls with a single comb and unfeathered legs, originally bred in England. [After Orpington, a district of SE England.]

or·re·ry (ôr′ə-rē, ŏr′-) n., pl. -**ries** A mechanical model of the solar system. [After Charles Boyle, 4th Earl of Orrery (1676–1731), for whom one was made.]

or·ris (ôr′ĭs, ŏr′-) n. **1.** Any of several species of iris having a fragrant rootstock, esp. a variety of the hybrid Iris germanica. **2.** The fragrant rootstock of the orris, used in perfumes and cosmetics. [Prob. alteration of ME yreos < Med.Lat., alteration of Lat. īris. See IRIS.]

or·ris·root (ôr′ĭs-rōōt′, -rŏŏt′, ŏr′-) n. See orris 2.

Orsk (ôrsk) A city of W Russia on the Ural R. ESE of Orenburg. Pop. 274,601.

ort (ôrt) n. **1.** A small scrap or leaving of food after a meal is completed. Often used in the plural. **2.** A scrap; a bit. [ME orte, food left by animals, prob. < MDu. : oor, out; see **ud–** in App. + eten, to eat; see **ed–** in App.]

Or·te·ga (ôr-tā′gə, -tĕ′gä), **Daniel** b. 1945. Nicaraguan revolutionary leader who served as president (1984–90).

Ortega y Gas·set (ē gä-sĕt′), **José** 1883–1955. Spanish philosopher whose works include The Revolt of the Masses (1929).

or·thi·con (ôr′thĭ-kŏn′) n. A television camera pickup tube, more sensitive than the iconoscope, that scans a photoactive mosaic with a low-velocity electron beam. [ORTH(O)– + ICON(OSCOPE).]

or·tho (ôr′thō) adj. Orthochromatic. [< ORTHO–.]

ortho– or **orth–** pref. **1.** Straight; upright; vertical: orthotropous. **2.** Perpendicular: orthorhombic. **3.** Correct; correction: orthopsychiatry. **4.** The most fully hydrated form of an acid: orthoboric acid. **5.** Diatomic molecules in which the nuclei have the same spin direction: orthohydrogen. **6.** Of or relating to an isomer of a

Daniel Ortega

George Orwell

benzene ring with chemical groups attached to two adjacent carbon atoms: *ortho-dibromobenzene.* [ME < OFr. < Lat. < Gk. < *orthos*, straight, correct, right.]

or•tho•cen•ter (ôr′thō-sĕn′tər) *n.* The point of intersection of the three altitudes of a triangle.

or•tho•chro•mat•ic (ôr′thō-krō-măt′ĭk) *adj. Photography* **1.** Of, relating to, or accurately reproducing the colors of the subject. **2.** Sensitive to all colors except red. —**or′tho•chro′ma•tism** (-krō′mə-tĭz′əm) *n.*

or•tho•clase (ôr′thə-klās′, -klāz′) *n.* A monoclinic variety of feldspar, potassium aluminum silicate, KAlSi₃O₈, commonly found in many igneous rocks. [Gk. *ortho-*, ortho- + Gk. *klasis*, a breaking (< *klān*, to break).]

or•tho•don•tia (ôr′thə-dŏn′shə) or **or•tho•don•ture** (-dŏn′chər) *n.* Orthodontics.

or•tho•don•tics (ôr′thə-dŏn′tĭks) *n.* (*used with a sing. verb*) The dental specialty and practice of preventing and correcting irregularities of the teeth, as with braces. —**or′tho•don′tic** *adj.* —**or′tho•don′ti•cal•ly** *adv.* —**or′tho•don′tist** *n.*

or•tho•dox (ôr′thə-dŏks′) *adj.* **1.** Adhering to the accepted or traditional and established faith, esp. in religion. **2.** Adhering to the Christian faith as expressed in the early Christian ecumenical creeds. **3.** **Orthodox a.** Of or relating to any of the churches or rites of the Eastern Orthodox Church. **b.** Of or relating to Orthodox Judaism. **4.** Adhering to what is commonly accepted, customary, or traditional. ❖ *n.* **1.** One that is orthodox. **2. Orthodox** A member of an Eastern Orthodox church. [ME *orthodoxe* < OFr. < LLat. *orthodoxus* < L.Gk. *orthodoxos* : Gk. *ortho-*, ortho- + Gk. *doxa*, opinion (< *dokein*, to think; see **dek-** in App.).] —**or′tho•dox′ly** *adv.*

Orthodox Church *n.* The Eastern Orthodox Church.

Orthodox Judaism *n.* The branch of Judaism that is governed by adherence to the Torah as interpreted in the Talmud.

orthodox sleep *n.* Sleep characterized by a slow alpha rhythm and the absence of REM.

or•tho•dox•y (ôr′thə-dŏk′sē) *n., pl.* **-ies 1.** The quality or state of being orthodox. **2.** Orthodox practice, custom, or belief. **3. Orthodoxy a.** The beliefs and practices of the Eastern Orthodox Church. **b.** Orthodox Judaism.

or•tho•e•py (ôr-thō′ə-pē, ôr′thō-ĕp′ē) *n.* **1.** The study of pronunciation of words. **2.** The study of the relationship between the pronunciation of words and their orthography. **3.** The customary pronunciation of words. [Gk. *orthoepeia*, correctness of diction : *ortho-*, ortho- + *epos*, *epe-*, word; see **wekʷ-** in App.] —**or′tho•ep′ic** (-ĕp′ĭk), **or′tho•ep′i•cal** *adj.* —**or′tho•e′pist** *n.*

or•tho•gen•e•sis (ôr′thō-jĕn′ĭ-sĭs) *n.* **1.** *Biology* The theory that the evolution of a species is influenced by internal factors and not by external forces of natural selection. **2.** The theory that all cultures pass through sequential periods in the same order. —**or′tho•ge•net′ic** (-jə-nĕt′ĭk) *adj.* —**or′tho•ge•net′i•cal•ly** *adv.*

or•thog•o•nal (ôr-thŏg′ə-nəl) *adj. Mathematics* Relating to or composed of right angles. [< Gk. *orthogōnios* : *ortho-*, ortho- + *gōnia*, angle; see **genu-** in App.] —**or•thog′o•nal′i•ty** (-năl′ĭ-tē) *n.* —**or•thog′o•nal•ly** *adv.*

orthogonal projection *n.* The two-dimensional graphic representation of an object by the perpendicular intersections of lines drawn from points on the object to a plane of projection.

or•tho•graph•ic (ôr′thə-grăf′ĭk) also **or•tho•graph•i•cal** (-ĭ-kəl) *adj.* **1.** Of or relating to orthography. **2.** Spelled correctly. **3.** *Mathematics* Having perpendicular lines.

orthographic projection *n.* See orthogonal projection.

or•thog•ra•phy (ôr-thŏg′rə-fē) *n., pl.* **-phies 1.** The art or study of standard spelling. **2.** The aspect of language study concerned with letters and spelling. **3.** A method of representing a language or the sounds of language by written symbols; spelling. —**or•thog′ra•pher, or•thog′ra•phist** *n.*

or•tho•mo•lec•u•lar (ôr′thō-mə-lĕk′yə-lər) *adj.* Of, relating to, or being a theory holding that mental diseases or abnormalities can be cured by restoring proper levels of chemical substances, such as vitamins and minerals, in the body.

or•tho•pe•dics also **or•tho•pae•dics** (ôr′thə-pē′dĭks) *n.* (*used with a sing. verb*) The branch of medicine that treats injuries or disorders of the skeletal system and associated muscles, joints, and ligaments. [< *orthopedic* < Fr. *orthopédique* < *orthopédie*, orthopedic surgery : Gk. *ortho-*, ortho- + Gk. *paideia*, child-rearing (< *pais*, *paid-*, child).] —**or′tho•pe′dic** *adj.* —**or′tho•pe′di•cal•ly** *adv.* —**or′tho•pe′dist** *n.*

or•tho•psy•chi•a•try (ôr′thō-sī-kī′ə-trē, -sī-) *n.* The psychiatric study, treatment, and prevention of emotional and behavioral problems, esp. of those that arise during early development. —**or′tho•psy′chi•at′ric** (-sī′kē-ăt′rĭk), **or′tho•psy′chi•at′ri•cal** (-ĭ-kəl) *adj.* —**or′tho•psy•chi′a•trist** *n.*

or•thop•ter•an (ôr-thŏp′tər-ən) also **or•thop•ter•on** (-tə-rŏn′, -tər-ən) *n.* An insect of the order Orthoptera, characterized by folded membranous hind wings covered by narrow leathery forewings and including the locusts and cockroaches. [< NLat. *Orthoptera*, order name : Gk. *ortho-*, ortho- + Gk. *ptera*, neut. pl. of *pteron*, wing; see **pet-** in App.] —**or•thop′ter•an, or•thop′ter•ous, or•thop′ter•al** *adj.*

or•tho•rhom•bic (ôr′thō-rŏm′bĭk) *adj.* Of or relating to a crystalline structure of three mutually perpendicular axes of different length.

or•tho•scop•ic (ôr′thə-skŏp′ĭk) *adj.* **1.** Having normal vision; free from visual distortion. **2.** Giving an undistorted image. Used of an optical instrument.

or•tho•stat•ic (ôr′thə-stăt′ĭk) *adj.* Relating to or caused by standing upright: *orthostatic hypotension.* [ORTHO- + Gk. *statos*, standing; see STATIC + –IC.]

or•thot•ics (ôr-thŏt′ĭks) *n.* (*used with a sing. verb*) The science that deals with the use of specialized mechanical devices to support or supplement weakened or abnormal joints or limbs. [< NLat. *orthōsis, orthōt-*, artificial support, brace < Gk., a straightening < *orthoun*, to straighten < *orthos*, straight.] —**or•thot′ic** *adj. & n.* —**or•thot′ist** (ôr-thŏt′ĭst, ôr′thə-tĭst) *n.*

or•tho•trop•ic (ôr′thə-trŏp′ĭk, -trō′pĭk) *adj.* **1.** Tending to grow or form along a vertical axis. **2.** Of or relating to a bridge deck consisting of steel plates supported by ribs underneath. —**or′tho•trop′i•cal•ly** *adv.* —**or•thot′ro•pism** (ôr-thŏt′rə-pĭz′əm) *n.*

or•thot•ro•pous (ôr-thŏt′rə-pəs) *adj. Botany* Growing straight, so that the micropyle is at the end opposite the stalk. Used of an ovule.

Ort•les (ôrt′läs) also **Ort•ler** (-lər) A range of the Alps in N Italy rising to 3,901.6 m (12,792 ft) at **Ortles** peak.

or•to•lan (ôr′tl-ən) *n.* **1.** A small brownish Old World bunting (*Emberiza hortulana*) eaten as a delicacy. **2.** Any of several New World birds, such as the bobolink and the sora. [Fr. < Provençal, gardener, ortolan < Lat. *hortulānus* < *hortulus*, dim. of *hortus*, garden. See **gher-** in App.]

ORV *abbr.* off-road vehicle

Or•well (ôr′wĕl′, -wəl), **George** Pen name of Eric Arthur Blair. 1903–50. British writer whose works include *Animal Farm* (1945) and *1984* (1949). —**Or•well′i•an** *adj.*

–ory *suff.* **1.** Of, relating to, or characterized by: *advisory.* **2.** A place or thing used for or connected with: *crematory.* [ME *-orie* < ONFr. and AN < Lat. *-ōrius*, adj. suff., and *-ōrium*, n. suff.]

o•ryx (ôr′ĭks, ōr′-, ŏr′-) *n., pl.* **oryx** or **o•ryx•es** Any of several African antelopes of the genus *Oryx*, including the gemsbok, having long straight or slightly curved horns and a hump above the shoulders. [Lat. < Gk. *orux*, pickax, gazelle (< its sharp horns), perh. < *orussein*, to dig.]

or•zo (ôr′zō) *n.* A pasta shaped like grains of rice, frequently used in soups. [Ital., barley, orzo < Lat. *hordeum*.]

os¹ (ŏs) *n., pl.* **o•ra** (ôr′ə, ōr′ə) A mouth or an opening. [Lat. *ōs*, mouth. See **ōs-** in App.]

os² (ŏs) *n., pl.* **os•sa** (ŏs′ə) A bone. [Lat., bone. See **ost-** in App.]

os³ (ŏs) *n., pl.* **os•ar** (ō′sär′) See esker. [Swed. *ås*, ridge < ON *āss*.]

Os The symbol for the element osmium.

OS *abbr.* **1.** *Latin* oculus sinister (left eye) **2.** or **O/S** Old Style **3.** ordinary seaman

O•sage (ō′sāj′, ō-sāj′) *n., pl.* **Osage** or **O•sag•es 1.** A member of a Native American people formerly inhabiting western Missouri and southeast Kansas, with a present-day population in Oklahoma. **2.** The Siouan language of the Osage. [Fr. < Osage *wazházhe*, tribal name.] —**O′sage′** *adj.*

Osage orange *n.* A dioecious spiny tree (*Maclura pomifera*) native to Arkansas and Texas and having pulpy, inedible, orangelike multiple fruit.

Osage River A river of central MO flowing c. 579 km (360 mi) through the Lake of the Ozarks to the Missouri R.

O•sa•ka (ō-sä′kə, ō′sä-kä′) A city of S Honshu, Japan, on **Osaka Bay,** an inlet of the Pacific Ocean. Pop. 2,588,989.

O•sas•co (oo-säs′koo) A city of SE Brazil, a suburb of São Paulo. Pop. 566,949.

Os•borne (ŏz′bərn, -bôrn′, -bōrn′), **John James** 1929–94. British playwright noted for *Look Back in Anger* (1956).

Os•can (ŏs′kən) *n.* **1.** A member of an ancient people of Campania. **2.** The Italic language of the Oscans. —**Os′can** *adj.*

Os•car (ŏs′kər) A trademark for an award for excellence in the creation and production of movies.

Oscar II also **Os•kar II** (ŏs′kär) 1829–1907. King of Sweden from 1872 to 1907 and of Norway from 1872 to 1905.

Os•ce•o•la (ŏs′ē-ō′lə, ō′sē-) 1804?–38. Seminole leader who resisted the removal of his people from Florida.

os•cil•late (ŏs′ə-lāt′) *intr.v.* **-lat•ed, -lat•ing, -lates 1.** To swing back and forth with a steady uninterrupted rhythm. **2.** To waver, as between conflicting opinions or courses of action; vacillate. **3.** *Physics* To vary between alternate extremes, usu. within a definable period of time. [Lat. *ōscillāre, ōscillāt-* < *ōscillum*, swing, prob. < *ōscillum*, small mask of Bacchus, dim. of *ōs*, mouth. See **ōs-** in App.] —**os′cil•la′tor** *n.* —**os′cil•la•to′ry** (-lə-tôr′ē, -tōr′ē) *adj.*

os•cil•lat•ing universe (ŏs′ə-lā′tĭng) *n.* A model of the universe in which its expansion slows and reverses, causing a collapse into a singularity that then explodes into a new universe, repeating the cycle.

os•cil•la•tion (ŏs′ə-lā′shən) *n.* **1.** The act or state of oscillating. **2.** A single oscillatory cycle. —**os′cil•la′tion•al** *adj.*

os•cil•lo•gram (ə-sĭl′ə-grăm′) *n.* **1.** The graph traced by an os-

oryx
Arabian oryx
Oryx leucoryx

Osceola
1838 portrait by
George Catlin

ă pat	oi boy
ā pay	ou out
âr care	oo took
ä father	oo boot
ĕ pet	ŭ cut
ē be	ûr urge
ĭ pit	th thin
ī pie	th this
îr pier	hw which
ŏ pot	zh vision
ō toe	ə about,
ô paw	item

Stress marks:
′ (primary);
′ (secondary), as in
lexicon (lĕk′sĭ-kŏn′)

cillograph. **2.** An instantaneous oscilloscope trace or photograph. [OSCILLO(GRAPH) + −GRAM.]

os·cil·lo·graph (ə-sĭl′ə-grăf′) *n.* A device that records oscillations, as of an electric current and voltage. [OSCILL(ATION) + −GRAPH.] —**os·cil′lo·graph′ic** —**os·cil′lo·graph′i·cal·ly** *adv.* —**os′cil·log′ra·phy** (ŏs′ə-lŏg′rə-fē) *n.*

os·cil·lo·scope (ə-sĭl′ə-skōp′) *n.* An electronic instrument that produces an instantaneous trace on the screen of a cathode-ray tube corresponding to oscillations of voltage and current. —**os·cil′lo·scop′ic** (-skŏp′ĭk) *adj.*

os·cine (ŏs′īn′) *adj.* Of, relating to, or belonging to the Oscines, a suborder of passerine birds that includes most songbirds. [< NLat. Oscinēs, suborder name < Lat. oscinēs, pl. of oscen, bird used in augury. See **kan-** in App.] —**os′cine** *n.*

os·ci·tance (ŏs′ĭ-təns) *n.* Oscitancy.

os·ci·tan·cy (ŏs′ĭ-tən-sē) *n., pl.* **-cies 1.** The act of yawning. **2.** The state of being drowsy or inattentive; dullness. [< oscitant, yawning < Lat. ōscitāns, ōscitant-, pr. part. of ōscitāre, to yawn : ōs, mouth; see **ōs-** in App. + citāre, to set in motion; see **kei-**[2] in App.]

Os·co-Um·bri·an (ŏs′kō-ŭm′brē-ən) *n.* See **Sabellic.**

os·cu·late (ŏs′kyə-lāt′) *v.* **-lat·ed, -lat·ing, -lates** —*tr.* **1.** To kiss. **2.** *Mathematics* To have three or more points coincident with. —*intr.* To come together; contact. [Lat. ōsculārī, ōsculāt- < ōsculum, kiss, dim. of ōs, mouth. See **ōs-** in App.]

os·cu·la·tion (ŏs′kyə-lā′shən) *n.* **1a.** The act of kissing. **b.** A kiss. **2.** *Mathematics* A contact, as between two curves or surfaces, at three or more common points.

os·cu·lum (ŏs′kyə-ləm) also **os·cule** (-kyōōl′) *n., pl.* **-cu·la** (-kyə-lə) also **-cules** The mouthlike opening in a sponge, used to expel water. [Lat. ōsculum, dim. of ōs, mouth. See **ōs-** in App.]

-ose[1] *suff.* Possessing; having the characteristics of; full of: *cymose.* [ME, var. of *-ous* < Lat. *-ōsus.*]

-ose[2] *suff.* **1.** Carbohydrate: *fructose.* **2.** Product of protein hydrolysis: *proteose.* [Fr. < *glucose*, glucose. See GLUCOSE.]

OSHA (ō′shə) *abbr.* Occupational Safety and Health Administration

Osh·a·wa (ŏsh′ə-wä′, -wə) A city of SE Ontario, Canada, on Lake Ontario ENE of Toronto. Pop. 134,364.

O·shog·bo (ō-shŏg′bō) A city of SW Nigeria NE of Ibadan. Pop. 336,000.

o·sier (ō′zhər) *n.* **1a.** Any of several willows having long rodlike twigs used in basketry, esp. the Eurasian *Salix viminalis* and *S. purpurea.* **b.** A twig of one of these trees. **2.** Any of various similar or related trees. [ME < OE oser and OFr. osier, both < Med.Lat. osera, osiera.]

O·si·ris (ō-sī′rĭs) *n. Mythology* The ancient Egyptian god whose annual death and resurrection personified the self-renewing vitality and fertility of nature.

-osis *suff.* **1.** Condition; process; action: *osmosis.* **2.** Diseased or abnormal condition: *neurosis.* **3.** Increase; formation: *leukocytosis.* [Lat. *-ōsis* < Gk., n. suff.]

Os·kar II (ŏs′kär) See **Oscar II.**

Ös·ke·men (ōōs′kə-mĕn′, œs′-) or **Ust-Ka·me·no·gorsk** (ōōst′kə-mĕn′ə-gôrsk′) A city of NE Kazakhstan on the Irtysh R. SE of Semey; founded 1720. Pop. 334,000.

Os·lo (ŏz′lō, ŏs′-) Formerly (1624–1925) **Chris·ti·a·ni·a** (krĭs′tē-ăn′ē-ə, -än′-, krĭs′chē-) The cap. of Norway, in the SE part at the head of the **Oslo Fjord,** a deep inlet of the Skagerrak; founded c. 1050 and rebuilt and renamed in 1624 by Christian IV (1577–1648). Pop. 473,454.

Os·man I (ŏz′mən, ŏs′-, ōs-män′) also **Oth·man I** (ŏth′mən, ōōth-män′) 1258–1326? Founder of the Ottoman dynasty that controlled most of NW Asia Minor.

Os·man·li (ŏz-măn′lē, ŏs-) *n., pl.* **-lis 1.** An Ottoman Turk. **2.** Ottoman Turkish. ❖ *adj.* Ottoman. [Turk. osmanli : OSMAN (I) + -li, adj. suff.]

os·mat·ic (ŏz-măt′ĭk) *adj.* Having or characterized by a well-developed sense of smell. [< Gk. osmē, smell.]

os·mic[1] (ŏz′mĭk) *adj.* Of, relating to, or containing osmium, esp. in a compound with valence 4 or a valence higher than that in a comparable osmous compound. [OSM(IUM) + −IC.]

os·mic[2] (ŏz′mĭk) *adj.* Of or relating to odors or the sense of smell. [Gk. osmē, smell + −IC.] —**os′mi·cal·ly** *adv.*

osmic acid *n.* See **osmium tetroxide.**

os·mics (ŏz′mĭks) *n.* (used with a sing. verb) The science that deals with smells and the olfactory sense.

os·mi·rid·i·um (ŏz′mə-rĭd′ē-əm) *n.* A mineral that is a natural alloy of osmium and iridium with small inclusions of platinum, rhodium, and other metals. [OSM(IUM) + IRIDIUM.]

os·mi·um (ŏz′mē-əm) *n. Symbol* **Os** A hard metallic element, found in small amounts in osmiridium and platinum ores and used as a platinum hardener and in making pen points and instrument pivots. Atomic number 76; atomic weight 190.2; melting point 3,000°C; boiling point 5,000°C; specific gravity 22.57; valence 2, 3, 4, 8. See table at **element.** [< Gk. osmē, smell (< the odor of osmium tetroxide).]

osmium tetroxide *n.* A poisonous compound, OsO₄, with a pungent smell, used as a stain and a tissue fixative.

os·mom·e·ter (ŏz-mŏm′ĭ-tər, ŏs-) *n.* A device for measuring osmotic pressure. [OSMO(SIS) + −METER.] —**os′mo·met′ric** (ŏz′mə-mĕt′rĭk, ŏs′-) *adj.* —**os·mom′e·try** *n.*

Osman I
portrait from a 16th-century
illuminated manuscript

osprey
Pandion haliaetus

os·mo·reg·u·la·tion (ŏz′mə-rĕg′yə-lā′shən, ŏs′-) *n.* Maintenance of an optimal constant osmotic pressure in the body of a living organism. [OSMO(SIS) + REGULATION.]

os·mose (ŏz′mōs′, ŏs′-) *intr. & tr.v.* **-mosed, -mos·ing, -mos·es** To diffuse or cause to diffuse by osmosis.

os·mo·sis (ŏz-mō′sĭs, ŏs-) *n., pl.* **-ses** (-sēz) **1a.** Diffusion of fluid through a semipermeable membrane from a solution with a low solute concentration to a solution with a higher solute concentration until there is an equal concentration of fluid on both sides of the membrane. **b.** The tendency of fluids to diffuse in such a manner. **2.** A gradual, often unconscious process of absorption or learning. [< osmose < earlier endosmose < Fr. : Gk. endo-, endo- + Gk. ōsmos, thrust, push (< ōthein, to push).] —**os·mot′ic** (-mŏt′ĭk) *adj.* —**os·mot′i·cal·ly** *adv.*

osmotic pressure *n.* The pressure exerted by the flow of water through a semipermeable membrane separating two solutions with different concentrations of solute.

osmotic shock *n.* The rupture of bacterial or other cells in a solution following a sudden reduction in osmotic pressure.

os·mous (ŏz′məs) also **os·mi·ous** (-mē-əs) *adj.* Of, relating to, or containing osmium in a compound with a valence lower than that in a comparable osmic compound.

os·mun·da (ŏz-mŭn′də) also **os·mund** (ŏz′mənd) *n.* Any of several ferns of the genus Osmunda, having bipinnately compound fronds and edible crosiers. [NLat. Osmunda, genus name < ME osmunde, a fern < OFr. osmonde.]

Os·na·brück (ŏz′nə-brōōk′, ŏs′nä-brük′) A city of NW Germany NE of Münster. Pop. 168,078.

os·na·burg (ŏz′nə-bûrg′) *n.* A heavy coarse cotton fabric, used for grain sacks, upholstery, and draperies. [After Osnaburg (Osnabrück).]

os·prey (ŏs′prē, -prā) *n., pl.* **-preys 1.** A fish-eating hawk (*Pandion haliaetus*) having plumage that is dark on the back and white below. **2.** A plume formerly used to trim women's hats. [ME osprai < AN ospreit < Med.Lat. avis praedae, bird of prey : Lat. avis, bird; see **awi-** in App. + Lat. praedae, genitive of praeda, booty, prey; see **ghend-** in App.]

OSS *abbr.* Office of Strategic Services

os·sa (ŏs′ə) *n.* Plural of **os**[2].

Os·sa (ŏs′ə), **Mount** A peak, 1,979.1 m (6,489 ft), of the Olympus Mts. in N Greece.

os·sa·ture (ŏs′ə-chōōr′, -chər) *n.* A framework or skeleton, as for a building. [Fr. < Lat. os, oss-, bone. See OS[2].]

os·se·in (ŏs′ē-ĭn) *n.* The collagen component of bone. [OSSE(OUS) + −IN.]

os·se·ous (ŏs′ē-əs) *adj.* Composed of, containing, or resembling bone; bony. [< Lat. osseus < os, oss-, bone. See **ost-** in App.] —**os′se·ous·ly** *adv.*

Os·set (ŏs′ĭt, ŏ-sĕt′) also **Os·sete** (ŏs′ēt′, ŏ-sĕt′) *n.* A member of a people of mixed Iranian and Caucasian origin inhabiting Ossetia.

Os·se·tia (ŏ-sē′shə) A region of the central Caucasus in Georgia and SW Russia; annexed by Russia between 1801 and 1806. —**Os·se′tian** *adj. & n.*

Os·set·ic (ŏ-sĕt′ĭk) *adj.* Of or relating to Ossetia, the Ossets, or their language or culture. ❖ *n.* Their Iranian language.

os·si·a (ŏ-sē′ə) *conj. Music* Or else. Used to designate an alternate section or passage. [Ital. < o sia, or let it be : o, or (< Lat. aut) + sia, third pers. sing. pr. subjunctive of essere, to be (< Lat. esse; see **es-** in App.)]

Os·sian (ŏsh′ən, ŏs′ē-ən) *n.* A legendary Gaelic hero and bard of the third century A.D.

os·si·cle (ŏs′ĭ-kəl) *n.* A small bone, esp. of the middle ear. [Lat. ossiculum, dim. of os, bone. See **ost-** in App.] —**os·sic′u·lar** (ŏ-sĭk′yə-lər), **os·sic′u·late** (-lĭt) *adj.*

Os·si·etz·ky (ŏs′ē-ĕt′skē ō′sē-), **Carl von** 1889–1938. German journalist who won the 1935 Nobel Peace Prize.

os·si·fi·ca·tion (ŏs′ə-fĭ-kā′shən) *n.* **1.** The natural process of bone formation. **2a.** The hardening or calcification of soft tissue into a bonelike material. **b.** A mass or deposit of such material. **3a.** The process of becoming set in a rigid conventionalism, as of behavior. **b.** Rigid unimaginative convention.

os·si·frage (ŏs′ə-frĭj, -frāj′) *n.* **1.** See **lammergeier. 2.** *Archaic* An osprey. [Lat. ossifraga < ossifragus, bone-breaking : os, oss-, bone; see **ost-** in App. + frangere, to break; see **bhreg-** in App.]

os·si·fy (ŏs′ə-fī′) *v.* **-fied, -fy·ing, -fies** —*intr.* **1.** To change into bone; become bony. **2.** To become set in a rigid conventionalism. —*tr.* **1.** To convert (a membrane or cartilage, for example) into bone. **2.** To mold into a rigidly conventional pattern. [Lat. os, oss-, bone; see **ost-** in App. + −FY.] —**os·sif′ic** (ŏ-sĭf′ĭk) *adj.*

os·so bu·co (ō′sō bōō′kō, ô′sō) *n., pl.* **osso bu·cos** An Italian dish consisting of braised veal shanks in white wine. [Ital. osso-buco, marrowbone : osso, bone + buco, hole.]

os·su·ar·y (ŏsh′ōō-ĕr′ē, ŏs′yōō-) *n., pl.* **-ies** A container or receptacle for the bones of the dead. [LLat. ossuārium < neut. of Lat. ossuārius, of bones < os, oss-, bone. See **ost-** in App.]

os·te·al (ŏs′tē-əl) *adj.* **1.** Bony; osseous. **2.** Relating to bone or to the skeleton.

os·te·i·tis (ŏs′tē-ī′tĭs) *n.* Inflammation of bone or bony tissue.

Ost·end (ŏs-tĕnd′, ŏs′tĕnd′) also **Oost·en·de** (ō-stĕn′də) A city of NW Belgium WSW of Bruges. Pop. 69,129.

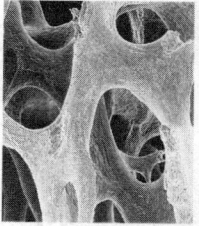

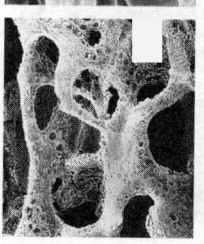

os·ten·si·ble (ŏ-stĕn′sə-bəl) *adj.* Represented or appearing as such; professed. [Fr. < Med.Lat. *ostensibilis* < Lat. *ostēnsus*, p. part. of *ostendere*, to show : *ob-*, ob- + *tendere*, to stretch; see **ten-** in App.] —**os·ten′si·bly** *adv.*

os·ten·sive (ŏ-stĕn′sĭv) *adj.* Seeming or professed; ostensible. —**os·ten′sive·ly** *adv.*

os·ten·so·ri·um (ŏs′tĕn-sôr′ē-əm, -sōr′-) also **os·ten·so·ry** (ŏ-stĕn′sə-rē) *n., pl.* -**so·ri·a** (-sôr′ē-ə, -sōr′-) also -**so·ries** *Roman Catholic Church* See **monstrance.** [Med.Lat. *ostēnsōrium* < Lat. *ostēnsus*, p. part. of *ostendere*, to show. See OSTENSIBLE.]

os·ten·ta·tion (ŏs′tĕn-tā′shən, -tən-) *n.* **1.** Pretentious display meant to impress others; boastful showiness. **2.** *Archaic* The act or an instance of showing; an exhibition. [ME *ostentacioun* < OFr. *ostentacion* < Lat. *ostentātiō, ostentātiōn-* < *ostentāre*, freq. of *ostendere*, to show. See OSTENSIBLE.]

os·ten·ta·tious (ŏs′tĕn-tā′shəs, -tən-) *adj.* Characterized by or given to ostentation; pretentious. See Syns at **showy.** —**os′ten·ta′tious·ly** *adv.*

osteo- or **oste-** *pref.* Bone: *osteoarthritis.* [Gk. < *osteon,* bone. See **ost-** in App.]

os·te·o·ar·thri·tis (ŏs′tē-ō-är-thrī′tĭs) *n.* A form of arthritis, occurring mainly in older persons, that is characterized by chronic degeneration of the cartilage of the joints. —**os′te·o·ar·thrit′ic** (-thrĭt′ĭk) *adj.*

os·te·o·blast (ŏs′tē-ō-blăst′) *n.* A cell from which bone develops; a bone-forming cell. —**os′te·o·blas′tic** *adj.*

os·te·oc·la·sis (ŏs′tē-ŏk′lə-sĭs) *n., pl.* -**ses** (-sēz′) **1.** The process of dissolution and resorption of bony tissue. **2.** Surgical fracture of a bone, performed to correct a deformity. [OSTEO- + Gk. *klasis,* breakage < *klān,* to break).]

os·te·o·clast (ŏs′tē-ə-klăst′) *n.* **1.** A large multinucleate cell found in growing bone that resorbs bony tissue, as in the formation of cavities. **2.** An instrument used in surgical osteoclasis. [OSTEO- + Med.Lat. *-clastēs,* breaker (< L.Gk. *-klastēs* < Gk. *klastos,* broken < *klān,* to break).]

os·te·o·cyte (ŏs′tē-ə-sīt′) *n.* A branched cell embedded in the matrix of bone tissue.

os·te·o·gen·e·sis (ŏs′tē-ə-jĕn′ĭ-sĭs) *n., pl.* -**ses** (-sēz′) The formation and development of bony tissue. —**os′te·o·ge·net′ic** (-ō-jə-nĕt′ĭk), **os′te·og′e·nous** (-ŏj′ə-nəs) *adj.*

os·te·o·gen·ic (ŏs′tē-ə-jĕn′ĭk) *adj.* **1.** Derived from or composed of bone-forming tissue. **2.** Of osteogenesis.

os·te·oid (ŏs′tē-oid′) *adj.* Resembling bone. ❖ *n.* The bone matrix, esp. before calcification.

os·te·ol·o·gy (ŏs′tē-ŏl′ə-jē) *n., pl.* -**gies 1.** The anatomical study of bones. **2.** The bone structure or system of an animal. —**os′te·o·log′i·cal** (-ə-lŏj′ĭ-kəl) *adj.* —**os′te·o·log′i·cal·ly** *adv.* —**os′te·ol′o·gist** *n.*

os·te·o·ma (ŏs′tē-ō′mə) *n., pl.* -**mas** or -**ma·ta** (-mə-tə) A benign tumor of bony tissue, often developing on the skull.

os·te·o·ma·la·cia (ŏs′tē-ō-mə-lā′shəs, -shē-ə) *n.* A disease occurring mostly in adult women as a result of a deficiency in vitamin D or calcium and characterized by a softening of the bones, pain, and weakness. [NLat. : OSTEO- + Gk. *malakiā,* softness (< *malakos,* soft).]

os·te·o·my·e·li·tis (ŏs′tē-ō-mī′ə-lī′tĭs) *n.* A usu. bacterial infection of bone and bone marrow.

os·te·o·path (ŏs′tē-ə-păth′) also **os·te·op·a·thist** (ŏs′tē-ŏp′ə-thĭst) *n.* A physician who practices osteopathy.

os·te·op·a·thy (ŏs′tē-ŏp′ə-thē) *n.* A system of medicine based on the theory that disturbances in the musculoskeletal system affect other bodily parts, causing disorders that can be corrected by various manipulative techniques in conjunction with conventional therapeutic procedures. —**os′te·o·path′ic** (-ə-păth′ĭk) *adj.* —**os′te·o·path′i·cal·ly** *adv.*

os·te·o·phyte (ŏs′tē-ə-fīt′) *n.* A small abnormal bony outgrowth. —**os′te·o·phyt′ic** (-fĭt′ĭk) *adj.*

os·te·o·plas·tic (ŏs′tē-ə-plăs′tĭk) *adj.* **1.** Of or relating to osteoplasty. **2.** Relating to or functioning in bone formation.

os·te·o·plas·ty (ŏs′tē-ə-plăs′tē) *n., pl.* -**ties** Surgical repair or alteration of bone.

os·te·o·po·ro·sis (ŏs′tē-ō-pə-rō′sĭs) *n., pl.* -**ses** (-sēz) A disease in which the bones become extremely porous, are subject to fracture, and heal slowly, occurring esp. in women after menopause and often leading to curvature of the spine. [NLat. : OSTEO- + Gk. *poros,* passage, pore; see PORE² + -OSIS.] —**os′te·o·po·rot′ic** (-rŏt′ĭk) *adj.*

os·te·o·sar·co·ma (ŏs′tē-ō-sär-kō′mə) *n., pl.* -**ma·ta** (-mə-tə) or -**mas** A malignant bone tumor.

os·te·ot·o·my (ŏs′tē-ŏt′ə-mē) *n., pl.* -**mies** Surgical division or sectioning of bone. —**os′te·ot′o·mist** *n.*

Os·ti·a (ŏs′tē-ə, ô′styä) An ancient city of W-central Italy at the mouth of the Tiber R.; developed as a port after the 1st cent. B.C.

Os·ti·ak (ŏs′tē-ăk′) *n.* Variant of **Ostyak.**

os·ti·na·to (ŏs′tĭ-nä′tō) *n., pl.* -**tos** A short melody or pattern that is constantly repeated, usu. in the same part at the same pitch. [Ital. *obstinātus,* stubborn, p. part. of *obstināre,* to persist. See OBSTINATE.]

os·ti·ole (ŏs′tē-ōl′) *n.* A small opening or pore, as of a fruiting body. [Lat. *ostiolum,* dim. of *ostium,* opening. See OSTIUM.] —**os′ti·o·lar** (ŏs′tē-ō′lər, ŏ-stī′ə-) *adj.*

os·ti·um (ŏs′tē-əm) *n., pl.* -**ti·a** (-tē-ə) **1.** A small orifice, as in a body organ. **2.** Any of the small pores in a sponge. [Lat. *ōstium,* door, opening < *ōs,* mouth. See **ōs-** in App.]

os·tler (ŏs′lər) *n.* Variant of **hostler.**

ost·mark (ŏst′märk, ôst′-) *n.* A former monetary unit of East Germany worth 100 pfennigs. [Ger. : *Ost,* east (< MHGer. *ōst,* east < OHGer. *ōstan;* see **aus-** in App.) + *Mark,* mark (< MHGer. *marke, marc;* see MARK²).]

os·to·mate (ŏs′tə-māt′) *n.* One who has undergone an ostomy.

os·to·my (ŏs′tə-mē) *n., pl.* -**mies** Surgical construction of an artificial excretory opening. [< (COL)OSTOMY.]

os·tra·cism (ŏs′trə-sĭz′əm) *n.* **1a.** The act of banishing or excluding. **b.** Banishment or exclusion from a group; disgrace. **2.** In ancient Greece, the temporary banishment by popular vote of one deemed a threat to the state.

os·tra·cize (ŏs′trə-sīz′) *tr.v.* -**cized,** -**ciz·ing,** -**ciz·es 1.** To exclude from a group. **2.** To banish by ostracism. [Gk. *ostrakizein* < *ostrakon,* shell, potsherd (< the potsherds used as ballots in voting for ostracism). See **ost-** in App.]

os·tra·cod (ŏs′trə-kŏd′) *n.* Any of various minute, chiefly freshwater crustaceans of the subclass Ostracoda, having a bivalve carapace. [NLat. *Ostracōda,* subclass name < Gk. *ostrakōdēs, testaceous < ostrakon,* shell. See **ost-** in App.]

os·tra·co·derm (ŏs′trə-kō-dûrm′) *n.* Any of several groups of extinct primitive jawless fishes of the Paleozoic, having bodies covered with bony plates. [Gk. *ostrakon,* shell; see **ost-** in App. + -DERM.]

os·tra·con (ŏs′trə-kŏn′) *n., pl.* -**ca** (-kə) An inscribed potsherd. [Gk. *ostrakon,* shell. See **ost-** in App.]

Os·tra·va (ô′strä-vä) A city of NE Czech Republic near the Oder R. Pop. 327,159.

os·trich (ŏs′trĭch, ôs′-) *n., pl.* **ostrich** or -**trich·es 1a.** A large swift-running flightless bird (*Struthio camelus*) of Africa having a long bare neck, small head, and two-toed feet. **b.** A rhea. **2.** One who tries to avoid disagreeable situations by refusing to face them. [ME < OFr. *ostrusce, ostrice* and Med.Lat. *ostrica,* both < VLat. **avis strūthiō* : Lat. *avis,* bird; see **awi-** in App. + LLat. *strūthiō,* ostrich; see STRUTHIOUS.]

ostrich fern *n.* A fern (*Matteuccia struthiopteris*) of northern temperate regions having long fronds that form a crown.

Os·tro·goth (ŏs′trə-gŏth′) *n.* One of a tribe of eastern Goths that conquered and ruled Italy from A.D. 493 to 555. [< ME *Ostrogotes,* Ostrogoths < LLat. *Ostrogothī : ostro-,* eastern (of Gmc. orig.; see **aus-** in App.) + *Gothī,* Goths; see GOTH.]

Ost·wald (ŏst′wôld′, ôst′vält), **Wilhelm** 1853–1932. German chemist who won a 1909 Nobel Prize.

Os·ty·ak also **Os·ti·ak** (ŏs′tē-ăk′) *n.* **1.** A member of a Finno-Ugric people inhabiting western Siberia. **2.** The Ugric language of this people. [Russ. < Ostyak *āsyakh,* pl. of *āskho,* person from the Ob River < *Ās,* the Ob River.]

Os·wald (ŏz′wôld′), **Lee Harvey** 1939–63. Amer. alleged assassin of President John F. Kennedy (Nov. 22, 1963) who was shot while under arrest (Nov. 24).

Oś·wię·cim (ôsh-vyĕn′chĕm) Formerly **Ausch·witz** (oush′vĭts′) A city of S Poland W of Kraków; site of the largest Nazi concentration camp. Pop. 45,700.

OT *abbr.* **1.** occupational therapy **2.** Old Testament **3.** overtime

ot- *pref.* Variant of **oto-.**

O·ta·hei·te orange (ō′tə-hē′tē, -hā′-) *n.* A widely cultivated house plant, considered a hybrid between *Citrus limon* and *C. reticulata,* having lemon-shaped insipid fruit. [After *Otaheite* (Tahiti).]

o·tal·gi·a (ō-tăl′jē-ə, -jə) *n.* Pain in the ear; earache. —**o·tal′gic** *adj.*

OTB *abbr.* off-track betting

OTC *abbr.* **1.** Officers' Training Corps **2.** over-the-counter

oth·er (ŭth′ər) *adj.* **1a.** Being the remaining one or more: *the other ear.* **b.** Being the remaining ones of several: *His other books are packed.* **2.** Different from that or those implied or specified: *Any other person would go.* **3.** Of a different character or quality. **4.** Of a different time or era either future or past: *other centuries.* **5.** Additional; extra: *I have no other shoes.* **6.** Opposite or contrary; reverse: *the other side.* **7.** Alternate; second: *every other day.* **8.** Of the recent past: *just the other day.* ❖ *n.* **1a.** The remaining one of two or more: *One wept, and the other giggled.* **b. others** The remaining ones of several: *After she left, the others sighed.* **2a.** A different person or thing: *one hurricane after the other.* **b.** An additional person or thing: *How many others will come?* ❖ *pron.* **1.** A different or additional person or thing: *someone or other.* **2. others** People aside from oneself: *what others think.* ❖ *adv.* In another way; differently: *other than perfectly.* [ME < OE *ōther.* See **al-** in App.]

oth·er·ness (ŭth′ər-nĭs) *n.* The quality or condition of being or seeming other or different, esp. if exotic or strange.

other than *prep.* With the exception of; except for; besides: *Other than one sister, she has no close relatives.*

oth·er·wise (ŭth′ər-wīz′) *adv.* **1.** In another way; differently: *She thought otherwise.* **2.** Under other circumstances: *Otherwise I might go.* **3.** In other respects: *an otherwise logical mind.* ❖ *adj.* Other than supposed; different: *The evidence is otherwise.* [ME < OE (*on*) *ōthere wīsan,* (in) another manner : *ōthre,* dative of

osteoporosis
top: scanning electron micrograph of healthy bone
bottom: scanning electron micrograph of porous bone

ostrich
male ostrich
Struthio camelus

otoscope

otter hound

ōther, other + *wīsan*, dative of *wīse*, manner; see WISE[2].]

oth·er·world (ŭth′ər-wûrld′) *n.* A world or existence beyond earthly reality.

oth·er·world·ly (ŭth′ər-wûrld′lē) *adj.* **1.** Of or relating to another world, esp. a mystical or transcendental one. **2.** Devoted to the world of the mind and intellectual or imaginative things. **3.** Concerned with an afterlife, esp. when inattentive to the present. —**oth′er·world′li·ness** *n.*

Oth·man (ŏth′mən) *n., pl.* **-mans** *Archaic* An Ottoman Turk; a Turk. [After *Othman*, var. of OSMAN (I).]

Oth·man I (ŏth′mən, ōth-män′) See **Osman I.**

O·tho I (ō′thō, ō′tō) See **Otto I.**

o·tic (ō′tĭk, ŏt′ĭk) *adj.* Of, relating to, or located near the ear; auricular. [Gk. *ōtikos* < *ous*, *ōt*-, ear. See **ous-** in App.]

-otic *suff.* **1.** Of, relating to, or characterized by a specified condition or process: *anabiotic.* **2.** Having a specified disease or abnormal condition: *epizootic.* **3.** Characterized by an increase or formation of a specified kind: *leukocytotic.* [Fr. *-otique* < Lat. *-ōticus* < Gk. *-ōtikos*, adj. suff.]

o·ti·ose (ō′shē-ōs′, ō′tē-) *adj.* **1.** Lazy; indolent. **2.** Of no use. **3.** Ineffective; futile. [Lat. *ōtiōsus*, idle < *ōtium*, leisure.] —**o′ti·ose′ly** *adv.* —**o′ti·os′i·ty** (-ŏs′ĭ-tē) *n.*

O·tis (ō′tĭs), **Elisha Graves** 1811–61. Amer. inventor of the first passenger elevator (installed 1857).

Otis, James 1725–83. Amer. Revolutionary politician who influenced sentiment against the British.

o·ti·tis (ō-tī′tĭs) *n.* Inflammation of the ear. —**o·tit′ic** (-tĭt′ĭk) *adj.*

otitis media *n.* Inflammation of the middle ear, common in children and often causing pain and temporary hearing loss. [NLat. : OTITIS + Lat. *media*, fem. of *medius*, middle.]

O·to (ō′tō) *n., pl.* **Oto** or **O·tos** **1.** A member of a Native American people formerly inhabiting eastern Nebraska along the Platte River, with present-day descendants in north-central Oklahoma. **2.** The Siouan language of the Oto. [Missouri *wat′ota*, lechers.]

oto- or **ot-** *pref.* Ear: *otology.* [NLat. < Gk. *ous*, *ōt*-, ear. See **ous-** in App.]

o·to·cyst (ō′tə-sĭst′) *n.* **1.** The structure formed by invagination of the embryonic ectodermal tissue that develops into the inner ear. **2.** See **statocyst.** —**o′to·cys′tic** *adj.*

o·to·lar·yn·gol·o·gy (ō′tō-lăr′ĭng-gŏl′ə-jē) *n.* The branch of medicine that deals with diagnosis and treatment of diseases of the ear, nose, and throat. —**o′to·lar′yn·go·log′i·cal** (-lə-rĭng′gə-lŏj′ĭ-kəl) *adj.* —**o′to·lar′yn·gol′o·gist** *n.*

o·to·lith (ō′tə-lĭth′) *n.* One of many minute calcareous particles found in the inner ear of certain lower vertebrates and in the statocysts of many invertebrates. —**o′to·lith′ic** *adj.*

o·tol·o·gy (ō-tŏl′ə-jē) *n.* The branch of medicine that deals with the structure, function, and pathology of the ear. —**o′to·log′i·cal** (ō′tə-lŏj′ĭ-kəl) *adj.* —**o·tol′o·gist** *n.*

o·to·rhi·no·lar·yn·gol·o·gy (ō′tō-rī′nō-lăr′ĭng-gŏl′ə-jē) *n.* See **otolaryngology.** —**o′to·rhi′no·la·ryn′go·log′i·cal** (-lə-rĭng′gə-lŏj′ĭ-kəl) *adj.* —**o′to·rhi′no·lar′yn·gol′o·gist** *n.*

o·to·scle·ro·sis (ō′tō-sklə-rō′sĭs) *n.* A disease of the ear in which abnormal deposits of spongy bone in the inner ear cause a progressive loss of hearing. —**o′to·scle·rot′ic** (-rŏt′ĭk) *adj.*

o·to·scope (ō′tə-skōp′) *n.* An instrument for examining the interior of the ear, esp. the eardrum, consisting essentially of a magnifying lens and a light.

o·to·tox·ic (ō′tə-tŏk′sĭk) *adj.* Having a toxic effect on the structures of the ear, esp. on its nerve supply.

O·tran·to (ō-trän′tō), **Strait of** A passage between SE Italy and W Albania connecting the Adriatic Sea with the Ionian Sea.

OTS *abbr.* Officers' Training School

ot·tar (ŏt′ər) *n.* Variant of **attar.**

ot·ta·va (ō-tä′və) *adv. & adj. Music* At an octave higher or lower than the notes written. [Ital. *(all′)ottava*, (at the) octave < Med.Lat. *octāva* < Lat., fem. of *octāvus*, eighth. See OCTAVE.]

ottava ri·ma (rē′mə) *n.* A stanza of verse consisting of eight lines in iambic pentameter rhyming *ababbcc.* [Ital. : *ottava*, fem. of *ottavo*, eighth + *rima*, rhyme.]

Ot·ta·wa¹ (ŏt′ə-wə, -wä′, -wô′) *n., pl.* **Ottawa** or **-was** **1.** A member of a Native American people formerly inhabiting the northern shore of Lake Huron, with present-day populations mainly in southern Ontario, northern Michigan, and Oklahoma. **2.** Their Ojibwa dialect. [Ojibwa *odaawaa*.]

Ot·ta·wa² (ŏt′ə-wə) The cap. of Canada, in SE Ontario at the confluence of the Ottawa R. and the Rideau Canal; founded as Bytown during the construction of the Rideau Canal and renamed Ottawa in 1854. Pop. 323,340.

Ottawa River A river rising in the Laurentian Plateau of SW Quebec, Canada, and flowing c. 1,126 km (700 mi) to the St. Lawrence R. near Montreal.

ot·ter (ŏt′ər) *n., pl.* **otter** or **-ters** **1.** Any of various aquatic carnivorous mammals of the genus *Lutra* and allied genera, having webbed feet and dense, dark brown fur. **2.** The fur of this mammal. [ME *oter* < OE *otor.* See **wed-** in App.]

otter hound *n.* Any of a breed of hardy dog developed in England for hunting otters, having slightly webbed feet and a thick coarse coat with an oily undercoat.

ot·to (ŏt′ō) *n.* Variant of **attar.**

Ot·to I (ŏt′ō, ŏt′ō) also **O·tho I** (ō′thō, ō′tō) Known as "Otto the Great." 912–973. King of Germany (936–973) and first Holy Roman emperor (962–973).

ot·to·man (ŏt′ə-mən) *n., pl.* **-mans** **1a.** An upholstered sofa or divan without arms or a back. **b.** An upholstered low seat or cushioned footstool. **2.** A heavy silk or rayon fabric with a corded texture, usu. used for coats and trimmings. [Fr. *ottomane*, fem. of *ottoman*, Ottoman. See OTTOMAN.]

Ottoman *n., pl.* **-mans** A Turk, esp. a member of the family or tribe of Osman I. ❖ *adj.* **1.** Of or relating to the Ottoman Empire or its people, language, or culture. **2.** Ottoman Turkish. [Fr. < Ital. *ottomano* < Ar. *'uṭmānī*, of Uthman < *'uṭmān*, Osman I.]

Ottoman Empire also **Turkish Empire** A vast Turkish sultanate of SW Asia, NE Africa, and SE Europe; founded in the 13th cent. by Osman I and dissolved after World War I.

Ottoman Turkish *n.* The form of the Turkish language used as the administrative and literary language of the Ottoman Empire.

oua·ba·in (wä-bā′ĭn) *n.* A poisonous glycoside, $C_{29}H_{44}O_{12}$, extracted from the seeds of the African trees *Strophanthus gratus* and *Acokanthera ouabaio* and used as a heart stimulant. [< Fr. *ouabaïo* < Somali *wabayo.*]

Ouach·i·ta Mountains (wŏsh′ĭ-tô′) A mountain range extending c. 322 km (200 mi) from central AR to SE OK and rising to 839.7 m (2,753 ft).

Ouachita River A river rising in the Ouachita Mts. of W AR and flowing c. 965 km (600 mi) into E LA.

Oua·ga·dou·gou (wä′gə-dōō′gōō) The cap. of Burkina Faso, in the central part. Pop. 634,479.

ou·bli·ette (ōō′blē-ĕt′) *n.* A dungeon with a trapdoor in the ceiling as its only means of entrance or exit. [Fr. < *oublier*, to forget < OFr. *oblier* < VLat. **oblītāre* < Lat. *oblitus*, p. part. of *oblīvīscī.*]

ouch¹ (ouch) *interj.* Used to express sudden pain or displeasure.

ouch² (ouch) *n.* **1.** A setting for a precious stone. **2.** A brooch or buckle set with jewels. **3.** *Obsolete* A clasp; a brooch. [ME *ouche* < AN *(une) ouche*, alteration of *(une) nouch*, (a) brooch, of Gmc. orig.]

oud (ōōd) *n.* A musical instrument of northern Africa and southwest Asia resembling a lute. [Ar. *'ūd*, wood, stem, lute, oud.]

Oudh (oud) A historical region of N-central India dating from at least the 4th cent. A.D.; ruled by the Moguls after the 16th cent. and annexed by Great Britain in 1856.

ought¹ (ôt) *aux.v.* **1.** Used to indicate obligation or duty: *You ought to help.* **2.** Used to indicate advisability or prudence: *You ought to wear a raincoat.* **3.** Used to indicate desirability: *You ought to have been there; it was great fun.* **4.** Used to indicate probability or likelihood: *She ought to finish by next week.* [ME *oughten*, to be obliged to < *oughte*, owned < OE *āhte*, p. t. of *āgan*, to possess.]

ought² (ôt) *pron. & adv.* Variant of **aught¹.**

ought³ (ôt) *n.* Variant of **aught².**

ought⁴ (ôt) *v. Obsolete* A past participle of **owe.**

ou·gui·ya (ōō-gē′yə) *n.* See table at **currency.** [Native word in Mauritania.]

Oui·ja (wē′jə, -jə) A trademark used for a board with the alphabet and other symbols on it and a planchette that is thought, when touched with the fingers, to move so as to spell spiritualistic and telepathic messages on the board.

Ouj·da (ōōj-dä′) A city of NE Morocco near the Algerian border; founded 944. Pop. 331,000.

ounce¹ (ouns) *n.* **1a.** A unit of weight in the US Customary System, an avoirdupois unit equal to 437.5 grains (28.35 grams). See table at **measurement.** **b.** A unit of apothecary weight, equal to 480 grains (31.10 grams). **2.** A fluid ounce. See table at **measurement.** **3.** A tiny bit: *not an ounce of sympathy.* [ME *unce* < OFr. < Lat. *ūncia.* See **oi-no-** in App.]

ounce² (ouns) *n.* See **snow leopard.** [ME *unce* < OFr. *once*, alteration of *lonce* < VLat. **luncea* < Lat. *lynx*, *lync*-, lynx < Gk. *lunx.* See **leuk-** in App.]

our (our) *adj.* The possessive form of **we.** Used as a modifier before a noun: *our street.* [ME < OE *ūre.* See **nes-²** in App.]

Our Father *n.* See **Lord's Prayer.**

Our Lady *n.* The Virgin Mary.

ours (ourz) *pron.* (*used with a sing. or pl. verb*) Used to indicate the one or ones belonging to us: *This notebook is ours. Their apples are red, but ours are green.* [ME *oures < oure*, our < OE *ūre.* See **nes-²** in App.]

our·self (our-sĕlf′, är-) *pron.* **1.** Myself. Used as a reflexive when *we* is used instead of *I* by a singular speaker or author, as in an editorial or a royal proclamation. See Usage Note at **myself.**

2. *Nonstandard* Ourselves. See Note at **hisself.**

our·selves (our-sĕlvz′, är-) *pron.* **1.** Those ones identical with us. **a.** Used reflexively as the object of a verb or the object of a preposition: *We bought ourselves lunch.* **b.** Used for emphasis: *We ourselves were certain.* **c.** Used in an absolute construction: *Feeling chilly ourselves, we went indoors.* **2.** Our normal or healthy condition or state: *We're feeling ourselves again after our colds.* See Usage Note at **myself.**

–ous *suff.* **1.** Possessing; full of; characterized by: *joyous.* **2.** Having a valence lower than that of a specified element in compounds or ions named with adjectives ending in *-ic: ferrous.* [ME < OFr. *-ous, -eus, -eux* < Lat. *-ōsus* and *-us,* adj. suff.]

ou·sel (ōō′zəl) *n.* Variant of **ouzel.**

Ouse River (ōōz) **1.** also **Great Ouse River** A river, c. 249 km (155 mi), flowing from S-central England to the Wash, an inlet of the North Sea. **2.** A river, c. 97 km (60 mi), of NE England joining the Trent R. to form the Humber R.

oust (oust) *tr.v.* **oust·ed, oust·ing, ousts** **1.** To eject from a position or place; force out: *ousted him from power.* See Syns at **eject. 2.** To take the place of, esp. by force; supplant. [ME *ousten* < AN *ouster* < Lat. *obstāre,* to hinder. See OBSTACLE.]

oust·er (ou′stər) *n.* **1a.** The act of ousting. **b.** The state of being ousted. **2.** One that ousts. **3.** *Law* The act of forcing one out of possession or occupancy of material property to which that one is entitled; illegal or wrongful dispossession. [AN, to oust, ouster. See OUST.]

out (out) *adv.* **1.** In a direction away from the inside: *Let's go out and look at the stars.* **2.** Away from the center or middle: *The troops fanned out.* **3a.** Away from a usual place: *went out for the evening.* **b.** Out of normal position: *threw his back out.* **c.** Out-of-bounds. **4a.** From inside a building or shelter into the open air; outside: *went out to play.* **b.** In the open air; outside: *Is it snowing out?* **5a.** From within a container or source: *drained the water out.* **b.** From among others: *picked out the thief in the crowd.* **6a.** To exhaustion or depletion: *Supplies ran out.* **b.** Into extinction or imperceptibility: *The fire has gone out.* **c.** To a finish or conclusion: *Play the game out.* **d.** To the fullest extent or degree: *all decked out for the dance.* **e.** In or into competition or directed effort: *went out for golf.* **7.** In or into a state of unconsciousness: *The drug put him out for two hours.* **8a.** Into being or evident existence: *The new car models have come out.* **b.** Into public circulation: *The paper came out early today.* **9.** Into view: *The moon came out.* **10.** Without inhibition; boldly: *Speak out.* **11.** Into possession of another or others; into distribution: *giving out free passes.* **12a.** Into disuse or an unfashionable status: *Narrow ties have gone out.* **b.** Into a state of deprivation or loss: *voted the governor out.* **13.** In the time following; afterward: *six months out.* **14.** *Baseball* So as to be retired, or counted as an out: *He grounded out.* **15.** On strike. ❖ *adj.* **1.** Exterior; external: *the out surface of a ship's hull.* **2.** Directed away from a place or center; outgoing: *the out doorway.* **3.** Traveling or landing out-of-bounds. **4a.** Not operating or operational: *The power is out.* **b.** Extinguished: *The lights are out next door.* **5.** Unconscious: *was out for an hour after surgery.* **6.** Not to be considered or permitted: *Eating candy before dinner is out.* **7.** No longer fashionable. **8.** No longer possessing or supplied with something: *I'd offer you coffee but we're out.* **9.** *Informal* Openly gay, lesbian, or bisexual: *an out performer.* **10.** *Baseball* Not allowed to continue to bat or run; retired. ❖ *prep.* **1.** Forth from; through: *He fell out the window.* **2.** Beyond or outside of: *Out this door is the garage.* **3.** Within the area of: *The house has a garden out back.* ❖ *n.* **1.** One that is out, esp. one who is out of power. **2.** *Informal* A means of escape. **3.** *Baseball* **a.** A play in which a batter or base runner is retired. **b.** The player retired in such a play. **4.** *Sports* A serve or return that falls out of bounds in a court game. **5.** *Printing* A word or other part of a manuscript omitted from the printed copy. ❖ *v.* **out·ed, out·ing, outs** *—intr.* To be disclosed or revealed; come out. *—tr.* **1.** *Sports* To send (a tennis ball, for example) outside the court or playing area. **2.** To expose (one considered to be heterosexual) as being gay, lesbian, or bisexual: *outed a well-known politician* **3.** *Chiefly British* To knock unconscious. ❖ *interj.* Used in a two-way radio to indicate that a transmission is complete and no reply is expected. **—idiom: on the outs** *Informal* Not on friendly terms; disagreeing. [ME < OE *ūt.* See **ud-** in App.]

out– *pref.* **1.** In a way that surpasses, exceeds, or goes beyond: *outdistance.* [< OUT.]

out·age (ou′tij) *n.* **1.** A quantity or portion of something lacking after shipping or storage. **2.** A temporary suspension of operation, esp. of electric power.

out and away *adv.* By far: *She's out and away the best.*

out-and-out (out′n-out′) *adj.* Complete; thoroughgoing.

out-and-out·er (out′ən-ou′tər) *n.* One given to extremes.

out·back (out′băk′) *n.* The remote rural part of a country, esp. of Australia or New Zealand. ❖ *adv.* (out′băk′) Out to or in the outback. **—out′back′er** *n.*

out·bal·ance (out-băl′əns) *tr.v.* **-anced, -anc·ing, -anc·es** To exceed in influence or significance; outweigh.

out·bid (out-bĭd′) *tr.v.* **-bid, -bid·den** (-bĭd′n) or **-bid, -bid·ding, -bids** To bid higher than: *We outbid our rivals.*

out·board (out′bôrd′, -bōrd′) *adj.* **1.** *Nautical* **a.** Situated or positioned outside the hull of a vessel. **b.** Being in a position that is away from the center line of a ship. **2.** Situated or positioned toward the end of an aircraft wing. ❖ *n.* **1.** An outboard motor. **2.** A boat with an outboard motor. **—out′board′** *adv.*

outboard motor *n.* A detachable engine mounted on outboard brackets or on the transom of a boat.

out·bound (out′bound′) *adj.* Outward bound; headed away.

out·break (out′brāk′) *n.* **1.** A sudden increase: *a flu outbreak.* **2.** A sudden eruption; an outburst: *a violent outbreak.*

out·breed (out′brēd′) *tr.v.* **-bred** (-brĕd′), **-breed·ing, -breeds** To subject to outbreeding.

out·breed·ing (out′brē′dĭng) *n.* **1.** The breeding of distantly related or unrelated individuals, often producing a superior hybrid. **2.** *Anthropology* The mating of persons from different groups, often as a result of marriage proscriptions within the group.

out·build·ing (out′bĭl′dĭng) *n.* A building separate from but associated with a main building.

out·burst (out′bûrst′) *n.* A sudden violent display, as of activity or emotion: *an outburst of indignation.*

out·call (out′kôl′) *n.* A visit by a professional person to a client or patient's home; a house call.

out·cast (out′kăst′) *n.* One that has been excluded from a society or system. **—out′cast′** *adj.*

out·caste (out′kăst′) *n.* An Untouchable.

out·class (out-klăs′) *tr.v.* **-classed, -class·ing, -class·es** To surpass decisively, so as to appear of a higher class.

out·come (out′kŭm′) *n.* An end result; a consequence. See Syns at **effect.**

out·crop (out′krŏp′) *n.* A portion of bedrock or other stratum protruding through the soil level. ❖ *intr.v.* (out-krŏp′) **-cropped, -crop·ping, -crops** To protrude above the soil. [OUT + CROP, to appear on the surface.]

out·cross (out′krôs′, -krŏs′) *tr.v.* **-crossed, -cross·ing, -cross·es** To cross (animals or plants) by breeding individuals of different strains but usu. of the same breed. ❖ *n.* **1.** The process of outcrossing. **2.** Offspring thus produced.

out·cry (out′krī′) *n., pl.* **-cries 1.** A loud cry or clamor. **2.** A strong protest or objection: *public outcry over prices.*

out·date (out-dāt′) *tr.v.* **-dat·ed, -dat·ing, -dates** To replace or make obsolete or old-fashioned.

out·dat·ed (out-dā′tĭd) *adj.* Out-of-date; old-fashioned.

out·dis·tance (out-dĭs′təns) *tr.v.* **-tanced, -tanc·ing, -tanc·es** **1.** To outrun, esp. in a long-distance race. **2.** To surpass by a wide margin, esp. through superior skill or endurance.

out·do (out-dōō′) *tr.v.* **-did** (-dĭd′), **-done** (-dŭn′), **-do·ing, -does** (-dŭz′) To do more or better than.

out·door (out′dôr′, -dōr′) *also* **out-of-door** (out′əv-dôr′, -dōr′) *adj.* Located in, done in, or suited to the open air.

out·doors (out-dôrz′, -dōrz′) *also* **out-of-doors** (out′əv-dôrz′, -dōrz′) *adv.* In or into the open; outside. ❖ *n.* **1.** The open air. **2.** An area away from human settlements.

out·doors·man (out-dôrz′mən, -dōrz′-) *n.* A man who spends considerable time pursuing outdoor activities.

out·doors·wo·man (out-dôrz′wōōm′ən, -dōrz′-) *n.* A woman who spends considerable time pursuing outdoor activities.

out·door·sy (out-dôr′zē, -dōr′-) *adj. Informal* **1.** Associated with the outdoors. **2.** Showing a liking for the outdoors.

out·er (ou′tər) *adj.* **1.** Located on the outside; external. **2.** Farther than another from the center or middle. **3.** Relating to the body or its appearance rather than the mind or spirit.

out·er·course (ou′tər-kôrs′, -kōrs′) *n.* Sexual stimulation or activity between partners without anal or vaginal penetration. [OUTER + (INTER)COURSE.]

outer ear *n.* See **external ear.**

Outer Hebrides See **Hebrides.**

Outer Mongolia See **Mongolia** 2.

out·er·most (ou′tər-mōst′) *adj.* Most distant from the center or inside; outmost.

outer planet *n.* Any of the five planets, Jupiter, Saturn, Uranus, Neptune, and Pluto, with orbits outside that of Mars.

outer space *n.* **1.** The region of space immediately beyond Earth's atmosphere. **2.** Interplanetary or interstellar space.

out·er·wear (ou′tər-wâr′) *n.* Clothing, such as hats, coats, and gloves, for use outdoors.

out·face (out-fās′) *tr.v.* **-faced, -fac·ing, -fac·es** **1.** To overcome with a bold or self-assured look; stare down. **2.** To defy or resist.

out·fall (out′fôl′) *n.* The place where a sewer, drain, or stream discharges.

out·field (out′fēld′) *n. Baseball* **1.** The playing area extending outward from the diamond, divided into left, center, and right field. **2.** The position played by an outfielder. **3.** The members of a team playing in the outfield.

out·field·er (out′fēl′dər) *n. Baseball* A player who defends left, center, or right field.

out·fit (out′fĭt′) *n.* **1.** A set of tools or equipment for a specialized purpose. **2.** A set of clothing. **3.** *Informal* An association of persons, esp. a military or business group. **4.** The act of equipping. ❖ *tr.v.* **-fit·ted, -fit·ting, -fits** To provide with necessary equipment. **—out′fit′ter** *n.*

out·flank (out-flăngk′) *tr.v.* **-flanked, -flank·ing, -flanks** **1.** To maneuver around and behind the flank of (an opposing force).

outcrop

ă pat　oi boy
ā pay　ou out
âr care　ōō took
ä father　ōō boot
ĕ pet　ŭ cut
ē be　ûr urge
ĭ pit　th thin
ī pie　th this
îr pier　hw which
ŏ pot　zh vision
ō toe　ə about,
ô paw　　item

Stress marks: ′ (primary);
′ (secondary), as in
lexicon (lĕk′sĭ-kŏn′)

2. To gain a tactical advantage over.

out·flow (out′flō′) *n.* **1.** The act or the process of flowing out. **2a.** Something that flows out. **b.** The amount flowing out: *a heavy outflow of cash.* ❖ *intr.v.* **-flowed, -flow·ing, -flows** To issue or stream out, in or as if in a flow.

out·fox (out-fŏks′) *tr.v.* **-foxed, -fox·ing, -fox·es** To surpass (another) in cleverness or cunning; outsmart.

out-front (out′frŭnt′) *adj. Informal* Straightforward; frank.

out·gas (out′găs′) *v.* **-gassed, -gas·sing, -gas·ses** —*tr.* To remove embedded gas from (a solid), as by heating or reducing the pressure. —*intr.* To lose gas, as from a solid.

out·gen·er·al (out-jĕn′ər-əl) *tr.v.* **-aled, -al·ing, -als** To surpass (another, esp. an opponent) in leadership.

out·giv·ing (out′gĭv′ĭng) *adj.* Friendly and responsive; outgoing.

out·go (out-gō′) *tr.v.* **-went** (-wĕnt′), **-gone** (-gôn′, -gŏn′), **-go·ing, -goes** (-gōz′) To go beyond; exceed or surpass. ❖ *n.* (out′gō′) *pl.* **-goes 1.** Something that goes out, esp. an expenditure or a cost. **2.** The act or process of going out.

out·go·ing (out′gō′ĭng) *adj.* **1a.** Going out or away; departing. **b.** Retiring from or relinquishing a place, position, or office. **c.** Addressed for sending: *outgoing mail.* **2.** Sociable and responsive to others; friendly. **3.** Intended to be taken out, as from a restaurant. —**out′go′ing·ness** *n.*

out-group (out′groop′) *n.* A group of people excluded from or not belonging to one's own group, esp. when viewed as subordinate or contemptibly different.

out·grow (out-grō′) *tr.v.* **-grew** (-groo′), **-grown** (-grōn′), **-grow·ing, -grows 1.** To grow too large for. **2.** To lose or discard in the course of maturation. **3.** To surpass in growth.

out·growth (out′grōth′) *n.* **1.** The act or process of growing out. **2.** A product of growing out; a projecting part or offshoot. **3.** A result or consequence.

out·guess (out-gĕs′) *tr.v.* **-guessed, -guess·ing, -guess·es 1.** To anticipate correctly the actions of. **2.** To gain the advantage over (another) by cleverness or forethought; outwit.

out·gun (out′gŭn′) *tr.v.* **-gunned, -gun·ning, -guns 1.** To surpass in military force. **2.** To overwhelm or defeat.

out·haul (out′hôl′) *n. Nautical* A line used to extend a sail along a spar or boom.

out·house (out′hous′) *n.* **1.** An enclosed structure having a seat with one or two holes over a pit and serving as an outdoor toilet. **2.** An outbuilding, as on a farm.

out·ing (ou′tĭng) *n.* **1.** An excursion, typically a pleasure trip. **2.** A walk outdoors. **3.** The exposing of one assumed to be or wishing to be considered heterosexual as being gay, lesbian, or bisexual. **4.** An athletic competition or an appearance therein.

outing flannel *n.* A soft lightweight cotton fabric, usu. with a short nap on both sides.

out·land (out′lănd′, -lənd) *n.* **1.** A foreign land. **2. outlands** A country's outlying areas; the provinces. —**out′land′** *adj.*

out·land·er (out′lăn′dər) *n.* **1.** A person from a foreign country; a foreigner. **2.** A stranger.

out·land·ish (out-lăn′dĭsh) *adj.* **1.** Conspicuously unconventional; bizarre. See Syns at **strange. 2.** Strikingly unfamiliar. **3.** Located far from civilized areas. **4.** *Archaic* Of foreign origin. —**out·land′ish·ly** *adv.* —**out·land′ish·ness** *n.*

out·last (out-lăst′) *tr.v.* **-last·ed, -last·ing, -lasts** To last longer than.

out·law (out′lô′) *n.* **1a.** A fugitive from the law. **b.** A habitual criminal. **c.** A rebel; a nonconformist. **2.** A person excluded from normal legal protection and rights. **3.** A wild or vicious horse or other animal. ❖ *tr.v.* **-lawed, -law·ing, -laws 1.** To declare illegal. **2.** To place under a ban; prohibit. **3.** To deprive (one declared to be a criminal fugitive) of the protection of the law. [ME *outlaue* < OE *ūtlaga* < ON *ūtlagi* < *ūtlagr*, outlawed, banished : *ūt*, out; see **ud-** in App. + *lög*, law; see **legh-** in App.] —**out′law′** *adj.*

out·law·ry (out′lô′rē) *n., pl.* **-ries 1.** The act or process of outlawing or the state of having been outlawed. **2.** Defiance of the law. [ME *outlawrie* < AN *utlagerie* and < Med.Lat. *ūtlagāria*, both < OE *ūtlaga*, outlaw. See OUTLAW.]

out·lay (out′lā′) *n.* **1.** The spending or disbursement of money. **2.** An amount spent; an expenditure. ❖ *tr.v.* (out-lā′) **-laid** (-lād′), **-lay·ing, -lays** To spend or disburse (money).

out·let (out′lĕt′, -lĭt) *n.* **1a.** A passage for escape or exit; a vent. **b.** A means of release or gratification, as for energies, drives, or desires. **2a.** A stream that flows out of a lake or pond. **b.** The mouth of a river where it flows into a larger body of water. **c.** The point of intersection of a driveway and a road. **3a.** A commercial market for goods or services. **b.** A store that sells the goods of a particular manufacturer or wholesaler. **4.** A receptacle connected to a power supply and equipped with a socket for a plug.

out·li·er (out′lī′ər) *n.* **1.** One whose domicile is distant from his or her place of business. **2.** A value far from most others in a set of data. **3.** *Geology* A portion of stratified rock separated from a main formation by erosion.

out·line (out′līn′) *n.* **1a.** A line marking the outer contours or boundaries of an object or figure. **b.** The shape of an object or figure. **2a.** A style of drawing in which objects are delineated in contours without shading. **b.** A sketch done in this style. **3a.** A general description covering the main points of a subject. **b.** A

statement summarizing the important points of a text. **c.** A summary of a written work or speech, usu. analyzed in headings and subheadings. **4.** A preliminary draft or plan, as of a project. ❖ *tr.v.* **-lined, -lin·ing, -lines 1.** To draw an outline of. **2.** To display or accentuate the outline of. **3.** To give the main features or various aspects of; summarize.

SYNONYMS *outline, contour, profile, silhouette* These nouns refer to a line that defines the boundary and shape of an object, mass, or figure: *the outline of the mountains against the sunset; saw the island's contour from the airplane; a monarch's profile on an ancient coin; saw the dark silhouette of the family waving farewell.*

out·live (out-lĭv′) *tr.v.* **-lived, -liv·ing, -lives 1.** To live longer than: *She outlived her son.* **2.** To continue in use or existence long enough to survive (something else).

out·look (out′lŏok′) *n.* **1.** A point of view; an attitude: *a positive outlook.* **2.** Expectation for the future. **3a.** A place where something can be viewed. **b.** The view seen from such a place. **4.** The act of looking out.

out loud *adv.* Loud enough to be audible; aloud.

out·ly·ing (out′lī′ĭng) *adj.* Relatively distant or remote from a center or middle: *outlying regions.*

out·man (out-măn′) *tr.v.* **-manned, -man·ning, -mans 1.** To exceed in human resources; outnumber. **2.** To get the better of; overwhelm or defeat.

out·ma·neu·ver (out′mə-noo′vər, -nyoo′-) *tr.v.* **-vered, -ver·ing, -vers 1.** To overcome (an opponent) by artful, clever maneuvering. **2.** To excel in maneuverability.

out·match (out-măch′) *tr.v.* **-matched, -match·ing, -match·es** To prove greater or better than; surpass.

out·mi·grant (out′mī′grənt) *n.* One that out-migrates.

out·mi·grate (out′mī′grāt) *intr.v.* **-grat·ed, -grat·ing, -grates** To move out of one community, region, or country in order to reside in another. —**out′-mi·gra′tion** *n.*

out·mode (out-mōd′) *tr.v.* **-mod·ed, -mod·ing, -modes** To cause to become unfashionable or obsolete.

out·mod·ed (out-mō′dĭd) *adj.* **1.** Not in fashion: *outmoded ideas.* **2.** No longer usable or practical; obsolete.

out·most (out′mōst′) *adj.* Farthest out; outermost.

out·mus·cle (out-mŭs′əl) *tr.v.* **-cled, -cling, -cles** *Informal* To dominate or defeat by superior strength or power.

out·num·ber (out-nŭm′bər) *tr.v.* **-bered, -ber·ing, -bers** To exceed the number of; be more numerous than.

out of *prep.* **1a.** From within to the outside of: *got out of the car.* **b.** From a given condition: *came out of her trance.* **c.** From an origin, source, or cause: *made out of wood; did it out of spite.* **d.** In, esp. intermittently in: *works out of the main office.* **2a.** In a position or situation beyond the range, boundaries, limits, or sphere of: *out of sight.* **b.** In a state or position away from the expected or usual: *out of practice.* **3.** From among: *five out of six votes.* **4.** In or into a condition of no longer having: *out of coffee.* —*idiom:* **out of it** *Informal* **1.** Not aware of or participating in a particular group, pursuit, or trend. **2.** Disoriented or inebriated.

out-of-bod·y (out′əv-bŏd′ē) *adj.* Of or marked by the psychological sensation of perceiving oneself from an external perspective, as if from outside the physical body.

out-of-bounds (out′əv-boundz′) *adv.* Beyond the designated boundaries or limits.

out-of-court (out′əv-kôrt′, -kōrt′) *adj.* Managed or agreed upon without a judicial decision.

out-of-date (out′əv-dāt′) *adj.* Out of style or use; outmoded.

out-of-door (out′əv-dôr′, -dōr′) *adj.* Variant of **outdoor.**

out-of-doors (out′əv-dôrz′, -dōrz′) *adv. & n.* Variant of **outdoors.**

out of pocket *adv.* **1.** Without funds or assets. **2.** In a state of having experienced a loss, esp. a financial one.

out-of-pock·et (out′əv-pŏk′ĭt) *adj.* **1.** Calling for the spending of cash: *out-of-pocket expenses.* **2.** Lacking funds.

out-of-state (out′əv-stāt′) *adj.* Of, relating to, or being from another state.

out-of-stat·er (out′əv-stā′tər) *n.* **1.** A visitor from another state. **2.** A legal resident of one state who lives for a period of time in another, as to attend school.

out-of-the-way (out′əv-thə-wā′) *adj.* **1.** Being in a remote or secluded location: *an out-of-the-way resort.* **2.** Being out of the ordinary; unusual. **3.** Improper; offensive.

out-of-town (out′əv-toun′) *adj.* Of, relating to, being from, or happening in another town or city. —**out′-of-town′er** *n.*

out·pace (out-pās′) *tr.v.* **-paced, -pac·ing, -pac·es** To surpass or outdo (another), as in speed, growth, or performance.

out·pa·tient (out′pā′shənt) *n.* A patient in a hospital or clinic whose treatment does not require an overnight stay.

out·per·form (out′pər-fôrm′) *tr.v.* **-formed, -form·ing, -forms** To surpass (another) in performance.

out·place (out-plās′) *tr.v.* **-placed, -plac·ing, -plac·es** To discontinue the employment of. —**out′placed′** *adj.*

out·place·ment (out′plās′mənt) *n.* The process of helping a terminated employee search for a new job by provision of professional services, such as counseling.

out·play (out-plā′) *tr.v.* **-played, -play·ing, -plays** To surpass (an opponent) in skill, technique, or score.

out·point (out-point′) *tr.v.* **-point·ed, -point·ing, -points 1.** *Nautical* To sail closer to the wind than (another vessel). **2.** *Sports* To surpass (an opponent, esp. a boxer) in the number of points won.

out·poll (out-pōl′) *tr.v.* **-polled, -poll·ing, -polls** To win more votes than: *She outpolled her rival by a wide margin.*

out·post (out′pōst′) *n.* **1a.** A detachment of troops stationed at a distance from a main force to guard against surprise attacks. **b.** The station occupied by such troops. **c.** A military base in another country. **2.** An outlying settlement.

out·pour (out-pôr′, -pōr′) *intr. & tr.v.* **-poured, -pour·ing, -pours** To flow out rapidly or pour out. ❖ *n.* (out′pôr′, -pōr′) A rapid outflow; an outpouring. —**out·pour′er** *n.*

out·pour·ing (out′pôr′ĭng, -pōr′-) *n.* **1.** The act of pouring out. **2.** Something that pours out or is poured out; an outflow.

out·put (out′pŏot′) *n.* **1.** The act or process of producing; production. **2a.** An amount produced or manufactured during a certain time. **b.** Intellectual or creative production: *literary output.* **3a.** The energy, power, or work produced by a system. **b.** *Computer Science* The information produced by a program or process from a specific input. ❖ *tr.v.* **-put·ted** or **-put, -put·ting, -puts** To produce or manufacture an output.

output device *n.* A device, such as a video display, that presents data from a computer to a user.

out·race (out-rās′) *tr.v.* **-raced, -rac·ing, -rac·es** To surpass in speed or performance.

out·rage (out′rāj′) *n.* **1.** An act of extreme violence or viciousness. **2.** An act grossly offensive to decency, morality, or good taste. **3.** A deplorable insult. **4.** Resentful anger aroused by a violent or offensive act. ❖ *tr.v.* **-raged, -rag·ing, -rag·es 1.** To offend grossly against (standards of decency or morality); commit an outrage on. **2.** To produce anger or resentment in. [ME < OFr. < *outre,* beyond. See OUTRÉ.]

out·ra·geous (out-rā′jəs) *adj.* **1a.** Grossly offensive to decency or morality. **b.** Being well beyond the bounds of good taste: *outrageous epithets.* **2.** Having no regard for morality. **3.** Violent or unrestrained in temperament or behavior. **4a.** Extremely unusual or unconventional; extraordinary. **b.** Being beyond all reason; extravagant or immoderate: *spent an outrageous amount on airfare.* —**out·ra′geous·ly** *adv.* —**out·ra′geous·ness** *n.*

out·range (out-rānj′) *tr.v.* **-ranged, -rang·ing, -rang·es** To exceed (another) in range.

out·rank (out-răngk′) *tr.v.* **-ranked, -rank·ing, -ranks** To rank higher than.

ou·tré (ōō-trā′) *adj.* Highly unconventional; eccentric or bizarre. [Fr. < OFr., defeated, p. part. of *outrer,* to pass someone < *outre,* beyond < Lat. *ultrā.* See **al-** in App.]

out·reach (out-rēch′) *v.* **-reached, -reach·ing, -reach·es** —*tr.* **1.** To surpass (another) in reach. **2.** To be more or greater than; exceed. —*intr.* **1.** To go too far. **2.** To reach out. ❖ *n.* (out′rēch′) **1.** The act or process of reaching out. **2.** Extent or length of reach. **3.** A systematic attempt to provide services beyond conventional limits, as to particular segments of a community.

out·ride (out-rīd′) *tr.v.* **-rode** (-rōd′), **-rid·den** (-rĭd′n), **-rid·ing, -rides 1.** To ride faster, farther, or better than; outstrip. **2.** To withstand successfully; ride out: *outride a storm at sea.* ❖ *n.* An unstressed syllable or cluster of syllables within a given metrical unit that is omitted from the scansion pattern in sprung rhythm. [N., coined by Gerard Manley Hopkins.]

out·rid·er (out′rī′dər) *n.* **1.** A guide; an escort. **2.** One that goes in advance; a forerunner. **3.** A mounted attendant who rides in front of or beside a carriage.

out·rig·ger (out′rĭg′ər) *n.* **1.** *Nautical* **a.** A projecting beam or spar run out from the side of a vessel to secure the masts or from a mast to extend a rope or sail. **b.** A long thin float attached parallel to a seagoing canoe by projecting spars to prevent capsizing. **c.** A vessel with such a float or beam. **d.** A support for an oarlock projecting from the side of a racing shell. **e.** A racing shell with such a support. **2.** A projecting frame extending laterally from a vehicle, aircraft, or machine to stabilize it or support an extending part.

out·right (out′rīt′, -rīt′) *adv.* **1.** Without reservation or qualification; openly. **2.** Completely and entirely; wholly: *denied the charges outright.* **3.** At once; straightway. **4.** Without additional payments owing, constraints, or stipulations. ❖ *adj.* (out′rīt′) **1.** Presented without reservation; unqualified. **2a.** Complete; total. **b.** Thoroughgoing; out-and-out. **3.** Made without constraints, stipulations, or additional payments owed. **4.** *Archaic* Moving straight onward. —**out′right·ly** *adv.* —**out′right′ness** *n.*

out·run (out-rŭn′) *tr.v.* **-ran** (-răn′), **-run, -run·ning, -runs 1a.** To run faster than. **b.** To escape from: *outrun one's creditors.* **2.** To go beyond; exceed.

out·sell (out-sĕl′) *tr.v.* **-sold** (-sōld′), **-sell·ing, -sells 1.** To surpass (another) in amount sold: *The book outsold its competitors.* **2.** To outdo (another) in selling.

out·set (out′sĕt′) *n.* The initial stage of something; the start.

out·shine (out-shīn′) *v.* **-shone** (-shōn′), **-shin·ing, -shines** —*tr.* **1a.** To shine brighter than. **b.** To be more beautiful, splendid, or flamboyant than. **2.** To surpass in obvious excellence; outdo. —*intr.* To shine forth.

out·shoot (out-shōōt′) *tr.v.* **-shot** (-shŏt′), **-shoot·ing, -shoots**

To shoot better than (another). ❖ *n.* (out′shōōt′) A protuberance, projection, or outgrowth.

out·side (out-sīd′, out′sīd′) *n.* **1.** The part or parts that face out; the outer surface. **2a.** The part or side of an object that is presented to the viewer; the external aspect. **b.** Outward aspect or appearance. **3.** The space beyond a boundary or limit. **4.** *Sports* A position at a distance from the inside or center, as of a playing field or racetrack. **5.** The utmost limit; the maximum: *in ten days at the outside.* ❖ *adj.* **1a.** Of, relating to, or being on or near the outer side; outer: *the outside margin.* **b.** Of, restricted to, or situated on the outer side of an enclosure or a boundary; external: *an outside door lock.* **2.** Located away from the inside or center: *the outside traffic lane.* **3a.** Acting, occurring, originating, or being at a place beyond certain limits: *the outside world.* **b.** Gaining or providing access to the external side: *an outside telephone line.* **4a.** Not belonging to or originating in a certain group or association: *outside assistance.* **b.** Being beyond the limits of one's usual work or responsibilities. **5.** Extreme, uttermost: *our outside estimates.* **6.** Very unlikely; remote. **7.** *Baseball* Passing on the side of home plate away from the batter. Used of a pitch. ❖ *adv.* **1.** On or to the outer or external side. **2.** Outdoors. ❖ *prep.* **1.** On or to the outer or external side of. **2.** Beyond the limits of: *outside the city.* **3.** With the exception of; except.

outside of *prep.* Outside; aside from.

out·sid·er (out-sī′dər) *n.* **1a.** One who is excluded from a party, association, or set. **b.** One who is isolated or detached from the activities or concerns of one's own community. **2.** A contestant given little chance of winning.

out·sight (out′sīt′) *n.* The faculty or act of clearly perceiving and understanding external things.

out·size (out′sīz′) *n.* **1.** An unusual size, esp. a very large size. **2.** A garment of unusual size. ❖ *adj.* also **out·sized** (-sīzd′) Unusually large, weighty, or extensive.

out·skirt (out′skûrt′) *n.* The part or region remote from a central district, as of a city or town. Often used in the plural.

out·smart (out-smärt′) *tr.v.* **-smart·ed, -smart·ing, -smarts** To gain the advantage over by cunning; outwit.

out·soar (out-sôr′, -sōr′) *tr.v.* **-soared, -soar·ing, -soars** To soar beyond or to a higher place than.

out·sold (out-sōld′) *v.* Past tense and past participle of **outsell.**

out·sole (out′sōl′) *n.* The outer sole of a shoe or boot.

out·source (out′sôrs′, -sōrs′) *tr.v.* **-sourced, -sourc·ing, -sourc·es** To send out (work, for example) to an outside provider or manufacturer in order to cut costs.

out·speak (out-spēk′) *v.* **-spoke** (-spōk′), **-spo·ken** (-spō′kən), **-speak·ing, -speaks** —*tr. Archaic* To speak better or more cogently than (another). —*intr.* To speak out.

out·spend (out-spĕnd′) *tr.v.* **-spent** (-spĕnt′), **-spend·ing, -spends 1.** To spend beyond the limits of: *outspends his earnings.* **2.** To outdo in spending: *outspend their relatives.*

out·spent (out-spĕnt′) *adj.* Completely exhausted.

out·spo·ken (out-spō′kən) *adj.* **1.** Spoken without reserve; candid. **2.** Frank and unreserved in speech. See Syns at **frank¹.** —**out·spo′ken·ly** *adv.* —**out·spo′ken·ness** *n.*

out·spread (out-sprĕd′) *tr. & intr.v.* **-spread, -spread·ing, -spreads** To stretch or extend or to be stretched or extended. ❖ *n.* (out′sprĕd′) **1.** The act of spreading out. **2.** Something spread out; an expanse. ❖ *adj.* Spread out; extended.

out·stand (out-stănd′) *intr.v.* **-stood** (-stōōd′), **-stand·ing, -stands** To stand out plainly.

out·stand·ing (out-stăn′dĭng, out′stăn′-) *adj.* **1.** Standing out among others of its kind; prominent. **2.** Superior to others of its kind; distinguished. **3.** Projecting upward or outward; standing out. **4.** Still in existence; not settled. **5.** Publicly issued and sold. —**out·stand′ing·ly** *adv.*

out·stare (out-stâr′) *tr.v.* **-stared, -star·ing, -stares** To overcome by or as if by staring; stare down.

out·sta·tion (out′stā′shən) *n.* A remote station or post.

out·stay (out-stā′) *tr.v.* **-stayed, -stay·ing, -stays 1.** To stay longer than; overstay. **2.** To show more endurance than.

out·stretch (out-strĕch′) *tr.v.* **-stretched, -stretch·ing, -stretch·es** To stretch out; extend.

out·strip (out-strĭp′) *tr.v.* **-stripped, -strip·ping, -strips 1.** To leave behind; outrun. **2.** To exceed or surpass.

out·stroke (out′strōk′) *n.* An outward stroke, esp. the stroke of an engine piston moving toward the crankshaft.

out·take (out′tāk′) *n.* **1a.** A shot, section, or scene, as of a movie, filmed but not used in the final version. **b.** A complete version, as of a recording, dropped in favor of another version. **2.** An opening for outward discharge; a vent.

out·talk (out-tôk′) *tr.v.* **-talked, -talk·ing, -talks 1.** To outdo (another) in talking. **2.** To outwit by talking.

out·think (out-thĭngk′) *tr.v.* **-thought** (-thôt′), **-think·ing, -thinks 1.** To outdo (another) in thinking. **2.** To outwit by thinking.

out·thrust (out-thrŭst′) *intr. & tr.v.* **-thrust·ed, -thrust·ing, -thrusts** To extend or cause to extend outward. ❖ *n.* (out′thrŭst′) Something that extends outward.

out·turn (out′tûrn′) *n.* A total amount produced during a given period; output.

out·vote (out-vōt′) *tr.v.* **-vot·ed, -vot·ing, -votes 1.** To outdo

outrigger

in voting: *The city outvoted the suburbs.* **2.** To defeat (an opponent or proposal, for example) in voting.

out·wait (out-wāt′) *tr.v.* **-wait·ed, -wait·ing, -waits 1.** To delay until the end of; wait out. **2.** To get the better of or overcome by refraining from action: *outwaited my opponent.*

out·ward (out′wərd) *adj.* **1.** Of, located on, or approaching the outside or exterior; outer. **2.** Relating to the physical self: *outward beauty.* **3.** Purely external; superficial. ❖ *adv.* **1.** also **out·wards** (-wərdz) Toward the outside; away from the center. **2.** *Archaic* On the outside; externally. ❖ *n.* The material or external world. **—out′ward·ness** *n.*

out·ward-bound (out′wərd-bound′) *adj.* Headed out, as toward the open sea: *an outward-bound tanker.*

out·ward·ly (out′wərd-lē) *adv.* **1.** On the outside or exterior; externally. **2.** Toward the outside. **3.** In regard to outward condition, conduct, or manifestation.

out·wash (out′wŏsh′, -wôsh′) *n.* Sediment deposited by streams flowing away from a melting glacier.

out·wear (out-wâr′) *tr.v.* **-wore** (-wôr′, -wōr′), **-worn** (-wôrn′, -wōrn′), **-wears 1.** To last longer than; outlast: *Denim outwears other fabric.* **2.** To get over (something) by the passage of time; outgrow.

out·weigh (out-wā′) *tr.v.* **-weighed, -weigh·ing, -weighs 1.** To weigh more than. **2.** To be more significant than; exceed in value or importance: *The benefits outweigh the risks.*

out·went (out-wĕnt′) *v.* Past tense of **outgo.**

out·wit (out-wĭt′) *tr.v.* **-wit·ted, -wit·ting, -wits 1.** To surpass in cleverness or cunning; outsmart. **2.** *Archaic* To surpass in intelligence.

out·work (out-wûrk′) *tr.v.* **-worked** or **-wrought** (-rôt′), **-work·ing, -works 1.** To work better or faster than. **2.** To complete (something); work (something) out. ❖ *n.* (out′wûrk′) A minor fortification constructed beyond a main defensive position or fortification.

out·worn (out-wôrn′, -wōrn′) *adj.* No longer acceptable, usable, or practical.

ou·zel also **ou·sel** (oo′zəl) *n.* A water ouzel. [ME *osel* < OE *ōsle.*]

ou·zo (oo′zō) *n., pl.* **-zos** A colorless unsweetened Greek liqueur flavored with anise. [Mod.Gk.]

ov– *pref.* Variant of **ovi-.**

o·va (ō′və) *n.* Plural of **ovum.**

o·val (ō′vəl) *adj.* **1.** Resembling an egg in shape. **2.** Resembling an ellipse in shape; elliptical. ❖ *n.* **1.** An egg-shaped or elliptical form or figure. **2.** An elliptical track, as for racing or athletic events. [Med.Lat. *ōvālis* < Lat. *ōvum,* egg. See **awi–** in App.] **—o′val·ly** *adv.* **—o′val·ness** *n.*

o·val·bu·min (ō′vəl-byoō′mĭn, ō′vəl-) *n.* The albumin of egg white. [Alteration of LLat. *ōvī albūmen* : Lat. *ōvī,* genitive sing. of *ōvum,* egg; see OVUM + Lat. *albūmen,* white of an egg; see ALBUMEN.]

Oval Office *n.* **1.** The office of the US President, located in the White House. **2.** The office, authority, or executive power of the US President; the presidency.

oval window *n.* The oval opening in the middle ear to which the base of the stapes is connected and through which the ossicles of the ear transmit sound vibrations to the cochlea.

o·var·i·ec·to·my (ō-vâr′ē-ĕk′tə-mē) *n., pl.* **-mies** See **oophorectomy.**

o·var·i·ot·o·my (ō-vâr′ē-ŏt′ə-mē) *n., pl.* **-mies 1.** An ovariectomy. **2.** Surgical incision into an ovary.

o·va·ri·tis (ō′və-rī′tĭs) *n.* See **oophoritis.**

o·va·ry (ō′və-rē) *n., pl.* **-ries 1.** The usu. paired female or hermaphroditic reproductive organ that produces ova and in vertebrates estrogen and progesterone. **2.** *Botany* The ovule-bearing lower part of a pistil that ripens into a fruit. [NLat. *ōvārium* < Lat. *ōvum,* egg. See **awi–** in App.] **—o·var′i·an** (ō-vâr′ē-ən) *adj.*

o·vate (ō′vāt′) *adj.* **1.** Shaped like an egg; oval. **2.** *Botany* Broad and rounded at the base and tapering toward the end. [Lat. *ōvātus* < *ōvum,* egg. See **awi–** in App.] **—o′vate·ly** *adv.*

o·va·tion (ō-vā′shən) *n.* **1.** Prolonged enthusiastic applause. **2.** A show of public homage or welcome. **3.** An ancient Roman victory ceremony of somewhat less importance than a triumph. [Lat. *ovātiō, ovātiōn-,* a Roman victory ceremony < *ovātus,* p. part. of *ovāre,* to rejoice.] **—o·va′tion·al** *adj.*

ov·en (ŭv′ən) *n.* A chamber or enclosed compartment for heating, baking, or roasting food, as in a stove, or for firing, baking, or drying objects, as in a kiln. [ME < OE *ofen.*]

ov·en·bird (ŭv′ən-bûrd′) *n.* **1.** A thrushlike North American warbler (*Seiurus aurocapillus*) having a shrill call and building a domed oven-shaped nest on the ground. **2.** Any of various South American birds of the family Furnariidae, esp. of the genus *Furnarius.*

ov·en·proof (ŭv′ən-proōf′) *adj.* Capable of resisting the heat produced in a kitchen oven: *an ovenproof casserole dish.*

ov·en·ware (ŭv′ən-wâr′) *n.* Heat-resistant dishes used for baking and serving food.

o·ver (ō′vər) *prep.* **1.** In or at a position above or higher than: *a sign over the door.* **2a.** Above and across from one end or side to the other: *a jump over the fence.* **b.** To the other side of; across: *strolled over the bridge.* **c.** Across the edge of and down: *fell over the cliff.* **3.** On the other side of: *over the border.* **4a.** Upon the

surface of: *varnish over the woodwork.* **b.** On top of or down upon: *tripped over the toys.* **5a.** Through the extent of; all through: *walked over the grounds.* **b.** Through the medium of; via: *spoke over the phone.* **6.** So as to cover: *a shawl over her shoulders.* **7.** Up to or higher than the level or height of: *The water was over my shoulders.* **8a.** Through the period or duration of: *records maintained over two years.* **b.** Until or beyond the end of: *stayed over the holidays.* **9.** More than in degree, quantity, or extent: *over ten miles.* **10a.** In superiority to: *a victory over her rival.* **b.** In preference to: *selected over the others.* **11.** In a position to rule or control: *presiding over the meeting.* **12.** So as to have an effect or influence on: *the change that came over you.* **13.** While occupied with or engaged in: *a chat over coffee.* **14.** With reference to; concerning: *an argument over methods.* ❖ *adv.* **1.** Above the top or surface: *climbed up and peered over.* **2a.** Across to another or opposite side: *stopped at the curb, then crossed over.* **b.** Across the edge, brink, or brim: *The coffee spilled over.* **c.** Across an intervening space: *Throw the ball over.* **3a.** Across a distance in a particular direction or at a location: *lives over in England.* **b.** To another often specified place or position: *Move over.* **c.** To one's place of residence or business: *invited us over.* **4.** Throughout an entire area or region: *wandered all over.* **5a.** To a different opinion or allegiance: *win someone over.* **b.** So as to be comprehensible, acceptable, or effective; across: *got my point over.* **6.** To a different person, condition, or title: *sign the property over.* **7.** So as to be completely enclosed or covered: *The river froze over.* **8.** Completely through; from beginning to end: *Think it over.* **9a.** From an upright position: *kicked the stool over.* **b.** From an upward position to an inverted or reversed position: *turn the paper over.* **10.** Another time; again: *had to do it over.* **11.** In repetition: *said it over.* **12.** In addition or excess; in surplus: *food left over.* **13.** Beyond or until a specified time: *stay a day over.* **14.** At an end: *Fall is over.* ❖ *adj.* **1.** External; outer. **2.** Excessive; extreme. **3a.** Not yet used up; remaining. **b.** Extra; surplus. ❖ *n. Sports* A series of six balls bowled from one end of a cricket pitch. ❖ *tr.v.* **o·vered, o·ver·ing, o·vers** To jump over. ❖ *interj.* Used in two-way radio to indicate that a transmission is complete and a reply is awaited. **—idioms: over against** As opposed to; contrasted with. **over and above** In addition to. **over and over** Again and again; repeatedly. **over with** Completely finished; done. [ME < OE *ofer.* See **uper** in App.]

over– *pref.* **1.** Above or upon in position: *overpass; overcoat.* **2.** Superior in rank or importance: *overlord.* **3.** To an inverted or reverse position: *overturn.* **4.** Excessively: *overcharge.* [ME < OE *ofer-.* See **uper** in App.]

USAGE NOTE In forming compounds, *over–* is joined with the following element without space or a hyphen: *overachieve.* When *over* combines with other words as a unit modifier, however, the words are joined by hyphens: *over-the-counter medication.*

---

o·ver·a·bun·dance (ō′vər-ə-bŭn′dəns) *n.* A going or being beyond what is needed, desired, or appropriate; an excess. **—o′ver·a·bun′dant** *adj.* **—o′ver·a·bun′dant·ly** *adv.*

o·ver·a·chieve (ō′vər-ə-chēv′) *intr.v.* **-chieved, -chiev·ing, -chieves** To perform better or achieve more success than expected. **—o′ver·a·chieve′ment** *n.* **—o′ver·a·chiev′er** *n.*

o·ver·act (ō′vər-ăkt′) *v.* **-act·ed, -act·ing, -acts** *—tr.* To act (a dramatic role) with unnecessary exaggeration. *—intr.* **1.** To exaggerate a role; overplay. **2.** To act over and above what is required; overdo in acting. **—o′ver·ac′tion** *n.*

o·ver·ac·tive (ō′vər-ăk′tĭv) *adj.* Active to an excessive or abnormal degree: *an overactive child.* **—o′ver·ac·tiv′i·ty** *n.*

o·ver·age[1] (ō′vər-ĭj) *n.* **1.** An amount, as of money or goods, that is actually on hand and exceeds the listed amount in records or books. **2.** A surplus; an excess.

o·ver·age[2] (ō′vər-āj′) *adj.* **1.** Beyond the proper or required age. **2.** Older than usual for a particular position or activity. **3.** Too old to be of use or service: *an overage vehicle.*

o·ver·all (ō′vər-ôl′) *adj.* **1.** From one end to the other. **2.** Including everything; comprehensive. **3.** Regarded as a whole; general. ❖ *adv.* (ō′vər-ôl′) On the whole; generally. ❖ *n.* **1.** *Chiefly British* A loose-fitting protective outer garment; a smock. **2.** **overalls** Loose-fitting trousers, usu. of strong fabric, with a bib front and shoulder straps, often worn over regular clothing as protection from dirt.

o·ver·arch (ō′vər-ärch′) *tr.v.* **-arched, -arch·ing, -arch·es** To form an arch over: *Grape vines overarched the garden path.*

o·ver·arch·ing (ō′vər-är′chĭng) *adj.* **1.** Forming an arch overhead or above. **2.** Extending over or throughout: *overarching enthusiasm.* **—o′ver·arch′ing·ly** *adv.*

o·ver·arm[1] (ō′vər-ärm′) *adj. Sports* **1.** Executed with the arm raised above the shoulder; overhand: *an overarm throw.* **2.** Of, relating to, or being a stroke in swimming that is begun with the arm lifted and stretched forward over the shoulder.

o·ver·arm[2] (ō′vər-ärm′) *tr.v.* **-armed, -arm·ing, -arms** To supply with an excess of weaponry, esp. nuclear missiles.

o·ver·awe (ō′vər-ô′) *tr.v.* **-awed, -aw·ing, -awes** To control or subdue by inspiring awe.

o·ver·bal·ance (ō′vər-băl′əns) *v.* **-anced, -anc·ing, -anc·es** *—tr.* **1.** To have greater weight or importance than. **2.** To throw off balance. *—intr.* To lose one's balance. ❖ *n.* (ō′vər-băl′əns) **1.**

ovate
ovate leaf

overalls

An excess in weight or quantity. **2.** Something that overbalances or more than equals something else.

o·ver·bear (ō′vər-bâr′) v. **-bore** (-bôr′, -bōr′), **-borne** (-bôrn′), **-bear·ing, -bears** —tr. **1.** To crush or press down on with physical force. **2.** To prevail over, as if by superior weight or force; dominate. **3.** To be more important than; outweigh. —intr. To bear an overabundance of fruit or offspring.

o·ver·bear·ing (ō′vər-bâr′ĭng) adj. **1.** Domineering in manner; arrogant: an overbearing person. **2.** Overwhelming in power or significance; predominant. —**o′ver·bear′ing·ly** adv. —**o′ver·bear′ing·ness** n.

o·ver·bid (ō′vər-bĭd′) v. **-bid, -bid·den** (-bĭd′n) or **-bid, -bid·ding, -bids** —tr. **1.** To outbid (a person) for something, as at an auction. **2.** Games To bid more than the value of (one's hand in bridge, for example). —intr. To bid higher than the actual value of something. ❖ n. (ō′vər-bĭd′) A bid higher than another bid. —**o′ver·bid′der** n.

o·ver·bite (ō′vər-bīt′) n. A malocclusion in which the front upper incisor and canine teeth project over the lower.

o·ver·blouse (ō′vər-blous′, -blouz′) n. A blouse fashioned for wearing outside the waistband of a skirt or slacks.

o·ver·blow (ō′vər-blō′) tr.v. **-blew** (-blōō′), **-blown** (-blōn′), **-blow·ing, -blows** To blow (a wind instrument) so as to produce an overtone instead of a fundamental tone.

o·ver·blown (ō′vər-blōn′) adj. **1a.** Done to excess; overdone. **b.** Full of empty or pretentious language; bombastic. **2.** Past the stage of full bloom. **3.** Very fat; obese. **4.** Having been blown down or over.

o·ver·board (ō′vər-bôrd′, -bōrd′) adv. Over or as if over the side of a boat or ship. **—idiom: go overboard** To go to extremes, esp. as a result of enthusiasm.

o·ver·book (ō′vər-bŏŏk′) v. **-booked, -book·ing, -books** —tr. To take reservations for (a restaurant, for example) beyond the capacity for accommodation. —intr. To take reservations beyond the capacity for accommodation. —**o′ver·book′ing** n.

o·ver·borne (ō′vər-bôrn′) adj. Overpowered or overcome.

o·ver·bought (ō′vər-bôt′) adj. Characterized by excessively high prices owing to prior heavy buying.

o·ver·build (ō′vər-bĭld′) v. **-built** (-bĭlt′), **-build·ing, -builds** —tr. **1.** To build over or on top of. **2.** To construct more buildings in (an area) than necessary. **3.** To build with excessive size or elaboration. —intr. To overbuild an area.

o·ver·bur·den (ō′vər-bûr′dn) tr.v. **-dened, -den·ing, -dens 1.** To burden with too much weight; overload. **2.** To subject to an excessive burden or strain; overtax. ❖ n. (ō′vər-bûr′dn) **1.** An excessive burden or load. **2.** Geology **a.** Material overlying a useful mineral deposit. **b.** Sedimentary rock covering older crystalline layers.

o·ver·buy (ō′vər-bī′) v. **-bought** (-bôt′), **-buy·ng, -buys** —tr. **1.** To buy in excess. **2.** To buy (stock) on margin in excess of one's ability to provide further security if prices drop. —intr. To buy goods beyond one's means or needs.

o·ver·call (ō′vər-kôl′) v. **-called, -call·ing, -calls** Games —tr. To bid beyond or in excess of (a previous bid or player) in a game of cards. —intr. To bid higher than one's opponent when one's partner has not bid in bridge. ❖ n. (ō′vər-kôl′) Games **a.** An overbid. **b.** An instance of overcalling in bridge.

o·ver·ca·pac·i·ty (ō′vər-kə-păs′ĭ-tē) n. Too great a capacity for production of commodities or delivery of services in relation to actual need.

o·ver·cap·i·tal·ize (ō′vər-kăp′ĭ-tl-īz′) tr.v. **-ized, -iz·ing, -iz·es 1.** To provide excess capital for (a business enterprise). **2.** To overestimate the value of (property). **3.** To put an unlawfully or unreasonably high value on the nominal capital of (a corporation). —**o′ver·cap′i·tal·i·za′tion** (-ĭ-zə′shən) n.

o·ver·cast (ō′vər-kăst′, ō′vər-kăst′) adj. **1a.** Covered or obscured, as with mist. **b.** Clouded over. **2.** Gloomy; melancholy. **3.** Sewn with long overlying stitches to prevent raveling, as of the raw edges of fabric. ❖ n. (ō′vər-kăst′) **1.** A covering, as of mist

or clouds. **2.** An arch or support for one passage over another in a mine. **3.** An overcast stitch or seam. ❖ v. (ō′vər-kăst′, ō′vər-kăst′) **-cast, -cast·ing, -casts** —tr. **1.** To make cloudy or gloomy. **2.** To sew with long overlying stitches. —intr. To become cloudy or gloomy.

o·ver·cast·ing (ō′vər-kăs′tĭng) n. **1a.** The act of overcasting raw edges of fabric. **b.** Overcast stitching. **2.** An overcast stitch.

o·ver·charge (ō′vər-chärj′) v. **-charged, -charg·ing, -charg·es** —tr. **1.** To charge (a party) an overcharge. **2.** To fill too full; overload. **3.** To overstate or exaggerate. —intr. To charge too much. ❖ n. (ō′vər-chärj′) **1.** An excessive charge or price. **2.** A load or burden that is too full or heavy.

o·ver·class (ō′vər-klăs′) n. The upper social stratum of a society, esp. when viewed as controlling economic power.

o·ver·cloud (ō′vər-kloud′) v. **-cloud·ed, -cloud·ing, -clouds** —tr. **1.** To cover with clouds. **2.** To make dark and gloomy. —intr. To become cloudy.

o·ver·coat (ō′vər-kōt′) n. **1.** A heavy winter coat worn over clothing. **2.** An additional protective coating, as of paint.

o·ver·coat·ing (ō′vər-kō′tĭng) n. An overcoat, as of paint.

o·ver·come (ō′vər-kŭm′) v. **-came** (-kām′), **-come, -com·ing, -comes** —tr. **1.** To defeat (another) in competition or conflict; conquer. See Syns at **defeat**. **2.** To prevail over; surmount. **3.** To overpower, as with emotion; affect deeply. —intr. To surmount opposition; be victorious.

o·ver·com·mit (ō′vər-kə-mĭt′) v. **-mit·ted, -mit·ting, -mits** —tr. **1.** To bind or obligate (oneself, for example) beyond the capacity for realization. **2.** To allocate or apportion (money, goods, or resources) in amounts incapable of replacement. —intr. To be or become overcommitted. —**o′ver·com·mit′ment** n.

o·ver·com·pen·sate (ō′vər-kŏm′pən-sāt′) v. **-sat·ed, -sat·ing, -sates** —intr. To engage in overcompensation. —tr. To pay (someone) too much; compensate excessively. —**o′ver·com·pen′sa·to·ry** (-kəm-pĕn′sə-tôr′ē, -tōr′ē) adj.

o·ver·com·pen·sa·tion (ō′vər-kŏm′pən-sā′shən) n. Excessive compensation, esp. for a physical or psychological characteristic or defect.

o·ver·cor·rect (ō′vər-kə-rĕkt′) v. **-rect·ed, -rect·ing, -rects** —tr. To correct beyond what is needed, appropriate, or usual, esp. when causing a mistake. —intr. To correct something to an excessive or unusual degree. —**o′ver·cor·rec′tion** n.

o·ver·crop (ō′vər-krŏp′) tr.v. **-cropped, -crop·ping, -crops** To exhaust the fertility of by continuous cultivation of crops.

o·ver·de·vel·op (ō′vər-dĭ-vĕl′əp) v. **-oped, -op·ing, -ops 1.** To develop to excess: overdeveloped muscles. **2.** To process (a photographic plate or film) too long or in too concentrated a solution. —**o′ver·de·vel′op·ment** n.

o·ver·do (ō′vər-dōō′) v. **-did** (-dĭd′), **-done** (-dŭn′), **-do·ing, -does** (-dŭz′) —tr. **1a.** To do, use, or stress to excess; carry (something) too far. **b.** To exaggerate. **2.** To wear out the strength of; overtax. **3.** To cook (food) too long. —intr. To do too much; go to extremes. —**o′ver·do′er** n.

o·ver·dog (ō′vər-dôg′, -dŏg′) n. Informal One that has a significant advantage. [OVER + (UNDER)DOG.]

overdose n. An excessive dose, esp. of a narcotic. —intr. To take an overdose. —tr. To administer too large a dose or too many doses to.

o·ver·draft (ō′vər-drăft′) n. **1a.** The act of overdrawing a bank account. **b.** The amount overdrawn. **c.** The maximum amount of credit extended to a customer. **2.** also **o·ver·draught** (-drăft′) **a.** A current of air made to pass over the ignited fuel in a furnace. **b.** A series of flues in a brick kiln designed to force air down from the top. **c.** The air so forced.

o·ver·draw (ō′vər-drô′) v. **-drew** (-drōō′), **-drawn** (-drôn′), **-draw·ing, -draws** —tr. **1.** To draw against (a bank account) in excess of credit. **2.** To pull back too far: overdraw a bow. **3.** To spoil the effect of by exaggeration in telling or describing. —intr. To make an overdraft.

o·ver·dress (ō′vər-drĕs′) v. **-dressed, -dress·ing, -dress·es**

ă	pat	oi	boy
ā	pay	ou	out
âr	care	ōō	took
ä	father	ōō	boot
ĕ	pet	ŭ	cut
ē	be	ûr	urge
ĭ	pit	th	thin
ī	pie	th	this
îr	pier	hw	which
ŏ	pot	zh	vision
ō	toe	ə	about,
ô	paw		item

Stress marks:
′ (primary);
′ (secondary), as in
lexicon (lĕk′sĭ-kŏn′)

—*intr.* To overdress oneself. —*tr.* To dress (oneself) more formally or elaborately than appropriate or desirable. ❖ *n.* (ō′vər-drĕs′) A skirted garment worn over outer clothing.

o•ver•drive (ō′vər-drīv′) *n.* **1.** A gearing mechanism of a motor vehicle engine that reduces the power output required to maintain driving speed in a specific range by lowering the gear ratio. **2.** *Informal* A state of heightened activity or concentration. ❖ *tr.v.* (ō′vər-drīv′) **-drove** (-drōv′), **-driv•en** (-drĭv′ən), **-driv•ing, -drives 1.** To drive (a vehicle) too far or too long. **2.** To push (oneself) too far, as with tasks.

o•ver•dub (ō′vər-dŭb′) *tr.v.* **-dubbed, -dub•bing, -dubs** To add (an overdub) to a previously taped musical recording esp. in order to heighten the effect. ❖ *n.* Additional recorded sound blended into a musical recording.

o•ver•due (ō′vər-do͞o′, -dyo͞o′) *adj.* **1.** Being unpaid when due. **2.** Coming or arriving after the scheduled or expected time. **3a.** Expected or required but not yet having occurred. **b.** Being something that should have occurred earlier.

o•ver•es•ti•mate (ō′vər-ĕs′tə-māt′) *tr.v.* **-mat•ed, -mat•ing, -mates 1.** To estimate too highly. **2.** To esteem too greatly. —**o′ver•es′ti•mate** (-mĭt) *n.* —**o′ver•es′ti•ma′tion** *n.*

o•ver•ex•ert (ō′vər-ĭg-zûrt′) *tr.v.* **-ert•ed, -ert•ing, -erts** To exert (oneself) too much; overtax. —**o′ver•ex•er′tion** *n.*

o•ver•ex•pose (ō′vər-ĭk-spōz′) *tr.v.* **-posed, -pos•ing, -pos•es 1.** To expose too long or too much: *overexposed to TV.* **2.** To expose (a photographic film or plate) too long or to too much light. —**o′ver•ex•po′sure** (-ĭk-spō′zhər) *n.*

o•ver•ex•tend (ō′vər-ĭk-stĕnd′) *tr.v.* **-tend•ed, -tend•ing, -tends 1.** To expand or disperse beyond a safe or reasonable limit: *overextended their defenses.* **2.** To obligate (oneself) beyond a limit, esp. a financial one. —**o′ver•ex•ten′sion** *n.*

o•ver•fa•mil•iar (ō′vər-fə-mĭl′yər) *adj.* Too familiar, as: **a.** Exceedingly common or ordinary. **b.** Unduly forward or brash; offensively presumptuous: *overfamiliar behavior.* —**o′ver•fa•mil′iar′i•ty** (-mĭl′yăr′ĭ-tē, -mĭl′ē-ăr′-) *n.*

o•ver•fish (ō′vər-fĭsh′) *v.* **-fished, -fish•ing, -fish•es** —*tr.* To fish (a body of water) to such a degree as to upset the ecological balance or cause depletion of living creatures. —*intr.* To overfish a body of water.

o•ver•flight (ō′vər-flīt′) *n.* An aircraft flight over a particular area, esp. over foreign territory.

o•ver•flow (ō′vər-flō′) *v.* **-flowed, -flow•ing, -flows** —*intr.* **1.** To flow or run over the top, brim, or banks. **2.** To be filled beyond capacity, as a container. **3.** To have a boundless supply; be superabundant. See Syns at **teem**[1]. —*tr.* **1.** To flow over the top, brim, or banks of. **2.** To spread or cover over; flood. **3.** To cause to fill beyond capacity. ❖ *n.* (ō′vər-flō′) **1.** The act of overflowing. **2.** Something that flows over; an excess. **3.** An outlet or vent through which excess liquid may escape. **4.** *Computer Science* A condition in which the result of a calculation is too large to be stored in the allotted location.

o•ver•fly (ō′vər-flī′) *tr.v.* **-flew** (-flo͞o′), **-flown** (-flōn′), **-fly•ing, -flies 1.** To fly over (a particular area or territory) in an aircraft or spacecraft. **2.** To fly beyond or past; overshoot.

o•ver•gar•ment (ō′vər-gär′mənt) *n.* An outer garment.

o•ver•glaze (ō′vər-glāz′) *n.* **1.** An outer coat of glaze on a piece of pottery. **2.** A painted or printed decoration applied over a glaze. ❖ *tr.v.* (ō′vər-glāz′, ō′vər-glāz′) **-glazed, -glaz•ing, -glaz•es** To apply an overglaze to. ❖ *adj.* Applied or designed for applying over a ceramic glaze.

o•ver•graze (ō′vər-grāz′) *tr.v.* **-grazed, -graz•ing, -graz•es** To permit animals to graze (vegetation cover) excessively, to the detriment of the vegetation.

o•ver•grow (ō′vər-grō′, ō′vər-grō′) *v.* **-grew** (-gro͞o′), **-grown** (-grōn′), **-grow•ing, -grows** —*tr.* **1.** To grow over with herbage or foliage. **2.** To grow beyond or too large for. —*intr.* **1.** To grow beyond normal or usual size. **2.** To become grown over, as with unwanted vegetation or weeds.

o•ver•growth (ō′vər-grōth′) *n.* A usu. abundant growth over or on something else: *an overgrowth of ivy on the wall.*

o•ver•hand (ō′vər-hănd′) also **o•ver•hand•ed** (ō′vər-hăn′dĭd) *adj.* **1.** Executed with the hand brought forward and down from above the level of the shoulder. **2.** Sewn with close vertical stitches drawing two edges together, with each stitch passing over the seam formed by the edges. ❖ *adv.* In an overhand manner. ❖ *n.* **1.** An overhand throw, stroke, or delivery. **2.** An overhand stitch or seam. ❖ *tr.v.* **-hand•ed, -hand•ing, -hands** To sew with overhand stitches.

overhand knot

overhand knot *n.* A knot formed by making a loop in a piece of cord and pulling the end through it.

overhang
Fallingwater by Frank Lloyd Wright, near Mill Run, Pennsylvania

o•ver•hang (ō′vər-hăng′) *v.* **-hung** (-hŭng′), **-hang•ing, -hangs** —*tr.* **1.** To project or extend beyond. **2.** To loom over; menace. **3.** To ornament with hangings. —*intr.* To project over something that lies beneath. ❖ *n.* (ō′vər-hăng′) **1.** A projecting part, such as a rock formation. **2.** An amount of projection: *an overhang of six inches.* **3.** *Nautical* The part of a bow or stern that projects over the water. **4.** A supply of a commodity in excess of what can easily be disposed of.

o•ver•haul (ō′vər-hôl′, ō′vər-hôl′) *tr.v.* **-hauled, -haul•ing, -hauls 1a.** To examine or go over carefully for needed repairs. **b.** To dismantle in order to make repairs. **c.** *Nautical* To pull (a line) through the hands from one end to the other. **2.** To make extensive renovations or revisions on; renovate. **3.** To catch up with; overtake. ❖ *n.* (ō′vər-hôl′) **1.** An act of overhauling. **2.** A repair job. —**o′ver•haul′er** *n.*

o•ver•head (ō′vər-hĕd′) *adj.* **1.** Located, functioning, or originating from above. **2.** Of or relating to the overhead of a business. ❖ *n.* **1.** The operating expenses of a business, including rent, utilities, interior decoration, and taxes, exclusive of labor and materials. **2.** *Nautical* The top surface in an enclosed space of a ship. **3.** Something, such as a light, that is located above head height. **4.** *Sports* A stroke in a game, such as tennis, that is made with a hard downward motion from above the head. **5a.** An overhead projector. **b.** The image projected by an overhead projector. ❖ *adv.* (ō′vər-hĕd′) Over or above the level of the head; high or higher up.

overhead projector

overhead projector *n.* A projector that projects enlarged images, as onto a screen, from a transparency placed horizontally below the projector and lighted from underneath.

o•ver•hear (ō′vər-hîr′) *v.* **-heard** (-hûrd′), **-hear•ing, -hears** —*tr.* To hear (speech or a speaker) without the speaker's awareness or intent. —*intr.* To overhear something or someone. —**o′ver•hear′er** *n.*

o•ver•heat (ō′vər-hēt′) *v.* **-heat•ed, -heat•ing, -heats** —*tr.* **1.** To heat too much. **2.** To cause to become excited, agitated, or overstimulated. —*intr.* To become too hot or very excited.

o•ver•joy (ō′vər-joi′) *tr.v.* **-joyed, -joy•ing, -joys** To fill with joy; delight. —**o′ver•joyed′** (-joid′) *adj.*

o•ver•kill (ō′vər-kĭl′) *n.* **1.** Destructive nuclear capacity exceeding the amount needed to destroy an enemy. **2.** Excessive killing. **3.** An excess of what is necessary or appropriate for a particular end. ❖ *tr.v.* (ō′vər-kĭl′) **-killed, -kill•ing, -kills** To destroy (an enemy or enemy target) with overkill.

o•ver•lad•en (ō′vər-lād′n) *adj.* Loaded or burdened too heavily.

o•ver•lain (ō′vər-lān′) *v.* Past participle of **overlie.**

o•ver•land (ō′vər-lănd′, -lənd) *adj.* Accomplished, traversing, or passing over the land instead of the ocean: *an overland route.* ❖ *adv.* By way of land: *traveled overland.*

O•ver•land Park (ō′vər-lənd) A city of NE KS, a suburb of Kansas City. Pop. 149,080.

Overland Trail Any of several trails, such as the Oregon Trail or the Santa Fe Trail, of westward migration in the US.

o•ver•lap (ō′vər-lăp′) *v.* **-lapped, -lap•ping, -laps** —*tr.* **1.** To lie or extend over and cover part of. **2.** To have an area or range in common with. —*intr.* **1.** To lie over and partly cover something. **2.** To correspond in character or function: *Their duties overlap.* **3.** *Mathematics* To have one or more elements in common. Used of sets. ❖ *n.* (ō′vər-lăp′) **1.** A part or portion that overlaps or is overlapped. **2.** An instance of overlapping.

o•ver•lay[1] (ō′vər-lā′) *tr.v.* **-laid** (-lād′), **-lay•ing, -lays 1.** To lay or spread over or on. **2a.** To cover the surface of with a decorative overlay. **b.** To embellish superficially. **3.** *Printing* To put an overlay on. **4.** To create (a new area code) having the same boundaries as another. ❖ *n.* (ō′vər-lā′) **1.** Something that is laid over or covers something else. **2.** A layer of decoration applied to a surface. **3.** *Printing* A piece of paper used on a press tympan to vary the pressure that produces light and dark tones. **4.** A transparent sheet containing graphic matter placed on illustrative matter to be incorporated into it. **5.** An area code whose boundaries are the same as another area code.

o•ver•lay[2] (ō′vər-lā′) *v.* Past tense of **overlie.**

o•ver•leaf (ō′vər-lēf′) *adv.* On the other side of the page or leaf.

o•ver•leap (ō′vər-lēp′) *tr.v.* **-leaped** or **-leapt** (-lĕpt′), **-leap•ing, -leaps 1.** To leap across or over. **2.** To defeat (oneself or one's purpose) by going too far.

o•ver•learn (ō′vər-lûrn′) *tr.v.* **-learned** also **-learnt** (-lûrnt′), **-learn•ing, -learns** To continue studying or practicing (something) after initial proficiency has been achieved so as to reinforce or ingrain the learned material or skill.

o•ver•lie (ō′vər-lī′) *tr.v.* **-lay** (-lā′), **-lain** (-lān′), **-ly•ing, -lies 1.** To lie over or on. **2.** To suffocate (a baby, for example) by accidentally lying on top of it.

o•ver•load (ō′vər-lōd′) *tr.v.* **-load•ed, -load•ing, -loads** To load too heavily. ❖ *n.* (ō′vər-lōd′) An excessive load.

o•ver•long (ō′vər-lông′, -lŏng′) *adj.* Excessively long: *an overlong play.* ❖ *adv.* For too long: *talked overlong.*

o•ver•look (ō′vər-lo͝ok′) *tr.v.* **-looked, -look•ing, -looks 1a.** To look over or at from a higher place. **b.** To rise above, esp. with a view over. **2a.** To fail to notice or consider; miss. **b.** To ignore deliberately or indulgently; disregard. **3.** To look over; examine. **4.** To watch over; oversee. ❖ *n.* (ō′vər-lo͝ok′) An elevated place with an extensive view.

o•ver•lord (ō′vər-lôrd′) *n.* **1.** A lord having power or supremacy over other lords. **2.** One in a position of supremacy or domination over others. —**o′ver•lord′ship** *n.*

o•ver•ly (ō′vər-lē) *adv.* To an excessive degree: *overly stern.*

o•ver•man (ō′vər-mən) *n.* **1.** A person with authority over others, esp. an overseer or shift supervisor. **2.** (ō′vər-măn′) See **superman** 2. ❖ *tr.v.* (ō′vər-măn′) **-manned, -man•ning, -mans** To provide with excess personnel. [N., sense 2, transl. of Ger. *Übermensch* : *über,* over, higher + *Mensch,* man.]

o·ver·mas·ter (ō′vər-măs′tər) *tr.v.* **-tered, -ter·ing, -ters** To overpower by superior force; overcome.

o·ver·match (ō′vər-măch′) *tr.v.* **-matched, -match·ing, -match·es** 1. To be more than a match for; exceed or defeat. 2. To match with a superior opponent. ❖ *n.* (ō′vər-măch′) A contest in which one opponent is distinctly superior.

o·ver·much (ō′vər-mŭch′) *adj.* Too much. ❖ *adv.* In excess. ❖ *n.* (ō′vər-mŭch′, ō′vər-mŭch′) An excessive amount.

o·ver·night (ō′vər-nīt′) *adj.* 1. Lasting for, extending over, or remaining during a night. 2. For use over a single night or for a short journey. 3. Mailed for guaranteed delivery on the next day. 4. Happening as if in a single night; sudden. ❖ *adv.* (ō′vər-nīt′) 1. During or for the length of the night. 2. In or as if in the course of one night; suddenly. ❖ *n.* An overnight stay or trip. ❖ *v.* (ō′vər-nīt′) **-night·ed, -night·ing, -nights** —*intr.* To spend the night. —*tr.* To send by mail or other courier for delivery the next day.

overnight bag *n.* A small piece of luggage used to carry items needed for an overnight stay.

o·ver·night·er (ō′vər-nī′tər) *n.* 1. An overnight. 2. One making an overnight stay or trip. 3. Something relating to or used for overnight travel.

o·ver·pass (ō′vər-păs′) *n.* A passage, roadway, or bridge that crosses above a roadway or thoroughfare. ❖ *tr.v.* (ō′vər-păs′) **-passed** or **-past** (-păst′), **-pass·ing, -pass·es** 1. To pass over or across; traverse. 2. To go beyond; surpass. 3. To go over (a limit or boundary); transgress. 4. To overlook or disregard.

o·ver·per·suade (ō′vər-pər-swād′) *tr.v.* **-suad·ed, -suad·ing, -suades** To persuade (someone) to act contrary to inclination or choice. —**o′ver·per·sua′sion** *n.*

o·ver·play (ō′vər-plā′) *v.* **-played, -play·ing, -plays** —*tr.* 1a. To present (a dramatic role, for example) in an exaggerated manner. b. To emphasize or stress unduly. 2. To overestimate the strength of (one's holding or position) with resulting defeat: *overplayed his hand.* 3. *Sports* To hit (a golf ball) beyond the green. —*intr.* To overdo a role or an effect.

o·ver·plus (ō′vər-plŭs′) *n.* An excess amount; a surplus.

o·ver·pop·u·late (ō′vər-pŏp′yə-lāt′) *v.* **-lat·ed, -lat·ing, -lates** —*tr.* To fill with excessive population to the detriment of the inhabitants, resources, or environment. —*intr.* To breed to excess. —**o′ver·pop′u·la′tion** *n.*

o·ver·pow·er (ō′vər-pou′ər) *tr.v.* **-ered, -er·ing, -ers** 1. To overcome or vanquish by superior force; subdue. 2. To affect so strongly as to make helpless or ineffective; overwhelm. 3. To supply with excessive mechanical power.

o·ver·pow·er·ing (ō′vər-pou′ər-ĭng) *adj.* So strong as to be overwhelming. —**o′ver·pow′er·ing·ly** *adv.*

o·ver·pres·sure (ō′vər-prĕsh′ər) *n.* A transient air pressure, such as the shock wave from an explosion, that is greater than the surrounding atmospheric pressure. ❖ *tr.v.* **-sured, -sur·ing, -sures** To cause or subject to overpressure. —**o′ver·pres′sur·i·za′tion** (-ī-zā′shən) *n.*

o·ver·print (ō′vər-prĭnt′) *tr.v.* **-print·ed, -print·ing, -prints** To imprint over something with something more, esp. to print over with another color. ❖ *n.* (ō′vər-prĭnt′) 1. A mark or impression made by overprinting. 2a. A mark or words printed over a postage stamp to note a change in use or a special occasion. b. A stamp so marked.

o·ver·proof (ō′vər-prōōf′) *adj.* Containing a greater proportion of alcohol than proof spirit, esp. containing more than 50 percent alcohol by volume.

o·ver·pro·por·tion (ō′vər-prə-pôr′shən, -pōr′-) *tr.v.* **-tioned, -tion·ing, -tions** To make larger and out of proportion to what is normal, desired, or appropriate. —**o′ver·pro·por′tion** *n.* —**o′ver·pro·por′tion·ate** (-shə-nĭt) *adj.* —**o′ver·pro·por′tion·ate·ly** *adv.*

o·ver·qual·i·fied (ō′vər-kwŏl′ə-fīd′) *adj.* Educated or skilled beyond what is needed or desired for a given job.

o·ver·reach (ō′vər-rēch′) *v.* **-reached, -reach·ing, -reach·es** —*tr.* 1. To reach or extend over or beyond. 2. To miss by reaching too far or attempting too much. 3. To defeat (oneself) by going too far or by attempting too much. 4. To get the better of, esp. by deceitful cleverness; outwit. —*intr.* 1. To reach or go too far. 2. To overreach oneself. 3. To outwit or cheat others. 4. To strike the front part of a hind foot against the corresponding rear or side part of a forefoot or foreleg. Used of a horse. —**o′ver·reach′** *n.* —**o′ver·reach′er** *n.*

o·ver·re·act (ō′vər-rē-ăkt′) *intr.v.* **-act·ed, -act·ing, -acts** To react with unnecessary or inappropriate force, emotion, or violence. —**o′ver·re·ac′tion** *n.* —**o′ver·re·ac′tive** *adj.*

o·ver·rep·re·sent·ed (ō′vər-rĕp′rĭ-zĕn′tĭd) *adj.* Represented in excessive or disproportionately large numbers. —**o′ver·rep′re·sen·ta′tion** (-zĕn-tā′shən, -zən-) *n.*

o·ver·ride (ō′vər-rīd′) *tr.v.* **-rode** (-rōd′), **-rid·den** (-rĭd′n), **-rid·ing, -rides** 1a. To ride across. b. To ride beyond. 2. To trample on. 3. To ride (a horse) too hard. 4a. To prevail over; conquer. b. To declare null and void; set aside: *overrode the veto.* c. To counteract the normal operation of (an automatic control). 5. To extend over; overlap. ❖ *n.* (ō′vər-rīd′) 1. A sales commission collected by an executive in addition to that received by a subordinate salesperson. 2. See **royalty** 9. 3. A mechanism or system used to override an automatic control. 4. The act or an instance of nullifying.

o·ver·rid·ing (ō′vər-rī′dĭng) *adj.* First in priority; more important than all others. —**o′ver·rid′ing·ly** *adv.*

o·ver·ripe (ō′vər-rīp′) *adj.* 1. Too ripe. 2. Marked by decay or decline. —**o′ver·ripe′ly** *adv.* —**o′ver·ripe′ness** *n.*

o·ver·ruff (ō′vər-rŭf′) *intr. & tr.v.* **-ruffed, -ruff·ing, -ruffs** *Games* To overtrump. —**o′ver·ruff′** *n.*

o·ver·rule (ō′vər-rōōl′) *tr.v.* **-ruled, -rul·ing, -rules** 1a. To disallow the action or arguments of, esp. by virtue of higher authority. b. To decide or rule against. c. To declare null and void; reverse. 2. To dominate by strong influence; prevail over.

o·ver·run (ō′vər-rŭn′) *v.* **-ran** (-răn′), **-run, -run·ning, -runs** —*tr.* 1a. To seize the positions of and defeat conclusively. b. To spread or swarm over destructively. 2. To spread swiftly throughout. 3. To overflow. 4a. To run beyond or past; overshoot. b. To run or extend beyond (a limit); exceed. 5. *Printing* a. To rearrange or move (set type or pictures) from one column, line, or page to another. b. To set too much type for. c. To print (a job order) in a quantity larger than that ordered. —*intr.* 1. To run over; overflow. 2. To go beyond the normal or desired limit. ❖ *n.* (ō′vər-rŭn′) 1. An act of overrunning. 2. The amount by which something overruns. 3a. The exceeding of estimated costs for product development and manufacture covered by contract. b. The amount by which actual costs exceed estimates. 4. *Printing* A run beyond the quantity ordered by a customer.

o·ver·scale (ō′vər-skāl′) or **o·ver·scaled** (-skāld′) *adj.* Being greater in size or scope than usual; unusually large.

o·ver·score (ō′vər-skôr′, -skōr′) *tr.v.* **-scored, -scor·ing, -scores** To cross out with a line or lines.

o·ver·sea (ō′vər-sē′, ō′vər-sē′) *adv. & adj.* Overseas.

o·ver·seas (ō′vər-sēz′, ō′vər-sēz′) *adv.* Beyond the sea; abroad. ❖ *adj.* Of, relating to, originating in, or situated in countries across the sea.

overseas cap *n.* See **garrison cap.**

o·ver·see (ō′vər-sē′) *tr.v.* **-saw** (-sô′), **-seen** (-sēn′), **-see·ing, -sees** 1. To watch over and direct; supervise. 2. To subject to scrutiny; examine or inspect.

o·ver·se·er (ō′vər-sē′ər) *n.* 1. One who keeps watch over and directs the work of others, esp. laborers. 2. A supervisor or superintendent.

o·ver·sell (ō′vər-sĕl′) *tr.v.* **-sold** (-sōld′), **-sell·ing, -sells** 1. To contract to sell more of (a stock or commodity) than can be delivered. 2. To be too eager or insistent in attempting to sell something to. 3. To present with excessive or unwarranted enthusiasm; overpraise. —**o′ver·sell′** *n.*

o·ver·set (ō′vər-sĕt′) *v.* **-set, -set·ting, -sets** —*tr.* 1. To throw into a confused or disturbed state; upset: *The accident overset him.* 2. *Printing* a. To set (type or copy) in excess of what is needed. b. To set too much type for (a given space). —*intr. Printing* To set too much material for a given space. ❖ *n.* (ō′vər-sĕt′) *Printing* Too much typeset matter.

o·ver·sew (ō′vər-sō′, ō′vər-sō′) *tr.v.* **-sewed, -sewn** (-sōn′) or **-sewed, -sew·ing, -sews** To sew with overhand stitches.

o·ver·sexed (ō′vər-sĕkst′) *adj.* Having or showing an excessive sexual appetite or interest in sexual matters.

o·ver·shad·ow (ō′vər-shăd′ō) *tr.v.* **-owed, -ow·ing, -ows** 1. To cast a shadow over; darken or obscure. 2. To make insignificant by comparison; dominate.

o·ver·shoe (ō′vər-shōō′) *n.* An article of footwear worn over a shoe as protection from water, snow, or cold.

o·ver·shoot (ō′vər-shōōt′) *v.* **-shot** (-shŏt′), **-shoot·ing, -shoots** —*tr.* 1. To shoot or pass over or beyond. 2. To miss by or as if by shooting, hitting, or propelling something too far. 3. To fly beyond or past; overrun. 4. To go beyond; exceed. —*intr.* To shoot or go too far. —**o′ver·shoot′** *n.*

o·ver·shot (ō′vər-shŏt′) *adj.* 1. Having an upper part projecting beyond the lower: *an overshot jaw.* 2. Operated by water that flows over the top from above: *an overshot water wheel.* ❖ *n.* A pattern in weaving made when filling threads are passed over two or more warp threads.

o·ver·sight (ō′vər-sīt′) *n.* 1. An unintentional omission or mistake. 2. Watchful care or management; supervision.

o·ver·sim·pli·fy (ō′vər-sĭm′plə-fī′) *v.* **-fied, -fy·ing, -fies** —*tr.* To simplify to the point of causing misrepresentation, misconception, or error. —*intr.* To cause distortion or error by extreme simplification of a subject. —**o′ver·sim′pli·fi·ca′tion** (-fĭ-kā′shən) *n.* —**o′ver·sim′pli·fi′er** *n.*

o·ver·size (ō′vər-sīz′) *n.* 1. A size that is larger than usual. 2. An oversize article or object. ❖ *adj.* **o·ver·size** (ō′vər-sīz′) also **o·ver·sized** (-sīzd′) Larger in size than usual or necessary.

o·ver·skirt (ō′vər-skûrt′) *n.* An outer skirt, esp. a shorter one worn draped over another skirt.

o·ver·sleep (ō′vər-slēp′) *v.* **-slept** (-slĕpt′), **-sleep·ing, -sleeps** —*intr.* To sleep beyond one's usual or intended time for waking. —*tr.* To sleep beyond the time for.

o·ver·sold (ō′vər-sōld′) *v.* Past tense and past participle of **oversell.** ❖ *adj.* Characterized by prices regarded as excessively low because of prior heavy selling: *an oversold stock market.*

o·ver·soul (ō′vər-sōl′) *n.* In New England transcendentalism, a spiritual essence or force in the universe in which all souls partici-

ă	pat	oi	boy
ā	pay	ou	out
âr	care	ōō	took
ä	father	ōō	boot
ĕ	pet	ŭ	cut
ē	be	ûr	urge
ĭ	pit	th	thin
ī	pie	th	this
îr	pier	hw	which
ŏ	pot	zh	vision
ō	toe	ə	about,
ô	paw		item

Stress marks:
′ (primary);
′ (secondary), as in
lexicon (lĕk′sĭ-kŏn′)

pate and that transcends individual consciousness.

o·ver·spend (ō′vər-spĕnd′) v. **-spent** (-spĕnt′), **-spend·ing, -spends** —intr. To spend more than is prudent or necessary. —tr. **1.** To spend in excess of: *overspend one's income.* **2.** To tire out; exhaust: *overspent with toil.* —**o′ver·spend′er** n.

o·ver·spill (ō′vər-spĭl′) intr.v. **-spilled** or **-spilt** (-spĭlt), **-spill·ing, -spills** To spill over. ❖ n. (ō′vər-spĭl′) **1.** The act of spilling over. **2.** Something that spills over. **3.** *Chiefly British* Movement from cities to less populated areas.

o·ver·spread (ō′vər-sprĕd′) tr.v. **-spread, -spread·ing, -spreads** To spread or extend over the surface of: *Dark clouds are overspreading the sky.* —**o′ver·spread′** n.

o·ver·state (ō′vər-stāt′) tr.v. **-stat·ed, -stat·ing, -states** To state in exaggerated terms. See Syns at **exaggerate.** —**o′ver·state′ment** n.

o·ver·stay (ō′vər-stā′) tr.v. **-stayed, -stay·ing, -stays** To stay beyond the set limits or expected duration of; outstay.

o·ver·steer (ō′vər-stîr′) intr.v. **-steered, -steer·ing, -steers** To turn more sharply than the operator would expect. Used of vehicles, esp. automobiles. ❖ n. **1.** An instance of oversteering. **2.** A tendency to oversteer.

o·ver·step (ō′vər-stĕp′) tr.v. **-stepped, -step·ping, -steps** To go beyond (a limit); exceed: *overstepped the bounds.*

o·ver·stock (ō′vər-stŏk′) tr.v. **-stocked, -stock·ing, -stocks** To stock more of (something) than necessary or desirable. ❖ n. (ō′vər-stŏk′) An excessive supply.

o·ver·sto·ry (ō′vər-stôr′ē, -stōr′ē) n. The uppermost layer of foliage that forms a forest canopy.

o·ver·strain (ō′vər-strān′) v. **-strained, -strain·ing, -strains** —tr. To subject to excessive strain, esp. to force beyond a natural or proper limit: *overstraining the environment.* —intr. To put forth too much physical effort.

o·ver·stress (ō′vər-strĕs′) tr.v. **-stressed, -stress·ing, -stress·es** **1.** To place too much emphasis on. **2.** To subject to excessive physical or emotional stress. **3.** To deform by excessive mechanical force or pressure. —**o′ver·stress′** n.

o·ver·stretch (ō′vər-strĕch′) v. **-stretched, -stretch·ing, -stretch·es** —tr. **1.** To stretch excessively; overstrain. **2.** To stretch or extend over. —intr. To stretch one's body or muscles to the point of strain or injury.

o·ver·stride (ō′vər-strīd′) v. **-strode** (-strōd′), **-strid·den** (-strĭd′n), **-strid·ing, -strides** —tr. **1.** To stride over, across, or farther than: *overstride a stream.* **2.** To sit or stand astride. **3.** To stride faster than or beyond, as in a competition. **4.** To go beyond; surpass. —intr. To run with an overly long stride for one's leg length.

o·ver·strung (ō′vər-strŭng′) adj. **1.** Too sensitive, nervous, or tense. **2.** Too tightly strung: *an overstrung archery bow.*

o·ver·stuff (ō′vər-stŭf′) tr.v. **-stuffed, -stuff·ing, -stuffs** **1.** To stuff too much into: *overstuff a suitcase.* **2.** To upholster (an armchair, for example) deeply and thickly.

o·ver·sub·scribe (ō′vər-səb-skrīb′) tr.v. **-scribed, -scrib·ing, -scribes** To subscribe for (something) in excess of available supply. —**o′ver·sub·scrip′tion** (-skrĭp′shən) n.

o·ver·sup·ply (ō′vər-sə-plī′) n., pl. **-plies** A supply in excess of what is appropriate or required. ❖ tr.v. (ō′vər-sə-plī′) **-plied, -ply·ing, -plies** To give an oversupply.

o·vert (ō-vûrt′, ō′vûrt′) adj. **1.** Open and observable; not hidden, concealed, or secret: *overt hostility.* **2.** Of, relating to, or being military or intelligence operations sanctioned or mandated by Congress. [ME < OFr., p. part. of *ovrir*, to open < VLat. *ōperīre*, alteration of Lat. *aperīre.*] —**o·vert′ly** adv. —**o·vert′ness** n.

o·ver·take (ō′vər-tāk′) tr.v. **-took** (-tŏŏk′), **-tak·en** (-tā′kən), **-tak·ing, -takes** **1a.** To catch up with; draw even or level with. **b.** To pass after catching up with. **2.** To come upon unexpectedly; take by surprise.

o·ver-the-air (ō′vər-thē-âr′) adj. Of, relating to, or being a medium of broadcast transmission, such as radio.

o·ver-the-count·er (ō′vər-thə-koun′tər) adj. **1.** Not listed or available on an officially recognized stock exchange but traded directly between buyers and sellers. **2.** That can be sold legally without a prescription.

o·ver-the-hill (ō′vər-thə-hĭl′) adj. *Informal* **1.** Past one's peak of youthful vigor and freshness. **2.** Far along in life; old.

o·ver·throw (ō′vər-thrō′) tr.v. **-threw** (-thrōō′), **-thrown** (-thrōn′), **-throw·ing, -throws** **1.** To throw over; overturn. **2.** To cause the downfall or destruction of, esp. by force or concerted action. **3.** *Sports* To throw an object over and beyond (an intended mark). ❖ n. (ō′vər-thrō′) **1.** An instance of overthrowing, esp. one that results in downfall or destruction. **2.** *Sports* The overthrowing of a ball.

SYNONYMS *overthrow, overturn, subvert, topple, upset* These verbs mean to cause the downfall, destruction, abolition, or undoing of: *overthrow an empire; overturn existing institutions; subverting civil order; toppled the government; upset all our plans.*

o·ver·time (ō′vər-tīm′) n. **1.** Time beyond an established limit, as: **a.** Working hours in addition to those of a regular schedule. **b.** *Sports* A period of playing time added after the expiration of the set time limit. **2.** Payment for work done overtime. ❖ adv.

Beyond the established time limit, esp. that of the normal working day. ❖ tr.v. (ō′vər-tīm′) **-timed, -tim·ing, -times** To exceed the desired timing for.

o·ver·tone (ō′vər-tōn′) n. **1.** An ulterior, usu. implicit meaning or quality; an implication or a hint. Often used in the plural. **2.** See **harmonic** 1.

o·ver·top (ō′vər-tŏp′) tr.v. **-topped, -top·ping, -tops** **1.** To extend or rise above or beyond; tower over. **2.** To take precedence over; override. **3.** To be greater or better than; surpass.

o·ver·trick (ō′vər-trĭk′) n. *Games* A card trick won in excess of game or of contract, as in bridge.

o·ver·trump (ō′vər-trŭmp′, ō′vər-trŭmp′) v. **-trumped, -trump·ing, -trumps** *Games* —intr. To overtrump a card. —tr. To trump with a higher trump card than one previously played on a trick.

o·ver·ture (ō′vər-chŏŏr′) n. **1.** *Music* **a.** An instrumental composition intended esp. as an introduction to an extended work. **b.** A similar orchestral work intended for independent concert performance. **2.** An introductory section or part, as of a poem; a prelude. **3.** An act, offer, or proposal indicating readiness for a course of action or a relationship. ❖ tr.v. **-tured, -tur·ing, -tures** **1.** To present as an introduction or proposal. **2.** To present an offer or proposal to. [ME, opening < OFr. < VLat. *ōpertūra*, alteration of Lat. *apertūra < apertus*, p. part. of *aperīre*, to open.]

o·ver·turn (ō′vər-tûrn′) v. **-turned, -turn·ing, -turns** —tr. **1.** To cause to turn over or capsize; upset. **2a.** To cause the ruin or destruction of. See Syns at **overthrow. b.** *Law* To invalidate or reverse (a decision) by legal means. —intr. To turn over or capsize. ❖ n. (ō′vər-tûrn′) **1.** The act or process of overturning. **2.** The state of having been overturned.

o·ver·view (ō′vər-vyōō′) n. **1.** A broad comprehensive view; a survey. **2.** A summary or review.

o·ver·vote (ō′vər-vōt′) n. **1.** A ballot showing the selection of more candidates or choices than are allowed in a given race or referendum. **2.** The number of such ballots cast in an election.

o·ver·ween·ing (ō′vər-wē′nĭng) adj. **1.** Presumptuously arrogant; overbearing: *overweening manners.* **2.** Excessive; immoderate: *overweening ambition.* —**o′ver·ween′ing·ly** adv.

o·ver·weigh (ō′vər-wā′) tr.v. **-weighed, -weigh·ing, -weighs** **1.** To have more weight than. **2.** To weigh down excessively; overburden or oppress.

o·ver·weight (ō′vər-wāt′) adj. Weighing more than is normal, necessary, or allowed, esp. having more body weight than is considered normal or healthy for one's age or build. ❖ n. (ō′vər-wāt′) **1.** More weight than is normal, necessary, or allowed. **2.** Greater weight or importance; preponderance. ❖ tr.v. (ō′vər-wāt′) **-weight·ed, -weight·ing, -weights** **1.** To weigh down too heavily; overload. **2.** To give too much emphasis, importance, or consideration to.

o·ver·whelm (ō′vər-hwĕlm′, -wĕlm′) tr.v. **-whelmed, -whelm·ing, -whelms** **1.** To surge over and submerge; engulf. **2a.** To defeat completely and decisively. **b.** To affect deeply in mind or emotion. **3.** To present with an excessive amount. **4.** To turn over; upset.

o·ver·whelm·ing (ō′vər-hwĕl′mĭng, -wĕl′-) adj. Overpowering in effect or strength. —**o′ver·whelm′ing·ly** adv.

o·ver·win·ter (ō′vər-wĭn′tər) intr.v. **-tered, -ter·ing, -ters** **1.** To remain alive through the winter: *sheep that overwintered on the steppe.* **2.** To pass or spend the winter. ❖ adj. (ō′vər-wĭn′tər) Occurring during the period of winter.

o·ver·with·hold (ō′vər-wĭth-hōld′, -wĭth-) v. **-held** (-hĕld′), **-hold·ing, -holds** —tr. **1.** To deduct (an amount in withholding tax) beyond the tax owed. **2.** To subject to overwithholding. —intr. To deduct too much withholding tax.

o·ver·work (ō′vər-wûrk′) v. **-worked, -work·ing, -works** —tr. **1.** To force to work too hard or too long. **2a.** To rework to excess. **b.** To use too often: *overworked clichés.* **3.** To decorate the entire surface of. —intr. To work too long or too hard. ❖ n. (ō′vər-wûrk′) Excessive work.

o·ver·write (ō′vər-rīt′) v. **-wrote** (-rōt′), **-writ·ten** (-rĭt′n), **-writ·ing, -writes** —tr. **1.** To cover (something) with writing. **2.** To write about in an artificial or an excessively elaborate, wordy style. **3.** *Computer Science* **a.** To destroy or lose (old data) by recording new data over it. **b.** To record (new data) on top of already stored data, thus destroying the old data. —intr. To write artificial, excessively elaborate, or wordy prose.

o·ver·wrought (ō′vər-rôt′) adj. **1.** Excessively nervous or excited; agitated. **2.** Extremely elaborate or ornate; overdone.

ovi- or **ovo-** or **ov-** pref. Egg; ovum: *oviferous.* [Lat. *ōvi- < ōvum*, egg. See **awi-** in App.]

o·vi·cide (ō′vĭ-sīd′) n. A chemical agent that kills eggs, esp. the eggs of insects. —**o′vi·cid′al** (-sīd′l) adj.

Ov·id (ŏv′ĭd) 43 B.C.–A.D. 17. Roman poet known for his explorations of love, esp. in *Metamorphoses* (c. A.D. 8). —**O·vid′i·an** (ō-vĭd′ē-ən) adj.

o·vi·duct (ō′vĭ-dŭkt′) n. A tube through which ova pass from the ovary to the uterus or to the outside. —**o′vi·duc′tal** adj.

O·vie·do (ō-vyā′dō, ō-vyĕ′thō) A city of NW Spain near the Cantabrian Mts.; founded c. 760 and the cap. of Asturian kings until 910. Pop. 195,651.

o·vif·er·ous (ō-vĭf′ər-əs) adj. Bearing or producing ova.

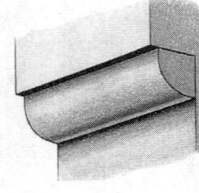

ovolo

Jesse Owens
at the 1936 Olympics
in Berlin

o·vi·form (ō'və-fôrm') *adj.* Shaped like an egg; ovoid.

O·vim·bun·du (ō'vĭm-bo͞on'do͞o) *n., pl.* **Ovimbundu** or **-dus** See Mbundu 1.

o·vine (ō'vīn') *adj.* Of, relating to, or characteristic of sheep; sheeplike. ❖ *n.* An ovine animal. [LLat. *ovīnus* < Lat. *ovis*, sheep. See owi- in App.]

o·vip·a·rous (ō-vĭp'ər-əs) *adj.* Producing eggs that hatch outside the body. **—o'vi·par'i·ty** (ō'və-păr'ĭ-tē) *n.* **—o·vip'a·rous·ly** *adv.*

o·vi·pos·it (ō'və-pŏz'ĭt) *intr.v.* **-it·ed, -it·ing, -its** To lay eggs, esp. by means of an ovipositor. **—o'vi·po·si'tion** (-pə-zĭsh'ən) *n.* **—o'vi·po·si'tion·al** *adj.*

o·vi·pos·i·tor (ō'və-pŏz'ĭ-tər) *n.* **1.** A tubular structure, usu. concealed, with which many female insects deposit eggs. **2.** A similar organ of certain fishes.

o·vi·sac (ō'vĭ-săk') *n.* An egg-containing capsule, such as an ootheca or a Graafian follicle.

ovo– *pref.* Variant of ovi–.

o·void (ō'void') also **o·voi·dal** (ō-void'l) *adj.* Shaped like an egg; ovate. ❖ *n.* Something that is shaped like an egg.

o·vo·lac·to·veg·e·tar·i·an (ō'vō-lăk'tō-vĕj'ĭ-târ'ē-ən) *n.* A vegetarian whose diet includes eggs and milk or milk products.

o·vo·lo (ō'və-lō) *n., pl.* **-li** (-lī') A rounded convex molding, often a quarter section of a circle or ellipse. [Obsolete Ital., dim. of *uovo*, *ovo*, egg < Lat. *ōvum*. See awi- in App.]

o·von·ic (ō-vŏn'ĭk) *adj.* Of or relating to a device whose operation is based on the Ovshinsky effect. [OV(SHINSKY EFFECT) + (ELECTR)ONIC.]

o·vo·tes·tis (ō'vō-tĕs'tĭs) *n., pl.* **-tes** (-tēz') A hermaphroditic reproductive organ that produces both sperm and eggs, found in certain gastropods.

o·vo·vi·vip·a·rous (ō'vō-vī-vĭp'ər-əs) *adj.* Producing eggs that hatch within the female's body without obtaining nourishment from it. Used of certain fishes and reptiles and many invertebrates. **—o'vo·vi·vi·par'i·ty** (-vī'və-păr'ĭ-tē), **o'vo·vi·vip'a·rous·ness** (-vĭp'ər-əs-nĭs) *n.* **—o'vo·vi·vip'a·rous·ly** *adv.*

Ov·shin·sky effect (ŏv-shĭn'skē, ôv-) *n.* The effect by which a specific glassy thin film switches from a nonconductor to a semiconductor upon application of a minimum voltage. [After Stanford Robert *Ovshinsky* (born 1922), American inventor.]

o·vu·late (ō'vyə-lāt', ŏv'yə-) *intr.v.* **-lat·ed, -lat·ing, -lates** To produce ova; discharge eggs from the ovary. [< OVULE.] **—o'vu·la'tion** *n.* **—o'vu·la·to'ry** (-lə-tôr'ē, -tōr'-) *adj.*

o·vule (ō'vyo͞ol, ŏv'yo͞ol) *n.* **1.** *Botany* A minute structure in seed plants, containing the embryo sac and surrounded by the nucellus, that develops into a seed after fertilization. **2.** *Zoology* A small or immature ovum. [NLat. *ōvulum*, dim. of Lat. *ōvum*, egg. See awi- in App.] **—o'vu·lar** (ō'vyə-lər, ŏv'yə-), **o'vu·lar'y** (-lĕr'ē) *adj.*

o·vum (ō'vəm) *n., pl.* **o·va** (ō'və) The female reproductive cell or gamete of animals; egg. [Lat. *ōvum*, egg. See awi- in App.]

ow (ou) *interj.* Used esp. in response to sudden pain.

owe (ō) *v.* **owed, ow·ing, owes** **—tr. 1.** To be indebted to the amount of. **2.** To have a moral obligation to render or offer for. **3.** To be in debt to. **4.** To be indebted or obliged for. **5.** To bear (a certain feeling) toward someone. **6.** *Archaic* To have as a possession; own. **—intr.** To be in debt. [ME *owen* < OE *āgan*, to possess.]

Ow·en (ō'ĭn), **Robert** 1771–1858. Welsh-born British manufacturer and social reformer who attempted to establish a cooperative community at New Harmony IN (1825–28).

Owen, Wilfred 1893–1918. British poet whose work reflects his experiences in World War I.

Ow·ens (ō'ĭnz), **Jesse** 1913–80. Amer. track star who won four gold medals at the 1936 Olympics.

Owen Sound A city of SE Ontario, Canada, on **Owen Sound**, an inlet of Georgian Bay. Pop. 21,390.

Owens River A river of E CA rising in the Sierra Nevada and flowing c. 193 km (120 mi) via aqueduct to Los Angeles.

Owen Stanley Range A mountain range extending c. 483 km (300 mi) SE on New Guinea I. in Papua New Guinea and rising to 4,075.7 m (13,363 ft).

ow·ing (ō'ĭng) *adj.* Still to be paid; due.

owing to *prep.* Because of; on account of.

owl (oul) *n.* **1.** Any of various often nocturnal birds of prey of the order Strigiformes, having hooked talons, large heads with short hooked beaks, and large eyes set forward. **2.** Any of a breed of domestic pigeons resembling owls. [ME *owle* < OE *ūle*, of imit. orig.]

owl·et (ou'lĭt) *n.* A small or young owl.

owlet moth *n.* See noctuid.

owl·ish (ou'lĭsh) *adj.* Resembling or characteristic of an owl. **—owl'ish·ly** *adv.* **—owl'ish·ness** *n.*

owl's clover (oulz) *n.* Any of various New World plants of the genus *Orthocarpus*, having spikes of variously colored flowers enclosed in prominent bracts.

own (ōn) *adj.* Of or belonging to oneself or itself: *her own clothes.* ❖ *n.* That which belongs to one: *a room of my own.* ❖ *v.* **owned, own·ing, owns** **—tr. 1a.** To possess as property: *owns two cars.* **b.** To have control over: *Enemy planes owned the skies.* **2.** To admit as being in accordance with fact, truth, or a claim; acknowledge. **—intr.** To make a full confession or acknowledgment: *The thief owned up.* **—idiom: on (one's) own 1.** By one's own efforts. **2.** Responsible for oneself; independent of outside help or control. [ME *owen* < OE *āgen.*] **—own'er** *n.*

own·er·ship (ō'nər-shĭp') *n.* **1.** The state or fact of being an owner. **2.** Legal right to the possession of a thing.

O·wy·hee (ō-wī'ē, -hē) A river, c. 483 km (300 mi), of SW ID, N NV, and SE OR emptying into the Snake R.

ox (ŏks) *n., pl.* **ox·en** (ŏk'sən) **1.** An adult castrated bull of the genus *Bos*, esp. *B. taurus*, used chiefly as a draft animal. **2.** A bovine mammal. [ME < OE *oxa.*]

ox– *pref.* Variant of oxo–.

ox·a·cil·lin (ŏk'sə-sĭl'ĭn) *n.* A semisynthetic penicillin, $C_{19}H_{19}N_3O_5S$, used esp. against penicillin-resistant staphylococcal infections. [OX(O)– + A(ZOLE) + (PENI)CILLIN.]

ox·a·late (ŏk'sə-lāt') *n.* A salt or ester of oxalic acid. ❖ *tr.v.* **-lat·ed, -lat·ing, -lates** To treat (a specimen) with an oxalate or oxalic acid. [OXAL(IC ACID) + –ATE[2].]

ox·al·ic acid (ŏk-săl'ĭk) *n.* A poisonous crystalline organic acid, $H_2C_2O_4\cdot 2H_2O$, found in many plants, such as spinach, and used as a bleach and rust remover. [Lat. *oxalis*, wood sorrel; see OXALIS + –IC.]

ox·a·lis (ŏk'sə-lĭs, ŏk-săl'ĭs) *n.* Any of numerous plants of the genus *Oxalis*, having often cloverlike compound leaves with three leaflets and flowers usu. clustered in umbels. [Lat. *oxalis*, wood sorrel < Gk. < *oxus*, sour. See ak- in App.]

ox·a·lo·ac·e·tate (ŏk'sə-lō-ăs'ĭ-tāt') or **ox·al·ac·e·tate** (-ăs'ĭ-tāt') *n.* A salt or ester of oxaloacetic acid. [OXAL(IC ACID) + ACET(IC ACID) + –ATE[2].]

ox·a·lo·a·ce·tic acid (ŏk'sə-lō-ə-sē'tĭk, ŏk-săl'ō-) or **ox·al·a·ce·tic acid** (ŏk-sĕl'ə-sē'tĭk, ŏk'səl-) *n.* A colorless crystalline dicarboxylic acid, $C_4H_4O_5$, that is formed by oxidation of malic acid in the Krebs cycle and is an intermediate in the metabolism of carbohydrates. [OXAL(IC ACID) + ACETIC ACID.]

ox·blood red (ŏks'blŭd') *n.* A dark or deep red to medium reddish brown.

ox·bow (ŏks'bō') *n.* **1.** A U-shaped piece of wood that fits under and around the neck of an ox, with its upper ends attached to the bar of the yoke. **2a.** A U-shaped bend in a river. **b.** The land within an oxbow. **—ox'bow'** *adj.*

oxbow lake *n.* A crescent-shaped lake formed when a meander of a river or stream is cut off from the main channel.

Ox·bridge (ŏks'brĭj') *n.* Oxford and Cambridge universities. [OX(FORD) + (CAM)BRIDGE.] **—Ox'bridge'** *adj.*

ox·en (ŏk'sən) *n.* Plural of ox.

ox·eye (ŏks'ī') *n.* **1.** Either of two Eurasian plants of the genus *Buphthalum*, having flowers with yellow rays and dark centers. **2.** Any of various New World plants of the genus *Heliopsis*, having similar flowers. **3.** A round or oval dormer window.

oxeye daisy *n.* See daisy 1.

ox·ford (ŏks'fərd) *n.* **1.** A low sturdy shoe that laces over the instep. **2.** A cotton cloth of a tight basket weave, used primarily for shirts. [After OXFORD, England.]

Oxford A borough of S-central England on the Thames R. WNW of London; chartered 1605. Oxford University was founded in the 12th cent. and still dominates the center of the city. Pop. 131,967.

Oxford, 17th Earl of. Title of Edward de Vere. 1550–1604. English courtier and poet who is believed by some to have written Shakespeare's plays.

oxford gray *n.* A dark gray. [After OXFORD, England.]

Oxford movement *n.* A 19th-century Anglican movement, originating in Oxford, England, for restoration of High-Church ideals.

ox·heart (ŏks'härt') *n.* A variety of cultivated cherry having sweet juicy fruit. [< its shape.]

ox·i·dant (ŏk'sĭ-dənt) *n.* A substance that oxidizes another substance; an oxidizing agent. [Fr. *oxidant*, pr. part. of *oxider*, to oxidize < *oxide*, oxide. See OXIDE.]

ox·i·dase (ŏk'sĭ-dās', -dāz') *n.* Any of a group of enzymes that catalyze oxidation, esp. one that reacts with molecular oxygen to catalyze the oxidation of a substrate. [OXID(ATION) + –ASE.] **—ox'i·da'sic** *adj.*

ox·i·da·tion (ŏk'sĭ-dā'shən) *n.* **1.** The combination of a substance with oxygen. **2.** A reaction in which the atoms in an element lose electrons and the valence of the element is correspondingly increased. [Fr. < *oxider*, to oxidize < *oxide*, oxide. See OXIDE.] **—ox'i·da'tive** *adj.*

ox·i·da·tion-re·duc·tion (ŏk'sĭ-dā'shən-rĭ-dŭk'shən) *n.* A chemical reaction in which an atom or ion loses electrons to another atom or ion.

oxidative phosphorylation *n.* The process of cell metabolism by which ATP is synthesized from ADP and inorganic phosphate during the oxidation of NADH by molecular oxygen.

oxidative stress *n.* A condition of increased oxidant production in animal cells that results in cellular degeneration.

ox·ide (ŏk'sīd') *n.* A binary compound of an element or radical with oxygen. [Fr. : *ox(ygène)*, oxygen; see OXYGEN + *(ac)ide*, acid (< Lat. *acidus*, tart, acid; see ACID).] **—ox·id'ic** (ŏk-sĭd'ĭk) *adj.*

ox·i·dize (ŏk'sĭ-dīz') *v.* **-dized, -diz·ing, -diz·es** **—tr. 1.** To

owl
snowy owl
Nyctea scandiaca

owl's clover
Orthocarpus purpurascens

ă	pat	oi	boy
ā	pay	ou	out
âr	care	o͝o	took
ä	father	o͞o	boot
ĕ	pet	ŭ	cut
ē	be	ûr	urge
ĭ	pit	th	thin
ī	pie	th	this
îr	pier	hw	which
ŏ	pot	zh	vision
ō	toe	ə	about,
ô	paw		item

Stress marks:
' (primary);
' (secondary), as in
lexicon (lĕk'sĭ-kŏn')

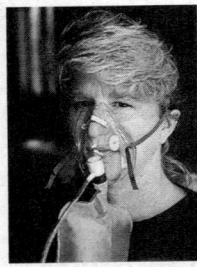

oxygen mask

oyster mushroom
Pleurotus ostreatus

Seiji Ozawa

combine with oxygen; make into an oxide. **2.** To increase the positive charge or valence of (an element) by removing electrons. **3.** To coat with oxide. —*intr.* To become oxidized. —**ox′i·diz′a·ble** *adj.* —**ox′i·di·za′tion** (-dī-zǝ′shǝn) *n.*

ox·i·diz·er (ŏk′sĭ-dī′zǝr) *n.* A substance that oxidizes another substance, esp. one that supports the combustion of fuel; an oxidizing agent.

ox·i·do·re·duc·tase (ŏk′sĭ-dō-rĭ-dŭk′tās′, -tāz′) *n.* An enzyme that catalyzes an oxidation-reduction reaction. [OXID(ATION) + REDUCT(ION) + -ASE.]

ox·ime (ŏk′sēm) *n.* Any of a group of compounds containing a CNOH group, formed by treating aldehydes or ketones with hydroxylamine. [OX(O)- + IM(ID)E.]

ox·lip (ŏks′lĭp′) *n.* A Eurasian primrose (*Primula elatior*) having yellow flowers clustered in a one-sided umbel. [ME *oxeslippe* < OE *oxanslyppe* : *oxan*, genitive sing. of *oxa*, ox + *slyppe*, slimy substance.]

Ox·nard (ŏks′närd′) A city of S CA WNW of Los Angeles on the Pacific coast. Pop. 170,358.

oxo- or **ox-** *pref.* Oxygen: *oxime*. [< OXYGEN.]

Ox·o·ni·an (ŏk-sō′nē-ǝn) *adj.* Of or relating to Oxford, England, or Oxford University. ❖ *n.* **1.** A native or inhabitant of Oxford, England. **2.** One who studies or has studied at Oxford University. [< Med.Lat. *Oxōnia*, Oxford < OE *Oxnaford* : *oxena*, genitive pl. of *oxa*, ox + *ford*, ford; see FORD.]

ox·peck·er (ŏks′pĕk′ǝr) *n.* Either of two African starlings (*Buphagus africanus* or *B. erythrorhyncus*) that eat ticks on the hides of large wild or domestic animals.

ox·tail (ŏks′tāl′) *n.* The tail of an ox, esp. when used for food.

Ox·us (ŏk′sǝs) See **Amu Darya.**

oxy- *pref.* Oxygen, esp. additional oxygen: *oxyacetylene.* [< OXYGEN.]

ox·y·a·cet·y·lene (ŏk′sē-ǝ-sĕt′l-ĭn, -ēn′) *adj.* Of or using a mixture of acetylene and oxygen: *an oxyacetylene torch.*

ox·y·ac·id (ŏk′sē-ăs′ĭd) *n.* An oxygen-containing acid.

ox·y·ceph·a·ly (ŏk′sē-sĕf′ǝ-lē) *n., pl.* **-lies** A congenital abnormality of the skull in which the top of the head assumes a conical or pointed shape. [< Gk. *oxukephalos*, sharp-headed : *oxus*, sharp; see OXYGEN + *-kephalos*, -cephalous.] —**ox′y·ce·phal′ic** (-sǝ-făl′ĭk), **ox′y·ceph′a·lous** *adj.*

ox·y·co·done (ŏk′sĭ-kō′dōn′) *n.* A narcotic alkaloid, $C_{18}H_{21}NO_4$, related to codeine and used as an analgesic and a sedative chiefly in the form of its hydrochloride salt. [(HYDR)OXY + COD(EINE) + -ONE.]

ox·y·gen (ŏk′sĭ-jǝn) *n.* *Symbol* **O** An element constituting 21 percent of the atmosphere by volume that occurs as a diatomic gas, O_2, combines with most elements, is essential for plant and animal respiration, and is required for nearly all combustion. Atomic number 8; atomic weight 15.9994; melting point −218.4°C; boiling point −183.0°C; gas density at 0°C 1.429 grams per liter; valence 2. See table at **element.** [Fr. *oxygène* < Gk. *oxus*, sharp, acid; see *ak-* in App. + Fr. *-gène*, -gen.] —**ox′y·gen′ic** (-jĕn′ĭk) *adj.* —**ox·yg′e·nous** (ŏk-sĭj′ǝ-nǝs) *adj.*

ox·y·gen·ase (ŏk′sĭ-jǝ-nās′, -nāz′) *n.* An oxidoreductase that catalyzes the incorporation of molecular oxygen into its substrate.

ox·y·gen·ate (ŏk′sĭ-jǝ-nāt′) also **ox·y·gen·ize** (-jǝ-nīz′) *tr.v.* **-at·ed, -at·ing, -ates** also **-ized, -iz·ing, -iz·es** To treat, combine, or infuse with oxygen. —**ox′y·gen·a′tion** *n.* —**ox′y·gen·a′tor** *n.*

oxygen debt *n.* The amount of extra oxygen required by muscle tissue during recovery from vigorous exercise.

oxygen mask *n.* A device placed over the mouth and nose, through which oxygen is supplied from a storage tank.

oxygen tent *n.* A canopy placed over the head and shoulders or over the entire body of a patient to provide oxygen at a higher level than normal.

ox·y·he·mo·glo·bin (ŏk′sē-hē′mǝ-glō′bĭn) *n.* A bright red chemical complex of hemoglobin and oxygen that transports oxygen to the tissues.

ox·y·hy·dro·gen (ŏk′sē-hī′drǝ-jǝn) *adj.* Of or using a mixture of hydrogen and oxygen: *an oxyhydrogen torch.*

ox·y·mo·ron (ŏk′sē-môr′ŏn′, -môr′-) *n., pl.* **-mo·ra** (-môr′ǝ, -môr′ǝ) or **-rons** A rhetorical figure in which incongruous or contradictory terms are combined, as in *deafening silence.* [Gk. *oxumōron* < neut. of *oxumōros*, pointedly foolish : *oxus*, sharp; see OXYGEN + *mōros*, foolish, dull.] —**ox′y·mo·ron′ic** (-mǝ-rŏn′ĭk) *adj.* —**ox′y·mo·ron′i·cal·ly** *adv.*

ox·y·sul·fide (ŏk′sē-sŭl′fīd′) *n.* A sulfide compound in which part of the sulfur has been replaced by oxygen.

ox·y·to·cic (ŏk′sĭ-tō′sĭk) *adj.* Hastening or facilitating childbirth, esp. by stimulating contractions of the uterus. Used of a drug. ❖ *n.* An oxytocic drug. [< alteration (influenced by L.Gk.

oxutokiă, sudden delivery) of Gk. *ōkutokios*, oxytocic : *ōkus*, swift + *tokos*, birth; see *tek-* in App.]

ox·y·to·cin (ŏk′sĭ-tō′sĭn) *n.* A short polypeptide hormone, $C_{43}H_{66}N_{12}O_{12}S_2$, released from the posterior lobe of the pituitary gland, that stimulates the contraction of smooth muscle of the uterus during labor and facilitates ejection of milk during nursing.

ox·y·tone (ŏk′sĭ-tōn′) *adj.* **1.** Relating to or being a Greek word with an acute accent on its last syllable. **2.** Relating to or being a word with a heavy stress on its last syllable. ❖ *n.* An oxytone word. [Gk. *oxutonos* : *oxus*, sharp; see *ak-* in App. + *tonos*, tone; see TONE.]

ox·y·u·ri·a·sis (ŏk′sē-yōō-rī′ǝ-sĭs) *n.* Infestation with pinworms. [NLat. *Oxyūris*, type genus (Gk. *oxus*, sharp; see *ak-* in App. + Gk. *ourā*, tail; see *ors-* in App.) + -IASIS.]

oy·er and ter·mi·ner (oi′ǝr; tûr′mǝ-nǝr) *n.* *Law* **1.** A hearing or trial. **2.** A court of general criminal jurisdiction in some states of the United States. [ME, partial transl. of Anglo-Norman *oyer et terminer*, to hear and determine : *oyer*, to hear + *terminer*, to determine.]

o·yez (ō′yĕs, ō′yĕz′, ō′yā′) also **o·yes** (ō′yĕs) *interj.* Used three times in succession to introduce the opening of a court of law. [ME < AN, hear ye, imper. pl. of *oyer* to hear < Lat. *audīre*.]

oys·ter (oi′stǝr) *n.* **1a.** Any of several edible bivalve mollusks of the family Ostreidae, esp. of the genera *Crassostrea* and *Ostrea*, that live chiefly in shallow marine waters and have a rough, irregularly shaped shell. **b.** Any of various similar or related bivalve mollusks. **2.** An edible bit of muscle found in the hollow of the pelvic bone of a fowl. **3a.** A special delicacy. **b.** Something from which benefits may be extracted. **4.** *Slang* A close-mouthed person. ❖ *intr.v.* **-tered, -ter·ing, -ters** To gather, dredge for, or raise oysters. [ME *oistre* < OFr. < Lat. *ostreum, ostrea* < Gk. *ostreon*. See *ost-* in App.]

oyster bed *n.* A place where oysters breed or are raised.

oys·ter·catch·er (oi′stǝr-kăch′ǝr) *n.* Any of several wading birds of the genus *Haematopus*, having black and white plumage and a long orange bill and feeding on oysters and clams.

oyster crab *n.* A small crab (*Pinnotheres ostreum*) that lives commensally inside the shell of a bivalve mollusk.

oyster cracker *n.* A small, dry, usu. round soda cracker.

oys·ter·man (oi′stǝr-mǝn) *n.* **1.** One who gathers, cultivates, or sells oysters. **2.** *Nautical* An oyster-dredging vessel.

oyster mushroom *n.* Any of several edible mushrooms of the genus *Pleurotus*, having a soft flavorful grayish cap.

oyster plant *n.* See **salsify.**

oys·ters Rockefeller (oi′stǝrz) *pl.n.* Oysters cooked with spinach and a cream sauce. [Perh. after John D. ROCKEFELLER.]

oyster white *n.* A pale yellowish green to light gray.

oz also **oz.** *abbr.* ounce

Oz[1] (ŏz) *n.* An unreal, magical, often bizarre place. [After *Oz* in *The Wonderful World of Oz* by L. Frank Baum.]

Oz[2] (ŏz) *n. Slang* Australia. [Alteration of AUS(TRALIAN).]

O·zark Plateau or **O·zark Mountains** (ō′zärk′) An upland region of the S-central US extending from SW MO across NW AR into E OK.

O·zarks (ō′zärks′), **Lake of the** A lake of central MO formed by Bagnell Dam (completed 1931) on the Osage R.

O·za·wa (ō-zä′wǝ), **Seiji** b. 1935. Japanese-born conductor and director of the Boston Symphony Orchestra (since 1973).

o·zo·ce·rite (ō′zō-sîr′īt′) also **o·zo·ke·rite** (-kîr′-) *n.* A yellow-brown to black or green hydrocarbon wax, found in irregular veins in sandstones and used in making electrical insulation and polishes. [Gk. *ozein*, to smell + Gk. *kēros*, wax + -ITE[1].]

o·zone (ō′zōn′) *n.* **1.** An unstable, poisonous allotrope of oxygen, O_3, that is formed naturally in the ozone layer and by the photochemical reaction of certain pollutants in the lower atmosphere. It is a highly reactive oxidizing agent used to deodorize air, purify water, and treat industrial wastes. **2.** *Informal* Fresh pure air. [Ger. *Ozon* < Gk. *ozon*, neut. pr. part. of *ozein*, to smell.] —**o·zo′nic** (ō-zō′nĭk, ō-zŏn′ĭk), **o′zon′ous** (ō′zō′nǝs) *adj.*

ozone hole *n.* An area of the ozone layer, such as the large area over Antarctica, that periodically becomes depleted of ozone.

ozone layer *n.* A region of the upper atmosphere, between about 15 and 30 kilometers (10 and 20 miles) in altitude, containing a relatively high concentration of ozone that absorbs solar ultraviolet radiation in a wavelength range not screened by other atmospheric components.

o·zo·nide (ō′zō-nīd′, -zǝ-) *n.* Any of various, often explosive chemicals formed by attachment of ozone to the double bond of an unsaturated compound.

o·zo·nize (ō′zō-nīz′, -zǝ-) *tr.v.* **-nized, -niz·ing, -niz·es 1.** To treat or impregnate with ozone. **2.** To convert (oxygen) to ozone. —**o′zon·iz′er** *n.*

o·zo·no·sphere (ō-zō′nǝ-sfîr′) *n.* See **ozone layer.** —**o·zo′no·spher′ic** (-sfîr′ĭk, -sfĕr′-), **o·zo′no·spher′i·cal** *adj.*

Pp

p¹ or **P** (pē) *n., pl.* **p's** or **P's** also **ps** or **Ps 1.** The 16th letter of the modern English alphabet. **2.** Any of the speech sounds represented by the letter *p*. **3.** The 16th in a series. **4.** Something shaped like the letter P.

p² *Physics* The symbol for **momentum** 1.

p³ *abbr.* **1.** piano (musical direction) **2.** proton

P¹ The symbol for the element **phosphorus.**

P² *abbr.* **1.** *Genetics* parental generation **2.** *Physics* parity **3.** pass **4.** pawn (chess) **5.** *Bible* Peter **6.** petite **7.** *Physics* pressure

p. *abbr.* **1.** page **2.** part **3.** participle **4.** past **5.** penny **6.** peseta **7.** peso **8.** pint **9.** population **10.** *Economics* principal

pa (pä) *n. Informal* Father; papa. [Short for PAPA.]

Pa¹ The symbol for the element **protactinium.**

Pa² *abbr.* pascal

PA *abbr.* **1.** or **Pa.** Pennsylvania **2.** physician's assistant **3.** or **P/A** power of attorney **4.** press agent **5.** production assistant **6.** prosecuting attorney **7.** public-address system

p.a. *abbr.* per annum

pa'an·ga (päng'gə, pä-äng'-) *n., pl.* **pa'anga** See table at **currency.** [Tongan.]

PA·BA (pä'bə) *n.* A crystalline para form of aminobenzoic acid that is part of the vitamin B complex and is often used in sunscreens to absorb ultraviolet light. [P(ARA-)A(MINO)B(ENZOIC) A(CID).]

pab·lum (păb'ləm) *n.* Trite, insipid, or simplistic writing, speech, or conceptualization. [< PABLUM.]

Pablum A trademark used for a bland soft cereal for infants.

pab·u·lum (păb'yə-ləm) *n.* **1.** A substance that gives nourishment; food. **2.** Insipid intellectual nourishment. [Lat. *pābulum.* See **pā-** in App. Sense 2, by confusion with PABLUM.]

pac also **pack** (păk) *n.* **1.** A moccasin or soft shoe designed to be worn inside a boot. **2.** A shoepac. [Short for *shoepac,* alteration (influenced by SHOE) of pidgin Delaware *seppock,* shoe < Unami Delaware *chípahko,* shoes.]

PAC *abbr.* political action committee

Pac. *abbr.* Pacific

pa·ca (pä'kə, păk'ə) *n.* A large nocturnal burrowing rodent of the genus *Cuniculus,* found in South and Central America and similar to the agouti, esp. the edible spotted species *C. paca.* [Port. and Am.Sp., both < Tupi *páca.*]

pace¹ (pās) *n.* **1.** A step made in walking; a stride. **2.** A unit of length equal to 30 inches (0.76 meter). **3.** The distance spanned by a step or stride, esp.: **a.** The modern version of the Roman pace, measuring five English feet. **b.** Thirty inches at quick marching time or 36 at double time. **c.** Five Roman feet or 58.1 English inches, measured from the point at which the heel of one foot is raised to the point at which it is set down again after a step by the other foot. **4a.** The rate of speed at which a person, animal, or group walks or runs. **b.** The rate of speed at which an activity or movement proceeds. **5.** A manner of walking or running: *a jaunty pace.* **6.** A gait of a horse in which both feet on one side are lifted and put down together. ❖ *v.* **paced, pac·ing, pac·es** —*tr.* **1.** To walk or stride back and forth across. **2.** To measure by counting the number of steps needed to cover a distance. **3.** To set or regulate the rate of speed for. **4.** To advance or develop (something) at a particular rate or tempo. **5.** To train (a horse) in a particular gait, esp. the pace. —*intr.* **1.** To walk with long deliberate steps. **2.** To go at the pace. Used of a horse or rider. [ME < OFr. *pas* < Lat. *passus* < p. part. of *pandere,* to stretch, spread out.]

pa·ce² (pä'chā, -kā, pā'sē) *prep.* With permission of or deference to. Used in polite, sometimes ironic disagreement. [Lat. *pāce,* ablative of *pāx,* peace.] —**pa'ce** *adv.*

pace car (pās) *n.* A usu. high-performance automobile that leads a group of competing cars through the pace lap.

pace lap (pās) *n.* The initial lap of an auto race in which the racers warm up their engines and prepare for a fast start.

pace·mak·er (pās'mā'kər) *n.* **1.** *Sports* One who sets the pace in a race. **2.** A leader in a field. **3a.** *Biology* A part of the body, such as the mass of muscle fibers of the sinoatrial node, that sets the pace or rhythm of physiological activity. **b.** *Medicine* Any of several usu. miniaturized and surgically implanted electronic devices used to stimulate or regulate contractions of the heart muscle. **4.** *Biochemistry* A substance that regulates a series of related reactions. —**pace'mak'ing** *adj. & n.*

pac·er (pā'sər) *n.* **1.** A horse trained to pace. **2.** *Sports* See **pacemaker** 1.

pace·set·ter (pās'sĕt'ər) *n.* **1.** *Sports* See **pacemaker** 1. **2.** See **pacemaker** 2. —**pace'set'ting** *adj. & n.*

pa·cha (pä'shə, păsh'ə, pə-shä') *n.* Variant of **pasha.**

pa·chin·ko (pə-chǐng'kō) *n.* A Japanese gambling game played on a vertical pinball machine. [J.]

pa·chi·si (pə-chē'zē) *n.* An ancient game of India similar to backgammon that uses cowrie shells instead of dice. [Hindi *pacīsī* < *pacīs,* twenty-five : Skt. *pañca,* five; see **penk**ʷe in App. + Skt. *viṃśatiḥ,* twenty; see **wīkṃti** in App.]

Pa·chu·ca (pə-chōō'kə, pä-chōō'kä) also **Pachuca de So·to** (dǐ sō'tō, dĕ) A city of central Mexico NNE of Mexico City; founded 1534 on an ancient Toltec site. Pop. 110,351.

pa·chu·co (pə-chōō'kō) *n., pl.* **-cos** A Mexican-American youth or teenager, esp. one who dresses in flamboyant clothes and belongs to a neighborhood gang. [Am.Sp., poss. alteration of *pa-yuco,* yokel < *payo,* rustic, prob. < VLat. *pāgius.*]

pach·y·ceph·a·lo·saur (păk'ĭ-sĕf'ə-lə-sôr') *n.* A medium-sized herbivorous dinosaur of the genus *Pachycephalosaurus* of the late Cretaceous period of North America, having a domed skull up to ten inches (25.4 centimeters) thick. [NLat. *Pachycephalosaurus,* genus name : Gk. *pakhus,* thick + Gk. *kephalē,* head; see **ghebh-el-** in App. + Gk. *sauros,* lizard.]

pach·y·derm (păk'ĭ-dûrm') *n.* Any of various large thick-skinned hoofed mammals such as the elephant, rhinoceros, or hippopotamus. [Fr. *pachyderme* < NLat. **Pachyderma,* sing. of *Pachydermata,* obsolete order name < Gk. *pakhudermos,* thick-skinned : *pakhus,* thick + *derma,* skin.] —**pach'y·der'mal, pach'y·der'mic, pach'y·der'mous** *adj.*

pach·y·der·ma·tous (păk'ĭ-dûr'mə-təs) *adj.* **1.** Of or relating to a pachyderm. **2.** Thick-skinned; insensitive.

pach·y·san·dra (păk'ĭ-săn'drə) *n.* Any of several plants of the genus *Pachysandra,* esp. the evergreen *P. terminalis* native to Japan, having toothed leaves and white flowers. [NLat. *Pachysandra,* genus name : Gk. *pakhus,* thick + NLat. *-andrus,* -androus (< its thick stamens).]

pach·y·tene (păk'ĭ-tēn') *n.* The stage of the prophase of meiosis during which chromosome pairs shorten, thicken, and divide into four distinct chromatids. [Fr. *pachytène* : Gk. *pakhus,* thick + *-tène,* ribbon (< Lat. *taenia;* see TAENIA).]

pa·cif·ic (pə-sĭf'ĭk) also **pa·cif·i·cal** (-ĭ-kəl) *adj.* **1.** Tending to diminish or put an end to conflict; appeasing. **2.** Of a peaceful nature; tranquil. [Fr. *pacifique* < OFr. *pacifice* < Lat. *pācificus* : *pāx, pāc-,* peace + *-ficus, -fic.*] —**pa·cif'i·cal·ly** *adv.*

pac·i·fi·ca·tion (păs'ə-fĭ-kā'shən) *n.* **1.** The act of pacifying or the condition of being pacified; appeasement. **2a.** Reduction to peaceful submission. **b.** Practical measures or policy aiming to effect this type of submission. **3.** often **Pacification** A peace treaty. —**pa·cif'i·ca'tor** (pə-sĭf'ĭ-kā'tər) *n.* —**pa·cif'i·ca·to'ry** (-kə-tôr'ē, -tōr'ē) *adj.*

Pacific Islander *n.* **1.** A native or inhabitant of any of the Polynesian, Micronesian, or Melanesian islands of Oceania. **2.** A person of Polynesian, Micronesian, or Melanesian descent. See Usage Note at **Asian.**

Pacific Islands, Trust Territory of the A group of more than 2,000 islands and islets of the NW Pacific Ocean administered by the US as a United Nations trust territory (1947–78); orig. included the Caroline, Marianas (excluding Guam), and Marshall islands. —**Pacific Islander** *n.*

pa·cif·i·cism (pə-sĭf'ĭ-sĭz'əm) *n.* Pacifism. —**pa·cif'i·cist** *n.*

Pacific Northwest A region usu. including WA and OR and sometimes also SW British Columbia, Canada.

Pacific Ocean The world's largest ocean, divided into the **North Pacific** and the **South Pacific** and extending from the W Americas to E Asia and Australia.

Pacific Rim The countries and landmasses surrounding the Pacific Ocean, often considered as a socioeconomic region.

Pacific Standard Time *n.* Standard time in the eighth time zone west of Greenwich, England, reckoned at 120° west and used, for example, on the Pacific coast of the United States.

Pacific yew *n.* A yew (*Taxus brevifolia*) of western North America having bark that is a source of the drug paclitaxel.

pac·i·fi·er (păs'ə-fī'ər) *n.* A rubber or plastic nipple or teething ring for a baby to suck or chew on.

pac·i·fism (păs'ə-fĭz'əm) *n.* **1.** The belief that disputes between nations should be settled peacefully. **2a.** Opposition to the use of war or violence to resolve disputes. **b.** Such opposition demonstrated by refusal to participate in military action. [Fr. *pacifisme* < *pacifique,* pacific; see PACIFIC.] —**pac'i·fist** *n.* —**pac'i·fis'tic** *adj.* —**pac'i·fis'ti·cal·ly** *adv.*

pac·i·fy (păs'ə-fī') *tr.v.* **-fied, -fy·ing, -fies 1.** To ease the anger or agitation of. **2.** To end war, fighting, or violence in; establish

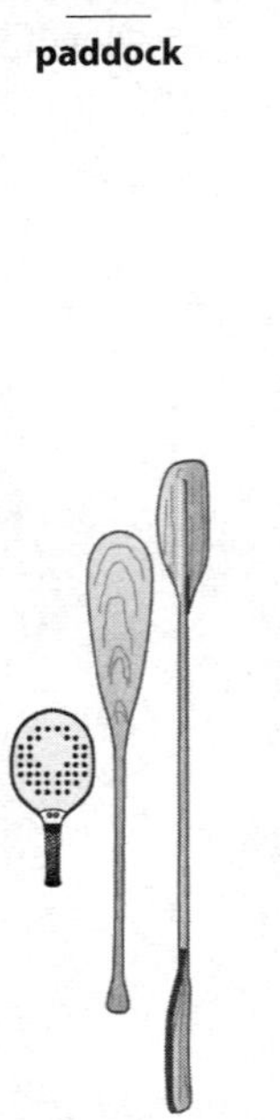

paddle¹
left to right: paddleball, canoe, and kayak paddles

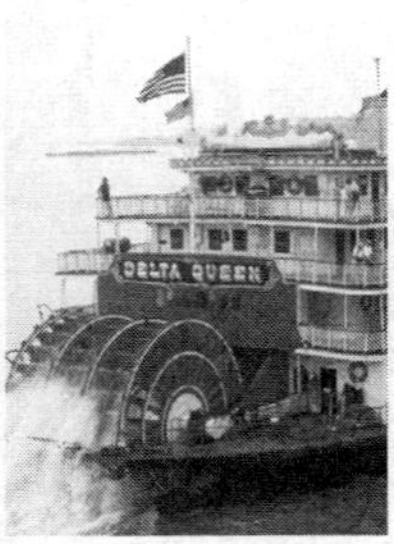

paddle wheel

peace in. [ME *pacifien* < OFr. *pacifier* < Lat. *pācificāre* : *pāx*, *pāc-*, peace + *-ficāre*, -fy.] —**pac′i•fi′a•ble** *adj.*

SYNONYMS *pacify, mollify, conciliate, appease, placate* These verbs refer to allaying another's anger, belligerence, discontent, or agitation. To *pacify* is to restore calm to or establish peace in: *"The explanation . . . was merely an invention framed to pacify his guests"* (Charlotte Brontë). *Mollify* stresses the soothing of hostile feelings: *The therapist mollified the angry teenager by speaking gently. Conciliate* implies winning over, often by reasoning and with mutual concessions: *"A wise government knows how to enforce with temper or to conciliate with dignity"* (George Grenville). *Appease* and *placate* suggest the satisfaction of claims or demands or the tempering of antagonism, often by concessions: *I appeased my friend's anger with a compliment. An apology placated the indignant customer.*

Pa•cin•i•an corpuscle (pə-sĭn′ē-ən) *n.* An encapsulated receptor in the skin that senses vibratory pressure and touch. [After Filippo *Pacini* (1812–83), Italian anatomist.]

pack¹ (păk) *n.* **1a.** A collection of items tied up or wrapped; a bundle. **b.** A container made to be carried on the body of a person or animal. **2.** The amount, as of food, processed and packaged at one time or in one season. **3.** A small package containing a standard number of identical or similar items: *a pack of matches.* **4a.** A complete set of related items: *a pack of cards.* **b.** *Informal* A large amount; a heap: *earned a pack of money.* **5a.** A group of animals, such as wolves, that run and hunt together. **b.** A gang of people: *a pack of hoodlums.* **c.** An organized troop having common interests: *a Cub Scout pack.* **6.** A mass of large pieces of floating ice driven together. **7.** *Medicine* **a.** The swathing of a patient or a body part in hot, cold, wet, or dry materials, such as cloth towels. **b.** The materials so used. **c.** A material, such as gauze, therapeutically inserted into a body cavity or wound; packing. **8.** An ice pack. **9.** A cosmetic paste applied to the skin, allowed to dry, and then rinsed off. ❖ *v.* **packed, pack•ing, packs** —*tr.* **1.** To fold, roll, or combine into a bundle; wrap up. **2a.** To put into a receptacle for transporting or storing: *pack one's belongings.* **b.** To fill up with items: *packed the trunk.* **3.** To process and put into containers to preserve, transport, or sell: *packed the fruit in jars.* **4a.** To bring together (persons or things) closely; crowd together: *packed 300 students into the lecture hall.* **b.** To fill up tight; cram. **5.** *Medicine* **a.** To wrap (a patient) in a pack. **b.** To insert a pack into a body cavity or wound. **6.** To wrap tightly for protection or to prevent leakage: *pack a valve stem.* **7.** To press together; compact firmly: *packed the clay and straw into bricks.* **8.** *Informal* To carry, deliver, or have available for action: *a fighter who packs a hard punch.* **9.** To send unceremoniously: *packed them off to bed.* **10.** To constitute (a voting panel) by appointment, selection, or arrangement so that it is favorable to one's interests; rig. —*intr.* **1.** To place one's belongings in boxes or luggage for transporting or storing. **2.** To be susceptible of compact storage: *Dishes pack more easily than glasses.* **3.** To form lumps or masses; become compacted. —***idiom:* pack it in** *Informal* To cease work or activity. [ME *pak*, poss. of LGer. orig.] —**pack′a•bil′i•ty** *n.* —**pack′a•ble** *adj.*

pack² (păk) *n.* Variant of **pac**.

pack•age (păk′ĭj) *n.* **1.** A wrapped or boxed object; a parcel. **2.** A container in which something is packed. **3a.** A preassembled unit. **b.** A commodity, such as food, processed and containerized. **4.** An offer composed of several items, each of which must be accepted. ❖ *tr.v.* **-aged, -ag•ing, -ag•es** To place into a package or make a package of. —**pack′ag•er** *n.*

package store *n.* A store that sells bottles or cans of alcoholic beverages for consumption off the premises.

pack•ag•ing (păk′ə-jĭng) *n.* **1.** The act, process, industry, art, or style of packing. **2.** Material used for making packages. **3.** The manner in which something, such as a product, or someone, such as a candidate, is presented to the public.

pack animal *n.* An animal, such as a mule, used to carry loads.

packed (păkt) *adj.* **1.** Crowded to capacity. **2.** Compressed. **3.** *Informal* Filled with. Often used in combination: *a thrill-packed trip.*

pack•er (păk′ər) *n.* **1.** One that packs. **2.** One whose occupation is the processing and packing of wholesale goods.

pack•et (păk′ĭt) *n.* **1.** A small package or bundle. **2.** *Informal* A sizable sum of money. **3.** A boat, usu. a coastal or river steamer, that plies a regular route and carries passengers, freight, and mail. **4.** *Computer Science* A short block of data transmitted as a unit over a channel dedicated to the connection only for the duration of the transmission. [ME *pekette*, prob. dim. of *pak*, pack. See PACK¹.]

pack•horse (păk′hôrs′) *n.* A horse used as a pack animal.

pack ice *n.* Floating ice driven together into a single mass.

pack•ing (păk′ĭng) *n.* **1.** The act or process of one that packs. **2.** The processing and packaging of manufactured products, esp. food products. **3.** A material used to prevent leakage or seepage, as around a pipe joint. **4a.** The insertion of gauze or other material into a body cavity or wound for therapeutic purposes. **b.** The material so used; a pack.

pack•ing•house (păk′ĭng-hous′) *n.* **1.** A firm that slaughters livestock and processes and packs meat and meat products. **2.** A firm that processes and packs other food products.

pack•man (păk′măn′, -mən) *n.* A peddler.

pack rat *n.* **1.** Any of various small North American rodents of the genus *Neotoma* that collect a great variety of small objects in or around their nests. **2.** *Western US* A petty thief. **3.** *Slang* A collector or accumulator of miscellaneous objects.

pack•sack (păk′săk′) *n.* A canvas or leather traveling bag designed to be carried while strapped to the shoulders.

pack•sad•dle (păk′săd′l) *n.* A saddle on which loads can be secured.

pack•thread (păk′thrĕd′) *n.* A strong two-ply or three-ply twine for sewing or tying packages or bundles.

pack train *n.* A line of animals, such as horses or mules, loaded with supplies for an expedition.

pac•li•tax•el (păk′lĭ-tăk′səl) *n.* A drug derived from the bark of the Pacific yew tree, used in the treatment of certain cancers, esp. of the breast or ovary. [PAC(IFIC YEW) + NLat. *(Taxus brevifō)li(a)*, scientific name of Pacific yew (Lat. *brevis*, short + Lat. *fōlium*, leaf; see FOLIUM) + alteration of TAXOL.]

pact (păkt) *n.* **1.** A formal agreement, as between nations; a treaty. **2.** A compact; a bargain. [Ult. < Lat. *pactum* < neut. sing. p. part. of *pacīscī*, to agree.]

pad¹ (păd) *n.* **1.** A thin cushionlike mass of soft material used to fill, give shape, or protect against jarring, scraping, or other injury. **2.** A flexible saddle without a frame. **3.** An ink-soaked cushion used to ink a rubber stamp. **4.** A number of sheets of paper of the same size stacked one on top of the other and glued together at one end; a tablet. **5a.** The broad floating leaf of an aquatic plant such as the water lily. **b.** The flattened fleshy stem of a cactus. **6a.** The cushionlike flesh on the underpart of the toes and feet of many animals. **b.** The foot of such an animal. **7.** The fleshy underside of the end of a finger or toe. **8a.** A launch pad. **b.** A helipad. **9.** A keypad. **10.** *Slang* One's apartment or room. ❖ *tr.v.* **pad•ded, pad•ding, pads 1.** To line or stuff with soft material. **2.** To lengthen or increase, esp. with extraneous or false information. —***idiom:* on the pad** *Slang* Taking bribes. [?]

pad² (păd) *v.* **pad•ded, pad•ding, pads** —*intr.* **1.** To go about on foot. **2.** To move about quietly. —*tr.* To go along (a route) on foot. ❖ *n.* **1.** A muffled sound like soft footsteps. **2.** A horse with a plodding gait. [Perh. < MDu. *paden*, tread a path < *pad*, *pat*, path. See **pent-** in App.] —**pad′der** *n.*

Pa•dang (pä′däng′, pä-däng′) A city of W Indonesia on the W-central coast of Sumatra. Pop. 631,543.

pa•dauk (pə-dôk′) also **pa•douk** (-do͝ok′) *n.* **1.** A southeast Asian tree *(Pterocarpus indicus)* having reddish wood with a black grain. **2.** The wood of this tree. [Burmese.]

pad•ding (păd′ĭng) *n.* **1.** The act of stuffing, filling, or lining. **2.** A soft material used to make pads or a pad. **3.** Something added, esp. extraneously or fraudulently: *a resumeé with lots of padding.*

pad•dle¹ (păd′l) *n.* **1.** A usu. wooden implement having a blade at one or both ends, used without an oarlock to propel a canoe or small boat. **2.** Any of various implements resembling the paddle of a boat or canoe, as: **a.** An iron tool for stirring molten ore in a furnace. **b.** A tool with a shovellike blade used to mix materials in glassmaking. **c.** A potter's pallet. **d.** A narrow board used to beat clothes when laundering by hand. **e.** A flat board for administering physical punishment. **f.** *Sports* A light wooden or plastic racket used in playing table tennis, platform tennis, and similar games. **3.** A board on a paddle wheel. **4.** A flipper or flat appendage of certain animals. **5.** The act of paddling. ❖ *v.* **-dled, -dling, -dles** —*intr.* **1.** *Nautical* **a.** To propel a watercraft with paddles or a paddle. **b.** To row slowly and gently. **2.** To move through water by repeated short strokes of the limbs. —*tr.* **1.** *Nautical* **a.** To propel (a watercraft) with paddles or a paddle. **b.** To convey in a watercraft propelled by paddles. **2.** To spank or beat with a paddle, esp. as a punishment. **3.** To stir or shape (material) with a paddle. [ME *padell*, tool used to clean plowshares, perh. < Med.Lat. *padela.*] —**pad′dler** *n.*

pad•dle² (păd′l) *intr.v.* **-dled, -dling, -dles 1.** To dabble about in shallow water; splash gently with the hands or feet. **2.** To move with a waddling motion; toddle. [Perh. of LGer. orig.]

pad•dle•ball (păd′l-bôl′) *n.* **1.** A game for two to four participants played with a perforated paddle and a ball similar to a tennis ball on a court having one, three, or four walls. **2.** The ball used in this game.

pad•dle•board (păd′l-bôrd′, -bōrd′) *n.* A long narrow floatable board used esp. in surfing.

pad•dle•boat (păd′l-bōt′) *n.* A boat, esp. a steamship, propelled through the water by paddle wheels on each side or by one paddle wheel astern.

pad•dle•fish (păd′l-fĭsh′) *n., pl.* **paddlefish** or **-fish•es** A fish of the family Polyodontidae, having a long paddle-shaped snout, esp. *Polyodon spathula* of the Mississippi River basin.

paddle wheel *n.* A wheel with boards or paddles affixed around its circumference, usu. driven by steam to propel a ship. —**pad′dle-wheel′** (păd′l-hwēl′, -wēl′) *adj.*

paddle wheeler *n.* See **paddleboat.**

pad•dling (păd′lĭng, păd′l-ĭng) *n.* **1.** Moving a boat with a paddle. **2.** A spanking or beating with a paddle.

pad•dock (păd′ək) *n.* **1.** A fenced area, usu. near a stable, used chiefly for grazing horses. **2.** *Sports* **a.** An enclosure at a racetrack where the horses are assembled, saddled, and paraded before each race. **b.** An area of an automobile racetrack where cars are prepared. **3.** *Australian* A piece of fenced-in land. ❖ *tr.v.* **-docked, -dock•ing, -docks** To confine in a paddock. [Alteration of ME *parrok* < OE *pearroc.*]

pad•dy (păd′ē) *n., pl.* **-dies** **1.** Rice, esp. in the husk, whether gathered or still in the field. **2.** A specially irrigated or flooded field where rice is grown. [Malay *padi.*]

Paddy *n. Offensive Slang* Used as a disparaging term for a person, esp. a man, of Irish birth or descent. [Nickname for Ir.Gael. *Pádraig,* Patrick.]

paddy field *n.* A rice paddy.

paddy wagon *n. Slang* A van used by police for taking suspects into custody. [Perh. < *paddy,* policeman < PADDY.]

Pa•de•rew•ski (păd′ə-rĕf′skē, -rĕv′-, pä′də-), **Ignace Jan** 1860–1941. Polish pianist and prime minister (1919–20) who led (1940–41) the exiled Polish government.

Pa•di•shah (pä′dĭ-shä′) *n.* **1.** Used formerly as a title for the monarch of Iran. **2.** Used formerly as a title for the sultan of Turkey. [Pers. *pādshāh* : OPers. *pati-,* master; see **poti-** in App. + Pers. *shāh,* king; see SHAH.]

pad•lock (păd′lŏk′) *n.* A detachable lock with a U-shaped bar hinged at one end, designed to be passed through the staple of a hasp or a link in a chain and then snapped shut. ❖ *tr.v.* **-locked, -lock•ing, -locks** To lock up with or as if with a padlock. [ME *padlok* : *pad-,* of unknown meaning + *lok,* lock; see LOCK[1].]

pa•douk (pə-do͞ok′) *n.* Variant of **padauk.**

pa•dre (pä′drā, -drē) *n.* **1.** Father. Used as a form of address for a priest in Italy, Spain, Portugal, and Latin America. **2.** *Informal* A military chaplain. **3.** *Chiefly British* A parson. [Sp., Ital., or Port., all < Lat. *pater, patr-,* father. See **pəter-** in App.]

pa•dro•ne (pə-drō′nē, -nā) *n., pl.* **-nes** (-nēz, -nāz) or **-ni** (-nē) **1.** An owner or manager, esp. of an inn; a proprietor. **2.** A man who exploitatively employs or finds work for Italian immigrants in America. [Ital. < Lat. *patrōnus,* patron. See PATRON.] —**pa•dro′nism** *n.*

pad thai (päd′ tī′, päd′) *n.* A Thai dish of stir-fried rice noodles, egg, bean sprouts, shrimp, peanuts, and seasonings. [Thai *phàd thaj :* *phàd,* fried, fried dish + *thaj,* Thai.]

Pad•u•a (păj′o͞o-ə, păd′yo͞o-ə) A city of NE Italy W of Venice; an important cultural center during the Middle Ages. Pop. 215,025. —**Pad′u•an** *adj. & n.*

pad•u•a•soy (păj′o͞o-ə-soi′) *n.* **1.** A rich heavy silk fabric with a corded effect. **2.** A hanging or garment made of this fabric. [Alteration of *pou-de-soie* < OFr. *pou-de-soie :* *pout,* of uncertain meaning + *de,* of (< Lat. *dē;* see DE–) + *soie,* silk (< VLat. **sēta* < LLat. *saeta,* raw silk < Lat., bristle).]

pae•an also **pe•an** (pē′ən) *n.* **1.** A song of joyful praise or exultation. **2.** A fervent expression of joy or praise. **3.** An ancient Greek hymn of thanksgiving or invocation, esp. to Apollo. [Lat. *paeān,* Gk. *paian* < *Paiān,* a title of Apollo.] —**pae′an•is′tic** (-ĭs′tĭk) *adj.*

paed– and **paedo–** *pref.* Variants of **pedo–**[2].

pa•el•la (pä-ĕl′ə, -āl′yä, -ā′yä) *n.* A Spanish dish made with rice, vegetables, meat, chicken, and seafood and spiced with saffron. [Catalan, frying pan < OFr. *paele,* frying pan, pot < Lat. *patella,* dim. of *patina,* pan. See PATEN.]

pae•on (pē′ən, -ŏn′) *n.* In quantitative verse, a foot of one long syllable and three short syllables occurring in any order. [Lat. *paeōn* < Gk. *paiōn, paiān, paiōn,* paean. See PAEAN.]

Paes•tum (pĕs′təm, pē′stəm) An ancient city of S Italy on the Gulf of Salerno; founded as a Greek colony before 600 B.C.

pa•gan (pā′gən) *n.* **1.** One who is not a Christian, Muslim, or Jew, esp. a worshiper of a polytheistic religion. **2.** One who has no religion. **3.** A non-Christian. **4.** A hedonist. **5.** A Neo-Pagan. ❖ *adj.* **1.** Not Christian, Muslim, or Jewish. **2.** Professing no religion; heathen. **3.** Neo-Pagan. [ME < LLat. *pāgānus* < Lat., country dweller, civilian < *pāgus,* country, rural district.] —**pa′gan•dom** (-dəm) *n.* —**pa′gan•ish** *adj.* —**pa′gan•ism** *n.* —**pa′gan•i•za′tion** (-gə-nĭ-zā′shən) *n.* —**pa′gan•ize′** *v.*

Pa•ga•ni•ni (păg′ə-nē′nē, pä′gä-), **Niccolò** 1782–1840. Italian violinist and composer whose works include six violin concertos.

page[1] (pāj) *n.* **1a.** A leaf or one side of a leaf, as of a book, newspaper, or manuscript. **b.** The writing or printing on one side of a leaf. **c.** The type set for printing one side of a leaf. **2.** A noteworthy or memorable event. **3.** *Computer Science* A quantity of memory storage equal to between 512 and 4,096 bytes. **4.** *Computer Science* A webpage. **5. pages** A source or record of knowledge. ❖ *tr.v.* **paged, pag•ing, pag•es** **1.** To number the pages of; paginate. **2.** To turn the pages of. [Fr., alteration of OFr. *pagine* < Lat. *pāgina.*] —**page′ful′** *n.*

page[2] (pāj) *n.* **1.** A boy who acted as a knight's attendant as the first stage of training for knighthood. **2.** A youth in ceremonial employment or attendance at court. **3a.** One employed to run errands, carry messages, or act as a guide in a hotel, theater, or club. **b.** One similarly employed in the US Congress or another legislature. **4.** A boy who holds the bride's train at a wedding. ❖ *tr.v.* **paged, pag•ing, pag•es** **1.** To summon or call (a person) by name. **2.** To summon or call (a person) by means of a beeper. **3.** To attend as a page. [ME < OFr., poss. < Ital. *paggio,* perh. ult. < Gk. *paidion,* dim. of *pais, paid-,* child. See **pau–** in App.]

pag•eant (păj′ənt) *n.* **1.** An elaborate public dramatic presentation, usu. of a historical or traditional event. **2.** A spectacular procession or celebration. **3.** Colorful showy display; pageantry or pomp. [ME *pagin, pagent,* mystery play, alteration of Med.Lat. *pāgina,* prob. < Lat., page.]

pag•eant•ry (păj′ən-trē) *n., pl.* **-ries** **1.** Pageants and their presentation. **2a.** Grand display; pomp. **b.** Empty pomp or show; flashy display.

page•boy (pāj′boi′) *n.* **1.** One, usu. a boy, who acts or serves as a page. **2.** A hairstyle, usu. shoulder-length, with the ends of the hair curled under smoothly in a loose roll.

page-jack (pāj′jăk′) *tr.v.* **-jacked, -jack•ing, -jacks** To copy keywords, metatags, or content from (a website) and insert this material into another website so that a search engine will direct unwitting users to that site. [(WEB)PAGE + (HI)JACK.]

pag•er (pā′jər) *n.* See **beeper** 2.

Pag•et (păj′ĭt), **Sir James** 1814–99. British surgeon and pathologist who discovered (1834) the cause of trichinosis and described (1874) Paget's disease of the breast.

Pag•et's disease (păj′ĭts) *n.* **1.** A disease, chiefly of old age, in which the bones become enlarged and weakened, often resulting in fracture or deformation. **2.** A form of breast cancer affecting the nipple. [After Sir James PAGET.]

pag•i•nal (păj′ə-nəl) *adj.* **1.** Of, relating to, or consisting of pages. **2.** Page for page: *a paginal facsimile.* [LLat. *pāginālis* < Lat. *pāgina,* page. See PAGE[1].]

pag•i•nate (păj′ə-nāt′) *tr.v.* **-nat•ed, -nat•ing, -nates** To number the pages of; page. [< Lat. *pāgina,* page. See PAGE[1].]

pag•i•na•tion (păj′ə-nā′shən) *n.* **1.** The system by which pages are numbered. **2.** The arrangement and number of pages in a book, as noted in a catalog or bibliography.

pa•go•da (pə-gō′də) *n.* **1a.** A religious building of the Far East, esp. a multistory Buddhist tower, erected as a memorial or shrine. **b.** A stupa. **2.** A structure, such as a garden pavilion, built in imitation of such a tower. [Port. *pagode,* perh. < Tamil *pagavadi* < Skt. *bhagavatī,* goddess < fem. of *bhagavat-,* blessed < *bhagaḥ,* good fortune. See **bhag-** in App.]

Pa•go Pa•go (päng′ō päng′ō, păng′gō păng′gō, päng′gō päng′gō, pä′gō pä′gō, päng′ō päng′ō, păng′gō păng′gō, päng′gō päng′gō, pä′gō pä′gō) also **Pan•go Pan•go** (päng′ō päng′ō, păng′gō päng′gō, päng′gō päng′gō, pä′gō pä′gō) The cap. of American Samoa, on Tutuila I. Pop. 3,519.

pah (pä) *interj.* Used to express disgust or irritation.

Pa•ha•ri (pə-här′ē) *n., pl.* **Pahari** or **-ris** **1.** A member of any of various, mostly Hindu peoples of Nepal and the Himalayan foothills of India. **2.** The group of Indo-Aryan languages spoken by these peoples, including Nepali. [Hindi *Pahāṛī,* of the mountains, Pahari < *pahāṛ,* mountain.]

Pah•la•vi (pä′lə-vē′, -hlə-) also **Peh•le•vi** (pā′-) *n.* An Iranian language used in Persia during the reign of the Sassanids. [Pers. *pahlawī* < *Pahlav,* Parthia < OPers. *Parthava-.*]

Pahlavi, Muhammed Reza 1919–80. Shah of Iran from 1941 to 1979, when he was deposed by Islamic fundamentalists.

pa•hoe•hoe (pə-hoi′hoi′) *n.* Lava with a smooth, ropy or billowy surface. [Hawaiian *pāhoehoe :* *pā-,* pref. + *hoehoe,* redup. of *hoe,* to paddle (prob. < the swirls on its surface).]

paid[1] (pād) *v.* Past tense and past participle of **pay**[1].

paid[2] (pād) *v. Nautical* A past tense and past participle of **pay**[2].

Paige (pāj), **Leroy Robert** Known as "Satchel." 1906–82. Amer. baseball player who became the first African-American pitcher in the American League (1948).

pail (pāl) *n.* **1.** A watertight cylindrical vessel, open at the top and fitted with a handle; a bucket. **2.** The amount that a pail can hold. [ME *paile* prob. < OFr. *paele,* warming pan, perh. < Lat. *patella,* small pan. See PAELLA.] —**pail′ful′** *n.*

pail•lard (pī-yär′) *n.* A slice of veal, chicken, or beef that is pounded until very thin and cooked quickly. [?]

pail•lasse also **pal•liasse** (păl-yăs′, păl′yăs′) *n.* A thin mattress filled with straw or sawdust. [Fr. < OFr. < *paille,* straw < LLat. *palea* < Lat., chaff.]

pail•lette (pä-yĕt′, pā-, pă-lĕt′) *n.* **1.** A small piece of metal or foil used in painting with enamel. **2.** A spangle used to ornament a dress or costume. [Fr. < OFr., dim. of *paille,* straw. See PAILLASSE.] —**pail′let′ted** *adj.*

pain (pān) *n.* **1.** An unpleasant sensation varying in severity, resulting from injury, disease, or emotional disorder. **2.** Suffering or distress. **3. pains** The pangs of childbirth. **4. pains** Great care or effort. **5.** *Informal* A source of annoyance; a nuisance. ❖ *v.* **pained, pain•ing, pains** —*tr.* To cause pain to; hurt or injure. —*intr.* To be the cause of pain. —*idiom:* **on** (or **under**) **pain of** Subject to the penalty of (a specified punishment). [ME < OFr. *peine* < Lat. *poena,* penalty, pain < Gk. *poinē,* penalty. See **kwei-** in App.]

Paine (pān), **Robert Treat** 1731–1814. Amer. Revolutionary leader and jurist who signed the Declaration of Independence.

Paine, Thomas 1737–1809. British-born Amer. writer and Revolutionary leader who wrote *Common Sense* (1776) and *The Rights of Man* (1791–92).

pain•ful (pān′fəl) *adj.* **1.** Causing pain. **2.** Full of pain. **3.** Requiring care and labor; irksome: *a painful task.* **4.** *Archaic* Diligent; careful. —**pain′ful•ly** *adv.* —**pain′ful•ness** *n.*

pain•kill•er (pān′kĭl′ər) *n.* An agent, such as an analgesic drug,

paddy
rice paddy

pagoda

Satchel Paige

ă	pat	oi	boy
ā	pay	ou	out
âr	care	o͝o	took
ä	father	o͞o	boot
ĕ	pet	ŭ	cut
ē	be	ûr	urge
ĭ	pit	th	thin
ī	pie	th	this
îr	pier	hw	which
ŏ	pot	zh	vision
ō	toe	ə	about,
ô	paw		item

Stress marks:
′ (primary),
′ (secondary), as in
lexicon (lĕk′sĭ-kŏn′)

that relieves pain. **—pain′kill′ing** *adj.*

pains·tak·ing (pānz′tā′kĭng) *adj.* Marked by or requiring great pains; careful and diligent. ❖ *n.* Careful and diligent work or effort. **—pains′tak′ing·ly** *adv.*

paint (pānt) *n.* **1a.** A liquid mixture, usu. of a solid pigment in a liquid vehicle, used as a decorative or protective coating. **b.** The thin dry film formed by such a mixture applied to a surface. **c.** The solid pigment before it is mixed with a vehicle. **2.** A cosmetic, such as rouge, used to give color to the face; makeup. **3.** See **pinto.** ❖ *v.* **paint·ed, paint·ing, paints** *—tr.* **1.** To make (a picture) with paints. **2a.** To represent in a picture with paints. **b.** To depict vividly in words. **3.** To coat or decorate with paint. **4.** To apply cosmetics to. **5.** To apply medicine to; swab. *—intr.* **1.** To practice the art of painting pictures. **2.** To cover something with paint. **3.** To apply cosmetics to oneself. **4.** To serve as a surface to be coated with paint. **—idiom: paint the town red** *Slang* To go on a spree. [< ME *painten,* to paint < OFr. *peintier* < *peint,* p. part. of *peindre* < Lat. *pingere.*] **—paint′a·bil′i·ty** *n.* **—paint′a·ble** *adj.*

paint·ball (pānt′bôl′) *n.* **1.** A game in which players on one team seek to eliminate those on an opposing team by marking them with a water-soluble dye shot in capsules from air guns. **2.** The dye-filled gelatinous capsule shot from guns in this game.

paint·brush (pānt′brŭsh′) *n.* **1.** A brush for applying paint. **2.** The Indian paintbrush.

paint·ed (pān′tĭd) *adj.* **1.** Represented in paint. **2a.** Covered or decorated with paint. **b.** Brightly colored; gaudy. **3.** Excessively made up with cosmetics.

painted bunting *n.* A small finch (*Passerina ciris*) of the southern United States and Mexico, the male of which has brilliant multicolored plumage.

painted cup *n.* See **Indian paintbrush.**

Painted Desert A plateau region of N-central AZ E of the Colorado and Little Colorado rivers. Eroded layers of sediment and clay have left striking bands of color.

painted lady *n.* A widely distributed butterfly (*Vanessa cardui*) having brown, black, and orange markings.

paint·er[1] (pān′tər) *n.* One who paints, either as an artist or worker.

paint·er[2] (pān′tər) *n.* A rope attached to the bow of a boat, esp. a small boat or dinghy, used for tying up, as when docking or towing. [ME *peintour,* prob. < OFr. *pentoir,* strong rope < *pendre,* to hang < VLat. *pendere* < Lat. *pendēre.*]

paint·er[3] (pān′tər) *n. Chiefly Upper Southern US* See **mountain lion.** [Alteration of PANTHER.]

paint·er·ly (pān′tər-lē) *adj.* **1.** Of, relating to, or characteristic of a painter; artistic. **2a.** Having qualities unique to the art of painting. **b.** Of, relating to, or being a style of painting marked by openness of form, with shapes distinguished by variations of color rather than by outline or contour.

painter's colic (pān′tərz) *n.* Chronic intestinal pains and constipation caused by lead poisoning. [So called because the disease is often caused by exposure to lead-based paint.]

paint·ing (pān′tĭng) *n.* **1.** The process, art, or occupation of coating surfaces with paint for a utilitarian or artistic effect. **2.** A picture or design in paint.

pair (pâr) *n., pl.* **pair** or **pairs 1.** Two corresponding persons or items, similar in form or function and matched or associated. **2.** One object composed of two joined similar parts dependent upon each other: *a pair of pliers.* **3a.** Two persons who are married, engaged, or dating. **b.** Two persons who have something in common and are considered together. **c.** Two mated animals. **d.** Two animals joined together in work. **4.** *Games* Two playing cards of the same denomination. **5.** Two members of a deliberative body in opposition on a given issue who offset each other's vote by abstention. **6.** *Chemistry* An electron pair. ❖ *v.* **paired, pair·ing, pairs** *—tr.* **1.** To arrange in sets of two; couple. **2.** To join in a pair; mate. **3.** To provide a partner to. *—intr.* **1.** To form pairs or a pair. **2.** To join in marriage; mate. [ME < OFr. *paire* < Lat. *paria,* equals, pl. of *pār,* a pair < *pār,* equal. See **perə-** in App.]

USAGE NOTE *Pair* as a noun can be followed by a singular or plural verb. The singular is always used when *pair* denotes the set taken as a single entity: *This pair of shoes is on sale.* A plural verb is used when the members are considered as individuals: *The pair are working together.* After a number other than one, *pair* can be either singular or plural, but the plural is now more common: *She bought six pairs* (or *pair*) *of stockings.*

pair bond *n.* The association formed between a female and male animal during courtship and mating. **—pair bonding** *n.*

pair of compasses *n.* See **compass 2.**

pair of virginals *n.* See **virginal**[2].

pair production *n.* The simultaneous creation of a positron and an electron from a gamma ray photon in a strong electric field, such as that near a nucleus.

pai·sa·no (pī-zä′nō) *also* **pai·san** (-zän′) *n., pl.* **-sa·nos** *also* **-sans 1.** A countryman; a compatriot. **2.** *Slang* A friend; a pal. [Sp. < Fr. *paysan* < OFr. *paisant,* peasant. See PEASANT.]

pais·ley (pāz′lē) *adj.* **1.** Made of a soft wool fabric with a colorful, woven or printed swirled pattern of abstract curved shapes. **2.** Marked with this pattern. ❖ *n., pl.* **-leys** An article of clothing made of paisley fabric. [After PAISLEY.]

Paisley A burgh of SW Scotland W of Glasgow; became famous in the 19th cent. for its colorful patterned shawls. Pop. 86,100.

Pai·ute *also* **Pi·ute** (pī′yōōt′) *n., pl.* **Paiute** or **-utes** *also* **Piute** or **-utes 1.** A member of a Native American people occupying eastern Oregon, western Nevada, and adjacent areas of northeast California. **2.** A member of a Native American people occupying southern Utah and Nevada, northern Arizona, and adjacent areas of southeast California.

pa·ja·ma (pə-jä′mə, -jăm′ə) *n.* **1.** A loose-fitting garment consisting of trousers and a jacket, worn for sleeping or lounging. Often used in the plural. **2.** Loose-fitting trousers worn in the Far East by men and women. Often used in the plural. [Hindi *pāijāma,* loose-fitting trousers : Pers. *pāī,* leg (< MPers.; see ped- in App.) + Pers. *jāmah,* garment.]

Pak. *abbr.* Pakistan

pak choi (bŏk′ choi′) *n.* Variant of **bok choy.**

Pak·i (păk′ē) *n., pl.* **Pak·is** *Chiefly British Offensive Slang* Used as a disparaging term for a person from Pakistan or neighboring countries or for the descendant of such a person. [Short for PAKISTANI.]

Pak·i·stan (păk′ĭ-stăn′, pä′kĭ-stän′) A country of S Asia; home of the prehistoric Indus Valley civilization that flourished until overrun by Aryans c. 1500 B.C. Pakistan passed to the British as part of India and became a separate Muslim state in 1947. Cap. Islamabad. Pop. 126,610,000. **—Pak′i·stan′i** (-stăn′ē, -stä′nē) *adj. & n.*

WORD HISTORY Many central and south Asian states and regions end with the element *–stan,* such as *Afghanistan, Pakistan, Baluchistan, Kurdistan,* and *Turkistan.* This *–stan* is formed from the Iranian root **stā–,* "to stand, stay," and means "place (where one stays), home, country." Iranian peoples have been the principal inhabitants of the geographical region occupied by these states for over a thousand years. The names are compounds of *–stan* and the name of the people living there. Pakistan is a bit of an exception; its name was coined in 1933 using the suffix *–istan* from Baluch*istan* preceded by the initial letters of Punjab, Afghanistan, and Kashmir.

pal (păl) *Informal n.* A friend; a chum. ❖ *intr.v.* **palled, pal·ling, pals** To associate as friends or chums. Often used with *around.* [Romany *phral, phal* < Skt. *bhrātā, bhrātr-,* brother. See **bhrāter-** in App.] **—pal′ly** *adj.*

Pal. *abbr.* Palestine

pal·ace (păl′ĭs) *n.* **1.** An official royal residence. **2.** *Chiefly British* The official residence of a high dignitary, such as a bishop. **3a.** A large or splendid residence. **b.** A large, often gaudy building used for entertainment or exhibitions. [ME < OFr. *palais* < *Palātium,* Palatine, imperial residence.]

pal·a·din (păl′ə-dĭn) *n.* **1.** A paragon of chivalry; a heroic champion. **2.** A strong supporter or defender of a cause. **3.** Any of the 12 peers of Charlemagne's court. [Fr. < Ital. *paladino* < LLat. *palātīnus,* imperial servant. See PALATINE[1].]

palae– *or* **palaeo–** *pref.* Variants of **paleo-.**

pa·laes·tra (pə-lĕs′trə) *n.* Variant of **palestra.**

pal·an·quin *also* **pal·an·keen** (păl′ən-kēn′) *n.* A covered litter carried on poles on the shoulders of four or more bearers, formerly used in eastern Asia. [Port. *palanquim* < Javanese *pelangki* < Pali *pallanko* < Skt. *paryaṅkaḥ, palyaṅkaḥ,* couch, bed.]

pa·la·pa (pə-lä′pə) *n.* An open-sided dwelling or structure with a thatched roof of dried palm leaves. [Perh. < Am.Sp., a palm tree.]

pal·at·a·ble (păl′ə-tə-bəl) *adj.* **1.** Acceptable to the taste; sufficiently agreeable in flavor to be eaten. **2.** Acceptable or agreeable to the mind or sensibilities. **—pal′at·a·bil′i·ty, pal′at·a·ble·ness** *n.* **—pal′at·a·bly** *adv.*

pal·a·tal (păl′ə-təl) *adj.* **1.** Of or relating to the palate. **2.** *Linguistics* **a.** Produced with the front of the tongue near or against the hard palate, as the (y) in English *young.* **b.** Produced with the blade of the tongue near the hard palate, as the (ch) in English *chin.* **c.** Produced with the front of the tongue in a forward position. Used of a vowel. ❖ *n. Linguistics* A palatal sound. **—pal′a·tal·ly** *adv.*

pal·a·tal·ize (păl′ə-tə-līz′) *tr.v.* **-ized, -iz·ing, -iz·es** To pronounce as or alter to a palatal sound. **—pal′a·tal·i·za′tion** (-tə-lĭ-zā′shən) *n.*

pal·ate (păl′ĭt) *n.* **1.** The roof of the mouth in vertebrates having separate oral and nasal cavities and consisting of the hard palate and the soft palate. **2.** The sense of taste. [ME < OFr. *palat* < Lat. *palātum,* perh. of Etruscan orig.]

pa·la·tial (pə-lā′shəl) *adj.* **1.** Of or suitable for a palace: *palatial furnishings.* **2.** Of the nature of a palace, as in spaciousness: *a palatial yacht.* [< Lat. *Palātium,* imperial residence. See PALACE.] **—pa·la′tial·ly** *adv.* **—pa·la′tial·ness** *n.*

pa·lat·i·nate (pə-lăt′n-āt′, -ĭt) *n.* The office, powers, or territory of a palatine.

Palatinate Either of two historical districts and former states of S Germany: the **Lower Palatinate** in SW Germany between Luxembourg and the Rhine R. and the **Upper Palatinate** in E Bavaria.

painted lady
Vanessa cardui

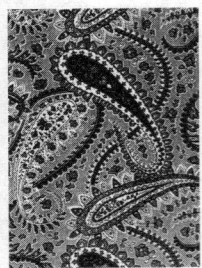

paisley

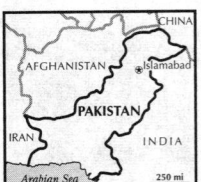

Pakistan

palapa
Lhohifushi Island, Maldives

pal•a•tine[1] (păl′ə-tīn′) *n.* **1a.** A soldier of the imperial palace guard formed under Diocletian. **b.** A Roman soldier in the time of Constantine I. **2.** Used as a title for various administrative officials of the late Roman and Byzantine empires. **3.** A feudal lord exercising sovereign power over his lands. ❖ *adj.* **1.** Belonging to or fit for a palace. **2.** Of or relating to a palatine or palatinate. [< ME, ruled by an independent lord < OFr. *palatin* < LLat. *palātīnus*, palace official < Lat. *palātīnus* < *Palātium*, imperial residence. See PALACE.]

pal•a•tine[2] (păl′ə-tīn′) *adj.* **1.** Of or relating to the palate. **2.** Of or relating to either of two bones that make up the hard palate. ❖ *n.* Either of the palatine bones.

Palatine The most important of the seven hills of ancient Rome; traditionally the earliest to be settled and later the site of many imperial palaces. —**Palatine** *adj.*

Pa•lau (pä-lou′, pə-) also **Be•lau** (bə-) A group of about 200 islands in the Caroline Is. of the W Pacific Ocean; self-governing under a compact of free association with the US. Cap. Koror. Pop. 16,952.

pa•lav•er (pə-lăv′ər, -lä′vər) *n.* **1a.** Idle chatter. **b.** Talk intended to charm or beguile. **2.** *Obsolete* A parley between European explorers and representatives of local populations, esp. in Africa. ❖ *v.* **-ered, -er•ing, -ers** —*tr.* To flatter or cajole. —*intr.* To chatter idly. [Port. *palavra*, speech, alteration of LLat. *parabola*, speech, parable. See PARABLE.]

Pa•la•wan (pə-lä′wən, pä-lä′wän) A long narrow island of the SW Philippines N of Borneo between the Sulu Sea and the **Palawan Passage** of the South China Sea.

pa•laz•zo (pə-lät′sō) *n., pl.* **-zi** (-sē) or **-zos** A large splendid residence or public building, such as a palace or museum. [Ital. < Lat. *Palātium*, imperial residence. See PALACE.]

pale[1] (pāl) *n.* **1.** A stake or pointed stick; a picket. **2.** A fence enclosing an area. **3.** The area enclosed by a fence or boundary. **4a.** A region or district lying within an imposed boundary or constituting a separate jurisdiction. **b. Pale** The medieval dominions of the English in Ireland. Used with *the.* **5.** *Heraldry* A wide vertical band in the center of an escutcheon. ❖ *tr.v.* **paled, pal•ing, pales** To enclose with pales; fence in. ***—idiom:* beyond the pale** Irrevocably unacceptable or unreasonable. [ME < OFr. *pal* < Lat. *pālus.*]

pale[2] (pāl) *adj.* **pal•er, pal•est 1.** Whitish in complexion; pallid. **2a.** Of a low intensity of color; light. **b.** Having high lightness and low saturation. **3.** Of a low intensity of light; dim or faint. **4.** Feeble; weak: *a pale rendition of the aria.* ❖ *v.* **paled, pal•ing, pales** —*tr.* To cause to turn pale. —*intr.* **1.** To become pale; blanch. **2.** To decrease in relative importance. [ME < OFr. < Lat. *pallidus* < *pallēre*, to be pale.] —**pale′ly** *adv.* —**pale′ness** *n.*

pale– *pref.* Variant of **paleo–**.

pa•le•a (pā′lē-ə) *n., pl.* **-le•ae** (-lē-ē′) **1.** A small chafflike bract enclosing the flower of a grass. **2.** The chaffy scales on the receptacle of a flower head in a plant of the composite family. [Lat., chaff.]

Pa•le•arc•tic (pā′lē-ärk′tĭk, -är′tĭk) *adj.* Of or relating to the biogeographic region that includes Europe, the northwest coast of Africa, and Asia north of the Himalaya Mountains, esp. with respect to distribution of animals.

pale-dry (pāl′drī′) *adj.* Light in color and dry in flavor.

pale•face (pāl′fās′) *n.* *Offensive Slang* A white person.

Pa•lem•bang (pä′ləm-bäng′, -lĕm-) A city of Indonesia on SE Sumatra; center of a powerful Hindu kingdom in the 7th and 8th cent. Pop. 787,187.

Pa•len•que (pä-lĕng′kĕ) An ancient Mayan city of S Mexico SE of Villahermosa; noted for its Temple of Inscriptions.

paleo– or **pale–** or **palaeo–** or **palae–** *pref.* **1.** Ancient; prehistoric; old: *paleobotany.* **2.** Early; primitive: *Paleozoic.* [Gk. *palaio-* < *palaios*, ancient < *palai*, long ago.]

pa•le•o•an•throp•ic (pā′lē-ō-ăn-thrŏp′ĭk) *adj.* Of or relating to extinct members of the genus *Homo.*

pa•le•o•an•thro•pol•o•gy (pā′lē-ō-ăn′thrə-pŏl′ə-jē) *n.* The study of extinct members of the genus *Homo sapiens.* —**pa′le•o•an′thro•po•log′ic** (-pə-lŏj′ĭk), **pa′le•o•an′thro•po•log′i•cal** (-ĭ-kəl) *adj.* —**pa′le•o•an′thro•pol′o•gist** *n.*

pa•le•o•bi•o•ge•og•ra•phy (pā′lē-ō-bī′ō-jē-ŏg′rə-fē) *n.* The study of the geographic distribution of fossil organisms. —**pa′le•o•bi′o•ge′o•graph′ic** (-jē′ə-grăf′ĭk), **pa′le•o•bi′o•ge′o•graph′i•cal** (-ĭ-kəl) *adj.*

pa•le•o•bi•ol•o•gy (pā′lē-ō-bī-ŏl′ə-jē) *n.* The branch of paleontology that focuses on fossils as organisms rather than as features of the geological record. —**pa′le•o•bi•o•log′ic** (-ə-lŏj′ĭk), **pa′le•o•bi•o•log′i•cal** (-ĭ-kəl) *adj.* —**pa′le•o•bi•o•log′i•cal•ly** *adv.* —**pa′le•o•bi•ol′o•gist** *n.*

pa•le•o•bot•a•ny (pā′lē-ō-bŏt′n-ē) *n.* The paleontology of plant fossils and ancient vegetation. —**pa′le•o•bo•tan′ic** (-bə-tăn′ĭk), **pa′le•o•bo•tan′i•cal** (-ĭ-kəl) *adj.* —**pa′le•o•bo•tan′i•cal•ly** *adv.* —**pa′le•o•bot′a•nist** *n.*

Pa•le•o•cene (pā′lē-ə-sēn′) *adj.* Of or belonging to the geologic time of the earliest epoch of the Tertiary Period, characterized by the appearance of placental mammals. See table at **geologic time.** ❖ *n.* The Paleocene Epoch or its deposits.

pa•le•o•cli•ma•tol•o•gy (pā′lē-ō-klī′mə-tŏl′ə-jē) *n.* The study of climatic conditions of the past, using evidence found in the geologic record, esp. in glacial deposits. —**pa′le•o•cli′ma•tol′o•gist** *n.*

pa•le•o•e•col•o•gy (pā′lē-ō-ĭ-kŏl′ə-jē) *n.* The branch of ecology that deals with the interaction between ancient organisms and their environment. —**pa′le•o•ec′o•log′i•cal** (-ĕk′ə-lŏj′ĭ-kəl, -ē′kə-), **pa′le•o•ec′o•log′ic** (-lŏj′ĭk) *adj.* —**pa′le•o•e•col′o•gist** *n.*

pa•le•og•ra•phy (pā′lē-ŏg′rə-fē) *n.* **1.** The study and scholarly interpretation of earlier, esp. ancient, writing and forms of writing. **2.** The documents so studied. —**pa′le•og′ra•pher** *n.* —**pa′le•o•graph′ic** (-ə-grăf′ĭk), **pa′le•o•graph′i•cal** (-ĭ-kəl) *adj.*

Pa•le•o-In•di•an (pā′lē-ō-ĭn′dē-ən) *adj.* Of or relating to prehistoric human culture in the Western Hemisphere from the earliest habitation to around 5000 B.C. —**Pa′le•o-In′di•an** *n.*

pa•le•o•lith (pā′lē-ə-lĭth′) *n.* A stone implement of the Paleolithic Period. [Back-formation < PALEOLITHIC.]

Pa•le•o•lith•ic (pā′lē-ə-lĭth′ĭk) *adj.* Of or relating to the cultural period of the Stone Age from the earliest chipped stone tools, about 750,000 years ago, to the beginning of the Mesolithic, about 15,000 years ago. ❖ *n.* The Paleolithic Period.

pa•le•o•mag•net•ism (pā′lē-ō-măg′nĭ-tĭz′əm) *n.* **1.** The study of the remanent magnetization in rocks. **2.** The earth's magnetic field as it existed in the past.

pa•le•on•tol•o•gy (pā′lē-ŏn-tŏl′ə-jē) *n.* The study of the forms of life existing in prehistoric or geologic times. —**pa′le•on′to•log′ic** (-ŏn′tə-lŏj′ĭk), **pa′le•on′to•log′i•cal** (-ĭ-kəl) *adj.* —**pa′le•on•tol′o•gist** *n.*

Pa•le•o•si•be•ri•an (pā′lē-ō-sī-bîr′ē-ən) *adj.* Of or relating to a grouping of mostly unrelated languages and language isolates spoken primarily in Siberia, including Chukchi. ❖ *n.* The Paleosiberian languages.

Pa•le•o•zo•ic (pā′lē-ə-zō′ĭk) *adj.* Of or belonging to the first era of geologic time, between approx. 570 and 245 million years ago, characterized by the appearance of marine invertebrates, primitive fishes and reptiles, and land plants. See table at **geologic time.** ❖ *n.* The Paleozoic Era or its deposits.

pa•le•o•zo•ol•o•gy (pā′lē-ō-zō-ŏl′ə-jē) *n.* The paleontology of animal fossils and ancient animal life. —**pa′le•o•zo′o•log′i•cal** (-zō′ə-lŏj′ĭ-kəl) *adj.* —**pa′le•o•zo•ol′o•gist** *n.*

Pa•ler•mo (pə-lûr′mō, -lâr′-, pä-lĕr′-) A city of NW Sicily, Italy, on the Tyrrhenian Sea; founded by Phoenicians c. 8th cent. B.C. and cap. of the kingdom of Sicily (1072–1194). Pop. 697,162.

Pal•es•tine (păl′ĭ-stīn′) Often called "the Holy Land." A historical region of SW Asia between the E Mediterranean shore and the Jordan R. roughly coextensive with modern Israel and the West Bank. —**Pal′es•tin′i•an** (-stĭn′ē-ən) *adj. & n.*

pa•les•tra also **pa•laes•tra** (pə-lĕs′trə) *n., pl.* **-trae** (-trē) or **-tras** A public place in ancient Greece for training in wrestling and other athletics. [ME *palestre* < OFr. < Lat. *palaestra* < Gk. *palaistra* < *palaiein*, to wrestle.] —**pa•les′tral, pa•les′tri•an** *adj.*

Pa•le•stri•na (păl′ĭ-strē′nə, pä′lĕ-strē′nä), **Giovanni Pierluigi da** 1526?–94. Italian composer known for his Masses.

pal•ette (păl′ĭt) *n.* **1.** A board, usu. with a hole for the thumb, which an artist can hold while painting and on which colors are mixed. **2a.** The range of colors used in a particular painting or by a particular artist. **b.** The range of qualities inherent in nongraphic art forms such as music and literature. [Fr. < OFr., small potter's shovel, dim. of *pale*, shovel, spade < Lat. *pāla.*]

palette knife *n.* A knife with a thin flexible blade, used by artists for mixing, scraping, or applying paint.

pal•frey (pôl′frē) *n., pl.* **-freys** *Archaic* A saddle horse, esp. one for a woman to ride. [ME < OFr. *palefrei* < Med.Lat. *palafrēdus*, alteration of LLat. *paraverēdus*, post horse for secondary routes, extra horse : Gk. *para*, extra, beyond; see **per**[1] in App. + Lat. *verēdus*, post horse, of Celt. orig.]

Pa•li (pä′lē) *n.* A Prakit language that is a scriptural and liturgical language of Theravada Buddhism. [Short for Skt. *pālibhāṣā*, language of the row, series of Buddhist sacred texts < *pāliḥ*, row, perh. of Dravidian orig.]

Pal•i•kir (păl′ĭ-kər) The capital of the Federated States of Micronesia.

pal•i•mo•ny (păl′ə-mō′nē) *n.* *Informal* An allowance for support made under court order and given usu. by one person to a former lover or live-in companion after separation.

pal•imp•sest (păl′ĭmp-sĕst′) *n.* **1.** A manuscript, usu. of papyrus or parchment, written on more than once, with the earlier writing incompletely erased and often legible. **2.** An object, place, or area that reflects its history. [Lat. *palimpsēstum* < Gk. *palimpsēston*, neut. of *palimpsēstos*, scraped again : *palin*, again; see **kʷel-** in App. + *psēn*, to scrape.]

pal•in•drome (păl′ĭn-drōm′) *n.* A word, phrase, verse, or sentence that reads the same backward or forward, as *Madam, I'm Adam.* [< Gk. *palindromos*, running back again, recurring : *palin*, again; see **kʷel-** in App. + *dromos*, a running.] —**pal′in•dro′mic** (-drō′mĭk, -drŏm′ĭk) *adj.*

pal•ing (pā′lĭng) *n.* **1.** One of a row of upright pointed sticks forming a fence; a pale. **2.** Pointed sticks used in making fences; pales. **3.** A fence made of pales or pickets.

pal•in•gen•e•sis (păl′ĭn-jĕn′ĭ-sĭs) *n., pl.* **-ses** (-sēz′) **1.** The doctrine of transmigration of souls; metempsychosis. **2.** *Biology*

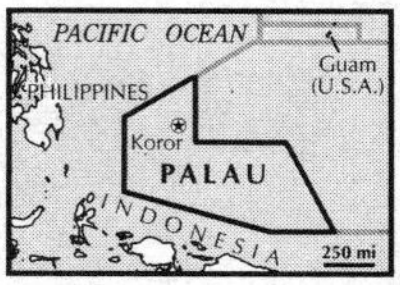

Palau

Palenque
Temple of Inscriptions, constructed seventh century A.D.

palette

ă	pat	oi	boy
ā	pay	ou	out
âr	care	ŏŏ	took
ä	father	ōō	boot
ĕ	pet	ŭ	cut
ē	be	ûr	urge
ĭ	pit	th	thin
ī	pie	*th*	this
îr	pier	hw	which
ŏ	pot	zh	vision
ō	toe	ə	about, item
ô	paw		

Stress marks:
′ (primary);
′ (secondary), as in
lexicon (lĕk′sĭ-kŏn′)

The repetition by a single organism of various stages in the evolution of its species during embryonic development. [Gk. *palin*, again; see **kʷel-¹** in App. + —GENESIS.] —**pal′in·ge·net′ic** (-jə-nĕt′ĭk) *adj.* —**pal′in·ge·net′i·cal·ly** *adv.*

pal·i·node (păl′ə-nōd′) *n.* **1.** A poem in which the author retracts something said in a previous poem. **2.** A formal statement of retraction. [< LLat. *palinōdia* < Gk. *palinōidiā* : *palin*, again; see **kʷel-¹** in App. + *ōidē*, song; see PARODY.]

pal·i·sade (păl′ĭ-sād′) *n.* **1a.** A fence of pales forming a defense barrier or fortification. **b.** A pale of such a fence. **2. palisades** A line of lofty steep cliffs, usu. by a river. ❖ *tr.v.* **-sad·ed, -sad·ing, -sades** To equip or fortify with palisades or a palisade. [Fr. *palissade* < OFr. < O Provençal *palissada* < *palissa*, stake < VLat. **pālīcea* < Lat. *pālus*.]

palisade parenchyma *n.* A leaf tissue composed of columnar cells containing numerous chloroplasts in which the long axis of each cell is perpendicular to the leaf surface.

Pal·i·sades (păl′ĭ-sādz′) A row of cliffs in NE NJ along the W bank of the Hudson R.

pal·ish (pā′lĭsh) *adj.* Slightly pale.

Palk Strait (pôk, pôlk) A waterway between SE India and N Sri Lanka.

pall¹ (pôl) *n.* **1.** A cover for a coffin, bier, or tomb, often made of black, purple, or white velvet. **2.** A coffin, esp. one being carried to a grave or tomb. **3a.** A covering that darkens or obscures. **b.** A gloomy effect or atmosphere. **4.** *Ecclesiastical* **a.** A linen cloth or a square of cardboard faced with cloth used to cover the chalice. **b.** See **pallium** 2. ❖ *tr.v.* **palled, pall·ing, palls** To cover with or as if with a pall. [ME *pal* < OE *pæll*, cloak, covering < Lat. *pallium*.]

pall² (pôl) *v.* **palled, pall·ing, palls** —*intr.* **1.** To become insipid, boring, or wearisome. **2.** To have a dulling, wearisome, or boring effect. **3.** To become cloyed or satiated. —*tr.* **1.** To cloy; satiate. **2.** To make vapid or wearisome. [ME *pallen*, to grow feeble, prob. short for APPALL. See APPALL.]

Pal·la·di·an¹ (pə-lā′dē-ən) *adj.* **1.** *Greek Mythology* Of, relating to, or characteristic of Athena. **2.** Of, relating to, or characterized by wisdom or study. [< Lat. *Palladius* < Gk. *Palladios* < *Pallas, Pallad-*, Pallas Athena.]

Pal·la·di·an² (pə-lā′dē-ən) *adj.* **1.** Of or characteristic of the Renaissance architectural style of Andrea Palladio. **2.** Of or characteristic of an architectural style of the mid-18th century derived from that of Andrea Palladio, esp. in Britain.

Palladian²
Villa Barbaro, Maser, Italy
c. 1555 by Andrea Palladio

pal·la·dic (pə-lā′dĭk, -lăd′ĭk) *adj.* Of or being compounds that contain palladium, esp. with valence 4.

Pal·la·dio (pə-lā′dē-ō, pä-lä′dyō), **Andrea** 1508–80. Italian architect whose style was based on the classicism of ancient Rome.

pal·la·di·um¹ (pə-lā′dē-əm) *n. Symbol* **Pd** A soft ductile metallic element occurring naturally with platinum, esp. in gold, nickel, and copper ores, used as a catalyst in hydrogenation and alloyed for use in electric contacts, jewelry, nonmagnetic watch parts, and surgical instruments. Atomic number 46; atomic weight 106.4; melting point 1,552°C; boiling point 3,140°C; specific gravity 12.02 (20°C); valence 2, 3, 4. See table at **element**. [< PALLAS (discovered at the same time).]

pal·la·di·um² (pə-lā′dē-əm) *n., pl.* **-di·a** (-dē-ə) or **-di·ums** **1.** A safeguard, esp. of the integrity of social institutions. **2.** A sacred object having the power to preserve a city or state possessing it. [ME *Palladion*, a statue of Pallas Athena believed to protect Troy < OFr. *palladion* < Lat. *Palladium* < Gk. *Palladion* < *Pallas, Pallad-*, Pallas Athena.]

pal·la·dous (pə-lā′dəs, păl′ə-dəs) *adj.* Of or being compounds that contain palladium, esp. with valence 2. [PALLAD(IUM)¹ + -OUS.]

Pal·las (păl′əs) *n.* **1.** A large asteroid, the second to be discovered. **2.** *Greek Mythology* Athena. [After PALLAS (ATHENA).]

Pallas Athena also **Pallas Athene** *n. Greek Mythology* Athena. [Gk. *Pallas Athēnē* : *Pallas*, epithet of Athena + *Athēnē*, Athena.]

pall·bear·er (pôl′bâr′ər) *n.* One of the persons carrying or attending a coffin at a funeral.

pal·let¹ (păl′ĭt) *n.* **1.** A projection on a machine part that engages the teeth of a ratchet wheel to convert reciprocating motion to rotary motion or vice versa. **2.** A wooden shovellike potter's tool for working clay. **3.** A metal tool for printing on book bindings. **4.** A fine brush for taking up and applying gold leaf. **5.** A portable platform for storing or moving cargo or freight. **6.** A painter's palette. [ME *palet*, tongue depressor < OFr. *palete*, small potter's shovel. See PALETTE.]

pal·let² (păl′ĭt) *n.* **1.** A narrow hard bed or straw-filled mattress. **2.** *Chiefly Southern US* A temporary bed made from bedding arranged on the floor. [ME *paillet* < AN, bundle of straw < *paille*, straw < LLat. *palea*. See PAILLASSE.]

pal·let·ize (păl′ĭ-tīz′) *tr.v.* **-ized, -iz·ing, -iz·es** To store or move (freight, for example) by means of pallets. —**pal′let·i·za′tion** (-lĭ-tĭ-zā′shən) *n.* —**pal′let·iz′er** *n.*

pal·li·al (păl′ē-əl) *adj.* **1.** Of or relating to the cerebral cortex. **2.** Of the mantle of a mollusk, brachiopod, or bird.

pal·liasse (păl-yăs′, păl′yăs′) *n.* Variant of PAILLASSE.

pal·li·ate (păl′ē-āt′) *tr.v.* **-at·ed, -at·ing, -ates** **1.** To make (an offense or crime) seem less serious; extenuate. **2.** To make less severe or intense; mitigate. See Syns at **relieve**. **3.** To relieve the

palmette

symptoms of a disease or disorder. [ME *palliaten* < LLat. *palliāre, palliāt-*, to cloak, palliate < Lat. *pallium*, cloak.] —**pal′li·a′tion** *n.* —**pal′li·a′tor** *n.*

pal·li·a·tive (păl′ē-ā′tĭv, -ē-ə-tĭv) *adj.* **1.** Tending or serving to palliate. **2.** Relieving or soothing the symptoms of a disease or disorder without effecting a cure. ❖ *n.* One that palliates, esp. a palliative drug or medicine. —**pal′li·a′tive·ly** *adv.*

pal·lid (păl′ĭd) *adj.* **1.** Having an abnormally pale or wan complexion: *the invalid's pallid face.* **2.** Lacking intensity of color or luminousness. **3.** Lacking in radiance or vitality; dull: *pallid prose.* [Lat. *pallidus* < *pallēre*, to be pale.] —**pal′lid·ly** *adv.* —**pal′lid·ness** *n.*

pal·li·um (păl′ē-əm) *n., pl.* **pal·li·ums** or **pal·li·a** (ē-ə) **1.** A cloak or mantle worn by the ancient Greeks and Romans. **2.** *Ecclesiastical* A vestment worn by the pope and conferred by him on archbishops and sometimes on bishops. **3a.** The mantle of gray matter forming the cerebral cortex. **b.** The mantle of a mollusk, brachiopod, or bird. [Lat.]

pall-mall (pĕl′mĕl′, păl′măl′, pôl′môl′) *n.* **1.** A 17th-century game in which a ball was struck with a mallet to drive it through an iron ring suspended at the end of an alley. **2.** This alley. [Obsolete Fr. *pallemaille* < Ital. *pallamaglio* : *palla*, ball (of Gmc. orig.; see **bhel-²** in App.) + *maglio*, mallet (< Lat. *malleus*; see **melə-** in App.).]

pal·lor (păl′ər) *n.* Extreme or unnatural paleness. [ME *pallour* < OFr. *palor* < Lat. *pallor* < *pallēre*, to be pale.]

palm¹ (päm) *n.* **1a.** The inner surface of the hand that extends from the wrist to the base of the fingers. **b.** The similar part of the forefoot of a quadruped. **2.** A unit of length equal to either the width or the length of the hand. **3.** The part of a glove or mitten that covers the palm of the hand. **4.** *Nautical* A leather shield worn by sailmakers over the palm of the hand and used to force a needle through heavy canvas. **5.** *Nautical* The blade of an oar or paddle. **6.** The flattened part of the antlers of certain animals, such as the moose. ❖ *tr.v.* **palmed, palm·ing, palms 1a.** To hold in the palm of the hand. **b.** To touch or stroke with the palm of the hand. **2.** To conceal (something) in the palm of the hand, as in a sleight-of-hand trick. **3.** To pick up furtively. **4.** *Basketball* To commit a violation by letting (the ball) rest momentarily in the palm of the hand while dribbling. —*phrasal verb:* **palm off** To dispose of or pass off by deception. [ME *paume* < OFr. < Lat. *palma*, palm tree, palm of the hand. See **pelə-²** in App.] —**palm′ful** *n.*

palm² (päm) *n.* **1.** Any of various chiefly tropical evergreen trees, shrubs, or woody vines of the family Palmae (or Arecaceae), having unbranched trunks with a crown of large pinnate or palmate leaves having conspicuous parallel venation. **2.** A leaf of a palm tree, carried as an emblem of victory, success, or joy. **3.** Triumph; victory. **4.** A small metallic representation of a palm leaf added to a military decoration awarded more than one time. [ME < OE and < OFr. *palme*, both < Lat. *palma*, palm of the hand, palm tree (< the shape of the fronds). See **pelə-²** in App.]

Pal·ma (päl′mä) also **Palma de Mal·lor·ca** (də mä-yôr′kä, thĕ mä-lyôr′kä) A city of W Majorca I., Spain, on the **Bay of Palma**, an inlet of the Mediterranean Sea. Pop. 298,971.

pal·mar (păl′mər, päl′-, pä′mər) *adj.* Of, relating to, or corresponding to the palm of the hand or an animal's paw.

pal·ma·ry (păl′mə-rē, päl′-, pä′mə-) *adj.* Of first-rate importance; principal. [Lat. *palmārius*, decorated with the palm of victory < *palma*, palm. See PALM².]

pal·mate (păl′māt′, päl′-, pä′māt′) also **pal·mat·ed** (-mā′tĭd) *adj.* **1.** Having a shape similar to that of a hand with the fingers extended. **2.** *Botany* Having three or more veins, leaflets, or lobes radiating from one point; digitate. **3.** *Zoology* Having webbed toes. —**pal′mate·ly** *adv.*

Palm Beach A city of SE FL on a barrier beach of the Atlantic Ocean N of Fort Lauderdale. Pop. 10,468.

Pal·me (päl′mə), **Olaf** 1927–86. Swedish politician who served as premier (1969–76 and 1982–86).

palm·er (pä′mər) *n.* A medieval European pilgrim who carried a palm branch as a token of having visited the Holy Land.

Pal·mer (pä′mər, päl′-), **Alice Elvira Freeman** 1855–1902. Amer. educator who was president of Wellesley College (1882–88).

Palmer, Arnold b. 1929. Amer. golfer who was the first to win four Masters championships (1958, 1960, 1962, and 1964).

Palmer Archipelago Formerly **Antarctic Archipelago.** An island group between the S tip of South America and the NW coast of the Antarctic Peninsula.

Palmer Peninsula See **Antarctic Peninsula.**

Pal·mer·ston (pä′mər-stən, päl′-), 3rd Viscount. Title of Henry John Temple. 1784–1865. British politician and prime minister (1855–58 and 1859–65).

palm·er·worm (pä′mər-wûrm′) *n.* Any of several caterpillars that injure fruit trees by feeding on their leaves, esp. the small green caterpillar of the North American moth *Dichomeris ligulella.* [< appearing like a throng of pilgrims.]

pal·mette (păl-mĕt′) *n.* A stylized palm leaf used as a decorative element, notably in Persian rugs and in classical moldings, reliefs, frescoes, and vase paintings. [Fr., dim. of *palme*, palm < OFr. < Lat. *palma*. See PALM².]

pal·met·to (păl-mĕt′ō) *n., pl.* **-tos** or **-toes** **1.** Any of several small tropical palms with fan-shaped leaves, esp. one of the genus *Sabal*, such as *S. palmetto* of the southeast United States. **2.** Leaf strips of any of these plants, used in weaving. [Sp. *palmito*, dim. of *palma*, palm < Lat. See PALM².]

Pal·mi·ra (păl-mîr′ə, -mē′rä) A city of W Colombia SW of Bogotá on the Pan-American Highway. Pop. 181,157.

palm·ist (pä′mĭst) also **palm·is·ter** (-mĭ-stər) *n.* One who practices palmistry. [Prob. back-formation < PALMISTRY.]

palm·is·try (pä′mĭ-strē) *n.* The practice or art of telling fortunes from the lines, marks, and patterns on the palms of the hands. [ME *palmestrie* < *palme, paume*, palm. See PALM¹.]

pal·mi·tate (păl′mĭ-tāt′, päl′-, pä′mĭ-) *n.* A salt or ester of palmitic acid. [PALMIT(IC) ACID + -ATE².]

pal·mit·ic acid (păl-mĭt′ĭk, päl-, pä-mĭt′-) *n.* A fatty acid, $C_{16}H_{32}O_2$, occurring in many natural oils and fats and used in making soaps. [Fr. *palmitique* < *palmite*, pith of the palm tree. See PALMITIN.]

pal·mi·tin (păl′mĭ-tĭn, päl′-, pä′mĭ-) *n.* The glyceryl ester, $C_3H_5(OOC_{16}H_{31})_3$, of palmitic acid, found in palm oil and animal fats and used to manufacture soap. [Fr. *palmitine*, perh. < *palmite*, pith of the palm tree < Port. *palmito*, dim. of *palma*, palm < Lat. *palma*. See PALM².]

palm oil *n.* A yellowish fatty oil obtained esp. from the crushed nuts of an African palm (*Elaeis guineensis*) and used in the manufacture of soaps, chocolates, cosmetics, and candles.

Palm Springs A resort city of SE CA ESE of Riverside. Pop. 42,807.

palm sugar *n.* Sugar made from the sap of various palm trees.

Palm Sunday *n.* The Sunday before Easter, observed by Christians in commemoration of Jesus's entry into Jerusalem, when palm fronds were strewn before him.

palm·top (päm′tŏp′) *n.* A computer small enough to fit in one's palm. [PALM¹ + (LAP)TOP.]

palm·y (pä′mē) *adj.* **-i·er, -i·est** **1.** Of or relating to palm trees. **2.** Covered with palm trees. **3.** Prosperous; flourishing.

pal·my·ra (păl-mī′rə) *n.* A tall dioecious palm (*Borassus flabellifer*) of tropical Africa and Asia having large fanlike leaves. [Alteration (influenced by PALMYRA) of Port. *palmeira* < *palma*, palm tree < Lat. See PALM².]

Palmyra An ancient city of central Syria NE of Damascus; said to have been built by Solomon.

Pal·o Al·to (păl′ō ăl′tō) A city of W CA NW of San Jose. Pop. 58,598.

Pal·o·mar (păl′ə-mär′), **Mount** A peak, 1,868.4 m (6,126 ft) of S CA NE of San Diego; site of an observatory with one of the world's largest reflecting telescopes.

pal·o·mi·no (păl′ə-mē′nō) *n., pl.* **-nos** A horse with a golden or tan coat and a white or cream-colored mane and tail. [Am.Sp. < Sp., young dove, perh. < Ital. *palombino*, dove-colored < Lat. *palumbīnus*, pertaining to ringdoves < *palumbēs*, ringdove.]

pa·loo·ka (pə-loo′kə) *n.* **1.** *Sports* An incompetent or easily defeated athlete, esp. a prizefighter. **2.** *Slang* A stupid or clumsy person. [?]

Pa·louse (pə-loos′) *n., pl.* **Palouse** or **Pa·louses** A member of a Sahaptin-speaking Native American people formerly inhabiting an area of southeast Washington and northwest Idaho, with present-day descendants in northeast Washington.

Palouse River A river rising in NW ID and flowing c. 225 km (140 mi) to the Snake R. in SE WA.

pa·lo ver·de (päl′ō vûr′dē, vûrd′) *n.* **1.** A spiny, nearly leafless bushy tree (*Cercidium floridum*, syn. *Parkinsonia florida*) of the southwest United States having yellow flowers and blue-green bark. **2.** Any of several similar shrubs. [Am.Sp. : Sp. *palo*, tree (< Lat. *pālus*, stake; see PALE¹) + Sp. *verde*, green (< Lat. *viridis*).]

palp (pălp) *n.* An elongated, often segmented appendage usu. near the mouth in invertebrate organisms such as insects, used for sensation, locomotion, or feeding. [Fr. *palpe* < NLat. *palpus* < Lat.]

pal·pa·ble (păl′pə-bəl) *adj.* **1.** Capable of being handled, touched, or felt. **2.** Easily perceived; obvious. See Syns at **perceptible**. **3.** *Medicine* That can be felt by palpating. [ME < OFr. < LLat. *palpābilis* < Lat. *palpāre*, to touch gently.] —**pal′pa·bil′i·ty** *n.* —**pal′pa·bly** *adv.*

pal·pal (păl′pəl) *adj.* Of, relating to, or characteristic of a palp.

pal·pate¹ (păl′pāt′) *tr.v.* **-pat·ed, -pat·ing, -pates** To examine or explore by touching (an organ or area of the body), usu. as a diagnostic aid. [Lat. *palpāre, palpāt-*, to touch gently.] —**pal′pa′tion** *n.* —**pal′pa′tor** *n.* —**pal′pa·to′ry** (-ə-tôr′ē, -tōr′ē) *adj.*

pal·pate² (păl′pāt′) *adj.* Having a palp or palps.

pal·pe·bra (păl′pə-brə, păl-pē′-) *n., pl.* **-brae** (-brē′) also **-bras** An eyelid. [Lat.] —**pal′pe·bral** (păl′pə-brəl, păl-pē′brəl, -pĕb′rəl) *adj.*

pal·pi·tant (păl′pĭ-tənt) *adj.* **1.** Shaking; trembling. **2.** Undergoing pulsation; pulsating. [Lat. *palpitāns, palpitant-*, pr. part. of *palpitāre*, to palpitate. See PALPITATE.]

pal·pi·tate (păl′pĭ-tāt′) *intr.v.* **-tat·ed, -tat·ing, -tates** **1.** To move with a slight tremulous motion; tremble, shake, or quiver. **2.** To beat with excessive rapidity; throb. [Lat. *palpitāre, palpitāt-*, freq. of *palpāre*, to touch gently.] —**pal′pi·tat′ing·ly** *adv.*

pal·pi·ta·tion (păl′pĭ-tā′shən) *n.* **1.** A trembling or shaking. **2.** Irregular rapid beating or pulsation of the heart.

pal·pus (păl′pəs) *n., pl.* **-pi** (-pī) See palp. [Lat., a toweling, the soft palm of the hand. See PALP.]

pals·grave¹ (pôlz′grāv′) *n.* See palatine¹ 3. [Obsolete Du. *paltsgrave* < MDu. *palsgrēve, palsgrāve : pals*, palatine (< VLat. *palatia*, palace < Lat. *palātia*, pl. of *Palātium*, imperial palace; see PALACE) + MDu. *grēve, grāve*, count; see MARGRAVE.]

pal·sied (pôl′zēd) *adj.* **1.** Affected with palsy. **2.** Trembling or shaking.

pal·sy (pôl′zē) *n., pl.* **-sies** **1.** Complete or partial muscle paralysis, often accompanied by loss of sensation and uncontrollable body movements or tremors. **2a.** A weakening or debilitating influence. **b.** An enfeebled condition or debilitated state thought to result from such an influence. **3.** A fit of strong emotion marked by the inability to act. ❖ *tr.v.* **-sied, -sy·ing, -sies 1a.** To paralyze. **b.** To deprive of strength. **2.** To make helpless, as with fear. [ME *palsie*, alteration of OFr. *paralisie*, alteration of Lat. *paralysis*. See PARALYSIS.]

pal·sy-wal·sy (păl′zē-wăl′zē) *adj. Slang* Having or appearing to have a close friendly relationship. [Reduplication of *palsy* : pl. of PAL + -Y¹.]

pal·ter (pôl′tər) *intr.v.* **-tered, -ter·ing, -ters** **1.** To talk or act insincerely or misleadingly; equivocate. **2.** To be capricious; trifle. **3.** To quibble, esp. in bargaining. [?] —**pal′ter·er** *n.*

pal·try (pôl′trē) *adj.* **-tri·er, -tri·est** **1.** Lacking in importance or worth; trivial. **2.** Wretched or contemptible. [Prob. < obsolete and dialectal *paltry*, trash, pert. < LGer. *paltrig*, ragged < *palte, rag*.] —**pal′tri·ly** *adv.* —**pal′tri·ness** *n.*

pa·lu·dal (pə-lood′l, păl′yə-dəl) *adj.* Of or relating to a swamp; marshy. [< Lat. *palūs, palūd-*, marsh. See **pelə-¹** in App.]

pal·y¹ (pā′lē) *adj.* **-i·er, -i·est** *Archaic* Pale.

pal·y² (pā′lē) *adj. Heraldry* Divided into several equal parts by perpendicular lines. Used of a field. [ME < OFr. *pale* < *pal*, stake. See PALE¹.]

pal·y·nol·o·gy (păl′ə-nŏl′ə-jē) *n.* The scientific study of spores and pollen. [Gk. *palunein*, to sprinkle + -LOGY.] —**pal′y·no·log′i·cal** (-nə-lŏj′ĭ-kəl), **pal′y·no·log′ic** *adj.* —**pal′y·no·log′i·cal·ly** *adv.* —**pal′y·nol·o·gist** *n.*

pam (păm) *n.* The jack of clubs and highest trump in certain variations of loo. [Probably ultimately < the Greek name *Pamphilos*, beloved of all. See PAMPHLET.]

Pa·ma-Nyun·gan (pä′mə-nyŏŏng′gən) *n.* A family of Australian aboriginal languages, spoken throughout Australia except in the extreme north, and including Warlpiri. [*pama*, man (in northeast languages) + *nyunga*, man (in southwest languages).]

Pa·mir (pə-mîr′, pä-) A mountainous region of S-central Asia mostly in Tajikistan with extensions in N Afghanistan, N Kashmir, and W China and rising to 7,500 m (24,590 ft).

Pam·li·co Sound (păm′lĭ-kō′) An inlet of the Atlantic Ocean between the E coast of NC and a row of sandy barrier islands.

pam·pa (păm′pə) *n., pl.* **-pas** (-pəz, -pəs) An extensive treeless grassland area, as found in southern South America. [Am.Sp. < Quechua, flat field.]

Pam·pas (păm′pəz, păm′pəs) A vast plain of S-central South America from the lower Paraná R. to S-central Argentina.

pam·pas grass (păm′pəs) *n.* A grass (*Cortaderia selloana*) of southern South America having silvery plumes and growing in large clumps more than three meters (ten feet) tall. [After the PAMPAS.]

pam·pe·an also **Pam·pe·an** (păm′pē-ən, păm-pē′ən) *adj.* Of or relating to a pampa or the Pampas or their inhabitants.

pam·per (păm′pər) *tr.v.* **-pered, -per·ing, -pers** **1.** To treat with excessive indulgence. **2.** To give in to; gratify. **3.** *Archaic* To indulge with rich food; glut. [ME *pamperen*, prob. of LGer. orig.] —**pam′per·er** *n.*

pam·pe·ro (păm-pâr′ō, päm-) *n., pl.* **-ros** A strong cold southwest wind that blows across the Pampas. [Am.Sp. < *pampa*, pampa. See PAMPA.]

pam·phlet (păm′flĭt) *n.* **1.** An unbound printed work, usu. with a paper cover. **2.** A short essay or treatise, usu. on a current topic, published without a binding. [ME *pamflet* < Med.Lat. *pamfletus* < *Pamphiletus*, dim. of *Pamphilus*, amatory Latin poem of the 12th cent. < Gk. *pamphilos*, beloved by all : *pan-*, pan- + *philos*, beloved.] —**pam′phlet·ar′y** (păm′flĭ-tĕr′ē) *adj.*

pam·phlet·eer (păm′flĭ-tîr′) *n.* A partisan writer of pamphlets or other short works. —**pam′phlet·eer′** *v.*

Pam·plo·na (păm-plō′nə, päm-plō′nä) A city of N Spain ESE of Bilbao; an ancient Basque city and cap. of the kingdom of Navarre (824-1512). Pop. 181,349.

pam·pro·dac·ty·lous (păm′prō-dăk′tə-ləs) *adj.* Having all toes pointing forward. Used of certain birds. [PAN- + PRO-² + DACTYL(O)- + -OUS.]

pan¹ (păn) *n.* **1.** A shallow wide open container, usu. of metal and without a lid, for cooking and other domestic purposes. **2.** A vessel similar to a pan, esp.: **a.** An open metal dish for separating gold or other metal from gravel or waste by washing. **b.** Either of the receptacles on a balance or pair of scales. **c.** A vessel for boiling and evaporating liquids. **3a.** A basin or depression in the earth, often containing mud or water. **b.** A basin for obtaining salt by evaporating brine. **c.** Hardpan. **4.** A freely floating piece

palomino

pampas grass
Cortaderia selloana

pan²

pane

of ice that has broken off a larger floe. **5.** The small cavity in the lock of a flintlock used to hold powder. **6.** *Music* A steel drum. **7.** *Slang* The face. **8.** *Informal* Severe criticism, esp. a negative review. ❖ *v.* **panned, pan·ning, pans** —*tr.* **1.** To wash (gravel, for example) in a pan for gold or other precious metal. **2.** To cook (food) in a pan. **3.** *Informal* To criticize or review harshly. —*intr.* **1.** To wash gravel, sand, or other sediment in a pan. **2.** To yield gold as a result of washing in a pan. —*phrasal verb:* **pan out** To turn out well; be successful. [ME < OE *panne* < West Gmc. **panna*, prob. < VLat. **patna* < Lat. *patina*, shallow pan, platter < Gk. *patanē*.]

pan² (păn) *n.* **1.** A leaf of the betel vine. **2.** A chewing preparation of this leaf with betel nuts, spices, and lime. [Hindi *pān* < Skt. *parṇam*, feather, betel leaf. See **per-²** in App.]

pan³ (păn) *v.* **panned, pan·ning, pans** —*intr.* To pan a movie or television camera. —*tr.* To move (a camera) to follow an object or create a panoramic effect.

Pan (păn) *n. Greek Mythology* **1.** The god of woods, fields, and flocks, having a man's torso and head with a goat's legs, horns, and ears. **2.** A satellite of Saturn. [ME < Lat. *Pān* < Gk.]

Pan. *abbr.* Panama

pan– *pref.* **1.** All: *panorama.* **2.** also **Pan–** Involving all of or the union of a specified group: *Pan-Hellenic.* **3.** General; whole: *panleukopenia.* [Gk. < *pan,* neut. of *pās, pant-.*]

pan·a·ce·a (păn´ə-sē´ə) *n.* A remedy for all diseases, evils, or difficulties; a cure-all. [Lat. *panacēa* < Gk. *panakeia* < *panakēs,* all-healing : *pan-, pan-* + *akos,* cure.] —**pan´a·ce´an** *adj.*

pa·nache (pə-năsh´, -näsh´) *n.* **1.** Dash; verve. **2.** A bunch of feathers or a plume, esp. on a helmet. [Fr., plume, verve < Ital. *pinnacchio,* plume < LLat. *pinnāculum,* dim. of Lat. *pinna,* feather, wing. See **pet-** in App.]

pa·na·da (pə-nä´də) *n.* A paste or gruel of bread crumbs, toast, or flour combined with milk, stock, or water and used for making soups, binding forcemeats, or thickening sauces. [Sp. < *pan,* bread < Lat. *pānis.* See **pā-** in App.]

Pan·a·ma (păn´ə-mä´) **1.** A country of SE Central America; gained independence in 1903. Cap. Panama. Pop. 2,583,000. **2.** also **Panama City** The cap. of Panama, in the central part on the Gulf of Panama. Pop. 445,902. —**Pan´a·ma´ni·an** (-mä´nē-ən) *adj. & n.*

Panama, Gulf of A wide inlet of the Pacific Ocean on the S coast of Panama.

Panama, Isthmus of Formerly **Isthmus of Da·ri·én** (dăr´ē-ĕn´, där-yĕn´) An isthmus of Central America connecting North and South America and separating the Pacific Ocean from the Caribbean Sea; first crossed by Balboa in 1513.

Panama Canal A ship canal, c. 82 km (51 mi), crossing the Isthmus of Panama in the Canal Zone and connecting the Caribbean Sea with the Pacific Ocean; opened to traffic on Aug. 15, 1914. Panama gained full rights of sovereignty over the canal on Dec. 31, 1999.

Panama Canal Zone See **Canal Zone.**

Panama hat *n.* A natural-colored hand-plaited hat made from leaves of the jipijapa plant of South and Central America.

Pan-A·mer·i·can (păn´ə-mĕr´ĭ-kən) *adj.* Of or relating to North, South, and Central America.

Pan-American Highway A system of roadways, about 25,744 km (16,000 mi) long, extending from AK to Chile and linking the nations of the Western Hemisphere.

Pan·a·mint Range (păn´ə-mĭnt´) A range of E CA between Death Valley and the **Panamint Valley** rising to 3,370 m (11,049 ft).

pan and scan (păn) *n.* A method of printing movies for presentation on television that modifies the rectangular theater image by trimming the sides and focusing on significant action within the newly truncated image. —**pan´-and-scan´** (păn´ənd-skăn´) *adj.*

pan·a·tel·a (păn´ə-tĕl´ə) also **pan·e·tel·a** or **pan·e·tel·la** (păn´ĭ-) *n.* A long slender cigar. [Sp., biscuit, cigar < Am.Sp., long thin biscuit < Ital. *panatella,* dim. of *panata,* panada < *pane,* bread < Lat. *pānis.* See **pā-** in App.]

Pa·nay (pə-nī´, pä-) An island of the central Philippines in the Visayan Is. NW of Negros.

pan-broil (păn´broil´) *tr.v.* **-broiled, -broil·ing, -broils** To cook (steak, for example) over direct heat in an uncovered, usu. ungreased skillet.

pan·cake (păn´kāk´) *n.* A thin cake made of batter that is poured onto a hot greased surface and cooked until brown.

Pan-Cake A trademark used for a semisolid cosmetic or theatrical makeup pressed into a flat cake and usu. applied with a damp sponge.

pancake landing *n.* An irregular or emergency landing in which an aircraft drops flat to the ground from a low altitude.

pan·cet·ta (păn-chĕt´ə) *n.* Italian bacon that has been cured in salt and spices and then air-dried. [Ital., dim. of *pancia,* belly < Lat. *pantex, pantic-.*]

pan·chax (păn´chăks´) *n.* Any of various small, brightly colored Old World tropical fishes of the genus *Aplocheilus* and related genera, often kept in home aquariums. [NLat. *Panchax,* former genus name.]

Pan·chen La·ma (păn´chən lä´mə) *n.* One of Tibet's two grand lamas, the other being the Dalai Lama. [Tibetan *paṇchen bla-ma* : *paṇchen,* great scholar (< Skt. *paṇḍitaḥ,* scholar; see PUNDIT + Tibetan *chen-po,* great) + Tibetan *bla-ma,* monk; see LAMA.]

pan·chro·mat·ic (păn´krō-măt´ĭk) *adj.* Sensitive to all colors. —**pan·chro´ma·tism** (-krō´mə-tĭz´əm) *n.*

pan·cra·ti·um (păn-krā´shē-əm) *n.* An athletic contest in ancient Greece that involved boxing and wrestling. [Lat. < Gk. *pankration* : *pan-, pan-* + *kratos,* strength; see –CRACY.]

pan·cre·as (păng´krē-əs, păn´-) *n.* A long, irregularly shaped gland in vertebrates, lying behind the stomach, that secretes pancreatic juice into the duodenum and insulin, glucagon, and somatostatin into the bloodstream. [Gk. *pankreas* : *pan-, pan-* + *kreas,* flesh; see **kreuə-** in App.] —**pan´cre·at´ic** (păng´krē-ăt´ĭk, păn´-) *adj.*

pan·cre·a·tec·to·my (păng´krē-ə-tĕk´tə-mē, păn´-) *n., pl.* **-mies** Surgical removal of all or part of the pancreas.

pancreatic duct *n.* The duct by which pancreatic juice is secreted into the duodenum.

pancreatic juice *n.* A clear alkaline secretion of the pancreas containing enzymes that aid in the digestion of proteins, carbohydrates, and fats.

pan·cre·a·tin (păng´krē-ə-tĭn, păn´-, păn-krē´ə-tĭn) *n.* A mixture of the enzymes of pancreatic juice, such as amylase, lipase, and trypsin, extracted from animals such as cattle or hogs and used as a digestive aid.

pan·cre·a·ti·tis (păng´krē-ə-tī´tĭs, păn´-) *n.* Inflammation of the pancreas.

pancreato– or **pancreat–** *pref.* Pancreas: *pancreatin.* [< Gk. *pankreas, pankreat-,* pancreas. See PANCREAS.]

pan·cy·to·pe·ni·a (păn´sī-tə-pē´nē-ə) *n.* See **aplastic anemia.**

pan·da (păn´də) *n.* **1.** A rare bearlike mammal (*Ailuropoda melanoleuca*) of the mountains of China and Tibet (Xizang) having woolly fur with distinctive black and white markings. **2.** A small raccoonlike mammal (*Ailurus fulgens*) of northeast Asia having reddish fur, white face markings, and a long ringed tail. [Fr., perh. of Nepalese orig.]

pan·da·nus (păn-dā´nəs, -dăn´əs) *n.* Any of numerous palmlike trees and shrubs of the genus *Pandanus* of the Old World tropics, having large prop roots and narrow spiny leaves that yield a fiber used in weaving mats and similar articles. [NLat. *Pandanus,* genus name < Malay *pandan,* screw pine.] —**pan´da·na´ceous** (păn´də-nā´shəs) *adj.*

Pan·da·rus (păn´dər-əs) also **Pan·dar** (-dər) *n.* **1.** The leader of the Lycians, slain by Diomedes in the *Iliad.* **2.** The procurer of Cressida for Troilus in medieval romance.

Pan·de·an pipe (păn-dē´ən) *n.* See **panpipe.** [< PAN.]

pan·dect (păn´dĕkt´) *n.* **1.** A comprehensive digest or complete treatise. **2. pandects** A complete body of laws; a legal code. **3. Pandects** A digest of Roman civil law, compiled for the emperor Justinian in the sixth century A.D. and part of the Corpus Juris Civilis. [Lat. *pandectēs,* encyclopedia < Gk. *pandektēs,* all-receiving : *pan-, pan-* + *dektēs,* receiver (< *dekhesthai,* to receive, accept; see **dek-** in App.).]

pan·dem·ic (păn-dĕm´ĭk) *adj.* **1.** Widespread; general. **2.** *Medicine* Epidemic over a wide geographic area and affecting a large proportion of the population: *pandemic influenza.* ❖ *n.* A pandemic disease. [< LLat. *pandēmus* < Gk. *pandēmos,* of all the people : *pan-, pan-* + *dēmos,* people; see **dā-** in App.]

pan·de·mo·ni·um (păn´də-mō´nē-əm) *n.* **1.** A very noisy and often chaotic place. **2.** Wild uproar or noise; tumult. [< *Pandæmonium,* capital of Hell in *Paradise Lost* by John Milton : Gk. *pan-, pan-* + LLat. *daemonium,* demon (< Gk. *daimonion* < *daimōn,* lesser god, demon; see DEMON).] —**pan´de·mo´ni·ac** (-nē-ăk´) *adj.*

pan·der (păn´dər) *intr.v.* **-dered, -der·ing, -ders 1.** To act as a go-between in sexual intrigues; function as a procurer. **2.** To cater to the lower tastes and desires of others or exploit their weaknesses. [Ult. < Gk. *Pandaros,* Pandarus.] —**pan´der** *n.*

pan·der·er (păn´dər-ər) *n.* **1.** A sexual procurer. **2.** One who caters to or exploits the lower tastes and desires of others.

pan·dit (păn´dĭt) or **pun·dit** (pŭn´-) *n.* **1.** A Brahman scholar or learned man. **2.** Used as a title of respect for a learned man in India. [Hindi *paṇḍit* < Skt. *paṇḍitaḥ.* See PUNDIT.]

Pan·do·ra (păn-dôr´ə, -dōr´ə) *n. Greek Mythology* **1.** The first woman, who was bestowed upon humankind as punishment for Prometheus's theft of fire and who out of curiosity opened a box containing all human ills and released them. **2.** A satellite of Saturn. [Gk. *Pandōra,* having all gifts : *pan-, pan-* + *dōron,* gift; see **dō-** in App.]

pan·dore (păn´dôr´, -dōr´) *n.* See **bandore.** [Ult. < Gk. *pandoura.*]

pan·dow·dy (păn-dou´dē) *n., pl.* **-dies** Sliced fruit with sugar, spices, and a thick top crust, in a deep dish. [Perh. < obsolete dialectal *pandoulde,* custard < PAN¹ + dialectal *dowl,* to mix dough in a hurry (prob. var. of DOUGH).]

pane (pān) *n.* **1a.** A framed section of a window or door that is usu. filled with a sheet of glass or other transparent material. **b.** The transparent material used to fill such a section. **2.** A panel, as of a door or wall. **3.** One of the flat surfaces or facets of an object, such as a bolt, having many sides. [ME, section, pane of glass

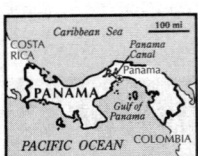

Panama

Panama Canal
the Gaillard Cut, which crosses the continental divide

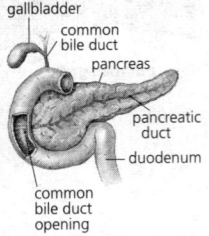

gallbladder
common bile duct
pancreas
pancreatic duct
duodenum
common bile duct opening

pancreas

panda
giant panda
Ailuropoda melanoleuca

< OFr. *pan*, piece of cloth, panel < Lat. *pannus*, cloth.]

paned (pānd) *adj.* Having a specified kind or number of panes. Often used in combination: *clear-paned windows.*

pan·e·gyr·ic (păn′ə-jĭr′ĭk, -jī′rĭk) *n.* **1.** A formal public eulogy. **2.** Elaborate praise or laudation. [Lat. *panēgyricus* < Gk. *panēgurikos (logos)*, (speech) at a public assembly, panegyric < *panēguris*, public assembly : *pan-*, pan- + *aguris*, assembly, marketplace; akin to *agorā*, marketplace.] —**pan′e·gyr′i·cal** *adj.*

pan·e·gyr·ist (păn′ə-jĭr′ĭst, -jī′rĭst) *n.* One who writes or delivers panegyrics; a eulogist. —**pan′e·gy·rize** (-jə-rīz′) *v.*

pan·el (păn′əl) *n.* **1.** A flat, usu. rectangular piece forming a raised, recessed, or framed part of the surface in which it is set. **2.** The space or section in a fence or railing between two posts. **3.** A vertical section of fabric; a gore. **4a.** A thin wooden board, used as a surface for an oil painting. **b.** A painting on such a board. **5a.** A board having switches or buttons to control an electric device. **b.** An instrument panel. **6.** A section of a telephone switchboard. **7.** A cartoon drawing in a sequence of cartoons that form a narrative. **8.** *Law* **a.** The complete list of persons summoned for jury duty. **b.** Those persons selected from this list to compose a jury. **c.** A jury. **9a.** A group of people gathered to plan or discuss an issue, judge a contest, or act as a team on a quiz program. **b.** A discussion by such a group. ❖ *tr.v.* **-eled, -el·ing, -els** or **-elled, -el·ling, -els** **1.** To cover or furnish with panels. **2.** To decorate with panels. **3.** To separate into panels. **4.** *Law* To select or impanel (a jury). [ME, piece of cloth < OFr., prob. < VLat. *pannellus*, dim. of Lat. *pannus*, cloth.]

panel discussion *n.* A discussion of a subject of public interest by a panel of persons, often before an audience.

pan·el·ing (păn′ə-lĭng) *n.* A section of panels or paneled wall.

pan·el·ist (păn′ə-lĭst) *n.* A member of a panel.

pan·el·ized (păn′ə-līzd′) *adj.* Consisting of or characterized by prefabricated wall, floor, and roof sections.

panel truck *n.* A small truck with a fully enclosed body.

pan·e·tel·a or **pan·e·tel·la** (păn′ĭ-tĕl′ə) *n.* Variants of **panatela.**

pan·et·to·ne (păn′ĭ-tō′nē) *n., pl.* **-nes** or **-ni** (-nē) An Italian yeast cake made with candied fruit peels and raisins. [Ital., augmentative of *panetto*, a small loaf, dim. of *pane*, bread < Lat. *pānis*. See PANADA.]

pan fish (păn) *n.* A fish small enough to be fried whole in a pan.

pan·fry also **pan·fry** (păn′frī′) *tr.v.* **-fried, -fry·ing, -fries** To fry in a frying pan or skillet with a small amount of fat.

pan·ful (păn′fŏŏl′) *n.* The amount that a pan can hold.

pang (păng) *n.* **1.** A sudden sharp spasm of pain. **2.** A sudden sharp twinge of emotional distress. ❖ *tr.v.* **panged, pang·ing, pangs** To cause to feel pangs; distress acutely. [?]

Pan·gae·a also **Pan·ge·a** (păn-jē′ə) *n.* A hypothetical supercontinent that included all the landmasses of the earth before the Triassic Period. [PAN- + Gk. *gaia*, earth.]

pan·gen·e·sis (păn-jĕn′ĭ-sĭs) *n.* A theory of heredity proposed by Charles Darwin in which gemmules of hereditary information from every part of the body coalesce in the gonads and are incorporated into the reproductive cells.

Pan·gloss·i·an (păn-glŏs′ē-ən, -glôs′-, păng-) *adj.* Blindly or naively optimistic. [After *Pangloss*, the naively optimistic philosopher in *Candide* by Voltaire.]

pan·go·lin (păng′gə-lĭn, păn-) *n.* Any of several long-tailed, scale-covered mammals of the order Pholidota of tropical Africa and Asia, having a long snout and a sticky tongue. [Malay *penggu-ling* : *peng-*, instrumental pref. + *guling*, to roll over (< its rolling into a ball when frightened).]

Pan·go Pan·go (păng′ō păng′ō, păng′gō păng′gō, păng′gō păng′gō) See Pago Pago.

pan·gram (păn′grăm′, -grəm, păng′-) *n.* A sentence that uses all the letters of the alphabet.

pan·han·dle[1] (păn′hăn′dl) *v.* **-dled, -dling, -dles** *Informal* —*intr.* To approach strangers and beg for money or food. —*tr.* **1.** To approach and beg from (a stranger). **2.** To obtain by panhandling. [Back-formation < *panhandler*, beggar : perh. PAN[1] + HANDLER.] —**pan′han′dler** *n.*

pan·han·dle[2] (păn′hăn′dl) *n.* **1.** The handle of a pan. **2.** often **Panhandle** A narrow strip of territory projecting from a larger, broader area, as in Alaska or Texas.

Pan-Hel·len·ic also **Pan-hel·len·ic** (păn′hə-lĕn′ĭk) *adj.* **1.** Of or relating to all Greek peoples or a movement to unify them. **2.** Of or relating to all Greek-letter fraternities and sororities.

pan·hu·man (păn-hyŏŏ′mən) *adj.* Of or relating to all humanity.

pan·ic (păn′ĭk) *n.* **1.** A sudden overpowering terror, often affecting many people at once. See Syns at **fear.** **2.** A sudden widespread alarm concerning finances, often resulting in a rush to sell. **3.** *Slang* One that is uproariously funny. ❖ *adj.* **1.** Of, relating to, or resulting from sudden overwhelming terror. **2.** Of or resulting from a financial panic. **3.** often **Panic** *Mythology* Of or relating to Pan. ❖ *tr. & intr.v.* **-icked, -ick·ing, -ics** To affect or be affected with panic. [< Fr. *panique*, terrified < Gk. *Pānikos*, of Pan (a source of terror, as in flocks), groundless (used of fear) < *Pān*, Pan. See PAN.] —**pan′ick·y** *adj.*

panic attack *n.* The sudden onset of intense anxiety, accompanied by physical signs such as rapid heartbeat, shortness of

breath, sweating, and trembling.

panic disorder *n.* A psychological disorder characterized by recurrent panic attacks and the development of one or more phobias.

panic grass *n.* Any of numerous grasses of the genus *Panicum*, many of which are grown for grain and fodder. [ME *panik* < OFr. < Lat. *pānicum*.]

pan·i·cle (păn′ĭ-kəl) *n.* A branched cluster of flowers in which the branches are racemes. [Lat. *pānicula*, fem. dim. of *pānus*, a swelling, main stalk of a panicle.] —**pan′i·cled** *adj.*

pan·ic-strick·en (păn′ĭk-strĭk′ən) also **pan·ic-struck** (-strŭk′) *adj.* Overcome by panic; terrified.

pa·nic·u·late (pə-nĭk′yə-lĭt, -lāt′) also **pa·nic·u·lat·ed** (-lā′tĭd) *adj. Botany* Growing or arranged in a panicle. [NLat. *pāniculātus* < Lat. *pānicula*, panicle. See PANICLE.] —**pa·nic′u·late·ly** *adv.*

pan·ier (păn′yər, -ē-ər) *n.* Variant of **pannier.**

Pa·ni·ni (pä′nə-nē) fl. 400 B.C. Indian grammarian whose *Ashtadhyayi* describes grammatical rules for Sanskrit.

pa·ni·no (pə-nē′nō) *n., pl.* **pa·ni·ni** (-nē) An Italian sandwich made usu. with vegetables, cheese, and grilled or cured meat. [Short for Ital. *panino imbottito*, stuffed bread, sandwich < *panino*, dim. of *pane*, bread.]

Pan·ja·bi (pŭn-jä′bē, -jäb′ē) *n. & adj.* Variant of **Punjabi.**

pan·jan·drum (păn-jăn′drəm) *n.* An important or self-important person. [After the Grand *Panjandrum*, a character in a nonsense farrago by Samuel Foote (1720–77).]

Pank·hurst (păngk′hûrst′), **Emmeline Goulden** 1858–1928. British suffrage leader who with her daughters **Christabel Pankhurst** (1880–1958) and **Sylvia Pankhurst** (1882–1960) founded (1903) the Women's Social and Political Union.

pan·leu·ko·pe·ni·a also **pan·leu·co·pe·ni·a** (păn′lōō-kə-pē′nē-ə) *n.* See **distemper**[1] 1b.

pan·mix·i·a (păn-mĭk′sē-ə) also **pan·mix·is** (-mĭk′sĭs) *n.* Random mating within a breeding population. [NLat. : PAN- + Gk. *mixis*, act of mingling (< *mignunai*, to mix; see meik- in App.).] —**pan·mic′tic** (-mĭk′tĭk) *adj.*

Pan·mun·jom (păn′mŏŏn′jŭm′) A village of NW South Korea just S of the 38th parallel where the truce ending the Korean War was officially signed on Jul. 27, 1953.

panne (păn) *n.* A special finish for velvet and satin that produces a high luster. [Fr., a soft cloth < OFr. *penne, pane*, fur lining < Lat. *pinna, penna*, feather. See PENNA.]

pan·nier or **pan·ier** (păn′yər, -ē-ər) *n.* **1.** A large wicker basket, esp.: **a.** One of a pair of baskets carried on either side of a pack animal. **b.** A basket carried on a person's back. **2.** A basket or pack that fastens to the rack of a bicycle. **3a.** A framework of wire, bone, or other material formerly used to expand a woman's skirt at the hips. **b.** A skirt or overskirt puffed out at the hips. [ME *panier* < OFr. < Lat. *pānārium*, breadbasket < *pānis*, bread. See pā- in App.] —**pan′niered** *adj.*

Pan·no·ni·a (pə-nō′nē-ə) An ancient Roman province of central Europe including present-day W Hungary and the NW Balkan Peninsula. —**Pan·no′ni·an** *adj. & n.*

pa·no·cha (pə-nō′chə) also **pa·no·che** (-chē) *n.* **1.** A coarse grade of Mexican sugar. **2.** Variants of **penuche.** [Am.Sp., prob. < Sp. *panoja, panocha*, ear of grain, panicle < Lat. *pānicula*. See PANICLE.]

pan·o·ply (păn′ə-plē) *n., pl.* **-plies** **1.** A splendid or striking array. **2.** Ceremonial attire with all accessories. **3.** Something that covers and protects. **4.** The complete arms and armor of a warrior. [Gk. *panopliā* : *pan-*, pan- + *hopla*, arms, armor, pl. of *hoplon*, weapon.]

pan·op·tic (păn-ŏp′tĭk) also **pan·op·ti·cal** (-tĭ-kəl) *adj.* Including everything visible in one view. [< Gk. *panoptos*, fully visible : *pan-*, with respect to everything, fully; see PAN- + *optos*, visible; see ok"- in App.]

pan·o·ram·a (păn′ə-răm′ə, -rä′mə) *n.* **1.** An unbroken view of an entire surrounding area. **2.** A comprehensive presentation; a survey. **3.** A picture or series of pictures representing a continuous scene. **4.** A mental vision of a series of events. [PAN- + Gk. *horāma*, sight (< *horān*, to see).] —**pan′o·ram′ic** (-răm′ĭk) *adj.* —**pan′o·ram′i·cal·ly** *adv.*

pan·pipe (păn′pīp′) *n.* A primitive wind instrument consisting of a series of pipes or reeds of graduated length bound together, played by blowing across the top open ends. Often used in the plural. [PAN + PIPE.]

pan·psy·chism (păn-sī′kĭz′əm) *n.* The view that all matter has consciousness.

pan·sex·u·al (păn-sĕk′shŏŏ-əl) *adj.* Relating to, having, or open to sexual activity of many kinds. ❖ *n.* A pansexual person. —**pan′sex·u·al′i·ty** (-ăl′ĭ-tē) *n.*

pan·sy (păn′zē) *n., pl.* **-sies** **1.** Any of various plants of the genera *Achimenes* or *Viola*, having flowers with velvety petals of various colors. **2.** A deep to strong violet. **3.** *Offensive Slang* **a.** Used as a disparaging term for a man or boy who is considered effeminate. **b.** Used as a disparaging term for a homosexual man. [ME *pancy* < OFr. *pensee* < fem. p. part. of *penser*, to think. See PENSIVE.]

pant[1] (pănt) *v.* **pant·ed, pant·ing, pants** —*intr.* **1.** To breathe rapidly in short gasps, as after exertion. **2.** To beat loudly or heavily; throb or pulsate. **3.** To give off short puffs, esp. while moving.

pangolin

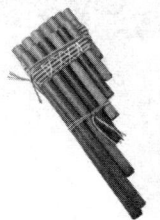
panpipe
double-row panpipe

ă pat	oi boy	
ā pay	ou out	
âr care	ŏŏ took	
ä father	ŏŏ boot	
ĕ pet	ŭ cut	
ē be	ûr urge	
ĭ pit	th thin	
ī pie	th this	
îr pier	hw which	
ŏ pot	zh vision	
ō toe	ə about,	
ô paw	item	

Stress marks:
′ (primary);
′ (secondary), as in
lexicon (lĕk′sĭ-kŏn′)

4. To long demonstratively; yearn. —*tr.* To utter hurriedly or breathlessly. ❖ *n.* **1.** A short labored breath; a gasp. **2.** A throb; a pulsation. **3.** A short loud puff. [ME *panten,* perh. alteration of OFr. *pantaisier* < VLat. **pantasiāre* < Gk. *phantasioun,* to form images < *phantasiā,* appearance. See FANTASY.] —**pant′ing·ly** *adv.*

pant² (pănt) *n.* **1.** Trousers. Often used in the plural. **2.** Underpants. Often used in the plural. —*idiom:* **with (one's) pants down** *Slang* In an embarrassing position. [Short for *pantaloon.*]

pan·ta·let also **pan·ta·lette** (păn′tə-lĕt′) *n.* **1.** Long underpants trimmed with ruffles extending below the skirt, worn by women in the mid-19th century. Often used in the plural. **2.** A frill attached to the leg of underpants. Often used in the plural. [< PANTALOON.]

pan·ta·loon (păn′tə-lo͞on′) *n.* **1a.** Men's wide breeches extending from waist to ankle, worn esp. in England in the late 17th century. Often used in the plural. **b.** Tight trousers extending from waist to ankle with straps passing under the instep, worn esp. in the 19th century. Often used in the plural. **2.** Trousers; pants. Often used in the plural. [Fr. *pantalon,* a kind of trouser < *Pantalon,* Pantaloon. See PANTALOON.]

Pan·ta·loon (păn′tə-lo͞on′) *n.* **1.** often **Pan·ta·lo·ne** (păn′tə-lō′nä, păn′tä-lō′nĕ) A character in the commedia dell'arte, portrayed as a foolish old man in tight trousers and slippers. **2.** A stock character in modern pantomime, the butt of a clown's jokes. [Fr. *Pantalon* < Ital. *Pantalone,* after San *Pantalone,* or St. Pantaleon (died A.D. 303), Roman martyr.]

pan·the·ism (păn′thē-ĭz′əm) *n.* **1.** A doctrine identifying the Deity with the universe and its phenomena. **2.** Belief in and worship of all gods. —**pan′the·ist** *n.* —**pan′the·is′tic, pan′the·is′ti·cal** *adj.* —**pan′the·is′ti·cal·ly** *adv.*

pan·the·on (păn′thē-ŏn′, -ən) *n.* **1.** **Pantheon** A circular temple in Rome, completed in 27 B.C. and dedicated to all the gods. **2.** A temple dedicated to all gods. **3.** All the gods of a people considered as a group: *Jupiter is head of the Roman pantheon.* **4.** A public building commemorating and dedicated to a nation's heroes and heroines. **5.** A group of persons most highly regarded for contributions to a field or endeavor. [ME *Panteon,* Pantheon < Lat. *Panthēum, Panthēon* < Gk. *Pantheion,* shrine of all the gods < neut. sing. of *pantheios,* of all the gods : *pan-,* pan- + *theos,* god; see **dhēs-** in App.]

pan·ther (păn′thər) *n.* **1.** The leopard, esp. in its black unspotted form. **2.** See **mountain lion.** [ME *pantere* < OFr. and < OE *panthera,* both < Lat. *panthēra* < Gk. *panthēr.*]

pant·ie or **pant·y** (păn′tē) *n., pl.* **pant·ies** Short underpants for women or children. Often used in the plural. [Dim. of PANT².]

pan·tile (păn′tīl′) *n.* A roofing tile with an S-shaped profile, laid so that the down curve of one tile overlaps the up curve of the next one. [PAN¹ + TILE.] —**pan′tiled′** *adj.*

pan·tof·fle also **pan·to·fle** (păn-tŏf′əl, -tō′fəl, -to͞o′fəl, păn′tə-fəl) *n.* A slipper. [ME *pantufle* < OFr. *pantoufle.*]

pan·to·graph (păn′tə-grăf′) *n.* **1.** An instrument for copying a plane figure to a desired scale, consisting of styluses mounted on four jointed rods in the form of a parallelogram with extended sides. **2.** A similarly jointed framework, such as an extensible telephone arm. [Gk. *panto-,* all (< *pās, pant-;* see PAN–) + –GRAPH.] —**pan′to·graph′ic** *adj.*

pan·to·mime (păn′tə-mīm′) *n.* **1.** Communication by means of gesture and facial expression. **2a.** The telling of a story without words, by means of bodily movements and facial expressions. **b.** A theatrical performance characterized by such storytelling. **c.** An ancient Roman theatrical performance in which one actor played all the parts by means of gesture and movement, accompanied by a narrative chorus. **d.** Such an actor. **3.** A British light musical comedy for children at Christmas time, usu. based on nursery tales and featuring audience participation. ❖ *v.* **-mimed, -mim·ing, -mimes** —*tr.* To represent or express by pantomime. —*intr.* To express oneself in pantomime. [Lat. *pantomīmus,* a pantomimic actor < Gk. *pantomīmos : panto-,* all (< *pās, pant-;* see PAN–) + *mīmos,* mime.] —**pan′to·mim′ic** (-mĭm′ĭk) *adj.* —**pan′to·mim′ist** (-mī′mĭst) *n.*

pan·to·then·ate (păn′tə-thĕn′āt′, păn-tŏth′ə-nāt′) *n.* A salt or ester of pantothenic acid. [PANTOTHEN(IC ACID) + -ATE².]

pan·to·then·ic acid (păn′tə-thĕn′ĭk) *n.* A yellow oily acid, C₉H₁₇NO₅, found widely in plant and animal tissues. [< Gk. *pantothen,* from all sides : *panto-,* all (< *pās, pant-;* see PAN–) + *-othen,* adv. suff.]

pan·trop·ic (păn-trŏp′ĭk, -trō′pĭk) *adj.* Having an affinity for or indiscriminately affecting many kinds of tissue.

pan·try (păn′trē) *n., pl.* **-tries 1.** A small room or closet, usu. off a kitchen, where food, tableware, and similar items are stored. **2.** A small room where cold foods are prepared. [ME *pantrie* < OFr. *paneterie,* bread closet < *panetier,* pantry servant < *pan,* bread < Lat. *pānis.* See **pā-** in App.]

pant·suit also **pants suit** (pănt′so͞ot′) *n.* A woman's suit having pants and a matching jacket. —**pant′suit′ed** *adj.*

pant·y·hose or **pant·y hose** (păn′tē-hōz′) *pl.n.* A woman's one-piece undergarment consisting of underpants and stretchable stockings.

pant·y·waist (păn′tē-wāst′) *n.* **1.** A child's undergarment consisting of a shirt and pants buttoned together at the waist. **2.** *Slang*

papaya
Carica papaya

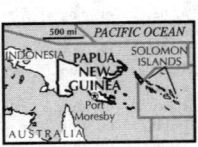

Papua New Guinea

A boy or man who is considered weak or effeminate. —**pant′y· waist′** *adj.*

pan·zer (păn′zər, pänt′sər) *n.* A German armored vehicle, such as a tank, esp. of the type used during World War II. ❖ *adj.* **1.** Of or equipped with armored vehicles. **2.** Of or relating to an armored division. [Ger., short for *Panzerdivision,* armored unit < *Panzer,* tank < MHGer. *panzier,* armor < OFr. *pancier,* belly armor < *pance,* belly. See PAUNCH.]

Pao·ting (bou′dĭng′) See **Baoding.**
Pao·tow (bou′tō′) See **Baotou.**

pap¹ (păp) *n.* **1.** *Midland US* A teat or nipple. **2.** Something resembling a nipple. [ME *pappe,* prob. < Lat. *papilla.* See PAPILLA.]

pap² (păp) *n.* **1.** Soft or semiliquid food, as for infants. **2.** Material lacking real value or substance. **3.** *Slang* Money and favors obtained as political patronage. [ME < OFr. *papa* < Lat., children's word for food.]

pa·pa (pä′pə, pə-pä′) also **pop·pa** (pä′pə) *n. Informal* Father. [Fr.]

pa·pa·cy (pä′pə-sē) *n., pl.* **-cies 1.** The office and jurisdiction of a pope. **2.** The period of time during which a pope is in office. **3.** A succession or line of popes: *the Medici papacy.* **4.** **Papacy** *Roman Catholic Church* The system of church government headed by the pope. [ME *papacie* < Med.Lat. *pāpātia* < LLat. *pāpa,* pope. See POPE.]

Pa·pa·go (päp′ə-gō′, pä′pə-) *n., pl.* **Papago** or **-gos 1.** A member of a Native American people inhabiting desert regions of southern Arizona and northwest Mexico. **2.** The Uto-Aztecan language of this people.

pa·pa·in (pə-pā′ĭn, -pī′ĭn) *n.* An enzyme capable of digesting protein, obtained from unripe papaya fruit and used as a meat tenderizer and in medicine as a digestive aid. [PAPA(YA) + –IN.]

pa·pal (pä′pəl) *adj.* **1.** Of, relating to, or issued by a pope: *a papal bull.* **2.** Of or relating to the Roman Catholic Church. [ME < OFr. < Med.Lat. *pāpālis* < LLat. *pāpa,* pope. See POPE.] —**pa′pal·ly** *adv.*

Papal States A group of territories in central Italy ruled by the popes from 754 until 1870; orig. given to the papacy by Pepin the Short.

Pap·an·dre·ou (päp′ən-drā′o͞o, pä′pän-drĕ′-), **Andreas George** 1919–96. Greek politician and premier (1981–89 and 1993–96).

Pa·pa·ni·co·laou test (pä′pə-nē′kə-lou′, păp′ə-nĭk′ə-lou′) *n.* A Pap smear.

pa·pa·raz·zo (pä′pə-rät′sō) *n., pl.* **-zi** (-sē) A freelance photographer who pursues celebrities to take candid pictures for sale to magazines and newspapers. [Ital. *Paparazzo,* a character in *La Dolce Vita,* a film by Federico Fellini.]

pa·pav·er·ine (pə-păv′ə-rēn′, -ər-ĭn) *n.* A nonaddictive opium derivative, C₂₀H₂₁NO₄, used medicinally to relieve spasms of smooth muscle. [Lat. *papāver,* poppy + –INE².]

pa·paw also **paw·paw** (pô′pô′) *n.* **1.** A deciduous tree (*Asimina triloba*) of the eastern and southeast United States having flowers with three sepals and three petals and fleshy edible fruit. **2.** The fruit of this tree. **3.** See **papaya.** [Ult. < Sp. and obsolete Port. *papaya,* papaya; see PAPAYA.]

pa·pa·ya (pə-pä′yə) *n.* **1.** An evergreen tropical American tree (*Carica papaya*) having a crown of palmately divided leaves and large edible yellow fruit. **2.** The fruit of this tree. [Sp. and Port., both of Cariban orig.]

Pa·pe·e·te (pä′pē-ā′tä, pə-pē′tē) The cap. of the overseas territory of French Polynesia, a port on the NW coast of Tahiti in the Society Is. of the S Pacific. Pop. 23,496.

Pa·pen (pä′pən), **Franz von** 1879–1969. German politician and diplomat who served as vice chancellor (1933–34).

pa·per (pä′pər) *n.* **1.** A material made of cellulose pulp, derived mainly from wood and rags, processed into flexible sheets or rolls by deposit from an aqueous suspension, and used for writing, printing, drawing, wrapping, and covering walls. **2.** A single sheet of this material. **3.** One or more sheets of paper bearing writing or printing, esp.: **a.** A formal written composition intended to be published or read aloud; a scholarly essay or treatise. **b.** A piece of written work for school; a report or theme. **c.** An official document, esp. one establishing the identity of the bearer. Often used in the plural. **4.** **papers** A collection of letters, diaries, and other writings, esp. by one person. **5.** Commercial documents that represent value and have transferable ownership; negotiable instruments considered as a group. **6.** A newspaper. **7.** Wallpaper. **8.** A wrapper made of paper, often with its contents. **9.** *Slang* **a.** A free pass to a theater. **b.** The audience admitted with free passes. ❖ *tr.v.* **-pered, -per·ing, -pers 1.** To cover, wrap, or line with paper. **2.** To cover with wallpaper. **3.** To supply with paper. **4.** *Slang* To issue free passes for (a theater, for example). ❖ *adj.* **1.** Made of paper. **2.** Resembling paper, as in flimsiness. **3.** Of or relating to clerical work. **4a.** Existing only in printed or written form. **b.** Planned but not realized; theoretical. —*phrasal verb:* **paper over 1.** To put or keep out of sight; conceal: *paper over a deficit.* **2.** To downplay or gloss over (differences, for example). —*idioms:* **in paper** With a paperback binding; as a paperback. **on paper 1.** In writing or print. **2.** In theory, as opposed to actual performance or fact. [ME < OFr. *papier* < Lat. *papȳrus,* papyrus plant, papyrus paper < Gk. *papūros.*] —**pa′per·er** *n.*

pa·per·back (pā′pər-băk′) n. A book having a flexible paper binding. —**pa′per·back′, pa′per·backed′** adj.

paper birch n. A North American birch tree (Betula papyrifera) having paperlike white bark.

pa·per·board (pā′pər-bôrd′, -bōrd′) n. Cardboard; pasteboard.

pa·per·bound (pā′pər-bound′) adj. Bound in paper; paperback.

pa·per·boy (pā′pər-boi′) n. A boy who sells or delivers newspapers.

paper clip also **pa·per·clip** (pā′pər-klĭp′) n. A wire or plastic clip for papers.

paper cutter n. A device for trimming paper, typically a ruled board with a long pivoted cutting knife attached to one side.

pa·per·girl (pā′pər-gûrl′) n. A girl who sells or delivers newspapers.

pa·per·hang·er (pā′pər-hăng′ər) n. **1.** One whose occupation is covering or decorating walls with wallpaper; a paperer. **2.** Slang One who passes bad checks. —**pa′per·hang′ing** n.

pa·per·knife (pā′pər-nīf′) n. A thin dull knife used for opening sealed envelopes and slitting uncut pages of books.

pa·per·less (pā′pər-lĭs) adj. Not requiring paper to record, convey, and store information: a paperless office.

pa·per·mak·ing (pā′pər-mā′kĭng) n. The process or craft of making paper. —**pa′per·mak′er** n.

paper money n. Currency in the form of government notes and bank notes.

paper mulberry n. An eastern Asian ornamental deciduous tree (Broussonetia papyrifera) having bark that can be processed into a paperlike fabric.

paper nautilus n. A cephalopod mollusk (Argonauta argo) with eight tentacles, the female of which inhabits a paper-thin shell that later acts as an egg case.

paper plant n. See **papyrus** 1.

paper tiger n. One only seemingly dangerous and powerful.

paper trail n. Informal Documentary evidence of one's actions: "Judges leave a paper trail, a track record of opinions that tell, literally, where they are coming from" (Ellen Goodman).

pa·per-train (pā′pər-trān′) tr.v. **-trained, -train·ing, -trains** To train (a pet) to urinate and defecate on paper.

paper wasp n. Any of various social wasps, such as the hornet, that build papery nests from chewed wood pulp.

pa·per·weight (pā′pər-wāt′) n. A small, heavy, often decorative object placed on loose papers to hold them down.

paper white n. A daffodil (Narcissus papyraceus) having star-shaped, pure white flowers

pa·per·work (pā′pər-wûrk′) n. Work involving the handling of reports, letters, and records.

pa·per·y (pā′pə-rē) adj. Resembling paper, as in thickness or texture. —**pa′per·i·ness** n.

pap·e·terie (păp′ĭ-trē, păp-trē′) n. A box used to hold stationery and other writing materials. [Fr. < OFr. papetier, papermaking < papier, paper. See PAPER.]

Pa·pia·men·tu (pä′pyä-mĕn′tōō) also **Pa·pia·men·to** (-tō) n. A creole of the Netherlands Antilles based on Portuguese and pidgin Spanish. [< Papiamentu papia, talk, prob. < Port. papaguear, papear, to chatter < papagaio, parrot.]

pa·pier-mâ·ché (pā′pər-mə-shā′, pă-pyä′-) n. A material, made from paper pulp or shreds mixed with glue or paste, that can be molded when wet and becomes hard and suitable for painting and varnishing when dry. [Fr. : papier, paper; see PAPER + mâché, p. part. of mâcher, to chew (< OFr. maschier < Lat. masticāre; see MASTICATE).] —**pa′pier-mâ·ché′** adj.

pa·pil·i·o·na·ceous (pə-pĭl′ē-ə-nā′shəs) adj. Having a bilaterally symmetrical corolla somewhat resembling a butterfly, characteristic of most plants of the pea family. [Lat. pāpiliō, pāpiliōn-, butterfly + -ACEOUS.]

pa·pil·la (pə-pĭl′ə) n., pl. **-pil·lae** (-pĭl′ē) **1.** A small nipplelike projection, such as a protuberance at the root of a hair. **2.** One of the small protuberances on the top of the tongue that contain taste buds. **3.** A pimple or pustule. **4.** Botany A minute projection on the surface of a stigma, petal, or leaf. [Lat., nipple, dim. of papula, swelling, pimple.] —**pap′il·lar′y** (păp′ĭ-lĕr′ē, pə-pĭl′ə-rē) adj. —**pap′il·late′** (păp′ĭ-lāt′, pə-pĭl′ĭt) adj.

pap·il·lo·ma (păp′ə-lō′mə) n., pl. **-mas** or **-ma·ta** (-mə-tə) A small benign epithelial tumor, such as a wart, consisting of an overgrowth of cells on a core of smooth connective tissue. —**pap′il·lo′ma·tous** adj.

pap·il·lon (păp′ə-lŏn′, pä′pē-yôn′) n. Any of a breed of small dog related to the spaniel, having a long silky coat and large ears shaped like the wings of a butterfly. [Fr. < OFr., butterfly < Lat. pāpiliō, pāpiliōn-.]

pap·il·lote (pä′pē-yōt′, păp′ē-) n. **1.** A paper frill used to decorate a bone end, as on a rack of lamb. **2.** An oiled paper or foil wrapper in which certain foods are baked. [Fr. < OFr., ornament for the hair < fem. of papillot, dim. of papillon, butterfly < Lat. pāpiliō, pāpiliōn-.]

pa·pist (pā′pĭst) n. Offensive Used as a disparaging term for a Roman Catholic. [NLat. pāpista < LLat. pāpa. See POPE.] —**pa′pist, pa·pis′tic** (pə-pĭs′tĭk) adj. —**pa′pist·ry** n.

pa·poose (pă-pōōs′, pə-) n. A Native American infant or very young child. [Narragansett papoòs, child.]

pa·po·va·vi·rus (pə-pō′və-vī′rəs) n., pl. **-rus·es** Any of a group of DNA-containing viruses that are associated with or cause papillomas or polyomas in animals. [PA(PILLOMA) + poly·oma, small form of the papovavirus (POLY– + –OMA) + VA(CU·OLATION) + VIRUS.]

Papp, Joseph (păp), 1921–91. Amer. producer and director best known for Hair (1967), A Chorus Line (1975), and the New York Shakespeare Festival.

pap·pa·dam (pä′pə-dəm) n. A very thin flatbread made with lentil flour, often crisped by deep-frying or grilling. [Tamil : Hindi pāpaṛ (< Prakrit pappaḍa- < Skt. parpaṭaḥ) + -am, n. suff.]

pap·pus (păp′əs) n., pl. **pap·pi** (păp′ī) A modified calyx, composed of scales, bristles, or fine hairs, in plants of the composite family. [Lat., old man, seed down < Gk. pappos.] —**pap′pose** (-ōs), **pap′pous** (-əs) adj.

pap·py[1] (păp′ē) adj. **-pi·er, -pi·est** Paplike; mushy.

pap·py[2] (păp′ē) n., pl. **-pies** Informal Father. [Dim. of PAPA.]

pa·pri·ka (pă-prē′kə, pä-, păp′rĭ-kə) n. **1.** A mild powdered seasoning made from sweet red peppers. **2.** A dark to deep or vivid reddish orange. [Hung. < Serbian < papar, ground pepper < Slav. *pipŭrŭ < Lat. piper. See PEPPER.]

Pap smear (păp) n. A test for cancer, esp. of the female genital tract, in which a smear of exfoliated cells is specially stained and examined under a microscope for pathological changes. [After George Papanicolaou (1883–1962), American anatomist.]

Pap·u·a (păp′yōō-ə, pä′pōō-ä′), **Gulf of** A large inlet of the Coral Sea on the SE coast of New Guinea.

Pap·u·an (păp′yōō-ən) adj. Of or relating to the peoples, languages, or cultures of Papua New Guinea or New Guinea. ❖ n. **1.** A native or inhabitant of Papua New Guinea or New Guinea. **2.** A member of any of the indigenous peoples of New Guinea and neighboring islands. **3.** Any of the indigenous languages of New Guinea, New Britain, and the Solomon Islands.

Papua New Guinea A country of the SW Pacific comprising the E half of New Guinea, the Bismarck Archipelago, the W Solomons, and adjacent islands; became fully independent from Australia in 1975. Cap. Port Moresby. Pop. 3,997,000. —**Papua New Guinean** adj. & n.

pap·ule (păp′yōōl) also **pap·u·la** (-yə-lə) n., pl. **-ules** also **-u·lae** (-yə-lē′) A small, solid, usu. inflammatory elevation of the skin that does not contain pus. [Lat. papula.] —**pap′u·lar** (-yə-lər) adj.

pap·y·rol·o·gy (păp′ə-rŏl′ə-jē) n. The study of papyrus manuscripts. —**pap′y·ro·log′ic** (păp′ər-ə-lŏj′ĭk, pə-pī′rə-), **pap′y·ro·log′i·cal** (-ĭ-kəl) adj.

pa·py·rus (pə-pī′rəs) n., pl. **-rus·es** or **-ri** (-rī′) **1.** A tall aquatic Mediterranean sedge (Cyperus papyrus) having numerous drooping rays grouped in umbels. **2a.** A material on which to write made from the pith or the stems of this sedge, used esp. by the ancient Egyptians, Greeks, and Romans. **b.** A document written on this material. [ME papirus < Lat. papȳrus < Gk. papūros.]

par (pär) n. **1.** An amount or level considered to be average; a standard. **2.** An equality of status, level, or value; equal footing. **3.** The established value of a monetary unit expressed in terms of a monetary unit of another country using the same metal standard. **4.** The face value of a stock, bond, or other negotiable instrument. **5.** Sports The number of golf strokes considered necessary to complete a hole or course in expert play. ❖ tr.v. **parred, par·ring, pars** Sports To score par on (a hole or course) in golf. ❖ adj. **1.** Equal to the standard; normal. **2.** Of or relating to monetary face value. —**idiom: par for the course** Usual; typical. [< Lat. pār, equal, that which is equal. See perə– in App.]

par. abbr. **1.** paragraph **2.** parallel **3.** parenthesis **4.** parish

Par. abbr. Paraguay

para–[1] or **par–** pref. **1.** Beside; near; alongside: parathyroid. **2.** Beyond: paranormal. **3.** Incorrect; abnormal: paresthesia. **4.** Similar to; resembling: paratyphoid fever. **5.** Subsidiary; assistant: paraprofessional. **6.** Isomeric; polymeric: paraldehyde. **7.** A diatomic molecule in which the nuclei have opposite spin directions: parahydrogen. **8.** Of or relating to an isomer of a benzene ring in which the two carbon atoms with attached groups are separated by two unsubstituted carbon atoms: para-aminobenzoic acid. [Gk. < para, beside. See per[1] in App.]

para–[2] pref. Parachute; parachutist: paratroops. [< PARACHUTE.]

Pa·rá (pə-rä′) See **Belém**.

par·a·a·mi·no·ben·zo·ic acid (păr′ə-ə-mē′nō-bĕn-zō′ĭk, -äm′ə-) n. PABA.

par·a·bi·o·sis (păr′ə-bī-ō′sĭs) n., pl. **-ses** (-sēz) **1.** The union of anatomical parts of two organisms, usu. involving exchange of blood, as in Siamese twins or certain transplant operations. **2.** A temporary suspension of conductivity or excitability in a nerve. —**par′a·bi·ot′ic** (-ŏt′ĭk) adj.

par·a·blast (păr′ə-blăst′) n. The nutritive yolk of a meroblastic egg. —**par′a·blas′tic** adj.

par·a·ble (păr′ə-bəl) n. A simple story that illustrates a moral or religious lesson. [ME < OFr. < LLat. parabola < Gk. parabolē < paraballein, to compare : para-, beside; see PARA–[1] + ballein, to throw; see gʷelə– in App.]

pa·rab·o·la (pə-răb′ə-lə) n. A plane curve formed by the intersection of a right circular cone and a plane parallel to an element

papyrus
Cyperus papyrus

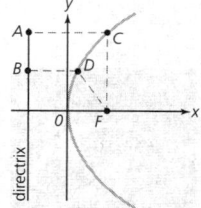

parabola
Any point on a parabola is the same distance from the directrix as it is from the focus. AC equals CF and BD equals DF.

ă pat	oi boy	
ā pay	ou out	
âr care	ŏŏ took	
ä father	ōō boot	
ĕ pet	ŭ cut	
ē be	ûr urge	
ĭ pit	th thin	
ī pie	th this	
îr pier	hw which	
ŏ pot	zh vision	
ō toe	ə about,	
ô paw		item

Stress marks:
′ (primary);
′ (secondary), as in
lexicon (lĕk′sĭ-kŏn′)

of the cone or by the locus of points equidistant from a fixed line and a fixed point not on the line. [NLat. < Gk. *parabolē*, comparison, application, parabola (< the relationship between the line joining the vertices of a conic and the line through its focus and parallel to its directrix) < *paraballein*, to compare. See PARABLE.]

par•a•bol•ic (păr′ə-bŏl′ĭk) also **par•a•bol•i•cal** (-ĭ-kəl) *adj.* **1.** Of or similar to a parable. **2.** Of or having the form of a parabola or paraboloid. [Ult. < Gk. *parabolē*, comparison. See PARABLE. Sense 2 < PARABOLA.] **—par′a•bol′i•cal•ly** *adv.*

pa•rab•o•loid (pə-răb′ə-loid′) *n.* A surface having parabolic sections parallel to a coordinate axis and elliptic sections perpendicular to that axis. **—pa•rab′o•loi′dal** (-loid′l) *adj.*

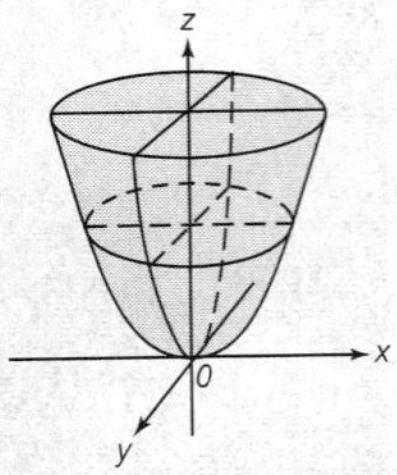

paraboloid
The equation for a circular paraboloid is:
$\frac{x^2}{a^2}+\frac{y^2}{b^2}=z$

Par•a•cel•sus (păr′ə-sĕl′səs) Orig. Philippus Aureolus Theophrastus Bombast von Hohenheim. 1493–1541. German-Swiss alchemist and physician who held that illness was caused by external agents rather than imbalances within the body.

par•a•chute (păr′ə-sho͞ot′) *n.* **1.** An apparatus used to retard free fall from an aircraft, consisting of a usu. hemispherical canopy attached to a harness. **2.** Any of various similar unpowered devices used to retard free-speeding or free-falling motion. ❖ *v.* **-chut•ed, -chut•ing, -chutes** *—tr.* To drop by means of a parachute. *—intr.* To descend by means of a parachute. [Fr. : *para(sol)*, parasol; see PARASOL + *chute*, fall; see CHUTE.] **—par′a•chut′ic** *adj.* **—par′a•chut′ist, par′a•chut′er** *n.*

parachute spinnaker *n.* An oversize spinnaker used on racing yachts.

Par•a•clete (păr′ə-klēt′) *n.* The Holy Spirit. [ME *Paraclit* < OFr. *Paraclet* < Lat. *Paraclētus* < Gk. *Paraklētos* < *parakalein*, to invoke : *para-*, to the side of; see PARA–[1] + *kalein*, *klē-*, to call; see **kelə-** in App.]

pa•rade (pə-rād′) *n.* **1a.** An organized public procession on a festive or ceremonial occasion. **b.** The participants in such a procession. **2a.** A place where troops are reviewed. **b.** A ceremonial review of troops. **3.** A line or extended group of moving persons or things. **4.** An extended, usu. showy succession. **5.** An ostentatious show; an exhibition. **6.** A public square or promenade. ❖ *v.* **-rad•ed, -rad•ing, -rades** *—intr.* **1.** To take part in a parade; march in a public procession. **2.** To assemble for a military parade. **3.** To stroll in public, esp. so as to be seen; promenade. **4.** To behave so as to attract attention; show off. *—tr.* **1.** To cause to take part in a parade. **2.** To assemble (troops) for a parade. **3.** To march or walk through or around. **4.** To exhibit ostentatiously; flaunt. [Prob. Fr., action of stopping a horse < OSpan., parada < VLat. **parāta* < fem. p. part. of Lat. *parāre*, to prepare.] **—pa•rad′er** *n.*

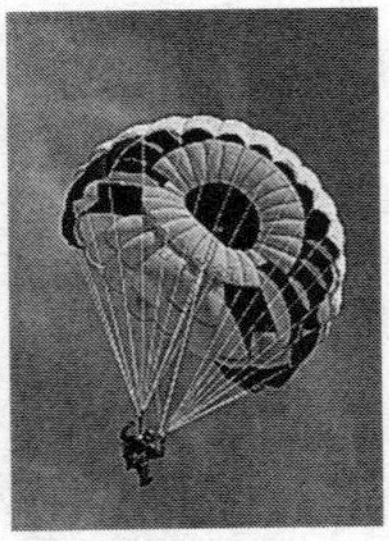

parachute

par•a•di•chlo•ro•ben•zene (păr′ə-dī-klôr′ə-bĕn′zēn′, -bĕn-zēn′, -klōr′-) *n.* A white crystalline compound, $C_6H_4Cl_2$, used as a germicide and an insecticide.

par•a•did•dle (păr′ə-dĭd′l) *n.* A pattern of drumbeats characterized by four basic beats and alternating left-handed and right-handed strokes on the successive primary beats. [Prob. imit.]

par•a•digm (păr′ə-dīm′, -dĭm′) *n.* **1.** One that serves as pattern or model. **2.** A set or list of all the inflectional forms of a word or of one of its grammatical categories. **3.** A set of assumptions, concepts, values, and practices that constitutes a way of viewing reality for the community that shares them, esp. in an intellectual discipline. [ME, example < LLat. *paradīgma* < Gk. *paradeigma* < *paradeiknunai*, to compare : *para-*, alongside; see PARA–[1] + *deiknunai*, to show; see **deik-** in App.]

par•a•dig•mat•ic (păr′ə-dĭg-măt′ĭk) *adj.* **1.** Of or relating to a paradigm. **2.** *Linguistics* Of or relating to the set of substitutional or oppositional relationships a linguistic unit has with other units, such as the relationship between (n) in *not* and other sounds that could be substituted for it in the same context, like (t) and (p). [Fr. *paradigmatique* < Gk. *paradeigmatikos*, serving as a model < *paradeigma, paradeigmat-*, example. See PARADIGM.]

par•a•dise (păr′ə-dīs′, -dīz′) *n.* **1.** often **Paradise** The Garden of Eden. **2.** *Christianity* **a.** The abode of the righteous after death; heaven. **b.** An intermediate resting place for righteous souls awaiting the Resurrection. **3.** A place of ideal beauty or loveliness. **4.** A state of delight. [ME *paradis* < OFr. < LLat. *paradīsus* < Gk. *paradeisos*, garden, enclosed park, paradise < Avestan *pairidaēza-*, enclosure, park : *pairi-*, around; see **per**[1] in App. + *daēza-*, wall; see **dheigh-** in App.] **—par′a•di•si′a•cal** (-dĭ-sī′ə-kəl, -zī′-), **par′a•di•si′ac** (-ăk), **par′a•di•sa′i•cal** (-dĭ-sā′ĭ-kəl, -zā′-), **par′a•di•sa′ic** (-ĭk), **par′a•dis′al** (-dī′səl, -zəl) *adj.*

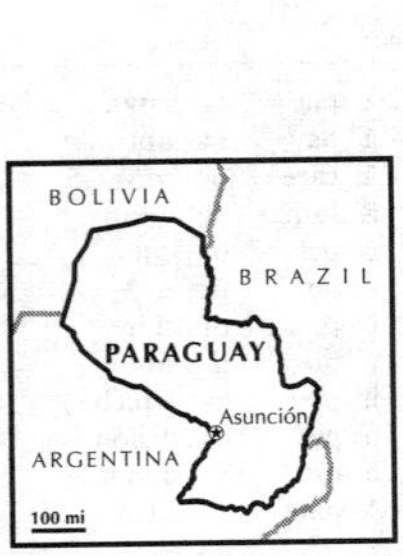

Paraguay

par•a•dor (păr′ə-dôr, pä′rä-*thôr*′, -dôr′) *n., pl.* **-dors** or **-dor•es** (-*thō*′rĕs, -dō′-) A government-run country hotel in Spain or Latin America. [Sp. < *parar*, to stop < Lat. *parāre*, to prepare. See PARADE.]

par•a•dox (păr′ə-dŏks′) *n.* **1.** A seemingly contradictory statement that may nonetheless be true. **2.** One exhibiting inexplicable or contradictory aspects. **3.** An assertion that is essentially self-contradictory, though based on a valid deduction from acceptable premises. **4.** A statement contrary to received opinion. [Lat. *paradoxum* < Gk. *paradoxon* < neut. sing. of *paradoxos*, conflicting with expectation : *para-*, beyond; see PARA–[1] + *doxa*, opinion (< *dokein*, to think; see **dek-** in App.).] **—par′a•dox′i•cal** *adj.* **—par′a•dox′i•cal•ly** *adv.* **—par′a•dox′i•cal•ness** *n.*

paradoxical sleep *n.* See **REM sleep.**

par•a•drop (păr′ə-drŏp′) *n.* Delivery of supplies to a place by parachute. **—par′a•drop′** *v.*

par•aes•the•sia (păr′ĭs-thē′zhə) *n.* Variant of **paresthesia.**

par•af•fin (păr′ə-fĭn) *n.* **1.** A waxy solid hydrocarbon mixture used to make candles, wax paper, lubricants, and sealing materials. **2.** *Chemistry* A member of the alkane series. **3.** *Chiefly British* Kerosene. ❖ *tr.v.* **-fined, -fin•ing, -fins** To saturate, impregnate, or coat with paraffin. [Ger. : Lat. *parum*, little + Lat. *affīnis*, associated with (< its lack of affinity with other materials); see AFFINED.] **—par′af•fin′ic** *adj.*

paraffin series *n.* See **alkane series.**

paraffin wax *n.* See **paraffin** 1.

par•a•foil (păr′ə-foil′) *n.* A nonrigid, parachutelike, usu. nylon airfoil of ribbed or cellular construction, used esp. in kites and paragliders. [PARA(CHUTE) + (AIR)FOIL.]

par•a•for•mal•de•hyde (păr′ə-fôr-măl′də-hīd′) *n.* A solid polymer of formaldehyde, $(HCHO)_n$, where *n* is at least 6, used as a disinfectant, fumigant, and fungicide.

par•a•gen•e•sis (păr′ə-jĕn′ĭ-sĭs) also **par•a•ge•ne•sia** (-jə-nē′zhə, -zhē-ə) *n.* The order of formation of associated minerals in a rock or vein. **—par′a•ge•net′ic** (-jə-nĕt′ĭk) *adj.*

par•a•glid•er (păr′ə-glī′dər) *n.* **1.** A recreational aircraft consisting of a large parafoil equipped with a harness from which a rider hangs while gliding from a height. **2.** One who engages in paragliding. [PARA(FOIL) + GLIDER.]

par•a•glid•ing (păr′ə-glī′dĭng) *n.* The sport or activity of flying by means of a paraglider. [PARA(FOIL) + *gliding*, gerund of GLIDE.]

par•a•gon (păr′ə-gŏn′, -gən) *n.* **1.** A model of excellence or perfection of a kind; a peerless example. **2a.** An unflawed diamond weighing at least 100 carats. **b.** A very large spherical pearl. **3.** *Printing* A type size of 20 points. ❖ *tr.v.* **-goned, -gon•ing, -gons 1.** To compare; parallel. **2.** To equal; match. [Obsolete Fr. < OFr. < OItal. *paragone* < *paragonare*, to test on a touchstone, perh. < Gk. *parakonān*, to sharpen : *para-*, alongside; see PARA–[1] + *akonē*, whetstone; see **ak-** in App.]

par•a•graph (păr′ə-grăf′) *n.* **1.** A division of written or printed matter that begins on a new, usu. indented line, has one or more sentences, and typically deals with one topic or quotes one speaker's continuous words. **2.** A mark (¶) used to indicate where a new paragraph should begin or serve as a reference mark. **3.** A brief article, notice, or announcement, as in a newspaper. ❖ *tr.v.* **-graphed, -graph•ing, -graphs** To divide or arrange into paragraphs. [ME *paragraf* < OFr. *paragrafe* < Med.Lat. *paragraphus* < Gk. *paragraphos*, line showing a break in sense or a change of speakers in a dialogue < *paragraphein*, to write beside : *para-*, beside; see PARA–[1] + *graphein*, to write; see **gerbh-** in App.] **—par′a•graph′ic, par′a•graph′i•cal** *adj.*

Par•a•guay (păr′ə-gwī′, -gwā′) A country of S-central South America; achieved independence from Spain in 1811. Cap. Asunción. Pop. 4,700,000. **—Par′a•guay′an** *adj. & n.*

Paraguay River A river rising in SW Brazil and flowing c. 2,574 km (1,600 mi) to the Paraná R. in SW Paraguay.

Paraguay tea *n.* See **maté** 2.

Pa•ra•í•ba (păr′ə-ē′bə, pä′rä-ē′bä) also **Paraíba do Sul** (do͞o so͞ol′) A river, c. 1,046 km (650 mi), of SE Brazil emptying into the Atlantic Ocean.

par•a•in•flu•en•za (păr′ə-ĭn′flo͞o-ĕn′zə) *adj.* Of, relating to, or being any of a group of paramyxoviruses that are similar to the influenza viruses and cause respiratory infections.

par•a•jour•nal•ism (păr′ə-jûr′nə-lĭz′əm) *n.* Subjective journalism that uses some of the techniques or license of fiction.

par•a•keet (păr′ə-kēt′) *n.* Any of various small slender parrots, usu. having long tapering tails and often kept as pets. [Sp. *periquito*, prob. dim. of *Perico*, dim. of *Pedro*, Peter.]

par•al•de•hyde (pə-răl′də-hīd′) *n.* A colorless liquid polymer, $C_6H_{12}O_3$, of acetaldehyde, used as a solvent and a sedative.

par•a•le•gal (păr′ə-lē′gəl) *adj.* Of, relating to, or being a person with specialized training who assists an attorney. **—par′a•le′gal** *n.*

par•al•lax (păr′ə-lăks′) *n.* An apparent change in the direction of an object, caused by a change in observational position that provides a new line of sight. [Fr. *parallaxe* < Gk. *parallaxis* < *parallassein*, to change : *para-*, among; see PARA–[1] + *allassein*, to exchange (< *allos*, other; see **al-** in App.).] **—par′al•lac′tic** (-lăk′tĭk) *adj.*

par•al•lel (păr′ə-lĕl′) *adj.* **1.** Being an equal distance apart everywhere. **2.** *Mathematics* Of, relating to, or being lines, curves, or surfaces that are everywhere equidistantly apart, such as nonintersecting coplanar lines or nonintersecting planes. **3a.** Having comparable parts, analogous aspects, or readily recognized similarities. See Usage Note at **unique. b.** Having the same tendency or direction. **4.** *Grammar* Having identical or equivalent syntactic constructions in corresponding clauses or phrases. **5.** *Music* **a.** Moving in the same direction at a fixed interval: *parallel fifths.* **b.** Having the same tonic. Used of scales and keys. **6.** *Electronics* Of or being a circuit or part of a circuit connected in parallel. **7.** *Computer Science* **a.** Of or relating to the simultaneous transmission of all the bits of a byte over separate wires: *a parallel port.* **b.** Of or relating to the simultaneous performance of multiple operations: *parallel processing.* ❖ *adv.* In a parallel relationship or manner. ❖ *n.* **1.** *Mathematics* One of a set of parallel geometric figures, such as lines or planes. **2a.** One that closely resembles or is analogous to another. **b.** A comparison indicating likeness; an analogy. **3.** The condition of being parallel; near similarity or exact agreement in particulars; parallelism. **4.** Any of the imaginary lines representing degrees of latitude that encircle the earth parallel to the plane of the equator. **5.** *Printing* A sign indicating material referred to in a note or reference. **6.** *Electronics* An arrangement of components in a circuit that splits the current into two or more paths. ❖ *tr.v.* **-leled, -lel•ing, -lels** also **-lelled, -lel•ling, -lels 1.** To make or place parallel to something else. **2.** To be or extend parallel to. **3.** To be similar or analogous to. **4.** To be or provide an equal for; match. **5.** To show to be analogous; compare or liken. [Lat. *parallēlus* < Gk. *parallēlos* : *para-*, beside; see PARA–¹ + *allēlōn*, of one another (< *allos*, other; see **al-** in App.).]

parallel bars *pl.n.* An apparatus for gymnastic exercises consisting of two horizontal bars set parallel to each other in adjustable upright supports and used mainly for swinging maneuvers.

parallel cousin *n.* A cousin who is the child of one's mother's sister or one's father's brother.

par•al•lel•e•pi•ped (păr′ə-lĕl′ə-pī′pĭd, -pĭp′ĭd) *n.* A solid with six faces, each a parallelogram and each being parallel to the opposite face. [Gk. *parallēlepipedon* : *parallēlos*, parallel; see PARALLEL + *epipedon*, plane surface < neut. sing. of *epipedos*, level (*epi-*, epi- + *pedon*, ground; see **ped-** in App.).]

par•al•lel•ism (păr′ə-lĕ-lĭz′əm) *n.* **1.** The quality or condition of being parallel. **2.** Likeness, correspondence, or similarity in aspect, course, or tendency. **3.** *Grammar* The use of identical syntactic constructions in corresponding phrases or clauses. **4.** *Philosophy* The doctrine that to every mental change there corresponds a concomitant but causally unconnected physical alteration.

par•al•lel•o•gram (păr′ə-lĕl′ə-grăm′) *n.* A four-sided plane figure with opposite sides parallel. [LLat. *parallēlogrammum* < Gk. *parallēlogrammon* < neut. sing. of *parallēlogrammos*, bounded by parallel lines : *parallēlos*, parallel; see PARALLEL + *grammē*, line; see **gerbh-** in App.]

pa•ral•o•gism (pə-răl′ə-jĭz′əm) *n.* A fallacious or illogical argument or conclusion. [LLat. *paralogismus* < Gk. *paralogismos* < *paralogos*, unreasonable : *para-*, beyond; see PARA–¹ + *logos*, reason; see **leg-** in App.] **—pa•ral′o•gist** *n.* **—pa•ral′o•gis′tic** *adj.*

par•a•lyse (păr′ə-līz′) *v. Chiefly British* Variant of **paralyze.**

pa•ral•y•sis (pə-răl′ĭ-sĭs) *n., pl.* **-ses** (-sēz′) **1a.** Loss or impairment of the ability to move a body part, usu. as a result of damage to its nerve supply. **b.** Loss of sensation over a region of the body. **2.** Inability to move or function; total stoppage or severe impairment of activity. [Lat. < Gk. *paralusis* < *paraluein*, to disable, loosen : *para-*, on one side; see PARA–¹ + *luein*, to release; see **leu-** in App.]

paralysis ag•i•tans (ăj′ĭ-tănz′) *n.* See **Parkinson's disease.** [NLat. *paralysis agitāns* : Lat. *paralysis*, palsy + Lat. *agitāns*, pr. part. of *agitāre*, to shake.]

par•a•lyt•ic (păr′ə-lĭt′ĭk) *adj.* **1.** Of or relating to paralysis. **2.** Characteristic of or resembling paralysis. **3.** Affected with paralysis; paralyzed. ❖ *n.* One affected with paralysis. **—par′a•lyt′i•cal•ly** *adv.*

par•a•lyze (păr′ə-līz′) *tr.v.* **-lyzed, -lyz•ing, -lyz•es 1.** To affect with paralysis; make paralytic. **2.** To make unable to move or act. **3.** To impair the progress or functioning of; make inoperative or powerless. [Fr. *paralyser* < *paralysie*, paralysis < OFr. < Lat. *paralysis.* See PARALYSIS.] **—par′a•ly•za′tion** (-lĭ-zā′shən) *n.* **—par′a•lyz′er** *n.* **—par′a•lyz′ing•ly** *adv.*

par•a•mag•net (păr′ə-măg′nĭt) *n.* A paramagnetic substance.

par•a•mag•net•ic (păr′ə-măg-nĕt′ĭk) *adj.* Relating to or being a substance in which an induced magnetic field is parallel and proportional to the magnetizing field but is much weaker than in ferromagnetic materials. **—par′a•mag•net′i•cal•ly** *adv.* **—par′a•mag′net•ism** (-măg′nĭ-tĭz′əm) *n.*

Par•a•mar•i•bo (păr′ə-măr′ə-bō′) The cap. of Suriname, on the Suriname R.; under Dutch rule after 1815. Pop. 67,905.

par•a•mat•ta or **par•ra•mat•ta** (păr′ə-măt′ə) *n.* A fine, lightweight silk and wool or cotton and wool dress fabric. [After PARRAMATTA.]

par•a•me•ci•um (păr′ə-mē′sē-əm, -shē-əm) *n., pl.* **-ci•a** (-sē-ə, -shē-ə) or **-ci•ums** Any of various freshwater ciliate protozoans of the genus *Paramecium*, usu. oval and having an oral groove for feeding. [NLat. *Paramēcium*, genus name < Gk. *paramēkēs*, oblong in shape : *para-*, alongside; see PARA–¹ + *mēkos*, length.]

par•a•med•ic (păr′ə-mĕd′ĭk) *n.* A person who is trained to give emergency medical treatment or assist medical professionals. **—par′a•med′i•cal** (-ĭ-kəl) *adj.*

par•a•ment (păr′ə-mənt) *n., pl.* **-ments** or **-men•ta** (-mĕn′tə) An ecclesiastical vestment or hanging. [< ME *paramentes*, adornments < OFr. *parement*, ornament < Med.Lat. *parāmentum* < *parāre*, to decorate < Lat., to ready. See PARE.]

pa•ram•e•ter (pə-răm′ĭ-tər) *n.* **1.** *Mathematics* **a.** A constant in an equation that varies in other equations of the same general form, esp. in the equation of a curve or surface that can be varied to represent a family of curves or surfaces. **b.** One of a set of independent variables that express the coordinates of a point. **2a.** One of a set of measurable factors, such as temperature, that define a system and determine its behavior and are varied in an experiment. **b.** A factor that restricts what is possible or what results. **c.** A factor that determines a range of variations; a boundary. **3.** *Statistics* A quantity, such as a mean, that is calculated from data and describes a population. **4.** A distinguishing characteristic or feature. [NLat. *parametrum*, a line through the focus and parallel to the directrix of a conic : Gk. *para-*, beside; see PARA–¹ + Gk. *metron*, measure; see –METER.] **—par′a•met′ric** (păr′ə-mĕt′rĭk), **par′a•met′ri•cal** *adj.* **—par′a•met′ri•cal•ly** *adv.*

pa•ram•e•ter•ize (pə-răm′ĭ-tə-rīz′) also **pa•ram•e•trize** (-ĭ-trīz′) *tr.v.* **-ized, -iz•ing, -iz•es** also **-trized, -triz•ing, -triz•es** To describe in terms of parameters. **—pa•ram′e•ter•i•za′tion** (-tə-rĭ-zā′shən) *n.*

par•a•mil•i•tar•y (păr′ə-mĭl′ĭ-tĕr′ē) *adj.* Of, relating to, or being a group of civilians organized in a military fashion, esp. to operate in place of or assist regular army troops. ❖ *n., pl.* **-ies** A member of a paramilitary force.

par•am•ne•sia (păr′ăm-nē′zhə) *n.* **1.** A distortion of memory in which fantasy and objective experience are confused. **2.** An inability to recall the meanings of common words.

pa•ra•mo (pä′rə-mō′, păr′ə-) *n., pl.* **-mos** A treeless alpine plateau of the Andes and tropical South America. [Am.Sp. *páramo* < Sp., wasteland.]

par•a•morph (păr′ə-môrf′) *n.* A mineral crystal formed or affected by paramorphism.

par•a•mor•phine (păr′ə-môr′fēn′) *n.* See **thebaine.**

par•a•mor•phism (păr′ə-môr′fĭz′əm) *n.* Structural alteration of a mineral without change of chemical composition. **—par′a•mor′phic** (-fĭk), **par′a•mor′phous** (-fəs) *adj.*

par•a•mount (păr′ə-mount′) *adj.* **1.** Of chief concern or importance. **2.** Supreme in rank, power, or authority. ❖ *n.* One that has the highest rank, power, or authority. [AN *paramont*, above : *par*, by (< Lat. *per*; see **per**¹ in App.) + *amont*, above, upward; see AMOUNT.] **—par′a•mount′cy** *n.* **—par′a•mount′ly** *adv.*

par•a•mour (păr′ə-mo͝or′) *n.* A lover, esp. one in an adulterous relationship. [ME < *par amour*, by way of love, passionately < AN : *par*, by (< Lat. *per*; see **per**¹ in App.) + *amour*, love (< Lat. *amor* < *amāre*, to love).]

par•a•myx•o•vi•rus (păr′ə-mĭk′sə-vī′rəs) *n., pl.* **-rus•es** Any of a group of viruses that contain RNA, are related to the myxoviruses, and include the parainfluenza viruses.

Pa•ra•ná (păr′ə-nä′, pä′rä-) A city of NE Argentina on the Paraná R. N of Rosario. Pop. 206,848.

Pa•ra•na•í•ba (păr′ə-nə-ē′bə, pä′rä-nä-ē′bä) A river of S-central Brazil flowing c. 805 km (500 mi) to the Paraná R.

Paraná River A river of central South America rising in E-central Brazil and flowing c. 2,896 km (1,800 mi) to the Río de la Plata estuary in E Argentina.

pa•rang (pä′răng′) *n.* A short heavy straight-edged knife used in Malaysia and Indonesia as a tool and weapon. [Malay.]

par•a•noi•a (păr′ə-noi′ə) *n.* **1.** A psychotic disorder characterized by delusions of persecution with or without grandeur, often strenuously defended with apparent logic and reason. **2.** Extreme irrational distrust of others. [Gk., madness < *paranoos*, demented : *para-*, beyond; see PARA–¹ + *nous, noos*, mind.]

par•a•noi•ac (păr′ə-noi′ăk′, -noi′ĭk) *n.* A paranoid. ❖ *adj.* Of, relating to, or resembling paranoia.

par•a•noid (păr′ə-noid′) *adj.* **1.** Relating to, characteristic of, or affected with paranoia. **2.** Exhibiting or characterized by extreme and irrational fear or distrust of others. ❖ *n.* One affected with paranoia.

par•a•nor•mal (păr′ə-nôr′məl) *adj.* Beyond the range of normal experience or scientific explanation. **—par′a•nor•mal′i•ty** (-nôr-măl′ĭ-tē) *n.* **—par′a•nor′mal•ly** *adv.*

par•a•pa•re•sis (păr′ə-pə-rē′sĭs, -păr′ĭ-sĭs) *n., pl.* **-ses** (-sēz) Partial paralysis of the lower limbs.

par•a•pet (păr′ə-pĭt, -pĕt′) *n.* **1.** A low protective wall or railing along the edge of a raised structure such as a roof. **2.** An earthen or stone embankment protecting soldiers from enemy fire. [Fr. < Ital. *parapetto* : *parare*, to shield; see PARASOL + *petto*, chest (< Lat. *pectus*).]

par•aph (păr′əf, pə-ră′) *n.* A flourish made after or below a signature, originally to prevent forgery. [Fr. *paraphe* < OFr. *paraffe*, abbreviated signature < Med.Lat. *paraphus*, paragraph sign, short for *paragraphus.* See PARAGRAPH.]

par•a•pher•na•lia (păr′ə-fər-nāl′yə, -fə-nāl′yə) *pl.n.* (*used with a sing. or pl. verb*) **1.** Personal belongings. **2.** The articles used in a particular activity; equipment. **3.** A married woman's personal property exclusive of her dowry, according to common law. [Med.Lat. *paraphernālia*, neut. pl. of *paraphernālis*, pertaining to the *parapherna*, a married woman's property exclusive of her dowry < LLat. < Gk. : *para-*, beyond; see PARA–¹ + *phernē*, dowry; see **bher-**¹ in App.]

par•a•phil•i•a (păr′ə-fĭl′ē-ə, -fēl′yə) *n.* Any of a group of psychosexual disorders characterized by sexual fantasies, feelings, or activities involving an object, a nonconsenting partner such as a child, or pain or humiliation. **—par′a•phil′i•ac** *n.*

par•a•phrase (păr′ə-frāz′) *n.* **1.** A restatement of a text or passage in another form or other words. **2.** The restatement of texts in other words as a studying or teaching device. ❖ *v.* **-phrased, -phras•ing, -phras•es** *—tr.* To restate in a paraphrase. *—intr.*

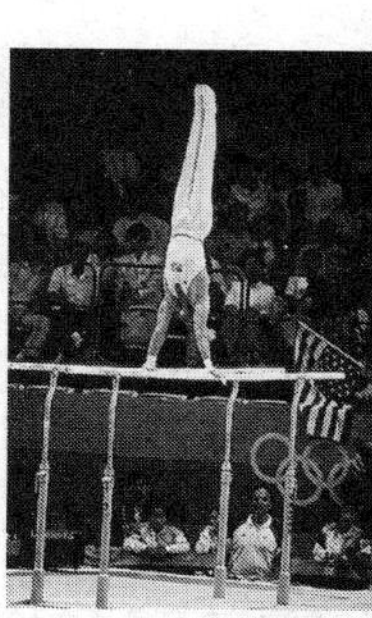

parallel bars

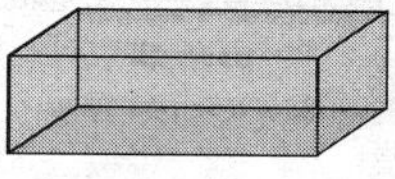

parallelipiped
rectangular parallelipiped

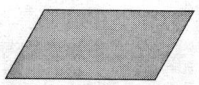

parallelogram

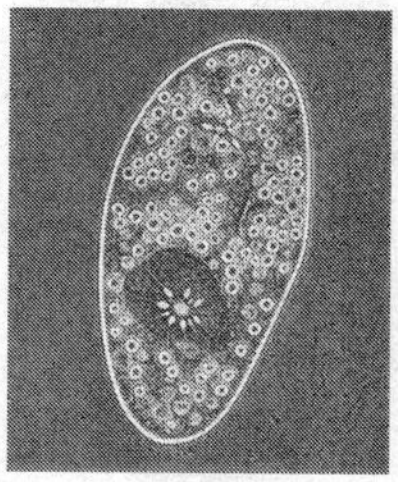

paramecium
photomicrograph

ă	pat	oi	boy
ā	pay	ou	out
âr	care	o͝o	took
ä	father	o͞o	boot
ĕ	pet	ŭ	cut
ē	be	ûr	urge
ĭ	pit	th	thin
ī	pie	*th*	this
îr	pier	hw	which
ŏ	pot	zh	vision
ō	toe	ə	about, item
ô	paw		

Stress marks:
′ (primary);
′ (secondary), as in
lexicon (lĕk′sĭ-kŏn′)

To compose a paraphrase. [Fr. < Lat. *paraphrasis* < Gk. < *paraphrazein*, to paraphrase : *para-*, alongside; see PARA–[1] + *phrazein*, to show, explain.] **—par′a•phras′a•ble** *adj.* **—par′a•phras′er** *n.*

par•a•phras•tic (păr′ə-frăs′tĭk) or **par•a•phras•ti•cal** (-tĭ-kəl) *adj.* Of, relating to, or having the nature of paraphrase. [Med.Lat. *paraphrasticus* < Gk. *paraphrastikos* < *paraphrazein*, to paraphrase. See PARAPHRASE.]

pa•raph•y•sis (pə-răf′ĭ-sĭs) *n., pl.* **-ses** (-sēz′) One of the erect sterile filaments often occurring among the reproductive organs of certain fungi, algae, and mosses. [NLat. : PARA–[1] + Gk. *phusis*, nature, growth; see PHYSIC.]

par•a•ple•gi•a (păr′ə-plē′jē-ə, -jə) *n.* Complete paralysis of the lower half of the body, usu. caused by damage to the spinal cord. [Gk. dialectal *paraplēgiē*, hemiplegia < *paraplēssesthai*, to be paralyzed < *paraplēssein*, to strike on one side : *para-*, beside; see PARA–[1] + *plēssein*, to strike; see **plāk-** in App.] **—par′a•ple′gic** (-plē′jĭk) *adj. & n.*

par•a•po•di•um (păr′ə-pō′dē-əm) *n., pl.* **-di•a** (-dē-ə) One of the fleshy paired appendages of polychete annelids that function in locomotion and breathing.

par•a•prax•is (păr′ə-prăk′sĭs) *n., pl.* **-prax•es** (-prăk′sēz) *Psychology* A minor error, such as a slip of the tongue, thought to reveal a repressed motive. [PARA–[1] + Gk. *praxis*, act, action; see PRAXIS.]

par•a•pro•fes•sion•al (păr′ə-prə-fĕsh′ə-nəl) *n.* A worker trained to assist a professional. ❖ *adj.* Of, relating to, or performing the work of a paraprofessional.

par•a•psy•chol•o•gy (păr′ə-sī-kŏl′ə-jē) *n.* The study of the evidence for psychological phenomena, such as telepathy, that are inexplicable by science. **—par′a•psy′cho•log′i•cal** (-sī′kə-lŏj′ĭ-kəl) *adj.* **—par′a•psy•chol′o•gist** *n.*

par•a•quat (păr′ə-kwŏt′) *n.* A yellow compound, $C_{12}H_{14}N_2 \cdot 2CH_3SO_4$, used as a herbicide. [PARA–[1] + QUAT(ERNARY).]

Pa•rá rubber (pä-rä′, pär′ə) *n.* Rubber obtained from various tropical South American trees of the genus *Hevea*, esp. *H. brasiliensis*. [After *Pará*, a state of northern Brazil.]

par•a•sail (păr′ə-sāl′) *n.* A parachute that lifts a rider in its harness up and through the air when towed by an automobile or a motorboat. [PARA(CHUTE) + SAIL.] **—par′a•sail′** *v.* **—par′a•sail′er** *n.*

parasail

par•a•sang (păr′ə-săng′) *n.* An ancient Persian unit of distance, usu. estimated at 3.5 miles (5.6 kilometers). [Lat. *parasanga* < Gk. *parasangēs*, of Iran. orig.]

par•a•se•le•ne (păr′ə-sĭ-lē′nē) *n., pl.* **-nae** (-nē) A luminous spot on a lunar halo. [PARA–[1] + Gk. *selēnē*, moon.]

par•a•sen•so•ry (păr′ə-sĕn′sə-rē) *adj.* Extrasensory. **—par′a•sen•so′ri•ly** (-sôr′ə-lē, -sōr′-) *adv.*

par•a•sex•u•al (păr′ə-sĕk′shoō-əl) *adj.* Of, relating to, or involving a form of reproduction in which recombination of genes from different individuals occurs without meiosis and fertilization. **—par′a•sex′u•al′i•ty** (-ăl′ĭ-tē) *n.*

par•a•site (păr′ə-sīt′) *n.* **1.** *Biology* An organism that grows, feeds, and lives on or in another organism to whose survival it contributes nothing. **2a.** One who habitually takes advantage of generosity without making any useful return. **b.** One who lives off and flatters the rich; a sycophant. **3.** A professional dinner guest, esp. in ancient Greece. [Lat. *parasītus*, a person who lives by amusing the rich < Gk. *parasītos*, person who eats at someone else's table, parasite : *para-*, beside; see PARA–[1] + *sītos*, grain, food.]

par•a•sit•ic (păr′ə-sĭt′ĭk) also **par•a•sit•i•cal** (-ĭ-kəl) *adj.* **1.** Of, relating to, or characteristic of a parasite. **2.** Caused by a parasite: *parasitic diseases*. **—par′a•sit′i•cal•ly** *adv.*

par•a•sit•i•cide (păr′ə-sĭt′ĭ-sīd′) *n.* An agent or preparation used to destroy parasites. **—par′a•sit′i•cid′al** (-sīd′l) *adj.*

par•a•sit•ism (păr′ə-sī-tĭz′əm, -sī-) *n.* **1.** The characteristic behavior or mode of existence of a parasite or parasitic population. **2.** Parasitosis.

par•a•sit•ize (păr′ə-sī-tīz′, -sī-) *tr.v.* **-ized, -iz•ing, -iz•es** To live on or in (a host) as a parasite.

par•a•sit•oid (păr′ə-sī-toid′, -sī′toid) *n.* Any of various insects whose parasitic larvae eventually kill their hosts. ❖ *adj.* Of or relating to a parasitic insect of this kind.

par•a•si•tol•o•gy (păr′ə-sī-tŏl′ə-jē, -sī-) *n.* The scientific study of parasitism. **—par′a•si′to•log′ic** (-sī′tə-lŏj′ĭk), **par′a•si′to•log′i•cal** (-ĭ-kəl) *adj.* **—par′a•si•tol′o•gist** *n.*

par•a•si•to•sis (păr′ə-sī-tō′sĭs, -sī-) *n., pl.* **-ses** (-sēz) A disease resulting from parasitic infestation.

par•a•sol (păr′ə-sôl′, -sŏl′) *n.* A light, usu. small umbrella carried as protection from the sun. [Fr. < Ital. *parasole* : *parare*, to shield (< Lat. *parāre*, to prepare) + *sole*, sun (< Lat. *sōl*; see **sāwel-** in App.).] **—par′a•soled′** *adj.*

parasol
lacquered paper parasol

par•a•som•ni•a (păr′ə-sŏm′nē-ə) *n.* Any of several disorders that may interfere with sleep, occurring esp. in children and including bed-wetting. [Prob. PARA–[1] + (IN)SOMNIA.]

par•a•sym•pa•thet•ic (păr′ə-sĭm′pə-thĕt′ĭk) *adj.* Of, relating to, or affecting the parasympathetic nervous system. ❖ *n.* **1.** The parasympathetic nervous system. **2.** Any of the nerves of this system. **—par′a•sym′pa•thet′i•cal•ly** *adv.*

parasympathetic nervous system *n.* The part of the auto-nomic nervous system originating in the brain stem and the lower part of the spinal cord that in general inhibits or opposes the physiological effects of the sympathetic nervous system, as in tending to slow the heart and dilate blood vessels.

par•a•sym•pa•tho•mi•met•ic (păr′ə-sĭm′pə-thō-mĭ-mĕt′ĭk, -mī-) *adj.* Producing effects similar to those produced by a parasympathetic nerve. ❖ *n.* A drug or agent that produces such effects.

par•a•syn•the•sis (păr′ə-sĭn′thĭ-sĭs) *n., pl.* **-ses** (-sēz′) The formation of words by both compounding and adding an affix, as in *downhearted*, formed from *down* plus *heart* plus *-ed*, not *down* plus *hearted*. **—par′a•syn•thet′ic** (-thĕt′ĭk) *adj.*

par•a•tax•is (păr′ə-tăk′sĭs) *n.* The juxtaposition of clauses or phrases without conjunctions, as *It was cold; it snowed*. [Gk., a placing side by side < *paratassein*, to arrange side by side : *para-*, beside; see PARA–[1] + *tassein, tag-*, to arrange.] **—par′a•tac′tic** (-tăk′tĭk), **par′a•tac′ti•cal** (-tĭ-kəl) *adj.* **—par′a•tac′ti•cal•ly** *adv.*

par•a•thi•on (păr′ə-thī′ŏn) *n.* A liquid insecticide, $C_8H_{10}NO_5PS$. [PARA–[1] + *thio(phosphate)*, phosphoric acid salt (THIO– + PHOSPHATE) + –ON[3].]

par•a•thy•roid (păr′ə-thī′roid) *adj.* Of, relating to, or obtained from the parathyroid glands. ❖ *n.* **1.** The parathyroid gland. **2.** A parathyroid hormone.

parathyroid gland *n.* Any of usu. four small kidney-shaped glands that lie in pairs near or within the posterior surface of the thyroid gland and secrete parathyroid hormone.

parathyroid hormone *n.* A hormone produced by the parathyroid glands that regulates the metabolism of calcium and phosphorus in the body.

par•a•troop•er (păr′ə-troō′pər) *n.* A member of the paratroops.

par•a•troops (păr′ə-troōps′) *pl.n.* Infantry trained and equipped to parachute. **—par′a•troop′** *adj.*

par•a•ty•phoid fever (păr′ə-tī′foid′) *n.* An acute intestinal disease, similar to typhoid fever but less severe, caused by certain bacteria of the genus *Salmonella*.

par•a•vane (păr′ə-vān′) *n.* A device equipped with sharp teeth and towed alongside a ship to cut the mooring cables of submerged mines. [< its vanes that keep it at a constant depth.]

par•boil (pär′boil′) *tr.v.* **-boiled, -boil•ing, -boils 1.** To cook partially by boiling for a brief period. **2.** To subject to intense, often uncomfortable heat. [ME *parboilen*, to boil partly, to boil thoroughly (influenced by *part*, part) < OFr. *parbouillir*, to boil thoroughly < LLat. *perbullīre* : Lat. *per-*, thoroughly; see PER– + Lat. *bullīre*, to boil.]

par•buck•le (pär′bŭk′əl) *n.* **1.** A rope sling for rolling cylindrical objects up or down an inclined plane. **2.** A sling for raising or lowering an object vertically. ❖ *tr.v.* **-led, -ling, -les** To raise or lower with such a sling. [Alteration (influenced by BUCKLE) of *parbunkel*.]

Par•cae (pär′sē) *pl.n. Roman Mythology* The Fates. [Lat.]

par•cel (pär′səl) *n.* **1.** Something wrapped up or packaged; a package. **2.** A plot of land, usu. a division of a larger area. **3.** A quantity of merchandise offered for sale. **4.** A group or company; a pack: *"this youthful parcel of noble bachelors"* (Shakespeare). ❖ *tr.v.* **-celed, -cel•ing, -cels** also **-celled, -cel•ling, -cels 1.** To divide into parts and distribute. **2.** To make into a parcel; package. **3.** *Nautical* To wind protective strips of canvas around (rope). [ME < OFr., portion < VLat. *particella*, dim. of Lat. *particula*, dim. of *pars, part-*, part. See **pera-** in App.]

parcel post *n.* A postal service or department that handles and delivers packages.

par•ce•ner (pär′sə-nər) *n.* See coparcener. [ME < AN < *parcen*, portion, division < VLat. *partiō, *partiōn-* < Lat. *partītiō, partitiōn-*. See PARTITION.]

parch (pärch) *v.* **parched, parch•ing, parch•es** *—tr.* **1.** To make extremely dry, esp. by exposure to heat. **2.** To make thirsty. **3.** To dry or roast (corn, for example) by exposing to heat. *—intr.* **1.** To become very dry. **2.** To become thirsty. [ME *parchen*.]

Par•chee•si (pär-chē′zē) A trademark used for a board game based on the ancient game of pachisi.

parch•ment (pärch′mənt) *n.* **1.** The skin of a sheep or goat prepared as a material on which to write or paint. **2.** A written text or drawing on parchment. **3.** Paper made in imitation of this material. [ME *parchemin, parchement* < OFr. *parchemin* < LLat. *pergamīna*, var. of Lat. *pergamēna* < fem. of *Pergamēnus*, of Pergamum < Gk. *Pergamēnos*, after *Pergamon* (Pergamum).]

pard (pärd) *n.* A leopard or other large cat. [ME *parde* < OFr. < Lat. *pardus* < Gk. *pardos*, prob. of Iran. orig.; akin to Sogdian *purdhank*.]

pard•ner (pärd′nər) *n. Regional* A partner, companion, or friend. [Variant of PARTNER.]

par•don (pär′dn) *tr.v.* **-doned, -don•ing, -dons 1.** To release (a person) from punishment; exempt from penalty. **2.** To let (an offense) pass without punishment. **3.** To make courteous allowance for; excuse: *Pardon me*. See Syns at **forgive**. ❖ *n.* **1.** The act of pardoning. **2.** *Law* **a.** Exemption of a convicted person from the penalties of an offense or crime by the power of the executor of the laws. **b.** An official document or warrant declaring such an exemption. **3.** Allowance or forgiveness for an offense or discourtesy. [ME *pardonen* < OFr. *pardoner* < VLat. **perdōnāre*, to give wholeheartedly : Lat. *per-*, intensive pref.; see PER- + Lat. *dōnāre*, to give, forgive (< *dōnum*, gift; see **dō-** in App.).] —**par·don·a·ble** *adj.* —**par·don·a·bly** *adv.*

par·don·er (pär′dn-ər) *n.* **1.** One that pardons. **2.** A medieval cleric authorized to grant papal indulgences to contributors.

pare (pâr) *tr.v.* **pared, par·ing, pares** **1.** To remove the outer covering or skin of with a knife or similar instrument. **2.** To remove by or as if by cutting, clipping, or shaving: *pared off the excess dough.* **3.** To reduce as if by cutting off outer parts; trim. [ME *paren* < OFr. *parer*, to prepare, trim < Lat. *parāre*, to prepare.] —**par′er** *n.*

par·e·gor·ic (păr′ə-gôr′ĭk, -gŏr′-) *n.* A camphorated tincture of opium, taken internally for the relief of diarrhea and intestinal pain. [LLat. *parēgoricus*, soothing < Gk. *parēgorikos* < *parēgorein*, to talk over, soothe < *parēgoros*, consoling : *para-*, beside; see PARA-¹ + *agorā*, agora; see AGORA.]

paren. *abbr.* parenthesis

pa·ren·chy·ma (pə-rĕng′kə-mə) *n.* **1.** *Anatomy* The tissue characteristic of an organ, as distinguished from associated connective or supporting tissues. **2.** *Botany* The primary tissue of higher plants, composed of thin-walled cells and forming the greater part of leaves, roots, the pulp of fruit, and the pith of stems. [NLat. < Gk. *parenkhuma*, visceral flesh < *parenkhein*, to pour in beside : *para-*, beside; see PARA-¹ + *en-*, in; see **en** in App. + *khein*, to pour; see **gheu-** in App.] —**pa·ren′chy·mal**, **par′en·chym′a·tous** (păr′ĕn-kĭm′ə-təs) *adj.*

par·ent (pâr′ənt, păr′-) *n.* **1.** One who begets, gives birth to, or nurtures and raises a child; a father or mother. **2.** An ancestor; a progenitor. **3.** An organism that produces or generates offspring. **4.** A guardian; a protector. **5.** A parent company. **6.** A source or cause; an origin: *the parent of rebellion.* ❖ *v.* **-ent·ed, -ent·ing, -ents** *—tr.* **1.** To act as a parent to; raise and nurture. **2.** To cause to come into existence; originate. *—intr.* To act as a parent. [ME < OFr. < Lat. *parēns, parent-* < pr. part. of *parere*, to give birth.] —**par′ent·hood**′ *n.*

par·ent·age (pâr′ən-tĭj, păr′-) *n.* **1.** Descent from parents; lineage: *of humble parentage.* **2.** The state or relationship of being a parent. **3.** Derivation from a source; origin.

pa·ren·tal (pə-rĕn′tl) *adj.* **1.** Of, relating to, or characteristic of a parent. **2.** *Genetics* Of or being the generation from which hybrid offspring are produced. —**pa·ren′tal·ly** *adv.*

parental leave *n.* A leave of absence granted to a parent to care for a new baby.

parent company *n.* A company that controls or owns another company or companies.

par·en·ter·al (pă-rĕn′tər-əl) *adj.* **1.** *Physiology* Located outside the alimentary canal. **2.** *Medicine* Taken into the body or administered in a manner other than through the digestive tract, as by intravenous injection. —**par·en′ter·al·ly** *adv.*

par·en·the·sis (pə-rĕn′thĭ-sĭs) *n., pl.* **-ses** (-sēz′) **1.** Either or both of the upright curved lines, ( ), used to mark off explanatory or qualifying remarks in writing or printing or enclose a sum, product, or other expression treated as a collective entity in a mathematical operation. **2a.** A qualifying or amplifying word, phrase, or sentence inserted within written matter so as to be independent of the surrounding grammatical structure. **b.** A comment departing from the theme of discourse; a digression. **3.** An interruption of continuity; an interval. [LLat., insertion of a letter or syllable in a word < Gk. < *parentithenai*, to insert : *para-*, beside; see PARA-¹ + *en-*, in; see **en** in App. + *tithenai*, to put; see **dhē-** in App.]

par·en·thet·i·cal (păr′ən-thĕt′ĭ-kəl) *adj.* also **par·en·thet·ic** (-ĭk) **1.** Set off within or as if within parentheses; qualifying or explanatory: *a parenthetical remark.* **2.** Using or containing parentheses. ❖ *n.* A parenthetical word, phrase, or remark. —**par·en·thet′i·cal·ly** *adv.*

parent language *n.* A language from which a later language is derived: *Latin is the parent language of Italian and French.*

pa·re·sis (pə-rē′sĭs, păr′ĭ-sĭs) *n., pl.* **-ses** (-sēz) **1.** Slight or partial paralysis. **2.** General paresis. [Gk., act of letting go, paralysis < *parienai*, to let fall : *para-*, beside; see PARA-¹ + *hienai*, to throw.] —**pa·ret′ic** (pə-rĕt′ĭk) *adj. & n.*

par·es·the·sia also **par·aes·the·sia** (păr′ĭs-thē′zhə) *n.* A skin sensation, such as burning or tingling, with no apparent physical cause. [NLat. *paraesthēsia* : PARA-¹ + Gk. *aisthēsis*, feeling; see AN-ESTHESIA.] —**par′es·thet′ic** (-thĕt′ĭk) *adj.*

pa·re·u (pä′rā-ōō′) *n.* A rectangular piece of cloth worn esp. in Polynesia as a wraparound skirt. [Tahitian.]

pa·reve (pä′rə-və) also **par·ve** (pär′və) *adj. Judaism* Prepared without meat, milk, or their derivatives and therefore permissible to be eaten with both meat and dairy dishes according to dietary laws. [Yiddish *pareve*.]

par ex·cel·lence (pär ĕk-sə-läns′) *adj.* Being the best or truest of a kind; quintessential. [Fr. : *par*, by + *excellence*, preeminence.]

par·fait (pär-fā′) *n.* **1.** A dessert made of cream, eggs, sugar, and flavoring frozen together and served in a tall glass. **2.** A dessert made of several layers of different flavors of ice cream or ices served in a tall glass. [Fr. < OFr., perfect < Lat. *perfectus.* See PER-FECT.]

parfait glass *n.* A tall slender glass with a short stem.

par·fleche (pär′flĕsh′) *n.* **1.** An untanned animal hide soaked in lye and water to remove the hair and then dried on a stretcher. **2.** An article, such as a shield, made of this hide. [Canadian Fr. *parflèche* : Fr. *parer*, to parry, defend; see PARRY + Fr. *flèche*, arrow; see FLÈCHE.]

par·get (pär′jĭt) *n.* **1.** A mixture, such as plaster, used to coat walls and line chimneys. **2.** Ornamental work in plaster. **3.** A cement mixture used to waterproof outer walls. ❖ *tr.v.* **par·get·ed, -get·ing, -gets** also **-get·ted, -get·ting, -gets** To cover or adorn with parget. [ME, prob. < *pargetten*, to parget < OFr. *pargeter, parjeter*, to throw about (*par-*, intensive pref. < Lat. *per*; see **per¹** in App. + *jeter*, to throw < Lat. *iactāre*, freq. of *iacere*) and < OFr. *porgeter*, to roughcast a wall (*por-*, forward, ult. < Lat. *porrō*; see **per¹** in App. + *iactāre*, to throw).] —**par′get·ing** *n.*

par·he·lic circle (pär-hē′lĭk) *n.* A luminous halo visible at the height of the sun and parallel to the horizon, caused by the sun's rays reflecting off atmospheric ice crystals.

par·he·li·on (pär-hē′lē-ən, -hēl′yən) *n., pl.* **-he·li·a** (-hē′lē-ə, -hēl′yə) A bright spot sometimes appearing on either side of the sun, often on a luminous ring or halo. [Lat. *parēlion* < Gk. : *para-*, beside; see PARA-¹ + *hēlios*, sun; see **sāwel-** in App.] —**par·he′lic** (-hē′lĭk) *adj.*

pa·ri·ah (pə-rī′ə) *n.* **1.** A social outcast. **2.** An Untouchable. [Tamil *paraiyar*, pl. of *paraiyan*, pariah caste < *parai*, festival drum.]

Par·i·an (pâr′ē-ən, păr′-) *adj.* **1.** Of or relating to the island of Páros or its inhabitants. **2.** Of or being a type of white semitranslucent marble quarried at Páros and highly valued in ancient times for making sculptures. **3.** Of or being a fine white porcelain. ❖ *n.* **1.** A native or inhabitant of Páros. **2.** Parian marble. **3.** Parian porcelain.

Pa·rí·cu·tin (pä-rē′kōō-tēn′) A volcano, 2,272.3 m (7,450 ft), of W-central Mexico W of Mexico City; first erupted in Feb. 1943.

pa·ri·es (pâr′ē-ĕz′) *n., pl.* **pa·ri·e·tes** (pə-rī′ĭ-tēz′) A wall of a body part, organ, or cavity. Often used in the plural. [Lat. *pariēs*, wall.]

pa·ri·e·tal (pə-rī′ĭ-təl) *adj.* **1.** Relating to or forming the wall of a body part, organ, or cavity. **2.** Of or relating to either of the parietal bones. **3.** *Botany* Borne on the inside of the ovary wall. Used of the ovules or placentas in flowering plants. **4.** Dwelling within or having authority within the walls or buildings of a college. ❖ *n.* A parietal part, such as a wall or bone. **2. parietals** The rules governing visits from members of the opposite sex in college or university dormitories. [ME < LLat. *parietālis*, of a wall < Lat. *pariēs, pariet-*, wall.]

parietal bone *n.* Either of two large, irregularly quadrilateral bones between the frontal and occipital bones that together form the sides and top of the skull.

parietal lobe *n.* The division of each hemisphere of the brain that lies beneath each parietal bone.

par·i-mu·tu·el also **par·i·mu·tu·el** (păr′ĭ-myōō′chōō-əl) *n.* **1.** A system of betting on races whereby winnings are divided in proportion to the sums individually wagered. **2.** A machine that records such bets and computes the payoffs. [Fr. : *pari*, wager (< *parier*, to wager < Lat. *pariāre*, to settle a debt < *pār, par-*, equal; see **perə-** in App.) + *mutuel*, mutual (< OFr.; see MUTUAL).]

par·ing (pâr′ĭng) *n.* **1.** Something pared off, such as a peel. **2.** The act of removing the outer covering or skin.

paring knife *n.* A small knife for paring fruits and vegetables.

pa·ri pas·su (pär′ē pås′ōō, pär′ī, pâr′ē) *adv.* At an equal pace; side by side. [Lat. *parī passū* : *parī*, ablative of *pār*, equal + *passū*, ablative of *passus*, step.]

par·i·pin·nate (păr′ĭ-pĭn′āt, -ĭt) *adj. Botany* Pinnately compound with two terminal leaflets: *paripinnate leaves.* [Lat. *pār, par-*, equal, a pair + PINNATE.]

Par·is¹ (păr′ĭs) *n. Greek Mythology* The prince of Troy whose abduction of Helen provoked the Trojan War.

Par·is² (păr′ĭs) *n.* The cap. of France, in the N-central part on the Seine R.; founded as a fishing village on the Île de la Cité and est. as the cap. of France by Hugh Capet in 987. Pop. 2,149,900. —**Pa·ris′ian** (pə-rē′zhən, -rĭz′ē-ən) *adj. & n.*

Paris, Matthew 1200?–59. English monk known for his *Chronica Majora.*

Paris daisy *n.* See **marguerite** 1.

Paris green *n.* A poisonous green powder consisting largely of copper and arsenic, formerly used as an insecticide.

par·ish (păr′ĭsh) *n.* **1a.** An administrative part of a diocese with its own church in the Anglican, Roman Catholic, and some other churches. **b.** The members of such a parish. **2.** A political subdivision of a British county, usu. corresponding to parish boundaries. **3.** An administrative subdivision in Louisiana that corresponds to a county in other US states. [ME < OFr. *parroche* < LLat. *parochia*, diocese, alteration of *paroecia* < L.Gk. *paroikiā* < Gk., a sojourning < *paroikos*, neighboring, neighbor, sojourner : *para-*, near; see PARA-¹ + *oikos*, house; see **weik-** in App.]

pa·rish·ion·er (pə-rĭsh′ə-nər) *n.* A member of a parish. [ME < *parishon*, parishioner < OFr. *parochien* < *parroche*, parish. See PARISH.]

par·i·ty¹ (păr′ĭ-tē) *n., pl.* **-ties** **1.** Equality, as in amount, status,

ă **pat**	oi **boy**
ā **pay**	ou **out**
âr **care**	ōō **took**
ä **father**	ōō **boot**
ĕ **pet**	ŭ **cut**
ē **be**	ûr **urge**
ĭ **pit**	th **thin**
ī **pie**	th **this**
îr **pier**	hw **which**
ŏ **pot**	zh **vision**
ō **toe**	ə **about,**
ô **paw**	**item**

Stress marks:
′ (primary);
′ (secondary), as in
lexicon (lĕk′sĭ-kŏn′)

parka

Rosa Parks
1990 bronze bust by Artis
Lane (b. 1927)

or value. **2.** Functional equivalence, as in the military strength of adversaries. **3.** The equivalent in value of a sum of money expressed in terms of a different currency at a fixed official rate of exchange. **4.** Equality of prices of goods or securities in two different markets. **5.** A level for farm-product prices maintained by governmental support in order to give farmers the same purchasing power they had during a chosen base period. **6.** *Mathematics* The even or odd quality of an integer; for example, 1 and 7 have the same parity, but 3 and 4 do not. **7.** *Physics* **a.** An intrinsic symmetry property of a wave function that determines its behavior under reflection through the origin of spatial coordinates. **b.** A quantum number, either +1 (even) or −1 (odd), that describes this property. **8.** *Computer Science* **a.** The even or odd quality of the number of 1's or 0's in a binary code, often used to determine the integrity of data, esp. after transmission. **b.** A bit added to a binary code that indicates parity. [Fr. *parité* < OFr. *parite* < LLat. *paritās* < *pār*, equal. See PAIR.]

par·i·ty² (păr′ĭ-tē) *n.* **1.** The condition of having given birth. **2.** The number of children borne by one woman. [Lat. *parere*, to give birth, bring forth + -ITY.]

park (pärk) *n.* **1.** An area of land set aside for public use, as: **a.** A piece of land with few or no buildings within or adjoining a town, maintained for recreational and ornamental purposes. **b.** A landscaped city square. **c.** A large tract of rural land kept in its natural state and usu. reserved for the enjoyment and recreation of visitors. **2.** A broad, fairly level valley between mountain ranges. **3.** A tract of land attached to a country house, esp. when including extensive gardens, woods, pastures, or a game preserve. **4.** *Sports* A stadium or an enclosed playing field. **5a.** An area where military vehicles or artillery are stored and serviced. **b.** The materiel kept in such an area. **6.** An area in or near a town designed and usu. zoned for a certain purpose. **7.** A parking lot. **8.** A position in an automatic transmission that disengages the gears and sets the brake so the vehicle cannot move. ❖ *v.* **parked, park·ing, parks** —*tr.* **1.** To put or leave (a vehicle) for a time in a certain location. **2.** *Aerospace* To place (a spacecraft or satellite) in a usu. temporary orbit. **3.** *Informal* To place or leave temporarily. **4.** To assemble (artillery or other equipment) in a military park. —*intr.* **1.** To park a motor vehicle. **2.** *Slang* To engage in kissing or caressing in a vehicle stopped in a secluded spot. [ME, enclosed tract of land < OFr. *parc*, of Gmc. orig.] —**park′er** *n.*

Park, Mungo 1771–1806. Scottish explorer in Africa known for his expeditions on the Niger R. (1795–96 and 1805).

par·ka (pär′kə) *n.* **1.** A hooded fur outer garment worn in the Arctic, originally of pullover design but now generally having a front closure. **2.** A coat or jacket with a hood and usu. a warm lining for cold-weather wear. [Alaskan Russ., pelt, ult. of Nenets orig.]

park·ade (pär-kād′) *n.* *Canadian* A multilevel structure for parking motor vehicles. [Blend of PARK and ARCADE.]

Park Avenue A wide thoroughfare extending N to S on the East Side of Manhattan.

Par·ker (pär′kər), **Charlie** Known as "Bird." 1920–55. Amer. jazz musician and composer best remembered for his improvisations.

Parker, Dorothy Rothschild 1893–1967. Amer. writer noted for her satirical wit in poems such as "Resumé" (1926).

Parker, Matthew 1504–75. English prelate who, as archbishop of Canterbury (1559–75), helped establish ecclesiastical forms for the Anglican Church.

park·ing (pär′kĭng) *n.* **1.** The act or practice of parking a vehicle. **2.** Space in which to park vehicles or a vehicle: *can't find parking.* **3.** *Upper Midwest & Western US* The grass strip, often planted with shade trees, between a sidewalk and a street.

REGIONAL NOTE The grassy strip between the sidewalk and the street has acquired specific names in some parts of the United States. In the Midwest and West, it is often called the *parking* or *parkway*, and in Washington State it is the *parking strip*, according to the survey conducted by the *Dictionary of American Regional English*. In the Upper Midwest, it is also known as the *boulevard* or *boulevard strip*; around the Great Lakes, it is sometimes a *terrace;* around the Great Lakes and in especially northeastern Ohio, it is also called a *tree lawn.* In Massachusetts it is a *tree belt*; in the Atlantic states, sometimes a *grass-plot*; and in Louisiana and Mississippi, *neutral ground.* Some of these words are also used for the grassy strip in the middle of a street or highway. See Regional Note at **neutral ground.**

parking lot *n.* An area for parking motor vehicles.

parking meter *n.* A coin-operated device that registers the amount of time purchased for the parking of a motor vehicle, at the expiration of which the driver is liable for a fine.

parking strip *n.* *Washington State* See **parking** 3.

Par·kin·son·ism (pär′kĭn-sə-nĭz′əm) *n.* **1.** Any of a group of nervous disorders similar to Parkinson's disease, marked by muscular rigidity, tremor, and impaired motor control and often having a specific cause, such as frequent exposure to toxic chemicals. **2.** Parkinson's disease. [< PARKINSON'S DISEASE.] —**Par′kin·so′ni·an** (-sō′nē-ən) *adj.*

Par·kin·son's disease (pär′kĭn-sənz) *n.* A progressive nervous disease usu. occurring after the age of 50, associated with the destruction of brain cells that produce dopamine and characterized

by muscular tremor, slowing of movement, partial facial paralysis, and weakness. [After James *Parkinson* (1755–1824), British physician.]

Parkinson's Law *n.* Any of several satirical observations propounded as economic laws, esp. "Work expands to fill the time available for its completion." [After Cyril Northcote *Parkinson* (1909–93), British historian.]

Parkinson's syndrome *n.* See **Parkinsonism** 1.

park·land (pärk′lănd′) *n.* **1.** Land within or suitable for public parks. **2.** Grassland with scattered clusters of trees or shrubs.

Park·man (pärk′mən), **Francis** 1823–93. Amer. historian who wrote *The California and Oregon Trail* (1849).

Park Range A range of the Rocky Mts. in N-central CO and S WY rising to 4,357.2 m (14,286 ft).

Parks (pärks), **Rosa** b. 1913. Amer. civil rights leader whose refusal to give up her seat on a bus to a white man in Montgomery AL stirred the civil rights movement across the nation.

park·way (pärk′wā′) *n.* **1.** A broad landscaped highway, often divided by a planted median strip. **2.** *Mississippi Valley, Ohio Valley, & Western US* See **parking** 3. See Regional Note at **parking.**

Parl. *abbr.* Parliament

par·lance (pär′ləns) *n.* **1.** A particular manner of speaking; idiom: *terms associated with legal parlance.* **2.** Speech, esp. a conversation or parley. [M Fr. < OFr. < *parler*, to speak. See PARLEY.]

par·lan·do (pär-län′dō) also **par·lan·te** (-tā) *adv. & adj. Music* To be sung in a style suggestive of speech. [Ital., pr. part. of *parlare*, to speak < VLat. *paraulāre*. See PARLEY.]

par·lay (pär′lā′, -lē) *tr.v.* **-layed, -lay·ing, -lays 1.** To bet (an original wager and its winnings) on a subsequent event. **2.** To maneuver (an asset) to great advantage. ❖ *n.* A bet comprising the sum of a prior wager plus its winnings or a series of such bets. [Alteration of *paroli*, staking of double a prior stake in faro < Fr. < obsolete Ital., prob. < Ital. *parare*, to place a bet < Lat. *parāre*, to prepare. See PARE.]

par·ley (pär′lē) *n., pl.* **-leys** A discussion or conference, esp. one between enemies over terms of truce or other matters. ❖ *intr.v.* **-leyed, -ley·ing, -leys** To have a discussion, esp. with an enemy. [ME < OFr. *parlee* < fem. p. part. of *parler*, to talk < VLat. *paraulāre* < LLat. *parabolāre* < *parabola*, discourse. See PARABLE.]

par·lia·ment (pär′lə-mənt) *n.* **1.** A national representative body having supreme state legislative powers. **2. Parliament** The national legislature of various countries, esp. that of the United Kingdom. [ME, a meeting about national concerns < OFr. *parlement* < *parler*, to talk. See PARLEY.]

par·lia·men·tar·i·an (pär′lə-mĕn-târ′ē-ən) *n.* **1.** One who is expert in parliamentary procedures, rules, or debate. **2.** A member of a parliament. **3. Parliamentarian** A Roundhead.

par·lia·men·ta·ry (pär′lə-mĕn′tə-rē, -mĕn′trē) *adj.* **1.** Of, relating to, or resembling a parliament. **2.** Enacted or decreed by a parliament. **3.** Being in accord with the rules and customs of a parliament. **4a.** Having a parliament. **b.** Characterized by an executive branch consisting of cabinet ministers selected from and responsible to the parliament.

parliamentary law *n.* A body of rules governing procedure in legislative and deliberative assemblies.

par·lor (pär′lər) *n.* **1.** A room in a private home set apart for the entertainment of visitors. **2.** A small lounge or sitting room affording limited privacy, as at a tavern. **3.** A room equipped and furnished for a special function or business. [ME *parlur* < OFr. < *parler*, to talk. See PARLEY.]

parlor car *n.* A railroad car for day travel fitted with individual reserved seats.

parlor game *n.* A game that can be played indoors.

par·lour (pär′lər) *n. Chiefly British* Variant of **parlor.**

par·lous (pär′ləs) *adj.* **1.** Perilous; dangerous: *a parlous journey.* **2.** *Obsolete* Dangerously cunning. [ME, var. of *perilous*, perilous < *peril*, peril. See PERIL.] —**par′lous·ly** *adv.*

Par·ma (pär′mə) **1.** A city of N-central Italy SE of Milan; founded by Romans in 183 B.C. Pop. 168,905. **2.** A city of NE OH, a suburb of Cleveland. Pop. 85,655.

Par·men·i·des (pär-mĕn′ĭ-dēz′) b. 515? B.C. Greek philosopher and a founder of the Eleatic tradition.

Par·me·san (pär′mə-zän′, -zän′, -zən) *n.* A sharp dry hard Italian cheese made from skim milk and usu. served grated as a garnish. [Fr. < OFr. *permigean*, of Parma < OItal. *parmigiano.* See PARMIGIANA.]

par·mi·gia·na (pär′mĭ-zhä′nə, -jä′-) *adj.* Made or covered with Parmesan cheese: *eggplant parmigiana.* [Ital., fem. of *parmigiano,* of Parma, after PARMA, Italy.]

Par·mi·gia·ni·no (pär′mĭ-jä-nē′nō, -mē-) or **Par·mi·gia·no** (-jä′nō), **Il** 1503–40. Italian Mannerist painter and etcher whose works include *Vision of Saint Jerome* (1527).

Par·na·í·ba (pär′nə-ē′bə, -nä-ē′bä) A river of NE Brazil flowing c. 1,287 km (800 mi) to the Atlantic.

Par·nas·si·an (pär-năs′ē-ən) *adj.* **1.** Of or relating to poetry. **2.** Of or relating to the Parnassians or their style of poetry. ❖ *n.* A member of a school of late 19th-century French poets whose work is characterized by detachment and emphasis on metrical form. [< Lat. *Parnassius,* of Parnassus < Gk. *parnāsios,* after *Parnāsos* (Parnassus), sacred to Apollo and the Muses. N. < Fr. *parnassien,* after *Le Parnasse contemporain,* the group's first anthology of poetry (1866) < *Parnasse*, Parnassus, ult. < Gk. *Parnāsos*.]

Par•nas•sus (pär-năs′əs) also **Par•nas•sós** (-nä-sôs′) A mountain, c. 2,458 m (8,060 ft), of central Greece N of the Gulf of Corinth.

Par•nell (pär-něl′, pär′nəl), **Charles Stewart** 1846–91. Irish politician who led the Home Rule Movement.

pa•ro•chi•al (pə-rō′kē-əl) *adj.* **1.** Of, relating to, supported by, or located in a parish. **2.** Of or relating to a parochial school. **3.** Narrowly restricted in scope or outlook; provincial: *parochial attitudes.* [ME < OFr. < LLat. *parochiālis* < *parochia*, diocese. See PARISH.] —**pa•ro′chi•al•ism** *n.* —**pa•ro′chi•al•ist** *n.* —**pa•ro′chi•al•ly** *adv.*

parochial school *n.* A school supported by a religious organization.

par•o•dy (păr′ə-dē) *n., pl.* **-dies 1a.** A literary or artistic work that imitates the characteristic style of an author or a work for comic effect or ridicule. **b.** The genre of literature comprising such works. **2.** Something so bad as to be equivalent to intentional mockery; a travesty: *The trial was a parody of justice.* ❖ *tr.v.* **-died, -dy•ing, -dies** To make a parody of. See Syns at **imitate.** [Lat. *parōdia* < Gk. *parōidia* : *para-*, subsidiary to; see PARA-[1] + *ōidē*, song.] —**pa•rod′ic** (pə-rŏd′ĭk), **pa•rod′i•cal** (-ĭ-kəl) *adj.* —**par′o•dist** *n.* —**par′o•dis′tic** *adj.*

pa•rol (pə-rōl′, păr′əl) *Law n.* An oral statement or utterance. ❖ *adj.* Expressed or evidenced by word of mouth; not written. [ME *parole* < AN < VLat. **paraula*. See PAROLE.]

pa•role (pə-rōl′) *n.* **1.** *Law* **a.** The release of a prisoner whose term has not expired on condition of sustained lawful behavior that is subject to monitoring by an officer of the law for a set period of time. **b.** The duration of such conditional release. **2.** A password used by an officer of the day, an officer on guard, or the personnel commanded by such an officer. **3.** Word of honor, esp. that of a prisoner of war who is granted freedom only after promising to lay down arms until being exchanged. **4.** *Linguistics* The act of speaking; a particular utterance or word. ❖ *tr.v.* **-roled, -rol•ing, -roles** To release (a prisoner) on parole. [Fr., promise, word < VLat. **paraula* < Lat. *parabola*, discourse. See PARABLE.]

pa•rol•ee (pə-rō′lē′) *n.* One who is released on parole.

par•o•no•ma•sia (păr′ə-nō-mā′zhə, -zhē-ə) *n.* **1.** Word play; punning. **2.** A pun. [Lat. < Gk. *paronomasia* < *paronomazein*, to call by a different name : *para-*, beside; see PARA-[1] + *onomazein*, to name; see ONOMASTIC.] —**par′o•no•mas′tic** (-măs′tĭk), **par′o•no•ma′sial** (-mā′zhəl, -zhē-əl) *adj.*

par•o•nych•i•a (păr′ə-nĭk′ē-ə) *n.* Inflammation of the tissue surrounding a fingernail or toenail. [Lat. *parōnychia* < Gk. *parōnukhiā* : *para-*, around; see PARA-[1] + *onux, onukh-*, nail.] —**par′o•nych′i•al** *adj.*

par•o•nym (păr′ə-nĭm′) *n.* A paronymous word. [Gk. *parōnumon* < neut. sing. of *parōnumos*, derivative. See PARONYMOUS.] —**par•o•nym′ic** *adj.*

pa•ron•y•mous (pə-rŏn′ə-məs) *adj.* Allied by derivation from the same root; having the same stem; for example, *beautiful* and *beauteous.* [Gk. *parōnumos*, derivative : *para-*, beside; see PARA-[1] + *onuma*, name; see **nō-men-** in App.]

Pá•ros also **Par•os** (pâr′ŏs, pä′rôs) An island in the Cyclades of SE Greece in the Aegean Sea; settled by Ionians and held by the Ottoman Turks from 1537 to 1832.

pa•ros•mi•a (pə-rŏz′mē-ə) *n.* A distortion of the sense of smell, as in smelling odors that are not present. [NLat. : PAR(A)-[1] + Gk. *osmē*, smell.]

pa•rot•id (pə-rŏt′ĭd) *n.* A parotid gland. ❖ *adj.* **1.** Situated near the ear. **2.** Of or relating to a parotid gland.

parotid gland *n.* Either of the pair of salivary glands situated below and in front of each ear. [NLat. *parōtis, parōtid-* < Lat., tumor near the ear < Gk. : *para-*, beside; see PARA-[1] + *ous, ōt-*, ear; see **ous-** in App.]

par•o•ti•tis (păr′ə-tī′tĭs) also **pa•rot•i•di•tis** (pə-rŏt′ĭ-dī′tĭs) *n.* Inflammation of the parotid glands, as in mumps.

par•ous (păr′əs, pâr′-) *adj.* Having given birth one or more times. [< −PAROUS.]

−parous *suff.* Giving birth to; producing: *multiparous.* [< Lat. *-parus* < *parere*, to give birth.]

Par•ou•si•a (pə-rōō′sē-ə, -rōō′zē-ə) *n.* The Second Coming. [Gk. *parousia*, presence, Parousia < *parousa*, fem. pr. part. of *pareinai*, to be present : *para-*, beside; see PARA-[1] + *einai*, to be; see **es-** in App.]

par•ox•e•tine (pă-rŏk′sĭ-tēn′) *n.* An oral antidepressant of the SSRI class of drugs. [PAR(A)-[1] + OX(Y)- + (M)ET(HYL) + (PIPERID)INE.]

par•ox•ysm (păr′ək-sĭz′əm) *n.* **1.** A sudden outburst of emotion or action. **2.** *Medicine* **a.** A sudden attack, recurrence, or intensification of a disease. **b.** A spasm or fit; a convulsion. [ME *paroxism*, periodic attack of a disease < Med.Lat. *paroxysmus* < Gk. *paroxusmos* < *paroxūnein*, to stimulate, irritate : *para-*, intensive pref.; see PARA-[1] + *oxūnein*, to goad, sharpen (< *oxus*, sharp; see App.).] —**par′ox•ys′mal** (-ək-sĭz′məl) *adj.* —**par′ox•ys′mal•ly** *adv.*

par•ox•y•tone (pă-rŏk′sĭ-tōn′) *adj.* Having an acute accent on the next to last syllable. Used of some words in Greek and certain Romance languages. ❖ *n.* A paroxytone word. [Gk. *paroxutonos* :

para-, beside; see PARA-[1] + *oxutonos*, oxytone; see OXYTONE.]

par•quet (pär-kā′) *n.* **1.** A floor made of parquetry. **2.** The art or process of making parquetry. **3a.** The part of the main floor of a theater between the orchestra pit and the parquet circle. **b.** The entire main floor of a theater. ❖ *tr.v.* **-queted** (-kād′), **-quet•ing** (-kā′ĭng), **-quets** (-kāz′) **1.** To furnish with a floor of parquetry. **2.** To make (a floor, for example) of parquetry. [Fr., parquetry < OFr., dim. of *parc*, enclosure. See PARK.]

parquet circle *n.* The part of the main floor of a theater that lies under the balcony section.

par•quet•ry (pär′kĭ-trē) *n., pl.* **-ries** Inlay of wood in a geometric pattern or mosaic, used esp. for floors. [Fr. *parqueterie* < *parquet*. See PARQUET.]

parr (pär) *n., pl.* **parr** or **parrs 1.** A young salmon during its first two years of life, when it lives in fresh water. **2.** The young of various other fishes. [?]

Parr, Catherine 1512–48. Queen of England as the sixth and last wife of Henry VIII.

par•ra•mat•ta (păr′ə-măt′ə) *n.* Variant of **paramatta.**

Parramatta A city of SE Australia, a suburb of Sydney; founded 1788. Pop. 131,800.

par•rel also **par•ral** (păr′əl) *n.* A sliding loop of rope or metal by which a running yard or gaff is connected to, while still being able to move vertically along, the mast. [ME *perel, parrail*, short for *appareil*, apparel, rigging. See APPAREL.]

par•ri•cide (păr′ĭ-sīd′) *n.* **1.** The murdering of one's father, mother, or other near relative. **2.** One who commits such a murder. [Lat. *parricīda* and *parricīdium* : *parri-, parri-*, kin + *-cīda, -cīdium, -cide.*] —**par′ri•cid′al** (-sīd′l) *adj.*

Par•rish (păr′ĭsh), **Maxfield Frederick** 1870–1966. Amer. artist noted for his murals, magazine covers, and book illustrations.

Par•ris Island (păr′ĭs) An island of the Sea Is. off S SC.

par•rot (păr′ət) *n.* **1.** Any of numerous tropical and semitropical birds of the order Psittaciformes, characterized by a short hooked bill, brightly colored plumage, and in some species the ability to mimic human speech. **2.** One who imitates the words or actions of another, esp. without understanding them. ❖ *tr.v.* **-rot•ed, -rot•ing, -rots** To repeat or imitate, esp. without understanding. [Prob. < Fr. dialectal *Perrot*, dim. of *Pierre*, Peter.] —**par′rot•er** *n.*

parrot fever *n.* See **psittacosis.**

par•rot•fish (păr′ət-fĭsh′) *n., pl.* **parrotfish** or **-fish•es** Any of various tropical marine fishes, esp. of the family Scaridae, having fused teeth resembling a parrot's beak.

par•ry (păr′ē) *v.* **-ried, -ry•ing, -ries** —*tr.* **1.** To deflect or ward off (a fencing thrust, for example). **2.** To deflect, evade, or avoid. —*intr.* To parry a thrust or blow. ❖ *n., pl.* **-ries 1.** The parrying of a thrust or blow. **2.** An evasive answer or action. [Prob. < Fr. *parez*, imper. of *parer*, to defend < Ital. *parare* < Lat. *parāre*, to prepare.]

Parry, Sir William Edward 1790–1855. British navigator who commanded three expeditions in search of the Northwest Passage between 1819 and 1825.

parse (pärs) *v.* **parsed, pars•ing, pars•es** —*tr.* **1.** To break (a sentence) down into its component parts of speech with an explanation of the form, function, and syntactical relationship of each part. **2.** To describe (a word) by stating its part of speech, form, and syntactical relationships in a sentence. **3a.** To examine closely or subject to detailed analysis, esp. by breaking into components. **b.** To make sense of; comprehend. **4.** *Computer Science* To analyze or separate (input, for example) into more easily processed components. —*intr.* To admit of being parsed. [Prob. < ME *pars*, part of speech < Lat. *pars (ōrātiōnis)*, part (of speech). See **pera-** in App.] —**pars′er** *n.*

par•sec (pär′sĕk′) *n.* A unit of astronomical length based on the distance from Earth at which stellar parallax is one second of arc and equal to 3.258 light-years, 3.086 × 10^13 kilometers, or 1.918 × 10^13 miles. [PAR(ALLAX) + SEC(OND)[1].]

Par•si also **Par•see** (pär′sē, pär-sē′) *n., pl.* **-sis** also **-sees** A member of a Zoroastrian religious sect in India. [Pers. *Pārsī* < *Pārs*, Persia < OPers. *Pārsā*.] —**Par′sism** (-sĭz′əm) *n.*

par•si•mo•ni•ous (pär′sə-mō′nē-əs) *adj.* Excessively sparing or frugal. —**par′si•mo′ni•ous•ly** *adv.* —**par′si•mo′ni•ous•ness** *n.*

par•si•mo•ny (pär′sə-mō′nē) *n.* **1.** Unusual or excessive frugality; stinginess. **2.** Adoption of the simplest assumption, as in the formulation of a theory. [ME *parcimony* < Lat. *parsimōnia* < *parsus*, p. part. of *parcere*, to spare.]

pars•ley (pär′slē) *n., pl.* **-leys 1.** A member of the parsley family. **2.** A Eurasian herb (*Petroselinum crispum*) having flat or curled, ternately compound leaves that are used for seasoning or as a garnish. [ME *persely* < OE *petersilie* and OFr. *persil*, both ult. < LLat. *petrosillum*, alteration of Lat. *petroselīnum* < Gk. *petroselīnon* : *petrā*, rock; see **per-**[2] in App. + *selīnon*, celery.]

parsley family *n.* A large family of aromatic herbs, the Umbelliferae (Apiaceae), having compound leaves and small flowers grouped in umbels and including vegetables such as carrots, celery, and parsley and spices such as cumin.

pars•nip (pär′snĭp) *n.* **1.** A strong-scented plant (*Pastinaca sativa*) cultivated for its white edible root. **2.** The root of this plant. [ME *pasnepe*, alteration of OFr. *pasnaie* < Lat. *pastināca*

parsley
common (*left*)
Italian parsley (*right*)

parsnip
Pastinaca sativa

ă	pat	oi	boy
ā	pay	ou	out
âr	care	ŏŏ	took
ä	father	ōō	boot
ĕ	pet	ŭ	cut
ē	be	ûr	urge
ĭ	pit	th	thin
ī	pie	th	this
îr	pier	hw	which
ŏ	pot	zh	vision
ō	toe	ə	about,
ô	paw		item

Stress marks:
′ (primary);
′ (secondary), as in
lexicon (lĕk′sĭ-kŏn′)

< *pastinum*, a kind of two-pronged dibble.]

par·son (pär′sən) *n.* **1.** An Anglican cleric with full legal control of a parish under ecclesiastical law; a rector. **2.** A member of the clergy, esp. a Protestant minister. [ME, parish priest < OFr. *persone* < Med.Lat. *persōna* < Lat., character. See PERSON.]

par·son·age (pär′sə-nĭj) *n.* The official residence usu. provided by a church for its parson; a rectory.

parson bird *n.* See **tui.**

Par·sons (pär′sənz), **Talcott** 1902–79. Amer. sociologist noted for developing the structural-functional approach to studying social systems. —**Par·son′i·an** (pär-sō′nē-ən) *adj.*

parson's nose *n. Informal* See **pope's nose.**

Parsons table *n.* A usu. rectangular table with straight legs that are equal in thickness to the top of the table and form its four corners. [After the *Parsons* School of Design in New York.]

part (pärt) *n.* **1.** A portion, division, piece, or segment of a whole. **2.** Any of several equal portions or fractions that can constitute a whole or into which a whole can be divided: *a mixture of two parts flour to one part sugar.* **3.** A division of a literary work. **4a.** An organ, member, or other division of an organism. **b. parts** The external genitals. **5.** A component that can be separated from or attached to a system; a detachable piece. **6.** A role: *the main part in the play.* **7.** One's responsibility, duty, or obligation; share. **8.** Individual endowment or ability; talent. Often used in the plural. **9.** A region, area, land, or territory. Often used in the plural: *It's easy to get lost in these parts.* **10.** The line where the hair on the head is parted. **11.** *Music* **a.** The music or score for a particular instrument, as in an orchestra. **b.** One of the melodic divisions or voices of a contrapuntal composition. ❖ *v.* **part·ed, part·ing, parts** —*tr.* **1.** To divide or break into separate parts. **2.** To break up the relationship or association of. **3.** To put or keep apart: *No one could part the two friends.* See Syns at **separate. 4.** To comb (hair, for example) away from a dividing line, as on the scalp. **5.** *Archaic* To divide into shares or portions. —*intr.* **1.** To become divided or separated: *The curtain parted in the middle.* **2.** To go apart from one another; separate. **3.** To separate or divide into ways going in different directions. **4.** To go away; depart. **5.** To disagree by factions. **6.** *Archaic* To die. ❖ *adv.* Partially; in part: *part yellow, part green.* ❖ *adj.* Not full or complete; partial: *a part owner of the business.* —***phrasal verb:*** **part with** To give up or let go of; relinquish. —***idioms:*** **for (one's) part** So far as one is concerned. **for the most part** To the greater extent; generally or mostly. **in good part** Good-naturedly or with good grace. **in part** To some extent; partly. **on the part of** Regarding or with respect to. **part and parcel** A basic or essential part. **part company** To leave another's presence. **take part** To join in; participate. **take (someone's) part** To side with in a disagreement; support. [ME < OFr. < Lat. *pars, part-.* See **perə-** in App.]

part. *abbr.* **1.** particle **2.** particular **3.** partitive

par·take (pär-tāk′) *v.* **-took** (-tŏŏk′), **-tak·en** (-tā′kən), **-tak·ing, -takes** —*intr.* **1.** To take or have a part or share; participate. **2.** To take or be given part or portion. **3.** To have part of the quality, nature, or character of something. —*tr.* To take or have a part in; share in. [Back-formation < *partaker*, one who partakes < ME *part-taker.*] —**par·tak′er** *n.*

part·ed (pär′tĭd) *adj.* **1.** Separated or divided into parts. **2.** Being or kept apart; separated. **3.** *Botany* Cleft almost to the base, so as to have distinct divisions or lobes. **4.** *Archaic* Deceased.

par·terre (pär-târ′) *n.* **1.** An ornamental flower garden having the beds and paths arranged to form a pattern. **2.** See **parquet circle.** [Fr. < OFr., ornamental garden < *par terre*, on the ground : *par*, over, on; see PARAMOUNT + *terre*, ground (< OFr. < Lat. *terra*, earth; see **ters-** in App.).]

parterre

par·the·no·car·py (pär′thə-nō-kär′pē) *n.* The production of fruit without fertilization. [Gk. *parthenos*, virgin + Gk. *karpos*, fruit; see **-CARP** + -Y².] —**par′the·no·car′pic** *adj.*

par·the·no·gen·e·sis (pär′thə-nō-jĕn′ĭ-sĭs) *n.* A form of reproduction in which an unfertilized egg develops into a new individual, occurring commonly among insects and certain other arthropods. [NLat. : Gk. *parthenos*, virgin + GENESIS.] —**par′the·no·ge·net′ic** (-jə-nĕt′ĭk) *adj.* —**par′the·no·ge·net′i·cal·ly** *adv.*

Par·the·non (pär′thə-nŏn′, -nən) *n.* The chief temple of the goddess Athena built on the acropolis at Athens between 447 and 432 B.C. and considered a supreme example of Doric architecture. [Lat. *Parthenōn* < Gk. < *parthenos*, virgin.]

Parthenon
view of the west end

Par·thi·a (pär′thē-ə) An ancient country and kingdom of SW Asia corresponding to modern NE Iran; reached the height of its influence at the beginning of the 1st cent. B.C.

Par·thi·an (pär′thē-ən) *adj.* **1.** Of or relating to Parthia or its people, language, or culture. **2.** Delivered in or as if in retreat. ❖ *n.* **1.** A native or inhabitant of Parthia. **2.** The Iranian language of the Parthians.

par·tial (pär′shəl) *adj.* **1.** Of, relating to, being, or affecting only a part; not total; incomplete. **2.** Favoring one person or side over another or others; biased or prejudiced. **3.** Having a special liking or fondness for something or someone: *partial to spicy food.* ❖ *n.* **1.** *Music* See **harmonic** 1. **2.** *Mathematics* A partial derivative. [ME *parcial* < OFr. < LLat. *partiālis* < Lat. *pars, part-.* See PART.] —**par′tial·ness** *n.*

par·tial-birth abortion (pär′shəl-bûrth′) *n.* A late-term abor-

tion involving partial delivery of a viable fetus before extraction. Not in technical use.

partial derivative *n.* The derivative with respect to a single variable of a function of two or more variables, regarding other variables as constants.

partial differential equation *n.* A differential equation containing at least one partial derivative.

partial differentiation *n.* Differentiation with respect to a single variable in a function of several variables, regarding other variables as constants.

partial fraction *n.* One of a set of fractions having a sum equal to a specified fraction.

par·ti·al·i·ty (pär′shē-ăl′ĭ-tē, pär-shăl′-) *n., pl.* **-ties 1.** The state of being partial. **2.** Favorable prejudice or bias. **3.** A special fondness; a predilection. See Syns at **predilection.**

par·tial·ly (pär′shə-lē) *adv.* To a degree; not totally.

partial pressure *n.* The pressure that one component of a mixture of gases would exert if it were alone in a container.

partial tone *n.* See **harmonic** 1.

par·ti·ble (pär′tə-bəl) *adj.* That can be parted, divided, or separated; divisible: *a partible estate.*

par·tic·i·pant (pär-tĭs′ə-pənt) *n.* One that participates, shares, or takes part in something. ❖ *adj.* Sharing in or taking part; participating. —**par·tic′i·pance** *n.*

par·tic·i·pate (pär-tĭs′ə-pāt′) *v.* **-pat·ed, -pat·ing, -pates** —*intr.* **1.** To take part in something. **2.** To share in something. —*tr. Archaic* To partake of. [Lat. *participāre, participāt-* < *particeps, particip-*, partaker : *pars, part-*, part; see PART + *capere*, to take; see **kap-** in App.] —**par·tic′i·pa′tive** *adj.* —**par·tic′i·pa′tor** *n.*

par·tic·i·pa·tion (pär-tĭs′ə-pā′shən) *n.* The act of taking part or sharing in something. —**par·tic′i·pa′tion·al** *adj.*

par·tic·i·pa·to·ry (pär-tĭs′ə-pə-tôr′ē, -tōr′ē) *adj.* Marked by, requiring, or involving participation, esp. individually.

par·ti·cip·i·al (pär′tĭ-sĭp′ē-əl) *adj.* Of, relating to, consisting of, or formed with a participle. ❖ *n.* A participle. [Lat. *participiālis* < *participium*, part. See PART.] —**par′ti·cip′i·al·ly** *adv.*

par·ti·ci·ple (pär′tĭ-sĭp′əl) *n.* A form of a verb that in some languages, such as English, can function independently as an adjective, as *baked* in *We had some baked beans*, and is used with an auxiliary verb to indicate tense, aspect, or voice, as *baked* in *The beans were baked too long.* [ME < OFr., var. of *participe* < Lat. *participium* (transl. of Gk. *metokhē*, sharing, partaking, participle) < *particeps, particip-*, partaker. See PARTICIPATE.]

USAGE NOTE Readers will ordinarily associate participial phrases with the noun, noun phrase, or pronoun adjacent to it, and misplacement may produce comic effects, as in *Coming in for a landing, the control tower contacted the plane.* A correctly placed participial phrase leaves no doubt about what is being modified: *Sitting at her desk, Jane read the letter carefully.* • Another pitfall in using participial phrases is illustrated in the following sentence: *Turning the corner, the view was quite different.* Here there is no noun or pronoun in the sentence that the participial phrase could logically modify. Moving the phrase will not solve the problem (as it would in the sentence about the control tower). To avoid distracting the reader, it would be better to recast the sentence as *When we turned the corner, the view was quite different* or *Turning the corner, we had a different view.* • Several originally participial expressions have become prepositions, such as *concerning, considering*, and *speaking of*; these may be used without criticism to introduce phrases that are not associated with the immediately adjacent noun phrase, as in *Considering the hour, it is surprising that he arrived at all.*

par·ti·cle (pär′tĭ-kəl) *n.* **1.** A very small piece or part; a tiny portion or speck. **2.** A very small or the smallest possible amount or degree: *a particle of doubt.* **3.** *Physics* **a.** A body whose spatial extent and internal motion and structure, if any, are irrelevant in a specific problem. **b.** An elementary particle. **c.** A subatomic particle. **4.** *Linguistics* **a.** An uninflected item that has grammatical function but does not clearly belong to one of the major parts of speech, such as *to* in English infinitives. **b.** In some systems of grammatical analysis, any of various short function words, including articles, prepositions, and conjunctions. **5.** *Roman Catholic Church* **a.** A small piece of a consecrated host. **b.** One of the smaller, individual hosts. **6.** *Archaic* A small division or section of something written, such as a clause of a document. [ME < Lat. *particula*, dim. of *pars, part-*, part. See PART.]

particle accelerator *n.* A device, such as a cyclotron or linear accelerator, that accelerates charged subatomic particles or nuclei to high energies.

par·ti·cle·board or **particle board** (pär′tĭ-kəl-bôrd′, -bōrd′) *n.* A structural material made of wood fragments that are mechanically pressed into sheet form and bonded together with resin.

particle physics *n.* The branch of physics that deals with subatomic particles.

par·ti-col·ored (pär′tē-kŭl′ərd) *adj.* Having parts, sections, or areas colored differently from each other; pied. [< Obsolete *party*, variegated < ME *parti* < OFr., divided, striped, p. part. of *partir*, to divide. See PARTY.]

par·tic·u·lar (pər-tĭk′yə-lər, pə-tĭk′-) *adj.* **1.** Of, belonging to, or associated with a specific person, group, thing, or category; not general or universal: *has a particular preference for Chinese art.* **2.** Separate and distinct from others of the same group, category, or nature: *made an exception in this particular case.* **3.** Worthy of note; exceptional. **4a.** Of, relating to, or providing details: *a particular description.* **b.** Attentive to or concerned with details or niceties, often excessively so; meticulous or fussy. **5.** *Logic* Encompassing some but not all of the members of a class or group. Used of a proposition. ❖ *n.* **1.** An individual item, fact, or detail. See Syns at **item. 2.** An item or detail of information or news. Often used in the plural. **3.** A separate case or an individual thing or instance, esp. one that can be distinguished from a larger category or class. Often used in the plural: *"What particulars were ambushed behind these generalizations?"* (Aldous Huxley). **4.** *Logic* A particular proposition. —*idiom:* **in particular** Particularly; especially. [ME *particuler* < OFr. < LLat. *particulāris* < Lat. *particula,* dim. of *pars, part-,* part. See PART.]

par·tic·u·lar·ism (pər-tĭk′yə-lə-rĭz′əm, pə-tĭk′-) *n.* **1.** Exclusive adherence to or interest in one's own group, party, sect, or nation. **2.** A principle of allowing each state in a nation or federation to act independently of the central authority. —**par·tic′u·lar·ist** *n.* —**par·tic′u·lar·is′tic** *adj.*

par·tic·u·lar·i·ty (pər-tĭk′yə-lăr′ĭ-tē, pə-tĭk′-) *n., pl.* **-ties 1.** The quality or state of being particular rather than general. **2.** Exactitude of detail, esp. in description. **3.** Attention to or concern with detail; fastidiousness. **4.** A specific point or detail; a particular. **5.** An individual characteristic; a peculiarity.

par·tic·u·lar·ize (pər-tĭk′yə-lə-rīz′, pə-tĭk′-) *v.* **-ized, -iz·ing, -iz·es** —*tr.* **1.** To mention, describe, or treat individually; itemize or specify. **2.** To make particular as opposed to general or universal. —*intr.* To go into or give details or particulars. —**par·tic′u·lar·i·za′tion** (-lər-ĭ-zā′shən) *n.* —**par·tic′u·lar·iz′er** *n.*

par·tic·u·lar·ly (pər-tĭk′yə-lər-lē, pə-tĭk′-) *adv.* **1.** To a great degree. **2.** With particular reference or emphasis; individually or specifically. **3.** With regard to particulars; in detail.

par·tic·u·late (pər-tĭk′yə-lĭt, -lāt′, pär-) *adj.* Of, relating to, or formed of separate particles. ❖ *n.* **1.** A minute separate particle, as of a granular substance or powder. **2.** Particulate matter. Often used in the plural: *atmospheric particulates.* [< Lat. *particula,* a small part. See PARTICLE.]

part·ing (pär′tĭng) *n.* **1a.** The act or process of separating or dividing. **b.** The state of being separated or divided. **2.** A departure or leave-taking. ❖ *adj.* Given, received, or done on departing or separating: *a parting gift.* —*idiom:* **parting of the ways** A point of divergence, esp. an important one.

parting shot *n.* An act of aggression or retaliation, such as a retort or threat, that is made upon one's departure or at the end of a heated discussion.

par·ti pris (pär′tē prē′) *n., pl.* **par·tis pris** (pär′tē) An inclination for or against something or someone that affects judgment; bias. [Fr. : *parti,* decision, side + *pris,* taken.]

par·ti·san[1] (pär′tĭ-zən) *n.* **1.** A fervent, sometimes militant supporter or proponent of a party, cause, person, or idea. **2.** A member of an organized body of fighters who attack or harass an enemy; a guerrilla. ❖ *adj.* **1.** Of, relating to, or characteristic of a partisan or partisans. **2.** Devoted to or biased in support of a party, group, or cause. [Fr. < OFr. < OItal. dialectal *partisano,* var. of OItal. *partigiano* < *parte,* part < Lat. *pars, part-.* See PART.] —**par′ti·san·ship′** *n.*

par·ti·san[2] *also* **par·ti·zan** (pär′tĭ-zən) *n.* A weapon having a blade with lateral projections mounted on the end of a long shaft, used chiefly in the 16th and 17th centuries. [Fr. *partizane* < Ital. dialectal *(arma) partisana,* partisan (weapon), fem. sing. of *partisano,* supporter. See PARTISAN[1].]

par·ti·ta (pär-tē′tə) *n. Music* **1.** An instrumental piece, such as a suite, composed of a series of variations. **2.** One of the variations contained in such a piece. [Ital. < fem. p. part. of *partire,* divide < Lat. *partīre.* See PARTITE.]

par·tite (pär′tīt′) *adj.* Divided into parts. [Lat. *partītus,* p. part. of *partīre,* to divide < *pars, part-,* part. See PART.]

par·ti·tion (pär-tĭsh′ən) *n.* **1a.** The act or process of dividing something into parts. **b.** The state of being so divided. **2a.** Something that divides or separates, as a wall dividing one room or cubicle from another. **b.** A wall, septum, or other separating membrane in an organism. **3.** A part or section into which something has been divided. **4.** Division of a country into separate autonomous nations. **5.** *Mathematics* **a.** The representation of a positive integer as a sum of positive integers. **b.** The decomposition of a set into a family of disjoint sets. **6.** *Computer Science* A section of storage space on a hard disk. **7.** *Law* Division of property, esp. real estate. ❖ *tr.v.* **-tioned, -tion·ing, -tions 1.** To divide into parts, pieces, or sections. **2.** To divide or separate by means of a partition. **3.** To divide (a country) into separate autonomous nations. [ME *particioun* < OFr. *partition* < Lat. *partītiō, partītiōn-* < *partītus,* p. part. of *partīre,* to divide < *pars, part-,* part. See PART.] —**par·ti′tion·er** *n.* —**par·ti′tion·ment** *n.*

par·ti·tion·ist (pär-tĭsh′ə-nĭst) *n.* One who advocates partition of a country.

par·ti·tive (pär′tĭ-tĭv) *adj.* **1.** Dividing or serving to divide something into parts; marked by division. **2.** *Grammar* Indicating

a part as distinct from a whole, as *some of the coffee* in the sentence *She drank some of the coffee.* ❖ *n. Grammar* **1.** A partitive word, such as *many* or *less.* **2.** A partitive construction or case. [ME < OFr. *partitif* < LLat. *partītīvus* < Lat. *partītus,* p. part. of *partīre,* to divide. See PARTITE.]

part·let (pärt′lĭt) *n.* A collared, usu. ruffled covering for the neck and shoulders, popular in 16th-century Europe and worn esp. by women. [Alteration of ME *patelet* < OFr. *patelete,* band of cloth, dim. of *pate,* paw. See PATOIS.]

part·ly (pärt′lē) *adv.* In part or in some degree; not completely.

part·ner (pärt′nər) *n.* **1.** One that is united or associated with another or others in an activity or a sphere of common interest, esp.: **a.** A member of a business partnership. **b.** A spouse. **c.** A domestic partner. **d.** Either of two persons dancing together. **e.** One of a pair or team in a sport or game, such as tennis or bridge. **2.** *Nautical* A wooden framework used to strengthen a ship's deck at the point where a mast or other structure passes through it. Often used in the plural. ❖ *v.* **-nered, -ner·ing, -ners** —*tr.* **1.** To make a partner of. **2.** To bring together as partners. **3.** To be the partner of. —*intr.* To work or perform as a partner. [ME *partener,* alteration (influenced by *part,* part) of *parcener,* parcener; see PARCENER.]

SYNONYMS *partner, colleague, ally, confederate* These nouns denote one who is united or associated with another, as in a relationship. A *partner* participates in a relationship in which each member has equal status: *a partner in a firm.* A *colleague* is an associate in an occupation or profession: *a colleague and fellow professor.* An *ally* is one who associates with another, at least temporarily, in a common cause: *countries that were allies.* A *confederate* is a member of a confederacy, league, or alliance or sometimes a collaborator in a suspicious venture: *confederates in a scheme to oust the chairman.*

part·ner·ship (pärt′nər-shĭp′) *n.* **1.** The state of being a partner. **2a.** A legal contract entered into by two or more persons in which each agrees to furnish a part of the capital and labor for a business enterprise, and by which each shares a fixed proportion of profits and losses. **b.** The persons bound by such a contract. **3.** A relationship of individuals or groups marked by mutual cooperation and responsibility.

part of speech *n., pl.* **parts of speech 1.** One of a group of traditional classifications of words according to their functions in context, including the noun, pronoun, verb, adjective, adverb, preposition, conjunction, and interjection and sometimes the article. **2.** A word considered as a part of speech.

par·ton (pär′tŏn′) *n.* A hypothetical elementary particle formerly believed to be a constituent of hadrons. [PART(ICLE) + -ON[1].]

par·took (pär-tŏŏk′) *v.* Past tense of **partake.**

par·tridge (pär′trĭj) *n., pl.* **partridge** *or* **-tridg·es 1.** Any of several plump-bodied Old World game birds, esp. of the genera *Perdix* and *Alectoris,* related to the pheasants and grouse. **2.** Any of several birds, such as the bobwhite, similar or related to the partridge. [ME *partrich* < OFr. *perdriz,* alteration of *perdis* < Lat. *perdīx* < Gk. See **perd-** in App.]

par·tridge·ber·ry (pär′trĭj-bĕr′ē) *n.* A creeping evergreen perennial plant *(Mitchella repens)* of eastern North America having small white flowers and scarlet berries.

part song *n.* **1.** An unaccompanied secular, usu. homophonic choral composition, esp. of the 19th century. **2.** An unaccompanied secular polyphonic song predating the madrigal.

part-time (pärt′tīm′) *adj.* For or during less than the customary or standard time: *a part-time job.* —**part′-time′** *adv.* —**part′-tim′er** *n.*

par·tu·ri·ent (pär-tŏŏr′ē-ənt, -tyŏŏr′-) *adj.* **1.** About to bring forth young; being in labor. **2.** Of or relating to giving birth. **3.** About to produce or come forth with something, such as an idea. [Lat. *parturiēns, parturient-,* pr. part. of *parturīre,* to be in labor < *partus,* p. part. of *parere,* to give birth.] —**par·tu′ri·en·cy** *n.*

par·tu·ri·fa·cient (pär-tŏŏr′ə-fā′shənt, -tyŏŏr′-) *adj.* Inducing or facilitating childbirth. ❖ *n.* A parturifacient drug. [Lat. *parturīre,* to be in labor; see PARTURIENT + -FACIENT.]

par·tu·ri·tion (pär′tyŏŏ-rĭsh′ən, -tŏŏ-, pär′chə-) *n.* The act or process of giving birth; childbirth. [LLat. *parturītiō, parturītiōn-* < Lat. *parturītus,* p. part. of *parturīre,* to be in labor. See PARTURIENT.]

part·way (pärt′wā′) *adv. Informal* To a certain degree or distance; in part.

par·ty (pär′tē) *n., pl.* **-ties 1a.** A social gathering esp. for pleasure or amusement. **b.** A group of people who have gathered to participate in an activity. **2.** An established political group organized to promote and support its principles and candidates for public office. **3a.** A person or group involved in an enterprise; a participant or an accessory. **b.** *Law* A person or group involved in a legal proceeding as a litigant. **4a.** A subscriber to a telephone party line. **b.** A person using a telephone. **5.** A person. **6.** A selected group of soldiers. **7.** *Slang* **a.** An act of sexual intercourse. **b.** An orgy. ❖ *adj.* **1.** Of, relating to, or participating in an established political organization. **2.** Suitable for use at a social gathering. **3.** Characteristic of a pleasurable social gathering. ❖ *intr.v.* **-tied, -ty·ing, -ties** *Informal* To celebrate or carouse at or as if at a party. [ME *partie*, group < OFr. < fem. p. part. of *partir*, to divide < Lat. *par-tīre* < *pars*, *part-*, part. See PART.]

party line *n.* **1.** A telephone circuit connecting subscribers with the same exchange. **2.** One or more of the policies or principles of a political party to which members are expected to adhere. —**party liner, par′ty-lin′er** (pär′tē-lī′nər) *n.*

par·ty poop·er also **par·ty-poop·er** (pär′tē-pōō′pər) *n. Slang* One who declines to participate with enthusiasm, esp. in the recreational activities of a group.

party wall *n.* A wall built on the boundary line of adjoining properties and shared by both owners. [Obsolete *party*, shared, divided < OFr. *parti*. See PARTI-COLORED.]

pa·rure (pə-rōōr′) *n.* A set of matched jewelry or other ornaments. [Fr. < OFr., adornment < *parer*, to adorn. See PARE.]

par value *n.* The value imprinted on a security, such as a stock certificate or bond, used to calculate a payment, such as a dividend or interest; face value.

par·ve (pär′və) *adj.* Variant of **pareve.**

par·ve·nu (pär′və-nōō′, -nyōō′) *n.* A person who has suddenly risen to a higher social and economic class and has not yet gained social acceptance in that class. [Fr. < p. part. of *parvenir*, to arrive < Lat. *pervenīre* : *per*, through; see PER¹ in App. + *venīre*, to come; see gⸯā- in App.] —**par′ve·nu′** *adj.*

par·vis (pär′vĭs) *n.* **1.** An enclosed courtyard or space at the entrance to a building, esp. a cathedral, that is sometimes surrounded by porticoes or colonnades. **2.** Such a portico or colonnade. [ME < OFr., alteration of *pareis*, paradise < LLat. *paradīsus*, garden, paradise. See PARADISE.]

par·vo (pär′vō) *n., pl.* **-vos** A parvovirus.

par·vo·vi·rus (pär′vō-vī′rəs) *n., pl.* **-rus·es** Any of a group of small viruses that contain DNA in an icosahedral protein shell and cause disease in many vertebrates, esp. mammals. [Lat. *parvus*, small + VIRUS.]

pas (pä) *n., pl.* **pas** (pä) **1.** A step or dance. **2.** The right of precedence. [Fr. < OFr. < Lat. *passus*, step. See PACE¹.]

Pas·a·de·na (păs′ə-dē′nə) **1.** A city of S CA NE of Los Angeles; noted for its annual Tournament of Roses parade. Pop. 133,936. **2.** A city of SE TX, a suburb of Houston. Pop. 141,674.

Pa·sar·ga·dae (pə-sär′gə-dē′) A ruined city of ancient Persia NE of Persepolis; said to have been founded by Cyrus the Great in 550 B.C.

pas·cal (pă-skäl′, pä-skäl′) *n.* **1.** A unit of pressure equal to one newton per square meter. **2.** **Pascal** or **PASCAL** A high-level programming language for support of structured programming, used in applications and systems programming. [After Blaise PASCAL.]

Pascal, Blaise 1623–62. French mathematician who co-developed, with Fermat, the modern theory of probability.

pas·cal celery also **Pas·cal celery** (pă-skäl′) *n.* Any of several types of celery having unblanched green stalks. [?]

Pas·cal's triangle (pă-skälz′, pä-skälz′) *n.* A triangle of numbers in which a row represents the coefficients of the binomial series. [After Blaise PASCAL.]

Pascal's wager *n.* An argument that belief in God is rational whether or not God exists, since falsely denying the existence of God may lead to damnation whereas falsely believing that God exists leads to no harm. [After Blaise PASCAL.]

Pasch (păsk) *n.* **1.** Passover. **2.** Easter. [ME < OFr. *pasche* < LLat. *pascha*, Passover, Easter < L.Gk. *paskha* < Aram. *pashā*, passover; akin to Heb. *pesaḥ*. See PESACH.] —**Pas′chal, pas′chal** *adj.*

paschal lamb *n.* **1.** The lamb sacrificed at the first Passover. **2. Paschal Lamb** Jesus. **3. Paschal Lamb** See **Agnus Dei** 1.

pas de bour·rée (pä də bōō-rā′, bōō-) *n., pl.* **pas de bourrée** A small stepping movement in ballet, often executed on pointe. [Fr. : *pas*, step + *de*, of + *bourrée*, bourrée.]

Pas de Ca·lais (pä də kä-lā′, käl′ā, kä-lĕ′) The Strait of Dover.

pas de chat (shä) *n., pl.* **pas de chat** A ballet jump in which the feet are lifted, one after the other, to the level of the opposite knee. [Fr. : *pas*, step + *de*, of + *chat*, cat.]

pas de deux (dœ) *n., pl.* **pas de deux** **1.** A dance for two, esp. in ballet. **2.** A close relationship between two people or things, as during an activity. [Fr. : *pas*, step + *de*, of, for + *deux*, two.]

pas de quat·re (kät′rə) *n., pl.* **pas de quatre** A dance for four. [Fr. : *pas*, step + *de*, of, for + *quatre*, four.]

pas de trois (trwä) *n., pl.* **pas de trois** A dance for three. [Fr. : *pas*, step + *de*, of, for + *trois*, three.]

pa·se (pä′sā) *n.* One of several usu. one-handed maneuvers in bullfighting in which the matador presents and moves the cape to attract a close passing charge of the bull. [Sp. < *pasar*, to pass < VLat. *passāre*. See PASS.]

pa·se·o (pä-sā′ō) *n., pl.* **-os** **1.** A slow easy stroll or walk outdoors. **2.** The street, series of streets, or walkway along which

Blaise Pascal
portrait by Philippe de
Champaigne (1602–74)

pasqueflower
American pasqueflower
Anemone patens

such a walk is taken. **3.** In bullfighting, the formal procession into the ring of the players, including the matadors, banderilleros, and horses, that occurs just before the first bull is fought. [Sp. < *pasear*, to take a stroll, freq. of *pasar*, to go, pass. See PASE.]

pash (păsh) *n. Slang* **1.** A romantic infatuation. **2.** The object of such an infatuation. [Short for PASSION.]

pa·sha also **pa·cha** (pä′shə, păsh′ə, pə-shä′) *n.* Used formerly as a title for military and civil officers, esp. in Turkey and northern Africa. [Turk. *paşa* < Pers. *pādshāh*. See PADISHAH.]

pash·mi·na (păsh-mē′nə) *n.* **1.** Fine, downy wool growing beneath the outer hair of feral Himalayan goats. **2.** A soft fabric made of this wool. [Pers. *pashmīne*, woolen garment, pashmina < *pashmīn*, made of wool < *pashm*, wool, down.]

Pash·to (pŭsh′tō) also **Push·tu** (pŭsh′tōō) *n.* An Iranian language that is the principal vernacular language of Afghanistan and parts of western Pakistan. [Pers. *pashtu* < Pashto *pašto*, perh. ult. < Iran. *parsāwa-*, border, border people.]

Pash·tun (pŭsh′tōōn) *n.* A member of the predominant ethnic group of Afghanistan and parts of western Pakistan. [Pashto *Paštūn*. See PATHAN.]

Pa·siph·a·ë (pə-sĭf′ə-ē′) *n. Greek Mythology* **1.** The wife of Minos and mother, by a white bull, of the Minotaur. **2.** A satellite of Jupiter.

pa·so do·ble also **pa·so·do·ble** (pä′sō-dō′blä, -vlĕ) *n., pl.* **-bles** (-bläz, -vlĕs) **1.** A moderately fast Spanish dance. **2.** Music for or in the rhythm of this dance, set in march time and often played at bullfights. [Sp. : *paso*, step + *doble*, double.]

Pa·so·li·ni (pä′sō-lē′ne), **Pier Paolo** 1922–75. Italian writer and director whose films include *The Decameron* (1971).

pasque·flow·er (păsk′flou′ər) *n.* Any of several plants of the genus *Anemone*, esp. *A. patens*, having large blue, purple, or white flowers. [Alteration (influenced by *pasque*, Easter < their flowering in April) of obsolete *passeflower* < Fr. *passefleur* : *passer*, to pass; see PASS + *fleur*, flower; see FLOWER.]

pas·qui·nade (păs′kwə-nād′) *n.* A satire or lampoon, esp. one that ridicules a specific person, traditionally written and posted in a public place. [Fr. < Ital. *pasquinata*, after *Pasquino*, nickname of a Roman statue used for lampoons.] —**pas′qui·nade′** *v.*

pass (păs) *v.* **passed, pass·ing, pass·es** —*intr.* **1.** To move on or ahead; proceed. **2.** To extend; run: *The river passes through our land.* **3a.** To move by: *The band passed and the crowd cheered.* **b.** To move past another vehicle: *The sports car passed on the right.* **4.** To gain passage despite obstacles: *passed through difficulties.* **5.** To move past in time; elapse: *The days passed quickly.* **6a.** To be transferred from one to another; circulate. **b.** *Sports* To propel a ball or puck to a teammate. **7.** To be communicated or exchanged between persons. **8.** To be transferred or conveyed to another by will or deed: *The title passed to the older heir.* **9.** To undergo transition from one condition, form, quality, or characteristic to another: *Daylight passed into darkness.* **10.** To come to an end: *The headache finally passed.* **11.** To cease to exist; die. Often used with *on.* **12.** To happen; take place. **13a.** To be allowed to happen without notice or challenge: *Let the rude remark pass.* **b.** *Games* To decline one's turn to play or bid, draw, bet, compete, or play. **c.** To decline an offer: *We offered him dessert, but he passed.* **14.** To undergo an examination or trial with favorable results. **15a.** To serve as a barely acceptable substitute. **b.** To be accepted as a member of a group by denying one's own ancestry or background. **16.** To be approved or adopted: *The motion to adjourn passed.* **17.** *Law* **a.** To pronounce an opinion, judgment, or sentence. **b.** To sit in adjudication. **18.** To be voided: *Her kidney stone passed.* **19.** *Sports* To thrust or lunge in fencing. —*tr.* **1.** To go by without stopping; leave behind. **2a.** To go by without paying attention to; disregard or ignore. **b.** To fail to pay (a dividend). **3.** To go beyond; surpass. **4.** To go across; go through: *We passed the border.* **5a.** To undergo (a trial or examination) with favorable results: *passed the test.* **b.** To cause or allow to go through a trial, test, or examination successfully: *The instructor passed all the candidates.* **6a.** To cause to move: *We passed our hands over the fabric.* **b.** To cause to move into a certain position. **c.** To cause to move as part of a process: *pass liquid through a filter.* **d.** To cause to go by. **e.** *Baseball* To walk (a batter). **f.** To maneuver (the bull) by means of a pase in bullfighting. **7.** To allow to go by or elapse; spend: *He passed his winter in Vermont.* **8.** To allow to cross a barrier: *The border guard passed the tourists.* **9a.** To cause to be transferred from one to another; circulate. **b.** To hand over to someone else. **c.** *Sports* To propel (a ball, for example) to a teammate, as by throwing. **d.** To cause to be accepted; circulate fraudulently. **e.** *Law* To transfer title or ownership of. **10.** To discharge (body waste, for example); void. **11a.** To approve; adopt: *The legislature passed the bill.* **b.** To be sanctioned, ratified, or approved by: *The bill passed the House of Representatives.* **12.** To pronounce; utter: *pass sentence on an offender.* ❖ *n.* **1.** The act of passing; passage. **2.** A way or means of passage, as through a barrier. See Syns at **way.** **3a.** A permit, ticket, or authorization to come and go at will. **b.** A free ticket entitling one to transportation or admission. **c.** Written leave of absence from military duty. **4a.** A sweep or run by an aircraft over an area or target. **b.** A single complete cycle of operations, as by a computer program. **5.** A condition or situation, often critical in nature; a predicament. **6.** A sexual invitation or overture. **7.** A motion of the hand or the waving of a wand.

8a. *Sports* A transfer of a propelled ball or puck between teammates. **b.** *Sports* A lunge or thrust in fencing. **c.** *Baseball* A base on balls. **9.** *Games* A refusal to bid, draw, bet, compete, or play. **10.** *Games* A winning throw of the dice in craps. **11.** A pase in bullfighting. —***phrasal verbs:*** **pass away** 1. To pass out of existence; end. 2. To die. **pass for** To be accepted as or believed to be. **pass off** 1. To offer, sell, or put into circulation (an imitation) as genuine. 2. To present (one's self) as other than what one is. **pass out** To lose consciousness. **pass over** To leave out; disregard. **pass up** *Informal* To let go by; reject. —***idioms:*** **bring to pass** To cause to happen. **come to pass** To occur. **pass muster** To pass an examination or inspection; measure up to a given standard. **pass (one's) lips** 1. To be eaten or drunk. 2. To issue or be spoken. **pass the buck** *Slang* To shift responsibility or blame to another. **pass the hat** To take up a collection of money. **pass the time of day** To exchange greetings or engage in pleasantries. **pass the torch** To relinquish (responsibilities, for example) to another or others. [ME *passen* < OFr. *passer* < VLat. *passāre* < Lat. *passus*, step. See PACE[1].] —**pass′er** *n.*

pass. *abbr.* **1.** passage **2.** passive

pass·a·ble (păs′ə-bəl) *adj.* **1.** That can be passed, traversed, or crossed; navigable. **2.** Acceptable for general circulation. **3.** Satisfactory but not outstanding; adequate. **4.** That can be legislated. —**pass′a·ble·ness** *n.* —**pass′a·bly** *adv.*

pas·sa·ca·glia (pä′sə-käl′yə, päs′ə-käl′yə) *n.* **1.** A musical form of the 17th and 18th centuries consisting of continuous variations on a ground bass and similar to the chaconne. **2.** A dance of the period performed to such music. [Ital. < Sp. *pasacalle* : *pasar*, to pass, step; see PASE + *calle*, street (< Lat. *callis*, call-), path).]

pas·sade (pə-säd′) *n.* **1.** A dressage technique in which the horse is made to course repeatedly over the same spot. **2.** A passing flirtation or romance. [Fr., passado, passade < Ital. *passata* < *passare*, to pass. See PASSAGE[2].]

pas·sa·do (pə-sä′dō) *n., pl.* **-dos** or **-does** A fencing maneuver in which the foil is thrust forward and one foot advanced at the same time. [Alteration of French *passade*. See PASSADE.]

pas·sage¹ (păs′ij) *n.* **1.** The act or process of passing, esp.: **a.** A movement from one place to another, as by going by or across; transit or migration. **b.** The process of elapsing: *the passage of time.* **c.** The process of passing from one condition or stage to another; transition. **d.** Enactment into law of a legislative measure. **2.** A journey, esp. one by air or water. **3.** The right to travel as a passenger, esp. on a ship. **4.** The right, permission, or power to come and go freely. **5a.** A path, channel, or duct through, over, or along which something may pass. **b.** A corridor. See Syns at **way. 6a.** An occurrence or event. **b.** Something, such as an exchange of words, that occurs between two persons. **7a.** A segment of a written work or speech. **b.** *Music* A segment of a composition. **c.** A section of a painting or other piece of artwork; a detail. **8.** *Physiology* An act of emptying, as of the bowels. **9.** *Biology* The process of passing or maintaining a group of microorganisms or cells through a series of hosts or cultures. **10.** *Obsolete* Death. [ME < OFr. < *passer*, to pass. See PASS.]

pas·sage² (păs′ij, pə-säzh′) *n.* A slow cadenced trot in which the horse raises and returns to the ground first one diagonal pair of feet, then the other. ❖ *v.* **-saged, -sag·ing, -sag·es** —*intr.* To execute a passage. —*tr.* To cause (a horse) to execute a passage. [Fr. < *passager*, to execute a passage, alteration of *passéger* < Ital. *passeggiare* < *passare*, to pass < VLat. **passāre* < Lat. *passus*, step. See PACE[1].]

pas·sage grave (păs′ij) *n.* A Neolithic tomb consisting of a passageway and burial chamber made of large stones, originally buried in the earthen mound.

pas·sage·way (păs′ij-wā′) *n.* A way allowing passage, esp. a corridor.

pas·sage·work (păs′ij-wûrk′) *n.* **1.** A portion of a musical composition that permits a performer to make a display of technique. **2.** A musician's performance of a passagework.

Pas·sa·ic (pə-sā′ĭk) A city of NE NJ S of Paterson on the **Passaic River**, c. 129 km (80 mi); settled in 1678. Pop. 67,861.

pass-a·long also **pass·a·long** (păs′ə-lông′, -lŏng′) *n.* The policy, practice, or act of paying for an increased cost by raising the price charged to one's customers or clients.

Pas·sa·ma·quod·dy (păs′ə-mə-kwŏd′ē) *n., pl.* **Passamaquoddy** or **-dies** **1.** A member of a Native American people formerly inhabiting parts of coastal Maine and New Brunswick, with present-day descendants in eastern Maine. **2.** Their Algonquian language. [Of Micmac orig.]

Passamaquoddy Bay An arm of the Bay of Fundy between S New Brunswick, Canada, and E ME.

pas·sant (păs′ənt) *adj. Heraldry* Being a beast facing and walking toward the viewer's left with one front leg raised. [ME < OFr. pr. part. of *passer*, to pass. See PASS.]

pass·band (păs′bănd′) *n.* The range of frequencies transmitted by a bandpass filter.

pass·book (păs′bŏŏk′) *n.* **1.** See bankbook. **2.** A book in which a merchant records credit sales.

pas·sé (pă-sā′) *adj.* **1.** No longer current or in fashion; out-of-date. **2.** Past the prime; faded or aged. [Fr., p. part. of *passer*, to pass < OFr. See PASS.]

passed ball (păst) *n. Baseball* A pitch that the catcher should field but misses, allowing a runner to advance a base or more.

pas·sel (păs′əl) *n. Informal* A large quantity or group. [Alteration of PARCEL.]

passe·men·terie (păs-mĕn′trē) *n.* Trimming, such as braid or lace, for a garment. [Fr. < *passement*, braid, cloth < OFr., a passing < *passer*, to pass. See PASS.]

pas·sen·ger (păs′ən-jər) *n.* **1.** A person who travels in a conveyance, such as a car or train, without participating in its operation. **2.** *Informal* A person who participates only passively in an activity. **3.** A wayfarer or traveler. [ME *passinger*, alteration of *passager* < OFr. *passageor* < *passager*, passing < *passage*, passage. See PASSAGE[1].]

passenger pigeon *n.* An extinct migratory bird (*Ectopistes migratorius*) abundant in eastern North America until the latter part of the 19th century.

passe-par·tout (păs-pär-tōō′) *n.* **1.** Something, such as a master key, that permits one to pass or go at will. **2a.** A border, such as a mat, that is used to frame or mount a picture. **b.** An adhesive tape or a gummed paper used for a similar purpose. [Fr. : *passer*, to pass + *partout*, everywhere.]

passe·pied (păs-pyä′) *n.* **1.** A spirited dance in triple meter, popular in France and England in the 17th and 18th centuries, resembling a minuet but faster. **2.** Music for or in the rhythm of this dance. [Fr. : *passer*, to pass; see PASS + *pied*, foot (< OFr. < Lat. *pēs, ped-*; see PEDAL).]

pas·ser·by also **pas·ser-by** (păs′ər-bī′, -bī′) *n., pl.* **pas·sers·by** also **pas·sers-by** (păs′ərz-) A person who passes by.

pas·ser·ine (păs′ə-rīn′) *adj.* Of or relating to birds of the order Passeriformes, which includes perching birds and songbirds such as the finches and sparrows. [Lat. *passerīnus*, of sparrows < *passer*, sparrow.] —**pas′ser·ine** *n.*

pas seul (pä sœl′) *n., pl.* **pas seuls** (pä sœl′) A dance for one person. [Fr. : *pas*, step + *seul*, solo.]

pass-fail (păs′fāl′) *adj.* Of, relating to, or being a system of grading in which a student passes or fails instead of receiving a letter grade. ❖ *n.* This kind of a grading system.

pas·si·ble (păs′ə-bəl) *adj.* Capable of feeling or suffering; sensitive. [ME < OFr. < Lat. *passibilis* < Lat. *passus*, p. part. of *patī*, to suffer.] —**pas′si·bil′i·ty** *n.*

pas·sim (păs′ĭm) *adv.* Throughout or frequently; here and there. Used in textual annotation to indicate that something occurs frequently in the work cited. [Lat. < *passus*, p. part. of *pandere*, to scatter, spread out.]

pass·ing (păs′ĭng) *adj.* **1.** Moving by; going past. **2.** Of brief duration; transitory: *a passing fancy.* **3.** Cursory or superficial; casual: *a passing glance.* **4.** Allowing one to pass something such as a test or inspection; satisfactory: *a passing grade.* **5.** *Archaic* Extreme or great; surpassing. ❖ *adv.* Very; surpassingly. ❖ *n.* **1.** The act of one that passes or the fact of having passed. **2.** A place where or a means by which one can pass. **3.** Death. —***idiom:*** **in passing** While going by; incidentally. —**pass′ing·ly** *adv.*

passing note *n. Music* A note that connects two consonant pitches by stepwise motion and usu. occurs on a weak beat.

passing shot *n.* A forceful shot, as in tennis, that travels to one side out of the reach of one's opponent.

passing tone *n.* See passing note.

pas·sion (păsh′ən) *n.* **1.** A powerful emotion, such as love, joy, hatred, or anger. See Syns at **feeling. 2a.** Ardent love. **b.** Strong sexual desire; lust. **c.** The object of such love or desire. **3a.** Boundless enthusiasm. **b.** The object of such enthusiasm. **4.** An abandoned display of emotion, esp. of anger. **5. Passion a.** The sufferings of Jesus in the period following the Last Supper and the Crucifixion. **b.** A narrative, musical setting, or pictorial representation of Jesus's sufferings. **6.** *Archaic* Martyrdom. **7.** *Archaic* Passivity. [ME < OFr. < Med.Lat. *passiō, passiōn-*, sufferings of Jesus < LLat., physical suffering, sinful desire < Lat., an undergoing < *passus*, p. part. of *patī*, to suffer.]

pas·sion·al (păsh′ə-nəl) *adj.* Of, relating to, or filled with passion. ❖ *n.* A book of the sufferings of saints and martyrs.

pas·sion·ate (păsh′ə-nĭt) *adj.* **1.** Capable of, having, or dominated by powerful emotions. **2.** Wrathful by temperament; choleric. **3.** Marked by strong sexual desire; amorous or lustful. **4.** Showing or expressing strong emotion; ardent. **5.** Arising from or marked by passion. —**pas′sion·ate·ly** *adv.* —**pas′sion·ate·ness** *n.*

pas·sion·flow·er (păsh′ən-flou′ər) *n.* Any of various climbing, chiefly tropical American vines of the genus *Passiflora*, having showy flowers with a fringelike crown and a conspicuous stalk that bears the stamens and pistil. [< the resemblance of its parts to the instruments of the Passion.]

passion fruit *n.* The edible fruit of the passionflower.

pas·sion·less (păsh′ən-lĭs) *adj.* **1.** Lacking strong emotion or feeling. **2.** Unbiased or impartial; detached.

Passion play *n.* A dramatic performance of medieval origin that represents the events associated with the Passion of Jesus.

Passion Sunday *n.* The second Sunday before Easter.

Pas·sion·tide (păsh′ən-tīd′) *n.* The two weeks between Passion Sunday and Easter.

Passion Week *n.* The week between Passion Sunday and Palm Sunday.

passionflower

ă	pat	oi	boy
ā	pay	ou	out
âr	care	ŏŏ	took
ä	father	ōō	boot
ĕ	pet	ŭ	cut
ē	be	ûr	urge
ĭ	pie	*th*	thin
ī	pie	*th*	this
îr	pier	hw	which
ŏ	pot	zh	vision
ō	toe	ə	about,
ô	paw		item

Stress marks:
′ (primary);
′ (secondary), as in
lexicon (lĕk′sĭ-kŏn′)

pas•si•vate (păs′ə-vāt′) *tr.v.* **-vat•ed, -vat•ing, -vates 1.** To treat or coat (a metal) in order to reduce the chemical reactivity of its surface. **2.** To coat (a semiconductor, for example) with an oxide layer to protect against contamination and increase electrical stability. **—pas′si•va′tion** *n.* **—pas′si•va•tor** *n.*

pas•sive (păs′ĭv) *adj.* **1.** Receiving or subjected to an action without responding or initiating an action in return. See Syns at **inactive. 2.** Accepting or submitting without objection or resistance; submissive. **3.** Existing, conducted, or experienced without active or concerted effort: "[Many parents believe] *that computers are educational and . . . less passive than television*" (Tamar Lewin). **4.** Of or relating to certain bonds or shares that do not bear financial interest. **5.** Of or relating to a solar heating or cooling system that uses no external mechanical power. **6.** *Grammar* Indicating that the subject of the sentence is the object of the action or the effect of the verb. For example, in *They were impressed by his manner, were impressed* is in the passive voice. **7.** *Chemistry* Unreactive except under special or extreme conditions; inert. **8.** *Electronics* Exhibiting no gain or contributing no energy. **9.** *Psychology* Relating to or characteristic of an inactive or submissive role in a relationship, esp. a sexual relationship. ❖ *n.* **1.** *Grammar* **a.** The passive voice. **b.** A verb or construction in the passive voice. **2.** One that is submissive or inactive. Often used in the plural. [ME < OFr. *passif* < Lat. *passīvus*, subject to emotion, the passive < *passus*, p. part. of *patī*, to suffer.] **—pas′sive•ly** *adv.* **—pas′sive•ness** *n.*

pas•sive-ag•gres•sive (păs′ĭv-ə-grĕs′ĭv) *adj.* Of or characterized by habitual passive resistance to demands for adequate performance in occupational or social situations, as by procrastination, sullenness, or inefficiency.

passive immunity *n.* Immunity acquired by the transfer of antibodies from another individual, as through injection or placental transfer to a fetus. **—passive immunization** *n.*

pas•sive-ma•trix (păs′ĭv-mā′trĭks) *adj.* Of or relating to a liquid-crystal display that controls an entire row of cells in the liquid-crystal layer with a single transistor.

passive resistance *n.* Resistance by nonviolent methods to a government, an occupying power, or specific laws, as refusing to comply or demonstrating in protest. **—passive resister** *n.*

passive restraint *n.* An automatic safety device, such as an air bag, in a motor vehicle that protects a person during a crash.

passive smoking *n.* The involuntary inhalation of tobacco smoke by a person who occupies an area with a smoker.

pas•siv•ism (păs′ə-vĭz′əm) *n.* Passive character, attitude, quality, or behavior. **—pas′siv•ist** *n.*

pas•siv•i•ty (pă-sĭv′ĭ-tē) *n.* The condition or quality of being passive; inactivity, quiescence, or submissiveness.

pass•key (păs′kē′) *n.* **1.** See **master key. 2.** See **skeleton key.**

Pass•o•ver (păs′ō′vər) *n.* *Judaism* A holiday beginning on the 14th of Nisan and continuing for eight days or seven days, commemorating the exodus of the Jews from Egypt. [Transl. of Heb. *pesaḥ* (< *pāsaḥ*, to pass over).]

pass pattern *n.* *Football* A predetermined course that a receiver runs in order to be in position to catch a pass.

pass•port (păs′pôrt′, -pōrt′) *n.* **1.** An official government document that certifies one's identity and citizenship and permits a citizen to travel abroad. **2.** An official permit issued by a foreign country allowing one to transport goods or travel through that country. **3.** An official document issued by an allied foreign government to a ship, esp. a neutral merchant ship in time of war, authorizing it to enter and travel through certain waters freely. **4.** Something that gives one the right or privilege of passage, entry, or acceptance. [Fr. *passeport* < OFr. : *passer*, to pass; see PASS + *port*, port; see PORT[1].]

pass-through (păs′thro͞o′) *n.* **1.** An opening between two rooms, esp. a shelved space between a kitchen and dining room that is used for passing food. **2.** A route through which something is permitted to pass. **3.** A security that passes through payments made by debtors, thus providing investors with regular returns. **4.** See **pass-along. —pass′-through′** *adj.*

pass•word (păs′wûrd′) *n.* **1.** A secret word or phrase giving admittance or access to information. **2.** *Computer Science* A sequence of characters that one must input to gain access to a file, application, or computer system.

Pas•sy (pă-sē′, pä-), **Frédéric** 1822–1912. French economist who shared the first Nobel Peace Prize (1901).

Passy, Paul Édouard 1859–1940. French philologist who founded the International Phonetic Association (1894).

past (păst) *adj.* **1.** No longer current; gone by; over. **2.** Having existed or occurred in an earlier time; bygone. **3a.** Earlier than the present time; ago: *40 years past.* **b.** Just gone by or elapsed. **4.** Having served formerly in a given capacity, esp. an official one. **5.** *Grammar* Of, relating to, or being a verb tense or form used to express an action or condition prior to the time it is expressed. ❖ *n.* **1.** The time before the present. **2a.** Previous background, career, experiences, and activities. **b.** A former period of someone's life kept secret or thought to be shameful. **3.** *Grammar* **a.** The past tense. **b.** A verb form in the past tense. ❖ *adv.* So as to pass by or go beyond. ❖ *prep.* **1.** Beyond in time; later than or after: *a quarter past two.* **2.** Beyond in position; farther than. **3a.** Beyond the power, scope, extent, or influence of. **b.** Beyond in development or appropriateness. **4.** Beyond the number or amount of. [ME < p. part. of *passen*, to pass. See PASS.]

pas•ta (päs′tə) *n.* **1.** Unleavened dough, made of wheat flour, water, and sometimes eggs, that is molded into any of a variety of shapes and boiled. **2.** A prepared dish containing pasta as its main ingredient. [Ital. < LLat., paste, pastry cake. See PASTE[1].]

paste[1] (pāst) *n.* **1.** A soft, smooth, thick mixture or material, as: **a.** A smooth viscous mixture, as of flour and water or of starch and water, that is used as an adhesive for joining light materials, such as paper. **b.** The moist clay or clay mixture used in making porcelain or pottery. **c.** A smooth dough of water, flour, and butter or other shortening, used in making pastry. **d.** A food that has been pounded until it is reduced to a smooth creamy mass. **e.** A sweet doughy candy or confection. **2a.** A hard brilliant lead-containing glass used in making artificial gems. **b.** A gem made of this glass. ❖ *tr.v.* **past•ed, past•ing, pastes 1.** To cause to adhere by or as if by applying paste. **2.** To cover with something by or as if by pasting. **3.** *Computer Science* To insert (text, graphics, or other data) into a document or file. [ME < OFr. < LLat. *pasta* < Gk., barley porridge < neut. pl. of *pastos*, sprinkled, salted < *passein*, to sprinkle.]

paste[2] (pāst) *Slang tr.v.* **past•ed, past•ing, pastes 1.** To strike forcefully. **2.** To defeat soundly. ❖ *n.* A hard blow. [Prob. alteration of BASTE[3].]

paste•board (pāst′bôrd′, -bōrd′) *n.* **1.** A thin firm board made of sheets of paper pasted together or of pressed paper pulp. **2.** A card, esp.: **a.** A ticket. **b.** *Games* A playing card. **c.** A visiting card. ❖ *adj.* **1.** Made of pasteboard. **2.** Of inferior quality; flimsy or unsubstantial.

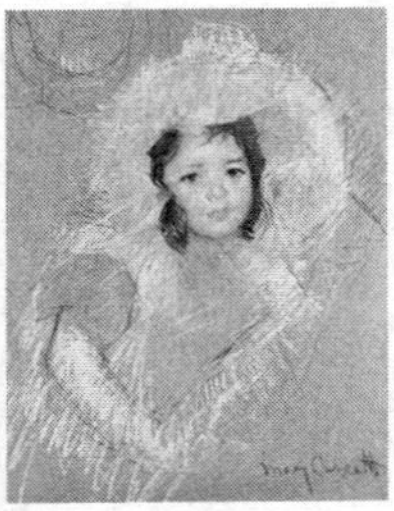

pastel
Margot Lux with a Large Hat
by Mary Cassatt

pas•tel (pă-stĕl′) *n.* **1a.** A drawing medium of dried paste made of ground pigments and a water-based binder that is manufactured in crayon form. **b.** A crayon of this material. **2a.** A picture or sketch drawn with this type of crayon. **b.** The art or process of drawing with pastels. **3.** A soft delicate hue; a pale color. **4.** A sketchy or brief prose work. ❖ *adj.* **1.** Of, relating to, or made of pastel. **2.** Pale and soft in color. [Fr. < Ital. *pastello*, material made into a paste < LLat. *pastellus*, woad dye, dim. of *pasta*, paste. See PASTE[1].] **—pas•tel′ist, pas•tel′list** *n.*

past•er (pā′stər) *n.* **1.** One that applies or covers with paste. **2.** A paper sticker.

pas•tern (păs′tərn) *n.* **1.** The part of a horse's foot between the fetlock and hoof. **2.** An analogous part of the leg of a dog or other quadruped. [Alteration of ME *pastron*, hobble, pastern < OFr. *pasturon*, dim. of *pasture*, pasture, tether, alteration of **pastoire* < Lat. *pāstōria*, fem. sing. of *pāstōrius*, of herdsmen < *pāstor*, shepherd. See PASTOR.]

Pas•ter•nak (păs′tər-năk′, pə-styĭr-näk′), **Boris Leonidovich** 1890–1960. Russian writer, best known for *Doctor Zhivago* (1957), who was forced to refuse the 1958 Nobel Prize for literature.

paste-up (pāst′ŭp′) *n.* **1.** A composition of light flat objects pasted onto a sheet of paper, board, or other backing. **2.** The art or process of making such a composition.

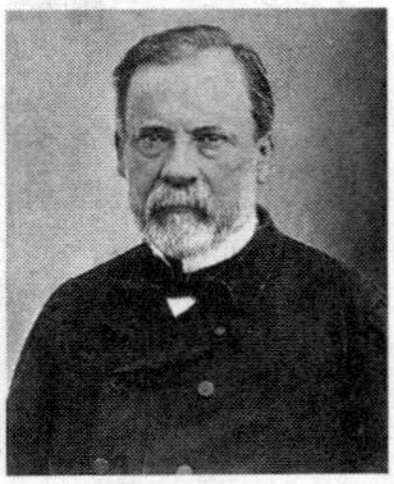

Louis Pasteur
photographed in the late 1880s

Pas•teur (păs-tûr′, pä-stœr′), **Louis** 1822–95. French chemist who invented the process of pasteurization and developed vaccines for anthrax and rabies. **—Pas•teur′i•an** *adj.*

Pasteur effect *n.* The inhibiting effect of oxygen on the process of fermentation. [After Louis PASTEUR.]

pas•teur•i•za•tion (păs′chər-ĭ-zā′shən, păs′tər-) *n.* **1.** The act or process of heating a beverage or other food, such as milk or beer, to a specific temperature for a specific period of time in order to kill microorganisms that could cause disease, spoilage, or undesired fermentation. **2.** The act or process of destroying most microorganisms in certain foods by irradiating them to prevent spoilage. [After Louis PASTEUR.]

pas•teur•ize (păs′chə-rīz′, păs′tə-) *tr.v.* **-ized, -iz•ing, -iz•es** To subject (a beverage or other food) to pasteurization. **—pas′teur•iz′er** *n.*

Pasteur treatment *n.* A treatment for rabies in which a series of increasingly strong inoculations with attenuated virus is given to stimulate antibody production during the incubation period of the disease. [After Louis PASTEUR.]

pas•tic•cio (pă-stē′chō, -chē-ō, pä-) *n., pl.* **-ci** (-chē) A work or style produced by borrowing fragments, ingredients, or motifs from various sources; a potpourri. [Ital. < VLat. **pastīcium*, pasty. See PATISSERIE.]

pas•tiche (pă-stēsh′, pä-) *n.* **1.** A dramatic, literary, or musical piece openly imitating the previous works of other artists, often with satirical intent. **2.** A pasticcio of incongruous parts; a hodgepodge. [Fr. < Ital. *pasticcio*. See PASTICCIO.]

past•ies (pā′stēz′) *pl.n.* A pair of adhesive patches that conceal a woman's nipples, worn usu. by erotic dancers. [PASTE[1].]

pas•tille (pă-stēl′) also **pas•til** (păs′tĭl) *n.* **1.** A small medicated or flavored tablet; a troche. **2.** A tablet containing aromatic substances that is burned to fumigate or deodorize the air. **3.** A pastel paste or crayon. [Fr. < Sp. *pastilla*, perfume pellet, and Ital. *pastillo*, pastille, both < Lat. *pāstillus*, little loaf, medicine tablet, dim. of *pānis*, bread. See **pā-** in App.]

pas•time (păs′tīm′) *n.* An activity that occupies one's spare time pleasantly. [ME *passe tyme*, transl. of Fr. *passe temps* : *passer*, to pass + *temps*, time.]

pas•ti•na (pă-stē′nə) *n.* Tiny pieces of pasta, often cooked in soup. [Ital., dim. of *pasta,* pasta. See PASTA.]

pas•tis (pă-stēs′) *n.* A French licorice-flavored liqueur, usu. drunk as an apéritif. [Fr., muddle, pastis < O Provençal *pastitz,* paste, pasty < VLat. *pastīcium.* See PATISSERIE.]

past master *n.* **1.** One who has formerly held the position of master in an organization, esp. a social one such as a lodge or club. **2.** One who is experienced and skilled in a particular craft or activity.

past•ness (păst′nĭs) *n.* **1.** The quality or condition of being past. **2.** The emotion or feeling evoked by memory.

Pas•to (păs′tō) A city of SW Colombia near the Ecuadorian border; founded 1539. Pop. 203,742.

pas•tor (păs′tər) *n.* **1.** A Christian minister or priest having spiritual charge over a congregation or other group. **2.** A layperson having spiritual charge over a person or group. **3.** A shepherd. ❖ *tr.v.* **-tored, -tor•ing, -tors** To serve or act as pastor of. [ME < OFr. < Lat. *pāstor,* shepherd. See pā- in App.] —**pas′tor•ship′** *n.*

pas•tor•al (păs′tər-əl, pă-stôr′-, -stōr′-) *adj.* **1a.** Of or relating to shepherds or herders. **b.** Of or used for animal husbandry. **2a.** Of or relating to the country or country life; rural. **b.** Charmingly simple and serene; idyllic. **3.** Of, relating to, or being a literary or other artistic work that portrays or evokes rural life, usu. in an idealized way. **4.** Of or relating to a pastor or the duties of a pastor. ❖ *n.* **1.** A pastoral literary or other artistic work. **2.** *Music* A pastorale. [ME < OFr. < Lat. *pāstōrālis < pāstor,* shepherd. See PASTOR.] —**pas′tor•al•ly** *adv.*

pas•to•rale (păs′tə-räl′, -răl′, -rä′lē, pä′stə-) *n., pl.* **-ra•li** (-rä′lē) or **-rales** **1.** An instrumental or vocal composition with a tender melody in a moderately slow rhythm, suggestive of traditional shepherds' music and rural life. **2.** A dramatic performance or opera, popular in the 16th and 17th centuries, based on a rural theme or subject. [Ital. < Lat. *pāstōrālis,* of herdsmen. See PASTORAL.]

Pastoral Epistles *n. Bible* The three New Testament Epistles, two addressed to Timothy and one to Titus, that are attributed to Saint Paul and concerned with the duties of ministers and certain issues of Church doctrine.

pas•tor•al•ism (păs′tər-ə-lĭz′əm, pă′stər-) *n.* **1.** The quality or state of being pastoral. **2.** A social and economic system based on raising livestock. —**pas′tor•al•ist** *n.*

pas•tor•ate (păs′tər-ĭt) *n.* **1.** The office, rank, or jurisdiction of a pastor. **2.** A pastor's term of office with one congregation. **3.** A body of pastors.

pas•to•ri•um (pă-stôr′ē-əm, -stōr′-) *n., pl.* **-ums** *Chiefly Southern US* The residence of a pastor; a parsonage. [PAST(OR) + Lat. *-ōrium,* n. suff.; see -ORY.]

past participle *n.* A verb form indicating past or completed action or time that is used as a verbal adjective in phrases such as *baked beans* and with auxiliaries to form the passive voice or perfect and pluperfect tenses in constructions such as *The work was finished* and *She had baked the beans.*

past perfect *n.* See pluperfect.

pas•tra•mi (pə-strä′mē) *n., pl.* **-mis** A highly seasoned smoked cut of beef, usu. taken from the shoulder. [Yiddish *pastrame* < Rom. *pastramă < păstra,* to preserve < VLat. *parsitāre,* to spare, save < Lat. *parsus,* p. part. of *parcere,* to be thrifty with.]

pas•try (pā′strē) *n., pl.* **-tries** **1.** Dough or paste consisting primarily of flour, water, and shortening that is baked and often used as a crust for foods such as pies and tarts. **2a.** Baked sweet foods made with pastry. **b.** One of these baked foods. [ME *pastree* < *paste,* dough. See PASTE¹.]

past tense *n.* A verb tense used to express an action or a condition that occurred in or during the past.

pas•tur•age (păs′chər-ĭj) *n.* **1.** The grass or other vegetation eaten by grazing animals. **2.** Land covered with vegetation suitable for grazing animals. **3.** The business of grazing cattle.

pas•ture (păs′chər) *n.* **1a.** A tract of land that supports grass or other vegetation eaten by domestic grazing animals. **b.** Such vegetation, esp. that eaten by domestic grazing animals. **2.** The feeding or grazing of animals. ❖ *v.* **-tured, -tur•ing, -tures** —*tr.* **1.** To herd (animals) into a pasture to graze. **2.** To provide (animals) with pasturage. Used of land. **3a.** To graze on (land or vegetation). **b.** To use (land) as pasture. —*intr.* To graze in a pasture. —*idiom:* **put out to pasture 1.** To herd (grazing animals) into pasturable land. **2.** *Informal* To retire or compel to retire from work or a full workload. [ME < OFr. < LLat. *pāstūra* < Lat. *pāstus,* p. part. of *pāscere,* to feed. See pā- in App.] —**pas′tur•a•ble** *adj.* —**pas′tur•er** *n.*

pas•ture•land (păs′chər-lănd′) *n.* Land suitable for grazing.

past•y¹ (pā′stē) *adj.* **-i•er, -i•est 1.** Resembling paste in consistency. **2.** Having a pale lifeless appearance; pallid: *an unhealthy pasty complexion.* —**past′i•ness** *n.*

pas•ty² (păs′tē) *n., pl.* **-ties** *Chiefly British* A pie or turnover, esp. one filled with seasoned meat or fish. [ME *pastey* < OFr. *paste* < VLat. *pastātum* < LLat. *pasta,* paste. See PASTE¹.]

PA system *n.* A public-address system.

pat¹ (păt) *v.* **pat•ted, pat•ting, pats** —*tr.* **1a.** To tap gently with the open hand or with something flat. **b.** To stroke lightly as a gesture of affection. **2.** To mold by tapping gently with the hands

or a flat implement. —*intr.* **1.** To run or walk with a tapping sound. **2.** To hit something or against something gently or lightly. ❖ *n.* **1.** A light gentle stroke or tap. **2.** The sound made by a light stroke or tap or by light footsteps. **3.** A small mass shaped by or as if by patting: *a pat of butter.* —*idiom:* **pat on the back** A word or gesture of praise or approval. [< ME, a blow, perh. of imit. orig.]

pat² (păt) *adj.* **1.** Trite or glib; superficially complete or satisfactory. **2a.** Timely or opportune. **b.** Suitable; fitting. **3.** *Games* Being a poker hand that is strong enough to make drawing cards unlikely to improve it. ❖ *adv. Informal* Completely, exactly, or perfectly. [< PAT¹.] —**pat′ly** *adv.* —**pat′ness** *n.*

pat. *abbr.* patent

pa•ta•ca (pə-tä′kə) *n.* See table at **currency.** [Port. < Ar. 'abū ṭāqa : 'abū, father of, possessing, bound form of 'ab, father + ṭāqa, window (< ṭāqa, to be able, sustain).]

pa•ta•gi•um (pə-tā′jē-əm) *n., pl.* **-gi•a** (-jē-ə) **1.** A thin membrane extending between the body and a limb to form a wing or winglike extension, as in bats. **2.** An expandable membranous fold of skin between the wing and body of a bird. [Lat. *patagium,* gold tunic edging, perh. < Gk. *patageion < patagos,* clatter, of imit. orig.] —**pa•ta′gi•al** (-jē-əl) *adj.*

Pat•a•go•ni•a (păt′ə-gō′nē-ə, -gōn′yə) A tableland region of South America in S Argentina and Chile extending from the Colorado R. to the Straits of Magellan and the Andes to the Atlantic Ocean. —**Pat′a•go′ni•an** *adj. & n.*

Patagonian hare *n.* See mara.

pa•ta•phys•ics (pă′tə-fĭz′ĭks) *n.* (*used with a sing. verb*) The French absurdist concept of a philosophy or science dedicated to studying what lies beyond the realm of metaphysics, often expressed in nonsensical language. [Fr. *pataphysique,* alteration of Gk. *ta epi ta metaphusika,* the (works) after the metaphysics (pseudo-title of a work by Aristotle modeled on *ta meta ta phusika,* the (works) after the Physics, Aristotle's Metaphysics) : *epi,* after; see EPI– + *metaphusika,* metaphysics; see METAPHYSICS.] —**pa′ta•phys′i•cal** (-ĭ-kəl) *adj.*

patch¹ (păch) *n.* **1a.** A small piece of material affixed to another larger piece to conceal, reinforce, or repair a worn area, hole, or tear. **b.** A small piece of cloth used for patchwork. **2.** A small cloth badge affixed to a garment as a decoration or an insignia, as of a military unit. **3a.** A dressing or covering applied to protect a wound or sore. **b.** A pad or shield of cloth worn over an eye socket or an injured eye. **c.** A transdermal patch. **4.** A beauty spot applied to the skin. **5a.** A small piece, part, or section, esp. that which differs from or contrasts with the whole. **b.** A small plot or piece of land, esp. one that produces specific vegetation. **6.** An indefinite period of time; a spell. **7.** A temporary, removable electronic connection, as one between two components in a communications system. **8.** A piece of code added to software in order to fix a bug. ❖ *v.* **patched, patch•ing, patch•es** —*tr.* **1.** To put a patch or patches on. **2.** To make by sewing scraps of material together: *patch a quilt.* **3.** To mend, repair, or put together, esp. hastily, clumsily, or poorly: *patched up their friendship.* **4.** To connect (electronic components) temporarily, as with a patch cord. **5.** To correct a bug in (an item of software). —*intr. Electronics* To be connected temporarily. [ME *pacche,* perh. alteration of *pece, pieche,* piece. See PIECE.] —**patch′a•ble** *adj.* —**patch′er** *n.*

patch² (păch) *n.* A fool or clown; a dolt. [Perh. < Ital. dialectal *paccio* < OItal.]

patch cord *n.* A conductor with a plug at each end that is used to temporarily connect components of an electronic system.

patch•ou•li also **patch•ou•ly** (pə-choo′lē, păch′oo-lē) *n., pl.* **-lis** also **-lies** **1.** A small southeast Asian shrub (*Pogostemon cablin*) in the mint family, having leaves that yield a fragrant oil. **2.** A perfume made from this oil. [Tamil *paccuḷi.*]

patch pocket *n.* An unfitted flat pocket on the outside of a garment.

patch test *n.* A test for allergic sensitivity in which a suspected allergen is applied to the skin on a small surgical pad.

patch•work (păch′wûrk′) *n.* **1.** Needlework consisting of varicolored patches of material sewn together, as in a quilt. **2.** A collection of miscellaneous or incongruous parts; a jumble.

patchwork
detail of a patchwork quilt

patch•y (păch′ē) *adj.* **-i•er, -i•est 1.** Made up of or marked by patches: *patchy trousers.* **2.** Uneven in quality or performance. —**patch′i•ly** *adv.* —**patch′i•ness** *n.*

patd. *abbr.* patented

pate (pāt) *n.* **1.** The human head, esp. the top of the head. **2.** The intellect; one's brains. [ME.] —**pat′ed** *adj*

pâte (pät) *n.* See paste¹ 1b. [Fr. < OFr. *paste,* paste. See PASTE¹.]

pâ•té (pä-tā′) *n.* **1.** A meat paste, such as pâté de foie gras. **2.** A small pastry filled with meat or fish. [Fr. < OFr. *paste,* paste, pâté. See PASTE¹.]

pâté de foie gras (də fwä grä′) *n., pl.* **pâ•tés de foie gras** (pä-tā′) A paste made from goose liver, pork fat, onions, mushrooms, and often truffles. [Fr. : *pâté,* pâté + *de,* of + *foie,* liver + *gras,* fat.]

pa•tel•la (pə-tĕl′ə) *n., pl.* **-tel•lae** (-tĕl′ē) **1a.** A flat triangular bone located at the front of the knee joint. **b.** A dish-shaped anatomical formation. **2.** A pan or dish in ancient Rome. [Lat., dim. of *patina,* plate, pan. See PATEN.] —**pa•tel′lar, pa•tel′late** (-tĕl′ĭt, -āt′) *adj.*

pa•tel•li•form (pə-tĕl′ə-fôrm′) *adj.* Shaped like a pan, dish, or cup. [Lat. *patella*, small plate, pan; see PATELLA + −FORM.]

pat·en also **pat·in** (păt′n) *n.* **1.** A plate, usu. of gold or silver, that is used to hold the host during the celebration of the Eucharist. **2.** A plate or shallow dish, esp. an artifact from an ancient civilization. **3.** A thin disk of or resembling metal. [ME < OFr. *patene* < Med.Lat. *patina* < Lat., pan < Gk. *patanē*, platter.]

pa·ten·cy (pāt′n-sē) *n.* **1.** The state or quality of being obvious. **2.** *Biology* The state or quality of being open, expanded, or unblocked.

pat·ent (păt′nt) *n.* **1a.** A grant made by a government that confers upon the creator of an invention the sole right to make, use, and sell that invention for a set period of time. **b.** Letters patent. **c.** An invention protected by such a grant. **2a.** A grant made by a government that confers on an individual fee-simple title to public lands. **b.** The official document of such a grant. **c.** The land so granted. **3.** An exclusive right or title. ❖ *adj.* **1a.** Protected or conferred by a patent or letters patent: *a patent right.* **b.** Of, relating to, or dealing in patents: *patent law.* **2.** (*also* pāt′nt) Obvious; plain: *a patent falsehood.* See Syns at **apparent. 3.** (pāt′nt) *Biology* **a.** Not blocked; open. **b.** Spreading open; expanded. **4.** Of, relating to, or being a nonprescription drug or other medical preparation that is often protected by a trademark. **5.** Of high quality. Used of flour. **6.** (*also* pāt′nt) *Archaic* Open to general inspection. Used esp. of documents. ❖ *tr.v.* **-ent·ed, -ent·ing, -ents 1.** To obtain a patent on or for (an invention, for example). **2.** To invent, originate, or be the proprietor of (an idea, for example). **3.** To grant a patent to or for. [ME, document granting a right, short for *(lettre) patent*, open (letter) < OFr. *(lettre) patente* < Lat. *patēns, patent-*, open, pr. part. of *patēre*, to be open.] —**pat′ent·a·bil′i·ty** *n.* —**pat′ent·a·ble** *adj.*

pat·ent·ed (păt′n-tĭd) *adj.* **1.** Characteristic of, unique to, or originated by a particular person or group. **2.** Protected or conferred by a patent or letters patent.

pat·ent·ee (păt′n-tē′) *n.* The party that possesses or has been granted a patent.

patent leather *n.* Black leather finished to a hard glossy surface and used esp. for shoes and clothing accessories.

patent log *n. Nautical* A torpedo-shaped instrument with rotary fins that is dragged from the stern of a vessel to measure the speed or distance traveled.

pat·ent·ly (pāt′nt-lē, păt′-) *adv.* In a patent manner.

patent office *n.* A government bureau that studies claims for, grants, and maintains records of patents.

pat·en·tor (păt′n-tər, păt′n-tôr′) *n.* One that grants a patent.

pa·ter (pā′tər) *n. Chiefly British* Father. [Lat. See **pəter-** in App.]

Pater, Walter Horatio 1839–94. British writer of *Studies in the History of the Renaissance* (1873).

pa·ter·fa·mil·i·as (pā′tər-fə-mĭl′ē-əs, pä′-, păt′ər-) *n., pl.* **pa·tres·fa·mil·i·as** (pā′trēz-, pä′-, păt′rēz-) A man who is the head of a household or the father of a family. [Lat. *paterfamiliās : pater,* father; see PATER + *familiās,* archaic genitive of *familia,* family; see FAMILY.]

pa·ter·nal (pə-tûr′nəl) *adj.* **1.** Relating to or characteristic of a father or fatherhood; fatherly. **2.** Received or inherited from a father: *a paternal trait.* **3.** Related through one's father: *my paternal aunt.* [ME < OFr. < LLat. *paternālis* < Lat. *paternus* < *pater,* father. See **pəter-** in App.] —**pa·ter′nal·ly** *adv.*

pa·ter·nal·ism (pə-tûr′nə-lĭz′əm) *n.* A policy or practice of treating or governing people in a fatherly way, esp. by providing for them without giving them rights or responsibilities. —**pa·ter′nal·ist** *adj. & n.* —**pa·ter′nal·is′tic** *adj.*

pa·ter·ni·ty (pə-tûr′nĭ-tē) *n., pl.* **-ties 1.** The state of being a father; fatherhood. **2.** Descent on a father's side; paternal descent. **3.** Authorship; origin. ❖ *adj.* Of or relating to a lawsuit brought by a woman attempting to establish that a particular man is the father of her child and so must provide the child with financial support. [ME *paternite* < OFr. < LLat. *paternitās* < Lat. *paternus,* paternal. See PATERNAL.]

paternity leave *n.* A leave of absence from work granted to a father to care for an infant.

paternity test *n.* A test using blood group identification in a mother, child, and putative father to establish the probability of paternity. —**paternity testing** *n.*

pa·ter·nos·ter (pā′tər-nŏs′tər, pä′-, păt′ər-) *n.* **1.** often **Paternoster** The Lord's Prayer. **2.** One of the large beads on a rosary on which the Lord's Prayer is said. **3.** A sequence of words spoken as a prayer or a magic formula. **4.** An elevator constructed of a series of doorless compartments hung on chains that move slowly and continuously, allowing passengers to step on and off at will. [ME < OE < LLat. : Lat. *pater,* father; see PATER + Lat. *noster,* our; see **nes-²** in App.]

Pat·er·son (păt′ər-sən) A city of NE NJ at the falls of the Passaic R. N of Newark; founded 1791. Pop. 149,222.

path (păth, päth) *n., pl.* **paths** (păthz, päthz, păths, päths) **1.** A trodden track or way. **2.** A road, way, or track made for a particular purpose. **3.** The route or course along which something travels or moves. **4.** A course of action or conduct: *the path of righteousness.* **5.** *Computer Science* **a.** A sequence of commands or a link between points that is needed to reach a particular goal. **b.** A pathname. [ME < OE *pæth.* See **pent-** in App.]

–path *suff.* **1.** A practitioner of a specified kind of medical treatment: *naturopath.* **2.** One affected by a specified kind of disorder: *sociopath.* [Back-formation < −PATHY.]

Pa·than (pə-tän′) *n.* A member of a Pashto-speaking people of eastern Afghanistan and northwest Pakistan, constituting the majority population of Afghanistan. [Hindi *Paṭhān* < Pashto *Pəštana,* pl. of *Pəštūn,* an Afghan < *pašto,* Pashto. See PASHTO.]

pa·thet·ic (pə-thĕt′ĭk) also **pa·thet·i·cal** (-ĭ-kal) *adj.* **1.** Arousing or capable of arousing sympathetic sadness and compassion. **2.** Arousing or capable of arousing scornful pity. [Fr. *pathétique* < LLat. *patheticus* < Gk. *pathētikos,* sensitive < *pathētos,* liable to suffer < *pathos,* suffering.] —**pa·thet′i·cal·ly** *adv.*

pathetic fallacy *n.* The attribution of human emotions or characteristics to inanimate objects or to nature.

path·find·er (păth′fīn′dər, päth′-) *n.* One that discovers a new course or way, esp. through or into unexplored regions.

patho– or **path–** *pref.* Disease; suffering: *pathogen.* [NLat. < Gk. < *pathos,* suffering.]

path·o·bi·ol·o·gy (păth′ō-bī-ŏl′ə-jē) *n.* See **pathology** 1.

path·o·gen (păth′ə-jən) *n.* An agent that causes disease, esp. a living microorganism such as a bacterium or fungus.

path·o·gen·e·sis (păth′ə-jĕn′ĭ-sĭs) also **pa·thog·e·ny** (pă-thŏj′ə-nē) *n.* The development of a diseased condition.

path·o·gen·ic (păth′ə-jĕn′ĭk) also **path·o·ge·net·ic** (-jə-nĕt′ĭk) *adj.* **1.** Capable of causing disease. **2.** Originating or producing disease. **3.** Of or relating to pathogenesis. —**path′o·gen′i·cal·ly** *adv.* —**path′o·ge·nic′i·ty** (-jə-nĭs′ĭ-tē) *n.*

pa·thog·no·mon·ic (pə-thŏg′nə-mŏn′ĭk, păth′ŏg-nō-) *adj.* Characteristic or symptomatic of a particular disease or condition. [Gk. *pathognōmonikos : patho-,* patho- + *gnōmonikos,* able to judge (< *gnōmōn,* interpreter; see **gnō-** in App.).]

path·o·log·i·cal (păth′ə-lŏj′ĭ-kal) also **path·o·log·ic** (-ĭk) *adj.* **1.** Of or relating to pathology. **2.** Relating to or caused by disease. **3.** Of, relating to, or manifesting behavior that is habitual and compulsive. —**path′o·log′i·cal·ly** *adv.*

pa·thol·o·gy (pă-thŏl′ə-jē) *n., pl.* **-gies 1.** The scientific study of the nature of disease and its causes. **2.** The anatomic or functional manifestations of a disease: *the pathology of cancer.* **3.** A departure or deviation from a normal condition. —**pa·thol′o·gist** *n.*

path·o·phys·i·ol·o·gy (păth′ō-fĭz′ē-ŏl′ə-jē) *n.* **1.** The functional changes associated with or resulting from disease or injury. **2.** The scientific study of such changes. —**path′o·phys′i·o·log′ic** (-ə-lŏj′ĭk), **path′o·phys′i·o·log′i·cal** (-ĭ-kal) *adj.* —**path′o·phys′i·ol·o·gist** *n.*

pa·thos (pā′thŏs′, -thôs′) *n.* **1.** A quality, as of an experience or a work of art, that arouses feelings of pity, sympathy, tenderness, or sorrow. **2.** The feeling, as of sympathy or pity, so aroused. [Gk., suffering.]

path·way (păth′wā′, päth′-) *n.* **1.** A path. **2.** *Physiology* **a.** A course usu. followed by a body part. **b.** A chain of nerve fibers along which impulses normally travel. **c.** A sequence of enzymatic or other reactions by which one biological material is converted to another.

–pathy *suff.* **1.** Feeling; suffering; perception: *telepathy.* **2a.** Disease: *neuropathy.* **b.** A system of treating disease: *homeopathy.* [Gk. *-patheia* < *pathos.*]

pa·tience (pā′shəns) *n.* **1.** The capacity, quality, or fact of being patient. **2.** *Chiefly British* The game solitaire.

SYNONYMS *patience, long-suffering, resignation, forbearance* These nouns denote the capacity to endure hardship, difficulty, or inconvenience without complaint. *Patience* emphasizes calmness, self-control, and the willingness or ability to tolerate delay: *"Our patience will achieve more than our force"* (Edmund Burke). *Long-suffering* is long and patient endurance, as of wrong or provocation: *The general, a man not known for docility and long-suffering, flew into a rage. Resignation* implies acceptance of or submission to something trying, as out of despair or necessity: *undertook the job with an air of resignation. Forbearance* denotes restraint, as in retaliating, demanding what is due, or voicing disapproval: *"It is the mutual duty of all to practice Christian forbearance, love, and charity towards each other"* (Patrick Henry).

pa·tient (pā′shənt) *adj.* **1.** Bearing or enduring pain, difficulty, provocation, or annoyance with calmness. **2.** Marked by or exhibiting calm endurance of pain, difficulty, provocation, or annoyance. **3.** Tolerant; understanding. **4.** Persevering; constant. **5.** Capable of calmly awaiting an outcome or result; not hasty or impulsive. **6.** Capable of patience. ❖ *n.* **1.** One who receives medical attention, care, or treatment. **2.** *Linguistics* A noun or noun phrase identifying one that is acted upon or undergoes an action. **3.** *Archaic* One who suffers. [ME *pacient* < OFr. < Lat. *patiēns, patient-,* pr. part. of *patī,* to endure.] —**pa′tient·ly** *adv.*

pat·in (păt′n) *n.* Variant of **paten.**

pat·i·na¹ (păt′n-ə) *n., pl.* **pat·i·nae** (păt′n-ē) See **paten** 1. [Med.Lat. < Lat., plate. See PATEN.]

pat·i·na² (păt′n-ə, pə-tē′nə) also **pa·tine** (pă-tēn′) *n.* **1.** A thin greenish layer, usu. basic copper sulfate, that forms on copper or copper alloys, such as bronze, as a result of corrosion. **2.** The sheen on any surface, produced by age and use. **3.** A change in appearance produced by long-standing behavior, practice, or use. [Ital. < Lat., plate. See PATEN.]

pat·i·naed (păt′n-īd, pə-tē′nĭd) *adj.* Having a coating, covering, or sheen; patinated.

pat·i·nate (păt′n-āt′) *v.* **-nat·ed, -nat·ing, -nates** —*tr.* To furnish with a patina. —*intr.* To acquire a patina.

pa·tine (pă-tēn′) *tr.v.* **-tined, -tin·ing, -tines** To coat with a patina. [Fr. *patiner* < *patine*, patina < Ital. *patina*. See PATINA².]

pat·i·o (păt′ē-ō′, pä′tē-ō′) *n., pl.* **-os 1.** An outdoor space for dining or recreation that adjoins a residence and is often paved. **2.** A roofless inner courtyard, typically found in Spanish and Spanish-style dwellings. [Sp. < OSpan., poss. < O Provençal *patu, pati*, pasture, perh. < Lat. *pactum*, agreement. See PACT.]

pa·tis·se·rie (pə-tĭs′ə-rē, pä-tēs-rē′) *n.* A bakery specializing in French pastry. [Fr. *pâtisserie* < OFr. *pastiserie* < *pasticier*, to make pastry < *pastitz*, pastry < VLat. *pastīcium* < LLat. *pasta*, dough. See PASTE¹.]

Pát·mos also **Pat·mos** (păt′mŏs, -məs, păt′môs) An island of SE Greece in the Dodecanese Is. of the Aegean Sea.

Pat·na (pŭt′nə) A city of NE India on the Ganges R. NW of Calcutta; Asoka's cap. in the 3rd cent. B.C. Pop. 917,243.

pat·ois (păt′wä′, pä-twä′) *n., pl.* **pat·ois** (păt′wäz′, pä-twä′). **1.** A regional dialect, esp. one without a literary tradition. **2a.** A creole. **b.** Nonstandard speech. **3.** The special jargon of a group; cant. [Fr. < OFr., poss. < *pate*, paw < VLat. *patta*, perh. of imit. orig.]

Pa·ton (pāt′n), **Alan Stewart** 1903–88. South African writer noted for *Cry, the Beloved Country* (1948).

Pa·tos (pä′əs, pä′tōōs), **Lagoa dos** A shallow tidal lagoon of SE Brazil separated from the Atlantic Ocean by a wide sandbar.

Pá·trai (pä′trē) also **Pa·tras** (pə-träs′, păt′rəs), **Gulf of** also **Gulf of Patras,** A city of S Greece in the NW Peloponnesus on the **Gulf of Pátrai,** or **Gulf of Patras,** an inlet of the Ionian Sea. Pop. 142,163.

pa·tres·fa·mil·i·as (pä′trēz-fə-mĭl′ē-əs, pä′-, păt′rēz-) *n.* Plural of **paterfamilias.**

patri– or **patr–** *pref.* Father, paternal: *patrilineal.* [Lat. (< *pater, patr*-, father) and Gk. (< *patēr, patr*-, father; see **pəter-** in App.]

pa·tri·arch (pā′trē-ärk′) *n.* **1.** A man who rules a family, clan, or tribe. **2.** *Bible* **a.** One of the progenitors of the human race, from Adam to Noah. **b.** Abraham, Isaac, Jacob, or any of Jacob's 12 sons, the eponymous progenitors of the 12 tribes of Israel. **3.** Used formerly as a title for the bishops of Rome, Constantinople, Jerusalem, Antioch, and Alexandria. **4.** *Roman Catholic Church* A bishop who holds the highest episcopal rank after the pope. **5.** *Eastern Orthodox Church* Any one of the bishops of the sees of Constantinople, Antioch, Alexandria, Moscow, and Jerusalem who has authority over other bishops. **6.** *Judaism* The head of the Sanhedrin in Syrian Palestine from about 180 B.C. to A.D. 429. **7.** *Mormon Church* A high dignitary of the priesthood empowered to invoke blessings. **8.** One who is regarded as the founder or original head of an enterprise, organization, or tradition. **9.** A very old, venerable man; an elder. **10.** The oldest member of a group. [ME *patriarche* < OFr. < LLat. *patriarcha* < Gk. *patriarkhēs* : *patriā*, lineage (< *patēr, patr*-, father; see **pəter-** in App.) + *-arkhēs*, ruler.]

pa·tri·ar·chal (pā′trē-är′kəl) also **pa·tri·ar·chic** (-är′kĭk) *adj.* **1.** Of, relating to, or characteristic of a patriarch. **2.** Of or relating to a patriarchy. **3.** Ruled by a patriarch. —**pa·tri·ar′chal·ism** *n.* —**pa·tri·ar′chal·ly** *adv.*

patriarchal cross *n.* A Latin cross having two horizontal bars, of which the upper is the shorter.

pa·tri·ar·chate (pā′trē-är′kĭt, -kāt′) *n.* **1.** The territory, rule, or rank of a patriarch. **2.** See **patriarchy.**

pa·tri·ar·chy (pā′trē-är′kē) *n., pl.* **-chies 1.** A social system in which the father is the head of the family and men have authority over women and children. **2.** A family, community, or society based on this system or governed by men.

pa·tri·cian (pə-trĭsh′ən) *n.* **1.** A person of refined upbringing, manners, and tastes. **2.** A member of an aristocracy; an aristocrat. **3.** A member of one of the noble families of the ancient Roman Republic, which before the third century B.C. had exclusive rights to the Senate and the magistracies. **4.** Used as a title for members of a class of honorary nobility appointed by the Byzantine emperors. **5.** A member of the hereditary ruling class in the medieval free cities of Italy and Germany. [ME *patricion* < OFr. *patricien* < Lat. *patricius* < *patrēs* (cōnscrīptī), enrolled fathers, senators, pl. of *pater, patr*-, father. See **pəter-** in App.] —**pa·tri′cian** *adj.*

pa·tri·ci·ate (pə-trĭsh′ē-ĭt, -āt′) *n.* **1.** Nobility or aristocracy. **2.** The rank, position, or term of office of a patrician. [Lat. *patriciātus* < *patricius*, patrician. See PATRICIAN.]

pat·ri·cide (păt′rĭ-sīd′) *n.* **1.** The act of murdering one's father. **2.** One who murders one's father. [LLat. *patricīdium* and *patricīda* : Lat. *patri-*, patri- + *-cīdium, -cīda*, -cide.]

Pat·rick (păt′rĭk), **Saint.** A.D. 389?–461? Christian missionary and patron saint of Ireland.

pat·ri·lin·e·age (păt′rə-lĭn′ē-ĭj) *n.* Line of descent as traced through men on the paternal side of a family.

pat·ri·lin·e·al (păt′rə-lĭn′ē-əl) *adj.* Relating to, based on, or tracing ancestral descent through the paternal line.

pat·ri·lo·cal (păt′rə-lō′kəl) *adj. Anthropology* Of or relating to the residence of a husband's kin group or clan.

pat·ri·mo·ny (păt′rə-mō′nē) *n., pl.* **-nies 1a.** An inheritance from a father or other ancestor. **b.** An inheritance or legacy; heri-

tage. **2.** An endowment or estate of an institution, esp. a church. [ME < OFr. *patrimoine* < Lat. *patrimōnium* < *pater, patr*-, father. See **pəter-** in App.]

pa·tri·ot (pā′trē-ət, -ŏt′) *n.* One who loves, supports, and defends one's country. [Fr. *patriote* < OFr., compatriot < LLat. *patriōta* < Gk. *patriōtēs* < *patrios*, of one's fathers < *patēr, patr*-, father. See **pəter-** in App.]

pa·tri·ot·ic (pā′trē-ŏt′ĭk) *adj.* Feeling, expressing, or inspired by love for one's country. —**pa′tri·ot′i·cal·ly** *adv.*

pa·tri·ot·ism (pā′trē-ə-tĭz′əm) *n.* Love of and devotion to one's country.

Pa·tri·ots′ Day (pā′trē-əts, -ŏts′) *n.* The third Monday in April, a holiday in Maine and Massachusetts commemorating the battles of Lexington and Concord in 1775.

pa·tris·tic (pə-trĭs′tĭk) also **pa·tris·ti·cal** (-tĭ-kəl) *adj.* Of or relating to the fathers of the early Christian church or their writings. —**pa·tris′ti·cal·ly** *adv.*

pa·tris·tics (pə-trĭs′tĭks) *n. (used with a sing. verb)* **1.** The study of the lives, writings, and doctrines of the Church fathers. **2.** The writings of the Church fathers.

Pa·tro·clus (pə-trō′kləs) *n. Greek Mythology* A Greek warrior and friend to Achilles, killed by Hector in the Trojan War.

pa·trol (pə-trōl′) *n.* **1.** The act of moving about an area esp. by an authorized and trained person or group, for purposes of observation, inspection, or security. **2.** A person or group of persons who perform such an act. **3a.** A military unit sent out on a reconnaissance or combat mission. **b.** One or more military vehicles, boats, ships, or aircraft assigned to guard or reconnoiter a given area. **4.** A division of a Boy Scout troop or Girl Scout troop consisting of between six and eight children. ❖ *v.* **-trolled, -trol·ling, -trols** —*tr.* To engage in a patrol of. —*intr.* To engage in a patrol. [Fr. *patrouille* < *patrouiller*, to patrol, alteration of OFr. *patouiller*, to paddle about in mud, patrol, prob. < *pate*, paw. See PATOIS.] —**pa·trol′ler** *n.*

patrol car *n.* See **squad car.**

pa·trol·man (pə-trōl′mən) *n.* **1.** A policeman who patrols or polices an assigned area. **2.** One who patrols an assigned area.

patrol wagon *n.* An enclosed police truck for prisoners.

pa·trol·wom·an (pə-trōl′wŏŏm′ən) *n.* A policewoman who patrols or polices an assigned area.

pa·tron (pā′trən) *n.* **1.** One that supports, protects, or champions someone or something; a sponsor or benefactor: *a patron of the arts.* **2.** A customer, esp. a regular customer. **3.** *(also* pä-trōn′*)* The owner or manager of an establishment, esp. a French or Spanish restaurant or inn. **4a.** A noble or wealthy person in ancient Rome who granted favor and protection to someone in exchange for certain services. **b.** A slave owner in ancient Rome who freed a slave without relinquishing all legal claim to him. **5.** One who possesses the right to grant an ecclesiastical benefice to a member of the clergy. **6.** A patron saint. [ME < OFr. < Med.Lat. *patrōnus* < Lat. < *pater, patr*-, father. See **pəter-** in App.] —**pa′tron·al** (pā′trə-nəl) *adj.*

pa·tron·age (pā′trə-nĭj, păt′rə-) *n.* **1.** The support or encouragement of a patron, as for an institution or cause. **2.** Support or encouragement proffered in a condescending manner. **3.** The trade given to a commercial establishment by its customers. **4.** Customers or patrons considered as a group; clientele. **5a.** The power to distribute or appoint people to governmental or political positions. **b.** The act of distributing or appointing people to such positions. **c.** The positions so distributed or filled. **6.** The right to grant an ecclesiastical benefice to a member of the clergy.

pa·tron·ess (pā′trə-nĭs) *n.* **1.** A woman who supports, protects, or champions someone or something; a sponsor or benefactor. **2.** A woman who possesses the right to grant an ecclesiastical benefice to a member of the clergy. See Usage Note at **-ess.**

pa·tron·ize (pā′trə-nīz′, păt′rə-) *tr.v.* **-ized, -iz·ing, -iz·es 1.** To act as a patron to; support or sponsor. **2.** To go to as a customer, esp. on a regular basis. **3.** To treat in a condescending manner. —**pa′tron·i·za′tion** (-trə-nĭ-zā′shən) *n.*

patron saint *n.* A saint who is regarded as the intercessor and advocate in heaven of a nation, place, craft, class, or person.

pat·ro·nym·ic (păt′rə-nĭm′ĭk) *adj.* Of, relating to, or derived from the name of one's father or a paternal ancestor. ❖ *n.* A name so derived. [LLat. *patrōnymicus* < Gk. *patrōnumikos* < *patrōnumos*, named after one's father : *patēr, patr*-, father + *onuma*, name; see **nŏ-men-** in App.] —**pat′ro·nym′i·cal·ly** *adv.*

pa·troon (pə-trōōn′) *n.* A landholder in New Netherland who, under Dutch colonial rule, was granted proprietary and manorial rights to a large tract of land in exchange for bringing 50 new settlers to the colony. [Du. < Fr. *patron*, patron, master < OFr. PATRON.]

pat·sy (păt′sē) *n., pl.* **-sies** *Slang* A person easily taken advantage of, cheated, blamed, or ridiculed. [Perh. < Ital. *pazzo*, fool < OItal. *paccio.*]

pat·ten (păt′n) *n.* Any one of various types of wooden-soled footwear, such as a sandal or clog, worn to increase one's height or keep one's feet out of the mud. [ME *patin* < OFr., perh. < *pate*, paw, hoof. See PATOIS.]

pat·ter¹ (păt′ər) *v.* **-tered, -ter·ing, -ters** —*intr.* **1.** To make a quick series of light soft tapping sounds. **2.** To move with quick, light, softly audible steps. —*tr.* To cause to patter. ❖ *n.* A quick succession of pattering sounds. [Frequentative of PAT¹.]

pat·ter² (pătʹər) *v.* **-tered, -ter·ing, -ters** —*intr.* **1.** To speak or chatter glibly and rapidly. **2.** To mumble prayers in a mechanical manner. —*tr.* To utter in a pattering manner. ❖ *n.* **1.** The jargon of a particular group; cant. **2.** Glib rapid speech, as of a salesperson. **3.** Meaningless talk; chatter. [ME *patren*, shortening and alteration of *paternoster*, paternoster (< its mechanical and rapid recitation). See PATERNOSTER.] —**patʹter·er** *n.*

pat·tern (pătʹərn) *n.* **1a.** A model or original used as an archetype. **b.** A person or thing considered worthy of imitation. **2.** A plan, diagram, or model to be followed in making things. **3.** A representative sample; a specimen. **4a.** An artistic or decorative design. **b.** A design of natural or accidental origin. **5.** A consistent characteristic form, style, or method, as: **a.** A composite of traits or features characteristic of an individual or a group. **b.** Form and style in an artistic work or body of artistic works. **6a.** The configuration of gunshots upon a target that is used as an indication of skill in shooting. **b.** The distribution and spread, around a targeted region, of spent shrapnel, bomb fragments, or shot from a shotgun. **7.** Enough material to make a complete garment. **8.** A test pattern. **9.** The flight path of an aircraft about to land. **10.** *Football* A pass pattern. ❖ *v.* **-terned, -tern·ing, -terns** —*tr.* **1.** To make, mold, or design by following a pattern. **2.** To cover or ornament with a design or pattern. —*intr.* To make a pattern. [ME *patron* < OFr. See PATRON.]

pat·tern·ing (pătʹər-nĭng) *n.* **1.** Design, structure, or configuration of a form, style, or method. **2.** Physical therapy in which a pattern of exercises is imposed to stimulate weak or paralyzed nerves and muscles to act on their own.

pat·tern·mak·er also **pattern maker** (pătʹərn-māʹkər) *n.* One who makes patterns, as for sewing, carpentry, or industrial machinery. —**patʹtern·makʹing** *n.*

Pat·ti (pătʹē, pätʹē), **Adelina** 1843–1919. Spanish-born Italian coloratura soprano.

Pat·ton (pătʹn), **Charley** 1881–1934. Amer. blues singer and guitarist who helped pioneer the Mississippi blues style.

Patton, George Smith, Jr. 1885–1945. Amer. general who led the Allied armies in Germany (1944–45).

pat·ty (pătʹē) *n., pl.* **-ties 1.** A small rounded flattened cake of food, esp. one made from ground ingredients. **2.** A patty shell. **3.** A small pie; a pasty. [Fr. *pâté*, *pâté*. See PÂTÉ.]

pat·ty-cake (pătʹē-kākʹ) *n.* A child's game in which two players pat each other's palms together in rhythmic beat, often accompanied by a nursery rhyme. [Alteration of *pat-a-cake*, the first words of the nursery rhyme accompanying the game.]

pat·ty·pan squash (pătʹē-pănʹ) *n.* A variety of squash (*Cucurbita Pepo*) having a flat round fruit with a scalloped edge, ribbed white skin, and creamy white flesh.

patty shell *n.* An edible shell of baked puff pastry that is made to be filled with other food, such as fruit or creamed seafood.

pat·u·lous (păchʹə-ləs) also **pat·u·lent** (-lənt) *adj. Botany* Spreading or expanded. [< Lat. *patulus* < *patēre*, to be open.] —**patʹu·lous·ness** *n.*

pat·zer (pătʹsər, pätʹ-) *n. Slang* A poor or amateurish chess player. [Prob. < Ger., bungler < *patzen*, to bungle.]

PAU *abbr.* Pan American Union

pau·ci·ty (pôʹsĭ-tē) *n.* **1.** Smallness of number; fewness. **2.** Scarcity; dearth. [ME *paucite* < OFr. < Lat. *paucitās* < *paucus*, few.]

Paul (pôl), Saint. A.D. 5?–67? Apostle to the Gentiles whose life and teachings appear in the Acts of the Apostles. —**Paulʹine** (- īn, -ēn) *adj.*

Paul I¹ 1754–1801. Russian czar (1796–1801) who led military campaigns against France (1798–1800).

Paul I² 1901–64. King of Greece (1947–64) who took refuge in South Africa during World War II.

Paul III 1468–1549. Pope (1534–49) who initiated the Catholic Reformation.

Paul VI 1897–1978. Pope (1963–78) noted for easing regulations on fasting and interfaith marriages.

Paul, Alice 1885–1977. Amer. feminist who wrote (1923) the first equal rights amendment considered by Congress.

Paul Bunyan *n.* A giant lumberjack noted for superhuman acts in American folklore.

Pau·li (pouʹlē), **Wolfgang** 1900–58. Austrian-born Amer. physicist who won a 1945 Nobel Prize.

Pauli exclusion principle (pôʹlē, pouʹ-) *n.* See **exclusion principle.** [After Wolfgang PAULI.]

Pau·ling (pôʹlĭng), **Linus Carl** 1901–94. Amer. chemist who won a 1954 Nobel Prize and the 1962 Nobel Peace Prize.

Paul·ist (pôʹlĭst) *n.* A member of the Roman Catholic Missionary Society of Saint Paul the Apostle, founded in New York in 1858.

pau·low·ni·a (pô-lōʹnē-ə) *n.* Any of several Chinese deciduous trees of the genus *Paulownia*, having large heart-shaped opposite leaves and pyramidal flower panicles. [NLat. *Paulownia*, genus name, after Anna Paulovna (1795–1865), Russian princess.]

paunch (pônch, pänch) *n.* **1.** The belly, esp. a potbelly. **2.** See **rumen.** [ME *paunche* < OFr. *panche* < Lat. *pantex.*]

paunch·y (pônʹchē, pänʹ-) *adj.* **-i·er, -i·est** Having a potbelly. —**paunchʹi·ness** *n.*

pau·per (pôʹpər) *n.* **1.** One who is extremely poor. **2.** One living on or eligible for public charity. [< Lat., poor.] —**pauʹper·ism** *n.*

pau·per·ize (pôʹpə-rīzʹ) *tr.v.* **-ized, -iz·ing, -iz·es** To make a pauper of. —**pauʹper·i·zaʹtion** (-pər-ĭ-zāʹshən) *n.*

pau·piette (pō-pyĕtʹ) *n.* A thin slice of meat or fish wrapped around a forcemeat or vegetable filling. [Fr., prob. < obsolete *poulpe*, fleshy part < OFr. *polpe* < Lat. *pulpa.*]

Pau·sa·ni·as (pô-sāʹnē-əs) *fl.* 2nd cent. A.D. Greek geographer and historian who wrote *Periegesis of Greece.*

pause (pôz) *v.* **paused, paus·ing, paus·es** —*intr.* **1.** To cease or suspend an action temporarily. **2.** To linger; tarry. **3.** To hesitate: *He paused before replying.* —*tr.* To cease or suspend the action of temporarily: *paused the videotape.* ❖ *n.* **1.** A temporary cessation. **2.** A delay or suspended reaction, as from uncertainty; a hesitation. **3.** A break, stop, or rest, often for a calculated purpose or effect. **4a.** *Music* A sign indicating that a note or rest is to be held. **b.** A caesura in poetry. **5.** Reason for hesitation: *The task's immensity gave me pause.* [< ME, pause < OFr. < Lat. *pausa* < Gk. *pausis* < *pauein*, to stop.]

SYNONYMS pause, intermission, recess, respite, suspension These nouns denote a temporary stop, as in activity: *a short pause in the conversation; a concert with a 15-minute intermission; the legislature's summer recess; toiling without respite; a suspension of work.*

pa·vane also **pa·van** (pə-vänʹ, -vănʹ) *n.* **1.** A slow, stately court dance of the 16th and 17th centuries, usu. in duple meter. **2.** Its music. [Fr. *pavane* < Ital. *pavana* < fem. of *pavano*, of Padua < dialectal *pavàn* < *Pava*, dialectal var. of *Padova*, Padua.]

Pav·a·rot·ti (păvʹə-rŏtʹē, pä-vä-rōtʹtē), **Luciano** b. 1935. Italian-born operatic tenor.

pave (pāv) *tr.v.* **paved, pav·ing, paves 1.** To cover with a pavement. **2.** To cover uniformly, as if with pavement. **3.** To be or compose the pavement of. —**idiom: pave the way** To make progress or development easier. [ME *paven* < OFr. *paver* < Lat. *pavīre*, to beat, tread down.] —**pavʹer** *n.*

pa·vé (pă-vāʹ, păvʹā) *n.* A setting of precious stones placed together so closely that no metal shows: *diamonds in pavé.* [Fr. < p. part. of *paver*, to pave < OFr. See PAVE.] —**pa·véʹ** *adj.*

pave·ment (pāvʹmənt) *n.* **1a.** A hard smooth surface, esp. of a public area or way, that will bear travel. **b.** Material for making such a surface. **2.** *Chiefly British* A sidewalk.

Pa·vi·a (pə-vēʹə, pä-vēʹä) A city of NW Italy S of Milan; orig. a Roman stronghold known as Ticinum. Pop. 85,056.

pav·id (păvʹĭd) *adj.* Exhibiting or experiencing fear; timid. [Lat. *pavidus* < *pavēre*, to fear.]

pa·vil·ion (pə-vĭlʹyən) *n.* **1.** An ornate tent. **2a.** A light roofed structure for amusement or shelter, as at parks. **b.** A usu. temporary structure housing an exhibition at a fair or show. **c.** A large structure housing sports or entertainment facilities; an arena. **3.** A structure or building connected to a larger building; an annex. **4.** One of the buildings in a complex. **5.** The lower surface of a brilliant-cut gem, slanting outward from the culet to the girdle. ❖ *tr.v.* **-ioned, -ion·ing, -ions 1.** To cover or furnish with or as if with a pavilion. **2.** To put in or as if in a pavilion. [ME *pavilon* < OFr. *pavillon* < Lat. *pāpiliō*, *pāpiliōn-*, butterfly, tent. See **pāl-** in App.]

pav·ing (pāʹvĭng) *n.* **1.** The act or process of laying pavement. **2.** A pavement. **3.** Material used for pavement.

pav·is also **pav·isse** (păvʹĭs) *n.* A medieval shield large enough to protect the whole body. [ME < OFr. *pavais* < OItal. *pavese* < PAVIA.]

Pav·lo·dar (păvʹlə-därʹ, pə-vlə-) A town of NE Kazakhstan on the Irtysh R. SE of Omsk. Pop. 349,000.

Pav·lov (păvʹlôfʹ, -lŏvʹ, păvʹləf), **Ivan Petrovich** 1849–1936. Russian physiologist who won a 1904 Nobel Prize for his research on digestion. —**Pav·loʹvi·an** (păv-lōʹvē-ən, -lōʹ-) *adj.*

Pav·lo·va (păvʹlô-və, păv-, päv-, păvʹlə-), **Anna** 1882–1931. Russian ballerina famous for her role in *Swan Lake.*

Pavlovian conditioning *n.* Classical conditioning.

Pa·vo (pāʹvō) *n.* A constellation in the Southern Hemisphere near Apus and Indus. [Lat. *pāvō*, peacock.]

pav·o·nine (păvʹə-nīnʹ) *adj.* **1.** Of or resembling a peacock. **2.** Resembling a peacock's tail in color, design, or iridescence. [Lat. *pāvōnīnus* < *pāvō*, *pāvōn-*, peacock.]

paw (pô) *n.* **1.** The foot of an animal, esp. a quadruped, that has claws or nails. **2.** *Informal* A human hand, esp. a large clumsy one: *"Lennie dabbled his big paw in the water"* (John Steinbeck). ❖ *v.* **pawed, paw·ing, paws** —*tr.* **1.** To strike with the paw or paws. **2.** To strike or scrape with a beating motion. **3.** To handle clumsily, rudely, or with too much familiarity. —*intr.* **1.** To scrape the ground with the forefeet. **2.** To paw someone or something as in rudeness. [ME *pawe* < OFr. *powe.*] —**pawʹer** *n.*

pawk·y (pôʹkē) *adj.* **-i·er, -i·est** *Chiefly British* Shrewd and cunning, often humorously. [< E. dialectal *pawk*, a trick.]

pawl (pôl) *n.* A hinged or pivoted device that fits into a notch of a ratchet wheel to impart forward motion or prevent backward motion. [Prob. < Du. *pal* < Lat. *pālus*, stake.]

pawn¹ (pôn) *n.* **1.** Something given as security for a loan; a pledge or guaranty. **2.** The condition of being held as a pawn: *jewels in pawn.* **3.** A person serving as security; a hostage. **4.** The act of

pattypan squash

Alice Paul
photographed in 1920

Linus Pauling

pawning. ❖ *tr.v.* **pawned, pawn•ing, pawns 1.** To give or deposit (property) as security for the payment of money borrowed. **2.** To risk; hazard: *pawn one's honor.* ***—phrasal verb:* pawn off** To dispose or get rid of deceptively. [ME *paun* < OFr. *pan,* of Gmc. orig.] **—pawn′a•ble** *adj.* **—pawn′age** *n.* **—pawn′er** (pô′nər), **paw′nor′** (-nôr′) *n.*

pawn[2] (pôn) *n.* **1.** *Games* A chess piece of the lowest value. **2.** A person or an entity used to further the purposes of another: *treated as a political pawn.* [ME < OFr. *pedon, paon* < Med.Lat. *pedō, pedōn-,* foot soldier < LLat., one who has wide feet < Lat. *pēs, ped-,* foot. See **ped-** in App.]

pawn•bro•ker (pôn′brō′kər) *n.* One that lends money at interest in exchange for personal property deposited as security. **—pawn′bro′king** *n.*

Paw•nee (pô-nē′) *n., pl.* **Pawnee** or **-nees 1.** A member of a Native American people formerly inhabiting the Platte River valley in south-central Nebraska and northern Kansas, with a present-day population in north-central Oklahoma. **2.** The Caddoan language of the Pawnee. [N.Amer.Fr. *Pani,* of Illinois orig., ult. of Siouan orig.]

pawn•shop (pôn′shŏp′) *n.* The shop of a pawnbroker.

pawn ticket *n.* A receipt for goods pawned.

paw•paw (pô′pô) *n.* Variant of **papaw.**

Paw•tuck•et (pô-tŭk′ĭt, pə-) A city of NE RI, a suburb of Providence. Pop. 72,958.

pax (păks) *n.* **1.** *Ecclesiastical* **a.** A small flat tablet adorned with a sacred image that worshipers kiss when offered the kiss of peace. **b.** The kiss of peace. **2. Pax** A time of wide-ranging stability when there is only a single dominant power. Used with a Latinized name: *Pax Britannica.* [Med.Lat. *pāx* < Lat., peace. Sense 2, on the model of LLat. *pāx (Rōmāna),* the Roman peace, state of security obtaining under Roman rule, alteration of Lat. *(Rōmāna) pāx.*]

Pax•il (păk′sĭl) A trademark used for the drug paroxetine.

pay[1] (pā) *v.* **paid** (pād), **pay•ing, pays** *—tr.* **1.** To give money to in return for goods or services rendered: *pay the cashier.* **2.** To give (money) in exchange for goods or services: *paid $10 for the book; paid an hourly wage.* **3.** To discharge or settle (a debt or obligation): *paid the tax.* **4a.** To give recompense for; requite: *pay back a kindness.* **b.** To give recompense to; reward or punish: *paid him back for his insult.* **5.** To bear (a cost or penalty, for example) in recompense. **6.** To yield as a return: *paid six percent interest.* **7.** To afford an advantage to; profit. **8.** To give or bestow: *paid a compliment; paid attention.* **9.** To make (a visit or call). **10.** *past tense and past participle* **paid** or **payed** (pād) To let out (a line or cable) by slackening. *—intr.* **1.** To give money in exchange for goods or services. **2.** To discharge a debt or obligation. **3.** To bear a cost or penalty in recompense. **4.** To be profitable or worthwhile: *It doesn't pay to get angry.* ❖ *adj.* **1.** Of, relating to, giving, or receiving payments. **2.** Requiring payment to use or operate: *a pay toilet.* **3.** Yielding valuable metal in mining. ❖ *n.* **1.** The act of paying or state of being paid. **2.** Money given in return for work done; salary; wages. **3a.** Recompense or reward. **b.** Retribution or punishment. **4.** Paid employment. **5.** One considered with regard to one's credit or reliability in discharging debts. ***—phrasal verbs:* pay off 1.** To pay the full amount on (a debt). **2.** To effect profit. **3.** To get revenge for or on; requite. **4.** To pay the wages due to (an employee) upon discharge. **5.** *Informal* To bribe. **pay out 1.** To give (money) out; spend. **2.** To let out (a line or rope) by slackening. **pay up** To give over the full monetary amount demanded. ***—idioms:* pay (one's) dues** To earn a position through hard work, long-term experience, or suffering. **pay (one's) way** To contribute one's own share; pay for oneself. **pay the piper** To bear the consequences of something. **pay through the nose** *Informal* To pay excessively. [ME *paien* < OFr. *paiier* < LLat. *pācāre,* to appease < Lat., to pacify < *pāx, pāc-,* peace.]

pay[2] (pā) *tr.v.* **payed** or **paid** (pād), **pay•ing, pays** To coat or cover (seams of a ship, for example) with waterproof material such as tar or asphalt. [Obsolete Fr. *peier* < OFr. < Lat. *picāre* < *pix, pic-,* pitch.]

pay•a•ble (pā′ə-bəl) *adj.* **1.** Requiring payment on a certain date; due. **2.** Requiring payment to a particular person or entity. **3.** Capable of producing profit: *a payable business.* ❖ *n.* Money owed to a creditor. Often used in the plural.

pay-as-you-go also **pay as you go** (pā′əz-yōō-gō′) *n.* The system or practice of paying debts as they are incurred. **—pay′-as-you-go′** *adj.*

pay•back (pā′băk′) *n.* **1a.** The return gained from or paid on an investment. **b.** The return on an investment that is equal to the amount invested. **2.** A benefit gained as the result of a previous action. **3.** The act or process of paying back.

pay•check (pā′chĕk′) *n.* **1.** A check issued to an employee in payment of salary or wages. **2.** Salary or wages.

pay•day (pā′dā′) *n.* The day on which employees' salaries or wages are paid.

pay dirt *n.* **1.** Earth, ore, or gravel that is profitable to mine. **2.** *Informal* A useful or profitable discovery or venture.

pay•ee (pā-ē′) *n.* One to whom money is paid.

pay equity *n.* Comparable worth.

pay•er (pā′ər) *n.* **1.** One that pays: *a prompt payer of bills.* **2.** One named responsible for paying a bill or note.

pay•load (pā′lōd′) *n.* **1.** The revenue-producing part of a cargo. **2a.** The total weight of passengers and cargo that an aircraft carries or can carry. **b.** The total weight of the instruments, crew, and life-support systems that a spacecraft carries or can carry. **c.** The passengers, crew, instruments, or equipment carried by an aircraft, spacecraft, or rocket. **3.** The explosive charge carried in the warhead of a missile.

pay•mas•ter (pā′măs′tər) *n.* A person in charge of paying wages and salaries.

pay•ment (pā′mənt) *n.* **1.** The act of paying or the state of being paid. **2.** An amount paid: *received a large payment.* **3.** One's due, reward, or punishment; requital.

pay•nim (pā′nĭm) *n. Archaic* **1.** A non-Christian, esp. a Muslim. **2.** A pagan or heathen. [ME *painim* < OFr. *paienime,* heathendom < LLat. *pāgānismus* < *pāgānus,* pagan. See PAGAN.]

pay•off (pā′ôf′, -ŏf′) *n.* **1a.** Full payment of a salary or wages. **b.** The time of such payment. **2.** *Informal* **a.** A final settlement or reckoning. **b.** The climax of a narrative or sequence of events. **3.** Final retribution or revenge. **4.** *Informal* A bribe.

pay•o•la (pā-ō′lə) *n.* **1.** Bribery of an influential person in exchange for the promotion of a product or service, as of disc jockeys for the promotion of records. **2.** A payment constituting such bribery. [Prob. PAY(OFF) + *-ola,* suff.; see CRAPOLA.]

pay•out (pā′out′) *n.* **1.** The act or an instance of paying out. **2.** A percentage of corporate earnings that is paid as dividends to shareholders.

pay•roll also **pay roll** (pā′rōl′) *n.* **1.** A list of employees receiving wages or salaries, with the amounts due to each. **2.** The total amount paid to employees in a given period.

payt. *abbr.* payment

Pay•ton (pāt′n), **Walter** 1954–99. Amer. football player who set an NFL record for career rushing yards (16,726).

pay-TV (pā′tē-vē′) *n.* A system for receiving television broadcasts by making subscription payments, as by renting a device that unscrambles the broadcaster's scrambled signal.

Paz (päz, päs), **Octavio** 1914–98. Mexican writer who won the 1990 Nobel Prize for literature.

Pb The symbol for the element **lead[2]** 1. [< Lat. *plumbum,* lead.]

PBS *abbr.* Public Broadcasting Service

PBX *abbr.* private branch exchange

PC *abbr.* **1.** Past Commander **2.** personal computer **3.** police constable **4.** politically correct **5.** post commander **6.** Privy Council

p.c. *abbr.* **1.** percent **2.** *Latin* post cibum (after meals)

p/c or **P/C** *abbr.* **1.** petty cash **2.** prices current

PCB (pē′sē-bē′) *n.* Any of a family of industrial chemical compounds produced by chlorination of biphenyl, noted primarily as an environmental pollutant that accumulates in animal tissue with resultant pathogenic and teratogenic effects. [P(OLY)-C(HLORINATED) B(IPHENYL).]

P-Cel•tic (pē′kĕl′tĭk, -sĕl′-) *n.* Brittonic. [< the change of the Common Celt. labiovelar stops to labial stops in Brittonic.]

PCP[1] (pē′sē-pē′) *n.* Phencyclidine. [< the chemical name *p(henyl)c(yclohexyl)p(iperidine).*]

PCP[2] *abbr.* pneumocystis pneumonia

PCR *abbr.* polymerase chain reaction

pct. *abbr.* percent

Pd The symbol for the element **palladium[1].**

PD *abbr.* **1.** police department **2.** postal district **3.** potential difference

pd. *abbr.* paid

p.d. *abbr.* per diem

PDA *abbr.* **1.** personal digital assistant **2.** public display of affection

PDT *abbr.* Pacific Daylight Time

pe (pā) *n.* The 17th letter of the Hebrew alphabet. [Heb. *pē* < Phoenician **pē,* mouth, 17th letter of the Phoenician alphabet.]

PE *abbr.* **1.** physical education **2.** Prince Edward Island **3.** probable error **4.** professional engineer

pea (pē) *n.* **1.** A member of the pea family. **2.** A Eurasian climbing annual vine *(Pisum sativum)* cultivated in temperate zones and having compound leaves with terminal leaflets modified into tendrils and globose edible seeds enclosed in a green pod. **3.** The seed of this plant, used as a vegetable. **4.** The unopened pod of this plant. Also used in the plural. **5.** Any of several plants of the genus *Lathyrus,* such as the sweet pea. [Back-formation < ME *pease* (mistaken for pl.) < OE *pise, piose* < LLat. *pīsa,* var. of Lat. *pīsum* < Gk. *pisos, pison.*]

pea bean *n.* The navy bean.

Pea•bod•y (pē′bŏd′ē, -bə-dē), **Elizabeth Palmer** 1804–94. Amer. educator who founded the first kindergarten in the US (1860).

peace (pēs) *n.* **1.** The absence of war or other hostilities. **2.** An agreement or a treaty to end hostilities. **3.** Freedom from quarrels and disagreement; harmonious relations. **4.** Public security and order. **5.** Inner contentment; serenity. ❖ *interj.* Used as a greeting or farewell and as a request for silence. ***—idioms:* at peace 1.** In a state of tranquillity; serene. **2.** Free from strife. **keep (or hold) (one's) peace** To be silent. **keep the peace** To maintain or observe law and order. [ME *pes* < OFr. *pais, pes* < Lat. *pāx, pāc-.* See PAX.]

peace•a•ble (pē′sə-bəl) *adj.* **1.** Inclined or disposed to peace; promoting calm: *They met in a peaceable spirit.* **2.** Peaceful; un-

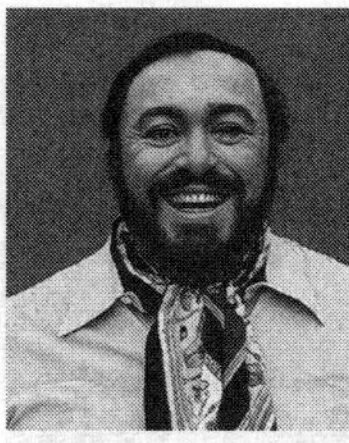

Luciano Pavarotti

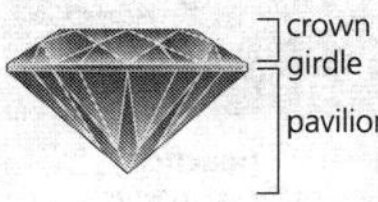

pavilion
brilliant-cut gemstone

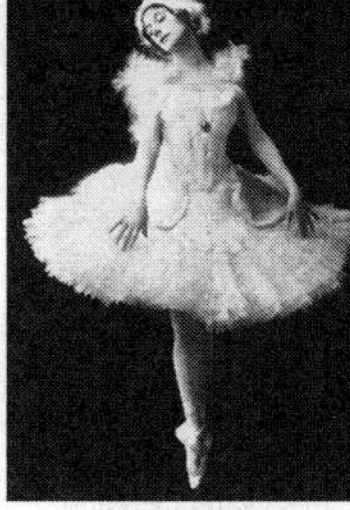

Anna Pavlova
photographed c. 1910 in costume for *The Dying Swan*

ă	pat	oi	boy
ā	pay	ou	out
âr	care	ŏŏ	took
ä	father	ōō	boot
ĕ	pet	ŭ	cut
ē	be	ûr	urge
ĭ	pit	th	thin
ī	pie	*th*	this
îr	pier	hw	which
ŏ	pot	zh	vision
ō	toe	ə	about, item
ô	paw		

Stress marks:
′ (primary);
′ (secondary), as in
lexicon (lĕk′sĭ-kŏn′)

disturbed. **—peace′a•ble•ness** *n.* **—peace′a•bly** *adv.*

Peace Corps *n.* A US government organization that sends volunteers to work on technological, agricultural, and educational projects in developing countries.

peace•ful (pēs′fəl) *adj.* **1.** Undisturbed by strife, turmoil, or disagreement; tranquil. See Syns at **calm. 2.** Inclined or disposed to peace; peaceable. **3.** Of or characteristic of a condition of peace. **—peace′ful•ly** *adv.* **—peace′ful•ness** *n.*

peace•keep•er (pēs′kē′pər) *n.* **1.** One that preserves or promotes peace. **2.** A member of a military force engaged in peacekeeping, often under international sanction.

peace•keep•ing (pēs′kē′pĭng) *adj.* Of or relating to the preservation of peace, esp. the supervision by international forces of a truce between hostile nations. **—peace′keep′ing** *n.*

peace•mak•er (pēs′mā′kər) *n.* One that makes peace, esp. by settling disputes. **—peace′mak′ing** *adj. & n.*

peace•nik (pēs′nĭk) *n. Informal* A person against war or the proliferation of weapons; a pacifist.

peace offering *n.* An offering made to an adversary in the interests of peace or reconciliation.

peace officer *n.* A law enforcement officer, such as a sheriff, who is responsible for maintaining civil peace.

peace pipe *n.* A calumet.

Peace River A river, c. 1,521 km (945 mi), rising in central British Columbia, Canada, and flowing E to Alberta then NE to the Slave River near Lake Athabasca.

peace sign *n.* A hand sign made with the palm forward and the middle and index fingers forming a V to express peace.

peace•time (pēs′tīm′) *n.* A time free from war. **—peace′time′** *adj.*

peach¹ (pēch) *n.* **1a.** A small Chinese tree (*Prunus persica*) widely cultivated in temperate regions and having pink flowers and edible fruit. **b.** The soft juicy fruit of this tree, having yellow flesh, downy red-tinted yellow skin, and a stone containing a single seed. **2.** A light yellowish pink to light orange. **3.** *Informal* A particularly admirable or pleasing person or thing. [ME *peche* < OFr., a peach < Lat. *persica*, peach tree < Gk. *persikē* < fem. of *Persikos*, Pers. See PERSE.]

peach² (pēch) *v.* **peached, peach•ing, peach•es** *—intr.* To inform on someone; turn informer. *—tr.* To inform against. [ME *pechen* < *apechen*, to accuse (prob. < AN *anpecher* < LLat. *impedicāre*, to entangle; see IMPEACH) and < *empechen*, to accuse; see IMPEACH.]

peach palm *n.* A densely spiny, widely cultivated Amazonian palm (*Bactris gasipaes*) having an edible heart and a highly nutritious, mealy fruit wall.

peach•y (pē′chē) *adj.* **-i•er, -i•est 1.** Resembling a peach, esp. in color or texture. **2.** *Informal* Splendid; fine. **—peach′i•ness** *n.*

pea coat *n.* See **pea jacket.**

pea•cock (pē′kŏk′) *n.* **1a.** A male peafowl, distinguished by its crested head, brilliant blue or green plumage, and long modified back feathers that are marked with iridescent eyelike spots and can be spread in a fanlike form. **b.** A peafowl, either male or female. **2.** A vain person; a dandy. ❖ *intr.v.* **-cocked, -cock•ing, -cocks** To strut about like a peacock; exhibit oneself vainly. [ME *pocock, pecok* : *po*, peacock (< OE *pawa, pēa*, peafowl < Lat. *pāvō*, peacock) + ME *cok*; see COCK¹.] **—pea′cock′ish, pea′cock′y** *adj.*

peacock
Pavo cristatus

Peacock, Thomas Love 1785–1866. British writer whose satirical novels include *Nightmare Abbey* (1818).

peacock blue *n.* A moderate to dark or strong greenish blue. **—pea′cock-blue′** (pē′kŏk-blōō′) *adj.*

peacock orchid *n.* See **acidanthera.**

pea family *n.* A large and widespread family of plants, the Leguminosae (Fabaceae), characterized by stipulate, usu. compound leaves, often bilaterally symmetrical flowers, and legume fruits and including such food plants as beans and peas.

pea•fowl (pē′foul′) *n., pl.* **peafowl** or **-fowls** Either of two large pheasants, *Pavo cristatus* of India and Sri Lanka or *P. muticus* of southeast Asia. [PEA(COCK) + FOWL.]

peag also **peage** (pēg) *n.* See **wampum** 1. [Short for WAMPUMPEAG.]

pea green *n.* A moderate, strong, or brilliant yellow green. **—pea′-green′** (pē′grēn′) *adj.*

pea•hen (pē′hĕn′) *n.* A female peafowl. [ME *pohen, pehenne* : *po*, peacock; see PEACOCK + *hen*, female bird; see HEN.]

pea jacket *n.* A short double-breasted coat of heavy wool, worn esp. by sailors. [Prob. partial transl. of Du. *pijjekker* : *pij*, a kind of coarse cloth (< MDu. *pīe*) + *jekker*, jacket.]

peak¹ (pēk) *n.* **1.** A tapering, projecting point; a pointed extremity: *the peak of the roof.* **2a.** The pointed summit of a mountain. **b.** The mountain itself. **3a.** The point of a beard. **b.** A widow's peak. **4.** The point of greatest development, value, or intensity: *at the peak of her career.* **5.** *Physics* The highest value attained by a varying quantity. **6.** *Nautical* **a.** The narrow portion of a ship's hull at the bow or stern. **b.** The upper after corner of a gaff-headed sail. **c.** The outermost end of a gaff. ❖ *v.* **peaked, peak•ing, peaks** *—tr.* **1.** *Nautical* To raise (a gaff) above the horizontal. **2.** To bring to a maximum of development, value, or intensity. *—intr.* **1.** To be formed into a peak or peaks. **2.** To achieve a maximum of development, value, or intensity: *Sales tend to peak just before the holidays.* ❖ *adj.* Approaching or constituting the

maximum. [Prob. ME *pike, peke.* See PIKE⁵.]

peak² (pēk) *intr.v.* **peaked, peak•ing, peaks** To become sickly, emaciated, or pale. [?]

peaked¹ (pēkt, pē′kĭd) *adj.* Ending in a peak; pointed.

peak•ed² (pē′kĭd) *adj.* Having a sickly appearance.

peal (pēl) *n.* **1.** A ringing of a set of bells, esp. a change or set of changes rung on bells. **2.** A set of bells tuned to each other; a chime. **3.** A loud burst of noise. ❖ *v.* **pealed, peal•ing, peals** *—intr.* To sound in a peal; ring. *—tr.* To sound loudly and sonorously. [ME *pele*, a bell peal, esp. a summons to church, short for *apel*, appeal. See APPEAL.]

Peale (pēl) Amer. family of painters, including **Charles Willson Peale** (1741–1827) and his brother **James** (1749–1831). Four of Charles's children became painters: **Raphael** (1774–1825), **Rembrandt** (1778–1860), **Rubens** (1784–1865), and **Titian** (1799–1885).

pe•an (pē′ən) *n.* Variant of **paean.**

pea•nut (pē′nŭt′) *n.* **1.** A prostrate southern Brazilian plant (*Arachis hypogaea*) widely cultivated in warm regions and having yellow flowers on stalks that bend over so that the seed pods ripen underground. **2.** The edible, nutlike oily seed of this plant, used for food and as a source of oil. **3.** A peanut-shaped piece of polystyrene, used in cushioning items during shipment. **4.** *Slang* **a.** A person small in stature. **b.** An insignificant person. **5. peanuts** *Informal* A very small amount of money; a trifling sum. ❖ *adj. Slang* Of no importance; insignificant.

peanut brittle *n.* A hard toffee containing peanuts.

peanut butter *n.* A paste made from ground roasted peanuts.

peanut gallery *n.* **1.** The hindmost or uppermost section of seating in a theater balcony, where the seats are cheapest. **2.** A group of people whose opinions are considered unimportant.

peanut oil *n.* The oil pressed from peanuts, used for cooking, in soaps, and as a solvent for pharmaceutical preparations.

pear (pâr) *n.* **1.** A widely cultivated tree (*Pyrus communis*) in the rose family, having glossy leaves, white flowers grouped in a corymb, and edible fruit. **2.** The fruit of this tree, spherical at the base and tapering toward the stalk. [ME *pere* < OE *peru*, a pear, ult. < VLat. **pira* < Lat., pl. of *pirum*.]

pearl¹ (pûrl) *n.* **1.** A smooth, lustrous, variously colored deposit, chiefly calcium carbonate, formed around a grain of sand or other foreign matter in the shells of certain mollusks and valued as a gem. **2.** Mother-of-pearl; nacre. **3.** One that is prized for beauty or value. **4.** *Printing* A type size measuring approximately five points. **5.** A yellowish white. ❖ *v.* **pearled, pearl•ing, pearls** *—tr.* **1.** To decorate or cover with or as if with pearls. **2.** To make into the shape or color of pearls. *—intr.* **1.** To dive or fish for pearls or pearl-bearing mollusks. **2.** To form beads resembling pearls. [ME *perle* < OFr. < Lat. **pernula*, dim. of *perna*, ham, seashell.]

pearl² (pûrl) *v. & n.* Variant of **purl².**

pearl¹
freshwater (*left*) and
cultured pearls (*right*)

pearl ash *n.* An impure form of potassium carbonate.

pearl danio *n.* A slender freshwater tropical fish (*Brachydanio albolineatus*) that has silvery scales and is a popular aquarium fish.

pearl•er (pûr′lər) *n.* **1.** One who dives for pearls. **2.** A boat engaged in seeking or trading pearls.

pearl•es•cent (pûr-lĕs′ənt) *adj.* Having a pearly luster or gloss.

pearl gray *n.* A light gray, from yellowish to light bluish gray. **—pearl′-gray′** (pûrl′grā′) *adj.*

Pearl Harbor An inlet of the Pacific Ocean on the S coast of Oahu HI W of Honolulu; site of a naval base that was attacked by the Japanese on Dec. 7, 1941.

pearl•ite (pûr′līt′) *n.* **1.** A mixture of ferrite and cementite forming distinct layers or bands in slowly cooled carbon steels. **2.** Variant of **perlite.**

pearl•ized (pûr′līzd) *adj.* Having a pearlescent finish.

pearl millet *n.* A tropical Old World grass (*Pennisetum americanum*) having long dense flowering panicles and whitish grains that are used as food.

pearl oyster *n.* Any of several bivalve marine mollusks of the genus *Pinctada* and related genera of tropical waters, esp. *P. margaritifera*, a major commercial source of pearls.

Pearl River A river of central and S MS flowing c. 780 km (485 mi) generally S to the Gulf of Mexico.

pearl•y (pûr′lē) *adj.* **-i•er, -i•est 1.** Resembling pearls. **2.** Covered or decorated with pearls or mother-of-pearl.

pearly everlasting *n.* A rhizomatous plant (*Anaphalis margaritacea*) with long-lasting whitish flower heads.

Pearly Gates *n. Informal* The gateway to heaven. [< the description of heaven in Revelation 21.]

pearly nautilus *n.* See **nautilus** 1.

pear psylla *n.* A small plant louse (*Psylla pyricola*) that is a destructive pest of pear trees.

Pear•son (pîr′sən), **Lester Bowles** 1897–1972. Canadian politician who served as prime minister (1963–68) and won the 1957 Nobel Peace Prize.

Pea•ry (pîr′ē), **Robert Edwin** 1856–1920. Amer. naval officer who led the expedition credited with first reaching the North Pole (1909).

peas•ant (pĕz′ənt) *n.* **1.** A member of the class comprising small farmers and tenants, sharecroppers, and laborers on the land where they form the main agricultural labor force. **2.** A country person; a rustic. **3.** An uncouth, crude, or ill-bred person; a boor. [ME *paissaunt* < OFr. *paisant* < *pais*, country < LLat. *pāgēnsis*, inhabitant of a district < Lat. *pāgus*, district.]

peas·ant·ry (pĕz′ən-trē) *n.* **1.** The social class comprising peasants. **2.** The condition, rank, or conduct of a peasant.

pease (pēz) *n., pl.* **pease** or **peas·en** (pē′zən) *Archaic* A pea. [ME. See PEA.]

pease·cod also **peas·cod** (pēz′kŏd′) *n.* The pod of the pea.

pea·shoot·er (pē′shōō′tər) *n.* A toy consisting of a small tube through which dried peas or other pellets are blown.

pea soup *n.* **1.** A purée or soup made of cooked dried peas. **2.** *Informal* Dense fog.

peat (pēt) *n.* Partially carbonized vegetable matter, usu. mosses, found in bogs and used as fertilizer and fuel. [ME *pete*, perh. < Med.Lat. *peta*.] —**peat′y** *adj.*

peat bog *n.* See **bog** 1.

peat moss *n.* **1.** Any of various mosses of the genus *Sphagnum*, growing in very wet places. **2.** The partly carbonized remains of these plants, used as a mulch and plant food.

peau de soie (pō′ də swä′) *n.* A silk fabric of satin weave having a dull finish. [Fr. : *peau*, skin + *de*, of + *soie*, silk.]

pea·vey also **pea·vy** (pē′vē) *n., pl.* **-veys** also **-vies** An implement consisting of a wooden shaft with a metal point and a hinged hook near the end, used to handle logs. [After Joseph *Peavey* (fl. 1875), American inventor.]

peb·ble (pĕb′əl) *n.* **1.** A small stone, esp. one worn smooth by erosion. **2a.** Clear colorless quartz; rock crystal. **b.** A lens made of such quartz. **3.** *Geology* A rock fragment between 4 and 64 millimeters in diameter, esp. one that has been naturally rounded. **4.** An irregularly rough grainy surface, as on leather or paper. ❖ *tr.v.* **-bled, -bling, -bles 1.** To pave with pebbles. **2.** To impart an irregularly rough grainy surface to (leather or paper). **3.** To pelt with pebbles. [ME *pobble, pibel, pebul* < OE *papol-* (as in *papolstān*, pebblestone).] —**peb′bly** *adj.*

pebble plant *n.* See **fig marigold.**

pe·can (pĭ-kän′, -kăn′, pē′kăn) *n.* **1.** A deciduous tree (*Carya illinoinensis*) of southern North America having deeply furrowed bark, pinnately compound leaves, and edible nuts. **2.** The smooth thin-shelled oval nut of this tree. [N.Amer.Fr. *pacane* < Illinois *pakani.*]

pec·ca·dil·lo (pĕk′ə-dĭl′ō) *n., pl.* **-loes** or **-los** A small sin or fault. [Sp. *pecadillo*, dim. of *pecado*, sin, and Ital. *peccadiglio*, dim. of *peccato*, sin, both < Lat. *peccātum* < neut. of *peccātus*, p. part. of *peccāre*, to sin. See **ped-** in App.]

pec·cant (pĕk′ənt) *adj.* **1.** Sinful; guilty. **2.** Violating a rule or an accepted practice; erring. [Lat. *peccāns, peccant-*, pr. part. of *peccāre*, to sin. See **ped-** in App.] —**pec′can·cy** *n.*

pec·ca·ry (pĕk′ə-rē) *n., pl.* **-ries** Any of several piglike hoofed mammals of the family Tayassuidae, found in the Americas and having long dark dense bristles. [Ult. < Carib *pakira*.]

pec·ca·vi (pĕ-kä′wē, -vē, -kä′vī′) *n., pl.* **-vis** A confession of sin. [Lat. *peccāvī*, I have sinned, first pers. sing. perfect t. of *peccāre*, to sin. See PECCABLE.]

Pe·cho·ra (pə-chôr′ə, -chôr′ə, pyĭ-) A river of N-central Russia flowing c. 1,802 km (1,120 mi) N to **Pechora Bay**, an arm of the Barents Sea.

peck¹ (pĕk) *v.* **pecked, peck·ing, pecks** —*tr.* **1.** To strike with the beak or a pointed instrument. **2.** To make (a hole, for example) by striking repeatedly with the beak or a pointed instrument. **3.** To grasp and pick up with the beak. **4.** *Informal* To kiss briefly and casually. —*intr.* **1.** To make strokes with the beak or a pointed instrument. **2.** To eat in sparing bits; nibble: *pecked at dinner.* **3.** To criticize repeatedly; carp. ❖ *n.* **1a.** A stroke or light blow with the beak or a pointed instrument. **b.** A mark or hole made by such a stroke. **2.** *Informal* A light quick kiss. [ME *pecken*, prob. var. of *piken*, to peck (perh. influenced by MLGer. *pekken*). See PICK¹.]

peck² (pĕk) *n.* **1a.** A unit of dry volume or capacity in the US Customary System equal to 8 quarts or approx. 537.6 cubic inches. **b.** A unit of dry volume or capacity in the British Imperial System equal to 8 quarts or approx. 554.8 cubic inches. See table at **measurement. 2.** A container holding or measuring a peck. **3.** *Informal* A large quantity; a lot. [ME.]

peck·er (pĕk′ər) *n.* **1.** One that pecks, as a beak. **2.** *Chiefly British Slang* Courage; pluck. **3.** *Vulgar Slang* The penis.

peck·er·wood (pĕk′ər-wōōd′) *n.* *Chiefly Southern US* See **woodpecker.** See Regional Note at **everywhere.**

peck·ing order (pĕk′ĭng) *n.* **1.** A hierarchy among a group, as of people, classes, or nations. **2.** The social hierarchy in a flock of domestic fowl in which each bird pecks subordinate birds and submits to being pecked by dominant birds.

peck·ish (pĕk′ĭsh) *adj.* **1.** Ill-tempered; irritable. **2.** *Chiefly British* Somewhat hungry. [< PECK¹, to eat.]

Peck's bad boy (pĕks) *n.* A person whose bad behavior embarrasses and annoys others. [After *Peck's Bad Boy and His Pa*, by George Wilbur Peck (1840–1916), American writer.]

Peck·sniff·i·an (pĕk-snĭf′ē-ən) *adj.* Hypocritically benevolent; sanctimonious. [After Seth *Pecksniff*, a character in *Martin Chuzzlewit*, a novel by Charles Dickens.]

pe·co·ri·no (pĕk′ə-rē′nō) *n., pl.* **-nos** An Italian cheese, esp. Ro-

---

mano, made from ewe's milk. [Ital., of ewes, pecorino < *pecora*, ewe, sheep < Lat., cattle, pl. of *pecus.* See **peku-** in App.]

Pe·cos (pā′kəs) A river of E NM and W TX flowing c. 1,490 km (926 mi) to the Rio Grande.

Pécs (pāch) A city of SW Hungary near the Croatian border SSW of Budapest; orig. a Celtic settlement. Pop. 171,870.

pec·tate (pĕk′tāt′) *n.* A salt or ester of pectic acid. [PECT(IC ACID).]

pec·ten (pĕk′tən) *n., pl.* **-tens** or **-ti·nes** (-tə-nēz′) **1.** A body structure or organ resembling a comb. **2.** A scallop of the genus *Pecten.* [Lat. *pecten, pectin-*, comb.]

pec·tic acid (pĕk′tĭk) *n.* A transparent gelatinous acid, $C_{17}H_{24}O_{16}$, insoluble in water and formed by the hydrolysis of certain esters of pectin. [Fr. *pectique*, related to pectin < Gk. *pēktikos*, coagulating < *pēktos*, coagulated. See PECTIN.]

pec·tin (pĕk′tĭn) *n.* Any of a group of water-soluble colloidal carbohydrates of high molecular weight found in ripe fruits and used to jell various foods, drugs, and cosmetics. [Fr. *pectine* < Gk. *pēktos*, coagulated < *pēgnunai*, to coagulate.] —**pec′tic, pec′tin·ous** *adj.*

pec·ti·nate (pĕk′tə-nāt′) also **pec·ti·nat·ed** (-nā′tĭd) *adj.* Having projections resembling the teeth of a comb; comblike. —**pec′ti·na′tion** *n.*

pec·to·ral (pĕk′tər-əl) *adj.* **1.** Relating to or situated in the breast or chest. **2.** Useful in relieving disorders of the chest or respiratory tract. **3.** Worn on the chest or breast. ❖ *n.* **1.** A muscle or organ of the chest. **2.** A pectoral fin. **3.** A pectoral medicine. **4.** An ornament or decoration worn on the chest. [Prob. Lat. *pectorālis* < *pectus, pector-*, breast. N., sense 4, ME < OFr. < Lat. *pectorāle*, breastplate < neut. of *pectorālis.*]

pectoral arch *n.* See **pectoral girdle.**

pectoral fin *n.* Either of the anterior pair of fins attached to the pectoral girdle of fishes.

pectoral girdle *n.* A bony or cartilaginous structure in vertebrates, attached to and supporting the forelimbs or anterior fins.

pectoral sandpiper *n.* A New World sandpiper (*Calidris melanotos*) with brownish streaks on the upper part of the breast.

pec·u·late (pĕk′yə-lāt′) *tr. & intr.v.* **-lat·ed, -lat·ing, -lates** To embezzle (funds) or engage in embezzlement. [Lat. *pecūlārī, pecūlāt-* < *pecūlium*, private property. See **peku-** in App.] —**pec′u·la′tion** *n.* —**pec′u·la′tor** *n.*

pe·cu·liar (pĭ-kyōol′yər) *adj.* **1.** Unusual or eccentric; odd. **2.** Distinct from all others. See Syns at **strange. 3.** Belonging distinctively or primarily to one person, group, or kind; special or unique: *rights peculiar to the rich.* ❖ *n.* **1.** One's exclusive privilege or property. **2.** *Chiefly British* A church or parish under the jurisdiction of a diocese different from that in which it lies. [ME *peculier*, personal < Lat. *pecūliāris* < *pecūlium*, private property. See **peku-** in App.] —**pe·cu′liar·ly** *adv.*

pe·cu·li·ar·i·ty (pĭ-kyōō′lē-ăr′ĭ-tē, -kyōol-yăr′-) *n., pl.* **-ties 1.** The quality or state of being peculiar. **2.** A notable or distinctive feature or characteristic. **3.** An eccentricity; an idiosyncrasy.

pe·cu·ni·ar·y (pĭ-kyōō′nē-ĕr′ē) *adj.* **1.** Of or relating to money. **2.** Requiring payment of money. [Latin *pecūniārius* < *pecūnia*, wealth. See **peku-** in App.]

ped-¹ *pref.* Variant of **pedo-**¹.

ped-² *pref.* Variant of **pedo-**².

-ped or **-pede** *suff.* Foot: *maxilliped.* [< Lat. *pēs, ped-*, foot. See **ped-** in App.]

ped·a·gog·ic (pĕd′ə-gŏj′ĭk, -gōj′ĭk) also **ped·a·gog·i·cal** (-gŏj′ĭ-kəl, -gōj′ĭ-) *adj.* **1.** Of, relating to, or characteristic of pedagogy. **2.** Characterized by pedantic formality.

ped·a·gog·ics (pĕd′ə-gŏj′ĭks, -gōj′ĭks) *n. (used with a sing. verb)* The art of teaching; pedagogy.

ped·a·gogue also **ped·a·gog** (pĕd′ə-gŏg′, -gŏg′) *n.* **1.** A schoolteacher; an educator. **2.** One who instructs in a pedantic or dogmatic manner. [ME *pedagoge* < OFr. < Lat. *paedagōgus*, slave who supervised children and took them to and from school < Gk. *paidagōgos* : *paido-*, boy; see PEDO-² + *agōgos*, leader (< *agein*, to lead; see **ag-** in App.).] —**ped′a·gogu′ish** *adj.*

ped·a·go·gy (pĕd′ə-gō′jē, -gŏj′ē) *n.* **1.** The art or profession of teaching. **2.** Training or instruction. [Fr. *pédagogie* < OFr. < Gk. *paidagōgia* < *paidagōgos*, slave who took children to and from school. See PEDAGOGUE.]

ped·al (pĕd′l) *n.* **1a.** A foot-operated lever used for actuating or controlling a mechanism, as in a loom or piano. **b.** A similar foot-operated part attached to a crank and used for powering various devices, such as a bicycle. **2.** *Music* **a.** A pedal point. **b.** A pedal keyboard. ❖ *adj.* **1.** Of or relating to a pedal. **2.** (also pĕd′l) Of or relating to a foot or footlike part. ❖ *v.* **-aled, -al·ing, -als** or **-alled, -al·ling, -als** —*intr.* **1.** To use or operate a pedal or pedals. **2.** To ride a bicycle. —*tr.* To operate the pedals of. [Fr. *pédale* < Ital. *pedale* < Lat. *pedālis*, one foot long < *pēs, ped-*, foot. See **ped-** in App.]

ped·al·er also **ped·al·ler** (pĕd′l-ər) *n.* One who rides a pedal-driven vehicle, such as a bicycle.

pe·dal·fer (pĭ-dăl′fər) *n.* Soil rich in alumina and iron and deficient in carbonates, found in characteristic of humid regions. [PED(O)-¹ + AL(UMINUM) + Lat. *ferrum*, iron.]

pedal keyboard *n.* A keyboard of pedals in an instrument such as a pipe organ.

---

peasantry

pedal keyboard

Robert E. Peary
photographed in 1909
aboard the USS *Roosevelt*

ă	pat	oi	boy
ā	pay	ou	out
âr	care	ōō	took
ä	father	ōō	boot
ĕ	pet	ŭ	cut
ē	be	ûr	urge
ĭ	pit	th	thin
ī	pie	th	this
îr	pier	hw	which
ŏ	pot	zh	vision
ō	toe	ə	about,
ô	paw		item

Stress marks:
′ (primary);
′ (secondary), as in
lexicon (lĕk′sĭ-kŏn′)

pedal piano *n.* A piano with a pedal keyboard.

pedal point *n. Music* A note, usu. in the bass and on the tonic or dominant, sustained through harmonic changes in the other parts. [POINT, musical note.]

pedal pushers *pl.n.* Calf-length slacks worn by women and girls. [< their orig. being worn by bicyclists.]

pedal steel *n.* An electronically amplified guitar mounted on legs, with up to ten strings whose pitch can be altered by sliding a steel bar or by depressing pedals.

ped·ant (pĕd′nt) *n.* **1.** One who pays undue attention to book learning and formal rules. **2.** One who exhibits learning or scholarship ostentatiously. **3.** *Obsolete* A schoolmaster. [Fr. *pédant* or Ital. *pedante* (Fr. < Ital.), poss. < VLat. **paedēns, *paedent-,* pr. part. of **paedere,* to instruct, prob. < Gk. *paideuein* < *pais, paid-,* child.]

pe·dan·tic (pǝ-dăn′tĭk) *adj.* Characterized by a narrow, often ostentatious concern for book learning and formal rules: *a pedantic attention to details.* —**pe·dan′ti·cal·ly** *adv.*

ped·ant·ry (pĕd′n-trē) *n., pl.* **-ries** **1.** Pedantic attention to detail or rules. **2.** An instance of pedantic behavior. **3.** The habit of mind or manner characteristic of a pedant.

ped·ate (pĕd′āt′) *adj.* **1.** Resembling or functioning as a foot: *pedate appendages.* **2.** *Zoology* Having feet: *pedate larvae.* **3.** *Botany* Having palmately divided lobes with the lateral lobes cleft or divided. [Lat. *pedātus,* p. part. of *pedāre,* to furnish with feet < *pēs, ped-,* foot. See **ped-** in App.]

ped·dle (pĕd′l) *v.* **-dled, -dling, -dles** —*tr.* **1a.** To travel about selling (wares). **b.** To sell (narcotics) illicitly. **2.** *Informal* To seek to disseminate; give out. —*intr.* **1.** To peddle wares. **2.** To occupy oneself with trifles. [Back-formation < PEDDLER. V., intr., sense 2, prob. influenced by PIDDLE.]

ped·dler (pĕd′lǝr) *n.* One who peddles for a living. [ME *pedlere,* prob. alteration of *peddere* < Med.Lat. *pedārius,* crozier bearer < Lat. *pēs, ped-,* foot. See PEDI-.]

–pede *suff.* Variant of **–ped.**

ped·er·ast (pĕd′ǝ-răst′) *n.* A man who has sexual relations with a boy. [Gk. *paiderastēs : pais, paid-,* child + *erastēs,* lover (< *erasthai,* to love).] —**ped′er·as′ty** *n.*

pe·des (pē′dēz) *n.* Plural of **pes.**

ped·es·tal (pĕd′ĭ-stǝl) *n.* **1.** An architectural support or base, as for a column. **2.** A support or foundation. **3.** A position of high regard or adoration. ❖ *tr.v.* **-taled, -tal·ing, -tals** or **-talled, -tal·ling, -tals** To place on or provide with a pedestal. [Obsolete Fr. *pedestal* < Ital. *piedistallo : piè,* foot (< Lat. *pēs;* see PEDI-) + *di* (< Lat. *dē;* see DE–) + *stallo,* stall (of Gmc. orig.; see stel- in App.).]

pe·des·tri·an (pǝ-dĕs′trē-ǝn) *n.* One who travels on foot; a walker. ❖ *adj.* **1.** Of, relating to, or made for pedestrians: *a pedestrian crossing.* **2.** Going or performed on foot. **3.** Undistinguished; ordinary: *pedestrian prose.* [< Lat. *pedester, pedestr-,* going on foot < *pedes,* a pedestrian < *pēs, ped-,* foot. See **ped-** in App.] —**pe·des′tri·an·ism** *n.*

pedi– *pref.* Foot: *pediform.* [Lat. < *pēs, ped-,* foot. See **ped-** in App.]

pe·di·a·tri·cian (pē′dē-ǝ-trĭsh′ǝn) also **pe·di·at·rist** (-ăt′rĭst) *n.* A physician who specializes in pediatrics.

pe·di·at·rics (pē′dē-ăt′rĭks) *n.* (*used with a sing. verb*) The branch of medicine that deals with the care and treatment of infants and children. —**pe·di·at′ric** *adj.*

ped·i·cab (pĕd′ĭ-kăb′) *n.* A small three-wheeled vehicle having a seat, pedals, and handlebars in front for the operator and a usu. hooded cab in back for passengers.

ped·i·cel (pĕd′ĭ-sǝl, -sĕl′) *n.* **1.** *Botany* **a.** A stalk bearing one flower in an inflorescence. **b.** A support for a fern sporangium or moss capsule. **2.** *Anatomy* See **pedicle** 1. [NLat. *pedicellus,* dim. of Lat. *pediculus,* dim. of *pēs, ped-,* foot. See **ped-** in App.]

ped·i·cel·late (pĕd′ĭ-sĕl′ĭt, -āt′) *adj. Biology* Having or supported by a pedicel.

ped·i·cle (pĕd′ĭ-kǝl) *n.* **1.** *Anatomy* A small stalk or stalklike structure, esp. one supporting an organ or other body part. **2.** *Botany* See **pedicel** 1. **3.** *Medicine* A piece of temporarily attached skin or grafted tissue. [Lat. *pediculus,* dim. of *pēs, ped-,* foot. See PEDICEL.]

pe·dic·u·lar (pǝ-dĭk′yǝ-lǝr) *adj.* Of or caused by lice. [Lat. *pēdiculāris < pēdiculus,* dim. of *pēdis,* louse.]

pe·dic·u·late (pǝ-dĭk′yǝ-lĭt, -lāt′) *adj.* Of or relating to the marine teleost fishes of the order Pediculati, characterized by pectoral fins extending from an armlike process and a dorsal fin ray that serves as a lure for prey. [< NLat. *Pediculātī,* order name < Lat. *pediculus,* dim. of *pēs, ped-,* foot. See PEDI–.] —**pe·dic′u·late′** *n.*

pe·dic·u·lo·sis (pǝ-dĭk′yǝ-lō′sĭs) *n.* Infestation with lice. [Lat. *pēdiculus,* dim. of *pēdis,* louse; see PEDICULAR + –OSIS.] —**pe·dic′u·lous** (-lǝs) *adj.*

ped·i·cure (pĕd′ĭ-kyoŏr′) *n.* **1.** Cosmetic care or a cosmetic treatment of the feet and toenails. **2.** A podiatrist. [Fr. *pédicure : Lat. pēs, ped-,* foot; see PEDI– + Lat. *cūra,* care; see CURE.] —**ped′i·cure′** *v.* —**ped′i·cur′ist** *n.*

ped·i·form (pĕd′ǝ-fôrm′) *adj.* Shaped like a foot.

ped·i·gree (pĕd′ĭ-grē′) *n.* **1a.** A line of ancestors; a lineage. **b.** A list of ancestors; a family tree. **2.** A chart of an individual's ances-

pedicab
Mumbai, India

pediment

tors used in human genetics to analyze Mendelian inheritance, esp. of familial diseases. **3.** A list of the ancestors of a purebred animal. [ME *pedegru* < AN *pe de grue : pe,* foot (< Lat. *pēs;* see PEDI–) + *de,* of (< Lat. *dē;* see DE–) + *grue,* crane (< VLat. **grūa* < Lat. *grūs* < the resemblance of a crane's foot to the lines of succession on a genealogical chart).] —**ped′i·greed′** *adj.*

ped·i·ment (pĕd′ǝ-mǝnt) *n.* **1a.** A wide low-pitched gable surmounting the façade of a building in the Grecian style. **b.** A similar triangular element, used in architecture and decoration. **2.** *Geology* A broad, gently sloping rock surface at the base of a steeper slope, often covered with alluvium and formed primarily by erosion. [Alteration of earlier *perement,* prob. alteration of PYRAMID.] —**ped′i·men′tal** (-mĕn′tl) *adj.* —**ped′i·ment′ed** *adj.*

ped·i·palp (pĕd′ǝ-pălp′) *n.* One of the second pair of appendages near the mouth of an arachnid that are modified for various reproductive, predatory, or sensory functions.

ped·lar (pĕd′lǝr) *n. Chiefly British* Variant of **peddler.**

pedo–[1] or **ped–** *pref.* Soil: *pedocal.* [< Gk. *pedon,* soil, earth. See **ped-** in App.]

pedo–[2] or **ped–** or **paed–** or **paedo–** *pref.* Child; children: *pedodontics.* [Gk. *paido- < pais, paid-,* child.]

ped·o·cal (pĕd′ǝ-kăl′) *n.* A soil of semiarid and arid regions that is rich in calcium carbonate and lime. [PEDO–[1] + CAL(CIUM).] —**ped′o·cal′ic** *adj.*

pe·do·don·tia (pē′dǝ-dŏn′shǝ) *n.* Pedodontics.

pe·do·don·tics (pē′dǝ-dŏn′tĭks) *n.* (*used with a sing. verb*) The branch of dentistry that deals with the care and treatment of children's teeth. —**pe′do·don′tist** (-dŏn′tĭst) *n.*

ped·o·gen·e·sis[1] (pĕd′ǝ-jĕn′ĭ-sĭs) *n.* The process of soil formation. [PEDO–[1] + GENESIS.]

pe·do·gen·e·sis[2] (pē′dō-jĕn′ĭ-sĭs) *n.* Reproduction of young during the larval or preadult stage, esp. in insects. [PEDO–[2] + GENESIS.] —**pe′do·ge·net′ic** (-jǝ-nĕt′ĭk) *adj.*

pe·dol·o·gy[1] (pē-dŏl′ǝ-jē) *n.* The study of the physical and mental development and characteristics of children. [PEDO–[2] + –LOGY.] —**pe′do·log′ic** (-dǝ-lŏj′ĭk), **pe′do·log′i·cal** (-ĭ-kǝl) *adj.* —**pe′do·log′i·cal·ly** *adv.* —**pe·dol′o·gist** *n.*

pe·dol·o·gy[2] (pĭ-dŏl′ǝ-jē, pē-) *n.* The scientific study of soils, including their origins, characteristics, and uses. [PEDO–[1] + –LOGY.] —**ped′o·log′ic** (pĕd′l-ŏj′ĭk), **ped′o·log′i·cal** (-ĭ-kǝl) *adj.* —**ped′o·log′i·cal·ly** *adv.* —**ped·ol′o·gist** *n.*

pe·dom·e·ter (pĭ-dŏm′ĭ-tǝr) *n.* An instrument that gauges the distance traveled on foot by counting the steps taken.

ped·o·mor·phism (pĕd′ǝ-môr′fĭz′ǝm, pē′dǝ-) *n.* Retention of juvenile characteristics in the adult, occurring in mammals. —**ped′o·mor′phic** (-fĭk) *adj.*

ped·o·phil·i·a (pĕd′ǝ-fĭl′ē-ǝ, pē′dǝ-) *n.* The act or fantasy on the part of an adult of engaging in sexual activity with a child. —**ped′o·phile′** (-fīl′) *n.* —**ped′o·phil′i·ac** (-ăk) *adj. & n.* —**ped′o·phil′ic** (fĭl′ĭk) *adj.*

Pe·dro I (pā′drō, pĕd′drŏŏ) 1798–1834. Brazilian political leader who was the country's first emperor (1822–31).

Pedro II 1825–91. Brazilian emperor (1831–89) who abolished slavery.

pe·dun·cle (pĭ-dŭng′kǝl, pē′dŭng′kǝl) *n.* **1.** *Botany* The stalk of an inflorescence or a stalk bearing a solitary flower. **2.** *Zoology* A stalklike structure in invertebrate animals, usu. serving as an attachment for a larger part or structure. **3.** *Anatomy* A stalklike bundle of nerve fibers connecting different parts of the brain. **4.** *Medicine* The stalklike base to which a polyp or tumor is attached. [NLat. *pedunculus,* dim. of Lat. *pēs, ped-,* foot. See **ped-** in App.] —**pe·dun′cu·lar** (pĭ-dŭng′kyǝ-lǝr) *adj.*

pe·dun·cu·late (pĭ-dŭng′kyǝ-lĭt, -lāt′) also **pe·dun·cu·lat·ed** (-lā′tĭd) *adj.* Having or supported on a peduncle.

pee[1] (pē) *n.* The letter *p.*

pee[2] (pē) *Slang intr.v.* **peed, pee·ing, pees** To urinate. ❖ *n.* **1.** Urine. **2.** An act of urination. [< the first letter of PISS.]

Pee Dee (pē′ dē′) also **Great Pee Dee** A river, c. 375 km (233 mi), of S-central NC and NE SC.

peek (pēk) *intr.v.* **peeked, peek·ing, peeks** **1.** To glance quickly. **2.** To look or peer furtively, as from a place of concealment. **3.** To be only partially visible, as if peering or emerging from hiding: *Tiny crocuses peeked through the snow.* ❖ *n.* A brief or furtive look. [ME *piken,* perh. alteration of MDu. *kieken,* var. of *kīken.*]

peek·a·boo (pēk′ǝ-bōō′) *n.* A game for amusing a small child, in which one covers one's face or hides and then returns to view saying "Peekaboo!" ❖ *adj.* **1.** Decorated with embroidered holes or eyelets. **2.** Made of a sheer or transparent fabric. [PEEK + BOO.]

peel[1] (pēl) *n.* **1.** The skin or rind of certain fruits and vegetables. **2.** A chemical peel. ❖ *v.* **peeled, peel·ing, peels** —*tr.* **1.** To strip or cut away the skin, rind, or bark from; pare. **2.** To strip away; pull off: *peeled the label from the jar.* —*intr.* **1.** To lose or shed skin, bark, or other covering. **2.** To come off in thin strips or pieces, as bark, skin, or paint. **3.** *Slang* To remove one's clothes; undress. —*phrasal verb:* **peel off** **1.** To leave flight formation in order to land or make a dive. Used of an aircraft. **2.** To leave or depart. [< ME *pilen, pelen,* to peel < OFr. *peler* and OE *pilian* (both < Lat. *pilāre,* to deprive of hair < *pilus,* hair) and < OFr. *pillier,* to tug, pull, plunder (< Lat. *pilleum,* felt cap).]

peel[2] (pēl) *n.* **1.** A long-handled shovellike tool used by bakers to move bread or pastries into and out of an oven. **2.** *Printing* A T-shaped pole used for hanging up freshly printed sheets of paper to dry. [ME < OFr. *pele* < Lat. *pāla*, spade, peel.]

peel[3] (pēl) *n.* A fortified house or tower of a kind constructed in the borderland of Scotland and England in the 16th century. [ME *pel*, stake, small castle < AN, stockade, var. of OFr., stake < Lat. *pālus*.]

Peel, Sir Robert 1788–1850. British politician who served as prime minister (1834–35 and 1841–46).

peel•a•ble (pē′lə-bəl) *adj.* **1.** Having a peel or rind that can be peeled off. **2.** Capable of being removed and reused: *peelable address labels.*

peel•er[1] (pē′lər) *n.* **1.** One that peels, esp. a kitchen implement for peeling fruits and vegetables. **2.** One that can be readily peeled, esp. a crab that is about to molt. **3.** *Slang* A stripteaser.

peel•er[2] (pē′lər) *n. Chiefly British* A police officer. [After Sir Robert PEEL.]

peel•ing (pē′lĭng) *n.* A peeled piece or strip, as of a fruit rind.

Peel River A river of N Yukon Terr. and W Northwest Terrs., Canada, flowing c. 644 km (400 mi) to the Mackenzie R.

peen (pēn) *n.* The end of a hammerhead opposite the flat striking surface, used for chipping, indenting, and metalworking. ❖ *tr.v.* **peened, peen•ing, peens** To hammer, bend, or shape with a peen. [Prob. of Scand. orig.]

peep[1] (pēp) *intr.v.* **peeped, peep•ing, peeps 1.** To utter short high-pitched sounds, like those of a baby bird; cheep. **2.** To speak in a hesitant, thin, high-pitched voice. ❖ *n.* **1.** A peeping sound or utterance. **2.** A slight sound or utterance. **3.** Any of various small North American sandpipers. [ME **pepen*, prob. alteration of *pipen* < OE *pīpian*, to pipe < *pīpe*, tube, musical instrument and < Lat. *pīpāre*, to peep; see PIPE.]

peep[2] (pēp) *v.* **peeped, peep•ing, peeps** —*intr.* **1.** To peek furtively; steal a quick glance. **2.** To peer through a small aperture or from behind something. **3.** To appear as though emerging from a hiding place. —*tr.* To cause to emerge or become partly visible. ❖ *n.* **1.** A quick or furtive look or glance. **2.** A first glimpse or appearance: *the peep of dawn.* [ME *pepen*, perh. alteration of *piken*, to peek. See PEEK.]

peep•er[1] (pē′pər) *n.* A creature that makes short high-pitched sounds, esp. a frog.

peep•er[2] (pē′pər) *n.* **1.** One who peeks furtively. **2.** *Slang* An eye.

peep•hole (pēp′hōl′) *n.* A small hole or crevice for peeping.

peep•ing Tom (pē′pĭng) *n.* A person who gets pleasure, esp. sexual pleasure, from secretly watching others; a voyeur. [After the legendary *Peeping Tom* of Coventry, England, who was the only person to see the naked Lady Godiva.]

peep•show also **peep show** (pēp′shō′) *n.* **1.** An exhibit viewed through a small hole or magnifying glass. **2.** A short pornographic film seen usu. in a coin-operated booth.

peep sight *n.* A rear sight of a firearm consisting of an adjustable eyepiece with a small opening through which the front sight and the target are aligned.

pee•pul (pē′pəl) *n.* Variant of **pipal.**

peer[1] (pîr) *intr.v.* **peered, peer•ing, peers 1.** To look intently, searchingly, or with difficulty. **2.** To be partially visible; show: *Stars peered through the clouds.* [ME *piren* (prob. < Frisian *piren*) and *peren* (short for *aperen*, to appear; see APPEAR).]

peer[2] (pîr) *n.* **1.** One who has equal standing with another or others, as in rank, class, or age: *influenced by their peers.* **2a.** A nobleman. **b.** A man who holds a peerage by descent or appointment. **3.** *Archaic* A companion; comrade. [ME < OFr. *per*, equal, peer < Lat. *pār.* See **perə-** in App.]

peer•age (pîr′ĭj) *n.* **1.** The rank, title, or jurisdiction of a noble; a duchy, marquisate, county, viscountcy, or barony. **2.** Nobles considered as a group. **3.** A listing of nobles and their families.

peer•ess (pîr′ĭs) *n.* **1a.** A noblewoman. **b.** A woman who holds a peerage by descent or appointment. **2.** A woman who holds a title by association, as the wife or widow of a peer.

peer•less (pîr′lĭs) *adj.* Being such as to have no match; incomparable. —**peer′less•ly** *adv.* —**peer′less•ness** *n.*

peer pressure *n.* Pressure from one's peers to behave in a manner similar or acceptable to them.

peeve (pēv) *tr.v.* **peeved, peev•ing, peeves** To cause to be annoyed or resentful. ❖ *n.* **1.** A vexation; a grievance. **2.** A resentful mood: *in a peeve.* [Back-formation < PEEVISH.]

pee•vish (pē′vĭsh) *adj.* **1a.** Querulous or discontented. **b.** Ill-tempered. **2.** Contrary; fractious. [ME *pevish*, poss. < PERVERSE.] —**pee′vish•ly** *adv.* —**pee′vish•ness** *n.*

pee•wee[1] (pē′wē) *n. Informal* One, such as a child, that is notably small. [Prob. redup. of WEE.] —**pee′wee** *adj.*

pee•wee[2] (pē′wē) *n.* Variant of **pewee.**

pee•wit (pē′wĭt, pyōō′ĭt) *n.* Variant of **pewit.**

peg (pĕg) *n.* **1a.** A small cylindrical or tapered pin, as of wood, used to fasten things or plug a hole. **b.** A similar pin forming a projection that may be used as a support or boundary marker. **2.** *Music* One of the pins of a stringed instrument that are turned to tighten or slacken the strings so as to regulate their pitch. **3.** A degree or notch, as in estimation. **4.** *Chiefly British* A drink of liquor. **5.** *Baseball* A low and fast throw made to put a base runner out. **6.** *Informal* A leg, esp. a wooden one. ❖ *v.* **pegged, peg•ging, pegs** —*tr.* **1.** To fasten or plug with a peg or pegs. **2.** To

designate or mark by means of a peg or pegs. **3.** To fix (a price) at a certain level or within a certain range. **4.** *Informal* To classify; categorize. **5.** *Informal* To throw. —*intr.* To work steadily; persist: *pegged away in school.* —*idiom:* **take (someone) down a peg** To reduce the pride of; humble. [ME *pegge* < MDu.]

Peg•a•sus (pĕg′ə-səs) *n.* **1.** *Greek Mythology* A winged horse that with a stroke of his hoof caused the fountain Hippocrene to spring forth from Mount Helicon. **2.** A constellation in the Northern Hemisphere near Aquarius and Andromeda. [ME < Lat. *Pēgasus* < Gk. *Pēgasos.*]

peg•board (pĕg′bôrd′, -bōrd′) *n.* **1.** *Games* **a.** A game board perforated with a pattern of holes into which pegs can be fitted. **b.** A game played by fitting pegs into such holes. **2.** A board fitted with pegs for hanging clothing.

Peg-Board A trademark used for a type of hardboard with rows of regularly spaced holes into which hooks may be inserted for storing or displaying objects.

peg leg *n. Informal* An artificial leg.

peg•ma•tite (pĕg′mə-tīt′) *n.* An unusually coarse-grained igneous rock, esp. granite, often occurring in dikes, and sometimes containing rare elements such as uranium. [Gk. *pēgma, pēgmat-*, something fastened together (< *pēgnunai*, to fasten) + -ITE[1].]

Peh•le•vi (pā′lə-vē′) *n.* Variant of **Pahlavi.**

Pei (pā), I(eoh) M(ing) b. 1917. Chinese-born Amer. architect whose designs include the Pyramide at the Louvre in Paris (1989).

P.E.I. *abbr.* Prince Edward Island

pei•gnoir (pān-wär′, pēn-) *n.* A woman's loose-fitting dressing gown. [Fr. < OFr. *peignouer*, linen covering used while combing oneself < *peigner*, to comb the hair < Lat. *pectināre* < *pecten, pectin-*, comb.]

Pei•ping (pā′pĭng′) See **Beijing.**

Pei•pus (pī′pəs), **Lake** A lake bordering on E Estonia amd NW Russia.

Peirce (pîrs, pûrs), **Charles Sanders** 1839–1914. Amer. philosopher and scientist who cofounded pragmatism and was one of the original developers of semiotics.

Pei•sis•tra•tus (pī-sĭs′trə-təs, pī-) See **Pisistratus.**

pej•o•ra•tion (pĕj′ə-rā′shən, pē′jə-) *n.* **1.** The process or condition of worsening or degenerating. **2.** *Linguistics* The process by which the meaning of a word becomes negative or less elevated over time. [Med.Lat. *pēiōrātiō, pēiōrātiōn-* < LLat. *pēiōrātus*, p. part. of *pēiōrāre*, to make worse < Lat. *pēior*, worse. See **ped-** in App.]

pe•jor•a•tive (pĭ-jôr′ə-tĭv, -jōr′-, pĕj′ə-rā′tĭv, pē′jə-) *adj.* **1.** Tending to make or become worse. **2.** Disparaging; belittling. ❖ *n.* A pejorative word or expression. —**pe•jor′a•tive•ly** *adv.*

pek•an (pĕk′ən) *n.* See **fisher** 2a. [Canadian Fr. *pékan* < Eastern Abenaki *pékané*.]

pe•kin (pē′kĭn) *n.* **1.** A striped or figured silk fabric. **2.** also **Pekin** A large white duck of a Chinese breed, widely raised for food. [Fr. *pékin*, after *Pékin* (Beijing), China.]

Pe•king (pē′kĭng′, pā′-) See **Beijing.**

Peking duck *n.* A Chinese dish of roast duck with crispy skin.

Pe•king•ese (pē′kĭng-ēz′, -ēs′) also **Pe•kin•ese** (pē′kə-nēz′, -nēs′) *n., pl.* **Pekingese** also **Pekinese 1.** A native or resident of Peking (Beijing). **2.** The Chinese dialect of Peking. **3.** Any of a breed of small dog developed in China having a flat nose, a long-haired coat, and a tail that curls over its back. —**Pe′king•ese′** *adj.*

Peking man *n.* An early member of an extinct species of humans, considered a subspecies of *Homo erectus* and known from Pleistocene fossils found in China. [After *Peking* (Beijing), China.]

pe•koe (pē′kō) *n.* A grade of black tea consisting of the leaves around the buds. [Chin. (Amoy) *pek ho* : *pek*, white + *ho*, down, fine feathers.]

pel•age (pĕl′ĭj) *n.* **1.** The coat of a mammal, consisting of hair, fur, wool, or other soft covering, as distinct from bare skin. **2.** Something resembling the coat of a mammal. [Fr. < OFr. < *peil, pel*, hair < Lat. *pilus.*]

Pe•la•gi•an•ism (pə-lā′jē-ə-nĭz′əm) *n.* The theological doctrine of Pelagius, a British monk, denying original sin and affirming the exercise of free will to achieve righteousness, condemned as heresy by the Roman Catholic Church in A.D. 416. —**Pe•la′gi•an** *adj. & n.*

pe•lag•ic (pə-lăj′ĭk) *adj.* Of, relating to, or living in open oceans or seas rather than waters adjacent to land or inland waters: *pelagic birds.* [Lat. *pelagicus* < Gk. *pelagikos* < *pelagos*, sea.]

pel•ar•go•ni•um (pĕl′är-gō′nē-əm) *n.* Any of various herbs and shrubs of the genus *Pelargonium*, including the geraniums. [NLat. *Pelargonium*, genus name < Gk. *pelargos*, stork (its capsules being like a stork's bill).]

Pe•las•gi•an (pə-lăz′jē-ən) *n.* A member of a people living in the region of the Aegean Sea before the Greeks. [ME < Lat. *Pelasgus* < Gk. *Pelasgos.*] —**Pe•las′gi•an, Pe•las′gic** (-jĭk) *adj.*

pe•lec•y•pod (pə-lĕs′ə-pŏd′) *n.* Any of the bivalve mollusks of the class Pelecypoda, including the clams, scallops, and oysters. [< NLat. *Pelecypoda*, class name : Gk. *pelekus*, ax + NLat. *-poda*, -pod.]

Pe•lée (pə-lā′), **Mount** A volcano, c. 1,373 m (4,500 ft), on N Martinique; erupted violently in 1902, killing 40,000 people.

pel•er•ine (pĕl′ə-rēn′, pĕl′ər-ĭn) *n.* A woman's cape, usu. short,

I.M. Pei

ă	pat	oi	boy
ā	pay	ou	out
âr	care	ŏŏ	took
ä	father	ōō	boot
ĕ	pet	ŭ	cut
ē	be	ûr	urge
ĭ	pit	th	thin
ī	pie	th	this
îr	pier	hw	which
ŏ	pot	zh	vision
ō	toe	ə	about,
ô	paw		item

Stress marks:
′ (primary),
′ (secondary), as in
lexicon (lĕk′sĭ-kŏn′)

with points in front. [Fr. *pèlerine* < fem. of *pèlerin*, pilgrim < LLat. *pelegrīnus*. See PILGRIM.]

Pe·le·us (pēʹlē-əs, pēlʹyoōs′) *n. Greek Mythology* A king of the Myrmidons and the father of Achilles.

pelf (pĕlf) *n.* Wealth or riches, esp. when dishonestly acquired. [ME < Med.Lat. *pelfra, pelfa*, prob. < OFr. *pelfre.*]

pel·i·can (pĕlʹĭ-kən) *n.* Any of various large web-footed birds of the genus *Pelecanus* of warm regions, having a pouch of skin hanging from a long bill for catching and holding fish. [ME < OE *pellican* and < OFr. *pelican*, both < LLat. *pelicānus* < Gk. *pelekan*.]

Pe·li·on (pēʹlē-ən, -ŏn′), Mount A peak, 1,601.9 m (5,252 ft), of NE Greece; legendary home of the centaurs.

pe·lisse (pə-lēs′) *n.* **1.** A long cloak or outer robe, usu. of fur or with a fur lining. **2.** A woman's loose light cloak, often with arm holes. [Fr. < OFr. *pelice* < LLat. *pellīcia* < Lat., fem. of *pellīcius*, made of skin < *pellis*, skin. See **pel-¹** in App.]

pe·lite (pēʹlīt′) *n.* Sedimentary rock composed of fine fragments, as of clay or mud. [Gk. *pēlos*, clay + -ITE¹.] **—pe·litʹic** (pĭ-lĭtʹĭk) *adj.*

Pel·la (pĕlʹə) An ancient city of Greek Macedonia; cap. of Macedonia from the 4th cent. to 168 B.C.

pel·la·gra (pə-lăgʹrə, -lāʹgrə, -lăʹ-) *n.* A disease caused by a dietary deficiency of niacin and protein and characterized by skin eruptions, digestive and nervous system disturbances, and mental deterioration. [Ital. : *pelle*, skin (< Lat. *pellis*; see **pel-¹** in App.) + *-agra*, a seizure (< Lat. < Gk. *-agrā* < *agrā*, a seizing; see **ag-** in App.).] **—pel·lagʹrous** *adj.*

pel·la·grin (pə-lăgʹrĭn, -lāʹ-, -lăʹgrĭn) *n.* A person affected with pellagra. [< PELLAGRA.]

pel·let (pĕlʹĭt) *n.* **1.** A small solid or densely packed ball or mass, as of food. **2a.** A bullet or piece of small shot. **b.** A stone ball used as a catapult missile or a primitive cannonball. ❖ *tr.v.* **-let·ed, -let·ing, -lets** **1.** To make or form into pellets. **2.** To strike with pellets. [ME *pelet* < OFr. *pelote* < VLat. **pilotta*, dim. of Lat. *pila*, ball.]

pel·li·cle (pĕlʹĭ-kəl) *n.* A thin skin or film, such as an organic membrane or liquid film. [Fr. < Lat. *pellicula*, husk, dim. of *pellis*, skin. See **pel-¹** in App.] **—pel·licʹu·lar** (-lĭkʹyə-lər) *adj.*

pel·li·to·ry (pĕlʹĭ-tôr′ē, -tōr′ē) *n., pl.* **-ries** **1.** A small Mediterranean plant (*Anacyclus pyrethrum*) containing a volatile oil that relieves toothache and facial neuralgia. **2.** Any of various monoecious plants of the genus *Parietaria*, having long narrow leaves with hairy tufts at the base and apetalous flowers. [ME *peletre, peletori* < OFr. *piretre, peletre* < Lat. *pyrethrum*. See PYRETHRUM.]

pell-mell also **pell·mell** (pĕlʹmĕlʹ) *adv.* **1.** In a jumbled, confused manner; helter-skelter. **2.** In frantic disorderly haste; headlong. [Fr. *pêle-mêle* < OFr. *pesle mesle*, prob. redup. of *mesle*, imper. of *mesler*, to mix. See MEDDLE.] **—pellʹ-mellʹ** *adj. & n.*

pel·lu·cid (pə-loōʹsĭd) *adj.* **1.** Admitting the passage of light; transparent or translucent. **2.** Transparently clear in style or meaning. [Lat. *pellūcidus* < *pellūcēre*, to shine through : *per-*, through; see PER-+ *lūcēre*, to shine; see **leuk-** in App.] **—pel·luʹcid·i·ty, pel·luʹcid·ness** *n.* **—pel·luʹcid·ly** *adv.*

Pel·ly (pĕlʹē) A river of central Yukon Terr., Canada, flowing c. 531 km (330 mi) generally NW to the Yukon R.

Pel·o·pon·ne·sus (pĕlʹə-pə-nēʹsəs) or **Pel·o·pon·ne·sos** (pĕlʹə-pə-nēʹsəs) also **Pel·o·pon·nese** (pĕlʹə-pə-nēz′, -nēs′) A peninsula forming the S part of Greece S of the Gulf of Corinth; dominated by Sparta until the 4th cent. B.C. **—Pelʹo·pon·neʹsian** (-nēʹzhən, -shən) *adj. & n.*

Pe·lops (pēʹlŏps′) *n. Greek Mythology* The son of Tantalus and father of Atreus. [Lat. < Gk. : *pelios*, dark + *ōps*, face, eye; see **okʷ-** in App.]

pe·lo·ri·a (pə-lôrʹē-ə, -lōrʹ-) *n.* Regularity in form of a normally irregular flower. [NLat. < Gk. *pelōros*, monstrous < *pelōr*, monster.] **—pe·lorʹic** (-lôrʹĭk, -lōrʹ-) *adj.*

pe·lo·rus (pə-lôrʹəs, -lōrʹ-) *n., pl.* **-rus·es** A fixed compass card on which bearings relative to a ship's heading are taken. [?]

pe·lo·ta (pə-lōʹtə) *n.* **1.** Jai alai. **2.** The ball used in jai alai. [Sp. < OFr. *pelote*, ball. See PELLET.]

Pe·lo·tas (pə-lōʹtəs, pĭ-lôʹtäs) A city of SE Brazil on a lagoon SSW of Pôrto Alegre. Pop. 290,660.

pelt¹ (pĕlt) *n.* **1.** The skin of an animal with the fur or hair still on it. **2.** A stripped animal skin ready for tanning. [ME, prob. < OFr. *pelete*, dim. of *pel*, skin < Lat. *pellis*. See **pel-¹** in App.]

pelt² (pĕlt) *v.* **pelt·ed, pelt·ing, pelts** *—tr.* **1.** To strike or assail repeatedly with or as if with blows or missiles; bombard. **2.** To cast, hurl, or throw (missiles). **3.** To strike repeatedly. *—intr.* **1.** To beat or strike heavily and repeatedly. **2.** To move at a vigorous gait. ❖ *n.* **1.** A sharp blow; a whack. **2.** A rapid pace. [ME *pelten*, var. of *pilten*, perh. ult. < Lat. *pultāre*, to beat, var. of *pulsāre*, freq. of *pellere*, to strike. See **pel-²** in App.] **—peltʹer** *n.*

pel·tate (pĕlʹtāt′) *adj.* Having a flat circular structure attached to a stalk near the center rather than the margin; shield-shaped: *a peltate leaf.* [Lat. *peltātus*, armed with a small shield < *pelta*, small shield < Gk. *peltē*. See **pel-¹** in App.]

pelt·ing (pĕlʹtĭng) *adj. Archaic* Paltry; petty. [Perh. < dialectal *pelt*, trash.]

pel·try (pĕlʹtrē) *n.* Undressed pelts considered as a group. [ME < OFr. *peleterie < peletier*, furrier < *pel*, skin < Lat. *pellis*. See PELT¹.]

pelican
Brown pelican
Pelecanus occidentalis

pendant¹
turquoise and silver
thunderbird design
pendant

pel·vic (pĕlʹvĭk) *adj.* Of, in, near, or relating to the pelvis.

pelvic arch *n.* See **pelvic girdle.**

pelvic fin *n.* Either of a pair of lateral hind fins of fishes, attached to the pelvic girdle.

pelvic girdle *n.* A bony or cartilaginous structure in vertebrates, attached to and supporting the hind limbs or fins.

pelvic inflammatory disease *n.* Inflammation of the female genital tract, esp. of the fallopian tubes, caused by any of several microorganisms, chiefly chlamydia and gonococci, and marked by abdominal pain, fever, and vaginal discharge.

pel·vis (pĕlʹvĭs) *n., pl.* **-vis·es** or **-ves** (-vēz) **1a.** A basin-shaped structure of the vertebrate skeleton, composed of the innominate bones on the sides, the pubis in front, and the sacrum and coccyx behind and resting on the lower limbs and supporting the spinal column. **b.** The cavity formed by this structure. **2.** The funnel in the outlet of the kidney, through which urine passes to the ureter. [Lat. *pēlvis*, basin.]

Pem·ba (pĕmʹbə) An island of Tanzania in the Indian Ocean N of Zanzibar; under British control after 1890.

pem·mi·can also **pem·i·can** (pĕmʹĭ-kən) *n.* **1.** A Native American food prepared from lean dried strips of meat pounded into paste, mixed with fat and berries, and pressed into small cakes. **2.** A food made from beef, dried fruit, and suet used as emergency rations. [Cree *pimihkaam*.]

pem·phi·gus (pĕmʹfĭ-gəs, pĕm-fīʹgəs) *n.* Any of several skin diseases characterized by itching blisters. [NLat. *pemphigus* < Gk. *pemphīx, pemphīg-*, pustule.] **—pem·phiʹgous** *adj.*

pen¹ (pĕn) *n.* **1.** An instrument for writing or drawing with ink or similar fluid, esp.: **a.** A ballpoint pen. **b.** A fountain pen. **c.** A pen point. **d.** A penholder and its pen point. **e.** A quill. **2.** An instrument for writing regarded as a means of expression. **3.** A writer or author. **4.** A style of writing: *a witty pen.* **5. pens** Pinions. **6.** The chitinous internal shell of a squid. ❖ *tr.v.* **penned, pen·ning, pens** To write or compose with or as if with a pen. [ME *penne* < OFr. < LLat. *penna* < Lat., feather. See **pet-** in App.] **—penʹner** *n.*

pen² (pĕn) *n.* **1a.** A fenced enclosure for animals. **b.** The animals kept in a pen. **2.** Any of various enclosures, such as a bullpen or playpen. **3.** A repair dock for submarines. ❖ *tr.v.* **penned** or **pent** (pĕnt), **pen·ning, pens** To confine in or as if in a pen. [ME < OE *penn.*]

pen³ (pĕn) *n.* A female swan. [?]

pen⁴ (pĕn) *n. Informal* A penitentiary; a prison.

Pen. *abbr.* peninsula

pe·nal (pēʹnəl) *adj.* **1.** Of, relating to, or prescribing punishment, as for breaking the law. **2.** Subject to punishment; legally punishable: *a penal offense.* **3.** Serving as or constituting a means or place of punishment: *a penal colony.* [ME < OFr. *peinal* and < Med.Lat. *pēnālis*, both < Lat. *poenālis < poena*, penalty < Gk. *poinē*. See **kʷei-** in App.] **—peʹnal·ly** *adv.*

penal code *n.* A body of laws relating to crimes and offenses and the penalties for their commission.

pe·nal·ize (pēʹnə-līz′, pĕnʹə-) *tr.v.* **-ized, -iz·ing, -iz·es** **1.** To subject to a penalty, esp. for infringement of a law or regulation. **2.** To impose a handicap on; place at a disadvantage. **—peʹnal·i·zaʹtion** (-lĭ-zāʹshən) *n.*

pen·al·ty (pĕnʹəl-tē) *n., pl.* **-ties** **1.** A punishment established by law or authority for an offense. **2.** Something, esp. a sum of money, required as a forfeit for an offense. **3.** The disadvantage or painful consequences resulting from an action or condition: *rarely slept and paid the penalty.* **4.** *Sports* **a.** A punishment, handicap, or loss of advantage imposed on a team or competitor for infraction of a rule. **b.** An infraction of a rule; a foul. **5.** *Games* Points scored in contract bridge by the opponents when the declarer fails to make a bid. [ME *penalte* < OFr. *penalite* < Med.Lat. *poenālitās* < Lat. *poenālis*, penal. See PENAL.]

penalty area *n.* An area marked on a soccer field in front of each goal within which a violation of the rules by a defending player results in a penalty kick.

penalty box *n.* An area to the side of an ice hockey rink where penalized players wait out their penalties.

penalty kick *n.* In soccer, a free kick on the goal defended only by the goalkeeper, awarded when a defensive player has committed a foul in the penalty area.

penalty killer *n.* In ice hockey, any of the players other than the goalie who attempt to prevent the opposition from scoring on a power play. **—penalty killing** *adj. & n.*

penalty shot *n.* An unhindered shot on the goal defended only by the goalkeeper, usu. awarded to an offensive player who has been illegally obstructed on a scoring chance, as in ice hockey.

pen·ance (pĕnʹəns) *n.* **1.** A voluntary act of self-mortification or devotion expressing sorrow for sin. **2.** A sacrament in some Christian churches that includes contrition, confession to a priest, acceptance of punishment, and absolution. ❖ *tr.v.* **-anced, -anc·ing, -anc·es** To impose penance upon. [ME < OFr. < Lat. *paenitentia*, penitence < *paenitēns, paenitent-*, penitent. See PENITENT.]

Pe·nang (pĭ-năngʹ, pēʹnăng′) See **George Town** 1.

Pe·na·tes (pə-nāʹtēz, -năʹ-) *pl.n. Roman Mythology* The household deities whose cult was connected with that of the Lares. [Lat. *Penātēs < penus*, foodstuff, interior of a house.]

pen-based (pĕn′bāst′) *adj. Computer Science* Using a stylus to input or retrieve data.

pence (pĕns) *n. Chiefly British* A plural of **penny** 2.

pen·cel also **pen·sil** (pĕn′səl) *n.* A narrow flag, streamer, or pennon, esp. one carried at the top of a lance or spear. [ME < OFr. *penoncel*, dim. of *penon*, pennon. See PENNON.]

pen·chant (pĕn′chənt) *n.* A definite liking; a strong inclination. See Syns at **predilection**. [Fr. < pr. part. of *pencher*, to incline < OFr. < VLat. *pendicāre* < Lat. *pendēre*, to hang.]

pen·cil (pĕn′səl) *n.* **1.** A narrow, usu. cylindrical implement for writing, drawing, or marking, consisting of a thin rod of graphite, colored wax, or similar substance encased in wood or held in a mechanical holder. **2.** Something shaped or used like a pencil, esp. a narrow medicated or cosmetic stick: *an eyebrow pencil.* **3a.** Style, technique, or skill in drawing, delineating, or describing. **b.** An artist's brush, esp. a fine one. **4.** *Physics* A beam of radiant energy in the form of a narrow cone or cylinder. **5.** *Mathematics* A family of geometric objects that have a common property, such as all lines passing through a given point. ❖ *tr.v.* **-ciled, -cil·ing, -cils** also **-cilled, -cil·ling, -cils** **1.** To write, edit, or produce by using a pencil. **2.** To mark or color with or as if with a pencil. —*phrasal verb:* **pencil in** **1.** To schedule tentatively: *penciled in a meeting for 1:00.* **2.** To schedule a tentative appointment with: *penciled him in for lunch.* [ME *pencel*, artist's brush < OFr. *pincel*, *peincel* < VLat. *pēnicellus*, alteration of Lat. *pēnicillus*, dim. of *pēniculus*, dim. of *pēnis*, tail, brush. See **pes-** in App.] —**pen′cil·er, pen′cil·ler** *n.*

pencil pusher *n. Informal* One whose job involves paperwork.

pen computer *n.* A computer that allows the user to input and retrieve data by writing with a stylus directly on a display screen.

pen·dant[1] also **pen·dent** (pĕn′dənt) *n.* **1.** Something suspended from something else, esp. an ornament or piece of jewelry attached to a necklace or bracelet. **2.** A hanging lamp or chandelier. **3.** A sculptured ornament suspended from a vaulted Gothic roof or ceiling. **4.** One of a matched pair; a companion piece. [ME *pendaunt* < OFr. *pendant* < pr. part. of *pendre*, to hang < VLat. *pendere* < Lat. *pendēre*.]

pen·dant[2] (pĕn′dənt) *adj.* Variant of **pendent**[1].

Pen·del·i·kón (pĕn-dĕl′ĭ-kŏn′, pĕn′dĕ-lē-kôn′) A mountain, c. 1,119 m (3,670 ft), of E-central Greece NE of Athens.

pen·dent[1] also **pen·dant** (pĕn′dənt) *adj.* **1.** Hanging down; dangling; suspended. **2.** Projecting; overhanging. **3.** Awaiting settlement; pending. [ME *pendant* (influenced by Lat. *pendēns, pendent-*, pr. part. of *pendēre*, to hang) < OFr. See PENDANT[1].] —**pen′dent·ly** *adv.*

pen·dent[2] (pĕn′dənt) *n.* Variant of **pendant**[1].

pen·den·tive (pĕn-dĕn′tĭv) *n.* A triangular section of vaulting between the rim of a dome and each adjacent pair of the arches that support it. [Fr. *pendentif* < Lat. *pendēns, pendent-*, hanging, pr. part. of *pendēre*, to hang.]

pend·ing (pĕn′dĭng) *adj.* **1.** Not yet decided or settled; awaiting conclusion or confirmation. **2.** Impending; imminent. ❖ *prep.* **1.** While in the process of; during. **2.** While awaiting; until. [Fr. *pendant*, pendant, pending (< OFr.; see PENDANT[1]) + -ING[1].]

Pend O·reille (pŏn′də-rā′) A river rising in **Pend Oreille Lake** in N ID and flowing c. 161 km (100 mi) to the Columbia R. just N of the British Columbia, Canada, border.

pen·du·lar (pĕn′jə-lər, pĕn′dyə-, -də-) *adj.* Of or resembling the motion of a pendulum; swinging back and forth.

pen·du·lous (pĕn′jə-ləs, pĕn′dyə-, -də-) *adj.* **1.** Hanging loosely; suspended so as to swing or sway. **2.** Wavering; undecided. [< Lat. *pendulus* < *pendēre*, to hang.] —**pen′du·lous·ly** *adv.* —**pen′du·lous·ness** *n.*

pen·du·lum (pĕn′jə-ləm, pĕn′dyə-, pĕn′də-) *n.* **1.** A body suspended from a fixed support so that it swings freely back and forth under the influence of gravity, used to regulate various devices, esp. clocks. **2.** Something that swings back and forth from one course, opinion, or condition to another. [NLat., prob. < Ital. *pendolo*, pendulous, pendulum < Lat. *pendulus*, hanging. See PENDULOUS.]

Pe·nel·o·pe (pə-nĕl′ə-pē) *n. Greek Mythology* The wife of Odysseus and mother of Telemachus.

pe·ne·plain also **pe·ne·plane** (pē′nə-plān′) *n.* A nearly flat land surface representing an advanced stage of erosion. [*pene-*, almost (< Lat. *paene*) + PLAIN.]

pe·nes (pē′nēz) *n.* A plural of **penis**.

pen·e·tra·ble (pĕn′ĭ-trə-bəl) *adj.* Capable of being penetrated. —**pen′e·tra·bil′i·ty** *n.* —**pen′e·tra·bly** *adv.*

pen·e·tra·li·a (pĕn′ĭ-trā′lē-ə) *pl.n.* **1.** The innermost parts of a building, esp. the sanctuary of a temple. **2.** The most private or secret parts; recesses. [Lat. *penetrālia* < neut. pl. of *penetrālis*, inner < *penetrāre*, to penetrate. See PENETRATE.]

pen·e·trance (pĕn′ĭ-trəns) *n.* The frequency, under given environmental conditions, with which a specific phenotype is expressed by those individuals with a specific genotype.

pen·e·trant (pĕn′ĭ-trənt) *adj.* Penetrating; piercing. ❖ *n.* Something that penetrates or is capable of penetrating.

pen·e·trate (pĕn′ĭ-trāt′) *v.* **-trat·ed, -trat·ing, -trates** —*tr.* **1.** To enter or force a way into; pierce. **2a.** To enter into and permeate. **b.** To cause to be permeated or diffused; steep. **3.** To insert the penis into the vagina or anus of. **4.** To enter (an organization, for example), usu. surreptitiously, so as to gain influence or information; infiltrate. **5.** To enter and gain a share of (a market). **6.** To grasp the inner significance of; understand. **7.** To see through. **8.** To affect deeply, as by piercing the consciousness or emotions. —*intr.* **1.** To pierce, enter into, or make a way in or through something. **2.** To gain admittance or access. **3.** To gain insight. [Lat. *penetrāre, penetrāt-* < *penitus*, deeply.] —**pen′e·tra′tor** *n.*

pen·e·trat·ing (pĕn′ĭ-trā′tĭng) *adj.* **1.** Capable of penetrating or seeming to penetrate. **2.** Keenly perceptive or understanding; acute. —**pen′e·trat′ing·ly** *adv.*

pen·e·tra·tion (pĕn′ĭ-trā′shən) *n.* **1.** The act or process of piercing or penetrating something, esp.: **a.** The act of entering a country or organization so as to establish influence or gain information. **b.** An attack that penetrates enemy territory or a military front. **c.** Insertion of the penis into the vagina or anus. **2.** The power or ability to penetrate. **3.** The depth reached by a projectile after hitting its target. **4a.** The degree to which something is sold or recognized in a particular market. **b.** The influence that one culture or nation has on another. **5.** The capacity or action of understanding; insight.

pen·e·tra·tive (pĕn′ĭ-trā′tĭv) *adj.* **1.** Tending to penetrate; penetrant. **2.** Displaying keen insight; acute.

pen·e·trom·e·ter (pĕn′ĭ-trŏm′ĭ-tər) also **pen·e·tram·e·ter** (-trăm′ĭ-tər) *n.* **1.** A device for measuring the penetrating power of radiation, esp. x-rays. **2.** A device for measuring the penetrability of semisolids.

Peng·hu (pŭng′hoo′) See **Pescadores**.

Peng·pu (pŭng′poo′) See **Bengbu**.

pen·guin (pĕng′gwĭn, pĕn′-) *n.* **1.** Any of various flightless marine birds of the family Spheniscidae, native to cool regions of the Southern Hemisphere and having flipperlike wings and webbed feet adapted for swimming. **2.** *Obsolete* The great auk. [Poss. < Welsh *pen gwyn*, White Head (name of an island in Newfoundland), great auk : *pen*, chief, head + *gwynn*, white; see **weid-** in App.]

pen·hold·er (pĕn′hōl′dər) *n.* **1.** A holder for a pen point. **2.** A rack or cup for holding a pen or pens.

–penia *suff.* Lack; deficiency: *leukopenia.* [NLat. < Gk. *peniā*, poverty, lack.]

pen·i·cil·la·mine (pĕn′ĭ-sĭl′ə-mēn′) *n.* A degradation product of penicillin, $C_5H_{11}NO_2S$, used in medicine as a chelating agent and in the treatment of rheumatoid arthritis. [PENICILL(IN) + -AMINE.]

pen·i·cil·late (pĕn′ĭ-sĭl′ĭt, -āt′) *adj.* Having or resembling a tuft or brush of fine hairs, as those on caterpillars and certain grasses. [Lat. *pēnicillus*, brush; see PENCIL + -ATE[2].]

pen·i·cil·lin (pĕn′ĭ-sĭl′ĭn) *n.* Any of a group of broad-spectrum antibiotic drugs obtained from penicillium molds or produced synthetically and used in the treatment of various infections and diseases. [PENICILL(IUM) + -IN.]

pen·i·cil·li·um (pĕn′ĭ-sĭl′ē-əm) *n.,* pl. **-cil·li·ums** or **-cil·li·a** (-sĭl′ē-ə) Any of various characteristically bluish-green fungi of the genus *Penicillium* that are used in the production of penicillin and in making cheese. [NLat. *Pēnicillium*, genus name < Lat. *pēnicillus*, brush. See PENCIL.]

pe·nile (pē′nīl′, -nəl) *adj.* Of or relating to the penis.

pen·in·su·la (pə-nĭn′syə-lə, -sə-lə) *n.* A piece of land that projects into a body of water and is connected with the mainland by an isthmus. [Lat. *paenīnsula* : *paene*, almost + *īnsula*, island.] —**pen·in′su·lar** *adj.*

pe·nis (pē′nĭs) *n.,* pl. **-nis·es** or **-nes** (-nēz) **1.** The male organ of copulation in higher vertebrates that in mammals also serves as the male organ of urinary excretion. **2.** Any of various copulatory organs in males of lower animals. [Lat. *pēnis*. See **pes-** in App.]

penis envy *n.* The supposed wish of a girl or woman to have a penis, postulated by Sigmund Freud as a cause of feelings of inferiority and psychic conflict.

pen·i·tence (pĕn′ĭ-təns) *n.* The condition or quality of being penitent; regret for wrongdoing.

pen·i·tent (pĕn′ĭ-tənt) *adj.* Feeling or expressing remorse for one's misdeeds or sins. ❖ *n.* **1.** One who is penitent. **2.** A person performing penance under the direction of a confessor. [ME < OFr. < Med.Lat. *pēnitēns, pēnitent-* < Lat. *paenitēns*, pr. part. of *paenitēre*, to repent.] —**pen′i·tent·ly** *adv.*

pen·i·ten·tial (pĕn′ĭ-tĕn′shəl) *adj.* **1.** Of, relating to, or expressing penitence. **2.** Of or relating to penance. ❖ *n.* **1.** A book or set of church rules concerning the sacrament of penance. **2.** A penitent. —**pen′i·ten′tial·ly** *adv.*

pen·i·ten·tia·ry (pĕn′ĭ-tĕn′shə-rē) *n.,* pl. **-ries** **1.** A prison for those convicted of major crimes. **2.** *Roman Catholic Church* **a.** A tribunal of the Roman Curia having jurisdiction in matters relating to penance, dispensations, and papal absolutions. **b.** A priest whose special function is the administration of the sacrament of penance in a particular church or diocese. ❖ *adj.* **1.** Of or for the purpose of penance; penitential. **2.** Relating to or used for punishment or reform of criminals or wrongdoers. **3.** Resulting in or punishable by imprisonment in a penitentiary. [ME *penitenciarie*, penance officer, episcopal prison < Med.Lat. *pēnitentiāria*, fem. of *pēnitentiārius* < Lat. *paenitentia*, penitence < *paenitēns, penitent.* See PENITENT.]

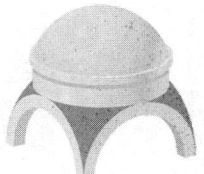

pendentive

penguin
Magellanic penguin
Spheniscus magellanicus

Pen·ki (bŭn′jē′) See **Benxi.**

pen·knife (pĕn′nīf′) n. A small pocketknife.

pen·light (pĕn′līt′) n. A small flashlight having the size and shape of a fountain pen.

pen·man (pĕn′mən) n. **1.** A copyist; a scribe. **2.** An expert in penmanship. **3.** An author; a writer.

pen·man·ship (pĕn′mən-shĭp′) n. The art, skill, style, or manner of handwriting; calligraphy.

Penn, **William** 1644–1718. English Quaker colonizer in America who founded Pennsylvania in 1681.

Penn, Sir **William** 1621–70. English admiral who led the English fleet during the Dutch War (1665–67).

Penn. or **Penna.** abbr. Pennsylvania

pen·na (pĕn′ə) n., pl. **pen·nae** (pĕn′ē) A contour feather of a bird, as distinguished from a down feather or a plume. [Lat., feather. See **pet-** in App.] —**pen·na′ceous** (pē-nā′shəs) adj.

pen name also **pen·name** (pĕn′nām′) n. A pseudonym.

pen·nant (pĕn′ənt) n. **1.** Nautical A long, usu. triangular flag, used on ships for signaling or identification. **2.** A flag or an emblem similar in shape to a ship's pennant. **3.** Sports **a.** A flag that symbolizes the championship of a league, esp. in professional baseball. **b.** The championship so symbolized. [Blend of PEN-DANT¹ and PENNON.]

pen·nate (pĕn′āt′) also **pen·nat·ed** (pĕn′ā′tĭd) adj. **1.** Having feathers or wings. **2.** Botany Pinnate. **3.** Of diatoms of the class Pennales, distinguished by bilaterally symmetrical form. [Lat. pennātus < penna, feather. See **pet-** in App.]

pen·ne (pĕn′ā) n., pl. **penne** Pasta in small short tubes with diagonally cut ends. [Ital., pl. of penna, quill pen < Lat. See PENNA.]

pen·ni·less (pĕn′ē-lĭs, pĕn′ə-) adj. **1.** Entirely without money. **2.** Very poor. See Syns at **poor.** —**pen′ni·less·ness** n.

Pen·nine Alps (pĕn′īn′) A range of the Alps along the Swiss-Italian border rising to 4,636.9 m (15,203 ft).

Pen·nines (pĕn′īnz′) also **Pennine Chain** A range of hills extending c. 257 km (160 mi) from the Scottish border to central England and rising to 893.7 m (2,930 ft).

pen·non (pĕn′ən) n. **1.** A long narrow banner borne upon a lance. **2.** A pennant, banner, or flag. **3.** A pinion; a wing. [ME < OFr. penon, streamer, feather of an arrow, augmentative of penne, feather < Lat. penna. See **pet-** in App.] —**pen′noned** adj.

pen·non·cel also **pen·on·cel** or **pen·non·celle** (pĕn′ən-sĕl′) n. A small pennon or flag borne on a lance. [ME penoncel < OFr., dim. of penon, pennon. See PENNON.]

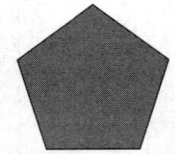

Penn·syl·va·nia (pĕn′səl-vān′yə, -vā′nē-ə) A state of the E US; admitted as one of the original Thirteen Colonies in 1787. Cap. Harrisburg. Pop. 12,281,054.

Pennsylvania Dutch n. **1.** (used with a pl. verb) The descendants of German and Swiss immigrants who settled in Pennsylvania in the 17th and 18th centuries. **2.** The dialect of High German spoken by the Pennsylvania Dutch. **3.** The style of folk art and decorative arts developed by the Pennsylvania Dutch. [Alteration of Ger. Deutsch, German. See PLATTDEUTSCH.]

Penn·syl·va·nian (pĕn′səl-vān′yən, -vā′nē-ən) adj. **1.** Of or relating to Pennsylvania. **2.** Of or belonging to the geologic time of the sixth period of the Paleozoic Era, characterized by the deposition of coal-bearing rock. See table at **geologic time.** ❖ n. **1.** A native or resident of Pennsylvania. **2.** The Pennsylvanian Period or its deposits.

pen·ny (pĕn′ē) n., pl. **-nies 1.** In the United States and Canada, the coin worth one cent. **2.** pl. **pence** (pĕns) **a.** A coin used in Great Britain since 1971, worth ¹⁄₁₀₀ of a pound. **b.** A coin formerly used in Great Britain, worth ¹⁄₂₄₀ of a pound. **c.** A coin used in the Republic of Ireland, worth ¹⁄₁₀₀ of a pound. **d.** A coin used in various dependent territories of the United Kingdom. **3.** Any of various coins of small denomination. **4.** A sum of money. —**idiom: pretty penny** A considerable sum of money. [ME, a coin < OE penig.]

penny ante n. **1.** A poker game in which the highest bet is limited to a penny or another small sum. **2.** Informal A business transaction on a trivial scale. —**pen′ny-an′te** (pĕn′ē-ăn′tē) adj.

pen·ny·cress (pĕn′ē-krĕs′) n. Any of several plants of the genus Thlaspi, having small flattened seed pods with winglike margins, esp. the Eurasian species T. arvense.

penny pincher n. Informal A very stingy person.

pen·ny-pinch·ing (pĕn′ē-pĭn′chĭng) adj. Giving or spending money grudgingly; niggardly. —**pen′ny-pinch′ing** n.

pen·ny·roy·al (pĕn′ē-roi′əl) n. **1.** A Eurasian mint (Mentha pulegium) having ovate or nearly orbicular leaves that yield a useful, aromatic oil. **2.** An aromatic plant (Hedeoma pulegioides) of eastern North America having glabrous leaves that yield an oil used as an insect repellent. [Prob. by folk ety. < ME puliol real < AN : puliol, thyme (< Lat. pūlegium) + real, royal (< Lat. rēgālis; see REGAL).]

pen·ny·weight (pĕn′ē-wāt′) n. A unit of troy weight equal to 24 grains, ¹⁄₂₀ of a troy ounce or approx. 1.555 grams.

pen·ny·whis·tle also **pen·ny whis·tle** (pĕn′ē-hwĭs′əl, -wĭs′-) n. An inexpensive fipple flute, usu. having a plastic mouthpiece and a tin body.

pen·ny-wise or **pen·ny·wise** (pĕn′ē-wīz′) adj. Careful in dealing with small sums of money or small matters.

pen·ny·wort (pĕn′ē-wûrt′, -wôrt′) n. Any of several plants hav-

pentagon
top: geometric figure
bottom: The Pentagon,
Arlington, Virginia

ing rounded leaves suggestive of pennies, as: **a.** A Eurasian plant (Umbilicus rupestris) having thick peltate leaves and yellowish-green flowers. **b.** A North American plant (Obolaria virginica) having small white or purplish flowers.

pen·ny·worth (pĕn′ē-wûrth′) n. **1.** As much as a penny will buy. **2.** A small amount; a modicum. **3.** A bargain.

Pe·nob·scot (pə-nŏb′skət, -skŏt′) n., pl. **Penobscot** or **-scots 1.** A member of a Native American people inhabiting Penobscot Bay and the Penobscot River valley in Maine. **2.** The Algonquian language of the Penobscot, a dialect of Eastern Abenaki. [< a Penobscot place name.]

Penobscot River A river rising in several lakes and tributaries in W and central ME and flowing c. 563 km (350 mi) to **Penobscot Bay,** an inlet of the Atlantic Ocean.

pe·nol·o·gy also **poe·nol·o·gy** (pē-nŏl′ə-jē) n. The study, theory, and practice of prison management and criminal rehabilitation. [Lat. poena, penalty (< Gk. poinē; see kʷei- in App.) + -LOGY.] —**pe′no·log′i·cal** (pē′nə-lŏj′ĭ-kəl) adj. —**pe′no·log′i·cal·ly** adv. —**pe·nol′o·gist** n.

pen·on·cel (pĕn′ən-sĕl′) n. Variant of **pennoncel.**

pen pal n. A person with whom one becomes acquainted through regular correspondence.

pen point n. **1.** A tapering metal device with a split point that fits into a holder and is used for writing; a nib. **2.** The point or tip of a pen.

Pen·sa·co·la (pĕn′sə-kō′lə) A city of extreme NW FL on **Pensacola Bay,** an inlet of the Gulf of Mexico; settled by the Spanish in 1559. Pop. 56,255.

pen·sil (pĕn′səl) n. Variant of **pencel.**

pen·sile (pĕn′sīl′) adj. **1.** Hanging loosely; suspended. **2.** Having or building a hanging nest. Used of birds. [Lat. pēnsilis < pēnsus, p. part. of pendēre, to hang.]

pen·sion¹ (pĕn′shən) n. A sum of money paid regularly as a retirement benefit or by way of patronage. ❖ tr.v. **-sioned, -sion·ing, -sions 1.** To grant a pension to. **2.** To retire or dismiss with a pension. [ME pensioun, payment < OFr. pension < Lat. pēnsiō, pēnsiōn- < pēnsus, p. part. of pendere, to weigh, pay.] —**pen′sion·a·ble** adj.

pen·sion² (pän-syôN′) n. **1.** A boarding house or small hotel in Europe. **2.** Accommodations or the payment for accommodations, esp. at a pension. **3.** Room and board. [Fr. < OFr., payment. See PENSION¹.]

pen·sion·ar·y (pĕn′shə-nĕr′ē) adj. **1.** Constituting a pension. **2.** Mercenary; venal. ❖ n., pl. **-ies 1.** A pensioner. **2.** A hireling.

pen·sion·er (pĕn′shə-nər) n. **1.** One who receives a pension. **2.** One who is dependent on the bounty of another. **3.** Obsolete **a.** A gentleman-at-arms. **b.** An attendant; a retainer.

pen·sion plan (pĕn′shən) n. An arrangement for paying a pension to an employee, esp. one funded fully or in large part by an employer.

pen·sive (pĕn′sĭv) adj. **1.** Deeply, often wistfully or dreamily thoughtful. **2.** Suggestive or expressive of melancholy thoughtfulness. [ME pensif < OFr. < penser, to think < Lat. pēnsāre, freq. of pendere, to weigh.] —**pen′sive·ly** adv. —**pen′sive·ness** n.

SYNONYMS pensive, contemplative, reflective, meditative, thoughtful These adjectives mean characterized by or disposed to thought, especially serious or deep thought. Pensive often connotes a wistful, dreamy, or sad quality: "while pensive poets painful vigils keep" (Alexander Pope). Contemplative implies slow, directed consideration, often with conscious intent of achieving better understanding or spiritual or aesthetic enrichment: "The Contemplative Atheist is rare . . . And yet they seem to be more than they are" (Francis Bacon). Reflective suggests careful, analytical deliberation, as in reappraising past experience: "Cromwell was of the active, not the reflective temper" (John Morley). Meditative implies earnest, sustained thought: the meditative scholar. Thoughtful can refer to absorption in thought or to the habit of reflection and circumspection: thoughtful voters.

pen·ste·mon (pĕn-stē′mən, pĕn′stə-mən) n. Any of numerous plants of the genus Penstemon of North America and eastern Asia, having flowers with a usu. two-lipped, variously colored corolla. [NLat. Pēnstēmon, genus name : Gk. pente, five; see **penkʷe** in App. + Gk. stēmōn, thread; see **stā-** in App.]

pen·stock (pĕn′stŏk′) n. **1.** A sluice or gate used to control a flow of water. **2.** A pipe or conduit used to carry water to a water wheel or turbine.

pent (pĕnt) v. A past tense and a past participle of **pen².** ❖ adj. Penned or shut up; closely confined.

penta– or **pent–** pref. Five: pentamerous. [Gk. < pente, five. See **penkʷe** in App.]

pen·ta·chlo·ro·phe·nol (pĕn′tə-klôr′ə-fē′nôl′, -nŏl′, -nōl′, -klōr′-) n. A toxic white crystalline compound, C_6Cl_5OH, used in solution as a fungicide and wood preservative.

pen·ta·cle (pĕn′tə-kəl) n. A pentagram. [Med.Lat. *pentāculum : Gk. penta-, penta- + Lat. -culum, diminutive suff.]

pen·tad (pĕn′tăd′) n. A group of five. [Gk. pentas, pentad-, group of five < pente, five. See **penkʷe** in App.]

pen·ta·dac·tyl (pĕn′tə-dăk′təl) also **pen·ta·dac·ty·late** (-tə-lĭt, -lāt′) adj. Having five fingers or toes on each hand or foot. [Lat. pentadactylus < Gk. pentadaktulos : penta-, penta- + dak-

tulos, finger.] —**pen′ta•dac′tyl•ism** *n.*

pen•ta•gon (pĕn′tə-gŏn′) *n.* **1.** A polygon having five sides and five interior angles. **2. Pentagon** The US military establishment. Used with *the.* —**pen•tag′o•nal** (pĕn-tăg′ə-nəl) *adj.* —**pen•tag′o•nal•ly** *adv.*

pen•ta•gram (pĕn′tə-grăm′) *n.* A five-pointed star, often held to have magical or mystical significance.

pen•ta•he•dron (pĕn′tə-hē′drən) *n.,* pl. **-drons** or **-dra** (-drə) A solid having five plane faces. —**pen′ta•he′dral** (-drəl) *adj.*

pen•tam•er•ous (pĕn-tăm′ər-əs) *adj.* **1.** Having five similar parts. **2.** Having flower parts, such as petals and stamens, in sets of five, as in the geranium. —**pen•tam′er•ism** *n.*

pen•tam•e•ter (pĕn-tăm′ĭ-tər) *n.* **1.** A line of verse consisting of five metrical feet. **2.** English verse composed in iambic pentameter. [Lat. < Gk. *pentametros* : *penta-,* penta- + *metron,* measure; see METER¹.]

pen•tane (pĕn′tān′) *n.* Any of three colorless flammable isomeric hydrocarbons, C₅H₁₂, derived from petroleum and used as solvents.

pen•ta•gu•lar (pĕn-tăng′gyə-lər) *adj.* Having five angles.

pen•ta•ploid (pĕn′tə-ploid′) *adj.* Having five haploid sets of chromosomes. ❖ *n.* A pentaploid individual.

pen•tar•chy (pĕn′tär′kē) *n.,* pl. **-chies 1.** Government by five rulers. **2.** A body of five joint rulers. **3.** An association or federation of five governments, each ruled by a different leader. [Gk. *pentarkhiā* : *penta-,* penta- + *-arkhiā,* -archy.] —**pen•tar′chi•cal** (pĕn-tär′kĭ-kəl) *adj.*

pen•ta•stich (pĕn′tə-stĭk′) *n.* A poem or stanza having five lines. [< L.Gk. *pentastikhos,* of five lines : *penta-,* penta- + *stikhos,* line; see **steigh-** in App.]

Pen•ta•teuch (pĕn′tə-tōōk′, -tyōōk′) *n.* The first five books of the Hebrew Scriptures. [ME *Pentateuke* < LLat. *Pentateuchus* < Gk. *Pentateukhos* : *penta-,* penta- + *teukhos,* implement, vessel, scroll case.] —**Pen′ta•teuch′al** *adj.*

pen•tath•lete (pĕn-tăth′lēt′) *n.* An athlete who participates in a pentathlon.

pen•tath•lon (pĕn-tăth′lən, -lŏn′) *n.* **1.** A track-and-field event usu. for women that includes the 200-meter and 1500-meter runs, the long jump, and the discus and javelin throws. **2.** The modern pentathlon. [Gk. *pentāthlon* : *penta-,* penta- + *āthlon,* contest.]

pen•ta•ton•ic (pĕn′tə-tŏn′ĭk) *adj.* Music Of or using only five tones, usu. the first, second, third, fifth, and sixth tones of a diatonic scale.

pen•ta•va•lent (pĕn′tə-vā′lənt) *adj.* Having valence 5.

Pen•te•cost (pĕn′tĭ-kôst′, -kŏst′) *n.* **1.** The seventh Sunday after Easter, commemorating the descent of the Holy Spirit upon the disciples. **2.** *Judaism* See **Shavuot.** [ME *pentecoste* < OE *Pentecosten* < LLat. *Pentēcostē* < Gk. *pentēkostē* (*hēmera*), fiftieth (day), fem. of *pentēkostos,* fiftieth < *pentēkonta,* fifty. See **penkᵂe** in App.]

Pen•te•cos•tal (pĕn′tĭ-kŏs′təl, -kô′stəl) *adj.* **1.** Of, relating to, or occurring at Pentecost. **2.** Of, relating to, or being any of various Christian congregations whose members seek to be filled with the Holy Spirit, in emulation of the Apostles at Pentecost. ❖ *n.* A member of a Pentecostal congregation. —**Pen′te•cos′tal•ism** *n.* —**Pen′te•cos′tal•ist** *adj. & n.*

pent•house (pĕnt′hous′) *n.* **1a.** An apartment or dwelling situated on the roof of a building. **b.** A residence, often with a terrace, on the top floor or floors of a building. **c.** A structure housing machinery on the roof of a building. **2.** A shed or sloping roof attached to the side of a building or wall. [Alteration of ME *pentis, pentace,* a shed attached to a wall of a building < AN *pentiz,* penthouses < OFr. *apentiz,* penthouse < *apent,* p. part. of *apendre,* to belong, depend < Med.Lat. *appendere* < Lat., to hang, suspend. See APPEND.]

WORD HISTORY The word *penthouse* is a good example of a folk-etymology. It goes back ultimately to Latin *appendere,* "to cause to be suspended." In Medieval Latin *appendere* developed the sense "to belong, depend," a sense continued by its Old French descendant *apendre.* From *apent,* the past participle of *apendre,* came the derivative *apentiz,* "low building behind or beside a house," shortened in Anglo-Norman to *pentiz.* This was then borrowed into Middle English as *pentis* (first recorded about 1300), which was applied to sheds or lean-tos added on to buildings. Because these structures often had sloping roofs, the word was connected with the French word *pente,* "slope," and the second part of the word changed by folk-etymology to *house;* the whole thing meant simply "a building for human use." The use of the term with reference to fancy apartments developed from its application to a structure built on a roof to cover such things as a stairway or an elevator shaft. *Penthouse* then came to mean an apartment built on a rooftop and finally the top floor of an apartment building.

pen•ti•men•to (pĕn′tə-mĕn′tō) *n.,* pl. **-ti** (-tē) An underlying image in a painting, as an earlier painting, part of a painting, or original draft, that shows through, usu. when the top layer of paint has become transparent with age. [Ital., correction, pentimento < *pentire,* to repent < Lat. *paenitēre.*]

Pent•land Firth (pĕnt′lənd) A narrow channel between NE Scotland and the Orkney Is.

pent•land•ite (pĕnt′lən-dīt′) *n.* A yellowish-brown nickel iron sulfide that is the principal ore of nickel. [Fr., after Joseph Barclay *Pentland* (1797–1873), Irish scientist.]

pen•to•bar•bi•tal sodium (pĕn′tə-bär′bĭ-tôl′, -tăl′) *n.* A white crystalline or powdery derivative of nickel, C₁₁H₁₇N₂O₃Na, used as a hypnotic, a sedative, and an anticonvulsive drug.

pen•to•san (pĕn′tə-săn′) *n.* Any of a group of polysaccharides found with cellulose in many woody plants and yielding pentoses on hydrolysis.

pen•tose (pĕn′tōs′, -tōz′) *n.* Any of a class of monosaccharides having five carbon atoms per molecule and including ribose and several other sugars.

Pen•to•thal (pĕn′tə-thôl′) A trademark used for thiopental sodium.

pent•ox•ide (pĕnt-ŏk′sīd′) *n.* A compound having five atoms of oxygen combined with another element or radical.

pent-up (pĕnt′ŭp′) *adj.* Not given expression; repressed.

pen•tyl (pĕn′təl) *n.* See **amyl.**

pe•nu•che also **pe•nu•chi** (pə-nōō′chē) or **pa•no•cha** (-nō′chə) or **pa•no•che** (-chē) *n.* A fudgelike confection of brown sugar, cream or milk, and chopped nuts. [Variant of PANOCHA.]

pe•nuch•le or **pe•nuck•le** (pē′nŭk′əl) *n.* Variants of **pinochle.**

pe•nult (pē′nŭlt′, pĭ-nŭlt′) also **pe•nul•ti•ma** (pĭ-nŭl′tə-mə) *n.* **1.** The next to the last item in a series. **2.** The next to the last syllable in a word. [Short for *penultima* < Lat. *paenultima,* from of *paenultimus,* next to last : *paene,* almost + *ultimus,* last; see ULTIMATE.]

pe•nul•ti•mate (pĭ-nŭl′tə-mĭt) *adj.* **1.** Next to last. **2.** Of or relating to the penult of a word. ❖ *n.* The next to the last. [< Lat. *paenultimus.* See PENULT.] —**pe•nul′ti•mate•ly** *adv.*

pe•num•bra (pĭ-nŭm′brə) *n.,* pl. **-brae** (-brē) or **-bras 1.** A partial shadow, as in an eclipse, between regions of complete shadow and complete illumination. **2.** The grayish outer part of a sunspot. **3.** An area in which something exists to a lesser or uncertain degree. **4.** An outlying surrounding region; a periphery. [NLat. *pēnumbra* : Lat. *paene,* almost + Lat. *umbra,* shadow.] —**pe•num′bral, pe•num′brous** *adj.*

pe•nu•ri•ous (pə-nōōr′ē-əs, -nyōōr′-) *adj.* **1.** Unwilling to spend money; stingy. **2.** Yielding little; barren. **3.** Poverty-stricken; destitute. [< Med.Lat. *pēnūriōsus* < Lat. *pēnūria,* want.] —**pe•nu′ri•ous•ness** *n.*

pen•u•ry (pĕn′yə-rē) *n.* **1.** Extreme want or poverty; destitution. **2.** Extreme dearth; barrenness or insufficiency. [ME *penurie* < Lat. *pēnūria,* want.]

Pe•nu•ti•an (pə-nōō′tē-ən, -shən) *n.* A proposed stock of North American Indian languages spoken in Pacific coastal areas from California into British Columbia.

Pen•za (pĕn′zə, pyĕn′-) A city of W-central Russia SSW of Kazan; founded 1666. Pop. 547,623.

pe•on (pē′ŏn′, pē′ən) *n.* **1a.** An unskilled laborer or farm worker of Latin America or the southwest United States. **b.** Such a worker bound in servitude to a landlord creditor. **2.** A menial worker; a drudge. **3.** (*also* pyōōn) A person of menial position, such as a servant or messenger, in southern Asia. [Sp., day laborer < Med.Lat. *pedō, pedōn-,* foot soldier. See PIONEER.]

pe•on•age (pē′ə-nĭj) *n.* **1.** The condition of being a peon. **2.** A system by which debtors are bound in servitude to their creditors until their debts are paid.

pe•o•ny (pē′ə-nē) *n.,* pl. **-nies** Any of various plants of the genus *Paeonia,* having large, variously colored flowers with numerous stamens and several pistils. [ME *pione,* ult. < Med.Lat. *peōnia* < Lat. *paeōnia* < Gk. *paiōniā,* perh. < *Paiōn,* Apollo, physician of the gods.]

peo•ple (pē′pəl) *n.,* pl. **people 1.** Humans considered as a group or in indefinite numbers. **2.** A body of persons living in the same country under one national government; a nationality. **3.** *pl.* **peo•ples** A body of persons sharing a religion, culture, language, or inherited condition of life. **4.** Persons with regard to their residence, class, profession, or group. **5.** The mass of ordinary persons; the populace. **6.** The citizens of a political unit, such as a nation or state; the electorate. **7.** Persons subordinate to or loyal to a ruler, superior, or employer. **8.** Family, relatives, or ancestors. **9.** *Informal* Animals or other beings distinct from humans. ❖ *tr.v.* **-pled, -pling, -ples** To furnish with or as if with people; populate. [ME *peple* < OFr. *pueple* < Lat. *populus,* of Etruscan orig.] —**peo′pler** *n.*

people mover *n.* A means of mass transit, such as a monorail, used to transport people, usu. along a fixed route.

Peo•ple's Party (pē′pəlz) *n.* See **Populist Party.**

People's Republic *n.* A political organization founded and controlled by a national Communist party.

Pe•or•i•a¹ (pē-ôr′ē-ə, -ōr′-) *n.,* pl. **Peoria** or **-as** A member of a

peony

Native American people in the Illinois confederacy.

Pe·or·i·a² (pē-ôr′ē-ə, -ôr′-) A city of NW-central IL on the Illinois R. N of Springfield; founded on the site of a French fort est. by La Salle in 1680. Pop. 112,936.

pep (pĕp) *Informal n.* Energy and high spirits; vim. ❖ *tr.v.* **pepped, pep·ping, peps** To bring energy or liveliness to; invigorate. [Short for PEPPER.]

pep·er·o·mi·a (pĕp′ə-rō′mē-ə) *n.* Any of numerous succulent tropical herbs of the genus *Peperomia*, having palmately veined leaves and minute flowers densely grouped in cylindrical spikes. [NLat. *Peperomia*, genus name : Gk. *peperi*, pepper; see PEPPER + Gk. *homos*, same; see HOMO–.]

Pep·in the Short (pĕp′ĭn) also **Pepin III** 714?–768. King of the Franks (751–768) who established the Papal States.

pep·los (pĕp′ləs, -lŏs′) also **pep·lus** (-ləs) *n., pl.* **-los·es** also **-lus·es** A loose outer robe worn by women in ancient Greece. [Gk.]

pep·lum (pĕp′ləm) *n., pl.* **-lums** 1. A short overskirt or ruffle attached at the waistline of a jacket, blouse, or dress. 2. See **peplos**. [Lat., robe of state < Gk. *peplon*, neut. of *peplos*, peplos.] —**pep′lumed** *adj.*

pe·po (pē′pō) *n., pl.* **-pos** The fruit of any of various related plants, such as the watermelon, cucumber, squash, and melon, having a hard or leathery rind, fleshy pulp, and flattened seeds. [Lat. *pepō*, a kind of melon < Gk. *pepōn*, ripe. See **pekʷ-** in App.]

pep·per (pĕp′ər) *n.* 1. Black pepper. 2. Any of several plants of the genus *Piper*, such as cubeb, betel, and kava. **3a.** Any of several tropical American cultivated forms of *Capsicum frutescens* or *C. annuum* having podlike many-seeded berries. **b.** The podlike fruit of any of these plants, varying in size, shape, and degree of pungency. 4. Any of various condiments made from the more pungent varieties of *Capsicum frutescens*, such as cayenne pepper or chili. 5. *Baseball* A warm-up exercise in which players standing a short distance from a batter field the ball and toss it to the batter, who hits each toss back to the fielders. ❖ *tr.v.* **-pered, -per·ing, -pers** 1. To season or sprinkle with pepper. 2. To sprinkle liberally; dot. 3. To shower with or as if with small missiles. 4. To make (a speech, for example) lively and vivid with wit or invective. [ME *peper* < OE *pipor* < Lat. *piper* < Gk. *peperi*, of Indic orig.; akin to Prakrit *pippari* < Skt. *pippalī* < *pippalam*, pipal.]

pep·per-and-salt (pĕp′ər-ən-sôlt′) *adj.* Salt-and-pepper.

pep·per·box (pĕp′ər-bŏks′) *n.* See **peppershaker**.

pep·per·bush (pĕp′ər-bŏosh′) *n.* Sweet pepperbush.

pep·per·corn (pĕp′ər-kôrn′) *n.* 1. A dried berry of the pepper vine *Piper nigrum.* 2. A small or insignificant thing.

pep·per·cress (pĕp′ər-krĕs′) *n.* See **peppergrass**.

pep·per·grass (pĕp′ər-grăs′) *n.* Any of several plants of the genus *Lepidium*, esp. the North American species *L. virginicum*, having white flowers and pungent foliage and seeds.

pep·per·idge (pĕp′ər-ĭj) *n.* See **sour gum**. [?]

pepper mill *n.* A utensil for grinding peppercorns.

pep·per·mint (pĕp′ər-mĭnt′) *n.* 1. A plant (*Mentha piperita*) having downy leaves that yield a pungent oil. 2. The oil from this plant or a preparation made from it, used as a flavoring. 3. A candy or lozenge flavored with this oil.

pep·per·o·ni (pĕp′ə-rō′nē) *n., pl.* **-nis** 1. A highly spiced pork and beef sausage. 2. A slice of this type of sausage. [Ital. *peperoni*, pl. of *peperone*, pimento, red pepper, augmentative of *pepe*, pepper < Lat. *piper.* See PEPPER.]

pepper pot *n.* 1. A soup made with vegetables and tripe or other meat, seasoned with pepper and often containing dumplings. 2. A thick West Indian stew of meat or fish, vegetables, and regional condiments. 3. See **peppershaker**.

pep·per·shak·er (pĕp′ər-shā′kər) *n.* A container with small holes in the top for sprinkling ground pepper.

pepper tree also **pep·per·tree** (pĕp′ər-trē′) *n.* Any of several evergreen trees of the genus *Schinus*, esp. *S. molle* of South America, having compound leaves, yellowish-white flowers, and small rose-colored drupes.

pep·per·wood (pĕp′ər-wŏod′) *n.* See **Hercules' club** 2.

pep·per·wort (pĕp′ər-wûrt′, -wôrt′) *n.* 1. Any of various aquatic or marsh ferns of the genus *Marsilea*, having floating, four-parted palmate leaves rising from long runners. 2. See **peppergrass**.

pep·per·y (pĕp′ə-rē) *adj.* 1. Of, containing, or resembling pepper; sharp or pungent in flavor. 2. Vigorously sharp-tempered. 3. Sharp and stinging in style or content; vivid or fiery: *peppery criticism.* —**pep′per·i·ness** *n.*

pep pill *n. Slang* A tablet or capsule containing a stimulant drug, esp. an amphetamine.

pep·py (pĕp′ē) *adj.* **-i·er, -i·est** *Informal* Full of or characterized by energy and high spirits; lively. —**pep′pi·ly** *adv.* —**pep′pi·ness** *n.*

pep·sin also **pep·sine** (pĕp′sĭn) *n.* 1. A digestive enzyme found in gastric juice that catalyzes the breakdown of protein to peptides. 2. A substance containing pepsin, found in hog and calf stomachs and used as a digestive aid. [Gk. *pepsis*, digestion (< *peptein*, to digest; see **pekʷ-** in App.) + –IN.]

pep talk *n. Informal* A speech of exhortation, as to a team or staff, meant to instill enthusiasm or bolster morale.

pep·tic (pĕp′tĭk) *adj.* **1a.** Of, relating to, or assisting digestion. **b.**

Induced by or associated with the action of digestive secretions. 2. Of, relating to, or involving pepsin. 3. Capable of digesting. ❖ *n.* A digestive agent. [Lat. *pepticus* < Gk. *peptikos*, digested < *peptos* < *peptein*, to digest. See **pekʷ-** in App.]

pep·ti·dase (pĕp′tĭ-dās′, -dāz′) *n.* An enzyme that catalyzes the hydrolysis of peptides into amino acids.

pep·tide (pĕp′tīd′) *n.* Any of various natural or synthetic compounds containing two or more amino acids linked by the carboxyl group of one amino acid to the amino group of another. [PEPT(ONE) + –IDE.] —**pep·tid′ic** (-tĭd′ĭk) *adj.*

peptide bond *n.* The chemical bond formed between the carboxyl groups and amino groups of neighboring amino acids, constituting the primary linkage of all protein structures.

pep·tize (pĕp′tīz′) *tr.v.* **-tized, -tiz·ing, -tiz·es** To disperse (a precipitate) to form a colloid. [Gk. *peptein*, to digest; see **pekʷ-** in App. + –IZE.] —**pep′ti·za′tion** (-tĭ-zā′shən) *n.* —**pep′tiz′er** *n.*

pep·tone (pĕp′tōn′) *n.* Any of various compounds obtained by partial hydrolysis of a protein by an acid or enzyme during digestion and used in culture media in bacteriology. [Ger. *Pepton* < Gk. *peptos*, digested < *peptein*, to digest. See **pekʷ-** in App.] —**pep·ton′ic** (-tŏn′ĭk) *adj.*

pep·to·nize (pĕp′tə-nīz′) *tr.v.* **-nized, -niz·ing, -niz·es** 1. To convert (protein) into a peptone. 2. To dissolve (food) by means of a proteolytic enzyme. 3. To combine with peptone. —**pep′to·ni·za′tion** (-nī-zā′shən) *n.*

Pepys (pēps, pĕp′ĭs), **Samuel** 1633–1703. English civil servant whose diary includes descriptions of the Great Plague (1665) and the Great Fire of London (1666). —**Pepys′i·an** *adj.*

Pe·quot (pē′kwŏt′) *n., pl.* **Pequot** or **-quots** 1. A member of a Native American people formerly inhabiting eastern Connecticut, with present-day descendants in the same area. 2. The Algonquian language of the Pequot.

per (pûr) *prep.* 1. To, for, or by each; for every: *40 cents per gallon.* 2. According to; by: *changes made per instructions.* 3. By means of; through. ❖ *adv. Informal* 1. For each one; apiece: *cookies for one dollar per.* 2. Per hour: *driving at 60 miles per.* [Lat. See **per**¹ in App.]

per. *abbr.* 1. period 2. person

per– *pref.* 1. Thoroughly; completely; intensely: *perfervid.* 2. Containing an element in its highest oxidation state: *perchloric acid.* 3. Containing a large or the largest possible proportion of an element: *peroxide.* 4. Containing the peroxy group: *peracid.* [Lat. < *per*, through. See **per**¹ in App.]

per·ac·id (pûr′ăs′ĭd) *n.* 1. Any of various acids containing the peroxy group. 2. An inorganic acid containing the largest proportion of oxygen in a series of related acids.

per·ad·ven·ture (pûr′əd-vĕn′chər, pĕr′-) *adv. Archaic* Perhaps; perchance. ❖ *n.* Chance or uncertainty; doubt. [ME *per aventure* < OFr., by chance : *per*, through (< Lat.; see PER) + *aventure*, chance; see ADVENTURE.]

per·am·bu·late (pə-răm′byə-lāt′) *v.* **-lat·ed, -lat·ing, -lates** —*tr.* 1. To walk through. 2. To inspect (an area) on foot. —*intr.* To walk about; roam or stroll. [Lat. *perambulāre, perambulāt-* : *per-,* per- + *ambulāre*, to walk; see **ambhi** in App.] —**per·am′bu·la′tion** *n.* —**per·am′bu·la·to′ry** (-lə-tôr′ē, -tōr′ē) *adj.*

per·am·bu·la·tor (pə-răm′byə-lā′tər) *n. Chiefly British* A baby carriage.

per an·num (pər ăn′əm) *adv.* By the year; annually. [Lat.]

P/E ratio (pē′ē′) *n.* Price-earnings ratio.

per·bo·rate (pər-bôr′āt′, -bôr′-) *n.* A salt containing the radical BO_3, formed from a borate and hydrogen peroxide.

per·cale (pər-kāl′) *n.* A closely woven cotton fabric used for sheets and clothing. [Fr. < Pers. *pargālah*, rag.]

per·ca·line (pûr′kə-lēn′) *n.* A fine cotton fabric, usu. glazed, used esp. for linings and in the bindings of books. [Fr., dim. of *percale*, percale. See PERCALE.]

per cap·i·ta (pər kăp′ĭ-tə) *adv. & adj.* 1. Per unit of population. 2. Equally to each individual. [Med.Lat., by heads : Lat. *per*, per + Lat. *capita*, heads.]

per·ceive (pər-sēv′) *tr.v.* **-ceived, -ceiv·ing, -ceives** 1. To become aware of directly through any of the senses, esp. sight or hearing. 2. To achieve understanding of; apprehend. See Syns at **see**¹. [ME *perceiven* < OFr. *perceivre* < Lat. *percipere* : *per-,* per- + *capere*, to seize; see **kap-** in App.] —**per·ceiv′a·ble** *adj.* —**per·ceiv′a·bly** *adv.* —**per·ceiv′er** *n.*

per·cent also **per cent** (pər-sĕnt′) *adv.* Out of each hundred; per hundred. ❖ *n. pl.* **percent** One part in a hundred: *fifty percent of the alumni.* 2. *pl.* **percents** A percentage or portion. 3. **percents** *Chiefly British* Public securities yielding interest at a specified percentage. ❖ *adj.* Paying or demanding interest at a specified percentage. [< *per cent*, abbr. of *per centum*, by the hundred : *per*, per; see PER + *centum*, hundred; see **dekm** in App.]

USAGE NOTE Phrases expressing percentages take singular verbs if they are conceived as single entities; otherwise they take plural verbs. Typically the number of the last noun in the phrase determines whether the verb is singular or plural. Thus one might say *Eighty percent of the legislators are going to vote against the bill* but *Eighty percent of the legislature is set to vote the bill down.* When *percent* is used without a following prepositional phrase, either a singular or plural verb is acceptable, depending on the context:

Eighty percent is a large majority. Eighty percent are saying they will vote against the bill.

per·cent·age (pər-sĕn′tĭj) *n.* **1a.** A fraction or ratio with 100 understood as the denominator; for example, 0.98 equals a percentage of 98. **b.** The result obtained by multiplying a quantity by a percent. **2.** A proportion or share in relation to a whole; a part: *a small percentage of the audience.* **3.** An amount, such as a commission, that varies in proportion to a larger sum, such as total sales. **4.** *Informal* Advantage; gain.

USAGE NOTE *Percentage,* when preceded by *the,* takes a singular verb: *The percentage of unskilled workers is small.* When preceded by *a,* it takes either a singular or plural verb, depending on the number of the noun in the prepositional phrase that follows: *A small percentage of the workers are unskilled. A large percentage of the crop has spoiled.*

per·cen·tile (pər-sĕn′tīl′) *n.* One of a set of points on a scale arrived at by dividing a group into parts in order of magnitude. For example, a score equal to or greater than 97 percent of those attained on an examination is in the 97th percentile.

per cen·tum (pər sĕn′təm) *n.* See **percent** 1. [Lat. See PERCENT.]

per·cept (pûr′sĕpt′) *n.* **1.** The object of perception. **2.** A mental impression of something perceived by the senses, viewed as the basic component in the formation of concepts; a sense datum. [< Lat. *perceptum,* neut. p. part. of *percipere,* to perceive. See PERCEIVE.]

per·cep·ti·ble (pər-sĕp′tə-bəl) *adj.* Capable of being perceived by the senses or the mind. —**per·cep′ti·bil′i·ty** *n.* —**per·cep′ti·bly** *adv.*

SYNONYMS *perceptible, palpable, appreciable, noticeable, discernible* These adjectives apply to what is capable of being apprehended as being real by the mind or through the senses. *Perceptible* is the least specific: *a perceptible pause in his speech. Palpable* applies both to what is perceptible by means of the sense of touch and to what is readily perceived by the mind: *"The advantages Mr. Falkland possessed . . . are palpable"* (William Godwin). What is *appreciable* is capable of being estimated or measured: *dumping appreciable amounts of waste. Noticeable* means easily observed: *noticeable shadows under your eyes. Discernible* means distinguishable, especially by the faculty of vision or the intellect: *no discernible progress.*

per·cep·tion (pər-sĕp′shən) *n.* **1.** The process, act, or faculty of perceiving. **2.** The effect or product of perceiving. **3.** *Psychology* **a.** Recognition and interpretation of sensory stimuli based chiefly on memory. **b.** The neurological processes by which such recognition and interpretation are effected. **4a.** Insight, intuition, or knowledge gained by perceiving. **b.** The capacity for such insight. [ME *percepcioun* < OFr. *percepcion* < Lat. *perceptiō, perceptiōn-* < *perceptus,* p. part. of *percipere,* to perceive. See PERCEIVE.] —**per·cep′tion·al** *adj.*

per·cep·tive (pər-sĕp′tĭv) *adj.* **1.** Of or relating to perception: *perceptive faculties.* **2a.** Having the ability to perceive; keen in discernment. **b.** Marked by discernment and understanding; sensitive. —**per·cep′tive·ly** *adv.* —**per·cep·tiv′i·ty** (pûr′sĕp-tĭv′ĭ-tē), per·cep′tive·ness (pər-sĕp′tĭv-nĭs) *n.*

per·cep·tu·al (pər-sĕp′chōō-əl) *adj.* Of, based on, or involving perception. —**per·cep′tu·al·ly** *adv.*

perch¹ (pûrch) *n.* **1.** A rod or branch serving as a roost for a bird. **2a.** An elevated place for resting or sitting. **b.** A position that is secure, advantageous, or prominent. **3.** A pole, stick, or rod. **4.** *Chiefly British* **a.** A linear measure equal to 5.50 yards or 16.5 feet (5.03 meters); a rod. **b.** One square rod of land. **5.** A unit of cubic measure used in stonework, usu. 16.5 feet by 1.0 foot by 1.5 feet, or 24.75 cubic feet (0.70 cubic meter). **6.** A frame on which cloth is laid for examination of quality. ❖ *v.* **perched, perch·ing, perch·es** —*intr.* **1.** To alight or rest on a perch; roost. **2.** To stand, sit, or rest on an elevated place or position. —*tr.* **1.** To place on or as if on a perch. **2.** To lay (cloth) on a perch in order to examine it. [ME *perche* < OFr. < Lat. *pertica,* stick, pole.]

perch² (pûrch) *n., pl.* **perch** or **perch·es 1.** Any of various spiny-finned freshwater fishes of the genus *Perca,* esp. *P. flavescens* of North America and *P. fluviatilis* of Europe. **2.** Any of various similar or related fishes, such as the pike perch. [ME *perche* < OFr. < Lat. *perca* < Gk. *perkē.*]

per·chance (pər-chăns′) *adv.* Perhaps; possibly.

perch·er (pûr′chər) *n.* **1.** One that perches. **2.** A bird whose feet are adapted for perching.

Per·che·ron (pûr′chə-rŏn′, -shə-) *n.* Any of a breed of gray or black draft horse originally used in France. [Fr. < *Perche,* a historical region of NW France.]

per·chlo·rate (pər-klôr′āt′, -klôr′-) *n.* A salt or ester of perchloric acid.

per·chlo·ric acid (pər-klôr′ĭk, -klôr′-) *n.* A clear colorless liquid, HClO₄, explosively unstable under some conditions, that is a powerful oxidant used as a catalyst and in explosives.

per·chlo·ride (pər-klôr′īd′, -klôr′-) also **per·chlo·rid** (-klôr′ĭd, -klôr′-) *n.* A chloride having more chlorine than other chlorides of the same element.

per·chlo·ro·eth·yl·ene (pər-klôr′ō-ĕth′ə-lēn′, -klôr′-) *n.* A

colorless nonflammable organic solvent, Cl₂C:CCl₂, used in dry-cleaning solutions and as an industrial solvent.

per·cip·i·ent (pər-sĭp′ē-ənt) *adj.* Having the power of perceiving, esp. keenly and readily. ❖ *n.* One that perceives. [Lat. *percipiēns, percipient-,* pr. part. of *percipere,* to perceive. See PERCEIVE.] —**per·cip′i·ence, per·cip′i·en·cy** *n.*

per·coid (pûr′koid′) also **per·coi·de·an** (pər-koi′dē-ən) *adj.* Of or relating to the Percoidea, a large suborder of spiny-finned fishes that includes the perches, sunfishes, and groupers. [< NLat. *Percoīdea,* suborder name : Lat. *perca,* perch; see PERCH² + NLat. *-oīdea,* pl. of *-oīdēs,* resembling (< Gk. *-oeidēs;* see –OID).] —**per′coid′** *n.*

per·co·late (pûr′kə-lāt′) *v.* **-lat·ed, -lat·ing, -lates** —*tr.* **1.** To cause (liquid, for example) to pass through a porous substance or small holes; filter. **2.** To pass or ooze through. **3.** To make (coffee) in a percolator. —*intr.* **1.** To drain or seep through a porous material or filter. **2.** *Informal* To become lively or active. **3.** *Informal* To spread slowly or gradually. ❖ *n.* (-lĭt, -lāt′) A liquid that has been percolated. [Lat. *percōlāre, percōlāt-* : *per-,* per- + *cōlāre,* to filter (< *cōlum,* sieve).] —**per′co·la′tion** *n.*

per·co·la·tor (pûr′kə-lā′tər) *n.* A coffeepot in which boiling water is forced repeatedly up through a central tube to filter back down through a basket of ground coffee beans.

per con·tra (pər kŏn′trə) *adv.* **1.** On the contrary. **2.** By way of contrast. [Lat. *per contrā* : *per,* per + *contrā,* against.]

per·cuss (pər-kŭs′) *tr.v.* **-cussed, -cuss·ing, -cuss·es** To strike or tap firmly. [Lat. *percutere, percuss-,* to strike hard : *per-,* per- + *quatere,* to strike.]

per·cus·sion (pər-kŭsh′ən) *n.* **1.** The striking together of two bodies, esp. when noise is produced. **2.** The sound, vibration, or shock caused by the striking together of two bodies. **3.** The act of detonating a percussion cap in a firearm. **4.** A method of medical diagnosis in which various areas of the body, esp. the chest, back, and abdomen, are tapped to determine by resonance the condition of internal organs. **5.** *Music* **a.** The section of a band or orchestra composed of percussion instruments. **b.** Percussion instruments or their players considered as a group. [Lat. *percussiō, percussiōn-* < *percussus,* p. part. of *percutere,* to percuss. See PERCUSS.]

percussion cap *n.* A thin metal cap containing an explosive substance that explodes on being struck.

percussion instrument *n.* An instrument, such as a drum, xylophone, piano, or maraca, in which sound is produced by one object striking another or by being scraped or shaken.

per·cus·sion·ist (pər-kŭsh′ə-nĭst) *n.* One who plays percussion instruments.

per·cus·sive (pər-kŭs′ĭv) *adj.* Of, relating to, or marked by percussion. —**per·cus′sive·ly** *adv.* —**per·cus′sive·ness** *n.*

per·cu·ta·ne·ous (pûr′kyoō-tā′nē-əs) *adj. Medicine* Passed, done, or effected through the skin.

Per·cy (pûr′sē), Sir **Henry** Known as "Hotspur." 1364–1403. English soldier killed leading an uprising against Henry IV (1403).

Percy, Walker 1916–90. Amer. novelist whose works include *The Moviegoer* (1961).

per di·em (pər dē′əm, dī′əm) *adv.* By the day; per day. ❖ *adj.* **1.** Reckoned on a daily basis; daily. **2.** Paid by the day. ❖ *n., pl.* **per diems** An allowance for daily expenses. [Lat.]

per·di·tion (pər-dĭsh′ən) *n.* **1a.** Loss of the soul; eternal damnation. **b.** Hell. **2.** *Archaic* Utter ruin. [ME *perdicion* < OFr. < LLat. *perditiō, perditiōn-* < Lat. *perditus,* p. part. of *perdere,* to lose : *per-,* per- + *dare,* to give; see dō- in App.]

per·du or **per·due** (pər-doō′, -dyoō′) *n. Obsolete* A soldier sent on an esp. dangerous mission. [< Fr. *sentinelle perdue,* forward sentry : *sentinelle,* sentinel + *perdu,* p. part. of *perdre,* to lose (< Lat. *perdere;* see PERDITION).]

per·du·ra·ble (pər-doōr′ə-bəl, -dyoōr′-) *adj.* Extremely durable; permanent. [ME < OFr. < LLat. *perdūrābilis* < Lat. *perdūrāre,* to endure : *per-,* per- + *dūrāre,* to last.] —**per·du′ra·bil′i·ty** *n.* —**per·du′ra·bly** *adv.*

per·dure (pər-doōr′, -dyoōr′) *intr.v.* **-dured, -dur·ing, -dures** To last permanently; endure. [ME *perduren* < OFr. *pardurer* < Lat. *perdūrāre.* See PERDURABLE.]

père (pĕr) *n.* **1.** Used after a man's surname to distinguish a father from a son. **2.** Père *Roman Catholic Church* Used as a title for some priests. [Fr. < OFr. *pedre* < Lat. *pater.* See pəter- in App.]

per·e·gri·nate (pĕr′ĭ-grə-nāt′) *v.* **-nat·ed, -nat·ing, -nates** —*intr.* To journey or travel from place to place, esp. on foot. —*tr.* To travel through or over; traverse. [Lat. *peregrīnārī, peregrīnāt-* < *peregrīnus,* foreigner. See PEREGRINE.] —**per′e·gri·na′tion** *n.* —**per′e·gri·na′tor** *n.*

per·e·grine (pĕr′ĭ-grĭn, -grēn′) *adj.* **1.** Foreign; alien. **2.** Roving or wandering; migratory. ❖ *n.* A peregrine falcon. [ME < OFr. < Med.Lat. *peregrīnus,* wandering, pilgrim < Lat., foreigner < *pereger,* being abroad : *per-,* through; see PER– + *ager,* land; see agro- in App.]

peregrine falcon *n.* A widely distributed swift-flying bird of prey (*Falco peregrinus*) having gray and white plumage and much used in falconry. [ME, transl. of Med.Lat. *falcōperegrīnus* (so called because they were caught in passage).]

Pe·rei·ra (pə-rĕr′ə, pĕ-rā′rä) A city of W-central Colombia

Percheron

peregrine falcon
Falco peregrinus

ă	pat	oi	boy
ā	pay	ou	out
âr	care	oō	took
ä	father	oō	boot
ĕ	pet	ŭ	cut
ē	be	ûr	urge
ĭ	pit	th	thin
ī	pie	th	this
îr	pier	hw	which
ŏ	pot	zh	vision
ō	toe	ə	about,
ô	paw		item

Stress marks:
′ (primary);
′ (secondary), as in
lexicon (lĕk′sĭ-kŏn′)

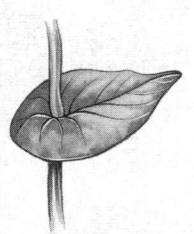

perfoliate
perfoliate leaf

west of Bogotá. Pop. 241,927.

Per·el·man (pĕr′əl-mən), **S(idney) J(oseph)** 1904–79. Amer. writer known for his satirical pieces in *The New Yorker.*

per·emp·to·ry (pə-rĕmp′tə-rē) *adj.* **1.** Putting an end to all debate or action. **2.** Not allowing contradiction or refusal; imperative. **3.** Having the nature of or expressing a command; urgent: *a peremptory tone.* **4.** Offensively self-assured; dictatorial. [Lat. *perēmptōrius < perēmptus,* p. part. of *perimere,* to take away : *per-, per-* + *emere,* to obtain.] **—per·emp′to·ri·ly** *adv.* **—per·emp′to·ri·ness** *n.*

per·en·nate (pĕr′ə-nāt′, pə-rĕn′āt) *intr.v.* **-nat·ed, -nat·ing, -nates** To survive from one growing season to the next, often with a period of reduced or arrested growth between seasons. [Lat. *perennāre, perennāt-,* to last many years < *perennis,* lasting for years. See PERENNIAL.] **—per′en·na′tion** *n.*

per·en·ni·al (pə-rĕn′ē-əl) *adj.* **1.** Lasting or active through the year or through many years. **2a.** Lasting an indefinitely long time; enduring. **b.** Appearing again and again; recurrent. See Syns at **continual. 3.** *Botany* Living three or more years. ❖ *n.* **1.** *Botany* A perennial plant. **2.** Something that recurs or seems to recur yearly or continually. [Lat. *perennis* (per-, throughout; see PER- + *annus,* year; see **at-** in App.) + *-AL*[1].] **—per·en′ni·al·ly** *adv.*

Per·es (pâr′ĕs), **Shimon** b. 1923. Polish-born Israeli political leader who served as prime minister (1977, 1984–86, and 1995–96). He shared the 1994 Nobel Peace Prize.

per·e·stroi·ka (pĕr′ĭ-stroi′kə) *n.* The restructuring of the Soviet economy and bureaucracy that began in the mid 1980s. [Russ. *perestroĭka : pere-,* around, again (< ORuss.; see **per**[1] in App.) + *stroĭka,* construction (< *stroit′,* to build < ORuss. *stroiti < stroji,* order).]

Pé·rez de Cué·llar (pĕr′əz də kwä′yär, pĕ′rĕs dĕ kwĕ′yär), **Ja·vier** b. 1920. Peruvian diplomat who served as secretary-general of the United Nations (1982–91).

Pe·rez Es·qui·vel (pĕr′əs ĕs′kē-vĕl′, pĕr′ĕs), **Adolfo** b. 1931. Argentine civil rights leader who won the 1980 Nobel Peace Prize.

per·fect (pûr′fĭkt) *adj.* **1.** Lacking nothing essential to the whole; complete of its nature or kind. See Usage Notes at **complete, unique. 2.** Being without defect or blemish: *a perfect specimen.* **3.** Thoroughly skilled or talented in a certain field or area; proficient. **4.** Completely suited for a particular purpose or situation. **5a.** Completely corresponding to a description, standard, or type: *a perfect circle.* **b.** Accurately reproducing an original. **6.** Complete; thorough; utter: *a perfect fool.* **7.** Pure; undiluted; unmixed: *perfect red.* **8.** Excellent and delightful in all respects: *a perfect day.* **9.** *Botany* Having both stamens and pistils in the same flower; monoclinous. **10.** *Grammar* Of, relating to, or constituting a verb form expressing action completed prior to a fixed point of reference in time. **11.** *Music* Designating the three basic intervals of the octave, fourth, and fifth. ❖ *n.* **1.** *Grammar* The perfect tense. **2.** A verb or verb form in the perfect tense. ❖ *tr.v.* (pər-fĕkt′) **-fect·ed, -fect·ing, -fects** To bring to perfection or completion. [ME *perfit < OFr. parfit < Lat. perfectus,* p. part. of *perficere,* to finish : *per-, per-* + *facere,* to do; see **dhē-** in App.] **—per·fect′er** *n.* **—per′fect·ness** *n.*

SYNONYMS *perfect, consummate, faultless, flawless, impeccable* These adjectives mean being wholly without flaw: *a perfect diamond; a consummate performer; faultless logic; a flawless instrumental technique; speaks impeccable French.* **ANTONYM** *imperfect*

per·fec·ta (pər-fĕk′tə) *n.* See **exacta.** [< Am.Sp. (*quiniela*) *perfecta,* perfect (quinella), fem. of *perfecto,* perfect < Lat. *perfectus.* See PERFECT.]

perfect game *n.* **1.** *Baseball* A complete game in which no opposing batter reaches first base. **2.** *Sports* A game in bowling in which a player bowls 12 successive strikes.

per·fect·i·ble (pər-fĕk′tə-bəl) *adj.* Capable of becoming perfect or being made perfect. **—per·fect′i·bil′i·ty** *n.*

per·fec·tion (pər-fĕk′shən) *n.* **1.** The quality or condition of being perfect. **2.** The act or process of perfecting. **3.** A person or thing considered to be perfect. **4.** An instance of excellence.

per·fec·tion·ism (pər-fĕk′shə-nĭz′əm) *n.* **1.** A propensity for being displeased with anything that is not perfect or does not meet extremely high standards. **2.** A belief in certain religions that moral or spiritual perfection can be achieved before the soul has passed into the afterlife. **—per·fec′tion·ist** *adj. & n.* **—per·fec′tion·is′tic** *adj.*

per·fec·tive (pər-fĕk′tĭv) *adj.* **1.** Tending toward perfection. **2.** *Grammar* Of, related to, or being the aspect that expresses the completion or the result of the action denoted by the verb. ❖ *n. Grammar* The perfective aspect. **2.** A verb having a perfective form. **—per·fec′tive·ly** *adv.* **—per·fec′tive·ness, per′fec·tiv′i·ty** (pûr′fĕk-tĭv′ĭ-tē) *n.*

per·fect·ly (pûr′fĭkt-lē) *adv.* **1.** In a perfect manner or to a perfect degree. **2.** To a complete or full degree or extent.

perfect number *n.* A positive integer that is equal to the sum of its positive integral factors, including 1 but excluding itself.

per·fec·to (pər-fĕk′tō) *n., pl.* **-tos** A cigar of standard length, thick in the center and tapered at each end. [< Sp., perfect < Lat. *perfectus.* See PERFECT.]

perfect participle *n.* See **past participle.**

perfect pitch *n.* See **absolute pitch** 2.

perfect rhyme *n.* **1.** Rhyme in which the final accented vowel and all succeeding consonants or syllables are identical, while the preceding consonants are different, for example, *rider, beside her.* **2.** Rime riche.

perfect square *n.* An integer that is the square of an integer.

per·fer·vid (pər-fûr′vĭd) *adj.* Extremely eager; impassioned or zealous. **—per·fer′vid·ly** *adv.* **—per·fer′vid·ness** *n.*

per·fid·i·ous (pər-fĭd′ē-əs) *adj.* Of, relating to, or marked by perfidy; treacherous. **—per·fid′i·ous·ly** *adv.*

per·fi·dy (pûr′fĭ-dē) *n., pl.* **-dies 1.** Deliberate breach of faith; calculated violation of trust; treachery. **2.** The act or an instance of treachery. [Lat. *perfidia < perfidus,* treacherous : *per-,* to destruction; see PER– + *fidēs,* faith; see **bheidh-** in App.]

per·fo·li·ate (pər-fō′lē-ĭt) *adj.* Of or relating to a sessile leaf or bract that completely clasps the stem and is apparently pierced by it. [NLat. *perfoliātus :* Lat. *per-, per-* + Lat. *foliātus,* bearing leaves (< *folium,* leaf; see **bhel-** in App.).] **—per·fo′li·a′tion** *n.*

per·fo·rate (pûr′fə-rāt′) *v.* **-rat·ed, -rat·ing, -rates** —*tr.* **1.** To pierce, punch, or bore a hole or holes in; penetrate. **2.** To pierce or stamp with rows of holes, as those between postage stamps, to allow easy separation. —*intr.* To pass into or through something. ❖ *adj.* (pûr′fər-ĭt, -fə-rāt′) Having been perforated. [Lat. *perforāre, perforāt- : per-, per-* + *forāre,* to bore.] **—per′fo·ra·ble** (-fər-ə-bəl) *adj.* **—per′fo·ra′tor** *n.*

per·fo·rat·ed (pûr′fə-rā′tĭd) *adj.* Having a hole or holes, esp. a row of small holes.

per·fo·ra·tion (pûr′fə-rā′shən) *n.* **1.** A hole or series of holes punched or bored through something, esp. a hole in a series, separating sections in a sheet or roll. **2a.** The act of perforating. **b.** The state of being perforated.

per·force (pər-fôrs′, -fōrs′) *adv.* By necessity; by force of circumstance. [ME *par force < OFr. : par,* by (< Lat. *per;* see PER) + *force;* see FORCE.]

per·form (pər-fôrm′) *v.* **-formed, -form·ing, -forms** —*tr.* **1.** To begin and carry through to completion; do: *The surgeon performed the operation.* **2.** To take action in accordance with the requirements of; fulfill: *perform one's contractual obligations.* **3a.** To enact (a feat or role) before an audience. **b.** To give a public presentation of; present: *performed a one-act play.* —*intr.* **1.** To carry on; function: *a car that performs well on curves.* **2.** To fulfill an obligation or requirement; accomplish something as promised or expected. **3.** To portray a role or demonstrate a skill before an audience: *The juggler performed atop a unicycle.* **4.** To present a dramatic or musical work or other entertainment before an audience. [ME *performen < AN performer < OFr. parfornir : par-,* intensive pref. (< Lat. *per-, per-*) + *fournir,* to furnish; see FURNISH.] **—per·form′a·ble** *adj.* **—per·form′er** *n.*

per·for·mance (pər-fôr′məns) *n.* **1.** The act of performing or the state of being performed. **2.** The act or style of performing a work or role before an audience. **3.** The way in which someone or something functions. **4.** A presentation before an audience. **5.** Something performed; an accomplishment. **6.** *Linguistics* One's actual use of language in actual situations.

performance art *n.* A form of theatrical art featuring the activity of the artist and works presented in a variety of media. **—performance artist** *n.*

per·for·ma·tive (pər-fôr′mə-tĭv) *adj.* Relating to or being an utterance that performs an act or creates a state of affairs by the fact of its being uttered, as in uttering *I now pronounce you husband and wife* at a wedding ceremony, thus creating a legal union. ❖ *n.* A performative utterance.

per·form·ing arts (pər-fôr′mĭng) *pl.n.* Arts, such as dance, drama, and music, that are performed before an audience.

per·fume (pûr′fyōōm′, pər-fyōōm′) *n.* **1.** A substance that emits and diffuses a fragrant odor, esp. a volatile liquid distilled from flowers or prepared synthetically. **2.** A pleasing, agreeable scent or odor. ❖ *tr.v.* (pər-fyōōm′) **-fumed, -fum·ing, -fumes** To fill or permeate with fragrance; impart a pleasant odor to. [Fr. *parfum < OItal. parfumo < parfumare,* to fill with smoke : *par-,* intensive pref. (< Lat. *per-, per-*) + *fumare,* to smoke (< Lat. *fūmāre < fūmus,* smoke).]

per·fum·er (pər-fyōō′mər) *n.* A maker or seller of perfumes.

per·fum·er·y (pər-fyōō′mə-rē) *n., pl.* **-ies 1.** Perfumes. **2.** An establishment that makes or sells perfume. **3.** The art of making perfume.

per·func·to·ry (pər-fŭngk′tə-rē) *adj.* **1.** Done routinely and with little interest or care. **2.** Showing little interest or care. [LLat. *perfūnctōrius < Lat. perfūnctus,* p. part. of *perfungī,* to get through with : *per-, per-* + *fungī,* to perform.] **—per·func′to·ri·ly** *adv.* **—per·func′to·ri·ness** *n.*

per·fuse (pər-fyōōz′) *tr.v.* **-fused, -fus·ing, -fus·es 1.** To coat or permeate with liquid, color, or light; suffuse. **2.** To pour or diffuse (a liquid, for example) over or through something. [Lat. *perfundere, perfūs-,* to pour over : *per-, per-* + *fundere,* to pour; see **gheu-** in App.] **—per·fu′sive** (pər-fyōō′sĭv, -zĭv) *adj.*

per·fu·sion (pər-fyōō′zhən) *n.* **1.** The act of perfusing. **2.** The injection of fluid into a blood vessel in order to reach an organ or tissues, usu. to supply nutrients and oxygen.

Per·ga·mum (pûr′gə-məm) An ancient Greek city and kingdom of W Asia Minor in modern-day W Turkey; noted for its library, which Mark Antony gave to Cleopatra.

per·go·la (pûr′gə-lə) *n.* An arbor or a passageway of columns supporting a roof of trelliswork on which climbing plants are trained to grow. [Ital. < Lat. *pergula.*]

Per·go·le·si (pĕr′gə-lā′zē, -gō-lĕ′-), Giovanni Battista 1710–36. Italian composer known for his comic operas.

per·haps (pər-hăps′) *adv.* Maybe; possibly. [< ME *perhap* : *per*, by (< Lat.; see PER) + *hap*, chance; see HAP.]

pe·ri (pîr′ē) *n., pl.* **-ris** In Persian mythology, a beautiful and benevolent supernatural being or fairy, earlier regarded as malevolent. [Pers. *parī* < MPers. *parīk*, malevolent sprite < Avestan *pairikā*, a kind of female demon.]

peri– *pref.* 1. Around; about; enclosing: *perimysium.* 2. Near: *perinatal.* [Gk. < *peri.* See **per**[1] in App.]

per·i·anth (pĕr′ē-ănth′) *n.* The outer envelope of a flower, consisting of either the calyx or the corolla or both. [Fr. *périanthe* < NLat. *perianthum* : Gk. *peri-*, peri- + Gk. *anthos*, flower.]

per·i·apt (pĕr′ē-ăpt′) *n.* A charm worn as protection against mischief and disease; an amulet. [Fr. *périapte* < Gk. *periapton* < *periaptos*, hung around : *peri-*, peri- + *haptos*, fastened (< *haptein*, to fasten).]

Per·i·bon·ca (pĕr′ə-bŏng′kə) A river of central Quebec, Canada, flowing c. 451 km (280 mi) through **Peribonca Lake** to Lake St. John.

per·i·car·di·tis (pĕr′ĭ-kär-dī′tĭs) *n.* Inflammation of the pericardium.

per·i·car·di·um (pĕr′ĭ-kär′dē-əm) *n., pl.* **-di·a** (-dē-ə) The membranous sac filled with serous fluid that encloses the heart and the roots of the aorta and other large blood vessels. [NLat. < Gk. *perikardion* < *perikardios*, around the heart : *peri-*, peri- + *kardia*, heart; see **kerd-** in App.] —**per′i·car′di·al** (-dē-əl), **per′i·car′di·ac′** (-dē-ăk′) *adj.*

per·i·carp (pĕr′ĭ-kärp′) *n.* 1. *Botany* The wall of a ripened ovary; fruit wall. 2. A membranous structure surrounding the cystocarp of red algae. —**per′i·car′pi·al** *adj.*

per·i·chon·dri·um (pĕr′ĭ-kŏn′drē-əm) *n., pl.* **-dri·a** (-drē-ə) The fibrous membrane of connective tissue covering the surface of cartilage except at joint endings. [NLat. : PERI– + Gk. *khondros*, cartilage; see CHONDRO–.] —**per′i·chon′dri·al** (-drē-əl) *adj.*

Per·i·cles (pĕr′ĭ-klēz′) d. 429 B.C. Athenian leader noted for advancing democracy. —**Per′i·cle′an** (-klē′ən) *adj.*

pe·ric·o·pe (pə-rĭk′ə-pē) *n., pl.* **-pes** or **-pae** (-pē′) An extract or selection from a book, esp. a Scripture reading that is part of a church service. [LLat. *pericopē* < Gk. *perikopē*, a cutting around, section < *perikoptein*, to cut around : *peri-*, peri- + *koptein*, to cut.] —**pe·ric′o·pal** (pə-rĭk′ə-pəl), **per′i·cop′ic** (pĕr′ĭ-kŏp′ĭk) *adj.*

per·i·cy·cle (pĕr′ĭ-sī′kəl) *n.* A plant tissue characteristic of the roots, located between the endodermis and phloem. [Fr. *péricycle* < Gk. *perikuklos*, spherical : *peri-*, peri- + *kuklos*, circle; see CYCLE.] —**per′i·cy′clic** (-sī′klĭk, -sĭk′lĭk) *adj.*

per·i·derm (pĕr′ĭ-dûrm′) *n.* The outer layers of tissue of woody roots and stems, consisting of the cork cambium and the tissues produced by it. —**per′i·der′mal, per′i·der′mic** *adj.*

pe·rid·i·um (pə-rĭd′ē-əm) *n., pl.* **-i·a** (-ē-ə) The covering of the spore-bearing organ in many fungi. [NLat. *pērīdium* < Gk. *pērīdion*, dim. of *pērā*, leather pouch.] —**pe·rid′i·al** (-ē-əl) *adj.*

per·i·dot (pĕr′ĭ-dŏt′, -dō′) *n.* A yellowish-green variety of olivine used as a gem. [ME < OFr.]

per·i·do·tite (pĕr′ĭ-dō-tīt′, pə-rĭd′ə-) *n.* Any of a group of igneous rocks composed mainly of olivine and various pyroxenes and having a granitelike texture.

per·i·gee (pĕr′ə-jē) *n.* 1. The point nearest the earth's center in the orbit of the moon or a satellite. 2. The point in any orbit nearest to the body being orbited. [Fr. *périgée* < Med.Lat. *perigēum* < L.Gk. *perigeion* : Gk. *peri-*, peri- + Gk. *gē*, earth.] —**per′i·ge′al** (-jē′əl), **per′i·ge′an** (-jē′ən) *adj.*

pe·rig·y·nous (pə-rĭj′ə-nəs) *adj.* 1. Having sepals, petals, and stamens around the edge of a cuplike receptacle containing the ovary, as in flowers of the rose or cherry. 2. Of or being perigynous flower parts. —**pe·rig′y·ny** (-ə-nē) *n.*

per·i·he·li·on (pĕr′ə-hē′lē-ən, -hēl′yən) *n., pl.* **-he·li·a** (-hē′lē-ə, -hēl′yə) The point nearest the sun in the orbit of a planet or other celestial body. [Alteration of NLat. *perihēlium* : PERI–, *hēlios*, sun; see **sāwel-** in App.] —**per′i·he′li·al** (-hē′lē-əl, -hēl′yəl) *adj.*

per·i·kar·y·on (pĕr′ĭ-kăr′ē-ŏn′, -ən) *n., pl.* **-kar·y·a** (-kăr′ē-ə) The cell body of a neuron, containing the nucleus and organelles. [PERI– + Gk. *karuon*, nut; see KARYO–.] —**per′i·kar′y·al** (-ē-əl) *adj.*

per·il (pĕr′əl) *n.* 1a. Imminent danger. b. Exposure to the risk of harm or loss. 2. Something that endangers or involves risk. ❖ *tr.v.* **-iled, -il·ing, -ils** also **-illed, -il·ling, -ils** To expose to danger or the chance of injury; imperil. [ME < OFr. < Lat. *perīculum.*]

pe·ril·la (pə-rĭl′ə) *n.* 1. An annual Asian plant (*Perilla frutescens*) having opposite leaves and flowers with a white tubular corolla. 2. The oil from the seeds of this plant, used in the manufacture of paint, varnish, and artificial leather and as a substitute for linseed oil. [NLat., genus name.]

per·il·ous (pĕr′ə-ləs) *adj.* Full of or involving peril; dangerous. —**per′il·ous·ly** *adv.* —**per′il·ous·ness** *n.*

per·i·lymph (pĕr′ə-lĭmf′) *n.* The fluid in the space between the membranous and bony labyrinths of the inner ear.

pe·rim·e·ter (pə-rĭm′ĭ-tər) *n.* 1. *Mathematics* a. A closed curve bounding a plane area. b. The length of such a boundary. 2. The outer limits of an area. 3. A fortified strip or boundary usu. protecting a military position. [ME *perimetre* < Lat. *perimetros* < Gk. : *peri-*, peri- + *metron*, measure; see METER[2].] —**per′i·met′ric** (pĕr′ə-mĕt′rĭk), **per′i·met′ri·cal** (-kəl) *adj.*

per·i·morph (pĕr′ə-môrf′) *n.* A mineral that encloses a different mineral. —**per′i·mor′phic, per′i·mor′phous** *adj.* —**per′i·mor′phism** *n.*

per·i·my·si·um (pĕr′ə-mĭzh′ē-əm, -mĭz′ē-əm) *n., pl.* **-my·si·a** (-mĭzh′ē-ə, -mĭz′ē-ə) The sheath of connective tissue enveloping bundles of muscle fibers. [NLat. : PERI– + Gk. *mūs*, muscle; see **mūs-** in App.]

per·i·na·tal (pĕr′ə-nāt′l) *adj.* Of, relating to, or being the period around childbirth, esp. the five months before and one month after birth. —**per′i·na′tal·ly** *adv.*

per·i·ne·um (pĕr′ə-nē′əm) *n., pl.* **-ne·a** (-nē′ə) 1. The portion of the body in the pelvis occupied by urogenital passages and the rectum, bounded in front by the pubic arch, in the back by the coccyx, and laterally by part of the hipbone. 2. The region between the scrotum and the anus in males and between the posterior vulva junction and the anus in females. [ME < Med.Lat. *perinaeon* < Gk. *perinaion* : *peri-*, peri- + *inān*, to excrete.] —**per′i·ne′al** (-nē′əl) *adj.*

per·i·neu·ri·um (pĕr′ə-noŏr′ē-əm, -nyoŏr′-) *n., pl.* **-neu·ri·a** (-noŏr′ē-ə, -nyoŏr′-) The sheath of connective tissue enclosing a bundle of nerve fibers. [NLat. : PERI– + Gk. *neuron*, nerve; see NEURON.] —**per′i·neu′ri·al** *adj.*

pe·ri·od (pîr′ē-əd) *n.* 1. An interval of time characterized by the occurrence of a certain condition, event, or phenomenon: *a period of economic prosperity.* 2. An interval of time characterized by the prevalence of a specified culture, ideology, or technology: *artifacts of the pre-Columbian period.* 3. An interval regarded as a distinct evolutionary or developmental phase. 4. *Geology* A unit of time, longer than an epoch and shorter than an era. 5. Any of various arbitrary units of time, esp.: a. Any of the divisions of the academic day. b. *Sports & Games* A division of the playing time of a game. 6. *Physics & Astronomy* The time interval between two successive occurrences of a recurrent event or phases of an event; a cycle. 7. An instance or occurrence of menstruation. 8. A point or portion of time at which something is ended; a completion or conclusion. 9. The full pause at the end of a spoken sentence. 10. A punctuation mark (.) indicating a full stop, placed at the end of declarative sentences and other statements thought to be complete and after many abbreviations. 11. A sentence of several carefully balanced clauses in formal writing. 12a. A metrical unit of quantitative verse consisting of two or more cola. b. An analogous unit or division of classical Greek or Latin prose. 13. *Music* A group of two or more phrases within a composition, made up of 8 or 16 measures and terminating with a cadence. 14. *Mathematics* a. The least interval in the range of the independent variable of a periodic function of a real variable in which all possible values of the dependent variable are assumed. b. A group of digits separated by commas in a written number. c. The number of digits that repeat in a repeating decimal. For example, $\frac{1}{7}$ = 0.142857142857 . . . has a six-digit period. 15. *Chemistry* A sequence of elements arranged in order of increasing atomic number and forming one of the horizontal rows in the periodic table. ❖ *adj.* Of, belonging to, or representing a certain historical age or time. ❖ *interj.* Used to emphasize finality, as when expressing a decision or opinion: *You're not going to the movies tonight, period!* [ME *periode* < OFr. < Med.Lat. *periodus* < Lat. *perihodos*, rhetorical period < Gk. *periodos*, circuit : *peri-*, peri- + *hodos*, way.]

pe·ri·od·ic (pîr′ē-ŏd′ĭk) *adj.* 1. Having or marked by repeated cycles. 2. Happening or appearing at regular intervals. 3. Recurring or reappearing from time to time. 4. Characterized by periodic sentences. —**pe′ri·od′i·cal·ly** *adv.*

SYNONYMS *periodic, sporadic, intermittent, occasional, fitful* These adjectives mean recurring now and then. Something *periodic* occurs at regular or at least generally predictable intervals: *periodic anxiety. Sporadic* implies scattered, irregular, unpredictable, or isolated instances: *sporadic bombings. Intermittent* describes something that stops and starts at intervals: *intermittent rain.* What is *occasional* happens at random and irregularly: *occasional anger.* Something *fitful* occurs in spells and often abruptly: *fitful activity.*

per·i·od·ic acid (pûr′ī-ŏd′ĭk) *n.* A white crystalline inorganic acid, $HIO_4 \cdot 2H_2O$, used as an oxidizer.

pe·ri·od·i·cal (pîr′ē-ŏd′ĭ-kəl) *adj.* 1. Periodic. 2a. Published at regular intervals of more than one day. b. Of a publication issued at such intervals. ❖ *n.* A periodical publication.

periodical cicada *n.* A cicada of the genus *Magicicada* of the eastern United States whose 17-year or 13-year life cycle consists almost entirely of a nymphal stage spent underground.

pe·ri·o·dic·i·ty (pîr′ē-ə-dĭs′ĭ-tē) *n., pl.* **-ties** 1. The quality or state of being periodic; recurrence at regular intervals. 2. The repetition of similar properties in chemical elements, as indicated by their positioning in the periodic table.

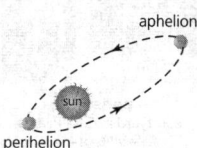

perihelion

pe•ri•od•ic law (pĭr′ē-ŏd′ĭk) *n. Chemistry* The principle that the properties of the elements recur periodically as their atomic numbers increase.

pe•ri•od•ic sentence (pĭr′ē-ŏd′ĭk) *n.* A sentence in which the main clause or its predicate is withheld until the end; for example, *Despite heavy winds and ground fog, we landed.*

pe•ri•od•ic table (pĭr′ē-ŏd′ĭk) *n. Chemistry* A tabular arrangement of the elements in rows according to their atomic numbers so that elements with similar properties are in the same column. See table at **element.**

per•i•o•don•tal (pĕr′ē-ə-dŏn′tl) *adj.* **1.** Surrounding or encasing a tooth. **2.** Relating to or affecting periodontal tissue and structures. **—per′i•o•don′tal•ly** *adv.*

per•i•o•don•tia (pĕr′ē-ə-dŏn′shə) *n.* Periodontics.

per•i•o•don•tics (pĕr′ē-ə-dŏn′tĭks) *n.* (*used with a sing. verb*) The branch of dentistry that deals with the study and treatment of periodontal disease. **—per′i•o•don′tic, per′i•o•don′ti•cal** *adj.* **—per′i•o•don′tist** *n.*

per•i•o•nych•i•um (pĕr′ē-ō-nĭk′ē-əm) *n., pl.* **-i•a** (-ē-ə) The border of epidermal tissue surrounding a fingernail or toenail. [NLat. : PERI– + Gk. *onux, onukh-*, nail.]

per•i•os•te•um (pĕr′ē-ŏs′tē-əm) *n., pl.* **-te•a** (-tē-ə) The dense fibrous membrane covering the surface of bones except at the joints and serving as an attachment for muscles and tendons. [NLat. < LLat. *periosteon* < Gk. < *periosteos*, around the bone : *peri-*, peri- + *osteon*, bone; see **ost-** in App.] **—per′i•os′te•al** (-tē-əl), **per′i•os′te•ous** (-tē-əs) *adj.*

per•i•os•ti•tis (pĕr′ē-ŏs-tī′tĭs) *n.* Inflammation of the periosteum. **—per′i•os•tit′ic** (-tĭt′ĭk) *adj.*

per•i•o•tic (pĕr′ē-ō′tĭk) *adj.* **1.** Situated around the ear. **2.** Of or relating to the bones immediately around the inner ear.

per•i•pa•tet•ic (pĕr′ə-pə-tĕt′ĭk) *adj.* **1.** Walking about or from place to place; traveling on foot. **2. Peripatetic** Of or relating to the philosophy of Aristotle, who conducted discussions while walking about in the Lyceum of ancient Athens. ❖ *n.* **1.** One who walks from place to place; an itinerant. **2. Peripatetic** A follower of the philosophy of Aristotle. [ME *peripatetik* < Lat. *peripatēticus* < Gk. *peripatētikos* < *peripatein*, to walk about, or < *peripatos*, covered walk (where Aristotle allegedly lectured) : *peri-*, peri- + *patein*, to walk; see **pent-** in App.]

per•i•pe•te•ia also **per•i•pe•ti•a** (pĕr′ə-pə-tē′ə, -tī′ə) *n.* A sudden change of events or reversal of circumstances, esp. in a literary work. [Gk. < *peripiptein*, to change suddenly : *peri-*, peri- + *piptein, pet-*, to fall; see **pet-** in App.]

pe•rip•e•ty (pə-rĭp′ĭ-tē) *n.* Peripeteia. [Fr. *péripétie* < Gk. *peripeteia.* See PERIPETEIA.]

pe•riph•er•al (pə-rĭf′ər-əl) *adj.* **1.** Relating to, located in, or constituting an outer boundary or periphery. **2.** Perceived or perceiving near the outer edges of the retina. **3.** *Anatomy* **a.** Of the surface or outer part of a body or organ; external. **b.** Of or relating to the peripheral nervous system. **4.** Of minor relevance or importance. **5.** Auxiliary. ❖ *n. Computer Science* An auxiliary device, such as a modem, that works in conjunction with a computer. **—pe•riph′er•al•ly** *adv.*

peripheral nervous system *n.* The part of the vertebrate nervous system constituting the nerves outside the central nervous system and including the cranial nerves, spinal nerves, and sympathetic and parasympathetic nervous systems.

pe•riph•er•y (pə-rĭf′ə-rē) *n., pl.* **-ies 1.** A line that forms the boundary of an area; a perimeter. **2.** The surface of a solid. **3a.** The outermost part or region within a precise boundary. **b.** A zone constituting an imprecise boundary. [ME *periferie* < Med.Lat. *periferia* < LLat. *peripherīa* < Gk. *periphereia* < *peripherēs*, carrying around : *peri-*, peri- + *pherein*, to carry; see **bher-**[1] in App.]

pe•riph•ra•sis (pə-rĭf′rə-sĭs) *n., pl.* **-ses** (-sēz′) **1.** The use of circumlocution. **2.** A circumlocution. [Lat. < Gk. < *periphrazein*, to express periphrastically : *peri-*, peri- + *phrazein*, to say.]

per•i•phras•tic (pĕr′ə-frăs′tĭk) *adj.* **1.** Having the nature of or characterized by periphrasis. **2.** *Grammar* Constructed by using an auxiliary word rather than an inflected form; for example, *did say* is the periphrastic past tense of *say,* but *said* is the inflected past tense. **—per′i•phras′ti•cal•ly** *adv.*

pe•riph•y•ton (pə-rĭf′ĭ-tŏn′) *n.* Sessile organisms, such as algae and small crustaceans, that live attached to surfaces projecting from the bottom of a freshwater aquatic environment. [NLat. < Gk. *periphuton* < neut. sing. of *periphutos*, planted all over < *periphuein*, to grow around, cling to : *peri-*, peri- + *phuein*, to grow; see **bheuə-** in App.]

pe•rip•ter•al (pə-rĭp′tər-əl) *adj. Architecture* Having a single row of columns on all sides. [< Lat. *peripteros* < Gk. : *peri-*, peri- + *pteron*, wing; see **pet-** in App.]

pe•rique (pə-rēk′) *n.* A strongly flavored black tobacco grown in Louisiana and used in blends. [Louisiana Fr., perhaps from *Périque*, a nickname of *Pierre Chenet*, a Louisiana tobacco grower.]

per•i•sarc (pĕr′ĭ-särk′) *n.* A horny external covering that encloses the polyp colonies of certain hydrozoans. [PERI– + Gk. *sarx, sark-*, flesh.] **—per′i•sar′cal, per′i•sar′cous** *adj.*

per•i•scope (pĕr′ĭ-skōp′) *n.* Any of various tubular optical instruments that contain reflecting elements, such as mirrors and prisms, to permit observation from a position displaced from a direct line of sight. **—per′i•scop′ic** (-skŏp′ĭk), **per′i•scop′i•cal** (-ĭ-kəl) *adj.*

per•ish (pĕr′ĭsh) *v.* **-ished, -ish•ing, -ish•es** *—intr.* **1.** To die or be destroyed, esp. in a violent or untimely manner. **2.** To pass from existence; disappear gradually. **3.** *Chiefly British* To spoil or deteriorate. *—tr.* To bring to destruction; destroy. ***—idiom:*** **perish the thought** Used to express the wish that one not even think about something. [ME *perishen* < OFr. *perir, periss-*, to perish < Lat. *perīre* : *per-*, per- + *īre*, to go; see **ei-** in App.]

per•ish•a•ble (pĕr′ĭ-shə-bəl) *adj.* Subject to decay, spoilage, or destruction. ❖ *n.* Something, esp. food, subject to decay or spoilage. Often used in the plural. **—per′ish•a•bil′i•ty, per′ish•a•ble•ness** *n.* **—per′ish•a•bly** *adv.*

pe•ris•so•dac•tyl (pə-rĭs′ō-dăk′təl) *adj. Zoology* **1.** Having an uneven number of toes. **2.** Of or relating to certain hoofed mammals, such as horses and rhinoceroses, of the order Perissodactyla, having an uneven number of toes. [NLat. *perissodactylus* < Gk. *perissodaktulos* : *perissos*, irregular, uneven (< *peri*, beyond; see **per**[1] in App.) + *daktulos*, finger.] **—pe•ris′so•dac′tyl** *n.* **—pe•ris′so•dac′ty•lous** (-dăk′tə-ləs) *adj.*

per•i•stal•sis (pĕr′ĭ-stôl′sĭs, -stăl′-) *n., pl.* **-ses** (-sēz) The wavelike muscular contractions of the alimentary canal or other tubular structures by which contents are forced onward toward the opening. [NLat. < Gk. *peristaltikos*, peristaltic < *peristellein*, to wrap around : *peri-*, peri- + *stellein*, to place; see **stel-** in App.] **—per′i•stal′tic** (-stôl′tĭk, -stăl′-) *adj.* **—per′i•stal′ti•cal•ly** *adv.*

per•i•stome (pĕr′ĭ-stōm′) *n.* **1.** *Botany* A fringe of toothlike appendages around the mouth of a moss capsule. **2.** *Zoology* The area or parts around the mouth in some invertebrates. **—per′i•sto′mal** (-stō′məl), **per′i•sto′mi•al** (-stō′mē-əl) *adj.*

per•i•style (pĕr′ĭ-stīl′) *n.* **1.** A series of columns surrounding a building or enclosing a court. **2.** A court enclosed by columns. [Fr. *péristyle* < Lat. *peristȳlum* < Gk. *peristūlon* < neut. of *peristūlos*, surrounded by columns : *peri-*, peri- + *stūlos*, pillar; see **stā-** in App.] **—per′i•sty′lar** (-stī′lər) *adj.*

per•i•the•ci•um (pĕr′ə-thē′shē-əm, -sē-əm) *n., pl.* **-ci•a** (-shē-ə, -sē-ə) A small flask-shaped fruiting body in ascomycetous fungi that contains the ascospores. [NLat. : PERI– + Gk. *thēkion*, dim. of *thēkē*, case; see **dhē-** in App.]

per•i•to•ne•um also **per•i•to•nae•um** (pĕr′ĭ-tn-ē′əm) *n., pl.* **-to•ne•a** also **-to•nae•a** (-tn-ē′ə) The serous membrane that lines the walls of the abdominal cavity and folds inward to enclose the viscera. [ME < LLat. *peritonaeum* < Gk. *peritonaion* : ult. *peri-*, peri- + *teinein*, to stretch; see **ten-** in App.] **—per′i•to•ne′al** *adj.* **—per′i•to•ne′al•ly** *adv.*

per•i•to•ni•tis (pĕr′ĭ-tn-ī′tĭs) *n.* Inflammation of the peritoneum.

per•i•trich (pĕr′ĭ-trĭk′) *n., pl.* **pe•rit•richs** also **pe•rit•ri•cha** (pə-rĭt′rĭ-kə) Any of various protozoans, such as the vorticella, having a wide oral opening surrounded by cilia. [< NLat. *Peritrichida*, former order name : PERI– + Gk. *thrix, trikh-*, hair.]

pe•rit•ri•chous (pə-rĭt′rĭ-kəs) *adj.* **1.** Having flagella uniformly distributed over the body surface, as certain bacteria. **2.** Having a band of cilia around the mouth, as certain protozoans. **—pe•rit′ri•chous•ly** *adv.*

per•i•wig (pĕr′ĭ-wĭg′) *n.* A wig, esp. a peruke. [By folk-ety. < OFr. *perruque.* See PERUKE.]

per•i•win•kle[1] (pĕr′ĭ-wĭng′kəl) *n.* **1.** Any of several small, often edible marine snails, esp. of the genus *Littorina*, having thick, cone-shaped whorled shells. **2.** Their shell. [ME **periwinkle*, prob. alteration of OE *pīnewincle* : Lat. *pīna*, mussel (< Gk. *pīnē*) + OE *-wincel*, snail shell.]

per•i•win•kle[2] (pĕr′ĭ-wĭng′kəl) *n.* **1.** Any of several shrubby, trailing evergreen plants of the genus *Vinca*, esp. *V. minor*, having dark green opposite leaves and flowers with a blue funnel-shaped corolla. **2.** A pale purplish blue. [ME *pervinkle*, dim. of *pervinke* < OE *pervince* < Lat. *(vinca) pervinca* < *pervincīre*, to wind about.]

per•jure (pûr′jər) *tr.v.* **-jured, -jur•ing, -jures** *Law* To make (oneself) guilty of perjury by deliberately testifying falsely under oath. [ME *perjuren* < OFr. *perjurer* < Lat. *periūrāre* : *per-*, per- + *iūrāre*, to swear.] **—per′jur•er** *n.*

per•ju•ry (pûr′jə-rē) *n., pl.* **-ries 1.** *Law* The deliberate, willful giving of false, misleading, or incomplete testimony under oath. **2.** The breach of an oath or promise. [ME *periurie* < AN < Lat. *periūrium* < *periūrāre*, to perjure. See PERJURE.] **—per•ju′ri•ous** (pər-jo͝or′ē-əs) *adj.* **—per•ju′ri•ous•ly** *adv.*

perk[1] (pûrk) *v.* **perked, perk•ing, perks** *—intr.* **1.** To stick up or jut out. **2.** To carry oneself in a lively and jaunty manner. *—tr.* To cause to stick up quickly. ❖ *adj.* Perky. ***—phrasal verb:*** **perk up 1.** To regain or cause to regain one's good spirits or liveliness. **2.** To refresh the appearance of. [Poss. ME *perken*, to perch < *perk*, rod, perch, prob. < Med.Lat. *perca* and < OFr. *perche, perce*, both < Lat. *pertica*, rod. See PERCH[1].]

perk[2] (pûrk) *n. Informal* A perquisite.

perk[3] (pûrk) *intr.v.* **perked, perk•ing, perks** *Informal* To percolate: *The coffee was perking on the stove.*

Per•kins (pûr′kĭnz), **Frances** 1882–1965. Amer. social reformer who served as US secretary of labor (1933–45).

Perkins, Maxwell Evarts 1884–1947. Amer. editor who helped writers such as F. Scott Fitzgerald.

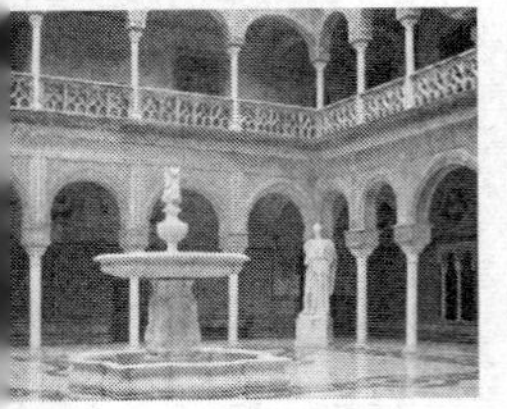

peristyle
courtyard in Casa Pilatos, Seville, Spain

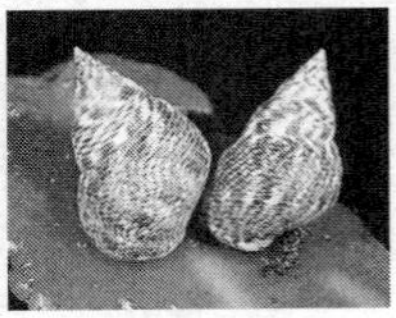

periwinkle[1]
angulate periwinkles
Littorina angulifera

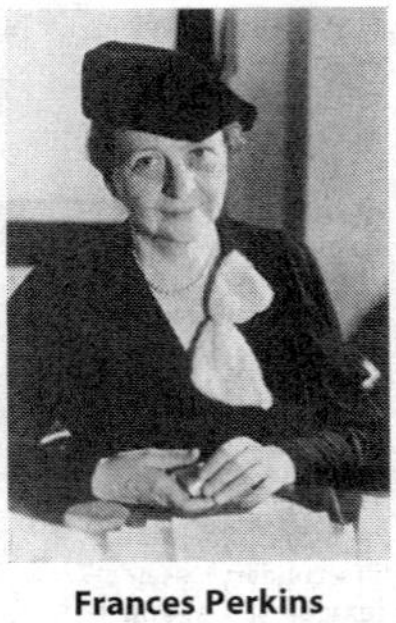

Frances Perkins

perk·y (pûr′kē) *adj.* **-i·er, -i·est 1.** Having a buoyant or self-confident air; briskly cheerful. **2.** Jaunty; sprightly. **—perk′i·ly** *adv.* **—perk′i·ness** *n.*

per·lite also **pearl·ite** (pûr′līt′) *n.* A volcanic glass having distinctive concentric cracks and a relatively high water content, used in a heat-expanded form as a lightweight aggregate in insulation and potting soil. [Fr. (< *perle*, pearl < OFr.; see PEARL[1]), or Ger. *Perlit* (< *Perle*, pearl, ult. < VLat. **pernula*).]

perm (pûrm) *Informal n.* A permanent. ❖ *tr.v.* **permed, perm·ing, perms** To give (hair) a permanent.

Perm (pĕrm, pyĕrm) A city of W-central Russia on the Kama R. in the foothills of the Ural Mts. Pop. 1,091,056.

per·ma·frost (pûr′mə-frôst′, -frŏst′) *n.* Permanently frozen subsoil, occurring throughout the Polar Regions and locally in perennially frigid areas. [PERMA(NENT) + FROST.]

Perm·al·loy (pûr′mə-loi′, pûrm-ăl′oi′) A trademark used for any of several alloys of nickel and iron having high magnetic permeability.

per·ma·nence (pûr′mə-nəns) *n.* The quality or condition of being permanent.

per·ma·nen·cy (pûr′mə-nən-sē) *n.* Permanence.

per·ma·nent (pûr′mə-nənt) *adj.* **1.** Lasting or remaining without essential change: *"the universal human yearning for something permanent, enduring, without shadow of change"* (Willa Cather). **2.** Not expected to change in status, condition, or place: *a permanent address.* ❖ *n.* Any of several long-lasting hair styles usu. achieved by chemical applications which straighten, curl, or wave the hair. [ME < OFr. < Lat. *permanēns, permanent-*, pr. part. of *permanēre*, to endure < *per-*, throughout; see PER- + *manēre*, to remain.] **—per′ma·nent·ly** *adv.* **—per′ma·nent·ness** *n.*

permanent magnet *n.* A piece of magnetic material that retains its magnetism after it is removed from a magnetic field.

permanent press *n.* **1.** A chemical process in which fabrics are permanently shaped and treated for wrinkle resistance. **2.** A fabric treated by permanent press. **—per′ma·nent-press′** (pûr′mə-nənt-prĕs′) *adj.*

permanent tooth *n.* One of the second set of teeth in mammals. Humans have 32 permanent teeth.

per·man·ga·nate (pər-măng′gə-nāt′) *n.* Any of the salts of permanganic acid, all of which are strong oxidizing agents.

per·man·gan·ic acid (pûr′măn-găn′ĭk, -măng-) *n.* An unstable inorganic acid, HMnO₄, existing only in dilute solution.

per·me·a·bil·i·ty (pûr′mē-ə-bĭl′ĭ-tē) *n., pl.* **-ties 1.** The property or condition of being permeable. **2.** The rate of flow of a liquid or gas through a porous material.

per·me·a·ble (pûr′mē-ə-bəl) *adj.* That can be permeated or penetrated, esp. by liquids or gases.

per·me·ance (pûr′mē-əns) *n.* A measure of the ability of a magnetic circuit to conduct magnetic flux; the reciprocal of reluctance. [< Lat. *permeāre*, to penetrate. See PERMEATE.]

per·me·ase (pûr′mē-ās′) *n.* Any of several cell-membrane proteins that function as channels for the transport of a specific molecule in or out of the cell.

per·me·ate (pûr′mē-āt′) *v.* **-at·ed, -at·ing, -ates** *—tr.* **1.** To spread or flow throughout; pervade. **2.** To pass through the openings or interstices of: *liquid permeating a membrane.* *—intr.* To spread through or penetrate something. [Lat. *permeāre, permeāt-*, to penetrate : *per-*, through; see PER- + *meāre*, to pass.] **—per′me·ant** (-ənt), **per′me·a′tive** (-ā′tĭv) *adj.* **—per′me·a′tion** *n.*

per·meth·rin (pər-mĕth′rĭn) *n.* A topical insecticide, C₂₁H₂₀Cl₂O₃, used to treat head lice, mites, and ticks. [PER- + *(res)methrin*, a pyrethroid (*resm-*, of unknown orig. + (PYR)ETHRIN).]

Per·mi·an (pûr′mē-ən, pĕr′-) *adj.* Of or belonging to the geologic time of the seventh and last period of the Paleozoic Era, characterized by the rise of conifers and the diversification of reptiles, and ending with the largest known mass extinction in the history of life. See table at **geologic time.** ❖ *n.* The Permian Period or its deposits. [After *Perm* Oblast, in W-central Russia.]

per mil also **per mill** *adv.* Per thousand. [PER + *mil* (short for Lat. *mīlle*, thousand).]

per·mis·si·ble (pər-mĭs′ə-bəl) *adj.* Permitted; allowable: *permissible tax deductions.* **—per·mis′si·bil′i·ty, per·mis′si·ble·ness** *n.* **—per·mis′si·bly** *adv.*

per·mis·sion (pər-mĭsh′ən) *n.* **1.** The act of permitting. **2.** Consent, esp. formal consent; authorization. [ME < OFr. < Lat. *permissiō, permissiōn-* < *permissus*, p. part. of *permittere*, to permit. See PERMIT.]

per·mis·sive (pər-mĭs′ĭv) *adj.* **1.** Granting or inclined to grant permission; tolerant or lenient. **2.** Permitting discretion; optional. **3.** *Archaic* Not forbidden; permitted. **—per·mis′sive·ly** *adv.* **—per·mis′sive·ness** *n.*

per·mit (pər-mĭt′) *v.* **-mit·ted, -mit·ting, -mits** *—tr.* **1.** To allow the doing of (something); consent to. **2.** To grant leave or consent to (someone); authorize: *permitted him to explain.* **3.** To afford opportunity or possibility. *—intr.* To afford opportunity; allow. ❖ *n.* (pûr′mĭt, pər-mĭt′) **1.** Permission, esp. in written form. **2.** A document or certificate giving permission to do something; a license or warrant. [ME *permitten* < Lat. *permittere* : *per-*, through; see PER- + *mittere*, to let go.] **—per′mit·tee′**

(pûr′mĭ-tē′) *n.* **—per·mit′ter** *n.*

per·mit·tiv·i·ty (pûr′mĭ-tĭv′ĭ-tē) *n., pl.* **-ties** A measure of the ability of a material to resist the formation of an electric field within it, often quantified relative to the permittivity of a vacuum.

per·mu·ta·tion (pûr′myōō-tā′shən) *n.* **1.** A complete change; a transformation. **2.** The act of altering a given set of objects in a group. **3.** *Mathematics* A rearrangement of the elements of a set. **—per′mu·ta′tion·al** *adj.*

per·mute (pər-myōōt′) *tr.v.* **-mut·ed, -mut·ing, -mutes 1.** To change the order of. **2.** *Mathematics* To subject to permutation. [ME *permuten* < OFr. *permuter* < Lat. *permūtāre* : *per-*, per- + *mūtāre*, to change.] **—per·mut′a·bil′i·ty** *n.* **—per·mut′a·ble** *adj.* **—per·mut′a·bly** *adv.*

per·ni·cious (pər-nĭsh′əs) *adj.* **1a.** Tending to cause death or serious injury; deadly: *a pernicious virus.* **b.** Causing great harm; destructive: *pernicious rumors.* **2.** *Archaic* Evil; wicked. [ME < OFr. *pernicios* < Lat. *perniciōsus* < *perniciēs*, destruction : *per-*, per- + *nex, nec-*, violent death; see nek- in App.] **—per·ni′cious·ly** *adv.* **—per·ni′cious·ness** *n.*

pernicious anemia *n.* A severe anemia caused by failure of the stomach to absorb vitamin B₁₂ and characterized by abnormally large red blood cells and gastrointestinal disturbances.

per·nick·e·ty (pər-nĭk′ĭ-tē) *adj.* Persnickety. [?]

Pe·rón (pə-rōn′, pĕ-), **Juan Domingo** 1895–1974. Argentine soldier who served as president (1946–55 and 1973–74). His second wife, **(Maria) Eva Duarte de Perón** (1919–52), "Evita," was popular for her charitable works. Perón was succeeded by his third wife, **Maria Estela Martínez de Perón** (b. 1931), "Isabelita," who was ousted in 1976.

Eva and Juan Perón
photographed in 1951

per·o·ne·al (pĕr′ə-nē′əl) *adj.* Of or relating to the fibula or to the outer portion of the leg. [< Gk. *peronē*, pin of a brooch, fibula. See per-² in App.]

per·o·ral (pər-ôr′əl, -ōr′-) *adj.* Through or by way of the mouth: *a peroral infection.* **—per·o′ral·ly** *adv.*

per·o·rate (pĕr′ə-rāt′) *intr.v.* **-rat·ed, -rat·ing, -rates 1.** To conclude a speech with a formal recapitulation. **2.** To speak at great length, often in a grandiloquent manner; declaim. [Lat. *perōrāre, perōrāt-* : *per-*, per- + *ōrāre*, to speak.] **—per′o·ra′tion** *n.* **—per′o·ra′tion·al** *adj.*

per·ox·i·dase (pə-rŏk′sĭ-dās′, -dāz′) *n.* Any of a group of enzymes that occur esp. in plant cells and catalyze the oxidation of a substance by a peroxide.

per·ox·ide (pə-rŏk′sīd′) *n.* **1.** A compound, such as sodium peroxide, Na₂O₂, that contains a peroxyl group and yields hydrogen peroxide when treated with an acid. **2.** Hydrogen peroxide. ❖ *tr.v.* **-id·ed, -id·ing, -ides 1.** To treat with peroxide. **2.** To bleach (hair) with hydrogen peroxide. **—per·ox′ide′** *adj.* **—per·ox·id′ic** (pûr′ŏk-sĭd′ĭk) *adj.*

per·ox·i·some (pə-rŏk′sĭ-sōm′) *n.* A cell organelle containing enzymes, such as catalase and oxidase, that catalyze the production and breakdown of hydrogen peroxide.

peroxy– *pref.* Containing the bivalent group O₂: *peroxybenzoic acid.* [PER- + OXY-.]

perp (pûrp) *n. Slang* One who perpetrates a crime.

perp. *abbr.* perpendicular

per·pend (pər-pĕnd′) *v.* **-pend·ed, -pend·ing, -pends** *—tr.* To consider carefully; ponder. *—intr.* To be attentive; reflect. [Lat. *perpendere* : *per-*, per- + *pendere*, to weigh.]

per·pen·dic·u·lar (pûr′pən-dĭk′yə-lər) *adj.* **1.** *Mathematics* Intersecting at or forming right angles. **2.** Being at right angles to the horizontal; vertical. **3.** often **Perpendicular** Of or relating to a style of English Gothic architecture of the 14th and 15th centuries characterized by emphasis of the vertical element. ❖ *adv.* In a perpendicular position. ❖ *n.* **1.** *Mathematics* A line or plane perpendicular to a given line or plane. **2.** A perpendicular position. **3.** A device, such as a plumb line, used in marking the vertical from a given point. **4.** A vertical or nearly vertical line or plane. [ME *perpendiculer* < OFr. < Lat. *perpendiculāris* < *perpendiculum*, plumb line < *perpendere*, to weigh carefully : *per-*, per- + *pendere*, to weigh.] **—per′pen·dic′u·lar′i·ty** (-lăr′ĭ-tē) *n.* **—per′pen·dic′u·lar·ly** *adv.*

Perpendicular
King's College Chapel, constructed c. 1446–1515, Cambridge University, England

per·pe·trate (pûr′pĭ-trāt′) *tr.v.* **-trat·ed, -trat·ing, -trates** To be responsible for; commit. [Lat. *perpetrāre, perpetrāt-*, to accomplish : *per-*, per- + *patrāre*, to bring about (< *pater*, father; see pəter- in App.).] **—per′pe·tra′tion** *n.* **—per′pe·tra′tor** *n.*

per·pet·u·al (pər-pĕch′ōō-əl) *adj.* **1.** Lasting for eternity. **2.** Continuing or lasting for an indefinitely long time. **3.** Instituted to be in effect or have tenure for an unlimited duration: *perpetual friendship.* **4.** Continuing without interruption. See Syns at **continual. 5.** Flowering throughout the growing season. [ME *perpetuel* < OFr. < Lat. *perpetuālis* < *perpetuus*, continuous : *per-*, per- + *petere*, to go toward; see pet- in App.] **—per·pet′u·al·ly** *adv.*

perpetual calendar *n.* A chart or device that indicates the day of the week corresponding to a date over a period of years.

perpetual motion *n.* The hypothetical continuous operation of an isolated mechanical device or other closed system without a sustaining energy source.

per·pet·u·ate (pər-pĕch′ōō-āt′) *tr.v.* **-at·ed, -at·ing, -ates 1.** To cause to continue indefinitely; make perpetual. **2.** To prolong the existence of; cause to be remembered. [Lat. *perpetuāre,*

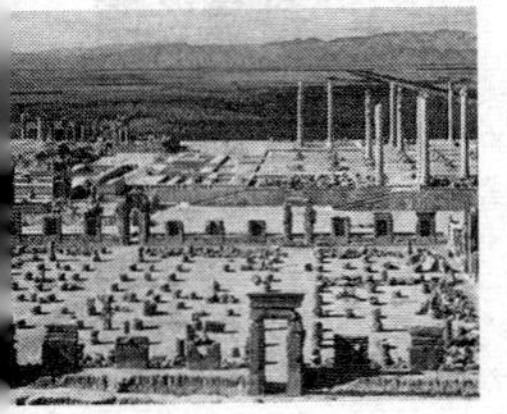

Persepolis

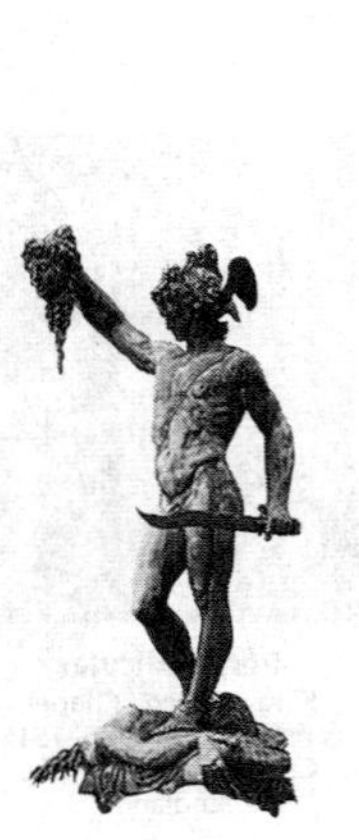

Perseus
Perseus with the Head of Medusa, 1545–54 bronze sculpture by Benvenuto Cellini, Loggia dei Lanzi, Florence, Italy

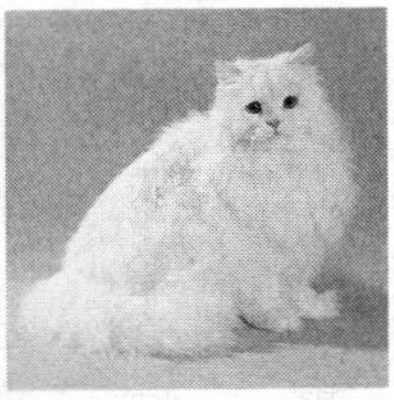

Persian cat

perpetuāt- < *perpetuus,* continuous. See PERPETUAL.] —**per•pet′u•ance, per•pet′u•a′tion** *n.* —**per•pet′u•a′tor** *n.*

per•pe•tu•i•ty (pûr′pĭ-to͞o′ĭ-tē, -tyo͞o′-) *n., pl.* **-ties 1.** The quality or condition of being perpetual. **2.** Time without end; eternity. **3.** *Law* A property interest granted contingent upon the fulfillment of a condition that may not be fulfilled until more than 21 years after the death of a person alive at the time of the creation of the interest, thus void under the classic rule against perpetuities. ***—idiom:* in perpetuity** For an indefinite period of time; forever.

per•phen•a•zine (pər-fĕn′ə-zēn′) *n.* A crystalline compound, $C_{21}H_{26}ClN_3OS$, used as a tranquilizer and in treating nausea and vomiting. [PER– + PHEN(YL) + (PIPER)AZINE.]

Per•pi•gnan (pĕr-pē-nyäN′) A city of S France near the Spanish border and the Mediterranean Sea. Pop. 105,869.

per•plex (pər-plĕks′) *tr.v.* **-plexed, -plex•ing, -plex•es 1.** To confuse or trouble with uncertainty or doubt. **2.** To make confusedly intricate; complicate. —**per•plex′ing•ly** *adv.*

per•plexed (pər-plĕkst′) *adj.* **1.** Filled with confusion or bewilderment; puzzled. **2.** Full of complications or difficulty; involved. [ME < *perplex,* confused < OFr. *perplexe* < Lat. *perplexus* : *per-,* per- + *plexus,* p. part. of *plectere,* to entwine; see **plek-** in App.] —**per•plex′ed•ly** (-plĕk′sĭd-lē) *adv.*

per•plex•i•ty (pər-plĕk′sĭ-tē) *n., pl.* **-ties 1.** The state of being perplexed or puzzled. **2.** The state of being intricate or complicated. **3.** Something that perplexes.

perp walk *n.* The deliberate escorting of an arrested suspect by police in front of the news media, esp. as a means of pressuring or humiliating the suspect.

per•qui•site (pûr′kwĭ-zĭt) *n.* **1.** A payment or profit received in addition to a regular wage or salary, esp. a benefit expected as one's due. See Syns at **right. 2.** A tip; a gratuity. **3.** Something claimed as an exclusive right. [< ME *perquisites,* property acquired otherwise than by inheritance < Med.Lat. *perquīsītum,* acquisition < Lat., neut. p. part. of *perquīrere,* to search diligently for : *per-,* per- + *quaerere,* to seek.]

Per•rault (pə-rō′, pĕ-), **Charles** 1628–1703. French writer best known for his *Contes de ma Mère l'Oye* (c. 1697), a collection of retold fairy tales including "Sleeping Beauty."

per•ry (pĕr′ē) *n., pl.* **-ries** A fermented, often effervescent beverage made from pears. [ME *pere* < OFr. *pere* < VLat. **pirātum* < Lat. *pirum,* pear.]

Perry, Matthew Calbraith 1794–1858. Amer. naval officer who opened diplomatic relations with Japan (1854).

Perry, Oliver Hazard 1785–1819. Amer. naval officer who led the fleet that defeated the British in the Battle of Lake Erie (1813) during the War of 1812.

pers. *abbr.* person

Pers. *abbr.* **1.** Persia **2.** Persian

perse (pûrs) *adj.* Dark grayish blue or purple. [ME *pers* < OFr. < Med.Lat. *persus,* back-formation < Lat. *Persicus,* Persian < Gk. *Persikos,* a Persian < *Persē* < OPers. *Pārsa,* of Median orig.; akin to OPers. *Parthava-,* Parthian.]

per se (pər sā′, sē′) *adv.* Of, in, or by itself or oneself; intrinsically. [Lat. *per sē* : *per,* per + *sē,* itself.]

Perse (pĕrs, pûrs), **Saint-John** See Alexis Saint-Léger **Léger.**

per•se•cute (pûr′sĭ-kyo͞ot′) *tr.v.* **-cut•ed, -cut•ing, -cutes 1.** To oppress or harass with ill-treatment, esp. because of race, religion, gender, sexual orientation, or beliefs. **2.** To annoy persistently; bother. [Ult. < LLat. *persecūtus,* p. part. of *persequī,* to persecute < Lat., to pursue : *per-,* per- + *sequī,* to follow; see **sek**ʷ-¹ in App.] —**per′se•cu•tee′** (-kyo͞o-tē′) *n.* —**per′se•cu′tive, per′se•cu•to′ry** (-kyo͞o-tôr′ē, -tōr′ē, -kyo͞o′tə-rē) *adj.* —**per′se•cu′tor** *n.*

per•se•cu•tion (pûr′sĭ-kyo͞o′shən) *n.* **1.** The act or practice of persecuting on the basis of race, religion, gender, sexual orientation, or beliefs that differ from those of the persecutor. **2.** The condition of being persecuted. —**per′se•cu′tion•al** *adj.*

Per•se•id (pûr′sē-ĭd) *n., pl.* **Per•se•ids** or **Per•se•i•des** (pər-sē′ĭ-dēz′) One of a shower of meteors that appears to originate in the vicinity of the constellation Perseus during the second week of August. [< Lat. *Perseus,* the constellation Perseus; see PERSEUS, or < Gk. *Perseīdes,* pl. of *Perseïs,* offspring of Perseus (< *Perseus,* Perseus).]

Per•seph•o•ne (pər-sĕf′ə-nē) *n. Greek Mythology* The daughter of Demeter and Zeus who was abducted by Hades but was rescued by her mother and thereafter spent six months of the year on earth and six in the underworld.

Per•sep•o•lis (pər-sĕp′ə-lĭs) An ancient city of Persia NE of modern Shiraz in SW Iran; ceremonial cap. of Darius I and his successors.

Per•se•us (pûr′sē-əs, -syo͞os′) *n.* **1.** *Greek Mythology* Andromeda's husband, who killed Medusa. **2.** A constellation in the Northern Hemisphere near Andromeda and Auriga. [Lat. < Gk.]

per•se•ver•ance (pûr′sə-vîr′əns) *n.* **1.** Steady persistence in adhering to a course of action, a belief, or a purpose; steadfastness. **2.** *Christianity* The Calvinistic doctrine that God's chosen will continue in a state of grace to the end and will be saved.

per•sev•er•ate (pər-sĕv′ə-rāt′) *intr.v.* **-at•ed, -at•ing, -ates** *Psychology* To manifest or experience perseveration. [Back-formation < PERSEVERATION.] —**per•sev′er•a′tive** *adj.*

per•sev•er•a•tion (pər-sĕv′ə-rā′shən) *n.* **1.** *Psychology* **a.** Uncontrollable repetition of a particular response, such as a word or gesture, despite the absence of a stimulus, usu. caused by an organic disorder. **b.** The tendency to continue or repeat an act or activity after the cessation of the original stimulus. **2.** The act or an instance of persevering; perseverance.

per•se•vere (pûr′sə-vîr′) *intr.v.* **-vered, -ver•ing, -veres** To persist in a purpose, idea, or task in the face of obstacles or discouragement. [ME *perseveren* < OFr. *perseverer* < Lat. *persevērāre* < *persevērus,* very serious : *per-,* per- + *sevērus,* severe; see **segh-** in App.] —**per′se•ver′ing•ly** *adv.*

Per•shing (pûr′shĭng, -zhĭng), **John Joseph** Known as "Black Jack." 1860–1948. Amer. general who commanded the American Expeditionary Force in Europe during World War I.

Per•sia (pûr′zhə, -shə) **1.** also **Persian Empire** A vast empire of SW Asia founded by Cyrus II after 546 B.C., brought to its height by Darius I and his son Xerxes, and conquered by Alexander the Great in 334 B.C. **2.** See **Iran.**

Per•sian (pûr′zhən, -shən) *adj.* Of Persia or Iran or their peoples, languages, or cultures. ❖ *n.* **1.** A native or inhabitant of Persia or Iran. **2.** Any of the western Iranian dialects or languages of ancient or medieval Persia and modern Iran.

Persian cat *n.* A stocky domestic cat having long silky fur, short legs, and a broad round head with small ears.

Persian Gulf also **Arabian Gulf** An arm of the Arabian Sea between the Arabian Peninsula and SW Iran.

Persian Gulf War *n.* See **Gulf War.**

Persian lamb *n.* **1.** The lamb of the karakul sheep of Asia. **2.** The pelt of a Persian lamb, having glossy, tightly curled fur.

Persian melon *n.* A variety of melon *(Cucumis melo)* having a netted unridged rind and musky orange-colored flesh.

per•si•flage (pûr′sə-fläzh′) *n.* **1.** Light good-natured talk; banter. **2.** A light or frivolous manner of discussing a subject. [Fr. < *persifler,* to banter : *per-,* intensive pref. (< Lat.; see PER–) + *siffler,* to whistle (< OFr. < LLat. *sīfilāre,* alteration of Lat. *sībilāre*).]

per•sim•mon (pər-sĭm′ən) *n.* **1.** Any of various chiefly tropical trees of the genus *Diospyros,* having orange-red fruit that is edible only when completely ripe. **2.** The fruit of any of these trees. [Of Virginia Algonquian orig.]

per•sist (pər-sĭst′, -zĭst′) *intr.v.* **-sist•ed, -sist•ing, -sists 1.** To be obstinately repetitious, insistent, or tenacious. **2.** To hold firmly and steadfastly to a purpose, state, or undertaking despite obstacles, warnings, or setbacks. **3.** To continue in existence; last. [Lat. *persistere* : *per-,* per- + *sistere,* to stand; see **stā-** in App.] —**per•sis′ter** *n.*

per•sis•tence (pər-sĭs′təns, -zĭs′-) *n.* **1.** The act of persisting. **2.** The state or quality of being persistent; persistency. **3.** Continuance of an effect after the cause is removed. —**per•sis′ten•cy** *n.*

per•sis•tent (pər-sĭs′tənt, -zĭs′-) *adj.* **1.** Refusing to give up or let go; persevering obstinately. **2.** Insistently repetitive or continuous. **3.** Existing or remaining in the same state for an indefinitely long time; enduring: *persistent rumors.* **4.** *Botany* Lasting past maturity without being shed. **5.** *Zoology* Retained permanently, rather than disappearing in an early stage of development. —**per•sis′tent•ly** *adv.*

per•snick•e•ty (pər-snĭk′ĭ-tē) *adj.* **1a.** Overparticular about trivial details; fastidious. **b.** Snobbish; pretentious. **2.** Requiring strict attention to detail; demanding. [Alteration of PERNICKETY.] —**per•snick′e•ti•ness** *n.*

per•son (pûr′sən) *n.* **1.** A living human. Often used in combination: *chairperson; spokesperson; salesperson.* **2.** An individual of specified character. **3.** The composite of characteristics that make up an individual personality; the self. **4.** The living body of a human. **5.** Physique and general appearance. **6.** *Law* A human or an organization with legal rights and duties. **7.** *Christianity* Any of the separate individualities of the Father, Son, and Holy Spirit. **8.** *Grammar* **a.** Any of three groups of pronoun forms with corresponding verb inflections that distinguish the speaker (first person), the individual addressed (second person), and the individual or thing spoken of (third person). **b.** Any of the different forms or inflections expressing these distinctions. **9.** A character or role, as in a play; a guise. ***—idiom:* in person** In one's physical presence; personally. [ME < OFr. *persone* < Lat. *persōna,* prob. < Etruscan *phersu,* mask.]

USAGE NOTE The word *person* has found widespread use in recent decades as a gender-neutral alternative to *man* in the names of occupational and social roles, such as *businessperson, chairperson,* and *layperson.* In addition, a variety of entirely new, more inclusive phrases have arisen to compete with or supplant *-man* compounds. Now we often hear *first-year student* instead of *freshman* and *letter carrier* instead of *mailman.* In other cases, a clipped form, such as *chair* for *chairman,* or a phrase, such as *member of the clergy* for *clergyman,* has found widespread use as a neutral alternative. Reflecting this trend, many government agencies have adopted such words in their documents.

per•so•na (pər-sō′nə) *n.* **1.** *pl.* **-nas** or **-nae** (-nē) A voice or character representing the speaker in a literary work. **2. personae** The characters in a dramatic or literary work. **3.** *pl.* **personas** The role that one assumes in public. [Lat. *persōna.* See PERSON.]

per•son•a•ble (pûr′sə-nə-bəl) *adj.* Pleasing in personality or appearance. **—per′son•a•ble•ness** *n.* **—per′son•a•bly** *adv.*

per•son•age (pûr′sə-nĭj) *n.* **1.** A character in a literary work. **2a.** A person. **b.** A person of distinction. [ME, person < OFr. < *persone.* See PERSON.]

persona gra•ta (grä′tə, grăt′ə) *adj.* Fully acceptable or welcome, esp. to a foreign government. [LLat. *persōna grāta* : Lat. *persōna,* person + *grāta,* fem. of *grātus,* acceptable.]

per•son•al (pûr′sə-nəl) *adj.* **1.** Of or relating to a particular person; private. **2a.** Done, made, or performed in person. **b.** Done to or for or directed toward a particular person: *a personal favor.* **3.** Concerning a particular person and his or her private business, interests, or activities; intimate. **4a.** Aimed pointedly at the most intimate aspects of a person, esp. in a critical or hostile manner. **b.** Tending to make remarks, or be unduly questioning, about another's affairs. **5.** Of or relating to the body or physical being. **6.** Relating to or having the nature of a person or self-conscious being. **7.** *Law* Relating to a person's movable property. **8.** *Grammar* Indicating grammatical person. ❖ *n.* **1.** A personal item or notice in a newspaper. **2. personals** A column in a newspaper or magazine featuring personal notices.

personal computer *n.* A computer built around a microprocessor for use by an individual.

personal digital assistant *n.* A lightweight, hand-held, usu. pen-based computer used as a personal organizer.

personal effects *pl.n.* Privately owned items, such as a wallet, regularly worn on one's person.

personal equation *n. Psychology* **1.** Personal characteristics that cause variation in observation, judgment, and reasoning. **2.** An allowance or adjustment made for such variation.

personal foul *n.* A foul in a game that usu. involves bodily contact with or willful roughing of an opponent.

per•son•a•li•a (pûr′sə-nā′lē-ə, -nāl′yə) *pl.n.* **1.** Personal allusions or references. **2.** Personal belongings or affairs. [Lat. *persōnālia,* neut. pl. of *persōnālis,* relating to a person. See PERSONALITY.]

per•son•al•ism (pûr′sə-nə-lĭz′əm) *n.* **1.** The quality of being characterized by purely personal modes of expression or behavior; idiosyncrasy. **2.** *Philosophy* Any of various theories of subjective idealism regarding personality as the key to the interpretation of reality. **—per′son•al•ist** *adj. & n.* **—per′son•al•is′tic** *adj.*

per•son•al•i•ty (pûr′sə-năl′ĭ-tē) *n., pl.* **-ties 1.** The quality or condition of being a person. **2.** The totality of qualities and traits, as of character or behavior, peculiar to a specific person. **3.** The pattern of collective character, behavioral, temperamental, emotional, and mental traits of a person. **4.** Distinctive qualities of a person, esp. those distinguishing personal characteristics that make one socially appealing. **5a.** A person as the embodiment of distinctive traits of mind and behavior. **b.** A person of prominence or notoriety: *television personalities.* **6.** An offensively personal remark. Often used in the plural: *Let's not engage in personalities.* **7.** The distinctive characteristics of a place or situation. [ME *personalite* < OFr. < LLat. *persōnālitās* < Lat. *persōnālis,* personal < *persōna,* person. See PERSON.]

per•son•al•ize (pûr′sə-nə-līz) *tr.v.* **-ized, -iz•ing, -iz•es 1.** To take (a general remark) in a personal manner. **2.** To attribute human or personal qualities to; personify. **3.** To have printed, engraved, or monogrammed with one's name or initials. **—per′son•al•i•za′tion** (-lĭ-zā′shən) *n.*

per•son•al•ly (pûr′sə-nə-lē) *adv.* **1.** Without the intervention of another; in person. **2.** As far as oneself is concerned. **3.** As a person. **4.** In a personal manner: *took it personally.*

personal pronoun *n.* A pronoun designating the person speaking (*I, me, we, us*), the person spoken to (*you*), or the person or thing spoken about (*he, she, it, they, him, her, them*).

personal property *n. Law* Temporary or movable property.

per•son•al•ty (pûr′sə-nəl-tē) *n., pl.* **-ties** *Law* Personal property; chattels. [AN *personalte* < LLat. *persōnālitās,* personality. See PERSONALITY.]

personal watercraft *n.* **1.** A motorized recreational water vehicle normally ridden by straddling a seat. **2.** (*used with a pl. verb*) Such water vehicles considered as a group.

persona non gra•ta (nŏn grä′tə, grăt′ə) *adj.* Fully unacceptable or unwelcome, esp. to a foreign government. [LLat. *persōna nōn grāta* : Lat. *persōna,* person + Lat. *nōn,* not + Lat. *grāta,* fem. of *grātus,* acceptable.]

per•son•ate[1] (pûr′sə-nāt′) *tr.v.* **-at•ed, -at•ing, -ates 1.** To play the role or portray the part of (a character); impersonate. **2.** To endow with personal qualities; personify. **3.** *Law* To assume the identity of, with intent to deceive. [LLat. *persōnāre, persōnāt-,* to bear the character of, represent < Lat. *persōna,* person. See PERSON.] **—per′son•a′tion** *n.* **—per′son•a′tive** *adj.* **—per′son•a′tor** *n.*

per•son•ate[2] (pûr′sə-nĭt) *adj. Botany* Having two lips, with the throat closed by a prominent palate. [Lat. *persōnātus,* masked < *persōna,* mask. See PERSON.]

per•son•i•fi•ca•tion (pər-sŏn′ə-fĭ-kā′shən) *n.* **1.** The act of personifying. **2.** A person or thing typifying a certain quality or idea; an embodiment. **3.** A figure of speech in which inanimate objects or abstractions are represented with human qualities or form. **4.** Artistic representation of an abstract quality or idea as a person.

per•son•i•fy (pər-sŏn′ə-fī′) *tr.v.* **-fied, -fy•ing, -fies 1.** To think of or represent (an inanimate object or abstraction) as having personality or the qualities, thoughts, or movements of a living being: *"To make history or psychology alive I personify it"* (Anaïs Nin). **2.** To represent (an object or abstraction) by a human figure. **3.** To represent (an abstract quality or idea). **4.** To be the embodiment or perfect example of. [Fr. *personnifier* < *personne,* person < OFr. *persone.* See PERSON.] **—per•son′i•fi′er** *n.*

per•son•nel (pûr′sə-nĕl′) *n.* **1a.** The people employed by or active in an organization. **b.** (*used with a pl. verb*) Persons. **2.** An administrative division of an organization concerned with its personnel. [Fr. < OFr., personal < Lat. *persōnālis.* See PERSONALITY.]

per•son-to-per•son (pûr′sən-tə-pûr′sən) *adj.* **1.** Of or relating to a telephone call chargeable only when an indicated person is reached. **2.** Involving direct communication or contact between persons. **—per′son-to-per′son** *adv.*

per•spec•tive (pər-spĕk′tĭv) *n.* **1a.** A view or vista. **b.** A mental view or outlook. **2.** The appearance of objects in depth as perceived by normal binocular vision. **3a.** The relationship of aspects of a subject to each other and to a whole. **b.** Subjective evaluation of relative significance; a point of view. **c.** The ability to perceive things in their actual interrelations or comparative importance. **4.** The technique of representing three-dimensional objects and depth relationships on a two-dimensional surface. ❖ *adj.* Of, relating to, seen, or represented in perspective. [ME, science of optics (influenced by Fr. *perspective,* perspective) < Med.Lat. *perspectīva (ars),* fem. of *perspectīvus,* optical < *perspectus,* p. part. of *perspicere,* to inspect : *per-,* per- + *specere,* to look; see **spek-** in App.] **—per•spec′tiv•al** *adj.* **—per•spec′tive•ly** *adv.*

per•spi•ca•cious (pûr′spĭ-kā′shəs) *adj.* Having or showing penetrating mental discernment; clear-sighted. [< Lat. *perspicāx, perspicāc-* < *perspicere,* to look through. See PERSPECTIVE.] **—per′spi•ca′cious•ly** *adv.* **—per′spi•ca′cious•ness** *n.*

per•spi•cac•i•ty (pûr′spĭ-kăs′ĭ-tē) *n.* Acuteness of perception, discernment, or understanding.

per•spi•cu•i•ty (pûr′spĭ-kyōō′ĭ-tē) *n.* **1.** The quality of being perspicuous; clearness and lucidity. **2.** Perspicacity.

per•spic•u•ous (pər-spĭk′yōō-əs) *adj.* Clearly expressed or presented; easy to understand. [< Lat. *perspicuus* < *perspicere,* to see through. See PERSPICACIOUS.] **—per•spic′u•ous•ly** *adv.* **—per•spic′u•ous•ness** *n.*

per•spi•ra•tion (pûr′spə-rā′shən) *n.* **1.** The fluid, consisting of water with small amounts of urea and salts, excreted through the pores of the skin by the sweat glands; sweat. **2.** The act or process of perspiring. **—per•spir′a•to′ry** (pər-spīr′ə-tôr′ē, -tōr′ē, pûr′spər-ə-) *adj.*

per•spire (pər-spīr′) *v.* **-spired, -spir•ing, -spires** *—intr.* To excrete perspiration through the pores of the skin. *—tr.* To expel through external pores; exude. [Lat. *perspīrāre,* to blow steadily : *per-,* through; see PER– + *spīrāre,* to breathe.]

per•suade (pər-swād′) *tr.v.* **-suad•ed, -suad•ing, -suades** To induce to undertake a course of action or embrace a point of view by means of argument, reasoning, or entreaty. [Lat. *persuādēre* : *per-,* per- + *suādēre,* to urge; see **swād-** in App.] **—per•suad′a•ble** *adj.* **—per•suad′er** *n.*

per•sua•si•ble (pər-swā′zə-bəl, -sə-bəl) *adj.* Capable of being persuaded. **—per•sua′si•bil′i•ty, per•sua′si•ble•ness** *n.*

per•sua•sion (pər-swā′zhən) *n.* **1.** The act of persuading or the state of being persuaded. **2.** The ability or power to persuade. **3.** A strongly held opinion; a conviction. **4a.** A body of religious beliefs; a religion. **b.** A party, faction, or group holding to a particular set of ideas or beliefs. **5.** *Informal* Kind; sort: *invited politicians of any persuasion.* [ME < OFr. < Lat. *persuāsiō, persuāsiōn-* < *persuāsus,* p. part. of *persuādēre,* to persuade. See PERSUADE.]

per•sua•sive (pər-swā′sĭv, -zĭv) *adj.* Tending or having the power to persuade. **—per•sua′sive•ness** *n.*

pert (pûrt) *adj.* **pert•er, pert•est 1.** Trim and stylish in appearance; jaunty. **2.** High-spirited; vivacious. **3.** Impudently bold; saucy. [ME, unconcealed, bold, short for *apert,* obvious, frank < OFr. < Lat. *apertus,* open, p. part. of *aperīre,* to open.] **—pert′ly** *adv.* **—pert′ness** *n.*

per•tain (pər-tān′) *intr.v.* **-tained, -tain•ing, -tains 1.** To have reference; relate: *evidence that pertains to the accident.* **2.** To belong as an adjunct, part, holding, or quality. **3.** To be fitting or suitable. [ME *pertenen, pertainen* < OFr. *partenir* < Lat. *pertinēre* : *per-,* per- + *tenēre,* to hold; see **ten-** in App.]

Perth (pûrth) **1.** A city of SW Australia near the Indian Ocean; founded 1829. Pop. 1,018,702. **2.** A burgh of central Scotland on the Tay R. NNW of Edinburgh; cap. of Scotland from the 11th to the mid-15th cent. Pop. 42,000.

per•ti•na•cious (pûr′tn-ā′shəs) *adj.* **1.** Holding tenaciously to a purpose, belief, opinion, or course of action. **2.** Stubbornly or perversely persistent. See Syns at **obstinate.** [< Lat. *pertināx, pertināc-* : *per-,* per- + *tenāx,* tenacious (< *tenēre,* to hold; see **ten-** in App.).] **—per′ti•na′cious•ly** *adv.* **—per′ti•nac′i•ty** (-tn-ăs′ĭ-tē) *n.*

per•ti•nent (pûr′tn-ənt) *adj.* Having precise logical relevance to the matter at hand. [ME < OFr. < Lat. *pertinēns, pertinent-,* pr. part. of *pertinēre,* to pertain. See PERTAIN.] **—per′ti•nence,**

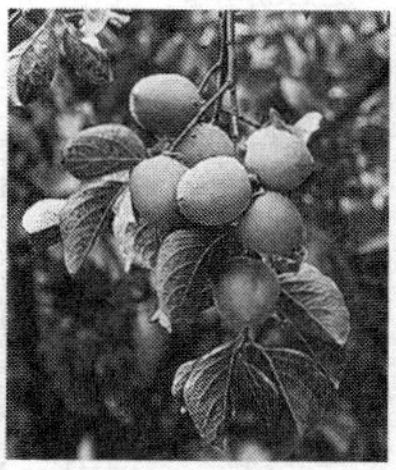

persimmon
Japanese persimmon
Diospyros kaki

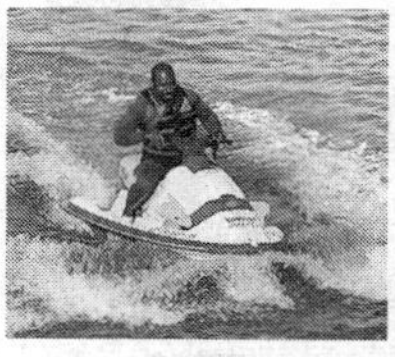

personal watercraft

ă	pat	oi	boy
ā	pay	ou	out
âr	care	ŏŏ	took
ä	father	ōō	boot
ĕ	pet	ŭ	cut
ē	be	ûr	urge
ĭ	pit	th	thin
ī	pie	*th*	this
îr	pier	hw	which
ŏ	pot	zh	vision
ō	toe	ə	about, item
ô	paw		

Stress marks:
′ (primary);
′ (secondary), as in
lexicon (lĕk′sĭ-kŏn′)

per'ti·nen·cy *n.* —**per'ti·nent·ly** *adv.*
per·turb (pər-tûrb') *tr.v.* **-turbed, -turb·ing, -turbs 1.** To disturb greatly; make uneasy or anxious. **2.** To throw into great confusion. **3.** *Physics & Astronomy* To cause perturbation, as of a celestial orbit. [ME *perturben* < OFr. *perturber* < Lat. *perturbāre* : *per-*, per- + *turbāre*, to throw into disorder (< *turba*, confusion, perh. < Gk. *turbē*).] —**per·turb'a·ble** *adj.*
per·tur·ba·tion (pûr'tər-bā'shən) *n.* **1a.** The act of perturbing. **b.** The state of being perturbed; agitation. **2a.** A small change in a physical system. **b.** *Physics & Astronomy* Variation in a designated orbit, as of a planet, resulting from the influence of one or more external bodies. —**per'tur·ba'tion·al** *adj.*
per·tus·sis (pər-tŭs'ĭs) *n.* See **whooping cough.** [NLat. : Lat. *per-*, thorough; see PER– + Lat. *tussis*, cough.]
Pe·ru (pə-rōō') A country of W South America on the Pacific; inhabited since at least the 9th millennium B.C. and the center of an Incan empire established after the 12th cent. A.D. The Spanish under Pizarro conquered the empire in 1533. Peru achieved full independence in 1824. Cap. Lima. Pop. 23,088,000. —**Pe·ru'vi·an** (-vē-ən) *adj. & n.*
Peru Current *n.* See **Humboldt Current.**
Pe·ru·gia (pə-rōō'jə, -jē-ə, pĕ-rōō'jä) A city of central Italy on a hill overlooking the Tiber R. N of Rome; orig. an Etruscan settlement. Pop. 143,698. —**Pe·ru'gian** *adj. & n.*
Pe·ru·gi·no (pĕr'ə-jē'nō, pĕr'ō-), Il 1445?–1523? Italian painter known for his religious frescoes.
pe·ruke (pə-rōōk') *n.* A wig, esp. one worn by men in the 17th and 18th centuries; a periwig. [Fr. *perruque* < OFr., head of hair < OItal. *perrucca*.]
pe·ruse (pə-rōōz') *tr.v.* **-rused, -rus·ing, -rus·es** To read or examine, typically with great care. [ME *perusen*, to use up : Lat. *per-*, per- + Lat. *ūsus*; see USE.] —**pe·rus'a·ble** *adj.* —**pe·rus'al** *n.* —**pe·rus'er** *n.*

Peru

USAGE NOTE *Peruse* has long meant "to read thoroughly." Seventy-eight percent of the Usage Panel accepts *She perused the pages, carefully looking for errors.* But the word is sometimes used loosely as a highfalutin synonym for *read,* and some people even use it to mean "to glance over, skim," as in *I only had a moment to peruse the manual quickly.* This sentence was unacceptable to 58 percent of the Panel in our 1999 survey, down somewhat from 66 percent in 1988, suggesting that resistance is still quite strong to this usage.

Per·utz (pə-rōōts', pĕr'əts), Max Ferdinand b. 1914. Austrian-born biochemist who shared a 1962 Nobel Prize.
Peruvian bark *n.* See **cinchona 2.**
per·vade (pər-vād') *tr.v.* **-vad·ed, -vad·ing, -vades** To be present throughout; permeate. [Lat. *pervādere* : *per-*, through; see PER– + *vādere*, to go.] —**per·vad'er** *n.* —**per·va'sion** (-vā'zhən) *n.*
per·va·sive (pər-vā'sĭv, -zĭv) *adj.* Having the quality or tendency to pervade or permeate: *the pervasive odor of garlic.* [< Lat. *pervāsus,* p. part. of *pervādere,* to pervade. See PERVADE.] —**per·va'sive·ly** *adv.* —**per·va'sive·ness** *n.*
pervasive developmental disorder *n.* Any of several disorders, such as autism or Asperger's syndrome, characterized by impaired development in certain areas, such as social interaction and communication, often by the presence of stereotyped behaviors, and usu. by varying degrees of mental retardation.
per·verse (pər-vûrs', pûr'vûrs') *adj.* **1.** Directed away from what is right or good; perverted. **2.** Obstinately persisting in an error or fault. **3a.** Marked by a disposition to oppose and contradict. **b.** Arising from such a disposition. **4.** Cranky; peevish. [ME *pervers* < OFr. < Lat. *perversus,* p. part. of *pervertere,* to pervert. See PERVERT.] —**per·verse'ly** *adv.* —**per·verse'ness** *n.*
per·ver·sion (pər-vûr'zhən, -shən) *n.* **1a.** The act of perverting. **b.** The state of being perverted. **2.** A sexual practice or act considered deviant. —**per·ver'sive** (-sĭv, -zĭv) *adj.*
per·ver·si·ty (pər-vûr'sĭ-tē) *n., pl.* **-ties 1.** The quality or state of being perverse. **2.** An instance of being perverse.
per·vert (pər-vûrt') *tr.v.* **-vert·ed, -vert·ing, -verts 1.** To cause to turn away from what is right, proper, or good; corrupt. **2.** To bring to a worse condition; debase. **3.** To put to a wrong or improper use; misuse. **4.** To interpret incorrectly; misconstrue or distort. ❖ *n.* (pûr'vûrt') One who practices sexual perversion. [ME *perverten* < OFr. *pervertir* < Lat. *pervertere* : *per-*, per- + *vertere*, to turn; see wer-² in App.] —**per·vert'er** *n.* —**per·vert'i·ble** *adj.*
per·vert·ed (pər-vûr'tĭd) *adj.* **1.** Deviating from what is considered right and correct. **2.** Of, relating to, or practicing sexual perversion. **3.** Marked by misinterpretation or distortion. —**per·vert'ed·ly** *adv.* —**per·vert'ed·ness** *n.*
per·vi·ous (pûr'vē-əs) *adj.* **1.** Open to passage or entrance; permeable. **2.** Open to arguments, ideas, or change; approachable. [< Lat. *pervius* : *per-*, through; see PER– + *via*, way; see **wegh-** in App.] —**per'vi·ous·ness** *n.*
pes (pās) *n., pl.* **pe·des** (pĕd'ās') A foot or footlike part, esp. the foot of a four-footed vertebrate. [Lat. *pēs.* See **ped-** in App.]
Pe·sach (pä'säkH', pĕ'-) *n. Judaism* See **Passover.** [Heb. *pesaḥ* < *pāsaḥ,* to pass over.]
pe·sade (pə-säd', -zäd') *n.* The act or position of a horse when

pestle
mortar and pestle

rearing on its hind legs with its forelegs in the air. [Fr., alteration of obsolete *posade* < OItal. *posata,* a pause < *posare,* to pause < LLat. *pausāre.* See POSE¹.]
Pes·ca·do·res (pĕs'kə-dôr'ēz, -ĭs, -dôr'-) In Pinyin **Peng·hu** (pŭng'hōō') An island group of Taiwan in Taiwan Strait between the W coast of Taiwan and mainland China; ceded to Japan in 1895 and returned to China after World War II.
pe·se·ta (pə-sā'tə) *n.* See table at **currency.** [Sp., dim. of *peso,* peso. See PESO.]
Pe·sha·war (pə-shä'wər) A city of NW Pakistan NW of Lahore near the Khyber Pass. Pop. 566,248.
pes·ky (pĕs'kē) *adj.* **-ki·er, -ki·est** *Informal* Troublesome; annoying: *a pesky mosquito.* [Prob. alteration of PEST.] —**pes'ki·ly** *adv.* —**pes'ki·ness** *n.*
pe·so (pā'sō) *n., pl.* **-sos** See table at **currency.** [Sp. < Lat. *pēnsum,* something weighed < neut. p. part. of *pendere,* to weigh.]
pes·sa·ry (pĕs'ə-rē) *n., pl.* **-ries 1.** A device worn in the vagina to support or correct the position of the uterus or rectum. **2.** A contraceptive diaphragm. **3.** A medicated vaginal suppository. [ME *pessarie* < LLat. *pessārium* < *pessus, pessum* < Gk. *pessos,* oval-shaped stone, pessary.]
pes·si·mism (pĕs'ə-mĭz'əm) *n.* **1.** A tendency to stress the negative or take the gloomiest possible view. **2.** The doctrine or belief that this is the worst of all possible worlds and that all things ultimately tend toward evil. **3.** The doctrine or belief that the evil in the world outweighs the good. [Fr. *pessimisme* (as Fr. *optimisme,* optimism) < Lat. *pessimus,* worst. See **ped-** in App.] —**pes'si·mist** *n.* —**pes'si·mis'tic** *adj.* —**pes'si·mis'ti·cal·ly** *adv.*
pest (pĕst) *n.* **1.** An annoying person or thing; a nuisance. **2.** An injurious plant or animal, esp. one harmful to humans. **3.** A deadly epidemic disease; a pestilence. [Fr. *peste,* pestilence < OFr. < Lat. *pestis.*]
Pest (pĕst, pĕsht) A former town of N-central Hungary on the left bank of the Danube R.; part of Budapest since 1873.
Pes·ta·loz·zi (pĕs'tə-lŏt'sē, -tä-lŏt'-), **Johann Heinrich** 1746–1827. Swiss educational reformer whose teaching theories are based on respect and attention to the individual.
pes·ter (pĕs'tər) *tr.v.* **-tered, -ter·ing, -ters** To harass with petty annoyances; bother. See Syns at **harass.** [Prob. short for Fr. *empestrer,* to constrain, embarrass < OFr. < VLat. **impāstōriāre* < Lat. *in-,* in; see IN–² + VLat. **pāstōria,* a hobble < Lat., fem. of *pāstōrius,* of a herdsman < Lat. *pāstor,* herdsman. See **pā-** in App.] —**pes'ter·er** *n.*
pest·hole (pĕst'hōl') *n.* A place that is considered a breeding ground for epidemic disease.
pest house (pĕst) *n.* A hospital for people affected with plague or other infectious disease.
pes·ti·cide (pĕs'tĭ-sīd') *n.* A chemical used to kill pests, esp. insects. —**pes'ti·cid'al** (-sīd'l) *adj.*
pes·tif·er·ous (pĕ-stĭf'ər-əs) *adj.* **1a.** Producing or breeding infectious disease. **b.** Infected with or contaminated by an epidemic disease. **2.** Morally evil or deadly; pernicious. **3.** Bothersome; annoying. [ME < Lat. *pestiferus,* var. of *pestifer* : *pestis,* pestilence; see PEST + *-fer,* -fer.] —**pes·tif'er·ous·ly** *adv.* —**pes·tif'er·ous·ness** *n.*
pes·ti·lence (pĕs'tə-ləns) *n.* **1.** A usu. fatal epidemic disease, esp. bubonic plague. **2.** A pernicious, evil influence or agent.
pes·ti·lent (pĕs'tə-lənt) *adj.* **1.** Tending to cause death; deadly. **2.** Likely to cause an epidemic disease. **3.** Infected with or contaminated with a contagious disease. **4.** Morally, socially, or politically harmful; pernicious. **5.** Causing annoyance or disapproval. [ME < OFr. < Lat. *pestilēns, pestilent-* < *pestis,* pestilence. See PEST.] —**pes'ti·len'tial** (-lĕn'shəl) *adj.* —**pes'ti·len'tial·ly** *adv.*
pes·tle (pĕs'əl, pĕs'təl) *n.* **1.** A club-shaped tool for grinding or mashing substances in a mortar. **2.** A large bar moved vertically to stamp or pound, as in a mill. ❖ *v.* **-tled, -tling, -tles** —*tr.* To pound, grind, or mash with or as if with a pestle. —*intr.* To use a pestle. [ME *pestel* < OFr. < Lat. *pistillum.*]
pes·to (pĕs'tō) *n.* A sauce typically consisting of fresh basil, garlic, pine nuts, olive oil, and grated cheese. [Ital. < p. part. of *pistare, pestare,* to pound. See PISTON.]
pet¹ (pĕt) *n.* **1.** An animal kept for amusement or companionship. **2.** An object of the affections. **3.** A person esp. loved or indulged; a favorite: *the teacher's pet.* ❖ *adj.* **1.** Kept as a pet: *a pet cat.* **2a.** Particularly cherished or indulged. **b.** Expressing or showing affection. **3.** Being a favorite. ❖ *v.* **pet·ted, pet·ting, pets** —*tr.* To stroke or caress gently; pat. —*intr. Informal* To make love by fondling and caressing. [Sc. Gael. *peata,* tame animal, pet < OIr.] —**pet'ter** *n.*
pet² (pĕt) *n.* A fit of bad temper or pique. ❖ *intr.v.* **pet·ted, pet·ting, pets** To be sulky and peevish. [?]
PET *abbr.* positron emission tomography
Pet. *abbr. Bible* Peter
peta– *pref.* One quadrillion (10¹⁵): *petahertz.* [Alteration of PENTA– (< its representing the fifth power of a thousand).]
pet·a·byte (pĕt'ə-bīt') *n. Computer Science* **1.** A unit of storage capacity equal to 1,024 terabytes (2⁵⁰ bytes). **2.** One quadrillion bytes.
pet·a·hertz (pĕt'ə-hûrts') *n.* One quadrillion (10¹⁵) hertz.
Pé·tain (pā-tăN'), **Henri Philippe** 1856–1951. French soldier who led the government of Vichy France (1940–44).

Peter the Great

pet·al (pĕt′l) *n.* One of the often brightly colored parts of a flower immediately surrounding the reproductive organs; a division of the corolla. [NLat. *petalum* < Gk. *petalon,* leaf.] —**pet′aled, pet′alled** *adj.*

-petal *suff.* Moving toward: *basipetal.* [< NLat. *-petus* < Lat. *petere,* to seek. See **pet-** in App.]

pet·al·oid (pĕt′l-oid′) *adj.* Resembling a petal.

pet·al·ous (pĕt′l-əs) *adj.* Having petals.

pe·tard (pĭ-tärd′) *n.* **1.** A small bell-shaped bomb used to breach a gate or wall. **2.** A loud firecracker. [Fr. *pétard* < OFr. < *peter,* to break wind < *pet,* a breaking of wind < Lat. *pēditum* < neut. p. part. of *pēdere,* to break wind.]

pet·a·sos or **pet·a·sus** (pĕt′ə-səs) *n.* **1.** A wide-brimmed hat worn by ancient Greeks and Romans. **2.** *Greek Mythology* The winged hat of Hermes. [Gk.]

pet·cock (pĕt′kŏk′) *n.* A small valve or faucet used to drain or reduce pressure, as from a boiler. [Perh. PET¹ + COCK¹.]

pe·te·chi·a (pə-tē′kē-ə) *n., pl.* **-chi·ae** (-kē-ī′) A small purplish spot on a body surface, such as the skin, caused by a minute hemorrhage and often seen in typhus. [NLat. < Ital. *petecchie,* pl. of *petecchia,* spot on skin, perh. ult. < Lat. *impetīx, impetīc-,* var. of *impetīgō.* See IMPETIGO.]

pe·ter¹ (pē′tər) *intr.v.* **-tered, -ter·ing, -ters** **1.** To diminish slowly and come to an end; dwindle. Often used with *out: My strength petered out.* **2.** To become exhausted. Used with *out.* [Perh. < Fr. *peter,* to break wind < OFr. See PETARD.]

pe·ter² (pē′tər) *n. Vulgar Slang* The penis. [< the name *Peter.*]

Pe·ter³ (pē′tər) *n.* See table at **Bible.**

Peter, Saint. d. c. A.D. 67. The chief of the 12 Apostles who is traditionally regarded as the first bishop of Rome.

Peter I Known as "Peter the Great." 1672–1725. Russian czar (1682–1725) who extended his territory around the Baltic and Caspian shores and reformed the administration of the state.

Peter II 1923–70. Yugoslavian king (1934–45) who was forced to abdicate by the Communist government.

Pe·ter·bor·ough (pē′tər-bûr′ə, -bər-ə, -bŭr′ō) A municipal borough of E-central England E of Leicester. Pop. 156,375.

Peter Pan collar *n.* A small, close-fitting, usu. flat collar with rounded ends. [After *Peter Pan,* in the play of the same name by J.M. Barrie.]

Peter Principle *n.* The theory that employees within an organization will advance to their highest level of competence and then be promoted to and remain at a level at which they are incompetent. [After Laurence Johnston *Peter* (1919–90).]

Pe·ters·burg (pē′tərz-bûrg′) An independent city of SE VA S of Richmond; the site of a prolonged siege (Jun. 15, 1864–Apr. 3, 1865) during the Civil War. Pop. 33,740.

Pe·ter·son (pē′tər-sən), **Oscar Emmanuel** b. 1925. Canadian jazz pianist known esp. for work produced with his own trio (1953–65).

Pe·ter's pence (pē′tərz) *n. Roman Catholic Church* **1.** A tax of one penny per household paid in medieval England to the Papal See. **2.** An annual voluntary contribution made toward the expenses of the Holy See. [ME *Peteres pens,* pl. of *Peteres peni* : *Peteres,* genitive of *Peter,* St. Peter (who is said to have founded the papacy) + *peni,* penny; see PENNY.]

pet·i·o·lar (pĕt′ē-ō′lər) *adj.* Of, relating to, or growing on a petiole: *a petiolar sheath.*

pet·i·o·late (pĕt′ē-ə-lāt′, pĕt′ē-ə-lĭt) *adj.* Having a petiole.

pet·i·ole (pĕt′ē-ōl′) *n.* **1.** *Botany* The stalk by which a leaf is attached to a stem. **2.** *Zoology* A slender stalklike part, as that connecting the thorax and abdomen in certain insects. [Lat. *petiolus,* var. of *peciolus,* little foot, fruit stalk, prob. < **pediciolus,* dim. of *pediculus.* See PEDICEL.] —**pet′i·oled** *adj.*

pet·i·o·lule (pĕt′ē-ō-lōōl′, pĕt′ē-ō-lŏōl′yōōl) *n.* The stalk of a leaflet in a compound leaf.

pet·it also **pet·ty** (pĕt′ē) *adj. Law* Lesser; minor. [ME < OFr.]

pet·it bourgeois (pĕt′ē, pə-tē′) *n.* A member of the petite bourgeoisie. [Fr. *petit-bourgeois* : *petit,* small + *bourgeois,* bourgeois.] —**pet·it·bour·geois′** *adj.*

pe·tite (pə-tēt′) *adj.* Small and slender. Used of a girl or woman. See Syns at **small.** ❖ *n.* A clothing size for women 5′4″ and under. [Fr., fem. of *petit.* See PETIT.]

petite bourgeoisie *n.* The lower middle class, including minor businesspeople, tradespeople, and craftworkers. [Fr. *petite-bourgeoisie* : *petite,* fem. of *petit,* small + *bourgeoisie,* bourgeoisie.]

pet·it four (pĕt′ē fôr′, fōr′) *n., pl.* **pe·tits fours** or **pet·it fours** (pĕt′ē fôrz′, fōrz′) A small, square-cut, frosted and decorated piece of cake. [Fr. : *petit,* little + *four,* oven.]

pe·ti·tion (pə-tĭsh′ən) *n.* **1.** A supplication or request to a superior authority; an entreaty. **2.** A formal document requesting a right or benefit from an authority. **3.** *Law* **a.** A formal written application requesting a court for a specific judicial action. **b.** The judicial action asked for in any such request. **4.** Something requested or entreated. ❖ *v.* **-tioned, -tion·ing, -tions** —*tr.* **1.** To address a petition to. **2.** To ask for by petition; request formally. —*intr.* To make a request, esp. formally. [ME *peticion* < OFr. *petition* < Lat. *petītiō, petītiōn-* < *petītus,* p. part. of *petere,* to request. See **pet-** in App.] —**pe·ti′tion·ar′y** (-tĭsh′ə-nĕr′ē) *adj.* —**pe·ti′tion·er** *n.*

pe·ti·ti·o prin·ci·pi·i (pə-tĭsh′ē-ō′ prĭn-sĭp′ē-ē′, -ē-ī′) *n.*

Logic The fallacy of assuming in the premise of an argument that which one wishes to prove in the conclusion; a begging of the question. [Med.Lat. *petītiō prīncipiī* : Lat. *petītiō,* request + Lat. *prīncipiī,* genitive of *prīncipium,* beginning.]

pet·it jury also **pet·ty jury** (pĕt′ē) *n.* A jury that sits at civil and criminal trials.

pet·it larceny also **pet·ty larceny** (pĕt′ē) *n.* The theft of objects whose value is below a certain arbitrary standard.

pet·it mal (pĕt′ē mäl′, măl′) *n.* A form of epilepsy, occurring most often in adolescents and children, characterized by frequent but transient lapses of consciousness and only rare spasms or falling. [Fr. : *petit,* small + *mal,* illness.]

pet·it point (pĕt′ē point′) *n.* **1.** A small stitch used in needlepoint. **2.** Needlepoint done with a small stitch. [Fr.]

pet·nap·ping (pĕt′năp′ĭng) *n.* The stealing of a pet, such as a dog or cat. [PET¹ + (KID)NAP.] —**pet′nap′per** *n.*

Pe·tö·fi (pĕt′ə-fē, pĕt′tœ-), **Sándor** 1823–49. Hungarian poet best known for the epic *Janos the Hero* (1845).

petr– *pref.* Variant of **petro-.**

Pe·tra (pē′trə, pĕt′rə) An ancient ruined city of Edom in present-day SW Jordan; captured by Muslims in the 7th cent. and by Crusaders in the 12th cent.

Pe·trarch (pē′trärk′, pĕt′rärk′) or **Pe·trar·ca** (pē-trär′kä), **Francesco** 1304–74. Italian poet, scholar, and humanist famous for his love lyrics. —**Pe·trarch′an** (pĭ-trär′kən) *adj.*

Petrarchan sonnet *n.* A sonnet containing an octave with the rhyme pattern *abbaabba* and a sestet of various rhyme patterns such as *cdecde* or *cdcdcd.* [After Francesco PETRARCH.]

pet·rel (pĕt′rəl) *n.* Any of numerous black, gray, or white sea birds of the order Procellariiformes, esp. the storm petrel. [Perh. alteration of earlier *pitteral* (perhaps influenced by St. *Peter* walking on the water, because the bird flies so close to the water as to appear to walk on it).]

pe·tri dish (pē′trē) *n.* A shallow circular dish with a loose-fitting cover, used to culture microorganisms. [After Julius Richard *Petri* (1852–1921), German bacteriologist.]

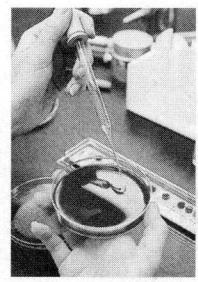

petri dish

Pe·trie (pē′trē), Sir **(William Matthew) Flinders** 1853–1942. British Egyptologist who excavated at Memphis and Thebes.

pet·ri·fac·tion (pĕt′rə-făk′shən) also **pet·ri·fi·ca·tion** (-fĭ-kā′shən) *n.* **1.** A process of fossilization in which dissolved minerals replace organic matter. **2.** The state of being stunned or paralyzed with fear.

Pet·ri·fied Forest (pĕt′rə-fīd′) A section of the Painted Desert in E AZ reserved as a national park for its fossilized trees dating from the Triassic Period.

pet·ri·fy (pĕt′rə-fī′) *v.* **-fied, -fy·ing, -fies** —*tr.* **1.** To convert (wood or other organic matter) into a stony replica by petrifaction. **2.** To cause to become stiff or stonelike; deaden. **3.** To stun or paralyze with terror; daze. —*intr.* To become stony, esp. by petrifaction. [ME *petrifien,* to harden < OFr. *petrifier* : Lat. *petra,* rock; see PETROUS + OFr. *-fier,* -fy.]

Pe·trine (pē′trīn′) *adj.* Of or relating to Saint Peter. [LLat. *Petrus,* Saint Peter + –INE¹.]

petro– or **petri–** or **petr–** *pref.* **1.** Rock; stone: *petroglyph.* **2.** Petroleum: *petrochemistry.* [Gk. < *petros,* stone. See **per-²** in App.]

pet·ro·chem·i·cal (pĕt′rō-kĕm′ĭ-kəl) *n.* A chemical derived from petroleum or natural gas. —**pet′ro·chem′i·cal** *adj.*

pet·ro·chem·is·try (pĕt′rō-kĕm′ĭ-strē) *n.* **1.** The chemistry of petroleum and its derivatives. **2.** The branch of geochemistry that deals with the chemical composition of rocks.

pet·ro·dol·lars (pĕt′rō-dŏl′ərz) *pl.n.* Money paid to oil-producing countries that is then deposited in Western banks.

pet·ro·gen·e·sis (pĕt′rō-jĕn′ĭ-sĭs) *n.* The branch of petrology that deals with the origin of rocks, esp. igneous rocks. —**pet′ro·ge·net′ic** (-jə-nĕt′ĭk) *adj.*

pet·ro·glyph (pĕt′rə-glĭf′) *n. Archaeology* A carving or line drawing on rock, esp. one made by prehistoric people. —**pet′ro·glyph′ic** *adj.*

Pet·ro·grad (pĕt′rə-grăd′) See **Saint Petersburg** 1.

pe·trog·ra·phy (pə-trŏg′rə-fē) *n.* The description and classification of rocks. —**pe·trog′ra·pher** *n.* —**pet′ro·graph′ic** (pĕt′rə-grăf′ĭk), **pet′ro·graph′i·cal** (-ĭ-kəl) *adj.*

pet·rol (pĕt′rəl) *n. Chiefly British* Gasoline. [Fr. *(essence de) pétrole,* (essence of) petroleum, gasoline < OFr. *petrole,* petroleum < Med.Lat. *petrōleum.* See PETROLEUM.]

pet·ro·la·tum (pĕt′rə-lā′təm, -lä′təm) *n.* See **petroleum jelly.** [< PETROL.]

pe·tro·le·um (pə-trō′lē-əm) *n.* A thick, flammable, yellow to black mixture of gaseous, liquid, and solid hydrocarbons that occurs naturally beneath the earth's surface, can be separated into fractions including natural gas, gasoline, fuel and lubricating oils, paraffin, and asphalt, and is used as raw material for many derivative products. [ME < Med.Lat. *petrōleum* < Lat. *petra,* rock; see PETROUS + Lat. *ōleum,* oil; see OIL.]

petroleum jelly *n.* A semisolid mixture of hydrocarbons obtained from petroleum, used in lubricants and ointments.

pe·trol·ic (pə-trŏl′ĭk) *adj.* Of or relating to petroleum.

pe·trol·o·gy (pə-trŏl′ə-jē) *n.* The branch of geology that deals with the origin, composition, structure, and alteration of rocks. —**pet′ro·log′ic** (pĕt′rə-lŏj′ĭk), **pet′ro·log′i·cal** (-ĭ-kəl) *adj.* —**pet′ro·log′i·cal·ly** *adv.* —**pe·trol′o·gist** *n.*

petroglyph
Newspaper Rock State
Historical Monument,
Indian Creek Canyon, Utah

ă	pat	oi	boy
ā	pay	ou	out
âr	care	ōō	took
ä	father	ōō	boot
ĕ	pet	ŭ	cut
ē	be	ûr	urge
ĭ	pit	th	thin
ī	pie	th	this
îr	pier	hw	which
ŏ	pot	zh	vision
ō	toe	ə	about,
ô	paw		item

Stress marks:
′ (primary);
′ (secondary), as in
lexicon (lĕk′sĭ-kŏn′)

peyote
Lophophora williamsii

Pe·tro·ni·us (pĭ-trō′nē-əs), **Gaius** Known as "Petronius Arbiter." d. A.D. 66. Roman courtier credited with writing the *Satyricon.*

Pet·ro·pav·lovsk-Kam·chat·ski (pĕt′rə-păv′lôfsk′kăm-chät′skē) A city of E Russia on the Pacific coast of the Kamchatka Peninsula. Pop. 265,254.

Pe·tróp·o·lis (pə-trŏp′ə-lĭs, pĭ-trô′pōō-) A city of SE Brazil N of Rio de Janeiro. Pop. 255,261.

pe·tro·sal (pə-trō′səl) *adj.* Relating to or located near the petrous portion of the temporal bone. [< Lat. *petrosus,* rocky. See PETROUS.]

pet·rous (pĕt′rəs) *adj.* **1.** Of, relating to, or resembling rock, esp. in hardness; stony. **2.** Of or relating to the very dense hard portion of the temporal bone that forms a protective case for the inner ear. [ME < OFr. *petros* < Lat. *petrōsus,* rocky < *petra,* rock < Gk. *petrā.* See per-² in App.]

Pet·ro·za·vodsk (pĕt′rə-zə-vŏtsk′) A city of NW Russia NE of St. Petersburg. Pop. 278,986.

pe·tsai (bä′tsī′) *n.* See **Chinese cabbage** 1. [Chin. (Mandarin) *bái cài.* See BOK CHOY.]

PET scan (pĕt) *n.* A cross-sectional image produced by a PET scanner.

PET scanner *n.* A device that produces cross-sectional x-rays of metabolic processes by means of positron emission tomography. [P(OSITRON) E(MISSION) T(OMOGRAPHY).]

pet·ti·coat (pĕt′ē-kōt′) *n.* **1.** A woman's slip or underskirt, often full and trimmed with ruffles or lace. **2.** Something, such as a valance, that resembles a woman's underskirt. ❖ *adj. Offensive* **1.** Female; feminine. **2.** Of, relating to, or carried out by women. [ME *peticote : peti,* small; see PETTY + *cote,* coat; see COAT.]

pet·ti·fog (pĕt′ē-fŏg′, -fôg′) *intr.v.* **-fogged, -fog·ging, -fogs** To act like a pettifogger.

pet·ti·fog·ger (pĕt′ē-fŏg′ər, -fô′gər) *n.* **1.** A petty, quibbling, unscrupulous lawyer. **2.** One who quibbles over trivia. [Prob. PETTY + obsolete *fogger,* pettifogger.] **—pet′ti·fog′ger·y** *n.*

pet·ting (pĕt′ĭng) *n. Informal* The act or practice of amorously embracing, kissing, and caressing one's partner.

petting zoo *n.* A collection of farm and docile wild animals, such as goats and deer, for children to feed and pet.

pet·tish (pĕt′ĭsh) *adj.* Ill-tempered; peevish. [Prob. < PET².] **—pet′tish·ly** *adv.* **—pet′tish·ness** *n.*

pet·ti·skirt (pĕt′ē-skûrt′) *n.* See **petticoat** 1.

pet·ti·toes (pĕt′ē-tōz′) *pl.n.* **1.** The feet of a pig used as food. **2.** Human feet or toes, esp. those of a child. [Poss. < earlier *pettytoe,* offal, poss. < OFr. *petite oye,* giblets of a goose : *petite,* small + *oye,* goose (< LLat. *auca;* see OCARINA).]

pet·ty (pĕt′ē) *adj.* **-ti·er, -ti·est 1.** Of small importance; trivial. **2.** Marked by narrowness of mind, ideas, or views. **3.** Marked by meanness or lack of generosity, esp. in trifling matters. **4.** Secondary in importance or rank; subordinate. **5.** *Law* Variant of **petit.** [ME *peti* < OFr., var. of *petit.* See PETIT.] **—pet′ti·ly** *adv.* **—pet′ti·ness** *n.*

petty cash *n.* A small fund of money for incidental expenses.

petty jury *n.* Variant of **petit jury.**

petty larceny *n.* Variant of **petit larceny.**

petty officer *n.* A noncommissioned naval officer ranking between enlisted personnel and commissioned officers.

pet·u·lant (pĕch′ə-lənt) *adj.* **1.** Unreasonably irritable or ill-tempered; peevish. **2.** Contemptuous in speech or behavior. [Lat. *petulāns, petulant-,* insolent < *petere,* to assail. See pet- in App.] **—pet′u·lance, pet′u·lan·cy** *n.*

pe·tu·nia (pĭ-tōōn′yə, -tyōōn′-) *n.* **1.** Any of various widely cultivated South American plants of the genus *Petunia,* having funnel-shaped flowers in colors from white to purple. **2.** A moderate to dark purple. [NLat. *Petunia,* genus name < obsolete Fr. *pétun,* tobacco < Port. *petum,* of Tupi-Guarani orig.]

pe·tun·tze or **pe·tun·tse** (pə-tōōn′tsĕ) *n.* A variety of feldspar sometimes mixed with kaolin and used in Chinese porcelain. [Chin. (Mandarin) *bái dūnzi : bái,* white + *dūnzi,* block of stone (*dūn,* mound, block + *-zi,* n. suff. < *zǐ,* son, child).]

Pevs·ner (pĕvz′nər, pyĕf′snĭr), **Antoine** 1886–1962. Russian artist who was a founder of constructivism.

pew (pyōō) *n.* **1.** One of the long, fixed, backed benches used as seats in a church. **2.** An enclosed compartment in a church that provides seating for a number of people. [ME *pewe* < OFr. *puie,* balcony < Lat. *podia,* pl. of *podium,* balcony. See PODIUM.]

pe·wee also **pee·wee** (pē′wē) *n.* Any of various small olive-gray North American flycatchers of the genus *Contopus.* [Imit. of its call.]

pe·wit also **pee·wit** (pē′wĭt, pyōō′ĭt) *n.* See **lapwing.** [Imit. of its call.]

pew·ter (pyōō′tər) *n.* **1.** Any of numerous silver-gray alloys of tin with various amounts of antimony, copper, and sometimes lead, used widely for fine kitchen utensils and tableware. **2.** Pewter articles considered as a group. [ME *pewtre* < OFr. *peutre* < VLat. **peltrum.*] **—pew′ter** *adj.*

pe·yo·te also **pe·yo·tl** (-ōt′l) *n.* **1.** A spineless dome-shaped cactus (*Lophophora williamsii*) native to Mexico and the southwest United States and having buttonlike tubercles that can be chewed as a hallucinogenic drug. **2.** See **mescal button. 3.** See

mescaline. [Am.Sp. < Nahuatl *peyotl.*]

pf. *abbr.* **1.** or **pfd.** preferred (stock) **2.** pfennig

PFC *abbr.* private first class

pfen·nig (fĕn′ĭg) *n., pl.* **pfennig** or **-nigs** A coin equal to ¹⁄₁₀₀ of the deutsche mark. [Ger. < MHGer. *pfennic* < OHGer. *pfenning.*]

pfft (ft, pft) *interj.* Used to express or indicate a usu. sudden disappearance or ending.

Pforz·heim (fôrts′hīm, fôrts′-, pfôrts′-) A city of SW Germany WNW of Stuttgart; chartered c. 1195. Pop. 117,450.

PG (pē′jē′) A trademark used for a movie rating indicating that admission will be granted to persons of all ages but that parental guidance is advised in the case of children.

pg. *abbr.* page

Pg. *abbr.* Portuguese

PG-13 (pē′jē′thûr-tēn′) A trademark used for a movie rating indicating that admission will be granted to persons of all ages but that parental guidance is suggested in the case of children under the age of 13.

PGA *abbr.* Professional Golfers' Association

PGP *abbr.* pretty good privacy (data encryption)

pH (pē′āch′) *n.* A measure of the acidity or alkalinity of a solution, equal to 7 for neutral solutions and increasing to 14 with increasing alkalinity and decreasing to 0 with increasing acidity. [*p(otential of) h(ydrogen).*]

Ph *abbr.* Bible Philippians

PH *abbr.* **1.** penthouse **2.** public health **3.** Purple Heart

phac·o·e·mul·si·fi·ca·tion (făk′ō-ĭ-mŭl′sə-fĭ-kā′shən) *n.* Removal of a cataract by emulsifying the lens ultrasonically. [Gk. *phakos,* lentil, lentil-shaped object; see bha-bhā- in App. + EMULSIFICATION.]

Phae·dra (fē′drə, fĕd′rə) *n. Greek Mythology* The wife of Theseus who killed herself after accusing Hippolytus of rape.

Pha·ë·thon (fā′ə-thŏn′, -thən) *n. Greek Mythology* A son of Helios who was killed while driving the sun's chariot across the sky. [Lat. *Phaëtōn, Phaëthōn* < Gk. *Phaethōn* < *phaethein,* pr. part. of *phaethein,* to shine.]

pha·e·ton (fā′ĭ-tn) *n.* **1.** A light four-wheeled open carriage, usu. drawn by a pair of horses. **2.** A touring car. [Fr. *phaéton* < *Phaeton,* Phaethon < OFr. < Lat. *Phaethōn.* See PHAËTHON.]

phage (fāj) *n.* A bacteriophage.

–phage *suff.* One that eats: *macrophage.* [< Gk. *-phagos,* eating < *phagein,* to eat. See bhag- in App.]

–phagia or **–phagy** *suff.* The eating of a specified substance or eating in a specified manner: *dysphagia.* [Gk. *-phagiā* < *phagein,* to eat. See bhag- in App.]

phago– *pref.* Eating; consuming: *phagocyte.* [Gk. < *phagein,* to eat. See bhag- in App.]

phag·o·cyte (făg′ə-sīt′) *n.* A cell, such as a white blood cell, that engulfs and absorbs foreign bodies in the bloodstream and tissues. **—phag′o·cyt′ic** (-sĭt′ĭk) *adj.*

phagocytic index *n.* The average number of bacteria ingested by each phagocyte in an individual's blood as observed in a mixture of the blood serum, bacteria, and phagocytes.

phag·o·cy·tize (făg′ə-sĭ-tīz′, -sī′-) *tr.v.* **-tized, -tiz·ing, -tiz·es** To ingest by phagocytosis.

phag·o·cy·to·sis (făg′ə-sī-tō′sĭs) *n.* The engulfing and ingestion of bacteria or other foreign bodies by phagocytes. **—phag′o·cy·tot′ic** (-tŏt′ĭk) *adj.*

–phagous *suff.* Eating; feeding on: *ichthyophagous.* [< Lat. *-phagus* < Gk. *-phagos* < *phagein,* to eat. See bhag- in App.]

pha·lange (fā′lănj′, fə-lănj′) *n.* Anatomy A phalanx **3.** [Ult. < Gk. *phalanx, phalang-,* log, battle array, bone between the finger and toe joints. See PHALANX.]

pha·lan·ge·al (fə-lăn′jē-əl, fā-) also **pha·lan·gal** (fə-lăng′gəl, fā-) or **pha·lan·ge·an** (fə-lăn′jē-ən, fā-) *adj. Anatomy* Of or relating to a phalanx or phalanges.

pha·lan·ger (fə-lăn′jər) *n.* Any of various small arboreal marsupials of the family Phalangeridae of Australia, having a long tail and dense woolly fur. [NLat. < Gk. *phalanx, phalang-,* toe bone (< its fused hind toes). See PHALANX.]

phal·an·ster·y (făl′ən-stĕr′ē) *n., pl.* **-ies 1a.** A self-sustaining cooperative community of the followers of Fourierism. **b.** The buildings in such a community. **2.** An association resembling a Fourierist phalanstery. [Fr. *phalanstère : phalange,* phalanx (< Lat. *phalanx, phalang-;* see PHALANX) + *(mona)stère,* monastery (< LLat. *monastērium;* see MONASTERY).] **—phal′an·ste′ri·an** (-stîr′ē-ən) *adj. & n.*

pha·lanx (fā′lăngks′, făl′ăngks′) *n. pl.* **pha·lanx·es** or **pha·lan·ges** (fə-lăn′jēz, fā-) **1.** A compact or close-knit body of people. **2.** A formation of infantry carrying overlapping shields and long spears, used in classical Greece. **3.** *pl.* **phalanges** *Anatomy* A bone of a finger or toe. **4.** See **phalanstery** 1a. [Lat. *phalanx, phalang-* < Gk.]

phal·a·rope (făl′ə-rōp′) *n.* Any of several small wading birds of the family Phalaropodidae, resembling sandpipers but having lobed toes that enable them to swim. [Fr. < NLat. *phalaropus :* Gk. *phalaris,* coot (< *phalaros,* having a white spot; see bhel-¹ in App.) + Gk. *pous,* foot; see ped- in App.]

phal·lic (făl′ĭk) *adj.* **1.** Of, relating to, or resembling a phallus. **2.** Of or relating to the cult of the phallus as an embodiment of generative power. **3.** In psychoanalytic theory, of or relating to the third stage of psychosexual development during which gratification is focused on sensations associated with the genital organs. [Gk. *phallikos* < *phallos*, phallus.] —**phal′li·cal·ly** *adv.*

phal·lo·cen·tric (făl′ō-sĕn′trĭk) *adj.* Centered on men or on a male viewpoint, esp. one held to entail the domination of women by men. [PHALL(US) + −CENTRIC.] —**phal′lo·cen′trism** *n.*

phal·lus (făl′əs) *n., pl.* **phal·li** (făl′ī′) or **phal·lus·es 1.** *Anatomy* **a.** The penis. **b.** The sexually undifferentiated tissue in an embryo that becomes the penis or clitoris. **2.** A representation of the penis and testes as an embodiment of generative power. **3.** The immature penis considered in psychoanalysis as the libidinal object of infantile sexuality in the male. [LLat. < Gk. *phallos*.]

–phane or **–phan** *suff.* A substance resembling something specified: *tryptophan*. [< Gk. *-phanēs*, appearing < *phainesthai*, to appear.]

phan·er·o·gam (făn′ər-ə-găm′, fə-nâr′ə-) *n.* A plant that produces seeds. [NLat. *phanerogamus* : Gk. *phaneros*, visible (< *phainein*, to cause to appear; see bhā-¹ in App.) + Gk. *gamos*, marriage; see –GAMOUS.] —**phan′er·o·gam′ic, phan′er·og′a·mous** (făn′ə-rŏg′ə-məs) *adj.*

Phan·er·o·zo·ic (făn′ər-ə-zō′ĭk) *adj.* Of or belonging to the period of geologic time from approx. 570 million years ago to the present, comprising the Paleozoic, Mesozoic, and Cenozoic eras, and marked by an abundance of fossil evidence of life, esp. higher forms, in the corresponding rocks. See table at **geologic time.** ❖ *n.* The Phanerozoic Eon or its deposits. [Gk. *phaneros*, visible (< *phainein*, to cause to appear; see bhā-¹ in App.) + –ZOIC.]

phan·tasm (făn′tăz′əm) *n.* **1.** Something apparently seen but having no physical reality; a phantom or an apparition. **2.** An illusory mental image. **3.** In Platonic philosophy, objective reality as perceived and distorted by the five senses. [Ult. < Gk. *phantazein*, to make visible < *phantos*, visible < *phainein*, to show.] —**phan·tas′mal** (făn-tăz′məl), **phan·tas′mic** (-tăz′mĭk) *adj.*

phan·tas·ma (făn-tăz′mə) *n., pl.* **-ma·ta** (-mə-tə) See **phantasm** 1, 2. [Ult. < Gk. See PHANTASM.]

phan·tas·ma·go·ri·a (făn-tăz′mə-gôr′ē-ə, -gôr′-) also **phan·tas·ma·go·ry** (făn-tăz′mə-gôr′ē, -gôr′ē) *n.* **1.** pl. **-ri·as** also **-ries a.** A fantastic sequence of haphazardly associative imagery, as seen in dreams or fever. **b.** A constantly changing scene composed of numerous elements. **2.** Fantastic imagery as represented in art. [Alteration of obsolete Fr. *phantasmagorie*, art of creating supernatural illusions : perh. *fantasme*, illusion (< OFr., ult. < Gk. *phantasma*; see PHANTASM) + *allégorie*, allegory, allegorical visual representation (< OFr., allegory < Lat. *allēgoria*; see ALLEGORY).] —**phan′tas′ma·gor′ic** (-gôr′ĭk, -gôr′-) *adj.*

phan·tom also **fan·tom** (făn′təm) *n.* **1a.** Something apparently seen, heard, or sensed but having no physical reality; a ghost or an apparition. **b.** Something elusive or delusive. **2.** An image that appears only in the mind; an illusion. **3.** Something dreaded or despised. ❖ *adj.* **1.** Resembling, characteristic of, or being a phantom; illusive. **2.** Fictitious; nonexistent: *phantom employees on the payroll.* [ME *fantom* < OFr. *fantosme*, prob. < VLat. **phantauma* < Gk. dialectal **phantagma* < Gk. *phantasma*. See PHANTASM.]

phantom limb pain *n.* Pain or discomfort felt by an amputee in the area of the missing limb.

Phar·aoh also **phar·aoh** (fâr′ō, fā′rō) *n.* **1.** A king of ancient Egypt. **2.** A tyrant. [ME *Pharao* < LLat. *Pharaō* < Gk. < Heb. *par′ō* < Egypt. *pr-ˁ* : *pr*, house + *ˁ*, great.] —**Phar′a·on′ic** (fâr′ā-ŏn′ĭk) *adj.*

pharaoh ant *n.* A tiny yellowish-red ant (*Monomorium pharaonis*) that infests human dwellings throughout the world.

phar·i·sa·ic (fâr′ĭ-sā′ĭk) also **phar·i·sa·i·cal** (-sā′ĭ-kəl) *adj.* **1.** **Pharisaic** Of, relating to, or characteristic of the Pharisees. **2.** Hypocritically self-righteous and condemnatory. —**phar′i·sa′i·cal·ly** *adv.* —**phar′i·sa′i·cal·ness** *n.*

phar·i·sa·ism (fâr′ĭ-sā-ĭz′əm) also **phar·i·see·ism** (-sē-ĭz′əm) *n.* **1. Pharisaism** The doctrines and practices of the Pharisees. **2.** Hypocritical observance of the letter of religious or moral law without regard for the spirit.

phar·i·see (fâr′ĭ-sē) *n.* **1. Pharisee** A member of an ancient Jewish sect that emphasized strict interpretation and observance of the Mosaic law. **2.** A hypocritically self-righteous person. [ME *pharise* < OE *fariseus* and < OFr. *pharise*, both < LLat. *pharīsaeus* < Gk. *pharīsaios* < Aram. *pərīšayyā*, pl. of *pərīš*, separate < *pəraš*, to separate.]

phar·ma·ceu·ti·cal (fär′mə-sōō′tĭ-kəl) also **phar·ma·ceu·tic** (-tĭk) *adj.* Of or relating to pharmacy or pharmacists. ❖ *n.* A pharmaceutical product or preparation. [< LLat. *pharmaceuticus* < Gk. *pharmakeutikos* < *pharmakeutēs*, preparer of drugs, var. of *pharmakeus* < *pharmakon*, drug.] —**phar′ma·ceu′ti·cal·ly** *adv.*

phar·ma·ceu·tics (fär′mə-sōō′tĭks) *n.* **1.** (*used with a sing. verb*) The science of preparing and dispensing drugs. **2.** (*used with a pl. verb*) Pharmaceutical preparations; medicinal drugs.

phar·ma·cist (fär′mə-sĭst) *n.* One trained in pharmacy.

pharmaco– *pref.* Drug; medicine: *pharmacognosy.* [Gk. < *pharmakon*, poison, drug.]

phar·ma·co·dy·nam·ics (fär′mə-kō′dī-năm′ĭks) *n.* (*used with a sing. verb*) The study of the action or the effects of drugs on living organisms. —**phar′ma·co′dy·nam′ic** *adj.* —**phar′-**

ma·co′dy·nam′i·cal·ly *adv.*

phar·ma·cog·no·sy (fär′mə-kŏg′nə-sē) *n.* The branch of pharmacology that deals with drugs in their crude or natural state and with medicinal herbs. [PHARMACO- + Gk. *gnōsis*, knowledge; see GNOSIS.] —**phar′ma·cog·nos′tic** (-kŏg-nŏs′tĭk) *adj.*

phar·ma·co·ki·net·ics (fär′mə-kō-kə-nĕt′ĭks, -kī-) *n.* (*used with a sing. verb*) **1.** The process by which a drug is absorbed, distributed, metabolized, and eliminated by the body. **2.** The study of this process. —**phar′ma·co·ki·net′ic** *adj.*

phar·ma·col·o·gy (fär′mə-kŏl′ə-jē) *n.* **1.** The science of drugs, including their composition, uses, and effects. **2.** The characteristics or properties of a drug, esp. those that make it medically effective. —**phar′ma·co·log′ic** (-kə-lŏj′ĭk), **phar′ma·co·log′i·cal** (-ĭ-kəl) *adj.* —**phar′ma·co·log′i·cal·ly** *adv.* —**phar′ma·col′o·gist** *n.*

phar·ma·co·poe·ia also **phar·ma·co·pe·ia** (fär′mə-kə-pē′ə) *n.* **1.** A book containing an official list of medicinal drugs together with articles on their preparation and use. **2.** A collection or stock of drugs. [NLat. < Gk. *pharmakopoiiā*, preparation of drugs < *pharmakopoios*, preparing drugs : *pharmako-*, pharmaco- + *poiein*, to make.] —**phar′ma·co·poe′ial** (-pē′əl) *adj.*

phar·ma·co·ther·a·py (fär′mə-kō-thĕr′ə-pē) *n., pl.* **-pies** Treatment of disease through the use of drugs.

phar·ma·cy (fär′mə-sē) *n., pl.* **-cies 1.** The art of preparing and dispensing drugs. **2.** A place where drugs are sold; a drugstore. [Ult. < Med.Lat. *pharmacīa*, a medicine < Gk. *pharmakeia*, use of drugs < *pharmakon*, drug.]

pharm·ing (fär′mĭng) *n.* The production of pharmaceuticals from genetically altered plants or animals. [Blend of PHARMACEUTICAL and *farming*, gerund of FARM.]

pha·ros (fâr′ŏs′) *n.* A lighthouse. [Lat. < Gk., after *Pharos*, near Alexandria, Egypt, site of an ancient lighthouse.]

Phar·sa·lus (fär-sā′ləs) or **Phar·sa·la** (fär′sä-lä) An ancient city of Thessaly in NE Greece; site of Julius Caesar's defeat of Pompey (48 B.C.).

pha·ryn·ge·al (fə-rĭn′jē-əl, -jəl, fär′ĭn-jē′əl) also **pha·ryn·gal** (fə-rĭng′gəl) *adj.* Of, relating to, located in, or coming from the pharynx. ❖ *n.* A speech sound produced in the pharynx. [< NLat. *pharyngeus* < *pharynx, pharyng-*, pharynx. See PHARYNX.]

phar·yn·gi·tis (fär′ĭn-jī′tĭs) *n.* Inflammation of the pharynx.

pharyngo– or **pharyng–** *pref.* Pharynx: *pharyngoscope.* [NLat. < Gk. *pharungo-* < *pharunx, pharung-*. See PHARYNX.]

pha·ryn·go·scope (fə-rĭng′gə-skōp′) *n.* An instrument used in examining the pharynx. —**phar′yn·gos′co·py** (fär′ĭn-gŏs′kə-pē, fär′ĭng-) *n.*

phar·ynx (fär′ĭngks) *n., pl.* **pha·ryn·ges** (fə-rĭn′jēz) or **phar·ynx·es** The section of the alimentary canal that extends from the mouth and nasal cavities to the larynx, where it joins the esophagus. [NLat. *pharynx, pharyng-* < Gk. *pharunx*.]

phase (fāz) *n.* **1.** A distinct stage of development: *a comprehensive plan with three phases.* **2.** A temporary manner, attitude, or pattern of behavior: *just a passing phase.* **3.** An aspect; a part: *in control of every phase of the operation.* **4.** *Astronomy* One of the cyclically recurring apparent forms of the moon or a planet. **5.** *Physics* **a.** A stage in a periodic process or phenomenon. **b.** The fraction of a complete cycle elapsed as measured from a reference point and often expressed as an angle. **6.** *Chemistry* **a.** Any of the forms or states, solid, liquid, gas, or plasma, in which matter can exist, depending on temperature and pressure. **b.** A discrete homogeneous part of a material system that is separable from the rest, as ice is from water. **7.** *Biology* A characteristic form, appearance, or stage of development that occurs in a cycle or distinguishes some individuals of a group: *the swarming phase of locusts.* ❖ *tr.v.* **phased, phas·ing, phas·es 1.** To plan or carry out systematically by phases. **2.** To set or regulate so as to be synchronized. —***phrasal verbs:*** **phase in** To introduce one stage at a time. **phase out** To bring or come to an end one stage at a time. —***idioms:*** **in phase** In a correlated or synchronized way. **out of phase** In an unsynchronized or uncorrelated way. [Back-formation < NLat. *phasēs*, phases of the moon < Gk. *phaseis*, pl. of *phasis*, appearance < *phainein*, to show.] —**pha′sic** (fā′zĭk) *adj.*

phase contrast microscope *n.* A microscope that uses the differences in the phase of light transmitted or reflected by a specimen to form distinct, contrasting images of the specimen.

phased array (fāzd) *n.* An arrangement of dipoles on a radar antenna, in which the phase of each dipole is controlled by a computer so that the beam can scan very rapidly.

phase modulation *n.* A type of modulation in which the phase of a carrier wave is varied in proportion to the amplitude of the signal.

–phasia *suff.* A speech disorder of a specified kind: *dysphasia.* [Gk. *-phasiā*, speech < *phasis*, utterance < *phanai*, to say, speak. See bhā- in App.]

phas·mid (făz′mĭd) *n.* Any of various insects of the order Phasmida, including the leaf insects and walking sticks, common esp. in tropical areas and resembling foliage in color and form. [< NLat. *Phasmida*, order name < *Phasma*, type genus < Gk. *phasma*, apparition < *phainein* to show.]

phat (făt) *adj.* **-ter, -test** *Slang* Excellent; first-rate: *phat fashion.* [Earlier, sexy (said of a woman), of unknown orig.]

phat·ic (făt′ĭk) *adj.* Of, relating to, or being speech used to share

ă	pat	oi	boy
ā	pay	ou	out
âr	care	ŏŏ	took
ä	father	ōō	boot
ĕ	pet	ŭ	cut
ē	be	ûr	urge
ĭ	pit	th	thin
ī	pie	th	this
îr	pier	hw	which
ŏ	pot	zh	vision
ō	toe	ə	about,
ô	paw		item

Stress marks:
′ (primary);
′ (secondary), as in
lexicon (lĕk′sĭ-kŏn′)

feelings or establish a mood of sociability rather than communicate information or ideas. [< Gk. *phatos*, spoken < *phanai*, to speak. See –PHASIA.] —**phat′i·cal·ly** *adv.*

PhB *abbr.* Latin Philosophiae Baccalaureus (Bachelor of Philosophy)

PhC *abbr.* pharmaceutical chemist

PhD *abbr. Latin* Philosophiae Doctor (Doctor of Philosophy)

pheas·ant (fĕz′ənt) *n., pl.* **pheas·ants** or **pheasant 1.** Any of various Old World birds of the family Phasianidae, esp. the ring-necked pheasant, having long tails and in the males of many species brilliantly colored plumage. **2.** Any of several birds that resemble the pheasant, such as the partridge. [ME *fesaunt* < OFr. *fesan* < Lat. *phāsiānus* < Gk. *phāsiānos* (*ornis*), (bird) of the Phasis River, pheasant < *Phāsis*, Rioni River (Georgia).]

phel·lem (fĕl′əm, -ĕm′) *n.* See **cork 4.** [Ger. : Gk. *phellos*, cork + -*em* (as in *Phloëm*, phloem; see PHLOEM).]

phel·lo·derm (fĕl′ə-dûrm′) *n.* A tissue produced inwardly by the cork cambium. [Gk. *phellos*, cork + –DERM.]

phel·lo·gen (fĕl′ə-jən) *n.* See **cork cambium.** [Gk. *phellos*, cork + –GEN.]

phe·nac·e·tin (fə-năs′ĭ-tĭn) *n.* A white powder or crystalline solid, CH₃CONHC₆H₄OC₂H₅, derived from coal tar and used to reduce fever and relieve pain until its removal from the US market for its potential harmful effects. [Rearrangement of chemical name ACETOPHENETIDIN.]

phen·a·cite (fĕn′ə-sīt′) or **phen·a·kite** (-kīt′) *n.* A natural beryllium silicate, Be₂SiO₄, occurring as vitreous crystals used as gems. [Gk. *phenāx, phenāk-*, impostor + –ITE¹.]

phe·nan·threne (fə-năn′thrēn′) *n.* A colorless crystalline hydrocarbon, C₁₄H₁₀, obtained by fractional distillation of coal tar oils and used in dyes, drugs, and explosives. [PHEN(O)– + ANTHR(AC)ENE.]

phen·a·zine (fĕn′ə-zēn′) also **phen·a·zin** (-zĭn) *n.* A crystalline compound, C₆H₄N₂C₆H₄, used in making dyes.

phen·cy·cli·dine (fĕn-sī′klĭ-dēn′, -dĭn, -sĭk′lĭ-) *n.* A drug, C₁₇H₂₅N, used as a hallucinogen and in veterinary medicine as an anesthetic; PCP. [PHEN(O)– + CYCL(O)– + ID(E) + –INE².]

phe·net·ic (fĭ-nĕt′ĭk) *adj.* Of, relating to, or being a system of classification of organisms based on overall or observable similarities rather than on phylogenetic or evolutionary relationships. [PHEN(OTYPE) + –ETIC.] —**phe·net′i·cal·ly** *adv.*

phe·net·ics (fĭ-nĕt′ĭks) *n.* (*used with a sing. verb*) The phenetic system of taxonomic classification.

phe·nix (fē′nĭks) *n.* Variant of **phoenix.**

pheno– or **phen–** *pref.* **1.** Showing; displaying: *phenotype.* **2a.** Related to or derived from benzene: *phenyl.* **b.** Containing phenyl: *phenothiazine.* [Gk. *phaino-* < *phainein,* to show.]

phe·no·bar·bi·tal (fē′nō-bär′bĭ-tôl′, -tăl′) *n.* A crystalline barbiturate, C₁₂H₁₂N₂O₃, used medicinally as a sedative, a hypnotic, and an anticonvulsant.

phe·no·bar·bi·tone (fē′nō-bär′bĭ-tōn′) *n. Chiefly British* Phenobarbital.

phe·no·cop·y (fē′nə-kŏp′ē) *n., pl.* -**ies** An environmentally induced, nonhereditary variation in an organism, closely resembling a genetically determined trait. [PHENO(TYPE) + COPY.]

phe·no·cryst (fē′nə-krĭst′) *n.* A conspicuous, usu. large crystal embedded in porphyritic igneous rock. [PHENO– + CRYST(AL).] —**phe·no·crys′tic** *adj.*

phe·nol (fē′nôl′, -nōl′, -nŏl′) *n.* **1.** A caustic poisonous crystalline compound, C₆H₅OH, derived from benzene and used in resins, plastics, and pharmaceuticals. **2.** Any of a class of aromatic organic compounds having at least one hydroxyl group attached directly to the benzene ring.

phe·no·late (fē′nə-lāt′) *n.* A salt of phenol.

phe·no·lic (fĭ-nō′lĭk, -nŏl′ĭk) *adj.* Of, relating to, containing, or derived from phenol. ❖ *n.* Any of various synthetic thermosetting resins, obtained by the reaction of phenols with simple aldehydes and used in molded products and coatings.

phe·nol·o·gy (fĭ-nŏl′ə-jē) *n.* **1.** The relationship between a periodic biological phenomenon and climatic conditions. **2.** The scientific study of phenology. [PHENO(MENON) + –LOGY.] —**phe′no·log′i·cal** (fē′nə-lŏj′ĭ-kəl) *adj.*

phe·nol·phthal·ein (fē′nôl-thăl′ēn′, -thăl′ē-ĭn, -thă′lēn′, -thă′lē-ĭn) *n.* A crystalline powder, C₂₀H₁₄O₄, used as an acid-base indicator, in making dyes, and formerly as an ingredient in laxatives.

phenol red *n.* A red water-soluble dye, C₁₉H₁₄O₅S, used as an acid-base indicator and in medicine to test kidney function.

phe·nom (fē′nŏm′, fĭ-nŏm′) *n. Slang* A phenomenon, esp. a remarkable or outstanding person.

phe·nom·e·nal (fĭ-nŏm′ə-nəl) *adj.* **1.** Of, relating to, or constituting phenomena or a phenomenon. **2.** Extraordinary; outstanding. **3.** *Philosophy* Known or derived through the senses rather than through the mind. —**phe·nom′e·nal·ly** *adv.*

phe·nom·e·nal·ism (fĭ-nŏm′ə-nə-lĭz′əm) *n. Philosophy* The doctrine, set forth by David Hume and his successors, that percepts and concepts constitute the sole objects of knowledge, with the objects of perception and the nature of the mind itself remaining unknowable. —**phe·nom′e·nal·ist** *n.* —**phe·nom′e·nal·is′tic** *adj.* —**phe·nom′e·nal·is′ti·cal·ly** *adv.*

phe·nom·e·nol·o·gy (fĭ-nŏm′ə-nŏl′ə-jē) *n.* **1.** A philosophy

or method of inquiry based on the premise that reality consists of objects and events as they are perceived or understood in human consciousness and not of anything independent of human consciousness. **2.** A movement based on this, originated about 1905 by Edmund Husserl. —**phe·nom′e·no·log′i·cal** (-nə-lŏj′ĭ-kəl) *adj.* —**phe·nom′e·no·log′i·cal·ly** *adv.* —**phe·nom′e·nol′o·gist** *n.*

phe·nom·e·non (fĭ-nŏm′ə-nŏn′, -nən) *n., pl.* -**na** (-nə) **1.** An occurrence, circumstance, or fact that is perceptible by the senses. **2.** *pl.* -**nons a.** An unusual, significant, or unaccountable fact or occurrence; a marvel. **b.** A remarkable or outstanding person; a paragon. See Syns at **wonder. 3.** *Philosophy* In the philosophy of Kant, an object as it is perceived by the senses, as opposed to a noumenon. **4.** *Physics* An observable event. [LLat. *phaenomenon* < Gk. *phainomenon* < neut. pr. part. of *phainesthai*, to appear.]

> **USAGE NOTE** *Phenomenon* is the only singular form of this noun; *phenomena* is the usual plural. *Phenomenons* may also be used as the plural in nonscientific writing when the meaning is "extraordinary things, occurrences, or persons."

phe·no·thi·a·zine (fē′nō-thī′ə-zēn′, -nə-) *n.* **1.** An organic compound, C₁₂H₉NS, used in insecticides, livestock anthelmintics, and dyes. **2.** Any of a group of drugs derived from this compound and used in the treatment of psychiatric disorders such as schizophrenia.

phe·no·type (fē′nə-tīp′) *n.* **1a.** The observable physical or biochemical traits of an organism, as determined by both genetics and environment. **b.** The expression of a given trait based on phenotype. **2.** An individual or group of organisms with a particular phenotype. —**phe′no·typ′ic** (-tĭp′ĭk), **phe′no·typ′i·cal** (-ĭ-kəl) *adj.* —**phe′no·typ′i·cal·ly** *adv.*

phe·nox·ide (fĭ-nŏk′sīd′) *n.* See **phenolate.**

phen·yl (fĕn′əl, fē′nəl) *n.* The univalent organic radical C₆H₅, derived from benzene by removal of one hydrogen atom. —**phe·nyl′ic** (fĭ-nĭl′ĭk) *adj.*

phen·yl·al·a·nine (fĕn′əl-ăl′ə-nēn′, fē′nəl-) *n.* An essential amino acid, C₉H₁₁NO₂, that occurs as a constituent of many proteins.

phen·yl·ene (fĕn′ə-lēn′, fē′nə-) *n.* A bivalent organic radical, C₆H₄, derived from benzene by removal of two hydrogen atoms.

phen·yl·eph·rine (fĕn′əl-ĕf′rĭn, fē′nəl-) *n.* An adrenergic drug, C₉H₁₃NO₂, that is a powerful vasoconstrictor and is used to relieve nasal congestion, dilate the pupils, and maintain blood pressure during anesthesia. [PHENYL + (EPIN)EPHRINE.]

phen·yl·ke·to·nu·ri·a (fĕn′əl-kēt′n-ōōr′ē-ə, -yŏōr′-, fē′nəl-) *n.* A genetic disorder in which the body lacks the enzyme necessary to metabolize phenylalanine, causing possible brain damage and progressive mental retardation. —**phen′yl·ke′to·nu′ric** *adj.*

phen·yl·pro·pa·nol·a·mine (fĕn′əl-prō′pə-nŏl′ə-mēn′, fē′nəl-) *n.* An adrenergic drug, C₉H₁₃NO, that acts as a vasoconstrictor and is used as a nasal decongestant, bronchodilator, appetite suppressant, and mild stimulant.

phen·yl·thi·o·car·ba·mide (fĕn′əl-thī′ō-kär′bə-mīd′, -kär-băm′īd, fē′nəl-) *n.* A crystalline compound, C₆H₅NHCSNH₂, that tastes bitter to people with a specific dominant gene, used to test for the presence of the gene.

phen·yl·thi·o·u·re·a (fĕn′əl-thī′ō-yŏō-rē′ə, fē′nəl-) *n.* See **phenylthiocarbamide.**

phen·y·to·in (fĕn′ĭ-tō′ĭn, fə-nĭt′ō-) *n.* An anticonvulsant drug, C₁₅H₁₂N₂O₂, used in the treatment of epilepsy. [(DI)PHENY(LHYDAN)TOIN.]

phe·re·sis (fə-rē′sĭs, fĕr′ə-) *n. Informal* Apheresis.

pher·o·mone (fĕr′ə-mōn′) *n.* A chemical secreted by an animal, esp. an insect, that influences the behavior or development of others of the same species, as in mating. [Gk. *pherein,* to carry; see bher-¹ in App. + (HOR)MONE.] —**pher′o·mon′al** *adj.*

phew (fyŏō) *interj.* Used to express relief, fatigue, surprise, or disgust.

PhG *abbr.* Graduate in Pharmacy

phi (fī, fē) *n.* The 21st letter of the Greek alphabet. [LGk. *phi* < Gk. *phei.*]

phi·al (fī′əl) *n.* A vial. [ME *fiole* < OFr. < LLat. *fiola*, shallow vessel, alteration of Lat. *phiala* < Gk. *phialē.*]

Phi Beta Kappa (fī′) *n.* **1.** An honorary society of college students and graduates chosen on the basis of high academic standing. **2.** A member of this society. [< the initials of the society's Greek motto *philosophiā biou kubernētēs*, philosophy (is) the guide of life.]

Phid·i·as (fĭd′ē-əs) fl. 5th cent. B.C. Athenian sculptor whose Olympian Zeus was one of the Seven Wonders of the World.

Phil. *abbr.* **1.** *Bible* Philippians **2.** Philippines

phil– *pref.* Variant of **philo–.**

–phil *suff.* Variant of **–phile.**

Phil·a·del·phi·a (fĭl′ə-dĕl′fē-ə) **1.** An ancient city of Asia Minor NE of the Dead Sea in modern-day Jordan; chief city of the Ammonites. **2.** A city of SE PA on the Delaware R.; founded in 1681 and the second cap. of the US (1790–1800). Pop. 1,517,550. —**Phil′a·del′phi·an** *adj. & n.*

Philadelphia lawyer *n.* An attorney adept at the discovery and manipulation of legal technicalities.

Philae
Trajan's Kiosk, now on Agilika Island, Egypt

Philip II³
portrait of Philip II of Spain, attributed to Titian

Philadelphia pepper pot *n.* See **pepper pot** 1.

Phi·lae (fī′lē) A former island in the Nile R. of SE Egypt; noted for its temple dedicated to Isis.

phi·lan·der (fĭ-lăn′dər) *intr.v.* **-dered, -der·ing, -ders** To carry on a sexual affair or many affairs, esp. with a frivolous or casual attitude. Used of a man. [< *philander,* lover, ult. < Gk. *philandros,* loving men : *phil-, philo-,* philo- + *anēr, andr-,* man; see **ner-** in App.] —**phi·lan′der·er** *n.*

phil·an·throp·ic (fĭl′ən-thrŏp′ĭk) also **phil·an·throp·i·cal** (-ĭ-kəl) *adj.* **1.** Of, relating to, or marked by philanthropy; humanitarian. **2.** Organized to provide humanitarian or charitable assistance. —**phil′an·throp′i·cal·ly** *adv.*

phi·lan·thro·py (fĭ-lăn′thrə-pē) *n., pl.* **-pies 1.** The effort or inclination to increase human well-being, as by charitable aid. **2.** Love of humankind in general. **3.** Something intended to promote human welfare. [LLat. *philanthrōpia* < Gk. < *philanthrōpos,* humane, benevolent : *phil-, philo-,* philo- + *anthrōpos,* man, mankind.] —**phi·lan′thro·pist** *n.*

phi·lat·e·ly (fĭ-lăt′l-ē) *n.* The collection and study of postage stamps, postmarks, and related materials; stamp collecting. [Fr. *philatélie* : Gk. *phil-, philo-,* philo- + Gk. *ateleia,* exemption from payment (*a-,* without; see A⁻¹ + *telos,* tax, charge; see **telə-** in App.).] —**phil′a·tel′ic** (fĭl′ə-tĕl′ĭk), **phil′a·tel′i·cal** (-ĭ-kəl) *adj.* —**phi·lat′e·list** *n.*

–phile or **–phil** *suff.* **1.** One that loves or has a strong affinity or preference for: *audiophile.* **2.** Loving; having a strong affinity or preference for: *Francophile.* [NLat. *-philus* < Gk. *-philos,* beloved, dear < *philos,* beloved, loving.]

Phi·le·mon¹ (fĭ-lē′mən, fī-) *n.* See table at **Bible.**

Phi·le·mon² (fĭ-lē′mən, fī-) *n. Greek Mythology* The husband of Baucis.

phil·har·mon·ic (fĭl′här-mŏn′ĭk, fĭl′ər-) *adj.* **1.** Devoted to or appreciative of music. **2.** Relating to a symphony orchestra. ❖ *n.* also **Philharmonic** A symphony orchestra or the group that supports it. [Fr. *philharmonique* < Ital. *filarmonico* : Gk. *phil-, philo-,* philo- + Gk. *harmonia,* theory of music < neut. pl. of *harmonikos,* musical; see HARMONIC.]

phil·hel·lene (fĭl-hĕl′ēn′) also **phil·hel·len·ist** (-hĕl′ə-nĭst) One who admires Greece or the Greeks. [Gk. *philellēn* : *phil-, philo-,* philo- + *Hellēn,* Greek.] —**phil·hel·len′ic** (fĭl′hĕ-lĕn′ĭk) *adj.* —**phil·hel′len·ism** *n.*

Phil. I. *abbr.* Philippine Islands

–philia *suff.* **1.** Tendency toward: *hemophilia.* **2.** Abnormal attraction to: *necrophilia.* [NLat. < Gk. *-philia* : *-philos, -phile* + *-iā, -ia.*]

–philiac *suff.* **1.** One that has a tendency toward: *hemophiliac.* **2.** One that has an abnormal attraction to: *coprophiliac.* [—PHILI(A) + –AC.]

–philic *suff.* Variant of **–philous.**

Phil·ip (fĭl′ĭp) See **Metacom.**

Philip, Prince. Duke of Edinburgh. b. 1921. Husband of Elizabeth II of Great Britain; given the title Prince in 1957.

Philip, Saint. fl. 1st cent. A.D. One of the 12 Apostles, who was present at the feeding of the 5,000.

Philip II¹ 382–336 B.C. King of Macedon (359–336) whose army defeated a Greek coalition at Chaeronea (338).

Philip II² or **Philip Augustus** 1165–1223. King of France (1180–1223) whose reign was marked by an expansion of royal territories.

Philip II³ 1527–98. King of Spain (1556–98), of Naples and Sicily (1554–98), and of Portugal (1580–98) as Philip I. In 1588 he launched the Spanish Armada.

Philip IV Known as "Philip the Fair." 1268–1314. King of France (1285–1314) and of Navarre (1284–1305) as the husband of Joan I (1273–1305).

Philip V 238–179 B.C. King of Macedon (221–179) who won the First Macedonian War with Rome (205) but was defeated in the Second Macedonian War (197).

Philip VI 1293–1350. King of France (1328–50) whose reign was dominated by the Hundred Years' War.

Phi·lip·pi (fĭ-lĭp′ī) An ancient town of N-central Macedonia; site of Antony and Octavian's defeat of Brutus and Cassius in 42 B.C. —**Phi·lip′pi·an** (-lĭp′ē-ən) *adj. & n.*

Phi·lip·pi·ans (fĭ-lĭp′ē-ənz) *pl.n.* (*used with a sing. verb*) See table at **Bible.**

Phi·lip·pic (fĭ-lĭp′ĭk) *n.* **1.** Any of the orations of Demosthenes against Philip of Macedon in the fourth century B.C. **2.** Any of the orations of Cicero against Antony in 44 B.C. **3. philippic** A harsh, often insulting verbal denunciation; a tirade.

Philippine mahogany *n.* Any of various southeast Asian hardwood trees of the genus *Shorea* and related genera. **2.** The wood of any of these trees.

Phil·ip·pines (fĭl′ə-pēnz′, fĭl′ə-pēnz′) A country of E Asia consisting of the **Philippine Islands,** an archipelago in the W Pacific Ocean SE of China; came under US control in 1898 after the Spanish-American War and achieved independence in 1946. Cap. Manila. Pop. 67,038,000. —**Phil′ip·pine′** *adj.*

Philippine Sea A section of the W Pacific Ocean E of the Philippines and W of the Marianas.

Phil·ips (fĭl′ĭps), **Ambrose** Called "Namby Pamby." 1674–1749. British poet known esp. for his collection *Pastorals* (1709).

Phil. Is. *abbr.* Philippine Islands

Phi·lis·ti·a (fĭ-lĭs′tē-ə) An ancient region of SW Palestine; strategically important in biblical times.

Phil·is·tine (fĭl′ĭ-stēn′, fĭ-lĭs′tĭn, -tēn′) *n.* **1.** A member of an Aegean people who settled ancient Philistia around the 12th century B.C. **2a.** A smug, ignorant, esp. middle-class person seen as indifferent or antagonistic to artistic and cultural values. **b.** One who lacks knowledge in a given area. ❖ *adj.* **1.** Of ancient Philistia. **2.** often **philistine** Boorish; barbarous. [< ME *Philistines,* Philistines < LLat. *Philistīnī* < Gk. *Philistīnoi* < Heb. *Pəlištîm* < *Pəlešet,* Philistia.]

Phil·is·tin·ism also **phi·lis·tin·ism** (fĭl′ĭ-stē-nĭz′əm, fĭ-lĭs′tə-nĭz′əm, -tē-nĭz′əm) *n.* An attitude of smug ignorance and conventionalism, esp. toward artistic and cultural values.

Phil·lips (fĭl′ĭps) A trademark used for a screw with a head having two intersecting perpendicular slots and for a screwdriver with a tip shaped to fit into these slots.

Phillips, Wendell 1811–84. Amer. abolitionist who was president of the American Antislavery Society (1865–70).

phil·lu·men·ist (fə-lōō′mə-nĭst) *n.* One who collects matchbooks or matchboxes. [PHIL(O)– + Lat. *lūmen,* light; see **leuk-** in App. + –IST.]

philo– or **phil–** *pref.* Having a strong affinity or preference for; loving: *philoprogenitive.* [Gk. < *philos,* beloved, loving.]

phil·o·den·dron (fĭl′ə-dĕn′drən) *n., pl.* **-drons** or **-dra** (-drə) Any of various climbing tropical American plants of the genus *Philodendron,* many of which are cultivated as houseplants. [NLat. *Philodendron,* genus name < Gk., neut. of *philodendros,* fond of trees (because it twines around trees) : *philo-, philo-* + *dendron,* tree; see **deru-** in App.]

Phi·lo Ju·dae·us (fĭ′lō jōō-dē′əs, -dā′-) also **Philo of Alexandria** 30? B.C.–A.D. 45? Alexandrian Jewish philosopher who attempted to interpret the Hebrew Scriptures in the terms of Neo-Platonist philosophy.

phi·lol·o·gy (fĭ-lŏl′ə-jē) *n.* **1.** Literary study or classical scholarship. **2.** See **historical linguistics.** [ME *philologie* < Lat. *philologia,* love of learning < Gk. *philologiā* < *philologos,* fond of learning or of words : *philo-, philo-* + *logos,* reason, speech; see –LOGY.] —**phi·lol′o·ger, phi·lol′o·gist** *n.* —**phil′o·log′ic** (fĭl′ə-lŏj′ĭk), **phil′o·log′i·cal** (-ĭ-kəl) *adj.* —**phil′o·log′i·cal·ly** *adv.*

phil·o·mel (fĭl′ə-mĕl′) *n.* A nightingale. [Alteration of ME *phylomene* < Med.Lat. *philomēna* < Lat. *Philomēla.* See PHILOMELA.]

Phil·o·me·la (fĭl′ə-mē′lə) *n. Greek Mythology* A princess of Athens who, after being raped by her brother-in-law Tereus, was avenged by her sister Procne and was later turned into a swallow or nightingale. [Lat. *Philomēla* < Gk. *Philomēlē.*]

phil·o·pro·gen·i·tive (fĭl′ō-prō-jĕn′ĭ-tĭv) *adj.* **1.** Producing many offspring; prolific. **2.** Loving children or one's own children. **3.** Of or relating to love of children.

phi·lo·sophe (fĭl′ə-sŏf′, fē′lô-zôf′) *n.* Any of the philosophical, political, and social writers of the 18th-century French Enlightenment. [Fr. < OFr., philosopher. See PHILOSOPHER.]

phi·los·o·pher (fĭ-lŏs′ə-fər) *n.* **1.** A student of or specialist in philosophy. **2.** One who lives and thinks according to a particular philosophy. **3.** One who is invariably calm and rational. [ME *philosophre* < alteration of OFr. *philosophe* < Lat. *philosophus* < Gk. *philosophos,* lover of wisdom, philosopher : *philo-, philo-* + *sophiā,* knowledge, learning.]

phi·los·o·phers' stone also **phi·los·o·pher's stone** (fĭ-lŏs′ə-fərz) *n.* A substance that was believed to have the power of transmuting base metal into gold.

phil·o·soph·i·cal (fĭl′ə-sŏf′ĭ-kəl) also **phil·o·soph·ic** (-ĭk) *adj.* **1.** Of, relating to, or based on a system of philosophy. **2.** Characteristic of a philosopher, as in equanimity, enlightenment, and wisdom. —**phil′o·soph′i·cal·ly** *adv.*

phi·los·o·phize (fĭ-lŏs′ə-fīz′) *v.* **-phized, -phiz·ing, -phiz·es** —*intr.* **1.** To speculate in a philosophical manner. **2.** To set forth or express a moralistic, often superficial philosophy. —*tr.* To consider (a matter) from a philosophical standpoint. —**phi·los′o·phiz′er** *n.*

phi·los·o·phy (fĭ-lŏs′ə-fē) *n., pl.* **-phies 1a.** Love and pursuit of wisdom. **b.** Investigation of the nature, causes, or principles of reality, knowledge, or values, based on logical reasoning rather than empirical methods. **c.** A system of thought based on or involving such investigation. **2.** The critical analysis of fundamental assumptions or beliefs. **3.** The disciplines presented in university curriculums of science and the liberal arts, except medicine, law, and theology. **4.** The discipline comprising logic, ethics, aesthetics, metaphysics, and epistemology. **5.** A set of ideas or beliefs relating to a particular field or activity; an underlying theory: *a philosophy of advertising.* **6.** A system of values by which one lives. [ME *philosophie* < OFr. < Lat. *philosophia* < Gk. *philosophiā* < *philosophos,* lover of wisdom, philosopher. See PHILOSOPHER.]

–philous or **–philic** *suff.* Having a strong affinity or preference for; loving: *anemophilous.* [< NLat. *-philus.* See –PHILE.]

phil·ter also **phil·tre** (fĭl′tər) *n.* **1.** A love potion. **2.** A magic potion or charm. ❖ *tr.v.* **-tered, -ter·ing, -ters** also **-tred, -tring, -tres** To enchant with or as if with a philter. [Fr. *philtre* < OFr. < Lat. *philtrum* < Gk. *philtron* < *philein,* to love < *philos,* beloved, loving.]

phi·mo·sis (fī-mō′sĭs, fĭ-) *n., pl.* **-ses** (-sēz) An abnormal con-

Philippines

philodendron

striction of the foreskin of the penis that prevents it from being drawn back to uncover the glans. [NLat. *phīmōsis* < Gk., a muzzling, phimosis < *phīmoun*, to muzzle < *phīmos*, muzzle.]

phle·bi·tis (flĭ-bī′tĭs) *n.* Inflammation of a vein. —**phle·bit′ic** (-bĭt′ĭk) *adj.*

phlebo– or **phleb–** *pref.* Vein: phlebology. [Gk. < *phleps*, *phleb–*, blood vessel, vein.]

phle·bog·ra·phy (flĭ-bŏg′rə-fē) *n.* See **venography.** —**phle′bo·gram** (flē′bə-grăm′) *n.*

phle·bol·o·gy (flĭ-bŏl′ə-jē) *n.* The branch of medicine that deals with veins and their diseases. —**phle·bol′o·gist** *n.*

phleb·o·scle·ro·sis (flĕb′ō-sklə-rō′sĭs) *n.* The thickening or hardening of the walls of veins.

phle·bot·o·mist (flĭ-bŏt′ə-mĭst) *n.* **1.** One who practices phlebotomy. **2.** One who draws blood for analysis or transfusion.

phle·bot·o·my (flĭ-bŏt′ə-mē) *n., pl.* **-mies** The act or practice of opening a vein by incision or puncture to remove blood as a therapeutic treatment. [ME *flebotomie* < OFr. *flebothomie* < LLat. *phlebotomia* < Gk. *phlebotomiā* < *phlebotomos*, opening a vein : *phlebo–*, *phlebo–* + *-tomos*, cutting; see –TOME.] —**phleb′o·tom′ic** (flĕb′ə-tŏm′ĭk), **phleb′o·tom′i·cal** (-ĭ-kəl) *adj.* —**phle·bot′o·mize′** *v.*

Phleg·e·thon (flĕg′ə-thŏn′) *n. Greek Mythology* A river of fire, one of the five rivers of Hades. [ME *Flegeton* < Lat. *Phlegethōn* < Gk. < the pr. part. of *phlegethein*, to blaze, var. of *phlegein*, to burn.]

phlegm (flĕm) *n.* **1.** Thick, sticky, stringy mucus secreted by the mucous membrane of the respiratory tract, as during a cold. **2.** One of the four humors of ancient and medieval physiology, thought to cause sluggishness, apathy, and evenness of temper. **3.** Sluggishness of temperament. **4.** Calm self-possession; equanimity. [ME *fleume*, mucous discharge, the humor phlegm < OFr. < Med.Lat. *phlegma, flegma* < LLat. *phlegma*, the humor phlegm < Gk., heat, the humor phlegm < *phlegein*, to burn.] —**phlegm′y** *adj.*

phleg·mat·ic (flĕg-măt′ĭk) also **phleg·mat·i·cal** (-ĭ-kəl) *adj.* **1.** Of or relating to phlegm. **2.** Having or suggesting a calm sluggish temperament; unemotional. [ME *fleumatik* < OFr. *fleumatique* < LLat. *phlegmaticus*, full of phlegm < Gk. *phlegmatikos* < *phlegma, phlegmat–*, heat, the humor phlegm < *phlegein*, to burn.] —**phleg·mat′i·cal·ly** *adv.*

phlo·em (flō′ĕm′) *n.* The food-conducting tissue of vascular plants, consisting of sieve tubes, fibers, parenchyma, and sclereids. [Ger. < Gk. *phloios*, bark.]

phlo·gis·tic (flō-jĭs′tĭk) *adj.* **1.** Of or relating to phlogiston. **2.** Of, relating to, or inducing inflammation or fever.

phlo·gis·ton (flō-jĭs′tŏn′, -tən) *n.* A hypothetical substance formerly thought to be a volatile constituent of all combustible substances, released as flame in combustion. [< Gk., neut. of *phlogistos*, inflammable < *phlogizein*, to set on fire < *phlox, phlog–*, flame.]

phlog·o·pite (flŏg′ə-pīt′) *n.* A yellow to dark brown mica, K(Mg,Fe)₃AlSi₃O₁₀(OH)₂, used in insulation. [Gk. *phlogōpos*, fiery-looking (*phlox, phlog–*, flame + *ōps*, eye, face; see **okʷ-** in App.) + –ITE¹.]

phlox (flŏks) *n., pl.* **phlox** or **phlox·es** Any of various North American plants of the genus *Phlox*, having opposite leaves and a salverform corolla. [Lat., a kind of flame-colored flower < Gk., flame, wallflower.]

phlyc·te·na also **phlyc·tae·na** (flĭk-tē′nə) *n., pl.* **-nae** (-nē) A small blister or vesicle, esp. from a mild burn. [NLat. < Gk. *phluktaina*, blister < *phlūzein*, to boil over, var. of *phlūein*.]

Phm *abbr. Bible* Philemon

Phnom Penh (pə-nôm′ pĕn′, nŏm′) The cap. of Cambodia, in the SW part on the Mekong R.; founded in the 14th cent. and the cap. of Cambodia after 1867. Pop. 400,000.

–phobe *suff.* One that fears or is averse to a specified thing: *ailurophobe*. [Fr. < Lat. *-phobus* < Gk. *-phobos*, fearing < *phobos*, fear.]

pho·bi·a (fō′bē-ə) *n.* **1.** A persistent, abnormal, or irrational fear of a specific thing or situation that compels one to avoid it, despite the awareness that it is not dangerous. **2.** A strong fear, dislike, or aversion. [< –PHOBIA.]

–phobia *suff.* An intense, abnormal, or illogical fear of a specified thing: *xenophobia*. [LLat. < Gk. *-phobia* < *phobos*, fear.]

pho·bic (fō′bĭk) *adj.* Of, relating to, arising from, or having a phobia. ❖ *n.* One who has a phobia.

–phobic or **–phobous** *suff.* **1.** Having a fear of or an aversion for: *xenophobic*. **2.** Lacking an affinity for: *lyophobic*. [LLat. *-phobicus* < Gk. *-phobikos* < *-phobiā*, -phobia.]

Pho·bos (fō′bŏs) *n.* One of the two satellites of Mars. [Gk., fear, deity of fear < *phobos*, fear. See –PHOBE.]

Pho·cae·a (fō-sē′ə) An ancient Ionian Greek city of W Asia Minor on the Aegean Sea in present-day Turkey; an important maritime state c. 1000 to 600 B.C.

pho·cine (fō′sīn) *adj. Zoology* Of, relating to, or resembling seals. [< Lat. *phōca*, seal < Gk. *phōkē*.]

Pho·cis (fō′sĭs) A region of ancient Greece N of the Gulf of Corinth; controlled the oracle at Delphi before 590 B.C.

phoe·be (fē′bē) *n.* Any of several medium-sized birds of the genus *Sayornis* of North America, noted for the flicking motion

phoebe
Say's phoebe
Sayornis saya

of the tail. [Imit. of its song.]

Phoe·be *n.* **1.** *Greek Mythology* Artemis. **2.** The moon. **3.** A satellite of Saturn. [ME *phebe* < Lat. *Phoebē* < Gk. *Phoibē* < fem. of *phoibos*, shining.]

Phoe·bus (fē′bəs) *n.* **1.** *Greek Mythology* Apollo. **2.** The sun. [ME *phebus* < Lat. *Phoebus* < Gk. *phoibos*, shining, Apollo.]

Phoe·ni·cia (fĭ-nĭsh′ə, -nē′shə) An ancient country of city-states of SW Asia along the E Mediterranean Sea in present-day Syria and Lebanon. Its people became the foremost navigators and traders of the Mediterranean by 1250 B.C.

Phoe·ni·cian (fĭ-nĭsh′ən, -nē′shən) *adj.* Of or relating to ancient Phoenicia or its people, language, or culture. ❖ *n.* **1.** A native or inhabitant of ancient Phoenicia. **2.** The Semitic language of ancient Phoenicia.

phoe·nix also **phe·nix** (fē′nĭks) *n.* **1.** *Mythology* A bird in Egyptian mythology that lived in the desert for 500 years and then consumed itself by fire, later to rise renewed from its ashes. **2.** A person or thing of unsurpassed excellence or beauty; a paragon. **3.** *Phoenix* A constellation in the Southern Hemisphere near Tucana and Sculptor. [ME *fenix* < OE and < OFr., both < Med.Lat. *fēnix* < Lat. *phoenix* < Gk. *phoinix*.]

Phoenix The cap. of AZ, in the S-central part NW of Tucson; settled c. 1868. Pop. 1,321,045.

Phoenix Islands A group of eight small islands of Kiribati in the central Pacific N of Samoa.

phon (fŏn) *n.* A unit of apparent loudness, equal in number to the intensity in decibels of a 1,000-hertz tone judged to be as loud as the sound being measured. [Ger. < Gk. *phōnē*, sound. See PHONE¹.]

pho·nate (fō′nāt′) *intr.v.* **-nat·ed, -nat·ing, -nates** To utter speech sounds; vocalize. —**pho·na′tion** *n.*

phon·a·thon (fŏn′ə-thŏn′) *n.* An intensive fundraising campaign in which callers solicit donations by telephone.

phone¹ (fōn) *n.* A telephone. ❖ *v.* **phoned, phon·ing, phones** —*intr.* To telephone. —*tr.* **1.** To get in touch with by telephone. **2.** To impart (news, for example) by telephone. [Short for TELEPHONE.]

phone² (fōn) *n.* A speech sound considered without reference to its status as a phoneme or an allophone in a language. [Gk. *phōnē*, sound, voice. See **bhā-** in App.]

–phone *suff.* **1.** Sound: *homophone*. **2.** Device that receives or emits sound: *geophone*. **3.** Speaker of a language: *Anglophone*. [< Gk. *phōnē*, sound, voice. See **bhā-** in App.]

phone card *n.* A prepaid card or a credit card that can be used to pay for telephone calls.

pho·ne·mat·ic (fō′nĭ-mät′ĭk) *adj.* Phonemic.

pho·neme (fō′nēm′) *n.* The smallest phonetic unit in a language capable of conveying a distinction in meaning, as the *m* of *mat* and the *b* of *bat*. [Fr. *phonème* < Gk. *phōnēma, phōnēmat–*, utterance, sound produced < *phōnein*, to produce a sound < *phōnē*, sound, voice. See **bhā-** in App.]

pho·ne·mic (fə-nē′mĭk, fō-) *adj.* **1.** Of or relating to phonemes. **2.** Of or relating to phonemics. **3.** Serving to distinguish phonemes or distinctive features. —**pho·ne′mi·cal·ly** *adv.*

pho·ne·mics (fə-nē′mĭks, fō-) *n.* (*used with a sing. verb*) The study and establishment of the phonemes of a language. —**pho·ne′mi·cist** (-mĭ-sĭst) *n.*

phone sex *n.* Sexually explicit talk engaged in by telephone, esp. to enhance autoerotic pleasure.

pho·net·ic (fə-nĕt′ĭk) *adj.* **1.** Of or relating to phonetics. **2.** Representing the sounds of speech with a set of distinct symbols for every sound: *phonetic spelling*. **3.** Of, relating to, or being features of pronunciation that are not phonemically distinctive in a language, as aspiration of consonants in English. [NLat. *phōnēticus*, representing speech sounds < Gk. *phōnētikos*, vocal < *phōnētos*, to be spoken < *phōnein*, to produce a sound < *phōnē*, sound, voice. See **bhā-** in App.] —**pho·net′i·cal** *adj.* —**pho·net′i·cal·ly** *adv.*

phonetic alphabet *n.* **1.** A standardized set of symbols used in phonetic transcription. **2.** Any of various systems of code words for identifying letters in voice communication.

pho·ne·ti·cian (fō′nĭ-tĭsh′ən) also **pho·net·i·cist** (fə-nĕt′ĭ-sĭst) *n.* An expert in phonetics.

pho·net·ics (fə-nĕt′ĭks) *n.* (*used with a sing. verb*) **1.** The branch of linguistics dealing with speech sounds and their production, combination, description, and representation by written symbols. **2.** The system of sounds of a given language.

pho·ney (fō′nē) *adj. & n.* Variant of **phony.**

phon·ic (fŏn′ĭk) *adj.* Of, relating to, or having the nature of sound, esp. speech sounds. —**phon′i·cal·ly** *adv.*

phon·ics (fŏn′ĭks) *n.* (*used with a sing. verb*) **1.** A method of teaching elementary reading and spelling based on the phonetic interpretation of ordinary spelling. **2.** Phonetics.

phono– or **phon–** *pref.* Sound; voice; speech: *phonology*. [Gk. *phōno–* < *phōnē*, sound, voice. See **bhā-** in App.]

pho·no·car·di·o·gram (fō′nə-kär′dē-ə-grăm′) *n.* A graphic record of heart sounds and murmurs that is produced by a phonocardiograph.

pho·no·car·di·o·graph (fō′nə-kär′dē-ə-grăf′) *n.* An instrument consisting of microphones and recording equipment used to make phonocardiograms. —**pho′no·car′di·o·graph′ic** *adj.*

—**pho′no·car′di·og′ra·phy** (-ŏg′rə-fē) *n.*

pho·no·gram (fō′nə-grăm′) *n.* A character or symbol, as in a phonetic alphabet, representing a word or phoneme in speech.

pho·no·graph (fō′nə-grăf′) *n.* A machine that reproduces sound by a stylus in contact with a grooved rotating disk. —**pho′no·graph′ic** *adj.* —**pho′no·graph′i·cal·ly** *adv.*

pho·nog·ra·phy (fə-nŏg′rə-fē, fō-) *n.* **1.** The science or practice of transcribing speech by means of symbols representing elements of sound; phonetic transcription. **2.** A system of shorthand based on phonetic transcription.

pho·no·lite (fō′nə-līt′) *n.* A light-colored volcanic rock composed largely of feldspars. —**pho′no·lit′ic** (-lĭt′ĭk) *adj.*

pho·nol·o·gy (fə-nŏl′ə-jē, fō-) *n., pl.* -**gies** **1.** The study of speech sounds in language or a language with reference to their distribution and patterning and to pronunciation rules. **2.** The sound system of a language: *the phonology of English.* —**pho′no·log′ic** (fō′nə-lŏj′ĭk), **pho′no·log′i·cal** (-ĭ-kəl) *adj.* —**pho′no·log′i·cal·ly** *adv.* —**pho·nol′o·gist** *n.*

pho·non (fō′nŏn′) *n.* The quantum of acoustic or vibrational energy, considered a discrete particle and used esp. in mathematical models to calculate thermal and vibrational properties of solids.

pho·no·re·cep·tion (fō′nō-rĭ-sĕp′shən) *n.* Perception of or response to sound waves. —**pho′no·re·cep′tor** (-tər) *n.*

pho·no·scope (fō′nə-skōp′) *n.* A device that produces a visible display of the mechanical properties of a sounding body.

pho·no·tac·tics (fō′nə-tăk′tĭks) *n.* (*used with a sing. verb*) The set of allowed arrangements or sequences of speech sounds in a given language. [PHONO- + *tactics,* arrangement of linguistic units; see TACTICS.]

pho·no·type (fō′nə-tīp′) *n.* **1.** A phonetic symbol used in printing. **2.** Text printed in phonetic symbols. —**pho′no·typ′ic** (fō′nə-tĭp′ĭk), **pho′no·typ′i·cal** (-ĭ-kəl) *adj.*

pho·no·typ·y (fō′nə-tī′pē) *n.* The practice of transcribing speech sounds by means of phonetic symbols. —**pho′no·typ′ist** *n.*

pho·ny also **pho·ney** (fō′nē) *adj.* -**ni·er,** -**ni·est** **1a.** Not genuine or real; counterfeit. **b.** False; spurious. **2.** Not honest or truthful; deceptive. **3a.** Insincere or hypocritical. **b.** Giving a false impression of truth or authenticity; specious. ❖ *n., pl.* -**nies** also -**neys** **1.** Something not genuine; a fake. **2a.** One who is insincere or pretentious. **b.** An impostor; a hypocrite. [Alteration of *fawney,* swindler's ring < Ir.Gael. *fáinne,* ring < OIr.] —**pho′ni·ly** *adv.* —**pho′ni·ness** *n.*

-**phony** *suff.* Sound: *telephony.* [Gk. *-phōnia* < *phōnē,* sound, voice. See **bhā-** in App.]

phoo·ey (fōō′ē) *interj.* Used to express disgust, disbelief, or contempt.

pho·rate (fôr′āt′, fōr′-) *n.* A toxic liquid, $C_7H_{17}O_2PS_3$, used as an insecticide esp. in soil treatment. [(PHOS)PHOR(US) + *(dithio)ate* (DI-¹ + THIO- + -ATE²).]

-**phore** *suff.* Bearer; carrier: *chromatophore.* [< Gk. *-phoros,* bearing < *pherein,* to carry. See **bher-¹** in App.]

-**phoresis** *suff.* Transmission: *electrophoresis.* [< Gk. *phorēsis,* a carrying < *phorein,* freq. of *pherein,* to bear. See **bher-¹** in App.]

phor·e·sy (fôr′ĭ-sē) *n.* A symbiotic relationship, esp. among arthropods and some fishes, in which one organism transports another organism of a different species. [NLat. *phoresia* < Gk. *phorēsis,* a carrying. See —PHORESIS.]

pho·ro·nid (fə-rō′nĭd) *n.* Any of the small, wormlike marine animals of the phylum Phoronida, inhabiting a chitinous tube and having a U-shaped digestive tract. [< NLat. *Phorōnida,* phylum name < *Phorōnis,* type genus, prob. < Lat., Phoronean, Argive (name of Io, priestess of Argos) < *Phorōneus,* son of Inachus, king of Argos < Gk.] —**pho·ro′nid** *adj.*

-**phorous** *suff.* Bearing: *gonophorous.* [< Gk. *-phoros* < *pherein,* to carry. See **bher-¹** in App.]

phos- *pref.* Light: *phosgene.* [Gk. *phōs,* light.]

phos·gene (fŏs′jēn′, fŏz′-) *n.* A volatile liquid or gas, $COCl_2$, used as a poison gas in World War I and in making plastics. [Fr. *phosgène* : Gk. *phōs,* light + Fr. *-gène,* -gen.]

phos·pham·i·don (fŏs-făm′ĭ-dŏn′) *n.* An insecticide, $C_{10}H_{19}ClNO_5P$, used to control mites and other plant pests. [PHOSPH(ATE) + AMID(E) + -ON³.]

phos·pha·tase (fŏs′fə-tās′, -tāz′) *n.* Any of numerous enzymes that catalyze the hydrolysis of esters of phosphoric acid. [PHOSPHAT(E) + -ASE.]

phos·phate (fŏs′fāt′) *n.* **1.** A salt or ester of phosphoric acid. **2.** A fertilizer containing phosphorus compounds. **3.** A soda fountain drink made by blending carbonated water with flavored syrup. —**phos·phat′ic** (-făt′ĭk) *adj.*

phosphate rock *n.* Any of various rocks composed largely of phosphate minerals, esp. apatite, used as fertilizer and as a source of phosphorous compounds.

phos·pha·tide (fŏs′fə-tīd′) *n.* See **phospholipid.**

phos·pha·tize (fŏs′fə-tīz′) *tr.v.* -**tized,** -**tiz·ing,** -**tiz·es** **1.** To change into phosphates or a phosphate. **2.** To treat with phosphate or phosphoric acid. —**phos′pha·ti·za′tion** (-tĭ-zā′shən) *n.*

phos·pha·tu·ri·a (fŏs′fə-tŏŏr′ē-ə, -tyŏŏr′-) *n.* An excess of phosphates in the urine.

phos·phene (fŏs′fēn′) *n.* A sensation of light caused by excitation of the retina by mechanical or electrical means rather than by light, as when the eyeballs are pressed through closed lids. [Fr. *phosphène* : Gk. *phōs,* light; see PHOS- + Gk. *phainein,* to cause to appear, to show.]

phos·phide (fŏs′fīd′) also **phos·phid** (-fĭd) *n.* A compound of phosphorus and a more electropositive element or radical.

phos·phine (fŏs′fēn′) also **phos·phin** (-fĭn) *n.* **1.** A spontaneously flammable poisonous gas, PH_3, used as a doping agent for solid-state components. **2.** Any of several analogues of an amine with phosphorus in place of nitrogen.

phos·phite (fŏs′fīt′) *n.* A salt or ester of phosphorous acid.

phospho- or **phosph-** *pref.* **1.** Phosphorus: *phosphine.* **2.** Phosphate: *phospholipid.* [< PHOSPHORUS.]

phos·pho·cre·a·tine (fŏs′fō-krē′ə-tēn′) also **phos·pho·cre·a·tin** (-tĭn) *n.* An organic compound, $C_4H_{10}N_3O_5P$, found in muscle tissue and capable of storing and providing energy for muscular contraction.

phos·pho·lip·id (fŏs′fō-lĭp′ĭd) *n.* A phosphorous-containing lipid composed mainly of fatty acids, a phosphate group, and a simple organic molecule.

phos·pho·ni·um (fŏs-fō′nē-əm) *n.* A univalent radical, PH_4, derived from phosphine. [PHOSPH(O)- + (AMM)ONIUM.]

phos·pho·pro·tein (fŏs′fō-prō′tēn′, -tē-ĭn) *n.* Any of a group of proteins with chemically bound phosphoric acid.

phos·phor (fŏs′fər, -fôr′) *n.* **1.** A substance that exhibits phosphorescence. **2.** The phosphorescent coating inside the screen of a cathode-ray tube. [Lat. *Phōsphorus,* the morning star. See PHOSPHORUS.]

phosphor bronze *n.* A hard corrosion-resistant bronze containing tin and some phosphorus, used in machine parts.

phos·pho·resce (fŏs′fə-rĕs′) *intr.v.* -**resced,** -**resc·ing,** -**resc·es** To persist in emitting light, unaccompanied by sensible heat or combustion, after exposure to and removal of a source of radiation. [Prob. back-formation < PHOSPHORESCENT.]

phos·pho·res·cence (fŏs′fə-rĕs′əns) *n.* **1.** Persistent emission of light following exposure to and removal of incident radiation. **2.** Emission of light with no burning or very slow burning without appreciable heat. —**phos′pho·res′cent** *adj.* —**phos′pho·res′cent·ly** *adv.*

phos·phor·ic (fŏs-fôr′ĭk, -fŏr′-) *adj.* Of, relating to, or containing phosphorus, esp. with valence 5 or a valence higher than that of a comparable phosphorous compound.

phosphoric acid *n.* A clear colorless liquid, H_3PO_4, used in fertilizers, detergents, food flavoring, and pharmaceuticals.

phos·pho·rism (fŏs′fə-rĭz′əm) *n.* Chronic phosphorus poisoning.

phos·pho·rite (fŏs′fə-rīt′) *n.* A sedimentary rock consisting predominantly of apatite and other phosphates.

phos·pho·rous (fŏs′fər-əs, fŏs-fôr′əs, -fōr′-) *adj.* Of, relating to, or containing phosphorus, esp. with valence 3 or a valence lower than that of a comparable phosphoric compound.

phosphorous acid *n.* A hygroscopic crystalline solid, H_3PO_3, used as a reducing agent and to produce phosphite salts.

phos·pho·rus (fŏs′fər-əs) *n.* **1.** *Symbol* **P** A highly reactive poisonous nonmetallic element occurring naturally in phosphates, esp. apatite, and existing in three allotropic forms, white, red, and black. An essential constituent of protoplasm, it is used in safety matches, pyrotechnics, incendiary shells, and fertilizers. Atomic number 15; atomic weight 30.9738; melting point (white) 44.1°C; boiling point 280°C; specific gravity (white) 1.82; valence 3, 5. See table at **element. 2.** A phosphorescent substance. [Lat. *Phōsphorus* < Gk. *phōsphoros,* bringing light, morning star : *phōs,* light + *-phoros,* -phorous.]

phos·pho·ryl·ase (fŏs′fər-ə-lās′, -lāz′) *n.* An enzyme that catalyzes the production of glucose phosphate from glycogen and inorganic phosphate.

phos·pho·ryl·ate (fŏs′fər-ə-lāt′) *tr.v.* -**at·ed,** -**at·ing,** -**ates** To add a phosphate group to (an organic molecule). —**phos′pho·ryl·a′tion** *n.* —**phos′pho·ryl·a′tive** *adj.*

phot (fōt) *n.* A unit of illumination equal to one lumen per square centimeter. [Gk. *phōs, phōt-,* light.]

pho·tic (fō′tĭk) *adj.* **1.** Of or relating to light. **2.** Penetrated by or receiving light. **3.** Being or relating to the layer of a body of water that receives sufficient sunlight for photosynthesis.

pho·to (fō′tō) *Informal n., pl.* -**tos** A photograph. ❖ *tr. & intr.v.* -**toed,** -**to·ing,** -**tos** To photograph or take photographs.

photo- or **phot-** *pref.* **1.** Light; radiant energy: *photosynthesis.* **2.** Photographic: *photomontage.* **3.** Photoelectric: *photoemission.* [Gk. *phōto-* < *phōs, phōt-.*]

pho·to·ac·tive (fō′tō-ăk′tĭv) *adj.* **1.** Capable of responding to light photoelectrically. **2.** Capable of responding to sunlight or ultraviolet radiation by chemical reaction.

pho·to·ag·ing (fō′tō-ā′jĭng) *n.* Damage to the skin as a result of exposure to ultraviolet radiation, manifested as wrinkles, discoloration, or susceptibility to cancer.

pho·to·au·to·troph (fō′tō-ô′tō-trŏf′, -trŏf′) *n.* An organism, such as a green plant, that can synthesize its own food from inorganic substances using light as an energy source. —**pho′to·au′to·troph′ic** *adj.*

pho·to·bi·ol·o·gy (fō′tō-bī-ŏl′ə-jē) *n.* The study of the ef-

phonograph

fects of light on living organisms. —**pho·to·bi·o·log·ic** (-bī′ə-lŏj′ĭk), **pho·to·bi·o·log′i·cal** (-ĭ-kəl) adj.

pho·to·bi·ot·ic (fō′tō-bī-ŏt′ĭk) adj. Biology Depending on light for life and growth.

pho·to·cell (fō′tō-sĕl′) n. A photoelectric cell.

photochemical smog n. Air pollution produced by the action of sunlight on hydrocarbons and other pollutants.

pho·to·chem·is·try (fō′tō-kĕm′ĭ-strē) n. The chemistry of the effects of light on chemical systems. —**pho′to·chem′i·cal** (-ĭ-kəl) adj. —**pho′to·chem′i·cal·ly** adv.

pho·to·co·ag·u·la·tion (fō′tō-kō-ăg′yə-lā′shən) n. Surgical coagulation of tissue by means of intense light energy, such as a laser beam, so as to destroy abnormal tissues or form adhesive scars, esp. in ophthalmology. —**pho′to·co·ag′u·late** v.

pho·to·com·pose (fō′tō-kəm-pōz′) tr.v. **-posed, -pos·ing, -pos·es** To prepare (written matter) for printing by photocomposition. —**pho′to·com·pos′er** n.

pho·to·com·po·si·tion (fō′tō-kŏm′pə-zĭsh′ən) n. The preparation of manuscript for printing by the projection of type characters on photographic film, from which printing plates are made.

pho·to·con·duc·tiv·i·ty (fō′tō-kŏn′dŭk-tĭv′ĭ-tē) n., pl. **-ties** Electrical conductivity enhanced by exposure to light. —**pho′to·con·duc′tion** n. —**pho′to·con·duc′tive** adj.

pho·to·cop·i·er (fō′tə-kŏp′ē-ər) n. A machine for photocopying.

pho·to·cop·y (fō′tə-kŏp′ē) tr.v. **-cop·ied, -cop·y·ing, -cop·ies** To make a photographic reproduction of (written, printed, or graphic material), esp. by xerography. ❖ n., pl. **-cop·ies** A photographic or xerographic reproduction.

pho·to·cur·rent (fō′tō-kûr′ənt, -kŭr′-) n. An electric current produced by illumination of a photoelectric material.

pho·to·de·com·po·si·tion (fō′tō-dē-kŏm′pə-zĭsh′ən) n. Chemical breakdown caused by radiant energy.

pho·to·de·grad·a·ble (fō′tō-dĭ-grā′də-bəl) adj. Capable of being chemically broken down by light.

pho·to·dis·in·te·gra·tion (fō′tō-dĭs-ĭn′tĭ-grā′shən) n. Nuclear disintegration or transformation caused by absorption of high-energy radiation, as of gamma rays.

pho·to·dra·ma (fō′tə-drä′mə, -drăm′ə) n. See **photoplay**.

pho·to·dy·nam·ic (fō′tō-dī-năm′ĭk) adj. **1.** Of or relating to the energy of light. **2.** Enhancing the effects of or inducing a toxic reaction to light, esp. to ultraviolet light.

pho·to·dy·nam·ics (fō′tō-dī-năm′ĭks) n. (used with a sing. verb) The science that deals with the activating effects of light on living organisms.

pho·to·e·lec·tric (fō′tō-ĭ-lĕk′trĭk) also **pho·to·e·lec·tri·cal** (-trĭ-kəl) adj. Of or relating to the electric effects caused by light. —**pho′to·e·lec′tri·cal·ly** adv.

photoelectric cell n. An electronic device having an electrical output that varies in response to incident radiation, esp. to visible light.

pho·to·e·lec·tron (fō′tō-ĭ-lĕk′trŏn′) n. An electron released or ejected from a substance by photoelectric effect.

pho·to·e·mis·sion (fō′tō-ĭ-mĭsh′ən) n. Emission of photoelectrons, esp. from metallic surfaces.

pho·to·en·grave (fō′tō-ĕn-grāv′) tr.v. **-graved, -grav·ing, -graves** To reproduce by photoengraving; make a photoengraving of. —**pho′to·en·grav′er** n.

pho·to·en·grav·ing (fō′tō-ĕn-grā′vĭng) n. **1.** The process of reproducing graphic material by transferring the image photographically to a plate or another surface, which is then etched for printing. **2.** A plate prepared by this process. **3.** A reproduction made by this process.

pho·to·es·say also **pho·to es·say** (fō′tō-ĕs′ā′) n. A series of photographs that conveys a story, usu. accompanied by a written text. —**pho′to·es′say·ist** n.

photo finish n. **1.** A race in which the leading contestants finish so close together that the winner must be determined by a photograph. **2.** Informal An extremely close competition.

pho·to·fin·ish·ing (fō′tō-fĭn′ĭ-shĭng) n. The act or business of developing camera films and printing photographs for customers. —**pho′to·fin′ish·er** n.

pho·to·flash (fō′tō-flăsh′) n. See **flashbulb**.

pho·to·flood (fō′tō-flŭd′) n. An electric lamp that produces a bright continuous light for photographic illumination.

pho·to·fluor·o·gram (fō′tə-floor′ə-grăm′, -flôr′-, -flōr′-) n. A photograph made by photofluorography.

pho·to·fluo·rog·ra·phy (fō′tə-floo-rŏg′rə-fē, -flô-, -flō-) n. The photographic record of x-ray images from a fluoroscope.

pho·tog (fə-tŏg′) n. Informal A photographer.

pho·to·gel·a·tin process (fō′tə-jĕl′ə-tĭn) n. See **collotype** 1.

pho·to·gene (fō′tə-jēn′) n. See **afterimage**.

pho·to·gen·ic (fō′tə-jĕn′ĭk) adj. **1.** Attractive as a subject for photography. **2.** Biology Producing or emitting light; phosphorescent. **3.** Caused or produced by light. —**pho′to·gen′i·cal·ly** adv.

pho·to·gram (fō′tə-grăm′) n. An image made by placing an object on photosensitive paper and exposing it to light.

pho·to·gram·me·try (fə-tŏg′rə-grăm′ĭ-trē) n. **1.** The process of making maps or scale drawings from photographs, esp. aerial photographs. **2.** The process of making precise measurements by means of photography. —**pho′to·gram·met′ric** (-grə-mĕt′rĭk) adj. —**pho′to·gram′me·trist** n.

pho·to·graph (fō′tə-grăf′) n. An image, esp. a positive print, recorded by a camera and reproduced on a photosensitive surface. ❖ v. **-graphed, -graph·ing, -graphs** —tr. To take a photograph of. —intr. **1.** To practice photography. **2.** To be the subject for photographs: She photographs well. —**pho′to·graph′a·ble** adj. —**pho·tog′ra·pher** (fə-tŏg′rə-fər) n.

pho·to·graph·ic (fō′tə-grăf′ĭk) also **pho·to·graph·i·cal** (-ĭ-kəl) adj. **1.** Of, relating to, or consisting of photography or a photograph. **2.** Used in photography. **3.** Resembling a photograph, esp. representing or simulating something with great accuracy and fidelity of detail. **4.** Capable of retaining accurate or vivid impressions: a photographic memory. —**pho′to·graph′i·cal·ly** adv.

pho·tog·ra·phy (fə-tŏg′rə-fē) n. **1.** The art or process of producing photographs. **2.** The art, practice, or occupation of taking and printing photographs. **3.** A body of photographs.

pho·to·gra·vure (fō′tō-grə-vyoor′) n. The process of printing from an intaglio plate, etched according to a photographic image.

pho·to·he·li·o·graph (fō′tō-hē′lē-ə-grăf′) n. A telescope equipped to photograph the sun.

pho·to·jour·nal·ism (fō′tō-jûr′nə-lĭz′əm) n. Journalism in which photographs supplemented by texts present a story.

pho·to·ki·ne·sis (fō′tō-kə-nē′sĭs, -kī-) n. Movement as a response to light. —**pho′to·ki·net′ic** (-nĕt′ĭk) adj.

pho·to·lith·o·graph (fō′tō-lĭth′ə-grăf′) n. A picture made by photolithography. ❖ tr.v. **-graphed, -graph·ing, -graphs** To reproduce by means of photolithography; make a photolithograph of. —**pho′to·li·thog′ra·pher** (-lĭ-thŏg′rə-fər) n.

pho·to·li·thog·ra·phy (fō′tō-lĭ-thŏg′rə-fē) n. A planographic printing process using plates made according to a photographic image. —**pho′to·lith′o·graph′ic** (-lĭth′ə-grăf′ĭk) adj. —**pho′to·lith′o·graph′i·cal·ly** adv.

pho·tol·y·sis (fō-tŏl′ĭ-sĭs) n. Chemical decomposition induced by light or other radiant energy. —**pho′to·lyt′ic** (fō′tə-lĭt′ĭk) adj. —**pho′to·lyt′i·cal·ly** adv.

pho·to·map (fō′tə-măp′) n. A map made by superimposing orienting data and markings on an aerial photograph. —**pho′to·map′** v.

pho·to·me·chan·i·cal (fō′tō-mĭ-kăn′ĭ-kəl) adj. Of, relating to, or involving any of various methods by which plates are prepared for printing by means of photography. —**pho′to·me·chan′i·cal·ly** adv.

pho·tom·e·ter (fō-tŏm′ĭ-tər) n. An instrument for measuring a property of light, esp. luminous intensity or flux.

pho·tom·e·try (fō-tŏm′ĭ-trē) n. Measurement of the properties of light, esp. luminous intensity. —**pho′to·met′ric** (fō′tə-mĕt′rĭk), **pho′to·met′ri·cal** (-rĭ-kəl) adj. —**pho′to·met′ri·cal·ly** adv. —**pho·tom′e·trist** n.

pho·to·mi·cro·graph (fō′tō-mī′krə-grăf′) n. A photograph made through a microscope. ❖ tr.v. **-graphed, -graph·ing, -graphs** To photograph (an object) through a microscope. —**pho′to·mi·crog′ra·pher** (-mī-krŏg′rə-fər) n. —**pho′to·mi′cro·graph′ic** adj. —**pho′to·mi·crog′ra·phy** n.

pho·to·mon·tage (fō′tō-mŏn-täzh′, -mŏn-) n. **1.** The technique of combining photographs in a montage. **2.** The picture produced by this technique.

pho·to·mul·ti·pli·er (fō′tō-mŭl′tə-plī′ər) n. An electronic sensing device used to detect electromagnetic energy of a wide range of frequencies and intensity levels.

pho·ton (fō′tŏn′) n. **1.** The quantum of electromagnetic energy, regarded as a discrete particle having zero mass, no electric charge, and an indefinitely long lifetime. **2.** A unit of retinal illumination, equal to the amount of light that reaches the retina through 1 square millimeter of pupil area from a surface having a brightness of 1 candela per square meter. —**pho·ton′ic** adj.

pho·to·neg·a·tive (fō′tō-nĕg′ə-tĭv) adj. Biology Exhibiting a negative phototactic or phototropic response.

pho·ton·ics (fō-tŏn′ĭks) n. (used with a sing. verb) The study or application of electromagnetic energy whose basic unit is the photon, incorporating optics, laser technology, materials science, and information storage.

pho·to·nu·cle·ar (fō′tō-noo′klē-ər, -nyoo′-) adj. Of or relating to a nuclear reaction induced by photons.

pho·to·off·set (fō′tō-ôf′sĕt′, -ŏf′-) n. A method of offset printing using photomechanical plates.

photo opportunity n. A brief period reserved for the press to photograph the participants in a newsworthy event.

pho·to·pe·ri·od (fō′tō-pîr′ē-əd) n. The duration of an organism's daily exposure to light, considered esp. with regard to its effect on growth and development. —**pho′to·pe′ri·od′ic** (-ŏd′ĭk), **pho′to·pe′ri·od′i·cal** (-ĭ-kəl) adj.

pho·to·pe·ri·od·ism (fō′tō-pîr′ē-ə-dĭz′əm) also **pho·to·pe·ri·o·dic·i·ty** (-dĭs′ĭ-tē) n., pl. **-isms** The response of an organism to changes in its photoperiod, esp. as indicated by vital processes.

pho·to·phil·ic (fō′tə-fĭl′ĭk) also **pho·toph·i·lous** (fō-tŏf′ə-ləs) adj. Biology Growing or functioning best in strong light.

pho·to·pho·bi·a (fō′tə-fō′bē-ə) n. **1.** An abnormal sensitivity to or intolerance of light, esp. by the eyes, as may be caused by eye inflammation, lack of pigmentation in the iris, or various diseases. **2.** An abnormal or irrational fear of light.

pho•to•pho•bic (fō'tə-fō'bĭk) *adj.* **1.** Exhibiting photophobia. **2.** Avoiding light. **3.** Growing best in the absence of light; photonegative.

pho•to•phore (fō'tə-fôr', -fōr') *n.* A light-producing organ found esp. in marine fishes that emits light from specialized structures or derives light from luminescent bacteria.

pho•to•phos•phor•y•la•tion (fō'tō-fŏs'fôr-ə-lā'shən, -fər-) *n.* Phosphorylation induced by radiant energy in photosynthesis.

pho•to•pi•a (fō-tō'pē-ə) *n.* Vision in bright light, mediated by cone cells of the retina; daylight vision. —**pho•to•pic** (-tō'pĭk, -tŏp'ĭk) *adj.*

pho•to•play (fō'tə-plā') *n.* A play filmed as a movie.

pho•to•pos•i•tive (fō'tō-pŏz'ĭ-tĭv) *adj. Biology* Drawn to light; exhibiting a positive phototactic or phototropic response.

pho•to•re•al•ism (fō'tō-rē'ə-lĭz'əm) *n.* A style of painting that is like photography in its attention to realistic detail. —**pho'to•re'al•ist** *adj. & n.* —**pho'to•re'al•is'tic** *adj.*

pho•to•re•cep•tion (fō'tō-rĭ-sĕp'shən) *n.* The detection, absorption, and use of light, as for vision in animals or photosynthesis in plants. —**pho'to•re•cep'tive** *adj.*

pho•to•re•cep•tor (fō'tō-rĭ-sĕp'tər) *n.* A nerve ending, cell, or group of cells specialized to sense or receive light.

pho•to•re•con•nais•sance (fō'tō-rĭ-kŏn'ə-səns, -zəns) *n.* Photographic aerial reconnaissance esp. of military targets.

pho•to•re•frac•tive (fō'tō-rĭ-frăk'tĭv) *adj.* Of or relating to a material that undergoes a change in refractive index when subjected to light or an electric field.

pho•to•res•pi•ra•tion (fō'tō-rĕs'pə-rā'shən) *n.* Oxidation of carbohydrates in plants with the release of carbon dioxide during photosynthesis.

pho•to•sen•si•tive (fō'tō-sĕn'sĭ-tĭv) *adj.* **1.** Sensitive or responsive to light or other radiant energy. **2.** *Medicine* Abnormally sensitive or reactive to light.

pho•to•sen•si•tiv•i•ty (fō'tō-sĕn'sĭ-tĭv'ĭ-tē) *n., pl.* **-ties 1.** Sensitivity or responsiveness to light. **2.** *Medicine* An abnormally heightened response, esp. of the skin, to sunlight or ultraviolet radiation, caused by certain disorders or chemicals.

pho•to•sen•si•ti•za•tion (fō'tō-sĕn'sĭ-tĭ-zā'shən) *n.* The act or process of inducing photosensitivity.

pho•to•sen•si•tize (fō'tō-sĕn'sĭ-tīz') *tr.v.* **-tized, -tiz•ing, -tiz•es** To make (an organism, for example) photosensitive.

pho•to•set (fō'tō-sĕt') *tr.v.* **-set, -set•ting, -sets** To photocompose. —**pho'to•set'ter** *n.*

pho•to•sphere (fō'tə-sfîr') *n.* The visible outer layer of a star, esp. of the sun. —**pho'to•spher'ic** (-sfîr'ĭk, -sfĕr'ĭk) *adj.*

Pho•to•stat (fō'tə-stăt') A trademark used for a photographic device for making positive or negative copies of graphic matter.

pho•to•syn•the•sis (fō'tō-sĭn'thĭ-sĭs) *n.* The process by which green plants and certain other organisms synthesize carbohydrates from carbon dioxide and water using light as an energy source and usu. releasing oxygen as a byproduct. —**pho'to•syn'the•size'** (-sīz') *v.* —**pho'to•syn•thet'ic** (-sĭn-thĕt'ĭk) *adj.* —**pho'to•syn•thet'i•cal•ly** *adv.*

pho•to•tax•is (fō'tō-tăk'sĭs) *n.* The movement of an organism or a cell toward or away from a source of light. —**pho'to•tac'tic** (-tăk'tĭk) *adj.*

pho•to•tox•ic (fō'tō-tŏk'sĭk) *adj.* Making the skin susceptible to damage by light. —**pho'to•tox•ic'i•ty** (-tŏk-sĭs'ĭ-tē) *n.*

pho•to•tran•sis•tor (fō'tō-trăn-zĭs'tər) *n.* A transistor having highly photosensitive electrical characteristics.

pho•tot•ro•pism (fō-tŏt'rə-pĭz'əm, fō'tō-trō'-) *n.* Growth or movement of a sessile organism toward or away from a source of light. —**pho•to•trop•ic** (fō'tə-trō'pĭk, -trŏp'ĭk) *adj.* —**pho'to•trop'i•cal•ly** *adv.*

pho•to•tube (fō'tō-tōōb', -tyōōb') *n.* An electron tube with a photosensitive cathode.

pho•to•type•set•ter (fō'tō-tīp'sĕt'ər) *n.* **1.** Any of various machines used in photocomposition. **2.** The operator of one of these machines.

pho•to•type•set•ting (fō'tō-tīp'sĕt'ĭng) *n.* See **photocomposition.**

pho•to•ty•pog•ra•phy (fō'tō-tī-pŏg'rə-fē) *n.* Photomechanical printing that resembles metal typography. —**pho'to•ty'po•graph'ic** (-tī'pə-grăf'ĭk), **pho'to•ty'po•graph'i•cal** (-ĭ-kəl) *adj.*

pho•to•vol•ta•ic (fō'tō-vŏl-tā'ĭk, -vōl-) *adj.* Capable of producing a voltage when exposed to radiant energy, esp. light. —**pho'to•vol•ta'ic** *n.*

photovoltaic cell *n.* See **solar cell.**

phr. *abbr.* phrase

phrag•mi•tes (frăg-mī'tēz) *n.* Any of several perennial long-stemmed reeds of the genus *Phragmites* in the grass family, found in wetlands. [Lat. *phragmītēs,* a hedge reed < Gk., fencing in < *phragma,* fence < *phrassein,* to fence in.]

phrasal verb *n.* An English verb complex consisting of a verb and one or more following particles that act as a complete syntactic and semantic unit, as *go on* in *What's going on?*

phrase (frāz) *n.* **1.** A meaningful sequence of words. **2a.** A char-

acteristic way or mode of expression. **b.** A brief, apt, and cogent expression. **3.** A word or group of words read or spoken as a unit and separated by pauses or other junctures. **4.** *Grammar* Two or more words in sequence forming a syntactic unit that is less than a complete sentence. **5.** *Music* A short passage or segment, often consisting of four measures or forming part of a larger unit. **6.** A series of dance movements forming a unit in a choreographic pattern. ❖ *v.* **phrased, phras•ing, phras•es** —*tr.* **1.** To express orally or in writing: *prose that is clearly phrased.* **2.** To pace or mark off (something read aloud or spoken) by pauses. **3.** *Music* **a.** To divide (a passage) into phrases. **b.** To combine (notes) in a phrase. —*intr.* **1.** To make or render phrases, as in reading aloud. **2.** *Music* To perform a passage with the correct phrasing. [Lat. *phrasis,* diction < Gk., speech, diction, phrase < *phrazein,* to point out, show.] —**phras'al** *adj.* —**phras'al•ly** *adv.*

phrase book *n.* A book of foreign language expressions and their translations.

phra•se•o•gram (frā'zē-ə-grăm') *n.* A symbol, such as one used in shorthand, that designates a particular phrase.

phra•se•o•graph (frā'zē-ə-grăf') *n.* A phrase represented by a phraseogram. —**phra'se•o•graph'ic** *adj.*

phra•se•ol•o•gy (frā'zē-ŏl'ə-jē) *n., pl.* **-gies 1.** The way in which words and phrases are used in speech or writing; style. **2.** A set of expressions used by a particular person or group: *was familiar with nautical phraseology.* —**phra'se•o•log'i•cal** (-ə-lŏj'ĭ-kəl) *adj.* —**phra'se•ol'o•gist** *n.*

phras•ing (frā'zĭng) *n.* **1.** The act of making phrases. **2.** The manner in which an expression is phrased. **3.** *Music* The manner in which a phrase is rendered.

phra•try (frā'trē) *n., pl.* **-tries 1.** A kinship group among the ancient Greeks of several patrilinear clans. **2.** *Anthropology* An exogamous subdivision of the tribe, constituting two or more related clans. [Gk. *phrātria* < *phrātēr, phrātr-,* fellow member of a clan. See **bhrāter-** in App.] —**phra'tric** *adj.*

phreak (frēk) *intr.v. Slang* **phreaked, phreak•ing, phreaks** To manipulate a telephone system illicitly to allow one to make calls without paying for them. [Alteration of FREAK[1] (influenced by PHONE).]

phre•at•ic (frē-ăt'ĭk) *adj.* Of or relating to ground water. [< Gk. *phrear, phreat-,* well, spring.]

phre•at•o•phyte (frē-ăt'ə-fīt') *n.* A deep-rooted plant that obtains water from a permanent ground supply or from the water table. [Gk. *phrear, phreat-,* well, spring + –PHYTE.] —**phre•at'o•phyt'ic** (-fĭt'ĭk) *adj.*

phre•net•ic (frə-nĕt'ĭk) or **phre•net•i•cal** (-ĭ-kəl) *adj.* Variants of **frenetic.**

–phrenia *suff.* Mental disorder: *schizophrenia.* [< Gk. *phrēn,* mind.]

phren•ic (frĕn'ĭk, frē'nĭk) *adj.* **1.** Of or relating to the mind. **2.** *Anatomy* Of or relating to the diaphragm: *the phrenic nerve.*

phre•ni•tis (frĭ-nī'tĭs) *n.* **1.** Inflammation of the diaphragm. **2.** Encephalitis. Not in scientific use.

phreno– or **phren–** *pref.* **1.** Mind: *phrenology.* **2.** Diaphragm: *phrenic.* [Gk. < *phrēn, phren-,* diaphragm, midriff, heart, mind.]

phre•nol•o•gy (frĭ-nŏl'ə-jē) *n.* The study of the shape and protuberances of the skull, based on the now discredited belief that they reveal character and mental capacity. —**phren'o•log'ic** (frĕn'ə-lŏj'ĭk, frē'nə-), **phren'o•log'i•cal** (-ĭ-kəl) *adj.* —**phre•nol'o•gist** *n.*

Phryg•i•a (frĭj'ē-ə) An ancient region of central Asia Minor in modern-day central Turkey; settled c. 1200 B.C. and flourished from the 8th to the 6th cent.

Phryg•i•an (frĭj'ē-ən) *adj.* Of or relating to Phrygia or its people, language, or culture. ❖ *n.* **1.** A native or inhabitant of Phrygia. **2.** The Indo-European language of the Phrygians.

Phrygian cap *n.* See **liberty cap.**

PHS *abbr.* Public Health Service

phthal•ein also **phthal•eine** (thăl'ēn', thăl'ē-ĭn, thā'lēn', thā'lē-ĭn, fthăl'-) *n.* Any of a group of chemical compounds formed by a reaction of phthalic anhydride with a phenol, from which certain synthetic dyes are derived.

phthal•ic (thăl'ĭk, fthăl'-) *adj.* Of, relating to, or derived from naphthalene. **2.** Relating to phthalic acid. [Short for *naphthalic acid* : NAPHTHAL(ENE) + –IC.]

phthalic acid *n.* A colorless crystalline organic acid, $C_6H_4(COOH)_2$, prepared from naphthalene and used in the synthesis of dyes, perfumes, and other organic compounds.

phthalic anhydride *n.* A crystalline compound, $C_6H_4(CO)_2O$, prepared by oxidizing naphthalene and used in the manufacture of dyes, resins, plasticizers, and insecticides.

phthal•in (thăl'ĭn, fthăl'-) *n.* Any of various colorless compounds derived from the reduction of phthaleins.

phthal•o•cy•a•nine (thăl'ō-sī'ə-nēn', fthăl'-) *n.* Any of several stable light-fast blue or green organic pigments derived from the basic compound $(C_6H_4C_2N)_4N_4$ and used in enamels, printing inks, linoleum, and plastics. [PHTHAL(IC) + CYANINE.]

phthi•ri•a•sis (thĭ-rī'ə-sĭs, thī-) *n.* Infestation with lice, esp. crab lice; pediculosis. [Lat. *phthīriāsis* < Gk. *phtheiríāsis* < *phtheiriān,* to be lousy < *phtheir,* louse.]

phthi•sis (thī'sĭs, tĭ'-, thĭs'ĭs, tĭs'-) *n.* **1.** A disease marked by the wasting away or atrophy of the body or a body part. **2.** Tuberculosis of the lungs. No longer in scientific use. [Lat. < Gk. *phthinein*, to waste away.] —**phthis'ic** *adj.*

phyco– *pref.* Seaweed; algae: *phycology.* [Gk. *phūko-* < *phūkos,* seaweed.]

phy·co·cy·a·nin (fī'kō-sī'ə-nĭn) *n.* A blue protein pigment occurring esp. in the cells of cyanobacteria.

phy·co·er·y·thrin (fī'kō-ĕr'ĭ-thrĭn) *n.* A red protein pigment occurring esp. in the cells of red algae.

phy·col·o·gy (fī-kŏl'ə-jē) *n.* The branch of botany that deals with algae. —**phy'co·log'i·cal** (fī'kə-lŏj'ĭ-kəl) *adj.* —**phy·col'o·gist** *n.*

phy·co·my·cete (fī'kō-mī'sēt', -mī-sēt') *n.* Any of various fungi that resemble algae, including certain molds and mildews. [< NLat. *Phȳcomycētēs,* class name : PHYCO- + –MYCETE.] —**phy'co·my·ce'tous** *adj.*

Phyfe (fīf), Duncan 1768?–1854. Scottish-born Amer. cabinetmaker who pioneered factory methods of construction.

phy·la (fī'lə) *n.* Plural of **phylum.**

phy·lac·ter·y (fī-lăk'tə-rē) *n., pl.* **-ies 1.** *Judaism* Either of two small leather boxes, each containing strips of parchment inscribed with quotations from the Hebrew Scriptures, traditionally worn by Jewish men during morning worship, except on the Sabbath and holidays. **2a.** An amulet. **b.** A reminder. [Ult. < LLat. *phylactērium* < Gk. *phulaktērion* < *phulaktēr,* guard < *phulax, phulak-*.]

phy·le (fī'lē) *n., pl.* **-lae** (-lē) A large citizens' organization based on kinship, constituting the largest political subdivision of an ancient Greek city-state. [Gk. *phūlē,* tribe, phyle. See **bheuə-** in App.] —**phy'lic** *adj.*

phy·let·ic (fī-lĕt'ĭk) *adj.* Of or relating to the evolutionary descent and development of a species or group of organisms; phylogenetic. [< Gk. *phūletikos,* of a tribesman < *phūletēs,* tribesman < *phūlē,* tribe. See **bheuə-** in App.] —**phy·let'i·cal·ly** *adv.*

-phyll *suff.* Leaf: *chlorophyll; sporophyll.* [< Gk. *phullon,* leaf. See PHYLLO-.]

phyl·lite (fīl'īt') *n.* A green, gray, or red metamorphic rock, similar to slate but often having a wavy surface and a distinctive micaceous luster. —**phyl·lit'ic** (fī-lĭt'ĭk) *adj.*

phyl·lo also **fi·lo** (fē'lō, fī'-) *n.* A pastry dough layered in very thin sheets that become flaky when baked, used esp. in Greek and Middle Eastern dishes. [Mod.Gk. *phullon* < Gk., leaf. See PHYLLO-.]

phyllo– or **phyll–** *pref.* Leaf: *phylloid.* [Gk. < *phullon,* leaf. See **bhel-** in App.]

phyl·lo·clade (fīl'ə-klād') also **phyl·lo·clad** (-klăd') *n.* A flattened photosynthetic branch or stem that resembles or performs the function of a leaf, as in certain cacti. [NLat. *phyllocladium* : PHYLLO- + Gk. *klados,* branch.]

phyl·lode (fīl'ōd) also **phyl·lo·di·um** (fī-lō'dē-əm) *n., pl.* **-lodes** also **-lo·di·a** (-lō'dē-ə) A flattened leafstalk that functions as a leaf, as in an acacia. [NLat. *phyllōdium* < Gk. *phullōdēs,* leaflike : *phullon,* leaf; see PHYLLO- + *-ōdēs,* adj. suff.; see COLLODION.] —**phyl'lo·di·al** *adj.*

phyl·loid (fīl'oid') *adj.* Resembling a leaf; leaflike.

phyl·lome (fīl'ōm') *n.* A leaf or a plant part that evolved from a leaf. —**phyl·lo'mic** (fī-lō'mĭk, -lŏm'ĭk) *adj.*

phyl·loph·a·gous (fī-lŏf'ə-gəs) *adj.* Feeding on leaves.

phyl·lo·pod (fīl'ə-pŏd') *n.* Any of various branchiopod crustaceans having phylloid swimming and respiratory appendages. ❖ *adj.* also **phyl·lop·o·dous** (fī-lŏp'ə-dəs) Of or relating to the phyllopods. —**phyl'lop·o·dan** (fī-lŏp'ə-dən) *adj. & n.*

phyl·lo·tax·y (fīl'ə-tăk'sē) also **phyl·lo·tax·is** (fīl'ə-tăk'sĭs) *n., pl.* **-tax·ies** also **-tax·es 1.** The arrangement of leaves on a stem. **2.** The principles governing leaf arrangement. —**phyl'lo·tac'tic** (-tăk'tĭk), **phyl'lo·tac'ti·cal** *adj.*

-phyllous *suff.* Having a specified kind or number of leaves: *gamophyllous.* [< NLat. *-phyllus* < Gk. *-phullos* < *phullon,* leaf. See **bhel-** in App.]

phyl·lox·e·ra (fīl'ŏk-sîr'ə, fī-lŏk'sər-ə) *n., pl.* **-rae** (-rē) Any of several small insects of the genus *Phylloxera* related to aphids, esp. *P. vitifoliae,* a widely distributed species harmful to grape crops. [NLat. *Phyllōxēra,* genus name : Gk. *phullo-,* phyllo- + Gk. *xēros,* dry.] —**phyl·lox'e·ran** *adj. & n.*

phy·lo·gen·e·sis (fī'lō-jĕn'ĭ-sĭs) *n.* See **phylogeny** 1.

phy·lo·ge·net·ic (fī'lō-jə-nĕt'ĭk) *adj.* **1.** Of phylogeny or phylogenetics. **2.** Relating to or based on evolutionary development or history. —**phy'lo·ge·net'i·cal·ly** *adv.*

phy·lo·ge·net·ics (fī'lō-jə-nĕt'ĭks) *n.* (used with a sing. verb) The study of phylogeny.

phy·log·e·ny (fī-lŏj'ə-nē) *n., pl.* **-nies 1.** The evolutionary development and history of a species or higher taxonomic grouping of organisms. **2.** The evolutionary development of an organ or other part of an organism. **3.** The historical development of a tribe or racial group. [Gk. *phūlon,* race, class; see **bheuə-** in App. + -GENY.] —**phy'lo·gen'ic** (-jĕn'ĭk) *adj.*

phy·lum (fī'ləm) *n., pl.* **-la** (-lə) **1.** *Biology* A primary division of a kingdom, as of the animal kingdom, ranking next above a class in size. See table at **taxonomy. 2.** *Linguistics* A large group of possibly related languages or language families. [NLat. *phȳlum* < Gk. *phūlon,* class. See **bheuə-** in App.]

phys– or **physi–** *pref.* Variants of **physio-.**

phylactery

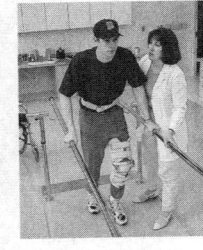
physical therapy

phys ed (fīz' ĕd') *n. Informal* Physical education.

phys·i·at·rics (fīz'ē-ăt'rĭks) *n.* (used with a sing. verb) **1.** See **physical medicine. 2.** Physical therapy.

phys·i·a·trist (fīz'ē-ăt'rĭst, fĭ-zī'ə-trĭst) *n.* **1.** A physician specializing in physical medicine. **2.** A physical therapist.

phys·i·a·try (fīz'ē-ăt'rē, fĭ-zī'ə-trē) *n.* **1.** See **physical medicine. 2.** Physical therapy.

phys·ic (fīz'ĭk) *n.* **1.** A medicine or drug, esp. a cathartic. **2.** *Archaic* The art or profession of medicine. ❖ *tr.v.* **-icked, -ick·ing, -ics 1.** To act on as a cathartic. **2.** To cure or heal. **3.** To treat with or as if with medicine. [ME *phisik* < OFr. *fisique,* medical science, natural science < Lat., natural science < Gk. *phusikē,* fem. of *phusikos,* of nature < *phusis,* nature. See **bheuə-** in App.]

phys·i·cal (fīz'ĭ-kəl) *adj.* **1a.** Of or relating to the body as distinguished from the mind or spirit. See Syns at **bodily. b.** Involving or marked by vigorous bodily activity. **c.** *Slang* Involving or characterized by violence. **2.** Of or relating to material things: *our physical environment.* **3.** Of or relating to matter and energy or the sciences dealing with them, esp. physics. ❖ *n.* A physical examination. [ME *phisical,* medical < Med.Lat. *physicālis* < Lat. *physica,* physics. See PHYSICS.] —**phys'i·cal'i·ty** (-kăl'ĭ-tē) *n.* —**phys'i·cal·ly** *adv.*

physical anthropology *n.* The branch of anthropology that deals with human evolutionary biology, physical variation, and classification. —**physical anthropologist** *n.*

physical chemistry *n.* Scientific analysis of the properties and behavior of chemical systems primarily by physical theory and technique.

physical education *n.* Education in the care and development of the human body, stressing athletics and including hygiene.

physical examination *n.* A medical examination to determine the condition of a person's health or physical fitness.

physical geography *n.* The study of the natural features of the earth's surface, esp. in its current aspects, including land formation, climate, currents, and distribution of flora and fauna.

phys·i·cal·ism (fīz'ĭ-kə-lĭz'əm) *n. Philosophy* The view that all that exists is ultimately physical. —**phys'i·cal·ist** *n.* —**phys'i·cal·is'tic** *adj.*

physically challenged *adj.* Having a physical disability or impairment, esp. one that limits mobility. See Usage Note at **challenged.** ❖ *n.* (used with a pl. verb) People who have physical disabilities or impairments considered as a group. Used with *the.*

physical medicine *n.* The branch of medicine that deals with the treatment, prevention, and diagnosis of disease by essentially physical means, including manipulation and exercise.

physical science *n.* Any of the sciences, such as physics, chemistry, astronomy, and geology, that analyze the nature and properties of energy and nonliving matter.

physical therapy *n.* The treatment of physical dysfunction or injury by the use of therapeutic exercise and the application of modalities, intended to restore or facilitate normal function or development. —**physical therapist** *n.*

phy·si·cian (fĭ-zĭsh'ən) *n.* **1.** A person licensed to practice medicine; a medical doctor. **2.** A person who practices general medicine as distinct from surgery. **3.** A person who heals or exerts a healing influence. [ME *fisicien* < OFr. < *fisique,* medical science. See PHYSIC.]

phy·si·cian's assistant (fĭ-zĭsh'ənz) *n., pl.* **physicians' assistants** A person trained to provide basic medical services, usu. under the supervision of a physician.

phys·i·cist (fīz'ĭ-sĭst) *n.* A scientist who specializes in physics.

phys·i·co·chem·i·cal (fīz'ĭ-kō-kĕm'ĭ-kəl) *adj.* **1.** Relating to both physical and chemical properties. **2.** Relating to physical chemistry.

phys·ics (fīz'ĭks) *n.* **1.** (used with a sing. verb) The science of matter and energy and of interactions between the two, grouped in traditional fields such as acoustics, optics, mechanics, and thermodynamics, as well as in modern extensions including atomic and nuclear physics, cryogenics, and particle physics. **2.** (used with a pl. verb) Physical properties, interactions, processes, or laws: *the physics of supersonic flight.* **3.** (used with a sing. verb) *Archaic* The study of the natural or material world and phenomena; natural philosophy. [< Lat. *physica* < Gk. *(ta) phusika,* (the things) of nature < neut. pl. of *phusikos* < *phusis,* nature. See **bheuə-** in App.]

physio– or **physi–** or **phys–** *pref.* **1.** Nature; natural: *physiography.* **2.** Physical: *physiotherapy.* [Gk. *phusio-* < *phusis,* nature. See **bheuə-** in App.]

phys·i·og·no·my (fīz'ē-ŏg'nə-mē, -ŏn'ə-mē) *n., pl.* **-mies 1a.** The art of judging human character from facial features. **b.** Divination based on this art. **2a.** Facial features, esp. when seen as revealing character. **b.** Aspect and character of an inanimate or abstract entity. [Ult. < LLat. *physiognōmia,* var. of *phusiognōmia* : Gk. *phusiognōmiā,* var. of *phusiognōmonia* : *phusio-,* physio- + *gnōmōn, gnōmon-,* interpreter; see **gnō-** in App.] —**phys'i·og·nom'ic** (-ŏg-nŏm'ĭk, -ə-nŏm'ĭk), **phys'i·og·nom'i·cal** (-ĭ-kəl) *adj.* —**phys'i·og'no·mist** *n.*

phys·i·og·ra·phy (fīz'ē-ŏg'rə-fē) *n.* See **physical geography.** —**phys'i·o·graph'ic** (-ə-grăf'ĭk), **phys'i·o·graph'i·cal** (-ĭ-kəl) *adj.*

phys·i·o·log·i·cal (fīz'ē-ə-lŏj'ĭ-kəl) also **phys·i·o·log·ic**

(-ĭk) *adj.* **1.** Of or relating to physiology. **2.** Consistent with or characteristic of the normal functioning of a living organism. **3.** Of or being an additive primary color. —**phys′i·o·log′i·cal·ly** *adv.*

physiological psychology *n.* The branch of psychology that studies the biological and physiological basis of behavior. —**physiological psychologist** *n.*

physiological saline *n.* A sterile solution of sodium chloride that is isotonic to body fluids, used to maintain living tissue temporarily and as a solvent for parenterally administered drugs.

phys·i·ol·o·gy (fĭz′ē-ŏl′ə-jē) *n.* **1.** The biological study of the functions of living organisms and their parts. **2.** All the functions of a living organism or any of its parts. —**phys′i·ol′o·gist** *n.*

phys·i·o·pa·thol·o·gy (fĭz′ē-ō-pə-thŏl′ə-jē) *n.* See patho-physiology. —**phys′i·o·path′o·log′ic** (-păth′ə-lŏj′ĭk), **phys′i·o·path′o·log′i·cal** (-ĭ-kəl) *adj.* —**phys′i·o·pa·thol′o·gist** *n.*

phys·i·o·ther·a·py (fĭz′ē-ō-thĕr′ə-pē) *n.* See physical therapy. —**phys′i·o·ther′a·peu′tic** (-thĕr′ə-pyōō′tĭk) *adj.* —**phys′i·o·ther′a·pist** *n.*

phy·sique (fĭ-zēk′) *n.* The body considered with reference to its proportions, muscular development, and appearance. [Fr., physical, physique < Lat. *physicus,* of nature < Gk. *phusikos < phusis,* nature. See bheuə- in App.] —**phy·siqued′** *adj.*

phy·so·stig·mine (fī′sō-stĭg′mēn′) also **phy·so·stig·min** (-mĭn) *n.* A crystalline alkaloid, $C_{15}H_{21}N_3O_2$, extracted from the Calabar bean and used in medicine as a miotic and cholinergic agent and to enhance memory in patients with Alzheimer's disease. [NLat. *Physostigma,* genus name of the Calabar bean (Gk. *phūsa,* bellows + STIGMA) + -INE².]

phy·sos·to·mous (fī-sŏs′tə-məs) *adj.* Having a connecting tube between the air bladder and a part of the alimentary canal. [< Gk. *phūsa,* bladder + Gk. *stoma,* mouth.]

–phyte *suff.* **1.** A plant with a specified character or habitat: *halophyte.* **2.** A pathological growth: *osteophyte.* [< Gk. *phuton,* plant < *phuein,* to make grow. See bheuə- in App.]

phyto– or **phyt–** *pref.* Plant: *phytogenesis.* [NLat. < Gk. *phuto-, phuton,* plant. See -PHYTE.]

phy·to·chem·i·cal (fī′tō-kĕm′ĭ-kəl) *adj.* Of or relating to phytochemistry or phytochemicals. ❖ *n.* A nonessential bioactive plant substance, such as a flavonoid, considered to have health benefits. —**phy′to·chem′i·cal·ly** *adv.*

phy·to·chem·is·try (fī′tō-kĕm′ĭ-strē) *n.* The chemistry of plants. —**phy′to·chem′ist** *n.*

phy·to·chrome (fī′tə-krōm′) *n.* A cytoplasmic pigment of green plants that absorbs light and regulates dormancy, seed germination, and flowering.

phy·to·es·tro·gen (fī′tō-ĕs′trə-jən) *n.* A compound occurring naturally in plants that acts like estrogen in the body.

phy·to·gen·e·sis (fī′tō-jĕn′ĭ-sĭs) *n.* The origin and evolutionary development of plants. —**phy′to·ge·net′ic** (-jə-nĕt′ĭk) *adj.*

phy·to·gen·ic (fī′tō-jĕn′ĭk) also **phy·tog·e·nous** (fī-tŏj′ə-nəs) *adj.* Having a plant origin, as coal.

phy·to·ge·og·ra·phy (fī′tō-jē-ŏg′rə-fē) *n.* The study of the geographic distribution of plants. —**phy′to·ge·og′ra·pher** *n.* —**phy′to·ge′o·graph′i·cal** (-jē′ə-grăf′ĭ-kəl), **phy′to·ge′o·graph′ic** (-grăf′ĭk) *adj.*

phy·tog·ra·phy (fī-tŏg′rə-fē) *n.* The science of plant description; descriptive botany.

phy·to·he·mag·glu·ti·nin (fī′tō-hē′mə-glōōt′n-ĭn) *n.* A hemagglutinin extracted from a plant.

phy·to·hor·mone (fī′tō-hôr′mōn′) *n.* See **plant hormone.**

phy·tol·o·gy (fī-tŏl′ə-jē) *n.* The study of plants; botany. —**phy′to·log′ic** (fī′tə-lŏj′ĭk), **phy′to·log′i·cal** (-ĭ-kəl) *adj.*

phy·ton (fī′tŏn′) *n.* The smallest unit of plant structure. [NLat. < Gk. *phuton,* plant. See PHYTO–.] —**phy·ton′ic** *adj.*

phy·to·nu·tri·ent (fī′tō-nōō′trē-ənt, -nyōō′-) *n.* See phytochemical.

phy·to·pa·thol·o·gy (fī′tō-pə-thŏl′ə-jē) *n.* The science of plant diseases. —**phy′to·path′o·log′ic** (-păth′ə-lŏj′ĭk), **phy′to·path′o·log′i·cal** (-ĭ-kəl) *adj.*

phy·toph·a·gous (fī-tŏf′ə-gəs) *adj.* Feeding on plants, including shrubs and trees. Used esp. of certain insects.

phy·to·plank·ton (fī′tō-plăngk′tən) *n.* Minute free-floating aquatic plants, algae, and other organisms. —**phy′to·plank′ton′ic** (-plăngk-tŏn′ĭk) *adj.*

phy·to·re·me·di·a·tion (fī′tō-rĭ-mē′dē-ā′shən) *n.* The use of plants to remove or neutralize contaminants, as in polluted soil or water.

phy·to·so·ci·ol·o·gy (fī′tō-sō′sē-ŏl′ə-jē, -shē-) *n.* The branch of ecology that deals with the traits, classification, relationships, and distribution of plant communities.

phy·to·tox·ic (fī′tō-tŏk′sĭk) *adj.* Poisonous to plants. —**phy′to·tox·ic′i·ty** (-tŏk-sĭs′ĭ-tē) *n.*

PHz *abbr.* petahertz

pi¹ (pī) *n.* **1.** (*also* pē) The 16th letter of the Greek alphabet. **2.** *Mathematics* A transcendental number, approx. 3.14159, represented by the symbol π, that expresses the ratio of the circumference to the diameter of a circle and appears as a constant in many mathematical expressions. [L.Gk. *pī* < Gk. *pei* < Phoenician *pē,* mouth, 17th letter of the Phoenician alphabet.]

pi² also **pie** (pī) *Printing n., pl.* **pis** also **pies** An amount of type that has been jumbled or thrown together at random. ❖ *v.* **pied** (pīd), **pi·ing, pies** also **pied, pie·ing, pies** —*tr.* To jumble or mix up (type). —*intr.* To become jumbled. [?]

pi·a (pī′ə, pē′ə) *n.* The pia mater. —**pi′al** *adj.*

Pia·cen·za (pyä-chĕn′zə, -tsä) A town of N Italy on the Po R. SE of Milan; founded as Placentia in 218 B.C. Pop. 102,252.

pi·ac·u·lar (pī-ăk′yə-lər) *adj.* **1.** Making expiation or atonement for a sacrilege: *piacular sacrifice.* **2.** Requiring expiation; wicked or blameworthy. [Lat. *piāculāris < piāculum,* propitiatory sacrifice < *piāre,* to appease < *pius,* dutiful.]

Pi·af (pē-äf′, pē′äf′), **Edith** 1915–63. French cabaret singer whose songs include *Non, je ne regrette rien.*

piaffe (pyäf) *intr.v.* **piaffed, piaf·fing, piaffes** To perform the piaffer. [Fr. *piaffer.*]

piaf·fer (pyäf′ər) *n.* A movement in which a horse trots in place with high action of the legs. [Fr. < *piaffer,* to strut, piaffe.]

Pia·get (pē′ə-zhā′, pyä-), **Jean** 1896–1980. Swiss psychologist noted for his studies of mental development in children.

pia ma·ter (mā′tər, mä′tər) *n.* The fine vascular membrane that closely envelops the brain and spinal cord under the arachnoid and the dura mater. [ME < Med.Lat. *pia māter* : Lat. *pia,* fem. of *pius,* tender + Lat. *māter,* mother (transl. of Ar. *'umm raqīqa* : *'umm,* mother + *raqīqa,* tender).]

pi·an·ism (pē-ăn′ĭz′əm, pē′ə-nĭz′əm) *n.* The technique or execution of piano playing.

pi·a·nis·si·mo (pē′ə-nĭs′ə-mō′) *Music adv. & adj.* In a very soft or quiet tone. ❖ *n., pl.* **-mos** A part of a composition played very softly or quietly. [Ital., superl. of *piano,* soft. See PIANO².]

pi·an·ist (pē-ăn′ĭst, pē′ə-nĭst) *n.* One who plays the piano.

pi·a·nis·tic (pē′ə-nĭs′tĭk) *adj.* **1.** Of or relating to the piano. **2.** Well adapted to the piano. —**pi′a·nis′ti·cal·ly** *adv.*

pi·an·o¹ (pē-ăn′ō, pyăn′ō) *n., pl.* **-os** A musical instrument with a manual keyboard actuating hammers that strike wire strings, creating sounds that may be softened or sustained by means of pedals. [Ital., short for *pianoforte.* See PIANOFORTE.]

pi·a·no² (pē-ä′nō, pyä′-) *Music adv. & adj.* In a soft or quiet tone. ❖ *n., pl.* **-nos** A passage to be played softly or quietly. [Ital. < LLat. *plānus,* smooth, graceful < Lat., flat. See pelə-² in App.]

pi·an·o·for·te (pē-ăn′ō-fôr′tā, -fôr′tē, pē-ăn′ō-fôrt′) *n.* A piano. [Ital. < (*gravecembalo col*) *piano* (*e*) *forte,* (harpsichord with) soft (and) loud : *piano,* soft; see PIANO² + *forte,* loud; see FORTE².]

pi·a·no hinge (pē-ăn′ō, pyăn′ō) *n.* A long narrow hinge with a pin running the entire length of its joint.

pi·as·sa·va (pē′ə-sä′və) also **pi·as·sa·ba** (-sä′bə) *n.* **1.** Either of two South American palm trees, *Attalea funifera* or *Leopoldinia piassaba,* from which a strong coarse fiber is obtained. **2.** The fiber of either of these plants, used for making ropes, brushes, and brooms. [Port. < Tupi *plaçaba.*]

pi·as·ter also **pi·as·tre** (pē-ăs′tər, -ä′stər) *n.* Piece of eight. [Fr. *piastre* < Ital. *piastra,* thin metal plate < Lat. *emplastrum,* medical dressing. See PLASTER.]

pi·az·za (pē-ăz′ə, -ä′zə) *n., pl.* **-zas 1.** (*also* pē-ät′sə, pyät′sä), *pl.* **pi·az·ze** (pē-ät′sə, pyät′sĕ) A public square in an Italian town. **2.** A roofed and arcaded passageway; a colonnade. **3.** *New England & Southern Atlantic US* A veranda. [Ital. < Lat. *platēa,* street < Gk. *plateia* (*hodos*), broad (way), fem. of *platus,* broad.]

pi·broch (pē′brŏкн) *n.* A series of variations on a martial theme or traditional dirge for the highland bagpipes. [Sc. Gael. *piobaireachd,* pipe music < *piobair,* piper < *piob,* pipe < MIr. *píp* < Med.Lat. *pīpa* < VLat. **pīpa.* See PIPE.]

pic (pĭk) *n., pl.* **pics** or **pix** (pĭks) *Slang* **1.** A photograph. **2.** A movie. [Short for PICTURE.]

pi·ca¹ (pī′kə) *n.* **1a.** A printer's unit of type size, equal to 12 points or about ⅙ of an inch. **b.** An equivalent unit of composition measurement used to determine the dimensions of lines, illustrations, or printed pages. **2.** A type size for typewriters, providing ten characters to the inch. [Prob. < Med.Lat. *pīca,* list of church services.]

pi·ca² (pī′kə) *n.* An abnormal craving or appetite for nonfood substances, such as dirt, paint, or clay. [NLat. *pīca* < Lat., magpie (< its omnivorous nature).]

pic·a·dor (pĭk′ə-dôr′, pē′kä-dôr′) *n., pl.* **-dors** or **pic·a·do·res** (pē′kä-dô′rĕs) A horseman in a bullfight who lances the bull's neck muscles so that it will tend to keep its head low for the later stages of the fight. [Sp. < *picar,* to prick. See PICARO.]

pi·can·te (pī-kän′tä) *adj.* **1.** Prepared so as to be spicy. **2.** Having a sauce typically containing tomatoes, onions, peppers, and vinegar. [Sp., pr. part. of *picar,* to bite, prick. See PICARO.]

pi·ca·ra (pē′kä-rä′) *n., pl.* **-ras** (-räz′, -räs′) **1.** A woman who is a rogue or adventurer. **2.** The main character in a picaresque novel when that character is a woman or girl. [Sp. *pícara,* fem. of *pícaro,* rogue. See PICARO.]

Pi·card (pē-kär′), **Jean** 1620–82. French astronomer who calculated the circumference of the earth (1668–70).

Pic·ar·dy (pĭk′ər-dē) A historical region of N France bordering on the English Channel; became part of the French crown lands in 1477.

pic·a·resque (pĭk′ə-rĕsk′, pē′kə-) *adj.* **1.** Of or involving clever rogues or adventurers. **2.** Of or relating to a genre of usu. satiric

Edith Piaf

Pablo Picasso
photographed in 1950

Piccadilly Circus

pickax

fiction that originated in Spain and depicts the adventures of a roguish hero in a corrupt society. ❖ *n.* One that is picaresque. [Fr. < Sp. *picaresco* < *pícaro*, picaro. See PICARO.]

pi•ca•ro (pē′kä-rō) *n., pl.* **-ros** (-rōz′, -rōs′) **1.** A rogue or adventurer. **2.** The main character in a picaresque work when that character is a man or boy. [Sp. *pícaro*, perh. < *picar*, to prick < VLat. **piccāre*. See PIQUE.]

pic•a•roon (pĭk′ə-ro͞on′) *n.* **1a.** A pirate. **b.** A pirate ship. **2.** See **picaro 1.** ❖ *intr.v.* **-rooned, -roon•ing, -roons** To act as a pirate. [Sp. *picarón*, augmentative of *pícaro*, picaro. See PICARO.]

Pi•cas•so (pĭ-kä′sō, -kăs′ō), **Pablo** 1881–1973. Spanish artist. One of the most prolific and influential artists of the 20th century, he excelled in painting, sculpture, etching, and ceramics. Picasso introduced the technique of collage and launched cubism with Georges Braque (1906–25).

pic•a•yune (pĭk′ə-yo͞on′) *adj.* **1.** Of little value or importance; paltry. **2.** Petty; mean. ❖ *n.* **1.** A Spanish-American half-real piece formerly used in parts of the southern United States. **2.** A five-cent piece. **3.** Something of very little value; a trifle. [Louisiana Fr. *picaillon*, small coin < Fr. < Provençal *picaioun* < *picaio*, money, perh. < O Provençal *piquar*, to jingle, clink < VLat. **piccāre*, to pierce. See PIQUE.] **—pic′a•yun′ish** *adj.*

Pic•ca•dil•ly Circus (pĭk′ə-dĭl′ē) A traffic junction and meeting place in central London, England, noted for the statue *Eros.*

pic•ca•lil•li (pĭk′ə-lĭl′ē) *n., pl.* **-lis** A pickled relish made of various chopped vegetables and hot spices. [Prob. alteration of PICKLE.]

Pic•card (pē-kärd′, -kär′), **Auguste** 1884–1962. Swiss physicist noted for extreme altitude and depth experiments.

pic•ca•ta (pĭ-kä′tə) *adj.* Sliced, sautéed, and served in a sauce containing lemon, butter, and spices. Used of meat or fish. [Ital., fem. of *piccato*, larded, p. part. of *piccare*, to prick (transl. of Fr. *piqué*, p. part. of *piquer*, to prick, lard) < VLat. **piccāre*. See PIQUE.]

pic•co•lo[1] (pĭk′ə-lō′) *n., pl.* **-los** A small flute pitched an octave above a regular flute. [Fr. < Ital., short for *(flauto) piccolo*, small (flute).] **—pic′co•lo′ist** *n.*

pic•co•lo[2] (pĭk′ə-lō′) *adj.* Of or being a musical instrument considerably smaller than the usual size. [Ital., small.]

pice (pīs) *n., pl.* **pice** A monetary unit worth 1/64 of a rupee, formerly used in India. [Hindi *paisā* < Skt. **padāṁśaḥ*, quarter part : *padam*, foot; see **ped-** in App. + *aṁśaḥ*, portion.]

pi•ce•ous (pī′sē-əs) *adj.* **1.** *Botany* Of or relating to pitch. **2.** Glossy black. [< Lat. *piceus* < *pix*, *pic-*, pitch.]

pick[1] (pĭk) *v.* **picked, pick•ing, picks** *—tr.* **1.** To select from a group; choose: *picked the best painting.* **2a.** To gather in; harvest. **b.** To gather the harvest from: *pick a row of corn.* **3a.** To remove the outer covering of; pluck. **b.** To tear off bit by bit: *pick meat from the bones.* **4.** To remove extraneous matter from (the teeth). **5.** To poke and pull at (something) with the fingers. **6.** To break up, separate, or detach by means of a sharp pointed instrument: *picked the clay.* **7.** To pierce or make (a hole) with a sharp pointed instrument. **8.** To take up (food) with the beak; peck. **9.** To steal the contents of: *picked his pocket.* **10.** To open (a lock) without the use of a key. **11.** To provoke: *pick a fight.* **12.** *Music* **a.** To pluck (an instrument's strings). **b.** To play (an instrument) by plucking its strings. **c.** To play (a tune) in this manner. *—intr.* **1.** To decide with care or forethought. **2.** To work with a pick. **3.** To find fault or make petty criticisms; carp. **4.** To be harvested or gathered. ❖ *n.* **1.** The act of picking, esp. with a sharp pointed instrument. **2.** The act of selecting or choosing; choice. **3.** Something selected as the most desirable; the best or choicest part. **4.** The amount or quantity of a crop that is picked by hand. **5.** *Basketball* A screen. ***—phrasal verbs:*** **pick apart** To refute or find flaws in by close examination. **pick at 1.** To pluck or pull at, esp. with the fingers. **2.** To eat sparingly or without appetite. **3.** *Informal* To nag. **pick off 1.** To shoot after singling out. **2.** *Baseball* To catch (a base runner) off base and put out with a quick throw, as from the pitcher or catcher. **3.** *Sports* To intercept, as a football pass. **pick on** To tease or bully. **pick out 1.** To choose or select. **2.** To discern from the surroundings; distinguish. **pick over** To sort out or examine item by item. **pick up 1a.** To take up (something) by hand. **b.** To collect or gather. **c.** To tidy up. **2.** To take on (passengers or freight, for example). **3.** *Informal* **a.** To acquire casually or by accident. **b.** To acquire (knowledge) by learning or experience. **c.** To claim: *picked up her shoes.* **d.** To buy. **e.** To accept (a bill or charge) in order to pay it. **f.** To come down with (a disease). **g.** To gain. **4.** *Informal* To take into custody. **5.** *Slang* To make casual acquaintance with, usu. in anticipation of sexual relations. **6a.** To come upon and follow. **b.** To come upon and observe. **7.** To continue after a break. **8.** *Informal* To improve in condition or activity. **9.** *Slang* To prepare a sudden departure: *She just picked up and left.* ***—idioms:*** **pick and choose** To select with great care. **pick holes in** To seek and discover flaws or a flaw in. **pick (one's) way** To find passage and make careful progress through it. **pick (someone) to pieces** To criticize sharply. **pick up on** *Informal* **1.** To take into the mind and understand, typically with speed. **2.** To notice. [ME *piken*, to prick < OE **pīcian*, to prick, and < OFr. *piquer*, to pierce (< VLat. **piccāre*; see PIQUE).] **—pick′er** *n.*

pick[2] (pĭk) *n.* **1.** A tool for breaking hard surfaces, consisting of a curved bar sharpened at both ends and fitted to a long handle. **2a.** A tool for picking, such as an ice pick or toothpick. **b.** A long-toothed comb, usu. designed for curly hair. **c.** A pointed projection on the front of the blade of a figure skate. **3.** *Music* A plectrum. [ME *pik*, var. of *pike*, sharp point. See PIKE[5].]

pick[3] (pĭk) *n.* **1.** A weft thread. **2.** A throw of the shuttle in a loom. ❖ *tr.v.* **picked, pick•ing, picks 1.** To throw (a shuttle) across a loom. **2.** *Archaic* To cast; pitch. [Dialectal < *pick*, to pitch, thrust, var. of PITCH[2].]

pick-and-roll (pĭk′ən-rōl′) *n. Basketball* An offensive play in which a player stops to block a defender for a teammate handling the ball and then slips behind the defender to accept a pass.

pick•a•nin•ny (pĭk′ə-nĭn′ē) *n., pl.* **-nies** *Offensive* Used as a disparaging term for a young Black child. [Poss. < Sp. *pequeño*, small + *niño*, child, or < Port. *pequenino*, dim. of *pequeno*, small.]

pick•ax or **pick•axe** (pĭk′ăks′) *n.* A pick, esp. with one end of the head pointed and the other end with a chisel edge for cutting through roots. [ME *picax*, alteration (influenced by *ax*, ax) of *picas* < OFr. *picois* (< *pic*, pick), and < Med.Lat. *pīcōsa*, both prob. < Lat. *pīcus*, woodpecker.] **—pick′ax′** *v.*

picked[1] (pĭkt) *adj.* **1.** Chosen by careful selection. **2.** Gathered, harvested, or plucked: *picked berries.*

picked[2] (pĭkt) *adj. Regional* Pointed: *a picked cap.* [< PICK[2].]

pick•er•el (pĭk′ər-əl, pĭk′rəl) *n., pl.* **pickerel** or **-els 1.** Any of several small North American freshwater game and food fishes of the genus *Esox*, esp. *E. reticulatus*, of the eastern and southern United States. **2.** Any of various fishes, such as the walleye, similar to the pickerel. **3.** *Chiefly British* A young pike. [ME *pikerel*, dim. of *pike*, pike. See PIKE[2].]

pick•er•el•weed (pĭk′ər-əl-wēd′, pĭk′rəl-) *n.* A freshwater plant *(Pontederia cordata)* of eastern North America having heart-shaped leaves with spikes of violet-blue flowers.

Pick•er•ing (pĭk′ər-ĭng), **Edward Charles** 1846–1919. Amer. astronomer noted for his work on photometry. His brother **William Henry** (1858–1938) discovered the ninth moon of Saturn (1899).

pick•et (pĭk′ĭt) *n.* **1.** A pointed stake often driven into the ground to support a fence, secure a tent, tether animals, mark points in surveying, or, when pointed at the top, serve as a defense. **2.** A military detachment held in readiness or advanced to warn of an enemy's approach. **3a.** A person or group of persons stationed outside a place of employment, usu. during a strike, to express grievance or protest and discourage entry by customers or nonstriking employees. **b.** A person or group of persons present outside a building to protest. ❖ *v.* **-et•ed, -et•ing, -ets** *—tr.* **1.** To enclose, secure, tether, mark out, or fortify with pickets. **2a.** To post as a picket. **b.** To guard with a picket. **3.** To post a picket or pickets during a strike or demonstration. *—intr.* To act or serve as a picket. [Fr. *piquet* < OFr. < *piquer*, to prick. See PIQUE.] **—pick′et•er** *n.*

picket fence *n.* A fence of upright pointed pickets.

picket line *n.* A line or procession of picketing protesters.

Pick•ett (pĭk′ĭt), **George Edward** 1825–75. Amer. Confederate general known for leading Pickett's Charge at Gettysburg (1863), in which three fourths of his troops were lost.

Pick•ford (pĭk′fərd), **Mary** 1893–1979. Canadian-born Amer. actress who appeared in numerous silent films.

pick•ing (pĭk′ĭng) *n.* **1.** The act of one that picks. **2. pickings** Something or a group of things that are or may be picked. **3a.** Leftovers. **b.** A share of spoils. In both senses often used in the plural.

pick•le (pĭk′əl) *n.* **1.** An edible product, esp. a cucumber, that has been preserved and flavored in a solution of brine or vinegar. **2.** A solution of brine or vinegar for preserving and flavoring food. **3.** A chemical solution, such as an acid, used as a bath to remove scale and oxides from the surface of metals before plating or finishing. **4.** *Informal* A disagreeable or troublesome situation; a plight. **5.** *Baseball* A rundown. ❖ *tr.v.* **-led, -ling, -les 1.** To preserve or flavor (food) in a brine or vinegar solution. **2.** To treat (metal) in a chemical bath. [ME *pikle*, highly seasoned sauce, prob. < MDu. *pekel*, pickle, brine.]

WORD HISTORY Trade with the Low Countries across the North Sea was important to England in the later Middle Ages, and it is probably because of this trade that we have the word *pickle.* Middle English *pikel*, the ancestor of our word, is first recorded around 1400 with the meaning "a spicy sauce or gravy served with meat or fowl." This sense is somewhat related to our word's possible Middle Dutch source *pekel*, a solution, such as spiced brine, for preserving and flavoring food. After coming into English the word *pickle* expanded its sense range in several ways. It was applied, as in Middle Dutch, to a pickling solution. Later *pickle* was used to refer to something so treated, such as a cucumber.

pick•led (pĭk′əld) *adj.* **1.** Preserved in or treated with pickle. **2.** *Slang* Intoxicated; drunk.

pick•le•worm (pĭk′əl-wûrm′) *n.* The larva of a pyralid moth *(Diaphania nitidalis)* of southern North America that feeds destructively on cucumbers and gourds.

pick•lock (pĭk′lŏk′) *n.* **1.** A person who picks locks, esp. a thief. **2.** An instrument for picking a lock.

pick-me-up (pĭk′mē-ŭp′) *n. Informal* A drink, often an alcoholic beverage, taken as a stimulant or a cure for a hangover.
pick•off (pĭk′ôf′, -ŏf′) *n.* **1.** *Baseball* A play in which a runner is caught off base and is put out by a throw, as from the pitcher. **2.** *Sports* An interception, as in football.
pick•pock•et (pĭk′pŏk′ĭt) *n.* One who steals from pockets.
pick•up (pĭk′ŭp′) *n.* **1a.** The act or process of picking up. **b.** *Sports* The act of striking or fielding a ball after it has touched the ground. **c.** Capacity for acceleration. **d.** *Informal* An improvement in condition or activity. **e.** *Slang* An arrest by a law enforcement officer. **2.** One that is picked up, esp.: **a.** Passengers or freight. **b.** *Informal* A hitchhiker. **c.** *Slang* A stranger with whom casual acquaintance is made, usu. in anticipation of sexual relations. **3.** *Accounting* A balance brought forward. **4.** Previous journalistic copy to which succeeding copy is added. **5.** *Music* See **upbeat** 1. **6.** That picks up, esp.: **a.** A pickup truck. **b.** The rotary rake on a piece of machinery, such as a harvester, that picks up windrowed hay or straw. **7.** *Electronics* **a.** A device that converts the oscillations of a phonograph needle into electrical impulses for subsequent conversion into sound. **b.** The tone arm of a record player. **8a.** The reception of light or sound waves for conversion to electrical impulses. **b.** The apparatus used for such reception. **c.** A telecast from outside a studio. **d.** The apparatus for transmitting a broadcast from an outside place to the broadcasting station. ❖ *adj.* Being, relating to, or involving people assembled informally for a temporary purpose.
pickup truck *n.* A light truck with an open body and low sides.
Pick•wick•i•an (pĭk-wĭk′ē-ən) *adj.* **1.** Simple and kind: *a Pickwickian uncle.* **2.** Meant or understood in an idiosyncratic or unusual way. [After Mr. *Pickwick,* central character in *The Posthumous Papers of the Pickwick Club* by Charles Dickens.]
pick•y (pĭk′ē) *adj.* **-i•er, -i•est** *Informal* Excessively meticulous; fussy.
pic•lo•ram (pĭk′lə-răm′, pī′klə-) *n.* A compound, $C_6H_3Cl_3N_2O_2$, used as a herbicide. [PIC(OLINE) + (CH)LOR(O)– + AM(INE).]
pic•nic (pĭk′nĭk) *n.* **1.** A meal eaten outdoors, as on an outing. **2.** *Slang* An easy task or a pleasant experience. **3.** A smoked section of pork foreleg and shoulder. ❖ *intr.v.* **-nicked, -nick•ing, -nics** To go on or hold a picnic. [Fr. *pique-nique,* prob. redup. of *piquer,* to pick. See PIQUE.] **—pic′nick•er** *n.*
pico– *pref.* **1.** One trillionth (10^{-12}): *picosecond.* **2.** Very small: *picornavirus.* [Sp. *pico,* beak, small quantity < Lat. *beccus,* beak, of Celt. orig.]
Pi•co del•la Mi•ran•do•la (pē′kō dĕl′ə mə-răn′də-lə, dĕl′lä mē-rän′dō-lä), Count **Giovanni** 1463–94. Italian philosopher and humanist famous for his 900 theses (1486).
pi•co•far•ad (pē′kə-făr′əd, -ăd, pī′-) *n.* One trillionth (10^{-12}) of a farad.
pic•o•line (pĭk′ə-lēn′, pī′kə-) *n.* Any of three isomeric liquids, $C_5H_4N(CH_3)$, found in coal tar, tobacco smoke, and bone oil and used as a solvent. [Lat. *pix, pic-,* pitch + –OL¹ + –INE².]
pi•cor•na•vi•rus (pē-kôr′nə-vī′rəs, pĭ-) *n., pl.* **-rus•es** Any of a group of small viruses that infect animals and consist of RNA surrounded by an icosahedral protein shell. [PICO– + RNA + VIRUS.]
pi•co•sec•ond (pē′kə-sĕk′ənd, pī′-) *n.* One trillionth (10^{-12}) of a second.
pi•cot (pē′kō, pē-kō′) *n.* A series of small embroidered loops forming an ornamental edging on some ribbon and lace. ❖ *tr.v.* **-coted** (-kō′tĭd), **-cot•ing** (-kō-ĭng), **-cots** (-kōz) To trim with picots. [Fr. < OFr. < *pic,* point < *piquer,* to prick. See PIQUE.]
pic•o•tee (pĭk′ə-tē′) *n.* A carnation having pale petals bordered by a darker color. [Fr. *picoté,* p. part. of *picoter,* to mark with points < *picot,* point, picot. See PICOT.]
pi•co•wave (pē′kə-wāv′, pī′-) *tr.v.* **-waved, -wav•ing, -waves** To irradiate (food) with gamma rays in order to kill insects or worms.
pic•quet (pĭ-kā′) *n.* Variant of **piquet.**
pic•rate (pĭk′rāt′) *n.* A salt or ester of picric acid.
pic•ric acid (pĭk′rĭk) *n.* A poisonous, explosive crystalline solid, $C_6H_2(NO_2)_3OH$, used in explosives, dyes, and antiseptics.
picro– or **picr–** *pref.* **1.** Bitter: *picrotoxin.* **2.** Picric acid: *picrate.* [Gk. *pikro–* < *pikros,* bitter.]
pic•ro•tox•in (pĭk′rə-tŏk′sĭn) *n.* A bitter crystalline compound, $C_{30}H_{34}O_{13}$, derived from the seed of an East Indian woody vine (*Animirta cocculus*) and used as a stimulant, esp. in treating barbiturate poisoning. **—pic′ro•tox′ic** *adj.*
Pict (pĭkt) *n.* One of an ancient people of northern Britain who in the ninth century joined with the Scots to form a kingdom that later became Scotland. [< ME *Pictes,* Picts < LLat. *Pictī* < Lat. *pictī,* pl. of *pictus,* painted. See PICTURE.]
Pict•ish (pĭk′tĭsh) *adj.* Of or relating to the Picts or their language or culture. ❖ *n.* The language of the Picts, of uncertain affiliation and extinct by the tenth century.
pic•to•gram (pĭk′tə-grăm′) *n.* See **pictograph.** [Lat. *pictus,* p. part. of *pingere,* to paint; see PICTOGRAPH + –GRAM.]
pic•to•graph (pĭk′tə-grăf′) *n.* **1.** A picture representing a word or idea; a hieroglyph. **2.** A record in hieroglyphic symbols. **3.** A pictorial representation of numerical data, esp. a graph, in which a given value is represented by a picture. [Lat. *pictus,* p. part. of *pingere,* to paint + –GRAPH.] **—pic′to•**

graph′i•cal•ly *adv.* **—pic•tog′ra•phy** (pĭk-tŏg′rə-fē) *n.*
Pic•tor (pĭk′tər) *n.* A constellation in the Southern Hemisphere near Columba and Dorado. [Lat. *pictor,* painter < *pingere,* to paint.]
pic•to•ri•al (pĭk-tôr′ē-əl, -tōr′-) *adj.* **1.** Relating to, characterized by, or composed of pictures. **2.** Represented as if in a picture. **3.** Illustrated by pictures. ❖ *n.* An illustrated periodical. [< Lat. *pictōrius* < *pictor,* painter. See PICTOR.] **—pic•to′ri•al′i•ty** (-ăl′ĭ-tē) *n.* **—pic•to′ri•al•i•za′tion** (-ə-lĭ-zā′shən) *n.* **—pic•to′ri•al•ize′** (-ə-līz′) *v.* **—pic•to′ri•al•ly** *adv.*
pic•ture (pĭk′chər) *n.* **1.** A visual representation or image drawn, photographed, or otherwise rendered on a flat surface. **2.** A visible image, esp. one on a flat surface or screen: *the picture reflected in the lake; focused the picture on the movie screen.* **3a.** A vivid or realistic verbal description. **b.** A vivid mental image. **4.** A person or object bearing a marked resemblance to another. **5.** A person or object that typifies or embodies an emotion or a state of mind. **6.** The chief circumstances of an event or time; a situation. **7.** A movie. **8.** A tableau vivant. ❖ *tr.v.* **-tured, -tur•ing, -tures 1.** To make a visible representation of. **2.** To form a mental image of; visualize. **3.** To describe vividly; make a verbal picture of. [ME < Lat. *pictūra* < *pictus,* painted, p. part. of *pingere,* to paint.]
picture card *n.* See **face card.**
picture hat *n.* A decorated broad-brimmed hat for women.
pic•tur•esque (pĭk′chə-rĕsk′) *adj.* **1.** Of, suggesting, or suitable for a picture. **2.** Striking or interesting in an unusual way; irregularly or quaintly attractive. **3.** Strikingly expressive or vivid. [Alteration of Fr. *pittoresque* < Ital. *pittoresco* < *pittore,* painter < Lat. *pictor.* See PICTOR.] **—pic′tur•esque′ness** *n.*
picture tube *n.* A cathode-ray tube in a television receiver that translates electrical signals into a picture on a luminescent screen.
picture window *n.* A large, usu. single-paned window that provides a broad outside view.
pic•ul (pĭk′əl) *n.* Any of various units of weight used in southeast Asia and China and equal to 100 catties. [Malay *pikul,* to carry the heaviest load a man can carry.]
PID *abbr.* pelvic inflammatory disease
pid•dle (pĭd′l) *v.* **-dled, -dling, -dles** *—tr.* To use triflingly; squander: *piddle away one's time.* *—intr.* **1.** To spend time aimlessly; diddle. **2.** *Informal* To urinate. [?]
pid•dling (pĭd′lĭng) *adj.* Trifling; trivial.
pid•dock (pĭd′ək) *n.* A marine bivalve mollusk of the family Pholadidae, having a long shell with which it bores into wood, rock, and clay, often destroying wharf pilings. [?]
pidg•in (pĭj′ən) *n.* A simplified form of speech that is usu. a mixture of two or more languages, has a rudimentary grammar and vocabulary, is used for communication between speakers of different languages, and is no one's native language. [< PIDGIN ENGLISH.] **—pidg′in•i•za′tion** *n.* **—pidg′in•ize′** *v.*
Pidgin English also **pidgin English** *n.* Any of several pidgins based on English and now spoken mostly on the Pacific islands and in West Africa. [Alteration of *pigeon English* < Pidgin E. *pigeon,* business, perh. < a Chinese pronunciation of E. BUSINESS.]
pi-dog (pī′dôg′, -dŏg′) *n.* Variant of **pye-dog.**
pie¹ (pī) *n.* **1.** A baked food composed of a pastry shell filled with fruit, meat, cheese, or other ingredients, and usu. covered with a pastry crust. **2.** A layer cake having cream, custard, or jelly filling. **3.** A whole that can be shared. **—idiom: pie in the sky** An empty wish or promise. [ME.]
pie² (pī) *n.* See **magpie** 1. [ME < OFr. < Lat. *pīca.*]
pie³ (pī) *n.* A monetary unit formerly used in India and Pakistan. [Hindi *pā'ī* < Skt. *pādikā,* quarter < *pāt, pad-,* foot, leg. See ped- in App.]
pie⁴ (pī) *n.* An almanac of services used in the English church before the Reformation. [Med.Lat. *pīca.*]
pie⁵ (pī) *n. & v. Printing* Variant of **pi².**
PIE *abbr.* Proto-Indo-European
pie•bald (pī′bôld′) *adj.* Spotted or patched, esp. in black and white. ❖ *n.* A piebald animal, esp. a horse. [PIE² + BALD.]
piece (pēs) *n.* **1.** A thing considered as a unit or element of a larger thing, quantity, or class; a portion: *a piece of string.* **2.** A portion or part separated from a whole: *a piece of cake.* **3.** An object that is one member of a group or class: *a piece of furniture.* **4.** An artistic, musical, or literary work or composition. **5.** An instance; a specimen: *a piece of sheer folly.* **6.** A declaration of one's opinions or findings: *spoke my piece.* **7.** A coin: *a ten-cent piece.* **8.** *Games* **a.** One of the counters or figures used in various board games. **b.** Any one of the chess figures other than a pawn. **9.** *Slang* A firearm, esp. a rifle. **10.** *Informal* A given distance: *"There was farm country down the road on the right a piece"* (James Agee). **11.** *Vulgar Slang* A sexually attractive person. ❖ *tr.v.* **pieced, piec•ing, piec•es 1.** To mend by adding pieces or a piece to. **2.** To join or unite the pieces of: *pieced together the vase.* **—idioms: a piece of (one's) mind** Frank and severe criticism; censure. **of a piece** Belonging to the same class or kind. **piece by piece** In stages: *took the clock apart piece by piece.* **piece of cake** *Informal* Something very easy to do. **piece of the action** *Slang* A share of an activity or of profits. [ME *pece* < OFr. < VLat. **pettia,* prob. of Celt. orig.]
pièce de ré•sis•tance (pyĕs də rə-zē-stäNs′) *n., pl.* **pièces de ré•sis•tance** (pyĕs) **1.** An outstanding accomplishment. **2.** The

picket fence

principal dish of a meal. [Fr. : *pièce*, piece + *de*, of, with + *résistance*, staying power, lastingness.]

piece goods *pl.n.* Fabrics made and sold in standard lengths.

piece·meal (pēs′mēl′) *adv.* **1.** By a small amount at a time; in stages: *articles acquired piecemeal.* **2.** In pieces; apart. ❖ *adj.* Accomplished or made in stages. [ME *pecemeale* : *pece*, piece; see PIECE + -*mele*, by a fixed measure (< OE -*mǣlum*, at a time < dative pl. of *mǣl*, appointed time; see **mē-**¹ in App.).]

piece of eight *n., pl.* **pieces of eight** An old Spanish silver coin. [< its original value of eight reals.]

piece·work (pēs′wûrk′) *n.* Work paid for according to the number of units turned out. —**piece′work′er** *n.*

pie chart *n.* A circular graph having radii dividing the circle into sectors proportional in angle and area to the relative size of the quantities represented.

pied¹ (pīd) *adj.* Patchy in color; splotched or piebald. [ME < *pie*, magpie. See PIE¹.]

pied² (pīd) *v. Printing* Past tense and past participle of **pi**².

pied-à-terre (pyā-dä-târ′) *n., pl.* **pieds-à-terre** (pyā-dä-târ′) A secondary or temporary place of lodging. [Fr. : *pied*, foot + *à*, to, on + *terre*, ground.]

pied-billed grebe (pīd′bĭld′) *n.* A small brown North American diving bird (*Podilymbus podiceps*) found in freshwater ponds and having a short heavy whitish bill.

pied·mont (pēd′mŏnt′) *n.* An area of land formed or lying at the foot of a mountain or mountain range. [After PIEDMONT.]

Piedmont 1. A historical region of NW Italy bordering on France and Switzerland; occupied by Rome in the 1st cent. B.C. **2.** A plateau region of the E US from NY to AL between the Appalachian Mts. and the Atlantic coastal plain. —**Pied′mon·tese′** (-tēz′, -tēs′) *adj. & n.*

pied piper *n.* **1.** A person who offers others strong yet delusive enticements. **2.** One who makes irresponsible promises. [After *The Pied Piper of Hamelin*, a poem by Robert Browning.]

pie-eyed (pī′īd′) *adj. Slang* Intoxicated; drunk.

Pie·gan (pē-găn′) *n., pl.* **Piegan** or **-gans** A member of the southernmost tribe of the Blackfoot confederacy, inhabiting northwest Montana and southern Alberta.

pie plant *n.* See **rhubarb** 1.

pier (pîr) *n.* **1a.** A platform extending from a shore over water and supported by piles or pillars, used to secure, protect, and provide access to ships or boats. **b.** Such a platform used esp. for entertainment. **2.** A supporting structure at the junction of connecting spans of a bridge. **3.** *Architecture* Any of various vertical supporting structures, esp.: **a.** A pillar, generally rectangular in cross section, supporting an arch or roof. **b.** The portion of a wall between windows, doors or other openings. **c.** A reinforcing structure that projects from a wall; a buttress. [ME *per*, bridge support, partly < Norman Fr. *pere*, piere (< OFr. *puiere*, a support < *puie* < *puier*, to support < VLat. **podiāre* < Lat. *podium*, platform; see PODIUM) and partly < Med.Lat. *pera* (< ONFr. *pire*, *piere*, breakwater, poss. < Lat. *petra*, rock; see PETROUS).]

pierce (pîrs) *v.* **pierced, pierc·ing, pierc·es** —*tr.* **1.** To cut or pass through with or as if with a sharp instrument; stab or penetrate. **2.** To make a hole or opening in; perforate. **3.** To make a way through: *The path pierced the woods.* **4.** To sound sharply through: *Shouts pierced the din.* **5.** To succeed in penetrating (something) with the eyes or the intellect. —*intr.* To penetrate into or through something. [ME *percen* < OFr. *percer*, prob. < VLat. **pertūsiāre* < Lat. *pertūsus*, p. part. of *pertundere*, to bore through : *per-*, per- + *tundere*, to beat.] —**pierc′er** *n.* —**pierc′ing** *adj.* —**pierc′ing·ly** *adv.*

Pierce, Franklin 1804–69. The 14th President of the US (1853–57), who failed to resolve the issue of slavery.

pierced (pîrst) *adj.* **1.** Cut through with a sharp instrument; perforated. **2.** Of or relating to a body part that has been perforated for the purpose of attaching a piece of jewelry. **3.** Of or relating to a piece of jewelry designed to be worn in a such a body part: *a pierced earring.*

Pi·e·ri·a (pī-îr′ē-ə) A region of ancient Macedonia including Mt. Olympus and Mt. Pierus.

Pi·e·ri·an Spring (pī-îr′ē-ən) *n.* **1.** *Greek Mythology* A spring in Macedonia, sacred to the Muses. **2.** A source of inspiration. [< Lat. *Pīerius*, sacred to the Muses < Gk. *Pīeriā*, Pieria. See **peiə-** in App.]

Pie·ro del·la Fran·ce·sca (pyâr′ō dĕl′ə frän-chĕs′kə, frän-) 1420?–92. Italian painter whose works show a mastery of geometric perspective.

pie·ro·gi also **pi·ro·gi** (pĭ-rō′gē) *n., pl.* **pierogi** also **pirogi** or **-gies** A semicircular dumpling with any of various fillings, such as finely chopped meat or vegetables, that is often sautéed after being boiled. [Pol., pl. of *pieróg*, dumpling, and Russ. *pirogi*, pl. of *pirog*.]

Pierre (pîr) The cap. of SD, in the central part on the Missouri R.; chosen as state cap. in 1889. Pop. 13,876.

Pier·rot (pē′ə-rō′, pyĕ-rō′) *n.* A character in French pantomime, dressed in a floppy white outfit. [Fr., dim. of the name *Pierre*, Peter < OFr. *Petrus*.]

pie·tà also **Pie·tà** (pyā-tä′) *n.* A painting or sculpture of the Virgin Mary holding and mourning over the dead body of Jesus. [Ital., pity, a pietà < Lat. *pietās*. See PIETY.]

pi·e·tism (pī′ĭ-tĭz′əm) *n.* **1.** Stress on the emotional and personal aspects of religion. **2.** Affected or exaggerated piety. **3.** Pietism A 17th- and 18th-century reform movement in the German Lutheran Church. [Ger. *Pietismus* < Lat. *pietās*. See PIETY.] —**pi′e·tist** *adj.* —**pi′e·tis′tic** *adj.* —**pi′e·tis′ti·cal·ly** *adv.*

pi·e·ty (pī′ĭ-tē) *n., pl.* **-ties 1.** The state or quality of being pious, esp.: **a.** Religious devotion and reverence to God. **b.** Devotion and reverence to parents and family. **2.** A devout act, thought, or statement. **3.** A conventional or hypocritical position or statement. [ME *piete*, mercy, pity < OFr. < Lat. *pietās*, dutiful conduct < *pius*, dutiful.]

piezo– *pref.* Pressure: *piezoelectricity.* [< Gk. *piezein*, to press tight, squeeze. See **sed-** in App.]

pi·e·zo·e·lec·tric·i·ty (pī-ē′zō-ĭ-lĕk-trĭs′ĭ-tē, -ē′lĕk-, pē-ā′zō-) *n.* The generation of electricity or of electric polarity in dielectric crystals subjected to mechanical stress or the generation of stress in such crystals subjected to an applied voltage. —**pi·e′zo·e·lec′tric, pi·e′zo·e·lec′tri·cal** *adj.*

pi·e·zom·e·ter (pī′ĭ-zŏm′ĭ-tər, pē′ĭ-) *n.* An instrument for measuring pressure, esp. high pressure. —**pi·e′zo·met′ric** (pī-ē′ĭ-zə-mĕt′rĭk, pē-ā′zə-) *adj.* —**pi′e·zom′e·try** *n.*

pif·fle (pĭf′əl) *intr.v.* **-fled, -fling, -fles** To talk or act feebly or futilely. ❖ *n.* Foolish or futile talk or ideas. [?]

pig (pĭg) *n.* **1a.** Any of several mammals of the family Suidae, having short legs, cloven hooves, bristly hair, and a cartilaginous snout used for digging. **b.** The edible parts of one of these mammals. **2.** *Informal* A person considered piglike, greedy, or gross. **3a.** A crude block of metal, chiefly iron or lead, poured from a smelting furnace. **b.** A mold in which such metal is cast. **c.** Pig iron. **4.** *Offensive Slang* Used as a disparaging term for a police officer. **5.** *Slang* A person holding sexist or racist views. ❖ *intr.v.* **pigged, pig·ging, pigs** To give birth to pigs; farrow. —*phrasal verb:* **pig out** *Slang* To eat ravenously; gorge oneself. —*idioms:* **in a pig's eye** *Slang* Under no condition; never. **pig in a poke** Something that is offered in a manner that conceals its true nature or value. [ME *pigge*, young pig, prob. < OE **picga.*]

pig bed *n.* A bed of sand in which pigs of iron are cast.

pig-boat (pĭg′bōt′) *n. Slang* A submarine.

pi·geon (pĭj′ən) *n.* **1.** Any of various birds of the widely distributed family Columbidae, typically having plump bodies, small heads, and short legs, esp. the rock dove. **2.** *Slang* One who is easily swindled; a dupe. [ME < OFr. *pijon*, prob. < VLat. **pībiō*, *pībiōn-*, alteration of LLat. *pīpiō*, young chirping bird, squab < *pīpīre*, to chirp.]

pigeon breast *n.* A chest deformity marked by a projecting sternum, often occurring as a result of infantile rickets.

pigeon hawk *n.* See **merlin**.

pi·geon·hole (pĭj′ən-hōl′) *n.* **1.** A small compartment or recess, as in a desk, for papers. **2.** A specific, often oversimplified category. **3.** The hole or holes in a pigeon loft for nesting. ❖ *tr.v.* **-holed, -hol·ing, -holes 1.** To place or file in a pigeonhole. **2.** To classify mentally. **3.** To put aside and ignore.

pigeon pea *n.* **1.** A tropical African shrub (*Cajanus cajan*) of the pea family, having hairy pods and edible seeds. **2.** A seed of this plant. [< the use of its seeds as pigeon feed.]

pi·geon-toed (pĭj′ən-tōd′) *adj.* Having the toes turned inward.

pig·fish (pĭg′fĭsh′) *n., pl.* **pigfish** or **-fish·es** A North American grunt (*Orthopristis chrysoptera*) with a piglike mouth, found along the Atlantic and Gulf coasts and important as a food fish. [< the grunting sound it makes.]

pig·ger·y (pĭg′ə-rē) *n., pl.* **-ies 1.** A place where pigs are raised or kept. **2.** Piggish conduct.

pig·gish (pĭg′ĭsh) *adj.* **1.** Greedy: *a piggish appetite.* **2.** Stubborn; pigheaded. —**pig′gish·ly** *adv.* —**pig′gish·ness** *n.*

pig·gy (pĭg′ē) *n., pl.* **-gies** *Informal* A little pig.

pig·gy·back (pĭg′ē-băk′) *adv. & adj.* **1.** On the shoulders or back. **2.** By or relating to a method of transportation, such as one by which truck trailers are carried on trains. **3.** In connection with something larger or more important. ❖ *n.* The act of transporting piggyback. ❖ *v.* **-backed, -back·ing, -backs** —*tr.* To cause to be aligned with an issue, for example, that is larger or more important. —*intr.* To function as if carried on the back of another. [Alteration of dialectal *pig back*, alteration of *pickaback*, *pickback*, *pick pack* : prob. dialectal *pick*, to throw (var. of PITCH²) + BACK¹ or PACK¹.]

piggy bank *n.* A child's coin bank, often shaped like a pig.

pig·head·ed (pĭg′hĕd′ĭd) *adj.* Stupidly obstinate. See Syns at **obstinate**. —**pig′head′ed·ly** *adv.* —**pig′head′ed·ness** *n.*

pig iron *n.* Crude iron cast in blocks.

pig Latin *n.* A code language formed by the transposition of the initial consonant to the end of the word and the suffixation of the vowel ā, as *igpay atinlay* for *pig Latin.*

pig lead (lĕd) *n.* Crude lead cast in blocks.

pig·let (pĭg′lĭt) *n.* A young pig.

pig·ment (pĭg′mənt) *n.* **1.** A substance that is used as coloring. **2.** Dry coloring matter, usu. an insoluble powder, that is mixed with water, oil, or another base to produce paint and similar products. **3.** A substance, such as chlorophyll or melanin, that produces a characteristic color in the tissue of plants or animals. ❖ *tr.v.* **-ment·ed, -ment·ing, -ments** To color with pigment. [ME, spice, red dye < Lat. *pigmentum* < *pingere*, to paint.] —**pig′**

men•tar′y (pĭg′mən-tĕr′ē) *adj.*

pig•men•ta•tion (pĭg′mən-tā′shən) *n. Biology* **1.** Coloration of tissues by pigment. **2.** Deposition of pigment by cells.

pigment cell *n. Biology* See **chromatophore** 1.

Pig•my or **pig•my** (pĭg′mē) *n. & adj.* Variants of **Pygmy.**

pi•gno•li (pēn-yō′lē) *pl.n.* Pine nuts. [Ital., pl. of *pignolo*, pine nut < *pigna*, pine cone, var. of *pina* < Lat. *pīnea*. See PINEAL.]

pig•nut (pĭg′nŭt′) *n.* **1.** Either of two deciduous trees *(Carya glabra* or *C. ovalis)* of the eastern United States having pinnately compound leaves and nuts with somewhat bitter kernels. **2.** The nut of a pignut. **3.** The wood of a pignut.

pig-out (pĭg′out′) *n. Slang* The act or an instance of voracious eating.

pig•pen (pĭg′pĕn′) *n.* **1.** A pen for pigs. **2.** *Slang* A dirty or very untidy place.

Pigs (pĭgz), **Bay of** An inlet of the Caribbean on the S coast of W Cuba; site of an ill-fated invasion by US-trained guerrilla troops on Apr. 17, 1961.

pig•skin (pĭg′skĭn′) *n.* **1.** The skin of a pig. **2.** Leather made from pigskin. **3.** *Sports* A football. **4.** *Informal* A saddle.

pigs•ney (pĭgz′nē) *n., pl.* **-neys** *Obsolete* **1.** A darling. **2.** An eye. [ME *piggesnye* : *pigges*, genitive of *pigge*, pig; see PIG + *nye* (< *an eye*, an eye; see EYE).]

pig•sty (pĭg′stī′) *n., pl.* **-sties 1.** A shelter where pigs are kept. **2.** *Slang* A dirty or very untidy place.

pig•tail (pĭg′tāl′) *n.* **1.** A plait of braided hair. **2.** A twisted roll of tobacco. **—pig′tailed′** *adj.*

pig•weed (pĭg′wēd′) *n.* **1.** See **goosefoot. 2.** See **amaranth** 1.

pi•ka (pī′kə, pē-) *n.* Any of several small tailless furry mammals of the genus *Ochotona* of the mountains of North America and Eurasia. [Evenki *piika*, perh. < Russ. *pikat'*, to squeak.]

pike[1] (pīk) *n.* A long spear formerly used by infantry. ❖ *tr.v.* **piked, pik•ing, pikes** To attack or pierce with a pike. [Fr. *pique* < OFr. < *piquer*, to prick. See PIQUE.] **—piked** *adj.*

pike[2] (pīk) *n., pl.* **pike** or **pikes 1.** A freshwater game and food fish *(Esox lucius)* of the Northern Hemisphere that has a long snout and attains a length of over 1.2 meters (4 feet). **2.** Any of various similar or related fishes. [ME, perh. < OE *pīc*, sharp point (< its shape).]

pike[3] (pīk) *n.* **1.** A turnpike. **2a.** A tollgate on a turnpike. **b.** A toll paid. ❖ *intr.v.* **piked, pik•ing, pikes** To move quickly. ***—idiom:* come down the pike** *Slang* To become prominent. [Short for TURNPIKE.]

pike[4] (pīk) *n. Chiefly British* A hill with a pointed summit. [ME, poss. of Scand. orig.]

pike[5] (pīk) *n.* A spike or sharp point, as on the tip of a spear. [ME < OE *pīc*.]

pike[6] (pīk) *n.* A mid-air position in sports such as diving and gymnastics in which the athlete bends to touch the toes or grab the calves while keeping the legs together and straight. [?]

Pike, Zebulon Montgomery 1779–1813. Amer. explorer noted for his expedition to the Rocky Mts. (1806–07).

piked whale (pīkt) *n.* A small dark gray whale *(Balaenoptera acutorostrata)* having a white underside.

pike•perch (pīk′pûrch′) *n., pl.* **pikeperch** or **-perch•es** A fish that is related to the perch and resembles the pike.

pik•er (pī′kər) *n. Slang* **1.** A cautious gambler. **2.** A person regarded as petty or stingy. [Poss. < *Piker*, a poor migrant to CA, after *Pike* County in eastern Missouri.]

Pikes Peak (pīks) A mountain, 4,303.6 m (14,110 ft), of the Rocky Mts. in central CO; named after Zebulon M. Pike.

pike•staff (pīk′stăf′) *n.* **1.** The shaft of a pike. **2.** A walking stick tipped with a metal spike.

pi•laf or **pi•laff** (pĭ-läf′, pē′läf′) also **pi•lau** (pĭ-läf′, -lô′, -lou′, pē′läf′, -lô′, -lou′) *n.* A steamed rice dish often with meat, shellfish, or vegetables. [Pers. *pilāw* < Turk. *pilâv*.]

pi•lar (pī′lər) *adj.* Of, relating to, or covered with hair. [NLat. *pilāris* < Lat. *pilus*, hair.]

pi•las•ter (pĭ-lăs′tər) *n. Architecture* A rectangular column with a capital and base, projecting only slightly from a wall as an ornamental motif. [Fr. *pilastre* < OFr. < OItal. *pilastro* < Med.Lat. *pīlaster* : Lat. *pīla*, pillar + Lat. *-aster*, n. suff., or blend of Lat. *pīla*, pillar, and LLat. *parastatēs*, pilaster (< Gk., stay, supporter : *para-*, beside; see PARA–[1] + *-statēs*, -stat).]

Pi•late (pī′lət), **Pontius** fl. 1st cent. A.D. Roman prefect of Judea who ordered Jesus's crucifixion.

Pi•la•tes (pĭ-lä′tēz) A trademark used for a system of conditioning exercises often performed on specialized apparatus.

Pi•la•tus (pĭ-lä′təs, pē-lä′to͞os) A peak, 2,121.3 m (6,955 ft), in the Alps of central Switzerland; so named supposedly because Pontius Pilate's body was thrown into a lake here.

pil•chard (pĭl′chərd) *n.* Any of various small marine fishes related to the herrings, esp. the edible species *Sardina pilchardus* of European waters. [?]

Pil•co•ma•yo (pĭl′kō-mä′yō, pēl′-) A river of central South America rising in central Bolivia and flowing c. 1,609 km (1,000 mi) SE to the Paraguay R.

pile[1] (pīl) *n.* **1.** A quantity of objects stacked or thrown together in a heap. **2.** *Informal* A large accumulation or quantity. **3.** *Slang* A large sum of money; a fortune. **4.** A funeral pyre. **5.** A very large building or complex of buildings. **6.** A voltaic pile. ❖ *v.* **piled, pil•ing, piles** *—tr.* **1a.** To place or lay in or as if in a pile or heap: *piled books onto the table.* **b.** To load (something) with a heap or pile: *piled the table with books.* **2.** To heap (something) in abundance. *—intr.* **1.** To form a heap or pile. **2.** To move in, out, or forward in a disorderly mass or group: *pile into a bus.* ***—phrasal verb:* pile up 1.** To accumulate. **2.** *Informal* To undergo a serious vehicular collision. [ME < OFr. < Lat. *pīla*, pillar.]

pile[2] (pīl) *n.* **1.** A heavy beam of timber, concrete, or steel, driven into the earth as a foundation or support for a structure. **2.** *Heraldry* A wedge-shaped charge pointing downward. **3.** A Roman javelin. ❖ *tr.v.* **piled, pil•ing, piles 1.** To drive piles into. **2.** To support with piles. [ME < OE *pīl*, shaft, stake < Lat. *pīlum*, spear, pestle.]

pile[3] (pīl) *n.* **1a.** Cut or uncut loops of yarn forming the surface of certain fabrics, such as velvet and carpeting. **b.** The surface so formed. **2.** Soft fine hair, fur, or wool. [< ME *piles*, hair, plumage, prob. < MDu. *pijl*, fine hair, and MLGer. *pile*, downy plumage, both < Lat. *pilus*, hair.] **—piled** *adj.*

pi•le•at•ed (pī′lē-ā′tĭd) also **pi•le•ate** (-ĭt) *adj.* **1.** *Botany* Having a pileus. **2.** Having a crest covering the pileum. Used of a bird. [< Lat. *pīleātus*, wearing a pileus < *pīleus*, felt cap.]

pileated woodpecker *n.* A large North American woodpecker *(Dryocopus pileatus)* having black and white plumage and a bright red crest.

pile driver *n.* A machine that drives a pile by raising a weight between guideposts and dropping it on the head of the pile.

piles (pīlz) *pl.n.* See **hemorrhoid** 2. [ME *piles* < Med.Lat. *pilī* < Lat. *pila*, ball.]

pi•le•um (pī′lē-əm) *n., pl.* **-le•a** (-lē-ə) The top of a bird's head, extending from the base of the bill to the nape. [NLat. *pīleum* < Lat. *pīleus*, felt cap.]

pile•up or **pile-up** (pīl′ŭp′) *n.* **1.** *Informal* A serious collision usu. involving several motor vehicles. **2.** An accumulation.

pi•le•us (pī′lē-əs) *n., pl.* **-le•i** (-lē-ī′) **1.** *Botany* The umbrellalike fruiting structure forming the top of a stalked fleshy fungus; the cap. **2.** A brimless skullcap worn by ancient Romans. **3.** See **caul** 1. [NLat. *pīleus* < Lat., cap.]

pile•wort (pīl′wûrt′, -wôrt′) *n.* Any of several plants, such as the lesser celandine and the fireweed, reputed to be effective in treating hemorrhoids. [< its use in treating piles.]

pil•fer (pĭl′fər) *v.* **-fered, -fer•ing, -fers** *—tr.* To steal (a small amount or item). *—intr.* To steal or filch. [< ME *pilfre*, spoils < OFr. *pelfre*.] **—pil′fer•age** (-ĭj) *n.* **—pil′fer•er** *n.*

pil•grim (pĭl′grəm) *n.* **1.** A religious devotee who journeys to a shrine or sacred place. **2.** One who embarks on a quest for something held sacred. **3.** A traveler. **4. Pilgrim** One of the English Separatists who founded Plymouth Colony in 1620. [ME < OFr. *peligrin* < LLat. *pelegrīnus*, alteration of Lat. *peregrīnus*, foreigner. See PEREGRINE.]

pil•grim•age (pĭl′grə-mĭj) *n.* **1.** A journey to a sacred place or shrine. **2.** A long journey or search, esp. one of exalted purpose or moral significance. **—pil′grim•age** *v.*

pilgrim bottle *n.* A costrel.

pi•li (pī′lī′) *n.* Plural of **pilus.**

pi•lif•er•ous (pī-lĭf′ər-əs) *adj.* Bearing or producing hair. [Lat. *pilus*, hair + –FEROUS.]

pil•i•form (pĭl′ə-fôrm′) *adj.* Having the form of a hair. [Lat. *pilus*, hair + –FORM.]

pil•ing (pī′lĭng) *n.* **1.** The act of driving piles. **2.** Piles considered as a group. **3.** A structure composed of piles.

Pil•i•pi•no (pĭl′ə-pē′nō) *n.* The Filipino language. [Tagalog < Sp. *filipino*. See FILIPINO.]

pill[1] (pĭl) *n.* **1.** A small, often coated pellet or tablet of medicine, taken by swallowing or by chewing. **2.** *Informal* An oral contraceptive. **3.** *Slang* Something, such as a baseball, that resembles a medicinal pill. **4.** Something distasteful but necessary. **5.** *Slang* An insipid or ill-natured person. ❖ *v.* **pilled, pil•ling, pills** *—tr.* **1.** To dose with pills. **2.** To make into pills. **3.** *Slang* To blackball. *—intr.* To form small balls resembling pills. [ME *pille* < MDu. or MLGer. *pille* and OFr. *pile*, all < Lat. *pilula*, dim. of *pila*, ball.]

pill[2] (pĭl) *v.* **pilled, pil•ling, pills** *—intr. Chiefly British* To come off, as in flakes or scales. *—tr. Archaic* To subject to extortion. [ME *pillen*, to plunder, peel < OE *pilian*; see PEEL[1], and < OFr. *piller*, to plunder. See PILLAGE.]

pil•lage (pĭl′ĭj) *v.* **-laged, -lag•ing, -lag•es** *—tr.* **1.** To rob of goods by force, esp. in wartime; plunder. **2.** To take as spoils. *—intr.* To take spoils by force. ❖ *n.* **1.** The act of pillaging. **2.** Something pillaged; spoils. [< ME, booty < OFr. < *piller*, to plunder < *peille*, rag (prob. < Lat. *pilleus*, *pīleus*, felt cap) or < VLat. **pīliāre*.] **—pil′lag•er** *n.*

pil•lar (pĭl′ər) *n.* **1a.** A slender freestanding vertical support; a column. **b.** Such a structure or one like it used for decoration. **2.** One who occupies a central or responsible position: *a pillar of the state.* ❖ *tr.v.* **-lared, -lar•ing, -lars** To support or decorate with pillars or a pillar. ***—idiom:* from pillar to post** From one place to another; hither and thither. [ME < OFr. *pilier* < Med.Lat. *pīlāre* < Lat. *pīla*.]

Pil•lars of Hercules (pĭl′ərz) Two promontories at the E end of the Strait of Gibraltar and the entrance to the Mediterranean Sea; usu. identified as Gibraltar in Europe and Jebel Musa in North Africa.

pike[2]
Northern pike
Esox lucius

pileated woodpecker
female pileated woodpecker
Dryocopus pileatus

ă	pat	oi	boy
ā	pay	ou	out
âr	care	o͝o	took
ä	father	o͞o	boot
ĕ	pet	ŭ	cut
ē	be	ûr	urge
ĭ	pit	th	thin
ī	pie	*th*	this
îr	pier	hw	which
ŏ	pot	zh	vision
ō	toe	ə	about, item
ô	paw		

Stress marks:
′ (primary);
′ (secondary), as in
lexicon (lĕk′sĭ-kŏn′)

piñata

pill·box (pĭl′bŏks′) *n.* **1.** A small box for pills. **2.** A woman's small hat with upright sides and a flat crown. **3.** A low-roofed concrete emplacement for a machine gun or antitank gun.

pill bug *n.* **1.** A small terrestrial isopod crustacean of the genus *Armadillidium,* related to the sow bug and having a convex segmented body enabling it to curl up when disturbed. **2.** A sow bug.

> **USAGE NOTE** Many people, especially science teachers, like to make a distinction between pill bugs and sow bugs. According to this usage, a pill bug, or roly-poly, is a terrestrial isopod crustacean whose segmented body gives it the ability to curl up into a ball when disturbed. A sow bug is any of several similar looking creatures that lack this ability. In popular usage, however, the names *pill bug* and *sow bug,* along with a number of other popular names, are used to refer to any of these tiny segmented crustaceans that are often mistaken for insects.

pil·lion (pĭl′yən) *n.* **1.** A pad or cushion for an extra rider behind the saddle on a horse or motorcycle. **2.** A bicycle or motorcycle saddle. [Prob. < Sc. Gael. *pillean,* dim. of *peall,* rug, or Ir.Gael. *pillín,* dim. of *pell,* rug, both < OIr. *pell* < Lat. *pellis,* animal skin. See **pel-**[1] in App.]

pil·lo·ry (pĭl′ə-rē) *n., pl.* **-ries** A wooden framework on a post, with holes for the head and hands, in which offenders were formerly locked to be exposed to public scorn as punishment. ❖ *tr.v.* **-ried, -ry·ing, -ries 1.** To ridicule and abuse. **2.** To put in a pillory as punishment. [ME < OFr. *pilori,* prob. < Lat. *pīla,* pillar.]

pil·low (pĭl′ō) *n.* **1.** A cloth case, stuffed with something soft, such as down, used to cushion the head, esp. during sleep. **2.** A decorative cushion. **3.** The pad on which bobbin lace is made. ❖ *v.* **-lowed, -low·ing, -lows** —*tr.* **1.** To rest (one's head) on or as if on a pillow. **2.** To serve as a pillow for: *Grass pillowed my head.* —*intr.* **1.** To rest on or as if on a pillow. **2.** To assume the shape of a pillow. [ME < OE *pyle* < West Gmc. **pulwī* < Lat. *pulvīnus.*] —**pil′low·y** *adj.*

pillow block *n.* A block that encloses and supports a journal or shaft; a bearing.

pil·low·case (pĭl′ō-kās′) *n.* A removable pillow covering.

pillow lace *n.* See **bobbin lace.**

pillow sham *n.* A decorative covering for a pillow on a bed.

pil·low·slip (pĭl′ō-slĭp′) *n.* See **pillowcase.**

pillow talk *n.* Intimate conversation between lovers in bed.

pi·lo·car·pine (pī′lō-kär′pēn′) *n.* A poisonous compound, $C_{11}H_{16}N_2O_2$, obtained from the jaborandi and used to induce sweating, promote salivation, and treat glaucoma. [NLat. *Pilocarpus,* jaborandi genus (Gk. *pilos,* wool, felt + Gk. *karpos,* fruit; see —CARP[2]) + —INE[2].]

pi·lose (pī′lōs) also **pi·lous** (-ləs) *adj.* Covered with fine soft hair. [Lat. *pilōsus* < *pilus,* hair.] —**pi·los′i·ty** (-lŏs′ĭ-tē) *n.*

pi·lot (pī′lət) *n.* **1.** One who operates or is licensed to operate an aircraft in flight. **2.** *Nautical* **a.** One licensed to conduct a ship into and out of port or through dangerous waters. **b.** The helmsman of a ship. **3.** One who guides or directs others. **4.** The part of a tool, device, or machine that leads or guides the whole. **5.** A pilot light, as in a stove. **6.** A television program produced as a prototype of a series under consideration. ❖ *tr.v.* **-lot·ed, -lot·ing, -lots 1.** To serve as the pilot of. **2.** To steer or control the course of. ❖ *adj.* **1.** Serving as a tentative model for future experiment or development. **2.** Serving or leading as guide. [Obsolete Fr., helmsman < OFr. < OItal. *pilota,* alteration of *pedota* < Med.Gk. **pēdōtēs* < Gk. *pēdon,* steering oar, pl. of *pēdon,* blade of an oar. See **ped-** in App.]

pi·lot·age (pī′lə-tĭj) *n.* **1.** *Nautical* **a.** The technique or act of piloting. **b.** The fee paid to a pilot. **2.** Aerial navigation by visual identification of landmarks.

pilot balloon *n.* A balloon for determining wind velocity.

pilot bread *n.* Hardtack.

pilot burner *n.* **1.** A small service burner, as in a boiler system, kept lighted to ignite main fires. **2.** See **pilot light** 1.

pilot engine *n.* A locomotive sent ahead of a train to check the track for safety and clearance.

pilot fish *n.* A small slender marine fish (*Naucrates ductor*) that often swims with larger fishes, esp. sharks and mantas.

pi·lot·house (pī′lət-hous′) *n. Nautical* An enclosed area, usu. on a vessel's bridge, from which the vessel is controlled.

pi·lot·ing (pī′lə-tĭng) *n.* **1.** The occupation or service of a pilot. **2.** *Nautical* Coastal navigation, as by reference to buoys.

pilot lamp *n.* A small electric lamp used to indicate that an electric circuit is energized.

pilot light *n.* **1.** A small jet of gas that is kept burning in order to ignite a gas burner, as in a stove. **2.** See **pilot lamp.**

pilot whale *n.* Any of several large, usu. black dolphins of the genus *Globicephala,* having an outward-curving globular forehead and noted for their occasional mass strandings.

pi·lous (pī′ləs) *adj.* **1.** Variant of **pilose. 2.** Of the nature of hair; consisting of hair; hairlike. [< Lat. *pilōsus.* See PILOSE.]

pil·sner or **Pil·sner** (pĭlz′nər, pĭls′-) also **pil·sen·er** or **Pil·sen·er** (pĭlz′nər, pĭls′-) also **pil·sen·er** or **Pil·sen·er** (pĭlz′zə-nər, -sə-, pĭlz′nər, pĭls′-) *n.* **1.** A light, golden lager having a strong flavor of hops. **2.** A tall, thin, footed beer glass. [Ger. *Pilsner, Pilsener,* of Pilsen (Plzeň), Czech Republic, where the beer was first brewed.]

Pil·sud·ski (pĭl-sōōt′skē), Jozef 1867–1935. Polish politician and first president (1918–22) of independent Poland.

Pilt·down man (pĭlt′doun′) *n.* A supposed early species of human postulated from a skull allegedly found in a gravel bed in about 1912 but determined in 1953 to be a fake. [After *Piltdown* Common in SE England.]

pil·ule (pĭl′yōōl) *n.* A small pill or pellet. [Fr. < OFr. *pillule* < Lat. *pilula.*] —**pil′u·lar** (pĭl′yə-lər) *adj.*

pi·lus (pī′ləs) *n., pl.* **-li** (-lī′) A hair or hairlike structure, esp. on the surface of a cell or microorganism. [Lat.]

Pi·ma (pē′mə) *n., pl.* **Pima** or **-mas 1.** A member of a Native American people inhabiting south-central Arizona. **2.** The Uto-Aztecan language of the Pima. [< Am.Sp. *Pimahitos,* Pimas < obsolete Pima *pimahaitu,* nothing (misunderstood by missionaries as a tribal name).] —**Pi′man** *adj.*

pima cotton *n.* A very strong high-grade cotton of medium staple developed from Egyptian cottons in the southwest United States. [After *Pima* County in southern Arizona, where it was developed.]

pi·men·to (pĭ-mĕn′tō) *n., pl.* **-tos 1.** See **allspice. 2.** Variant of **pimiento.** [Sp. *pimiento,* red or green pepper, pepper plant < *pimienta,* black pepper, pepper fruit < LLat. *pigmenta,* pl. of *pigmentum,* vegetable juice, condiment, pigment < Lat., pigment < *pingere,* to paint.]

pi meson *n.* See **pion.**

pi·mien·to (pĭ-mĕn′tō, -myĕn′tō) also **pi·men·to** (-mĕn′tō) *n., pl.* **-tos 1.** A garden pepper (*Capsicum annuum*) having a mild red fruit. **2.** The fruit of this plant, used in cookery, salad, and as stuffing for green olives. [Sp. See PIMENTO.]

pimp (pĭmp) *n.* One who finds customers for a prostitute; a procurer. ❖ —**pimp** *v.*

pim·per·nel (pĭm′pər-nĕl′, -nəl) *n.* Any of various plants of the genus *Anagallis,* esp. the scarlet pimpernel (*A. arvensis*), having opposite entire leaves and small red flowers. [ME *pimpernelle* < OFr., alteration of *piprenelle* < LLat. *pimpinella,* perh. < Lat. *piper,* pepper. See PEPPER.]

pim·ple (pĭm′pəl) *n.* A small swelling of the skin, usu. caused by acne; a papule or pustule. [ME.] —**pim′pled, pim′ply** *adj.*

pin (pĭn) *n.* **1a.** A short, straight, stiff piece of wire with a blunt head and a sharp point, used esp. for fastening. **b.** Something, such as a safety pin, that resembles such a piece of wire in shape or use. **c.** A whit; a jot. **2.** A slender, usu. cylindrical piece of wood or metal for holding or fastening parts together or serving as a support for suspending one thing from another, as: **a.** A thin rod for securing the ends of fractured bones. **b.** A peg for fixing the crown to the root of a tooth. **c.** A cotter pin. **d.** The part of a key stem entering a lock. **e.** *Music* One of the pegs securing the strings and regulating their tension on a stringed instrument. **f.** *Nautical* A belaying pin. **g.** *Nautical* A thole pin. **3.** An ornament fastened to clothing by means of a clasp. **4.** A rolling pin. **5.** *Sports* **a.** One of the wooden clubs at which the ball is aimed in bowling. **b.** A flagstick on a golf course. **c.** See **fall** 14a. **6. pins** *Informal* The legs. **7.** *Electronics* The part of a device that plugs into the socket or receptor of another component of a system. ❖ *tr.v.* **pinned, pin·ning, pins 1.** To fasten or secure with or as if with a pin or pins. **2.** To transfix. **3.** To place in a position of trusting dependence. **4a.** To hold fast; immobilize. **b.** *Sports* To win a fall from in wrestling. ❖ *adj.* Having a grain suggestive of the heads of pins. Used of leather. —*phrasal verbs:* **pin down 1.** To fix or establish clearly. **2.** To force (someone) to give firm opinions or precise information. **pin on** To attribute (a crime) to (someone). [ME < OE *pinn,* perh. < Lat. *pinna,* feather. See **pet-** in App.]

PIN *abbr.* personal identification number

pi·ña cloth (pēn′yə) *n.* A soft sheer fabric made from the fibers of pineapple leaves. [Sp. *piña,* pine cone, pineapple < Lat. *pīnea,* pine cone < *pīnus,* pine. See **peiə-** in App.]

pi·ña co·la·da (pēn′yə kō-lä′də, kə-, pĭn′yə, pēn′ə) *n.* A drink made of rum, coconut cream, and unsweetened pineapple juice. [Sp., strained pineapple : *piña,* pineapple + *colada,* strained.]

pin·a·fore (pĭn′ə-fôr′, -fōr′) *n.* A sleeveless garment similar to an apron, worn esp. by girls as a dress or an overdress. [PIN + AFORE (formerly pinned to the front of the dress).]

Pi·nang (pə-näng′, pē′näng′) See **George Town** 1.

pi·nas·ter (pī-năs′tər) *n.* A Mediterranean pine tree (*Pinus pinaster*) having a characteristic pyramidal form and needles in fascicles of two. [Lat., wild pine < *pīnus,* pine. See PINE[1].]

pi·ña·ta (pēn-yä′tə) *n.* A decorated container filled with candy and toys and suspended from a height, intended to be broken by blindfolded players with sticks in a game of Latin-American origin. [Sp. < Ital. *pignatta,* a pot, prob. < dialectal *pigna,* pine cone < Lat. *pīnea.* See PINEAL.]

pin·ball (pĭn′bôl′) *n.* A game played on a device in which a ball rolls down a slanted surface having obstacles and targets, often equipped with flippers to keep the ball in play.

pince-nez (păns′nā′, pĭns′-) *n., pl.* **pince-nez** (-nāz′, -nā′) Eyeglasses clipped to the bridge of the nose. [Fr. : *pincer,* to pinch (< OFr. *pincier;* see PINCH) + *nez,* nose (< Lat. *nāsus;* see **nas-** in App.).]

pin·cer (pĭn′sər) *n.* **1.** An object resembling one of the grasping parts of a set of pincers. **2.** A maneuver in which an enemy force is attacked from two flanks and the front.

pin·cers (pĭn′sərz) also **pinch·ers** (pĭn′chərz) *pl.n.* (*used with a sing. or pl. verb*) **1.** A grasping tool having a pair of jaws and handles pivoted together to work in opposition. **2.** The prehensile claws of certain arthropods, such as the lobster. [ME *pinsours* < OFr. *pinceure* < OFr. *pincier*, to pinch. See PINCH.]

pinch (pĭnch) *v.* **pinched, pinch·ing, pinch·es** —*tr.* **1.** To squeeze between the thumb and a finger, the jaws of a tool, or other edges. **2.** To squeeze or bind (a part of the body) so as to cause discomfort or pain: *These shoes pinch my toes.* **3.** To nip, wither, or shrivel. **4.** To straiten. **5.** *Slang* To take (money or property) unlawfully; steal. **6.** *Slang* To take into custody; arrest. **7.** To move (something) with a pinch bar. **8.** *Nautical* To sail (a boat) so close to the wind that its sails shiver and its speed is reduced. —*intr.* **1.** To press, squeeze, or bind painfully. **2.** To be miserly. **3.** *Nautical* To drag an oar at the end of a stroke. ❖ *n.* **1.** The act or an instance of pinching. **2.** An amount that can be held between thumb and forefinger. **3.** A painful, difficult, or straitened circumstance. **4.** An emergency situation. **5.** A narrowing of a mineral deposit, as in a mine. **6.** *Informal* A theft. **7.** *Slang* An arrest by a law enforcement officer. ❖ *adj. Baseball* Relating to pinch-hitting or pinch runners. —*idiom:* **pinch pennies** *Informal* To be thrifty or miserly. [ME *pinchen* < ONFr. **pinchier*, var. of OFr. *pincier*, perh. < VLat. **pinctiāre.*]

pinch bar *n.* A crowbar with a pointed projection at one end.

pinch·beck (pĭnch′bĕk′) *n.* **1.** An alloy of zinc and copper used as imitation gold. **2.** A cheap imitation. ❖ *adj.* **1.** Made of pinchbeck. **2.** Imitation; spurious. [After Christopher *Pinchbeck* (1670?–1732), English watchmaker.]

pinch·cock (pĭnch′kŏk′) *n.* A clamp used to regulate or close a flexible tube, esp. in laboratory apparatus.

pinch effect *n.* Radial constriction of flowing plasma or other matter carrying an electric current, caused by the magnetic field that is produced by the current.

pinch-hit (pĭnch′hĭt′) *intr.v.* **-hit, -hit·ting, -hits 1.** *Baseball* To bat in place of the scheduled batter, esp. when a hit is needed. **2.** *Informal* To substitute for another in a time of need. —**pinch hit** *n.* —**pinch hitter** *n.*

pinch·pen·ny (pĭnch′pĕn′ē) *adj.* **1.** Miserly; penny-pinching. **2.** Marked by scarcity of money. —**pinch′pen′ny** *n.*

pinch runner *n. Baseball* A substitute base runner.

Pinck·ney (pĭngk′nē), **Charles Cotesworth** 1746–1825. Amer. minister to France (1797) who refused to bribe French negotiators, causing the conflict known as the XYZ Affair.

pin clover *n.* See **alfilaria.**

pin curl *n.* A usu. damp coiled strand of hair secured with a bobby pin or clip and combed into a wave or curl when dry.

pin·cush·ion (pĭn′koŏsh′ən) *n.* A small firm cushion into which pins are stuck when not in use.

Pin·dar (pĭn′dər) 522?–443? B.C. Greek lyric poet remembered esp. for his *Odes.*

Pin·dar·ic (pĭn-dăr′ĭk) *adj.* **1.** Relating to or characteristic of the poetic style of Pindar. **2.** Of or characteristic of a Pindaric ode. ❖ *n.* A Pindaric ode.

Pindaric ode *n.* An ode in the form used by Pindar, consisting of a series of triads in which the strophe and antistrophe have the same stanza form and the epode has a different form.

Pin·dus Mountains (pĭn′dəs) A range of mountains extending c. 161 km (100 mi) S from S Albania to NW Greece and rising to 2,638.3 m (8,650 ft).

pine¹ (pīn) *n.* **1.** Any of various evergreen trees of the genus *Pinus*, having fascicles of needle-shaped leaves and producing woody seed-bearing cones. **2.** Any of various other coniferous trees, such as the Norfolk Island pine. **3.** The wood of any of these trees. [ME < OE *pin-* (as in *pīntreow*, pine tree) < Lat. *pīnus*. See **peia-** in App.]

pine² (pīn) *v.* **pined, pin·ing, pines** —*intr.* **1.** To feel a lingering, often hopeless desire. **2.** To wither or waste away from longing or grief: *pined away.* —*tr. Archaic* To grieve or mourn for. ❖ *n. Archaic* Intense longing or grief. [ME *pinen* < OE *pīnian*, to cause to suffer < **pīne*, pain < VLat. **pēna*, penalty, var. of Lat. *poena* < Gk. *poinē.* See **kʷei-** in App.]

pin·e·al (pĭn′ē-əl, pī′nē-) *adj.* **1.** Having the form of a pine cone. **2.** Of or relating to the pineal gland. [Fr. *pinéal* < Lat. *pīnea*, pine cone < fem. of *pīneus*, of pine < *pīnus*, pine. See **peia-** in App.]

pineal body *n.* See **pineal gland.**

pineal gland *n.* A small cone-shaped organ in the brain of most vertebrates that secretes the hormone melatonin.

pine·ap·ple (pīn′ăp′əl) *n.* **1a.** A tropical American plant (*Ananas comosus*) having large swordlike leaves and a large edible multiple fruit with a terminal tuft of leaves. **b.** Its fruit. **2.** *Slang* A hand grenade. [ME *pinappel*, pine cone : *pine*, pine; see PINE¹ + *appel*, apple; see APPLE.]

pineapple weed *n.* A western North American plant (*Matricaria matricarioides*) having greenish-yellow discoid flower heads and an odor of pineapple when crushed.

Pine Barrens A coastal plain region of SE-central and S NJ.

pine·cone (pīn′kōn′) *n.* The cone of a pine tree.

pine·drops (pīn′drŏps′) *pl.n.* (*used with a sing. or pl. verb*) A purplish-brown, leafless North American plant (*Pterospora andromedea*) living as a parasite on roots and having reddish or

white flowers arranged in a terminal raceme.

pine finch *n.* See **pine siskin.**

pine·land (pīn′lănd′, -lənd) *n.* A forested area in which pine trees predominate. Also used in the plural.

pine mouse *n.* Any of various voles of the genus *Pitymys*, esp. *P. pinetorum*, of eastern North America.

pi·nene (pī′nēn′) *n.* Either of two isomeric terpene liquids, $C_{10}H_{16}$, used as solvents and in making resins.

pine nut *n.* The edible seed of certain pines, such as the piñon.

pin·er·y (pī′nə-rē) *n., pl.* **-ies 1.** A hothouse or plantation where pineapples are grown. **2.** A forest of pine trees.

pine·sap (pīn′săp′) *n.* A white or reddish plant (*Monotropa hypopithys*) growing as a saprophyte or parasite on tree roots and having racemes with drooping flowers.

pine siskin *n.* A North American finch (*Carduelis pinus*) having streaked brownish plumage.

pine snake *n.* Any of various bull snakes common in pine woods, esp. *Pituophis melanoleucus*, of the eastern United States.

pine straw *n. Chiefly Southern US* Yellowed fallen pine needles.

pine tar *n.* A viscous or semisolid brown-to-black substance produced by the destructive distillation of pine wood and used in roofing compositions and as an expectorant and antiseptic.

pi·ne·tum (pī-nē′təm) *n., pl.* **-ta** (-tə) An area planted with pine trees or related conifers, esp. for botanical study. [Lat. *pīnētum*, pine grove < *pīnus*, pine. See PINE¹.]

pine vole *n.* See **pine mouse.**

pine warbler *n.* A small yellow-breasted songbird (*Dendroica pinus*) found in pine forests of the eastern United States.

pine·wood (pīn′woŏd′) *n.* **1.** The wood of the pine tree. **2.** A forest of pines. Often used in the plural.

pin·e·y (pī′nē) *adj.* Variant of **piny.**

pin·feath·er (pĭn′fĕth′ər) *n.* A growing feather still enclosed in its horny sheath, esp. one just emerging through the skin.

pin·fish (pĭn′fĭsh′) *n., pl.* **pinfish** or **-fish·es** A small spiny-finned fish (*Lagodon rhomboides*) found along the southeast coast of the United States.

pin·fold (pĭn′fōld′) *n.* An enclosure where stray animals are confined. [ME *pynfold*, alteration of OE *pundfald* : *pund-*, enclosure + *fald*, fold.] —**pin′fold′** *v.*

ping¹ (pĭng) *n.* **1.** A sharp high-pitched sound, as that made by a bullet striking metal. **2.** See **knock** 3. ❖ *intr.v.* **pinged, ping·ing, pings** To make a ping. [Imit.]

ping² (pĭng) *n.* A protocol that sends a message to another computer and waits for acknowledgment, used esp. to determine if another computer is reachable. [*p(acket) in(formation) g(roper).*]

Ping A river, c. 563 km (350 mi), of W Thailand, a major tributary of the Chao Phraya.

ping·er (pĭng′ər) *n.* A device used underwater to produce pulses of sound, as for an echo sounder.

pin·go (pĭng′gō) *n., pl.* **-gos** or **-goes** An Arctic mound or conical hill consisting of an outer layer of soil covering a core of solid ice. [Inuit *pingu.*]

Ping-Pong (pĭng′pông′, -pŏng′) A trademark used for table tennis and associated equipment.

pin·guid (pĭn′gwĭd) *adj.* Fat; oily. [Lat. *pinguis* + *-id* (as in LIQUID).]

pin·head (pĭn′hĕd′) *n.* **1.** The head of a pin. **2.** Something very small or insignificant. **3.** *Slang* A stupid person; a dunce. —**pin′head′ed** *adj.*

pin·hole (pĭn′hōl′) *n.* A tiny puncture made by or as if by a pin.

pin·ion¹ (pĭn′yən) *n.* **1.** The wing of a bird. **2.** The outer rear edge of the wing of a bird, containing the primary feathers. **3.** A primary feather of a bird. ❖ *tr.v.* **-ioned, -ion·ing, -ions 1a.** To remove or bind the wing feathers of (a bird) to prevent flight. **b.** To cut or bind (the wings of a bird). **2a.** To restrain (a person) by binding the arms. **b.** To bind (a person's arms). **3.** To bind fast or hold down; shackle. [ME < OFr. *pignon* < VLat. **pinniō, pinniōn-* < Lat. *pinna*, feather. See PINNA.]

pin·ion² (pĭn′yən) *n.* A small cogwheel that engages or is engaged by a larger cogwheel or a rack. [Fr. *pignon* < OFr. *peignon*, prob. < *peigne*, comb < Lat. *pecten* < *pecten, pectinis*, comb.]

pink¹ (pĭngk) *n.* **1.** Any of a group of colors reddish in hue, of medium to high lightness, and of low to moderate saturation. **2a.** Any of various plants of the genus *Dianthus*, such as the carnation, having fragrant showy flowers. **b.** Any of various other plants, such as the wild pink. **c.** A flower of any of these plants. **3.** The highest or best degree. **4.** **pinks a.** Light-colored trousers formerly worn as part of the winter semidress uniform by US Army officers. **b.** The scarlet coat worn by fox hunters. **5.** *Slang* A pinko. **6.** A pink salmon. ❖ *adj.* **pink·er, pink·est 1.** Of the color pink. **2.** *Slang* Having moderately leftist political opinions. —**pink′ness** *n.*

pink² (pĭngk) *tr.v.* **pinked, pink·ing, pinks 1.** To stab lightly with a pointed weapon; prick. **2.** To decorate with a perforated pattern. **3.** To cut with pinking shears. [ME *pingen, pinken* < OE *pyngan* < Lat. *pungere.*]

pink³ (pĭngk) also **pink·ie** or **pink·y** (pĭng′kē) *n., pl.* **pinks** also **pink·ies** *Nautical* A small sailing vessel with a sharply narrowed stern and an overhanging transom. [ME < MDu. *pinke.*]

pink bollworm *n.* The pinkish larva of a moth (*Pectinophora gossypiella*) that is destructive to the cotton plant.

ă	pat	oi	boy
ā	pay	ou	out
âr	care	oŏ	took
ä	father	oō	boot
ĕ	pet	ŭ	cut
ē	be	ûr	urge
ĭ	pit	th	thin
ī	pie	th	this
îr	pier	hw	which
ŏ	pot	zh	vision
ō	toe	ə	about,
ô	paw		item

Stress marks:
′ (primary);
′ (secondary), as in
lexicon (lĕk′sĭ-kŏn′)

pinkroot
Spigelia marilandica

pinnacle
Bath Abbey, Bath, England

pinnate
top: simple pinnate leaf
bottom: bipinnate leaf

pintail
male Northern pintail
Anas acuta

pink-col•lar (pĭnk′kŏl′ər) *adj.* Of or relating to a class of jobs, such as typist, once traditionally filled by women.

Pin•ker•ton (pĭng′kər-tən), **Allan** 1819–84. Scottish-born Amer. detective whose agency was notorious for strikebreaking.

pink•eye (pĭngk′ī′) *n.* An acute contagious conjunctivitis, caused by the hemophilic bacterium *Hemophilus aegyptius* and characterized by inflammation of the eyelids and eyeballs.

pink•ie also **pink•y** (pĭng′kē) *n., pl.* **-ies** *Informal* The little finger. [Prob. < Du. *pinkje,* dim. of *pink,* little finger.]

pink•ing shears (pĭng′kĭng) *pl.n.* Shears with notched blades, used to finish edges of cloth with a zigzag cut.

pink•ish (pĭng′kĭsh) *adj.* Somewhat pink.

pink lady *n.* A cocktail of gin, brandy, lemon or lime juice, egg white, and grenadine, shaken with cracked ice and strained.

pink•o (pĭng′kō) *n., pl.* **-os** *Slang* A person who holds moderately leftist political views; a pink.

pink•root (pĭngk′ro͞ot′, -ro͝ot′) *n.* A perennial plant *(Spigelia marilandica)* of the southeast United States, having flowers with a tubular corolla that is red outside and yellow inside.

pink root *n.* A disease of onions and related bulbous plants caused by a fungus *(Pyrenochaeta terrestris)* and resulting in stunted growth and shriveled pink roots.

pink salmon *n.* A small salmon *(Oncorhynchus gorbuscha)* of Pacific waters, the male of which has a pink color and a conspicuous dorsal hump during the spawning season.

pink slip *n. Informal* A notice of termination of employment. —**pink′-slip′** (pĭngk′slĭp′) *v.*

pin money *n.* Money for incidental expenses.

pin•na (pĭn′ə) *n., pl.* **pin•nae** (pĭn′ē) or **pin•nas 1.** *Botany* A leaflet or primary division of a pinnately compound leaf. **2.** *Zoology* A feather, wing, fin, or similar appendage. **3.** *Anatomy* See **auricle** 1a. [Lat., feather. See **pet-** in App.] —**pin′nal** *adj.*

pin•nace (pĭn′ĭs) *n.* **1.** A light boat propelled by sails or oars, formerly used as a tender for merchant and war vessels. **2.** Any of various kinds of ship's boats. [Fr. *pinace* < OFr., prob. < OSpan. *pinaza* < *pino,* pine tree, boat < Lat. *pīnus.* See **peiə-** in App.]

pin•na•cle (pĭn′ə-kəl) *n.* **1.** *Architecture* A small turret or spire on a roof or buttress. **2.** A tall pointed formation, such as a mountain peak. **3.** The highest point; the culmination. ❖ *tr.v.* **-cled, -cling, -cles 1.** To furnish with a pinnacle. **2.** To place on or as if on a pinnacle. [ME < OFr. < LLat. *pinnāculum,* dim. of Lat. *pinna,* feather. See **pet-** in App.]

pin•nate (pĭn′āt′) also **pin•nat•ed** (-ā′tĭd) *adj.* Resembling a feather; having parts or branches arranged on each side of a common axis: *pinnate leaves.* [Lat. *pinnātus,* feathered < *pinna,* feather. See **pet-** in App.] —**pin′nate′ly** *adv.*

pinnati– *pref.* Resembling a feather: *pinnatifid.* [< Lat. *pinnātus,* feathered. See PINNATE.]

pin•nat•i•fid (pĭ-năt′ə-fĭd) *adj.* Divided or cleft in a pinnate fashion. Used of certain leaves. —**pin•nat′i•fid•ly** *adv.*

pin•nat•i•sect (pĭ-năt′ĭ-sĕkt′) *adj.* Divided pinnately nearly to the midrib. Used of certain leaves.

pin•ni•ped (pĭn′ə-pĕd′) *adj.* Of or belonging to the Pinnipedia, a suborder of carnivorous aquatic mammals that includes the seals, walruses, and similar animals having finlike flippers for locomotion. [< NLat. *Pinnipedia,* order name : Lat. *pinna,* feather; see PINNA + Lat. *pēs, ped-,* foot; see –PED.] —**pin′ni•ped′** *n.*

pin•nule (pĭn′yo͞ol) also **pin•nu•la** (pĭn′yə-lə) *n., pl.* **pin•nules** also **pin•nu•lae** (pĭn′yə-lē′) **1.** *Botany* Any of the ultimate leaflets of a bipinnately compound leaf. **2.** *Zoology* A featherlike or plumelike organ or part. [Lat. *pinnula,* dim. of *pinna,* feather. See **pet-** in App.] —**pin′nu•lar** *adj.*

pi•noch•le or **pi•noc•le** (pē′nŭk′əl, -nŏk′əl) also **pe•nuch•le** or **pe•nuck•le** (pē′nŭk′əl) *n.* **1.** A card game for two to four persons, played with a special deck of 48 cards. Points are scored by taking tricks and forming certain combinations. **2.** The combination of the queen of spades and jack of diamonds in this game. [Perh. < Ger. dialectal *Binokel,* beziquelike card game < Fr. dialectal *binocle,* spectacles < NLat. *bīnoculus,* the two eyes : Lat. *bīnī,* two each; see **dwo-** in App. + Lat. *oculus,* eye; see **okʷ-** in App.]

pin•o•cy•to•sis (pĭn′ə-sĭ-tō′sĭs, -sī-, pī′nə-) *n.* Introduction of fluids into a cell by the formation of vesicles in the cell membrane. [Gk. *pīnein,* to drink; see **pō(i)-** in App. + CYT(O)– + –OSIS.] —**pin′o•cy•tot′ic** (-tŏt′ĭk) *adj.*

pi•no•le (pĭ-nō′lē) *n.* Meal made of ground corn or wheat and mesquite beans. [Am.Sp. < Nahuatl *pinolli,* mixture of vanilla powder, spices, and ground toasted chocolate beans.]

pi•ñon also **pin•yon** (pĭn′yŏn′, -yən) *n., pl.* **pi•ñons** or **pi•ño•nes** (pĭn-yō′nēz) also **pin•yons** Any of several pine trees bearing edible nutlike seeds, esp. *Pinus edulis* of the western United States and Mexico. [Sp. *piñón,* pine nut, pine cone, augmentative of *piña* < Lat. *pīnea* < fem. of *pīneus,* of pine < *pīnus,* pine tree. See **peiə-** in App.]

piñon jay also **pinyon jay** *n.* A small, dull blue uncrested jay *(Gymnorhinus cyanocephala)* of western North America.

pi•not (pē′nō, pē-nō′) *n.* **1.** Any of several related white or red grapes chiefly grown on the West Coast and in France. **2.** A white or red wine made from these grapes. [Fr., var. of *pineau,* dim. of *pin,* pine tree < Lat. *pīnus.* See **peiə-** in App.]

pin•point (pĭn′point′) *n.* **1.** Something extremely small or trifling. **2.** A very small or sharp point. **3.** A point on a map marking a precise location or target. ❖ *tr.v.* **-point•ed, -point•ing, -points 1.** To locate or identify with precision. **2.** To take precise aim at. **3.** To direct attention to. ❖ *adj.* **1.** Meticulously precise. **2.** Extremely small; minuscule.

pin•prick (pĭn′prĭk′) *n.* **1.** A small puncture made by or as if by a pin. **2.** A slight wound. **3.** An annoyance. —**pin′prick′** *v.*

pins and needles *pl.n.* A tingling sensation felt in a part of the body numbed from lack of circulation. —***idiom:* on pins and needles** In a state of tense anticipation.

pin•scher (pĭn′shər) *n.* A Doberman pinscher.

pin•set•ter (pĭn′sĕt′ər) *n.* An employee or a mechanical apparatus that sets up pins in a bowling alley.

Pinsk (pĭnsk, pyĕnsk) A city of SW Belarus SSW of Minsk; cap. of the Pinsk duchy in the 13th cent. Pop. 128,300.

pin•stripe also **pin stripe** (pĭn′strīp′) *n.* **1.** A very thin stripe, esp. on a fabric. **2a.** A fabric with very thin stripes, often used for suits. **b.** A suit made of such fabric. Often used in the plural. —**pin′striped′** *adj.*

pint (pīnt) *n.* **1a.** A unit of volume or capacity in the US Customary System, used in liquid measure, equal to ⅛ gallon or 16 ounces (0.473 liter). **b.** A unit of volume or capacity in the US Customary System, used in dry measure, equal to 1⁄16 peck or ½ quart (0.551 liter). **c.** A unit of volume or capacity in the British Imperial System, used in dry and liquid measure, equal to 0.568 liter. See table at **measurement. 2a.** A container with a pint capacity. **b.** The amount that can be held in such a container. [ME *pinte,* a unit of volume < OFr. < VLat. **pīncta,* mark on a container < fem. of **pīnctus,* alteration of Lat. *pictus,* p. part. of *pingere,* to paint.]

pin•ta (pĭn′tə, pēn′tä) *n.* A contagious tropical American skin disease caused by a spirochete *(Treponema carateum)* and marked by extreme thickening and spotty discoloration of the skin. [Sp., colored spot < VLat. **pīncta.* See PINT.]

pin•tail (pĭn′tāl′) *n., pl.* **pintail** or **-tails** A duck *(Anas acuta)* of the Northern Hemisphere having gray, brown, and white plumage and a sharply pointed tail.

pin•ta•no (pĭn-tä′nō) *n., pl.* **pintano** or **-nos** Any of various brilliantly colored damselfishes of the genus *Abudefduf,* esp. the sergeant major. [Am.Sp. *píntano.*]

Pin•ter (pĭn′tər), **Harold** b. 1930. British playwright whose works include *The Dumbwaiter* (1957) and *Birthday Party* (1958). —**Pin′ter•esque′** (-ĕsk′) *adj.*

pin•tle (pĭn′tl) *n.* **1.** A pin or a bolt on which another part pivots. **2.** *Nautical* The pin on which a rudder turns. **3.** The pin on which a gun carriage revolves. **4.** A hook or a bolt on the rear of a towing vehicle for attaching a gun or trailer. [ME *pintel,* penis < OE.]

pin•to (pĭn′tō) *n., pl.* **-tos** or **-toes** A horse with patchy markings of white and another color. ❖ *adj.* Mottled; pied. [Sp., piebald, spotted < VLat. **pīnctus,* p. part. of Lat. *pingere,* to paint.]

pinto bean *n.* A form of the string bean that has mottled seeds and is grown esp. in the southwest United States.

pint•size (pīnt′sīz′) also **pint•sized** (-sīzd′) *adj. Informal* Of small dimensions; diminutive.

pin•up (pĭn′ŭp′) *n.* **1a.** A picture, esp. of a sexually attractive person, that is displayed on a wall. **b.** A person considered a suitable model for such a picture. **2.** Something intended to be affixed to a wall. —**pin′up′** *adj.*

pin•wale (pĭn′wāl′) *adj.* Made with narrow wales.

pin•weed (pĭn′wēd′) *n.* Any of various North American perennial plants of the genus *Lechea,* having narrow leaves and numerous small flowers.

pin•wheel (pĭn′hwēl′, -wēl′) *n.* **1.** A toy consisting of vanes of colored paper or plastic pinned to a stick so that they revolve when blown on. **2.** A firework that forms a rotating wheel of colored flames. **3.** A wheel with a circle of pins at right angles to its face, used as a tripping device.

pin•work (pĭn′wûrk′) *n.* Fine stitches raised from the surface of the design in the embroidery of needlepoint lace.

pin•worm (pĭn′wûrm′) *n.* Any of various small nematode worms of the family Oxyuridae that are parasitic on mammals, esp. *Enterobius vermicularis,* a species that infests the human intestines and rectum.

pin•wrench (pĭn′rĕnch′) *n.* A wrench having a projection designed to fit a hole in the object to be turned.

pinx. *abbr. Latin* pinxit (he painted it; she painted it)

pinx•ter flower (pĭngk′stər) *n.* A deciduous shrub *(Rhododendron periclymenoides)* of the southeast United States having a funnel-shaped pink or purple corolla and flowers that bloom before the leaves appear. [< *Pinkster, Pinxter,* Whitsuntide < obsolete Du. *pinxter* < MDu., ult. < Gk. *pentēkostē,* Pentecost. See PENTECOST.]

pin•y also **pine•y** (pī′nē) *adj.* **pin•i•er, pin•i•est** Relating to, suggestive of, or abounding in pines.

Pin•yin or **pin•yin** (pĭn′yĭn′, -yĭn) *n.* A system for transliterating Chinese ideograms into the Roman alphabet, officially adopted by China in 1979. [Chin. (Mandarin) *pīn yīn,* to combine sounds into syllables : *pīn,* to combine + *yīn,* sound.]

pin•yon (pĭn′yŏn′, -yən) *n.* Variant of **piñon.**

pinyon jay *n.* Variant of **piñon jay.**

Pin•zón (pĭn-zōn′, pēn-thōn′), **Martín Alonso** 1440?–93. Spanish navigator who commanded the *Pinta* on Christopher Columbus's first voyage to America (1492–93). His brother **Vicente Yáñez Pinzón** (1460?–1524) was the first European explorer of the Amazon R. (1500).

pi•o•let (pē′ə-lā′) *n.* See **ice ax.** [Fr. < Fr. dialectal, dim. of *piola,* small axe < OFr. **piola* < O Provençal, dim. of *apcha, apia,* of Gmc. orig.]

pi•on (pī′ŏn′) *n.* A semistable meson, existing either as a neutral particle with a mass 264 times that of an electron or as a positively or negatively charged particle with a mass 273 times that of an electron. [Contraction of PI MESON.]

pi•o•neer (pī′ə-nîr′) *n.* **1.** One who goes into unknown or unclaimed territory to settle. **2.** One who opens up new areas of thought, research, or development. **3.** A soldier who does construction and demolition work in the field to facilitate troop movements. **4.** *Ecology* An animal or plant species that establishes itself in a previously barren environment. ❖ *adj.* **1.** Of or characteristic of early settlers. **2.** Leading the way; trailblazing: *a pioneer treatment for cancer.* ❖ *v.* **-neered, -neer•ing, -neers** *—tr.* **1a.** To open up (an area) or prepare (a way). **b.** To settle (a region). **2.** To initiate or participate in the development of. *—intr.* To act as a pioneer. [Fr. *pionnier* < OFr. *peonier,* foot soldier < *peon* < Med.Lat. *pedō, pedōn-* < LLat., one with broad feet < Lat. *pēs, ped-,* foot. See **ped-** in App.]

pi•os•i•ty (pī-ŏs′ĭ-tē) *n., pl.* **-ties** An exaggerated display of piety. [< PIOUS.]

pi•ous (pī′əs) *adj.* **1.** Having or exhibiting religious reverence; earnestly compliant in the observance of religion; devout. **2a.** Marked by conspicuous devoutness. **b.** Marked by false devoutness; solemnly hypocritical. **3.** Devotional: *pious readings.* **4.** Professing or exhibiting a strict, traditional sense of virtue and morality; high-minded. **5.** Commendable; worthy. [< Lat. *pius,* dutiful.] **—pi′ous•ly** *adv.* **—pi′ous•ness** *n.*

Pioz•zi (pyôt′sē), **Hester Lynch** Known as "Mrs. Thrale." 1741–1821. British writer whose works include *Anecdotes of the Late Samuel Johnson* (1786).

pip¹ (pĭp) *n.* The small seed of a fruit. [Short for PIPPIN.]

pip² (pĭp) *tr.v.* **pipped, pip•ping, pips** *Chiefly British* **1.** To wound or kill with a bullet. **2.** To get the better of; defeat. **3.** To blackball. [Poss. < PIP³.]

pip³ (pĭp) *n.* **1.** *Games* **a.** A dot indicating a unit of numerical value on dice or dominoes. **b.** A mark indicating the suit or numerical value of a playing card. **2.** A spot or speck. **3.** A rootstock of certain flowering plants, esp. the lily of the valley. **4.** Any of the segments of the surface of a pineapple. **5.** *Informal* A shoulder insignia indicating the rank of certain officers, as in the British Army. **6.** See **blip** 1. [?]

pip⁴ (pĭp) *v.* **pipped, pip•ping, pips** *—tr.* To break through (the shell) in hatching. Used of a chick. *—intr.* To peep or chirp, as a chick does. ❖ *n.* A short high-pitched radio signal. [Variant of PEEP¹ and PEEP².]

pip⁵ (pĭp) *n.* **1a.** A disease of birds, characterized by a thick mucous discharge that forms a crust in the mouth and throat. **b.** The crust symptomatic of this disease. **2.** *Slang* A minor unspecified human ailment. [ME *pippe* < MDu., phlegm, pip < Med.Lat. **pippīta,* alteration of Lat. *pītuīta.* See **peiə-** in App.]

pi•pal or **pee•pul** (pē′pəl) *n.* A fig tree *(Ficus religiosa)* native to India, having broadly ovate leaves and sacred to Buddhists. [Hindi *pīpal* < Skt. *pippalam.*]

pipe (pīp) *n.* **1a.** A hollow cylinder or tube used to conduct a liquid, gas, or finely divided solid. **b.** A section or piece of such a tube. **2a.** A device for smoking, consisting of a tube of wood, clay, or other material with a small bowl at one end. **b.** An amount of smoking material, such as tobacco, needed to fill the bowl of a pipe; a pipeful. **3.** *Informal* **a.** A tubular part or organ of the body. **b. pipes** The passages of the human respiratory system. **4a.** A wine cask having a capacity of 126 gallons or 2 hogsheads (478 liters). **b.** This volume as a unit of liquid measure. **5.** *Music* **a.** A tubular wind instrument, such as a flute. **b.** Any of the tubes in an organ. **c. pipes** A small wind instrument, consisting of tubes of different lengths bound together. **d. pipes** A bagpipe. **6. pipes** *Informal* The vocal cords; the voice, esp. as used in singing. **7.** A birdcall. **8.** *Nautical* A whistle used for signaling crew members. **9.** *Geology* **a.** A vertical cylindrical vein of ore. **b.** One of the vertical veins of eruptive origin in which diamonds are found in South Africa. **10.** *Geology* An eruptive passageway opening into the crater of a volcano. **11.** *Metallurgy* A cone-shaped cavity in an ingot, formed during cooling by escaping gases. ❖ *v.* **piped, pip•ing, pipes** *—tr.* **1a.** To convey (liquid or gas) by means of pipes. **b.** To convey as if by pipes, esp. to transmit by wire or cable: *piped music.* **2.** To provide with pipes or connect with pipes. **3a.** To play (a tune) on a pipe or pipes. **b.** To lead by playing on pipes. **4.** *Nautical* **a.** To signal (crew members) with a boatswain's pipe. **b.** To receive aboard or mark the departure of by sounding a boatswain's pipe. **5.** To utter in a shrill reedy tone. **6.** To furnish (a garment or fabric) with piping. **7.** To force through a pastry tube, as frosting onto a cake. **8.** *Slang* To take a look at; notice. *—intr.* **1.** To play on a pipe. **2.** To speak shrilly; make a shrill sound. **3.** To chirp or whistle, as a bird does. **4.** *Nautical* To signal the crew with a boatswain's pipe. **5.** *Metallurgy* To develop pipes during solidification. ***—phrasal verbs:* pipe down** *Slang* To stop talking; be quiet. **pipe up** To speak up. [ME < OE *pīpe* < VLat. **pīpa* < Lat. *pīpāre,* to chirp.]

pipe bomb *n.* An explosive device contained in a metal pipe.

pipe clay *n.* A fine white clay used in making tobacco pipes and pottery and in whitening leather.

pipe cleaner *n.* A pliant tufted narrow rod used for cleaning the stem of a tobacco pipe.

pipe dream *n.* A fantastic notion or vain hope.

pipe•fish (pīp′fĭsh′) *n., pl.* **pipefish** or **-fish•es** Any of various slim elongated fishes of the family Syngnathidae, living in temperate and warm seas and characterized by a tubelike snout and an external covering of bony plates.

pipe fitter *n.* One that installs and repairs piping systems.

pipe•fit•ting (pīp′fĭt′ĭng) *n.* **1.** The act of connecting pipes. **2.** A trade that installs and repairs piping systems. **3.** A section of pipe used to connect two or more pipes.

pipe•ful (pīp′fo͝ol′) *n.* The amount of smoking material that a pipe can hold.

pipe•line (pīp′līn′) *n.* **1.** A conduit of pipe, esp. one used to convey water, gas, or petroleum products. **2.** A direct channel by which information is privately transmitted. **3.** A system through which something is conducted, esp. as a means of supply. ❖ *tr.v.* **-lined, -lin•ing, -lines 1.** To convey by or as if by piping. **2.** To lay piping through.

pipe organ *n.* See **organ** 1a.

pip•er (pī′pər) *n.* *Music* **1.** One who plays the bagpipe. **2.** One who plays on a pipe.

pi•per•a•zine (pī-pĕr′ə-zēn′, pĭ-) *n.* A crystalline compound, $C_4H_{10}N_2$, used as a hardener for epoxy resins, an antihistamine, and an anthelmintic. [PIPER(INE) + AZ(O)– + –INE².]

pi•per•i•dine (pī-pĕr′ĭ-dēn′, pĭ-) *n.* A strongly basic liquid, $C_5H_{10}NH$, used in the manufacture of rubber and as a curing agent in epoxy resins. [PIPER(INE) + –ID(E) + –INE².]

pip•er•ine (pĭp′ə-rēn′) *n.* A crystalline solid, $C_{17}H_{19}NO_3$, extracted from black pepper and used as flavoring and as an insecticide. [Lat. *piper,* pepper; see PEPPER + –INE².]

pi•per•o•nal (pī-pĕr′ə-năl′, pĭ-) *n.* A powder, $C_8H_6O_3$, used as flavoring and in perfume. [PIPER(INE) + –ON(E) + –AL³.]

pipe•stone (pīp′stōn′) *n.* A heat-hardened compacted red clay stone used in Native American tobacco pipes.

pi•pette also **pi•pet** (pī-pĕt′) *n.* A narrow, usu. calibrated glass tube into which small amounts of liquid are suctioned for transfer or measurement. [Fr. < OFr., tube, dim. of *pipe,* pipe < VLat. **pīpa.* See PIPE.] **—pi•pette′** *v.*

pipe vine *n.* A deciduous woody vine *(Aristolochia durior)* of the eastern United States having greenish, brown-mottled flowers shaped like a curved pipe.

pipe wrench *n.* A wrench with two serrated jaws, one adjustable, for gripping and turning pipe.

pip•ing (pī′pĭng) *n.* **1.** A system of pipes, such as those used in plumbing. **2.** *Music* **a.** The act of playing on a pipe. **b.** The music produced by a pipe when played. **3.** A shrill high-pitched sound. **4.** A narrow tube of fabric, sometimes enclosing a cord, used for trimming seams and edges, as of slipcovers. **5.** A tubular ribbon of icing on a pastry. ❖ *adj.* **1.** *Music* Playing on a pipe. **2.** Having a high-pitched sound. **3.** Tranquil; peaceful. ***—idiom:* piping hot** Very hot: *piping hot tea.*

pip•i•strelle also **pip•i•strel** (pĭp′ĭ-strĕl′, pĭp′ĭ-strĕl′) *n.* Any of various very small insectivorous cosmopolitan bats of the genus *Pipistrellus.* [Fr. < Ital. *pipistrello,* bat, alteration of OItal. *vipistrello* < Lat. *vespertiliō.* See VESPERTILIONID.]

pip•it (pĭp′ĭt) *n.* Any of various widely distributed songbirds of the genus *Anthus,* characteristically having brownish upper plumage and a streaked breast. [Imit. of its call.]

pip•kin (pĭp′kĭn) *n.* A small earthenware or metal cooking pot. [Poss. PIP(E), cask + –KIN.]

pip•pin (pĭp′ĭn) *n.* **1.** Any of several varieties of apple. **2.** The seed of a fleshy fruit; a pip. **3.** *Informal* A person or thing that is admired. [ME *pipin* < OFr. *pepin.*]

pip•sis•se•wa (pĭp-sĭs′ĭ-wô′, -wə) *n.* Any of several evergreen plants of the genus *Chimaphila,* esp. the Eurasian species *C. umbellata,* having a terminal corymb of white or pinkish flowers. [Perh. Eastern Abenaki *kpi-pskwáhsawe.*]

pip-squeak (pĭp′skwēk′) *n.* *Informal* One that is small or insignificant.

pi•quant (pē′kənt, -känt′, pē-känt′) *adj.* **1.** Pleasantly pungent or tart in taste; spicy. **2a.** Appealingly provocative: *a piquant wit.* **b.** Charming, interesting, or attractive. **3.** *Archaic* Causing hurt feelings; stinging. [Fr. < OFr., pr. part. of *piquer,* to prick. See PIQUE.] **—pi′quan•cy, pi′quant•ness** *n.* **—pi′quant•ly** *adv.*

pique (pēk) *n.* A state of vexation caused by a perceived slight or indignity; a feeling of wounded pride. ❖ *tr.v.* **piqued, piqu•ing, piques 1.** To cause to feel resentment or indignation. **2.** To provoke; arouse: *piqued her curiosity.* **3.** To pride (oneself). [Fr., a prick, irritation < OFr. < *piquer,* to prick < VLat. **piccāre,* ult. of imit. orig.]

pi•qué (pĭ-kā′, pē-) *n.* A tightly woven fabric with raised patterns, produced esp. by a double warp. [Fr., p. part. of *piquer,* to quilt < OFr., to backstitch, prick. See PIQUE.]

pi•quet also **pic•quet** (pĭ-kā′) *n.* A card game for two people, played with a deck from which all cards below the seven, aces being high, are omitted. [Fr.]

pinto

pipeline
Trans Alaska Pipeline

pipkin

ă	pat	oi	boy
ā	pay	ou	out
âr	care	o͝o	took
ä	father	o͞o	boot
ĕ	pet	ŭ	cut
ē	be	ûr	urge
ĭ	pit	th	thin
ī	pie	*th*	this
îr	pier	hw	which
ŏ	pot	zh	vision
ō	toe	ə	about, item
ô	paw		

Stress marks:
′ (primary);
′ (secondary), as in
lexicon (lĕk′sĭ-kŏn′)

Pi·ra·ci·ca·ba (pĭr′ə-sĭ-kä′bə, pē′rä-sĭ-kä′bä) A city of SE Brazil NW of São Paulo. Pop. 283,634.

pi·ra·cy (pī′rə-sē) *n., pl.* **-cies 1a.** Robbery committed at sea. **b.** A similar act of robbery, as the hijacking of an airplane. **2.** The unauthorized use or reproduction of copyrighted or patented material. **3.** The operation of an unlicensed, illegal radio or television station. [Med.Lat. *pīrātia* < L.Gk. *peirateia* < Gk. *peiratēs,* pirate. See PIRATE.]

Pi·rae·us (pī-rē′əs, pī-rā′-) A city of E-central Greece on the Saronic Gulf SW of Athens. Pop. 196,389.

pi·ra·gua (pĭ-rä′gwə) *n.* **1.** A canoe made by hollowing out a tree trunk; a dugout. **2.** A flatbottom sailing boat with two masts. [Sp. < Carib.]

Pi·ran·del·lo (pĭr′ən-dĕl′ō, pē′rän-dĕl′lō), **Luigi** 1867–1936. Italian writer of *Six Characters in Search of an Author* (1921) who won the 1934 Nobel Prize for literature.

Pi·ra·ne·si (pĭr′ə-nā′zē, pē′rä-nĕ′-), **Giambattista** 1720–78. Italian architect and artist whose etchings of Roman ruins aided the revival of neoclassicism. —**Pi′ra·ne′si·an** *adj.*

pi·ra·nha also **pi·ra·ña** (pĭ-rän′yə, -răn′yə, -rä′nə, -răn′ə) *n.* Any of several aggressive, voraciously carnivorous tropical American freshwater fishes of the genus *Serrasalmus.* [Port. < Tupi : *pirá,* fish + *ánha,* to cut.]

pi·ra·ru·cu (pĭ-rär′ə-kōō′) *n.* See **arapaima.** [Port. *pirarucú* < Tupi *pirá-rucú* : *pirá,* fish + *urucú,* red.]

pi·rate (pī′rĭt) *n.* **1a.** One who robs at sea or plunders the land from the sea without commission from a sovereign nation. **b.** A ship used for this purpose. **2.** One who preys on others; a plunderer. **3.** One who makes use of or reproduces the work of another without authorization. **4.** One that operates an unlicensed illegal television or radio station. ❖ *v.* **-rat·ed, -rat·ing, -rates** —*tr.* **1.** To attack and rob (a ship at sea). **2.** To take (something) by piracy. **3.** To make use of or reproduce (another's work) without authorization. —*intr.* To act as a pirate; practice piracy. [ME < OFr. < Lat. *pīrāta* < Gk. *peiratēs* < *peirān,* to master < *peira,* trial.] —**pi·rat′ic** (pī-răt′ĭk), **pi·rat′i·cal** (-ĭ-kəl) *adj.*

pirate perch *n.* A small North American freshwater fish (*Aphredoderus sayanus*) that has its anal opening near the throat.

pi·ro·gi (pĭ-rō′gē) *n., pl.* **pirogi** or **-gies** Variant of **pierogi.**

pi·rogue (pĭ-rōg′, pĭr′ō) *n.* A canoe made from a hollowed tree trunk; a piragua. [Fr. < Sp. *piragua.* See PIRAGUA.]

pir·o·plasm (pĭr′ə-plăz′əm) *n.* See **babesia.** [NLat. *Piroplasma,* genus name : Lat. *pirum,* pear + Gk. *plasma,* image; see PLASMA.]

pir·o·plas·mo·sis (pĭr′ə-plăz-mō′sĭs) *n.* See **babesiosis.**

pir·ou·ette (pĭr′ōō-ĕt′) *n.* A turn of the body on the point of the toe or the ball of the foot in ballet. [Fr. < OFr. *pirouet,* spinning top.] —**pir′ou·ette′** *v.*

pi·rozh·ki also **pi·rosh·ki** (pĭ-rôsh′kē, -rôsh′-) *pl.n.* Small pastries filled with finely chopped meat or cabbage, baked or fried. [Russ., pl. of *pirozhok,* dim. of *pirog,* dumpling. See PIEROGI.]

Pi·sa (pē′zə, -zä) A city of W Italy on the Arno R. near the Tyrrhenian Sea; noted for the campanile known as the Leaning Tower of Pisa. Pop. 98,006. —**Pi′san** *adj.* & *n.*

pis al·ler (pē zá-lā′) *n.* The final recourse or expedient; the last resort. [Fr. : *pis,* worse + *aller,* to go.]

Pi·sa·no (pē-zä′nō), **Nicola** or **Niccolò** 1220–84? Italian sculptor whose works include the hexagonal pulpit of the Baptistry in Pisa. Nicola's son **Giovanni** (1245?–1314?) designed the Church of the Franciscans in Naples (1268).

pis·ca·ry (pĭs′kə-rē) *n., pl.* **-ries** A fishery. [Med.Lat. *piscārium* < Lat. *piscis,* fish + Lat. *-ārium,* -arium.]

pis·ca·to·ri·al (pĭs′kə-tôr′ē-əl, -tōr′-) or **pis·ca·to·ry** (pĭs′kə-tôr′ē, -tōr′ē) *adj.* **1.** Of or relating to fish or fishing. **2.** Involved in or dependent on fishing. [< Lat. *piscātōrius* < *piscātor,* fisherman < *piscārī,* to fish < *piscis,* fish.]

Pi·sces (pī′sēz) *n.* **1.** A constellation in the Northern Hemisphere near Aries and Pegasus. **2a.** The 12th sign of the zodiac in astrology. **b.** *pl.* **Pisces** One born under this sign. [Ult. < Lat. *piscēs,* pl. of *piscis,* fish.]

pisci– *pref.* Fish: *piscivorous.* [< Lat. *piscis,* fish.]

pi·sci·cul·ture (pī′sĭ-kŭl′chər, pĭs′ĭ-) *n.* The breeding, hatching, and rearing of fish under controlled conditions. —**pi′sci·cul′tur·al** *adj.* —**pi′sci·cul′tur·ist** *n.*

pi·sci·form (pī′sĭ-fôrm′, pĭs′ĭ-) *adj.* Shaped like a fish.

pi·sci·na (pī-sē′nə, -sī′nə, -shē′nə) *n., pl.* **-nae** (-nē) *Ecclesiastical* A stone basin with a drain for carrying away the water used in ceremonial ablutions. [ME *piscine* < Med.Lat. *piscīna* < Lat. *fishpond,* pool < *piscis,* fish.] —**pis′ci·nal** (pĭs′ə-nəl) *adj.*

pi·scine (pī′sēn′, pĭs′ĭn′) *adj.* Of, relating to, or characteristic of a fish or fishes. [Med.Lat. *piscīnus* < Lat. *piscis,* fish.]

Pi·scis Aus·tri·nus (pī′sĭs ô-strī′nəs) *n.* A constellation in the Southern Hemisphere near Aquarius and Grus. [NLat. *Piscis Austrīnus* : Lat. *piscis,* fish + Lat. *austrīnus,* southern.]

pi·sciv·o·rous (pī-sĭv′ər-əs, pĭ-) *adj.* Fish-eating.

pish (pĭsh) *interj.* Used to express disdain.

pi·shogue also **pi·shoge** (pĭ-shōg′) *n. Irish* **1.** Black magic; sorcery. **2.** An evil spell; an incantation. [Ir.Gael. *píseog* < MIr. *pisóc, píseóc.*]

pi·si·form (pī′sə-fôrm′) *adj.* Resembling a pea in size or shape. ❖ *n.* A small bone at the junction of the ulna and the carpus. [Lat. *pīsum,* pea; see PEA + –FORM.]

Pi·sis·tra·tus or **Pei·sis·tra·tus** (pī-sĭs′trə-təs, pī-) d. 527 B.C. Athenian tyrant (560–527) remembered for encouraging athletic contests and literary efforts.

pis·mire (pĭs′mīr′, pĭz′-) *n.* An ant. [ME *pissemyre : pisse,* urine (< the smell of the formic acid that ants secrete); see PISS + *mire,* ant (prob. of Scand. orig.; akin to Dan. *myre*).]

pis·mo clam (pĭz′mō) *n.* A large thick-shelled edible marine clam (*Tivela stultorum*) off the southern Pacific coast of North America. [After *Pismo Beach,* a city of southwest California.]

pi·so·lite (pī′sə-līt′) *n.* **1.** Rock, usu. limestone, composed of pisoliths. **2.** See **pisolith.** [Gk. *pisos,* pea + –LITE.] —**pi′so·lit′ic** (-lĭt′ĭk) *adj.*

pi·so·lith (pī′sə-lĭth′, -zə-, pĭs′ə-, pĭz′ə-) *n. Geology* A small rounded accretionary mass, usu. of calcium carbonate, larger and less regular than an oolite. [Gk. *pisos,* pea + –LITH.]

piss (pĭs) *Vulgar Slang v.* **pissed, piss·ing, piss·es** —*intr.* To urinate. —*tr.* **1.** To urinate on or in. **2.** To discharge (blood, for example) in the urine. ❖ *n.* **1.** Urine. **2.** The act or an instance of urinating. —*phrasal verb:* **piss off 1.** To make or become angry. **2.** Used in the imperative as a signal of angry dismissal. [ME *pissen* < OFr. *pissier* < VLat. **pissiāre,* of imit. orig.]

piss·ant also **piss-ant** or **piss ant** (pĭs′ănt′) *n. Slang* One that is insignificant. **2.** *Obsolete* An ant. ❖ *adj. Slang* Not important; insignificant. [Modeled on PISMIRE.]

Pis·sar·ro (pĭ-sär′ō, pē-), **Camille** 1830–1903. French painter whose works include *Orchard in Blossom* (1877).

pissed (pĭst) *adj. Vulgar Slang* **1.** Extremely irritated or angry. Often used with *off.* **2.** *Chiefly British Slang* Intoxicated; drunk.

piss·er (pĭs′ər) *n. Vulgar Slang* **1.** One that is extremely disagreeable. **2.** One that is extraordinary or remarkable.

pis·soir (pē-swär′) *n.* A public urinal located on the street in some European countries. [Fr. < OFr. < *pissier,* to urinate. See PISS.]

pis·ta·chi·o (pĭ-stăsh′ē-ō′, -stä′shē-ō′) *n., pl.* **-os 1a.** A deciduous Asian tree (*Pistacia vera*) having pinnately compound leaves and nutlike fruits. **b.** The fruit of this tree, having an edible oily green or yellow kernel. **2.** The flavor of these nuts. [Ital. *pistacchio* < Lat. *pistacium,* pistachio nut < Gk. *pistakion* < *pistakē,* pistachio tree, perh. < MPers. **pistak.*]

pis·ta·reen (pĭs′tə-rēn′) *n.* A small silver coin used in America and the West Indies during the 18th century. [Prob. alteration of Sp. *peseta,* peseta. See PESETA.]

piste (pēst) *n.* A ski trail densely packed with snow. [Fr. < Ital. *pista* < obsolete *pistare,* to trample down, var. of *pestare.* See PISTON.]

pis·til (pĭs′təl) *n.* The female ovule-bearing organ of a flower, including the stigma, style, and ovary. [Fr. < NLat. *pistillum* < Lat., pestle (< its shape).]

pis·til·late (pĭs′tə-lāt′, -lĭt) *adj.* **1.** Having one or more pistils. **2.** Having pistils but no stamens: *pistillate flowers.*

Pis·to·ia (pĭ-stoi′ə, pē-stô′yä) A city of N-central Italy NW of Florence; settled in the 6th cent. B.C. Pop. 83,600.

pis·tol (pĭs′təl) *n.* A firearm held and fired with one hand. ❖ *tr.v.* **-toled, -tol·ing, -tols** To shoot with such a handgun. [Fr. *pistole* < Ger. *Pistole* < Czech *píšt′ala,* pipe, whistle, firearm < *píštěti,* to whistle, of imit. orig.]

pis·tole (pĭ-stōl′) *n.* **1.** A gold coin equal to two escudos, formerly used in Spain. **2.** Any of several gold coins used in various European countries until the late 19th century. [Fr., back-formation < *pistolet,* dim. of *pistole,* pistol. See PISTOL.]

pistol grip *n.* **1a.** The grip of a pistol, shaped to fit the hand. **b.** A similar grip sometimes used on a submachine gun or other firearm. **2.** A grip used on certain tools shaped to fit the hand.

pis·tol-whip (pĭs′təl-hwĭp′, -wĭp′) *tr.v.* **-whipped, -whip·ping, -whips** To beat with a pistol.

pis·ton (pĭs′tən) *n.* **1.** A cylinder or disk that fits into a larger cylinder and moves under fluid pressure, as in a reciprocating engine, or displaces or compresses fluids, as in a pump. **2.** *Music* A valve mechanism in brass instruments for altering the pitch. [Fr. < Ital. *pistone, pestone,* large pestle < *pestare,* to pound < LLat. *pistāre,* freq. of Lat. *pīnsere, pīnsāre.*]

piston ring *n.* An adjustable split metal ring that fits around a piston to seal the gap between it and the cylinder wall.

piston rod *n.* A connecting rod that transmits power to or is powered by a piston.

pis·tou (pē-stōō′) *n.* A sauce made of garlic, basil, Parmesan, and olive oil. [Fr. < Provençal < *pestar,* to crush < O Provençal < LLat. *pistāre.* See PISTON.]

pit¹ (pĭt) *n.* **1.** A natural or artificial hole or cavity in the ground. **2a.** An excavation for the removal of mineral deposits; a mine. **b.** The shaft of a mine. **3.** A concealed hole in the ground used as a trap; a pitfall. **4a.** Hell. **b.** A miserable or depressing place or situation. **c.** *pits Slang* The worst. **5.** A small indentation in a surface. **6a.** A natural hollow or depression in the body or an organ. **b.** A small indented scar left in the skin by smallpox or other eruptive disease; a pockmark. **c.** *Informal* An armpit. Often used in the plural. **7.** An enclosed, usu. sunken area in which animals, such as dogs or gamecocks, are placed for fighting. **8a.** The section directly in front of and below the stage of a theater, in which the musicians sit. **b.** *Chiefly British* The ground floor of a theater behind the stalls. **9a.** The section of an exchange where trading in a specific commodity is carried on. **b.** The gambling area of a casino. **10a.** A sunken area in a garage floor from which mechanics may work on cars. **b.** *Sports* An area beside an auto racecourse where cars may be refueled or serviced during a race. Often used in the plural. **11.** *Football* The middle areas of the defensive and offensive lines. **12.** *Botany* A cavity in the wall of a plant cell where there is no secondary wall, as in fibers, tracheids, and vessels. ❖ *v.* **pit•ted, pit•ting, pits** —*tr.* **1.** To mark with cavities, depressions, or scars. **2.** To set in direct opposition or competition. **3.** To place, bury, or store in a pit. —*intr.* **1.** To become marked with pits. **2.** To retain an impression after being indented. Used of the skin. **3.** To stop at a refueling area during an auto race. [ME < OE *pytt*, ult. < Lat. *puteus*, well.]

pit[2] (pĭt) *n.* The single central kernel or stone of certain fruits, such as a peach or cherry. ❖ *tr.v.* **pit•ted, pit•ting, pits** To extract the pit from (a fruit). [Du. < MDu.]

pi•ta[1] (pē′tə) *n.* A round flat bread of Middle Eastern origin that can be opened to form a pocket for filling. [Mod.Gk. *pētta, pita*, pie, cake, bread.]

pi•ta[2] (pē′tə) *n.* **1.** Any of several plants of the genus *Agave* that yield strong leaf fibers. **2.** This fiber, used in making cordage and paper. [Sp. < Quechua, to complicate.]

pit•a•pat (pĭt′ə-păt′) *intr.v.* **-pat•ted, -pat•ting, -pats 1.** To move with a series of quick tapping steps. **2.** To make a repeated tapping sound. ❖ *n.* A series of quick steps, taps, or beats. ❖ *adv.* With a rapid tapping sound. [Imit.]

pit boss *n.* One who supervises the gambling in a casino.

pit bull *n.* **1.** See **American Staffordshire terrier. 2.** *Slang* One who behaves in a markedly aggressive or ruthless manner.

pit bull terrier *n.* See **American Staffordshire terrier.**

Pit•cairn Island (pĭt′kârn′) A volcanic island of the S Pacific ESE of Tahiti; settled in 1790 by mutineers from H.M.S. *Bounty* and administered by the British since 1839.

pitch[1] (pĭch) *n.* **1.** Any of various thick, dark, sticky substances obtained from the distillation residue of coal tar, wood tar, or petroleum and used for waterproofing, roofing, caulking, and paving. **2.** Any of various natural bitumens, such as mineral pitch or asphalt. **3.** A resin derived from the sap of various coniferous trees. ❖ *tr.v.* **pitched, pitch•ing, pitch•es** To smear or cover with or as if with pitch. [ME *pich* < OE *pic* and < AN *piche*, both < Lat. *pix, pic-*.]

pitch[2] (pĭch) *v.* **pitched, pitch•ing, pitch•es** —*tr.* **1a.** To throw, usu. with careful aim. See Syns at **throw. b.** To discard by throwing. **2.** *Baseball* **a.** To throw (the ball) from the mound to the batter. **b.** To play (a game) as pitcher. **c.** To assign as pitcher. **3.** To erect or establish; set up: *pitched a tent; pitch camp.* **4.** To set firmly; implant; embed: *pitched stakes in the ground.* **5.** To set at a specified downward slant: *pitched the roof at a steep angle.* **6a.** To set at a particular level, degree, or quality. **b.** *Music* To set the pitch or key of. **c.** To adapt so as to be applicable; direct. **7.** *Informal* To attempt to promote or sell, often in a high-pressure manner. **8.** *Sports* To pitch a golf ball. —*intr.* **1.** To throw or toss something, such as a ball, horseshoe, or bale. **2.** *Baseball* To play in the position of pitcher. **3.** To plunge headlong. **4a.** To stumble around; lurch. **b.** To buck, as a horse. **5a.** *Nautical* To dip bow and stern alternately. **b.** To oscillate about a lateral axis so that the nose lifts or descends in relation to the tail. Used of an aircraft. **6.** To slope downward. **7.** To set up living quarters; encamp; settle. **8.** *Sports* To hit a golf ball in a high arc with backspin so that it does not roll very far after striking the ground. ❖ *n.* **1.** The act or an instance of pitching. **2.** *Baseball* **a.** A throw of the ball by the pitcher to the batter. **b.** A ball so thrown. **3.** *Sports* The rectangular area between the wickets in cricket, 22 yards (20.1 meters) by 10 feet (3.1 meters). **4a.** *Nautical* The pitching of a ship. **b.** The pitching of an airplane. **5a.** A steep downward slope. **b.** The degree of such a slope. **6.** *Architecture* **a.** The angle of a roof. **b.** The highest point of a structure: *the pitch of an arch.* **7.** A level or degree, as of intensity. **8a.** *Acoustics* The quality of highness or lowness of a sound, dependent primarily on the frequency of the sound waves produced by its source. **b.** *Music* The relative position of a tone within a range of musical sounds, as determined by pitch. **c.** *Music* Any of various standards for pitch associating each tone with a particular frequency. **9a.** The distance traveled by a machine screw in one revolution. **b.** The distance between two corresponding points on adjacent screw threads or gear teeth. **c.** The distance between two corresponding points on a helix. **10.** The distance that a propeller would travel in an ideal medium during one revolution, measured parallel to its shaft. **11.** *Informal* **a.** A line of talk designed to persuade. **b.** An advertisement. **12.** *Chiefly British* The stand of a vendor or hawker. **13.** *Games* See **seven-up. 14.** *Printing* The density of characters in a printed line, usu. expressed as characters per inch. ***—phrasal verbs:* pitch in** *Informal* **1.** To set to work vigorously. **2.** To join forces with others; help or cooperate. **pitch into** *Informal* To attack verbally or physically; assault. **pitch on (or upon)** *Informal* To succeed in choosing or achieving, usu. quickly. [ME *pichen*, prob. < OE **piccean*, causative of **pīcian*, to prick.]

pitch accent *n.* See **tonic accent.**

pitch-black (pĭch′blăk′) *adj.* Extremely dark.

pitch•blende (pĭch′blĕnd′) *n.* A massive variety of the mineral uraninite. [Partial transl. of Ger. *Pechblende* : *Pech*, pitch + *Blende*, blende; see BLENDE.]

pitch-dark (pĭch′därk′) *adj.* Extremely dark.

pitched battle (pĭcht) *n.* **1.** An intense battle fought in close contact by troops in a predetermined formation. **2.** A fiercely waged battle or struggle between opposing forces.

pitched roof *n.* A two-sided sloped roof having a gable at both ends.

pitch•er[1] (pĭch′ər) *n.* **1.** One that pitches. **2.** *Baseball* The player who throws the ball from the mound to the batter. **3.** *Sports* A seven iron used in golf.

pitch•er[2] (pĭch′ər) *n.* **1.** A container for liquids, usu. having a handle and a lip or spout for pouring. **2.** *Botany* A pitcherlike part, such as the leaf of a pitcher plant. [ME *picher* < OFr. *pichier*, alteration of *bichier* < Med.Lat. *bicārium*, drinking cup, prob. < Gk. *bikos*, jar, poss. < Egypt. *bik*, oil vessel.]

Pitcher, Molly See Mary Ludwig Hays **McCauley.**

pitcher plant *n.* Any of various insectivorous plants of the genera *Sarracenia, Nepenthes,* or *Darlingtonia*, having pitcherlike leaves that attract and trap insects.

pitch•fork (pĭch′fôrk′) *n.* A large long-handled fork with sharp, widely spaced prongs for lifting and pitching hay. [Alteration (influenced by *pichen*, to throw) of ME *pikforke* : *pik*, pick; see PICK[2], or *pik*, spike; see PIKE[5] + *forke*, fork; see FORK.] **—pitch′fork′** *v.*

pitch•man (pĭch′mən) *n.* **1.** A hawker of small wares, as on the streets or at a carnival. **2.** One who makes aggressive selling or promotional efforts. **3.** One who delivers commercials on radio or television.

pitch•out (pĭch′out′) *n.* **1.** *Baseball* A pitch deliberately thrown high and away from the batter to make it easier for the catcher to throw out a base runner who is standing off a base or attempting to steal. **2.** *Football* A lateral pass from the back receiving the snap from the center to another back behind the line of scrimmage.

pitch pine *n.* An eastern North American pine tree *(Pinus rigida)* that yields pitch or turpentine.

pitch pipe *n.* A small pipe that, when sounded, gives the initial pitch for a piece of music or the standard pitch for tuning an instrument.

pitch•stone (pĭch′stōn′) *n.* Any of various volcanic glasses distinguished by their dull pitchlike luster.

pitch•y (pĭch′ē) *adj.* **-i•er, -i•est 1.** Full of or covered with pitch. **2.** Resembling pitch in consistency. **3.** Extremely dark; black. **—pitch′i•ness** *n.*

pit•e•ous (pĭt′ē-əs) *adj.* **1.** Demanding or arousing pity. **2.** *Archaic* Pitying; compassionate. [ME < OFr. *piteus* < LLat. *pietōsus*, merciful < Lat. *pietās*, compassion. See PIETY.] **—pit′e•ous•ly** *adv.* **—pit′e•ous•ness** *n.*

pit•fall (pĭt′fôl′) *n.* **1.** An unapparent source of trouble or danger; a hidden hazard. **2.** A concealed hole in the ground that serves as a trap.

pith (pĭth) *n.* **1.** *Botany* The soft spongy parenchymatous center of the stems of most flowering plants. **2.** *Zoology* The soft inner substance of a feather or hair. **3.** The essential or central part; the heart or essence. **4.** Strength; vigor; mettle. **5.** Significance; importance. **6.** *Archaic* Spinal cord or bone marrow. ❖ *tr.v.* **pithed, pith•ing, piths 1.** To remove the pith from (a plant stem). **2.** To sever or destroy the spinal cord of, usu. by inserting a needle into the vertebral canal. **3.** To kill (cattle) by cutting the spinal cord. [ME < OE *pitha.*]

pith•e•can•thro•pus (pĭth′ĭ-kăn′thrə-pəs, -kăn-thrō′pəs) *n.* An extinct primate postulated from bones found in Java in 1891, now classified as *Homo erectus.* [NLat. *Pithēcanthrōpus*, former genus name : Gk. *pithēkos*, ape + Gk. *anthrōpos*, man.] **—pith′e•can•throp′ic** (-kən-thrŏp′ĭk) *adj.* **—pith′e•can′thro•pine** (-kăn′thrə-pīn′) *adj.*

pith•e•coid (pĭth′ĭ-koid′, pĭ-thē′koid) *adj.* **1.** Resembling or relating to the apes, esp. the anthropoid apes. **2.** Of or belonging to a genus *(Pithecia)* of small slender South American monkeys related to the titi. [Gk. *pithēkos*, ape + -OID.]

pith helmet *n.* A lightweight hat made from dried pith and worn in tropical countries for protection from the sun.

pith ray *n.* The parenchymatous tissue that extends between the vascular bundles of a stem or root.

pith•y (pĭth′ē) *adj.* **-i•er, -i•est 1.** Precisely meaningful; forceful and brief: *a pithy comment.* **2.** Consisting of or resembling pith. **—pith′i•ly** *adv.* **—pith′i•ness** *n.*

pit•i•a•ble (pĭt′ē-ə-bəl) *adj.* **1.** Arousing or deserving of pity or compassion; lamentable. **2.** Arousing disdainful pity. **—pit′i•a•ble•ness** *n.* **—pit′i•a•bly** *adv.*

pit•i•ful (pĭt′ĭ-fəl) *adj.* **1.** Inspiring or deserving pity. **2.** Arousing contemptuous pity, as through ineptitude or inadequacy. **3.** *Archaic* Filled with pity or compassion. **—pit′i•ful•ly** *adv.* **—pit′i•ful•ness** *n.*

pit•i•less (pĭt′ĭ-lĭs) *adj.* Having no pity; merciless. **—pit′i•less•ly** *adv.* **—pit′i•less•ness** *n.*

pit•man (pĭt′mən) *n.* **1.** *pl.* **pit•men** (-mĕn) A worker employed inside a pit in various industrial operations, as in a coal mine. **2.** *pl.* **pit•mans** (-mənz) See **connecting rod.**

Pi•to•cin (pĭ-tō′sĭn) A trademark used for preparations of oxytocin.

pi•ton (pē′tŏn′) *n.* A metal spike that is fitted at one end with an eye for securing a rope and is driven into rock or ice as a support

pitcher plant
Nepenthes × mixta

pitchfork

ă	pat	oi	boy
ā	pay	ou	out
âr	care	o͝o	took
ä	father	o͞o	boot
ĕ	pet	ŭ	cut
ē	be	ûr	urge
ĭ	pit	th	thin
ī	pie	*th*	this
îr	pier	hw	which
ŏ	pot	zh	vision
ō	toe	ə	about, item
ô	paw		

Stress marks:
′ (primary);
′ (secondary), as in
lexicon (lĕk′sĭ-kŏn′)

in mountain climbing. [Fr. < OFr., nail.]

Pi·tot-stat·ic tube (pē′tō-stăt′ĭk, pē-tō′-) *n.* A device consisting of a Pitot tube and a static tube, used in aircraft to determine relative wind speed.

Pi·tot tube (pē′tō, pē-tō′) *n.* A tube set parallel to the direction of fluid-stream movement and attached to a manometer, used to measure the total pressure of a fluid stream. [After Henri *Pitot* (1695–1771), French physicist.]

Pit River[1] *n.* See **Achomawi** 1.

Pit River[2] A river of N CA flowing c. 322 km (200 mi) to the Sacramento R.

pit·saw also **pit saw** (pĭt′sô′) *n.* A large saw for cutting logs, operated jointly by a person standing above the log and another in a pit underneath.

pit stop *n.* **1.** *Sports* A stop at a pit for refueling or service during an automobile race. **2.** *Informal* **a.** A brief stop for rest and refreshment, esp. during an automobile trip. **b.** A place where such a stop is made.

Pitt[1] (pĭt), **William.** 1st Earl of Chatham. Known as "the Elder." 1708–78. British politician who directed his country's military effort during the Seven Years' War (1756–63).

Pitt[2] (pĭt), **William.** 2nd Earl of Chatham. Known as "the Younger." 1759–1806. British prime minister (1783–1801 and 1804–06) who secured the Act of Union between Ireland and Great Britain (1800).

pit·ta (pĭt′ə) *n.* Any of several brightly colored perching birds of the family Pittidae of Asia, Australia, and Africa, having a strong bill, short tail, and long legs. [Telugu *piṭṭa,* bird.]

pitta

pit·tance (pĭt′ns) *n.* **1.** A meager monetary allowance, wage, or remuneration. **2.** A very small amount. [ME *pitance* < OFr., allowance of food < Med.Lat. *pietantia,* ult. < Lat. *pietās,* piety. See PITY.]

pit·ted (pĭt′ĭd) *adj.* **1.** Marked by pits. **2.** Having the pit removed: *pitted dates.*

pit·ter-pat·ter (pĭt′ər-păt′ər) *n.* A rapid series of light tapping sounds. [Imit.] —**pit′ter-pat′ter** *v.*

pit·tos·po·rum (pĭ-tŏs′pər-əm, pĭt′ə-spôr′əm, -spōr′-) *n.* Any of various Old World evergreen shrubs or plants of the genus *Pittosporum.* [NLat., genus name : Gk. *pissa, pitta,* pitch + NLat. *spora,* spore; see SPORE.]

Pitts·burgh (pĭts′bûrg′) A city of SW PA at the point where the confluence of the Allegheny and Monongahela rivers forms the Ohio R. Pop. 334,563.

pi·tu·i·tar·y (pĭ-tōō′ĭ-tĕr′ē, -tyōō′-) *n., pl.* **-ies 1.** The pituitary gland. **2.** *Medicine* An extract of the pituitary gland, prepared for therapeutic use. ❖ *adj.* **1.** Of or relating to the pituitary gland. **2.** Of or secreting phlegm or mucus; mucous. [< Lat. *pītuītārius,* of phlegm (< the early belief that it produced mucus) < *pītuīta,* phlegm. See peiə- in App.]

pituitary gland *n.* A small oval endocrine gland attached to the base of the vertebrate brain and consisting of an anterior and a posterior lobe, the secretions of which control the other endocrine glands and influence growth, metabolism, and maturation.

pit viper *n.* Any of various venomous snakes of the family Crotalidae, such as a copperhead, rattlesnake, or fer-de-lance, characterized by a small sensory pit below each eye.

pit·y (pĭt′ē) *n., pl.* **-ies 1.** Sympathy and sorrow aroused by the misfortune or suffering of another. **2.** A matter of regret: *It's a pity you can't attend.* ❖ *v.* **-ied, -y·ing, -ies** —*tr.* To feel pity for. —*intr.* To feel pity. —*idiom:* **have** (or **take**) **pity on** To show compassion for. [ME *pite* < OFr. < Lat. *pietās,* piety, compassion < *pius,* dutiful.] —**pit′y·ing·ly** *adv.*

pit·y·ri·a·sis (pĭt′ĭ-rī′ə-sĭs) *n., pl.* **-ses** (-sēz′) Any of various skin diseases characterized by shedding of flaky epidermal scales. [Gk. *pitūriasis* < *pitūron,* grain husk, dandruff.]

più (pyōō) *adv. Music* More. [Ital. < Lat. *plūs.* See peiə-[1] in App.]

Pi·us II (pī′əs) 1405–64. Pope (1458–64) noted for his unsuccessful attempt to lead a crusade against the Turks.

Pius V, Saint. 1504–72. Pope (1566–72) who excommunicated Elizabeth I of England.

Pius VII 1742–1823. Pope (1800–23) who was forced to crown Napoleon emperor in 1804.

Pius IX 1792–1878. Pope (1846–78) who summoned the First Vatican Council (1869–70).

Pius X, Saint. 1835–1914. Pope (1903–14) who was strongly opposed to religious modernism.

Pius XI 1857–1939. Pope (1922–39) who signed a treaty with Benito Mussolini granting papal sovereignty over the Vatican City.

Pius XII 1876–1958. Pope (1939–58) who maintained neutrality during World War II and was later criticized for not taking forceful measures to aid European Jews.

Pi·ute (pī′yōōt′) *n.* Variant of **Paiute.**

piv·ot (pĭv′ət) *n.* **1.** A short rod or shaft on which a related part rotates or swings. **2.** A person or thing on which something depends or turns; the central or crucial factor. **3.** The act of turning on or as if on a pivot. ❖ *v.* **-ot·ed, -ot·ing, -ots** —*tr.* **1.** To mount on, attach by, or provide with a pivot or pivots. **2.** To cause to rotate, revolve, or turn. —*intr.* To turn on or as if on a pivot. [Fr. < OFr.] —**piv′ot·a·ble** *adj.*

piv·ot·al (pĭv′ə-tl) *adj.* **1.** Of, relating to, or serving as a pivot. **2.** Being of vital importance; crucial. —**piv′ot·al·ly** *adv.*

pivot joint *n.* A joint in which a bone rotates around another.

pix[1] (pĭks) *n.* A plural of **pic.**

pix[2] (pĭks) *n.* Variant of **pyx.**

pix·el (pĭk′səl, -sĕl′) *n.* The basic unit of the composition of an image on a television screen, computer monitor, or similar display. [PIX[1] + EL(EMENT).]

pix·ie or **pix·y** (pĭk′sē) *n., pl.* **-ies** A fairylike or elfin creature, esp. one that is mischievous; a playful sprite. ❖ *adj.* Playfully mischievous. [?]

pix·i·lat·ed or **pix·il·lat·ed** (pĭk′sə-lā′tĭd) *adj.* **1.** Behaving as if mentally unstable; eccentric. **2.** Whimsical; prankish. **3.** *Slang* Intoxicated; drunk. [< PIXIE.] —**pix′i·la′tion** *n.*

Pi·zar·ro (pĭ-zär′ō, pē-thär′ō, -sär′-), **Francisco** 1475?–1541. Spanish explorer and conqueror of Peru (1531–33).

piz·za (pēt′sə) *n.* A baked pie of Italian origin consisting of a shallow breadlike crust with toppings such as seasoned tomato sauce, cheese, or olives. [Ital., pie, tart, pizza.]

piz·zazz or **pi·zazz** or **piz·zazz** (pĭ-zăz′) *n. Informal* **1.** Dazzling style; flamboyance; flair. **2.** Vigorous spirit; energy or excitement. [?]

piz·ze·ri·a (pēt′sə-rē′ə) *n.* A place where pizzas are made and sold. [Ital. < *pizza,* pie, pizza.]

piz·zi·ca·to (pĭt′sĭ-kä′tō) *Music adj.* Played by plucking rather than bowing the strings. ❖ *n., pl.* **-ti** (-tē) A pizzicato note or passage. [Ital., p. part. of *pizzicare,* to pluck < *pizzare,* to prick < *pizzo,* point.] —**piz′zi·ca′to** *adv.*

piz·zle (pĭz′əl) *n.* **1.** The penis of an animal, esp. a bull. **2.** A whip made from a bull's penis. [Poss. < LGer. *pēsel,* dim. of MLGer. *pese,* penis, tendon.]

PJs or **PJ's** or **pj's** (pē′jāz′) *pl.n. Informal* Pajamas. [*p(a)j(ama)s,* pl. of PAJAMA.]

pk. *abbr.* **1.** park **2.** also **Pk.** peak **3.** peck

pkg. *abbr.* package

pkt. *abbr.* packet

PKU *abbr.* phenylketonuria

Pkwy or **Pky** *abbr.* parkway

pl. *abbr.* **1.** or **Pl.** place **2.** *Printing & Photography* plate **3.** plural

plac·a·ble (plăk′ə-bəl, plā′kə-) *adj.* Easily calmed or pacified; tolerant. [ME, agreeable < OFr. < Lat. *plācābilis* < *plācāre,* to calm.] —**plac′a·bil′i·ty** *n.* —**plac′a·bly** *adv.*

plac·ard (plăk′ärd′, -ərd) *n.* **1.** A sign or notice for display in a public place. **2.** A small card or plaque, such as a nameplate on a door. ❖ *tr.v.* **-ard·ed, -ard·ing, -ards 1.** To announce or advertise by means of placards. **2.** To post placards on or in. **3.** To display as a placard. [ME, official document < OFr. < *plaquier,* to plaster, piece together < MDu. *placken,* to patch.]

pla·cate (plā′kāt′, plăk′āt′) *tr.v.* **-cat·ed, -cat·ing, -cates** To allay the anger of, esp. by making concessions; appease. See Syns at **pacify.** [Lat. *plācāre, plācāt-,* to calm.] —**pla′cat′er** *n.* —**pla·ca′tion** (plā-kā′shən) *n.* —**pla·ca·to·ry** (-tôr′ē, -tōr′ē), **pla·ca′·tive** (-kā′tĭv) *adj.*

place (plās) *n.* **1a.** A bounded area; a portion of space. **b.** Room or space, esp. adequate space. **2a.** The given portion of space occupied by or allocated to a person or thing. **b.** A building or area set aside for a specified purpose: *a place of worship.* **3a.** A dwelling; a house. **b.** A business establishment or office. **c.** A locality, such as a town or city. **4.** often **Place** A public square or street with houses in a town. **5a.** A space in which one person, such as a passenger, can sit or stand. **b.** A setting for one person at a table. **6.** A position regarded as belonging to someone or something else; stead. **7.** A particular point reached, as in a book. **8.** A particular spot, as on the body. **9a.** The proper or designated role or function. **b.** The proper or customary position or order: *These files are out of place.* **c.** A suitable setting or occasion. **d.** The appropriate right or duty: *not your place to criticize.* **10.** Social station. **11.** A particular situation or circumstance: *Put yourself in my place.* **12.** High rank or status. **13.** A job, post, or position: *found a place at the firm.* **14.** Relative position in a series; standing. **15.** *Games* Second position for betting purposes, as in a horserace. **16.** The specified stage in a list of points to be made, as in an argument: *in the first place.* **17.** *Mathematics* A position in a numeral or series. ❖ *v.* **placed, plac·ing, plac·es** —*tr.* **1.** To put in or as if in a particular place or position; set. **2.** To put in a specified relation or order: *Place the words in alphabetical order.* **3.** To offer for consideration: *placed the matter before the board.* **4.** To find accommodation or employment for. **5.** To put into a particular condition: *placed him under arrest.* **6.** To arrange for the publication or display of. **7.** To appoint to a post: *placed her in a key position.* **8a.** To rank in an order or sequence. **b.** To estimate: *placed the distance at 100 feet.* **9.** To identify or classify in a particular context. **10a.** To give an order for: *place a bet.* **b.** To apply or arrange for: *place an order.* **11.** To adjust (one's voice) for the best effects. —*intr.* To be among those who finish a competition or race, esp. to finish second. —*phrasal verb:* **place out** To qualify for a waiver of a requirement or prerequisite. —*idioms:* **all over the place** In or to many locations; everywhere: *Film is sold all over the place.* **in place 1.** In the appropriate or usual position or order. **2.** In the same spot; without moving forward or backward. **in place of** Instead of. **keep** (or **know**) **(one's) place** To recognize one's social position and act accordingly. **place in the sun** A dominant or favorable position or situation. [ME < OE *plæce* and < OFr. *place*, open space (< Med.Lat. *placea* < VLat. **plattea*), both < Lat. *platēa*, broad street < Gk. *plateia (hodos)*, broad (street), fem. of *platus*.] —**place′a·ble** *adj.* —**plac′er** *n.*

pla·ce·bo (plə-sē′bō) *n., pl.* -**bos** or -**boes** **1a.** A substance containing no medication and given to reinforce a patient's expectation to get well. **b.** An inactive substance used as a control in an experiment or test to determine the effectiveness of a medicinal drug. **2.** Something of no intrinsic remedial value that is used to appease or reassure another. **3.** (plä-chā′bō) *Roman Catholic Church* The service or office of vespers for the dead. [ME, vespers for the dead < LLat. *placēbō*, I will please, first pers. sing. fut. t. of Lat. *placēre*, to please.]

placebo effect *n.* The beneficial effect in a patient following a treatment that arises from the patient's expectations concerning the treatment rather than from the treatment itself.

place·hold·er (plās′hōl′dər) *n.* **1.** One who holds an office or place, esp.: **a.** One who acts as a deputy or proxy. **b.** One who holds an appointed office in a government. **2.** A mathematical or logical symbol that may be replaced by the name of any element of a set. **3.** A nonsignificant digit in a decimal number.

place kick *n. Football* A kick, as for a kickoff or field goal, for which the ball is held or propped up in a fixed position on the ground. —**place′kick′** (plās′kĭk′) *v.* —**place′kick′er** *n.*

place·man (plās′mən) *n. Chiefly British* One who has a political appointment in the government.

place mat *n.* A protective table mat for a single place setting.

place·ment (plās′mənt) *n.* **1a.** The act of placing or arranging. **b.** The state of being placed or arranged. **2a.** The finding of suitable accommodation or employment for applicants. **b.** Assignment of students to appropriate classes or programs. **3.** *Football* **a.** The setting of the ball in position for a place kick. **b.** A place kick.

pla·cen·ta (plə-sĕn′tə) *n., pl.* -**tas** or -**tae** (-tē) **1a.** A membranous vascular organ that develops in female mammals during pregnancy, lining the uterine wall and partially enveloping the fetus, to which it is attached by the umbilical cord. **b.** An organ with similar functions in some nonmammals, such as certain sharks and reptiles. **2.** *Botany* The part within the ovary of a flowering plant to which the ovules are attached. [NLat. < Lat., flat cake, alteration of Gk. *plakoenta* < accusative of *plakoeis*, flat < *plax, plak-*, flat land, surface.] —**pla·cen′tal** *adj.*

plac·en·ta·tion (plăs′ən-tā′shən) *n.* **1a.** Formation of a placenta in the uterus. **b.** The type or structure of a placenta. **2.** *Botany* Arrangement of placentas within the ovary.

plac·er (plăs′ər) *n.* **1.** A glacial or alluvial deposit of sand or gravel containing eroded particles of valuable minerals. **2.** A place where a placer deposit is washed to extract its mineral content. [Sp., shoal, placer < Catalan, shoal < *plassa*, place < Med.Lat. *placea*. See PLACE.]

place setting *n.* A table service for one person.

plac·id (plăs′ĭd) *adj.* **1.** Undisturbed by tumult or disorder; calm or quiet. See Syns at **calm**. **2.** Satisfied; complacent. [Lat. *placidus* < *placēre*, to please.] —**pla·cid′i·ty** (plə-sĭd′ĭ-tē), **plac′id·ness** (plăs′ĭd-nĭs) *n.* —**plac′id·ly** *adv.*

Placid, Lake A lake of NE NY in the Adirondack Mts.

plack·et (plăk′ĭt) *n.* **1.** A slit in a dress, blouse, or skirt. **2.** A pocket, esp. in a woman's skirt. [?]

pla·co·derm (plăk′ə-dûrm′) *n.* Any of various extinct fishes of the Silurian and Devonian periods, having bony plates of armor, hinged jaws, and paired fins. [NLat. *Placodermī*, class name < Gk. *plax, plak-*, flat stone, plate + –DERM.]

plac·oid (plăk′oid′) *adj.* Platelike, as the hard toothlike scales of sharks, skates, and rays. [Gk. *plax, plak-*, flat stone, plate + –OID.]

pla·fond (plə-fôn′, plä-fôN′) *n.* A decorated ceiling. [Fr. : *plat*, flat; see PLATE + *fond*, base, bottom; see FOND².]

pla·gal (plā′gəl) *adj. Music* **1.** Of or being a medieval mode having a range from the fourth below to the fifth above its final tone. **2.** Of or being a cadence with the subdominant chord immediately preceding the tonic chord. [Med.Lat. *plagālis* < *plaga*, plagal mode < *plagius*, plagal < Med.Gk. *plagios (ēkhos)*, plagal (mode) < Gk., oblique < *plagos*, side.]

plage (pläzh) *n.* **1.** A sandy beach at a seaside resort. **2.** A bright and intensely hot area in the sun's chromosphere, usu. associated with a sunspot. [Fr. < Ital. *piaggia*, ult. < Gk. *plagia*, neut. pl. of *plagios*, oblique, slanting. See PLAGAL.]

pla·gia·rism (plā′jə-rĭz′əm) *n.* **1.** The act of plagiarizing. **2.** Something plagiarized. [< PLAGIARY.] —**pla′gia·rist** *n.* —**pla′gia·ris′tic** *adj.*

pla·gia·rize (plā′jə-rīz′) *v.* -**rized**, -**riz·ing**, -**riz·es** —*tr.* **1.** To use and pass off (the ideas or writings of another) as one's own. **2.** To appropriate for use as one's own passages or ideas from (another). —*intr.* To plagiarize the ideas or words of another. —**pla′gia·riz′er** *n.*

pla·gia·ry (plā′jə-rē) *n., pl.* -**ries** **1.** Plagiarism. **2.** *Archaic* One who plagiarizes. [Lat. *plagiārius*, kidnapper, plagiarist < *plagium*, kidnapping < *plaga*, net.]

plagio– *pref.* Slanting; inclining: *plagiotropism*. [Gk., oblique < *plagios* < *plagos*, side.]

pla·gi·o·clase (plā′jē-ə-klās′, -klāz′, plăj′ē-) *n.* Any of a common rock-forming series of triclinic feldspars, consisting of mix-

---

tures of sodium and calcium aluminum silicates. [Gk. *plagio-*, plagio- + Gk. *klasis*, breaking (< its oblique cleavage) (< *klān*, to break).]

pla·gi·ot·ro·pism (plā′jē-ŏt′rə-pĭz′əm) *n. Botany* The tendency to grow at an oblique or horizontal angle, as roots or branches. —**pla′gi·o·tro′pic** (-ə-trō′pĭk, -trŏp′ĭk) *adj.*

plague (plāg) *n.* **1.** A widespread affliction or calamity, esp. one seen as divine retribution. **2.** A sudden destructive influx or injurious outbreak: *a plague of accidents*. **3.** A cause of annoyance; a nuisance. **4.** A highly infectious, usu. fatal epidemic disease, esp. bubonic plague. ❖ *tr.v.* **plagued, plagu·ing, plagues 1.** To pester or annoy persistently or incessantly. See Syns at **harass. 2.** To afflict with or as if with a disease or calamity. [ME *plage*, blow, calamity, plague < LLat. *plāga* < Lat., blow, wound. See **plāk-** in App.] —**plagu′er** *n.*

pla·guy also **pla·guey** (plā′gē) *adj.* Vexatious; bothersome. —**pla′guy, pla′gui·ly** *adv.*

plaice (plās) *n., pl.* **plaice** or **plaic·es 1.** A large edible marine flatfish (*Pleuronectes platessa*) of western European waters. **2.** Any of various flatfishes, such as *Hippoglossoides platessoides* of North American Atlantic waters, related to the plaice. [ME < OFr. *plais* < VLat. **platix*, alteration of LLat. *platessa*, prob. ult. < Gk. *platus*, broad.]

plaid (plăd) *n.* **1.** A rectangular woolen scarf of a tartan pattern worn over the left shoulder by Scottish Highlanders. **2a.** Cloth with a tartan or checked pattern. **b.** A pattern of this kind. [Sc. Gael. *plaide*.] —**plaid** *adj.*

plaid·ed (plăd′ĭd) *adj.* **1.** Made of plaid or having a plaid pattern. **2.** Wearing a plaid.

plain (plān) *adj.* **plain·er, plain·est 1.** Free from obstructions; open; clear: *in plain view.* **2.** Obvious to the mind; evident: *make one's intention plain.* See Syns at **apparent. 3.** Not elaborate or complicated; simple: *plain food.* **4.** Straightforward; frank or candid: *plain talk.* **5.** Not mixed with other substances; pure: *plain water.* **6.** Common in rank or station; average; ordinary: *a plain man.* **7.** Not pretentious; unaffected. **8.** Marked by little or no ornamentation or decoration. **9.** Not dyed, twilled, or patterned: *a plain fabric.* **10.** Lacking beauty or distinction: *a plain face.* **11.** Sheer; utter; unqualified: *plain stupidity.* **12.** *Archaic* Having no visible elevation or depression; flat; level. ❖ *n.* **1a.** An extensive, level, usu. treeless area of land. **b.** A broad level expanse, as part of the sea floor or a lunar mare. **2.** Something free of ornamentation or extraneous matter. ❖ *adv. Informal* Clearly; simply: *plain stubborn.* [ME < OFr. < Lat. *plānus.* See **pelə-²** in App.] —**plain′ly** *adv.* —**plain′ness** *n.*

plain·chant (plān′chănt′) *n.* See **plainsong** 2. [Fr. *plain-chant* (transl. of Med.Lat. *cantus plānus*) : *plain*, plain; see PLAIN + *chant*, song; see CHANT.]

plain·clothes or **plain-clothes** (plān′klōz′, -klōthz′) *adj.* Wearing civilian clothes while on duty to avoid being identified as police or security: *a plainclothes detective.*

plain·clothes·man or **plain-clothes man** (plān′klōz′mən, -klōthz′-) *n.* A member of a police force, esp. a detective, who wears civilian clothes on duty.

plain-Jane (plān′jān′) *adj.* Lacking adornment or pretension; basic or simple.

plain-laid (plān′lād′) *adj.* Made of three strands laid together with a right-hand twist. Used of a rope.

Plain People *pl.n.* Members of the Mennonites, Amish, or Dunkers, noted for their plain dress and simple style of life.

Plains Indian (plānz) *n.* A member of any of the Native American peoples inhabiting the Great Plains.

plains·man (plānz′mən) *n.* An inhabitant or a settler of the plains, esp. of the prairie regions of the United States.

plain·song (plān′sông′, -sŏng′) *n. Roman Catholic Church* **1.** Gregorian chant. **2.** Any monophonic medieval liturgical music without strict meter and traditionally sung without accompaniment. [Transl. of Med.Lat. *cantus plānus*.]

plain·spo·ken (plān′spō′kən) *adj.* Frank; straightforward; blunt. —**plain′spo′ken·ness** *n.*

plaint (plānt) *n.* **1.** A complaint. **2.** An utterance of grief or sorrow; a lamentation. [ME < OFr. *plainte* < Lat. *plānctus*, lament < p. part. of *plangere*, to strike one's breast, lament. See **plāk-** in App.]

plain text or **plain-text** (plān′tĕkst′) *n.* The unencrypted form of an encrypted message.

plain·tiff (plān′tĭf) *n. Law* The party that institutes a suit in a court. [ME *plaintif* < AN *pleintif* < OFr. *plaintif*, aggrieved. See PLAINTIVE.]

plain·tive (plān′tĭv) *adj.* Expressing sorrow; mournful or melancholy. [ME *plaintif* < OFr., lamenting < *plaint*, complaint. See PLAINT.] —**plain′tive·ly** *adv.* —**plain′tive·ness** *n.*

plain vanilla *adj. Informal* Lacking adornments or special features; basic or ordinary: *plain vanilla stock options.*

plain weave *n.* A weave in which the filling threads and the warp threads interlace alternately, forming a checkerboard pattern.

plain-wo·ven (plān′wō′vən) *adj.* Made in plain weave.

plait (plāt, plăt) *n.* **1.** A braid, esp. of hair. **2.** A pleat. ❖ *tr.v.* **plait·ed, plait·ing, plaits 1.** To braid. **2.** To pleat. **3.** To make by braiding. [ME *pleit*, fold, braid, poss. < *pleiten*, to fold, braid, alteration (influenced by OFr. *pleit*, fold) of OFr. *plier, pleiir* < Lat.

plaid

plicāre, to fold. See **plek-** in App.] —**plait′**er *n.*

plan (plăn) *n.* **1.** A scheme, program, or method worked out beforehand to accomplish an objective. **2.** A tentative project or course of action. **3.** A systematic arrangement of parts; a configuration or outline. **4.** A drawing or diagram made to scale showing the structure or arrangement of something. **5.** In perspective rendering, one of several imaginary planes perpendicular to the line of vision between the viewer and the object being depicted. **6.** A program or policy stipulating a service or benefit: *a pension plan.* ❖ *v.* **planned, plan•ning, plans** —*tr.* **1.** To form a scheme or program for the accomplishment or attainment of. **2.** To have as a specific aim or purpose; intend. **3.** To draw or make a graphic representation of. —*intr.* To make plans. [Fr., alteration of *plant*, ground plan, map < *planter*, to plant < Lat. *plantāre* < *planta*, sole of the foot.] —**plan′**ner *n.*

SYNONYMS *plan, blueprint, design, project, scheme, strategy* These nouns denote a method or program in accordance with which something is to be done or accomplished: *has no vacation plans; a blueprint for reorganization; social conventions of human design; an urban-renewal project; a scheme for conservation; a strategy for survival.*

---

plan– *pref.* Variant of **plano–**.

pla•nar (plā′nər, -när′) *adj.* **1.** Of, relating to, or situated in a plane. **2.** Flat: *a planar surface.* **3.** Having a two-dimensional quality. [LLat. *plānāris*, flat < Lat. *plānus.* See PLAIN.] —**pla•nar′i•ty** (plā-năr′ĭ-tē) *n.*

pla•nar•i•an (plə-nâr′ē-ən) *n.* Any of various small, chiefly freshwater turbellarian flatworms of the order Tricladida, having soft broad ciliated bodies. [< NLat. *Plānāria*, genus name < fem. of LLat. *plānārius*, on level ground < *plānus*, flat. See pelə-² in App.]

pla•na•tion (plā-nā′shən) *n.* The process of erosion and deposition in which a level surface is produced, as by streams or wind. [Lat. *plānum*, flat surface; see PLANE¹ + –ATION.]

planch•et (plăn′chĭt) *n.* **1.** A flat disk of metal ready for stamping as a coin; a coin blank. **2.** A small shallow metal container in which a radioactive substance is deposited for measurement of its activity. [Dim. of *planch*, flat plate, slab < ME *plaunche*, plank < OFr. *planche* < LLat. *planca* < fem. of Lat. *plancus*, flat.]

plan•chette (plăn-shĕt′) *n.* A small triangular board supported by two casters and a vertical pencil that, when lightly touched by the fingertips, is said to spell out subconscious or supernatural messages. [Fr. < OFr., dim. of *planche*, board. See PLANCHET.]

Planck (plängk), **Max Karl Ernst Ludwig** 1858–1947. German physicist who won a 1918 Nobel Prize.

Planck's constant (plängks) *n. Symbol* **h** The constant of proportionality relating the energy of a photon to its frequency, equal to approx. 6.626 ×10⁻³⁴ joule-seconds. [After Max Karl Ernst Ludwig PLANCK.]

plane¹ (plān) *n.* **1.** *Mathematics* A surface containing all the straight lines that connect any two points on it. **2.** A flat or level surface. **3.** A level of development, existence, or achievement. **4.** An airplane or hydroplane. **5.** A supporting surface of an airplane; an airfoil or wing. ❖ *adj. Mathematics* Of or being a figure lying in a plane: *a plane curve.* **2.** Flat; level. [Lat. *plānum*, flat surface < neut. of *plānus*, flat. See pelə-² in App.] —**plane′**ness *n.*

plane² (plān) *n.* **1.** A carpenter's tool with an adjustable blade for smoothing and leveling wood. **2.** A trowel-shaped tool for smoothing the surface of clay, sand, or plaster in a mold. ❖ *v.* **planed, plan•ing, planes** —*tr.* **1.** To smooth or finish with or as if with a plane. **2.** To remove with a plane. —*intr.* **1.** To work with a plane. **2.** To act as a plane. [ME < OFr. < LLat. *plāna* < *plānāre*, to plane < *plānus*, flat. See pelə-² in App.]

plane³ (plān) *intr.v.* **planed, plan•ing, planes** **1.** To rise partly out of the water, as a boat does at high speeds. **2.** To soar or glide. **3.** To travel by airplane. [ME *planen*, to glide, soar < OFr. *planer* < *plain*, flat, level. See PLAIN.]

plane⁴ (plān) *n.* The plane tree. [ME < OFr. < Lat. *platanus* < Gk. *platanos*, perh. < *platus*, broad.]

plane angle *n.* An angle formed by two straight lines in the same plane.

plane geometry *n.* The geometry of planar figures.

plane•load (plān′lōd′) *n.* The load an airplane can carry.

plan•er (plā′nər) *n.* **1.** One that planes, esp. a machine tool that is used to smooth or finish the surfaces of wood or metal. **2.** *Printing* A smooth block of wood used to level a form of type.

pla•ner tree (plā′nər) *n.* A small, deciduous elmlike swamp tree (*Planera aquatica*) of the southern United States, having small ribbed nutlike fruit. [After Johann Jacob *Planer* (1743–89), German botanist.]

plane•side (plān′sīd′) *n.* The area adjacent to an airplane.

plan•et (plăn′ĭt) *n.* **1.** A nonluminous celestial body larger than an asteroid or comet that revolves around a star. **2.** One of the seven celestial bodies, Mercury, Venus, the moon, the sun, Mars, Jupiter, and Saturn, thought by ancient astronomers to revolve in the heavens about a fixed Earth and among fixed stars. **3.** One of the seven revolving astrological celestial bodies that in conjunction with the stars are believed to influence human affairs. [ME < OFr. *planete* < LLat. *planēta* < Gk. *planētēs*,

plane²
carpenter's plane

var. of *planēs, planēt-* < *planāsthai*, to wander. See pelə-² in App.]

plane table *n.* A portable surveying instrument consisting essentially of a drawing board and a ruler mounted on a tripod and used to sight and map topographic details.

plan•e•tar•i•um (plăn′ĭ-târ′ē-əm) *n., pl.* **-i•ums** or **-i•a** (-ē-ə) **1.** An apparatus or model representing the solar system. **2a.** An optical device for projecting images of celestial bodies and other astronomical phenomena onto the inner surface of a hemispherical dome. **b.** A building or room containing a planetarium, with seats for an audience.

plan•e•tar•y (plăn′ĭ-tĕr′ē) *adj.* **1.** Of, relating to, or resembling the physical or orbital characteristics of a planet or the planets. **2a.** Of or relating to the earth; terrestrial or earthly. **b.** Of or affecting the entire world; global. **3.** Wandering; erratic. **4.** Being or relating to a gear train having a central gear with an internal ring gear and one or more pinions.

planetary nebula *n.* A nebula consisting of a hot blue-white central star surrounded by an envelope of expanding gas.

plan•e•tes•i•mal (plăn′ĭ-tĕs′ə-məl) *n.* Any of innumerable small bodies thought to have orbited the sun and aggregated into the planets. [PLANET + (INFINIT)ESIMAL.]

plan•e•toid (plăn′ĭ-toid′) *n. Astronomy* See **asteroid** 1. —**plan′e•toi′dal** (-toid′l) *adj.*

plan•e•tol•o•gy (plăn′ĭ-tŏl′ə-jē) *n.* The branch of astronomy that deals with the planets of the solar system. —**plan′e•to•log′i•cal** (plăn′ĭ-tl-ŏj′ĭ-kəl) *adj.* —**plan′e•tol′o•gist** *n.*

plane tree *n.* Any of several trees of the genus *Platanus*, having ball-shaped fruit clusters and usu. outer bark that flakes off in patches. [PLANE⁴ + TREE.]

planet wheel *n.* A small gear wheel in an epicyclic train.

plan•gent (plăn′jənt) *adj.* **1.** Loud and resounding: *plangent bells.* **2.** Expressing or suggesting sadness; plaintive. [Lat. *plangēns, plangent-*, pr. part. of *plangere*, to strike, lament. See plāk- in App.] —**plan′gen•cy** *n.* —**plan′gent•ly** *adv.*

pla•nim•e•ter (plə-nĭm′ĭ-tər, plā-) *n.* An instrument that measures the area of a plane figure as a mechanically coupled pointer traverses the perimeter of the figure. —**pla′ni•met′ric** (plā′nə-mĕt′rĭk), **pla′ni•met′ri•cal** (-rĭ-kəl) *adj.* —**pla′ni•met′ri•cal•ly** *adv.* —**pla•nim′e•try** *n.*

plan•ish (plăn′ĭsh) *tr.v.* **-ished, -ish•ing, -ish•es** To smooth (metal) by rolling or hammering. [ME *planisen* < OFr. *planir, planiss-*, to make smooth < *plan*, level < Lat. *plānus.* See pelə-² in App.] —**plan′ish•er** *n.*

pla•ni•sphere (plā′nĭ-sfîr′) *n.* **1.** A representation of a sphere or part of a sphere on a plane surface. **2.** *Astronomy* A polar projection of half or more of the celestial sphere on a chart with an adjustable overlay to show the stars visible at a given time and place. —**pla′ni•spher′ic** (-sfîr′ĭk, -sfĕr′-) *adj.*

plank (plăngk) *n.* **1a.** A piece of lumber cut thicker than a board. **b.** Planking. **2.** A foundation; a support. **3.** One of the articles of a political platform. ❖ *tr.v.* **planked, plank•ing, planks** **1.** To furnish or cover with planks. **2.** To bake or broil and serve (fish or meat) on a plank. **3.** To put or set down, often emphatically or with force. [ME < ONFr. *planke* < LLat. *planca* < *plancus*, flat.]

plank•ing (plăng′kĭng) *n.* **1.** Planks considered as a group; plank. **2.** An object or structure made of planks.

plank•ter (plăngk′tər) *n.* One of the many organisms that collectively constitute plankton. [Gk. *planktēr*, wanderer < *planktos*, wandering. See PLANKTON.]

plank•ton (plăngk′tən) *n.* The collection of small or microscopic organisms, including algae, that float or drift in great numbers in fresh or salt water, esp. at or near the surface, and serve as food for larger organisms. [Ger. < Gk., neut. of *planktos*, wandering < *plazein*, to turn aside. See plāk- in App.] —**plank•ton′ic** (-tŏn′ĭk) *adj.*

Pla•no (plā′nō) A city of NE TX, a suburb of Dallas. Pop. 222,030.

plano– or **plani–** or **plan–** *pref.* Flat: *planoconvex.* [< Lat. *plānus*, flat. See pelə-² in App.]

plan•o•blast (plăn′ə-blăst′) *n.* The medusa of certain hydrozoans. [Gk. *planos*, wandering (< *planāsthai*, to wander; see PLANET) + –BLAST.]

pla•no•con•cave (plā′nō-kŏn-kāv′, -kŏn′kāv′) *adj.* Flat on one side and concave on the other: *a planoconcave lens.*

pla•no•con•vex (plā′nō-kŏn-vĕks′, -kŏn′vĕks′) *adj.* Flat on one side and convex on the other: *a planoconvex lens.*

plan•o•gam•ete (plăn′ō-găm′ĕt, -gə-mēt′) *n.* A motile gamete, esp. one having undulipodia. [Gk. *planos*, wandering; see PLANO-BLAST + GAMETE.]

pla•nog•ra•phy (plə-nŏg′rə-fē, plā-) *n.* A process for printing from a smooth surface, as lithography or offset. —**pla′no•graph′ic** (plā′nə-grăf′ĭk) *adj.* —**pla′no•graph′i•cal•ly** *adv.*

pla•nom•e•ter (plə-nŏm′ĭ-tər, plā-) *n.* A flat metal plate for gauging the accuracy of a plane surface in precision metalworking. —**pla•nom′e•try** *n.*

plant (plănt) *n.* **1.** *Botany* **a.** Any of various photosynthetic, eukaryotic multicellular organisms of the kingdom Plantae, characteristically producing embryos, containing chloroplasts, having cellulose cell walls, and lacking locomotion. **b.** A plant having no permanent woody stem; an herb. **2a.** A building or group of buildings for manufacture; a factory. **b.** The equipment, includ-

Listed below are the nine planets that have been identified in our solar system and their respective satellites. The **sidereal period** of a planet is the amount of time required for that planet to make one revolution about the sun with respect to the stars. The **rotational period** of a planet is the amount of time required for the planet to perform one complete rotation about its own axis. If the planet rotates on its axis in a manner opposite to that of Earth, the rotation is called **retrograde** and the number is given with a – sign in front of it.

PLANETS: PHYSICAL PROPERTIES

PLANET	EQUATORIAL RADIUS kilometers	EQUATORIAL RADIUS miles	MASS x 10^{24} kilograms	SIDEREAL PERIOD days	ROTATIONAL PERIOD days	AVERAGE SURFACE TEMPERATURE degrees Celsius	AVERAGE SURFACE TEMPERATURE degrees Fahrenheit	MEAN DISTANCE FROM SUN x 10^6 kilometers	MEAN DISTANCE FROM SUN x 10^6 miles
Mercury	2,440	1,516	0.3302	87.97	58.6462	179	354	57.909	35.983
Venus	6,052	3,761	4.869	224.7	−243.01	453	847	108.21	67.239
Earth	6,378.14	3,963	5.9742	365.2564	0.99727	7.9	46	149.5979	92.956
Mars	3,397	2,111	0.64191	686.98	1.025957	−63	−81	227.941	141.63
Jupiter	71,492	44,423	1,899.00	4,332.71	0.41354	−153	−244	778.332	483.63
Saturn	60,268	37,449	568.8	10,759.22	0.4375	−185	−301	1,426.98	886.69
Uranus	25,559	15,882	86.6	30,685.40	−0.65	−215	−355	2,870.99	1,783.95
Neptune	24,764	15,388	102.78	60,189.00	0.768	−225	−373	4,497.072	2,794.36
Pluto	1,151	715	0.013	90,780.80	−6.3872	−236	−393	5,913.514	3,674.5

PLANETARY SATELLITES (BY PLANET, FROM NEAREST SATELLITE TO FURTHEST SATELLITE)

Planet	Satellite	Planet	Satellite	Planet	Satellite	Planet	Satellite
Earth	Moon		Carme		Rhea		Ariel
Mars	Phobos		Pasiphae		Titan		Umbriel
	Deimos		Sinope		Hyperion		Titania
Jupiter	Metis	Saturn	Pan		Iapetus		Oberon
	Adrastea		Atlas		Phoebe		Caliban
	Amalthea		Prometheus	Uranus	Cordelia		Sycorax
	Thebe		Pandora		Ophelia	Neptune	Naiad
	Io		Epimetheus*		Bianca		Thalassa
	Europa		Janus*		Cressida		Despina
	Ganymede		Mimas		Desdemona		Galatea
	Callisto		Enceladus		Juliet		Larissa
	Leda		Tethys**		Portia		Proteus
	Himalia		Telesto**		Rosalind		Triton
	Lysithea		Calypso**		Belinda		Nereid
	Elara		Dione***		Puck	Pluto	Charon
	Ananke		Helene***		Miranda		

*The satellites Epimetheus and Janus orbit so closely together that gravitational interactions cause them to regularly exchange orbits.
**The satellites Tethys, Telesto, and Calypso have been determined to be the same distance from Saturn to within current experimental accuracy.
***The satellites Dione and Helene have been determined to be the same distance from Saturn to within current experimental accuracy.

ing machinery, tools, and fixtures and the buildings containing them, necessary for an industrial or manufacturing operation. **3.** The buildings, equipment, and fixtures of an institution. **4.** A person or thing put into place in order to mislead or function secretly, esp.: **a.** A person placed in a group of spectators to influence behavior. **b.** A spy or observer stationed in a given location. **c.** A misleading piece of evidence placed so as to be discovered. **d.** A remark or action in a play or narrative that becomes important later. **5.** *Slang* A scheming trick; a swindle. ❖ *tr.v.* **plant•ed, plant•ing, plants 1a.** To place or set (seeds, for example) in the ground to grow. **b.** To place seeds or young plants in (land); sow. **2a.** To place (spawn or young fish) in water or an underwater bed for cultivation. **b.** To stock with spawn or fish. **3.** To introduce (an animal) into an area. **4.** To set firmly in position; fix: *planted both feet on the ground.* **5.** To establish; found. **6.** To fix firmly in the mind; implant. **7a.** To station (a person) for the purpose of functioning in secret, as by spying. **b.** To place secretly or deceptively so as to be discovered or made public. **c.** To conceal; hide: *planted the stolen goods in the warehouse.* **8.** *Slang* To deliver (a blow or punch). [ME *plante* < OE and OFr., both < Lat. *planta*, shoot, sole of the foot.] —**plant′a•ble** *adj.*

Plan•tag•e•net (plăn-tăj′ə-nĭt) Royal house of English kings from Henry II to Richard III (1154–1485).

plan•tain¹ (plăn′tən) *n.* Any of various plants of the genus *Plantago* that produce dense spikes of small greenish flowers, esp. either of two Eurasian weeds, *P. major* or *P. lanceolata*. [ME < OFr. < Lat. *plantāgō, plantāgin-* < *planta*, sole of the foot (< its broad leaves).]

plan•tain² (plăn′tən) *n.* **1.** A large southeast Asian treelike herb (*Musa paradisiaca*) resembling the banana and bearing similar fruit. **2.** The fruit of this plant, used as a staple food. [Sp. *plátano, plántano*, plane tree, plantain < Lat. *platanus*. See PLANE⁴.]

plantain lily *n.* Any of several eastern Asian plants of the genus *Hosta*, cultivated for their foliage and their white, blue, or lilac flowers borne in a one-sided raceme.

plan•tar (plăn′tər, -tär′) *adj.* Of or occurring on the sole of the foot. [Lat. *plantāris* < *planta*, sole.]

plan•ta•tion (plăn-tā′shən) *n.* **1.** An area under cultivation. **2.** A group of cultivated trees or plants. **3.** A large estate or farm on which crops are raised, often by resident workers. **4.** A newly established settlement; a colony.

plant bug *n.* An insect of the order Hemiptera, having mouthparts adapted for piercing plants and sucking their juices.

plant•er (plăn′tər) *n.* **1a.** One who plants. **b.** A machine or tool for planting seeds. **2.** The owner or manager of a plantation. **3.** An early settler or colonist. **4.** A decorative container for a plant or small tree.

plant•er's punch (plăn′tərz) *n.* A drink of rum with lemon or lime juice, sugar syrup, water or soda, bitters, and grenadine.

plant hormone *n.* Any of various hormones produced by plants that control or regulate physiological activities.

plan•ti•grade (plăn′tĭ-grād′) *adj.* Walking with the entire sole of the foot on the ground. ❖ *n.* A plantigrade animal. [Fr. : Lat. *planta*, sole of the foot + Lat. *-gradus*, going (< *gradī*, to walk, go; see ghredh- in App.).]

plant kingdom *n.* A main classification of living organisms that includes all plants.

plant•let (plănt′lĭt) *n.* A young or small plant.

plant louse *n.* See aphid.

plan•u•la (plăn′yə-lə) *n., pl.* **-lae** (-lē′) The flat free-swimming ciliated larva of a cnidarian. [NLat. *plānula* < Lat., fem. dim. of *plānus*, flat (< its shape). See pelə-² in App.]

plaque (plăk) *n.* **1.** A flat plate, slab, or disk ornamented or engraved for mounting, as on a wall for decoration. **2.** A small pin or brooch worn as an ornament or a membership badge. **3a.** *Pathology* A small disk-shaped formation or growth; a patch. **b.** A deposit of fatty material on the inner lining of an arterial wall, characteristic of atherosclerosis. **c.** A scaly patch formed on the skin by psoriasis. **d.** A film of mucus and bacteria on a tooth surface. **e.** A clear patch of lysed cells in an otherwise opaque layer of a bacteria or cell culture. [Fr. < OFr., metal plate, perh. < MDu. *placke*, disk, patch.]

plash (plăsh) *n.* **1.** A light splash. **2.** The sound of a light splash. ❖ *v.* **plashed, plash•ing, plash•es** —*tr.* To spatter (liquid) about; splash. —*intr.* To cause a light splash. [Poss. < ME *plashe*, pool of water < OE *plæsc*.]

plantain lily

–plasia or **–plasy** *suff.* Growth; development: *achondroplasia.* [NLat. < Gk. *plasis,* molding < *plassein,* to mold. See **pelə-²** in App.]

plasm (plăz′əm) *n.* See **germ plasm** 2.

plasm– *pref.* Variant of **plasmo-**.

–plasm *suff.* Material forming cells or tissue: *cytoplasm.* [< PLASMA.]

plas·ma (plăz′mə) also **plasm** (plăz′əm) *n.* **1a.** The clear yellowish fluid portion of blood, lymph, or intramuscular fluid in which cells are suspended. **b.** Blood plasma. **2.** *Medicine* Cell-free sterilized blood plasma, used in transfusions. **3.** Protoplasm or cytoplasm. **4.** The fluid portion of milk from which the curd is separated by coagulation; whey. **5.** *Physics* A highly ionized gas containing nearly equal numbers of positive ions and electrons. [NLat. < LLat., image, figure < Gk. < *plassein,* to mold. See **pelə-²** in App.] —**plas·mat′ic** (plăz-măt′ĭk), **plas′mic** (-mĭk) *adj.*

plasma cell *n.* Any of the antibody-producing cells found in lymphoid tissue and derived from B cells upon reaction with a specific antigen.

plas·ma·cyte (plăz′mə-sīt′) *n.* See **plasma cell.**

plas·ma·gel (plăz′mə-jĕl′) *n.* A jellylike state of cytoplasm, characteristically occurring in the pseudopod of the amoeba.

plas·ma·gene (plăz′mə-jēn′) *n.* A self-replicating hereditary structure thought to exist in cytoplasm and function in a manner analogous to but independent of chromosomal genes.

plas·ma·lem·ma (plăz′mə-lĕm′ə) *n.* See **cell membrane.** [PLASMA + Gk. *lemma,* husk; see LEMMA².]

plasma membrane *n.* See **cell membrane.**

plas·ma·pher·e·sis (plăz′mə-fĕr′ĭ-sĭs, -fə-rē′-) *n.* A process in which plasma is taken from donated blood and the remaining components are returned to the donor. [PLASM(A) + Gk. *aphairesis,* removal; see APHAERESIS.]

plas·ma·sol (plăz′mə-sôl′, -sōl′, -sŏl′) *n.* A state of cytoplasm that is more liquid than plasmagel.

plas·mid (plăz′mĭd) *n.* A circular double-stranded unit of DNA that replicates within a cell independently of the chromosomal DNA and is most often found in bacteria.

plas·min (plăz′mĭn) *n.* A proteolytic enzyme that is formed from plasminogen in blood plasma and dissolves the fibrin in blood clots.

plas·min·o·gen (plăz-mĭn′ə-jən) *n.* The inactive precursor to plasmin that is found in body fluids and blood plasma.

plasmo– or **plasm–** *pref.* Plasma: *plasmin.* [< PLASMA.]

plas·mo·des·ma (plăz′mə-dĕz′mə) also **plas·mo·desm** (plăz′mə-dĕz′əm) *n., pl.* **-ma·ta** (-mə-tə) or **-mas** also **-desms** A strand of cytoplasm that passes through openings in cell walls and connects the protoplasts of adjacent living plant cells. [PLASMO- + Gk. *desma,* bond (< *dein,* to bind).]

plas·mo·di·um (plăz-mō′dē-əm) *n., pl.* **-di·a** (-dē-ə) **1.** A multinucleate mass of cytoplasm formed by the fusion of a number of amoeboid cells. **2.** A protozoan of the genus *Plasmodium,* which includes the parasites that cause malaria. [NLat. *Plasmodium,* genus name < PLASM(O)– + Gk. *-ōdēs,* resembling; see COLLODION.] —**plas·mo′di·al** (-dē-əl) *adj.*

plas·mol·y·sis (plăz-mŏl′ĭ-sĭs) *n., pl.* **-ses** (-sēz′) Shrinkage or contraction of the protoplasm away from the wall of a living plant or bacterial cell, caused by water loss. —**plas′mo·lyt′ic** (plăz′mə-lĭt′ĭk) *adj.* —**plas′mo·lyt′i·cal·ly** *adv.* —**plas′mo·lyze′** (-mō-līz′) *v.*

–plast *suff.* A small body, structure, particle, or granule, esp. of living matter; cell: *chloroplast.* [< Gk. *plastos,* molded < *plassein,* to mold. See **pelə-²** in App.]

plastron

plas·ter (plăs′tər) *n.* **1.** A mixture of lime or gypsum, sand, and water that hardens to a smooth solid, used for coating walls and ceilings. **2.** Plaster of Paris. **3.** A pastelike mixture applied to a part of the body for healing or cosmetic purposes. **4.** *Chiefly British* An adhesive bandage. ❖ *v.* **-tered, -ter·ing, -ters** —*tr.* **1.** To cover, coat, or repair with plaster. **2.** To cover or hide with or as if with a coat of plaster: *plastered over differences.* **3.** To apply a plaster to. **4a.** To cover conspicuously, as with things pasted on; overspread. **b.** To affix conspicuously, usu. with a paste. **5.** To make smooth by applying a sticky substance. **6.** To make adhere to another surface. **7.** *Informal* **a.** To inflict heavy damage or injury on. **b.** To defeat decisively. —*intr.* To apply plaster. [ME < OE, medical dressing, and < OFr. *plastre,* cementing material, both < Lat. *emplastrum,* medical dressing < Gk. *emplastron* < *emplassein,* to plaster on : *en-,* in, on; see EN-² + *plassein,* to mold; see **pelə-²** in App.] —**plas′ter·er** *n.* —**plas′ter·y** *adj.*

plas·ter·board (plăs′tər-bôrd′, -bōrd′) *n.* A board of layers of fiberboard or paper bonded to a gypsum plaster core, used instead of plaster or wood panels for walls.

plaster cast *n.* **1.** A sculptured mold or cast in plaster of Paris. **2.** See **cast** 11.

plas·tered (plăs′tərd) *adj. Slang* Intoxicated; drunk.

plas·ter·ing (plăs′tər-ĭng) *n.* **1.** A layer or coating of plaster. **2.** *Informal* A resounding defeat; a beating.

plaster of Paris *n.* Any of a group of gypsum cements, essentially hemihydrated calcium sulfate, $CaSO_4 \cdot \frac{1}{2}H_2O$, a powder that forms a paste when mixed with water and hardens into a solid, used in making casts, molds, and sculpture. [ME, after PARIS², France.]

plas·ter·work (plăs′tər-wûrk′) *n.* Construction or ornamental work done with plaster.

plas·tic (plăs′tĭk) *adj.* **1.** Capable of being shaped or formed. **2.** Relating to or dealing with shaping or modeling. **3.** Having the qualities of sculpture; well-formed. **4.** Giving form or shape to a substance. **5.** Easily influenced; impressionable. **6.** Made of a plastic or plastics. **7.** *Physics* Capable of undergoing continuous deformation without rupture or relaxation. **8.** *Biology* Capable of building tissue; formative. **9.** Marked by artificiality or superficiality; synthetic. **10.** *Informal* Of or obtained by means of credit cards. ❖ *n.* **1.** Any of various organic compounds produced by polymerization and capable of being molded, extruded, cast into shapes and films, or drawn into filaments used as textile fibers. **2.** An object or objects made of plastic. **3.** *Informal* A credit card or credit cards. [Lat. *plasticus* < Gk. *plastikos* < *plastos,* molded < *plassein,* to mold. See **pelə-²** in App.] —**plas′ti·cal·ly** *adv.* —**plas·tic′i·ty** (plăs-tĭs′ĭ-tē) *n.*

–plastic *suff.* Forming; growing; changing; developing: *metaplastic.* [Gk. *plastikos,* fit for molding. See PLASTIC.]

plastic explosive *n.* A moldable explosive substance used in bombs detonated by fuse or electrical impulse.

plas·ti·cize (plăs′tĭ-sīz′) *tr. & intr. v.* **-cized, -ciz·ing, -ciz·es** To make or become plastic. —**plas′ti·ci·za′tion** (-sĭ-zā′shən) *n.*

plas·ti·ciz·er (plăs′tĭ-sī′zər) *n.* Any of various substances added, as to plastics, for softness or pliability.

plastic surgery *n.* Surgery to remodel, repair, or restore body parts, esp. by the transfer of tissue. —**plastic surgeon** *n.*

plas·tid (plăs′tĭd) *n.* Any of several pigmented cytoplasmic organelles found in plant cells and other organisms and having various functions such as food synthesis and storage. [< Gk. *plastis,* plastid-, fem. of *plastēs,* molder < *plastos,* molded. See PLASTIC.] —**plas·tid′i·al** (plăs-tĭd′ē-əl) *adj.*

plas·tron (plăs′trən) *n.* **1.** A metal breastplate worn under a coat of mail. **2.** A quilted pad worn by fencers to protect the torso and side. **3.** A trimming on a bodice. **4.** The front of a man's dress shirt. **5.** The front panel of the tunic of a uniform, usu. of a different color than the rest. **6.** *Zoology* The ventral part of the shell of a turtle or tortoise. [Fr. < OFr. < OItal. *piastrone,* augmentative of *piastra,* thin metal plate. See PIASTER.] —**plas′tral** (-trəl) *adj.*

–plasty *suff.* Molding or forming surgically; plastic surgery: *dermatoplasty.* [Gk. *-plastiā* < *plastos,* molded < *plassein,* to mold. See **pelə-²** in App.]

–plasy *suff.* Variant of **–plasia.**

plat¹ (plăt) *tr.v.* **plat·ted, plat·ting, plats** To plait or braid. ❖ *n.* A braid. [ME *platen,* alteration of *plaiten,* to fold, braid. See PLAIT.]

plat² (plăt) *n.* **1.** A piece of land; a plot. **2.** A map showing actual or planned features, such as streets. ❖ *tr.v.* **plat·ted, plat·ting, plats** To make a plat of. [ME, prob. alteration (influenced by *plat,* something flat), of *plot.* See PLOT.]

plat. *abbr.* **1.** plateau **2.** platoon

Pla·ta (plä′tə, -tä), **Río de la** A wide estuary of SE South America between Argentina and Uruguay formed by the Paraná and Uruguay rivers and opening on the Atlantic.

Pla·tae·a (plə-tē′ə) An ancient city of Greece SW of Thebes; site of a Greek victory over the Persians in 479 B.C.

plate (plāt) *n.* **1.** A smooth, flat, thin, rigid body of uniform thickness. **2a.** A sheet of hammered, rolled, or cast metal. **b.** A very thin applied or deposited coat of metal. **3a.** A flat piece of metal forming part of a machine: *a boiler plate.* **b.** A flat piece of metal on which something is engraved. **4a.** A license plate. **4a.** A thin piece of metal used for armor. **b.** Armor made of such pieces. **5.** *Printing* **a.** A sheet of metal, rubber, or other material prepared for use as a printing surface, such as an electrotype. **b.** A print of a woodcut or other engraved material, esp. when reproduced in a book. **c.** A full-page book illustration, often in color and printed on paper different from that used for the text pages. **6.** *Photography* A light-sensitive sheet of glass or metal on which a photographic image can be recorded. **7.** *Dentistry* A thin metallic or plastic support fitted to the gums to anchor artificial teeth. **8.** *Architecture* In wood-frame construction, a horizontal member, capping the exterior wall studs, upon which the roof rafters rest. **9.** *Baseball* Home plate. **10a.** A shallow dish for food. **b.** The contents of such a dish: *ate a plate of spaghetti.* **c.** A whole course served on such a dish. **11.** Service and food for one person at a meal: *dinner at a set price per plate.* **12.** Household articles, such as hollowware, covered with a precious metal, such as gold. **13.** A dish passed, as in a congregation, for offerings. **14.** *Sports* **a.** A dish or other article of silver or gold offered as a prize. **b.** A contest, esp. a horserace, offering such a prize. **15.** A thin cut of beef from the brisket. **16.** *Biology* **a.** A thin flat layer or scale, as that of a fish. **b.** A platelike part, organ, or structure, such as that covering some reptiles. **17.** *Electricity* **a.** An electrode, as in a storage battery or capacitor. **b.** The anode in an electron tube. **18.** *Geology* In the theory of plate tectonics, one of the sections of the earth's lithosphere, constantly moving in relation to the other sections. **19.** *Informal* A schedule of matters to be dealt with: *had a lot on my plate at work.* ❖ *tr.v.* **plat·ed, plat·ing, plates** **1.** To coat or cover with a thin layer of metal. **2.** To cover with armor plate: *plate a warship.* **3.** *Printing* To make a plate from. **4.** To give a glossy finish to (paper) by pressing between metal sheets or rollers. **5.** To arrange (food) on a plate, as for serving. [ME < OFr. < fem. of *plat*, flat < VLat. **plattus* < Gk. *platus*.] —**plat′er** *n.*

pla·teau (plă-tō′) *n., pl.* **-teaus** or **-teaux** (-tōz′) **1.** An elevated, relatively level expanse of land; a tableland. **2.** A relatively stable level, period, or state. ❖ *intr.v.* **-teaued, -teau·ing, -teaus** To reach a stable level; level off. [Fr. < OFr. *platel*, platter < *plat*, flat. See PLATE.]

plat·ed (plā′tĭd) *adj.* **1.** Coated with a thin adherent layer of metal. Often used in combination: *a gold-plated pen.* **2.** Covered with protective plates or sheets of metal. Often used in combination: *a steel-plated safe.* **3.** Knitted with two kinds of yarn, one on the face and one on the back.

plate·ful (plāt′fŏol′) *n., pl.* **-fuls 1.** The amount that a plate can hold. **2.** A generous portion of food.

plate glass *n.* A strong rolled and polished glass containing few impurities, used for mirrors and large windows.

plate·let (plāt′lĭt) *n.* **1.** A minute, flattened body, as of ice. **2.** Blood platelet.

plat·en (plăt′n) *n.* **1.** The roller in a typewriter that serves as the backing for the paper against which the type bars strike. **2.** The roller in a computer printer against which the print head strikes. **3.** A flat plate or rolling cylinder in a printing press that positions the paper and holds it against the inked type. **4.** The glass surface of a flatbed scanner. [ME *plateine*, paten < OFr. *platine*, metal plate < *plat*, flat. See PLATE.]

plate proof *n. Printing* A proof taken from a master plate.

plate tectonics *n.* **1.** (*used with a sing. verb*) A theory that explains the global distribution of geological phenomena such as seismicity, volcanism, continental drift, and mountain building in terms of the formation, destruction, movement, and interaction of the earth's lithospheric plates. **2.** (*used with a sing. or pl. verb*) The dynamics of plate movement. —**plate′-tec·ton′ic** (plăt′tĕk-tŏn′ĭk) *adj.*

plat·form (plăt′fôrm′) *n.* **1a.** A horizontal surface raised above the level of the adjacent area, as a stage for public speaking. **b.** A vessel, such as a submarine, from which weapons can be deployed. **c.** An oil platform. **2.** A place, means, or opportunity for public expression of opinion. **3.** A vestibule at the end of a railway car. **4.** A formal declaration of the principles on which a group makes its appeal to the public. **5a.** A thick layer, as of cork, between the inner and outer soles of a shoe, giving added height. **b.** A shoe having such a construction. **6.** *Computer Science* The basic technology of a computer system's hardware and software that defines how a computer is operated and determines what other kinds of software can be used. **7.** *Geology* **a.** A flat, elevated surface. **b.** The stable, interior portion of continental craton composed of igneous and metamorphic rocks usu. covered by sedimentary strata. [Fr. *plate-forme*, diagram < OFr. : *plat*, flat; see PLATE + *forme*, form (< Lat. *fōrma*; see FORM).]

platform scale *n.* An industrial weighing instrument consisting of a platform coupled to an automatic system of levers and adjustable weights, used to weigh large or heavy objects.

platform tennis *n.* A variation of tennis played with paddles and a rubber ball on a raised wooden floor that is fenced with a wire screen.

Plath (plăth), **Sylvia** 1932–63. Amer. writer whose poems are noted for their images of alienation.

pla·ti·na (plə-tē′nə) *n.* Platinum, esp. as found naturally in impure form. [Sp., dim. of *plata*, silver, plate < VLat. **plattus.* See PLATE.]

plat·ing (plā′tĭng) *n.* **1.** A thin layer of metal deposited on or applied to a surface. **2.** A coating of metal sheets or plates.

pla·tin·ic (plə-tĭn′ĭk) *adj.* Of, relating to, or containing platinum, esp. with valence 4.

plat·i·nize (plăt′n-īz′) *tr.v.* **-nized, -niz·ing, -niz·es** To electroplate with platinum.

platino– or **platini–** or **platin–** *pref.* Platinum: *platinotype.* [< PLATINUM.]

plat·i·no·cy·a·nide (plăt′n-ō-sī′ə-nīd′) *n.* A double salt of platinous cyanide and another cyanide.

plat·i·noid (plăt′n-oid′) *adj.* Resembling platinum. ❖ *n.* **1.** An alloy of copper, nickel, tungsten, and zinc, formerly used in electric coils. **2.** A metal chemically resembling platinum, esp. osmium, iridium, or palladium.

plat·i·no·type (plăt′n-ō-tīp′) *n.* **1.** A process formerly used for making photographic prints, using a platinum salt and an iron salt in the sensitizing solution to produce prints in platinum black. **2.** A print produced by platinotype.

plat·i·nous (plăt′n-əs) *adj.* Of, relating to, or containing platinum, esp. with valence 2.

plat·i·num (plăt′n-əm) *n.* **1.** *Symbol* **Pt** A ductile malleable metallic element usu. occurring mixed with other metals such as iridium, osmium, or nickel and used as a catalyst and in electrical components, jewelry, dentistry, and electroplating. Atomic number 78; atomic weight 195.08; melting point 1,772°C; boiling point 3,827°C; specific gravity 21.45; valence 2, 3, 4. See table at **element. 2.** A medium to light gray. [NLat. < Sp. *platina*, platinum. See PLATINA.]

platinum black *n.* A fine black powder of metallic platinum, used as a catalyst and as a gas absorbent.

platinum blond *n.* **1.** A very light silver-blond hair color, esp.

when artificially produced. **2.** One with hair of this color.

plat·i·tude (plăt′ĭ-tōod′, -tyōod′) *n.* **1.** A trite or banal remark or statement, esp. one expressed as if it were original or significant. **2.** Lack of originality; triteness. [Fr. < *plat*, flat < OFr. See PLATE.] —**plat′i·tu′di·nous** (-tōod′n-əs, -tyōod′-), **plat′i· tu′di·nal** (-tōod′n-əl, -tyōod′-) *adj.* —**plat′i·tu′di·nous·ly** *adv.*

plat·i·tu·di·nar·i·an (plăt′ĭ-tōod′n-âr′ē-ən, -tyōod′-) *n.* One who habitually uses platitudes.

plat·i·tu·di·nize (plăt′ĭ-tōod′n-īz′, -tyōod′-) *intr.v.* **-nized, -niz·ing, -niz·es** To speak or write with platitudes.

Pla·to (plā′tō) 427?–347? B.C. Greek philosopher who presented his ideas in dramatic dialogues, as in *The Republic.*

Pla·ton·ic (plə-tŏn′ĭk, plā-) *adj.* **1.** Of, relating to, or characteristic of Plato or his philosophy. **2.** often **platonic** Transcending physical desire and tending toward the purely spiritual or ideal. **3.** often **platonic** Speculative or theoretical. —**Pla·ton′i·cal·ly** *adv.*

Pla·to·nism (plāt′n-ĭz′əm) *n.* The philosophy of Plato, esp. insofar as it asserts ideal forms as an absolute reality of which the phenomena of the world are an imperfect and transitory reflection. —**Pla′to·nist** *n.* —**Pla′to·nis′tic** *adj.*

pla·toon (plə-tōon′) *n.* **1.** A subdivision of a company of troops consisting of two or more squads or sections and usu. commanded by a lieutenant. **2.** A group of people working, traveling, or assembled together: *a platoon of firefighters.* **3.** *Sports* A group of players within a team, esp. a football team, that is trained and sent into or withdrawn from play as a unit. ❖ *tr.v.* **-tooned, -toon·ing, -toons** *Sports* To play (a player) in alternation with another player in the same position. [Fr. *peloton* < OFr., dim. of *pelote*, ball. See PELLET.]

platoon sergeant *n.* The senior noncommissioned officer in an army platoon or comparable unit.

Platt·deutsch (plăt′doich′) *n.* See **Low German 1.** [Ger. (partial transl. of Du. *Platduits*, Low German) : Du. *platt*, low, flat (< MDu. *plat* < OFr.; see PLATE) + Ger. *Deutsch*, German (< MHGer. *diutsch* < OHGer. *diutisc*, of the people; see **teutã–** in App.).]

Platte (plăt) A river of central NE flowing c. 499 km (310 mi) to the Missouri R. at the IA border.

plat·ter (plăt′ər) *n.* **1.** A large shallow dish or plate, used esp. for serving food. **2.** A meal or course served on a platter. **3.** *Slang* A phonograph record. —**idiom: on a platter** Without exertion; effortlessly. [ME *plater* < AN < OFr. *plate*, plate. See PLATE.]

Platts·burgh (plăts′bûrg′) A city of extreme NE NY on Lake Champlain; site of a major naval battle during the War of 1812. Pop. 18,816.

plat·y[1] (plā′tē) *adj.* **-i·er, -i·est** Relating to or being soil or minerals occurring in flaky layers.

plat·y[2] (plăt′ē) *n., pl.* **-ys** or **-ies** Any of several small freshwater live-bearing fishes of the genus *Xiphophorus* of southern North America, popular in aquariums for their bright and variable colors. [Short for NLat. *Platypoecilus*, former genus name : PLATY– + Gk. *poikilos*, many-colored; see **peig–** in App.]

platy– *pref.* Flat: *platyhelminth.* [Gk. *platu–* < *platus.*]

plat·y·fish (plăt′ē-fĭsh′) *n., pl.* **platyfish** or **-fish·es** See **platy**[2].

plat·y·hel·minth (plăt′ĭ-hĕl′mĭnth) *n.* See **flatworm**. [< NLat. *Platyhelminthēs*, phylum name : PLATY– + Gk. *helmīs, helminth–*, parasitic worm; see **wel–** in App.] —**plat′y·hel·min′thic** *adj.*

plat·y·pus (plăt′ĭ-pəs) *n., pl.* **-pus·es** A semiaquatic egg-laying mammal (*Ornithorhynchus anatinus*) of Australia and Tasmania having a broad flat tail, webbed feet, and a snout resembling a duck's bill. [NLat. *Platypūs*, former genus name < Gk. *platupous*, flat-footed : *platu–*, platy– + *pous*, foot; see **ped–** in App.]

plat·yr·rhine (plăt′ĭ-rīn′) also **plat·yr·rhin·i·an** (plăt′ĭ-rĭn′ē-ən) *adj.* **1.** Having a broad flat nose. **2.** Of or being the New World monkeys, distinguished from the Old World monkeys by widely separated nostrils that generally open to the side. ❖ *n.* A platyrrhine animal. [NLat. *Platyrrhīna*, group name < Gk. *platurrhīs*, broad-nosed : *platu–*, platy– + *rhīs, rhīn–*, nose.]

plau·dit (plô′dĭt) *n.* Enthusiastic praise or approval. [Short for Lat. *plaudite*, pl. imper. of *plaudere*, to applaud (used at the end of Roman plays).]

plau·si·ble (plô′zə-bəl) *adj.* **1.** Seemingly or apparently valid, likely, or acceptable; credible: *a plausible excuse.* **2.** Giving a deceptive impression of truth, acceptability, or reliability; specious. **3.** Disingenuously smooth; fast-talking. [Lat. *plausibilis*, deserving applause < *plausus*, p. part. of *plaudere*, to applaud.] —**plau′si·bil′i·ty, plau′si·ble·ness** *n.* —**plau′si·bly** *adv.*

SYNONYMS *plausible, believable, colorable, credible* These adjectives mean appearing to merit belief or acceptance: *a plausible pretext; a believable excuse; a colorable story; a credible hint.*

plau·sive (plô′zĭv, -sĭv) *adj.* **1.** Showing or expressing praise or approbation; applauding. **2.** *Obsolete* Plausible. [< Lat. *plaudere, plaus–*, to applaud.]

Plau·tus (plô′təs), **Titus Maccius** 254?–184 B.C. Roman comic playwright whose works influenced Shakespeare.

play (plā) *v.* **played, play·ing, plays** —*intr.* **1.** To occupy oneself in amusement, sport, or other recreation: *played with toys.* **2a.** To take part in a game: *was eligible to play.* **b.** To participate in bet-

platypus
Ornithorhynchus anatinus

ă	pat	oi	boy
ā	pay	ou	out
âr	care	ŏŏ	took
ä	father	ōō	boot
ĕ	pet	ŭ	cut
ē	be	ûr	urge
ĭ	pit	th	thin
ī	pie	th	this
îr	pier	hw	which
ŏ	pot	zh	vision
ō	toe	ə	about,
ô	paw		item

Stress marks:
′ (primary);
′ (secondary), as in
lexicon (lĕk′sĭ-kŏn′)

ting; gamble. **3.** To act in jest or sport. **4.** To deal or behave carelessly or indifferently; toy. **5.** To behave or converse in a sportive or playful way. **6.** To act or conduct oneself in a specified way: *played fair.* **7.** To act, esp. in a dramatic production. **8.** *Music* **a.** To perform on an instrument. **b.** To emit sound or be sounded in performance. **9.** To be performed, as in a theater or on television: *A good movie is playing tonight.* **10.** To be received or accepted: *a speech that played poorly with the voters.* **11.** To move or seem to move quickly, lightly, or irregularly: *The breeze played on the water.* **12.** To function or discharge uninterruptedly: *The fountains played in the courtyard.* **13.** To move or operate freely within a bounded space, as machine parts do. —*tr.* **1a.** To perform or act (a role or part) in a dramatic performance. **b.** To assume the role of; act as: *played the peacemaker at the meeting.* **2.** To perform (a theatrical work) on or as if on the stage. **3.** To present a theatrical performance in (a given place). **4.** To pretend to be; mimic the activities of. **5a.** To engage in (a game or sport): *play chess; play hockey.* **b.** To compete against in a game or sport. **c.** To occupy or work at (a position) in a game: *play first base.* **d.** To employ (a player) in a game or position. **e.** To use or move (a card or piece) in a game: *play the ace of clubs.* **f.** To make (a shot or stroke), as in tennis: *played a strong backhand.* **g.** To attempt to keep or gain possession or control of. **6a.** To bet; wager. **b.** To make bets on. **7.** To perform or put into effect, esp. as a jest or deception. **8.** To handle; manage. **9.** To use or manipulate, esp. for one's own interests. **10.** *Music* **a.** To perform on (an instrument). **b.** To perform (a piece) on instruments or an instrument. **11.** To cause (a compact disk, for example) to emit recorded sounds. **12.** To discharge or direct in or as if in a continuous stream. **13.** To cause to move rapidly, lightly, or irregularly: *play lights over the floor.* **14.** To exhaust (a hooked fish) by allowing it to pull on the line. ❖ *n.* **1a.** A literary work written for performance on the stage; a drama. **b.** The performance of such a work. **2.** Activity engaged in for enjoyment or recreation. **3.** Fun or jesting. **4a.** The act or manner of engaging in a game or sport. **b.** The act or manner of using a card, piece, or ball in a game or sport. **c.** A move or action in a game. **5.** Participation in betting; gambling. **6.** Manner of dealing with others; conduct. **7.** An attempt to obtain something; a bid. **8a.** Action, motion, or use. **b.** Freedom or occasion for action; scope. **9.** Movement or space for movement, as of mechanical parts. **10.** Quick, often irregular movement or action, esp. of light or color. —*phrasal verbs:* **play along** *Informal* To cooperate or pretend to cooperate. **play around** To philander. **play at 1.** To participate in; engage in. **2.** To do or take part in halfheartedly. **play back** To replay (a recently recorded tape, for example). **play down** To minimize the importance of; make little of. **play off 1.** *Sports* **a.** To establish the winner of (a tie) by playing in an additional game or series of games. **b.** To participate in a playoff. **2.** To set (one individual or party) in opposition to another so as to advance one's own interests. **play on** (or **upon**) To take advantage of (another's attitudes or feelings) for one's own interests. **play out** To use up; exhaust. **play up** To emphasize or publicize. —*idioms:* **in play 1.** *Sports* In a position to be legally or feasibly played. **2.** In a position to be rumored to be in a position of possible corporate takeover. **out of play** *Sports* Not in a position to be legally or feasibly played. **play ball** *Slang* To cooperate. **play both ends against the middle** To set opposing parties or interests against one another so as to advance one's own goals. **play fast and loose** To behave in a recklessly irresponsible or deceitful manner. **play for time** To use delaying tactics; temporize. **play games** *Slang* To be evasive or deceptive. **play hard to get** To pretend to be inaccessible or uninterested, as when flirting. **play into the hands of** To act or behave so as to give an advantage to (an opponent). **play (one's) cards** *Informal* To use the resources or strategies at one's disposal. **play possum** To pretend to be sleeping or dead. **play the field** *Informal* To date more than one person. **play the game** *Informal* To behave according to the accepted customs or standards. **play up to** To curry favor with. **play with a full deck** *Slang* To be of sound mind: *didn't seem to be playing with a full deck.* **play with fire** To take part in a dangerous or risky undertaking. **play with (oneself)** *Vulgar Slang* To masturbate. [ME *playen* < OE *plegian.* See **dlegh-** in App.] —**play′a•bil′i•ty** *n.* —**play′a•ble** *adj.*

pla•ya (plī′ə) *n.* A nearly level area at the bottom of an undrained desert basin, sometimes temporarily covered with water. [Sp. < LLat. *plagia,* hillside, shoreline, prob. < Gk., sides < neut. pl. of *plagios,* oblique. See PLAGIO–.]

play-act (plā′ăkt′) *intr.v.* **-act•ed, -act•ing, -acts 1.** To play a role in a dramatic performance. **2.** To play a pretended role; make believe. **3.** To behave overdramatically or artificially.

play-ac•tion pass (plā′ăk′shən) *n. Football* A pass play in which the quarterback fakes a handoff to a running back before throwing the ball.

play•back (plā′băk′) *n.* **1.** The act or process of replaying a newly made audio or video recording. **2.** A method of or an apparatus for reproducing sound recordings.

play•bill (plā′bĭl′) *n.* A poster announcing a theatrical performance.

play•book (plā′bŏŏk′) *n.* **1.** A book containing the scripts of dramatic plays. **2.** *Sports* A notebook containing descriptions and diagrams of the plays of a team, esp. a football team.

play•boy (plā′boi′) *n.* A man given to sexual promiscuity and the pursuit of pleasure.

play-by-play (plā′bī-plā′) *adj.* Being or giving a detailed running account of the action of an event, esp. a sports event, as it occurs. ❖ *n.* A play-by-play account of an event.

play•er (plā′ər) *n.* **1.** One that plays, esp.: **a.** A participant in a game or sport. **b.** A gambler. **c.** One who performs in theatrical roles. **d.** *Music* One who plays a musical instrument. **2.** An active participant. **3.** The mechanism actuating a player piano. **4.** A machine that plays recorded audio or audiovisual material. **5.** *Slang* One who has sexual affairs outside one's primary relationship.

player piano *n.* A mechanically operated piano that uses a perforated paper roll to actuate the keys.

play•fel•low (plā′fĕl′ō) *n.* A playmate.

play•ful (plā′fəl) *adj.* **1.** Full of fun and high spirits; frolicsome or sportive: *a playful kitten.* **2.** Humorous; jesting. —**play′ful•ly** *adv.* —**play′ful•ness** *n.*

play•girl (plā′gûrl′) *n.* A woman given to sexual promiscuity and the pursuit of pleasure.

play•go•er (plā′gō′ər) *n.* One who attends the theater. —**play′-go′ing** *n.*

play•ground (plā′ground′) *n.* **1.** An outdoor area for recreation and play, esp. one having items such as swings. **2.** A field or sphere of unrestricted pleasurable activity.

play•house (plā′hous′) *n., pl.* **-hous•es** (-hou′zĭz, -sĭz) **1.** A theater. **2.** A small house for children to play in. **3.** A child's toy house; a dollhouse.

play•ing card (plā′ĭng) *n.* A card marked with its rank and suit and belonging to any of several decks used in games.

playing field *n.* **1.** A field for games such as soccer. **2.** The conditions or circumstances in which competition takes place.

play•let (plā′lĭt) *n.* A short play.

play•list also **play list** (plā′lĭst′) *n.* A list of musical selections for broadcast or performance.

play•mak•er (plā′mā′kər) *n.* A player in a sport with goals, such as a guard in basketball, who initiates offensive plays. —**play′-mak′ing** *n.*

play•mate (plā′māt′) *n.* A companion in play or recreation.

play•off also **play-off** (plā′ôf′, -ŏf′) *n. Sports* **1.** A final game or series of games played to break a tie. **2.** A series of games played to determine a championship.

play•pen (plā′pĕn′) *n.* A portable enclosure in which a baby or young child can be safely left to play.

play•room (plā′rŏŏm′, -rŏŏm′) *n.* A room designed or set aside for recreation or playing.

play•suit (plā′sŏōt′) *n.* A play outfit usu. consisting of shorts and a blouse, sometimes in one piece, that is often worn by children.

play therapy *n.* A form of psychotherapy used with children that makes use of dolls, toys, and other playthings under the guidance of a therapist. —**play therapist** *n.*

play•thing (plā′thĭng′) *n.* **1.** Something to play with; a toy. **2.** One treated as a toy: *a plaything of fate.*

play•wear (plā′wâr′) *n.* Garments suitable for recreation.

play•wright (plā′rīt′) *n.* One who writes plays; a dramatist.

pla•za (plä′zə, plăz′ə) *n.* **1.** A public square or similar open area in a town or city. **2a.** A widened roadway providing the approach to tollbooths on a highway. **b.** A parking or service area next to a highway. **3.** A shopping center. [Sp. < VLat. *plattea* < Lat. *platea,* broad street. See PLACE.]

plea (plē) *n.* **1.** An earnest request; an appeal. **2.** An excuse; a pretext. **3.** *Law* **a.** An allegation offered in pleading a case. **b.** A defendant's answer to the plaintiff's declaration in a civil action. **c.** The answer of the accused to a criminal charge or indictment. **d.** A special answer depending on or demonstrating one or more reasons for avoiding, dismissing, or barring a suit in equity law. **e.** An action or suit. [ME *plai,* lawsuit < OFr. *plai, plaid* < LLat. *placitum,* decree < Lat. < neut. p. part. of *placēre,* to please.]

plea-bar•gain (plē′bär′gən) *intr.v.* **-gained, -gain•ing, -gains** To make an agreement in which a defendant pleads guilty to a lesser charge and the prosecutor in return drops more serious charges. —**plea′ bar′gain** *n.* —**plea′ bar′gain•ing** *n.*

pleach (plēch, plăch) *tr.v.* **pleached, pleach•ing, pleach•es 1.** To plait or interlace (vines, for example), esp. in making a hedge or an arbor. **2.** To shade or border with interlaced branches or vines. [ME *plechen* < ONFr. *plechier,* prob. < Lat. *plectere.* See **plek-** in App.]

plead (plēd) *v.* **plead•ed** or **pled** (plĕd), **plead•ing, pleads** —*intr.* **1.** To appeal earnestly; beg: *plead for more time.* **2.** To offer reasons for or against something; argue earnestly: *plead against a bill.* **3.** To provide an argument or appeal. **4.** *Law* **a.** To put forward a plea of a specific nature in court: *plead guilty.* **b.** To make or answer an allegation in a legal proceeding. **c.** To address a court as a lawyer or advocate. —*tr.* **1.** To assert as defense, vindication, or excuse; claim as a plea. **2.** *Law* **a.** To present as an answer to a charge, indictment, or declaration made against one. **b.** To argue or present (a case) in a court or similar tribunal. [ME *pleden* < OFr. *plaidier* < Med.Lat. *placitāre,* to appeal to the law < LLat. *placitum,* decree, opinion. See PLEA.] —**plead′a•ble** *adj.* —**plead′er** *n.* —**plead′ing•ly** *adv.*

plead•ing (plē′dĭng) *n.* **1.** A plea; an entreaty. **2.** *Law* Advocacy of causes in court. **3.** *Law* **a.** A formal statement, generally written, propounding the cause of action or the defense in a case. **b. pleadings** The consecutive statements, allegations, and counter-allegations made by plaintiff and defendant, or prosecutor and accused, in a legal proceeding.

pleas•ance (plĕz′əns) *n.* **1.** A secluded garden or landscaped area. **2.** *Archaic* Pleasure or a source of pleasure.

pleas•ant (plĕz′ənt) *adj.* **-er, -est 1.** Giving or affording pleasure or enjoyment; agreeable: *a pleasant scene.* **2.** Pleasing in manner, behavior, or appearance. **3.** Fair and comfortable: *pleasant weather.* **4.** Merry; lively. [ME *plesaunt* < OFr. *plaisant*, pr. part. of *plaisir*, to please < Lat. *placēre*.] **—pleas′ant•ly** *adv.* **—pleas′ant•ness** *n.*

Pleasant Island See **Nauru.**

pleas•ant•ry (plĕz′ən-trē) *n., pl.* **-ries 1.** A humorous remark or act; a jest. **2.** A polite social utterance; a civility: *exchanged pleasantries.* **3.** A good-humored or playful manner in conversation or social relations. [Fr. *plaisanterie* < OFr. *plesanterie* < *plaisant*, pleasant. See PLEASANT.]

please (plēz) *v.* **pleased, pleas•ing, pleas•es** *—tr.* **1.** To give enjoyment, pleasure, or satisfaction to; make glad or contented. **2.** To be the will or desire of: *May it please the court to admit this evidence.* *—intr.* **1.** To give satisfaction or pleasure; be agreeable: *We aim to please.* **2.** To have the will or desire; wish: *Do as you please.* ❖ *adv.* **1.** If it is your desire or pleasure; if you please. Used in polite requests: *Please stand back.* **2.** Yes. Used in polite affirmative replies to offers: *May I help you? Please.* [ME *plesen* < OFr. *plaisir*. See PLEASANT.] **—pleas′er** *n.*

pleas•ing (plē′zĭng) *adj.* Giving pleasure or enjoyment; agreeable. **—pleas′ing•ly** *adv.* **—pleas′ing•ness** *n.*

pleas•ur•a•ble (plĕzh′ər-ə-bəl) *adj.* Agreeable; gratifying. **—pleas′ur•a•bil′i•ty, pleas′ur•a•ble•ness** *n.* **—pleas′ur•a•bly** *adv.*

pleas•ure (plĕzh′ər) *n.* **1.** The state or feeling of being pleased or gratified. **2.** A source of enjoyment or delight. **3.** Amusement, diversion, or worldly enjoyment. **4.** Sensual gratification or indulgence. **5.** One's preference or wish. ❖ *v.* **-ured, -ur•ing, -ures** *—tr.* To give pleasure or enjoyment to; gratify. *—intr.* **1.** To take pleasure; delight. **2.** To go in search of pleasure or enjoyment. [ME < OFr. *plaisir* < *plaisir*, to please. See PLEASE.] **—pleas′ure•less** *adj.*

pleasure principle *n.* In psychoanalysis, the tendency or drive to achieve pleasure and avoid pain as the chief motivating force in behavior.

pleat (plēt) *n.* A fold in cloth made by doubling the material upon itself and then pressing or stitching it into place. ❖ *tr.v.* **pleat•ed, pleat•ing, pleats** To press or arrange in pleats. [ME *plet*, var. of *plait*, pleat, fold. See PLAIT.] **—pleat′er** *n.*

pleb (plĕb) *n.* A commoner; a plebeian. [Short for PLEBEIAN or perh. back-formation < PLEBS.]

plebe (plēb) *n.* A first-year student at the US Military or Naval Academy. [Prob. short for PLEBEIAN.]

ple•be•ian (plĭ-bē′ən) *adj.* **1.** Of or relating to the common people of ancient Rome. **2.** Of, belonging to, or characteristic of commoners. **3.** Unrefined or coarse in nature or manner. ❖ *n.* **1.** One of the common people of ancient Rome. **2.** A member of the lower classes. **3.** A vulgar or coarse person. [< Lat. *plēbius* < *plēbs*, *plēb-*, the common people. See **pelə-**[1] in App.] **—ple•be′ian•ism** *n.* **—ple•be′ian•ly** *adv.*

pleb•i•scite (plĕb′ĭ-sīt′, -sĭt) *n.* **1.** A direct vote in which the entire electorate is invited to accept or refuse a proposal. **2.** A vote in which a population exercises the right of national self-determination. [Fr. *plébiscite* < Lat. *plēbiscītum* : *plēbis*, genitive of *plēbs*, the people; see **pelə-**[1] in App. + *scītum*, decree < neut. p. part. of *scīscere*, to vote for, inchoative of *scīre*, to know.] **—ple•bis′ci•tar′y** (plə-bĭs′ĭ-tĕr′ē, plĕb′ĭ-sīt′ə-rē) *adj.*

plebs (plĕbz) *n., pl.* **ple•bes** (plē′bēz) **1.** The common people of ancient Rome: *the plebs and the patricians.* **2.** The common people; the populace. [Lat. *plēbs*. See **pelə-**[1] in App.]

ple•cop•ter•an (plĭ-kŏp′tər-ən) *n.* See **stonefly.** [< NLat. *Plecoptera*, order name : Gk. *plekein*, to plait, twist; see **plek-** in App. + Gk. *pteron*, wing; see **pet-** in App.] **—ple•cop′ter•an** *adj.*

plec•tog•nath (plĕk′tŏg-năth′) *n.* Any of various tropical marine fishes of the order Tetraodontiformes or Plectognathi, which includes the puffers. [< NLat. *Plectognathī*, order name : Gk. *plektos*, twisted; see **plek-** in App. + Gk. *gnathos*, jaw; see –GNATHOUS.] **—plec′tog•nath′** *adj.*

plec•trum (plĕk′trəm) *n., pl.* **-trums** or **-tra** (-trə) A small device used to pluck the strings of certain instruments, such as the guitar or lute. [Lat. *plēctrum* < Gk. *plēktron* < *plēssein*, *plēg-*, to strike. See **plāk-** in App.]

pled (plĕd) *v.* A past tense and a past participle of **plead.**

pledge (plĕj) *n.* **1.** A solemn binding promise to do, give, or refrain from doing something. **2a.** Something given or held as security to guarantee payment of a debt or fulfillment of an obligation. **b.** The condition of something thus given or held. **3.** *Law* **a.** Delivery of goods or personal property as security for a debt or obligation. **b.** The contract by which such delivery is made. **4.** A token or sign. **5.** A person about to join a fraternity, sorority, or similar organization. **6.** The act of drinking in honor of someone; a toast. **7.** A vow to abstain from alcoholic liquor. ❖ *v.* **pledged, pledg•ing, pledg•es** *—tr.* **1.** To offer or guarantee by a solemn binding promise. **2.** To bind or secure by or as if by a pledge. **3.** To deposit as security; pawn. **4a.** To promise to join (a fraternity or similar organization). **b.** To accept as a prospective member of such an organization. **5.** To drink a toast to. *—intr.* **1.** To make a solemn binding promise; swear. **2.** To drink a toast. [ME < OFr. *plege*, prob. < LLat. *plevium*, a security, of Gmc. orig. See **dlegh-** in App.]

pledg•ee (plĕj-ē′) *n.* **1.** A person to whom something is pledged. **2.** A person with whom a pledge is deposited.

pledg•er (plĕj′ər) *n.* One who makes or gives a pledge.

pled•get (plĕj′ĭt) *n.* A small flat absorbent pad used to medicate, drain, or protect a wound or sore. [?]

pledg•or also **pledge•or** (plĕj′ər, plĕj-ôr′) *n.* *Law* A person who deposits property as a pledge.

–plegia *suff.* Paralysis: *monoplegia.* [Gk. *-plēgiā* < *plēgē*, a blow < *plēssein*, *plēg-*, to strike. See **plāk-** in App.]

Ple•iad (plē′əd, -ăd′, plī′-) *n., pl.* **Ple•ia•des** (plē′ə-dēz′, plī′-) **1.** One of the Pleiades. **2.** often **pleiad** A group of seven illustrious persons. [Back-formation < PLEIADES.]

Ple•ia•des (plē′ə-dēz′, plī′-) *pl.n.* **1.** *Greek Mythology* The seven daughters of Atlas who were metamorphosed into stars. **2.** An open star cluster in the constellation Taurus, consisting of several hundred stars, of which six are visible to the naked eye. [ME *Pliades* < Lat. *Plēïades* < Gk. *Plēiades*.]

plein air or **plein-air** (plān′âr′, plĕ-nĕr′) *adj.* **1.** Of or being a style of painting produced out of doors in natural light. **2.** Taking place outdoors: *plein air dining.* [< Fr. *(en) plein air*, (in) the open air : *en*, in + *plein*, full + *air*, air.]

plein air
The Fountain, Villa Torlonia, Frascati, Italy, 1907, by John Singer Sargent

pleio– *pref.* Variant of **pleo–.**

plei•o•tax•y (plī′ə-tăk′sē) *n.* *Botany* An increase in the number of whorls in an inflorescence. [Gk. *pleiōn*, more; see **pelə-**[1] in App. + –TAXY.]

plei•ot•ro•pism (plī-ŏt′rə-pĭz′əm) also **plei•ot•ro•py** (-pē) *n.* The control by a single gene of several distinct and seemingly unrelated phenotypic effects. [Gk. *pleiōn*, more; see **pelə-**[1] in App. + –TROPISM.] **—plei′o•tro′pic** (plī′ə-trō′pĭk, -trŏp′ĭk) *adj.* **—plei′o•tro′pi•cal•ly** *adv.*

Pleis•to•cene (plī′stə-sēn′) *adj.* Of or belonging to the geologic time of the earlier of the two epochs of the Quaternary Period, characterized by a succession of northern glaciations and the appearance of humans. See table at **geologic time.** ❖ *n.* The Pleistocene Epoch or its deposits. [Gk. *pleistos*, most; see **pelə-**[1] in App. + –CENE.]

ple•na•ry (plē′nə-rē, plĕn′ə-) *adj.* **1.** Complete in all respects; unlimited or full: *plenary powers.* **2.** Fully attended by all qualified members. [LLat. *plēnārius* < Lat. *plēnus*, full. See **pelə-**[1] in App.] **—ple′na•ri•ly** *adv.* **—ple′na•ri•ness** *n.*

plenary indulgence *n.* *Roman Catholic Church* An indulgence that remits the full temporal punishment incurred by a sinner.

plen•i•po•ten•ti•ar•y (plĕn′ə-pə-tĕn′shē-ĕr′ē, -shə-rē) *adj.* Invested with or conferring full powers: *a plenipotentiary deputy.* ❖ *n., pl.* **-ies** A diplomat with full authority. [Med.Lat. *plēnipotentiārius* < LLat. *plēnipotēns*, *plēnipotent-*, invested with full power : Lat. *plēnus*, full; see **pelə-**[1] in App. + Lat. *potēns*, powerful; see POTENT.]

plen•i•tude (plĕn′ĭ-to͞od′, -tyo͞od′) *n.* **1.** An ample amount or quantity; an abundance: *an area blessed with a plenitude of natural resources.* **2.** The condition of being full, ample, or complete. [ME < OFr. < Lat. *plēnitūdō* < *plēnus*, full. See **pelə-**[1] in App.] **—plen′i•tu′di•nous** (-to͞od′n-əs, -tyo͞od′-) *adj.*

plen•te•ous (plĕn′tē-əs) *adj.* **1.** Abundant; copious. **2.** Producing or yielding in abundance. [ME, alteration of *plentivous* < OFr. *plentiveus* < *plentif* < *plente*, plenty. See PLENTY.] **—plen′te•ous•ly** *adv.* **—plen′te•ous•ness** *n.*

plen•ti•ful (plĕn′tĭ-fəl) *adj.* **1.** Existing in great quantity or ample supply. **2.** Providing or producing an abundance. **—plen′ti•ful•ly** *adv.* **—plen′ti•ful•ness** *n.*

plen•ty (plĕn′tē) *n.* **1.** A full or completely adequate amount or supply. **2.** A large quantity or amount; an abundance. **3.** A condition of general abundance or prosperity. ❖ *adj.* Plentiful; abundant. ❖ *adv.* *Informal* Sufficiently; very. [ME < OFr. *plente* < Lat. *plēnitās* < *plēnus*, full. See **pelə-**[1] in App.]

ple•num (plē′nəm, plĕn′əm) *n., pl.* **ple•nums** or **ple•na** (plē′nə, plĕn′ə) **1.** An assembly or meeting with all members present. **2.** A condition, space, or enclosure in which air or other gas is at a pressure greater than that of the outside atmosphere. **3.** The condition of being full; fullness. **4.** A space completely filled with matter. [Lat. *plēnum (spatium)*, full (space), neut. of *plēnus*. See **pelə-**[1] in App.]

pleo– or **pleio–** or **plio–** *pref.* More: *pleopod.* [< Gk. *pleiōn*, *pleōn*, more. See **pelə-**[1] in App.]

ple•och•ro•ism (plē-ŏk′rō-ĭz′əm) *n.* The property possessed by some crystals of exhibiting different colors, esp. three different colors, when viewed along different axes. [PLEO– + Gk. *khrōs*, color + –ISM.] **—ple′o•chro′ic** (plē′ə-krō′ĭk) *adj.*

ple•o•mor•phism (plē′ə-môr′fĭz′əm) *n.* **1.** *Chemistry* See **polymorphism** 2. **2.** *Biology* The occurrence of two or more structural forms during a life cycle, esp. of certain plants. **—ple′o•mor′phic** *adj.*

ple•o•nasm (plē′ə-năz′əm) *n.* **1a.** The use of more words than

ă	pat	oi	boy
ā	pay	ou	out
âr	care	o͝o	took
ä	father	o͞o	boot
ĕ	pet	ŭ	cut
ē	be	ûr	urge
ĭ	pit	th	thin
ī	pie	*th*	this
îr	pier	hw	which
ŏ	pot	zh	vision
ō	toe	ə	about, item
ô	paw		

Stress marks:
′ (primary);
′ (secondary), as in
lexicon (lĕk′sĭ-kŏn′)

are required to express an idea; redundancy. **b.** An instance of pleonasm. **2.** A superfluous word or phrase. [LLat. *pleonasmus* < Gk. *pleonasmos* < *pleonazein*, to be excessive < *pleōn*, more. See **pelə-**[1] in App.] —**ple·o·nas·tic** (-năs′tĭk) *adj.* —**ple′o·nas′ti·cal·ly** *adv.*

ple·o·pod (plē′ə-pŏd′) *n.* See **swimmeret.**

ple·ro·cer·coid (plĭr′ō-sûr′koid′) *n.* The infective larva of some tapeworms, characterized by its solid elongated body. [Gk. *plērēs*, full, infected; see **pelə-**[1] in App. + *kerkos*, tail + -OID.]

ple·si·o·saur (plē′sē-ə-sôr′, plē′zē-) also **ple·si·o·sau·rus** (plē′sē-ə-sôr′əs, plē′zē-) *n., pl.* **-saurs** also **-saur·i** (-sôr′ī) A large extinct marine reptile having paddlelike limbs that was common in Europe and North America during the Mesozoic Era. [NLat. *Plēsiosaurus*, type genus : Gk. *plēsios*, near; see **pel-**[2] in App. + Gk. *sauros*, lizard.]

pleth·o·ra (plĕth′ər-ə) *n.* **1.** A superabundance; an excess. **2.** An excess of blood in the circulatory system or in one organ or area. [LLat. *plēthōra* < Gk. *plēthein*, to be full. See **pelə-**[1] in App.]

ple·thor·ic (plĕ-thôr′ĭk, -thŏr′-, plĕth′ə-rĭk) *adj.* **1a.** Excessive in quantity; superabundant. **b.** Excessive in style; turgid: *plethoric prose.* **2.** Characterized by an overabundance of blood. —**ple·thor′i·cal·ly** *adv.*

ple·thys·mo·gram (plĕ-thĭz′mə-grăm′, plə-) *n.* A record or tracing produced by a plethysmograph.

ple·thys·mo·graph (plĕ-thĭz′mə-grăf′, plə-) *n.* An instrument that measures variations in the size of an organ or body part on the basis of the amount of blood passing through or present in the part. [Gk. *plēthusmos*, increase (< *plēthūnein*, to increase < *plēthūs*, quantity < *plēthein*, to be full; see **pelə-**[1] in App.) + -GRAPH.] —**pleth′ys·mo·graph′ic** *adj.* —**pleth′ys·mog′ra·phy** (plĕth′ĭz-mŏg′rə-fē) *n.*

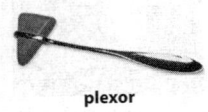

plexor

pleu·ra[1] (plŏŏr′ə) *n., pl.* **pleu·rae** (plŏŏr′ē) A thin serous membrane in mammals that envelops each lung and folds back to make a lining for the chest cavity. [ME < Med.Lat. < Gk., side, rib.] —**pleu′ral** *adj.*

pleu·ra[2] (plŏŏr′ə) *n.* Plural of **pleuron.**

pleu·ri·sy (plŏŏr′ĭ-sē) *n.* Inflammation of the pleura, usu. occurring as a complication of a disease such as pneumonia, accompanied by accumulation of fluid in the pleural cavity, chills, fever, and painful breathing and coughing. [ME *pluresy* < OFr. *pleuresie* < LLat. *pleurīsis*, alteration of Lat. *pleurītis* < Gk. : *pleura*, side + -*ītis*, -itis.] —**pleu·rit′ic** (plŏŏ-rĭt′ĭk) *adj.*

pleurisy root *n.* See **butterfly weed.**

pleuro– or **pleur–** *pref.* **1.** Side; lateral: *pleurodont.* **2.** Pleura; pleural: *pleurotomy.* [Gk. < *pleura*, side, rib.]

pleu·ro·dont (plŏŏr′ə-dŏnt′) *adj.* Having the teeth attached by their sides to the inner side of the jaw, as in some lizards. ❖ *n.* A lizard with pleurodont teeth.

pleu·ro·dyn·i·a (plŏŏr′ə-dĭn′ē-ə) *n.* **1.** Paroxysmal pain and soreness of the muscles between the ribs. **2.** A disease caused by a coxsackievirus, characterized by paroxysmal pain in the lower chest, fever, headache, and malaise. [NLat. : PLEUR(O)– + Gk. *odunē*, pain; see **ed-** in App.]

pleu·ron (plŏŏr′ŏn′) *n., pl.* **pleu·ra** (plŏŏr′ə) An external lateral plate of the body segments of arthropods. [NLat. < Gk., side, rib.]

pleu·ro·pneu·mo·nia (plŏŏr′ō-nŏŏ-mōn′yə, -nyŏŏ-) *n.* **1.** Pneumonia aggravated by pleurisy. **2.** An infectious febrile disease of cattle, caused by a mycoplasma and characterized by inflammation of the pleura and lungs.

pleu·ro·pneu·mo·nia-like organism (plŏŏr′ō-nŏŏ-mōn′yə-lĭk′, -nyŏŏ-) *n.* See **mycoplasma.**

pleu·rot·o·my (plŏŏ-rŏt′ə-mē) *n., pl.* **-mies** Surgical incision of the pleura.

pleus·ton (plŏŏ′stən, -stŏn′) *n.* Plants that float on the surface of bodies of fresh water. [Gk. *pleusis*, sailing; see **pleu-** in App. + (PLANK)TON.] —**pleus·ton′ic** (plŏŏ-stŏn′ĭk) *adj.*

–plex *suff.* Divided into a specified number of parts: *fourplex.* [< Lat. -*plex*, -fold (as in *duplex*, twofold). See **plek-** in App.]

plex·i·form (plĕk′sə-fôrm′) *adj.* Similar to or having the form of a plexus. [PLEX(US) + -FORM.]

Plex·i·glas (plĕk′sĭ-glăs′) A trademark used for a light transparent weather-resistant thermoplastic.

plex·or (plĕk′sər) *n.* A small rubber-headed hammer used in examination or diagnosis by percussion. [< Gk. *plēxis*, a blow < *plēssein*, *plēg*, to strike. See **plāk-** in App.]

plex·us (plĕk′səs) *n., pl.* **plexus** or **-us·es 1.** A structure in the form of a network, esp. of nerves, blood vessels, or lymphatics. **2.** A combination of interlaced parts; a network. [NLat. < Lat., braid < p. part. of *plectere*, to plait. See **plek-** in App.]

pli·a·ble (plī′ə-bəl) *adj.* **1.** Easily bent or shaped. **2.** Receptive to change; adaptable. **3.** Easily influenced, persuaded, or swayed; tractable. [ME < OFr. < *plier*, to bend. See **PLIANT.**] —**pli′a·bil′i·ty, pli′a·ble·ness** *n.* —**pli′a·bly** *adv.*

pli·ant (plī′ənt) *adj.* **1.** Easily bent or flexed; pliable. **2.** Easily altered or modified to fit conditions; adaptable. **3.** Yielding readily to influence or domination; compliant. [ME < OFr., pr. part. of *plier*, to bend < Lat. *plicāre*. See **plek-** in App.] —**pli′an·cy, pli′ant·ness** *n.* —**pli′ant·ly** *adv.*

pli·ca (plī′kə) *n., pl.* **pli·cae** (plī′sē, -kē) A fold or ridge, as of skin, membrane, or shell. [Med.Lat., fold < Lat. *plicāre*, to fold. See **plek-** in App.] —**pli′cal** *adj.*

pli·cate (plī′kāt′) also **pli·cat·ed** (-kā′tĭd) *adj.* Arranged in folds like those of a fan; pleated. [Lat. *plicātus*, p. part. of *plicāre*, to fold. See **plek-** in App.] —**pli′cate·ly** *adv.* —**pli′cate·ness** *n.*

pli·ca·tion (plī-kā′shən) also **plic·a·ture** (plĭk′ə-chŏŏr′) *n.* **1a.** The act or process of folding. **b.** The state of being folded. **2.** A fold.

pli·é (plē-ā′) *n.* A ballet movement in which the knees are bent while the back is held straight. [Fr. < p. part. of *plier*, to fold, bend < OFr. See **PLIANT.**]

plied[1] (plīd) *v.* Past tense and past participle of **ply**[1].

plied[2] (plīd) *v.* Past tense and past participle of **ply**[2].

pli·er also **ply·er** (plī′ər) *n.* **1.** One who plies a trade. **2. pliers** A variously shaped hand tool having a pair of pivoted jaws, used for holding, bending, or cutting.

plies[1] (plīz) *v.* Third person singular present tense of **ply**[1]. ❖ *n.* Plural of **ply**[1].

plies[2] (plīz) *v.* Third person singular present tense of **ply**[2].

plight[1] (plīt) *n.* A situation, esp. a bad or unfortunate one. [ME, alteration of *plit*, fold, wrinkle, situation < AN < Lat. *plicitum*, neut. p. part. of *plicāre*, to fold. See **plek-** in App.]

plight[2] (plīt) *tr.v.* **plight·ed, plight·ing, plights 1.** To promise or bind by a solemn pledge, esp. to betroth. **2.** To give or pledge (one's word or oath, for example). **3.** A solemn pledge, as of faith. —*idiom:* **plight (one's) troth 1.** To become engaged to marry. **2.** To give one's solemn oath. [ME *plighten* < OE *plihtan*, to endanger, put at risk < *pliht*, danger, risk. See **dlegh-** in App.] —**plight′er** *n.*

plim·soll (plĭm′səl, -sôl′) also **plim·sol** or **plim·sole** (-sōl′) *n.* Chiefly British A rubber-soled cloth shoe; a sneaker. [Prob. < the resemblance of its mudguard to a PLIMSOLL MARK.]

Plimsoll line *n.* See **Plimsoll mark.**

Plimsoll mark *n. Nautical* Any of a set of lines on the hull of a merchant ship that indicate the depth to which it may be legally loaded under specified conditions. [After Samuel *Plimsoll* (1824–98), British merchant and shipping reformer.]

plink (plĭngk) *v.* **plinked, plink·ing, plinks** —*tr.* **1.** To cause to make a soft sharp metallic sound; clink. **2.** To shoot at casually. —*intr.* **1.** To make a soft sharp metallic sound. **2.** To shoot casually at random targets. [Imit.]

plinth (plĭnth) *n.* **1.** A block or slab on which a pedestal, column, or statue is placed. **2.** The base block at the intersection of the baseboard and the vertical trim around an opening. **3.** A continuous course of stones supporting a wall. **4.** A square base, as for a vase. [Fr. *plinthe* < Lat. *plinthus* < Gk. *plinthos*, tile, plinth.]

Plin·y (plĭn′ē) Originally Gaius Plinius Secundus. Known as "the Elder." A.D. 23–79. Roman scholar and naturalist who wrote the 37-volume *Historia Naturalis.* His nephew **Pliny** (originally Gaius Plinius Caecilius Secundus, A.D. 62?–113?), known as "the Younger," was a consul and writer whose letters provide valuable information about Roman life.

plio– *pref.* Variant of **pleo–**.

Pli·o·cene (plī′ə-sēn′) *adj.* Of or belonging to the geologic time of the last epoch of the Tertiary Period, characterized by the appearance of distinctly modern animals. See table at **geologic time.** ❖ *n.* The Pliocene Epoch or its deposits. [Gk. *pleiōn*, more; see **pelə-**[1] in App. + -CENE.]

plis·sé also **plis·se** (plĭ-sā′) *n.* **1.** A puckered finish given to fabric by treating it with a caustic soda. **2.** Fabric with a plissé. [Fr. < p. part. of *plisser*, to pleat < OFr. < *pli*, fold < *plier*, to fold < Lat. *plicāre*. See **plek-** in App.]

PLO *abbr.* Palestine Liberation Organization

plod (plŏd) *v.* **plod·ded, plod·ding, plods** —*intr.* **1.** To move or walk heavily or laboriously; trudge. **2.** To work or act perseveringly or monotonously; drudge: *plodding through paperwork.* —*tr.* To trudge along or over. ❖ *n.* **1.** The act of moving or walking heavily and slowly. **2.** The sound made by a heavy step. [Perh. imit.] —**plod′der** *n.* —**plod′ding·ly** *adv.*

–ploid *suff.* Having a number of chromosomes that is a multiple of, or has a specified relationship to, the basic number of chromosomes of a group: *heteroploid.* [< DIPLOID and HAPLOID.]

ploi·dy (ploi′dē) *n.* A multiple of the basic number of chromosomes in a cell. [< DIPLOIDY and HAPLOIDY.]

Plo·ieş·ti or **Plo·eş·ti** (plô-yĕsht′, -yĕsh′tē) A city of SE-central Romania N of Bucharest. Pop. 254,304.

plonk[1] (plŏngk, plŭngk) *v., n.,* & *adv.* Variant of **plunk.**

plonk[2] (plŏngk) *n. Chiefly British Slang* Cheap or inferior wine. [Short for earlier *plink-plonk*, perh. alteration of Fr. *vin blanc*, white wine : *vin*, wine (< OFr.; see VINEGAR) + *blanc*, white (< OFr.; see BLANK).]

plop (plŏp) *v.* **plopped, plop·ping, plops** —*intr.* **1.** To fall with a sound like that of an object falling into water without splashing. **2.** To let the body drop heavily. —*tr.* To drop or set heavily, with or as if with a plop: *plopped the child into the stroller.* ❖ *n.* A plopping sound or movement. [Imit.] —**plop** *adv.*

plo·sion (plō′zhən) *n.* **1.** The articulation of a plosive sound. **2.** The sudden release of occluded air characteristic of plosives. [< EXPLOSION.]

plo·sive (plō′sĭv, -zĭv) *adj.* Of or being a speech sound produced by complete closure of the oral passage and subsequent release with a burst of air, as in the sound (p) in *pit.* ❖ *n.* A plosive speech sound. [< EXPLOSIVE.]

plot (plŏt) *n.* **1a.** A small piece of ground, generally used for a specific purpose. **b.** A measured area of land; a lot. **2.** A ground plan, as for a building; a diagram. **3.** See **graph**¹ 1. **4.** The pattern of events or main story in a narrative or drama. **5.** A secret plan to accomplish a hostile or illegal purpose; a scheme. ❖ *v.* **plot•ted, plot•ting, plots** —*tr.* **1.** To represent graphically, as on a chart. **2.** *Mathematics* **a.** To locate (points or other figures) on a graph by means of coordinates. **b.** To draw (a curve) connecting points on a graph. **3.** To conceive and arrange the action and incidents of. **4.** To form a plot for; prearrange secretly or deviously. —*intr.* **1.** To be located by means of coordinates, as on a chart or with data. **2.** To form or take part in a plot; scheme. [ME < OE.]

Plo•ti•nus (plō-tī′nəs) A.D. 205–270. Egyptian-born Roman philosopher and writer who founded Neo-Platonism.

plot line or **plot•line** (plŏt′līn′) *n.* **1.** A literary or dramatic plot; a story line. **2.** Dialogue essential to the development of a plot in a drama. Often used in the plural.

plot•tage (plŏt′ĭj) *n.* The area of land in a plot or group of plots.

plot•ter (plŏt′ər) *n.* **1.** One who plots. **2.** A computer output device that draws graphs or pictures, usu. by moving a pen.

Plov•div (plôv′dĭf′) A city of S-central Bulgaria on the Maritsa R. SE of Sofia; orig. built by Thracians. Pop. 341,374.

plov•er (plŭv′ər, plō′vər) *n., pl.* **plover** or **-ers 1.** Any of various widely distributed wading birds of the family Charadriidae, having rounded bodies, short tails, and short bills. **2.** Any of various similar or related birds. [ME < AN < VLat. **pluviārius* < Lat. *pluvia*, rain. See PLUVIAL.]

plow also **plough** (plou) *n.* **1.** A farm implement consisting of a heavy blade at the end of a beam, usu. hitched to a draft team or motor vehicle and used for breaking up soil and cutting furrows in preparation for sowing. **2.** An implement of similar function, such as a snowplow. **3. Plow** See **Big Dipper.** ❖ *v.* **plowed, plow•ing, plows** also **ploughed, plough•ing, ploughs** —*tr.* **1a.** To break and turn over (earth) with a plow. **b.** To form (a furrow, for example) with a plow. **c.** To form furrows in with or as if with a plow. **2.** To make or form with driving force. **3.** To cut through (water). —*intr.* **1.** To break and turn up earth with a plow. **2.** To admit of plowing. **3.** To move or progress with driving force. **4.** To proceed laboriously; plod. ***—phrasal verbs:* plow back** To reinvest (earnings or profits) in one's business. **plow into** *Informal* **1.** To strike with force. **2.** To undertake (a task, for example) with eagerness and vigor. **plow under 1.** To cause to vanish under something piled up. **2.** To overwhelm, as with burdens. [ME *plough, plouw* < OE *plōh, plōg*, plow, plowland.] **—plow′a•ble** *adj.* **—plow′er** *n.*

plow•back (plou′băk′) *n.* **1.** The plowing back of profits. **2.** An amount of profits plowed back.

plow•boy (plou′boi′) *n.* **1.** A boy who leads or guides a team of animals in plowing. **2.** A country boy.

plow•man (plou′mən) *n.* **1.** A man who plows. **2.** A farmer or rustic.

plow•share (plou′shâr′) *n.* The cutting blade of a plow.

plow steel *n.* A high-strength steel having a carbon content of 0.5 to 0.95 percent and used primarily to make wire rope.

ploy (ploi) *n.* An action calculated to frustrate an opponent or gain an advantage indirectly or deviously; a maneuver. [Perh. < EMPLOY, employment (obsolete).]

PLSS *abbr.* portable life-support system

pluck (plŭk) *v.* **plucked, pluck•ing, plucks** —*tr.* **1.** To remove or detach by grasping and pulling abruptly with the fingers; pick. **2.** To pull out the hair or feathers of. **3.** To remove abruptly or forcibly. **4.** To give an abrupt pull to; tug at. **5.** *Music* To sound (the strings of an instrument) by pulling and releasing them. —*intr.* To give an abrupt pull; tug. ❖ *n.* **1.** The act or an instance of plucking. **2.** Resourceful courage and daring in the face of difficulties; spirit. **3.** The heart, liver, windpipe, and lungs of a slaughtered animal. [ME *plukken* < OE *pluccian*, prob. < VLat. **piluccāre*, ult. < Lat. *pilāre* < *pilus*, hair.] **—pluck′er** *n.*

pluck•y (plŭk′ē) *adj.* **-i•er, -i•est** Having or showing courage and spirit in trying circumstances. See Syns at **brave.** **—pluck′i•ly** *adv.* **—pluck′i•ness** *n.*

plug (plŭg) *n.* **1.** An object, such as a cork, used to fill a hole tightly; a stopper. **2.** A dense mass of material that obstructs a passage. **3.** A usu. cylindrical or conic piece cut from something larger, often as a sample. **4.** *Electricity* **a.** A fitting, commonly with two metal prongs for insertion in a fixed socket, used to connect an appliance to a power supply. **b.** A spark plug. **5.** A hydrant. **6a.** A flat cake of pressed or twisted tobacco. **b.** A piece of chewing tobacco. **7.** *Geology* A mass of igneous rock filling the vent of a volcano. **8.** *Informal* A favorable public mention of a commercial product, business, or performance, esp. when broadcast. **9.** *Slang* Something inferior, useless, or defective, esp. an old horse. **10.** *Slang* A gunshot or bullet. **11.** A lure to which hooks are attached, used esp. in angling. ❖ *v.* **plugged, plug•ging, plugs** —*tr.* **1.** To fill (a hole) tightly with or as if with a plug; stop up. **2.** To insert (something) as a plug. **3.** *Slang* **a.** To hit with a bullet; shoot. **b.** To hit with the fist; punch. **4.** *Informal* To publicize (a product, for example) favorably, as by mentioning on a broadcast. —*intr.* **1.** To become stopped up or obstructed. **2.** *Informal* To work doggedly and persistently. ***—phrasal verbs:* plug in 1.** To connect (an appliance) to an electrical outlet. **2.** To function by being connected to an electrical outlet. **plug into 1.** To connect or be connected to in the manner of an electrical appliance. **2.** *Slang* To cause to be closely attuned or responsive to. [Du. < MDu. *plugge.*] **—plug′ger** *n.*

plug board *n.* **1.** A control panel or wiring panel. **2.** A removable panel in a computing device that may be rewired at will to sort data by a prescribed pattern.

plug-com•pat•i•ble (plŭg′kəm-păt′ə-bəl) *adj.* Capable of being connected peripherally to a computer without modification. Used of hardware.

plug-in (plŭg′ĭn′) *n.* See **add-in** 2.

plug•o•la (plŭg-ō′lə) *n. Informal* Advertising or publicity that is intended for self-promotion and not paid for or underwritten by an independent sponsor. [PLUG + *-ola*, suff. prob. modeled on trade names like *Shinola*, a brand of shoe polish.]

plug-ug•ly (plŭg′ŭg′lē) *n., pl.* **-lies** *Slang* A gangster or ruffian. [< the *Plug Uglies*, an East Coast gang in the 1850s.]

plum¹ (plŭm) *n.* **1a.** Any of several shrubs or small trees of the genus *Prunus*, bearing smooth-skinned fleshy edible fruit with a single hard-shelled stone that encloses the seed. **b.** The fruit of any of these trees. **2a.** Any of several trees bearing plumlike fruit. **b.** The fruit of such a tree. **3.** A raisin, when added to a pudding or cake. **4.** A sugarplum. **5.** A dark purple to deep reddish purple. **6.** An esp. desirable position, assignment, or reward. [ME < OE *plūme* < VLat. **prūna* < neut. pl. of Lat. *prūnum.*]

plum² (plŭm) *Informal adv.* Variant of **plumb** 3. ❖ *adj.* Variant of **plumb** 2.

plum•age (plo͞o′mĭj) *n.* **1.** The covering of feathers on a bird. **2.** Feathers used ornamentally. **3.** Elaborate dress; finery. [ME < OFr. < *plume*, plume < Lat. *plūma.*] **—plum′aged** *adj.*

plu•mate (plo͞o′māt′) *adj.* Resembling a plume or feather. [Lat. *plūmātus*, feathered < *plūma*, feather.]

plumb (plŭm) *n.* **1.** A weight on the end of a line, used to determine water depth. **2.** A weight on the end of a line, used esp. by masons and carpenters to establish a vertical. ❖ *adv.* **1.** In a vertical or perpendicular line. **2.** *Informal* Directly; squarely: *fell plumb in the middle of the puddle.* **3.** also **plum** *Informal* Utterly; completely: *plumb worn out.* ❖ *adj.* **1.** Exactly vertical. **2.** also **plum** *Informal* Utter; absolute; sheer: *a plumb fool.* ❖ *v.* **plumbed, plumb•ing, plumbs** —*tr.* **1.** To determine the depth of with a plumb; sound. **2.** To test the verticality or alignment of with a plumb. **3.** To straighten or make perpendicular: *plumb up the wall.* **4.** To examine closely or deeply; probe. **5.** To seal with lead. —*intr.* To work as a plumber. ***—idiom:* off** (or **out of) plumb** Not vertical. [ME, lead, a plumb < OFr. *plomb* < Lat. *plumbum*, lead.] **—plumb′a•ble** *adj.* **—plumb′ness** *n.*

plum•ba•go (plŭm-bā′gō) *n., pl.* **-gos 1.** See **graphite. 2.** Any of various plants of the genus *Plumbago*; leadwort. [Lat. *plumbāgō*, lead ore < *plumbum*, lead.]

plumb bob *n.* A weight attached to the end of a plumb line.

plumb•er (plŭm′ər) *n.* **1.** One that installs and repairs pipes and plumbing. **2.** *Slang* One assigned to investigate and stop leaks of sensitive information. [ME *plummer* < OFr. *plomier* < Lat. *plumbārius*, lead worker < Lat. *plumbum*, lead.]

plumb•er's helper (plŭm′ərz) *n.* See **plunger** 2.

plumber's snake *n.* See **snake** 3.

plumb•er•y (plŭm′ə-rē) *n., pl.* **-ies 1.** A plumber's workshop or place of business. **2.** A plumber's work; plumbing.

plum•bif•er•ous (plŭm-bĭf′ər-əs) *adj.* Containing lead. [Lat. *plumbum*, lead + -FEROUS.]

plumb•ing (plŭm′ĭng) *n.* **1.** The pipes, fixtures, and other apparatus of a water, gas, or sewage system in a building. **2.** The work or trade of a plumber. **3.** *Informal* An arrangement of vessels or ducts in the body.

plum•bism (plŭm′bĭz′əm) *n.* Chronic lead poisoning. [< Lat. *plumbum*, lead.]

plumb line *n.* **1.** A line from which a weight is suspended to determine verticality or depth. **2.** A line regarded as directed exactly toward the earth's center of gravity.

plumb rule *n.* A narrow strip of wood with a plumb line hanging from it, used to test verticality.

plume (plo͞om) *n.* **1.** A feather, esp. a large and showy one. **2.** A large feather or cluster of feathers worn as an ornament or symbol of rank. **3.** A token of honor or achievement. **4.** A structure or form that is like a long feather. **5.** *Ecology* A space in air, water, or soil containing pollutants released from a point source. **6.** *Geology* An upwelling of molten material from the earth's mantle. ❖ *tr.v.* **plumed, plum•ing, plumes 1.** To decorate, cover, or supply with or as if with plumes. **2.** To smooth (feathers); preen. **3.** To congratulate (oneself) in a self-satisfied way. [ME < OFr. < Lat. *plūma.*]

plume•let (plo͞om′lĭt) *n.* A small plume.

plum•met (plŭm′ĭt) *n.* **1.** See **plumb bob. 2.** Something that weighs down or oppresses; a burden. ❖ *intr.v.* **-met•ed, -met•ing, -mets 1.** To fall straight down; plunge. **2.** To decline suddenly and steeply. [ME *plomet* < OFr., ball of lead, dim. of *plom, plomb*, sounding lead < Lat. *plumbum.*]

plum•my (plŭm′ē) *adj.* **-mi•er, -mi•est 1a.** Filled with plums. **b.** Smelling or tasting of plums. **2.** Choice; desirable. **3.** Exceedingly or affectedly mellow and rich.

plu•mose (plo͞o′mōs′) *adj.* **1.** Having feathers or featherlike

plover
Egyptian plover
Pluvianus aegyptius

plume

ă	**pat**	oi	**boy**
ā	**pay**	ou	**out**
âr	**care**	o͝o	**took**
ä	**father**	o͞o	**boot**
ĕ	**pet**	ŭ	**cut**
ē	**be**	ûr	**urge**
ĭ	**pit**	th	**thin**
ī	**pie**	*th*	**this**
îr	**pier**	hw	**which**
ŏ	**pot**	zh	**vision**
ō	**toe**	ə	**about, item**
ô	**paw**		

Stress marks:
′ (primary);
′ (secondary), as in
lexicon (lĕk′sĭ-kŏn′)

growths; feathered. **2.** Resembling a plume; feathery. [Lat. *plūmōsus* < *plūma*, feather.] —**plu•mos′i•ty** (-mŏs′ĭ-tē) *n.*

plump[1] (plŭmp) *adj.* **plump•er, plump•est 1.** Well-rounded and full in form; chubby. See Syns at **fat. 2.** Abundant; ample: *a plump reward.* ❖ *v.* **plumped, plump•ing, plumps** —*tr.* To make well-rounded or full in form: *plumped up the pillows.* —*intr.* To become well-rounded, chubby, or full in form. [ME, dull, prob. < MLGer. *plomp*, blunt, thick.] —**plump′ish** *adj.* —**plump′ly** *adv.* —**plump′ness** *n.*

plump[2] (plŭmp) *v.* **plumped, plump•ing, plumps** —*intr.* **1.** To drop abruptly or heavily. **2.** To give full support or praise. —*tr.* To throw down or drop (something) abruptly or heavily. ❖ *n.* **1.** A heavy or abrupt fall or collision. **2.** The sound of a heavy fall or collision. ❖ *adj.* Blunt; direct. ❖ *adv.* **1.** With a heavy or abrupt drop. **2.** Directly; straight: *walked plump into the pole.* **3.** Without qualification; bluntly. [ME *plumpen*, to immerse quickly, perh. < MLGer., prob. of imit. orig.]

plum pudding *n.* A rich boiled or steamed pudding made with flour, suet, raisins, currants, citron, and spices.

plu•mule (plo͞om′yo͞ol) *n.* **1.** A down feather. **2.** *Botany* The rudimentary bud of a plant embryo situated at the end of the hypocotyl, consisting of the epicotyl and often of immature leaves. [Lat. *plūmula*, dim. of *plūma*, feather.] —**plu′mu•lose′** (plo͞om′yə-lōs′) *adj.*

plum•y (plo͞o′mē) *adj.* **-i•er, -i•est 1.** Consisting of or covered with feathers. **2.** Resembling a feather or plume.

plun•der (plŭn′dər) *v.* **-dered, -der•ing, -ders** —*tr.* **1.** To rob of goods by force, esp. in time of war; pillage: *plunder a village.* **2.** To seize wrongfully or by force; steal: *plundered supplies.* —*intr.* To take booty; rob. ❖ *n.* **1.** The act or practice of plundering. **2.** Property stolen by fraud or force; booty. [Ger. *plündern* < MHGer. *plundern* < MLGer. *plunder*, household goods.] —**plun′der•a•ble** *adj.* —**plun′der•er** *n.* —**plun′der•ous** *adj.*

plus fours
golfer Payne Stewart

plunge (plŭnj) *v.* **plunged, plung•ing, plung•es** —*tr.* **1.** To thrust or throw forcefully into a substance or place. **2.** To cast suddenly, violently, or deeply into a given state or situation. —*intr.* **1.** To fall or throw oneself into a substance or place: *The swimmer plunged into the lake.* **2.** To throw oneself earnestly or wholeheartedly into an activity or situation: *plunged into my studies.* **3.** To enter or move headlong through something. **4.** To descend steeply; fall precipitously. **5.** To move forward and downward violently. **6.** To become suddenly lower; decrease dramatically: *stock prices plunged.* **7.** To speculate or gamble extravagantly. ❖ *n.* **1.** The act or an instance of plunging. **2a.** A place or area, such as a swimming pool, for diving or plunging. **b.** A swim; a dip. —***idiom:* take the plunge** *Informal* To begin an unfamiliar venture, esp. after hesitating. [ME *plungen* < OFr. *plongier* < VLat. **plumbicāre*, to heave a sounding lead < Lat. *plumbum*, lead.]

plung•er (plŭn′jər) *n.* **1.** One who plunges or dives. **2.** A device consisting of a rubber suction cup attached to the end of a stick, used to unclog drains and pipes. **3.** A machine part that operates with a thrusting or plunging movement.

plunk (plŭngk) also **plonk** (plŏngk, plŭngk) *v.* **plunked, plunk•ing, plunks** also **plonked, plonk•ing, plonks** —*tr.* **1.** To throw or place heavily or abruptly: *plunked the money down.* **2.** To strum or pluck (a stringed instrument). —*intr.* **1.** To drop or fall abruptly or heavily; plump. **2.** To emit a hollow twanging sound. ❖ *n.* **1.** *Informal* A heavy blow or stroke. **2.** A short hollow twanging sound. ❖ *adv. Informal* **1.** With a short hollow thud. **2.** Exactly; precisely. [Imit.] —**plunk′er** *n.* —**plunk′y** *adj.*

plu•per•fect (plo͞o-pûr′fĭkt) *adj.* **1.** Of or being a verb tense used to express action completed before a specified or implied past time. **2.** More than perfect; ideal. ❖ *n.* **1.** The pluperfect tense, formed in English with the past participle of a verb and the auxiliary *had*, as *had learned* in the sentence *He had learned to type by that time.* **2.** A verb or form in the pluperfect tense. [ME *pluperfyth*, alteration of Lat. *plūs quam perfectum*, more than perfect : *plūs*, more; see **pelə-[1]** in App. + *quam*, than + *perfectum*, neut. p. part. of *perficere*, to complete; see PERFECT.]

plu•ral (plo͝or′əl) *adj.* **1.** Relating to or composed of more than one member, set, or kind. **2.** *Grammar* Of, relating to, or being a grammatical form that designates more than one of the things specified. ❖ *n. Grammar* **1.** The plural number or form. **2.** A word or term in the plural form. [Ult. < Lat. *plūrālis* < *plūs, plūr-*, more. See **pelə-[1]** in App.] —**plu′ral•ly** *adv.*

plu•ral•ism (plo͝or′ə-lĭz′əm) *n.* **1.** The condition of being multiple or plural. **2a.** A condition in which numerous distinct ethnic, religious, or cultural groups are present and tolerated within a society. **b.** The belief that such a condition is desirable or socially beneficial. **3.** *Ecclesiastical* The holding by one person of two or more positions or offices, esp. two or more ecclesiastical benefices, at the same time. **4.** *Philosophy* **a.** The doctrine that reality is composed of many ultimate substances. **b.** The belief that no single explanatory system or view of reality can account for all the phenomena of life. —**plu′ral•is′tic** *adj.* —**plu′ral•is′ti•cal•ly** *adv.*

plu•ral•ist (plo͝or′ə-lĭst) *n.* **1.** An adherent of social or philosophical pluralism. **2.** *Ecclesiastical* A person who holds two or more offices, esp. two or more benefices, at the same time.

plu•ral•i•ty (plo͞o-răl′ĭ-tē) *n., pl.* **-ties 1.** The state or fact of being plural. **2.** A large number or amount; a multitude. **3.** *Ecclesiastical* **a.** Pluralism. **b.** The offices or benefices held by a pluralist. **4a.** In a contest of more than two choices, the number of votes cast for the winning choice if this number is not more than one half of the total votes cast. **b.** The number by which the vote of the winning choice in such a contest exceeds that of the closest opponent. **5.** The larger or greater part.

plu•ral•ize (plo͝or′ə-līz′) *v.* **-ized, -iz•ing, -iz•es** —*tr.* **1.** To make plural. **2.** *Grammar* To express in the plural. —*intr.* **1.** To become plural. **2.** *Ecclesiastical* To engage in pluralism. —**plu′ral•i•za′tion** (plo͝or′ə-lĭ-zā′shən) *n.*

plus (plŭs) *conj.* **1.** *Mathematics* Increased by the addition of: *Two plus two is four.* **2.** Added to; along with. **3.** *Usage Problem* And. ❖ *adj.* **1.** Positive or on the positive part of a scale: *a plus value.* **2.** Added or extra. **3.** *Informal* Increased to a further degree or number. **4.** Ranking on the higher end of a designated scale: *a grade of C plus.* **5.** *Physics* Positive. ❖ *n., pl.* **plus•es** or **plus•ses 1.** *Mathematics* The plus sign (+). **2.** A positive quantity. **3.** A favorable condition or factor. [Lat. *plūs*, more. See **pelə-[1]** in App.]

USAGE NOTE When mathematical equations involving the + sign are pronounced as English sentences, the verb is usually in the singular: *Two plus two* is (or *equals*) *four.* By the same token, subjects containing two noun phrases joined by *plus* are usually construed as singular: *The construction slowdown plus the bad weather has made for a weak market.* • The usage *plus which* in *The construction industry has seen a rise in rates. Plus which, bad weather has affected it* is not well established in formal writing, nor is the use of *plus* introducing an independent clause, as in *She has a great deal of talent, plus she works hard.*

plus fours *pl.n.* Loose knickers bagging below the knees, worn formerly for sports. [< the fact that they were four inches longer than ordinary knickers.]

plush (plŭsh) *n.* A fabric, as of silk, having a thick deep pile. ❖ *adj.* **plush•er, plush•est 1.** Made of or covered with plush. **2.** Luxurious. [Fr. *pluche*, var. of *peluche* < *pelucher*, to become fluffy, shed < OFr. *peluchier*, to pluck, prob. < VLat. **piluccāre*. See PLUCK.] —**plush′ly** *adv.* —**plush′ness** *n.*

plush•y (plŭsh′ē) *adj.* **-i•er, -i•est 1.** Resembling plush in texture. **2.** *Informal* Ostentatiously luxurious: *a plushy office.* —**plush′i•ly** *adv.* —**plush′i•ness** *n.*

plus sign *n.* The symbol (+), as in 2 + 2 = 4, that is used to indicate addition or a positive quantity.

plus-size (plŭs′sīz′) *n.* **1.** An extra large or oversize clothing size. **2.** A garment of such a size. —**plus′-sized′** (-sīzd′) *adj.*

Plu•tarch (plo͞o′tärk′) A.D. 46?–120? Greek biographer and Neo-Platonist philosopher who wrote *Parallel Lives.* —**Plu•tarch′an** (-tär′kən), **Plu•tarch′i•an** (-tär′kē-ən) *adj.*

Plu•to (plo͞o′tō) *n.* **1.** *Roman Mythology* The god of the dead and the ruler of the underworld. **2.** The ninth and usu. farthest planet from the sun. See table at **planet.** [Lat. *Plūtō, Plūtōn-* < Gk. *Ploutōn* < *ploutos*, wealth (because the underworld was thought to be the source of wealth from the ground). See **pleu-** in App.]

plu•toc•ra•cy (plo͞o-tŏk′rə-sē) *n., pl.* **-cies 1.** Government by the wealthy. **2.** A wealthy class that controls a government. **3.** A government or state in which the wealthy rule. [Gk. *ploutokratiā* : *ploutos*, wealth; see **pleu-** in App. + *-kratiā*, -cracy.] —**plu′to•crat′** (plo͞o′tə-krăt′) *n.* —**plu′to•crat′ic, plu′to•crat′i•cal** *adj.* —**plu′to•crat′i•cal•ly** *adv.*

plu•ton (plo͞o′tŏn′) *n.* A body of igneous rock formed beneath the surface of the earth by consolidation of magma. [Ger., back-formation < *plutonisch*, plutonic < Lat. *Plūtō, Plūtōn-*, Pluto. See PLUTO.] —**plu•ton′ic** *adj.*

Plu•to•ni•an (plo͞o-tō′nē-ən) also **Plu•ton•ic** (-tŏn′ĭk) *adj.* **1.** Of or relating to the god Pluto or the underworld; infernal. **2.** Of or relating to the planet Pluto.

plu•to•ni•um (plo͞o-tō′nē-əm) *n. Symbol* **Pu** A naturally radioactive, metallic transuranic element, occurring in uranium ores or produced artificially by neutron bombardment of uranium and used, esp. the highly fissionable isotope Pu 239, as a reactor fuel and in nuclear weapons. Its longest-lived isotope is Pu 244 with a half-life of 76 million years. Atomic number 94; melting point 640°C; boiling point 3,235°C; specific gravity 19.84; valence 3, 4, 5, 6. See table at **element.** [After the planet PLUTO (following neptunium in the periodic table).]

plu•vi•al (plo͞o′vē-əl) *adj.* **1.** Of or relating to precipitation, esp. rain. **2.** *Geology* Marked by or resulting from rain or its effects. ❖ *n.* An extended period of abundant rainfall, esp. during the Pleistocene Epoch. [Lat. *pluviālis* < *pluvia*, rain. See PLUVIOUS.]

plu•vi•ous (plo͞o′vē-əs) also **plu•vi•ose** (-ōs′) *adj.* Characterized by heavy rainfall; rainy. [Ult. < Lat. *pluviōsus* < *(aqua) pluvia*, rain (water), fem. of *pluvius*, of rain < *pluere*, to rain. See **pleu-** in App.] —**plu′vi•os′i•ty** (-ŏs′ĭ-tē) *n.*

ply[1] (plī) *tr.v.* **plied** (plīd), **ply•ing, plies** (plīz) **1.** To join together, as by molding or twisting. **2.** To double over (cloth, for example). ❖ *n., pl.* **plies** (plīz) **1.** A layer, as of paperboard. **2.** One of the sheets of wood glued together to form plywood. **3.** A layer of rubber-coated, usu. synthetic fabric forming the body of an automobile tire. **4.** One of the strands twisted together to make yarn, rope, or thread. Often used in combination: *three-ply* *cord.* **5.** A bias; an inclination. [ME *plien* < OFr. *plier,* alteration of *pleier* < Lat. *plicāre,* to fold. See **plek-** in App.]

ply[2] (plī) *v.* **plied** (plīd), **ply•ing, plies** (plīz) —*tr.* **1.** To use diligently; wield: *ply a knitting needle.* **2.** To engage in diligently; practice: *plied the carpenter's trade.* **3.** To traverse or sail over regularly. **4.** To continue offering something to; ensure that (another) is abundantly served. **5.** To assail vigorously. —*intr.* **1.** To traverse a route or course regularly. **2.** To perform or work diligently or regularly. **3.** *Nautical* To work against the wind by a zigzag course; tack. [ME *plien* < *applien,* to apply. See APPLY.]

Plym•outh (plĭm′əth) **1.** A borough of SW England on **Plymouth Sound,** an inlet of the English Channel. Pop. 250,300. **2.** A town of SE MA on **Plymouth Bay,** an inlet of the Atlantic Ocean SE of Boston; founded 1620 by Pilgrims, who supposedly set foot on **Plymouth Rock** when disembarking from the *Mayflower,* and the center of **Plymouth Colony,** absorbed by Massachusetts in 1691. Pop. 51,701.

Plymouth Rock *n.* Any of an American breed of medium-sized chicken raised for both meat and eggs.

ply•wood (plī′wo͝od′) *n.* A structural material made of layers of wood glued together, usu. with the grains of adjoining layers at right angles to each other. [PLY[1] + WOOD[1].]

Plzeň (pəl′zĕn′, -zĕn′yə) A city of W Czech Republic WSW of Prague; famed for its beer. Pop. 175,000.

pm or **p-m** *abbr.* phase modulation

Pm The symbol for the element **promethium.**

PM *abbr.* **1.** particulate matter **2.** past master **3.** police magistrate **4a.** postmaster **b.** postmistress **5.** prime minister **6.** provost marshal

P.M. also **p.m.** or **p.m.** *abbr.* post meridiem. See Usage Note at **A.M.**

PMG *abbr.* postmaster general

PMS *abbr.* premenstrual syndrome

PMSA *abbr.* Primary Metropolitan Statistical Area

pmt. *abbr.* payment

p.n. or **P/N** *abbr.* promissory note

pneu•ma (no͞o′mə, nyo͞o′-) *n.* The soul or vital spirit. [Gk.]

pneu•mat•ic (no͞o-măt′ĭk, nyo͞o-) also **pneu•mat•i•cal** (-ĭ-kəl) *adj.* **1.** Of or relating to air or other gases. **2.** Of or relating to pneumatics. **3a.** Run by or using compressed air. **b.** Filled with air, esp. compressed air. **4.** *Zoology* Having cavities filled with air, as the bones of certain birds. **5.** Of or relating to the pneuma; spiritual. [Fr. *pneumatique* < Lat. *pneumaticus* < Gk. *pneumatikos* < *pneuma, pneumat-,* wind.] —**pneu•mat′i•cal•ly** *adv.* —**pneu′ma•tic′i•ty** (no͞o′mə-tĭs′ĭ-tē, nyo͞o′-) *n.*

pneu•mat•ics (no͞o-măt′ĭks, nyo͞o-) *n.* (*used with a sing. verb*) The study of the mechanical properties of air and other gases.

pneumato– or **pneumat–** *pref.* **1.** Air; gas: *pneumatolysis.* **2.** Breath; respiration: *pneumatophore.* [< Gk. *pneuma, pneumat-,* wind, breath.]

pneu•ma•tol•o•gy (no͞o′mə-tŏl′ə-jē, nyo͞o′-) *n.* **1.** The doctrine or study of spiritual beings and phenomena, esp. the belief in spirits intervening between humans and God. **2.** The Christian doctrine of the Holy Ghost. —**pneu′ma•to•log′ic** (-tə-lŏj′ĭk), **pneu′ma•to•log′i•cal** (-ĭ-kəl) *adj.* —**pneu′ma•tol′o•gist** *n.*

pneu•ma•tol•y•sis (no͞o′mə-tŏl′ĭ-sĭs, nyo͞o′-) *n.* A process of rock alteration or mineral formation brought about by the action of gases emitted from solidifying magma. —**pneu′ma•to•lyt′ic** (-tə-lĭt′ĭk) *adj.*

pneu•mat•o•phore (no͞o-măt′ə-fôr′, -fōr′, nyo͞o-, no͞o′mə-tə-, nyo͞o′-) *n.* **1.** A gas-filled sac serving as a float in some colonial marine hydrozoans, such as the Portuguese man-of-war. **2.** *Botany* A specialized respiratory root structure in certain aquatic plants, such as the bald cypress.

pneumo– or **pneum–** *pref.* **1.** Air; gas: *pneumothorax.* **2.** Lung; pulmonary: *pneumoconiosis.* **3.** Respiration: *pneumograph.* **4.** Pneumonia: *pneumococcus.* [< Gk. *pneuma,* wind, breath; see **pneu-** in App., and < Gk. *pneumōn,* alteration (influenced by *pneuma*) of *pleumōn,* lung; see **pleu-** in App.]

pneu•mo•ba•cil•lus (no͞o′mō-bə-sĭl′əs, nyo͞o′-) *n., pl.* **-cil•li** (-sĭl′ī′) A nonmotile gram-negative bacterium *(Klebsiella pneumoniae)* that causes a severe form of pneumonia and is associated with other respiratory infections.

pneu•mo•coc•cus (no͞o′mə-kŏk′əs, nyo͞o′-) *n., pl.* **-coc•ci** (-kŏk′sī′, -kŏk′ī′) A nonmotile gram-positive bacterium *(Streptococcus pneumoniae)* that is the most common cause of bacterial pneumonia. —**pneu′mo•coc′cal** (-kŏk′əl) *adj.*

pneu•mo•co•ni•o•sis (no͞o′mō-kō′nē-ō′sĭs, nyo͞o′-) *n.* Any of several, usu. occupational diseases of the lungs, such as asbestosis or silicosis, caused by prolonged inhalation of esp. mineral or metallic dust particles. [PNEUMO– + Gk. *konis, koniā,* dust + –OSIS.] —**pneu′mo•co′ni•ot′ic** (-ŏt′ĭk) *adj. & n.*

pneu•mo•cys•tis (no͞o′mə-sĭs′tĭs, nyo͞o′-) *n.* A severe lung infection caused by the parasitic protozoan *Pneumocystis carinii* and affecting primarily individuals with an immunodeficiency disease, such as AIDS. [< NLat. *Pneumocystis,* genus name : PNEUMO– + NLat. *cystis,* cyst; see CYST.]

pneu•mo•graph (no͞o′mə-grăf′, nyo͞o′-) also **pneu•mat•o•graph** (no͞o-măt′ə-grăf′, nyo͞o-) *n.* A device for recording the force and speed of chest movements during respiration. —**pneu′mo•graph′ic** *adj.*

pneu•mo•nec•to•my (no͞o′mə-nĕk′tə-mē, nyo͞o′-) also **pneu•mec•to•my** (no͞o-mĕk′tə-mē, nyo͞o-) *n., pl.* **-mies** Surgical removal of all or part of a lung. [Gk. *pneumōn,* lung; see PNEUMONIC + –ECTOMY.]

pneu•mo•nia (no͞o-mōn′yə, nyo͞o-) *n.* An acute or chronic disease marked by inflammation of the lungs and caused by viruses, bacteria, or other microorganisms and sometimes by physical and chemical irritants. [NLat. < Gk. *pneumoniā,* lung disease, alteration (influenced by *pneuma,* breath) of *pleumoniā* < *pleumōn,* lung. See **pleu-** in App.]

pneu•mon•ic (no͞o-mŏn′ĭk, nyo͞o-) *adj.* **1.** Of, affecting, or relating to the lungs; pulmonary. **2.** Relating to, affected by, or similar to pneumonia. [NLat. *pneumonicus* < Gk. *pneumonikos,* of the lungs < *pneumōn,* lung. See **pleu-** in App.]

pneu•mo•tho•rax (no͞o′mō-thôr′ăks′, -thōr′-, nyo͞o′-) *n.* Accumulation of air or gas in the pleural cavity, occurring as a result of disease or injury or sometimes induced to collapse the lung in the treatment of lung diseases.

Po[1] (pō) A river of N Italy flowing c. 652 km (405 mi) to the Adriatic Sea.

Po[2] The symbol for the element **polonium.**

PO *abbr.* **1.** personnel officer **2.** petty officer **3.** postal order **4.** post office **5.** putout

poach[1] (pōch) *tr.v.* **poached, poach•ing, poach•es** To cook in a boiling or simmering liquid. [Back-formation < ME *poched,* poached < *poche,* dish of poached eggs < OFr. < p. part. of *pochier,* to poach eggs < *poche,* pocket, bag (< their appearance), of Gmc. orig.] —**poach′a•ble** *adj.*

poach[2] (pōch) *v.* **poached, poach•ing, poach•es** —*tr.* **1.** To trespass on (another's property) for fishing or hunting. **2.** To take (fish or game) illegally. **3.** To make (land) muddy or broken up by trampling. **4.** To take or appropriate unfairly or illegally. —*intr.* **1.** To poach another's property. **2.** To poach fish or game. **3.** To become poached. Used of land. **4.** To sink into soft earth when walking. **5.** To poach something. [Obsolete Fr. *pocher,* to poke, thrust, intrude < OFr. *pochier,* to poke, gouge, of Gmc. orig.] —**poach′a•ble** *adj.*

poach•er[1] (pō′chər) *n.* A vessel or dish designed for the poaching of food, such as eggs or fish.

poach•er[2] (pō′chər) *n.* **1.** One who hunts or fishes illegally on the property of another. **2.** Any of various elongated marine fishes of the family Agonidae, chiefly of northern Pacific waters and having an external covering of bony plates.

Po•be•da Peak (pō-bĕd′ə, pə-byĕ′də) A mountain, 7,443.8 m (24,406 ft), of the Tian Shan on the border between E Kirghiz and W China.

po•boy (pō′boi′) *n. Gulf Coast US* Variant of **poor boy.**

Po•ca•hon•tas (pō′kə-hŏn′təs) 1595?–1617. Powhatan princess who befriended the English colonists at Jamestown and is said to have saved Capt. John Smith from execution.

Po•ca•tel•lo (pō′kə-tĕl′ō, -tĕl′ə) A city of SE ID SSW of Idaho Falls. Pop. 51,466.

po•chard (pō′chərd) *n.* Any of various diving ducks of the genus *Aythya,* esp. *A. ferina* of Europe and Asia, having gray and black plumage and a reddish head. [?]

pock (pŏk) *n.* **1.** A pustule caused by smallpox or a similar eruptive disease. **2.** A mark or scar left in the skin by such a pustule; a pockmark. ❖ *tr.v.* **pocked, pock•ing, pocks** To mark with pocks; pit. [ME *pokke* < OE *pocc.*] —**pock′y** *adj.*

pock•et (pŏk′ĭt) *n.* **1.** A small baglike attachment forming part of a garment and used to carry small articles, as a flat pouch sewn inside a pair of pants or a piece of material sewn on its sides and bottom to the outside of a shirt. **2.** A small sack or bag. **3.** A receptacle, cavity, or opening. **4.** Financial means; money supply. **5a.** A small cavity in the earth, esp. one containing ore. **b.** A small body or accumulation of ore. **6.** A pouch in an animal body, such as the cheek pouch of a rodent or the abdominal pouch of a marsupial. **7.** *Games* One of the pouchlike receptacles at the corners and sides of a billiard or pool table. **8.** *Baseball* The deepest part of a baseball glove, just below the web, where the ball is normally caught. **9.** *Sports* A racing position in which a contestant has no room to pass a group of contestants. **10.** A small, isolated, or protected area or group: *pockets of dissatisfied voters.* **11.** *Football* The area behind the line of scrimmage that blockers attempt to keep clear so that the quarterback can pass the ball. **12.** An air pocket. **13.** A bin for storing ore, grain, or other materials. ❖ *adj.* **1.** Suitable for or capable of being carried in one's pocket. **2.** Small; miniature. ❖ *tr.v.* **-et•ed, -et•ing, -ets 1.** To place in or as if in a pocket. **2.** To take possession of for oneself, esp. dishonestly. **3a.** To accept or tolerate (an insult, for example). **b.** To conceal or suppress. **4.** To prevent (a bill) from becoming law by failing to sign until the adjournment of the legislature. **5.** *Sports* To hem in (a competitor) in a race. **6.** *Games* To hit (a ball) into a pocket of a pool or billiard table. —***idioms:* in (one's) pocket** In one's power, influence, or possession. **in pocket 1.** Having funds. **2.** Having gained or retained funds of a specified amount. [ME, pouch, small bag < AN *pokete,* dim. of ONFr. *poke,* bag, of Gmc. orig.] —**pock′et•a•ble** *adj.* —**pock′et•less** *adj.*

pocket billiards *pl.n.* (*used with a sing. or pl. verb*) See **pool[2]** 7.

pock•et•book (pŏk′ĭt-bo͝ok′) *n.* **1.** A purse; a handbag. **2.** A pocket-sized folder or case used to hold money and papers; a billfold. **3.** Financial resources; money supply. **4.** often **pocket book**

Plymouth Rock
White Plymouth Rock rooster

Pocahontas
1616 portrait by an unknown artist

ă pat	oi boy
ā pay	ou out
âr care	o͝o took
ä father	o͞o boot
ĕ pet	ŭ cut
ē be	ûr urge
ĭ pit	th thin
ī pie	*th* this
îr pier	hw which
ŏ pot	zh vision
ō toe	ə about, item
ô paw	

Stress marks:
′ (primary);
′ (secondary), as in
lexicon (lĕk′sĭ-kŏn′)

A pocket-sized, usu. paperbound book.

pocket borough *n.* A borough in England, before the parliamentary reform of 1832, whose representation was controlled by a single person or family.

pocket edition *n.* See **pocketbook** 4.

pock·et·ful (pŏk′ĭt-fŏol′) *n., pl.* **pock·et·fuls** or **pock·ets·ful** (pŏk′ĭts-fŏol′) The amount that a pocket can hold.

pocket gopher *n.* See **gopher** 1.

pock·et·knife (pŏk′ĭt-nīf′) *n.* A small knife with blades or a blade that can fold into the handle when not in use.

pocket money *n.* Money for incidental or minor expenses.

pocket mouse *n.* Any of various small nocturnal North American burrowing rodents of the genus *Perognathus,* having furlined external cheek pouches, small ears, and a long tail.

pock·et-sized (pŏk′ĭt-sīzd′) or **pock·et·size** (-sīz′) *adj.* 1. Of a size suitable to be carried in a pocket. 2. Small.

pocket veto *n.* 1. The indirect veto of a bill received by the President within ten days of the adjournment of Congress, effected by retaining the bill unsigned until Congress adjourns. 2. A similar action exercised by a state governor or other chief executive. —**pock′et-ve′to** (pŏk′ĭt-vē′tō) *v.*

pock·mark (pŏk′märk′) *n.* 1. A pitlike scar left on the skin by smallpox or another eruptive disease. 2. A small pit on a surface. —**pock′mark′** *v.* —**pock′marked′** *adj.*

po·co (pō′kō) *adv. Music* To a slight degree or amount; somewhat. [Ital. < Lat. *paucus.*]

podium

po·co a po·co (pō′kō ä pō′kō) *adv. Music* Little by little; gradually. [Ital. : *poco,* little + *a,* by + *poco,* little.]

po·co·cu·ran·te (pō′kō-kŏo-rän′tē, -rän′tĕ) *adj.* Indifferent; apathetic. ❖ *n.* One who does not care. [Ital. : *poco,* little; see POCO + *curante,* pr. part. of *curare,* to care for (< Lat. *cūrāre* < *cūra,* care).] —**po′co·cu·ran′tism** *n.*

Po·co·no Mountains (pō′kə-nō′) A range of the Appalachian system in NE PA rising to c. 488 m (1,600 ft).

po·co·sin (pə-kō′sĭn) *n. Chiefly South Atlantic US* A swamp in an upland coastal region. [Poss. of Virginia Algonquian orig.]

pod[1] (pŏd) *n.* 1. *Botany* a. A dehiscent fruit of a leguminous plant such as the pea. b. A dry several-seeded dehiscent fruit. 2. *Zoology* A protective covering that encases the eggs of some insects and fish. 3. A casing or housing forming part of a vehicle, as: a. A streamlined external housing that encloses engines, machine guns, or fuel. b. *Aerospace* A detachable compartment on a spacecraft for carrying personnel or instrumentation. 4. Something resembling a pod, as in compactness. ❖ *v.* **pod·ded, pod·ding, pods** —*intr.* 1. To bear or produce pods. 2. To expand or swell like a pod. —*tr.* To remove (seeds) from a pod. [?]

pod[2] (pŏd) *n.* A school of marine mammals, such as seals, whales, or dolphins. [?]

Edgar Allan Poe

pod[3] (pŏd) *n.* 1. The lengthwise groove in boring tools such as augers. 2. The socket for holding the bit in a boring tool. [?]

–pod or **–pode** *suff.* Foot; footlike part: *pleopod.* [< NLat. *-podium* (< Gk. *podion;* see PODIUM) and < NLat. *-poda* (< Gk., pl. of *pous, pod-,* foot; see **ped-** in App.).]

po·dag·ra (pə-dăg′rə) *n.* Gout, esp. of the big toe. [ME < Lat. < Gk. *podagrā* : *pous, pod-,* foot; see **ped-** in App. + *agrā,* trap, seizing; see **ag-** in App.] —**po·dag′ral, po·dag′ric** *adj.*

po·des·ta (pō-dĕs′tə, pō′dĕ-stä′) *n.* The chief magistrate of a republic in medieval Italy. [Ital. *podestà* < OItal. *podestate* < Lat. *potestās,* power < *potis,* powerful, able. See **poti-** in App.]

Pod·go·ri·ca (pŏd′gə-rēt′sə) The cap. of Montenegro, in the SE part near the Albanian border. Pop. 118,059.

Pod·gor·ny (pŏd-gôr′nē), **Nikolai Viktorovich** 1903–83. Soviet politician who was president of the USSR (1965–77).

po·di·a·try (pə-dī′ə-trē) *n.* The branch of medicine that deals with the diagnosis, treatment, and prevention of diseases of the human foot. [Gk. *pous, pod-,* foot; see **ped-** in App. + –IATRY.] —**po′di·at′ric** (pō′dē-ăt′rĭk) *adj.* —**po·di′a·trist** *n.*

pod·ite (pŏd′īt′) *n.* A segment of the limb of an arthropod. [Gk. *pous, pod-,* foot; see **ped-** in App. + –ITE[1].]

po·di·um (pō′dē-əm) *n., pl.* **-di·a** (-dē-ə) or **-di·ums** 1. An elevated platform, as for a public speaker. 2. A stand for holding the notes of a public speaker; a lectern. 3. *Architecture* a. A low wall serving as a foundation. b. A wall circling the arena of an ancient amphitheater. 4. *Biology* A structure resembling or functioning as a foot. [Lat. < Gk. *podion,* base, dim. of *pous, pod-,* foot. See **ped-** in App.]

pod·o·phyl·lin (pŏd′ə-fĭl′ĭn) *n.* A bitter-tasting resin obtained from the dried root of the May apple and used as a cathartic and caustic. [< NLat. *Podophyllum,* genus name : Gk. *pous, pod-,* foot; see **ped-** in App. + Gk. *phullon,* leaf; see **bhel-** in App. + –IN.]

–podous *suff.* Having a specified kind or number of feet or footlike parts: *polypodous.*

Po·dunk (pō′dŭngk′) *n. Slang* A small isolated town, region, or place regarded as unimportant. [After *Podunk,* name of two New England towns.]

pod·zol (pŏd′zŏl′) also **pod·sol** (-sŏl′) *n.* A leached soil formed mainly in cool humid climates. [Russ. : *pod,* under; see **ped-** in App. + *zola,* ashes; see **ghel-** in App.] —**pod·zol′ic** *adj.*

pod·zol·i·za·tion (pŏd′zō-lĭ-zā′shən) also **pod·sol·i·za·tion** (pŏd′sŏl-) *n.* 1. The process by which soils are depleted of bases and become acidic. 2. The development of a podzol.

Poe (pō), **Edgar Allan** 1809–49. Amer. writer whose works include "The Gold Bug" (1843) and "The Raven" (1845).

POE *abbr.* port of entry

PO′ed (pē′ŏd′) *adj. Informal* Extremely irritated or angry. [P(ISS) O(FF) : –ED[2].]

po·em (pō′əm) *n.* 1. A verbal composition designed to convey experiences, ideas, or emotions, characterized by the use of language chosen for its sound and suggestive power and by the use of literary techniques such as meter, metaphor, and rhyme. 2. A composition in verse rather than in prose. 3. A literary composition written with an intensity or beauty of language more characteristic of poetry than of prose. 4. A creation, object, or experience having beauty suggestive of poetry. [Fr. *poème* < OFr. < Lat. *poēma* < Gk. *poiēma,* creation < *poiein,* to create.]

poe·nol·o·gy (pē-nŏl′ə-jē) *n.* Variant of **penology.**

po·e·sy (pō′ĭ-zē, -sē) *n., pl.* **-sies** 1. Poetical works; poetry. 2. The art or practice of composing poems. 3. The inspiration involved in composing poetry. [ME *poesie* < OFr. < Lat. *poēsis* < Gk. *poiēsis* < *poiein,* to create.]

po·et (pō′ĭt) *n.* 1. One who composes poems. 2. One who is esp. gifted in the perception and expression of the beautiful or lyrical. [ME < OFr. *poete* < Lat. *poēta* < Gk. *poiētēs,* maker, composer < *poiein,* to create.]

po·et·as·ter (pō′ĭt-ăs′tər) *n.* A writer of insignificant, meretricious, or shoddy poetry. [NLat. *poētaster* : Lat. *poēta,* poet; see POET + *-aster,* pejorative suff.]

po·et·ess (pō′ĭ-tĭs) *n.* A woman who is a writer of poems. See Usage Note at **–ess.**

po·et·ic (pō-ĕt′ĭk) *adj.* 1. Of or relating to poetry. 2. Having a quality or style characteristic of poetry. 3. Suitable as a subject for poetry. 4. Of, relating to, or befitting a poet: *poetic insight.* 5. Characterized by romantic imagery. ❖ *n.* The theory or practice of writing poetry; poetics. [Lat. *poēticus* < Gk. *poiētikos,* inventive < *poiein,* to make.]

po·et·i·cal (pō-ĕt′ĭ-kəl) *adj.* 1. Poetic. 2. Fancifully depicted or embellished; idealized. —**po·et′i·cal·ly** *adv.* —**po·et′i·cal·ness, po·et′i·cal·i·ty** (-kăl′ĭ-tē) *n.*

po·et·i·cism (pō-ĕt′ĭ-sĭz′əm) *n.* A poetic expression that is hackneyed, archaic, or excessively artificial.

po·et·i·cize (pō-ĕt′ĭ-sīz′) *v.* **-cized, -ciz·ing, -ciz·es** —*tr.* To describe or express in poetry or in a poetic manner. —*intr.* To write poetry.

poetic justice *n.* The rewarding of virtue and the punishment of vice, often in an esp. appropriate or ironic manner.

poetic license *n.* The liberty taken by an artist or a writer in deviating from convention to achieve a desired effect.

po·et·ics (pō-ĕt′ĭks) *n.* (*used with a sing. or pl. verb*) 1. Literary criticism that deals with the nature, forms, and laws of poetry. 2. A treatise on or study of poetry or aesthetics. 3. The practice of writing poetry; poetic composition.

po·et·ize (pō′ĭ-tīz′) *v.* **-ized, -iz·ing, -iz·es** —*tr.* To describe or express in poetry or a poetic manner. —*intr.* To write poetry.

poet laureate *n., pl.* **poets laureate** or **poet laureates** 1. A poet appointed for life by a British monarch as a member of the royal household and expected to write patriotic poems. 2. A poet appointed to a similar honorary position or honored for artistic excellence. 3. A poet acclaimed as the most excellent or most representative of a locality or group.

po·et·ry (pō′ĭ-trē) *n.* 1. The art or work of a poet. 2a. Poems regarded as forming a division of literature. b. The poetic works of a given author, group, nation, or kind. 3. A piece of literature written in meter; verse. 4. Prose that resembles a poem in some respect, as in form or sound. 5. The essence or characteristic quality of a poem. 6. A quality that suggests poetry, as in grace, beauty, or harmony. [ME *poetrie* < OFr. < Med.Lat. *poētria* < Lat. *poēta,* poet. See POET.]

poetry slam *n.* A spoken-word poetry competition.

pog·o·nip (pŏg′ə-nĭp′) *n.* See **ice fog.** [Shoshone *pakenappeh.*]

po·go stick (pō′gō) *n.* A stick with footrests and a spring set into the bottom end, used to propel oneself along the ground by hopping. [< *Pogo,* a former trademark.]

po·grom (pə-grŏm′, pō′grəm) *n.* An organized, often officially encouraged massacre or persecution, esp. one against Jews. [Russ., outrage, havoc < *pogromit',* to wreak havoc : *po-,* adverbial pref. (< *po,* next to; see **apo-** in App.) + *gromit',* wreak havoc (< *grom,* thunder).] —**po·grom′** *v.*

po·gy (pō′gē) *n., pl.* **pogy** or **-gies** See **menhaden.** [Alteration of dialectal *poghaden,* perh. of Eastern Abenaki orig.]

Po Hai (bō′ hī′) See **Bo Hai.**

poi (poi) *n.* A Hawaiian food made from the tuber of the taro that is cooked, pounded to a paste, and fermented. [Hawaiian.]

–poiesis *suff.* Production; creation; formation: *hematopoiesis.* [< Gk. *poiēsis,* creation < *poiein,* to make.]

–poietic *suff.* Productive; formative: *galactopoietic.* [< Gk. *poiētikos,* creative < *poiētēs,* maker < *poiein,* to make.]

poign·ant (poin′yənt) *adj.* 1a. Profoundly moving; touching: *a poignant memory.* b. Keenly distressing to the mind or feelings: *poignant anxiety.* c. Physically painful. 2. Piercing; incisive: *poignant criticism.* 3a. Neat, skillful, and to the point. b. Astute and pertinent; relevant: *poignant suggestions.* 4. Agreeably intense or stimulating: *poignant delight.* 5. *Archaic* a. Sharp or sour to the taste; piquant. **b.** Sharp or pungent to the smell. [ME *poinaunt* < OFr. *poignant*, pr. part. of *poindre*, to prick < Lat. *pungere*.] **—poign′ance, poign′an•cy** *n.* **—poign′ant•ly** *adv.*

poi•kil•o•therm (poi-kĭl′ə-thûrm′) *n.* An organism, such as a fish or reptile, having a body temperature that varies with the temperature of its surroundings; an ectotherm. [Gk. *poikilos*, spotted, various + –THERM.] **—poi′ki•lo•ther′mi•a** (-thûr′mē-ə) *n.* **—poi′ki•lo•ther′mic** (-mĭk) *adj.*

poi•lu (pwä-lü′) *n. Slang* A French soldier, esp. in World War I. [Fr., hairy, tough, poilu < OFr. *pelu*, hairy < VLat. **pilūtus* < Lat. *pilus*, hair.]

Poin•ca•ré (pwăN-kä-rā′), **Jules Henri** 1854–1912. French mathematician and physicist who made a number of contributions to the field of celestial mechanics.

Poincaré, Raymond 1860–1934. French president (1913–20) and premier (1912–13, 1922–23, and 1926–29).

poin•ci•an•a (poin′sē-ăn′ə, -ä′nə) *n.* See **royal poinciana.** [NLat. *Poinciāna*, genus name, after M. De *Poinci*, 17th-cent. governor of the French West Indies.]

poin•set•ti•a (poin-sĕt′ē-ə, -sĕt′ə) *n.* A tropical American shrub *(Euphorbia pulcherrima)* that has showy, usu. scarlet bracts beneath the small yellow inflorescences. [NLat., after Joel Roberts *Poinsett* (1779–1851), American diplomat.]

point (point) *n.* **1.** A sharp or tapered end: *the point of a knife.* **2.** An object having a sharp or tapered end. **3.** A tapering extension of land projecting into water; a peninsula, cape, or promontory. **4.** A mark formed by or as if by a sharp end. **5.** A mark or dot used in printing or writing for punctuation, esp. a period. **6.** A decimal point. **7.** *Linguistics* A vowel point. **8.** One of the protruding marks used in certain methods of writing and printing for the blind. **9.** *Mathematics* **a.** A dimensionless geometric object having no properties except location. **b.** An element in a geometrically described set. **10a.** A place or locality considered with regard to its position: *the train to Chicago and points west.* **b.** A narrowly particularized and localized position or place; a spot. **11.** A specified degree, condition, or limit, as in a scale or course: *the melting point of a substance.* **12a.** Any of the 32 equal divisions marked at the circumference of a mariner's compass card that indicate direction. **b.** The interval of 11°15′ between any two adjacent markings. **13a.** A distinct condition or degree: *reached the point of exhaustion.* **b.** The interval of time immediately before a given occurrence; the verge: *at the point of death.* **14.** A specific moment in time. **15.** An objective or purpose to be reached or achieved, or one that is worth reaching or achieving. **16.** The major idea or essential part of a concept or narrative: *missed the point of the novel.* **17.** A significant, outstanding, or effective idea, argument, or suggestion: *Your point is well taken.* **18.** A separate distinguishing item or element; a detail: *not his strong point.* **19.** A quality or characteristic that is important or distinctive, esp. a standard characteristic used to judge an animal. **20.** A single unit, as in counting, rating, or measuring. **21a.** A unit of academic credit usu. equal to one hour of class work per week during one semester. **b.** A numerical unit of academic achievement equal to a letter grade. **22.** *Sports & Games* A unit of scoring or counting. **23a.** A unit equal to one dollar, used to quote or state variations in the current prices of stocks or commodities. **b.** A unit equal to one percent, used to quote or state interest rates or shares in gross profits. **24.** One percent of the total principal of a loan, paid up front to the lender and considered separately from the interest. **25.** *Music* A phrase, such as a fugue subject, in contrapuntal music. **26.** *Printing* A unit of type size equal to 0.01384 inch, or approx. 1⁄72 of an inch. **27.** A jeweler's unit of weight equal to 2 milligrams or 0.01 carat. **28a.** The act or an instance of pointing. **b.** The stiff and attentive stance taken by a hunting dog. **29a.** Needlepoint. **b.** See **bobbin lace. 30a.** A reconnaissance or patrol unit that moves ahead of an advance party or guard, or that follows a rear guard. **b.** The position occupied by such a unit or guard. **31a.** An electrical contact, esp. one in the distributor of an automobile engine. **b.** *Chiefly British* An electrical socket or outlet. **32.** *Sports* Either of two positions in ice hockey just inside the offensive zone near the boards, usu. assumed by defenders on the attacking team. **33.** *Basketball* A position in the forecourt beyond the top of the key, usu. taken by the point guard. **34. points** The extremities of an animal, such as a horse or dog. **35a.** A movable rail, tapered at the end, such as that used in a railroad switch. **b.** The vertex of the angle created by the intersection of rails in a frog or switch. **36.** A ribbon or cord with a metal tag at the end, used to fasten clothing in the 16th and 17th centuries. ❖ *v.* **point•ed, point•ing, points** *—tr.* **1.** To direct or aim: *pointed the weapon.* **2.** To bring (something) to notice: *pointed out an error.* **3.** To indicate the position or direction of: *pointed them out over there.* **4.** To sharpen (a pencil, for example); provide with a point. **5.** To separate with decimal points: *pointed off the tenths place.* **6.** To mark (text) with points; punctuate. **7.** *Linguistics* To mark (a consonant) with a vowel point. **8.** To give emphasis to; stress: *pointing up my error.* **9.** To indicate the presence and position of (game) by standing immobile and directing the muzzle toward it. Used of a hunting dog. **10.** To fill and finish the joints of (masonry) with cement or mortar. *—intr.* **1.** To direct attention or indicate position with or as if with the finger. **2.** To turn the mind or thought in a particular direction or to a particular conclusion: *All signs point to an early spring.* **3.** To be turned or faced in a given direction; aim. **4.** To point game. **5.** *Nautical* To sail close to the wind. ***—idioms:* beside the point** Irrelevant to the matter at hand. **in point** Having relevance or pertinence. **in point of** With reference to; in the matter of. **make a point of** To consider or treat (an action or activity) as indispensable. **stretch a point** To make an exception. **to the point** Concerning or with relevance to the matter at hand. [ME, partly < OFr. *point*, prick, mark, moment (< VLat. **punctum* < Lat. *pūnctum* < neut. p. part. of *pungere*, to prick) and partly < OFr. *pointe*, sharp end (< VLat. **puncta* < Lat. *pūncta*, fem. p. part. of *pungere*, to prick).]

point-and-click (point′ənd-klĭk′) *adj. Computer Science* Relating to an interface or design having icons that are activated by clicking with a pointing device.

point-blank (point′blăngk′) *adj.* **1.** Aimed straight at the mark or target without allowing for the drop in a projectile's course. **2a.** So close to a target that a weapon may be aimed directly at it. **b.** Close enough so that missing the target is unlikely or impossible. **3.** Straightforward; blunt: *a point-blank question.* ❖ *adv.* **1.** With a straight aim; directly. **2.** Without hesitation, deliberation, or equivocation. [Perh. < Fr. *point (de tir)*, (firing) point, or *point (visé)*, (aiming) point (< OFr.; see POINT) + Fr. *blanc*, bull's-eye, target (< OFr., white; see BLANK).]

point-de-vice (point′dĭ-vīs′) *adj.* Scrupulously correct or neat; precise or meticulous. [ME *at point devis*, prob. < OFr. **a point devis* : *a*, to + *point*, point, moment + *devis*, fixed, arranged.] **—point′-de-vice′** *adv.*

pointe (pwăNt) *n.* In ballet, dancing that is performed on the tips of the toes. [< Fr. *pointe (des pieds)*, point (of the feet), tiptoe. See POINT.]

point•ed (poin′tĭd) *adj.* **1.** Having an end coming to a point. **2.** Sharp; cutting: *pointed criticism.* **3.** Obviously directed at or making reference to a particular person or thing. **4.** Clearly evident or conspicuous; marked. **5.** Characterized by the use of a pointed crown, as in Gothic architecture. **6.** Having a rough finish produced by a pointed tool. Used of masonry. **—point′ed•ly** *adv.* **—point′ed•ness** *n.*

point•er (poin′tər) *n.* **1.** One that directs, indicates, or points. **2.** A scale indicator on a watch or other measuring instrument. **3.** A long tapered stick for indicating objects, as on a chart. **4.** Any of a breed of hunting dogs that points game, typically having a smooth short-haired coat, usu. white with dark spots. **5a.** A piece of advice; a suggestion. **b.** A piece of indicative information. **6.** *Computer Science* **a.** A variable that holds the address of a core storage location. **b.** A symbol appearing on a display screen in a GUI that lets the user select a command, as by clicking with a pointing device. **7.** Either of the two stars in the Big Dipper that point to Polaris.

point guard *n. Basketball* A guard who runs the team's offense, usu. from the point.

poin•til•lism (pwăN′tē-ĭz′əm, point′l-ĭz′-) *n.* A postimpressionist school of painting flourishing in late 19th-century France, characterized by the application of paint in small dots and brush strokes. [Fr. *pointillisme* < *pointiller*, to paint small dots, stipple < OFr. **pointille*, engraved with small dots < *point*, point < Lat. *pūnctum* < neut. p. part. of *pungere*, to prick.] **—poin′til•list** *adj. & n.*

poin•til•lis•tic (pwăn′tē-ĭs′tĭk, point′l-ĭs′-) *adj.* **1.** Of or relating to pointillism. **2.** Minutely detailed or particularized.

point•ing device (poin′tĭng) *n. Computer Science* An input device, such as a mouse, with which one can move or manipulate a cursor or pointer on a GUI.

point lace *n.* See **needlepoint** 2.

point•less (point′lĭs) *adj.* **1.** Lacking meaning; senseless. **2.** Ineffectual. **—point′less•ly** *adv.* **—point′less•ness** *n.*

point man *n.* **1.** A soldier assigned to a position some distance ahead of a patrol as a lookout. **2.** A man who has a crucial, often hazardous role in the forefront of an enterprise.

point of accumulation *n.* See **limit** 6.

point of honor *n., pl.* **points of honor** A matter that affects one's honor or reputation.

point of no return *n., pl.* **points of no return 1.** The point in a course of action when it cannot be reversed. **2.** The point in an aircraft flight when the fuel amount precludes return to the starting point.

point of order *n., pl.* **points of order** A question as to whether the present proceedings are in order or allowed by the rules of parliamentary procedure.

point of view *n., pl.* **points of view 1.** A manner of viewing things; an attitude. **2a.** A position from which something is observed or considered. **b.** The attitude or outlook of a narrator or character, as in a piece of literature or a movie.

point-shav•ing (point′shā′vĭng) *n.* The illegal practice of deliberately limiting the number of points scored by one's team in an athletic contest, as in return for a payment from gamblers to ensure winnings.

point source *n.* A source, esp. of pollution or radiation, occupying a very small area and having a concentrated output.

point spread *n.* See **spread** 10.

Point Success A peak, 4,318.2 m (14,158 ft), in the Cascade Range of W-central WA near Mt. Rainier.

poinsettia
Euphorbia pulcherrima

pointe

pointillism
detail of *Women at the Well*, 1892, by Paul Signac (1863–1935)

ă	pat	oi	boy
ā	pay	ou	out
âr	care	o͝o	took
ä	father	o͞o	boot
ĕ	pet	ŭ	cut
ē	be	ûr	urge
ĭ	pit	th	thin
ī	pie	*th*	this
îr	pier	hw	which
ŏ	pot	zh	vision
ō	toe	ə	about, item
ô	paw		

Stress marks:
′ (primary);
′ (secondary), as in
lexicon (lĕk′sĭ-kŏn′)

poison ivy
Toxicodendron radicans syn.
Rhus radicans

Poland

polar bear
Ursus maritimus

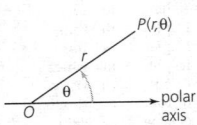

polar coordinate
The polar coordinates of
point *P* are (r,θ).

point system *n.* **1.** A system of evaluating academic achievement based on grade points. **2.** Any of various printing or writing systems for the blind, such as Braille, that use an alphabet of raised symbols or dots. **3.** *Printing* A system of graduating sizes of type in multiples of the point. **4.** A system of assigning points to drivers for each type of traffic violation and revoking a license for a certain number of points.

point woman *n.* A woman who has a crucial, often hazardous role in the forefront of an enterprise.

point·y (poin′tē) *adj.* **-i·er, -i·est** Having an end tapering to a point.

poise¹ (poiz) *v.* **poised, pois·ing, pois·es** —*tr.* To carry or hold in equilibrium; balance. —*intr.* To be balanced or held in suspension; hover. ❖ *n.* **1.** A state of balance or equilibrium; stability. **2.** Freedom from affectation or embarrassment; composure. **3.** The bearing or deportment of the head or body; mien. **4.** A state or condition of hovering or being suspended. [ME *poisen,* to balance, weigh < OFr. *peser, pois-* < VLat. **pēsāre* < Lat. *pēnsāre,* freq. of *pendere,* to weigh.]

poise² (poiz, pwäz) *n.* A centimeter-gram-second unit of dynamic viscosity equal to one dyne-second per square centimeter. [Fr., after Jean Louis Marie *Poiseuille* (1799–1869), French physician and physiologist.]

poised (poizd) *adj.* **1.** Assured; composed. **2.** Held balanced or steady in readiness: *stood poised for the jump.*

poi·son (poi′zən) *n.* **1.** A substance that causes injury, illness, or death, esp. by chemical means. **2.** Something destructive or fatal. **3.** *Chemistry & Physics* A substance that inhibits another substance or a reaction. ❖ *tr.v.* **-soned, -son·ing, -sons** **1.** To kill or harm with poison. **2.** To put poison on or into. **3a.** To pollute. **b.** To have a harmful influence on; corrupt: *Jealousy poisoned the friendship.* **4.** *Chemistry & Physics* To inhibit (a substance or reaction). ❖ *adj.* Poisonous. [ME < OFr. < Lat. *pōtiō, pōtiōn-,* drink. See *pō(i)-* in App.] —**poi′son·er** *n.*

poi·son-ar·row frog (poi′zən-ăr′ō) *n.* Any of several small, often brightly colored terrestrial frogs that inhabit the rainforests of Central and South America and secrete poisonous biological toxins from their skin. [< using its toxic secretions to coat arrowheads.]

poison gas *n.* A gas or vapor used esp. in chemical warfare to injure, disable, or kill upon inhalation or contact.

poison hemlock *n.* A deadly poisonous European plant (*Conium maculatum*) having bipinnately compound leaves and compound umbels of small white flowers.

poison ivy *n.* **1.** A North American shrub or vine (*Toxicodendron radicans* syn. *Rhus radicans*) that has compound leaves with three leaflets, small green flowers, and whitish berries and causes a rash on contact. **2.** A skin rash caused by contact with this plant.

poison oak *n.* **1.** Either of two shrubs, *Toxicodendron toxicarium* (syn. *Rhus toxicodendron*) of the southeast United States or *T. diversilobum* (syn. *R. diversiloba*) of western North America, related to poison ivy and causing a rash on contact. **2.** See **poison ivy. 3.** A skin rash caused by contact with one of these plants.

poi·son·ous (poi′zə-nəs) *adj.* **1.** Capable of harming or killing by or as if by poison; toxic or venomous. **2.** Containing a poison. **3.** Marked by apparent ill will. —**poi′son·ous·ly** *adv.*

poi·son-pen letter (poi′zən-pĕn′) *n.* A usu. anonymous letter or note containing abusive or malicious statements or accusations about the recipient or a third party.

poison sumac *n.* **1.** A swamp shrub (*Toxicodendron vernix* syn. *Rhus vernix*) of eastern North America that has compound leaves and greenish-white berries and causes a skin rash on contact. **2.** A skin rash caused by contact with this plant.

Pois·son distribution (pwä-sôn′) *n. Statistics* A probability distribution which arises when counting the occurrences of a rare event in a long series of trials. [After Siméon Denis *Poisson* (1781–1840), French mathematician.]

Poi·tou (pwä-tōō′) A historical region of W-central France bordering on the Bay of Biscay; frequently contested by France and England until the end of the Hundred Years' War.

poke¹ (pōk) *v.* **poked, pok·ing, pokes** —*tr.* **1.** To push or jab at, as with a finger or an arm; prod. **2.** To make (a hole or pathway, for example) by or as if by prodding, elbowing, or jabbing. **3.** To push; thrust. **4.** To stir (a fire) by prodding the wood or coal with a poker or stick. **5.** *Slang* To strike; punch. —*intr.* **1.** To make thrusts or jabs, as with a stick or poker. **2.** To pry or meddle; intrude. **3.** To search or look curiously in a desultory manner. **4.** To proceed in a slow or lazy manner; putter. **5.** To thrust forward; appear. ❖ *n.* **1.** A push, thrust, or jab. **2.** *Slang* A punch or blow with the fist. **3.** One who moves slowly or aimlessly; a dawdler. —*idiom:* **poke fun at** To ridicule in a mischievous manner; tease. [ME *poken,* prob. < MLGer. or MDu.]

poke² (pōk) *n.* **1.** A projecting brim at the front of a bonnet. **2.** A large bonnet having a projecting brim. [< POKE¹.]

poke³ (pōk) *n. Chiefly Southern US* A sack; a bag. [ME, prob. < ONFr. See POCKET.]

REGIONAL NOTE The noun *poke*—meaning a bag or sack—dates from the 14th century in English. In many parts of Scotland *poke* means a little paper bag for carrying purchases or a cone-shaped piece of paper for an ice-cream cone.

poke⁴ (pōk) *n.* Pokeweed. [Short for dialectal *pocan,* of Virginia Algonquian orig.; akin to PUCCOON.]

poke·ber·ry (pōk′bĕr′ē) *n.* **1.** The blackish-red berry of the pokeweed. **2.** See **pokeweed.**

poke check *n.* A check in ice hockey in which a defender uses the blade of the stick to push the puck off the stick of an opponent. —**poke′-check′** (pōk′chĕk′) *v.*

pok·er¹ (pō′kər) *n.* One that pokes, esp. a metal rod used to stir a fire.

pok·er² (pō′kər) *n.* Any of various card games played by two or more who bet on the value of their hands. [?]

poker face *n.* A face lacking any expression, as that of an expert poker player. —**pok′er·faced′** (pō′kər-fāst′) *adj.*

poke sal·lit (săl′ĭt) *n. Chiefly Southern US* Greens of the wild pokeweed eaten boiled. [Variant of *poke salad.*]

poke·weed (pōk′wēd′) *n.* A tall North American plant (*Phytolacca americana*) having small white flowers, blackish-red berries, and a poisonous root. [POKE⁴ + WEED¹.]

po·key (pō′kē) *n., pl.* **-keys** also **-kies** *Slang* A jail or prison. [?]

poke·y² also **po·ky** (pō′kē) *adj. Informal* Variant of **poky¹.**

pok·y¹ also **poke·y** (pō′kē) *adj.* **pok·i·er, pok·i·est** *Informal* **1.** Dawdling; slow. **2.** Frumpish; shabby. **3.** Small and cramped. [< POKE¹.] —**pok′i·ly** *adv.* —**pok′i·ness** *n.*

po·ky² (pō′kē) *n. Slang* Variant of **pokey¹.**

pol (pŏl) *n. Informal* A politician.

Pol. *abbr.* **1.** Poland **2.** Polish

Po·lack (pō′lŏk′, -lăk′) *n.* **1.** *Offensive Slang* Used as a disparaging term for a person of Polish birth or descent. **2.** *Obsolete* A Pole. [Pol. *Polak.* See **pelə-²** in App.]

Po·land (pō′lənd) A country of central Europe bordering on the Baltic Sea; unified as a kingdom in the 10th cent., carved up among other states in three partitions (1772, 1793, and 1795), and reconstituted as a republic in 1918. Cap. Warsaw. Pop. 38,544,000.

Poland China *n.* Any of a breed of large black-and-white hogs developed in North America.

po·lar (pō′lər) *adj.* **1a.** Of or relating to a pole. **b.** Measured from or referred to a pole. **2.** Relating to or located near the North Pole or South Pole. **3a.** Passing over a planet's north and south poles: *a polar orbit.* **b.** Traveling in a polar orbit. **4.** Serving as a guide or polestar. **5.** Occupying or marked by opposite extremes. **6.** Central or pivotal. **7.** *Chemistry* **a.** Relating to or characterized by a dipole: *a polar molecule.* **b.** Ionizing when dissolved or fused: *polar bonds.*

polar angle *n.* The angle formed by the polar axis and the radius vector in a polar coordinate system.

polar axis *n.* The fixed reference axis from which the polar angle is measured in a polar coordinate system.

polar bear *n.* A large white-furred bear (*Ursus maritimus* or *Thalarctos maritimus*) living in Arctic regions.

polar body *n.* A minute cell produced and ultimately discarded in the development of an oocyte, containing one of the nuclei derived from the first or second meiotic division.

polar cap *n.* **1a.** Either of the regions around the poles of the earth that are permanently covered with ice. **b.** A high-altitude icecap. **2.** *Astronomy* Either of the polar regions of Mars covered with frozen carbon dioxide and water.

polar circle *n.* **1.** The Arctic Circle. **2.** The Antarctic Circle.

polar coordinate *n.* Either of two coordinates, the radius or the polar angle, that together specify the position of a point in a plane.

po·lar·im·e·ter (pō′lə-rĭm′ĭ-tər) *n.* An instrument used to measure the rotation of the plane of polarization of polarized light passing through an optical structure or sample. —**po′lar·i·met′ric** (-lər-ə-mĕt′rĭk) *adj.* —**po′lar·im′e·try** *n.*

Po·lar·is (pə-lăr′ĭs) *n.* A star of the second magnitude, at the end of the handle of the Little Dipper and almost at the north celestial pole. [NLat. *(Stēlla) Polāris,* polar (star) < Lat. *polus,* pole. See POLE¹.]

po·lar·i·scope (pō-lăr′ĭ-skōp′) *n.* Any of several instruments for studying the interactions of polarized light with optically transparent media.

po·lar·i·ty (pō-lăr′ĭ-tē, pə-) *n., pl.* **-ties** **1.** Intrinsic polar separation, alignment, or orientation, esp. of a physical property: *magnetic polarity.* **2.** An indicated polar extreme: *an electric terminal with positive polarity.* **3.** The possession or manifestation of two opposing attributes, tendencies, or principles.

po·lar·i·za·tion (pō′lər-ĭ-zā′shən) *n.* **1.** The production or condition of polarity, as: **a.** A process or state in which rays of light exhibit different properties in different directions, esp. the state in which all the vibration takes place in one plane. **b.** The partial or complete polar separation of the positive and negative electric charges in a nuclear, atomic, molecular, or chemical system. **2.** A concentration, as of groups, about two conflicting or contrasting positions.

po·lar·ize (pō′lə-rīz′) *v.* **-ized, -iz·ing, -iz·es** —*tr.* **1.** To induce polarization in; impart polarity to. **2.** To cause to concentrate about two conflicting or contrasting positions: *polarized the electorate.* —*intr.* **1.** To acquire polarity. **2.** To cause polarization of light. —**po′lar·iz′a·ble** *adj.* —**po′lar·iz′er** *n.*

polar nucleus *n.* Either of two nuclei in a flowering plant embryo sac that fuse to form the endosperm nucleus.

po·lar·og·ra·phy (pō′lə-rŏg′rə-fē) *n.* An electrochemical method of quantitative or qualitative analysis based on measuring a current passing through the solution being analyzed as an applied voltage is increased. [POLAR(IZATION) + –GRAPHY.] —**po·lar′o·graph′ic** (-lăr′ə-grăf′ĭk) *adj.*

Po·lar·oid (pō′lə-roid′) 1. A trademark used for a specially treated transparent plastic capable of polarizing light passing through it, used in glare-reducing optical devices. 2. A trademark used for a camera and film that produce instant photographs.

Polar Regions The various lands and waters surrounding the North Pole and the South Pole, known respectively as the **North Polar Region** and the **South Polar Region**.

polar star *n.* See **Polaris**.

Po·lar·tec (pō′lər-tĕk′) A trademark used for a fleecy synthetic fabric that is warm, lightweight, and water-resistant.

pol·der (pōl′dər) *n.* An area of low-lying land, esp. in the Netherlands, that has been reclaimed from a body of water and is protected by dikes. [Du. < MDu.]

pole¹ (pōl) *n.* 1. Either extremity of an axis through a sphere. 2. Either of the regions contiguous to the extremities of the earth's rotational axis, the North Pole or the South Pole. 3. *Physics* A magnetic pole. 4. Either of two oppositely charged terminals, as in an electric cell or battery. 5. *Astronomy* A celestial pole. 6. *Biology* **a.** Either extremity of the main axis of a nucleus, cell, or organism. **b.** Either end of the spindle formed in a cell during mitosis. **c.** The point on a cell where a process originates, such as a flagellum. 7. Either of two antithetical ideas, propensities, forces, or positions. 8. A fixed point of reference. 9. *Mathematics* The origin in a polar coordinate system; the vertex of a polar angle. [ME < OFr. < Lat. *polus* < Gk. *polos*, axis, sky. See **kʷel-** in App.]

pole² (pōl) *n.* 1. A long, relatively slender, generally rounded piece of wood or other material. 2. The long tapering wooden shaft extending up from the front axle of a vehicle to the collars of the animals drawing it; a tongue. **3a.** See **rod** 6a. **b.** A unit of area equal to a square rod. 4. *Sports* The inside position on the starting line of a racetrack. ❖ *v.* **poled, pol·ing, poles** —*tr.* **1a.** To propel with a pole: *poled the barge up the river.* **b.** To propel (oneself) or make (one's way) by the use of ski poles. 2. To support (plants) with a pole. 3. To strike, poke, or stir with a pole. —*intr.* 1. To propel a boat or raft with a pole. 2. To use ski poles to maintain or gain speed. [ME < OE *pāl* < Lat. *pālus*, stake.]

Pole *n.* 1. A native or inhabitant of Poland. 2. A person of Polish descent.

Pole, Reginald 1500–58. English prelate who was the last Roman Catholic archbishop of Canterbury (1556).

pole·ax or **pole·axe** (pōl′ăks′) *n.* 1. An ax having a hammer face opposite the blade, used to slaughter cattle. 2. A battle-ax used in the Middle Ages, consisting of a long shaft topped with an ax or a combination of an ax, hammer, and pick. ❖ *tr.v.* **-axed, -ax·ing, -ax·es** To strike or fell with or as if with a poleax. [ME, alteration of *pollax* : *poll*, head; see POLL + *ax*, ax; see AX¹.]

pole bean *n.* Any of various cultivated climbing beans that grow on poles or supports.

pole·cat (pōl′kăt′) *n.* **1a.** A chiefly nocturnal European carnivorous mammal (*Mustela putorius*) of the weasel family that ejects a malodorous fluid to mark its territory and ward off enemies. **b.** Any of various related mammals of Asia, esp. *Mustela eversmanni* of central Asia. 2. See **skunk** 1a. [ME *polcat* : poss. OFr. *poll*, *poule*, fowl, hen; see PULLET + ME *cat*, cat; see CAT.]

pole horse *n.* A horse harnessed to the pole of a vehicle.

po·leis (pō′lās′) *n.* Plural of **polis**.

po·lem·ic (pə-lĕm′ĭk) *n.* 1. A controversial argument, esp. one refuting or attacking an opinion or a doctrine. 2. One engaged in or inclined to polemical matters. ❖ *adj.* also **po·lem·i·cal** (-ĭ-kəl) Of or relating to a controversy, argument, or refutation. [Fr. *polémique* < Gk. *polemikos*, hostile < *polemos*, war.] —**po·lem′i·cal·ly** *adv.*

po·lem·i·cist (pə-lĕm′ĭ-sĭst) also **po·lem·ist** (pə-lĕm′ĭst, pōl′ə-mĭst) *n.* A person skilled or involved in polemics.

po·lem·i·cize (pə-lĕm′ĭ-sīz′) *intr.v.* **-cized, -ciz·ing, -ciz·es** To write or deliver an argument; engage in controversy.

po·lem·ics (pə-lĕm′ĭks) *n.* (*used with a sing. or pl. verb*) 1. The art or practice of argumentation or controversy. 2. The practice of theological controversy to refute errors of doctrine.

po·len·ta (pō-lĕn′tə) *n.* A thick mush made of boiled cornmeal. [Ital. < Lat., crushed grain, barley meal.]

pol·er (pō′lər) *n.* 1. One that propels, supports, conveys, or strikes with a pole. 2. A vault.

pole·star (pōl′stär′) *n.* 1. See **Polaris**. 2. A guiding principle.

pole vault *n.* 1. A field event in which an athlete vaults over a high crossbar with the aid of a long pole. 2. A vault made with the aid of a long pole. —**pole′-vault′** (pōl′vôlt′) *v.* —**pole′-vault′er** *n.*

po·lice (pə-lēs′) *n., pl.* **police** 1. The governmental department charged with the regulation and control of the affairs of a community, now chiefly the department established to maintain order, enforce the law, and prevent and detect crime. **2a.** A body of persons making up such a department. **b.** A body of persons

having similar organization and function: *campus police*. 3. (*used with a pl. verb*) Police officers considered as a group. 4. Regulation and control of the affairs of a community, esp. with respect to maintenance of such things as order, law, health, morals, and safety. 5. *Informal* A group that admonishes, cautions, or reminds: *grammar police*. **6a.** The cleaning of a military base or other military area. **b.** The soldiers assigned to a specified maintenance duty. ❖ *tr.v.* **-liced, -lic·ing, -lic·es** 1. To regulate, control, or keep in order with or as if with a law enforcement agency. 2. To make (a military area, for example) neat in appearance. [Fr. < OFr. *policie*, civil organization < LLat. *polītīa* < Lat., the State < Gk. *polīteia* < *polītēs*, citizen < *polis*, city.] —**po·lice′a·ble** *adj.* —**po·lic′er** *n.*

police action *n.* A localized military action undertaken without a formal declaration of war.

police dog *n.* 1. A dog trained to aid the police, as in detecting controlled substances. 2. See **German shepherd**.

police force *n.* See **police** 2.

po·lice·man (pə-lēs′mən) *n.* A man on a police force.

police officer *n.* A policeman or policewoman.

police power *n.* The inherent authority of a government to impose restrictions on private rights for the sake of public welfare, order, and security.

police state *n.* A state in which the government exercises rigid and repressive controls over the social, economic, and political life of the people, esp. by means of a secret police force.

police station *n.* The headquarters of a unit of a police force, where those under arrest are first charged.

po·lice·wom·an (pə-lēs′wŏŏm′ən) *n.* A woman on a police force.

pol·i·clin·ic (pŏl′ē-klĭn′ĭk) *n.* The department esp. of a European hospital or health care facility that treats outpatients. [Ger. *Poliklinik* : Gk. *polis*, city + *Klinik*, clinic (< Gk. *klīnikos*, of a bed; see CLINIC).]

pol·i·cy¹ (pŏl′ĭ-sē) *n., pl.* **-cies** 1. A plan or course of action, as of a government, political party, or business, intended to influence and determine decisions, actions, and other matters. **2a.** A course of action, guiding principle, or procedure considered expedient, prudent, or advantageous. **b.** Prudence, shrewdness, or sagacity in practical matters. [ME *policie*, art of government, civil organization < OFr. See POLICE.]

pol·i·cy² (pŏl′ĭ-sē) *n., pl.* **-cies** 1. A written contract or certificate of insurance. 2. A numbers game. [Obsolete *police* < Fr., contract, bill of lading < OFr. < OItal. *polizza*, alteration of Med. Lat. *apodixa*, receipt < Med.Gk. *apodeixis* < Gk., proof < *apodeiknunai*, to prove : *apo-*, intensive pref.; see APO- + *deiknunai*, to show; see **deik-** in App.]

pol·i·cy·hol·der (pŏl′ĭ-sē-hōl′dər) *n.* One that holds an insurance contract or policy.

pol·i·cy·mak·ing or **pol·i·cy-mak·ing** (pŏl′ĭ-sē-mā′kĭng) *n.* High-level development of policy, esp. government policy. —**pol′i·cy·mak′er** *n.* —**pol′i·cy·mak′ing** *adj.*

po·li·o (pō′lē-ō′) *n.* Poliomyelitis.

po·li·o·my·e·li·tis (pō′lē-ō-mī′ə-lī′tĭs) *n.* A highly infectious viral disease that chiefly affects children and in its acute forms causes inflammation of motor neurons of the spinal cord and brain stem, leading to paralysis, muscular atrophy, and often deformity. [NLat. : Gk. *polios*, gray + MYELITIS.] —**po′li·o·my′e·lit′ic** (-lĭt′ĭk) *adj.*

po·li·o·vi·rus (pō′lē-ō-vī′rəs) *n., pl.* **-rus·es** Any of three enteroviruses that cause poliomyelitis.

po·lis (pō′lĭs) *n., pl.* **-leis** (-lās′) A city-state of ancient Greece. [Gk.]

pol·ish (pŏl′ĭsh) *v.* **-ished, -ish·ing, -ish·es** —*tr.* 1. To make smooth and shiny by rubbing or chemical action. 2. To remove the outer layers from (grains of rice) by rotation in drums. 3. To free from coarseness; refine: *polish one's manners.* 4. To remove flaws from; perfect or complete. —*intr.* 1. To become smooth and shiny by or as if by being rubbed. 2. To become perfect or refined. ❖ *n.* 1. Smoothness or shininess of surface or finish. 2. A substance containing chemical agents or abrasive particles and applied to smooth or shine a surface. 3. The act or process of polishing. 4. Elegance of style or manners; refinement. —*phrasal verb:* **polish off** *Informal* To finish or dispose of quickly and easily. [ME *polisshen* < OFr. *polir, poliss-* < Lat. *polīre*. See **pel-²** in App.] —**pol′ish·er** *n.*

Po·lish (pō′lĭsh) *adj.* Of or relating to Poland, the Poles, their language, or their culture. ❖ *n.* The Slavic language of the Poles.

Polish Corridor (pō′lĭsh) A strip of land between the German territories of Pomerania and East Prussia awarded to Poland by the Treaty of Versailles (1919) to afford access to the Baltic Sea.

pol·ished (pŏl′ĭsht) *adj.* **1a.** Made smooth and shiny by or as if by rubbing or chemical action. **b.** Naturally shiny and smooth. 2. Having the husk or outer layers removed. Used of grains of rice. 3. Refined; cultured: *polished manners.* 4. Having no imperfections or errors; flawless.

pol·it·bu·ro (pŏl′ĭt-byŏŏr′ō, pə-lĭt′-) *n., pl.* **-ros** The chief political and executive committee of a Communist party. [Russ., contraction of *Polit(icheskoe) Byuro*, political bureau.]

po·lite (pə-līt′) *adj.* **-lit·er, -lit·est** 1. Marked by or showing consideration for others, tact, and observance of accepted social

pole vault

Polish Corridor

usage. **2.** Refined; elegant: *polite society.* [ME *polit,* polished < Lat. *politus,* p. part. of *polīre,* to polish. See POLISH.] —**po•lite′ly** *adv.* —**po•lite′ness** *n.*

SYNONYMS *polite, mannerly, civil, courteous, genteel* These adjectives mean mindful of, conforming to, or marked by good manners. *Polite* and *mannerly* imply consideration for others and the adherence to conventional social standards of good behavior: "*It costs nothing to be polite*" (Winston S. Churchill). *The child was scolded for not being more mannerly. Civil* suggests only the barest observance of accepted social usages; it often means merely neither polite nor rude: *gave a civil reply to every question. Courteous* implies courtliness and dignity: "*If a man be gracious and courteous to strangers, it shows he is a citizen of the world*" (Francis Bacon). *Genteel,* which originally meant well-bred, now usually suggests excessive and affected refinement: "*A man, indeed, is not genteel when he gets drunk*" (James Boswell).

pol•i•tesse (pŏl′ĭ-tĕs′, pô′lē-) *n.* Courteous formality; politeness. [Fr. < OFr., cleanliness < Ital. *pulitezza, politezza < pulire,* to polish, clean < Lat. *polīre.* See POLITE.]

pol•i•tic (pŏl′ĭ-tĭk) *adj.* **1.** Using or marked by prudence, expedience, and shrewdness; artful. **2.** Using, displaying, or proceeding from policy; judicious: *a politic decision.* **3.** Crafty; cunning. [ME *politik* < OFr. *politique* < Lat. *polīticus,* political < Gk. *polītikos < polītēs,* citizen < *polis,* city.] —**pol′i•tic•ly** *adv.*

po•lit•i•cal (pə-lĭt′ĭ-kəl) *adj.* **1.** Of, relating to, or dealing with the structure or affairs of government, politics, or the state. **2.** Relating to, involving, or characteristic of politics, parties, or politicians. **3.** Relating to or involving acts regarded as damaging to a government or state: *political crimes.* **4.** Interested or active in politics. **5.** Having or influenced by partisan interests: *The court should never become a political institution.* **6.** Based on or motivated by partisan or self-serving objectives. —**po•lit′i•cal•i•za′tion** (-īzā′shən) *n.* —**po•lit′i•cal•ize** (-kə-līz′) *v.* —**po•lit′i•cal•ly** *adv.*

political action committee *n.* A committee formed by special-interest groups to raise money and make contributions to the campaigns of political candidates whom they support.

political economy *n.* **1.** The social science that deals with political science and economics as one subject; the study of the interrelationships between political and economic processes. **2.** The science of economics through the 19th century.

politically correct *adj.* **1.** Of, relating to, or supporting a program of broad social, political, and educational change, esp. to redress historical injustices in matters such as race, class, gender, and sexual orientation. **2.** Being or perceived as being overconcerned with such change, esp. in the avoidance of giving offense. —**political correctness** *n.*

political science *n.* The study of the processes, principles, and structure of government and political institutions.

pol•i•ti•cian (pŏl′ĭ-tĭsh′ən) *n.* **1a.** One who is actively involved in politics, esp. party politics. **b.** One who holds or seeks a political office. **2.** One who seeks personal or partisan gain, often by maneuvering. **3.** One who is skilled or experienced in the science or administration of government.

po•lit•i•cize (pə-lĭt′ĭ-sīz′) *v.* **-cized, -ciz•ing, -ciz•es** —*intr.* To engage in or discuss politics. —*tr.* To make political. —**po•lit′i•ci•za′tion** (-sĭ-zā′shən) *n.*

pol•i•tick (pŏl′ĭ-tĭk) *intr.v.* **-ticked, -tick•ing, -ticks** To engage in or discuss politics. [Back-formation < *politicking* < POLITIC.] —**pol′i•tick′er** *n.*

po•lit•i•co (pə-lĭt′ĭ-kō′) *n., pl.* **-cos** A politician. [< Ital. or < Sp. *político,* both < Lat. *polīticus,* political. See POLITIC.]

pol•i•tics (pŏl′ĭ-tĭks) *n.* **1.** (*used with a sing. verb*) **a.** The art or science of government or governing, esp. the governing of a political entity, such as a nation, and the administration and control of its internal and external affairs. **b.** Political science. **2.** (*used with a sing. or pl. verb*) **a.** The activities or affairs engaged in by a government, politician, or political party. **b.** The methods or tactics involved in managing a state or government. **3.** (*used with a sing. or pl. verb*) Political life. **4.** (*used with a sing. or pl. verb*) Intrigue or maneuvering within a political unit or group in order to gain control or power. **5.** (*used with a sing. or pl. verb*) Political attitudes and positions. **6.** (*used with a sing. or pl. verb*) The often internally conflicting relationships among people in a society.

USAGE NOTE *Politics,* although plural in form, takes a singular verb when used to refer to the art or science of governing or to political science: *Politics has been a concern of philosophers since Plato.* But in its other senses *politics* can take either a singular or plural verb. Many other nouns that end in *-ics* behave similarly, and the user is advised to consult specific entries for precise information.

pol•i•ty (pŏl′ĭ-tē) *n., pl.* **-ties 1.** The form of government of a nation, state, church, or organization. **2.** An organized society, such as a nation, having a specific form of government. [Obsolete Fr. *politie* < OFr. < LLat. *polītīa,* the Roman government. See POLICE.]

Polk (pōk), **James Knox** 1795–1849. The 11th President of the US (1845–49).

pol•ka (pōl′kə, pō′kə) *n.* **1.** A lively dance for couples, originat-

James K. Polk
detail from an 1846 portrait
by George Peter Alexander
Healy (1813–94)

ing in Bohemia. **2.** Music for this dance, having duple meter. —*intr.* **-kaed, -ka•ing, -kas** To dance the polka. [Czech, prob. < Polish < *Polka,* Polish woman, fem. of *Polak,* Pole. See **pelə-²** in App.]

polka dot *n.* **1.** One of a number of dots or round spots forming a pattern. **2.** A pattern or fabric with such dots.

poll (pōl) *n.* **1.** The casting and registering of votes in an election. **2.** The number of votes cast or recorded. **3.** The place where votes are cast and registered. Used with *the.* Often used in the plural. **4.** A survey of the public or of a sample of public opinion to acquire information. **5.** The head, esp. the top of the head where hair grows. **6.** The blunt or broad end of a tool such as an ax. ❖ *v.* **polled, poll•ing, polls** —*tr.* **1.** To receive (a given number of votes). **2.** To receive or record the votes of. **3.** To cast (a vote or ballot). **4.** To question in a survey; canvass. **5.** To cut off or trim (hair or wool, for example); clip. **6.** To trim or cut off the hair, wool, branches, or horns of. —*intr.* To vote at the polls in an election. [ME *pol,* head < MLGer. or MDu.] —**poll′er** *n.*

pol•lack also **pol•lock** (pŏl′ək) *n., pl.* **pollack** or **-lacks** also **pollock** or **-locks** A marine food fish (*Pollachius virens*) of northern Atlantic waters, related to the cod. [Alteration of Sc. *podlok.*]

pol•lard (pŏl′ərd) *n.* **1.** A tree whose top branches have been cut back to the trunk so that it may produce a dense growth of new shoots. **2.** An animal, such as an ox, goat, or sheep, that no longer has its horns. ❖ *tr.v.* **-lard•ed, -lard•ing, -lards** To convert or make into a pollard. [< POLL.]

polled (pōld) *adj.* Having no horns; hornless.

pol•len (pŏl′ən) *n.* The fine powderlike material whose individual grains contain the male reproductive cells of seed-bearing plants. [Lat., fine flour.]

pollen count *n.* The average number of pollen grains, usu. of ragweed, in a cubic yard or other standard volume of air over a 24-hour period at a specified time and place.

pollen grain *n.* A microspore of seed plants, containing a male gametophyte.

pollen tube *n.* The slender tube formed by the pollen grain that penetrates an ovule and releases the male gametes.

pol•lex (pŏl′ĕks′) *n., pl.* **pol•li•ces** (pŏl′ĭ-sēz′) See **thumb** 1. [Lat., thumb, big toe.]

pol•li•nate also **pol•len•ate** (pŏl′ə-nāt′) *tr.v.* **-li•nat•ed, -li•nat•ing, -li•nates** also **-len•at•ed, -len•at•ing, -len•ates** To transfer pollen from an anther to (a female flower) or from a male one to (a female cone). [NLat. *pollen, pollin-,* pollen (< Lat., fine flour) + -ATE¹.] —**pol′li•na′tion** *n.* —**pol′li•na′tor** *n.*

pollini- or **pollin-** *pref.* Pollen: *polliniferous.* [< NLat. *pollen, pollin-,* pollen. See POLLINATE.]

pol•li•nif•er•ous also **pol•len•if•er•ous** (pŏl′ə-nĭf′ər-əs) *adj.* **1.** Producing or yielding pollen. **2.** Adapted for carrying pollen.

pol•lin•i•um (pŏ-lĭn′ē-əm) *n., pl.* **-i•a** (-ē-ə) A mass of coherent pollen grains, found in the flowers of orchids and milkweeds. [NLat. < *pollen, pollin-,* pollen. See POLLINATE.]

pol•li•nize (pŏl′ə-nīz′) *tr.v.* **-nized, -niz•ing, -niz•es** To pollinate. —**pol′li•ni•za′tion** (-nĭ-zā′shən) *n.* —**pol′li•niz′er** *n.*

pol•li•no•sis also **pol•len•o•sis** (pŏl′ə-nō′sĭs) *n.* See **hay fever.**

pol•li•wog also **pol•ly•wog** (pŏl′ē-wŏg′, -wôg′) *n.* See **tadpole.** [Variant of *polliwig* < ME *polwigle* < *pol,* head; see POLL + *wiglen,* to wiggle; see WIGGLE.]

pol•lock (pŏl′ək) *n.* Variant of **pollack.**

Pollock, Jackson 1912–56. Amer. artist who was a leader of abstract expressionism.

poll•ster (pōl′stər) *n.* One that takes public-opinion surveys.

WORD HISTORY The suffix *-ster* is nowadays most familiar in words like *pollster, jokester, huckster,* where it forms agent nouns that are unspecified as to gender. Originally in Old English, however, the suffix (then spelled *-estre*) was used to form feminine agent nouns. *Hoppestre,* for example, meant "female dancer." But in Old English *-estre* was occasionally applied to men, though mostly to translate Latin masculine nouns denoting occupations that were usually held by women in Anglo-Saxon society. An example is *bæcester,* "baker," glossing Latin *pistor;* it survives as the Modern English name *Baxter.* In Middle English, use of the suffix with nouns denoting men was more common in northern England, while the old associations with females predominated in the southern parts of the country. In time the masculine usage became dominant throughout the country, and old feminines in *-ster* were refashioned by adding the newer feminine suffix *-ess* (borrowed from French) to them, such as *seamstress* remade from *seamster.* In Modern English, the only noun ending in *-ster* with a feminine referent is *spinster,* which originally meant "a woman who spins thread."

poll•tak•er (pōl′tā′kər) *n.* See **pollster.**

poll tax *n.* A tax levied on people rather than on property, often as a requirement for voting.

pol•lut•ant (pə-lōōt′nt) *n.* Something that pollutes, esp. a waste material that contaminates air, soil, or water.

pol•lute (pə-lōōt′) *tr.v.* **-lut•ed, -lut•ing, -lutes 1.** To make unfit or harmful to living things, esp. by the addition of waste matter. **2.** To make less suitable for an activity, esp. by the introduction of unwanted factors. **3.** To render impure or morally harmful; corrupt. **4.** To make ceremonially impure; profane. [ME *polluten* < Lat. *polluere, pollūt-.*] —**pol·lut′er** *n.*

pol·lu·tion (pə-lōō′shən) *n.* **1.** The act or process of polluting or the state of being polluted, esp. the contamination of soil, water, or the atmosphere by the discharge of harmful substances. **2.** Something that pollutes; a pollutant.

Pol·lux (pŏl′əks) *n. Greek Mythology* **1.** One of the Dioscuri. **2.** A bright star in the constellation Gemini. [Lat. *Pollūx* < Gk. *Poludeukēs.*]

Pol·ly·an·na (pŏl′ē-ăn′ə) *n.* One held to be foolishly or blindly optimistic. [After the heroine of the novel *Pollyanna*, by Eleanor Hodgman Porter (1868–1920), American writer.]

po·lo (pō′lō) *n.* **1.** A game played by two teams of three or four players on horseback equipped with long-handled mallets for driving a small wooden ball through the opponents' goal. **2.** Water polo. [Balti (Tibeto-Burman language of Pakistan), ball.] —**po′lo·ist** *n.*

Polo, Marco 1254–1324. Venetian traveler who explored Asia (1271–95) and wrote the only account of the Far East available to Europeans until the 17th cent.

polo coat *n.* A loose-fitting tailored overcoat made from camel's hair or a similar material.

pol·o·naise (pŏl′ə-nāz′, pō′lə-) *n.* **1.** A stately marchlike Polish dance, primarily a promenade by couples. **2.** Music for or based on the rhythm of this dance, having triple meter. **3.** A woman's dress of the 18th century, having a fitted bodice and draped cutaway skirt and worn over an elaborate underskirt. [Fr. < fem. of *polonais*, Polish < Med.Lat. *Polōnia*, Poland.]

po·lo·ni·um (pə-lō′nē-əm) *n. Symbol* **Po** A naturally radioactive metallic element, occurring in minute quantities in uranium ores and produced by bombarding bismuth with neutrons; its most readily available isotope is Po 210, with a half-life of 138.39 days. Atomic number 84; melting point 254°C; boiling point 962° C; specific gravity 9.32; valence 2, 4. See table at **element.** [< Med.Lat. *Polōnia*, Poland (the native country of Pierre and Marie Curie, who discovered it).]

polo shirt *n.* A pullover sport shirt of knitted cotton.

Pol Pot (pŏl pŏt′) 1928–98. Cambodian political leader whose Khmer Rouge movement overthrew the Cambodian government in 1975.

Pol·ta·va (pəl-tä′və) A city of central Ukraine WSW of Kharkiv; a Cossack stronghold in the 17th cent. Pop. 323,600.

pol·ter·geist (pōl′tər-gīst′) *n.* A ghost that makes its presence known by noises and the moving of objects. [Ger. : *poltern*, to make noises (< MHGer. *boldern*) + *Geist*, ghost (< MHGer. < OHGer.).]

pol·troon (pŏl-trōōn′) *n.* A base coward. [Fr. *poltron* < OItal. *poltrone*, coward, idler, perh. augmentative of *poltro*, unbroken colt (< VLat. **pulliter* < Lat. *pullus*, young animal), or < *poltro*, bed, lazy.] —**pol·troon′er·y** *n.*

pol·y (pŏl′ē) *n.* **1.** Polyester. **2.** Polyethylene.

poly– *pref.* **1.** More than one; many; much: *polyandry.* **2.** More than usual; excessive; abnormal: *polydipsia.* **3.** Polymer; polymeric: *polyethylene.* [Gk. *polu-* < *polus*, much, many. See **pelə-¹** in App.]

pol·y·a·cryl·a·mide (pŏl′ē-ə-krĭl′ə-mīd′) *n.* A white polyamide related to acrylic acid. [POLY- + ACRYLAMIDE.]

pol·y·ad·e·nyl·ic acid (pŏl′ē-ăd′n-ĭl′ĭk) *n.* A polymer of adenylic acid attached to messenger RNA that stabilizes the molecule before transport from the nucleus into the cytoplasm.

pol·y·am·ide (pŏl′ē-ăm′īd′) *n.* A polymer containing repeated amide groups, as in various kinds of nylon.

pol·y·an·drous (pŏl′ē-ăn′drəs) *adj.* **1.** Relating to, characterized by, or practicing polyandry. **2.** *Botany* Having an indefinite number of stamens.

pol·y·an·dry (pŏl′ē-ăn′drē) *n.* **1.** The condition or practice of having more than one husband at one time. **2.** *Zoology* A mating pattern in which a female mates with more than one male in a single breeding season. **3.** *Botany* The condition of being polyandrous. —**pol′y·an′dric** *adj.*

pol·y·an·thus (pŏl′ē-ăn′thəs) *n., pl.* **-thus·es** Any of a group of hybrid garden primroses having clusters of variously colored flowers. [NLat. < Gk. *poluanthos*, having many flowers : *polu-*, poly- + *anthos*, flower.]

polyanthus narcissus *n.* A bulbous Mediterranean plant (*Narcissus tazetta*) having fragrant white and yellow flowers.

pol·y·ba·sic (pŏl′ē-bā′sĭk) *adj.* Of or relating to an acid that has two or more hydrogen atoms that can be replaced by basic atoms or radicals.

pol·y·ba·site (pŏl′ē-bā′sīt′) *n.* A black mineral with a metallic luster, (Ag,Cu)₁₆Sb₂S₁₁, that is an ore of silver. [POLY- + BAS(IS) + -ITE¹.]

Po·lyb·i·us (pə-lĭb′ē-əs) 200?–118? B.C. Greek historian known for the 5 extant books of his history of Rome.

pol·y·car·bon·ate (pŏl′ē-kär′bə-nāt′) *n.* Any of a group of thermoplastics characterized by flexibility and strength, and used as shatter-resistant substitutes for glass.

Pol·y·carp (pŏl′ē-kärp′), Saint. A.D. 69?–155? Christian martyr who was burned at the stake.

pol·y·car·pel·lar·y (pŏl′ē-kär′pə-lĕr′ē) *adj. Botany* Having

or consisting of many carpels.

pol·y·car·pous (pŏl′ē-kär′pəs) also **po·ly·car·pic** (-pĭk) *adj.* Having fruit or pistils with two or more carpels. —**pol′y·car′py** *n.*

pol·y·cen·tric (pŏl′ē-sĕn′trĭk) *adj.* **1.** Having many centers, esp. of authority or control. **2.** Having several central parts, such as centrosomes or chromatids. ❖ *n.* A polycentric chromosome. —**pol′y·cen′trism** *n.*

pol·y·chete also **pol·y·chaete** (pŏl′ĭ-kēt′) *n.* Any of various annelid worms of the class Polychaeta, including mostly marine worms such as the lugworm and characterized by fleshy paired appendages tipped with bristles on each body segment. [NLat. *Polychaeta*, class name < Gk. *polukhaitēs*, with much hair : *polu-*, poly- + *khaitē*, long hair.] —**pol′y·chete′, pol′y·che′tous** *adj.*

pol·y·chlo·rin·at·ed biphenyl (pŏl′ē-klôr′ə-nā′tĭd, -klōr′-) *n.* PCB.

pol·y·chro·mat·ic (pŏl′ē-krō-măt′ĭk) also **pol·y·chro·mic** (-krō′mĭk) or **pol·y·chro·mous** (-krō′məs) *adj.* **1.** Having or exhibiting many colors. **2.** Of or composed of radiation of more than one wavelength: *polychromatic light.*

pol·y·chrome (pŏl′ē-krōm′) *adj.* **1.** Having many or various colors; polychromatic. **2.** Made or decorated in many or various colors. ❖ *n.* A polychrome object or work.

pol·y·chro·my (pŏl′ē-krō′mē) *n.* The use of many colors in decoration, esp. in architecture and sculpture.

Pol·y·cli·tus or **Pol·y·clei·tus** (pŏl′ĭ-klī′təs) fl. 5th cent. B.C. Greek sculptor known for his statues of athletes.

pol·y·clo·nal (pŏl′ē-klō′nəl) *adj.* Descended from more than one group of cells, esp. of genetically different origins. —**pol′y·clo′nal·ly** *adv.*

pol·y·con·ic projection (pŏl′ē-kŏn′ĭk) *n.* A conic map projection having distances between meridians along every parallel equal to those distances on a globe.

pol·y·cot·y·le·don (pŏl′ē-kŏt′l-ēd′n) also **pol·y·cot** (-kŏt′) *n.* A plant whose seed contains more than two cotyledons. —**pol′y·cot′y·le′don·ous** *adj.*

pol·y·cy·clic (pŏl′ĭ-sī′klĭk, -sĭk′lĭk) *adj.* Having two or more atomic rings in a molecule.

polycyclic aromatic hydrocarbon *n.* Any of a class of carcinogenic organic molecules that consist of three or more rings containing carbon and hydrogen and that are commonly produced by fossil fuel combustion.

pol·y·cy·the·mi·a (pŏl′ē-sī-thē′mē-ə) *n.* A condition marked by an abnormally large number of red blood cells. [POLY- + CYT(O)- + -HEMIA.]

pol·y·dac·tyl (pŏl′ē-dăk′təl) also **pol·y·dac·ty·lous** (-tə-ləs) *Biology adj.* Having more than the normal number of digits. ❖ *n.* A polydactyl person or animal.

pol·y·dip·si·a (pŏl′ē-dĭp′sē-ə) *n.* Excessive or abnormal thirst. [POLY- + Gk. *dipsa*, thirst + -IA¹.]

pol·y·e·lec·tro·lyte (pŏl′ē-ĭ-lĕk′trə-līt′) *n.* An electrolyte, such as a polysaccharide, having a high molecular weight.

pol·y·em·bry·o·ny (pŏl′ē-ĕm′brē-ə-nē, -ĕm-brī′-) *n.* Development of more than one embryo from a single egg or ovule. —**pol′y·em′bry·on′ic** (-brē-ŏn′ĭk) *adj.*

pol·y·ene (pŏl′ē-ēn′) *n.* An organic compound containing many double bonds.

pol·y·es·ter (pŏl′ē-ĕs′tər, pŏl′ē-ĕs′tər) *n.* **1.** Any of numerous synthetic polymers produced by reaction of dibasic acids with dihydric alcohols and used as light, strong, weather-resistant resins in boat hulls, textile fibers, and molded parts. **2.** A wrinkle-resistant fabric of fibers made from any of these resins. —**pol′y·es′ter** *adj.* —**pol′y·es′ter·i·fi·ca′tion** (-ə-fĭ-kā′shən) *n.*

pol·y·es·trous (pŏl′ē-ĕs′trəs) *adj.* **1.** Having several estrous cycles during a single breeding season. **2.** Ovulating more than once a year.

pol·y·eth·yl·ene (pŏl′ē-ĕth′ə-lēn′) *n.* A polymerized ethylene resin, used esp. for containers, kitchenware, and tubing or in the form of films and sheets for packaging.

polyethylene glycol *n.* Any of a family of colorless liquids with high molecular weight that are soluble in water and in many organic solvents and are used as emulsifiers and plasticizers.

po·lyg·a·la (pə-lĭg′ə-lə) *n.* Any of various plants of the genus *Polygala*, which constitutes the milkworts. [NLat. *Polygala*, genus name < Gk. *polugalon*, milkwort : *polu-*, poly- + *gala*, milk; see **melg–** in App.]

po·lyg·a·mist (pə-lĭg′ə-mĭst) *n.* A practicer of polygamy.

po·lyg·a·mous (pə-lĭg′ə-məs) *adj.* **1.** Of, characterized by, or practicing polygamy. **2.** *Botany* Having hermaphroditic and unisexual flowers on the same plant or on separate plants of the same species. —**po·lyg′a·mous·ly** *adv.*

po·lyg·a·my (pə-lĭg′ə-mē) *n.* **1.** The condition or practice of having more than one spouse at one time. **2.** *Zoology* A mating pattern in which a single individual mates with more than one individual of the opposite sex. [Fr. *polygamie* < LLat. *polygamia* < Gk. *polugamia* : *polu-*, poly- + *-gamia*, -gamy.]

pol·y·gene (pŏl′ē-jēn′) *n.* Any of a group of nonallelic genes, each having a small quantitative effect, that together produce a wide range of phenotypic variation. —**pol′y·gen′ic** (-jĕn′ĭk) *adj.*

pol·y·gen·e·sis (pŏl′ē-jĕn′ĭ-sĭs) *n.* Derivation of a species or

polo

Marco Polo

ă	pat	oi	boy
ā	pay	ou	out
âr	care	ŏŏ	took
ä	father	ōō	boot
ĕ	pet	ŭ	cut
ē	be	ûr	urge
ĭ	pit	th	thin
ī	pie	*th*	this
îr	pier	hw	which
ŏ	pot	zh	vision
ō	toe	ə	about,
ô	paw		item

Stress marks:
′ (primary);
′ (secondary), as in
lexicon (lĕk′sĭ-kŏn′)

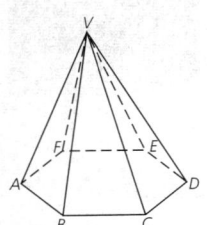

polyhedral angle
Lateral faces *VAB, VBC, VCD, VDE,* and *VEF* join at the common vertex *V* to form a polyhedral angle.

type from more than one ancestor or germ cell. —**pol′y•gen′e• sist** *n.* —**pol′y•ge•net′ic** (-jə-nĕt′ĭk) *adj.*

pol•y•glot (pŏl′ē-glŏt′) *adj.* Speaking, writing, written in, or composed of several languages. ❖ *n.* **1.** A person having a knowledge of several languages. **2.** A book, esp. a Bible, containing several versions of the same text in different languages. **3.** A mixture or confusion of languages. [Fr. *polyglotte* < Gk. *poluglōttos* : *polu-,* poly- + *glōtta,* tongue, language.] —**pol′y•glot′ism, pol′y• glot′tism** *n.*

pol•y•gon (pŏl′ē-gŏn′) *n. Mathematics* A closed plane figure bounded by three or more line segments. —**po•lyg′o•nal** (pə-lĭg′ə-nəl) *adj.* —**po•lyg′o•nal•ly** *adv.*

po•lyg•o•num (pə-lĭg′ə-nəm) *n.* Any of numerous plants of the widely distributed genus *Polygonum,* characterized by stems with knotlike joints and conspicuous sheathlike stipules. [NLat. *Polygonum,* genus name < Gk. *polugonon,* knotgrass : *polu-,* poly- + *gonu,* knee; see **genu-** in App.]

pol•y•graph (pŏl′ē-grăf′) *n.* An instrument that simultaneously records changes in physiological processes such as blood pressure and respiration, often used as a lie detector. ❖ *tr.v.* **-graphed, -graph•ing, -graphs** To test (a suspect, for example) with a polygraph. —**po•lyg′ra•pher** (pə-lĭg′rə-fər), **po•lyg′ra•phist** (-fĭst) *n.* —**pol′y•graph′ic** *adj.*

po•lyg•y•ny (pə-lĭj′ə-nē) *n.* **1.** The condition or practice of having more than one wife at one time. **2.** *Zoology* A mating pattern in which a male mates with more than one female in a single breeding season. —**po•lyg′y•nous** *adj.*

polyhedral angle *n.* A shape formed by three or more planes intersecting at a common point.

pol•y•he•dron (pŏl′ē-hē′drən) *n., pl.* **-drons** or **-dra** (-drə) A solid bounded by polygons. —**pol′y•he′dral** *adj.*

pol•y•his•tor (pŏl′ē-hĭs′tər) *n.* A person with broad knowledge. [Lat. *Polyhistōr* < Gk. *poluistōr,* very learned : *polu-,* poly- + *histōr,* learned; see **weid-** in App.]

Pol•y•hym•ni•a (pŏl′ē-hĭm′nē-ə) also **Po•lym′ni•a** (pə-lĭm′nē-ə) *n. Greek Mythology* The Muse of sacred song and oratory.

pol•y•im•ide (pŏl′ē-ĭm′īd′) *n.* A synthetic polymeric resin of a class resistant to high temperatures, wear, and corrosion, used primarily as a coating or film on a substrate substance.

pol•y•math (pŏl′ē-măth′) *n.* A person of great or varied learning. [Gk. *polumathēs* : *polu-,* poly- + *manthanein, math-,* to learn.] —**pol′y•math′, pol′y•math′ic** *adj.* —**po•lym′a•thy** (pə-lĭm′ə-thē) *n.*

pol•y•mer (pŏl′ə-mər) *n.* Any of numerous natural or synthetic compounds of usu. high molecular weight consisting of repeated linked units, each a relatively light and simple molecule. [Gk. *polumerēs,* consisting of many parts : *polu-,* poly- + *meros,* part.]

pol•y•mer•ase (pŏl′ə-mə-rās′, -rāz′) *n.* Any of various enzymes that catalyze the formation of polynucleotides of DNA or RNA using an existing strand of DNA or RNA as a template.

polymerase chain reaction *n.* A technique for amplifying DNA sequences in vitro by repeatedly separating paired DNA strands and using each strand as a template for a new DNA segment.

pol•y•mer•ic (pŏl′ə-mĕr′ĭk) *adj.* Of, relating to, or consisting of a polymer. —**pol′y•mer′i•cal•ly** *adv.* —**po•lym′er•ism** (pə-lĭm′ə-rĭz′əm, pŏl′ə-mə-) *n.*

po•lym•er•i•za•tion (pə-lĭm′ər-ĭ-zā′shən, pŏl′ə-mər-) *n.* **1.** The bonding of two or more monomers to form a polymer. **2.** A chemical process that effects this bonding. —**pol′y•mer•ize** (pŏl′ə-mə-rīz′, pə-lĭm′ə-) *v.*

pol•y•morph (pŏl′ē-môrf′) *n.* **1.** *Biology* An organism characterized by polymorphism. **2.** *Chemistry* A specific crystalline form of a compound that can crystallize in different forms.

pol•y•mor•phism (pŏl′ē-môr′fĭz′əm) *n.* **1.** *Biology* The occurrence of different forms in organisms of the same species, independent of sexual variations. **2.** *Chemistry* Crystallization of a compound in at least two distinct forms. —**pol′y•mor′phic, pol′y•mor′phous** *adj.* —**pol′y•mor′phous•ly** *adv.*

pol•y•mor•pho•nu•cle•ar (pŏl′ē-môr′fə-nōō′klē-ər, -nyōō′-) *adj.* Having a lobed nucleus. Used esp. of neutrophil white blood cells. ❖ *n.* A polymorphonuclear cell.

polymorphous perverse *adj.* Characterized by or displaying sexual tendencies that have no specific direction, as in an infant or young child.

pol•y•myx•in (pŏl′ē-mĭk′sĭn) *n.* Any of various mainly toxic antibiotics derived from strains of the soil bacterium *Bacillus polymyxa* and used to treat various infections with gram-negative bacteria. [NLat. *polymyxa,* species name (POLY- + Gk. *muxa,* slime) + -IN.]

Pol•y•ne•sia (pŏl′ə-nē′zhə, -shə) A division of Oceania including volcanic and coral islands of the central and S Pacific roughly between New Zealand, Hawaii, and Easter I.

Pol•y•ne•sian (pŏl′ə-nē′zhən, -shən) *adj.* Of or relating to Polynesia or its peoples, languages, or cultures. ❖ *n.* **1.** A native or inhabitant of Polynesia. **2.** A subfamily of the Austronesian language family spoken in Polynesia.

Pol•y•ni•ces (pŏl′ə-nī′sēz) *n. Greek Mythology* A son of Oedipus and Jocasta who, with six other men, launched an unsuccessful expedition against Thebes to dethrone his brother Eteocles.

pol•y•no•mi•al (pŏl′ē-nō′mē-əl) *adj.* Of, relating to, or consisting of more than two names or terms. ❖ *n.* **1.** A taxonomic designation consisting of more than two terms. **2.** *Mathematics* An algebraic expression consisting of one or more summed terms, each term being the product of a constant and one or more variables raised to integral powers, for example, $2p^3q + y$. [POLY– + (BI)NOMIAL.]

pol•y•nu•cle•o•tide (pŏl′ē-nōō′klē-ə-tīd′, -nyōō′-) *n.* A polymeric compound, usu. DNA or RNA, consisting of a sequence of nucleotides.

po•lyn•ya (pŏl′ən-yä′, pə-lĭn′yə) *n.* An area of open water surrounded by sea ice. [Russ. *polyn'ya* < *polyĭ,* open, hollow. See **pelə-²** in App.]

pol•y•o•ma•vi•rus (pŏl′ē-ō′mə-vī′rəs) also **pol•y•o•ma** (pŏl′ē-ō′mə) *n.* A papovavirus that contains DNA and causes various tumors in rodents.

pol•yp (pŏl′ĭp) *n.* **1.** A cnidarian having a cylindrical body and an oral opening usu. surrounded by tentacles, and existing, as in coral, as a sedentary organism or, as in jellyfish, in a sedentary phase before developing into a medusa. **2.** A usu. nonmalignant growth or tumor protruding from the mucous lining of an organ such as the nose, often causing obstruction. [ME *polip,* nasal tumor < OFr. *polipe* < Lat. *pōlypus,* cuttlefish, nasal tumor < Gk. *polupous, poulupous* : *polu-,* poly- + *pous,* foot; see **ped-** in App.] —**pol′yp•oid′** *adj.*

pol•y•par•y (pŏl′ə-pĕr′ē) also **pol•y•par•i•um** (pŏl′ə-pâr′ē-əm) *n., pl.* **-ies** also **-i•a** (-ē-ə) The common supporting framework of a colony of polyps, esp. of coral.

pol•y•pep•tide (pŏl′ē-pĕp′tīd′) *n.* A peptide, such as a small protein, containing amino acid molecules typically numbering between 10 and 100.

pol•y•pet•al•ous (pŏl′ē-pĕt′l-əs) *adj.* Having separate petals, as on the corolla of a rose or carnation.

pol•y•pha•gi•a (pŏl′ē-fā′jē-ə, -jə) **po•lyph•a•gy** (pə-lĭf′ə-jē) *n.* **1.** An excessive or pathological desire to eat. **2.** *Zoology* The habit of feeding on many different kinds of food. —**pol′y• pha′gi•an** *adj.*

po•lyph•a•gous (pə-lĭf′ə-gəs) *adj.* Feeding on many different kinds of food: *polyphagous insects or birds.*

Pol•y•phe•mus (pŏl′ē-fē′məs) *n. Greek Mythology* The Cyclops who confined Odysseus in a cave until Odysseus blinded him and escaped. [Lat. < Gk. *Poluphēmos* < *poluphēmos,* famous : *polu-,* much; see POLY– + *phēmē,* saying, report; see **bhā-** in App.]

polyphemus moth *n.* A large North American silkworm moth (*Antheraea polyphemus*) having an eyelike spot on each hind wing. [After POLYPHEMUS.]

pol•y•phone (pŏl′ē-fōn′) *n.* A written character or combination of characters having two or more phonetic values, such as the letter *a* in English.

pol•y•phon•ic (pŏl′ē-fŏn′ĭk) *adj.* **1.** *Music* Of, relating to, or characterized by polyphony. **2.** *Linguistics* Having two or more phonetic values. —**pol′y•phon′i•cal•ly** *adv.*

po•lyph•o•ny (pə-lĭf′ə-nē) *n., pl.* **-nies** Music with two or more independent melodic parts sounded together. —**po•lyph′o• nous** *adj.* —**po•lyph′o•nous•ly** *adv.*

pol•y•phy•let•ic (pŏl′ē-fī-lĕt′ĭk) *adj.* Of or characterized by development from more than one ancestral type.

pol•y•ploid (pŏl′ē-ploid′) *adj.* Having one or more extra sets of chromosomes. —**pol′y•ploid** *n.* —**pol′y•ploi′dy** *n.*

pol•yp•ne•a (pŏl′ĭp-nē′ə) *n.* Very rapid breathing; panting. [NLat. : POLY– + Gk. *pnoiā, -pnoia,* breath, breathing (< *pnein,* to breathe).] —**pol′yp•ne′ic** (-nē′ĭk) *adj.*

pol•y•pod (pŏl′ē-pŏd′) also **po•lyp•o•dous** (pə-lĭp′ə-dəs) *adj. Biology* Having numerous feet.

pol•y•po•dy (pŏl′ē-pō′dē) *n., pl.* **-dies** Any of various ferns of the genus *Polypodium,* having simple or compound fronds, round sori arranged in one or more rows along the midrib, and creeping rootstocks. [ME *polypodie* < Lat. *polypodium* < Gk. *polupodion* < dim. of *polupous,* many-footed : *polu-,* poly- + *pous, pod-,* foot; see —POD.]

pol•y•pore (pŏl′ē-pôr′, -pōr′) *n.* See **pore fungus.**

pol•y•pro•pyl•ene (pŏl′ē-prō′pə-lēn′) *n.* **1.** Any of various thermoplastic resins that are polymers of propylene and used to make molded articles and fibers. **2.** A fabric of fibers made from any of these resins. —**pol′y•pro′pyl•ene′** *adj.*

pol•yp•tych (pŏl′ĭp-tĭk′) *n.* A work consisting of four or more painted or carved panels hinged together. [< LLat. *polyptycha,* registers, account books < Gk. *poluptukha* < neut. pl. of *poluptukhos,* having many folds : *polu-,* poly- + *ptukhē,* fold; see DIP-TYCH.]

pol•y•rhythm (pŏl′ē-rĭth′əm) *n. Music* The use or an instance of simultaneous contrasting rhythms. —**pol′y•rhyth′mic** *adj.*

pol•y•ri•bo•some (pŏl′ē-rī′bə-sōm′) *n.* A cluster of ribosomes that is connected by a strand of messenger RNA and is active in protein synthesis.

pol•y•sac•cha•ride (pŏl′ē-săk′ə-rīd′) also **pol•y•sac•cha•rid** (-rĭd) or **pol•y•sac•cha•rose** (-rōs′, -rōz′) *n.* Any of a class of carbohydrates, such as starch and cellulose, consisting of a number of monosaccharides joined by glycosidic bonds.

pol•y•se•mous (pŏl′ē-sē′məs) *adj.* Having or characterized by many meanings, as the word *table.* [< LLat. *polysēmus* < Gk. *polu-*

sēmos : polu-, poly- + *sēma*, sign.] —**pol′y•se′my** (pŏl′ē-sē′mē, pə-lĭs′ə-).]

pol•y•sep•al•ous (pŏl′ē-sĕp′ə-ləs) *adj.* Having separate sepals.

pol•y•some (pŏl′ē-sōm′) *n.* See **polyribosome.**

pol•y•so•mic (pŏl′ē-sō′mĭk) *adj.* Having an extra copy of one or more chromosomes: *a polysomic cell.* ❖ *n.* A polysomic organism or cell. [POLY– + (CHROMO)SOM(E) + –IC.]

po•lys•ti•chous (pə-lĭs′tĭ-kəs) *adj. Botany* Arranged in two or more series or rows. [Gk. *polustikhos*, of many lines : *polu-*, poly- + *stikhos*, row; see STICH.]

pol•y•sty•rene (pŏl′ē-stī′rēn) *n.* A rigid clear thermoplastic polymer that can be molded into objects or made into a foam used in insulation and packaging. —**pol′y•sty′rene** *adj.*

pol•y•sul•fide (pŏl′ē-sŭl′fīd) *n.* A sulfide compound containing at least two sulfur atoms per molecule.

pol•y•syl•lab•ic (pŏl′ē-sĭ-lăb′ĭk) *adj.* **1.** Having more than two and usu. more than three syllables. **2.** Characterized by polysyllabic words. —**pol′y•syl•lab′i•cal•ly** *adv.*

pol•y•syl•la•ble (pŏl′ē-sĭl′ə-bəl) *n.* A word of more than three syllables.

pol•y•syn•de•ton (pŏl′ē-sĭn′dĭ-tŏn′) *n.* The repetition of conjunctions in close succession for rhetorical effect, as in *here and there and everywhere.* [L.Gk. *polusundeton*, neut. of *polusundetos*, using many connectives : Gk. *polu-*, poly- + Gk. *sundetos*, bound together; see SYNDETIC.]

pol•y•syn•thet•ic (pŏl′ē-sĭn-thĕt′ĭk) *adj.* Of or relating to a language such as Eskimo or Mohawk, characterized by long, morphologically complex words with a large number of affixes that express syntactic relationships and meanings usu. expressed as phrases or sentences in other languages.

pol•y•tech•nic (pŏl′ē-tĕk′nĭk) *adj.* Offering, receiving, or dealing with instruction in many industrial arts and applied sciences. ❖ *n.* A polytechnic school.

pol•y•tet•ra•fluor•o•eth•yl•ene (pŏl′ē-tĕt′rə-flŏŏr′ō-ĕth′ə-lēn′, -flôr′-, -flōr′-) *n.* A thermoplastic resin, (C₂F₄)ₙ, that is resistant to heat and chemicals, has a low coefficient of friction, and is used as a coating, as on cookware.

pol•y•the•ism (pŏl′ē-thē-ĭz′əm, pŏl′ē-thē′ĭz-əm) *n.* The worship of or belief in more than one god. [Fr. *polythéisme* < Gk. *polutheos*, polytheistic : *polu-*, poly- + *theos*, god; see **dhēs-** in App.] —**pol′y•the′ist** *n.* —**pol′y•the•is′tic** *adj.*

pol•y•thene (pŏl′ə-thēn′) *n. Chiefly British* Variant of **polyethylene.** [POLY(E)TH(YL)ENE.]

po•lyt•o•cous (pə-lĭt′ə-kəs) *adj.* Producing many offspring in a single birth. [Gk. *polutokos*, bearing many offspring : *polu-*, poly- + *tokos*, offspring, birth; see **tek-** in App.]

pol•y•to•nal•i•ty (pŏl′ē-tō-năl′ĭ-tē) *n.* Simultaneous use of two or more tonalities in a musical composition. —**pol′y•to′nal** (-tō′nəl) *adj.*

pol•y•tro•phic (pŏl′ē-trō′fĭk, -trŏf′ĭk) *adj.* Subsisting on various types of organic material. Used of certain bacteria.

pol•y•typ•ic (pŏl′ē-tĭp′ĭk) also **pol•y•typ•i•cal** (-ĭ-kəl) *adj.* Having several variant forms, esp. subspecies or varieties.

pol•y•un•sat•u•rat•ed (pŏl′ē-ŭn-săch′ə-rā′tĭd) *adj.* Of or relating to an organic compound, esp. a fatty acid, having two or more double bonds between carbon atoms.

pol•y•u•re•thane (pŏl′ē-yŏŏr′ə-thān′) *n.* Any of various resins, widely varying in flexibility, used in chemical-resistant coatings, adhesives, and foams. —**pol′y•u′re•thane′** *adj.*

pol•y•u•ri•a (pŏl′ē-yŏŏr′ē-ə) *n.* Excessive passage of urine, as in diabetes. —**pol′y•u′ric** *adj.*

pol•y•va•lent (pŏl′ē-vā′lənt) *adj.* **1.** Acting against or interacting with more than one kind of antigen or toxin. **2.** *Chemistry* **a.** Having more than one valence. **b.** Having a valence of 3 or higher. —**pol′y•va′lence, pol′y•va′len•cy** *n.*

pol•y•vi•nyl (pŏl′ē-vī′nəl) *adj.* Being any of a group of polymerized thermoplastic vinyls, such as polyvinyl chloride.

polyvinyl chloride *n.* PVC.

pol•y•zo•an (pŏl′ē-zō′ən) *n.* See **bryozoan.** [< NLat. *Polyzōa*, phylum name : POLY– + –ZŌA, pl. of –*zōon*; see –ZOON.] —**pol′y•zo′an** *adj.*

pol•y•zo•ar•i•um (pŏl′ē-zō-âr′ē-əm) also **pol•y•zo•a•ry** (-zō′ə-rē) *n., pl.* **-ar•i•a** (-âr′ē-ə) also **-a•ries** A bryozoan colony or its supporting skeletal structure. [NLat. *polyzōārium* < *Polyzōa*, phylum name; see POLYZOAN + –ARIUM.]

pom•ace (pŭm′ĭs, pŏm′-) *n.* **1.** The pulpy material remaining after the juice has been pressed from fruit. **2.** Pulpy material remaining after the extraction of oil from nuts, seeds, or fish. [ME *pomis* < Med.Lat. *pōmācium*, cider < VLat. **pōma*, apple, fruit. See POME.]

pomace fly *n.* See **fruit fly** 1.

po•ma•ceous (pō-mā′shəs) *adj.* Of, relating to, bearing, or characteristic of apples or pomes. [< NLat. *pōmāceus* < LLat. *pōmum*, apple. See POME.]

po•made (pō-mād′, -mäd′) *n.* A perfumed ointment, esp. one used to groom the hair. ❖ *tr.v.* **-mad•ed, -mad•ing, -mades** To anoint with pomade. [Fr. *pommade* < Ital. *pomata* < *pomo*, apple < Lat. *pōmum*. See POME.]

po•man•der (pō′măn′dər, pō-măn′-) *n.* **1.** A mixture of aromatic substances enclosed in a bag or box as a protection against odor or infection. **2.** A case, box, or bag for holding this mixture.

[ME *pomendambre*, alteration of OFr. *pome d'ambre*, apple of amber < Med.Lat. *pōmum dē ambrā* : *pōmum*, apple, ball (< Lat., fruit) + Lat. *dē*, of; see DE– + *ambrā*, ablative of *ambra*, amber; see AMBER.]

pome (pōm) *n.* A fleshy fruit, such as an apple, having several seed chambers and an outer fleshy part largely derived from the hypanthium. [ME < OFr., apple, fruit < VLat. **pōma* < neut. pl. of Lat. *pōmum* < Lat., fruit.]

pome•gran•ate (pŏm′grăn′ĭt, pŏm′ĭ-, pŭm′-, pŭm′ĭ-) *n.* **1.** A deciduous shrub or small tree (*Punica granatum*) native to Asia and widely cultivated for its edible fruit. **2.** The fruit of this tree, having a tough reddish rind and containing many seeds, each enclosed in a juicy, mildly acidic red pulp. [ME *pome granate* < OFr. *pome grenate* : *pome*, apple; see POME + *grenate*, having many seeds (< Lat. *grānātus* < *grānum*, grain, seed; see **gr̥ə-no-** in App.).]

pom•e•lo (pŏm′ə-lō′) *n., pl.* **-los** See **shaddock.** [Alteration of POMPELMOUS.]

Pom•er•a•ni•a (pŏm′ə-rā′nē-ə, -rān′yə) A historical region of N-central Europe on the Baltic Sea in present-day NW Poland and NE Germany; inhabited since the 10th cent.

Pom•er•a•ni•an (pŏm′ə-rā′nē-ən, -rān′yən) *adj.* Of or relating to Pomerania or its people. ❖ *n.* **1.** A native or inhabitant of Pomerania. **2.** Any of a breed of small dogs having long hair, a foxlike face, and a tail curling over the back.

Pomeranian

po•mif•er•ous (pō-mĭf′ər-əs) *adj.* Bearing pomes. [Lat. *pōmifer*, fruit-bearing : *pōmum*, fruit + *-fer*, -fer) + –OUS.]

pom•mel (pŭm′əl, pŏm′-) *tr.v.* **-meled, -mel•ing, -mels** also **-melled, -mel•ling, -mels** To beat; pummel. ❖ *n.* **1.** The upper front part of a saddle; a saddlebow. **2.** Either of the two rounded handles on top of a pommel horse. **3.** A knob on the hilt of a sword or similar weapon. [< ME *pomel*, a pommel < OFr., dim. of *pom*, ball, fruit < Lat. *pōmum*, fruit.]

pommel horse *n.* **1.** An apparatus for gymnastic exercises that consists of a padded, loaf-shaped object with two pommels on top and stands horizontal to the floor, usu. on adjustable legs. **2.** An athletic event in which the pommel horse is used.

pom•my or **pom•mie** (pŏm′ē) *n., pl.* **-mies** *Australian & New Zealand Offensive Slang* Used as a disparaging term for a British person, esp. a recent immigrant. [Short for *pomegranate*, *Pummy Grant*, alterations of *Jimmy Grant*, prob. rhyming alteration of IMMIGRANT.]

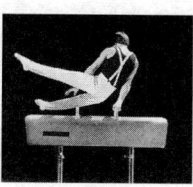

pommel horse

Po•mo (pō′mō) *n., pl.* **Pomo** or **-mos 1.** A member of a group of Native American peoples inhabiting an area of the Coast Ranges of northern California. **2.** Any of the seven languages of the Pomo.

po•mol•o•gy (pō-mŏl′ə-jē) *n.* The scientific study and cultivation of fruit. [Lat. *pōmum*, fruit + –LOGY.] —**po′mo•log′i•cal** (pō′mə-lŏj′ĭ-kəl) *adj.* —**po•mol′o•gist** *n.*

Po•mo•na (pə-mō′nə) A city of S CA, a suburb of Los Angeles. Pop. 149,473.

pomp (pŏmp) *n.* **1.** Dignified or magnificent display; splendor: *the pomp of a funeral.* **2.** Vain or ostentatious display. [ME < OFr. *pompe* < Lat. *pompa*, pomp, procession < Gk. *pompē*, procession < *pempein*, to send.]

pom•pa•dour (pŏm′pə-dôr′, -dōr′) *n.* **1.** A woman's hairstyle formed by sweeping the hair straight up from the forehead into a high, turned-back roll. **2.** A man's hairstyle formed by brushing the hair up from the forehead. [After the Marquise de POMPADOUR.]

Pom•pa•dour (pŏm′pə-dôr′, -dōr′, -dōr′, pôn-pä-dōōr′), Marquise de. Title of Jeanne Antoinette Poisson. Known as "Madame de Pompadour." 1721–64. The lover of Louis XV who was blamed for establishing France's alliance with Austria, which led to the Seven Years' War (1756–63).

pom•pa•no (pŏm′pə-nō′) *n., pl.* **pompano** or **-nos** Any of several marine food fishes of the genus *Trachinotus*, esp. *T. carolinus*, of tropical and temperate Atlantic waters, having a silvery oblong body with a bluish back. [Am.Sp. *pámpano*, a fish < Sp. < Lat. *pampinus*, vine tendril.]

Pompano Beach A city of SE FL on the Atlantic coast N of Miami. Pop. 78,191.

pompano dolphin *n.* See **dolphin** 2b.

Pompeian red *n.* A grayish to moderate red.

Pom•pe•ii (pŏm-pā′, -pā′ē) A city of S Italy SE of Naples; founded c. 6th cent. B.C. and destroyed by an eruption of Mt. Vesuvius in A.D. 79. —**Pom•pe′ian, Pom•pei′ian** *adj. & n.*

pom•pel•mous (pŏm′pəl-mōōs′) *n.* See **shaddock.** [Du. *pompelmoes*, prob. ult. < Tamil *pampalimāsu*.]

Pom•pey (pŏm′pē) Originally Gnaeus Pompeius Magnus 106–48 B.C. Roman general and politician who was defeated by Caesar and murdered in Egypt.

Pom•pi•dou (pŏm′pĭ-dōō′, pôn-pē-dōō′), Georges Jean Raymond 1911–74. French politician who served as premier (1962–68) and president (1969–74).

pom•pon (pŏm′pŏn′) also **pom•pom** (-pŏm′) *n.* **1.** A tuft or ball of material used as a decoration, esp. on shoes, caps, and curtains. **2.** A small buttonlike flower of some chrysanthemums and dahlias. **3.** *pompom* A ball of fluffy material waved by cheerleaders and sports fans. [Fr.]

pom•pous (pŏm′pəs) *adj.* **1.** Marked by excessive self-esteem or

pontoon
pontoons on a seaplane

pontoon bridge

poodle
standard poodle

exaggerated dignity; pretentious. **2.** Full of high-sounding phrases; bombastic. **3.** Marked by pomp or stately display; ceremonious. [ME < OFr. *pompeux* < LLat. *pompōsus* < Lat. *pompa*, pomp. See POMP.] —**pom·pos′i·ty** (-pŏs′ĭ-tē), **pom′pous·ness** (-pəs-nĭs) *n.* —**pom′pous·ly** *adv.*

Pon·ca (pŏng′kə) *n., pl.* **Ponca** or **-cas 1.** A member of a Native American people formerly inhabiting northeast Nebraska, with present-day populations also in Oklahoma. **2.** The Siouan language of the Ponca.

Pon·ce (pŏn′sā, -sē) A city of S Puerto Rico SW of San Juan. Pop. 155,038.

Ponce de Le·ón (pŏns′ də lē′ən, lē-ōn′, pŏn′thē thē lĕ-ōn′, pŏn′sē), **Juan** 1460–1521. Spanish explorer of Florida (1513) who was searching for the legendary Fountain of Youth.

Pon·chiel·li (pŏng-kyĕl′lē), **Amilcare** 1834–86. Italian composer noted for the opera *La Gioconda* (1876).

pon·cho (pŏn′chō) *n., pl.* **-chos 1.** A blanketlike cloak having a hole in the center for the head. **2.** A similar garment having a hood and used as a raincoat. [Am.Sp. < Sp., cape, perh. var. of *pocho*, faded, discolored.]

pond (pŏnd) *n.* A still body of water smaller than a lake. [ME *ponde* < OE *pund-*, enclosure.]

pon·der (pŏn′dər) *v.* **-dered, -der·ing, -ders** —*tr.* To weigh in the mind with thoroughness and care. —*intr.* To reflect or consider with thoroughness and care. [ME *ponderen* < OFr. *ponderer* < Lat. *ponderāre* < *pondus, ponder-*, weight.] —**pon′der·er** *n.*

pon·der·a·ble (pŏn′dər-ə-bəl) *adj.* Considerable enough to be weighed or assessed; appreciable. —**pon′der·a·bil′i·ty** *n.*

pon·der·o·sa pine (pŏn′də-rō′sə) *n.* A tall timber tree (*Pinus ponderosa*) of western North America having long dark green needles grouped in fascicles of three. [< NLat. *ponderōsa*, specific epithet < Lat. *ponderōsa*, fem. of *ponderōsus*, heavy. See PONDEROUS.]

pon·der·ous (pŏn′dər-əs) *adj.* **1.** Having great weight. **2.** Clumsy or unwieldy due to size, weight, bulk, or complexity. **3.** Lacking grace or fluency; labored and dull. [Ult. < Lat. *ponderōsus* < *pondus, ponder-*, weight.] —**pon′der·ous·ly** *adv.* —**pon′der·ous·ness, pon′der·os′i·ty** (-ŏs′ĭ-tē) *n.*

Pon·di·cher·ry (pŏn′dĭ-chĕr′ē, -shĕr′ē) A city of SE India on the Bay of Bengal SSW of Chennai (Madras). Pop. 203,065.

pond lily *n.* See **water lily.**

pond scum *n.* Any of various freshwater algae that form a usu. greenish film on the surface of stagnant water.

pond·weed (pŏnd′wĕd′) *n.* Any of various submerged or floating aquatic plants of the genus *Potamogeton*, having inconspicuous flowers borne in small spikes.

pone (pōn) *n. Chiefly Southern US* See **johnnycake.** See Regional Note at **johnnycake.** [Virginia Algonquian *poan, appoans*, cornbread.]

REGIONAL NOTE *Pone* is one of several Virginia Algonquian words (including *hominy* and *tomahawk*) borrowed into the English of the Atlantic seaboard. The word *pone*, usually in the compound *cornpone*, is now used mainly in the South, where it means cakes of cornbread baked on a griddle or in hot ashes.

pon·gee (pŏn-jē′, pŏn′jē) *n.* A soft thin cloth woven from Chinese or Indian raw silk or an imitation thereof. [Chin. (Mandarin) *bĕn zhī*, homemade fabric : *bĕn*, one's own + *zhī*, to weave, spin.]

pon·gid (pŏn′jĭd) *n.* An anthropoid ape of the family Pongidae, which includes the chimpanzee, gorilla, and orangutan. [< NLat. *Pongidae*, family name < *Pongo*, type genus, of African orig.; akin to Kikongo *im-pongo*.] —**pon′gid** *adj.*

pon·iard (pŏn′yərd) *n.* A dagger typically having a slender square or triangular blade. ❖ *tr.v.* **-iard·ed, -iard·ing, -iards** To stab with such a dagger. [Fr. *poignard* < *poing*, fist < OFr. < Lat. *pugnus*.]

pons (pŏnz) *n., pl.* **pon·tes** (pŏn′tēz) **1.** A slender tissue joining two parts of an organ. **2.** A band of nerve fibers on the ventral surface of the brain stem that links the medulla oblongata and the cerebellum with upper portions of the brain. [Lat. *pōns*, bridge. See pent- in App.]

pons as·i·no·rum (pŏnz′ ăs′ə-nôr′əm, -nōr′əm) *n.* A problem that severely tests the ability of an inexperienced person. [NLat. *pōns asinōrum*, bridge of fools (nickname of the Fifth Proposition in Euclid's *Elements*, due to its difficulty) : Lat. *pōns*, bridge + Lat. *asinōrum*, genitive pl. of *asinus*, ass, fool.]

Pon·selle (pŏn-sĕl′), **Rosa Melba** 1897–1981. Amer. soprano who performed with the Metropolitan Opera.

pons Va·ro·li·i (pŏnz′ və-rō′lē-ī′) *n.* See **pons** 2. [NLat. *pōns Varoliī*, bridge of Varoli, after Costanzo *Varolio* (1543?–75), Italian anatomist.]

Pont·char·train (pŏn′chər-trān′), **Lake** A lake of SE LA N of New Orleans.

Pon·ti·ac¹ (pŏn′tē-ăk′) 1720?–69. Ottawa leader who led a revolt against the British (1763–66).

Pon·ti·ac² (pŏn′tē-ăk′) A city of SE MI NW of Detroit. Pop. 66,337.

Pon·ti·a·nak (pŏn′tē-ä′näk) A city of W Borneo, Indonesia, at the N edge of the Kapuas R. delta. Pop. 304,778.

pon·ti·fex (pŏn′tə-fĕks′) *n., pl.* **pon·tif·i·ces** (pŏn-tĭf′ĭ-sēz′)

A man on the highest council of priests in ancient Rome. [Lat. See pent- in App.]

pon·tiff (pŏn′tĭf) *n.* **1a.** The pope. **b.** A bishop. **2.** A pontifex. [Fr. *pontife* < OFr. *pontif* < Lat. *pontifex*, pontifex. See pent- in App.]

pon·tif·i·cal (pŏn-tĭf′ĭ-kəl) *adj.* **1.** Relating to, characteristic of, or suitable for a pope or bishop. **2.** Having the dignity, pomp, or authority of a pontiff or bishop. **3.** Pompously dogmatic or self-important; pretentious. ❖ *n.* **1. pontificals** The vestments and insignia of a pontiff or bishop. **2.** A book of forms for ceremonies performed by a bishop. [ME < OFr. < Lat. *pontificālis*, of a pontifex < *pontifex, pontific-*, pontifex. See PONTIFEX.] —**pon·tif′i·cal·ly** *adv.*

pon·tif·i·cate (pŏn-tĭf′ĭ-kĭt, -kāt′) *n.* The office or term of office of a pontiff. ❖ *intr.v.* (-kāt′) **-cat·ed, -cat·ing, -cates 1.** To express opinions or judgments in a dogmatic way. **2.** To administer the office of a pontiff. [Lat. *pontificātus < pontifex, pontific-*, pontifex. See PONTIFEX. V., Med.Lat. *pontificāre, pontificāt-*, to act as an ecclesiastic < Lat. *pontifex*.] —**pon·tif′i·ca′tion** *n.* —**pon·tif′i·ca′tor** *n.*

pon·til (pŏn′tĭl) *n.* See **punty.** [Fr., poss. < Ital. *puntello*, dim. of *punto*, point < Lat. *pūnctum* < neut. p. part. of *pungere*, to prick.]

pon·tine (pŏn′tīn′, -tēn′) *adj.* **1.** Of or relating to bridges. **2.** Of or relating to a pons, esp. the pons Varolii. [Lat. *pōns, pont-*, bridge; see pent- in App. + -INE¹.]

Pon·tine Marshes (pŏn′tēn, -tĭn) An area of central Italy between the Tyrrhenian Sea and the Apennine foothills; drained during the 1930s to produce fertile farmland.

Pon·tius Pi·late (pŏn′chəs pī′lət) See **Pontius Pilate.**

Pont l'É·vêque (pŏnt′l'ĕ-vĕk′, pôn′lā-vĕk′) *n.* A pale yellow, semisoft French cheese made of whole or partially skimmed cow's milk. [After *Pont l'Évêque*, a town of northwest France.]

pon·to·nier (pŏn′tə-nîr′) *n.* One who is in charge of pontoons or is engaged in the construction of pontoon bridges. [Fr. *pontonnier* < OFr. < *ponton*, pontoon. See PONTOON.]

pon·toon (pŏn-tōōn′) *n.* **1.** A floating structure, such as a flat-bottom boat, used to support a bridge. **2.** A floating structure serving as a dock. **3.** A float on a seaplane. [Fr. *ponton* < OFr. < Lat. *pontō, pontōn-*, floating bridge < *pōns, pont-*, bridge. See pent- in App.]

pontoon bridge *n.* A temporary floating bridge that uses pontoons for support.

Pon·top·pi·dan (pŏn-tŏp′ĭ-dän′, -dän′), **Henrik** 1857–1943. Danish writer who shared the 1917 Nobel Prize for literature.

Pon·tus (pŏn′təs) An ancient country of NE Asia Minor along the S coast of the Black Sea. —**Pon′tic** (-tĭk) *adj.*

po·ny (pō′nē) *n., pl.* **-nies 1.** Any of several types or breeds of horses that are small in size when full grown, such as the Shetland pony. **2a.** *Informal* A racehorse. **b.** *Sports* A polo horse. **3.** Something small for its kind, esp. a small glass for beer or liqueur. **4.** A word-for-word translation of a foreign language text, esp. one used secretly by students as an aid. **5.** *Chiefly British* The sum of 25 pounds. ❖ *tr. & intr.v.* **-nied, -ny·ing, -nies** To study with the aid of a pony. —*phrasal verb:* **pony up** *Slang* To pay (money owed or due). [Prob. < obsolete Fr. *poulenet*, dim. of *poulain*, colt < LLat. *pullāmen*, young of an animal < Lat. *pullus*.]

pony express *n.* A system of rapid mail transportation by relays of horses in use in the western US in 1860–61.

po·ny·tail (pō′nē-tāl′) *n.* A hairstyle in which the hair is held back so as to hang down like a pony's tail.

Pon·zi scheme (pŏn′zē) *n.* An investment swindle in which high profits are promised from fictitious sources and early investors are paid off with funds raised from later ones. [After Charles *Ponzi* (1882?–1949), Italian-born speculator.]

poo (pōō) *Slang intr.v.* **pooed, poo·ing, poos** To defecate. ❖ *n.* **1.** Excrement. **2.** An act of defecating. [Prob. < POOH.]

pooch¹ (pōōch) *n. Slang* A dog. [?]

pooch² (pōōch) *intr.v.* **pooched, pooch·ing, pooch·es** To bulge, protrude. Used with *out*. [Alteration of POUCH.]

pood (pōōd) *n.* A Russian unit of weight equivalent to about 16.4 kilograms (36.1 pounds) avoirdupois. [Russ. *pud* < ON *pund*, pound, ult. < Lat. *pondō*. See POUND¹.]

poo·dle (pōōd′l) *n.* Any of a breed of dogs originally developed in Europe as hunting dogs, having thick curly hair and classified by shoulder height into standard, miniature, and toy varieties. [Ger. *Pudel*, short for *Pudelhund* : LGer. *pudeln*, to splash about (< *pudel*, puddle) + *Hund*, dog.]

poof¹ (pōōf) *interj.* Used to indicate a sudden vanishing. [Imit.]

poof² (pōōf) *n. Offensive Slang* Used as a disparaging term for an effeminate or homosexual male. [Prob. alteration of *puff*, braggart, homosexual man < PUFF (influenced by POOF¹).]

pooh (pōō) *interj.* Used to express disdain or disbelief.

Pooh-Bah or **pooh-bah** (pōō′bä′) *n.* **1.** A pompous ostentatious official, esp. one who performs none of many offices held. **2.** A person who holds high office. [After *Pooh-Bah* in *The Mikado* by W.S. Gilbert and Arthur Sullivan.]

pooh-pooh (pōō′pōō′) *tr.v.* **-poohed, -pooh·ing, -poohs** *Informal* To express contempt for or impatience about; make light of. [Reduplication of POOH.]

pool¹ (pōōl) *n.* **1.** A small body of still water. **2.** An accumulation of standing liquid, as a puddle. **3.** A deep or still place in a stream.

4. A swimming pool. **5.** An underground accumulation of petroleum or gas in porous sedimentary rock. ❖ *intr.v.* **pooled, pool·ing, pools 1.** To form pools or a pool. **2.** To accumulate in a body part. [ME < OE *pōl*.]

pool² (pōol) *n.* **1a.** A game of chance, resembling a lottery, in which the contestants put staked money into a common fund that is later paid to the winner. **b.** A fund containing all the money bet in a game of chance or on the outcome of an event. **2.** A grouping of resources for the common advantage of the participants. **3.** An available supply, the use of which is shared by a group. **4.** A group of journalists who cover an event and then share their reports with participating news media. **5.** A mutual fund established by a group of stockholders for speculating in or manipulating prices of securities. **6.** An agreement between competing business concerns to establish controls over production, market, and prices for common profit. **7.** Any of several games played on a six-pocket billiards table usu. with 15 object balls and a cue ball. ❖ *v.* **pooled, pool·ing, pools** —*tr.* To put into a fund for use by all. —*intr.* To join or form a pool. [Fr. *poule*, hen, stakes, booty < OFr., hen, young chicken < Lat. *pullus*, young of an animal.] —**pool′er** *n.*

Poole (pōol) A municipal borough of S England WSW of Southampton; chartered 1248. Pop. 137,159.

pool·room (pōol′rōom′, -rōom′) *n.* A commercial establishment or room for the playing of pool or billiards.

pool·side (pōol′sīd′) *n.* The area near a swimming pool.

pool table *n.* A six-pocket billiards table for pool.

poon (pōon) *n.* Any of several trees of the genus *Calophyllum* of southern Asia, having light hard wood used for masts and spars. [Sinhalese *pūna*, perh. of Dravidian orig.]

Poo·na (pōo′nə) See **Pune.**

poop¹ (pōop) *n.* **1.** An enclosed superstructure at the stern of a ship. **2.** A poop deck. ❖ *v.* **pooped, poop·ing, poops 1.** To break over the stern of (a ship). **2.** To take (a wave) over the stern. [ME *poupe* < OFr. < Lat. *puppis*.]

poop² (pōop) *tr.v.* **pooped, poop·ing, poops** *Slang* To cause to become fatigued; tire. —*phrasal verb:* **poop out** *Slang* **1.** To quit because of exhaustion: *poop out of a race.* **2.** To decide not to participate, esp. at the last moment. [?]

poop³ (pōop) *n. Slang* Inside information. [?]

poop⁴ (pōop) *n. Slang* A person regarded as very disagreeable. [Perh. short for NINCOMPOOP.]

poop⁵ (pōop) *Slang n.* Excrement. ❖ *intr.v.* **pooped, poop·ing, poops** To defecate. [Poss. < obsolete *poop*, to break wind < ME *poupen*, to blow a horn, toot, of imit. orig.]

poop deck *n.* An exposed partial deck on the stern superstructure of a ship.

poop·er-scoop·er (pōo′pər skōo′pər) *n.* A scoop for picking up and removing the feces of a pet.

poor (pōor) *adj.* **poor·er, poor·est 1.** Having little or no wealth and few or no possessions. **2.** Lacking in a specified resource or quality: *a diet poor in calcium.* **3.** Not adequate in quality; inferior: *a poor performance.* **4a.** Lacking in value; insufficient: *poor wages.* **b.** Lacking in quantity: *poor attendance.* **5.** Lacking fertility: *poor soil.* **6.** Undernourished; lean. **7.** Humble: *a poor spirit.* **8.** Eliciting or deserving pity; pitiable. ❖ *n.* People with little or no wealth and possessions considered as a group. [ME *poure* < OFr. *povre* < Lat. *pauper*.] —**poor′ness** *n.*

SYNONYMS *poor, indigent, needy, impecunious, penniless, impoverished, poverty-stricken, destitute* These adjectives mean lacking the money or the means for an adequate or comfortable life. *Poor* is the most general: "*Resolve not to be poor: whatever you have, spend less.*" (Samuel Johnson). *Indigent* and *needy* refer to one in need or want: *indigent people living on the street; distributed food to needy families. Impecunious* and *penniless* mean having little or no money: "*Certainly an impecunious Subaltern was not a catch*" (Rudyard Kipling). *Poor investments left the family penniless.* One who is *impoverished* has been reduced to poverty: *an impoverished country. Poverty-stricken* means suffering from extreme poverty and therefore miserable: *poverty-stricken refugees. Destitute* means lacking any means of subsistence: *The fire left many tenants destitute.*

USAGE NOTE In informal speech *poor* is sometimes used as an adverb, as in *They never played poorer.* In formal usage *more poorly* would be required in this example.

poor box *n.* A box, as one in a church, for collecting alms.

poor boy also **po·boy** (pō′boi′) *n. Gulf Coast US* See **submarine 2.** See Regional Note at **submarine.** [Prob. < Fr. *pour bois*, for a drink. See POURBOIRE.]

poor farm *n.* A farm that houses, supports, and employs the poor at public expense.

poor·house (pōor′hous′) *n.* An establishment maintained at public expense as housing for the homeless.

poo·ri also **pu·ri** (pōor′ē) *n., pl.* **-ris** A puffy deep-fried bread of Pakistan and India. [Hindi *pūrī* < Skt. *pūraḥ*, cake. See pelə-¹ in App.]

poor law *n.* A law or system of laws providing for public relief and support of the poor.

poor·ly (pōor′lē) *adv.* In a poor manner. See Usage Note at **poor.**

❖ *adj. Chiefly Southern US* In poor health; ill: *feeling poorly.* See Usage Note at **bad¹.**

poor·mouth (pōor′mouth′, -mouth′) *v.* **-mouthed, -mouth·ing, -mouths** —*tr.* To speak ill of. —*intr.* To claim poverty as an excuse or a defense. ❖ *n.* An exaggerated assertion of poverty.

poor white *n.* A member of a class of low-income white farmers and laborers, esp. in the southern United States.

pop¹ (pŏp) *v.* **popped, pop·ping, pops** —*intr.* **1.** To make a pop. **2.** To burst open with a pop. **3.** To move quickly or unexpectedly; appear abruptly. **4.** To open wide suddenly. **5.** *Baseball* To hit a short high fly ball. **6.** To shoot a firearm, such as a pistol. —*tr.* **1.** To cause to make a sharp bursting sound. **2.** To cause to explode with a sharp bursting sound. **3.** To put or thrust suddenly or unexpectedly. **4a.** To discharge (a firearm). **b.** To fire at; shoot. **5.** To hit or strike. **6.** *Baseball* To hit (a ball) high in the air but not far. **7.** *Slang* To take (drugs), esp. orally. **b.** To have (a drink). ❖ *n.* **1.** A sudden sharp explosive sound. **2.** A shot with a firearm. **3.** *Chiefly Midwestern US* See **soft drink.** See Regional Note at **tonic. 4.** *Baseball* A pop fly. ❖ *adv.* **1.** With a popping sound. **2.** Abruptly or unexpectedly. —*phrasal verbs:* **pop in** (or **by**) *Informal* To visit briefly. **pop off** *Informal* **1.** To leave abruptly or hurriedly. **2.** To die suddenly. **3.** To speak thoughtlessly in a burst of anger. —*idioms:* **a pop** *Slang* Apiece; each. **pop the question** *Informal* To propose marriage. [ME *poppen* < *pop*, a blow, stroke, of imit. orig.]

pop² (pŏp) *n. Informal* Father. [Short for PAPA.]

pop³ (pŏp) *Informal adj.* **1.** Of or for the general public; popular or popularized: *pop culture.* **2.** Of, relating to, or specializing in popular music: *a pop singer.* **3.** Of or suggestive of pop art: *a pop style.* ❖ *n.* **1.** Popular music. **2.** Pop art.

POP *abbr.* **1.** point of purchase **2.** proof of purchase

pop. *abbr.* population

pop art or **Pop Art** *n.* A form of art that depicts everyday life and employs techniques of commercial art and popular illustration.

pop·corn (pŏp′kôrn′) *n.* **1a.** A variety of corn, *Zea mays everta,* having hard kernels that burst to form white, irregularly shaped puffs when heated. **b.** The edible popped kernels of this variety of corn. **2.** A small piece, as of polystyrene, used in quantity to protect items in shipping. [Contraction of *popped corn.*]

pope (pōp) *n.* **1.** often **Pope** *Roman Catholic Church* The bishop of Rome and head of the Roman Catholic Church on earth. **2.** *Eastern Orthodox Church* The patriarch of Alexandria. **3.** The Coptic patriarch of Alexandria. **4.** A person considered to have unquestioned authority. [ME < OE *pāpa* < LLat. < Lat., father (title of bishops) < Gk. *pappās*.]

Pope, Alexander 1688–1744. English poet whose works include *The Dunciad* (1728).

Pope, John 1822–92. Amer. Union general who was defeated at the Second Battle of Bull Run (1862).

pop·er·y (pō′pə-rē) *n. Offensive* The doctrines, practices, and rituals of the Roman Catholic Church.

pope's nose (pōps) *n. Informal* The tail of a cooked fowl.

pop·eyed (pŏp′īd′) *adj.* **1.** Having bulging eyes. **2.** Amazed; astonished: *popeyed with wonder.*

pop fly *n. Baseball* A short high fly ball.

pop·gun (pŏp′gŭn′) *n.* A toy gun that makes a popping noise.

pop·in·jay (pŏp′ĭn-jā′) *n.* A vain talkative person. [ME, parrot < OFr. *papegai* < Sp. *papagayo* or O Provençal *papagai,* both < Ar. *babḡā′, babaḡā′* < Pers. *babbaghā.*]

pop·ish (pō′pĭsh) *adj. Offensive* Of or relating to the Roman Catholic Church. —**pop′ish·ly** *adv.* —**pop′ish·ness** *n.*

pop·lar (pŏp′lər) *n.* **1a.** Any of several fast-growing deciduous trees of the genus *Populus,* having unisexual flowers borne in catkins. **b.** The wood of these trees. **2.** See **tulip tree.** [ME *popler* < OFr. *poplier* < *pouple* < Lat. *pōpulus.*]

pop·lin (pŏp′lĭn) *n.* A ribbed fabric of silk, rayon, wool, or cotton, used in making clothing and upholstery. [Obsolete Fr. *papeline,* perh. < Provençal *papalino,* fem. of *papalin,* papal (so called because it was first made at the papal town of Avignon) < Med.Lat. *pāpālis* < LLat. *pāpa,* pope. See POPE.]

pop·lit·e·al (pŏp-lĭt′ē-əl, pŏp′lĭ-tē′əl) *adj.* Of or relating to the hollow part of the leg behind the knee joint. [< NLat. *popliteus* < Lat. *poples, poplit-,* ham of the knee.]

Po·po·ca·té·petl (pō′pə-kăt′ə-pĕt′l, -pō-kä-tĕ′-) A volcano, 5,455.5 m (17,887 ft), of central Mexico W of Puebla.

Po·pol Vuh (pō-pōl′ vōo′) *n.* An epic describing the cosmogony, mythology, and history of the Quiché Maya of Guatemala. [Quiché Maya, Book of the Community: *popol,* together, common house (< *pop,* to gather, join) + *vuh,* paper, book.]

pop·o·ver (pŏp′ō′vər) *n.* A very light hollow muffin made with eggs, milk, and flour.

pop·pa (pä′pə) *n.* Variant of **papa.**

pop·per (pŏp′ər) *n.* **1.** One that pops. **2.** A container or pan for making popcorn. **3.** *Slang* An ampoule of amyl nitrite or butyl nitrite, used illicitly to induce euphoria and enhance sexual stimulation.

pop·pet (pŏp′ĭt) *n.* **1.** A poppet valve. **2.** *Nautical* **a.** A small wooden strip on a gunwale that forms or supports an oarlock. **b.** One of the beams of a launching cradle supporting a ship's hull. **3.** *Chiefly British* A darling. [ME *popet,* small child, doll, puppet. See PUPPET.]

pop art
Campbell's Soup I (Tomato),
1968, by Andy Warhol

poplar
balsam poplar
Populus balsamifera

ă	pat	oi	boy
ā	pay	ou	out
âr	care	ŏŏ	took
ä	father	ōō	boot
ĕ	pet	ŭ	cut
ē	be	ûr	urge
ĭ	pit	th	thin
ī	pie	*th*	this
îr	pier	hw	which
ŏ	pot	zh	vision
ō	toe	ə	about,
ô	paw		item

Stress marks:
′ (primary);
′ (secondary), as in
lexicon (lĕk′sĭ-kŏn′)

porcupine
common porcupine
Erethizon dorsatum

porcupine fish
Diodon hystrix

porringer

poppet valve *n.* An intake or exhaust valve, operated by springs and cams, that opens and closes by axial motion.

pop·ple¹ (pŏp′əl) *intr.v.* **-pled, -pling, -ples** To move in a tossing, bubbling, or rippling manner, as choppy water. ❖ *n.* **1.** Choppy water. **2.** The motion or sound of boiling liquid. [ME *poplen*, prob. of MDu. orig.]

pop·ple² (pŏp′əl) *n. Informal* A poplar. [ME *popel* (perh. < OE *popul*-) < Lat. *pōpulus*.]

pop·py (pŏp′ē) *n., pl.* **-pies 1.** Any of numerous plants of the genus *Papaver*, having nodding buds with four crumpled petals, showy red, orange, or white flowers, a milky juice, and capsules that dehisce through terminal pores. **2.** Any of several similar or related plants, such as the California poppy. **3.** An extract from poppy seedpods, used in medicine and narcotics. **4.** A vivid red to reddish orange. [ME *popi* < OE *popig*, prob. alteration of VLat. *papāvum*, alteration of Lat. *papāver*.]

pop·py·cock (pŏp′ē-kŏk′) *n.* Senseless talk; nonsense. [Du. dialectal *pappekak* : *pap*, pap (< MDu. *pappe*, perh. < Lat. *pappa*, food) + *kak*, dung (< *kakken*, to defecate < MDu. *kacken* < Lat. *cacāre*).]

Pop·si·cle (pŏp′sĭ-kəl, -sĭk′əl) A trademark used for a colored, flavored ice confection with one or two flat sticks for a handle.

pop-top (pŏp′tŏp′) *adj.* Having a tab that can be pulled up or off to make an opening in a container. —**pop′-top′** *n.*

pop·u·lace (pŏp′yə-lĭs) *n.* **1.** The general public; the masses. **2.** A population. [Fr. < Ital. *popolaccio*, rabble < *popolo*, the people < Lat. *populus*. See POPULAR.]

pop·u·lar (pŏp′yə-lər) *adj.* **1.** Widely liked or appreciated. **2.** Liked by acquaintances; sought after for company. **3.** Of, representing, or carried on by the people at large. **4.** Fit for, adapted to, or reflecting the taste of the people at large. **5.** Accepted by or prevalent among the people in general. **6.** Suited to or within the means of ordinary people. **7.** Originating among the people: *popular legend.* [ME < OFr. *populaire*, of the people, commonly known < OFr. *populaire*, of the people < Lat. *populāris* < *populus*, the people, of Etruscan orig.] —**pop′u·lar·ly** *adv.*

popular front *n.* A political coalition of leftist parties against fascism, such as that in European countries during the 1930s.

pop·u·lar·i·ty (pŏp′yə-lăr′ĭ-tē) *n.* The quality or state of being popular, esp. of being widely admired or sought after.

pop·u·lar·ize (pŏp′yə-lə-rīz′) *tr.v.* **-ized, -iz·ing, -iz·es 1.** To make popular: *popularized the hairstyle.* **2.** To present in a widely understandable or acceptable form. —**pop′u·lar·i·za′tion** (-lər-ĭ-zā′shən) *n.* —**pop′u·lar·iz′er** *n.*

pop·u·late (pŏp′yə-lāt′) *tr.v.* **-lat·ed, -lat·ing, -lates 1.** To supply with inhabitants, as by colonization; people. **2.** To live in; inhabit: *creatures that populate the ocean.* [Med.Lat. *populāre, populāt-* < Lat. *populus*, the people. See POPULAR.]

pop·u·la·tion (pŏp′yə-lā′shən) *n.* **1a.** All of the people inhabiting a specified area. **b.** The total number of such people. **2.** The total number of inhabitants constituting a particular race, class, or group in a specified area. **3.** The act or process of furnishing with inhabitants. **4.** *Ecology* All the organisms that constitute a specific group or occur in a specified habitat. **5.** *Statistics* The set of individuals, items, or data from which a statistical sample is taken.

population explosion *n.* The geometric expansion of a biological population, esp. the unchecked growth in human population resulting from a decrease in infant mortality and an increase in longevity.

pop·u·lism (pŏp′yə-lĭz′əm) *n.* **1a.** A political philosophy supporting the rights and power of the people in their struggle against the elite. **b.** The movement organized around this philosophy. **2. Populism** The philosophy of the Populist Party.

pop·u·list (pŏp′yə-lĭst) *n.* **1.** A supporter of the rights and power of the people. **2. Populist** A supporter of the Populist Party. ❖ *adj.* **1.** Of or relating to populism or its advocates. **2. Populist** Of or relating to the Populist Party.

Populist Party *n.* A US political party in the 1890s that advocated free silver and a graduated federal income tax.

pop·u·lous (pŏp′yə-ləs) *adj.* Containing many people or inhabitants. [ME < Lat. *populōsus* < *populus*, the people. See POPULAR.] —**pop′u·lous·ly** *adv.* —**pop′u·lous·ness** *n.*

pop-up (pŏp′ŭp′) *adj.* Rising to form a three-dimensional structure when a page is opened. ❖ *n.* **1.** A device or illustration that pops up. **2.** *Baseball* See **pop fly.**

por·bea·gle (pôr′bē′gəl) *n.* A mackerel shark (*Lamna nasus*) of temperate Atlantic waters. [Cornish *porbugel*.]

por·ce·lain (pôr′sə-lĭn, pôr′-, pôrs′lĭn, pōrs′-) *n.* **1.** A hard white translucent ceramic made by firing a pure clay and then glazing it with fusible materials; china. **2.** An object made of porcelain. [Fr. *porcelaine*, cowry shell, porcelain < OItal. *porcellana* < fem. of *porcellano*, of a young sow (< the shell's resemblance to a pig's back) < *porcella*, young sow, dim. of *porca* < Lat., fem. of *porcus*, pig. See porko- in App.] —**por′ce·la′ne·ous** (-lā′nē-əs) *adj.*

porcelain enamel *n.* A glass coating fired on metal.

porcelain flower *n.* See **hoya.**

porch (pôrch, pōrch) *n.* **1.** A covered platform, usu. having a separate roof, at an entrance to a building. **2.** An open or enclosed gallery or room attached to the outside of a building; a veranda.

3. *Obsolete* A portico or covered walk. [ME *porche* < OFr. *porticus*, portico < *porta*, gate. See per-² in App.]

por·cine (pôr′sīn′) *adj.* Of or resembling swine or a pig: *"a bald porcine old man"* (Vladimir Nabokov). [ME < OFr. *porcin* < Lat. *porcīnus* < *porcus*, pig. See porko- in App.]

por·ci·no (pôr-chē′nō) *n., pl.* **-ni** (-nē) A large edible mushroom (*Boletus edulis*) widely distributed in woodlands, having a thick rounded brown cap. [Ital., short for *fungo porcino*, porcine mushroom < Lat. *porcīnus*. See PORCINE.]

por·cu·pine (pôr′kyə-pīn′) *n.* Any of various rodents of the Old World family Hystricidae or the New World family Erethizontidae, having long sharp erectile quills interspersed with coarse hair. [ME *porke despine* < OFr. *porc espin* : Lat. *porcus*, pig; see porko- in App. + Lat. *spīna*, thorn, spine.]

porcupine fish *n.* Any of various tropical marine fishes of the family Diodontidae, having strong spines on the body.

Porcupine River A river rising in NW Yukon Terr., Canada, and flowing c. 721 km (448 mi) to the Yukon R. in NE AK.

pore¹ (pôr, pōr) *intr.v.* **pored, por·ing, pores 1.** To read or study carefully and attentively: *pored over the ads.* **2.** To gaze intently. **3.** To meditate deeply; ponder. [ME *pouren.*]

pore² (pôr, pōr) *n.* **1.** A minute opening in tissue, as in the skin of an animal, serving as an outlet for perspiration, or in a plant leaf or stem, serving as a means of absorption and transpiration. **2.** A space in rock, soil, or unconsolidated sediment that is not occupied by mineral matter and allows the passage or absorption of fluids: *pores of a rock.* [ME < OFr. < LLat. *porus*, passage < Gk. *poros*. See per-² in App.]

pore fungus *n.* Any of various basidiomycetous fungi of the families Boletaceae and Polyporaceae, whose basidia line the inside of tubes that lead to exterior pores.

por·gy (pôr′gē) *n., pl.* **porgy** or **-gies 1.** Any of various deep-bodied marine food fishes of the family Sparidae, esp. the common species *Pagrus pagrus* of Mediterranean and Atlantic waters. **2.** Any of several fishes similar to the porgy. [Alteration of Sp. and Port. *pargo*, both alteration of Lat. *phager*, a kind of fish < Gk. *phagros*, sea bream.]

po·rif·er·an (pə-rĭf′ər-ən) *n.* Any of various members of the phylum Porifera constituting the sponges. [< NLat. *Porifera*, phylum name : NLat. *porus*, pore (< Lat., passage; see PORE²) + Lat. *-fera*, neut. pl. of *-fer*, -fer.] —**po·rif′er·al, po·rif′er·an** *adj.*

po·rif·er·ous (pə-rĭf′ər-əs) *adj.* **1.** Having pores. **2.** Of or relating to the poriferans. [NLat. *porus*, pore; see PORIFERAN + -FEROUS.]

pork (pôrk, pōrk) *n.* **1.** The flesh of a pig or hog used as food. **2.** *Slang* Government funds, appointments, or benefits dispensed or enacted by politicians to gain favor with their constituents. ❖ *intr.v.* **porked, pork·ing, porks** *Slang* **1.** To eat ravenously; gorge oneself. Used with *out.* **2.** To become fat. Used with *out.* [ME < OFr. *porc*, pig < Lat. *porcus*. See porko- in App.]

pork barrel *n. Slang* A government project or appropriation that yields jobs or other benefits to a specific locale and patronage opportunities to its political representative. [< *pork barrel*, barrel for storing pork, supply of money.]

pork belly *n.* A side of fresh pork.

pork·er (pôr′kər, pōr′-) *n.* **1.** A fattened young pig. **2.** *Slang* A fat person.

pork·pie (pôrk′pī′, pōrk′-) *n.* A man's hat having a low flat crown and a flexible brim.

pork·y¹ (pôr′kē, pōr′-) *adj.* **-i·er, -i·est 1.** Of or like pork: *a porky flavor.* **2.** *Slang* Fat or corpulent. —**pork′i·ness** *n.*

pork·y² (pôr′kē, pōr′-) *n., pl.* **-kies** *Informal* A porcupine.

porn (pôrn) also **por·no** (pôr′nō) *Slang n.* Pornography. ❖ *adj.* Pornographic. —**porn′y** *adj.*

por·nog·ra·phy (pôr-nŏg′rə-fē) *n.* **1.** Sexually explicit pictures, writing, or other material whose primary purpose is to cause sexual arousal. **2.** The presentation or production of this material. [Fr. *pornographie* < *pornographe*, pornographer < L.Gk. *pornographos*, writing about prostitutes : *pornē*, prostitute; see per-⁵ in App. + *graphein*, to write; see -GRAPHY.] —**por·nog′ra·pher** *n.* —**por′no·graph′ic** (pôr′nə-grăf′ĭk) *adj.* —**por′no·graph′i·cal·ly** *adv.*

po·ros·i·ty (pə-rŏs′ĭ-tē, pô-) *n., pl.* **-ties 1.** The state or property of being porous. **2.** A structure or part that is porous. **3.** The ratio of the volume of all the pores in a material to the volume of the whole. [ME *porosite* < OFr. < Med.Lat. *porōsitās* < *porōsus*, porous. See POROUS.]

po·rous (pôr′əs, pōr′-) *adj.* **1.** Full of or having pores. **2.** Admitting the passage of gas or liquid through pores or interstices. **3.** Easily crossed or penetrated. [ME < OFr. *poreux, poros* < Med.Lat. *porōsus* < Lat. *porus*, passage. See PORE².] —**po′rous·ly** *adv.* —**po′rous·ness** *n.*

por·phyr·i·a (pôr-fîr′ē-ə) *n.* Any of several disorders of porphyrin metabolism, usu. hereditary, characterized by the presence of large amounts of porphyrins in the blood and urine. [NLat. : PORPHYR(IN) + -IA¹.]

por·phy·rin (pôr′fə-rĭn) *n.* Any of various nitrogen-containing organic compounds, derived from pyrrole and occurring in protoplasm. [Gk. *porphurā*, purple + -IN.]

por·phy·rit·ic (pôr′fə-rĭt′ĭk) also **por·phy·rit·i·cal** (-ĭ-kəl) *adj.* **1.** Containing relatively large isolated crystals in a mass of fine texture. **2.** Of or containing porphyry.

por•phy•roid (pôr′fə-roid′) *n.* Metamorphic rock having porphyritic texture.

por•phy•rop•sin (pôr′fə-rŏp′sĭn) *n.* A purple pigment similar to rhodopsin, found in the rods of the retinas of freshwater fishes and certain frogs. [Gk. *porphurā*, purple + OPSIN.]

por•phy•ry (pôr′fə-rē) *n., pl.* **-ries** Igneous rock having porphyritic texture. [ME *porphiri, porfurie* < OFr. *porfire* < Ital. *porfiro* < Med.Lat. *porphyrium* < Lat. *porphyrītēs* < Gk. *porphurītēs* < *porphurā*, purple (< its color).]

por•poise (pôr′pəs) *n., pl.* **porpoise** or **-pois•es 1.** Any of several gregarious toothed whales of the genus *Phocaena* and related genera of oceanic waters, having a blunt snout and a triangular dorsal fin. **2.** Any of several related mammals, such as the dolphin. [ME *porpeis* < OFr. (prob. transl. of a Gmc. compound meaning sea pig) : *porc*, pig (< Lat. *porcus*; see **porko-** in App.) + *peis*, fish (< Lat. *piscis*).]

por•rect (pə-rĕkt′, pô-) *adj. Zoology* Stretched out or forth; extended, esp. forward: *porrect mandibles.* [Lat. *porrēctus*, p. part. of *porrigere*, to stretch out : *por-*, forward, out; see **per**[1] in App. + *regere*, to direct, rule; see DIRECT.]

por•ridge (pôr′ĭj, pŏr′-) *n.* A soft food made by boiling oatmeal or another meal in water or milk. [Alteration of POTTAGE (influenced by obsolete *porray*, vegetable soup, ult. < Lat. *porrum*).] **—por′ridg•y** *adj.*

por•rin•ger (pôr′ĭn-jər, pŏr′-) *n.* A shallow cup or bowl with a handle. [ME, alteration of *potinger, potager* < OFr. *potager* < *potage*, soup. See POTTAGE.]

port[1] (pôrt, pōrt) *n.* **1a.** A place on a waterway with facilities for loading and unloading ships. **b.** A city or town on a waterway with such facilities. **c.** The waterfront district of a city. **2.** A place along a coast that gives ships and boats protection; a harbor. **3.** A port of entry. [ME < OE < Lat. *portus*. See **per-**[2] in App.]

port[2] (pôrt, pōrt) *n.* The left-hand side of a ship or aircraft facing forward. ❖ *adj.* Of, relating to, or on the port side. ❖ *tr. & intr.v.* **port•ed, port•ing, ports** To turn (a craft) or make a shift to the port side. [Prob. < *port side* < PORT[1].]

port[3] (pôrt, pōrt) *n.* **1.** *Nautical* **a.** An opening in a ship's side providing access to the interior. **b.** A porthole. **c.** *Archaic* A cover for a porthole. **2.** An opening, as in a cylinder or valve face, for the passage of steam or fluid. **3.** A hole in an armored vehicle or a fortified structure for viewing or for firing weapons. **4.** *Computer Science* **a.** An entrance to or exit for a data network. **b.** A connection point for a peripheral device. **5.** *Scots* A gateway or portal, as to a town. ❖ *tr.v.* **port•ed, port•ing, ports** *Computer Science* To modify (software) for use on a different machine or platform. [ME, gate, porthole < OFr. *porte*, gate < Lat. *porta*. See **per-**[2] in App.]

port[4] also **Port** (pôrt, pōrt) *n.* A rich sweet fortified wine. [After OPORTO.]

port[5] (pôrt, pōrt) *tr.v.* **port•ed, port•ing, ports** To hold or carry (a weapon) diagonally across the body, with the muzzle or blade near the left shoulder. ❖ *n.* **1.** The position of a weapon when ported. **2.** The manner in which one carries oneself; bearing. [Fr. *porter*, to carry < OFr. < Lat. *portāre*. See **per-**[2] in App.]

Port. *abbr.* **1.** Portugal **2.** Portuguese

por•ta•bel•la (pôr′tə-bĕl′ə, pōr′-) *n.* Variant of **portobello.**

por•ta•ble (pôr′tə-bəl, pōr′-) *adj.* **1.** Carried or moved with ease. **2.** Capable of being transferred from one employer to another: *portable insurance.* **3.** Of or being software that can run on two or more kinds of computers or with two or more kinds of operating systems. **4.** *Obsolete* Bearable; endurable. ❖ *n.* Something portable, such as a light typewriter. [ME < OFr. < LLat. *portābilis* < Lat. *portāre*, to carry. See **per-**[2] in App.] **—por′ta•bil′i•ty, por′ta•ble•ness** *n.* **—por′ta•bly** *adv.*

port•age (pôr′tĭj, pōr′-, pôr-täzh′) *n.* **1a.** The act or an instance of carrying. **b.** A charge for carrying. **2.** *Nautical* **a.** The carrying of boats and supplies overland between two waterways or around an obstacle to navigation. **b.** A track or route used for such carrying. ❖ *tr. & intr.v.* **-aged, -ag•ing, -ag•es** *Nautical* To transport or travel by portage. [ME < OFr. < *porter*, to carry < Lat. *portāre*. See **per-**[2] in App.]

por•tal (pôr′tl, pōr′-) *n.* **1.** A doorway, entrance, or gate, esp. a large and imposing one. **2.** A website considered as an entry point to other websites, often by being or providing access to a search engine. ❖ *adj. Anatomy* Of or relating to a point of entrance to an organ, esp. the transverse fissure of the liver, through which the blood vessels enter. [ME < OFr. < Med.Lat. *portāle*, city gate < neut. of *portālis*, of a gate < Lat. *porta*, gate; see **per-**[2] in App. Adj. < NLat. *porta (hepatis)*, transverse fissure (of the liver) < Lat., gate, perh. ult. transl. of Akkadian *bāb (ekalli)*, gate (of the palace), umbilical fissure of the liver (next to the transverse fissure).]

portal system *n.* A system of blood vessels that begins and ends in capillaries.

portal tomb *n.* A Neolithic tomb consisting of two or more upright stones with a capstone, believed to have been buried in earth except for a central opening.

por•tal-to-por•tal (pôr′tl-tə-pôr′tl, pōr′tl-tə-pōr′tl) *adj.* Of or based on the time a worker spends on the employer's property, calculated from arrival to departure.

portal vein *n.* A vein that conducts blood from the digestive organs, spleen, pancreas, and gallbladder to the liver.

por•ta•men•to (pôr′tə-mĕn′tō, pōr′-) *n., pl.* **-ti** (-tē) or **-tos** A smooth uninterrupted glide in passing from one tone to another, esp. with the voice or a bowed stringed instrument. [Ital. < *portare*, to carry < Lat. *portāre*. See **per-**[2] in App.]

por•ta•tive (pôr′tə-tĭv, pōr′-) *adj.* **1.** Portable. **2.** Capable of or used in carrying. [ME *portatif* < OFr. < Lat. *portāre*, to carry. See **per-**[2] in App.]

Port-au-Prince (pôrt′ō-prĭns′, pōrt′-, pôr-tō-prăɴs′) The cap. of Haiti, in the SW part on an arm of the Caribbean; founded by French sugar planters in 1749. Pop. 690,168.

port•cul•lis (pôrt-kŭl′ĭs, pōrt-) *n.* A grating of iron or wooden bars or slats, suspended in the gateway of a fortified place and lowered to block passage. [ME *port-colice* < OFr. *porte coleice*, sliding gate : *porte*, gate (< Lat. *porta*; see **per-**[2] in App.) + *coleice*, fem. of *coleis*, sliding (< VLat. **cōlāticius* < Lat. *cōlātus*, p. part. of *cōlāre*, to filter, strain < *cōlum*, sieve).]

port de bras (pôr′ də brä′) *n.* The technique or practice of positioning and moving the arms in ballet.

Port du Sa•lut (pôrt′ də să-lo͞o′, pōrt′, pôr′ dü să-lü′) *n.* Variant of **Port Salut.**

Porte (pôrt, pōrt) *n.* The government of the Ottoman Empire. [Fr., short for *la Sublime Porte*, the High Gate < OFr. *porte*, gate. See PORT[3].]

porte-co•chère or **porte-co•chere** (pôrt′kō-shâr′, pōrt′-) *n.* **1.** A carriage entrance leading through a building or wall into an inner courtyard. **2.** A roofed structure covering a driveway at the entrance of a building to provide shelter while entering or leaving a vehicle. [Fr. *porte cochère* : *porte*, door + *cochère*, for coaches.]

Port Elizabeth (pôrt, pōrt) A city of SE South Africa on an inlet of the Indian Ocean. Pop. 303,353.

por•tend (pôr-tĕnd′, pōr-) *tr.v.* **-tend•ed, -tend•ing, -tends 1.** To serve as an omen or a warning of; presage: *Clouds portend a storm.* **2.** To indicate by prediction; forecast. [ME *portenden* < Lat. *portendere*. See **ten-** in App.]

por•tent (pôr′tĕnt′, pōr′-) *n.* **1.** A prophecy of something important or calamitous; an omen. **2.** Prophetic or threatening significance. **3.** Something amazing or marvelous; a prodigy. [Lat. *portentum* < neut. p. part. of *portendere*, to portend. See PORTEND.]

por•ten•tous (pôr-tĕn′təs, pōr-) *adj.* **1.** Of the nature of or constituting a portent; foreboding. **2.** Full of unspecifiable significance; exciting wonder and awe. **3.** Marked by pompousness; pretentiously weighty. **—por•ten′tous•ly** *adv.* **—por•ten′tous•ness** *n.*

por•ter[1] (pôr′tər, pōr′-) *n.* **1.** A person employed to carry burdens, esp. an attendant who carries baggage at a hotel or transportation station. **2.** A railroad employee who waits on passengers in a sleeping car or parlor car. **3.** A maintenance worker for a building or institution. [ME *portour* < AN < LLat. *portātor* < Lat. *portāre*, to carry. See **per-**[2] in App.]

por•ter[2] (pôr′tər, pōr′-) *n. Chiefly British* One in charge of a gate or door. [ME < AN < LLat. *portārius* < Lat. *porta*, gate. See **per-**[2] in App.]

por•ter[3] (pôr′tər, pōr′-) *n.* A dark beer made from malt dried at a high temperature. [Short for *porter's ale.*]

Porter, Cole Albert 1891?–1964. Amer. composer and lyricist remembered for his witty scores.

Porter, Edwin Stanton 1869–1941. Amer. filmmaker whose works include the first edited film, *The Life of an American Fireman* (1903).

Porter, Katherine Anne 1890–1980. Amer. writer known for her short stories and her novel *Ship of Fools* (1962).

Porter, William Sydney Pen name O. Henry. 1862–1910. Amer. writer whose works include *Cabbages and Kings* (1904).

por•ter•age (pôr′tər-ĭj, pōr′-) *n.* **1.** The carrying of burdens or goods as done by porters. **2.** The charge for this activity.

por•ter•ess (pôr′tər-ĭs, pōr′-) *n.* Variant of **portress.**

por•ter•house (pôr′tər-hous′, pōr′-) *n.* **1.** A cut of beef from the thick end of the short loin, having a T-shaped bone and a sizable piece of tenderloin. **2.** *Archaic* An alehouse or chophouse.

port•fo•li•o (pôrt-fō′lē-ō′, pōrt-) *n., pl.* **-os 1a.** A portable case for holding material, such as photographs or drawings. **b.** The materials collected in such a case, esp. when representative of a person's work. **2.** The office or post of a cabinet member or minister of state. **3.** A group of investments held by an investor or financial institution. [Ital. *portafoglio* : *portare*, to carry (< Lat. *portāre*; see **per-**[2] in App.) + *foglio*, sheet (< Lat. *folium*, leaf; see **bhel-** in App.).]

port•hole (pôrt′hōl′, pōrt′-) *n.* **1.** *Nautical* A small, usu. circular window that can be opened in a ship's side. **2.** An opening in a fortified wall; an embrasure.

por•ti•co (pôr′tĭ-kō′, pōr′-) *n., pl.* **-coes** or **-cos** A porch or walkway with a roof supported by columns, often leading to the entrance of a building. [Ital. < Lat. *porticus* < *porta*, gate. See **per-**[2] in App.] **—por′ti•coed′** *adj.*

por•tière or **por•tiere** (pôr-tyâr′, pōr-) *n.* A heavy curtain hung across a doorway. [Fr., fem. of *portier*, porter < OFr. < LLat. *portārius* < Lat. *porta*, gate. See **per-**[2] in App.]

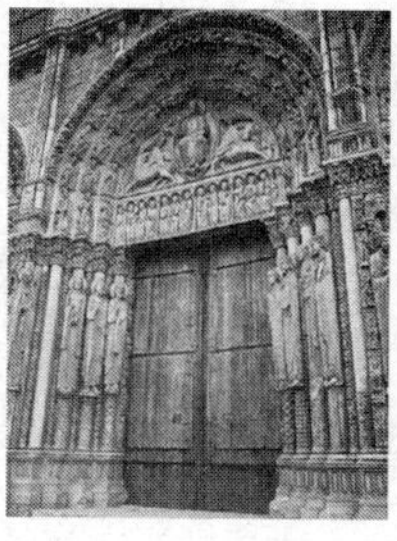

portal
central royal portal, Chartres Cathedral, France

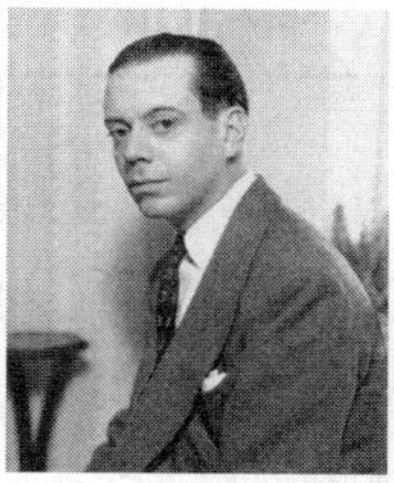

Cole Porter

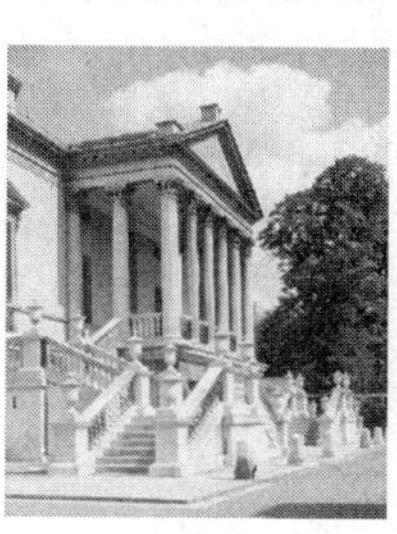

portico
Chiswick House, London; designed by Lord Burlington (1694–1753)

ă	pat	oi	boy
ā	pay	ou	out
âr	care	o͝o	took
ä	father	o͞o	boot
ĕ	pet	ŭ	cut
ē	be	ûr	urge
ĭ	pit	th	thin
ī	pie	*th*	this
îr	pier	hw	which
ŏ	pot	zh	vision
ō	toe	ə	about,
ô	paw		item

Stress marks:
′ (primary);
′ (secondary), as in
lexicon (lĕk′sĭ-kŏn′)

por·tion (pôr′shən, pōr′-) *n.* **1.** A section or quantity within a larger thing; a part of a whole. **2.** A part separated from a whole. **3.** A part allotted to a person or group, as: **a.** A helping of food. **b.** The part of an estate received by an heir. **c.** A woman's dowry. **4.** A person's lot or fate. ❖ *tr.v.* **-tioned, -tion·ing, -tions 1.** To divide into parts for distribution; parcel. **2.** To provide with a share, inheritance, or dowry. [ME < OFr. < Lat. *portiō, portiōn-.* See **perə-** in App.] —**por′tion·a·ble** *adj.* —**por′tion·er** *n.* —**por′tion·less** *adj.*

Port·land (pôrt′lənd, pōrt′-) **1.** A city of SW ME on an arm of the Gulf of Maine S of Lewiston; settled c. 1632. Pop. 64,249. **2.** A city of NW OR on the Willamette R.; founded 1845. Pop. 529,121. —**Port′land·er** *n.*

Portland cement or **portland cement** *n.* A hydraulic cement made by heating a limestone and clay mixture in a kiln and pulverizing the resulting material. [After *Portland,* an urban district of southern England.]

Port Lou·is (loo′ĭs, loo′ē, loo-ē′) The cap. of Mauritius, in the NW on the Indian Ocean; founded 1735. Pop. 136,812.

port·ly (pôrt′lē, pōrt′-) *adj.* **-li·er, -li·est 1.** Comfortably stout; corpulent. See Syns at **fat. 2.** *Archaic* Stately; majestic; imposing. [< PORT⁵.] —**port′li·ness** *n.*

port·man·teau (pôrt-măn′tō, pōrt-, pôrt′măn-tō′, pōrt′-) *n.,* *pl.* **-teaus** or **-teaux** (-tōz, -tōz′) A large leather suitcase with two hinged compartments. ❖ *adj.* General or generalized: *a portmanteau description.* [Fr. *portemanteau : porte* (< *porter,* to carry < OFr.; see PORT⁵) + *manteau,* cloak (< OFr. *mantel* < Lat. *mantellum*).]

portmanteau word *n.* A word formed by merging the sounds and meanings of two different words, as *chortle,* from *chuckle* and *snort.*

Port Mores·by (môrz′bē, mōrz′-) The cap. of Papua New Guinea, on SE New Guinea. Pop. 173,500.

Por·to or **Pôr·to** (pôr′tōō) See **Oporto.**

Pôrto A·le·gre (ə-lĕ′grə) A city of SE Brazil on a lagoon near the Atlantic Ocean; founded c. 1742. Pop. 1,263,239.

por·to·bel·lo (pôr′tə-bĕl′ō, pōr′-) or **por′ta·bel·la** (-bĕl′ə) or **por·to·bel·la** (-bĕl′ə) *n., pl.* **-los** or **-las** A mature, very large cremini mushroom. [?]

port of call *n., pl.* **ports of call** A port where ships dock to load or unload cargo, obtain supplies, or undergo repairs.

port of entry *n., pl.* **ports of entry** A place where travelers or goods may enter or leave a country under official supervision.

Port of Spain or **Port-of-Spain** (pôrt′əv-spän′, pōrt′-) The cap. of Trinidad and Tobago, on the NW coast of Trinidad on an arm of the Atlantic. Pop. 50,878.

Por·to-No·vo (pôr′tō-nō′vō, pōr′-) The cap. of Benin, in the SE part on an inlet of the Gulf of Guinea; settled as a slave-trading center in the 17th cent. Pop. 179,138.

Pôr·to Vel·ho (pôr′tōō vĕl′yōō) A city of NW Brazil on the Madeira R. near the Bolivian border. Pop. 286,471.

Port Phil·lip Bay (fĭl′əp) A large deep-water inlet of Bass Strait on the SE coast of Australia.

por·trait (pôr′trĭt, -trāt′, pōr′-) *n.* **1.** A likeness of a person, esp. of the face. **2.** A verbal picture or description, esp. of a person. **3.** The orientation of a page such that the longer side runs from top to bottom. [Fr. < OFr., image < p. part. of *portraire,* to portray. See PORTRAY.]

por·trait·ist (pôr′trə-tĭst, pōr-) *n.* A person who makes portraits, esp. a painter or photographer.

por·trai·ture (pôr′trĭ-chōōr′, pōr′-) *n.* **1.** The art or practice of making portraits. **2.** A portrait. **3.** Portraits as a group.

por·tray (pôr-trā′, pōr-) *tr.v.* **-trayed, -tray·ing, -trays 1.** To depict or represent pictorially; make a picture of. **2.** To depict or describe in words. **3.** To represent dramatically, as on the stage. [ME *portraien* < OFr. *portraire < por-,* forth (< Lat. *prō-,* forth; see PRO-¹) + *traire,* to draw (< Lat. *trahere,* to drag).] —**por·tray′a·ble** *adj.* —**por·tray′er** *n.*

por·tray·al (pôr-trā′əl, pōr-) *n.* **1.** The act or process of depicting or portraying. **2.** A representation or description.

por·tress (pôr′trĭs, pōr′-) also **por·ter·ess** (-tər-ĭs) *n.* A woman doorkeeper or porter, esp. in a convent.

Port Royal See **Annapolis Royal.**

Port Sa·id (sä-ēd′) A city of NE Egypt on the Mediterranean Sea at the N entrance to the Suez Canal; founded by the builders of the canal in 1859. Pop. 460,000.

Port Sa·lut (pôr′ sä-lōō′, -lü′) also **Port du Sa·lut** (pôr′ də sä-lōō′, pôrt′, pôr dü sä-lü′) *n.* A semihard fermented cheese. [After Notre Dame de *Port-du-Salut,* a Trappist abbey in northwest France.]

port·side (pôrt′sīd′, pōrt′-) *adv. & adj.* **1.** On a port waterfront. **2.** *Nautical* On the port side of a ship or boat.

Ports·mouth (pôrt′sməth, pōrt′-) **1.** A borough of S England on the English Channel opposite the Isle of Wight; chartered 1194. Pop. 187,900. **2.** An independent city of SE VA opposite Norfolk. Pop. 100,565.

Port Stanley (pôrt, pōrt) See **Stanley.**

Port Sudan A city of NE Sudan on the Red Sea NE of Khartoum; est. 1905. Pop. 305,385.

Por·tu·gal (pôr′chə-gəl, pōr′-) A country of SW Europe on the W Iberian Peninsula, including the Madeira Is. and the Azores in

Portugal

the N Atlantic Ocean; an independent kingdom after 1143. Cap. Lisbon. Pop. 9,830,000.

Por·tu·guese (pôr′chə-gēz′, -gēs′, pôr′-) *adj.* Of or relating to Portugal or its people, language, or culture. ❖ *n., pl.* **Portuguese 1a.** A native or inhabitant of Portugal. **b.** A person of Portuguese descent. **2.** The Romance language of Portugal and Brazil. [Port. *português* < VLat. **portugalēnsis,* ult. < LLat. *Portus Cale,* the ancient port of Gaya (Oporto).]

Portuguese man-of-war *n.* A complex colonial siphonophore of the genus *Physalia* of warm seas, having a broad saillike float from which hang numerous long stinging tentacles.

por·tu·lac·a (pôr′chə-lăk′ə, pōr′-) *n.* Any of various fleshy plants of the genus *Portulaca,* esp. *P. grandiflora* of South America, having colorful flowers that open in sunlight. [ME < Lat. *portulāca,* purslane < *portula,* dim. of *porta,* gate (< the gatelike covering of the seed capsule). See **per-²** in App.]

Port-Vi·la (pôrt′vē′lə, pōrt′-, pôr-vē-lä′) or **Vi·la** (vē′lə, vē-lä′) The cap. of Vanuatu, in the SW Pacific. Pop. 13,067.

po·sa·da (pō-sä′də, -dä) *n.* A Christmas festival originating in Latin America that dramatizes Joseph and Mary's search for lodging. [Am.Sp. < Sp., lodging < *posar,* to lodge < LLat. *pausāre,* to rest < Lat. *pausa,* pause. See PAUSE.]

pose¹ (pōz) *v.* **posed, pos·ing, pos·es** —*intr.* **1.** To assume or hold a particular position or posture, as for a portrait. **2.** To affect a particular mental attitude. **3.** To represent oneself falsely; pretend to be other than what one is. —*tr.* **1.** To place (a model, for example) in a specific position. **2.** To set forth in words; propound: *pose a question.* **3.** To put forward; present: *pose a threat.* ❖ *n.* **1.** A bodily attitude or position, esp. one assumed for a portrait. **2.** A studied attitude assumed for effect. [ME *posen,* to place < OFr. *poser* < VLat. **pausāre* < LLat. *pausāre,* to rest < Lat. *pausa,* pause. See PAUSE.] —**pos′a·ble** *adj.*

pose² (pōz) *tr.v.* **posed, pos·ing, pos·es** To puzzle, confuse, or baffle. [Short for *appose,* to examine closely (< ME *apposen,* alteration of *opposen;* see OPPOSE) and < Fr. *poser,* to assume (obsolete) (< OFr.; see POSE¹).]

Po·sei·don (pō-sīd′n, pə-) *n. Greek Mythology* The brother of Zeus and god of the waters, earthquakes, and horses.

pos·er¹ (pō′zər) *n.* **1.** One who poses. **2.** A poseur.

pos·er² (pō′zər) *n.* A baffling question or problem.

po·seur (pō-zœr′, pō′zər) *n.* One who affects a particular attribute, attitude, or identity to impress or influence others. [Fr. < *poser,* to pose < OFr. See POSE¹.]

posh (pŏsh) *adj.* **posh·er, posh·est** Smart and fashionable. [Perh. *posh,* halfpenny, money, dandy < Romany *pǎsh.*] —**posh′ly** *adv.* —**posh′ness** *n.*

pos·it (pŏz′ĭt) *tr.v.* **-it·ed, -it·ing, -its 1.** To assume the existence of; postulate. See Syns at **presume. 2.** To put forward, as for study; suggest. **3.** To place firmly in position. [< Lat. *positus,* p. part. of *pōnere,* to place. See POSITION.]

po·si·tion (pə-zĭsh′ən) *n.* **1.** A place or location. **2a.** The right or appropriate place. **b.** An area occupied by members of a force for a strategic purpose. **3a.** The way in which something is placed: *the position of the clock's hands.* **b.** The arrangement of body parts; posture: *a standing position.* **4.** An advantageous place or location: *jockeys maneuvering for position.* **5.** A situation relative to the surrounding circumstances: *in a position to bargain.* **6.** A point of view or attitude on a certain question: *the mayor's position on taxes.* **7.** Social standing or status; rank. **8.** A post of employment; a job. **9a.** *Sports* The area for which a particular player is responsible. **b.** *Games* The arrangement of the pieces or cards at any particular time in a game such as chess or bridge. **10a.** The act or process of positing. **b.** A principle or proposition posited. **11a.** A commitment to buy or sell a given amount of securities or commodities. **b.** The amount of securities or commodities held by a person, firm, or institution. **c.** The ownership status of a person's or an institution's investments. ❖ *tr.v.* **-tioned, -tion·ing, -tions 1.** To put in place or position. **2.** To determine the position of; locate. [ME *posicioun* < OFr. *posicion* < Lat. *positiō, positiōn-* < *positus,* p. part. of *pōnere,* to place. See apo- in App.] —**po·si′tion·al** *adj.* —**po·si′tion·al·ly** *adv.* —**po·si′tion·er** *n.*

positional notation *n.* A system of writing numbers in which the value of a digit depends on its position.

position paper *n.* **1.** A detailed policy report that usu. explains, justifies, or recommends a particular course of action. **2.** See **aide-mémoire** 1.

pos·i·tive (pŏz′ĭ-tĭv) *adj.* **1.** Marked by or displaying certainty, acceptance, or affirmation: *a positive answer; positive criticism.* **2.** Measured or moving forward or in a direction of increase or progress. **3.** Explicitly or openly expressed or laid down: *a positive demand.* **4.** Admitting of no doubt; irrefutable: *positive proof.* **5a.** Very sure; confident: *I'm positive she's right.* **b.** Overconfident; dogmatic. **6.** Formally or arbitrarily determined; prescribed. **7.** Concerned with practical rather than theoretical matters. **8.** Composed of or marked by the presence of particular qualities or attributes. **9.** *Philosophy* **a.** Of or relating to positivism. **b.** Of or relating to laws imposed by human authority rather than by nature or reason alone. **c.** Of or relating to religion based on revelation rather than on nature or reason alone. **10.** *Informal* Utter; absolute: *a positive darling.* **11.** *Mathematics* **a.** Relating to or being a quantity greater than zero. **b.** Relating to or being the sign

(+). **c.** Relating to or being a quantity, number, angle, or direction opposite to another designated as negative. **12.** *Physics* Relating to or being an electric charge of a sign opposite to that of an electron. **13.** *Medicine* Indicating the presence of a particular disease, condition, or organism: *positive test results.* **14.** *Biology* Indicating or marked by response or motion toward the source of a stimulus, such as light. **15.** Having the areas of light and dark in their original and normal relationship, as in a photographic print made from a negative. **16.** *Grammar* Of, relating to, or being the simple uncompared degree of an adjective or adverb, as opposed to either the comparative or superlative. **17.** Driven by or generating power directly through intermediate machine parts having little or no play: *positive drive.* ❖ *n.* **1.** An affirmative element or characteristic. **2.** *Mathematics* A quantity greater than zero. **3.** *Physics* A positive electric charge. **4.** A photographic image in which the lights and darks appear as in nature. **5.** *Grammar* **a.** The uncompared degree of an adjective or adverb. **b.** A word in this degree. **6.** *Music* A division of some pipe organs, similar in sound to the great but smaller and less powerful. [ME, having a specified quality < OFr. *positif* < Lat. *positīvus*, formally laid down < *positus*, p. part. of *pōnere*, to place. See **apo-** in App.] —**pos′i·tive·ly** *adv.* —**pos′i·tive·ness, pos′i·tiv′i·ty** *n.*

pos·i·tiv·ism (pŏz′ĭ-tĭ-vĭz′əm) *n.* **1.** *Philosophy* **a.** A doctrine contending that sense perceptions are the only admissible basis of human knowledge and precise thought. **b.** The application of this doctrine in logic, epistemology, and ethics. **c.** The system of Auguste Comte designed to supersede theology and metaphysics and depending on a hierarchy of the sciences, beginning with mathematics and culminating in sociology. **d.** Any of several doctrines or viewpoints that stress attention to actual practice over consideration of what is ideal. **2.** The state or quality of being positive. —**pos′i·tiv·ist** *n.* —**pos′i·tiv·is′tic** *adj.* —**pos′i·tiv·ist·ly** *adv.*

pos·i·tron (pŏz′ĭ-trŏn′) *n.* An elementary particle having the same mass and magnitude of charge as an electron but exhibiting a positive charge; the antiparticle of the electron.

positron emission tomography *n.* Tomography in which a computer-generated image of a biological activity within the body is produced through the detection of gamma rays that are emitted when introduced radionuclides decay and release positrons.

pos·i·tro·ni·um (pŏz′ĭ-trō′nē-əm) *n.* A short-lived association of an electron and a positron bound together in a configuration resembling the hydrogen atom.

po·so·le (pə-zō′lā, -sō′-) or **po·zo·le** (-zō′-) *n.* **1.** Kernels of corn that have been soaked in lime water, hulled, and dried. **2.** A stew or soup made with posole, pork, chili, and other seasonings. [Am.Sp. *pozole* < Nahuatl *pozolli*.]

po·sol·o·gy (pə-sŏl′ə-jē, pō-) *n.* The study of the dosages of medicines and drugs. [Gk. *posos,* what quantity + –LOGY.]

poss. *abbr.* possessive

pos·se (pŏs′ē) *n.* **1.** A group of people summoned by a sheriff to aid in law enforcement. **2.** A search party. **3.** *Slang* A group of friends or associates. [Short for Med.Lat. *posse comitātūs* : *posse,* power, body of men (< Lat., to be able; see POTENT) + *comitātūs,* genitive of *comitātus,* county.]

pos·sess (pə-zĕs′) *tr.v.* **-sessed, -sess·ing, -sess·es 1.** To have as property; own. **2.** To have as a quality, characteristic, or other attribute. **3.** To acquire command of or have knowledge of. **4a.** To gain or exert influence or control over; dominate. **b.** To control or maintain (one's nature) in a particular condition. **5.** To cause to own, hold, or be proficient in something, such as property or knowledge. **6.** To cause to be influenced or controlled, as by an idea or emotion. **7.** *Obsolete* To gain or seize. [ME *possessen* < OFr. *possesser* < Lat. *possidēre, possess-* : *pos-,* as master; see **poti-** full in App. + *sedēre,* to sit; see **sed-** in App.] —**pos·ses′sor** *n.*

pos·sessed (pə-zĕst′) *adj.* **1.** Owning or mastering something. Used with *of.* **2.** Controlled by or as if by a spirit or other force; obsessed. **3.** Calm; collected.

pos·ses·sion (pə-zĕsh′ən) *n.* **1a.** The act or fact of possessing. **b.** The state of being possessed. **2.** Something owned or possessed. **3. possessions** Wealth or property. **4.** *Law* Actual holding or occupancy with or without rightful ownership. **5.** A territory subject to foreign control. **6.** Self-control. **7.** The state of being dominated by or as if by evil spirits or an obsession. **8.** *Sports* **a.** Physical control of the ball or puck by a player or team. **b.** The condition of being on offense. —**pos·ses′sion·al** *adj.*

pos·ses·sive (pə-zĕs′ĭv) *adj.* **1.** Of or relating to ownership or possession. **2.** Having or manifesting a desire to control or dominate: *a possessive parent.* **3.** *Grammar* Of, relating to, or being a noun or pronoun case that indicates possession. ❖ *n. Grammar* **1.** The possessive case. **2.** A possessive form or construction. —**pos·ses′sive·ly** *adv.* —**pos·ses′sive·ness** *n.*

pos·ses·so·ry (pə-zĕs′ə-rē) *adj.* **1.** Of, relating to, or having possession. **2.** *Law* Depending on or arising from possession.

pos·set (pŏs′ĭt) *n.* A spiced drink of hot sweetened milk curdled with wine or ale. [ME *poshet, possot* : perh. OFr. **posce* (Lat. *pōsca,* drink of vinegar and water < *potāre,* to drink; see POTABLE + Lat. *ēsca,* food < *edere,* to eat; see EDIBLE) + ME *hot*; see HOT.]

pos·si·bil·i·ty (pŏs′ə-bĭl′ĭ-tē) *n., pl.* **-ties 1.** The fact or state of being possible. **2.** Something that is possible. **3. possibilities** Potentiality for favorable or interesting results.

pos·si·ble (pŏs′ə-bəl) *adj.* **1.** Capable of happening, existing, or being true without contradicting facts, laws, or circumstances. **2.** Capable of occurring or being done without offense to character, nature, or custom. **3.** Capable of favorable development; potential: *a possible building site.* **4.** Of uncertain likelihood. [ME < OFr. < Lat. *possibilis* < *posse,* to be able. See **poti-** in App.] —**pos′si·bly** *adv.*

pos·sum (pŏs′əm) *n. Chiefly Southern US* An opossum.

post¹ (pōst) *n.* **1.** A long piece of wood or other material set upright into the ground to serve as a marker or support. **2.** A similar vertical support or structure, as: **a.** A support for a beam in the framework of a building. **b.** A terminal of a battery. **3.** *Sports* A goal post. **4.** The starting point at a racetrack. **5.** An electronic message sent to and displayed on an online forum. **6.** The part of a stud earring that passes through the ear. ❖ *tr.v.* **post·ed, post·ing, posts 1a.** To display (an announcement) in a place of public view. **b.** To cover (a wall, for example) with posters. **2.** To announce by or as if by posters. **3.** To make (an electronic message) available by sending it to an online forum. **4.** To put up signs on (property) warning against trespassing. **5.** To denounce publicly. **6.** To publish (a name) on a list. **7.** *Games* To gain (points or a point) in a game or contest; score. [ME < OE < Lat. *postis.* See **stā-** in App.]

post² (pōst) *n.* **1.** A military base. **2.** A local organization of military veterans. **3.** Either of two bugle calls sounded as a tattoo in the British Army. **4.** An assigned position or station, as of a guard or sentry. **5.** A position of employment, esp. an appointed public office. **6.** *Basketball* A position usu. taken by the center, near either the basket or the foul line, serving as the focus of the team's offense. **7.** A place to which someone is assigned for duty. **8.** A trading post. ❖ *tr.v.* **post·ed, post·ing, posts 1.** To assign to a specific position or station: *post a sentry at the gate.* **2.** To appoint to a naval or military command. **3.** To put forward; present: *post bail.* [Fr. *poste* < Ital. *posto* < OItal. < VLat. **postum* < Lat. *positum,* neut. p. part. of *pōnere,* to place. See **apo-** in App.]

post³ (pōst) *n.* **1a.** A delivery of mail. **b.** The mail delivered. **2.** *Chiefly British* **a.** A governmental system for transporting and delivering the mail. **b.** A post office. **3a.** *Archaic* One of a series of relay stations along a fixed route, furnishing fresh riders and horses for the delivery of mail on horseback. **b.** *Obsolete* A rider on such a mail route; a courier. ❖ *v.* **post·ed, post·ing, posts —tr. 1.** To mail (a letter or package). **2.** To send by mail in a system of relays on horseback. **3.** To inform of the latest news: *Keep us posted.* **4a.** To transfer (an item) to a ledger in bookkeeping. **b.** To make the necessary entries in (a ledger). **5.** *Computer Science* To enter (a unit of information) on a record or into a section of storage. —*intr.* **1.** To travel in stages or relays. **2.** To travel with speed or in haste. **3.** To bob up and down in the saddle in rhythm with a horse's trotting gait. ❖ *adv.* **1.** By mail. **2.** With great speed; rapidly. **3.** By post horse. [Fr. *poste* < OFr., relay station for horses < OItal. *posta* < VLat. **posta,* station < Lat. *posita,* fem. p. part. of *pōnere,* to place. See **apo-** in App.]

Post, Emily Price 1872–1960. Amer. etiquette authority who wrote *Etiquette: The Blue Book of Social Usage* (1922).

Post, Wiley 1899–1935. Amer. aviator who made the first solo flight around the world (1933).

post– *pref.* **1.** After; later: *postdate.* **2.** Behind; posterior to: *postaxial.* [Lat. < *post,* behind, after. See **apo-** in App.]

post·age (pō′stĭj) *n.* **1.** The charge for mailing an item. **2.** The stamps, labels, or printing placed on an item to be mailed as evidence of payment of this charge.

postage meter *n.* A machine used in bulk mailing to print the correct amount of postage for each piece of mail.

postage stamp *n.* A small, usu. adhesive label issued by a government and sold in various denominations to be affixed to items of mail as evidence of the payment of postage.

post·al (pō′stəl) *adj.* Of or relating to a post office or mail service. —*idiom:* **go postal** *Slang* To become extremely angry or deranged, esp. in an outburst of violence. —**post′al·ly** *adv.*

postal card *n.* A plain card printed with the image of a postage stamp, issued by a government and used for sending messages.

postal order *n. Chiefly British* A money order.

postal service *n.* See **post office** 1.

post·ax·i·al (pōst-ăk′sē-əl) *adj.* Located behind an axis of the body, as the lateral aspect of the lower leg or the medial aspect of the upper arm. —**post·ax′i·al·ly** *adv.*

post·bel·lum (pōst-bĕl′əm) *adj.* Of the period after a war, esp.

the US Civil War. [Lat. *post*, after + *bellum*, war.]

post·box (pōst′bŏks′) *n.* See **mailbox** 1.

post card also **post·card** (pōst′kärd′) *n.* **1.** A commercially printed card with space on one side for an address and a postage stamp, used for sending messages. **2.** See **postal card.**

post chaise *n.* A closed four-wheeled horse-drawn carriage, formerly used to transport mail and passengers.

post·con·sum·er (pōst′kən-sōō′mər) *adj.* Of or relating to products that have been purchased and recycled by consumers.

post·cra·ni·al (pōst-krā′nē-əl) *adj.* **1.** Situated behind the cranium. **2.** Consisting of the parts or structures behind the cranium. —**post′cra′ni·al·ly** *adv.*

post·date (pōst-dāt′, pōst′-) *tr.v.* **-dat·ed, -dat·ing, -dates 1.** To put a date on (a check, for example) that is later than the actual date. **2.** To occur later than; follow in time.

post·di·lu·vi·an (pōst′dĭ-lōō′vē-ən) also **post·di·lu·vi·al** (-əl) *Bible adj.* Existing or occurring after the Flood. ❖ *n.* A person or thing living after the Flood. [POST- + Lat. *dīluvium*, flood; see DILUVIAL + -AN¹.]

post·doc (pōst′dŏk′) *Informal adj.* Postdoctoral. ❖ *n.* **1.** A postdoctoral program of study. **2.** A grant or award funding postdoctoral study or research. **3.** A postdoctoral scholar or researcher.

post·doc·tor·al (pōst-dŏk′tər-əl) also **post·doc·tor·ate** (-ĭt) *adj.* Of, relating to, or engaged in academic study beyond the level of a doctoral degree.

post·er¹ (pō′stər) *n.* **1a.** A large, usu. printed placard, bill, or announcement, often illustrated, that advertises or publicizes something. **b.** An artistic work, often a reproduction, printed on a large sheet of paper. **2.** One that posts bills or notices.

post·er² (pō′stər) *n. Archaic* One that travels rapidly.

poster boy *n.* A male poster child.

poster child *n.* **1.** A child who appears on a poster as a member of a group benefited by a charitable organization. **2.** A person who is a prominent example or type of something.

poster color *n.* See **tempera** 1.

poster girl *n.* A female poster child.

poste res·tante (pōst′ rĕ-stänt′) *n.* A notation written on a letter indicating that the letter should be held at the post office until claimed by the addressee. [Fr. : *poste*, mail + *restante*, fem. pr. part. of *rester*, to remain.]

pos·te·ri·or (pŏ-stîr′ē-ər, pō-) *adj.* **1.** Located behind a part or toward the rear of a structure. **2.** Relating to the caudal end of the body in quadrupeds or the dorsal side in humans and other primates. **3.** *Botany* Next to or facing the main stem or axis. **4.** Coming later in order; following. **5.** Following in time; subsequent. ❖ *n.* The buttocks. [Lat., comp. of *posterus*, coming after < *post*, afterward. See APO- in App.] —**pos·te′ri·or·ly** *adv.*

pos·te·ri·or·i·ty (pŏ-stîr′ē-ôr′ĭ-tē, -ŏr′-, pō-) *n.* The condition of being posterior in location or time.

pos·ter·i·ty (pŏ-stĕr′ĭ-tē) *n.* **1.** Future generations. **2.** All of a person's descendants. [ME *posterite* < OFr. < Lat. *posteritās* < *posterus*, coming after. See POSTERIOR.]

pos·tern (pō′stərn, pŏs′tərn) *n.* A small rear gate, esp. one in a fort or castle. ❖ *adj.* Situated in the back or at the side. [ME *posterne* < OFr., alteration of *posterle* < LLat. *posterula*, dim. of Lat. *posterus*, behind. See POSTERIOR.]

poster paint *n.* See **tempera** 1.

Post Exchange A service mark used for a store on a military base that sells goods to military personnel and their families or to authorized civilians.

post·ex·il·ic (pōst′ĕg-zĭl′ĭk, -ĕk-sĭl′-) also **post·ex·il·i·an** (-ĕg-zĭl′ē-ən, -zĭl′yən, -ĕk-sĭl′ē-ən, -sĭl′yən) *adj.* Of or relating to the period of Jewish history following the Babylonian captivity (after 586 B.C.).

post·fix (pōst-fĭks′) *tr.v.* **-fixed, -fix·ing, -fix·es** To suffix. ❖ *n.* (pōst′fĭks′) A suffix. —**post·fix′al, post·fix′i·al** *adj.*

post·fron·tal (pōst-frŭn′tl) *adj.* **1.** At the back of the frontal bone; behind the forehead: *a postfrontal suture.* **2.** Toward the rear of the frontal lobe.

post·gan·gli·on·ic (pōst′găng-glē-ŏn′ĭk) *adj.* Posterior or distal to a ganglion.

post·grad·u·ate (pōst-grăj′ōō-ĭt, -āt′) *adj.* Of, relating to, or pursuing advanced study after graduation from high school or college. ❖ *n.* One who is engaged in postgraduate study.

post·haste (pōst′hāst′) *adv.* With great speed; rapidly. ❖ *n. Archaic* Great speed; rapidity. [< the phrase *haste, post, haste*, a direction on letters.]

post hoc (hŏk, hōk) *adv. & adj.* In or of the form of an argument in which one event is asserted to have caused a later event simply because it happened earlier. [Lat., short for *post hoc, ergō propter hoc*, after this, therefore because of this : *post*, after + *hoc*, neut. of *hic*, this.]

post·hole (pōst′hōl′) *n.* A hole dug in the ground to hold a fence post.

post·hu·mous (pŏs′chə-məs) *adj.* **1.** Occurring or continuing after one's death. **2.** Published after the writer's death. **3.** Born after the death of the father: *a posthumous child.* [ME *posthumus* < LLat., alteration (perh. influenced by Lat. *humus*, earth, or *humāre*, to bury) of *postumus*, coming after; see POSTERIOR.] —**post′hu·mous·ly** *adv.* —**post′hu·mous·ness** *n.*

post·hyp·not·ic suggestion (pōst′hĭp-nŏt′ĭk) *n.* A sugges-

postimpressionism
Vahine no te tiare, 1891, by
Paul Gauguin

tion made to a hypnotized person that specifies an action to be performed after awakening, often in response to a cue.

pos·tiche (pŏ-stēsh′) *n.* **1.** Something false; a sham. **2.** A small hairpiece; a toupee. [Fr. < Ital. *posticcio* < *posto*, added (< Lat. *positus*, p. part. of *pōnere*, to place) or < VLat. *appostīcius* (alteration of Lat. *appositus*, p. part. of *appōnere*, to place by, to add : *ad-*, ad- + *pōnere*, to place; see APO- in App.).]

pos·til·ion also **pos·til·lion** (pō-stĭl′yən, pŏ-) *n.* One who rides the near horse of the leaders to guide the horses drawing a coach. [Fr. *postillon* < Ital. *postiglione* < *posta*, mail < OItal., mail station. See POST³.]

post·im·pres·sion·ism (pōst′ĭm-prĕsh′ə-nĭz′əm) *n.* A school of painting in France in the late 19th century that rejected the objective naturalism of impressionism and used form and color in more personally expressive ways. —**post′im·pres′sion·ist** *adj. & n.* —**post′im·pres′sion·is′tic** *adj.*

post·in·dus·tri·al (pōst′ĭn-dŭs′trē-əl) *adj.* Of or relating to an economic period in which manufacturing lessens in importance in relation to services, information, and research.

Post-It (pōst′ĭt′) A trademark for a slip of notepaper with an adhesive edge that allows it to be attached and removed from a document without causing damage.

post·lude (pōst′lōōd′) *n.* **1.** *Music* **a.** An organ voluntary played at the end of a church service. **b.** A concluding piece. **2.** A final chapter or phase. [POST- + (PRE)LUDE.]

post·man (pōst′mən) *n.* See **mailman.**

post·mark (pōst′märk′) *n.* An official mark printed over a postage stamp, esp. one that cancels the stamp and records the date and place of mailing. ❖ *tr.v.* **-marked, -mark·ing, -marks** To stamp with such a mark.

post·mas·ter (pōst′măs′tər) *n.* A man in charge of the operations of a local post office. —**post′mas′ter·ship′** *n.*

postmaster general *n., pl.* **postmasters general** The executive head of a national postal service.

post·me·rid·i·an (pōst′mə-rĭd′ē-ən) *adj.* Of, relating to, or taking place in the afternoon.

post me·rid·i·em (mə-rĭd′ē-əm) *adv. & adj.* After noon. Used chiefly in abbreviated form to tell time: *10:30 P.M.* See Usage Note at **A.M.** [Lat. *post merīdiem* : *post*, after + *merīdiem*, accusative of *merīdiēs*, midday.]

post·mil·le·nar·i·an (pōst′mĭl-ə-nâr′ē-ən) *adj.* Of or relating to postmillennialism. ❖ *n.* One who believes in postmillennialism.

post·mil·le·nar·i·an·ism (pōst′mĭl-ə-nâr′ē-ə-nĭz′əm) *n.* Postmillennialism.

post·mil·len·ni·al (pōst′mə-lĕn′ē-əl) also **post·mil·len·ni·an** (-ən) *adj.* Happening or existing after the millennium.

post·mil·len·ni·al·ism (pōst′mə-lĕn′ē-ə-lĭz′əm) *n.* The doctrine that Jesus's Second Coming will follow the millennium. —**post′mil·len′ni·al·ist** *n.*

post·mis·tress (pōst′mĭs′trĭs) *n.* A woman in charge of the operations of a local post office.

post·mod·ern (pōst-mŏd′ərn) *adj.* Of or relating to art, architecture, or literature that reacts against earlier modernist principles, as by using traditional, classical, or extreme modernist styles or practices. —**post·mod′ern·ism** *n.* —**post·mod′ern·ist** *adj. & n.*

post·mor·tem (pōst-môr′təm) *adj.* **1.** Occurring or done after death. **2.** Of or relating to a medical examination of a dead body. ❖ *n.* **1.** See **autopsy** 1. **2.** *Informal* An analysis or review of a finished event. [Lat. *post mortem* : *post*, afterward; see POST- + *mortem*, accusative of *mors*, death; see **mer-** in App.] —**post·mor′tem** *adv.*

post·na·sal drip (pōst-nā′zəl) *n.* The chronic secretion of mucus from the posterior nasal cavities, often caused by a cold or allergy.

post·na·tal (pōst-nāt′l) *adj.* Of or occurring after birth, esp. immediately after birth. —**post·na′tal·ly** *adv.*

post office *n.* **1.** The public department responsible for the transportation and delivery of the mails. **2.** A local office where mail is received, sorted, and delivered, and where postal materials are sold. **3.** A game in which kisses are exchanged for pretended letters.

post office box *n.* A container at a central mailing location, in which incoming mail is held for one renting the container.

post·op also **post·op** (pōst′ŏp′) *Informal adj.* Postoperative: *post-op care; post-op complications.* ❖ *n.* **1.** A postoperative patient. **2.** A section of a hospital providing postoperative treatment.

post·op·er·a·tive (pōst-ŏp′ər-ə-tĭv, -ŏp′rə-, -ŏp′ə-rā′-) *adj.* Happening or done after a surgical operation. —**post·op′er·a·tive·ly** *adv.*

post·or·bi·tal (pōst-ôr′bĭ-tl) *adj.* Situated behind the socket of the eye: *a postorbital bone.*

post·paid (pōst′pād′) *adj.* With the postage having been paid in advance.

post·par·tum (pōst-pär′təm) *adj.* Of or occurring in the period shortly after childbirth. [Lat. *post partum* : *post*, after; see POST- + *partum*, accusative of *partus*, birth < p. part. of *parere*, to beget.]

post·po·li·o syndrome (pōst-pō′lē-ō′) *n.* A condition affecting poliomyelitis patients several decades after the initial attack, characterized by fatigue, muscular deterioration, pain in the joints, and respiratory problems.

post·pone (pōst-pōn′, pōs-pōn′) *tr.v.* **-poned, -pon·ing, -pones** **1.** To delay until a future time; put off. **2.** To place after in importance; subordinate. [Lat. *postpōnere* : *post-*, post- + *pōnere*, to put; see POST².] —**post·pon′a·ble** *adj.* —**post·pone′ment** *n.* —**post·pon′er** *n.*

post·pose (pōst-pōz′) *v.* **-posed, -pos·ing, -pos·es** —*tr.* To place (a word or phrasal constituent) after other constituents in a sentence, as the direct object noun phrase *all he had seen* in the sentence *He described to them all he had seen.* —*intr.* To become postposed.

post·po·si·tion (pōst′pə-zĭsh′ən) *n.* **1.** The placing of a word or suffixed element after the word to which it is grammatically related, as *notwithstanding* in *these facts notwithstanding.* **2.** A word or element placed in such a manner. —**post′po·si′tion·al** *adj.* —**post′po·si′tion·al·ly** *adv.*

post·pos·i·tive (pōst-pŏz′ĭ-tĭv) *adj.* Occurring or placed after a word. ❖ *n.* A word or particle occurring or placed after another word. [LLat. *postpositīvus* < Lat. *postpositus*, p. part. of *postpōnere*, to put after. See POSTPONE.] —**post·pos′i·tive·ly** *adv.*

post·pran·di·al (pōst-prăn′dē-əl) *adj.* Following a meal, esp. dinner. —**post·pran′di·al·ly** *adv.*

post·pro·duc·tion (pōst′prə-dŭk′shən) *n.* A final stage in the production of a film or television program, occurring after filming or videotaping and typically involving editing, special effects, titling, and the addition of soundtracks.

post·script (pōst′skrĭpt′, pōs′skrĭpt′) *n.* **1.** A message appended to a letter after the writer's signature. **2.** Additional information appended to the manuscript, as of a book. [Med.Lat. *postscrīptum* < neut. p. part. of Lat. *postscrībere*, to write after : *post-*, post- + *scrībere*, to write; see skrībh- in App.]

Post·Script (pōst′skrĭpt′) A trademark used for an object-oriented computer language for describing the layout of documents, used to print high-resolution text and graphics.

post·struc·tur·al·ism (pōst′strŭk′chər-ə-lĭz′əm) *n.* Any of various theories, such as deconstruction, that deny the validity of structuralism's method of binary opposition and maintain that meanings are shifting and unstable.

post·syn·ap·tic (pōst′sĭ-năp′tĭk) *adj.* Situated behind or occurring after a synapse. —**post′syn·ap′ti·cal·ly** *adv.*

post time *n. Sports* The time set immediately before the official start of a race after which no betting is allowed.

post·tran·scrip·tion·al (pōst′trăn-skrĭp′shə-nəl) *adj.* Occurring or formed after genetic transcription.

post·trans·la·tion·al (pōst′trăns-lā′shə-nəl, -trănz-) *adj.* Occurring or formed after genetic translation.

post·trau·mat·ic (pōst′trô-măt′ĭk, -trou-) *adj.* Following injury or resulting from it: *posttraumatic amnesia.*

posttraumatic stress disorder *n.* A psychological disorder of individuals who have experienced profound trauma, such as torture, marked by recurrent flashbacks, nightmares, eating disorders, anxiety, fatigue, forgetfulness, and withdrawal.

pos·tu·lant (pŏs′chə-lənt) *n.* **1.** A person submitting a request or application; a petitioner. **2.** A candidate for admission into a religious order. [Fr. < OFr. < Lat. *postulāns, postulant-*, pr. part. of *postulāre*, to request. See POSTULATE.] —**pos′tu·lan·cy, pos′tu·lant·ship′** *n.*

pos·tu·late (pŏs′chə-lāt′) *tr.v.* **-lat·ed, -lat·ing, -lates** **1.** To make claim for; demand. **2.** To assume or assert the truth, reality, or necessity of, esp. as a basis of an argument. **3.** To assume as a premise or axiom; take for granted. See Syns at **presume.** ❖ *n.* (-lĭt, -lāt′) **1.** Something assumed without proof as being self-evident or generally accepted, esp. when used as a basis for an argument. **2.** A fundamental element; a basic principle. **3.** *Mathematics* An axiom. **4.** A requirement; a prerequisite. [Med.Lat. *postulāre, postulāt-*, to nominate to a bishopric, to assume < Lat., to request. See prek- in App.] —**pos′tu·la′tion** *n.*

pos·tu·la·tor (pŏs′chə-lā′tər) *n.* **1.** One who postulates. **2.** *Roman Catholic Church* A church official who presents a plea for canonization or beatification.

pos·ture (pŏs′chər) *n.* **1a.** A position of the body or of body parts. **b.** An attitude; a pose. **2.** A characteristic way of bearing one's body; carriage. **3.** Relative placement or arrangement. **4.** A stance or disposition with regard to something. **5.** A frame of mind affecting one's thoughts or behavior; an overall attitude. ❖ *v.* **-tured, -tur·ing, -tures** —*intr.* **1.** To assume an exaggerated or unnatural pose or mental attitude; attitudinize. **2.** To assume a pose. —*tr.* To put into a specific posture; pose. [Fr. < Ital. *postura* < Lat. *positūra*, position < *positus*, p. part. of *pōnere*, to place. See apo- in App.] —**pos′tur·al** *adj.* —**pos′tur·er, pos′tur·ist** *n.*

post·ver·te·bral (pōst-vûr′tə-brəl, pōst′vər-tē′-) *adj.* Situated behind the vertebrae: *postvertebral muscles.*

post·vo·cal·ic (pōst′vō-kăl′ĭk) *adj.* **1.** Being a consonant or consonantal sound directly following a vowel. **2.** Of, relating to, or being a form of a linguistic element, such as a suffix or word, that occurs only after vowels.

po·sy (pō′zē) *n., pl.* **-sies** **1.** A flower or bunch of flowers; a nosegay. **2.** *Archaic* A brief verse or sentimental phrase, esp. one inscribed on a trinket. [Alteration of POESY, motto or line of verse (archaic).]

---

pot¹ (pŏt) *n.* **1.** Any of various usu. domestic containers made of pottery, metal, or glass, as: **a.** A round, fairly deep cooking vessel with a handle and often a lid. **b.** A short round pot for storing or serving food: *a jam pot.* **c.** A coffeepot. **d.** A teapot. **2a.** Such a container and its contents: *a pot of stew.* **b.** A potful. **3a.** A large drinking cup; a tankard. **b.** A drink of liquor contained in such a cup. **4.** An artistic or decorative ceramic vessel of any shape. **5.** A flowerpot. **6.** Something, such as a chimney pot, that resembles a round cooking vessel in appearance or function. **7.** A trap for fish or crustaceans, typically a wicker or wire basket or cage. **8.** *Games* **a.** The total amount staked by all the players in one hand at cards. See Syns at **bet.** **b.** The area on a card table where stakes are placed. **c.** A shot in billiards or related games intended to send a ball into a pocket. **9.** *Informal* A common fund to which members of a group contribute. **10.** *Informal* A large amount. Often used in the plural: *pots of money.* **11.** *Informal* A potshot. **12.** *Informal* A potbelly. **13.** *Informal* A potty or toilet. **14.** See potentiometer 2. ❖ *v.* **pot·ted, pot·ting, pots** —*tr.* **1.** To place or plant in a pot. **2.** To preserve (food) in a pot. **3.** To cook in a pot. **4.** To shoot (game) for food rather than for sport. **5.** *Informal* To shoot with a potshot. **6.** *Games* To hit (a ball) into a pocket. —*intr.* **1.** *Informal* To take a potshot. **2.** To make or shape objects from clay, as on a potter's wheel. [ME < OE *pott* < VLat. **pottus.*]

pot² (pŏt) *n. Slang* Marijuana. [?]

po·ta·ble (pō′tə-bəl) *adj.* Fit to drink. ❖ *n.* A beverage, esp. an alcoholic beverage. [ME < OFr. < LLat. *potābilis* < Lat. *pōtāre*, to drink < *pōtus*, a drink. See pō(i)- in App.] —**po′ta·bil′i·ty, po′ta·ble·ness** *n.*

po·tage (pō-tăzh′) *n.* A thick, often creamy soup. [Fr. < OFr. See POTTAGE.]

pot·a·mol·o·gy (pŏt′ə-mŏl′ə-jē) *n.* The scientific study of rivers. [Gk. *potamos*, river; see pet- in App. + –LOGY.]

Po·ta·ro (pə-tär′ō, pō-) A river, c. 161 km (100 mi), of central Guyana; site of Kaieteur Falls.

pot·ash (pŏt′ăsh′) *n.* **1.** See **potassium carbonate. 2.** See **potassium hydroxide. 3.** Any of several compounds containing potassium, esp. potassium oxide, potassium chloride, and various potassium sulfates, used chiefly in fertilizers. [Sing. of obsolete *pot ashes*, transl. of obsolete Du. *potaschen* (this substance orig. being obtained by leaching wood ashes and evaporating the leach in a pot).]

potash feldspar *n.* See **orthoclase.**

potash mu·ri·ate (myŏŏr′ē-ĭt, -āt′) *n.* See **potassium chloride.**

po·tas·si·um (pə-tăs′ē-əm) *n. Symbol* **K** A soft, highly or explosively reactive metallic element that occurs in nature only in compounds and is found in or converted to a wide variety of salts used esp. in fertilizers and soaps. Atomic number 19; atomic weight 39.098; melting point 63.65°C; boiling point 774°C; specific gravity 0.862; valence 1. See table at **element.** [< POTASH.] —**po·tas′sic** *adj.*

po·tas·si·um-ar·gon (pə-tăs′ē-əm-är′gŏn′) *adj.* Of, relating to, or being a geologic dating method relying on the percentage of potassium that has radioactively decayed to argon in a specimen.

potassium bicarbonate *n.* A compound, $KHCO_3$, in the form of a white powder or colorless crystals, used in baking powder and as an antacid medicine.

potassium bitartrate *n.* A white acid crystalline solid or powder, $KHC_4H_4O_6$, used in baking powder, in the tinning of metals, and as a component of laxatives.

potassium bromide *n.* A crystalline solid or powder, KBr, used as a sedative, in photography, and in lithography.

potassium carbonate *n.* A transparent, deliquescent granular powder, K_2CO_3, used in making glass, enamels, and soaps.

potassium chlorate *n.* A poisonous crystalline compound, $KClO_3$, used as an oxidizing agent, a bleach, and a disinfectant and in making explosives, matches, and fireworks.

potassium chloride *n.* A crystalline solid or powder, KCl, used in fertilizers and in the preparation of most potassium salts.

potassium cyanide *n.* A poisonous compound, KCN, used in the extraction of gold and silver from ores, in electroplating and photography, and as a fumigant and insecticide.

potassium dichromate *n.* A crystalline compound, $K_2Cr_2O_7$, used as an oxidizing agent and in explosives.

potassium hydroxide *n.* A caustic white solid, KOH, used as a bleach and in the manufacture of soaps, dyes, alkaline batteries, and many potassium compounds.

potassium iodide *n.* A white crystalline compound, KI, used in photography and medicine and as an analytical reagent.

potassium mu·ri·ate (myŏŏr′ē-ĭt, -āt′) *n.* See **potassium chloride.**

potassium nitrate *n.* A crystalline compound, KNO_3, used to pickle meat and in the manufacture of pyrotechnics, explosives, matches, rocket propellants, and fertilizers.

potassium permanganate *n.* A dark purple crystalline compound, $KMnO_4$, used as an oxidizing agent and disinfectant and in deodorizers and dyes.

potassium sodium tartrate *n.* An effervescent crystalline compound, $KNaC_4H_4O_6 \cdot 4H_2O$, that is used in making mirrors, in

ă	pat	oi	boy
ā	pay	ou	out
âr	care	ŏŏ	took
ä	father	ōō	boot
ĕ	pet	ŭ	cut
ē	be	ûr	urge
ĭ	pit	th	thin
ī	pie	*th*	this
îr	pier	hw	which
ŏ	pot	zh	vision
ō	toe	ə	about,
ô	paw		item

Stress marks:
′ (primary);
′ (secondary), as in
lexicon (lĕk′sĭ-kŏn′)

potbelly stove

electronics, and as a laxative.

potassium sulfate *n.* A crystalline compound, K₂SO₄, used in glassmaking and fertilizers and as an analytical reagent.

po·ta·tion (pō-tā′shən) *n.* **1.** The act of drinking. **2.** A drink, esp. of an alcoholic beverage. [ME *potacion* < OFr. < Lat. *pōtātiō*, *pōtātiōn*-, a drinking party < *pōtātus*, p. part. of *pōtāre*, to drink < *pōtus*, a drink. See **pō(i)-** in App.]

po·ta·to (pə-tā′tō) *n., pl.* **-toes 1.** A South American plant (*Solanum tuberosum*) widely cultivated for its starchy edible tubers. **2.** A tuber of this plant. **3.** A sweet potato. See Regional Note at **possum.** [Sp. *patata*, alteration (prob. influenced by Quechua *papa*, white potato) of Taino *batata*, sweet potato.]

potato beetle *n.* The Colorado potato beetle.

potato bug *n.* The Colorado potato beetle.

potato chip *n.* A thin slice of potato fried in deep fat until crisp and then usu. seasoned. Often used in the plural.

po·ta·to·ry (pō′tə-tôr′ē, -tōr′ē) *adj.* Of, relating to, or given to drinking. [LLat. *pōtātōrius* < Lat. *pōtātus*, p. part. of *pōtāre*, to drink < *pōtus*. See **pō(i)-** in App.]

potato skin *n.* An appetizer made of a piece of baked potato skin spread with a topping and broiled or baked. Often used in the plural.

potato yam *n.* See **air potato.**

pot-au-feu (pô-tō-fœ′) *n., pl.* **pot-au-feu** A French dish of boiled meats and vegetables. [Fr. : *pot*, pot + *au*, on the + *feu*, fire.]

Pot·a·wat·o·mi (pŏt′ə-wŏt′ə-mē) *n., pl.* **Potawatomi** or **-mis 1.** A member of a Native American people formerly located in Michigan, Wisconsin, Illinois, and Indiana, with present-day populations in Oklahoma, Kansas, Michigan, and Ontario. **2.** Their Algonquian language.

potbellied pig *n.* A small domesticated pig native to Vietnam, having a saddle-shaped back and usu. dark coloration.

pot·bel·ly (pŏt′bĕl′ē) *n., pl.* **-lies 1.** A protruding abdominal region. **2.** A potbelly stove. —**pot′bel′lied** *adj.*

potbelly stove or **potbellied stove** *n.* A short rounded stove in which wood or coal is burned.

pot·boil (pŏt′boil′) *intr.v.* **-boiled, -boil·ing, -boils** To produce potboilers. [Back-formation < POTBOILER.]

pot·boil·er (pŏt′boi′lər) *n.* A literary or artistic work of poor quality, produced quickly for profit. [< the phrase *boil the pot*, to provide one's livelihood.]

pot·bound (pŏt′bound′) *adj.* Having grown too large for its container, resulting in matted or tangled roots.

pot·boy (pŏt′boi′) *n. Chiefly British* A boy or man who works in an inn or a public house.

pot cheese *n.* See **cottage cheese.**

po·teen (pō-tēn′, pŏ-, pə-chēn′) *n.* Unlawfully distilled Irish whiskey. [Ir.Gael. *poitín*, small pot, poteen < *pota*, pot < E. POT¹.]

Po·tem·kin (pō-tĕm′kĭn, pə-, pə-tyôm′-), **Grigori Aleksandrovich** 1739–91. Russian army officer who helped Catherine II seize power in 1762.

Potemkin village *n.* Something that appears elaborate and impressive but in actual fact lacks substance. [After Grigori Aleksandrovich POTEMKIN, who had elaborate fake villages constructed for some of Catherine the Great's tours.]

po·tence (pōt′ns) *n.* Potency.

po·ten·cy (pōt′n-sē) *n., pl.* **-cies 1.** The quality or condition of being potent. **2.** Inherent capacity for growth and development; potentiality.

po·tent (pōt′nt) *adj.* **1.** Possessing inner or physical strength; powerful. **2a.** Exerting or capable of exerting strong physiological or chemical effects: *potent liquor.* **b.** Exerting or capable of exerting strong influence; cogent: *potent arguments.* **3.** Having great control or authority. **4.** Able to have sexual intercourse. Used of a male. [ME < Lat. *potēns, potent-*, pr. part. of *posse*, to be able. See **poti-** in App.] —**po′tent·ly** *adv.* —**po′tent·ness** *n.*

po·ten·tate (pōt′n-tāt′) *n.* **1.** One who has the power and position to rule over others; a monarch. **2.** One who dominates or leads a group or an endeavor: *industrial potentates.* [ME *potentat* < OFr. < LLat. *potentātus* < Lat., power < *potēns*, pr. part. of *posse*, to be able. See POTENT.]

po·ten·tial (pə-tĕn′shəl) *adj.* **1.** Capable of being but not yet in existence; latent: *a potential problem.* **2.** Having possibility, capability, or power. **3.** *Grammar* Of, relating to, or being a verbal construction with auxiliaries such as *may* or *can*; for example, *It may snow.* ❖ *n.* **1.** The inherent ability or capacity for growth, development, or realization. **2.** Something possessing the capacity for growth or development. **3.** *Grammar* A potential verb form. **4.** *Physics* The work required to move a unit of positive charge, a magnetic pole, or an amount of mass from a reference point to a designated point in a static electric, magnetic, or gravitational field; potential energy. **5.** See **potential difference.** [ME *potencial* < OFr. *potenciel* < LLat. *potentiālis*, powerful < Lat. *potentia*, power < *potēns, potent-*, pr. part. of *posse*, to be able. See POTENT.] —**po·ten′tial·ly** *adv.*

potential difference *n. Symbol* V The amount of energy per unit charge needed to move a charged particle from a reference point to a designated point in a static electric field; voltage.

potential energy *n.* The energy of a particle or system of particles derived from position, or condition, rather than motion.

po·ten·ti·al·i·ty (pə-tĕn′shē-ăl′ĭ-tē) *n., pl.* **-ties 1.** The state of being potential. **2a.** Inherent capacity for growth, development, or realization. **b.** Something with such capacity.

po·ten·ti·ate (pə-tĕn′shē-āt′) *tr.v.* **-at·ed, -at·ing, -ates 1.** To make potent or powerful. **2.** To enhance or increase the effect of (a drug). **3.** To promote or strengthen (a biochemical or physiological action or effect). [< Lat. *potentia*, power. See POTENTIAL.] —**po·ten′ti·a′tion** *n.*

po·ten·til·la (pōt′n-tĭl′ə) *n.* Any of numerous herbs or shrubs of the genus *Potentilla* of the North Temperate Zone, having compound leaves and flowers with many pistils. [Med.Lat., garden valerian < Lat. *potēns, potent-*, pr. part. of *posse*, to be able. See POTENT.]

po·ten·ti·om·e·ter (pə-tĕn′shē-ŏm′ĭ-tər) *n.* **1.** An instrument for measuring an unknown voltage by comparison to a standard voltage. **2.** A three-terminal resistor with an adjustable center connection, widely used for volume control in radio and television receivers. [POTENTI(AL) + -METER.] —**po·ten′ti·o·met′ric** (-ə-mĕt′rĭk) *adj.*

pot·ful (pŏt′fo͝ol′) *n.* **1.** The amount that a pot can hold. **2.** *Informal* A large amount: *won a potful of money.*

pot·head (pŏt′hĕd′) *n. Slang* A regular marijuana smoker.

poth·er (pŏth′ər) *n.* **1.** A commotion; a disturbance. **2.** A state of nervous activity; a fuss. **3.** A cloud of smoke or dust that chokes or smothers. ❖ *v.* **-ered, -er·ing, -ers** —*tr.* To make confused; trouble; worry. —*intr.* To be overconcerned with trifles; fuss. [?]

pot·herb (pŏt′ûrb′, -hûrb′) *n.* A plant whose leaves, stems, or flowers are cooked and eaten or used as seasoning.

pot·hold·er (pŏt′hōl′dər) *n.* A small fabric pad used to handle hot cooking utensils.

pot·hole (pŏt′hōl′) *n.* **1.** A hole or pit, esp. one in a road surface. **2.** A deep round hole worn in rock by stones whirling in strong rapids or waterfalls. **3.** *Western US* A place filled with mud or quicksand and hazardous to cattle.

pot·hook (pŏt′ho͝ok′) *n.* **1.** A bent or hooked piece of iron for hanging a pot or kettle over a fire. **2.** A curved iron rod with a hooked end used for lifting hot pots, irons, or stove lids. **3.** A curved S-shaped mark made in writing. **4a.** Illegible handwriting or aimless scribbling. **b.** *Informal* Stenographic writing. In both senses often used in the plural.

pot·house (pŏt′hous′) *n. Chiefly British* A tavern.

pot·hunt·er (pŏt′hŭn′tər) *n.* **1.** One who hunts game for food, ignoring the rules of sport. **2.** One who participates in contests simply to win prizes. **3.** One who seeks archaeological artifacts for personal use, sometimes illegally, without adhering to professional standards. —**pot′hunt′ing** *n.*

po·tiche (pô-tēsh′) *n.* A vase or jar with a round or polygonal body tapering at the neck and having a removable cover. [Fr. < *pot*, pot < OFr. < VLat. *pottus*.]

po·tion (pō′shən) *n.* A liquid or liquid mixture, esp. one that is medicinal, poisonous, or magical. [ME *pocion* < OFr. < Lat. *pōtiō*, *pōtiōn*-. See **pō(i)-** in App.]

pot·latch (pŏt′lăch′) *n.* A ceremonial feast among certain Native American peoples of the northwest Pacific coast, as for a marriage or accession, at which the host distributes gifts according to each guest's rank or status. [Chinook Jargon < Nootka *p'achitl*, to make a potlatch gift.]

pot liquor *n.* See **liquor** 2.

pot·luck (pŏt′lŭk′) *n.* **1.** Whatever food happens to be available, esp. when offered to a guest: *Unannounced guests got potluck.* **2.** A meal at which each guest brings food to be shared. **3.** Whatever is available at a particular time.

pot marigold *n.* See **calendula.**

pot marjoram *n.* Marjoram.

Po·to·mac River (pə-tō′mək) A river of the E-central US rising in NE WV and flowing c. 459 km (285 mi) to Chesapeake Bay.

Po·to·sí (pō-tə-sē′, -tō-) A city of S-central Bolivia SW of Sucre in the Andes at an altitude of c. 4,203 m (13,780 ft); founded after silver was discovered in 1545. Pop. 113,380.

pot·pie (pŏt′pī′) *n.* **1.** A mixture of meat or poultry and vegetables covered with a pastry crust and baked in a deep dish. **2.** A meat or poultry stew with dumplings.

pot·pour·ri (pō′po͝o-rē′) *n., pl.* **-ris 1.** An incongruous combination. **2.** A miscellaneous anthology or collection. **3.** A mixture of dried flower petals and spices used to scent the air. [Fr. *pot pourri* (transl. of Sp. *olla podrida*, rotten pot, olla podrida) : *pot*, pot; see POTICHE + *pourri*, p. part. of *pourrir*, to rot (< OFr. *purir* < VLat. *putrīre* < Lat. *putrēscere*; see PUTRID).]

pot roast *n.* A cut of beef that is browned and then cooked until tender, often with vegetables, in a covered pot.

Pots·dam (pŏts′dăm′) A city of NE Germany on the Havel R. near Berlin; site of the Potsdam Conference (Jul.–Aug. 1945), at which Allied leaders drew up plans for the postwar administration of Germany. Pop. 139,262.

pot·sherd (pŏt′shûrd′) also **pot·shard** (-shärd′) *n.* A pottery fragment, esp. one found in an archaeological excavation.

pot·shot also **pot shot** (pŏt′shŏt′) *n.* **1.** A random or easy shot. **2.** A criticism made without careful thought and aimed at a handy target for attack. [< a pothunter's shot.]

pot sticker *n.* A dumpling filled with ground meat, vegetables, and seasonings that is browned on one side and then simmered.

pot•stone (pŏtʹstōnʹ) *n.* A variety of steatite once used to make cooking vessels.

pot•tage (pŏtʹĭj) *n.* **1.** A thick soup or stew of vegetables and sometimes meat. **2.** *Archaic* Porridge. [ME *potage* < OFr. < *pot,* pot. See POTICHE.]

pot•ted (pŏtʹĭd) *adj.* **1a.** Placed in a pot. **b.** Grown in a pot. **2.** Preserved in a pot, can, or jar. **3.** *Slang* **a.** Intoxicated; drunk. **b.** Under the influence of a hallucinogen.

pot•ter[1] (pŏtʹər) *n.* One who makes pottery.

pot•ter[2] (pŏtʹər) *v. Chiefly British* Variant of **putter**[2].

Potter, (Helen) Beatrix 1866–1943. British writer and illustrator of *The Tale of Peter Rabbit* (1900).

Pot•ter•ies (pŏtʹə-rēz) A district of W-central England in the Trent R. valley; a center for the manufacture of china and earthenware since the 16th cent.

pot•ter's clay (pŏtʹərz) *n.* A clay free of iron, suitable for making pottery or for modeling.

potter's field *n.* A place for the burial of unknown or indigent persons. [< the potter's field mentioned in Matthew 27:7.]

potter's wheel *n.* A revolving, often treadle-operated horizontal disk on which clay is shaped manually.

potter wasp *n.* Any of various small black and yellow solitary wasps of the genus *Eumenes,* characteristically building pot-shaped nests of clay. See Regional Note at **mud dauber.**

pot•ter•y (pŏtʹə-rē) *n., pl.* **-ies 1.** Ware, such as pots, shaped from moist clay and hardened by heat. **2.** The craft or work of a potter. **3.** The place where a potter works. [Fr. *poterie* < OFr. < *potier,* potter < *pot,* pot. See POTICHE.]

pot•tle (pŏtʹl) *n.* **1.** A pot or drinking vessel with a capacity of 2.0 quarts (1.9 liters). **2.** The liquid contained in a pottle. **3.** An old English liquid measure equal to 2.0 quarts (1.9 liters). [ME *potel* < OFr. < *pot,* pot. See POTICHE.]

pot•to (pŏtʹō) *n., pl.* **-tos** Any of several small nocturnal African primates of the genera *Perodicticus* and *Arctocebus,* having a pointed snout and a stumplike tail. [Of Niger-Congo orig.; perh. akin to Wolof *pata,* a tailless monkey; or Akan (Twi) *apɔsɔ,* a fierce monkeylike animal.]

Pott's disease (pŏts) *n.* Partial destruction of the vertebral bones, usu. caused by a tuberculous infection and often producing curvature of the spine. [After Percival *Pott* (1714–88), British surgeon.]

pot•ty[1] (pŏtʹē) *adj.* **-ti•er, -ti•est** *Chiefly British* **1.** Of little importance; trivial. **2.** Slightly intoxicated. **3.** Somewhat silly or crazy; addlebrained. [Poss. < POT[1].]

pot•ty[2] (pŏtʹē) *n., pl.* **-ties** A small pot for use as a toilet by an infant or young child.

pot•ty-chair (pŏtʹē-chârʹ) *n.* A small chair with an opening in the seat and a receptacle beneath, used in toilet training.

POTUS *abbr.* President of the United States

pouch (pouch) *n.* **1.** A small bag often closing with a drawstring and used esp. for carrying loose items in one's pocket. **2.** A bag or sack used to carry mail or diplomatic dispatches. **3.** A leather bag or case for carrying powder or small-arms ammunition. **4.** A sealed plastic or foil container used in packaging frozen or dehydrated food. **5.** Something resembling a bag in shape. **6.** *Zoology* A saclike structure, such as the abdominal pocket of marsupials. **7.** *Anatomy* A pocketlike space in the body. **8.** *Scots* A pocket. **9.** *Archaic* A purse for small coins. ❖ *v.* **pouched, pouch•ing, pouch•es** *—tr.* **1.** To place in or as if in a pouch; pocket. **2.** To cause to resemble a pouch. **3.** To swallow. Used of certain birds or fishes. *—intr.* To assume the form of a pouch or pouchlike cavity. [ME < OFr., of Gmc. orig.] **—pouchʹy** *adj.*

pouched (poucht) *adj.* Having a pouch, as a gopher or pelican.

pouf (po͞of) *n.* **1.** A woman's hairstyle popular in the 18th century, marked by high rolled puffs. **2.** A part of a garment that is gathered into a puff. **3.** A rounded ottoman. [Fr. < OFr., interj. for a fall, of imit. orig.] **—poufʹfy** *adj.*

pouil•ly-fuis•sé (po͞o-yēʹfwē-sāʹ) *n.* A dry white Burgundy wine. [After *Solutré-Pouilly* and *Fuissé* in east-central France.]

pou•lard also **pou•larde** (po͞o-lärdʹ) *n.* A young hen spayed for fattening. [Fr. *poularde* < *poule,* hen < OFr. < Lat. *pulla,* fem. of *pullus,* young of an animal, chicken.]

Pou•lenc (po͞o-lĕnkʹ), **Francis** 1899–1963. French composer and pianist whose works include the ballet *Les Biches* (1924).

poult (pōlt) *n.* A young fowl, esp. a turkey, chicken, or pheasant. [ME *pult,* short for *polet* < OFr. *poulet,* dim. of *poule, polle,* hen. See POULARD.]

poul•ter's measure (pōlʹtərz) *n.* A metrical pattern employing couplets in which the first line is in iambic hexameter and the second is in iambic heptameter. [< obsolete *poulter,* a poultry dealer (< the practice of giving a few extra eggs in the dozen) < ME *pulter* < OFr. *pouletier.* See POULTRY.]

poul•tice (pōlʹtĭs) *n.* A soft moist mass of bread, meal, clay, or other adhesive substance, usu. heated, spread on cloth, and applied to warm, moisten, or stimulate an aching or inflamed part of the body. ❖ *tr.v.* **-ticed, -tic•ing, -tic•es** To apply a poultice to. [ME *pultes* < Med.Lat. *pultēs,* thick paste < Lat., pl. of *puls, pult-,* pottage. See PULSE[2].]

poul•try (pōlʹtrē) *n.* Domestic fowls, such as chickens or turkeys, raised for meat or eggs. [ME *pultrie* < OFr. *pouletrie* < *pouletier,* poultry dealer < *poulet,* pullet. See PULLET.]

pounce[1] (pouns) *v.* **pounced, pounc•ing, pounc•es** *—intr.* **1.** To spring or swoop with intent to seize someone or something. **2.** To attack suddenly. **3.** To seize something swiftly and eagerly. *—tr.* To seize with or as if with talons. ❖ *n.* **1.** The act or an instance of pouncing. **2.** The talon or claw of a bird of prey. [< ME, talon of a hawk, perh. var. of *ponson,* pointed tool. See PUNCHEON[1].] **—pouncʹer** *n.*

pounce[2] (pouns) *n.* **1.** A fine powder formerly used to smooth and finish writing paper and soak up ink. **2.** A fine powder, such as pulverized charcoal, dusted over a stencil to transfer a design. ❖ *tr.v.* **pounced, pounc•ing, pounc•es 1.** To sprinkle, smooth, or treat with pounce. **2.** To transfer (a stenciled design) with pounce. [Fr. *ponce* < OFr. < VLat. **pōmex,* **pōmic-* < Lat. *pūmex,* pumice.] **—pouncʹer** *n.*

pounce[3] (pouns) *tr.v.* **pounced, pounc•ing, pounc•es** To ornament (metal, for example) by perforating from the back with a pointed implement. [ME *pouncen,* prob. < OFr. *poinssonner* < *poinson,* pointed tool. See PUNCHEON[1].]

pounce box *n.* A small box with a perforated top, formerly used to sprinkle sand or pounce on writing paper.

poun•cet box (pounʹsĭt) *n.* A small perfume box with a perforated top. [Perh. alteration of **pounced-box* < POUNCE[3].]

pound[1] (pound) *n.* **1a.** A unit of weight equal to 16 ounces (453.592 grams). See table at **measurement. b.** A unit of apothecary weight equal to 12 ounces (373.242 grams). **2.** A unit of weight differing in various countries and times. **3.** A British unit of force equal to the weight of a standard one-pound mass where the local acceleration of gravity is 9.817 meters (32.174 feet) per second per second. **4a.** The basic monetary unit of the United Kingdom, worth 20 shillings or 240 old pence before the decimalization of 1971. **b.** See table at **currency. 5.** A monetary unit of Scotland before 1707. **6.** The pound key on a telephone. [ME < OE *pund* < West Gmc. **punda-* < Lat. *(lībra) pondō,* (a pound) by weight.]

pound[2] (pound) *v.* **pound•ed, pound•ing, pounds** *—tr.* **1.** To strike repeatedly and forcefully. **2.** To beat to a powder or pulp; pulverize or crush. **3.** To instill by persistent, emphatic repetition. **4.** To assault with heavy gunfire. *—intr.* **1.** To strike repeated vigorous blows. **2.** To move along heavily and noisily. **3.** To pulsate rapidly and heavily; throb. **4.** To move or work laboriously. ❖ *n.* **1.** A heavy blow. **2.** The sound of a heavy blow; a thump. **3.** The act of pounding. ***—idiom:* pound the pavement** *Slang* To travel the streets on foot, esp. in search of work. [ME *pounden,* alteration of *pounen* < OE *pūnian.*] **—poundʹer** *n.*

pound[3] (pound) *n.* **1.** A public enclosure for stray dogs or livestock. **2.** A place in which impounded property is held. **3.** An enclosure for trapping or keeping animals or fish. **4.** A place of confinement for lawbreakers. ❖ *tr.v.* **pound•ed, pound•ing, pounds** To confine in or as if in a pound; impound. [ME < OE *pund-,* enclosure (as in *pundfall,* pen).]

Pound, Ezra Loomis 1885–1972. Amer. writer whose influential poetic works include *Cantos* (1925–60).

Pound, Roscoe 1870–1964. Amer. jurist who wrote *The Spirit of the Common Law* (1921).

pound•age[1] (pounʹdĭj) *n.* **1.** A tax or commission based on value per pound sterling. **2.** A rate or charge based on weight in pounds. **3.** Weight measured in pounds.

pound•age[2] (pounʹdĭj) *n.* **1.** Confinement of animals in a pound. **2.** A fee charged for the redemption of impounded animals or other property.

pound•al (pounʹdl) *n.* A unit of force in the foot-pound-second system of measurement, equal to the force required to accelerate a standard one-pound mass one foot per second per second (approx. 0.138 newton). [POUND[1] + *-al* (as in QUINTAL).]

pound cake *n.* A rich, finely textured yellow cake containing eggs, flour, butter, and sugar. [< the original recipe, calling for a pound each of butter, sugar, and flour.]

pound-fool•ish (poundʹfo͞oʹlĭsh) *adj.* Unwise in dealing with large sums of money or large matters. [< the phrase *penny-wise, pound-foolish.*]

pound key *n.* The pushbutton in the lower right corner on the dialing pad of a standard pushbutton telephone, marked with a pound sign (#).

pound scots *n.* See **pound**[1] 5.

pound sign *n.* **1.** The symbol (£) for a unit of currency, esp. the pound sterling. **2.** The symbol (#) for a pound as a unit of weight.

pound sterling *n.* See **pound**[1] 4a.

pour (pôr, pōr) *v.* **poured, pour•ing, pours** *—tr.* **1.** To make (a liquid or granular solid) stream or flow, as from a container. **2.** To send forth, produce, express, or utter copiously, as if in a stream or flood: *poured out my thoughts. —intr.* **1.** To stream or flow continuously or profusely. **2.** To rain hard or heavily. **3.** To pass or proceed in large numbers or quantity: *Students poured into the auditorium.* **4.** To serve a beverage to a gathering. ❖ *n.* A pouring or flowing forth, esp. a downpour of rain. ***—idiom:* pour it on** *Informal* **1.** To move or perform an activity at maximum speed or intensity. **2.** To speak or express oneself continuously or elaborately. [ME *pouren,* perh. < ONFr. *purer,* to sift, pour out < Lat. *pūrāre,* to purify < *pūrus,* pure.] **—pourʹer** *n.*

pour•boire (po͝or-bwärʹ) *n.* Money given as a gratuity; a tip. [Fr. < *pour boire,* for drinking : *pour,* for (< OFr. < Lat. *prō;* see PRO–[1])

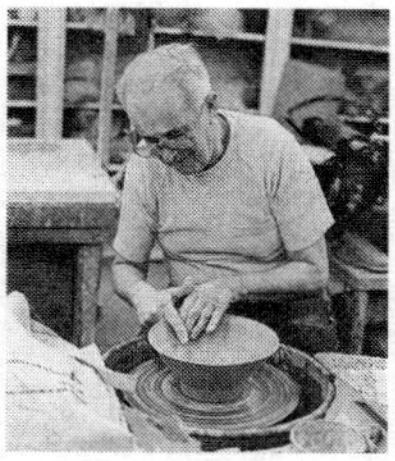

potter's wheel

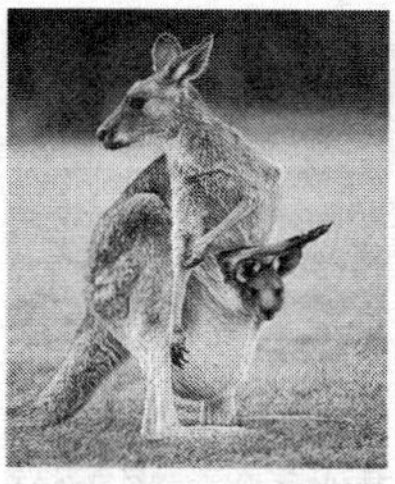

pouch
Eastern gray kangaroo with joey in pouch

ă pat	oi boy	ā pay	ou out
âr care	o͝o took	ä father	o͞o boot
ĕ pet	ŭ cut	ē be	ûr urge
ĭ pit	th thin	ī pie	*th* this
îr pier	hw which	ŏ pot	zh vision
ō toe	ə about, item	ô paw	

Stress marks:
ʹ (primary);
ʹ (secondary), as in
lexicon (lĕkʹsĭ-kŏnʹ)

+ *boire*, to drink (< OFr. *boivre* < Lat. *bibere*; see BEVERAGE).]

pour•par•ler (pŏŏr′pär-lā′) *n.* Conversation or discussion preliminary to negotiation. [Fr. < OFr. : *pour*, for, before (< OFr. < Lat. *prō*; see PRO-¹) + *parler*, to talk; see PARLEY.]

pour point *n.* The lowest temperature at which an oil or other liquid will pour under given conditions.

pousse-ca•fé (pŏŏs′kă-fā′) *n.* **1.** A drink consisting of several liqueurs of different densities, poured to form differently colored layers. **2.** A brandy or liqueur served after dinner with coffee. [Fr. : *pousser*, to push (< OFr.; see POUSSETTE) + *café*, coffee; see CAFÉ.]

pous•sette (pŏŏ-sĕt′) *n.* A country-dance figure in which couples or a couple join hands and swing around the floor. [Fr., pushpin, dim. of obsolete *pousse*, a push < *pousser*, to push < OFr. *poulser*, *pousser*, to push < Lat. *pulsāre*, freq. of *pellere*, to push. See pel-² in App.]

Pous•sin (pŏŏ-săn′), **Nicolas** 1594–1665. French painter whose works include *Landscape with Diogenes* (1648).

pout¹ (pout) *v.* **pout•ed, pout•ing, pouts** —*intr.* **1.** To show displeasure or disappointment; sulk. **2.** To protrude the lips in displeasure or sulkiness. **3.** To project or protrude. —*tr.* **1.** To protrude (the lips). **2.** To utter or express with a pout. ❖ *n.* **1.** A protrusion of the lips, esp. as an expression of sullen discontent. **2.** A fit of petulant sulkiness. Often used in the plural. [ME *pouten*, perh. of Scand. orig.] —**pout′y** *adj.*

pout² (pout) *n., pl.* **pout** or **pouts** Any of various freshwater or marine fishes, esp. the eelpout or hornpout. [ME **poute* < OE -*pūte* (as in *ǣlepūte*, eelpout).]

pout•er (pou′tər) *n.* **1.** One that pouts. **2.** One of a breed of pigeons capable of distending the crop until the breast becomes puffed out.

pov•er•ty (pŏv′ər-tē) *n.* **1.** The state of being poor; lack of the basic material goods. **2.** Deficiency in amount; scantiness. **3.** Unproductiveness; infertility. **4.** Renunciation by a member of a religious order of the right to own property. [ME *poverte* < OFr. < Lat. *paupertās* < *pauper*, poor.]

poverty grass *n.* Any of several North American grasses that grow in poor or sandy soil.

poverty level *n.* A minimum income level below which a person is officially considered to be living in poverty.

pov•er•ty-strick•en (pŏv′ər-tē-strĭk′ən) *adj.* Suffering from poverty; miserably poor. See Syns at **poor**.

POW (pē′ō-dŭb′əl-yōō, -yōō) *n.* A prisoner of war.

pow•der (pou′dər) *n.* **1.** A substance of ground, pulverized, or otherwise finely dispersed solid particles. **2.** Any of various preparations in powder form, as certain medicines. **3.** An explosive mixture, such as gunpowder. **4.** Light dry snow. ❖ *v.* **-dered, -der•ing, -ders** —*tr.* **1.** To reduce to powder; pulverize. **2.** To dust or cover with or as if with powder. —*intr.* **1.** To become powder; be pulverized. **2.** To use powder as a cosmetic. —*idioms:* **keep (one's) powder dry** To be ready for a challenge with little warning. **take a powder** To make a quick departure; run away. [ME *poudre* < OFr. < Lat. *pulvis, pulver-*.] —**pow′der•er** *n.*

powder blue *n.* A moderate to pale blue or purplish blue. [< the color of powdered smalt.]

powder horn *n.* An animal's horn capped at the open end, used to carry gunpowder.

powder keg *n.* **1.** A small cask for holding gunpowder or other explosives. **2.** A potentially explosive situation or thing.

powder metallurgy *n.* The technology of powdered metals, esp. as used for fabricating massive materials and shaped objects.

powder monkey *n. Slang* One who carries or sets explosives.

powder puff *n.* A soft pad for applying powder to the skin.

Powder River A river rising in the Bighorn Mts. of central WY and flowing c. 782 km (486 mi) into S MT.

powder room *n.* **1.** A lavatory for women. **2.** A lavatory for guests in a private home.

pow•der•y (pou′də-rē) *adj.* **1.** Composed of or similar to powder. **2.** Dusted or covered with or as if with powder. **3.** Easily made into powder; friable.

powdery mildew *n.* **1.** Any of various fungi, esp. of the family Erysiphaceae, that produce powdery conidia on the host surface. **2.** A plant disease caused by any of these fungi.

Pow•ell (pou′əl), **Adam Clayton, Jr.** 1908–72. Amer. politician from NY who was an outspoken advocate of civil rights.

Powell, Cecil Frank 1903–69. British physicist who won a 1950 Nobel Prize.

Powell, Colin Luther b. 1937. Amer. general who has served as US secretary of state (since 2001) and as chairman of the Joint Chiefs of Staff (1989–96).

Powell, Earl Known as "Bud." 1924–66. Amer. jazz pianist and composer who was a key figure in the bop movement.

Powell, John Wesley 1834–1902. Amer. geologist and ethnologist who directed the US Geological Survey (1881–94) and classified many Native American languages.

Powell, Lewis Franklin, Jr. 1907–98. Amer. jurist; associate justice of the US Supreme Court (1971–87).

Powell, Lake A reservoir of S UT and N-central AZ formed by the Glen Canyon Dam on the Colorado R.

pow•er (pou′ər) *n.* **1.** The ability or capacity to perform or act

powder horn

Colin Powell

effectively. **2.** A specific capacity, faculty, or aptitude. Often used in the plural. **3.** Strength or force exerted or capable of being exerted; might. See Syns at **strength**. **4.** The ability or official capacity to exercise control; authority. **5.** A person, group, or nation having great influence or control over others. **6.** The might of a nation, political organization, or similar group. **7.** Forcefulness; effectiveness. **8.** *Chiefly Upper Southern US* A large number or amount. **9a.** The energy or motive force by which a physical system or machine is operated. **b.** The capacity of a system or machine to operate. **c.** Electrical or mechanical energy, esp. as used to assist or replace human energy. **d.** Electricity supplied to a home, building, or community. **10.** *Physics* The rate at which work is done, expressed as the amount of work per unit time and commonly measured in units such as the watt and horsepower. **11.** *Electricity* **a.** The product of applied potential difference and current in a direct-current circuit. **b.** The product of the effective values of the voltage and current with the cosine of the phase angle between current and voltage in an alternating-current circuit. **12.** *Mathematics* **a.** See **exponent** 3. **b.** The number of elements in a finite set. **13.** *Statistics* The probability of rejecting the null hypothesis where it is false. **14.** A measure of the magnification of an optical instrument, such as a telescope. **15. powers** *Christianity* The sixth of the nine orders of angels. **16.** *Archaic* An armed force. ❖ *adj.* **1.** Of or relating to political, social, or economic control. **2.** Operated with mechanical or electrical energy in place of bodily exertion: *a power tool.* **3.** Of or relating to the generation or transmission of electricity. **4.** *Informal* Of or relating to influential business or professional practices. ❖ *tr.v.* **-ered, -er•ing, -ers** To supply with power, esp. mechanical power. —*idiom:* **powers that be** Those who hold effective power in a system or situation. [ME < OFr. *pooir*, to be able, power < VLat. **potēre*, to be able < Lat. *potis*, able, powerful. See poti- in App.]

pow•er•boat (pou′ər-bōt′) *n.* See **motorboat**.

power broker or **pow•er•brok•er** (pou′ər-brō′kər) *n.* A person who exerts strong political or economic influence, esp. by virtue of the individuals and votes he or she controls.

power dive *n.* A downward plunge of an aircraft accelerated by both gravity and engine power. —**pow′er-dive**′ *v.*

power drill *n.* **1.** A portable electric drill. **2.** A large drilling machine having a vertical motorized drill set in a table stand.

pow•er•ful (pou′ər-fəl) *adj.* **1.** Having or capable of exerting power. **2.** Effective or potent. **3.** *Chiefly Upper Southern US* Great. ❖ *adv. Chiefly Upper Southern US* Very. —**pow′er•ful•ly** *adv.* —**pow′er•ful•ness** *n.*

pow•er•house (pou′ər-hous′) *n.* **1.** See **power plant** 2. **2.** One with great force or energy.

pow•er•less (pou′ər-lĭs) *adj.* **1.** Lacking strength or power; helpless and totally ineffectual. **2.** Lacking legal or other authority. —**pow′er•less•ly** *adv.* —**pow′er•less•ness** *n.*

power mower *n.* A lawn mower powered by a gasoline or electric motor.

power of appointment *n., pl.* **powers of appointment** Authority granted to one person by another to transfer property upon the death of the latter.

power of attorney *n., pl.* **powers of attorney** A legal instrument authorizing one to act as another's attorney or agent.

power pack *n.* A usu. compact portable device that converts supply current to direct or alternating current as required by specific equipment.

power plant *n.* **1.** All the equipment, including structural members, that constitutes a unit power source: *the power plant of a truck.* **2.** A complex of structures, machinery, and associated equipment for generating electric energy from another source of energy, such as a hydroelectric dam.

power play *n.* **1.** *Sports* **a.** An offensive maneuver in a team game, esp. in football, using massive concentration of players in a certain area. **b.** A temporary numerical advantage of one ice hockey team because the other team has one or more players in the penalty box. **2.** A strategic maneuver, as in politics, based on the use or threatened use of power for coercion.

power politics *n. (used with a sing. or pl. verb)* International diplomacy in which each nation uses or threatens to use military or economic power to further its own interests.

Powers, Hiram 1805–73. Amer. sculptor whose works include *Greek Slave* (1843).

power series *n.* A sum of successively higher integral powers of a variable or combination of variables, each multiplied by a constant coefficient.

power shovel *n.* A large, usu. mobile earthmoving machine having a boom and a hinged bucket for excavating.

power station *n.* See **power plant** 2.

power steering *n.* A device driven by the engine of a vehicle that facilitates the turning of the steering wheel by the driver.

power structure *n.* **1.** An elite group of people in influential positions within a government, society, or organization. **2.** A hierarchy of managerial authority.

power takeoff *n.* A mechanism attached to a motor vehicle engine that supplies power to a nonvehicular device, such as a pump or pneumatic hammer.

power train *n.* An assembly of gears and associated parts by which power is transmitted from an engine to a driving axle.

power trip *n. Slang* An action undertaken chiefly for the gratification of exercising power over another or others. **—pow′er·trip′** (pou′ər-trĭp′) *v.* **—power tripper** *n.*

Pow·ha·tan[1] (pou′ə-tăn′, pou-hăt′n) Orig. Wahunsonacock. 1550?–1618. Algonquian leader and father of Pocahontas who founded the Powhatan confederacy.

Pow·ha·tan[2] (pou′ə-tăn′, pou-hăt′n) *n., pl.* **Powhatan** or **-tans** **1.** A member of a confederacy of Native American peoples of eastern Virginia in the 16th and 17th centuries, with present-day descendants in the same area. **2.** The Algonquian language of the Powhatan. [After POWHATAN[1].]

pow·wow (pou′wou′) *n.* **1.** A council or meeting with or of Native Americans. **2a.** A Native American shaman. **b.** A ceremony conducted by a shaman, as in the performance of healing or hunting rituals. **3.** *Informal* A conference or gathering. ❖ *intr.v.* **-wowed, -wow·ing, -wows** *Informal* To hold a powwow. [Narragansett *powwaw*, shaman.]

WORD HISTORY Because trances were so important to the Native American shaman, the title *powwaw*, literally meaning "one who has visions," was accorded him. The word whose spelling was eventually settled in English as *powwow* was also used as the name for ceremonies and councils, probably because of the shaman's important role in both. Eventually the newcomers decided that they could have powwows too, the first reference to one of these being recorded in the Salem, Massachusetts, *Gazette* of 1812: "The Warriors of the Democratic Tribe will hold a powwow at Agawam on Tuesday next."

Pow·ys (pō′ĭs) Family of British writers including the brothers **John Cowper Powys** (1872–1963), whose novels, such as *Wolf Solent* (1929), glorify nature; and **Theodore Francis Powys** (1875–1953), who wrote allegorical novels, such as *Mr. Weston's Good Wine* (1927).

pox (pŏks) *n.* **1.** A disease such as smallpox, characterized by pustulent skin eruptions that may leave pockmarks. **2.** Syphilis. **3.** *Archaic* Misfortune and calamity. [Alteration of *pocks* < ME, pl. of *pocke, pokke.* See POCK.]

pox·vi·rus (pŏks′vī′rəs) *n., pl.* **-rus·es** Any of a group of DNA-containing viruses, including those that cause smallpox, cowpox, and other poxlike diseases in vertebrates.

Po·yang (pō′yäng′) A lake of E China SE of Wuhan; connected to the Chang Jiang (Yangtze River) by canal.

Poz·nań (pôz′năn′, -nän′, pôz′hän′yə) A city of W-central Poland W of Warsaw. Pop. 590,087.

poz·zo·lan (pŏt′sə-län′) also **poz·zo·la·na** (-sə-lä′nə) or **poz·zuo·la·na** (-swä-) *n.* **1.** Any of several siliceous materials, such as volcanic ash, used to produce cements. **2.** Any of various artificially produced substances resembling pozzuolana ash. [Ital. *pozzolana,* after POZZUOLI.] **—poz′zuo·la′nic** *adj.*

po·zo·le (pə-zō′lā) *n.* Variant of **posole.**

Poz·zuo·li (pŏt-swō′lē) A city of S Italy W of Naples on the **Bay of Pozzuoli,** a section of the Bay of Naples. Pop. 61,300.

pp or **pp.** *abbr.* pianissimo

PP *abbr.* prepositional phrase

pp. *abbr.* **1.** pages **2.** prepaid **3.** postpaid

p.p. *abbr.* **1.** parcel post **2.** past participle **3.** *Latin* per procurationem (by proxy) **4.** postpaid

ppb *abbr.* parts per billion

ppm *abbr.* parts per million

PPO *abbr.* preferred provider organization

PPP *abbr. Computer Science* point to point protocol

PPS *abbr. Latin* post postscriptum (additional postscript)

ppt *abbr.* **1.** parts per thousand **2.** parts per trillion **3.** precipitate

PPV *abbr.* pay-per-view

PQ *abbr.* **1.** Parti Québécois **2.** Quebec

Pr[1] The symbol for the element **praseodymium.**

Pr[2] *abbr.* **1.** propyl **2.** *Bible* Proverbs

PR *abbr.* **1.** payroll **2.** proportional representation **3.** public relations **4.** or **P.R.** Puerto Rico

pr. *abbr.* **1.** pair **2.** present **3a.** printed **b.** printing **4.** pronoun

prac·ti·ca·ble (prăk′tĭ-kə-bəl) *adj.* **1.** Capable of being effected, done, or put into practice; feasible. **2.** Usable for a specified purpose: *a practicable way of entry.* [Med.Lat. *prăcticābilis,* capable of being used < *prăcticāre,* to practice < *prăctica, practicable* < Gk. *prāktikē,* practical science < fem. of *prāktikos,* fit for action, practical < *prāssein, prāk-,* to make, do.] **—prac′ti·ca·bil′i·ty** *n.* **—prac′ti·ca·bly** *adv.*

USAGE NOTE *Practicable* means "feasible, possible" as well as "usable"; it is never applied to persons. *Practical* has a wider range of meanings and can be applied to persons when meaning "level-headed, efficient." It can also mean "capable of being put into effect, useful," and here it is very close in meaning to *practicable:* We came up with some practical (or practicable) suggestions for improving the company's performance. Even so, it is worth noting the subtle distinction between these words. Someone with a practical knowledge of French may be able to order coffee in a Parisian café, but it may not be practicable to learn French solely by visiting Parisian cafés.

prac·ti·cal (prăk′tĭ-kəl) *adj.* **1.** Of, relating to, governed by, or acquired through practice or action, rather than theory, speculation, or ideals: *practical experience.* **2.** Manifested in or involving practice: *practical applications of calculus.* **3.** Actually engaged in a specified occupation or a certain kind of work; practicing. **4.** Capable of or suitable to being used or put into effect; useful: *practical knowledge of Japanese.* See Usage Note at **practicable. 5.** Concerned with the production or operation of something useful: *Woodworking is a practical art.* **6.** Level-headed, efficient, and unspeculative. **7.** Being actually so in almost every respect; virtual: *a practical disaster.* [ME *practicale* < Med.Lat. *prăcticālis* < *prăctica.* See PRACTICABLE.] **—prac′ti·cal′i·ty** (-kăl′ĭ-tē), **prac′ti·cal·ness** *n.*

practical joke *n.* A mischievous trick, esp. one that causes embarrassment, indignity, or discomfort. **—practical joker** *n.*

prac·ti·cal·ly (prăk′tĭk-lē) *adv.* **1.** In a practical way. **2.** For all practical purposes; virtually. **3.** All but; nearly; almost.

practical nurse *n.* **1.** A licensed practical nurse. **2.** One with practical experience but no degree in nursing.

prac·tice (prăk′tĭs) *v.* **-ticed, -tic·ing, -tic·es** **—***tr.* **1.** To do or perform habitually or customarily; make a habit of: *practices courtesy in social situations.* **2.** To do or perform (something) repeatedly in order to acquire or polish a skill: *practice a dance step.* **3.** To give lessons or repeated instructions to; drill. **4.** To work at, esp. as a profession: *practice law.* **5.** To carry out in action; observe. **6.** *Obsolete* To plot (something evil). **—***intr.* **1.** To do or perform something habitually or repeatedly. **2.** To do something repeatedly in order to acquire or polish a skill. **3.** To work at a profession. **4.** *Archaic* To intrigue or plot. ❖ *n.* **1.** A habitual or customary action or way of doing something: *makes a practice of being punctual.* **2a.** Repeated performance of an activity in order to learn or perfect a skill: *Practice will make you a good musician.* **b.** A session of preparation or performance undertaken to acquire or polish a skill: *has soccer practice on Monday.* **c.** *Archaic* The skill so learned or perfected. **d.** The condition of being skilled through repeated exercise: *out of practice.* **3.** The act or process of doing something; performance or action. **4.** Exercise of an occupation or profession: *the practice of law.* **5.** The business of a professional person: *an obstetrician with her own practice.* **6.** A habitual or customary action or act. Often used in the plural: *engaged in questionable business practices.* **7.** *Law* The methods of procedure used in a court of law. **8.** *Archaic* **a.** The act of tricking or scheming, esp. with malicious intent. **b.** A trick, scheme, or intrigue. [ME *practisen* < OFr. *practiser,* alteration of *practiquer* < *practique,* practice < LLat. *prăctica,* practical. See PRACTICABLE.] **—prac′tic·er** *n.*

SYNONYMS *practice, exercise, rehearse* These verbs mean to do repeatedly to acquire or maintain proficiency: *practice the shot put; exercising one's wits; rehearsed the play for 14 days.* See also Syns at **habit.**

prac·ticed (prăk′tĭst) *adj.* **1.** Skilled or expert; proficient. **2.** Acquired or brought to perfection by practice.

practice teacher *n.* See **student teacher.** **—prac′tice-teach′** (prăk′tĭs-tēch′) *v.* **—practice teaching** *n.*

prac·tic·ing (prăk′tĭ-sĭng) *adj.* Actively engaged in or observing, esp. a given profession or religion: *a practicing attorney.*

prac·ti·cum (prăk′tĭ-kəm) *n.* A school or college course, esp. one in a specialized field, designed to give students supervised practical experience. [Ger. *Praktikum* < LLat. *prăcticum,* neut. of *prăcticus,* practical. See PRACTICAL.]

prac·tise (prăk′tĭs) *v. & n. Chiefly British* Variant of **practice.**

prac·ti·tion·er (prăk-tĭsh′ə-nər) *n.* One who practices something, esp. an occupation, profession, or technique. [Alteration of *practician* < OFr. *practicien* < *practiser,* to practice. See PRACTICE.]

prae·di·al also **pre·di·al** (prē′dē-əl) *adj.* **1.** Relating to, containing, or possessing land; landed. **2.** Attached to, bound to, or arising from the land: *praedial serfs.* [ME < Med.Lat. *praediālis,* of an estate < Lat. *praedium,* estate < *praes, praed-,* surety, bondsman : *prae-,* pre- + *vas-, vad-,* guarantor.]

prae·mu·ni·re (prē′myŏŏ-nī′rē) *n.* **1.** The offense under English law of appealing to or obeying a foreign court or authority, thus challenging the supremacy of the Crown. **2.** The writ charging this offense. **3.** The penalty for it. [Short for ME *premunire facias,* a writ of premunire < Med.Lat. *praemūnīre faciās : prae-mūnīre,* to warn (< Lat., to fortify : *prae-,* pre- + *mūnīre,* to defend) + Lat. *faciās,* that you cause, second pers. sing. pr. subjunctive of *facere,* to do (words used in the writ).]

prae·no·men (prē-nō′mən) *n., pl.* **-no·mens** or **-nom·i·na** (-nŏm′ə-nə, -nō′mə-) **1.** A first or given name. **2.** The first name of a citizen of ancient Rome, as *Gaius* in *Gaius Julius Caesar.* [Lat. *praenōmen : prae-,* pre- + *nōmen,* name; see **nō-men-** in App.] **—prae·nom′i·nal** (-nŏm′ə-nəl) *adj.*

prae·tor also **pre·tor** (prē′tər) *n.* An annually elected magistrate of the ancient Roman Republic, ranking below but having approximately the same functions as a consul. [ME *pretor* < OFr. < Lat. *praetor,* perh. < *praeīre,* to go before : *prae-,* pre- + *īre,* to go; see **ei-** in App.] **—prae·to′ri·al** (prē-tôr′ē-əl, -tōr′-) *adj.* **—prae′tor·ship′** *n.*

ă	pat	oi	boy
ā	pay	ou	out
âr	care	ŏŏ	took
ä	father	ōō	boot
ĕ	pet	ŭ	cut
ē	be	ûr	urge
ĭ	pit	th	thin
ī	pie	th	this
îr	pier	hw	which
ŏ	pot	zh	vision
ō	toe	ə	about,
ô	paw		item

Stress marks:
′ (primary);
′ (secondary), as in
lexicon (lĕk′sĭ-kŏn′)

prairie dog
black-tailed prairie dog
Cynomys ludovicianus

prayer rug

prae·to·ri·an also **pre·to·ri·an** (prē-tôr′ē-ən, -tōr′-) *adj.* **1.** Of or relating to a praetor or the praetorship. **2. Praetorian** Of or belonging to the Praetorian Guard. **3.** Venal; corruptible. ❖ *n.* **1.** A praetor or ex-praetor. **2. Praetorian** A member of the Praetorian Guard.

Praetorian Guard *n.* **1.** The elite bodyguard of a Roman emperor. **2.** A member of this bodyguard. [Orig. the bodyguard of a praetor or a general.]

prag·mat·ic (prăg-măt′ĭk) *adj.* **1.** Concerned with facts or actual occurrences; practical. **2.** *Philosophy* Of or relating to pragmatism. **3.** Relating to or being the study of cause and effect in historical or political events with emphasis on the practical lessons to be learned from them. **4.** *Archaic* **a.** Active; busy. **b.** Active in an officious or meddlesome way. **c.** Dogmatic; dictatorial. ❖ *n.* **1.** A pragmatic sanction. **2.** *Archaic* A meddler; a busybody. [Lat. *prāgmaticus*, skilled in business < Gk. *prāgmatikos* < *prāgma*, *prāgmat-*, deed < *prāssein*, *prāg-*, to do.] —**prag·mat′i·cal** *adj.* —**prag·mat′i·cal·ly** *adv.*

prag·mat·ics (prăg-măt′ĭks) *n. (used with a sing. verb)* The study of language as it is used in a social context, including its effect on the interlocutors.

pragmatic sanction *n.* An edict or decree issued by a sovereign that becomes part of the fundamental law of the land. [Transl. of LLat. *prāgmatica sānctiō*, imperial decree referring to the affairs of a community.]

prag·ma·tism (prăg′mə-tĭz′əm) *n.* **1.** *Philosophy* A movement consisting of various related theories and distinguished by the doctrine that the meaning of an idea or a proposition lies in its observable practical consequences. **2.** A practical matter-of-fact way of approaching or assessing situations or of solving problems. —**prag′ma·tist** *n.* —**prag′ma·tis′tic** *adj.*

Prague (präg) The cap. of the Czech Republic, in the W part on the Vltava R.; came under Hapsburg rule in 1526 and was the cap. of Czechoslovakia from the country's formation in 1918 until its dissolution in 1993. Pop. 1,216,513.

pra·hu (prä′ōō) *n.* Variant of **proa.**

Prai·a (prī′ə) The cap. of Cape Verde, on the SE coast of São Tiago I. Pop. 61,644.

prai·rie (prâr′ē) *n.* An extensive area of flat or rolling grassland, esp. the large plain of central North America. [Fr. < OFr. *praierie* < VLat. *prātāria* < Lat. *prāta*, meadow.]

prairie chicken *n.* Either of two birds (*Tympanuchus cupido* or *T. pallidicinctus*) of the grouse family, found in western North America and having mottled brownish plumage.

prairie dog *n.* Any of several burrowing rodents of the genus *Cynomys* in the squirrel family, having light brown fur and a warning call similar to a dog's bark.

prairie oyster *n.* **1.** *Slang* A drink made from a whole raw egg yolk, Worcestershire sauce, hot sauce, salt, and pepper that is taken as a palliative for a hangover or as a cure for hiccups. **2.** *Chiefly Western US* The testis of a calf, cooked and served as food.

prairie potato *n.* See **breadroot.**

Prairie Provinces The Canadian provinces of Manitoba, Saskatchewan, and Alberta.

prairie schooner *n.* A covered wagon drawn by horses or oxen and used by pioneers in crossing North America.

prairie wolf *n.* See **coyote** 1.

praise (prāz) *n.* **1.** Expression of approval, commendation, or admiration. **2.** The extolling or exaltation of a deity, ruler, or hero. **3.** *Archaic* A reason for praise; merit. ❖ *tr.v.* **praised, prais·ing, prais·es 1.** To give praise to or for. **2.** To extol or exalt; worship. [ME *preise* < *preisen*, to praise < OFr. *preisier* < LLat. *pretiāre*, to prize < Lat. *pretium*, price.] —**prais′er** *n.*

SYNONYMS *praise, acclaim, commend, extol, laud* These verbs mean to express approval or admiration. To *praise* is to voice approbation, commendation, or esteem: *"She was enthusiastically praising the beauties of Gothic architecture"* (Francis Marion Crawford). *Acclaim* usually implies hearty approbation warmly and publicly expressed: *Critics acclaimed the film highly. Commend* suggests moderate or restrained approval, as from a superior: *The judge commended the jury for their work. Extol* suggests exaltation or glorification: *"that sign of old age, extolling the past"* (Sydney Smith). *Laud* connotes respectful, often inordinate praise: *"aspirations which are lauded up to the skies"* (Charles Kingsley).

praise·wor·thy (prāz′wûr′thē) *adj.* **-thi·er, -thi·est** Meriting praise; highly commendable. —**praise′wor′thi·ly** *adv.* —**praise′wor′thi·ness** *n.*

Pra·krit (prä′krĭt) *n.* Any of various vernacular and literary Indic languages recorded from the third century B.C. to the fourth century A.D. [Skt. *prākṛtam* < neut. sing. of *prākṛta-*, natural, vulgar, vernacular : *pra-*, before, forward; see **per**[1] in App. + *karoti*, he makes; see SANSKRIT.] —**Pra·krit′ic** *adj.*

pra·line (prä′lēn′, prā′-) *n.* A confection made of nut kernels, esp. almonds or pecans, stirred in boiling sugar syrup until crisp and brown. [Fr., after César de Choiseul, Comte du Plessis-*Praslin* (1598–1675), French army officer.]

prall·tril·ler (präl′trĭl′ər) *n. Music* A trill consisting of alternation between a written note and the note immediately above it.

[Ger. : *prallen*, to rebound (alteration of MHGer. *prellen*) + *Triller*, trill (< Ital. *trillo* < *trillare*, to trill, prob. of imit. orig.).]

pram[1] (prăm) *n. Chiefly British* A baby carriage. [Shortening and alteration of PERAMBULATOR.]

pram[2] (prăm) *n. Chiefly New England* A small dinghy having a flat snub-nosed bow. **2.** A flatbottom boat used chiefly in the Baltic Sea as a barge. [Du. *praam*, flat bottom boat < MDu. *praem* < Czech *prám*. See **per**[1] in App.]

prance (prăns) *v.* **pranced, pranc·ing, pranc·es** —*intr.* **1a.** To spring forward on the hind legs. Used of a horse. **b.** To spring or bound forward in a manner reminiscent of a spirited horse. **2.** To ride a prancing horse. **3.** To walk or move about spiritedly; strut. —*tr.* To cause (a horse) to prance. ❖ *n.* The act or an instance of prancing. [ME *prauncen*.] —**pranc′er** *n.* —**pranc′ing·ly** *adv.*

pran·di·al (prăn′dē-əl) *adj.* Of or relating to a meal. [< Lat. *prandium*, late breakfast. See **ed-** in App.] —**pran′di·al·ly** *adv.*

prang (prăng) *tr.v.* **pranged, prang·ing, prangs** *Chiefly British* **1.** To crash (an airplane, for example). **2.** To damage (a car, for example) in a collision. **3.** To bomb from the air. [Imit.]

prank[1] (prăngk) *n.* A mischievous trick or practical joke. [?]

prank[2] (prăngk) *v.* **pranked, prank·ing, pranks** —*tr.* To decorate or dress ostentatiously or gaudily. —*intr.* To make an ostentatious display. [< ME *pranken*, to show off, perh. < MDu. *pronken* (< *pronk*, show, display) and < MLGer. *prunken* (< *prank*, display).]

prank·ish (prăng′kĭsh) *adj.* Impishly playful; mischievous. —**prank′ish·ly** *adv.* —**prank′ish·ness** *n.*

prank·ster (prăngk′stər) *n.* One who plays tricks or pranks.

pra·se·o·dym·i·um (prā′zē-ō-dĭm′ē-əm, prā′sē-) *n. Symbol* **Pr** A soft malleable ductile rare-earth element that develops a characteristic green tarnish in air, occurs naturally in monazite, and is used to color glass and ceramics yellow and in metallic alloys and the cores of carbon arcs. Atomic number 59; atomic weight 140.908; melting point 935°C; boiling point 3,127°C; specific gravity 6.8; valence 3, 4. See table at **element.** [NLat. < Ger. *Praseodym* : Gk. *prasios, praseos*, leek-green (< *prason*, leek) + (DI)DYMIUM.]

prat (prăt) *n. Slang* The buttocks. [?]

prate (prāt) *v.* **prat·ed, prat·ing, prates** —*intr.* To talk idly or at length; chatter. —*tr.* To utter idly or to little purpose. ❖ *n.* Empty, foolish, or trivial talk; idle chatter. [ME *praten* < MDu. *prāten*.] —**prat′er** *n.* —**prat′ing·ly** *adv.*

prat·fall (prăt′fôl′) *n.* **1.** A fall on the buttocks. **2.** A humiliating error, failure, or defeat.

prat·in·cole (prăt′n-kōl′, prăt′-, prăt′ĭng-, prā′tĭng-) *n.* Any of several Old World shore birds of the genera *Glareola* and *Stiltia*, having brown and black plumage, long pointed wings, a forked tail, and a tapered bill. [NLat. *prātincola* : Lat. *prātum*, meadow + Lat. *incola*, inhabitant; see kʷel- in App.]

pra·tique (prā-tēk′) *n.* Clearance granted to a ship to proceed into port after compliance with health regulations or quarantine. [Fr. < OFr. *practique* < Med.Lat. *prāctica*, ult. < Gk. *prāktikē* < fem. of *prāktikos*, practical. See PRACTICAL.]

Pra·to (prä′tō) A city of central Italy NW of Florence. Pop. 165,364.

prat·tle (prăt′l) *v.* **-tled, -tling, -tles** —*intr.* To talk or chatter idly or meaninglessly; babble or prate. —*tr.* To utter or express by prattling. ❖ *n.* **1.** Idle or meaningless chatter; babble. **2.** A sound suggestive of such chattering; a babbling noise. [Frequentative of PRATE.] —**prat′tler** *n.* —**prat′tling·ly** *adv.*

prau (prou) *n.* Variant of **proa.**

prawn (prôn) *n.* Any of various edible crustaceans similar to the shrimps. ❖ *intr.v.* **prawned, prawn·ing, prawns** To fish for prawns. [ME *praine, prane.*] —**prawn′er** *n.*

prax·e·ol·o·gy also **prax·i·ol·o·gy** (prăk′sē-ŏl′ə-jē) *n.* The study of human conduct. [PRAX(IS) + -LOGY.] —**prax′e·o·log′i·cal** (-ə-lŏj′ĭ-kəl) *adj.*

prax·is (prăk′sĭs) *n., pl.* **prax·es** (prăk′sēz′) **1.** Practical application or exercise of a branch of learning. **2.** Habitual or established practice; custom. [Med.Lat. *prāxis* < Gk. < *prāssein, prāg-*, to do.]

Prax·it·e·les (prăk-sĭt′l-ēz′) fl. 4th cent. B.C. Greek sculptor whose works include *Hermes Carrying Dionysius.*

pray (prā) *v.* **prayed, pray·ing, prays** —*intr.* **1.** To utter a prayer or prayers. **2.** To make a fervent request or entreaty. —*tr.* **1.** To utter or say a prayer or prayers to; address by prayer. **2.** To ask (someone) imploringly; beseech. **3.** To make a devout or earnest request for: *I pray your permission to speak.* **4.** To move or bring by prayer or entreaty. [ME *preien* < OFr. *preier* < Lat. *precārī* < *precēs*, pl. of **prex*, prayer. See **prek-** in App.]

prayer[1] (prâr) *n.* **1a.** A reverent petition made to God or another object of worship. **b.** The act of making such a reverent petition. **2.** An act of communion with one worshiped, as in devotion or thanksgiving. **3.** A specially worded form of address used in worship. **4. prayers** A religious observance in which praying predominates: *morning prayers.* **5a.** A fervent request. **b.** The thing requested. **6.** The slightest chance or hope. **7.** *Law* **a.** The request of a complainant, as stated in a complaint or in equity, that the court grant the aid or relief solicited. **b.** The section of the complaint or bill that contains this request. [ME *preiere* < OFr. < Med.Lat. *precāria* < fem. of Lat. *precārius*, obtained by entreaty < *precārī*, to entreat. See PRAY.]

pray·er² (prā′ər) *n.* One who prays.

prayer beads *pl.n.* A string of beads for keeping count of the prayers one is saying.

prayer book *n.* **1.** A book containing religious prayers. **2. Prayer Book** The Book of Common Prayer.

prayer·ful (prâr′fəl) *adj.* **1.** Inclined or given to praying frequently; devout. **2.** Typical or indicative of prayer, as a mannerism, gesture, or facial expression. —**prayer′ful·ly** *adv.* —**prayer′ful·ness** *n.*

prayer meeting *n.* An evangelical service, esp. one held on a weekday evening, in which laypersons participate by singing, praying, or testifying their faith.

prayer rug *n.* A small rug used by Muslims to kneel and prostrate themselves upon during devotions.

prayer shawl *n.* See **tallith.**

prayer wheel *n.* A cylinder containing or inscribed with prayers or litanies that is revolved on its axis in devotions, esp. by Tibetan Buddhists.

pray·ing mantis (prā′ĭng) *n.* A green or brownish predatory insect (*Mantis religiosa*) that while at rest folds its front legs as if in prayer.

PRC *abbr.* People's Republic of China

pre– *pref.* **1a.** Earlier; before; prior to: *prehistoric.* **b.** Preparatory; preliminary: *premedical.* **c.** In advance: *prepay.* **2.** Anterior; in front of: *preaxial.* [ME < OFr. < Lat. *prae-* < *prae,* before, in front. See **per¹** in App.]

preach (prēch) *v.* **preached, preach·ing, preach·es** —*tr.* **1.** To proclaim or put forth in a sermon. **2.** To advocate, esp. to urge acceptance of or compliance with. **3.** To deliver (a sermon). —*intr.* **1.** To deliver a sermon. **2.** To give religious or moral instruction, esp. in a tedious manner. [ME *prechen* < OFr. *preechier* < LLat. *praedicāre* < Lat., to proclaim : *prae-,* pre- + *dicāre,* to proclaim; see **deik-** in App.]

preach·er (prē′chər) *n.* **1.** One who preaches, esp. one who publicly proclaims the gospel for an occupation. **2.** *Alaska* A submerged tree or log that creates a hazard for riverboats.

preach·i·fy (prē′chə-fī′) *intr.v.* **-fied, -fy·ing, -fies** *Informal* To preach tediously and didactically.

preach·ment (prēch′mənt) *n.* **1.** The act of preaching. **2.** A tiresome or unwelcome moral discourse; tedious sermonizing.

preach·y (prē′chē) *adj.* **-i·er, -i·est** Given to tedious moralizing; didactic. —**preach′i·ly** *adv.* —**preach′i·ness** *n.*

pre·ad·ap·ta·tion (prē′ăd-ăp-tā′shən, -əp-) *n.* A characteristic evolved from an ancestral species or population that serves an adaptive though different function in a descendant one.

pre·am·ble (prē′ăm′bəl, prē-ăm′-) *n.* **1.** A preliminary statement, esp. one that explains the purpose of a formal document. **2.** An introductory occurrence or fact; a preliminary. [ME < OFr. *preambule* < Med.Lat. *praeambulum* < neut. of LLat. *praeambulus,* walking in front : Lat. *prae-,* pre- + Lat. *ambulāre,* to walk; see **AMBULATE.**] —**pre·am′bu·lar′y** (-byə-lĕr′ē) *adj.*

pre·amp (prē′ămp) *n. Informal* A preamplifier.

pre·am·pli·fi·er (prē-ăm′plə-fī′ər) *n.* An electronic circuit or device that detects and strengthens weak signals, as from a radio receiver, for subsequent amplification stages.

pre·ap·prove (prē′ə-prōōv′) *tr.v.* **-proved, -prov·ing, -proves** To approve or qualify before the usual procedures or formalities have taken place: *preapprove an application.*

pre·a·tom·ic (prē′ə-tŏm′ĭk) *adj.* Of or belonging to the time before the use of, existence of, or capability for atomic energy or weapons.

pre·ax·i·al (prē-ăk′sē-əl) *adj.* Situated in front of or superior to the median axis of the body or a body part. —**pre·ax′i·al·ly** *adv.*

preb·end (prĕb′ənd) *n.* **1.** A stipend drawn from the endowment or revenues of an Anglican church by a presiding cleric; a benefice. **2.** The property or tithe providing the endowment for such a stipend. **3.** A prebendary. [ME *prebende* < OFr. < Med.Lat. *praebenda* < LLat., state allowance < Lat., neut. pl. gerundive of *praebēre,* to grant < *praehibēre* : *prae-,* pre- + *habēre,* to hold; see **ghabh-** in App.]

preb·en·dar·y (prĕb′ən-dĕr′ē) *n., pl.* **-ies 1.** A member of the Anglican clergy who receives a prebend. **2.** An Anglican cleric holding the honorary title of prebend without a stipend.

pre·bi·o·log·i·cal (prē′bī-ə-lŏj′ĭ-kəl) *adj.* Of, relating to, or being the time before the appearance of living things.

pre·bi·ot·ic (prē′bī-ŏt′ĭk) *adj.* Prebiological.

pre·board (prē′bôrd′, -bōrd′) *v.* **-board·ed, -board·ing, -boards** —*tr.* **1.** To board (an aircraft, for example) ahead of the regular time or before other passengers. **2.** To allow (one or more passengers) to board ahead of the regular time or before other passengers. —*intr.* To preboard an aircraft or other conveyance.

Pre·cam·bri·an (prē-kăm′brē-ən) *adj.* Of or belonging to the period of geologic time from approx. 3.8 billion years ago to approx. 570 million years ago, often subdivided into the Archean and Proterozoic eons, comprising most of the earth's history, and marked by the appearance of primitive forms of life. See table at **geologic time.** ❖ *n.* The Precambrian Eon or its deposits.

pre·can·cel (prē-kăn′səl) *tr.v.* **-celed, -cel·ing, -cels** or **-celled, -cel·ling, -cels** To cancel (a postage stamp) before mailing. ❖ *n.* A precanceled stamp or envelope. —**pre′can·cel·la′tion** *n.*

pre·can·cer (prē-kăn′sər) *n.* A precancerous condition.

pre·can·cer·ous (prē-kăn′sər-əs) *adj.* Of, relating to, or being a condition that typically precedes or develops into a cancer.

pre·car·i·ous (prĭ-kâr′ē-əs) *adj.* **1.** Dangerously lacking in security or stability. **2.** Subject to chance or unknown conditions. **3.** Based on uncertain, unwarranted, or unproved premises. **4.** *Archaic* Dependent on the will or favor of another. [< Lat. *precārius,* obtained by entreaty, uncertain < *precārī,* to entreat. See **PRAY.**] —**pre·car′i·ous·ly** *adv.* —**pre·car′i·ous·ness** *n.*

pre·cast (prē-kăst′) *adj.* Relating to or being a structural member, esp. of concrete, that has been cast into form before being transported to its site of installation. —**pre·cast′** *v.*

prec·a·to·ry (prĕk′ə-tôr′ē, -tōr′ē) also **prec·a·tive** (-tĭv) *adj.* Relating to or expressing entreaty or supplication. [LLat. *precātōrius* < Lat. *precārī,* to entreat. See **PRAY.**]

pre·cau·tion (prĭ-kô′shən) *n.* **1.** An action taken in advance to protect against possible danger, failure, or injury; a safeguard. **2.** Caution practiced in advance; forethought or circumspection. [LLat. *praecautiō, praecautiōn-* < *praecautus,* p. part. of Lat. *praecavēre,* to guard against : *prae-,* pre- + *cavēre,* to beware.] —**pre·cau′tion·ar′y, pre·cau′tion·al** *adj.*

pre·cede (prĭ-sēd′) *v.* **-ced·ed, -ced·ing, -cedes** —*tr.* **1.** To come, exist, or occur before in time. **2.** To come before in order or rank; surpass or outrank. **3.** To be in a position in front of; go in advance of. **4.** To preface; introduce: *She preceded her lecture with a joke.* —*intr.* To come or go before in time, order, rank, or position. [ME *preceden* < OFr. *preceder* < Lat. *praecēdere* : *prae-,* pre- + *cēdere,* to go.]

prec·e·dence (prĕs′ĭ-dəns, prĭ-sēd′ns) also **prec·e·den·cy** (prĕs′ĭ-dən-sē, prĭ-sēd′n-sē) *n.* **1.** The fact, state, or right of preceding; priority. **2.** Priority claimed or received because of preeminence or superiority. **3.** A ceremonial order of rank or preference, esp. as observed on formal occasions.

prec·e·dent (prĕs′ĭ-dənt) *n.* **1a.** An act or instance that may be used as an example in dealing with subsequent similar instances. **b.** *Law* A judicial decision that may be used as a standard in subsequent similar cases. **2.** Convention or custom arising from long practice. ❖ *adj.* (prĭ-sēd′nt, prĕs′ĭ-dənt) Preceding. [ME < OFr. < Lat. *praecēdēns, praecēdent-,* pr. part. of *praecēdere,* to go before. See **PRECEDE.**]

prec·e·den·tial (prĕs′ĭ-dĕn′shəl) *adj.* **1.** Of, relating to, or constituting a precedent. **2.** Having precedence.

pre·ced·ing (prĭ-sē′dĭng) *adj.* Existing or coming before another or others in time, place, rank, or sequence; previous.

pre·cen·tor (prĭ-sĕn′tər) *n.* A cleric who directs the choral services of a church or cathedral. [Lat. *praecentor* < *praecentus,* p. part. of *praecinere,* to sing before : *prae-,* pre- + *canere,* to sing; see **kan-** in App.] —**pre′cen·to′ri·al** (prē′sĕn-tôr′ē-əl, -tōr′-) *adj.*

pre·cept (prē′sĕpt′) *n.* A rule or principle prescribing a particular course of action or conduct. [ME < OFr. < Lat. *praeceptum* < neut. p. part. of *praecipere,* to advise, teach : *prae-,* pre- + *capere,* to take; see **kap-** in App.]

pre·cep·tive (prĭ-sĕp′tĭv) *adj.* **1.** Of, relating to, or expressing a precept. **2.** Instructive; didactic. —**pre·cep′tive·ly** *adv.*

pre·cep·tor (prĭ-sĕp′tər, prē′sĕp′tər) *n.* **1.** A teacher; an instructor. **2.** A specialist, such as a physician, who gives practical experience and training to a student. **3.** The head of a preceptory. [ME < Lat. *praeceptor* < *praecipere,* to teach. See **PRECEPT.**] —**pre′cep·to′ri·al** (prē′sĕp-tôr′ē-əl, -tōr′-) *adj.*

prayer wheel

praying mantis
Mantis religiosa

pre′ad·o·les′cence *n.*	**pre·heat′er** *n.*	**pre·or·dain′** *tr.v.*	**pre′re·cord′** *tr.v.*
pre′ad·o·les′cent *adj. & n.*	**pre·hom′i·nid** *n. & adj.*	**pre·or·dain′ment** *n.*	**pre′reg·is′ter** *intr.v.*
pre′a·dult′ *adj.*	**pre′in·dus′tri·al** *adj.*	**pre·or′di·na′tion** *n.*	**pre′reg·is·tra′tion** *n.*
pre′ag·ri·cul′tur·al *adj.*	**pre·judge′** *tr.v.*	**pre·owned′** *adj.*	**pre′re·tire′ment** *adj. & n.*
pre′ar·range′ *tr.v.*	**pre·judg′er** *n.*	**pre·pay′** *tr.v.*	**pre′se·lect′** *tr.v.*
pre′ar·range′ment *n.*	**pre·judg′ment** *n.*	**pre·pay′ment** *n.*	**pre′se·lec′tion** *n.*
pre′built′ *adj.*	**pre·launch′** *adj.*	**pre′pro·fes′sion·al** *adj.*	**pre·set′** *tr.v.*
pre-Chris′tian *adj.*	**pre·mar′i·tal** *adj.*	**pre′pro′gram′** *tr.v.*	**pre·set′ta·ble** *adj.*
pre·cook′ *tr.v.*	**pre·mar′i·tal·ly** *adv.*	**pre·pu′ber·al** *adj.*	**pre·sig′ni·fy′** *tr.v.*
pre·dawn′ *n. & adj.*	**pre′men·o·paus′al** *adj.*	**pre·pu′ber·tal** *adj.*	**pre·treat′** *tr.v.*
pre′de·cease′ *tr.v.*	**pre·mix′** *n. & tr.v.*	**pre·pu′bes·cence** *n.*	**pre·treat′ment** *n.*
pre′des·ig′nate *tr.v.*	**pre·mod′ern** *adj.*	**pre·pu′bes·cent** *adj. & n.*	**pre·war′** *adj.*
pre′des·ig·na′tion *n.*	**pre·na′tal** *adj.*	**pre′pub′li·ca′tion** *n.*	
pre·heat′ *tr.v.*	**pre·na′tal·ly** *adv.*		

pre•cep•tor•ship (prĭ-sĕp′tər-shĭp′) *n.* A period of practical experience and training under a preceptor.

pre•cep•to•ry (prĭ-sĕp′tə-rē, prē′sĕp-) *n., pl.* **-ries** A community of medieval Knights Templars located on a provincial estate and subordinate to the temples at Paris and London.

pre•cess (prē-sĕs′, prē′sĕs′) *intr.v.* **-cessed, -cess•ing, -cess•es** To move in or be subjected to precession.

pre•ces•sion (prē-sĕsh′ən) *n.* **1.** The act or state of preceding; precedence. **2.** *Physics* The motion of the axis of a spinning body, such as the wobble of a top, due to an applied external force. **3.** *Astronomy* **a.** Precession of the equinoxes. **b.** A slow gyration of the earth's axis around the pole of the ecliptic, caused mainly by the gravitational pull of the sun and moon on Earth's equatorial bulge. [LLat. *praecessiō, praecessiōn-* < Lat. *praecessus*, p. part. of *praecēdere*, to go before. See PRECEDE.] **—pre•ces′sion•al** *adj.*

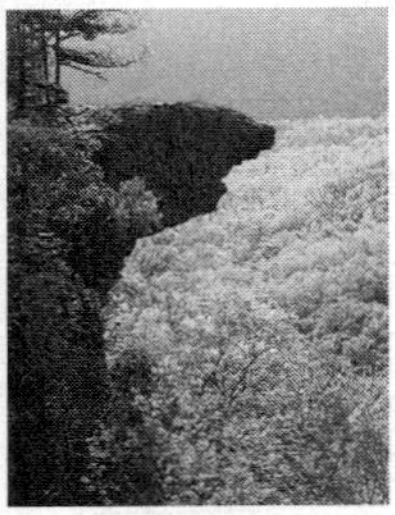

precipice
Hawksbill Crag in the Ozark Mountains, Arkansas

precession of the equinoxes *n.* A slow westward shift of the equinoxes along the plane of the ecliptic, resulting from precession of the earth's axis of rotation and causing the equinoxes to occur earlier each sidereal year. A complete precession requires 25,800 years.

pre•cinct (prē′sĭngkt′) *n.* **1a.** A district of a city or town under the jurisdiction of or patrolled by a specific unit of its police force. **b.** The police station situated in and having jurisdiction over a precinct. **2.** An election district of a city or town. **3a.** A place or enclosure marked off by definite limits. **b.** A boundary. In both senses often used in the plural. **4. precincts** The neighborhood or surrounding area; the environs. **5.** An area of thought or action; a province or domain. Often used in the plural. [ME *precincte*, a defined district or area < Med.Lat. *praecīnctum* < Lat., neut. p. part. of *praecingere*, to encircle : *prae-*, pre- + *cingere*, to gird.]

pre•ci•os•i•ty (prĕsh′ē-ŏs′ĭ-tē, prĕs′-) *n., pl.* **-ties 1.** Extreme meticulousness or overrefinement, as in taste. **2.** An instance of preciosity. [ME *preciousite*, preciousness < OFr. *preciosite* < Lat. *pretiōsitās* < *pretiōsus*, precious < *pretium*, price. See PRECIOUS.]

pre•cious (prĕsh′əs) *adj.* **1.** Of high cost or worth; valuable. **2.** Highly esteemed; cherished. **3.** Dear; beloved. **4.** Affectedly dainty or overrefined. **5.** *Informal* Thoroughgoing; unmitigated. ❖ *n.* One who is dear or beloved; a darling. ❖ *adv.* Used as an intensive: *precious little time.* [ME < OFr. *precios* < Lat. *pretiōsus* < *pretium*, price.] **—pre′cious•ly** *adv.* **—pre′cious•ness** *n.*

precious stone *n.* Any of several gems, such as the diamond, that are valuable because of their rarity or appearance.

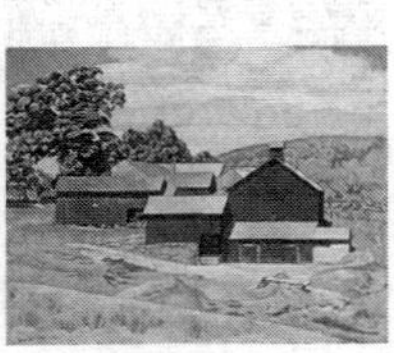

precisionism
Connecticut Barns in Landscape, 1934, by Charles Sheeler (1883–1965)

prec•i•pice (prĕs′ə-pĭs) *n.* **1.** An overhanging or extremely steep mass of rock, such as a crag. **2.** The brink of a dangerous or disastrous situation. [Fr. *précipice* < Lat. *praecipitium* < *praeceps, praecipit-*, headlong. See PRECIPITATE.]

pre•cip•i•ta•ble (prĭ-sĭp′ĭ-tə-bəl) *adj.* Capable of being precipitated.

pre•cip•i•tan•cy (prĭ-sĭp′ĭ-tən-sē) also **pre•cip•i•tance** (-təns) *n.* **1.** The quality of being precipitant. **2.** Action or thought marked by impulsiveness or rash haste.

pre•cip•i•tant (prĭ-sĭp′ĭ-tənt) *adj.* **1.** Rushing or falling headlong. **2.** Acting with or marked by impulsiveness in thought or action; rash. See Usage Note at **precipitate. 3.** Abrupt or unexpected; sudden. ❖ *n. Chemistry* A substance that causes a precipitate to form when it is added to a solution. [Lat. *praecipitāns, praecipitant-*, pr. part. of *praecipitāre*, to throw headlong. See PRECIPITATE.] **—pre•cip′i•tant•ly** *adv.*

pre•cip•i•tate (prĭ-sĭp′ĭ-tāt′) *v.* **-tat•ed, -tat•ing, -tates** *—tr.* **1.** To throw from or as if from a great height; hurl downward. **2.** To cause to happen, esp. suddenly or prematurely. **3.** *Meteorology* To cause (water vapor) to precipitate. **4.** *Chemistry* To cause (a solid substance) to be separated from a solution. *—intr.* **1.** *Meteorology* To condense and fall from the air as rain, snow, sleet, or hail. **2.** *Chemistry* To be separated from a solution as a solid. **3.** To fall or be thrown headlong. ❖ *adj.* (-tĭt) **1.** Moving rapidly and heedlessly; speeding headlong. **2.** Acting with or marked by excessive haste and lack of due deliberation. **3.** Occurring suddenly or unexpectedly. ❖ *n.* (-tāt′, -tĭt) **1.** *Chemistry* A solid or solid phase separated from a solution. **2.** A product resulting from a process, event, or course of action. [Lat. *praecipitāre, praecipitāt-*, to throw headlong < *praeceps, praecipit-*, headlong : *prae-*, pre- + *caput, capit-*, head; see **kaput-** in App.] **—pre•cip′i•tate•ly** (-tĭt-lē) *adv.* **—pre•cip′i•tate•ness** *n.* **—pre•cip′i•ta′tive** *adj.* **—pre•cip′i•ta′tor** *n.*

USAGE NOTE The adjective *precipitate* and the adverb *precipitately* were once applied to physical steepness but are now used primarily of rash, headlong actions: *They made a precipitate decision. He withdrew precipitately from the race. Precipitous* currently means "steep" in both literal and figurative senses. But *precipitous* and *precipitously* are also frequently applied to abruptness and hastiness. This usage is a natural extension of the use of *precipitous* to describe a rise or fall in a quantity over time, but though well attested in the work of reputable writers, it is still widely regarded as an error.

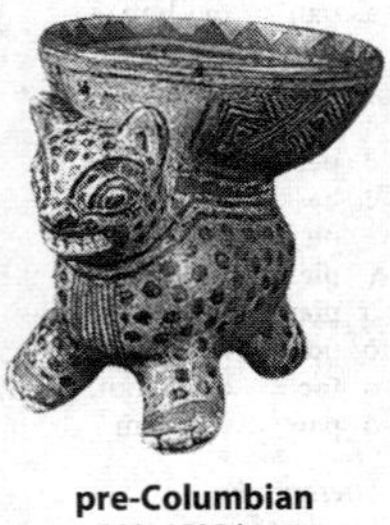

pre-Columbian
c. 800–1525 jaguar effigy vessel

pre•cip•i•ta•tion (prĭ-sĭp′ĭ-tā′shən) *n.* **1.** A headlong fall or rush. **2.** Abrupt or impulsive haste. **3.** A hastening or acceleration, esp. one that is sudden or unexpected. **4.** *Meteorology* **a.** Any form of water, such as rain or snow, that falls to the earth's surface. **b.** The quantity of such water falling in a specific area within a specific period. **5.** *Chemistry* The process of separating a substance from a solution as a solid.

pre•cip•i•tin (prĭ-sĭp′ĭ-tĭn) *n.* An antibody that reacts with a specific soluble antigen to produce a precipitate.

pre•cip•i•tin•o•gen (prĭ-sĭp′ĭ-tĭn′ə-jən) *n.* An antigen that induces the production of a precipitin.

pre•cip•i•tous (prĭ-sĭp′ĭ-təs) *adj.* **1.** Resembling a precipice; extremely steep. See Syns at **steep**[1]. **2.** Having several precipices: *a precipitous bluff.* **3.** *Usage Problem* Extremely rapid or abrupt; precipitate. See Usage Note at **precipitate.** [Prob. < obsolete *precipitious* < Lat. *praecipitium*, precipice. See PRECIPICE.] **—pre•cip′i•tous•ly** *adv.* **—pre•cip′i•tous•ness** *n.*

pré•cis (prā′sē, prā-sē′) *n., pl.* **pré•cis** (prā′sēz, prā-sēz′) A concise summary of a book, article, or other text; an abstract. ❖ *tr.v.* **-cised, -cis•ing, -cis•es** To make a précis of. [Fr. < OFr. *precis*, condensed. See PRECISE.]

pre•cise (prĭ-sīs′) *adj.* **1.** Clearly expressed or delineated; definite. **2.** Exact, as in performance or amount; accurate or correct: *a precise instrument.* **3.** Strictly distinguished from others; very. **4.** Distinct and correct in sound or meaning. **5.** Conforming strictly to rule or proper form. [ME, exact < OFr. *precis*, condensed, precisely fixed < Lat. *praecīsus*, p. part. of *praecīdere*, to shorten : *prae-*, pre- + *caedere*, to cut.] **—pre•cise′ness** *n.*

pre•cise•ly (prĭ-sīs′lē) *adv.* **1.** In a precise manner. **2.** Used as an intensive: *That's precisely the reason I'm angry.*

pre•ci•sian (prĭ-sĭzh′ən) *n.* **1.** One who is strict and precise in adherence to rules or standards, esp. with regard to religion or morals. **2.** A Puritan. [< PRECISE.] **—pre•ci′sian•ism** *n.*

pre•ci•sion (prĭ-sĭzh′ən) *n.* **1.** The state or quality of being precise; exactness. **2a.** The ability of a measurement to be consistently reproduced. **b.** The number of significant digits to which a value has been reliably measured. ❖ *adj.* **1.** Used or intended for accurate or exact measurement. **2.** Made so as to vary minimally from a set standard: *precision components.* **3.** Of or characterized by accurate action. [Lat. *praecīsiō, praecīsiōn-*, a cutting off < *praecīsus*, p. part. of *praecīdere*, to cut off. See PRECISE.]

pre•ci•sion•ism also **Pre•ci•sion•ism** (prĭ-sĭzh′ə-nĭz′əm) *n.* A style of early 20th-century painting in which a subject is reduced or simplified to elemental structural forms and rendered by abstractionism and realism.

pre•ci•sion•ist (prĭ-sĭzh′ə-nĭst) *n.* **1.** One who values precision; a purist. **2.** often **Precisionist** A painter whose work is marked by precisionism.

pre•clin•i•cal (prē-klĭn′ĭ-kəl) *adj.* Of or relating to the period of a disease before the appearance of symptoms.

pre•clude (prĭ-klo͞od′) *tr.v.* **-clud•ed, -clud•ing, -cludes 1.** To make impossible, as by action taken in advance; prevent. **2.** To exclude or prevent (someone) from a given condition or activity. [Lat. *praeclūdere* : *prae-*, pre- + *claudere*, to close.] **—pre•clu′sion** (-klo͞o′zhən) *n.* **—pre•clu′sive** (-klo͞o′sĭv, -zĭv) *adj.* **—pre•clu′sive•ly** *adv.*

pre•co•cial (prĭ-kō′shəl) *adj.* Covered with down and capable of moving about when hatched. Used of wading birds and domestic fowl. [< NLat. *praecocēs*, precocial birds < pl. of Lat. *praecox*, premature. See PRECOCIOUS.]

pre•co•cious (prĭ-kō′shəs) *adj.* **1.** Manifesting or characterized by unusually early development or maturity, esp. in mental aptitude. **2.** *Botany* Blossoming before the appearance of leaves. [< Lat. *praecox, praecoc-*, premature < *praecoquere*, to boil before, ripen fully : *prae-*, pre- + *coquere*, to cook, ripen; see **pek^w-** in App.] **—pre•co′cious•ly** *adv.* **—pre•coc′i•ty** (-kŏs′ĭ-tē), **pre•co′cious•ness** *n.*

pre•cog•ni•tion (prē′kŏg-nĭsh′ən) *n.* Knowledge of something in advance of its occurrence, esp. by extrasensory perception; clairvoyance. **—pre•cog′ni•tive** *adj.*

pre•co•lo•ni•al or **pre-co•lo•ni•al** (prē′kə-lō′nē-əl) *adj.* Of, relating to, or being the period of time before colonization of a region or territory.

pre-Co•lum•bi•an also **pre•co•lum•bi•an** (prē′kə-lŭm′bē-ən) *adj.* Of, relating to, or originating in the Americas before the arrival of Columbus.

pre•con•ceive (prē′kən-sēv′) *tr.v.* **-ceived, -ceiv•ing, -ceives** To form (an opinion, for example) before possessing full or adequate knowledge or experience.

pre•con•cep•tion (prē′kən-sĕp′shən) *n.* A preconceived opinion or conception; a prejudice or bias.

pre•con•cert (prē′kən-sûrt′) *tr.v.* **-cert•ed, -cert•ing, -certs** To agree on, settle, or arrange in advance.

pre•con•di•tion (prē′kən-dĭsh′ən) *n.* A condition that must exist or be established before something can occur or be considered; a prerequisite. ❖ *tr.v.* **-tioned, -tion•ing, -tions** To condition, train, or accustom in advance.

pre•con•scious (prē-kŏn′shəs) *n.* Memories or feelings of which one is not immediately aware but that are consciously recallable. **—pre•con′scious** *adj.* **—pre•con′scious•ly** *adv.*

pre•con•tract (prē-kŏn′trăkt) *n.* An existing contract that obviates the making of another contract of the same kind: *a precontract of marriage.* **—pre′con•tract′** (-kən-trăkt′) *v.*

pre•cool (prē-ko͞ol′) *tr.v.* **-cooled, -cool•ing, -cools** To reduce the temperature of (produce or meat, for example) by artificial means before packaging or shipping.

pre·crit·i·cal (prē-krĭt′ĭ-kəl) *adj.* Coming before a critical state or phase.

pre·cur·sive (prĭ-kûr′sĭv) *adj.* Precursory.

pre·cur·sor (prĭ-kûr′sər, prē′kûr′sər) *n.* **1.** One that indicates, suggests, or announces someone or something to come. **2.** One that precedes another; a forerunner or predecessor. **3.** A biochemical substance that gives rise to a more stable or definitive product. [ME *precursoure* < OFr. *precurseur* < Lat. *praecursor* < *praecursus*, p. part. of *praecurrere*, to run before : *prae-*, pre- + *currere*, to run.]

pre·cur·so·ry (prĭ-kûr′sə-rē) *adj.* **1.** Preceding or preliminary; introductory: *a precursory statement.* **2.** Suggesting or indicating something to follow.

pre·cut (prē′kŭt′) *adj.* Cut into size or shape before being marketed, assembled, or used. —**pre·cut′** *v.*

pred. *abbr.* predicate

pre·da·cious also **pre·da·ceous** (prĭ-dā′shəs) *adj.* **1.** Living by seizing or taking prey; predatory. **2.** Given to victimizing, plundering, or destroying for one's own gain. [< Lat. *praedārī*, to plunder. See PREDATORY.] —**pre·dac′i·ty** (-dăs′ĭ-tē) *n.*

pre·date (prē-dāt′) *tr.v.* **-dat·ed, -dat·ing, -dates** **1.** To mark or designate with a date earlier than the actual one: *predated the check.* **2.** To precede in time; antedate.

pre·da·tion (prĭ-dā′shən) *n.* **1.** The act or practice of plundering or marauding. **2.** The capturing of prey as a means of maintaining life. [ME *predacion* < Lat. *praedātiō, praedātiōn-* < *praedātus*, p. part. of *praedārī*, to plunder. See PREDATORY.]

pred·a·tor (prĕd′ə-tər, -tôr′) *n.* **1.** An organism that lives by preying on other organisms. **2.** One that victimizes, plunders, or destroys, esp. for one's own gain. [Lat. *praedātor*, pillager < *praedārī*, to plunder. See PREDATORY.]

pred·a·to·ry (prĕd′ə-tôr′ē, -tōr′ē) *adj.* **1.** Living by preying on other organisms. **2a.** Of, relating to, or marked by predation. **b.** Living by or given to exploiting or destroying others for one's own gain. [Lat. *praedātōrius*, plundering < *praedārī*, to plunder < *praeda*, booty. See **ghend-** in App.] —**pred′a·to′ri·ly** *adv.* —**pred′a·to′ri·ness** *n.*

pred·e·ces·sor (prĕd′ĭ-sĕs′ər, prē′dĭ-) *n.* **1.** One who precedes another in time, esp. in an office or position. **2.** Something that has been succeeded by another. **3.** *Archaic* An ancestor; a forebear. [ME *predecessoure* < OFr. *predecesseur* < LLat. *praedēcessor* : Lat. *prae-*, pre- + Lat. *dēcessor*, a retiring magistrate (< *dēcessus*, p. part. of *dēcēdere*, to depart : *dē-*, away; see DE- + *cēdere*, to go).]

pre·des·ti·nar·i·an (prē-dĕs′tə-nâr′ē-ən) *adj.* **1.** Of or relating to predestination. ❖ *n.* One who believes in the doctrine of predestination. —**pre·des′ti·nar′i·an·ism** *n.*

pre·des·ti·nate (prē-dĕs′tə-nāt′) *tr.v.* **-nat·ed, -nat·ing, -nates** **1.** *Theology* To predestine. **2.** *Archaic* To destine or determine in advance; foreordain. ❖ *adj.* (-nĭt, -nāt′) Foreordained; predestined. [ME *predestinaten* < LLat. *praedēstināre, praedēstināt-*. See PREDESTINE.]

pre·des·ti·na·tion (prē-dĕs′tə-nā′shən) *n.* **1.** The act of predestining or the condition of being predestined. **2.** *Theology* **a.** The doctrine that God has foreordained all things, esp. salvation of certain souls. **b.** The divine decree foreordaining all souls to either salvation or damnation. **c.** The act of God foreordaining all things past and future. **3.** Destiny; fate.

pre·des·tine (prē-dĕs′tĭn) *tr.v.* **-tined, -tin·ing, -tines** **1.** To fix upon, decide, or decree in advance; foreordain. **2.** *Theology* To foreordain or elect by divine will or decree. [ME *predestinen* < OFr. *predestiner* < LLat. *praedēstināre* : Lat. *prae-*, pre- + Lat. *dēstināre*, to determine; see DESTINY.]

pre·de·ter·mine (prē′dĭ-tûr′mĭn) *v.* **-mined, -min·ing, -mines** —*tr.* **1.** To determine, decide, or establish in advance. **2.** To influence or sway toward an action or opinion; predispose. —*intr.* To determine or decide in advance. —**pre′de·ter′mi·nate** (-mə-nĭt) *adj.* —**pre′de·ter′mi·na′tion** *n.*

pre·de·ter·min·er (prē′dĭ-tûr′mə-nər) *n.* An adjectival word that can stand before an article, a possessive pronoun, or another determiner, as *all* in *all the flowers.*

pre·di·al (prē′dē-əl) *adj.* Variant of **praedial.**

pred·i·ca·ble (prĕd′ĭ-kə-bəl) *adj.* That can be stated or predicated: *a predicable conclusion.* ❖ *n.* **1.** Something that can be predicated. **2.** *Logic* Any of the general attributes of a subject or class. In scholastic thought, the attributes are genus, species, property, differentia, and accident; in Aristotelian thought, they are definition, genus, proprium, and accident. [LLat. *praedicābilis* < *praedicāre*, to proclaim publicly, preach, predicate. See PREACH.] —**pred′i·ca·bil′i·ty, pred′i·ca·ble·ness** *n.*

pre·dic·a·ment (prĭ-dĭk′ə-mənt) *n.* **1.** A situation, esp. an unpleasant or trying one, from which extrication is difficult. See Usage Note at **dilemma.** **2.** *Logic* One of the basic Aristotelian states or classifications into which all things can be placed; a category. [ME, class, category < OFr. < LLat. *praedicāmentum* (transl. of Gk. *katēgoria* < *katēgoreuein*, to speak against, signify, predicate < *praedicāre*, to proclaim publicly, predicate. See PREACH.] —**pre·dic′a·men′tal** (-mĕn′tl) *adj.*

pred·i·cate (prĕd′ĭ-kāt′) *v.* **-cat·ed, -cat·ing, -cates** —*tr.* **1.** To base or establish (a statement or action, for example): *predicated*

---

my argument on facts. **2.** To state or affirm as an attribute or quality of something. **3.** To carry the connotation of; imply. **4.** *Logic* To make (a term or expression) the predicate of a proposition. **5.** To proclaim or assert; declare. —*intr.* To make a statement or assertion. ❖ *n.* (-kĭt) **1.** *Grammar* One of the two main constituents of a sentence or clause, modifying the subject and including the verb, objects, or phrases governed by the verb, as *is red* in *The door is red.* **2.** *Logic* That part of a proposition that is affirmed or denied about the subject, as, for example, *mortal* in the proposition *We are mortal.* ❖ *adj.* (-kĭt) **1.** *Grammar* Of or belonging to a predicate. **2.** Stated or asserted; predicated. [LLat. *praedicāre, praedicāt-* < Lat., to proclaim : *prae-*, pre- + *dicāre*, to proclaim; see **deik-** in App.] —**pred′i·ca′tion** *n.* —**pred′i·ca′tion·al** *adj.* —**pred′i·ca′tive·ly** *adv.*

predicate calculus *n.* The branch of symbolic logic that deals not only with relations between propositions as a whole but also with their internal structure, esp. the relation between subject and predicate.

predicate nominative *n.* A noun or pronoun that follows a linking verb and refers back to the subject of the verb.

pred·i·ca·to·ry (prĕd′ĭ-kə-tôr′ē, -tōr′ē) *adj.* Of, relating to, or characteristic of preaching or a preacher. [LLat. *praedicātōrius*, praising < Lat. *praedicātor*, one who makes known < *praedicāre*, to proclaim. See PREACH.]

pre·dict (prĭ-dĭkt′) *v.* **-dict·ed, -dict·ing, -dicts** —*tr.* To state, tell about, or make known in advance, esp. on the basis of special knowledge. —*intr.* To foretell something; prophesy. [Lat. *praedicere, praedict-* : *prae-*, pre- + *dīcere*, to say; see **deik-** in App.] —**pre·dict′a·bil′i·ty** *n.* —**pre·dict′a·ble** *adj.* —**pre·dict′a·bly** *adv.* —**pre·dic′tive** *adj.* —**pre·dic′tive·ly** *adv.* —**pre·dic′tive·ness** *n.* —**pre·dic′tor** *n.*

pre·dic·tion (prĭ-dĭk′shən) *n.* **1.** The act of predicting. **2.** Something foretold or predicted; a prophecy.

pre·di·gest (prē′dī-jĕst′, -dĭ-) *tr.v.* **-gest·ed, -gest·ing, -gests** **1.** To subject (food) to partial digestion, usu. through an enzymatic or chemical process, before ingestion. **2.** To render in a simpler style or form. —**pre′di·ges′tion** *n.*

pred·i·lec·tion (prĕd′l-ĕk′shən, prēd′l-) *n.* A partiality or disposition in favor of something; a preference. [Fr. *prédilection* < OFr. < Med.Lat. *prēdīlēctus*, p. part. of *prēdīligere*, to prefer : Lat. *prae-*, pre- + Lat. *dīligere*, to love; see DILIGENT.]

SYNONYMS *predilection, bias, leaning, partiality, penchant, prejudice, proclivity, propensity* These nouns denote a predisposition to favor someone or something particular: *a predilection for jazz; a pro-American bias; conservative leanings; a partiality for liberal friends; a penchant for exotic foods; a prejudice in favor of the poor; a proclivity for action; a propensity for lies.*

---

pre·dis·pose (prē′dĭ-spōz′) *v.* **-posed, -pos·ing, -pos·es** —*tr.* **1a.** To make (someone) inclined to something in advance. See Syns at **incline.** **b.** To make susceptible or liable. **2.** *Archaic* To settle or dispose of in advance. —*intr.* To provide an inclination or susceptibility.

pre·dis·po·si·tion (prē′dĭs-pə-zĭsh′ən) *n.* The state of being predisposed; tendency, inclination, or susceptibility.

pred·nis·o·lone (prĕd-nĭs′ə-lōn′) *n.* A synthetic steroid, $C_{21}H_{28}O_5$, similar to hydrocortisone and used in various compounds as an anti-inflammatory, immunosuppressive, and antiallergic drug. [Blend of PREDNISONE and –OL¹.]

pred·ni·sone (prĕd′nĭ-sōn′, -zōn′) *n.* A synthetic steroid, $C_{21}H_{26}O_5$, that is similar to cortisone and used as an antiallergic, anti-inflammatory, and immunosuppressive drug. [*pre*(gnane), a steroid (from PREGNANT) + D(I–)¹ + –(E)N(E) + (CORT)ISONE.]

pre·dom·i·nance (prĭ-dŏm′ə-nəns) also **pre·dom·i·nan·cy** (-nən-sē) *n.* The state or quality of being predominant; preponderance.

pre·dom·i·nant (prĭ-dŏm′ə-nənt) *adj.* **1.** Having greatest ascendancy, importance, influence, authority, or force. **2.** Most common or conspicuous; main or prevalent. [Med.Lat. *prēdomināns, prēdominant-*, pr. part. of *prēdominārī*, to predominate. See PREDOMINATE.] —**pre·dom′i·nant·ly** *adv.*

pre·dom·i·nate (prĭ-dŏm′ə-nāt′) *v.* **-nat·ed, -nat·ing, -nates** —*intr.* **1.** To have or gain controlling power or influence; prevail. **2.** To be of or have greater quantity or importance; preponderate. —*tr.* To dominate or prevail over. [Med.Lat. *prēdominārī, prēdomināt-*: Lat. *prae-*, pre- + Lat. *dominārī*, to rule (< *dominus*, master; see **dem-** in App.).] —**pre·dom′i·nate·ly** (-nĭt-lē) *adv.* —**pre·dom′i·na′tion** *n.* —**pre·dom′i·na′tor** *n.*

pre·e·clamp·si·a (prē′ĭ-klămp′sē-ə) *n.* A condition of hypertension occurring in pregnancy, typically accompanied by edema and proteinuria. —**pre′e·clamp′tic** (-tĭk) *adj.*

pre·em·bry·o (prē-ĕm′brē-ō′) *n., pl.* **-os** A fertilized ovum up to 14 days old, before it becomes implanted in the uterus. —**pre·em′bry·on′ic** (-ŏn′ĭk) *adj.*

pree·mie (prē′mē) *n. Informal* A prematurely born infant.

pre·em·i·nent or **pre-em·i·nent** (prē-ĕm′ə-nənt) *adj.* Superior to or notable above all others; outstanding. See Syns at **noted.** [ME < Lat. *praeēminēns*, pr. part. of *praeēminēre*, to excel : *prae-*, pre- + *ēminēre*, to stand out; see EMINENT.] —**pre·em′i·nence** *n.* —**pre·em′i·nent·ly** *adv.*

pre·empt or **pre-empt** (prē-ĕmpt′) *v.* **-empt·ed, -empt·ing,**

ă pat | oi boy
ā pay | ou out
âr care | ŏŏ took
ä father | ōō boot
ĕ pet | ŭ cut
ē be | ûr urge
ĭ pit | th thin
ī pie | th this
îr pier | hw which
ŏ pot | zh vision
ō toe | ə about,
ô paw | item

Stress marks:
′ (primary);
′ (secondary); as in
lexicon (lĕk′sĭ-kŏn′)

-empts —*tr.* **1.** To appropriate, seize, or take for oneself before others. **2a.** To take the place of; displace. **b.** To have precedence or predominance over. **3.** To gain possession of by prior right or opportunity, esp. to settle on (public land) to obtain the right to buy first. —*intr. Games* To make a preemptive bid in bridge. —**pre·emp'tor'** (-ĕmp'tôr') *n.* —**pre·emp'to·ry** (-ĕmp'tə-rē) *adj.*

pre·emp·tion or **pre-emp·tion** (prē-ĕmp'shən) *n.* **1a.** The right to purchase something before others, esp. the right to purchase public land that is granted to one who has settled on that land. **b.** A purchase made by such a right. **2.** Prior seizure of, appropriation of, or claim to something, such as property. [PRE– + Lat. *ĕmptiō, ĕmptiōn-*, buying (< *ĕmptus,* p. part. of *emere,* to buy).]

pre·emp·tive or **pre-emp·tive** (prē-ĕmp'tĭv) *adj.* **1.** Of, relating to, or characteristic of preemption. **2.** Having or granted by the right of preemption. **3a.** Relating to or constituting a military strike made so as to gain the advantage when an enemy strike is believed imminent. **b.** Initiated to deter or prevent an anticipated, usu. unpleasant situation or occurrence. **4.** Having or marked by the power to preempt or take precedence: *preemptive authority.* **5.** *Games* Relating to or being a bid in bridge at a high level that is intended to interfere with the opponents' bidding. —**pre·emp'tive·ly** *adv.*

preemptive right *n.* The right of certain stockholders to maintain ownership of a constant percentage of a firm's stock.

preen (prēn) *v.* **preened, preen·ing, preens** —*tr.* **1a.** To smooth or clean (feathers) with the beak or bill. **b.** To trim or clean (fur) with the tongue, as cats do. **2.** To dress or groom (oneself) with elaborate care; primp. **3.** To take pride or satisfaction in (oneself); gloat. —*intr.* **1.** To dress up; primp. **2.** To swell with pride; gloat or exult. [ME *proinen, preinen,* blend of OFr. *proignier,* to prune; see PRUNE², and OFr. *poroindre,* to anoint before (*por-,* before < Lat. *prō-;* see PRO–¹ + *oindre,* to anoint < Lat. *unguere*).] —**preen'er** *n.*

pre·en·gi·neered or **pre-en·gi·neered** (prē'ĕn-jə-nîrd') *adj.* Built of or using prefabricated sections or parts.

pre·ex·il·i·an or **pre-ex·il·i·an** (prē'ĕg-zĭl'ē-ən, -zĭl'yən, -ĕk-sĭl'ē-ən, -sĭl'yən) also **pre·ex·il·ic** or **pre-ex·il·ic** (-ĕg-zĭl'ĭk, -ĕk-sĭl'-) *adj.* Relating to the history of the Jews before their exile in Babylonia in the sixth century B.C.

pre·ex·ist or **pre-ex·ist** (prē'ĭg-zĭst') *v.* **-ist·ed, -ist·ing, -ists** —*tr.* To exist before; precede. —*intr.* To exist beforehand. —**pre'ex·is'tence** *n.* —**pre'ex·is'tent** *adj.*

pref. *abbr.* **1.** preface **2.** preferred (stock) **3.** prefix

pre·fab (prē'făb') *Informal adj.* Prefabricated. ❖ *n.* Something prefabricated. —**pre'fab'** *v.*

prefab

pre·fab·ri·cate (prē-făb'rĭ-kāt') *tr.v.* **-cat·ed, -cat·ing, -cates** **1.** To manufacture (a building, for example) in advance, esp. in sections to be shipped and assembled. **2.** To make up, construct, or develop in an artificial, unoriginal, or stereotypic manner. —**pre·fab'ri·ca'tion** *n.* —**pre·fab'ri·ca'tor** *n.*

pref·ace (prĕf'ĭs) *n.* **1a.** An explanatory statement or essay introducing a book, usu. written by the author. **b.** An introductory section, as of a speech. **2.** Something introductory; a preliminary. **3.** often **Preface** The words introducing the central part of the Eucharist in several Christian churches. ❖ *tr.v.* **-aced, -ac·ing, -ac·es** **1.** To introduce by or provide with a preliminary statement or essay. **2.** To serve as an introduction to. [ME < OFr. < Lat. *praefātiō, praefātiōn-* < *praefātus,* p. part. of *praefārī,* to say before : *prae-,* pre- + *fārī,* to speak; see **bhā-** in App.] —**pref'ac·er** *n.*

pre·fad·ed (prē-fā'dĭd) *adj.* Artificially given a faded, weathered, or aged look. Used of clothing or fabric.

pref·a·to·ry (prĕf'ə-tôr'ē, -tōr'ē) *adj.* Of or constituting a preface; introductory. [< Lat. *praefātus,* p. part. of *praefārī,* to say before. See PREFACE.] —**pref'a·to'ri·ly** *adv.*

pre·fect (prē'fĕkt') *n.* **1.** A high administrative official or chief officer, as: **a.** Any of several high officials in ancient Rome. **b.** The chief of police of Paris, France. **c.** A chief administrative official of a department of France. **d.** The administrator in charge of discipline at a Jesuit school. **2.** A student monitor or officer, esp. in a private school. [ME < OFr. < Lat. *praefectus* < p. part. of *praeficere,* to place at the head of : *prae-,* pre- + *facere,* to make; see **dhē-** in App.]

pre·fec·ture (prē'fĕk'chər) *n.* **1.** The district administered or governed by a prefect. **2.** The office or authority of a prefect. **3.** The residence or housing of a prefect. —**pre·fec'tur·al** (prī-fĕk'chər-əl) *adj.*

pre·fer (prĭ-fûr') *tr.v.* **-ferred, -fer·ring, -fers** **1.** To choose or habitually choose as more desirable or more valuable. **2.** *Law* **a.** To give priority or preference to (a creditor). **b.** To file, prosecute, or offer for consideration or resolution before a magistrate, court, or other legal authority. **3.** *Archaic* To recommend for advancement or appointment; promote. [ME *preferren* < OFr. *preferer* < Lat. *praeferre* : *prae-,* pre- + *ferre,* to carry; see **bher-¹** in App.] —**pre·fer'rer** *n.*

pref·er·a·ble (prĕf'ər-ə-bəl, prĕf'rə-) *adj.* More desirable or worthy than another; preferred. —**pref'er·a·bil'i·ty, pref'er·a·ble·ness** *n.* —**pref'er·a·bly** *adv.*

pref·er·ence (prĕf'ər-əns, prĕf'rəns) *n.* **1a.** The selecting of

someone or something over another or others. **b.** The right or chance to so choose. **c.** Someone or something so chosen. Syns at **choice. 2.** The state of being preferred. **3.** *Law* **a.** A priority of payment given to one or more creditors by an insolvent debtor. **b.** The right of a creditor to precedence. **4.** The granting of precedence or advantage to one or more countries in international trade. [ME *preferraunce,* preferment < OFr. *preference* < *preferer,* to prefer. See PREFER.]

pref·er·en·tial (prĕf'ə-rĕn'shəl) *adj.* **1.** Of, relating to, or giving advantage or preference: *preferential treatment.* **2.** Manifesting or originating from partiality or preference. —**pref'er·en'tial·ism** *n.* —**pref'er·en'tial·ist** *n.* —**pref'er·en'tial·ly** *adv.*

preferential voting *n.* A system of voting in which the voter ranks candidates in order of preference.

pre·fer·ment (prĭ-fûr'mənt) *n.* **1.** The act of advancing to a higher position or office; promotion. **2.** A position, appointment, or rank giving advancement, as of profit or prestige. **3.** The act of preferring or the state of being preferred.

preferred stock *n.* Capital stock having priority over a corporation's common stock in the distribution of dividends and often of assets.

pre·fig·u·ra·tion (prē-fĭg'yə-rā'shən) *n.* **1.** The act of representing, suggesting, or imagining in advance. **2.** Something that prefigures; a foreshadowing.

pre·fig·ure (prē-fĭg'yər) *tr.v.* **-ured, -ur·ing, -ures** **1.** To suggest, indicate, or represent by an antecedent form or model; presage or foreshadow: *Cézanne prefigured cubism.* **2.** To imagine or picture to oneself in advance. [ME *prefiguren* < OFr. *prefigurer* < LLat. *praefigūrāre* : Lat. *prae-,* pre- + Lat. *figūrāre,* to shape (< *figūra,* shape; see **dheigh-** in App.).] —**pre·fig'ur·a·tive** (-fĭg'yər-ə-tĭv) *adj.* —**pre·fig'ur·a·tive·ly** *adv.* —**pre·fig'ure·ment** *n.*

pre·fin·ished (prē-fĭn'ĭsht) *adj.* Coated or treated before being sold or distributed: *prefinished wood paneling.*

pre·fix (prē'fĭks') *tr.v.* **-fixed, -fix·ing, -fix·es** **1.** To put or attach before or in front of. **2.** (prē-fĭks') To settle or arrange in advance. **3.** *Grammar* **a.** To add as a prefix. **b.** To add a prefix to. ❖ *n.* **1.** *Grammar* An affix, such as *dis-* in *disbelieve,* attached to the front of a word to produce a derivative word or an inflected form. **2.** A title placed before a person's name. [ME *prefixen* < OFr. *prefixer* : *pre-,* before (< Lat. *prae-;* see PRE–) + *fixer,* to place (< Lat. *fixus,* p. part. of *figere,* to fasten). N. < NLat. *praefixum* < neut. sing. of Lat. *praefīxus,* p. part. of *praefīgere,* to fix in front : *prae-,* pre- + *figere,* to fasten.] —**pre'fix'al** *adj.* —**pre'fix'al·ly** *adv.* —**pre·fix·a'tion** (-fĭk-sā'shən), **pre·fix'ion** (-fĭk'shən) *n.*

pre·flight (prē'flīt') *adj.* Preparing for or occurring before flight. ❖ *tr.v.* **-flight·ed, -flight·ing, -flights** To check (an aircraft) for airworthiness before flight. —**pre'flight'** *n.*

pre·form (prē'fôrm') *tr.v.* **-formed, -form·ing, -forms** **1.** To shape or form beforehand. **2.** To determine the shape or form of beforehand. ❖ *n.* **1.** An object that has been subjected to preliminary shaping or molding before being completed. **2.** *Linguistics* A reconstructed ancestral word or form.

pre·for·ma·tion (prē'fôr-mā'shən) *n.* **1.** The act of shaping or forming in advance; prior formation. **2.** A theory popular in the 18th century that all parts of an organism exist completely formed in the germ cell and develop only by increasing in size.

pre·fron·tal (prē-frŭn'tl) *adj.* **1.** Of, relating to, or situated in the anterior part of the frontal lobe. **2.** Situated anterior to the frontal bone.

prefrontal lobotomy *n.* A lobotomy in which the white fibers that connect the thalamus to the prefrontal and frontal lobes of the brain are severed, performed as a treatment for extremely violent behavior.

pre·gan·gli·on·ic (prē-găng'glē-ŏn'ĭk) *adj.* Of, relating to, or being the nerve fibers that supply a ganglion, esp. a ganglion of the autonomic nervous system.

preg·na·ble (prĕg'nə-bəl) *adj.* Being such that attack or capture is possible; vulnerable or assailable. [ME *preignable, pregnabul* < OFr. *prenable, pregnauble* < *prendre,* to grasp < Lat. *prehendere, prĕndere.* See **ghend-** in App.] —**preg'na·bil'i·ty** *n.*

preg·nan·cy (prĕg'nən-sē) *n., pl.* **-cies 1a.** The condition of being pregnant. **b.** An instance of being pregnant. **c.** The period during which one is pregnant. **2.** Richness of significance, import, or implication. **3.** Creativity; inventiveness.

preg·nant¹ (prĕg'nənt) *adj.* **1.** Carrying developing offspring within the body. **2a.** Weighty or significant; full of meaning. **b.** Of great or potentially great import, implication, or moment. **3.** Filled or fraught; replete. **4.** Having a profusion of ideas; creative or inventive. **5.** Producing results; fruitful. [ME < OFr. < Lat. *praegnāns, praegnant-,* var. of *praegnās.* See **genə-** in App.] —**preg'nant·ly** *adv.*

preg·nant² (prĕg'nənt) *adj. Archaic* Convincing; cogent. Used of an argument or a proof. [ME, prob. < OFr. *preignant,* pr. part. of *prembre,* to press < Lat. *premere.*]

pre·hen·sile (prē-hĕn'səl, -sīl') *adj.* **1.** Adapted for seizing, grasping, or holding, esp. by wrapping around an object. **2.** Having keen intellect; insightful. **3.** Greedy; grasping. [Fr. *préhensile* < Lat. *prehēnsus,* p. part. of *prehendere,* to grasp. See **ghend-** in App.] —**pre·hen·sil'i·ty** (-sĭl'ĭ-tē) *n.*

pre·hen·sion (prē-hĕn′shən) *n.* **1.** The act of grasping or seizing. **2a.** Apprehension by the senses. **b.** Understanding. [Lat. *prehēnsiō, prehēnsiōn-* < *prehēnsus,* p. part. of *prehendere,* to seize. See **ghend-** in App.]

pre·his·tor·ic (prē′hĭ-stôr′ĭk, -stôr′-) also **pre·his·tor·i·cal** (-ĭ-kəl) *adj.* **1.** Of, relating to, or belonging to the era before recorded history. **2.** Of or relating to a language before it is first recorded in writing. —**pre′his·tor′i·cal·ly** *adv.*

pre·his·to·ry (prē-hĭs′tə-rē) *n., pl.* **-ries** **1.** History of humankind in the period before recorded history. **2.** The circumstances or developments leading up to or surrounding a situation, event, or development; background. —**pre·his·tor′i·an** (-hĭ-stôr′ē-ən, -stôr′-) *n.*

pre·ig·ni·tion (prē′ĭg-nĭsh′ən) *n.* The ignition of fuel in an internal-combustion engine before the spark passes through the fuel, resulting from a hot spot in the cylinder or from too great a compression ratio for the fuel.

prej·u·dice (prĕj′ə-dĭs) *n.* **1a.** An adverse judgment or opinion formed beforehand or without knowledge or examination of the facts. **b.** A preconceived preference or idea. See Syns at **predilection.** **2.** The act or state of holding unreasonable preconceived judgments or convictions. **3.** Irrational suspicion or hatred of a particular group, race, or religion. **4.** Detriment or injury caused to a person by the preconceived, unfavorable conviction of another or others. ❖ *tr.v.* **-diced, -dic·ing, -dic·es** **1.** To cause (someone) to judge prematurely and irrationally. **2.** To affect injuriously or detrimentally by a judgment or act. [ME < OFr. < Lat. *praeiūdicium : prae-, pre- + iūdicium,* judgment (< *iūdex, iūdic-,* judge; see **deik-** in App.).]

prej·u·di·cial (prĕj′ə-dĭsh′əl) *adj.* **1.** Detrimental; injurious. **2.** Causing or tending to preconceived judgment or convictions. —**prej′u·di′cial·ly** *adv.* —**prej′u·di′cial·ness** *n.*

prej·u·di·cious (prĕj′ə-dĭsh′əs) *adj.* Prejudicial. —**prej′u·di′cious·ly** *adv.*

prel·a·cy (prĕl′ə-sē) *n., pl.* **-cies** **1a.** The office or station of a prelate. **b.** Prelates considered as a group. **2.** Church government administered by prelates.

pre·lap·sar·i·an (prē′lăp-sâr′ē-ən) *adj.* Of or relating to the period before the fall of Adam and Eve. [PRE- + Lat. *lāpsus,* fall; see LAPSE + -ARIAN.]

prel·ate (prĕl′ĭt) *n.* A high-ranking member of the clergy, esp. a bishop. [ME *prelat* < OFr. < Med.Lat. *praelātus* < Lat., p. part. of *praeferre,* to carry before, to prefer : *prae-, pre- + lātus,* brought; see **telə-** in App.] —**pre·lat′ic** (prĭ-lăt′ĭk) *adj.*

prel·a·ture (prĕl′ə-chər, -choŏr′) *n.* See **prelacy** 1.

pre·law (prē′lô′) *adj.* Of, relating to, or being the studies that prepare one for the study of law.

pre·lect (prĭ-lĕkt′) *intr.v.* **-lect·ed, -lect·ing, -lects** To lecture or discourse in public. [Lat. *praelegere, praelēct- : prae-, pre- + legere,* to read; see **leg-** in App.] —**pre·lec′tion** *n.* —**pre·lec′tor** *n.*

pre·li·ba·tion (prē′lī-bā′shən) *n.* A foretaste. [Lat. *praelībātiō, praelībātiōn-* < *praelibātus,* p. part. of *praelibāre,* to taste beforehand : *prae-, pre- + lībāre,* pour out, to taste.]

pre·lim (prē′lĭm′, prĭ-lĭm′) *n.* A preliminary: *a team that won in the prelims; studied for my prelims.*

pre·lim·i·nar·y (prĭ-lĭm′ə-nĕr′ē) *adj.* Prior to or preparing for the main matter, action, or business; introductory or prefatory. ❖ *n., pl.* **-ies** **1.** Something that is preliminary. **2.** An academic test or examination preparatory to another one. **3.** *Sports* A contest to determine the finalists in a competition. **4.** *Sports* An event that precedes the main event of a program, esp. in boxing or wrestling. **5.** *Printing* The front matter of a book. Often used in the plural. [< NLat. *praelīmināris* : Lat. *prae-, pre- + Lat. līmen, līmin-,* threshold.] —**pre·lim′i·nar′i·ly** (-nâr′ə-lē) *adv.*

pre·lit·er·ate (prē-lĭt′ər-ĭt) *adj.* Of, relating to, or being a culture not having a written language. —**pre·lit′er·ate** *n.*

Pre·log (prĕl′ôg′), **Vladimir** 1906–98. Bosnian-born Swiss chemist who shared a 1975 Nobel Prize.

prel·ude (prĕl′yoŏd′, prā′loŏd′, prē′-) *n.* **1.** An introductory performance, event, or action preceding a more important one; a preliminary or preface. **2.** *Music* **a.** A piece or movement that serves as an introduction to another section or composition and establishes the key, such as one that precedes a fugue, opens a suite, or precedes a church service. **b.** A similar but independent composition for the piano. **c.** The overture to an oratorio, opera, or act of an opera. **d.** A short composition of the 15th and early 16th centuries written in a free style, usu. for keyboard. ❖ *v.* **-ud·ed, -ud·ing, -udes** —*tr.* **1.** To serve as a prelude to. **2.** To introduce with or as if with a prelude. —*intr.* To serve as a prelude or introduction. [Med.Lat. *praelūdium* < Lat. *praelūdere,* to play beforehand : *prae-, pre- + lūdere,* to play.] —**prel′ud′er** *n.* —**pre·lu′di·al** (prĭ-loŏ′dē-əl) *adj.*

pre·lu·sion (prĭ-loŏ′zhən) *n.* A prelude or introduction. [Lat. *praelūsiō, praelūsiōn-* < *praelūsus,* p. part. of *praelūdere,* to play beforehand. See PRELUDE.]

pre·lu·sive (prĭ-loŏ′sĭv) *adj.* Of or serving as a prelude; introductory. —**pre·lu′sive·ly** *adv.*

pre·ma·lig·nant (prē′mə-lĭg′nənt) *adj.* Precancerous.

pre·ma·ture (prē′mə-tyoŏr′, -toŏr′, -choŏr′) *adj.* **1.** Occurring, growing, or existing before the customary, correct, or assigned time; uncommonly or unexpectedly early. **2.** Born after a gesta-

tion period of less than the normal time: *a premature infant.* [ME, ripe < Lat. *praemātūrus,* ripe too early : *prae-, pre- + mātūrus,* ripe.] —**pre′ma·ture′ly** *adv.* —**pre′ma·ture′ness, pre′ma·tu′ri·ty** *n.*

pre·max·il·la (prē′măk-sĭl′ə) *n., pl.* **-max·il·lae** (-măk-sĭl′ē) Either of two bones located in front of and between the maxillary bones in the upper jaw of vertebrates. —**pre·max′il·lar′y** (-măk′sə-lĕr′ē) *adj.*

pre·med (prē′mĕd′) *Informal adj.* Premedical. ❖ *n.* **1.** A premedical student. **2.** A premedical program of study.

pre·med·i·cal (prē-mĕd′ĭ-kəl) *adj.* Being or relating to studies that prepare one for medical school.

pre·med·i·tate (prē-mĕd′ĭ-tāt′) *v.* **-tat·ed, -tat·ing, -tates** —*tr.* To plan, arrange, or plot (a crime, for example) in advance. —*intr.* To reflect, ponder, or deliberate beforehand. —**pre·med′i·ta′tive** *adj.* —**pre·med′i·ta′tor** *n.*

pre·med·i·tat·ed (prē-mĕd′ĭ-tā′tĭd) *adj.* Marked by deliberate purpose, previous consideration, and some degree of planning. —**pre·med′i·tat′ed·ly** *adv.*

pre·med·i·ta·tion (prē-mĕd′ĭ-tā′shən) *n.* **1.** The act of speculating, arranging, or plotting in advance. **2.** *Law* The contemplation of a crime well enough in advance to show deliberate intent to commit the crime; forethought.

pre·men·stru·al (prē-mĕn′stroŏ-əl) *adj.* Of or occurring just before menstruation. —**pre·men′stru·al·ly** *adv.*

premenstrual syndrome *n.* A group of symptoms, including abdominal bloating, breast tenderness, headache, fatigue, irritability, and depression, that occur in many women from 2 to 7 days before the onset of menstruation.

pre·mier (prĭ-mîr′, -myîr′, prē′mîr′) *adj.* **1.** First in status or importance; principal or chief. **2.** First to occur or exist; earliest. ❖ *n.* (prĭ-mîr′) **1.** A prime minister. **2.** A chief administrative officer, as of a Canadian province. [ME *primier* < OFr. < Lat. *prīmārius* < *prīmus,* first. See **per¹** in App.] —**pre·mier′ship** *n.*

pre·mier dan·seur (prə-myä′ dän-sœr′) *n., pl.* **pre·miers dan·seurs** (prə-myä′ dän-sœr′) A man who is the principal dancer in a ballet company. [Fr.]

pre·miere or **pre·mière** (prĭ-mîr′, -myâr′) *n.* The first public performance, as of a movie or play. ❖ *v.* **-miered, -mier·ing, -mieres** or **-mièred, -mièr·ing, -mières** —*tr.* To present the premiere of. —*intr.* **1.** To have the premiere. **2.** To make a first appearance in a public performance. ❖ *adj.* First or paramount; premier. [Fr. *première* < fem. of *premier,* first. See PREMIER.]

> **USAGE NOTE** In entertainment contexts the verb *premiere* has by now become the standard way of saying "to introduce to the public," though some Panelists do not like this usage. The example *The Philharmonic will premiere works by two young Americans* was acceptable to 77 percent of the Panelists in 1999, up from 14 percent in 1969 and 51 percent in 1987. But only 25 percent of the Panelists in 1999 (up from 10 percent in 1987) accepted extension of the verb to nonentertainment contexts, as in *Last fall the school premiered several new degree programs.*

pre·mière dan·seuse (prĭ-mîr′ dän-sœz′, -myâr′) *n., pl.* **pre·mières dan·seuses** (prĭ-myâr′ dän-sœz′) A woman who is the principal dancer in a ballet company. [Fr. : *première,* fem. of *premier,* first + *danseuse,* fem. of *danseur,* dancer.]

pre·mil·le·nar·i·an (prē-mĭl′ə-nâr′ē-ən) *adj.* Of or relating to premillennialism. ❖ *n.* A person who believes in premillennialism. —**pre·mil′le·nar′i·an·ism** *n.*

pre·mil·len·ni·al (prē′mĭ-lĕn′ē-əl) *adj.* Of or happening in the time before the millennium. —**pre′mil·len′ni·al·ly** *adv.*

pre·mil·len·ni·al·ism (prē′mĭ-lĕn′ē-ə-lĭz′əm) *n.* The belief that the Second Coming of Jesus will immediately precede the millennium. —**pre′mil·len′ni·al·ist** *n.*

prem·ise (prĕm′ĭs) *n.* also **prem·iss** (prĕm′ĭs) **1.** A proposition upon which an argument is based or from which a conclusion is drawn. **2.** *Logic* **a.** One of the propositions in a deductive argument. **b.** Either the major or the minor proposition of a syllogism, from which the conclusion is drawn. **3. premises** *Law* The preliminary or explanatory statements or facts of a document, as in a deed. **4. premises a.** Land and the buildings on it. **b.** A building or part of a building. ❖ *v.* **-ised, -is·ing, -is·es** —*tr.* **1.** To state in advance as an introduction or explanation. **2.** To state or assume as a proposition in an argument. —*intr.* To make a premise. [ME *premisse* < OFr. < Med.Lat. *praemissa (propositiō),* (proposition) put before, premise < Lat., fem. p. part. of *praemittere,* to set in front : *prae-, pre- + mittere,* to send.]

pre·mi·um (prē′mē-əm) *n.* **1.** A prize or award. **2.** Something offered free or at a reduced price as an inducement to buy something else. **3.** A sum of money or bonus paid in addition to a regular price, salary, or other amount. **4.** The amount paid, often in addition to the interest, to obtain a loan. **5.** The amount paid or payable, often in installments, for an insurance policy. **6.** The amount at which something is valued above its par or nominal value, as money or securities. **7.** The amount at which a securities option is bought or sold. **8.** Payment for training in a trade or profession. **9.** An unusual or high value. ❖ *adj.* Of superior quality or value. —***idiom:* at a premium** More valuable than usual, as from scarcity. [Lat. *praemium,* inducement, reward : *prae-, pre- + emere,* to take, buy.]

ă	pat	oi	boy
ā	pay	ou	out
âr	care	oŏ	took
ä	father	oō	boot
ĕ	pet	ŭ	cut
ē	be	ûr	urge
ĭ	pit	th	thin
ī	pie	th	this
îr	pier	hw	which
ŏ	pot	zh	vision
ō	toe	ə	about,
ô	paw		item

Stress marks:
′ (primary);
′ (secondary), as in
lexicon (lĕk′sĭ-kŏn′)

pre·mo·lar (prē-mō′lər) *n.* One of eight bicuspid teeth located in pairs on each side of the upper and lower jaws behind the canines and in front of the molars. —**pre·mo′lar** *adj.*

pre·mo·ni·tion (prē′mə-nĭsh′ən, prĕm′ə-) *n.* **1.** A presentiment of the future; a foreboding. **2.** A forewarning. [LLat. *praemonitiō, praemonitiōn-* < Lat. *praemonitus,* p. part. of *praemonēre,* to forewarn : *prae-,* pre- + *monēre,* to warn; see **men-**[1] in App.] —**pre·mon′i·to′ri·ly** (-mŏn′ĭ-tôr′ə-lē, -tōr′-) *adv.* —**pre·mon′i·to′ry** *adj.*

pre·morse (prĭ-môrs′) *adj.* Abruptly truncated, as though bitten or broken off: *a premorse leaf.* [Lat. *praemorsus,* p. part. of *praemordēre,* to bite off in front : *prae-,* pre- + *mordēre,* to bite; see **mer-** in App.]

pre·mu·ni·tion (prē′myōō-nĭsh′ən) *n.* Relative immunity to severe infection by a pathogen as a result of a chronic low-grade infection induced by the same pathogen. [Fr. *prémunition* < Lat. *praemūnītiō, praemūnītiōn-,* fortification beforehand < *praemūnītus,* p. part. of *praemūnīre,* to fortify in advance : *prae-,* pre- + *mūnīre,* to fortify; see **MUNITION**.] —**pre·mune′** (prē-myōōn′) *adj.*

pre·name (prē′nām′) *n.* A forename.

pren·tice (prĕn′tĭs) *n. Archaic* An apprentice.

pre·nup·tial (prē-nŭp′shəl, -chəl) *adj.* Before marriage or a wedding: *a prenuptial celebration.*

pre·oc·cu·pan·cy (prē-ŏk′yə-pən-sē) *n.* **1.** The act or right of occupying a place beforehand or in advance. **2.** The state of being preoccupied or engrossed; preoccupation.

pre·oc·cu·pa·tion (prē-ŏk′yə-pā′shən) *n.* **1.** The state of being preoccupied; absorption of the attention or intellect. **2.** Something that preoccupies or engrosses the mind. **3.** Occupation of a place in advance; preoccupancy.

pre·oc·cu·pied (prē-ŏk′yə-pīd′) *adj.* **1a.** Absorbed in thought; engrossed. **b.** Excessively concerned with something; distracted. **2.** Formerly or already occupied. **3.** Already used and therefore unavailable for further use. Used of taxonomic names.

pre·oc·cu·py (prē-ŏk′yə-pī′) *tr.v.* **-pied, -py·ing, -pies 1.** To occupy completely the mind or attention of; engross. **2.** To occupy or take possession of in advance or before another.

pre-op also **pre·op** (prē′ŏp′) *Informal adj.* Preoperative: *pre-op testing; a pre-op patient.* ❖ *n.* **1.** A preoperative patient. **2.** A section of a hospital providing preoperative treatment.

pre·op·er·a·tive (prē-ŏp′ər-ə-tĭv, -ŏp′rə-, -ŏp′ə-rā′-) *adj.* Occurring before surgery. —**pre·op′er·a·tive·ly** *adv.*

pre·o·ral (prē-ôr′əl, -ōr′-) *adj.* Situated in front of the mouth.

pre·or·bit·al (prē-ôr′bĭ-tl) *adj.* Occurring before the orbit, as of an artificial satellite, has been established.

prep (prĕp) *adj. Informal* Preparatory. ❖ *n.* **1.** *Informal* A preparatory school. **2.** *Informal* Preparation. **3.** *Chiefly British* The preparing of lessons; homework. **4.** *Informal* A preppy. ❖ *v.* **prepped, prep·ping, preps** *Informal* —*intr.* **1.** To be enrolled in and attend a preparatory school. **2.** To study or train in preparation for something. —*tr.* **1.** To prepare (someone) for a medical examination or surgical procedure. **2.** To prepare or prime: *prep a surface for painting.*

prep. *abbr.* preposition

pre·pack·age (prē-păk′ĭj) *tr.v.* **-aged, -ag·ing, -ag·es** To wrap or package (a product) before marketing.

prep·a·ra·tion (prĕp′ə-rā′shən) *n.* **1.** The act or process of preparing. **2.** The state of having been made ready beforehand; readiness. **3.** A preliminary measure that serves to make ready for something. Often used in the plural. **4.** A substance, such as a medicine, prepared for a particular purpose. **5.** *Music* **a.** The anticipation of a dissonant tone by means of its introduction as a consonant tone in the preceding chord. **b.** The dissonant tone so anticipated.

pre·par·a·tive (prĭ-păr′ə-tĭv, -pâr′-) *adj.* Serving or tending to prepare or make ready; preliminary. ❖ *n.* Something that is preparative. —**pre·par′a·tive·ly** *adv.*

pre·par·a·tor (prĭ-păr′ə-tər, -pâr′-) *n.* One who prepares specimens or exhibits for scientific study or display.

pre·par·a·to·ry (prĭ-păr′ə-tôr′ē, -tōr′ē, -pâr′-, prĕp′ər-ə-) *adj.* **1.** Serving to make ready or prepare. **2.** Relating to or engaged in study or training as preparation for advanced education. ❖ *adv.* In preparation. Used with *to: cleaned the house preparatory to our departure.* —**pre·par′a·to′ri·ly** *adv.*

preparatory school *n.* **1.** A usu. private secondary school that prepares students for college. **2.** A usu. private British elementary school that prepares students for public school.

pre·pare (prĭ-pâr′) *v.* **-pared, -par·ing, -pares** —*tr.* **1.** To make ready for a specific purpose, as for an event or occasion: *The teacher prepared the students for the exams.* **2.** To put together or make by combining various elements or ingredients; manufacture or compound: *prepare a meal.* **3.** To fit out; equip: *prepared the ship for an arctic expedition.* **4.** *Music* To lead up to and soften (a dissonance or its impact) by means of a preparation. —*intr.* **1.** To make things or oneself ready. **2.** To study or complete a course of study at a preparatory school. [ME *preparen* < OFr. *preparer* < Lat. *praeparāre : prae-,* pre- + *parāre,* prepare, equip.] —**pre·par′ed·ly** (-pâr′ĭd-lē) *adv.* —**pre·par′er** *n.*

pre·par·ed·ness (prĭ-pâr′ĭd-nĭs) *n.* The state of being prepared, esp. military readiness for combat.

pre·pense (prĭ-pĕns′) *adj.* Contemplated or arranged in advance; premeditated: *malice prepense.* [< ME, p. part. of *purpensen,* to premeditate < AN *purpenser : pur-,* before (< Lat. *pro-;* see **PRO-**[1]) + *penser,* to think (< Lat. *pēnsāre.*)] —**pre·pense′ly** *adv.*

pre·pon·der·ance (prĭ-pŏn′dər-əns) also **pre·pon·der·an·cy** (-ən-sē) *n.* Superiority in weight, force, importance, or influence.

pre·pon·der·ant (prĭ-pŏn′dər-ənt) *adj.* Having superior weight, force, importance, or influence. —**pre·pon′der·ant·ly** *adv.*

pre·pon·der·ate (prĭ-pŏn′də-rāt′) *intr.v.* **-at·ed, -at·ing, -ates 1.** To exceed something else in weight. **2.** To be greater than something else, as in quantity or importance; predominate. ❖ *adj.* (-dər-ĭt) Preponderant. [Lat. *praeponderāre, praeponderāt- : prae-,* pre- + *ponderāre,* to weigh.] —**pre·pon′der·ate·ly** *adv.* —**pre·pon′der·a′tion** *n.*

prep·o·si·tion[1] (prĕp′ə-zĭsh′ən) *n.* A word or phrase placed typically before a substantive and indicating the relation of that substantive to a verb, an adjective, or another substantive, as English *at, by, with, from,* and *in regard to.* [ME *preposicioun* < OFr. *preposicion* < Lat. *praepositiō, praepositiōn-,* a putting before, preposistion (transl. of Gk. *prothesis*) < *praepositus,* p. part. of *praepōnere,* to put in front : *prae-,* pre- + *pōnere,* to put; see **apo-** in App.]

USAGE NOTE The doctrine that a preposition may not be used to end a sentence has become one of the most venerated maxims of schoolroom grammatical lore. However, English syntax allows and sometimes requires final placement of the preposition. Such placement is the only possible one in a sentence such as *We have much to be thankful for.* • Even sticklers for the traditional rule can have no grounds for criticizing sentences such as *Where will she end up?* or *It's the most curious book I've ever run across.* In these examples, *up* and *across* are used as adverbs, not prepositions.

pre·po·si·tion[2] also **pre·po·si·tion** (prē′pə-zĭsh′ən) *tr.v.* **-tioned, -tion·ing, -tions** To place in position in advance.

prep·o·si·tion·al (prĕp′ə-zĭsh′ə-nəl) *adj.* Relating to or used as a preposition. —**prep′o·si′tion·al·ly** *adv.*

prepositional phrase *n.* A phrase that consists of a preposition and its object and has adjectival or adverbial value, such as *in the house in the people in the house.*

pre·pos·i·tive (prĭ-pŏz′ĭ-tĭv) *Grammar adj.* Occurring or placed before another word. ❖ *n.* A prepositive word or particle. [LLat. *praepositīvus* < Lat. *praepositus,* p. part. of *praepōnere,* to put in front. See **PREPOSITION**[1].]

pre·pos·sess (prē′pə-zĕs′) *tr.v.* **-sessed, -sess·ing, -sess·es 1.** To preoccupy the mind of to the exclusion of other thoughts or feelings. **2a.** To influence beforehand against or in favor of someone or something; prejudice. **b.** To impress favorably in advance.

pre·pos·sess·ing (prē′pə-zĕs′ĭng) *adj.* **1.** Serving to impress favorably; pleasing: *a prepossessing appearance.* **2.** *Archaic* Causing prejudice. —**pre′pos·sess′ing·ly** *adv.*

pre·pos·ses·sion (prē′pə-zĕsh′ən) *n.* **1.** A preconception or prejudice. **2.** The state of being preoccupied with thoughts, opinions, or feelings.

pre·pos·ter·ous (prĭ-pŏs′tər-əs) *adj.* Contrary to nature, reason, or common sense; absurd. [< Lat. *praeposterus,* inverted, unseasonable : *prae-,* pre- + *posterus,* coming behind (< *post,* behind; see **apo-** in App.).] —**pre·pos′ter·ous·ly** *adv.* —**pre·pos′ter·ous·ness** *n.*

pre·po·ten·cy (prē-pōt′n-sē) *n.* **1.** The condition of being greater in power, influence, or force than another or others; predominance. **2.** *Genetics* The ability of one parent, variety, or strain to transmit traits to an offspring, apparently to the exclusion of the other parent, variety, or strain.

pre·po·tent (prē-pōt′nt) *adj.* **1.** Greater in power, influence, or force than another or others; predominant. **2.** *Genetics* Of, having, or exhibiting prepotency. [ME < Lat. *praepotēns, praepotent-,* pr. part. of *praeposse,* to be more powerful : *prae-,* pre- + *posse,* to be able or powerful; see **poti-** in App.] —**pre·po′tent·ly** *adv.*

prep·py or **prep·pie** (prĕp′ē) *Informal n., pl.* **-pies 1.** A student or former student of a preparatory school. **2.** A person whose manner and dress are deemed typical of traditional preparatory schools. ❖ *adj.* **-pi·er, -pi·est** Of or relating to a preppy or a preparatory school. [PREP(ARATORY SCHOOL) + -Y[1].] —**prep′pi·ly** *adv.* —**prep′pi·ness** *n.*

pre·pran·di·al (prē-prăn′dē-əl) *adj.* Before a meal, esp. dinner: *a preprandial walk.*

pre·print (prē′prĭnt′) *n.* Something printed and often distributed in partial or preliminary form in advance of official publication: *a preprint of a scientific article.* ❖ *tr.v.* (prē-prĭnt′) **-print·ed, -print·ing, -prints** To print in advance.

pre·proc·ess (prē-prŏs′ĕs′, -prō′sĕs′) *tr.v.* **-essed, -ess·ing, -ess·es** To perform preliminary processing on (data, for example). —**pre·proc′es·sor** *n.*

prep school *n. Informal* A preparatory school.

pre·puce (prē′pyōōs′) *n.* **1.** See **foreskin. 2.** A loose fold of skin covering the glans clitoridis. [ME < OFr. < Lat. *praepūtium : poss.*

prae-, pre- + *pūtos, penis.] —**pre·pu′tial** (-pyo͞o′shəl) *adj.*

pre·pu·pa (prē-pyo͞o′pə) *n. pl* **-pae** (-pē) or **-pas 1.** An inactive stage just before the pupa in the development of certain insects. **2.** The prepupal form of an insect. —**pre·pu′pal** *adj.*

pre·quel (prē′kwəl) *n.* A literary, dramatic, or cinematic work whose narrative takes place before that of a preexisting work or a sequel. [PRE– + (SE)QUEL.]

Pre-Raph·a·el·ite also **pre-Raph·a·el·ite** (prē-răf′ē-ə-līt′, -rā′fē-) *n.* A painter or writer belonging to or influenced by the Pre-Raphaelite Brotherhood, a society founded in England in 1848 to advance the style and spirit of Italian painting before Raphael. ❖ *adj.* Of, relating to, or characteristic of the Pre-Raphaelites. —**Pre-Raph′a·el·it′ism** *n.*

pre·re·lease (prē′rĭ-lēs′) *n.* Something released before a scheduled date. —**pre′re·lease′** *adj.*

pre·req·ui·site (prē-rĕk′wĭ-zĭt) *adj.* Required or necessary as a prior condition. ❖ *n.* Something that is prerequisite, as a course that is required prior to taking an advanced course.

pre·rog·a·tive (prĭ-rŏg′ə-tĭv) *n.* **1.** An exclusive right or privilege held by a person or group, esp. a hereditary or official right. See Syns at **right. 2.** The exclusive right and power to command, decide, rule, or judge. **3.** A special quality that confers superiority. ❖ *adj.* Of, arising from, or exercising a prerogative. [ME < OFr. < Lat. *praerogātīva*, fem. of *praerogātīvus*, asked first < *praerogātus*, p. part. of *praerogāre*, to ask before : *prae-*, pre- + *rogāre*, to ask; see **reg-** in App.] —**pre·rog′a·tived** *adj.*

pres. *abbr.* **1.** present **2.** or **Pres.** president

pres·age (prĕs′ĭj) *n.* **1.** An indication or warning of a future occurrence; an omen. **2.** A feeling or intuition of what is going to occur; a presentiment. **3.** Prophetic significance or meaning. **4.** *Archaic* A prediction. ❖ *v.* **pre·sage** (prĭ-sāj′, prĕs′ĭj) **-saged, -sag·ing, -sag·es** —*tr.* **1.** To indicate or warn of in advance; portend. **2.** To have a presentiment of. **3.** To foretell or predict. —*intr.* To make or utter a prediction. [ME < Lat. *praesāgium* < *praesāgīre*, to perceive beforehand : *prae-*, pre- + *sāgīre*, to perceive.] —**pre·sage′ful** (prĭ-sāj′fəl) *adj.*

Presb. or **Presby.** *abbr.* Presbyterian

pres·by·ope (prĕz′bē-ōp′, prĕs′-) *n.* A person affected with presbyopia.

pres·by·o·pi·a (prĕz′bē-ō′pē-ə, prĕs′-) *n.* Inability of the eye to focus sharply on nearby objects, resulting from loss of elasticity of the crystalline lens with advancing age. [NLat. : Gk. *presbus*, old man; see **per**[1] in App. + –OPIA.] —**pres′by·op′ic** (-ŏp′ĭk, -ō′pĭk) *adj.*

pres·by·ter (prĕz′bĭ-tər, prĕs′-) *n.* **1.** A priest in various hierarchical churches. **2a.** A teaching elder in the Presbyterian Church. **b.** A ruling elder in the Presbyterian Church. **3.** An elder of the congregation in the early Christian church. [LLat. < Gk. *presbuteros* < comp. of *presbus*, old man. See **per**[1] in App.]

pres·byt·er·ate (prĕz-bĭt′ər-ĭt, -ə-rāt′, prĕs-) *n.* **1.** The office of a presbyter. **2.** A body or an order of presbyters.

pres·by·te·ri·al (prĕz′bĭ-tîr′ē-əl, prĕs′-) *adj.* Of or relating to a presbyter or the presbytery. —**pres′by·te′ri·al·ly** *adv.*

pres·by·te·ri·an (prĕz′bĭ-tîr′ē-ən, prĕs′-) *adj.* **1.** Of or relating to ecclesiastical government by presbyters. **2. Presbyterian** Of or relating to a Presbyterian Church. ❖ *n.* **Presbyterian** A member or an adherent of a Presbyterian Church. —**pres′by·te′ri·an·ism** *n.*

Presbyterian Church *n.* Any of various Protestant churches governed by presbyters and traditionally Calvinist in doctrine.

pres·by·ter·y (prĕz′bĭ-tĕr′ē, prĕs′-) *n., pl.* **-ies 1a.** A court composed of Presbyterian Church ministers and representative elders of a particular locality. **b.** The district represented by this court. **2.** Presbyters considered as a group. **3.** Government of a church by presbyters. **4.** The section of a church reserved for the clergy. **5.** *Roman Catholic Church* The residence of a priest. [ME *presbetory*, priests' bench < LLat. *presbyterium*, council of elders < Gk. *presbuterion* < *presbuteros*, elder. See PRESBYTER.]

pre·school (prē′sko͞ol′) *adj.* Of, for, relating to, or being the early years of childhood before elementary school. ❖ *n.* (prē′sko͞ol′) A school for preschoolers; a nursery school.

pre·school·er (prē′sko͞o′lər) *n.* **1.** A child who is not old enough to attend kindergarten. **2.** A child who is enrolled in a preschool.

pre·school·ing (prē′sko͞o′lĭng) *n.* Early childhood education, esp. when received at a preschool.

pre·science (prĕsh′əns, -ē-əns, prē′shəns, -shē-əns) *n.* Knowledge of actions or events before they occur; foresight.

pre·scient (prĕsh′ənt, -ē-ənt, prē′shənt, -shē-ənt) *adj.* **1.** Of or relating to prescience. **2.** Possessing prescience. [Fr. < OFr. < Lat. *praesciēns, praescient-*, pr. part. of *praescīre*, to know beforehand : *prae-*, pre- + *scīre*, to know.] —**pre′scient·ly** *adv.*

pre·sci·en·tif·ic (prē-sī′ən-tĭf′ĭk) *adj.* **1.** Of, relating to, or occurring at a time before the advent of modern science and the application of its methods. **2.** Prior to testing or formulation in scientific terms; preliminary.

pre·scind (prĭ-sĭnd′) *v.* **-scind·ed, -scind·ing, -scinds** —*tr.* To separate or divide in thought; consider individually. —*intr.* To withdraw one's attention. [Lat. *praescindere*, to cut off in front : *prae-*, pre- + *scindere*, to cut off, split.]

Pres·cott (prĕs′kət, -kŏt′), **William Hickling** 1796–1859. Amer. historian noted for his lively studies of the conquistadors, including *History of the Conquest of Mexico* (1843).

pre·screen (prē-skrēn′) *tr.v.* **-screened, -screen·ing, -screens 1.** To view (a movie) before release for public showing. **2.** To examine or interview before further selection processes.

pre·scribe (prĭ-skrīb′) *v.* **-scribed, -scrib·ing, -scribes** —*tr.* **1.** To set down as a rule or guide; enjoin. See Syns at **dictate. 2.** To order the use of (a medicine or other treatment). —*intr.* **1.** To establish rules, laws, or directions. **2.** To order a medicine or other treatment. [ME *prescriben* < Lat. *praescrībere* : *prae-*, pre- + *scrībere*, to write; see **skrībh-** in App.] —**pre·scrib′er** *n.*

pre·script (prē′skrĭpt′) *n.* Something prescribed, esp. a rule or regulation of conduct. ❖ *adj.* (prē′skrĭpt′, prĭ-skrĭpt′) Having been established as a rule; prescribed. [< ME, prescribed < Lat. *praescrīptum*, neut. p. part. of *praescrībere*, to order, prescribe. See PRESCRIBE.]

pre·scrip·ti·ble (prĭ-skrĭp′tə-bəl) *adj.* **1.** That can be prescribed. **2.** Requiring or derived from prescription. —**pre·scrip′ti·bil′i·ty** *n.*

pre·scrip·tion (prĭ-skrĭp′shən) *n.* **1a.** The act of establishing official rules, laws, or directions. **b.** Something prescribed as a rule. **2a.** A written order, esp. by a physician, for the preparation and administration of a medicine or other treatment. **b.** A prescribed medicine or other treatment. **c.** An ophthalmologist's or optometrist's written instruction, as for the grinding of corrective lenses. **3.** A formula directing the preparation of something. **4.** *Law* The process of acquiring title to property by reason of uninterrupted possession of specified duration. **5.** *Law* The limitation of time beyond which an action, debt, or crime is no longer valid or enforceable. [ME *prescripcion*, establishment of a claim < OFr. *prescription* < Med.Lat. *praescrīptiō, praescrīptiōn-* < Lat., introduction, precept < *praescrīptus*, p. part. of *praescrībere*, to order. See PRESCRIBE.]

pre·scrip·tive (prĭ-skrĭp′tĭv) *adj.* **1.** Sanctioned or authorized by long-standing custom or usage. **2.** Making or giving injunctions, directions, laws, or rules. **3.** *Law* Acquired by or based on uninterrupted possession. **4.** *Linguistics* Based on or establishing norms or rules indicating how a language should or should not be used rather than describing the ways in which a language is used. —**pre·scrip′tive·ly** *adv.* —**pre·scrip′tive·ness** *n.*

pre·scrip·tiv·ism (prĭ-skrĭp′tə-vĭz′əm) *n.* The support or promotion of prescriptive grammar. —**pre·scrip′tiv·ist** *adj. & n.*

pres·ence (prĕz′əns) *n.* **1.** The state or fact of being present; current existence or occurrence. **2.** Immediate proximity in time or space. **3.** The area immediately surrounding a great personage, esp. a sovereign. **4.** A person who is present. **5a.** A person's bearing, esp. when it commands respectful attention. **b.** The quality of self-assurance and effectiveness that permits a performer to achieve a rapport with the audience: *stage presence.* **6.** A supernatural influence felt to be nearby. **7.** The diplomatic, political, or military influence of a nation in a foreign country.

presence of mind *n.* The ability to think and act calmly and efficiently, esp. in an emergency.

pres·ent[1] (prĕz′ənt) *n.* **1.** A moment or period in time perceptible as intermediate between past and future; now. **2.** *Grammar* **a.** The present tense. **b.** A verb form in the present tense. **3. presents** *Law* The document or instrument in question: *Be it known by these presents.* ❖ *adj.* **1.** Existing or happening now; current: *the present leader; present trends.* **2a.** Being at hand or in attendance: *Thirty guests were present at the ceremony.* **b.** Existing in something specified: *Oxygen is present in the bloodstream.* **3.** Now being considered; actually here or involved: *present company excepted.* **4.** *Grammar* Being a verb tense or form that expresses current time. **5.** *Archaic* Readily available; immediate. **6.** *Obsolete* Alert to circumstances; attentive. —***idioms:* at present** At the present time; right now. **for the present** For the time being; temporarily. [ME < OFr. < Lat. *praesēns, praesent-*, pr. part. of *praeesse*, to be present : *prae-*, pre- + *esse*, to be; see **es-** in App.] —**pres′ent·ness** *n.*

pre·sent[2] (prĭ-zĕnt′) *v.* **-sent·ed, -sent·ing, -sents** —*tr.* **1a.** To introduce, esp. with formal ceremony. **b.** To introduce (a young woman) to society with conventional ceremony. **2.** To bring before the public: *present a play.* **3a.** To make a gift or award of. **b.** To make a gift to. **4a.** To offer for observation, examination, or consideration; show or display. See Syns at **offer. b.** To afford or furnish: *Dinner presented a chance to talk.* **c.** To turn or position in the direction of another: *presented his face to the camera.* **d.** To attach or be capable of attaching (an antigen, for example) on the surface of a molecule for detection by other molecules. **5.** To salute with (a weapon). **6.** *Ecclesiastical* To recommend (a cleric) for a benefice. **7.** *Law* To bring a charge or indictment against. —*intr.* **1.** To display as part of a disease or disease process. **2.** To make a presentation. ❖ *n.* **1. pres·ent** (prĕz′ənt) Something presented; a gift. **2. pre·sent** (prĭ-zĕnt′) The position of a rifle or other weapon when presented. [ME *presenten* < OFr. *presenter* < Lat. *presentāre*, to show < *praesēns, praesent-*, pr. part. of *praeesse*, to be in front of. See PRESENT[1].] —**pre·sent′er** *n.*

pre·sent·a·ble (prĭ-zĕn′tə-bəl) *adj.* **1.** That can be given, displayed, or offered: *presentable attire.* **2.** Fit for introduction to others: *presentable relatives.* —**pre·sent′a·bil′i·ty, pre·sent′a·ble·ness** *n.* —**pre·sent′a·bly** *adv.*

pre·sent arms (prĭ-zĕnt′) *n.* **1.** A position in the military manual

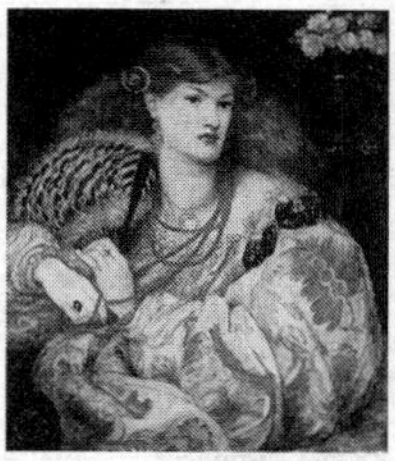

Pre-Raphaelite
Monna Vanna, 1866, by Dante Gabriel Rossetti

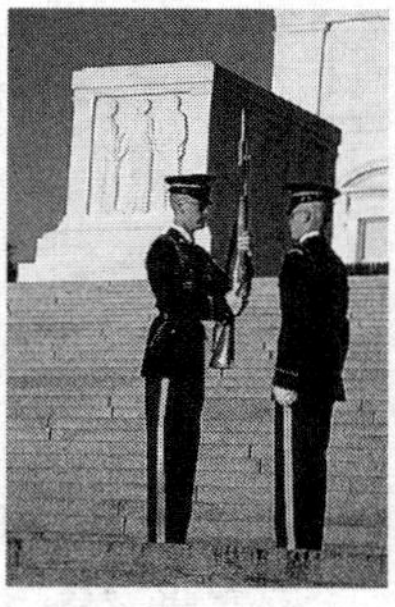

present arms
changing of the guard at the Tomb of the Unknown Soldier, Arlington National Cemetery, Arlington, Virginia

ă **pat**	oi **boy**
ā **pay**	ou **out**
âr **care**	o͝o **took**
ä **father**	o͞o **boot**
ĕ **pet**	ŭ **cut**
ē **be**	ûr **urge**
ĭ **pit**	th **thin**
ī **pie**	*th* **this**
îr **pier**	hw **which**
ŏ **pot**	zh **vision**
ō **toe**	ə **about, item**
ô **paw**	

Stress marks:
′ (primary);
′ (secondary), as in
lexicon (lĕk′sĭ-kŏn′)

of arms in which the rifle is held vertically in front of the body. **2.** A command to assume present arms or give a hand salute.

pres•en•ta•tion (prĕz′ən-tā′shən, prē′zən-) *n.* **1a.** The act of presenting. **b.** The state of being presented. **2.** A performance, as of a drama. **3a.** Something, such as a gift, that is offered or given. **b.** Something, such as a speech, that is set forth for an audience. **4a.** A formal introduction. **b.** A social debut. **5.** *Ecclesiastical* The act or right of naming a cleric to a benefice. **6.** The process of offering for consideration or display. **7.** *Medicine* The position of the fetus in the uterus at birth with respect to the mouth of the uterus. **—pres′en•ta′tion•al** *adj.*

pre•sent•a•tive (prĭ-zĕn′tə-tĭv) *adj.* **1a.** Perceived or capable of being perceived directly rather than through association. **b.** Having the ability to perceive something directly. **2.** *Ecclesiastical* Capable of naming or of being named to a benefice. **—pre•sent′a•tive•ness** *n.*

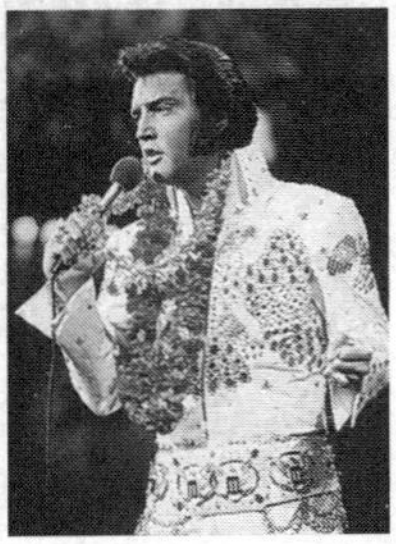

Elvis Presley

pres•ent-day (prĕz′ənt-dā′) *adj.* Now in existence or progress; current: *present-day attitudes about the family.*

pres•ent•ee (prĕz′ən-tē′, prĭ-zĕn′-) *n.* **1.** One who is presented. **2.** One to whom something is given.

pre•sen•tient (prē-sĕn′shənt, -shē-ənt) *adj.* Having a presentiment. [Lat. *praesentiēns, praesentient-*, pr. part. of *praesentīre*, to feel beforehand. See PRESENTIMENT.]

pre•sen•ti•ment (prĭ-zĕn′tə-mənt) *n.* A sense that something is about to occur; a premonition. [Obsolete Fr. < *presentir*, to feel before < Lat. *praesentīre* : *prae-*, pre- + *sentīre*, to feel.] **—pre•sen′ti•men′tal** (-mĕn′tl) *adj.*

pres•ent•ly (prĕz′ənt-lē) *adv.* **1.** In a short time; soon. **2.** *Usage Problem* At this time or period; now. **3.** *Archaic* At once.

USAGE NOTE There is some prejudice against the use of *presently* in the sense "at the present time; currently," even though that was an original meaning of the word in the 17th century and is widely found in literate speech and writing. In the 1999 survey, only 48 percent of the Usage Panel accepted this usage.

pre•sent•ment (prĭ-zĕnt′mənt) *n.* **1a.** The act of presenting to view or to the mind. **b.** Something expressed, presented, or exhibited. **c.** The light in which something is presented. **2.** *Law* **a.** The act of submitting or presenting a formal statement of a legal matter to a court or an authorized person. **b.** The report written by a grand jury concerning an offense and based on the jury's knowledge and observation. **3.** The act of presenting a bill or note for payment.

pres•ent participle (prĕz′ənt) *n.* A participle expressing present action, in English formed by the infinitive plus *-ing* and used to express present action in relation to the time indicated by the finite verb in its clause, to form progressive tenses with the auxiliary *be*, and to function as a verbal adjective.

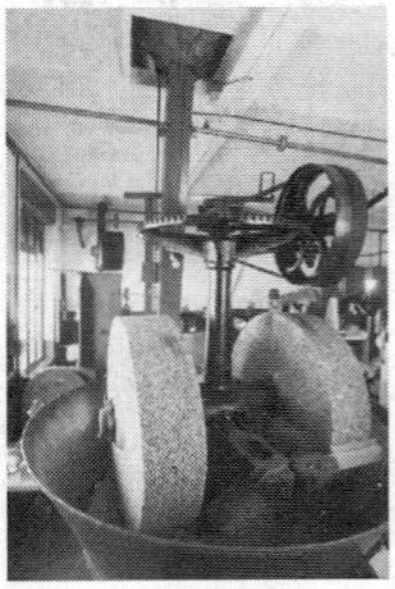

press[1]
olive press

pres•ent per•fect (prĕz′ənt pûr′fĭkt) *n.* **1.** The verb tense expressing action completed at the present time, formed in English by combining the present tense of *have* with a past participle, as in *He has spoken.* **2.** A verb in the present perfect tense.

pres•ent tense (prĕz′ənt) *n.* The verb tense expressing action in the present time, as in *She writes; she is writing.*

pres•er•va•tion•ist (prĕz′ər-vā′shə-nĭst) *n.* One who advocates preservation, esp. of natural areas, historical sites, or endangered species. **—pres′er•va′tion•ism** *n.*

pre•ser•va•tive (prĭ-zûr′və-tĭv) *adj.* Tending to preserve or capable of preserving. ❖ *n.* Something used to preserve, esp. a chemical added to foods to inhibit spoilage.

pre•serve (prĭ-zûrv′) *v.* **-served, -serv•ing, -serves** *—tr.* **1.** To maintain in safety from injury, peril, or harm; protect. **2.** To keep in perfect or unaltered condition; maintain unchanged. **3.** To keep or maintain intact: *preserving family harmony.* See Syns at **defend. 4.** To prepare (food) for future use, as by canning or salting. **5.** To prevent (organic bodies) from decaying or spoiling. **6.** To keep (game or fish) for one's private hunting or fishing. *—intr.* **1.** To treat fruit or other foods so as to prevent decay. **2.** To maintain a private area stocked with game or fish. ❖ *n.* **1.** Something that acts to preserve; a preservative. **2.** Fruit cooked with sugar to prevent decay or fermentation. Often used in the plural. **3.** An area maintained for the protection of wildlife or natural resources. **4.** Something considered as being the exclusive province of certain persons: *Ancient Greek is the preserve of scholars.* [ME *preserven* < OFr. *preserver* < Med.Lat. *praeservāre* < LLat., to observe beforehand : Lat. *prae-*, pre- + Lat. *servāre*, to guard, preserve.] **—pre•serv′a•bil′i•ty** *n.* **—pre•serv′a•ble** *adj.* **—pres′er•va′tion** (prĕz′ər-vā′shən) *n.* **—pre•serv′er** *n.*

pre•shrunk also **pre-shrunk** (prē′shrŭngk′) *adj.* Of, relating to, or being fabric or a garment that has been shrunk during manufacture to minimize subsequent shrinkage.

pre•side (prĭ-zīd′) *intr.v.* **-sid•ed, -sid•ing, -sides 1.** To hold the position of authority; act as chairperson or president. **2.** To possess or exercise authority or control. **3.** *Music* To be the featured instrumental performer: *presided at the keyboard.* [Fr. *présider* < OFr. < Lat. *praesidēre* : *prae-*, pre- + *sedēre*, to sit; see **sed-** in App.] **—pre•sid′er** *n.*

pres•i•den•cy (prĕz′ĭ-dən-sē, -dĕn′-) *n., pl.* **-cies 1.** The office, function, or term of a president. **2a.** often **Presidency** The office of president of a republic. **b. Presidency** The office of the President of the United States. **3.** *Mormon Church* **a.** A governing body consisting of three men. **b.** often **Presidency** The chief administrative body of the church.

pres•i•dent (prĕz′ĭ-dənt, -dĕnt′) *n.* **1.** One appointed or elected to preside over an organized body of people, such as an assembly or meeting. **2a.** often **President** The chief executive of a republic. **b. President** The chief executive of the United States, serving as both chief of state and chief political executive. **3.** The chief officer of a branch of government, corporation, board of trustees, university, or similar body. [ME < OFr. < Lat. *praesidēns, praesident-* < pr. part. of *praesidēre*, to preside. See PRESIDE.] **—pres′i•dent•ship′** *n.*

pres•i•dent-e•lect (prĕz′ĭ-dənt-ĭ-lĕkt′) *n., pl.* **pres•i•dents-e•lect** (-dənts-) A person who has been elected president but has not yet been inducted into office.

pres•i•den•tial (prĕz′ĭ-dĕn′shəl) *adj.* **1.** Of, relating to, or befitting a president or presidency. **2.** Of or relating to a political system in which the chief officer is a president elected independently of the legislature. **—pres′i•den′tial•ly** *adv.*

president pro tem (prō tĕm′) *n., pl.* **presidents pro tem** *Informal* A president pro tempore.

president pro tem•po•re (tĕm′pə-rē) *n., pl.* **presidents pro tempore** The senator who presides over the US Senate in the absence of the Vice President.

Pres•i•dents' Day (prĕz′ĭ-dənts, -dĕnts) *n.* The third Monday in February, observed in the United States as a legal holiday in commemoration of the birthdays of George Washington and Abraham Lincoln.

pre•sid•i•al (prĭ-sĭd′ē-əl) also **pre•sid•i•ar•y** (-ĕr′ē) *adj.* Of, relating to, possessing, or being a garrison.

pre•si•di•o (prĭ-sē′dē-ō′, -sĭd′ē-ō′) *n., pl.* **-os** A garrison, esp. a fortress of the kind established in the southwest United States by the Spanish to protect their holdings and missions. [Sp. < Lat. *praesidium*, guard, defense < *praesidēre*, to guard. See PRESIDE.]

pre•sid•i•um (prĭ-sĭd′ē-əm) *n., pl.* **-i•a** (-ē-ə) or **-i•ums** Any of various permanent executive committees in Communist countries having power to act for a larger governing body. [Russ. *prezidium* < Lat. *praesidium*, garrison. See PRESIDIO.]

Pres•ley (prĕs′lē, prĕz′-), **Elvis Aron** 1935–77. Amer. singer whose rock 'n' roll records and charismatic manner greatly influenced popular culture.

pre•soak (prē-sōk′) *tr.v.* **-soaked, -soak•ing, -soaks** To soak (laundry) before washing. ❖ *n.* (prē′sōk′) **1.** The act or an instance of presoaking. **2.** A liquid preparation in which laundry is presoaked. **3.** A cycle on an automatic washing machine for presoaking laundry.

pre-So•crat•ic (prē′sō-krăt′ĭk, -sə-) *adj.* Of or relating to the Greek philosophers or philosophical systems of thought before Socrates. ❖ *n.* A pre-Socratic philosopher.

pre•sort (prē-sôrt′) *tr.v.* **-sort•ed, -sort•ing, -sorts** To sort (mail) by Zip Code before delivery to a post office.

press[1] (prĕs) *v.* **pressed, press•ing, press•es** *—tr.* **1.** To exert steady weight or force against; bear down on. **2a.** To squeeze the juice or other contents from. **b.** To extract (juice, for example) by squeezing or compressing. **3a.** To reshape or make compact by applying steady force; compress. **b.** To iron (clothing, for example). **4.** To clasp in fondness or politeness. **5.** To try to influence, as by insistent arguments; importune or entreat: *He pressed me for a reply.* **6.** To urge or force to action; impel. **7.** To place in trying or distressing circumstances; harass or oppress. **8.** To move (keys on a keyboard, for example) by applying pressure. **9.** To lay stress on; emphasize. **10.** To advance or carry on vigorously. **11.** To put forward importunately or insistently: *press an argument.* **12.** To make (a phonograph record or videodisk) from a mold or matrix. **13.** *Sports* To lift (a weight) to a position above the head without moving the legs. *—intr.* **1.** To exert force or pressure. **2.** To weigh heavily, as on the mind. **3.** To advance eagerly; push forward. **4.** To require haste; be urgent. **5.** To iron clothes or other material. **6.** To assemble closely and in large numbers; crowd. **7.** To employ urgent persuasion or entreaty. **8.** *Sports* To raise or lift a weight in a press. **9.** *Basketball* To employ a press. ❖ *n.* **1.** Any of various machines or devices that apply pressure. **2.** A printing press. **3.** A place or establishment where matter is printed. **4.** The art, method, or business of printing. **5a.** The collecting and transmitting of news; journalism in general. **b.** The entirety of media and agencies that collect, publish, transmit, or broadcast the news. **c.** The people involved in the media, as news reporters, photographers, publishers, and broadcasters. **d.** Commentary or coverage esp. in newspapers or periodicals: *It received good press.* **6.** The act of gathering in large numbers or of pushing forward. **7.** A large gathering; a throng. **8a.** The act of applying pressure. **b.** The state of being pressed. **9.** The haste or urgency of business or matters. **10.** The set of proper creases in a garment or fabric, formed by ironing. **11.** *Chiefly Northeastern US* An upright closet or case used for storing clothing, books, or other articles. **12.** A viselike device for keeping a racket from warping. **13.** *Sports* A lift in weightlifting in which the weight is raised to shoulder level and then steadily pushed straight overhead without movement of the legs. **14.** *Basketball* An aggressive defense tactic in which players guard opponents closely, often over the entire court. ***—idioms:*** **go to press** To be submitted for printing. **in press** Submitted for printing; in the process of being printed.

pressed for time In a hurry; under time pressure. **press the flesh** *Informal* To shake hands and mingle with many people, esp. while campaigning for public office. [ME *pressen* < OFr. *presser* < Lat. *pressāre*, freq. of *premere*, to press.]

press² (prĕs) *tr.v.* **pressed, press•ing, press•es** **1.** To force into service in the army or navy; impress. **2a.** To take arbitrarily or by force, esp. for public use. **b.** To use in a manner different from the usual or intended, esp. in an emergency. ❖ *n.* **1.** Conscription, esp. into the army or navy. **2.** *Obsolete* An official warrant for impressing men into military service. [Alteration of obsolete *prest*, to hire for military service by advance payment < ME, enlistment money, loan < OFr. < *prester*, to lend < Med.Lat. *praestāre* < Lat., to furnish < *praestō*, present, at hand. See **ghes-** in App.]

press agency *n.* See **news agency**.

press agent *n.* A person employed to arrange advertising and publicity, as for a performer. —**press a′gent•ry** *n.*

press•board (prĕs′bôrd′, -bōrd′) *n.* **1.** A heavy glazed paper or pasteboard used esp. to cover the platen or cylinder of a printing press. **2.** A small ironing board.

press box *n.* A section for reporters, as in a stadium.

press conference *n.* An interview held for news reporters by a political figure or famous person.

press•er (prĕs′ər) *n.* **1.** One who presses clothes. **2.** Any of various devices that apply pressure to a product in manufacturing or canning.

press gang also **press•gang** (prĕs′găng′) *n.* A company of men under an officer detailed to force men into military or naval service.

press-gang (prĕs′găng′) *tr.v.* **-ganged, -gang•ing, -gangs** **1.** To force into military or naval service. **2.** To force or coerce.

press•ing (prĕs′ĭng) *adj.* **1.** Demanding immediate attention; urgent: *a pressing need.* See Syns at **urgent**. **2.** Very earnest or persistent; insistent: *a pressing invitation.* ❖ *n.* **1.** The process or an instance of applying pressure by means of a press. **2a.** A phonograph record pressed from a master mold or matrix. **b.** A number of recordings pressed at the same time. **3.** Urgent solicitation; insistence. —**press′ing•ly** *adv.*

press kit *n.* A packaged set of promotional materials for distribution to the press.

press•man (prĕs′mən, -măn′) *n.* **1.** A man who operates a printing press. **2.** *Chiefly British* A newspaper reporter.

press•mark (prĕs′märk′) *n.* **1.** *Printing* A notation or figure in the margin of a printed sheet indicating the press on which it was printed. **2.** *Chiefly British* A notation in or on a book indicating where it should be placed in a library.

press of sail *n.* The greatest amount of sail that a ship can carry safely under prevailing conditions.

pres•sor (prĕs′ôr′, -ər) *adj.* Causing an increase in blood pressure. [LLat., one who presses < Lat. *pressus*, p. part. of *premere*, to press. See PRESS¹.]

press release *n.* An announcement of an event, performance, or other newsworthy item that is issued to the press.

press•room (prĕs′rōōm′, -rōōm′) *n.* The room in a printing or newspaper publishing establishment for the presses.

press run or **press•run** (prĕs′rŭn′) *n.* **1.** Continuous operation of a printing press for a specific job. **2.** The number of copies printed in one such continuous operation.

press secretary *n.* One who officially manages the public affairs and press conferences of a public figure.

pres•sure (prĕsh′ər) *n.* **1a.** The act of pressing. **b.** The condition of being pressed. **2.** The application of continuous force by one body on another that it is touching; compression. **3.** *Physics* Force applied uniformly over a surface, measured as force per unit of area. **4.** *Meteorology* Atmospheric pressure. **5.** A compelling or constraining influence, such as a moral force, on the mind or will. **6.** Urgent claim or demand. **7.** An oppressive condition of physical, mental, social, or economic distress. **8.** A physical sensation produced by compression of a part of the body. **9.** *Archaic* A mark made by application of force or weight; an impression. ❖ *tr.v.* **-sured, -sur•ing, -sures** **1.** To force, as by overpowering influence. **2.** To pressurize. **3.** To pressure-cook. [ME < OFr. < Lat. *pressūra* < *pressus*, p. part. of *premere*, to press.]

pressure cabin *n.* A pressurized section of an aircraft.

pres•sure-cook (prĕsh′ər-kŏŏk′) *tr.v.* **-cooked, -cook•ing, -cooks** To cook in a pressure cooker.

pressure cooker *n.* **1.** An airtight metal pot that uses steam under pressure at high temperature to cook food quickly. **2.** *Informal* A stressful situation or atmosphere.

pressure gauge *n.* **1.** A device for measuring the pressure of a gas or liquid. **2.** A device for measuring the pressure of explosions.

pressure group *n.* An interest group that endeavors to influence public policy and government legislation.

pressure point *n.* **1.** Any of several points on the body at which an underlying artery can be pressed against a bone to stop distal bleeding. **2.** An area on the skin that is highly sensitive to the application of pressure.

pressure suit *n.* A garment worn in high-altitude aircraft or spacecraft to compensate for low-pressure conditions.

pres•sur•ize (prĕsh′ə-rīz′) *tr.v.* **-ized, -iz•ing, -iz•es** **1.** To

maintain normal air pressure in (an enclosure). **2.** To put (gas or liquid) under a greater than normal pressure. **3.** To design to resist pressure. **4.** To pressure-cook. **5.** *Informal* To subject to excessive stress, strain, or vexation. —**pres′sur•i•za′tion** (-ər-ĭ-zā′shən) *n.* —**pres′sur•iz′er** *n.*

press•work (prĕs′wûrk′) *n.* **1.** Management or operation of a printing press. **2.** The matter printed by such a press.

Pres•ter John (prĕs′tər) *n.* A legendary medieval Christian priest and king thought to have reigned over a Christian kingdom in the Far East and Ethiopia. [ME *prestre*, priest < OFr. < LLat. *presbyter*. See PRESBYTER.]

pre•ster•num (prē-stûr′nəm) *n.* See **manubrium** 1.

pres•ti•dig•i•ta•tion (prĕs′tĭ-dĭj′ĭ-tā′shən) *n.* **1.** Performance of or skill in performing magic or conjuring tricks with the hands; sleight of hand. **2.** A show of skill or deceitful cleverness. [Fr. < *prestidigitateur*, conjurer : *preste*, nimble (< Ital. *presto*; see PRESTO) + Lat. *digitus*, finger; see DIGIT.] —**pres′ti•dig′i•ta′tor** *n.*

pres•tige (prĕ-stēzh′, -stēj′) *n.* **1.** The level of respect at which one is regarded by others; standing. **2.** A person's high standing among others; honor or esteem. **3.** Widely recognized prominence, distinction, or importance: *a position of prestige.* [Fr., illusion < Lat. *praestīgiae*, tricks, prob. alteration of **praestrīgiae* < *praestringere*, to touch, blunt, blind : *prae-*, pre- + *stringere*, to draw tight.]

pres•ti•gious (prĕ-stē′jəs, -stĭj′əs) *adj.* Having prestige; esteemed. —**pres•ti′gious•ly** *adv.* —**pres•ti′gious•ness** *n.*

pres•tis•si•mo (prĕ-stĭs′ə-mō′) *Music adv. & adj.* In as fast a tempo as possible. ❖ *n., pl.* **-mos** A prestissimo passage or movement. [Ital., superl. of *presto*, presto. See PRESTO.]

pres•to (prĕs′tō) *adv.* **1.** *Music* In a very fast tempo, usu. considered to be faster than allegro but slower than prestissimo. **2.** So suddenly that magic seems involved; right away. ❖ *n., pl.* **-tos** *Music* A passage or movement that is performed presto. [Ital. < LLat. *praestus*, quick < Lat. *praestō*, at hand. See **ghes-** in App.] —**pres′to** *adj.*

Pres•ton (prĕs′tən) A borough of NW England NNE of Liverpool; site of a Jacobite defeat (1715). Pop. 132,166.

pre•sum•a•ble (prĭ-zōō′mə-bəl) *adj.* That can be presumed or taken for granted; reasonable as a supposition: *presumable causes of the disaster.* —**pre•sum′a•bly** *adv.*

pre•sume (prĭ-zōōm′) *v.* **-sumed, -sum•ing, -sumes** —*tr.* **1.** To take for granted as being true in the absence of proof to the contrary: *We presumed she was innocent.* **2.** To constitute reasonable evidence for assuming; appear to prove: *A signed hotel bill presumes occupancy of a room.* **3.** To venture without authority or permission; dare. —*intr.* **1.** To act overconfidently; take liberties. **2.** To take unwarranted advantage of something; go beyond the proper limits: *Don't presume on their hospitality.* **3.** To take for granted that something is true or factual; suppose. [ME *presumen* < OFr. *presumer* < LLat. *praesūmere* < Lat., to anticipate : *prae-*, pre- + *sūmere*, to take.] —**pre•sum′ed•ly** (-zōō′mĭd-lē) *adv.* —**pre•sum′er** *n.*

SYNONYMS presume, presuppose, postulate, posit, assume These verbs signify to take something for granted or as being a fact. To *presume* is to suppose that something is reasonable or possible in the absence of proof to the contrary: *"I presume you're tired after the long ride"* (Edith Wharton). *Presuppose* can mean to believe or suppose in advance: *It is unrealistic to presuppose that kind of knowledge in a beginner. Postulate* and *posit* denote the assertion of the existence, reality, necessity, or truth of something as the basis for reasoning or argument: *"We can see individuals, but we can't see providence; we have to postulate it"* (Aldous Huxley). *Scientists* posit a common ancestor for the two species. To *assume* is to accept something as existing or being true without proof or on inconclusive grounds: *"We must never assume that which is incapable of proof"* (G.H. Lewes).

---

pre•sum•ing (prĭ-zōō′mĭng) *adj.* Having or showing excessive and arrogant self-confidence; presumptuous. —**pre•sum′ing•ly** *adv.*

pre•sump•tion (prĭ-zŭmp′shən) *n.* **1.** Behavior or attitude that is boldly arrogant or offensive; effrontery. **2.** The act of presuming or accepting as true. **3.** Acceptance or belief based on reasonable evidence; assumption or supposition. **4.** A condition or basis for accepting or presuming. **5.** *Law* A conclusion derived from a particular set of facts based on law, rather than probable reasoning. [ME *presumpcion* < OFr. < LLat. *praesūmptiō, praesūmptiōn-* < Lat., anticipation < *praesūmptus*, p. part. of *praesūmere*, to anticipate. See PRESUME.]

pre•sump•tive (prĭ-zŭmp′tĭv) *adj.* **1.** Providing a reasonable basis for belief or acceptance. **2.** Founded on probability or presumption. —**pre•sump′tive•ly** *adv.*

pre•sump•tu•ous (prĭ-zŭmp′chōō-əs) *adj.* Going beyond what is right or proper; excessively forward. [ME < OFr. *presumptueux* < LLat. *presūmptuōsus*, var. of *praesūmptiōsus* < *praesūmptiō*, presumption. See PRESUMPTION.] —**pre•sump′tu•ous•ly** *adv.* —**pre•sump′tu•ous•ness** *n.*

pre•sup•pose (prē′sə-pōz′) *tr.v.* **-posed, -pos•ing, -pos•es** **1.** To believe or suppose in advance. See Syns at **presume**. **2.** To require or involve necessarily as an antecedent condition. —**pre•**

ă	pat	oi	boy
ā	pay	ou	out
âr	care	ŏŏ	took
ä	father	ōō	boot
ĕ	pet	ŭ	cut
ē	be	ûr	urge
ĭ	pit	th	thin
ī	pie	*th*	this
îr	pier	hw	which
ŏ	pot	zh	vision
ō	toe	ə	about,
ô	paw		item

Stress marks:
′ (primary);
′ (secondary), as in
lexicon (lĕk′sĭ-kŏn′)

sup•po•si•tion (-sŭp′ə-zĭsh′ən) n. —pre•sup′po•si′tion•al adj.

pre•syn•ap•tic (prē′sĭ-năp′tĭk) adj. Situated in front of or occurring before a synapse: a presynaptic nerve fiber.

pret. abbr. preterit

prêt-à-por•ter (prĕt′ä-pôr-tā′, -pōr-) n. Ready-to-wear clothing. [Fr. : prêt, ready + à, to + porter, to wear.]

pre•tax (prē′tăks′) adj. Existing before tax deductions.

pre•teen (prē′tēn′) adj. 1. Being a child esp. between the ages of 9 and 12; preadolescent. 2. Relating to or designed for preteen children. ❖ n. A preadolescent boy or girl.

pre•teen•ag•er (prē′tēn′ā′jər) n. A preteen.

pre•tence (prē′tĕns′, prĭ-tĕns′) n. Chiefly British Variant of pretense.

pre•tend (prĭ-tĕnd′) v. -tend•ed, -tend•ing, -tends —tr. 1. To give a false appearance of; feign. 2. To claim or allege insincerely or falsely; profess: doesn't pretend to be an expert. 3. To represent fictitiously in play; make believe: pretended they were on a cruise. 4. To take upon oneself; venture: I cannot pretend to say that you are wrong. —intr. 1. To feign an action or character, as in play. 2. To put forward a claim. 3. To make pretensions: pretends to gourmet tastes. ❖ adj. Informal Imitation; make-believe. [ME pretenden < OFr. pretendre < Lat. praetendere : prae-, pre- + tendere, to extend; see ten- in App.]

pre•tend•ed (prĭ-tĕn′dĭd) adj. 1. Not genuine or sincere; feigned. 2. Supposed; alleged. —pre•tend′ed•ly adv.

pre•tend•er (prĭ-tĕn′dər) n. 1. One who simulates, pretends, or alleges falsely; a hypocrite or dissembler. 2. One who sets forth a claim, esp. a claimant to a throne.

pre•tense (prē′tĕns′, prĭ-tĕns′) n. 1. The act of pretending; a false appearance or action intended to deceive. 2. A false or studied show; an affectation. 3. A professed but feigned reason or excuse; a pretext. 4. Something imagined or pretended. 5. Mere show without reality; outward appearance. 6. A right asserted with or without foundation; a claim. 7. The quality or state of being pretentious; ostentation. [ME < OFr. pretensse < Med.Lat. *praetensa < LLat., fem. of praetensus, alteration of Lat. praetentus, p. part. of praetendere, to pretend, assert. See PRETEND.]

pre•ten•sion (prĭ-tĕn′shən) n. 1. A specious allegation; a pretext. 2. A claim to something, such as a right. 3. The advancing of a claim. 4. Ostentatious display; pretentiousness.

pre•ten•tious (prĭ-tĕn′shəs) adj. 1. Claiming or demanding a position of distinction or merit, esp. when unjustified. 2. Outwardly extravagant; ostentatious. See Syns at showy. —pre•ten′tious•ly adv. —pre•ten′tious•ness n.

pret•er•it or **pret•er•ite** (prĕt′ər-ĭt) adj. Of, relating to, or being the verb tense that describes a past action or state. ❖ n. 1. The verb form expressing or describing a past action or condition. 2. A preterit verb. [ME < OFr. < Lat. (tempus) praeteritum, past (tense), neut. p. part. of praeterīre, to go by : praeter, beyond, comp. of prae, before; see per¹ in App. + īre, to go; see ei- in App.]

pret•er•i•tion (prĕt′ə-rĭsh′ən) n. 1. The act of passing by, disregarding, or omitting. 2. Law Neglect of a testator to mention a legal heir in his or her will. 3. Christianity The Calvinist doctrine that God neglected to designate those who would be damned, positively determining only the elect. [LLat. praeteritiō, praeteritiōn-, a passing over < Lat. praeteritus, p. part. of praeterīre, to go by. See PRETERIT.]

pre•term (prē′tûrm′, prē-tûrm′) adj. Occurring or appearing before the expected time at the end of a full-term pregnancy: preterm labor. ❖ n. An infant born prematurely.

pre•ter•mit (prē′tər-mĭt′) tr.v. -mit•ted, -mit•ting, -mits 1. To disregard intentionally or allow to pass unnoticed or unmentioned. 2. To fail to do or include; omit. 3. To interrupt or terminate. [Lat. praetermittere : praeter, beyond; see PRETERIT + mittere, to let go.] —pre′ter•mis′sion (-mĭsh′ən) n. —pre′ter•mit′ter n.

pre•ter•nat•u•ral (prē′tər-năch′ər-əl, -năch′rəl) adj. 1. Out of or being beyond the normal course of nature; differing from the natural. 2. Surpassing the normal or usual; extraordinary. 3. Transcending the natural or material order; supernatural. [Med. Lat. praeternātūrālis < Lat. praeter nātūram, beyond nature : praeter, beyond; see PRETERIT + nātūra, nature; see NATURE.] —pre′ter•nat′u•ral•ism, pre′ter•nat′u•ral•ness n. —pre′ter•nat′u•ral•ly adv.

pre•test (prē′tĕst′) n. 1a. A preliminary test for determining a student's baseline knowledge or preparedness for an educational experience or course of study. b. A test taken for practice. 2. Advance testing; test of an idea. ❖ tr. & intr.v. (prē-tĕst′) -test•ed, -test•ing, -tests To subject to or conduct a pretest.

pre•text (prē′tĕkst′) n. 1. An ostensible or professed purpose; an excuse. 2. An effort or strategy intended to conceal something. ❖ tr.v. -text•ed, -text•ing, -texts To allege as an excuse. [Lat. praetextum < neut. p. part. of praetexere, to disguise : prae-, pre- + texere, to weave.]

pre•tor (prē′tər) n. Variant of praetor.

Pre•to•ri•a (prĭ-tôr′ē-ə, -tōr′-) The administrative cap. of South Africa, in the NE part N of Johannesburg; founded 1855. Pop. 435,100.

pre•to•ri•an (prĭ-tôr′ē-ən, -tōr′-) adj. Variant of praetorian.

Pre•to•ri•us (prĭ-tôr′ē-əs, -tōr′-), **Andries Wilhelmus Jacobus** 1798–1853. Afrikaner soldier and politician who led the defeat of the Zulus (1838). His son **Marthinus Wessels Pretorius** (1819–1901) founded Pretoria.

pre•tri•al (prē-trī′əl, -trī′l) n. A proceeding held before an official trial, esp. to clarify points of law and facts. ❖ adj. 1. Of or relating to a pretrial. 2. Existing or occurring before a trial: pretrial hearings.

pret•ti•fy (prĭt′ĭ-fī′) tr.v. -fied, -fy•ing, -fies To make pretty or prettier, esp. in a superficial way. —pret′ti•fi•ca′tion (-fĭ-kā′shən) n. —pret′ti•fi′er n.

pret•ty (prĭt′ē) adj. -ti•er, -ti•est 1. Pleasing or attractive in a graceful or delicate way: a pretty dress. 2. Clever; adroit: a pretty maneuver. 3. Very bad; terrible: in a pretty predicament. 4. Ostensibly or superficially attractive but lacking substance or conviction: full of pretty phrases. 5. Informal Considerable in size or extent. ❖ adv. 1. To a fair degree; moderately: a pretty good student. 2. In a pretty manner; prettily or pleasingly. ❖ n., pl. -ties 1. One that is pretty. 2. pretties Delicate clothing, esp. lingerie. ❖ tr.v. -tied, -ty•ing, -ties To make pretty: pretty up the house. —idiom: pretty much For the most part; mostly. [ME prety, clever, fine, handsome < OE prættig, cunning < prætt, trick.] —pret′ti•ly adv. —pret′ti•ness n.

pret•zel (prĕt′səl) n. A glazed brittle biscuit that is usu. salted on the outside and baked in the form of a loose knot or a stick. [Ger. Brezel, Pretzel < MHGer. brëzel, prëzel < OHGer. brezitella < Med.Lat. *brāchitellum, dim. of Lat. bracchiātus, branched < bracchium, arm < Gk. brakhīōn, upper arm.]

pre•vail (prĭ-vāl′) intr.v. -vailed, -vail•ing, -vails 1. To be greater in strength or influence; triumph. 2. To be or become effective; win out. 3. To be most common or frequent; be predominant. 4. To be in force, use, or effect; be current. 5. To use persuasion or inducement successfully. Often used with on, upon, or with. [ME prevailen < OFr. prevaloir, prevaill- < Lat. praevalēre, to be stronger : prae-, pre- + valēre, to be strong.] —pre•vail′er n.

pre•vail•ing (prĭ-vā′lĭng) adj. 1. Most frequent or common; predominant. 2. Generally current; widespread. —pre•vail′ing•ly adv. —pre•vail′ing•ness n.

Pré•val (prā-väl′), **René García** b. 1942. Haitian politician who served as prime minister (1991–95) and president (since 1996).

prev•a•lence (prĕv′ə-ləns) n. 1. The condition of being prevalent. 2. Medicine The total number of cases of a disease in a given population at a specific time.

prev•a•lent (prĕv′ə-lənt) adj. Widely or commonly occurring, existing, accepted, or practiced. [ME, very strong < Lat. praevalēns, praevalent-, pr. part. of praevalēre, to be stronger. See PREVAIL.] —prev′a•lent•ly adv.

pre•var•i•cate (prĭ-văr′ĭ-kāt′) intr.v. -cat•ed, -cat•ing, -cates To stray from or evade the truth; equivocate. [Lat. praevāricārī, praevāricāt- : prae-, pre- + vāricāre, to straddle (< vāricus, straddling < vārus, bent).] —pre•var′i•ca′tion n. —pre•var′i•ca′tor n.

pre•ve•nience (prĭ-vēn′yəns) n. 1. The act or state of being antecedent or prevenient. 2. Attention to another's needs.

pre•ve•nient (prĭ-vēn′yənt) adj. 1. Coming before; preceding. 2. Expectant; anticipatory. [Lat. praeveniēns, praevenient-, pr. part. of praevenīre, to precede : prae-, pre- + venīre, to come; see gʷā- in App.] —pre•ven′ient•ly adv.

pre•vent (prĭ-vĕnt′) v. -vent•ed, -vent•ing, -vents —tr. 1. To keep from happening. 2. To keep (someone) from doing something; impede. 3. Archaic To anticipate or counter in advance. 4. Archaic To come before; precede. —intr. To present an obstacle. [ME preventen, to anticipate < Lat. praevenīre, praevent- : prae-, pre- + venīre, to come; see gʷā- in App.] —pre•vent′a•bil′i•ty, pre•vent′i•bil′i•ty n. —pre•vent′a•ble, pre•vent′i•ble adj. —pre•vent′er n.

pre•ven•tion (prĭ-vĕn′shən) n. 1. The act of preventing or impeding. 2. A hindrance; an obstacle.

pre•ven•tive (prĭ-vĕn′tĭv) also **pre•ven•ta•tive** (-tə-tĭv) adj. 1. Intended or used to prevent or hinder. 2. Carried out to deter expected aggression by hostile forces. 3. Preventing or slowing the course of an illness or disease; prophylactic. ❖ n. 1. Something that prevents; an obstacle. 2. Something that prevents or slows the course of an illness or disease. —pre•ven′tive•ly adv. —pre•ven′tive•ness n.

pre•verb (prē′vûrb′) n. A prefix or particle preceding the root or stem of a verb, as for- in forget. —pre•verb′ adj.

pre•verb•al (prē-vûr′bəl) adj. 1. Preceding the verb. 2a. Having not yet learned to speak: preverbal children. b. Marked by the absence of spoken language.

pre•view also **pre•vue** (prē′vyōō′) n. 1. A showing, as of art, to which a selected audience is invited before public presentation. 2. An advance viewing or exhibition, esp. of scenes advertising a forthcoming movie; a trailer. 3. An introductory or preliminary message, sample, or overview; a foretaste. ❖ tr.v. -viewed, -view•ing, -views also -vued, -vu•ing, -vues 1. To view or exhibit in advance. 2. To provide a preliminary sample or overview of.

pre•vi•ous (prē′vē-əs) adj. 1. Existing or occurring before something else in time or order; prior. 2. Informal Acting, occurring, or done too soon; premature. [< Lat. praevius, going before :

prae-, pre- + via, way; see **wegh-** in App.] —**pre′vi·ous·ly** adv. —**pre′vi·ous·ness** n.

previous question n. A parliamentary motion to take a vote on the main question being considered.

previous to prep. Prior to; before.

pre·vise (prĭ-vīz′) tr.v. **-vised, -vis·ing, -vis·es** 1. To know in advance; foresee. 2. To notify in advance; forewarn. [ME *previsen* < Lat. *praevidēre, praevīs-* : *prae-,* pre- + *vidēre,* to see; see **weid-** in App.] —**pre·vi′sor** n.

pre·vi·sion (prĭ-vĭzh′ən) n. 1. Prescience; foresight. 2. A prediction. ❖ tr.v. **-sioned, -sion·ing, -sions** To foresee. —**pre·vi′sion·al, pre·vi′sion·ar′y** (-vĭzh′ə-nĕr′ē) adj.

pre·vo·cal·ic (prē′vō-kăl′ĭk) adj. 1. Preceding a vowel. 2. Of or relating to a form of a linguistic element, such as a prefix, that occurs only before a vowel.

pre·vo·ca·tion·al (prē′vō-kā′shə-nəl) adj. Of or relating to instruction given in preparation for vocational school.

Pré·vost d'Ex·iles (prā-vō′ dĕg-zēl′), **Antoine Françoise** Known as "**Abbé Prévost.**" 1697–1763. French writer and cleric known for the novel *Manon Lescaut* (1731).

pre·washed (prē′wŏsht′, -wôsht′) adj. Washed by the manufacturer so as to impart a softer texture or faded appearance.

pre·writ·ing (prē′rī′tĭng) n. The creation and arrangement of ideas preliminary to writing.

prex·y (prĕk′sē) n., pl. **-ies** Slang A president, esp. of a college or university. [Shortening and alteration of PRESIDENT.]

prey (prā) n. 1. An animal hunted or caught for food; quarry. 2. One that is defenseless, esp. in the face of attack; a victim. 3. The act or practice of preying. ❖ intr.v. **preyed, prey·ing, preys** 1. To hunt, catch, or eat prey: *Owls prey on mice.* 2. To victimize someone or make a profit at someone else's expense. 3. To plunder or pillage. 4. To exert a baneful or injurious effect: *Remorse preyed on his mind.* [ME *preie* < OFr. < Lat. *praeda,* booty, prey. See **ghend-** in App.]

Pri·am (prī′əm) n. Greek Mythology The father of Paris, Hector, and Cassandra and king of Troy, who was killed when his city fell to the Greeks.

pri·a·pic (prī-ā′pĭk, -ăp′ĭk) also **pri·a·pe·an** (prī′ə-pē′ən) adj. 1. Of, relating to, or resembling a phallus; phallic. 2. Relating to or overly concerned with masculinity. [< PRIAPUS.]

pri·a·pism (prī′ə-pĭz′əm) n. Persistent, usu. painful erection of the penis, esp. as a consequence of disease. [Fr. *priapisme* < LLat. *priāpismus* < Gk. *priāpismos* < *priāpizein,* to have an erection < *Priāpos,* Priapus.]

pri·a·pus (prī-ā′pəs) n. 1. **Priapus** Greek & Roman Mythology The god of procreation, guardian of gardens and vineyards, and personification of the erect phallus. 2. An image of this god, often used as a scarecrow in ancient gardens. 3. A representation of a phallus. [Lat. *Priāpus* < Gk. *Priāpos.*]

Prib·i·lof Islands (prĭb′ə-lôf′) A group of islands off SW AK in the Bering Sea; named by a Russian explorer in 1786.

price (prīs) n. 1. The amount as of money or goods, asked for or given in exchange for something else. 2. The cost at which something is obtained. 3. The cost of bribing someone. 4. A reward offered for the capture or killing of a person: *a felon with a price on his head.* 5. Archaic Value or worth. ❖ tr.v. **priced, pric·ing, pric·es** 1. To fix or establish a price for: *shoes that are priced at sixty dollars.* 2. To find out the price of: *spent the day pricing cars.* —**idiom: price out of the market** To eliminate the demand for (goods or services) by setting prices too high. [ME *pris* < OFr. < Lat. *pretium.*] —**price′a·ble** adj. —**pric′er** n.

Price, (Mary) Leontyne b. 1927. Amer. soprano who performed with the Metropolitan Opera (1961–85).

price-earn·ings ratio (prīs′ûr′nĭngz) n. The ratio of the market price of a common stock to its earnings per share.

price fix·ing also **price-fix·ing** (prīs′fĭk′sĭng) n. 1. The setting of commodity prices by a government. 2. The result of an unlawful agreement between manufacturers or dealers to set and maintain prices on typically competing products.

price index n. A number relating prices of a group of commodities to their prices during an arbitrarily chosen base period.

price·less (prīs′lĭs) adj. 1. Of inestimable worth; invaluable. 2. Highly amusing, absurd, or odd. —**price′less·ly** adv.

price point n. The retail price of a product, usu. when viewed as one of a series of competitive prices.

price support n. Maintenance of prices, as of a commodity, at a certain level usu. through government intervention.

price tag n. 1. A label attached to a piece of merchandise indicating its price. 2. The cost of something.

price war n. An intense competition for sales based on underselling.

pric·ey also **pric·y** (prī′sē) adj. **-i·er, -i·est** Informal Expensive: *a pricey restaurant.* —**pric′ey·ness** n. —**pric′i·ly** adv.

prick (prĭk) n. 1a. The act of piercing or pricking. b. The sensation of being pierced or pricked. 2a. A persistent or sharply painful feeling of sorrow or remorse. b. A small sharp local pain, such as that made by a needle. 3. A small mark or puncture made by a pointed object. 4. A pointed object, such as a goad or thorn. 5. A hare's track or footprint. 6. Vulgar Slang A penis. 7. Vulgar Slang A person regarded as highly unpleasant, esp. a male. ❖ v. **pricked, prick·ing, pricks** —tr. 1. To puncture lightly. 2. To af-

fect with a mental or emotional pang, as of sorrow or remorse. 3. To impel as if with a spur; urge on. 4. To mark or delineate on a surface by means of small punctures. 5. To pierce the quick of (a horse's hoof) while shoeing. 6. To transplant (seedlings, for example) before final planting. 7. To cause to stand erect or point upward: *The dogs pricked their ears.* —intr. 1. To pierce or puncture something or cause a pricking feeling. 2. To feel a pang or twinge from or as if from being pricked. 3a. To spur a horse on. b. To ride at a gallop. 4. To stand erect; point upward. —**phrasal verb: prick off** Nautical To measure with dividers on a chart. —**idiom: prick up (one's) ears** To listen with attentive interest. [ME < OE *prica,* puncture.]

prick·er (prĭk′ər) n. 1. One, such as a pricking tool, that pierces or pricks. 2. A prickle or thorn.

prick·et (prĭk′ĭt) n. 1a. A small point or spike for holding a candle upright. b. A candlestick having such a spike. 2. A buck in its second year, before the antlers show. [ME *priket,* dim. of *prik, prick,* prick. See PRICK.]

prick·le (prĭk′əl) n. 1. A small sharp point, spine, or thorn. 2. A tingling or pricking sensation. ❖ v. **-led, -ling, -les** —tr. 1. To prick as if with a thorn. 2. To cause a prickle in. —intr. 1. To feel a prickle. 2. To rise or stand up like prickles. [ME *prikel* < OE *pricel.*]

prick·ly (prĭk′lē) adj. **-li·er, -li·est** 1. Having prickles. 2. Marked by prickling, tingling, or smarting: *a prickly sensation in my foot.* 3a. Causing trouble or vexation; thorny: *a prickly situation.* b. Bristling or irritable. —**prick′li·ness** n.

prickly ash n. Any of numerous cosmopolitan deciduous or evergreen shrubs or trees of the genus *Zanthoxylum,* having alternate, mostly pinnate leaves. 2. See **Hercules' club** 1.

prickly heat n. See **heat rash.**

prickly juniper n. See **cade.**

prickly pear n. 1. Any of various cacti of the genus *Opuntia,* having bristly flat or terete joints, usu. yellow flowers, and ovoid, often prickly fruit. 2. The edible fruit of any of these plants.

prickly poppy n. Any of various plants of the genus *Argemone,* chiefly of tropical America, having large yellow, lavender, or white flowers and prickly leaves, stems, and pods.

prick·y (prĭk′ē) adj. **-i·er, -i·est** Prickly.

pride (prīd) n. 1. A sense of one's own proper dignity or value; self-respect. 2. Pleasure or satisfaction taken in an achievement, possession, or association. 3. Arrogant or disdainful conduct or treatment; haughtiness. 4a. A cause or source of pleasure or satisfaction; the best of a group or class. b. The most successful or thriving condition; prime: *the pride of youth.* 5. An excessively high opinion of oneself; conceit. 6. Mettle or spirit in horses. 7. A company of lions. 8. A flamboyant or impressive group: *a pride of acrobats.* ❖ tr.v. **prid·ed, prid·ing, prides** To indulge (oneself) in a feeling of pleasure or satisfaction: *I pride myself on this garden.* [ME < OE *prȳde < prūd,* proud. See PROUD.]

Pride, Thomas d. 1658. English Parliamentarian who led a regiment to Parliament and expelled those who opposed the condemnation of Charles I (1648).

pride·ful (prīd′fəl) adj. 1. Arrogant; disdainful. 2. Highly pleased; elated. —**pride′ful·ly** adv. —**pride′ful·ness** n.

pride of place n. The highest or most important position.

pried¹ (prīd) v. Past tense and past participle of **pry¹.**

pried² (prīd) v. Past tense and past participle of **pry².**

prie-dieu (prē-dyœ′) n., pl. **-dieus** or **-dieux** (-dyœz′) A desklike kneeling bench with space above for a book, for use by a person at prayer. [Fr. *prie-Dieu : prier,* to pray (< OFr. < Lat. *precārī;* see PRAY) + *Dieu,* God (< OFr.; see ADIEU).]

pri·er also **pry·er** (prī′ər) n. One who pries, esp. a person who is unduly interested in the affairs of others.

pries¹ (prīz) v. Third person singular present tense of **pry¹.** ❖ n. Plural of **pry¹.**

pries² (prīz) v. Third person singular present tense of **pry².** ❖ n. Plural of **pry².**

priest (prēst) n. 1. In many Christian churches, a member of the second grade of clergy ranking below a bishop but above a deacon and having authority to administer the sacraments. 2. One with authority to perform and administer religious rites. ❖ tr.v. **priest·ed, priest·ing, priests** To ordain or admit to the priesthood. [ME *preost* < OE *prēost,* perh. < VLat. **prester* (< LLat. *presbyter;* see PRESBYTER) or < West Gmc. **prevost* (< Lat. *praepositus,* superintendent; see PROVOST).]

priest·ess (prē′stĭs) n. A woman who presides over religious rites, esp. in pagan religions.

priest·hood (prēst′hŏod) n. 1. The character, office, or vocation of a priest. 2. The clergy.

Priest·ley (prēst′lē), **J(ohn) B(oynton)** 1894–1984. British writer known for *The Good Companions* (1929).

Priestley, Joseph 1733–1804. British chemist noted for work on the isolation of gases and his discovery of oxygen (1774).

priest·ly (prēst′lē) adj. **-li·er, -li·est** 1. Of or relating to a priest or the priesthood. 2. Characteristic of or suitable for a priest. —**priest′li·ness** n.

prig (prĭg) n. 1. A person who demonstrates an exaggerated conformity or propriety, esp. in an arrogant or smug manner. 2. Chiefly British A petty thief or pickpocket. 3. Archaic A conceited dandy; a fop. ❖ tr.v. **prigged, prig·ging, prigs** Chiefly British

pricket

To steal or pilfer. [?] —**prig′ger•y** n. —**prig′gish** adj. —**prig′- gish•ly** adv. —**prig′gish•ness** n.

Pri•go•gine (prĭ-gô′zhən, -gō-zhĕn′), Ilya b. 1917. Russian-born Belgian chemist who won a 1977 Nobel Prize.

prim¹ (prĭm) adj. **prim•mer, prim•mest 1a.** Precise or proper to the point of affectation; excessively decorous. **b.** Strait-laced; prudish. **2.** Neat and trim: *a prim hedgerow.* ❖ v. **primmed, prim•ming, prims** —*tr.* **1.** To fix (the face or mouth) in a prim expression. **2.** To make prim, as in appearance. —*intr.* To assume a prim expression. [Poss. < obsolete *prim,* formal or demure person, perh. < OFr. *prin,* first, delicate. See PRIME.] —**prim′ly** adv. —**prim′ness** n.

prim² (prĭm) n. A privet. [Short for obsolete *primprint,* of unknown orig.]

pri•ma ballerina (prē′mə) n. The leading woman dancer in a ballet company. [Ital.]

pri•ma•cy (prī′mə-sē) n., pl. **-cies 1.** The state of being first or foremost. **2.** *Ecclesiastical* The office, rank, or province of primate. [ME *primacie* < OFr. < Med.Lat. *prīmātia,* office of church primate < Lat. *prīmās, prīmāt-,* of first rank. See PRIMATE.]

pri•ma donna (prē′mə, prĭm′ə) n. **1.** The leading woman soloist in an opera company. **2.** A temperamental, conceited person. [Ital. : *prima,* fem. of *primo,* first + *donna,* lady.]

pri•ma fa•cie (prī′mə fā′shē -shə, -shē-ē) adv. At first sight; before closer inspection. ❖ adj. **1.** True, authentic, or adequate at first sight; ostensible. **2.** Evident without proof or reasoning; obvious. [ME, manifestly < Lat. *prīmāfaciē : prīmā,* fem. ablative of *prīmus,* first + *faciē,* ablative of *faciēs,* shape, face.]

prima facie case n. *Law* A case in which the evidence presented is sufficient for a judgment to be made unless the evidence is contested.

prima facie evidence n. *Law* Evidence that would, if uncontested, establish a fact or raise a presumption of a fact.

pri•mal (prī′məl) adj. **1.** Being first in time; original; primeval. **2.** Of first importance; primary. [Med.Lat. *prīmālis* < Lat. *prīmus,* first. See **per¹** in App.] —**pri•mal′i•ty** (-măl′ĭ-tē) n.

primal therapy n. *Psychology* A method for treating emotional problems that involves the reliving of early traumatic experiences and expression of feelings, as by angry screaming. —**primal therapist** n.

pri•mar•i•ly (prī-mâr′ə-lē, -mĕr′-) adv. **1.** Chiefly; mainly. **2.** At first; originally.

pri•mar•y (prī′mĕr′ē, -mə-rē) adj. **1.** First or highest in rank, quality, or importance; principal. **2.** Being or standing first in a list, series, or sequence. **3.** Occurring first in time or sequence; earliest. **4.** Being or existing as the first or earliest of a kind; primitive. **5.** *Geology* Characteristic of or existing in a rock at the time of its formation. **6.** Serving as or being an essential component, as of a system; basic. **7a.** Immediate; direct: *a primary effect.* **b.** Preliminary to a later stage in a continuing process. **c.** Of or relating to a primary school. **8.** Of or relating to a primary color or colors. **9.** *Linguistics* **a.** Having a word root or other linguistic element as a basis that cannot be further analyzed or broken down. **b.** Referring to present or future time. Used as a collective designation for various verb tenses. **10.** *Electronics* Of, relating to, or constituting an inducting current, circuit, or coil. **11.** Of, relating to, or being the main flight feathers projecting along the outer edge of a bird's wing. **12.** Of or relating to agriculture, forestry, the industries that extract natural materials from the earth, or the products so obtained. **13.** *Chemistry* **a.** Relating to the replacement of one of several atoms or radicals in a compound by another atom or radical. **b.** Having a carbon atom attached solely to one other carbon atom in a molecule. **14.** *Biochemistry* Of, relating to, or being the sequence of amino acids in a protein. **15.** *Botany* Of, relating to, or derived from a primary meristem. ❖ n., pl. **-ies 1a.** One that is first in time, order, or sequence. **b.** One that is first or best in degree, quality, or importance. **c.** One that is fundamental, basic, or elemental. **2a.** A meeting of the registered voters of a political party for the purpose of nominating candidates and for choosing delegates to their party convention. **b.** A primary election. **3.** A primary color. **4.** A primary flight feather. **5.** *Electronics* An inducting current, circuit, or coil, esp. the coil to which the input voltage is applied in a transformer. **6.** *Astronomy* **a.** A celestial body, esp. a star, relative to other bodies in orbit around it. **b.** The brighter of two stars that make up a double star. [ME < Lat. *prīmārius,* chief < *prīmus,* first. See **per¹** in App.]

primary accent n. See **primary stress.**

primary care n. The medical care a patient receives upon first contact with the health care system before referral. —**pri′mar•y- care′** (prī′mĕr′ē-kâr′, -mə-rē-) adj.

primary cell n. A cell in which an irreversible chemical reaction generates electricity; a cell that cannot be recharged.

primary color n. A color of any of three groups each of which is seen as generating all colors, the groups being: **a.** Additive, physiological, or light primaries red, green, and blue. **b.** Subtractive or colorant primaries magenta, yellow, and cyan. **c.** Psychological primaries red, yellow, green, and blue, as well as the achromatic pair black and white.

primary election n. A preliminary election in which voters nominate party candidates for office.

primary school n. **1.** A school usu. including the first three or

four grades of elementary school and sometimes kindergarten. **2.** See **elementary school.**

primary stress n. **1.** The strongest degree of stress placed on a syllable in the pronunciation of a word. **2.** The mark (′) used to indicate such stress.

primary tooth n. See **milk tooth.**

primary wall n. The wall layer of a plant cell deposited during cell expansion.

primary wave n. An earthquake wave in which rock particles vibrate parallel to the direction of wave travel.

pri•mate (prī′mĭt, -māt′) n. **1.** (prī′māt′) A mammal of the order Primates, which includes the anthropoids, characterized by refined development of the hands and feet, a shortened snout, and a large brain. **2.** A bishop of highest rank in a province or country. [< NLat. *Prīmātēs,* order name < Lat. *prīmātēs,* pl. of *prīmās,* principal, of first rank < *prīmus,* first. See **per¹** in App. Sense 2 < ME *primat* < OFr. < Med.Lat. *prīmās, prīmāt-* < Lat.] —**pri•ma′tial** (-mā′shəl) adj.

pri•ma•tol•o•gy (prī′mə-tŏl′ə-jē) n. The branch of zoology that deals with the study of primates. —**pri′ma•to•log′i•cal** (-tl-ŏj′ĭ-kəl) adj. —**pri′ma•tol′o•gist** n.

pri•ma•ve•ra¹ (prē′mə-vĕr′ə) n. **1.** A tree (*Cybistax donnellsmithii*) of Mexico and Guatemala having opposite, palmately compound leaves and close-grained light-colored wood. **2.** The wood of this tree. [Sp., spring, primavera < LLat. *prīma vēra,* early spring, pl. of *prīmum vēr* : Lat. *prīmus,* first; see **per¹** in App. + Lat. *vēr,* spring; see **wesr** in App.]

pri•ma•ve•ra² (prē′mə-vĕr′ə) adj. Garnished or served with assorted fresh vegetables. [< Ital. *(alla) primavera,* (in the) spring (style) < LLat. *prīma vēra.* See PRIMAVERA¹.]

prime (prīm) adj. **1.** First in excellence, quality, or value. **2.** First in degree or rank; chief. **3.** First or early in time, order, or sequence; original. **4.** Of the highest US government grade of meat. **5.** *Mathematics* Of, relating to, or being a prime number. ❖ n. **1.** The earliest hours of the day; dawn. **2.** Spring. **3.** The age of ideal physical perfection and intellectual vigor. **4.** The period or phase of ideal or peak condition. **5.** The first position of thrust and parry in fencing. **6.** A mark (′) appended above and to the right of a character, esp.: **a.** One used to distinguish different values of the same variable in a mathematical expression. **b.** One used to represent a unit of measurement, such as feet or minutes in latitude and longitude. **7.** also **Prime** *Ecclesiastical* The second of the seven canonical hours. No longer in liturgical use. **8.** *Mathematics* A prime number. **9.** A prime rate. **10.** See **primitive** 5b. ❖ v. **primed, prim•ing, primes** —*tr.* **1.** To make ready; prepare. **2.** To prepare (a gun or mine) for firing by inserting a charge of gunpowder or a primer. **3.** To prepare for operation, as by pouring water into a pump. **4.** To prepare (a surface) for painting by covering with primer. **5.** To inform or instruct beforehand; coach. —*intr.* To become prepared for future action or operation. —*idiom:* **prime the pump** *Informal* To encourage the growth or action of something. [ME, first in occurrence < OFr., fem. of *prin* < Lat. *prīmus.* See **per¹** in App.] —**prime′ly** adv. —**prime′ness** n.

prime interest rate n. See **prime rate.**

prime meridian n. The zero meridian (0°), used as a reference line from which longitude east and west is measured.

prime minister n. **1.** A chief minister appointed by a ruler. **2.** The head of the cabinet and often also the chief executive of a parliamentary democracy. —**prime ministerial** adj. —**prime ministership,** **prime ministry** n.

prime mover n. **1a.** One regarded as the initial source of energy directed toward a goal. **b.** The initial force, such as wind, that engages or moves a machine. **c.** A machine or mechanism that converts natural energy into work. **2.** Any of various heavy-duty trucks or tractors. **3.** *Philosophy* In Aristotelian philosophy, the self-moved being causing all motion.

prime number n. A positive integer not divisible without a remainder by any positive integer other than itself and one.

prim•er¹ (prĭm′ər) n. **1.** An elementary textbook for teaching children to read. **2.** A book that covers the basic elements of a subject. [ME, devotional manual < Norman Fr. < Med.Lat. *prīmārium* < neut. of *prīmārius,* first < Lat. < *prīmus.* See PRIME.]

prim•er² (prī′mər) n. **1.** A cap or tube containing a small amount of explosive used to detonate the main explosive charge of a firearm or mine. **2.** An undercoat of paint or size applied to prepare a surface, as for painting. **3.** A segment of DNA or RNA that is complementary to a given DNA sequence and needed to initiate replication by DNA polymerase.

prime rate n. The lowest rate of interest on bank loans at a given time and place, offered to preferred borrowers.

prime time n. The evening hours, generally between 7 and 11 P.M., when the largest television audience is available. —**prime′- time′** (prīm′tīm′) adj.

pri•me•val (prī-mē′vəl) adj. Belonging to the first or earliest age or ages; original or ancient: *a primeval forest.* [< Lat. *prīmaevus,* early in life : *prīmus,* first; see **per¹** in App. + *aevum,* age; see **aiw-** in App.] —**pri•me′val•ly** adv.

prim•ing (prī′mĭng) n. **1.** The act of one that primes. **2.** The explosive used to ignite a charge. **3.** A preliminary coat of paint or size applied to a surface.

pri·mip·a·ra (prī-mĭp'ər-ə) n., pl. **-a·ras** or **-a·rae** (-ə-rē') **1.** A woman who is pregnant for the first time. **2.** A woman who has given birth to only one child. [Lat. *prīmipara* : *prīmus*, first; see **per**¹ in App. + *-para*, fem. of *-parus*, having given birth; see MULTIPARA.] **—pri'mi·par'i·ty** (-mĭ-păr'ĭ-tē) n. **—pri·mip'a·rous** adj.

prim·i·tive (prĭm'ĭ-tĭv) adj. **1.** Not derived from something else; primary. **2a.** Of or relating to an earliest or original stage or state; primeval. **b.** Being little evolved from an early ancestral type. **3.** Characterized by simplicity or crudity; unsophisticated. **4.** *Anthropology* Of or relating to a nonindustrial, often tribal culture, esp. one marked by a low level of economic complexity. **5.** *Linguistics* **a.** Serving as the basis for derived or inflected forms. **b.** Being a protolanguage: *primitive Germanic.* **6.** *Mathematics* An algebraic or geometric expression from which another expression is derived. **7.** Relating or belonging to forces of nature; elemental. **8a.** Of or created by an artist without formal training; simple or naive in style. **b.** Of or relating to the work of an artist from a primitive culture. **9.** Of or relating to late medieval or pre-Renaissance European painters or sculptors. **10.** *Biology* Occurring in or characteristic of an early stage of development or evolution. ❖ n. **1.** A person belonging to a primitive society. **2.** An unsophisticated person. **3.** One that is at a low or early stage of development. **4a.** One belonging to an early stage in the development of an artistic trend, esp. a pre-Renaissance painter. **b.** An artist having or affecting an unschooled style, as of painting. **c.** A self-taught artist. **d.** A work of art by a primitive artist. **5.** *Linguistics* **a.** A primitive word or word element. **b.** A basic and indivisible unit of linguistic analysis. **6.** *Computer Science* A basic or fundamental unit of machine instruction or translation. [ME < OFr. *primitif*, primitive < Lat. *prīmitīvus* < *prīmitus*, at first < *prīmus*, first. See **per**¹ in App.] **—prim'i·tive·ly** adv. **—prim'i·tive·ness, prim'i·tiv'i·ty** n.

prim·i·tiv·ism (prĭm'ĭ-tĭ-vĭz'əm) n. **1.** The condition or quality of being primitive. **2.** The style of a primitive artist. **3a.** A belief that it is best to live simply and in a natural environment. **b.** A belief that the acquisitions of civilization are evil or that the earliest period of human history was the best. **—prim'i·tiv·ist** adj. & n. **—prim'i·tiv·is'tic** adj.

pri·mo (prē'mō) n., pl. **-mi** (-mē) also **-mos** (-mōz) *Music* The principal part in a duet or ensemble composition. ❖ adj. **1.** First. **2.** *Slang* **a.** Exceptionally good of its kind; first-class. **b.** Highly or most valuable. [Ital. < OItal., first < Lat. *prīmus*. See **per**¹ in App.]

Pri·mo de Ri·ve·ra y Or·ba·ne·ja (prē'mō dā rĭ-vĕr'ə ē ôr'bə-nā'hä, thē rē-vĕr'rä ē ôr'vä-nā'hä), **Miguel.** Marqués de Estella. 1870–1930. Spanish general and politician who ruled as dictator (1923–30). His son **José Antonio Primo de Rivera** (1903–36) founded the Spanish Fascist Party (1933).

pri·mo·gen·i·tor (prī'mō-jĕn'ĭ-tər) n. **1.** The earliest ancestor. **2.** An ancestor or forebear. [LLat. *prīmōgenitor* : Lat. *prīmō*, at first (< *prīmus*, first; see **per**¹ in App.) + Lat. *genitor*, begetter (< *gignere, genit-*, to beget; see **genə-** in App.).]

pri·mo·gen·i·ture (prī'mō-jĕn'ĭ-chŏŏr') n. **1.** The state of being the first-born or eldest child of the same parents. **2.** *Law* The right of the eldest child, esp. the eldest son, to inherit the entire estate of one or both parents. [LLat. *prīmōgenitūra* : Lat. *prīmō*, at first (< *prīmus*, first; see **per**¹ in App.) + Lat. *genitūra*, birth (< *genitus*, p. part. of *gignere*, to beget; see **genə-** in App.).] **—pri'mo·gen'i·tar'y** (-jĕn'ĭ-tĕr'ē), **pri'mo·gen'i·tal** (-təl) adj.

pri·mor·di·al (prī-môr'dē-əl) adj. **1.** Being or happening first in sequence of time; original. **2.** Primary or fundamental: *a primordial role.* **3.** *Biology* Belonging to or characteristic of the earliest stage of development of an organism or part. ❖ n. A basic principle. [ME < LLat. *prīmōrdiālis* < Lat. *prīmōrdium*, origin : *prīmus*, first; see **per**¹ in App. + *ōrdīrī*, to begin to weave.] **—pri·mor'di·al·ly** adv.

primordial soup n. A liquid rich in organic compounds and providing favorable conditions for the emergence and growth of life forms.

pri·mor·di·um (prī-môr'dē-əm) n., pl. **-di·a** (-dē-ə) An organ or a part in its most rudimentary form or stage of development. [Lat. *prīmōrdium*. See PRIMORDIAL.]

primp (prĭmp) v. **primped, primp·ing, primps** —*tr.* To dress or groom (oneself) with meticulous or excessive care. —*intr.* To primp oneself; preen. [Perh. alteration of PRIM.¹]

prim·rose (prĭm'rōz') n. **1.** Any of numerous plants of the genus *Primula*, having well-developed basal leaves and tubular, variously colored flowers grouped in umbels or heads. **2.** An evening primrose. [ME *primerose* < OFr. < Med.Lat. *prīma rosa* : Lat. *prīma*, fem. of *prīmus*, first; see PRIME + Lat. *rosa*, rose.]

primrose path n. **1.** A way of life of worldly ease or pleasure. **2.** A course of action that seems easy and appropriate but can actually end in calamity.

pri·mum mo·bi·le (prī'məm mō'bə-lē', prē'məm mō'bĭ-lā') n. **1.** In Ptolemaic astronomy, the tenth and outermost concentric sphere of the universe, revolving around the earth from east to west in 24 hours and causing the other nine spheres to revolve with it. **2.** See **prime mover** 1. [Med.Lat. *prīmum mōbile* : *prīmum*, neut. of *prīmus*, first + *mōbile* < neut. of *mōbilis*, mova-

ble (transl. of Ar. *al-muharrik al-'awwal* : *al-*, the + *muharrik*, mover + *'awwal*, first).]

pri·mus or **Pri·mus** (prī'məs) n., pl. **-mus·es** The first in rank of the bishops of Scotland. [Med.Lat. *prīmus* < Lat., first. See **per**¹ in App.]

pri·mus in·ter pa·res (prī'məs ĭn'tər pâr'ēz, prē'mŏŏs ĭn'tər pä'rĕs') n. pl. **pri·mi inter pares** (-mī, -mē) The first among equals. [Lat. *prīmus inter parēs*.]

prince (prĭns) n. **1.** A male member of a royal family other than the monarch, esp. a son of the monarch. **2a.** A man who is a ruler of a principality. **b.** A hereditary male ruler; a king. **3.** A nobleman of varying status or rank. **4.** An outstanding man, esp. in a particular group: *a merchant prince.* [ME < OFr. < Lat. *prīnceps.* See **per**¹ in App.] **—prince'ship'** n.

Prince Albert n. A man's long double-breasted frock coat. [After *Prince Albert* Edward, later Edward VII.]

Prince Charming also **prince charming** n. **1.** A man who fulfills all the romantic expectations of a woman. **2.** A man who ardently seeks the company and affection of women. [After *Prince Charming*, hero of *Cinderella*.]

prince consort n. The husband of a sovereign queen.

prince·dom (prĭns'dəm) n. **1.** The territory, jurisdiction, sovereignty, rank, or estate of a prince. **2.** princedoms *Christianity* See **principality** 3.

Prince Edward Island A province of SE Canada consisting of **Prince Edward Island** in the S Gulf of St. Lawrence; joined the confederacy in 1873. Cap. Charlottetown. Pop. 134,557.

Prince George A city of central British Columbia, Canada, at the confluence of the Fraser and Nechako rivers. Pop. 75,150.

prince·ling (prĭns'lĭng) n. A prince judged to be of minor status or importance.

prince·ly (prĭns'lē) adj. **-li·er, -li·est 1.** Of or relating to a prince; royal. **2.** Befitting a prince, as: **a.** Noble. **b.** Munificent; lavish. **—prince'li·ness** n. **—prince'ly** adv.

Prince of Wales n. **1.** The male heir to the British throne. **2.** Used as the title for the male heir to the British throne, conferred by the sovereign.

Prince of Wales Island 1. An island of central Nunavut, Canada, NE of Victoria I. **2.** An island of extreme SE AK in the Alexander Archipelago.

prince regent n., pl. **prince regents** or **princes regent** A prince who rules during the minority, absence, or incapacity of a sovereign.

prince's feather (prĭn'sĭz) n. Either of two plants (*Amaranthus hybridus* var. *erythrostachys* or *A. cruentus*) having reddish foliage and dense panicles of brownish-red flowers.

prince's pine n. See **pipsissewa.**

prin·cess (prĭn'sĭs, -sĕs', prĭn-sĕs') n. **1.** A woman member of a royal family other than the monarch, esp. a daughter of a monarch. **2a.** A woman who is ruler of a principality. **b.** A woman hereditary ruler; a queen. **3.** A noblewoman of varying status or rank. **4.** The wife of a prince. **5.** A woman regarded as having the status or qualities of a princess. ❖ adj. Designed to hang in smooth, close-fitting unbroken lines from shoulder to flared hem: *a princess dress.* [ME *princesse* < OFr., fem. of *prince*, prince. See PRINCE.]

prin·cesse (prĭn-sĕs') adj. Princess: *a gown cut on princesse lines.* [Fr. < OFr., princess. See PRINCESS.]

princess royal n. **1.** The eldest daughter of a British sovereign, who has had the title conferred on her for life by the sovereign. **2.** Used as the title for such a woman.

princess tree n. See **paulownia.** [After *Princess* Anna Paulovna (1795–1865), queen of William II of the Netherlands.]

Princeton, Mount A mountain, 4,330 m (14,197 ft), in the Sawatch Range of the Rocky Mts. in central CO.

Prince William Sound An arm of the Gulf of Alaska E of the Kenai Peninsula; site of the worst US oil spill (Mar. 1989).

prin·ci·pal (prĭn'sə-pəl) adj. **1.** First, highest, or foremost in importance, rank, worth, or degree; chief. **2.** Of, relating to, or being financial principal, or a principal in a financial transaction. ❖ n. **1.** One who holds a position of presiding rank, esp. the head of a school. **2.** A main participant in a situation. **3.** A person having a leading or starring role. **4a.** The capital or main body of an estate or financial holding as distinguished from the interest or revenue from it. **b.** A sum of money owed as a debt, upon which interest is calculated. **5.** *Law* **a.** One who empowers another to act as one's representative. **b.** One with prime responsibility for an obligation as distinguished from one who acts as surety or as an endorser. **c.** One who commits or is an accomplice to a crime. **6.** Either of a pair of timbers forming the sides of a triangular truss for a pitched roof. [ME < OFr. < Lat. *prīncipālis* < *prīnceps, prīncip-*, leader, emperor. See **per**¹ in App.] **—prin'ci·pal·ly** adv. **—prin'ci·pal·ship'** n.

USAGE NOTE *Principal* and *principle* are often confused but have no meanings in common. *Principle* is only a noun, and usually refers to a rule or standard. *Principal* is both a noun and an adjective. As a noun (aside from its specialized meanings in law and finance) it generally denotes a person who holds a high position or plays an important role. As an adjective it has the sense of "chief" or "leading."

primitive
Landscape with Monkeys,
c. 1910 by Henri Rousseau

ă	pat	oi	boy
ā	pay	ou	out
âr	care	ŏŏ	took
ä	father	ōō	boot
ĕ	pet	ŭ	cut
ē	be	ûr	urge
ĭ	pit	th	thin
ī	pie	th	this
îr	pier	hw	which
ŏ	pot	zh	vision
ō	toe	ə	about,
ô	paw		item

Stress marks:
' (primary);
' (secondary), as in
lexicon (lĕk'sĭ-kŏn')

prin·ci·pal·i·ty (prĭn'sə-păl'ĭ-tē) *n., pl.* **-ties 1.** A territory ruled by or giving the title to a prince or princess. **2.** The position, authority, or jurisdiction of a prince or princess; sovereignty. **3.** **principalities** *Christianity* The seventh of the nine orders of angels.

principal parts *pl.n.* **1.** In inflected languages, the verb forms traditionally considered basic, from which all other verb forms can be derived. **2.** In English, the present infinitive (*eat*), the past tense (*ate*), the present participle (*eating*), and the past participle (*eaten*).

Prín·ci·pe (prĭn'sə-pə, prĕn'sĭ-) An island of W Africa in the Gulf of Guinea, part of São Tomé and Príncipe.

prin·cip·i·um (prĭn-sĭp'ē-əm) *n., pl.* **-i·a** (-ē-ə) A principle, esp. a basic one. [Lat. *principium.* See PRINCIPLE.]

prin·ci·ple (prĭn'sə-pəl) *n.* **1.** A basic truth, law, or assumption: *the principles of democracy.* **2a.** A rule or standard, esp. of good behavior. **b.** The collectivity of moral or ethical standards or judgments. **3.** A fixed or predetermined policy or mode of action. **4.** A quality or element determining intrinsic nature or characteristic behavior. **5.** A rule or law concerning the functioning of natural phenomena or mechanical processes. **6.** *Chemistry* One of the elements that compose a substance, esp. one that gives some special quality or effect. **7.** A basic source. See Usage Note at **principal.** **—idioms: in principle** With regard to the basics. **on principle** According to or because of principle. [ME, alteration of OFr. *principe* < Lat. *principium* < *princeps, princip-,* leader, emperor. See **per¹** in App.]

prin·ci·pled (prĭn'sə-pəld) *adj.* Based on, marked by, or manifesting principle: *a principled decision.*

prink (prĭngk) *v.* **prinked, prink·ing, prinks** —*tr.* To adorn (oneself) in a showy manner. —*intr.* To dress or groom oneself with elaborate care or vanity; primp. [Prob. alteration of PRANK².] **—prink'er** *n.*

print (prĭnt) *n.* **1.** A mark or impression made in or on a surface by pressure: *the print of footsteps in the sand.* **2a.** A device or implement, such as a seal, used to press markings onto or into a surface. **b.** Something formed or marked by such a device. **3a.** Lettering or other impressions produced in ink from type by a printing press or other means. **b.** Matter so produced; printed material. **c.** Printed state or form. **4a.** A printed publication, such as a magazine or newspaper. **b.** Printed matter. **5.** A design or picture transferred from an engraved plate, wood block, or other medium. **6.** A photographic image transferred to paper or a similar surface, usu. from a negative. **7.** A copy of a film or movie made from a negative. **8a.** A fabric or garment with a dyed pattern that has been pressed onto it, usu. by engraved rollers. **b.** The pattern itself. ❖ *v.* **print·ed, print·ing, prints** —*tr.* **1.** To press (a mark or design, for example) onto or into a surface. **2a.** To make an impression on or in (a surface) with a device such as a seal. **b.** To press (a stamp or similar device) onto or into a surface to leave a marking. **3a.** To produce (a document, for example) on a paper surface by means of pressed type, an electronic printer, or similar means. **b.** To offer in printed form; publish. **4.** To write (something) in characters similar to those commonly used in print. **5.** To impress firmly in the mind or memory. **6.** To produce a photographic image from (a negative, for example) by passing light through film onto a photosensitive surface, esp. sensitized paper. —*intr.* **1a.** To work as a printer. **b.** To produce printed material. **2.** To produce something in printed form by means of a printing press or other reproduction process. **3.** To write characters similar to those commonly used in print. **4.** To produce or receive an impression, marking, or image. ❖ *adj.* Of, relating to, writing for, or constituting printed publications: *a print journalist; print coverage.* **—idioms: in print 1.** In printed or published form. **2.** Offered for sale by a publisher. **out of print** No longer offered for sale by a publisher. [ME *preinte* < OFr. < fem. p. part. of *preindre,* to press, alteration of *prembre* < Lat. *premere.*]

print·a·ble (prĭn'tə-bəl) *adj.* **1.** Capable of being printed or of producing a print: *printable negatives.* **2.** Fit for publication: *printable language.* **—print'a·bil'i·ty** *n.*

print bar *n.* A mechanism in a printing device that carries the template of the final form of the alphanumeric characters to be printed.

print·ed circuit (prĭn'tĭd) *n.* An electric circuit in which the conducting connections have been printed or otherwise deposited in predetermined patterns on an insulating base.

printed circuit
printed circuit board

printed matter *n.* Printed material, such as a book, that is not considered first-class mail and has a special postal rate.

print·er (prĭn'tər) *n.* **1.** One that prints, esp. one whose occupation is printing. **2.** A device that prints text or graphics on paper.

print·er's devil (prĭn'tərz) *n.* An apprentice in a printing establishment. [< the apprentice becoming black from the ink.]

print head *n.* The element of a printer that applies the mark or image to the paper.

print·ing (prĭn'tĭng) *n.* **1.** The art, process, or business of producing printed material by means of inked type and a printing press or by similar means. **2a.** The act of one that prints. **b.** Matter that is printed. **3.** All the copies of a publication, such as a book, that are printed at one time. **4.** Written characters not con-

nected to one another and resembling those appearing in print.

printing office *n.* An establishment where printed material is produced, esp. one that is officially authorized.

printing press *n.* A machine that transfers lettering or images by contact with various forms of inked surface onto paper or similar material fed into it in various ways.

print·mak·ing (prĭnt'mā'kĭng) *n.* The artistic design and manufacture of prints, such as woodcuts. **—print'mak'er** *n.*

print·out (prĭnt'out') *n.* A document printed from a printing device, esp. one using continuously fed paper.

print wheel *n.* A disk-shaped mechanism in a printing device that carries the template of the characters to be printed around its rim and revolves to print one character at a time.

pri·on (prē'ŏn) *n.* A microscopic protein particle similar to a virus but lacking nucleic acid, thought to be the infectious agent of certain diseases of the nervous system. [Alteration of *pro(teinaceous) in(fectious particle).*]

pri·or¹ (prī'ər) *adj.* **1.** Preceding in time or order. **2.** Preceding in importance or value: *a prior consideration.* [Lat. See PRIOR².] **—pri'or·ly** *adv.*

pri·or² (prī'ər) *n.* **1.** A monastic officer in charge of a priory or ranking next below the abbot of an abbey. **2.** One of the ruling magistrates of the medieval republic of Florence. [ME *priour* < OE and OFr. *prior,* both < Med.Lat. < Lat., superior. See **per¹** in App.] **—pri'or·ate** (-ĭt), **pri'or·ship'** (-shĭp') *n.*

pri·or·ess (prī'ər-ĭs) *n.* A nun in charge of a priory or ranking next below the abbess of an abbey. [ME *prioresse* < OFr., fem. of *prior,* a prior. See PRIOR².]

pri·or·i·tize (prī-ôr'ĭ-tīz', -ŏr'-) *v.* **-tized, -tiz·ing, -tiz·es** *Usage Problem* —*tr.* To arrange or deal with in order of importance. —*intr.* To put things in order of importance. [PRIORIT(Y) + –IZE.] **—pri·or'i·ti·za'tion** (-tĭ-zā'shən) *n.*

USAGE NOTE It can be argued that *prioritize* serves a useful function in providing a single word to mean "arrange according to priority," but it is often regarded as corporate or bureaucratic jargon. Resistance to *prioritize,* however, has fallen dramatically in recent decades. In 1976, 97 percent of the Usage Panel rejected its use in the phrase *a first attempt to prioritize the tasks facing the new administration.* By 1997, however, 53 percent of the Panel approved the use of *prioritize* in the sentence *Overwhelmed with work, the lawyer was forced to prioritize his caseload.* This suggests that, like *finalize, prioritize* is rapidly securing a place in our everyday vocabulary. See Usage Note at **finalize.**

pri·or·i·ty (prī-ôr'ĭ-tē, -ŏr'-) *n., pl.* **-ties 1.** Precedence, esp. established by order of importance or urgency. **2a.** An established right to precedence. **b.** An authoritative rating that establishes such precedence. **3.** A preceding or coming earlier in time. **4.** Something afforded or deserving prior attention. [ME *priorite* < OFr. < Med.Lat. *prioritās* < Lat. *prior,* first. See PRIOR².]

prior to *prep.* Preceding; before.

pri·or·y (prī'ə-rē) *n., pl.* **-ies** A monastery governed by a prior or a convent governed by a prioress.

Prip·et (prĭp'ĕt) or **Pri·pyat** (-yət) A river, c. 708 km (440 mi), of N Ukraine and S Belarus flowing generally E through the **Pripet Marshes** to the Dnieper R.

Pris·cian (prĭsh'ən, -ē-ən) fl. A.D. 500. Latin grammarian at Constantinople known for his *Institutiones Grammaticae.*

prise (prīz) *v. & n.* Variant of **prize³.**

prism (prĭz'əm) *n.* **1.** A solid figure whose bases or ends have the same size and shape and are parallel to one another and each of whose sides is a parallelogram. **2.** A transparent body of this form, often of glass and usu. with triangular ends, used to separate white light passed through it into a spectrum or to reflect light beams. **3.** A cut-glass object, such as a chandelier. **4.** A crystal form consisting of three or more similar faces parallel to a single axis. **5.** A medium that misrepresents whatever is seen through it. [LLat. *prisma* < Gk. *prisma,* thing sawed off, prism < *priein, prizein,* to saw.]

pris·mat·ic (prĭz-măt'ĭk) also **pris·mat·i·cal** (-ĭ-kəl) *adj.* **1.** Of, relating to, resembling, or being a prism. **2.** Formed by refraction of light through a prism. Used of a spectrum of light. **3.** Brilliantly colored; iridescent. [Gk. *prisma, prismat-,* prism; see PRISM + –IC.] **—pris·mat'i·cal·ly** *adv.*

pris·ma·toid (prĭz'mə-toid') *n.* A polyhedron all of whose vertices lie in one of two parallel planes. [Gk. *prisma, prismat-,* prism + –OID.] **—pris'ma·toi'dal** (-toid'l) *adj.*

pris·moid (prĭz'moid') *n.* A prismatoid having polygons with the same number of sides as bases and faces that are parallelograms or trapezoids. **—pris·moi'dal** (-moid'l) *adj.*

pris·on (prĭz'ən) *n.* **1.** A place for the confinement of persons in lawful detention, esp. persons convicted of crimes. **2.** A place or condition of confinement or forcible restraint. **3.** A state of imprisonment or captivity. ❖ *tr.v.* **-oned, -on·ing, -ons** To imprison. [ME < OFr., alteration of **prehensio* < OFr. *pris,* taken) of Lat. *prēnsiō, prēnsiōn-,* a seizing < *prehēnsiō < prehēnsus,* p. part. of *prehendere,* to seize. See **ghend-** in App.]

prison camp *n.* **1.** A camp for detaining and confining prisoners of war. **2.** A camp detaining and confining political dissidents and other prisoners. **3.** A minimum security facility for the internment of prisoners.

pris•on•er (prĭz′ə-nər, prĭz′nər) n. **1.** A person held in custody, captivity, or a condition of forcible restraint, esp. while on trial or serving a prison sentence. **2.** One deprived of freedom of expression or action.

prisoner of war n., pl. **prisoners of war** A person taken by or surrendering to enemy forces in wartime.

pris•on•er's base (prĭz′ə-nərz, prĭz′nərz) n. A children's game in which two teams try to capture opposing players by tagging them and bringing them to a base.

prison fever n. See **typhus**. [So called because it formerly prevailed in prisons.]

pris•sy (prĭs′ē) adj. **-si•er, -si•est** Excessively or affectedly prim and proper. [Perh. blend of PRI(M)[1] and (SI)SSY.] —**pris′si•ly** adv. —**pris′si•ness** n.

Priš•ti•na (prĭsh′tə-nä′) A city of S Yugoslavia, the chief city of the Kosovo region. Pop. 155,000.

pris•tine (prĭs′tēn′, prĭ-stēn′) adj. **1a.** Remaining in a pure state; uncorrupted by civilization. **b.** Remaining free from dirt or decay; clean: *pristine mountain snow.* **2.** Of, relating to, or typical of the earliest time or condition; primitive or original. [Lat. *prīstinus.* See **per**[1] in App.] —**pris′tine•ly** adv.

prith•ee (prĭth′ē, prĭth′ē) interj. Archaic Used to express a polite request. [Alteration of *(I) pray thee.*]

priv. abbr. **1.** private **2.** privative

pri•va•cy (prī′və-sē) n. **1a.** The quality or condition of being secluded from the presence or view of others. **b.** The state of being free from unsanctioned intrusion: *a person's right to privacy.* **2.** The state of being concealed; secrecy.

pri•vate (prī′vĭt) adj. **1a.** Secluded from the sight, presence, or intrusion of others: *a private hideaway.* **b.** Designed or intended for one's exclusive use: *a private room.* **2a.** Of or confined to the individual; personal: *a private joke; private opinions.* **b.** Undertaken on an individual basis: *private studies; private research.* **c.** Of, relating to, or receiving special hospital services and privileges: *a private patient.* **3.** Not available for public use, control, or participation: *a private club.* **4a.** Belonging to a particular person or persons, as opposed to the public or the government: *private property.* **b.** Of, relating to, or derived from nongovernment sources: *private funding.* **c.** Conducted and supported primarily by private individuals or by a nongovernmental agency or corporation: *a private college.* **d.** Enrolled in or attending a private school: *a private student.* **5.** Not holding an official or public position: *a private citizen.* **6a.** Not for public knowledge or disclosure; secret: *private papers.* **b.** Not appropriate for use or display in public; intimate: *private behavior.* **c.** Placing a high value on personal privacy. ❖ n. **1a.** A noncommissioned rank in the US Army or Marine Corps that is below private first class. **b.** One who holds this rank or a similar rank in a military organization. **2. privates** Private parts. —**idiom: in private** Not in public; confidentially. [ME *privat* < Lat. *prīvātus,* not in public life, p. part. of *prīvāre,* to release, deprive < *prīvus,* single, alone. See **per**[1] in App.] —**pri′vate•ly** adv. —**pri′vate•ness** n.

private detective n. See **private investigator**.

private enterprise n. **1.** Business activities not controlled or owned by any state; privately owned business. **2.** A privately owned business, esp. one operating under capitalism.

pri•va•teer (prī′və-tîr′) n. **1.** A privately owned ship authorized by a government during wartime to attack and capture enemy vessels. **2.** The commander or one of the crew of such a ship. ❖ intr.v. **-teered, -teer•ing, -teers** To sail as a privateer.

private eye n. See **private investigator**.

private first class n., pl. **privates first class** A noncommissioned officer in the US Army ranking above private and below corporal or in the US Marine Corps ranking above private and below lance corporal.

private investigator n. A person privately hired to do investigative or detective work.

private law n. The branch of law that deals with the legal rights and relationships of private individuals.

private parts pl.n. The external organs of sex and excretion.

private school n. A secondary or elementary school run and supported by private individuals or a corporation rather than by a government or public agency.

pri•va•tion (prī-vā′shən) n. **1a.** Lack of the basic necessities or comforts of life. **b.** The condition resulting from such lack. **2.** An act, condition, or result of deprivation or loss. [ME *privacion* < OFr. *privation* < Lat. *prīvātiō, prīvātiōn-* < *prīvātus,* p. part. of *prīvāre,* to deprive. See PRIVATE.]

pri•vat•ism (prī′və-tĭz′əm) n. The social position of being noncommittal to or uninvolved with anything other than one's own immediate interests. —**pri′va•tist** adj. & n. —**pri′va•tis′tic** adj.

priv•a•tive (prĭv′ə-tĭv) adj. **1.** Causing deprivation, lack, or loss. **2.** Grammar Altering the meaning of a term from positive to negative. ❖ n. Grammar A privative prefix or suffix, such as a-, non-, un-, or -less. [ME *privatif* < Lat. *prīvātīvus* < *prīvātus,* p. part. of *prīvāre,* to deprive. See PRIVATE.] —**priv′a•tive•ly** adv.

pri•va•tize (prī′və-tīz′) tr.v. **-tized, -tiz•ing, -tiz•es** To change (an industry or business, for example) from government or public ownership or control to private enterprise. —**pri′va•ti•za′tion** (-tĭ-zā′shən) n.

priv•et (prĭv′ĭt) n. **1.** Any of several shrubs of the genus *Ligus-*

trum, having white flowers and widely used for hedges. **2.** Any of several similar or related plants. [?]

priv•i•lege (prĭv′ə-lĭj, prĭv′lĭj) n. **1a.** A special advantage, immunity, permission, right, or benefit granted to or enjoyed by an individual, class, or caste. See Syns at **right. b.** Such a privilege held as a prerogative of status or rank and exercised to the exclusion or detriment of others. **2.** The principle of granting and maintaining a special right or immunity: *a society based on privilege.* **3.** Law The right to privileged communication in a confidential relationship, as between patient and physician. **4.** An option to buy or sell a stock, including put, call, spread, and straddle. ❖ tr.v. **-leged, -leg•ing, -leg•es 1.** To grant a privilege to. **2.** To free or exempt. [ME < OFr. < Lat. *prīvilēgium,* a law affecting one : *prīvus,* single, alone; see **per**[1] in App. + *lēx, lēg-,* law; see **leg-** in App.]

priv•i•leged (prĭv′ə-lĭjd, prĭv′lĭjd) adj. **1.** Enjoying a privilege or having privileges. **2.** Confined to an exclusive or chosen group of individuals. ❖ n. (used with a pl. verb) Privileged people considered as a group. Often used with the.

privileged communication n. **1.** A confidential communication that one cannot be forced to divulge. **2.** A communication that is not subject to charges of slander or libel.

priv•i•ly (prĭv′ə-lē) adv. Privately or secretly.

priv•i•ty (prĭv′ĭ-tē) n., pl. **-ties 1.** Knowledge of something private or secret shared between individuals, esp. with the implication of approval or consent. **2.** Law A relation between parties that is held to be sufficiently close and direct to support a legal claim on behalf of or against another person with whom this relation exists. **b.** A successive or mutual interest in or relationship to the same property. [ME *privete,* secrecy, privacy < OFr. < Med.Lat. *prīvitās* < Lat. *prīvus,* single, alone. See **per**[1] in App.]

priv•y (prĭv′ē) adj. **1.** Made a participant in knowledge of something private or secret. **2.** Belonging or proper to a person, such as a sovereign, in a private rather than official capacity. **3.** Secret; concealed. ❖ n., pl. **-ies 1a.** An outdoor toilet; an outhouse. **b.** A toilet. **2.** Law One of the parties having an interest in the same matter. [ME *prive* < OFr. < Lat. *prīvātus,* private < *prīvus,* single, alone. See **per**[1] in App.]

Privy Council n. **1.** A council of the British sovereign that until the 17th century was the supreme legislative body, now consists of cabinet ministers, and has no important function except that its Judicial Committee sometimes acts as a supreme appellate court. **2. privy council** An advisory council to an executive. —**privy councilor** n.

prix fixe (prē′ fĕks′) n., pl. **prix fixes** (prē′ fĕks′) **1.** A complete meal of several courses offered by a restaurant at a fixed price. **2.** A fixed price charged for such a meal. **3.** See **table d'hôte**. [Fr. : *prix,* price + *fixe,* fixed.]

prize[1] (prīz) n. **1.** Something offered or won as an award for superiority or victory, as in a contest or competition. **2.** Something worth striving for; a highly desirable possession. ❖ adj. **1.** Offered or given as a prize: *a prize cup.* **2.** Given a prize, or likely to win a prize: *a prize cow.* **3.** Worthy of a prize; first-class. ❖ tr.v. **prized, priz•ing, priz•es 1.** To value highly; esteem or treasure. See Syns at **appreciate. 2.** To estimate the worth of; evaluate. [Alteration of ME *pris,* value, price, reward. See PRICE.]

prize[2] (prīz) n. **1.** Something seized by force or taken as booty, esp. an enemy ship and its cargo. **2.** The act of seizing; capture. [Alteration of ME *prise* < OFr. < fem. p. part. of *prendre* < Lat. *prehendere, prēndere,* to seize. See **ghend-** in App.]

prize[3] also **prise** (prīz) tr.v. **prized, priz•ing, priz•es** also **prised, pris•ing, pris•es** To move or force with or as if with a lever; pry. ❖ n. **1.** Leverage. **2.** Chiefly Southern US Something used as a lever or for prying. [< ME *prise,* instrument for prying, prob. < *prise,* the taking of something. See PRIZE[2].]

prize•fight (prīz′fīt′) n. A professional boxing match for money. —**prize′fight′er** n. —**prize′fight′ing** n.

prize•win•ner (prīz′wĭn′ər) n. One that wins a prize.

prize•win•ning also **prize-win•ning** (prīz′wĭn′ĭng) adj. Having won or worthy of winning a prize: *the prizewinning entry.*

p.r.n. abbr. Latin pro re nata (as the situation demands; as needed)

pro[1] (prō) n., pl. **pros 1.** An argument or consideration in favor of something: *the pros and cons.* **2.** One who supports a proposal or takes the affirmative side in a debate. ❖ adv. In favor; affirmatively: *arguing pro and con.* ❖ adj. Affirmative; supporting: *a pro vote.* [ME < Lat. *prō,* for. See **per**[1] in App.]

pro[2] (prō) Informal n., pl. **pros 1.** A professional, esp. in sports. **2.** An expert in a field of endeavor. ❖ adj. Professional.

pro-[1] pref. **1.** Acting in the place of; substituting for: *proform.* **2.** Supporting; favoring: *prorevolutionary.* [ME < OFr. < Lat. *prō-,* for < *prō,* for. See **per**[1] in App.]

pro-[2] pref. **1a.** Earlier; before; prior to: *procambium.* **b.** Rudimentary: *pronucleus.* **2.** Anterior; in front of: *procephalic.* [ME < OFr. < Gk. < *pro,* before, in front. See **per**[1] in App.]

pro•a (prō′ə) also **prau** (prou) or **prah•u** (prä′ōō) n. A swift Malayan sailboat with a triangular sail and single outrigger. [Malay *perahu* < Marathi *paḍāv.*]

pro-a•bor•tion (prō′ə-bôr′shən) adj. Favoring or supporting legalized abortion. —**pro′a•bor′tion•ist** n.

pro•ac•tive or **pro-ac•tive** (prō-ăk′tĭv) adj. Acting in advance

ă	pat	oi	boy
ā	pay	ou	out
âr	care	ŏŏ	took
ä	father	ōō	boot
ĕ	pet	ŭ	cut
ē	be	ûr	urge
ĭ	pit	th	thin
ī	pie	th	this
îr	pier	hw	which
ŏ	pot	zh	vision
ō	toe	ə	about,
ô	paw		item

Stress marks:
′ (primary);
′ (secondary), as in
lexicon (lĕk′sĭ-kŏn′)

to deal with an expected difficulty; anticipatory: *proactive steps to prevent terrorism.* —**pro•ac′tion** *n.* —**pro•ac′tive•ly** *adv.*

pro-am (prō′ăm′) *n.* A sports event in which professionals and amateurs compete. —**pro′-am′** *adj.*

prob•a•bi•lism (prŏb′ə-bə-lĭz′əm) *n.* **1.** *Philosophy* The doctrine that probability is a sufficient basis for belief and action. **2.** *Roman Catholic Church* The moral system that allows one to follow advice favoring personal liberty, even though opposing advice, favoring law, is more probable. —**prob′a•bi•list** *adj. & n.*

prob•a•bil•is•tic (prŏb′ə-bə-lĭs′tĭk) *adj.* **1.** Of, relating to, or based on probabilism. **2.** Of, based on, or affected by probability, randomness, or chance.

prob•a•bil•i•ty (prŏb′ə-bĭl′ĭ-tē) *n.*, *pl.* **-ties 1.** The quality or condition of being probable; likelihood. **2.** A probable situation, condition, or event. **3a.** The likelihood that a given event will occur: *a great probability of rain.* **b.** *Statistics* The ratio of the number of actual occurrences of a specific event to the total number of possible occurrences. —**idiom: in all probability** Most probably; very likely.

probability density *n. Statistics* **1.** A function whose integral over a given interval gives the probability that the values of a random variable will fall within the interval. **2.** The calculated value of a probability density.

probability distribution *n. Statistics* **1.** See **probability density. 2.** A function of a discrete random variable yielding the probability that the variable will have a given value.

probability theory *n.* The branch of mathematics that studies the likelihood of occurrence of random events in order to predict the behavior of defined systems.

prob•a•ble (prŏb′ə-bəl) *adj.* **1.** Likely to happen or to be true. **2.** Likely but uncertain; plausible. **3.** *Theology* Of or relating to advice or action in ethics and morals whose lawfulness can be justified by intrinsic reasons or extrinsic authority. [ME, plausible < OFr. < Lat. *probābilis* < *probāre*, to prove. See PROVE.]

probable cause *n.* Reasonable grounds for belief that an accused person may be subject to arrest or the issuance of a warrant.

prob•a•bly (prŏb′ə-blē) *adv.* Most likely; presumably.

pro•bang (prō′băng′) *n.* A long flexible rod having a tuft or sponge at the end, used in cleaning or medicating the larynx or esophagus. [Alteration of *provang.*]

pro•bate (prō′bāt′) *n.* **1.** The process of legally establishing the validity of a will before a judicial authority. **2.** Judicial certification of the validity of a will. **3.** An authenticated copy of a will so certified. ❖ *tr.v.* **-bat•ed, -bat•ing, -bates** To establish the validity of (a will) by probate. [ME *probat* < Lat. *probātum*, neut. p. part. of *probāre*, to prove. See PROVE.]

probate court *n.* A court limited to the jurisdiction of probating wills and administering estates.

pro•ba•tion (prō-bā′shən) *n.* **1.** A process or period in which a person's fitness, as for work or membership in a social group, is tested. **2a.** *Law* The act of suspending the sentence of a person convicted of a criminal offense and granting that person provisional freedom on the promise of good behavior. **b.** A discharge from commitment as an insane person on condition of continued sanity and not being recommitted upon the reappearance of insanity. **3.** A trial period in which a student is given time to try to redeem failing grades or bad conduct. **4.** The status of a person on probation. [ME *probacion*, a testing < OFr. *probation* < Lat. *probātiō, probātiōn-* < *probātus*, p. part. of *probāre*, to test. See PROVE.] —**pro•ba′tion•al, pro•ba′tion•ar′y** *adj.* —**pro•ba′tion•al•ly** *adv.*

pro•ba•tion•er (prō-bā′shə-nər) *n.* A person on probation.

probation officer *n.* **1.** An official charged with the care of juvenile delinquents. **2.** An official charged with supervising convicts at large on suspended sentence or probation.

pro•ba•tive (prō′bə-tĭv) also **pro•ba•to•ry** (-tôr′ē, -tōr′ē) *adj.* **1.** Furnishing evidence or proof. **2.** Serving to test, try, or prove.

probe (prōb) *n.* **1.** An exploratory action, expedition, or device, esp. one designed to investigate and obtain information on a remote or unknown region. **2.** A slender, flexible instrument used to explore a wound or body cavity. **3.** A substance that is radioactively labeled or otherwise marked and used to detect or identify another substance in a sample. **4.** The act of exploring or searching with or as if with a device or an instrument. **5.** An investigation into unfamiliar matters or questionable activities. **6.** A space probe. ❖ *v.* **probed, prob•ing, probes** —*tr.* **1.** To explore with or as if with a probe: *probe a wound; probe one's motives.* **2.** To delve into; investigate. —*intr.* To conduct an exploratory investigation; search. [ME, examination < Med.Lat. *proba* < LLat., proof < Lat. *probāre*, to test < *probus*, good. See **per**¹ in App.] —**prob′er** *n.* —**prob′ing•ly** *adv.*

pro•bi•ty (prō′bĭ-tē) *n.* Complete and confirmed integrity; uprightness. [ME *probite* < OFr. < Lat. *probitās* < *probus*, upright, good. See **per**¹ in App.]

prob•lem (prŏb′ləm) *n.* **1.** A question to be considered, solved, or answered. **2.** A situation, matter, or person that presents perplexity or difficulty. See Usage Note at **dilemma. 3.** A misgiving, objection, or complaint: *I have a problem with your cynicism.* ❖ *adj.* **1.** Difficult to deal with or control: *a problem child.* **2.** Dealing with a moral or social problem. —**idiom: no problem** *Informal* **1.** Used to express confirmation of or compliance with a re-

proboscis
African elephant

quest. **2.** Used to acknowledge an expression of gratitude. [ME *probleme* < OFr. < Lat. *problēma, problēmat-* < Gk. < *proballein*, to throw before, put forward : *pro-*, before; see PRO-² + *ballein*, *blē-*, to throw; see g*ʷ*elə- in App.]

prob•lem•at•ic (prŏb′lə-măt′ĭk) also **prob•lem•at•i•cal** (-ĭ-kəl) *adj.* **1.** Posing a problem; difficult to solve. **2.** Open to doubt; debatable. **3.** Not settled; unresolved or dubious: *a problematic future.* —**prob′lem•at′i•cal•ly** *adv.*

pro bo•no (prō bō′nō) *adj.* Done without compensation for the public good. [Lat. *prō bonō (publicō)*, for the (public) good : *prō*, for + *bonō*, ablative of *bonum*, the good.]

pro•bos•cid•i•an (prō′bə-sĭd′ē-ən) also **pro•bos•ci•de•an** (prō-bŏs′ĭ-dē′ən) *n.* A mammal of the order Proboscidea, such as the elephant or its extinct relatives, having a long trunk, large tusks, and a massive body. [< NLat. *Proboscidea*, order name < Lat. *proboscis, proboscid-*, proboscis. See PROBOSCIS.] —**pro′bos•cid′i•an** *adj.*

pro•bos•cis (prō-bŏs′ĭs) *n.*, *pl.* **-bos•cis•es** or **-bos•ci•des** (-bŏs′ĭ-dēz′) **1.** A long flexible snout or trunk. **2.** The slender tubular feeding and sucking organ of certain invertebrates. **3.** A human nose, esp. a prominent one. [Lat. < Gk. *proboskis* : *pro-*, in front; see PRO-² + *boskein*, to feed.]

pro•caine (prō′kān′) *n.* A white crystalline powder, $C_{13}H_{20}N_2O_2$, used chiefly in its hydrochloride form as a local anesthetic in medicine and dentistry. [PRO-² + (CO)CAINE (it being the precursor of cocaine).]

pro•cam•bi•um (prō-kăm′bē-əm) *n.* The primary meristem that gives rise to vascular tissue. —**pro•cam′bi•al** (-əl) *adj.*

pro•car•y•ote (prō-kăr′ē-ōt′) *n.* Variant of **prokaryote.**

pro•ce•dur•al (prə-sē′jər-əl) *adj.* Of or concerning procedure, esp. of a court of law or parliamentary body. ❖ *n.* A police procedural. —**pro•ce′dur•al•ly** *adv.*

pro•ce•dure (prə-sē′jər) *n.* **1.** A manner of proceeding; a way of performing or effecting something: *standard procedure.* **2.** A series of steps taken to accomplish an end: *a medical procedure.* **3.** A set of established forms or methods for conducting the affairs of an organized body such as a business, club, or government. **4.** *Computer Science* A set of instructions that performs a specific task. [Fr. *procédure* < OFr. < *proceder*, to proceed. See PROCEED.]

pro•ceed (prō-sēd′, prə-) *intr.v.* **-ceed•ed, -ceed•ing, -ceeds 1.** To go forward or onward, esp. after an interruption; continue. **2.** To begin to carry on an action or a process. **3.** To move on in an orderly manner. **4.** To come from a source; originate or issue. See Syns at **stem**¹. **5.** *Law* To institute and conduct legal action. ❖ *pl.n.* **pro•ceeds** (prō′sēdz′) The amount of money derived from a commercial or fundraising venture; the yield. [ME *proceden* < OFr. *proceder* < Lat. *prōcēdere* : *prō-*, forward; see PRO-¹ + *cēdere*, to go.] —**pro•ceed′er** *n.*

pro•ceed•ing (prō-sē′dĭng, prə-) *n.* **1.** A course of action; a procedure. **2. proceedings** A sequence of events occurring at a particular place or occasion. **3. proceedings** A record of business carried on by a society or other organization; minutes. **4.** *Law* **a.** Legal action; litigation. **b.** The instituting or conducting of legal action. In both senses, often used in the plural.

pro•ce•phal•ic (prō′sə-făl′ĭk) *adj.* Of, relating to, or located on or near the front of the head.

pro•cer•coid (prō-sûr′koid) *n.* A larval stage of certain tapeworms that typically develops in the body cavity of a copepod. [PRO-² + Gk. *kerkos*, tail + -OID.]

proc•ess¹ (prŏs′ĕs′, prō′sĕs′) *n.*, *pl.* **proc•ess•es** (prŏs′ĕs′ĭz, prō′sĕs′-, prŏs′ĭ-sēz′, prō′sĭ-) **1.** A series of actions, changes, or functions bringing about a result: *the process of digestion.* **2.** A series of operations performed in the making or treatment of a product: *a manufacturing process.* **3.** Progress; passage: *the process of time.* **4.** *Law* The entire course of a judicial proceeding. **5.** *Law* **a.** A summons or writ ordering a defendant to appear in court. **b.** The total quantity of summonses or writs issued in a particular proceeding. **6.** *Biology* An outgrowth of tissue; a projecting part: *a bony process.* **7.** Any of various photomechanical or photoengraving methods. **8.** *Computer Science* **a.** A running program or other computing operation. **b.** A part of a running program or other computing operation that does a single task. **9.** See **conk**³. ❖ *tr.v.* **-essed, -ess•ing, -ess•es 1.** To put through the steps of a prescribed procedure: *processing newly arrived immigrants; process an order.* **2.** To prepare, treat, or convert by subjecting to a special process: *process ore to obtain minerals.* **3.** *Law* **a.** To serve with a summons or writ. **b.** To institute legal proceedings against; prosecute. **4.** *Computer Science* To perform operations on (data). **5.** To straighten (hair) by a chemical process; conk. ❖ *adj.* **1.** Prepared or converted by a special process: *process cheese.* **2.** Made by or used in any of several photomechanical or photoengraving processes: *a process print.* [ME *proces* < OFr. < Lat. *prōcessus* < p. part. of *prōcēdere*, to advance. See PROCEED.]

USAGE NOTE In recent years there has been a tendency to pronounce the plural ending of *processes* as (-ēz) rather than (-ĭz), perhaps by analogy to the plurals of Greek origin like *analysis* and *neurosis.* But there is no etymological justification for pronouncing *processes* in this way, and in a recent survey 79 percent of the Usage Panel preferred the traditional pronunciation.

pro·cess² (prə-sĕs′) *intr.v.* **-cessed, -cess·ing, -cess·es** To move along in or as if in a procession.

pro·ces·sion (prə-sĕsh′ən) *n.* **1.** The act of moving along or forward; progression. **2.** Origination; emanation; rise. **3a.** A group of persons, vehicles, or objects moving along in an orderly, formal manner. **b.** The movement of such a group. **4.** An orderly succession. ❖ *intr.v.* **-sioned, -sion·ing, -sions** To form or go in a procession. [ME < OFr. < LLat. *prōcessiō, prōcessiōn-* < Lat., an advance < *prōcessus,* p. part. of *prōcēdere,* to advance. See PROCEED.]

pro·ces·sion·al (prə-sĕsh′ə-nəl) *adj.* Of, relating to, or suitable for a procession. ❖ *n.* **1.** A book containing the rituals observed during a religious procession. **2.** *Music* **a.** A piece played or sung at the entrance of the clergy in a church service. **b.** Music played or sung during a procession. **—pro·ces′sion·al·ly** *adv.*

proc·es·sor (prŏs′ĕs′ər, prō′sĕs′-) *n.* **1.** One that processes, esp. an apparatus for preparing, treating, or converting material. **2.** *Computer Science* **a.** A computer. **b.** A central processing unit. **c.** A program that translates another program into a form acceptable by the computer being used.

proc·ess printing (prŏs′ĕs′, prō′sĕs′) *n.* Printing from multiple halftone images, each inked with a different color such that the composite impression will reproduce the colors of the original.

pro·cès-ver·bal (prō-sä′vĕr-bäl′) *n., pl.* **-ver·baux** (-vĕr-bō′) A detailed official record of diplomatic, deliberative, or legal proceedings. [Fr. : *procès,* proceedings + *verbal,* oral.]

pro-choice (prō-chois′) *adj.* Favoring or supporting the legal right to choose whether or not to continue a pregnancy to term. **—pro-choic′er** *n.*

pro·claim (prō-klām′, prə-) *tr.v.* **-claimed, -claim·ing, -claims** **1.** To announce officially and publicly; declare. **2.** To indicate conspicuously; make plain: *wearing a button that proclaimed my choice for president.* **3.** To praise; extol. [ME *proclamen, proclaimen* (influenced by *claimen,* to claim) < OFr. *proclamer* < Lat. *prōclāmāre* : *prō-,* forward; see PRO-¹ + *clāmāre,* to cry out; see kelə- in App.] **—pro·claim′er** *n.* **—pro·clam′a·to·ry** (prō-klăm′ə-tôr′ē, -tōr′ē) *adj.*

proc·la·ma·tion (prŏk′lə-mā′shən) *n.* **1.** The act of proclaiming or the condition of being proclaimed. **2.** Something proclaimed, esp. an official public announcement.

pro·clit·ic (prō-klĭt′ĭk) *n.* A clitic that is attached to the beginning of another word. ❖ *adj.* Of, relating to, or forming a proclitic. [NLat. *procliticus* : PRO-² + LLat. *encliticus,* enclitic; see ENCLITIC.] **—pro·clit′i·cize′** (-ə-sīz′) *v.* **—pro·clit′i·ci·za′tion** (-ə-sī-zā′shən), **pro·clis′is** (-klĭs′ĭs) *n.*

pro·cliv·i·ty (prō-klĭv′ĭ-tē) *n., pl.* **-ties** A natural propensity or inclination; predisposition. See Syns at **predilection.** [Lat. *prōclīvitās* < *prōclīvis,* inclined : *prō-,* forward; see PRO-¹ + *clīvus,* slope; see klei- in App.]

Proc·ne (prŏk′nē) *n. Greek Mythology* An Athenian princess who avenged the cruelty of her husband, Tereus, by killing their son and with her sister Philomela became a swallow or nightingale.

pro·con·sul (prō-kŏn′səl) *n.* **1.** A provincial governor of consular rank in the Roman Republic and Roman Empire. **2.** A high administrator in a modern colonial empire. [ME < Lat. *prōcōnsul* < *prōcōnsule,* in place of the consul : *prō,* instead of; see PRO-¹ + *cōnsule,* ablative of *cōnsul,* consul; see CONSUL.] **—pro·con′su·lar** (-sə-lər) *adj.* **—pro·con′su·late** (-sə-lĭt), **pro·con′sul·ship′** *n.*

Pro·co·pi·us (prə-kō′pē-əs) *fl.* 6th cent. A.D. Byzantine historian who wrote about the Persian, Vandal, and Gothic wars.

pro·cras·ti·nate (prō-krăs′tə-nāt′, prə-) *v.* **-nat·ed, -nat·ing, -nates** *—intr.* To put off doing something, esp. out of habitual carelessness or laziness. *—tr.* To postpone or delay needlessly. [Lat. *prōcrāstināre, prōcrāstināt-* : *prō-,* forward; see PRO-¹ + *crāstinus,* of tomorrow (< *crās,* tomorrow).] **—pro·cras′ti·na′tion** *n.* **—pro·cras′ti·na′tor** *n.*

pro·cre·ate (prō′krē-āt′) *v.* **-at·ed, -at·ing, -ates** *—tr.* **1.** To beget and conceive (offspring). **2.** To produce or create; originate. *—intr.* To beget and conceive offspring. [Lat. *prōcreāre, prōcreāt-* : *prō-,* forward; see PRO-¹ + *creāre,* to create; see ker-² in App.] **—pro′cre·ant** (-ənt) *adj.* **—pro′cre·a′tive** *adj.* **—pro′cre·a′tor** *n.*

Pro·crus·te·an also **pro·crus·te·an** (prō-krŭs′tē-ən) *adj.* Producing or designed to produce strict conformity by ruthless or arbitrary means. [After *Procrustes,* a mythical Greek giant who stretched or shortened captives to make them fit his beds < Lat. *Procrustēs* < Gk. *Prokroustēs* < *prokrouein,* to stretch out : *pro-,* forth; see PRO-² + *krouein,* to beat.]

pro·cryp·tic (prō-krĭp′tĭk) *adj. Zoology* Having a pattern or coloration adapted for natural camouflage. [Prob. PRO(TECTIVE) + CRYPTIC.]

proc·ti·tis (prŏk-tī′tĭs) *n.* Inflammation of the rectum or anus. [Gk. *prōktos,* anus + -ITIS.]

proc·tol·o·gy (prŏk-tŏl′ə-jē) *n.* The branch of medicine that deals with the diagnosis and treatment of disorders that affect the colon, rectum, and anus. [Gk. *prōktos,* anus + -LOGY.] **—proc·to·log′ic** (-tə-lŏj′ĭk), **proc·to·log′i·cal** (-ĭ-kəl) *adj.* **—proc·to·log′i·cal·ly** *adv.* **—proc·tol′o·gist** *n.*

proc·tor (prŏk′tər) *n.* A supervisor, esp. of an examination or dormitory in a school. ❖ *tr.v.* **-tored, -tor·ing, -tors** To supervise (an examination). [ME *procutor, proctour,* university officer, manager < *procuratour.* See PROCURATOR.] **—proc·to′ri·al** (-tôr′ē-əl, -tōr′-) *adj.* **—proc′tor·ship′** *n.*

proc·to·scope (prŏk′tə-skōp′) *n.* An instrument consisting of a tube or speculum equipped with a light, used to examine the rectum. [Gk. *prōktos,* anus + -SCOPE.] **—proc′to·scop′ic** (-skŏp′ĭk) *adj.* **—proc·tos′co·py** (-tŏs′kə-pē) *n.*

pro·cum·bent (prō-kŭm′bənt) *adj.* **1.** Lying face down; prone. **2.** *Botany* Trailing along the ground but not rooting. [Lat. *prōcumbēns, prōcumbent-,* pr. part. of *prōcumbere,* to bend down : *prō-,* forward; see PRO-¹ + *-cumbere,* to lie down.]

proc·u·ra·tor (prŏk′yə-rā′tər) *n.* **1.** One authorized to manage the affairs of another; an agent. **2.** An employee of the Roman emperor in civil affairs. [ME *procuratour* < OFr. < Lat. *prōcūrātor* < *prōcūrāre,* to take care of. See PROCURE.] **—proc′u·ra·to′ri·al** (-yər-ə-tôr′ē-əl, tōr′-) *adj.*

pro·cure (prō-kyoŏr′, prə-) *v.* **-cured, -cur·ing, -cures** *—tr.* **1.** To get by special effort; obtain or acquire. **2.** To bring about; effect: *procure a solution to a knotty problem.* **3.** To obtain (a sexual partner) for another. *—intr.* To obtain sexual partners for others. [ME *procuren* < OFr. *procurer,* to take care of < Lat. *prōcūrāre* : *prō-,* for; see PRO-¹ + *cūrāre,* to care for (< *cūra,* care; see CURE).] **—pro·cur′a·ble** *adj.* **—pro·cur′ance, pro·cure′ment** *n.*

pro·cur·er (prō-kyoŏr′ər, prə-) *n.* **1.** One that procures. **2.** A pander.

Pro·cy·on (prō′sē-ŏn′) *n.* A binary star in the constellation Canis Minor. [Lat. *Procyōn* < Gk. *Prokuōn* : *pro-,* before; see PRO-² + *kuōn,* dog; see kwon- in App.]

prod (prŏd) *tr.v.* **prod·ded, prod·ding, prods** **1.** To jab or poke, as with a pointed object. **2.** To goad to action; incite. ❖ *n.* **1.** A pointed object used to prod. **2.** An incitement; a stimulus. [?] **—prod′der** *n.*

prod·i·gal (prŏd′ĭ-gəl) *adj.* **1.** Rashly or wastefully extravagant: *prodigal expenditures.* **2.** Giving or given in abundance; lavish or profuse: *prodigal praise.* ❖ *n.* One given to wasteful luxury or extravagance. [Prob. back-formation < PRODIGALITY.] **—prod′i·gal·ly** *adv.*

prod·i·gal·i·ty (prŏd′ĭ-găl′ĭ-tē) *n., pl.* **-ties 1.** Extravagant wastefulness. **2.** Profuse generosity. **3.** Extreme abundance; lavishness. [ME *prodigalite* < OFr. < LLat. *prōdigālitās* < Lat. *prōdigus,* prodigal < *prōdigere,* to drive away, squander : *prōd-, prō-,* forth; see PROUD + *agere,* to drive; see ag- in App.]

pro·di·gious (prə-dĭj′əs) *adj.* **1.** Impressively great in size, force, or extent; enormous. **2.** Extraordinary; marvelous: *a prodigious talent.* **3.** *Obsolete* Portentous; ominous. [Lat. *prōdigiōsus,* portentous < *prōdigium,* omen.] **—pro·di′gious·ly** *adv.* **—pro·di′gious·ness** *n.*

prod·i·gy (prŏd′ə-jē) *n., pl.* **-gies 1.** A person with exceptional talents or powers. **2.** An act or event so extraordinary or rare as to inspire wonder. See Syns at **wonder.** **3.** A portentous sign or event; an omen. [ME *prodige,* portent < Lat. *prōdigium.*]

pro·drome (prō′drōm′) *n., pl.* **-dromes** or **-dro·ma·ta** (-drō′mə-tə) An early symptom indicating the onset of an attack of a disease. [Fr. < Lat. *prodromus,* precursor < Gk. *prodromos,* precursor : *pro-,* forward; see PRO-² + *dromos,* running.] **—pro·dro′mal** (-drō′məl), **pro·drom′ic** (-drŏm′ĭk) *adj.*

pro·drug (prō′drŭg′) *n.* An inactive precursor of a drug, converted into its active form in the body by metabolic processes.

pro·duce (prə-dōōs′, -dyōōs′, prō-) *v.* **-duced, -duc·ing, -duc·es** *—tr.* **1.** To bring forth; yield: *a plant that produces pink flowers.* **2a.** To create by physical or mental effort: *produce a tapestry; produce a poem.* **b.** To manufacture: *factories that produce cars and trucks.* **3.** To cause to occur or exist; give rise to: *chemicals that produce a noxious vapor when mixed.* **4.** To bring forth; exhibit: *produced an eyewitness.* **5.** To supervise and finance the making and public presentation of: *produce a videotape.* **6.** *Mathematics* To extend (an area or volume) or lengthen (a line). *—intr.* **1.** To make or yield products or a product: *an apple tree that produces well.* **2.** To manufacture or create economic goods and services. ❖ *n.* (prŏd′ōōs, prō′dōōs) **1.** Something produced; a product. **2.** Farm products, esp. fresh fruits and vegetables. [ME *producen,* to proceed, extend < Lat. *prōdūcere,* to extend, bring forth : *prō-,* forward; see PRO-¹ + *dūcere,* to lead; see deuk- in App.] **—pro·duc′i·ble, pro·duce′a·ble** *adj.*

SYNONYMS *produce, bear, yield* These verbs mean to bring forth as a product: *a mine that produces gold; a seed that bore fruit; a plant that yields medicinal oil.*

pro·duc·er (prə-dōō′sər, -dyōō′-, prō-) *n.* **1.** One that produces, esp. a person or organization that produces goods or services for sale. **2.** One who supervises and controls the finances, creation, and public presentation of a play, film, program, or similar work. **3.** A furnace that manufactures producer gas. **4.** *Ecology* A photosynthetic green plant or chemosynthetic bacterium, constituting the first trophic level in a food chain; an autotrophic organism.

producer gas *n.* A combustible mixture of nitrogen, carbon monoxide, and hydrogen, generated by passing air with steam over burning coke or coal in a furnace and used as fuel.

producer goods *pl.n.* Goods, such as raw materials and tools, used to make consumer goods.

ă	pat	oi	boy
ā	pay	ou	out
âr	care	ŏŏ	took
ä	father	ōō	boot
ĕ	pet	ŭ	cut
ē	be	ûr	urge
ĭ	pit	th	thin
ī	pie	*th*	this
îr	pier	hw	which
ŏ	pot	zh	vision
ō	toe	ə	about,
ô	paw		item

Stress marks:
′ (primary);
′ (secondary); as in
lexicon (lĕk′sĭ-kŏn′)

profile
detail from *Portrait of a Young Woman* by Botticelli

producer price index *n.* A comprehensive index of wholesale price changes, often viewed as an indicator of future retail price changes.

prod•uct (prŏd′əkt) *n.* **1.** Something produced by human or mechanical effort or by a natural process. **2.** A direct result; a consequence. **3.** *Chemistry* A substance resulting from a chemical reaction. **4.** *Mathematics* **a.** The number or quantity obtained by multiplying two or more numbers together. **b.** A scalar product. **c.** A vector product. [ME, result of multiplication, produced < Med.Lat. *prōductum*, result of multiplication < neut. p. part. of Lat. *prōdūcere*, to bring forth. See PRODUCE.]

pro•duc•tion (prə-dŭk′shən, prō-) *n.* **1a.** The act or process of producing: *timber used for the production of lumber.* **b.** The fact or process of being produced: *a movie in production.* **2.** The creation of value or wealth by producing goods and services. **3.** The total output, as of a commodity: *increased production at the factory.* **4.** Something produced; a product. **5a.** A work of art or literature. **b.** A work produced for the stage, screen, television, or radio. **c.** A staging or presentation of a theatrical work. **6.** An exaggerated or unduly complicated spectacle or display. —**pro•duc′tion•al** *adj.*

production line *n.* See **assembly line** 1.

pro•duc•tive (prə-dŭk′tĭv, prō-) *adj.* **1.** Producing or capable of producing. **2.** Producing abundantly; fertile. **3.** Yielding favorable or useful results; constructive. **4.** *Economics* Of or involved in the creation of goods and services to produce wealth or value. **5.** Effective in achieving specified results; originative. **6.** *Medicine* **a.** Producing mucus or sputum. **b.** Forming new tissue: *a productive inflammation.* **7.** *Linguistics* **a.** Of or relating to the linguistic skills of speaking and writing. **b.** Of or relating to a linguistic element or rule that can be used to form further examples of a particular feature or pattern. —**pro•duc′tive•ly** *adv.* —**pro•duc′tive•ness** *n.*

pro•duc•tiv•i•ty (prō′dŭk-tĭv′ĭ-tē, prŏd′ək-) *n.* **1.** The quality of being productive. **2.** *Economics* The rate at which goods or services are produced, esp. output per unit of labor. **3.** *Ecology* The rate at which radiant energy is used by producers to form organic substances as food for consumers.

pro•em (prō′ĕm′) *n.* An introduction; a preface. [ME *proheme* < OFr. < Lat. *prooemium* < Gk. *prooimion* : *pro-*, before; see PRO-[2] + *oimē*, song.] —**pro•e′mi•al** (prō-ē′mē-əl, -ĕm′ē-) *adj.*

pro•en•zyme (prō-ĕn′zīm′) *n.* The precursor of an enzyme, converted into an active enzyme by proteolysis.

pro•es•trus (prō-ĕs′trəs) *n.* The period immediately before estrus in most female mammals, characterized by development of the endometrium and ovarian follicles.

prof (prŏf) *n. Informal* A professor.

pro•fam•i•ly also **pro•fam•i•ly** (prō-făm′ə-lē, -făm′lē) *adj.* Favoring or supporting values held to promote traditional family life, typically values identified with social conservatism.

prof•a•na•tion (prŏf′ə-nā′shən) *n.* The act or an instance of profaning; desecration.

pro•fane (prō-fān′, prə-) *adj.* **1.** Marked by contempt or irreverence for what is sacred. **2.** Nonreligious in subject matter, form, or use; secular. **3.** Not admitted into a body of secret knowledge or ritual; uninitiated. **4.** Vulgar; coarse. ❖ *tr.v.* **-faned, -fan•ing, -fanes** **1.** To treat with irreverence: *profane the name of God.* **2.** To put to an improper, unworthy, or degrading use; abuse. [ME *prophane* < OFr. < Lat. *profānus*, in front of the temple : *prō-*, before, outside; see PRO-[1] + *fānō*, ablative of *fānum*, temple; see **dhēs-** in App.] —**pro•fan′a•to′ry** (prō-făn′ə-tôr′ē, -tōr′ē, prə-) *adj.* —**pro•fane′ly** *adv.* —**pro•fan′er** *n.*

pro•fan•i•ty (prō-făn′ĭ-tē, prə-) *n., pl.* **-ties** **1.** The condition or quality of being profane. **2a.** Abusive, vulgar, or irreverent language. **b.** The use of such language.

pro•fess (prə-fĕs′, prō-) *v.* **-fessed, -fess•ing, -fess•es** —*tr.* **1.** To affirm openly; declare or claim. **2.** To make a pretense of; pretend. **3a.** To practice as a profession or claim knowledge of: *profess medicine.* **b.** To teach (a subject) as a professor. **4.** To affirm belief in: *profess Catholicism.* **5.** To receive into a religious order or congregation. —*intr.* **1.** To make an open affirmation. **2.** To take the vows of a religious order or congregation. [ME *professen*, to take vows < OFr. *profes*, that has taken a religious vow (< Med.Lat. *professus*, avowed) and < Med.Lat. *professāre*, to administer a vow, both < Lat. *professus*, p. part. of *profitērī*, to affirm openly : *pro-*, forth; see PRO-[1] + *fatērī*, to acknowledge; see **bhā-** in App.] —**pro•fess′ed•ly** (-fĕs′ĭd-lē) *adv.*

pro•fes•sion (prə-fĕsh′ən) *n.* **1a.** An occupation or career. **b.** An occupation such as law that requires considerable training and specialized study. **2.** The body of qualified persons in an occupation or field. **3.** An act or instance of professing; a declaration. **4.** An avowal of faith or belief. **5.** A faith or belief.

pro•fes•sion•al (prə-fĕsh′ə-nəl) *adj.* **1a.** Of, relating to, engaged in, or suitable for a profession: *lawyers, doctors, and other professional people.* **b.** Conforming to the standards of a profession: *professional behavior.* **2.** Engaging in a given activity as a source of livelihood or as a career. **3.** Performed by persons receiving pay. **4.** Having or showing great skill; expert. ❖ *n.* **1.** A person following a profession, esp. a learned profession. **2.** One who earns a living in a given or implied occupation. **3.** A skilled practitioner; an expert. —**pro•fes′sion•al•ly** *adv.*

pro•fes•sion•al•ism (prə-fĕsh′ə-nə-lĭz′əm) *n.* **1.** Professional status, methods, character, or standards. **2.** The use of professional performers, as in athletics or in the arts.

pro•fes•sion•al•ize (prə-fĕsh′ə-nə-līz′) *tr.v.* **-ized, -iz•ing, -iz•es** To make professional. —**pro•fes′sion•al•i•za′tion** (-lī-zā′shən) *n.*

pro•fes•sor (prə-fĕs′ər) *n.* **1a.** A college or university teacher who ranks above an associate professor. **b.** A teacher or instructor. **2.** One who professes. [ME *professour* < OFr. *professeur* < Lat. *professor* < *professus*, p. part. of *profitērī*, to profess. See PROFESS.] —**pro′fes•so′ri•al** (prō′fĭ-sôr′ē-əl, -sōr′-, prŏf′ĭ-) *adj.* —**pro′fes•so′ri•al•ly** *adv.* —**pro•fes′sor•ship′** *n.*

pro•fes•so•ri•ate or **pro•fes•so•ri•at** (prō′fĭ-sôr′ē-ət, -sōr′-, prŏf′ĭ-) *n.* **1.** The rank or office of a professor. **2.** College or university professors considered as a group.

prof•fer (prŏf′ər) *tr.v.* **-fered, -fer•ing, -fers** To offer for acceptance; tender. See Syns at **offer.** ❖ *n.* The act of proffering; an offer. [ME *profren* < OFr. *poroffrir, profrir* : *por-*, forth (< Lat. *prō-*; see PRO-[1]) + *offrir*, to offer (< Lat. *offerre*; see OFFER).] —**prof′fer•er** *n.*

pro•fi•cien•cy (prə-fĭsh′ən-sē) *n., pl.* **-cies** The state or quality of being proficient; competence.

pro•fi•cient (prə-fĭsh′ənt) *adj.* Having or marked by an advanced degree of competence, as in an art. ❖ *n.* An expert; an adept. [Lat. *prōficiēns, prōficient-*, pr. part. of *prōficere*, to make progress. See PROFIT.] —**pro•fi′cient•ly** *adv.*

SYNONYMS *proficient, adept, skilled, skillful, expert* These adjectives mean having or showing knowledge, ability, or skill, as in a profession or field of study. *Proficient* implies an advanced degree of competence acquired through training: *proficient in Greek and Latin.* *Adept* suggests a natural aptitude improved by practice: *adept at cutting straight.* *Skilled* implies sound, thorough competence and often mastery, as in a craft: *a skilled potter.* *Skillful* adds to *skilled* the idea of natural dexterity in performance or achievement: *skillful in the use of the loom.* *Expert* applies to one with consummate skill and command: *an expert violinist.*

pro•file (prō′fīl′) *n.* **1a.** A side view of an object or structure, esp. of the human head. **b.** A representation of an object or structure seen from the side. **2.** An outline of an object. See Syns at **outline.** **3.** Degree of exposure to public notice; visibility: *kept a low profile.* **4.** A biographical essay presenting the subject's most noteworthy characteristics and achievements. **5.** A formal summary or analysis of data representing distinctive features or characteristics. **6.** *Geology* A vertical section of soil or rock showing the sequence of the various layers. ❖ *tr.v.* **-filed, -fil•ing, -files** **1.** To draw or shape a profile of. **2.** To produce a profile of. [Ital. *profilo* < *profilare*, to draw in outline : *pro-*, forward (< Lat. *prō-*; see PRO-[1]) + *filare*, to draw a line (< Med.Lat. *fīlāre*, to spin < Lat. *fīlum*, thread).] —**pro′fil•er** *n.*

prof•it (prŏf′ĭt) *n.* **1.** An advantageous gain or return; benefit. **2.** The return on a business undertaking after all operating expenses have been met. **3a.** The return on an investment after all charges have been paid. **b.** The rate of increase in the net worth of a business enterprise in a given accounting period. **c.** Income from investments or property. **d.** The amount received for a commodity or service in excess of the original cost. ❖ *v.* **-it•ed, -it•ing, -its** —*intr.* **1.** To make a gain or profit. **2.** To derive advantage; benefit: *profiting from the other team's mistakes.* —*tr.* To be beneficial to. [ME < OFr. < Lat. *prōfectus* < p. part. of *prōficere*, make progress, to profit : *prō-*, forward; see PRO-[1] + *facere*, to make; see **dhē-** in App.] —**prof′it•less** *adj.*

prof•it•a•ble (prŏf′ĭ-tə-bəl) *adj.* Yielding profit; advantageous or lucrative. See Syns at **beneficial.** —**prof′it•a•bil′i•ty, prof′it•a•ble•ness** *n.* —**prof′it•a•bly** *adv.*

profit and loss *n.* An account showing net profit and loss over a given period.

prof•it•eer (prŏf′ĭ-tîr′) *n.* One who makes excessive profits on goods in short supply. —**prof′it•eer′** *v.*

pro•fit•er•ole (prə-fĭt′ə-rōl′) *n.* A small round cream puff. [Fr., perh. dim. of *profiter*, to profit < OFr. < *profit*, profit. See PROFIT.]

profit sharing *n.* A system by which employees receive a share of the profits of a business enterprise.

prof•li•gate (prŏf′lĭ-gĭt, -gāt′) *adj.* **1.** Given over to dissipation; dissolute. **2.** Recklessly wasteful; wildly extravagant. ❖ *n.* A profligate person; a wastrel. [Lat. *prōflīgātus*, p. part. of *prōflīgāre*, to ruin, cast down : *prō-*, forward; see PRO-[1] + *-flīgāre*, intensive of *flīgere*, to strike down.] —**prof′li•ga•cy** (-gə-sē) *n.* —**prof′li•gate•ly** *adv.*

pro for•ma (prō fôr′mə) *adj.* **1.** Done as a formality; perfunctory. **2.** Provided in advance so as to prescribe form or describe items. [NLat. *prō fōrmā* : *prō*, for the sake of + *fōrmā*, ablative of *fōrma*, form.]

pro•found (prə-found′, prō-) *adj.* **-er, -est** **1.** Situated at, extending to, or coming from a great depth; deep. **2.** Coming as if from the depths of one's being: *profound contempt.* **3.** Thoroughgoing; far-reaching: *profound social changes.* **4.** Penetrating beyond what is superficial or obvious: *a profound insight.* **5.** Unqualified; absolute: *a profound silence.* [ME *profounde* < OFr. *profond* < Lat. *profundus* : *prō-*, before; see PRO-[1] + *fundus*, bottom.] —**pro·found′ly** *adv.* —**pro·found′ness** *n.*

pro·fun·di·ty (prə-fŭn′dĭ-tē, prō-) *n., pl.* **-ties 1.** Great depth. **2.** Depth of intellect, feeling, or meaning. **3.** Something profound or abstruse. [ME *profundite* < OFr. < LLat. *profunditās* < Lat. *profundus*, deep. See PROFOUND.]

pro·fuse (prə-fyōōs′, prō-) *adj.* **1.** Plentiful; copious. **2.** Giving or given freely and abundantly; extravagant. [ME, lavish < Lat. *profūsus*, p. part. of *profundere*, to pour forth : *pro-*, forth; see PRO-¹ + *fundere*, to pour; see **gheu-** in App.] —**pro·fuse′ly** *adv.* —**pro·fuse′ness** *n.*

pro·fu·sion (prə-fyōō′zhən, prō-) *n.* **1.** The state of being profuse; abundance. **2.** Lavish or unrestrained expense; extravagance. **3.** A profuse outpouring or quantity.

pro·gen·i·tor (prō-jĕn′ĭ-tər) *n.* **1.** A direct ancestor. See Syns at **ancestor. 2.** An originator of a line of descent; a precursor. **3.** An originator; a founder. [Ult. < Lat. *prōgenitor* < *prōgenitus*, p. part. of *prōgignere*, to beget : *prō-*, forward; see PRO-¹ + *gignere*, *gen-*, to beget; see **genə-** in App.]

prog·e·ny (prŏj′ə-nē) *n., pl.* **progeny** or **-nies 1a.** One born of, begotten by, or derived from another; an offspring or a descendant. **b.** Offspring or descendants considered as a group. **2.** A result of creative effort; a product. [ME *progeni* < OFr. *progenie* < Lat. *prōgeniēs* < *prōgignere*, to beget. See PROGENITOR.]

pro·ger·i·a (prō-jîr′ē-ə) *n.* A rare congenital disorder of childhood, characterized by rapid onset of the physical changes typical of old age, usu. resulting in death before age 20. [PRO-² + Gk. *gēras*, old age; see GERIATRICS + -IA¹.]

pro·ges·ta·tion·al (prō′jĕs-tā′shə-nəl) *adj.* **1.** Of or relating to the phase of the menstrual cycle immediately following ovulation, characterized by secretion of progesterone. **2a.** Of or relating to progesterone and its actions. **b.** Having actions similar to progesterone. Used of a drug.

pro·ges·ter·one (prō-jĕs′tə-rōn′) *n.* **1.** A steroid hormone, C₂₁H₃₀O₂, secreted by the corpus luteum of the ovary and by the placenta, that acts to prepare the uterus for implantation of the fertilized ovum, maintain pregnancy, and promote development of the mammary glands. **2.** A drug prepared from natural or synthetic progesterone, used in the prevention of miscarriage, in the treatment of menstrual disorders, and as a constituent of some oral contraceptives. [PRO-¹ + GEST(ATION) + (ST)ER(OL) + -ONE.]

pro·ges·tin (prō-jĕs′tĭn) *n.* **1.** A progestational substance that mimics progesterone. **2.** A crude hormone of the corpus luteum from which progesterone can be isolated in pure form. Not in scientific use. [PRO-¹ + GEST(ATION) + -IN.]

pro·ges·to·gen (prō-jĕs′tə-jən) *n.* Any of various substances having progestational effects; a progestin. [PRO-¹ + GEST(ATION) + -GEN.]

pro·glot·tid (prō-glŏt′ĭd) also **pro·glot·tis** (-glŏt′ĭs) *n., pl.* **-glot·tids** also **-glot·ti·des** (-glŏt′ĭ-dēz′) One of the segments of a tapeworm, containing both male and female reproductive organs. [Gk. *proglōttis, proglōttid-*, tip of the tongue (< its shape) : *pro-*, before; see PRO-² + *glōtta*, tongue.] —**pro·glot′tic, pro·glot·ti·de·an** (-glŏt-ĭ-dē′ən, -glō-tĭd′ē-ən) *adj.*

prog·na·thous (prŏg′nə-thəs, prŏg-nā′-) also **prog·nath·ic** (prŏg-năth′ĭk, -nā′thĭk) *adj.* Having jaws that project forward to a marked degree. —**prog′na·thism** (-nə-thĭz′əm) *n.*

prog·no·sis (prŏg-nō′sĭs) *n., pl.* **-ses** (-sēz) **1a.** A prediction of the probable course and outcome of a disease. **b.** The likelihood of recovery from a disease. **2.** A forecast or prediction. [LLat. *prognōsis* < Gk. < *prognōskein*, to foreknow : *pro-*, before; see PRO-² + *gignōskein*, to know; see **gnō-** in App.]

prog·nos·tic (prŏg-nŏs′tĭk) *adj.* **1.** Of, relating to, or useful in prognosis. **2.** Of or relating to prediction; predictive. ❖ *n.* **1.** A sign or symptom indicating the future course of a disease. **2.** A sign of a future happening; a portent. [ME *pronostik*, prognosticating, omen (< Med.Lat. *prognōsticus*, prognosticating), and < Lat. *prognōsticum*, omen < neut. of *prognōsticus*, both < Gk. *prognōstikos < prognōsis*, foreknowledge; see PROGNOSIS. N. < Lat. *prognōsticum*, omen < Gk. *prognōstikon* < neut. of *prognōstikos*.]

prog·nos·ti·cate (prŏg-nŏs′tĭ-kāt′) *tr.v.* **-cat·ed, -cat·ing, -cates 1.** To predict according to present indications or signs; foretell. **2.** To foreshadow; portend. [ME *pronosticaten* < Med.Lat. *prognōsticāre, prognōsticāt-* < Lat. *prognōsticum*, sign of the future < Gk. *prognōstikon* < neut. of *prognōstikos*, foreknowing. See PROGNOSTIC.] —**prog·nos′ti·ca′tion** *n.* —**prog·nos′ti·ca′tive** *adj.* —**prog·nos′ti·ca′tor** *n.*

pro·gram (prō′grăm′, -grəm) *n.* **1a.** A listing of the order of events and other pertinent information for a public presentation. **b.** The presentation itself. **2.** A scheduled radio or television show. **3.** An ordered list of events to take place or procedures to be followed; a schedule. **4.** A system of services, opportunities, or projects, usu. designed to meet a social need. **5a.** A course of academic study; a curriculum. **b.** A plan or system of academic and related or ancillary activities: *a work-study program.* **c.** A plan or system of nonacademic extracurricular activities. **6.** A set of coded instructions that enables a machine, esp. a computer, to perform a desired sequence of operations. **7.** An instruction sequence in programmed instruction. ❖ *tr.v.* **-grammed, -gram·ming, -grams** or **-gramed, -gram·ing, -grams 1.** To include or schedule in a program: *program a new musical composition.* **2.** To design a program for; schedule the activities of. **3.** To provide (a

machine) with a set of coded working instructions. **4.** To train to perform automatically in a desired way, as if programming a machine. **5.** To prepare an instructional sequence for (material to be taught) in programmed instruction. [LLat. *programma*, public notice < Gk. *programma, programmat-* < *programphein*, to write publicly : *pro-*, forth; see PRO-² + *graphein*, to write; see **gerbh-** in App.] —**pro·gram′ma·bil′i·ty** *n.* —**pro′gram′ma·ble** *adj.*

program director *n.* A radio or television station director who selects, plans, and schedules programs.

pro·gram·mat·ic (prō′grə-măt′ĭk) *adj.* **1.** Of, relating to, or having a program. **2.** *Music* Of, resembling, or constituting program music. —**pro′gram·mat′i·cal·ly** *adv.*

pro·gramme (prō′grăm′, -grəm) *n. & v. Chiefly British* Variant of **program.**

pro·grammed instruction (prō′grămd′, -grəmd) *n.* A method of teaching in which the information to be learned is presented in discrete sequential units, with a correct response to each unit required.

pro·gram·mer or **pro·gram·er** (prō′grăm′ər) *n.* One who programs, esp. one who writes computer programs.

pro·gram·ming or **pro·gram·ing** (prō′grăm′ĭng, -grə-mĭng) *n.* **1.** The designing, scheduling, or planning of a program, as in broadcasting. **2.** The writing of a computer program.

programming language *n.* An artificial language used to write instructions that can be translated into machine language and then executed by a computer.

program music *n.* Music intended to depict or suggest nonmusical incidents, ideas, or images.

program trading *n.* Large-scale computer-assisted trading of stocks or other securities according to systems in which decisions to buy and sell are triggered automatically by fluctuations in price. —**program trader** *n.*

prog·ress (prŏg′rĕs′, -rəs, prō′grĕs′) *n.* **1.** Movement, as toward a goal; advance. **2.** Development or growth. **3.** Steady improvement, as of a society or civilization. See Syns at **development. 4.** A ceremonial journey made by a sovereign through his or her realm. ❖ *intr.v.* **pro·gress** (prə-grĕs′) **-gressed, -gress·ing, -gress·es 1.** To advance; proceed. **2.** To advance toward a higher or better stage; improve steadily. —*idiom:* **in progress** Going on; under way. [ME *progresse* < Lat. *prōgressus* < p. part. of *prōgredī*, to advance : *prō-*, forward; see PRO-¹ + *gradī*, to go, walk; see **ghredh-** in App.]

pro·gres·sion (prə-grĕsh′ən) *n.* **1.** The process of progressing; progress. **2.** Movement from one member of a continuous series to the next. **3.** A continuous series; a sequence. **4.** *Mathematics* A series of numbers or quantities in which there is always the same relation between each quantity and the one succeeding it. **5.** *Music* **a.** A succession of tones or chords. **b.** A series of repetitions of a phrase, each in a new position on the scale. —**pro·gres′sion·al** *adj.*

pro·gres·sive (prə-grĕs′ĭv) *adj.* **1.** Moving forward; advancing. **2.** Proceeding in steps; continuing steadily by increments: *progressive change.* **3.** Promoting or favoring progress toward better conditions or new policies, ideas, or methods. **4. Progressive** Of or relating to a Progressive Party. **5.** Of or relating to progressive education. **6.** Increasing in rate as the taxable amount increases: *a progressive tax.* **7.** *Pathology* Tending to become more severe or wider in scope. **8.** *Grammar* Relating to or being a verb form that expresses an action or condition in progress. ❖ *n.* **1.** A person who favors or strives for progress toward better conditions, as in society or government. **2. Progressive** A member or supporter of a Progressive Party. **3.** *Grammar* A progressive verb form. —**pro·gres′sive·ly** *adv.* —**pro·gres′sive·ness** *n.*

Pro·gres·sive-Con·ser·va·tive Party (prə-grĕs′ĭv-kən-sûr′və-tĭv) *n.* A major political party in Canada advocating economic nationalism and close ties with Great Britain and the Commonwealth.

progressive education *n.* A set of reformist educational philosophies and methods that emphasize individual instruction and informality in the classroom.

Progressive Party *n.* **1.** A US political party organized by Republican insurgents in 1911. **2.** A US political party organized in 1924 that was active in Wisconsin until 1946. **3.** A US political party formed in 1948 to support the presidential candidacy of Henry A. Wallace.

pro·gres·siv·ism (prə-grĕs′ĭ-vĭz′əm) *n.* **1.** The principles and practices of political progressives. **2.** Progressive education. —**pro·gres′siv·ist** *n.* —**pro·gres′siv·is′tic** *adj.*

pro·gres·siv·i·ty (prō′grĕ-sĭv′ĭ-tē, prŏg′rĕ-) *n., pl.* **-ties** The quality or degree of being progressive.

pro·hib·it (prō-hĭb′ĭt) *tr.v.* **-it·ed, -it·ing, -its 1.** To forbid by authority: *Smoking is prohibited.* See Syns at **forbid. 2.** To prevent; preclude. [ME *prohibiten* < Lat. *prohibēre, prohibit-* : *pro-*, in front; see PRO-¹ + *habēre*, to hold; see **ghabh-** in App.]

pro·hi·bi·tion (prō′ə-bĭsh′ən) *n.* **1.** The act of prohibiting or the condition of being prohibited. **2.** A law, order, or decree that forbids something. **3a.** The forbidding by law of the manufacture, transportation, and possession of alcoholic beverages. **b. Prohibition** The period (1920–33) during which the manufacture and sale of alcoholic beverages was forbidden in the United States.

pro·hi·bi·tion·ist (prō′ə-bĭsh′ə-nĭst) *n.* **1.** One in favor of outlawing the manufacture and sale of alcoholic beverages. **2.** often **Prohibitionist** A member or supporter of the Prohibition Party. **—pro′hi·bi′tion·ism** *n.*

Prohibition Party *n.* A US political party organized in 1869 that advocated prohibition.

pro·hib·i·tive (prō-hĭb′ĭ-tĭv) also **pro·hib·i·to·ry** (-tôr′ē, -tōr′ē) *adj.* **1.** Prohibiting; forbidding. **2.** So high or burdensome as to discourage purchase or use: *prohibitive prices.* **3.** So likely to win as to discourage competition. **—pro·hib′i·tive·ly** *adv.* **—pro·hib′i·tive·ness** *n.*

pro·in·su·lin (prō-ĭn′sə-lĭn) *n.* A single-chain polypeptide that is the precursor of insulin.

proj·ect (prŏj′ĕkt′, -ĭkt) *n.* **1.** A plan or proposal; a scheme. See Syns at **plan. 2.** An undertaking requiring concerted effort: *a cleanup project.* **3.** An extensive task undertaken by a student or group of students to apply, illustrate, or supplement classroom lessons. **4.** A housing project. ❖ *v.* **pro·ject** (prə-jĕkt′) **-ject·ed, -ject·ing, -jects** —*tr.* **1.** To thrust outward or forward: *project one's jaw.* **2.** To throw forward; hurl: *project an arrow.* **3.** To send out into space; cast: *project a light beam.* **4.** To cause (an image) to appear on a surface: *projected the slide onto a screen.* **5.** *Mathematics* To produce (a projection). **6.** To direct (one's voice) so as to be heard clearly at a distance. **7.** *Psychology* To externalize and attribute (an emotion, for example) to someone or something else. **8.** To convey an impression of to an audience or to others: *a posture that projects defeat.* **9.** To form a plan or intention for: *project a new business enterprise.* **10.** To calculate, estimate, or predict (something in the future), based on present data or trends: *projecting next year's expenses.* —*intr.* **1.** To extend forward or out; jut out: *beams that project beyond the eaves.* **2.** To direct one's voice so as to be heard clearly at a distance. [ME *projecte* < Lat. *prōiectum*, projecting structure < neut. p. part. of *prōicere*, to throw out : *prō-*, forth; see PRO-¹ + *iacere*, to throw.] **—pro·ject′a·ble** *adj.*

pro·jec·tile (prə-jĕk′təl, -tīl′) *n.* **1.** A propelled object, such as a bullet, having no capacity for self-propulsion. **2.** A self-propelled missile, such as a rocket. ❖ *adj.* **1.** Capable of being impelled or hurled forward. **2.** Driving forward; impelling. **3.** *Zoology* Capable of being thrust outward; protrusile. [NLat. *proiectile*, neut. of *prōiectilis*, that can be thrown < Lat. *prōiectus*, p. part. of *prōicere*, to throw out. See PROJECT.]

pro·jec·tion (prə-jĕk′shən) *n.* **1.** The act of projecting or the condition of being projected. **2.** A thing or part that extends outward beyond a prevailing line or surface. **3.** A plan for an anticipated course of action. **4.** A prediction or estimate of something in the future, based on present data or trends. **5a.** The process of projecting a filmed image onto a screen, for example. **b.** An image so projected. **6.** *Mathematics* The image of a geometric figure reproduced on a line, plane, or surface. **7.** A system of intersecting lines, such as the grid of a map, on which part or all of the globe or another spherical surface is represented as a plane surface. **8.** *Psychology* The attribution of one's own attitudes, feelings, or desires to someone or something. **—pro·jec′tion·al** *adj.*

projection booth *n.* A booth, as in a theater, in which a movie projector is operated.

pro·jec·tion·ist (prə-jĕk′shə-nĭst) *n.* **1.** One who operates a movie or slide projector. **2.** A maker of map projections.

pro·jec·tive (prə-jĕk′tĭv) *adj.* **1.** Extending outward; projecting. **2.** Relating to or made by projection. **3.** *Mathematics* Relating to or being a property of a geometric figure that does not vary when the figure undergoes projection. **—pro·jec′tive·ly** *adv.*

projective geometry *n.* The study of geometric properties that are invariant under projection.

projective test *n.* A psychological test in which responses to unstructured stimuli, such as abstract patterns or incomplete sentences, are analyzed to determine personality traits, feelings, or attitudes.

pro·jec·tor (prə-jĕk′tər) *n.* **1.** A device for projecting a beam of light. **2.** A machine for projecting an image onto a screen. **3.** One who devises plans or projects.

pro·kar·y·ote also **pro·car·y·ote** (prō-kăr′ē-ōt′) *n.* An organism of the kingdom Monera (or Prokaryotae), comprising the bacteria and cyanobacteria, characterized by the absence of a nuclear membrane and by DNA that is not organized into chromosomes. [Fr. *procaryote* : Gk. *pro-*, before; see PRO-² + Gk. *karuōtos*, having nuts (< *karuon*, nut).] **—pro·kar′y·ot·ic** (-ŏt′ĭk) *adj.*

Pro·kho·rov (prō′KHə-rôf), **Aleksandr Mikhailovich** 1916–2002. Russian physicist who shared a 1964 Nobel Prize.

Pro·kof·iev (prə-kô′fē-ĕf, -əf, -kō′-, -kôf′yĭf), **Sergei Sergeyevich** 1891–1953. Russian composer whose works include the symphonic fairy tale *Peter and the Wolf* (1936).

Pro·ko·pyevsk (prə-kôp′yəfsk) A city of S-central Russia ESE of Novosibirsk. Pop. 264,959.

pro·lac·tin (prō-lăk′tĭn) *n.* A pituitary hormone that stimulates and maintains the secretion of milk.

pro·la·mine also **pro·la·min** (prō′lə-mĭn, -mēn′) *n.* Any of a class of simple proteins having a high proline content and found in the seeds of wheat, rye, and other grains. [PROL(INE) + AM(MONIA) + −INE².]

pro·lapse (prō-lăps′) *Medicine intr.v.* **-lapsed, -laps·ing, -laps·es** To fall or slip out of place. ❖ *n.* **prolapse** (prō′lăps′, prō-lăps′) also **pro·lap·sus** (prō-lăp′səs) The falling down or slipping out of place of an organ or part. [Lat. *prōlābī, prōlaps-*, to fall down : *prō-*, forward; see PRO-¹ + *lābī*, to fall.]

pro·late (prō′lāt′) *adj.* **1.** Having the shape of a spheroid generated by rotating an ellipse about its longer axis. **2.** Having the polar axis longer than the equatorial diameter. [Lat. *prōlātus*, p. part. of *prōferre*, to stretch out : *prō-*, forth; see PRO-¹ + *lātus*, brought; see **telə-** in App.] **—pro′late′ly** *adv.* **—pro′late′ness** *n.*

prole (prōl) *n.* A proletarian.

pro·leg (prō′lĕg′) *n.* One of the stubby limbs on the abdominal segments of caterpillars and certain other insect larvae.

pro·le·gom·e·non (prō′lĭ-gŏm′ə-nŏn′, -nən) *n.*, *pl.* **-na** (-nə) **1.** A preliminary discussion, esp. a formal essay introducing a lengthy or complex work. **2.** **prolegomena** (*used with a sing. or pl. verb*) Prefatory remarks or observations. [Gk. < neut. pr. passive part. of *prolegein*, to say beforehand : *pro-*, before; see PRO-² + *legein*, to speak; see **leg-** in App.] **—pro′le·gom′e·nous** *adj.*

pro·lep·sis (prō-lĕp′sĭs) *n.*, *pl.* **-ses** (-sēz) **1.** The anachronistic representation of something as existing before its proper or historical time, as in *the precolonial United States.* **2a.** The assignment of something, such as an event or name, to a time that precedes it, as in *If you tell the cops, you're a dead man.* **b.** The use of a descriptive word in anticipation of the act or circumstances that would make it applicable, as *dry* in *They drained the lake dry.* **3.** The anticipation and answering of an objection or argument before one's opponent has put it forward. [LLat. *prolēpsis* < Gk. < *prolambanein*, to anticipate : *pro-*, before; see PRO-² + *lambanein*, *lēp-*, to take.] **—pro·lep′tic** (-lĕp′tĭk), **pro·lep′ti·cal** (-tĭ-kəl) *adj.*

pro·le·tar·i·an (prō′lĭ-târ′ē-ən) *adj.* Of, relating to, or characteristic of the proletariat. ❖ *n.* A member of the proletariat. [< Lat. *prōlētārius*, of the lowest class of Roman citizens (seen as contributing to the state only by having children) < *prōlēs*, offspring.] **—pro′le·tar′i·an·ism** *n.*

pro·le·tar·i·at (prō′lĭ-târ′ē-ĭt) *n.* **1a.** The class of industrial wage earners who must earn their living by selling their labor. **b.** The poorest class of working people. **2.** The propertyless class of ancient Rome, constituting the lowest class of citizens. [Fr. *prolétariat* < Lat. *prōlētārius*, of the Roman proletariat. See PROLETARIAN.]

pro-life (prō-līf′) *adj.* Advocating legal protection of human embryos or fetuses, esp. by opposing legal abortion. **—pro-lif′er** *n.*

pro·lif·er·ate (prə-lĭf′ə-rāt′) *v.* **-at·ed, -at·ing, -ates** —*intr.* **1.** To grow or multiply by rapidly producing new tissue, parts, cells, or offspring. **2.** To increase or spread at a rapid rate. —*tr.* To cause to grow or increase rapidly. [Back-formation < PROLIFERATION, the act of proliferating < Fr. *prolifération* < *prolifère*, procreative : Lat. *prōlēs*, *prōl-*, offspring + Lat. *-fer*, *-fer*.] **—pro·lif′er·a′tion** *n.* **—pro·lif′er·a′tive** *adj.* **—pro·lif′er·a′tor** *n.*

pro·lif·er·ous (prə-lĭf′ər-əs) *adj.* *Zoology* Reproducing freely by means of buds and side branches, as corals do. **2.** *Botany* Freely producing buds or offshoots, esp. from unusual places, as fruits from fruits. [< Med.Lat. *prōlifer* : Lat. *prōlēs*, *prōl-*, offspring + *-fer*, *-fer*.] **—pro·lif′er·ous·ly** *adv.*

pro·lif·ic (prə-lĭf′ĭk) *adj.* **1.** Producing offspring or fruit in great abundance; fertile. **2.** Producing abundant works or results. [Fr. *prolifique* < Med.Lat. *prōlificus* : Lat. *prōlēs*, *prōl-*, offspring + Lat. *-ficus*, *-fic*.] **—pro·lif′i·ca·cy** (-ĭ-kə-sē), **pro·lif′ic·ness** (-ĭk-nĭs) *n.* **—pro·lif′i·cal·ly** *adv.*

pro·line (prō′lēn′) *n.* An amino acid, C_4H_8NCOOH, found in most proteins and a major constituent of collagen. [Short for *pyrrolidine*, one of its constituents : PYRROL(E) + −ID(E) + −INE².]

pro·lix (prō-lĭks′, prō′lĭks′) *adj.* **1.** Tediously prolonged; wordy. **2.** Tending to speak or write at excessive length. [ME < OFr. *prolixe* < Lat. *prōlixus*, poured forth, extended.] **—pro·lix′i·ty** (-lĭk′sĭ-tē) *n.* **—pro·lix′ly** *adv.*

pro·logue also **pro·log** (prō′lôg′, -lŏg′) *n.* **1.** An introduction or preface, esp. a poem recited to introduce a play. **2.** An introduction or introductory chapter, as to a novel. **3.** An introductory act, event, or period. [ME *prolog* < OFr. *prologue* < Lat. *prologus* < Gk. *prologos* : *pro-*, before; see PRO-² + *logos*, speech; see **leg-** in App.]

pro·long (prə-lông′, -lŏng′) *tr.v.* **-longed, -long·ing, -longs 1.** To lengthen in duration; protract. **2.** To lengthen in extent. [Ult. < LLat. *prōlongāre* : Lat. *prō-*, forth; see PRO-¹ + Lat. *longus*, long; see **del-** in App.] **—pro·long′er** *n.*

pro·lon·gate (prə-lông′gāt′, -lŏng′-, prō-) *tr.v.* **-gat·ed, -gat·ing, -gates** To prolong. **—pro′lon·ga′tion** (prō′lông-gā′shən, -lŏng-) *n.*

pro·lu·sion (prō-lōō′zhən) *n.* **1.** A preliminary exercise; a prelude. **2.** An essay written as a preface to a more detailed work. [Lat. *prōlūsiō, prōlūsiōn-* < *prōlūsus*, p. part. of *prōlūdere*, to practice beforehand : *prō-*, before; see PRO-¹ + *lūdere*, to play.] **—pro·lu′so·ry** (-sə-rē, -zə-) *adj.*

prom (prŏm) *n.* A formal dance held for a high-school or college class typically at or near the end of the academic year. [Short for PROMENADE.]

PROM (prŏm) *n. Computer Science* Memory hardware that can be programmed only once. [*p(rogrammable) r(ead-)o(nly) m(emory).*]

prom. *abbr.* promontory

prom•e•nade (prŏm′ə-nād′, -näd′) *n.* **1a.** A leisurely walk, esp. one taken in a public place. **b.** A public place for such walking. **2a.** A formal dance; a ball. **b.** A march of all the guests at the opening of a ball. **3.** A square-dance figure in which couples march counterclockwise in a circle. ❖ *v.* **-nad•ed, -nad•ing, -nades** —*intr.* **1.** To go on a leisurely walk. **2.** To execute a promenade. —*tr.* **1.** To take a promenade along or through. **2.** To take or display on or as if on a promenade. [Fr. < *promener,* to take for a walk < Lat. *prōmināre,* to drive forward : *prō-,* forward; see PRO–[1] + *mināre,* to drive with shouts (< *minārī,* to threaten < *minae,* threats).] —**prom′e•nad′er** *n.*

promenade deck *n.* The upper deck or a section of the upper deck on a ship where the passengers can promenade.

Pro•me•the•an (prə-mē′thē-ən) *adj.* **1.** *Greek Mythology* Relating to or suggestive of Prometheus. **2.** Boldly creative; defiantly original. ❖ *n.* One who is boldy creative or defiantly original.

Pro•me•the•us (prə-mē′thē-əs, -thyo͞os′) *n. Greek Mythology* **1.** A Titan who stole fire from Olympus and gave it to the human race, for which Zeus chained him to a rock and sent an eagle to eat his liver, which grew back daily. **2.** A satellite of Saturn. [Lat. *Promētheus* < Gk.]

pro•me•thi•um (prə-mē′thē-əm) *n. Symbol* **Pm** A radioactive rare-earth element prepared by fission of uranium. Pm 147, the longest-lived isotope with a half-life of 2.5 years, is used as a source of beta rays. Atomic number 61; melting point 1,168°C; boiling point 2,460°C; valence 3. See table at **element.** [< PROMETHEUS.]

prom•i•nence (prŏm′ə-nəns) *n.* **1.** The quality or condition of being prominent. **2.** Something prominent, esp. an area of land raised above its surroundings. **3.** *Anatomy* A small projection or protuberance. **4.** *Astronomy* A tonguelike cloud of flaming gas rising from the sun's surface.

prom•i•nen•cy (prŏm′ə-nən-sē) *n.* Prominence.

prom•i•nent (prŏm′ə-nənt) *adj.* **1.** Projecting outward or upward from a line or surface; protuberant. **2.** Immediately noticeable; conspicuous. **3.** Widely known; eminent. [ME < Lat. *prōminēns, prōminent-,* pr. part. of *prōminēre,* to jut out : *prō-,* forth; see PRO–[1] + *-minēre,* to jut, threaten.] —**prom′i•nent•ly** *adv.*

prom•is•cu•i•ty (prŏm′ĭ-skyo͞o′ĭ-tē, prō′mĭ-) *n., pl.* **-ties 1.** The state or character of being promiscuous. **2.** Promiscuous sexual relations. **3.** A mixture of diverse or unrelated parts or individuals; a hodgepodge.

pro•mis•cu•ous (prə-mĭs′kyo͞o-əs) *adj.* **1.** Relating to or having casual sexual relations frequently with different partners. **2.** Lacking standards of selection; indiscriminate. **3.** Casual; random. **4.** Consisting of diverse unrelated parts or individuals. [< Lat. *prōmiscuus,* possessed equally : *prō-,* intensive pref.; see PRO–[1] + *miscēre,* to mix; see **meik-** in App.] —**pro•mis′cu•ous•ly** *adv.* —**pro•mis′cu•ous•ness** *n.*

prom•ise (prŏm′ĭs) *n.* **1a.** A declaration assuring that one will or will not do something; a vow. **b.** Something promised. **2.** Indication of something favorable to come; expectation. **3.** Indication of future excellence or success. ❖ *v.* **-ised, -is•ing, -is•es** —*tr.* **1.** To commit oneself by a promise to do or give; pledge. **2.** To afford a basis for expecting. —*intr.* **1.** To make a declaration assuring that something will or will not be done. **2.** To afford a basis for expectation. [ME *promis* < OFr. *promise* < Med.Lat. *prōmissa,* alteration of Lat. *prōmissum* < neut. p. part. of *prōmittere,* to send forth, promise : *prō-,* forth; see PRO–[1] + *mittere,* to send.] —**prom′is•er** *n.*

Prom•ised Land (prŏm′ĭst) *n.* The land of Canaan, promised by the Lord to Abraham's descendants in the Bible.

prom•is•ee (prŏm′ĭ-sē′) *n. Law* The party to which a promise is made.

prom•is•ing (prŏm′ĭ-sĭng) *adj.* Likely to develop in a desirable manner. —**prom′is•ing•ly** *adv.*

prom•i•sor (prŏm′ĭ-sôr′) *n. Law* One that makes a promise.

prom•is•so•ry (prŏm′ĭ-sôr′ē, -sōr′ē) *adj.* Containing, involving, or having the nature of a promise. [Med.Lat. *prōmissōrius* < Lat. *prōmissor,* one who promises < *prōmissus,* p. part. of *prōmittere,* to promise. See PROMISE.]

promissory note *n.* A written promise to pay or repay a specified sum of money at a stated time or on demand.

pro•mo (prō′mō) *n., pl.* **-mos** *Informal* A promotional presentation, such as a television spot or radio announcement.

prom•on•to•ry (prŏm′ən-tôr′ē, -tōr′ē) *n., pl.* **-ries 1.** A high ridge of land or rock jutting out into a body of water; a headland. **2.** *Anatomy* A projecting part. [Lat. *prōmontorium,* alteration (influenced by *mōns, mont-,* mount) of *prōmunturium,* prob. < *prōminēre,* to jut out. See PROMINENT.]

pro•mote (prə-mōt′) *tr.v.* **-mot•ed, -mot•ing, -motes 1a.** To raise to a more important or responsible job or rank. **b.** To advance (a student) to the next higher grade. **2.** To contribute to the progress or growth of; further. See Syns at **advance. 3.** To urge the adoption of; advocate: *promote a constitutional amendment.* **4.** To attempt to sell or popularize by advertising or publicity: *commercials promoting a new product.* **5.** To help establish or organize (a new enterprise), as by securing financial backing: *promote a Broadway show.* [Ult. < Lat. *prōmovēre, prōmōt-* : *prō-,* forward; see PRO–[1] + *movēre,* to move.] —**pro•mot′a•bil′i•ty** *n.* —**pro•mot′a•ble** *adj.*

pro•mot•er (prə-mō′tər) *n.* **1.** One that promotes, esp. an active supporter or advocate. **2.** A financial and publicity organizer. **3.** *Genetics* The region of an operon that acts as the initial binding site for RNA polymerase.

pro•mo•tion (prə-mō′shən) *n.* **1.** Advancement in rank or responsibility. **2.** Encouragement of the progress, growth, or acceptance of something; furtherance. **3.** Advertising; publicity. —**pro•mo′tion•al** *adj.* —**pro•mo′tion•al•ly** *adv.*

pro•mo•tive (prə-mō′tĭv) *adj.* Tending to promote. —**pro•mo′tive•ness** *n.*

prompt (prŏmpt) *adj.* **prompt•er, prompt•est 1.** Being on time; punctual. **2.** Carried out or performed without delay: *a prompt reply.* ❖ *tr.v.* **prompt•ed, prompt•ing, prompts 1.** To move to act; spur; incite: *A noise prompted the guard to go back and investigate.* **2.** To give rise to; inspire: *The accident prompted a review of school safety policy.* **3.** To assist with a reminder; remind. **4.** To assist (an actor or reciter) by providing the next words of a forgotten passage; cue. ❖ *n.* **1a.** The act of prompting or giving a cue. **b.** A reminder or cue. **2.** *Computer Science* A symbol that appears on a monitor to indicate that the computer is ready to receive input. [ME, ready < OFr. < Lat. *prōmptus* < p. part. of *prōmere,* to bring forth : *prō-,* forth; see PRO–[1] + *emere,* to take, obtain.] —**prompt′er** *n.* —**promp′ti•tude′** (prŏmp′tĭ-to͞od′, -tyo͞od′), **prompt′ness** (prŏmpt′nĭs) *n.* —**prompt′ly** *adv.*

prompt•book (prŏmpt′bo͝ok′) *n.* An annotated script used by a theater prompter.

prom•ul•gate (prŏm′əl-gāt′, prō-mŭl′gāt′) *tr.v.* **-gat•ed, -gat•ing, -gates 1.** To make known (a decree, for example) by public declaration; announce officially. **2.** To put (a law) into effect by formal public announcement. [Lat. *prōmulgāre, prōmulgāt-.*] —**prom′ul•ga′tion** (prŏm′əl-gā′shən, prō′məl-) *n.* —**prom′ul•ga′tor** *n.*

pron. *abbr.* **1.** pronoun **2.** pronounced **3.** pronunciation

pro•na•tal•ism (prō-nāt′l-ĭz′əm) *n.* An attitude or policy that encourages childbearing. —**pro•na′tal•ist** *n.* —**pro•na′tal•is′tic** *adj.*

pro•nate (prō′nāt′) *v.* **-nat•ed, -nat•ing, -nates** —*tr.* **1a.** To turn or rotate (the hand or forearm) so that the palm faces down or back. **b.** To turn or rotate (the foot) so that the inner edge of the sole bears the body's weight. **2.** To place in a prone position. —*intr.* **1.** To become pronated. **2.** To assume a prone position. [LLat. *prōnāre, prōnāt-,* to bend forward < *prōnus,* turned forward. See PRONE.] —**pro•na′tion** *n.*

pro•na•tor (prō′nā′tər) *n.* A muscle that effects or assists in pronation.

prone (prōn) *adj.* **1.** Lying with the front or face downward. **2.** Having a tendency; inclined. ❖ *adv.* In a prone manner. [ME, inclined, disposed < Lat. *prōnus,* leaning forward. See **per**[1] in App.] —**prone′ly** *adv.* —**prone′ness** *n.*

pro•neph•ros (prō-nĕf′rəs, -rŏs′) *n., pl.* **-roi** (-roi) or **-ra** (-rə) A kidneylike organ, being either part of the most anterior pair of three pairs of organs in a vertebrate embryo or functioning as a kidney in some simple vertebrates, such as the lamprey. [PRO–[2] + Gk. *nephros,* kidney.] —**pro•neph′ric** (-rĭk) *adj.*

prong (prông, prŏng) *n.* **1.** A thin pointed projecting part. **2.** A branch; a fork. ❖ *tr.v.* **pronged, prong•ing, prongs** To pierce with or as if with a prong. [ME *pronge,* pointed instrument, pain < Med.Lat. *pronga,* of Gmc. orig.]

prong•horn (prông′hôrn′, prŏng′-) *n., pl.* **pronghorn** or **-horns** A small ruminant mammal *(Antilocapra americana)* found on western North American plains, resembling an antelope and having small forked horns.

pro•no•grade (prō′nə-grād′) *adj.* Walking with the long axis of the body parallel to the ground. Used of quadrupeds. [Lat. *prōnus,* leaning forward; see PRONE + *-gradus,* walking (< *gradī,* to move; see RETROGRADE).]

pro•nom•i•nal (prō-nŏm′ə-nəl) *adj.* **1.** Of, relating to, or functioning as a pronoun. **2.** Resembling a pronoun, as by specifying a person, place, or thing, while functioning primarily as another part of speech. *His* in *his choice* is a pronominal adjective. [LLat. *prōnōminālis* < Lat. *prōnōmen, prōnōmin-,* pronoun : *prō-,* in place of; see PRO–[1] + *nōmen,* name; see NOUN.] —**pro•nom′i•nal•ly** *adv.*

pro•noun (prō′noun′) *n.* **1.** The part of speech that substitutes for nouns or noun phrases and designates persons or things asked for, previously specified, or understood from the context. **2.** Any of the words belonging to this part of speech, such as *he.* [Late ME *pronoun, pronoune,* partial transl. of Lat. *prōnōmen* (transl. of Gk. *antōnumiā,* interchange of names, pronoun) : *prō-,* pro- + *nōmen,* name, noun.]

pro•nounce (prə-nouns′) *v.* **-nounced, -nounc•ing, -nounc•es** —*tr.* **1a.** To use the organs of speech to make heard (a word or speech sound); utter. **b.** To say clearly, correctly, or in a given manner: *pronounce French.* **2.** To represent (a word) in phonetic symbols. **3.** To declare officially or formally. —*intr.* **1.** To say words; speak. **2.** To declare one's opinion; make a pronouncement. [ME *pronouncen* < OFr. *prononcier* < Lat. *prōnūntiāre* :

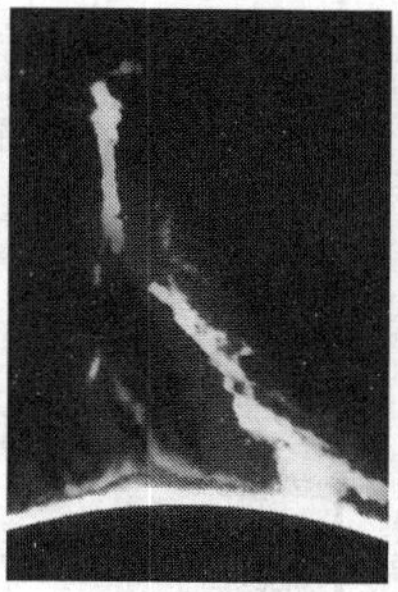

prominence
solar prominence

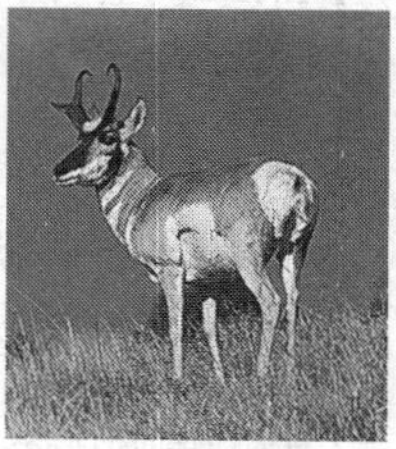

pronghorn
Antilocapra americana

ă	pat	oi	boy
ā	pay	ou	out
âr	care	o͝o	took
ä	father	o͞o	boot
ĕ	pet	ŭ	cut
ē	be	ûr	urge
ĭ	pit	th	thin
ī	pie	*th*	this
îr	pier	hw	which
ŏ	pot	zh	vision
ō	toe	ə	about, item
ô	paw		

Stress marks:
′ (primary);
′ (secondary), as in
lexicon (lĕk′sĭ-kŏn′)

prŏ-, forth; see PRO-[1] + nūntiāre, to announce (< nūntius, messenger).] —**pro·nounce′a·ble** adj. —**pro·nounc′er** n.

pro·nounced (prə-nounst′) adj. **1.** Spoken; voiced. **2.** Strongly marked; distinct: a pronounced limp. —**pro·nounc′ed·ly** (-noun′sĭd-lē) adv. —**pro·nounc′ed·ness** n.

pro·nounce·ment (prə-nouns′mənt) n. **1.** A formal expression

PROOFREADER'S MARKS

Instruction	Mark in Margin	Mark on Proof	Corrected Type
GENERAL			
delete	⌒	the best word	the word
delete and close up space	⌒	the wo~~r~~d	the word
insert indicated material	best	the ^word	the best word
let it stand	stet	the ~~best~~ word	the best word
spell out	SP	②words	two words
POSITION AND SPACING			
new paragraph	¶	"Where is it?"/"It's on the shelf."	"Where is it?" "It's on the shelf."
flush paragraph	⊡	"Where is it?"/"It's on the shelf."	"Where is it?" "It's on the shelf."
transpose	tr	the word/best	the best word
move left	⊏	⊏the word	the word
move right	⊐	⊐the word	the word
move down	⎵	the word	the word
move up	⎴	the word	the word
align	‖	the word the word	the word the word
straighten line	=	the word	the word
insert space	#	theword	the word
equalize space	eq #	the best word	the best word
close up	⌒	the wo⌒rd	the word
en space	⊠	the word	the word
em space	⊠	the word	the word
PUNCTUATION			
period	⊙	This is the word^	This is the word.
comma	⋀	words^words, words	words, words, words
hyphen	=	word^for^word test	word-for-word test
colon	⊙	The following words^	The following words:
semicolon	⋀	Scan the words/skim the words.	Scan the words; skim the words.
apostrophe	⩔	Johns words	John's words
double quotation marks	⩔/⩔	the word word	the word "word"
single quotation marks	⩔/⩔	the "good word"	the "good 'word'"
parentheses	{ / }	The list of words in the dictionary^on page 101^ is useful.	The list of words in the dictionary (on page 101) is useful.
brackets	[/]	He read the list of words from the dictionary^	He read the list of words [from the dictionary].
en dash	⊥/N	1984^1992	1984–1992
em dash	⊥/M	The dictionary^how often it is needed^belongs in every home.	The dictionary—how often it is needed—belongs in every home.
asterisk	⩔	word^	word*
dagger	⩔	word^	word†
section symbol	§	^Book Reviews	§Book Reviews
virgule (slash)	/	either/or	either/or
three ellipses	|⊙|⊙|	the^word	the...word
four ellipses	⌒⊙|⊙|⊙|	the word^	the word....
STYLE OF TYPE			
uppercase	uc	the ^word	The Word
lowercase	lc	⧸The ⧸Word	the word
small capitals	sc	the word	THE WORD
italic	ital	the entry word	the entry *word*
roman	rom	the entry *word*	the entry word
boldface	bf	the entry word	the entry **word**
lightface	lf	the entry word	the entry word
superior	⩔	2²=4	2²=4
inferior	⩕	H2O	H₂O

of opinion; a judgment. **2.** An authoritative statement.

pro·nounc·ing (prə-noun′sĭng) adj. Relating to, designed for, or showing pronunciation: a pronouncing dictionary.

pron·to (prŏn′tō) adv. Informal Without delay; quickly. [Sp. < Lat. prōmptus. See PROMPT.]

pro·nu·cle·us (prō-no̅o̅′klē-əs, -nyo̅o̅′-) n., pl. **-cle·i** (-klē-ī′) The haploid nucleus of a sperm or egg before fusion of the nuclei in fertilization. —**pro·nu′cle·ar** adj.

pro·nun·ci·a·men·to (prō-nŭn′sē-ə-měn′tō) n., pl. **-tos** or **-toes** An official or authoritarian declaration. [Sp. pronunciamiento < pronunciar, to pronounce < Lat. prōnūntiāre. See PRONOUNCE.]

pro·nun·ci·a·tion (prə-nŭn′sē-ā′shən) n. **1.** The act or manner of pronouncing words; utterance of speech. **2.** A way of speaking a word, esp. a way that is accepted or generally understood. **3.** A graphic representation of the way a word is spoken, using phonetic symbols. [Ult. < Lat. prōnūntiātiō, prōnūntiātiōn- < prōnūntiātus, p. part. of prōnūntiāre, to pronounce. See PRONOUNCE.] —**pro·nun′ci·a′tion·al** adj.

pronunciation spelling n. A spelling that is supposed to represent a pronunciation more closely than a traditional spelling, as lite for light, or wanna for want to.

proof (pro̅o̅f) n. **1.** The evidence or argument that compels the mind to accept an assertion as true. **2a.** The validation of a proposition by application of specified rules, as of induction or deduction, to axioms and previously derived conclusions. **b.** An argument used in such a validation. **3.** Convincing or persuasive demonstration: proof of his identity. **4.** Determination of the quality of something by testing; trial. **5.** Law The whole body of evidence that determines the verdict or judgment in a case. **6.** The alcoholic strength of a liquor, expressed by a number that is twice the percentage by volume of alcohol present. **7.** Printing a. A trial sheet of printed material that is made to be checked and corrected. **b.** A trial impression of a plate, stone, or block taken at any of various stages in engraving. **8a.** A trial photographic print. **b.** Any of a limited number of newly minted coins or medals struck as specimens and for collectors from a new die on a polished planchet. **9.** Archaic Proven impenetrability. ❖ adj. **1.** Fully or successfully resistant; impervious. Often used in combination: waterproof watches. **2.** Of standard alcoholic strength. **3.** Used in proving or making corrections. ❖ v. **proofed, proof·ing, proofs** —tr. **1.** Printing a. To make a trial impression of (printed or engraved matter). **b.** To proofread (copy). **2a.** To activate (dormant dry yeast) by adding water. **b.** To work (dough) into proper lightness. **3.** To treat so as to make resistant: proof a fabric against shrinkage. —intr. **1.** Printing To proofread. **2.** To become properly light for cooking. [ME prove, preve < AN prove and < OFr. prueve, both < LLat. proba < Lat. probāre, to prove. See PROVE.] —**proof′er** n.

proof·read (pro̅o̅f′rēd′) v. **-read** (-rĕd′), **-read·ing, -reads** —tr. To read (copy or proof) to find and correct errors. —intr. To proofread copy or proof. —**proof′read·er** n.

proof sheet n. Printing See **proof** 7a.

proof spirit n. An alcohol-water mixture or a beverage containing a standard amount of alcohol, the US standard being 100 proof of ethyl alcohol by volume at 60°F (approx. 15.6°C).

prop[1] (prŏp) n. **1.** An object placed beneath or against a structure to keep it from falling or shaking; a support. **2.** One that serves as a means of support or assistance. ❖ tr.v. **propped, prop·ping, props** To support by placing something beneath or against; shore up. [ME proppe, prob. < MDu.]

prop[2] (prŏp) n. A theatrical property.

prop[3] (prŏp) n. Informal A propeller.

prop. abbr. **1.** proper **2.** property **3.** proposition

prop- pref. Related to or derived from propionic acid: propane. [< PROPIONIC ACID.]

pro·pae·deu·tic (prō′pĭ-do̅o̅′tĭk, -dyo̅o̅′-) adj. Providing introductory instruction. ❖ n. Preparatory instruction. [< Gk. propaideuein, to teach beforehand : pro-, before; see PRO-[2] + paideuein, to teach (< pais, paid-, child; see PEDO-[2]).]

prop·a·gan·da (prŏp′ə-găn′də) n. **1.** The systematic propagation of a doctrine or cause or of information reflecting the views and interests of its propagators. **2.** Material disseminated by the advocates or opponents of a doctrine or cause: published wartime propaganda. **3. Propaganda** Roman Catholic Church A division of the Roman Curia that has authority over missions. [NLat., short for Sacra Congregātiō dē Prōpagandā Fidē, Sacred Congregation for Propagating the Faith (est. 1622) < ablative fem. gerundive of Lat. prōpāgāre, to propagate. See PROPAGATE.] —**prop′a·gan′dism** n. —**prop′a·gan·dist′ic** adj. —**prop′a·gan·dis′ti·cal·ly** adv.

prop·a·gan·dize (prŏp′ə-găn′dīz′) v. **-dized, -diz·ing, -diz·es** —tr. **1.** To engage in propaganda for (a doctrine or cause). **2.** To subject (a person or group) to propaganda. —intr. To spread propaganda. —**prop′a·gan·diz′er** n.

prop·a·gate (prŏp′ə-gāt′) v. **-gat·ed, -gat·ing, -gates** —tr. **1.** To cause (an organism) to multiply or breed. **2.** To breed (offspring). **3.** To transmit (characteristics) from one generation to another. **4.** To cause to extend to a broader area or larger number; spread: propagate the faith. **5.** To make widely known; publicize. **6.** Physics To cause (a wave, for example) to move in some direction or through a medium; transmit. —*intr.* **1.** To have off-spring; multiply. **2.** To extend to a broader area or larger number; spread. **3.** *Physics* To move through a medium. [Lat. *prōpagāre, prōpagāt-.*] —**prop′a•ga•ble** (-gə-bəl) *adj.* —**prop′a•ga′tive** *adj.* —**prop′a•ga′tor** *n.*

prop•a•ga•tion (prŏp′ə-gā′shən) *n.* **1.** Multiplication or increase, as by natural reproduction. **2.** The process of spreading to a larger area or greater number. **3.** *Physics* The act or process of propagating, esp. the process by which electromagnetic or sound waves are transmitted through a medium. —**prop′a•ga′tion•al** *adj.*

prop•a•gule (prŏp′ə-gyōōl′) *n.* Any of various usu. vegetative portions of a plant, such as a bud or other offshoot, that aid in dispersal of the species and from which a new individual may develop. [NLat. *prōpāgulum,* dim. of Lat. *prōpāgō,* shoot < *prōpāgāre,* to propagate. See PROPAGATE.]

pro•pane (prō′pān′) *n.* A colorless gas, C_3H_8, found in natural gas and petroleum and widely used as a fuel.

pro•pa•no•ic acid (prō′pə-nō′ĭk) *n.* See **propionic acid.**

pro•pel (prə-pĕl′) *tr.v.* **-pelled, -pel•ling, -pels** To cause to move forward or onward. See Syns at **push.** [ME *propellen* < Lat. *prōpellere* : *prō-,* forward; see PRO-[1] + *pellere,* to drive; see **pel-**[2] in App.]

pro•pel•lant *also* **pro•pel•lent** (prə-pĕl′ənt) *n.* **1.** Something, such as an explosive charge or a rocket fuel, that propels or provides thrust. **2.** A compressed inert gas that acts as a vehicle for discharging the contents of an aerosol container. ❖ *adj.* Serving to propel; propelling.

pro•pel•ler *also* **pro•pel•lor** (prə-pĕl′ər) *n.* A machine for propelling an aircraft or boat, consisting of a power-driven shaft with radiating blades placed so as to thrust air or water in a desired direction when spinning.

pro•pend (prō-pĕnd′) *intr.v.* **-pend•ed, -pend•ing, -pends** *Obsolete* To have a propensity. [Lat. *prōpendēre* : *prō-,* forward; see PRO-[1] + *pendēre,* to hang.]

pro•pen•si•ty (prə-pĕn′sĭ-tē) *n., pl.* **-ties** An innate inclination; a tendency. See Syns at **predilection.** [< *propense,* inclined < Lat. *prōpensus,* p. part. of *prōpendēre,* to be inclined. See PROPEND.]

prop•er (prŏp′ər) *adj.* **1.** Characterized by appropriateness or suitability; fitting: *the proper knife for cutting bread.* **2.** Called for by rules or conventions; correct: *the proper form for a business letter.* **3.** Strictly following rules or conventions, esp. in social behavior; seemly: *a proper lady; a proper gentleman.* **4a.** Belonging to one; own: *restored to his proper shape by the magician.* **b.** Characteristically belonging to the being or thing in question; peculiar: *an optical effect proper to fluids.* **5.** Being within the strictly limited sense, as of a term: *the town proper, excluding the suburbs.* **6.** *Ecclesiastical* For use in the liturgy of a particular feast or season of the year. **7.** *Mathematics* Of or relating to a subset of a given set when the set has at least one element not in the subset. **8.** Worthy of the name; true: *wanted a proper dinner, not just a snack.* **9.** Out-and-out; thorough: *a proper whipping.* ❖ *adv.* Thoroughly: *beat the eggs good and proper.* ❖ *n. also* **Proper** *Ecclesiastical* The parts of the liturgy that vary according to the feast or season. [ME *propre* < OFr. < Lat. *proprius.* See **per**[1] in App.] —**prop′er•ly** *adv.* —**prop′er•ness** *n.*

proper adjective *n.* An adjective formed from a proper noun.

pro•per•din (prō-pûr′dn) *n.* A protein in blood serum that participates in the body's immune response by working in conjunction with the complement system. [Prob. PRO-[1] + Lat. *perdere,* to destroy; see PERDITION + -IN.]

proper fraction *n.* **1.** A fraction in which the numerator is less than the denominator. **2.** A polynomial fraction in which the numerator is of a lower degree than the denominator.

proper name *n.* See **proper noun.**

proper noun *n.* A noun belonging to the class of words used as names for unique individuals, events, or places.

prop•er•tied (prŏp′ər-tēd) *adj.* Owning land or securities as a principal source of revenue.

Pro•per•tius (prō-pûr′shəs, -shē-əs), **Sextus** 50?–15? B.C. Roman poet whose extant works include *Cynthia.*

prop•er•ty (prŏp′ər-tē) *n., pl.* **-ties 1a.** Something owned; a possession. **b.** A piece of real estate. **c.** Something tangible or intangible to which its owner has legal title: *properties such as copyrights.* **d.** Possessions considered as a group. **2.** The right of ownership; title. **3.** An article, except costumes and scenery, that appears on the stage or on screen during a dramatic performance. **4a.** A characteristic trait or peculiarity, esp. one serving to define or describe its possessor. **b.** A characteristic attribute possessed by all members of a class. **5.** A special capability or power; a virtue: *the chemical properties of a metal.* [ME < OFr. *propriete* < Lat. *prōprietās,* ownership < *proprius,* one's own. See **per**[1] in App.] —**prop′er•ty•less** *adj.*

property tax *n.* A tax levied against the owner of real or personal property.

pro•phage (prō′fāj′) *n.* The latent form of a bacteriophage in which the viral genes are incorporated into the bacterial chromosomes without causing disruption of the bacterial cell. [Short for Fr. *probactériophage* : Gk. *pro-,* before; see PRO-[2] + Fr. *bactériophage,* bacteriophage (BACTERIO- + Gk. *-phagos,* -phage).]

pro•phase (prō′fāz′) *n.* **1.** The first stage of mitosis, during

which the chromosomes condense and become visible, the nuclear membrane breaks down, and the spindle apparatus forms at opposite poles of the cell. **2.** The first stage of meiosis, characterized by the thickening and coiling of the chromosomes, synapsis of homologous chromosomes, tetrad formation, and crossing over. —**pro•pha′sic** (-fā′zĭk) *adj.*

proph•e•cy (prŏf′ĭ-sē) *n., pl.* **-cies** (-sēz) **1a.** An inspired utterance of a prophet, viewed as a revelation of divine will. **b.** A prediction of the future made under divine inspiration. **c.** Such an inspired message transmitted orally or in writing. **2.** The vocation or condition of a prophet. **3.** A prediction. [ME *prophecie* < OFr. < Lat. *prophētīa* < Gk. *prophēteia* < *prophētēs,* prophet. See PROPHET.]

proph•e•sy (prŏf′ĭ-sī′) *v.* **-sied** (-sīd′), **-sy•ing** (-sī′ĭng), **-sies** (-sīz′) —*tr.* **1.** To reveal by divine inspiration. **2.** To predict with certainty as if by divine inspiration. **3.** To prefigure; foreshow. —*intr.* **1.** To reveal the will or message of God. **2.** To predict the future as if by divine inspiration. **3.** To speak as a prophet. [ME *prophecien* < OFr. *prophecier* < *prophecie,* prophecy. See PROPHECY.]

proph•et (prŏf′ĭt) *n.* **1.** One who speaks by divine inspiration or as the interpreter through whom the will of God or a god is expressed. **2.** One gifted with profound moral insight and exceptional powers of expression. **3.** A predictor; a soothsayer. **4.** The chief spokesperson of a movement or cause. **5a. Prophets** (*used with a sing. or pl. verb*) The second of the three divisions of the Hebrew Scriptures, comprising the books of Joshua, Judges, Samuel, Kings, Isaiah, Jeremiah, Ezekiel, and the Twelve. Used with *the.* See table at **Bible. b. Prophet** One of the prophets mentioned in the Bible, esp. one believed to be the author of one of these books. Used with *the.* **6. Prophet** *Islam* Muhammad. Used with *the.* [ME *prophete* < OFr. < Lat. *propheta* < Gk. *prophētēs* : *pro-,* before; see PRO-[2] + *-phētēs,* speaker (< *phanai,* to speak; see **bhā-** in App.).] —**proph′et•hood′** *n.*

proph•et•ess (prŏf′ĭ-tĭs) *n.* **1.** A woman who speaks by divine inspiration or as the interpreter through whom the will of a god is expressed. **2.** A woman predictor; a woman soothsayer. **3.** The chief spokeswoman of a movement or cause. See Usage Note at **-ess.**

pro•phet•ic (prə-fĕt′ĭk) *also* **pro•phet•i•cal** (-ĭ-kəl) *adj.* **1.** Of, belonging to, or characteristic of a prophet or prophecy. **2.** Foretelling events as if by divine inspiration. —**pro•phet′i•cal•ly** *adv.* —**pro•phet′i•cal•ness** *n.*

pro•phy•lac•tic (prō′fə-lăk′tĭk, prŏf′ə-) *adj.* Acting to defend against or prevent something, esp. disease; protective. ❖ *n.* **1.** A prophylactic agent, device, or measure, such as a vaccine or drug. **2.** A contraceptive device, esp. a condom. [Fr. *prophylactique* < Gk. *prophulaktikos* < *prophulassein,* to take precautions against : *pro-,* before; see PRO-[2] + *phulassein,* to protect (< *phulax,* guard).] —**pro′phy•lac′ti•cal•ly** *adv.*

pro•phy•lax•is (prō′fə-lăk′sĭs, prŏf′ə-) *n., pl.* **-lax•es** (-lăk′sēz′) Prevention of or protective treatment for disease. [NLat. < Gk. *prophulaktikos,* prophylactic. See PROPHYLACTIC.]

pro•pin•qui•ty (prə-pĭng′kwĭ-tē) *n.* **1.** Proximity; nearness. **2.** Kinship. **3.** Similarity in nature. [ME *propinquite* < OFr. < Lat. *propinquitās* < *propinquus,* near. See **per**[1] in App.]

pro•pi•o•nate (prō′pē-ə-nāt′) *n.* A salt or ester of propionic acid. [PROPION(IC ACID) + -ATE[2].]

pro•pi•on•ic acid (prō′pē-ŏn′ĭk) *n.* A liquid fatty acid, CH_3CH_2COOH, found naturally in sweat or synthesized and used in the form of its propionates to inhibit mold in baked goods. [Gk. *pro-,* first; see PRO-[2] + Gk. *pīon,* fat (being first in order among the fatty acids); see **peiə-** in App. + -IC.]

pro•pi•ti•ate (prō-pĭsh′ē-āt′) *tr.v.* **-at•ed, -at•ing, -ates** To conciliate; appease. [Lat. *propitiāre, propitiāt-* < *propitius,* propitious. See PROPITIOUS.] —**pro•pi′ti•a•ble** (-pĭsh′ē-ə-bəl, -pĭsh′ə-bəl) *adj.* —**pro•pi′ti•at′ing•ly** *adv.* —**pro•pi′ti•a′tive** *adj.* —**pro•pi′ti•a′tor** *n.*

pro•pi•ti•a•tion (prō-pĭsh′ē-ā′shən) *n.* **1.** The act of propitiating. **2.** Something that propitiates, esp. a conciliatory offering to a god.

pro•pi•ti•a•to•ry (prō-pĭsh′ē-ə-tôr′ē, -tōr′ē, -pĭsh′ə-) *adj.* Of or offered in propitiation. —**pro•pi′ti•a•to′ri•ly** *adv.*

pro•pi•tious (prə-pĭsh′əs) *adj.* **1.** Presenting favorable circumstances; auspicious. See Syns at **favorable. 2.** Kindly; gracious. [ME *propicius* < OFr. *propicieux* < Lat. *propitius.* See **pet-** in App.] —**pro•pi′tious•ly** *adv.* —**pro•pi′tious•ness** *n.*

prop•jet (prŏp′jĕt′) *n.* See **turboprop.**

prop•o•lis (prŏp′ə-lĭs) *n.* A resinous substance collected from the buds of certain trees by bees and used in the construction of their hives. [Lat. < Gk., suburb, bee glue (orig. a structure around the hive opening) : *pro-,* before; see PRO-[2] + *polis,* city.]

pro•po•nent (prə-pō′nənt) *n.* One who argues in support of something; an advocate. [Lat. *prōpōnēns, prōpōnent-,* pr. part. of *prōpōnere,* to set forth. See PROPOSE.]

pro•por•tion (prə-pôr′shən, -pōr′-) *n.* **1.** A part considered in relation to the whole. **2.** A relationship between things or parts of things with respect to comparative magnitude, quantity, or degree. **3.** A relationship between quantities such that if one varies then another varies in a manner dependent on the first. **4.** Agreeable or harmonious relation of parts within a whole; balance or

propeller

symmetry. **5.** Dimensions; size. Often used in the plural. **6.** *Mathematics* A statement of equality between two ratios. Four quantities, *a, b, c, d,* are in proportion if $\frac{a}{b} = \frac{c}{d}$. ❖ *tr.v.* **-tioned, -tioning, -tions 1.** To adjust so that proper relations between parts are attained. **2.** To form the parts of with balance or symmetry. [Ult. < Lat. *prōportiō, prōportiōn-* < *prō portiōne,* according to (each) part : *prō,* according to; see PRO-[1] + *portiōne,* ablative of *portiō,* part; see **perə-** in App.] **—pro·por'tion·a·ble** *adj.* **—pro·por'tion·a·bly** *adv.* **—pro·por'tion·er** *n.* **—pro·por'tion·ment** *n.*

> **SYNONYMS** *proportion, harmony, symmetry, balance* These nouns mean aesthetic arrangement marked by proper distribution of elements. *Proportion* is the agreeable relation of parts within a whole: *a house with rooms of gracious proportion. Harmony* is the pleasing interaction or appropriate combination of elements: *the harmony of your facial features. Symmetry* and *balance* both imply an arrangement of parts and details on either side of a dividing line, but *symmetry* frequently emphasizes mirror-image correspondence of parts, while *balance* often suggests dissimilar parts that offset each other to make a harmonious and satisfying whole: *Flowers were planted in perfect symmetry around the pool. "In all perfectly beautiful objects, there is found the opposition of one part to another, and a reciprocal balance"* (John Ruskin).

pro·por·tion·al (prə-pôr'shə-nəl, -pōr'-) *adj.* **1.** Forming a relationship with other parts or quantities; being in proportion. **2.** Properly related in size, degree, or other measurable characteristics; corresponding. **3.** *Mathematics* Having the same or a constant ratio. ❖ *n.* One of the quantities in a mathematical proportion. **—pro·por'tion·al'i·ty** (-shə-năl'ĭ-tē) *n.* **—pro·por'tion·al·ly** *adv.*

proportional representation *n.* Representation of all parties in a legislature in proportion to their popular vote.

pro·por·tion·ate (prə-pôr'shə-nĭt, -pōr'-) *adj.* Being in due proportion; proportional. ❖ *tr.v.* (-shə-nāt') **-at·ed, -at·ing, -ates** To make proportionate. **—pro·por'tion·ate·ly** *adv.* **—pro·por'tion·ate·ness** *n.*

pro·pos·al (prə-pō'zəl) *n.* **1.** The act of proposing. **2.** A plan that is proposed. **3.** An offer of marriage.

pro·pose (prə-pōz') *v.* **-posed, -pos·ing, -pos·es** *—tr.* **1.** To put forward for consideration, discussion, or adoption; suggest. **2.** To recommend (a person) for a position, office, or membership; nominate. **3.** To offer (a toast) to be honored. **4.** To make known as one's intention; purpose or intend. *—intr.* To form or make a proposal, esp. of marriage. [ME *proposen* < OFr. *proposer,* alteration (influenced by *poser,* to put, place), of Lat. *prōpōnere* : *prō-,* forth; see PRO-[1] + *pōnere,* to put; see **apo-** in App.] **—pro·pos'er** *n.*

prop·o·si·tion (prŏp'ə-zĭsh'ən) *n.* **1.** A plan suggested for acceptance; a proposal. **2.** *Informal* A matter to be dealt with; a task. **3.** *Informal* An offer of a private bargain, esp. a request for sexual relations. **4.** A subject for discussion or analysis. **5.** *Logic* **a.** A statement that affirms or denies something. **b.** The meaning expressed in such a statement, as opposed to the way it is expressed. **6.** *Mathematics* A theorem. ❖ *tr.v.* **-tioned, -tion·ing, -tions** *Informal* To offer a proposition to. [Ult. < Lat. *prōpositiō, prōpositiōn-,* setting out in words < *prōpositus,* p. part. of *prōpōnere,* to set forth. See PROPOSE.] **—prop'o·si'tion·al** *adj.* **—prop'o·si'tion·al·ly** *adv.*

propositional calculus *n.* The branch of symbolic logic that deals with the relationships formed between propositions by connectives such as *and, or,* and *if* as opposed to their internal structure.

propositional function *n. Logic* An expression having the form of a proposition but containing undefined symbols for the substantive elements and becoming a proposition when appropriate values are assigned to the symbols.

pro·pos·i·tus (prō-pŏz'ĭ-təs) *n., pl.* **-ti** (-tī') The person immediately concerned about or affected by an action. [Lat. *prōpositus,* p. part. of *prōpōnere,* to set forth. See PROPOSE.]

pro·pound (prə-pound') *tr.v.* **-pound·ed, -pound·ing, -pounds** To put forward for consideration; set forth. [Alteration of *propoune* < ME *proponen* < Lat. *prōpōnere,* to set forth. See PROPOSE.] **—pro·pound'er** *n.*

pro·pox·y·phene (prō-pŏk'sə-fēn') *n.* A nonnarcotic analgesic drug, $C_{22}H_{29}NO_2$. [PROP(IONATE) + OXY- + -*phene* (alteration of PHENYL).]

pro·prae·tor (prō-prē'tər) *n.* An ancient Roman official, appointed as the chief administrator of a province after serving as praetor. [Lat. *prōpraetor* : *prō-,* for; see PRO-[1] + *praetor,* praetor; see PRAETOR.] **—pro'prae·to'ri·al** (prō'prī-tôr'ē-əl, -tōr'-), **pro'prae·to'ri·an** (-ən) *adj.*

pro·pri·e·tar·y (prə-prī'ĭ-tĕr'ē) *adj.* **1.** Of, relating to, or suggestive of a proprietor or to proprietors as a group: *has proprietary rights.* **2.** Exclusively owned; private: *a proprietary hospital.* **3.** Owned by a private individual or corporation under a trademark or patent: *a proprietary drug.* ❖ *n., pl.* **-ies 1.** A proprietor. **2.** A group of proprietors. **3.** Ownership; proprietorship. **4.** A proprietary medicine. **5.** One granted ownership of a proprietary colony. [< ME *proprietarie,* owner of property < OFr. *proprietaire* and

< Med.Lat. *proprietārius,* both < LLat., of a property owner < Lat. *proprietās,* ownership. See PROPERTY.] **—pro·pri'e·tar'i·ly** *adv.*

proprietary colony *n.* Any of certain early North American colonies, such as Pennsylvania, granted by the English Crown to one or more proprietors who had governing power.

pro·pri·e·tor (prə-prī'ĭ-tər) *n.* **1.** One who has legal title to something; an owner. **2.** One who owns or owns and manages a business or other such establishment. [Prob. alteration of ME *proprietarie.* See PROPRIETARY.] **—pro·pri'e·to'ri·al** (-tôr'ē-əl, -tōr'-) *adj.* **—pro·pri'e·to'ri·al·ly** *adv.* **—pro·pri'e·tor·ship'** *n.*

pro·pri·e·tress (prə-prī'ĭ-trĭs) *n.* **1.** A woman who has legal title to something; an owner. **2.** A woman who owns or owns and manages a business or other such establishment. See Usage Note at **-ess.**

pro·pri·e·ty (prə-prī'ĭ-tē) *n., pl.* **-ties 1.** The quality of being proper; appropriateness. **2.** Conformity to prevailing customs and usages. **3. proprieties** The usages and customs of polite society. [ME *propriete,* ownership, particular character < OFr. See PROPERTY.]

pro·pri·o·cep·tion (prō'prē-ō-sĕp'shən) *n.* The unconscious perception of movement and spatial orientation arising from stimuli within the body itself. [Lat. *proprius,* one's own; see **per**[1] in App. + (RE)CEPTION.]

pro·pri·o·cep·tor (prō'prē-ō-sĕp'tər) *n.* A sensory receptor, found in muscles and the inner ear, that detects the motion or position of the body or a limb by responding to stimuli arising within the organism. [Lat. *proprius,* one's own; see **per**[1] in App. + (RE)CEPTOR.] **—pro'pri·o·cep'tive** *adj.*

pro·pri·um (prō'prē-əm) *n., pl.* **-pri·a** (-prē-ə) In Aristotelian thought, a predicable property common to all members of a kind but not constituting part of the definition of that kind. [Med.Lat. < neut. of Lat. *proprius,* proper (to) (transl. of Gk. *idion*). See **per**[1] in App.]

prop root *n.* An adventitious root that arises from the stem, penetrates the soil, and helps support the plant, as in corn.

prop·to·sis (prŏp-tō'sĭs) *n., pl.* **-ses** (-sēz) Forward displacement of an organ, esp. an eyeball. [LLat. *proptōsis,* prolapse < Gk. < *propiptein,* to fall forward : *pro-,* forward; see PRO-[2] + *piptein, ptō-,* to fall; see **pet-** in App.]

pro·pul·sion (prə-pŭl'shən) *n.* **1.** The process of driving or propelling. **2.** A driving or propelling force. [Med.Lat. *prōpulsiō, prōpulsiōn-,* onslaught, urging on < Lat. *prōpulsus,* p. part. of *prōpellere,* to drive forward. See PROPEL.] **—pro·pul'sive, pro·pul'so·ry** (-sə-rē) *adj.*

pro·pyl (prō'pĭl) *n.* A univalent organic radical with composition $C_3H_7,$ derived from propane. [PROP(ANE) + -YL.] **—pro·pyl'ic** *adj.*

prop·y·lae·um (prŏp'ə-lē'əm, prō'pə-) *n., pl.* **-lae·a** (-lē'ə) An entrance or vestibule to a temple or group of buildings. [Lat. < Gk. *propulaion* : *pro-,* before; see PRO-[2] + *pulē,* gate.]

propyl alcohol *n.* A clear colorless liquid, $CH_3CH_2CH_2OH,$ used as a solvent and an antiseptic.

pro·pyl·ene (prō'pə-lēn') *n.* A flammable gas, $CH_3CH:CH_2,$ derived from petroleum and used in organic synthesis.

propylene glycol *n.* A viscous liquid, $CH_3CHOHCH_2OH,$ used in antifreeze solutions and as a solvent.

pro ra·ta (prō rā'tə, rä'-, răt'ə) *adv.* In proportion, according to a factor that can be calculated exactly. [Lat. *prō ratā (parte),* according to the calculated (share) : *prō,* according to + *ratā,* fem. ablative of *ratus,* calculated.] **—pro·ra'ta** *adj.*

pro·rate (prō-rāt', prō'rāt') *v.* **-rat·ed, -rat·ing, -rates** *—tr.* To divide, distribute, or assess proportionately. *—intr.* To settle affairs on the basis of proportional distribution. [< PRO RATA.] **—pro·rat'a·ble** *adj.* **—pro·ra'tion** *n.*

pro·rogue (prō-rōg') *tr.v.* **-rogued, -rogu·ing, -rogues 1.** To discontinue a session of (a parliament, for example). **2.** To postpone; defer. [ME *prorogen* < OFr. *proroguer,* to postpone < Lat. *prōrogāre* : *prō-,* forward; see PRO-[1] + *rogāre,* to ask; see **reg-** in App.] **—pro'ro·ga'tion** *n.*

pros- *pref.* **1.** Near; toward: *prosenchyma.* **2.** In front of: *prosencephalon.* [Gk. < *pros,* near, at. See **per**[1] in App.]

pro·sa·ic (prō-zā'ĭk) *adj.* **1.** Consisting of or characteristic of prose. **2.** Lacking in imagination; dull. [LLat. *prōsaicus* < Lat. *prōsa,* prose. See PROSE.] **—pro·sa'i·cal·ly** *adv.* **—pro·sa'ic·ness** *n.*

pro·sa·ism (prō'zā-ĭz'əm) *n.* **1.** A quality or style that is prosaic. **2.** A prosaic word, phrase, or other expression.

pro·sce·ni·um (prō-sē'nē-əm, prə-) *n., pl.* **-ni·ums** or **-ni·a** (-nē-ə) **1.** The area of a modern theater located between the curtain and the orchestra. **2.** The stage of an ancient theater, located between the background and the orchestra. **3.** The arch that frames a stage, separating it from the auditorium. [Lat. *proscēnium* < Gk. *proskēnion* : *pro-,* before; see PRO-[2] + *skēnē,* buildings at the back of the stage.]

pro·sciut·to (prō-shoō'tō) *n., pl.* **-ti** (-tē) or **-tos** An aged Italian ham usu. served in thin slices. [Ital., alteration of *presciutto* < VLat. **perexsūctus,* thoroughly dried up : Lat. *per-,* per- + Lat. *exsūctus,* p. part. of *exsūgere,* to suck out (*ex-,* ex- + *sūgere,* to suck).]

pro·scribe (prō-skrīb') *tr.v.* **-scribed, -scrib·ing, -scribes 1.** To denounce or condemn. **2.** To prohibit; forbid. See Syns at **forbid. 3a.** To banish or outlaw (a person). **b.** To publish the name of (a person) as outlawed. [ME *proscriben* < Lat. *prōscrībere*, to put up someone's name as outlawed : *prō-*, in front; see PRO-¹ + *scrībere*, to write; see **skribh-** in App.] —**pro·scrib′er** *n.*

pro·scrip·tion (prō-skrĭp′shən) *n.* **1.** The act of proscribing; prohibition. **2.** The condition of having been proscribed. [ME *proscripcion* < Lat. *prōscrīptiō*, *prōscrīptiōn-*, public notice of outlawry < *prōscrīptus*, p. part. of *prōscrībere*, to proscribe. See PRO-SCRIBE.] —**pro·scrip′tive** *adj.* —**pro·scrip′tive·ly** *adv.*

prose (prōz) *n.* **1.** Ordinary speech or writing, without metrical structure. **2.** Commonplace expression or quality. ❖ *intr.v.* **prosed, pros·ing, pros·es 1.** To write prose. **2.** To speak or write in a dull tiresome style. [ME < OFr. < Lat. *prōsa* (*ōrātiō*), straightforward (discourse), fem. of *prōsus*, alteration of *prōrsus* < *prōversus*, p. part. of *prōvertere*, to turn forward : *prō-*, forward; see PRO-¹ + *vertere*, to turn; see **wer-²** in App.]

pro·sec·tor (prō-sĕk′tər) *n.* One who dissects cadavers for anatomical instruction or pathological examination. [Lat. *prōsector*, anatomist < *prōsecāre*, to cut off or up : *prō-*, before; see PRO-¹ + *secāre*, to cut; see SECTOR.]

pros·e·cute (prŏs′ĭ-kyōōt′) *v.* **-cut·ed, -cut·ing, -cutes** —*tr.* **1.** *Law* **a.** To initiate civil or criminal court action against. **b.** To seek to obtain or enforce by legal action. **2.** To pursue (an undertaking, for example) until completion; follow to the very end. **3.** To carry on, engage in, or practice. —*intr. Law* **1.** To initiate and conduct legal proceedings. **2.** To act as prosecutor. [ME *prosecuten* < Lat. *prōsequī, prōsecūt-* : *prō-*, forward; see PRO-¹ + *sequī*, to follow; see **sekw-¹** in App.] —**pros′e·cut′a·ble** *adj.*

pros·e·cut·ing attorney (prŏs′ĭ-kyōō′tĭng) *n.* A lawyer empowered to prosecute cases on behalf of a government and its people.

pros·e·cu·tion (prŏs′ĭ-kyōō′shən) *n.* **1.** The act of prosecuting. **2.** The institution and conduct of a legal proceeding. **3.** See **prosecuting attorney.**

pros·e·cu·tor (prŏs′ĭ-kyōō′tər) *n.* **1.** One that prosecutes. **2.** One that initiates and carries out a legal action, esp. criminal proceedings. **3.** See **prosecuting attorney.**

pros·e·cu·to·ri·al (prŏs′ĭ-kyōō-tôr′ē-əl, -tōr′-) *adj.* Of, relating to, or concerned with prosecution.

pros·e·lyte (prŏs′ə-līt′) *n.* A new convert to a doctrine or religion. ❖ *v.* **-lyt·ed, -lyt·ing, -lytes** —*tr.* To proselytize (a person). —*intr.* To engage in proselytization. [ME *proselite* < OFr. < LLat. *prosēlytus* < Gk. *prosēlutos*, stranger, proselyte : *pros-*, *pros-* + *ēluth-*, aorist t. stem of *erkhesthai*, to go.] —**pros′e·lyt′er** *n.*

pros·e·ly·tism (prŏs′ə-lĭ-tĭz′əm, -lī-) *n.* **1.** The practice of proselytizing. **2.** The state of being a proselyte. —**pros′e·lyt′i·cal** (-lĭt′ĭ-kəl) *adj.*

pros·e·ly·tize (prŏs′ə-lĭ-tīz′) *v.* **-tized, -tiz·ing, -tiz·es** —*intr.* **1.** To convert someone to one's own religious faith. **2.** To induce someone to join one's own political party or to espouse one's doctrine. —*tr.* To convert (a person) from one belief, doctrine, cause, or faith to another. —**pros′e·ly·ti·za′tion** (-tĭ-zā′shən) *n.* —**pros′e·ly·tiz′er** *n.*

pro·sem·i·nar (prō-sĕm′ə-när′) *n.* A course of study for graduate and advanced undergraduate students in a college or university, conducted as a seminar. [PRO-² + SEMINAR.]

pros·en·ceph·a·lon (prŏs′ĕn-sĕf′ə-lŏn′) *n.* The forebrain. —**pros′en·ce·phal′ic** (-sə-făl′ĭk) *adj.*

pros·en·chy·ma (prŏ-sĕng′kĭ-mə) *n.* A type of plant tissue consisting of elongated cells with tapering ends, occurring in supporting and conducting tissue. —**pros′en·chym′a·tous** (-kĭm′ə-təs) *adj.*

prose poem *n.* A prose work that has poetic characteristics such as vivid imagery and concentrated expression.

Pro·ser·pi·na (prō-sûr′pə-nə) *also* **Pro·ser·pi·ne** (prō-sûr′pə-nē, prŏs′ər-pīn′) *n. Roman Mythology* The daughter of Ceres who, after being abducted by Pluto, became the goddess of the underworld.

pro·sit (prōst, prō′zĭt) *or* **prost** (prōst) *interj.* Used as a toast to someone's health while drinking. [Ger. < Lat. *prōsit*, may it benefit, third pers. sing. pr. subjunctive of *prōdesse*, to benefit. See PROUD.]

pro·slav·er·y (prō-slā′və-rē, -slāv′rē) *adj.* Advocating the practice of slavery.

pros·o·dy (prŏs′ə-dē) *n., pl.* **-dies 1.** The study of the metrical structure of verse. **2.** A particular system of versification. [ME *prosodie* < Lat. *prosōdia*, accent < Gk. *prosōidiā*, song sung to music, accent : *pros-*, *pros-* + *ōidē*, song; see ODE.] —**pro·sod′ic** (prə-sŏd′ĭk) *adj.* —**pro·sod′i·cal·ly** *adv.* —**pros′o·dist** *n.*

pro·so·ma (prō-sō′mə) *n.* The anterior or cephalic portion of the body of certain invertebrates, such as arachnids, in which segmentation is not evident. [PRO-² + Gk. *sōma*, body.] —**pro·so′mal** *adj.*

pros·o·pog·ra·phy (prŏs′ə-pŏg′rə-fē) *n.* A study, often using statistics, that identifies and draws relationships between various characters or people within a specific historical, social, or literary context. [Gk. *prosōpon*, character; see PROSOPOPEIA + -GRAPHY.] —**pros′o·po·graph′i·cal** (-pə-grăf′ĭ-kəl) *adj.*

pro·so·po·pe·ia *also* **pro·so·po·poe·ia** (prə-sō′pə-pē′ə) *n.* **1.** A figure of speech in which an absent or imaginary person is

represented as speaking. **2.** See **personification** 3. [Lat. *prosōpopoeia* < Gk. *prosōpopoiiā* : *prosōpon*, face, mask, dramatic character (*pros-*, *pros-* + *ōpon*, face < *ōps*, *ōp-*, eye; see **okʷ-** in App.) + *poiein*, to make; see **kʷei-²** in App.] —**pro·so′po·pe′ial** *adj.*

pros·pect (prŏs′pĕkt′) *n.* **1.** Something expected; a possibility. **2.** **prospects a.** Chances. **b.** Financial expectations, esp. of success. **3a.** A potential customer, client, or purchaser. **b.** A candidate deemed likely to succeed. **4.** The direction in which an object, such as a building, faces; an outlook. **5.** Something presented to the eye; a scene: *a pleasant prospect.* **6a.** The location or probable location of a mineral deposit. **b.** An actual or probable mineral deposit. **c.** The mineral yield obtained by working an ore. ❖ *v.* **-pect·ed, -pect·ing, -pects** —*tr.* To search for or explore (a region) for mineral deposits or oil. —*intr.* To explore for mineral deposits or oil. [ME *prospecte* < Lat. *prōspectus*, distant view < p. part. of *prōspicere*, to look out : *prō-*, forward; see PRO-¹ + *specere*, to look at; see **spek-** in App.]

pro·spec·tive (prə-spĕk′tĭv) *adj.* **1.** Likely or expected to happen. **2.** Likely to become or be. —**pro·spec′tive·ly** *adv.*

pros·pec·tor (prŏs′pĕk′tər) *n.* One who explores an area for mineral deposits or oil.

pro·spec·tus (prə-spĕk′təs) *n.* **1.** A formal summary of a proposed venture or project. **2.** A document describing the chief features of something, esp. a stock offering or mutual fund, for prospective buyers, investors, or participants. [Lat. *prōspectus*, distant view. See PROSPECT.]

pros·per (prŏs′pər) *intr.v.* **-pered, -per·ing, -pers** To be fortunate or successful, esp. in terms of one's finances; thrive. [ME *prosperen* < OFr. *prosperer* < Lat. *prosperāre*, to render fortunate < *prosperus*, favorable.]

pros·per·i·ty (prŏ-spĕr′ĭ-tē) *n.* The condition of being prosperous.

pros·per·ous (prŏs′pər-əs) *adj.* **1.** Having success; flourishing. **2.** Well-to-do; well-off. **3.** Propitious; favorable. —**pros′per·ous·ly** *adv.* —**pros′per·ous·ness** *n.*

prost (prōst) *interj.* Variant of **prosit.**

pros·ta·glan·din (prŏs′tə-glăn′dĭn) *n.* Any of a group of hormonelike substances that mediate a wide range of physiological functions, such as control of blood pressure, contraction of smooth muscle, and modulation of inflammation. [PROSTA(TE) + GLAND¹ + -IN.]

pros·tate (prŏs′tāt′) *n.* The prostate gland. [NLat. *prostata* < Gk. *prostatēs* (*adēn*), prostate (gland) < *proïstanai*, to set before : *pro-*, in front; see PRO-² + *histanai*, to set, place; see **stā-** in App.] —**pros′tate′, pro·stat′ic** (prō-stăt′ĭk) *adj.*

pros·ta·tec·to·my (prŏs′tə-tĕk′tə-mē) *n., pl.* **-mies** Surgical removal of all or part of the prostate gland.

prostate gland *n.* A partly muscular gland in male mammals surrounding the urethra at the base of the bladder that secretes a fluid that is a major constituent of semen.

pros·tate-spe·cif·ic antigen (prŏs′tāt′spĭ-sĭf′ĭk) *n.* A protein produced by the prostate gland, used in blood testing as a screen for prostate cancer.

pros·ta·tism (prŏs′tə-tĭz′əm) *n.* A disorder characterized by decreased force of urination and dysuria, usu. resulting from enlargement of the prostate gland.

pros·ta·ti·tis (prŏs′tə-tī′tĭs) *n.* Inflammation of the prostate gland.

pros·the·sis (prŏs-thē′sĭs) *n., pl.* **-ses** (-sēz) **1.** An artificial device used to replace a missing body part, such as a limb, tooth, eye, or heart valve. **2.** Replacement of a missing body part with such a device. **3.** *Linguistics* Prothesis. [Gk., addition < *prostithenai*, to add : *pros-*, *pros-* + *tithenai*, the-, to put; see **dhē-** in App.]

pros·thet·ic (prŏs-thĕt′ĭk) *adj.* **1.** Serving as or relating to a prosthesis. **2.** Of or relating to prosthetics.

prosthetic group *n.* The nonprotein component of a conjugated protein, as the heme group in hemoglobin.

pros·thet·ics (prŏs-thĕt′ĭks) *n.* (*used with a sing. verb*) The branch of medicine or surgery that deals with prostheses. —**pros·the′tist** (prŏs′thĭ-tĭst) *n.*

pros·tho·don·tia (prŏs′thə-dŏn′shə) *n.* Prosthodontics.

pros·tho·don·tics (prŏs′thə-dŏn′tĭks) *n.* (*used with a sing. verb*) The branch of dentistry that deals with the replacement of missing teeth and related mouth or jaw structures by artificial devices. [PROSTH(ESIS) + -ODONT(IA) + -ICS.] —**pros′tho·don′tic** *adj.* —**pros′tho·don′tist** *n.*

pros·ti·tute (prŏs′tĭ-tōōt′, -tyōōt′) *n.* **1.** One who solicits and accepts payment for sex. **2.** One who sells one's abilities, talent, or name for an unworthy purpose. ❖ *tr.v.* **-tut·ed, -tut·ing, -tutes 1.** To offer (oneself or another) for sexual hire. **2.** To sell (one's talent, for example) for an unworthy purpose. [Lat. *prōstitūta* < fem. p. part. of *prōstituere*, to prostitute : *prō-*, in front; see PRO-¹ + *statuere*, to cause to stand; see **stā-** in App.] —**pros′ti·tu′tor** *n.*

pros·ti·tu·tion (prŏs′tĭ-tōō′shən, -tyōō′-) *n.* **1.** The act or practice of engaging in sex acts for hire. **2.** The act or an instance of offering or devoting one's talent unworthily.

pro·sto·mi·um (prō-stō′mē-əm) *n., pl.* **-mi·a** (-mē-ə) The portion of the head in earthworms and other annelids that is situated anterior to the mouth. [NLat. < Gk. *prostomion*, mouth, lips :

prosthesis

pro-, in front of; see PRO-² + *stoma*, mouth.] —**pro•sto′mi•al** (-əl) *adj.*

pros•trate (prŏs′trāt′) *tr.v.* **-trat•ed, -trat•ing, -trates** **1.** To put or throw flat with the face down, as in submission or adoration: *"He did not simply sit and meditate, he also knelt down, sometimes even prostrated himself"* (Iris Murdoch). **2.** To cause to lie flat: *The wind prostrated the young trees.* **3.** To reduce to extreme weakness or incapacitation; overcome. ❖ *adj.* **1.** Lying face down, as in submission or adoration. **2.** Lying flat or at full length. **3.** Reduced to extreme weakness or incapacitation; overcome. **4.** *Botany* Growing flat along the ground. [ME *prostraten* < *prostrat*, prostrate < Lat. *prōstrātus*, p. part. of *prōsternere*, to throw down : *prō-*, forward; see PRO-¹ + *sternere*, to spread, cast down.] —**pros′tra′tor** *n.*

pros•tra•tion (prŏ-strā′shən) *n.* **1a.** The act of prostrating oneself. **b.** The state of being prostrate. **2.** Total exhaustion or weakness; collapse.

pro•style (prō′stīl′) *adj.* Having a row of columns across the front only. [Lat. *prostylos* < Gk. *prostūlos* : *pro-*, in front; see PRO-² + *stūlos*, pillar; see **stā-** in App.]

pros•y (prō′zē) *adj.* **-i•er, -i•est** **1.** Matter-of-fact and dry; prosaic. **2.** Dull; commonplace. [< PROSE.] —**pros′i•ly** *adv.* —**pros′i•ness** *n.*

Prot. *abbr.* Protestant

prot– *pref.* Variant of **proto–**.

pro•tac•tin•i•um (prō′tăk-tĭn′ē-əm) *n. Symbol* **Pa** A rare, extremely toxic radioactive element having 13 known isotopes, the most stable of which is protactinium 231 with a half-life of 32,480 years. Atomic number 91; melting point 1,230°C; specific gravity 15.37; valence 4, 5. See table at **element.** [PROT(O)– + AC-TINIUM (so called because it decays into actinium).]

pro•tag•o•nist (prō-tăg′ə-nĭst) *n.* **1.** The main character in a literary work. **2.** In ancient Greek drama, the first actor to engage in dialogue with the chorus, in later dramas playing the main character and some minor characters as well. **3a.** A leading or principal figure. **b.** The leader of a cause; a champion. **4.** *Usage Problem* A proponent; an advocate. [Gk. *prōtagōnistēs* : *prōto-*, proto- + *agōnistēs* < *agōnizesthai*, to contend < *agōnia*, contest < *agōn* < *agein*, to drive, lead; see **ag-** in App.).]

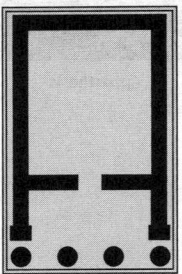

prostyle
plan of Greek Temple B,
Selinunte, Sicily

USAGE NOTE The *protagonist* of a Greek drama was its leading actor, of whom there could be but one in any play. Thus when the members of the Usage Panel were asked "How many protagonists are there in *Othello* ?" the great majority answered "One" and offered substitutes such as *antagonist, villain, principal,* and *deuteragonist* to describe Desdemona and Iago. But there is reputable precedent from the 17th century on for using *protagonist* to mean simply "important actor" or "principal party," with no implication of uniqueness. • The use of *protagonist* to refer to a proponent is likely to strike many as an error.

Pro•tag•o•ras (prō-tăg′ər-əs) fl. 5th cent. B.C. Greek philosopher who is considered the first Sophist. —**Pro•tag′o•re′an** (-ə-rē′ən) *adj.*

pro•ta•mine (prō′tə-mēn′, -mĭn) also **pro•ta•min** (-mĭn) *n.* Any of a group of simple proteins found in fish sperm that are strongly basic, are soluble in water, are not coagulated by heat, and yield chiefly arginine upon hydrolysis.

pro•ta•no•pi•a (prō′tə-nō′pē-ə) *n.* A form of colorblindness characterized by defective perception of red. [PROT(O)– + AN– + –OPIA.] —**pro′ta•nop′ic** (-nŏp′ĭk) *adj.*

prot•a•sis (prŏt′ə-sĭs) *n., pl.* **-ses** (-sēz′) **1.** *Grammar* The dependent clause of a conditional sentence, as *if it rains* in *The game will be canceled if it rains.* **2.** The first part of an ancient Greek or Roman drama, in which the characters and subject are introduced. [LLat. *protasis*, proposition, first part of a play < Gk., premise of a syllogism, conditional clause < *proteinein*, to propose : *pro-*, forward; see PRO-² + *teinein, ta-*, to stretch; see **ten-** in App.] —**pro•tat′ic** (prō-tăt′ĭk, prō-) *adj.*

prote– *pref.* Variant of **proteo–**.

pro•te•an (prō′tē-ən, prō-tē′-) *adj.* **1.** Readily taking on varied shapes, forms, or meanings. **2.** Exhibiting considerable variety or diversity. [< PROTEUS.]

pro•te•ase (prō′tē-ās′, -āz′) *n.* Any of various enzymes that catalyze the hydrolytic breakdown of proteins into peptides or amino acids.

protease inhibitor *n.* An anti-HIV drug that blocks the action of the enzyme protease, which is needed for viral replication.

pro•tect (prə-tĕkt′) *tr.v.* **-tect•ed, -tect•ing, -tects** **1.** To keep from being damaged, attacked, stolen, or injured; guard. See Syns at **defend. 2.** To help (domestic industry) with tariffs or quotas on imported goods. **3.** To assure payment of (drafts or notes, for example) by setting aside funds. **4.** *Sports* To attempt to hold (a lead) by playing careful defense and avoiding risky plays. **5.** *Baseball* **a.** To swing at a pitch near (home plate) in order to avoid being called out on strikes. **b.** To swing at a pitch so as to give (a base runner) a better chance of advancing. [ME *protecten* < Lat. *prōtegere, prōtēct-*: *prō-*, in front; see PRO-¹ + *tegere*, to cover; see **(s)teg-** in App.] —**pro•tect′ing•ly** *adv.*

pro•tec•tant (prə-tĕk′tənt) *n.* One that protects.

pro•tect•ed sex (prə-tĕk′tĭd) *n.* Sexual activity in which a condom or similar device is used to minimize the risk of pregnancy

or of spreading or contracting disease.

pro•tec•tion (prə-tĕk′shən) *n.* **1a.** The act of protecting. **b.** The condition of being protected. **2.** One that protects. **3.** A pass guaranteeing safe-conduct to travelers. **4.** A system of tariffs or other measures protecting domestic producers from foreign competition. **5.** A contraceptive or barrier, esp. a condom, that lowers the risk of pregnancy or infection. **6.** *Slang* **a.** Money extorted by racketeers threatening violence for nonpayment. **b.** Bribes paid to officials by racketeers for immunity from prosecution. —**pro•tec′tion•al** *adj.*

pro•tec•tion•ism (prə-tĕk′shə-nĭz′əm) *n.* The advocacy, system, or theory of protecting domestic producers by impeding or limiting, as by tariffs or quotas, the importation of foreign goods and services. —**pro•tec′tion•ist** *n.*

pro•tec•tive (prə-tĕk′tĭv) *adj.* Adapted or intended to afford protection. ❖ *n.* Something that protects. —**pro•tec′tive•ly** *adv.* —**pro•tec′tive•ness** *n.*

pro•tec•tor also **pro•tect•er** (prə-tĕk′tər) *n.* **1.** A person or a thing that protects. **2. Protector a.** One who rules a kingdom during the minority of a sovereign. **b.** The head of the Commonwealth of England, Scotland, and Ireland from 1653 to 1659. —**pro•tec′tor•al** *adj.* —**pro•tec′tor•ship′** *n.*

pro•tec•tor•ate (prə-tĕk′tər-ĭt) *n.* **1a.** A relationship of protection and partial control assumed by a superior power over a dependent country or region. **b.** The protected country or region. **2. Protectorate a.** The government, office, or term of a protector. **b.** The government of England under Oliver Cromwell and his son Richard.

pro•tec•to•ry (prə-tĕk′tə-rē) *n., pl.* **-ries** An institution providing for homeless, destitute, or delinquent children.

pro•té•gé (prō′tə-zhā′, prō′tə-zhā′) *n.* One whose welfare, training, or career is promoted by an influential person. [Fr., p. part. of *protéger*, to protect < OFr. < Lat. *prōtegere*. See PROTECT.]

pro•té•gée (prō′tə-zhā′, prō′tə-zhā′) *n.* A woman or girl whose welfare, training, or career is promoted by an influential person. [Fr., fem. of *protégé*, protégé. See PROTÉGÉ.]

pro•te•i (prō′tē-ī′) *n.* Plural of **proteus.**

pro•tein (prō′tēn′, -tē-ĭn) *n.* Any of a group of complex organic macromolecules that contain carbon, hydrogen, oxygen, nitrogen, and usu. sulfur, are composed of one or more chains of amino acids, and include many substances, such as enzymes, hormones, and antibodies, that are necessary for the proper functioning of an organism. [Fr. *protéine* < L.Gk. *prōteios*, of the first quality < Gk. *prōtos*, first. See **per**¹ in App.] —**pro′tein•a′ceous** (prōt′n-ā′shəs, prō′tē-nā′-), **pro′tein•ic** (prō-tē′nĭk) *adj.*

pro•tein•ase (prōt′n-ās′, -āz′, prō′tē-nās′, -nāz′) *n.* An endopeptidase, such as pepsin, trypsin, or papain.

pro•tein•u•ri•a (prōt′n-ŏor′ē-ə, -yŏor′-, prō′tē-nŏor′-, -nyŏor′-) *n.* The presence of excessive amounts of protein in the urine.

pro tem (prō tĕm′) *adv.* Pro tempore.

pro tem•po•re (prō tĕm′pə-rē) *adv.* For the time being; temporarily. [Lat. *prō tempore* : *prō*, for + *tempore*, ablative of *tempus*, time.]

proteo– or **prote–** *pref.* Protein: *proteolysis.* [< PROTEIN.]

pro•te•ol•y•sis (prō′tē-ŏl′ĭ-sĭs) *n.* The hydrolytic breakdown of proteins into simpler soluble substances such as peptides and amino acids, as occurs in digestion. —**pro′te•o•lyt′ic** (-tē-ə-lĭt′ĭk) *adj.* —**pro′te•o•lyt′i•cal•ly** *adv.*

pro•te•ose (prō′tē-ōs′, -ōz′) *n.* Any of various water-soluble compounds produced by the hydrolytic breakdown of proteins during digestion.

Prot•er•o•zo•ic (prŏt′ər-ə-zō′ĭk, prō′tər-) *adj.* Of or belonging to the later of the two divisions of Precambrian time, from approx. 2.5 billion years ago to approx. 570 million years ago, characterized by the buildup of oxygen and the appearance of the first multicellular eukaryotic life forms. See table at **geologic time.** ❖ *n.* The Proterozoic Eon or its deposits. [Gk. *proteros*, earlier, former; see **per**¹ in App. + –ZOIC.]

pro•test (prə-tĕst′, prō′tĕst′, prō′tĕst′) *v.* **-test•ed, -test•ing, -tests** —*tr.* **1.** To object to, esp. in a formal statement. See Syns at **object. 2.** To promise or affirm with earnest solemnity. **3.** *Archaic* To proclaim or make known: *"unrough youths that even now/ Protest their first of manhood"* (Shakespeare). —*intr.* **1.** To express strong objection. **2.** To make an earnest avowal or affirmation. ❖ *n.* (prō′tĕst′) **1.** A formal declaration of disapproval or objection issued by a concerned person, group, or organization. **2.** An individual or collective gesture or display of disapproval. [ME *protesten* < OFr. *protester* < Lat. *prōtestārī* : *prō-*, forth; see PRO-¹ + *testārī*, to testify (< *testis*, witness; see **trei-** in App.).] —**pro•test′er** *n.*

Prot•es•tant (prŏt′ĭ-stənt) *n.* **1.** A member of a Western Christian church whose faith and practice are founded on the principles of the Reformation, especially in the acceptance of the Bible as the sole source of revelation, in justification by faith alone, and in the universal priesthood of all the believers. **2.** One who supported the protestation presented by the German Lutheran states against the revocation of the decree of the Diet of Speyer (1529). **3. protestant** (prə-tĕs′tənt) One who makes a declaration or avowal. [Fr. < Ger. < Lat. *prōtestāns, prōtestant-*, pr. part. of *prōtestārī*, to protest. See PROTEST.] —**Prot′es•tant** *adj.*

Protestant Episcopal Church *n.* The Episcopal Church.

Prot·es·tant·ism (prŏt′ĭ-stən-tĭz′əm) *n.* **1.** Adherence to the religion and beliefs of a Protestant church. **2.** The religion and religious beliefs fostered by the Protestant movement. **3.** Protestants considered as a group.

prot·es·ta·tion (prŏt′ĭ-stā′shən, prō′tĭ-, -tĕ-) *n.* **1.** An emphatic declaration. **2.** A strong or formal expression of dissent.

pro·te·us (prō′tē-əs) *n., pl.* **-te·i** (-tē-ī′) Any of various gramnegative rod-shaped bacteria of the genus *Proteus,* certain species of which are associated with human enteritis and urinary tract infections. [NLat. *Prōteus,* genus name < Lat., Proteus. See PROTEUS.]

Pro·te·us (prō′tē-əs, -tyŏŏs′) *n. Greek Mythology* **1.** A sea god who could change his shape at will. **2.** A satellite of Neptune. [Lat. *Prōteus* < Gk.]

pro·tha·la·mi·on (prō′thə-lā′mē-ən, -ŏn′) *n., pl.* **-mi·a** (-mē-ə) A song in celebration of a wedding. [PRO–² + Gk. *(epi)thalamion,* epithalamium; see EPITHALAMIUM.]

pro·thal·lus (prō-thăl′əs) *or* **pro·thal·li·um** (-thăl′ē-əm) *n., pl.* **-thal·li** (-thăl′ī) *or* **-thal·li·a** (-thăl′ē-ə) A small flat delicate structure produced by a germinating spore of a fern and bearing sex organs. [NLat. : PRO–² + Gk. *thallos,* shoot (< *thallein,* to sprout).] **—pro·thal′li·al** (-lē-əl) *adj.*

proth·e·sis (prŏth′ĭ-sĭs) *n., pl.* **-ses** (-sēz′) The addition of a phoneme or syllable at the beginning of a word, as in Spanish *espina,* "thorn," from Latin *spina.* [Gk., prefixing < *protithenai,* to put before : pro-, before; see PRO–² + *tithenai, the-,* to put; see **dhē-** in App.] **—pro·thet′ic** (prŏ-thĕt′ĭk) *adj.* **—pro·thet′i·cal·ly** *adv.*

pro·thon·o·tar·y (prō-thŏn′ə-tĕr′ē, prō′thə-nō′tə-rē) *also* **pro·ton·o·tar·y** (prō-thŏn′ə-tĕr′ē, prō′thə-nō′tə-rē) *n., pl.* **-ies 1.** The principal clerk in certain courts of law. **2.** *Roman Catholic Church* One of a college of 12 ecclesiastics charged with the registry of important pontifical proceedings. [ME *prothonotarie* < Med.Lat. *prōthonotārius* < LLat. *prōtonotārius* : Gk. *prōto-,* proto- + Lat. *notārius,* secretary (< *nota,* mark; see **gnō-** in App.).]

prothonotary warbler *n.* A small North American bird (*Prothonotaria citrea*) having a deep yellow head and breast and inhabiting wooded swamps.

prothoracic gland *n.* Either of a pair of glands located in the prothorax of certain insects and regulating molting.

pro·tho·rax (prō-thôr′ăks′, -thōr′-) *n., pl.* **-tho·rax·es** *or* **-tho·ra·ces** (-thôr′ə-sēz′, -thōr′-) The anterior division of the thorax of an insect, bearing the first pair of legs. **—pro′tho·rac′ic** (-thə-răs′ĭk) *adj.*

pro·throm·bin (prō-thrŏm′bĭn) *n.* A plasma protein that is converted into thrombin during blood clotting.

pro·tist (prō′tĭst) *n.* Any of the eukaryotic unicellular organisms of the former kingdom Protista, which now belong to the kingdom Protoctista. [< NLat. *Prōtista,* former kingdom name < Gk. *prōtista,* neut. pl. of *prōtistos,* the very first, superl. of *prōtos,* first. See **per¹** in App.]

pro·ti·um (prō′tē-əm, prō′shē-) *n.* The most abundant isotope of hydrogen, H¹, with atomic mass 1.

proto– *or* **prot–** *pref.* **1.** First in time; earliest: *protolithic.* **2.** First formed; primitive; original: *protohuman.* **3. Proto–** Being a form of a language that is the ancestor of a language or group of related languages: *Proto-Germanic.* **4.** Having the least amount of a specified element or radical: *protoporphyrin.* [Gk. *prōto-* < *prōtos.* See **per¹** in App.]

Pro·to-Al·gon·qui·an (prō′tō-ăl-gŏng′kwē-ən, -kē-ən) *n.* The reconstructed protolanguage of Algonquian.

pro·to·col (prō′tə-kôl′, -kŏl′, -kōl′) *n.* **1a.** The forms of ceremony and etiquette observed by diplomats and heads of state. **b.** A code of correct conduct. **2.** The first copy of a treaty or other such document before its ratification. **3.** A preliminary draft or record of a transaction. **4.** The plan for a course of medical treatment or for a scientific experiment. **5.** *Computer Science* A standard procedure for regulating data transmission between computers. ❖ *intr.v.* **-coled, -col·ing, -cols** *or* **-colled, -col·ling, -cols** To form or issue protocols. [Fr. *protocole* < OFr. *prothocolle,* draft of a document < Med.Lat. *prōtocollum* < L.Gk. *prōtokollon,* table of contents, first sheet : Gk. *prōto-,* proto- + Gk. *kollēma,* sheets of a papyrus glued together (< *kollān,* to glue together < *kolla,* glue).] **—pro′to·col′ar** (-kŏl′ər), pro′to·col′a·ry** (-kŏl′ə-rē) *adj.*

pro·toc·tist (prə-tŏk′tĭst) *n.* Any of the unicellular protists and their descendant multicellular organisms, considered as a separate taxonomic kingdom in most modern classification systems. [< NLat. *Prōtoctista,* kingdom name : Gk. *prōto-,* proto- + Gk. *ktistos,* created (< *ktizein,* to create; see **tkei-** in App.).]

pro·to·derm (prō′tə-dûrm′) *n. Botany* The primary meristem that gives rise to epidermis. **—pro′to·derm′al** *adj.*

pro·to·gal·ax·y (prō′tō-găl′ək-sē) *n., pl.* **-ies** An accumulation of gas, dust, and dark matter with sufficient mass to form a galaxy.

Pro·to-Ger·man·ic (prō′tō-jûr-măn′ĭk) *n.* The reconstructed prehistoric ancestor of the Germanic languages.

pro·tog·y·nous (prō-tŏj′ə-nəs, prō′tə-jī′nəs, -gĭ′-) *adj.* Of or relating to a flower in which the stigma is receptive before the pollen is shed from the anthers of the same flower.

pro·to·his·to·ry (prō′tō-hĭs′tə-rē, -hĭs′trē) *n.* The study of a culture just before the time of its earliest recorded history. **—pro′to·his·tor′i·an** (-hĭ-stôr′ē-ən, -stōr′-) *n.* **—pro′to·his·tor′ic** (-hĭ-stôr′ĭk, -stōr′-) *adj.*

pro·to·hu·man (prō′tō-hyōō′mən) *adj.* Of or relating to various extinct hominids or other primates that resemble modern humans. **—pro′to·hu′man** *n.*

Pro·to-In·do-Eur·o·pe·an (prō′tō-ĭn′dō-yŏŏr′ə-pē′ən) *n.* The reconstructed language that was the ancestor of the Indo-European languages. **—Pro′to-In′do-Eur′o·pe′an** *adj.*

pro·to·lan·guage (prō′tō-lăng′gwĭj) *n.* A language that is the recorded or hypothetical ancestor of another language or group of languages.

pro·to·lith·ic (prō′tə-lĭth′ĭk) *adj.* Of, relating to, or characteristic of the very beginning of the Stone Age; Eolithic.

pro·to·mar·tyr (prō′tō-mär′tər) *n.* The first martyr in a cause. Used esp. of the first Christian martyr, Saint Stephen.

pro·ton (prō′tŏn′) *n.* A stable, positively charged subatomic particle in the baryon family having a mass 1,836 times that of the electron. [< Gk. *prōton,* neut. of *prōtos,* first. See **per¹** in App.] **—pro·ton′ic** *adj.*

pro·to·ne·ma (prō′tə-nē′mə) *n., pl.* **-ne·ma·ta** (-nē′mə-tə, -nĕm′ə-) The filamentous growth that arises from spore germination in mosses and gives rise to a mature gametophyte. [PROTO– + Gk. *nēma,* thread; see **(s)nē-** in App.] **—pro′to·ne′mal** (-nē′məl), pro′to·ne′ma·tal** (-nĕm′ə-təl, -nē′mə-) *adj.*

pro·ton·o·tar·y (prō-tŏn′ə-tĕr′ē, prō′tə-nō′tə-rē) *n.* Variant of *prothonotary.*

proton synchrotron *n.* A synchrotron that accelerates protons to energies of several hundred billion electron volts.

pro·to·path·ic (prō′tə-păth′ĭk) *adj.* Sensing stimuli in a nonspecific manner. Used esp. of certain sensory nerves. [< Med.Gk. *prōtopathēs,* affected first < Gk. *prōtopathein,* to feel first : *prōto-,* proto- + *pathos,* experience, feeling.]

pro·to·plasm (prō′tə-plăz′əm) *n.* The semifluid translucent substance that constitutes the living matter of plant and animal cells, is composed of proteins, fats, and other molecules suspended in water, and includes the nucleus and cytoplasm. **—pro′to·plas′mic** (-plăz′mĭk), pro′to·plas′mal** (-plăz′məl), pro′to·plas·mat′ic** (-plăz-măt′ĭk) *adj.*

pro·to·plast (prō′tə-plăst′) *n.* **1.** *Biology* The living material of a plant or bacterial cell, including the protoplasm and plasma membrane after the cell wall has been removed. **2.** One that is first made or formed; a prototype. [Fr. *protoplaste* < OFr., the first man < LLat. *prōtoplastus* < Gk. *prōtoplastos* : *prōto-,* proto- + *plastos,* formed, molded; see –PLAST.] **—pro′to·plas′tic** *adj.*

pro·to·por·phy·rin (prō′tō-pôr′fə-rĭn) *n.* A metal-free porphyrin, $C_{34}H_{34}N_4O_4$, that combines with iron to form the heme of hemoglobin and other iron-containing proteins.

pro·to·stele (prō′tə-stēl′, prō′tə-stē′lē) *n. Botany* A stele that forms a solid core of xylem encased by phloem.

pro·to·tro·phic (prō′tə-trō′fĭk, -trŏf′ĭk) *adj.* Having the same metabolic capabilities and nutritional requirements as the wild type parent strain: *prototrophic bacteria.* **—pro′to·troph′, pro′to·troph′y** *n.*

pro·to·type (prō′tə-tīp′) *n.* **1.** An original type, form, or instance serving as a basis or standard for stages. **2.** An original, full-scale, and usu. working model of a new product. **3.** An early typical example. **4.** *Biology* A form or species that serves as an original type or example. [Fr. < Gk. *prōtotupon* < neut. of *prōtotupos,* original : *prōto-,* proto- + *tupos,* model.] **—pro′to·typ′al** (-tī′pəl), pro′to·typ′ic** (-tĭp′ĭk), pro′to·typ′i·cal** (-ĭ-kəl) *adj.*

pro·to·xy·lem (prō′tə-zī′ləm) *n.* The first formed xylem that differentiates from the procambium.

pro·to·zo·an (prō′tə-zō′ən) *also* **pro·to·zo·on** (-ŏn′) *n., pl.* **-zo·ans** *or* **-zo·a** (-zō′ə) *also* **-zo·ons** Any of a large group of single-celled, usu. microscopic eukaryotic organisms, such as amoebas. [< NLat. *Prōtozoa,* former subkingdom name : PROTO– + NLat. *-zōa,* pl. of *-zōon,* -zoon.] **—pro′to·zo′an, pro′to·zo′al, pro′to·zo′ic** *adj.*

pro·to·zo·ol·o·gy (prō′tə-zō-ŏl′ə-jē) *n.* The biological study of protozoans. **—pro′to·zo′o·log′i·cal** (-zō′ə-lŏj′ĭ-kəl) *adj.* **—pro′to·zo·ol′o·gist** *n.*

pro·tract (prō-trăkt′, prə-) *tr.v.* **-tract·ed, -tract·ing, -tracts 1.** To draw out or lengthen in time; prolong. **2.** *Mathematics* To draw to scale by means of a scale and protractor; plot. **3.** *Anatomy* To extend or protrude (a body part). [Lat. *prōtrahere, prōtract-* : *prō-,* forth; see PRO–¹ + *trahere,* to drag.] **—pro·tract′ed·ly** (-trăk′tĭd-lē) *adv.* **—pro·tract′ed·ness** *n.* **—pro·trac′tive** *adj.*

pro·trac·tile (prō-trăk′təl, -tīl′, prə-) *also* **pro·tract·i·ble** (-tə-bəl) *adj.* That can be protracted; extensible: *protractile limbs and claws.* **—pro′trac·til′i·ty** (prō′trăk-tĭl′ĭ-tē) *n.*

pro·trac·tion (prō-trăk′shən, prə-) *n.* **1a.** The act of protracting. **b.** The state of being protracted. **2.** *Linguistics* The irregular lengthening of a normally short syllable.

pro·trac·tor (prō-trăk′tər, prə-) *n.* **1.** A semicircular instrument for measuring and constructing angles. **2.** An adjustable pattern used by tailors. **3.** *Anatomy* A muscle that extends a limb or other part.

pro·trude (prō-trōōd′) *v.* **-trud·ed, -trud·ing, -trudes** *—tr.* To push or thrust outward. *—intr.* To jut out; project: *teeth that pro-*

trude. [Lat. *prōtrūdere* : *prō-*, forward; see PRO-[1] + *trūdere*, to thrust.] —**pro•trud′ent** (-trōo′dnt) *adj.*

pro•tru•sile (prō-trōo′səl, -sīl′) also **pro•tru•si•ble** (-sə-bəl) *adj.* Capable of being thrust outward. [Lat. *prōtrūsus*, p. part. of *prōtrūdere*, to protrude; see PROTRUDE + -ILE[1].] —**pro′tru•sil′i•ty** (prō′trōo-sĭl′ĭ-tē) *n.*

pro•tru•sion (prō-trōo′zhən) *n.* **1a.** The act of protruding. **b.** The state of being protruded. **2.** Something that protrudes.

pro•tru•sive (prō-trōo′sĭv, prə-) *adj.* **1.** Tending to protrude; protruding. **2.** Unduly or disagreeably conspicuous; obtrusive. —**pro•tru′sive•ly** *adv.* —**pro•tru′sive•ness** *n.*

pro•tu•ber•ance (prō-tōo′bər-əns, -tyōo′-, prə-) *n.* **1.** Something, such as a bulge, knob, or swelling, that protrudes. **2.** The condition of being protuberant.

pro•tu•ber•an•cy (prō-tōo′bər-ən-sē, -tyōo′-, prə-) *n.,* pl. **-cies** **1.** Protuberance. **2.** Something that is protuberant.

pro•tu•ber•ant (prō-tōo′bər-ənt, -tyōo′-, prə-) *adj.* Swelling outward; bulging. —**pro•tu′ber•ant•ly** *adv.*

pro•tu•ber•ate (prō-tōo′bə-rāt′, -tyōo′-, prə-) *intr.v.* **-at•ed, -at•ing, -ates** To swell or bulge. [LLat. *prōtūberāre, prōtūberāt-* < Lat. *prō-*, forth; see PRO-[1] + Lat. *tūber*, a swelling.] —**pro•tu′ber•a′tion** *n.*

proud (proud) *adj.* **proud•er, proud•est** **1.** Feeling pleasurable satisfaction over an act, possession, quality, or relationship used to measure one's stature or self-worth. **2.** Occasioning or being a reason for pride. **3.** Feeling or showing justifiable self-respect. Filled with or showing excessive self-esteem. **5.** Of great dignity; honored. **6.** Majestic; magnificent. **7.** Spirited. Used of an animal. [ME < OE *prūd* < OFr. *prou, prud*, brave, virtuous, oblique case of *prouz* < VLat. **prōdis* < LLat. *prōde*, advantageous < Lat. *prōdesse*, to be good : *prōd-*, for (var. of *prō-*, on the model of *re-, red-*, again; see PRO-[1]) + *esse*, to be; see **es-** in App.] —**proud′ly** *adv.* —**proud′ness** *n.*

SYNONYMS proud, arrogant, haughty, disdainful, supercilious These adjectives mean characterized by an inflated ego and contempt for what one considers inferior. *Proud* can suggest justifiable self-satisfaction but often implies conceit: *"There is such a thing as a man being too proud to fight"* (Woodrow Wilson). One who is *arrogant* is overbearingly proud and demands excessive power or consideration: *an arrogant professor*. *Haughty* suggests proud superiority, as by reason of high status: *"Her laugh was satirical, and so was the habitual expression of her arched and haughty lip"* (Charlotte Brontë). *Disdainful* emphasizes scorn or contempt: *"Nor* [let] *grandeur hear with a disdainful smile/The short and simple annals of the poor"* (Thomas Gray). *Supercilious* implies haughty disdain and aloofness: *"His mother eyed me in silence with a supercilious air"* (Tobias Smollett).

proud flesh *n.* The swollen flesh surrounding a healing wound. [< its swelling up.]

proud•ful (proud′fəl) *n. Chiefly Southern US* Full of pride; proud.

proud-heart•ed (proud′här′tĭd) *adj.* **1.** Full of pride; proud. **2.** Arrogant; disdainful.

Prou•dhon (prōo-dôN′), **Pierre Joseph** 1809–65. French anarchist who believed that human moral development would ultimately eliminate the need for laws and government.

Proust (prōost), **Marcel** 1871–1922. French writer noted for *Remembrance of Things Past* (1913–27). —**Proust′i•an** *adj.*

Prov. *abbr.* **1.** Provençal **2.** *Bible* Proverbs **3.** province **4.** provost

prove (prōov) *v.* **proved, proved** or **prov•en** (prōo′vən), **prov•ing, proves** —*tr.* **1.** To establish the truth or validity of by presentation of argument or evidence. **2.** *Law* To establish the authenticity of (a will). **3.** To determine the quality of by testing; try out. **4.** *Mathematics* **a.** To demonstrate the validity of (a hypothesis or proposition). **b.** To verify (the result of a calculation). **5.** *Printing* To make a sample impression of (type). **6.** *Archaic* To find out or learn (something) through experience. —*intr.* To be shown to be such; turn out. [ME *proven* < OFr. *prover* < Lat. *probāre*, to test < *probus*, good. See **per-**[1] in App.] —**prov′a•bil′i•ty, prov′a•ble•ness** *n.* —**prov′a•ble** *adj.* —**prov′a•bly** *adv.* —**prov′er** *n.*

USAGE NOTE *Proved* is actually the older form of the past participle of *prove. Proven* is a Scottish variant that was first introduced into wider usage in legal contexts: *The jury ruled that the charges were not proven.* Both forms are now well established in written English as participles: *He has proved* (or *proven*) *his point.* However, when used as an adjective before a noun, *proven* is now the more common word: *a proven talent.*

prov•en (prōo′vən) *adj.* Having been demonstrated or verified without doubt. See Usage Note at **prove.** —**prov′en•ly** *adv.*

prov•e•nance (prŏv′ə-nəns, -näns′) *n.* **1.** Place of origin; derivation. **2.** Proof of authenticity or of past ownership. Used of artworks and antiques. [Fr. < *provenant*, pr. part. of *provenir*, to originate < OFr. < Lat. *provenīre* : *prō-*, forth; see PRO-[1] + *venīre*, to come; see **gʷā-** in App.]

Pro•ven•çal (prō′vän-säl′, prŏv′ən-) *n.* **1.** The Romance language of Provence. **2.** *pl.* **-çals** or **-çaux** (-sō′) A native or inhabitant of Provence. [Fr. < Lat. *provinciālis* < *provincia*, province.] —**Pro′ven•çal′** *adj.*

Marcel Proust
detail from an 1892 portrait
by Jacques-Émile Blanche
(1861–1942)

Pro•vence (prə-väns′, prô-väns′) A historical region and former province of SE France on the Mediterranean Sea; settled c. 600 B.C. by Greeks and part of France since 1486.

prov•en•der (prŏv′ən-dər) *n.* **1.** Dry food, such as hay, used as feed for livestock. **2.** Food or provisions. [ME *provendre* < OFr., alteration of *provende* < VLat. **provenda*, alteration of LLat. *praebenda*. See PREBEND.]

pro•ve•nience (prə-vēn′yəns, -vē′nē-əns) *n.* A source or origin. [Alteration of PROVENANCE.]

pro•ven•tric•u•lus (prō′vĕn-trĭk′yə-ləs) *n.,* pl. **-li** (-lī′) **1.** The division of the stomach in birds that secretes digestive enzymes and passes food from the crop to the gizzard. **2.** A similar digestive chamber in certain insects and worms. [PRO-[2] + Lat. *ventriculus*, stomach, dim. of *venter*, belly.] —**pro•ven•tric′u•lar** (-lər) *adj.*

prov•erb (prŏv′ûrb′) *n.* **1.** A short pithy saying in frequent and widespread use that expresses a basic truth or practical precept. **2. Proverbs** (*used with a sing. verb*) See table at **Bible.** [ME *proverbe* < OFr. < Lat. *proverbium* : *prō-*, forth; see PRO-[1] + *verbum*, word; see **wer-**[1] in App.]

pro•ver•bi•al (prə-vûr′bē-əl) *adj.* **1.** Of the nature of a proverb. **2.** Expressed in a proverb. **3.** Widely referred to, as if the subject of a proverb; famous. —**pro•ver′bi•al•ly** *adv.*

pro•vide (prə-vīd′) *v.* **-vid•ed, -vid•ing, -vides** —*tr.* **1.** To furnish; supply. **2.** To make available; afford. **3.** To set down as a stipulation. **4.** *Archaic* To make ready ahead of time; prepare. —*intr.* **1.** To take measures in preparation. **2.** To supply means of subsistence. **3.** To make a stipulation or condition. [ME *proviten* < Lat. *providēre*, to provide for : *prō-*, forward; see PRO-[1] + *vidēre*, to see; see **weid-** in App.]

pro•vid•ed (prə-vī′dĭd) *conj.* On the condition; if: *will pay the bonus provided the job is completed on time.*

prov•i•dence (prŏv′ĭ-dəns, -dĕns′) *n.* **1.** Care or preparation in advance; foresight. **2.** Prudent management; economy. **3.** The care, guardianship, and control exercised by a deity; divine direction. **4. Providence** God.

Providence The cap. of RI, in the NE part on Narragansett Bay; founded by Roger Williams in 1636. Pop. 173,618.

prov•i•dent (prŏv′ĭ-dənt, -dĕnt′) *adj.* **1.** Providing for future needs or events. **2.** Frugal; economical. [ME < Lat. *providēns, provident-*, pr. part. of *providēre*, to provide for. See PROVIDE.] —**prov′i•dent•ly** *adv.*

prov•i•den•tial (prŏv′ĭ-dĕn′shəl) *adj.* **1.** Of or resulting from divine providence. **2.** Happening as if through divine intervention; opportune. —**prov′i•den′tial•ly** *adv.*

pro•vid•er (prə-vī′dər) *n.* **1.** One who supplies a means of subsistence. **2.** One that makes something available.

pro•vid•ing (prə-vī′dĭng) *conj.* On the condition; provided.

prov•ince (prŏv′ĭns) *n.* **1.** A territory governed as an administrative or political unit of a country or empire. **2.** A division of territory under the jurisdiction of an archbishop. **3. provinces** Areas of a country situated away from the capital or population center. **4.** A comprehensive area of knowledge, activity, or interest. **5.** The range of one's proper duties and functions; scope or jurisdiction. **6.** *Ecology* An area of land, less extensive than a region, having a characteristic plant and animal population. **7.** Any of various lands outside Italy conquered by the Romans and administered as self-contained units. [ME < OFr. < Lat. *provincia.*]

Prov•ince•town (prŏv′ĭns-toun′) A town of SE MA on the tip of Cape Cod. Pilgrims first landed on the site in 1620 before sailing on to Plymouth. Pop. 3,192.

pro•vin•cial (prə-vĭn′shəl) *adj.* **1.** Of or relating to a province. **2.** Of or characteristic of people from the provinces; not fashionable or sophisticated. **3.** Limited in perspective; narrow and self-centered. ❖ *n.* **1.** A native or inhabitant of the provinces. **2.** A person who has provincial ideas or habits. —**pro•vin′cial•ism, pro•vin′ci•al′i•ty** (-shē-ăl′ĭ-tē) *n.* —**pro•vin′cial•ly** *adv.*

pro•vin•cial•ism (prə-vĭn′shə-lĭz′əm) *n.* **1.** A regional word, phrase, pronunciation, or usage. **2.** The condition of being provincial; lack of sophistication or perspective. **3.** The act or an instance of placing the interests of one's province before one's nation.

pro•vin•cial•ize (prə-vĭn′shə-līz′) *tr.v.* **-ized, -iz•ing, -iz•es** To make provincial. —**pro•vin′cial•i•za′tion** (-shə-lĭ-zā′shən) *n.*

prov•ing ground (prōo′vĭng) *n.* A place for testing new devices, weapons, or theories.

pro•vi•rus (prō′vī′rəs, prō-vī′-) *n.,* pl. **-rus•es** The precursor or latent form of a virus that is capable of being integrated into the genetic material of a host cell and replicated with it.

pro•vi•sion (prə-vĭzh′ən) *n.* **1.** The act of supplying or fitting out. **2.** Something provided. **3.** A preparatory action or measure. **4. provisions** A stock of necessary supplies, esp. food. **5.** A stipulation or qualification, esp. a clause in a document or agreement. ❖ *tr.v.* **-sioned, -sion•ing, -sions** To supply with provisions. [ME < OFr., forethought < Lat. *prōvīsiō, prōvīsiōn-* < *prōvīsus*, p. part. of *prōvidēre*, to foresee, provide for. See PROVIDE.] —**pro•vi′sion•er** *n.*

pro•vi•sion•al (prə-vĭzh′ə-nəl) *adj.* **1.** Provided or serving only for the time being; temporary. **2. Provisional** Of or relating to any of the extremist factions of the Irish Republican Army established in 1970. ❖ *n.* **1.** A person hired temporarily for a job, typically before having taken a qualifying examination. **2. Provisional** A member of a Provisional faction of the Irish Republican Army. —**pro•vi′sion•al•ly** *adv.*

pro•vi•so (prə-vī′zō) *n., pl.* **-sos** or **-soes** A clause in a document making a qualification, condition, or restriction. [ME < Med.Lat. *prōvīsō (quod),* provided (that) < Lat. *prōvīsō,* ablative of *prōvīsus,* p. part. of *prōvidēre,* to provide. See PROVIDE.]

pro•vi•so•ry (prə-vī′zə-rē) *adj.* Depending on a proviso; conditional. [Fr. *provisoire* < OFr. < Med.Lat. *prōvīsōrius* < Lat. *prōvīsus,* p. part. of *prōvidēre,* to provide for. See PROVIDE.] —**pro•vi′so•ri•ly** *adv.*

pro•vi•ta•min (prō-vī′tə-mĭn) *n.* A vitamin precursor that is converted to its active form through normal metabolism. Carotene, for example, is a provitamin of vitamin A.

Pro•vo[1] (prō′vō) A city of N-central UT SSE of Salt Lake City; settled by Mormons in 1849. Pop. 105,166.

Pro•vo[2] (prō′vō) *n., pl.* **-vos** A member of a Provisional faction of the Irish Republican Army.

pro•vo•ca•teur (prō-vŏk′ə-tûr′) *n.* An agent provocateur.

prov•o•ca•tion (prŏv′ə-kā′shən) *n.* **1.** The act of provoking or inciting. **2.** Something that provokes. [Ult. < Lat. *prōvocātiō, prōvocātiōn-,* a challenging < *prōvocātus,* p. part. of *prōvocāre,* to challenge. See PROVOKE.]

pro•voc•a•tive (prə-vŏk′ə-tĭv) *adj.* Tending to provoke or stimulate. —**pro•voc′a•tive** *n.* —**pro•voc′a•tive•ly** *adv.* —**pro•voc′a•tive•ness** *n.*

pro•voke (prə-vōk′) *tr.v.* **-voked, -vok•ing, -vokes** **1.** To incite to anger or resentment. **2.** To stir to action or feeling. **3.** To give rise to; bring about deliberately; induce: *provoke a fight.* [ME *provoken* < OFr. *provoquer* < Lat. *prōvocāre,* to challenge : *prō-,* forth; see PRO-[1] + *vocāre,* to call; see **wek**ʷ- in App.]

pro•vok•ing (prə-vō′kĭng) *adj.* Troubling the nerves or peace of mind, as by repeated vexations. —**pro•vok′ing•ly** *adv.*

pro•vo•lo•ne (prō′və-lō′nē) *n.* A hard, usu. smoked Italian cheese. [Ital., augmentative of *provola,* a kind of cheese.]

pro•vost (prō′vōst′, -vəst, prŏv′əst) *n.* **1.** A university administrator of high rank. **2.** The highest official in certain cathedrals or collegiate churches. **3.** The keeper of a prison. **4.** The chief magistrate of certain Scottish cities. [ME < OE *profost* and OFr. *provost,* both < Med.Lat. *prōpositus,* alteration of Lat. *praepositus,* superintendent < p. part. of *praepōnere,* to place over : *prae-, pre-* + *pōnere,* to put; see **apo-** in App.]

pro•vost marshal (prō′vō) *n.* The head of a unit of military police.

prow (prou) *n.* **1.** The forward part of a ship's hull; the bow. **2.** A projecting forward part, such as the front end of a ski. [Fr. *proue* < OFr. < Ital. dialectal *prua* < VLat. **prōda,* alteration of Lat. *prōra* < Gk. *prōira.* See **per**[1] in App.]

prow•ess (prou′ĭs) *n.* **1.** Superior skill or ability. **2.** Superior strength, courage, or daring, esp. in battle. [ME *prowesse* < OFr. *proesse* < *prud, prou,* brave. See PROUD.]

prowl (proul) *v.* **prowled, prowl•ing, prowls** —*tr.* To roam through stealthily, as in search of prey. —*intr.* To rove furtively or with predatory intent. ❖ *n.* The act or an instance of prowling. —*idiom:* **on the prowl** Actively looking for something. [ME *prollen,* to move about.] —**prowl′er** *n.*

prowl car *n.* See **squad car.**

prox. *abbr.* proximo

prox•i•mal (prŏk′sə-məl) *adj.* **1.** Nearest; proximate. **2.** *Anatomy* Nearer to a point of reference such as an origin, a point of attachment, or the midline of the body. [< Lat. *proximus,* nearest. See PROXIMATE.] —**prox′i•mal•ly** *adv.*

prox•i•mate (prŏk′sə-mĭt) *adj.* **1.** Very near or next, as in space, time, or order. See Syns at **close. 2.** Approximate. [Lat. *proximātus,* p. part. of *proximāre,* to come near < *proximus,* nearest. See **per**[1] in App.] —**prox′i•mate•ly** *adv.* —**prox′i•mate•ness** *n.*

prox•im•i•ty (prŏk-sĭm′ĭ-tē) *n.* The state, quality, sense, or fact of being near or next; closeness. See Usage Note at **redundancy.** [ME < OFr. *proximite* < Lat. *proximitās* < *proximus,* nearest. See PROXIMATE.]

proximity fuze *n.* An electronic device for detonating a warhead as it approaches a target, used in antiaircraft shells.

prox•i•mo (prŏk′sə-mō′) *adv.* Archaic Of or in the following month. [Lat. *proximō (mēnse),* in the next (month).]

prox•y (prŏk′sē) *n., pl.* **-ies** **1.** A person authorized to act for another; an agent or substitute. **2.** The authority to act for another. **3.** The written authorization to act in place of another. [ME *procy,* contraction of earlier *procuracie,* annual payment to a prelate < AN *procuracie* < Med.Lat. *prōcūrātia,* alteration of Lat. *prōcūrātiō* < *prōcūrātus,* p. part. of *prōcūrāre,* to take care of. See PROCURE.]

Pro•zac (prō′zăk′) A trademark used for fluoxetine hydrochloride.

prude (prood) *n.* One who is excessively concerned with being or appearing proper, modest, or righteous. [Fr., short for *prude femme,* virtuous woman : OFr. *prude,* fem. of *prud,* virtuous; see PROUD + Fr. *femme,* woman (< Lat. *fēmina.*)]

WORD HISTORY Being called a prude is rarely considered a compliment, but if we dig into the history of the word *prude,* we find that it has a noble past. The change for the worse took place in French. French *prude* first had a good sense, "wise woman," but apparently a woman could be too wise or, in the eyes of some, too observant of decorum and propriety. Thus *prude* took on the sense in French that was brought into English along with the word, first recorded in 1704. The French word *prude* was a shortened form of *prude femme* (earlier in Old French *prode femme*), a word modeled on earlier *preudomme,* "a man of experience and integrity." Despite this history filled with wisdom and integrity, *prude* has become a term of reproach.

pru•dence (prood′ns) *n.* **1.** The state, quality, or fact of being prudent. **2.** Careful management; economy.

SYNONYMS prudence, discretion, foresight, forethought, circumspection These nouns refer to the exercise of good judgment, common sense, and even caution, especially in the conduct of practical matters. *Prudence* is the most comprehensive: "She had been forced into prudence in her youth, she learned romance as she grew older" (Jane Austen). *Discretion* suggests wise self-restraint, as in resisting a rash impulse: "The better part of valor is discretion" (Shakespeare). *Foresight* implies the ability to foresee and make provision for what may happen: had the foresight to plan. *Forethought* suggests advance consideration of future eventualities: The empty refrigerator illustrated a lack of forethought. *Circumspection* implies discretion, as out of concern for moral or social repercussions: "The necessity of the times . . . calls for our utmost circumspection" (Samuel Adams).

pru•dent (prood′nt) *adj.* **1.** Wise in handling practical matters; exercising good judgment or common sense. **2.** Careful in regard to one's own interests; provident. **3.** Careful about one's conduct; circumspect. [ME < OFr. < Lat. *prūdēns, prūdent-,* contraction of *prōvidēns,* pr. part. of *prōvidēre,* to provide. See PROVIDE.] —**pru′dent•ly** *adv.*

pru•den•tial (proo-dĕn′shəl) *adj.* **1.** Arising from or characterized by prudence. **2.** Exercising prudence, good judgment, or common sense. —**pru•den′tial•ly** *adv.*

prud•er•y (prood′ə-rē) *n., pl.* **-ies** **1.** The state or quality of being prudish. **2.** An instance of prudish behavior or talk. [Fr. *pruderie* < *prude,* prude. See PRUDE.]

Prud•hoe Bay (prood′hō, prŭd′-) An inlet of the Arctic Ocean on the N coast of AK E of the Colville R. delta.

prud•ish (prood′ĭsh) *adj.* Marked by or having the characteristics of a prude; priggish. —**prud′ish•ly** *adv.* —**prud′ish•ness** *n.*

pru•i•nose (proo′ə-nōs′) *adj. Botany* Having a white powdery covering or bloom. [Lat. *pruīnōsus,* frosty < *pruīna,* hoarfrost.]

prune[1] (proon) *n.* **1a.** The partially dried fruit of any of several varieties of the common plum, *Prunus domestica.* **b.** Any kind of plum that can be dried without spoiling. **2.** *Slang* An ill-tempered, stupid, or incompetent person. ❖ *intr.v.* **pruned, prun•ing, prunes** *Slang* To make a facial expression exhibiting ill temper or disgust. [ME < OFr. < VLat. **prūna* < Lat. *prūnum,* plum.]

prune[2] (proon) *v.* **pruned, prun•ing, prunes** —*tr.* **1.** To cut off or remove dead or living parts or branches of (a plant, for example) to improve shape or growth. **2.** To remove or cut out as superfluous. **3.** To reduce: *prune a budget.* —*intr.* To remove what is superfluous or undesirable. [ME *prouinen* < OFr. *proignier,* perh. < VLat. **prōretundiāre* : Lat. *prō-,* in front; see PRO-[1] + Lat. *rotundus,* round (< *rota,* wheel).] —**prun′er** *n.*

pru•nel•la (proo-nĕl′ə) also **pru•nelle** (proo-nĕl′) *n.* A heavy fabric of worsted twill, used chiefly for shoe uppers, clerical robes, and academic gowns. [Alteration of Fr. *prunelle,* sloe < OFr., dim. of *prune,* prune. See PRUNE[1].]

prun•ing hook (proo′nĭng) *n.* A long pole with a curved saw blade and usu. a clipping mechanism on one end, used esp. for pruning small trees.

pru•ri•ent (proor′ē-ənt) *adj.* **1.** Inordinately interested in matters of sex; lascivious. **2a.** Characterized by an inordinate interest in sex: *prurient thoughts.* **b.** Arousing or appealing to an inordinate interest in sex. [Lat. *prūriēns, prūrient-,* pr. part. of *prūrīre,* to yearn for, itch.] —**pru′ri•ence, pru′ri•en•cy** *n.* —**pru′ri•ent•ly** *adv.*

pru•ri•go (proo-rī′gō) *n.* A chronic skin disease having various causes, marked by the eruption of pale papules that itch severely. [Lat. *prūrīgō,* an itching < *prūrīre,* to itch.] —**pru•rig′i•nous** (-rĭj′ə-nəs) *adj.*

pru•ri•tus (proo-rī′təs) *n.* Severe itching, often of undamaged skin. [Lat. *prūrītus* < p. part. of *prūrīre,* to itch.] —**pru•rit′ic** (-rĭt′ĭk) *adj.*

Prus•sia (prŭsh′ə) A historical region and former kingdom of N-central Europe including present-day N Germany and Poland. The kingdom of Prussia was proclaimed in 1701. It became a republic in 1918 and was formally abolished after World War II.

Prus•sian (prŭsh′ən) *adj.* **1.** Of or relating to Prussia or its Baltic or German inhabitants. **2.** Suggestive of or resembling the Junkers and the military class of Prussia. ❖ *n.* **1.** Any of the western Balts inhabiting the region between the Vistula and Neman rivers in ancient times. **2.** A Baltic inhabitant of Prussia. **3.** A German inhabitant of Prussia.

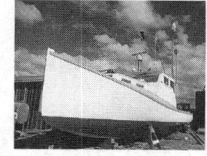

prow

ă	pat	oi	boy
ā	pay	ou	out
âr	care	o͝o	took
ä	father	o͞o	boot
ĕ	pet	ŭ	cut
ē	be	ûr	urge
ĭ	pit	th	thin
ī	pie	*th*	this
îr	pier	hw	which
ŏ	pot	zh	vision
ō	toe	ə	about,
ô	paw		item

Stress marks:
′ (primary);
′ (secondary); as in
lexicon (lĕk′sĭ-kŏn′)

Prussian blue *n.* **1.** An insoluble dark blue pigment and dye, ferric ferrocyanide or one of its modifications. **2.** See **iron blue. 3.** A moderate to strong blue or deep greenish blue. [< its being discovered in Berlin (then in Prussia).]

prus·si·ate (prŭs′ē-āt′) *n.* **1.** A ferrocyanide or ferricyanide. **2.** A salt of hydrocyanic acid; cyanide. [PRUSSI(C ACID) + –ATE².]

prus·sic acid (prŭs′ĭk) *n.* See **hydrocyanic acid.** [So called because it was first obtained from Prussian blue.]

Prut (prō̄ot) A river rising in SW Ukraine and flowing c. 885 km (550 mi) to the Danube R.

pru·tah (prō̄o-tä′) *n., pl.* **-toth** or **-tot** (-tōt′) A coin formerly used in Israel, equal to one thousandth of a pound. [Mod.Heb. *pruta* < Mishnaic Heb. *pərûṭâ,* a small coin, fem. passive part. of *pāraṭ,* to break.]

pry¹ (prī) *intr.v.* **pried** (prīd), **pry·ing, pries** (prīz) To look or inquire closely, curiously, or impertinently: *always prying into the affairs of others.* ❖ *n., pl.* **pries** (prīz) **1.** The act of prying. **2.** An excessively inquisitive person. [ME *prien.*]

pry² (prī) *tr.v.* **pried** (prīd), **pry·ing, pries** (prīz) **1.** To raise, move, or force open with a lever. **2.** To obtain with effort or difficulty. ❖ *n., pl.* **pries** (prīz) Something, such as a crowbar, that is used to apply leverage. [Alteration of PRIZE³.]

pry·er (prī′ər) *n.* Variant of **prier.**

pry·ing (prī′ĭng) *adj.* Insistently or impertinently curious or inquisitive. —**pry′ing·ly** *adv.*

ps *abbr.* picosecond

PS *abbr.* **1.** police sergeant **2.** postscript **3.** public school

Ps. *abbr. Bible* **1.** Psalm **2.** Psalms

PSA *abbr.* **1.** prostate-specific antigen **2.** public service announcement

psalm (säm) *n.* **1.** A sacred song; a hymn. **2. Psalms** (*used with a sing. verb*) See table at **Bible.** ❖ *tr.v.* **psalmed, psalm·ing, psalms** To sing of or celebrate in psalms. [ME < OE < Lat. *psalmus* < Gk. *psalmos* < *psallein,* to play the harp.]

psalm·ist (sä′mĭst) *n.* A writer or composer of psalms.

psalm·o·dy (sä′mə-dē, säl′mə-) *n., pl.* **-dies 1.** The act or practice of singing psalms in divine worship. **2.** The composition or arranging of psalms for singing. **3.** A collection of psalms. [ME *psalmodie* < LLat. *psalmōdia* < Gk. *psalmōidiā,* singing to the harp : *psalmos,* psalm; see PSALM + *aoidē, ōidē,* song; see ODE.] —**psalm′o·dist** *n.*

Psal·ter also **psal·ter** (sôl′tər) *n.* A book containing the Book of Psalms or a particular version of, musical setting for, or selection from it. [ME < OE *psaltere* and OFr. *psaultier,* both < LLat. *psaltērium* < Lat., psaltery < Gk. *psaltērion.* See PSALTERY.]

psal·te·ri·um (sôl-tîr′ē-əm) *n., pl.* **-te·ri·a** (-tîr′ē-ə) The omasum. [LLat. *psaltērium,* psalter (so called because when slit open its folds fall apart like the leaves of a book). See PSALTER.] —**psal·te′ri·al** *adj.*

psal·ter·y (sôl′tə-rē) also **psal·try** (sôl′trē) *n., pl.* **-ter·ies** also **-tries** An ancient stringed instrument played by plucking the strings with the fingers or a plectrum. [ME *psalterie* < OFr. < Lat. *psaltērium* < Gk. *psaltērion* < *psallein,* to play the harp.]

p's and q's *pl.n.* **1.** Socially correct behavior; manners. **2.** The way one acts; conduct: *was told to watch his p's and q's.*

PSAT/NMSQT A trademark used for a preliminary standardized college entrance examination.

psec. *abbr.* picosecond

pse·phol·o·gy (sē-fŏl′ə-jē) *n.* The study of political elections. [Gk. *psēphos,* pebble, ballot + –LOGY.] —**pse′pho·log′i·cal** (sē′fə-lŏj′ĭ-kəl) *adj.* —**pse·phol′o·gist** *n.*

pseud·e·pig·ra·pha (sō̄o′dĭ-pĭg′rə-fə) *pl.n.* **1.** Spurious writings, esp. writings that are falsely attributed to biblical characters or times. **2.** A body of texts written between 200 B.C. and A.D. 200 and spuriously ascribed to various prophets and kings of the Hebrew Scriptures. [Gk. < neut. pl. of *pseudepigraphos,* falsely ascribed : *pseudēs,* false; see PSEUDO– + *epigraphein,* to inscribe (*epi-, epi-* + *graphein,* to write; see gerbh- in App.).] —**pseud·e·pig′ra·phal** (-rə-fəl), **pseud′ep·i·graph′ic** (sō̄o′dĕp-ĭ-grăf′ĭk), **pseud′ep·i·graph′i·cal** (-ĭ-kəl), **pseud′e·pig′ra·phous** (-rə-fəs) *adj.*

pseu·do (sō̄o′dō) *adj.* False or counterfeit; fake. [< PSEUDO–.]

pseudo– or **pseud–** *pref.* **1.** False; deceptive; sham: *pseudoscience.* **2.** Apparently similar: *pseudocoel.* [Gk. < *pseudēs,* false < *pseudein,* to lie.]

pseu·do·carp (sō̄o′də-kärp′) *n.* See **accessory fruit.** —**pseu′do·car′pous** *adj.*

pseu·do·coel (sō̄o′də-sēl′) also **pseu·do·coe·lom** (sō̄o′də-sē′ləm) *n.* An internal body cavity of some primitive invertebrates, similar to a coelom but lacking a mesodermal lining.

pseu·do·coe·lo·mate (sō̄o′dō-sē′lə-māt′) *adj.* Having a pseudocoel. ❖ *n.* An animal having a pseudocoel.

pseu·do·cy·e·sis (sō̄o′dō-sī-ē′sĭs) *n.* See **false pregnancy.** [PSEUDO– + NLat. *cyēsis,* pregnancy (< Gk. *kuēsis* < *kuein,* to swell).]

pseu·do·force or **pseudo force** (sō̄o′dō-fôrs′, -fōrs&′) *n.* The apparent force needed by an observer in a noninertial frame to make Newton's laws of motion hold true. The centrifugal force is a pseudo-force.

pseu·do·mo·nad (sō̄o′də-mō′năd′) *n.* Any of various gram-negative rod-shaped bacteria of the genus *Pseudomonas.* [< NLat.

Pseudomonas, genus name : PSEUDO– + Lat. *monas, monad-,* unit (< Gk. < *monos,* single; see **men-²** in App.).]

pseu·do·morph (sō̄o′də-môrf′) *n.* **1.** A false, deceptive, or irregular form. **2.** A mineral that has the crystalline form of another mineral rather than the form normally characteristic of its own composition. —**pseu′do·mor′phic, pseu′do·mor′phous** *adj.* —**pseu′do·mor′phism** *n.*

pseu·do·nym (sō̄od′n-ĭm′) *n.* A fictitious name, esp. a pen name. [Fr. *pseudonyme,* neut. of *pseudonumos,* falsely named : *pseudēs,* false; see PSEUDO– + *onuma,* name; see **nŏ-men-** in App.] —**pseu′do·nym′i·ty** *n.* —**pseu·don′y·mous** (sō̄o-dŏn′ə-məs) *adj.* —**pseu·don′y·mous·ly** *adv.*

pseu·do·pod (sō̄o′də-pŏd′) *n.* A temporary projection of the cytoplasm of a cell, esp. an amoeba, that serves in locomotion and phagocytosis. —**pseu·dop′o·dal** (-dŏp′ə-dl), **pseu′do·po′di·al** (-pō′dē-əl) *adj.*

pseu·do·po·di·um (sō̄o′də-pō′dē-əm) *n., pl.* **-po·di·a** (-pō′dē-ə) A pseudopod.

pseu·do·preg·nan·cy (sō̄o′dō-prĕg′nən-sē) *n., pl.* **-cies** See **false pregnancy.** —**pseu′do·preg′nant** *adj.*

pseu·do·ran·dom (sō̄o′dō-răn′dəm) *adj.* Of, relating to, or being random numbers generated by a definite nonrandom computational process.

pseu·do·sci·ence (sō̄o′dō-sī′əns) *n.* A theory, methodology, or practice purported to be scientific. —**pseu′do·sci′en·tif′ic** (-ən-tĭf′ĭk) *adj.* —**pseu′do·sci′en·tist** *n.*

psf *abbr.* pounds per square foot

pshaw (shô) *interj.* Used to indicate impatience, irritation, disapproval, or disbelief.

psi¹ (sī, psī, psē) *n.* The 23rd letter of the Greek alphabet. [ME < L.Gk. < Gk. *psei.*]

psi² (sī) *n.* Parapsychological phenomena or abilities considered as a group. [Shortening and alteration of PARAPSYCHOLOGICAL.]

psi³ *abbr.* pounds per square inch

psil·o·cin (sīl′ə-sĭn, sĭl′ə-) *n.* A hallucinogenic compound, $C_{12}H_{16}N_2O$, related to psilocybin. [PSILOC(YBIN) + –IN.]

psil·o·cy·bin (sīl′ə-sī′bĭn, sĭl′ə-) *n.* A hallucinogenic compound, $C_{12}H_{17}N_2O_4P$, obtained from the mushroom *Psilocybe mexicana.* [NLat. *Psilocybē,* genus name (Gk. *psīlos,* bare + Gk. *kubē,* head) + –IN.]

psi·lom·e·lane (sī-lŏm′ə-lān′) *n.* A mixture of black manganese oxide minerals. [Gk. *psīlos,* bare + Gk. *melās, melan-,* black.]

psi particle *n.* See **J/psi particle.**

psit·ta·cine (sĭt′ə-sīn′) *adj.* **1.** Relating to, resembling, or characteristic of parrots. **2.** Of or belonging to the family Psittacidae, which includes the parrots, macaws, and parakeets. [Lat. *psittacīnus* < *psittacus,* parrot < Gk. *psittakos.*]

psit·ta·co·sis (sĭt′ə-kō′sĭs) *n.* An infectious disease of parrots and related birds caused by the bacterium *Chlamydia psittaci* and communicable to humans, in whom it produces high fever, severe headache, and symptoms similar to pneumonia. [NLat. *psittacōsis* : Lat. *psittacus,* parrot (< Gk. *psittakos*) + –OSIS.] —**psit′ta·cot′ic** (-kŏt′ĭk, -kō′tĭk) *adj.*

pso·as (sō′əs) *n.* Either of two muscles of the loin that rotate the hip joint and flex the spine. [NLat. < Gk. *psoa.*]

pso·cid (sō′sĭd, sŏs′ĭd) *n.* Any of various small, soft-bodied, sometimes winged insects of the order Psocoptera, which includes the booklice. [< NLat. *Psōcidae,* family name < *Psŏcus,* type genus < Gk. *psōkhos,* dust.]

pso·ri·a·sis (sə-rī′ə-sĭs) *n.* A noncontagious inflammatory skin disease characterized by recurring scaly reddish patches. [Gk. *psōriāsis,* itch, mange < *psōriān,* to have the itch < *psōrā,* itch.] —**pso′ri·at′ic** (sôr′ē-ăt′ĭk, sōr′-) *adj.*

psst (pst) *interj.* Used to capture someone's attention inconspicuously. [Imit.]

PST *abbr.* Pacific Standard Time

psych also **psyche** (sīk) *Informal v.* **psyched, psych·ing, psyches** —*tr.* **1a.** To put into the right psychological frame of mind: *psyched up the team before the game.* **b.** To excite emotionally. **2.** To undermine the confidence of by psychological means; intimidate. **3a.** To analyze, solve, or comprehend: *psyched out the test.* **b.** To anticipate or guess the intentions of. **4.** To psychoanalyze. —*intr.* To become confused or mentally deranged. ❖ *n.* **psych** Psychology.

psych– *pref.* Variant of **psycho-.**

psy·chas·the·ni·a (sī′kas-thē′nē-ə) *n.* A psychological disorder characterized by phobias, obsessions, compulsions, or excessive anxiety. Not in scientific use.

psy·che (sī′kē) *n.* **1.** The spirit or soul. **2.** *Psychology* The mind functioning as the center of thought, emotion, and behavior. [Lat. *psȳchē* < Gk. *psūkhē,* soul.]

Psy·che (sī′kē) *n. Greek Mythology* A young woman who loved and was loved by Eros and who became the personification of the soul.

psy·che·del·i·a (sī′kĭ-dē′lē-ə, -dĕl′yə) *n.* The subculture associated with psychedelic drugs.

psy·che·del·ic (sī′kĭ-dĕl′ĭk) *adj.* Of, characterized by, or generating hallucinations, distortions of perception, altered states of awareness, and occasionally states resembling psychosis. ❖ *n.* A drug, such as LSD or mescaline, that produces such effects. [PSY-

CHE + Gk. *dēloun*, to make visible (< *dēlos*, clear, visible; see **dyeu-** in App.) + **-IC.**] —**psy′che·del′i·cal·ly** *adv.*

psychiatric hospital *n.* A hospital for the care and treatment of people affected with acute or chronic mental illness.

psy·chi·a·try (sĭ-kī′ə-trē, sī-) *n.* The branch of medicine that deals with mental and emotional disorders. —**psy·chi·at′ric** (sī′kē-ăt′rĭk), **psy′chi·at′ri·cal** (-rĭ-kəl) *adj.* —**psy′chi·at′ri·cal·ly** *adv.* —**psy·chi′a·trist** (-trĭst) *n.*

psy·chic (sī′kĭk) *n.* **1.** A person apparently responsive to psychic forces. **2.** See **medium** 6. ❖ *adj.* also **psy·chi·cal** (-kĭ-kəl) **1.** Of, relating to, affecting, or influenced by the human mind or psyche; mental. **2a.** Capable of extraordinary mental processes, such as mental telepathy. **b.** Of or relating to such mental processes. [< Gk. *psūkhikos*, of the soul < *psūkhē*, soul.] —**psy′chi·cal·ly** *adv.*

psy·cho (sī′kō) *Slang n.*, *pl.* **-chos** A psychopath. ❖ *adj.* Crazy; insane.

psycho– or **psych–** *pref.* **1a.** Mind; mental: *psychogenic.* **b.** Mental activities or processes: *psychomotor.* **2.** Psychology; psychological: *psychohistory.* [Gk. *psūkho-*, soul, life < *psūkhē*.]

psy·cho·a·cous·tics (sī′kō-ə-koo′stĭks) *n.* (*used with a sing. verb*) The scientific study of the perception of sound. —**psy′cho·a·cous′tic, psy′cho·a·cous′ti·cal** *adj.*

psy·cho·ac·tive (sī′kō-ăk′tĭv) *adj.* Affecting the mind or mental processes. Used of a drug.

psy·cho·a·nal·y·sis (sī′kō-ə-năl′ĭ-sĭs) *n.*, *pl.* **-ses** (-sēz′) **1a.** The method of psychological therapy originated by Sigmund Freud in which free association, dream interpretation, and analysis of resistance and transference are used to explore repressed or unconscious impulses, anxieties, and internal conflicts. **b.** The theory of personality developed by Freud that focuses on repression and unconscious forces and includes the concepts of infantile sexuality and division of the psyche into the id, ego, and superego. **2.** Psychotherapy incorporating this method and theory. —**psy′cho·an′a·lyst** (-ăn′ə-lĭst) *n.* —**psy′cho·an′a·lyt′ic** (-ăn′ə-lĭt′ĭk), **psy′cho·an′a·lyt′i·cal** (-ĭ-kəl) *adj.*

psy·cho·an·a·lyze (sī′kō-ăn′ə-līz′) *tr.v.* **-lyzed, -lyz·ing, -lyz·es** To analyze and treat by psychoanalysis.

psy·cho·bab·ble (sī′kō-băb′əl) *n.* Language characterized by the use of jargon from psychiatry and psychotherapy. [Coined by Richard Dean Rosen (born 1949), American writer.] —**psy′cho·bab′bler** *n.*

psy·cho·bi·og·ra·phy (sī′kō-bī-ŏg′rə-fē) *n.*, *pl.* **-phies** A biography that analyzes the psychological character of its subject. —**psy′cho·bi·og′ra·pher** *n.*

psy·cho·bi·ol·o·gy (sī′kō-bī-ŏl′ə-jē) *n.* **1.** The branch of biology dealing with the application of biological methods to the study of cognitive processes. **2.** The school of psychology that emphasizes the interrelationship between psychological, biological, social, and cultural factors. —**psy′cho·bi′o·log′ic** (-bī′ə-lŏj′ĭk), **psy′cho·bi′o·log′i·cal** (-ĭ-kəl) *adj.* —**psy′cho·bi·ol′o·gist** *n.*

psy·cho·chem·i·cal (sī′kō-kĕm′ĭ-kəl) *n.* A psychoactive drug or substance. —**psy′cho·chem′i·cal** *adj.*

psy·cho·dra·ma (sī′kə-drä′mə, -drăm′ə) *n.* **1.** A psychotherapeutic technique in which people are assigned roles to be played spontaneously within a dramatic context devised by a therapist. **2.** A dramatization in which this technique is employed. **3.** An event, social interaction, or narrative that manifests psychological forces or problems. —**psy′cho·dra·mat′ic** (-drə-măt′ĭk) *adj.*

psy·cho·dy·nam·ics (sī′kō-dī-năm′ĭks, -dī-) *n.* **1.** (*used with a sing. or pl. verb*) The interaction of various conscious and unconscious mental or emotional processes, esp. as they influence personality and behavior. **2.** (*used with a sing. verb*) The study of personality and behavior in terms of such processes. —**psy′cho·dy·nam′ic** *adj.*

psy·cho·gen·e·sis (sī′kə-jĕn′ĭ-sĭs) *n.* **1.** The origin and development of psychological processes, personality, or behavior. **2.** Development of a medical disorder or illness resulting from psychological rather than physiological factors. —**psy′cho·ge·net′ic** (-jə-nĕt′ĭk), **psy′cho·ge·net′i·cal·ly** *adv.*

psy·cho·gen·ic (sī′kə-jĕn′ĭk) *adj.* Originating in the mind or in mental or emotional processes. Used of certain disorders. —**psy′cho·gen′i·cal·ly** *adv.*

psy·cho·graph (sī′kə-grăf′) *n.* A graphic representation or chart of personality traits. —**psy′cho·graph′ic** *adj.*

psy·cho·his·to·ry (sī′kō-hĭs′tə-rē) *n.*, *pl.* **-ries** A psychological or psychoanalytic interpretation or study of historical events or persons. —**psy′cho·his·tor′i·an** (-hĭ-stôr′ē-ən, -stôr′-) *n.*

psy·cho·ki·ne·sis (sī′kō-kə-nē′sĭs, -kī-) *n.*, *pl.* **-ses** (-sēz) The production or control of motion, esp. in inanimate objects, purportedly by psychic powers. —**psy′cho·ki·net′ic** (-kə-nĕt′ĭk, -kī-) *adj.* —**psy′cho·ki·net′i·cal·ly** *adv.*

psy·cho·lin·guis·tics (sī′kō-lĭng-gwĭs′tĭks) *n.* (*used with a sing. verb*) The study of the influence of psychological factors on the development, use, and interpretation of language. —**psy′cho·lin′guist** *n.* —**psy′cho·lin·guis′tic** *adj.*

psy·cho·log·i·cal (sī′kə-lŏj′ĭ-kəl) also **psy·cho·log·ic** (-lŏj′ĭk) *adj.* **1.** Of or relating to psychology. **2.** Of, relating to, or arising from the mind or emotions. **3.** Influencing or intended to influence the mind or emotions. **4.** Of or being any of certain primary colors whose mixture may be subjectively conceived as producing other colors. —**psy′cho·log′i·cal·ly** *adv.*

psychological moment *n.* The time at which the mental state of a person is most likely to produce a desired response.

psychological warfare *n.* The use of various techniques, such as propaganda and terror, to lower an enemy's morale.

psy·chol·o·gist (sī-kŏl′ə-jĭst) *n.* A person trained and educated to perform psychological research, testing, and therapy.

psy·chol·o·gize (sī-kŏl′ə-jīz′) *v.* **-gized, -giz·ing, -giz·es** —*tr.* To explain (behavior) in psychological terms. —*intr.* To investigate, reason, or speculate in psychological terms.

psy·chol·o·gy (sī-kŏl′ə-jē) *n.*, *pl.* **-gies 1.** The science that deals with mental processes and behavior. **2.** The emotional and behavioral characteristics of an individual, group, or activity. **3.** Subtle tactical action or argument used to manipulate or influence another. **4.** *Philosophy* The branch of metaphysics that studies the soul, the mind, and the relationship of life and mind to the functions of the body.

psy·cho·met·rics (sī′kə-mĕt′rĭks) *n.* (*used with a sing. verb*) The branch of psychology that deals with the design, administration, and interpretation of quantitative tests for the measurement of psychological variables such as intelligence, aptitude, and personality traits. —**psy′cho·met′ric, psy′cho·met′ri·cal** *adj.* —**psy′chom·e·tri′cian** (sī-kŏm′ĭ-trĭsh′ən), **psy·chom′e·trist** (sī-kŏm′ĭ-trĭst) *n.*

psy·chom·e·try (sī-kŏm′ĭ-trē) *n.* **1.** See **psychometrics. 2.** The ability or art of divining information about people or events associated with an object solely by touching or being near to it.

psy·cho·mo·tor (sī′kō-mō′tər) *adj.* Of or relating to movement or muscular activity associated with mental processes.

psy·cho·neu·ro·im·mu·nol·o·gy (sī′kō-noor′ō-ĭm′yə-nŏl′ə-jē, -nyoor′-) *n.* The study of the interaction of behavioral, neural, and endocrine factors and the functioning of the immune system.

psy·cho·neu·ro·sis (sī′kō-noo-rō′sĭs, -nyoo-) *n.*, *pl.* **-ses** (-sēz) See **neurosis.** —**psy′cho·neu·rot′ic** (-rŏt′ĭk) *adj. & n.*

psy·cho·path (sī′kə-păth′) *n.* A person with an antisocial personality disorder, manifested in aggressive, perverted, or criminal behavior without empathy or remorse. [Back-formation < PSYCHOPATHIC.]

psy·cho·path·ic (sī′kə-păth′ĭk) *adj.* **1.** Of, relating to, or characterized by psychopathy. **2.** Relating to or affected with an antisocial personality disorder. —**psy′cho·path′i·cal·ly** *adv.*

psy·cho·pa·thol·o·gy (sī′kō-pə-thŏl′ə-jē, -pă-) *n.* **1.** The study of the origin, development, and manifestations of mental or behavioral disorders. **2.** The manifestation of a mental or behavioral disorder. —**psy′cho·path′o·log′i·cal** (-păth′ə-lŏj′ĭ-kəl), **psy′cho·path′o·log′ic** (-lŏj′ĭk) *adj.* —**psy′cho·pa·thol′o·gist** *n.*

psy·chop·a·thy (sī-kŏp′ə-thē) *n.* Mental disorder, esp. when manifested by antisocial behavior.

psy·cho·phar·ma·col·o·gy (sī′kō-fär′mə-kŏl′ə-jē) *n.* The branch of pharmacology that deals with the study of the actions and effects of psychoactive drugs. —**psy′cho·phar′ma·co·log′ic** (-kə-lŏj′ĭk), **psy′cho·phar′ma·co·log′i·cal** (-ĭ-kəl) *adj.* —**psy′cho·phar′ma·col′o·gist** *n.*

psy·cho·phys·ics (sī′kō-fĭz′ĭks) *n.* (*used with a sing. verb*) The branch of psychology that deals with the relationships between physical stimuli and sensory response. —**psy′cho·phys′i·cal** *adj.*

psy·cho·phys·i·ol·o·gy (sī′kō-fĭz′ē-ŏl′ə-jē) *n.* The branch of physiology dealing with the relationship between physiological processes and thoughts, emotions, and behavior. —**psy′cho·phys′i·o·log′ic** (-ə-lŏj′ĭk), **psy′cho·phys′i·o·log′i·cal** (-ĭ-kəl) *adj.*

psy·cho·sex·u·al (sī′kō-sĕk′shoo-əl) *adj.* Of or relating to the mental and emotional aspects of sexuality. —**psy′cho·sex′u·al′i·ty** (-ăl′ĭ-tē) *n.* —**psy′cho·sex′u·al·ly** *adv.*

psy·cho·sis (sī-kō′sĭs) *n.*, *pl.* **-ses** (-sēz) A severe mental disorder, with or without organic damage, characterized by derangement of personality and loss of contact with reality.

psy·cho·so·cial (sī′kō-sō′shəl) *adj.* Involving aspects of social and psychological behavior. —**psy′cho·so′cial·ly** *adv.*

psy·cho·so·mat·ic (sī′kō-sō-măt′ĭk) *adj.* **1.** Of or relating to a disorder having physical symptoms but originating from mental or emotional causes. **2.** Relating to or concerned with the influence of the mind on the body, and the body on the mind, esp. with respect to disease. —**psy′cho·so·mat′i·cal·ly** *adv.*

psy·cho·sur·ger·y (sī′kō-sûr′jə-rē) *n.*, *pl.* **-ies** Brain surgery used to treat severe, intractable mental or behavioral disorders. —**psy′cho·sur′geon** (-sûr′jən) *n.* —**psy′cho·sur′gi·cal** (-jĭ-kəl) *adj.*

psy·cho·ther·a·peu·tics (sī′kō-thĕr′ə-pyoo′tĭks) *n.* (*used with a sing. verb*) Psychotherapy.

psy·cho·ther·a·py (sī′kō-thĕr′ə-pē) *n.*, *pl.* **-pies** The treatment of mental and emotional disorders with psychological techniques that encourage communication of and insight into conflicts and problems, intended to relieve symptoms and effect changes in behavior. —**psy′cho·ther′a·peu′tic** (-pyoo′tĭk) *adj.* —**psy′cho·ther′a·pist** *n.*

ă	pat	oi	boy
ā	pay	ou	out
âr	care	ŏŏ	took
ä	father	ōō	boot
ĕ	pet	ŭ	cut
ē	be	ûr	urge
ĭ	pit	th	thin
ī	pie	*th*	this
îr	pier	hw	which
ŏ	pot	zh	vision
ō	toe	ə	about,
ô	paw		item

Stress marks:
′ (primary);
′ (secondary), as in
lexicon (lĕk′sĭ-kŏn′)

psy·chot·ic (sī-kŏt′ĭk) *adj.* Of, relating to, or affected by psychosis. ❖ *n.* A person affected by psychosis.

psy·chot·o·mi·met·ic (sī-kŏt′ō-mə-mĕt′ĭk, -mī-) *adj.* Tending to induce hallucinations, delusions, or other symptoms of a psychosis. Used of a drug. [Alteration of *psychosomimetic* : PSYCHOS(IS) + MIMETIC.] —**psy·chot′o·mi·met′ic** *n.*

psy·cho·tron·ic (sī′kə-trŏn′ĭk) *adj.* Of or relating to a genre of film characterized by bizarre or shocking story lines, often shot on a low budget. [Prob. PSYCHO- + (ELEC)TRONIC.]

psy·cho·tro·pic (sī′kə-trō′pĭk, -trŏp′ĭk) *adj.* Having an altering effect on perception or behavior. Used esp. of a drug. ❖ *n.* A psychotropic drug or other agent.

psychro– *pref.* Cold: *psychrophilic*. [Gk. *psūkhro-* < *psūkhros*, cold.]

psy·chrom·e·ter (sī-krŏm′ĭ-tər) *n.* An instrument that uses the difference in readings between wet-bulb and dry-bulb thermometers to measure the relative humidity of air.

psy·chro·phil·ic (sī′krō-fĭl′ĭk) *adj.* Thriving at relatively low temperatures. Used of certain bacteria. —**psy′chro·phile′** (-fīl′) *n.*

psyl·la (sĭl′ə) also **psyl·lid** (sĭl′ĭd) *n.* Any of various jumping plant lice of the family Psyllidae, esp. of the genus *Psylla*. [NLat. *Psylla*, type genus < Gk. *psulla*, flea.]

psyl·li·um (sĭl′ē-əm) *n.* **1.** An annual Eurasian plant (*Plantago afra*) having opposite leaves and small flowers borne in dense spikes. **2.** The seeds of this plant, used as a mild bulk laxative. [NLat. < Gk. *psullion*, dim. of *psulla*, flea.]

Pt The symbol for the element **platinum** 1.

PT *abbr.* **1.** Pacific Time **2.** part-time **3.** patrol torpedo **4.** physical therapy **5.** physical training

pt. *abbr.* **1.** part **2.** payment **3.** pint **4.** point **5.** also **Pt.** port **6.** preterit

p.t. *abbr.* pro tempore

PTA *abbr.* Parent Teacher Association

Ptah (ptä, ptäн) *n. Mythology* The Egyptian creator god and patron deity of artisans.

ptar·mi·gan (tär′mĭ-gən) *n., pl.* **ptarmigan** or **-gans** Any of various grouses of the genus *Lagopus* of the Northern Hemisphere having plumage that is brown or gray in summer and white in winter. [Alteration of Sc. Gael. *tarmachan*.]

PT boat (pē-tē′) *n.* A fast, maneuverable, lightly armed vessel used to torpedo enemy shipping. [P(ATROL) + T(ORPEDO) BOAT.]

PTC *abbr.* phenylthiocarbamide

PTCA (pē′tē-sē-ā′) *n.* Angioplasty with a balloon-tipped catheter that is performed to open a narrowed coronary artery. [p(ercutaneous) t(ransluminal) c(oronary) a(ngioplasty).]

–pter *suff.* Wing; winglike part: *ornithopter*. [< Gk. *pteron*, feather, wing. See pet- in App.]

pter·an·o·don (tə-răn′ə-dŏn′) *n.* Any of several large pterosaurs of the genus *Pteranodon* of the Cretaceous Period, having a long pointed head and a wingspan upward of 6 meters (20 feet). [NLat. *Pteranodōn*, genus name : Gk. *pteron*, wing; see –PTER + Gk. *a-*, *an-*, without; see A–¹ + Gk. *-odōn*, -odon.]

pter·i·dol·o·gy (tĕr′ĭ-dŏl′ə-jē) *n.* The study of ferns. [Gk. *pteris*, *pterid-*, fern (< *pteron*, feather, wing; see pet- in App.) + -LOGY.] —**pter′i·do·log′i·cal** (-də-lŏj′ĭ-kəl) *adj.*

pte·rid·o·phyte (tə-rĭd′ə-fīt′, tĕr′ĭ-dō-) *n.* Any of various vascular plants that reproduce by means of spores, including the ferns. [< NLat. Pteridophyta, former division name : Gk. *pteris*, *pterid-*, fern; see PTERIDOLOGY + Gk. *phuton*, plant; see –PHYTE.] —**pte·rid′o·phyt′ic** (tə-rĭd′ə-fĭt′ĭk, tĕr′ĭ-dō-), **pter′i·doph′y·tous** (tĕr′ĭ-dŏf′ĭ-təs) *adj.*

pter·o·dac·tyl (tĕr′ə-dăk′təl) *n.* Any of various small, mostly tailless, extinct flying reptiles of the order Pterosauria that existed during the Jurassic and Cretaceous periods. [NLat. *Pterodactylus*, genus name : Gk. *pteron*, feather, wing; see –PTER + Gk. *daktulos*, finger.] —**pter′o·dac′ty·loid′** *adj.*

pter·o·pod (tĕr′ə-pŏd′) *n.* Any of various gastropod mollusks of the subclass Opisthobranchia that have winglike lobes on the feet. [< NLat. *Pteropoda*, order name : Gk. *pteron*, feather, wing; see –PTER + Gk. *-poda*, -pod.] —**pter′o·pod′** *adj.* —**pte·rop′o·dan** (tə-rŏp′ə-dən) *adj. & n.*

pter·o·saur (tĕr′ə-sôr′) *n.* Any of various extinct flying reptiles of the order Pterosauria of the Jurassic and Cretaceous periods, characterized by wings consisting of a flap of skin supported by the very long fourth digit on each forelimb. [< NLat. *Pterosauria*, order name : Gk. *pteron*, feather, wing; see –PTER + Gk. *sauros*, lizard.]

pte·ryg·i·um (tə-rĭj′ē-əm) *n., pl.* **-i·ums** or **-i·a** (-ē-ə) An abnormal mass of tissue arising from the conjunctiva of the eye that obstructs vision by growing over the cornea. [NLat. < Gk. *pterugion*, dim. of *pterux*, *pterug-*, wing. See PTERYGOID.] —**pte·ryg′i·al** (-əl) *adj.*

pter·y·goid (tĕr′ĭ-goid′) *adj.* **1.** Of, relating to, or located in the region of the sphenoid bone. **2.** Resembling a wing; winglike. ❖ *n.* Either of two processes descending from the body of the sphenoid bone. [Gk. *pterugoeidēs*, winglike : *pterux*, *pterug-*, wing; see pet- in App. + *-oeidēs*, -oid.]

pter·y·la (tĕr′ə-lə) *n., pl.* **-lae** (-lē′, -lī′) An area on the skin of a bird from which feathers grow. [NLat. : Gk. *pteron*, wing, feather; see –PTER + Gk. *hūlē*, forest, matter.]

PTH *abbr.* parathyroid hormone

ptis·an (tĭz′ən, tĭ-zăn′) *n.* A medicinal infusion, such as sweetened barley water. [ME *tisane*, peeled barley, barley water < OFr. < Lat. *ptisana*, *tisana* < Gk. *ptisanē* < *ptissein*, to crush.]

PTO *abbr.* **1.** Parent Teacher Organization **2.** or **p.t.o.** please turn over **3.** power takeoff

Ptol·e·ma·ic (tŏl′ə-mā′ĭk) *adj.* **1.** Of or relating to the astronomer Ptolemy. **2.** Of or relating to the Ptolemies or to Egypt during their rule.

Ptolemaic system *n.* The astronomical system of Ptolemy, in which the earth is at the center of the universe.

Ptol·e·my¹ (tŏl′ə-mē) An Egyptian dynasty of Macedonian kings (323–30 B.C.) including **Ptolemy I** (367?–283?), who succeeded Alexander the Great as ruler of Egypt (323–285), and **Ptolemy XV** (47–30), who ruled as coregent (44–30) with Cleopatra.

Ptol·e·my² (tŏl′ə-mē) fl. 2nd cent. A.D. Alexandrian astronomer and geographer who based his theories on the belief that all heavenly bodies revolve around the earth.

pto·maine (tō′mān′, tō-mān′) *n.* A nitrogenous organic compound produced by putrefaction of protein. [Ital. *ptomaina* < Gk. *ptōma*, corpse < *piptein*, *ptō-*, to fall. See pet- in App.]

ptomaine poisoning *n.* Food poisoning, erroneously believed to be the result of ptomaine ingestion. Not in scientific use.

pto·sis (tō′sĭs) *n., pl.* **-ses** (-sēz) Abnormal lowering or drooping of an organ or a part, as of the upper eyelid. [Gk. *ptōsis*, fall < *piptein*, *ptō-*, to fall. See pet- in App.] —**pto′tic** (-tĭk) *adj.*

PTSD *abbr.* posttraumatic stress disorder

pty·a·lin (tī′ə-lĭn) *n.* A form of amylase in the saliva of humans and some animals that catalyzes the hydrolysis of starch into maltose and dextrin. [Gk. *ptualon*, saliva (< *ptūein*, to spit) + –IN.]

pty·a·lism (tī′ə-lĭz′əm) *n.* Excessive flow of saliva. [Gk. *ptualismos*, salivation < *ptualizein*, to salivate < *ptualon*, saliva < *ptūein*, to spit.]

Pu The symbol for the element **plutonium**.

pub (pŭb) *n.* A place of business where alcoholic beverages are sold and drunk. [Short for PUBLIC HOUSE.]

pub. *abbr.* **1.** publication **2.** published **3.** publisher

pub-crawl (pŭb′krôl′) *intr.v.* **-crawled, -crawl·ing, -crawls** *Slang* To visit a series of bars.

pu·ber·ty (pyoo′bər-tē) *n.* The stage of adolescence in which an individual becomes physiologically capable of sexual reproduction. [ME *puberte* < OFr. < Lat. *pūbertās* < *pūbēs*, *pūber-*, adult.] —**pu′ber·tal, pu′ber·al** (-bər-əl) *adj.*

pu·ber·u·lent (pyoo-bĕr′yə-lənt, -bĕr′ə-) also **pu·ber·u·lous** (-bĕr′yə-ləs, -bĕr′ə-) *adj.* Covered with minute hairs or very fine down; finely pubescent. [Lat. *pūber*, downy, adult + *-ulentus*, abounding in.]

pu·bes (pyoo′bēz) *n., pl.* **pubes 1.** The lower part of the abdomen, esp. the region surrounding the external genital organs. **2.** The hair that appears on this region at puberty. [Lat. *pūbēs*.]

pu·bes·cence (pyoo-bĕs′əns) *n.* **1.** The state of being pubescent. **2.** The attainment or onset of puberty. **3.** A covering of soft down or short hairs, as on certain plants and insects.

pu·bes·cent (pyoo-bĕs′ənt) *adj.* **1.** Reaching or having reached puberty. **2.** Covered with short hairs or soft down. [Lat. *pūbēscēns*, *pūbēscent-*, pr. part. of *pūbēscere*, to reach puberty < *pūbēs*, adult.]

pu·bic (pyoo′bĭk) *adj.* Of, relating to, or located in the region of the pubis or the pubes. [< PUBES and PUBIS.]

pu·bis (pyoo′bĭs) *n., pl.* **-bes** (-bēz) The forward portion of either of the hipbones, at the juncture forming the front arch of the pelvis. [Short for NLat. *(os) pūbis*, (bone) of the groin < genitive of Lat. *pūbēs*, groin.]

pub·lic (pŭb′lĭk) *adj.* **1.** Of, concerning, or affecting the community or the people: *the public good*. **2.** Maintained for or used by the people or community: *a public park*. **3.** Capitalized in shares of stock that can be traded on the open market: *a public company*. **4.** Participated in or attended by the people or community: "*Opinions are formed in a process of open discussion and public debate*" (Hannah Arendt). **5.** Connected with or acting on behalf of the people, community, or government: *public office*. **6.** Enrolled in or attending a public school. **7.** Open to the knowledge or judgment of all: *a public scandal*. ❖ *n.* **1.** The community or the people as a whole. **2.** A group of people sharing a common interest: *the reading public*. **3.** Admirers or followers, esp. of a famous person. See Usage Note at **collective noun. —idioms: go public** To become publicly owned by launching shares of stock onto the open market. **go public with** *Informal* To reveal to the public a previously unknown or secret piece of information. **in public** In such a way as to be visible to the scrutiny of the people. [ME *publik* < OFr. *public* < Lat. *pūblicus*, alteration (influenced by *pūbēs*, adult population) of *poplicus* < *populus*, people, of Etruscan orig.] —**pub′lic·ness** *n.*

public access *n.* The availability of television or radio broadcast facilities, as provided by law, for use by the public for presentation of programs.

pub·lic-ad·dress system (pŭb′lĭk-ə-drĕs′) *n.* An electronic amplification apparatus for broadcasting in public areas.

pub·li·can (pŭb′lĭ-kən) *n.* **1.** *Chiefly British* The keeper of a public house or tavern. **2.** A collector of public taxes or tolls in the Roman Empire. **3.** A collector of taxes or tribute from the public. [ME, tax collector < OFr. < Lat. *pūblicānus* < *pūblicum*, public revenue < neut. of *pūblicus*, public. See PUBLIC.]

public assistance *n.* Aid given to the needy, the aged, or the inhabitants of a disaster-stricken area; relief.

pub·li·ca·tion (pŭb′lĭ-kā′shən) *n.* **1.** The act or process of publishing printed matter. **2.** An issue of printed material offered for sale or distribution. **3.** Communication of information to the public. [Ult. < Lat. *pūblicātiō, pūblicātiōn-*, making public < *pūblicātus*, p. part. of *pūblicāre*, to make public < *pūblicus*, public. See PUBLIC.]

public defender *n.* An attorney or a staff of attorneys, usu. publicly appointed, having responsibility for the defense of those unable to afford or obtain legal assistance.

public domain *n.* **1.** Land owned and controlled by the state or federal government. **2.** The status of publications, products, and processes not protected under patent or copyright.

public health *n.* The science and practice of protecting and improving the health of a community, as by preventive medicine, health education, and sanitary measures.

public house *n. Chiefly British* A place, such as a tavern or bar, that is licensed to sell alcoholic beverages.

public housing *n.* Housing built, operated, and owned by a government and usu. provided at nominal rent to the needy.

public interest *n.* **1.** The well-being of the general public; the commonweal. **2.** The attention of the people with respect to events.

pub·li·cist (pŭb′lĭ-sĭst) *n.* One who publicizes, esp. a press or publicity agent.

pub·lic·i·ty (pŭ-blĭs′ĭ-tē) *n.* **1a.** Information disseminated through various media to attract public notice, as of a person or product. **b.** Public interest, notice, or notoriety achieved by the spreading of such information. **c.** The act, process, or occupation of disseminating information to gain public interest. **2.** The condition of being public. [Fr. *publicité* < *public*, public < OFr. < PUBLIC.]

pub·li·cize (pŭb′lĭ-sīz) *tr.v.* **-cized, -ciz·ing, -ciz·es** To give publicity to.

public law *n.* **1.** The branch of law that deals with the state or government and its relationships with individuals or other governments. **2.** A law affecting the public.

public library *n.* A noncommercial library often supported with public funds, intended for use by the general public.

pub·lic·ly (pŭb′lĭk-lē) *adv.* **1.** In a public manner; openly. **2.** By or with consent of the public.

public offering *n.* The sale of a new securities issue to the public by way of an underwriter, a transaction that must be registered with the Securities and Exchange Commission.

public opinion *n.* Public consensus, as with respect to an issue. —**pub′lic·o·pin′ion** (pŭb′lĭk-ə-pĭn′yən) *adj.*

public policy *n.* The policy or set of policies forming the foundation of public laws, such policy not yet formally enunciated.

public prosecutor *n.* A government official who prosecutes criminal actions on behalf of the state or community.

public relations *pl.n.* **1.** (*used with a sing. verb*) The art or science of establishing and promoting a favorable relationship with the public. **2.** (*used with a pl. verb*) The methods and activities used to establish and promote such a relationship. **3.** (*used with a sing. or pl. verb*) The degree of success obtained in achieving such a relationship.

public sale *n.* An auction of property or merchandise.

public school *n.* **1.** An elementary or secondary school in the United States supported by public funds and providing free education for children of a community or district. **2.** A private boarding secondary school in Great Britain.

public servant *n.* A person who holds a government position by election or appointment.

public service *n.* **1.** Employment within a governmental system, esp. within the civil service. **2.** A service performed for the benefit of the public, esp. by a nonprofit organization. **3.** The business of supplying an essential commodity or service to the public. —**pub′lic-ser′vice** (pŭb′lĭk-sûr′vĭs) *adj.*

public-service corporation *n.* A corporation providing essential services, such as water or electricity, to the public.

public speaking *n.* The act, art, or process of making effective speeches before an audience. —**public speaker** *n.*

pub·lic-spir·it·ed (pŭb′lĭk-spĭr′ĭ-tĭd) *adj.* Motivated by or exhibiting devotion to the public welfare. —**pub′lic-spir′it·ed·ness** *n.*

public television *n.* Noncommercial television that provides programs, esp. of an educational nature, for the public.

public utility *n.* **1.** A private business organization, subject to governmental regulation, that provides an essential commodity or service to the public. **2.** Stock shares issued by such a company. Often used in the plural.

public works *pl.n.* Construction projects, such as highways or dams, financed by public funds and constructed by a government for the benefit or use of the general public.

pub·lish (pŭb′lĭsh) *v.* **-lished, -lish·ing, -lish·es** —*tr.* **1.** To prepare and issue (printed material) for public distribution or sale. **2.** To bring to the public attention; announce. —*intr.* **1.** To issue

a publication. **2.** To be the writer or author of published works or a work. [ME *publicen, publishen*, to make known publicly < OFr. *publier* < Lat. *pūblicāre*. See PUBLICATION.] —**pub′lish·a·ble** *adj.*

pub·lish·er (pŭb′lĭ-shər) *n.* One engaged in publishing printed material.

Puc·ci·ni (pōō-chē′nē), **Giacomo** 1858–1924. Italian composer whose operas include *Madame Butterfly* (1904).

puc·coon (pə-kōōn′) *n.* **1a.** Any of several North American plants of the genus *Lithospermum*, having orange or yellow flowers and roots that yield a red dye. **b.** Any of several plants, such as the bloodroot, whose roots yield a reddish dye. **2.** Any of these dyes. [Of Virginia Algonquian orig.]

puce (pyōōs) *n.* A deep red to dark grayish purple. [Fr. *(couleur) puce*, flea (color), puce < OFr., var. of *pulce*, flea < Lat. *pūlex, pūlic-*.] —**puce** *adj.*

puck (pŭk) *n.* A hard rubber disk used in ice hockey. [Perh. < dialectal *puck*, to strike.]

Puck *n.* **1.** A mischievous sprite in English folklore. **2.** A satellite of Uranus. [ME *pouke*, goblin < OE *pūca*. Sense 2, after the sprite in *A Midsummer Night's Dream* by Shakespeare.]

puck·a (pŭk′ə) *adj.* Variant of **pukka**.

puck·er (pŭk′ər) *v.* **-ered, -er·ing, -ers** —*tr.* To gather into small wrinkles or folds: *puckered my lips; puckered the curtains.* —*intr.* To become gathered, contracted, and wrinkled. ❖ *n.* **1.** A wrinkle or wrinkled part, as in tightly stitched cloth. **2.** A facial expression in which the lips are tightly pulled together and pushed outward. **3.** A tart flavor that causes one's lips to pucker: *the pucker of lemon.* [Prob. freq. of dialectal *pock*, bag, sack, var. of POKE[3].]

puck·ish (pŭk′ĭsh) *adj.* Mischievous; impish. —**puck′ish·ly** *adv.* —**puck′ish·ness** *n.*

pud·ding (pŏŏd′ĭng) *n.* **1a.** A sweet dessert, usu. containing flour or a cereal product, that has been boiled, steamed, or baked. **b.** A mixture with a soft puddinglike consistency. **2.** A sausagelike preparation stuffed into a bag or skin and boiled. [ME, a kind of sausage < OFr. *boudin*.]

pud·ding·stone (pŏŏd′ĭng-stōn′) *n. Geology* A conglomerate.

pud·dle (pŭd′l) *n.* **1a.** A small pool of water, esp. rainwater. **b.** A small pool of a liquid. **2.** A tempered paste of wet clay and sand that serves as waterproofing when dry. ❖ *v.* **-dled, -dling, -dles** —*tr.* **1.** To make muddy. **2.** To work (clay or sand) into puddle. **3.** To process (impure metal) by puddling. —*intr.* To splash or dabble in or as if in a pool of liquid. [ME *podel*, dim. of OE *pudd*, ditch.] —**pud′dly** *adj.*

pud·dler (pŭd′lər) *n.* One that puddles iron or clay.

pud·dling (pŭd′lĭng) *n.* **1.** Purification of impure metal, esp. pig iron, by heating and stirring in an oxidizing atmosphere. **2.** Tempering of wet material, such as clay, to make puddle.

pu·den·cy (pyōōd′n-sē) *n.* Modesty. [LLat. *pudentia* < Lat. *pudēre*, to make or be ashamed.]

pu·den·dum (pyōō-dĕn′dəm) *n., pl.* **-da** (-də) The human external genital organs, esp. of a woman. Often used in the plural. [Lat., neut. gerundive of *pudēre*, to make or be ashamed.] —**pu·den′dal** (-dĕn′dəl) *adj.*

pudg·y (pŭj′ē) *adj.* **-i·er, -i·est** Short and fat; chubby: *pudgy fingers.* See Syns at **fat**. [< *pudge*, something thick and short.] —**pudg′i·ness** *n.*

Pueb·la (pwĕb′lä) A city of E-central Mexico ESE of Mexico City; founded by the Spanish in 1532. Pop. 1,007,170.

Pueb·lo[1] (pwĕb′lō) *n., pl.* **Pueblo** or **-los 1.** A member of any of some 25 Native American peoples, including the Hopi, Zuni, and Taos, living in established villages in northern and western New Mexico and northeast Arizona. **2.** **pueblo,** *pl.* **-los** A permanent village or community of any of the Pueblo peoples, typically consisting of multilevel adobe or stone apartment dwellings of terraced design around a central plaza. [Am.Sp. < Sp., people, pueblo < Lat. *populus*, people. See PUBLIC.]

Pueblo[2] A city of SE-central CO SSE of Colorado Springs. Pop. 102,121.

pu·er·ile (pyōō′ər-əl, pyŏŏr′əl, -īl′) *adj.* **1.** Belonging to childhood; juvenile. **2.** Immature; childish. [Lat. *puerīlis < puer*, child, boy.] —**pu′er·ile·ly** *adv.* —**pu′er·il′i·ty** (-ĭl′ĭ-tē), **pu′er·ile·ness** (-ə-nĭs, -īl-) *n.*

pu·er·il·ism (pyōō′ər-ə-lĭz′əm, pyŏŏr′ə-) *n.* Childish behavior in an adult, esp. as a symptom of mental illness.

pu·er·per·al (pyōō-ûr′pər-əl) *adj.* Relating to, connected with, or occurring during childbirth or the period immediately following childbirth. [< Lat. *puerper*, a woman in childbed : *puer*, child, boy + *parere*, to bear; see –PAROUS.]

puerperal fever *n.* An illness resulting from infection of the endometrium following childbirth or abortion, marked by fever and septicemia and usu. caused by unsterile technique.

pu·er·pe·ri·um (pyōō′ər-pîr′ē-əm) *n., pl.* **-per·i·a** (-pîr′ē-ə) **1.** The state of a woman during childbirth or immediately thereafter. **2.** The approximate six-week period lasting from childbirth to the return of normal uterine size. [Lat., childbirth < *puerpera*, a woman in childbed. See PUERPERAL.]

Puer·to Ri·co (pwĕr′tə rē′kō, pôrt′ə, pōrt′ə, pwĕr′tō) A self-governing island commonwealth of the US in the Caribbean Sea E of Hispaniola; colonized by the Spanish in the 16th cent. and ceded to the US in 1898 after the Spanish-American War. Cap.

Giacomo Puccini

pueblo[1]
Taos Pueblo, New Mexico

ă	pat	oi	boy
ā	pay	ou	out
âr	care	ŏŏ	took
ä	father	ōō	boot
ĕ	pet	ŭ	cut
ē	be	ûr	urge
ĭ	pit	th	thin
ī	pie	th	this
îr	pier	hw	which
ŏ	pot	zh	vision
ō	toe	ə	about,
ô	paw		item

Stress marks:
′ (primary);
′ (secondary), as in
lexicon (lĕk′sĭ-kŏn′)

San Juan. Pop. 3,808,610. —**Puer'to Ri'can** *adj. & n.*

puff (pŭf) *n.* **1a.** A short forceful exhalation of breath. **b.** A short sudden gust of wind. **c.** A brief sudden emission of air, vapor, or smoke. **d.** A short sibilant sound produced by a puff. **2.** An amount of vapor, smoke, or similar material released in a puff. **3.** An act of drawing in and expelling the breath, as in smoking tobacco. **4.** A swelling or rounded protuberance. **5.** Puff pastry. **6.** A light soft pad for applying powder or lotion. **7.** A gathered protruding portion of fabric. **8.** A light padded bed covering. **9.** An approving or flattering recommendation. **10.** *Genetics* A localized region of swelling in certain chromosomes indicating the active synthesis of RNA. ❖ *v.* **puffed, puff·ing, puffs** —*intr.* **1.** To blow in puffs. **2.** To come forth in puffs. **3.** To breathe forcefully and rapidly. **4.** To emit puffs. **5.** To take puffs on smoking material: *puffing on a cigar.* **6.** To swell or seem to swell, with pride or air. Often used with *up.* —*tr.* **1.** To emit or give forth in puffs. **2.** To impel with puffs. **3.** To smoke (a cigar, for example). **4.** To inflate or distend. **5.** To fill with pride or conceit. **6.** To publicize with often exaggerated praise. [< ME *puffen,* to puff < OE *pyffan,* perh. of imit. orig.] —**puff'i·ly** *adv.* —**puff'i·ness** *n.* —**puff'y** *adj.*

puff adder *n.* **1.** A venomous African viper (*Bitis arietans*) having crescent-shaped yellowish markings. **2.** See **hognose snake.** [So called because it inflates its body when excited.]

puff·ball (pŭf'bôl') *n.* **1.** Any of various fungi of the genus *Lycoperdon* and related genera, having a ball-shaped fruiting body that releases spores in puffs of dust. **2.** *Informal* The rounded head of a dandelion that has gone to seed.

puffed-up (pŭft'ŭp') *adj.* Displaying exaggerated dignity or self-importance; pompous.

puff·er (pŭf'ər) *n.* Any of various prickly, often poisonous, chiefly marine fishes of the family Tetraodontidae that are capable of puffing up by swallowing water or air.

puff·er·y (pŭf'ə-rē) *n.* Flattering, often exaggerated praise and publicity, esp. when used for promotional purposes.

puf·fin (pŭf'ĭn) *n.* Any of several sea birds of the genera *Fratercula* and *Lunda* of northern regions, characteristically having black and white plumage and a vertically flattened triangular bill that is brightly colored during breeding season. [ME *poffoun, puffon,* perh. < *puf,* puff. See PUFF.]

puff pastry *n.* A light flaky pastry that is formed by rolling and folding the dough in layers so that it expands when baked.

pug[1] (pŭg) *n.* **1.** A small sturdy dog of an ancient breed originating in China, having a snub nose, wrinkled face, short smooth hair, and curled tail. **2.** A pug nose. [?]

pug[2] (pŭg) *n.* **1.** Clay ground and kneaded with water into a plastic consistency for forming bricks or pottery. **2.** A machine for grinding and mixing clay. ❖ *tr.v.* **pugged, pug·ging, pugs** **1.** To work or knead (clay) with water. **2.** To fill in with clay or mortar. **3.** To make soundproof by covering or packing with clay, mortar, sawdust, or felt. [?]

pug[3] (pŭg) *n.* A footprint, track, or trail, esp. of an animal. [Hindi *pag,* prob. < Skt. *padakam,* footstep, foot < *padam.* See **ped-** in App.]

pug[4] (pŭg) *n. Slang* A fighter, esp. a boxer. [Short for PUGILIST, boxer.]

Pu·get Sound (pyōō'jĭt) A deep inlet of the Pacific in W WA extending S from the Strait of Juan de Fuca through Admiralty Inlet; named by Capt. George Vancouver for his aide, Peter Puget, in 1792.

pu·gi·lism (pyōō'jə-lĭz'əm) *n.* The skill, practice, and sport of fighting with the fists; boxing. [< Lat. *pugil,* pugilist.] —**pu'gi·list** *n.* —**pu'gi·lis'tic** *adj.*

Pu·glia (pōō'lyä) See **Apulia.**

pug·mark (pŭg'märk') *n.* The pug of an animal.

pug·na·cious (pŭg-nā'shəs) *adj.* Combative in nature; belligerent. [< Lat. *pugnāx, pugnāc-* < *pugnāre,* to fight < *pugnus,* fist.] —**pug·na'cious·ly** *adv.* —**pug·na'cious·ness, pug·nac'i·ty** (-năs'ĭ-tē) *n.*

pug nose *n.* A short nose that is somewhat flattened and turned up at the end. [< PUG[1], ape (obsolete), pug.] —**pug'-nosed'** (pŭg'nōzd') *adj.*

puis·ne (pyōō'nē) *Chiefly British adj.* Lower in rank; junior. ❖ *n.* One of lesser rank than another, esp. an associate judge. [OFr. *puisne : puis,* afterward (ult. < Lat. *post*; see **apo-** in App.) + *ne,* born (< Lat. *nātus,* p. part. of *nāscī,* to be born; see **gena-** in App.).]

puis·sance (pwĭs'əns, pyōō'ĭ-səns, pyōō-ĭs'əns) *n.* Power; might. [ME < OFr. < *poissant,* powerful, pr. part. of *pooir, poeir,* to be able. See POWER.] —**puis'sant** *adj.*

puke (pyōōk) *Slang intr. & tr.v.* **puked, puk·ing, pukes** To vomit. ❖ *n.* **1.** The act of vomiting. **2.** Vomit. **3.** One regarded as disgusting or contemptible. [Perh. imit.]

puk·ka also **puck·a** (pŭk'ə) *adj.* **1.** Genuine; authentic. **2.** Superior; first-class. [Hindi *pakkā,* cooked, ripe < Skt. *pakva-* < *pacati,* he cooks. See **pek**[w]- in App.]

pu·la (pōō'lä) *n.* See table at **currency.** [Tswana, rain (used as a greeting for good fortune).]

Pu·las·ki (pōō-lăs'kē, pə-), Casimir or Kazimierz 1747–79. Polish patriot and general who aided Amer. forces in the Revolutionary War.

puffball
releasing spores

puffin
Atlantic puffin
Fratercula arctica

pug[1]

pul·chri·tude (pŭl'krĭ-tōōd', -tyōōd') *n.* Great physical beauty and appeal. [ME *pulcritude* < Lat. *pulchritūdō* < *pulcher, pulchr-,* beautiful.]

pul·chri·tu·di·nous (pŭl'krĭ-tōōd'n-əs, -tyōōd'-) *adj.* Characterized by or having great physical beauty and appeal.

pule (pyōōl) *intr.v.* **puled, pul·ing, pules** To whine; whimper. [Perh. < Fr. *piauler,* of imit. orig.] —**pul'er** *n.*

pu·li (pōō'lē, pyōō'lē) *n., pl.* **pu·lis** (pōō'lēk, pyōō'lĕk) A longhaired sheepdog of a Hungarian breed. [Hung.]

Pu·lit·zer (pōō'lĭt-sər, pyōō'lĭt-), **Joseph** 1847–1911. Hungarian-born Amer. journalist and publisher who established and endowed the Pulitzer Prizes.

Pulitzer Prize *n.* Any of several annual awards for accomplishment in American journalism, literature, and music.

pull (pōōl) *v.* **pulled, pull·ing, pulls** —*tr.* **1.** To apply force to so as to cause or tend to cause motion toward the source of the force. **2.** To remove from a fixed position; extract: *The dentist pulled the tooth.* **3.** To tug at; jerk or tweak. **4.** To rip or tear; rend. **5.** To stretch (taffy, for example) repeatedly. **6.** To strain (a muscle, for example) injuriously. **7.** *Informal* To attract; draw: *pulled a large crowd.* **8.** *Slang* To draw out (a weapon) in readiness for use: *The thief pulled a knife on me.* **9.** *Informal* To remove: *pulled the engine.* **10.** *Sports* To hit (a ball) so that it moves in the direction away from the dominant hand of the player propelling it, as to the left of a right-handed player. **11.** *Nautical* **a.** To operate (an oar) in rowing. **b.** To transport or propel by rowing. **c.** To be rowed by: *That boat pulls six oars.* **12.** To rein in (a horse) to keep it from winning a race. **13.** *Printing* To produce (a print or an impression) from type. —*intr.* **1.** To exert force in moving something toward the source of the force. **2.** To drink or inhale deeply: *pulled on the cold beer with gusto; pull on a cigarette.* **3.** *Nautical* To row a boat. **4.** *Informal* To express or feel great sympathy or empathy: *We're pulling for our new president.* ❖ *n.* **1.** The act or process of pulling. **2.** Force required to overcome resistance in pulling. **3.** A sustained effort: *a long pull across the mountains.* **4.** Something, such as a knob on a drawer, that is used for pulling. **5.** A deep inhalation or draft, as of a cigarette or beverage. **6.** *Slang* A means of gaining special advantage; influence: *The lobbyist has pull with the senator.* **7.** *Informal* Ability to draw or attract; appeal: *a star with pull at the box office.* —**phrasal verbs: pull away 1.** To move away or backward; withdraw: *The car pulled away from the curb.* **2.** To move ahead, as in a race. **pull back** To withdraw or retreat. **pull down 1.** To demolish; destroy. **2.** To reduce to a lower level. **3.** To depress, as in spirits or health. **4.** *Informal* To draw (money) as wages: *pulls down a hefty salary.* **pull in 1.** To arrive at a destination. **2.** To rein in; restrain. **3.** To arrest (a criminal suspect, for example). **pull off** *Informal* To perform in spite of difficulties or obstacles; bring off. **pull out 1.** To leave or depart. **2.** To withdraw, as from a situation or commitment. **pull over 1.** To bring a vehicle to a stop at a curb or at the side of a road. **2.** To instruct or force (a motorist) to pull over. **pull round** To restore or be restored to sound health. **pull through** To come or bring successfully through trouble or illness. **pull up 1.** To bring or come to a halt. **2.** To move to a position or place ahead, as in a race. —**idioms: pull a fast one** *Informal* To play a trick or perpetrate a fraud. **pull (oneself) together** To regain one's composure. **pull (one's) punches** To refrain from deploying all the resources or force at one's disposal. **pull (one's) weight** To do one's own share, as of work. **pull out all the stops** *Informal* To deploy all the resources or force at one's disposal. **pull (someone's) leg** To play a joke on; tease or deceive. **pull strings** (or **wires**) *Informal* To exert secret control or influence in order to gain an end. **pull the plug on** *Slang* To stop supporting or bring to an end. **pull the rug (out) from under** *Informal* To remove all support and assistance from, usu. suddenly. **pull the wool over (someone's) eyes** To deceive; hoodwink. **pull together** To make a joint effort. **pull up stakes** To clear out; leave. [ME *pullen* < OE *pullian.*] —**pull'er** *n.*

pull·back (pōōl'băk') *n.* **1.** The act or process of pulling back, esp. an orderly troop withdrawal. **2.** A device for holding or drawing back.

pul·let (pōōl'ĭt) *n.* A young domestic hen, usu. one less than one year old. [ME *pulet* < OFr. *polet, poulet,* dim. of *poul,* cock, and *poule,* hen, both < Lat. *pullus,* young fowl, young animal, chicken.]

pul·ley (pōōl'ē) *n., pl.* **-leys** **1.** A simple machine consisting essentially of a wheel with a grooved rim in which a pulled rope or chain can run to change the direction of the pull and thereby lift a load. **2.** A wheel turned by or driving a belt. [ME *poley* < OFr. *polie* and < Med.Lat. *poliva,* both ult. < Gk. *polos,* axis. See **kwel-** in App.]

pull·man (pōōl'mən) *adj.* Small, long, and narrow in architectural design. [From its resemblance to a PULLMAN railroad car.]

Pullman *n.* **1.** A railroad parlor car or sleeping car. **2.** A large suitcase. [After George Mortimer *Pullman* (1831–97), American industrialist and inventor.]

pull-on (pŏol′ŏn′, -ôn′) *n.* A garment, such as a sweater, designed to be easily pulled on.

pul·lo·rum disease (pə-lôr′əm, -lōr′-) *n.* A contagious, often fatal diarrheal disease of young poultry, caused by the bacterium *Salmonella pullorum,* specific epithet < genitive pl. of Lat. *pullus,* young fowl. See PULLET.]

pull·out (pŏol′out′) *n.* **1.** A withdrawal, esp. of troops. **2.** The change from a dive to level flight. Used of an aircraft. **3.** An object designed to be pulled out.

pull·o·ver (pŏol′ō′vər) *n.* A garment, such as a sweater, that is put on by being drawn over the head.

pul·lu·late (pŭl′yə-lāt′) *intr.v.* **-lat·ed, -lat·ing, -lates** **1.** To put forth sprouts or buds; germinate. **2.** To breed rapidly or abundantly. **3.** To teem; swarm. [Lat. *pullulāre, pullulāt- < pullulus,* dim. of *pullus,* young fowl. See PULLET.] —**pul′lu·la′tion** *n.* —**pul′lu·la′tive** *adj.*

pull-up (pŏol′ŭp′) *n.* See **chin-up.**

pul·mo·nar·y (pŏol′mə-nĕr′ē, pŭl′-) *adj.* **1.** Of, relating to, or affecting the lungs. **2.** Having lungs or lunglike organs. [Lat. *pulmōnārius < pulmō, pulmōn-,* lung. See pleu- in App.]

pulmonary artery *n.* An artery that carries venous blood from the right ventricle of the heart to the lungs.

pulmonary vein *n.* A vein that carries oxygenated blood from the lungs to the left atrium of the heart.

pul·mo·nate (pŏol′mə-nāt′, pŭl′-) *adj.* **1.** Having lungs or lunglike organs. **2.** Of or belonging to the Pulmonata, a subclass of gastropods, including slugs, that are capable of breathing air through lunglike sacs. [< Lat. *pulmō, pulmōn-,* lung. See PULMONARY.] —**pul′mo·nate′** *n.*

pul·mon·ic (pŏol-mŏn′ĭk, pŭl′-) *adj.* Of or relating to the lungs; pulmonary.

pul·mo·nol·o·gy (pŏol′mə-nŏl′ə-jē, pŭl′-) *n.* The branch of medicine that deals with diseases of the respiratory system. [Lat. *pulmō, pulmōn-,* lung; see pleu- in App. + -LOGY.] —**pul′mo·nol′o·gist** *n.*

pulp (pŭlp) *n.* **1.** A soft moist shapeless mass of matter. **2.** The soft moist part of fruit. **3.** A mass of pressed vegetable matter. **4.** The soft pith forming the contents of the stem of a plant. **5.** A mixture of cellulose material, such as wood, paper, and rags, ground up and moistened to make paper. **6.** The soft tissue forming the inner structure of a tooth. **7.** A mixture of crushed ore and water. **8.** A lurid publication. ❖ *v.* **pulped, pulp·ing, pulps** —*tr.* **1.** To reduce to pulp. **2.** To remove the pulp from. —*intr.* To be reduced to a pulpy consistency. [ME < Lat. *pulpa,* fleshy parts of the body, fruit pulp.] —**pulp′i·ness** *n.* —**pulp′ous** (pŭl′pəs) *adj.* —**pulp′y** *adj.*

pul·pit (pŏol′pĭt, pŭl′-) *n.* **1.** An elevated platform, lectern, or stand used in preaching or conducting a religious service. **2a.** Clerics considered as a group. **b.** The ministry of preaching. **3.** An elevated metal guardrail extending around the bow or stern of a yacht or other small vessel. **4.** An elevated platform, such as one used by harpooners in a whaling boat. [ME < OFr. < LLat. *pulpitum < Lat.,* wooden platform.]

pulp·wood (pŭlp′wŏod′) *n.* Soft wood, such as spruce, aspen, or pine, used in making paper.

pul·que (pŏol′kā′, -kē, pŏol′-) *n.* A thick fermented alcoholic beverage made in Mexico from various species of agave. [Am.Sp. < Nahuatl *poliuhqui,* decomposed, lost.]

pul·sar (pŭl′sär′) *n.* Any of a class of celestial objects believed to be rotating neutron stars, emitting intense regular bursts of radio waves. [< PULSE¹, by analogy with QUASAR.]

pul·sate (pŭl′sāt′) *intr.v.* **-sat·ed, -sat·ing, -sates** **1.** To expand and contract rhythmically; beat. **2.** To quiver; vibrate. [Lat. *pulsāre, pulsāt-,* freq. of *pellere,* to beat. See pel-² in App.]

pul·sa·tile (pŭl′sə-təl, -tīl′) *adj.* Undergoing pulsation.

pul·sa·tion (pŭl-sā′shən) *n.* **1.** The act of pulsating. **2.** A single beat, throb, or vibration.

pul·sa·tor (pŭl′sā′tər, pŭl-sā′-) *n.* A pulsating device.

pul·sa·to·ry (pŭl′sə-tôr′ē, -tōr′ē) *adj.* Having rhythmical vibration or movement.

pulse¹ (pŭls) *n.* **1.** The rhythmical throbbing of arteries produced by the regular contractions of the heart, esp. as palpated at the wrist or in the neck. **2a.** A regular or rhythmical beating. **b.** A single beat or throb. **3.** *Physics* **a.** A brief sudden change in a normally constant quantity: *a pulse of current.* **b.** Any of a series of intermittent occurrences characterized by such a change. **4.** The perceptible emotions or sentiments of a group of people. ❖ *intr.v.* **pulsed, puls·ing, puls·es** **1.** To pulsate; beat. **2.** *Physics* To undergo a series of intermittent occurrences characterized by pulses. [ME < OFr. < Lat. *pulsus* < p. part. of *pellere,* to beat. See pel-² in App.]

pulse² (pŭls) *n.* **1.** The edible seeds of certain pod-bearing plants, such as peas and beans. **2.** A plant yielding these seeds. [ME *pols* < OFr. < Lat. *puls,* pottage of meal and pulse, prob. ult. < Gk. *poltos.*]

pulse·jet (pŭls′jĕt′) *n.* A jet engine with intermittent air intake and combustion, producing rapid periodic bursts of thrust.

pulse modulation *n.* A type of modulation in which a train of pulses is varied in order to represent the signal.

pul·som·e·ter (pŭl-sŏm′ĭ-tər) *n.* A pump without pistons that operates by means of pulsed condensation of steam.

pul·ver·a·ble (pŭl′vər-ə-bəl) *adj.* That can be pulverized.

pul·ver·ize (pŭl′və-rīz′) *v.* **-ized, -iz·ing, -iz·es** —*tr.* **1.** To pound, crush, or grind to a powder or dust. **2.** To demolish. —*intr.* To be ground or reduced to powder or dust. [ME *pulverizen* < LLat. *pulverizāre < Lat. pulvis, pulver-,* dust.] —**pul′ver·iz′a·ble** *adj.* —**pul′ver·i·za′tion** (-vər-ĭ-zā′shən) *n.* —**pul′ver·iz′er** *n.*

pul·ver·u·lent (pŭl-vĕr′yə-lənt, -vĕr′ə-) *adj.* Made of, covered with, or crumbling to fine powder or dust. **2.** Dusty; crumbly. [Lat. *pulverulentus :* < *pulvis, pulver-,* dust + *-ulentus,* abounding in.]

pul·vil·lus (pŭl-vĭl′əs) *n., pl.* **-vil·li** (-vĭl′ī′) A soft pad on the foot of an insect by which it clings to a surface. [Lat., short for *pulvīnulus,* dim. of *pulvīnus,* cushion.]

pul·vi·nate (pŭl′və-nāt′) also **pul·vi·nat·ed** (-nā′tĭd) *adj.* **1.** Shaped like a cushion. **2.** *Botany* Swollen at the base. Used of a leafstalk. **3. pulvinated** *Architecture* Having a convex face or profile: *a pulvinated frieze.* [Lat. *pulvīnātus < pulvīnus,* cushion.]

pul·vi·nus (pŭl-vī′nəs, -vē′-) *n., pl.* **-ni** (-nī′) A pulvinate swelling. [Lat. *pulvīnus,* cushion.]

pu·ma (pyōo′mə, pōo′-) *n.* See **mountain lion.** [Sp. < Quechua.]

pum·e·lo (pŭm′ə-lō′) *n., pl.* **-los** See **shaddock.** [Variant of POMELO.]

pum·ice (pŭm′ĭs) *n.* A light, porous, glassy lava, used in solid form as an abrasive and in powdered form as a polish and an abrasive. ❖ *tr.v.* **-iced, -ic·ing, -ic·es** To clean, polish, or smooth with pumice. [ME < AN *pomis* < LLat. *pōmex < Lat. pūmex,* alteration of *spūma,* foam.] —**pu·mi′ceous** (pyōo-mĭsh′əs, pə-) *adj.* —**pum′ic·er** *n.*

pum·mel (pŭm′əl) *tr.v.* **-meled, -mel·ing, -mels** also **-melled, -mel·ling, -mels** To beat, as with the fists; pommel. ❖ *n.* The act of beating, as with the fists. [Alteration of POMMEL.]

pump¹ (pŭmp) *n.* **1.** A machine or device for raising, compressing, or transferring fluids. **2.** *Physiology* A molecular mechanism for the active transport of ions or molecules across a cell membrane. **3.** *Physics* Electromagnetic radiation used to raise atoms or molecules to a higher energy level. **4.** *Informal* The heart. ❖ *v.* **pumped, pump·ing, pumps** —*tr.* **1.** To raise or cause to flow by means of a pump. **2.** To draw, deliver, or pour forth as if with a pump. **3.** To remove the water from. **4.** To cause to move with the up-and-down motion of a pump handle. **5.** To propel, eject, or insert with or as if with a pump: *pumped new life into the economy.* **6.** *Physics* To raise (atoms or molecules) to a higher energy level by exposing them to electromagnetic radiation at a resonant frequency. **7.** *Physiology* To transport (ions or molecules) against a concentration gradient by the expenditure of chemically stored energy. **8.** To question closely or persistently. —*intr.* **1.** To operate a pump. **2.** To raise or move gas or liquid with a pump. **3.** To move up and down in the manner of a pump handle. **4.** *Sports* To fake a throw, pass, or shot by moving the arm or arms without releasing the ball. —*phrasal verb:* **pump up 1.** To inflate with gas by means of a pump. **2.** *Slang* To fill with enthusiasm, strength, and energy. **3.** *Sports* To be actively involved in a body-building program. —*idiom:* **pump iron** *Sports* To lift weights. [ME *pumpe.*] —**pump′er** *n.*

pump² (pŭmp) *n.* A woman's shoe that has medium or high heels and no fastenings. [?]

pumped storage (pŭmpt) *n.* A system of generating hydroelectric power, in which electricity is generated during hours of peak consumption by using water that has been pumped into an elevated reservoir during hours of low consumption.

pum·per·nick·el (pŭm′pər-nĭk′əl) *n.* A dark sourish bread made from whole, coarsely ground rye. [Ger., prob. < dialectal, term of abuse : obsolete *Pumper,* breaking wind (< dialectal *pumpern,* to break wind < MHGer., to knock, freq. of *pumpen,* of imit. orig.) + Ger. *Nickel,* goblin; see NICKEL.]

pump·kin (pŭmp′kĭn, pŭm′-, pŭng′-) *n.* **1a.** A coarse trailing vine (*Cucurbita pepo*) cultivated for its fruit. **b.** The large pulpy round fruit of this plant, having a thick orange-yellow rind. **c.** Any of several other vines of the genus *Cucurbita,* esp. *C. maxima* or *C. moschata,* bearing large pumpkinlike squashes. **2.** A moderate to strong orange. [Alteration (influenced by -KIN) of obsolete *pumpion* < obsolete Fr. *pompon, popon* < OFr. *pepon* < LLat. *pepōn < Lat.,* watermelon or gourd < Gk., ripe, large melon. See pekʷ- in App.]

pump·kin·seed (pŭmp′kĭn-sēd′, pŭm′-, pŭng′-) *n.* **1.** The seed of a pumpkin. **2.** A North American sunfish (*Lepomis gibbosus*) having a rounded, mostly orange body with a bright red spot on each gill cover.

pump-prim·ing or **pump priming** (pŭmp′prī′mĭng) *n.* Government action taken to stimulate the economy, as cutting taxes or reducing interest rates.

pun (pŭn) *n.* A play on words, sometimes on different senses of the same word and sometimes on the similar sense or sound of different words. ❖ *intr.v.* **punned, pun·ning, puns** To make puns or a pun. [?] —**pun′ning·ly** *adv.*

punch¹ (pŭnch) *n.* **1.** A tool for circular or other piercing. **2.** A tool for forcing a pin, bolt, or rivet in or out of a hole. **3.** A tool for stamping a design on a surface. **4.** A tool for making a countersink. ❖ *intr. & tr.v.* **punched, punch·ing, punch·es** To use

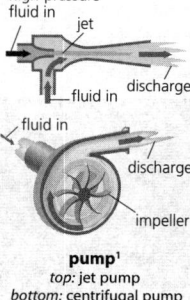

pump¹
top: jet pump
bottom: centrifugal pump

high-pressure fluid in
jet
discharge
fluid in
fluid in
discharge
impeller

a punch or use a punch on. [ME *pounce, punche* < OFr. *poinçon, ponchon*; see PUNCHEON¹. V. < ME *pouncen, punchen,* to prick < OFr. *poinçoner, ponchoner,* to emboss with a punch. See PUNCH².] —**punch′er** n.

punch² (pŭnch) tr.v. **punched, punch•ing, punch•es 1.** To hit with a sharp blow of the fist. **2a.** To poke or prod with a stick. **b.** *Western US* To herd (cattle). **3.** To depress (a key or button, for example) in order to activate a device or perform an operation. **4.** *Baseball* To hit (a ball) with a quick short swing. ❖ n. **1.** A blow with the fist. **2.** Vigor or drive. —**phrasal verbs: punch in** To check in formally at a job upon arrival. **punch out 1.** To check out formally at a job upon leaving. **2.** To knock unconscious with a punch. **3.** *Slang* To eject from a military aircraft. —**idiom: beat to the punch** To make the first decisive move. [ME *punchen,* to thrust, prod, prick < OFr. *poinçonner, ponchonner,* to emboss with a punch < *poinçon, ponchon,* pointed tool. See PUNCHEON¹.] —**punch′less** adj.

punch³ (pŭnch) n. A beverage of fruit juices and sometimes a soft drink or carbonated water, often spiced and mixed with wine or liquor. [Perh. < Hindi *pañc,* five < Skt. *pañca* (it orig. being prepared from five ingredients). See **penkʷe** in App.]

Punch n. The quarrelsome hook-nosed husband of Judy in the comic puppet show *Punch and Judy.* —**idiom: pleased as Punch** Highly pleased; gratified. [Short for PUNCHINELLO.]

punch•board (pŭnch′bôrd′, -bōrd′) n. A small, usu. rectangular board that contains holes each filled with a slip of paper that, when punched out, indicates a designated prize, win, or loss.

punch bowl n. A large serving bowl, as for punch.

punch card n. A medium for feeding data into a computer, essentially a card punched with holes or notches to represent letters and numbers or with a pattern of holes to represent related data.

punch-drunk (pŭnch′drŭngk′) adj. **1.** Showing signs of brain damage caused by blows to the head. Used esp. of a boxer. **2.** Behaving in a bewildered, confused, or dazed manner.

pun•cheon¹ (pŭn′chən) n. **1.** A short wooden upright used in structural framing. **2.** A piece of broad, heavy, roughly dressed timber with one face finished flat. **3.** A punching, perforating, or stamping tool, esp. one used by a goldsmith. [ME *punchon* < OFr. *ponçon, ponchon* < VLat. **pūnctiō, *pūnctiōn-,* punch < **pūnctiāre,* to pierce < Lat. *pūnctus,* p. part. of *pungere,* to prick.]

pun•cheon² (pŭn′chən) n. **1.** A cask with a capacity of from 72 to 120 gallons (273 to 454 liters). **2.** The amount of liquid contained in a puncheon. [ME *punchon* < OFr. *poinçon, poinchon,* punch, cask (prob. because inspected casks were marked with a punch). See PUNCHEON¹.]

Pun•chi•nel•lo (pŭn′chə-nĕl′ō) n., pl. **-los** or **-loes 1.** The short fat buffoon or clown in an Italian puppet show. **2.** One who resembles a short fat clown. [Variant of *Polichinello* < Ital. dialectal *Pollecinella,* dim. of *pollecena,* turkey pullet (< the resemblance between its beak and Punchinello's nose), ult. < Lat. *pullus,* young chicken.]

punch•ing bag (pŭn′chĭng) n. A stuffed or inflated leather bag that is punched with the fists for exercise.

punch line n. The climactic phrase or statement of a joke, producing a sudden humorous effect.

punch press n. A power press that can be fitted with various dies, as for metalworking.

punch-up (pŭnch′ŭp′) n. *Chiefly British* A fistfight.

punch•y (pŭn′chē) adj. **-i•er, -i•est 1.** Characterized by vigor or drive. **2.** Groggy or dazed from or as if from a punch or punches. —**punch′i•ly** adv. —**punch′i•ness** n.

punc•tate (pŭngk′tāt′) also **punc•tat•ed** (-tā′tĭd) adj. Having tiny spots, points, or depressions. [< Lat. *pūnctum,* prick mark < neut. p. part. of *pungere,* to prick. See PUNCTUATE.] —**punc•ta′tion** n.

punc•til•i•o (pŭngk-tĭl′ē-ō′) n., pl. **-os 1.** A fine point of etiquette. **2.** Precise observance of formalities. [Obsolete Ital. *punctiglio* < Sp. *puntillo,* dim. of *punto,* point < Lat. *pūnctum* < neut. p. part. of *pungere,* to prick.]

punc•til•i•ous (pŭngk-tĭl′ē-əs) adj. Strictly attentive to minute details of form in action or conduct. —**punc•til′i•ous•ly** adv. —**punc•til′i•ous•ness** n.

punc•tu•al (pŭngk′chōō-əl) adj. **1.** Acting or arriving exactly at the time appointed; prompt. **2.** Paid or accomplished at or by the appointed time. **3.** Precise; exact. **4.** Confined to or having the nature of a point in space. [ME, sharp-pointed < Med.Lat. *pūnctuālis* < Lat. *pūnctum,* point < neut. p. part. of *pungere,* to prick.] —**punc•tu•al′i•ty** (-ăl′ĭ-tē), **punc′tu•al•ness** (-əl-nĭs) n. —**punc′tu•al•ly** adv.

punc•tu•ate (pŭngk′chōō-āt′) v. **-at•ed, -at•ing, -ates** —tr. **1.** To provide (a text) with punctuation marks. **2.** To interrupt periodically. **3.** To stress or emphasize. —intr. To use punctuation. [Med.Lat. *pūnctuāre, pūnctuāt-* < Lat. *pūnctum,* point < neut. p. part. of *pungere,* to prick.] —**punc′tu•a′tive** adj. —**punc′tu•a′tor** n.

punc•tu•at•ed equilibrium (pŭngk′chōō-ā′tĭd) n. The theory that speciation occurs in spurts of major genetic alterations that punctuate long periods of little change.

punc•tu•a•tion (pŭngk′chōō-ā′shən) n. **1a.** The use of standard marks and signs in writing and printing to separate words

into sentences, clauses, and phrases to clarify meaning. **b.** These marks. **2.** The act or an instance of punctuating.

punctuation mark n. One of a set of marks or signs, such as the comma (,) or the period (.), used to punctuate texts.

punc•ture (pŭngk′chər) v. **-tured, -tur•ing, -tures** —tr. **1.** To pierce with a pointed object. **2.** To make (a hole) by piercing. **3.** To cause to collapse by piercing. **4.** To depreciate or deflate. —intr. To be pierced or punctured. ❖ n. **1.** The act or an instance of puncturing. **2.** A hole or depression made by a sharp object. [< ME, a pricking < LLat. *pūnctūra* < *pūnctus,* p. part. of *pungere,* to prick.] —**punc′tur•a•ble** adj.

puncture weed n. A prostrate weed (*Tribulus terrestris*) native to the Old World, and having opposite, pinnately compound leaves and woody fruit with stout divergent spines.

pun•dit (pŭn′dĭt) n. **1.** A source of opinion; a critic. **2.** A learned person. **3.** *Hinduism* Variant of **pandit.** [Hindi *paṇḍit,* learned man < Skt. *paṇḍitaḥ,* learned, scholar, perh. of Dravidian orig.] —**pun′dit•ry** n.

Pu•ne or **Poo•na** (pōō′nə) A city of W-central India ESE of Mumbai (Bombay); a Maratha cap. in the 17th and 18th cent. Pop. 1,203,351.

pung (pŭng) n. *New England* A low one-horse box sleigh. [Short for dialectal *tom-pung* < an Algonquian language.]

pun•gent (pŭn′jənt) adj. **1.** Affecting the organs of taste or smell with a sharp acrid sensation. **2a.** Penetrating, biting, or caustic: *pungent satire.* **b.** To the point; sharp. **3.** Pointed: *a pungent leaf.* [Lat. *pungēns, pungent-,* pr. part. of *pungere,* to sting.] —**pun′gen•cy** n. —**pun′gent•ly** adv.

Pu•nic (pyōō′nĭk) adj. **1.** Of or relating to ancient Carthage, its inhabitants, or their language. **2.** Having the character of treachery attributed to the Carthaginians by the Romans. ❖ n. The dialect of Phoenician spoken in ancient Carthage. [Lat. *Poenicus, Pūnicus* < *Poenus,* a Carthaginian < Gk. *Phoinix,* Phoenician.]

Punic War n. Any of the three wars (264–241, 218–201, and 149–146 B.C.) fought between Rome and Carthage, resulting ultimately in the destruction of Carthage.

pun•ish (pŭn′ĭsh) v. **-ished, -ish•ing, -ish•es** —tr. **1.** To subject to a penalty for an offense, sin, or fault. **2.** To inflict a penalty for (an offense). **3.** To handle roughly; hurt: *The heavy surf punished the small boat.* —intr. To exact or mete out punishment. [ME *punissen, punishen* < OFr. *punir, puniss-* < Lat. *poenīre, pūnīre* < *poena,* punishment < Gk. *poinē.* See **kʷei-** in App.] —**pun′ish•a•bil′i•ty** n. —**pun′ish•a•ble** adj. —**pun′ish•er** n.

pun•ish•ment (pŭn′ĭsh-mənt) n. **1a.** The act or an instance of punishing. **b.** The condition of being punished. **2.** A penalty for wrongdoing. **3.** Rough handling; mistreatment.

pu•ni•tive (pyōō′nĭ-tĭv) adj. Inflicting or aiming to inflict punishment; punishing. [Med.Lat. *pūnītīvus* < Lat. *poenīre, pūnīre,* to punish. See PUNISH.] —**pu′ni•tive•ly** adv. —**pu′ni•tive•ness** n.

punitive damages pl.n. Damages awarded by a court against a defendant as a deterrent or punishment to redress an egregious wrong perpetrated by the defendant.

pu•ni•to•ry (pyōō′nĭ-tôr′ē, -tōr′ē) adj. Inflicting or intended to inflict punishment. [< Lat. *pūnītus* < p. part. of *pūnīre,* to punish. See PUNISH.]

Pun•jab (pŭn′jăb′, pŭn-jäb′) A historical region of NW India and N Pakistan bounded by the Indus and Yamuna rivers. A center of the Indus Valley civilization, it was controlled by Sikhs from 1799 to 1849, when it was annexed by Great Britain, and partitioned between India and Pakistan in 1947.

Pun•ja•bi also **Pan•ja•bi** (pŭn-jä′bē, -jäb′ē) adj. Of or relating to the Punjab or Punjabi. ❖ n., pl. **-bis 1.** A native or inhabitant of the Punjab. **2.** An Indic language spoken in the Punjab.

pun•ji stick (pōōn′jē, pŭn′-) n. A very sharp bamboo stake that is concealed at an angle in high grass, in a hole, or in deep mud, often coated with excrement, and planted to wound and infect the feet of enemy soldiers. [?]

punk¹ (pŭngk) n. **1.** *Slang* **a.** An unproductive or antisocial young person, esp. one given to disruptive or violent behavior. **b.** An inexperienced young man. **2.** *Music* **a.** Punk rock. **b.** A performer or follower of punk rock. **3a.** *Slang* A young man who is the sexual partner of an older man. **b.** *Archaic* A prostitute. [?] —**punk′er** n.

punk² (pŭngk) n. **1.** Dry decayed wood, used as tinder. **2.** Any of various substances that smolder when ignited, used to light fireworks. **3.** Chinese incense. ❖ adj. **1.** Of poor quality; worthless. **2.** Weak in spirits or health. [Prob. of eastern Algonquian orig.]

pun•ka or **pun•kah** (pŭng′kə) n. A fan used esp. in India, made of a palm frond or strip of cloth hung from the ceiling. [Hindi *paṅkhá* < Skt. *pakṣakaḥ,* fan < *pakṣaḥ,* wing.]

punk•ie also **punk•y** (pŭng′kē) n., pl. **-ies** Any of various minute biting flies of the family Ceratopogonidae. [Of North American Du. orig. < Munsee *pónkwəs.*]

pun•kin (pŭng′kĭn) n. *Informal* Variant of **pumpkin.**

punk rock n. Rock 'n' roll characterized by extremely fast tempos and lyrics expressing emotional isolation and antisocial attitudes. —**punk rocker** n.

punk•ster (pŭn′stər) n. A maker of puns.

punt¹ (pŭnt) n. An open flatbottom boat with squared ends, used in shallow waters and usu. propelled by a long pole. ❖ v. **punt**

punching bag

punt¹
punting on the river Cam,
Cambridge, England

ed, punt•ing, punts —*tr.* **1.** To propel (a boat) with a pole. **2.** To carry in a punt. —*intr.* To go in a punt. [Prob. ME **punt* < OE *punt* < Lat. *pontō*, pontoon, flatbottom boat < *pōns, pont-*, bridge. See **pent-** in App.] —**punt′er** *n.*

punt[2] (pŭnt) *Football n.* A kick in which the ball is dropped from the hands and kicked before it touches the ground. ❖ *v.* **punt•ed, punt•ing, punts** —*tr.* To propel (a ball) by means of a punt. —*intr.* **1.** To execute a punt. **2.** *Informal* To cease doing something; give up. [Perh. < dialectal *punt*, to strike, push, perh. alteration of *bunt.*] —**punt′er** *n.*

punt[3] (pŭnt) *intr.v.* **punt•ed, punt•ing, punts 1.** *Games* To lay a bet against the bank, as in roulette. **2.** *Chiefly British Slang* To gamble. [Fr. *ponter* < obsolete *pont*, p. part. of *pondre*, to put (obsolete), lay an egg < OFr., to lay an egg < Lat. *pōnere*. See **apo-** in App.] —**punt′er** *n.*

punt[4] (pŭnt) *n.* The indentation in the bottom of a champagne or wine bottle. [Perh. < PUNTY.]

Pun•ta A•re•nas (po͞on′tə ə-rĕn′əs, po͞on′tä ä-rĕ′näs) A city of S Chile on the Strait of Magellan; founded in the 1840s and the southernmost city in the world. Pop. 120,030.

pun•ty (pŭn′tē) *n., pl.* **-ties** An iron rod on which molten glass is handled when being shaped and worked. [Prob. < Fr. *pontil.* See PONTIL.]

Punx•su•taw•ney (pŭngk′sə-tô′nē) A city of W-central PA NE of Pittsburgh; noted for its annual observance of Groundhog Day, Feb. 2. Pop. 6,271.

pu•ny (pyo͞o′nē) *adj.* **-ni•er, -ni•est 1.** Of inferior size, strength, or significance; weak. **2.** *Chiefly Southern US* Sickly; ill. [Variant of PUISNE.] —**pu′ni•ly** *adv.* —**pu′ni•ness** *n.*

pup (pŭp) *n.* **1a.** A young dog; a puppy. **b.** The young of various other canine animals, such as the wolf. **c.** The young of certain other animals, such as the seal. **2.** An inexperienced or conceited young person. ❖ *intr.v.* **pupped, pup•ping, pups** To give birth to pups. [Short for PUPPY.]

pu•pa (pyo͞o′pə) *n., pl.* **-pae** (-pē) or **-pas** An insect in the nonfeeding stage between the larva and adult, during which it typically undergoes complete transformation within a protective cocoon or hardened case. Only insects that undergo complete metamorphosis have pupal stages. [Lat. *pūpa*, girl, doll.] —**pu′pal** *adj.*

pu•pate (pyo͞o′pāt′) *intr.v.* **-pat•ed, -pat•ing, -pates 1.** To become a pupa. **2.** To go through a pupal stage. —**pu•pa′tion** *n.*

pup•fish (pŭp′fĭsh′) *n., pl.* **pupfish** or **-fish•es** Any of various small killifishes of the genus *Cyprinodon* of Mexico and the southwest United States.

pu•pil[1] (pyo͞o′pəl) *n.* **1.** A student under the direct supervision of a teacher or professor. **2.** *Law* A minor under the supervision of a guardian. [ME *pupille*, orphan < OFr. < Lat. *pūpillus*, dim. of *pūpus*, boy.]

pu•pil[2] (pyo͞o′pəl) *n.* The circular opening in the center of the iris of the eye, through which light passes to the retina. [ME < OFr. *pupille* < Lat. *pūpilla*, little doll, pupil (< the tiny image reflected in it). See PUPIL[1].] —**pu′pi•lar** *adj.*

pu•pil•age also **pu•pil•lage** (pyo͞o′pə-lĭj) *n.* The state or period of being a pupil.

pu•pil•lar•y[1] (pyo͞o′pə-lĕr′ē) *adj.* Of or relating to a student or ward.

pu•pil•lar•y[2] (pyo͞o′pə-lĕr′ē) *adj.* Of or affecting the pupil.

pu•pip•a•rous (pyo͞o-pĭp′ər-əs) *adj.* Producing well-developed young that are ready to pupate. Used of an insect.

pup•pet (pŭp′ĭt) *n.* **1.** A small figure having a hollow head and often a cloth body, designed to be fitted over and manipulated by the hand. **2.** A figure having jointed parts animated from above by strings or wires; a marionette. **3.** A toy representing a human figure; a doll. **4.** One whose behavior is determined by the will of others: *a political puppet.* [ME *poppet*, doll, poss. < AN *poppe*, doll. See PUPPY.]

pup•pet•eer (pŭp′ĭ-tîr′) *n.* One who entertains with and operates puppets or marionettes.

pup•pet•ry (pŭp′ĭ-trē) *n., pl.* **-ries 1.** The art of making puppets and presenting puppet shows. **2.** The actions of puppets. **3.** A stilted or artificial dramatic performance.

Pup•pis (pŭp′ĭs) *n.* A constellation in the Southern Hemisphere near Canis Major and Pyxis. [Lat. *puppis*, stern, poop.]

pup•py (pŭp′ē) *n., pl.* **-pies** A young dog; a pup. [ME *popi*, small pet dog, perh. < AN *poppe*, doll < VLat. **puppa* < Lat. *pūpa.*]

pup•py•ish (pŭp′ē-ĭsh) *adj.* Resembling a puppy.

puppy love *n.* Adolescent love or infatuation.

pup tent *n.* See **shelter tent.**

pur•blind (pûr′blīnd′) *adj.* **1.** Having poor vision; nearly or partly blind. **2.** Slow in understanding or discernment; dull. **3.** *Obsolete* Completely blind. [ME *pur blind*, totally blind, nearsighted : *pur*, pure; see PURE + *blind*, blind; see BLIND.] —**pur′blind′ly** *adv.* —**pur′blind′ness** *n.*

Pur•cell (pûr′səl, pûr-sĕl′), **Henry** 1659?–95. English composer known for his opera *Dido and Aeneas* (1689).

pur•chas•a•ble (pûr′chĭ-sə-bəl) *adj.* **1.** That can be bought. **2.** Capable of being bribed; venal. —**pur′chas•a•bil′i•ty** *n.*

pur•chase (pûr′chĭs) *tr.v.* **-chased, -chas•ing, -chas•es 1.** To obtain in exchange for money or its equivalent; buy. **2.** To acquire by effort; earn. **3.** To move or hold with a mechanical device, such as a lever. ❖ *n.* **1a.** The act or an instance of buying. **b.** Something bought. **c.** Acquisition through the payment of money or its equivalent. **2.** A grip applied manually or mechanically to move something or prevent it from slipping. **3.** A device, such as a lever, used to obtain mechanical advantage. **4.** A position, as of a lever, affording means to move or secure a weight. **5a.** A means of increasing power or influence. **b.** An advantage that is used in exerting one's power. [ME *purchasen*, to pursue, purchase < OFr. *purchacier* : *pur-*, forth (< Lat. *prō-*; see **per[1]** in App.) + *chacier*, to chase; see CHASE[1].] —**pur′chas•er** *n.*

pur•dah (pûr′də) *n.* **1a.** A curtain or screen, used mainly in India to keep women separate from men or strangers. **b.** The Hindu or Muslim system of sex segregation, practiced esp. by keeping women in seclusion. **2.** Social seclusion. [Urdu *pardah*, veil < Pers. < MPers. *pardak* < OPers. **paridaka-* < *pari-dā-*, to place over : *pari*, around, over; see **per[1]** in App. + *dā-*, to place; see **dhē-** in App.]

pure (pyo͝or) *adj.* **pur•er, pur•est 1.** Having a homogeneous or uniform composition; not mixed: *pure oxygen.* **2.** Free from adulterants or impurities: *pure chocolate.* **3.** Free of dirt, defilement, or pollution: *"A memory without blot or contamination must be . . . an inexhaustible source of pure refreshment"* (Charlotte Brontë). **4.** Free of foreign elements. **5.** Containing nothing inappropriate or extraneous: *a pure literary style.* **6.** Complete; utter: *pure folly.* **7.** Having no faults; sinless: *"I felt pure and sweet as a new baby"* (Sylvia Plath). **8.** Chaste; virgin. **9.** Of unmixed ancestry; purebred. **10.** *Genetics* Produced by self-fertilization or continual inbreeding; homozygous: *a pure line.* **11.** *Music* Free from discordant qualities. **12.** *Linguistics* Articulated with a single unchanging speech sound; monophthongal: *a pure vowel.* **13.** Theoretical: *pure science.* **14.** *Philosophy* Free of empirical elements: *pure reason.* [ME *pur* < OFr. < Lat. *pūrus.*] —**pure′ly** *adv.* —**pure′ness** *n.*

SYNONYMS *pure, absolute, sheer, simple, unadulterated* These adjectives mean free of extraneous elements: *pure gold; absolute oxygen; sheer alcohol; a simple substance; unadulterated coffee.*

pure•blood (pyo͝or′blŭd′) also **pure•blood•ed** (-blŭd′ĭd) *adj.* Of unmixed ancestry; purebred. —**pure′blood′** *n.*

pure•bred (pyo͝or′brĕd′) *adj.* Of a recognized strain established by breeding individuals of unmixed lineage over many generations. ❖ *n.* (pyo͝or′brĕd′) A purebred animal.

pu•rée or **pu•ree** (pyo͞o-rā′, pyo͝or′ā) *tr.v.* **-réed, -réing, -rées** To rub through a sieve or process (food) in a blender. ❖ *n.* Food prepared by straining or blending. [< Fr., purée < OFr. < fem. p. part. of *purer*, to strain, clean < Lat. *pūrāre*, to purify < *pūrus*, clean.]

pur•fle (pûr′fəl) *tr.v.* **-fled, -fling, -fles** To finish or decorate the border or edge of. ❖ *n.* also **pur•fling** (-flĭng) An ornamental border or edging. [ME *purfilen* < OFr. *porfiler* < VLat. **prōfīlāre* : Lat. *prō-*, forth; see PRO-[1] + Lat. *fīlum*, thread.]

pur•ga•tion (pûr-gā′shən) *n.* The act of purging or purifying.

pur•ga•tive (pûr′gə-tĭv) *adj.* Tending to cleanse or purge, esp. causing evacuation of the bowels. ❖ *n.* A purgative agent or medicine; a cathartic.

Pur•ga•toire (pûr′gə-twär′, -tôr′ē, -tōr′ē) A river of SE CO flowing c. 299 km (186 mi) to the Arkansas R.

pur•ga•to•ri•al (pûr′gə-tôr′ē-əl, -tōr′-) *adj.* **1.** Serving to purify of sin; expiatory. **2.** Of or resembling purgatory.

pur•ga•to•ry (pûr′gə-tôr′ē, -tōr′ē) *n., pl.* **-ries 1.** *Roman Catholic Church* A state in which the souls of those who have died in grace must expiate their sins. **2.** A place or condition of suffering, expiation, or remorse. ❖ *adj.* Tending to cleanse or purge. [ME *purgatorie* < OFr. *purgatoire* < Med.Lat. *pūrgātōrium* < LLat., means of purgation < neut. of *pūrgātōrius*, cleansing < Lat. *pūrgāre*, to cleanse. See PURGE.]

purge (pûrj) *v.* **purged, purg•ing, purg•es** —*tr.* **1a.** To free from impurities; purify. **b.** To remove (impurities and other elements) by or as if by cleansing. **2.** To rid of sin, guilt, or defilement. **3.** *Law* To clear (a person) of a charge or an imputation. Often used with respect to contempt of court. **4a.** To rid (a nation, for example) of people considered undesirable. **b.** To get rid of (people considered undesirable). **5.** *Medicine* **a.** To cause evacuation of (the bowels or stomach). **b.** To induce evacuation of the bowels or stomach in (an individual). —*intr.* **1.** To become pure or clean. **2.** *Medicine* To undergo or cause an emptying of the bowels or stomach. ❖ *n.* **1.** The act or process of purging. **2.** Something that purges, esp. a medicinal purgative. [ME *purgen* < OFr. *purgier* < Lat. *pūrgāre* < *pūrus*, pure.] —**purg′er** *n.*

pu•ri (po͝or′ē) *n.* Variant of **poori.**

pu•ri•fi•ca•tion (pyo͝or′ə-fĭ-kā′shən) *n.* The act or an instance of cleansing or purifying.

pu•ri•fi•ca•tor (pyo͝or′ə-fĭ-kā′tər) *n.* *Ecclesiastical* A cloth used to clean the chalice after the celebration of the Eucharist.

pu•ri•fy (pyo͝or′ə-fī′) *v.* **-fied, -fy•ing, -fies** —*tr.* **1.** To rid of impurities; cleanse. **2.** To rid of foreign or objectionable elements. **3.** To free from sin, guilt, or other defilement. —*intr.* To become clean or pure. [ME *purifien* < OFr. *purifier* < Lat. *pūrificāre* : *pūrus*, clean; see PURE + *-ficāre*, -fy.] —**pu•rif′i•ca•to′ry** (pyo͞o-rĭf′ĭ-kə-tôr′ē, -tōr′ē) *adj.* —**pu′ri•fi′er** *n.*

Pu•rim (po͝or′ĭm, po͞o-rēm′) *n.* *Judaism* The 14th of Adar, ob-

punty

pupa
of a monarch butterfly

ă	pat	oi	boy
ā	pay	ou	out
âr	care	o͝o	took
ä	father	o͞o	boot
ĕ	pet	ŭ	cut
ē	be	ûr	urge
ĭ	pit	th	thin
ī	pie	*th*	this
îr	pier	hw	which
ŏ	pot	zh	vision
ō	toe	ə	about, item
ô	paw		

Stress marks:
′ (primary);
′ (secondary), as in
lexicon (lĕk′sĭ-kŏn′)

served in celebration of the delivery by Esther of the Persian Jews from massacre. [Heb. *pûrîm*, pl. of *pûr*, lot (< the lots Haman cast to decide the day of the massacre, Esther 9:24–26) < Akkadian *pūru*, lot.]

pu•rine (pyŏŏr′ēn′) *n.* **1.** A crystalline organic base, $C_5H_4N_4$, that is the parent compound of various biologically important derivatives. **2.** Any of a group of organic compounds derived from or structurally related to purine, including uric acid and the nucleic acid constituents adenine and guanine. [Ger. *Purin*, blend of Lat. *pūrus*, clean; see PURE, and NLat. *ūricus*, uric (< Gk. *ouron*, urine) + Ger. *-in*, -in, -ine.]

pur•ism (pyŏŏr′ĭz′əm) *n.* **1.** Strict observance of or insistence on traditional correctness, esp. of language. **2.** An example of purism.

pur•ist (pyŏŏr′ĭst) *n.* One who practices or urges strict correctness, esp. in the use of words. —**pu•ris′tic** (pyŏŏ-rĭs′tĭk) *adj.* —**pu•ris′ti•cal•ly** *adv.*

Pu•ri•tan (pyŏŏr′ĭ-tn) *n.* **1.** A member of a group of English Protestants who in the 16th and 17th centuries advocated strict religious discipline and simplification of the ceremonies and creeds of the Church of England. **2. puritan** One who lives in accordance with strict religious or moral precepts, esp. one who regards pleasure as sinful. ❖ *adj.* **1.** Of or relating to the Puritans or Puritanism. **2. puritan** Characteristic of a puritan; puritanical. [< LLat. *pūritās*, purity < Lat. *pūrus*, pure.]

pu•ri•tan•i•cal (pyŏŏr′ĭ-tăn′ĭ-kəl) *adj.* **1.** Rigorous in religious observance; marked by stern morality. **2. Puritanical** Of, relating to, or characteristic of the Puritans. —**pu′ri•tan′i•cal•ly** *adv.*

Pu•ri•tan•ism (pyŏŏr′ĭ-tn-ĭz′əm) *n.* **1.** The practices and doctrines of the Puritans. **2. puritanism** Scrupulous moral rigor, esp. hostility to social pleasures and indulgences.

pu•ri•ty (pyŏŏr′ĭ-tē) *n.* **1.** The quality or condition of being pure. **2.** Freedom from sin or guilt; innocence; chastity. **3.** The absence in speech or writing of elements deemed inappropriate to good style. **4.** The degree to which a color is free from being mixed with other colors.

Pur•kin•je cell (pûr-kĭn′jē) *n.* A large, drop-shaped, densely branching neuron that is the characteristic cell of the cerebellar cortex. [After Johannes Evangelista von *Purkinje* (1787–1869), Bohemian physiologist.]

Purkinje fiber *n.* One of a network of specialized cardiac muscle fibers that rapidly transmit impulses from the atrioventricular node to the ventricles. [After Johannes Evangelista von *Purkinje* (1787–1869), Bohemian physiologist.]

purl¹ (pûrl) *intr.v.* **purled, purl•ing, purls** To flow or ripple with a murmuring sound. ❖ *n.* The sound made by rippling water. [Prob. of Scand. orig.]

purl² also **pearl** (pûrl) *v.* **purled, purl•ing, purls** also **pearled, pearl•ing, pearls** —*tr.* **1.** To knit (yarn) with a purl stitch. **2.** To edge or finish (a handkerchief, for example) with lace or embroidery. —*intr.* **1.** To do knitting with a purl stitch. **2.** To edge or finish with lace or embroidery. ❖ *n.* **1.** Inversion of a knit stitch; purl stitch. **2.** A decorative edging of lace or embroidery. **3.** Gold or silver wire used in embroidery. [?]

pur•lieu (pûr′lyŏŏ, pûrl′yŏŏ) *n.* **1.** An outlying or neighboring area. **2. purlieus** Outskirts; the environs. **3.** A place one frequents. [ME *purlewe*, piece of land on the edge of a forest, prob. alteration of *porale, purale*, royal perambulation < OFr. *porale* < *poraler*, to traverse : *por-*, forth (< Lat. *prō-*; see PRO-¹) + *aler*, *aller*, to go; see ALLEY¹.]

pur•lin also **pur•line** (pûr′lĭn) *n.* One of several horizontal timbers supporting the rafters of a roof. [ME.]

pur•loin (pər-loin′, pûr′loin′) *v.* **-loined, -loin•ing, -loins** —*tr.* To steal, often in a violation of trust. —*intr.* To commit theft. [ME *purloinen*, to remove < AN *purloigner* : *pur-*, away (< Lat. *prō-*; see PRO-¹) + *loign*, far (< Lat. *longē < longus*, long; see **del-** in App.).] —**pur•loin′er** *n.*

purl stitch *n.* An inverted knitting stitch, often alternated with the knit stitch to produce a ribbed effect.

pu•ro•my•cin (pyŏŏr′ə-mī′sĭn) *n.* An antibiotic, $C_{22}H_{29}N_7O_5$, obtained from the soil bacterium *Streptomyces alboniger* and used experimentally as an inhibitor of protein synthesis. [PUR(INE) + –MYCIN.]

pur•ple (pûr′pəl) *n.* **1.** Any of a group of colors with a hue between that of violet and red. **2.** Cloth of a color between violet and red, once a symbol of royalty or high office. **3.** Imperial power; high rank. ❖ *adj.* **1.** Of the color purple. **2.** Royal or imperial; regal. **3.** Elaborate and ornate. ❖ *tr. & intr.v.* **-pled, -pling, -ples** To make or become purple. [ME < OE *purpul < purpure*, purple garment < Lat. *purpura* < Gk. *porphūrā*, a shellfish yielding purple dye, purple.]

purple grackle *n.* A type of common grackle (*Quiscalus quiscula*) of eastern North America having iridescent blackish-purple plumage and a long keel-shaped tail.

pur•ple•heart (pûr′pəl-härt′) *n.* **1.** A tropical tree (*Peltogyne paniculata*) native to Guiana and Trinidad and having very hard durable brown wood that turns a purple color on exposure. **2.** The purplish heartwood of this tree.

Purple Heart *n.* A US military decoration awarded to members of the armed forces wounded in action.

purple loosestrife *n.* An Old World marsh plant (*Lythrum*

Purple Heart

salicaria) having long spikes of purple flowers and naturalized in the United States.

purple martin *n.* A large North American swallow (*Progne subis*) having glossy blue-black plumage and a light-colored breast in the female.

pur•plish (pûr′plĭsh) *adj.* Somewhat purple.

pur•port (pər-pôrt′, -pōrt′) *tr.v.* **-port•ed, -port•ing, -ports 1.** To have or present the often false appearance of being or intending; profess. **2.** To have the intention of doing; purpose. ❖ *n.* (pûr′pôrt′, -pōrt′) **1.** Meaning presented, intended, or implied; import. **2.** Intention; purpose. [ME *purporten*, to set forth < AN *purporter* : *pur-*, forth (< Lat. *prō-*; see PRO-¹) + *porter*, to carry (< Lat. *portāre*; see **per-²** in App.).]

pur•port•ed (pər-pôr′tĭd, -pōr′-) *adj.* Assumed to be such; supposed. —**pur•port′ed•ly** *adv.*

pur•pose (pûr′pəs) *n.* **1.** The object toward which one strives or for which something exists; an aim or goal. **2.** A result or effect that is intended or desired; an intention. See Syns at **intention**. **3.** Determination; resolution. **4.** The matter at hand; the point at issue. ❖ *tr.v.* **-posed, -pos•ing, -pos•es** To intend or resolve to perform or accomplish. —*idioms:* **on purpose** Intentionally; deliberately. **to good purpose** With good results. **to little** (or **no**) **purpose** With few or no results. [ME *purpos < AN < purposer*, to intend < *pur-*, forth (< Lat. *prō-*; see PRO-¹) + *poser*, to put; see POSE¹.]

pur•pose•ful (pûr′pəs-fəl) *adj.* **1.** Having a purpose; intentional. **2.** Having or manifesting purpose; determined. —**pur′pose•ful•ly** *adv.* —**pur′pose•ful•ness** *n.*

pur•pose•less (pûr′pəs-lĭs) *adj.* Lacking a purpose; meaningless or aimless.

pur•pose•ly (pûr′pəs-lē) *adv.* With specific purpose.

pur•po•sive (pûr′pə-sĭv) *adj.* **1.** Having or serving a purpose. **2.** Purposeful. —**pur′po•sive•ness** *n.*

pur•pu•ra (pûr′pə-rə, -pyə-) *n.* A condition characterized by hemorrhages in the skin and mucous membranes that result in the appearance of purplish spots or patches. [Lat., purple. See PURPLE.] —**pur•pu′ric** (-pyŏŏr′ĭk) *adj.*

pur•pu•rin (pûr′pyə-rĭn′) *n.* A reddish crystalline compound, $C_{14}H_5O_2(OH)_3$, used as a biological stain and commercial dye. [Lat. *purpura*, purple; see PURPLE + –IN.]

purr (pûr) *n.* **1.** The soft vibrant sound made by a cat. **2.** A sound similar to that made by a cat. ❖ *v.* **purred, purr•ing, purrs** —*intr.* To make or utter a purr. —*tr.* To express by a purr. [Imit.]

purse (pûrs) *n.* **1.** A woman's bag for carrying personal items; a handbag. **2.** A small bag or pouch for carrying money. **3.** Something that resembles a bag or pouch. **4.** Available wealth or resources; money. **5.** A sum of money collected as a present or offered as a prize. ❖ *tr.v.* **pursed, purs•ing, purs•es** To gather or contract (the lips or brow) into wrinkles or folds; pucker. [ME < OE < LLat. *bursa*. See BURSA.]

purs•er (pûr′sər) *n.* The officer in charge of money matters on a ship or commercial aircraft. [ME < *purse*, purse. See PURSE.]

purse seine *n.* A fishing seine that is drawn into the shape of a bag to enclose the catch.

purse strings or **purse•strings** (pûrs′strĭngz′) *pl.n.* Financial support or resources, or control over them.

purs•lane (pûrs′lĭn, -lān′) *n.* A trailing Asian weed (*Portulaca oleracea*) having small yellow flowers, reddish stems, and fleshy obovate edible leaves. [ME < AN *purcelane, alteration of Lat. *portulāca, porcilāca*. See PORTULACA.]

pur•su•ance (pər-sŏŏ′əns) *n.* A carrying out or putting into effect; prosecution.

pur•su•ant (pər-sŏŏ′ənt) *adj.* Proceeding from and conformable to; in accordance with. ❖ *adv.* Accordingly; consequently. [Prob. < ME *pursuant*, aspirant < AN, pr. part. of *pursure*, to pursue. See PURSUE.]

pur•sue (pər-sŏŏ′) *v.* **-sued, -su•ing, -sues** —*tr.* **1.** To follow in an effort to overtake or capture; chase. **2.** To strive to gain or accomplish. **3.** To proceed along the course of; follow. **4.** To carry further; advance. **5.** To be engaged in (a vocation or hobby, for example). **6.** To court. **7.** To continue to torment or afflict; haunt. —*intr.* **1.** To follow in an effort to overtake or capture; chase. **2.** To carry on; continue. [ME *pursuen < AN pursure < VLat. *prōsequere < Lat. *prōsequī. See PROSECUTE.] —**pur•su′a•ble** *adj.* —**pur•su′er** *n.*

pur•suit (pər-sŏŏt′) *n.* **1.** The act or an instance of chasing or pursuing. **2.** The act of striving. **3.** An activity, such as a vocation or hobby, engaged in regularly. [ME < AN *pursuite < pursure*, to pursue. See PURSUE.]

pursuit plane *n.* A high-speed fighter plane designed and equipped to pursue and attack enemy aircraft.

pur•sui•vant (pûr′swĭ-vənt) *n.* **1.** An officer in the British Colleges of Heralds who ranks below a herald. **2.** A follower or attendant. [ME *pursevant*, attendant < OFr. *poursuivant < pr. part. of *poursuivre*, to follow < VLat. *prōsequere.*]

pur•te•nance (pûr′tn-əns) *n.* An animal's viscera or internal organs, esp. the heart, liver, and lungs. [ME *pertenaunce, purtenaunce*, adjunct < OFr. *partenance, pertinence < partenir*, to pertain. See PERTAIN.]

pur•ty (pûr′tē) *adj.* Regional Variant of **pretty**.

REGIONAL NOTE *Purty* is probably the most common American example of metathesis, a linguistic process in which two adjacent sounds are reversed in order. Metathesis in English often involves the consonant *r* and a vowel. For example, the word *third* used to be *thrid.* By the same process, English *pretty* often became *purty* in regional speech.

pu•ru•lence (pyo͝or′ə-ləns, pyo͝or′yə-) *n.* **1.** The condition of containing or discharging pus. **2.** Pus.

pu•ru•lent (pyo͝or′ə-lənt, pyo͝or′yə-) *adj.* Containing, discharging, or causing the production of pus. [ME *purulente* < OFr. *purulent* < Lat. *pūrulentus* < *pūs, pūr-*, pus. See **pū-** in App.] **—pu′ru•lent•ly** *adv.*

Pu•rus (pə-ro͞os′, po͞o-) A river of E-central Peru and W Brazil flowing c. 3,379 km (2,100 mi) to the Amazon R.

pur•vey (pər-vā′, pûr′vā′) *tr.v.* **-veyed, -vey•ing, -veys 1.** To supply (food, for example); furnish. **2.** To advertise or circulate. [ME *purveien* < AN *purveier* < Lat. *prōvidēre.* See PROVIDE.] **—pur•vey′ance** *n.*

pur•vey•or (pər-vā′ər) *n.* **1.** One that furnishes provisions, esp. food. **2.** One that promulgates something.

pur•view (pûr′vyo͞o′) *n.* **1.** The extent or range of function, power, or competence; scope. **2.** Range of vision, comprehension, or experience; outlook. [Alteration of ME *purveu*, proviso < AN *purveu est*, it is provided (introducing a proviso), p. part. of *purveier*, to provide. See PURVEY.]

pus (pŭs) *n.* A generally viscous yellowish-white fluid formed in infected tissue, consisting of white blood cells, cellular debris, and necrotic tissue. [Lat. *pūs.* See **pū-** in App.]

Pu•san (po͞o′sän′) also **Fu•san** (fo͞o′-) A city of SE South Korea on Korea Strait SE of Seoul. Pop. 3,814,000.

Pu•sey (pyo͞o′zē), **Edward Bouverie** 1800–82. British theologian who led the Oxford movement after 1845.

Pu•sey•ism (pyo͞o′zē-ĭz′əm, pyo͞o′sē-) *n.* Tractarianism. [After Edward Bouverie PUSEY.] **—Pu′sey•ite′** (-īt′) *n.*

push (po͝osh) *v.* **pushed, push•ing, push•es** *—tr.* **1a.** To apply pressure against (something), esp. for the purpose of moving it: *pushed the door but couldn't budge it.* **b.** To move (something) by exerting force against it; thrust or shove: *pushed the crate aside.* **2.** To force (one's way): *pushed our way through the crowd.* **3.** To urge forward or urge insistently; pressure: *pushed him to study harder.* **4.** To exert downward pressure on (a button or keyboard, for example); press. **5.** To extend or enlarge: *pushed sales into the millions.* **6.** *Informal* To approach in age: *is pushing 40.* **7.** *Slang* **a.** To promote or sell (a product): *pushed her latest book during the interview.* **b.** To sell (a narcotic) illegally: *pushed drugs.* **8.** *Sports* To hit (a ball) in the direction toward the dominant hand of the player propelling it, as to the right of a right-handed player. *—intr.* **1.** To exert outward pressure or force against something. **2.** To advance despite difficulty or opposition; press forward. **3.** To expend great or vigorous effort. ❖ *n.* **1.** The act of pushing; a thrust: *gave the door a swift push.* **2.** A vigorous or insistent effort toward an end; a drive: *a push to democracy.* **3.** A provocation to action; a stimulus. **4.** *Informal* Persevering energy; enterprise. ***—phrasal verbs:*** **push around** *Informal* To treat or threaten to treat roughly; intimidate. **push off** *Informal* To set out; depart. **push on** To continue or proceed along one's way. ***—idioms:*** **push up daisies** *Slang* To be dead and buried. **when** (or **if**) **push comes to shove** At a point when or if all else has been taken into account and matters must be confronted. [ME *pusshen* < OFr. *poulser, pousser* < Lat. *pulsāre*, freq. of *pellere*, to strike, push. See **pel-**[2] in App.]

SYNONYMS *push, propel, shove, thrust* These verbs mean to press against something in order to move it forward or aside: *push a baby carriage; wind propelling a sailboat; shove a tray across a table; thrust the stick into the ground.* **ANTONYM** *pull*

push•ball (po͝osh′bôl′) *n.* **1.** A game in which two opposing teams attempt to push a heavy ball, 6 feet (1.8 meters) in diameter, across a goal. **2.** The ball used in this game.

push broom *n.* A broom having a wide brush perpendicular to the end of a long handle, designed to be pushed in sweeping.

push•but•ton (po͝osh′bŭt′n) *n.* also **push button** A small button that activates an electric circuit when pushed. ❖ *adj.* also **push-button** Equipped with or operated by a push button.

push•cart (po͝osh′kärt′) *n.* A light cart pushed by hand.

push•er (po͝osh′ər) *n. Slang* One who sells drugs illegally.

push•ful (po͝osh′fo͝ol′) *adj.* Pushing. **—push′ful•ness** *n.*

push•ing (po͝osh′ĭng) *adj.* **1.** Energetic; enterprising. **2.** Aggressive; forward; presuming. **—push′ing•ly** *adv.*

Push•kin (po͝osh′kĭn, po͝osh′-), **Aleksandr Sergeyevich** 1799–1837. Russian writer whose works include the play *Boris Godunov* (1831) and the novel *Eugene Onegin* (1833).

push•o•ver (po͝osh′ō′vər) *n.* **1.** One easily defeated or taken advantage of. **2.** Something easily done or attained.

push•pin (po͝osh′pĭn′) *n.* **1.** A tacklike pin with a large head that is easily inserted into a wall or board. **2.** A game played by children with pins.

Push•tu (pŭsh′to͞o) *n.* Variant of **Pashto.**

push•up (po͝osh′ŭp′) *n.* An exercise for strengthening arm muscles performed by lying face down with the palms on the floor and moving the body up and down with the arms.

push•y (po͝osh′ē) *adj.* **-i•er, -i•est** Disagreeably aggressive or forward. **—push′i•ly** *adv.* **—push′i•ness** *n.*

pu•sil•la•nim•i•ty (pyo͞o′sə-lə-nĭm′ĭ-tē) *n.* The state or quality of being pusillanimous; cowardice.

pu•sil•lan•i•mous (pyo͞o′sə-lăn′ə-məs) *adj.* Lacking courage; cowardly. [ME *pusillanimus* < LLat. *pusillanimis* : Lat. *pusillus*, weak, dim. of *pullus*, young of an animal + *animus*, reason, mind; see **anə-** in App.] **—pu′sil•lan′i•mous•ly** *adv.*

puss[1] (po͝os) *Informal n.* **1.** A cat. **2.** A girl or young woman. [Prob. of Gmc. orig.]

puss[2] (po͝os) *n. Slang* **1.** The mouth. **2.** The human face. [Ir.Gael. *pus*, mouth < MIr. *bus*, lip.]

puss•ley (pŭs′lē) *n.* Purslane. [Alteration of *pursley*, alteration of PURSLANE.]

puss•y[1] (po͝os′ē) *n., pl.* **-ies 1.** *Informal* A cat. **2.** *Botany* A fuzzy catkin, esp. of the pussy willow. **3.** *Vulgar Slang* **a.** The vulva. **b.** Sexual intercourse with a woman. **4.** *Offensive Slang* Used as a disparaging term for a woman. **5.** *Slang* A man regarded as weak, timid, or unmanly.

pus•sy[2] (pŭs′ē) *adj.* **-si•er, -si•est** Containing or resembling pus.

puss•y•cat (po͝os′ē-kăt′) *n.* **1.** A cat. **2.** *Informal* One who is regarded as easygoing, mild-mannered, or amiable.

puss•y•foot (po͝os′ē-fo͝ot′) *intr.v.* **-foot•ed, -foot•ing, -foots 1.** To move stealthily or cautiously. **2.** *Informal* To act or proceed cautiously or timidly to avoid committing oneself. **—puss′y•foot′er** *n.*

puss•y•toes (po͝os′ē-tōz′) *pl.n.* (*used with a sing. or pl. verb*) Any of several low-growing perennial plants of the genus *Antennaria*, having downy leaves and clusters of white flower heads.

puss•y willow (po͝os′ē) *n.* **1.** A deciduous North American shrub or small tree *(Salix discolor)* having large silky catkins. **2.** Any of several willows similar to this plant.

pus•tu•lant (pŭs′chə-lənt, pŭs′tyə-) *adj.* Causing the formation of pustules. ❖ *n.* A pustulant agent.

pus•tu•lar (pŭs′chə-lər, pŭs′tyə-) *adj.* Of, relating to, or consisting of pustules.

pus•tu•late (pŭs′chə-lāt′, pŭs′tyə-) *v.* **-lat•ed, -lat•ing, -lates** *—tr.* To cause to form pustules. *—intr.* To form pustules. ❖ *adj.* (*also* -lĭt) Covered with pustules. **—pus′tu•la′tion** *n.*

pus•tule (pŭs′cho͞ol, pŭs′tyo͞ol) *n.* **1.** A small inflamed elevation of the skin that is filled with pus; a pimple. **2.** A small swelling similar to a blister or pimple. **3.** Something likened to an inflamed pus-filled lesion. [ME < OFr. < Lat. *pūstula*, blister.]

put (po͝ot) *v.* **put, put•ting, puts** *—tr.* **1.** To place in a specified location; set: *She put the books on the table.* **2.** To cause to be in a specified condition: *His manners put me at ease.* **3.** To cause (one) to undergo something; subject: *put the prisoner to torture.* **4.** To assign; attribute: *put a false interpretation on events.* **5.** To estimate: *We put the time at 5:00.* **6.** To impose or levy: *put a tax on cigarettes.* **7.** *Games* To wager (a stake); bet: *put $50 on a horse.* **8.** *Sports* To hurl with an overhand pushing motion: *put the shot.* **9.** To bring up for consideration or judgment: *put a question to the judge.* **10.** To express; state: *I put my objections bluntly.* **11.** To render in a specified language or literary form: *put prose into verse.* **12.** To adapt: *put lyrics to music.* **13.** To urge or force to an action: *a mob that put the thief to flight.* **14.** To apply: *We must put our minds to it.* **15.** To force the purchase of (a stock or commodity) by exercising a put option. *—intr.* **1.** To begin to move, esp. in a hurry. **2.** *Nautical* To proceed: *The ship put into the harbor.* ❖ *n.* **1.** *Sports* An act of putting the shot. **2.** An option to sell a stipulated amount of stock or securities within a specified time and at a fixed price. ❖ *adj. Informal* Fixed; stationary: *stay put.* ***—phrasal verbs:*** **put about** *Nautical* To change or cause to change direction; go or cause to go from one tack to another. **put across 1.** To state so as to be understood clearly or accepted readily. **2.** To attain or carry through by deceit or trickery. **put away 1.** To renounce; discard: *put all negative thoughts away.* **2.** *Informal* To consume (food or drink) readily and quickly. **3.** *Informal* To confine to a mental health facility. **4a.** *Informal* To kill. **b.** To bury. **put by** To save for later use. **put down 1a.** To write down. **b.** To enter in a list. **2a.** To end by force; repress: *put down a rebellion.* **b.** To render ineffective: *put down rumors.* **3.** To subject (an animal) to euthanasia. **4.** *Slang* **a.** To criticize: *put me down for failing the course.* **b.** To belittle; disparage: *put down their knowledge of literature.* **c.** To humiliate. **5a.** To assign to a category: *put him down as a sneak.* **b.** To attribute: *put the mistake down to inexperience.* **6.** To consume (food or drink) readily; put away. **put forth 1.** To grow: *Plants put forth new growth in the spring.* **2.** To bring to bear; exert: *put forth effort.* **3.** To offer for consideration: *put forth an idea.* **put forward** To propose for consideration: *put forth an idea.* **put in 1.** To make a formal offer of: *put in a plea of guilty.* **2.** To interpose: *He put in a good word for me.* **3.** To spend (time) at a location or job: *put in eight hours at the office.* **4.** To plant: *put in 20 rows of trees.* **5.** To apply: *put in for early retirement.* **6.** *Nautical* To enter a port or harbor. **put off 1a.** To delay; postpone: *put off paying the bills.* **b.** To persuade to delay further action: *put off creditors.* **2.** To take off; discard: *put off a sweater.* **3.** To repel or repulse, as from bad manners. **4.** To pass (money) or sell (merchandise) fraudulently. **put on 1.** To clothe oneself with; don. **2.** To apply; activate: *put on the*

Aleksandr S. Pushkin
detail of a painting by Orest Kiprensky (1773?–1836)

pussy willow
Salix discolor

ă	**pat**	oi	**boy**
ā	**pay**	ou	**out**
âr	**care**	o͝o	**took**
ä	**father**	o͞o	**boot**
ĕ	**pet**	ŭ	**cut**
ē	**be**	ûr	**urge**
ĭ	**pit**	th	**thin**
ī	**pie**	*th*	**this**
îr	**pier**	hw	**which**
ŏ	**pot**	zh	**vision**
ō	**toe**	ə	**about, item**
ô	**paw**		

Stress marks:
′ (primary);
′ (secondary), as in
lexicon (lĕk′sĭ-kŏn′)

brakes. **3.** To assume affectedly: *put on airs.* **4.** *Slang* To tease or mislead (another). **5.** To add: *put on weight.* **6.** To produce; perform. **put out 1.** To extinguish: *put out a fire.* **2.** *Nautical* To leave, as a port or harbor; depart. **3.** To expel: *put out a drunk.* **4.** To publish. **5a.** To inconvenience: *Did our early arrival put you out?* **b.** To offend or irritate. **6.** To make an effort. **7.** *Baseball* To retire a runner. **8.** *Vulgar Slang* To be sexually active. Used of a woman. **put over 1.** To postpone; delay. **2.** To put across, esp. in order to deceive. **put through 1.** To bring to a successful end. **2.** To cause to undergo: *put us through an ordeal.* **3a.** To make a telephone connection for. **b.** To obtain a connection for (a telephone call). **put to** *Nautical* To head for shore. **put together** To construct; create. **put up 1.** To erect; build. **2.** To preserve; can. **3.** To nominate. **4.** To provide (funds) in advance. **5.** To provide lodgings for. **6.** *Sports* To startle (game animals) from cover. **7.** To offer for sale. **8a.** To make a display or the appearance of. **b.** To engage in; carry on: *put up a good fight.* **put upon** To impose on; overburden. —*idioms:* **put an end (or a halt or a stop) to** To bring to an end; terminate. **put down roots** To establish a permanent residence in a locale. **put it to (someone)** *Slang* **1.** To overburden with tasks or work. **2.** To put blame on. **3.** To take unfair advantage of. **4.** To lay out the facts of a situation to (another) in a forceful, candid manner. **5.** To defeat soundly; trounce. **put (one) in mind** To remind. **put (oneself) out:** To make a considerable effort; go to trouble or expense. **put (one's) finger on** To identify. **put (one's) foot down** To take a firm stand. **put (one's) foot in (one's) mouth** To make a tactless remark. **put paid to** *Chiefly British* To finish off; put to rest. **put (someone) in (someone's) place** To lower the dignity of (someone); humble. **put (someone) through (someone's) paces** To cause to demonstrate ability or skill; test. **put (someone) up to** To cause to commit a funny, mischievous, or malicious act. **put something over on** To deceive, cheat, or trick. **put the arm (or bite or squeeze) on** *Slang* To ask another for money. **put the finger on** *Slang* To inform on. **put the make (or moves) on** *Slang* To make sexual advances to. **put the screws to (or on)** *Slang* To pressure (another) in an extreme manner. **put the skids on** *Slang* To bring to a halt. **put to bed** *Informal* **1.** To make final preparations for the printing of (a newspaper, for example). **2.** To make final preparations for completing (a project). **put to it** To cause extreme difficulty for: *put to it to finish the deal.* **put to sleep 1.** To make weary; bore. **2.** To subject to euthanasia. **3.** To subject to general anesthesia. **put two and two together** To draw the proper conclusions from existing evidence or indications. **put up or shut up** *Slang* To have to endure (something unpleasant) without complaining or take the action necessary to remove the source of the unpleasantry. **put up with** To endure without complaint. [ME *putten,* back-formation < OE **pūtte,* p. t. of *pȳtan,* to put out.]

pu·ta·men (pyōo-tā′mən) *n.,* pl. **-tam·i·na** (-tăm′ə-nə) A hard shell-like covering, such as that enclosing the kernel of a peach. [Lat. *putāmen,* that which falls off in pruning, shell, husk < *putāre,* to prune.] —**pu·tam′i·nous** (-tăm′ə-nəs) *adj.*

pu·ta·tive (pyōo′tə-tĭv) *adj.* Generally regarded as such; supposed. [ME < OFr. *putatif* < LLat. *putātīvus* < Lat. *putāre,* to prune, think.] —**pu·ta·tive·ly** *adv.*

put·down or **put-down** (pōōt′doun′) *n. Slang* **1.** A dismissal or rejection, esp. in the form of a critical or slighting remark. **2.** A typically good-natured parody, esp. in theater.

put·log (pōōt′lôg′, -lŏg′, pŭt′-) *n.* One of the short pieces of lumber supporting the floor of a scaffold. [Alteration (influenced by LOG[1]) of obsolete *putlock* : perh. PUT + LOCK[1].]

Put·nam (pŭt′nəm), *Israel* 1718–90. Amer. soldier who during the Battle of Bunker Hill (Jun. 17, 1775) supposedly issued the order, "Don't one of you shoot until you see the whites of their eyes."

Putnam, Rufus 1738–1824. Amer. Revolutionary soldier who helped force the British to evacuate Boston (1775).

put·off (pōōt′ôf′, -ŏf′) *n.* A pretext for inaction; an excuse.

put-on (pōōt′ŏn′, -ôn′) *adj.* Pretended; feigned. ❖ *n. Slang* **1.** A deceptive outward appearance. **2.** The act of teasing or misleading someone, esp. for amusement. **3.** Something, such as a prank, intended as a hoax or joke; a spoof.

Pu·tong·hua also **Pu tong hua** (pōō′tông′hwä′, -wä′, -tŏng′-) *n.* See **Mandarin** 4. [Chin. (Mandarin) *pǔtōnghuà* : *pǔtōng,* ordinary (*pǔ,* general, widespread + *tōng,* through) + *huà,* language.]

put·out (pōōt′out′) *abbr. Baseball* A play in which a batter or base runner is retired.

put-put (pŭt′pŭt′) *n. Slang* **1.** A small gasoline engine. **2.** A vehicle, such as a boat, that is operated by a small gasoline engine. [Imit. of a running engine.]

pu·tre·fac·tion (pyōo′trə-făk′shən) *n.* **1.** Decomposition of organic matter, esp. protein, by microorganisms, resulting in production of foul-smelling matter. **2.** Putrefied matter. **3.** The condition of being putrefied.

pu·tre·fac·tive (pyōo′trə-făk′tĭv) *adj.* **1.** Bringing about putrefaction. **2.** Of, relating to, or characterized by putrefaction.

pu·tre·fy (pyōo′trə-fī′) *v.* **-fied, -fy·ing, -fies** —*tr.* **1.** To cause to decay and have a foul odor. **2.** To make gangrenous. —*intr.* **1.** To become decayed and have a foul odor. **2.** To become gangrenous. [ME *putrefien* < OFr. *putrefier* < Lat. *putrefacere* : *puter,*

putr-, rotten; see **pū-** in App. + *facere,* to make; see **dhē-** in App.]

pu·tres·cence (pyōo-trĕs′əns) *n.* **1.** A putrescent character or condition. **2.** Putrid matter.

pu·tres·cent (pyōo-trĕs′ənt) *adj.* **1.** Becoming putrid; putrefying. **2.** Of or relating to putrefaction. [Lat. *putrēscēns, putrēscent-,* pr. part. of *putrēscere,* to rot, inchoative of *putrēre,* to be rotten < *puter, putr-,* rotten. See **pū-** in App.]

pu·tres·ci·ble (pyōo-trĕs′ə-bəl) *adj.* Subject to putrefaction. [Fr. < OFr. < LLat. *putrēscibilis* < Lat. *putrēscere,* to rot. See PUTRESCENT.]

pu·tres·cine (pyōo-trĕs′ēn) *n.* A colorless foul-smelling ptomaine, $NH_2(CH_2)_4NH_2$, produced in decaying animal tissue by the decarboxylation of ornithine. [Lat. *putrēscere,* to rot; see PUTRESCENT + -INE[2].]

pu·trid (pyōo′trĭd) *adj.* **1.** Decomposed and foul-smelling; rotten. **2.** Proceeding from, relating to, or exhibiting putrefaction. **3.** Morally rotten; corrupt. **4.** Extremely objectionable; vile. [ME *putred* < OFr. *putride* < Lat. *putridus* < *putrēre,* to be rotten < *puter, putr-,* rotten. See **pū-** in App.] —**pu·trid′i·ty** (-trĭd′ĭ-tē), **pu′trid·ness** (-trĭd-nĭs) *n.* —**pu′trid·ly** *adv.*

putsch also **Putsch** (pōōch) *n.* A sudden attempt by a group to overthrow a government. [Ger. < Ger. dialectal < MHGer., thrust, of imit. orig.] —**putsch′ist** *n.*

putt (pŭt) *n.* A light golf stroke made on the putting green in an effort to place the ball into the hole. ❖ *v.* **putt·ed, putt·ing, putts** —*tr.* To hit (a golf ball) with a light stroke on the green. —*intr.* To putt a golf ball. [Variant of PUT.]

putt
golfer Tiger Woods

put·tee (pŭ-tē′, pŭt′ē) *n.* **1.** A strip of cloth wound spirally around the leg from ankle to knee. Often used in the plural. **2.** A gaiter covering the lower leg. Often used in the plural. [Hindi *paṭṭī* < Skt. *paṭṭikā* < *paṭṭakaḥ,* bandage, ribbon < *paṭṭaḥ,* strip of cloth.]

putt·er[1] (pŭt′ər) *n.* **1.** A short golf club used for putting. **2.** A golfer who is putting.

putt·er[2] (pŭt′ər) *v.* **-tered, -ter·ing, -ters** —*intr.* To occupy oneself in an aimless or ineffective manner. —*tr.* To waste (time) in idling: *puttered away the hours.* [Prob. alteration of *potter,* prob. freq. of ME *poten,* to poke, push < OE *potian.*] —**putt′er·er** *n.*

put·to (pōō′tō) *n.,* pl. **-ti** (-tē) A representation of a small child, often naked and having wings, used esp. in the art of the European Renaissance. [Ital., boy < VLat. **puttus* < Lat. *putus.*]

put·ty (pŭt′ē) *n.,* pl. **-ties 1a.** A doughlike cement made by mixing whiting and linseed oil, used to fill holes in woodwork and secure panes of glass. **b.** A substance with a similar consistency or function. **2.** A fine lime cement used as a finishing coat on plaster. **3.** A yellowish or light brownish gray to grayish yellow or light grayish brown. ❖ *tr.v.* **-tied, -ty·ing, -ties** To fill, cover, or secure with putty. [Fr. *potée,* polishing powder < OFr., a potful < *pot,* pot < VLat. **pottus.*]

putty knife *n.* A tool having a flat flexible blade, used for scraping and applying putty.

put·ty·root (pŭt′ē-rōōt′, -rŏŏt′) *n.* A North American orchid (*Aplectrum hyemale*) bearing a single leaf and yellowish-brown flowers clustered in a raceme.

Pu·tu·ma·yo (pōō′tə-mī′ō, pōō′tōō-mä′yô) A river of NW South America rising in SW Colombia and flowing c. 1,609 km (1,000 mi) to the Amazon R. in NW Brazil.

put-up (pōōt′ŭp′) *adj. Informal* Prearranged secretly.

putz (pŭts) *n.* **1.** *Slang* A fool; an idiot. **2.** *Vulgar Slang* A penis. ❖ *intr.v.* **putzed, putz·ing, putz·es** *Slang* To behave in an idle manner; putter. [Yiddish *pots,* penis, fool.]

Pu·vis de Cha·vannes (pyōo-vē′ də shä-vän′, -vēs′, pü-vē′), **Pierre** 1824–98. French artist noted for his decorative and allegorical murals, such as *Work* (1863).

puz·zle (pŭz′əl) *v.* **-zled, -zling, -zles** —*tr.* **1.** To baffle or confuse mentally by presenting or being a difficult problem or matter. **2.** To clarify or solve (something confusing) by reasoning or study: *I puzzled it out.* —*intr.* **1.** To be perplexed. **2.** To ponder over a problem in an effort to solve or understand it. ❖ *n.* **1.** Something, such as a game, toy, or problem, that requires ingenuity in solving or assembling. **2.** Something that baffles or confuses. **3.** The condition of being perplexed; bewilderment. [?] —**puz′zler** *n.*

puz·zle·ment (pŭz′əl-mənt) *n.* The state of being confused or baffled; perplexity.

PV *abbr.* polyvinyl

PVC (pē′vē-sē′) *n.* A common thermoplastic resin, used in a wide variety of manufactured products, including rainwear, garden hoses, and floor tiles. [P(OLY)V(INYL) C(HLORIDE).]

PVT or **Pvt** *abbr.* private

PWA *abbr.* **1.** person with AIDS **2.** Public Works Administration

pwt. *abbr.* pennyweight

pxt. *abbr. Latin* pinxit (he painted this; she painted this)

py– *pref.* Variant of **pyo–.**

pyc·nid·i·um (pĭk-nĭd′ē-əm) *n.,* pl. **-i·a** (-ē-ə) A flask-shaped asexual structure containing conidia, found in certain fungi. [NLat. : Gk. *puknos,* thick + Lat. *-idium,* diminutive suff. (< Gk. *-idion*).] —**pyc·nid′i·al** *adj.*

pyc·nog·o·nid (pĭk-nŏg′ə-nĭd, pĭk′nə-gŏn′ĭd) *n.* See **sea spider.** [< NLat. Pycnogonidae, family name < *Pycnogonum,* type

putto
detail from *The Triumph of Galatea,* c. 1512–14 fresco in the Villa Farnesina, Rome

genus : Gk. *puknos*, thick + Gk. *gonu*, knee; see **genu-** in App.]

pyc·nom·e·ter (pĭk-nŏm′ĭ-tər) *n.* A standard vessel used in measuring the density or specific gravity of materials. [Gk. *puknos*, dense + –METER.]

pye-dog also **pi-dog** (pī′dôg′, -dŏg′) *n.* A stray dog. [Perh. Hindi *pāhī*, outsider.]

py·e·li·tis (pī′ə-lī′tĭs) *n.* Acute inflammation of the pelvis of the kidney, caused by bacterial infection. [NLat. *pyelitis* : Gk. *puelos*, basin; see **pleu-** in App. + –ITIS.] —**py′e·lit′ic** (-lĭt′ĭk) *adj.*

py·e·lo·gram (pī′ə-lə-grăm′) *n.* An x-ray obtained by pyelography. [Gk. *puelos*, basin; see PYELITIS + –GRAM.]

py·e·log·ra·phy (pī′ə-lŏg′rə-fē) *n.* X-ray photography of the pelvis of the kidney after injection with a radiopaque dye. [Gk. *puelos*, basin; see PYELITIS + –GRAPHY.]

py·e·lo·ne·phri·tis (pī′ə-lō-nĭ-frī′tĭs) *n.* Inflammation of the kidney and its pelvis, caused by bacterial infection. [NLat. *pyelonephritis* : Gk. *puelos*, basin; see PYELITIS + NEPHRITIS.]

py·e·mi·a (pī-ē′mē-ə) *n.* Septicemia caused by pyogenic microorganisms in the blood, often resulting in the formation of multiple abscesses. —**py·e′mic** *adj.*

py·gid·i·um (pī-jĭd′ē-əm) *n., pl.* -i·a (-ē-ə) The posterior body region or caudal segment of certain insects and other invertebrates. [NLat. < Gk. *pugidion*, dim. of *pugē*, buttocks.] —**py·gid′i·al** (-ē-əl) *adj.*

pyg·mae·an or **pyg·me·an** (pĭg-mē′ən, pĭg′mē-) *adj.* Pygmy. [< Lat. *pygmaeus*, sing. of *Pygmaeī*, the Pygmies. See PYGMY.]

Pyg·ma·lion (pĭg-māl′yən, -mā′lē-ən) *n. Greek Mythology* A king of Cyprus who carved and then fell in love with a statue of a woman, which Aphrodite brought to life as Galatea.

Pyg·my also **Pig·my** (pĭg′mē) *n., pl.* -mies 1. *Greek Mythology* A member of a race of dwarfs. 2. also **pygmy** A member of any of various peoples, as members of equatorial Africa and parts of southeast Asia, having an average height less than 5 feet (1.27 m). Not in scientific use. 3. **pygmy a.** An individual of unusually small size. b. An individual considered to be of little or no importance. ❖ *adj.* 1. also **pygmy** *Anthropology* Of or relating to the Pygmies. 2. **pygmy a.** Unusually or atypically small. b. Unimportant; trivial. [ME *pigmie* < Lat. *Pygmaeī*, the Pygmies < Gk. *Pugmaioi* < *pugmē*, cubit, fist.] —**pyg′moid** (-moid′) *adj.*

pygmy chimpanzee *n.* See bonobo.

pygmy hippopotamus *n.* A small hippopotamus (*Choeropsis liberiensis*) of Liberia and and Côte d'Ivoire.

py·ja·ma (pə-jä′mə, -jăm′ə) *n. Chiefly British* Variant of pajama.

pyk·nic (pĭk′nĭk) *adj.* Having a short stocky physique. [< Gk. *puknos*, dense.] —**pyk′nic** *n.*

Pyle (pīl), **Ernest Taylor** Known as "Ernie." 1900–45. Amer. journalist noted for his stories about World War II soldiers.

py·lon (pī′lŏn′) *n.* 1. A steel tower supporting high-tension wires. 2. A tower marking a turning point in a race among aircraft. 3. A large structure or group of structures marking an entrance or approach. 4. A monumental gateway in the form of a pair of truncated pyramids serving as the entrance to an ancient Egyptian temple. [Gk. *pulōn*, gateway < *pulē*, gate.]

py·lo·rus (pī-lôr′əs, -lōr′-, pĭ-) *n., pl.* -lo·ri (-lôr′ī′, -lōr′ī′) The passage at the lower end of the stomach that opens into the duodenum. [LLat. *pylōrus* < Gk. *pulōros* : *pulē*, gate + *ouros*, guard.] —**py·lo′ric** (-ĭk) *adj.*

Pym (pĭm), **John** 1584–1643. English Parliamentarian who moved for the impeachment of the advisers to Charles I, precipitating the English Civil War.

pyo- or **py-** *pref.* Pus: *pyogenic.* [Gk. *puo-* < *puon*, pus. See **pǔ-** in App.]

py·o·der·ma (pī′ə-dûr′mə) *n.* A pyogenic skin disease. —**py′o·der′mic** *adj.*

py·o·gen·e·sis (pī′ə-jĕn′ĭ-sĭs) *n.* Formation of pus.

py·o·gen·ic (pī′ə-jĕn′ĭk) *adj.* 1. Producing pus. 2. Of, relating to, or characterized by pyogenesis.

py·oid (pī′oid) *adj.* Of or resembling pus.

Pyong·yang (pyŭng′yäng′, -yăng′, pyông′-) The cap. of North Korea, in the SW-central part; an important cultural center and Chinese culture after 108 B.C. Pop. 2,355,000.

py·or·rhe·a or **py·or·rhoe·a** (pī′ə-rē′ə) *n.* 1. Purulent inflammation of the gums and tooth sockets, often causing loose teeth. 2. A discharge of pus. —**py′or·rhe′al** *adj.*

py·o·sis (pī-ō′sĭs) *n.* Pyogenesis.

pyr– *pref.* Variant of pyro-.

py·ra·can·tha (pī′rə-kăn′thə) *n.* A shrub of the genus *Pyracantha*; the fire thorn. [NLat. *Pyracantha*, genus name < Lat. *pyracantha*, a shrub < Gk. *purakantha* : *pūr*, fire; see PYRE + *akantha*, thorn.]

py·ral·id (pī-răl′ĭd, pīr′ə-lĭd) also **py·ral·i·did** (pī-răl′ĭ-dĭd) *n.* Any of numerous small or medium-sized moths of the family Pyralidae. [< NLat. *Pyralidae*, family name < *Pyralis*, type genus < Gk. *puralis, puralid-*, an insect said to live in fire < *pūr*, fire. See PYRE.] —**py·ral′id** *adj.*

pyr·a·mid (pîr′ə-mĭd) *n.* **1a.** A solid figure with a polygonal base and triangular faces that meet at a common point. **b.** Something shaped like this polyhedron. **2a.** A massive monument of ancient Egypt having a rectangular base and four triangular faces culminating in a single apex, built over or around a crypt or

tomb. **b.** Any of various similar constructions, esp. a four-sided Mesoamerican temple having stepped sides and a flat top surmounted by chambers. **3.** The transactions involved in pyramiding stock. **4.** *Anatomy* A structure or part suggestive of a pyramid in shape. ❖ *v.* -**mid·ed**, -**mid·ing**, -**mids** —*tr.* **1.** To place or build in the shape of a pyramid. **2.** To build (an argument, for example) progressively from a basic general premise. **3.** To speculate in (stock) using paper profits as margin for buying more stock. —*intr.* **1.** To assume the shape of a pyramid. **2.** To increase rapidly and on a widening base. **3.** To pyramid stocks. [Lat. *pȳramis, pȳramid-* < Gk. *pūramis*, prob. orig.] —**py·ram′i·dal** (pī-răm′ĭ-dl), **pyr′a·mid′ic** (-mĭd′ĭk), **pyr′a·mid′i·cal** (-ĭ-kəl) *adj.* —**py·ram′i·dal·ly** *adv.*

pyramidal tract *n.* A major motor pathway of the central nervous system, originating in the cerebral cortex and generally descending through the brain stem to the spinal cord.

Pyramid Peak A mountain, 4,275.5 m (14,018 ft), in the Elk Mts. of W-central CO.

pyramid scheme *n.* A fraudulent moneymaking scheme in which people are recruited to make payments to others above them in a hierarchy while expecting to receive payments from people recruited below them. Eventually the number of new recruits fails to sustain the payment structure, and the scheme collapses with most people losing the money they paid in.

Pyr·a·mus (pîr′ə-məs) *n. Roman Mythology* A young man of Babylonia who committed suicide when he mistakenly thought his lover Thisbe was dead.

py·ran (pī′răn′) *n.* Either of two isomers with the formula C_5H_6O, having a ring of five carbon atoms and one oxygen atom. [*pyrone*, heterocyclic compound (PYR(O)– + –ONE) + –AN².]

py·rar·gy·rite (pī-rär′jə-rīt′, pĭ-) *n.* A deep red to black silver ore with composition Ag_3SbS_3. [Ger. *Pyrargyrit* < Gk. *puro-*, pyro- + Gk. *arguros*, silver; see ARGENT.]

pyre (pīr) *n.* **1.** A heap of combustibles for burning a corpse as a funeral rite. **2.** A pile of combustibles. [Lat. *pyra* < Gk. *purā* < *pūr*, fire. See **paəwṛ** in App.]

py·rene (pī′rēn′, pī-rēn′) *n.* The stone of certain fruits, such as the cherry. [NLat. *pȳrēna* < Gk. *purēna* < *pūr*, fire.]

Pyr·e·nees (pîr′ə-nēz′) A mountain range of SW Europe extending from the Bay of Biscay to the Mediterranean Sea and rising to 3,406.2 m (11,168 ft). —**Pyr′e·ne′an** *adj.*

py·re·noid (pī-rē′noid′, pīr′ə-) *n.* A proteinaceous structure found within the chloroplast of certain algae and hornworts that is associated with starch deposition. [NLat. *pȳrēna*, fruit stone; see PYRENE + –OID.]

py·re·thrin (pī-rē′thrĭn, -rĕth′rĭn) *n.* Either of two viscous liquid esters, $C_{21}H_{28}O_3$ or $C_{22}H_{28}O_5$, that are extracted from pyrethrum flowers and used as insecticides.

py·re·thrum (pī-rē′thrəm, -rĕth′rəm) *n.* **1.** Any of several Old World plants of the genus *Chrysanthemum* cultivated for their showy flower heads. **2.** An insecticide made from the dried flower heads of *Chrysanthemum cinerariifolium* or *C. coccineum.* [Lat., pellitory < Gk. *purethron*, feverfew < *pūr*, fire (< its warming effect). See PYRETIC.]

py·ret·ic (pī-rĕt′ĭk) *adj.* Relating to, producing, or affected by fever. [NLat. *pyreticus* < Gk. *puretos*, fever < *pūr*, fire. See **paəwṛ** in App.]

Py·rex (pī′rĕks′) A trademark used for any of various types of heat-resistant and chemical-resistant glass.

py·rex·i·a (pī-rĕk′sē-ə) *n.* Fever. [NLat. < Gk. *purexis < puressein*, to have a fever < *puretos*, fever. See PYRETIC.] —**py·rex′i·al, py·rex′ic** *adj.*

pyr·he·li·om·e·ter (pîr′hē-lē-ŏm′ĭ-tər, pîr′-) *n.* Any of various devices that measure the intensity of solar radiation striking a surface. —**pyr′he·li·o·met′ric** (-ə-mĕt′rĭk) *adj.*

py·ric (pī′rĭk, pîr′ĭk) *adj.* Of, relating to, or resulting from burning.

pyr·i·dine (pîr′ĭ-dēn′) *n.* A flammable colorless or yellowish liquid base, C_5H_5N, that has a penetrating odor, serves as the parent compound of many biologically important derivatives, and is used as a solvent and waterproofing agent and in the manufacture of various drugs and vitamins. [PYR(O)– + –ID(E) + –INE².] —**py·rid′ic** (pī-rĭd′ĭk) *adj.*

pyr·i·dox·al (pîr′ĭ-dŏk′səl) *n.* An aldehyde, $C_8H_9NO_3$, one of several active forms of pyridoxine, important in amino acid synthesis. [PYRIDOX(INE) + –AL³.]

pyr·i·dox·a·mine (pîr′ĭ-dŏk′sə-mēn′) *n.* A crystalline amine, $C_8H_{12}N_2O_2$, one of several active forms of pyridoxine, important in protein metabolism. [PYRIDOX(INE) + –AMINE.]

pyr·i·dox·ine (pîr′ĭ-dŏk′sēn, -sĭn) also **pyr·i·dox·in** (-dŏk′sĭn) *n.* A pyridine derivative, $C_{18}H_{11}NO_3$, occurring esp. in cereals, yeast, liver, and fish and acting as a coenzyme in amino acid synthesis. [PYRID(INE) + OX(O)– + –INE².]

py·ri·form (pîr′ə-fôrm′) *adj.* Shaped like a pear. [Med.Lat. *pyrum*, pear (alteration of Lat. *pirum*) + –FORM.]

py·rim·i·dine (pī-rĭm′ĭ-dēn′, pĭ-) *n.* **1.** A crystalline organic base, $C_4H_4N_2$, that is the parent substance of many biologically important derivatives. **2.** Any of several compounds derived from or structurally related to pyrimidine, esp. the nucleic acid constituents uracil, cytosine, and thymine. [Alteration of PYRIDINE.]

pygmy hippopotamus
Choeropsis liberiensis

pylon
Temple of Luxor, Egypt

pyramid
El Castillo, Chichén Itzá,
Mexico

ă	pat	oi	boy
ā	pay	ou	out
âr	care	ŏŏ	took
ä	father	ōō	boot
ĕ	pet	ŭ	cut
ē	be	ûr	urge
ĭ	pit	th	thin
ī	pie	th	this
îr	pier	hw	which
ŏ	pot	zh	vision
ō	toe	ə	about,
ô	paw		item

Stress marks:
′ (primary),
′ (secondary), as in
lexicon (lĕk′sĭ-kŏn′)

py·rite (pī′rīt′) *n.* A brass-colored mineral, FeS_2, used as an iron ore and in producing sulfur dioxide for sulfuric acid. [ME *perides, pirite* < OFr. *pirite* < Lat. *pyrītēs*, flint. See PYRITES.] —**py·rit′ic** (-rĭt′ĭk), **py·rit′i·cal** (-ĭ-kəl) *adj.*

py·ri·tes (pī-rī′tēz, pĭ-rīts′) *n., pl.* **pyrites** Any of various natural metallic sulfide minerals, esp. of iron. [Lat. *pyrītēs* < Gk. *purītēs (lithos),* fire (stone), flint < *pūr,* fire. See **paəwr̥** in App.]

py·ro (pī′rō) *n., pl.* **-ros** *Slang* A person who has a compulsion to set fires; a pyromaniac.

pyro– or **pyr–** *pref.* **1.** Fire; heat: *pyrotechnic.* **2.** Relating to the action of fire or heat: *pyrometallurgy.* **3.** Fever: *pyrogen.* **4.** Derived from an acid by the loss of a water molecule: *pyrosulfuric acid.* [NLat. < Gk. *puro-* < *pūr,* fire. See **paəwr̥** in App.]

py·ro·chem·i·cal (pī′rō-kĕm′ĭ-kəl) *adj.* Relating to or being chemical activity at elevated temperatures.

py·ro·clas·tic (pī′rō-klăs′tĭk) *adj.* Composed chiefly of rock fragments of volcanic origin.

py·ro·e·lec·tric·i·ty (pī′rō-ĭ-lĕk-trĭs′ĭ-tē, -ē′lĕk-) *n.* Generation of electric charge on a crystal by change of temperature.

py·ro·gal·lic acid (pī′rō-găl′ĭk, -gô′lĭk) *n.* See **pyrogallol.**

py·ro·gal·lol (pī′rō-găl′ôl′, -ōl′, -ōl′, -gô′lôl′, -lôl′, -lōl′) *n.* A toxic crystalline phenol, $C_6H_3(OH)_3$, used as a photographic developer and to treat certain skin diseases. [PYRO– + GALL(IC ACID) + –OL[1].] —**py·ro·gal′lic** (-găl′ĭk, -gô′lĭk) *adj.*

py·ro·gen (pī′rə-jən) *n.* A substance that produces fever.

py·ro·gen·ic (pī′rō-jĕn′ĭk) also **py·rog·e·nous** (pī-rŏj′ə-nəs) *adj.* **1.** Producing or produced by fever. **2.** Caused by or generating heat. **3.** Of or relating to solid rock formed from molten rock; igneous.

py·ro·lig·ne·ous (pī′rō-lĭg′nē-əs) *adj.* Made by the destructive distillation of wood.

pyroligneous acid *n.* A reddish-brown wood distillate containing acetic acid, methyl alcohol, acetone, and a tarry residue.

py·ro·lu·site (pī′rō-lōo′sīt) *n.* A soft black to dark gray mineral, MnO_2, the commonest and most important secondary ore of manganese. [Ger. *Pyrolusit* : Gk. *puro-,* pyro- + Gk. *lousis,* a washing (< *louein,* to wash; see **leu(ə)-** in App.).]

py·rol·y·sis (pī-rŏl′ĭ-sĭs) *n.* Decomposition or transformation of a compound caused by heat. —**py·ro·lyt′ic** (-rə-lĭt′ĭk) *adj.* —**py·ro·lyt′i·cal·ly** *adv.*

py·ro·lyze (pī′rə-līz′) *tr.v.* **-lyzed, -lyz·ing, -lyz·es** To subject (something) to pyrolysis.

py·ro·man·cy (pī′rə-măn′sē) *n.* Divination by fire or flames. [ME *piromancie* < OFr. *pyromancie* < LLat. *pyromantīa* < Gk. *puromanteia* : *puro-,* pyro- + *manteia,* divination; see –MANCY.] —**py·ro·man′tic** (-măn′tĭk) *adj.*

py·ro·ma·ni·a (pī′rō-mā′nē-ə, -mān′yə) *n.* The irresistible urge to start fires. —**py′ro·ma′ni·ac′** (-mā′nē-ăk′) *adj. & n.* —**py′ro·ma′ni·a·cal** (-mə-nī′ə-kəl) *adj.*

py·ro·met·al·lur·gy (pī′rō-mĕt′l-ûr′jē) *n., pl.* **-gies** An ore-refining process, such as smelting, dependent on the action of heat. —**py′ro·met′al·lur′gi·cal** (-mĕt′l-ûr′jĭ-kəl) *adj.*

py·rom·e·ter (pī-rŏm′ĭ-tər) *n.* Any of various thermometers used for measuring high temperatures. —**py′ro·met′ric** (-rə-mĕt′rĭk), **py′ro·met′ri·cal** (-rĭ-kəl) *adj.* —**py·rom′e·try** *n.*

py·ro·mor·phite (pī′rə-môr′fīt′) *n.* A green, brown, or yellow mineral, $Pb_5(PO_4)_3Cl$, a minor ore of lead. [Ger. *Pyromorphit* : Gk. *puro-,* pyro- + Gk. *morphē,* form.]

py·ro·nine (pī′rə-nēn′) *n.* Any of a group of red dyes used as a biological stain, esp. to detect the presence of RNA. [Ger. *Pyronin,* orig. a trademark.]

py·rope (pī′rōp′) *n.* A deep red garnet, $Mg_3Al_2Si_3O_{12}$, used as a gem. [ME *pirope* < OFr. < Lat. *pyrōpum,* gold-bronze alloy < Gk. *purōpos,* fiery, kind of red bronze : *puro-,* pyro- + *ōps, ōp,* eye, face; see **okʷ-** in App.]

py·ro·phor·ic (pī′rə-fôr′ĭk, -fŏr′-) *adj.* **1.** Spontaneously igniting in air. **2.** Producing sparks by friction. [< *pyrophorus,* substance that ignites spontaneously : < Gk. *purophoros,* fire-bearing : *puro-,* pyro- + *-phoros,* -phorous.]

py·ro·phos·phate (pī′rō-fŏs′fāt′) *n.* A salt or ester of pyrophosphoric acid. —**py′ro·phos·phat′ic** (-făt′ĭk) *adj.*

py·ro·phos·phor·ic acid (pī′rō-fŏs-fôr′ĭk, -fŏr′-) *n.* A syrupy viscous liquid, $H_4P_2O_7$, used as a catalyst and in organic chemical manufacture.

py·ro·phyl·lite (pī′rō-fĭl′īt′, pī-rŏf′ə-līt′) *n.* A silvery white or pale green aluminum silicate mineral, $Al_2Si_4O_{10}(OH)_2$, occurring naturally in soft compact masses.

py·ro·sis (pī-rō′sĭs) *n.* See **heartburn.** [NLat. *pyrōsis* < Gk. *purōsis,* a burning < *puroun,* to burn < *pūr,* fire. See **paəwr̥** in App.]

py·ro·stat (pī′rə-stăt′) *n.* A high-temperature thermostat.

py·ro·sul·fate (pī′rō-sŭl′fāt′) *n.* A salt of pyrosulfuric acid.

py·ro·sul·fu·ric acid (pī′rō-sŭl-fyŏŏr′ĭk) *n.* A heavy oily fuming liquid, $H_2S_2O_7$, used in petroleum refining and explosives.

py·ro·tech·nic (pī′rō-tĕk′nĭk) also **py·ro·tech·ni·cal** (-nĭ-kəl) *adj.* **1.** Of or relating to fireworks. **2.** Resembling fireworks; brilliant. —**py′ro·tech′ni·cal·ly** *adv.*

py·ro·tech·nics (pī′rō-tĕk′nĭks) *n.* (*used with a sing. verb*) **1.** The art of manufacturing or setting off fireworks. **2.** A fireworks display. **3.** A brilliant display, as of rhetoric or wit, or of virtuosity in the performing arts. —**py′ro·tech′nist** *n.*

pyrrhuloxia
Cardinalis sinuatus

Pythagoras
marble bust

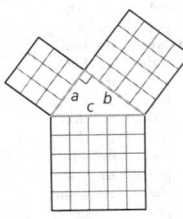

Pythagorean theorem
The Pythagorean theorem
is: $a^2 + b^2 = c^2$

py·ro·tech·ny (pī′rə-tĕk′nē) *n.* See **pyrotechnics** 1. [NLat. *pyrotechnia* : Gk. *puro-,* pyro- + Gk. *tekhnē,* craft; see TECHNIQUE.]

py·rox·ene (pī-rŏk′sēn′) *n.* Any of a group of crystalline silicate minerals common in igneous and metamorphic rocks and containing two metallic oxides, as of magnesium, iron, or calcium. [Fr. *pyroxène* : Gk. *puro-,* pyro- + Gk. *xenos,* stranger; see **ghosti-** in App.] —**py′rox·en′ic** (-rŏk-sĕn′ĭk, -sĕn′ĭk) *adj.*

py·rox·e·nite (pī-rŏk′sə-nīt′) *n.* An igneous rock consisting chiefly of pyroxenes. —**py·rox′e·nit′ic** (-nĭt′ĭk) *adj.*

py·rox·y·lin (pī-rŏk′sə-lĭn) also **py·rox·y·line** (-lĕn′, -lĭn) *n.* A highly flammable nitrocellulose used in the manufacture of collodion, plastics, and lacquers.

pyr·rhic (pĭr′ĭk) *n.* A metrical foot having two short or unaccented syllables. ❖ *adj.* Of or characterized by pyrrhics. [Lat. *pyrrhicius* < Gk. *purrikhios* < *purrikhē,* a war dance, perhaps from *Purrikhos,* supposed inventor of the dance.]

Pyrrhic victory *n.* A victory that is offset by staggering losses. [After PYRRHUS.]

pyr·rho·tite (pĭr′ə-tīt′) also **pyr·rho·tine** (-tīn′) *n.* A brownish-bronze, weakly magnetic iron sulfide mineral, FeS, used as an iron ore and in making sulfuric acid. [Alteration (influenced by –ITE[1]) of Ger. *Pyrrhotin* < Gk. *purrotēs,* redness < *purros,* fiery < *pūr,* fire. See **paəwr̥** in App.]

pyr·rhu·lox·i·a (pĭr′ə-lŏk′sē-ə, pĭr′yə-) *n.* A large crested finch (*Cardinalis sinuatus*) of Mexico and the southwest United States having gray and red plumage and a short thick bill. [NLat. *Pyrrhūloxia,* former genus name : *Pyrrhūla,* finch genus (< Gk. *purroulas,* red-colored bird < *purros,* red < *pūr,* fire; see PYRE) + *Loxia,* crossbill genus (< Gk. *loxos,* oblique).]

Pyr·rhus (pĭr′əs) 319–272 B.C. King of Epirus (306–302 and 297–272) who defeated the Romans at Heraclea (280) and Asculum (279) despite his own staggering losses.

pyr·role (pĭr′ōl′) *n.* A five-membered heterocyclic ring compound, C_4H_5N, that has an odor similar to chloroform and is the parent compound of protoporphyrin. [Gk. *purros,* red (< *pūr,* fire; see PYRE) + –OLE.] —**pyr·rol′ic** (pĭ-rō′lĭk) *adj.*

py·ru·vate (pī-rōo′vāt, pĭ-) *n.* A salt or ester of pyruvic acid.

py·ru·vic acid (pī-rōo′vĭk, pĭ-) *n.* A colorless organic liquid, $C_3H_4O_3$, formed as an intermediate in carbohydrate metabolism and as an end product in glycolysis. [PYR(O)– + Lat. *ūva,* grape (< its being produced by the dry distillation of racemic acid, orig. derived from grapes) + –IC.]

Py·thag·o·ras (pĭ-thăg′ər-əs) fl. 6th cent. B.C. Greek philosopher and mathematician who proved the universal validity of the Pythagorean theorem.

Py·thag·o·re·an·ism (pĭ-thăg′ə-rē′ə-nĭz′əm) *n.* The syncretistic philosophy expounded by Pythagoras, distinguished chiefly by its description of reality in terms of arithmetical relationships. —**Py·thag′o·re′an** *adj. & n.*

Pythagorean theorem *n.* The theorem that the sum of the squares of the lengths of the sides of a right triangle is equal to the square of the length of the hypotenuse.

Pyth·i·an (pĭth′ē-ən) also **Pyth·ic** (pĭth′ĭk) *adj.* **1.** *Greek Mythology* Of or relating to Delphi, the temple of Apollo at Delphi, or its oracle. **2.** Of or relating to the Pythian games. [< Lat. *Pȳthius* < Gk. *Pūthios* < *Pūthō,* ancient name of Delphi.]

Pythian games *pl.n.* A pan-Hellenic festival of athletic games held every four years at Delphi in honor of the god Apollo.

Pyth·i·as (pĭth′ē-əs) *n.* A Greek who rescued his friend Damon, who stood bail for Pythias when he was condemned to die.

py·thon (pī′thŏn′, -thən) *n.* Any of various nonvenomous snakes of the family Pythonidae, found chiefly in Asia, Africa, and Australia, that often attain lengths of 6 meters (20 feet) or more. [Prob. Fr. < Lat. *Pȳthōn,* mythical serpent killed by Apollo near Delphi. See PYTHON.]

Python *n. Greek Mythology* A dragon or serpent that was the tutelary demon of the oracular cult at Delphi until killed by Apollo. [Lat. *Pȳthōn* < Gk. *Pūthōn.* See **dheub-** in App.]

py·tho·ness (pī′thə-nĭs, pĭth′ə-) *n.* **1.** *Greek Mythology* A priestess of Apollo at Delphi. **2.** A prophetess. [ME *phitonesse* < OFr. *phitonise* < LLat. *pȳthonissa* < Gk. *Pūthōn,* Python. See PYTHON.]

py·thon·ic (pī-thŏn′ĭk) *adj.* **1.** Oracular; prophetic. **2.** Of or resembling a python. **3.** Of extraordinary size and power.

py·u·ri·a (pī-yŏŏr′ē-ə) *n.* The presence of pus in the urine.

pyx also **pix** (pĭks) *n.* **1.** *Ecclesiastical* **a.** A container in which wafers for the Eucharist are kept. **b.** A container in which the Eucharist is carried to the sick. **2.** A chest in a mint in which specimen coins are placed to await assay. [ME *pyxe* < Lat. *pyxis,* box < Gk. *puxis.*]

pyx·id·i·um (pĭk-sĭd′ē-əm) *n., pl.* **-i·a** (-ē-ə) A pyxis. [NLat. < Gk. *puxidion,* dim. of *puxis,* box.]

pyx·ie (pĭk′sē) *n.* A creeping evergreen shrub (*Pyxidanthera barbulata*) native to pine barrens of the eastern United States and having small white or pinkish flowers. [Shortening and alteration of NLat. *Pyxidanthera,* genus name : Gk. *puxis, puxid-,* box + Gk. *anthera,* pollen; see ANTHER.]

pyx·is (pĭk′sĭs) *n., pl.* **pyx·i·des** (pĭk′sĭ-dēz′) *Botany* A capsule dehiscing transversely by a lid that falls off to release the seeds. [Lat. *pyxis,* box < Gk. *puxis.*]

Pyxis *n.* A constellation in the Southern Hemisphere near Antlia. [NLat. *Pyxis (nautica),* (mariner's) compass < Gk. *puxis,* box.]

Qq

q¹ or **Q** (kyōō) *n., pl.* **q's** or **Q's** also **qs** or **Qs 1.** The 17th letter of the modern English alphabet. **2.** Any of the speech sounds represented by the letter *q*. **3.** The 17th in a series. **4.** Something shaped like the letter Q.

q² *Physics* The symbol for **charge** 13.

Q *abbr.* **1.** quarter (of a year) **2.** *Games* queen

q. *abbr.* **1.** quart **2.** quarterly **3.** also **Q.** quarto **4.** question **5.** quintal **6.** quire

qab·a·lah or **qab·a·la** (kăb′ə-lə, kə-bä′lə) *n.* Variant of **kabbalah.**

Qad·da·fi or **Qa·dha·fi** (kə-dä′fē), **Muammar al-** or **el-** b. 1942. Libyan political leader who seized power (1969) and imposed socialist policies and Islamic orthodoxy.

Q and A *abbr.* question and answer

Qan·da·har or **Kandahar** (kŭn′də-här′, kän′-) A city of SE Afghanistan near the Pakistan border SW of Kabul; probably founded in the 4th cent. B.C. Pop. 225,500.

Qa·ra·ghan·dy or **Ka·ra·gan·da** (kăr′ə-gən-dä′, kə-rə-) A city of central Kazakhstan NNE of Tashkent; founded 1857. Pop. 596,000.

Qa·tar (kä′tər, кнŭt′ər) A country of E Arabia on the Persian Gulf; achieved independence from Great Britain in 1971. Cap. Doha. Pop. 540,000. —**Qa·tar′i** *adj. & n.*

Qaz·vin also **Kaz·vin** (käz-vēn′) A city of NW Iran NW of Tehran; founded in the 4th cent. A.D. Pop. 298,705.

QB *abbr.* quarterback

QC *abbr.* **1.** quality control **2.** Queen's Counsel

Q-Cel·tic (kyōō′kĕl′tĭk, -sĕl′-) *n.* Goidelic. [On the model of P-CELTIC (< its changing the Common Celt. labiovelar stops to velar stops, symbolized by the letter Q).]

QED *abbr. Latin* quod erat demonstrandum (which was to be demonstrated)

QEF *abbr. Latin* quod erat faciendum (which was to have been done)

Q fever *n.* An infectious disease caused by the rickettsia *Coxiella burnetii* and characterized by fever, malaise, and muscular pains. [Q(UERY) (because orig. the infectious agent was unknown) + FEVER.]

Qi or **qi** (chē) *n.* Variants of **chi²**.

Qian·long (chyän′lōong′) also **Ch'ien-lung** (chyĕn′lōong′) 1711–99. Chinese emperor (1735–96) of the Qing dynasty.

q.i.d. *abbr. Latin* quater in die (four times a day)

Qi Gong (gŭng, gŏng) *n.* A Chinese system of prescribed physical exercises or movements performed in a meditative state. [Chin. (Mandarin) *qìgōng : qì*, air, breath + *gōng*, skill.]

Qi·lian Shan (chē′lyän′ shän′) also **Nan Shan** (nän′) A mountain range of N-central China extending NW to SE and rising to more than 6,100 m (20,000 ft).

Qin also **Ch'in** (chĭn) A Chinese dynasty (221–206 B.C.) that organized the first centralized imperial government in China. [Chin. (Mandarin) *Qín*, after *Qín*, alternate name for Shanxi Province.]

Qing also **Ch'ing** (chĭng) Also called **Manchu.** The last Chinese dynasty (1644–1912), overthrown by nationalist revolutionaries.

Qing·dao (chĭng′dou′) also **Tsing·tao** (tsĭng′tou′) A city of E China on the Yellow Sea NNW of Shanghai; leased to Germany in 1898. Pop. 2,060,000.

Qing·hai also **Ching·hai** (chĭng′hī′) or **Tsing·hai** (tsĭng′-) A province of NW-central China, bordered on the N by the Qilian Shan. Cap. Xining. Pop. 4,456,946.

Qinghai Hu (hōō) also **Ko·ko Nor** (kō′kō′ nôr′, nōr′) A salt lake of N-central China S of the Qilian Shan.

Qin·huang·dao (chĭn′hwäng′dou′) also **Chin·wang·tao** (-wäng′tou′) A city of NE China on the Gulf of Bo Hai E of Beijing; formerly a treaty port. Pop. 518,912.

qin·tar (kĭn-tär′) *n.* A coin formerly used in Albania and worth one one-hundredth of a lek. [Albanian. See QINDARKA.]

Qi·qi·har (chē′chē′här′) also **Tsi·tsi·har** (tsē′tsē′-) A city of NE China NW of Harbin; founded 1691. Pop. 1,400,591.

qi·vi·ut (kē′vē-ət, -ōōt′) *n.* The soft wool lying beneath the long coat of the muskox, valued for its use as a fiber. [Inuit, *pl.* of *qiviuq*, down, underhair.]

ql. *abbr.* quintal

QM *abbr.* quartermaster

QMC *abbr.* quartermaster corps

QMG *abbr.* quartermaster general

Qom (kōm) also **Qum** (kōōm) A city of W-central Iran SSW of Tehran; a Shiite Muslim center and a pilgrimage site since 17th cent. Pop. 780,453.

qoph (kôf) *n.* The 19th letter of the Hebrew alphabet. [Heb. *qôp*, of Phoenician orig.; akin to Heb. *qôp*, ape, and perh. Skt. *kapiḥ*, ape.]

q.p. *abbr. Latin* quantum placet (as much as you please)

qq. *abbr.* questions

qq.v. *abbr. Latin* quae vide (which [things] see)

qr. *abbr.* **1.** quarter **2.** quarterly **3.** quire

q.s. *abbr. Latin* quantum sufficit (as much as suffices)

Q-ship (kyōō′shĭp′) *n.* A decoy ship, esp. an armed ship disguised as a merchant ship to entice submarines to surface so that they may be attacked with gunfire. [Q, naval classification.]

qt. or **qt** *abbr.* quart

q.t. (kyōō′tē′) *n. Slang* Quiet: *spoke on the q.t.* [Short for QUIET.]

Q-Tip (kyōō′tĭp′) A trademark used for a cotton-tipped swab.

qto. *abbr.* quarto

qty. *abbr.* quantity

qua (kwä, kwā) *prep.* In the capacity or character of; as. [Lat. *quā*, fem. ablative sing. of *quī*, who. See **kʷo-** in App.]

Quaa·lude (kwä′lōōd′) A trademark used for the drug methaqualone.

quack¹ (kwăk) *n.* The characteristic sound uttered by a duck. ❖ *intr.v.* **quacked, quack·ing, quacks** To utter a quack. [ME *quek*, of imit. orig.] —**quack′y** *adj.*

quack² (kwăk) *n.* **1.** An untrained person who pretends to be a physician and dispenses medical advice and treatment. **2.** A charlatan; a mountebank. ❖ *adj.* Relating to or characteristic of a quack: *a quack cure.* ❖ *intr.v.* **quacked, quack·ing, quacks** To act as a quack. [Short for QUACKSALVER.] —**quack′er·y** *n.* —**quack′ish** *adj.* —**quack′ish·ly** *adv.*

quack grass *n.* See **couch grass.** [Variant of QUITCH GRASS.]

quack·sal·ver (kwăk′săl′vər) *n. Archaic* A quack or charlatan. [Obsolete Du. : MDu. *quac-*, unguent, or *quacken* (to quack, boast + MDu. *salven*, to salve.]

quad¹ (kwŏd) *n.* A quadrangle: *the campus quad.*

quad² (kwŏd) *n. Printing* See **quadrat** 1.

quad³ (kwŏd) *adj. & n. Informal* Quadruple.

quad⁴ (kwŏd) *n.* A quadruplet.

quad⁵ (kwŏd) *adj.* Quadraphonic.

quad⁶ (kwŏd) *n. Informal* A quadriceps muscle. Often used in the plural.

quadr– or **quadra–** *pref.* Variants of **quadri–.**

quad·ran·gle (kwŏd′răng′gəl) *n.* **1.** *Mathematics* A quadrilateral. **2a.** A rectangular area surrounded on all four sides by buildings. **b.** The buildings bordering this area. **3.** The area of land shown on one atlas sheet charted by the US Geological Survey. [ME < OFr. < LLat. *quadrangulum* < Lat., neut. of *quadrangulus*, four-cornered : *quadri-*, quadri- + *angulus*, angle.] —**quad·ran′gu·lar** (-răng′gyə-lər) *adj.* —**quad·ran′gu·lar·ly** *adv.* —**quad·ran′gu·lar·ness** *n.*

quad·rant (kwŏd′rənt) *n.* **1.** *Mathematics* **a.** A circular arc of 90°; one fourth of the circumference of a circle. **b.** The plane area bounded by such an arc and two perpendicular radii. **c.** Any of the four areas into which a plane is divided by the reference axes in a Cartesian coordinate system. **2.** A machine part or other mechanical device that is shaped like a quarter circle. **3.** An early instrument for measuring altitude of celestial bodies, consisting of a 90° graduated arc with a movable radius for measuring angles. [ME, quarter of a day < Lat. *quadrāns, quadrant-*, a fourth part. See **kʷetwer-** in App.]

quad·ra·phon·ic also **quad·ri·phon·ic** (kwŏd′rə-fŏn′ĭk) *adj.* Of or for a four-channel sound system in which speakers are positioned at all four corners of the listening space, reproducing signals that are independent of each other. —**qua·draph′o·ny** *n.*

quad·ra·son·ic (kwŏd′rə-sŏn′ĭk) *adj.* Quadraphonic.

quad·rat (kwŏd′rət, -răt′) *n.* **1.** *Printing* A piece of type metal lower than the raised typeface, used for filling spaces and blank lines. **2.** *Ecology* A rectangular plot of land designated for studying the distribution of plants or animals in an area. [ME, a square geometric instrument, rectangular area. See QUADRATE.]

quad·rate (kwŏd′rāt′, -rĭt) *n.* **1a.** A square or cube. **b.** An approx. square or cubic area, space, or object. **2.** *Zoology* A bone or cartilaginous structure of the skull, joining the upper and lower jaws in birds, fish, reptiles, and amphibians. ❖ *adj.* **1.** Having four sides and four angles; square or rectangular. **2.** *Zoology* Being the quadrate bone or cartilage. ❖ *intr.v.* **-rat·ed, -rat·ing, -rates** *Archaic* To correspond; agree. [ME *quadrat*, something square < Lat. *quadrātum* < neut. p. part. of *quadrāre*, to make square < *quadrum*, square. See **kʷetwer-** in App.]

Muammar al-Qaddafi

Qatar

ă	pat	oi	boy
ā	pay	ou	out
âr	care	ŏŏ	took
ä	father	ōō	boot
ĕ	pet	ŭ	cut
ē	be	ûr	urge
ĭ	pit	th	thin
ī	pie	*th*	this
îr	pier	hw	which
ŏ	pot	zh	vision
ō	toe	ə	about,
ô	paw		item

Stress marks:
′ (primary);
′ (secondary), as in
lexicon (lĕk′sĭ-kŏn′)

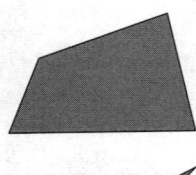

quadrilateral
top: convex quadrilateral
bottom: nonconvex
quadrilateral

quadripartite
quadripartite vault,
Washington National
Cathedral, Washington, DC

quad·rat·ic (kwŏ-drăt′ĭk) *adj. Mathematics* Of, relating to, or containing quantities of the second degree. [< QUADRATE.] —**quad·rat′ic** *n.* —**quad·rat′i·cal·ly** *adv.*

quadratic equation *n.* An equation of the second degree having the general form $ax^2 + bx + c = 0$, where *a*, *b*, and *c* are constants.

quadratic formula *n.* The formula $x = [-b \pm \sqrt{(b^2 - 4ac)}]/2a$, used to compute the roots of a quadratic equation.

quad·rat·ics (kwŏ-drăt′ĭks) *n.* (*used with a sing. verb*) The algebraic study of quadratic equations.

quad·ra·ture (kwŏd′rə-chŏŏr′) *n.* **1.** The process of making something square. **2.** *Mathematics* The process of constructing a square equal in area to a given surface. **3.** *Astronomy* A configuration in which the position of one celestial body is 90° from another celestial body, as measured from a third.

quad·ren·ni·al (kwŏ-drĕn′ē-əl) *adj.* **1.** Happening once in four years. **2.** Lasting for four years. —**quad·ren′ni·al** *n.* —**quad·ren′ni·al·ly** *adv.*

quad·ren·ni·um (kwŏ-drĕn′ē-əm) *n., pl.* **quad·ren·ni·ums** or **quad·ren·ni·a** (kwŏ-drĕn′ē-ə) A period of four years. [Lat. *quadriennium : quadri-, quadri- + annus, year.*]

quadri– or **quadr–** or **quadra–** or **quadru–** *pref.* **1.** Four: *quadrilateral.* **2.** Square: *quadrate.* [ME < Lat. See k**ʷ**etwer- in App.]

quad·ric (kwŏd′rĭk) *adj.* Of or relating to geometric surfaces that are defined by quadratic equations.

quad·ri·cen·ten·a·ry (kwŏd′rĭ-sĕn-tĕn′ə-rē, -sĕn′tə-nĕr′ē) *n., pl.* **-ries** A 400th anniversary or celebration. ❖ *adj.* Of or relating to a span of 400 years or to a 400th anniversary. [< alteration of Lat. *quadringentī, quadrigentī,* four hundred (on the model of such words as TERCENTENARY). See k**ʷ**etwer- in App.]

quad·ri·cen·ten·ni·al (kwŏd′rĭ-sĕn-tĕn′ē-əl) *adj.* Quadricentenary. ❖ *n.* A quadricentenary event or celebration.

quad·ri·ceps (kwŏd′rĭ-sĕps′) *n.* The large four-part extensor muscle at the front of the thigh. [QUADRI– + (BI)CEPS.] —**quad′ri·cip′i·tal** (-sĭp′ĭ-tl) *adj.*

quad·ri·ga (kwŏd-rē′gə, -rī′-) *n., pl.* **-gae** (-gē) A two-wheeled chariot drawn by four horses abreast. [Lat. *quadrīga,* sing. of *quadrīgae,* team of four horses, contraction of *quadriiugae,* fem. pl. of *quadriiugus,* of a team of four : *quadri-, quadri- + iugum,* yoke; see JUGUM.]

quad·ri·lat·er·al (kwŏd′rə-lăt′ər-əl) *n.* A polygon having four sides. ❖ *adj.* Having four sides.

qua·drille[1] (kwŏ-drĭl′, kwə-, kə-) *n.* **1.** A square dance of French origin composed of five sections and performed by four couples. **2.** Music for this dance in 6/8 and 2/4 time. [Fr. < *quadrille,* team, crew, one of four groups of horsemen < Sp. *cuadrilla,* prob. dim. of *cuadro,* square < Lat. *quadrum.* See k**ʷ**etwer- in App.]

qua·drille[2] (kwŏ-drĭl′, kwə-, kə-) *n.* A card game popular during the 18th century, played by four people with a deck of 40 cards. [Fr., perh. < Sp. *cuartillo,* dim. of *cuarto,* fourth < Lat. *quārtus.* See k**ʷ**etwer- in App.]

quad·ril·lion (kwŏ-drĭl′yən) *n.* **1.** The cardinal number equal to 10^{15}. **2.** *Chiefly British* The cardinal number equal to 10^{24}. [QUADR(I)– + (M)ILLION.] —**quad·ril′lion** *adj.*

quad·ril·lionth (kwŏ-drĭl′yənth) *n.* **1.** The ordinal number matching the number quadrillion in a series. **2.** One of a quadrillion equal parts. —**quad·ril′lionth** *adv. & adj.*

quad·ri·par·tite (kwŏd′rə-pär′tīt′) *adj.* **1.** Consisting of or divided into four parts. **2.** Involving four participants.

quad·ri·phon·ic (kwŏd′rə-fŏn′ĭk) *adj.* Variant of **quadraphonic.** —**quad′ri·phon′y** *n.*

quad·ri·ple·gi·a (kwŏd′rə-plē′jē-ə, -jə) *n.* Total paralysis of the body from the neck down. —**quad′ri·ple′gic** *adj. & n.*

quad·ri·va·lent (kwŏd′rə-vā′lənt) *adj. Chemistry* **1.** Having four valences. **2.** Having a valence of four; tetravalent. —**quad′ri·va′lence, quad′ri·va′len·cy** *n.*

quad·riv·i·um (kwŏ-drĭv′ē-əm) *n., pl.* **-i·a** (-ē-ə) The higher division of the seven liberal arts in the Middle Ages, composed of geometry, astronomy, arithmetic, and music. [LLat. < Lat., place where four roads meet : *quadri-, quadri- + via,* road; see VIA.]

quad·roon (kwŏ-drōōn′) *n.* A person having one-quarter Black ancestry. [Alteration of Sp. *cuarterón < cuarto,* quarter < Lat. *quārtus.* See k**ʷ**etwer- in App.]

quadru– *pref.* Variant of **quadri–.**

quad·ru·ma·nous (kwŏ-drōō′mə-nəs) also **quad·ru·ma·nal** (-nəl) *adj.* Having four feet with opposable first digits, as primates other than humans. [QUADRU– + Lat. *manus,* hand; see man-[2] in App.] —OUS.]

quad·rum·vi·rate (kwŏ-drŭm′vər-ĭt) *n.* A group of four people joined in authority or office, esp. a government of four people. [QUADR(I)– + (TRI)UMVIRATE.]

quad·ru·ped (kwŏd′rə-pĕd′) *n.* A four-footed animal. ❖ *adj.* Four-footed: *a quadruped mammal.* —**quad·ru′pe·dal** (kwŏ-drōō′pə-dəl, kwŏd′rə-pĕd′l) *adj.*

quad·ru·ple (kwŏ-drōō′pəl, -drŭp′əl, kwŏd′rŏŏ-pəl) *adj.* **1.** Consisting of four parts or members. **2.** Four times as much in size, strength, number, or amount. **3.** *Music* Having four beats to the measure. ❖ *n.* A number four times larger than another. ❖ *tr. & intr.v.* **-pled, -pling, -ples** To multiply or be multiplied by four; *quadrupled in size.* [< ME *quadrible,* fourfold amount, and *quadruple,* tooth with four roots, both < OFr. *quadruple* < Lat. *quadruplum* < neut. of *quadruplus,* four-

fold : *quadru-, quadri-,* quadri- + *-plus,* -fold.] —**quad·ru′ply** *adv.*

quad·ru·plet (kwŏ-drŭp′lĭt, -drōō′plĭt, kwŏd′rə-plĭt) *n.* **1.** One of four offspring born in a single birth. **2.** A group or combination of four associated by common properties or behavior. **3.** *Music* A group of four notes having the time value of three notes of the same kind. [< QUADRUPLE, modeled on TRIPLET.]

quad·ru·pli·cate (kwŏ-drōō′plĭ-kĭt) *adj.* **1.** Multiplied by four; quadruple. **2.** Fourth in a group of four identical things. ❖ *n.* **1.** One of a group of four identical things. **2.** A set of four copies. ❖ *tr. & intr.v.* (-kāt′) **-cat·ed, -cat·ing, -cates** To multiply or be multiplied by four. [Lat. *quadruplicātus,* p. part. of *quadruplicāre,* to multiply by four < *quadruplex,* fourfold : *quadru-, quadri-, quadri- + -plex,* -fold; see DUPLEX.] —**quad·ru′pli·cate·ly** (-kĭt-lē) *adv.* —**quad·ru′pli·ca′tion** *n.*

quaes·tor (kwĕs′tər, kwē′stər) *n.* Any of various public officials in ancient Rome responsible chiefly for government and military finance. [ME *questor* < Lat. *quaestor* < **quaestus,* obs. p. part. of *quaerere,* to inquire.] —**quaes·to′ri·al** (kwĕ-stôr′ē-əl, -stōr′-, kwē-) *adj.* —**quaes′tor·ship′** *n.*

quaff (kwŏf, kwăf, kwôf) *v.* **quaffed, quaff·ing, quaffs** —*tr.* To drink (a beverage) heartily. —*intr.* To drink heartily: *quaffed from the spring.* ❖ *n.* A hearty draft of liquid. [?] —**quaff′er** *n.*

quag (kwăg, kwŏg) *n.* A quagmire. [Perh. var. of ME *quabbe* < OE **cwabba.*]

quag·ga (kwăg′ə, kwŏg′ə) *n.* A zebralike mammal (*Equus quagga*) of southern Africa, extinct since the late 19th century. [Afr. < Xhosa (*i-*)*qwaxa,* something striped, perh. < Khoikhoin !*ua-xa.*]

quag·gy (kwăg′ē, kwŏg′ē) *adj.* **-gi·er, -gi·est** **1.** Resembling a marsh; soggy. **2.** Soft and flabby.

quag·mire (kwăg′mīr′, kwŏg′-) *n.* **1.** Land with a soft muddy surface. **2.** A difficult or precarious situation; a predicament.

qua·hog also **qua·haug** (kō′hôg′, -hŏg′, kō′hŏg, kwô′-) *n.* An edible clam (*Venus mercenaria*) of the Atlantic coast of North America having a hard rounded shell. [Narragansett *poquaûhock.*]

quaich also **quaigh** (kwăKH) *n. Scots* A two-handled drinking cup. [Sc. Gael. *cuach* < OIr. *cúach,* alteration of *cuäch.*]

Quai d'Or·say (kā′ dôr-sā′, kĕ′ dôr-sĕ′) A street paralleling the S bank of the Seine R. in Paris, France, notable for its governmental ministries.

quail[1] (kwāl) *n., pl.* **quail** or **quails** **1.** Any of various small Old World chickenlike birds of the genus *Coturnix,* esp. *C. coturnix,* having mottled brown plumage and a short tail. **2.** Any of various similar or related New World birds, such as the bobwhite. [ME *quaille* < OFr., perh. < VLat. **coacula,* of imit. orig.]

quail[2] (kwāl) *intr.v.* **quailed, quail·ing, quails** To shrink back in fear; cower. [ME *quailen,* to give way, prob. < MDu. *quelen,* to suffer, be ill. See g**ʷ**elə- in App.]

quaint (kwānt) *adj.* **quaint·er, quaint·est** **1.** Charmingly odd, esp. in an old-fashioned way. **2.** Unfamiliar or unusual in character; strange. **3.** Cleverly made; artful. [ME, clever, cunning, peculiar < OFr. *queinte, cointe* < Lat. *cognitus,* p. part. of *cognōscere,* to learn. See COGNITION.] —**quaint′ly** *adv.* —**quaint′ness** *n.*

quake (kwāk) *intr.v.* **quaked, quak·ing, quakes** **1.** To shake or tremble, as from instability or shock. **2.** To shiver, as with cold or from strong emotion. ❖ *n.* **1.** An instance of quaking. **2.** An earthquake. [ME *quaken* < OE *cwacian.*] —**quak′y** *adj.*

quake·proof (kwāk′prōōf′) *adj.* Designed to withstand an earthquake. —**quake′proof′** *v.*

Quak·er (kwā′kər) *n.* A member of the Society of Friends. [< QUAKE (< an early leader's admonishment to "tremble at the word of the Lord").] —**Quak′er·ism** *n.* —**Quak′er·ly** *adv. & adj.*

Quaker gun *n.* A dummy gun made of wood.

Quak·er·la·dies (kwā′kər-lā′dēz) *pl.n.* See **bluets.**

quak·ing aspen (kwā′kĭng) *n.* A North American deciduous tree (*Populus tremuloides*) having broadly ovate, finely toothed leaves with a truncate base.

quaking bog *n.* A floating mat of thickly woven mosses, rushes, and shrubs that forms across the surface of shallow ponds and shakes when walked on.

qua·le (kwä′lē) *n., pl.* **-li·a** (-lē-ə) A property, such as whiteness, considered independently from things having the property. [< Lat. *quāle,* neut. of *quālis,* of what kind. See QUALITY.]

qual·i·fi·ca·tion (kwŏl′ə-fĭ-kā′shən) *n.* **1.** The act of qualifying or the condition of being qualified. **2.** A quality, ability, or accomplishment that makes a person suitable for a particular position or task. **3.** A condition or circumstance that must be met or complied with: *met the qualifications for residence.* **4.** A restriction or modification.

qual·i·fied (kwŏl′ə-fīd′) *adj.* **1.** Having the appropriate qualifications for an office, position, or task. **2.** Limited, restricted, or modified. —**qual′i·fied′ly** (-fīd′lē, -fī′ĭd-lē) *adv.*

qual·i·fi·er (kwŏl′ə-fī′ər) *n.* **1.** One that qualifies, esp. one that has or fulfills all appropriate qualifications, as for a position or task. **2.** *Grammar* A word or phrase that qualifies, limits, or modifies the meaning of another word or phrase.

qual·i·fy (kwŏl′ə-fī′) *v.* **-fied, -fy·ing, -fies** —*tr.* **1.** To describe by enumerating the characteristics or qualities of; characterize. **2.**

To make competent or eligible for an office, position, or task. **3a.** To declare competent or capable; certify. **b.** To make legally capable; license. **4.** To modify, limit, or restrict, as by giving exceptions. **5.** To make less harsh or severe; moderate. **6.** *Grammar* To modify the meaning of (a noun, for example). —*intr.* **1.** To be or become qualified. **2.** To reach the later stages of a selection process or contest by succeeding in earlier rounds. [< Fr. *qualifier* (< OFr.) and < ME *qualifien*, to specify the time and place of a document's execution, both < Med.Lat. *qualificāre*, to attribute a quality to : Lat. *quālis*, of such a kind; see QUALITY + Lat. *-ficāre*, -fy.] —**qual′i·fi′a·ble** *adj.*

qual·i·ta·tive (kwŏl′ĭ-tā′tĭv) *adj.* Of, relating to, or concerning quality. [ME, producing a primary quality < Med.Lat. *qualitā-tivus* < LLat., qualitative < Lat. *quālitās, quālitāt-*, quality. See QUALITY.] —**qual′i·ta′tive·ly** *adv.*

qualitative analysis *n.* The testing of a substance or mixture to determine its chemical constituents.

qual·i·ty (kwŏl′ĭ-tē) *n., pl.* **-ties** **1a.** An inherent or distinguishing characteristic; a property. **b.** A personal trait, esp. a character trait: *"The most vital quality a soldier can possess is self-confidence"* (George S. Patton). **2.** Essential character; nature: *"The quality of mercy is not strain'd"* (Shakespeare). **3a.** Superiority of kind: *an intellect of quality.* **b.** Degree or grade of excellence: *goods of low quality.* **4a.** High social position. **b.** Those in a high social position. **5.** *Music* Timbre, as determined by harmonics: *a voice with a metallic quality.* **6.** *Linguistics* The character of a vowel sound determined by the size and shape of the oral cavity and the amount of resonance with which the sound is produced. **7.** *Logic* The positive or negative character of a proposition. ❖ *adj.* Having a high degree of excellence: *the importance of quality health care.* [ME *qualite* < OFr. < Lat. *quālitās, quālitāt-* < *quālis*, of what kind. See kʷo- in App.]

quality control *n.* A system for ensuring the maintenance of proper standards in manufactured goods, esp. by random inspection. —**qual′i·ty-con·trol′** (kwŏl′ĭ-tē-kən-trōl′) *adj.*

quality time *n.* Time during which one focuses on or dedicates oneself to a person or activity.

qualm (kwäm, kwôm) *n.* **1.** A sudden feeling of sickness, faintness, or nausea. **2.** A sudden disturbing feeling: *qualms of homesickness.* **3.** An uneasy feeling about the propriety or rightness of a course of action. [?] —**qualm′ish** *adj.* —**qualm′ish·ly** *adv.*

quam·ash (kwŏm′ăsh′) *n.* See **camas** 1. [NLat., species name, var. of Chinook Jargon *kamass*. See CAMAS.]

quan·da·ry (kwŏn′də-rē, -drē) *n., pl.* **-ries** A state of uncertainty or perplexity. [?]

Quandary Peak A mountain, 4,350.8 m (14,265 ft), in the Park Range of the Rocky Mts. in central CO.

quan·go (kwăng′gō) *n., pl.* **-gos** An organization or agency that is financed by a government but acts independently of it. [*qua(si) n(on)g(overnmental) o(rganization).*]

Quant (kwŏnt), **Mary** b. 1934. British fashion designer who is credited with designing the first miniskirt (1960) and hot pants (c. 1970).

quan·ta (kwŏn′tə) *n.* Plural of **quantum.**

quan·tal (kwŏn′tl) *adj.* *Physics* **a.** Of or relating to a quantum or a quantized system. **b.** Existing in only one of two possible states. **2.** *Biology* Of or being an all-or-none response or effect: *a quantal reaction.* —**quan′tal·ly** *adv.*

quan·ta·some (kwŏn′tə-sōm′) *n.* One of numerous particles located on the inner lamellar surface of a chloroplast and sometimes considered to be the functional unit of photosynthesis. [QUANTA + -SOME³.]

quan·tic (kwŏn′tĭk) *n.* A homogeneous polynomial having two or more variables. [Lat. *quantus*, how much; see QUANTITY + -IC.]

quan·ti·fi·er (kwŏn′tə-fī′ər) *n.* **1.** *Logic* An operator that limits the variables of a proposition, as *some* or *all.* **2.** A linguistic form that expresses a contrast in quantity, as *some, all,* or *many.*

quan·ti·fy (kwŏn′tə-fī′) *tr.v.* **-fied, -fy·ing, -fies** **1.** To determine or express the quantity of. **2.** *Logic* To limit the variables of (a proposition) by prefixing an operator such as *all* or *some.* [Med.Lat. *quantificāre* : Lat. *quantus*, how great; see QUANTITY + Lat. *-ficāre*, -fy.] —**quan′ti·fi′a·ble** *adj.* —**quan′ti·fi·ca′tion** (-fĭ-kā′shən) *n.*

quan·ti·tate (kwŏn′tĭ-tāt′) *tr.v.* **-tat·ed, -tat·ing, -tates** To determine or measure the quantity of. [Back-formation < QUANTITATIVE (ANALYSIS).] —**quan′ti·ta′tion** *n.*

quan·ti·ta·tive (kwŏn′tĭ-tā′tĭv) *adj.* **1a.** Expressed or expressible as a quantity. **b.** Of, relating to, or susceptible of measurement. **c.** Of or relating to number or quantity. **2.** Of or relating to a metrical system based on the duration of syllables rather than on stress. [Med.Lat. *quantitātivus* < Lat. *quantitās, quantitāt-*, quantity < *quantus*, how great. See QUANTITY.] —**quan′ti·ta′tive·ly** *adv.* —**quan′ti·ta′tive·ness** *n.*

quantitative analysis *n.* The testing of a substance or mixture to determine the amounts and proportions of its chemical constituents.

quantitative trait *n.* A phenotype that is influenced by multiple genes.

quan·ti·ty (kwŏn′tĭ-tē) *n., pl.* **-ties** **1a.** A specified or indefinite number or amount. **b.** A considerable amount or number: *sells food in quantity.* **c.** An exact number or amount. **2.** The

measurable, countable, or comparable property or aspect of a thing. **3.** *Mathematics* Something that serves as the object of an operation. **4a.** *Linguistics* The relative amount of time needed to pronounce a vowel, consonant, or syllable. **b.** The duration of a syllable in quantitative verse. **5.** *Logic* The exact character of a proposition in reference to its universality, singularity, or particularity. [ME *quantite* < OFr. < Lat. *quantitās, quantitāt-* < *quantus*, how great. See kʷo- in App.]

quan·tize (kwŏn′tīz′) *tr.v.* **-tized, -tiz·ing, -tiz·es** *Physics* **1.** To limit the possible values of (a magnitude or quantity) to a discrete set of values by quantum mechanical rules. **2.** To apply quantum mechanics or the quantum theory to. —**quan′ti·za′tion** (-tĭ-zā′shən) *n.*

quan·tum (kwŏn′təm) *n., pl.* **-ta** (-tə) **1.** A quantity or amount. **2.** A specified portion. **3.** Something that can be counted or measured. **4.** *Physics* **a.** The smallest amount by which certain physical quantities can change, esp. a discrete quantity of electromagnetic radiation. **b.** This amount of energy regarded as a unit. ❖ *adj.* Relating to or based upon quantum mechanics. [Lat. < neut. of *quantus*, how great. See QUANTITY.]

quantum bit *n.* The smallest unit of information in a computer designed to manipulate or store information through effects predicted by quantum physics.

quantum chromodynamics *n.* (*used with a sing. verb*) See chromodynamics.

quantum electrodynamics *n.* (*used with a sing. verb*) The quantum theory of the properties and behavior of muons, photons, and electrons and the electromagnetic field.

quantum jump *n.* **1.** Abrupt change from one energy level to another, esp. such a change in the state of an electron with the loss or gain of a quantum of energy. **2.** A quantum leap.

quantum leap *n.* An abrupt change or advance, esp. in method, information, or knowledge.

quantum mechanics *n.* (*used with a sing. or pl. verb*) Quantum theory, esp. the quantum theory of the structure and behavior of atoms and molecules.

quantum number *n.* Any of a set of discrete values that individually characterize the properties and collectively specify the state of a particle or of a physical system.

quantum physics *n.* (*used with a sing. verb*) The branch of physics that uses quantum theory to describe and predict the properties of a physical system.

quantum system *n.* A physical or theoretical system that cannot be correctly described without the use of quantum physics.

quantum theory *n.* **1.** A theory in physics based on the principle that matter and energy have the properties of both particles and waves, and used to explain the radiation of energy from a blackbody, the photoelectric effect, and the Bohr theory, and to account for such physical phenomena as the existence of discrete packets of energy and matter, the uncertainty principle, and the exclusion principle. **2.** Any of various specific applications of this theory.

Quan·zhou (chwän′jō′) Formerly **Tsin·kiang** (tsĭn′kyäng′, chĭn′jyäng′) A city of SE China SW of Fuzhou. Pop. 444,000.

Qua·paw (kwô′pô) *n., pl.* Quapaw or -paws **1.** A member of a Native American people formerly inhabiting parts of Arkansas along the Arkansas River, with a present-day population in Oklahoma. **2.** The Siouan language of the Quapaw.

Qu′Ap·pelle (kwə-pĕl′) A river of S Saskatchewan and SW Manitoba, Canada, flowing c. 434 km (270 mi) to the Assiniboine R.

quar·an·tine (kwôr′ən-tēn′, kwŏr′-) *n.* **1a.** A period of time during which a vehicle, person, or material suspected of carrying a contagious disease is detained at a port of entry under enforced isolation to prevent disease from entering a country. **b.** A place for such detention. **2.** Enforced isolation or restriction of free movement imposed to prevent the spread of contagious disease. **3.** A condition of enforced isolation. **4.** A period of 40 days. ❖ *tr.v.* **-tined, -tin·ing, -tines** **1.** To isolate in or as if in quarantine. **2.** To isolate politically or economically. [Ital. *quarantina* < *quaranta (giorni)*, forty (days) < Lat. *quadrāgintā*. See kʷetwer- in App.] —**quar′an·tin′a·ble** *adj.*

quark¹ (kwôrk, kwärk) *n.* Any of a group of six elementary particles having electric charges of a magnitude one-third or two-thirds that of the electron, regarded as constituents of all hadrons. [Possibly from *Three quarks for Muster Mark!*, a line in *Finnegans Wake* by James Joyce.]

WORD HISTORY *"Three quarks for Muster Mark!/Sure he hasn't got much of a bark/And sure any he has it's all beside the mark."* This passage from James Joyce's *Finnegans Wake*, part of a scurrilous 13-line poem directed against King Mark, the cuckolded husband in the Tristan legend, has left its mark on modern physics. The poem and the accompanying prose are packed with names of birds and words suggestive of birds, and the poem is a squawk against the king that suggests the cawing of a crow. The word *quark* comes from the standard English verb *quark*, meaning "to caw, croak," and also from the dialectal verb *quawk*, meaning "to caw, screech like a bird." It is easy to see why Joyce chose the word, but why should it have become the name for a group of hypothetical subatomic particles proposed as the fundamental units of matter? Murray Gell-Mann, the physicist who

quail¹
Gambel's quail
Callipepla gambeii

proposed this name for these particles, said in a private letter of June 27, 1978, to the editor of the *Oxford English Dictionary* that he had been influenced by Joyce's words: *"The allusion to three quarks seemed perfect"* (originally there were only three subatomic quarks). Gell-Mann, however, wanted to pronounce the word with (ô), not (ä), as Joyce seemed to indicate by rhyming words in the vicinity such as *Mark*. Gell-Mann got around that *"by supposing that one ingredient of the line 'Three quarks for Muster Mark' was a cry of 'Three quarts for Mister . . .' heard in H.C. Earwicker's pub,"* a plausible suggestion given the complex punning in Joyce's novel. It seems appropriate that this perplexing and humorous novel should have supplied the term for particles that come in six "flavors" and three "colors."

quarry²
marble quarry

quartet

quark² (kwôrk, kwärk) *n.* A soft creamy acid-cured cheese of central Europe made from whole milk. [Ger. < MHGer. *quarc* < Lower Sorbian *twarog* < O Church Slavonic *tvarogŭ.*]

quark star *n.* A hypothetical celestial object that is the remnant of a massive star that has collapsed with a force sufficient to reduce all particles to strange quarks.

Quarles (kwärlz, kwôrlz), **Francis** 1592–1644. English metaphysical poet known for *Emblems, Divine and Moral* (1635).

quar·rel¹ (kwôr′əl, kwŏr′-) *n.* **1.** An angry dispute; an altercation. **2.** A cause of a dispute or argument. ❖ *intr.v.* **-reled, -rel·ing, -rels** or **-relled, -rel·ling, -rels 1.** To engage in a quarrel; dispute angrily. **2.** To disagree; differ. **3.** To find fault; complain. [ME *querele* < OFr., complaint < Lat. *querella, querēla* < *querī,* to complain.] —**quar′rel·er, quar′rel·ler** *n.*

quar·rel² (kwôr′əl, kwŏr′-) *n.* **1.** A bolt for a crossbow. **2.** A tool, such as a stonemason's chisel, that has a squared head. **3.** A small diamond-shaped or square pane of glass in a latticed window. [ME *quarel* < OFr. < VLat. **quadrellus,* dim. of LLat. *quadrus,* square < Lat. *quadrum.* See k***ʷ**etwer- in App.]

quar·rel·some (kwôr′əl-səm, kwŏr′-) *adj.* **1.** Given to quarreling; contentious. See Syns at **argumentative. 2.** Marked by quarreling.

quar·ry¹ (kwôr′ē, kwŏr′ē) *n., pl.* **-ries 1a.** A hunted animal; a prey. **b.** Hunted animals considered as a group; game. **2.** An object of pursuit: *The police lost their quarry in the crowd.* [ME *querre,* entrails of a deer given to hounds as a reward < OFr. *cuiriee,* alteration (influenced by *cuir,* skin) of *coree* < VLat. **corāta,* viscera < Lat. *cor,* heart. See kerd- in App.]

quar·ry² (kwôr′ē, kwŏr′ē) *n., pl.* **-ries 1.** An open excavation or pit from which stone is quarried. **2.** A rich or productive source. ❖ *tr.v.* **-ried, -ry·ing, -ries 1.** To obtain (stone) from a quarry, as by cutting, digging, or blasting. **2.** To extract (facts, for example) by long careful searching. **3.** To use (land) as a quarry. [ME *quarey* < Med.Lat. *quareria, quareia,* alteration of OFr. *quarriere* < **quarre,* cut stone < Lat. *quadrum,* square. See k***ʷ**etwer- in App.] —**quar′ri·er** *n.*

quar·ry³ (kwôr′ē, kwŏr′ē) *n., pl.* **-ries 1.** A square or diamond shape. **2.** A pane of glass having this shape. [Variant of QUARREL².]

quart (kwôrt) *n.* **1a.** A unit of volume or capacity in the US Customary System, used in liquid measure, equal to ¼ gallon or 32 ounces (0.946 liter). **b.** A unit of volume or capacity in the US Customary System, used in dry measure, equal to ⅛ peck or 2 pints (1.101 liters). **c.** A unit of volume or capacity in the British Imperial System, used in liquid and dry measure, equal to 1.201 US liquid quarts or 1.032 US dry quarts (1.136 liters). See table at **measurement. 2a.** A container that can hold one quart. **b.** The contents of such a container. [ME < OFr. *quarte* < Lat. *quārta,* fem. of *quārtus,* fourth. See k***ʷ**etwer- in App.]

quar·tan (kwôr′tn) *adj.* Occurring every fourth day, counting inclusively, or every 72 hours. Used of a fever. ❖ *n.* A malarial fever recurring every 72 hours. [ME *quartaine* < OFr. < Lat. *quārtāna,* of the fourth < *quārtus,* fourth. See k***ʷ**etwer- in App.]

quar·ter (kwôr′tər) *n.* **1.** One of four equal parts. **2.** A coin equal to one fourth of the dollar of the United States and Canada. **3.** One fourth of an hour; 15 minutes. **4a.** One fourth of a year; three months: *Sales were up in the second quarter.* **b.** An academic term lasting approximately three months. **5.** *Astronomy* **a.** One fourth of the period of the moon's revolution around Earth. **b.** One of the four phases of the moon. **6.** *Sports* One of four equal periods of playing time into which some games, such as basketball, are divided. **7.** One fourth of a yard; nine inches. **8.** One fourth of a mile; two furlongs. **9.** One fourth of a pound; four ounces. **10.** One fourth of a ton; 500 pounds. Used as a measure of grain. **11.** *Chiefly British* A measure of grain equal to approx. eight bushels. **12a.** One fourth of a hundredweight; 25 pounds. **b.** One fourth of a British hundredweight; 28 pounds. **13a.** One of the four major divisions of the compass. **b.** One fourth of the distance between any two of the 32 points of the compass. **c.** One of the four major divisions of the horizon as determined by the four major points of the compass. **d.** A region or an area of the earth thought of as falling into such a specific division of the compass. **e.** *Nautical* The general direction on either side of a ship located 45° off the stern. **14.** *Nautical* The upper portion of the after side of a ship, usu. from the mainmast or mizzen aft to the stern. **15.** *Heraldry* Any of four equal divisions of a shield. **16.** One leg of an animal's carcass, usu. including the adjoining parts.

17. Either side of a horse's hoof. **18.** The part of the side of a shoe between the heel and the vamp. **19. quarters** A place of residence, esp. for military personnel or their dependents. **20.** A proper or assigned station or place, as for officers and crew on a warship. Often used in the plural. **21.** often **Quarter** A specific district or section, as of a city: *the French Quarter.* **22.** An unspecified person or group. Often used in the plural: *information from the highest quarters.* **23.** Mercy or clemency, esp. when displayed or given to an enemy. ❖ *adj.* **1.** Being one of four equal or equivalent parts. **2.** Being one fourth of a standard or usual value. ❖ *v.* **-tered, -ter·ing, -ters** —*tr.* **1.** To divide into four equal or equivalent parts. **b.** To quartersaw. **2.** To divide or separate into a number of parts. **3.** To dismember (a human body) into four parts. **4.** *Heraldry* To divide (a shield) into four equal areas with vertical and horizontal lines. **5a.** To mark or place (holes, for example) a fourth of a circle apart. **b.** To locate and adjust (one machine part) at right angles to its connecting part within the machine. **6.** To furnish with housing: *quartered the troops in an old factory.* **7.** To traverse (an area of ground) laterally back and forth while slowly advancing forward. —*intr.* **1.** To take up or be assigned lodgings. **2.** To cover an area of ground by ranging over it from side to side. [ME < OFr. *quartier* < Lat. *quārtārius* < *quārtus,* fourth. See k***ʷ**etwer- in App.]

quar·ter·age (kwôr′tər-ĭj) *n.* A monetary allowance, wage, or payment made or received quarterly.

quar·ter·back (kwôr′tər-băk′) *n. Football* The backfield player who usu. calls the signals for the plays. ❖ *v.* **-backed, -back·ing, -backs** —*tr.* **1.** *Football* To direct the offense of. **2.** *Slang* To lead or direct. —*intr. Football* To play quarterback.

quarter day *n.* Any of the four days of the year regarded as the beginning of a new season or quarter, when most quarterly payments are due.

quar·ter·deck (kwôr′tər-dĕk′) *n.* The after part of the upper deck of a ship, usu. reserved for officers.

quar·ter·fi·nal (kwôr′tər-fī′nəl) *adj.* Of or relating to one of four competitions in a tournament, whose winners go on to play in semifinal competitions. ❖ *n.* **1. quarterfinals** A quarterfinal round. **2.** A quarterfinal match. —**quar′ter·fi′nal·ist** *n.*

quarter horse *n.* One of a breed of strong saddle horses developed in the western United States. [< its formerly being trained for races up to a quarter mile.]

quar·ter-hour also **quar·ter hour** (kwôr′tər-our′) *n.* **1.** Fifteen minutes. **2.** The point on a clock's face marking either 15 minutes after or 15 minutes before an hour.

quar·ter·ly (kwôr′tər-lē) *adj.* **1.** Made up of four parts. **2.** Being one of four parts. **3.** Occurring or appearing at three-month intervals: *a quarterly magazine.* **4.** *Heraldry* Having four sections. Used of a shield. ❖ *n., pl.* **-lies 1.** A publication issued every three months. **2.** An examination given every three months in some colleges. ❖ *adv.* In or by quarters.

quar·ter·mas·ter (kwôr′tər-măs′tər) *n.* **1.** An officer responsible for the food, clothing, and equipment of troops. **2.** A petty officer responsible for the steering of a ship.

quar·tern (kwôr′tərn) *n.* **1.** One fourth of something, esp. of some weights and measures. **2.** *Chiefly British* A loaf of bread weighing about 4 pounds (1.81 kilograms). [ME *quartron* < OFr. *quarteron* < *quartier,* quarter. See QUARTER.]

quarter note *n. Music* A note having one-fourth the time value of a whole note.

quar·ter-phase (kwôr′tər-fāz′) *adj. Electricity* Two-phase.

quar·ter·saw (kwôr′tər-sô′) *tr.v.* **-sawed, -sawed** or **-sawn** (-sôn′), **-saw·ing, -saws** To saw (a log) into quarters lengthwise along its axis.

quarter section *n.* A land unit equal to a quarter of a section and measuring ½ of a mile on a side.

quar·ter·staff (kwôr′tər-stăf′) *n., pl.* **-staves** (-stāvz′) A long wooden staff formerly used as a weapon.

quar·ter·tone (kwôr′tər-tōn′) *n.* Half a semitone.

quar·tet also **quar·tette** (kwôr-tĕt′) *n.* **1.** *Music* **a.** A composition for four voices or four instruments. **b.** A group of four singers or four instrumentalists. **2.** A group of four. [Fr. *quartette* < Ital. *quartetto,* dim. of *quarto,* fourth < Lat. *quārtus.* See QUART.]

quar·tic (kwôr′tĭk) *adj. Mathematics* Of or relating to the fourth degree. [Lat. *quārtus,* fourth; see QUART + -IC.] —**quar′tic** *n.*

quar·tile (kwôr′tīl′, -tĭl) *n.* The value of the boundary at the 25th, 50th, or 75th percentiles of a frequency distribution divided into four parts, each containing a quarter of the population. [ME, 90 degrees apart (of the relative position of two celestial bodies) < OFr. *quartil* < Med.Lat. *quārtīlis,* of a quartile < Lat. *quārtus,* fourth. See QUART.]

quar·to (kwôr′tō) *n., pl.* **-tos 1.** The page size obtained by folding a whole sheet into four leaves. **2.** A book composed of pages of this size. [Short for ME *(in) quarto,* (in) the fourth part (of a sheet) < Med.Lat. *(in) quārtō* < Lat., ablative of *quārtus,* fourth. See k***ʷ**etwer- in App.]

quartz (kwôrts) *n.* A very hard mineral composed of silica, SiO_2, found worldwide in many different types of rocks, including sandstone and granite. [Ger. *Quarz* < MHGer. *quarc,* of Slav. orig.] —**quartz′ose′** (kwôrt′sōs′) *adj.*

quartz crystal *n.* A small crystal of quartz accurately cut along certain axes so that it can be vibrated at a particular frequency, used for its piezoelectric properties to produce an electric signal of constant known frequency.

quartz glass *n.* A clear vitreous solid, formed by melting pure quartz, that can withstand high temperatures and is extremely transparent to infrared, visible, and ultraviolet radiations.

quartz·if·er·ous (kwôrt-sĭf′ər-əs) *adj.* Containing quartz.

quartz·ite (kwôrt′sīt′) *n.* A rock formed from the metamorphism of quartz sandstone.

quartz lamp *n.* A mercury-vapor lamp enclosed by an envelope made from quartz rather than glass.

qua·sar (kwā′zär′, -sär′, -zər, -sər) *n.* An extremely distant celestial object whose power output is thousands of times that of our entire galaxy. [*quas*(i-stellar) + (ST)AR.]

quash¹ (kwŏsh) *tr.v.* **quashed, quash·ing, quash·es** To set aside or annul, esp. by judicial action. [ME *quassen* < OFr. *casser*, *quasser* < Med.Lat. *quassāre*, alteration (influenced by *quassāre*, to shatter) of *cassāre* < Lat. *cassus*, empty, void.]

quash² (kwŏsh) *tr.v.* **quashed, quash·ing, quash·es** To put down or suppress forcibly and completely: *quash a rebellion.* [ME *quashen* < OFr. *quasser* < Med.Lat. *quassāre*, to shatter < Lat. See SQUASH².]

qua·si (kwā′zī′, -sī′, kwä′zē, -sē) *adj.* Having a likeness to something; resembling: *a quasi success.* [ME, as if < OFr. < Lat. : *quam*, as; see K*o- in App. + *sī*, if; see **swo-** in App.]

quasi– *pref.* To some degree; in some manner: *quasi-stellar object.* [Lat. *quasi*, as if. See *quasi*.]

Qua·si·mo·do (kwä′zē-mō′dō), **Salvatore** 1901–68. Italian poet who won the 1959 Nobel Prize for literature.

qua·si-stel·lar object (kwä′zī-stĕl′ər, -sī′-, kwä′zē-, -sē-) *n.* A quasar.

quas·sia (kwŏsh′ə) *n.* **1a.** A tropical American shrub or small tree (*Quassia amara*) yielding a fine-grained wood. **b.** The wood of this plant. **2a.** A bitter substance obtained from the wood of this plant, used in medicine and as an insecticide. [NLat., after Graman *Quassi*, an 18th-cent. Surinamese.]

qua·ter·cen·ten·a·ry (kwŏt′ər-sĕn-tĕn′ə-rē, -sĕn′tə-nĕr′ē) *n., pl.* **-ries** A quadricentennial. [Lat. *quater*, four times; see QUATERNARY + CENTENARY.]

qua·ter·nar·y (kwŏt′ər-nĕr′ē, kwə-tûr′nə-rē) *adj.* **1.** Consisting of four; in fours. **2. Quaternary** Of or belonging to the geologic time of the second and last period of the Cenozoic Era, characterized by the appearance of humans. See table at **geologic time. 3.** *Chemistry* Relating to an atom bonded to four carbon atoms. ❖ *n., pl.* **-nar·ies 1.** The number four. **2.** The member of a group that is fourth in order. **3. Quaternary** The Quaternary Period or its deposits. [Lat. *quaternārius* < *quaternī*, by fours < *quater*, four times. See K*etwer- in App.]

quaternary ammonium compound *n.* Any of a group of compounds in which a central nitrogen atom is joined to four organic radicals and one acid radical, used in making plastics.

qua·ter·ni·on (kwə-tûr′nē-ən) *n.* **1.** A set of four persons or items. **2.** *Mathematics* Any number of the form $a + bi + cj + dk$ where a, b, c, and d are real numbers, $ij = k$, $i^2 = j^2 = -1$, and $ij = -ji$. [ME *quaternioun* < LLat. *quaterniō, quaterniōn-* < Lat. *quaternī*, by fours < *quater*, four times. See K*etwer- in App.]

quat·rain (kwŏt′rān′, kwŏ-trān′) *n.* A stanza or poem of four lines. [Fr. < OFr. < *quatre*, four < Lat. *quattuor*. See K*etwer- in App.]

quat·re·foil (kăt′ər-foil′, kăt′rə-) *n.* **1.** A representation of a flower with four petals or a leaf with four leaflets, esp. in heraldry. **2.** *Architecture* Tracery or an ornament with four foils or lobes. [ME *quaterfoile* < OFr. *quatre*, four; see QUATRAIN + OFr. *foil*, leaf; see FOIL².]

quat·tro·cen·to (kwŏt′rō-chĕn′tō) *n.* The 15th-century period of Italian art and literature. [Ital., short for *(mil) quattrocento*, one thousand four hundred < *quattro*, four (< Lat. *quattuor*; see K*etwer- in App.) + *cento*, hundred (< Lat. *centum*; see **dekm** in App.).]

quat·tu·or·de·cil·lion (kwŏt′oo-ôr-dĭ-sĭl′yən, kwŏt′yoo-) *n.* **1.** The cardinal number equal to 10^{45}. **2.** *Chiefly British* The cardinal number equal to 10^{84}. [Lat. *quattuordecim*, fourteen (*quattuor*, four; see K*etwer- in App. + *decem*, ten; see DECI–) + (M)ILLION.] —**quat′tu·or·di·cil′lion** *adj.* —**quat′tu·or·di·cil′lionth** *adj., adv. & n.*

qua·ver (kwā′vər) *v.* **-vered, -ver·ing, -vers** —*intr.* **1.** To quiver, as from weakness; tremble. **2.** To speak in a quivering voice; utter a quivering sound. **3.** *Music* To produce a trill on an instrument or with the voice. —*tr.* To utter or sing in a trilling voice. ❖ *n.* **1.** A quivering sound. **2.** A trill. **3.** *Chiefly British* An eighth note. [ME *quaveren*, prob. freq. of *cwavien, quaven*, to tremble.] —**qua′ver·y** *adj.*

quay (kē, kā) *n.* A wharf or reinforced bank where ships are loaded or unloaded. [ME *keye* < ONFr. *cai*, of Celt. orig.]

quay·age (kē′ĭj) *n.* **1.** A charge for the use of a quay. **2.** A group of quays. **3.** The space available on a system of quays.

Quayle (kwāl), **James Danforth** Known as "**Dan.**" b. 1947. Vice President of the US (1989–93).

qu·bit (kyōo′bĭt′) *n.* A quantum bit.

qu·byte (kyōo′bīt′) *n.* A sequence of eight quantum bits operated on as a unit by a computer. [QU(ANTUM) + BYTE.]

Que. *abbr.* Quebec

quean (kwēn) *n.* **1.** A woman regarded as being disreputable, esp. a prostitute. **2.** *Scots* A young woman. [ME *quene* < OE *cwene*, woman. See g*en- in App.]

quea·sy also **quea·zy** (kwē′zē) *adj.* **-si·er, -si·est** also **-zi·er, -zi·est 1.** Experiencing nausea; nauseated. **2.** Easily nauseated. **3.** Causing nausea; sickening: *an airplane's queasy lurch.* **4a.** Causing uneasiness. **b.** Uneasy; troubled. **5a.** Easily troubled. **b.** Ill at ease; squeamish. [ME *coisy*, perh. of Scand. orig.] —**quea′si·ly** *adv.* —**quea′si·ness** *n.*

Que·bec (kwĭ-bĕk′) or **Qué·bec** (kā-) **1.** A province of E Canada; joined the confederacy in 1867. The region was made a royal colony of France in 1663 and came under British sovereignty in 1763. Cap. Quebec. Pop. 7,138,795. **2.** also **Quebec City** or **Québec City** The cap. of Quebec, Canada, in the S part on the St. Lawrence R. Pop. 167,264. —**Que·beck′er, Que·bec′er** *n.*

Qué·be·cois or **Que·be·cois** (kā′bĕ-kwä′) *adj.* Of or relating to Quebec and esp. to its French-speaking inhabitants or their culture. ❖ *n., pl.* **Québecois** or **Quebecois** A native or inhabitant of Quebec, esp. a French-speaking one. [Fr. *québecois* < *Québec*, Quebec.]

que·bra·cho (kā-brä′chō) *n., pl.* **-chos 1.** Either of two South American trees, *Aspidosperma quebracho-blanco*, whose bark is used in medicine, or *Schinopsis lorentzii*, whose wood is one of the richest sources of tannin. **2.** The bark or wood of either of these trees. [Sp., alteration of *quiebrahacha* : *quebrar*, to break (< Lat. *crepāre*, to crack) + *hacha*, ax (< Fr. *hache* < OFr., of Gmc. orig.).]

Que·chan (kĕch′ən) *n.* See **Yuma¹**. [Yuma *kʷacán*, those who descended (< the sacred mountain of creation).]

Quech·ua also **Kech·ua** (kĕch′wä, -wä′) or **Quich·ua** (kĕch′-) *n., pl.* **Quechua** or **-uas** also **Kechua** or **-uas** or **Quichua** or **-uas 1.** The Quechuan language of the Inca empire, now widely spoken throughout the Andes highlands from southern Colombia to Chile. **2a.** A member of a South American Indian people originally constituting the ruling class of the Inca empire. **b.** A member of a Quechuan-speaking people. [Sp. < Quechua *kkechuwa*, plunderer.]

Quech·uan (kĕch′wən) *n.* A subgroup of the Quechumaran languages. ❖ *adj.* Of or relating to the Quechua or their language or culture.

Quech·u·ma·ran (kĕch′oo-mä-rän′) *n.* A group of languages found mostly in the Andes highlands from southern Colombia to northern Chile and Argentina, composed of the Quechuan and Aymaran languages.

queen (kwēn) *n.* **1a.** The wife or widow of a king. **b.** A woman sovereign. **2.** Something having eminence or supremacy in a given domain and personified as a woman: *Paris is the queen of cities.* **3.** *Games* **a.** The most powerful chess piece, able to move in any direction over any number of empty squares in a straight line. **b.** A playing card bearing the figure of a queen, ranking above the jack and below the king. **4.** The fertile, fully developed female in a colony of social bees, ants, or termites. **5.** *Offensive Slang* Used as a disparaging term for a homosexual man. ❖ *v.* **queened, queen·ing, queens** —*tr.* **1.** To make (a woman) a queen. **2.** *Games* To raise (a pawn) to queen in chess. —*intr. Games* To become a queen in chess. —*idiom:* **queen it** To act like a queen; domineer. [ME *quene* < OE *cwēn*. See g*en- in App.]

WORD HISTORY *Queen* and *quean* sound alike, are spelled almost identically, and both refer to women, but of wildly different kinds. *Queen* comes from Old English *cwēn*, pronounced (kwān), "queen, wife of a king," which comes from Germanic **kwēn-iz*, "woman, wife, queen." *Quean* comes from Old English *cwene*, pronounced (kwĕn′ə), "woman, female, female serf"; from the eleventh century on it was also used to mean "prostitute." The Germanic source of *cwene* is **kwen-ōn-*, "woman, wife." Once established, the pejorative sense of *quean* drove out its neutral senses and especially in the 16th and 17th centuries it was used almost solely to refer to prostitutes. Around the same time, in many English dialects the pronunciation of *queen* and *quean* became identical, leading to the obsolescence of the latter term except in some regions. • The Germanic root for both words, **kwen–*, "woman," comes by Grimm's Law from the Indo-European root **gʷen–*, "woman," which appears in at least two other English words borrowed from elsewhere in the Indo-European family. One is *gynecology*, from Greek *gunē*, "woman." Another, less obvious, one is *banshee*, "woman of the fairies," the wailing female spirit attendant on a death, from Old Irish *ben*, "woman."

Queen Anne *n.* **1.** The style in English architecture and furniture typical of the reign of Queen Anne (1702–14). **2.** A style of architecture and furniture reviving elements of the original Queen Anne design.

Queen Anne's lace *n.* A widely naturalized Eurasian herb (*Daucus carota* var. *carota*) having white nonfleshy fusiform compound umbels of small white or yellowish flowers.

Queen Char·lotte Islands (shär′lət) An archipelago off the W coast of British Columbia, Canada, separated from Vancouver I. by **Queen Charlotte Sound,** an inlet of the Pacific Ocean.

quatrefoil

Queen Anne's lace
Daucus carota var. *carota*

ă pat	oi boy
ā pay	ou out
âr care	ŏŏ took
ä father	ōō boot
ĕ pet	ŭ cut
ē be	ûr urge
ĭ pit	th thin
ī pie	th this
îr pier	hw which
ŏ pot	zh vision
ō toe	ə about,
ô paw	item

Stress marks:
′ (primary);
′ (secondary), as in
lexicon (lĕk′sĭ-kŏn′)

queen consort *n., pl.* **queens consort** The wife of a reigning king.

queen cup *n.* A perennial stemless plant (*Clintonia uniflora*) of Pacific North America having one white flower and a blue berry.

Queen Elizabeth Islands A group of islands of N Canada, in the Arctic Archipelago N of Parry Channel.

queen•ly (kwēn′lē) *adj.* **-li•er, -li•est** **1.** Having the status or rank of queen. **2.** Of, resembling, or befitting a queen; majestic and regal. ❖ *adv.* In a royal way; regally. —**queen′li•ness** *n.*

Queen Maud Land (môd) A region of Antarctica between the Weddell Sea and Enderby Land; claimed by Norway in 1939.

Queen Maud Mountains A mountain range of Antarctica extending c. 805 km (500 mi) near the South Pole.

queen mother *n.* A dowager queen who is the mother of a reigning monarch.

queen-of-the-prai•rie (kwēn′əv-thə-prâr′ē) *n.* A rhizomatous plant (*Filipendula rubra*) of the prairies and meadows of the eastern and central United States, having aromatic, pinnately compound leaves and showy pannicles of small pink flowers.

queen olive *n.* A large edible variety of olive not used as a source of oil.

queen post *n.* One of two upright supporting posts set vertically between the rafters and the tie beam at equal distances from the apex of a roof.

queen regnant *n., pl.* **queens regnant** A queen reigning in her own right.

Queens (kwēnz) A borough of New York City on W Long I.; first settled in 1635. Pop. 2,229,379.

Queen's Bench (kwēnz) *n.* A division of the British superior courts system that hears criminal and civil cases. Used when the sovereign is a woman.

Queens•ber•ry (kwēnz′bĕr′ē, -bə-rē), 8th Marquis of. Title of Sir John Sholto Douglas. 1844–1900. British aristocrat who formulated rules (1867) to govern boxing.

Queensberry rules *pl.n.* Marquis of Queensberry rules.

Queen's Counsel *n.* A barrister appointed as counsel to the British crown. Used when the sovereign is a woman.

Queen's English *n.* English speech or usage that is considered standard or accepted; Received Standard English.

queen•ship (kwēn′shĭp′) *n.* **1.** The rank or state of being a queen. **2.** A noble or regal quality, as of a queen.

queen-size (kwēn′sīz′) also **queen-sized** (-sīzd′) *adj.* **1.** Extra large in size. **2a.** Measuring about 60 inches by 80 inches (1.5 meters by 2.0 meters). Used of a bed. **b.** Being of a size that will fit such a bed: *queen-size sheets.*

queen substance *n.* A pheromone secreted by queen bees and given to worker bees to prevent them from producing more queens.

queen truss *n.* A building truss using queen posts.

queer (kwîr) *adj.* **queer•er, queer•est** **1.** Deviating from the expected or normal; strange: *a queer situation.* **2.** Odd or unconventional, as in behavior; eccentric. See Syns at **strange**. **3.** Of a questionable nature or character; suspicious. **4.** *Slang* Fake; counterfeit. **5.** Feeling slightly ill; queasy. **6.** *Offensive Slang* Homosexual. **7.** *Usage Problem* Of or relating to lesbians, gay men, bisexuals, or transgendered people. ❖ *n.* **1.** *Offensive Slang* Used as a disparaging term for a homosexual person. **2.** *Usage Problem* A lesbian, gay male, bisexual, or transgendered person. ❖ *tr.v.* **queered, queer•ing, queers** *Slang* **1.** To ruin or thwart. **2.** To put (someone) in a bad position. [Perh. < LGer., oblique, off-center < MLGer. *dwer.*] —**queer′ish** *adj.* —**queer′ly** *adv.* —**queer′ness** *n.*

USAGE NOTE A reclaimed word is a word that was once used solely as a slur but has been semantically overturned by members of the maligned group, who use it as a term of defiant pride. *Queer* is an example of a word undergoing this process. For decades *queer* was used solely as a derogatory adjective for gays and lesbians, but in the 1980s the term began to be used by gay and lesbian activists as a term of self-identification. Eventually, it came to be used as an umbrella term that included gay men, lesbians, bisexuals, and transgendered people. Nevertheless, a sizable percentage of people to whom this term might apply still hold *queer* to be a hateful insult, and its use by heterosexuals is often considered offensive. Similarly, other reclaimed words are usually offensive to the in-group when used by outsiders, so extreme caution must be taken concerning their use when one is not a member of the group.

que•le•a (kwē′lē-ə) *n.* An African weaverbird of the genus *Quelea*, esp. *Q. quelea*, a small red-billed bird that is destructive to grain crops. [NLat. *Quelea*, genus name, perh. alteration of Med. Lat. *qualea*, quail, ult. < VLat. *coacula*, of imit. orig.]

quell (kwĕl) *tr.v.* **quelled, quell•ing, quells** **1.** To put down forcibly; suppress: *quelled the riot.* **2.** To pacify; quiet: *quelled the children's fears.* [ME *quellen*, to kill < OE *cwellan.* See **gʷelǝ-** in App.]

Que•moy (kĭ-moi′) In Pinyin **Jin•men** (jĭn′mĕn′) An island and group of 2 islands and 12 islets off SE China in Taiwan Strait; administered by Taiwan since 1949.

quench (kwĕnch) *tr.v.* **quenched, quench•ing, quench•es** **1.** To put out (a fire, for example); extinguish. **2.** To suppress; squelch. **3.** To put an end to; destroy. **4.** To slake; satisfy:

quenched our thirst with a cold glass of pop. **5.** To cool (hot metal) by thrusting into water or other liquid. [ME *quenchen* < OE *-cwencan* (in *ācwencan*, to quench).] —**quench′a•ble** *adj.* —**quench′er** *n.* —**quench′less** *adj.*

que•nelle (kə-nĕl′) *n.* A ball or dumpling of finely chopped meat or seafood bound with eggs and poached in stock or water. [Fr. < Ger. *Knödel* < MHGer., dim. of *knode*, knot, knob < OHGer. *knodo.*]

quer•ce•tin (kwûr′sĭ-tĭn) *n.* A yellow powdered crystalline compound, $C_{15}H_{10}O_7$, synthesized or occurring as a glycoside in the rind and bark of numerous plants, and used medicinally to treat abnormal capillary fragility. [Lat. *quercētum*, oak forest (< *quercus*, oak; see **perkʷu-** in App.) + –IN.]

quer•ci•tron (kwûr′sĭ-trən, -trŏn′, kwər-sĭt′rən) *n.* **1.** The bright orange inner bark of the black oak. **2.** The yellow dye obtained from this bark. [Blend of Lat. *quercus*, oak; see **perkʷu-** in App., and CITRON.]

Que•ré•ta•ro (kə-rĕt′ə-rō′, kĕ-rē′tä-rō′) A city of central Mexico NW of Mexico City; site of an ancient pre-Aztec settlement. Pop. 215,976.

que•rist (kwîr′ĭst) *n.* One who asks questions; an inquirer. [< obsolete *quere*, question < QUERY.]

quern (kwûrn) *n.* A simple hand-turned grain mill. [ME *querne* < OE *cweorn.* See **gʷerǝ-** in App.]

quer•u•lous (kwĕr′ə-ləs, kwĕr′yə-) *adj.* **1.** Given to complaining; peevish. **2.** Expressing a complaint or grievance; grumbling: *querulous comments.* [ME *querulose*, litigious, quarrelsome < OFr. *querelos* < LLat. *querulōsus*, querulous < Lat. *querulus* < *querī*, to complain.] —**quer′u•lous•ly** *adv.* —**quer′u•lous•ness** *n.*

que•ry (kwîr′ē) *n., pl.* **-ries** **1.** A question; an inquiry. **2.** A doubt in the mind; a mental reservation. **3.** A notation, usu. a question mark, calling attention to an item in order to question its validity or accuracy. ❖ *tr.v.* **-ried, -ry•ing, -ries** **1.** To express doubt or uncertainty about; question: *query someone's motives.* **2.** To put a question to (a person). See Syns at **ask**. **3.** To mark (an item) with a notation in order to question its validity or accuracy. [Alteration of obsolete *quaere, quere* < Lat. *quaere*, sing. imper. of *quaerere*, to ask, to seek.] —**que′ri•er** *n.*

que•sa•dil•la (kā′sə-dē′yə) *n.* A dish consisting of a flour tortilla folded in half around a savory filling, as of cheese or beans, then fried or toasted. [Am.Sp. < Sp., dim. of *quesada*, type of cheesecake < *queso*, cheese < Lat. *cāseus.*]

Ques•nay (kā-nā′, kĕ-), François 1694–1774. French physician and pioneer political economist.

quest (kwĕst) *n.* **1.** The act or an instance of seeking or pursuing something; a search. **2.** An expedition undertaken in medieval romance by a knight in order to perform a prescribed feat: *the quest for the Holy Grail.* **3.** *Archaic* A jury of inquest. ❖ *v.* **quest•ed, quest•ing, quests** —*intr.* **1.** To go on a quest. **2.** To search for game. —*tr.* To search for; seek. [ME *queste* < OFr., ult. < Lat. *quaesta* < fem. of *quaestus, obs. p. part. of *quaerere*, to seek.] —**quest′er** *n.*

ques•tion (kwĕs′chən) *n.* **1a.** An expression of inquiry that invites or calls for a reply. **b.** An interrogative sentence, phrase, or gesture. **2.** A subject or point open to controversy; an issue. **3.** A difficult matter; a problem: *a question of ethics.* **4.** A point or subject under discussion or consideration. **5a.** A proposition brought up for consideration by an assembly. **b.** The act of bringing a proposal to vote. **6.** Uncertainty; doubt: *no question about his competence.* ❖ *v.* **-tioned, -tion•ing, -tions** —*tr.* **1.** To put a question to. See Syns at **ask**. **2.** To examine (a witness, for example) by questioning; interrogate. **3.** To express doubt about; dispute. **4.** To analyze; examine. —*intr.* To ask questions. —**idioms: in question** Under consideration or discussion. **out of the question** Not worth considering; impossible. [ME < OFr., legal inquiry < Lat. *quaestiō, quaestiōn-* < *quaesitus, obs. p. part. of *quaerere*, to ask, seek.] —**ques′tion•er** *n.* —**ques′tion•ing•ly** *adv.*

ques•tion•a•ble (kwĕs′chə-nə-bəl) *adj.* **1a.** Open to doubt or challenge; problematic. **b.** Not yet determined or specified. **2.** Of dubious morality or respectability. —**ques′tion•a•ble•ness**, **ques′tion•a•bil′i•ty** *n.* —**ques′tion•a•bly** *adv.*

question mark *n.* A punctuation symbol (?) written at the end of a sentence or phrase to indicate a direct question.

ques•tion•naire (kwĕs′chə-nâr′) *n.* A form containing a set of questions often used to gather information for a statistical survey. [Fr. < *questionner*, to ask < OFr. < *question*, legal inquiry. See QUESTION.]

Quet•ta (kwĕt′ə) A city of W-central Pakistan WSW of Lahore. Pop. 285,719.

quet•zal (kĕt-säl′) *n., pl.* **-zals** or **-za•les** (-sä′lās) **1.** A Central American bird (*Pharomachrus mocino*) that has brilliant bronze-green and red plumage and long flowing tail feathers in the male. **2.** See table at **currency**. [Am.Sp. < Nahuatl *quetzalli*, large brilliant tail feather.]

Quet•zal•co•a•tl (kĕt-säl′kō-ät′l) *n. Mythology* A god of the Toltecs and Aztecs, represented as a plumed serpent.

queue (kyoō) *n.* **1.** A line of waiting people or vehicles. **2.** A long braid of hair worn hanging down the back of the neck; a pigtail. **3.** *Computer Science* **a.** A sequence of stored data or programs awaiting processing. **b.** A data structure from which the first item that can be retrieved is the one stored earliest. ❖ *intr.v.* **queued,**

queu•ing, queues To get in line: *We queued up.* [Fr. < OFr. *cue,* tail < Lat. *cauda, cōda.*]

Que•zon City (kāʹsôn′, -sōn′) A city of central Luzon, Philippines, adjoining Manila; official cap. from 1948 to 1976. Pop. 1,676,644.

Quezon y Mo•li•na (ē mə-lēʹnə, mō-lēʹnä), **Manuel Luis** 1878–1944. Philippine politician who served as the first president of the Philippines (1935–44).

quib•ble (kwĭbʹəl) *intr.v.* **-bled, -bling, -bles 1.** To evade the truth of an issue with trivial distinctions and objections. **2.** To find fault or criticize for petty reasons; cavil. ❖ *n.* **1.** A petty distinction or an irrelevant objection. **2.** *Archaic* A pun. [Prob. dim. of obsolete *quib,* equivocation, perh. < Lat. *quibus,* dative and ablative pl. of *quī,* who (< its frequent use in legal documents). See **kʷo-** in App.] **—quibʹbler** *n.*

quiche (kēsh) *n.* A rich unsweetened custard pie often containing ingredients such as vegetables, cheese, or seafood. [Fr. < Ger. dialectal *Küche,* dim. of Ger. *Kuchen,* cake. See KUCHEN.]

Qui•ché (kē-chāʹ) *n., pl.* **Quiché** or **-chés 1.** A member of a Mayan people of Guatemala. **2.** The Mayan language of the Quiché.

quiche Lor•raine (lə-rānʹ, lô-) *n.* A quiche made with cheese and pieces of bacon. [Fr., after LORRAINE.]

Quich•ua (kēchʹwə, -wä′) *n.* Variant of **Quechua.**

quick (kwĭk) *adj.* **quick•er, quick•est 1.** Moving or functioning rapidly and energetically; speedy. **2.** Learning, thinking, or understanding with speed and dexterity; bright: *a quick mind.* **3a.** Perceiving or responding with speed and sensitivity; keen. **b.** Reacting immediately and sharply: *a quick temper.* **4.** Occurring, acquired, or done in a relatively brief period of time: *a quick inspection.* See Syns at **fast**[1]. **5.** Tending to react hastily: *quick to find fault.* **6.** *Archaic* **a.** Alive. **b.** Pregnant. ❖ *n.* **1.** Sensitive or raw exposed flesh, as under the fingernails. **2.** The most personal and sensitive aspect of the emotions. **3.** The living: *the quick and the dead.* **4.** The vital core; the essence: *the quick of the matter.* ❖ *adv.* Quickly; promptly. [ME, alive, lively, quick < OE *cwicu,* alive. See **gʷeiə-** in App.] **—quickʹly** *adv.* **—quickʹness** *n.*

USAGE NOTE In speech *quick* is commonly used as an adverb in phrases such as *Come quick.* In formal writing, however, *quickly* is required.

quick-and-dirt•y (kwĭkʹən-dûrʹtē) *adj.* Cheaply made or done; of inferior quality: *a quick-and-dirty report.*

quick assets *pl.n.* Liquid assets, including cash on hand and assets readily convertible to cash.

quick bread *n.* A bread made with a leavening agent, such as baking powder, that expands during baking and requires no leavening period beforehand.

quick•en (kwĭkʹən) *v.* **-ened, -en•ing, -ens** *—tr.* **1.** To make more rapid; accelerate. **2.** To make alive; vitalize. **3.** To excite and stimulate; stir: *Such stories quicken the imagination.* **4.** To make steeper. *—intr.* **1.** To become more rapid. **2.** To come or return to life: *"And the weak spirit quickens"* (T.S. Eliot). **3.** To reach the stage of pregnancy when the fetus can be felt to move. **—quickʹen•er** *n.*

quick fix *n. Slang* A hastily contrived temporary remedy for a problem.

quick-freeze (kwĭkʹfrēz′) *tr.v.* **-froze** (-frōzʹ), **-fro•zen** (-frōʹzən), **-freez•ing, -freez•es** To freeze (food) rapidly so as to retain flavor, nutritional value, or other properties.

quick•ie (kwĭkʹē) *n. Informal* Something made or done rapidly. **—quickʹie** *adj.*

quick•lime (kwĭkʹlīm′) *n.* See **lime**[3] 1b. [ME *qwyke lime* (transl. of Lat. *calx vīva*) : *quick, qwyke,* living; see QUICK + *lime, lyme,* lime; see LIME[3].]

quick•sand (kwĭkʹsănd′) *n.* **1.** A bed of loose sand and water forming a soft shifting mass that yields easily to pressure and tends to engulf any object resting on its surface. **2.** A place or situation similar to quicksand. [ME *quyksond,* living sand : *quick, quyk,* living; see QUICK + *sand, sond,* sand; see SAND.]

quick•set (kwĭkʹsĕt′) *n. Chiefly British* **1.** Cuttings or slips of a plant suitable for hedges. **2.** A hedge consisting of these plant cuttings or slips. [QUICK, alive + SET[1].]

quick•sil•ver (kwĭkʹsĭl′vər) *n.* See **mercury** 1. ❖ *adj.* Unpredictable; mercurial. [ME < OE *cwicseolfor,* living silver (transl. of Lat. *argentum vīvum*) : *cwic, cwicu,* alive; see **gʷeiə-** in App. + *seolfor,* silver; see SILVER.]

quick•step (kwĭkʹstĕp′) *n.* A march for accompanying quick time.

quick study *n.* One who is able to memorize or understand something quickly.

quick-tem•pered (kwĭkʹtĕmʹpərd) *adj.* Easily angered.

quick time *n.* A marching pace of 120 steps per minute.

quick-wit•ted (kwĭkʹwĭtʹĭd) *adj.* Mentally alert and sharp; keen. See Syns at **intelligent. —quickʹ-witʹted•ly** *adv.* **—quickʹ-witʹted•ness** *n.*

quid[1] (kwĭd) *n.* A cut or piece, as of chewing tobacco. [ME *quide,* cud < OE *cwidu.*]

quid[2] (kwĭd) *n., pl.* **quid** or **quids** *Chiefly British* A pound sterling. [Poss. < Lat., something, what. See QUIDDITY.]

Quid•de (kvĭdʹə), **Ludwig** 1858–1941. German politician who shared the 1927 Nobel Peace Prize.

quid•di•ty (kwĭdʹĭ-tē) *n., pl.* **-ties 1.** The real nature of a thing; the essence. **2.** A hairsplitting distinction; a quibble. [Med.Lat. *quidditās* < Lat. *quid,* what. See **kʷo-** in App.]

quid•nunc (kwĭdʹnŭngk′) *n.* A nosy person; a busybody. [Lat. *quid nunc?,* what now? : *quid,* what; see **kʷo-** in App. + *nunc,* now; see **nu-** in App.]

quid pro quo (kwĭdʹ prō kwōʹ) *n., pl.* **quid pro quos** or **quids pro quo** An equal exchange or substitution. [Lat. *quid prō quō* : *quid,* something + *prō,* for + *quō,* ablative of *quid,* something.]

qui•es•cent (kwē-ĕsʹənt, kwī-) *adj.* Being quiet, still, or at rest; inactive. [Lat. *quiēscēns, quiēscent-,* pr. part. of *quiēscere,* to rest < *quiēs,* quiet. See QUIET.] **—qui•esʹcence** *n.* **—qui•esʹcent•ly** *adv.*

qui•et (kwīʹĭt) *adj.* **-et•er, -et•est 1.** Making no noise; silent: *quiet neighbors; a quiet engine.* **2.** Free of noise; hushed: *a quiet street.* **3.** Calm and unmoving; still: *a quiet lake.* **4.** Free of turmoil and agitation; untroubled. **5.** Restful; soothing: *a quiet afternoon nap.* **6.** Tranquil; serene: *a quiet place in the country.* **7.** Not showy or garish; restrained: *quiet colors.* **8.** Restrained in style; understated: *a quiet strength; a quiet life.* ❖ *n.* The quality or condition of being quiet. ❖ *v.* **-et•ed, -et•ing, -ets** *—tr.* **1.** To cause to become quiet. **2.** *Law* To make (a title) secure by freeing from all questions or challenges. *—intr.* To become quiet: *The child wouldn't quiet down.* [ME < OFr. < Lat. *quiētus,* p. part. of *quiēscere,* to rest.] **—quiʹet•ly** *adv.* **—quiʹet•ness** *n.*

qui•et•en (kwīʹĭ-tn) *Chiefly British tr. & intr.v.* **-ened, -en•ing, -ens** To make or become quiet.

qui•et•ism (kwīʹĭ-tĭz′əm) *n.* **1.** A form of Christian mysticism enjoining passive contemplation and the beatific annihilation of the will. **2.** A state of quietness and passivity. **—quiʹet•ist** *n.* **—qui′et•isʹtic** *adj.*

qui•e•tude (kwīʹĭ-to͞od′, -tyo͞od′) *n.* Tranquillity. [LLat. *quiētūdō* < Lat. *quiētus,* resting < p. part. of *quiēscere,* to rest. See QUIET.]

qui•e•tus (kwī-ēʹtəs) *n.* **1.** Something that serves to suppress, check, or eliminate. **2.** Release from life; death. **3.** A final discharge, as of a duty. [Short for ME *quietus (est),* (he is) discharged (of an obligation) < Med.Lat. *quiētus (est)* < Lat., (he is) at rest. See QUIET.]

quiff[1] (kwĭf) *n. Chiefly British* A tuft of hair, esp. a forelock. [?]

quiff[2] (kwĭf) *n.* A woman regarded as promiscuous. [?]

quill (kwĭl) *n.* **1.** The hollow stemlike main shaft of a feather. **2.** Any of the larger wing or tail feathers of a bird. **3.** A writing pen made from the shaft of a feather. **4.** *Music* **a.** A plectrum for a stringed instrument of the clavichord type. **b.** A pipe with a hollow stem. **5.** A toothpick made from the stem of a feather. **6.** One of the sharp hollow spines of a porcupine or hedgehog. **7.** A bobbin around which yarn is wound in weaving. **8.** A hollow shaft that rotates on a solid shaft when gears are engaged. ❖ *tr.v.* **quilled, quill•ing, quills 1.** To wind (thread or yarn) onto a quill. **2.** To make or press small ridges in (fabric). [ME *quil.*]

quill•back (kwĭlʹbăk′) *n., pl.* **quillback** or **-backs** A North American freshwater fish *(Carpiodes cyprinus)* with one dorsal fin ray extending conspicuously beyond the others.

quill•work (kwĭlʹwûrk′) *n.* Decoration, as of leather articles, with porcupine quills.

quill•wort (kwĭlʹwûrt′, -wôrt′) *n.* Any of several vascular spore-bearing aquatic or marsh plants of the genus *Isoetes,* having short rhizomes and quill-like leaves.

Quil•mes (kēlʹmĕs′) A city of E Argentina, a suburb of Buenos Aires on the Río de la Plata. Pop. 509,445.

quilt (kwĭlt) *n.* **1.** A coverlet or blanket made of two layers of fabric with a layer of cotton, wool, feathers, or down in between, all stitched firmly together. **2.** A thick protective cover similar to a quilt. ❖ *v.* **quilt•ed, quilt•ing, quilts** *—tr.* **1.** To make into a quilt by stitching (layers of fabric) together. **2.** To construct like a quilt. **3.** To pad and stitch ornamentally. *—intr.* **1.** To make a quilt. **2.** To do quilted work. [ME *quilte* < AN < Lat. *culcita,* mattress.] **—quiltʹer** *n.*

quilt•ing (kwĭlʹtĭng) *n.* **1.** The process of doing quilted work. **2a.** Material used for quilts. **b.** Quilted material.

quin– *pref.* Variant of **quino–.**

quin•a•crine hydrochloride (kwĭnʹə-krēn′) *n.* A crystalline compound, $C_{23}H_{30}ClN_3O \cdot 2H_2O$, used primarily to treat malaria and giardiasis. [QUIN– + ACR(ID)INE.]

qui•nate (kwīʹnāt′) *adj.* Arranged in groups of five: *quinate leaflets.* [Lat. *quīnī,* five each; see **penkʷe** in App. + –ATE[1].]

quince (kwĭns) *n.* **1.** A western Asian shrub or tree *(Cydonia oblonga)* having white flowers and hard applelike fruit. **2.** The many-seeded fruit of this plant, edible only when cooked. [ME *quynce,* pl. of *quyn,* quince < OFr. *cooin* < Lat. *cotōneum (mālum),* quince (fruit), prob. var. of *cydōnium* < Gk. dialectal *kudōnion (mālon),* alteration (influenced by *Kudōniā,* Cydonia, an ancient city of NW Crete) of *kodumālon.*]

quin•cen•ten•a•ry (kwĭn′sĕn-tĕnʹə-rē, kwĭn-sĕnʹtə-nĕr′ē) *n., pl.* **-ries** A 500th anniversary or celebration. ❖ *adj.* Of or relating to a span of 500 years or to a 500th anniversary. [< alteration of Lat. *quīngentī, quīncentī,* five hundred (on the model of such words as TERCENTENARY). See **penkʷe** in App.]

quin•cen•ten•ni•al (kwĭn′sĕn-tĕnʹē-əl) *adj.* Quincentenary. ❖

Manuel Quezon y Molina

quillwork
quillwork on buckskin

quilt
detail of a patchwork quilt

ă	pat	oi	boy
ā	pay	ou	out
âr	care	o͝o	took
ä	father	o͞o	boot
ĕ	pet	ŭ	cut
ē	be	ûr	urge
ĭ	pit	th	thin
ī	pie	*th*	this
îr	pier	hw	which
ŏ	pot	zh	vision
ō	toe	ə	about,
ô	paw		item

Stress marks:
ʹ (primary);
′ (secondary), as in
lexicon (lĕkʹsĭ-kŏn′)

n. A quincentenary event or celebration.

quin·cun·cial also **quin·cunx·ial** (kwĭn-kŭn′shəl) *adj.* Of, relating to, or forming a quincunx. —**quin·cun′cial·ly** *adv.*

quin·cunx (kwĭn′kŭngks′) *n.* An arrangement of five objects with one at each corner of a rectangle or square and one at the center. [Lat. *quīncūnx, quīncūnc-,* five twelfths : *quīnque,* five; see **penkʷe** in App. + *ūncia,* twelfth part of a unit; see OUNCE[1].]

Quin·cy (kwĭn′zē) A city of E MA, a suburb of Boston. Pop. 88,025.

Quin·cy (kwĭn′zē, -sē), **Josiah** 1744–75. Amer. Revolutionary patriot who traveled to England (1774–75) to present the colonists' grievances.

quin·de·cen·ni·al (kwĭn′dĭ-sĕn′ē-əl) *adj.* 1. Occurring once every 15 years. 2. Lasting 15 years. ❖ *n.* A 15th anniversary. [< Lat. *quīndecim,* fifteen; see **penkʷe** in App. + Lat. *-ennium* (< *annus,* year; see **at-** in App.).]

quin·de·cil·lion (kwĭn′dĭ-sĭl′yən) *n.* 1. The cardinal number equal to 10⁴⁸. 2. *Chiefly British* The cardinal number equal to 10⁹⁰. [Lat. *quīndecim,* fifteen (*quīnque,* five; see **penkʷe** in App. + *decem,* ten; see DECI-) + (M)ILLION.] —**quin′de·cil′lion** *adj.* —**quin′de·cil′lionth** *adj., adv. & n.*

Quine (kwīn), **Willard van Orman** 1908–2000. Amer. analytic philosopher and logician whose writings include *Word and Object* (1960).

qui·nel·la (kwĭ-nĕl′ə, kē-) also **qui·nie·la** (kēn-yĕl′ə) *n.* A system of betting in which the bettor must pick the first two finishers of a race but not necessarily in the correct sequence. [Am.Sp. *quiniela,* dim. of Sp. *quina,* keno < Fr. *quine.* See KENO.]

quin·i·dine (kwĭn′ĭ-dēn′) *n.* A colorless crystalline alkaloid, $C_{20}H_{24}N_2O_2$, resembling quinine and used in treating malaria and certain heart disorders.

qui·nine (kwī′nīn′) *n.* 1. A bitter colorless amorphous powder or crystalline alkaloid, $C_{20}H_{24}N_2O_2 \cdot 3H_2O$, derived from certain cinchona barks and used in medicine to treat malaria. 2. Any of various compounds or salts of quinine.

quinine water *n.* See **tonic water.**

quin·nat salmon (kwĭn′ăt′) *n.* See **Chinook salmon.** [Chinook *ikwanat.*]

quino– or **quin–** *pref.* 1. Cinchona; cinchona bark: *quinoidine.* 2. Quinone: *quinoid.* [< Sp. *quina,* cinchona bark < Quechua *kina.*]

qui·no·a (kĭ-nō′ə, kēn′wä) *n.* A goosefoot (*Chenopodium quinoa*) native to the Andes and cultivated for its edible seeds. 2. The dried fruits and seeds of this plant, used as a food staple and ground into flour. [Am.Sp. *quínoa* < Quechua *kinua, kinoa.*]

quin·oid (kwĭn′oid′) *n.* A substance resembling quinone in structure or physical properties.

qui·noi·dine (kwĭ-noi′dēn′, -dĭn) *n.* A brownish-black mixture of alkaloids remaining after extraction of crystalline alkaloids from cinchona bark, used as a quinine substitute.

quin·o·line (kwĭn′ə-lēn′, -lĭn) *n.* An organic base, C_9H_7N, having a tarlike odor, synthesized or obtained from coal tar, and used as a food preservative and in antiseptics and dyes.

qui·none (kwĭ-nōn′, kwĭn′ōn′) *n.* Any of a class of aromatic compounds found widely in plants, esp. the yellow form, $C_6H_4O_2$, used in making dyes, tanning hides, and photography.

quin·o·noid (kwĭn′ə-noid′, kwĭ-nō′-) *adj.* Of or containing quinone or resembling it in structure or properties.

quin·qua·ge·nar·i·an (kwĭng′kwə-jə-nâr′ē-ən) *n.* A person 50 years old or in his or her fifties. ❖ *adj.* Of or characteristic of a quinquagenarian. [< Lat. *quīnquāgēnārius,* containing fifty < *quīnquāgēnī,* fifty each < *quīnquāgintā,* fifty. See **penkʷe** in App.]

quinque– *pref.* Five: *quinquevalent.* [Lat. *quīnque- < quīnque,* five. See **penkʷe** in App.]

quin·quen·ni·al (kwĭn-kwĕn′ē-əl, kwĭng-) *adj.* 1. Happening once every five years. 2. Lasting for five years. ❖ *n.* A fifth anniversary. 2. A period of five years. —**quin′quen′ni·al·ly** *adv.*

quin·quen·ni·um (kwĭn-kwĕn′ē-əm, kwĭng-) *n., pl.* **-quen·ni·ums** or **-quen·ni·a** (-kwĕn′ē-ə) A period of five years. [Lat. *quīnquennium* : *quīnque, quinque-* + *annus,* year.]

quin·que·va·lent (kwĭng′kwə-vā′lənt) *adj.* Pentavalent. —**quin′que·va′lence** *n.*

quin·sy (kwĭn′zē) *n.* Acute inflammation of the tonsils and the surrounding tissue, often leading to the formation of an abscess. [ME < Med.Lat. *quinancia* and OFr. *quinancie,* both < Gk. *kunankhē,* dog quinsy, dog collar : *kuōn, kun-,* dog; see **kwon-** in App. + *ankhein,* to squeeze.]

quint[1] (kwĭnt) *n.* A sequence of five cards of the same suit in one hand in piquet. [Fr. *quinte* < OFr., interval of a fifth (in music), fem. of *quint,* fifth < Lat. *quīntus.* See **penkʷe** in App.]

quint[2] (kwĭnt) *n.* A quintuplet.

quin·tain (kwĭn′tən) *n.* A post or an object mounted on a post, used as a target in tilting exercises. [ME *quintaine* < OFr., prob. < Lat. *quīntāna (via),* fifth (street in a Roman camp, supposedly used for military exercises) < *quīntus,* fifth. See **penkʷe** in App.]

quin·tal (kwĭnt′l) *n.* 1. A unit of mass in the metric system equal to 100 kilograms. 2. See **hundredweight** 2. [ME, a unit of weight < OFr. < Med.Lat. *quintāle* < Ar. *qinṭār* < L.Gk. *kentēnarion* < LLat. *centēnārium (pondus),* hundred(weight) < Lat. *centēnārius,* of a hundred. See CENTENARY.]

quin·tes·sence (kwĭn-tĕs′əns) *n.* 1. The pure, highly concentrated essence of a thing. 2. The purest or most typical instance: *the quintessence of evil.* 3. In ancient and medieval philosophy, the fifth and highest essence after the four elements of earth, air, fire, and water, thought to be the substance of the heavenly bodies and latent in all things. [ME < OFr. *quinte essence,* fifth essence < Med.Lat. *quīnta essentia* : Lat. *quīnta,* fem. of *quīntus,* fifth; see **penkʷe** in App. + Lat. *essentia,* essence; see ESSENCE.]

quin·tes·sen·tial (kwĭn′tə-sĕn′shəl) *adj.* Of, relating to, or having the nature of a quintessence; being the most typical: "*Liszt was the quintessential romantic*" (Musical Heritage Review). —**quin′tes·sen′tial·ly** *adv.*

quin·tet also **quin·tette** (kwĭn-tĕt′) *n.* 1. *Music* **a.** A composition for five voices or five instruments. **b.** A group of five singers or five instrumentalists. 2. A group of five. [Prob. < Ital. *quintetto,* dim. of *quinto,* fifth < Lat. *quīntus.* See **penkʷe** in App.]

quin·tile (kwĭn′tīl′, kwĭn′tĭl) *n.* 1. The astrological aspect of planets distant from each other by 72° or one fifth of the zodiac. 2. *Statistics* The value at any of the boundaries that divide a frequency distribution into five parts, each containing one fifth of the population. [Lat. *quīntus,* fifth; see **penkʷe** in App. + *-ile,* as in QUARTILE.]

Quin·til·ian (kwĭn-tĭl′yən, -ē-ən) 1st cent. A.D. Roman rhetorician known for his *Institutio Oratoria.*

quin·til·lion (kwĭn-tĭl′yən) *n.* 1. The cardinal number equal to 10¹⁸. 2. *Chiefly British* The cardinal number equal to 10³⁰. [Lat. *quīntus,* fifth; see **penkʷe** in App. + (M)ILLION.] —**quin·til′lion** *adj.*

quin·til·lionth (kwĭn-tĭl′yənth) *n.* 1. The ordinal number matching the number quintillion in a series. 2. One of a quintillion equal parts. —**quin·til′lionth** *adv. & n.*

quin·tu·ple (kwĭn-tōō′pəl, -tŭp′-, -tŭp′əl, kwĭn′tə-pəl) *adj.* 1. Consisting of five parts or members. 2. Five times as much in size, strength, number, or amount. ❖ *n.* A number five times larger than another. ❖ *tr. & intr.v.* **-pled, -pling, -ples** To multiply or be multiplied by five. [Fr. < OFr. : Lat. *quīntus,* fifth; see **penkʷe** in App. + *-ple,* -fold (< Lat. *-plus*).] —**quin·tup′ly** *adv.*

quin·tu·plet (kwĭn-tŭp′lĭt, -tōō′plĭt, -tyōō′-, kwĭn′tə-plĭt) *n.* 1. One of five offspring born in a single birth. 2. A group or combination of five associated by common properties or behavior. [< QUINTUPLE (modeled on TRIPLET).]

quin·tu·pli·cate (kwĭn-tōō′plĭ-kĭt, -tyōō′-) *adj.* 1. Multiplied by five; fivefold. 2. Fifth of a group of five identical things. ❖ *n.* 1. One of a set of five identical things. 2. A set of five copies. ❖ *tr. & intr.v.* (-kāt′) **-cat·ed, -cat·ing, -cates** To multiply or be multiplied by five. [Lat. *quīntus,* fifth; see QUINTUPLE + (QUADRU)PLICATE.]

quip (kwĭp) *n.* 1. A clever, witty, usu. impromptu remark. 2. A clever, often sarcastic remark; a gibe. 3. A petty distinction or objection; a quibble. 4. Something curious or odd. ❖ *intr.v.* **quipped, quip·ping, quips** To make quips or a quip. [Alteration of obsolete *quippy,* perh. < Lat. *quippe,* indeed < *quid,* what. See **kʷo-** in App.] —**quip′py** *adj.* —**quip′ster** *n.*

qui·pu (kē′pōō) *n.* A record-keeping device of the Inca empire consisting of a series of variously colored strings attached to a base rope and knotted so as to encode information, esp. accounts. [Am.Sp. < Quechua *kipu.*]

quire[1] (kwīr) *n.* 1. A set of 24 or sometimes 25 sheets of paper of the same size and stock; one twentieth of a ream. 2. A collection of leaves of parchment or paper, folded one within the other, in a manuscript or book. [ME *quayer,* four double sheets of paper < OFr. *quaer* < VLat. **quaternus* < Lat. *quaternī,* set of four, four each < *quater,* four times. See **kʷetwer-** in App.]

quire[2] (kwīr) *n. & v.* *Archaic* Variant of **choir.**

Quir·i·nal (kwĭr′ə-nəl) One of the seven hills of ancient Rome; traditional home of the Sabines. —**Quir′i·nal** *adj.*

quirk (kwûrk) *n.* 1. A peculiarity of behavior; an idiosyncrasy: "*Every man had his own quirks and twists*" (Harriet Beecher Stowe). 2. An unpredictable or unaccountable act or event; a vagary: *a quirk of fate.* 3. A sudden sharp turn or twist. 4. An equivocation; a quibble. 5. *Architecture* A lengthwise groove on a molding between the convex upper part and the soffit. [?] —**quirk′i·ly** *adv.* —**quirk′i·ness** *n.* —**quirk′y** *adj.*

quirt (kwûrt) *n.* A riding whip with a short handle and a lash of braided rawhide. [Prob. < Am.Sp. *cuarta,* whip, ult. < Lat. *quārta,* fourth. See QUART.]

quis·ling (kwĭz′lĭng) *n.* A traitor who serves as the puppet of the enemy occupying his or her country. [After Vidkun *Quisling* (1887–1945), head of Norway's government during the Nazi occupation (1940–45).]

quit (kwĭt) *v.* **quit** or **quit·ted** (kwĭt′ĭd), **quit·ting, quits** —*tr.* 1. To depart from; leave. 2. To leave the company of: *quit the gathering.* 3. To give up; relinquish: *quit a job.* 4. To abandon or put aside; forsake: *quit smoking.* 5. To cease or discontinue: *quit talking.* 6. *Computer Science* To exit (an application). 7a. To rid oneself of by paying: *quit a debt.* **b.** To release from a burden or responsibility. 8. To conduct (oneself) in a specified way: *Quit yourselves like adults.* —*intr.* 1. To cease performing an action. See Syns at **stop.** 2. To give up, as in defeat; stop. 3. To leave a job. ❖ *adj.* Absolved of a duty or an obligation; free. [ME *quiten,* to release < OFr. *quiter* < Med.Lat. *quiētāre, quītāre* < Lat. *quiētus,* at rest. See QUIET.]

quipu

quitch grass (kwĭch) *n.* Couch grass. [ME *quich* < OE *cwice*. See gʷeiə- in App.]

quit·claim (kwĭt′klām′) *Law n.* The transfer of a title, right, or claim to another. ❖ *tr.v.* **-claimed, -claim·ing, -claims** To renounce all claim to (a possession or right). [ME *quitclaime* < AN *quiteclame* < *quiteclamer*, to release : *quite*, free; see QUITE + *clamer*, to proclaim (< Lat. *clāmāre*; see CLAIM).]

quite (kwīt) *adv.* **1.** To the greatest extent; completely: *quite alone.* **2.** Actually; really: *I'm quite positive.* **3.** To a degree; rather: *quite soon.* [ME < *quite*, clear, free < OFr. < Lat. *quiētus*, freed. See QUIET.]

Qui·to (kē′tō) The cap. of Ecuador, in the N-central part; captured by the Incas in 1487 and held by the Spanish from 1534 until 1822. Pop. 890,355.

quit·rent (kwĭt′rĕnt′) *n.* A rent paid by a freeman in lieu of the services required by feudal custom. [ME *quiterent* : *quite*, free; see QUITE + *rent*, rent; see RENT[1].]

quits (kwĭts) *adj.* On even terms with by payment or requital: *quits with the loan.* [ME, prob. alteration (influenced by Med.Lat. *quittus, quītus*, p. part. of *quītāre*, to free) of *quit*, rid of a debt < OFr. *quiter*. See QUIT.]

quit·tance (kwĭt′ns) *n.* **1a.** Release from a debt, obligation, or penalty. **b.** A document or receipt certifying such release. **2.** Something given as requital or recompense; a repayment. [ME *quitance* < OFr. < *quiter*, to free. See QUIT.]

quit·ter (kwĭt′ər) *n.* One who gives up easily.

quit·tor (kwĭt′ər) *n.* An inflammation of the hoof cartilage of horses and other solid-hoofed animals, characterized by degeneration of hoof tissue, formation of a slough, and fistulous sores. [ME *quiture*, perh. < OFr., act of boiling < Lat. *coctūra*, boiling liquid < *coctus*, p. part. of *coquere*, to cook. See pekʷ- in App.]

quiv·er[1] (kwĭv′ər) *intr.v.* **-ered, -er·ing, -ers** To shake with a slight, rapid, tremulous movement. ❖ *n.* The act or motion of quivering. [ME *quiveren*, perh. < *quiver*, nimble (< OE *cwifer-*; see gʷeiə- in App.).] —**quiv′er·ing·ly** *adv.* —**quiv′er·y** *adj.*

quiv·er[2] (kwĭv′ər) *n.* **1.** A portable case for holding arrows. **2.** A case full of arrows. [ME < AN *quiveir*, var. of OFr. *cuivre* < O Low Franconian *cocar*, prob. < Med.Lat. *cucurum*, prob. < Hunnish; akin to Mongolian *kökür*.]

qui vive (kē vēv′) *n.* A sentry's challenge. —**idiom: on the qui vive** On the alert; vigilant. [Fr., (long) live who? (a sentry's challenge to determine a person's political sympathies) : *qui*, who + *vive*, third pers. sing. pr. subjunctive of *vivre*, to live.]

quix·ot·ic (kwĭk-sŏt′ĭk) also **quix·ot·i·cal** (-ĭ-kəl) *adj.* **1.** Caught up in the pursuit of unreachable goals; idealistic without regard to practicality. **2.** Capricious; impulsive. [After Don *Quixote*, hero of a romance by Miguel de Cervantes.] —**quix·ot′i·cal·ly** *adv.* —**quix′o·tism** (kwĭk′sə-tĭz′əm) *n.*

quiz (kwĭz) *tr.v.* **quizzed, quiz·zing, quiz·zes** **1.** To question closely or repeatedly; interrogate. **2.** To test the knowledge of by posing questions: *quizzed the class on state capitals.* See Syns at **ask**. **3.** *Chiefly British* To poke fun at; mock. ❖ *n., pl.* **quiz·zes** **1.** A questioning or inquiry. **2.** A short oral or written test. **3.** A practical joke. [?] —**quiz′zer** *n.*

quiz show *n.* A television or radio program in which the contestants are quizzed and winners receive money or prizes.

quiz·zi·cal (kwĭz′ĭ-kəl) *adj.* **1.** Suggesting puzzlement; questioning. **2.** Teasing; mocking. **3.** Eccentric; odd. —**quiz′zi·cal′i·ty** (-kăl′ĭ-tē) *n.* —**quiz′zi·cal·ly** *adv.*

Qum (ko͞om) See **Qom.**

Qum·ran (ko͞om-rän′) also **Khir·bet Qumran** (kîr′bĕt) An ancient village of Palestine on the NW shore of the Dead Sea E of Jerusalem. The Dead Sea Scrolls were found here.

quod·li·bet (kwŏd′lə-bĕt′) *n.* **1a.** A theological or philosophical issue presented for formal argument or disputation. **b.** Formal disputation of such an issue. **2.** *Music* A usu. humorous medley. [ME < Med.Lat. *quodlibetum* < Lat. *quod libet*, anything at all : *quod*, what; see kʷo- in App. + *libet*, it pleases, third pers. sing. pr. t. of *libēre*, to be pleasing.]

quoin also **coign** (koin, kwoin) *n.* **1a.** An exterior angle of a wall or other piece of masonry. **b.** Any of the stones used in forming such an angle, often being of large size and dressed or arranged so as to form a decorative contrast with the adjoining wall. **2.** A keystone. **3.** *Printing* A wedge-shaped block used to lock type in a chase. **4.** A wedge used to raise the level of a gun. ❖ *tr.v.* **quoined, quoin·ing, quoins** also **coigned, coign·ing, coigns** To provide, secure, or raise with a quoin or quoins. [Variant of COIN.]

quoit (kwoit, koit) *n. Upper Northern US* **1. quoits** (used with a sing. verb) A game in which flat rings of iron or rope are pitched at a stake, with points awarded for encircling it. **2.** One of the rings used in this game. [ME *coyte*, flat stone, quoit < OFr. *coilte, coite* < Lat. *culcita*, cushion.]

REGIONAL NOTE The game *quoits* derives its name from *quoit*, specifically denoting a heavy iron ring slightly convex on the outside and concave inside, configured so as to give it an edge for cutting into the ground. Both the game and the term are associated almost exclusively with the Upper North (the northernmost tier of states from New York westward to North Dakota).

quok·ka (kwŏk′ə) *n.* A small short-tailed wallaby (*Setonix brachyurus*) living in coastal areas of SW Australia. [Nyungar (Aboriginal language of southwest Australia) *gwaga*.]

quon·dam (kwŏn′dəm, -dăm′) *adj.* That once was; former: "*the quondam drunkard, now perfectly sober*" (Bret Harte). [Lat. < *quom*, when. See kʷo- in App.]

Quon·set (kwŏn′sĭt) A trademark used for a prefabricated portable hut having a semicircular roof of corrugated metal that curves down to form walls.

quo·rum (kwôr′əm, kwōr′-) *n.* **1.** The minimal number of officers and members of a committee or organization who must be present for valid transaction of business. **2.** A select group. [ME, quorum of justices of the peace < Lat. *quōrum*, of whom (< the wording of a commission naming certain persons as members of a body), genitive pl. of *quī*, who. See kʷo- in App.]

quo·ta (kwō′tə) *n.* **1.** A proportional share, as of goods, assigned to a group or to each member of a group; an allotment. **2.** A production assignment. **3a.** A number or percentage, esp. of people, constituting or designated as an upper limit: *strict annual immigration quotas.* **b.** A number or percentage, esp. of people, constituting a required or targeted minimum: *a system of quotas for hiring minority applicants.* [Med.Lat. < Lat. *quota (pars)*, how large (a part), fem. of *quotus*, of what number. See QUOTE.]

quot·a·ble (kwō′tə-bəl) *adj.* Suitable for or worthy of quoting: *a quotable slogan.* —**quot′a·bil′i·ty** *n.*

quo·ta·tion (kwō-tā′shən) *n.* **1.** The act of quoting. **2.** A passage quoted. **3.** An explicit reference or allusion in an artistic work to another, usu. well-known work. **4a.** The quoting of current prices and bids for securities and goods. **b.** The prices or bids cited. —**quo·ta′tion·al** *adj.*

quotation mark *n.* Either of a pair of punctuation marks used to mark the beginning and end of a passage attributed to another and repeated word for word and also to indicate glosses. They appear in the form of double quotation marks (" ") and single quotation marks (' ').

quote (kwōt) *v.* **quot·ed, quot·ing, quotes** —*tr.* **1.** To repeat or copy the words of (another), usu. with acknowledgment of the source. **2.** To cite or refer to for illustration or proof. **3.** To repeat a brief passage or excerpt from: *quoted a Duke Ellington melody.* **4.** To state (a price) for securities, goods, or services. —*intr.* To give a quotation, as from a book. ❖ *n.* **1.** *Informal* A quotation. **2.** A quotation mark. **3.** Used by a speaker to indicate the beginning of a quotation. **4.** A dictum; a saying. [ME *coten*, to mark a book with numbers or marginal references < OFr. *coter* < Med.Lat. *quotāre*, to number chapters < Lat. *quotus*, of what number < *quot*, how many. See kʷo- in App.] —**quot′er** *n.*

quoth (kwōth) *tr.v. Archaic* Uttered; said. Used only in the first and third persons, with the subject following: "*Quoth the Raven, 'Nevermore!'*" (Edgar Allan Poe). [ME < OE *cwæth*, third pers. sing. p. t. of *cwethan*, to say.]

quo·tha (kwō′thə) *interj. Archaic* Used to express surprise or sarcasm, after quoting the word or phrase of another. [Alteration of *quoth he.*]

quo·tid·i·an (kwō-tĭd′ē-ən) *adj.* **1.** Everyday; commonplace. **2.** Recurring daily. Used esp. of attacks of malaria. [ME *cotidien* < OFr. < Lat. *quōtīdiānus* < *quōtīdiē*, each day : *quot*, how many, as many as; see kʷo- in App. + *diē*, ablative of *diēs*, day; see dyeu- in App.]

quo·tient (kwō′shənt) *n.* The number obtained by dividing one quantity by another; for example, in 45 ÷ 3 = 15, 15 is the quotient. [ME *quocient*, alteration of Lat. *quotiēns*, how many times < *quot*, how many. See kʷo- in App.]

Qŭ·qon (ko͞o-kôn′, кнōо-кнōн′) or **Ko·kand** (kō-känd′) A city of E Uzbekistan SE of Tashkent; center of a powerful khanate in the 18th cent. Pop. 176,000.

Qur·'an (kə-rän′, -răn′, kô-, kō-) *n.* Variant of **Koran.**

q.v. *abbr. Latin* quod vide (which see)

QWER·TY (kwûr′tē) *adj.* Of, relating to, or being the traditional configuration of typewriter or computer keyboard keys. [< the first six letters at the upper left on such a keyboard.]

quiver[2]
belt model

quoin
smooth-cut quoins

Rr

r¹ or **R** (är) *n., pl.* **r's** or **R's** also **rs** or **Rs** **1.** The 18th letter of the modern English alphabet. **2.** Any of the speech sounds represented by the letter *r*. **3.** The 18th in a series. **4.** Something shaped like the letter R.

r² *abbr.* **1.** radius **2.** or **R** *Electricity* resistance

R¹ A trademark used for a movie rating indicating that admission will be granted only to persons of or over a certain age, usu. 17, unless accompanied by a parent or guardian.

R² **1.** The symbol for **gas constant. 2.** The symbol for **radical.**

R³ *abbr.* **1.** range (surveying) **2.** Réaumur (scale) **3.** registered trademark **4.** Republican **5.** *Ecclesiastical* response **6.** right **7.** or **r** roentgen **8.** rook (chess) **9.** *Baseball* run

r. *abbr.* **1.** rare **2.** recto **3.** retired **4.** rod (unit of length) **5.** *Games* rubber

R. *abbr.* **1.** rabbi **2.** rector **3.** river

Ra¹ (rä) also **Re** (rā) *n. Mythology* The ancient Egyptian sun god, the supreme deity represented as a man with the head of a hawk crowned with a solar disk and uraeus.

Ra² The symbol for the element **radium.**

RA *abbr.* **1.** regular army **2.** residence assistant **3.** right ascension **4.** Royal Academy

Ra. *abbr.* range

ra•bat (răb′ĕ, rə-băt′) *n.* A piece of cloth fitted to the collar and covering the shirt front, worn chiefly by Roman Catholic and Anglican clergy. [Fr. < OFr. See REBATO.]

Ra•bat (rə-bät′, rä-) The cap. of Morocco, on the Atlantic Ocean NE of Casablanca. Pop. 1,220,000.

ra•ba•to (rə-bä′tō) *n.* Variant of **rebato.**

rab•bet (răb′ĭt) also **re•bate** (rē′băt′, răb′ĭt) *n.* **1.** A cut or groove along or near the edge of a piece of wood that allows another piece to fit into it to form a joint. **2.** A joint so made. ❖ *v.* **-bet•ed, -bet•ing, -bets** also **-bat•ed, -bat•ing, -bates** *—tr.* **1.** To cut a rabbet in. **2.** To join by a rabbet. *—intr.* To be joined by a rabbet. [ME *rabet* < OFr. *rabat*, recess in a wall < *rabattre*, to beat down again. See REBATE¹.]

rab•bi (răb′ī) *n., pl.* **-bis 1.** A person trained in Jewish law, ritual, and tradition and ordained for leadership of a Jewish congregation. **2.** A scholar qualified to interpret Jewish law. [ME *rabi* < OFr. < LLat. *rabbī*, master < Gk. *rhabbi*, O my master < Heb. and Aram. *rabbî*, my master : *rab*, master (< *rab*, to become great) + *-î*, my.]

rab•bin•ate (răb′ə-nāt′, -nĭt) *n.* **1.** The office or function of a rabbi. **2.** Rabbis considered as a group. [< obsolete *rabbin*, rabbi. See RABBINICAL.]

rab•bin•i•cal (rə-bĭn′ĭ-kəl) also **rab•bin•ic** (-ĭk) *adj.* Of, relating to, or characteristic of rabbis. [< obsolete *rabbin*, rabbi < Fr. < OFr. *rabain*, prob. < Aram. *rabbīn*, pl. of *rab*, master. See RABBI.] **—rab•bin′i•cal•ly** *adv.*

Rabbinic Hebrew *n.* See **Mishnaic Hebrew.**

rab•bin•ism (răb′ə-nĭz′əm) *n.* Rabbinical teachings and traditions.

rabbet

rab•bit (răb′ĭt) *n., pl.* **-bits** or **rabbit 1.** Any of various long-eared, short-tailed, burrowing mammals of the family Leporidae, such as the commonly domesticated Old World species *Oryctolagus cuniculus.* **2.** A hare. **3.** The fur of a rabbit or hare. ❖ *intr.v.* **-bit•ed, -bit•ing, -bits** To hunt rabbits or hares. [ME *rabet,* young rabbit, prob. < OFr. < MDu. *robbe,* rabbit.] **—rab′bit•er** *n.*

rabbit ears *pl.n. Informal* An indoor television antenna consisting of two usu. adjustable rods connected to a base.

rabbit fever *n.* See **tularemia.**

rabbit punch *n.* A chopping blow to the back of the neck. **—rab′bit-punch′** (răb′ĭt-pŭnch′) *v.*

rab•ble¹ (răb′əl) *n.* **1.** A tumultuous crowd; a mob. **2.** The lowest or coarsest class of people. **3.** A group of persons regarded with contempt. [ME.]

rab•ble² (răb′əl) *n.* **1.** An iron bar used to stir and skim molten iron in puddling. **2.** Any of various similar tools used in roasting or refining furnaces. ❖ *tr.v.* **-bled, -bling, -bles** To stir or skim (molten iron) with an iron bar. [Fr. *râble,* fire shovel < OFr. *roable* < Med.Lat. *rotābulum* < Lat. *rutābulum* < *rutus,* p. part. of *ruere,* to rake up, tumble down.] **—rab′bler** *n.*

rab•ble-rous•er (răb′əl-rou′zər) *n.* A leader or speaker who stirs up the passions of the masses; a demagogue. **—rab′ble-rous′ing** *adj. & n.*

Ra•be•lais (răb′ə-lā′, răb′ə-lā′, răb-lĕ′), François 1494?–1553. French humanist known for his satires, most notably *Pantagruel* (1532) and *Gargantua* (1534).

Rab•e•lai•si•an (răb′ə-lā′zē-ən, -zhən) *adj.* **1.** Of or relating to

raccoon
Procyon lotor

Rabelais or his works. **2.** Characterized by coarse humor or bold caricature.

Ra•bi (rŭ′bē) also **Ra•bi•a** (rə-bē′ə) *n.* Either the third or the fourth month of the year in the Islamic calendar. See table at **calendar.** [Ar. *rabī',* spring, fourth.]

Ra•bi (rä′bē), **Isidor Isaac** 1898–1988. Austrian-born Amer. physicist who won a 1944 Nobel Prize.

rab•id (răb′ĭd) *adj.* **1.** Of or affected by rabies. **2.** Raging; uncontrollable: *rabid thirst.* **3.** Extremely zealous or enthusiastic; fanatical. [Lat. *rabidus* < *rabere,* to rave.] **—ra•bid′i•ty** (rə-bĭd′ĭ-tē, rā-), **rab′id•ness** (răb′ĭd-nĭs) *n.* **—rab′id•ly** *adv.*

ra•bies (rā′bēz) *n.* An acute infectious, often fatal viral disease of most warm-blooded animals that attacks the central nervous system and is transmitted by the bite of infected animals. [Lat. *rabiēs,* rage < *rabere,* to rave.] **—ra′bi•et′ic** (-ĕt′ĭk) *adj.*

Ra•bin (rä-bēn′, rä′bēn), **Yitzhak** or **Itzhak** 1922–95. Israeli leader who served as prime minister (1974–77 and 1992–95) and shared the 1994 Nobel Peace Prize.

rac•coon also **ra•coon** (ră-kōōn′) *n., pl.* **rac•coons** or **raccoon** also **ra•coons** or **racoon 1.** A carnivorous North American mammal (*Procyon lotor*) having grayish-brown fur, black mask-like facial markings, and a black-ringed bushy tail. **2.** The fur of this mammal. **3.** Any of various similar or related animals. [Of Virginia Algonquian orig.]

race¹ (rās) *n.* **1.** A local geographic or global human population distinguished as a more or less distinct group by genetically transmitted physical characteristics. **2.** A group of people united or classified together on the basis of common history, nationality, or geographic distribution: *the Celtic race.* **3.** A genealogical line; a lineage. **4.** Humans considered as a group. **5.** *Biology* **a.** An interbreeding, usu. geographically isolated population of organisms differing from other populations of the same species in the frequency of hereditary traits. A race that has been given formal taxonomic recognition is known as a subspecies. **b.** A breed or strain, as of domestic animals. **6.** A distinguishing or characteristic quality, such as the flavor of a wine. [Fr. < OFr. < OItal. *razza,* race, lineage.]

USAGE NOTE The notion of race is nearly as problematic from a scientific point of view as it is from a social one. The biological basis for race is described today not in observable physical features but in the study of mitochondrial DNA and Y chromosomes, and the groupings outlined by earlier physical anthropologists seldom coincide with findings at the genetic level. Citing this and other points, many cultural anthropologists now consider race to be more a social or mental construct than an objective biological fact. The traditional terms *Caucasoid* or *Caucasian, Mongoloid, Negroid,* and *Australoid* still see use in physical anthropology, but these words may well be considered offensive in other contexts.

race² (rās) *n.* **1.** *Sports* **a.** A competition of speed, as in running. **b. races** A series of such competitions held at a regular time and place: *a fan of the dog races.* **2.** An extended competition similar to a race: *the presidential race.* **3.** Steady or rapid onward movement: *the race of time.* **4a.** A strong or swift current of water. **b.** The channel of such a current. **c.** An artificial channel built to transport water and use its energy. **5.** A groovelike part of a machine in which a moving part slides or rolls. **6.** See **slipstream.** ❖ *v.* **raced, rac•ing, rac•es** *—intr.* **1.** *Sports* To compete in a race. **2.** To move rapidly or at top speed: *We raced home. My heart was racing with fear.* **3.** To run too rapidly because of decreased resistance or unnecessary provision of fuel. *—tr.* **1.** *Sports* **a.** To compete against in a race. **b.** To cause to compete in a race; enter in a contest: *She races horses for a living.* **2.** To transport rapidly or at top speed; rush: *raced the injured motorist to the hospital.* **3.** To cause (an engine with the gears disengaged, for example) to run swiftly or too swiftly. [ME *ras* < ON *rās,* rush, running.]

race•course (rās′kôrs′, -kōrs′) *n. Sports* A course for racing.

race•horse (rās′hôrs′) *n.* A horse bred and trained to race.

ra•ceme (rā-sēm′, rə-) *n.* An inflorescence having stalked flowers arranged singly along an elongated unbranched axis, as in the lily of the valley. [Lat. *racēmus,* a bunch of grapes.]

ra•ce•mic (rā-sē′mĭk, rə-) *adj.* Of or relating to a chemical compound that contains equal quantities of dextrorotatory and levorotatory forms and therefore does not rotate the plane of incident polarized light.

racemic acid *n.* An optically inactive form of tartaric acid, $C_4H_6O_6$, that can be separated into dextrorotatory and levorotatory components and is found in grapes.

ra·ce·mi·form (rā-sē′mə-fôrm′) *adj.* Having the form of a raceme.

rac·e·mism (răs′ə-mĭz′əm, rā-sē′-) *n.* The condition or state of being racemic.

rac·e·mi·za·tion (răs′ə-mĭ-zā′shən) *n.* Conversion of an optically active substance to a racemic form.

rac·e·mose (răs′ə-mōs′) *adj.* **1.** *Botany* Resembling or borne in a raceme. **2.** *Anatomy* Having a structure of clustered parts. Used of glands. —**rac′e·mose′ly** *adv.*

race norm·ing (nôr′mĭng) *n.* The practice of adjusting scores on a standardized test by using separate curves for different racial groups. —**race′-normed** (-nôrmd) *adj.*

rac·er (rā′sər) *n.* **1.** One that races or takes part in a race. **2.** A vehicle used in racing. **3.** Any of various fast-moving North American snakes of the genus *Coluber.*

race riot *n.* A riot caused by racial hatred or dissension.

race·run·ner (rās′rŭn′ər) *n.* Any of several fast-moving New World lizards of the genus *Cnemidophorus.*

race·track (rās′trăk′) *n. Sports* A usu. oval, specially surfaced course on which races are held.

race·walk·ing (rās′wô′kĭng) *n.* The sport of walking for speed, the rules of which require the racer to maintain continual foot contact with the ground and to keep the supporting leg straight at the knee when that leg is directly below the body. —**race′walk′** *v.* —**race′walk′er** *n.*

race·way (rās′wā′) *n.* **1.** A course or track for racing, esp. harness racing. **2.** A tube that encloses and protects electric wires. **3.** See **race**[2] 4c.

Ra·chel (rā′chəl) In the Bible, the second wife of Jacob and the mother of Joseph and Benjamin. [Heb. *rāḥēl,* ewe.]

ra·chil·la (rə-kĭl′ə) *n., pl.* **-chil·lae** (-kĭl′ē) A diminutive axis of a spikelet that bears the florets, as in grasses and sedges. [NLat., dim. of *rachis,* rachis. See RACHIS.]

ra·chis (rā′kĭs) *n., pl.* **ra·chis·es** or **rach·i·des** (răk′ĭ-dēz′, rā′kĭ-) *Biology* A main axis or shaft, such as the main stem of an inflorescence or the spinal column. [NLat. < Gk. *rhakhis,* spine, ridge.] —**ra′chi·al** *adj.*

ra·chi·tis (rə-kī′tĭs) *n.* See **rickets.** [NLat. *rachītis,* inflammation of the spine (adopted because of its similarity in sound to RICKETS) < L.Gk. *rhakhītis* : Gk. *rhakhis,* spine + Gk. *-ītis,* -itis.] —**ra·chit′ic** (-kĭt′ĭk) *adj.*

Rach·ma·ni·noff (răk-mä′nə-nôf′, räκн-mä′nyĭ-nəf), **Sergei Vasilievich** 1873–1943. Russian-born composer and pianist who interpreted the later romantic composers.

ra·cial (rā′shəl) *adj.* **1.** Of, relating to, or characteristic of race or races. **2.** Arising from or based on differences among human racial groups: *racial discrimination.* —**ra′cial·ly** *adv.*

ra·cial·ism (rā′shə-lĭz′əm) *n.* **1a.** An emphasis on race or racial considerations. **b.** Policy or practice based on racial considerations. **2.** *Chiefly British* Variant of **racism.** —**ra′cial·ist** *adj. & n.* —**ra′cial·is′tic** *adj.*

ra·cial·ize (rā′shə-līz′) *tr.v.* **-ized, -iz·ing, -iz·es** **1a.** To differentiate or categorize according to race. **b.** To impose a racial character or context on. **2.** To perceive or experience in racial terms. —**ra′cial·i·za′tion** (-lĭ-zā′shən) *n.*

Ra·cine (rə-sēn′, ră-) A city of SE WI on Lake Michigan S of Milwaukee. Pop. 81,855.

Ra·cine (rə-sēn′, ră-), **Jean Baptiste** 1639–99. French playwright whose works include *Phèdre* (1677).

rac·ing form (rā′sĭng) *n.* An information sheet about horseraces.

ra·cism (rā′sĭz′əm) *n.* **1.** The belief that race accounts for differences in human character or ability and that a particular race is superior to others. **2.** Discrimination or prejudice based on race. —**rac′ist** *adj. & n.*

rack[1] (răk) *n.* **1a.** A framework or stand in or on which to hold, hang, or display various articles: *a laundry rack.* **b.** *Games* A triangular frame for arranging billiard balls at the start of a game. **c.** A receptacle for livestock feed. **d.** A frame for holding bombs in an aircraft. **2.** *Slang* A bunk; a bed. **3.** A toothed bar that meshes with a gearwheel or other toothed machine part. **4a.** A state of intense anguish. **b.** A cause of intense anguish. **5.** An instrument of torture on which the victim's body was stretched. **6.** A pair of antlers. ❖ *tr.v.* **racked, rack·ing, racks** **1.** To place (billiard balls, for example) in a rack. **2.** To cause great physical or mental suffering to: *Pain racked his body.* **3.** To torture by means of the rack. —*phrasal verb:* **rack up** *Informal* To accumulate or score: *rack up points.* [ME *rakke,* prob. < MDu. *rec,* framework. See **reg-** in App.] —**rack′er** *n.*

rack[2] (răk) *n.* A fast, flashy, four-beat gait of a horse in which each foot touches the ground separately and at equal intervals. ❖ *intr.v.* **racked, rack·ing, racks** To move in a rack. [?]

rack[3] (răk) *n.* A thin mass of wind-driven clouds. ❖ *intr.v.* **racked, rack·ing, racks** To be driven by the wind; scud. [ME *rak,* prob. of Scand. orig.; akin to Swed. *rak,* wreckage.]

rack[4] (răk) *n.* Variant of **wrack**[1].

rack[5] (răk) *n.* Variant of **wrack**[2].

rack[6] (răk) *tr.v.* **racked, rack·ing, racks** To drain (wine or cider) from the dregs. [ME *rakken* < O Provençal *arracar* < *raca,* stems and husks of grapes.]

rack[7] (răk) *n.* **1a.** A wholesale rib cut of lamb or veal between the

shoulder and the loin. **b.** A retail rib cut of lamb or veal, prepared for roasting or for rib chops. **2.** The neck and upper spine of mutton, pork, or veal. [Prob. < RACK[1].]

rack and pinion *n.* A device for the conversion of rotary and linear motion, consisting of a pinion and a mated rack. —**rack′-and-pin′ion** (răk′ən-pĭn′yən) *adj.*

rack·et[1] also **rac·quet** (răk′ĭt) *n.* **1.** A device consisting of an oval frame with tight interlaced strings and a handle, used to strike a ball or shuttlecock. **2.** A paddle, as for table tennis. [ME *raket,* a kind of handball < OFr. *rachette,* palm of the hand, racket < Med.Lat. *rascheta,* palm < Ar. *rāḥat (al-yad),* palm (of the hand), bound form of *rāḥa.*]

rack·et[2] (răk′ĭt) *n.* **1.** A loud distressing noise. See Syns at **noise.** **2.** A dishonest business or practice, esp. one using fraud or extortion. **3a.** An easy, profitable means of livelihood. **b.** *Slang* A business or occupation. ❖ *intr.v.* **-et·ed, -et·ing, -ets** **1.** To make or move with a loud distressing noise. **2.** To lead an active social life. [?]

rack·et·eer (răk′ĭ-tîr′) *n.* A person who commits crimes such as extortion, loansharking, bribery, and obstruction of justice in furtherance of illegal business activities. —**rack′et·eer′** *v.*

rack·et·y (răk′ĭ-tē) *adj.* Noisy; raucous.

rack railway *n.* See **cog railway.**

rack-rent (răk′rĕnt′) *n.* Exorbitant rent. ❖ *tr.v.* **-rent·ed, -rent·ing, -rents** To exact rack-rent for or from. [< RACK[1].] —**rack′-rent′er** *n.*

ra·clette (rä-klĕt′, ră-) *n.* **1.** A Swiss dish of cheese melted over high heat and served with boiled potatoes or bread and various garnishes. **2.** A firm cheese used in this dish. [Fr. < *racler,* to scrape < Provençal *rasclar,* to rake < O Provençal < VLat. **rāscu-lāre* < **rāsculum,* dim. of Lat. *rāstrum,* rake.]

rac·on·teur (răk′ŏn-tûr′) *n.* One who tells stories and anecdotes with skill and wit. [Fr. < *raconter,* to relate < OFr. : *re-,* re- + *aconter,* to count up, reckon; see ACCOUNT.]

ra·coon (ră-kōōn′) *n.* Variant of **raccoon.**

rac·quet·ball (răk′ĭt-bôl′) *n.* A game played on a four-walled handball court by two or four players with short-handled rackets and a small hollow rubber ball.

rac·quets also **rack·ets** (răk′ĭts) *pl.n.* (*used with a sing. verb*) A game played on a large netless four-walled court by two or four players with long-handled rackets and a hard fast-moving ball.

rac·y (rā′sē) *adj.* **-i·er, -i·est** **1.** Having a distinctive and characteristic quality or taste. **2.** Strong and sharp in flavor or odor; piquant or pungent. **3.** Risqué; ribald. **4.** Vigorous; lively. [< RACE[1].] —**rac′i·ly** *adv.* —**rac′i·ness** *n.*

rad[1] (răd) *n.* A unit of energy absorbed from ionizing radiation, equal to 100 ergs per gram or 0.01 joule per kilogram of irradiated material. It has been replaced as a standard scientific unit by the gray. [r(adiation) a(bsorbed) d(ose).]

rad[2] (răd) *adj. Slang* Excellent; wonderful. [Short for RADICAL.]

rad[3] *abbr.* radian

rad. *abbr. Mathematics* **1.** radical **2.** radius **3.** radix

ra·dar (rā′där) *n.* **1.** A method of detecting distant objects and determining their position, velocity, or other characteristics by analysis of very high frequency radio waves reflected from their surfaces. **2.** The equipment used in radar. [ra(dio) d(etecting) a(nd) r(anging).]

radar astronomy *n.* The branch of astronomy that studies bodies in the solar system by analyzing the reflections of radio waves sent from Earth.

radar beacon *n.* A fixed device that sends or receives, amplifies, alters, and returns a radar signal, permitting a distant receiver to determine its bearing and sometimes its range.

radar gun *n.* A usu. hand-held device that measures the velocity of a moving object by sending out a continuous radio wave and measuring the frequency of reflected waves.

ra·dar·scope (rā′där-skōp′) *n.* The oscilloscope viewing screen of a radar receiver.

radar telescope *n.* A large radar antenna used in radar astronomy.

Rad·cliffe (răd′klĭf′), **Ann Ward** 1764–1823. British Gothic novelist known for *The Mysteries of Udolpho* (1794).

rad·dle[1] (răd′l) *tr.v.* **-dled, -dling, -dles** To twist together; interweave. [< dialectal *raddle,* stick interwoven with others in a fence < AN *reidele,* stout pole, poss. < MHGer. *reidel,* rod.]

rad·dle[2] (răd′l) *n. & v.* Variant of **ruddle.**

rad·dled (răd′ld) *adj.* Worn-out and broken-down. [?]

radi– *pref.* Variant of **radio–.**

ra·di·al (rā′dē-əl) *adj.* **1a.** Of, relating to, or arranged like rays or radii. **b.** Radiating from or converging to a common center. **c.** Having or characterized by parts so arranged or so radiating. **2.** Moving or directed along a radius. **3.** *Anatomy* Of, relating to, or near the radius or forearm. **4.** Developing symmetrically about a central point. ❖ *n.* **1.** A radial part, such as a ray or radius. **2.** A radial tire. [ME < Med.Lat. *radiālis* < Lat. *radius,* ray.] —**ra′di·al·ly** *adv.*

radial engine *n.* An internal-combustion engine, formerly used in propeller-driven aircraft, with cylinders arranged radially around the crankshaft.

radial keratotomy *n.* Keratotomy involving a radial pattern of incisions, used to reduce or correct myopia.

racket[1]
top: tennis and racquetball rackets
bottom: squash racket

radar
aircraft radar system

ă	pat	oi	boy
ā	pay	ou	out
âr	care	ŏŏ	took
ä	father	ōō	boot
ĕ	pet	ŭ	cut
ē	be	ûr	urge
ĭ	pit	th	thin
ī	pie	th	this
îr	pier	hw	which
ŏ	pot	zh	vision
ō	toe	ə	about,
ô	paw		item

Stress marks:
′ (primary);
′ (secondary), as in
lexicon (lĕk′sĭ-kŏn′)

radio telescope
one of twenty-seven radio telescopes comprising the Very Large Array near Socorro, New Mexico

radial symmetry *n.* Symmetrical arrangement of constituents, esp. of radiating parts, about a central point. —**radially symmet·rical** *adj.*

radial tire *n.* A pneumatic tire in which the ply cords extending to beads are laid at approximately right angles to the center line of the tread.

ra·di·an (rā′dē-ən) *n.* A unit of angular measure equal to the angle subtended at the center of a circle by an arc equal in length to the radius of the circle, approx. 57°17′44.6″. See table at **measurement**. [RADI(US) + -AN[1].]

ra·di·ance (rā′dē-əns) also **ra·di·an·cy** (-ən-sē) *n.* **1.** The quality or state of being radiant. **2.** *Physics* The radiant energy emitted per unit time in a specified direction by a unit area of an emitting surface.

ra·di·ant (rā′dē-ənt) *adj.* **1.** Emitting heat or light. **2.** Consisting of or emitted as radiation: *radiant heat.* **3a.** Filled with light; bright. **b.** Glowing; beaming. See Syns at **bright.** ❖ *n.* **1.** An object or point from which light or heat rays are emitted. **2.** *Astronomy* The apparent celestial origin of a meteoric shower. —**ra′di·ant·ly** *adv.*

radiant energy *n.* Energy transferred by radiation, esp. by an electromagnetic wave.

radiant flux *n.* The rate of flow of radiant energy.

ra·di·ate (rā′dē-āt′) *v.* **-at·ed, -at·ing, -ates** —*intr.* **1.** To send out rays or waves. **2.** To issue or emerge in rays or waves: *Heat radiated from the stove.* **3.** To extend in straight lines from or toward a center; diverge or converge like rays: *Spokes radiate from the wheel's hub.* **4.** *Ecology* To spread into new habitats and thereby diverge or diversify. Used of a group of organisms. —*tr.* **1.** To emit (light, for example) in or as if in rays. **2.** To send or spread out from or as if from a center. **3.** To irradiate or illuminate (an object). **4.** To manifest in a glowing manner. ❖ *adj.* (-ĭt) **1.** *Botany* Having rays or raylike parts, as daisies. **2.** *Biology* Marked by radial symmetry. **3.** Surrounded with rays. [Lat. *radiāre, radiāt-,* to emit beams < *radius,* ray.] —**ra′di·a′tive** *adj.*

ra·di·a·tion (rā′dē-ā′shən) *n.* **1.** The act or process of radiating: *the radiation of heat from a fire.* **2.** *Physics* **a.** Emission and propagation of energy in the form of rays or waves. **b.** Energy radiated or transmitted in the form of rays, waves, or particles. **c.** A stream of particles or electromagnetic waves emitted by the atoms and molecules of a radioactive substance as a result of nuclear decay. **3a.** The act of exposing or the condition of being exposed to such energy. **b.** The application of such energy, as in medical treatment. **4.** *Anatomy* Radial arrangement of parts, as of a group of nerve fibers connecting different areas of the brain. **5a.** *Ecology* The spread of a group of organisms into new habitats. **b.** Adaptive radiation. —**ra′di·a′tion·al, ra′di·a′tive** *adj.*

radiational cooling *n.* The cooling of the earth's surface and the nearby air, occurring chiefly at night and due to heat lost through terrestrial radiation.

radiation sickness *n.* Illness induced by exposure to ionizing radiation, ranging in severity from vomiting, headache, and diarrhea to loss of hair and teeth, reduction in blood counts, and death.

ra·di·a·tor (rā′dē-ā′tər) *n.* **1.** A heating device consisting of connected pipes, typically inside an upright metal structure, through which steam or hot water is circulated so as to radiate heat into the surrounding space. **2.** A cooling device, as in automotive engines, through which fluid circulates as a coolant. **3.** *Physics* A body that emits radiation. **4.** A transmitting antenna.

rad·i·cal (răd′ĭ-kəl) *adj.* **1.** Arising from or going to a root or source; basic. **2.** Departing markedly from the usual or customary; extreme. **3.** Favoring or effecting fundamental or revolutionary changes in current practices, conditions, or institutions. **4.** *Linguistics* Of or being a root: *a radical form.* **5.** *Botany* Arising from the root or its crown: *radical leaves.* **6.** *Slang* Excellent; wonderful. ❖ *n.* **1.** One who advocates radical changes. **2.** *Mathematics* The root of a quantity as indicated by the radical sign. **3.** *Symbol* **R** An atom or a group of atoms with at least one unpaired electron. **4.** *Linguistics* See **root**[1] 8. [ME, of a root < LLat. *rādīcālis,* having roots < Lat. *rādix, rādīc-,* root. See **wrād-** in App.] —**rad′i·cal·ly** *adv.* —**rad′i·cal·ness** *n.*

radical expression *n.* *Mathematics* An expression or form in which radical signs appear.

rad·i·cal·ism (răd′ĭ-kə-lĭz′əm) *n.* **1.** The doctrines or practices of radicals. **2.** The quality of being radical.

rad·i·cal·ize (răd′ĭ-kə-līz′) *tr.v.* **-ized, -iz·ing, -iz·es** To make radical or more radical. —**rad′i·cal·i·za′tion** (-kə-lĭ-zā′shən) *n.*

radical sign *n.* *Mathematics* **1.** The sign $\sqrt{}$ placed before a quantity, indicating extraction of either the square root or the root designated by a raised integer. **2.** The radical sign together with a horizontal bar extending from its top to the end of the expression from which a root is to be extracted.

rad·i·cand (răd′ĭ-kănd′) *n.* The quantity under a radical sign. For example, 3 is the radicand of $\sqrt{3}$. [Lat. *rādīcandum,* neut. gerundive of *rādīcāre,* to take root < *rādix, rādīc-,* root. See RADICAL.]

ra·dic·chi·o (rə-dē′kē-ō, rä-) *n., pl.* **-os** Any of several varieties of chicory, having red or red-spotted leaves. [Ital. < OItal., chicory < VLat. **rādīculum* < Lat. *rādīcula,* dim. of *rādix, rādīc-,* root. See RADISH.]

rad·i·ces (răd′ĭ-sēz′, rā′dĭ-) *n.* A plural of **radix.**

rad·i·cle (răd′ĭ-kəl) *n.* **1.** *Botany* The part of a plant embryo that develops into a root. **2.** *Anatomy* A small structure, such as a fibril of a nerve, that resembles a root. [Lat. *rādīcula,* dim. of *rādix, rādīc-,* root. See **wrād-** in App.]

ra·di·i (rā′dē-ī′) *n.* A plural of **radius.**

ra·di·o (rā′dē-ō) *n., pl.* **-os 1.** The wireless transmission through space of electromagnetic waves in the approximate frequency range from 10 kilohertz to 300,000 megahertz. **2.** Communication of audible signals encoded in electromagnetic waves. **3.** Transmission of programs for the public by radio broadcast. **4a.** An apparatus used to transmit radio signals; a transmitter. **b.** An apparatus used to receive radio signals; a receiver. **c.** A complex of equipment capable of transmitting and receiving radio signals. **5a.** A station for radio transmitting. **b.** A radio broadcasting organization or network of affiliated organizations. **c.** The radio broadcasting industry. **6.** A message sent by radio. ❖ *v.* **-oed, -o·ing, -os** —*tr.* **1.** To transmit by radio: *radio a message.* **2.** To transmit a message to by radio. —*intr.* To radio messages or a message. [Short for RADIOTELEGRAPHY.]

radio- or **radi-** *pref.* **1.** Radiation; radiant energy: *radiometer.* **2.** Radioactive: *radiochemistry.* **3.** Radio: *radiotelephone.* [< RADIATION.]

ra·di·o·ac·tive (rā′dē-ō-ăk′tĭv) *adj.* Of or exhibiting radioactivity. —**ra′di·o·ac′tive·ly** *adv.*

radioactive decay *n.* Spontaneous disintegration of a radionuclide accompanied by the emission of ionizing radiation in the form of alpha or beta particles or gamma rays.

radioactive series *n.* A group of isotopes representing various stages of radioactive decay in which the heavier members of the group are transformed into successively lighter ones, the lightest being stable.

ra·di·o·ac·tiv·i·ty (rā′dē-ō-ăk-tĭv′ĭ-tē) *n.* **1.** The emission of radiation, either spontaneously from unstable atomic nuclei or as a consequence of a nuclear reaction. **2.** The radiation emitted, including alpha particles, electrons, and gamma rays.

radio astronomy *n.* The branch of astronomy that deals with the origin and nature of radio waves emitted from celestial sources. —**radio astronomer** *n.*

radio beacon *n.* A fixed radio transmitter that broadcasts distinctive signals as a navigational aid.

radio beam *n.* A focused beam of radio signals transmitted by a radio beacon to guide aircraft or ships.

ra·di·o·bi·ol·o·gy (rā′dē-ō-bī-ŏl′ə-jē) *n.* **1.** The study of the effects of radiation on living organisms. **2.** The use of radioactive tracers to study biological processes. —**ra′di·o·bi′o·log′i·cal** (-ə-lŏj′ĭ-kəl) *adj.* —**ra′di·o·bi·ol′o·gist** *n.*

ra·di·o·broad·cast (rā′dē-ō-brôd′kăst′) *tr.* & *intr.v.* **-cast** or **-cast·ed, -cast·ing, -casts** To broadcast or be broadcast by radio. —**ra′di·o·broad′cast′er** *n.*

ra·di·o·car·bon (rā′dē-ō-kär′bən) *n.* A radioactive isotope of carbon, esp. carbon 14.

radiocarbon dating *n.* The determination of the approximate age of an ancient object, such as a geologic specimen, by the amount of carbon 14 it contains.

ra·di·o·chem·is·try (rā′dē-ō-kĕm′ĭ-strē) *n.* The chemistry of radioactive materials. —**ra′di·o·chem′i·cal** (-ĭ-kəl) *adj.*

radio collar *n.* A collar fitted with a radio transmitter used to track the movements of an animal wearing it by means of radio telemetry.

radio compass *n.* A navigational aid consisting of an automatic radio receiver and a directional antenna that determine the transmission direction of incoming radio waves.

ra·di·o·el·e·ment (rā′dē-ō-ĕl′ə-mənt) *n.* A naturally occurring or artificially produced radioactive element.

radio frequency *n.* **1.** The frequency of the waves transmitted by a specific radio station. **2.** A frequency in the range within which radio waves may be transmitted, from about 3 kilohertz to about 300,000 megahertz.

radio galaxy *n.* A galaxy that strongly emits radio energy.

ra·di·o·gen·ic (rā′dē-ō-jĕn′ĭk) *adj.* Relating to or caused by radioactivity.

ra·di·o·gram (rā′dē-ō-grăm′) *n.* **1.** A message transmitted by wireless telegraphy. **2.** A radiograph.

ra·di·o·graph (rā′dē-ō-grăf′) *n.* An image produced on a radiosensitive surface, such as a photographic film, by radiation other than visible light, esp. by x-rays passed through an object or by photographing a fluoroscopic image. ❖ *tr.v.* **-graphed, -graph·ing, -graphs** To make a radiograph of. —**ra′di·og′ra·pher** (-ŏg′rə-fər) *n.* —**ra′di·o·graph′ic** *adj.*

ra·di·og·ra·phy (rā′dē-ŏg′rə-fē) *n.* The process by which radiographs are made.

ra·di·o·im·mu·no·as·say (rā′dē-ō-ĭm′yə-nō-ăs′ā, -ĭm′yōō′-) *n.* The immunoassay of a radiolabeled substance, such as a hormone or a drug.

ra·di·o·im·mu·nol·o·gy (rā′dē-ō-ĭm′yə-nŏl′ə-jē) *n.* The study of immunity, as by radiolabeling. —**ra′di·o·im′mu·no·log′i·cal** (-nə-lŏj′ĭ-kəl) *adj.*

ra·di·o·i·o·dine (rā′dē-ō-ī′ə-dīn′) *n.* A radioactive isotope of iodine widely used as a tracer in medical diagnosis.

ra·di·o·i·so·tope (rā′dē-ō-ī′sə-tōp′) *n.* A naturally or artificially produced radioactive isotope of an element.

ra·di·o·la·bel (rā′dē-ō-lā′bəl) *tr.v.* **-beled, -bel·ing, -bels** or **-belled, -bel·ling, -bels** To tag (a hormone, enzyme, or other substance) with a radioactive tracer. ❖ *n.* A radioactive isotope used as a tracer; a radiotracer.

ra·di·o·lar·i·an (rā′dē-ō-lâr′ē-ən) *n.* Any of various marine protozoans of the order Radiolaria, having rigid siliceous skeletons and spicules. [< NLat. *Radiolāria*, order name < LLat. *radiolus*, dim. of Lat. *radius*, ray.]

ra·di·o·lo·ca·tion (rā′dē-ō-lō-kā′shən) *n.* Detection of distant objects, such as ships or aircraft, by radar.

ra·di·ol·o·gy (rā′dē-ŏl′ə-jē) *n.* **1.** The branch of medicine that deals with the use of radioactive substances in diagnosis and treatment of disease. **2.** The use of ionizing radiation for medical diagnosis, esp. the use of x-rays in medical radiography or fluoroscopy. **3.** The use of radiation for the scientific examination of material structures; radioscopy. —**ra′di·o·log′i·cal** (-ə-lŏj′ĭ-kəl), **ra′di·o·log′ic** (-lŏj′ĭk) *adj.* —**ra′di·o·log′i·cal·ly** *adv.* —**ra′di·ol′o·gist** *n.*

ra·di·o·lu·cent (rā′dē-ō-lōō′sənt) *adj.* Transparent to x-rays or other radiation; not radiopaque. —**ra′di·o·lu′cen·cy** *n.*

ra·di·ol·y·sis (rā′dē-ŏl′ĭ-sĭs) *n., pl.* **-ses** (-sēz′) Molecular decomposition of a substance as a result of radiation. —**ra′di·o·lyt′ic** (-ə-lĭt′ĭk) *adj.*

ra·di·o·man (rā′dē-ō-măn′) *n.* A radio technician or operator.

ra·di·om·e·ter (rā′dē-ŏm′ĭ-tər) *n.* **1.** Any of various instruments that measure the intensity of radiant energy. **2.** Any of various instruments that detect electromagnetic radiation. —**ra′di·o·met′ric** (-ō-mĕt′rĭk) *adj.* —**ra′di·om′e·try** *n.*

ra·di·o·mi·met·ic (rā′dē-ō-mĭ-mĕt′ĭk) *adj.* Having effects on living tissue similar to those produced by radiation.

ra·di·o·nu·clide (rā′dē-ō-nōō′klīd′, -nyōō′-) *n.* A nuclide that exhibits radioactivity.

ra·di·o·paque (rā′dē-ō-pāk′) *adj.* Not transparent to x-rays or other radiation. —**ra′di·o·pac′i·ty** (-ō-păs′ĭ-tē) *n.*

ra·di·o·phar·ma·ceu·ti·cal (rā′dē-ō-fär′mə-sōō′tĭ-kəl) *n.* A radioactive compound used in radiotherapy or diagnosis.

ra·di·o·phone (rā′dē-ō-fōn′) *n.* A radiotelephone. —**ra′di·o·phon′ic** (-fŏn′ĭk) *adj.*

ra·di·o·pho·to (rā′dē-ō-fō′tō) *n.* A radiophotograph.

ra·di·o·pho·to·graph (rā′dē-ō-fō′tə-grăf′) *n.* A photograph transmitted by radio waves, each image point being reproduced by a received electric impulse. —**ra′di·o·pho·tog′ra·phy** (-fə-tŏg′rə-fē) *n.*

ra·di·os·co·py (rā′dē-ŏs′kə-pē) *n.* Examination of the inner structure of optically opaque objects by x-rays or other penetrating radiation; radiology. —**ra′di·o·scop′ic** (-ō-skŏp′ĭk), **ra′di·o·scop′i·cal** (-ĭ-kəl) *adj.*

ra·di·o·sen·si·tive (rā′dē-ō-sĕn′sĭ-tĭv) *adj.* Sensitive to the action of radiation. —**ra′di·o·sen′si·tiv′i·ty** *n.*

ra·di·o·sonde (rā′dē-ō-sŏnd′) *n.* An instrument carried aloft, chiefly by balloon, to gather and transmit meteorological data. [RADIO + Fr. *sonde*, sounding line (< OFr. < OE *sund(rāp)*, sounding (line) < *sund*, sea.)]

radio spectrum *n.* The entire range of electromagnetic communications frequencies; the radio-frequency spectrum.

ra·di·o·tel·e·graph (rā′dē-ō-tĕl′ĭ-grăf′) *n.* Transmission of messages by radiotelegraphy. —**ra′di·o·tel′e·graph′ic** *adj.*

ra·di·o·te·leg·ra·phy (rā′dē-ō-tə-lĕg′rə-fē) *n.* Telegraphy in which messages are transmitted by radio instead of wire.

ra·di·o·tel·e·phone (rā′dē-ō-tĕl′ə-fōn′) *n.* A telephone in which audible communication is established by use of a two-way radio transmitter and receiver. —**ra′di·o·tel′e·phon′ic** (-fŏn′ĭk) *adj.* —**ra′di·o·te·leph′o·ny** (-tə-lĕf′ə-nē) *n.*

radio telescope *n.* A device for detecting and recording radio waves coming from celestial objects, consisting of a radio receiver with an antenna fixed on a wide bowl-shaped reflector.

ra·di·o·ther·a·py (rā′dē-ō-thĕr′ə-pē) *n., pl.* **-pies** Treatment of disease with radiation, esp. by selective irradiation with x-rays or other ionizing radiation and by ingestion of radioisotopes. —**ra′di·o·ther′a·pist** *n.*

ra·di·o·trac·er (rā′dē-ō-trā′sər) *n.* A radioactive tracer.

radio wave *n.* An electromagnetic wave within the range of radio frequencies.

rad·ish (răd′ĭsh) *n.* **1.** A Eurasian plant (*Raphanus sativus*) having an edible root and white to purple flowers in a terminal raceme. **2.** The pungent root of this plant, eaten raw. [ME *radiche* < OE *rædic* < Lat. *rādīx, rādīc-*, root. See **wrād-** in App.]

ra·di·um (rā′dē-əm) *n. Symbol* **Ra** A luminescent, highly radioactive metallic element found in minute amounts in uranium ores, used as a neutron source for some research purposes, and formerly used in cancer radiotherapy and in luminescent paints; its most stable isotope is Ra 226 with a half-life of 1,622 years. Atomic number 88; melting point 700°C; boiling point 1,737°C; valence 2. See table at **element**. [Lat. *radius*, ray + –IUM.]

ra·di·us (rā′dē-əs) *n., pl.* **-di·i** (-dē-ī′) or **-di·us·es** **1.** *Mathematics* **a.** A line segment that joins the center of a circle with any point on its circumference. **b.** A line segment that joins the center of a sphere with any point on its surface. **c.** A line segment that joins the center of a regular polygon with any of its vertices. **d.** The length of any such line segment. **2.** A circular area measured by a given radius. **3.** A bounded range of effective activity or influence: *the operating radius of a helicopter.* **4.** A radial part or structure, such as a mechanically pivoted arm or the spoke of a wheel. **5.** *Anatomy* **a.** A long, prismatic, slightly curved bone, the shorter and thicker of the two forearm bones, located on the lateral side of the ulna. **b.** A similar bone in many vertebrates. [Lat., ray, spoke of a wheel, radius.]

radius vector *n.* **1.** *Mathematics* **a.** A line segment that joins the origin and any point in a system of polar or spherical coordinates. **b.** The length of such a line segment. **2.** *Astronomy* A line connecting the center of the sun or another body with the center of a planet or other body orbiting around it.

ra·dix (rā′dĭks) *n., pl.* **rad·i·ces** (răd′ĭ-sēz′, rā′dĭ-) or **ra·dix·es** **1.** *Biology* A root or point of origin. **2.** *Mathematics* The base of a system of numbers, such as 10 in the decimal system. [Lat. *rādīx*, root. See **wrād-** in App.]

RADM *abbr.* rear admiral (upper half)

Ra·dom (rä′dôm) A city of E-central Poland S of Warsaw; founded in the 14th cent. Pop. 229,250.

ra·dome (rā′dōm) *n.* A domelike shell transparent to radio-frequency radiation, used to house a radar antenna.

ra·don (rā′dŏn) *n. Symbol* **Rn** A radioactive, largely inert gaseous element formed by the radioactive decay of radium and used as a radiation source in radiotherapy and research; its most stable isotope is Rn 222 with a half-life of 3.82 days. Atomic number 86; melting point −71°C; boiling point −61.8°C; specific gravity (solid) 4. See table at **element**. [RAD(IUM) + −ON².]

rad·u·la (răj′ōō-lə) *n., pl.* **-lae** (-lē′) A flexible tonguelike organ in certain mollusks, having rows of horny teeth on the surface. [Lat. *rādula*, scraper < *rādere*, to scrape.] —**rad′u·lar** *adj.*

Rae (rā), **John** 1813–93. British explorer who charted much of the Canadian Arctic coast.

Rae·burn (rā′bərn), **Sir Henry** 1756–1823. British portrait painter of Sir Walter Scott and James Boswell, among others.

RAF *abbr.* Royal Air Force

raf·fi·a also **raph·i·a** (răf′ē-ə) *n.* **1.** An African palm tree (*Raphia ruffia*) having large leaves. **2.** The leaf fibers of this plant, used for mats and other products. [Malagasy *rafia*.]

raf·fi·nate (răf′ə-nāt′) *n.* The portion of a liquid that remains after other components have been dissolved by a solvent. [Fr. *raffiner*, to refine; see RAFFINOSE + -ATE².]

raf·fi·nose (răf′ə-nōs′) *n.* A white crystalline sugar, $C_{18}H_{32}O_{16} \cdot 5H_2O$, obtained from cottonseed meal, sugar beets, and molasses. [Fr. < *raffiner*, to refine : *re-*, again (< OFr.; see RE-) + *affiner*, to refine (*a-*, to < Lat. *ad-*; see AD- + *fin*, fine < OFr.; see FINE¹).]

raff·ish (răf′ĭsh) *adj.* **1.** Cheaply or showily vulgar in appearance or nature; tawdry. **2.** Characterized by a carefree or fun-loving unconventionality; rakish. [Prob. < dialectal *raff*, rubbish < ME *raf*, perh. of Scand. orig.] —**raff′ish·ly** *adv.* —**raff′ish·ness** *n.*

raf·fle¹ (răf′əl) *n.* A lottery in which chances to win a prize are sold. ❖ *v.* **-fled, -fling, -fles** —*tr.* To dispose of in a raffle. Often used with *off.* —*intr.* To conduct or take part in a raffle. [ME *rafle*, a game using dice < OFr., act of seizing, dice game, perh. of Gmc. orig.] —**raf′fler** *n.*

raf·fle² (răf′əl) *n.* Rubbish; debris. [Prob. < Fr. *rafle*, act of seizing < OFr. See RAFFLE¹.]

Raf·fles (răf′əlz), **Sir Thomas Stamford** 1781–1826. British colonial administrator in Singapore.

raf·fle·sia (ră-flē′zhə) *n.* Any of various parasitic plants of the genus *Rafflesia* of tropical Asia, having small brownish scalelike leaves and foul-smelling fleshy apetalous flowers. [NLat. *Rafflesia*, genus name, after Sir Thomas Stamford RAFFLES.]

Raf·san·ja·ni (răf′săn-jä′nē), **Ali Akbar Hashemi** b. 1934. Iranian religious and political leader who served as president (1989–97).

raft¹ (răft) *n.* **1.** A flat structure, typically made of planks, logs, or barrels, that floats on water and is used for transport or as a platform for swimmers. **2.** A flatbottom inflatable craft for floating or drifting on water. ❖ *v.* **raft·ed, raft·ing, rafts** —*tr.* **1.** To convey on a raft. **2.** To make into a raft. —*intr.* To travel by raft. [ME < ON *raptr*, beam, rafter.]

raft² (răft) *n. Informal* A great number, amount, or collection. [Alteration of dialectal *raff*, rubbish. See RAFFISH.]

raft·er¹ (răf′tər) *n.* One who travels by raft.

raft·er² (răf′tər) *n.* One of the sloping beams that supports a pitched roof. [ME < OE *ræfter*.] —**raf′tered** *adj.*

rag¹ (răg) *n.* **1a.** A scrap of cloth. **b.** A piece of cloth used for cleaning, washing, or dusting. **2. rags** Threadbare or tattered clothing. **3.** Cloth converted to pulp for making paper. **4.** A scrap; a fragment. **5.** *Slang* A newspaper, esp. one specializing in sensationalism or gossip. **6.** The stringy central portion and membranous walls of a citrus fruit. [ME *ragge* < OE *ragg* < ON *rögg*, woven tuft of wool.]

rag² (răg) *tr.v.* **ragged, rag·ging, rags** **1.** *Slang* To tease or taunt. **2.** *Slang* To berate; scold. **3.** *Chiefly British* To play a joke on. ❖ *n. Chiefly British* A practical joke; a prank. [?]

rag³ (răg) *n.* **1.** A roofing slate with one rough surface. **2.** *Chiefly British* A coarsely textured rock. [?]

rag⁴ (răg) *tr.v.* **ragged, rag·ging, rags** To compose or play (a piece) in ragtime. ❖ *n.* A piece written in ragtime. [Perh. < RAGGED.]

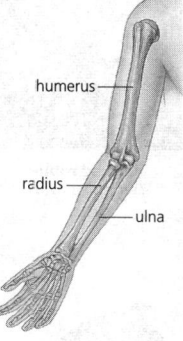

humerus

radius

ulna

radius

rafflesia

ragged robin
Lychnis flos-cuculi

raglan
raglan sleeve jacket

ragwort
tansy ragwort
Senecio jacobaea

ra·ga (rä′gə) *n.* A traditional melodic type in Hindu music, consisting of a theme that expresses religious feeling and sets forth a tonal system on which variations are improvised within a prescribed framework, as of rhythmic patterns. [Skt. *rāgaḥ,* color, musical mode.]

rag·a·muf·fin or **rag·ga·muf·fin** (rǎg′ə-mǔf′ĭn) *n.* A shabbily clothed, dirty child. [ME *Ragamuffyn,* a personal name : prob. *raggi* (< *ragge,* rag; see RAG¹) + MDu. *moffel, muffe,* mitten; see MUFF².]

rag·bag (rǎg′bǎg′) *n.* **1.** A bag for storing rags. **2.** A motley collection; a hodgepodge.

rage (rāj) *n.* **1a.** Violent, explosive anger. See Syns at **anger. b.** A fit of anger. **2.** Furious intensity, as of a storm or disease. **3.** A burning desire; a passion. **4.** A current, eagerly adopted fashion; a fad or craze: *torn jeans were all the rage.* ❖ *intr.v.* **raged, rag·ing, rag·es 1.** To speak or act in violent anger. **2.** To move with great violence or intensity: *A storm raged.* **3.** To spread or prevail forcefully: *The plague raged for months.* [ME < OFr. < LLat. *rabia* < Lat. *rabiēs < rabere,* to be mad.]

rag·ged (rǎg′ĭd) *adj.* **1.** Tattered, frayed, or torn: *ragged clothes.* **2.** Dressed in tattered or threadbare clothes. **3.** Unkempt or shaggy. **4.** Having an irregular surface or edge; uneven or jagged in outline: *text set with a ragged right margin.* **5.** Imperfect; uneven: *a ragged performance.* **6.** Harsh; rasping: *a ragged cough.* [ME < *ragge,* rag. See RAG¹.] —**rag′ged·ly** *adv.* —**rag′ged·ness** *n.*

ragged edge *n.* **1.** The edge of a cliff. **2.** A dangerous or precarious position; a brink.

ragged robin *n.* A European perennial plant (*Lychnis flos-cuculi*) with opposite clasping leaves and lobed flowers.

rag·ged·y (rǎg′ĭ-dē) *adj.* **-i·er, -i·est** Tattered or worn-out.

ra·gi (rǎg′ē) *n., pl.* **ra·gis** See **finger millet.** [Hindi *rāgī* < Skt., perh. of Dravidian orig.]

rag·lan (rǎg′lən) *adj.* Having or being a sleeve that extends in one piece to the neckline of the garment, with slanted seams from the armhole to the neck. ❖ *n.* A garment, such as a sweater, that has raglan sleeves. [After Fitzroy James Henry Somerset (1788–1855), 1st Baron *Raglan,* British field marshal.]

rag·man (rǎg′mǎn′) *n.* A man who collects and sells rags.

ra·gout (rǎ-gōō′) *n.* A well-seasoned meat or fish stew, usu. with vegetables. [Fr. *ragoût < ragoûter,* to revive the taste < OFr. *ragouster : re-,* re- + *a-,* to (< Lat. *ad-;* see AD–) + *gost,* taste (< Lat. *gustus;* see **geus-** in App.).]

rag·pick·er (rǎg′pĭk′ər) *n.* One who makes a living scavenging rags and other refuse.

rag·tag (rǎg′tǎg′) *adj.* **1.** Shaggy or unkempt; ragged. **2.** Diverse and disorderly in appearance or composition.

ragtag and bobtail *n.* The lowest social class; the rabble.

rag·time (rǎg′tīm′) *n.* A style of jazz characterized by elaborately syncopated rhythm in the melody and a steadily accented accompaniment. [< RAG⁴.]

rag·top (rǎg′tŏp′) *n.* Slang A convertible automobile.

Ra·gu·sa (rə-gōō′zə, rä-gōō′zä) See **Dubrovnik.**

rag·weed (rǎg′wēd′) *n.* **1.** Any of various weeds of the genus *Ambrosia,* having small greenish unisexual flower heads and producing abundant pollen that causes hay fever. **2.** Chiefly British Ragwort. [< the ragged shape of its leaves.]

rag·wort (rǎg′wûrt′, -wôrt′) *n.* Any of several plants of the very large genus *Senecio* in the composite family, having yellow flower heads. *S. jacobaea,* a European species poisonous to livestock, is widely naturalized in North America. [< the ragged shape of its leaves.]

rah (rä) *interj.* Used as an exclamation of approval or encouragement. [Short for HURRAH.]

rah-rah (rä′rä′) *adj. Informal* Ardently enthusiastic.

rai (rī) *n.* A form of popular Algerian music combining traditional Arabic vocal styles with elements of popular Western music. [Algerian Fr. *raï,* perh. < dialectal Ar. *(ha er-)ray,* (here is the) view (frequently heard in the songs) < Ar. *ra′y,* view < *ra′ā,* to observe.]

Ra·ia·te·a (rī′ə-tā′ə) A volcanic island in the Society Is. of French Polynesia in the S Pacific Ocean WNW of Tahiti.

raid (rād) *n.* **1.** A surprise attack by a small armed force. **2.** A sudden forcible entry into a place by police: *a raid on a gambling den.* **3.** An attempt to lure away the personnel or membership of a competing organization. **4.** An attempt to seize control of a company, as by acquiring a majority of its stock. **5.** An attempt by speculators to drive stock prices down by coordinated selling. ❖ *v.* **raid·ed, raid·ing, raids** —*tr.* To make a raid on. —*intr.* To conduct a raid or participate in one. [Sc., raid on horseback < ME *rade* < OE *rād,* a riding, road.] —**raid′er** *n.*

WORD HISTORY *Raid* and *road* descend from the same Old English word *rād.* The *ai* in *raid* represents the standard development in the northern dialects of Old English long *ā,* while the *oa* in *road* represents the standard development of Old English long *ā* in the rest of the English dialects. Old English *rād* meant "the act of riding" and "the act of riding with a hostile intent; that is, a raid," senses that no longer exist for our word *road* except in the compound *inroad,* "a riding on or in." It was left to Sir Walter Scott to revive the Scots form *raid* with the sense "a military expedition on horseback."

rail¹ (rāl) *n.* **1a.** A bar extending horizontally between supports, as in a fence. **b.** A structure made of such bars and supports and forming a barrier or guard; a railing. **2.** A steel bar used, usu. in pairs, as a track for railroad cars or other wheeled vehicles. **3.** The railroad as a means of transportation: *transported by rail.* **4.** A horizontal framing member in a door or in paneling. ❖ *tr.v.* **railed, rail·ing, rails** To supply or enclose with rails or a rail. [ME *raile* < OFr. *reille* < Lat. *rēgula,* straight piece of wood, ruler. See **reg-** in App.]

rail² (rāl) *n.* Any of various marsh birds of the family Rallidae, characteristically having brownish plumage and short wings adapted only for short flights. [ME *raile* < OFr. *raale,* perh. < OFr. *raler, racler,* to scrape < O Provençal *rasclar.* See RACLETTE.]

rail³ (rāl) *intr.v.* **railed, rail·ing, rails** To express objections or criticisms in bitter, harsh, or abusive language. [ME *railen* < OFr. *railler,* to tease, joke < O Provençal *ralhar,* to chat, joke < VLat. **ragulāre,* to bray < LLat. *ragere.*] —**rail′er** *n.*

rail·bird (rāl′bûrd′) *n. Slang* A horseracing enthusiast, esp. one who watches races at the outer rail of the track.

rail·car (rāl′kär′) *n.* A railroad car.

rail fence *n.* A fence of split logs secured to stakes or laid across each other at an angle.

rail·head (rāl′hĕd′) *n.* **1.** The farthest point on a railroad to which rails have been laid. **2.** A place on a railroad where military supplies are unloaded.

rail·ing (rā′lĭng) *n.* **1a.** A structure made of rails and upright members that is used as a guard or barrier or for support. **b.** The upper rail of such a structure. **2.** Rails considered as a group.

rail·ler·y (rā′lə-rē) *n., pl.* **-ies 1.** Good-natured teasing or ridicule; banter. **2.** An instance of bantering or teasing. [Fr. < OFr. *railler,* to tease.]

rail·road (rāl′rōd′) *n.* **1.** A road composed of parallel steel rails supported by ties and providing a track for wheeled vehicles. **2.** A system of railroad track, together with the land, stations, and other related property under one management. ❖ *v.* **-road·ed, -road·ing, -roads** —*tr.* **1.** To transport by railroad. **2.** To supply (an area) with railroads. **3.** Informal a. To rush or push (something) through quickly to prevent careful consideration and obstruction: *railroad a special-interest bill through Congress.* **b.** To convict (an accused person) without a fair trial or on trumped-up charges. —*intr.* To work for a railroad company. —**rail′road·er** *n.*

railroad flat *n.* An apartment in which the rooms are connected in a line.

rail·road·ing (rāl′rō′dĭng) *n.* The construction or operation of railroads.

rail·split·ter (rāl′splĭt′ər) *n.* One that splits logs for fences.

rail·way (rāl′wā′) *n.* **1.** A railroad, esp. one operated over a limited area: *a commuter railway.* **2.** A track providing a runway for wheeled equipment.

rai·ment (rā′mənt) *n.* Clothing; garments. [ME, short for *araiment* < OFr. *areement,* array < *areer, arrayer,* to array. See ARRAY.]

rain (rān) *n.* **1a.** Water condensed from atmospheric vapor and falling in drops. **b.** A fall of rain; a rainstorm. **c.** The descent of rain. **d.** Rainy weather. **e.** A rainy season. **2.** A heavy or abundant fall: *a rain of insults.* ❖ *v.* **rained, rain·ing, rains** —*intr.* **1.** To fall in drops of water from the clouds. **2.** To fall like rain: *Praise rained down on the composer.* **3.** To release rain. —*tr.* **1.** To send or pour down. **2.** To give abundantly; shower: *rain gifts.* —**phrasal verb: rain out** To force the cancellation or postponement of (an outdoor event) because of rain. Used in passive constructions: *The ball game was rained out.* —**idiom: rain cats and dogs** *Informal* To rain very heavily. [ME < OE *regn, rēn.*] —**rain′less** *adj.*

rain·bow (rān′bō′) *n.* **1a.** An arc of spectral colors, usu. identified as red, orange, yellow, green, blue, indigo, and violet, that appears in the sky opposite the sun as a result of the refractive dispersion of sunlight in drops of rain or mist. **b.** A similar arc or band, as one produced by a prism. **c.** A graded display of colors. **2.** An illusory hope: *chasing the rainbow of overnight success.* **3.** A diverse assortment or collection. [ME < OE *rēnboga : rēn,* rain + *boga,* bow.]

rainbow cactus *n.* Either of two tall spiny cylindrical varieties of cactus of the southwest United States and Mexico, *Echinocereus pectinatus* var. *neomexicanus,* having yellow flowers, or *E. pectinatus* var. *rigidissimus,* having showy magenta flowers.

rainbow trout *n.* A North American food fish (*Oncorhynchus mykiss*) having a reddish longitudinal band and black spots.

rain check *n.* **1.** A ticket stub entitling the holder to admission to a future event if the scheduled event is rained out. **2.** An assurance to a customer that an item on sale that is sold out or out of stock may be purchased later at the sale price. **3.** A promise that an unaccepted offer will be renewed.

rain·coat (rān′kōt′) *n.* A waterproof or water-resistant coat.

rain date *n.* A second date scheduled for an outdoor event in case rain forces cancellation of the first date.

rain·drop (rān′drŏp′) *n.* A drop of rain.

Rai·ney (rā′nē), **Gertrude Pridgett** Known as "Ma Rainey." 1886–1939. Amer. singer considered the first great blues vocalist.

rain•fall (rān′fôl′) *n.* **1.** A shower or fall of rain. **2.** The quantity of water, expressed in inches, precipitated as rain, snow, hail, or sleet in a specified area and time interval.
rain•for•est or **rain forest** (rān′fôr′ĭst, fŏr′-) *n.* A dense evergreen forest occupying a tropical region with an annual rainfall of at least 2.5 meters (100 inches).
rain gauge also **rain gage** *n.* A device for measuring rainfall.
Rai•nier III (rā-nîr′, rĕ-, rə-, rĕ-nyā′) b. 1923. Prince of Monaco (since 1949) who married Grace Kelly in 1956.
Rai•nier (rə-nîr′, rā-), **Mount** A volcanic peak, 4,395.1 m (14,410 ft), of the Cascade Range in W-central WA.
rain•mak•er (rān′mā′kər) *n.* **1.** *Slang* One who is known for achieving excellent results in a profession or field. **2.** One who is believed to be capable of producing rain, as through magical or ritual actions.
rain shadow *n.* An area having relatively little precipitation due to the effect of a barrier, such as a mountain range, that causes the prevailing winds to lose their moisture before reaching it.
rain•spout (rān′spout′) *n. Chiefly Pennsylvania & New Jersey* See **gutter** 2. See Regional Note at **gutter.**
rain•squall (rān′skwôl′) *n.* A squall accompanied by rain.
rain•storm (rān′stôrm′) *n.* A storm accompanied by rain.
rain-wash (rān′wŏsh′, -wôsh′) *n.* Rock debris transported downhill by rain. **—rain′-wash′** *v.*
rain•wa•ter (rān′wô′tər, -wŏt′ər) *n.* Water that has fallen as rain and contains little dissolved mineral matter.
rain•wear (rān′wâr′) *n.* Waterproof clothing.
rain•y (rā′nē) *adj.* **-i•er, -i•est** Characterized by, full of, or bringing rain. **—rain′i•ness** *n.*
rainy day *n.* A time of need or trouble.
Rai•pur (rī′po͝or) A city of E-central India E of Nagpur. Pop. 438,639.
raise (rāz) *v.* **raised, rais•ing, rais•es** *—tr.* **1.** To move to a higher position; elevate: *raised the loads with a crane.* See Syns at **lift. 2.** To set in an upright or erect position: *raise a flagpole.* **3.** To erect or build: *raise a new building.* **4.** To cause to arise, appear, or exist: *The slap raised a welt.* **5.** To increase in size, quantity, or worth: *raise an employee's salary.* **6.** To increase in intensity, degree, strength, or pitch: *raised his voice.* **7.** To improve in rank or dignity; promote: *raised her to management level.* **8a.** To grow, esp. in quantity; cultivate: *raise corn.* **b.** To breed and care for to maturity: *raise children.* **c.** To bring up; rear: *raise children.* **d.** To accustom to something from an early age: *was raised on cartoons and comic books.* **9.** To put forward for consideration: *raise a question.* **10.** To voice; utter: *raise a shout.* **11a.** To awaken; arouse: *noise that would raise the dead.* **b.** To stir up; instigate: *raise a revolt.* **c.** To bring about; provoke: *raised a laugh.* **12.** To make contact with by radio: *couldn't raise the control tower after dark.* **13.** To gather together; collect: *raise money.* **14.** To cause (dough) to puff up. **15.** To end (a siege) by withdrawing troops or forcing the enemy troops to withdraw. **16.** To remove or withdraw (an order). **17.** *Games* **a.** To increase (a poker bet). **b.** To bet more than (a preceding bettor in poker). **c.** To increase the bid of (one's bridge partner). **18.** *Nautical* To bring into sight by approaching nearer: *raised the Cape.* **19.** To alter and increase fraudulently the written value of (a check, for example). **20.** To cough up (phlegm). **21.** *Scots* To make angry; enrage. *—intr. Games* To increase a poker bet or a bridge bid. ❖ *n.* **1.** The act of raising or increasing. **2.** An increase in salary. ***—idioms:* raise Cain (or hell) 1.** To behave in a rowdy or disruptive fashion. **2.** To reprimand someone angrily. **raise eyebrows** To cause surprise or mild disapproval. [ME *raisen* < ON *reisa.* See **er-** in App.] **—rais′er** *n.*
raised (rāzd) *adj.* **1.** Projecting from a flat background; in relief; embossed: *a raised design.* **2.** Made light and high by yeast or other leaven.
rai•sin (rā′zĭn) *n.* **1.** A sweet dried grape. **2.** A deep brownish purple. [ME < OFr., grape < VLat. **racīmus* < Lat. *racēmus,* bunch of grapes.]
rai•son d'ê•tre (rā′zōn dĕt′rə, rĕ-zôɴ) *n., pl.* **rai•sons d'être** (rā′zōn, rĕ-zôɴ) Reason or justification for existing. [Fr. : *raison,* reason + *de,* of, for + *être,* to be.]
rai•ta (rī′tə) *n.* An Indian salad made with yogurt and chopped vegetables or fruits, such as cucumbers or bananas. [Hindi *rāytā* < Skt. **rājikātiktakaḥ,* mustard pickle : *rājikā,* black mustard (prob. < *rājiḥ,* streak, line < *ṛjyati,* he stretches out; see **reg-** in App.) + *tiktaka-,* bitter (< *tikta-,* p. part. of *tejate,* it is sharp).]
raj also **Raj** (räj) *n.* Dominion or rule, esp. the British rule over India (1757–1947). [Hindi *rāj* < Skt. *rājā,* king. See **reg-** in App.]
Raj•ab (rŭj′əb) *n.* The seventh month of the year in the Islamic calendar. See table at **calendar.** [Ar. *rajab* < *rajaba,* to fear, revere.]
ra•jah or **ra•ja** (rä′jə) *n.* A prince, chief, or ruler in India or the East Indies. [Hindi *rājā* < Skt., king. See **reg-** in App.]
Ra•jah•mun•dry (rä′jə-mo͞on′drē) A city of E India on the Godavari R. E of Hyderabad. Pop. 324,851.
Raj•kot (räj′kōt′) A city of W India WSW of Ahmadabad; formerly cap. of a princely state. Pop. 559,407.
Raj•put also **Raj•poot** (räj′po͝ot) *n.* A member of any of several powerful Hindu landowning and military lineages inhabiting northern and central India. [Hindi *rājpūt* < Skt. *rājaputraḥ,* king's son : *rājā,* king; see RAJAH + *putraḥ,* son.]
rake¹ (rāk) *n.* **1.** A long-handled implement with a row of projecting teeth at its head, used esp. to gather leaves or to loosen or smooth earth. **2.** A device that resembles a rake. ❖ *v.* **raked, rak•ing, rakes** *—tr.* **1.** To gather or move with or as if with a rake. **2.** To smooth, scrape, or loosen with a rake or similar implement. **3.** *Informal* To gain in abundance. Often used with *in: raking in the money.* **4.** To search or examine thoroughly; ransack. **5.** To scrape; scratch. **6.** To aim heavy gunfire along the length of. *—intr.* **1.** To use a rake. **2.** To conduct a thorough search. ***—phrasal verb:* rake up** To revive or bring to light; uncover. ***—idiom:* rake over the coals** To reprimand severely. [ME < OE *raca.* See **reg-** in App.] **—rak′er** *n.*
rake² (rāk) *n.* An immoral or dissolute person; a libertine. [Short for RAKEHELL.]
rake³ (rāk) *intr. & tr.v.* **raked, rak•ing, rakes** To slant or cause to incline from the perpendicular: *rake a ship's mast.* ❖ *n.* **1.** Inclination from the perpendicular. **2.** The angle between the cutting edge of a tool and a plane perpendicular to the working surface to which the tool is applied. [?]
rake•hell (rāk′hĕl′) *n.* A dissolute person; a rake. [Poss. by folk-ety. < obsolete *rackle,* headstrong < ME *rakel,* perh. < *raken,* to go.]
rake-off (rāk′ôf′, -ŏf′) *n. Informal* A percentage or share of the profits of an enterprise, esp. one given or accepted as a bribe. [< the rake used by a croupier.]
rak•i also **rak•ee** (răk′ē, rä′kē, rä′kə) *n., pl.* **-is** also **-ees** A brandy of Turkey and the Balkans, made from grapes or plums and flavored with anise. [Turk. *rāqī* < Ar. *ʿaraq,* arrack. See ARRACK.]
rak•ish¹ (rā′kĭsh) *adj.* **1.** *Nautical* Having a trim streamlined appearance. **2.** Dashingly or sportingly stylish; jaunty. [Prob. < RAKE³ (< the raking masts of pirate ships).]
rak•ish² (rā′kĭsh) *adj.* Of the character of a rake; dissolute.
rale also **râle** (räl) *n.* An abnormal respiratory sound characterized by fine crackles. [Fr. *râle* < *râler,* to make a rattling sound in the throat < OFr. *racler,* to scrape, rattle. See RACLETTE.]
Ra•leigh (rô′lē, rä′-) The cap. of NC, in the E-central part SE of Durham; laid out in 1792. Pop. 276,093.
Raleigh or **Ra•legh** (rô′lē, rä′-), Sir **Walter** 1552?–1618. English courtier, navigator, colonizer, and writer who colonized Virginia, introduced tobacco and the potato to Europe, and was executed for treason during the reign of James I.
Ra•lik Chain (rä′lĭk) The W group of the Marshall Is. in the W Pacific Ocean, comprising 3 coral islands and 15 atolls.
ral•len•tan•do (räl′ən-tän′dō, räl′lĕn-tän′dō) *Music adv. & adj.* Gradually slackening in tempo; ritardando. ❖ *n., pl.* **-dos** A rallentando passage or movement. [Ital., pr. part. of *rallentare,* to slow down : *re-,* intensive pref. (< Lat.; see RE-) + *allentare,* to slow down (< LLat. *allentāre* : Lat. *ad-,* ad- + Lat. *lentus,* slow).]
ral•li•form (răl′ə-fôrm′) *adj.* Relating to or resembling the rail, a marsh bird. [NLat. *Rallus,* rail genus (< Fr. *râle,* rail < OFr. *raale*; see RAIL²) + –FORM.]
ral•ly¹ (răl′ē) *v.* **-lied, -ly•ing, -lies** *—tr.* **1.** To call together for a common purpose; assemble. **2.** To reassemble and restore to order: *rally scattered forces.* **3.** To rouse or revive from inactivity or decline. *—intr.* **1.** To come together for a common purpose. **2.** To join in an effort for a common cause. **3.** To recover abruptly from a setback or disadvantage: *The stock market declined, then rallied.* **4.** To show sudden improvement in health or spirits. **5.** *Sports* To exchange several strokes before a point is won, as in tennis. ❖ *n., pl.* **-lies 1.** A gathering, esp. one intended to inspire enthusiasm for a cause. **2a.** A reassembling, as of dispersed troops. **b.** The signal ordering this reassembly. **3.** An abrupt recovery from a setback or disadvantage. **4.** A sharp improvement in health, vigor, or spirits. **5.** A notable rise in stock market prices and trading volume after a decline. **6.** *Sports* **a.** An exchange of several strokes before a point is won, as in tennis. **b.** An automobile competition over public roads. [Fr. *rallier* < OFr. *ralier* : *re-,* re- + *alier,* to unite, ally; see ALLY.]
ral•ly² (răl′ē) *v.* **-lied, -ly•ing, -lies** *—tr.* To tease good-humoredly; banter. *—intr.* To engage in good-humored teasing or jesting. [Fr. *railler* < OFr., to tease. See RAIL³.]
ralph (rălf) *intr.v.* **ralphed, ralph•ing, ralphs** *Slang* To vomit. [Imit. use of the personal name *Ralph.*]
ram (răm) *n.* **1.** A male sheep. **2.** Any of several devices used to drive, batter, or crush by forceful impact, esp.: **a.** A battering ram. **b.** The weight that drops in a pile driver or steam hammer. **c.** The plunger or piston of a force pump or hydraulic press. **3.** A hydraulic ram. **4a.** A projection on the prow of a warship, used to batter or cut into enemy vessels. **b.** A ship having such a projection. **5. Ram** See **Aries.** ❖ *tr.v.* **rammed, ram•ming, rams 1.** To strike or drive against with a heavy impact; butt. **2.** To force or press into place. **3.** To cram; stuff. **4.** To force passage or acceptance of. [ME < OE *ramm.*] **—ram′mer** *n.*
RAM (răm) *n. Computer Science* A memory device in which information can be accessed in any order. [R(ANDOM-)A(CCESS) M(EMORY).]
Ra•ma (rä′mə) *n. Hinduism* A deified hero worshiped as an incarnation of Vishnu.
ra•ma•da (rə-mä′də) *n. Southwestern US* **1a.** An open or semienclosed shelter roofed with brush or branches, designed esp. to

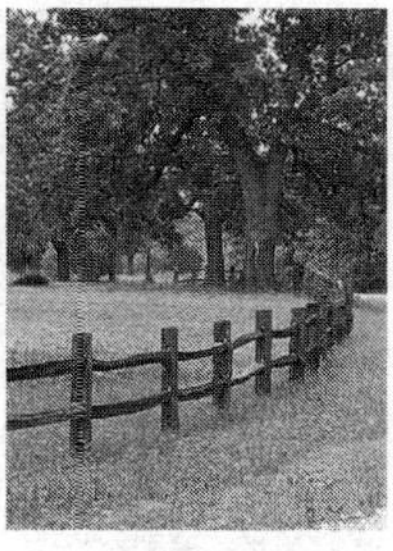

rail fence
two-rail post and rail fence

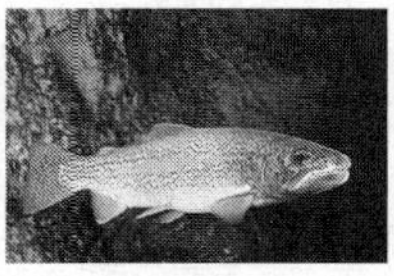

rainbow trout
Oncorhynchus mykiss

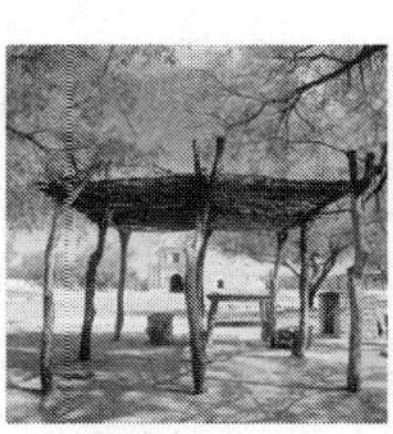

ramada
Tumacacori National Historical Park, Tumacacori, Arizona

ă	pat	oi	boy
ā	pay	ou	out
âr	care	o͝o	took
ä	father	o͞o	boot
ĕ	pet	ŭ	cut
ē	be	ûr	urge
ĭ	pit	th	thin
ī	pie	*th*	this
îr	pier	hw	which
ŏ	pot	zh	vision
ō	toe	ə	about, item
ô	paw		

Stress marks:
′ (primary);
′ (secondary), as in
lexicon (lĕk′sĭ-kŏn′)

Rameses II
detail of a colossus at the
Great Temple of Rameses II,
Abu Simbel, Egypt

ranch house

provide shade. **b.** An open porch or breezeway. **2.** An arbor or trellis made of twined branches. [Sp. < *rama*, branch < VLat. *rāma < Lat. *rāmus*. See RAMIFY.]

Ram·a·dan (răm′ə-dän′, răm′ə-dän′) *n.* **1.** The ninth month of the year in the Islamic calendar. See table at **calendar. 2.** A fast, held from sunrise to sunset, that is carried out during this period. [Ar. *ramaḍān* < *ramaḍ*, dryness < *ramiḍa*, to be scorched.]

Ra·man (rä′mən), Sir **Chandrasekhara Venkata** 1888–1970. Indian physicist who won a 1930 Nobel Prize.

Raman effect *n. Physics* The alteration in frequency and random alteration in phase of light passing through a transparent medium. [After Sir Chandrasekhara Venkata RAMAN.]

Ra·ma's Bridge (rä′məz) See **Adam's Bridge.**

ra·mate (rä′māt′) *adj.* Having branches; branched. [Lat. *rāmus*, branch; see RAMUS + –ATE[1].]

Ra·ma·ya·na (rə-mä′yə-nə) *n.* A Sanskrit epic concerning the banishment of Rama from his kingdom and his eventual restoration to the throne. [Skt. *Rāmāyaṇam*, the going of Rama : *Rāmaḥ*, Rama + *ayanam*, a going, way (< *eti, ay–*, he goes; see **ei–** in App.).]

ram·ble (răm′bəl) *intr.v.* **-bled, -bling, -bles 1.** To move about aimlessly. See Syns at **wander. 2.** To walk about casually or for pleasure. **3.** To follow an irregularly winding course of motion or growth. **4.** To speak or write at length and with many digressions. ❖ *n.* A leisurely, sometimes lengthy walk. [Prob. < MDu. *rammelen, to wander about in a state of sexual desire < *rammen*, to copulate with.]

ram·bler (răm′blər) *n.* **1.** One that rambles: *ramblers about town.* **2.** A type of climbing rose having numerous red, pink, or white flowers.

ram·bling (răm′blĭng) *adj.* **1.** Often or habitually roaming; wandering. **2.** Extended over an irregular area; sprawling. **3.** Lengthy and digressive. **—ram′bling·ly** *adv.*

Ram·bouil·let (răm′bʊʊ-lā, răm′bʊʊ-yā′) *n.* Any of a breed of merino sheep of French origin, raised for wool and meat. [After *Rambouillet*, a town in N-central France.]

ram·bunc·tious (răm-bŭngk′shəs) *adj.* Boisterous and disorderly. [Prob. alteration of *robustious, rumbustious* < ROBUST.] **—ram·bunc′tious·ly** *adv.* **—ram·bunc′tious·ness** *n.*

ram·bu·tan (răm-bōōt′n) *n.* **1.** A tree (*Nephelium lappaceum*) of southeast Asia bearing edible oval red fruit with soft spines. **2.** This fruit. [Malay < *rambut*, hair (< its hairy covering).]

Ra·meau (rä-mō′), **Jean Philippe** 1683–1764. French music theorist and composer of ballets and operas.

ram·e·kin also **ram·e·quin** (răm′ĭ-kĭn) *n.* **1.** A baked cheese preparation made with eggs and bread crumbs or unsweetened puff pastry and served in individual dishes. **2.** A small dish used for baking and serving. [Fr. *ramequin,* perh. < Du. dialectal *rammeken*, toasted bread, or < LGer. *ramken*, dim. of *ram*, cream (< MLGer. *rōme*).]

ra·men (rä′mən) *n.* **1.** A Japanese dish of noodles in broth, often garnished with small pieces of meat and vegetables. **2.** A thin white noodle served in this dish. [J. *ramen* < Chin. (Mandarin) *lā miàn*, pulled noodles : *lā*, pull + *miàn*, noodle.]

Ram·e·ses II also **Ram·es·ses II** (răm′ĭ-sēz′) or **Ram·ses II** (răm′sēz′) 14th–13th cent. B.C. King of Egypt (1304–1237 B.C.) who was probably king during the Jewish exodus.

ra·met (rä′mĭt) *n.* An individual member of a clone. [Lat. *rāmus*, branch; see RAMUS + –ET.]

ra·mi (rä′mī′) *n.* Plural of **ramus.**

ram·ie (răm′ē, rä′mē) *n.* **1.** A tropical Asian perennial herb (*Boehmeria nivea*) having broad leaves and small unisexual apetalous flowers. **2.** The flaxlike fiber from the stem of this plant, used in making fabrics and cordage. [Malay *rami*.]

ram·i·fi·ca·tion (răm′ə-fĭ-kā′shən) *n.* **1.** A development or consequence growing out of and sometimes complicating a problem, plan, or statement. **2a.** The act or process of branching out or dividing into branches. **b.** A subordinate part extending from a main body; a branch. **c.** An arrangement of branches or branching parts.

ram·i·form (răm′ə-fôrm′) *adj.* Branching or branchlike. [Lat. *rāmus*, branch; see RAMUS + –FORM.]

ram·i·fy (răm′ə-fī′) *v.* **-fied, -fy·ing, -fies** *—intr.* **1.** To have complicating consequences or outgrowths. **2.** To send out branches or subordinate branchlike parts. *—tr.* To divide into or cause to extend in branches or subordinate branchlike parts. [ME *ramifien,* to branch out < OFr. *ramifier* < Med.Lat. *ramificāre* : Lat. *rāmus*, branch; see **wrād–** in App. + Lat. *-ficāre,* -fy.]

ram·jet (răm′jĕt′) *n.* A jet engine that propels aircraft by igniting fuel mixed with air taken and compressed by the engine in a way that produces great exhaust from intake velocity.

ra·mo·na (rə-mō′nə) *n.* See **sage²** 1a. [Possibly after *Ramona*, heroine of a novel by Helen Hunt Jackson.]

ra·mose (rä′mōs′, rə-mōs′) *adj.* Having many branches. [Lat. *rāmōsus* < *rāmus*. See **wrād–** in App.]

Ra·mos-Hor·ta (rä′mōs-ôr′tä), **José** b. 1945. East Timorese resistance leader who shared the 1996 Nobel Peace Prize.

ra·mous (rä′məs) *adj.* **1.** Of or resembling branches. **2.** Branching; ramose. [< Lat. *rāmōsus*, ramose. See RAMOSE.]

ramp¹ (rămp) *n.* **1.** An inclined surface or roadway connecting different levels. **2.** A mobile staircase for boarding and leaving an

aircraft. **3.** A concave bend of a handrail where a sharp change in level or direction occurs, as at a stair landing. [Fr. *rampe* < *ramper*, to slope, rise up < OFr. See RAMP².]

ramp² (rămp) *intr.v.* **ramped, ramp·ing, ramps 1.** To act threateningly or violently; rage. **2.** To assume a threatening stance. **3.** *Heraldry* To stand in the rampant position. [ME *rampen* < OFr. *ramper*, to rear, rise up < Gmc. orig.] **—ramp** *n.*

ramp³ (rămp) also **ramps** (rămps) *n.* A plant, *Allium tricoccum,* related to onions and leeks and having edible underground stems. [Variant of *rams* < ME *ramse* < OE *hramsa.*]

ram·page (răm′pāj′) *n.* A course of violent frenzied action or behavior. ❖ *intr.v.* (also răm-pāj′) **-paged, -pag·ing, -pag·es** To move about wildly or violently. [Sc., poss. < RAMP².] **—ram·pag′er** *n.*

ram·pa·geous (răm-pā′jəs) *adj.* Raging; frenzied. **—ram·pa′geous·ly** *adv.*

ram·pant (răm′pənt) *adj.* **1.** Extending unchecked; unrestrained: *a rampant growth of weeds* **2.** Occurring without restraint and frequently, widely, or menacingly; rife: *rampant corruption.* **3a.** Rearing on the hind legs. **b.** *Heraldry* Rearing on the left hind leg with the forelegs elevated, the right above the left, and usu. with the head in profile. **4.** *Architecture* Springing from a support or an abutment that is higher at one side than at the other: *a rampant arch.* [ME *rampaunt* < OFr. *rampant,* pr. part. of *ramper,* to ramp. See RAMP².] **—ram′pan·cy** *n.* **—ram′pant·ly** *adv.*

ram·part (răm′pärt′, -pərt) *n.* **1.** A fortification consisting of an embankment, often with a parapet built on top. **2.** A means of protection or defense; a bulwark. ❖ *tr.v.* **-part·ed, -part·ing, -parts** To defend with a rampart. [Fr. *rempart* < OFr. < *remparer,* to fortify : *re–,* re- + *emparer,* to fortify, take possession of (< O Provençal *amparar* < VLat. **ante parāre,* to prepare : Lat. *ante-,* ante- + Lat. *parāre,* to prepare).]

ram·pike (răm′pīk′) *n.* A standing dead tree or tree stump, esp. one killed by fire. [?]

ram·pi·on (răm′pē-ən) *n.* **1.** A biennial Eurasian plant (*Campanula rapunculus*) having rosette leaves with winged stalks, lilac-colored flowers, and an edible root used in salads. **2.** Any of various similar plants of the genus *Phyteuma.* [Prob. alteration of Fr. *raiponce* < OFr. *responce* < OItal. *raponzo,* prob. < *rapa,* turnip < Lat. *rāpum.*]

ram·rod (răm′rŏd′) *n.* **1.** A rod for forcing the charge into a muzzleloading firearm. **2.** A rod for cleaning the barrel of a firearm. **3.** An overseer. ❖ *tr.v.* **-rod·ded, -rod·ding, -rods 1.** To control strictly; supervise closely. **2.** To force passage or acceptance of: *ramrodded the bill through Congress.*

Ram·say (răm′zē), **Allan** 1686–1758. Scottish poet whose works include *The Gentle Shepherd* (1725).

Ramsay, James Andrew Brown See 10th Earl and 1st Marquis of **Dalhousie.**

Ramsay, Sir William 1852–1916. British chemist who won a 1904 Nobel Prize.

Ram·ses II (răm′sēz′) See **Rameses II.**

ram·shack·le (răm′shăk′əl) *adj.* So poorly constructed or kept up that disintegration is likely; rickety. [Ult. < *ransackle,* to ransack, freq. of ME *ransaken,* to pillage. See RANSACK.]

ram's horn (rămz) *n. Judaism* A shofar.

ram·son (răm′zən, -sən) *n.* A Eurasian garlic (*Allium ursinum*) having broad, stalked, oblong to lance-shaped leaves and bulbous roots used in salads and relishes. Often used in the plural. [ME *ramsyn* < OE *hramsan,* pl. of *hramsa.*]

ram·til (răm′tĭl) or **ram·til·la** (răm-tĭl′ə) *n.* An Ethiopian plant (*Guizotia abyssinica*) having opposite leaves and rayed yellow flower heads, grown for its oil-rich seeds. [Hindi *rāmtil* : Skt. *rāma-,* dark + Skt. *tilaḥ,* sesame.]

ram·u·lose (răm′yə-lōs′) *adj.* Having numerous small branches. [Lat. *rāmulōsus* < *rāmulus,* dim. of *rāmus,* branch. See RAMUS.]

ra·mus (rä′məs) *n., pl.* **-mi** (-mī′) **1.** A branch, as of a plant or nerve. **2.** A bony process extending like a branch from a larger bone, esp. the ascending part of the lower jaw that makes a joint at the temple. [Lat. *rāmus,* branch. See **wrād–** in App.]

ran (răn) *v.* Past tense of **run.**

Ran (rän) *n. Mythology* The Norse goddess of the sea.

ranch (rănch) *n.* **1.** An extensive farm, esp. in the western United States, on which large herds of cattle, sheep, or horse are raised. **2.** A large specialized farm: *a mink ranch.* **3.** A house in which a rancher lives. ❖ *intr.v.* **ranched, ranch·ing, ranch·es** To manage or work on a ranch. [Am.Sp. *rancho,* small farm < Sp., hut, group of people who eat together < OSpan. *rancharse,* to be billeted < OFr. *se ranger,* to be arranged < *renc, reng,* row, line, of Gmc. orig.]

ranch·er (răn′chər) *n.* **1.** One that owns or manages a ranch. **2.** A rectangular house of one story; a ranch house.

ran·che·ri·a (răn′chə-rē′ə) *n. Southwestern US* **1a.** A Mexican herder's hut. **b.** A village of these huts. **2.** A rural Native American settlement. [Am.Sp. *ranchería* < *rancho,* small farm. See RANCH.]

ran·che·ro (răn-châr′ō) *n., pl.* **-ros** *Southwestern US* A ranch owner; a rancher. [Am.Sp. < *rancho,* small ranch. See RANCH.]

ranch house *n.* **1.** The house of a rancher. **2.** A rectangular one-story house with a low-pitched roof.

Ran·chi (rän′chē) A city of NE India WNW of Calcutta. It is a manufacturing center and a health resort. Pop. 599,306.

ranch·man (rănch′mən) *n.* The owner or manager of a ranch; a rancher.

ranch mink *n.* A mink bred in captivity from Alaskan and Labrador strains for special pelt colors and qualities.

ran·cho (răn′chō) *n., pl.* **-chos** *Southwestern US* **1.** A hut or group of huts for housing ranch workers. **2.** A ranch. [Am.Sp., small ranch. See RANCH.]

Rancho Cu·ca·mon·ga (ko͞o′kə-mŭng′gə, -mŏng′-) A city of SW CA W of San Bernardino. Pop. 127,743.

ran·cid (răn′sĭd) *adj.* **1.** Having the disagreeable odor or taste of decomposing oils or fats; rank: *rancid butter.* **2.** Repugnant; nasty: *rancid remarks.* [Lat. *rancidus,* from *rancēre,* to stink, be rotten.] **—ran·cid′i·ty, ran′cid·ness** *n.*

ran·cor (răng′kər) *n.* Bitter long-lasting resentment; deep-seated ill will. [ME < OFr. < LLat., rancid smell < Lat. *rancēre,* to stink, be rotten.] **—ran′cor·ous** *adj.* **—ran′cor·ous·ly** *adv.* **—ran′cor·ous·ness** *n.*

ran·cour (răng′kər) *n. Chiefly British* Variant of **rancor.**

rand (rănd, ränd) *n.* See table at **currency.** [Afr., after (WITWATERS)RAND.]

Rand (rănd, ränd) See **Witwatersrand.**

Rand (rănd), **Ayn** 1905–82. Russian-born Amer. writer whose novels include *The Fountainhead* (1943).

R & B *abbr.* rhythm and blues

R & D *abbr.* research and development

Ran·dolph (răn′dŏlf′), **A(sa) Philip** 1889–1979. Amer. labor and civil rights leader who campaigned for an end to racial discrimination in organized labor.

Randolph, Edmund Jennings 1753–1813. Amer. Revolutionary leader who was a member of the Constitutional Convention (1787) and served as US secretary of state (1794–95).

Randolph, John Called "Randolph of Roanoke." 1773–1833. Amer. politician who served as a US representative (12 terms between 1799 and 1829) and senator (1825–27) from VA.

ran·dom (răn′dəm) *adj.* **1.** Having no specific pattern, purpose, or objective: *random movements.* See Syns at **chance. 2.** *Mathematics & Statistics* Of or relating to a type of circumstance or event that is described by a probability distribution. **3.** Of or relating to an event in which all outcomes are equally likely, as in the testing of a blood sample for the presence of a substance. **—idiom: at random** Without a governing design, method, or purpose; unsystematically. [< *at random,* by chance, at great speed < ME *randon,* speed, violence < OFr. < *randir,* to run, of Gmc. orig.] **—ran′dom·ly** *adv.* **—ran′dom·ness** *n.*

ran·dom-ac·cess memory (răn′dəm-ăk′sĕs) *n.* See **RAM.**

ran·dom·ize (răn′də-mīz′) *tr.v.* **-ized, -iz·ing, -iz·es** To make random in arrangement, esp. in order to control the variables in an experiment. **—ran′dom·i·za′tion** (-də-mĭ-zā′shən) *n.* **—ran′dom·iz′er** *n.*

random variable *n.* A variable whose values are random but whose statistical distribution is known.

random walk *n. Statistics* A series of sequential movements in which the direction and size of each move is randomly determined.

R and R *abbr.* rest and recreation

ran·dy (răn′dē) *adj.* **-di·er, -di·est** **1a.** Lascivious; lecherous. **b.** Of or characterized by frank uninhibited sexuality. **2.** *Scots* Ill-mannered. [Poss. < obsolete *rand,* to rant < obsolete Du. *randen, ranten.*]

ra·nee (rä′nē) *n.* Variant of **rani.**

rang (răng) *v.* Past tense of **ring**[2].

range (rānj) *n.* **1a.** Extent of perception, knowledge, experience, or ability. **b.** The area or sphere in which an activity takes place. **c.** The full extent covered: *the range of possibilities.* **2a.** An amount or extent of variation. **b.** *Music* The gamut of tones that a voice or an instrument is capable of producing. **3a.** The maximum extent or distance limiting operation, action, or effectiveness, as of an aircraft or a sound. **b.** The maximum distance that can be covered by a vehicle with a specified payload before its fuel supply is exhausted. **c.** The distance between a projectile weapon and its target. **4.** A place equipped for practice in shooting at targets. **5.** *Aerospace* A testing area for rockets and missiles. **6.** An extensive area of open land for livestock. **7.** The geographic region in which a plant or animal normally lives or grows. **8.** The act of wandering or roaming over a large area. **9.** *Mathematics* The set of all values a given function may take on. **10.** *Statistics* The difference or interval between the smallest and largest values in a frequency distribution. **11.** A class, rank, or order. **12.** An extended group or series, esp. a row or chain of mountains. **13.** One of a series of double-faced bookcases in a library stack room. **14.** A north-south strip of townships, each six miles square, numbered east and west from a specified meridian in a US public land survey. **15.** A stove with spaces for cooking a number of things at the same time. ❖ *v.* **ranged, rang·ing, rang·es** *—tr.* **1.** To arrange or dispose in a particular order, esp. in rows or lines. **2.** To assign to a particular category; classify. **3.** To align (a gun, for example) with a target. **4a.** To determine the distance of (a target). **b.** To be capable of reaching (a maximum distance). **5.** To pass over or through (an area or region). **6.** To turn (livestock) onto an extensive area of open land for grazing. **7.** *Nautical* To

uncoil (a line or rode) along the deck so that it will pay out smoothly. *—intr.* **1.** To vary within specified limits. **2.** To extend in a particular direction. **3.** To extend or lie in the same direction. **4.** To pass over or through an area or region in or as if in exploration. See Syns at **wander. 5.** To wander freely; roam. **6.** To live or grow within a particular region. [ME, row, rank < OFr. < *rangier,* to put in a row < *rang, reng,* line, of Gmc. orig.]

range finder also **range·find·er** (rānj′fīn′dər) *n.* Any of various optical, electronic, or acoustical instruments used to determine the distance of an object from the observer.

range·land (rānj′lănd′, -lənd) *n.* An expanse of land suitable for livestock to wander and graze on.

Range·ley Lake (rānj′lē) A lake of W-central ME near the NH border.

rang·er (rān′jər) *n.* **1.** A wanderer; a rover. **2.** A member of an armed troop that patrols a given region. **3. Ranger** A member of a group of US soldiers trained to make raids. **4a.** A warden who maintains and protects a natural area, such as a forest or park. **b.** *Chiefly British* The keeper of a royal forest or park.

Ran·goon (răng-go͞on′, răng-) See **Yangon.**

rang·y (rān′jē) *adj.* **-i·er, -i·est** **1.** Having long slender limbs. **2.** Inclined to rove. **3.** Providing ample range; roomy.

ra·ni also **ra·nee** (rä′nē) *n., pl.* **-nis** also **-nees** **1.** The wife of a rajah. **2.** A princess or queen in India or the East Indies. [Hindi *rānī* < Skt. *rājñī,* fem. of *rājā, rājñ-,* rajah. See RAJAH.]

rank[1] (răngk) *n.* **1a.** A relative position in a scale. **b.** An official position or grade: *the rank of sergeant.* **c.** A relative position or degree of value in a graded group. **d.** High or eminent station or position. **2.** A row, line, series, or range. **3a.** A line, as of soldiers, standing side by side in close order. **b. ranks** The armed forces. **c. ranks** Personnel, esp. enlisted military personnel. **4. ranks** A body of people classed together; numbers: *joined the ranks of the unemployed.* **5.** *Games* Any of the rows of squares running crosswise to the files on a playing board in chess or checkers. ❖ *v.* **ranked, rank·ing, ranks** *—tr.* **1.** To place in a row or rows. **2.** To give a particular order or position to; classify. **3.** To outrank or take precedence over. *—intr.* **1.** To hold a particular rank: *ranked first in the class.* **2.** To form or stand in a row or rows. **3.** *Slang* **a.** To complain. **b.** To engage in carping criticism. Often used with *on.* **—idiom: pull rank** To use one's superior rank to gain an advantage. [ME, line, row < OFr. *ranc, renc,* of Gmc. orig.]

rank[2] (răngk) *adj.* **rank·er, rank·est** **1.** Growing profusely or with excessive vigor: *rank vegetation.* **2.** Yielding a profuse, often excessive crop; highly fertile: *rank earth.* **3.** Strong and offensive in odor or flavor. **4.** Conspicuously offensive: *rank treachery.* **5.** Absolute; complete: *a rank amateur.* [ME *ranc* < OE, strong, overbearing. See *reg-* in App.] **—rank′ly** *adv.* **—rank′ness** *n.*

rank and file *n.* **1.** The enlisted troops, excluding noncommissioned officers, in an army. **2.** The ordinary members of a group, organization, or society excluding the leaders and officers. **—rank′-and-file′** (răngk′ən-fīl′) *adj.*

Ran·ke (räng′kə), **Leopold von** 1795–1886. German historian who pioneered the analysis of firsthand documentation in works such as *The History of the Popes* (1834–36).

rank·er (răng′kər) *n. Chiefly British* **1.** An enlisted soldier. **2.** A commissioned officer who has been promoted from enlisted status.

Ran·kin (răng′kĭn), **Jeannette** 1880–1973. Amer. politician who served as the first woman US representative (1917–19 and 1941–43).

Ran·kine scale (răng′kĭn) *n.* A scale of absolute temperature having the same degree increments as those of the Fahrenheit scale, and in which the freezing point of water is 491.69° and the boiling point is 671.69°. [After William John Macquorn *Rankine* (1820–72), Scottish physicist.]

rank·ing (răng′kĭng) *adj.* Of the highest rank; preeminent. ❖ *n.* **1. rankings** A list of items in a group, such as schools or sports teams, according to a system of rating or a record of performance. **2.** A position in such a list.

ran·kle (răng′kəl) *v.* **-kled, -kling, -kles** *—intr.* **1.** To cause persistent irritation or resentment. **2.** To become sore or inflamed; fester. *—tr.* To embitter; irritate. [ME *ranclen* < OFr. *rancler,* alteration of *draoncler* < *draoncle,* festering sore < Lat. *dracunculus,* dim. of *dracō, dracōn-,* serpent. See DRAGON.]

Rann of Kutch (rŭn; kŭch) A salt marsh of W India and SE Pakistan between the Gulf of Kutch and the Indus R. delta.

ran·sack (răn′săk′) *tr.v.* **-sacked, -sack·ing, -sacks 1.** To search or examine thoroughly. **2.** To search carefully for plunder; pillage. [ME *ransaken* < ON *rannsaka* : *rann,* house + **saka,* to search, seek.] **—ran′sack′er** *n.*

ran·som (răn′səm) *n.* **1a.** The release of property or a person in return for payment of a demanded price. **b.** The price or payment for such release. **2.** A redemption from sin and its consequences. ❖ *tr.v.* **-somed, -som·ing, -soms 1a.** To obtain the release of for a certain price. **b.** To release after receiving such a payment. **2.** To deliver from sin and its consequences. [ME *ransome* < OFr. *rançon* < Lat. *redēmptiō, redēmptiōn-,* a buying back. See REDEMPTION.] **—ran′som·er** *n.*

Ransom, John Crowe 1888–1974. Amer. writer whose collections of poetry include *Chills and Fevers* (1924).

rant (rănt) *v.* **rant·ed, rant·ing, rants** *—intr.* To speak or an

Jeannette Rankin

ă pat	oi boy
ā pay	ou out
âr care	o͝o took
ä father	o͞o boot
ĕ pet	ŭ cut
ē be	ûr urge
ĭ pit	th thin
ī pie	th this
îr pier	hw which
ŏ pot	zh vision
ō toe	ə about,
ô paw	item

Stress marks:
′ (primary);
′ (secondary); as in
lexicon (lĕk′sĭ-kŏn′)

angry or violent manner; rave. —*tr.* To utter or express with violence or extravagance. ❖ *n.* **1.** Violent or extravagant speech or writing. **2.** A speech or piece of writing that incites anger or violence. **3.** *Chiefly British* Wild or uproarious merriment. [Prob. < obsolete Du. *ranten.*] —**rant′er** *n.*

ran·u·la (răn′yə-lə) *n.* A cyst on the underside of the tongue caused by the obstruction of a salivary gland duct. [Lat. *rānula,* tongue swelling, dim. of *rāna,* frog. See RANUNCULUS.]

ra·nun·cu·lus (rə-nŭng′kyə-ləs) *n., pl.* **-lus·es** or **-li** (-lī′) Any of numerous plants of the genus *Ranunculus,* including the buttercups. [NLat. *Rānunculus,* genus name < Lat. *rānunculus,* a kind of medicinal plant, dim. of *rāna,* frog, perh. of imit. orig.]

rap¹ (răp) *v.* **rapped, rap·ping, raps** —*tr.* **1.** To hit sharply and swiftly; strike. **2.** To utter sharply: *raps out an order.* **3.** To criticize or blame. —*intr.* To strike a quick light blow. ❖ *n.* **1.** A quick light blow or knock. **2.** A knocking or tapping sound. **3.** *Slang* **a.** A reprimand. **b.** A prison sentence. **4.** *Slang* A negative quality or characteristic associated with a person or an object. —*idioms:* **beat the rap** *Slang* To escape punishment or be acquitted of a charge. **take the rap** *Slang* To accept punishment or blame for an error or error. [ME *rappen,* poss. of imit. orig.]

rap² (răp) *tr.v.* **rapt** or **rapped** (răpt), **rap·ping, raps** *Archaic* **1.** *past participle* **rapt** To enchant or seize with rapture. **2.** To snatch. [Back-formation < RAPT.]

rap³ (răp) *n. Informal* The least bit. [< obsolete *rap,* counterfeit halfpenny < Ir.Gael., alteration of *ropaire.* See RAPPAREE.]

rap⁴ (răp) *n.* **1.** *Slang* A talk or discussion. **2.** *Music* A form of popular music developed esp. in African-American urban communities and characterized by spoken or chanted rhyming lyrics with a strong rhythmic accompaniment. ❖ *intr.v.* **rapped, rap·ping, raps 1.** *Slang* To discuss freely and at length. **2.** To perform rap music. [Poss. < RAP¹.]

OUR LIVING LANGUAGE The culture of hip-hop has been the source of dozens of words and expressions in American English, of which *rap* is one of the most familiar. The word is probably a development ultimately of *rap,* meaning "to hit." It shows up in the early 1900s in the extended meaning "to express orally," as used by so notable a figure as Winston Churchill in 1933. Over the next few decades it came to mean "to discuss or debate informally," a meaning that was well established in the African-American community by the late 1960s. A decade later the word was applied to an evolving style of music characterized by, among other things, beat-driven rhymes of an often improvisatory nature. The slang that is integral to the lyrics of rap continues to be a source of borrowings into colloquial American English; recent examples include *chill,* meaning "to calm down," and *dis,* meaning "to show disrespect to." These are but the latest examples in a long series of such borrowings from African American Vernacular English stretching back a century or more, many of them directly from popular music lyrics or from musicians' lingo.

Raphael²
c. 1506 self-portrait

ra·pa·cious (rə-pā′shəs) *adj.* **1.** Taking by force; plundering. **2.** Greedy; ravenous. **3.** Subsisting on live prey. [< Lat. *rapāx, rapāc-* < *rapere,* to seize.] —**ra·pa′cious·ly** *adv.* —**ra·pac′i·ty** (rə-pǎs′ǐ-tē), **ra·pa′cious·ness** *n.*

Ra·pa Nu·i (rä′pə nōō′ē) See **Easter Island.**

rape¹ (rāp) *n.* **1.** The crime of forcing another person to submit to sex acts, esp. sexual intercourse. **2.** The act of seizing and carrying off by force; abduction. **3.** Abusive or improper treatment; violation. ❖ *tr.v.* **raped, rap·ing, rapes 1.** To commit the crime of rape on. **2.** To seize and carry off by force. **3.** To plunder or pillage. [ME < *rapen,* to rape < OFr. *raper,* to abduct < Lat. *rapere,* to seize.] —**rap′er** *n.*

rape² (rāp) *n.* A European plant *(Brassica napus)* of the mustard family, cultivated as fodder and for its seed. [ME < OFr. < Lat. *rāpa,* pl. of *rāpum,* turnip.]

rape³ (rāp) *n.* The refuse of grapes left after the extraction of the juice in winemaking. [Fr. *râpe,* grape stalk < OFr. < *rasper,* to scrape. See RASP.]

rape oil *n.* See **rapeseed oil.**

rape·seed (rāp′sēd′) *n.* The seed of the rape plant.

rapeseed oil *n.* The edible oil extracted from rapeseed, also used as a lubricant and in the manufacture of various products.

rape shield law *n.* A law that prohibits the defense in a rape case from cross-examination regarding the plaintiff's prior sexual conduct.

Raph·a·el¹ (răf′ē-əl, rā′fē-, rä′fē-ĕl′) *n.* One of the archangels of Hebrew tradition.

Raph·a·el² (răf′ē-əl, rā′fē-, rä′fē-ĕl′) 1483–1520. Italian painter whose works, including religious subjects, portraits, and frescoes, exemplify the ideals of the High Renaissance.

ra·phe also **rha·phe** (rā′fē) *n., pl.* **-phae** (-fē′) **1.** *Anatomy* A seamless line or ridge between two similar parts of a body organ, as in the scrotum. **2.** *Botany* The portion of the funiculus that is united to the ovule wall, commonly visible as a line or ridge on the seed coat. **3.** The median groove of a bivalve diatom valve. [NLat. < Gk. *rhaphē,* seam, suture < *rhaptein,* to sew. See wer-² in App.]

raph·i·a (răf′ē-ə) *n.* Variant of **raffia.**

ra·phide (rā′fīd) also **ra·phis** (-fĭs) *n., pl.* **raph·i·des** (răf′ĭ-dēz′) One of a bundle of needlelike crystals of calcium oxalate occurring in many plant cells. [Fr., sing. of *raphides* < NLat. < Gk.

rhaphides, pl. of *rhaphis,* needle < *rhaptein,* to sew. See wer-² in App.]

rap·id (răp′ĭd) *adj.* **-er, -est** Moving, acting, or occurring with great speed. See Syns at **fast¹.** ❖ *n.* An extremely fast-moving part of a river, caused by a steep descent in the riverbed. Often used in the plural. [Lat. *rapidus* < *rapere,* to seize.] —**ra·pid′i·ty** (rə-pĭd′ĭ-tē), **rap′id·ness** (răp′ĭd-nĕs) *n.* —**rap′id·ly** *adv.*

Rapid City A city of SW SD WSW of Pierre in the E part of the Black Hills. Pop. 59,607.

rapid eye movement *n.* REM.

rap·id-fire (răp′ĭd-fīr′) *adj.* **1.** Designed to fire shots in rapid succession. **2.** Marked by continuous rapid occurrence.

rapid transit *n.* An urban passenger transportation system using elevated or underground trains or a combination of both.

ra·pi·er (rā′pē-ər, rāp′yər) *n.* **1.** A long slender two-edged sword with a cuplike hilt, used in the 16th and 17th centuries. **2.** A light sharp-pointed sword lacking a cutting edge and used only for thrusting. [Fr. *rapière* < OFr. (*espee*) *rapiere,* rapier (sword).]

rap·ine (răp′ĭn) *n.* Forcible seizure of another's property. [ME < OFr. < Lat. *rapīna* < *rapere,* to seize.]

rap·ist (rā′pĭst) *n.* One who commits rape.

Rap·pa·han·nock (răp′ə-hăn′ək) A river of NE VA flowing c. 341 km (212 mi) to Chesapeake Bay.

rap·pa·ree (răp′ə-rē′) *n.* **1.** A freebooting soldier of 17th-century Ireland. **2.** A bandit or robber. [Ir.Gael. *rapaire,* var. of *ropaire,* cutpurse < *ropaid,* he stabs.]

rap·pee (ră-pē′) *n.* A strong snuff made from a coarse dark tobacco. [< Fr. (*tabac*) *râpé,* grated (tobacco), p. part. of *râper,* to grate < OFr. *rasper,* to scrape. See RASP.]

rap·pel (ră-pĕl′) *n.* A descent of a vertical surface, as of a cliff, by means of a secured rope that is passed under one thigh and over the opposite shoulder or through a device that provides friction. ❖ *intr.v.* **-pelled, -pel·ling, -pels** To make such a descent. [Fr., recall, return, rappel < OFr., recall < *rapeler,* to recall : *re-,* re- + *apeler,* to summon; see APPEAL.]

rap·per¹ (răp′ər) *n.* One that raps or strikes, esp. a door knocker.

rap·per² (răp′ər) *n. Music* One who performs rap.

rap·port (ră-pôr′, -pōr′, rə-) *n.* Relationship, esp. one of mutual trust or emotional affinity. [Fr. < OFr. < *raporter,* to bring back : *re-,* re- + *aporter,* to bring (< Lat. *apportāre : ad-,* ad- + *portāre,* to carry; see per-² in App.).]

rap·por·teur (răp′ôr-tûr′, -tœr′) *n.* One who is designated to give a report, as at a meeting. [ME *raportour,* judge < OFr. *raporteur* < *raporter,* to bring back. See RAPPORT.]

rap·proche·ment (rä′prôsh-mäN′) *n.* **1.** A reestablishing of cordial relations, as between countries. **2.** The state of reconciliation or of cordial relations. [Fr. < *rapprocher,* to bring together : *re-,* re- + *approcher,* to approach (< OFr. *aprochier;* see APPROACH).]

rap·scal·lion (răp-skăl′yən) *n.* A rascal; a scamp. [Alteration of obsolete *rascallion* < RASCAL.]

rap session *n. Slang* An informal discussion held esp. by a group of people with similar concerns.

rap sheet *n. Slang* A police arrest record.

rapt (răpt) *v.* Past participle of **rap².** ❖ *adj.* **1.** Deeply moved or delighted; enraptured: *listened with rapt admiration.* **2.** Deeply absorbed; engrossed. [ME, carried away < Lat. *raptus,* p. part. of *rapere,* to seize.] —**rapt′ly** *adv.*

rap·tor (răp′tər) *n.* A bird of prey. [Lat., one who seizes < *rapere,* to seize. See RAPT.]

rap·to·ri·al (răp-tôr′ē-əl, -tōr′-) *adj.* **1.** Subsisting by seizing prey; predacious. **2.** Adapted for the seizing of prey. **3.** Of, relating to, or characteristic of birds of prey.

rap·ture (răp′chər) *n.* **1.** The state of being transported by a lofty emotion; ecstasy. **2.** An expression of ecstatic feeling. Often used in the plural. **3.** The transporting of a person from one place to another, esp. to heaven. ❖ *tr.v.* **-tured, -tur·ing, -tures** To enrapture. [Obsolete Fr., carrying off < *rapt,* carried away < OFr. *rat* < Lat. *raptus.* See RAPT.]

rap·tur·ous (răp′chər-əs) *adj.* Filled with great joy or rapture; ecstatic. —**rap′tur·ous·ly** *adv.* —**rap′tur·ous·ness** *n.*

ra·ra a·vis (râr′ə ā′vĭs) *n., pl.* **ra·ra a·vis·es** or **ra·rae a·ves** (râr′ē ā′vēz) A rare or unique person or thing. [Lat. *rāra avis : rāra,* fem. of *rārus,* rare + *avis,* bird.]

rare¹ (râr) *adj.* **rar·er, rar·est 1.** Infrequently occurring; uncommon: *a rare event; a plant that is rare in this region.* **2.** Excellent; extraordinary: *a rare sense of honor.* **3.** Thin in density; rarefied: *rare air.* [ME < OFr. < Lat. *rārus.*] —**rare′ness** *n.*

rare² (râr) *adj.* **rar·er, rar·est** Cooked just a short time so as to retain juice and redness: *a rare steak.* [ME *rere,* lightly boiled < OE *hrēr.*] —**rare′ness** *n.*

rare·bit (râr′bĭt) *n.* Welsh rabbit. [Prob. alteration of (WELSH) RABBIT.]

rare earth *n.* **1.** Any of various oxides of the rare-earth elements. **2.** A rare-earth element.

rare-earth element (râr′ûrth′) *n.* Any of the abundant metallic elements of atomic number 57 through 71. [So called because they were orig. thought to be rare.]

rar·ee show (râr′ē) *n.* **1.** See peepshow 1. **2.** A street show. [Alteration of RARE¹ + SHOW.]

rar·e·fac·tion (râr′ə-fǎk′shən) *n.* **1.** A decrease in density and pressure in a medium, such as air, caused by a sound wave. **2.** The region in which this occurs.

rar•e•fied also **rar•i•fied** (râr′ə-fīd′) *adj.* **1.** Of or reserved for an elite; esoteric. **2.** Elevated in character or style; lofty.

rar•e•fy also **rar•i•fy** (râr′ə-fī′) *v.* **-fied, -fy•ing, -fies** —*tr.* **1.** To make thin, less compact, or less dense. **2.** To purify or refine. —*intr.* To become thin, less compact, or less dense. [ME *rarefien* < OFr. *rarefier* < Med.Lat. *rārificāre*, alteration of Lat. *rārēfacere* : *rārus*, rare + *facere*, to make; see **dhē-** in App.] —**rar′e•fi′a•ble** *adj.*

rare•ly (râr′lē) *adv.* **1.** Not often; infrequently. **2.** In an unusual degree; exceptionally. **3.** With uncommon excellence.

rare•ripe (râr′rīp′) *adj.* Ripening early. ❖ *n.* A rareripe fruit or vegetable. [Dialectal *rare*, early (var. of RATHE) + RIPE.]

rar•ing (râr′ĭng) also **rar•in′** (-ĭn) *adj. Informal* Full of eagerness; enthusiastic. [Pr. part. of dialectal *rare*, to rear, var. of REAR[2].]

Rar•i•tan (răr′ĭ-tən) A river formed by the confluence of two tributaries in N-central NJ and flowing c. 129 km (80 km) to **Raritan Bay,** the W arm of Lower New York Bay.

rar•i•ty (râr′ĭ-tē) *n., pl.* **-ties 1.** Something rare. **2.** The quality or state of being rare; infrequency of occurrence.

Rar•o•ton•ga (răr′ə-tŏng′gə) A volcanic island of the S Pacific Ocean in the SW Cook Is.

ras•bo•ra (răz-bôr′ə, -bōr′ə) *n.* Any of various brightly colored tropical fishes of the genus *Rasbora.* [NLat. *Rasbora*, genus name < a native word in the East Indies.]

ras•cal (răs′kəl) *n.* **1.** One that is playfully mischievous. **2.** An unscrupulous, dishonest person; a scoundrel. ❖ *adj. Archaic* Made up of, belonging to, or relating to the common people. [ME *rascaile*, rabble, commoners < OFr. *rascaille*, prob. < *rasque*, mud < VLat. **rāsicāre*, to scrape. See RASH[2].] —**ras′cal•ly** *adj.*

ras•cal•i•ty (răs-kăl′ĭ-tē) *n., pl.* **-ties 1.** Behavior or character typical of a rascal. **2.** A base or mischievous act.

rase[1] (rāz) *tr.v.* **rased, ras•ing, ras•es** To erase. [ME *rasen*, to scrape off, erase. See RAZE.]

rase[2] (rāz) *v.* Variant of **raze.**

rash[1] (răsh) *adj.* **rash•er, rash•est 1.** Characterized by or resulting from ill-considered haste or boldness. **2.** *Archaic* Quick in producing a strong or marked effect. [ME *rasch*, active, unrestrained, perh. < OE *-raesc* (in *līgræsc*, lightning) or < MDu. or MLGer. *rasch*, fast.] —**rash′ly** *adv.* —**rash′ness** *n.*

rash[2] (răsh) *n.* **1.** A skin eruption. **2.** An outbreak of many instances within a brief period. [Poss. < obsolete Fr. *rache*, a sore < OFr. *rasche*, scurf < *raschier*, to scrape, scratch < VLat. **rāsicāre* < Lat. *rāsus*, p. part. of *rādere.*]

rash•er (răsh′ər) *n.* **1.** A thin slice of cooked bacon. **2.** A dish or an order of rashers. [?]

Rasht (răsht) also **Resht** (rĕsht) A city of NW Iran near the Caspian Sea ESE of Tabriz. Pop. 260,000.

Rask (răsk, räsk), **Rasmus Christian** 1787–1832. Danish philologist who was a founder of comparative linguistics.

Ras•mus•sen (răs′mə-sən, räs′mo͝os-ən), **Knud Johan Victor** 1879–1933. Danish ethnologist and Arctic explorer who conducted extensive research on Eskimo and Inuit culture and heritage.

ra•so•ri•al (rə-zôr′ē-əl, -zōr′-, -sôr′-, -sōr′-) *adj.* Characteristically scratching the ground for food. Used of chickens and similar birds. [< LLat. *rāsor*, scraper < Lat. *rāsus*, p. part. of *rādere*, to scrape.]

rasp (răsp) *n.* **1.** A coarse file with sharp pointed projections. **2.** The act of filing with a rasp. **3.** A harsh grating sound. ❖ *v.* **rasped, rasp•ing, rasps** —*tr.* **1.** To file or scrape with a rasp. **2.** To utter in a grating voice. **3.** To grate on (feelings). —*intr.* **1.** To scrape harshly; grate. **2.** To make a grating sound. [OFr. *raspe* < *rasper*, to rasp, of Gmc. orig. V., ME *raspen* < MDu. *raspen* and < OFr. *rasper.*] —**rasp′er** *n.* —**rasp′ing•ly** *adv.*

rasp•ber•ry (răz′bĕr′ē) *n.* **1.** Any of various shrubby, usu. prickly plants of the genus *Rubus* in the rose family that bear edible fruit. **2.** The aggregate fruit of any of these plants, consisting of many small, fleshy, usu. red drupelets. **3.** A moderate to dark or deep purplish red. **4.** *Slang* A derisive or contemptuous sound made by vibrating the extended tongue and the lips while exhaling. [Obs. *raspis*, raspberry + BERRY.]

Ras•pu•tin (răs-pyo͞o′tĭn, rə-spo͞o′tyĭn), **Grigori Efimovich** 1872?–1916. Russian starets known for his influence over the court of Nicholas II.

rasp•y (răs′pē) *adj.* **-i•er, -i•est** Rough; grating.

ras•sle (răs′əl) *intr. & tr.v.* **-sled, -sling, -sles** *Nonstandard* To wrestle. [Dialectal alteration of WRESTLE.]

Ras•ta (rä′stə, răs′tə) *n.* **1.** A Rastafarian. **2.** Rastafarianism. ❖ *adj.* Rastafarian.

Ras•ta•far•i•an (räs′tə-fär′ē-ən, răs′tə-får′-) *n.* An adherent of Rastafarianism. ❖ *adj.* Of or relating to Rastafarianism or its adherents.

Ras•ta•far•i•an•ism (rä′stə-fär′ē-ə-nĭz′əm, răs′tə-fâr′-) *n.* A religious and political movement originating in Jamaica in the 1930s that regards Ethiopia as the Promised Land and Haile Selassie as a messiah. [After *Ras Tafari* Makonnen, former name of Haile Selassie, proclaimed a divine being by adherents : Amharic *ras*, head, prince + Amharic *täfäri*, to be feared, p. part. of *täfärra*, to be feared, derived stem of *färra*, to fear, respect.]

ras•ter (răs′tər) *n.* A scanning pattern of parallel lines that form an image projected on the display screen of a cathode-ray tube. [Ger. < Lat. *rāstrum*, rake (< the resemblance of the parallel lines to a rake's path).]

rat (răt) *n.* **1a.** Any of various long-tailed rodents resembling mice but larger, esp. one of the genus *Rattus.* **b.** Any of various similar animals. **2.** *Informal* **a.** A despicable sneaky person, esp. one who betrays or informs upon associates. **b.** A scab laborer. **3.** A pad of material, typically hair, worn as part of a woman's coiffure to puff out her own hair. ❖ *intr.v.* **rat•ted, rat•ting, rats 1.** To hunt for or catch rats, esp. with the aid of dogs. **2.** *Slang* To betray one's associates by giving information. **3.** *Slang* To work as a scab laborer. [ME < OE *ræt.*]

rat•a•ble (rā′tə-bəl) *adj.* **1.** That can be rated, estimated, or appraised: *ratable income.* **2.** Proportional. **3.** *Chiefly British* Liable to assessment; taxable. —**rat′a•bil′i•ty, rat′a•ble•ness** *n.* —**rat′a•bly** *adv.*

rat•a•bles (rā′tə-bəlz) *pl.n.* **1.** Income from property taxes. **2.** Properties or buildings, esp. those used for commercial purposes, that provide tax income for local government.

rat•a•fi•a (răt′ə-fē′ə) also **rat•a•fee** (-ə-fē′) *n.* **1.** A sweet cordial flavored with fruit kernels or almonds. **2.** A biscuit flavored with ratafia. [Fr., perh. of West Indian Creole orig.]

Ra•tak Chain (rä′täk′) The E group of the Marshall Is. in the W Pacific Ocean.

rat•a•plan (răt′ə-plăn′) *n.* A tattoo, as of a drum, the hooves of a galloping horse, or gun fire. [Fr., of imit. orig.]

rat-a-tat-tat (răt′ə-tăt′tăt′) *n.* A series of short sharp sounds, as that made by knocking on a door. [Imit.]

ra•ta•touille (răt′ə-to͞o′ē, rä′tä-) *n.* A vegetable stew, usu. made of eggplant, zucchini, tomatoes, peppers, and onions. [Fr. < alteration of *toillier, touiller*, to stir, mix. See TOIL[1].]

rat-bite fever (răt′bīt′) *n.* Either of two infectious diseases contractible from a rat bite, caused by the bacterium *Streptobacillus moniliformis* or *Spirillum minus* and marked by skin inflammation, back and joint pains, and fever.

rat cheese *n.* Cheddar.

ratch•et (răch′ĭt) *n.* **1.** A mechanism consisting of a pawl that engages the sloping teeth of a wheel or bar, permitting motion in one direction only. **2.** The pawl, wheel, or bar of this mechanism. ❖ *tr. & intr.v.* **-et•ed, -et•ing, -ets** To increase or decrease by increments. Often used with *up, upward, down,* or *downward.* [Fr. *rochet* < OFr. *rocquet*, head of a lance (< the shape of the teeth), of Gmc. orig.]

rate[1] (rāt) *n.* **1.** A quantity measured with respect to another measured quantity: *a rate of speed of 60 miles an hour.* **2.** A measure of a part with respect to a whole; a proportion: *a tax rate.* **3.** The cost per unit of a commodity or service: *postal rates.* **4.** A charge or payment calculated in relation to a particular sum or quantity: *interest rates.* **5.** Level of quality. **6.** *Chiefly British* A locally assessed property tax. Often used in the plural. ❖ *v.* **rat•ed, rat•ing, rates** —*tr.* **1.** To calculate the value of; appraise. See Syns at **estimate. 2.** To place in a particular rank or grade. **3.** To regard or account: *rated the movie excellent.* **4.** To value for purposes of taxation. **5.** To set a rate for (goods to be shipped). **6.** To specify the performance limits of. **7.** *Informal* To merit or deserve. See Syns at **earn[1].** —*intr.* **1.** To be ranked in a particular class. **2.** *Informal* To have status, importance, or influence. —***idiom:* at any rate 1.** Whatever the case may be. **2.** At least. [ME < OFr. < Med.Lat. *rata*, proportion, short for Lat. *(prō) ratā (parte)*, (according to a) fixed (part) < fem. ablative p. part. of *rērī*, to consider, reckon.]

rate[2] (rāt) *v.* **rat•ed, rat•ing, rates** —*tr.* To berate. —*intr.* To express reproof. [ME *raten*, perh. of Scand. orig.]

ra•tel (rāt′l, rät′l) *n.* A carnivorous mammal *(Mellivora capensis)* of Africa and Asia having short legs and a thick coat that is dark below and whitish above. [Afr. < MDu., rattle, honeycomb (either < its cry or its taste for honey).]

rate•mak•ing (rāt′mā′kĭng) *n.* The practice of establishing rates of payment, as for public transportation or utilities.

rate of exchange *n., pl.* **rates of exchange** The ratio at which the unit of currency of one country is or may be exchanged for the unit of currency of another country.

rate•pay•er (rāt′pā′ər) *n.* One that pays rates.

rat•er (rā′tər) *n.* **1.** One that rates, esp. one that sets a rating. **2.** One with an indicated rating. Often used in combination: *a first-rater.*

rat•fink (răt′fĭngk′) *n. Slang* **1.** A contemptible, obnoxious, or otherwise undesirable person. **2.** An informer.

rat•fish (răt′fĭsh′) *n., pl.* **ratfish** or **-fish•es** A fish *(Hydrolagus collei)* of Pacific waters having a long narrow tail.

rathe (rāth, răth) *adj. Archaic* Appearing or ripening early in the year, as flowers or fruit. [ME, quick < OE *hræd, hræth.*]

rath•er (răth′ər, rä′thər) *adv.* **1.** More readily; preferably: *I'd rather go home.* **2.** With more reason or other justification. **3.** More exactly; more accurately: *He's my friend, or rather he was.* **4.** To a certain extent; somewhat: *rather cold.* **5.** On the contrary. **6.** (răˈthûr′, rä′-) *Chiefly British* Most certainly. Used as an emphatic affirmative reply. [ME < OE *hrathor*, comp. of *hræthe*, quickly, soon < *hræth*, quick.]

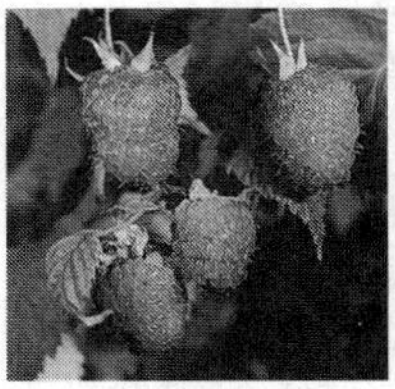

raspberry
cluster of raspberries

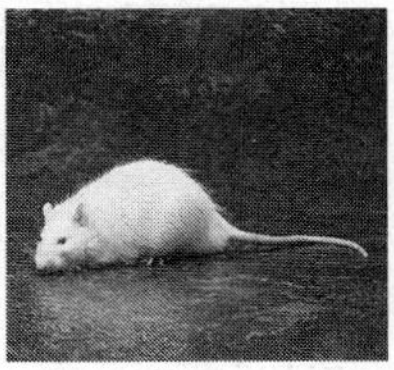

rat
albino Norway rat
Rattus norvegicus

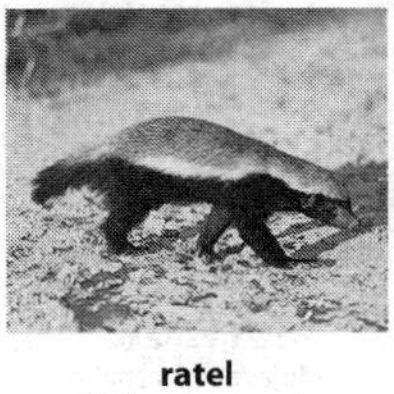

ratel
Mellivora capensis

ă	pat	oi	boy
ā	pay	ou	out
âr	care	o͝o	took
ä	father	o͞o	boot
ĕ	pet	ŭ	cut
ē	be	ûr	urge
ĭ	pit	th	thin
ī	pie	*th*	this
îr	pier	hw	which
ŏ	pot	zh	vision
ō	toe	ə	about, item
ô	paw		

Stress marks:
′ (primary);
′ (secondary), as in
lexicon (lĕk′sĭ-kŏn′)

rather than *conj.* And not: *The cheap book's binding was glued rather than sewn.* ❖ *prep.* Instead of: *Rather than idling about, you should find work.*

raths·kel·ler (răt′skĕl′ər, răth′-, răth′-) *n.* A restaurant or tavern, usu. below street level, that serves beer. [Ger. *Ratskeller, Rathskeller,* city hall basement restaurant : Ger. *Rat,* council (< MHGer. *rāt* < OHGer.; see **ar-** in App.) + Ger. *Keller,* cellar (< MHGer. < OHGer. *kellāri* < Lat. *cellārium;* see CELLAR).]

rat·i·fy (răt′ə-fī′) *tr.v.* **-fied, -fy·ing, -fies** To approve and give formal sanction to; confirm. See Syns at **approve.** [ME *ratifien* < OFr. *ratifier* < Med.Lat. *ratificāre* : Lat. *ratus,* fixed, p. part. of *rērī,* to reckon, consider + Lat. *-ficāre,* -fy.] —**rat′i·fi·ca′tion** (-fĭ-kā′shən) *n.* —**rat′i·fi′er** *n.*

rat·i·né (răt′ə-nā′) *n.* A loosely woven fabric with a rough nubby texture. [Fr., p. part. of *ratiner,* to adorn < *ratine,* ratteen. See RATTEEN.]

rat·ing[1] (rā′tĭng) *n.* **1.** A position assigned on a scale; a standing. **2a.** A classification according to specialty or proficiency, as of a member of the armed forces. **b.** *Chiefly British* An enlisted person in the navy. **3.** An evaluation of the financial status of a business or person: *a credit rating.* **4.** A specified performance limit, as of capacity, range, or operational capability: *the power rating of a light fixture.* **5.** The popularity of a television or radio program as estimated by a poll.

rat·ing[2] (rā′tĭng) *n.* A harsh scolding.

ra·tio (rā′shō, rā′shē-ō′) *n., pl.* **-tios 1.** Relation in degree or number between two similar things. **2.** The relative value of silver and gold in a bimetallic currency. **3.** *Mathematics* The relation between two quantities expressed as the quotient of one divided by the other. [Lat. *ratiō,* calculation < *ratus,* p. part. of *rērī,* to reckon, consider.]

ra·ti·oc·i·nate (răsh′ē-ŏs′ə-nāt′) *intr.v.* **-nat·ed, -nat·ing, -nates** To reason methodically and logically. [Lat. *ratiōcinārī, ratiōcināt-* < *ratiō,* calculation. See RATIO.] —**ra′ti·oc′i·na′tion** *n.* —**ra′ti·oc′i·na′tor** *n.*

ra·ti·oc·i·na·tive (răsh′ē-ŏs′ə-nā′tĭv) *adj.* Of, relating to, marked by, or skilled in methodical and logical reasoning.

ra·tion (răsh′ən, rā′shən) *n.* **1.** A fixed portion, esp. of food. **2. rations** Food issued or available to members of a group. ❖ *tr.v.* **-tioned, -tion·ing, -tions 1.** To supply with rations. **2.** To distribute as rations: *rationed out flour.* See Syns at **distribute. 3.** To restrict to limited allotments, as during wartime. [Fr. < Lat. *ratiō, ratiōn-,* calculation. See RATIO.]

ra·tion·al (răsh′ə-nəl) *adj.* **1.** Having or exercising the ability to reason. **2.** Of sound mind; sane. **3.** Consistent with or based on reason; logical. **4.** *Mathematics* Capable of being expressed as a quotient of integers. ❖ *n. Mathematics* A rational number. [ME *racional* < Lat. *ratiōnālis* < *ratiō, ratiōn-,* reason. See REASON.] —**ra′tion·al·ly** *adv.* —**ra′tion·al·ness** *n.*

ra·tion·ale (răsh′ə-năl′) *n.* **1.** Fundamental reasons; the basis. **2.** An exposition of principles or reasons. [LLat. *ratiōnāle* < neut. of Lat. *ratiōnālis,* rational. See RATIONAL.]

rational function *n.* A function that can be expressed as a quotient of polynomials, excluding division by zero.

rational horizon *n.* See **celestial horizon.**

ra·tion·al·ism (răsh′ə-nə-lĭz′əm) *n.* **1.** Reliance on reason as the best guide for belief and action. **2.** *Philosophy* The theory that the exercise of reason, rather than experience, authority, or spiritual revelation, provides the primary basis for knowledge. —**ra′tion·al·ist** *n.* —**ra′tion·al·is′tic** *adj.* —**ra′tion·al·is′ti·cal·ly** *adv.*

ra·tion·al·i·ty (răsh′ə-năl′ĭ-tē) *n., pl.* **-ties 1.** The quality or condition of being rational. **2.** A rational belief or practice.

ra·tion·al·i·za·tion (răsh′ə-nə-lĭ-zā′shən) *n.* **1.** The act, process, or practice of rationalizing. **2.** An instance of rationalizing.

ra·tion·al·ize (răsh′ə-nə-līz′) *v.* **-ized, -iz·ing, -iz·es** —*tr.* **1.** To make rational. **2.** To interpret rationally. **3.** To devise self-satisfying but incorrect reasons for (one's behavior). **4.** *Mathematics* To remove radicals, such as from a denominator, without changing the value of (an expression) or roots of (an equation). **5.** *Chiefly British* To bring modern, efficient methods to (an industry, for example). —*intr.* **1.** To think rationally or rationalistically. **2.** To devise self-satisfying but incorrect reasons for one's behavior. —**ra′tion·al·iz′er** *n.*

rational number *n.* A number capable of being expressed as an integer or a quotient of integers, excluding zero as a denominator.

Rat Islands A group of islands in the W Aleutian Is. of SW AK.

rattlesnake
Mojave rattlesnake
Crotalus scutulatus scutulatus

rat·ite (răt′īt′) *adj.* Relating to or being any of a group of flightless birds having a flat breastbone with no keellike prominence. ❖ *n.* A ratite bird, such as the emu. [< Lat. *ratītus,* marked with the figure of a raft < *ratis,* raft.]

rat·line also **rat·lin** (răt′lĭn) *n.* **1.** Any of the small ropes fastened horizontally to the shrouds of a ship and forming a ladder for going aloft. **2.** The material used for these ropes. [ME *ratheline (line),* wattling, ratline (cord).]

ra·toon also **rat·toon** (ră-tōōn′) *n.* A shoot sprouting from a plant base, as in the banana. ❖ *v.* **-tooned, -toon·ing, -toons** —*intr.* To produce or grow as a ratoon. —*tr.* To propagate (a crop) from ratoons. [Sp. *retoño,* sprout < *retoñar,* to sprout : *re-,* again (< Lat.; see RE–) + *otoñar,* to grow in autumn (< *otoño,* autumn < Lat. *autumnus;* see AUTUMN).]

rat race *n. Informal* A difficult, tiring, often competitive activity or routine.

rats·bane (răts′bān′) *n.* **1.** Rat poison. **2.** Arsenic trioxide.

rat snake *n.* Any of several nonvenomous snakes of the genus *Elaphe* that eat rats and other rodents.

rat's nest (răts) *n. Informal* A place of great clutter or disorder.

rat-tail (răt′tāl′) *n.* See **grenadier** 2. ❖ *adj.* also **rat·tailed** (-tāld′) or **rat·tail** (răt′tāl′) Shaped like or having a part shaped like a rat's tail: *a rat-tail file.*

rattail cactus or **rat's tail cactus** *n.* A Mexican cactus (*Aporocactus flagelliformis*) having thin creeping or hanging stems and brilliant crimson-pink flowers.

rat·tan (ră-tăn′, rə-) *n.* **1.** Any of various climbing palms of the genera *Calamus, Daemonorops,* or *Plectomia* of tropical Asia, having long tough slender stems. **2a.** The stems of any of these palms, used in wickerwork, canes, and furniture. **b.** Work made of the stems of these palms. **3.** A switch or cane made from these palms. [Malay *rōtan,* perh. < *raut,* to pare or trim for use.]

rat·teen (ră-tēn′) *n. Archaic* A thick twilled woolen cloth. [Fr. *ratine* < OFr. *rastin* < **raster,* to scrape, ult. < Lat. *rādere.*]

rat·ter (răt′ər) *n.* **1.** One that catches or kills rats: *Is the dog a ratter?* **2.** *Slang* One who betrays or deserts another.

rat·tle[1] (răt′l) *v.* **-tled, -tling, -tles** —*intr.* **1a.** To make or emit a quick succession of short percussive sounds. **b.** To move with such sounds: *A train rattled by.* **2.** To talk rapidly and at length, usu. without much thought: *rattled on.* —*tr.* **1.** To cause to make a quick succession of short percussive sounds: *rattled the dishes.* **2.** To utter or perform rapidly or effortlessly: *rattled off a list of complaints.* **3.** *Informal* To fluster; unnerve. ❖ *n.* **1.** A rapid succession of short percussive sounds. **2.** A device, such as a baby's toy, that produces short percussive sounds. **3.** A rattling sound in the throat caused by obstructed breathing, esp. near the time of death. **4.** The series of horny structures at the end of a rattlesnake's tail. **5.** Loud or rapid talk; chatter. [ME *ratelen,* perh. < MDu., prob. of imit. orig.]

rat·tle[2] (răt′l) *tr.v.* **-tled, -tling, -tles** To secure ratlines to (shrouds). [Back-formation < *rattling,* ratline, var. of RATLINE.]

rat·tle·box (răt′l-bŏks′) *n.* Any of various plants of the genus *Crotalaria,* having inflated pods containing seeds that rattle when the stem is moved.

rat·tle·brained (răt′l-brānd′) *adj.* Giddy and talkative; foolish. —**rat′tle·brain′** (-brān′) *n.*

rat·tler (răt′lər) *n.* **1.** One that rattles: *a rattler of pots and pans.* **2.** *Informal* A rattlesnake. **3.** *Informal* A freight train.

rat·tle·snake (răt′l-snāk′) *n.* Any of various venomous New World snakes of the genera *Crotalus* and *Sistrurus,* having at the end of the tail a series of loosely attached horny segments that can be vibrated to make a rattling or buzzing sound.

rattlesnake plantain *n.* Any of various rhizomatous orchids of the genus *Goodyera,* having mottled or striped leaves and spikes of small whitish flowers.

rattlesnake root *n.* Any of various plants of the genus *Prenanthes,* having bitter tuberous roots and white to purple flowers.

rattlesnake weed *n.* A North American plant (*Hieracium venosum*) having basal leaves with reddish-purple veins and yellow flower heads borne in open corymbose panicles.

rat·tle·trap (răt′l-trăp′) *n.* A rickety worn-out vehicle.

rat·tling (răt′lĭng) *adj. Informal* Animated; brisk: *a rattling conversation.* ❖ *adv.* Used as an intensive: *rattling good.*

rat·tly (răt′l-ē) *adj.* Rattling or likely to rattle; clattering.

rat·toon (ră-tōōn′) *n. & v.* Variant of **ratoon.**

rat·trap (răt′trăp′) *n.* **1.** A device for trapping rats. **2.** *Informal* A dilapidated or unsanitary dwelling.

rat·ty (răt′ē) *adj.* **-ti·er, -ti·est 1.** Of or characteristic of rats. **2.** Infested with rats. **3.** Dilapidated; shabby.

rau·cous (rô′kəs) *adj.* **1.** Rough-sounding and harsh: *heard raucous laughter.* **2.** Boisterous and disorderly. [< Lat. *raucus.*] —**rau′cous·ly** *adv.* —**rau′cous·ness** *n.* —**rau·cos′i·ty** (rô-sī-tē) *n.*

raunch (rônch, ränch) *n. Slang* **1.** Lewdness; vulgarity; obscenity. **2.** Material or a performance that is sexual. [Back-formation < RAUNCHY.]

raun·chy (rôn′chē, rän′-) *adj.* **-chi·er, -chi·est** *Slang* **1a.** Obscene, lewd, or vulgar. **b.** Sexually explicit. **c.** Exhibiting lust. **2.** Grimy; unkempt. [?] —**raun′chi·ly** *adv.* —**raun′chi·ness** *n.*

Rausch·en·berg (rou′shən-bûrg′), **Robert** b. 1925. Amer. artist noted for his paintings that incorporate photographs and real objects.

rau•wol•fi•a (rou-wo͝ol′fē-ə, rô-) *n.* Any of various tropical trees and shrubs of the genus *Rauvolfia,* esp. *R. serpentina* of southeast Asia, the root of which is the source of tranquilizing alkaloid drugs such as reserpine. [Variant of NLat. *Rauvolfia,* genus name, after Leonhard *Rauwolf* (1535–96), German botanist.]

rav•age (răv′ĭj) *v.* **-aged, -ag•ing, -ages** —*tr.* **1.** To bring heavy destruction on; devastate. **2.** To pillage; sack. —*intr.* To wreak destruction. ❖ *n.* **1.** The act or practice of pillaging, destroying, or devastating. **2.** Grievous damage; havoc: *the ravages of disease.* [Fr. *ravager* < OFr., to uproot < *ravir,* to ravish.] —**rav′ag•er** *n.*

rave (rāv) *v.* **raved, rav•ing, raves** —*intr.* **1.** To speak wildly, irrationally, or incoherently. **2.** To roar; rage: *The storm raved along the coast.* **3.** To speak or write with wild enthusiasm. **4.** To attend a rave. —*tr.* To utter in a frenzied manner. ❖ *n.* **1.** The act or an instance of raving. **2.** *Informal* An extravagantly enthusiastic opinion or review. **3.** An all-night dance party, usu. featuring electronically synthesized music. ❖ *adj. Informal* Relating to or being such an opinion or review. [ME *raven* < ONFr. *raver,* var. of *resver,* to dream, wander, rave.]

rav•el (răv′əl) *v.* **-eled, -el•ing, -els** also **-elled, -el•ling, -els** —*tr.* **1.** To separate the fibers or threads of (cloth, for example); unravel. **2.** To clarify by separating the aspects of. **3.** To tangle or complicate. —*intr.* **1.** To become separated into its component threads; unravel or fray. **2.** To become tangled or confused. ❖ *n.* **1.** A raveling. **2.** A broken or discarded thread. **3.** A tangle. [Obsolete Du. *ravelen* < *ravel,* loose thread.] —**rav′el•er, rav′el•ler** *n.*

Ra•vel (rə-vĕl′, rä-), **Maurice Joseph** 1875–1937. French composer whose works include *Boléro* (1928).

rav•el•ing also **rav•el•ling** (răv′ə-lĭng) *n.* A thread or fiber that has become separated from a woven material.

ra•ven[1] (rā′vən) *n.* A large bird *(Corvus corax)* having black plumage and a croaking cry. ❖ *adj.* Black and shiny: *raven tresses.* [ME < OE *hræfn.*]

rav•en[2] (răv′ən) *v.* **-ened, -en•ing, -ens** —*tr.* **1.** To consume greedily; devour. **2.** To seek or seize as prey or plunder. —*intr.* **1.** To seek or seize prey or plunder. **2.** To eat ravenously. [< ME *ravin, raven,* rapine, plunder, prey. See RAVIN.] —**rav′en•er** *n.*

rav•en•ing (răv′ə-nĭng) *adj.* Greedily predacious; voracious or rapacious. —**rav′en•ing•ly** *adv.*

Ra•ven•na (rə-vĕn′ə, rä-vĕn′nä) A city of NE Italy near the Adriatic Sea NE of Florence; center of Byzantine power in Italy from the late 6th cent. until c. 750. Pop. 135,435.

rav•en•ous (răv′ə-nəs) *adj.* **1.** Extremely hungry; voracious. **2.** Rapacious; predatory. **3.** Greedy for gratification. [ME < OFr. *ravineux* < *raviner,* to take by force < VLat. **rapīnāre* < Lat. *rapīna,* plunder. See RAPINE.] —**rav′en•ous•ly** *adv.* —**rav′en•ous•ness** *n.*

Ra•vi (rä′vē) A river, c. 764 km (475 mi), of NW India and NE Pakistan; one of the five rivers of the Punjab.

ra•vi•gote also **ra•vi•gotte** (ră-vē-gôt′) *n.* A vinegar sauce seasoned with onion, capers, and herbs. [Fr. < *ravigoter,* to add new vigor, alteration of obsolete *ravigorer* < OFr. : *re-,* re- + *a-,* to (< Lat. *ad-*; see AD–) + *vigeur,* vigor; see VIGOR.]

rav•in also **rav•en** (răv′ən) *n.* **1.** Voracity; rapaciousness. **2.** Something taken as prey. **3.** The act or practice of preying. [ME *ravin, raven* < OFr. *ravine,* rapine < Lat. *rapīna* < *rapere,* to seize.]

ra•vine (rə-vēn′) *n.* A deep narrow valley or gorge in the earth's surface worn by running water. [Fr. < OFr., violent rush < Lat. *rapīna,* rapine. See RAVIN.]

rav•ing (rā′vĭng) *adj.* **1.** Talking or behaving irrationally; wild: *a raving maniac.* **2.** Exciting admiration: *a raving beauty.* ❖ *n.* Delirious, irrational speech. —**rav′ing•ly** *adv.*

rav•i•o•li (răv′ē-ō′lē) *n., pl.* **ravioli** or **-lis 1.** A small casing of pasta with any of various fillings, such as chopped meat or cheese. **2.** A dish made with ravioli. [Ital., pl. of *raviolo,* perh. < dialectal *rava,* turnip < Lat. *rāpa,* pl. of *rāpum.*]

rav•ish (răv′ĭsh) *tr.v.* **-ished, -ish•ing, -ish•es 1.** To seize and carry off by force. **2.** To rape; violate. **3.** To overwhelm with emotion; enrapture. [ME *ravisshen* < OFr. *ravir, raviss-,* ult. < Lat. *rapere,* to seize.] —**rav′ish•er** *n.*

rav•ish•ing (răv′ĭ-shĭng) *adj.* Extremely attractive; entrancing. —**rav′ish•ing•ly** *adv.*

rav•ish•ment (răv′ĭsh-mənt) *n.* **1.** The act of seizing by force. **2.** Sexual rape. **3.** Rapture; entrancement.

raw (rô) *adj.* **raw•er, raw•est 1.** Uncooked: *raw meat.* **2a.** Being in a natural condition; not processed or refined: *raw wool.* **b.** Not finished, covered, or coated: *raw wood.* **c.** Not having been adjusted, treated, or analyzed: *raw data.* **3.** Untrained and inexperienced: *raw recruits.* **4.** Recently finished; fresh: *raw plaster.* **5.** Having subcutaneous tissue exposed: *a raw wound.* **6.** Inflamed; sore: *a raw throat.* **7.** Unpleasantly damp and chilly: *raw weather.* **8.** Cruel and unfair: *a raw punishment.* **9.** Outspoken; crude: *a raw portrayal of truth.* **10.** Powerfully impressive; stark: *raw talent.* **11.** Nude; naked. ***—idiom:* in the raw 1.** In a crude or unrefined state. **2.** Nude; naked. [ME < OE *hrēaw.* See **kreuə-** in App.] —**raw′ly** *adv.* —**raw′ness** *n.*

Ra•wal•pin•di (rä′wəl-pĭn′dē) A city of NE Pakistan NNW of Lahore; settled by Sikhs in 1765. Pop. 794,843.

raw bar *n.* A bar or counter at which raw shellfish is served.

raw•boned (rô′bōnd′) *adj.* Having a lean gaunt frame with prominent bones. See Syns at **lean**[2].

raw•hide (rô′hīd′) *n.* **1.** The untanned hide of cattle or other animals. **2.** A whip or rope made of rawhide. ❖ *tr.v.* **-hid•ed, -hid•ing, -hides** To beat with a rawhide whip.

ra•win•sonde (rā′wĭn-sŏnd′) *n.* A radiosonde used to observe the velocity and direction of upper-air winds and tracked by a radio direction-finding instrument or radar. [RA(DAR) + WIN(D)[1] + (RADIO)SONDE.]

Raw•lings (rô′lĭngz), **Marjorie Kinnan** 1896–1953. Amer. writer best known for her novel *The Yearling* (1938).

raw material *n.* **1.** An unprocessed natural product used in manufacture. **2.** Unprocessed material of any kind.

raw sienna *n.* **1.** A brownish-yellow pigment. **2.** A brownish orange to light brown.

raw silk *n.* **1.** Untreated silk as reeled from a cocoon. **2.** Fabric or yarn made from untreated silk.

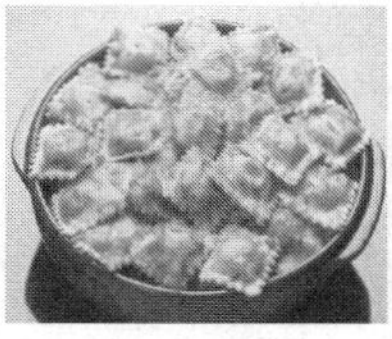

ravioli

ray[1] (rā) *n.* **1a.** A thin line or narrow beam of light or other radiant energy. **b.** A graphic or other representation of such a line. **2.** Radiance; light. **3.** A small amount; a trace: *a ray of hope.* **4.** *Mathematics* A straight line extending from a point. **5.** A structure or part with the form of such a straight line. **6.** Any of the bright streaks that are seen radiating from some craters on the moon. **7.** *Botany* **a.** A ray flower or the corolla of a ray flower. **b.** A branch of an umbel. **8.** *Zoology* **a.** One of the bony spines supporting the membrane of a fish's fin. **b.** One of the arms of a starfish or other radiate animal. **9. rays** *Slang* Sunshine. ❖ *tr.v.* **rayed, ray•ing, rays 1.** To send out as rays; emit. **2.** To supply with rays or radiating lines. **3.** To cast rays on; irradiate. [ME < OFr. *rai* < Lat. *radius.*]

ray[2] (rā) *n.* Any of various marine fishes of the order Rajiformes or Batoidei, having cartilaginous skeletons, horizontally flattened bodies, and narrow tails. [ME *raye* < OFr. *raie* < Lat. *raia.*]

Ray, John 1627–1705. English naturalist who introduced "species" as the basic classification of living things.

Ray, Man 1890–1976. Amer. artist best known for his photographs and later experiments with surrealism.

Ray (rī), **Satyajit** 1921–92. Bengali filmmaker whose works include *The World of Apu* (1958).

ray-finned fish (rā′fĭnd′) *n.* Any of various bony fishes belonging to the subclass Actinopterygii, having fins supported by dermal rays.

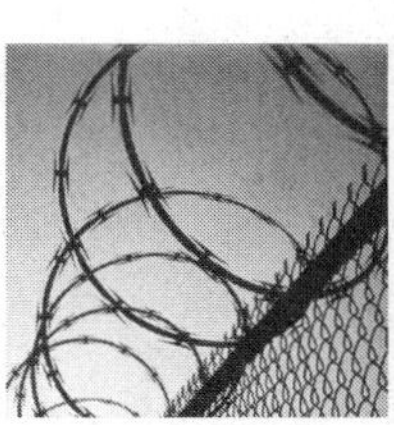

razor wire

ray flower (rā) *n.* A flattened flower found in members of the composite family, as the units of a flower head of the dandelion.

Ray•leigh (rā′lē), 3rd Baron. Title of John William Strutt. 1842–1919. British physicist who won a 1904 Nobel Prize.

Rayleigh scattering *n.* The scattering of electromagnetic radiation by particles with dimensions much smaller than the wavelength of the radiation, resulting in angular separation of colors and responsible for the reddish color of sunset and the blue of the sky. [After 3rd Baron RAYLEIGH.]

ray•less (rā′lĭs) *adj.* **1.** Lacking rays. **2.** Lacking light.

Ray•naud's disease (rā-nōz′) *n.* A circulatory disorder caused by insufficient blood supply to the hands and feet and resulting in cyanosis, numbness, and pain. [After Maurice *Raynaud* (1834–81), French physician.]

ray•on (rā′ŏn) *n.* **1.** Any of several synthetic textile fibers produced by forcing a cellulose solution through fine spinnerets and solidifying the resulting filaments. **2.** A fabric so woven or knit. [Perh. < Fr. *rayon,* ray of light (< its sheen) < *rai* < OFr. See RAY[1].]

raze also **rase** (rāz) *tr.v.* **razed, raz•ing, raz•es** also **rased, ras•ing, ras•es 1.** To level to the ground; demolish. See Syns at **ruin. 2.** To scrape or shave off. **3.** *Archaic* To erase. [ME *rasen,* to scrape off < OFr. *raser* < VLat. **rāsāre,* freq. of Lat. *rādere.*]

ra•zor (rā′zər) *n.* **1.** A sharp-edged cutting instrument used esp. for shaving the face or other body parts. **2.** A device for holding a razorblade, with guards to prevent cutting of the skin. **3.** An electric instrument with vibrating or rotating blades used for shaving. ❖ *tr.v.* **-zored, -zor•ing, -zors** To shave, cut, or remove with or as with a razor. [ME *rasor* < OFr. < *raser,* to scrape. See RAZE.]

ra•zor•back (rā′zər-băk′) *n.* **1.** A semiwild hog of the southeast United States having a narrow body with a ridged back. **2.** See **rorqual. 3.** A sharp ridged hill.

ra•zor•bill (rā′zər-bĭl′) *n.* A razor-billed auk.

ra•zor-billed auk (rā′zər-bĭld′) *n.* A sea bird *(Alca torda)* of the northern Atlantic Ocean having black-and-white plumage and a white-ringed flattened bill.

ra•zor•blade also **razor blade** (rā′zər-blād′) *n.* A thin sharp-edged piece of steel that can be fitted into a razor.

razor bump *n.* A small swelling that develops when the sharpened point of a razor-cut hair shaft grows back into the skin, sometimes resulting in inflammation and infection.

razor clam *n.* Any of various clams of the family Solenidae, characteristically having long narrow shells.

razor wire *n.* A sharp-edged wire used for fences and barriers.

razz (răz) *Slang n.* A raspberry sound; a Bronx cheer. ❖ *tr.v.* **razzed, razz•ing, razz•es** To deride, heckle, or tease. [Shortening and alteration of RASPBERRY.]

raz•zle-daz•zle (răz′əl-dăz′əl) *n. Informal* **1.** Dazzling excitement. **2.** Extravagant or showy display, as of technique. [Reduplication of DAZZLE.]

ă	pat	oi	boy
ā	pay	ou	out
âr	care	o͝o	took
ä	father	o͞o	boot
ĕ	pet	ŭ	cut
ē	be	ûr	urge
ĭ	pit	th	thin
ī	pie	*th*	this
îr	pier	hw	which
ŏ	pot	zh	vision
ō	toe	ə	about, item
ô	paw		

Stress marks:
′ (primary);
′ (secondary), as in
lexicon (lĕk′sĭ-kŏn′)

razz·ma·tazz (răz′mə-tăz′) *n. Slang* **1.** A flashy action or display intended to bewilder, confuse, or deceive. **2.** Ambiguous or evasive language; double talk. **3.** Ebullient energy; vim. [Perh. alteration of RAZZLE-DAZZLE.]

Rb The symbol for the element **rubidium**.

RBC *abbr.* **1.** red blood cell **2.** red blood cell count

RBI *abbr. Baseball* runs batted in

RC *abbr.* **1.** Red Cross **2.** Roman Catholic

RCAF *abbr.* Royal Canadian Air Force

RCC *abbr.* Roman Catholic Church

RCMP *abbr.* Royal Canadian Mounted Police

RCP *abbr.* Royal College of Physicians

rcpt. *abbr.* receipt

RCS *abbr.* Royal College of Surgeons

rct. *abbr.* recruit

rd *abbr.* **1.** rod (unit of measure) **2.** rutherford

RD *abbr.* rural delivery

Rd. *abbr.* road

RDA *abbr.* recommended daily allowance

RDML *abbr.* rear admiral (lower half)

re[1] (rā) *n. Music* The second tone of the diatonic scale in solfeggio. [ME < Med.Lat. See GAMUT.]

re[2] (rē) *prep.* In reference to; in the case of; concerning. [Lat. *rē*, ablative of *rēs*, thing.]

Re[1] (rā) *n. Mythology* Variant of **Ra**[1].

Re[2] The symbol for the element **rhenium**.

RE *abbr.* real estate

re– *pref.* **1.** Again; anew: *rebuild*. **2.** Backward; back: *react*. **3.** Used as an intensive: *refine*. [ME < OFr. < Lat.]

're Contraction of *are: They're not at home.*

re·ab·sorb (rē′əb-sôrb′, -zôrb′) *v.* **-sorbed, -sorb·ing, -sorbs** —*tr.* **1.** To absorb again. **2.** To accommodate or accept again, as into a group or category. —*intr.* To undergo resorption. —**re′ab·sorp′tion** (-sôrp′shən, -zôrp′-) *n.*

re·ac·cred·i·ta·tion (rē′ə-krĕd′ĭ-tā′shən) *n.* **1.** The process of reviewing the accreditation of an institution. **2.** Renewal of accreditation status.

reach (rēch) *v.* **reached, reach·ing, reach·es** —*tr.* **1.** To stretch out or put forth (a body part); extend: *reached out an arm.* **2.** To touch or grasp by stretching out or extending: *can't reach the shelf.* **3.** To arrive at; attain: *reached a conclusion; reached their destination.* **4a.** To succeed in getting in contact with or communicating with: *reached her by phone.* **b.** To succeed in having an effect on. **5a.** To extend as far as: *The property reaches the shore.* **b.** To project as far as: *A cry reached our ears.* **c.** To travel as far as. **6.** To aggregate or amount to: *Sales reached the millions.* **7.** *Informal* To grasp and hand over to another: *Reach me the sugar.* —*intr.* **1.** To thrust out or extend something. **2.** To try to grasp or touch something: *reached for a book.* **3a.** To have extension in space or time. **b.** To be extensive in influence or effect. **4.** To make an excessive effort, as in drawing a conclusion or making a joke; overreach. **5.** *Nautical* To sail a course between close-hauled and dead downwind. ❖ *n.* **1.** The act or an instance of stretching or thrusting out. **2.** The extent or distance something can reach. **3a.** Range of understanding; comprehension. **b.** Range or scope of influence or effect. **4.** An expanse: *a reach of prairie.* **5.** A pole connecting the rear axle of a vehicle with the front. **6.** *Nautical* Any course of a sailing vessel between close-hauled and dead downwind. **7.** The stretch of water visible between bends in a river or channel. [ME *rechen* < OE *rǣcan*.] —**reach′a·ble** *adj.* —**reach′er** *n.*

SYNONYMS *reach, achieve, attain, gain, compass* These verbs mean to succeed in arriving at a goal or objective. *Reach* is the least specific: *reach an understanding. Achieve* suggests the application of skill or initiative: *achieved recognition. Attain* often implies the impelling force of ambition, principle, or ideals: *trying to attain self-confidence. Gain* connotes considerable effort in surmounting obstacles: *gained the workers' trust. Compass* implies succeeding by circumventing impediments: *will compass the task.*

re·act (rē-ăkt′) *intr.v.* **-act·ed, -act·ing, -acts** **1.** To act in response to or under the influence of a stimulus or prompting: *reacted strongly to my sarcasm.* **2.** To act in opposition to a former condition or act: *reacted against romanticism.* **3.** To act reciprocally or in return. **4.** *Chemistry* To undergo a reaction.

re·ac·tance (rē-ăk′təns) *n. Symbol* X *Electricity* Opposition to the flow of alternating current caused by the inductance and capacitance in a circuit rather than by resistance.

re·ac·tant (rē-ăk′tənt) *n.* A substance participating in a chemical reaction, esp. a directly reacting substance present at the initiation of the reaction.

re·ac·tion (rē-ăk′shən) *n.* **1a.** A response to a stimulus. **b.** The state resulting from such a response. **2.** A reverse or opposing action. **3a.** A tendency to revert to a former state. **b.** Opposition to progress or liberalism; extreme conservatism. **4.** *Chemistry* A change or transformation in which a substance decomposes, combines with other substances, or interchanges constituents with other substances. **5.** *Physics* A nuclear reaction. **6.** *Physics* An equal and opposite force exerted by a body against a force acting upon it. **7.** The response of cells or tissues to an antigen.

re·ac·tion·ar·y (rē-ăk′shə-nĕr′ē) *adj.* Characterized by political reaction, esp. opposition to progress or liberalism; extremely conservative. —**re·ac′tion·ar′y** *n.*

reaction engine *n.* An engine that develops thrust by the focused expulsion of matter, esp. ignited fuel gases.

reaction formation *n. Psychology* A defense mechanism in which the opposite of an objectionable impulse is expressed.

re·ac·ti·vate (rē-ăk′tə-vāt′) *tr.v.* **-vat·ed, -vat·ing, -vates** **1.** To make active again. **2.** To restore the ability to function or the effectiveness of. —**re·ac′ti·va′tion** *n.*

re·ac·tive (rē-ăk′tĭv) *adj.* **1.** Tending to be responsive or to react to a stimulus. **2.** Characterized by reaction. **3.** *Chemistry & Physics* Tending to participate readily in reactions. —**re·ac′tive·ly** *adv.* —**re·ac′tive·ness, re′ac·tiv′i·ty** *n.*

re·ac·tor (rē-ăk′tər) *n.* **1.** One that reacts to a stimulus. **2.** *Electronics* A circuit element, such as a coil, used to introduce reactance. **3.** *Physics* A nuclear reactor.

reactor core *n.* The central part of a nuclear reactor where atomic fission occurs.

read (rēd) *v.* **read** (rĕd), **read·ing, reads** —*tr.* **1.** To examine and grasp the meaning of (written or printed characters, words, or sentences). **2.** To utter or render aloud (written or printed material): *read poems to the students.* **3.** To have the ability to examine and grasp the meaning of (written or printed material in a given language or notation): *reads Chinese.* **4a.** To examine and grasp the meaning of (language not in writing): *reading sign language.* **b.** To examine and grasp the meaning of (a graphic representation): *reading a map.* **5a.** To discern and interpret the nature or significance of through close examination or sensitive observation: *read the trail for signs of deer.* **b.** To discern or anticipate through examination or observation; descry. **6.** To determine the intent or mood of: *I can read your mind.* **7a.** To attribute a certain interpretation or meaning to: *read my words differently.* **b.** To consider (something written or printed) as having a particular meaning or significance. **8.** To foretell or predict (the future). **9.** To receive or comprehend (a radio message, for example). **10.** To study or make a study of. **11.** To learn or get knowledge of from something written or printed. **12.** To proofread. **13.** To have or use as a preferred reading in a particular passage: *For* change *read* charge. **14.** To indicate, register, or show: *The dial reads 32°.* **15.** *Computer Science* To obtain (information) from a storage medium. —*intr.* **1.** To examine and grasp the meaning of printed or written characters, as of words or music. **2.** To speak aloud the words that one is reading: *read to the children every night.* **3.** To learn by reading: *read about the storm in the paper.* **4.** To study. **5.** To have a particular wording: *Recite the poem exactly as it reads.* **6.** To contain a specific meaning. **7.** To indicate, register, or show a measurement or figure. **8.** To have a specified character or quality for the reader: *Your poems read well.* ❖ *n. Informal* Something that is read: *a good read.* ❖ *adj.* (rĕd) Informed by reading; learned. —*phrasal verbs:* **read out** To read aloud. **read up** To study or learn by reading. —*idioms:* **read a lecture** (or **lesson**) To issue a reprimand. **read between the lines** To perceive or detect an obscure or unexpressed meaning. **read out of** To expel by proclamation from a social, political, or other group. [ME *reden* < OE *rǣdan*, to advise.]

read·a·ble (rē′də-bəl) *adj.* **1.** Easily read; legible. **2.** Pleasurable or interesting to read: *a readable story.* —**read′a·bil′i·ty, read′a·ble·ness** *n.* —**read′a·bly** *adv.*

read·er (rē′dər) *n.* **1.** One that reads. **2.** One who publicly recites literary works. **3a.** One who reads and evaluates manuscripts for a publisher. **b.** A proofreader. **4.** A teaching assistant who grades examination papers. **5.** *Chiefly British* A university teacher, esp. one ranking next below a professor. **6a.** A textbook of reading exercises. **b.** An anthology, esp. of literature. **7.** A layperson or minor cleric who reads lessons or prayers in church services.

re·cal′cu·late′ *tr.v.*	**re·for′est** *tr.v.*	**re·in′vog′o·ra′tion** *n.*	**re·trac′er** *n.*
re·cal′cu·la′tion *n.*	**re·for′es·ta′tion** *n.*	**re·in′vig′o·ra′tor** *n.*	**re·train′** *tr. & intr.v.*
re′com·pose′ *tr.v.*	**re·house′** *tr.v.*	**re·num′ber** *tr.v.*	**re·train′a·ble** *adj.*
re′com·po·si′tion *n.*	**re·in′te·grate′** *tr.v.*	**re·pack′age** *tr.v.*	**re·train′ee′** *n.*
re′con·fig′ure *tr.v.*	**re·in′te·gra′tion** *n.*	**re·pack′ag·er** *n.*	**re·us′a·bil′i·ty** *n.*
re′con·firm′ *tr.v.*	**re·in′te·gra′tive** *adj.*	**re·stock′** *tr.v.*	**re·us′a·ble** *adj. & n.*
re′con·fir·ma′tion *n.*	**re·in′ter·pret** *tr.v.*	**re′sup·ply′** *tr.v. & n.*	**re·use′** *tr. & n.*
re′con·sid′er *tr. & intr.v.*	**re·in′ter·pre·ta′tion** *n.*	**re·test′** *tr.v.*	**re·val′i·date′** *tr.v.*
re′con·sid′er·a′tion *n.*	**re·in′vest′** *tr.v.*	**re·trace′** *tr.v.*	**re·val′i·da′tion** *n.*
re′dis·trib′ute *tr.v.*	**re·in′vest′ment** *n.*	**re·trace′able** *adj.*	**re·wak′en** *tr. & intr.v.*
re′dis′trict *tr.v.*	**re·in′vig′o·rate′** *tr.v.*	**re·trace′ment** *n.*	

read•er•ship (rē′dər-shĭp′) *n.* **1.** The readers of a publication considered as a group. **2.** *Chiefly British* The office of a reader at a university.

read•i•ly (rĕd′ə-lē, rĕd′l-ē) *adv.* **1.** In a prompt manner. **2.** In a cooperative manner; willingly. **3.** In a manner indicating or connoting ease; easily.

read•ing (rē′dĭng) *n.* **1.** The act or activity of one that reads. **2.** The act or practice of rendering texts aloud. **3.** An official or public recitation of written material: *the reading of a will.* **4a.** The specific form of a particular passage in a text. **b.** The distinctive interpretation of a work of performing art given by the person or persons performing it. **5.** A personal interpretation or appraisal. **6.** Written or printed material. **7.** The information given by a gauge or graduated instrument.

Read•ing (rĕd′ĭng) **1.** A borough of S-central England W of London; chartered 1253. Pop. 137,749. **2.** A city of SE PA NW of Philadelphia; settled in 1748. Pop. 81,207.

read•ing desk (rē′dĭng) *n.* A desk or stand, usu. with a slanted top, for holding a book or papers for a standing reader.

re•ad•just (rē′ə-jŭst′) *tr.v.* **-just•ed, -just•ing, -justs** To adjust again. **—re′ad•just′er** *n.* **—re′ad•just′ment** *n.*

read-on•ly memory (rēd′ōn′lē) *n.* See **ROM.**

read•out or **read-out** (rēd′out′) *n. Computer Science* Presentation of data, usu. in digital form, from calculations or storage.

read•y (rĕd′ē) *adj.* **-i•er, -i•est 1.** Prepared or available for service, action, or progress: *The soup will be ready in a minute.* **2.** Mentally disposed; willing: *He was ready to believe her.* **3.** Likely or about to do something: *She is ready to retire.* **4.** Prompt in apprehending or reacting: *a ready response.* **5.** Available: *ready money.* ❖ *tr.v.* **read•ied, read•y•ing, read•ies** To cause to be ready. ***—idioms:* at the ready** Available for immediate use. **make ready** To make preparations. [ME *redy* < OE *rǣde.*] **—read′i•ness** *n.*

read•y-made or **read•y•made** (rĕd′ē-mād′) *adj.* **1.** Already made, prepared, or available. **2.** Handy or expedient, esp. because of familiarity or preplanning.

read•y-mix (rĕd′ē-mĭks′) *n.* A mixture in proper proportions of two or more ingredients, as of a food, marketed for convenience; a premix. **—read′y-mix′, read′y-mixed′** *adj.*

read•y-to-wear (rĕd′ē-tə-wâr′) *adj.* **1.** Marketed in a finished condition in standard sizes. Used of clothing. **2.** Of, relating to, or doing business in ready-to-wear clothing. ❖ *n.* Clothing marketed in a finished condition in standard sizes.

re•af•firm (rē′ə-fûrm′) *tr.v.* **-firmed, -firm•ing, -firms** To affirm or assert again. **—re′af•fir•ma′tion** (rē′ăf-ər-mā′shən) *n.*

Rea•gan (rā′gən), **Nancy Davis** b. 1921. First Lady of the US (1981–89) who established a nationwide antidrug campaign.

Reagan, Ronald Wilson b. 1911. The 40th President of the US (1981–89) whose administration was marked by improved relations with the Soviet Union.

re•a•gent (rē-ā′jənt) *n.* A substance used in a chemical reaction to detect, analyze, or produce other substances.

re•a•gin (rē-ā′jĭn) *n.* **1.** An antibody found in the blood of individuals having a genetic predisposition to allergies such as asthma and hay fever. **2.** A substance present in the blood of individuals having a positive serological test for syphilis. [REAG(ENT) + –IN.] **—re′a•gin′ic** (rē′ə-jĭn′ĭk) *adj.*

re•al[1] (rē′əl, rēl) *adj.* **1a.** Being or occurring in fact or actuality; having verifiable existence: *real objects.* **b.** True and actual; not imaginary, alleged, or ideal: *real people, not ghosts.* **c.** Of or founded on practical matters and concerns: *a recent graduate entering the real world.* **2.** Genuine and authentic; not artificial or spurious: *real mink.* See Syns at **authentic. 3.** Being no less than what is stated; worthy of the name: *a real friend.* **4.** Free of pretense, falsehood, or affectation. **5.** Not to be taken lightly; serious: *real trouble.* **6.** *Philosophy* Existing regardless of being perceived or thought of. **7.** Relating to, being, or having value reckoned by actual purchasing power: *real income.* **8.** *Physics* Of, relating to, or being an image formed by light rays that converge in space. **9.** *Mathematics* Of, relating to, or being a real number. **10.** *Law* Of or relating to stationary or fixed property, such as land. ❖ *adv. Informal* Very: *I'm real sorry.* ❖ *n.* **1.** A thing or whole having actual existence. Often used with *the.* **2.** *Mathematics* A real number. ***—idiom:* for real** *Slang* Truly so in fact or actuality. [ME < OFr. < LLat. *reālis* < Lat. *rēs,* thing.] **—real′ness** *n.*

re•al[2] (rā-äl′) *n., pl.* **-als** or **-al•es** (-ä′lĕs) A silver coin formerly used in Spain and Latin America. [Sp., royal, real < Lat. *rēgālis,* royal < *rēx, rēg-,* king. See **reg-** in App.]

re•al[3] (rā-äl′) *n., pl.* **re•ais** (-īsh′) **1.** See table at **currency. 2.** A monetary unit formerly used in Portugal. [Port., royal, real < Lat. *rēgālis,* royal. See REAL[2].]

re•al estate (rē′əl, rēl) *n.* Land, including all the natural resources and permanent buildings on it. **—re′al-es•tate′** (rē′əl-ĭ-stāt′, rēl′-) *adj.*

re•al•gar (rē-ăl′gär′, -gər) *n.* A soft orange-red arsenic ore, As_2S_2, used in pyrotechnics and tanning and as a pigment. [ME < Med.Lat. < Catalan < Ar. *rahj al-ġār,* powder (of) the mine or cave : *rahj,* powder + *al-,* the + *ġār,* cave.]

re•a•lign (rē′ə-līn′) *tr.v.* **-ligned, -lign•ing, -ligns 1.** To put back into order or alignment. **2.** To make new groupings of or working arrangements between. **—re′a•lign′ment** *n.*

re•al•ism (rē′ə-lĭz′əm) *n.* **1.** An inclination toward literal truth and pragmatism. **2.** The representation in art or literature of objects, actions, or social conditions as they actually are, without idealization or presentation in abstract form. **3.** *Philosophy* **a.** The scholastic doctrine, opposed to nominalism, that universals exist independently of their being thought. **b.** The modern philosophical doctrine, opposed to idealism, that physical objects exist independently of perception.

re•al•ist (rē′ə-lĭst) *n.* **1.** One who is inclined to literal truth and pragmatism. **2.** A practitioner of artistic or philosophic realism.

re•al•is•tic (rē′ə-lĭs′tĭk) *adj.* **1.** Tending to or expressing an awareness of things as they really are: *a realistic appraisal of our chances.* **2.** Of or relating to the representation of objects, actions, or social conditions as they actually are: *a realistic novel.* See Syns at **graphic. —re′al•is′ti•cal•ly** *adv.*

re•al•i•ty (rē-ăl′ĭ-tē) *n., pl.* **-ties 1.** The quality or state of being actual or true. **2.** One, such as a person or an event, that is actual. **3.** The totality of all things possessing actuality, existence, or essence. **4.** That which exists objectively and in fact. ***—idiom:* in reality** In fact; actually.

reality check *n.* An assessment to determine if one's circumstances or expectations conform to reality.

reality principle *n.* In psychoanalysis, the satisfaction of instinctual needs through awareness of and adjustment to environmental demands.

re•al•i•za•tion (rē′ə-lĭ-zā′shən) *n.* **1.** The act of realizing or the condition of being realized. **2.** The result of realizing.

re•al•ize (rē′ə-līz′) *v.* **-ized, -iz•ing, -iz•es** *—tr.* **1.** To comprehend completely or correctly. **2.** To bring into reality; make real: *realized his lifelong ambition to learn French.* **3.** To make realistic: *a film that realizes court life of the 17th century.* **4.** To obtain or achieve, as gain or profit: *realized a substantial return on her investment.* **5.** To bring in (a sum) as profit by sale. *—intr.* To exchange holdings or goods for money. [Fr. *réaliser* < OFr. < *real,* real. See REAL[1].] **—re′al•iz′a•ble** *adj.* **—re′al•iz′er** *n.*

real-life (rē′əl,-līf′ rēl′-) *adj.* Actually happening or having happened; not fictional.

re•al•ly (rē′ə-lē′, rē′lē) *adv.* **1.** In actual truth or fact: *The horseshoe crab isn't really a crab.* **2.** Truly; genuinely: *That was really fun.* **3.** Indeed: *Really, you shouldn't have done it.*

realm (rĕlm) *n.* **1.** A community or territory over which a sovereign rules; a kingdom. **2.** A field, sphere, or province: *the realm of science.* [ME *realme* < OFr., alteration (influenced by OFr. *reial,* royal) of Lat. *regimen,* government < *regere,* to rule. See **reg-** in App.]

re•al number (rē′əl, rēl) *n.* A number that is rational or irrational, not imaginary.

re•al•po•li•tik (rā-äl′pō′lĭ-tēk′) *n.* A usu. expansionist national policy having as its sole principle advancement of the national interest. [Ger. : *real,* practical (< LLat. *reālis,* real; see REAL[1]) + *Politik,* politics (< Fr. *politique,* political, policy; see POLITIC).] **—re•al′po′li•tik′er** *n.*

re•al time (rē′əl, rēl) *n.* The actual time in which a physical process under computer study or control occurs.

re•al-time (rē′əl-tīm′, rēl′-) *adj.* Of or relating to computer systems that update output at the same rate as they receive data, enabling them to direct or control a process such as an automatic pilot.

Re•al•tor (rē′əl-tər, -tôr′) A service mark used for a real-estate agent affiliated with the National Association of Realtors.

re•al•ty (rē′əl-tē) *n., pl.* **-ties** Real estate.

ream[1] (rēm) *n.* **1.** A quantity of paper, formerly 480 sheets, now 500 sheets or, in a printer's ream, 516 sheets. **2.** A very large amount. Often used in the plural. [ME *reme* < OFr. *reime* < OSpan. *resma* < Ar. *rizma,* bundle < *razama,* to bundle.]

ream[2] (rēm) *tr.v.* **reamed, ream•ing, reams 1.** To form, shape, taper, or enlarge (a hole or bore) with or as if with a reamer. **2.** To remove (material) by this process. **3.** To squeeze the juice out of (fruit) with a reamer. [Poss. < ME *remen,* to make room, var. of *rimen* < OE *rȳman.*]

ream•er (rē′mər) *n.* **1.** Any of various tools used to shape or enlarge holes or bores. **2.** A utensil with a conical ridged projection, used for extracting citrus-fruit juice.

re•an•i•mate (rē-ăn′ə-māt′) *tr.v.* **-mat•ed, -mat•ing, -mates 1.** To give new life to: *This work reanimates the classics.* **2.** To bring to life; evoke powerfully or effectively.

reap (rēp) *v.* **reaped, reap•ing, reaps** *—tr.* **1.** To cut (grain or pulse) for harvest with a scythe, sickle, or reaper. **2.** To harvest (a crop). **3.** To harvest a crop from: *reaped the field.* **4.** To obtain by effort. *—intr.* **1.** To cut or harvest grain or pulse. **2.** To obtain a return or reward. [ME *repen* < OE *rīpan.*]

reap•er (rē′pər) *n.* One that reaps, esp. a machine for harvesting grain or pulse crops.

re•ap•por•tion (rē′ə-pôr′shən) *tr.v.* **-tioned, -tion•ing, -tions** To distribute anew.

re•ap•por•tion•ment (rē′ə-pôr′shən-mənt) *n.* **1.** The act of reapportioning or the state of being reapportioned. **2.** Redistribution of representation in a legislative body, esp. the periodic reallotment of US congressional seats according to changes in the census figures as required by the Constitution.

re•ap•prais•al (rē′ə-prā′zəl) *n.* A new appraisal or evaluation.

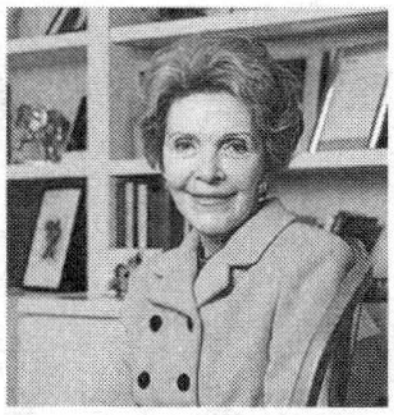

Nancy Reagan

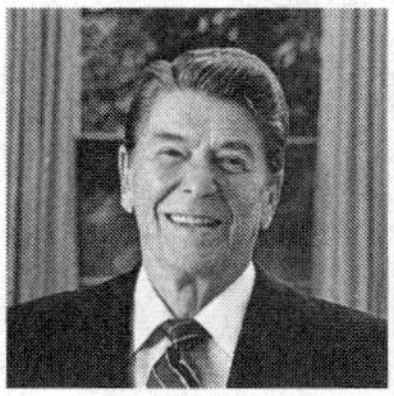

Ronald Reagan

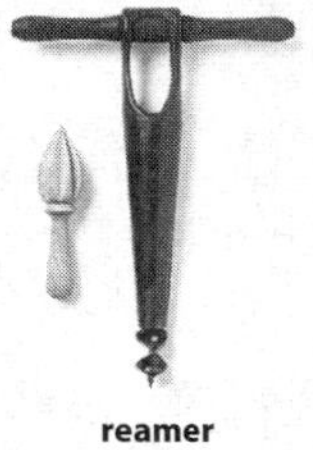

reamer
citrus (*left*) and wood-boring reamers

ă	pat	oi	boy
ā	pay	ou	out
âr	care	o͝o	took
ä	father	o͞o	boot
ĕ	pet	ŭ	cut
ē	be	ûr	urge
ĭ	pit	th	thin
ī	pie	*th*	this
îr	pier	hw	which
ŏ	pot	zh	vision
ō	toe	ə	about, item
ô	paw		

Stress marks:
′ (primary);
′ (secondary), as in
lexicon (lĕk′sĭ-kŏn′)

rebozo

re·ap·praise (rē′ə-prāz′) *tr.v.* **-praised, -prais·ing, -prais·es** To make a fresh appraisal or evaluation of.

rear[1] (rîr) *n.* **1.** A hind part. **2.** The point or area farthest from the front. **3.** The part of a military deployment usu. farthest from the fighting front. **4.** *Informal* The buttocks. ❖ *adj.* Of, at, or located in the rear. [ME *rere*, rear of an army, short for *rerewarde*, rear guard. See REARWARD[2].]

rear[2] (rîr) *v.* **reared, rear·ing, rears** —*tr.* **1.** To care for (children or a child) during the early stages of life; bring up. **2.** To lift upright; raise. **3.** To build; erect. **4.** To tend (growing plants or animals). —*intr.* **1.** To rise on the hind legs, as a horse. **2.** To rise high in the air; tower. [ME *reren*, to raise < OE *rǣran*. See **er-** in App.] —**rear′er** *n.*

rear admiral *n.* A commissioned officer in the US Navy or Coast Guard ranking above captain and below vice admiral.

rear end *n.* **1.** The rear part. **2.** *Informal* The buttocks.

rear-end (rîr′ĕnd′) *tr.v.* **-end·ed, -end·ing, -ends** *Slang* To run into (a motor vehicle) from behind. —**rear′-end′er** *n.*

rear guard *n.* A detachment of troops that protects the rear of a military force. [ME *reregarde* < OFr. : *rere*, backward (< Lat. *retrō*) + *guarde*, guard (< *guarder*, to defend; see GUARD).]

rear-guard (rîr′gärd′) *adj.* **1.** Of or relating to a rear guard. **2.** Of or relating to economic, political, or social resistance.

re·ar·gue (rē-är′gyōō) *tr.v.* **-gued, -gu·ing, -gues 1.** To argue again or repeatedly. **2.** To debate again or present additional arguments for (a case, for example), esp. in a court of law.

re·arm (rē-ärm′) *v.* **-armed, -arm·ing, -arms** —*tr.* **1.** To arm again. **2.** To equip with better weapons. —*intr.* To arm oneself again. —**re·ar′ma·ment** (rē-är′mə-mənt) *n.*

rear·most (rîr′mōst′) *adj.* Farthest in the rear; last.

re·ar·range (rē′ə-rānj′) *tr.v.* **-ranged, -rang·ing, -rang·es** To change the arrangement of. —**re′ar·range′ment** *n.*

rear·view mirror (rîr′vyōō′) *n.* A mirror, such as one attached to a motor vehicle, that provides a view of what is behind.

rear·ward[1] (rîr′wərd) *adv.* Toward, to, or at the rear. ❖ *adj.* Being at or in the rear. ❖ *n.* A rearward direction, point, or position. —**rear′wards** *adv.*

rear·ward[2] (rîr′wôrd′) *n.* The rear guard of an armed force. [ME *rerewarde* < AN : *rere*, behind (< Lat. *retrō*) + *warde*, guard (of Gmc. orig.).]

rea·son (rē′zən) *n.* **1.** The basis or motive for an action, decision, or conviction. See Usage Note at **why. 2.** A declaration made to explain or justify an action, decision, or conviction. **3.** An underlying fact or cause: *reason for doubt.* **4.** The capacity for logical, rational, and analytic thought; intelligence. **5.** Good judgment; sound sense. **6.** A normal mental state; sanity. **7.** *Logic* A premise, usu. the minor premise, of an argument. ❖ *v.* **-soned, -son·ing, -sons** —*intr.* **1.** To use the faculty of reason; think logically. **2.** To talk or argue logically and persuasively. **3.** *Obsolete* To engage in conversation or discussion. —*tr.* **1.** To determine or conclude by logical thinking: *reasoned out a solution.* **2.** To persuade or dissuade (someone) with reasons. —**idioms: by reason of** Because of. **in reason** With good sense or justification; reasonably. **within reason** Within the bounds of good sense or practicality. **with reason** With good cause; justifiably. [ME < OFr. *raison* < Lat. *ratiō, ratiōn-* < *ratus,* p. part. of *rērī,* to consider, think.] —**rea′son·er** *n.*

rea·son·a·ble (rē′zə-nə-bəl) *adj.* **1.** Capable of reasoning; rational. **2.** Governed by or being in accordance with reason or sound thinking. **3.** Being within the bounds of common sense. **4.** Not excessive or extreme; fair: *reasonable prices.* —**rea′son·a·bil′i·ty, rea′son·a·ble·ness** *n.* —**rea′son·a·bly** *adv.*

rea·son·ing (rē′zə-nĭng) *n.* **1.** Use of reason, esp. to form conclusions, inferences, or judgments. **2.** Evidence or arguments used in thinking or argumentation.

re·as·sem·ble (rē′ə-sĕm′bəl) *v.* **-bled, -bling, -bles** —*tr.* **1.** To bring or gather together again. **2.** To fit or join the parts of (something) together again. —*intr.* To gather together again, esp. in a different place.

re·as·sign (rē′ə-sīn′) *tr.v.* **-signed, -sign·ing, -signs** To assign to a new position, distribution, or function: *reassigned the ambassador to a new post.* —**re·as·sign′ment** *n.*

re·as·sure (rē′ə-shōōr′) *tr.v.* **-sured, -sur·ing, -sures 1.** To restore confidence to. **2.** To assure again. **3.** To reinsure. —**re′as·sur′ance** *n.* —**re′as·sur′ing·ly** *adv.*

re·a·ta (rē-ä′tə) *n.* Variant of **riata.**

Ré·au·mur or **Re·au·mur** (rā′ō-myōōr′) *adj.* Relating to, being, or indicated on a thermometer scale that registers the freezing point of water as 0° and the boiling point as 80°.

Ré·au·mur (rā′ə-myōōr′, -ō-, rā-ō-mür′), **René Antoine Ferchault de** 1683–1757. French physicist who invented the alcohol thermometer and devised the Réaumur scale.

reave[1] (rēv) *v.* **reaved** or **reft** (rĕft), **reav·ing, reaves** *Archaic* —*tr.* **1.** To seize and carry off forcibly. **2.** To deprive (one) of something. —*intr.* To rob, plunder, or pillage. [ME *reven,* to plunder < OE *rēafian* in App.] —**reup-** in App.]

reave[2] (rēv) *tr.v.* **reaved** or **reft** (rĕft), **reav·ing, reaves** *Archaic* To break or tear apart. [ME *reven,* poss. alteration (influenced by *reven,* to plunder) of ON *rifa,* to rive.]

Reb[1] also **reb** (rĕb) *n. Informal* A Confederate soldier. [Short for REBEL.]

Reb[2] (rĕb) *n. Judaism* Used with the given name as a title of respect for a man. [Yiddish < Heb. *rabbî,* my master. See RABBI.]

re·bar (rē′bär′) *n.* **1.** A rod or bar used for reinforcement in concrete or asphalt pourings. **2.** A group of such rods forming a grid. [*re(inforcing) bar.*]

re·bar·ba·tive (rĭ-bär′bə-tĭv) *adj.* Tending to irritate; repellent. [Fr. *rébarbatif* < OFr. < *(se) rebarber,* to confront : *re-, re-* + *barbe,* beard < Lat. *barba;* see **bhardh-ā-** in App.).]

re·bate[1] (rē′bāt′) *n.* A deduction from or a return of part of a payment. ❖ *tr.v.* (rē′bāt′, rĭ-bāt′) **-bat·ed, -bat·ing, -bates 1.** To deduct or return (an amount) from a payment or bill. **2.** To lessen; diminish. [< ME *rebaten,* to deduct < OFr. *rabattre, rebattre,* to reduce, to beat down again : *re-, re-* + *abattre,* to beat down; see ABATE.] —**re′bat′er** *n.*

re·bate[2] (rē′bāt′, răb′ĭt) *n. & v.* Variant of **rabbet.**

re·ba·to (rĭ-bä′tō) also **ra·ba·to** (rə-) *n., pl.* **-tos** A stiff flaring collar wired to stand up at the back of the head, worn in the 16th and early 17th century. [Obsolete Fr. *rebateau,* alteration of Fr. *rabat* < OFr. < *rabattre,* to turn down again, reduce. See REBATE[1].]

reb·be (rĕb′ə, rĕb′ē) *n.* A Jewish spiritual leader or rabbi, esp. of a Hasidic sect. [Yiddish < Heb. *rabbî,* rabbi. See RABBI.]

re·bec also **re·beck** (rē′bĕk′) *n. Music* A pear-shaped two-stringed or three-stringed medieval instrument, played with a bow. [Fr. < OFr., alteration (influenced by *bec,* beak < its shape) of *rebebe* < O Provençal *rebeb* < Ar. *rabāb* < *rabba,* to be master, control.]

Re·bec·ca also **Re·bek·ah** (rĭ-bĕk′ə) In the Bible, the wife of Isaac and the mother of Jacob and Esau.

reb·el (rĭ-bĕl′) *intr.v.* **-belled, -bel·ling, -bels 1.** To refuse allegiance to and oppose by force an established government or ruling authority. **2.** To resist or defy an authority or a generally accepted convention. **3.** To feel or express strong unwillingness or repugnance: *rebelled at the suggestion.* ❖ *n.* **reb·el** (rĕb′əl) **1.** One who rebels or is in rebellion. **2. Rebel** A Confederate soldier. [ME *rebellen* < OFr. *rebeller* < Lat. *rebellāre : re-, re-* + *bellāre,* to make war (< *bellum,* war). N. < ME, rebellious, rebel < OFr. *rebelle* < Lat. *rebellis* < *rebellāre.*]

re·bel·lion (rĭ-bĕl′yən) *n.* **1.** Open, armed, and organized resistance to a constituted government. **2.** An act or a show of defiance toward an authority or a convention. [ME < OFr. < Lat. *rebelliō, rebelliōn-* < *rebellāre.* See REBEL.]

re·bel·lious (rĭ-bĕl′yəs) *adj.* **1.** Prone to or engaged in rebellion. **2.** Of, relating to, or characteristic of a rebel or rebellion: *rebellious acts.* **3.** Resisting treatment or control; unruly. —**re·bel′lious·ly** *adv.* —**re·bel′lious·ness** *n.*

rebel yell *n. Chiefly Southern US* See **wahoo**[4].

re·bid (rē-bĭd′) *v.* **-bid, -bid·den** (-bĭd′n) or **-bid, -bid·ding, -bids** —*tr.* **1.** *Games* To bid (a previously bid suit) again in bridge. **2.** To offer a revised bid for (a contract). —*intr.* **1.** *Games* To bid again in the auction in bridge. **2.** To rebid a contract. —**re′bid′** *n.*

re·bind (rē-bīnd′) *tr.v.* **-bound** (-bound′), **-bind·ing, -binds** To bind again, esp. to put a new binding on (a book). ❖ *n.* (rē′bīnd′) A book that has been rebound.

re·birth (rē-bûrth′, rē′bûrth′) *n.* **1.** A second or new birth; reincarnation. **2.** A renaissance; a revival.

re·book (rē-bōōk′) *v.* **-booked, -book·ing, -books** —*tr.* **1.** To book again. **2.** To change a booking for (a performance or reservation). —*intr.* To make a new booking.

re·boot (rē-bōōt′) *tr.v.* **-boot·ed, -boot·ing, -boots** To restart (a computer).

re·born (rē-bôrn′) *adj.* Emotionally or spiritually revived or regenerated.

re·bound[1] (rē′bound′, rĭ-) *v.* **-bound·ed, -bound·ing, -bounds** —*intr.* **1.** To spring or bounce back after hitting or colliding with something. **2.** To recover, as from depression. **3.** To reecho; resound. **4.** *Basketball* To retrieve and gain possession of the ball as it bounces off the backboard or rim. —*tr.* **1.** To cause to rebound. **2.** *Basketball* To gain possession of (the ball) off the backboard or rim. ❖ *n.* (rē′bound′, rĭ-bound′) **1.** A springing or bounding back; a recoil. **2a.** *Sports* A rebounding or caroming ball or hockey puck. **b.** *Basketball* The act or an instance of rebounding. **3.** A quick recovery from or reaction to disappointment or depression: *is on the rebound following a tumultuous breakup.* [ME *rebounden* < OFr. *rebondir : re-, re-* + *bondir,* to leap; see BOUND[1].] —**re·bound′er** *n.*

re·bound[2] (rē-bound′) *v.* Past tense and past participle of **rebind.**

re·bo·zo (rĭ-bō′sō, -zō) *n., pl.* **-zos** A long scarf worn over the head and shoulders chiefly by Mexican women. [Sp. < *rebosar,* to muffle with a shawl : *re-,* back (< Lat.; see RE–) + *bozo,* muzzle, mouth (ult. < Lat. *bucca,* cheek).]

re·broad·cast (rē-brôd′kăst′) *tr.v.* **-cast** or **-cast·ed, -cast·ing, -casts 1.** To repeat the broadcast of (a program). **2.** To receive and send out (a broadcast) again. ❖ *n.* A broadcast that is repeated or that is relayed from another station.

re·buff (rĭ-bŭf′) *n.* **1.** A blunt or abrupt repulse or refusal, as to an offer. **2.** A check or an abrupt setback to progress or action. ❖ *tr.v.* **-buffed, -buff·ing, -buffs 1.** To reject bluntly, often disdainfully; snub. See Syns at **refuse**[1]. **2.** To repel or drive back. [< obsolete Fr. *rebuffer,* to reject < Ital. *ribuffare* < *ribuffo,* reprimand : *ri-*, back (< Lat. *re-*; see RE–) + *buffo*, gust, puff (of imit. orig.).]

re•build (rē-bĭld′) *tr.v.* **-built** (-bĭlt′), **-build•ing, -builds 1.** To build again. **2.** To make extensive structural repairs on. **3.** To remodel or make extensive changes in: *tried to rebuild society.*

re•buke (rĭ-byo͞ok′) *tr.v.* **-buked, -buk•ing, -bukes 1.** To criticize or reprove sharply; reprimand. See Syns at **admonish. 2.** To check or repress. ❖ *n.* A sharp reproof. [ME *rebuken* < ONFr. *rebuker* : *re-*, back (< Lat.; see RE–) + **buker*, to strike, chop wood (var. of OFr. *buschier* < *busche*, firewood, of Gmc. orig.).]

re•bus (rē′bəs) *n., pl.* **-bus•es** A representation of words in the form of pictures or symbols, often presented as a puzzle. [Lat. *rēbus*, ablative pl. of *rēs*, thing.]

re•but (rĭ-bŭt′) *v.* **-but•ted, -but•ting, -buts** —*tr.* **1.** To refute, esp. by offering opposing evidence or arguments. **2.** To repel. —*intr.* To present opposing evidence or arguments. [ME *reboten, rebutte*, to rebuke, repel < OFr. *rebouter* : *re-*, re- + *bouter*, to push (of Gmc. orig.; see **bhau-** in App.).]

re•but•tal (rĭ-bŭt′l) *n.* **1.** The act of rebutting. **2.** A statement made in rebutting.

re•but•ter (rĭ-bŭt′ər) *n.* One who refutes or rebuts.

rec (rĕk) *n. Informal* Recreation.

re•cal•ci•trant (rĭ-kăl′sĭ-trənt) *adj.* Marked by stubborn resistance to and defiance of authority or guidance. See Syns at **unruly.** ❖ *n.* A recalcitrant person. [LLat. *recalcitrāns, recalcitrant-*, pr. part. of *recalcitrāre*, to be disobedient < Lat., to deny access : *re-*, re- + *calcitrāre*, to kick (< *calx, calc-*, heel).] **—re•cal′ci•trance, re•cal′ci•tran•cy** *n.*

re•ca•les•cence (rē′kə-lĕs′əns) *n.* A sudden glowing in a cooling metal caused by liberation of the latent heat of transformation. [< Lat. *recalēscēns, recalēscent-*, pr. part. of *recalēscere*, to grow warm again : *re-*, re- + *calēscere*, to become warm, inchoative of *calēre*, to be warm.] **—re′ca•les′cent** *adj.*

re•call (rĭ-kôl′) *tr.v.* **-called, -cal•ling, -calls 1.** To ask or order to return. **2.** To summon back to awareness of or concern with the subject or situation at hand. **3.** To remember; recollect. See Syns at **remember. 4.** To cancel, take back, or revoke. **5.** To bring back; restore. **6.** To request return (of a product) to the manufacturer, as for necessary repairs or adjustments. ❖ *n.* (*also* rē′kôl′) **1.** The act of recalling or summoning back, esp. an official order to return. **2.** A signal, such as a bugle call, used to summon troops back to their posts. **3.** The ability to remember information or experiences. **4.** The act of revoking. **5a.** The procedure by which a public official may be removed from office by popular vote. **b.** The right to employ this procedure. **6.** The recalling of a product by its manufacturer. **—re•call′a•ble** *adj.*

Ré•ca•mi•er (rā′kəm-yā′, rā-käm-), **Jeanne Françoise Julie Adélaïde Bernard** 1777–1849. French socialite whose Parisian salon attracted noted literary and political figures.

re•cant (rĭ-kănt′) *v.* **-cant•ed, -cant•ing, -cants** —*tr.* To make a formal retraction or disavowal of (a previously held statement or belief). —*intr.* To recant a previously held statement or belief. [Lat. *recantāre* : *re-*, re- + *cantāre*, to sing, freq. of *canere*; see **kan-** in App.] **—re′can•ta′tion** (rē′kăn-tā′shən) *n.* **—re•cant′er** *n.*

re•cap¹ (rē-kăp′) *tr.v.* **-capped, -cap•ping, -caps 1.** To replace a cap or caplike covering on: *recapped the bottle.* **2.** To restore (a used tire of a motor vehicle) to usable condition by bonding new rubber onto the worn tread and lateral surface. ❖ *n.* (rē′kăp′) A tire that has been recapped.

re•cap² (rē′kăp′) *Informal tr.v.* **-capped, -cap•ping, -caps** To recapitulate. ❖ *n.* A recapitulation, as of a news report.

re•cap•i•tal•ize (rē-kăp′ĭ-tl-īz′) *tr.v.* **-ized, -iz•ing, -iz•es** To change the capital structure of (a corporation). **—re•cap′i•tal•i•za′tion** (-ĭ-zā′shən) *n.*

re•ca•pit•u•late (rē′kə-pĭch′ə-lāt′) *v.* **-lat•ed, -lat•ing, -lates** —*tr.* **1.** To repeat in concise form. **2.** *Biology* To appear to repeat (the evolutionary stages of the species) during the embryonic development of the individual organism. —*intr.* To make a summary. [Lat. *recapitulāre, recapitulāt-* : *re-*, re- + *capitulum*, main point, heading, dim. of *caput, capit-*, head. See **kaput-** in App.] **—re•ca•pit′u•la′tive, re•ca•pit′u•la•to′ry** (-lə-tôr′ē, -tōr′ē) *adj.*

re•ca•pit•u•la•tion (rē′kə-pĭch′ə-lā′shən) *n.* **1.** The act or process of recapitulating. **2.** A summary or concise review. **3.** See **biogenesis** 4. **4.** *Music* Restatement of the exposition in the tonic, constituting the third and final section of the typical sonata form.

recapitulation theory *n.* See **biogenetic law.**

re•cap•ture (rē-kăp′chər) *n.* **1a.** The act of retaking or recovering. **b.** The condition of having been retaken or recovered. **2.** Something recaptured. **3.** The lawful taking by a government of a fixed amount of the profits of a public-service corporation in excess of a stipulated rate of return. ❖ *tr.v.* **-tured, -tur•ing, -tures 1.** To capture again. **2.** To recall: *tried to recapture the past.* **3.** To acquire by the government procedure of recapture.

re•cast (rē-kăst′) *tr.v.* **-cast, -cast•ing, -casts 1.** To mold again: *recast a bell.* **2.** To set down or present (ideas or words, for example) in a new or different arrangement. **3.** To change the cast of (a theatrical production). ❖ *n.* (rē′kăst′) **1.** The act or process of recasting. **2.** Something made by recasting.

recd. *abbr.* received

re•cede¹ (rĭ-sēd′) *intr.v.* **-ced•ed, -ced•ing, -cedes 1.** To move back or away from a limit, point, or mark: *The floodwaters receded.* **2.** To slope backward. **3.** To become or seem to become fainter or more distant: *With time, the memories receded.* **4.** To withdraw or retreat. [ME *receden* < OFr. *receder* < Lat. *recēdere* : *re-*, re- + *cēdere*, to go.]

re•cede² (rē-sēd′) *tr.v.* **-ced•ed, -ced•ing, -cedes** To yield or grant to one formerly in possession; cede (something) back. [RE– + CEDE.]

re•ceipt (rĭ-sēt′) *n.* **1a.** The act of receiving. **b.** The fact of being or having been received. **2.** A quantity or amount received. Often used in the plural. **3.** A written acknowledgment that a given article, sum of money, or shipment has been received. **4.** A recipe. ❖ *v.* **-ceipt•ed, -ceipt•ing, -ceipts** —*tr.* **1.** To mark (a bill) as having been paid. **2.** To give or write a receipt for (money, goods, or services delivered). —*intr.* To give a receipt. [ME *receite* < ONFr. < Med.Lat. *recepta*, medical prescription, money received < Lat., fem. p. part. of *recipere*, to receive. See RECEIVE.]

re•ceiv•a•ble (rĭ-sē′və-bəl) *adj.* **1.** Suitable for being received or accepted, esp. as payment. **2.** Awaiting or requiring payment; due or collectible. ❖ *n.* A business asset due to one business from another. Often used in the plural.

re•ceive (rĭ-sēv′) *v.* **-ceived, -ceiv•ing, -ceives** —*tr.* **1.** To take or acquire (something given, offered, or transmitted); get. **2.** To hear or see (information, for example): *received bad news.* **3.** To have (a title, for example) bestowed on oneself. **4.** To meet with; experience: *receive sympathetic treatment.* **5.** To have inflicted or imposed on oneself: *receive a penalty.* **6.** To bear the weight or force of; support. **7.** To take or intercept the impact of (a blow, for example). **8.** To take in, hold, or contain: *a tank that receives rainwater.* **9.** To admit: *receive new members.* **10.** To greet or welcome: *receive guests.* **11.** To perceive or acquire mentally. **12.** To regard with approval or disapproval. **13.** To listen to and acknowledge formally and authoritatively. —*intr.* **1.** To acquire or get something; be a recipient. **2.** To admit or welcome guests or visitors. **3.** To partake of the Eucharist. **4.** *Electronics* To convert incoming electromagnetic waves into visible or audible signals. **5.** *Football* To catch or take possession of a kicked ball. [ME *receiven* < ONFr. *receivre* < Lat. *recipere* : *re-*, re- + *capere*, to take; see **kap-** in App.]

re•ceived (rĭ-sēvd′) *adj.* Accepted as true or worthy.

Received Pronunciation *n.* A pronunciation of British English, originally based on the speech of the upper class of southeastern England, formerly taught as standard in British public schools.

Received Standard English *n.* British English characterized esp. by Received Pronunciation.

re•ceiv•er (rĭ-sē′vər) *n.* **1.** One that receives something: *a receiver of gifts.* **2.** *Electronics* A device, such as a part of a radio or telephone, that converts incoming radio or electric signals to perceptible forms, such as sound. **3.** An official appointed to receive and account for money due. **4.** *Law* A person appointed by a court administrator to take into custody the property or funds of others, pending litigation. **5.** One who knowingly buys or receives stolen goods. **6.** A receptacle intended for a specific purpose. **7.** *Football* A member of the offensive team eligible to catch a forward pass.

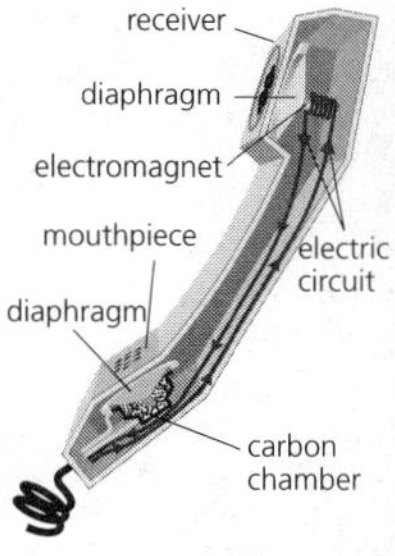
receiver
diaphragm
electromagnet
mouthpiece
electric circuit
diaphragm
carbon chamber

receiver
telephone handset

re•ceiv•er•ship (rĭ-sē′vər-shĭp′) *n. Law* **1.** The office or functions of a receiver. **2.** The state of being held by a receiver.

re•ceiv•ing blanket (rĭ-sē′vĭng) *n.* A lightweight blanket used to wrap a baby esp. after a bath.

receiving end *n.* The position in which one is subject to an often unpleasant action or effect.

receiving line *n.* A line of people formed to greet arriving guests individually, as at a formal gathering.

re•cen•sion (rĭ-sĕn′shən) *n.* **1.** A critical revision of a text incorporating the most plausible elements from varying sources. **2.** A text so revised. [Lat. *recēnsiō, recēnsiōn-*, a reviewing < *recēnsēre*, to review : *re-*, re- + *cēnsēre*, to estimate.]

re•cent (rē′sənt) *adj.* **1.** Of, belonging to, or occurring at a time immediately before the present. **2.** Modern; new. **3. Recent** *Geology* Of, belonging to, or being the Holocene Epoch. See table at **geologic time.** [ME, new, fresh < Lat. *recēns, recent-*.] **—re′cen•cy, re′cent•ness** *n.* **—re′cent•ly** *adv.*

re•cep•ta•cle (rĭ-sĕp′tə-kəl) *n.* **1.** A container that holds items or matter. **2.** *Botany* The expanded tip of a flower stalk or axis that bears the floral organs or the group of flowers in a head. **3.** *Electronics* A fitting connected to a power supply and equipped to receive a plug. [ME < OFr. < Lat. *receptāculum* < *receptāre*, to receive again, freq. of *recipere*, to receive. See RECEIVE.]

re•cep•tion (rĭ-sĕp′shən) *n.* **1a.** The act or process of receiving or of being received. **b.** *Football* The act or an instance of catching a forward pass. **2.** A welcome, greeting, or acceptance. **3.** A social function, esp. one intended to provide a welcome or greeting: *a wedding reception.* **4.** Mental approval or acceptance. **5.** *Electronics* **a.** Conversion of transmitted radio waves or electric signals into perceptible forms, such as light, by means of antennas and electronic equipment. **b.** The condition or quality of the waves or signals so received. [Ult. < Lat. *receptiō, receptiōn-* < *receptus*, p. part. of *recipere*, to receive. See RECEIVE.]

re•cep•tion•ist (rĭ-sĕp′shə-nĭst) *n.* An office worker employed chiefly to receive visitors and answer the telephone.

re•cep•tive (rĭ-sĕp′tĭv) *adj.* **1.** Capable of or qualifed for receiv-

ă	**pat**	oi	**boy**
ā	**pay**	ou	**out**
âr	**care**	o͝o	**took**
ä	**father**	o͞o	**boot**
ĕ	**pet**	ŭ	**cut**
ē	**be**	ûr	**urge**
ĭ	**pit**	th	**thin**
ī	**pie**	*th*	**this**
îr	**pier**	hw	**which**
ŏ	**pot**	zh	**vision**
ō	**toe**	ə	**about, item**
ô	**paw**		

Stress marks:
′ (primary);
′ (secondary), as in
lexicon (lĕk′sĭ-kŏn′)

ing. **2.** Ready or willing to receive favorably. **3.** Of or relating to the skills of listening and reading. —**re·cep′tive·ly** adv. —**re·cep′tive·ness, re′cep·tiv′i·ty** n.

re·cep·tor (rĭ-sĕp′tər) n. **1.** Physiology A specialized cell or group of nerve endings that responds to sensory stimuli. **2.** Biochemistry A molecular structure or site on the surface or inside a cell that binds with substances such as hormones or drugs.

re·cer·ti·fy (rē-sûr′tə-fī′) tr.v. **-fied, -fy·ing, -fies** To renew the certification of, esp. certification given by a licensing board. —**re′cer·ti·fi·ca′tion** (-fĭ-kā′shən) n.

re·cess (rē′sĕs′, rĭ-sĕs′) n. **1a.** A temporary cessation of the customary activities of an engagement, occupation, or pursuit. **b.** The period of such cessation. See Syns at **pause**. **2.** A remote, secret, or secluded place. Often used in the plural. **3a.** An indentation or small hollow. **b.** An alcove. ❖ v. **-cessed, -cess·ing, -cess·es** —tr. **1.** To place in a recess. **2.** To create a recess in: recessed the wall. **3.** To suspend for a recess: recessed the hearings. —intr. To take a recess. [Lat. recessus, retreat < p. part. of recēdere, to recede. See RECEDE¹.]

re·ces·sion¹ (rĭ-sĕsh′ən) n. **1.** The act of withdrawing or going back. **2.** An extended decline in business, typically at least two consecutive quarters of falling gross national product. **3.** The withdrawal in a line or file of participants in a ceremony, esp. clerics and choir members after a church service. [Lat. recessiō, recessiōn- < recessus, p. part. of recēdere, to recede. See RECEDE¹.] —**re·ces′sion·ar′y** adj.

re·ces·sion² (rē-sĕsh′ən) n. Law The act of restoring possession to a former owner.

re·ces·sion·al (rĭ-sĕsh′ə-nəl) n. **1.** A hymn that accompanies the exit of the clergy and choir after a service. **2.** A recession from a church. ❖ adj. Of or relating to a recession.

re·ces·sive (rĭ-sĕs′ĭv) adj. **1.** Tending to go backward or recede. **2a.** Genetics Of, relating to, or being an allele that does not produce a characteristic effect when present with a dominant allele. **b.** Of or relating to a trait that is expressed only when the determining allele is present in the homozygous condition. ❖ n. Genetics **1.** A recessive allele or trait. **2.** An organism having a recessive trait. —**re·ces′sive·ly** adv. —**re·ces′sive·ness** n.

re·charge (rē-chärj′) tr.v. **-charged, -charg·ing, -charg·es** To charge again, esp. to reenergize a storage battery. —**re′charge′** n. —**re·charge′a·ble** adj. —**re·charg′er** n.

ré·chauf·fé (rā′shō-fā′) n. **1.** Warmed leftover food. **2.** Revised old material. [Fr., p. part. of réchauffer, to reheat, warm over < OFr. rechaufer : re-, re- + echaufer, to warm < VLat. *excalefāre : Lat. ex-, intensive pref.; see EX- + Lat. calefacere, to warm; see CHAFE.]

re·cher·ché (rə-shĕr′shā′) adj. **1.** Uncommon; rare. **2.** Exquisite; choice. **3.** Overrefined; forced. **4.** Pretentious; overblown. [Fr., p. part. of rechercher, to research < OFr. recercher. See RESEARCH.]

re·cid·i·vate (rĭ-sĭd′ə-vāt′) intr.v. **-vat·ed, -vat·ing, -vates** To return to a previous pattern of behavior, esp. to return to criminal habits. [RECIDIV(ISM) + −ATE¹.]

re·cid·i·vism (rĭ-sĭd′ə-vĭz′əm) n. A tendency to recidivate. [< recidivist, one who recidivates < Fr. récidiviste < récidiver, to relapse < Med.Lat. recidīvāre < Lat. recidīvus, falling back < recidere, to fall back : re-, re- + cadere, to fall.] —**re·cid′i·vist** n. —**re·cid′i·vis′tic, re·cid′i·vous** adj.

Re·ci·fe (rə-sē′fə) A city of NE Brazil on the Atlantic Ocean S of Natal; first settled in 1535. Pop. 1,296,995.

rec·i·pe (rĕs′ə-pē′) n. **1.** A set of directions with a list of ingredients for making something, esp. food. **2.** A formula for or means to a goal. **3.** A medical prescription. [Lat., sing. imper. of recipere, to take, receive. See RECEIVE.]

re·cip·i·ence (rĭ-sĭp′ē-əns) also **re·cip·i·en·cy** (-ən-sē) n. Capacity to receive; receptivity.

re·cip·i·ent (rĭ-sĭp′ē-ənt) adj. Functioning as a receiver; receptive. ❖ n. **1.** One that receives or is receptive. **2.** One who receives blood, tissue, or an organ from a donor. [Lat. recipiēns, recipient-, pr. part. of recipere, to receive. See RECEIVE.]

re·cip·ro·cal (rĭ-sĭp′rə-kəl) adj. **1.** Concerning each of two or more persons or things. **2.** Interchanged, given, or owed to each other: a reciprocal invitation. **3.** Performed, experienced, or felt by both sides: reciprocal respect. **4.** Interchangeable; complementary: reciprocal electric outlets. **5.** Grammar Expressing mutual action or relationship. Used of some verbs and compound pronouns. **6.** Mathematics Of or relating to the reciprocal of a quantity. **7.** Physiology Of or relating to a neuromuscular phenomenon in which the inhibition of one group of muscles accompanies the excitation of another. **8.** Genetics Of or being a pair of crosses in which the male or female parent in one cross is of the same genotype or phenotype as the complementary female or male parent in the other cross. ❖ n. **1.** Something that is reciprocal to something else. **2.** Mathematics A number related to another so that when multiplied together their product is 1. For example, the reciprocal of 7 is ⅐. [< Lat. reciprocus, alternating. See per¹ in App.] —**re·cip′ro·cal′i·ty** (-kăl′ĭ-tē), **re·cip′ro·cal·ness** (-kəl-nĭs) n. —**re·cip′ro·cal·ly** adv.

reciprocal pronoun n. A pronoun or pronominal phrase, such as each other, that expresses mutual action or relationship.

re·cip·ro·cate (rĭ-sĭp′rə-kāt′) v. **-cat·ed, -cat·ing, -cates** —tr.

1. To give or take mutually; interchange. **2.** To show, feel, or give in return. —intr. **1.** To move back and forth alternately. **2.** To give and take something mutually. **3.** To make a return for something given or done. **4.** To be complementary or equivalent. [Lat. reciprocāre, reciprocāt-, to move back and forth < reciprocus, alternating. See RECIPROCAL.] —**re·cip′ro·ca′tive** adj. —**re·cip′ro·ca′tor** n.

re·cip·ro·cat·ing engine (rĭ-sĭp′rə-kā′tĭng) n. An engine whose crankshaft is turned by pistons moving up and down in a cylinder.

re·cip·ro·ca·tion (rĭ-sĭp′rə-kā′shən) n. **1.** An alternating back-and-forth movement. **2.** The act or fact of reciprocating.

rec·i·proc·i·ty (rĕs′ə-prŏs′ĭ-tē) n., pl. **-ties 1.** A reciprocal condition or relationship. **2.** A mutual or cooperative interchange of favors or privileges, esp. the exchange of trade privileges between nations.

re·ci·sion (rĭ-sĭzh′ən) n. The act of rescinding; annulment or cancellation. [Obsolete Fr. < OFr., annulment of a judgment < Lat. recīsiō, recīsiōn- < recīsus, p. part. of recīdere, to cut back : re-, re- + caedere, to cut.]

re·cit·al (rĭ-sīt′l) n. **1.** The act of reading or reciting before an audience. **2.** A very detailed account or report; a narration. **3.** A public music or dance performance, esp. a solo. —**re·ci′tal·ist** n.

rec·i·ta·tion (rĕs′ĭ-tā′shən) n. **1a.** The act of reciting memorized materials in a public performance. **b.** The material so presented. **2a.** Oral delivery of prepared lessons by a pupil. **b.** The class period within which this delivery occurs.

rec·i·ta·tive¹ (rĕs′ĭ-tā′tĭv, rĭ-sī′tə-tĭv) adj. Of, relating to, or having the character of a recital or recitation.

rec·i·ta·tive² (rĕs′ĭ-tə-tēv′, rĕch′-) n. Music **1.** A vocal style in which a text is declaimed in the rhythm of natural speech with slight melodic variation and little orchestral accompaniment. **2.** A passage thus rendered. [Ital. recitativo < recitare, to recite < Lat. recitāre. See RECITE.]

re·ci·ta·ti·vo (rĕs′ĭ-tə-tē′vō, rĕ′chē-tä-) n., pl. **-vi** (-vē) or **-vos** (-vōz) See **recitative²**. [Ital. See RECITATIVE².]

re·cite (rĭ-sīt′) v. **-cit·ed, -cit·ing, -cites** —tr. **1.** To repeat or utter aloud (something rehearsed or memorized), esp. before an audience. **2.** To relate in detail. **3.** To list or enumerate. —intr. **1.** To deliver a recitation. **2.** To repeat lessons prepared or memorized. [ME reciten < OFr. reciter < Lat. recitāre, to read out : re-, re- + citāre, to quote; see CITE.] —**re·cit′er** n.

reck (rĕk) tr. & intr.v. **recked, reck·ing, recks** To take heed of or to have caution. [ME recken < OE reccan. See **reg-** in App.]

reck·less (rĕk′lĭs) adj. **1a.** Heedless or careless. **b.** Headstrong; rash. **2.** Indifferent to or disregardful of consequences: a reckless driver. [ME reckeles < OE rēcelēas. See **reg-** in App.] —**reck′less·ly** adv. —**reck′less·ness** n.

reck·on (rĕk′ən) v. **-oned, -on·ing, -ons** —tr. **1.** To count or compute: reckon the cost. **2.** To consider as being; regard as. **3.** Informal To think or assume. —intr. **1.** To make a calculation; figure. **2.** To rely with confident expectancy. **3.** Informal To think or assume. —phrasal verbs: **reckon with** To take into account or deal with. **reckon without** To fail to consider or deal with; ignore. [ME reknen < OE gerecenian, to recount, arrange. See **reg-** in App.]

reck·on·ing (rĕk′ə-nĭng) n. **1.** The act of counting or computing. **2.** An itemized bill or statement of a sum due. **3.** A settlement of accounts. **4a.** The act or process of calculating the position of a ship or an aircraft. **b.** This position.

re·claim (rĭ-klām′) tr.v. **-claimed, -claim·ing, -claims 1.** To bring into or return to a suitable condition for use, as cultivation or habitation: reclaim marshlands. **2.** To procure (usable substances) from refuse or waste products. **3.** To bring back, as from error, to a right or proper course; reform. **4.** To tame (a falcon, for example). [ME reclamen, to call back < OFr. reclamer, to entreat < Lat. reclāmāre : re-, re- + clāmāre, to cry out; see **kelə-** in App.] —**re·claim′a·ble** adj. —**re·claim′ant, re·claim′er** n.

re-claim (rē-klām′) tr.v. **-claimed, -claim·ing, -claims** To demand the restoration or return of (a possession, for example); claim again or back.

rec·la·ma·tion (rĕk′lə-mā′shən) n. **1.** The act or process of reclaiming. **2.** A restoration, as to usefulness or morality. [ME reclamacion < OFr. reclamation < Lat. reclāmātiō, reclāmātiōn-, cry of opposition < reclāmātus, p. part. of reclāmāre, to exclaim against. See RECLAIM.]

ré·clame (rā-klăm′) n. **1.** Public acclaim. **2.** A taste or flair for publicity. [Fr., advertising < réclamer, to claim, beg for < OFr. reclamer, to exclaim against. See RECLAIM.]

rec·li·nate (rĕk′lə-nāt′) adj. Botany Bent or turned downward toward the base. [Lat. reclīnātus, p. part. of reclīnāre, to recline. See RECLINE.]

re·cline (rĭ-klīn′) v. **-clined, -clin·ing, -clines** —tr. To cause to assume a leaning or prone position. —intr. To lie back or down. [ME reclinen < OFr. recliner < Lat. reclīnāre : re-, re- + -clīnāre, to bend; see **klei-** in App.] —**rec′li·na′tion** (rĕk′lə-nā′shən) n.

re·clin·er (rĭ-klī′nər) n. One that reclines, as an armchair that reclines when its back is lowered and its front raised.

re·cluse (rĕk′lōōs′, rĭ-klōōs′) n. A person who withdraws from the world to live in seclusion and often in solitude. ❖ adj. Withdrawn from the world; reclusive. [ME < OFr. *reclus* < Lat. *reclūsus*, p. part. of *reclūdere*, to shut up : *re-*, re- + *claudere*, to close.]

re·clu·sion (rĭ-klōō′zhən) *n.* **1.** The condition of being a recluse. **2.** The state of being in solitary confinement.

re·clu·sive (rĭ-klōō′sĭv, -zĭv) *adj.* **1.** Seeking or preferring seclusion or isolation: *a reclusive hermit.* **2.** Providing seclusion: *a reclusive hut.* —**re·clu′sive·ly** *adv.* —**re·clu′sive·ness** *n.*

rec·og·ni·tion (rĕk′əg-nĭsh′ən) *n.* **1.** The act of recognizing or condition of being recognized. **2.** An awareness that something perceived has been perceived before. **3.** An acceptance as true or valid, as of a claim. **4.** Attention or favorable notice. **5.** Official acceptance of the national status of a new government by another nation. **6.** *Biology* The ability of one molecule to attach itself to another molecule having a complementary shape. [Ult. < Lat. *cognitiō, recognition-,* act of recognizing < *recognitus,* p. part. of *recognōscere,* to recognize. See RECOGNIZE.] —**re·cog′ni·to·ry** (rĭ-kŏg′nĭ-tôr′ē, -tōr′ē), **re·cog′ni·tive** (-tĭv) *adj.*

re·cog·ni·zance (rĭ-kŏg′nĭ-zəns, -kŏn′ĭ-) *n.* **1.** *Law* **a.** An obligation of record that is entered into before a court or magistrate, containing a condition to perform a particular act, such as appearing in court. **b.** A sum of money pledged to assure such an act. **2.** A recognition. **3.** *Archaic* A pledge; a token. [ME *recognisance* < OFr. *recognuissance,* alteration of *reconnoissance* < *reconoistre, reconoiss-,* to recognize. See RECOGNIZE.] —**re·cog′ni·zant** *adj.*

rec·og·nize (rĕk′əg-nīz′) *tr.v.* **-nized, -niz·ing, -niz·es** **1.** To know to be something that has been perceived before: *recognize a face.* **2.** To know or identify from past experience or knowledge: *recognize hostility.* **3.** To perceive or show acceptance of the validity or reality of: *recognized the tenants' concerns.* **4.** To permit to address a meeting. **5.** To accept officially the national status of as a new government. **6.** To show awareness of; approve of or appreciate. **7.** To admit the acquaintance of, as by salutation. **8.** *Biology* To exhibit recognition for (an antigen, for example). [ME *recognisen,* to resume possession of land, alteration (influenced by Med.Lat. *recognizāre,* to recognize) of OFr. *reconoistre, reconoiss-,* to know again < Lat. *recognōscere* : *re-*, re- + *cognōscere,* to get to know; see **gnō-** in App.] —**rec′og·niz·a·ble** *adj.* —**rec′og·niz′a·bly** *adv.* —**rec′og·niz′er** *n.*

re·coil (rĭ-koil′) *intr.v.* **-coiled, -coil·ing, -coils** **1.** To spring back, as upon firing. **2.** To shrink back, as in fear. **3.** To fall back; return. ❖ *n.* (*also* rē′koil′) **1.** The backward action of a firearm upon firing. **2.** The act or state of recoiling. [ME *recoilen* < OFr. *reculer* : *re-*, re- + *cul,* buttocks (< Lat. *cūlus;* see **(s)keu-** in App.).] —**re·coil′er** *n.*

re·coil·less (rĭ-koil′lĭs, rē′koil′-) *adj.* Designed to minimize the effect of recoil: *a recoilless rifle.*

rec·ol·lect (rĕk′ə-lĕkt′) *v.* **-lect·ed, -lect·ing, -lects** —*tr.* To recall to mind. See Syns at **remember.** —*intr.* To remember something; have a recollection. [Med.Lat. *recolligere, recollect-* < Lat., to gather up : *re-*, re- + *colligere,* to collect; see COLLECT¹.] —**rec′ol·lec′tive** *adj.*

re·col·lect (rē′kə-lĕkt′) *tr.v.* **-lect·ed, -lect·ing, -lects** **1.** To collect again. **2.** To calm or control (oneself).

rec·ol·lec·tion (rĕk′ə-lĕk′shən) *n.* **1.** The act or power of recollecting. **2.** Something recollected.

re·com·bi·nant (rē-kŏm′bə-nənt) *n.* **1.** An organism or a cell in which genetic recombination has taken place. **2.** Material produced by genetic engineering. ❖ *adj.* **1.** Formed by or showing recombination: *a recombinant chromosome.* **2.** Of or relating to recombinant DNA.

recombinant DNA *n.* Genetically engineered DNA prepared by transplanting or splicing genes from one species into the cells of a host organism of a different species.

re·com·bi·nase (rē-kŏm′bə-nās′, -nāz′) *n.* An enzyme that catalyzes the crossing over of homologous chromosomes in genetic recombination.

re·com·bi·na·tion (rē′kŏm-bə-nā′shən) *n.* The natural formation in offspring of genetic combinations not present in parents, by the processes of crossing over or independent assortment.

re·com·bine (rē′kəm-bīn′) *v.* **-bined, -bin·ing, -bines** —*tr.* To combine (things) again. —*intr.* **1.** To combine again. **2.** *Genetics* To undergo or cause recombination.

rec·om·mend (rĕk′ə-mĕnd′) *v.* **-mend·ed, -mend·ing, -mends** —*tr.* **1.** To praise or commend (one) to another as being worthy or desirable; endorse. **2.** To make (the possessor, as of an attribute) attractive or acceptable. **3.** To commit to the charge of another; entrust. **4.** To advise or counsel. —*intr.* To give advice or counsel. [ME *recomenden* < Med.Lat. *recommendāre* : Lat. *re-*, re- + Lat. *commendāre,* to entrust, commend; see COMMEND.] —**rec′om·mend′a·ble** *adj.* —**rec′om·mend′er** *n.*

rec·om·men·da·tion (rĕk′ə-mĕn-dā′shən) *n.* **1.** The act of recommending. **2.** Something that recommends, esp. a favorable statement concerning character or qualifications. **3.** Something, such as a course of action, that is recommended. See Syns at **advice.** —**rec′om·men′da·to′ry** (-mĕn′də-tôr′ē, -tōr′ē) *adj.*

rec·om·mit (rē′kə-mĭt′) *tr.v.* **-mit·ted, -mit·ting, -mits** **1.** To commit again. **2.** To refer (proposed bills, for example) to a committee again. —**re′com·mit′ment, re′com·mit′tal** (-mĭt′l) *n.*

rec·om·pense (rĕk′əm-pĕns′) *tr.v.* **-pensed, -pens·ing,**

-pens·es **1.** To award compensation to: *recompensed those injured.* **2.** To award compensation for; make a return for. ❖ *n.* **1.** Amends made, as for loss. **2.** Payment in return for something, such as a service. [ME *recompensen* < OFr. *recompenser* < LLat. *recompēnsāre* : Lat. *re-*, re- + Lat. *compēnsāre,* to compensate; see COMPENSATE.]

re·con¹ (rē′kŏn) *n.* The smallest genetic unit capable of recombination. [REC(OMBINATION) + -ON¹.]

re·con² (rē′kŏn) *n. Informal* Reconnaissance.

rec·on·cil·a·ble (rĕk′ən-sī′lə-bəl, rĕk′ən-sī′-) *adj.* Capable of or qualified for reconciliation. —**rec′on·cil′a·bil′i·ty, rec′on·cil′a·ble·ness** *n.* —**rec′on·cil′a·bly** *adv.*

rec·on·cile (rĕk′ən-sīl′) *v.* **-ciled, -cil·ing, -ciles** —*tr.* **1.** To reestablish a close relationship between. **2.** To settle or resolve. **3.** To bring (oneself) to accept: *reconciled himself to the change in management.* **4.** To make compatible or consistent. See Syns at **adapt.** —*intr.* **1.** To reestablish a close relationship, as in marriage. **2.** To become compatible or consistent. [ME *reconcilen* < OFr. *reconcilier* < Lat. *reconciliāre* : *re-*, re- + *conciliāre,* to conciliate; see CONCILIATE.] —**rec′on·cile′ment** *n.* —**rec′on·cil′er** *n.* —**rec′on·cil′i·a·to′ry** (-sīl′ē-ə-tôr′ē, -tōr′ē) *adj.*

rec·on·cil·i·a·tion (rĕk′ən-sĭl′ē-ā′shən) *n.* **1.** The act of reconciling. **2.** The condition of being reconciled. **3.** See **penance** 2. [Ult. < Lat. *reconciliātiō, reconciliātiōn-* < *reconciliātus,* p. part. of *reconciliāre,* to reconcile. See RECONCILE.]

rec·on·dite (rĕk′ən-dīt′, rĭ-kŏn′dīt′) *adj.* **1.** Not easily understood; abstruse. **2.** Concerned with or treating something abstruse or obscure. **3.** Concealed; hidden. [Lat. *reconditus,* p. part. of *recondere,* to put away : *re-*, re- + *condere,* to put together, preserve; see **dhē-** in App.] —**rec′on·dite′ly** *adv.*

re·con·di·tion (rē′kən-dĭsh′ən) *tr.v.* **-tioned, -tion·ing, -tions** To restore to good condition, esp. by repairing, renovating, or rebuilding.

re·con·nais·sance also **re·con·nois·sance** (rĭ-kŏn′ə-səns, -zəns) *n.* An inspection or exploration of an area, esp. one made to gather military information. [Fr. < OFr. *reconnoissance,* recognition < *reconoistre, reconoiss-,* to recognize. See RECOGNIZE.]

re·con·noi·ter (rē′kə-noi′tər, rĕk′ə-) *v.* **-tered, -ter·ing, -ters** —*tr.* To make a preliminary inspection of, esp. in order to gather military information. —*intr.* To make a reconnaissance. [Obsolete Fr. *reconnôitre* < OFr. *reconoistre,* to recognize. See RECOGNIZE.] —**re′con·noi′ter·er** *n.*

re·con·sti·tute (rē-kŏn′stĭ-tōōt′, -tyōōt′) *tr.v.* **-tut·ed, -tut·ing, -tutes** **1.** To provide with a new structure. **2.** To bring (a liquid in concentrated or powder form) to normal strength by adding water.

re·con·struct (rē′kən-strŭkt′) *tr.v.* **-struct·ed, -struct·ing, -structs** **1.** To construct again; rebuild. **2.** To assemble or build again mentally; re-create: *reconstructed the scene in his mind.* **3.** To cause to adopt a new attitude or outlook. —**re′con·struct′i·ble** *adj.*

re·con·struc·tion (rē′kən-strŭk′shən) *n.* **1.** The act or result of reconstructing. **2. Reconstruction** The period (1865–77) when the federal government controlled the states that had seceded to the Confederacy before readmitting them to the Union.

Re·con·struc·tion·ism (rē′kən-strŭk′shə-nĭz′əm) *n.* The branch of Judaism founded in the United States in the 20th century that regards Judaism as a religious civilization and questions the doctrine that the Jews are God's chosen people. —**Re′con·struc′tion·ist** *adj. & n.*

re·con·struc·tive (rē′kən-strŭk′tĭv) *adj.* **1.** Relating to or characterized by reconstruction. **2.** Of or relating to surgery that restores or corrects defective or misshaped body parts: *reconstructive surgery.*

re·con·vert (rē′kən-vûrt′) *intr. & tr.v.* **-vert·ed, -vert·ing, -verts** To undergo or cause to undergo conversion to a previous state or condition. —**re′con·ver′sion** (-vûr′zhən, -shən) *n.*

re·con·vey (rē′kən-vā′) *tr.v.* **-veyed, -vey·ing, -veys** To convey to a former owner or place. —**re′con·vey′ance** *n.*

re·cord (rĭ-kôrd′) *v.* **-cord·ed, -cord·ing, -cords** —*tr.* **1.** To set down for preservation in writing or other permanent form. **2.** To register or indicate: *recorded the votes.* **3a.** To register (sound or images) in permanent form by mechanical or electrical means for reproduction. **b.** To register the words, sound, appearance, or performance of by such means. —*intr.* To record something. ❖ *n.* **rec·ord** (rĕk′ərd) **1a.** An account, as of facts, set down esp. in writing as a means of preserving knowledge. **b.** Something on which such an account is based. **c.** Something that records: *a fossil record.* **2.** Information on a particular subject collected and preserved: *the coldest day on record.* **3.** The known history of performance, activities, or achievement: *a police record.* **4.** An unsurpassed measurement. **5.** *Computer Science* A collection of related, often adjacent items of data, treated as a unit. **6.** *Law* **a.** An account officially written and preserved as evidence or testimony. **b.** An account of judicial or legislative proceedings written and preserved as evidence. **c.** The documents or volumes containing such evidence. **7a.** A disk designed to be played on a phonograph. **b.** Something, such as magnetic tape, on which sound or visual images have been recorded. —**idioms: go on record** To embrace a certain position publicly. **off the record** Not for publication. **on record** Known to have been stated or to have taken a certain

position. [ME *recorden* < OFr. *recorder* < Lat. *recordārī*, to remember : *re-*, re- + *cor*, *cord-*, heart; see **kerd-** in App.]

re·cord·er (rĭ-kôr′dər) *n.* **1.** One, such as a tape recorder, that makes recordings or records. **2.** *Music* A flute with eight finger holes and a whistlelike mouthpiece. [Sense 2, prob. < RECORD, to practice a tune, warble.]

re·cord·ing (rĭ-kôr′dĭng) *n.* **1.** Something on which sound or visual images have been recorded. **2.** A recorded sound or image or group of sounds or images.

re·cord·ist (rĭ-kôr′dĭst) *n.* One that records sound electronically, as for films or at concerts.

re·count (rĭ-kount′) *tr.v.* **-count·ed, -count·ing, -counts 1.** To narrate the facts or particulars of. **2.** To enumerate. [ME *recounten* < OFr. *reconter* : *re-*, re- + *conter*, relate; see COUNT[1].] **—re·count′al** *n.*

re-count (rē-kount′) *tr.v.* **-count·ed, -count·ing, -counts** To count again. ❖ *n. (also* rē′kount′*)* An additional count, esp. a second count of votes cast in an election.

re·coup (rĭ-kōōp′) *v.* **-couped, -coup·ing, -coups** *—tr.* **1.** To receive an equivalent for; make up for: *recoup a loss.* See Syns at **recover**. **2.** To return as an equivalent for; reimburse. **3.** *Law* To deduct or withhold (part of something due) for an equitable reason. *—intr.* To regain a favorable position. ❖ *n.* The act of recouping. [ME *recoupen* < OFr. *recouper*, to cut back : *re-*, re- + *couper*, to cut (< *coup*, blow; see COUP).] **—re·coup′a·ble** *adj.* **—re·coup′ment** *n.*

re·course (rē′kôrs′, -kōrs′, rĭ-kôrs′, -kōrs′) *n.* **1.** The act or an instance of turning or applying to a person or thing for aid or security. **2.** One that is turned or applied to for aid or security: *His only recourse was the police.* **3.** *Law* The right to demand payment from the endorser of a commercial paper when the first party liable fails to pay. [ME *recours* < OFr. < Lat. *recursus*, a running back : *re-*, re- + p. part. of *currere*, to run back : *re-*, re- + *currere*, to run.]

re·cov·er (rĭ-kŭv′ər) *v.* **-ered, -er·ing, -ers** *—tr.* **1.** To get back; regain. **2.** To restore (oneself) to a normal state. **3.** To compensate for: *recovered her losses.* **4.** To procure (usable substances, such as metal) from unusable substances, such as ore or waste. **5.** To bring under observation again. *—intr.* **1.** To regain a normal or usual condition, as of health. **2.** To receive a favorable judgment in a lawsuit. [ME *recoveren* < OFr. *recoverer* < Lat. *recuperāre*. See RECUPERATE.] **—re·cov′er·a·ble** *adj.* **—re·cov′er·er** *n.*

SYNONYMS *recover, regain, recoup, retrieve* These verbs mean to get back something lost or taken away. *Recover* is the least specific: *"In a few days Mr. Barnstaple had recovered strength of body and mind"* (H.G. Wells). *Regain* suggests success in recovering something that has been taken from one: *"hopeful to regain/Thy Love"* (John Milton). To *recoup* is to get back the equivalent of something lost: *recouped her expenses. Retrieve* pertains to the effortful recovery of something (*retrieved the ball*) or to the making good of something gone awry: *"By a brilliant coup he has retrieved . . . a rather serious loss"* (Samuel Butler).

re-cov·er (rē-kŭv′ər) *tr.v.* **-ered, -er·ing, -ers** To cover anew: *recover an armchair.*

re·cov·ered memory (rĭ-kŭv′ərd) *n.* A memory of an experience, esp. a traumatic one, that is recalled after an often lengthy period of repression.

re·cov·er·y (rĭ-kŭv′ə-rē) *n., pl.* **-ies 1.** The act, process, duration, or an instance of recovering. **2.** A return to a normal condition. **3.** Something gained or restored in recovering. **4.** The act of obtaining usable substances from unusable sources.

recovery room *n.* A hospital room equipped for the care and observation of patients immediately following surgery.

rec·re·ant (rĕk′rē-ənt) *adj.* **1.** Unfaithful or disloyal to a belief, duty, or cause. **2.** Craven or cowardly. ❖ *n.* **1.** A faithless or disloyal person. **2.** A coward. [ME *recreaunt*, defeated < OFr. *recreant*, pr. part. of *recroire*, to yield in a trial by combat < Med.Lat. *recrēdere*, to yield, pledge : Lat. *re-*, re- + Lat. *crēdere*, to believe; see **kerd-** in App.] **—rec′re·ance, rec′re·an·cy** *n.* **—rec′re·ant·ly** *adv.*

rec·re·ate (rĕk′rē-āt′) *v.* **-at·ed, -at·ing, -ates** *—tr.* To impart fresh life to; refresh mentally or physically. *—intr.* To take recreation. [ME *recreaten* < Lat. *recreāre*, *recreāt-* : *re-*, re- + *creāre*, to create; see CREATE.] **—rec′re·a′tive** *adj.*

re-cre·ate (rē′krē-āt′) *tr.v.* **-at·ed, -at·ing, -ates** To create anew.

rec·re·a·tion (rĕk′rē-ā′shən) *n.* Refreshment of one's mind or body through activity that amuses or stimulates; play. **—rec′re·a′tion·al** *adj.* **—rec′re·a′tion·al·ly** *adv.*

recreational vehicle *n.* A vehicle, such as a motor home, used for traveling and recreational activities.

recreation room *n.* A room in a house or institution suited for games, dancing, or other kinds of recreation.

rec·re·ment (rĕk′rə-mənt) *n.* Waste matter; dross. [Lat. *recrēmentum* : *re-*, re- + *cernere*, *crē-*, to separate; see **krei-** in App.] **—rec′re·men′tal** (-mĕn′tl) *adj.*

re·crim·i·nate (rĭ-krĭm′ə-nāt′) *v.* **-nat·ed, -nat·ing, -nates** *—tr.* To accuse in return. *—intr.* To counter one accusation with another. [Med.Lat. *recrīminārī*, *recrīminat-* : Lat. *re-*, re- + Lat. *crīmināre*, to accuse (< *crīmen*, *crīmin-*, accusation, crime; see

krei- in App.).] **—re·crim′i·na·tive, re·crim′i·na·to′ry** (-nə-tôr′ē, -tōr′ē) *adj.* **—re·crim′i·na′tor** *n.*

re·crim·i·na·tion (rĭ-krĭm′ə-nā′shən) *n.* **1.** The act of recriminating. **2.** A countercharge.

rec room (rĕk) *n. Informal* A recreation room.

re·cru·desce (rē′krōō-dĕs′) *intr.v.* **-desced, -desc·ing, -desc·es** To break out anew or come into renewed activity, as after quiescence. [Lat. *recrūdēscere*, to grow raw again : *re-*, re- + *crūdēscere*, to get worse (< *crūdus*, raw; see **kreuə-** in App.).] **—re′cru·des′cence** *n.* **—re′cru·des′cent** *adj.*

re·cruit (rĭ-krōōt′) *v.* **-cruit·ed, -cruit·ing, -cruits** *—tr.* **1.** To engage (persons) for military service. **2.** To strengthen or raise (an armed force) by enlistment. **3.** To supply with new members or employees. **4.** To enroll or seek to enroll: *colleges recruiting students.* **5.** To replenish. **6.** To renew or restore the health, vitality, or intensity of. *—intr.* **1.** To raise a military force. **2.** To obtain replacements for or new supplies of something lost, wasted, or needed. **3.** To regain lost health or strength; recover. ❖ *n.* **1.** A newly engaged member of a military force, esp. of the lowest level. **2.** A new member of an organization or body. [Fr. *recruter* < obsolete *recrute*, recruit, var. of *recrue* < fem. p. part. of *recroître*, to grow again < OFr. *recroistre* : *re-*, re- + *croistre*, to grow (< Lat. *crēscere*; see **ker-²** in App.).] **—re·cruit′er** *n.* **—re·cruit′ment** *n.*

rec·ta (rĕk′tə) *n.* A plural of **rectum.**

rec·tal (rĕk′təl) *adj.* Of, relating to, or situated near the rectum. **—rec′tal·ly** *adv.*

rec·tan·gle (rĕk′tăng′gəl) *n.* A four-sided plane figure with four right angles. [Fr. < Med.Lat. *rectangulum*, a right triangle < LLat. *rēctiangulum* : Lat. *rēctus*, right; see **reg-** in App. + Lat. *angulus*, angle.]

rec·tan·gu·lar (rĕk-tăng′gyə-lər) *adj.* **1.** Having the shape of a rectangle. **2.** Having one or more right angles. **3.** Relating to or being a geometric coordinate system with mutually perpendicular axes. **—rec·tan′gu·lar′i·ty** (-lăr′ĭ-tē) *n.* **—rec·tan′gu·lar·ly** *adv.*

rectangular coordinate *n.* A coordinate in a rectangular Cartesian coordinate system.

rec·ti·fi·er (rĕk′tə-fī′ər) *n.* **1.** One that corrects errors or rights wrongs. **2.** *Electronics* A device that converts alternating current to direct current. **3.** One who rectifies alcoholic beverages.

rec·ti·fy (rĕk′tə-fī′) *tr.v.* **-fied, -fy·ing, -fies 1.** To set right; correct. **2.** To correct by calculation or adjustment. See Syns at **correct. 3.** *Chemistry* To refine or purify, esp. by distillation. **4.** *Electronics* To convert (alternating current) into direct current. **5.** To adjust (the proof of alcoholic beverages) by adding liquid. [ME *rectifien* < OFr. *rectifier* < Med.Lat. *rēctificāre* : Lat. *rēctus*, right; see **reg-** in App. + Lat. *-ficāre*, -fy.] **—rec′ti·fi′a·ble** *adj.* **—rec′ti·fi·ca′tion** (-fĭ-kā′shən) *n.*

rec·ti·lin·e·ar (rĕk′tə-lĭn′ē-ər) *adj.* Moving in, consisting of, bounded by, or characterized by a straight line or lines. [< LLat. *rēctilīneus* : Lat. *rēctus*, right; see **reg-** in App. + Lat. *līnea*, line; see LINE[1].] **—rec′ti·lin′e·ar·ly** *adv.*

rec·ti·tude (rĕk′tĭ-tōōd′, -tyōōd′) *n.* **1.** Moral uprightness; righteousness. **2.** The quality or condition of judging correctly. **3.** The quality of being straight. [ME < OFr. < LLat. *rēctitūdō* < *rēctus*, straight. See **reg-** in App.] **—rec′ti·tu′di·nous** *adj.*

rec·to (rĕk′tō) *n., pl.* **-tos** A right-hand page of a book or the front side of a leaf, on the other side of the verso. [< Lat. *(foliō) rēctō*, (the leaf) being right, ablative of *rēctus*, straight, right. See **reg-** in App.]

rec·tor (rĕk′tər) *n.* **1.** An Episcopalian cleric in charge of a parish. **2.** An Anglican cleric who has charge of a parish and owns the tithes from it. **3.** A Roman Catholic priest serving as managerial and spiritual head of a church or other institution. **4.** The principal of certain schools, colleges, and universities. [ME < OFr. < Lat. *rēctor*, director < *rēctus*, p. part. of *regere*, to rule. See **reg-** in App.] **—rec′tor·ate** (-ĭt) *n.* **—rec·to′ri·al** (rĕk-tôr′ē-əl, -tōr′-) *adj.*

rec·to·ry (rĕk′tə-rē) *n., pl.* **-ries 1.** The house in which a parish priest or minister lives. **2a.** An Anglican rector's dwelling. **b.** An Anglican rector's office and benefice.

rec·trix (rĕk′trĭks) *n., pl.* **rec·tri·ces** (rĕk′trĭ-sēz′, rĕk-trī′sēz) One of the stiff main feathers of a bird's tail, used to control flight direction. [Lat. *rēctrīx*, fem. of *rēctor*, director. See RECTOR.]

rec·tum (rĕk′təm) *n., pl.* **-tums** or **-ta** (-tə) The terminal portion of the large intestine, extending from the sigmoid colon to the anal canal. [ME < Lat. *(intestīnum) rēctum*, straight (intestine), neut. of *rēctus*, straight. See **reg-** in App.]

rec·tus (rĕk′təs) *n., pl.* **-ti** (-tī′) Any of various straight muscles, as of the abdomen, eye, neck, and thigh. [NLat. *(mūsculus) rēctus* < Lat., straight (muscle). See RECTUM.]

re·cum·bent (rĭ-kŭm′bənt) *adj.* **1.** Lying down, esp. for comfort or rest; reclining. **2.** Resting; idle. **3.** *Biology* Resting on the surface from which it arises. Used of an organ or other structure. [Lat. *recumbēns*, *recumbent-*, pr. part. of *recumbere*, to lie down : *re-*, re- + *cumbere*, to lie.] **—re·cum′bence, re·cum′ben·cy** *n.* **—re·cum′bent·ly** *adv.*

re·cu·per·ate (rĭ-kōō′pə-rāt′, -kyōō′-) *v.* **-at·ed, -at·ing, -ates** *—intr.* **1.** To return to health or strength; recover. **2.** To recover from financial loss. *—tr.* **1.** To restore to health or strength.

2. To regain. [Lat. *recuperāre, recuperāt-* : *re-, re-* + *capere,* to take; see **kap-** in App.] **—re·cu′per·a′tion** *n.* **—re·cu′per·a′tive** (-pə-rā′tĭv, -pər-ə-tĭv), **re·cu′per·a·to·ry** (-pər-ə-tôr′ē, -tōr′ē) *adj.*

re·cur (rĭ-kûr′) *intr.v.* **-curred, -cur·ring, -curs 1.** To happen, come up, or show up again or repeatedly. **2.** To return to one's attention or memory. **3.** To return in thought or discourse. **4.** To have recourse: *recur to force.* [Lat. *recurrere* : *re-, re-* + *currere,* to run.] **—re·cur′rence** *n.*

re·cur·rent (rĭ-kûr′ənt, -kûr′-) *adj.* **1.** Occurring or appearing again or repeatedly. **2.** *Anatomy* Turning in a reverse direction. Used of blood vessels and nerves. **—re·cur′rent·ly** *adv.*

re·cur·ring decimal (rĭ-kûr′ĭng, -kûr′-) *n.* See **repeating decimal.**

re·cur·sion (rĭ-kûr′zhən) *n. Mathematics* **1.** An expression, such as a polynomial, each term of which is determined by application of a formula to preceding terms. **2.** A formula that generates the successive terms of a recursion. [LLat. *recursiō, recursiōn-,* a running back < Lat. *recursus,* p. part. of *recurrere,* to run back. See RECUR.] **—re·cur′sive** *adj.*

re·cur·vate (rē-kûrv′, -vĭt) *adj.* Bent or curved backward.

re·curve (rē-kûrv′) *tr. & intr.v.* **-curved, -curv·ing, -curves** To curve (something) backward or downward or become so curved. [Lat. *recurvāre* : *re-, re-* + *curvāre,* to curve (< *curvus,* curve; see CURVE).] **—re′cur·va′tion** (rē′kûr-vā′shən) *n.*

rec·u·sant (rĕk′yə-zənt, rĭ-kyōo′-) *n.* **1.** One of the Roman Catholics in England formerly incurred legal and social penalties for refusing to attend Church of England services. **2.** A dissenter; a nonconformist. **—rec′u·san·cy** *n.* **—rec′u·sant** *adj.*

re·cuse (rĭ-kyōoz′) *tr.v.* **-cused, -cus·ing, -cus·es** To disqualify or seek to disqualify from participation in a decision on grounds such as prejudice or personal involvement. [ME *recusen* < OFr. *recusar* < Lat. *recūsāre* : *re-, re-* + *causa,* cause.]

re·cy·cle (rē-sī′kəl) *tr.v.* **-cled, -cling, -cles 1.** To put or pass through a cycle again, as in an industrial process. **2.** To start a different cycle in. **3a.** To extract useful materials from (waste). **b.** To extract and esp. reprocess (materials found in waste) for reuse. **4a.** To use again: *recycle paper.* **b.** To adapt to a new use or function. **—re·cy′cla·ble** *adj. & n.* **—re·cy′cler** *n.*

red (rĕd) *n.* **1a.** The hue of the long-wave end of the visible spectrum, evoked in the human observer by radiant energy with wavelengths of approx. 630 to 750 nanometers; any of a group of colors whose hue resembles that of blood; one of the additive or light primaries; one of the psychological primary hues. **b.** A pigment or dye having a red hue. **c.** Something that has a red hue. **2a.** often **Red** A Communist. **b.** A revolutionary activist. ❖ *adj.* **red·der, red·dest 1.** Having a color resembling that of blood. **2.** Reddish in color or having parts that are reddish in color: *a red dog.* **3a.** Having a reddish or coppery skin color. **b.** often **Red** Often Offensive Of or being a Native American. **4.** Having a ruddy or flushed complexion: *red with embarrassment.* **5.** often **Red** Communist. **—idiom: in the red** Operating at a loss; in debt. [ME < OE *rēad.* See reudh- in App.] **—red′ly** *adv.* **—red′ness** *n.*

re·dact (rĭ-dăkt′) *tr.v.* **-dact·ed, -dact·ing, -dacts 1.** To draw up or frame (a proclamation, for example). **2.** To prepare for publication; edit or revise. [ME *redacten* < Lat. *redigere, redāct-,* to drive back : *re-, red-, re-* + *agere,* to drive; see ACT.] **—re·dac′tor** (-dăk′tər, -tôr′) *n.*

re·dac·tion (rĭ-dăk′shən) *n.* **1.** The act or process of editing or revising; preparation for publication. **2.** An edited work; a new edition or revision.

red alga *n.* Any of various predominantly marine algae of the division Rhodophyta, characteristically red or reddish in color.

red·bait (rĕd′bāt′) *tr.v.* **-bait·ed, -bait·ing, -baits** To accuse, denounce, or attack (a person, for example) as a Communist or a Communist sympathizer. **—red′bait′er** *n.*

red·bird (rĕd′bûrd′) *n.* Any of various birds with red plumage.

red blood cell *n.* A cell in the blood of vertebrates that transports oxygen and carbon dioxide to and from the tissues.

red-blood·ed (rĕd′blŭd′ĭd) *adj.* Strong and highly spirited.

red·breast (rĕd′brĕst′) *n.* **1.** A bird, such as the robin, that has a red breast. **2.** A freshwater sunfish (*Lepomis auritus*) of the eastern United States having a reddish belly.

red·brick (rĕd′brĭk′) *adj.* Of, relating to, or being the British universities other than Oxford and Cambridge. [So called because many of the buildings of such universities were built of red bricks.]

red·bud (rĕd′bŭd′) *n.* Any of several shrubs or small trees of the genus *Cercis,* having flat pods and pinkish flowers.

red bug also **red-bug** (rĕd′bŭg′) *n.* See **chigger 1.**

red·cap (rĕd′kăp′) *n.* A porter, usu. in a railroad station.

red card *n.* A red-colored card shown by a referee to a player, esp. in soccer, to indicate that the player is being ejected from the game. **—red′-card′** (rĕd′kärd′) *v.*

red carpet *n.* A carpet laid down for important visitors. **—idiom: roll out the red carpet** To welcome with great hospitality or ceremony.

red cedar *n.* **1.** An eastern North American evergreen coniferous tree (*Juniperus virginiana*) having purplish-black seed cones. **2.** A tall Pacific North American evergreen tree (*Thuja plicata*) having

scalelike opposite leaves and ovoid seed cones. **3.** The reddish aromatic durable wood of these trees.

red cent *n. Informal* Insignificant value: *not worth a red cent.*

Red Cloud Originally Makhpyia-luta. 1822–1909. Oglala Sioux leader of the resistance against the development of a trail through WY and MT by the US government (1865–67).

Red·cloud Peak (rĕd′kloud′) A mountain, 4,280.4 m (14,034 ft), in the San Juan Mts. of SW CO.

red clover *n.* A Eurasian plant (*Trifolium pratense*) having trifoliate leaves and globular heads of rose-purple flowers, naturalized in North America and planted as a forage crop.

red·coat (rĕd′kōt′) *n.* A British soldier, esp. one serving during the American Revolution.

red corpuscle *n.* See **red blood cell.**

Red Crescent *n.* **1.** A branch of the Red Cross organization operating in a Muslim country. **2.** The crescent-shaped emblem of such a branch.

Red Cross *n.* **1a.** An international organization that cares for the wounded, sick, and homeless in wartime and during and following natural disasters. **b.** A national branch of this organization. **2.** The emblem of this organization, a Geneva cross or a red Greek cross on a white background.

redd[1] (rĕd) *tr.v.* **redd·ed** or **redd, redd·ing, redds** *Chiefly Pennsylvania* To clear: *redd the dinner table.* **—phrasal verb: redd up** To tidy: *redded up the front room.* [ME dialectal *redden,* to clear an area (influenced by *redden,* to rescue, free from) < ON *rydhja.* See RID.]

REGIONAL NOTE The terms *redd* and *redd up* came to the American Midlands from the Scottish immigrants who settled there. Meaning "to clear an area or make it tidy," *redd* is still used in Scotland and Northern Ireland; in the United States it is common in Pennsylvania as the phrasal verb *redd up.*

redd[2] (rĕd) *n.* A spawning nest made by a fish, esp. a salmon or trout. [?]

red deer *n.* **1.** A common deer (*Cervus elaphus*) of Europe and Asia having a reddish-brown coat. **2.** The summer morph of the white-tailed deer, having a reddish coat.

Red Deer River A river rising in the Rocky Mts. of SW Alberta, Canada, and flowing c. 619 km (385 mi) to the South Saskatchewan R. just across the Saskatchewan border.

red·den (rĕd′n) *v.* **-dened, -den·ing, -dens** —*tr.* To make red. —*intr.* **1.** To become red. **2.** To blush.

red·dish (rĕd′ĭsh) *adj.* Mixed or tinged with red; somewhat red. **—red′dish·ness** *n.*

red·dle (rĕd′l) *n. & v.* Variant of **ruddle.**

red-dog (rĕd′dôg′, -dŏg′) *Football n.* See **blitz 3.** ❖ *v.* **-dogged, -dog·ging, -dogs** —*tr.* To rush (the quarterback) in a blitz. —*intr.* To carry out a blitz.

red drum *n.* A large food fish (*Sciaenops ocellata*) of the Atlantic coastal waters of North America.

rede (rēd) *tr.v.* **red·ed, red·ing, redes 1.** To give advice to; counsel. **2.** To interpret; explain. ❖ *n.* **1.** Advice or counsel. **2.** *Archaic* A narration. [ME *reden* < OE *rǣdan.*]

re·dec·o·rate (rē-dĕk′ə-rāt′) *v.* **-rat·ed, -rat·ing, -rates** —*tr.* To change the appearance or furnishings of; refurbish. —*intr.* To change a decorative scheme. **—re·dec′o·ra′tion** *n.* **—re·dec′o·ra′tor** *n.*

re·deem (rĭ-dēm′) *tr.v.* **-deemed, -deem·ing, -deems 1.** To recover ownership of by paying a specified sum. **2.** To pay off (a promissory note, for example). **3.** To turn in (coupons, for example) and receive something in exchange. **4.** To fulfill (a pledge, for example). **5.** To convert into cash: *redeem stocks.* **6.** To set free; rescue or ransom. **7.** To save from a state of sinfulness and its consequences. **8.** To make up for; compensate for. **9.** To restore the honor, worth, or reputation of. [ME *redemen* < OFr. *redimer* < Lat. *redimere* : *re-, red-, re-* + *emere,* to buy.] **—re·deem′a·ble** *adj.*

re·deem·er (rĭ-dē′mər) *n.* **1.** One who redeems. **2. Redeemer** *Christianity* Jesus.

red eft *n.* The bright red terrestrial stage in the life cycle of the newt (*Notophthalmus viridescens*) of the eastern United States.

re·de·liv·er (rē′dĭ-lĭv′ər) *tr.v.* **-ered, -er·ing, -ers 1.** To deliver again. **2.** To deliver in return; give back.

re·demp·tion (rĭ-dĕmp′shən) *n.* **1.** The act of redeeming or the condition of having been redeemed. **2.** Recovery of something pawned or mortgaged. **3.** The payment of an obligation, as a government's payment of the value of its bonds. **4.** Deliverance upon payment of ransom; rescue. **5.** *Christianity* Salvation from sin through Jesus's sacrifice. [ME *redempcioun* < OFr. *redemption* < Lat. *redēmptiō, redēmptiōn-* < *redēmptus,* p. part. of *redimere,* to redeem. See REDEEM.] **—re·demp′tion·al, re·demp′tive, re·demp′to·ry** (-tə-rē) *adj.*

re·demp·tion·er (rĭ-dĕmp′shə-nər) *n.* A colonial emigrant from Europe to America who paid for the voyage by serving for a specified period as a bondservant.

Re·demp·tor·ist (rĭ-dĕmp′tər-ĭst) *n.* A member of the Congregation of the Most Holy Redeemer, a Roman Catholic order founded in 1732 by Saint Alphonsus Liguori (1696–1787). [Fr. *rédemptoriste* < LLat. *redēmptor,* redeemer < Lat., contractor < p. part. of *redimere,* to buy back. See REDEEM.]

Red Cloud

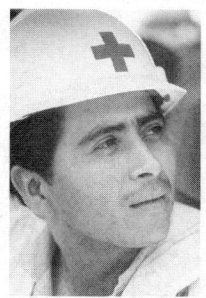

Red Cross

ă	pat	oi	boy
ā	pay	ou	out
âr	care	ŏŏ	took
ä	father	ōō	boot
ĕ	pet	ŭ	cut
ē	be	ûr	urge
ĭ	pit	th	thin
ī	pie	th	this
îr	pier	hw	which
ŏ	pot	zh	vision
ō	toe	ə	about,
ô	paw		item

Stress marks:
′ (primary);
′ (secondary), as in
lexicon (lĕk′sĭ-kŏn′)

red fox
Vulpes vulpes

red oak
northern red oak
Quercus rubra

re·de·ploy (rē′dĭ-ploi′) *tr.v.* **-ployed, -ploy·ing, -ploys** **1.** To move (military forces) from one combat zone to another. **2.** To shift (something) from one place or use to another for greater effectiveness. —**re′de·ploy′ment** *n.*

re·de·sign (rē′dĭ-zīn′) *tr.v.* **-signed, -sign·ing, -signs** To revise the appearance or function of. —**re′de·sign′** *n.*

re·de·vel·op (rē′dĭ-vĕl′əp) *v.* **-oped, -op·ing, -ops** —*tr.* **1.** To develop (something) again. **2.** To tone or intensify (a photographic print, for example) by a second developing process. **3.** To restore (buildings or neighborhoods, for example) to a better condition. —*intr.* To develop again. —**re′de·vel′op·er** *n.* —**re′de·vel′op·ment** *n.*

red·eye (rĕd′ī′) *n.* **1.** *Informal* A danger signal on a railroad. **2.** *Slang* A late-night or overnight flight. **3.** Any of several fishes with red eyes. **4.** *Slang* Inferior whiskey.

redeye gravy *n.* Gravy made from the juices of a cooked ham, thickened with flour and often containing black coffee.

red-faced (rĕd′fāst′) *adj.* Embarrassed.

red fir *n.* **1.** An evergreen tree (*Abies magnifica*) of California and Oregon having reddish wood valued as timber. **2.** The wood of this tree.

red fire *n.* Any of various combustible compounds, esp. salts of lithium or strontium, that burn bright red and are used in flares and fireworks.

red·fish (rĕd′fĭsh′) *n.*, *pl.* **redfish** or **-fish·es** Any of several fishes that are reddish in color, as the red drum.

red flag *n.* **1.** A warning signal. **2.** Something that demands attention or provokes an irritated reaction.

red fox *n.* A fox of the genus *Vulpes*, characteristically having reddish fur.

red giant *n.* A star of great size and brightness that has a relatively low surface temperature.

red grouse *n.* A grouse (*Lagopus lagopus* subsp. *scoticus*) of the British Isles that has chestnut plumage.

Red Guard *n.* **1.** A member of a Maoist youth movement in China, prominent during the Chinese Cultural Revolution of the late 1960s. **2.** A member of a radical political group with Maoist leanings. [Transl. of Chin. (Mandarin) *hóng wèibīng* : *hóng*, red + *wèi bīng*, guard (*wèi*, to defend + *bīng*, weapons, troops).]

red gum[1] *n.* Any of several Australian evergreen trees of the genus *Eucalyptus*, having lance-shaped aromatic leaves.

red gum[2] *n.* See **strophulus.**

red·hand·ed (rĕd′hăn′dĭd) *adv. & adj.* In the act of doing something wrong. [Earlier *red-hand*, with the hands red (from blood).] —**red′-hand′ed·ly** *adv.*

red·head (rĕd′hĕd′) *n.* **1.** A person with red hair. **2.** A North American duck (*Aythya americana*), the male of which has black and gray plumage and a reddish head.

red·head·ed (rĕd′hĕd′ĭd) *adj.* **1.** Having red hair. **2.** Having a red head: *a redheaded woodpecker.*

red heat *n.* **1.** The temperature of a red-hot substance. **2.** The physical condition of a red-hot substance.

red herring *n.* **1.** A smoked herring having a reddish color. **2.** Something that draws attention away from the central issue. [Sense 2 < being used to distract hunting dogs.]

red hind *n.* A reddish-brown grouper (*Epinephelus guttatus*) of the West Indies and the Gulf of Mexico.

red-hot (rĕd′hŏt′) *adj.* **1.** Glowing hot; very hot. **2.** Heated, as with excitement, anger, or enthusiasm. **3.** Very recent; new: *red-hot information.* ❖ *n.* **1.** See **hot dog.** **2.** A small, usu. round red candy strongly flavored with cinnamon.

re·di·a (rē′dē-ə) *n.*, *pl.* **-di·ae** (-dē-ē′) A larva of certain trematodes that is produced within the sporocyst and that can give rise to additional rediae or to cercariae. [NLat., after Francesco *Redi* (1626–97), Italian naturalist.]

re·did (rē-dĭd′) *v.* Past tense of **redo.**

re·dif·fer·en·ti·a·tion (rē′dĭf-ə-rĕn′shē-ā′shən) *n.* *Biology* A process by which a group of once differentiated cells return to their original specialized form.

red·in·gote (rĕd′ĭng-gōt′) *n.* **1.** A man's long double-breasted topcoat with full skirt. **2.** A woman's full-length unlined coat or dress open down the front to show a dress or underdress. [Fr., alteration of E. *riding coat.*]

red ink *n.* **1.** A financial loss in business. **2.** The condition of showing a fiscal deficit. [< the use of red ink to record debits and losses in financial records.]

red·in·te·gra·tion (rĕd-ĭn′tĭ-grā′shən, rĭ-dĭn′-) *n.* *Psychology* Evocation of a particular state of mind resulting from the recurrence of one of the elements that made up the original experience. [ME *redintegracion* < Lat. *redintegrātiō*, *redintegrātiōn-* < *redintegrāre*, to make whole again : *re-*, *red-*, re- + *integer*, whole, entire; see INTEGER.] —**red·in′te·gra′tive** *adj.* —**red·in′te·gra′tor** *n.*

re·di·rect (rē′dĭ-rĕkt′, -dī-) *tr.v.* **-rect·ed, -rect·ing, -rects** To change the direction or course of. ❖ *n.* (rē′dĭ-rĕkt′, -dī-) A redirect examination. —**re′di·rec′tion** *n.*

redirect examination *n.* Further examination of a witness after cross-examination, conducted by the party who first called the witness.

re·dis·count (rē-dĭs′kount′) *tr.v.* **-count·ed, -count·ing, -counts** To discount again. ❖ *n.* **1.** The act of rediscounting. **2.** Commercial paper that is discounted a second time. Often used in the plural.

re·dis·tri·bu·tion (rē′dĭs-trə-byōō′shən) *n.* **1.** The act or process of redistributing. **2.** An economic theory or policy that advocates reducing inequalities in the distribution of wealth. —**re′dis·tri·bu′tion·ist** *adj. & n.*

red·i·vi·vus (rĕd′ə-vī′vəs, -vē′-) *adj.* Come back to life; revived. [LLat. *redivīvus* < Lat., renewed : *re-*, red-, re- + *vīvus*, living; see VIVIFY.]

Red Jacket 1756?–1830. Seneca leader who advocated peace with the US while resisting the encroachment of settlers.

red lead (lĕd) *n.* A poisonous bright red powder, Pb_3O_4, used in paints, glass, pottery, and packing for pipe joints.

red-let·ter (rĕd′lĕt′ər) *adj.* Memorably happy. [< marking the holy days in church calendars in red.]

red light *n.* **1.** The red-colored light that signals traffic to stop. **2.** *Informal* A command to stop.

red-light district *n.* A neighborhood containing many brothels.

red·line (rĕd′līn′) *v.* **-lined, -lin·ing, -lines** —*intr.* **1.** To refuse home mortgages or home insurance to areas or neighborhoods deemed poor financial risks. **2.** *Computer Science* To mark or highlight edited text, as with a red line, to distinguish it from unedited portions of a document. —*tr.* **1.** To discriminate against by refusing to grant loans, mortgages, or insurance to. **2.** To remove from operational status because of mechanical defects or the need for scheduled maintenance. **3.** *Computer Science* To mark (edited text) by redlining.

red maple *n.* A medium-sized eastern North American maple (*Acer rubrum*) having reddish twigs and buds.

red meat *n.* Meat, esp. beef, that is red before being cooked.

Red·mond (rĕd′mənd) A city of W-central WA, a suburb of Seattle E of Lake Washington. Pop. 45,256.

red mulberry *n.* A deciduous eastern North American tree (*Morus rubra*) having irregularly lobed leaves and edible, red to purple fruit.

red mullet *n.* See **goatfish.**

red·neck (rĕd′nĕk′) *n.* *Offensive Slang* **1.** Used as a disparaging term for a member of the white rural laboring class, esp. in the southern United States. **2.** A white person regarded as having a provincial, conservative, often bigoted attitude.

re·do (rē-dōō′) *tr.v.* **-did** (-dĭd′), **-done** (-dŭn′), **-do·ing, -does** (-dŭz′) **1.** To do over again. **2.** To redecorate. ❖ *n.* (rē′dōō′) *pl.* **-dos** or **-do's** An act or instance of doing something again.

red oak *n.* Either of two eastern North American deciduous trees (*Quercus rubra* or *Q. falcata*) having deeply lobed leaves and a saucer-shaped cup enclosing part of the nut.

red ocher *n.* A form of hematite used as a pigment.

red·o·lence (rĕd′l-əns) also **red·o·len·cy** (-l-ən-sē) *n.* The quality or state of being redolent.

red·o·lent (rĕd′l-ənt) *adj.* **1.** Fragrant; aromatic. **2.** Suggestive; reminiscent: *redolent of politics.* [ME < OFr. < Lat. *redolēns*, *redolent-*, pr. part. of *redolēre*, to smell : *re-*, red-, re- + *olēre*, to smell.] —**red′o·lent·ly** *adv.*

Re·don (rə-dŏn′, -dôn′), **Odilon** 1840–1916. French artist who was a forerunner of surrealism.

red osier *n.* A North American shrub (*Cornus sericea*) often growing in dense clumps and having red branches, white flowers, and bluish-white drupes.

re·dou·ble (rē-dŭb′əl) *v.* **-bled, -bling, -bles** —*tr.* **1.** To double. **2.** To repeat. **3.** *Games* To double the doubling bid of (an opponent) in bridge. —*intr.* **1.** To become twice as great. **2.** *Games* To double a double in bridge. —**re·dou′ble** *n.*

re·doubt (rĭ-dout′) *n.* **1.** A small, often temporary defensive fortification. **2.** A reinforcing earthwork or breastwork within a permanent rampart. **3.** A protected place of refuge or defense. [Fr. *redoute* < Ital. *ridotto* < Med.Lat. *reductus*, concealed place < Lat., p. part. of *redūcere*, to withdraw, lead back. See REDUCE.]

Re·doubt (rĭ-dout′), **Mount** A volcano, 3,111 m (10,200 ft) of S AK; erupted in 1989 for the first time in 25 years.

re·doubt·a·ble (rĭ-dou′tə-bəl) *adj.* **1.** Arousing fear or awe; formidable. **2.** Worthy of respect or honor. [ME *redoubtabel* < OFr. *redoutable* < *redouter*, to dread : *re-*, re- + *douter*, to doubt, fear; see DOUBT.] —**re·doubt′a·bly** *adv.*

re·dound (rĭ-dound′) *intr.v.* **-dound·ed, -dound·ing, -dounds** **1.** To have an effect or consequence: *deeds that redound to one's credit.* **2.** To return; recoil: *Glory redounds upon the brave.* **3.** To contribute; accrue. [ME *redounden*, to flow abundantly < OFr. *redonder* < Lat. *redundāre*, to overflow. See REDUNDANT.]

red·out (rĕd′out′) *n.* A sudden reddening of the visual field accompanied by severe headache and caused by engorgement of the blood vessels of the head due to negative gravity, as in stunt flying.

re·dox (rē′dŏks′) *n.* Oxidation-reduction. [RED(UCTION) + OX(IDATION).]

red panda *n.* See **panda** 2.

red pepper *n.* **1.** The pungent red podlike fruit of any of several cultivars of the pepper plants, *Capsicum frutescens* and *C. annum.* **2.** See **cayenne pepper.**

red pine *n.* An evergreen timber tree (*Pinus resinosa*) of northeast North America, having long flexible glossy leaves that are grouped in fascicles of two.

red•poll (rĕd′pōl′) *n.* Any of several small finches of the genus *Carduelis* of northern North America and Eurasia, esp. *C. flammea,* having a red crown and black chin.

Red Poll or **Red Polled** *n.* Any of a breed of red hornless cattle developed in England and raised for milk and meat.

red puccoon *n.* See **bloodroot.**

re•dress (rĭ-drĕs′) *tr.v.* **-dressed, -dress•ing, -dress•es** **1.** To set right; remedy or rectify. **2.** To make amends to. **3.** To make amends for. See Syns at **correct. 4.** To adjust (a balance, for example). ❖ *n.* (*also* rē′drĕs) **1.** Satisfaction for wrong or injury; reparation. **2.** Correction or reformation. [ME *redressen* < OFr. *redrecier* : *re-,* re- + *drecier,* to arrange; see DRESS.] **—re•dress′er,** **re•dres′sor** *n.*

Red River 1. or in China **Yu•an Jiang** (yōō-än′ jyäng′, yü-) and in Vietnam **Hong Ha** (hông′ hä′) or **Song Hong** (sông′ hông′) A river of SE Asia rising in S China and flowing c. 1,175 km (730 mi) through N Vietnam to the Gulf of Tonkin. **2.** A river of the S-central US rising in two branches in the Texas Panhandle and flowing c. 1,638 km (1,018 mi) to the Mississippi R. **3.** also **Red River of the North** A river of the N-central US and S-central Canada formed by the confluence of two tributaries in W-central MN and flowing c. 499 km (310 mi) into SE Manitoba, Canada, where it empties into Lake Winnipeg.

red•root (rĕd′rōōt′, -rŏŏt′) *n.* **1.** An eastern North American bog plant (*Lachnanthes caroliana*) having red roots and woolly yellow flowers. **2.** A coarse cosmopolitan weed (*Amaranthus retroflexus*) having hairy leaves and stout terminal panicles with green flowers. **3.** See **ceanothus.**

red salmon *n.* See **sockeye salmon.**

Red Sea A sea between NE Africa and Arabia linked with the Mediterranean Sea by the Suez Canal and with the Gulf of Aden and the Arabian Sea through the Bab el Mandeb.

red•shank (rĕd′shăngk′) *n.* An Old World wading bird (*Tringa totanus*) having long red legs.

red shift or **red•shift** (rĕd′shĭft′) *n.* An increase in the wavelength of radiation emitted by a celestial body as a consequence of the Doppler effect. [< the fact that the longer wavelengths of light are at the red end of the visible spectrum.]

red•shirt (rĕd′shûrt′) *tr.v.* **-shirt•ed, -shirt•ing, -shirts** To keep (a college or school athlete) out of varsity competition for one year in order to extend the athlete's period of eligibility. [< the red jerseys worn by such athletes.] **—red′shirt′** *adj. & n.*

red•shoul•dered hawk (rĕd′shōl′dərd) *n.* A medium-sized North American hawk (*Buteo lineatus*) having rufous shoulder feathers and found in wet woodlands and savannas.

red•skin (rĕd′skĭn′) *n. Offensive Slang* Used as a disparaging term for a Native American.

red snapper *n.* Any of several marine food fishes of the genus *Lutjanus* of warm waters, having red or reddish bodies.

red snow *n.* Snow on which red-pigmented algae has grown, commonly found in Arctic and Alpine regions.

red spider *n.* Any of various small red mites of the family Tetranychidae that feed on vegetation, damaging the leaves.

red squill *n.* **1.** See **sea onion** 1. **2.** A powder prepared from the bulbs of the red squill and used as a rat poison.

red squirrel *n.* A North American squirrel (*Tamiasciurus hudsonicus*) having reddish or tawny fur.

red•start (rĕd′stärt′) *n.* **1.** A small North American bird (*Setophaga ruticilla*), the male of which has black plumage with orange patches on the wings and tail. **2.** A European bird (*Phoenicurus phoenicurus*) having grayish plumage and a rust-red breast and tail. [RED + obsolete *start,* tail (< ME *stert* < OE *steort*).]

red-tailed hawk (rĕd′tāld′) *n.* A heavy-bodied North American hawk (*Buteo jamaicensis*) that feeds primarily on rodents and has a conspicuous reddish-brown tail in the male.

red tape *n.* The collection or sequence of forms and procedures required to gain bureaucratic approval for something, esp. when oppressively complex and time-consuming. [< its former use in tying British official documents.]

red tide *n.* A bloom of dinoflagellates that cause reddish discoloration of coastal ocean waters and often produce toxins that kill fish and contaminate shellfish.

red•top (rĕd′tŏp′) *n.* A widely cultivated Eurasian grass (*Agrostis gigantea*) having reddish flower clusters.

re•duce (rĭ-dōōs′, -dyōōs′) *v.* **-duced, -duc•ing, -duc•es** *—tr.* **1.** To bring down, as in extent, amount, or degree; diminish. See Syns at **decrease. 2.** To bring to a humbler, weaker, difficult, or forced state or condition, esp.: **a.** To gain control of; conquer: "*a design to reduce them under absolute despotism*" (Declaration of Independence). **b.** To subject to destruction: *reduced the city to rubble.* **c.** To weaken bodily: *was reduced to emaciation.* **d.** To sap the spirit or mental energy of. **e.** To compel to desperate acts. **f.** To lower in rank or grade. **g.** To powder or pulverize. **h.** To thin (paint) with a solvent. **3.** To lower the price of. **4.** To put in order or arrange systematically. **5.** To separate into orderly components by analysis. **6.** *Chemistry* **a.** To decrease the valence of (an atom) by adding electrons. **b.** To remove oxygen from (a compound). **c.** To add hydrogen to (a compound). **d.** To change to a metallic state by removing nonmetallic constituents; smelt. **7.** *Mathematics* To simplify the form of (an expression, such as a fraction)

without changing the value. **8.** *Medicine* To restore (a fractured or displaced body part) to a normal condition or position. *—intr.* **1.** To become diminished. **2.** To lose weight, as by dieting. **3.** *Biology* To undergo meiosis. [ME *reducen,* to bring back < OFr. *reducier* < Lat. *redūcere* : *re-,* re- + *dūcere,* to lead; see **deuk-** in App.] **—re•duc′er** *n.* **—re•duc′i•bil′i•ty** *n.* **—re•duc′i•ble** *adj.* **—re•duc′i•bly** *adv.*

reducing agent *n.* A substance that chemically reduces other substances, esp. by donating an electron or electrons.

re•duc•tant (rĭ-dŭk′tənt) *n.* A reducing agent.

re•duc•tase (rĭ-dŭk′tās′, -tāz′) *n.* Any of various enzymes that catalyze the reduction of an organic compound. [REDUCT(ION) + −ASE.]

re•duc•ti•o ad ab•sur•dum (rĭ-dŭk′tē-ō ăd əb-sûr′dəm, -zûr′-, -shē-ō) *n., pl.* **-o•nes ad absurdum** (-ō′nēz, -nās) Disproof of a proposition by showing that it leads to absurd or untenable conclusions. [Med.Lat. *reductiō ad absurdum* : Lat. *reductiō,* a bringing back, reduction + Lat. *ad,* to + Lat. *absurdum,* absurdity < neut. of *absurdus,* absurd.]

re•duc•tion (rĭ-dŭk′shən) *n.* **1.** The act or process of reducing. **2.** The result of reducing. **3.** The amount by which something is lessened or diminished. **4.** *Biology* The first meiotic division, in which the chromosome number is reduced. **5.** *Chemistry* **a.** A decrease in positive valence or an increase in negative valence by the gaining of electrons. **b.** A reaction in which hydrogen is combined with a compound. **c.** A reaction in which oxygen is removed from a compound. **6.** *Mathematics* **a.** The canceling of common factors in the numerator and denominator of a fraction. **b.** The converting of a fraction to its decimal equivalent. **c.** The converting of an expression or equation to its simplest form. [Ult. < Lat. *reductiō, reductiōn-,* restoration < *reductus,* p. part. of *redūcere,* to bring back. See REDUCE.] **—re•duc′tion•al** *adj.*

re•duc•tion•ism (rĭ-dŭk′shə-nĭz′əm) *n.* An attempt or tendency to explain a complex set of facts, entities, phenomena, or structures by another, simpler set. **—re•duc′tion•ist** *adj. & n.* **—re•duc′tion•is′tic** *adj.*

re•duc•tive (rĭ-dŭk′tĭv) *adj.* **1.** Of or relating to reduction. **2.** Relating to or exhibiting reductionism. **3.** Relating to or being an instance of reductivism. **—re•duc′tive•ly** *adv.*

re•duc•tiv•ism (rĭ-dŭk′tə-vĭz′əm) *n.* See **minimalism** 1. **—re•duc′tiv•ist** *n.*

re•dun•dan•cy (rĭ-dŭn′dən-sē) *n., pl.* **-cies 1.** The state of being redundant. **2.** A superfluity; an excess. **3.** Repetition of linguistic information inherent in the structure of a language, as singularity in the sentence *It works.* **4.** Unnecessary repetition. **5.** *Electronics* Duplication or repetition of elements in electronic equipment to provide alternative functional channels in case of failure. **6.** Repetition of parts or all of a message to circumvent transmission errors.

USAGE NOTE The usages that critics have condemned as redundancies fall into several classes. In some cases, such as *consensus of opinion, close proximity, hollow tube,* and *refer back,* the use of what is regarded as an unnecessary modifier or qualifier can sometimes be justified on the grounds that it in fact makes a semantic contribution. Thus a *hollow tube* can be distinguished from one that has been blocked up with deposits, and a *consensus of opinion* can be distinguished from a consensus of judgments or practice. In other cases the use of the qualifier is harder to defend. Thus there is no way to *revert* without *reverting back* and no *consensus* that is not *general.* See Usage Note at **refer.**

---

re•dun•dant (rĭ-dŭn′dənt) *adj.* **1.** Exceeding what is necessary or natural; superfluous. **2.** Needlessly repetitive; verbose. **3.** Of or relating to linguistic redundancy. **4.** *Chiefly British* Dismissed or laid off from work, as for being no longer needed. **5.** *Electronics* Of or involving redundancy in electronic equipment. **6.** Of or involving redundancy in the transmission of messages. [Lat. *redundāns, redundant-,* pr. part. of *redundāre,* to overflow : *re-, red-,* re- + *undāre,* to surge (< *unda,* wave; see **wed-** in App.).] **—re•dun′dant•ly** *adv.*

re•du•pli•cate (rĭ-dōō′plə-kāt′, -dyōō′-) *v.* **-cat•ed, -cat•ing, -cates** *—tr.* **1.** To repeat over and again; redouble. **2.** *Linguistics* **a.** To double (the initial syllable or all of a root word) to produce an inflectional or derivational form. **b.** To form (a new word) by doubling all or part of a word. *—intr.* To be doubled. ❖ *adj.* (-plĭ-kĭt) Doubled. [LLat. *reduplicāre, reduplicāt-* : Lat. *re-,* re- + Lat. *duplicāre,* to duplicate; see DUPLICATE.] **—re•du•pli•ca•tion** (rĭ-dōō′plĭ-kā′shən, -dyōō′-) *n.* **1.** The act of reduplicating or the state of being reduplicated. **2.** The product or result of reduplicating. **3.** *Linguistics* **a.** A word formed by or containing a reduplicated element. **b.** The added element in a word form that is reduplicated. **—re•du′pli•ca′tive** *adj.* **—re•du′pli•ca′tive•ly** *adv.*

re•du•vi•id (rĭ-dōō′vē-ĭd, -dyōō′-) *n.* See **assassin bug.** [< NLat. *Reduviidae,* family name < *Reduvius,* type genus < Lat. *reduvia,* hangnail, fragment.]

re•dux (rē-dŭks′) *adj.* Brought back; returned. Used postpositively. [Lat. : *re-,* re- + *dux,* leader; see DUKE.]

red valerian *n.* A Mediterranean perennial plant (*Centranthus ruber*) having glabrous ovate leaves and fragrant, crimson to pale

---

red-tailed hawk
Buteo jamaicensis

ă	pat	oi	boy
ā	pay	ou	out
âr	care	ŏŏ	took
ä	father	ōō	boot
ĕ	pet	ŭ	cut
ē	be	ûr	urge
ĭ	pit	th	thin
ī	pie	*th*	this
îr	pier	hw	which
ŏ	pot	zh	vision
ō	toe	ə	about,
ô	paw		item

Stress marks:
′ (primary);
′ (secondary), as in
lexicon (lĕk′sĭ-kŏn′)

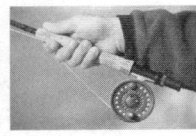

reel¹
top: reel of film
bottom: fishing reel

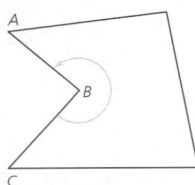

reentrant angle
Angle *CBA* is
a reentrant angle

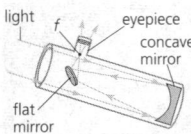

reflecting telescope
Newton's reflecting
telescope; *f* indicates the
focus

red flowers borne in dense terminal clusters.

red•wing (rĕd′wĭng′) *n.* **1.** See **red-winged blackbird. 2.** A European thrush (*Turdus iliacus*) having reddish feathers under the wings and a white eye stripe.

red-winged blackbird (rĕd′wĭngd′) *n.* A North American blackbird (*Agelaius phoeniceus*), the male of which has scarlet patches on the wings.

red wolf *n.* A small reddish wolf (*Canis rufus*) of the southeast United States that exists almost exclusively in captivity.

red•wood (rĕd′wo͝od′) *n.* **1a.** A tall evergreen tree (*Sequoia sempervirens*) native to Oregon and California and having small seed-bearing cones with peltate scales and unflattened branches. **b.** The soft reddish wood of this tree. **2.** Any of various woods having a reddish color or yielding a red dye.

re•ech•o (rĭ-ĕk′ō) *v.* **-oed, -o•ing, -oes** —*intr.* To sound back or reverberate. —*tr.* To echo back; repeat.

reed (rēd) *n.* **1a.** Any of various tall perennial grasses, esp. of the genera *Phragmites* or *Arundo*, having hollow stems, broad leaves, and large plumelike terminal panicles. **b.** The stalk of any of these plants. **c.** A collection of these stalks. **2.** *Music* A simple wind instrument made of a hollow reed stalk. **3.** *Music* **a.** A flexible strip of cane or metal set into the mouthpiece or air opening of certain instruments to produce tone by vibrating. **b.** An instrument, such as an oboe, that is fitted with a reed. **4.** A narrow frame fitted with reed or metal strips that separate the warp threads in weaving. **5.** *Architecture* A reeding. [ME *rede* < OE *hrēod*.]

Reed, John 1887–1920. Amer. journalist who wrote *Ten Days That Shook the World* (1919), an account of the Russian Revolution (1917).

Reed, Walter 1851–1902. Amer. physician who proved that yellow fever was transmitted by the *Aedes aegypti* mosquito.

reed•bird (rēd′bûrd′) *n.* See **bobolink.**

reed•buck (rēd′bŭk′) *n.* Any of several African antelopes of the genus *Redunca*, having long hooves, small horns that curve forward, and a short bushy tail. [Transl. of Afr. *rietbok*.]

reed•ing (rē′dĭng) *n.* **1.** *Architecture* A convex decorative molding having parallel strips resembling thin reeds. **2.** Parallel grooves cut into the edge of a coin at right angles to the faces.

reed mace *n.* See **cattail.**

reed organ *n.* A harmonium.

reed pipe *n.* *Music* An organ pipe with a reed that vibrates and produces a tone when air is forced through it.

reed stop *n.* *Music* A stop on an organ made up of or controlling reed pipes.

re•ed•u•cate (rē-ĕj′ə-kāt′) *tr.v.* **-cat•ed, -cat•ing, -cates 1.** To instruct again, esp. to change someone's behavior or beliefs. **2.** To retrain (a person) to function effectively; rehabilitate. —**re•ed′u•ca′tion** *n.*

reed•y (rē′dē) *adj.* **-i•er, -i•est 1.** Full of reeds. **2.** Made of reeds. **3.** Resembling a reed, esp. in being thin or fragile. **4.** *Music* Having a tone like that of a reed instrument. —**reed′i•ness** *n.*

reef¹ (rēf) *n.* **1.** A strip or ridge of rocks, sand, or coral that rises to or near the surface of a body of water. **2.** A vein of ore. [Obsolete Du. *rif*, poss. < ON, ridge.] —**reef′y** *adj.*

reef² (rēf) *Nautical n.* A portion of a sail rolled and tied down to lessen the area exposed to the wind. ❖ *tr.v.* **reefed, reef•ing, reefs** To reduce the size of (a sail) by tucking in a part and tying it to or rolling it around a yard or a boom. [ME *riff* < ON *rif*, ridge, reef.]

reef•er¹ (rē′fər) *n.* **1.** A short, heavy, close-fitting double-breasted jacket. **2.** A close-fitting single-breasted or double-breasted coat. **3.** *Nautical* A person, esp. a midshipman, who reefs.

reef•er² (rē′fər) *n.* *Slang* Marijuana, esp. a marijuana cigarette. [?]

ree•fer³ (rē′fər) *n.* *Slang* **1.** A conveyance, such as a railroad car or truck trailer, that carries cargo under refrigeration. **2.** A refrigerator. [Alteration of REFRIGERATOR.]

reef knot *n.* *Nautical* A square knot used in reefing sails.

reek (rēk) *v.* **reeked, reek•ing, reeks** —*intr.* **1.** To smoke, steam, or fume. **2.** To be pervaded by something unpleasant. **3.** To give off or become permeated with a strong unpleasant odor. —*tr.* **1.** To emit or exude (smoke, for example). **2.** To process or treat by exposing to smoke. ❖ *n.* **1.** A strong offensive odor. **2.** Vapor; steam. [ME *reken*, to emit smoke < OE *rēocan*, to emit smoke, and *rēcan*, to expose to smoke.] —**reek′er** *n.* —**reek′y** *adj.*

reel¹ (rēl) *n.* **1.** A device, such as a spool, that turns on an axis and is used for winding and storing rope, film, or other flexible materials. **2.** A cylindrical device attached to a fishing rod to let out or wind up the line. **3.** The quantity of wire, film, or other material wound on one reel. **4.** A set of curved lawnmower blades that rotate around a bar parallel to the ground, cutting grass while moving against a stationary straight blade. ❖ *tr.v.* **reeled, reel•ing, reels 1.** To wind on or let out from a reel. **2.** To recover by winding on a reel: *reel in a fish.* —*phrasal verb:* **reel off** To recite fluently and usu. at length: *reeled off names.* [ME < OE *hrēol*.] —**reel′a•ble** *adj.*

reel² (rēl) *v.* **reeled, reel•ing, reels** —*intr.* **1.** To be thrown off balance or fall back: *reeled from the sharp blow.* **2.** To stagger, lurch, or sway, as from drunkenness: *reeled down the alley.* **3.** To go round and round in a whirling motion: *gulls reeling and diving.* **4.** To feel dizzy. —*tr.* To cause to reel. ❖ *n.* **1.** A staggering, sway-

ing, or whirling movement. **2a.** A moderately fast dance of Scottish origin. **b.** The Virginia reel. **c.** The music for one of these dances. [ME *relen*, to whirl about, prob. < *reel*, spool. See REEL¹.] —**reel′er** *n.*

reel³ (rēl) *n.* *Maine* A hand-held hammer used in a quarry for shaping granite blocks.

re•e•lect (rē′ĭ-lĕkt′) *tr.v.* **-lect•ed, -lect•ing, -lects** To elect again. —**re′e•lec′tion** *n.*

reel•ing (rē′lĭng) *n.* *Maine* Sustained noise, as from hammering: *"Hark that reeling, now, you'll wake the baby!"* (Anonymous).

reel-to-reel (rēl′tə-rēl′) *adj.* Relating to or being sound recording equipment or sound recordings using magnetic tape that must be threaded through the equipment and onto an empty reel.

re•en•act (rē′ĕn-ăkt′, -ə-năkt′) *tr.v.* **-act•ed, -act•ing, -acts 1.** To enact again: *reenact a law.* **2.** To perform again: *reenact the scene.* **3.** To go through a second time. —**re′en•act′ment** *n.*

re•en•force (rē′ĭn-fôrs′, -fōrs′) *v.* Variant of **reinforce.**

re•en•ter (rē-ĕn′tər) *v.* **-tered, -ter•ing, -ters 1.** To enter or come in to again. **2.** To record again on a list or ledger. —*intr.* To come in or enter again. —**re•en′trance** *n.*

re•en•trant (rē-ĕn′trənt) *adj.* Reentering; pointing inward. ❖ *n.* A reentrant angle or part.

reentrant angle also **re-entrant angle** *n.* In an irregular polygon, an interior angle that is greater than 180° and whose apex faces into the polygon.

re•en•try (rē-ĕn′trē) *n., pl.* **-tries 1.** The act of reentering. **2.** The return of a missile or spacecraft into Earth's atmosphere.

reeve¹ (rēv) *n.* **1.** The elected president of a town council in some parts of Canada. **2.** Any of various minor officers of parishes or other local authorities. **3.** A bailiff or steward of a manor in the later medieval period. **4.** A high officer of local administration appointed by the Anglo-Saxon kings. [ME < OE *gerēfa.*]

reeve² (rēv) *tr.v.* **reeved** or **rove** (rōv), **reev•ing, reeves** *Nautical* **1.** To pass (a line or rod) through a hole, ring, fairlead, or block. **2.** To fasten by passing through or around. [?]

reeve³ (rēv) *n.* The female ruff. [Prob. alteration of RUFF¹.]

ref (rĕf) *n. Informal* A referee.

ref. *abbr.* **1.** reference **2.** referred

re•fect (rĭ-fĕkt′) *tr.v.* **-fect•ed, -fect•ing, -fects** *Archaic* To refresh with food and drink. [Lat. *reficere, refect-*, to refresh : *re-*, re- + *facere* to make; see **dhē-** in App.]

re•fec•tion (rĭ-fĕk′shən) *n.* **1.** Refreshment with food and drink. **2.** A light meal or repast.

re•fec•to•ry (rĭ-fĕk′tə-rē) *n., pl.* **-ries** A room where meals are served, esp. in a college or other institution.

refectory table *n.* A long table with straight heavy legs.

re•fer (rĭ-fûr′) *v.* **-ferred, -fer•ring, -fers** —*tr.* **1.** To direct to a source for help or information: *referred her to a heart specialist.* **2.** To assign or attribute to; regard as originated by. **3.** To assign to or regard as belonging within a particular kind or class. **4.** To submit (a matter in dispute) to an authority for arbitration, decision, or examination. **5.** To direct the attention of: *refer him to his actions.* —*intr.* **1.** To pertain; concern: *questions referring to yesterday's lecture.* **2.** To make mention or reference. **3.** To have recourse; turn: *refer to a dictionary.* [ME *referren* < OFr. *referer* < Lat. *referre* : *re-*, re- + *ferre*, to carry; see **bher-¹** in App.] —**ref′er•a•ble** (rĕf′ər-ə-bəl, rĭ-fûr′-) *adj.* —**re•fer′rer** *n.*

ref•e•ree (rĕf′ə-rē′) *n.* **1.** One to whom something is referred, esp. for settlement, decision, or an opinion as to the thing's quality. **2.** *Sports & Games* An official supervising the play; an umpire. **3.** *Law* A person appointed by a court to make a determination of a case or investigate and make a report on it. ❖ *v.* **-reed, -ree•ing, -rees** —*tr.* To judge as referee. —*intr.* To act as referee.

ref•er•ence (rĕf′ər-əns, rĕf′rəns) *n.* **1.** An act of referring. **2a.** Significance in a specified context: *Her speeches have special reference to environmental policy.* **b.** Meaning or denotation. **3.** The state of being related or referred: *in reference to.* **4.** A mention of an occurrence or situation. **5a.** A note in a publication referring the reader to another passage or source. **b.** The passage or source so referred to. **c.** A work frequently used as a source. **d.** A mark or footnote used to direct a reader elsewhere for additional information. **6a.** A person who is in a position to recommend another or vouch for his or her fitness, as for a job. **b.** A statement about a person's qualifications, character, and dependability. ❖ *tr.v.* **-enced, -enc•ing, -ences 1.** To supply references to. **2.** To mention in a reference; refer to: *He referenced her book.* See Usage Note at **allude.** —**ref′er•enc′er** *n.* —**ref′er•en′tial** (-ə-rĕn′shəl) *adj.* —**ref′er•en′tial•ly** *adv.*

reference book *n.* A book, such as a dictionary, to which one can refer for authoritative information.

reference frame *n.* See **frame of reference** 1.

ref•er•en•dum (rĕf′ə-rĕn′dəm) *n., pl.* **-dums** or **-da** (-də) **1a.**

The submission of a proposed public measure or actual statute to a direct popular vote. **b.** Such a vote. **2.** A note from a diplomat to the diplomat's government requesting instructions. [Lat., neut. gerundive of *referre*, to refer. See REFER.]

ref•er•ent (rĕf′ər-ənt, rĭ-fûr′ənt) *n.* A person or thing to which a linguistic expression refers.

re•ferred pain (rĭ-fûrd′) *n.* Pain that is felt in a part of the body at a distance from the area of pathology.

re•fill (rē-fĭl′) *tr.v.* **-filled, -fill•ing, -fills** To fill again. ❖ *n.* (rē′fĭl′) **1.** A product packaged to replace the used contents of a container. **2.** A second or subsequent filling.

re•fin•ance (rē′fə-năns′, rē-fī′năns′) *intr. & tr.v.* **-nanced, -nanc•ing, -nanc•es** To provide new financing or provide new financing for, as by discharging a mortgage with the proceeds from a new mortgage obtained at a lower interest rate. **—re•fi′nance′** *n.* **—re′fi•nan′cer, re′fin•an•cier′** (-fĭn-ən-sîr′, -fə-năn′-) *n.*

re•fine (rĭ-fīn′) *v.* **-fined, -fin•ing, -fines** *—tr.* **1.** To reduce to a pure state; purify. **2.** To remove by purifying. **3.** To free from coarse, unsuitable, or immoral characteristics: *refined his manners.* *—intr.* **1.** To become free of impurities. **2.** To acquire polish or elegance. **3.** To use precise distinctions and subtlety in thought or speech. **—re•fin′er** *n.*

re•fined (rĭ-fīnd′) *adj.* **1.** Free from coarseness or vulgarity; polite. **2.** Free of impurities; purified. **3.** Highly precise.

re•fine•ment (rĭ-fīn′mənt) *n.* **1.** The act of refining. **2.** The result of refining; an improvement or elaboration. **3.** The state or quality of being refined; cultivation, as in taste. **4.** A keen or precise phrasing; a subtle distinction.

re•fin•er•y (rĭ-fī′nə-rē) *n., pl.* **-ies** An industrial plant for purifying a crude substance, such as petroleum or sugar.

re•fin•ish (rē-fĭn′ĭsh) *tr.v.* **-ished, -ish•ing, -ish•es** To put a new finish on (furniture). **—re•fin′ish•er** *n.*

re•fit (rē-fĭt′) *v.* **-fit•ted, -fit•ting, -fits** *—tr.* To prepare and equip for additional use. *—intr.* To be made fit again. ❖ *n.* (rē′fĭt′, rē-fĭt′) **1.** Repair of damage or wear. **2.** A secondary or subsequent preparation of supplies and equipment.

re•flag (rē-flăg′) *tr.v.* **-flagged, -flag•ging, -flags** To give a new registered nationality to (a ship or an aircraft).

re•flect (rĭ-flĕkt′) *v.* **-flect•ed, -flect•ing, -flects** *—tr.* **1.** To throw or bend back (light, for example) from a surface. **2.** To give back or show an image of (an object); mirror. **3.** To make apparent; express or manifest: *Her work reflects intelligence.* **4.** To bring as a consequence: *The victory reflects credit on the coach.* **5.** *Archaic* To bend back. *—intr.* **1.** To be bent or thrown back: *Her voice reflected off the canyon walls.* **2.** To give something back, as light or sound: *a shiny surface that reflects well.* **3a.** To give evidence of the characteristics or qualities of someone or something. **b.** To bring blame or discredit. **4a.** To think seriously. **b.** To express carefully considered thoughts: *In the essay, he reflects on his career.* [ME *reflecten* < OFr. *reflecter* < Lat. *reflectere*, to bend back : *re-*, re- + *flectere*, to bend.]

re•flec•tance (rĭ-flĕk′təns) *n.* The ratio of the total amount of radiation, as of light, reflected by a surface to the total amount of radiation incident on the surface.

re•flect•ing telescope (rĭ-flĕk′tĭng) *n.* A telescope in which light from the object is gathered and focused by a concave mirror.

re•flec•tion (rĭ-flĕk′shən) *n.* **1.** The act of reflecting or the state of being reflected. **2.** Something, such as light, that is reflected. **3a.** Mental concentration; careful consideration. **b.** A thought or an opinion resulting from such consideration. **4.** An indirect expression of censure or discredit. **5.** A manifestation or result. **6.** *Anatomy* **a.** The folding of a membrane from the wall of a cavity over an organ. **b.** The folds so made. **—re•flec′tion•al** *adj.*

re•flec•tive (rĭ-flĕk′tĭv) *adj.* **1a.** Of, relating to, produced by, or resulting from reflection. **b.** Capable of or producing reflection. **2.** Characterized by or given to meditation or contemplation; thoughtful. See Syns at **pensive.** **—re•flec′tive•ly** *adv.* **—re•flec′tive•ness** *n.*

re•flec•tiv•i•ty (rē′flĕk-tĭv′ĭ-tē) *n., pl.* **-ties 1.** The quality of being reflective. **2.** The ability to reflect. **3.** *Physics* The ratio of the energy of a wave reflected from a surface to the energy possessed by the wave striking the surface.

re•flec•tom•e•ter (rē′flĕk-tŏm′ĭ-tər) *n.* An instrument for measuring the reflectance of a surface.

re•flec•tor (rĭ-flĕk′tər) *n.* **1.** Something, such as a surface, that reflects. **2.** A reflecting telescope.

re•flec•tor•ize (rĭ-flĕk′tə-rīz′) *tr.v.* **-ized, -iz•ing, -iz•es** To cause (a surface, for example) to reflect light, as by chemical treatment.

re•flex (rē′flĕks′) *adj.* **1.** Bent, turned, or thrown back; reflected. **2.** *Physiology* Being an involuntary action or response, such as a sneeze. **3.** Produced as an automatic response or reaction: *reflex opposition to change.* ❖ *n.* **1a.** Something, such as light, that is reflected. **b.** An image produced by reflection. **c.** A copy or reproduction. **2.** *Physiology* An involuntary response to a stimulus. **3.** *Psychology* An unlearned or instinctive response to a stimulus. **4.** *Linguistics* A form or feature that reflects or represents an earlier, often reconstructed form or feature having undergone phonetic or other change. ❖ *tr.v.* (rĭ-flĕks′) **-flexed, -flex•ing, -flex•es 1.** To bend, turn back, or reflect. **2.** To cause to undergo a reflex process. [< ME *reflexen*, to refract light, bend back < Lat. *reflexus*, p. part. of *reflectere*, to bend back. See REFLECT.]

reflex angle *n.* An angle between 180° and 360°.

reflex arc *n.* *Physiology* The neural path of a reflex.

reflex camera *n.* A camera with a mirror that reflects the image onto a viewing screen so that focus may be evaluated.

re•flex•ion (rĭ-flĕk′shən) *n.* *Chiefly British* Variant of **reflection.**

re•flex•ive (rĭ-flĕk′sĭv) *adj.* **1.** Directed back on itself. **2.** *Grammar* **a.** Of, relating to, or being a verb having an identical subject and direct object, as *dressed* in the sentence *She dressed herself.* **b.** Of, relating to, or being the pronoun used as the direct object of a reflexive verb, as *herself* in *She dressed herself.* **3.** Of or relating to a reflex. **4.** Elicited automatically; spontaneous. ❖ *n.* *Grammar* A reflexive verb or pronoun. See Usage Note at **myself.** **—re•flex′ive•ly** *adv.* **—re•flex′ive•ness, re′flex•iv′i•ty** (rē′flĕk-sĭv′ĭ-tē) *n.*

re•flex•ol•o•gy (rē′flĕk-sŏl′ə-jē) *n.* **1.** The study of reflex responses, esp. as they affect behavior. **2.** A method of massage that relieves nervous tension through the application of finger pressure, esp. to the feet. **—re′flex•ol′o•gist** *n.*

ref•lu•ent (rĕf′lo͞o-ənt) *adj.* Flowing back; ebbing. [Lat. *refluēns*, *refluent-*, pr. part. of *refluere*, to flow back : *re-*, re- + *fluere*, to flow; see FLUENT.] **—ref′lu•ence** *n.*

re•flux (rē′flŭks′) *n.* **1.** A flowing back; ebb. **2.** *Chemistry* The process of refluxing. ❖ *v.* **-fluxed, -flux•ing, -flux•es** *Chemistry* *—tr.* To boil (a liquid) in a vessel attached to a condenser so that the vapors continuously condense for reboiling. *—intr.* To be boiled in such a way. [Med.Lat. *reflūxus* : Lat. *re-*, re- + Lat. *flūxus*, flow < p. part. of *fluere*, to flow.]

re•form (rĭ-fôrm′) *v.* **-formed, -form•ing, -forms** *—tr.* **1.** To improve by alteration, correction of error, or removal of defects; put into a better form or condition. **2a.** To abolish abuse or malpractice in: *reform the government.* **b.** To put an end to (a wrong). See Syns at **correct.** **3.** To cause (a person) to give up harmful or immoral practices; persuade to adopt a better way of life. *—intr.* To change for the better. ❖ *n.* **1.** A change for the better; an improvement. **2.** Correction of evils, abuses, or errors. **3.** Action to improve social or economic conditions without radical or revolutionary change. ❖ *adj.* **1.** Relating to or favoring reform. **2. Reform** Of or relating to Reform Judaism. [ME *reformen* < OFr. *reformer* < Lat. *refōrmāre* : *re-*, re- + *fōrmāre*, to shape (< *fōrma*, form; see FORM).] **—re•form′a•bil′i•ty** *n.* **—re•form′a•ble** *adj.* **—re•for′ma•tive** (-fôr′mə-tĭv) *adj.* **—re•form′er** *n.*

re-form (rē-fôrm′) *v.* **-formed, -form•ing, -forms** *—tr.* To form again. *—intr.* To become formed again.

ref•or•ma•tion (rĕf′ər-mā′shən) *n.* **1.** The act of reforming or the state of being reformed. **2. Reformation** A 16th-century movement in Western Europe that aimed at reforming the Roman Catholic Church and resulted in the establishment of the Protestant churches. **—ref′or•ma′tion•al** *adj.*

re•for•ma•to•ry (rĭ-fôr′mə-tôr′ē, -tōr′ē) *n., pl.* **-ries** A penal institution for the discipline, reformation, and training of young or first offenders. ❖ *adj.* Reformative.

re•formed (rĭ-fôrmd′) *adj.* **1.** Improved by the removal of faults or abuses. **2.** Improved in conduct or character. **3. Reformed** Relating to or being the Protestant churches that follow the teachings of John Calvin and Ulrich Zwingli.

re•form•ism (rĭ-fôr′mĭz′əm) *n.* A doctrine or movement of reform. **—re•form′ist** *n.*

Reform Judaism *n.* The branch of Judaism that seeks to reconcile historical Judaism with modern life and does not require strict observance of traditional religious law and ritual.

reform school *n.* See **reformatory.**

re•fract (rĭ-frăkt′) *tr.v.* **-fract•ed, -fract•ing, -fracts 1.** To deflect (light, for example) from a straight path by refraction. **2.** To alter by viewing through a medium. **3.** *Medicine* To determine the refraction of (an eye, for example). [Lat. *refringere*, *refrāct-*, to break up : *re-*, re- + *frangere*, to break; see **bhreg-** in App.]

re•fract•ing telescope (rĭ-frăk′tĭng) *n.* A telescope in which light from an object is gathered and focused by lenses.

re•frac•tion (rĭ-frăk′shən) *n.* **1.** A change in the direction of a wave, such as a light wave, when it passes from one medium into another of different density. **2.** *Astronomy* The apparent change in position of celestial objects caused by the bending of light rays entering Earth's atmosphere. **3.** *Medicine* **a.** The ability of the eye to bend light to focus an image on the retina. **b.** Determination of the eye's refractive characteristics. **—re•frac′tion•al, re•frac′tive** *adj.* **—re•frac′tive•ly** *adv.* **—re•frac′tive•ness, re′frac•tiv′i•ty** (rē′frăk-tĭv′ĭ-tē) *n.*

refractive index *n.* See **index of refraction.**

re•frac•tom•e•ter (rē′frăk-tŏm′ĭ-tər) *n.* Any of several instruments used to measure the index of refraction of a substance.

re•frac•tor (rĭ-frăk′tər) *n.* **1.** One that refracts. **2.** A refracting telescope.

re•frac•to•ry (rĭ-frăk′tə-rē) *adj.* **1.** Obstinately resistant to authority or control. See Syns at **unruly.** **2.** Difficult to melt or work; resistant to heat. **3.** Resistant to treatment. ❖ *n., pl.* **-ries 1.** One that is refractory. **2.** Material that has a high melting point. [Alteration of obsolete *refractary* < Lat. *refrāctārius* < *refrāctus*, p.

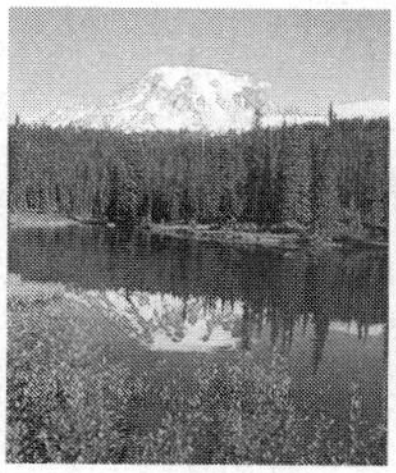

reflection
reflection of Mt. Rainier in Reflection Lake, Washington

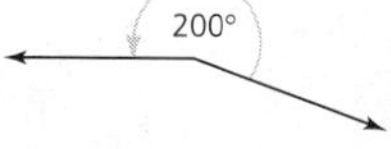

reflex angle

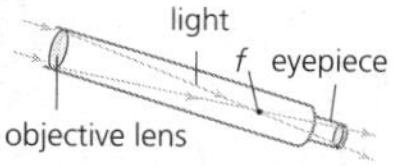

refracting telescope
a refracting telescope; *f* indicates the focus

ă	pat	oi	boy
ā	pay	ou	out
âr	care	o͝o	took
ä	father	o͞o	boot
ĕ	pet	ŭ	cut
ē	be	ûr	urge
ĭ	pit	th	thin
ī	pie	*th*	this
îr	pier	hw	which
ŏ	pot	zh	vision
ō	toe	ə	about, item
ô	paw		

Stress marks:
′ (primary);
′ (secondary), as in
lexicon (lĕk′sĭ-kŏn′)

part. of *refringere*, to break up. See REFRACT.] —re•frac′to•ri•ly *adv.* —re•frac′to•ri•ness *n.*

re•frain¹ (rĭ-frān′) *v.* -frained, -frain•ing, -frains —*intr.* To hold oneself back; forbear: *refrained from swearing.* —*tr. Archaic* To restrain or hold back; curb. [ME *refreinen* < OFr. *refrener*, to restrain < Lat. *refrēnāre* : *re-*, re- + *frēnāre*, to restrain (< *frēnum*, bridle < *frendere*, to grind; see ghrendh- in App.).] —re•frain′er *n.* —re•frain′ment *n.*

re•frain² (rĭ-frān′) *n.* **1a.** A phrase, verse, or group of verses repeated at intervals throughout a song or poem, esp. at the end of each stanza. **b.** Music for the refrain of a poem. **2.** A song or melody. **3.** A repeated utterance or theme. [ME *refrein* < OFr. *refrain*, alteration of *refrait*, p. part. of *refraindre*, to break off, repeat < VLat. *refrangere*, to break off, alteration of Lat. *refringere*. See REFRACT.]

re•fran•gi•ble (rĭ-frăn′jə-bəl) *adj.* That can be refracted. [< Lat. *refringere*, to refract (influenced by REFRACT).] —re•fran′gi•bil′i•ty *n.*

re•fresh (rĭ-frĕsh′) *v.* -freshed, -fresh•ing, -fresh•es —*tr.* **1.** To revive with or as if with rest, food, or drink. **2.** To give new freshness or brightness to; restore. **3.** To make cool, clean, or moist; freshen up. **4.** To renew by stimulation. **5.** To fill up again; replenish. **6.** *Computer Science* **a.** To renew (the image on a display screen) by renewing the flow of electrons from the cathode-ray tube. **b.** To maintain (data in a dynamic RAM) by sending a new electric pulse to recharge the chips. —*intr.* **1.** To take refreshment. **2.** To become fresh again; revive. [ME *refresshen* < OFr. *refreschir* : *re-*, re- + *fres, fresche*, fresh (of Gmc. orig.).]

re•fresh•er (rĭ-frĕsh′ər) *n.* **1.** One that refreshes. **2.** Instruction that serves to reacquaint one with material previously studied or to bring one's knowledge or skills up to date.

re•fresh•ing (rĭ-frĕsh′ĭng) *adj.* **1.** Serving to refresh. **2.** Pleasantly fresh and different. —re•fresh′ing•ly *adv.*

re•fresh•ment (rĭ-frĕsh′mənt) *n.* **1.** The act of refreshing or the state of being refreshed. **2.** Something, such as food, that refreshes. **3.** A snack, light meal, or drink. Often used in the plural.

re•fried beans (rē′frīd′) *pl.n.* Beans that have been cooked and then mashed and fried with seasonings. [Transl. of Sp. *frijoles fritos.*]

re•frig•er•ant (rĭ-frĭj′ər-ənt) *adj.* **1.** Cooling or freezing; refrigerating. **2.** *Medicine* Reducing fever. ❖ *n.* **1.** A substance, such as air or ammonia, used to provide cooling either as the working substance of a refrigerator or by direct absorption of heat. **2.** *Medicine* An agent used to reduce fever.

re•frig•er•ate (rĭ-frĭj′ə-rāt′) *tr.v.* -at•ed, -at•ing, -ates **1.** To cool or chill (a substance). **2.** To preserve (food) by chilling. [Lat. *refrigerāre, refrigerāt-* : *re-*, re- + *frīgerāre*, to make cool (< *frigus, frigor-*, coldness).] —re•frig′er•a′tive, re•frig′er•a•to′ry (-ər-ə-tôr′ē, -tōr′ē) *adj.*

re•frig•er•a•tor (rĭ-frĭj′ə-rā′tər) *n.* An appliance, cabinet, or room for storing substances at a low temperature.

re•frin•gence (rĭ-frĭn′jəns) *n.* Refractive power.

re•frin•gent (rĭ-frĭn′jənt) *adj.* Of, relating to, or producing refraction; refractive. [Lat. *refringēns, refringent-*, pr. part. of *refringere*, to break up. See REFRACT.]

reft¹ (rĕft) *v.* A past tense and a past participle of **reave**¹.

reft² (rĕft) *v.* A past tense and a past participle of **reave**².

re•fu•el (rē-fyo͞o′əl) *v.* -eled, -el•ing, -els also -elled, -el•ling, -els —*tr.* To supply again with fuel. —*intr.* To take on a fresh supply of fuel.

ref•uge (rĕf′yo͞oj) *n.* **1.** Protection or shelter, as from danger or hardship. **2.** A place providing protection or shelter. **3.** A source of help, relief, or comfort in times of trouble. ❖ *v.* -uged, -ug•ing, -ug•es *Archaic* —*tr.* To give refuge to. —*intr.* To take refuge. [ME < OFr. < Lat. *refugium* < *refugere*, to run away : *re-*, re- + *fugere*, to flee.]

ref•u•gee (rĕf′yo͞o-jē′) *n.* One who flees in search of refuge, as in times of war. [Fr. *réfugié* < p. part. of *réfugier*, to take refuge < OFr. < *refuge*, refuge. See REFUGE.]

re•fu•gi•um (rĭ-fyo͞o′jē-əm) *n., pl.* -gi•a (-jē-ə) An area that has escaped ecological changes occurring elsewhere and so provides a suitable habitat for relict species. [Lat., refuge. See REFUGE.]

re•ful•gent (rĭ-fo͞ol′jənt, -fŭl′-) *adj.* Shining radiantly; resplendent. [Lat. *refulgēns, refulgent-*, pr. part. of *refulgēre*, to flash back : *re-*, re- + *fulgēre*, to flash.] —re•ful′gence, re•ful′gen•cy *n.* —re•ful′gent•ly *adv.*

re•fund (rĭ-fŭnd′, rē′fŭnd′) *v.* -fund•ed, -fund•ing, -funds —*tr.* To give back, esp. money; return or repay. —*intr.* To make repayment. ❖ *n.* (rē′fŭnd′) **1.** A repayment of funds. **2.** An amount repaid. [ME *refunden* < OFr. *refunder* < Lat. *refundere* : *re-*, re- + *fundere*, to pour; see gheu- in App.] —re•fund′a•ble *adj.* —re•fund′er *n.* —re•fund′ment *n.*

re-fund (rē-fŭnd′) *tr.v.* -fund•ed, -fund•ing, -funds **1.** To fund anew. **2.** To pay back (a debt) with new borrowing.

re•fur•bish (rē-fûr′bĭsh) *tr.v.* -bished, -bish•ing, -bish•es To make clean, bright, or fresh again; renovate. —re•fur′bish•ment *n.*

re•fus•al (rĭ-fyo͞o′zəl) *n.* **1.** The act or an instance of refusing. **2.** The opportunity or right to accept or reject something before it is offered elsewhere.

re•fuse¹ (rĭ-fyo͞oz′) *v.* -fused, -fus•ing, -fus•es —*tr.* **1a.** To in-

dicate unwillingness to do, accept, give, or allow: *She was refused admittance. He refused treatment.* **b.** To indicate unwillingness (to do something): *refused to leave.* **2.** To decline to jump (an obstacle). Used of a horse. —*intr.* **1.** To decline to do, accept, give, or allow something. [ME *refusen* < OFr. *refuser* < VLat. *refūsāre*, prob. blend of Lat. *recūsāre*, to refuse; see RECUSE, and Lat. *refūtāre*, refute; see REFUTE.] —re•fus′er *n.*

SYNONYMS refuse, decline, reject, spurn, rebuff These verbs mean to be unwilling to accept, consider, or receive someone or something. *Refuse* usually implies determination and often brusqueness: *"The commander . . . refused to discuss questions of right"* (George Bancroft). To *decline* is to refuse courteously: *"Now I must decline the Pulitzer Prize"* (Sinclair Lewis). *Reject* suggests the discarding of someone or something as defective or useless; it implies categoric refusal: *"He again offered himself for enlistment and was again rejected"* (Arthur S.M. Hutchinson). To *spurn* is to reject scornfully or contemptuously: *"The more she spurns my love/The more it grows"* (Shakespeare). *Rebuff* pertains to blunt, often disdainful rejection: *"He had . . . gone too far in his advances, and had been rebuffed"* (Robert Louis Stevenson).

ref•use² (rĕf′yo͞os) *n.* Items or material discarded or rejected as useless or worthless; trash or rubbish. [ME < OFr. *refus*, rejection, refuse < *refuser*, to refuse. See REFUSE¹.]

re•fuse•nik (rĭ-fyo͞oz′nĭk) *n.* A Soviet citizen, usu. Jewish, denied permission to emigrate.

ref•u•ta•tion (rĕf′yo͞o-tā′shən) *also* re•fut•al (rĭ-fyo͞ot′l) *n.* **1.** The act of refuting. **2.** Something, such as an argument, that refutes someone or something.

re•fute (rĭ-fyo͞ot′) *tr.v.* -fut•ed, -fut•ing, -futes **1.** To prove to be false or erroneous; overthrow by argument or proof. **2.** To deny the accuracy or truth of: *refuted the results of the poll.* [Lat. *refūtāre.*] —re•fut′a•bil′i•ty (rĭ-fyo͞o′tə-bĭl′ĭ-tē, rĕf′yə-tə-) *n.* —re•fut′a•ble (rĭ-fyo͞o′tə-bəl, rĕf′yə-tə-) *adj.* —re•fut′a•bly *adv.* —re•fut′er *n.*

reg. *abbr.* **1.** regent **2.** regiment **3.** region **4.** registered **5.** registrar **6.** registry **7.** regular

re•gain (rē-gān′) *tr.v.* -gained, -gain•ing, -gains **1.** To recover possession of; get back again. See Syns at **recover**. **2.** To manage to reach again. —re•gain′er *n.*

re•gal (rē′gəl) *adj.* **1.** Of or relating to a monarch; royal. **2.** Belonging to or befitting a monarch. **3.** Magnificent; splendid. [ME < OFr. < Lat. *rēgālis* < *rēx, rēg-*, king. See reg- in App.] —re•gal′i•ty (rĭ-găl′ĭ-tē) *n.* —re′gal•ly *adv.*

re•gale (rĭ-gāl′) *v.* -galed, -gal•ing, -gales —*tr.* **1.** To provide with great enjoyment; entertain. **2.** To entertain sumptuously with food and drink; feast. —*intr.* To feast. ❖ *n.* **1.** A great feast. **2.** A choice food; a delicacy. **3.** Refreshment. [Fr. *régaler* < OFr. *regal*, feast < *gale* < *galer*, to make merry.] —re•gale′ment *n.*

re•ga•lia (rĭ-gāl′yə, -gā′lē-ə) *pl.n.* (*used with a sing. or pl. verb*) **1.** The emblems and symbols of royalty. **2.** The rights and privileges of royalty. **3.** The distinguishing symbols of a rank, office, order, or society. **4.** Magnificent attire; finery. [Med.Lat. *rēgālia* < Lat., neut. pl. of *rēgālis*, regal. See REGAL.]

re•gard (rĭ-gärd′) *v.* -gard•ed, -gard•ing, -gards —*tr.* **1.** To look at attentively; observe closely. **2.** To look upon or consider in a particular way: *I regard him as a fool.* **3.** To hold in esteem or respect: *She regards her teachers highly.* **4.** To relate or refer to; concern: *This item regards their liability.* **5.** To take into account; consider. **6.** *Obsolete* To take care of. —*intr.* **1.** To look or gaze. **2.** To give heed; pay attention. ❖ *n.* **1.** A look or gaze. **2.** Careful thought or attention; heed: *gave little regard for the laws.* **3a.** Respect, affection, or esteem: *has high regard for your work.* **b.** re•gards Good wishes expressing such sentiment: *Give them my best regards.* **4.** A particular point or aspect. **5.** Basis for action; motive. **6.** *Obsolete* Appearance or aspect. —*idioms:* as regards Concerning. in (or with) regard to With respect to. [ME *regarden* < OFr. *regarder* : *re-*, re- + *garder*, to guard; see GUARD.]

USAGE NOTE *Regard* is traditionally used in the singular in the phrase *in regard* (not *in regards*) *to. Regarding* and *as regards* are also standard in the sense "with reference to." In the same sense *with respect to* is acceptable, but *respecting* is not. • *Respects* is sometimes considered preferable to *regards* in the sense of "particulars": *In some respects* (not *regards*) *the books are alike.*

regardant

re•gar•dant (rĭ-gär′dnt) *adj. Heraldry* Looking backward in profile. [ME < OFr., pr. part. of *regarder*, to regard. See REGARD.]

re•gard•ful (rĭ-gärd′fəl) *adj.* **1.** Showing attention; heedful. **2.** Showing deference; respectful. —re•gard′ful•ly *adv.* —re•gard′ful•ness *n.*

re•gard•ing (rĭ-gär′dĭng) *prep.* In reference to; with respect to; concerning. See Usage Note at **regard.**

re•gard•less (rĭ-gärd′lĭs) *adv.* In spite of everything; anyway: *continues to work regardless.* ❖ *adj.* Heedless; unmindful. —re•gard′less•ly *adv.* —re•gard′less•ness *n.*

regardless of *prep.* **1.** In spite of. **2.** With no heed to.

re•gat•ta (rĭ-gä′tə, -găt′ə) *n.* A boat race or a series of boat races. [Ital. dialectal, a contention, regatta < *regattare*, to contend, perh. < *recatare*, to sell again, compete < VLat. *recaptāre*, to contend : Lat. *re-*, re- + Lat. *captāre*, to seek to catch, freq. of *capere*, to seize; see CATCH.]

regd. *abbr.* registered

re·ge·la·tion (rē′jə-lā′shən) *n.* **1.** The fusion of two ice blocks by pressure. **2.** Successive melting under pressure and freezing when pressure is relaxed at the interface of two ice blocks.

re·gen·cy (rē′jən-sē) *n., pl.* **-cies 1.** A person or group selected to govern in place of a ruler who is absent, disabled, or still in minority. **2.** The period during which a regent governs. **3.** The office, area of jurisdiction, or government of regents or a regent. ❖ *adj.* **1. Regency** Of, relating to, or characteristic of the style, esp. in furniture, prevalent in England during the regency (1811–20) of George, Prince of Wales (later George IV). **2. Regency** Of, relating to, or characteristic of the style prevalent in France during the regency (1715–23) of Philippe, Duc d'Orléans (1674–1723). **3.** Of a regency.

re·gen·er·a·cy (rĭ-jĕn′ər-ə-sē) *n.* The state of being regenerated.

re·gen·er·ate (rĭ-jĕn′ə-rāt′) *v.* **-at·ed, -at·ing, -ates** —*tr.* **1.** To reform spiritually or morally. **2.** To form, construct, or create anew, esp. in an improved state. **3.** To give new life or energy to; revitalize. **4.** *Biology* To replace (an organ or part) by formation of new tissue. —*intr.* **1.** To become formed or constructed again. **2.** To undergo spiritual conversion or rebirth; reform. **3.** To effect regeneration. ❖ *n.* (-ĭt) **1.** One who is spiritually reborn. **2.** *Biology* A regenerated organ or part. ❖ *adj.* (-ĭt) **1.** Spiritually or morally reformed. **2.** Formed or created anew. **3.** Restored to a better state; refreshed or renewed. [Lat. *regenerāre, regenerāt-,* to reproduce : *re-, re-* + *generāre,* to beget; see GENERATE.] —**re·gen′er·a·ble** (-ər-ə-bəl) *adj.* —**re·gen′er·ate·ly** *adv.* —**re·gen′er·a′tor** *n.*

re·gen·er·a·tion (rĭ-jĕn′ə-rā′shən) *n.* **1.** The act or process of regenerating or the state of being regenerated. **2.** Spiritual or moral revival or rebirth. **3.** *Biology* Regrowth of lost or destroyed parts or organs.

re·gen·er·a·tive (rĭ-jĕn′ə-rā′tĭv, -ər-ə-tĭv) *adj.* **1.** Of, relating to, or marked by regeneration. **2.** Tending to regenerate. —**re·gen′er·a′tive·ly** *adv.*

Re·gens·burg (rā′gənz-bûrg′, -gəns-bŏŏrk′) A city of SE Germany on the Danube R. NNE of Munich. Pop. 126,681.

re·gent (rē′jənt) *n.* **1.** One who rules during the minority, absence, or disability of a monarch. **2.** One acting as a ruler or governor. **3.** A member of a board that governs an institution, such as a university. [ME < OFr. < Lat. *regēns, regent-,* ruler < pr. part. of *regere,* to rule. See reg- in App.] —**re′gent·al** (-jən-tl) *adj.*

reg·gae (rĕg′ā) *n.* Popular music of Jamaican origin having elements of calypso and rhythm and blues, usu. with an accent placed on the offbeat. [Jamaican E., ult. < *rege-rege,* ragged clothing, prob. < E. RAG[1].]

Reg·gio di Ca·la·bri·a (rĕj′ē-ō dē kä-lä′brē-ä, rĕd′jō) also **Reggio Calabria** A city of extreme S Italy on the Strait of Messina opposite Sicily. Pop. 169,709.

reg·i·cide (rĕj′ĭ-sīd′) *n.* **1.** The killing of a king. **2.** One who kills a king. [Lat. *rēx, rēg-,* king; see reg- in App. + -CIDE.] —**reg′i·cid′al** (-sīd′l) *adj.*

re·gime also **ré·gime** (rā-zhēm′, rĭ-) *n.* **1a.** A form of government. **b.** A government in power; administration. **2.** A prevailing social system or pattern. **3.** The period during which a particular administration or system prevails. **4.** A regulated system, as of diet; a regimen. [Fr. *régime* < OFr. < Lat. *regimen* < *regere,* to rule. See reg- in App.]

reg·i·men (rĕj′ə-mən, -mĕn′) *n.* **1.** Governmental rule or control. **2.** The systematic procedure of a natural phenomenon or process. **3a.** A regulated system, as of diet, intended to achieve a beneficial effect. **b.** A course of intense physical training. [ME < Lat. See REGIME.]

reg·i·ment (rĕj′ə-mənt) *n.* **1.** A military unit of ground troops consisting of at least two battalions. **2.** A large group of people. ❖ *tr.v.* (rĕj′ə-mĕnt′) **-ment·ed, -ment·ing, -ments 1.** To form into a regiment. **2.** To put into systematic order; systematize. **3.** To subject to uniformity and rigid order. [ME, government, rule < OFr. < LLat. *regimentum,* rule < Lat. *regere,* to rule. See reg- in App.] —**reg′i·men′tal** (-mĕn′tl) *adj.* —**reg′i·men′tal·ly** *adv.* —**reg′i·men·ta′tion** *n.*

reg·i·men·tals (rĕj′ə-mĕnt′lz) *pl.n.* **1.** The uniform and insignia of a particular regiment. **2.** Military dress.

Re·gi·na (rĭ-jī′nə) The cap. of Saskatchewan, Canada, in the S part SE of Saskatoon. Pop. 180,400.

Re·gi·o·mon·ta·nus (rē′jē-ō-mŏn-tā′nəs, -tä′-, -tăn-əs, rĕj′ē-) See Johann Müller.

re·gion (rē′jən) *n.* **1.** A large, usu. continuous segment of a surface or space; area. **2.** A limited portion of the earth's surface. **3.** A specified district or territory. **4.** An area of interest or activity; a sphere. **5.** *Ecology* A part of the earth characterized by distinctive animal or plant life. **6.** An area of the body. [ME < OFr. < Lat. *regiō, region-* < *regere,* to rule. See reg- in App.]

re·gion·al (rē′jə-nəl) *adj.* **1.** Of or relating to a large geographic region. **2.** Of or relating to a particular region or district. **3.** Of or affecting a region of the body: *regional anesthesia.* **4.** Of or characteristic of a form of a language that is distinguishable in identifiable geographic areas and differs from the standard form; dialectal. ❖ *n.* Something, such as a magazine, that serves a region. —**re′gion·al·ly** *adv.*

re·gion·al·ism (rē′jə-nə-lĭz′əm) *n.* **1a.** Political division of an area into partially autonomous regions. **b.** Advocacy of such a political system. **2.** Loyalty to the interests of a particular region. **3.** A feature, such as an expression, that is characteristic of a geographic area. **4.** The use of regional characteristics in literature or art. —**re′gion·al·ist** *adj. & n.* —**re′gion·al·is′tic** *adj.*

re·gion·al·ize (rē′jə-nə-līz′) *tr.v.* **-ized, -iz·ing, -iz·es** To divide into regions, esp. for administrative purposes. —**re′gion·al·i·za′tion** (-lĭ-zā′shən) *n.*

ré·gis·seur (rā′zhē-sûr′, -scer′) *n., pl.* **-seurs** (-sûr′, -scer′) A stage director, esp. of a ballet. [Fr. < *régir, régiss-,* to direct < OFr. *regir* < Lat. *regere.* See REGENT.]

reg·is·ter (rĕj′ĭ-stər) *n.* **1a.** A formal or official recording of items, names, or actions. **b.** A book for such entries. **c.** An entry in such a record. **2.** The act of registering. **3.** A device that automatically records a quantity or number. **4.** *Computer Science* A part of the central processing unit used as a storage location. **5.** An adjustable grill-like device through which heated or cooled air is released into a room. **6.** A state of proper alignment. **7.** *Printing* **a.** Exact alignment of the lines and margins on the opposite sides of a leaf. **b.** Proper positioning of colors. **8.** *Music* **a.** The range of an instrument or a voice. **b.** A part of such a range. **c.** A group of matched organ pipes; a stop. **9.** A variety of language used in a specific social setting. ❖ *v.* **-tered, -ter·ing, -ters** —*tr.* **1a.** To enter in an official register. **b.** To enroll officially or formally, esp. in order to vote or attend classes. **2.** To set down in writing; record. **3.** To indicate on or as if on an instrument or a scale. **4.** To give outward signs of; express: *Her face registered surprise.* **5.** To attain or achieve. **6.** To cause (mail) to be officially recorded and specially handled by payment of a fee. **7.** To adjust so as to be properly aligned. —*intr.* **1.** To place or cause placement of one's name in a register. **2.** To have one's name officially placed on a list of eligible voters. **3.** To enroll as a student. **4.** To be indicated on or as if on an instrument or a scale. **5.** To be shown or expressed, as on the face. **6.** To make an impression; be recorded in the mind. **7.** To be in proper alignment. [ME *registre* < OFr. < Med.Lat. *registrum,* alteration of LLat. *regesta* < Lat., neut. pl. p. part. of *regerere,* to record : *re-, re-* + *gerere,* to carry.] —**reg′is·ter·er** *n.* —**reg′is·tra·ble** (-ĭ-strə-bəl) *adj.*

reg·is·tered (rĕj′ĭ-stərd) *adj.* **1.** Having the owner's name listed in a register. **2.** Having the pedigree recorded and verified by an authorized association of breeders. **3.** Officially qualified or certified: *a registered pharmacist.*

registered mail *n.* Mail recorded by the post office when sent and at each point on its route so as to assure safe delivery.

registered nurse *n.* A graduate trained nurse who has passed a state registration examination and has been licensed to practice nursing.

reg·is·trant (rĕj′ĭ-strənt) *n.* One who registers or is registered.

reg·is·trar (rĕj′ĭ-strär′, rĕj′ĭ-strär′) *n.* **1.** One who is in charge of official records. **2.** An officer in a college or university who keeps records of enrollment and academic standing. **3.** An officer of a corporation responsible for maintaining records of ownership of its securities. **4.** An admitting officer in a hospital. [Prob. < *registrary* < Med.Lat. *registrārius* < *registrum,* register. See REGISTER.]

reg·is·tra·tion (rĕj′ĭ-strā′shən) *n.* **1.** The act of registering. **2.** The number of persons registered; enrollment. **3.** An entry in a register. **4.** A document certifying an act of registering. **5.** *Music* **a.** A combination of organ stops used in playing a piece. **b.** The technique of selecting and adjusting organ stops.

reg·is·try (rĕj′ĭ-strē) *n., pl.* **-tries 1.** The act of registering; registration. **2.** The registered nationality of a ship. **3.** A place for registering. **4a.** A book for official records. **b.** The place where such records are kept.

re·gius professor (rē′jəs, -jē-əs) *n.* One holding a professorship established by royal subsidy at a British university. [< Lat. *rēgius,* royal < *rēx, rēg-,* king. See reg- in App.]

reg·let (rĕg′lĭt) *n.* **1.** *Architecture* A narrow flat molding. **2.** *Printing* A flat piece of wood used to separate lines of type. [Fr. *réglet* < OFr., dim. of *regle,* ruler < Lat. *regula,* rod. See reg- in App.]

reg·nal (rĕg′nəl) *adj.* Being a specified year of a monarch's reign calculated from the date of accession. [Med.Lat. *rēgnālis,* royal < Lat. *rēgnum,* reign. See REIGN.]

reg·nant (rĕg′nənt) *adj.* **1.** Reigning; ruling. **2.** Predominant. **3.** Widespread; prevalent. [Prob. < ME, a sovereign < OFr. < Lat. *rēgnāns, rēgnant-,* pr. part. of *rēgnāre,* to reign < *rēgnum,* reign. See REIGN.]

reg·o·lith (rĕg′ə-lĭth′) *n.* The layer of loose rock resting on bedrock, constituting the surface of most land. [Gk. *rhēgos,* blanket + -LITH.]

re·gorge (rē-gôrj′) *tr.v.* **-gorged, -gorg·ing, -gorg·es** To disgorge. [Fr. *regorger* < OFr. : *re-, re-* + *gorger,* to gorge (< *gorge,* throat; see GORGE).]

re·gress (rĭ-grĕs′) *v.* **-gressed, -gress·ing, -gress·es** —*intr.* **1.** To go back; move backward. **2.** To return to a previous, usu. worse or less developed state. **3.** To have a tendency to approach or go back to a statistical mean. ❖ *n.* (rē′grĕs′) **1.** The act of going or coming back; return. **2.** Passage back; reentry. [Lat. *regredī, regress-* : *re-, re-* + *gradī,* to go; see ghredh- in App.] —**re·gres′sor** *n.*

Regency
open armchair

William H. Rehnquist

re·gres·sion (rĭ-grĕsh′ən) n. **1.** Reversion; retrogression. **2.** Relapse to a less perfect or developed state. **3.** *Psychology* Reversion to a less mature pattern of feeling or behavior. **4.** *Medicine* A subsidence of the symptoms or progression of a disease. **5.** *Biology* The return of a population to an earlier or less complex physical type. **6.** *Statistics* The relationship between the mean value of a random variable and the corresponding values of one or more independent variables. **7.** *Astronomy* Retrograde motion of a celestial body. **8.** *Geology* A relative fall in sea level resulting in deposition of terrestrial strata over marine strata.

re·gres·sive (rĭ-grĕs′ĭv) adj. **1.** Tending to return or revert. **2.** Of or characterized by regression or a tendency to regress. **3.** Decreasing proportionately as the amount taxed increases. **4.** Of or relating to geological regression. —**re·gres′sive·ly** adv. —**re·gres′sive·ness** n.

re·gret (rĭ-grĕt′) v. **-gret·ted, -gret·ting, -grets** —tr. **1.** To feel sorry, disappointed, or distressed about: *regretted the error.* **2.** To remember with a feeling of loss or sorrow; mourn. —intr. To feel regret. ❖ n. **1.** A sense of loss and longing for someone or something gone. **2.** A feeling of disappointment or distress about something. **3. regrets** A courteous expression of regret, esp. at having to decline an invitation. [ME *regretten*, to lament < OFr. *regreter* : *re-*, re- + *-greter*, to weep (perh. of Gmc. orig.).] —**re·gret′ter** n.

re·gret·ful (rĭ-grĕt′fəl) adj. Full of regret; sorrowful or sorry. —**re·gret′ful·ly** adv. —**re·gret′ful·ness** n.

re·gret·ta·ble (rĭ-grĕt′ə-bəl) adj. Eliciting or deserving regret.

re·gret·ta·bly (rĭ-grĕt′ə-blē) adv. **1.** To an extent deserving of regret: *regrettably brief.* **2.** As a matter of regret.

re·group (rē-grōōp′) v. **-grouped, -group·ing, -groups** —tr. To arrange in a new grouping. —intr. **1.** To come back together in a tactical formation, as after a dispersal in a retreat. **2.** To reorganize for renewed effort, as after a setback.

regt. abbr. **1.** regent **2.** regiment

reg·u·lar (rĕg′yə-lər) adj. **1.** Customary, usual, or normal: *the train's regular schedule.* **2.** Orderly, even, or symmetrical: *regular teeth.* **3.** In conformity with a fixed procedure, principle, or discipline. **4.** Well-ordered; methodical: *regular habits.* **5.** Occurring at fixed intervals; periodic: *regular payments.* **6a.** Occurring with normal or healthy frequency. **b.** Having bowel movements or menstrual periods with normal or healthy frequency. **7.** Not varying; constant. **8.** Formally correct; proper. **9.** Having the required qualifications for an occupation: *not a regular lawyer.* **10.** *Informal* Complete; thorough: *a regular scoundrel.* **11.** *Informal* Good; nice: *a regular guy.* **12.** *Botany* Having symmetrically arranged parts of similar size and shape. **13.** *Grammar* Conforming to the usual pattern of inflection, derivation, or word formation. **14.** *Ecclesiastical* Belonging to a religious order and bound by its rules. **15.** *Mathematics* **a.** Having equal sides and equal angles. Used of polygons. **b.** Having faces that are congruent regular polygons and congruent polyhedral angles. Used of polyhedrons. **16.** Belonging to or constituting the permanent army of a nation. ❖ n. **1.** *Ecclesiastical* A member of the clergy or of a religious order. **2.** A soldier belonging to a regular army. **3.** A dependable loyal person: *a party regular.* **4.** A clothing size for persons of average height. **5.** A habitual customer. [ME *reguler*, living under religious rule < OFr. < LLat. *rēgulāris*, according to rule < Lat. *rēgula*, rod, rule. See **reg-** in App.] —**reg′u·lar′i·ty** (-lăr′ĭ-tē) n. —**reg′u·lar·ly** adv.

regular army n. The permanent standing army of a nation or state.

reg·u·lar·ize (rĕg′yə-lə-rīz′) tr.v. **-ized, -iz·ing, -iz·es** To make regular; cause to conform. —**reg′u·lar·i·za′tion** (-lər-ĭ-zā′shən) n. —**reg′u·lar·iz′er** n.

reg·u·late (rĕg′yə-lāt′) tr.v. **-lat·ed, -lat·ing, -lates 1.** To control or direct according to rule, principle, or law. **2.** To adjust to a particular specification or requirement: *regulate temperature.* **3.** To adjust (a mechanism) for accurate and proper functioning. **4.** To put or maintain in order. [ME < LLat. *rēgulāre, rēgulāt-* < Lat. *rēgula*, rod, rule. See **reg-** in App.] —**reg′u·la′tive, reg′u·la·to′ry** (-lə-tôr′ē, -tōr′ē) adj.

reg·u·la·tion (rĕg′yə-lā′shən) n. **1.** The act of regulating or the state of being regulated. **2.** A principle, rule, or law designed to control or govern conduct. **3.** A government order having the force of law. **4.** *Embryology* The capacity of an embryo to continue normal development following injury to or alteration of a structure. **5.** *Sports* The standard playing period for a timed game, prior to overtime or a shootout.

reg·u·la·tor (rĕg′yə-lā′tər) n. **1.** One that regulates, as: **a.** The mechanism in a watch by which its speed is governed. **b.** A clock used as a standard for timing other clocks. **c.** A device used to maintain uniform speed in a machine; a governor. **d.** A device used to control the flow of gases, liquids, or electric current. **e.** A substance that functions in the control of a biochemical process or reaction **2.** One that ensures compliance with laws and regulations.

regulatory gene n. A gene that represses the activity of another gene in an operon.

re·gu·lus (rĕg′yə-ləs) n., pl. **-li** (-lī) or **-lus·es 1.** The metallic mass that sinks to the bottom of a furnace or crucible during smelting. **2.** A relatively impure intermediate product of various

ores in smelting. [Lat. *rēgulus*, dim. of *rēx, rēg-*, king. See **reg-** in App.] —**reg′u·line** (rĕg′yə-lĭn, -lĭn′) adj.

Reg·u·lus (rĕg′yə-ləs) n. A bright double star in the constellation Leo. [Lat. *rēgulus*, dim. of *rēx, rēg-*, king. See REGULUS.]

re·gur·gi·tate (rē-gûr′jĭ-tāt′) v. **-tat·ed, -tat·ing, -tates** —intr. To rush or surge back. —tr. To cause to pour back, esp. to cast up (partially digested food). [Med.Lat. *regurgitāre, regurgitāt-*, to overflow : Lat. *re-*, re- + LLat. *gurgitāre*, to engulf, flood (< Lat. *gurges, gurgit-*, whirlpool).] —**re·gur′gi·tant** (-tənt) adj. —**re·gur′gi·ta′tion** n. —**re·gur′gi·ta·tive** adj.

re·hab (rē′hăb′) *Informal* n. **1.** Rehabilitation. **2.** Something, esp. a building, that has undergone rehabilitation. ❖ tr.v. **-habbed, -hab·bing, -habs** To rehabilitate. —**re′hab′ber** n.

re·ha·bil·i·tant (rē′hə-bĭl′ĭ-tənt) n. One who is undergoing rehabilitation, as for a disability.

re·ha·bil·i·tate (rē′hə-bĭl′ĭ-tāt′) tr.v. **-tat·ed, -tat·ing, -tates 1.** To restore to good health or useful life, as through therapy. **2.** To restore to good condition, operation, or capacity. **3.** To reinstate the good name of. **4.** To restore the former rank, privileges, or rights of. [Med.Lat. *rehabilitāre, rehabilitāt-*, to restore to a rank : Lat. *re-*, re- + LLat. *habilitāre*, to enable; see HABILITATE.] —**re′ha·bil′i·tat′a·ble** adj. —**re′ha·bil′i·ta′tion** n. —**re′ha·bil′i·ta′tive** adj.

re·hash (rē-hăsh′) tr.v. **-hashed, -hash·ing, -hash·es 1.** To bring forth again in another form without significant alteration. **2.** To discuss again. ❖ n. (rē′hăsh′) The act or result of rehashing.

re·hear (rē-hîr′) tr.v. **-heard** (-hûrd′), **-hear·ing, -hears 1.** To hear again. **2.** *Law* To give a new hearing to (a case) by the same court.

re·hear·ing (rē-hîr′ĭng) n. *Law* A new hearing of a case by the same court in which it was originally heard.

re·hears·al (rĭ-hûr′səl) n. **1.** The act of practicing in preparation for a public performance. **2.** A session of practice for a performance. **3.** A detailed enumeration or repetition.

re·hearse (rĭ-hûrs′) v. **-hearsed, -hears·ing, -hears·es** —tr. **1a.** To practice (a part in a play, for example) in preparation for a public performance. **b.** To direct in rehearsal: *rehearsed the orchestra.* **2.** To perfect or cause to perfect (an action) by repetition. See Syns at **practice. 3a.** To retell or recite. **b.** To list or enumerate. —intr. To practice something before presenting it publicly. [ME *rehercen*, to repeat < OFr. *rehercier* : *re-*, re- + *hercier*, to harrow (< *herce*, harrow; see HEARSE).] —**re·hears′er** n.

Rehn·quist (rĕn′kwĭst′), **William Hubbs** b. 1924. Amer. jurist; associate justice (1972–86) and chief justice of the US Supreme Court (since 1986).

Re·ho·bo·am (rē′ə-bō′əm) fl. 10th century B.C. Son and successor of Solomon and first king of Judah.

re·hy·drate (rē-hī′drāt′) tr.v. **-drat·ed, -drat·ing, -drates 1.** To cause (something dehydrated) to take up fluid. **2.** To replenish the body fluids of. —**re′hy·dra′tion** n.

Reich (rīk, rīкн) n. The territory or government of a German state, as the Holy Roman Empire, or First Reich (962–1806); the German Empire, or Second Reich (1871–1919); the Weimar Republic (1919–33); or the Third Reich (1933–45). [Ger., empire, realm < MHGer. *rīch, rīche* < OHGer. *rīhhi*. See **reg-** in App.]

Reich (rīk), **Stephen Michael ("Steve")** b. 1936. Amer. composer associated with the minimalist school.

Reich (rīk, rīкн), **Wilhelm** 1897–1957. Austrian psychoanalyst who theorized that sexual repression is the source of many psychological and social problems.

reichs·mark (rīks′märk′, rīкнs′-) n., pl. **reichsmark** or **-marks** A monetary unit of Germany from 1925 to 1948. [Ger. : *Reichs*, genitive of *Reich*, realm (< MHGer. *rich* < OHGer. *rīchi*; see **reg-** in App.) + *Mark*, unit of currency (< MHGer. *marke*; see MARK²).]

re·i·fy (rē′ə-fī′, rā′-) tr.v. **-fied, -fy·ing, -fies** To regard or treat (an abstraction) as if it had concrete or material existence. [Lat. *rēs, rē-*, thing + -FY.] —**re′i·fi·ca′tion** (-fĭ-kā′shən) n. —**re′i·fi′er** n.

reign (rān) n. **1.** Exercise of sovereign power. **2.** The period during which a monarch rules. **3.** Dominance or widespread influence. ❖ intr.v. **reigned, reign·ing, reigns 1.** To exercise sovereign power. **2.** To hold the title of monarch with limited authority. **3.** To be predominant or prevalent: *Panic reigned as the fire spread.* [ME *reigne* < OFr. < Lat. *rēgnum* < *rēx, rēg-*, king. See **reg-** in App.]

Reign of Terror n. **1.** The period (1793–94) of the French Revolution during which thousands of people were executed. **2. reign of terror,** pl. **reigns of terror** A period of brutal suppression or intimidation by those in power.

re·im·burse (rē′ĭm-bûrs′) tr.v. **-bursed, -burs·ing, -burs·es 1.** To repay (money spent); refund. **2.** To pay back or compensate (another party) for money spent or losses incurred. [RE- + *imburse*, to put in a purse, pay (< Fr. *embourser* < OFr. : *en-*, in < Lat. *in-*; see IN-² + *borser*, to get money < *borse*, purse < LLat. *bursa*, bag; see BURSA).] —**re′im·burs′a·ble** adj. —**re′im·burse′ment** n.

re·im·pres·sion (rē′ĭm-prĕsh′ən) n. A second impression, as of a book, that is identical to the original; a reprint.

Reims (rēmz, răNs) See **Rheims**.

rein (rān) *n.* **1.** A long narrow leather strap attached to each end of the bit of a bridle and used by a rider or driver to control a horse or other animal. Often used in the plural. **2.** A means of restraint, check, or guidance. **3.** A means or instrument by which power is exercised. Often used in the plural. ❖ *v.* **reined, rein·ing, reins** —*tr.* **1.** To check or hold back by or as if by the use of reins. Often with *in, back,* or *up.* **2.** To restrain or control. —*intr.* To control a horse, for example, with reins. —**idioms: draw in the reins** To slow down or stop by or as if by pressure on the reins. **give free (or full) rein to** Allow to go unchecked. **tight rein** Close control. [ME < OFr. *resne, reine* < VLat. **retina* < Lat. *retinēre,* to retain. See RETAIN.]

re·in·car·nate (rē′ĭn-kär′nāt) *tr.v.* **-nat·ed, -nat·ing, -nates** **1.** To cause to be reborn in another body; reincarnate again. **2.** To cause to appear in a new form; refurbish or revitalize.

re·in·car·na·tion (rē′ĭn-kär-nā′shən) *n.* **1.** Rebirth of the soul in another body. **2.** A reappearance or revitalization in another form; a new embodiment.

rein·deer (rān′dîr′) *n., pl.* **reindeer** or **-deers** A large deer (*Rangifer tarandus*) of the Arctic and northern regions of Eurasia and North America, having branched antlers in both sexes. [ME *reindere* : ON *hreinn,* reindeer; see **ker-**[1] in App. + ME *der,* animal; see DEER.]

WORD HISTORY Although Saint Nick uses reins on his reindeer and reindeer are used to pull sleds in Lapland and northern Siberia, the word *reindeer* has nothing to do with reins. The element *–deer* is indeed our word *deer,* but the *rein–* part is borrowed from an Old Norse word *hreinn,* "reindeer." The word *reindeer* is first recorded in Middle English in a work composed before 1400.

Reindeer Lake A lake of NE Saskatchewan and NW Manitoba, Canada, drained by the **Reindeer River,** flowing c. 230 km (143 mi) to the Churchill R.

reindeer moss *n.* An erect grayish branching lichen (*Cladonia rangiferina*) of Arctic regions.

re·in·fec·tion (rē′ĭn-fĕk′shən) *n.* A second infection that follows recovery from a previous infection of the same type.

re·in·force also **re·en·force** (rē′ĭn-fôrs′, -fōrs′) *tr.v.* **-forced, -forc·ing, -forc·es** **1.** To give more force or effectiveness to; strengthen. **2.** To strengthen (a military force) with additional personnel or equipment. **3.** To strengthen by adding extra support or material. **4.** To increase the number or amount of; augment. **5.** *Psychology* **a.** To reward (an experimental subject, for example) with a reinforcer subsequent to a desired response or performance. **b.** To encourage (a response) by means of a reinforcer. [RE– + *inforce* (var. of ENFORCE).] —**re′in·force′a·ble** *adj.*

re·in·forced concrete (rē′ĭn-fôrst′, -fōrst′) *n.* Poured concrete containing steel bars or metal netting to increase its tensile strength.

re·in·force·ment (rē′ĭn-fôrs′mənt, -fōrs′-) *n.* **1.** The act or process of reinforcing or the state of being reinforced. **2.** Something that reinforces. **3.** Additional personnel or equipment sent to support a military action. Often used in the plural. **4.** *Psychology* An event, circumstance, or condition that increases the likelihood that a given response will recur in a situation like that in which the reinforcing condition originally occurred.

re·in·forc·er (rē′ĭn-fôr′sər, -fōr′-) *n. Psychology* A stimulus, such as a reward, that in operant conditioning maintains or strengthens a desired response.

Rein·hardt (rīn′härt′), **Max** 1873–1943. Austrian theatrical director whose productions included *Oedipus Rex.*

reins (rānz) *pl.n.* **1.** The kidneys, loins, or lower back. **2.** The seat of the affections and passions. [ME < OFr. < Lat. *rēnēs.*]

re·in·state (rē′ĭn-stāt′) *tr.v.* **-stat·ed, -stat·ing, -states** **1.** To bring back into use or existence. **2.** To restore to a previous condition or position. —**re′in·state′ment** *n.*

re·in·sure (rē′ĭn-shŏŏr′) *tr.v.* **-sured, -sur·ing, -sures** To insure again, esp. by transferring all or part of the risk in a contract to a new contract with another insurance company. —**re′in·sur′ance** *n.* —**re′in·sur′er** *n.*

re·in·vent (rē′ĭn-vĕnt′) *tr.v.* **-vent·ed, -vent·ing, -vents** **1.** To make over completely. **2.** To bring back into existence or use. —**idiom: reinvent the wheel 1.** To do something over again, esp. needlessly or inefficiently. **2.** To recast something familiar or old into a different form.

re·is·sue (rē-ĭsh′ŏŏ) *v.* **-sued, -su·ing, -sues** —*tr.* To issue again, esp. to make available again. —*intr.* To come forth again. ❖ *n.* **1.** A second or subsequent issue, as of a book. **2.** A reprinting of postage stamps from unchanged plates.

REIT (rīt) *n.* A company that purchases and manages real estate or real estate loans, using money invested by its shareholders. [*r(eal) e(state) i(nvestment) t(rust).*]

re·it·er·ate (rē-ĭt′ə-rāt′) *tr.v.* **-at·ed, -at·ing, -ates** To say or do again or repeatedly. See Syns at **repeat.** —**re·it′er·a′tion** *n.* —**re·it′er·a′tive** (-ə-rā′tĭv, -ər-ə-tĭv) *adj.* —**re·it′er·a′tive·ly** *adv.* —**re·it′er·a′tor** *n.*

re·ject (rĭ-jĕkt′) *tr.v.* **-ject·ed, -ject·ing, -jects** **1.** To refuse to accept, submit to, believe, or make use of. **2.** To refuse to consider or grant; deny. **3.** To refuse to recognize or give affection to

(a person). **4.** To discard as defective or useless; throw away. See Syns at **refuse**[1]. **5.** To spit out or vomit. **6.** *Medicine* To resist immunologically the introduction of (a transplanted organ or tissue). ❖ *n.* (rē′jĕkt) One that has been rejected. [ME *rejecten* < Lat. *rēicere, rēiect-* : *re-, re-* + *iacere,* to throw.] —**re·ject′er** *n.* —**re·jec′tor** *n.* —**re·jec′tive** *adj.*

re·jec·tion (rĭ-jĕk′shən) *n.* **1.** The act of rejecting or the state of being rejected. **2.** Something rejected. **3.** *Medicine* The failure of a recipient's body to accept a transplanted tissue or organ as the result of immunological incompatibility.

rejection slip *n.* A printed note accompanying a manuscript rejected for publication and returned to the author.

re·jig·ger (rē-jĭg′ər) *tr.v.* **-gered, -ger·ing, -gers** *Informal* To readjust or rearrange.

re·joice (rĭ-jois′) *v.* **-joiced, -joic·ing, -joic·es** —*intr.* To feel joyful; be delighted. —*tr.* To fill with joy; gladden. —**phrasal verb: rejoice in** To have or possess. [ME *rejoicen* < OFr. *rejoir, rejoiss-* : *re-, re-* + *joir,* to be joyful (< VLat. **gaudīre* < Lat. *gaudēre*).] —**re·joic′er** *n.*

re·join[1] (rĭ-join′) *v.* **-joined, -join·ing, -joins** —*tr.* To say in reply, esp. in sharp response to a reply. —*intr.* To reply. [ME *rejoinen* < OFr. *rejoindre, rejoin-* : *re-, re-* + *joindre,* to join; see JOIN.]

re·join[2] (rē-join′) *v.* **-joined, -join·ing, -joins** **1.** To come again into the company of. **2.** To join together again; reunite. —*intr.* To become joined again.

re·join·der (rĭ-join′dər) *n.* An answer, esp. to a reply. [ME < OFr. *rejoindre,* to answer, rejoin. See REJOIN[1].]

re·ju·ve·nate (rĭ-jōō′və-nāt′) *tr.v.* **-nat·ed, -nat·ing, -nates** **1.** To restore to youthful vigor or appearance; make young again. **2.** To restore to an original or new condition. **3a.** To stimulate (a stream) to renewed erosive activity, as by uplift of the land. **b.** To develop youthful topographic features in (a previously leveled area). [RE– + Lat. *iuvenis,* young; see yeu- in App. + -ATE[1].] —**re·ju′ve·na′tor** (-tər) *n.*

re·ju·ve·nes·cence (rĭ-jōō′və-nĕs′əns) *n.* A renewal of youthful appearance or character. —**re·ju′ve·nes′cent** *adj.*

re·kin·dle (rē-kĭn′dl) *tr.v.* **-dled, -dling, -dles** **1.** To relight (a fire). **2.** To revive or renew.

re·lapse (rĭ-lăps′) *intr.v.* **-lapsed, -laps·ing, -laps·es** **1.** To fall or slide back into a former state. **2.** To regress after partial recovery from illness. **3.** To slip back into bad ways; backslide. ❖ *n.* (rē′lăps, rĭ-lăps′) A falling back into a former state, esp. after apparent improvement. [ME *relapsen,* to forswear < Lat. *relābī, relāps-,* to fall back gradually : *re-, re-* + *lābī,* to slide.] —**re·laps′er** *n.*

re·laps·ing fever (rĭ-lăp′sĭng) *n.* Any of several infectious diseases characterized by chills and fever and caused by spirochetes transmitted by lice and ticks.

re·late (rĭ-lāt′) *v.* **-lat·ed, -lat·ing, -lates** —*tr.* **1.** To narrate or tell. **2.** To bring into or link in logical or natural association. **3.** To establish or demonstrate a connection between. —*intr.* **1.** To have connection, relation, or reference. **2.** To have or establish a reciprocal relationship; interact. **3.** To react in response, esp. favorably: *I just can't relate to these new fashions.* [Obsolete Fr. *relater* < OFr. < Lat. *relātus,* p. part. of *referre* : *re-, re-* + *lātus,* brought; see telə- in App.] —**re·lat′a·ble** *adj.* —**re·lat′er** *n.*

re·lat·ed (rĭ-lā′tĭd) *adj.* **1.** Being connected; associated. **2.** Connected by kinship, common origin, or marriage. **3.** *Music* Having a close harmonic connection. —**re·lat′ed·ly** *adv.* —**re·lat′ed·ness** *n.*

re·la·tion (rĭ-lā′shən) *n.* **1.** A logical or natural association between two or more things; connection. **2.** The connection of people by blood or marriage; kinship. **3.** A person connected to another by blood or marriage; a relative. **4.** The way in which one person or thing is connected with another: *the relation of parent to child.* **5. relations a.** The mutual dealings or connections of persons, groups, or nations. **b.** Sexual intercourse. **6.** Reference; regard. **7a.** The act of telling or narrating. **b.** A narrative; an account.

re·la·tion·al (rĭ-lā′shə-nəl) *adj.* **1.** Of or arising from kinship. **2.** Relating to or constituting relation. **3.** *Grammar* Of, relating to, or being a word or particle, such as a conjunction or preposition, that expresses a syntactic relation between elements in a phrase or sentence. —**re·la′tion·al·ly** *adv.*

relational database *n.* A database system in which any database file can be a component of more than one of the database's tables.

re·la·tion·ship (rĭ-lā′shən-shĭp′) *n.* **1.** The condition or fact of being related; connection or association. **2.** Connection by blood or marriage; kinship. **3.** A particular type of connection between people related to or having dealings with each other. **4.** A romantic or sexual involvement.

rel·a·tive (rĕl′ə-tĭv) *adj.* **1.** Having pertinence or relevance; connected or related. **2.** Considered in comparison with something else: *the relative quiet of the suburbs.* **3.** Dependent on or interconnected with something else; not absolute. **4.** *Grammar* Referring to or qualifying an antecedent, as the pronoun *who* in *the man who left.* **5.** *Music* Having the same key signature. Used of major and minor scales and keys. ❖ *n.* **1.** One related by kinship, common origin, or marriage. **2.** Something having a relation or con-

reindeer
Rangifer tarandus

ă pat	oi	boy
ā pay	ou	out
âr care	ŏŏ	took
ä father	ōō	boot
ĕ pet	ŭ	cut
ē be	ûr	urge
ĭ pit	th	thin
ī pie	*th*	this
îr pier	hw	which
ŏ pot	zh	vision
ō toe	ə	about,
ô paw		item

Stress marks:
′ (primary);
′ (secondary); as in
lexicon (lĕk′sĭ-kŏn′)

nection to something else. **3.** *Grammar* A relative pronoun. [ME < OFr. *relatif* < LLat. *relātīvus* < Lat. *relātus*, p. part. of *referre*, to relate. See RELATE.] —**rel′a•tive•ness** *n.*

relative clause *n.* A dependent clause introduced by a relative pronoun, as *which is downstairs* in *The dining room, which is downstairs, is too dark.*

relative density *n.* See **specific gravity.**

relative humidity *n.* The ratio of the amount of water vapor in the air to the maximum amount that the air would hold at the same temperature, expressed as a percentage.

rel•a•tive•ly (rĕl′ə-tĭv-lē) *adv.* In a relative manner; in comparison.

relative pronoun *n.* A pronoun that introduces a relative clause and has reference to an antecedent, as *who* in *the child who is wearing a hat.*

relative to *prep.* With regard to; concerning.

rel•a•tiv•ism (rĕl′ə-tĭ-vĭz′əm) *n.* A theory, esp. in ethics or aesthetics, that conceptions of truth and moral values are not absolute but are relative to the persons or groups holding them.

rel•a•tiv•ist (rĕl′ə-tĭ-vĭst) *n.* **1.** *Philosophy* A proponent of relativism. **2.** A specialist in the theories of relativity.

rel•a•tiv•is•tic (rĕl′ə-tĭ-vĭs′tĭk) *adj.* **1.** Of or relating to relativism. **2.** *Physics* **a.** Of, relating to, or resulting from speeds approaching the speed of light. **b.** Having to do with or based on the theory of relativity.

rel•a•tiv•i•ty (rĕl′ə-tĭv′ĭ-tē) *n.* **1.** The quality or state of being relative. **2.** A state of dependence in which the existence or significance of one entity is solely dependent on that of another. **3.** *Physics* **a.** Special relativity. **b.** General relativity.

re•la•tor (rĭ-lā′tər) *n.* **1.** One who relates or narrates. **2.** *Law* A beneficially interested person on whose behalf an action is maintained by a sovereign power or a state.

re•lax (rĭ-lăks′) *v.* **-laxed, -lax•ing, -lax•es** —*tr.* **1.** To make lax or loose: *relax one's grip.* **2.** To make less severe or strict: *relax a curfew.* **3.** To reduce in intensity; slacken: *relax one's efforts.* **4.** To relieve from strain: *The warm bath relaxed me.* —*intr.* **1.** To take one's ease; rest. **2.** To become lax or loose. **3.** To become less severe or strict. **4.** To become less restrained or tense. [ME *relaxen* < OFr. *relaxer* < Lat. *relaxāre* : *re-*, re- + *laxāre*, to loosen (< *laxus*, loose).] —**re•lax′a•ble** *adj.*

re•lax•ant (rĭ-lăk′sənt) *n.* Something, such as a drug, that relaxes muscular or nervous tension. —**re•lax′ant** *adj.*

re•lax•a•tion (rē′lăk-sā′shən) *n.* **1.** The act of relaxing or the state of being relaxed. **2.** Refreshment of body or mind; recreation. **3.** A loosening or slackening. **4.** A reduction in strictness or severity. **5.** *Physiology* The lengthening of inactive muscle or muscle fibers. **6.** *Physics* The return of a system to equilibrium following displacement or abrupt change. **7.** *Mathematics* A method of solving equations in which the errors resulting from an initial approximation are reduced by succeeding approximations until all errors are within specified limits.

re•laxed (rĭ-lăkst′) *adj.* **1.** Not rigorous or strict. **2.** Free from strain or tension. **3.** Easy and informal in manner.

re•lax•er (rĭ-lăk′sər) *n.* One that relaxes, as a chemical solution used on tightly curled hair to soften or loosen the curls.

re•lax•in (rĭ-lăk′sĭn) *n.* A female hormone secreted by the corpus luteum that helps soften the cervix and relax the pelvic ligaments in childbirth.

re•lay (rē′lā) *n.* **1.** An act of passing something along from one person, group, or station to another. **2.** *Sports* **a.** A relay race. **b.** A division of a relay race. **3.** *Electronics* A device that responds to a small current or voltage change by activating switches or other devices in an electric circuit. **4.** A crew of workers who relieve another crew; a shift. **5.** A fresh team, as of horses, to relieve weary animals. ❖ *tr.v.* (rē′lā, rĭ-lā′) **-layed, -lay•ing, -lays 1.** To pass along by or as if by relay: *relayed the message to his boss.* **2.** To supply with fresh relays. **3.** *Electronics* To control or retransmit by means of a relay. [ME *relai*, fresh team of dogs for a hunt < OFr. < *relaier*, to relay : *re-*, re- + *laier*, to leave (< of Gmc. orig.).]

relay race *n.* A race between two or more teams, in which each team member participates in only a set part of the race and is then relieved by another member of the team.

re•leas•a•ble (rĭ-lē′sə-bəl) *adj.* **1.** That can be released. **2.** Intended or configured to release. —**re•leas•a•bil′i•ty** *n.* —**re•leas′a•bly** *adv.*

re•lease (rĭ-lēs′) *tr.v.* **-leased, -leas•ing, -leas•es 1.** To set free from confinement, restraint, or bondage. **2.** To free from something that binds, fastens, or holds back; let go: *released the balloons.* **3.** To dismiss, as from a job. **4.** To relieve of debt or obligation. **5.** To relieve of care and suffering. **6a.** To issue for performance, sale, publication, or distribution. **b.** To make known or available. **7.** To relinquish (a right or claim). ❖ *n.* **1.** A deliverance or liberation, as from confinement, restraint, or suffering. **2.** An authoritative discharge, as from an obligation or from prison. **3.** An unfastening or letting go of something caught or held fast. **4.** A device or catch for locking or releasing a mechanism. **5a.** The act or an instance of issuing something for publication, use, or distribution. **b.** Something thus released: *a new release of a software program.* **c.** The condition of being available, in use, or in publication: *a movie in wide release.* **6.** *Law* **a.** Relinquishment to another of a right, title, or claim. **b.** The document

authorizing such relinquishment. **7.** *Linguistics* The movement of a vocal organ or organs so as to end the closure of a stop consonant. [ME *relesen* < OFr. *relaissier*, alteration of *relacher* < Lat. *relaxāre*. See RELAX.]

re•leas•er (rĭ-lē′sər) *n.* **1.** One that releases. **2.** A stimulus that initiates a specific behavior pattern in an animal.

re•leas•ing factor (rĭ-lē′sĭng) *n.* Any of several hormones secreted by the hypothalamus that stimulate the anterior part of the pituitary gland to release certain hormones.

rel•e•gate (rĕl′ĭ-gāt) *tr.v.* **-gat•ed, -gat•ing, -gates 1.** To assign to an obscure place, position, or condition. **2.** To assign to a particular class or category; classify. **3.** To refer or assign (a matter or task, for example) for decision or action. **4.** To send to a place of exile; banish. [ME *relegaten*, to banish < Lat. *relēgāre*, *relēgāt-* : *re-*, re- + *lēgāre*, to send, depute; see **leg-** in App.] —**rel′e•ga′tion** *n.*

re•lent (rĭ-lĕnt′) *v.* **-lent•ed, -lent•ing, -lents** —*intr.* To become more lenient, compassionate, or forgiving. —*tr. Obsolete* **1.** To cause to slacken or abate. **2.** To cause to soften in attitude or temper. [ME *relenten*, to melt < AN *relenter* < *relent*, damp : Lat. *re-*, re- + Lat. *lentus*, sticky, slow.]

re•lent•less (rĭ-lĕnt′lĭs) *adj.* **1.** Unyielding in severity or strictness; unrelenting. **2.** Steady and persistent; unremitting. —**re•lent′less•ly** *adv.* —**re•lent′less•ness** *n.*

rel•e•vant (rĕl′ə-vənt) *adj.* Having a bearing on or connection with the matter at hand. [Med.Lat. *relevāns, relevant-* < Lat., pr. part. of *relevāre*, to relieve, raise up. See RELIEVE.] —**rel′e•vance, rel′e•van•cy** *n.* —**rel′e•vant•ly** *adv.*

re•li•a•ble (rĭ-lī′ə-bəl) *adj.* **1.** Capable of being relied on; dependable. **2.** Yielding the same or compatible results in different clinical experiments or statistical trials. —**re•li′a•bil′i•ty, re•li′a•ble•ness** *n.* —**re•li′a•bly** *adv.*

re•li•ance (rĭ-lī′əns) *n.* **1.** The act of relying or the state of being reliant. **2.** The faith, confidence, or trust felt by one who relies; dependence. **3.** One relied on; a mainstay.

re•li•ant (rĭ-lī′ənt) *adj.* Having or exhibiting reliance; dependent. —**re•li′ant•ly** *adv.*

rel•ic (rĕl′ĭk) *n.* **1.** Something that has survived the passage of time, esp. an object or custom whose original culture has disappeared. **2.** Something cherished for its age or historic interest. **3.** An object kept for its association with the past; a memento. **4.** An object of religious veneration, esp. a piece of the body or a personal item of a saint. **5.** or **relics** A corpse; remains. [ME *relik*, object of religious veneration < OFr. *relique* < LLat. *reliquiae*, sacred relics < Lat., remains < *reliquus*, remaining < *relinquere*, *reliqu-*, to leave behind. See RELINQUISH.]

rel•ict (rĕl′ĭkt, rĭ-lĭkt′) *n.* **1.** *Ecology* An organism or species of an earlier time surviving in an environment that has undergone considerable change. **2.** Something that has survived; a remnant. **3.** A widow. ❖ *adj. Geology* Of or relating to something that has survived, as structures after destructive processes. [< ME *relicte*, left undisturbed < Lat. *relictus*, p. part. of *relinquere*, to leave behind. See RELINQUISH. Sense 3, ME *relicte*, < Med.Lat. *relicta* < fem. passive part. of Lat. *relinquere*.]

re•lic•tion (rĭ-lĭk′shən) *n.* Gradual recession of water in a sea, lake, or stream, leaving permanently dry land.

re•lief (rĭ-lēf′) *n.* **1.** The easing of a burden or distress, such as pain, anxiety, or oppression. **2.** Something that alleviates pain or distress. **3a.** Public assistance. **b.** Aid in time of danger, esp. rescue from siege. **4a.** Release from a post or duty, as that of sentinel. **b.** One who releases another by taking over a post or duty. **5.** A pleasant or amusing change; a diversion. **6a.** The projection of figures or forms from a flat background, as in sculpture, or the apparent projection of such shapes in a painting or drawing. **b.** A work of art featuring such projection. **7.** *Geology* The variations in elevation of an area of the earth's surface. **8.** Distinction or prominence due to contrast. **9.** *Law* Redress awarded by a court. **10.** *Baseball* The pitching done by a relief pitcher. **11.** A payment made by the heir of a deceased tenant to a feudal lord for the privilege of succeeding to the tenant's estate. —*idiom:* **on relief** Receiving public assistance because of need or poverty. [ME < OFr. < *relever*, to relieve; see RELIEVE. Senses 6, 7, and 8, Fr. < Ital. *rilievo*; see BAS-RELIEF.]

relief map *n.* A map that depicts land configuration, usu. with contour lines.

relief pitcher *n. Baseball* A pitcher who replaces another during a game.

re•lieve (rĭ-lēv′) *tr.v.* **-lieved, -liev•ing, -lieves 1.** To cause a lessening or alleviation of: *relieved his symptoms; relieved the tension.* **2.** To free from pain, anxiety, or distress. **3.** To furnish assistance or aid to. **4.** To rescue from siege. **5.** To release (a person) from an obligation, restriction, or burden, as by law. **6a.** To free from a specified duty by providing or acting as a substitute. **b.** *Baseball* To take over for (a relief pitcher). **7.** To make less tedious, monotonous, or unpleasant: *A small candle relieved the gloom.* **8.** To make prominent or effective by contrast; set off. **9.** *Informal* To rob or deprive: *A mugger relieved him of his money.* —*idiom:* **relieve oneself** To urinate or defecate. [ME *releven* < OFr. *relever* < Lat. *relevāre* : *re-*, re- + *levāre*, to raise.] —**re•liev′a•ble** *adj.* —**re•liev′er** *n.*

SYNONYMS *relieve, allay, alleviate, assuage, lighten, mitigate, palliate* These verbs mean to make something less severe or more bearable. To *relieve* is to make more endurable something causing discomfort or distress: *"that misery which he strives in vain to relieve"* (Henry David Thoreau). *Allay* suggests at least temporary relief from what is burdensome or painful: *"This music crept by me upon the waters/Allaying both their fury and my passion/With its sweet air"* (Shakespeare). *Alleviate* connotes temporary lessening of distress without removal of its cause: *"No arguments shall be wanting on my part that can alleviate so severe a misfortune"* (Jane Austen). To *assuage* is to soothe or make milder: *assuaged his guilt by confessing to the crime. Lighten* signifies to make less heavy or oppressive: *Congress endeavored to lighten the taxpayers' burden. Mitigate* and *palliate* connote moderating the force or intensity of something that causes suffering: *"I . . . prayed to the Lord to mitigate a calamity"* (John Galt). *"His ability . . . made men turn to him in the hour of distress, as of all statesmen the most fitted to palliate it"* (William E.H. Lecky).

re·lie·vo (rĭ-lē′vō) *n., pl.* **-vos** See **relief** 6. [Ital. *rilievo.* See BAS-RELIEF.]

re·li·gion (rĭ-lĭj′ən) *n.* **1a.** Belief in and reverence for a supernatural power or powers regarded as creator and governor of the universe. **b.** A system grounded in such belief and worship. **2.** The life or condition of a person in a religious order. **3.** A set of beliefs, values, and practices based on the teachings of a spiritual leader. **4.** A cause, principle, or activity pursued with zeal or conscientious devotion. **—idiom: get religion** *Informal* **1.** To become religious or devout. **2.** To resolve to end one's immoral behavior. [ME *religioun* < OFr. *religion* < Lat. *religiō, religiōn-,* perh. < *religāre,* to tie fast. See RELY.]

re·li·gion·ism (rĭ-lĭj′ə-nĭz′əm) *n.* Excessive or affected religious zeal. **—re·li′gion·ist** *n.*

re·li·gi·ose (rĭ-lĭj′ē-ōs′) *adj.* Excessively religious, esp. in a conspicuous or sentimental manner.

re·li·gi·os·i·ty (rĭ-lĭj′ē-ŏs′ĭ-tē) *n.* **1.** The quality of being religious. **2.** Excessive or affected piety.

re·li·gious (rĭ-lĭj′əs) *adj.* **1.** Having or showing belief in and reverence for God or a deity. **2.** Of, concerned with, or teaching religion. **3.** Extremely scrupulous or conscientious. ❖ *n., pl.* **religious** A member of a monastic order, esp. a nun or monk. [ME < OFr. < Lat. *religiōsus* < *religiō,* religion. See RELIGION.] **—re·li′gious·ly** *adv.* **—re·li′gious·ness** *n.*

re·line (rē-līn′) *tr.v.* **-lined, -lin·ing, -lines 1.** To make new lines on. **2.** To put a new lining in.

re·lin·quish (rĭ-lĭng′kwĭsh) *tr.v.* **-quished, -quish·ing, -quish·es 1.** To retire from; give up or abandon. **2.** To put aside or desist from (something practiced, professed, or intended). **3.** To let go; surrender. **4.** To cease holding physically; release: *relinquish a grip.* [ME *relinquisshen* < OFr. *relinquir, relinquiss-* < Lat. *relinquere* : *re-, re-* + *linquere,* to leave; see **leik**ʷ- in App.] **—re·lin′quish·er** *n.* **—re·lin′quish·ment** *n.*

SYNONYMS *relinquish, yield, resign, abandon, surrender, cede, waive, renounce* These verbs mean letting something go or giving something up. *Relinquish,* the least specific, may connote regret: *can't relinquish the idea. Yield* implies giving way, as to pressure, often in the hope that such action will be temporary: *had to yield ground. Resign* suggests acquiescence arising from hopelessness: *resigned himself to forgoing his vacation. Abandon* and *surrender* both imply no expectation of recovery, but *surrender* also implies the operation of compulsion or force: *abandoned all hope; surrendering control. Cede* connotes formal transfer, as of territory: *ceded the province to the victor. Waive* implies a voluntary decision to dispense with something, such as a right: *waived all privileges.* To *renounce* is to relinquish formally and usually as a matter of principle: *renounced worldly goods.*

rel·i·quar·y (rĕl′ĭ-kwĕr′ē) *n., pl.* **-ies** A receptacle, such as a coffer or shrine, for keeping or displaying sacred relics. [Fr. *reliquaire* < OFr. < *relique,* relic < LLat. *reliquiae,* sacred relics. See RELIC.]

rel·ique (rĕl′ĭk) *n. Archaic* Variant of **relic.**

re·liq·ui·ae (rĭ-lĭk′wē-ē′) *pl.n.* Remains, as of fossil organisms. [Lat., remains. See RELIC.]

rel·ish (rĕl′ĭsh) *n.* **1.** An appetite for something; a strong appreciation or liking. **2a.** Hearty enjoyment; zest. **b.** Something that lends pleasure or zest. **3a.** A spicy or savory condiment or appetizer, such as chutney or olives. **b.** A condiment of chopped sweet pickle. **4.** The flavor of a food, esp. when appetizing. **5.** A trace or suggestion of a pleasurable quality. ❖ *v.* **-ished, -ish·ing, -ish·es** *—tr.* **1.** To take keen or zestful pleasure in. **2.** To enjoy the flavor of. **3.** To give spice or flavor to. *—intr.* To have a pleasing or distinctive taste. [Alteration of ME *reles,* taste < OFr., something remaining < *relaissier,* to leave behind. See RELEASE.]

re·live (rē-lĭv′) *v.* **-lived, -liv·ing, -lives** *—tr.* To undergo or experience again, esp. in the imagination. *—intr.* To live again.

re·lo·cate (rē-lō′kāt) *tr. & intr.v.* **-cat·ed, -cat·ing, -cates** To move or be moved to a new place. **—re′lo·ca′tion** *n.*

re·lu·cent (rĭ-lōō′sənt) *adj.* Reflecting light; shining. [Lat. *relūcēns, relūcent-,* pr. part. of *relūcēre,* to shine back : *re-, re-* + *lūcēre,* to shine; see **leuk**- in App.]

re·luct (rĭ-lŭkt′) *intr.v.* **-luct·ed, -luct·ing, -lucts** To show reluctance or repugnance. [Lat. *reluctārī* : *re-, re-* + *luctārī,* to struggle.]

re·luc·tance (rĭ-lŭk′təns) *also* **re·luc·tan·cy** (-tən-sē) *n.* **1.** The state of being reluctant. **2.** *Physics* A measure of the opposition to magnetic flux, analogous to electric resistance.

re·luc·tant (rĭ-lŭk′tənt) *adj.* **1.** Unwilling; disinclined: *reluctant to help.* **2.** Exhibiting or marked by unwillingness. **3.** Offering resistance; opposing. [Lat. *reluctāns, reluctant-,* pr. part. of *reluctārī,* to reluct. See RELUCT.] **—re·luc′tant·ly** *adv.*

rel·uc·tiv·i·ty (rĕl′ək-tĭv′ĭ-tē) *n.* A measure of the resistance of a material to magnetization, equal to the ratio of the intensity of the magnetic field to the magnetic induction of the material. [Blend of RELUCTANCE and CONDUCTIVITY.]

re·lume (rĭ-lōōm′) *tr.v.* **-lumed, -lum·ing, -lumes** To make bright or clear again; illuminate again. [RE- + (IL)LUME.]

re·ly (rĭ-lī′) *intr.v.* **-lied, -ly·ing, -lies 1.** To be dependent for support, help, or supply: *relies on her parents for tuition.* **2.** To place or have faith or confidence: *relied on them to tell him the truth.* [ME *relien,* to rally < OFr. *relier* < Lat. *religāre,* to bind fast : *re-, re-* + *ligāre,* to bind.] **—re·li′er** *n.*

rem (rĕm) *n.* **1.** The amount of ionizing radiation required to produce the same biological effect as one rad of high-penetration x-rays. **2.** A unit for measuring absorbed doses of radiation, equivalent to one roentgen of x-rays or gamma rays. [*r(oentgen) e(quivalent in) m(an).*]

REM (rĕm) *n.* The rapid periodic jerky movement of the eyes during certain stages of the sleep cycle when dreaming takes place. [R(APID) E(YE) M(OVEMENT).]

re·main (rĭ-mān′) *intr.v.* **-mained, -main·ing, -mains 1.** To continue in the same state or condition: *These matters remain in doubt.* **2.** To continue to be in the same place; stay or stay behind: *We are remaining at home.* **3.** To be left after the removal, loss, passage, or destruction of others: *Only a few trees remain.* See Syns at **stay¹. 4.** To be left as still to be dealt with: *A cure remains to be found.* **5.** To endure or persist. [ME *remainen* < OFr. *remanoir, remainer* < Lat. *remanēre* : *re-, re-* + *manēre,* to remain.]

re·main·der (rĭ-mān′dər) *n.* **1.** Something left over after other parts have been taken away. **2.** *Mathematics* **a.** The number left over when one integer is divided by another. **b.** The number obtained when one number is subtracted from another; the difference. **3.** *Law* An estate in land that is conveyed only after the natural termination of the preceding estate created by the same document. **4.** A book that remains with a publisher after sales have fallen off, usu. sold at a reduced price. ❖ *tr.v.* **-dered, -der·ing, -ders** To sell or dispose of as a remainder. [ME, second party's right of ownership < AN < *remeindre,* to remain, var. of OFr. *remaindre, remainer.* See REMAIN.]

re·mains (rĭ-mānz′) *pl.n.* **1.** All that is left after other parts have been taken away, used up, or destroyed. **2.** A corpse. **3.** The unpublished writings of a deceased author. **4.** Ancient ruins or fossils.

re·make (rē-māk′) *tr.v.* **-made** (-mād′), **-mak·ing, -makes** To make again or anew. ❖ *n.* (rē′māk′) **1.** The act of remaking. **2.** Something remade, esp. a new version of an earlier movie or song.

re·man (rē-măn′) *tr.v.* **-manned, -man·ning, -mans 1.** To supply with new personnel. **2.** To imbue with new manliness or courage.

re·mand (rĭ-mănd′) *tr.v.* **-mand·ed, -mand·ing, -mands 1.** To send or order back. **2.** *Law* **a.** To send back to custody. **b.** To send back (a case) to a lower court with instructions about further proceedings. [ME *remaunden* < OFr. *remander* < LLat. *remandāre,* to send back word : Lat. *re-, re-* + Lat. *mandāre,* to order; see **man-**² in App.] **—re·mand′, re·mand′ment** *n.*

rem·a·nence (rĕm′ə-nəns) *n.* The magnetic induction that remains in a material after removal of the magnetizing field. [< ME *remnant,* remaining < Lat. *remanēns, remanent-,* pr. part. of *remanēre,* to remain. See REMAIN.] **—rem′a·nent** *adj.*

re·mark (rĭ-märk′) *v.* **-marked, -mark·ing, -marks** *—tr.* **1.** To express briefly and casually as a comment. **2.** To take notice of; observe. *—intr.* To make a comment or observation. ❖ *n.* **1.** The act of noticing or observing. **2.** A casual or brief expression of opinion; a comment. See Syns at **comment.** [Alteration of Fr. *remarquer* : OFr. *re-, re-* + OFr. *marquer,* to mark (ult. < *merc,* sign < ON *merki,* mark; see **merg-** in App.).] **—re·mark′er** *n.*

re·mark·a·ble (rĭ-mär′kə-bəl) *adj.* **1.** Worthy of notice. **2.** Attracting notice as being unusual or extraordinary. **—re·mark′a·ble·ness** *n.* **—re·mark′a·bly** *adv.*

re·marque (rĭ-märk′) *n.* **1.** A small mark or sketch engraved in the margin of a plate to indicate its stage of development prior to completion. **2.** A print or proof from a plate carrying such a mark. [Fr. < *remarquer,* to remark. See REMARK.]

Re·marque (rə-märk′), **Erich Maria** 1898–1970. German-born Amer. writer known for his novel *All Quiet on the Western Front* (1929).

re·mas·ter (rē-măs′tər) *tr.v.* **-tered, -ter·ing, -ters** To master again, esp. to produce a new master sound recording of (an old recording) in order to improve the sound quality.

re·match (rē-măch′, rē′măch′) *n.* A second contest between the same opponents.

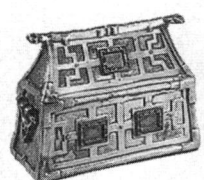

reliquary
wood, bronze, tinned
copper, and glass

Rembrandt van Rijn
1658–60 self-portrait

Rem·brandt van Rijn or **Rem·brandt van Ryn** (rĕm′brănt′ vän rīn′, -bränt′) 1606–69. Dutch painter whose works include *The Night Watch* (1642).

re·me·di·a·ble (rĭ-mē′dē-ə-bəl) *adj.* Possible to remedy. —**re·me′di·a·bly** *adv.*

re·me·di·al (rĭ-mē′dē-əl) *adj.* **1.** Supplying a remedy. **2.** Intended to correct or improve deficient skills in a specific subject: *remedial reading.* —**re·me′di·al·ly** *adv.*

re·me·di·a·tion (rĭ-mē′dē-ā′shən) *n.* The act or process of correcting a fault or deficiency. —**re·me′di·ate′** *v.*

rem·e·dy (rĕm′ĭ-dē) *n., pl.* **-dies 1.** Something, such as medicine, that relieves pain, cures disease, or corrects a disorder. **2.** Something that corrects an evil, fault, or error. **3.** *Law* A legal order of preventing or redressing a wrong or enforcing a right. **4.** The allowance by a mint for deviation from the standard weight or quality of coins. ❖ *tr.v.* **-died, -dy·ing, -dies 1.** To relieve or cure (a disease or disorder). **2.** To remove, counteract, or rectify. See Syns at **correct, cure.** [ME *remedie* < OFr. < Lat. *remedium* : *re-*, re- + *mederī*, to heal; see **med-** in App.]

re·mem·ber (rĭ-mĕm′bər) *v.* **-bered, -ber·ing, -bers** —*tr.* **1a.** To recall to the mind with effort; think of again: *I finally remembered the address.* **b.** To recall or become aware of suddenly or spontaneously: *Then I remembered that today is your birthday.* **2.** To retain in the memory: *Remember your appointment.* **3.** To keep (someone) in mind as worthy of consideration or recognition. **4.** To reward with a gift or tip. **5.** To give greetings from. **6.** *Engineering* To return to (an original shape or form) after being deformed or altered. **7.** *Electronics* To carry out (a programmed or preset activity). **8.** *Archaic* To remind. —*intr.* **1.** To have or use the power of memory. [ME *remembren* < OFr. *remembrer* < Lat. *rememorārī*, to remember again : *re-*, re- + *memor*, mindful; see **(s)mer-** in App.] —**re·mem′ber·a·bil′i·ty** *n.* —**re·mem′ber·a·ble** *adj.* —**re·mem′ber·er** *n.*

SYNONYMS *remember, recall, recollect* These verbs mean to bring an image or a thought back to the mind: *can't remember his name; recalling her kindness; recollected the events leading to the accident.* **ANTONYM** *forget*

re·mem·brance (rĭ-mĕm′brəns) *n.* **1a.** The act or process of remembering. **b.** The state of being remembered: *holds him in fond remembrance.* **2.** Something serving to celebrate or honor the memory of a person or event; a memorial. **3.** The length of time over which one's memory extends. **4.** Something remembered; a reminiscence. **5.** A souvenir. **6.** A greeting or token that is expressive of affection.

Remembrance Day *n.* The Sunday closest to November 11, observed in Canada and Great Britain in commemoration of those killed in the World Wars.

re·mem·branc·er (rĭ-mĕm′brən-sər) *n.* **1.** One that causes another to remember something. **2. Remembrancer a.** An officer of the British judiciary responsible for collecting debts owed to the Crown. **b.** An official who represents the City of London.

re·mex (rē′mĕks) *n., pl.* **rem·i·ges** (rĕm′ə-jēz′) A quill or flight feather of a bird's wing. [Lat. *rēmex, rēmig-*, rower : *rēmus*, oar + *agere*, to drive; see ACT.] —**re·mig′i·al** (rĭ-mĭj′ē-əl) *adj.*

re·mind (rĭ-mīnd′) *tr.v.* **-mind·ed, -mind·ing, -minds** To cause to remember; put in mind. —**re·mind′er** *n.*

Rem·ing·ton (rĕm′ĭng-tən), **Eliphalet** 1793–1861. Amer. firearms manufacturer whose company was a major supplier to the US government.

Remington, Frederic 1861–1909. Amer. artist and journalist best known for his sculptures and paintings of the West.

rem·i·nisce (rĕm′ə-nĭs′) *intr.v.* **-nisced, -nisc·ing, -nisc·es** To recollect and tell of past experiences or events. [Back-formation < REMINISCENCE.] —**rem′i·nisc′er** *n.*

rem·i·nis·cence (rĕm′ə-nĭs′əns) *n.* **1.** The act or process of recollecting past experiences or events. **2.** An experience or event recollected: *"Her mind seemed wholly taken up with reminiscences of past gaiety"* (Charlotte Brontë). **3.** A narration of past experiences. Often used in the plural. **4.** An event that brings to mind a similar former event.

rem·i·nis·cent (rĕm′ə-nĭs′ənt) *adj.* **1.** Having the quality of or containing reminiscence. **2.** Inclined to engage in reminiscence. **3.** Tending to recall or suggest something in the past. [Lat. *reminīscēns, reminīscent-*, pr. part. of *reminīscī*, to recollect. See **men-**[1] in App.] —**rem′i·nis′cent·ly** *adv.*

re·mint (rē-mĭnt′) *tr.v.* **-mint·ed, -mint·ing, -mints** To make into new coin by melting down and reprocessing.

re·miss (rĭ-mĭs′) *adj.* **1.** Lax in attending to duty; negligent. **2.** Exhibiting carelessness or slackness. [ME < Lat. *remissus*, p. part. of *remittere*, to remit, slacken. See REMIT.] —**re·miss′ly** *adv.* —**re·miss′ness** *n.*

re·mis·si·ble (rĭ-mĭs′ə-bəl) *adj.* Being such that forgiveness is possible. —**re·mis′si·bil′i·ty** *n.* —**re·mis′si·bly** *adv.*

re·mis·sion (rĭ-mĭsh′ən) *n.* **1a.** The act of remitting. **2.** A condition or period in which something is remitted. **2.** A lessening of intensity or degree; abatement. **3a.** *Medicine* Abatement or subsiding of the symptoms of a disease. **b.** The period during which the symptoms of a disease abate or subside. **4a.** Release, as from a debt. **b.** Forgiveness; pardon. [ME < OFr. < Lat. *remissiō, remissiōn-* < *remissus*, p. part. of *remittere*, to let go. See REMIT.]

re·mit (rĭ-mĭt′) *v.* **-mit·ted, -mit·ting, -mits** —*tr.* **1.** To transmit (money) in payment. **2a.** To refrain from exacting (a tax or penalty, for example); cancel. **b.** To pardon; forgive: *remit sins.* **3.** To restore to a former condition or position. **4.** *Law* **a.** To refer (a case) to another court for further consideration or action. **b.** To refer (a matter) to a committee or authority for decision. **5.** To allow to slacken: *The storm remitted its fury.* **6.** To desist from; give up. **7.** To put off; postpone. —*intr.* **1.** To transmit money. **2.** To diminish; abate. ❖ *n.* (rĭ-mĭt′, rē′mĭt) **1.** The act of remitting, esp. the referral of a case to another court. **2.** A matter remitted for further consideration. [ME *remitten*, to send back < Lat. *remittere* : *re-*, re- + *mittere*, to send.] —**re·mit′ment** *n.* —**re·mit′ta·ble** *adj.* —**re·mit′ter** *n.*

re·mit·tal (rĭ-mĭt′l) *n.* Remission.

re·mit·tance (rĭ-mĭt′ns) *n.* **1.** The sending of money to someone at a distance. **2.** The sum of money sent.

re·mit·tent (rĭ-mĭt′nt) *adj.* Characterized by temporary abatement in severity. Used esp. of diseases. —**re·mit′tence, re·mit′ten·cy** *n.* —**re·mit′tent·ly** *adv.*

re·mix (rē-mĭks′) *tr.v.* **-mixed, -mix·ing, -mix·es** To recombine (audio tracks or channels from a recording) to produce a new or modified audio recording. ❖ *n.* (rē′mĭks′) A recording produced by remixing.

rem·nant (rĕm′nənt) *n.* **1.** Something left over; a remainder. **2.** A piece of fabric remaining after the rest has been used or sold. **3.** A surviving trace or vestige: *a remnant of his past glory.* **4.** A small surviving group of people. Often used in the plural. [ME *remanant, remnant* < OFr. *remanant* < pr. part. of *remaindre*, to remain. See REMAIN.]

re·mod·el (rē-mŏd′l) *tr.v.* **-eled, -el·ing, -els** also **-elled, -el·ling, -els** To make over in structure or style; reconstruct. —**re·mod′el·er** *n.*

re·mon·strance (rĭ-mŏn′strəns) *n.* **1.** The act of remonstrating. **2.** An expression of protest, complaint, or reproof, esp. a formal statement of grievances.

re·mon·strant (rĭ-mŏn′strənt) *adj.* Characterized by remonstrance; expostulatory. ❖ *n.* **1.** One that remonstrates. **2. Remonstrant** One of the Dutch Arminians who in 1610 formally stated the grounds of their dissent from strict Calvinism. —**re·mon′strant·ly** *adv.*

re·mon·strate (rĭ-mŏn′strāt′, rĕm′ən-strāt′) *v.* **-strat·ed, -strat·ing, -strates** —*tr.* To say or plead in protest, objection, or reproof. —*intr.* To reason or plead in protest; present an objection. See Syns at **object.** [Med.Lat. *remōnstrāre, remōnstrāt-*, to demonstrate : Lat. *re-*, re- + Lat. *mōnstrāre*, to show (< *mōnstrum*, portent; see MONSTER).] —**re′mon·stra′tion** (rē′mŏn-strā′shən, rĕm′ən-) *n.* —**re·mon′stra·tive** (rĭ-mŏn′strə-tĭv) *adj.* —**re·mon′stra·tor** *n.*

rem·o·ra (rĕm′ər-ə) *n.* Any of several marine fishes of the family Echeneidae, having on the head a sucking disk with which they attach themselves to sharks, whales, sea turtles, or ships. [Lat., delay < *remorārī*, to delay : *re-*, re- + *morārī*, to delay (< *mora*, delay).]

re·morse (rĭ-môrs′) *n.* **1.** Moral anguish arising from repentance for past misdeeds; bitter regret. **2.** *Obsolete* Compassion. [ME *remors* < OFr. < Med.Lat. *remorsum* < neut. p. part. of Lat. *remordēre*, to torment : *re-*, re- + *mordēre*, to bite; see **mer-** in App.]

re·morse·ful (rĭ-môrs′fəl) *adj.* Marked by or filled with remorse. —**re·morse′ful·ly** *adv.* —**re·morse′ful·ness** *n.*

re·morse·less (rĭ-môrs′lĭs) *adj.* **1.** Having no pity or compassion; merciless. **2.** Unyielding; relentless. —**re·morse′less·ly** *adv.* —**re·morse′less·ness** *n.*

re·mote (rĭ-mōt′) *adj.* **-mot·er, -mot·est 1a.** Located far away; distant in space. **b.** Hidden away; secluded: *a remote hamlet.* **2.** Distant in time: *the remote past.* **3.** Faint; slight: *a remote possibility for success.* **4.** Far removed in connection or relevance: *a cause remote from everyday concerns.* **5.** Distantly related by blood or marriage: *a remote cousin.* **6.** Distant in manner; aloof. **7.** Operating or controlled from a distance: *remote sensors.* **8.** *Computer Science* Located at a distance from another computer that is accessible by cables or other communications links: *a remote terminal.* ❖ *n.* **1.** A radio or television broadcast originating from a point outside a studio. **2.** A remote-control device. [ME < OFr. *remot* < Lat. *remōtus*, p. part. of *removēre*, to remove. See REMOVE.] —**re·mote′ly** *adv.* —**re·mote′ness** *n.*

remote control *n.* **1.** The control of an activity, process, or machine from a distance, as by radioed instructions or coded signals. **2.** A device used to control an apparatus or machine from a distance. —**re·mote′-con·trol′** (rĭ-mōt′kən-trōl′), **re·mote′-con·trolled′** (-trōld′) *adj.*

re·mo·tion (rĭ-mō′shən) *n.* **1.** The act of removing; removal. **2.** The state of being remote. **3.** *Obsolete* Departure.

ré·mou·lade (rā′moo-läd′) *n.* A piquant cold sauce made with mayonnaise, chopped pickles, capers, anchovies, and herbs. [Fr. < dialectal *rémola*, large black radish < Lat. *armoracia*, wild radish.]

re·mount (rē-mount′) *tr.v.* **-mount·ed, -mount·ing, -mounts 1.** To mount again. **2.** To supply with a fresh horse. ❖ *n.* (rē′mount′, rē-mount′) A fresh horse.

re·mov·a·ble (rĭ-moo′və-bəl) *adj.* That can be removed. —**re·mov′a·bil′i·ty, re·mov′a·ble·ness** *n.*

removable cartridge *n.* A hard disk that is enclosed in a casing, can be removed from the drive, and has greater storage capacity than floppy disks.

re•mov•al (rĭ-mo͞o′vəl) *n.* **1a.** The act of removing. **b.** The fact of being removed. **2.** Relocation, as of a residence or business. **3.** Dismissal, as from office.

re•move (rĭ-mo͞ov′) *v.* **-moved, -mov•ing, -moves** —*tr.* **1.** To move from a place or position occupied: *removed the cups from the table.* **2.** To transfer or convey from one place to another: *removed the family to Texas.* **3.** To take off: *removed my boots.* **4.** To take away; withdraw: *removed the candidate's name from consideration.* **5.** To do away with; eliminate: *remove a stain.* **6.** To dismiss from an office or position. —*intr.* **1.** To change one's place of residence or business; move: *"In 1751, I removed from the country to the town"* (David Hume). **2.** To go away; depart. **3.** To be removable: *paint that removes with water.* ❖ *n.* **1.** The act of removing; removal. **2.** Distance or degree of separation or remoteness. [ME *removen* < OFr. *remouvoir* < Lat. *removēre* : *re-*, re- + *movēre*, to move.] —**re•mov′er** *n.*

re•moved (rĭ-mo͞ovd′) *adj.* **1.** Distant in space, time, or nature; remote. **2.** Separated in relationship by a given degree of descent: *a first cousin once removed.* —**re•mov′ed•ly** (-mo͞o′vĭd-lē) *adv.* —**re•mov′ed•ness** *n.*

REM sleep *n.* A stage in the normal sleep cycle during which dreams occur as well as rapid eye movement, loss of reflexes, and increased pulse rate and brain activity.

re•mu•da (rĭ-mo͞o′də) *n. Southwestern US* A herd of horses from which ranch hands select their mounts. [Am.Sp. < Sp., exchange < *remudar*, to exchange : *re-*, in return (< Lat.; see RE–) + *mudar*, to change (< Lat. *mūtāre*).]

re•mu•ner•ate (rĭ-myo͞o′nə-rāt′) *tr.v.* **-at•ed, -at•ing, -ates 1.** To pay (a person) a suitable equivalent in return for goods provided, services rendered, or losses incurred; recompense. **2.** To compensate for; make payment for. [Lat. *remūnerārī, remūnerāt-* : *re-*, re- + *mūnerārī*, to give (< *mūnus, mūner-*, gift).] —**re•mu′ner•a•bil′i•ty** (-nər-ə-bĭl′ĭ-tē) *n.* —**re•mu′ner•a•ble** *adj.* —**re•mu′ner•a′tor** *n.*

re•mu•ner•a•tion (rĭ-myo͞o′nə-rā′shən) *n.* **1.** The act of remunerating. **2.** Something that remunerates.

re•mu•ner•a•tive (rĭ-myo͞o′nər-ə-tĭv, -nə-rā′tĭv) *adj.* **1.** Yielding recompense; profitable. **2.** Serving to remunerate. —**re•mu′ner•a•tive•ly** *adv.* —**re•mu′ner•a•tive•ness** *n.*

Re•mus (rē′məs) *n. Roman Mythology* The twin brother of Romulus.

ren•ais•sance (rĕn′ĭ-säns′, -zäns′, rĕn′ĭ-säns′, -zäns′, rĭ-nā′səns) *n.* **1.** A rebirth or revival. **2. Renaissance a.** The humanistic revival of classical art, architecture, literature, and learning that originated in Italy in the 14th century. **b.** The period of this revival, roughly the 14th through the 16th century, marking the transition from medieval to modern times. **3.** often **Renaissance a.** A revival of intellectual or artistic achievement and vigor. **b.** The period of such a revival. ❖ *adj.* **Renaissance 1.** Of, relating to, or characteristic of the Renaissance or its artistic and intellectual works and styles. **2.** Of or being the style of architecture and decoration that was based on classical models and originated in Italy in the 15th century. [Fr. < OFr. < *renaistre*, to be born again < VLat. **renāscere* < Lat. *renāscī* : *re-*, re- + *nāscī*, to be born; see **genə-** in App.]

Renaissance man *n.* A man who has broad intellectual interests and is accomplished in both the arts and the sciences.

Renaissance woman *n.* A woman who has broad intellectual interests and is accomplished in both the arts and the sciences.

re•nal (rē′nəl) *adj.* Of, relating to, or in the region of the kidneys. [LLat. *rēnālis* < Lat. *rēnēs*, kidneys.]

renal clearance *n.* The volume of plasma completely cleared of a specific compound per unit time and measured as a test of kidney function.

renal corpuscle *n.* See **Malpighian corpuscle** 1.

renal pelvis *n.* See **pelvis** 2.

re•nas•cence (rĭ-năs′əns, -nā′səns) *n.* **1.** A new birth or life; a rebirth. **2.** A cultural revival; a renaissance. **3. Renascence** Renaissance.

re•nas•cent (rĭ-năs′ənt, -nā′sənt) *adj.* Coming again into being; showing renewed growth or vigor. [Lat. *renāscēns, renāscent-*, pr. part. of *renāscī*, to be born again. See RENAISSANCE.]

Re•nault (rə-nō′), **Jean Louis** 1843–1918. French jurist who shared the 1907 Nobel Peace Prize.

ren•coun•ter (rĕn-koun′tər) *Archaic n.* **1.** An unplanned meeting. **2.** A hostile encounter or contest. ❖ *tr. & intr.v.* **-tered, -ter•ing, -ters** To meet unexpectedly or have an unexpected meeting. [Fr. *rencontre* < OFr. < *rencontrer*, to meet : *re-*, re- + *encontrer*, to meet; see ENCOUNTER.]

rend (rĕnd) *v.* **rent** (rĕnt) or **rend•ed, rend•ing, rends** —*tr.* **1.** To tear or split apart or into pieces violently. See Syns at **tear**[1]. **2.** To tear (one's garments or hair) in anguish or rage. **3.** To tear away forcibly; wrest. **4.** To pull, split, or divide as if by tearing. **5.** To pierce or disturb with sound: *a scream rent the silence.* **6.** To cause pain or distress to: *tales that rend the heart.* —*intr.* To become torn or split; come apart. [ME *renden* < OE *rendan.*]

ren•der (rĕn′dər) *tr.v.* **-dered, -der•ing, -ders 1.** To submit or present, as for consideration or payment: *render a bill.* **2.** To give or make available; provide: *render assistance.* **3.** To give what is due or owed: *rendered thanks.* **4.** To give in return or retribution: *He rendered an apology for his rudeness.* **5.** To surrender or relinquish; yield. **6a.** To represent in verbal form; depict. **b.** To represent in a drawing or painting, esp. in perspective. **7.** *Computer Science* To convert (graphics) from a file into visual form, as on a video display. **8.** To perform an interpretation of (a musical piece, for example). **9.** To express in another language or form; translate. **10.** To deliver or pronounce formally: *The jury has rendered its verdict.* **11.** To cause to become; make: *The news rendered her speechless.* **12.** To reduce, convert, or melt down (fat) by heating. **13.** To coat (brick, for example) with plaster or cement. ❖ *n.* A payment in kind, services, or cash from a tenant to a feudal lord. [ME *rendren* < OFr. *rendre*, to give back < VLat. **rendere*, alteration of Lat. *reddere* : *red-*, *re-*, re- + *dare*, to give; see **dō-** in App.] —**ren′der•a•ble** *adj.* —**ren′der•er** *n.*

ren•der•ing (rĕn′dər-ĭng) *n.* **1.** A depiction or interpretation, as in painting. **2.** A drawing in perspective of a proposed structure. **3.** A translation. **4.** A coat of plaster or cement applied to a masonry surface.

ren•dez•vous (rän′dā-vo͞o′, -də-) *n., pl.* **ren•dez•vous** (-vo͞oz′) **1.** A meeting at a prearranged time and place. See Syns at **engagement. 2.** A prearranged meeting place, esp. an assembly point for troops or ships. **3.** A popular gathering place. **4.** *Aerospace* The process of bringing two spacecraft together. ❖ *tr. & intr.v.* **-voused** (-vo͞od′), **-vous•ing** (-vo͞o′ĭng), **-vous** (-vo͞oz′) To bring or come together at a rendezvous. [Fr. < the phrase *rendez vous*, present yourselves < OFr. : *rendez*, second pers. pl. imper. of *rendre*, to present; see RENDER + *vous*, yourselves, you (< Lat. *vōs*, you; see **wŏs** in App.).]

ren•di•tion (rĕn-dĭsh′ən) *n.* **1.** The act of rendering. **2.** An interpretation of a musical score or a dramatic piece. **3.** A performance of a musical or dramatic work. **4.** A translation, often interpretive. **5.** A surrender. [Obsolete Fr. < OFr. *rendre*, to give back. See RENDER.]

ren•dzi•na (rĕn-jē′nə) *n.* A dark soil that develops under grass on limestone and chalk. [Pol. *rędzina.*]

ren•e•gade (rĕn′ĭ-găd′) *n.* **1.** One who rejects a religion, cause, allegiance, or group for another; a deserter. **2.** An outlaw; a rebel. ❖ *adj.* Of, relating to, or resembling a renegade; traitorous. ❖ *intr.v.* **-gad•ed, -gad•ing, -gades** To become a deserter or an outlaw. [Sp. *renegado* < Med.Lat. *renegātus*, p. part. of *renegāre*, to deny : Lat. *re-*, re- + Lat. *negāre*, to deny; see **ne** in App.]

re•nege (rĭ-nĭg′, -nĕg′, -nēg′) *v.* **-neged, -neg•ing, -neges** —*intr.* **1.** To fail to carry out a promise or commitment: *reneged on the contract.* **2.** *Games* To fail to follow suit in cards when able and required to do so. —*tr.* To renounce; disown. ❖ *n.* The act of reneging. [Med.Lat. *renegāre*, to deny. See RENEGADE.] —**re•neg′er** *n.*

re•ne•go•ti•ate (rē′nĭ-gō′shē-āt′) *tr.v.* **-at•ed, -at•ing, -ates 1.** To negotiate anew. **2.** To revise the terms of (a contract) so as to limit or regain excess profits gained by the contractor. —**re′ne•go′ti•a•ble** (-shē-ə-bəl, -shə-bəl) *adj.* —**re′ne•go•ti•a′tion** *n.*

re•new (rĭ-no͞o′, -nyo͞o′) *v.* **-newed, -new•ing, -news** —*tr.* **1.** To make new or as if new again; restore: *renewed the antique chair.* **2.** To take up again; resume: *renew an old friendship.* **3.** To repeat so as to reaffirm: *renew a promise.* **4.** To regain or restore the vigor of; revive: *a vacation that renewed my spirits.* **5a.** To arrange for the extension of: *renew a contract.* **b.** To arrange to extend the loan of: *renewed the library books.* **6.** To replenish: *renewed the water in the humidifier.* **7.** To bring into being again; reestablish. —*intr.* **1.** To become new again. **2.** To start over. [ME *renewen* : *re-*, re- + *newen*, to renew (< *new*, new; see NEW).] —**re•new′er** *n.*

re•new•a•ble (rĭ-no͞o′ə-bəl, -nyo͞o′-) *adj.* **1.** That can be renewed: *renewable subscriptions.* **2.** Relating to or being a commodity or resource, such as solar energy, that is inexhaustible or replaceable by new growth. —**re•new′a•bil′i•ty** (-bĭl′ĭ-tē) *n.*

re•new•al (rĭ-no͞o′əl, -nyo͞o′-) *n.* **1.** The act of renewing or the state of having been renewed. **2.** Something renewed.

re•new•ed•ly (rĭ-no͞o′ĭd-lē, -nyo͞o′-) *adv.* Over again; anew.

Re•ni (rā′nē), **Guido** 1575–1642. Italian painter whose works include the *Crucifixion of Saint Peter* (1603).

ren•i•form (rĕn′ə-fôrm′, rē′nə-) *adj.* Shaped like a kidney: *a reniform leaf.* [Lat. *rēnēs*, kidneys + –FORM.]

re•nin (rē′nĭn, rĕn′ĭn) *n.* A protein-digesting enzyme that is released by the kidney and acts to raise blood pressure by activating angiotensin. [Lat. *rēnēs*, kidneys + –IN.]

ren•i•tent (rĕn′ĭ-tənt, rĭ-nīt′nt) *adj.* **1.** Resistant to physical pressure; not pliant. **2.** Reluctant to yield or be swayed; recalcitrant. [Lat. *renītēns, renītent-*, pr. part. of *renītī*, to resist : *re-*, re- + *nītī*, to press forward.] —**ren′i•tence, ren′i•ten•cy** *n.*

Rennes (rĕn) A city of NW France N of Nantes; became cap. of Brittany in 1196. Pop. 197,497.

ren•net (rĕn′ĭt) *n.* **1.** The inner lining of the fourth stomach of calves and other young ruminants. **2.** A dried extract made from the stomach lining of a ruminant, used in cheesemaking to curdle milk. **3.** See **rennin.** [ME, prob. < OE **rynet.*]

ren•nin (rĕn′ĭn) *n.* A milk-coagulating enzyme found in the gastric juice of the fourth stomach of young ruminants, used in

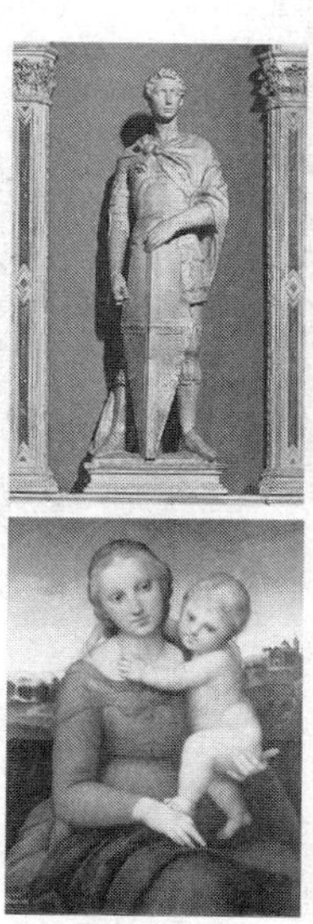

Renaissance
top: c. 1415–17 marble statue of Saint George, by Donatello
bottom: The Small Cowper Madonna, c. 1505, by Raphael

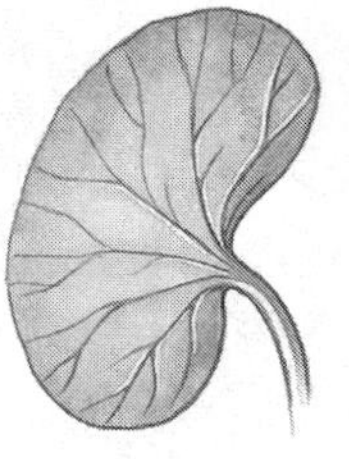

reniform

ă	pat	oi	boy
ā	pay	ou	out
âr	care	o͝o	took
ä	father	o͞o	boot
ĕ	pet	ŭ	cut
ē	be	ûr	urge
ĭ	pit	th	thin
ī	pie	*th*	this
îr	pier	hw	which
ŏ	pot	zh	vision
ō	toe	ə	about, item
ô	paw		

Stress marks:
′ (primary);
′ (secondary), as in
lexicon (lĕk′sĭ-kŏn′)

making cheeses. [RENN(ET) + –IN.]

Re•no (rē′nō′) A city of W NV near the CA border. Pop. 180,480.

Reno, Janet b. 1939. Amer. lawyer who became the first woman attorney general of the US (1993).

re•no•gram (rē′nə-grăm′) n. **1.** A graphic record of the passage of radiation through the renal system after injection of a radioactive tracer. **2.** A radiograph of a kidney. [Lat. *rēnēs*, kidneys + –GRAM.] —**re′nog′ra•phy** (rē-nŏg′rə-fē) n.

Ren•oir (rĕn′wär′, rən-wär′), **Jean** 1894–1979. French filmmaker whose films include *La Grande Illusion* (1937).

Renoir, Pierre Auguste 1841–1919. French impressionist painter whose works include *Le Moulin de la Galette* (1876).

Janet Reno

re•nom•i•nate (rē-nŏm′ə-nāt′) tr.v. **-nat•ed, -nat•ing, -nates** To nominate again, esp. for a subsequent term. —**re′nom•i•na′tion** n.

re•nor•mal•ize (rē-nôr′mə-līz′) tr.v. **-ized, -iz•ing, -iz•es** To bring into a normal or more normal state once again. —**re•nor′mal•i•za′tion** (-mə-lĭ-zā′shən) n.

re•nounce (rĭ-nouns′) v. **-nounced, -nounc•ing, -nounc•es** —tr. **1.** To give up (a title, for example), esp. by formal announcement. See Syns at **relinquish. 2.** To reject; disown. —intr. *Games* To revoke in cards. ❖ n. *Games* A revoke in cards. [ME *renouncen* < OFr. *renoncer* < Lat. *renūntiāre*, to report : *re-*, re- + *nūntiāre*, to announce (< *nūntius*, messenger).] —**re•nounce′ment** n. —**re•nounc′er** n.

ren•o•vate (rĕn′ə-vāt′) tr.v. **-vat•ed, -vat•ing, -vates 1.** To restore to an earlier condition, as by repairing or remodeling. **2.** To impart new vigor to; revive. [Lat. *renovāre, renovāt-* : *re-*, re- + *novāre*, to make new (< *novus*, new; see **newo-** in App.).] —**ren′o•va′tive** adj. —**ren′o•va′tor** n.

re•nown (rĭ-noun′) n. **1.** The quality of being widely honored and acclaimed; fame. **2.** *Obsolete* Report; rumor. [ME < AN < *renomer*, to make famous : *re-*, repeatedly (< Lat.; see RE–) + *nomer*, to name (< Lat. *nōmināre* < *nōmen, nōmin-*, name; see **nō-men-** in App.).]

re•nowned (rĭ-nound′) adj. Having renown; famous. See Syns at **noted.**

rent¹ (rĕnt) n. **1a.** Payment, usu. of an amount fixed by contract, made by a tenant at specified intervals in return for the right to occupy or use the property of another. **b.** A similar payment made for the use of a facility, equipment, or service provided by another. **2.** The return derived from cultivated or improved land after deduction of all production costs. **3.** The revenue yielded by a piece of land in excess of that yielded by the poorest or least favorably located land under equal market conditions. ❖ v. **rent•ed, rent•ing, rents** —tr. **1.** To obtain occupancy or use of (another's property) in return for regular payments. **2.** To grant temporary occupancy or use of (one's own property or a service) in return for regular payments: *rents out TV sets.* —intr. To be for rent: *The cottage rents for $1,200 a month.* —idiom: for rent Available for use or service in return for payment. [ME *rente* < OFr. < VLat. **rendita* < fem. p. part. of **rendere*, to yield, return. See RENDER.] —**rent′a•bil′i•ty** n. —**rent′a•ble** adj.

rent² (rĕnt) v. A past tense and a past participle of **rend.** ❖ n. **1.** An opening made by rending; a rip. **2.** A breach of relations; a rift.

rent³ (rĕnt) n. *Slang* A parent. Often used in the plural: *had to stay home with the rents.* [Short for PARENT.]

OUR LIVING LANGUAGE When young people talk about their *rents*, that is, their parents, they are using a slang term that is of interest to language historians. One of the fundamental characteristics of slang is its creation of novel ways of expressing what are often rather ordinary things (if parents may be considered ordinary things). Slang has recently produced two expressions for "parents" that have gained wide currency: *rents* and *parental units.* Both expressions demonstrate slang's use of unusual or creative linguistic means to achieve novelty of expression. While there are many slang terms, such as *bod* for "body" or *rad* for "radical," that result from the clipping of unstressed syllables, *rents* is a clipping that drops a stressed syllable, much like the similar term *za*, "pizza." The desire to coin new ways of referring to things also leads speakers of slang to use circumlocutions like *knuckle sandwich* for "punch." *Parental units* falls into this category. It plays on the jargon of bureaucrats and social science, in which the world is viewed as so much data waiting to be quantified. The appearance of terms such as *rents* and *parental units* also shows that all available styles and levels of language can be grist for slang's mill—so long as the material is perceived as irreverent, funny, or just plain cool. In fact, as if these two slang terms were not enough, speakers have recently taken them one step further, combining them, as it were, as *rental units.*

rent-a-car (rĕnt′ə-kär′) n. **1.** A rented car. **2.** An agency that offers cars and vans for rent.

rent•al (rĕn′tl) n. **1.** An amount paid or collected as rent. **2.** A piece of property available for renting. **3.** The act of renting. **4.** An agency that rents something. **5.** A list of tenants and schedule of rents. ❖ adj. Of, relating to, or available for rent.

rent control n. Governmental control and regulation of the amounts charged for rented housing.

rent•er (rĕn′tər) n. **1.** One that receives payment in exchange for

the use of one's property by another. **2.** One that pays rent for the use of another's property; a tenant.

rent-free (rĕnt′frē′) adj. Not being subject to rent. ❖ adv. Without having to pay or without paying rent.

ren•tier (răn-tyā′) n. A person who lives on income from property or investments. [Fr. < *rente*, yearly income < OFr. See RENT¹.]

rent strike n. An agreement among tenants to refuse to pay rent, often in protest of poor services.

re•nun•ci•a•tion (rĭ-nŭn′sē-ā′shən) n. **1.** The act or an instance of renouncing: *the renunciation of earthly pleasures.* **2.** A declaration in which something is renounced. [ME < AN *renunciacion* < Lat. *renūntiātiō, renūntiātiōn-* < *renūntiātus*, p. part. of *renūntiāre*, to renounce. See RENOUNCE.] —**re•nun′ci•a′tive, re•nun′ci•a•to′ry** (-ə-tôr′ē, -tōr′ē) adj.

Ren•wick (rĕn′wĭk), **James** 1818–95. Amer. architect who designed the Smithsonian Institution (1848).

re•o•pen (rē-ō′pən) tr. & intr.v. **-pened, -pen•ing, -pens 1.** To open or be opened again. **2.** To take up again or be taken up again; resume.

re•or•der (rē-ôr′dər) v. **-dered, -der•ing, -ders** —tr. **1.** To order (the same goods) again. **2.** To straighten out or put in order again. **3.** To rearrange. —intr. To order the same goods again. ❖ n. A further order of goods from the same supplier.

re•or•gan•i•za•tion (rē-ôr′gə-nĭ-zā′shən) n. **1.** The act or process of organizing again or differently. **2.** A thorough alteration of the structure of a business corporation. —**re•or′gan•i•za′tion•al** adj.

re•or•gan•ize (rē-ôr′gə-nīz′) v. **-ized, -iz•ing, -iz•es** —tr. To organize again or anew. —intr. To undergo or effect changes in organization. —**re•or′gan•iz′er** n.

re•o•vi•rus (rē′ō-vī′rəs) n., pl. **-rus•es** Any of a group of viruses that contain double-stranded RNA and are associated with various diseases, including gastrointestinal infections. [R(ESPIRATORY) + E(NTERIC) + O(RPHAN) + VIRUS.]

rep¹ also **repp** (rĕp) n. A ribbed or corded fabric of various materials, such as cotton, wool, or silk. [Alteration of Fr. *reps* < E. *ribs*, pl. of RIB.]

rep² (rĕp) n. *Informal* A representative.

rep³ (rĕp) n. A unit of absorbed radiation dose, equal to the amount of ionizing radiation that will transfer 93 ergs of energy to 1 gram of water or living tissue. [r(oentgen) e(quivalent) p(hysical).]

rep⁴ (rĕp) n. *Informal* **1.** A repertory company. **2.** A repertory theater.

rep⁵ (rĕp) n. *Informal* Reputation.

rep⁶ (rĕp) n. *Informal* A repetition of a particular movement done as exercise, esp. in weightlifting.

Rep. abbr. **1.** representative **2.** republic **3.** Republican

re•paid (rĭ-pād′) v. Past tense and past participle of **repay.**

re•pair¹ (rĭ-pâr′) v. **-paired, -pair•ing, -pairs** —tr. **1.** To restore to sound condition after damage or injury; fix: *repaired the broken watch.* **2.** To set right; remedy: *repair an oversight.* **3.** To renew or revitalize. **4.** To make up for or compensate for (a loss, for example). —intr. To make repairs. ❖ n. **1a.** The work, act, or process of repairing. **b.** An instance or a result of repairing. Often used in the plural: *My car is in the shop for repairs.* **2.** General condition after use or repairing: *in good repair.* **3.** Something that has been repaired. [ME *repairen* < OFr. *reparer* < Lat. *reparāre* : *re-*, re- + *parāre*, to prepare, put in order.] —**re•pair′a•bil′i•ty** n. —**re•pair′a•ble** adj. —**re•pair′a•bly** adv. —**re•pair′er** n.

re•pair² (rĭ-pâr′) intr.v. **-paired, -pair•ing, -pairs 1.** To betake oneself; go: *repair to the dining room.* **2.** To go frequently or habitually: *repairs to the café every week.* ❖ n. **1.** An act of going or sojourning. **2.** A place to which one goes frequently or habitually; a haunt. [ME *repairen*, to return < OFr. *repairier* < LLat. *repatriāre*, to return to one's country. See REPATRIATE.]

re•pair•man (rĭ-pâr′măn′, -mən) n. A man whose occupation is making repairs.

re•pair•per•son (rĭ-pâr′pûr′sən) n. A repairman or repairwoman.

re•pair•wom•an (rĭ-pâr′wŏom′ən) n. A woman whose occupation is making repairs.

re•pand (rĭ-pănd′) adj. *Botany* Having a somewhat wavy margin: *a repand leaf.* [Lat. *repandus*, bent backward : *re-*, re- + *pandus*, p. part. of *pandere*, to spread out.]

rep•a•ra•ble (rĕp′ər-ə-bəl) adj. Possible to repair. [Fr. *réparable* < Lat. *reparābilis* < *reparāre*, to repair. See REPAIR¹.] —**rep′a•ra•bil′i•ty** n. —**rep′a•ra•bly** adv.

rep•a•ra•tion (rĕp′ə-rā′shən) n. **1.** The act or process of repairing or the condition of being repaired. **2.** The act or process of making amends; expiation. **3.** Something done or paid to compensate or make amends. **4. reparations** Compensation or remuneration required from a defeated nation as indemnity for damage or injury during a war. [ME *reparacion* < OFr. < LLat. *reparātiō, reparātiōn-*, restoration < Lat. *reparātus*, p. part. of *reparāre*. See REPAIR¹.]

re•par•a•tive (rĭ-păr′ə-tĭv) also **re•par•a•to•ry** (-tôr′ē, -tōr′ē) adj. **1.** Tending to repair. **2.** Relating to or of the nature of reparations.

rep•ar•tee (rĕp′ər-tē′, -tā′, -är-tē′) n. **1.** A swift witty reply. **2.** Conversation marked by the exchange of witty retorts. [Fr. *repar-*

tie < fem. p. part. of *repartir*, to retort < OFr., to retort, to depart again : *re-*, re- + *partir*, to depart (< Lat. *partīre*, to divide < *pars*, *part-*, part; see **perə-** in App.).]

re·par·ti·tion (rē′pär-tĭsh′ən) *n.* **1.** Distribution; apportionment. **2.** A partitioning again or in a different way. ❖ *tr.v.* **-tioned, -tion·ing, -tions** To partition again; redivide.

re·pass (rē-păs′) *v.* **-passed, -pass·ing, -pass·es** —*tr.* **1.** To pass (something) again. —*intr.* To cause to pass again in the opposite direction. —*intr.* To pass again; go by again. —**re·pas′sage** (-ĭj) *n.*

re·past (rĭ-păst′) *n.* A meal or the food eaten or served at a meal. ❖ *v.* **-past·ed, -past·ing, -pasts** —*intr.* To eat or feast. —*tr.* *Obsolete* To give food to. [ME < OFr. < LLat. *repāstus* < p. part. of *repāscere*, to feed : *re-*, re- + Lat. *pāscere*, to feed; see **pā-** in App.]

re·pa·tri·ate (rē-pā′trē-āt′) *tr.v.* **-at·ed, -at·ing, -ates** To restore or return to the country of birth, citizenship, or origin. ❖ *n.* (-ĭt, -āt′) One who has been repatriated. [LLat. *repatriāre*, *repatriāt-*, to return to one's country : Lat. *re-*, re- + Lat. *patria*, native country; see **EXPATRIATE.**] —**re·pa′tri·a′tion** *n.*

re·pay (rĭ-pā′) *v.* **-paid** (-pād′), **-pay·ing, -pays** —*tr.* **1.** To pay back: *repaid a debt.* **2.** To give back, either in return or in compensation: *repay kindness with kindness.* **3.** To make a return or compensation for: *a company that repays hard work with bonuses.* **4.** To make or do in return: *repay a call.* —*intr.* To make repayment or requital. —**re·pay′a·ble** *adj.* —**re·pay′ment** *n.*

re·peal (rĭ-pēl′) *tr.v.* **-pealed, -peal·ing, -peals** **1.** To revoke or rescind, esp. by an official or formal act. **2.** *Obsolete* To summon back or recall, esp. from exile. ❖ *n.* The act or process of repealing. [ME *repelen*, *repealen* < AN *repeler*, alteration of OFr. *rapeler* : *re-*, re- + *apeler*, to appeal; see **APPEAL.**] —**re·peal′a·ble** *adj.* —**re·peal′er** *n.*

re·peat (rĭ-pēt′, rē′pēt′) *v.* **-peat·ed, -peat·ing, -peats** —*tr.* **1.** To say again: *repeat a question.* **2.** To duplicate another's utterance. **3.** To recite from memory. **4.** To tell to another. **5.** To do, experience, or produce again: *repeat past successes.* **6.** To express (oneself) in the same way or words. —*intr.* **1.** To do or say something again. **2.** To vote more than once in a single election. ❖ *n.* **1.** An act of repeating. **2.** Something repeated, as an interval in athletic training. **3.** A broadcast of a television or radio program that has been previously broadcast; a rerun. **4.** *Music* **a.** A passage or section that is repeated. **b.** A sign usu. consisting of two vertical dots that indicates a passage to be repeated. ❖ *adj.* Of, relating to, or being something that repeats or is repeated: *a repeat offender.* [ME *repeten* < OFr. *repeter* < Lat. *repetere*, to seek again : *re-*, re- + *petere*, to seek; see **pet-** in App.] —**re·peat′a·bil′i·ty** *n.* —**re·peat′a·ble** *adj.*

re·peat·ed (rĭ-pē′tĭd) *adj.* Said, done, or occurring again and again: *repeated knocks on the door.* —**re·peat′ed·ly** *adv.*

re·peat·er (rĭ-pē′tər) *n.* **1.** One that repeats. **2.** A watch or clock with a pressure-activated mechanism that strikes the hour. **3.** A repeating firearm. **4.** A student who repeats a course, usu. one that has been failed. **5.** One who repeats in an election. **6.** One who has been convicted of wrongdoing more than once, esp. for the same offense.

re·peat·ing decimal (rĭ-pē′tĭng) *n.* A decimal in which a pattern of one or more digits is repeated indefinitely, for example, 0.353535 . . .

repeating firearm *n.* A firearm capable of firing several times without being reloaded.

rep·e·chage (rĕp′ə-shäzh′) *n.* A trial heat, esp. in rowing, allowing competitors who have lost a heat another chance to qualify for the semifinals. [Fr. *repêchage*, rescuing, repechage < *repêcher*, to fish up again, rescue : *re-*, again (< OFr.; see **RE-**) : *pêcher*, to fish for (< OFr. *pescher* < VLat. *piscāre* < Lat. *piscārī*; see **PISCATORIAL**).]

re·pel (rĭ-pĕl′) *v.* **-pelled, -pel·ling, -pels** —*tr.* **1.** To ward off or keep away; drive back: *repel insects.* **2.** To offer resistance to; fight against: *repel an invasion.* **3.** To refuse to accept; reject. **4.** To turn away from; spurn. **5.** To cause aversion or distaste in. See Syns at **disgust.** See Usage Note at **repulse. 6.** To be resistant to; be incapable of absorbing or mixing with. **7.** *Physics* To present an opposing force to; push back or away by a force. —*intr.* **1.** To offer a resistant force to something. **2.** To cause aversion or distaste. [ME *repellen* < OFr. *repeller* < Lat. *repellere* : *re-*, re- + *pellere*, to drive; see **pel-²** in App.] —**re·pel′ler** *n.*

re·pel·lent also **re·pel·lant** (rĭ-pĕl′ənt) *adj.* **1a.** Serving or tending to repel. **b.** Able to repel. **2.** Inspiring aversion or distaste; repulsive. **3.** Resistant or impervious to a substance. Often used in combination: *water-repellent.* ❖ *n.* **1.** One that repels. **2a.** A substance used to repel insects. **b.** A substance or treatment for making a fabric or surface impervious or resistant to something else. —**re·pel′lence, re·pel′len·cy** *n.* —**re·pel′lent·ly** *adv.*

re·pent¹ (rĭ-pĕnt′) *v.* **-pent·ed, -pent·ing, -pents** —*intr.* **1.** To feel remorse or self-reproach for what one has done or failed to do; be contrite. **2.** To feel such regret for past conduct as to change one's mind regarding it: *repented of poor behavior.* **3.** To make a change for the better as a result of remorse or contrition

for one's sins. —*tr.* **1.** To feel regret or self-reproach for. **2.** To cause to feel remorse or regret. [ME *repenten* < OFr. *repentir* : *re-*, re- + *pentir*, to be sorry (< VLat. **paenitīre* < Lat. *paenitēre*).] —**re·pent′er** *n.*

re·pent² (rē′pənt) *adj.* *Biology* Creeping along the ground; prostrate. [Lat. *rēpēns, rēpent-*, pr. part. of *rēpere*, to creep.]

re·pen·tance (rĭ-pĕn′təns) *n.* **1.** The act or process of repenting. **2.** Remorse or contrition for past conduct or sin.

re·pen·tant (rĭ-pĕn′tənt) *adj.* Characterized by or demonstrating repentance; penitent. —**re·pen′tant·ly** *adv.*

re·per·cus·sion (rē′pər-kŭsh′ən, rĕp′ər-) *n.* **1.** An often indirect effect or result of an event or act. **2.** A recoil, rebounding, or reciprocal motion after impact. **3.** A reflection, esp. of sound. [Ult. < Lat. *repercussiō, repercussiōn-* < *repercussus*, p. part. of *repercutere*, to cause to rebound : *re-*, re- + *percutere*, to strike; see **PERCUSS.**] —**re′per·cus′sive** *adj.*

rep·er·toire (rĕp′ər-twär′) *n.* **1.** The stock of songs, plays, operas, or other pieces that a player or company is prepared to perform. **2.** The class of compositions in a genre. **3.** The range or number of skills, aptitudes, or accomplishments of a particular person or group. [Fr. *répertoire* < OFr. < LLat. *repertōrium.* See **REPERTORY.**]

rep·er·to·ry (rĕp′ər-tôr′ē, -tōr′ē) *n., pl.* **-ries 1.** A repertoire. **2a.** A theater in which a repertory company performs. **b.** A repertory company. **3a.** A place, such as a storehouse, where a stock of things is kept; a repository. **b.** Something stored in or as if in such a place; a stock or collection. [LLat. *repertōrium* < Lat. *repertus*, p. part. of *reperīre*, to find out : *re-*, re- + *parīre*, to get, beget.] —**rep′er·to′ri·al** *adj.*

repertory company *n.* A company that presents a number of plays or other works during a season, usu. in alternation.

rep·e·tend (rĕp′ĭ-tĕnd′, rĕp′ĭ-tĕnd′) *n.* **1.** A repeated word, sound, or phrase; a refrain. **2.** *Mathematics* The digit or group of digits that repeats infinitely in a repeating decimal. [< Lat. *repetendum*, neut. gerundive of *repetere*, to repeat. See **REPEAT.**]

rep·e·ti·tion (rĕp′ĭ-tĭsh′ən) *n.* **1.** The act or process or an instance of repeating or being repeated. **2.** A recitation or recital, esp. of prepared or memorized material. [Ult. < Lat. *repetitiō, repetitiōn-* < *repetitus*, p. part. of *repetere*, to repeat. See **REPEAT.**] —**rep′e·ti′tion·al** *adj.*

rep·e·ti·tious (rĕp′ĭ-tĭsh′əs) *adj.* Filled with repetition, esp. needless or tedious repetition. —**rep′e·ti′tious·ly** *adv.* —**rep′e·ti′tious·ness** *n.*

re·pet·i·tive (rĭ-pĕt′ĭ-tĭv) *adj.* Given to or characterized by repetition. —**re·pet′i·tive·ly** *adv.* —**re·pet′i·tive·ness** *n.*

repetitive strain injury *n.* Injury to a tendon, nerve, or other soft tissue caused by excessive repetition of a movement pattern and characterized by painful inflammation and weakness of the affected part.

re·phrase (rē-frāz′) *tr.v.* **-phrased, -phras·ing, -phras·es** To phrase again, esp. to state in a clearer or different way.

re·pine (rĭ-pīn′) *intr.v.* **-pined, -pin·ing, -pines 1.** To be discontented or low in spirits; complain or fret. **2.** To yearn after something. [ME *repinen*, to be aggrieved : *re-*, re- + *pinen*, to yearn; see **PINE².**] —**re·pin′er** *n.*

re·place (rĭ-plās′) *tr.v.* **-placed, -plac·ing, -plac·es 1.** To put back into a former position or place. **2.** To take or fill the place of. **3.** To be or provide a substitute for. **4.** To pay back or return; refund. —**re·place′a·ble** *adj.* —**re·plac′er** *n.*

re·place·ment (rĭ-plās′mənt) *n.* **1.** The act or process of replacing or of being replaced; substitution. **2.** One that replaces, esp. a person assigned to a vacant military position.

replacement therapy *n.* Administration of a body substance to compensate for the loss, as from disease or surgery, of a gland or tissue that would normally produce the substance.

re·plant (rē-plănt′) *tr.v.* **-plant·ed, -plant·ing, -plants 1.** To plant again or in a new place: *replanted the perennials.* **2.** To supply with new plants: *replant a window box.* **3.** To reattach (an organ, for example) surgically to the original site. ❖ *n.* (rē′plănt′) Something replanted. —**re′plan·ta′tion** *n.*

re·play (rē-plā′) *tr.v.* **-played, -play·ing, -plays** To play over again: *replay a tape.* ❖ *n.* (rē′plā′) **1.** The act or process of replaying. **2.** Something replayed. **3.** An instant replay.

re·plen·ish (rĭ-plĕn′ĭsh) *v.* **-ished, -ish·ing, -ish·es** —*tr.* **1.** To fill or make complete again; restock: *replenish the larder.* **2.** To inspire or nourish. —*intr.* To become full again. [ME *replenisshen* < OFr. *replenir, repleniss-* : *re-*, re- + *plenir*, to fill (< *plein*, full

ă	pat	oi	boy
ā	pay	ou	out
âr	care	ŏŏ	took
ä	father	ōō	boot
ĕ	pet	ŭ	cut
ē	be	ûr	urge
ĭ	pit	th	thin
ī	pie	th	this
îr	pier	hw	which
ŏ	pot	zh	vision
ō	toe	ə	about,
ô	paw		item

Stress marks:
′ (primary);
′ (secondary), as in
lexicon (lĕk′sĭ-kŏn′)

< Lat. *plēnus*; see **pelə-**[1] in App.).] **—re•plen′ish•er** *n.* **—re•plen′ish•ment** *n.*

re•plete (rĭ-plēt′) *adj.* **1.** Abundantly supplied; abounding: *a stream replete with trout.* **2.** Filled to satiation; gorged. **3.** *Usage Problem* Complete: *a computer system replete with color monitor, printer, and software.* [ME < OFr. < Lat. *replētus*, p. part. of *replēre*, to refill : *re-*, re- + *plēre*, to fill; see **pelə-**[1] in App.] **—re•plete′ness** *n.*

USAGE NOTE *Replete* means "abundantly supplied" and is not generally accepted as a synonym for *complete.*

re•ple•tion (rĭ-plē′shən) *n.* **1.** The condition of being fully supplied or completely filled. **2.** A state of excessive fullness.

re•plev•in (rĭ-plĕv′ĭn) *n.* **1.** An action to recover personal property said or claimed to be unlawfully taken. **2.** The writ or procedure of such an action. ❖ *tr.v.* **-ined, -in•ing, -ines** To replevy. [ME < AN *replevine* < *replevir*, to give as a security : *re-*, re- + *plevir*, to pledge (< LLat. *plebere*, of Gmc. orig.; see **dlegh-** in App.).]

re•plev•y (rĭ-plĕv′ē) *tr.v.* **-ied, -y•ing, -ies** To regain possession of by a writ of replevin. ❖ *n., pl.* **-ies** A replevin. [AN *replevir.* See REPLEVIN.]

rep•li•ca (rĕp′lĭ-kə) *n.* **1.** A copy or reproduction of a work of art, esp. one by the original artist. **2.** A copy or reproduction, esp. one smaller than the original. [Ital. < *replicare*, to repeat < LLat. *replicāre*. See REPLICATE.]

rep•li•case (rĕp′lĭ-kās′, -kāz′) *n.* An enzyme that catalyzes the synthesis of a complementary RNA molecule from an RNA template. [REPLIC(ATE) + -ASE.]

rep•li•cate (rĕp′lĭ-kāt′) *v.* **-cat•ed, -cat•ing, -cates** *—tr.* **1.** To duplicate, copy, reproduce, or repeat. **2.** *Biology* To reproduce or make an exact copy of (a cell, for example). **3.** To fold over or bend back. *—intr.* To become replicated; undergo replication. ❖ *n.* (-kĭt) A repetition of an experiment or procedure. ❖ *adj.* **replicate** (-kĭt) also **rep•li•cat•ed** (-kā′tĭd) Folded over or bent back upon itself: *a replicate leaf.* [ME *replicaten* < LLat. *replicāre*, *replicāt-*, to repeat < Lat., to fold back : *re-*, re- + *plicāre*, to fold; see **plek-** in App.] **—rep′li•ca′tive** *adj.*

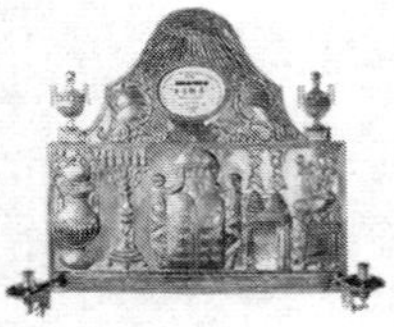

repoussé
brass and gilt repoussé on early 19th-century Shiviti

rep•li•ca•tion (rĕp′lĭ-kā′shən) *n.* **1.** A fold or a folding back. **2.** A reply to an answer; a rejoinder. **3.** *Law* The plaintiff's response to the defendant's answer or plea. **4.** An echo or a reverberation. **5.** A copy or reproduction. **6.** The act or process of duplicating or reproducing something, such as results in a scientific experiment. **7.** *Biology* The process by which genetic material, a single-celled organism, or a virus reproduces or makes a copy of itself.

rep•li•con (rĕp′lĭ-kŏn′) *n.* A genetic element that undergoes replication as an autonomous unit. [REPLIC(ATION) + -ON[1].]

re•ply (rĭ-plī′) *v.* **-plied, -ply•ing, -plies** *—intr.* **1.** To give an answer in speech or writing. **2.** To respond by an act or gesture. **3.** To echo. **4.** To return gunfire or an attack. **5.** *Law* To respond to a defendant's plea. *—tr.* To say or give as an answer: *I replied that I could.* See Syns at **answer.** ❖ *n., pl.* **-plies 1.** A written or spoken response. **2.** A response by an action or gesture. **3.** *Law* A plaintiff's formal response in answer to that of a defendant. [ME *replien* < OFr. *replier* < Lat. *replicāre*, to fold back. See REPLICATE.] **—re•pli′er** *n.*

re•po[1] (rē′pō′) *n., pl.* **-pos** *Informal* A repurchase agreement. [Shortening and alteration of REPURCHASE AGREEMENT.]

re•po[2] (rē′pō′) *n., pl.* **-pos** *Informal* **1.** Repossession of merchandise or property from a buyer who has defaulted on payment. **2.** Repossessed merchandise or property.

re•po•lar•i•za•tion (rē-pō′lər-ĭ-zā′shən) *n.* The restoration of a polarized state across a membrane, as in a muscle fiber following contraction.

re•po•lar•ize (rē-pō′lə-rīz′) *intr.v.* **-ized, -iz•ing, -iz•es** To return to a polarized state; undergo repolarization.

re•port (rĭ-pôrt′, -pōrt′) *n.* **1.** An account presented usu. in detail. **2.** A formal account of the proceedings or transactions of a group. **3.** *Law* A published collection of authoritative accounts of court cases or of judicial decisions. Often used in the plural. **4.** Common talk; rumor or gossip. **5.** Reputation; repute. **6.** An explosive noise. ❖ *v.* **-port•ed, -port•ing, -ports** *—tr.* **1.** To make or present an often official, formal, or regular account of. **2.** To relate or tell about; present. **3.** To write or provide an account or summation of for publication or broadcast. **4.** To submit or relate the results of considerations concerning: *reported the bill.* **5.** To carry back and repeat to another. **6.** To complain about or denounce: *reported them to the principal.* *—intr.* **1.** To make a report. **2.** To serve as a reporter for a publication, broadcasting company, or other news media. **3.** To present oneself. **4.** To be accountable. ***—idiom:* on report** Subject to disciplinary action. [ME < OFr. < *reporter*, to report < Lat. *reportāre* : *re-*, re- + *portāre*, to carry; see **per-**[2] in App.] **—re•port′a•ble** *adj.*

re•port•age (rĕp′ər-täzh′, rĭ-pôr′tĭj, -pōr′-) *n.* **1.** The act or process of reporting news or information. **2.** Something reported. [Fr. < *reporter*, to report < OFr. See REPORT.]

report card *n.* A report of a student's progress presented periodically to a parent or guardian.

re•port•ed•ly (rĭ-pôr′tĭd-lē, -pōr′-) *adv.* By report; supposedly.

re•port•er (rĭ-pôr′tər, -pōr′-) *n.* **1.** A writer, investigator, or presenter of news stories. **2.** *Law* A person who is authorized to write and issue official accounts of judicial or legislative proceedings. **—rep′or•to′ri•al** (rĕp′ər-tôr′ē-əl, -tōr′-, rē′pər-) *adj.* **—rep′or•to′ri•al•ly** *adv.*

re•pose[1] (rĭ-pōz′) *n.* **1.** The act of resting or the state of being at rest. **2.** Freedom from worry; peace of mind. **3.** Calmness; tranquillity. ❖ *v.* **-posed, -pos•ing, -pos•es** *—tr.* **1.** To lay (oneself) down. **2.** To rest or relax (oneself). *—intr.* **1.** To lie at rest. **2.** To lie dead. **3.** To lie while being supported by something. [< ME *reposen*, to be at rest < OFr. *reposer* < LLat. *repausāre*, to cause to rest : Lat. *re-*, re- + Lat. *pausāre*, to rest (< *pausa*, rest; see PAUSE).] **—re•pos′al** *n.* **—re•pos′er** *n.*

re•pose[2] (rĭ-pōz′) *tr.v.* **-posed, -pos•ing, -pos•es** To place (trust, for example): *reposed all his hopes in the new cure.* [ME *reposen*, to replace < Lat. *repōnere*, *repos-*, to put away. See REPOSIT.]

re•pose•ful (rĭ-pōz′fəl) *adj.* Marked by, conducive to, or expressing repose. **—re•pose′ful•ness** *n.*

re•pos•it (rĭ-pŏz′ĭt) *tr.v.* **-it•ed, -it•ing, -its 1.** To put away; store. **2.** To put back; replace. [Lat. *repōnere*, *reposit-* : *re-*, re- + *pōnere*, to place; see **apo-** in App.]

re•po•si•tion (rē′pə-zĭsh′ən, rĕp′ə-) *n.* **1.** The act of repositing or the condition of being reposited. **2.** The return of something, such as a bone, to its proper position. ❖ *tr.v.* (rē′pə-) **-tioned, -tion•ing, -tions 1.** To place or put in a new position; position again. **2.** To update or change the marketing of (a product or service).

re•pos•i•to•ry (rĭ-pŏz′ĭ-tôr′ē, -tōr′ē) *n., pl.* **-ries 1.** A place where things may be put for safekeeping. **2.** A warehouse. **3.** A museum. **4.** A burial vault; a tomb. **5.** One that contains or is a store of something specified. **6.** One who is entrusted with secrets or confidential information.

re•pos•sess (rē′pə-zĕs′) *tr.v.* **-sessed, -sess•ing, -sess•es 1a.** To regain possession of. **b.** To reclaim possession of for failure to pay installments due. **2.** To give back possession to. **—re′pos•ses′sion** (-zĕsh′ən) *n.* **—re′pos•ses′sor** *n.*

re•pous•sé (rə-po͞o-sā′) *adj.* **1.** Having patterns in relief formed by hammering and pressing on the reverse side. Used esp. of metal. **2.** Raised in relief. ❖ *n.* **1.** A design in relief. **2.** The technique of hammering and pressing designs in relief. [Fr., p. part. of *repousser*, to push back < OFr. : *re-*, re- + *pousser*, to push (< Lat. *pulsāre*, to beat, freq. of *pellere*, to push; see REPEL).]

repp (rĕp) *n.* Variant of **rep**[1].

rep•re•hend (rĕp′rĭ-hĕnd′) *tr.v.* **-hend•ed, -hend•ing, -hends** To reprove; censure. See Syns at **criticize.** [ME *reprehenden* < Lat. *reprehendere* : *re-*, re- + *prehendere*, to seize; see **ghend-** in App.]

rep•re•hen•si•ble (rĕp′rĭ-hĕn′sə-bəl) *adj.* Deserving rebuke or censure; blameworthy. [ME < OFr. < LLat. *reprehēnsibilis* < Lat. *reprehēnsus*, p. part. of *reprehendere*, to reprehend. See REPREHEND.] **—rep′re•hen′si•bil′i•ty, rep′re•hen′si•ble•ness** *n.* **—rep′re•hen′si•bly** *adv.*

rep•re•hen•sion (rĕp′rĭ-hĕn′shən) *n.* Reprehending. **—rep′re•hen′sive** (-sĭv) *adj.*

rep•re•sent (rĕp′rĭ-zĕnt′) *tr.v.* **-sent•ed, -sent•ing, -sents 1a.** To stand for; symbolize: *The bald eagle represents the United States.* **b.** To indicate or communicate by signs or symbols: *Letters of the alphabet represent sounds.* **2a.** To depict in art; portray. **b.** To describe in words; set forth. **3.** To present clearly to the mind. **4.** To draw attention to by way of remonstrance or protest. **5.** To describe or put forward (a person or thing) as manifesting a specified quality. **6a.** To serve as the official and authorized delegate or agent for. **b.** To act as a spokesperson for. **7.** To serve as an example of. **8.** To be the equivalent of. **9a.** To stage (a play, for example); produce. **b.** To act the part or role of. [ME *representen* < OFr. *representer* < Lat. *repraesentāre*, to show : *re-*, re- + *praesentāre*, to present; see PRESENT[2].] **—rep′re•sent′a•bil′i•ty** *n.* **—rep′re•sent′a•ble** *adj.* **—rep′re•sent′er** *n.*

rep•re•sen•ta•tion (rĕp′rĭ-zĕn-tā′shən, -zən-) *n.* **1.** The act of representing or the state of being represented. **2.** Something that represents, as: **a.** An image or likeness of something. **b.** An account or statement, as of facts or arguments. **c.** An expostulation; a protest. **d.** A presentation or production, as of a play. **3.** The state or condition of serving as an official delegate, agent, or spokesperson. **4.** The right or privilege of being represented by delegates having a voice in a legislative body. **5.** *Law* A statement of fact made by one party in order to induce another party to enter into a contract.

rep•re•sen•ta•tion•al (rĕp′rĭ-zĕn-tā′shə-nəl, -zən-) *adj.* Of or relating to representation, esp. to realistic graphic representation. **—rep′re•sen•ta′tion•al•ism** *n.*

rep•re•sen•ta•tive (rĕp′rĭ-zĕn′tə-tĭv) *n.* **1.** One that serves as an example or type for others of the same classification. **2.** One that serves as a delegate or agent for another. **3a.** A member of a governmental body, usu. legislative, chosen by popular vote. **b.** A member of the US House of Representatives or of the lower house of a state legislature. ❖ *adj.* **1.** Representing, depicting, or portraying or able to do so. **2.** Authorized to act as an official delegate or agent. **3.** Of, relating to, or characteristic of government by representation. **4.** Like or typical of others of the same class. **—rep′re•sen′ta•tive•ly** *adv.* **—rep′re•sen′ta•tive•ness** *n.*

re•press (rĭ-prĕs′) *v.* **-pressed, -press•ing, -press•es** *—tr.* **1.** To hold back by an act of volition: *repressed a smirk.* **2.** To put down by force; quell. **3.** *Psychology* To exclude (painful memories, for example) from the conscious mind. —*intr.* To take repressive action. [ME *repressen* < Lat. *reprimere, repress-* : *re-*, re- + *premere*, to press.] **—re•press′i•bil′i•ty** *n.* **—re•press′i•ble** *adj.*

re•pressed memory (rĭ-prĕst′) *n.* A memory that is repressed because of the anxiety it engenders.

re•pres•sion (rĭ-prĕsh′ən) *n.* **1.** The act of repressing or the state of being repressed. **2.** *Psychology* The unconscious exclusion of painful impulses, desires, or fears from the conscious mind. **—re•pres′sion•ist** *adj.*

re•pres•sive (rĭ-prĕs′ĭv) *adj.* Causing or inclined to cause repression. **—re•pres′sive•ly** *adv.* **—re•pres′sive•ness** *n.*

re•pres•sor (rĭ-prĕs′ər) *n.* **1.** also **re•press•er** One that represses. **2.** *Genetics* A protein that binds to an operator, blocking transcription of an operon and the enzymes for which it codes.

re•prieve (rĭ-prēv′) *tr.v.* **-prieved, -priev•ing, -prieves 1.** To postpone or cancel the punishment of. **2.** To bring relief to. ❖ *n.* **1a.** Postponement or cancellation of a punishment. **b.** A warrant for such an action. **2.** Temporary relief, as from danger. [Alteration of ME *reprien*, prob. < OFr. *repris*, p. part. of *reprendre*, to take back < Lat. *reprehendere, reprēndere*, to hold back. See REPREHEND.] **—re•priev′a•ble** *adj.*

rep•ri•mand (rĕp′rə-mănd′) *tr.v.* **-mand•ed, -mand•ing, -mands** To reprove severely, esp. in a formal or official way. See Syns at **admonish.** ❖ *n.* A severe, formal, or official rebuke or censure. [Fr. *réprimander* < *réprimande*, a reprimand, alteration (influenced by *mander*, to order) of obsolete *reprimende* < Lat. *reprimenda (culpa)*, (fault) to be repressed, fem. gerundive of *reprimere*, to restrain. See REPRESS.]

re•print (rē′prĭnt′) *n.* **1.** Something that has been printed again, esp.: **a.** A printing that is identical to an original; a reimpression. **b.** A separately printed excerpt; an offprint. **2.** A facsimile of a postage stamp printed after the original has been discontinued. ❖ *tr.v.* (rē-prĭnt′) **-print•ed, -print•ing, -prints** To make a new copy or edition of; print again. **—re•print′er** *n.*

re•pri•sal (rĭ-prī′zəl) *n.* **1.** Retaliation for an injury with the intent of injuring at least as much in return. **2.** Forcible seizure of an enemy's goods or subjects in retaliation for injuries. **3.** The practice of using political or military force outside of war. [ME *reprisail* < OFr. *reprisaille* < OItal. *ripresaglia* < *ripreso*, p. part. of *riprendere*, to take back < Lat. *reprehendere, reprēndere*, to take hold of. See REPREHEND.]

re•prise (rĭ-prēz′) *n.* **1.** *Music* **a.** A repetition of a phrase or verse. **b.** A return to an original theme. **2.** A recurrence or resumption of an action. ❖ *tr.v.* **-prised, -pris•ing, -pris•es** To repeat or resume an action; make a reprise of. [ME, act of taking back < OFr. < fem. p. part. of *reprendre*, to take back. See REPRIEVE.]

re•pro (rē′prō) *n., pl.* **-pros** *Informal* **1.** A reproduction proof. **2.** A copy or duplicate; a reproduction.

re•proach (rĭ-prōch′) *tr.v.* **-proached, -proach•ing, -proach•es 1.** To express disapproval of, criticism of, or disappointment in (someone). See Syns at **admonish. 2.** To bring shame upon; disgrace. ❖ *n.* **1.** Blame; rebuke. **2.** One that causes rebuke or blame. **3.** Disgrace; shame. ***—idiom:* beyond reproach** So good as to preclude criticism. [ME *reprochen* < OFr. *reprochier* < VLat. **repropiāre* : Lat. *re-*, re- + Lat. *prope*, near; see **per**[1] in App.] **—re•proach′a•ble** *adj.* **—re•proach′er** *n.*

re•proach•ful (rĭ-prōch′fəl) *adj.* Expressing reproach or blame. **—re•proach′ful•ly** *adv.* **—re•proach′ful•ness** *n.*

rep•ro•bate (rĕp′rə-bāt′) *n.* **1.** A morally unprincipled person. **2.** One who is predestined to damnation. ❖ *adj.* **1.** Morally unprincipled; shameless. **2.** Rejected by God and without hope of salvation. ❖ *tr.v.* **-bat•ed, -bat•ing, -bates 1.** To disapprove of; condemn. **2.** *Theology* To abandon to eternal damnation. [< ME, condemned < LLat. *reprobātus*, p. part. of *reprobāre*, to reprove : Lat. *re-*, opposite; see RE– + Lat. *probāre*, to approve; see PROVE.] **—rep′ro•ba′tion** *n.* **—rep′ro•ba′tive** *adj.*

re•proc•ess (rē-prŏs′ĕs′, -prō′sĕs′) *tr.v.* **-essed, -ess•ing, -ess•es** To cause to undergo special or further processing before reuse.

re•pro•duce (rē′prə-do͞os′, -dyo͞os′) *v.* **-duced, -duc•ing, -duc•es** —*tr.* **1.** To produce a counterpart, image, or copy of. **2.** *Biology* To generate (offspring). **3.** To produce again or anew; recreate. **4.** To bring (a memory, for example) to mind again; recall. —*intr.* **1.** To generate offspring. **2.** To undergo copying: *graphics that reproduce well.* **—re′pro•duc′er** *n.* **—re′pro•duc′i•bil′i•ty** *n.* **—re′pro•duc′i•ble** *adj.*

re•pro•duc•tion (rē′prə-dŭk′shən) *n.* **1.** The act of reproducing or the condition or process of being reproduced. **2.** Something reproduced. **3.** *Biology* The process by which organisms generate new individuals of the same kind.

reproduction proof *n.* A camera-ready proof of typeset material made through a photographic process such as photo-offset lithography.

re•pro•duc•tive (rē′prə-dŭk′tĭv) *adj.* Of, relating to, or capable of reproduction: *the reproductive organs.* ❖ *n. Zoology* A reproductive organism, esp. a sexually mature social insect. **—re′pro•duc′tive•ly** *adv.* **—re′pro•duc′tive•ness** *n.*

reproductive system *n.* The system of gonads, associated ducts, and external genitals concerned with sexual reproduction.

re•pro•graph•ics (rē′prə-grăf′ĭks) *n.* **1.** (*used with a sing. verb*) The technique of reprography. **2.** (*used with a sing. or pl. verb*) The materials, equipment, and processes of reprography.

re•prog•ra•phy (rĭ-prŏg′rə-fē) *n.* The process of reproducing graphic material, as by mechanical or electronic means. [REPRO(DUCTION) + –GRAPHY.] **—re•prog′ra•pher** *n.* **—re′pro•graph′ic** (rē′prə-grăf′ĭk, rĕp′rə-) *adj.*

re•proof (rĭ-pro͞of′) *n.* The act, an instance, or an expression of reproving; a rebuke. [ME *reprof*, var. of *reprove, repreve* < OFr. *reprueve* < *reprover*, to find fault with. See REPROVE.]

re•prove (rĭ-pro͞ov′) *tr.v.* **-proved, -prov•ing, -proves 1.** To voice or convey disapproval of; rebuke. See Syns at **admonish. 2.** To find fault with. [ME *reproven* < AN *repruver*, var. of OFr. *reprover* < LLat. *reprobāre*, to disapprove. See REPROBATE.] **—re•prov′a•ble** *adj.* **—re•prov′al** *n.* **—re•prov′er** *n.*

rep•tant (rĕp′tənt) *adj. Biology* Creeping or crawling; repent. [Lat. *rēptāns, reptant-*, pr. part. of *rēptāre*, to creep, freq. of *rēpere.*]

rep•tile (rĕp′tĭl′, -tīl) *n.* **1.** Any of various cold-blooded, usu. egg-laying vertebrates of the class Reptilia, such as a snake, turtle, or dinosaur, having an external covering of scales or horny plates and breathing by means of lungs. **2.** A person regarded as despicable or treacherous. [ME *reptil* < OFr. *reptile* < LLat. *rēptile* < neut. of Lat. *rēptilis*, creeping < *rēptus*, p. part. of *rēpere*, to creep.]

rep•til•i•an (rĕp-tĭl′ē-ən, -tĭl′yən) *adj.* **1.** Of or relating to reptiles. **2.** Resembling or characteristic of a reptile. **3.** Despicable; treacherous. ❖ *n.* A reptile.

rep•til•i•um (rĕp-tĭl′ē-əm) *n., pl.* **-i•a** (-ē-ə) A building or enclosure housing reptiles for public display.

re•pub•lic (rĭ-pŭb′lĭk) *n.* **1a.** A political order not headed by a monarch and in modern times led usu. by a president. **b.** A nation that has such a political order. **2a.** A political order in which the supreme power lies in a body of citizens who are entitled to vote for officers and representatives responsible to them. **b.** A nation that has such a political order. **3.** often **Republic** A specific republican government of a nation. **4.** An autonomous or partially autonomous political and territorial unit belonging to a sovereign federation. **5.** A group of people working as equals in the same sphere or field. [Fr. *république* < OFr. < Lat. *rēs pūblica* : *rēs*, thing + *pūblica*, fem. of *pūblicus*, of the people; see PUBLIC.]

re•pub•li•can (rĭ-pŭb′lĭ-kən) *adj.* **1.** Of, relating to, or characteristic of a republic. **2.** Favoring a republic as the best form of government. **3. Republican** Of, relating to, typical of, or belonging to the US Republican Party. ❖ *n.* **1.** One who favors a republic as the best form of government. **2. Republican** A member of the US Republican Party. **—re•pub′li•can•ism** *n.*

re•pub•li•can•ize (rĭ-pŭb′lĭ-kə-nīz′) *tr.v.* **-ized, -iz•ing, -iz•es** To make republican. **—re•pub′li•can•i•za′tion** (-kə-nĭ-zā′shən) *n.*

Republican Party *n.* **1.** One of the two primary political parties of the United States, organized in 1854 to oppose the extension of slavery. **2.** The Democratic-Republican Party.

Republican River A river rising in E CO and flowing c. 676 km (420 mi) to join the Smoky Hill R. and form the Kansas R.

re•pub•li•ca•tion (rē-pŭb′lĭ-kā′shən) *n.* **1.** The act or process of republishing. **2.** Something republished.

re•pub•lish (rē-pŭb′lĭsh) *tr.v.* **-lished, -lish•ing, -lish•es** To publish again. **—re•pub′lish•er** *n.*

re•pu•di•ate (rĭ-pyo͞o′dē-āt′) *tr.v.* **-at•ed, -at•ing, -ates 1.** To reject the validity or authority of. **2.** To reject strongly as unfounded, false, or unjust. **3.** To refuse to recognize or pay. **4a.** To disown (as a child). **b.** To refuse to have any dealings with. [Lat. *repudiāre, repudiāt-* < *repudium*, divorce.] **—re•pu′di•a′tive** *adj.* **—re•pu′di•a′tor** *n.*

re•pu•di•a•tion (rĭ-pyo͞o′dē-ā′shən) *n.* **1.** The act of repudiating or the state of being repudiated. **2.** The refusal, esp. by public authorities, to acknowledge a contract or debt. **—re•pu′di•a′tion•ist** *n.*

re•pugn (rĭ-pyo͞on′) *v.* **-pugned, -pugn•ing, -pugns** —*tr.* To oppose or contend against. —*intr. Archaic* To be opposed; conflict. [ME *repugnen* < OFr. *repugner* < Lat. *repugnāre*, to fight against : *re-*, re- + *pugnāre*, to fight with the fist.]

re•pug•nance (rĭ-pŭg′nəns) *n.* **1.** Great dislike; aversion. **2.** *Logic* The relationship of contradictory terms; inconsistency.

re•pug•nan•cy (rĭ-pŭg′nən-sē) *n., pl.* **-cies** Repugnance.

re•pug•nant (rĭ-pŭg′nənt) *adj.* **1.** Arousing disgust or aversion; repulsive: *repugnant behavior.* **2.** *Logic* Contradictory; inconsistent. [ME, antagonistic < OFr. < Lat. *repugnāns, repugnant-*, pr. part. of *repugnāre*, to fight against. See REPUGN.] **—re•pug′nant•ly** *adv.*

re•pulse (rĭ-pŭls′) *tr.v.* **-pulsed, -puls•ing, -puls•es 1.** To drive back; repel. **2.** To rebuff or reject with rudeness, coldness, or denial. **3.** *Usage Problem* To cause repugnance or distaste in. ❖ *n.* **1.** The act of repulsing or the state of being repulsed. **2.** Rejection; refusal. [ME *repulsen* < Lat. *repellere, repuls-*. See REPEL.] **—re•puls′er** *n.*

USAGE NOTE A number of critics have maintained that *repulse* should only be used to mean "to drive away, spurn," as in *He rudely repulsed their overtures,* and not to mean "to cause repulsion in," as in *Their hypocrisy repulsed me.* But reputable literary precedent exists for this usage, and given that the stigmatized use of *repulse* is parallel to the unexceptionable uses of *repulsion* and

ă	pat	oi	boy
ā	pay	ou	out
âr	care	o͝o	took
ä	father	o͞o	boot
ĕ	pet	ŭ	cut
ē	be	ûr	urge
ĭ	pit	th	thin
ī	pie	*th*	this
îr	pier	hw	which
ŏ	pot	zh	vision
ō	toe	ə	about, item
ô	paw		

Stress marks:
′ (primary);
′ (secondary), as in
lexicon (lĕk′sĭ-kŏn′)

repulsive, the frequency of its appearance is not surprising. Still, writers who want to avoid *repulse* may choose *repel*, a perfectly acceptable synonym.

re•pul•sion (rĭ-pŭl′shən) *n.* **1.** The act of repulsing or the condition of being repulsed. **2.** Aversion. **3.** *Physics* The tendency of particles or bodies of the same electric charge or magnetic polarity to separate.

re•pul•sive (rĭ-pŭl′sĭv) *adj.* **1.** Causing repugnance or aversion; disgusting. **2.** Tending to repel or drive off. **3.** *Physics* Opposing in direction: *a repulsive force.* —**re•pul′sive•ly** *adv.* —**re•pul′sive•ness** *n.*

re•pur•chase agreement (rē-pûr′chĭs) *n.* A contract giving the seller of an asset the right or obligation to buy back the asset at a specified price on a given date.

rep•u•ta•ble (rĕp′yə-tə-bəl) *adj.* Having a good reputation; honorable. —**rep′u•ta•bil′i•ty** *n.* —**rep′u•ta•bly** *adv.*

rep•u•ta•tion (rĕp′yə-tā′shən) *n.* **1.** The general estimation in which a person is held. **2.** The state or situation of being in high esteem. **3.** A specific characteristic or trait ascribed to a person or thing. [Ult. < Lat. *reputātiō, reputātiōn-*, a reckoning < *reputātus*, p. part. of *reputāre*, to reckon. See REPUTE.]

re•pute (rĭ-pyōōt′) *tr.v.* **-put•ed, -put•ing, -putes 1.** To ascribe a particular fact or characteristic to. **2.** To consider; suppose. ❖ *n.* **1.** Reputation. **2.** A good reputation. [ME *reputen* < OFr. *reputer* < Lat. *reputāre*, to think over : *re-*, re- + *putāre*, to think over.]

re•put•ed (rĭ-pyōō′tĭd) *adj.* Generally supposed to be such. —**re•put′ed•ly** *adv.*

re•quest (rĭ-kwĕst′) *tr.v.* **-quest•ed, -quest•ing, -quests 1.** To express a desire for; ask for. Often used with an infinitive or clause: *requested information about the proposal; requested to see the evidence; requested that the cab driver slow down.* **2.** To ask (a person) to do something: *He requested me to sit down.* ❖ *n.* **1.** The act of asking. **2.** Something asked for. —*idioms:* **by request** In response to a request. **in request** In great demand. **on** (or **upon**) **request** When asked for. [< ME *requeste*, the act of requesting < OFr. < VLat. **(rēs) requaesita*, (thing) requested < alteration of Lat. *requīsīta*, fem. p. part. of *requīrere*, to ask for. See REQUIRE.] —**re•quest′er** *n.*

req•ui•em (rĕk′wē-əm, rē′kwē-) *n.* **1. Requiem** *Roman Catholic Church* **a.** A Mass for a deceased person. **b.** A musical composition for such a Mass. **2.** A hymn, composition, or service for the dead. [ME < Lat., accusative of *requiēs*, rest, first word of the Requiem : *re-*, re- + *quiēs*, quiet.]

req•ui•es•cat (rĕk′wē-ĕs′kăt′, -kät′) *n.* A prayer for the repose of the souls of the dead. [Lat. *requiēscat*, third pers. sing. pr. subjunctive of *requiēscere*, to rest : *re-*, re- + *quiēscere*, to rest.]

re•quire (rĭ-kwīr′) *tr.v.* **-quired, -quir•ing, -quires 1.** To have as a requisite; need: *Most plants require sunlight.* **2.** To call for as obligatory or appropriate; demand. See Syns at **demand. 3.** To oblige; compel: *Students are required to attend classes.* [ME *requiren* < OFr. *requerre* < VLat. **requaerere*, alteration of Lat. *requīrere* : *re-*, re- + *quaerere*, to seek.] —**re•quir′a•ble** *adj.* —**re•quir′er** *n.*

re•quired (rĭ-kwīrd′) *adj.* **1.** Needed; essential. **2.** Obligatory.

re•quire•ment (rĭ-kwīr′mənt) *n.* **1.** Something that is required; a necessity. **2.** Something obligatory; a prerequisite.

req•ui•site (rĕk′wĭ-zĭt) *adj.* Required; essential. See Syns at **indispensable.** ❖ *n.* Something that is indispensable; a requirement. [ME < Lat. *requīsītus*, p. part. of *requīrere*, to require. See REQUIRE.] —**req′ui•site•ly** *adv.* —**req′ui•site•ness** *n.*

req•ui•si•tion (rĕk′wĭ-zĭsh′ən) *n.* **1.** A formal written request for something needed. **2.** A necessity; a requirement. **3.** The state or condition of being needed or put into service. ❖ *tr.v.* **-tioned, -tion•ing, -tions 1.** To demand, as for military needs. **2.** To make demands of.

re•quit•al (rĭ-kwīt′l) *n.* **1.** The act of requiting. **2.** Return, as for an injury or friendly act.

re•quite (rĭ-kwīt′) *tr.v.* **-quit•ed, -quit•ing, -quites 1.** To make repayment or return for: *requited love.* **2.** To avenge. [ME *requiten* : *re-*, re- + *quiten*, to pay; see QUIT.] —**re•quit′a•ble** *adj.* —**re•quit′er** *n.*

re•ra•di•ate (rē-rā′dē-āt′) *tr.v.* **-at•ed, -at•ing, -ates** To emit (radiation) following the absorption of incident radiation. —**re•ra′di•a′tion** *n.*

rere•dos (rĭr′dŏs′, rĭr′ĭ-, rĕr′ĭ-) *n.* **1.** A decorative screen or facing on the wall at the back of an altar; a retable. **2.** The back of an open hearth of a fireplace. [ME < AN < *areredos* : *arere*, behind (Lat. *ad-*, ad- + Lat. *retrō*, backward) + AN *dos*, back (< Lat. *dorsum*).]

re•re•lease (rē′rĭ-lēs′) *tr.v.* **-leased, -leas•ing, -leas•es** To release (a movie, for example) again. —**re′re•lease′** *n.*

re•run (rē′rŭn′) *n.* The act or an instance of rebroadcasting a recorded television program. ❖ *tr.v.* (rē-rŭn′) **-ran** (-răn′), **-run, -run•ning, -runs** To present a rerun of.

res. *abbr.* **1.** residence **2.** resolution

Res. *abbr.* **1.** reservation **2.** reserve **3.** reservoir

res ad•ju•di•ca•ta (rĕz′ ə-jōō′dĭ-kä′tə, räs′) *n.* Variant of **res judicata.**

re•sale (rē′sāl′, rē-sāl′) *n.* The act of selling again.

re•sched•ule (rē-skĕj′ōōl) *tr.v.* **-uled, -ul•ing, -ules** To schedule again or anew: *rescheduled the meeting.*

re•scind (rĭ-sĭnd′) *tr.v.* **-scind•ed, -scind•ing, -scinds** To make void; repeal or annul. [Lat. *rescindere* : *re-*, re- + *scindere*, to split.] —**re•scind′a•ble** *adj.* —**re•scind′er** *n.* —**re•scind′ment** *n.*

re•scis•sion (rĭ-sĭzh′ən) *n.* The act of rescinding. [Lat. *rescissiō, rescissiōn-* < *rescissus*, p. part. of *rescindere*, to rescind. See RESCIND.]

re•scis•so•ry (rĭ-sĭz′ə-rē, -sĭs′-) *adj.* Of, relating to, or having the power of rescission.

re•script (rē′skrĭpt′) *n.* **1a.** The act of rewriting. **b.** Something that has been rewritten. **2.** A formal decree or edict. **3.** *Roman Catholic Church* A response from an ecclesiastical superior to a question regarding discipline or doctrine. **4.** A reply from a Roman emperor to a magistrate's query about a point of law. [Lat. *rescrīptum* < neut. p. part. of *rescrībere*, to write back : *re-*, re- + *scrībere*, to write; see **skrib-** in App.]

res•cue (rĕs′kyōō) *tr.v.* **-cued, -cu•ing, -cues** To set free, as from danger; save. ❖ *n.* An act of rescuing; a deliverance. [ME *rescouen* < OFr. *rescourre* : *re-*, re- + *escourre*, to shake < Lat. *excutere* : *ex-*, ex- + *quatere*, to shake).] —**res′cu•a•ble** *adj.* —**res′cu•er** *n.*

rescue grass *n.* A tall South American grass (*Bromus unioloides*) cultivated for hay. [Prob. alteration of FESCUE.]

re•search (rĭ-sûrch′, rē′sûrch′) *n.* **1.** Scholarly or scientific investigation or inquiry. **2.** Close careful study. ❖ *v.* **-searched, -search•ing, -search•es** —*intr.* To engage in or perform research. —*tr.* **1.** To study (something) thoroughly so as to present in a detailed accurate manner. **2.** To do research for: *research a magazine article.* [Obsolete Fr. *recerche* < *recercher*, to search closely < OFr. : *re-*, re- + *cerchier*, to search; see SEARCH.] —**re•search′a•ble** *adj.* —**re•search′er, re•search′ist** *n.*

re•seat (rē-sēt′) *tr.v.* **-seat•ed, -seat•ing, -seats 1.** To provide with a new or different seat. **2.** To fit (a valve, for example) in a new seating.

ré•seau or **re•seau** (rā-zō′, rĭ-) *n., pl.* **-seaus** or **-seaux** (-zō′, -zō′) **1.** A net or mesh foundation for lace. **2.** *Astronomy* A reference grid of fine lines forming uniform squares on a photographic plate or print, used to aid in measurement. **3.** A mosaic screen of fine lines of three colors, used in color photography. [Fr. < OFr. *reseuil*, dim. of *raiz*, net < Lat. *rēte.*]

re•sect (rĭ-sĕkt′) *tr.v.* **-sect•ed, -sect•ing, -sects** To perform a resection on. [Lat. *resecāre, resect-*, to cut back : *re-*, re- + *secāre*, to cut; see **sek-** in App.] —**re•sect′a•bil′i•ty** *n.* —**re•sect′a•ble** *adj.*

re•sec•tion (rĭ-sĕk′shən) *n.* Surgical removal of all or part of an organ, tissue, or structure.

re•sec•to•scope (rĭ-sĕk′tə-skōp′) *n.* A surgical instrument for performing a resection without an opening or incision other than that made by the instrument.

re•se•da (rĭ-sē′də, -sĕd′ə) *n.* **1.** Any of various Mediterranean plants of the genus *Reseda*, including the mignonette, having flowered terminal racemes. **2.** A grayish or dark green to yellow green or light olive. [NLat. *Reseda*, genus name < Lat. *resēda*, plant.] —**re•se′da** *adj.*

re•sell (rē-sĕl′) *tr.v.* **-sold** (-sōld′), **-sell•ing, -sells 1.** To sell again. **2.** To sell (a product or service) to the public or to an end user, esp. as an authorized dealer.

re•sem•blance (rĭ-zĕm′bləns) *n.* **1.** The state or quality of resembling, esp. similarity in appearance or in external or superficial details. **2.** Something that resembles another; a likeness or semblance.

re•sem•ble (rĭ-zĕm′bəl) *tr.v.* **-bled, -bling, -bles** To exhibit similarity or likeness to. [ME *resemblen* < OFr. *resembler* : *re-*, re- + *sembler*, to appear (< Lat. *simulāre*, to imitate < *similis*, like; see **sem-¹** in App.).] —**re•sem′bler** *n.*

re•sent (rĭ-zĕnt′) *tr.v.* **-sent•ed, -sent•ing, -sents** To feel indignantly aggrieved at. [Fr. *ressentir*, to be angry < OFr. *resentir*, to feel strongly : *re-*, re- + *sentir*, to feel (< Lat. *sentīre*).]

re•sent•ful (rĭ-zĕnt′fəl) *adj.* Full of, marked by, or inclined to resentment. —**re•sent′ful•ly** *adv.* —**re•sent′ful•ness** *n.*

re•sent•ment (rĭ-zĕnt′mənt) *n.* Indignation or ill will felt as a result of a real or imagined grievance. See Syns at **anger.**

re•ser•pine (rĭ-sûr′pēn′, -pĭn, rĕs′ər-pĭn, -pēn′, rĕz′-) *n.* A powder, $C_{33}H_{40}N_2O_9$, isolated from the roots of certain species of rauwolfia and used as a sedative and an antihypertensive. [Ger. *Reserpin* < shortening and alteration of NLat. *Rauvolfia serpentīna*, species of snakeroot : RAUWOLFIA + LLat. *serpentīna*, fem. of *serpentīnus*, serpentine; see SERPENTINE.]

res•er•va•tion (rĕz′ər-vā′shən) *n.* **1.** The act of reserving; a keeping back or withholding. **2.** Something that is kept back or withheld. **3.** A limiting qualification or exception: *reservations about the plan.* **4.** A tract of land set apart by the federal government for a special purpose, esp. one for a Native American people. **5a.** An arrangement for securing accommodations in advance, as in a hotel. **b.** The accommodations so secured. **c.** The record or promise of such an arrangement. —**res′er•va′tion•ist** *n.*

re•serve (rĭ-zûrv′) *tr.v.* **-served, -serv•ing, -serves 1.** To keep back, as for future use or for a special purpose. **2.** To set or cause to be set apart for a particular person or use. **3.** To keep or secure for oneself; retain: *I reserve the right to disagree.* See Syns at **keep.** ❖ *n.* **1.** Something kept back or saved for future use or a special purpose. **2.** The act of reserving. **3.** The keeping of one's feelings, thoughts, or affairs to oneself. **4.** Self-restraint in expression; reticence. **5.** Lack of enthusiasm; skeptical caution. **6.** An amount of capital held back from investment in order to meet probable or possible demands. **7.** A reservation of public land: *a forest reserve.* **8.** An amount of a given resource known to exist in a particular location and to be exploitable. **9a.** A fighting force kept uncommitted until need arises. **b.** The part of a country's armed forces not on active duty but subject to call in an emergency. In both senses, often used in the plural. ❖ *adj.* Held in or forming a reserve. ***—idiom:* in reserve** Kept back, set aside, or saved. [ME *reserven* < OFr. *reserver* < Lat. *reservāre*, to keep back : *re-*, re- + *servāre*, to keep.] **—re•serv′a•ble** *adj.* **—re•serv′er** *n.*

reserve bank *n.* **1.** A central bank that holds the reserves of other banks. **2.** One of the 12 main banks of the US Federal Reserve System.

re•served (rĭ-zûrvd′) *adj.* **1.** Held in reserve; kept back or set aside. **2.** Self-restrained and reticent. See Syns at **silent.** **—re•serv′ed•ly** (-zûr′vĭd-lē) *adv.* **—re•serv′ed•ness** *n.*

re•serv•ist (rĭ-zûr′vĭst) *n.* A member of a military reserve.

res•er•voir (rĕz′ər-vwär′, -vwôr′, -vôr′) *n.* **1.** A pond or lake used for the storage and regulation of water. **2.** A receptacle or chamber for storing a fluid. **3.** An underground accumulation of petroleum or natural gas. **4.** *Anatomy* See **cisterna** 1. **5.** A large or extra supply; a reserve: *a reservoir of goodwill.* **6.** *Medicine* An organism or population that transmits a pathogen while being virtually immune to its effects. [Fr. *réservoir* < *réserver*, to reserve < OFr. *reserver*. See RESERVE.]

re•set (rē-sĕt′) *tr.v.* **-set, -set•ting, -sets 1.** To set again: *reset a broken bone.* **2.** To change the reading of: *reset a clock.* ❖ *n.* (rē′sĕt′) **1.** The act of setting again. **2.** Something set again. **—re•set′ta•ble** *adj.* **—re•set′ter** *n.*

res ges•tae (rās′ gĕs′tī′, rēz′ jĕs′tē) *pl.n.* **1.** Things done; deeds. **2.** *Law* The facts that are admissible in evidence as the surrounding circumstances of the event to be proved. [Lat. *rēs gestae* : *rēs*, pl. of *rēs*, thing + *gestae*, fem. pl. p. part. of *gerere*, to carry, show.]

resh (rĕsh) *n.* The 20th letter of the Hebrew alphabet. [Heb. *rêš* < Aram. *rēš* or Phoenician dialectal **rēš*, head, 20th letter of the Phoenician alphabet.]

Resht (rĕsht) See **Rasht.**

re•side (rĭ-zīd′) *intr.v.* **-sid•ed, -sid•ing, -sides 1.** To live in a place permanently or for a long period. **2.** To be inherently present; exist. **3.** To be vested, as a power or right. [ME *residen* < OFr. *resider* < Lat. *residēre*, to remain behind, reside : *re-*, re- + *sedēre*, to sit; see **sed-** in App.] **—re•sid′er** *n.*

res•i•dence (rĕz′ĭ-dəns, -dĕns′) *n.* **1.** The place in which one lives; a dwelling. **2.** The act or a period of residing in a place. **3.** A medical residency. **4.** The official home or location of a corporation. ***—idiom:* in residence** Committed to live and work in a specific place, often for a certain length of time.

res•i•den•cy (rĕz′ĭ-dən-sē, -dĕn′-) *n., pl.* **-cies 1.** The position or term of a medical resident. **2a.** The house of a colonial resident. **b.** The sphere of authority of a colonial resident. **3.** Residence.

res•i•dent (rĕz′ĭ-dənt, -dĕnt′) *n.* **1.** One who resides in a particular place permanently or for an extended period, as: **a.** A diplomatic official residing in a foreign seat of government. **b.** A colonial official acting as adviser to the ruler of a protected state. **c.** A physician receiving specialized clinical training in a hospital, usu. after completing an internship. **2.** A nonmigratory bird or other animal. ❖ *adj.* **1.** Dwelling in a particular place; residing: *resident aliens.* **2.** Living somewhere in connection with duty or work. **3.** Inherently present: *resident anxieties.* **4.** Nonmigratory: *resident fauna.*

res•i•den•tial (rĕz′ĭ-dĕn′shəl) *adj.* **1.** Of, relating to, or having residence. **2.** Of, suitable for, or limited to residences: *residential zoning.* **—res′i•den′tial•ly** *adv.*

res•i•den•ti•ar•y (rĕz′ĭ-dĕn′shē-ĕr′ē, -shə-rē) *adj.* **1.** Having a residence, esp. an official one. **2.** Involving or requiring official residence. ❖ *n., pl.* **-ies 1.** One residing in a certain place; a resident. **2.** A cleric required to live in an official residence.

re•sid•u•al (rĭ-zĭj′o͞o-əl) *adj.* **1.** Of, relating to, or characteristic of a residue. **2.** Remaining as a residue. ❖ *n.* **1.** The quantity left over at the end of a process; a remainder. **2.** A payment made to a performer, writer, or director for each repeat showing of a recorded television show or commercial. Often used in the plural. **—re•sid′u•al•ly** *adv.*

residual oil *n.* The low-grade oil products that remain after the distillation of petroleum, used in adhesives, roofing compounds, and asphalt manufacture.

re•sid•u•ar•y (rĭ-zĭj′o͞o-ĕr′ē) *adj.* **1.** Of, relating to, or constituting a residue. **2.** *Law* Entitled to the residue of an estate.

res•i•due (rĕz′ĭ-do͞o′, -dyo͞o′) *n.* **1.** The remainder of something after removal of parts or a part. **2.** Matter remaining after completion of an abstractive chemical or physical process, such as evaporation, distillation, or filtration; residuum. **3.** *Law* The remainder of a testator's estate after all claims, debts, and bequests are satisfied. [ME < OFr. *residu* < Lat. *residuum*, neut. of *residuus*, remaining < *residēre*, to remain behind. See RESIDE.]

re•sid•u•um (rĭ-zĭj′o͞o-əm) *n., pl.* **-u•a** (-o͞o-ə) **1.** Something remaining after removal of a part; a residue. **2.** *Law* See **residue** 3. [Lat., residue. See RESIDUE.]

re•sign (rĭ-zīn′) *v.* **-signed, -sign•ing, -signs** *—tr.* **1.** To submit (oneself) passively; accept as inevitable: *I resigned myself to a long wait.* **2.** To give up (a position, for example), esp. by formal notification. **3.** To relinquish (a privilege, right, or claim). See Syns at **relinquish.** *—intr.* To give up one's job or office; quit, esp. by formal notification. [ME *resignen* < OFr. *resigner* < Lat. *resignāre*, to unseal : *re-*, re- + *signāre*, to seal (< *signum*, mark, seal; see **sekʷ-¹** in App.).] **—re•sign′er** *n.*

res•ig•na•tion (rĕz′ĭg-nā′shən) *n.* **1.** The act or an instance of resigning. **2.** An oral or written statement that one is resigning a position or an office. **3.** Unresisting acceptance of something as inescapable; submission. See Syns at **patience.**

re•signed (rĭ-zīnd′) *adj.* Feeling or marked by resignation. **—re•sign′ed•ly** (-zī′nĭd-lē) *adv.* **—re•sign′ed•ness** *n.*

re•sile (rĭ-zīl′) *intr.v.* **-siled, -sil•ing, -siles 1.** To spring back, esp. to resume a former position or structure after being stretched or compressed. **2.** To draw back; recoil. [Obsolete Fr. *resilir* < Lat. *resilīre*, to leap back : *re-*, re- + *salīre*, to leap.]

re•sil•ience (rĭ-zĭl′yəns) *n.* **1.** The ability to recover quickly from illness, change, or misfortune; buoyancy. **2.** The property of a material that enables it to resume its original shape or position after being bent, stretched, or compressed; elasticity.

re•sil•ien•cy (rĭ-zĭl′yən-sē) *n.* Resilience.

re•sil•ient (rĭ-zĭl′yənt) *adj.* **1.** Able to recover readily, as from misfortune. **2.** Capable of returning to an original shape or position, as after having been compressed. [Lat. *resiliēns*, *resilient-*, pr. part. of *resilīre*, to leap back. See RESILE.] **—re•sil′ient•ly** *adv.*

res•i•lin (rĕz′ə-lĭn) *n.* An elastic substance consisting of cross-linked protein chains, found in the cuticles of many insects.

res•in (rĕz′ĭn) *n.* **1.** Any of numerous clear to translucent, yellow or brown, solid or semisolid viscous substances of plant origin, such as amber, used in lacquers, varnishes, inks, and synthetic plastics. **2.** Any of numerous physically similar polymerized synthetics or chemically modified natural resins including thermoplastic materials such as polyethylene and thermosetting materials such as polyesters that are used with stabilizers and other components to form plastics. ❖ *tr.v.* **-ined, -in•ing, -ines** To treat or rub with resin. [ME < OFr. *resine* < Lat. *rēsīna* < Gk. dialectal **rhēsīnā*, var. of Gk. *rhētīnē*.] **—res′in•ous** (rĕz′ə-nəs) *adj.*

res•in•ate (rĕz′ə-nāt′) *tr.v.* **-at•ed, -at•ing, -ates** To impregnate, permeate, or flavor with resin.

resin canal *n.* An intercellular tube lined with resin-secreting cells, found in the wood and leaves of many gymnosperms.

res•in•if•er•ous (rĕz′ə-nĭf′ər-əs) *adj.* Yielding resin.

res•in•oid (rĕz′ə-noid′) *adj.* Relating to, resembling, or containing resin. ❖ *n.* A synthetic resin, esp. a thermosetting one.

re•sist (rĭ-zĭst′) *v.* **-sist•ed, -sist•ing, -sists** *—tr.* **1.** To strive to fend off or offset the actions, effects, or force of. **2.** To remain firm against the actions, effects, or force of; withstand: *a bacterium that resisted the antibiotic.* **3.** To keep from giving in to or enjoying. *—intr.* To offer resistance. See Syns at **oppose.** ❖ *n.* A substance that can cover and protect a surface, as from corrosion. [ME *resisten* < OFr. *resister* < Lat. *resistere* : *re-*, re- + *sistere*, to place; see **stā-** in App.] **—re•sist′er** *n.*

re•sis•tance (rĭ-zĭs′təns) *n.* **1.** The act or an instance of resisting or the capacity to resist. **2.** A force tending to oppose or retard motion. **3.** often **Resistance** An underground organization struggling for national liberation in a country under military or totalitarian occupation. **4.** *Psychology* The opposition of the ego to the conscious recall of anxiety-producing experiences. **5.** *Biology* **a.** The capacity of an organism to fight a disease. **b.** The capacity of an organism or a tissue to withstand the effects of a harmful environmental agent. **6.** *Electricity* The opposition of a body or substance to current passing through it, dissipating electrical energy. **—re•sis′tant** *adj.*

re•sist•i•ble (rĭ-zĭs′tə-bəl) *adj.* Possible to resist: *resistible impulses.* **—re•sist′i•bil′i•ty** *n.* **—re•sist′i•bly** *adv.*

re•sis•tive (rĭ-zĭs′tĭv) *adj.* Of, tending toward, or marked by resistance. **—re•sis′tive•ly** *adv.* **—re•sis′tive•ness** *n.*

re•sis•tiv•i•ty (rē′zĭs-tĭv′ĭ-tē) *n., pl.* **-ties 1.** The capacity for or tendency toward resistance. **2.** *Electricity* The ability of a material to resist the flow of an electrical current, expressed in terms of a given length and cross-sectional area of the material.

re•sist•less (rĭ-zĭst′lĭs) *adj.* **1.** Impossible to resist; irresistible: *resistless force; resistless love.* **2.** Powerless to resist; unresisting.

re•sis•tor (rĭ-zĭs′tər) *n.* A device used to control current in an electric circuit by providing resistance.

res ju•di•ca•ta (rēz′ jo͞o′dĭ-kä′tə, rās′) also **res ad•ju•di•ca•ta** (ə-jo͞o′-) *n.* An adjudicated issue that cannot be relitigated. [Lat. *rēs iūdicāta*, thing decided.]

re•sole (rē-sōl′) *tr.v.* **-soled, -sol•ing, -soles** To put a new sole on (a shoe).

re•sol•u•ble (rĭ-zŏl′yə-bəl) *adj.* Possible to resolve; resolvable. [LLat. *resolūbilis* < Lat. *resolvere*, to resolve. See RESOLVE.] **—re•sol′u•bil′i•ty, re•sol′u•ble•ness** *n.*

res•o•lute (rĕz′ə-lo͞ot′, rĕz′ə-lo͞ot′) *adj.* Firm or determined; unwavering: *a resolute voice.* [ME, dissolved, dissolute < Lat. *resolūtus*, relaxed, p. part. of *resolvere*, to relax, untie. See RESOLVE.]

ă	pat	oi	boy
ā	pay	ou	out
âr	care	o͝o	took
ä	father	o͞o	boot
ĕ	pet	ŭ	cut
ē	be	ûr	urge
ĭ	pit	th	thin
ī	pie	*th*	this
îr	pier	hw	which
ŏ	pot	zh	vision
ō	toe	ə	about, item
ô	paw		

Stress marks:
′ (primary);
′ (secondary), as in
lexicon (lĕk′sĭ-kŏn′)

—**res′o•lute′ly** *adv.* —**res′o•lute′ness** *n.*

res•o•lu•tion (rĕz′ə-lo͞o′shən) *n.* **1.** The state or quality of being resolute; determination. **2.** A resolving to do something. **3.** A course of action resolved on. **4.** A formal statement of a decision or expression of opinion put before or adopted by an assembly or parliament. **5.** *Physics & Chemistry* The act or process of separating or reducing something into its constituent parts. **6.** The fineness of detail that can be distinguished in an image, as on a television. **7.** *Medicine* The subsiding or termination of an abnormal condition, such as a fever. **8.** *Law* A court decision. **9a.** An explanation, as of a problem; a solution. **b.** The part of a literary work in which the plot is resolved or simplified. **10.** *Music* **a.** The progression of a dissonant tone or chord to a consonant tone or chord. **b.** The tone or chord to which such a progression is made. **11.** The substitution of one metrical unit for another, esp. the substitution of two short syllables for one long syllable in quantitative verse.

re•solve (rĭ-zŏlv′) *v.* **-solved, -solv•ing, -solves** —*tr.* **1.** To make a firm decision about. **2.** To cause (a person) to reach a decision. See Syns at **decide. 3.** To decide or express by formal vote. **4.** To change or convert. **5.** To find a solution to; solve. See Syns at **solve. 6.** To remove or dispel (doubts). **7.** To bring to a usu. successful conclusion. **8.** *Medicine* To cause reduction of (an inflammation, for example). **9.** *Music* To cause (a tone or chord) to progress from dissonance to consonance. **10.** *Chemistry* To separate (an optically inactive compound or mixture) into its optically active constituents. **11.** To render parts of (an image) visible and distinct. **12.** *Mathematics* To separate (a vector, for example) into coordinate components. **13.** To melt or dissolve (something). **14.** *Archaic* To separate (something) into constituent parts. —*intr.* **1.** To decide or make a determination: *resolve on immediate action.* **2.** To become separated or reduced to constituents. **3.** *Music* To undergo resolution. ❖ *n.* **1.** Firmness of purpose; resolution. **2.** A determination or decision; a fixed purpose. **3.** A formal resolution made by a deliberative body. [ME *resolven,* to dissolve < OFr. *resolver* < Lat. *resolvere,* to untie : *re-*, re- + *solvere,* to untie; see **leu-** in App.] —**re•solv′a•ble** *adj.* —**re•solv′ed•ly** (-zŏl′vĭd-lē) *adv.* —**re•solv′er** *n.*

re•sol•vent (rĭ-zŏl′vənt) *adj.* Causing or able to cause separation into constituents; solvent. ❖ *n.* A resolvent substance, esp. a medicine that reduces inflammation or swelling.

res•o•nance (rĕz′ə-nəns) *n.* **1.** The quality or condition of being resonant. **2.** Richness or significance, esp. in evoking an association or strong emotion: *"a land of religious resonance"* (James Wolcott). **3.** *Physics* The increase in amplitude of oscillation of an electric or mechanical system due to a periodic force whose frequency is equal or very close to the natural undamped frequency of the system. **4.** *Acoustics* Intensification and prolongation of sound, esp. of a musical tone, produced by sympathetic vibration. **5.** *Physics* An unstable subatomic particle whose existence is usu. inferred from a peak in the energy distribution of its decay products. **6.** *Linguistics* Intensification of vocal tones during articulation, as by the air cavities of the mouth and nose. **7.** *Medicine* The sound produced by diagnostic percussion of the normal chest. **8.** *Chemistry* The property of a compound having simultaneously the characteristics of two or more structural forms that differ only in the distribution of electrons.

res•o•nant (rĕz′ə-nənt) *adj.* **1a.** Strong and deep in tone; resounding: *a resonant voice.* **b.** Having a lasting presence or effect; enduring: *resonant words of exhortation.* **c.** Strongly reminiscent; evocative: *a monument resonant of the nation's past glory.* **2.** Producing or exhibiting resonance: *resonant frequency excitation.* **3.** Resulting from or as if from resonance: *resonant amplification.* ❖ *n. Linguistics* A sonorant. [Lat. *resonāns, resonant-*, pr. part. of *resonāre,* to resound. See RESOUND.] —**res′o•nant•ly** *adv.*

resonant circuit *n.* An electric circuit with inductance and capacitance chosen to allow the greatest flow of current at a certain frequency.

res•o•nate (rĕz′ə-nāt′) *v.* **-nat•ed, -nat•ing, -nates** —*intr.* **1.** To exhibit or produce resonance or resonant effects. **2.** To have a profound emotional impact: *a theme that resonated with the voters.* **3.** To correspond closely or harmoniously. —*tr.* To cause to resonate; make resonant. [Lat. *resonāre, resonāt-*. See RESOUND.] —**res′o•na′tion** *n.*

res•o•na•tor (rĕz′ə-nā′tər) *n.* **1.** A resonating system. **2.** A hollow chamber or cavity with dimensions chosen to permit internal resonant oscillation of electromagnetic or acoustical waves of specific frequencies. **3.** A resonant circuit.

re•sorb (rē-sôrb′, -zôrb′) *v.* **-sorbed, -sorb•ing, -sorbs** —*tr.* **1.** To absorb again. **2.** *Biology* To dissolve and assimilate (bone tissue, for example). —*intr.* To undergo resorption. [Lat. *resorbēre,* to suck back : *re-*, re- + *sorbēre,* to suck up.]

res•or•cin•ol (rĭ-zôr′sə-nôl′, -nōl′, -nŏl′) also **res•or•cin** (rĭ-zôr′sĭn) *n.* A white crystalline compound, $C_6H_4(OH)_2$, used to treat certain skin diseases and in dyes, resin adhesives, and pharmaceuticals. [RES(IN) + ORC(HIL) + –IN + –OL[1].]

re•sorp•tion (rē-sôrp′shən, -zôrp′-) *n.* The act or process of resorbing.

re•sort (rĭ-zôrt′) *intr.v.* **-sort•ed, -sort•ing, -sorts 1.** To have recourse. **2.** To go customarily or frequently; repair. ❖ *n.* **1.** A place frequented by people for relaxation or recreation. **2.** A customary or frequent going or gathering. **3.** The act of turning to for aid or relief; recourse. **4.** One turned to for aid or relief. [ME *resorten,* to return < OFr. *resortir,* to go out again : *re-*, re- + *sortir,* to go out.]

re•sort•er (rĭ-zôr′tər) *n.* One who frequents resorts for vacations or recreation.

re•sound (rĭ-zound′) *v.* **-sound•ed, -sound•ing, -sounds** —*intr.* **1.** To be filled with sound; reverberate: *The room resounded with music.* **2.** To make a loud, long, or reverberating sound: *The music resounded through the hall.* **3.** To sound loudly; ring. **4.** To become famous or extolled. —*tr.* **1.** To send back (sound). **2.** To utter or emit loudly. **3.** To celebrate or praise, as in verse or song. [Alteration (influenced by SOUND[1]) of ME *resounen* < OFr. *resoner* < Lat. *resonāre* : *re-*, re- + *sonāre,* to sound.] —**re•sound′ing** *adj.* —**re•sound′ing•ly** *adv.*

re•source (rē′sôrs′, -sōrs′, -zôrs′, -zōrs′, rĭ-sôrs′, -sōrs′, -zôrs′, -zōrs′) *n.* **1.** Something that can be used for support or help. **2.** An available supply that can be drawn on when needed. Often used in the plural. **3.** The ability to deal with a difficult situation effectively; initiative. **4.** Means available in a difficult situation. Often used in the plural. **5a. resources** The total means available for economic and political development, such as mineral wealth and labor. **b. resources** The total means available to a company for increasing production or profit, including labor and raw material; assets. **c.** Such means considered individually. [Obsolete Fr. < OFr. < fem. p. part. of *resourdre,* to rise again < Lat. *resurgere* : *re-*, re- + *surgere,* to rise; see SURGE.]

re•source•ful (rĭ-sôrs′fəl, -sōrs′-, -zôrs′-, -zōrs′-) *adj.* Able to act effectively or imaginatively, esp. in difficult situations. —**re•source′ful•ly** *adv.* —**re•source′ful•ness** *n.*

resp. *abbr.* **1.** respective **2.** respectively

re•spect (rĭ-spĕkt′) *tr.v.* **-spect•ed, -spect•ing, -spects 1.** To feel or show deferential regard for; esteem. **2.** To avoid violation of or interference with: *respect the law.* **3.** To relate or refer to; concern. ❖ *n.* **1.** A feeling of appreciative, often deferential regard; esteem. **2.** The state of being regarded with honor or esteem. **3.** Willingness to show consideration or appreciation. **4. respects** Polite expressions of consideration or deference. **5.** A particular aspect, feature, or detail. **6.** *Usage Problem* Relation; reference. See Usage Note at **regard.** [< ME, regard < OFr. < Lat. *respectus* < p. part. of *respicere,* to look back at, regard : *re-*, re- + *specere,* to look at; see **spek-** in App.] —**re•spect′er** *n.*

re•spect•a•bil•i•ty (rĭ-spĕk′tə-bĭl′ĭ-tē) *n.* The quality, state, or characteristic of being respectable.

re•spect•a•ble (rĭ-spĕk′tə-bəl) *adj.* **1.** Meriting respect or esteem; worthy. **2.** Of or appropriate to good or proper behavior or conventional conduct. **3.** Of moderately good quality. **4.** Considerable in amount, number, or size. **5.** Acceptable in appearance; presentable. —**re•spect′a•ble•ness** *n.* —**re•spect′a•bly** *adv.*

re•spect•ful (rĭ-spĕkt′fəl) *adj.* Showing or marked by proper respect. —**re•spect′ful•ly** *adv.* —**re•spect′ful•ness** *n.*

re•spect•ing (rĭ-spĕk′tĭng) *prep. Usage Problem* With respect to; concerning. See Usage Note at **regard.**

re•spec•tive (rĭ-spĕk′tĭv) *adj.* Relating to two or more persons or things regarded individually; particular: *successful in their respective fields.* —**re•spec′tive•ness** *n.*

re•spec•tive•ly (rĭ-spĕk′tĭv-lē) *adv.* Singly in the order designated or mentioned: *I'm referring to each of you respectively.*

re•spell (rē-spĕl′) *tr.v.* **-spelled** or **-spelt** (-spĕlt′), **-spell•ing, -spells** To spell again or in a new way, esp. phonetically.

Re•spi•ghi (rĕ-spē′gē), **Ottorino** 1879–1936. Italian composer whose works include *Roman Festivals* (1929).

res•pi•ra•ble (rĕs′pər-ə-bəl, rĭ-spīr′-) *adj.* **1.** Fit for breathing: *respirable air.* **2.** Capable of undergoing respiration: *respirable organisms.* —**res′pi•ra•bil′i•ty** *n.*

res•pi•ra•tion (rĕs′pə-rā′shən) *n.* **1a.** The act or process of inhaling and exhaling; breathing. **b.** The act or process by which an organism without lungs, such as a plant, exchanges gases with its environment. **2a.** The oxidative process in living cells by which the chemical energy of organic molecules is released in metabolic steps involving the consumption of oxygen and the liberation of carbon dioxide and water. **b.** Any of various analogous metabolic processes by which certain organisms, such as fungi, obtain energy from organic molecules. —**res′pi•ra′tion•al** *adj.*

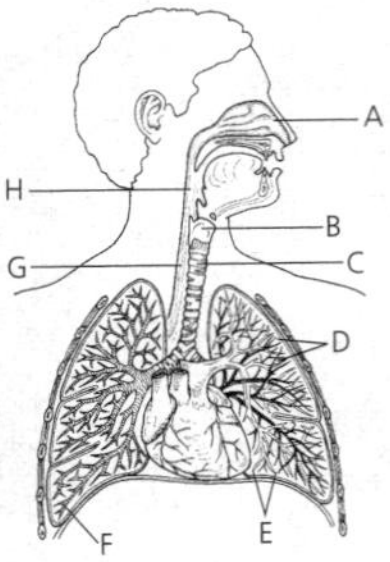

respiratory system
A. nasal passages
B. larynx
C. trachea
D. veins
E. arteries
F. bronchus
G. esophagus
H. throat

res•pi•ra•tor (rĕs′pə-rā′tər) *n.* **1.** A device that supplies oxygen or a mixture of oxygen and carbon dioxide for breathing, used esp. in artificial respiration. **2.** A screenlike device worn over the mouth or nose or both to protect the respiratory tract.

res•pi•ra•to•ry (rĕs′pər-ə-tôr′ē, -tōr′ē, rĭ-spīr′ə-) *adj.* Of, relating to, used in, or affecting respiration.

respiratory distress syndrome *n.* A respiratory disease of newborn babies, esp. premature babies, characterized by distressful breathing, cyanosis, and the formation of a glassy membrane over the alveoli of the lungs.

respiratory pigment *n.* Any of various colored conjugated proteins, such as hemoglobin, that occur in living organisms and function in oxygen transfer in cellular respiration.

respiratory quotient *n.* The ratio of the volume of carbon dioxide released to the volume of oxygen consumed by a body tissue or an organism in a given period.

respiratory syncytial virus *n.* An RNA-containing virus that causes respiratory infections, typically more severe in children.

respiratory system *n.* The integrated system of organs involved in the intake and exchange of oxygen and carbon dioxide between an organism and the environment.

re•spire (rĭ-spīr′) *v.* **-spired, -spir•ing, -spires** —*intr.* **1.** To breathe in and out; inhale and exhale. **2.** To undergo the metabolic process of respiration. **3.** To breathe easily again, as after a period of exertion or trouble. —*tr.* To inhale and exhale (air); breathe. [ME *respiren,* to breathe again < Lat. *respīrāre* : *re-,* re- + *spīrāre,* to breathe.]

res•pi•rom•e•ter (rĕs′pə-rŏm′ĭ-tər) *n.* An instrument for measuring the degree and nature of respiration. **—res′pi•ro•met′ric** (-rō-mĕt′rĭk) *adj.* **—res′pi•rom′e•try** *n.*

res•pite (rĕs′pĭt) *n.* **1.** A usu. short interval of rest or relief. See Syns at **pause. 2.** *Law* Temporary suspension of a death sentence; a reprieve. ❖ *tr.v.* **-pit•ed, -pit•ing, -pites** To delay; postpone. [ME < OFr. *respit* < Lat. *respectus,* refuge, looking back. See RESPECT.]

re•splen•dent (rĭ-splĕn′dənt) *adj.* Splendid or dazzling in appearance; brilliant. [ME < OFr. < Lat. *resplendēns, resplendent-,* pr. part. of *resplendēre,* to shine brightly : *re-,* re- + *splendēre,* to shine.] **—re•splen′dence, re•splen′den•cy** *n.* **—re•splen′dent•ly** *adv.*

re•spond (rĭ-spŏnd′) *v.* **-spond•ed, -spond•ing, -sponds** —*intr.* **1.** To make a reply; answer. See Syns at **answer. 2.** To act in return or in answer. **3.** To react positively or favorably: *The patient responded to the treatment.* —*tr.* To give as a reply; answer. ❖ *n. Architecture* A pilaster or half-pier engaged to a wall and carrying one end of an arch or groin, often at the end of an arcade. [ME *responden* < OFr. *respondre* < Lat. *respondēre* : *re-,* re- + *spondēre,* to promise; see **spend-** in App.] **—re•spond′er** *n.*

re•spon•dent (rĭ-spŏn′dənt) *adj.* **1.** Giving or given as an answer; responsive. **2.** *Law* Being a defendant. ❖ *n.* **1.** One who responds. **2.** *Law* A defendant, esp. in a divorce or equity case. **—re•spon′dence, re•spon′den•cy** *n.*

re•sponse (rĭ-spŏns′) *n.* **1.** The act of responding. **2.** A reply or an answer. **3.** A reaction, as that of an organism, to a specific stimulus. **4a.** *Ecclesiastical* Something that is spoken or sung by a congregation or choir in answer to the officiating cleric. **b.** A responsory. [ME *respons* < OFr. < Lat. *respōnsum* < neut. p. part. of *respondēre,* to respond. See RESPOND.]

re•spon•si•bil•i•ty (rĭ-spŏn′sə-bĭl′ĭ-tē) *n., pl.* **-ties 1.** The state, quality, or fact of being responsible. **2.** Something for which one is responsible; a duty, obligation, or burden.

re•spon•si•ble (rĭ-spŏn′sə-bəl) *adj.* **1.** Liable to be required to give account, as of one's actions. **2.** Involving personal accountability or ability to act without guidance or superior authority: *a responsible position.* **3.** Being a source or cause. **4.** Able to make moral or rational decisions and therefore answerable for one's behavior. **5.** Trustworthy or dependable; reliable. **6.** Based on or showing good judgment or sound thinking: *responsible journalism.* **7.** Having the means to pay debts or fulfill obligations. **8.** Required to render account; answerable. [Obsolete Fr., corresponding to < Lat. *respōnsus,* p. part. of *respondēre,* to respond. See RESPOND.] **—re•spon′si•ble•ness** *n.* **—re•spon′si•bly** *adv.*

SYNONYMS *responsible, answerable, liable, accountable, amenable* These adjectives share the meaning obliged to answer, as for one's actions, to an authority that may impose a penalty for failure. *Responsible* often implies the satisfactory performance of duties or the trustworthy care for or disposition of possessions: *"I am responsible for the ship's safety"* (Robert Louis Stevenson). *Answerable* suggests a moral or legal responsibility subject to review by a higher authority: *The court held the parents answerable for their child's acts. Liable* may refer to a legal obligation, as to pay damages or to perform jury duty: *Wage earners are liable to income tax. Accountable* emphasizes giving an account of one's discharge of a responsibility: *"The liberal philosophy holds that enduring governments must be accountable to someone beside themselves"* (Walter Lippmann). *Amenable* implies being subject to the control of an authority and therefore the absence of complete autonomy: *"There is no constitutional tribunal to which* [the king] *is amenable"* (Alexander Hamilton).

---

re•spon•sive (rĭ-spŏn′sĭv) *adj.* **1.** Answering or replying; responding. **2.** Readily reacting to suggestions, influences, appeals, or efforts. **3.** Containing or using responses: *responsive reading.* **—re•spon′sive•ly** *adv.* **—re•spon′sive•ness** *n.*

re•spon•so•ry (rĭ-spŏn′sə-rē) *n., pl.* **-ries** A chant or anthem recited or sung after a reading in a church service. [ME *responsorie* < LLat. *respōnsōrium* < Lat. *respōnsus,* p. part. of *respondēre,* to respond. See RESPOND.] **—re•spon•so′ri•al** (-sôr′ē-əl, -sōr′-) *adj.*

res pub•li•ca (rēz pŭb′lĭ-kə, rās po͞o′blē-kä′) *n., pl.* **-cae** (-kā, -kī) **1.** A state, republic, or commonwealth. **2.** The general public good or welfare. [Lat. *rēs pūblica.* See REPUBLIC.]

res•sen•ti•ment (rə-säN′tē-mäN′) *n.* A generalized feeling of resentment and often hostility harbored by one individual or group against another, esp. chronically and with no means of direct expression. [Fr., resentment < OFr. *ressentement* < *resentir,* to feel strongly. See RESENT.]

rest[1] (rĕst) *n.* **1.** Cessation of work, exertion, or activity. **2.** Peace, ease, or refreshment resulting from sleep or the cessation of an activity. **3.** Sleep or quiet relaxation. **4.** The repose of death: *eternal rest.* **5.** Relief or freedom from disquiet or disturbance. **6.** Mental or emotional tranquillity. **7.** Termination or absence of motion. **8.** *Music* **a.** An interval of silence corresponding to one of the possible time values within a measure. **b.** The mark or symbol indicating such a pause and its length. **9.** A short pause in a line of poetry; a caesura. **10.** A device used as a support: *a back rest.* **11.** *Games* See **bridge**[1] 7a. ❖ *v.* **rest•ed, rest•ing, rests** —*intr.* **1.** To cease motion, work, or activity. **2.** To lie down, esp. to sleep. **3.** To be at peace or ease; be tranquil. **4.** To be, become, or remain temporarily still, quiet, or inactive: *Let the issue rest.* **5.** To be supported or based; lie, lean, or sit: *The ladder rests firmly against the tree.* **6.** To be imposed or vested, as a responsibility or burden: *The final decision rests with the chairperson.* **7.** To depend or rely: *That argument rests on a false assumption.* **8.** To be located or be in a specified place: *The original manuscript rests in the museum.* **9.** To be fixed or directed on something: *Her eyes rested on the sunset.* **10.** To remain; linger. **11.** *Law* To cease voluntarily the presentation of evidence in a case: *The defense rests.* —*tr.* **1.** To give rest or repose to: *rested my eyes.* **2.** To place, lay, or lean for ease, support, or repose. **3.** To base or ground: *I rested my conclusion on that fact.* **4.** To fix or direct (the gaze, for example). **5.** To bring to rest; halt. **6.** *Law* To cease voluntarily the introduction of evidence in (a case). ***—idioms:* at rest 1a.** Asleep. **b.** Dead. **2.** Motionless; inactive. **3.** Free from anxiety or distress. **lay** (or **put**) **to rest 1.** To bury; inter. **2.** To settle (an issue, for example), esp. so as to be free of it. [ME < OE.] **—rest′er** *n.*

rest[2] (rĕst) *n.* **1.** The part that is left over after something has been removed; remainder. **2.** That or those remaining: *The beginning was boring, but the rest was interesting. The rest are arriving later.* ❖ *intr.v.* **rest•ed, rest•ing, rests 1.** To be or continue to be; remain: *Rest assured that I'll go.* **2.** To remain or be left over. [ME < OFr. *reste* < *rester,* to remain < Lat. *restāre,* to stay behind : *re-,* re- + *stāre,* to stand; see **stā-** in App.]

rest[3] (rĕst) *n.* A support for a lance on the side of the breastplate of medieval armor. [ME *reste,* short for *areste,* a stopping, holding < OFr. < *arester,* to stop. See ARREST.]

rest area *n.* A designated area, usu. along a major highway, where motorists can pause to relax.

re•start (rē-stärt′) *v.* **-start•ed, -start•ing, -starts** —*tr.* To start again or anew. —*intr.* To begin operation again. **—re′start′** *n.* **—re•start′a•ble** *adj.*

re•state (rē-stāt′) *tr.v.* **-stat•ed, -stat•ing, -states** To state again or anew. See Syns at **repeat. —re•state′ment** *n.*

res•tau•rant (rĕs′tər-ənt, -tə-ränt′) *n.* A place where meals are served to the public. [Fr., restorative soup, restaurant < pr. part. of *restaurer,* to restore < OFr. *restorer.* See RESTORE.]

res•tau•ra•teur (rĕs′tər-ə-tûr′) also **res•tau•ran•teur** (-tə-rän-tûr′) *n.* The manager or owner of a restaurant. [Fr. < *restaurer,* to restore. See RESTAURANT.]

rest energy *n.* The energy equivalent of the rest mass of a body, equal to the rest mass multiplied by the speed of light squared.

rest•ful (rĕst′fəl) *adj.* **1.** Affording, marked by, or suggesting rest; tranquil. **2.** Being at rest; quiet. **—rest′ful•ly** *adv.* **—rest′ful•ness** *n.*

rest•har•row (rĕst′hăr′ō) *n.* Any of several Old World plants of the genus *Ononis,* having woody stems, axillary pink or purplish flowers, and trifoliate leaves. [Obsolete *rest,* to check (short for ME *aresten;* see ARREST) + HARROW[1].]

rest home *n.* An establishment where the elderly or frail are housed and cared for.

res•ti•form body (rĕs′tə-fôrm′) *n.* A large cordlike bundle of nerve fibers lying on either side of the medulla oblongata and connecting it with the cerebellum. [Lat. *restis,* rope + –FORM.]

rest•ing (rĕs′tĭng) *adj.* **1a.** In a state of inactivity or rest. **b.** Dead. **2.** *Botany* Dormant. Used esp. of spores that germinate after a prolonged period.

resting cell *n.* A cell that is not actively dividing.

res•ti•tute (rĕs′tĭ-to͞ot′, -tyo͞ot′) *v.* **-tut•ed, -tut•ing, -tutes** —*tr.* **1.** To bring back to a former condition; restore. **2.** To refund. —*intr.* To undergo restitution. [Lat. *restituere, restitūt-* : *re-,* re- + *statuere,* to set up; see **stā-** in App.]

res•ti•tu•tion (rĕs′tĭ-to͞o′shən, -tyo͞o′-) *n.* **1.** The restoring to the rightful owner of something that has been taken away, lost, or surrendered. **2.** The act of making good or compensating for loss, damage, or injury; indemnification. **3.** A return to or restoration of a previous state or position.

res•tive (rĕs′tĭv) *adj.* **1.** Uneasily impatient under restriction, opposition, criticism, or delay. **2.** Resisting control; difficult to control. **3.** Refusing to move. Used of an animal. [ME *restif,* stationary < OFr. < *rester,* to remain < Lat. *restāre,* to keep back : *re-,* re- + *stāre,* to stand; see **stā-** in App.] **—res′tive•ly** *adv.* **—res′tive•ness** *n.*

rest•less (rĕst′lĭs) *adj.* **1.** Marked by a lack of quiet, repose, or rest. **2.** Not able to rest, relax, or be still. **3.** Never still or motionless. **—rest′less•ly** *adv.* **—rest′less•ness** *n.*

rest mass *n.* The physical mass of a body when it is regarded as being at rest.

res•to•ra•tion (rĕs′tə-rā′shən) *n.* **1a.** An act of restoring. **b.** An instance of restoring or of being restored. **c.** The state of being restored. **2.** Something, such as a renovated building, that has

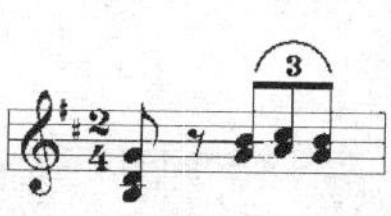

A B

rest[1]
A. note
B. rest

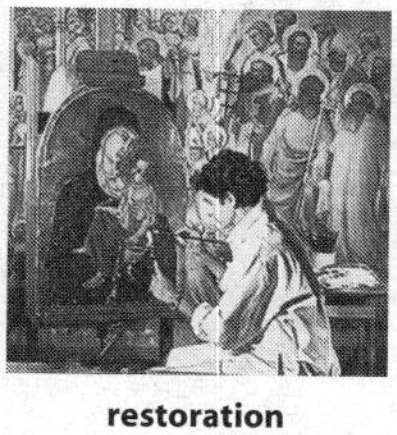

restoration
restoring a panel painting

ă	pat	oi	boy
ā	pay	ou	out
âr	care	o͝o	took
ä	father	o͞o	boot
ĕ	pet	ŭ	cut
ē	be	ûr	urge
ĭ	pit	th	thin
ī	pie	*th*	this
îr	pier	hw	which
ŏ	pot	zh	vision
ō	toe	ə	about,
ô	paw		item

Stress marks:
′ (primary);
′ (secondary), as in
lexicon (lĕk′sĭ-kŏn′)

been restored. **3. Restoration a.** The return of the monarchy to Great Britain in 1660 under Charles II. **b.** The period between the crowning of Charles II and the Revolution of 1688.

re•stor•a•tive (rĭ-stôr′ə-tĭv, -stōr′-) *adj.* **1.** Of or relating to restoration. **2.** Tending or having the power to restore. ❖ *n.* **1.** Something that restores. **2.** A medicine or other agent that helps restore health, strength, or consciousness. —**re•stor′a•tive•ly** *adv.* —**re•stor′a•tive•ness** *n.*

restorative justice *n.* A form of criminal justice that emphasizes reparation to the victim or the affected members of the community by the offender, as by cash payment or by community service.

re•store (rĭ-stôr′, -stōr′) *tr.v.* **-stored, -stor•ing, -stores 1.** To bring back into existence or use; reestablish. **2.** To bring back to an original condition. **3.** To put (someone) back in a former position. **4.** To make restitution of; give back. [ME *restoren* < OFr. *restorer* < Lat. *restaurāre.* See **stā-** in App.] —**re•stor′er** *n.*

re•strain (rĭ-strān′) *tr.v.* **-strained, -strain•ing, -strains 1a.** To hold back or keep in check; control: *restrained my tears.* **b.** To hold (a person) back; prevent: *restrained them from going.* **2.** To deprive of freedom or liberty. **3.** To limit or restrict. [ME *restreinen* < OFr. *restraindre, restreign-* < Lat. *restringere,* to bind back. See **RESTRICT.**] —**re•strain′a•ble** *adj.* —**re•strain′ed•ly** (-strā′nĭd-lē) *adv.* —**re•strain′er** *n.*

re•straint (rĭ-strānt′) *n.* **1.** The act of restraining or the condition of being restrained. **2.** Loss or abridgment of freedom. **3.** An influence that inhibits or restrains; a limitation. **4.** An instrument or a means of restraining. **5.** Control or repression of feelings; constraint. [ME *restreinte* < OFr. *restrainte* < fem. p. part. of *restraindre,* to restrain. See **RESTRAIN.**]

re•strict (rĭ-strĭkt′) *tr.v.* **-strict•ed, -strict•ing, -stricts** To keep or confine within limits. [Lat. *restringere, restrict-* : *re-, re-* + *stringere,* to draw tight.] —**re•stric′tor, re•strict′er** *n.*

re•strict•ed (rĭ-strĭk′tĭd) *adj.* **1.** Kept within limits; limited: *a restricted diet.* **2.** Excluding or unavailable to certain groups: *a restricted area.* **3.** Of, relating to, or being information available only to authorized persons. —**re•strict′ed•ly** *adv.*

re•stric•tion (rĭ-strĭk′shən) *n.* **1a.** The act of restricting. **b.** The state of being restricted. **2.** Something that restricts; a regulation or limitation.

restriction enzyme *n.* Any of a group of enzymes that cleave DNA at specific sites.

re•stric•tion•ism (rĭ-strĭk′shə-nĭz′əm) *n.* A view or policy approving restrictions, as on trade. —**re•stric′tion•ist** *n.*

re•stric•tive (rĭ-strĭk′tĭv) *adj.* **1.** Of or relating to restriction. **b.** Tending or serving to restrict; limiting. **2.** *Grammar* Of or being a subordinate clause or phrase that identifies the noun, phrase, or clause it modifies and limits or restricts its meaning, as the clause *who swim* in *People who swim have fun.* —**re•stric′tive•ly** *adv.* —**re•stric′tive•ness** *n.*

re•strike (rē′strīk′) *n.* A coin or medal freshly minted from an original die at a time after the first issue. —**re•strike′** *v.*

rest•room (rĕst′rōōm′, -rŏŏm′) *n.* A room equipped with toilets and lavatories for public use.

re•struc•ture (rē-strŭk′chər) *v.* **-tured, -tur•ing, -tures** —*tr.* **1.** To alter the makeup or pattern of. **2.** To make a basic change in (a system, for example). —*intr.* To alter the structure of something.

rest stop *n.* See **rest area.**

re•sult (rĭ-zŭlt′) *intr.v.* **-sult•ed, -sult•ing, -sults 1.** To come about as a consequence. See Syns at **follow. 2.** To end in a particular way. ❖ *n.* **1a.** The consequence of a particular action, operation, or course. See Syns at **effect. b.** A favorable or concrete outcome or effect. Often used in the plural. **2.** *Mathematics* The quantity or expression obtained by calculation. [ME *resulten* < Med.Lat. *resultāre* < Lat., to leap back, freq. of *resilīre* : *re-, re-* + *salīre,* to leap.] —**re•sult′ful** *adj.* —**re•sult′ful•ness** *n.* —**re•sult′less** *adj.*

re•sul•tant (rĭ-zŭl′tənt) *adj.* Issuing or following as a consequence or result. ❖ *n.* **1.** Something that results; an outcome. **2.** *Mathematics* A single vector that is the equivalent of a set of vectors. —**re•sul′tant•ly** *adv.*

re•sume (rĭ-zōōm′) *v.* **-sumed, -sum•ing, -sumes** —*tr.* **1.** To begin or take up again after interruption: *resumed his post.* **3.** To take on or take back again: *resumed my original name.* —*intr.* To begin again or continue after interruption. [ME *resumen* < OFr. *resumer* < Lat. *resūmere* : *re-, re-* + *sūmere,* to take.] —**re•sum′a•ble** *adj.* —**re•sum′er** *n.*

re•su•mé or **re•su•me** or **ré•su•mé** (rĕz′ŏŏ-mā′, rĕz′ŏŏ-mā′) *n.* **1.** A brief account of one's professional or work experience and qualifications, often submitted with a job application. **2.** A summary. [Fr. < p. part. of *résumer,* to summarize < OFr. *resumer,* to resume. See **RESUME.**]

re•sump•tion (rĭ-zŭmp′shən) *n.* The act or an instance of resuming. [ME < OFr. < LLat. *resūmptiō, resūmptiōn-,* recovery < Lat. *resūmptus,* p. part. of *resūmere,* to resume. See **RESUME.**]

re•su•pi•nate (rĭ-sōō′pə-nāt′, -nĭt) *adj. Biology* Inverted or seemingly turned upside down, as the flowers of most orchids. [Lat. *resupīnātus,* p. part. of *resupīnāre,* to bend back : *re-,* + *supīnus,* supine; see **SUPINE.**] —**re•su′pi•na′tion** *n.*

re•su•pine (rĕs′ə-pīn′) *adj.* Lying on the back; supine. [Lat. *resupīnus : re-,* + *supīnus,* supine; see **SUPINE.**]

retable

re•sur•face (rē-sûr′fəs) *v.* **-faced, -fac•ing, -fac•es** —*tr.* To cover with a new surface. —*intr.* To come to the surface again; reappear: *The rumor resurfaced.* —**re•sur′fac•er** *n.*

re•surge (rĭ-sûrj′) *intr.v.* **-surged, -surg•ing, -surg•es** To rise again; experience resurgence. [Lat. *resurgere : re-, re-* + *surgere,* to rise; see **SURGE.** Sense 2, RE– + SURGE.]

re•sur•gence (rĭ-sûr′jəns) *n.* **1.** A continuing after interruption; a renewal. **2.** A restoration to use, acceptance, activity, or vigor; a revival.

re•sur•gent (rĭ-sûr′jənt) *adj.* Experiencing or tending to cause renewal or revival.

res•ur•rect (rĕz′ə-rĕkt′) *v.* **-rect•ed, -rect•ing, -rects** —*tr.* **1.** To bring back to life; raise from the dead. **2.** To bring back into notice or use. —*intr.* To rise from the dead. [Back-formation < RESURRECTION.] —**res′ur•rec′tor** *n.*

res•ur•rec•tion (rĕz′ə-rĕk′shən) *n.* **1.** The act of rising from the dead or returning to life. **2.** The state of one who has returned to life. **3.** The act of bringing back to notice or use; revival. **4. Resurrection** *Christianity* **a.** The rising again of Jesus after the Crucifixion. **b.** The rising again of the dead at the Last Judgment. [ME < OFr. < LLat. *resurrēctiō, resurrēctiōn-* < Lat. *resurrēctus,* p. part. of *resurgere,* to rise again. See **RESURGE.**] —**res′ur•rec′tion•al** *adj.*

resurrection fern *n.* An epiphytic creeping American fern (*Polypodium polypodioides*) of warm regions having fronds that curl up and appear dead in prolonged dry weather and expand under moist conditions.

res•ur•rec•tion•ist (rĕz′ə-rĕk′shə-nĭst) *n.* **1.** One who steals bodies from graves to sell for dissection; a body snatcher. **2.** One who brings something back into use or notice again.

resurrection plant *n.* See **rose of Jericho.**

re•sur•vey (rē′sər-vā′, rē-sûr′vā) *tr.v.* **-veyed, -vey•ing, -veys** To survey or study anew. ❖ *n.* (rē-sûr′vā) A new survey or study.

re•sus•ci•tate (rĭ-sŭs′ĭ-tāt′) *v.* **-tat•ed, -tat•ing, -tates** —*tr.* To restore consciousness, vigor, or life to. —*intr.* To regain consciousness. [Lat. *resuscitāre, resuscitāt- : re-, re-* + *suscitāre,* to stir up (*sus-, sub-,* sub- + *citāre,* to move violently, freq. of *ciēre,* to set in motion; see **kei-²** in App.).] —**re•sus′ci•ta•ble** (-tə-bəl) *adj.* —**re•sus′ci•ta′tion** *n.* —**re•sus′ci•ta′tive** *adj.*

re•sus•ci•ta•tor (rĭ-sŭs′ĭ-tā′tər) *n.* One that resuscitates, as an apparatus that forces oxygen into the lungs of a person who has undergone partial asphyxiation.

ret (rĕt) *v.* **ret•ted, ret•ting, rets** —*tr.* To moisten or soak (flax, for example) in order to soften and separate the fibers by partial rotting. —*intr.* To become so moistened or soaked. [ME *reten,* prob. < MDu. *reeten.*]

ret. *abbr.* **1.** retired **2.** return

re•ta•ble (rē′tā′bəl, rĕt′ə-) *n.* A structure forming the back of an altar, esp.: **a.** An overhanging shelf for lights and ornaments. **b.** A frame enclosing painted panels. [Fr., ult. < Med.Lat. *retrōtabulum* : Lat. *retrō-,* retro- + Lat. *tabula,* tablet, board.]

re•tail (rē′tāl′) *n.* The sale of goods or commodities in small quantities directly to consumers. ❖ *adj.* Of, relating to, or engaged in retail. ❖ *adv.* **1.** In retail quantities. **2.** At a retail price. ❖ *v.* **-tailed, -tail•ing, -tails** —*tr.* **1.** To sell at retail. **2.** (*also* rĭ-tāl′) To tell or repeat (stories, for example) to others. —*intr.* To sell at retail. [ME < AN, var. of OFr., piece cut off < *retaillier,* to cut up : *re-, re-* + *tailler,* to cut; see **TAILOR.**] —**re′tail′er** *n.*

re•tain (rĭ-tān′) *tr.v.* **-tained, -tain•ing, -tains 1.** To maintain possession of. See Syns at **keep. 2.** To keep or hold in a particular place, condition, or position. **3.** To keep in mind; remember. **4.** To hire (an attorney, for example) by the payment of a fee. **5.** To keep in one's service or pay. [ME *retainen* < OFr. *retenir* < Lat. *retinēre : re-, re-* + *tenēre,* to hold; see **ten-** in App.] —**re•tain′a•bil′i•ty** *n.* —**re•tain′a•ble** *adj.* —**re•tain′ment** *n.*

re•tained earnings (rĭ-tānd′) *pl.n.* The accumulated net income retained for reinvestment in a business, rather than being paid out in dividends to stockholders.

retained object *n.* An object in a passive construction that is identical to the object in the corresponding active construction, as *story* in *Sue was told the story by Joan.*

re•tain•er¹ (rĭ-tā′nər) *n.* **1.** One that retains, as a device, frame, or groove that restrains or guides. **2.** *Dentistry* An appliance that holds teeth in position after orthodontic treatment. **3a.** An employee, typically a long-term employee. **b.** A servant or an attendant, esp. in the household of a person of high rank.

re•tain•er² (rĭ-tā′nər) *n.* **1.** The act of engaging the services of a professional adviser, such as an attorney, counselor, or consultant. **2.** The fee paid to retain a professional adviser.

re•tain•ing wall (rĭ-tā′nĭng) *n.* A wall built to support or prevent the advance of a mass of earth or water.

re•take (rē-tāk′) *tr.v.* **-took** (-tŏŏk′), **-tak•en** (-tā′kən), **-tak•ing, -takes 1.** To take back or again. **2.** To recapture. **3.** To photograph, film, or record again. ❖ *n.* (rē′tāk′) **1.** A taking again. **2.** The act or an instance of photographing, filming, or recording again.

re•tal•i•ate (rĭ-tăl′ē-āt′) *v.* **-at•ed, -at•ing, -ates** —*intr.* To return like for like, esp. evil for evil: *retaliate against an enemy attack.* —*tr.* To pay back (an injury) in kind. [LLat. *retāliāre, retāliāt- :* Lat. *re-, re-* + Lat. *tāliō,* punishment in kind; see **telə-** in App.] —**re•tal′i•a′tion** *n.* —**re•tal′i•a′tive, re•tal′i•a-**

to′ry (-ə-tôr′ē, -tōr′ē) *adj.* —**re•tal′i•a′tor** *n.*

re•tard[1] (rĭ-tärd′) *v.* **-tard•ed, -tard•ing, -tards** —*tr.* To cause to move or proceed slowly; delay or impede. —*intr.* To be delayed. ❖ *n.* **1.** A slowing down or hindering of progress; a delay. **2.** *Music* A slackening of tempo. [ME *retarden* < OFr. *retarder* < Lat. *retardāre* : *re-*, re- + *tardāre*, to delay (< *tardus*, slow).] —**re•tard′er** *n.*

re•tard[2] (rē′tärd′) *n. Offensive Slang* **1.** Used as a disparaging term for a mentally retarded person. **2.** A person considered to be foolish or socially inept. [Short for RETARDED.]

re•tar•dant (rĭ-tär′dnt) *adj.* Acting or tending to retard. Often used in combination. —**re•tar′dant** *n.*

re•tar•date (rĭ-tär′dāt′, -dĭt) *n. Often Offensive* A mentally retarded person.

re•tar•da•tion (rē′tär-dā′shən) *n.* **1a.** The act or process of retarding. **b.** The condition of being retarded. **2.** The extent to which something is held back or delayed. **3.** Something that retards; a delay or hindrance. **4.** Mental retardation. **5.** *Music* A diminishing of tempo; a retard.

re•tard•ed (rĭ-tär′dĭd) *adj.* **1.** *Often Offensive* Affected with mental retardation. **2.** Occurring or developing later than desired or expected; delayed.

retch (rĕch) *v.* **retched, retch•ing, retch•es** —*intr.* To try to vomit. —*tr.* To vomit. [Alteration of ME *rechen* < OE *hrǣcan*, to clear the throat, spit, bring up (phlegm).] —**retch** *n.*

re•te (rē′tē) *n., pl.* **re•ti•a** (rē′tē-ə, rē′shə) An anatomical mesh or network, as of veins or nerves. [Lat. *rēte*, net.]

re•tell (rē-tĕl′) *tr.v.* **-told** (-tōld′), **-tell•ing, -tells 1.** To relate or tell again or in a different form. **2.** To count again.

re•tell•ing (rē-tĕl′ĭng) *n.* A new account or an adaptation of a story: *a retelling of a Roman myth.*

re•tene (rē′tēn′, rĕt′ēn′) *n.* A crystalline compound, $C_{18}H_{18}$, derived from pine tar, fossil resins, and tar oils. [< Gk. *rhētīnē*, resin.]

re•ten•tion (rĭ-tĕn′shən) *n.* **1a.** The act of retaining. **b.** The condition of being retained. **2.** Capacity or power of retaining. **3.** Memory. **4.** Something retained. **5.** Involuntary withholding of body wastes or secretions that are normally eliminated. [ME *retencioun* < OFr. *retention* < Lat. *retentiō, retention-* < *retentus*, p. part. of *retinēre*, to retain. See RETAIN.]

re•ten•tive (rĭ-tĕn′tĭv) *adj.* **1.** Having the quality, power, or capacity of retaining. **2.** Having the ability or capacity to retain knowledge or information with ease: *a retentive memory.* —**re•ten′tive•ly** *adv.* —**re•ten′tive•ness** *n.*

re•ten•tiv•i•ty (rē′tĕn-tĭv′ĭ-tē) *n.* **1a.** The quality or state of being retentive. **b.** Capacity or power of retaining. **2.** *Physics* The capacity for a body to hold magnetization after the magnetizing field has been removed or no longer exists.

re•think (rē-thĭngk′) *tr. & intr.v.* **-thought** (-thôt′), **-think•ing, -thinks** To reconsider (something) or to involve oneself in reconsideration. —**re′think′** *n.* —**re•think′er** *n.*

re•ti•ar•y (rē′shē-ĕr′ē) *adj.* Of, resembling, or forming a net or web. [< Lat. *rēte*, net.]

ret•i•cence (rĕt′ĭ-səns) *n.* **1.** The state or quality of being reticent; reserve. **2.** The state or quality of being reluctant; unwillingness. **3.** An instance of being reticent.

ret•i•cent (rĕt′ĭ-sənt) *adj.* **1.** Inclined to keep one's thoughts, feelings, and personal affairs to oneself. See Syns at **silent. 2.** Restrained or reserved in style. **3.** *Usage Problem* Reluctant; unwilling. [Lat. *reticēns, reticent-*, pr. part. of *reticēre*, to keep silent : *re-*, re- + *tacēre*, to be silent.] —**ret′i•cent•ly** *adv.*

USAGE NOTE *Reticent* is generally used to indicate a reluctance to speak. Some commentators on usage have criticized its extended use as an all-purpose synonym for *reluctant.* In our 2001 survey, 83 percent of the Panel found unacceptable the sentence *A lot of out-of-towners are reticent to come to the Twin Cities for a ballgame if there's a chance the game will be rained out.*

ret•i•cle (rĕt′ĭ-kəl) *n.* A grid or pattern placed in the eyepiece of an optical instrument, used to establish scale or position. [Lat. *rēticulum*, dim. of *rēte*, net.]

re•tic•u•lar (rĭ-tĭk′yə-lər) *adj.* **1.** Resembling a net in form; netlike: *reticular tissue.* **2.** Marked by complexity; intricate. [< Lat. *rēticulum*, dim. of *rēte*, net.]

reticular formation *n.* A diffuse network of nerve fibers and cells in parts of the brain stem, important in regulating consciousness or wakefulness.

re•tic•u•late (rĭ-tĭk′yə-lĭt, -lāt′) *adj.* Resembling or forming a net or network: *reticulate veins of a leaf.* ❖ *v.* (-lāt′) **-lat•ed, -lat•ing, -lates** —*tr.* **1.** To make a net or network of. **2.** To mark with lines resembling a network. —*intr.* To form a net or network. [Lat. *rēticulātus* < *rēticulum*, dim. of *rēte*, net.] —**re•tic′u•late•ly** *adv.* —**re•tic′u•la′tion** *n.*

ret•i•cule (rĕt′ĭ-kyōōl′) *n.* **1.** A drawstring handbag or purse. **2.** A reticle. [Fr. *réticule* < Lat. *rēticulum*, dim. of *rēte*, net.]

re•tic•u•lo•cyte (rĭ-tĭk′yə-lō-sīt′) *n.* An immature red blood cell that contains a network of basophilic filaments. [RETICUL(UM) + -CYTE.] —**re•tic′u•lo•cyt′ic** (-sĭt′ĭk) *adj.*

re•tic•u•lo•en•do•the•li•al (rĭ-tĭk′yə-lō-ĕn′dō-thē′lē-əl) *adj.* Of, relating to, or being the widely diffused bodily system constituting all phagocytic cells except certain white blood cells.

[RETICUL(UM) + ENDOTHELIAL.]

re•tic•u•lum (rĭ-tĭk′yə-ləm) *n., pl.* **-la** (-lə) **1.** A netlike formation or structure; a network. **2.** *Zoology* The second compartment of the stomach of a ruminant, lined with a membrane having honeycombed ridges. **3.** **Reticulum** A constellation in the Southern Hemisphere near Dorado and Horologium. [Lat. *rēticulum*, dim. of *rēte*, net.]

re•ti•form (rē′tə-fôrm′, rĕt′ə-) *adj.* Arranged like a net; reticulate. [Lat. *rēte*, net + -FORM.]

ret•i•na (rĕt′n-ə) *n., pl.* **ret•i•nas** or **ret•i•nae** (rĕt′n-ē′) A delicate light-sensitive membrane lining the inner eyeball and connected by the optic nerve to the brain. [ME < Med.Lat. *rētina* < Lat. *rēte*, net.]

Ret•in-A (rĕt′n-ā′) A trademark for a preparation of retinoic acid, used in the topical treatment of acne.

ret•i•nac•u•lum (rĕt′n-ăk′yə-ləm) *n., pl.* **-la** (-lə) *Biology* A band or bandlike structure that holds a part in place. [Lat. *retināculum*, band : *retinēre*, to restrain; see RETAIN + -culum, suff. denoting instruments.] —**ret′i•nac′u•lar** (-lər) *adj.*

ret•i•nal[1] (rĕt′n-əl′) *adj.* Of or relating to the retina of the eye.

ret•i•nal[2] (rĕt′n-əl′, -ôl′) *n.* See **retinene.** [RETIN(OL) + -AL³.]

ret•i•nene (rĕt′n-ēn′) *n.* Either of two yellow to red retinal pigments, formed by oxidation of vitamin A alcohols.

ret•i•ni•tis (rĕt′n-ī′tĭs) *n.* Inflammation of the retina.

retinitis pig•men•to•sa (pĭg′mĕn-tō′sə, -mən-) *n.* A hereditary degenerative disease of the retina, characterized by night blindness, pigmentary changes within the retina, and eventual loss of vision. [NLat. *pigmentōsa*, fem. of *pigmentōsus*, pigmented.]

retino– or **retin–** *pref.* Retina: *retinoscopy.* [< RETINA.]

ret•i•no•blas•to•ma (rĕt′n-ō-blă-stō′mə) *n., pl.* **-mas** or **-ma•ta** (-mə-tə) A hereditary retinal malignant tumor transmitted as a dominant trait.

ret•i•no•ic acid (rĕt′n-ō′ĭk) *n.* **1.** A vitamin A derivative, $C_{20}H_{28}O_2$, that is active in morphogenesis, bone growth, and the maintenance of epithelium, and may reduce the proliferation of certain cancer cells. **2.** A preparation of this, used topically to treat acne and to modify the appearance of the skin. [RETIN(OL) + -OIC.]

ret•in•oid (rĕt′n-oid′) *n.* Any of various natural or synthetic derivatives of vitamin A. [RETIN(OL) + -OID.]

ret•i•nol (rĕt′n-ôl′, -ōl′, -ôl′) *n.* See **vitamin A.**

ret•i•nop•a•thy (rĕt′n-ŏp′ə-thē) *n., pl.* **-thies** A pathological disorder of the retina. —**ret′i•no•path′ic** (-ō-păth′ĭk) *adj.*

ret•i•no•scope (rĕt′n-ə-skōp′) *n.* An optical instrument for examining refraction of light in the eye. —**ret′i•nos′co•py** (rĕt′n-ŏs′kə-pē) *n.*

ret•i•nue (rĕt′n-ōō′, -yōō′) *n.* The retainers accompanying a high-ranking person. [ME *retenue* < OFr. < fem. p. part. of *retenir*, to retain. See RETAIN.]

re•tin•u•la (rĭ-tĭn′yə-lə) *n., pl.* **-lae** (-lē) A cluster of pigmented sensory cells in the compound eye of an arthropod. [NLat. *rētinula*, dim. of Med.Lat. *rētina*, retina. See RETINA.] —**re•tin′u•lar** *adj.*

re•tire (rĭ-tīr′) *v.* **-tired, -tir•ing, -tires** —*intr.* **1.** To withdraw, as for rest. **2.** To go to bed. **3.** To withdraw from one's occupation, business, or office; stop working. **4.** To fall back or retreat, as from battle. **5.** To move back or away; recede. —*tr.* **1.** To cause to withdraw from one's usual field of activity; withdraw. **2.** To lead (troops, for example) away from action; withdraw. **3.** To take out of circulation: *retired the bonds.* **4.** To withdraw from use or active service: *retiring an old ship.* **5.** *Baseball* **a.** To put out (a batter). **b.** To cause (the opposing team) to end a turn at bat. [Fr. *retirer*, to retreat < OFr., to take back : *re-*, re- + *tirer*, to draw; see TIER¹.]

re•tired (rĭ-tīrd′) *adj.* **1.** Withdrawn from one's occupation; having finished one's active working life. **2.** Received by a person in retirement: *retired pay.* **3.** Withdrawn; secluded. ❖ *n.* Retired people considered as a group. —**re•tired′ly** *adv.* —**re•tired′ness** *n.*

re•tir•ee (rĭ-tīr′ē′) *n.* One who has retired from active working life.

re•tire•ment (rĭ-tīr′mənt) *n.* **1.** The act of retiring. **2.** The state of being retired. **3.** Withdrawal from one's occupation, business, or office. **4.** Withdrawal into privacy or seclusion. **5.** A place of privacy or seclusion; a retreat.

re•tir•ing (rĭ-tīr′ĭng) *adj.* Shy and reserved; modest. —**re•tir′ing•ly** *adv.* —**re•tir′ing•ness** *n.*

re•told (rē-tōld′) *v.* Past tense and past participle of **retell.**

re•took (rē-tōōk′) *v.* Past tense of **retake.**

re•tool (rē-tōōl′) *v.* **-tooled, -tool•ing, -tools** —*tr.* **1.** To fit out (a factory, for example) with new machinery and tools for making a different product. **2.** To revise and reorganize, esp. in order to update or improve: *had to retool the city's economy.* —*intr.* To retool a factory, for example.

re•tor•sion or **re•tor•tion** (rĭ-tôr′shən) *n.* An act perpetrated by one nation upon another in retaliation or reprisal for a similar act. [Prob. Fr. *rétorsion* < Lat. *retortus*, p. part. of *retorquēre*, to cast back. See RETORT¹.]

re•tort[1] (rĭ-tôrt′) *v.* **-tort•ed, -tort•ing, -torts 1a.** To reply, esp. in a quick, caustic, or witty manner. See Syns at **answer. b.** To present a counterargument to. **2.** To return in

kind; pay back. —*intr.* **1.** To make a reply, esp. a quick, caustic, or witty one. **2.** To present a counterargument. **3.** To return like for like; retaliate. ❖ *n.* **1.** A quick incisive reply, esp. one that turns the first speaker's words to his or her own disadvantage. **2.** The act or an instance of retorting. [Lat. *retorquēre, retort-*, to bend back, retort : *re-*, re- + *torquēre*, to bend, twist.] —**re•tort′er** *n.*

re•tort[2] (rĭ-tôrt′, rē′tôrt′) *n.* A closed laboratory vessel with an outlet tube, used for distillation, sublimation, or decomposition by heat. [Fr. *retorte* < Med.Lat. *retorta* < fem. of Lat. *retortus*, p. part. of *retorquēre*, to bend back. See RETORT[1].]

re•touch (rē-tŭch′) *v.* **-touched, -touch•ing, -touch•es** —*tr.* **1.** To add new details or touches to for correction or improvement. **2.** To improve or change (a photographic negative or print), as by removing flaws. **3.** To color (recent growth of hair) to match hair that was tinted, dyed, or bleached at an earlier date. —*intr.* To give or make retouches. ❖ *n.* (rē′tŭch′, rē-tŭch′) The act or process or an instance of retouching. —**re•touch′er** *n.*

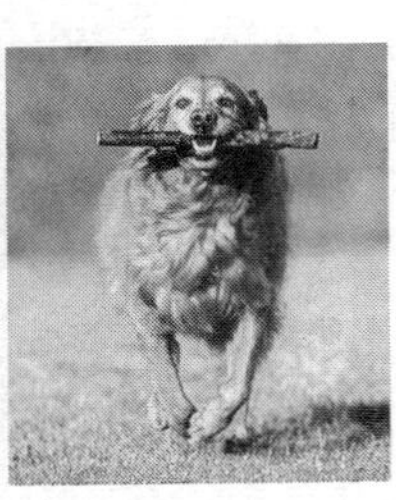

retriever
golden retriever

re•tract (rĭ-trăkt′) *v.* **-tract•ed, -tract•ing, -tracts** —*tr.* **1.** To take back; disavow. **2.** To draw back or in. **3.** *Linguistics* **a.** To utter (a sound) with the tongue drawn back. **b.** To draw back (the tongue). —*intr.* **1.** To take something back or disavow it. **2.** To draw back. [Lat. *retractāre*, to revoke, freq. of *retrahere*, to draw back : *re-*, re- + *trahere*, to draw. V., tr., senses 2 and 3, and v., intr., sense 2, ME *retracten* < OFr. *retracter* < Lat. *retractus*, p. part. of *retrahere*, to draw back.] —**re•tract′a•bil′i•ty, re•tract′i•bil′i•ty** *n.* —**re•tract′a•ble, re•tract′i•ble** *adj.* —**re′trac•ta′tion** (rē′trăk-tā′shən) *n.*

re•trac•tile (rĭ-trăk′tĭl, -tīl′) *adj.* That can be drawn back or in: *retractile claws.* —**re′trac•til′i•ty** (rē′trăk-tĭl′ĭ-tē) *n.*

re•trac•tion (rĭ-trăk′shən) *n.* **1.** The act of retracting or the state of being retracted. **2a.** The act of recanting or disavowing a previously held statement or belief. **b.** A formal statement of disavowal. **c.** Something recanted or disavowed. **3.** The power of drawing back or of being drawn back.

re•trac•tive (rĭ-trăk′tĭv) *adj.* Tending or serving to retract. —**re•trac′tive•ly** *adv.* —**re•trac′tive•ness** *n.*

re•trac•tor (rĭ-trăk′tər) *n.* One that retracts, as: **a.** *Anatomy* A muscle that retracts an organ or a part. **b.** *Medicine* A surgical instrument used to hold back organs, for example.

re•tral (rē′trəl, rĕt′rəl) *adj.* **1.** Situated at, located close to, or directed toward the back. **2.** Backward; reverse. [< Lat. *retrō*, back.] —**re′tral•ly** *adv.*

re•tread (rē-trĕd′) *tr.v.* **-tread•ed, -tread•ing, -treads 1.** To fit (a worn automotive tire) with a new tread. **2.** To make or do over again, esp. with minimal revision; rehash: *retreading an old story.* ❖ *n.* (rē′trĕd′) **1.** A tire that has a new tread. **2.** A revision or reworking; a remake or rehash. **3.** *Informal* A person who has been retrained for work.

re•treat (rĭ-trēt′) *n.* **1a.** The act or process of withdrawing, esp. from something hazardous or unpleasant. **b.** The process of receding from a position or condition gained. **2.** A place affording peace, quiet, privacy, or security. **3a.** A period of seclusion, retirement, or solitude. **b.** A period of withdrawal for prayer, meditation, or study. **4a.** Withdrawal of a military force from danger. **b.** The signal for such withdrawal. **c.** A bugle call or drumbeat signaling the lowering of the flag at sunset. **d.** The military ceremony of lowering the flag. ❖ *v.* **-treat•ed, -treat•ing, -treats** —*intr.* **1.** To fall or draw back; withdraw or retire. **2.** To slope backward. —*tr. Games* To move (a chess piece) back. [ME *retret* < OFr. *retrait, retret* < p. part. of *retraire, retrere*, to draw back < Lat. *retrahere*. See RETRACT.] —**re•treat′er** *n.*

re•treat•ant (rĭ-trēt′nt) *n.* A participant in a religious retreat.

re•trench (rĭ-trĕnch′) *v.* **-trenched, -trench•ing, -trench•es** —*tr.* **1.** To cut down; reduce. **2.** To remove, delete, or omit. —*intr.* To curtail expenses; economize. [Obsolete Fr. *retrencher* < OFr. *retrenchier* : *re-*, re- + *trenchier*, to cut; see TRENCH.] —**re•trench′er** *n.*

re•trench•ment (rĭ-trĕnch′mənt) *n.* **1.** A cutting down or back; reduction. **2.** A curtailment of expenses.

re•tri•al (rē′trī′əl, -trīl′, rē-trī′əl, -trīl′) *n.* A second trial, as of a legal case.

ret•ri•bu•tion (rĕt′rə-byo͞o′shən) *n.* **1.** Something deserved; recompense. **2.** Something given or demanded in repayment, esp. punishment. **3.** *Theology* Punishment or reward in a future life based on performance in this one. [Ult. < Lat. *retribūtiō, retribūtiōn-* < *retribūtus*, p. part. of *retribuere*, to pay back : *re-*, re- + *tribuere*, to grant; see TRIBUTE.]

re•trib•u•tive (rĭ-trĭb′yə-tĭv) *adj.* Of, involving, or characterized by retribution; retributory. —**re•trib′u•tive•ly** *adv.*

re•trib•u•to•ry (rĭ-trĭb′yə-tôr′ē, -tōr′ē) *adj.* Retributive.

re•tried (rē-trīd′) *v.* Past tense and past participle of **retry.**

re•tries (rē-trīz′) *v.* Third person singular present tense of **retry.**

re•triev•al (rĭ-trē′vəl) *n.* **1.** The act or process of retrieving. **2.** *Computer Science* The accessing of information from storage devices. **3.** The possibility of being retrieved or restored.

retrieval engine *n.* A search engine.

re•trieve (rĭ-trēv′) *v.* **-trieved, -triev•ing, -trieves** —*tr.* **1.** To get back; regain. **2a.** To rescue or save. **b.** *Sports* To make a difficult but successful return of (a ball or shuttlecock). **3.** To bring back again; revive or restore. **4.** To rectify the unfavorable consequences of; remedy. See Syns at **recover. 5.** To recall to mind; remember. **6.** To find and carry back; fetch. —*intr.* To find and bring back game. ❖ *n.* **1.** The act of retrieving; retrieval. **2.** *Sports* A difficult but successful return of a ball or shuttlecock. [ME *retreven* < OFr. *retrover, retruev-* : *re-*, re- + *trover*, to find; see TROVER.] —**re•triev′a•bil′i•ty** *n.* —**re•triev′a•ble** *adj.* —**re•triev′a•bly** *adv.*

re•triev•er (rĭ-trē′vər) *n.* One that retrieves, esp. any one of several breeds of dog that were bred to retrieve game.

ret•ro (rĕt′rō) *adj.* **1.** Retroactive. **2.** Involving, relating to, or reminiscent of things past; retrospective. ❖ *n., pl.* **-ros** A fashion, decor, or design reminiscent of things past.

retro– *pref.* **1.** Backward; back: *retrorocket.* **2.** Situated behind: *retrolental.* **3.** Contrary to a usual or natural course of action: *retrograde.* [Lat. *retrō-* < *retrō*, backward, behind.]

ret•ro•ac•tion (rĕt′rō-ăk′shən) *n.* **1.** An action, as of a law, that influences or applies to a prior time. **2.** An opposing or reciprocal action; a reaction. —**ret′ro•act′** *v.*

ret•ro•ac•tive (rĕt′rō-ăk′tĭv) *adj.* Influencing or applying to a period prior to enactment. [Fr. *rétroactif* < Lat. *retroāctus*, p. part. of *retroagere*, to drive back : *retrō-*, retro- + *agere*, to drive; see **ag-** in App.] —**ret′ro•ac′tive•ly** *adv.* —**ret′ro•ac•tiv′i•ty** *n.*

ret•ro•cede (rĕt′rō-sēd′) *v.* **-ced•ed, -ced•ing, -cedes** —*intr.* To go back; recede. —*tr.* To cede or give back (a territory, for example); return. [Lat. *retrōcēdere* : *retrō-*, retro- + *cēdere*, to go.] —**ret′ro•ces′sion** (-sĕsh′ən) *n.*

ret•ro•fire (rĕt′rō-fīr′) *v.* **-fired, -fir•ing, -fires** —*tr.* To ignite or fire (a retrorocket). —*intr.* To become ignited or fired. Used of a retrorocket.

ret•ro•fit (rĕt′rō-fĭt′) *n.* **1.** A modification of an existing product, facility, or structure with parts, equipment, or systems not available at the time of original manufacture or construction. **2.** Something, such as a structure, so modified. ❖ *v.* **-fit•ted** or **-fit, -fit•ting, -fits** —*tr.* **1.** To provide (a product, for example) with a retrofit. **2.** To install or fit (a new device, for example) during a retrofit. —*intr.* To undergo a retrofit. [*retro(active) (re)fit.*] —**ret′ro•fit′** *adj.* —**ret′ro•fit′ta•ble** *adj.* —**ret′ro•fit′ter** *n.*

ret•ro•flex (rĕt′rə-flĕks′) *adj.* also **ret•ro•flexed** (-flĕkst′) **1.** Bent, curved, or turned backward. **2.** Pronounced with the tip of the tongue turned back against the roof of the mouth. ❖ *n.* A sound pronounced with the tongue in retroflex position, as the sound (r) in some varieties of English. [Lat. **retrōflexus*, p. part. of *retrōflectere*, to bend back : *retrō*, retro- + *flectere*, to bend.] —**ret′ro•flex′ion, ret′ro•flec′tion** *n.*

ret•ro•grade (rĕt′rə-grād′) *adj.* **1.** Moving or tending backward. **2.** Opposite to the usual order; inverted or reversed. **3.** Reverting to an earlier or inferior condition. **4.** *Astronomy* **a.** Of or relating to the orbital revolution or axial rotation of a planetary body that moves clockwise from east to west, in the direction opposite to most celestial bodies. **b.** Of or relating to the brief, regularly occurring, apparently backward movement of a planetary body in its orbit as viewed against the fixed stars, caused by the differing orbital velocities of Earth and the body observed. **5.** *Archaic* Opposed; contrary. ❖ *intr.v.* **-grad•ed, -grad•ing, -grades 1.** To move or seem to move backward. **2.** To decline to an inferior state; degenerate. [ME < Lat. *retrōgradus* < *retrōgradī*, to go back : *retrō-*, retro- + *-gradus*, walking (< *gradī*, to go; see **ghredh-** in App.).] —**ret′ro•gra•da′tion** (-rō-grā-dā′shən) *n.* —**ret′ro•grade′ly** *adv.*

ret•ro•gress (rĕt′rə-grĕs′, rĕt′rə-grĕs′) *intr.v.* **-gressed, -gress•ing, -gress•es 1.** To return to an earlier, inferior, or less complex condition. **2.** To go or move backward. [Lat. *retrōgradī, *retrōgress-* : *retrō-*, retro- + *gradī*, to go; see **ghredh-** in App.] —**ret′ro•gres′sive** *adj.*

ret•ro•gres•sion (rĕt′rə-grĕsh′ən) *n.* **1.** The act or process of deteriorating or declining. **2.** *Biology* A return to a less complex or more primitive state or stage.

ret•ro•len•tal (rĕt′rō-lĕn′tl) *adj.* Situated or occurring behind a lens, as of the eye. [RETRO– + NLat. *lēns, lent-*, lens; see LENS + –AL[1].]

ret•ro•nym (rĕt′rə-nĭm′) *n.* A word or phrase created because an existing term that was once used alone needs to be distinguished from a term referring to a new development, as *acoustic guitar* in contrast to *electric guitar.* [RETR(O)– + –ONYM.]

ret•ro•oc•u•lar (rĕt′rō-ŏk′yə-lər) *adj.* Being behind the eye.

ret•ro•per•i•to•ne•al (rĕt′rō-pĕr′ĭ-tn-ē′əl) *adj.* Situated behind the peritoneum.

ret•ro•pha•ryn•ge•al (rĕt′rō-fə-rĭn′jē-əl, -jəl, -făr′ĭn-jē′əl) *adj.* Situated or occurring behind the pharynx.

ret•ro•rock•et (rĕt′rō-rŏk′ĭt) *n.* A rocket engine used to retard, arrest, or reverse the motion of a vehicle, such as an aircraft.

re•trorse (rĭ-trôrs′, rē′trôrs′) *adj.* Directed or turned back or down. [Lat. *retrōrsus* < *retrōversus* : *retrō-*, retro- + *versus*, p. part. of *vertere*, to turn; see **wer-**[2] in App.] —**re•trorse′ly** *adv.*

ret•ro•spect (rĕt′rə-spĕkt′) *n.* A review, survey, or contemplation of things in the past. ❖ *v.* **-spect•ed, -spect•ing, -spects** —*intr.* **1.** To contemplate the past. **2.** To refer back. —*tr.* To look back on or contemplate (things past). ***—idiom:* in retrospect** Looking backward or reviewing the past. [< Lat. **retrōspectus*, p. part. of *retrōspicere*, to look back at : *retrō-*, retro- + *specere*, to look at; see **spek-** in App.] —**ret′ro•spec′tion** *n.*

ret·ro·spec·tive (rĕt′rə-spĕk′tĭv) adj. 1. Directed to or retrospecting the past. 2. Looking or directed backward. 3. Applying to or influencing the past; retroactive. 4. Of, relating to, or being a retrospective: a retrospective exhibition. ❖ n. An exhibition or performance of works produced by an artist over a considerable period. —**ret′ro·spec′tive·ly** adv.

re·trous·sé (rə-trōō-sā′, rĕt′rōō-) adj. Turned up at the end. Used of the nose. [Fr., p. part. of retrousser, to turn back < OFr. : re-, re- + torser, trousser, to tie in a bundle (prob. < VLat. *torsāre < *torsus, twisted, var. of Lat. tortus, p. part. of torquēre, to twist; see TORQUE¹).]

ret·ro·ver·sion (rĕt′rō-vûr′zhən, -shən) n. 1. A turning or tilting backward. 2. The state of being turned or tilted back. [< Lat. retrōversus, retrorse. See RETRORSE.]

ret·ro·vi·rus (rĕt′rō-vī′rəs, rĕt′rə-vī′-) n., pl. -rus·es Any of a group of viruses that contain RNA and reverse transcriptase, including the AIDS virus. —**ret′ro·vi′ral** adj.

re·try (rē-trī′) tr.v. -tried, -try·ing, -tries To try again.

ret·si·na (rĕt′sĭ-nə, rĕt-sē′nə) n. A Greek white or rosé wine flavored with pine resin. [Mod.Gk., prob. < Ital. resina, resin < Lat. rēsīna. See RESIN.]

re·turn (rĭ-tûrn′) v. -turned, -turn·ing, -turns —intr. 1. To go or come back, as to an earlier condition or place. 2. To revert in speech, thought, or practice. 3. To revert to a former owner. 4. To answer or respond. —tr. 1. To send, put, or carry back. 2a. To give or send back in reciprocation. b. To give back to the owner. c. To reflect or send back. 3. To produce or yield (profit or interest) as a payment for labor, investment, or expenditure. 4. Law a. To submit (an official report, for example) to a judge or other person in authority. b. To render or deliver (a writ, for example) to the proper officer or court of law. 5. To elect or reelect, as to a legislative body. 6. Games To respond to (a partner's lead) by leading the same suit in cards. 7. Architecture To turn away from or place at an angle to the previous line of direction. 8a. Sports To send back (a tennis ball, for example) to one's opponent. b. Football To run with (the ball) after a kickoff, punt, interception, or fumble. ❖ n. 1a. The act or condition of going, coming, bringing, or sending back. b. The act of bringing or sending something back to a previous place, condition, or owner. 2a. Something brought or sent back. b. returns Merchandise returned, as to a retailer by a consumer. c. Something that goes or comes back. 3. A recurrence, as of a periodic event. 4. Something exchanged for that received; repayment. 5. A reply; a response. 6a. The profit made on an exchange of goods. b. A profit or yield, as from labor or investments. Often used in the plural. c. Output or yield per unit rather than cost per unit, as in manufacturing. 7a. A report, list, or set of statistics, esp. one that is formal or official. b. A report on the vote in an election. Often used in the plural. c. Chiefly British An election. 8. Games A lead in certain card games that responds to the lead of one's partner. 9. Sports In tennis and certain other sports: a. The act of returning the ball back to one's opponent. b. The ball thus sent back. 10. Football a. The act of returning the ball. b. The yardage so gained. 11. Architecture a. The extension of a molding, projection, or other part at an angle (usu. 90°) to the main part. b. A part of a building set at an angle to the façade. 12a. A turn, bend, or similar reversal of direction, as in a stream or road. b. A pipe or conduit for carrying something, esp. water, back to its starting point. 13. The key or mechanism on a machine, such as a typewriter or computer, that positions the carriage, cursor, or printing element at the beginning of a new line. 14. Chiefly British A roundtrip ticket. 15. Law a. The bringing or sending back of a writ or other document, generally with a short written report on it, by an officer to the court from which it was issued. b. A certified report, as by an election official. 16. A formal tax statement on the required official form indicating taxable income, allowed deductions, exemptions, and the computed tax that is due. ❖ adj. 1. Of, relating to, or bringing about a going or coming back to a place or situation. 2. Given, sent, or done in reciprocation or exchange. 3. Performed, presented, or taking place again. 4. Used on or for returning. 5. Returning or affording return or recirculation. 6. Relating to or being a roundtrip ticket. 7a. Reversing or changing direction. b. Having or formed by a reversal or change in direction; returning on itself, as a bend in a road or stream. —idiom: **in return** In repayment or reciprocation. [ME retornen < OFr. retourner < VLat. *retornāre : Lat. re-, re- + Lat. tornāre, to turn in a lathe; see TURN.] —**re·turn′er** n.

re·turn·a·ble (rĭ-tûr′nə-bəl) adj. That can be returned or brought back: returnable bottles. ❖ n. An empty beverage container that may be returned for refund of a deposit.

re·turn·ee (rĭ-tûr′nē′) n. 1. One who returns, as from a journey or to school after a long absence. 2. A person returning from military duty overseas. See Usage Note at -ee¹.

re·tuse (rĭ-tōōs′, -tyōōs′) adj. Botany Having a rounded or obtuse apex with a central shallow notch. [Lat. retūsus, p. part. of retundere, to beat back : re-, re- + tundere, to beat.]

Reu·ben¹ (rōō′bən) In the Bible, a son of Jacob and Leah and the forebear of one of the tribes of Israel.

Reu·ben² (rōō′bən) n. A hot sandwich consisting of corned beef, Swiss cheese, and sauerkraut usu. served on rye bread. [< name Reuben.]

re·u·ni·fy (rē-yōō′nə-fī′) tr.v. -fied, -fy·ing, -fies To cause (a group, party, state, or sect) to become unified again after being divided. —**re·u′ni·fi·ca′tion** (-fĭ-kā′shən) n.

re·un·ion (rē-yōōn′yən) n. 1a. The act of reuniting. b. The state of being reunited. 2. A gathering of the members of a group who have been separated: a high school reunion.

Ré·un·ion (rē-yōōn′yən, rā-ü-nyôN′) An island of France in the W Indian Ocean SW of Mauritius; colonized in the mid-1600s and an overseas department since 1946.

re·un·ion·ist (rē-yōōn′yə-nĭst) n. One who advocates reunion, as of divided parties or sects, esp. an advocate of the reunion of the Anglican Church with the Roman Catholic Church. —**re·un′ion·ism** n. —**re·un′ion·is′tic** adj.

re·u·nite (rē′yōō-nīt′) tr. & intr.v. -nit·ed, -nit·ing, -nites To bring or come together again.

re-up (rē-ŭp′) intr.v. -upped, -up·ping, -ups Informal 1. To enlist again for military service. 2. To sign a renewed contract for employment or service.

re·up·take (rē-ŭp′tāk′) n. The reabsorption of a neurotransmitter, such as serotonin, by brain tissue following transmission of a nerve impulse.

Reu·ter (roi′tər), Baron **Paul Julius von** 1816–99. German-born British journalist who founded (1848) Reuter's, one of the first international news agencies.

Reu·ther (rōō′thər), **Walter Philip** 1907–70. Amer. labor leader who was president of the United Auto Workers (1946–70) and the Congress of Industrial Organizations (1952–55).

rev (rĕv) Informal n. A revolution, as of a motor. ❖ v. **revved**, **rev·ving**, **revs** —tr. 1a. To increase the speed of (a motor, for example). b. To accelerate or increase: revving up output. 2. To make livelier or more productive: revving ourselves up for the game. —intr. 1. To operate at an increased speed. 2. To accelerate in quantity or activity.

rev. abbr. 1. revenue 2. reverse 3. review 4. revision 5. revolution

Rev. abbr. 1. Bible Revelation 2. reverend

re·val·u·ate (rē-văl′yōō-āt′) tr.v. -at·ed, -at·ing, -ates 1. To make a new valuation of. 2. To increase the exchange value of (a nation's currency). —**re·val′u·a′tion** n.

re·val·ue (rē-văl′yōō) tr.v. -ued, -u·ing, -ues 1. To revise the value of (a nation's currency). 2. To evaluate anew; reappraise.

re·vamp (rē-vămp′) tr.v. -vamped, -vamp·ing, -vamps 1. To patch up or restore; renovate. 2. To revise or reconstruct (a manuscript, for example). 3. To vamp (a shoe) anew. ❖ n. The act or an instance of revamping; a complete reorganization or revision. —**re·vamp′ment** n.

re·vanche (rə-vänch′, -vänsh′) n. 1. The act of retaliating; revenge. 2. A usu. political policy, esp. of a nation, intended to regain lost territory or standing. [Fr. < OFr. revancher, to revenge : re-, re- + vengier, vencher, to avenge; see REVENGE.] —**re·vanch′ism** (-vän′chĭz-əm, -vän′shĭz-) n. —**re·vanch′ist** adj. & n. —**re·vanch·is′tic** adj.

re·veal¹ (rĭ-vēl′) tr.v. -vealed, -veal·ing, -veals 1a. To make known (something concealed or secret). b. To bring to view; show. 2. To make known by supernatural or divine means. [ME revelen < OFr. reveler < Lat. revēlāre : re-, re- + vēlāre, to cover (< vēlum, veil).] —**re·veal′a·ble** adj. —**re·veal′er** n. —**re·veal′ment** n.

re·veal² (rĭ-vēl′) n. 1a. The part of the side of a window or door opening that is between the outer surface of a wall and the window or door frame. b. The whole side of such an opening; the jamb. 2. The framework of a motor vehicle window. [< ME revalen, to lower < OFr. revaler : re-, re- + avaler, to lower (< a val, down : a, to < Lat. ad + val, valley; see VALE¹).]

re·veal·ing (rĭ-vē′lĭng) adj. Permitting an elucidating glimpse or a perception of something intimate or concealed.

re·veg·e·tate (rē-vĕj′ĭ-tāt′) v. -tat·ed, -tat·ing, -tates —tr. To cause (eroded land, for example) to bear a new cover of vegetation. —intr. To bear a new cover of vegetation.

rev·eil·le (rĕv′ə-lē) n. 1a. The sounding of a bugle early in the morning to awaken and summon people in a camp or garrison. b. The first military formation of the day. 2. A signal to get up out of bed. [Alteration of Fr. réveillez, second pers. pl. imper. of réveiller, to wake < OFr. resveiller : re-, re- + esveiller, to awake (< VLat. *exvigilāre : Lat. ex-, ex- + Lat. vigilāre, to stay awake < vigil, awake).]

rev·el (rĕv′əl) intr.v. -eled, -el·ing, -els also -elled, -el·ling, -els 1. To take great pleasure or delight. 2. To engage in uproarious festivities; make merry. ❖ n. A boisterous festivity or celebration; merrymaking. Often used in the plural. [ME revelen, to carouse < OFr. reveler, to rebel, carouse < Lat. rebellāre, to rebel. See REBEL.] —**rev′el·er, rev′el·ler** n.

rev·e·la·tion (rĕv′ə-lā′shən) n. 1a. The act of revealing or disclosing. b. Something revealed, esp. a dramatic disclosure of something not previously known. 2. Theology A manifestation of divine will or truth. 3. Revelation Bible See table at Bible. [ME revelacion < OFr. revelation < Lat. revēlātiō, revēlātiōn- < revēlātus, p. part. of revēlāre, to reveal. See REVEAL¹.]

rev·e·la·tor (rĕv′ə-lā′tər) n. One who reveals, esp. one who reveals divine will.

rev·e·la·to·ry (rĕv′ə-lə-tôr′ē, -tōr′ē, rĭ-vĕl′ə-) adj. Of, relating to, or containing a revelation.

ă	pat	oi	boy
ā	pay	ou	out
âr	care	ŏŏ	took
ä	father	ōō	boot
ĕ	pet	ŭ	cut
ē	be	ûr	urge
ĭ	pit	th	thin
ī	pie	th	this
îr	pier	hw	which
ŏ	pot	zh	vision
ō	toe	ə	about,
ô	paw		item

Stress marks:
′ (primary);
′ (secondary); as in
lexicon (lĕk′sĭ-kŏn′)

rev•el•ry (rĕv′əl-rē) *n., pl.* **-ries** Boisterous merrymaking. —**rev′el•rous** (-rəs) *adj.*

rev•e•nant (rĕv′ə-nənt) *n.* **1.** One that returns after a lengthy absence. **2.** One who returns after death. [Fr. < pr. part. of *revenir,* to return < OFr. See REVENUE.]

re•venge (rĭ-vĕnj′) *tr.v.* **-venged, -veng•ing, -veng•es 1.** To punish in return for (injury or insult). **2.** To seek or take vengeance for (someone or oneself); avenge. ❖ *n.* **1.** The act of revenging injuries or wrongs; retaliation. **2.** Something done in vengeance; a retaliatory measure. **3.** A desire for revenge; vindictiveness. **4.** An opportunity to retaliate. [ME *revengen* < OFr. *revengier* : *re-,* re- + *vengier,* to take revenge (< Lat. *vindicāre,* to avenge < *vindex, vindic-,* avenger; see **deik-** in App.).] —**re•veng′er** *n.*

re•venge•ful (rĭ-vĕnj′fəl) *adj.* Full of or given to revenge. —**re•venge′ful•ly** *adv.* —**re•venge′ful•ness** *n.*

rev•e•nue (rĕv′ə-no͞o, -nyo͞o) *n.* **1.** The income of a government from all sources appropriated for the payment of public expenses. **2.** Yield from property or investment; income. **3.** All the income from a particular source. **4.** A governmental department set up to collect public funds. [ME < OFr. < fem. p. part. of *revenir,* to return < Lat. *revenīre* : *re-,* re- + *venīre,* to come; see g*w*ā- in App.]

revenue bond *n.* A bond issued by an agency commissioned to finance the building or improving of a public property, such as a bridge, the revenue from which will pay for the bond.

rev•e•nu•er (rĕv′ə-no͞o′ər, -nyo͞o′-) *n.* **1.** *Informal* A government agent in charge of collecting revenue, esp. one responsible for halting the unlawful distilling or bootlegging of alcohol. **2.** A lightly armed motorboat used by revenuers.

revenue sharing *n.* Distribution of a portion of federal tax revenues to state and municipal governments.

revenue stamp *n.* A stamp affixed to an item as proof that a government tax has been paid.

revenue tariff *n.* A tariff imposed chiefly to generate public revenue.

re•verb (rĭ-vûrb′) *Informal n.* (also rē′vûrb′) **1.** A reverberative effect produced in recorded music by electronic means. **2.** A device used for producing this effect. ❖ *intr.* & *tr.v.* **-verbed, -verb•ing, -verbs** To reverberate or cause to reverberate.

re•ver•ber•ant (rĭ-vûr′bər-ənt) *adj.* **1.** Having a tendency to reverberate. **2.** Characterized by reverberation; resounding. —**re•ver′ber•ant•ly** *adv.*

re•ver•ber•ate (rĭ-vûr′bə-rāt′) *v.* **-at•ed, -at•ing, -ates** —*intr.* **1.** To resound in a succession of echoes; reecho. **2.** To have a prolonged or continuing effect: *a friendship that reverberated throughout his life.* **3.** To be repeatedly reflected, as sound waves, heat, or light. **4.** To be forced or driven back; recoil or rebound. —*tr.* **1.** To reecho (a sound). **2.** To reflect (heat or light) repeatedly. **3.** To drive or force back; repel. **4.** To treat (a metal, for example) in a reverberatory furnace. [Lat. *reverberāre, reverberāt-,* to repel : *re-,* re- + *verberāre,* to beat (< *verber,* whip; see wer-² in App.).] —**re•ver′ber•a′tor** *n.*

re•ver•ber•a•tion (rĭ-vûr′bə-rā′shən) *n.* **1a.** The act of reverberating. **b.** The condition of being reverberated. **2a.** Something reverberated. **b.** An echolike trace or repercussion: *Reverberations from the stock market crash were still being felt months later.*

re•ver•ber•a•tive (rĭ-vûr′bə-rā′tĭv, -bər-ə-) *adj.* **1.** Having the nature of reverberation. **2.** Tending to reverberate; reverberant. —**re•ver′ber•a•tive•ly** *adv.*

re•ver•ber•a•to•ry (rĭ-vûr′bər-ə-tôr′ē, -tōr′ē) *adj.* **1.** Produced or operating by reverberation, esp. deflection or diversion, as of flame or heat, onto material being treated. **2.** Of, relating to, or being a reverberatory. ❖ *n., pl.* **-ies** A reverberatory furnace.

reverberatory furnace *n.* A furnace or kiln in which the material is heated by a flame deflected downward from the roof.

re•vere¹ (rĭ-vîr′) *tr.v.* **-vered, -ver•ing, -veres** To regard with awe, deference, and devotion. [Fr. *révérer* < Lat. *reverērī* : *re-,* re- + *verērī,* to respect; see wer-³ in App.]

Paul Revere
detail from a c. 1768–70
portrait by John Singleton
Copley

SYNONYMS *revere, worship, venerate, adore, idolize* These verbs mean to regard with the deepest respect, deference, and esteem. *Revere* suggests awe coupled with profound honor: *"At least one third of the population . . . reveres every sort of holy man"* (Rudyard Kipling). *Worship* implies reverent love and homage rendered to God or a god. In a more general sense it connotes an often uncritical devotion: *"She had worshiped intellect"* (Charles Kingsley). *Venerate* connotes reverence accorded by virtue especially of dignity, character, or age: *"I venerate the memory of my grandfather"* (Horace Walpole). To *adore* is to worship with deep, often rapturous love: *The students adored their caring teacher. Idolize* implies worship like that accorded an object of religious devotion: *He idolizes his wife.*

---

re•vere² (rĭ-vîr′, -vâr′) *n.* Variant of **revers.**

Re•vere (rĭ-vîr′), **Paul** 1735–1818. Amer. silversmith and engraver noted for his Apr. 18, 1775, ride to warn of the British advance on Lexington and Concord, MA.

rev•er•ence (rĕv′ər-əns) *n.* **1.** A feeling of profound awe and respect and often love; veneration. **2.** An act showing respect, esp. a bow or curtsy. **3.** The state of being revered. **4.** **Reverence** Used as a form of address for certain members of the Christian clergy:

Your Reverence. ❖ *tr.v.* **-enced, -enc•ing, -enc•es** To consider or treat with profound awe and respect; venerate. —**rev′er•enc•er** *n.*

rev•er•end (rĕv′ər-ənd) *adj.* **1.** Deserving reverence. **2.** Relating to or characteristic of the clergy; clerical. **3.** **Reverend** Used as a title and form of address for certain clerics in many Christian churches. In formal usage, preceded by *the.* ❖ *n.* *Informal* A cleric or minister. [ME < OFr. < Lat. *reverendus,* gerundive of *reverērī,* to revere. See REVERE¹.]

rev•er•ent (rĕv′ər-ənt) *adj.* Marked by, feeling, or expressing reverence. [ME < OFr. < Lat. *reverēns, reverent-,* pr. part. of *reverērī,* to revere.] —**rev′er•ent•ly** *adv.*

rev•er•en•tial (rĕv′ə-rĕn′shəl) *adj.* **1.** Expressing reverence; reverent. **2.** Inspiring reverence. —**rev′er•en′tial•ly** *adv.*

rev•er•ie (rĕv′ə-rē) *n.* **1.** A state of abstracted musing; daydreaming. **2.** A daydream. [ME, revelry < OFr. < *rever,* to dream.]

re•vers also **re•vere** (rĭ-vîr′, -vâr′) *n., pl.* **revers** also **-veres** (-vîrz′, -vârz′) A part of a garment, such as a lapel, turned back to show the reverse side. [Fr. < OFr., reverse. See REVERSE.]

re•ver•sal (rĭ-vûr′səl) *n.* **1a.** The act or an instance of reversing. **b.** The state of being reversed. **2.** A usu. adverse change in fortune. **3.** *Law* The act or an instance of changing or setting aside a lower court's decision by a higher court.

re•verse (rĭ-vûrs′) *adj.* **1a.** Turned backward in position, direction, or order. **b.** Having the back showing. **2.** Moving, acting, or organized in a manner contrary to the usual. **3.** Causing backward movement: *a reverse gear.* **4.** *Printing* Printed so that the normally colored part appears white against a colored or black background. ❖ *n.* **1.** The opposite or contrary. **2a.** The back or rear part. **b.** The side of a coin or medal that does not carry the principal design; the verso. **3.** A change to an opposite position, condition, or direction. **4.** A change in fortune from better to worse; a setback. **5a.** A mechanism, such as a car gear, that is used to reverse movement. **b.** The position or operating condition of such a mechanism. **c.** Movement in an opposite direction. **6.** *Football* An offensive play in which a back running in one direction executes a handoff to a back running in the opposite direction. ❖ *v.* **-versed, -vers•ing, -vers•es** —*tr.* **1.** To turn around to the opposite direction. **2.** To turn inside out or upside down. **3.** To exchange the positions of; transpose. **4.** *Law* To revoke or annul (a decree, for example). **5a.** To cause to adopt a contrary viewpoint. **b.** To change to the opposite. **6.** To cause (an engine or a mechanism) to function in reverse. —*intr.* **1.** To turn or move in the opposite direction. **2.** To reverse the action of an engine. —*idiom:* **reverse (one's) field** To turn and proceed in the opposite direction. [ME *revers* < OFr. < Lat. *reversus,* p. part. of *revertere,* to turn back. See REVERT.] —**re•verse′ly** *adv.* —**re•vers′er** *n.*

reverse discrimination *n.* Discrimination against members of a dominant or majority group, esp. when resulting from policies established to correct discrimination against members of a minority or disadvantaged group.

reverse dive *n.* A dive in which the diver leaves the springboard or platform facing the water and then rotates the body backward.

reverse fault *n.* A geologic fault in which the hanging wall has moved upward relative to the footwall.

reverse mortgage *n.* A mortgage in which a homeowner, usu. an elderly or retired person, borrows money in the form of annual payments which are charged against the equity of the home.

reverse osmosis *n.* A method of producing pure water by forcing saline or impure water through a semipermeable membrane across which salts or impurities cannot pass.

reverse transcriptase *n.* A polymerase found esp. in retroviruses that catalyzes the formation of DNA from an RNA template in the process of reverse transcription.

reverse transcription *n.* The process by which DNA is synthesized from an RNA template.

re•vers•i•ble (rĭ-vûr′sə-bəl) *adj.* **1.** That can be reversed, as: **a.** Finished so as to be usable on both sides. **b.** Wearable with either side turned outward. **2.** *Chemistry & Physics* **a.** Capable of assuming or producing either of two states: *a reversible cell.* **b.** Of or relating to a process, such as a chemical reaction or a phase change, in which the system undergoing the process can be returned to its original state. ❖ *n.* A reversible fabric or garment. —**re•vers′i•bil′i•ty** *n.* —**re•vers′i•bly** *adv.*

re•ver•sion (rĭ-vûr′zhən) *n.* **1.** A return to a former state, belief, or interest. **2.** A turning away or in the opposite direction; a reversal. **3.** *Genetics* A return to the normal phenotype, usu. by a second mutation. **4.** *Law* **a.** The return of an estate to the grantor or to the grantor's heirs after the grant has expired. **b.** The estate thus returned. **c.** The right to succeed to an estate.

re•ver•sion•er (rĭ-vûr′zhə-nər) *n.* *Law* A party entitled to receive an estate in reversion.

re•vert (rĭ-vûrt′) *intr.v.* **-vert•ed, -vert•ing, -verts 1.** To return to a former condition, practice, subject, or belief. See Usage Note at redundancy. **2.** *Law* To return to the former owner or his or her heirs. Used of money or property. **3.** *Genetics* To undergo reversion. [ME *reverten* < OFr. *revertir* < VLat. **revertīre,* var. of Lat. *revertere* : *re-,* re- + *vertere,* to turn; see wer-² in App.] —**re•vert′er** *n.* —**re•vert′i•ble** *adj.* —**re•vert′ive** *adj.*

re•ver•tant (rĭ-vûr′tnt) *adj.* Having reverted to the normal phenotype, usu. by a second mutation: *revertant cells.* ❖ *n.* A revertant organism, cell, or strain.

re•vest (rē-vĕst′) *tr.v.* **-vest•ed, -vest•ing, -vests 1.** To invest (someone) again with power or ownership; reinstate. **2.** To vest (power, for example) once again in a person or agency.

re•vet (rĭ-vĕt′) *v.* **-vet•ted, -vet•ting, -vets** —*tr.* To retain (an embankment, for example) with a layer of concrete or other supporting material. —*intr.* To construct a revetment. [Fr. *revêtir* < OFr. *revestir*, to clothe again < Lat. *revestīre* : *re-*, re- + *vestīre*, to clothe (< *vestis*, garment; see **wes-**[2] in App.).]

re•vet•ment (rĭ-vĕt′mənt) *n.* **1.** A facing, as of masonry, used to support an embankment. **2.** A barricade against explosives.

re•view (rĭ-vyo͞o′) *v.* **-viewed, -view•ing, -views** —*tr.* **1.** To look over, study, or examine again. **2.** To consider retrospectively; look back on. **3.** To examine critically. **4.** To write or give a critical report on (a new work, for example). **5.** *Law* To reexamine (an action or determination) judicially, esp. in a higher court, in order to correct possible errors. **6.** To subject to a formal inspection, esp. a military inspection. —*intr.* **1.** To go over or restudy material. **2.** To write critical reviews. ❖ *n.* **1.** A reexamination or reconsideration. **2.** A retrospective view or survey. **3a.** A restudying of subject matter. **b.** An exercise for use in restudying material. **4.** An inspection or examination for the purpose of evaluation. **5a.** A report or essay giving a critical estimate of a work or performance. **b.** A periodical devoted to current affairs, literature, or art. **6a.** A formal military inspection. **b.** A formal military ceremony honoring a person or occasion. **7.** *Law* A judicial reexamination, esp. by a higher court, of an action or determination. **8.** A revue. [Prob. < ME, inspection of military forces < OFr. *revue*, review < fem. p. part. of *reveeir*, to see again < Lat. *revidēre* : *re-*, re- + *vidēre*, to see; see **weid-** in App.] —**re•view′a•ble** *adj.*

re•view•er (rĭ-vyo͞o′ər) *n.* One who reviews, esp. one who writes critical reviews, as for a newspaper or magazine.

re•vile (rĭ-vīl′) *v.* **-viled, -vil•ing, -viles** —*tr.* To assail with abusive language; vituperate. —*intr.* To use abusive language. [ME *revilen* < OFr. *reviler* : *re-*, re- + *vil*, vile; see VILE.] —**re•vile′ment** *n.* —**re•vil′er** *n.* —**re•vil′ing•ly** *adv.*

re•vis•al (rĭ-vī′zəl) *n.* The act or an instance of revising.

re•vise (rĭ-vīz′) *tr.v.* **-vised, -vis•ing, -vis•es 1.** To prepare a newly edited version of (a text). **2.** To reconsider and change or modify: *I revised my opinion.* See Syns at **correct.** ❖ *n.* (rē′vīz′, rĭ-vīz′) *Printing* A proof made from an earlier proof on which corrections have been made. [Lat. *revīsere*, to visit again, look at again : *re-*, re- + *vīsere*, freq. of *vidēre*, to see; see REVIEW.] —**re•vis′a•ble** *adj.* —**re•vis′er, re•vi′sor** *n.*

Re•vised Standard Version (rĭ-vīzd′) *n.* A revision of the American Standard Version of the Bible, completed in 1952 and further revised in 1991.

Revised Version *n.* A British and American revision of the King James Version of the Bible, completed in 1885.

re•vi•sion (rĭ-vĭzh′ən) *n.* **1.** The act or process of revising. **2.** A revised or new version. —**re•vi′sion•ar′y** *adj.*

re•vi•sion•ism (rĭ-vĭzh′ə-nĭz′əm) *n.* Advocacy of the revision of an accepted, usu. long-standing view, theory, or doctrine, esp. a revision of a political doctrine or a view concerning history. —**re•vi′sion•ist** *adj.* & *n.*

re•vis•it (rē-vĭz′ĭt) *tr.v.* **-it•ed, -it•ing, -its** To visit again. ❖ *n.* A second or repeated visit. —**re′vis•i•ta′tion** *n.*

re•vi•so•ry (rĭ-vī′zə-rē) *adj.* Of, relating to, effecting, or having the power of revision.

re•vi•tal•ize (rē-vīt′l-īz′) *tr.v.* **-ized, -iz•ing, -iz•es** To impart new life or vigor to. —**re•vi′tal•i•za′tion** (-ĭ-zā′shən) *n.*

re•viv•al (rĭ-vī′vəl) *n.* **1a.** The act or an instance of reviving. **b.** The condition of being revived. **2.** A restoration to use, acceptance, activity, or vigor after obscurity or quiescence. **3.** A new presentation of a previously produced play, movie, opera, or similar work. **4a.** A time of reawakened interest in religion. **b.** A meeting or series of meetings held to revive religious faith, typified by impassioned preaching and public testimony. **5.** *Law* Renewal of validity or effect, as of a contract.

re•viv•al•ism (rĭ-vī′və-lĭz′əm) *n.* **1.** The spirit or activities characteristic of religious revivals. **2.** A desire or an inclination to revive what belongs to an earlier time.

re•viv•al•ist (rĭ-vī′və-lĭst) *n.* **1.** One who promotes or leads religious revivals. **2.** One who revives practices or ideas of an earlier time. —**re•viv′al•ist, re•viv′al•is′tic** *adj.*

re•vive (rĭ-vīv′) *v.* **-vived, -viv•ing, -vives** —*tr.* **1.** To restore to life or consciousness; resuscitate. **2.** To impart new health, vigor, or spirit to. **3.** To restore to use, currency, activity, or notice. **4.** To restore the validity or effectiveness of. **5.** To renew in the mind; recall. **6.** To present (an old play, for example) again. —*intr.* **1.** To return to life or consciousness. **2.** To regain health, vigor, or spirit. **3.** To return to use, currency, or notice. **4.** To return to validity, effectiveness, or operative condition. [ME *reviven* < OFr. *revivre* < Lat. *revīvere*, to live again : *re-*, re- + *vīvere*, to live; see **g^{w}eiə-** in App.] —**re•viv′a•ble** *adj.* —**re•viv′er** *n.*

re•viv•i•fy (rē-vĭv′ə-fī′) *tr.v.* **-fied, -fy•ing, -fies** To impart new life, energy, or spirit to. [Fr. *revivifier* < OFr., to come back to life < Lat. **revīvificāre*, to revivify : Lat. *re-*, re- + Lat. *vīvificāre*, to vivify; see VIVIFY.] —**re•viv′i•fi•ca′tion** (-fĭ-kā′shən) *n.*

rev•o•ca•ble (rĕv′ə-kə-bəl) also **re•vok•a•ble** (rĭ-vō′-) *adj.* That can be revoked: *a revocable order.*

rev•o•ca•tion (rĕv′ə-kā′shən) *n.* The act or an instance of revoking. [ME *revocacion* < OFr. < Lat. *revocātiō*, *revocātiōn-* < *revocātus*, p. part. of *revocāre*, to call back. See REVOKE.] —**rev′o•ca•to′ry** (rĕv′ə-kə-tôr′ē, -tōr′ē) *adj.*

re•voke (rĭ-vōk′) *v.* **-voked, -vok•ing, -vokes** —*tr.* To void or annul by recalling, withdrawing, or reversing. —*intr.* *Games* To fail to follow suit in cards when required and able to do so. [ME *revoken* < OFr. *revoquer* < Lat. *revocāre* : *re-*, re- + *vocāre*, to call; see **wek^w-** in App.] —**re•vok′er** *n.*

re•volt (rĭ-vōlt′) *v.* **-volt•ed, -volt•ing, -volts** —*intr.* **1.** To attempt to overthrow the authority of the state; rebel. **2.** To oppose or refuse to accept something. **3a.** To feel disgust or repugnance. **b.** To turn away in revulsion or abhorrence. —*tr.* To fill with disgust or abhorrence; repel. See Syns at **disgust.** ❖ *n.* **1.** An uprising, esp. against state authority; a rebellion. **2.** An act of protest or rejection. **3.** The state of being in rebellion. [Fr. *revolter* < Ital. *rivoltare*, to turn round < VLat. **revolvitāre*, freq. of Lat. *revolvere*, to turn over. See REVOLVE.] —**re•volt′er** *n.*

re•volt•ing (rĭ-vōl′tĭng) *adj.* Causing abhorrence or disgust. —**re•volt′ing•ly** *adv.*

rev•o•lute (rĕv′ə-lo͞ot′) *adj.* *Botany* Rolled backward from the tip or margins to the undersurface: *a revolute leaf.* [Lat. *revolūtus*, p. part. of *revolvere*, to roll back. See REVOLVE.]

rev•o•lu•tion (rĕv′ə-lo͞o′shən) *n.* **1a.** Orbital motion about a point, esp. as distinguished from axial rotation. **b.** A turning or rotational motion about an axis. **c.** A single complete cycle of such orbital or axial motion. **2.** The overthrow and replacement of a government. **3.** A sudden or momentous change in a situation. **4.** *Geology* A time of major crustal deformation, when folds and faults are formed. [Ult. < LLat. *revolūtiō*, *revolūtiōn-* < Lat. *revolūtus*, p. part. of *revolvere*, to turn over. See REVOLVE.]

rev•o•lu•tion•ar•y (rĕv′ə-lo͞o′shə-nĕr′ē) *adj.* **1a.** often **Revolutionary** Relating to or being a revolution: *revolutionary war.* **b.** Bringing about or supporting a political or social revolution. **2.** Characterized by or resulting in radical change. ❖ *n., pl.* **-ies 1.** A militant in the struggle for revolution. **2.** A supporter of revolutionary principles. —**rev′o•lu′tion•ar′i•ly** *adv.* —**rev′o•lu′tion•ar′i•ness** *n.*

Revolutionary War *n.* The American Revolution.

rev•o•lu•tion•ist (rĕv′ə-lo͞o′shə-nĭst) *n.* One who favors or is engaged in a revolution. —**rev′o•lu′tion•ist** *adj.*

rev•o•lu•tion•ize (rĕv′ə-lo͞o′shə-nīz′) *tr.v.* **-ized, -iz•ing, -iz•es 1.** To bring about a radical change in. **2.** To subject to a political or social revolution. **3.** To fill with revolutionary principles. —**rev′o•lu′tion•iz′er** *n.*

re•volve (rĭ-vŏlv′) *v.* **-volved, -volv•ing, -volves** —*intr.* **1.** To orbit a central point. **2.** To turn on an axis; rotate. **3.** To recur in cycles or periodically. **4.** To be held in the mind and considered in turn. **5.** To be centered. —*tr.* **1.** To cause to revolve. **2.** To ponder or reflect on. [ME *revolven*, to change direction < OFr. *revolver*, to reflect upon < Lat. *revolvere*, to turn over, roll back, reflect upon : *re-*, re- + *volvere*, to roll; see **wel-** in App.] —**re•volv′a•ble** *adj.*

re•volv•er (rĭ-vŏl′vər) *n.* **1.** A pistol having a revolving cylinder with several cartridge chambers that may be fired in succession. **2.** One that revolves, as a part of a mechanism.

re•volv•ing (rĭ-vŏl′vĭng) *adj.* **1.** Tending to revolve or happen repeatedly. **2.** Available at regular intervals.

revolving credit *n.* Credit repeatedly available up to a specified amount as periodic repayments are made.

revolving door *n.* **1.** A door, as in the entrance of a building, usu. consisting of four rigid upright sections interconnected at right angles and rotating about a central upright pivot. **2.** *Informal* An organization, institution, or place whose members or population remain only a short time.

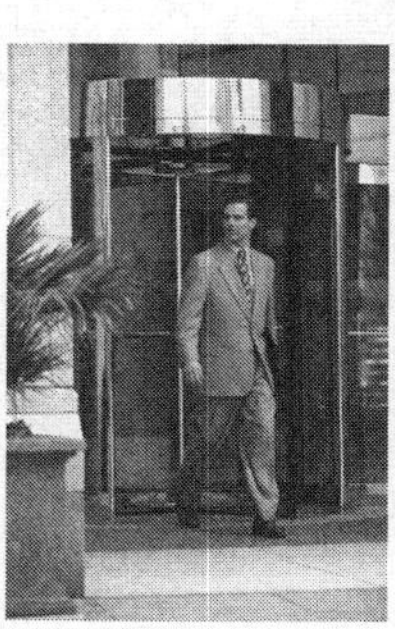

revolving door

revolving fund *n.* A fund established for a certain purpose, such as making loans, with the stipulation that repayments to the fund may be used anew for the same purpose.

re•vue (rĭ-vyo͞o′) *n.* An often satirical musical show consisting of skits, songs, and dances. [Fr. < OFr., review. See REVIEW.]

re•vul•sion (rĭ-vŭl′shən) *n.* **1.** A sudden strong change or reaction in feeling, esp. a feeling of violent disgust or loathing. **2.** A withdrawing or turning away from something. [Lat. *revulsiō*, *revulsiōn-* < *revulsus*, p. part. of *revellere*, to tear back : *re-*, re- + *vellere*, to tear.] —**re•vul′sive** *adj.*

Rev. Ver. *abbr.* *Bible* Revised Version

re•ward (rĭ-wôrd′) *n.* **1.** Something given or received in recompense for worthy behavior or in retribution for evil acts. **2.** Money offered or given for a special service, such as the return of a lost article. **3.** A satisfying return or result; profit. **4.** *Psychology* The return for performance of a desired behavior. ❖ *tr.v.* **-ward•ed, -ward•ing, -wards 1.** To give a reward to or for. **2.** To satisfy or gratify; recompense. [ME < AN < *rewarder*, to take notice of : *re-*, intensive pref. (< Lat.; see RE–) + *warder*, to guard, watch over (of Gmc. orig.).] —**re•ward′a•ble** *adj.* —**re•ward′er** *n.*

re•ward•ing (rĭ-wôr′dĭng) *adj.* **1.** Offering or likely to offer satisfaction or gratification. **2.** Affording profit; remunerative. **3.** Constituting a reward. —**re•ward′ing•ly** *adv.*

ă	pat	oi	boy
ā	pay	ou	out
âr	care	o͝o	took
ä	father	o͞o	boot
ĕ	pet	ŭ	cut
ē	be	ûr	urge
ĭ	pit	th	thin
ī	pie	*th*	this
îr	pier	hw	which
ŏ	pot	zh	vision
ō	toe	ə	about, item
ô	paw		

Stress marks:
′ (primary);
′ (secondary), as in
lexicon (lĕk′sĭ-kŏn′)

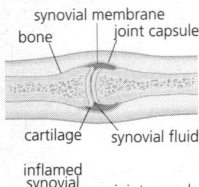

synovial membrane
bone — joint capsule

cartilage — synovial fluid

inflamed synovial membrane — joint capsule

eroded cartilage — synovial fluid

rheumatoid arthritis
top: normal finger joint
bottom: arthritic finger joint

rhinoceros
black rhinoceros
Diceros bicornis

rhinoceros beetle
male rhinoceros beetle

re•wind (rē-wīnd′) *tr.v.* **-wound** (-wound′), **-wind•ing, -winds** 1. To wind again or anew. 2. To reverse the winding of (audiotape, videotape, or film). ❖ *n.* (rē′wīnd′, rē-wīnd′) 1. The act or process of rewinding. 2. Something that rewinds or is rewound. 3. A control mechanism for rewinding (tape or film). —**re•wind′er** *n.*

re•wire (rē-wīr′) *v.* **-wired, -wir•ing, -wires** —*tr.* To provide with new wiring. —*intr.* To install new wiring.

re•word (rē-wûrd′) *tr.v.* **-word•ed, -word•ing, -words** 1a. To change the wording of. b. To express again in different words. 2. To express again in the same words; repeat.

re•work (rē-wûrk′) *tr.v.* **-worked, -work•ing, -works** 1. To work over again; revise. 2. To subject to a repeated or new process. ❖ *n.* (rē′wûrk′) Something reworked.

re•write (rē-rīt′) *v.* **-wrote** (-rōt′), **-writ•ten** (-rĭt′n), **-writ•ing, -writes** —*tr.* 1. To write again, esp. in a different or improved form; revise. 2. To put (material submitted to a newspaper or magazine) in a form suitable for publishing. 3. *Computer Science* To save (a usu. altered file) over its most recent version in the same storage location. —*intr.* To make revisions in written material. ❖ *n.* (rē′rīt′) 1. The act or an instance of rewriting. 2. Something rewritten. —**re•writ′a•ble, re•write′a•ble** *adj.* —**re•writ′er** *n.*

Reye's syndrome (rīz, rāz) *n.* An acute encephalopathy characterized by fever, vomiting, fatty infiltration of the liver, disorientation, and coma, occurring mainly in children and usu. following a viral infection, such as influenza or chicken pox. [After Ralph Douglas Kenneth *Reye* (1912–78), Australian pediatrician.]

Rey•kja•vík (rā′kyə-vēk′, -vīk′) The cap. of Iceland, in the SW part; traditionally founded 874. Pop. 101,418.

Rey•mont (rā′mônt′, -mônt′), **Wladyslaw Stanislaw** 1867–1925. Polish writer who won the 1924 Nobel Prize for literature.

Rey•nard or **rey•nard** (rā′nərd, -närd′, rĕn′ərd) *n.* A fox. [ME *Renard, Reynard* < OFr. *Renart* and MDu. *Reynaert,* the name of the fox in the beast epic *Roman de Renart.*]

Reyn•olds (rĕn′əldz), Sir **Joshua** 1723–92. British portrait painter whose subjects included the Prince of Wales (1783).

Rey•no•sa (rā-nō′sə) A city of E Mexico on the Rio Grande ENE of Monterrey. Pop. 194,693.

re•ze•ro (rē-zîr′ō, -zē′rō) *tr.v.* **-roed, -ro•ing, -roes** To reset (a gauge or control) back to zero.

re•zone (rē-zōn′) *tr.v.* **-zoned, -zon•ing, -zones** To change the zoning classification of (a neighborhood or property, for example). —**re′zone′** *n.*

Rf The symbol for the element **rutherfordium.**

RF *abbr.* 1. radio frequency 2a. right field b. right fielder

R factor *n.* Any of various plasmids that transmit genes involved in resistance to antibiotics from one bacterium to another. [R(ESISTANCE).]

RFD *abbr.* rural free delivery

Rh[1] (är′āch′) *adj.* Of or relating to the Rh factor.

Rh[2] The symbol for the element **rhodium.**

RH *abbr.* 1. relative humidity 2. right-hand

rhab•dom (răb′dəm, -dŏm′) *n.* A transparent rod in the center of each ommatidium in the compound eye of an arthropod. [< Gk. *rhabdōma,* bundle of rods < Gk. *rhabdos,* rod. See RHABDOMANCY.]

rhab•do•man•cy (răb′də-măn′sē) *n.* Divination by means of a wand or rod, esp. for discovering underground water or ores. [LGk. *rhabdomanteia* : Gk. *rhabdos,* rod; see **wer-²** in App. + Gk. *-manteia,* -mancy.] —**rhab′do•man′cer** *n.*

rhab•do•my•o•ma (răb′dō-mī-ō′mə) *n., pl.* **-mas** or **-ma•ta** (-mə-tə) A tumor in striated muscle fibers. [Gk. *rhabdos,* rod; see RHABDOMANCY + MYOMA.]

rhab•do•vi•rus (răb′dō-vī′rəs) *n., pl.* **-rus•es** Any of a group of RNA-containing plant and animal viruses, which includes the rabies virus. [Gk. *rhabdos,* rod; see **wer-²** in App. + VIRUS.]

Rhad•a•man•thine (răd′ə-măn′thĭn, -thĭn′) *adj.* Strictly and uncompromisingly just. [< RHADAMANTHUS.]

Rhad•a•man•thus also **Rhad•a•man•thys** (răd′ə-măn′thəs) *n. Greek Mythology* A son of Zeus and Europa who, in reward for his exemplary sense of justice, was made a judge of the underworld after his death.

Rhae•ti•a (rē′shē-ə, -shə) An ancient Roman province in present-day E Switzerland and W Austria. —**Rhae′tian** *adj. & n.*

Rhaetian Alps A range of the central Alps primarily in E Switzerland rising to 4,051.6 m (13,284 ft).

Rhae•to-Ro•mance (rē′tō-rō-măns′) *n.* A group of three Romance dialects, including Romansh, spoken in southern Switzerland, northern Italy, and the Tyrol. [Lat. *Rhaetus,* of Rhaetia, a Roman province + ROMANCE.]

rha•phe (rā′fē) *n.* Variant of **raphe.**

rhap•sod•ic (răp-sŏd′ĭk) also **rhap•sod•i•cal** (-ĭ-kəl) *adj.* 1. Of, like, or characteristic of a rhapsody. 2. Immoderately impassioned or enthusiastic. —**rhap•sod′i•cal•ly** *adv.*

rhap•so•dist (răp′sə-dĭst) *n.* 1. One who uses extravagantly enthusiastic or impassioned language. 2. also **rhap•sode** (-sōd′) One who recited epic and other poetry, esp. professionally, in ancient Greece.

rhap•so•dize (răp′sə-dīz′) *v.* **-dized, -diz•ing, -diz•es** —*intr.* To express oneself in an immoderately enthusiastic manner. —*tr.* To recite (something) in the manner of a rhapsody.

rhap•so•dy (răp′sə-dē) *n., pl.* **-dies** 1. Exalted or excessive enthusiasm in speech or writing. 2. A literary work written in an impassioned or exalted style. 3. A state of elated bliss; ecstasy. 4. *Music* A composition of irregular form and often improvisatory character. 5. An ancient Greek epic poem or a portion of one suitable for uninterrupted recitation. [Lat. *rhapsōdia,* section of an epic poem < Gk. *rhapsōidiā* < *rhapsōidein,* to recite poems : *rhaptein, rhaps-,* to sew; see **wer-²** in App. + *aoidē, ōidē,* song.]

rhat•a•ny (răt′n-ē) *n., pl.* **-nies** 1. Either of two South American shrubs (*Krameria lappacea* or *K. argentea*) having bilaterally symmetrical flowers, spiny globose fruits, and thick roots. 2. The dried root of either of these plants, used as an astringent and in dental preparations, such as toothpaste. [Am.Sp. *ratania,* poss. < Quechua *ratana,* to thin, unite.]

rhe•a (rē′ə) *n.* Any of several flightless South American birds of the genus *Rhea,* resembling the ostrich but somewhat smaller and having three toes instead of two. [NLat. *Rhea,* genus name, prob. < Lat., the wife of Cronus. See RHEA.]

Rhea *n.* 1. *Greek Mythology* The sister and wife of Cronus and the mother of Demeter, Hades, Hera, Hestia, Poseidon, and Zeus. 2. *Astronomy* A satellite of Saturn. [Lat. < Gk. *Rhea.*]

Rhee (rē), **Syngman** 1875–1965. South Korean politician who became president in 1948 and was forced into exile in 1960.

Rheims or **Reims** (rēmz, răns) A city of NE France ENE of Paris; long the coronation site of French kings. Pop. 180,611.

rheme (rēm) *n. Linguistics* See **comment** 2. [< Gk. *rhēma,* something said, word, subject of a speech (modeled on THEME). See **wer-²** in App.]

Rhen•ish (rĕn′ĭsh) *adj.* Of or relating to the Rhine River or the lands bordering on it. ❖ *n.* See **Rhine wine** 1. [Ult. < Lat. *Rhēnus,* the Rhine.]

rhe•ni•um (rē′nē-əm) *n. Symbol* **Re** A rare dense metallic element with a high melting point used for electrical contacts and with tungsten for high-temperature thermocouples. Atomic number 75; atomic weight 186.2; melting point 3,180°C; boiling point 5,627°C; specific gravity 21.02; valence 1, 2, 3, 4, 5, 6, 7. See table at **element.** [< Lat. *Rhēnus,* the Rhine.]

rheo- *pref.* Current; flow: *rheotaxis.* [< Gk. *rheos,* stream < *rhein,* to flow. See **sreu-** in App.]

rhe•ol•o•gy (rē-ŏl′ə-jē) *n.* The study of the deformation and flow of matter. —**rhe′o•log′i•cal** (rē′ə-lŏj′ĭ-kəl) *adj.* —**rhe′o•log′i•cal•ly** *adv.* —**rhe•ol′o•gist** *n.*

rhe•om•e•ter (rē-ŏm′ĭ-tər) *n.* An instrument for measuring the flow of viscous liquids, such as blood.

rhe•o•stat (rē′ə-stăt′) *n.* A continuously variable electrical resistor used to regulate current. —**rhe′o•stat′ic** *adj.*

rhe•o•tax•is (rē′ə-tăk′sĭs) *n.* Movement of an organism in response to a current of water or air. —**rhe′o•tac′tic** (-tăk′tĭk) *adj.*

rhe•sus (rē′səs) *n.* A rhesus monkey. [Lat. *Rhēsus,* a mythical king of Thrace < Gk. *Rhēsos.*]

Rhesus factor *n.* Rh factor. [Because it was first detected in the blood of the rhesus monkey.]

rhesus monkey *n.* A brownish monkey (*Macaca mulatta*) of India, used extensively in biological and medical research.

rhe•tor (rē′tôr′, -tər) *n.* 1. A teacher of rhetoric. 2. An orator. [ME *rether* < Lat. *rhētor* < Gk. *rhētōr.* See **wer-¹** in App.]

rhet•o•ric (rĕt′ər-ĭk) *n.* 1a. The art or study of using language effectively and persuasively. b. A treatise or book on this art. 2. Skill in using language effectively and persuasively. 3a. A style of speaking or writing, esp. the language of a particular subject: *political rhetoric.* b. Language that is elaborate, pretentious, insincere, or intellectually vacuous: *His talk is mere rhetoric.* 4. Verbal communication; discourse. [ME *rethorik* < OFr. *rethorique* < Lat. *rhētoricā* < Gk. *rhētorikē* (*tekhnē*), rhetorical (art), fem. of *rhētorikos,* rhetorical < *rhētōr.* See RHETOR.]

rhe•tor•i•cal (rĭ-tôr′ĭ-kəl, -tŏr′-) *adj.* 1. Of or relating to rhetoric. 2. Characterized by overelaborate or bombastic rhetoric. —**rhe•tor′i•cal•ly** *adv.*

rhetorical question *n.* A question to which no answer is expected, often used for rhetorical effect.

rhet•o•ri•cian (rĕt′ə-rĭsh′ən) *n.* 1. An expert in or teacher of rhetoric. 2. An eloquent speaker or writer. 3. A person given to verbal extravagance.

rheum (room) *n.* A watery or thin mucous discharge from the eyes or nose. [ME *reume* < OFr. < LLat. *rheuma* < Gk., a flowing, rheum. See **sreu-** in App.] —**rheum′y** *adj.*

rheu•mat•ic (roo-măt′ĭk) *adj.* Of, relating to, or having rheumatism. ❖ *n.* 1. One who has rheumatism. 2. **rheumatics** *Informal* Pains caused by rheumatism. [Ult. < Lat. *rheumaticus,* suffering from rheum < Gk. *rheumatikos* < *rheuma, rheumat-,* stream. See RHEUM.]

rheumatic fever *n.* A severe infectious disease occurring chiefly in children, marked by fever and painful inflammation of the joints and frequently causing permanent damage to the heart.

rheumatic heart disease *n.* Permanent damage to the heart valves caused esp. by repeated attacks of rheumatic fever.

rheu•ma•tism (roo′mə-tĭz′əm) *n.* 1. Any of several pathological conditions of the muscles, tendons, joints, bones, or nerves, characterized by discomfort and disability. **2.** Rheumatoid arthritis. [Lat. *rheumatismus*, rheum < Gk. *rheumatismos* < *rheumatizesthai*, to suffer from rheum < *rheuma, rheumat-*, flow, watery discharge < the body (thought to cause aches and pains). See RHEUM.]

rheu·ma·toid (rōō′mə-toid′) also **rheu·ma·toi·dal** (rōō′mə-toid′l) *adj.* **1.** Of or resembling rheumatism. **2.** Suffering from rheumatism. —**rheu′ma·toi′dal·ly** *adv.*

rheumatoid arthritis *n.* A chronic disease marked by stiffness and inflammation of the joints, weakness, loss of mobility, and deformity.

rheumatoid factor *n.* An immunoglobulin present in the blood serum of many individuals affected by rheumatoid arthritis, used as a means of diagnosing the disease.

rheu·ma·tol·o·gy (rōō′mə-tŏl′ə-jē) *n.* The medical science that deals with rheumatic diseases. —**rheu′ma·tol′o·gist** *n.*

Rh factor *n.* Any of several substances on the surface of red blood cells that induce a strong antigenic response in individuals lacking the substance. [RH(ESUS) FACTOR.]

rhi·nal (rī′nəl) *adj.* Of or relating to the nose; nasal.

Rhine (rīn) A river of W Europe formed by the confluence of two tributaries in E Switzerland and flowing c. 1,319 km (820 mi) through Germany and the Netherlands to the North Sea.

Rhine·land (rīn′lănd′, -lənd) A region along the Rhine R. in W Germany; noted for its vineyards.

rhi·nen·ceph·a·lon (rī′nĕn-sĕf′ə-lŏn′, -lən) *n., pl.* **-la** (-lə) The olfactory region of the brain, located in the cerebrum. —**rhi′nen′ce·phal′ic** (-sə-făl′ĭk) *adj.*

rhine·stone (rīn′stōn′) *n.* A colorless artificial gem of paste or glass, often with facets that sparkle in imitation of a diamond. [After the RHINE (transl. of Fr. *caillou du Rhin : caillou*, pebble + *du*, of the + *Rhin*, Rhine).] —**rhine′stoned′** *adj.*

Rhine wine *n.* **1.** Any of several dry white wines produced in the Rhine Valley. **2.** A similar light dry wine produced elsewhere.

rhi·ni·tis (rī-nī′tĭs) *n.* Inflammation of the nasal mucous membranes.

rhi·no (rī′nō) *n., pl.* **-nos** *Informal* A rhinoceros.

rhino– or **rhin–** *pref.* Nose; nasal: *rhinitis.* [Gk. *rhīno-* < *rhīs, rhīn-*, nose.]

rhi·noc·er·os (rī-nŏs′ər-əs) *n., pl.* **rhinoceros** or **-os·es** Any of several large thick-skinned herbivorous mammals of the family Rhinocerotidae of Africa and Asia, having one or two upright horns on the snout. [ME *rinoceros* < Lat. *rhīnocerōs* < Gk. *rhīnokerōs : rhīno-*, rhino- + *keras*, horn; see ker-¹ in App.]

rhinoceros beetle *n.* Any of various large scarabaeid beetles of the genus *Dynastes* and related genera, characterized by horns on the head and thorax and found in tropical regions.

rhi·nol·o·gy (rī-nŏl′ə-jē) *n.* The anatomy, physiology, and pathology of the nose. —**rhi·nol′o·gist** *n.*

rhi·no·phar·yn·gi·tis (rī′nō-făr′ĭn-jī′tĭs) *n.* Inflammation of the nasal and pharyngeal mucous membranes.

rhi·no·plas·ty (rī′nō-plăs′tē) *n., pl.* **-ties** Plastic surgery of the nose. —**rhi′no·plas′tic** *adj.*

rhi·nos·co·py (rī-nŏs′kə-pē) *n., pl.* **-pies** Examination of the nasal passages by means of a speculum or similar instrument.

rhi·no·vi·rus (rī′nō-vī′rəs) *n., pl.* **-rus·es** Any of a group of picornaviruses that are causative agents of disorders of the respiratory tract, such as the common cold.

rhi·zan·thous (rī-zăn′thəs) *adj.* Bearing flowers directly from the root.

rhizo– or **rhiz–** *pref.* Root: *rhizogenic.* [Greek < *rhiza*, root. See **wrād-** in App.]

rhi·zo·bi·um (rī-zō′bē-əm) *n., pl.* **-bi·a** (-bē-ə) Any of various nitrogen-fixing bacteria of the genus *Rhizobium* that form nodules on leguminous plant roots, as of beans. [NLat. *Rhizobium*, genus name : RHIZO- + Gk. *bios*, life; see gʷeiə- in App.]

rhi·zo·ceph·a·lan (rī′zō-sĕf′ə-lən) *n.* Any of various small aquatic crustaceans of the order Rhizocephala that are parasitic on other crustaceans. [< NLat. *Rhizocephala*, order name : RHIZO- + Gk. *kephalē*, head; see CEPHALO-.] —**rhi′zo·ceph′a·lous** (-ləs) *adj.*

rhi·zo·gen·ic (rī′zō-jĕn′ĭk) also **rhi·zo·ge·net·ic** (-jə-nĕt′ĭk) *adj. Botany* Giving rise to or producing roots.

rhi·zoid (rī′zoid′) *n.* **1.** A slender rootlike filament by which mosses, liverworts, and fern gametophytes attach to the substratum and absorb nourishment. **2.** A rootlike extension of the thallus of a fungus. —**rhi′zoid′, rhi·zoi′dal** (-zoid′l) *adj.*

rhi·zome (rī′zōm′) *n.* A horizontal, usu. underground stem that often sends out roots and shoots from its nodes. [Gk. *rhizōma*, mass of roots < *rhizoun*, to cause to take root < *rhiza*, root; see **wrād-** in App.] —**rhi·zom′a·tous** (-zŏm′ə-təs, -zō′mə-) *adj.* —**rhi·zom′ic** *adj.*

rhi·zoph·a·gous (rī-zŏf′ə-gəs) *adj.* Feeding on roots.

rhi·zo·pod (rī′zō-pŏd′, -zə-) *n.* A protozoan of the phylum Rhizopoda, such as an amoeba, characteristically moving and taking in food by means of pseudopods. [< NLat. *Rhizopoda*, phylum name : RHIZO- + NLat. *-poda, -pod*.] —**rhi′zop′o·dan** (-zŏp′ə-[ləs) *adj.* —**rhi′zop′o·dous** *adj.*

rhi·zo·pus (rī′zō-pəs, -zə-) *n.* Any of various rot-causing fungi of the genus *Rhizopus*. [NLat. *Rhizopūs*, genus name : RHIZO- + Gk. *pous, pod-*, foot; see –POD.]

rhi·zo·sphere (rī′zə-sfîr′) *n.* The soil zone that surrounds and is influenced by the roots of plants.

rhi·zot·o·my (rī-zŏt′ə-mē) *n., pl.* **-mies** Surgical severance of spinal nerve roots to relieve pain or hypertension.

Rh-neg·a·tive (är′ăch-nĕg′ə-tĭv) *adj.* Lacking an Rh factor.

rho (rō) *n.* The 17th letter of the Greek alphabet. [Gk. *rhō* < Phoenician *rōš*, head, 20th letter of the Phoenician alphabet.]

rhod– *pref.* Variant of rhodo–.

rho·da·mine (rō′də-mēn′) *n.* Any of several synthetic red to pink dyes having brilliant fluorescent qualities.

Rhode Island¹ (rōd) An island of RI at the entrance to Narragansett Bay.

Rhode Island² (rōd) A state of the NE US on the Atlantic Ocean; admitted as one of the original Thirteen Colonies in 1790. Cap. Providence. Pop. 1,048,319. —**Rhode Is′land·er** *n.*

Rhode Island Red *n.* Any of an American breed of domestic fowls having dark reddish-brown feathers.

Rhodes (rōdz) An island of SE Greece in the Aegean Sea off SW Turkey; colonized by Dorians before 1000 B.C. The ancient city of Rhodes, on the NE end of the island, was founded c. 408 B.C. and was the site of the Colossus of Rhodes, one of the Seven Wonders of the World.

Rhodes, Cecil John 1853–1902. British financier and colonizer who as prime minister of Cape Colony (1890–96) attempted to overthrow the Boer regime in the Transvaal.

Rho·de·sia (rō-dē′zhə) **1.** A region of S-central Africa S of Congo (formerly Zaire) and comprising modern-day Zambia and Zimbabwe. **2.** See Zimbabwe². —**Rho·de′sian** *adj. & n.*

Rhodesian man A fossil hominid specimen found in south-central Africa, previously classed as a distinct species but now generally regarded as an archaic example of *Homo sapiens.*

Rhodesian ridgeback (rĭj′băk′) *n.* Any of a breed of large dog developed in Africa and having short reddish-brown hair that forms a ridge along the back.

Rhodes scholar *n.* A student who holds a scholarship established by the will of Cecil Rhodes for study at Oxford University for a period of two or three years. —**Rhodes scholarship** *n.*

rho·di·um (rō′dē-əm) *n. Symbol* **Rh** A hard durable metallic element that is used to form high-temperature alloys with platinum and produce a corrosion-resistant coating on other metals. Atomic number 45; atomic weight 102.905; melting point 1,966°C; boiling point 3,727°C; specific gravity 12.41; valence 2, 3, 4, 5, 6. See table at **element.** [Gk. *rhodo-*, rhodo- + –IUM.]

rhodo– or **rhod–** *pref.* Rose; rosy; red: *rhodochrosite; rhodolite.* [Gk. < *rhodon*, rose.]

rho·do·chro·site (rō′də-krō′sīt′) *n.* A mineral consisting mainly of manganese carbonate, $MnCO_3$, light pink to rose-red in color with a pearly or vitreous luster, used as a manganese ore. [Ger. *Rhodochrosit* < Gk. *rhodokhrōs*, rose-colored : *rhodo-*, rhodo- + *khrōs*, color.]

rho·do·den·dron (rō′də-dĕn′drən) *n.* Any of numerous usu. evergreen ornamental shrubs of the genus *Rhododendron* of the North Temperate Zone, having variously colored flower clusters. [Lat., oleander < Gk. : *rhodo-*, rhodo- + *dendron*, tree; see **deru-** in App.]

rho·do·lite (rōd′l-īt′) *n.* A rose-red or pink variety of garnet, a silicate mineral used as a gem.

rho·do·nite (rōd′n-īt′) *n.* A pink to rose-red mineral, essentially a glassy crystalline manganese silicate, $MnSiO_3$, used as an ornamental stone. [< Gk. *rhodon*, rose.]

Rhod·o·pe Mountains (rŏd′ə-pē, rŏ-dō′-) A range in the Balkan Peninsula of SE Europe extending SE from SW Bulgaria to NE Greece and rising to 2,926.8 m (9,596 ft).

rho·dop·sin (rō-dŏp′sĭn) *n.* The pigment sensitive to red light in the retinal rods of the eyes, consisting of opsin and retinene. [RHOD(O)- + Gk. *opsis*, sight; see –OPSIS + –IN.]

rho·do·ra (rō-dôr′ə, -dōr′ə) *n.* A deciduous shrub (*Rhododendron canadense*) of northeast North America having rose-purple, two-lipped flowers that bloom before leaves appear. [Lat. *rhodōra*, var. of *rōdarum*, a plant, of Gaulish orig.]

rhom·ben·ceph·a·lon (rŏm′bĕn-sĕf′ə-lŏn′, -lən) *n.* The hindbrain.

rhom·bic (rŏm′bĭk) *adj.* **1.** Shaped like a rhombus. **2.** Orthorhombic.

rhombo– or **rhomb–** *pref.* Rhombus: *rhombohedron.* [Gk. < *rhombos.* See RHOMBUS.]

rhom·bo·he·dron (rŏm′bō-hē′drən) *n., pl.* **-drons** or **-dra** (-drə) A prism with six faces, each a rhombus. —**rhom′bo·he′dral** (-drəl) *adj.*

rhom·boid (rŏm′boid′) *n.* A parallelogram with unequal adjacent sides. ❖ *adj.* also **rhom·boi·dal** (-boid′l) Shaped like a rhombus or rhomboid.

rhom·bus (rŏm′bəs) *n., pl.* **-bus·es** or **-bi** (-bī) An equilateral parallelogram. [LLat. < Lat., flatfish, magician's circle < Gk. *rhombos*, rhombus. See wer-² in App.]

rhon·chus (rŏng′kəs) *n., pl.* **-chi** (-kī) A coarse rattling sound somewhat like snoring, usu. caused by a secretion in a bronchial tube. [Lat., a snoring < Gk. *rhonkhos*, var. of *rhenkos, rhenkhos* < *rhenkein*, to snore.] —**rhon′chal** (-kəl), **rhon′chi·al** (-kē-əl) *adj.*

Rhone or **Rhône** (rōn) A river rising in S-central Switzerland and

Rhodesian ridgeback

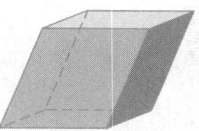

rhombohedron

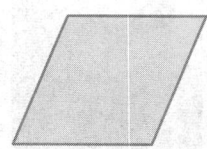

rhombus

ă pat	oi boy	
ā pay	ou out	
âr care	ŏŏ took	
ä father	ōō boot	
ĕ pet	ŭ cut	
ē be	ûr urge	
ĭ pit	th thin	
ī pie	*th* this	
îr pier	hw which	
ŏ pot	zh vision	
ō toe	ə about,	
ô paw	item	

Stress marks:
′ (primary);
′ (secondary), as in
lexicon (lĕk′sĭ-kŏn′)

flowing c. 813 km (505 mi) to E France, where it joins the Saône R. and continues to the Mediterranean Sea.

rhp *abbr.* rated horsepower

Rh-pos•i•tive (är′ăch-pŏz′ĭ-tĭv) *adj.* Containing an Rh factor.

rhu•barb (rōō′bärb′) *n.* **1.** Any of several plants of the genus *Rheum*, esp. *R. rhabarbarum*, having edible green or reddish leaf-stalks. **2.** The bitter-tasting dried rhizome and roots of *Rheum palmatum* or *R. officinale* of eastern Asia, used as a laxative. **3.** *Informal* A quarrel, fight, or heated discussion. [ME *rubarbe* < OFr. < LLat. *reubarbarum*, prob. alteration (influenced by Gk. *rhēon*) of *rhabarbarum* : *rha*, rhubarb (< Gk. *rhā*, perh. < *Rhā*, the Volga River) + Lat. *barbarum*, neut. of *barbarus*, barbarian, foreign; see BARBAROUS.]

rhumb (rŭm, rŭmb) *n.* **1.** A rhumb line. **2.** One of the points of the compass. [Poss. < Sp. or Port. *rumbo*, course, direction, ult. < Lat. *rhombus*, rhombus. See RHOMBUS.]

rhum•ba (rŭm′bə, rōōm′-, rŏŏm′-) *n.* Variant of **rumba.**

rhumb line *n.* The path of a ship that maintains a fixed compass direction, shown on a map as a line crossing all meridians at the same angle.

rhyme also **rime** (rīm) *n.* **1.** Correspondence of terminal sounds of words or of lines of verse. **2a.** A poem or verse having a regular correspondence of sounds, esp. at the ends of lines. **b.** Poetry or verse of this kind. **3.** A word that corresponds with another in terminal sound, as *behold* and *cold.* ❖ *v.* **rhymed, rhym•ing, rhymes** also **rimed, rim•ing, rimes** —*intr.* **1.** To form a rhyme. **2.** To compose rhymes or verse. **3.** To make use of rhymes in composing verse. —*tr.* **1.** To put into rhyme or compose with rhymes. **2.** To use (a word or words) as a rhyme. [Alteration (influenced by RHYTHM) of ME *rime* < OFr., < of Gmc. orig.] —**rhym′er, rim′er** *n.*

rhyme royal *n.* A form of verse having stanzas with seven lines in iambic pentameter rhyming *ababbcc.* **2.** One of these stanzas.

rhyme scheme *n.* The arrangement of rhymes in a poem or stanza.

rhyme•ster also **rime•ster** (rīm′stər) *n.* **1.** One who composes light verse. **2.** A minor or inferior poet.

rhy•ming slang (rī′mĭng) *n.* Slang in which a word is replaced by a word or phrase that rhymes with it, as *kiss* by *hit or miss.*

rhyn•cho•ce•pha•lian (rĭng′kō-sə-fāl′yən) *adj.* Of or belonging to the Rhynchocephalia, an order of mostly extinct lizardlike reptiles that includes the tuatara. [< NLat. *Rhynchocephalia*, order name : Gk. *rhunkhos*, beak + Gk. *kephalē*, head; see CEPHALIC.] —**rhyn′cho•ce•pha′lian** *n.*

rhy•o•lite (rī′ə-līt′) *n.* A fine-grained extrusive volcanic rock, similar to granite in composition and usu. exhibiting flow lines. [Gk. *rhuax*, stream (< *rhein*, to flow; see **sreu-** in App.) +—LITE.]

Rhys (rēs), **Jean** 1894–1979. West Indian–born British writer whose novels include *Wide Sargasso Sea* (1966).

rhythm (rĭth′əm) *n.* **1.** Movement or variation characterized by the regular recurrence or alternation of different quantities or conditions. **2.** The patterned recurring alternations of contrasting elements of sound or speech. **3.** *Music* **a.** The pattern of musical movement through time. **b.** A specific kind of such a pattern, formed by a series of notes differing in duration and stress: *a waltz rhythm.* **c.** A group of instruments supplying the rhythm in a band. **4a.** The pattern or flow of sound created by the arrangement of stressed and unstressed syllables in accentual verse or of long and short syllables in quantitative verse. **b.** The similar but less formal sequence of sounds in prose. **c.** A specific kind of metrical pattern or flow: *iambic rhythm.* **5a.** The sense of temporal development created in a work of literature or a film by the arrangement of formal elements such as the length of scenes, the nature and amount of dialogue, or the repetition of motifs. **b.** A regular or harmonious pattern created by lines, forms, and colors in painting, sculpture, and other visual arts. **6.** The pattern of development produced in a literary or dramatic work by repetition of elements such as words, phrases, incidents, themes, images, and symbols. **7.** Procedure or routine characterized by regularly recurring elements, activities, or factors. [Lat. *rhythmus* < Gk. *rhuthmos.* See **sreu-** in App.]

rhythm and blues *pl.n.* (*used with a sing. or pl. verb*) A style of music developed by African Americans that combines blues and jazz, characterized by a strong backbeat and repeated variations on syncopated instrumental phrases.

rhyth•mic (rĭth′mĭk) also **rhyth•mi•cal** (-mĭ-kəl) *adj.* Of, relating to, or having rhythm; recurring with measured regularity. —**rhyth′mi•cal•ly** *adv.*

rhythmic gymnastics *n.* (*used with a sing. verb*) A form of gymnastics in which dancelike movements are combined with the manipulation of a hand apparatus such as a rope, hoop, or ribbon.

rhyth•mics (rĭth′mĭks) *n.* (*used with a sing. verb*) *Music* The study of rhythm.

rhyth•mist (rĭth′mĭst) *n.* **1.** One who is an expert in or has a keen sense of rhythm. **2.** *Music* One who studies or produces rhythm.

rhythm method *n.* A birth-control method dependent on abstinence during the period of ovulation.

rhy•ton (rī′tŏn′) *n.* A hornlike drinking vessel of ancient times, having a pointed end shaped like an animal or animal's head. [Gk. *rhuton* < neut. of *rhutos*, fluid, liquid. See **sreu-** in App.]

rhyton
Persian, Achaemenid period

ribbing
Adirondack guideboat

RI or **R.I.** *abbr.* Rhode Island

ri•al¹ (rē-ôl′, -äl′) *n.* See table at **currency.** [Pers. < Ar. *riyāl* < Sp. *real.* See REAL².]

ri•al² (rē-ôl′, -äl′) *n.* Variant of **riyal.**

ri•al•to (rē-ăl′tō, rē-äl′-) *n., pl.* **-tos 1.** A theatrical district. **2.** A marketplace. [After *Rialto*, an island of Venice where a market was situated.]

ri•ant (rī′ənt, rē′-, rē-äN′) *adj.* Cheerful; mirthful. [Fr., pr. part. of *rire*, to laugh < OFr. < Lat. *rīdēre.*]

ri•a•ta also **re•a•ta** (rē-ä′tə) *n.* A lariat; a lasso. [Sp. *reata*, lasso, lariat. See LARIAT.]

Ri•au Archipelago (rē′ou) An island group of W Indonesia off the SE end of the Malay Peninsula.

rib (rĭb) *n.* **1.** *Anatomy* **a.** One of a series of long curved bones occurring in 12 pairs in humans and extending from the spine to or toward the sternum. **b.** A similar bone in most vertebrates. **2.** A part or piece similar to a rib and serving to shape or support: *the rib of an umbrella.* **3.** A cut of meat enclosing one or more rib bones. **4.** *Nautical* One of many curved members attached to a boat or ship's keel and forming the framework of the hull. **5.** One of many transverse pieces that provide an airplane wing with shape and strength. **6.** *Architecture* A long, narrow, usu. arched member projecting from a structure's surface, esp. such a member separating the webs of a vault. **7.** A raised ridge or wale in knitted material or in cloth. **8.** *Botany* The main vein or any of the prominent veins of a leaf or other plant organ. **9.** *Slang* A teasing remark or action; a joke. ❖ *tr.v.* **ribbed, rib•bing, ribs 1.** To shape, support, or provide with a rib or ribs. **2.** To make with ridges or raised markings. **3.** *Informal* To tease or make fun of. [ME < OE *ribb.*]

rib•ald (rĭb′əld, rī′bôld′) *adj.* Characterized by or indulging in vulgar, lewd humor. ❖ *n.* A vulgar, lewdly funny person. [< ME *ribaud*, ribald person < OFr. < *riber*, to be wanton, of Gmc. orig. See **wer-²** in App.]

rib•ald•ry (rĭb′əl-drē, rī′bə-) *n., pl.* **-ries** Vulgar, lewdly humorous language or joking or an instance of it.

rib•and (rĭb′ənd) *n.* A ribbon, esp. one used as a decoration. [ME, var. of *riban.* See RIBBON.]

rib•band (rĭb′ănd, -ənd, -ən) *n.* A length of flexible wood or metal used to hold the ribs of a ship in place while the exterior planking or plating is being applied. [RIB + BAND¹.]

ribbed vault (rĭbd) *n.* See **rib vault.**

rib•bing (rĭb′ĭng) *n.* **1.** Ribs considered as a group. **2.** An arrangement of ribs, as in a boat. **3.** *Informal* The act or an instance of joking or teasing.

rib•bon (rĭb′ən) *n.* **1.** A narrow strip or band of fine fabric, such as satin, finished at the edges and used for trimming, tying, or finishing. **2a.** Something, such as a tape measure, that resembles a ribbon. **b.** A long thin strip. **3.** **ribbons** Tattered or ragged strips: *a dress torn to ribbons.* **4.** An inked strip of cloth used for making an impression, as in a typewriter. **5a.** A band of colored cloth signifying membership in an order or the award of a prize. **b.** A strip of colored cloth worn on the left breast of a uniform to indicate the award of a medal or decoration. **6. ribbons** *Informal* Reins for driving horses. **7.** See **ledger board** 2. ❖ *tr.v.* **-boned, -bon•ing, -bons 1.** To decorate or tie with ribbons. **2.** To tear into ribbons or shreds. [ME *ribban, riban* < OFr. *ruban*, prob. of Gmc. orig. See **bhendh-** in App.] —**rib′bon•y** *adj.*

rib•bon•fish (rĭb′ən-fĭsh′) *n., pl.* **ribbonfish** or **-fish•es** Any of several marine fishes, chiefly of the genus *Trachipterus*, having long narrow compressed bodies.

ribbon worm *n.* See **nemertean.**

rib cage *n.* The enclosing structure formed by the ribs and the bones to which they are attached.

Ri•bei•rão Prê•to (rē′bā-rou₦′ prē′tōō) A city of SE Brazil NNW of São Paulo. Pop. 436,122.

rib•grass (rĭb′grăs′) *n.* A weedy Eurasian plant (*Plantago lanceolata*) having ribbed lance-shaped leaves.

ri•bo•fla•vin (rī′bō-flā′vĭn, -bə-) *n.* An orange-yellow crystalline compound, $C_{17}H_{20}N_4O_6$, the principal growth-promoting factor in the vitamin B complex, naturally occurring in milk, leafy vegetables, fresh meat, and egg yolks. [RIBO(SE) + FLAVIN.]

ri•bo•nu•cle•ase (rī′bō-nōō′klē-ās′, -āz′, -nyōō′-) *n.* Any of various enzymes that break down RNA.

ri•bo•nu•cle•ic acid (rī′bō-nōō-klē′ĭk, -klā′-, -nyōō-) *n.* See RNA. [RIBO(SE) + NUCLEIC ACID.]

ri•bo•nu•cle•o•pro•tein (rī′bō-nōō′klē-ō-prō′tēn, -tē-ĭn, -nyōō′-) *n.* A nucleoprotein that contains RNA.

ri•bo•nu•cle•o•side (rī′bō-nōō′klē-ə-sīd′, -nyōō′-) *n.* A nucleoside that contains ribose as its sugar component.

ri•bo•nu•cle•o•tide (rī′bō-nōōklē-ə-tīd′, -nyōō′-) *n.* A nucleotide that contains ribose as its sugar and is a component of RNA.

ri•bose (rī′bōs′) *n.* A pentose sugar, $C_5H_{10}O_5$, occurring as a component of riboflavin, nucleotides, and nucleic acids. [Ger., alteration of E. *arabinuse*, a kind of sugar : (GUM) ARAB(IC) + –IN + –OSE².]

ribosomal RNA *n.* The RNA that is a permanent structural part of a ribosome.

ri•bo•some (rī′bə-sōm′) *n.* A minute round particle composed of RNA and protein that is found in the cytoplasm of living cells and serves as the site of protein synthesis. [RIBO(NUCLEIC ACID) +

–SOME³.] —**ri′bo•so′mal** (-sō′məl) *adj.*

ri•bo•zyme (rī′bə-zīm′) *n.* An RNA segment that has the ability to catalyze the formation of covalent bonds in RNA strands. [RI-BO(NUCLEIC ACID) + (EN)ZYME.]

rib vault *n.* A vault in which the surface is divided into webs by a framework of diagonal arched ribs.

rib•wort (rĭb′wûrt′, -wôrt′) *n.* See **plantain¹**.

Ri•car•do (rĭ-kär′dō), **David** 1772–1823. British economist who wrote *Principles of Political Economy and Taxation* (1817).

rice (rīs) *n.* **1.** A cereal grass (*Oryza sativa*) that is cultivated extensively in warm climates for its edible grain. **2.** The starchy grain of this plant, used as a staple food throughout the world. ❖ *tr.v.* **riced, ric•ing, ric•es** To sieve (food) to the consistency of rice. [ME < OFr. *ris* < OItal. *riso* < Lat. *oryza* < Gk. *oruza*, of Indo-Iran. orig.]

Rice, Elmer Leopold 1892–1967. Amer. playwright whose works include *The Adding Machine* (1923).

rice•bird (rīs′bûrd′) *n.* **1.** *Chiefly Southern US* See **bobolink**. **2.** Any of various birds that frequent rice fields.

rice paper *n.* A thin paper made chiefly from the pith of the Chinese shrub or small tree *Tetrapanax papyriferus*.

ric•er (rī′sər) *n.* A kitchen utensil used for ricing soft foods by extrusion through small holes.

rich (rĭch) *adj.* **rich•er, rich•est 1.** Possessing great material wealth. **2.** Having great worth or value: *a rich harvest.* **3.** Magnificent; sumptuous. **4a.** Having an abundant supply: *rich in ideas.* **b.** Abounding, esp. in natural resources. **5.** Meaningful and significant. **6.** Very productive and therefore financially profitable. **7a.** Containing a large amount of choice ingredients, such as butter, sugar, or eggs, and therefore unusually heavy or sweet. **b.** Having or exuding a strong or pungent aroma. **8a.** Pleasantly full and mellow: *a rich bass voice.* **b.** Warm and strong in color. **9.** Containing a large proportion of fuel to air. **10.** *Informal* Highly amusing. ❖ *n. (used with a pl. verb)* Wealthy people considered as a group. [ME *riche* < OFr. (of Gmc. orig.) and < OE *rīce*, strong, powerful; see **reg-** in App.] —**rich′ly** *adv.* —**rich′ness** *n.*

Rich, Adrienne b. 1929. Amer. poet and essayist whose works include *Diving Into the Wreck* (1973).

Rich•ard I (rĭch′ərd) Known as "the Lion-Hearted" or "Coeur de Lion." 1157–99. King of England (1189–99) who was a leader of the Third Crusade (1190–92).

Richard II 1367–1400. King of England (1377–99) who quelled the Peasants' Revolt in 1381.

Richard III 1452–85. King of England (1483–85) who claimed the throne after imprisoning the sons of his deceased brother Edward IV. Richard's death at the Battle of Bosworth Field brought an end to the Wars of the Roses.

Ri•chard (rē-shärd′), **Joseph Henri Maurice** Known as "Rocket." 1921–2000. Canadian hockey player. A right wing for the Montreal Canadiens (1942–60), he was the first player to score 50 goals in a season.

Rich•ard Roe (rĭch′ərd) *n.* A name used in legal proceedings to designate an unknown or unidentified man.

Rich•ards (rĭch′ərdz), **I(vor) A(rmstrong)** 1893–1979. British critic who helped Charles Ogden develop Basic English.

Rich•ard•son (rĭch′ərd-sən) A city of NE TX, a suburb of Dallas. Pop. 91,802.

Richardson, Henry Hobson 1838–86. Amer. architect whose designs include Trinity Church in Boston (1872–77).

Richardson, Samuel 1689–1761. English writer whose epistolary novels include *Pamela* (1740).

Ri•che•lieu (rĭsh′ə-lōō′) A river of S Quebec, Canada, flowing c. 121 km (75 mi) to the St. Lawrence R.

Ri•che•lieu (rĭsh′ə-lōō′), Duc de. Title of Armand Jean du Plessis. 1585–1642. French prelate and politician who was chief minister of Louis XIII.

rich•en (rĭch′ən) *v.* **-ened, -en•ing, -ens** To make rich.

rich•es (rĭch′ĭz) *pl.n.* **1.** Abundant wealth. **2.** Valuable or precious possessions. [ME *richesse*, wealth < OFr. < *riche*, wealthy. See RICH.]

Rich•ler (rĭch′lər), **Mordecai** 1931–2001. Canadian writer whose novels include *The Apprenticeship of Duddy Kravitz* (1959).

Rich•mond (rĭch′mənd) **1.** A community of SW British Columbia, Canada, a suburb of Vancouver on the Strait of Georgia. Pop. 148,867. **2.** A city of W CA on an inlet of San Francisco Bay NNW of Oakland. Pop. 99,216. **3.** The cap. of VA, in the E-central part on the James R.; settled in the 17th cent. and the cap. of the Confederacy during the Civil War. Pop. 197,790.

Rich•ter (rĭk′tər), **Burton** b. 1931. Amer. physicist who shared a 1976 Nobel Prize.

Richter scale *n.* A logarithmic scale ranging from 1 to 10, used to express the total amount of energy released by an earthquake; the largest recorded quake measured 8.9. [After Charles Francis Richter (1900–85), American seismologist.]

ri•cin (rī′sĭn, rĭs′ĭn) *n.* A poisonous protein extracted from the castor bean and used as a biochemical reagent. [< Lat. *ricinus*, castor-oil plant.]

ric•in•o•le•ic acid (rĭs′ĭn-ō-lē′ĭk) *n.* An unsaturated fatty acid, $C_{18}H_{34}O_3$, prepared from castor oil and used in making soaps and in textile finishing. [< Lat. *ricinus*, castor-oil plant.]

rick (rĭk) *n.* A stack of hay, straw, or similar material, esp. when

covered or thatched for protection from the weather. ❖ *tr.v.* **ricked, rick•ing, ricks** To pile into ricks. [ME *reke* < OE *hrēac*.]

Rick•en•back•er (rĭk′ĭn-băk′ər), **Edward ("Eddie") Vernon** 1890–1973. Amer. aviator who was a highly decorated combat pilot in World War I.

rick•ets (rĭk′ĭts) *n. (used with a sing. or pl. verb)* A deficiency disease resulting from a lack of vitamin D and insufficient exposure to sunlight, characterized by defective bone growth and occurring chiefly in children. [?]

rick•ett•si•a (rĭ-kĕt′sē-ə) *n., pl.* **-si•ae** (-sē-ē′) Any of various bacteria of the genus *Rickettsia*, carried as parasites by many ticks, fleas, and lice and causing diseases such as typhus, scrub typhus, and Rocky Mountain spotted fever in humans. [NLat. *Rickettsia*, genus name, after Howard Taylor Ricketts (1871–1910), American pathologist.] —**rick•ett′si•al** *adj.*

rick•et•y (rĭk′ĭ-tē) *adj.* **-i•er, -i•est 1.** Likely to break or fall apart; shaky. **2.** Feeble with age; infirm. **3.** Of, having, or resembling rickets. [< RICKETS.] —**rick′et•i•ness** *n.*

rick•ey (rĭk′ē) *n., pl.* **-eys** A drink of soda water, lime or lemon juice, sugar, and usu. gin. [Prob. < the name *Rickey.*]

Rick•o•ver (rĭk′ō′vər), **Hyman George** 1900–86. Amer. admiral who advocated the development of nuclear-powered naval craft.

rick•rack (rĭk′răk′) *n.* A flat narrow braid woven in zigzag form, used to trim clothes or curtains. [Reduplication of RACK¹.]

rick•sha or **rick•shaw** (rĭk′shô) *n.* A jinriksha.

RICO *abbr.* Racketeer Influenced and Corrupt Organizations Act of 1970

ric•o•chet (rĭk′ə-shā′, rĭk′ə-shā′) *intr.v.* **-cheted** (-shād′), **-chet•ing** (-shā′ĭng), **-chets** (-shāz′) To rebound at least once from a surface. ❖ *n.* The act or an instance of ricocheting. [Fr.] ❖ *n.* give-and-take.]

ri•cot•ta (rĭ-kŏt′ə) *n.* **1.** A soft Italian cheese that resembles cottage cheese. **2.** A similar soft cheese made in the United States. [Ital. < Lat. *recocta*, fem. p. part. of *recoquere*, to cook again : *re-*, re- + *coquere*, to cook; see pekʷ- in App.]

ric•tus (rĭk′təs) *n., pl.* **rictus** or **-tus•es 1.** The expanse of an open mouth, a bird's beak, or a similar structure. **2.** A gaping grimace. [Lat. < p. part. of *ringī*, to gape.] —**ric′tal** *adj.*

rid (rĭd) *tr.v.* **rid** or **rid•ded, rid•ding, rids** To free from: *rid himself of all worry.* [ME *ridden* < ON *rydhja*, to clear land < *hrjōdha*, to strip, clear.] —**rid′der** *n.*

rid•dance (rĭd′ns) *n.* **1.** A deliverance from or removal of something unwanted or undesirable. **2.** The act of ridding.

rid•den (rĭd′n) *v.* Past participle of **ride**. ❖ *adj.* Dominated, harassed, or obsessed by. Often used in combination: *disease-ridden.*

rid•dle¹ (rĭd′l) *tr.v.* **-dled, -dling, -dles 1.** To pierce with numerous holes; perforate. **2.** To spread throughout. **3.** To put (gravel, for example) through a coarse sieve. **4.** To sift. ❖ *n.* A coarse sieve. [ME *ridelen*, to sift < *riddil*, sieve < OE *hriddel*. See krei- in App.] —**rid′dler** *n.*

rid•dle² (rĭd′l) *n.* **1.** A question or statement requiring thought to answer or understand; a conundrum. **2.** One that is perplexing; an enigma. ❖ *v.* **-dled, -dling, -dles** —*tr.* To solve or explain. —*intr.* **1.** To propound or solve riddles. **2.** To speak in riddles. [ME *redels* < OE *rǣdels*.] —**rid′dler** *n.*

ride (rīd) *v.* **rode** (rōd), **rid•den** (rĭd′n), **rid•ing, rides** —*intr.* **1.** To be carried or conveyed, as in a vehicle or on horseback. **2.** To travel over a surface. **3.** To move by way of an intangible force or impetus; move as if on water. **4.** *Nautical* To lie at anchor. **5.** To seem to float. **6.** To be sustained or supported on a pivot, axle, or other point. **7.** To be contingent; depend. **8.** To continue without interference: *Let matters ride.* **9.** To work or move from the proper place, esp. on the body: *pants that ride up.* —*tr.* **1.** To sit on and move in a given direction. **2.** To travel over, along, or through. **3.** To be supported or carried on. **4.** To take part in or do by riding: *rode his last race.* **5.** To cause to ride, esp. to cause to be carried. **6.** *Informal* **a.** To tease or ridicule. **b.** To harass with carping and criticism. **7.** To keep partially engaged by slightly depressing a pedal with the foot. ❖ *n.* **1.** The act or an instance of riding, as in a vehicle or on an animal. **2.** A path made for riding on horseback, esp. through woodlands. **3.** A device that one rides for pleasure or excitement. **4.** A means of transportation. —*phrasal verb:* **ride out** To survive or outlast. —*idioms:* **ride for a fall** To court danger or disaster. **ride herd on** To keep watch or control over. **ride high** To experience success. **ride shotgun 1.** To guard a person or thing while in transit. **2.** *Slang* To ride in the front passenger seat of a car or truck. **take for a ride** *Slang* **1.** To deceive or swindle. **2.** To transport to a place and kill. [ME *riden* < OE *rīdan.*] —**rid′a•ble, ride′a•ble** *adj.*

Ride, Sally b. 1951. Amer. astronaut who in 1983 became the first US woman to enter outer space.

Ri•deau Canal (rĭ-dō′) A waterway, c. 203 km (126 mi), of SE Ontario connecting the Ottawa R. with Lake Ontario.

rid•er (rī′dər) *n.* **1.** One that rides, esp. one who rides horses. **2.** A clause, usu. having little relevance to the main issue, that is added to a legislative bill. **3.** An amendment or addition to a document or record. **4.** Something, such as the top rail of a fence, that rests on or is supported by something else.

rid•er•ship (rī′dər-shĭp′) *n.* The number of passengers who ride a public transport system.

Sally Ride

ridge (rĭj) *n.* **1.** A long narrow upper section or crest. **2.** A long narrow chain of hills or mountains. **3.** A long narrow elevation on the ocean floor. **4.** An elongated zone of relatively high atmospheric pressure. **5.** A long, narrow, or crested part of the body. **6.** The horizontal line formed by the juncture of two sloping planes, esp. the line formed by the surfaces at the top of a roof. **7.** A narrow raised strip, as in cloth or on plowed ground. ❖ *v.* **ridged, ridg•ing, ridg•es** —*tr.* To mark with, form into, or provide with ridges. —*intr.* To form ridges. [ME *rigge* < OE *hrycg*.]

ridge•board (rĭj′bôrd′, -bōrd′) *n.* See **ridgepole** 1.

ridge•ling also **ridg•ling** (rĭj′lĭng) *n.* A male animal with one or two undescended testicles. [< obsolete *ridgel*, perh. < RIDGE (< the belief that they remained near the back).]

ridge•pole (rĭj′pōl′) *n.* **1.** A horizontal beam at the ridge of a roof to which the rafters are attached. **2.** The horizontal pole at the top of a tent.

Ridg•way (rĭj′wā′), **Matthew Bunker** 1895–1993. Amer. army officer who was commander of United Nations forces in Korea (1951–52) and NATO forces in Europe (1951–53).

ridg•y (rĭj′ē) *adj.* **-i•er, -i•est** Having or forming ridges.

rid•i•cule (rĭd′ĭ-kyōōl′) *n.* Words or actions intended to evoke contemptuous laughter at or feelings toward a person or thing. ❖ *tr.v.* **-culed, -cul•ing, -cules** To expose to ridicule; make fun of. [Fr. < Lat. *rīdiculum*, joke < neut. of *rīdiculus*, laughable. See RIDICULOUS.] —**rid′i•cul′er** *n.*

SYNONYMS *ridicule, mock, taunt, twit, deride* These verbs refer to making another the butt of amusement or mirth. *Ridicule* implies purposeful disparagement: "*My father discouraged me by ridiculing my performances*" (Benjamin Franklin). To *mock* is to poke fun at someone, often by mimicry and caricature: "*Seldom he smiles, and smiles in such a sort/As if he mock'd himself, and scorn'd his spirit*" (Shakespeare). *Taunt* suggests mocking, insulting, or scornful reproach: "*taunting him with want of courage to leap into the great pit*" (Daniel Defoe). To *twit* is to taunt by calling attention to something embarrassing: "*The schoolmaster was twitted about the lady who threw him over*" (J.M. Barrie). *Deride* implies scorn and contempt: "*Was all the world in a conspiracy to deride his failure?*" (Edith Wharton).

ri•dic•u•lous (rĭ-dĭk′yə-ləs) *adj.* Deserving or inspiring ridicule; absurd, preposterous, or silly. [< Lat. *rīdiculus*, laughable < *rīdēre*, to laugh.] —**ri•dic′u•lous•ly** *adv.* —**ri•dic′u•lous•ness** *n.*

rid•ing[1] (rī′dĭng) *n.* **1.** The act of riding. **2.** Horseback riding.

rid•ing[2] (rī′dĭng) *n.* **1.** An administrative division or electoral division in Canada. **2.** Any one of three former administrative divisions of Yorkshire, England. [ME, alteration of *trithing* < OE *thrithing* < ON *thridhjungr*, third part < *thridhi*, third. See **trei-** in App.]

rid•ley (rĭd′lē) *n.*, *pl.* **-leys 1.** A marine turtle (*Lepidochelys kempii*) of the Gulf of Mexico and Atlantic coastal waters. **2.** A related species (*L. olivaceae*) of the Pacific and Indian oceans. [?]

Ridley, Nicholas 1500?–55. English prelate who was executed for refusing to renounce his Protestantism after the accession of the Roman Catholic Mary I.

Rie•fen•stahl (rē′fən-stäl′, -shtäl′), **Helene Bertha Amalie** Known as "Leni." b. 1902. German filmmaker who gained notoriety for the Nazi-sponsored documentaries she made in the 1930s.

ri•el (rē-ĕl′) *n.* See table at **currency.** [?]

Ri•el (rē-ĕl′), **Louis** 1844–85. Canadian insurrectionist who organized métis settlers of the Red R. valley (1869) and Saskatchewan (1884–85) in uprisings over land rights.

Rie•mann (rē′män, -män′), **Georg Friedrich Bernhard** 1826–66. German mathematician who was a pioneer of non-Euclidean geometry.

Rie•mann•ian geometry (rē-män′ē-ən) *n.* A non-Euclidean system of geometry based on the postulate that within a plane every pair of lines intersects.

Ri•en•zi (rē-ĕn′zē) or **Ri•en•zo** (-zō), **Cola di** 1313?–54. Italian revolutionary leader who was dictator of Rome (1347).

Ries•ling (rēs′lĭng, rēz′-) *n.* **1.** A variety of grape grown in cool areas, esp. in Germany and the Pacific Northwest. **2.** A dry to sweet white wine made from this grape. [Ger., alteration of obsolete *Rüssling*.]

Rif (rĭf) See **Er Rif.**

ri•fam•pin (rĭ-făm′pĭn) also **ri•fam•pi•cin** (-pĭ-sĭn) *n.* A semisynthetic antibiotic that interferes with the synthesis of RNA and is used esp. in the treatment of tuberculosis. [Blend of RIFAM(YC)IN and P(IPERAZINE).]

rif•a•my•cin (rĭf′ə-mī′sĭn) *n.* Any of a group of antibiotics isolated from a strain of the soil microorganism *Streptomyces mediterranei*, used in the treatment of leprosy, tuberculosis, and other bacterial diseases. [Alteration of *rifomycin* : prob. Ital. *rifo(rmare*, to reform (*ri-*, again < Lat. *re-*; see RE– + *formare*, to form < Lat. *fōrmāre*; see REFORM) + –MYCIN.]

rife (rīf) *adj.* **rif•er, rif•est 1.** In widespread existence, practice, or use; increasingly prevalent. **2.** Abundant or numerous. [ME < OE *rȳfe*.]

riff (rĭf) *n.* **1.** *Music* A short rhythmic phrase, esp. one that is repeated in improvisation. **2.** A clever or inventive commentary or remark, as by a disc jockey. ❖ *intr.v.* **riffed, riff•ing, riffs** To play

rigging

or make riffs: *a comedian who riffed on politicians.* [?]

Riff or **Rif** (rĭf) *n., pl.* **Riff** or **Riffs** or **Rif** or **Rifs** also **Rif•fi** (rĭf′ē) **1.** A member of any of several Berber peoples inhabiting Er Rif. **2.** The Berber language of this people. —**Rif′fi•an** *adj. & n.*

rif•fle (rĭf′əl) *n.* **1a.** A rocky shoal or sandbar lying just below the surface of a waterway. **b.** A stretch of choppy water caused by such a shoal or sandbar; a rapid. **2a.** In mining, the sectional stone or wood bottom lining of a sluice, arranged for trapping mineral particles, as of gold. **b.** A groove or block in such a lining. **3.** *Games* The act or an instance of shuffling cards. ❖ *v.* **-fled, -fling, -fles** —*tr.* **1.** *Games* To shuffle (playing cards) by holding part of a deck in each hand and raising up the edges before releasing them to fall alternately in one stack. **2.** To thumb through (the pages of a book, for example). —*intr.* **1.** *Games* To shuffle cards. **2.** To become choppy, as water. [Poss. blend of RIPPLE[1] and RUFFLE[1].]

riff•raff (rĭf′răf′) *n.* **1.** People regarded as disreputable or worthless. **2.** Rubbish; trash. [ME *riffe raffe* < *rif and raf*, one and all < AN *rif et raf*, *rifle et rafle* : OFr. *rifler*, to rifle; see RIFLE[2] + OFr. *raffler*, to carry off (< *raffle*, act of seizing; see RAFFLE[1]).]

ri•fle[1] (rī′fəl) *n.* **1a.** A firearm with a rifled bore, designed to be fired from the shoulder. **b.** An artillery piece or naval gun with such spiral grooves. **2. rifles** Troops armed with rifles. ❖ *tr.v.* **-fled, -fling, -fles** To cut spiral grooves within (a gun barrel, for example). [< *rifle*, to cut spiral grooves in < Fr. *rifler* < OFr., to plunder, scratch. See RIFLE[2].]

ri•fle[2] (rī′fəl) *v.* **-fled, -fling, -fles** —*tr.* **1.** To search with intent to steal. **2.** To ransack or plunder; pillage. **3.** To rob: *rifle a safe.* —*intr.* To search vigorously. [ME *riflen*, to plunder < OFr. *rifler*, prob. of Gmc. orig.] —**ri′fler** *n.*

ri•fle•man (rī′fəl-mən) *n.* **1.** A soldier equipped with a rifle. **2.** One who shoots a rifle skillfully.

ri•fle•ry (rī′fəl-rē) *n.* **1.** The skill and practice of shooting a gun. **2.** Rifle fire: *distant riflery.*

ri•fling (rī′flĭng) *n.* **1.** The process or operation of cutting spiral grooves in a rifle barrel. **2.** Grooves cut in a rifle barrel.

rift[1] (rĭft) *n.* **1.** A narrow fissure in rock. **2.** A break in friendly relations. ❖ *v.* **rift•ed, rift•ing, rifts** —*intr.* To split open; break. —*tr.* To cause to split open or break. [ME, of Scand. orig.]

rift[2] (rĭft) *n.* **1.** A shallow area in a waterway. **2.** The backwash of a wave that has broken upon a beach. [Prob. alteration of dialectal *riff*, reef < Du. *rif*, *riffe*. See REEF[1].]

rift valley *n.* A valley that has developed along a rift. **2.** Any of the deep valleys that run along the center of the mid-ocean ridge.

rig (rĭg) *tr.v.* **rigged, rig•ging, rigs 1.** To provide with a harness or equipment; fit out. **2.** *Nautical* To equip (a ship) with spars, shrouds, and sails. **3.** *Informal* To dress, clothe, or adorn. **4.** To make or construct in haste or in a makeshift manner: *rig up a tent.* **5.** To manipulate dishonestly for personal gain. ❖ *n.* **1.** *Nautical* The configuration of masts, spars, and sails on a sailing vessel. **2.** Special equipment or gear used for a particular purpose. **3a.** A truck or tractor. **b.** A tractor-trailer. **c.** A vehicle with one or more horses harnessed to it. **4.** The special apparatus used for drilling oil wells. **5.** *Western US* See **saddle** 1a. **6.** *Informal* A costume or an outfit. **7.** Fishing tackle. [ME *riggen*, prob. of Scand. orig.]

Ri•ga (rē′gə) The cap. of Latvia, in the central part on the **Gulf of Riga**, an inlet of the Baltic Sea. Pop. 865,227.

rig•a•doon (rĭg′ə-dōōn′) or **ri•gau•don** (rē-gô-dōn′) *n.* **1.** A lively jumping quickstep for two couples. **2.** Music for this dance, usu. in rapid duple meter. [Fr. *rigaudon*, poss. < the name *Rigaud.*]

rig•a•ma•role (rĭg′ə-mə-rōl′) *n.* Variant of **rigmarole.**

rig•a•to•ni (rĭg′ə-tō′nē) *n.* Pasta in ribbed, slightly curved, large-sized tubes. [Ital. < *rigato*, p. part. of *rigare*, to draw a line < *riga*, line, of Gmc. orig.]

Ri•gel (rī′jəl) *n.* A bright double star in the constellation Orion. [Ar. *rijl*, foot.]

rig•ger (rĭg′ər) *n.* **1.** One that rigs. **2.** *Nautical* A ship with a specific kind of rigging.

rig•ging (rĭg′ĭng) *n.* **1.** *Nautical* The system of shrouds, stays, and control lines used to support and adjust the spars and sails of a sailing vessel. **2.** The supporting material for construction work.

right (rīt) *adj.* **right•er, right•est 1.** Conforming with or conformable to justice, law, or morality. **2.** In accordance with fact, reason, or truth; correct. **3.** Fitting, proper, or appropriate. **4.** Most favorable, desirable, or convenient: *the right time to act.* **5.** In or into a satisfactory state or condition: *put things right.* **6.** In good mental or physical health or order. **7.** Intended to be worn or positioned facing outward or toward an observer: *the right side of the dress.* **8a.** Of, belonging to, located on, or being the side of the body to the south when the subject is facing east. **b.** Of, relating to, directed toward, or located on the right side. **c.** Located on the right side of a person facing downstream. **9.** often **Right** Of or belonging to the political or intellectual right. **10.** *Mathematics* **a.** Formed by or in reference to a line or plane perpendicular to another line or plane. **b.** Having the axis perpendicular to the base: *right cone.* **c.** Having a right angle: *a right triangle.* **11.** Straight; uncurved; direct: *a right line.* **12.** *Archaic* Not spurious; genuine. ❖ *n.* **1.** That which is just, good, legal, proper, or fitting. **2a.** The direction or position on the right side. **b.** The right side. **c.** The right hand. **d.** A turn in the direction of the right hand or side. **3.** often **Right** *a.* The people and groups who advocate conservative or reactionary measures, esp. in government and politics. **b.** The opinion of those advocating such measures. **4.** *Sports* A blow delivered by a boxer's right hand. **5.** *Baseball* Right field. **6.** Something due to a person or community by law, tradition, or nature. **a.** Something due to a person or community by law, tradition, or nature. **b.** Something, esp. humane treatment, claimed to be due to animals by moral principle. **7.** A just or legal claim or title. **8a.** A stockholder's privilege of buying additional stock in a corporation at a special price, usu. at par or at a price below the current market value. **b.** The negotiable certificate on which this privilege is indicated. **c.** A privilege of subscribing for a particular stock or bond. Often used in the plural. ❖ *adv.* **1.** Toward or on the right. **2.** In a straight line; directly: *went right home.* **3.** In the proper or desired manner; well: *doesn't fit right.* **4.** Exactly; just: *happened right here.* **5.** Immediately: *right after dinner.* **6.** Completely; quite: *The wind blew right through me.* **7.** According to law, morality, or justice. **8.** Accurately; correctly. **9.** *Chiefly Southern US* Considerably; very: *They have a right nice place.* **10.** Used as an intensive: *kept right on going.* **11.** Used in titles: *The Right Reverend Jane Smith.* ❖ *v.* **right·ed, right·ing, rights** —*tr.* **1.** To put in or restore to an upright or proper position: *They righted their boat.* **2.** To put in order or set right; correct. **3.** To make reparation or amends for; redress. —*intr.* To regain an upright or proper position. —**idioms: by rights** In a just or proper manner; justly. **in (one's) own right** Through the force of one's own skills or qualifications. **right and left** From all directions or on every side. **right away (or off)** Immediately; at once; without delay. **right on** *Slang* Used as an exclamation of encouragement, support, or enthusiastic agreement. **to rights** In a satisfactory or orderly condition. [ME < OE *riht.* See **reg-** in App. N., sense 3, because conservatives sit on the right side of the legislative chamber in various assemblies.] —**right′er** *n.*

right angle *n.* An angle formed by the perpendicular intersection of two straight lines; an angle of 90°. —**right′-an′gled** (rīt′ăng′gəld) *adj.*

right ascension *n.* The angular distance of a celestial body or point on the celestial sphere, measured eastward from the vernal equinox along the celestial equator to the hour circle of the body or point and expressed in degrees or hours.

Right Bank A district of Paris on the N bank of the Seine R.

right brain *n.* The right portion of the cerebral hemisphere, controlling activity on the left side of the body, and in humans, involved in processing spatial and nonverbal concepts.

right-brained (rīt′brānd′) also **right-brain** (-brān′) *adj.* Of, relating to, or tending toward thought processes usu. associated with the right brain, esp. those involving creativity and imagination.

right circular cone *n.* A cone with a circular directrix whose base is perpendicular to its axis.

right-click (rīt′klĭk′) *intr.v.* **-clicked, -click·ing, -clicks** *Computer Science* To click the secondary button of a mouse having two buttons with different functions.

right·eous (rī′chəs) *adj.* **1.** Morally upright; without guilt or sin. **2.** In accordance with virtue or morality. **3.** Morally justifiable: *righteous anger.* See Syns at **moral.** ❖ *n.* Righteous people considered as a group. [ME *ryghtuous,* alteration of *rihtwise* < OE *rihtwīs* : *riht,* right; see RIGHT + *-wīse,* -wise.] —**right′eous·ly** *adv.* —**right′eous·ness** *n.*

right field *n.* *Baseball* **1.** The third of the outfield that is to the right, looking from home plate. **2.** The position played by the right fielder.

right fielder *n.* *Baseball* The player who defends right field.

right·ful (rīt′fəl) *adj.* **1.** Right or proper; just. **2.** Having a just or proper claim. **3.** Held or owned by just or proper claim. —**right′ful·ly** *adv.* —**right′ful·ness** *n.*

right-hand (rīt′hănd′) *adj.* **1.** Of, relating to, or located on the right. **2.** Relating to, designed for, or done with the right hand. **3.** Most helpful or reliable: *my right-hand assistant.*

right-hand·ed (rīt′hăn′dĭd) *adj.* **1a.** Using the right hand more skillfully or easily than the left. **b.** *Sports* Swinging from the right to the left. **2a.** Of, relating to, or done with the right hand. **b.** Intended for wear on or use by the right hand. **3a.** Turning or spiraling from left to right; clockwise. **b.** Rotating clockwise; dextrorotatory. ❖ *adv.* **1.** With the right hand. **2.** *Sports* From right to left. —**right′-hand′ed·ly** *adv.* —**right′-hand′ed·ness** *n.*

right-hand·er (rīt′hăn′dər) *n.* One who is right-handed.

right·ism also **Right·ism** (rī′tĭz′əm) *n.* **1.** The ideology of the political right. **2.** Belief in or support of the tenets of the political right. —**right′ist** *n.*

right·ly (rīt′lē) *adv.* **1.** In a correct manner; properly. **2.** With honesty; justly. **3.** *Informal* Really; I don't rightly know.

right-mind·ed (rīt′mīn′dĭd) *adj.* Having ideas and views based on what is right or intended to be right. —**right′-mind′ed·ness** *n.*

right of way also **right-of-way** (rīt′əv-wā′) *n., pl.* **rights of way** or **right of ways** also **rights-of-way** (rīts′-) or **right-of-ways** (-wāz′) **1a.** The right to pass over property owned by another party. **b.** The path or thoroughfare on which such passage is made. **2.** The strip of land over which facilities such as highways, railroads, or power lines are built. **3.** The customary or legal right of a person, vessel, or vehicle to pass in front of another.

right-on (rīt′ŏn′, -ôn′) *adj. Slang* **1.** Up-to-date and sophisticated. **2.** Absolutely right; perfectly true.

right-out (rīt′out′) *adj. Chiefly Southern US* Outright. See Regional Note at **everywhere.**

right-side up (rīt′sīd′) *adv. & adj.* **1a.** With the top facing upward. **b.** In or into the correct orientation. **2.** In or into a condition of order.

right-to-die (rīt′tə-dī′) *adj.* Relating to or advocating a person's right to refuse extraordinary measures intended to prolong life after a physician has deemed that person to be terminally or incurably ill.

right-to-life (rīt′tə-līf′) *adj.* Relating to or advocating full legal protection of human embryos or fetuses; pro-life. —**right-to-lif′er** *n.*

right-to-work law (rīt′tə-wûrk′) *n.* A state law that prohibits required union membership of workers.

right·ward (rīt′wərd) *adv. & adj.* To or on the right.

right whale *n.* Any of several whales of the family Balaenidae, characterized by a large head, whalebone plates in the mouth, and absence of a dorsal fin. [Because it was the "right" whale to kill.]

right wing or **Right Wing** *n.* **1.** The conservative or reactionary faction of a group. See **right** 3a. —**right′-wing′** (rīt′wĭng′) *adj.* —**right′-wing′er** *n.*

right·y (rī′tē) *Informal n., pl.* **-ies 1.** A right-handed person. **2.** An advocate or member of the political right. ❖ *adv.* With the right hand or in a right-handed manner.

rig·id (rĭj′ĭd) *adj.* **1.** Not flexible or pliant; stiff. **2.** Not moving; fixed. **3.** Marked by a lack of flexibility; rigorous and exacting. **4.** Scrupulously maintained or performed. See Syns at **stiff.** [ME *rigide* < Lat. *rigidus* < *rigēre,* to be stiff.] —**rig′id·ly** *adv.* —**rig′id·ness** *n.*

ri·gid·i·fy (rĭ-jĭd′ə-fī′) *intr. & tr.v.* **-fied, -fy·ing, -fies** To become or cause to become rigid. —**ri·gid′i·fi·ca′tion** (-fĭ-kā′shən) *n.*

ri·gid·i·ty (rĭ-jĭd′ĭ-tē) *n., pl.* **-ties 1.** The quality or state of being rigid. **2.** An instance of being rigid.

rig·ma·role (rĭg′mə-rōl′) also **rig·a·ma·role** (-ə-mə-rōl′) *n.* **1.** Confused, rambling, or incoherent discourse; nonsense. **2.** A complicated petty set of procedures. [Alteration of obsolete *ragman roll,* catalog < ME *ragmane roll,* scroll used in Ragman, a game of chance : perh. AN *Ragemon le bon,* Ragemon the Good, title of a set of verses about a character of this name + ME *rolle,* list (< OFr. < Lat. *rotula,* wheel; see ROLL).]

rig·or (rĭg′ər) *n.* **1.** Strictness or severity, as in temperament, action, or judgment. **2.** A harsh or trying circumstance; hardship. See Syns at **difficulty. 3.** A harsh or cruel act. **4.** *Medicine* Shivering or trembling, as caused by a chill. **5.** *Physiology* A state of rigidity in living tissues or organs that prevents response to stimuli. **6.** *Obsolete* Stiffness or rigidity. [ME *rigour* < OFr. < Lat. *rigor* < *rigēre,* to be stiff.]

rig·or·ism (rĭg′ə-rĭz′əm) *n.* Harshness or strictness, as in conduct or judgment. —**rig′or·ist** *n.* —**rig′or·is′tic** *adj.*

rigor mor·tis (môr′tĭs) *n.* Muscular stiffening following death. [Lat. : *rigor,* stiffness + *mortis,* genitive of *mors,* death.]

rig·or·ous (rĭg′ər-əs) *adj.* **1.** Characterized by or acting with rigor. **2.** Full of rigors; harsh. **3.** Rigidly accurate; precise. —**rig′or·ous·ly** *adv.* —**rig′or·ous·ness** *n.*

rig·our (rĭg′ər) *n. Chiefly British* Variant of **rigor.**

Rig-Ve·da also **Rig Ve·da** or **Rig·ve·da** (rĭg-vā′də, -vē′də) *n.* The most ancient collection of Hindu sacred verses. [Skt. *r̥gvedaḥ* : *r̥k,* verse, sacred text + *vedaḥ,* knowledge, veda; see **weid-** in App.]

Riis (rēs), **Jacob August** 1849–1914. Danish-born Amer. journalist known for his reports on conditions in city slums.

Ri·je·ka (rē-yĕk′ə) Formerly **Fi·u·me** (fyoō′mā, -mě) A city of W Croatia on the Adriatic Sea WSW of Zagreb; formerly an independent city. Pop. 167,964.

Rijs·wijk (rīs′vīk′) also **Rys·wick** (rĭz′wĭk′) A city of W Netherlands, a suburb of The Hague. The Treaty of Ryswick (1697) acknowledged William of Orange as William III of England. Pop. 49,790.

Riks·mål (rĭks′môl′, rĕks′-) *n.* See **Dano-Norwegian.** [Norw. : *riks,* genitive of *rik,* realm (< ON *rīki;* see **reg-** in App.) + *mål,* speech (< ON *māl*).]

rile (rīl) *tr.v.* **riled, ril·ing, riles 1.** To stir to anger. **2.** To stir up

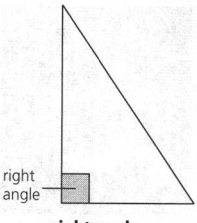

right angle

Jacob August Riis

ă	pat	oi	boy
ā	pay	ou	out
âr	care	ōō	took
ä	father	ōō	boot
ĕ	pet	ŭ	cut
ē	be	ûr	urge
ĭ	pit	th	thin
ī	pie	th	this
îr	pier	hw	which
ŏ	pot	zh	vision
ō	toe	ə	about,
ô	paw		item

Stress marks:
′ (primary);
′ (secondary), as in
lexicon (lĕk′sĭ-kŏn′)

(liquid); roil. [Variant of ROIL.]

Ri•ley (rī'lē), **James Whitcomb** 1849–1916. Amer. poet whose works include "The Raggedy Man" (1890).

Ril•ke (rĭl'kə), **Rainer Maria** 1875–1926. Austrian-born German poet who wrote *The Book of Hours* (1905).

rill also **rille** (rĭl) *n.* **1.** A small brook; a rivulet. **2.** A long narrow straight valley on the moon's surface. [LGer. *rille* or Du. *ril*, running stream.]

rill•et (rĭl'ĭt) *n.* A small rill.

rim (rĭm) *n.* **1.** The usu. curved or circular border or edge of an object. See Syns at **border**. **2.** The circular outer part of a wheel, furthest from the axle. **3.** A circular metal structure around which a wheel tire is fitted. ❖ *tr.v.* **rimmed, rim•ming, rims 1.** To furnish with a rim. **2.** *Sports* To roll around the rim of (a basket, for example) without falling in. **3.** *Vulgar Slang* To perform anilingus on. [ME < OE *rima*.]

Rim•baud (răm-bō', răn-), **Jean Nicholas Arthur** 1854–91. French poet whose work strongly influenced the surrealists.

rime[1] (rīm) *n.* **1.** A coating of ice, as on grass and trees, formed when water droplets freeze almost instantly on a cold surface. **2.** A coating, as of mud or slime, likened to a frosty film. ❖ *tr.v.* **rimed, rim•ing, rimes** To cover with or as if with frost or ice. [ME *rim* < OE *hrīm*.] —**rim'y** *adj.*

rime[2] (rīm) *n. & v.* Variant of **rhyme**.

rim•er (rī'mər) *n.* Variant of **rhymer**.

rime riche (rēm rēsh') *n., pl.* **rimes riches** (rēm rēsh') Rhyme using words or parts of words that are pronounced identically but have different meanings, for example, *write-right* or *port-deport*. [Fr. : *rime*, rhyme + *riche*, rich.]

rime•ster (rīm'stər) *n.* Variant of **rhymester**.

Ri•mi•ni (rĭm'ə-nē, rē'mē-) A city of N Italy on the Adriatic Sea SSE of Ravenna; founded by Umbrians and part of the Papal States from 1509 to 1860. Pop. 128,119.

Rimini, Francesca da See **Francesca da Rimini**.

ri•mose (rī'mōs', rī-mōs') *adj.* Full of chinks, cracks, or crevices. [Lat. *rīmōsus* < *rīma*, fissure.] —**ri'mose•ly** *adv.* —**ri•mos'i•ty** (-mŏs'ĭ-tē) *n.*

Rim•ski-Kor•sa•kov or **Rim•sky-Kor•sa•kov** (rĭm'skē-kôr'sə-kôf'), **Nikolai Andreyevich** 1844–1908. Russian composer whose works were heavily influenced by folk music.

rind (rīnd) *n.* A tough outer covering such as bark, the skin of some fruits, or the coating on cheese or bacon. [ME < OE.]

rin•der•pest (rĭn'dər-pĕst') *n.* An acute, often fatal contagious viral disease, chiefly of cattle, characterized by ulceration of the alimentary tract and resulting in diarrhea. [Ger. : *Rinder*, genitive pl. of *Rind*, head of cattle, ox (< MHGer. *rint* < OHGer. *hrind*; see *ker*-[1] in App.) + *Pest*, plague (< Lat. *pestis*).]

Rine•hart (rīn'härt'), **Mary Roberts** 1876–1958. Amer. writer whose mysteries include *The Circular Staircase* (1908).

ring[1] (rĭng) *n.* **1.** A circular object, form, line, or arrangement with a vacant circular center. **2.** A small circular band, usu. made of precious metal and often set with jewels, worn on the finger. **3.** A circular band used for carrying, holding, or containing something. **4. rings** *Sports* A pair of circular metal bands suspended in the air for gymnastic exercises, on which balancing and swinging maneuvers are performed while holding the bands as motionless as possible. **5.** A circular movement or course, as in dancing. **6.** An enclosed, usu. circular area in which exhibitions, sports, or contests take place. *Sports* **a.** A rectangular arena set off by stakes and ropes in which boxing or wrestling events are held. **b.** The sport of boxing. **8.** *Games* **a.** An enclosed area in which bets are placed at a racetrack. **b.** Bookmakers considered as a group. **9.** An exclusive group of people acting privately or illegally to advance their own interests. **10.** A political contest; a race. **11.** *Botany* An annual ring. **12.** *Mathematics* The area between two concentric circles; annulus. **13.** *Mathematics* A set of elements subject to the operations of addition and multiplication, in which the set is commutative under addition and associative under multiplication and in which the two operations are related by distributive laws. **14.** Any of the turns constituting a spiral or helix. **15.** *Chemistry* A group of atoms linked by bonds that may be represented graphically in circular or triangular form. ❖ *v.* **ringed, ring•ing, rings** —*tr.* **1.** To surround with or as if with a ring; encircle. **2.** To form into a ring or rings. **3.** To ornament or supply with a ring or rings. **4.** To remove a circular strip of bark around the circumference of (a tree trunk or branch); girdle. **5.** To put a ring in the nose of (an animal). **6.** To hem in (animals) by riding in a circle around them. **7.** *Games* To toss a ring over (a peg), as in horseshoes. —*intr.* **1.** To form a ring or rings. **2.** To move, run, or fly in a spiral or circular course. [ME < OE *hring*.]

ring[2] (rĭng) *v.* **rang** (răng), **rung** (rŭng), **ring•ing, rings** —*intr.* **1.** To give forth a clear resonant sound. **2.** To cause something to ring. **3.** To sound a bell in order to summon someone: *rang for the maid.* **4.** To have a sound or character suggestive of a particular quality: *a story that rings true.* **5.** To be filled with sound; resound. **6.** To hear a persistent humming or buzzing. **7.** To be filled with talk or rumor. —*tr.* **1.** To cause (a bell, for example) to ring. **2.** To produce (a sound) by or as if by ringing. **3.** To announce, proclaim, or signal by or as if by ringing. **4.** *Chiefly British* To call (someone) on the telephone. Often used with *up*: *Let's*

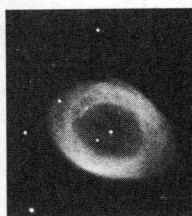

Ring Nebula

ring-necked pheasant
Phasianus colchicus

ring her up and invite her. **5.** To test (a coin, for example) for quality by the sound it produces when struck against something. ❖ *n.* **1.** The sound created by a bell or another sonorous vibrating object. **2.** A loud sound, esp. one repeated or continued. **3.** A telephone call: *Give me a ring when you get home.* **4.** A suggestion of a particular quality. **5.** A set of bells. **6.** The act or an instance of sounding a bell. —*phrasal verb:* **ring up 1.** To record, esp. by means of a cash register. **2.** To accomplish or achieve; win. —*idioms:* **ring a bell** *Informal* To arouse an often indistinct memory. **ring down the curtain** To end a performance, event, or action. **ring (someone's) chimes** (or **bells**) *Slang* To knock (an opponent) out by force. **ring up the curtain** To begin a performance, event, or action. [ME *ringen* < OE *hringan*.]

ring•bolt (rĭng'bōlt') *n.* A bolt having a ring fitted through its eye.

ring•bone (rĭng'bōn') *n.* A bony growth on the fetlock, pastern, or coffin bone of a horse's foot, usu. causing lameness.

ring•dove (rĭng'dŭv') *n.* **1.** An Old World pigeon (*Streptopelia risoria*) having black markings forming a half circle on the neck. **2.** See **wood pigeon**.

ringed (rĭngd) *adj.* **1.** Wearing or marked with a ring or rings. **2.** Encircled or surrounded by bands or rings. **3.** *Zoology* Formed from segmented rings; annulate.

rin•gent (rĭn'jənt) *adj.* Having gaping liplike parts, as the corolla of some flowers. [Lat. *ringēns, ringent-*, pr. part. of *ringī*, to open the mouth wide.]

ring•er[1] (rĭng'ər) *n. Games* A horseshoe or quoit thrown so that it encircles the peg.

ring•er[2] (rĭng'ər) *n.* **1.** One that rings, esp. one that sounds a bell or chime. **2.** *Slang* A contestant entered dishonestly into a competition. **3.** *Slang* One who bears a striking resemblance to another: *a ringer for his father.*

Ring•er's solution (rĭng'ərz) also **Ring•er solution** (-ər) *n.* An aqueous solution of the chlorides of sodium, potassium, and calcium that is isotonic to animal tissue and used topically as a physiological saline. [After Sydney *Ringer* (1835–1910), British physician.]

ring finger *n.* The third finger of the left hand.

ring•git (rĭng'gĭt) *n.* See table at **currency**. [Malay.]

ring•hals (rĭng'hăls') *n., pl.* **-hals•es** An African snake (*Hemachatus haemachatus*) that spits venom at the eyes of an attacker, sometimes causing blindness. [Obsolete Afr. : *ring*, ring (< MDu. *rinc*) + *hals*, neck (< MDu.; see *kwel-* in App.).]

ring•lead•er (rĭng'lē'dər) *n.* A person who leads others, esp. in illicit or informal activities.

ring•let (rĭng'lĭt) *n.* **1.** A long, spirally curled lock of hair. **2.** A small circle or ring. —**ring'let•ed** *adj.*

Ring•ling (rĭng'lĭng), **Charles** 1863–1926. Amer. circus owner who was a founder of the Ringling Brothers and Barnum & Bailey Circus (1907).

ring•mas•ter (rĭng'măs'tər) *n.* A person who is in charge of the performances in a circus ring.

Ring Nebula *n.* A planetary nebula in the constellation Lyra.

ring-necked duck (rĭng'nĕkt') *n.* A North American duck (*Aythya collaris*) having a distinctive light ring behind the tip of the bill and in the male a light chestnut ring around the neck.

ring-necked pheasant *n.* A widely distributed bird (*Phasianus colchicus*) native to the Old World, the male of which has brightly colored plumage and a white ring around the neck.

Ring of Fire *n.* An extensive zone of volcanic and seismic activity that coincides roughly with the borders of the Pacific Ocean.

ring•side (rĭng'sīd') *n.* **1.** The area or seats immediately outside an arena or ring, as at a prizefight. **2.** A place providing a close view of a spectacle.

ring•tail (rĭng'tāl') *n.* A small carnivorous raccoonlike mammal (*Bassariscus astutus*) of the southwest United States, having a black-banded tail.

ring-tailed (rĭng'tāld') *adj.* **1.** Having a tail with ringlike markings. **2.** Having a tail that curls to form a ring.

ring topology *n. Computer Science* A topology for a LAN in which all nodes are arranged in a circle.

ring•toss (rĭng'tôs') *n.* A game in which players toss rings at a stake so as to encircle it or come closer to it than the other players.

ring•worm (rĭng'wûrm') *n.* Any of a number of contagious skin diseases caused by several related fungi, characterized by ring-shaped scaly itching patches on the skin.

rink (rĭngk) *n.* **1.** An area surfaced with smooth ice for skating, hockey, or curling. **2.** A smooth floor suited for roller-skating. **3.** A building that houses a surface prepared for skating. **4.** A section of a bowling green large enough for holding a match. **5.** A team of players in quoits, bowling, or curling. [ME *renk*, racecourse, poss. < OFr. *renc*, line, of Gmc. orig.]

rin•ky-dink (rĭng'kē-dĭngk') *Slang adj.* **1.** Old-fashioned; worn out. **2.** Insignificant; unimportant. **3.** Of cheap or poor quality; makeshift. [?] —**rin'ky-dink'** *n.*

rinse (rĭns) *tr.v.* **rinsed, rins•ing, rins•es 1.** To wash lightly with water: *rinsed the dishes.* **2.** To remove (soap, for example) by washing lightly in water. ❖ *n.* **1.** The act of washing lightly. **2.** A solution, such as water, used in rinsing. **3.** A solution used in coloring or conditioning the hair. [ME *rincen* < OFr. *rincier* < VLat. *recentiāre* < Lat. *recēns, recent-*, fresh. See RECENT.]

—rins′a•ble, rins′i•ble adj. —rins′er n.

Rí•o or Ri•o (rē′ō) For names of South American rivers, see the specific element; for example, Plata, Río de la, or Roosevelt, Rio.

Ri•o•bam•ba (rē′ō-bäm′bə, -väm′bä) A city of central Ecuador in the Andes S of Quito; site of Ecuador's proclamation of independence (1830). Pop. 75,455.

Rio de Ja•nei•ro (dä zhə-nâr′ō, dē, dĭ) A city of SE Brazil on Guanabara Bay, an arm of the Atlantic Ocean; probably first visited by Portuguese explorers in Jan. 1502. Pop. 5,473,909.

Río de O•ro (dē ôr′ō, thē) The S part of Western Sahara in NW Africa.

Rio Grande (grănd′, grän′dä, grän′dē) or in Mexico Río Bra•vo (brä′vō) A river rising in SW CO and flowing c. 3,033 km (1,885 mi) to SW TX, where it forms the US-Mexico border before emptying into the Gulf of Mexico.

Río Mu•ni (mōō′nē) The mainland part of Equatorial Guinea, on the Bight of Biafra in W Africa.

ri•ot (rī′ət) n. 1. A wild or turbulent disturbance created by a large number of people. 2. Law A violent disturbance of the public peace by three or more persons assembled for a common purpose. 3. An unrestrained outbreak, as of laughter or passions. 4. A profusion. 5a. Unrestrained merrymaking; revelry. b. Debauchery. 6. Slang An irresistibly funny person or thing. ❖ v. -ot•ed, -ot•ing, -ots —intr. 1. To take part in a riot. 2. To live wildly or engage in uncontrolled revelry. —tr. To waste (money or time) in wild or wanton living. [ME < OFr., dispute < rioter, to quarrel, perh. < ruire, to roar < Lat. rūgīre.] —ri′ot•er n.

Riot Act n. An English law, enacted in 1715, providing that if 12 or more people unlawfully assemble and disturb the public peace, they must disperse upon proclamation or be considered guilty of felony. —idiom: read the riot act To warn or reprimand energetically or forcefully.

ri•ot•ous (rī′ət-əs) adj. 1. Of, relating to, or resembling a riot. 2. Participating in or inciting to riot or uproar. 3. Uproarious; boisterous. 4. Dissolute; wanton. 5. Abundant or luxuriant. —ri′ot•ous•ly adv. —ri′ot•ous•ness n.

rip¹ (rĭp) v. ripped, rip•ping, rips —tr. 1. To cut, tear apart, or tear away roughly or energetically. See Syns at tear¹. 2. To split or saw (wood) along the grain. 3. To subject to vehement criticism or attack: The critic ripped the tedious movie. 4. Informal To produce, display, or utter suddenly: rips out a yell. —intr. 1. To become torn or split apart. 2. Informal To move quickly or violently. ❖ n. 1. The act of ripping. 2. A torn or split place, esp. along a seam. 3. A ripsaw. —phrasal verbs: rip into To attack or criticize vehemently. rip off Slang 1. To steal from. 2. To steal. 3. To exploit, swindle, cheat, or defraud. [ME rippen < Flem. See reup- in App.] —rip′per n.

rip² (rĭp) n. 1. A stretch of water in a river, estuary, or tidal channel made rough by waves meeting an opposing current. 2. A rip current. [Prob. < RIP¹.]

rip³ (rĭp) n. 1. A dissolute person. 2. An old or worthless horse. [Poss. shortening and alteration of REPROBATE.]

RIP abbr. Latin requiescat in pace (may he rest in peace; may she rest in peace)

ri•par•i•an (rĭ-pâr′ē-ən) adj. Of, on, or relating to the banks of a natural course of water. [< Lat. rīpārius < rīpa, bank.]

riparian right n. The right, as to fishing or the use of a riverbed, of one who owns riparian land.

rip•cord (rĭp′kôrd′) n. 1. A cord pulled to release the pack of a parachute. 2. A cord pulled to release gas from a balloon.

rip current n. A strong narrow surface current that flows rapidly away from the shore.

ripe (rīp) adj. rip•er, rip•est 1. Fully developed; mature. 2. Resembling matured fruit, as in fullness. 3. Sufficiently advanced in preparation or aging to be used or eaten. 4. Thoroughly matured, as by study or experience; seasoned. 5. Advanced in years. 6. Fully prepared to do or undergo something; ready. 7. Sufficiently advanced; opportune. 8. Exhibiting overtones of or references to sex; scatological. 9. Emitting a foul odor, esp. body odor. [ME < OE rīpe.] —ripe′ly adv. —ripe′ness n.

rip•en (rī′pən) tr. & intr.v. -ened, -en•ing, -ens To make or become ripe or riper; mature. See Syns at mature.

Rip•ken (rĭp′kən), Calvin ("Cal") Edward, Jr. b. 1960. Amer. baseball player whose record-setting streak for consecutive games played (2,632) ended in 1998.

rip-off (rĭp′ôf′, -ŏf′) n. Slang 1. A theft. 2. A thief. 3. An act of exploitation. 4. Something, such as a film or story, that is clearly imitative of or based on something else.

ri•poste (rĭ-pōst′) n. 1. Sports A quick thrust given after parrying an opponent's lunge in fencing. 2. A retaliatory action, maneuver, or retort. ❖ intr.v. -post•ed, -post•ing, -postes 1. To make a return thrust. 2. To retort quickly. [Fr., alteration of obsolete risposte < Ital. risposta, answer < fem. p. part. of rispondere, to answer < Lat. respondēre. See RESPOND.]

ripped (rĭpt) adj. Slang 1. Having an extremely defined physique; toned: ripped, bulging muscles. 2. Intoxicated by alcohol or a drug.

rip•ping (rĭp′ĭng) adj. Informal Excellent; marvelous.

rip•ple (rĭp′əl) v. -pled, -pling, -ples —intr. 1a. To form or display small undulations or waves on the surface, as disturbed water does. b. To flow with such undulations or waves on the

surface. 2. To rise and fall gently in tone or volume. —tr. To cause to form small waves or undulations. ❖ n. 1. A small wave. 2. A wavelike motion; an undulation. 3. A sound like that made by rippling water. [ME ripplen, to wrinkle, crease, perh. of Scand. orig.] —rip′pler n. —rip′pling•ly adv.

rip•ple² (rĭp′əl) n. A comblike toothed instrument for removing seeds from flax and other fibers. ❖ tr.v. -pled, -pling, -ples To remove seeds from with a ripple. [ME < *ripelen, to remove seeds; akin to MLGer. repelen.]

ripple effect n. A gradually spreading effect or influence.

rip•plet (rĭp′lĭt) n. A small wave or ripple.

rip•ply (rĭp′lē) adj. -pli•er, -pli•est Characterized by or sounding in ripples.

rip•rap (rĭp′răp′) n. 1. A loose assemblage of broken stones erected in water or on soft ground as a foundation. 2. The broken stones used for such a foundation. ❖ tr.v. -rapped, -rap•ping, -raps 1. To construct a riprap in or on. 2. To strengthen with a riprap. [Reduplication of RAP¹.]

rip-roar•ing (rĭp′rôr′ĭng, -rōr′-) also rip-roar•i•ous (rĭp′rôr′rē-əs, -rōr′-) adj. Informal Noisy, lively, and exciting. [< RIP¹ + (UP)ROAR(IOUS).] —rip′-roar′ing•ly adv.

rip•saw (rĭp′sô′) n. A coarse-toothed saw used for cutting wood along the grain.

rip•snort•er (rĭp′snôr′tər) n. Slang One that is remarkable for strength, intensity, or excellence. —rip′snort′ing adj.

rip tide n. See rip current.

Rip•u•ar•i•an (rĭp′yōō-âr′ē-ən) adj. Of, relating to, or being a group of Franks who settled along the Rhine, near Cologne, in the fourth century A.D. [< Med.Lat. Ripuārius.] —Rip′u•ar′i•an n.

RISC abbr. reduced instruction set computer

rise (rīz) v. rose (rōz), ris•en (rĭz′ən), ris•ing, ris•es —intr. 1. To assume a standing position after lying, sitting, or kneeling. 2. To get out of bed: rose at dawn. 3. To move from a lower to a higher position; ascend: Hot air rises. 4. To increase in size, volume, or level: The river rises every spring. 5. To increase in number, amount, or value: Prices are rising. 6. To increase in intensity, force, or speed: The wind has risen. 7. To increase in pitch or volume: The sound of their voices rose. 8. To appear above the horizon: The sun rises later in the fall. 9. To extend upward; be prominent: The tower rose above the hill. 10. To slant or slope upward: Mt. McKinley rises to nearly 6,200 meters. 11. To come into existence; originate. See Syns at stem¹. 12. To be erected. 13. To appear at the surface of the water or the earth; emerge. 14. To puff up or become larger; swell up. 15. To become stiff and erect. 16. To attain a higher status. 17. To become apparent to the mind or senses. 18. To uplift oneself to meet a demand or challenge. 19. To return to life. 20. To rebel. 21. To close a session of an official assembly; adjourn. —tr. To cause to rise. ❖ n. 1. The act of rising; ascent. 2. The degree of elevation or ascent. 3. The appearance of the sun or other celestial body above the horizon. 4. An increase in height, as of the level of water. 5. A gently sloped hill. 6. A long broad elevation that slopes gently, as from the earth's surface. 7. An origin, beginning, or source. See Syns at beginning. 8. Occasion or opportunity. 9. The emergence of a fish seeking food or bait at the water's surface. 10. An increase in price, worth, quantity, or degree. 11. An increase in intensity, volume, or pitch. 12. Elevation in status, prosperity, or importance. 13. The height of a flight of stairs or of a single riser. 14. Chiefly British An increase in salary or wages; a raise. 15. Informal An angry or irritated reaction. 16. The distance between the crotch and waistband in pants, shorts, or underwear. [ME risen < OE rīsan. See er- in App.]

ris•er (rī′zər) n. 1. One who rises, esp. from sleep: a late riser. 2. The vertical part of a stair step. 3. A platform, as for elevating a group of people above a crowd, often arranged with similar platforms in tiers.

rish•i (rĭsh′ē, rē′shē) n., pl. -is A divinely inspired poet or sage in India. [Skt. ṛṣih.]

ris•i•bil•i•ty (rĭz′ə-bĭl′ĭ-tē) n., pl. -ties 1. The ability or tendency to laugh. 2. A sense of the ludicrous or amusing. Often used in the plural. 3. Laughter; hilarity.

ris•i•ble (rĭz′ə-bəl) adj. 1. Relating to laughter or used in eliciting laughter. 2. Eliciting laughter; ludicrous. 3. Capable of laughing or inclined to laugh. [LLat. rīsibilis < Lat. rīsus, p. part. of rīdēre, to laugh.] —ris′i•bly adv.

ris•ing (rī′zĭng) adj. 1. Ascending, sloping upward, or advancing. 2. Coming to maturity; emerging. ❖ n. 1. The action of one that rises. 2. An uprising; an insurrection. 3. A prominence or projection. 4. The leaven or yeast used to make dough rise in baking.

rising rhythm n. A rhythmic pattern in which the stress falls on the last syllable of each foot, as in "They danced by the light of the moon" (Edward Lear).

risk (rĭsk) n. 1. The possibility of suffering harm or loss; danger. 2. A factor, thing, element, or course involving uncertain danger; a hazard. 3a. The danger or probability of loss to an insurer. b. The amount that an insurance company stands to lose. 4a. The variability of returns from an investment. b. The chance of nonpayment of a debt. 5. One considered with respect to the possibility of loss. ❖ tr.v. risked, risk•ing, risks 1. To expose to a chance of loss or damage; hazard. See Syns at endanger. 2. To incur the

ă	pat	oi	boy
ā	pay	ou	out
âr	care	ŏŏ	took
ä	father	ōō	boot
ĕ	pet	ŭ	cut
ē	be	ûr	urge
ĭ	pit	th	this
ī	pie	th	this
îr	pier	hw	which
ŏ	pot	zh	vision
ō	toe	ə	about,
ô	paw		item

Stress marks:
′ (primary);
′ (secondary); as in
lexicon (lĕk′sĭ-kŏn′)

Diego Rivera

roadrunner
Geococcyx californianus

roadster
1929 Packard 640 Runabout

risk of. —*idiom:* **at risk** In an endangered state, esp. from lack of proper care. [Fr. *risque* < Ital. *risco, rischio.*] —**risk′er** *n.*

risk capital *n.* See **venture capital.**

risk•y (rĭs′kē) *adj.* **-i•er, -i•est** Accompanied by or involving risk or danger; hazardous. —**risk′i•ness** *n.*

Ri•sor•gi•men•to (rĭ-sôr′jə-mĕn′tō, rē-zôr′jē-) *n.* The period of or the movement for the liberation and political unification of Italy, beginning about 1750 and lasting until 1870. [Ital. < *risorgere,* to rise again < Lat. *resurgere.* See RESURGE.]

ri•sot•to (rē-zôt′tō, rĭ-) *n., pl.* **-tos** A dish of rice cooked in broth, often with saffron, and served with grated cheese. [Ital. < *riso,* rice < OItal. See RICE.]

ris•qué (rĭs-kā′) *adj.* Suggestive of or bordering on indelicacy or impropriety. [Fr. < p. part. of *risquer,* to risk < *risque,* risk. See RISK.]

ri•stra (rē′strə) *n.* A string on which foodstuffs, such as chilies, onions, or garlic, are threaded or tied for storage. [Sp. < OSpan. *riestra,* var. of *riesta, rieste* < Lat. *restis,* rope, cord.]

rit. *abbr.* ritardando

Rit•a•lin (rĭt′l-ĭn) A trademark used for methylphenidate.

ri•tar•dan•do (rē′tär-dän′dō) *adv. & adj. Music* Gradually slowing in tempo; retarding. [Ital., pr. part. of *ritardare,* to slow down < Lat. *retardāre.* See RETARD[1].]

rite (rīt) *n.* **1.** The prescribed or customary form for conducting a religious or other solemn ceremony. **2.** A ceremonial act or series of acts. **3. Rite** The liturgy or practice of a branch of the Christian church. [ME < Lat. *rītus.*]

rite of passage *n., pl.* **rites of passage** A ritual or ceremony signifying an event in a person's life indicative of a transition from one stage to another, as from adolescence to adulthood.

ri•tor•nel•lo (rē′tôr-nĕl′lō) *n., pl.* **-li** (-lē) or **-los 1.** An instrumental interlude recurring after each stanza in a vocal work. **2.** A passage or section for full orchestra in a concerto or aria. **3.** An instrumental interlude in early 17th-century opera. **4.** The refrain of a rondo. [Ital., dim. of *ritorno,* return < *ritornare,* to return < VLat. **retornāre.* See RETURN.]

Rit•ter (rĭt′ər), **Woodward Maurice** Known as "Tex." 1907–74. Amer. singer who played a singing cowboy in radio shows and motion-picture Westerns.

rit•u•al (rĭch′ōō-əl) *n.* **1a.** The prescribed order of a religious ceremony. **b.** The body of ceremonies or rites used in a place of worship. **2a.** The prescribed form of conducting a formal secular ceremony. **b.** The body of ceremonies used by a fraternal organization. **3.** A book of rites or ceremonial forms. **4. rituals a.** A ceremonial act or a series of such acts. **b.** The performance of such acts. **5a.** A detailed method of procedure faithfully or regularly followed. **b.** A state or condition characterized by the presence of established procedure or routine. ❖ *adj.* **1.** Associated with or performed according to a rite or ritual: *a ritual sacrifice.* **2.** Being part of an established routine: *a ritual glass of milk before bed.* [< Lat. *rītuālis,* of rites < *rītus,* rite.] —**rit′u•al•ly** *adv.*

rit•u•al•ism (rĭch′ōō-ə-lĭz′əm) *n.* **1.** The practice or observance of religious ritual. **2.** Insistence on or adherence to ritual.

rit•u•al•ist (rĭch′ōō-ə-lĭst) *n.* **1.** An authority on or a student of ritual. **2.** One who practices or advocates the observance of ritual.

rit•u•al•is•tic (rĭch′ōō-ə-lĭs′tĭk) *adj.* **1.** Relating to ritual or ritualism. **2.** Advocating or practicing ritual. —**rit′u•al•is′ti•cal•ly** *adv.*

rit•u•al•ize (rĭch′ōō-ə-līz′) *v.* **-ized, -iz•ing, -iz•es** —*tr.* **1.** To make a ritual of. **2.** To force a ritual on. —*intr.* To engage in ritualism. —**rit′u•al•i•za′tion** (-ə-lĭ-zā′shən) *n.*

ritz (rĭts) *n. Informal* Elegant, often ostentatious display. —*idiom:* **put on the ritz** *Informal* To behave or live in an elegant ostentatious manner. [Back-formation < RITZY.]

ritz•y (rĭt′sē) *adj.* **-i•er, -i•est** *Informal* Elegant; fancy. [After the *Ritz* hotels, established by César *Ritz* (1850–1918), Swiss hotelier.]

Riv. *abbr.* river

riv•age (rĭv′ĭj) *n. Archaic* A coast, shore, or bank. [ME < OFr. < *rive,* bank < Lat. *rīpa.*]

ri•val (rī′vəl) *n.* **1.** One who attempts to equal or surpass another or pursues the same object as another; a competitor. **2.** One that equals or almost equals another in a particular respect. **3.** *Obsolete* A companion or an associate in a particular duty. ❖ *v.* **-valed, -val•ing, -vals** or **-valled, -val•ling, -vals** —*tr.* **1.** To attempt to equal or surpass. **2.** To be the equal of; match. —*intr.* To be a competitor or rival; compete. [Lat. *rīvālis,* one using the same stream as another, a rival < *rīvus,* stream.]

ri•val•rous (rī′vəl-rəs) *adj.* Characterized by or given to rivalry or competition.

ri•val•ry (rī′vəl-rē) *n., pl.* **-ries 1.** The act of competing or emulating. **2.** The state or condition of being a rival.

rive (rīv) *v.* **rived, riv•en** (rĭv′ən) also **rived, riv•ing, rives** —*tr.* **1.** To rend or tear apart. **2.** To break into pieces, as by a blow; cleave or split asunder. **3.** To break or distress (the spirit, for example). —*intr.* To be broken or split. [ME *riven* < ON *rīfa.*]

riv•er (rĭv′ər) *n.* **1.** A large natural stream of water emptying into an ocean, lake, or other body of water and usu. fed along its course by converging tributaries. **2.** A stream or abundant flow. —*idiom:* **up the river** *Slang* In or into prison. [ME *rivere* < AN < VLat. *rīpāria < Lat., fem. of *rīpārius,* of a bank < *rīpa,* bank.]

Ri•ve•ra (rĭ-vĕr′ə, rē-vĕ′rä), **Diego** 1886–1957. Mexican painter noted for his murals.

Rivera y Or•ba•ne•ja (ē ôr′bä-nĕ′hä, ôr′vä-), **Miguel Primo de** See Miguel **Primo de Rivera y Orbaneja.**

riv•er•bank (rĭv′ər-băngk′) *n.* The bank of a river.

river basin *n.* The land area drained by a river and its tributaries.

riv•er•bed (rĭv′ər-bĕd′) *n.* The area between the banks of a river ordinarily covered by water.

river blindness *n.* See **onchocerciasis.**

riv•er•boat (rĭv′ər-bōt′) *n.* A boat suitable for use on a river.

riv•er•head (rĭv′ər-hĕd′) *n.* The source of a river.

river horse *n.* See **hippopotamus** 1.

riv•er•ine (rĭv′ə-rīn′, -rēn′) *adj.* **1.** Relating to or resembling a river. **2.** Located on or inhabiting the banks of a river; riparian. **3.** Operating on or equipped to operate on rivers.

Riv•ers (rĭv′ərz), **Larry** b. 1923. Amer. artist whose paintings combine bold brushwork and realistic images.

riv•er•side (rĭv′ər-sīd′) *n.* The bank or area alongside a river.

Riverside A city of S CA NE of Santa Ana. Pop. 255,166.

riv•er•ward (rĭv′ər-wərd) also **riv•er•wards** (-wərdz) *adv.* Toward a river.

riv•er•weed (rĭv′ər-wēd′) *n.* An eastern North American plant (*Podostemum ceratophyllum*) having olive-green foliage resembling seaweed and growing in rapidly flowing streams.

riv•et (rĭv′ĭt) *n.* A metal bolt or pin having a head on one end, inserted through aligned holes in the pieces to be joined and then hammered on the plain end so as to form a second head. ❖ *tr.v.* **-et•ed, -et•ing, -ets 1.** To fasten or secure with or as if with a rivet. **2.** To hammer the headless end of so as to form a head and fasten something. **3.** To fasten or secure firmly; fix. **4.** To engross or hold (the attention, for example). [ME < OFr. *river,* to attach.] —**riv′et•er** *n.*

riv•et•ing (rĭv′ĭ-tĭng) *adj.* Wholly absorbing or engrossing one's attention; fascinating. —**riv′et•ing•ly** *adv.*

Riv•i•er•a (rĭv′ē-ĕr′ə, rē-vyĕr′ä) A narrow coastal region between the Alps and the Mediterranean Sea extending from SE France to NW Italy.

ri•vière (rĭ-vyâr′) *n.* A necklace of precious stones, usu. set in one strand. [Fr. *rivière (de diamants),* river (of diamonds) < OFr. *rivere* < VLat. **rīpāria.* See RIVER.]

riv•u•let (rĭv′yə-lĭt) *n.* A small brook or stream; a streamlet. [Poss. < Ital. *rivoletto,* dim. of *rivolo,* small stream < Lat. *rīvulus,* dim. of *rīvus,* stream.]

Ri•yadh (rē-yäd′) The cap. of Saudi Arabia, in the E-central part ENE of Mecca. Pop. 1,400,000.

ri•yal also **ri•al** (rē-ôl′, -äl′) *n.* See table at **currency.** [Ar. *riyāl* < Sp. *real,* real. See REAL[2].]

Ri•zal (rĭ-zäl′, rē-säl′), **José** 1861–96. Philippine national leader and writer whose execution precipitated an insurrection against Spanish rule (1896–98).

Riz•zio (rĭt′sē-ō′, rēt′tsē-), **David** 1533?–66. Italian musician and secretary to Mary Queen of Scots.

RJ *abbr.* road junction

RK *abbr.* radial keratotomy

Rm *abbr. Bible* Romans

rm. *abbr.* **1.** ream **2.** room

rms *abbr.* root mean square

Rn The symbol for the element **radon.**

RN *abbr.* **1.** registered nurse **2.** Royal Navy

RNA (är′ĕn-ā′) *n.* A polymeric constituent of all living cells and many viruses, important in protein synthesis and the transmission of genetic information and consisting of a long, usu. single-stranded chain of alternating phosphate and ribose units with the bases adenine, guanine, cytosine, and uracil bonded to the ribose. [R(IBO)N(UCLEIC) A(CID).]

RNA polymerase *n.* A polymerase that catalyzes the synthesis of a complementary strand of RNA from a DNA template, or, in some viruses, from an RNA template.

RN•ase (är′ĕn-ās′, -āz′) also **RNA•ase** (är′ĕn-ā′ās′, -āz′) *n.* See **ribonuclease.**

RNA virus *n.* An RNA-containing virus; retrovirus.

roach[1] (rōch) *n., pl.* **roach** or **roach•es 1.** A freshwater fish (*Rutilus rutilus*) of northern Europe. **2.** Any of various similar or related fishes, such as some North American sunfishes. [ME *roche* < OFr. *roce, roche.*]

roach[2] (rōch) *n., pl.* **roach•es 1.** The cockroach. **2.** *Slang* The butt of a marijuana cigarette.

roach[3] (rōch) *n., pl.* **roach•es 1.** A roll of hair brushed up from the forehead or temple. **2.** A hairstyle esp. among certain Native American peoples in which the head is shaved except for a strip from front to back across the top. **3.** *Nautical* An outward curve in the leech of a fore-and-aft sail. ❖ *tr.v.* **roached, roach•ing, roach•es 1.** To brush (hair) into a roach. **2.** To shave (the mane of a horse) to a short bristle. [?]

Roach, Maxwell ("Max") b. 1924. Amer. jazz drummer who defined the role of the drummer in the development of bop.

road (rōd) *n.* **1a.** An open, usu. public way for the passage of vehicles, people, and animals. **b.** The surface of a road; a roadbed. **2.** A course or path: *the road to riches.* **3.** A railroad. **4.** *Nautical* A roadstead. Often used in the plural. —*idioms:* **down the road** In the future; at a later date. **on the road 1.** On tour, as a theatrical company. **2.** Traveling, esp. as a salesperson. **3.** Wandering, as a vagabond. [ME *rode*, *rade*, a riding, road < OE *rād*.]

road agent *n.* A stagecoach robber; a bandit.

road·bed (rōd′bĕd′) *n.* **1a.** The foundation upon which the ties, rails, and ballast of a railroad are laid. **b.** A layer of ballast directly under the ties. **2.** The foundation and surface of a road.

road·block (rōd′blŏk′) *n.* **1.** A barricade or obstruction across a road to prevent passage, as of a fugitive. **2.** An obstruction in a road, as fallen rocks. **3.** Something that prevents further progress toward an accomplishment. —**road′block′** *v.*

road hog *n. Informal* A motorist whose vehicle overlaps the traffic lane used by another motorist.

road·house (rōd′hous′) *n.* An inn, restaurant, or nightclub located on a road outside a town or city.

road·ie (rō′dē) *n.* A person engaged to load, unload, and set up equipment and perform errands for musicians on tour.

road·kill (rōd′kĭl′) *n.* An animal or animals killed by being struck by a motor vehicle.

road map *n.* **1.** A map, esp. one for motorists, showing and designating the roads of a region. **2.** A set of guidelines, instructions, or explanations.

road metal *n.* Crushed or broken stone, cinders, or similar material used in the construction and repair of roads and roadbeds.

road rage *n.* Violent behavior exhibited by drivers in traffic, often as a manifestation of stress.

road·run·ner (rōd′rŭn′ər) *n.* A swift-running crested bird (*Geococcyx californianus*) of southwest North America having streaked brownish plumage and a long tail.

road show *n.* **1.** A show presented by a touring theater company. **2.** A new movie shown at selected theaters usu. for higher ticket prices.

road·side (rōd′sīd′) *n.* The area bordering a road.

road·stead (rōd′stĕd′) *n.* A sheltered offshore anchorage area for ships. [Variant of *rodested* : RODE² + *sted*, place (var. of STEAD).]

road·ster (rōd′stər) *n.* **1.** An open automobile having a single seat in the front for two or three people and a rumble seat or luggage compartment in the back. **2.** A horse for riding on a road.

road test *n.* **1.** A test of a motor vehicle's operating capability under actual road conditions. **2.** A test of driving ability on the road required of a candidate for a driver's license. —**road′-test′** (rōd′tĕst′) *v.*

Road Town The cap. of the British Virgin Islands, on Tortola I. in the West Indies E of Puerto Rico. Pop. 2,479.

road warrior *n. Informal* A person who travels frequently, esp. on business.

road·way (rōd′wā′) *n.* A road, esp. the part vehicles travel over.

road·work (rōd′wûrk′) *n.* **1.** Outdoor long-distance running as a form of physical exercise or conditioning. **2.** Highway construction.

road·wor·thy (rōd′wûr′thē) *adj.* **-thi·er, -thi·est** Fit to be driven on the open road: *a roadworthy truck.*

roam (rōm) *v.* **roamed, roam·ing, roams** —*intr.* To move about without purpose or plan; wander. See Syns at **wander.** —*tr.* To wander over or through. ❖ *n.* The act or an instance of roaming. [ME *romen*.] —**roam′er** *n.*

roan (rōn) *adj.* Having a chestnut, bay, or sorrel coat thickly sprinkled with white or gray. ❖ *n.* **1a.** The characteristic coloring of a roan horse. **b.** A roan horse or other animal. **2.** A soft flexible sheepskin leather, often treated to resemble morocco and used in bookbinding. [Obsolete Fr. < OFr. < OSpan. *roano*, prob. of Gmc. orig.]

Ro·a·noke (rō′ə-nōk′) An independent city of SW VA WSW of Richmond. Pop. 94,911.

Roanoke Island An island of NE NC off the Atlantic coast between Albemarle and Pamlico sounds. A group of English colonists who landed on the island in Jul. 1587 vanished without a trace sometime before 1591.

Roanoke River A river rising in SW VA and flowing c. 660 km (410 mi) to Albemarle Sound in NE NC.

roar (rôr, rōr) *v.* **roared, roar·ing, roars** —*intr.* **1.** To utter a loud deep prolonged sound, esp. in distress, rage, or excitement. **2.** To laugh loudly or excitedly. **3.** To make or produce a loud noise or din. **4.** To be disorderly or rowdy. **5.** To breathe with a rasping sound. Used of a horse. —*tr.* **1.** To utter or express with a loud deep prolonged sound. See Syns at **shout.** **2.** To bring, force, or force into a specified state by roaring. ❖ *n.* **1.** A loud deep prolonged sound or cry, as of a person in distress or rage. **2.** The loud deep cry of a wild animal. **3.** A loud prolonged noise. **4.** A loud burst of laughter. —**phrasal verb: roar back** To have great success after a period of lackluster performance. [ME *roren* < OE *rārian*.] —**roar′er** *n.*

roar·ing (rôr′ĭng, rōr′-) *adj.* **1.** Very lively or successful; thriving. **2.** Used as an intensive. —**roar′ing·ly** *adv.*

roast (rōst) *v.* **roast·ed, roast·ing, roasts** —*tr.* **1.** To cook with dry heat, as in an oven or near hot coals. **2.** To dry, brown, or parch by exposing to heat. **3.** To expose to great or excessive heat. **4.** *Metallurgy* To heat (ores) in a furnace in order to dehydrate, purify, or oxidize before smelting. **5.** *Informal* **a.** To ridicule or criticize harshly. **b.** To honor at or subject to a roast. —*intr.* **1.** To cook food in an oven. **2.** To undergo roasting. ❖ *n.* **1a.** Some-

thing roasted. **b.** A cut of meat suitable or prepared for roasting. **2a.** The act or process of roasting. **b.** The state of being roasted. **3a.** Harsh ridicule or criticism. **b.** A facetious tribute, as at a banquet, in which the honoree is alternately praised and insulted. ❖ *adj.* Roasted. [ME *rosten* < OFr. *rostir*, of Gmc. orig.]

roast·er (rō′stər) *n.* **1.** One that roasts. **2.** A special pan or apparatus for roasting. **3.** Something, esp. a young chicken, that is fit for roasting.

rob (rŏb) *v.* **robbed, rob·bing, robs** —*tr.* **1.** *Law* To take property from (a person) illegally by using or threatening to use violence or force; commit robbery upon. **2.** To take valuable or desired articles unlawfully from. **3a.** To deprive unjustly of something belonging to, desired by, or legally due (someone). **b.** To deprive of something injuriously. **4.** To take as booty; steal. —*intr.* To engage in or commit robbery. —*idioms:* **rob (someone) blind** To rob in an unusually deceitful or thorough way. **rob the cradle** *Informal* To have a romantic or sexual relationship with someone much younger than oneself. [ME *robben* < OFr. *rober*, of Gmc. orig. See **reup-** in App.] —**rob′ber** *n.*

ro·ba·lo (rō-bä′lō) *n., pl.* **-los** or **robalo** Any of various chiefly tropical marine food fishes of the family Centropomidae, such as the snook. [Sp. *róbalo*, haddock, prob. alteration of Catalan *llobarro* < *lobo*, wolf < Lat. *lupus*. See LOBO.]

Robbe-Gril·let (rôb-grē-yā′), **Alain** b. 1922. French writer and exponent of the New Wave in French literature.

robber baron *n.* **1.** One of the American industrial or financial magnates of the late 19th century who became wealthy by unethical means. **2.** A feudal lord who robbed travelers passing through his domain.

robber fly *n.* Any of various predatory flies of the family Asilidae, characteristically having long bristly legs.

rob·ber·y (rŏb′ə-rē) *n., pl.* **-ies** The act or an instance of unlawfully taking the property of another by the use of violence or intimidation.

Rob·bins (rŏb′ĭnz), **Jerome** 1918–98. Amer. choreographer of ballets and musicals, including *West Side Story* (1957).

robe (rōb) *n.* **1.** A long loose flowing outer garment, esp.: **a.** An official garment worn on formal occasions to show office or rank, as by a judge or high church official. **b.** An academic gown. **c.** A dressing gown or bathrobe. **2. robes** Clothes; apparel. **3.** A blanket or covering made of material such as fur or cloth: *a lap robe.* ❖ *v.* **robed, rob·ing, robes** —*tr.* To cover or dress in or as if in a robe. —*intr.* To put on robes or a robe. [ME < OFr., of Gmc. orig. See **reup-** in App.]

Rob·ert I[1] (rŏb′ərt) Known as "Robert the Devil." d. 1035. Duke of Normandy (1027–35) who named as his heir his illegitimate son William, the future William I of England.

Robert I[2] Known as "Robert the Bruce." 1274–1329. King of Scotland (1306–29) who won Scottish independence from England in a battle at Bannockburn (1314).

Robert, Henry Martyn 1837–1923. Amer. army engineer and parliamentarian who wrote *Robert's Rules of Order* (1876).

Rob·erts (rŏb′ərts), **Richard John** b. 1943. British-born chemist who shared a 1993 Nobel Prize in medicine.

Robe·son (rŏb′sən), **Paul Bustill** 1898–1976. Amer. singer and actor noted for his performance in *Othello.*

Robes·pierre (rōbz′pîr′, -pē-âr′, rô-bĕs-pyĕr′), **Maximilien François Marie Isidore de** 1758–94. French revolutionary leader of the Jacobins and architect of the Reign of Terror.

rob·in (rŏb′ĭn) *n.* **1.** A North American songbird (*Turdus migratorius*) having a rust-red breast and gray and black upper plumage. **2.** A small Old World bird (*Erithacus rubecula*) having an orange breast and a brown back. **3.** Any of various birds resembling a robin. [Short for *Robin Redbreast* < ME *Robin*, personal name < OFr., dim. of *Robert.*]

Robin Good·fel·low (gŏod′fĕl′ō) *n.* A mischievous sprite in English folklore; Puck.

Robin Hood *n.* A legendary English outlaw of the 12th century, famous for his courage, chivalry, and practice of robbing the rich to aid the poor.

robin redbreast *n.* See **robin** 1, 2.

rob·in's-egg blue (rŏb′ĭnz-ĕg′) *n.* A pale bluish green to greenish or grayish blue.

Rob·in·son (rŏb′ĭn-sən), **Edwin Arlington** 1869–1935. Amer. poet whose works include "Miniver Cheevy" (1910).

Robinson, Jack Roosevelt ("Jackie") 1919–72. Amer. baseball player who was the first African-American player in the major leagues as a second baseman for the Brooklyn Dodgers (1947–56).

Robinson, Mary b. 1944. Irish lawyer and politician who was the first woman president of Ireland (1990–97).

Robinson, Ray Known as "Sugar Ray." 1921–89. Amer. prizefighter who was world champion six times, once as a welterweight (1946–51) and five times as a middleweight (1951–60).

Rob·in's plantain (rŏb′ĭnz) *n.* An eastern North American plant (*Erigeron pulchellus*) having many-rayed purplish flower heads grouped in a corymb.

ro·ble (rō′blä) *n.* **1.** A Californian oak (*Quercus lobata*) having leathery leaves and slender pointed acorns. **2.** Any of various similar or related trees. [Sp. and Port., oak, both < Lat. *rōbur*. See **reudh-** in App.]

Paul Robeson

robin
male American robin
Turdus migratorius

Jackie Robinson

ă	pat	oi	boy
ā	pay	ou	out
âr	care	ŏŏ	took
ä	father	ōō	boot
ĕ	pet	ŭ	cut
ē	be	ûr	urge
ĭ	pie	th	thin
ī	pie	*th*	this
îr	pier	hw	which
ŏ	pot	zh	vision
ō	toe	ə	about,
ô	paw		item

Stress marks:
′ (primary);
′ (secondary), as in
lexicon (lĕk′sĭ-kŏn′)

rob·o·rant (rŏb′ər-ənt) *adj.* Restoring vigor or strength. ❖ *n.* A roborant drug; a restorative or tonic. [Lat. *rōborāns, rōborant-*, pr. part. of *rōborāre*, to strengthen < *rōbur, rōbor-*, oak, strength. See **reudh-** in App.]

ro·bot (rō′bŏt′) *n.* **1.** A mechanical device that can perform a variety of often complex tasks on command or by being programmed in advance. **2.** A machine or device that operates automatically or by remote control. **3.** A person who works mechanically without original thought, esp. one who responds automatically to commands. [Czech < *robota*, drudgery. See **orbh-** in App.] —**ro·bot′ic** *adj.*

WORD HISTORY *Robot* is a word that is both a coinage by an individual person and a borrowing. It has been in English since 1923 when the Czech writer Karel Čapek's play *R.U.R.* was translated into English and presented in London and New York. *R.U.R.*, published in 1921, is an abbreviation of *Rossum's Universal Robots. Robot* itself comes from Czech *robota*, "servitude, forced labor," from *rab*, "slave." This word comes from an Indo-European root *orbh-* that meant "to separate from one's group" or "to pass from one sphere of ownership into another." Its other derivatives include Greek *orphanos*, the source of English *orphan*, and German *Erbe*, "inheritance." Czech *robota* is also similar to another German derivative of this root, namely *Arbeit*, "work" (its Middle High German form *arabeit* is even more like the Czech word). *Arbeit* may be descended from a word that meant "slave labor" and was later generalized to just "labor."

robot bomb *n.* A small winged missile loaded with explosives, jet-propelled and guided by a gyroscopic device.

ro·bot·ics (rō-bŏt′ĭks) *n.* (*used with a sing. verb*) The science or study of the technology associated with the design, fabrication, theory, and application of robots.

ro·bot·ize (rō′bə-tīz′) *tr.v.* **-ized, -iz·ing, -iz·es** **1.** To convert (a system, for example) to automation by the application of advanced scientific technology. **2.** To make (a person) act like a robot. —**ro′bot·i·za′tion** (-bə-tĭ-zā′shən) *n.*

rob roy (rŏb roi′) *n.* A cocktail made with Scotch whisky, sweet vermouth, and bitters. [After ROB ROY.]

Rob Roy Orig. Robert MacGregor. 1671–1734. Scottish clan leader whose banditry is the subject of Sir Walter Scott's novel *Rob Roy* (1817).

Rob·son (rŏb′sən), **Mount** A mountain, 3,956.5 m (12,972 ft), in the Canadian Rocky Mts. of E British Columbia, Canada, on the border with Alberta.

ro·bust (rō-bŭst′, rō′bŭst′) *adj.* **1.** Full of health and strength; vigorous. **2.** Powerfully built; sturdy. See Syns at **healthy**. **3.** Requiring or suited to physical strength or endurance: *robust labor*. **4.** Rough or crude; boisterous: *a robust tale*. **5.** Marked by richness and fullness; full-bodied: *a robust wine*. [Lat. *rōbustus* < *rōbur, rōbus*, oak, strength. See **reudh-** in App.] —**ro·bust′ly** *adv.* —**ro·bust′ness** *n.*

ro·bus·ta (rō-bŭs′tə) *n.* **1a.** A tropical shrub or small tree (*Coffea canephora*) of western Africa, having fragrant white flowers and red fruit. **b.** The seed of this plant. **2.** The coffee brewed from the seeds of this plant. [Lat. *rōbusta*, fem. of *rōbustus*, strong. See ROBUST.]

ro·bus·tious (rō-bŭs′chəs) *adj.* **1.** Boisterous; vigorous. **2.** Rough, coarse, or crude. —**ro·bus′tious·ly** *adv.*

roc (rŏk) *n.* A mythical bird of prey having enormous size and strength. [Ar. *ruḫḫ*.]

Ro·ca (rō′kə, rô′-), **Cape** A cape of W Portugal on the Atlantic Ocean WNW of Lisbon.

roc·am·bole (rŏk′əm-bōl′) *n.* **1.** A European plant (*Allium sativum* var. *ophioscordon*) having a garliclike bulb. **2.** The bulb of this plant used as a seasoning. [Fr. < Ger. *Rockenbolle* : *Rocken*, distaff (< MHGer. *rocke* < OHGer. *rocko* < VLat. **rotica* < Lat. *rotāre*, to turn; see ROTATE) + *Bolle*, bulb (< MHGer. *bolle* < OHGer. *bolla*, ball; see **bhel-²** in App.).]

Ro·cham·beau (rō′shăm-bō′, -shän-), **Comte de** Title of Jean Baptiste Donatien de Vimeur. 1725–1807. French army officer who commanded French forces in the American Revolution, most notably in the defeat of the British at Yorktown (1781).

Roch·dale (rŏch′dāl′) A borough of NW England NNE of Manchester. Pop. 288,400.

Ro·chelle salt or **Ro·chelle salts** (rə-shĕl′, rō-) *n.* See **potassium sodium tartrate**. [After *La Rochelle*, France.]

roche mou·ton·née (rôsh′ mōōt′n-ā′, mōō′tô-nā′) *n., pl.* **roches mou·ton·nées** (rôsh′ mōōt′n-ā′, -āz′, mōō′tô-nā′) An elongate mound of bedrock worn smooth and rounded by glacial abrasion. [Fr. : *roche*, rock + *moutonné*, fleecy.]

Roch·es·ter (rŏch′ĭ-stər, -ĕs′tər) **1.** A city of SE MN SE of St. Paul; site of the Mayo Clinic (founded 1889). Pop. 85,806. **2.** A city of W NY ENE of Buffalo on the New York State Barge Canal; first settled c. 1812. Pop. 219,773.

roch·et (rŏch′ĭt) *n.* A white ceremonial vestment made of linen or lawn, worn by bishops and other church dignitaries. [ME < OFr., of Gmc. orig.]

rock¹ (rŏk) *n.* **1.** Relatively hard, naturally formed mineral or petrified matter; stone. **2a.** A relatively small piece or fragment of such material. **b.** A relatively large body of such material, as a cliff. **3.** A naturally formed aggregate of mineral matter consti-

tuting a significant part of the earth's crust. **4.** One that is similar to or suggestive of a mass of stone, as in stability or firmness. **5.** **rocks** *Slang* Money. **6.** *Slang* A large gem, esp. a diamond. **7.** *Slang* Crack cocaine. **8a.** A varicolored stick candy. **b.** Rock candy. —*idioms:* **between a rock and a hard place** Faced with equally unpleasant alternatives and few or no opportunities to evade or circumvent them. **on the rocks 1.** In a state of difficulty, destruction, or ruin. **2.** Without money; bankrupt. **3.** Served over ice cubes. [ME < ONFr. *roque* < VLat. **rocca*.]

rock² (rŏk) *v.* **rocked, rock·ing, rocks** —*intr.* **1.** To move back and forth or from side to side, esp. gently or rhythmically. **2.** To sway violently, as from a blow. **3.** To be washed and panned in a cradle or rocker. Used of ores. **4.** *Music* To play or dance to rock 'n' roll. —*tr.* **1.** To move back and forth or from side to side, esp. in order to soothe or lull to sleep. **2.** To cause to shake or sway violently. **3.** To disturb the mental or emotional equilibrium of; upset: *News of the scandal rocked the town.* **4.** To wash or pan (ore) in a cradle or rocker. **5.** In mezzotint engraving, to roughen (a metal plate) with a rocker or roulette. ❖ *n.* **1a.** A rocking motion. **b.** The act of rocking. **2.** *Music* Rock 'n' roll. —*idiom:* **rock the boat** *Slang* To disturb the balance or routine of a situation. [ME *rokken* < OE *roccian*.] —**rock′ing·ly** *adv.*

rock·a·bil·ly (rŏk′ə-bĭl′ē) *n.* A form of popular music combining features of rock 'n' roll and bluegrass. [ROCK ('N' ROLL) + (HILL)BILLY.]

rock-a-bye also **rock·a·bye** or **rock·a·by** (rŏk′ə-bī′) *interj.* Used to lull an infant or child to sleep. [ROCK² + (LULL)ABY.]

rock-and-roll (rŏk′ən-rōl′) *n.* Variant of **rock 'n' roll**.

rock and rye *n.* A liqueur made of whiskey blended with powdered rock candy and sometimes fruit.

rock·a·way (rŏk′ə-wā′) *n.* A four-wheeled carriage with two seats and a standing top. [Prob. after *Rockaway*, a town of New Jersey.]

rock bass (băs) *n.* **1.** A freshwater food and game fish (*Ambloplites rupestris*) of eastern and central North America. **2.** Any of various similar or related fishes.

rock bottom *n.* The lowest possible level or absolute bottom. —**rock′-bot′tom** (rŏk′bŏt′əm) *adj.*

rock·bound also **rock-bound** (rŏk′bound′) *adj.* Hemmed in by or bordered with rocks.

rock brake *n.* Any of several ferns of the genus *Crytogramma* that usu. grow in rocky ground.

rock candy *n.* A hard confection made by cooling sugar syrup into large clear crystals around a piece of string or a stick.

rock climbing *n.* The sport or activity of climbing sheer rock faces, esp. by means of specialized techniques and equipment.

Rock Cornish *n.* A small fowl of a breed developed by crossing white Plymouth Rock and Cornish strains.

rock crab *n.* A crab found along rocky coasts, esp. one of the genus *Cancer*, whose hindmost pair of legs is adapted for running.

rock crystal *n.* Colorless transparent quartz, used in optical instruments and as a semiprecious gemstone.

rock dove *n.* The common pigeon (*Columba livia*), native to Europe, North Africa, and Asia but widely distributed and having variously colored plumage with iridescent markings on the neck.

Rock·e·fel·ler (rŏk′ə-fĕl′ər) *Amer.* family, including **John Davison** (1839–1937), who amassed great wealth through the Standard Oil Company. His son **John Davison, Jr.** (1874–1960), was a noted philanthropist, and his grandson **Nelson Aldrich** (1908–79) served as governor of NY (1959–73) and Vice President of the US (1974–77).

rock elm *n.* **1.** A deciduous eastern North American tree (*Ulmus thomasii*) having corky branches and coarsely toothed leaves. **2.** The wood of this tree.

rock·er (rŏk′ər) *n.* **1.** One that rocks, as: **a.** A rocking chair. **b.** A rocking horse. **2.** One of the two curved pieces upon which a cradle, rocking chair, or similar device rocks. **3.** A cradle used for washing or panning ores. **4.** A small curved blade with a toothed edge used in mezzotint engraving to roughen the surface of the metal plate. **5.** An object having a curved form, as the keel of a ship. **6.** A curved stripe at the bottom part of a chevron worn by noncommissioned officers above the rank of sergeant. **7.** *Music* **a.** A rock 'n' roll song, singer, or musician. **b.** A fan of rock 'n' roll. —*idiom:* **off (one's) rocker** *Slang* Out of one's mind; crazy.

rocker arm *n.* A pivoted lever used in an internal combustion engine to transfer cam or pushrod motion to a valve stem.

rock·er·y (rŏk′ə-rē) *n., pl.* **-ies** See **rock garden** 2.

rock·et¹ (rŏk′ĭt) *n.* **1a.** A rocket engine. **b.** A vehicle or device propelled by one or more rocket engines, esp. such a vehicle designed to travel through space. **2.** A projectile weapon carrying a warhead that is powered and propelled by rocket engines. **3.** A projectile firework having a cylindrical shape and a fuse that is lit from the rear. ❖ *v.* **-et·ed, -et·ing, -ets** —*intr.* **1.** To move swiftly and powerfully, as a rocket. **2.** To fly swiftly straight up, as a game bird frightened from cover. **3.** To soar or rise rapidly. —*tr.* **1.** To carry by means of a rocket. **2.** To assault with rockets. [Ital. *rocchetta*, dim. of *rocca*, spindle, distaff < Gmc. orig.]

rock·et² (rŏk′ĭt) *n.* **1.** See **arugula**. **2.** Any of several plants of the mustard family, esp. the dame's rocket and the sea rocket. [ME *rokette* < OFr. *roquette* < Ital. *rochetta*, var. of *ruchetta*, dim.

robot
camera-fitted robot designed to assist with fighting fires

John D. Rockefeller

of *ruca*, a cabbage < Lat. *ērūca*.]

rock·et·eer (rŏk′ĭ-tîr′) *n.* **1.** One who launches, rides in, or pilots rockets. **2.** An expert in rocketry.

rocket engine *n.* A reaction engine that operates independently of any outside substances, such as atmospheric oxygen, and thus is capable of operating in outer space.

rocket plane *n.* **1.** An aircraft powered by one or more rocket engines. **2.** An aircraft designed to carry and launch rockets.

rock·et·ry (rŏk′ĭ-trē) *n.* The science and technology of rocket design, construction, and flight.

rocket salad *n.* See **arugula**.

rocket science *n.* **1.** Rocketry. **2.** *Informal* An endeavor requiring great intelligence or technical ability.

rocket ship *n.* A spacecraft powered and propelled by rockets.

rocket sled *n.* A rocket-propelled sled that travels along rails and is used to study acceleration, deceleration, and crash survival techniques.

rock·et·sonde (rŏk′ĭt-sŏnd′) *n.* An instrument transported to the upper atmosphere by rocket, used to study meteorological conditions. [ROCKET¹ + (RADIO)SONDE.]

rock·fall (rŏk′fôl′) *n.* A fall of rocks, as from a cliff.

Rock fever *n.* See **brucellosis** 1. [After the *Rock* of Gibraltar, where it is endemic.]

rock·fish (rŏk′fĭsh′) *n.*, *pl.* **rockfish** or **-fish·es 1.** Any of various fishes living among rocks. **2.** Any of various fishes, chiefly of the genus *Sebastes*, of Pacific waters. **3.** See **striped bass**.

rock flour *n.* Finely ground rock particles produced by glacial abrasion.

Rock·ford (rŏk′fərd) A city of N IL WNW of Chicago; founded 1834. Pop. 150,115.

rock garden *n.* **1.** A rocky area in which plants particularly adapted to such terrain are cultivated. **2.** A garden that has a decorative scheme of rocks and cultivated plants.

rock hound *n.* *Informal* **1.** A specialist in geology. **2.** A collector of rocks and minerals, esp. gemstones, as a hobby. —**rock′hound′ing**, **rock′hound′ing** (rŏk′houn′dĭng) *n.*

rock hyrax *n.* See **rock rabbit** 1.

Rock·ies (rŏk′ēz) See **Rocky Mountains**.

rock·ing chair (rŏk′ĭng) *n.* A chair mounted on rockers or springs.

rocking horse *n.* A toy horse mounted on rockers or springs that is large enough for a child to ride.

rock·ling (rŏk′lĭng) *n.*, *pl.* **rockling** or **-lings** Any of various small marine fishes of the family Gadidae of North Atlantic coastal waters.

rock lobster *n.* See **spiny lobster**.

rock maple *n.* **1.** See **sugar maple**. **2.** The tough close-grained wood of the sugar maple.

rock music *n.* Rock 'n' roll.

Rock·ne (rŏk′nē), **Knute Kenneth** 1888–1931. Norwegian-born Amer. football coach at the University of Notre Dame (1918–31) who revolutionized the sport with the use of the forward pass and other offensive strategies.

rock 'n' roll or **rock-and-roll** (rŏk′ən-rōl′) *n.* A form of popular music arising from and incorporating a variety of musical styles, esp. rhythm and blues, country music, and gospel. —**rock 'n' roller**, **rock′-and-roll′er** *n.*

rock oil *n.* *Chiefly British* Petroleum.

rock·oon (rŏ-kōōn′) *n.* A device used for high-altitude sounding, composed of a small solid-propellant rocket that is launched from a balloon. [ROCK(ET)¹ + (BALL)OON.]

rock pigeon *n.* See **rock dove**.

rock rabbit *n.* **1.** A hyrax of the genus *Procavia* or *Dendrohyrax*, esp. the African species *P. capensis*. **2.** See **pika**.

rock-ribbed (rŏk′rĭbd′) *adj.* **1.** Having rocks or rock outcroppings; rocky. **2.** Firm and unyielding, esp. with regard to one's principles, loyalties, or beliefs: *a rock-ribbed conservative.*

Rock River A river rising in SE WI and flowing c. 459 km (285 mi) to the Mississippi R. in NW IL.

rock·rose (rŏk′rōz′) *n.* Any of various plants of the genera *Cistus* or *Helianthemum*, having small roselike yellow, white, or reddish flowers.

rock salt *n.* **1.** Rock containing halite as its main constituent. **2.** Coarsely ground common salt.

rock·shaft (rŏk′shăft′) *n.* A shaft that oscillates or rocks upon its bearings but does not revolve.

rock·slide (rŏk′slīd′) *n.* **1.** The usu. rapid downward movement of newly detached segments of bedrock. **2.** A rock mass that has undergone such a movement.

rock squirrel *n.* A large ground squirrel (*Spermophilus variegatus*) having variegated black and white upper parts and found in Mexico and the southwest United States.

rock·u·men·ta·ry (rŏk′yə-mĕn′tə-rē) *n.*, *pl.* **-ries** A documentary about rock music or rock musicians. [Blend of ROCK² and DOCUMENTARY.]

rock wallaby *n.* Any of several small agile wallabies, chiefly of the genus *Petrogale*, that live in rocky areas and have thick-soled feet and a slender tail.

rock·weed (rŏk′wēd′) *n.* Any of several coarse brownish seaweeds of the genera *Fucus* and *Ascophyllum* that grow on rocks in coastal areas.

Rock·well (rŏk′wĕl′), **Norman** 1894–1978. Amer. illustrator whose works offer a nostalgic view of everyday American life.

rock wool *n.* See **mineral wool**.

rock·work (rŏk′wûrk′) *n.* **1.** A natural mass or pile of rocks. **2.** Stonework imitating the irregular surface of natural rock.

rock wren *n.* **1.** Any of several wrens of the genus *Salpinctes*, esp. *S. obsoletus*, found in rocky regions of the western United States and Mexico. **2.** A small wren (*Xenicus gilviventris*) that inhabits New Zealand and feeds mostly among stones.

rock·y¹ (rŏk′ē) *adj.* **-i·er**, **-i·est 1.** Consisting of, containing, or abounding in rock or rocks. **2a.** Resembling or suggesting rock; firm or hard. **b.** Steadfast or stubborn; unyielding. **3.** Marked by obstructions. —**rock′i·ness** *n.*

rock·y² (rŏk′ē) *adj.* **-i·er**, **-i·est 1a.** Inclined or prone to sway or totter; unsteady or shaky. **b.** Appearing inclined to fail; discouraging or disappointing: *won the championship after a rocky start.* **2.** Weak, dizzy, or nauseated, as from excessive alcohol intake. —**rock′i·ness** *n.*

Rocky Mountain goat *n.* See **mountain goat**.

Rocky Mountains also **Rock·ies** (rŏk′ēz) A mountain system of W North America extending from NW AK to the Mexican border and rising to 4,402.1 m (14,433 ft) in central CO.

Rocky Mountain sheep *n.* See **bighorn**.

Rocky Mountain spotted fever *n.* An acute infectious disease caused by a microorganism (*Rickettsia rickettsii*) that is transmitted by ticks, is characterized by muscular pains, fever, and skin eruptions, and is endemic throughout North America.

ro·co·co (rə-kō′kō, rō′kə-kō′) *n.* **1a.** also **Rococo** A style of art and architecture that originated in France in the early 18th century and is marked by elaborate ornamentation. **b.** A very ornate style of speech or writing. **2.** also **Rococo** *Music* A style of composition arising in 18th-century France, usu. viewed as an extension of the baroque, and marked by a high degree of ornamentation. ❖ *adj.* **1.** also **Rococo** Of or relating to the rococo. **2.** Immoderately elaborate or complicated. [Fr., prob. alteration of *rocaille*, rockwork < *roc*, rock, var. of *roche* < VLat. *rocca.]

rod (rŏd) *n.* **1.** A thin straight piece or bar of material, such as metal, often having a particular use, as: **a.** A fishing rod. **b.** A piston rod. **c.** An often expandable horizontal bar used to suspend household items such as curtains. **d.** A leveling rod. **e.** A lightning rod. **f.** A divining rod. **g.** A measuring stick. **2.** A shoot or stem cut from or growing as part of a woody plant. **3a.** A stick or bundle of sticks or switches used to give punishment by whipping. **b.** Punishment; correction. **4.** A scepter, staff, or wand symbolizing power or authority. **5.** Power or dominion, esp. of a tyrannical nature. **6a.** A linear measure equal to 5.5 yards or 16.5 feet (5.03 meters). **b.** The square of this measure, equal to 30.25 square yards or 272.25 square feet (25.30 square meters). See table at **measurement**. **7.** *Bible* A line of family descent; a branch of a tribe. **8.** *Anatomy* Any of various rod-shaped cells in the retina that respond to dim light. **9.** *Microbiology* An elongated bacterium; a bacillus. **10.** *Slang* A pistol or revolver. **11.** A portion of the undercarriage of a train, esp. the drawbar under a freight car. Often used in the plural. [ME *rodd* < OE.]

rode¹ (rōd) *v.* Past tense of **ride**.

rode² (rōd) *n.* *Nautical* A cable, chain, or rope, esp. one attached to the anchor of a small boat. [< ME *at rode*, at an anchorage < *rode*, a riding. See ROAD.]

ro·dent (rōd′nt) *n.* Any of various mammals of the order Rodentia, such as a mouse, rat, squirrel, or beaver, characterized by large incisors adapted for gnawing or nibbling. ❖ *adj.* **1.** Gnawing. **2.** Of or relating to rodents. [< NLat. *Rōdentia*, order name < Lat. *rōdēns*, *rodent-*, pr. part. of *rōdere*, to gnaw.]

ro·den·ti·cide (rō-dĕn′tĭ-sīd′) *n.* A chemical substance used to kill rodents.

rodent ulcer *n.* A cancerous skin ulcer that derives from basal cells and usu. occurs on the face. [Lat. *rodēns*, *rodent-*, gnawing. See RODENT.]

ro·de·o (rō′dē-ō′, rō-dā′ō) *n.*, *pl.* **-os 1.** A public competition or exhibition in which skills such as riding broncos or roping calves are displayed. **2.** A cattle roundup. **3.** An enclosure for keeping cattle that have been rounded up. [Sp., corral, rodeo < *rodear*, to surround < *rueda*, wheel < Lat. *rota*.]

Rod·gers (rŏj′ərz), **Richard** 1902–79. Amer. composer known for his musical comedies, esp. his collaborations with Oscar Hammerstein II, including *The Sound of Music* (1959).

Ro·din (rō-dăn′, -dăN′), **François Auguste René** 1840–1917. French sculptor whose works include *The Thinker* (1880).

rod·man (rŏd′mən) *n.* One who carries and employs a leveling rod under the supervision of a surveyor.

rod·o·mon·tade (rŏd′ə-mŏn-tād′, -täd′, rō′də-) *n.* Pretentious boasting or bragging; bluster. ❖ *intr.v.* **-tad·ed**, **-tad·ing**, **-tades** To boast or brag; bluster. [Fr. < Ital. *rodomontada*, from *Rodomonte*, arrogant Saracen leader of Italian Renaissance epics.] —**rod′o·mon·tade′** *adj.*

roe¹ (rō) *n.* **1.** The eggs or the egg-laden ovary of a fish. **2.** The egg mass or spawn of certain crustaceans, such as the lobster. [ME *row* < MLGer. or MDu. *roge*.]

roe² (rō) *n.*, *pl.* **roe** or **roes** The roe deer. [ME *ro* < OE *rā*, *rāha*.]

Roeb·ling (rō′blĭng), **John Augustus** 1806–69. German-born Amer. engineer who designed the Brooklyn Bridge, completed

rocking chair

Knute Rockne

Richard Rodgers
photographed c. 1952

ă	pat	oi	boy
ā	pay	ou	out
âr	care	ŏŏ	took
ä	father	ōō	boot
ĕ	pet	ŭ	cut
ē	be	ûr	urge
ĭ	pit	th	thin
ī	pie	th	this
îr	pier	hw	which
ŏ	pot	zh	vision
ō	toe	ə	about,
ô	paw		item

Stress marks:
′ (primary);
′ (secondary); as in
lexicon (lĕk′sĭ-kŏn′)

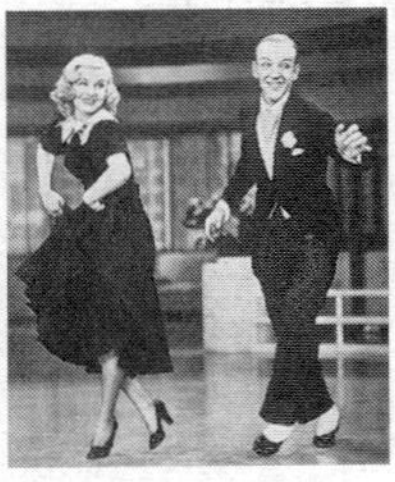

Ginger Rogers
dancing with Fred Astaire in *Swing Time*, 1936

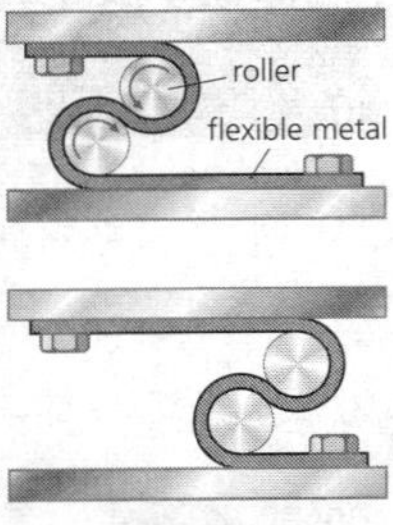

rolamite
When rotated as indicated in the top illustration, the rollers and metal strip will move to the right.

(1883) by his son **Washington Augustus** (1837–1926).

roe•buck (rō′bŭk′) *n.* A male roe deer.

roe deer *n.* A small, delicately formed Eurasian deer *(Capreolus capreolus)* having short branched antlers in the male and a brownish coat.

roent•gen also **rönt•gen** (rĕnt′gən, -jən, rŭnt′-) *n.* A unit of radiation exposure equal to the quantity of ionizing radiation that will produce one electrostatic unit of electricity in one cubic centimeter of dry air at 0°C and standard atmospheric pressure. **—roent′gen** *adj.*

Roent•gen (rĕnt′gən, -jən, rŭnt′-) or **Rönt•gen** (rœnt′gən), **Wilhelm Konrad** 1845–1923. German physicist who discovered x-rays and won a 1901 Nobel Prize.

roent•gen•ize (rĕnt′gə-nīz′, -jə-, rŭnt′-) *tr.v.* **-ized, -iz•ing, -iz•es** To subject to the action of x-rays.

roentgeno– *pref.* X-ray: *roentgenography.* [< ROENTGEN.]

roent•gen•o•gram (rĕnt′gə-nə-grăm′, -jə-, rŭnt′-) *n.* A photograph made with x-rays.

roent•gen•o•graph (rĕnt′gə-nə-grăf′, -jə-, rŭnt′-) *n.* See **roentgenogram.**

roent•gen•og•ra•phy (rĕnt′gə-nŏg′rə-fē, -jə-, rŭnt′-) *n.* Photography with the use of x-rays. **—roent′gen•o•graph′ic** (-gə-nə-grăf′ĭk, -jə-) *adj.*

roent•gen•ol•o•gy (rĕnt′gə-nŏl′ə-jē, -jə-, rŭnt′-) *n.* Radiology employing x-rays. **—roent′gen•o•log′ic** (-ə-lŏj′ĭk), **roent′gen•o•log′i•cal** (-ĭ-kəl) *adj.* **—roent′gen•ol′o•gist** *n.*

roent•gen•o•scope (rĕnt′gə-nə-skōp′, -jə-, rŭnt′-) *n.* See **fluoroscope. —roent′gen•o•scop′ic** (-skŏp′ĭk) *adj.* **—roent′gen•os′co•py** (-gə-nŏs′kə-pē, -jə-) *n.*

roent•gen•o•ther•a•py (rĕnt′gə-nə-thĕr′ə-pē, -jə-, rŭnt′-) *n., pl.* **-pies** The therapeutic use of x-rays in treating disease.

roentgen ray *n.* See **x-ray** 1.

Roeth•ke (rĕt′kē, -kə, rĕth′-), **Theodore** 1908–63. Amer. poet whose collections include *The Waking* (1953).

ro•ga•tion (rō-gā′shən) *n.* **1.** *Ecclesiastical* Solemn prayer or supplication, esp. as chanted during the rites of Rogation Day. Often used in the plural. **2a.** The formal proposal of a law in ancient Rome by a tribune or consul to the people for acceptance or rejection. **b.** A law proposed in this manner. [ME *rogacioun* < Lat. *rogātiō, rogātiōn-* < *rogātus*, p. part. of *rogāre*, to ask. See **reg-** in App.]

Rogation Day *n. Ecclesiastical* In western Christianity, one of the prescribed days of prayer and fasting traditionally for the harvest, usu. the three days before Ascension Day.

ro•ga•to•ry (rŏ′gə-tôr′ē, -tōr′ē) *adj. Law* Requesting information. Used esp. of a request by one court of another, often foreign court. [Fr. *rogatoire* < Med.Lat. *rogātōrius* < Lat. *rogātus*, p. part. of *rogāre*, to ask. See **reg-** in App.]

rog•er (rŏj′ər) *interj.* Used esp. in radio communications to indicate receipt of a message. [< *Roger*, spoken representation of the letter *r*, short for RECEIVED.]

Rog•ers (rŏj′ərz), **Ginger** 1911–95. Amer. dancer and actress whose motion pictures with Fred Astaire include *Swing Time* (1936).

Rogers, Robert 1731–95. Amer. soldier and pioneer who led (1758–63) the Rogers's Rangers on a series of missions during the French and Indian War.

Rogers, William Penn Adair ("Will") 1879–1935. Amer. humorist noted for his wry homespun commentary on society and politics.

Ro•get (rō-zhā′, rō′zhā), **Peter Mark** 1779–1869. British physician and scholar who compiled the *Thesaurus of English Words and Phrases* (1852).

rogue (rōg) *n.* **1.** An unprincipled, deceitful, and unreliable person; a scoundrel or rascal. **2.** One who is playfully mischievous; a scamp. **3.** A wandering beggar; a vagrant. **4.** A vicious and solitary animal, esp. an elephant that has separated itself from its herd. **5.** An organism, esp. a plant, that shows an undesirable variation from a standard. ❖ *v.* **rogued, rogu•ing, rogues** *—tr.* **1.** To defraud. **2.** To remove (diseased or abnormal specimens) from a group of plants of the same variety. *—intr.* To remove diseased or abnormal plants. [?]

Rogue River A river rising in the Cascade Range of SW OR and flowing c. 322 km (200 mi) to the Pacific Ocean.

rogu•er•y (rō′gə-rē) *n., pl.* **-ies 1.** Behavior characteristic of a rogue. **2.** A mischievous act.

rogues' gallery (rōgz) *n.* A collection of pictures of known and suspected criminals maintained in police files and used for making identifications.

rogu•ish (rō′gĭsh) *adj.* **1.** Deceitful; unprincipled. **2.** Playfully mischievous. **—rogu′ish•ly** *adv.* **—rogu′ish•ness** *n.*

Ro•hyp•nol (rō-hĭp′nôl′, -nōl′) A trademark used for the drug flunitrazepam.

roil (roil) *v.* **roiled, roil•ing, roils** *—tr.* **1.** To make (a liquid) muddy or cloudy by stirring up sediment. **2.** To displease or disturb; vex. *—intr.* To be in a state of turbulence or agitation. [?]

roil•y (roi′lē) *adj.* **-i•er, -i•est 1.** Full of sediment; muddy or cloudy. **2.** Turbulent; agitated.

rois•ter (roi′stər) *intr.v.* **-tered, -ter•ing, -ters 1.** To engage in boisterous merrymaking; revel noisily. **2.** To behave in a blustering manner; swagger. [< obsolete *roister*, roisterer, prob. < OFr. *rustre*, ruffian, alteration of *ruste* < Lat. *rūsticus*, rustic. See RUSTIC.] **—rois′ter•er** *n.* **—rois′ter•ous** *adj.*

ro•la•mite (rō′lə-mīt′) *n.* A mechanism consisting of two or more hard cylindrical rollers with a flexible nonstretching band looped around them, so that the rollers move against each other with very little friction. [ROL(L) + *-amite*, of unknown orig.]

Ro•land (rō′lənd, rô-läɴ′) *n.* A French hero in medieval chansons de geste, the nephew of Charlemagne and defender of Christianity, killed fighting the Saracens at Roncesvalles.

role (rōl) *n.* **1.** also **rôle** A character or part played by a performer. **2.** The characteristic and expected social behavior of an individual. **3.** A function or position. See Syns at **function.** [Fr. *rôle* < OFr. *rolle*, roll of parchment (on which an actor's part was written) < Lat. *rotula*, dim. of *rota*, wheel. See ROLL.]

role model *n.* A person who serves as a model in a particular behavioral or social role for another person to emulate.

role-play (rōl′plā′) *v.* **-played, -play•ing, -plays** *—tr.* To assume or represent in a drama; act out. *—intr.* To assume or act out a particular role. ❖ *n.* The acting out or assuming of a particular character or role, esp. as a therapeutic technique.

role player *n.* **1.** One who assumes or acts out a particular role. **2.** One who engages in role-playing. **3.** *Sports* A team athlete who plays mainly in specific situations.

Rolf (rŏlf) See **Rollo.**

Rolfe (rŏlf), **John** 1585–1622. English colonist in America and husband of Pocahontas.

roll (rōl) *v.* **rolled, roll•ing, rolls** *—intr.* **1.** To move forward along a surface by revolving on an axis or by repeatedly turning over. **2.** To travel or be moved on wheels or rollers. **3.** To travel around; wander. **4a.** To travel or be carried in a vehicle. **b.** To be carried on a stream. **5a.** To start to move or operate. **b.** To work or succeed in a sustained way; gain momentum. **6.** To go by; elapse: *The days rolled along.* **7.** To recur. Often used with *around: Summer has rolled around again.* **8.** To move in a periodic revolution, as a planet in its orbit. **9.** To turn over and over. **10.** To shift the gaze usu. quickly and continually. **11.** To turn around or revolve on or as if on an axis. **12.** To move or advance with a rising and falling motion; undulate. **13.** To extend or appear to extend in gentle rises and falls: *The dunes roll to the sea.* **14.** To move or rock from side to side. **15.** To walk with a swaying, unsteady motion. **16.** To take the shape of a ball or cylinder: *Yarn rolls easily.* **17.** To become flattened by or as if by pressure applied by a roller. **18.** To make a deep, prolonged, surging sound: *rolling thunder.* **19.** To make a sustained trilling sound, as certain birds do. **20.** To beat a drum in a continuous series of short blows. **21.** To pour or flow in or as if in a continual stream: *tourists rolling into the city.* **22.** To enjoy ample amounts: *rolled in the money.* *—tr.* **1.** To cause to move forward along a surface by revolving on an axis or by repeatedly turning over. **2.** To move or push along on wheels or rollers. **3.** To impel or send onward in a steady swelling motion. **4.** To impart a swaying, rocking motion to. **5.** To turn around or partly turn around; rotate. **6.** To cause to begin moving or operating: *roll the presses.* **7.** To extend or lay out: *rolled out a long rope.* **8.** To pronounce or utter with a trill. **9.** To utter or emit in full, swelling tones. **10.** To beat (a drum) with a continuous series of short blows. **11.** To wrap (something) round and round upon itself or around something else: *roll up a poster.* **12a.** To envelop or enfold in a covering: *roll laundry in a sheet.* **b.** To make by shaping into a ball or cylinder. **13.** To spread, compress, or flatten by applying pressure with a roller. **14.** *Printing* To apply ink to (type) with a roller or rollers. **15.** *Games* To throw (dice), as in craps. **16.** *Slang* To rob (a drunken, sleeping, or otherwise helpless person). ❖ *n.* **1.** The act or an instance of rolling. **2.** Something rolled up. **3.** A quantity, as of cloth, rolled into a cylinder and often considered as a unit of measure. **4.** A piece of parchment or paper that may be or is rolled up; a scroll. **5.** A register or a catalog. **6.** A list of names of persons belonging to a group. **7.** A mass in cylindrical or rounded form. **8a.** A small rounded portion of bread. **b.** A portion of food shaped like a tube with a filling. **9.** A rolling, swaying, or rocking motion. **10.** A gentle swell or undulation of a surface. **11.** A deep reverberation or rumble. **12.** A rapid succession of short sounds: *the roll of a drum.* **13.** A trill. **14.** A rhythmic resonant flow of words. **15.** A roller, esp. a cylinder on which to roll something up or with which to flatten something. **16.** A maneuver in which an airplane makes a single complete rotation about its longitudinal axis without changing direction or losing altitude. **17.** *Slang* Money, esp. a wad of paper money. ***—phrasal verbs:* roll back 1.** To reduce (prices or wages, for example) to a previous lower level. **2.** To cause to turn back or retreat. **roll out 1.** To get out of bed. **2.** *Football* To execute a rollout. **roll over 1.** To defer or postpone payment of (an obligation). **2.** To renegotiate the terms of (a financial deal). **3.** To reinvest (funds from a maturing security or from a tax-deferred account) into a similar security or account. **roll up 1.** To arrive in a vehicle. **2.** To accumulate; amass. ***—idioms:* on a roll** *Informal* Undergoing or experiencing sustained, even increasing good fortune or success. **roll in the hay** *Slang* Sexual intercourse. **roll the bones** *Games* To cast dice, esp. in craps. **roll with the punches** *Slang* To cope with and withstand adversity, esp. by being flexible. [ME *rollen* < OFr. *roler* < VLat. **rotulāre* < Lat. *rotula*, dim. of *rota*, wheel.]

Rol•land (rô-län′), **Romain** 1866–1944. French writer who won the 1915 Nobel Prize for literature.

roll•a•way (rōl′ə-wā′) *adj.* Set on rollers or casters for easy moving and storing: *a rollaway bed.* ❖ *n.* A piece of rollaway furniture.

roll•back (rōl′băk′) *n.* **1.** A reduction, esp. in prices or wages, to a previous lower level. **2.** A turning back or retreat, as from a previously held position.

roll bar *n.* A sturdy metal bar built into the inside roof of a motor vehicle to prevent or reduce injury in case of a rollover.

roll call *n.* **1.** The reading aloud of a list of names of people, as in a classroom or military post, to determine who is present or absent. **2.** The time fixed for such a reading.

roll•er[1] (rō′lər) *n.* **1.** One that rolls or performs a rolling operation or activity. **2.** Any of various cylindrical or spherical devices that roll or rotate, esp.: **a.** A small spokeless wheel, such as that of a roller skate. **b.** An elongated cylinder on which something is wound. **c.** A heavy revolving cylinder that is used to level, crush, or smooth. **d.** *Printing* A cylinder, usu. of hard rubber, used to ink the type before the paper is impressed. **e.** A cylinder of wire mesh, foam rubber, or other material around which a strand of hair is wound to produce a soft curl or wave. **3.** A long rolled bandage. **4.** A heavy swelling wave that breaks on a coast. **5.** A tumbler pigeon.

rol•ler[2] (rō′lər) *n.* **1.** Any of various Old World birds of the family Coraciidae, having bright blue wings and stocky bodies and noted for rolling and twisting in flight. **2.** A canary that trills. [Ger. < *rollen*, to roll, burble. See ROLLMOPS.]

roller bearing *n.* A bearing using rollers to reduce friction between machine parts.

Roll•er•blade (rō′lər-blād′) A trademark used for an in-line skate.

roller coaster *n.* **1.** A steep, sharply curving elevated railway with small open passenger cars that is operated at high speeds as a ride. **2.** Something that is marked by abrupt, extreme changes in circumstance, quality, or behavior.

roller skate *n.* A shoe or boot with two or four wheels or casters attached to its sole for skating on hard surfaces. —**roll′er-skate′** (rō′lər-skāt′) *v.* —**roller skater** *n.*

rol•lick (rōl′ĭk) *intr.v.* **-licked, -lick•ing, -licks** To behave or move in a carefree, frolicsome manner; romp. [?] —**rol′lick** *n.* —**rol′lick•some, rol′lick•y** *adj.*

rol•lick•ing (rōl′ĭ-kĭng) *adj.* Carefree and high-spirited; boisterous. —**rol′lick•ing•ly** *adv.*

roll•ing blackout (rō′lĭng) *n.* A series of intentional electrical blackouts affecting small areas in succession as a means of conserving electricity when supply is low.

rolling mill *n.* **1.** A factory in which metal is rolled into sheets, bars, or other forms. **2.** A machine used for rolling metal.

rolling pin *n.* A smooth, usu. wooden cylinder, often having a handle at each end, used for rolling out dough.

rolling stock *n.* The equipment available for transportation, such as automotive vehicles or railroad cars, owned by a particular company or carrier.

Rol•lins (rōl′ĭnz), **Theodore Walter** Known as "Sonny." b. 1930. Amer. jazz saxophonist and composer who originated the now standard practice of playing bop in three-quarter time.

roll•mops (rōl′mŏps′) *n., pl.* **rollmops** A marinated fillet of herring wrapped around a pickle or an onion and served as an hors d'oeuvre. [Ger. : *rollen*, to roll (< MHGer. < OFr. *roler*; see ROLL) + *Mops*, blockhead, pug dog (< LGer.; akin to Du. *moppen*, to make a sour face).]

Rol•lo (rōl′ō) also **Hrolf** (rōlf, hrōlf) or **Rolf** (rōlf) 860?–931? Norse chieftain and the first duke of Normandy.

roll-on (rōl′ŏn′, -ôn′) *adj.* Of or being a substance, such as a deodorant, that is dispensed from a container having a rolling ball at one end serving as an applicator. —**roll′-on′** *n.*

roll•out (rōl′out′) *n.* **1.** The inauguration or initial public exhibition of a new product, service, or policy. **2.** *Football* A play in which the quarterback runs toward a sideline after receiving the snap with the intention of passing the ball.

roll•o•ver (rōl′ō′vər) *n.* **1.** The act or process of rolling over. **2.** An accident in which a motor vehicle overturns. **3.** The act or an instance of rolling over funds: *an IRA rollover.*

roll-top desk or **roll•top desk** (rōl′tŏp′) *n.* A desk fitted with a flexible sliding top made of parallel slats.

roll•way (rōl′wā′) *n.* A surface along which cylindrical objects or objects on rollers may be moved, esp. an inclined surface used by lumberjacks to slide logs into a waterway.

Ro•lo•dex (rō′lə-dĕks′) A trademark used for a desktop rotary file of removable cards, usu. used for names, addresses, and telephone numbers.

Röl•vaag (rōl′väg′), **Ole Edvart** 1876–1931. Norwegian-born Amer. writer noted for *Giants in the Earth* (1927).

ro•ly-po•ly (rō′lē-pō′lē) *adj.* Short and plump; pudgy. ❖ *n., pl.* **-lies** **1.** A short plump person or thing. **2.** *Chiefly British* A pudding made of jam or fruit rolled up in pastry dough and baked or steamed until soft. **3.** See **pill bug 1.** [Alteration and redup. of ROLL.]

Rom (rŏm) *n., pl.* **Rom** or **Roma 1.** A Gypsy. **2.** A Gypsy man or boy. [Romany, man. See ROMANY.]

ROM (rŏm) *n. Computer Science* Memory hardware that allows fast access to permanently stored data but prevents addition to or modification of the data. [R(EAD-)O(NLY) M(EMORY).]

rom. *abbr. Printing* roman

Rom. *abbr.* **1.** Roman **2.** Romance (languages) **3.** Romania **4.** Romanian **5.** *Bible* Romans

Ro•ma•gna (rō-män′yə, -mä′nyä) A historical region of N-central Italy; a former center of Byzantine influence and now part of Emilia-Romagna.

Ro•ma•ic (rō-mā′ĭk) *n.* Modern Greek. [Mod.Gk. *Rhomaikos* < Gk. *Rhōmaikos*, Roman < *Rhōmē*, Rome < Lat. *Rōma*.] —**Ro•ma′ic** *adj.*

ro•maine (rō-mān′) *n.* A cultivar of lettuce (*Lactuca sativa*) having a slender head of oblong or obovate leaves with broad midribs. [Fr. < fem. of *Romain*, Roman < OFr. < Lat. *Rōmānus* < *Rōma*, Rome.]

ro•man (rō-män′) *n.* **1.** A narrative poem or a prose tale in medieval French literature. **2.** A novel. [Fr. < OFr. *romans*, romance. See ROMANCE.]

Ro•man (rō′mən) *adj.* **1a.** Of or relating to ancient or modern Rome or its people or culture. **b.** Of or relating to the Roman Empire. **2a.** Of, relating to, or composed in the Latin language. **b.** Of or using the Latin alphabet. **3.** Of or relating to the Roman Catholic Church. **4.** Of or being an architectural style developed by the ancient Romans and characterized by the round arch as chief structural element, the vault, concrete masonry construction, and classical ornamentation. **5. roman** Of or being a typeface characterized by upright letters having serifs and vertical lines thicker than horizontal lines. ❖ *n.* **1.** A native, inhabitant, or citizen of ancient or modern Rome. **2.** The Italian language as spoken in Rome. **3.** One belonging to the Roman Catholic Church. **4. roman** Roman print or typestyle. **5. Romans** (*used with a sing. verb*) See table at **Bible.** [ME < OE *Rōman* or < OFr. *romain*, both < Lat. *Rōmānus* < *Rōma*, Rome.]

ro•man à clef (rō-män′ ä klā′) *n., pl.* **ro•mans à clef** (rōmän′ zä klā′) A novel in which actual persons, places, or events are depicted in fictional guise. [Fr. : *roman*, novel + *à*, with + *clef*, key.]

Ro•man alphabet (rō′mən) *n.* See **Latin alphabet.**

Roman arch *n.* A semicircular arch. [< its being characteristic of Roman architecture.]

Roman calendar *n.* The lunar calendar used by the ancient Romans until the introduction of the Julian calendar in 46 B.C.

Roman candle *n.* A cylindrical firework that emits balls of fire and a shower of sparks.

Roman Catholic *adj.* Of, relating to, or being the Roman Catholic Church. ❖ *n.* A member of the Roman Catholic Church.

Roman Catholic Church *n.* The Christian church characterized by an episcopal hierarchy with the pope as its head and by belief in seven sacraments and the authority of tradition.

Roman Catholicism *n.* The doctrines, practices, and organization of the Roman Catholic Church.

ro•mance (rō-măns′, rō′măns′) *n.* **1a.** A love affair. **b.** Ardent emotional attachment or involvement between people; love. **c.** A strong, sometimes short-lived attachment, fascination, or enthusiasm for something. **2.** A mysterious or fascinating quality or appeal. **3a.** A long medieval narrative in prose or verse that tells of the adventures and heroic exploits of chivalric heroes. **b.** A long fictitious tale of heroes and extraordinary or mysterious events, usu. set in a distant time or place. **c.** The class of literature constituted by such tales. **4a.** An artistic work that deals with sexual love, esp. in an idealized form. **b.** The class or style of such works. **5.** A fictitiously embellished account or explanation. **6.** *Music* A lyrical, tender, usu. sentimental song or short instrumental piece. **7. Romance** The Romance languages. ❖ *adj.* **Romance** Of, relating to, or being any of the languages that developed from Latin, including Italian, French, Portuguese, Romanian, and Spanish. ❖ *v.* (rō-măns′) **-manced, -manc•ing, -manc•es** —*intr.* **1.** To invent, write, or tell romances. **2.** To think or behave in a romantic manner. —*tr. Informal* **1.** To make love to; court or woo. **2.** To have a love affair with. [ME < OFr. *romans*, romance, work written in French < VLat. **rōmānicē (scrībere)*, (to write) in the vernacular < Lat. *Rōmānicus*, Roman < *Rōmānus*. See ROMAN.] —**ro•manc′er** *n.*

Roman Empire also **Rome** (rōm) An empire that succeeded the Roman Republic during the reign of Augustus (27 B.C.–A.D. 14) and at its greatest extent stretched from Britain and Germany to North Africa and the Persian Gulf. After 395 it was split into the Byzantine Empire and the Western Roman Empire, which fell to the Goths in 476.

Ro•man•esque (rō′mə-nĕsk′) *adj.* **1.** Of, relating to, or being a style of European architecture containing both Roman and Byzantine elements, prevalent esp. in the 11th and 12th centuries and characterized by thick walls, round arches, and relatively simple ornamentation. **2.** Of, relating to, or being corresponding styles in painting and sculpture. —**Ro′man•esque′** *n.*

ro•man-fleuve (rō-män′flœv′) *n., pl.* **ro•mans-fleuves** (rō-män′flœv′) A long novel, often in many volumes, chronicling the history of several generations of a family, community, or other group. [Fr. : *roman*, novel + *fleuve*, river.]

Roman holiday *n.* **1.** Enjoyment or satisfaction derived from the suffering of others. **2.** A violent public spectacle or disturbance.

Romanesque
church of San Miniato al
Monte, Florence, Italy

[< the bloody Roman gladiatorial contests.]

Rom•a•ni (rŏm′ə-nē, rō′mə-) *n.* & *adj.* Variant of **Romany.**

Ro•ma•ni•a (rō-mā′nē-ə, -mān′yə) or **Ru•ma•ni•a** (rōō-) A country of SE Europe with a short coastline on the Black Sea; independent since 1878. Cap. Bucharest. Pop. 22,736,000.

Ro•ma•ni•an (rō-mā′nē-ən, -mān′yən) also **Ru•ma•ni•an** (rōō-) *adj.* Of or relating to Romania or its people, language, or culture. ❖ *n.* **1a.** A native or inhabitant of Romania. **b.** A person of Romanian descent. **2.** The Romance language of the Romanians.

Ro•man•ic (rō-măn′ĭk) *adj.* **1.** Of or derived from the ancient Romans. **2.** Of or relating to the Romance languages. —**Ro•man′ic** *n.*

Ro•man•ism (rō′mə-nĭz′əm) *n. Offensive* Roman Catholicism.

Ro•man•ist (rō′mə-nĭst) *n.* **1.** *Offensive* One who professes Roman Catholicism. **2.** A student of or authority on ancient Roman law, culture, and institutions.

Ro•man•ize (rō′mə-nīz′) *tr.v.* **-ized, -iz•ing, -iz•es** **1.** To convert (a person) to Roman Catholicism. **2.** To make Roman in character, allegiance, or style. **3.** often **romanize** To write or transliterate in the Latin alphabet. —**Ro′man•i•za′tion** (-mə-nĭ-zā′shən) *n.*

Roman law *n.* The legal system of ancient Rome, forming the basis for modern civil law.

Roman nose *n.* A nose with a high prominent bridge.

Roman numeral *n.* Any of the numerals in the ancient Roman system of numeration formed with the characters I, V, X, L, C, D, and M and still used in some formal contexts.

Ro•ma•no (rə-mä′nō, rō-) *n.* A sharp dry hard cheese of Italian origin that is made from cow's milk and usu. served grated as a garnish. [Ital., short for *(pecorino) romano,* Roman (sheep's milk cheese) < Lat. *Rōmānus.* See ROMAN.]

Ro•ma•nov also **Ro•ma•noff** (rō′mə-nŏf′, rō-mä′nəf, rə-) Russian ruling dynasty (1613–1917) that ended with the abdication of Nicholas II during the Russian Revolution.

Ro•mansh also **Ro•mansch** (rō-mänsh′, -mänsh′) *n.* The Rhaeto-Romance dialect that is an official language of Switzerland. [Romansch *Romonsch* < Lat. *Rōmānicus,* Roman. See RO-MANCE.]

ro•man•tic (rō-măn′tĭk) *adj.* **1.** Of, relating to, or characteristic of romance. **2.** Given to thoughts or feelings of romance. **3.** Displaying, expressive of, or conducive to love. **4.** Imaginative but impractical; visionary. **5.** Not based on fact; imaginary or fictitious. **6.** often **Romantic** Of or characteristic of romanticism in the arts. ❖ *n.* **1.** A romantic person. **2.** often **Romantic** A follower or adherent of romanticism. [Fr. *romantique* < obsolete *romant,* romance < OFr. *romans, romant-,* romance. See ROMANCE.] —**ro•man′ti•cal•ly** *adv.*

ro•man•ti•cism (rō-măn′tĭ-sĭz′əm) *n.* **1.** often **Romanticism** An artistic and intellectual movement originating in Europe in the late 18th century and characterized by a heightened interest in nature, emphasis on the expression of emotion and imagination, departure from classical art forms, and rebellion against established social conventions. **2.** Romantic quality or spirit in thought, expression, or action. —**ro•man′ti•cist** *n.*

ro•man•ti•cize (rō-măn′tĭ-sīz′) *v.* **-cized, -ciz•ing, -ciz•es** —*tr.* To view or interpret romantically; make romantic. —*intr.* To think in a romantic way. —**ro•man′ti•ci•za′tion** (-sĭ-zā′shən) *n.*

Rom•a•ny or **Rom•a•ni** (rŏm′ə-nē, rō′mə-) *n., pl.* **Romany** or **-nies** also **Romani** or **-nis** **1.** A Gypsy. **2.** The Indic language of the Gypsies. ❖ *adj.* Of or relating to the Gypsies or their language or culture. [Romany *romani,* fem. of *romano,* gypsy < *rom,* man < Prakrit *doma,* man of a low caste, of Dravidian orig.]

ro•maunt (rō-mônt′, -mônt′) *n. Archaic* A verse romance. [ME < OFr. *romans, romant-,* romance. See ROMANCE.]

Rom•berg (rŏm′bərg), **Sigmund** 1887–1951. Hungarian-born Amer. composer noted for *The Student Prince* (1924).

Rome¹ (rōm) **1.** The cap. of Italy, in the W-central part on the Tiber R.; traditionally founded by Romulus and Remus and cap. of the Roman Empire until A.D. 323. Pop. 2,693,383. **2.** See **Roman Empire.**

Rome² (rōm) *n.* A variety of apple having firm flesh with tough red skin. [After *Rome* Township, Ohio, where it was discovered.]

Ro•me•o (rō′mē-ō′) *n., pl.* **-os** A man devoted to lovemaking or the pursuit of love. [After *Romeo,* the hero of *Romeo and Juliet* by William Shakespeare.]

Rom•ish (rō′mĭsh) *adj. Offensive* Of or relating to the Roman Catholic Church. —**Rom′ish•ly** *adv.* —**Rom′ish•ness** *n.*

Rom•mel (rŏm′əl), **Erwin** Known as "the Desert Fox." 1891–1944. German general in France, Italy, and N Africa during World War II.

Rom•ney (rŏm′nē), **George** 1734–1802. British painter whose works include *Death of General Wolfe* (1763).

romp (rŏmp) *intr.v.* **romped, romp•ing, romps** **1.** To play or frolic boisterously. **2.** To run or advance in a rapid or easy manner. **3.** *Slang* To win a race or game easily. ❖ *n.* **1a.** Lively, merry play; frolic. **b.** Lively or frolicsome play that encompasses lovemaking. **2.** One, esp. a girl, that sports and frolics. **3.** A rapid or easy pace. **4.** *Slang* An easy win. [Alteration of RAMP².]

romp•er (rŏm′pər) *n.* **1.** One that romps. **2. rompers** A loosely

fitted one-piece garment having short bloomers that is worn esp. by small children for play.

Rom•u•lus (rŏm′yə-ləs) *n. Roman Mythology* The son of Mars and eponymous founder of Rome who with his twin brother, Remus, was reared and suckled by a wolf.

Ron•ces•valles (rŏn′sə-vălz′, rôn′thĕs-väl′yĕs) A mountain pass, 1,057.7 m (3,468 ft), through the W Pyrenees in N Spain; traditional site of the death of the hero Roland during the defeat of Charlemagne's army by the Saracens (778).

ron•deau (rŏn′dō, rŏn-dō′) *n., pl.* **-deaux** (-dōz, -dōz′) **1.** A lyrical poem of French origin having 13 or sometimes 10 lines with two rhymes throughout and with the opening phrase repeated twice as a refrain. **2.** A medieval French song, either monophonic or polyphonic in construction. [Fr., alteration of OFr. *rondel.* See RONDEL.]

ron•del (rŏn′dəl, rŏn-dĕl′) *n.* **1.** A poem similar to a rondeau, having 13 or 14 lines with two rhymes throughout, with the first and usu. second lines reappearing in the middle and at the end. **2.** often **ron•delle** (rŏn-dĕl′) A rounded or circular object. [ME < OFr., dim. of *ronde,* circle, round. See ROUND¹.]

ron•de•let (rŏn′dl-ĕt′, -dl-ā′) *n.* A poem similar to a rondeau, usu. having seven lines and always two rhymes, with the first line repeated as lines three and seven. [Fr. < OFr., dim. of *rondel,* rondel. See RONDEL.]

ron•do (rŏn′dō, rŏn-dō′) *n., pl.* **-dos** A musical composition built on the alternation of a principal recurring theme and contrasting episodes. [Ital. *rondò* < Fr. *rondeau,* rondeau. See RON-DEAU.]

ron•dure (rŏn′jər, -dyŏŏr′) *n.* A circular or gracefully rounded object. [Fr. *rondeur,* roundness < OFr. < *ronde,* round. See ROUND¹.]

Ron•sard (rôn-sär′), **Pierre de** 1524–85. French poet whose lyrical love poems include *Sonnets pour Hélène* (1578).

rönt•gen (rĕnt′gən, -jən, rŭnt′-) *n.* Variant of **roentgen.**

Rönt•gen (rœnt′gən), **Wilhelm Konrad** See Wilhelm Konrad Roentgen.

rood (rōōd) *n.* **1a.** A crucifix symbolizing the cross on which Jesus was crucified. **b.** A large crucifix surmounting the rood screen or rood beam of a medieval church. **2.** *Chiefly British* A measure of length that varies from 5½ to 8 yards (5.0 to 7.3 meters). [ME < OE *rōd.*]

rood beam *n.* A beam in a medieval church across the entrance to the choir, supporting the rood and usu. forming the head of the rood screen.

rood screen *n.* In medieval churches, an often openwork wall-like screen separating the choir from the nave and extending upward to the rood beam.

roof (rōōf, rŏŏf) *n.* **1a.** The exterior surface and its supporting structures on the top of a building. **b.** The upper exterior surface of a dwelling as a symbol of the home itself. **2.** The top covering of something. **3.** The upper surface of an anatomical structure, esp. one having a vaulted inner structure. **4.** The highest point or limit; the summit or ceiling. ❖ *tr.v.* **roofed, roof•ing, roofs** To furnish or cover with or as if with a roof. —*idioms:* **go through the roof** *Slang* **1.** To grow, intensify, or rise to an enormous, often unexpected degree. **2.** To become extremely angry. **raise the roof** *Slang* **1.** To be extremely noisy and boisterous. **2.** To complain loudly and bitterly. [ME < OE *hrōf.*]

roof•er (rōō′fər, rŏŏf′ər) *n.* One who lays or repairs roofs.

roof garden *n.* **1.** A garden on the roof of a building. **2.** The roof or top floor of a building designed for use by the public that often contains outdoor seating or dining facilities.

roof•ie (rōō′fē) *n. Slang* A tablet of the sedative flunitrazepam. [Prob. alteration (influenced by ROOF) of ROHYPNOL.]

roof•ing (rōō′fĭng, rŏŏf′ĭng) *n.* **1.** Materials used in building a roof. **2.** A roof.

roof•less (rōōf′lĭs, rŏŏf′-) *adj.* **1.** Lacking a roof. **2.** Having no home or shelter; homeless or destitute.

roof•line (rōōf′līn′, rŏŏf′-) *n.* The profile of or silhouette made by a roof or series of roofs.

roof•top (rōōf′tŏp′, rŏŏf′-) *n.* A roof, esp. its outer surface.

roof•tree (rōōf′trē′, rŏŏf′-) *n.* **1.** The ridgepole of a roof. **2.** A roof.

rook¹ (rŏŏk) *n.* **1.** An Old World bird (*Corvus frugilegus*) that resembles the North American crow and nests in colonies near the tops of trees. **2.** A swindler or cheat, esp. at games. ❖ *tr.v.* **rooked, rook•ing, rooks** To swindle; cheat. [ME *rok* < OE *hrōc.*]

rook² (rŏŏk) *n.* A chess piece that may move in a straight line over any number of empty squares in a rank or file. [ME *rok* < OFr. *roc* < Ar. *ruḥḥ* < Pers.]

rook•er•y (rŏŏk′ə-rē) *n., pl.* **-ies** **1a.** A place where rooks nest or breed. **b.** A colony of rooks. **2.** The breeding ground of certain other birds or animals, such as penguins and seals. **3.** *Informal* A crowded and dilapidated tenement.

rook•ie (rŏŏk′ē) *n.* **1.** *Slang* **a.** An untrained or inexperienced recruit, as in the army. **b.** An inexperienced person; a novice. **2.** *Sports* A first-year player, esp. in a professional sport. [Perh. alteration of RECRUIT.]

room (rōōm, rŏŏm) *n.* **1.** A space that is or may be occupied. **2a.** An area separated by walls or partitions from other similar parts of the structure or building in which it is located. **b.** The people

Romania

rood screen
Blagovestenska Church,
Szentendre, Hungary

rookery
emperor penguins, Cape
Crozier, Antarctica

present in such an area. **3. rooms** Living quarters; lodgings. **4.** Suitable opportunity; occasion. ❖ *intr.v.* **roomed, room•ing, rooms** To occupy a room; lodge. [ME *roum* < OE *rūm*.]

room and board *n.* Lodging and meals earned, purchased for a set fee, or otherwise provided.

room•er (ro͞o′mər, ro͝om′ər) *n.* One who rents a room or rooms in which to live; a lodger.

room•ette (ro͞o-mĕt′, ro͝om-ĕt′) *n.* A small private compartment in a railroad sleeping car.

room•ful (ro͞om′fo͝ol′, ro͝om′-) *n., pl.* **-fuls** The amount or number that a room can hold.

room•ie (ro͞o′mē, ro͝om′ē) *n. Informal* A roommate.

room•ing house (ro͞o′mĭng, ro͝om′ĭng) *n.* A house where lodgers may rent rooms.

room•mate (ro͞om′māt′, ro͝om′-) *n.* A person with whom one shares a room or rooms.

room temperature *n.* An indoor temperature of from 20 to 25°C (68 to 77°F).

room•y (ro͞o′mē, ro͝om′ē) *adj.* **-i•er, -i•est** Having plenty of room; spacious. —**room′i•ly** *adv.* —**room′i•ness** *n.*

roor•back (ro͝or′băk′) *n.* A false or slanderous story used for political advantage. [After Baron von *Roorback*, imaginary author of *Roorback's Tour Through the Western and Southern States*, from which a passage was purportedly quoted to disparage presidential candidate James K. Polk in 1844.]

Roo•se•velt (rō′zə-vĕlt′, rōz′vĕlt′, -vəlt, ro͞o′-), **(Anna) Eleanor** 1884–1962. Amer. diplomat, writer, and First Lady of the US (1933–45) who was a delegate to the United Nations (1945–52 and 1961–62).

Roosevelt, Edith Carow 1861–1948. First Lady of the US (1901–09) who oversaw a major renovation of the White House (1902).

Roosevelt, Franklin Delano 1882–1945. The 32nd President of the US (1933–45), whose administration was marked by measures to increase employment and assist recovery from the Depression and by US participation in World War II.

Roosevelt, Rio A river, c. 644 km (400 mi), of NW Brazil; orig. known as the River of Doubt and renamed in honor of Theodore Roosevelt, who explored it in 1913.

Roosevelt, Theodore 1858–1919. The 26th President of the US (1901–09), who oversaw the building of the Panama Canal and won the 1906 Nobel Peace Prize for his role in ending the Russo-Japanese War (1904–05).

Roosevelt Island 1. Formerly **Welfare Island.** An island in the East R. off the coast of central Manhattan. **2.** An island of Antarctica in the E part of the Ross Ice Shelf.

roost (ro͞ost) *n.* **1.** A perch on which domestic fowl or other birds rest or sleep. **2.** A place with perches for fowl or other birds. **3.** A place for temporary rest or sleep. ❖ *intr.v.* **roost•ed, roost•ing, roosts** To rest or sleep on or as if on a perch or roost. ***—idioms:* come home to roost** To have repercussions or aftereffects, esp. unfavorable ones. **rule the roost** *Informal* To be in charge; dominate. [ME *rooste* < OE *hrōst*.]

roost•er (ro͞o′stər) *n.* **1a.** An adult male chicken. **b.** An adult male of other birds. **2.** A person regarded as cocky or pugnacious.

roost•er•fish (ro͞o′stər-fĭsh′) *n., pl.* **roosterfish** or **-fish•es** A brightly colored food and game fish *(Nematistius pectoralis)* found from the Gulf of California to Panama.

rooster tail *n.* A projected mass of fine particles, as of water or snow, having an arced shape similar to that of a rooster's tail.

root¹ (ro͞ot, ro͝ot) *n.* **1.** The usu. underground portion of a plant that lacks buds, leaves, or nodes and serves as support, draws minerals and water from the surrounding soil, and sometimes stores food. **2.** Any of various other underground plant parts, esp. an underground stem such as a tuber. **3a.** The embedded part of an organ or structure such as a hair, tooth, or nerve, serving as a base or support. **b.** A base or support. **4.** An essential part or element; the basic core. **5.** A primary source; an origin. See Syns at **origin. 6.** A progenitor or ancestor from which a person or family is descended. **7a.** The condition of being settled and of belonging to a particular place or society. Often used in the plural. **b. roots** The state of having or establishing an indigenous relationship with or a personal affinity for a particular culture, society, or environment: *music with African roots.* **8.** *Linguistics* **a.** The element that carries the main component of meaning in a word and provides the basis from which a word is derived by adding affixes or inflectional endings or by phonetic change. **b.** Such an element reconstructed for a protolanguage. **9.** *Mathematics* **a.** A number that when multiplied by itself an indicated number of times equals a given product: *a fourth root of 4 is* $\sqrt{2}$. **b.** A number that reduces an equation in one variable to an identity when it is substituted for the variable. **c.** A number at which a polynomial has the value zero. **10.** *Music* **a.** The note from which a chord is built. **b.** Such a note occurring as the lowest note of a triad or other chord. ❖ *v.* **root•ed, root•ing, roots** *—intr.* **1.** To grow roots or a root. **2.** To become firmly established, settled, or entrenched. **3.** To come into existence; originate. *—tr.* **1.** To cause to put out roots and grow. **2.** To implant by or as if by the roots. **3.** To furnish a primary source or origin to. **4.** To remove by or as if by the roots. Often used with *up* or *out.* ***—idiom:* root and branch** Utterly; completely. [ME *rot* < OE *rōt* < ON. See **wrād-** in App.] —**root′er** *n.*

root² (ro͞ot, ro͝ot) *v.* **root•ed, root•ing, roots** *—tr.* To dig with or as if with the snout or nose. *—intr.* **1.** To dig in the earth with or as if with the snout or nose. **2.** To rummage for something. [ME *wroten* < OE *wrōtan*.] —**root′er** *n.*

root³ (ro͞ot, ro͝ot) *intr.v.* **root•ed, root•ing, roots 1.** To give audible encouragement or applause to a contestant or team; cheer. **2.** To lend support to someone or something. [Poss. alteration of ROUT³.] —**root′er** *n.*

Root (ro͞ot), **Elihu** 1845–1937. Amer. lawyer and public official who won the 1912 Nobel Peace Prize.

Root (ro͞ot), **John Wellborn** 1850–91. Amer. architect whose designs include the Monadnock Building (1889–91) in Chicago.

root•age (ro͞o′tĭj, ro͝ot′ĭj) *n.* **1.** A system or growth of roots. **2.** Establishment by or as if by roots.

root beer (ro͞ot, ro͝ot) *n.* A carbonated soft drink made from extracts of certain plant roots and herbs.

root canal *n.* **1.** A pulp-filled channel in a root of a tooth. **2.** A treatment in which diseased tissue from a root canal is removed and the resulting cavity filled with an inert material.

root cap *n. Botany* A thimble-shaped mass of cells that covers and protects the root tip.

root cellar *n.* An underground pit or cellar, usu. covered with earth, used for the storage of root crops and other vegetables.

root climber *n.* A vine, such as the ivy, that clings to its support by means of adventitious roots.

root crop *n.* A crop, as of yams, grown for its edible roots.

root•ed•ness (ro͞o′tĭd-nĭs, ro͝ot′ĭd-) *n.* The quality or state of having roots, esp. of being firmly established or entrenched.

root hair *n.* A hairlike outgrowth of an epidermal cell of a plant root that absorbs water and minerals from the soil.

root•hold (ro͞ot′hōld′, ro͝ot′-) *n.* Support or stabilization of a plant in the soil through the spreading of its roots.

root knot *n.* A disease of plants characterized by protuberant enlargements on the roots caused by a nematode.

root•less (ro͞ot′lĭs, ro͝ot′-) *adj.* **1.** Having no roots. **2.** Not belonging to a place or society. —**root′less•ness** *n.*

root•let (ro͞ot′lĭt, ro͝ot′-) *n.* A small root or division of a root.

root mean square *n. Statistics* The square root of the average of the squares of a set of numbers.

root pressure *n.* Pressure exerted in the roots of plants as the result of osmosis, causing exudation from cut stems and guttation of water from leaves.

root•stalk (ro͞ot′stôk′, ro͝ot′-) *n.* See **rhizome.**

root•stock (ro͞ot′stŏk′, ro͝ot′-) *n.* **1.** See **rhizome. 2.** A root or part of a root used as a stock for plant propagation. **3.** A source or origin.

root•worm (ro͞ot′wûrm′, ro͝ot′-) *n.* Any of several beetles of the genus *Diabrotica*, the larvae of which feed on the roots of various crop plants, esp. corn.

root•y (ro͞o′tē, ro͝ot′ē) *adj.* **-i•er, -i•est 1.** Full or consisting of roots. **2.** Resembling roots. —**root′i•ness** *n.*

rope (rōp) *n.* **1.** A flexible heavy cord of tightly intertwined hemp or other fiber. **2.** A string of items attached in one line by or as if by twisting or braiding. **3.** A sticky glutinous formation of stringy matter in a liquid. **4a.** A cord with a noose at one end for hanging a person. **b.** Execution or death by hanging. **5.** A lasso or lariat. **6. ropes** *Sports* Several cords strung between poles to enclose a boxing or wrestling ring. **7. ropes** *Informal* Specialized procedures or details. ❖ *v.* **roped, rop•ing, ropes** *—tr.* **1.** To tie or fasten with or as if with rope. **2.** To enclose, separate, or partition with or as if with a rope: *roped off the area.* **3.** To catch with a rope or lasso. **4.** *Informal* To trick or deceive. *—intr.* To become like a cord or rope. ***—idioms:* on the ropes 1.** *Sports* Knocked against the ropes that enclose a boxing ring. **2.** On the verge of defeat or collapse; hopeless or powerless. **the end of (one's) rope** The limit of one's patience, endurance, or resources. [ME < OE *rāp*.] —**rop′er** *n.*

rope tow *n.* A continuous rope conveyor used to pull skiers up a slope; a ski tow.

rope•walk (rōp′wôk′) *n.* **1.** An alley or covered pathway where strands of material, such as hemp fiber, are laid and twisted into rope. **2.** A long narrow building containing such a pathway.

rop•y also **rop•ey** (rō′pē) *adj.* **-i•er, -i•est 1.** Resembling a rope or ropes. **2.** Forming sticky glutinous strings or threads, as some liquids. —**rop′i•ly** *adv.* —**rop′i•ness** *n.*

roque (rōk) *n.* A variation of croquet played with short-handled mallets on a hard court that is bounded by a concrete wall against which a ball may rebound and be retrieved. [Alteration of ROQUET.]

Roque•fort (rōk′fərt) A trademark for a soft cheese made from sheep's milk and ripened in caves near Roquefort, France.

ro•que•laure (rō′kə-lôr′, -lōr′, rŏk′ə-) *n.* A knee-length cloak lined with brightly colored silk and often trimmed with fur, worn by European men in the 18th century. [After Antoine Gaston Jean Baptiste, Duc de *Roquelaure* (1656–1738), French marshal.]

ro•quet (rō-kā′) *tr.v.* **-queted** (-kād′), **-quet•ing** (-kā′ĭng), **-quets** (-kāz′) To hit (another player's ball) in croquet. [Alteration of CROQUET.]

ro•quette (rō-kĕt′) *n.* See **arugula.**

Ro•rem (rôr′əm, rōr′-), **Ned** b. 1923. Amer. composer whose

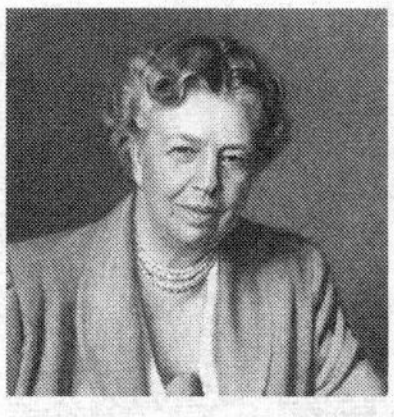

Eleanor Roosevelt
detail from a 1949 portrait by Douglas Chandor (1897–1953)

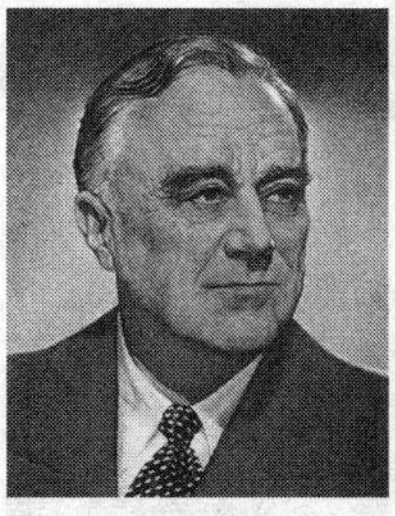

Franklin Delano Roosevelt

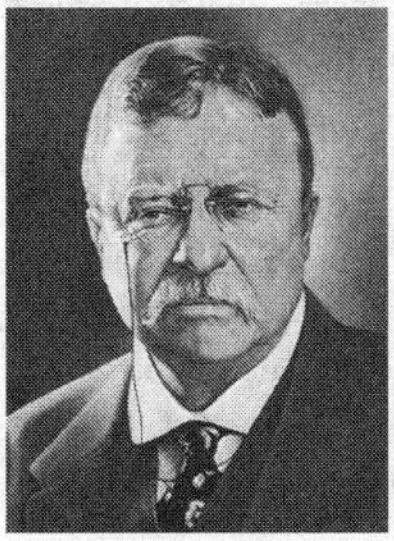

Theodore Roosevelt

ă	pat	oi	boy
ā	pay	ou	out
âr	care	o͝o	took
ä	father	o͞o	boot
ĕ	pet	ŭ	cut
ē	be	ûr	urge
ĭ	pit	th	thin
ī	pie	*th*	this
îr	pier	hw	which
ŏ	pot	zh	vision
ō	toe	ə	about, item
ô	paw		

Stress marks:
′ (primary);
′ (secondary), as in
lexicon (lĕk′sĭ-kŏn′)

works include the symphony *Air Music* (1976).

ror·qual (rôr'kwəl) *n.* Any of several baleen whales of the family Balaenopteridae, having longitudinal grooves on the throat and a small pointed dorsal fin. [Fr. < Norw. *rørhval* < ON *reydhar-hvalr* : *reydhr*, rorqual (< *raudhr*, red; see **reudh-** in App.) + *hvalr*, whale.]

Ror·schach test (rôr'shäk', -shäкн') *n.* A psychological test in which a subject's interpretations of a series of standard inkblots are analyzed as indicative of personality, preoccupations, and conflicts. [After Hermann *Rorschach* (1884–1922), Swiss psychiatrist.]

Ro·sa (rō'zä), **Monte** A mountain, 4,636.9 m (15,203 ft), in the Pennine Alps on the Swiss-Italian border.

ro·sa·ce·a (rō-zā'shē-ə) *n.* A chronic dermatitis of the face characterized by a red or rosy coloration and the appearance of acnelike pimples. [NLat. *rosācea*, rose-colored (acne) < Lat., fem. of *rosāceus*, made of roses. See ROSACEOUS.]

ro·sa·ceous (rō-zā'shəs) *adj.* **1.** Of or belonging to the rose family. **2.** Resembling the flower of a rose. [< Lat. *rosāceus*, made of roses < *rosa*, rose.]

ros·an·i·line also **ros·an·i·lin** (rō-zăn'ə-lĭn) *n.* A brownish-red crystalline aniline derivative, $C_{20}H_{21}N_3O$, used in the manufacture of dyes. [ROS(E)[1] + ANILINE.]

ro·sar·i·an (rō-zâr'ē-ən) *n.* A person with expertise or a special interest in the cultivation of roses.

Ro·sa·ri·o (rō-zär'ē-ō', -sär'-) A city of E-central Argentina on the Paraná R. NW of Buenos Aires. Pop. 894,645.

ro·sa·ry (rō'zə-rē) *n., pl.* **-ries 1.** *Roman Catholic Church* **a.** A form of devotion to the Virgin Mary, chiefly consisting of three sets of five decades each of the Hail Mary, each decade preceded by the Lord's Prayer and ending with a doxology. **b.** One of these sets of decades. **c.** A string of beads of 5 or 15 decades on which these prayers are counted. **2.** Similar beads used by other religious groups. [Ult. < Med.Lat. *rosārium* < Lat., rose garden < neut. of *rosārius*, of roses < *rosa*, rose.]

rosary pea *n.* A tropical woody vine (*Abrus precatorius*) widely naturalized in Florida and having scarlet and black poisonous seeds used as beads.

rose¹ (rōz) *n.* **1.** A member of the rose family. **2a.** Any of numerous shrubs or vines of the genus *Rosa*, having prickly stems, pinnately compound leaves, and variously colored, often fragrant flowers. **b.** The flower of any of these plants. **c.** Any of various similar or related plants. **2.** A dark pink to moderate red. **4.** An ornament, such as a decorative knot, resembling a rose in form; a rosette. **5.** A perforated nozzle for spraying water from a hose or sprinkling can. **6a.** A form of gem cut marked by a flat base and a faceted hemispheric upper surface. **b.** A gem, esp. a diamond, cut in this manner. **7.** A rose window. **8.** A compass card or its representation, as on a map. **9. roses** That which is marked by favor, success, or ease of execution. ❖ *adj.* **1.** Of the color rose. **2.** Relating to, containing, or used for roses. **3.** Scented or flavored with or as if with roses. —**idioms: come up roses** To result favorably or successfully. **under the rose** Sub rosa. [ME < OE < Lat. *rosa*.]

rose² (rōz) *v.* Past tense of **rise.**

ro·sé (rō-zā') *n.* A light pink wine made from purple grapes, with the skins being removed from the juice during fermentation as soon as the desired color has been attained. [Fr. *(vin) rosé*, pink (wine) < OFr. < *rose*, rose. See ROSE¹.]

rose acacia *n.* A shrub (*Robinia hispida*) of the southeast United States having bristly brittle branches and clusters of pale purple or rose flowers.

rose apple *n.* **1.** A southeast Asian evergreen tree (*Syzygium jambos*) having showy flowers and fragrant cream-yellow ovoid fruits. **2.** The fruit of this plant.

ro·se·ate (rō'zē-ĭt, -āt') *adj.* **1.** Rose-colored. **2.** Cheerful or bright; optimistic. [< Lat. *roseus*, rosy < *rosa*, rose.] —**ro'se·ate·ly** *adv.*

roseate spoonbill *n.* A New World species of spoonbill (*Ajaia ajaja*) having rosy or pinkish plumage.

Ro·seau (rō-zō') The cap. of Dominica, in the Windward Is. of the West Indies. Pop. 16,243.

rose·bay (rōz'bā') *n.* **1.** Any of several shrubs of the genus *Rhododendron*, esp. *R. maximum* of the southeast United States, having large glossy leaves and flowers with a rose-pink, bell-shaped corolla with green spots. **2.** See **oleander. 3.** *Chiefly British* The willow herb.

rose beetle *n.* See **rose chafer.**

rose-breast·ed grosbeak (rōz'brĕs'tĭd) *n.* A North American bird (*Pheucticus ludovicianus*), the male of which is black and white with a rose-red patch on the breast.

rose·bud (rōz'bŭd') *n.* The bud of a rose.

rose bug *n.* See **rose chafer.**

rose·bush (rōz'boosh') *n.* A flowering rose shrub.

rose campion *n.* A Eurasian plant (*Lychnis coronaria*) having a dense cover of white woolly down and rose-red flowers.

rose chafer *n.* A long-legged gray North American beetle (*Macrodactylus subspinosus*) that causes damage to the roots, leaves, and blossoms of garden plants, esp. roses.

rose cold *n.* See **rose fever.**

rose-col·ored (rōz'kŭl'ərd) *adj.* **1.** Having the color rose. **2.**

roseate spoonbill
Ajaia ajaja

rose window
13th-century rose (top) and lancet windows in Chartres Cathedral, France

Cheerful or optimistic, esp. to an excessive degree. —**idiom: through rose-colored glasses** With an unduly cheerful, optimistic, or favorable view of things.

Rose·crans (rōz'krănz'), **William Starke** 1819–98. Amer. Union general who was relieved of his command after the disastrous Battle of Chickamauga (1863).

rose family *n.* A large family of plants, the Rosaceae, characterized by showy flowers with five separated petals and numerous stamens borne on the margin of a cuplike structure, including fruit plants such as the apple, cherry, and strawberry and ornamentals such as the rose and spirea.

rose fever *n.* A spring or early summer hay fever.

rose·fish (rōz'fĭsh') *n., pl.* **rosefish** or **-fish·es** A bright red marine food fish (*Sebastes marinus*) of North Atlantic waters.

rose geranium *n.* A woody plant (*Pelargonium graveolens*) having rose-pink flowers and fragrant, deeply palmately lobed leaves used for flavoring and in perfumery.

rose hip or **rose·hip** (rōz'hĭp') *n.* The aggregate fruit of the rose plant, consisting of several dry fruitlets enclosed by an enlarged, fleshy, usu. red floral cup.

ro·selle (rō-zĕl') *n.* A tropical African plant (*Hibiscus sabdariffa*) having flowers with yellow petals and a persistent bright red calyx that has a pleasantly acid flavor. [?]

rose mallow *n.* A tall marsh plant (*Hibiscus moscheutos*) of eastern North America having leaves covered with whitish down and flowers with white, pink, or rose petals.

rose·mar·y (rōz'mâr'ē) *n., pl.* **-ies** An aromatic evergreen Mediterranean shrub (*Rosmarinus officinalis*) having light blue or pink flowers and grayish-green leaves used in cooking and perfume. [Alteration of ME *rosmarine* < Lat. *rōs marīnus*, sea dew : *rōs*, dew + *marīnus*, of the sea; see MARINE.]

rose moss *n.* **1.** Any of the various mosses of the genus *Rhodobryum*, esp. *R. roseum*, characterized by conspicuous terminal leaf rosettes. **2.** See **portulaca.**

Ro·sen·berg (rō'zĭn-bûrg'), **Julius** 1918–53. Amer. spy who with his wife, **Ethel** (1915–53), was convicted of helping pass information concerning nuclear weaponry to the Soviets. Both were executed despite questions regarding the fairness of their trial.

rose of heaven *n.* A glabrous Mediterranean annual plant (*Lychnis coeli-rosa*) having opposite linear or lance-shaped leaves and large rose-pink flowers.

rose of Jericho *n.* Either of two desert plants, *Anastatica hierochuntica* of the mustard family or *Selaginella lepidophylla*, that form a tight ball when dry and unfold when moistened.

rose of Shar·on (shăr'ən) *n.* **1.** A small eastern Asian tree or tall shrub (*Hibiscus syriacus*) having large reddish, purple, or white flowers and coarsely toothed leaves. **2.** A shrubby Eurasian evergreen plant (*Hypericum calycinum*) having oblong leaves and yellow flowers and usu. grown as a ground cover. [After the Plain of SHARON.]

ro·se·o·la (rō-zē'ə-lə, rō'zē-ō'lə) *n.* A rose-colored skin rash, sometimes occurring with diseases such as measles, syphilis, or scarlet fever. [NLat. < dim. of Lat. *roseus*, rosy < *rosa*, rose.] —**ro·se'o·lar** *adj.*

rose periwinkle *n.* See **Madagascar periwinkle.**

rose pink *n.* A moderate to dark pink.

rose quartz *n.* A pinkish variety of the mineral quartz, used as a gemstone or an ornamental stone.

rose·root (rōz'root', -root') *n.* A perennial plant (*Sedum rosea*) of the Northern Hemisphere having fleshy leaves and greenish-yellow or purple flowers.

rose slug *n.* The larva of either of two sawflies (*Cladius isomerus* or *Endelomyia aethiops*) that feeds destructively on the leaves of roses.

Ro·set·ta stone (rō-zĕt'ə) *n.* A basalt tablet bearing inscriptions in Greek and in Egyptian hieroglyphic and demotic scripts that was discovered in 1799 near Rosetta, a town of northern Egypt in the Nile River delta, and provided the key to the decipherment of Egyptian hieroglyphics.

ro·sette (rō-zĕt') *n.* **1.** An ornament or badge made of ribbon or silk that is pleated or gathered to resemble a rose. **2.** A roselike marking or formation, such as one of the clusters of spots on a leopard's fur. **3.** *Architecture* A painted, carved, or sculptured ornament having a circular arrangement of parts radiating out from the center and suggesting the petals of a rose. **4.** *Botany* A circular cluster of leaves that radiate from a center at or close to the ground. **5.** An ornamental circular band surrounding the central hole of an acoustic guitar. [Fr. < OFr., dim. of *rose*, rose. See ROSE¹.]

rose water *n.* A fragrant preparation made by steeping or distilling rose petals in water, used in cosmetics and in cookery.

rose window *n.* A circular window, usu. of stained glass, having tracery in intricate petallike patterns.

rose·wood (rōz'wood') *n.* **1.** Any of various tropical or semitropical leguminous trees of the genera *Tipuana*, *Pterocarpus*, or *Dalbergia*, having hard reddish or dark wood with a strongly marked grain. **2.** The wood of any of these trees.

Rosh Ha·sha·nah also **Rosh Ha·sha·na** or **Rosh Ha·sho·na** or **Rosh Ha·sho·nah** (rôsh' hə-shō'nə, -shär'-, hä-, hä-shä-nä') *n.* The Jewish New Year, observed on the first day or the first and second days of Tishri and marked by solemnity as well as festivity. [Heb. *rōʾš haš-šānâ* : *rōʾš*, head, beginning + *ha-*, the + *šānâ*, year.]

ro•shi (rō′shē) *n., pl.* **-shis** The spiritual leader of a group of Zen Buddhists. [J. *rōshi*, old master.]

Ro•si•cru•cian (rō′zĭ-kro͞o′shən, rŏz′ĭ-) *n.* **1.** A member of an international organization devoted to the study of ancient philosophy and religion. **2.** A member of any of several secret organizations or orders of the 17th and 18th centuries devoted to mysticism. ❖ *adj.* Of or relating to Rosicrucians or their philosophy. [< NLat. *(Fräter) Rosae Crucis*, (Brother) of the Cross of the Rose, transl. of Ger. *Rosenkreutz*, surname of the traditional founder of the society.] —**Ro′si•cru′cian•ism** *n.*

ros•in (rŏz′ĭn) *n.* A translucent yellowish to dark brown resin derived from the stumps or sap of various pine trees and used to increase sliding friction and to manufacture a wide variety of products. ❖ *tr.v.* **-ined, -in•ing, -ins** To coat or rub with rosin. [ME, var. of *resin*. See RESIN.] —**ros′in•y** *adj.*

rosin oil *n.* A white to brown viscous liquid obtained by fractional distillation of rosin and used in lubricants, adhesives, electrical insulation, and printing inks.

ros•in•weed (rŏz′ĭn-wēd′) *n.* Any of several North American plants of the genera *Grindelia* or *Silphium*, such as the compass plant, having a resinous juice.

Ross (rôs, rŏs), **Betsy Griscom** 1752–1836. Amer. seamstress who according to tradition made the first American flag (Jun. 1776) at the request of George Washington.

Ross, Harold Wallace 1892–1951. Amer. publisher who founded and edited (1925–51) *The New Yorker* magazine.

Ross, Sir **James Clark** 1800–62. British polar explorer who located the north magnetic pole (1831) and later explored Antarctica (1839–43).

Ross, John Orig. Kooweskoowe. 1790–1866. Cherokee leader who directed the forced removal of the Cherokee from GA to the Oklahoma Terr. (1838–39) along the Trail of Tears.

Ross, Sir **John** 1777–1856. British naval officer and Arctic explorer who led two expeditions (1818 and 1829–33) in search of the Northwest Passage.

Ross, Nellie Tayloe 1876–1977. Amer. politician who served as governor of WY (1925–27).

Ros•set•ti (rō-zĕt′ē), **Dante Gabriel** 1828–82. British poet and painter who was a founder (1848) of the Pre-Raphaelite Brotherhood. His sister **Christina Georgina Rossetti** (1830–94) is known for her verse collection *Goblin Market* (1862).

Ross Ice Shelf A vast area in Antarctica bordering on **Ross Sea,** an arm of the S Pacific Ocean including **Ross Island,** site of the active volcano Mt. Erebus.

Ros•si•ni (rō-sē′nē), **Gioacchino Antonio** 1792–1868. Italian composer whose operas include *William Tell* (1829).

Ros•tand (rôs-tän′), **Edmond** 1868–1918. French playwright noted esp. for *Cyrano de Bergerac* (1897).

ros•tel•late (rŏs′tə-lāt′, rō-stĕl′ĭt) *adj.* Having a rostellum.

ros•tel•lum (rō-stĕl′əm) *n., pl.* **ros•tel•la** (rō-stĕl′ə) *Biology* A small beaklike part. [Lat., dim. of *röstrum*, beak. See ROSTRUM.] —**ros•tel′lar** *adj.*

ros•ter (rŏs′tər, rô′stər) *n.* **1.** A list, esp. of names. **2.** A list of the names of military officers and enlisted personnel enrolled in a particular unit. [Du. *rooster*, gridiron, roster (< the ruled paper used for a roster) < *roosten*, to roast.]

Ros•tock (rŏs′tŏk′, rôs′tôk′) A city of NE Germany near the Baltic Sea NNW of Berlin; chartered 1218. Pop. 241,146.

Ros•tov (rə-stôf′) also **Ros•tov-on-Don** (-ŏn-dŏn′, -dôn′, -ôn-) A city of SW Russia on the Don R. near its outlet on an arm of the Sea of Azov; chartered 1797. Pop. 1,012,649.

ros•trate (rŏs′trāt, -trĭt, rō′strāt, -strĭt) *adj.* Having a beaklike part. [Lat. *röstrātus* < *röstrum*, beak. See ROSTRUM.]

ros•trum (rŏs′trəm, rô′strəm) *n., pl.* **ros•trums** or **ros•tra** (rŏs′trə, rô′strə) **1.** A dais, pulpit, or other elevated platform for public speaking. **2a.** The curved beaklike prow of an ancient Roman ship, esp. a war galley. **b.** The speaker's platform in an ancient Roman forum, which was decorated with the prows of captured enemy ships. **3.** *Biology* A beaklike or snoutlike projection. [Lat. *röstrum*, beak.] —**ros′tral** (-trəl) *adj.*

ros•y (rō′zē) *adj.* **-i•er, -i•est 1a.** Having the characteristic pink or red color of a rose. **b.** Flushed with a healthy glow. **2.** Consisting of, decorated with, or suggestive of a rose or roses. **3.** Bright or cheerful; optimistic. —**ros′i•ly** *adv.* —**ros′i•ness** *n.*

rot (rŏt) *v.* **rot•ted, rot•ting, rots** —*intr.* **1.** To undergo decomposition, esp. organic decomposition; decay. **2.** To become damaged, weakened, or useless because of decay. **3.** To languish; decline. **4.** To decay morally; become degenerate. —*tr.* To cause to decompose or decay. ❖ *n.* **1.** The process of rotting or the condition of being rotten. **2.** Foot rot. **3.** See **liver fluke** 2. **4.** Any of several plant diseases characterized by the breakdown of tissue and caused by various bacteria or fungi. **5.** Pointless talk; nonsense. **6.** *Archaic* Any disease causing the decay of flesh. ❖ *interj.* Used to express annoyance, contempt, or impatience. [ME *roten* < OE *rotian*.]

ro•ta (rō′tə) *n.* **1.** *Chiefly British* A roll call or a roster of names. **2.** *Chiefly British* A round or rotation of duties. **3. Rota** *Roman Catholic Church* A tribunal of prelates that serves as an ecclesi-

---

siastical court. [Lat., wheel.]

Ro•tar•i•an (rō-târ′ē-ən) *n.* A member of a Rotary Club, a major national and international service club.

ro•ta•ry (rō′tə-rē) *adj.* Of, relating to, causing, or characterized by rotation, esp. axial rotation. ❖ *n., pl.* **-ries 1.** A part or device that rotates around an axis. **2.** *Chiefly New England* See **traffic circle.** [Med.Lat. *rotärius* < Lat. *rota*, wheel.]

rotary engine *n.* An engine, such as a turbine, in which power is supplied directly to vanes or other rotary parts.

rotary plow *n.* A plow having a series of hoes arranged on a revolving power-driven shaft.

rotary press *n.* A printing press consisting of curved plates attached to a revolving cylinder that prints onto a continuous roll of paper.

rotary tiller *n.* See **rotary plow.**

ro•ta•ry-wing aircraft (rō′tə-rē-wĭng′) *n.* A rotorcraft.

ro•tate (rō′tāt) *v.* **-tat•ed, -tat•ing, -tates** —*intr.* **1.** To turn around on an axis or center. **2.** To proceed in sequence; take turns or alternate. —*tr.* **1.** To cause to turn on an axis or center. **2a.** To plant or grow (crops) in a fixed order of succession. **b.** To cause to alternate or proceed in sequence. ❖ *adj.* Having radiating parts; wheel-shaped. [Lat. *rotäre, rotät-* < *rota*, wheel.] —**ro′tat′a•ble** *adj.*

ro•ta•tion (rō-tā′shən) *n.* **1a.** The act or process of turning around a center or an axis. **b.** A single complete cycle of such motion. **2.** *Mathematics* A transformation of a coordinate system in which the axes are rotated through a given angle while the origin remains fixed. **3.** Regular and uniform variation in a sequence or series. **4.** *Games* An order of shooting balls in billiards in which the ball with the lowest number on the table is always pocketed first. —**ro•ta′tion•al** *adj.*

ro•ta•tive (rō′tā′tĭv) *adj.* **1.** Of, relating to, causing, or characterized by rotation. **2.** Characterized by or occurring in alternation or succession. —**ro′ta′tive•ly** *adv.*

ro•ta•tor (rō′tā′tər) *n.* **1.** One that rotates. **2.** *pl.* **ro•ta•tor•es** (rō′tə-tôr′ēz, -tōr-) *Anatomy* A muscle that serves to rotate a part of the body.

rotator cuff *n.* A set of muscles and tendons that secures the arm to the shoulder joint and permits rotation of the arm.

ro•ta•to•ry (rō′tə-tôr′ē, -tōr′ē) *adj.* **1.** Of, relating to, causing, or characterized by rotation. **2.** Occurring or proceeding in alternation or succession.

ro•ta•vi•rus (rō′tə-vī′rəs) *n., pl.* **-rus•es** Any of a group of wheel-shaped RNA viruses that cause gastroenteritis.

Rot•blat (rŏt′blăt′), **Joseph** b. 1908. Polish-born British physicist who won the 1995 Nobel Peace Prize.

ROTC (är′ō-tē-sē′, rŏt′sē) *abbr.* Reserve Officers' Training Corps

rote[1] (rōt) *n.* **1.** A memorizing process using routine or repetition, often without full attention or comprehension: *learn by rote.* **2.** Mechanical routine. [ME.] —**rote** *adj.*

rote[2] (rōt) *n.* The sound of surf breaking on the shore. [Prob. of Scand. orig.; akin to ON *rauta*, to roar.]

rote[3] (rōt) *n.* A medieval stringed instrument variably identified with a lyre, lute, or harp. [ME < OFr., prob. of Gmc. orig.]

ro•te•none (rōt′n-ōn′) *n.* A white crystalline compound, $C_{23}H_{22}O_6$, extracted from the roots of derris and cubé and used as an insecticide. [J. *röten*, derris + -ONE.]

rot•gut (rŏt′gŭt′) *n.* *Slang* Raw, inferior liquor.

Roth (rôth), **Philip Milton** b. 1933. Amer. writer whose novels include *Portnoy's Complaint* (1969).

Roth•er•ham (rŏth′ər-əm) A borough of N England NE of Sheffield. Pop. 255,727.

Roth IRA (ī′ar-ā′) *n.* An individual retirement account in which a person can set aside after-tax income up to a specified amount each year. Earnings on the account are tax-free, and tax-free withdrawals may be made after age 59½. [After William Victor Roth, Jr. (b. 1921), US congressman.]

Roth•ko (rŏth′kō), **Mark** 1903–70. Russian-born Amer. abstract expressionist painter whose works are characterized by horizontal bands of color with blurred edges.

Roth•schild (rŏth′chīld, rŏths′-, rôth′-, rŏths′-, rŏt′shīlt′) German family, including **Mayer Amschal** (1743–1812), who founded a bank at Frankfurt am Main. His sons, esp. **Salomon** (1774–1855) and **Nathan Mayer** (1774–1836), established branches of the bank throughout Europe.

ro•ti•fer (rō′tə-fər) *n.* Any of various minute multicellular aquatic organisms of the phylum Rotifera, having at the anterior end a wheellike ring of cilia. [< NLat. *Rotifera*, phylum name : Lat. *rota*, wheel; see ROTA + Lat. *-fer, -fer.*] —**ro•tif′er•al** (-tĭf′ər-əl), **ro•tif′er•ous** (-ər-əs) *adj.*

ro•ti•form (rō′tə-fôrm′) *adj.* Shaped like a wheel. [Lat. *rota*, wheel + -FORM.]

ro•tis•se•rie (rō-tĭs′ə-rē) *n.* **1.** A cooking device equipped with a rotating spit on which meat or other food is roasted. **2.** A shop or restaurant where meats are roasted to order. [Fr. *rôtisserie* < OFr. *rostisserie* < *rostir*, to roast, of Gmc. orig.]

rot•l (rŏt′l) *n.* A unit of weight used in countries bordering on the Mediterranean Sea and in nearby areas, varying in different regions from about 1 to 5 pounds (0.45 to 2.25 kilograms). [Ar. *raṭl, riṭl*, poss. < Gk. *litra*.]

ro•to•gra•vure (rō′tə-grə-vyo͞or′) *n.* **1.** An intaglio printing

---

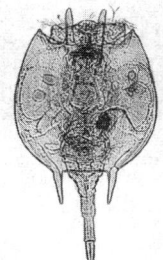

rotifer
photomicrograph of
Platyias quadricornis

ă	pat	oi	boy
ā	pay	ou	out
âr	care	o͞o	took
ä	father	o͞o	boot
ĕ	pet	ŭ	cut
ē	be	ûr	urge
ĭ	pit	th	thin
ī	pie	*th*	this
îr	pier	hw	which
ŏ	pot	zh	vision
ō	toe	ə	about,
ô	paw		item

Stress marks:
′ (primary);
′ (secondary), as in
lexicon (lĕk′sĭ-kŏn′)

process in which letters and pictures are transferred from an etched copper cylinder to a web of paper, plastic, or similar material in a rotary press. **2.** Printed material produced by this process. [Lat. *rota*, wheel + GRAVURE.]

ro•tor (rō′tər) *n.* **1.** A rotating part of an electrical or mechanical device. **2.** An assembly of rotating horizontal airfoils, as that of a helicopter. [Contraction of ROTATOR.]

ro•tor•craft (rō′tər-krăft′) *n.* An aircraft, esp. a helicopter, that is kept partially or completely airborne by airfoils rotating around a vertical axis.

rotor ship *n.* A ship propelled by one or more tall cylindrical rotors operated by wind power.

ro•to•till (rō′tə-tĭl′) *tr.v.* **-tilled, -till•ing, -tills** To cultivate or dig with a rototiller.

ro•to•till•er (rō′tə-tĭl′ər) *n.* A motorized rotary cultivator.

rot•ten (rŏt′n) *adj.* **-er, -est** **1.** Being in a state of putrefaction or decay; decomposed. **2.** Having a foul odor resulting from or suggestive of decay; putrid. **3.** Made weak or unsound by rot. **4.** Morally corrupt or despicable. **5.** Very bad; wretched. ❖ *adv.* To a very great degree. [ME *roten* < ON *rotinn*.] **—rot′ten•ly** *adv.* **—rot′ten•ness** *n.*

rotten borough *n.* An election district having only a few voters but the same voting power as other, more populous districts.

rot•ten•stone (rŏt′n-stōn′) *n.* A soft decomposed limestone used in powder form as a polishing material.

rot•ter (rŏt′ər) *n. Chiefly British Slang* A scoundrel.

Rot•ter•dam (rŏt′ər-dăm′) A city of SW Netherlands on the Rhine-Meuse delta SSE of The Hague; a major commercial power during the 16th and 17th centuries. Pop. 597,272.

rott•wei•ler (rŏt′wī′lər, rŏt′-) *n.* Any of a German breed of dog having a stocky body, short black fur, and tan face markings. [Ger., after *Rottweil*, a city of S Germany.]

ro•tund (rō-tŭnd′) *adj.* **1.** Rounded in figure; plump. See Syns at **fat. 2.** Having a full, rich sound; sonorous. [Lat. *rotundus*.] **—ro•tun′di•ty, ro•tund′ness** *n.* **—ro•tund′ly** *adv.*

ro•tun•da (rō-tŭn′də) *n.* **1.** A circular building, esp. one with a dome. **2a.** A large area with a high ceiling, as in a hotel lobby. **b.** A large round room. [Ital. *rotonda* < fem. of *rotondo*, round < Lat. *rotundus*.]

ro•tu•rier (rō-tōōr′ē-ā′, -tyōōr′-) *n.* A commoner. [Fr. < OFr. < *roture*, newly cultivated land < Lat. *ruptūra*, action of breaking. See RUPTURE.]

Rou•ault (rōō-ō′), **Georges** 1871–1958. French artist whose paintings are characterized by brilliant colors.

rou•ble (rōō′bəl) *n.* Variant of **ruble.**

rou•é (rōō-ā′) *n.* A lecherous dissipated man. [Fr. < p. part. of *rouer*, to break on a wheel (< the feeling that such a person deserves that) < OFr. < Lat. *rotāre*, to rotate. See ROTATE.]

Rou•en¹ (rōō-än′, -äɴ′) A city of N France on the Seine R. WNW of Paris; of pre-Roman origin and the cap. of medieval Normandy. Pop. 102,722.

Rou•en² (rōō-än′, -äɴ′) *n.* Any of a breed of domestic ducks descended from and resembling the mallard. [After ROUEN¹.]

rouge (rōōzh) *n.* **1.** A red or pink cosmetic for coloring the cheeks or lips. **2.** A reddish powder, chiefly ferric oxide, used to polish metals or glass. ❖ *v.* **rouged, roug•ing, roug•es** *—tr.* To put rouge onto. *—intr.* To use rouge. [Fr. < OFr., red < Lat. *rubeus*. See reudh- in App.]

Rou•get de Lisle (rōō-zhā′ də lēl′), **Claude Joseph** 1760–1836. French soldier who wrote "La Marseillaise" (1792), the French national anthem.

rough (rŭf) *adj.* **rough•er, rough•est** **1.** Having a surface marked by irregularities, protuberances, or ridges; not smooth. **2.** Coarse or shaggy to the touch. **3a.** Difficult to travel over or through. **b.** Characterized by violent motion; turbulent. **c.** Difficult to endure or live through, esp. because of harsh or inclement weather. **d.** Unpleasant or difficult. **4a.** Boisterous, unruly, uncouth, or rowdy. **b.** Lacking polish or finesse. **5.** Characterized by carelessness or force, as in manipulating. **6.** Harsh to the ear. **7.** Being in a natural state: *rough diamonds.* **8.** Not perfected, completed, or fully detailed. ❖ *n.* **1a.** Rugged overgrown terrain. **b.** *Sports* The part of a golf course left unmowed and uncultivated. **2.** The difficult or disagreeable aspect, part, or side. **3.** Something in an unfinished or hastily worked-out state. **4.** A crude unmannered person. ❖ *tr.v.* **roughed, rough•ing, roughs** **1a.** To treat roughly or with physical violence: *roughed him up.* **b.** *Sports* To treat (an opposing player) with unnecessary roughness, often in violation of the rules. **2.** To prepare or indicate in an unfinished form: *rough out a house plan.* ❖ *adv.* In a rough manner; roughly: *an engine running rough.* *—idiom:* **rough it** To live without the usual comforts and conveniences. [ME < OE *rūh*.] **—rough′er** *n.* **—rough′ly** *adv.* **—rough′ness** *n.*

rough•age (rŭf′ĭj) *n.* **1.** See **fiber** 6. **2.** Any rough or coarse material.

rough-and-read•y (rŭf′ən-rĕd′ē) *adj.* Rough or crude but effective for a purpose or use.

rough-and-tum•ble (rŭf′ən-tŭm′bəl) *adj.* Characterized by roughness and disregard for order or rules. ❖ *n.* A condition marked by rough disorderly struggle; infighting.

rough•back (rŭf′băk′) *n.* Any of several flatfish with rough skin, esp. a species of dab (*Hippoglossoides platessoides*).

rough breathing *n.* **1.** An aspirate sound in ancient Greek like that of the sound (h) in English. **2.** The symbol (ʽ) written over some initial vowels and the letter rho in ancient Greek to indicate that a word begins with the sound (h). **3.** In ancient Greek, a word beginning with the sound (h) plus a vowel or diphthong.

rough•cast (rŭf′kăst′) *n.* **1.** A coarse plaster of lime, shells, and pebbles used for outside wall surfaces. **2.** A rough preliminary model or form. ❖ *tr.v.* **-cast, -cast•ing, -casts** **1.** To plaster with roughcast. **2.** To shape or work into a rough or preliminary form. **—rough′cast′er** *n.*

rough-cut (rŭf′kŭt′) *n.* A print of a movie after assembly but before final editing.

rough•dry (rŭf′drī′) *tr.v.* **-dried, -dry•ing, -dries** To dry (laundry) without ironing or smoothing out.

rough•en (rŭf′ən) *tr. & intr.v.* **-ened, -en•ing, -ens** To make or become rough.

rough-hew (rŭf′hyōō′) *tr.v.* **-hewed, -hewed** or **-hewn** (-hyōōn′), **-hew•ing, -hews** **1.** To hew or shape roughly, without finishing. **2.** To make in rough form.

rough•house (rŭf′hous′) *n.* Rowdy, uproarious behavior or play. ❖ *v.* (also rŭf′houz′) **-housed, -hous•ing, -hous•es** *—intr.* To engage in rowdy, uproarious behavior or play. *—tr.* To handle or treat roughly, usu. in fun.

rough-leg•ged hawk (rŭf′lĕg′ĭd) *n.* An Arctic hawk (*Buteo lagopus*) that has dark plumage and whitish feathers covering the legs and feeds mainly on small rodents.

rough•neck (rŭf′nĕk′) *n.* **1.** An uncouth person. **2.** A rowdy. **3.** A member of the crew of an oil rig other than the driller.

rough•rid•er (rŭf′rī′dər) *n.* **1.** A skilled rider of little-trained horses, esp. one who breaks horses for riding. **2. Rough Rider** A member of the First US Volunteer Cavalry regiment under Theodore Roosevelt in the Spanish-American War.

rough•shod (rŭf′shŏd′) *adj.* **1.** Shod with horseshoes having projecting nails or points to prevent slipping. **2.** Marked by brutal force. *—idiom:* **ride roughshod over** To treat with brutal force.

rough trade *n. Slang* **1.** Violent, often brutal sex acts. **2.** One, esp. a male prostitute, who practices such acts.

rough•y (rŭf′ē) *n., pl.* **roughy** or **-ies** **1.** A perchlike food fish (*Arripis georgianus*) of Australia and New Zealand. **2.** A small fish (*Trachichthys australis*) having rough scales and found along the southeast coast of Australia. [Prob. < ROUGH.]

rou•lade (rōō-läd′) *n.* **1.** *Music* An embellishment consisting of a rapid run of several notes sung to one syllable. **2.** A slice of meat rolled around a filling and cooked. [Fr. < *rouler*, to roll < OFr. *roler*. See ROLL.]

rou•leau (rōō-lō′) *n., pl.* **-leaux** or **-leaus** (-lōz′) A small roll, esp. of coins wrapped in paper. [Fr. < OFr. *rolel*, dim. of *role*, roll < Lat. *rotula*, dim. of *rota*, wheel. See ROTA.]

rou•lette (rōō-lĕt′) *n.* **1.** A gambling game in which the players bet on which slot of a rotating disk a small ball will come to rest in. **2a.** A small toothed disk of tempered steel attached to a handle and used to make rows of dots, slits, or perforations, as on a sheet of postage stamps. **b.** Any of the short consecutive incisions made between individual stamps in a sheet. ❖ *tr.v.* **-lett•ed, -lett•ing, -lettes** To mark or divide with a roulette. [Fr. < OFr. *ruelete*, fem. of *ruele*, dim. of *ruele*, dim. of *rota*, wheel < Lat. *rota*.]

round¹ (round) *adj.* **round•er, round•est** **1a.** Being such that every part of the surface or the circumference is equidistant from the center: *a round ball.* **b.** Moving in or forming a circle. **c.** Shaped like a cylinder; cylindrical. **d.** Rather rounded in shape: *a round face.* **e.** Full in physique; plump. **2a.** *Linguistics* Formed or articulated with the lips in a rounded shape: *a round vowel.* **b.** Full in tone; sonorous. **3.** Whole or complete; full: *a round dozen.* **4a.** *Mathematics* Expressed or designated as a whole number or integer; not fractional. **b.** Not exact; approximate: *a round estimate.* **5.** Large; considerable: *a round sum of money.* **6.** Brought to satisfactory conclusion or completion; finished. **7a.** Outspoken; blunt: *a round scolding.* **b.** Done with full force; unrestrained. ❖ *n.* **1a.** Something, such as a circle, disk, globe, or ring, that is round. **b.** A circle formed of various things. **c.** Movement around a circle or about an axis. **2.** A rung or crossbar, as on a ladder. **3.** A cut of beef from the part of the thigh between the rump and the shank. **4.** An assembly of people; a group. **5.** A round dance. **6a.** A complete course, succession, or series: *a round of negotiations.* **b.** A course of customary or prescribed actions, duties, or places. Often used in the plural: *physicians' rounds.* **7.** A complete range or extent. **8.** One drink for each person in a gathering or group. **9.** A single outburst, as of applause. **10a.** A single shot or volley. **b.** Ammunition for a single shot or volley. **11.** A specified number of arrows shot from a specified distance to a target in archery. **12.** *Sports & Games* An interval of play that occupies a specified time, constitutes a certain number of plays, or allows each player a turn. **13.** *Music* A composition for two or more voices in which each voice enters at a different time with the same melody. ❖ *v.* **round•ed, round•ing, rounds** *—tr.* **1.** To make round. See Syns at **bend¹. 2.** To encompass; surround. **3.** To cause to proceed or move in a circular course. **4.** *Linguistics* To pronounce with rounded lips; labialize. **5.** To fill out; make plump. **6.** To bring to completion or perfection; finish. **7.** *Mathematics* To express as a round number. **8.** To make a complete circuit of; go or pass around. **9.** To make a turn about or to the other

rottweiler

rotunda
state capitol building,
Atlanta, Georgia

side of. —*intr.* **1.** To become round. **2.** To take a circular course; complete or partially complete a circuit. **3.** To turn about, as on an axis; reverse. **4.** To become curved, filled out, or plump. **5.** To come to satisfactory completion or perfection. ❖ *adv.* **1.** In a circular progression or movement; around. **2.** With revolutions. **3.** To a specific place or person. ❖ *prep.* **1.** Around. **2.** From the beginning to the end of; throughout. —*phrasal verb:* **round up 1.** To seek out and bring together; gather. **2.** To herd (cattle) together from various places. —*idioms:* **in the round 1.** With the stage in the center of the audience. **2.** Fully shaped so as to stand free of a background. **make** (or **go**) **the rounds 1.** To go from place to place, as on business. **2.** To be communicated or passed from person to person. [ME < AN *rounde*, var. of OFr. *rond*, ult. < VLat. **retundus* < Lat. *rotundus*.] —**round′ness** *n.*

round² (round) *tr.v.* **round•ed, round•ing, rounds** *Archaic* To whisper. [ME *rounden* < OE *rūnian* < *rūn*, a secret.]

round•a•bout (round′ə-bout′) *adj.* Indirect; circuitous. ❖ *n.* **1.** A short close-fitting jacket. **2.** *Chiefly British* A merry-go-round. **3.** *Chiefly British* A traffic circle.

round clam *n.* See **quahog.**

round dance *n.* **1.** A folk dance performed with the dancers arranged in a circle. **2.** A ballroom dance in which couples proceed in a circular direction around the room.

round•ed (roun′dĭd) *adj.* **1.** Shaped into a circle or sphere; made round. **2.** *Linguistics* Pronounced with the lips shaped ovally; labialized. **3.** Complete; balanced. —**round′ed•ness** *n.*

roun•del (roun′dəl) *n.* **1.** A curved form, esp. a semicircular panel, window, or recess. **2a.** A rondel. **b.** A rondeau. [ME < OFr. *rondel*, dim. of *rond*, circle, round. See ROUND¹.]

roun•de•lay (roun′dɪ-lā′) *n.* A poem or song with a regularly recurring refrain. [ME, alteration of OFr. *rondelet*, dim. of *rondel*, roundel. See ROUNDEL.]

round•er (roun′dər) *n.* **1.** One that rounds, esp. a tool for rounding corners and edges. **2.** One, such as a security guard, who makes rounds. **3.** A dissolute person. **4.** *Sports* **a.** A boxing match that goes on for a specified number of rounds. Often used in combination: *a five-rounder.* **b. rounders** (*used with a sing. verb*) An English ball game similar to baseball.

round hand *n.* A style of handwriting in which the letters are rounded and full rather than angular.

Round•head (round′hĕd′) *n.* A supporter of the Parliamentarians during the English Civil War and the Commonwealth. [< the close-cropped hair of the Puritans.]

round herring *n.* Any of the mostly tropical marine fishes of the family Dussumierlidae, having a rounded abdomen.

round•house (round′hous′) *n.* **1.** A circular building for housing and switching locomotives. **2.** *Nautical* A cabin on the after part of the quarterdeck of a ship. **3.** *Games* A meld of four kings and four queens in pinochle. **4.** *Slang* A punch or swing delivered with a sweeping sidearm movement.

round•ish (roun′dĭsh) *adj.* Somewhat round. —**round′ish•ness** *n.*

round•let (round′lĭt) *n.* **1.** A little circle. **2.** A small circular object. [ME < OFr. *rondelet*, dim. of *rondel*, roundel. See ROUNDEL.]

round•ly (round′lē) *adv.* **1.** In the form of a circle or sphere. **2.** With full force or vigor; thoroughly: *applauded roundly.*

round robin *n.* **1.** *Sports* A tournament in which each contestant is matched in turn against every other contestant. **2.** A petition or protest on which the signatures are arranged in a circle in order to conceal the order of signing. **3.** A letter sent among members of a group, often with comments added by each person.

round-shoul•dered (round′shōl′dərd) *adj.* Having the shoulders bent forward and drooping and the upper back rounded.

rounds•man (roundz′mən) *n.* **1.** A police officer in charge of several other officers. **2.** One who makes rounds.

round steak *n.* A cut of beef from between the rump and shank.

round-ta•ble (round′tā′bəl) *n.* **1.** often **round table** A conference or discussion involving several participants. **2. Round Table a.** In Arthurian legend, the circular table of King Arthur and his knights. **b.** The knights of King Arthur considered as a group.

round-the-clock (round′thə-klŏk′) also **a•round-the-clock** (ə-round′-) *adj.* Lasting or continuing throughout the entire 24 hours of the day; continuous.

round•trip or **round-trip** also **round trip** (round′trĭp′) *n.* A trip from one place to another and back, usu. the same way.

round•up (round′ŭp′) *n.* **1a.** The herding together of cattle for inspection, branding, or shipping. **b.** The cattle so herded. **c.** The workers and horses employed in such herding. **2.** A gathering up, as of suspects. **3.** A summary: *a news roundup.*

round•worm (round′wûrm′) *n.* See **nematode.**

roup (roop) *n.* An infectious disease of poultry and pigeons characterized by inflammation of the mouth and eyes. [?]

Rous (rous), **Francis Peyton** 1879–1970. Amer. pathologist who shared a 1966 Nobel Prize.

rouse (rouz) *v.* **roused, rous•ing, rous•es** —*tr.* **1.** To arouse from slumber, apathy, or depression. **2.** To excite, as to anger or action; stir up. —*intr.* **1.** To awaken. **2.** To become active. ❖ *n.* The act or an instance of arousing. [ME *rousen,* to shake the feathers (said of a hawk), perh. < OFr. *reuser, ruser,* to repel, push back < VLat. **recūsāre* < Lat., to refuse. See RECUSE.] —**rous′er** *n.*

rous•ing (rou′zĭng) *adj.* **1.** Inducing enthusiasm or excitement;

stirring. **2.** Lively; vigorous. **3.** Used as an intensive: *a rousing lie.* —**rous′ing•ly** *adv.*

Rous sarcoma *n.* A sarcoma produced in chickens by an RNA-containing virus. [After Francis Peyton ROUS.]

Rous•seau (roo-sō′), **Henri** Known as "Le Douanier." 1844–1910. French painter of primitive works, such as *The Snake Charmer* (1907).

Rousseau, Jean Jacques 1712–78. Swiss philosopher who held that the individual is essentially good but usu. corrupted by society. His works include *The Social Contract* (1762).

Rousseau, Théodore 1812–67. French landscape painter of the Barbizon school whose works include *Descent of the Cattle* (c. 1834).

Rous•sil•lon (roo-sē-yôn′) A historical region of S France bordering on Spain and the Mediterranean Sea; orig. inhabited by Iberians and formally awarded to France by the Treaty of the Pyrenees (1659).

roust (roust) *tr.v.* **roust•ed, roust•ing, rousts** To rout, esp. out of bed. [Prob. alteration of ROUSE.]

roust•a•bout (rous′tə-bout′) *n.* **1.** A laborer employed for temporary or unskilled jobs. **2.** A circus laborer. **3.** A deck or wharf laborer, esp. on the Mississippi River.

rout¹ (rout) *n.* **1a.** A disorderly retreat or flight following defeat. **b.** An overwhelming defeat. **2a.** A disorderly crowd of people; a mob. **b.** People of the lowest class; rabble. **3.** A public disturbance; a riot. **4.** A company, as of knights, that is in movement. **5.** A fashionable gathering. ❖ *tr.v.* **rout•ed, rout•ing, routs 1.** To put to disorderly flight or retreat. **2.** To defeat overwhelmingly. See Syns at **defeat.** [ME *route* < OFr., troop, defeat < VLat. **rupta* < fem. of Lat. *ruptus,* p. part. of *rumpere,* to break. See **reup-** in App.]

rout² (rout) *v.* **rout•ed, rout•ing, routs** —*intr.* **1.** To dig with the snout; root. **2.** To poke around; rummage. —*tr.* **1.** To expose to view as if by digging; uncover. **2.** To hollow, scoop, or gouge out. **3.** To drive or force out as if by digging; eject. **4.** *Archaic* To dig up with the snout. [Variant of ROOT².]

rout³ (rout, root) *intr.v.* **rout•ed, rout•ing, routs** *Chiefly British* To bellow. Used of cattle. [ME *routen,* to roar < ON *rauta.*]

route (root, rout) *n.* **1a.** A road, course, or way for travel from one place to another. **b.** A highway. **2.** A customary line of travel. See Syns at **way.** **3.** A fixed course or territory assigned to a salesperson or delivery person. **4.** *Football* A pass pattern. **5.** A means of reaching a goal. ❖ *tr.v.* **rout•ed, rout•ing, routes 1.** To send or forward by a specific route. **2.** To schedule the order of (a sequence of procedures). [ME < OFr. < Lat. *rupta (via),* broken (road), fem. p. part. of *rumpere,* to break. See ROUT¹.]

rout•er¹ (rou′tər) *n.* One that routs, esp. a machine tool that mills out the surface of metal or wood.

rout•er² (roo′tər, rou′-) *n.* **1.** One that routes, esp. one who prepares shipments for distribution and delivery. **2.** A device in a network that relays data packets transmitted between computers. **3.** See **gateway** 3.

rou•tine (roo-tēn′) *n.* **1.** A prescribed, detailed course of action to be followed regularly; a standard procedure. **2.** A set of customary procedures or activities. See Syns at **method.** **3.** A set piece of entertainment, esp. in a nightclub or theater. **4.** *Slang* A particular kind of behavior or activity. **5.** *Computer Science* A set of programming instructions designed to perform a specific limited task. ❖ *adj.* **1.** In accord with established procedure: *a routine check of passports.* **2.** Habitual; regular. **3.** Having no special quality; ordinary. [Fr. < *route,* route < OFr. See ROUTE.] —**rou•tine′ly** *adv.* —**rou•tine′ism** *n.* —**rou•tine′ist** *n.*

rou•tin•ize (roo-tē′nīz′, root′n-īz′) *tr.v.* **-ized, -iz•ing, -iz•es 1.** To establish a routine for. **2.** To reduce to a routine. —**rou•tin′i•za′tion** (-ĭ-zā′shən) *n.*

roux (roo) *n., pl.* **roux** A mixture of flour and fat cooked together and used as a thickening. [Fr. *(beurre) roux,* browned (butter) < OFr. *rous,* reddish brown < Lat. *russus,* red. See **reudh-** in App.]

rove¹ (rōv) *v.* **roved, rov•ing, roves** —*intr.* To wander about at random, esp. over a wide area; roam. —*tr.* To roam or wander around, over, or through. See Syns at **wander.** ❖ *n.* An act of wandering about, over, around, or through. [ME *roven,* to shoot arrows at a mark.]

rove² (rōv) *tr.v.* **roved, rov•ing, roves 1.** To card (wool). **2.** To put (fibers) through an eye or opening. **3.** To stretch and twist (fibers) before spinning; ravel out. ❖ *n.* A slightly twisted and extended fiber or sliver. [?]

rove³ (rōv) *v. Nautical* A past tense and a past participle of **reeve².**

rove beetle *n.* Any of numerous beetles of the family Staphylinidae, often found in decaying matter and having slender bodies and short wing covers. [Poss. < ROVE¹.]

rov•er¹ (rō′vər) *n.* **1a.** One that roves; a wanderer. **b.** A vehicle, with or without a crew, used esp. in exploring a planet and its satellites. **2.** *Sports* A mark in archery selected by chance.

ro•ver² (rō′vər) *n.* **1.** A pirate. **2.** A pirate vessel. [ME < MDu. or MLGer., robber < *roven,* to rob. See **reup-** in App.]

row¹ (rō) *n.* **1.** A series of objects placed next to each other, usu. in a straight line. **2.** A succession without a break or gap in time: *three years in a row.* **3.** A line of adjacent seats, as in a theater. **4.** A continuous line of buildings along a street. **5.** *Games* Any of the

Jean Jacques Rousseau
1753 pastel portrait by
Maurice-Quentin de la Tour
(1704–88)

row house
London row houses built c. 1850

Manuel Roxas y Acuña

royal lily
Lilium regale

lines of squares running crosswise to files on a playing board in chess or checkers. ❖ *tr.v.* **rowed, row•ing, rows** To place in a row. **—idiom: a tough row to hoe** *Informal* A difficult situation to endure. [ME < OE *rāw.*]

row² (rō) *v.* **rowed, row•ing, rows** *—intr. Nautical* To row a boat. *—tr.* **1.** *Nautical* **a.** To propel (a boat) with or as if with oars. **b.** To carry in or on a boat propelled by oars. **c.** To use (a specified number of oars or people deploying them.) **2.** To propel or convey in a manner resembling rowing of a boat. **3.** *Sports* **a.** To pull (an oar) as part of a racing crew. **b.** To race against by rowing. ❖ *n. Nautical* **1.** The act or an instance of rowing. **2.** A trip or an excursion in a rowboat. [ME *rowen* < OE *rōwan.*] **—row′er** *n.*

row³ (rou) *n.* **1.** A boisterous disturbance or quarrel; a brawl. **2.** An uproar; a great noise. ❖ *intr.v.* **rowed, row•ing, rows** To take part in a quarrel, brawl, or uproar. [?]

row•an (rō′ən, rou′-) *n.* A small deciduous tree (*Sorbus aucuparia*) of the rose family, having pinnately compound leaves, corymbs of white flowers, and orange-red berries. [Of Scand. orig. See **reudh-** in App.]

row•boat (rō′bōt′) *n.* **1.** A small boat propelled by oars. **2.** *Sports* A rowing machine.

row•dy (rou′dē) *n., pl.* **-dies** A rough, disorderly person. ❖ *adj.* **-di•er, -di•est** Disorderly; rough. [Prob. < ROW³.] **—row′di•ly** *adv.* **—row′di•ness** *n.* **—row′dy•ism** *n.*

row•el (rou′əl) *n.* A sharp-toothed wheel inserted into the end of the shank of a spur. [ME < OFr. *roelle*, dim. of *roue*, wheel < Lat. *rota.*] **—row′el** *v.*

row•en (rou′ən) *n. New England* A second crop, as of hay, in a season. [ME *rowein* < AN *rewain*, var. of OFr. *regain* : *re-*, re- + *gaaignier*, to till; see GAIN¹.]

row house (rō) *n.* One of a series of houses, often of similar or identical design, situated side by side and joined by common walls.

Row•land (rō′lənd), **F(rank) Sherwood** b. 1927. Amer. chemist who shared a 1995 Nobel Prize.

Row•land•son (rō′lənd-sən), **Thomas** 1756–1827. British caricaturist and illustrator of works by Laurence Sterne and Jonathan Swift.

row•lock (rō′lŏk′, rŏl′ək) *n. Chiefly British* An oarlock.

Ro•xas y A•cu•ña (rō′häs ē ä-kōōn′yə, -yä), **Manuel** 1892–1948. Philippine politician who was the first president of the Philippines (1946–48).

roy•al (roi′əl) *adj.* **1.** Of or relating to a monarch. **2.** Of the rank of a monarch. **3.** Of, relating to, or in the service of a kingdom. **4.** Issued or performed by a monarch. **5.** Founded, chartered, or authorized by a monarch. **6.** Befitting royalty; stately. **7a.** Superior, as in size or quality. **b.** Used as an intensive. ❖ *n.* **1.** *Informal* A member of a monarch's family. **2.** *Nautical* A sail set on a royalmast. **3.** A paper size, 20 by 25 inches for printing, 19 by 24 inches for writing. **—idiom: the royal road** A way or method that presents no difficulties. [ME < OFr. < Lat. *rēgālis* < *rēx, rēg-*, king. See **reg-** in App.] **—roy′al•ly** *adv.*

royal blue *n.* A deep to strong blue.

royal fern *n.* A deep-rooted fern (*Osmunda regalis*) of worldwide distribution having tall, bipinnately compound fronds.

royal flush *n.* A straight flush consisting of the five highest cards of one suit, ranked as the highest hand in certain games of poker.

roy•al•ism (roi′ə-lĭz′əm) *n.* Support of or adherence to the principle of rule by a monarch.

roy•al•ist (roi′ə-lĭst) *n.* **1.** A supporter of government by a monarch. **2. Royalist a.** See **cavalier** 3. **b.** An American loyal to British rule during the American Revolution; a Tory.

royal jelly *n.* A nutritious substance secreted by the pharyngeal glands of worker bees that serves as food for all young larvae and as the only food for larvae that will become queen bees.

royal lily *n.* A western Chinese lily (*Lilium regale*) having large, fragrant, horizontal, funnel-shaped flowers.

roy•al•mast also **roy•al mast** (roi′əl-mäst′) *n. Nautical* A small mast immediately above a topgallant mast.

royal palm *n.* Any of several tropical American palm trees of the genus *Roystonea*, having a tall naked trunk surmounted by a large tuft of pinnately compound leaves.

royal poinciana *n.* A tropical and semitropical tree (*Delonix regia*) native to Madagascar and having bipinnately compound leaves, clusters of large scarlet flowers, and long pods.

royal purple *n.* A moderate or strong violet to deep purple or dark reddish purple.

roy•al•ty (roi′əl-tē) *n., pl.* **-ties 1a.** A person of royal rank or lineage. **b.** Monarchs and their families considered as a group. **2.** The lineage or rank of a monarch. **3.** The power, status, or authority of a monarch. **4.** Royal quality or bearing. **5.** A kingdom or possession ruled by a monarch. **6.** A right or prerogative of the crown, as that of receiving a percentage of the proceeds from mines in the royal domain. **7a.** The granting of a right by a monarch to a corporation or an individual to exploit specified natural resources. **b.** The payment for such a right. **8a.** A share paid to a writer or composer out of the proceeds resulting from the sale or performance of his or her work. **b.** A share in the proceeds paid to an inventor or a proprietor for the right to use his or her invention or services. **9.** A share of the profit or product reserved

by the grantor, esp. of an oil or mining lease.

royal we *n.* The first-person plural pronoun used by a sovereign in formal address to refer to himself or herself.

RP *abbr.* Received Pronunciation

rpm *abbr.* revolutions per minute

rps *abbr.* revolutions per second

RQ *abbr.* respiratory quotient

RR *abbr.* **1.** railroad **2.** right reverend **3.** rural route

–rrhagia *suff.* Abnormal or excessive flow or discharge: *menorrhagia.* [Gk. *-rrhagiā* < *rhēgnunai, rhag-*, to burst forth.]

–rrhea or **–rrhoea** *suff.* Flow; discharge: *seborrhea.* [NLat. *-rrhoea* < Gk. *-rrhoia* < *rhoia*, a flowing < *rhein*, to flow. See **sreu-** in App.]

rRNA *abbr.* ribosomal RNA

RSI *abbr.* repetitive strain injury

RSV *abbr. Bible* Revised Standard Version

RSVP *abbr. French* répondez s'il vous plaît (please reply)

RT *abbr.* **1.** radiotelephone **2.** respiratory therapy **3.** room temperature

Rt *abbr. Bible* Ruth

Rt. or **Rte.** *abbr.* route

Rt. Hon. *abbr.* Right Honorable

Rt. Rev. *abbr.* Right Reverend

Ru¹ The symbol for the element **ruthenium.**

Ru² *abbr. Bible* Ruth

RU 486 *n.* A oral drug that prevents the attachment of a fertilized ovum to the wall of the uterus by interfering with the action of progesterone. [*R(oussel) U(CLAF)*, French pharmaceutical company that makes it + *486*, project number.]

Ru•an•da (rōō-än′də) See **Rwanda.**

Ru•an•da-U•run•di (rōō-än′də-ōō-rōōn′dē) A former colonial possession of central Africa; mandated to Belgium by the League of Nations after World War I and split into the present-day countries of Rwanda and Burundi in 1962.

rub (rŭb) *v.* **rubbed, rub•bing, rubs** *—tr.* **1.** To apply pressure and friction to (a surface). **2.** To clean, polish, or manipulate by the application of pressure and friction. **3.** To apply to a surface firmly and with friction: *rubbed lotion onto his hands.* **4.** To move (something) firmly along a surface, esp. repeatedly. **5.** To cause to become worn, chafed, or irritated. **6.** To remove, erase, or expunge. *—intr.* **1a.** To exert pressure or friction on something. **b.** To wear or chafe with friction. **c.** To cause irritation or annoyance. **2.** To move along in contact with a surface; graze or scrape. **3.** To be transferred or removed by contact or proximity: *newsprint that rubbed off on my fingers.* ❖ *n.* **1.** The act of rubbing. **2.** The application of friction and pressure: *a back rub.* **3.** A substance applied by rubbing, esp.: **a.** A liniment or balm. **b.** A seasoning made of ground spices and herbs, applied to the surface of meat, fish, or vegetables before cooking. **4.** An unevenness on a surface. **5.** An act or a remark that annoys or hurts another. **6.** A difficulty or obstacle. **—phrasal verbs: rub down** To perform a brisk rubbing of the body, as in massage. **rub in** To harp on (an unpleasant matter). **rub out 1.** To obliterate by or as if by rubbing. **2.** *Slang* To kill; murder. **—idioms: rub elbows** (or **shoulders**) To mix or socialize closely. **rub (one's) hands** To experience or display pleased anticipation, self-satisfaction, or glee. **rub (someone's) nose in** *Slang* To bring repeatedly and forcefully to another's attention. **rub (someone) the wrong way** To annoy; irritate. [ME *rubben.*]

Rub al Kha•li (rōōb′ äl kä′lē, äl кнä′lē) Sometimes called "the Empty Quarter." A desert region in the SE interior of Arabia.

ru•basse (rōō-băs′, rōō′băs′) *n.* A variety of quartz colored ruby red by its iron-oxide content. [Fr. *rubace* < *rubis*, ruby. See RUBY.]

ru•ba•to (rōō-bä′tō) *Music n., pl.* **-tos** Rhythmic flexibility within a phrase or measure; a relaxation of strict time. [Ital. (*tempo*) *rubato*, stolen (time), rubato, p. part. of *rubare*, to rob, of Gmc. orig. See **reup-** in App.] **—ru•ba′to** *adj.*

rub•ber¹ (rŭb′ər) *n.* **1.** A yellowish, amorphous elastic material obtained from the milky sap or latex of various tropical plants, esp. the rubber tree, and vulcanized and modified into products such as electric insulation, tires, and containers. **2.** Any of numerous synthetic elastic materials of varying chemical composition with properties similar to those of natural rubber. **3.** A low overshoe made of rubber. **4.** *Baseball* The rectangular piece of hard rubber that the pitcher must remain in contact with when making a pitch. **5.** Something made of rubber, as: **a.** An eraser. **b.** A tire. **c.** A set of tires on a vehicle. **6.** *Slang* A condom. **7.** One that rubs, esp. one that gives a massage. [< RUB.]

rub•ber² (rŭb′ər) *n.* **1.** A series of games of which two out of three or three out of five must be won to terminate the play. **2.** An odd game played to break a tie. [?]

rubber band *n.* An elastic loop of natural or synthetic rubber used to hold objects together.

rubber cement *n.* Nonvulcanized rubber in an organic solvent, used as an adhesive.

rubber check *n. Slang* A check returned by a bank because of insufficient funds in the account on which it is drawn.

rub•ber•ize (rŭb′ə-rīz′) *tr.v.* **-ized, -iz•ing, -iz•es** To coat, treat, or impregnate with rubber.

rub•ber•neck (rŭb′ər-nĕk′) *Slang intr.v.* **-necked, -neck•ing, -necks** To look about or survey with unsophisticated wonderment or curiosity. ❖ *n.* A rubbernecker.

rub•ber•neck•er (rŭb′ər-nĕk′ər) *n. Slang* One who rubbernecks.

rubber plant *n.* **1.** Any of several tropical plants yielding sap that can be coagulated to form crude rubber. **2.** A small tree *(Ficus elastica)* that has large, oblong, glossy, leathery leaves.

rubber stamp *n.* **1.** A piece of rubber affixed to a handle and bearing raised characters used to make ink impressions. **2.** also **rub•ber•stamp** (rŭb′ər-stămp′) **a.** One that gives perfunctory approval or endorsement of a policy without assessing its merit. **b.** Such approval or endorsement.

rub•ber-stamp (rŭb′ər-stămp′) *tr.v.* **-stamped, -stamp•ing, -stamps 1.** To mark with the imprint of a rubber stamp. **2.** To endorse, vote for, or approve without question or deliberation.

rubber tree *n.* A tropical South American tree *(Hevea brasiliensis)* widely cultivated throughout the Tropics and yielding a milky juice that is a major source of commercial rubber.

rub•ber•y (rŭb′ə-rē) *adj.* **-i•er, -i•est** Of or resembling rubber; elastic.

rub•bing (rŭb′ĭng) *n.* **1.** The act of polishing, cleaning, or drying. **2.** A representation of a textured surface made by rubbing a paper placed over the surface with a marking agent such as charcoal or chalk.

rubbing alcohol *n.* A mixture usu. consisting of 70 percent isopropyl or absolute alcohol, applied externally to relieve muscle and joint pain.

rub•bish (rŭb′ĭsh) *n.* **1.** Refuse; garbage. **2.** Worthless material. **3.** Foolish discourse; nonsense. [ME *robishe.*] **—rub′bish•y** *adj.*

rub•ble (rŭb′əl) *n.* **1.** A loose mass of angular fragments of rock or masonry crumbled by natural or human forces. **2a.** Irregular fragments or pieces of rock used in masonry. **b.** The masonry made with such rocks. [ME *rubel.*] **—rub′bly** *adj.*

rub•ble•work (rŭb′əl-wûrk′) *n.* Masonry made with rubble.

rub•down (rŭb′doun′) *n.* An energetic massage of the body.

rube (ro͞ob) *n. Slang* An unsophisticated country person. [Prob. < *Rube,* nickname for *Reuben.*]

ru•be•fa•cient (ro͞o′bə-fā′shənt) *adj.* Producing redness, as of the skin. ❖ *n.* A substance that irritates the skin, causing redness. [Lat. *rubefaciēns, rubefacient-,* pr. part. of *rubefacere,* to make red : *rubeus,* red; see **reudh-** in App. + *facere,* to make; see **dhē-** in App.] **—ru′be•fac′tion** (-făk′shən) *n.*

Rube Goldberg *adj.* Of, relating to, or being a contrivance that brings about by complicated means what apparently could have been accomplished simply. [After Reuben Lucius GOLDBERG.]

ru•bel•la (ro͞o-bĕl′ə) *n.* A mild, contagious, eruptive viral disease capable of producing congenital defects in infants born to mothers infected during the first three months of pregnancy. [< Lat., neut. pl. of *rubellus,* red < *ruber.* See **reudh-** in App.]

ru•bel•lite (ro͞o′bə-līt′, ro͞o-bĕl′īt) *n.* The red variety of tourmaline, used as a gemstone. [Lat. *rubellus,* red. See RUBELLA + –ITE[1].]

Ru•bens (ro͞o′bənz), **Peter Paul** 1577–1640. Flemish painter whose baroque works include *Descent from the Cross* (1611–14). **—Ru′ben•esque′** (ro͞o′bə-nĕsk′) *adj.*

ru•be•o•la (ro͞o-bē′ə-lə, ro͞o′bē-ō′lə) *n.* See **measles** 1a. [< Lat., neut. pl. dim. of *rubeus,* red. See **reudh-** in App.] **—ru•be′o•lar** *adj.*

ru•bes•cent (ro͞o-bĕs′ənt) *adj.* Turning red. [Lat. *rubēscēns, rubēscent-,* pr. part. of *rubēscere,* to grow red, inchoative of *rubēre,* to be red. See **reudh-** in App.] **—ru•bes′cence** *n.*

Ru•bi•con (ro͞o′bĭ-kŏn′) *n.* A limit that when passed or exceeded permits of no return. [Lat. *Rubicō, Rubicōn-,* Rubicon, a short river of N-central Italy, the crossing of which by Julius Caesar and his army in 49 B.C. began a civil war.]

ru•bi•cund (ro͞o′bĭ-kənd) *adj.* Inclined to a healthy rosiness; ruddy. [Lat. *rubicundus.* See **reudh-** in App.] **—ru′bi•cun′di•ty** (-kŭn′dĭ-tē) *n.*

ru•bid•i•um (ro͞o-bĭd′ē-əm) *n. Symbol* **Rb** A soft metallic element of the alkali group that ignites spontaneously in air and reacts violently with water, used in photocells. Atomic number 37; atomic weight 85.47; melting point 38.89°C; boiling point 688°C; specific gravity (solid) 1.532; valence 1, 2, 3, 4. See table at **element.** [< Lat. *rūbidus,* red. See **reudh-** in App.]

ru•big•i•nous (ro͞o-bĭj′ə-nəs) also **ru•big•i•nose** (-nōs′) *adj.* Rust-colored; reddish-brown. [Lat. *rūbīginōsus* < *rūbīgō, rūbīgin-,* rust < *rōbus,* red. See **reudh-** in App.]

Ru•bin•stein (ro͞o′bĭn-stīn′), **Anton Gregor** 1829–94. Russian pianist and composer who founded the St. Petersburg Conservatory (1862).

Rubinstein, Arthur or **Artur** 1887–1982. Polish-born Amer. pianist noted for his interpretations of the works of Chopin.

ru•bi•ous (ro͞o′bē-əs) *adj.* Of the color of a ruby; red.

ru•ble also **rou•ble** (ro͞o′bəl) *n.* See table at **currency.** [Russ. *rubl′* < ORuss. *rublĭ,* cut, piece (prob. orig. a piece cut from a silver bar) < *rubiti,* to chop, hew. See **reup-** in App.]

rub•out (rŭb′out′) *n. Slang* **1.** A murder or killing. **2.** Destruction or obliteration.

ru•bric (ro͞o′brĭk) *n.* **1a.** A class or category. **b.** A title; a name. **2.** A part of a manuscript or book that appears in decorative red lettering or is otherwise distinguished from the rest of the text. **3.** A title or heading of a statute or chapter in a code of law. **4.** *Ecclesiastical* A direction in a missal, hymnal, or other liturgical book. **5.** An authoritative rule or direction. **6.** A short commentary or explanation covering a broad subject. **7.** Red ocher. ❖ *adj.* **1.** Red or reddish. **2.** Written in red. [ME *rubrike,* heading, title < OFr. *rubrique* < Lat. *rubrīca,* red chalk < *ruber, rubr-,* red. See **reudh-** in App.] **—ru′bri•cal** *adj.*

ru•bri•cate (ro͞o′brĭ-kāt′) *tr.v.* **-cat•ed, -cat•ing, -cates 1.** To arrange, write, or print as a rubric. **2.** To provide with rubrics. **3.** To establish rules for. [LLat. *rūbrīcāre, rūbrīcāt-,* to color red < Lat. *rūbrīcātus,* rubricated < *rūbrīca,* rubric. See RUBRIC.] **—ru′bri•ca′tion** *n.* **—ru′bri•ca′tor** *n.*

ru•bri•cian (ro͞o-brĭsh′ən) *n. Ecclesiastical* A person learned in the rubrics of ritual.

ru•by (ro͞o′bē) *n., pl.* **-bies 1.** A deep red translucent variety of the mineral corundum, valued as a precious stone. **2.** Something, such as a watch bearing, that is made from a ruby. **3.** A dark or deep red to deep purplish red. ❖ *adj.* Of the color ruby. [ME < OFr. *rubi* < Med.Lat. *rubīnus (lapis),* red (stone), ruby < Lat. *rubeus,* red. See **reudh-** in App.]

ru•by-throat•ed hummingbird (ro͞o′bē-thrō′tĭd) *n.* A small bird *(Archilochus colubris)* of eastern North America having green upper plumage and in the male a brilliant red throat.

ruche (ro͞osh) *n.* A ruffle or pleat of fine fabric used for trimming women's garments. [Fr. < OFr. *rusche,* beehive < Med.Lat. *rūsca,* tree bark (used to make beehives), of Celt. orig.] **—ruched** (ro͞osht) *adj.*

ruck[1] (rŭk) *n.* **1.** A multitude; a throng. **2.** The undistinguished crowd or ordinary run of persons or things. [ME *ruke,* heap, prob. of Scand. orig.]

ruck[2] (rŭk) *v.* **rucked, ruck•ing, rucks** —*tr.* To make a fold in; crease. —*intr.* To become creased. ❖ *n.* A crease or pucker, as in cloth. [Ult. < ON *hrukka,* wrinkle, fold.]

ruck•sack (rŭk′săk′, ro͝ok′-) *n.* A knapsack. [Ger. : dialectal *Ruck,* back (< MHGer. *rück, ruck* < OHGer. *hrukki*) + *Sack,* sack (< MHGer. *sac* < OHGer. < Lat. *saccus;* see SACK[1]).]

ruck•us (rŭk′əs) *n.* A disturbance; a commotion. [Perh. blend of RUCTION and RUMPUS.]

ruc•tion (rŭk′shən) *n.* A riotous disturbance; a noisy quarrel. [Poss. alteration of INSURRECTION.]

Ru•da Śląs•ka (ro͞o′də shlôɴ′skə) A city of S-central Poland, a suburb of Katowice. Pop. 171,356.

rudd (rŭd) *n.* A European freshwater fish *(Scardinius erythrophthalmus)* related to the carp and having a brownish body and red fins. [Prob. < *rud,* red. See RUDDLE.]

rud•der (rŭd′ər) *n.* **1a.** A vertically hinged plate of metal, fiberglass, or wood mounted at the stern of a ship or boat for directing its course. **b.** A similar structure at the tail of an aircraft, used for effecting horizontal changes in course. **2.** A controlling agent or influence over direction; a guide. [ME *ruder* < OE *rōther,* steering oar.]

rud•der•post (rŭd′ər-pōst′) *n.* See **rudderstock.**

rud•der•stock (rŭd′ər-stŏk′) *n.* The vertical shaft of a rudder that allows it to pivot when the tiller or steering gear is operated.

rud•dle (rŭd′l) also **red•dle** (rĕd′l) or **rad•dle** (răd′l) *n.* Red ocherous iron ore, used in dyeing and marking. ❖ *tr.v.* **-dled, -dling, -dles** To dye or mark with or as if with red ocher. [Prob. dim. of *rud,* red < ME *rudde* < OE *rudu.* See **reudh-** in App.]

rud•dock (rŭd′ək) *n. Chiefly British* An Old World robin *(Erithacus rubecula)* having olive-brown upper plumage and a conspicuous orange breast. [ME *ruddok* < OE *rudduc.* See **reudh-** in App.]

rud•dy (rŭd′ē) *adj.* **-di•er, -di•est 1a.** Having a healthy reddish color. **b.** Reddish; rosy. **2.** *Chiefly British Slang* Used as an intensive: *"You ruddy liar!"* (John Galsworthy). [ME *rudi* < OE *rudig.* See **reudh-** in App.] **—rud′di•ly** *adv.* **—rud′di•ness** *n.*

ruddy duck *n.* A North American duck *(Oxyura jamaicensis)* having stiff pointed tail feathers and in the male brownish-red upper plumage and a black-and-white head.

rude (ro͞od) *adj.* **rud•er, rud•est 1a.** Lacking the graces and refinement of civilized life; uncouth. **b.** Lacking education or knowledge; unlearned. **c.** Ill-mannered; discourteous: *rude behavior.* **2.** Relatively undeveloped; primitive. **3a.** Being in a rough unfinished condition: *a rude thatched hut.* **b.** Exhibiting a marked lack of skill or precision in work. **c.** In a natural raw state: *bales of rude cotton.* **4.** Vigorous, robust, and sturdy. **5.** Abruptly and unpleasantly forceful: *a rude shock.* [ME < OFr. < Lat. *rudis.*] **—rude′ly** *adv.* **—rude′ness** *n.*

ru•der•al (ro͞o′dər-əl) *Botany adj.* Growing in rubbish, poor land, or waste. ❖ *n.* A ruderal plant. [NLat. *rūderālis* < Lat. *rūdus, rūder-,* rubbish.]

ru•di•ment (ro͞o′də-mənt) *n.* **1.** A fundamental element, principle, or skill, as of a field of learning. Often used in the plural. **2.** Something in an incipient or undeveloped form. Often used in the plural. **3.** *Biology* An imperfectly or incompletely developed organ or part. [Lat. *rudīmentum* < *rudis,* rough, unformed.] **—ru′di•men′tal** (-mĕn′tl) *adj.*

ru•di•men•ta•ry (ro͞o′də-mĕn′tə-rē, -mĕn′trē) *adj.* **1.** Of or relating to basic facts or principles; elementary. **2.** Being in the earliest stages of development; incipient. **3.** *Biology* Imperfectly or incompletely developed; embryonic. **—ru′di•men•tar′i•ly** (-târ′ə-lē) *adv.* **—ru′di•men′ta•ri•ness** *n.*

Ru•dolf I (ro͞o′dŏlf) 1218–91. Holy Roman emperor (1273–91)

royal palm
Cuban royal palm
Roystonea regia

rubber plant
Ficus elastica

Peter Paul Rubens
detail from a 1609 self-portrait entitled *The Artist and His First Wife, Isabella Brandt, in the Honeysuckle Bower*

ă	pat	oi	boy
ā	pay	ou	out
âr	care	o͝o	took
ä	father	o͞o	boot
ĕ	pet	ŭ	cut
ē	be	ûr	urge
ĭ	pit	th	thin
ī	pie	*th*	this
îr	pier	hw	which
ŏ	pot	zh	vision
ō	toe	ə	about, item
ô	paw		

Stress marks:
′ (primary);
′ (secondary), as in
lexicon (lĕk′sĭ-kŏn′)

and founder of the Hapsburg dynasty.

Rudolf, Lake See Lake Turkana.

Ru•dolph (rōo′dŏlf), **Wilma Glodean** 1940–94. Amer. athlete who won three gold medals in track at the 1960 Olympics.

rue[1] (rōo) v. **rued, ru•ing, rues** —tr. To feel regret, remorse, or sorrow for. —intr. To feel regret, remorse, or sorrow. ❖ n. Sorrow; regret. [ME *ruen* < OE *hrēowan*, to affect with grief, and *hrēowian*, to repent.] —**ru′er** n.

rue[2] (rōo) n. Any of various aromatic southwest Asian or Mediterranean plants of the genus *Ruta*, esp. the ornamental *R. graveolens*, having bipinnately compound leaves that yield an acrid volatile oil formerly used in medicine. [ME < OFr. < Lat. *rūta*, prob. < Gk. *rhūtē*.]

rue anemone n. A small North American woodland plant (*Anemonella thalictroides*) having white or pinkish apetalous flowers grouped in umbels.

rue•ful (rōo′fəl) adj. **1.** Inspiring pity or compassion. **2.** Causing, feeling, or expressing sorrow or regret. —**rue′ful•ly** adv. —**rue′ful•ness** n.

ru•fes•cent (rōo-fĕs′ənt) adj. Tinged with red. [Lat. *rūfēscēns, rūfēscent-*, pr. part. of *rūfēscere*, to become red < *rūfus*, red, reddish. See **reudh-** in App.] —**ru•fes′cence** n.

ruff[1] (rŭf) n. **1.** A stiffly starched, frilled or pleated circular collar of fine fabric, worn in the 16th and 17th centuries. **2.** A distinctive collarlike projection around the neck, as of feathers on a bird. **3.** A Eurasian sandpiper (*Philomachus pugnax*), the male of which has collarlike erectile feathers around the neck during the breeding season. [Perh. short for RUFFLE[1].] —**ruffed** adj.

ruff[2] (rŭf) *Games* n. **1.** The playing of a trump card when one cannot follow suit. **2.** An old game resembling whist. ❖ tr. & intr.v. **ruffed, ruff•ing, ruffs** To trump or play a trump. [Obsolete Fr. *ronfle, roffle*, a kind of card game < OFr. *ronfle* < *renfler*, to rise : *re-, re-* + *enfler*, to cause to swell (< Lat. *īnflāre*; see INFLATE).]

ruff[3] (rŭf) n. A small European freshwater fish (*Acerina cernua*) related to the perches. [ME *ruffe*, prob. < Med.Lat. *rufus*, a kind of fish.]

ruffed grouse (rŭft) n. A chickenlike North American game bird (*Bonasa umbellus*) with mottled brownish plumage, the male of which makes drumming sounds with its wings.

ruf•fi•an (rŭf′ē-ən, rŭf′yən) n. **1.** A tough or rowdy person. **2.** A thug or gangster. [Fr., pimp < OFr. *rufien* < O Provençal *rufian* < OItal. *ruffiano*.] —**ruf′fi•an•ism** n. —**ruf′fi•an•ly** adj.

ruf•fle[1] (rŭf′əl) n. **1.** A strip of frilled or closely pleated fabric used for trimming or decoration. **2.** A ruff on a bird. **3a.** A ruckus or fray. **b.** Annoyance; vexation. **4.** An irregularity or slight disturbance of a surface. ❖ v. **-fled, -fling, -fles** —tr. **1.** To disturb the smoothness or regularity of; ripple. **2.** To pleat or gather (fabric) into a ruffle. **3.** To erect (the feathers). Used of birds. **4.** To discompose; fluster. **5.** To flip through (the pages of a book). **6.** To shuffle (cards). —intr. **1.** To become irregular or rough. **2.** To flutter. **3.** To become flustered. [< ME *ruffelen*, to roughen.]

ruf•fle[2] (rŭf′əl) n. A low continuous beating of a drum that is not as loud as a roll. ❖ tr.v. **-fled, -fling, -fles** To beat a ruffle on (a drum). [Perh. < freq. of *ruff*, a drum roll, perh. of imit. orig.]

ruf•fle[3] (rŭf′əl) intr.v. **-fled, -fling, -fles** To behave arrogantly or roughly; swagger. [ME *ruffelen*, to quarrel.] —**ruf′fler** n.

ru•fi•yaa (rōo′fē-yä′) n. See table at **currency**. [Maldivean < Hindi *rupayā, rupiyā*. See RUPEE.]

ru•fous (rōo′fəs) adj. Strong yellowish pink to moderate orange; reddish. [< Lat. *rūfus*, red. See **reudh-** in App.]

rug (rŭg) n. **1.** A heavy fabric used to cover a floor. **2.** An animal skin used as a floor covering. **3.** *Chiefly British* A piece of thick warm fabric or fur used as a coverlet or lap robe. **4.** *Slang* A toupee. [Of Scand. orig.]

ru•ga (rōo′gə) n., pl. **-gae** (-gē′, -gī′) *Biology* A fold, crease, or wrinkle, as in the lining of the stomach. Often used in the plural. [Lat. *rūga*.] —**ru′gate** (-gāt′) adj.

Rug•by[1] (rŭg′bē) A municipal borough of central England ESE of Birmingham; site of Rugby School where the game of Rugby was developed in the 19th cent. Pop. 59,564.

Rug•by[2] (rŭg′bē) n. A game played by two teams of 15 players each on a rectangular field 110 yards long with goal lines and goal posts at either end, the object being to run with an oval ball across the opponent's goal line or kick it through the upper portion of the goal posts, with forward passing and time-outs not permitted. [After *Rugby* School, England.]

Rugby shirt n. A knit pullover shirt typically having long sleeves, a front button closure, and bold horizontal stripes.

Rü•gen (rōo′gən, rü′-) An island of NE Germany in the Baltic Sea, separated from the mainland by a narrow channel.

rug•e•lach or **rug•a•lach** (rŭg′ə-ləкн) n. A cookie of creamcheese dough spread with filling, such as jam or nuts, and then rolled up. [Yiddish *rugelekh*, pl. of *rugele*.]

rug•ged (rŭg′id) adj. **1.** Having a rough irregular surface. **2.** Having strong features marked with furrows or wrinkles. **3.** Having a sturdy build or strong constitution. **4.** Tempestuous; stormy. **5.** Demanding great effort, ability, or endurance: *rugged living conditions*. **6.** Lacking culture or polish; coarse and rude: *rugged manners*. [ME, shaggy, of Scand. orig.] —**rug′ged•ly** adv. —**rug′ged•ness** n.

ruff[1]
detail of a portrait of Maria d'Aviz of Portugal by Frans Pourbus the Younger (1569–1622)

Rugby[2]

rug•ger (rŭg′ər) n. *Chiefly British* Rugby.

ru•gose (rōo′gōs′) adj. **1.** Having many wrinkles or creases; ridged or wrinkled. **2.** *Botany* Having a rough wrinkled surface. [Lat. *rūgōsus* < *rūga*, wrinkle.] —**ru′gose′ly** adv. —**ru•gos′i•ty** (-gŏs′ĭ-tē) n.

Ruhr (rōor) A region of NW Germany along and N of the **Ruhr River**, which flows c. 233 km (145 mi) W to the Rhine R.

ru•in (rōo′ĭn) n. **1.** Total destruction or disintegration, either physical, moral, social, or economic. **2.** A cause of total destruction. **3a.** The act of destroying totally. **b.** A destroyed person, object, or building. **4.** The remains of something destroyed, disintegrated, or decayed. Often used in the plural: *the ruins of ancient Greece.* ❖ v. **-ined, -in•ing, -ins** —tr. **1.** To destroy completely; demolish. **2.** To harm irreparably. **3.** To reduce to poverty or bankruptcy. **4.** To deprive of chastity. —intr. To fall into ruin. [ME *ruine* < OFr. < Lat. *ruīna* < *ruere*, to rush, collapse.] —**ru′in•a•ble** adj. —**ru′in•er** n.

SYNONYMS *ruin, raze, demolish, destroy, wreck* These verbs mean to injure and deprive something—or, less often, someone—of usefulness, soundness, or value. *Ruin* usually implies irretrievable harm but not necessarily total destruction: "*You will ruin no more lives as you ruined mine*" (Arthur Conan Doyle). *Raze, demolish,* and *destroy* can all imply reduction to ruins or even complete obliteration: *Enemy forces razed the city. The prosecutor demolished the opposition's argument.* "*I saw the best minds of my generation destroyed by madness*" (Allen Ginsberg). To *wreck* is to ruin in or as if in a violent collision: "*The Boers had just wrecked a British military train*" (Arnold Bennett). When *wreck* is used in referring to the ruination of a person or his or her hopes or reputation, it implies irreparable shattering: "*Coleridge, poet and philosopher wrecked in a mist of opium*" (Matthew Arnold).

ru•in•ate (rōo′ə-nāt′) adj. Having been ruined. [Med.Lat. *ruīnātus* < Lat. *ruīna*, ruin. See RUIN.]

ru•in•a•tion (rōo′ə-nā′shən) n. **1.** The act of ruining or the condition of being ruined. **2.** A cause of ruin.

ru•in•ous (rōo′ə-nəs) adj. **1.** Causing or apt to cause ruin; destructive. **2.** Falling to ruin; dilapidated or decayed. —**ru′in•ous•ly** adv. —**ru′in•ous•ness** n.

Ruis•dael or **Ruys•dael** (rīz′däl′, rīs′-, rous′-), **Jacob** 1628?–82. Dutch landscape painter whose baroque works include *Windmill at Wijk* (c. 1665).

Ru•key•ser (rōo′kī-zər), **Muriel** 1913–80. Amer. writer whose collections of poetry include *The Gates* (1976).

rule (rōol) n. **1a.** Governing power or its possession or use; authority. **b.** The duration of such power. **2a.** An authoritative prescribed direction for conduct. **b.** The body of regulations prescribed by the founder of a religious order for governing the conduct of its members. **3.** A usual, customary, or generalized course of action or behavior. **4.** A generalized statement that describes what is true in most or all cases. **5.** *Mathematics* A standard method or procedure for solving a class of problems. **6.** *Law* **a.** A court order limited in application to a specific case. **b.** A subordinate regulation governing a particular matter. **7.** See **ruler** 2. **8.** *Printing* A thin metal strip of various widths and designs, used to print borders or lines, as between columns. ❖ v. **ruled, rul•ing, rules** —tr. **1.** To exercise control, dominion, or direction over; govern. **2.** To dominate by powerful influence. **3.** To decide or declare authoritatively or judicially; decree. See Syns at **decide**. **4a.** To mark with straight parallel lines. **b.** To mark (a straight line), as with a ruler. —intr. **1.** To be in total control or command; exercise supreme authority. **2.** To formulate and issue a decree or decision. **3.** To prevail at a particular level or rate. **4.** *Slang* To be excellent or superior: *That new movie rules!* —*phrasal verb:* **rule out** **1.** To prevent; preclude. **2.** To remove from consideration; exclude. —*idiom:* **as a rule** In general; for the most part. [ME *reule* < OFr. < VLat. **regula* < Lat. *rēgula*, rod, principle. See **reg-** in App.] —**rul′a•ble** adj.

ruled surface (rōold) n. A surface, such as a cone or cylinder, generated by the motion of a straight line.

rule of the road n., pl. **rules of the road** A set of customary practices, as for the operation of a motor vehicle, established to promote efficiency and safety. Often used in the plural.

rule of thumb n., pl. **rules of thumb** A useful principle having wide application but not intended to be strictly accurate.

rul•er (rōo′lər) n. **1.** One, such as a monarch, that rules or governs. **2.** A straightedged strip, as of wood or metal, for drawing straight lines and measuring lengths.

rul•ing (rōo′lĭng) adj. **1.** Exercising control or authority. **2.** Predominant: *a ruling principle.* ❖ n. **1.** The act of governing or controlling. **2.** An authoritative or official decision.

rum[1] (rŭm) n. **1.** An alcoholic liquor distilled from fermented molasses or sugar cane. **2.** Intoxicating beverages. [Prob. short for obsolete *rumbullion*.]

rum[2] (rŭm) adj. **rum•mer, rum•mest** *Chiefly British* **1.** Odd; strange. **2.** Presenting danger or difficulty. [?]

ru•ma•ki (rə-mä′kē) n., pl. **-kis** An appetizer of Japanese origin consisting of a piece of chicken liver and a water chestnut wrapped in a slice of bacon and grilled or broiled. [?]

Ru•ma•ni•a (rōo-mā′nē-ə, -mān′yə) See Romania.

Ru•ma•ni•an (ro͞o-mā′nē-ən, -mān′yən) *adj. & n.* Variant of **Romanian.**

rum•ba also **rhum•ba** (rŭm′bə, ro͝om′-, ro͞om′-) *n.* **1.** A dance of Cuban origin, combining complex footwork with a pronounced movement of the hips. **2.** A modern ballroom adaptation of this dance. **3.** Music for this dance or in this style. [Am.Sp. < Sp. *rumbo,* ship's course, revelry, pomp. See RHUMB.] —**rum′ba** *v.*

rum•ble (rŭm′bəl) *v.* **-bled, -bling, -bles** —*intr.* **1.** To make a deep long rolling sound. **2.** To move or proceed with a deep long rolling sound. **3.** *Slang* To engage in a gang fight. —*tr.* **1.** To utter with a deep long rolling sound. **2.** To polish or mix (metal parts) in a tumbling box. ❖ *n.* **1.** A deep long rolling sound. **2.** A tumbling box. **3.** A luggage compartment or servant's seat in the rear of a carriage. **4.** *Slang* **a.** Pervasive widespread expression of unrest or dissatisfaction. **b.** A gang fight. [ME *romblen,* perh. < MDu. *rommelen* or < M Low German *rummeln.*] —**rum′bler** *n.* —**rum′bly** *adj.*

rumble seat *n.* An uncovered passenger seat that opens out from the rear of an automobile.

rum•bus•tious (rŭm-bŭs′chəs) *adj.* Uncontrollably exuberant; unruly. [Prob. alteration of ROBUSTIOUS (influenced by RAMBUNCTIOUS).] —**rum•bus′tious•ly** *adv.* —**rum•bus′tious•ness** *n.*

ru•men (ro͞o′mən) *n., pl.* **-mi•na** (-mə-nə) or **-mens** The first division of the stomach of a ruminant animal, from which food is later returned to the mouth as cud. [Lat. *rūmen,* throat.] —**ru′mi•nal** *adj.*

ru•mi•nant (ro͞o′mə-nənt) *n.* Any of various hoofed, even-toed, usu. horned mammals of the suborder Ruminantia, such as cattle and sheep, characteristically having a stomach divided into four compartments and chewing a cud consisting of regurgitated, partially digested food. ❖ *adj.* **1.** Characterized by the chewing of cud. **2.** Of or belonging to the Ruminantia. **3.** Meditative; contemplative. [< Lat. *rūmināns, rūminant-,* pr. part. of *rūmināre,* to ruminate. See RUMINATE.]

ru•mi•nate (ro͞o′mə-nāt′) *v.* **-nat•ed, -nat•ing, -nates** —*intr.* **1.** To turn a matter over and over in the mind. **2.** To chew cud. —*tr.* To reflect on again and again. [Lat. *rūmināre, rūmināt-* < *rūmen, rūmin-,* throat.] —**ru′mi•na′tive** *adj.* —**ru′mi•na′tive•ly** *adv.* —**ru′mi•na′tor** *n.*

ru•mi•na•tion (ro͞o′mə-nā′shən) *n.* **1.** The act of pondering; meditation. **2.** The act or process of chewing cud.

rum•mage (rŭm′ĭj) *v.* **-maged, -mag•ing, -mag•es** —*tr.* **1.** To search thoroughly by handling, turning over, or disarranging the contents of. **2.** To discover by searching thoroughly. —*intr.* To make a search. ❖ *n.* **1.** A thorough search among a number of things. **2.** A confusion of miscellaneous articles. [< earlier *romage,* act of packing cargo < Fr. *arrumage* < OFr. < *arumer,* to stow < O Provençal *arumar* : *a-,* to (< Lat. *ad-*; see AD–) + perh. *run,* ship's hold (of Gmc. orig.).] —**rum′mag•er** *n.*

rummage sale *n.* **1.** A sale of assorted secondhand objects contributed by donors to raise money for a charity. **2.** A sale, esp. of unclaimed or excess goods, as at a warehouse.

rum•mer (rŭm′ər) *n.* A large drinking cup or glass. [Ger. *Römer* < Du. *roemer* < *roem,* praise < MDu.]

rum•my[1] (rŭm′ē) *n.* A card game, played in many variations, in which the object is to obtain sets of three or more cards of the same rank or suit. [?]

rum•my[2] (rŭm′ē) *n., pl.* **-mies** *Slang* A drunkard.

rum•my[3] (rŭm′ē) *adj.* **-mi•er, -mi•est** *Chiefly British* Odd, strange, or dangerous; rum.

ru•mor (ro͞o′mər) *n.* **1.** A piece of unverified information of uncertain origin usu. spread by word of mouth. **2.** Unverified information received from another; hearsay. ❖ *tr.v.* **-mored, -mor•ing, -mors** To spread or tell by rumor. [ME *rumour* < OFr. < Lat. *rūmor.*]

ru•mor•mon•ger (ro͞o′mər-mŭng′gər, -mŏng′-) *n.* One who spreads rumors. ❖ *intr.v.* **-gered, -ger•ing, -gers** To engage in the spreading of rumors.

ru•mour (ro͞o′mər) *n. & v. Chiefly British* Variant of **rumor.**

rump (rŭmp) *n.* **1.** The fleshy hindquarters of an animal. **2.** A cut of beef or veal from the rump. **3.** The buttocks. **4.** The part of a bird's back nearest the tail. **5.** The last or inferior part. **6.** A legislature having only a small part of its original membership. [ME *rumpe,* of Scand. orig.]

rum•ple (rŭm′pəl) *v.* **-pled, -pling, -ples** —*tr.* To wrinkle or form into folds or creases. —*intr.* To become wrinkled or creased. ❖ *n.* An irregular or untidy crease. [Perh. Du. *rompelen* < MDu. *rumpelen.*] —**rum′ply** *adj.*

rum•pus (rŭm′pəs) *n.* A noisy clamor. [?]

rumpus room *n.* A room for play and parties.

rum•run•ner (rŭm′rŭn′ər) *n.* **1.** One who illegally transports liquor across a border. **2.** A boat used by rumrunners.

run (rŭn) *v.* **ran** (răn), **run, run•ning, runs** —*intr.* **1a.** To move swiftly on foot so that both feet leave the ground during each stride. **b.** To move at a fast gallop. Used of a horse. **2.** To retreat rapidly; flee: *seized the money and ran.* **3a.** To move without hindrance or restraint: *dogs that always ran loose.* **b.** To go or move about from place to place; roam. **4.** To migrate, esp. to move in a shoal in order to spawn. Used of fish. **5a.** To move or go quickly; hurry: *ran for help.* **b.** To go when in trouble or distress: *is always running to his lawyer.* **c.** To make a short, quick trip or visit: *ran down to the store.* **6a.** To take part in a race or contest: *athletes who run for the gold medal.* **b.** To compete in a race for elected office: *ran for mayor.* **c.** To finish a race or contest in a specified position: *ran second.* **7.** To move freely, on or as if on wheels. **8.** To be in operation: *The engine is running.* **9.** To go back and forth esp. on a regular basis; ply: *The ferry runs every hour.* **10.** *Nautical* To sail directly before the wind. **11a.** To flow, esp. in a steady stream: *Fresh water runs from the spring.* **b.** To emit pus, mucus, or serous fluid: *Pollen makes my nose run.* **c.** To be wet or covered with a liquid: *The mourners' eyes ran with tears.* **12.** To melt and flow: *A hot flame will make the solder run.* **13.** To spread or dissolve, as dyes in fabric: *Colorfast garments are not supposed to run.* **14.** To extend, stretch, or reach in a certain direction or to a particular point: *This road runs to the next town.* **15.** To extend, spread, or climb as a result of growing: *Ivy ran up the wall.* **16.** To spread rapidly: *disease that ran rampant.* **17a.** To be valid in a given area: *The speed limit runs only to the town line.* **b.** To be present as a valid accompaniment: *Fishing rights run with ownership of the land.* **18.** To unravel along a line: *Her stocking ran.* **19.** To continue in effect or operation: *a lease with one year to run.* **20.** To pass: *Days ran into weeks.* **21.** To tend to persist or recur: *Stinginess seems to run in that family.* **22a.** To accumulate or accrue: *The interest runs from the first of the month.* **b.** To become payable. **23.** To take a particular form, order, or expression: *My reasoning runs thus.* **24.** To tend or incline: *Their taste in art runs to the bizarre.* **25.** To occupy or exist in a certain range: *The sizes run from small to large.* **26.** To be presented or performed for a continuous period of time: *The play ran for six months.* **27.** To pass into a specified condition: *We ran into debt.* **28.** *Informal* To leave; depart: *Sorry, I have to run.* —*tr.* **1a.** To travel over on foot at a pace faster than a walk: *ran the entire distance.* **b.** To cause (an animal) to move quickly or rapidly. **2.** To allow to move without restraint. **3.** To do or accomplish by or as if by running: *run errands.* **4.** To hunt or pursue; chase: *dogs running deer.* **5.** To bring to a given condition by or as if by running: *The toddlers ran me ragged.* **6.** To cause to move quickly. **7a.** To cause to compete in or as if in a race. **b.** To present or nominate for elective office: *The party ran her for senator.* **8.** To cause to move or progress freely. **9.** To cause to function; operate: *run a machine.* **10.** To convey or transport: *Run the garbage over to the dump.* **11.** *Football* To attempt to advance (the ball) by carrying it. **12.** To submit for consideration or review: *ran my idea by the committee.* **13.** *Nautical* To cause to move on a course. **14a.** To smuggle: *run guns.* **b.** To evade and pass through: *run a roadblock.* **15.** To pass over or through: *run the rapids.* **16.** To cause to flow: *run water into a tub.* **17.** To stream with: *The fountains ran champagne.* **18.** *Metallurgy* **a.** To melt, fuse, or smelt (metal). **b.** To mold or cast (molten metal): *run gold into ingots.* **19.** To cause to extend or pass: *run a rope between poles.* **20.** To mark or trace on a surface: *run a pencil line between two points.* **21.** To sew with a continuous line of stitches: *run a seam.* **22.** To cause to unravel along a line: *ran her stocking on a splinter.* **23a.** To cause to crash or collide: *ran the car into a fence.* **b.** To cause to penetrate: *I ran a pin into my thumb.* **24.** To continue to present or perform: *ran the film for a month.* **25.** To publish in a periodical: *run an advertisement.* **26.** To subject oneself or be subjected to: *run a risk.* **27.** To have as an ongoing financial obligation: *run a deficit.* **28.** *Games* **a.** To score (balls or points) consecutively in billiards. **b.** To clear (the table) in pool by consecutive scores. **29.** To conduct or perform: *run an experiment.* **30.** *Computer Science* To process or execute (a program or an instruction). **31.** To control, manage, or direct: *ran the campaign by himself.* ❖ *n.* **1a.** A pace faster than a walk. **b.** A fast gallop. Used of a horse. **2.** An act of running. **3a.** A distance covered by or as if by running. **b.** The time taken to cover such a distance. **4.** A quick trip or visit. **5a.** *Sports* A running race. **b.** A campaign for public office. **6.** *Baseball* A point scored by advancing around the bases and reaching home plate safely. **7.** *Football* A player's attempt to carry the ball past or through the opposing team, usu. for a specified distance. **8a.** The migration of fish, esp. in order to spawn. **b.** A group or school of fish ascending a river in order to spawn. **9.** Unrestricted freedom or use: *I had the run of the library.* **10.** A stretch or period of riding, as in a race or to the hounds. **11a.** A track or slope along or down which something can travel. **b.** *Sports* A particular type of passage down a hill or across country, as on skis. **12.** *Sports* The distance a golf ball rolls after hitting the ground. **13a.** A scheduled or regular route. **b.** The territory of a news reporter. **14a.** A continuous period of operation, as of a machine. **b.** The production achieved during such a period: *a press run of 20,000 copies.* **15.** A course of a sailing vessel directly before the wind. **16a.** A movement or flow. **b.** The duration of such a flow. **c.** The amount of such a flow. **17.** A pipe or channel through which something flows. **18.** *Eastern Lower Northern US* See **creek** 1. **19.** A fall or slide, as of sand or mud. **20.** Continuous length or extent. **21.** *Geology* A vein or seam, as of ore or rock. **22.** The direction, configuration, or lie: *the run of the grain in leather.* **23a.** A trail or way made or frequented by animals. **b.** An outdoor enclosure for domestic animals or poultry. **24a.** A length of torn or unraveled stitches in a knitted fabric. **b.** A blemish caused by excessive paint flow. **25a.**

ă	pat	oi	boy
ā	pay	ou	out
âr	care	o͝o	took
ä	father	o͞o	boot
ĕ	pet	ŭ	cut
ē	be	ûr	urge
ĭ	pit	th	thin
ī	pie	*th*	this
îr	pier	hw	which
ŏ	pot	zh	vision
ō	toe	ə	about, item
ô	paw		

Stress marks:
′ (primary);
′ (secondary), as in
lexicon (lĕk′sĭ-kŏn′)

An unbroken series or sequence. **b.** *Games* A continuous set or sequence, as of playing cards in one suit. **c.** An unbroken sequence of theatrical performances. **d.** *Sports* A successful sequence of shots or points. **e.** *Music* A rapid sequence of notes; a roulade. **f.** A series of unexpected and urgent demands, as by customers: *a run on a bank.* **26.** A sustained state or condition: *a run of good luck.* **27.** A trend or tendency: *the run of events.* **28.** The average type, group, or category. **29.** *Computer Science* An execution of a specific program or instruction. **30.** *Nautical* The immersed part of a ship's hull abaft of the middle body. **31.** runs *Slang* Diarrhea. Often used with *the.* ❖ *adj.* **1.** Being in a melted or molten state: *run butter; run gold.* **2.** Completely exhausted from running. —*phrasal verbs:* **run across** To find by chance; come upon. **run after 1.** To pursue; chase. **2.** To seek the company or attention of for purposes of courting. **run against 1.** To encounter unexpectedly; run into. **2.** To work against; oppose. **run along** To go away; leave. **run away 1.** To flee; escape. **2.** To leave one's home, esp. to elope. **3.** To stampede. **run back 1.** To stop because of lack of force or power. **2.** To become tired. **3a.** To collide with and knock down. **b.** *Nautical* To collide with and cause to sink. **4.** To chase and capture. **5.** To trace the source of. **6.** To disparage. **7.** To go over; review: *Run down the list once more.* **8.** *Baseball* To put a runner out after trapping him or her between two bases. **run in 1.** To insert or include as something extra. **2.** *Printing* To make a solid body of text without a break. **3.** *Slang* To take into legal custody. **4.** To go to or seek out someone's company in order to socialize; visit. **run into 1.** To meet or find by chance. **2.** To encounter (something): *ran into trouble.* **3.** To collide with. **4.** To amount to: *His net worth runs into seven figures.* **run off 1.** To print, duplicate, or copy. **2.** To run away; elope. **3.** To flow off; drain away. **4.** To decide (a contest or competition) by a runoff. **5.** To force or drive off (trespassers, for example). **run on 1.** To keep going; continue. **2.** To talk volubly, persistently, and usu. inconsequentially. **3.** To continue a text without a formal break. **run out 1.** To become used up; be exhausted. **2.** To put out by force; compel to leave. **3.** To become void, as through the passage of time. **run over 1.** To collide with, knock down, and often pass over. **2.** To read or review quickly. **3.** To flow over. **4.** To go beyond a limit. **run through 1.** To pierce. **2.** To use up quickly. **3.** To rehearse quickly. **4.** To go over the salient points or facts of. **run up** To make or become greater or larger. **run with 1.** To keep company: *runs with a wild crowd.* **2.** To take as one's own; adopt. —*idioms:* **a run for (one's) money** Strong competition. **in the long run** In the final analysis or outcome. **in the short run** In the immediate future. **on the run 1a.** In rapid retreat. **b.** In hiding. **2.** Hurrying busily from place to place. **run a temperature (or fever)** To have a fever. **run away with 1a.** To make off with hurriedly. **b.** To steal. **2.** To be greater or bigger than others in (a performance, for example). **run foul (or afoul) of 1.** To run into; collide with. **2.** To come into conflict with. **run in place** To go through the movements of running without leaving one's original position. **run off with** To capture or carry off. **run (one's) eyes over** To look at or read in a cursory manner. **run out of** To exhaust the supply of. **run out of gas** *Slang* **1.** To exhaust one's energy or enthusiasm. **2.** To falter or come to a stop because of a lack of capital, support, or enthusiasm. **run out on** To abandon. **run rings around** To be markedly superior to. **run scared** *Informal* To become intimidated or frightened. **run short** To become scanty or insufficient in supply. **run short of** To use up so that a supply becomes insufficient or scanty. **run to earth (or ground)** To pursue and successfully capture. [ME *ernen, runnen* < OE *rinnan, eornan, earnan* and < ON *rinna.*]

REGIONAL NOTE Terms for "a small, fast-flowing stream" vary, especially throughout the eastern United States. Speakers in Virginia, West Virginia, Delaware, Maryland, and southern Pennsylvania use the word *run.* In New York State, one finds the term *kill* (a Dutch borrowing); in the Northeast, *brook*; in the South, *branch*; and in the northern United States, *crick,* a variant of *creek.*

run•a•bout (rŭn'ə-bout') *n.* **1a.** A small motorboat. **b.** A light aircraft. **c.** A small open automobile or carriage. **2.** A vagabond or wanderer.

run•a•gate (rŭn'ə-gāt') *n.* **1.** A renegade or deserter. **2.** A vagabond. [Alteration (influenced by RUN and *agate,* on the way) of obsolete *renegate,* renegade < ME < Med.Lat. *renegātus.* See RENEGADE.]

run•a•round (rŭn'ə-round') *n.* **1.** *Informal* Deception, usu. in the form of evasive excuses. **2.** *Printing* Type set in a column narrower than the body of the text, as around a picture.

run•a•way (rŭn'ə-wā') *n.* **1.** A person or animal that has run away. **2.** Something that has escaped control or proper confinement. **3.** *Informal* An easy victory. ❖ *adj.* **1.** Escaping or having escaped restraint, captivity, or control: *runaway horses.* **2.** Out of control: *runaway inflation.* **3.** Easily won: *a runaway victory.*

run•back (rŭn'băk') *n. Football* The act of returning a kickoff, punt, or intercepted forward pass.

run•ci•ble spoon (rŭn'sə-bəl) *n.* A three-pronged fork, such as a pickle fork, curved like a spoon and having a cutting edge. [Coined by Edward Lear, perh. alteration of *rounceval,* big

runcinate
runcinate leaf

woman, large pea, wart, monster, huge, from *Roncevaux* (Roncesvalles), site where giant bones were found.]

run•ci•nate (rŭn'sə-nāt') *adj. Botany* Having saw-toothed divisions directed backward: *runcinate leaves.* [Lat. *runcinātus,* p. part. of *runcināre,* to plane < *runcina,* carpenter's plane, formerly taken to mean saw, alteration (influenced by *runcāre,* to weed, pluck) of Gk. *rhukanē,* carpenter's plane.]

run•down (rŭn'doun') *n.* **1.** A point-by-point summary. **2.** *Baseball* A play in which a runner is trapped between bases and is pursued by fielders. ❖ *adj. also* **run-down** (rŭn'doun') **1a.** In poor physical condition; weak or exhausted. **b.** Dirty and dilapidated. **2.** Unwound and not running.

rune[1] (rōōn) *n.* **1a.** Any of the characters in several alphabets used by ancient Germanic peoples from the 3rd to the 13th century. **b.** A similar character in another alphabet, sometimes believed to have magic powers. **2.** A poem or incantation of mysterious significance, esp. a magic charm. [ON or OE *rūn.*] —**run'ic** *adj.*

rune[2] (rōōn) *n.* A Finnish poem or section of a poem. [Finn. *runo,* of Gmc. orig.]

rung[1] (rŭng) *n.* **1.** A rod or bar forming a step of a ladder. **2.** A crosspiece between the legs of a chair. **3.** The spoke in a wheel. **4.** *Nautical* One of the spokes or handles on a ship's wheel. **5.** A level or degree in a hierarchy. [ME < OE *hrung.*]

rung[2] (rŭng) *v.* Past participle of **ring**[2].

run-in (rŭn'ĭn') *n.* **1.** A quarrel or an argument. **2.** *Printing* Matter added to a text. ❖ *adj. Printing* Having been added to or inserted into a text.

run•let (rŭn'lĭt) *n.* A rivulet.

run•nel (rŭn'əl) *n.* **1.** A rivulet; a brook. **2.** A narrow channel or course. [ME *rynel* < OE < *rinnan,* to run.]

run•ner (rŭn'ər) *n.* **1.** *Sports* One who competes in a race. **2a.** *Baseball* One who runs the bases. **b.** *Football* One who carries the ball. **3.** A fugitive. **4.** One who carries messages or runs errands. **5.** One who serves as an agent or collector, as for a bank. **6.** One who solicits business, as for a hotel. **7a.** A smuggler. **b.** A vessel engaged in smuggling. **8.** One who operates or manages something. **9.** A device in or on which something slides or moves, as: **a.** The blade of a skate. **b.** The supports on which a drawer slides. **10.** A long narrow carpet. **11.** A long narrow tablecloth. **12.** A roller towel. **13.** *Metallurgy* A channel along which molten metal is poured into a mold; a gate. **14.** *Botany* **a.** A slender creeping stem that puts forth roots from nodes spaced at intervals along its length. **b.** A plant, such as the strawberry, having such a stem. **c.** A twining vine, such as the scarlet runner. **15.** Any of several marine fishes of the family Carangidae, esp. the blue runner (*Caranx crysos*), of temperate waters of the American Atlantic coast. **16.** *Sports* See **flat**[1] 9.

run•ner-up (rŭn'ər-ŭp') *n., pl.* **run•ners-up** (rŭn'ərz-) One that takes second place in a competition.

run•ning (rŭn'ĭng) *n.* **1.** The act or an instance of running. **2.** The power or ability to run. **3.** *Sports* The exercise or sport of someone who runs. ❖ *adj.* **1.** Ongoing over a period of time: *a running conversation.* **2.** *Printing* **a.** Set in continuous or unbroken lines: *running text.* **b.** Printed at the top or bottom of every page or every other page: *a running header.* ❖ *adv.* In a consecutive way: *four years running.* —*idioms:* **in the running 1.** Entered as a contender in a competition. **2.** Having the possibility of winning or placing well in a competition. **out of the running 1.** Not entered as a contender in a competition. **2.** Having no possibility of winning or placing well in a competition.

running back *n. Football* An offensive back, such as a fullback or halfback, who has the responsibility of advancing the ball by running with it on plays from the line of scrimmage.

running board *n.* A narrow footboard extending under and beside the doors of some automobiles and other conveyances.

running gear *n.* The working parts of an automobile, locomotive, or other vehicle.

running hand *n.* Handwriting done rapidly without lifting the pen from the paper.

running knot *n.* See **slipknot.**

running light *n.* One of several lights on a vehicle or vessel turned on between dusk and dawn to indicate position and size.

running mate *n.* **1.** The candidate or nominee for the lesser of two closely associated political offices. **2.** A companion. **3.** A horse used to set the pace in a race for another horse.

running noose *n.* See **noose** 1.

running start *n.* See **flying start.**

running stitch *n.* One of a series of small even stitches.

run•ny (rŭn'ē) *adj.* **-ni•er, -ni•est** Inclined to run or flow.

Run•ny•mede (rŭn'ē-mēd') A meadow in SE England on the Thames R. W of London. King John accepted the Magna Carta here or on a nearby island in 1215.

run•off (rŭn'ôf', -ŏf') *n.* **1.** An overflow of fluid, as rainfall not absorbed by soil. **2.** Eliminated waste products from manufacturing processes. **3.** An extra competition to break a tie.

run-of-the-mill (rŭn'ŏv-thə-mĭl') *adj.* Not special or outstanding; average.

run-on (rŭn'ŏn', -ôn') *n. Printing* **1.** Matter that is appended or added without a formal break. **2.** A derived term, often formed by the addition of an affix, that is included undefined at the end of a dictionary entry. —**run'-on'** *adj.*

run-on sentence *n.* See **fused sentence.**

run·out (rŭn′out′) *n.* **1.** The act or an instance of fleeing so as to evade undesirable consequences. **2.** The area where one curved surface merges with another. **3.** The act or an instance of expiring or having expired.

runt (rŭnt) *n.* **1.** An undersized animal, esp. the smallest animal of a litter. **2.** *Slang* A short person. [?] —**runt′i·ness** *n.* —**runt′y** *adj.*

run-through (rŭn′thrōō′) *n.* **1.** An uninterrupted rehearsal. **2.** A brief outline or summary.

run·way (rŭn′wā′) *n.* **1.** A strip of level, usu. paved ground on which aircraft take off and land. **2.** A path, channel, or track over which something runs. **3.** The channel of a stream. **4.** A chute down which logs are skidded. **5.** A smooth ramp for wheeled vehicles. **6.** A narrow walkway extending from a stage into an auditorium.

Run·yon (rŭn′yən), **(Alfred) Damon** 1884–1946. Amer. writer known for his stories about Broadway and the New York underworld, such as "Guys and Dolls" (1931). —**Run′yon·esque′** (rŭn′yə-nĕsk′) *adj.*

ru·pee (rōō-pē′, rōō′pē) *n.* See table at **currency.** [Hindi *rupayā, rupiyā* < Skt. *rūpyam,* stamped silver coin < *rūpya-,* well-formed, stamped < *rūpam,* shape.]

Ru·pert (rōō′pərt), **Prince.** 1619–82. German-born English leader of the Royalists during the English Civil War.

Rupert River A river of W-central Quebec, Canada, rising in Lake Mistassini and flowing c. 611 km (380 mi) to James Bay.

ru·pi·ah (rōō-pē′ə) *n., pl.* **rupiah** See table at **currency.** [Hindi *rupayā, rupiyā.* See RUPEE.]

ru·pic·o·lous (rōō-pĭk′ə-ləs) *adj.* Thriving among or inhabiting rocks. [Lat. *rūpēs,* rock (< *ruptus,* p. part. of *rumpere,* to break; see **reup-** in App.) + -COLOUS.]

rup·ture (rŭp′chər) *n.* **1a.** The process or instance of breaking open or bursting. **b.** The state of being broken open. **2.** A break in friendly relations. **3.** *Pathology* **a.** A hernia, esp. of the groin or intestines. **b.** A tear in an organ or tissue. ❖ *v.* **-tured, -tur·ing, -tures** —*tr.* **1.** To break open; burst. —*intr.* **1.** To undergo or suffer a rupture. [ME < OFr. < Lat. *ruptūra* < *ruptus,* p. part. of *rumpere,* to break. See **reup-** in App.] —**rup′tur·a·ble** *adj.*

ru·ral (rōōr′əl) *adj.* **1.** Of, relating to, or characteristic of the country. **2.** Of or relating to people who live in the country. **3.** Of or relating to farming; agricultural. [ME < OFr. < Lat. *rūrālis* < *rūs, rūr-,* country.] —**ru′ral·ly** *adv.*

rural free delivery *n.* Free government delivery of mail in rural areas.

ru·ral·ism (rōōr′ə-lĭz′əm) *n.* Rurality.

ru·ral·ist (rōōr′ə-lĭst) *n.* **1.** One who resides in a rural area. **2.** An advocate of rural life.

ru·ral·i·ty (rōō-răl′ĭ-tē) *n., pl.* **-ties** **1.** The state or quality of being rural. **2.** A rural trait or characteristic.

ru·ral·ize (rōōr′ə-līz′) *tr. & intr.v.* **-ized, -iz·ing, -iz·es** To make or become rural. —**ru′ral·i·za′tion** (rōōr′ə-lĭ-zā′shən) *n.*

rural route *n.* A rural mail route.

Ru·rik (rōōr′ĭk, rōō′rĭk) d. c. 879. Scandinavian warrior and founder of the dynasty that ruled Russia until 1598.

Rus. *abbr.* **1.** Russia **2.** Russian

ruse (rōōs, rōōz) *n.* A crafty stratagem; a subterfuge. [ME, detour, dodging < OFr. < *ruser,* to drive back < Lat. *recūsāre,* to reject. See RUSH[1].]

Ru·se (rōō′sä) A city of NE Bulgaria on the Danube R. S of Bucharest; founded in the 2nd cent. A.D. Pop. 193,000.

rush[1] (rŭsh) *v.* **rushed, rush·ing, rush·es** —*intr.* **1.** To move or act swiftly; hurry. **2.** To make a sudden or swift attack or charge. **3.** To flow or surge rapidly, often with noise. **4.** *Football* To move the ball by running. —*tr.* **1.** To cause to move or act with unusual haste or violence. **2.** To perform with great haste. **3.** To attack swiftly and suddenly. **4.** To transport or carry hastily. **5.** To entertain or pay great attention to: *They rushed him for their fraternity.* **6.** *Football* To charge (a quarterback or passer) in order to block or prevent a play. ❖ *n.* **1.** A sudden forward motion. **2a.** Surging emotion. **b.** An anxious and eager movement to get to or from a place. **c.** A sudden, very insistent, generalized demand. **3.** General haste or busyness. **4.** A sudden attack; an onslaught. **5.** A rapid, often noisy flow or passage. **6.** *Football* **a.** An attempt to move the ball by running. **b.** An act of running at a passer or kicker in order to block or prevent a play. **7.** *Sports* A rapid advance of the ball or puck toward the opponent's goal. **8.** **rushes** The first, unedited print of a movie scene. **9a.** A time of attention, usu. one in which extensive social activity occurs. **b.** A drive by a Greek society on a college campus to recruit new members. **10a.** The intensely pleasurable sensation experienced immediately after use of a stimulant or a mind-altering drug. **b.** A sudden brief exhilaration. ❖ *adj.* Performed with or requiring great haste or urgency: *a rush job.* [ME *rushen* < AN *russher,* var. of OFr. *ruser,* to drive back < Lat. *recūsāre,* to reject < *re-,* re- + *causārī,* to give as a reason (< *causa,* cause).] —**rush′er** *n.*

rush[2] (rŭsh) *n.* **1a.** Any of various stiff marsh plants of the genus *Juncus,* having pliant hollow or pithy stems and small flowers with scalelike perianths. **b.** Any of various similar, usu. aquatic plants. **2.** The stem of one of these plants, used in making baskets, mats, and chair seats. [ME < OE *rysc.*]

Rush, Benjamin 1745–1813. Amer. physician and educator who signed the Declaration of Independence.

rush candle *n.* See **rushlight.**

Rush·die (rŭsh′dē), **Salman** b. 1947. Indian-born British writer whose works include *Midnight's Children* (1981) and *The Satanic Verses* (1988).

rush hour *n.* A period of heavy traffic. —**rush′-hour′** (rŭsh′our′) *adj.*

rush·light (rŭsh′līt′) *n.* A candle consisting of a rush wick in tallow.

Rush·more (rŭsh′môr′, -mōr′), **Mount** A mountain, 1,708 m (5,600 ft), in the Black Hills of W SD; site of a monument with massive likenesses of Washington, Jefferson, Lincoln, and Theodore Roosevelt.

rush·y (rŭsh′ē) *adj.* **-i·er, -i·est** **1.** Resembling or characteristic of rushes; rushlike. **2.** Abounding in rushes.

rusk (rŭsk) *n.* **1.** A light, soft-textured sweetened biscuit. **2.** Sweet raised bread dried and browned in an oven. [Sp. or Port. *rosca,* coil, rusk, perh. < VLat. **rotisca,* dim. of Lat. *rota,* wheel. See RO-TATE.]

Rus·ka (rōōs′kə, rōōsh′kä), **Ernst** 1906–88. German physicist who shared a 1986 Nobel Prize.

Rus·kin (rŭs′kĭn), **John** 1819–1900. British critic who wrote *Modern Painters* (1843–60). —**Rus′kin′i·an** *adj.*

Russ. *abbr.* **1.** Russia **2.** Russian

Rus·sell (rŭs′əl), **Bertrand Arthur William.** 3rd Earl Russell. 1872–1970. British philosopher, mathematician, social critic and writer who won the 1950 Nobel Prize for literature.

Russell, Charles Taze 1852–1916. Amer. religious leader who founded (1884) the sect now called Jehovah's Witnesses.

Russell, George William Pen name "A.E." 1867–1935. Irish writer and nationalist who was a leader of the Irish literary renaissance at the turn of the 20th cent.

Russell, Henry Norris 1877–1957. Amer. astronomer who developed a theory of stellar evolution.

Russell, John. 1st Earl Russell. 1792–1878. British politician who served as prime minister (1846–52 and 1865–66).

Russell, Lillian 1861–1922. Amer. entertainer known for her roles in comic operas.

Russell, Mount A peak, 4,296.8 m (14,088 ft), of the Sierra Nevada in E CA.

rus·set (rŭs′ĭt) *n.* **1.** A moderate to strong brown. **2.** A coarse reddish-brown to brown homespun cloth. **3.** A winter apple with a rough reddish-brown skin. **4.** A russet Burbank. ❖ *adj.* Moderate to strong brown. [ME < OFr. *rousset* < *rous,* red < Lat. *russus.* See **reudh-** in App.]

russet Burbank *n.* A long rounded potato with a rough brown skin. [After Luther BURBANK.]

Rus·sia (rŭsh′ə) **1.** A former empire of E Europe and N Asia. Orig. settled by Slavs, the region was a conglomerate of independent principalities until Moscow gained ascendancy in the 14th, 15th, and 16th cent. and lasted until the Revolution of 1917 and the formation of the USSR in 1922. **2.** A country of E Europe and N Asia bordering on the W on Finland, the Baltic States, Belarus, and Ukraine and stretching E to the Pacific Ocean. The Russian Soviet Federated Socialist Republic, coextensive with the region, was declared in 1917. Russia reemerged as an independent republic after the disintegration of the USSR in 1991. Cap. Moscow. Pop. 147,997,000. **3.** The Union of Soviet Socialist Republics.

Rus·sian (rŭsh′ən) *adj.* **1.** Of or relating to Russia or its people, language, or culture. **2.** Of or relating to the former Soviet Union. ❖ *n.* **1a.** A native or inhabitant of Russia. **b.** A person of Russian descent. **c.** A native or inhabitant of the former Soviet Union. **2.** The East Slavic language of the Russians and the official language of Russia. [Med.Lat. *Russiānus* < ORuss. *Rusĭ,* Vikings, Rus (medieval Russian state founded by Vikings) < ON **rōdhs(menn)* or *rōdhs(karlar),* seafarers < *rōdhr,* rowing.]

Russian dressing *n.* Salad dressing, such as mayonnaise, with chili sauce or ketchup, chopped pickles, and pimientos.

Rus·sian·ize (rŭsh′ə-nīz′) *tr.v.* **-ized, -iz·ing, -iz·es** To make Russian. —**Rus′sian·i·za′tion** (-ə-nĭ-zā′shən) *n.*

Russian olive *n.* See **oleaster.**

Russian Orthodox Church *n.* The Eastern Orthodox Church that is under the leadership of the patriarch of Russia and has autonomous branches in other countries.

Russian roulette *n.* **1.** A procedure in which one spins the cylinder of a revolver loaded with only one bullet, aims the muzzle at one's head, and pulls the trigger. **2.** An act of reckless bravado.

Russian thistle *n.* A red-stemmed prickly Eurasian plant (*Salsola kali* var. *tenuifolia*) that is a troublesome weed in western North America.

Russian wolfhound *n.* See **borzoi.**

Rus·si·fy (rŭs′ə-fī′) *tr.v.* **-fied, -fy·ing, -fies** To make Russian in character or quality. —**Rus′si·fi·ca′tion** (-fĭ-kā′shən) *n.*

Rus·sky (rŭs′kē, rōōs′-) *n., pl.* **-skies** *Offensive* A Russian. [Russ. *russkiĭ,* Russian < *Rus',* Rus (the medieval Russian state) < ORuss. *Rusĭ.* See RUSSIAN.] —**Rus′sky** *adj.*

Russo- *pref.* Russia; Russian: *Russophobe.* [< RUSSIA.]

Rus·so·phile (rŭs′ə-fīl′) *n.* An admirer of Russia or its people, language, or culture. —**Rus′so·phil′i·a** (-fĭl′ē-ə) *n.*

Rus·so·phobe (rŭs′ə-fōb′) *n.* One who fears or dislikes Russia or its people or culture. —**Rus′so·pho′bi·a** *n.*

Salman Rushdie

Mount Rushmore

Russia

rust (rŭst) *n.* **1.** Any of various powdery or scaly reddish-brown or reddish-yellow hydrated ferric oxides formed on iron and iron-containing materials by low-temperature oxidation in the presence of water. **2.** Any of various metallic coatings, esp. oxides, formed by corrosion. **3.** A stain or coating resembling iron rust. **4.** Deterioration, as of ability, resulting from inactivity or neglect. **5.** *Botany* **a.** Rust fungus. **b.** A plant disease caused by a rust fungus, characterized by reddish or brownish spots on leaves, stems, and other parts. **6.** A strong brown. ❖ *v.* **rust•ed, rust•ing, rusts** —*intr.* **1.** To become corroded. **2.** To deteriorate or degenerate through inactivity or neglect. **3.** To become the color of rust. **4.** *Botany* To develop a disease caused by a rust fungus. —*tr.* **1.** To corrode or subject (a metal) to rust formation. **2.** To impair or spoil, as by misuse. **3.** To color (something) rust. [ME < OE *rūst.* See **reudh-** in App.] —**rust** *adj.* —**rust′a•ble** *adj.*

Rus•ta•vi (rōō-stä′vē, -vyĭ) A city of S Georgia SE of Tbilisi. Pop. 143,000.

rust belt also **Rust Belt** *n.* A heavily industrialized area containing older factories, esp. those that are marginally profitable or that have been closed. —**rust′-belt′** *adj.*

rust fungus *n.* Any of various fungi of the order Uredinales that are injurious to a wide variety of plants.

rus•tic (rŭs′tĭk) *adj.* **1.** Of, relating to, or typical of country life or country people. **2a.** Lacking refinement or elegance; coarse. **b.** Charmingly simple or unsophisticated. **3.** Made of unfinished or roughly finished wood: *rustic furniture.* **4.** Having a rough or textured appearance; rusticated. Used of masonry. ❖ *n.* **1.** A rural person. **2.** A person regarded as crude, coarse, or simple. [ME *rustik* < OFr. *rustique* < Lat. *rūsticus* < *rūs,* country.] —**rus′ti•cal•ly** *adv.*

rus•ti•cate (rŭs′tĭ-kāt′) *v.* **-cat•ed, -cat•ing, -cates** —*intr.* To go to or live in the country. —*tr.* **1.** To send to the country. **2.** *Chiefly British* To suspend (a student) from a university. **3.** To cut or shape (masonry blocks) so as to create a rough-hewn or textured look. [Lat. *rūsticārī, rūsticāt-* < *rūsticus,* rustic. See **RUSTIC.**] —**rus′ti•ca′tion** *n.* —**rus′ti•ca′tor** *n.*

rus•tic•i•ty (rŭ-stĭs′ĭ-tē) *n., pl.* **-ties** **1.** The condition of being rustic. **2.** A rustic trait or mannerism.

rus•tle (rŭs′əl) *v.* **-tled, -tling, -tles** —*intr.* **1.** To move with soft fluttering or crackling sounds. **2.** To move or act energetically or with speed. **3.** To forage food. **4.** To rustle livestock. —*tr.* **1.** To cause to rustle. **2.** To obtain by rustling: *rustled up food.* **3.** To steal (livestock, esp. cattle). [ME *rustlen,* perh. of imit. orig.] —**rus′tler** *n.* —**rus′tling•ly** *adv.*

rust mite *n.* Any of various mites that cause a plant disease characterized by reddish or brownish spots on leaves and fruits.

rust•proof (rŭst′prōōf′) *adj.* Incapable of rusting. —**rust′proof′** *v.*

rust•y (rŭs′tē) *adj.* **-i•er, -i•est** **1.** Covered with rust; corroded. **2.** Consisting of or produced by rust. **3.** Of a yellowish-red or brownish-red color. **4.** Working or operating stiffly or incorrectly because of or as if because of rust. **5.** Weakened or impaired by neglect, disuse, or lack of practice. —**rust′i•ly** *adv.* —**rust′i•ness** *n.*

rut¹ (rŭt) *n.* **1.** A sunken track or groove made by the passage of vehicles. **2.** A fixed, usu. boring routine. ❖ *tr.v.* **rut•ted, rut•ting, ruts** To furrow. [Poss. alteration of ROUTE.]

rut² (rŭt) *n.* **1.** An annually recurring condition or period of sexual excitement and reproductive activity in male deer. **2.** A condition or period of mammalian sexual activity, such as estrus. ❖ *intr.v.* **rut•ted, rut•ting, ruts** To be in rut. [ME *rutte* < OFr. *rut* < VLat. **rūgitus* < **rūgere,* to roar < Lat. *rūgīre,* to roar.]

ru•ta•ba•ga (rōō′tə-bā′gə, rōōt′ə-, rōō′tə-bä′gə, rōōt′ə-) *n.* **1.** A European plant (*Brassica napus* var. *napobrassica*) having a thick edible bulbous root. **2.** The root of this plant. [Swed. dialectal *rotabagge* : *rot,* root (< ON *rōt;* see **wrād-** in App.) + *bagge,* bag (< ON *baggi*).]

ruth (rōōth) *n.* **1.** Compassion or pity for another. **2.** Sorrow or misery about one's own misdeeds or flaws. [ME *ruthe* < ON *hrygdh* (influenced by OE *hrēow,* sorrow, regret).]

Ruth¹ In the Bible, a Moabite widow who left home with her mother-in-law and went to Bethlehem, where she later married Boaz. [Heb. or Moabite *Rût;* perh. akin to *rāwâ,* to drink one's fill.]

Ruth² *n.* See table at **Bible.** [After RUTH¹.]

Ruth, George Herman Known as "Babe." 1895–1948. Amer. baseball player who hit 714 career home runs (1915–35).

Ru•the•nia (rōō-thēn′yə, -thē′nē-ə) A region of W Ukraine S of the Carpathian Mts.

Ru•the•ni•an (rōō-thē′nē-ən, -thēn′yən) *adj.* Of or relating to Ruthenia, the Ruthenians, or their language or culture. ❖ *n.* **1.** A native or inhabitant of Ruthenia. **2.** The variety of Ukrainian used by the Ruthenians.

Babe Ruth

Rwanda

ru•then•ic (rōō-thĕn′ĭk, -thē′nĭk) *adj.* Relating to or containing ruthenium with a high valence.

ru•the•ni•ous (rōō-thē′nē-əs) *adj.* Relating to or containing ruthenium with a low valence.

ru•the•ni•um (rōō-thē′nē-əm) *n.* *Symbol* **Ru** A hard acid-resistant metallic element that is found in platinum ores and is used in alloys for nonmagnetic wear-resistant instrument pivots and electrical contacts. Atomic number 44; atomic weight 101.07; melting point, 2,310°C; boiling point 3,900°C; specific gravity 12.41; valence 0, 1, 2, 3, 4, 5, 6, 7, 8. See table at **element.** [< Med.Lat. *Ruthenia,* Russia < *Ruthenī,* Russians < Russ. *Rusin* < ORuss. *Rusĭ,* Russian. See RUSSIAN.]

ruth•er•ford (rŭth′ər-fərd) *n.* A unit expressing the rate of decay of radioactive material, equal to one million disintegrations per second. [After Ernest RUTHERFORD.]

Rutherford, Daniel 1749–1819. British chemist and physician who is credited with the discovery of nitrogen.

Rutherford, Ernest. 1st Baron Rutherford of Nelson. 1871–1937. New Zealand–born physicist who discovered the atomic nucleus and won the 1908 Nobel Prize in chemistry.

ruth•er•ford•i•um (rŭth′ər-fôr′dē-əm, -fôr′-) *n.* *Symbol* **Rf** An artificially produced radioactive element with atomic number 104 whose longest-lived isotopes have mass numbers of 253, 255, 257, and 259 with half-lives of 1.8, 1.6, 4.7, and 3.4 seconds, respectively. See table at **element.** [After Ernest RUTHERFORD.]

ruth•ful (rōōth′fəl) *adj.* **1.** Full of sorrow; rueful. **2.** Causing sorrow or pity. —**ruth′ful•ly** *adv.* —**ruth′ful•ness** *n.*

ruth•less (rōōth′lĭs) *adj.* Having no compassion or pity; merciless. —**ruth′less•ly** *adv.* —**ruth′less•ness** *n.*

ru•ti•lant (rōōt′l-ənt) *adj.* Bright red. [ME *rutilaunt* < Lat. *rutilāns, rutilant-,* pr. part. of *rutilāre,* to make red, to be reddish < *rutilus,* red, reddish. See **reudh-** in App.]

ru•tile (rōō′tēl′, -tĭl′) *n.* A lustrous red, reddish-brown, or black mineral, TiO₂, used as a gemstone and an ore and in paints and fillers. [Fr. < Ger. *Rutil* < Lat. *rutilus,* red. See RUTILANT.]

Rut•ledge (rŭt′lĭj), **John** 1739–1800. Amer. jurist; associate justice (1789–91) and chief justice (1795) of the US Supreme Court.

rut•tish (rŭt′ĭsh) *adj.* Lustful; libidinous. —**rut′tish•ly** *adv.* —**rut′tish•ness** *n.*

rut•ty (rŭt′ē) *adj.* **-ti•er, -ti•est** Full of ruts. —**rut′ti•ness** *n.*

Ru•wen•zo•ri (rōō′wən-zôr′ē, -zōr′ē) A mountain range of E-central Africa on the Uganda-Zaire border; explored in 1889 by Henry M. Stanley.

Ruys•dael (rīz′däl′, rīs′-, rous′-), **Jacob van** See Jacob van **Ruisdael.**

RV *abbr.* **1.** recreational vehicle **2.** Revised Version

Rv. *abbr. Bible* Revelation

R-val•ue (är′văl′yōō) *n.* A measure of the capacity of a material, such as insulation, to impede heat flow, with increasing values indicating a greater capacity. [*r(esistance) value.*]

Rwan•da (rōō-än′də) Formerly **Ru•an•da** (rōō-än′də) A country of E-central Africa; part of the colonial territory of Ruanda-Urundi administered by Germany and Belgium until it achieved independence in 1962. Cap. Kigali. Pop. 5,109,000. —**Rwan′dan** *adj. & n.*

rwy. or **ry.** *abbr.* railway

Rx (är′ĕks′) *n.* **1.** A prescription for medicine or a medical appliance. **2.** A remedy, cure, or solution for a disorder or problem. [Alteration of ℞, symbol used in prescriptions, abbr. of Lat. *recipe,* sing. imper. of *recipere,* to take. See RECEIVE.]

–ry *suff.* Variant of **–ery.**

ry•a (rē′ə) *n.* **1.** A handwoven Scandinavian rug with a thick pile and usu. colorful abstract designs. **2.** The weaving pattern characteristic of such rugs. [After *Rya,* a village in SW Sweden.]

Rya•zan (ryĭ-zän′) A city of W-central Russia SE of Moscow; founded 1095. Pop. 494,000.

Ry•der (rī′dər), **Albert Pinkham** 1847–1917. Amer. painter whose works include *Toilers of the Sea* (c. 1884).

rye¹ (rī) *n.* **1.** A cereal grass (*Secale cereale*) widely cultivated for its grain. **2.** The grain of this plant, used in making flour and whiskey and for livestock feed. **3.** Whiskey made from the grains of this plant. [ME < OE *ryge.*]

rye² (rī) *n.* A Gypsy man. [Romany *rai* < Skt. *rājā,* king. See RAJAH.]

rye bread *n.* Bread made partially or entirely from rye flour.

rye•grass or **rye grass** (rī′grăs′) *n.* See **darnel.** [Alteration of *raygrass* : *ray,* darnel (< ME *rai,* perh. alteration of OFr. *ivraie* < Lat. *ēbriāca* < fem. of *ēbriācus,* drunk (< the plant's effects if ingested) < *ēbrius*) + GRASS.]

Rys•wick (rīz′wĭk) See **Rijswijk.**

Ryu•kyu Islands (rē-ōō′kyōō′, ryōō′kyōō′) An island group of SW Japan extending c. 1,046 km (650 mi) between Kyushu and Taiwan; incorporated into Japan in 1879.

Ss

¹ or S (ĕs) *n., pl.* **s's** or **S's** also **ss** or **Ss 1.** The 19th letter of the modern English alphabet. **2.** Any of the speech sounds represented by the letter *s*. **3.** The 19th in a series. **4.** Something shaped like the letter S.

² abbr. 1. second (unit of time) **2.** *Mathematics* second (of arc) **3.** stere **4.** strange quark

¹ 1. The symbol for the element **sulfur. 2.** The symbol for **entropy** 1.

² abbr. 1. *Bible* Samuel **2.** satisfactory **3.** Saturday **4.** siemens **5.** small **6.** soprano **7a.** south **b.** southern **8.** *Baseball* strike **9.** Sunday

abbr. 1. section **2.** shilling **3.** singular **4.** sire **5.** solo **6.** son

abbr. 1. saint **2.** sea **3.** *Medicine* signature **4a.** signor **b.** signore

s¹ or **-es** *suff.* Used to form plural nouns: *letters*. [ME -*es*, -*s* < OE -*es*, -*as*, nominative and accusative pl. suff.]

s² or **-es** *suff.* Used to form the third person singular present tense of all regular and most irregular verbs: *looks; holds*. [ME -*es*, -*s* < OE (Northumbrian) -*es*, -*as*, alteration (perh. influenced by ON) of -*eth*, -*eth*.]

s³ *suff.* Used to form adverbs: *They were caught unawares. He works nights*. [ME -*es*, -*s*, genitive sing. suff. < OE -*es*.]

's *suff.* Used to form the possessive case of singular nouns, plural nouns that do not end in *s*, certain pronouns, and phrases that function as nouns or pronouns: *nation's; women's; another's; the girl next door's cat*. [ME -*s*, -*es* < OE -*es*, genitive sing. suff.]

s. 1. Contraction of *is*: *She's here.* **2.** Contraction of *has*: *He's arrived.* **3.** Contraction of *does*: *What's he want?* **4.** Contraction of *us*: *Let's go.*

SA *abbr.* **1.** seaman apprentice **2.** South Africa **3.** South America

s.a. *abbr. Latin* sine anno (without date)

aa•le (zä′lə, sä′-) A river rising in central Germany and flowing c. 426 km (265 mi) N to the Elbe R.

aa•mi (sä′mē) *n.* Variant of **Sami.**

aar (sär, zär) A river rising in NE France and flowing c. 241 km (150 mi) NNW through the **Saar Basin** to the Moselle R. in W Germany.

aar•brück•en (zär-brook′ən, sär-, zär-brük′-) A city of SW Germany on the Saar R. S of Bonn. Pop. 188,763.

aa•re•maa also **Sa•re•ma** (sär′ə-mä′) An island of W Estonia in the Baltic Sea at the mouth of the Gulf of Riga.

aa•ri•nen (sär′ə-nən, -nĕn′), **Eero** 1910–61. Finnish-born Amer. architect whose designs include the Trans World Airlines terminal in New York City (1962).

aar•land (sär′länd′, zär′-, -länt′) or **Saar** (sär, zär) A region of SW Germany in the Saar R. valley on the border with France. —**Saar′land′er** *n.*

aa•ve•dra La•mas (sä-vä′drə lä′mäs, sä′ä-vĕ′drä), **Carlos** 1878?–1959. Argentinean diplomat who won the 1936 Nobel Peace Prize.

a•ba (sä′bə, sä′-) An island of the N Netherlands Antilles in the West Indies between St. Martin and St. Eustatius.

ab•a•dil•la (săb′ə-dĭl′ə, -dē′ə) *n.* **1.** A Mexican and Central American plant (*Schoenocaulon officinale*) of the lily family, having densely flowered spikelike racemes and brown seeds that are rich in veratrine. **2.** The seeds of this plant, used in insecticides and in medicinal preparations. [Sp. *cebadilla*, dim. of *cebada*, barley < Lat. *cibātus* < p. part. of *cibāre*, to feed < *cibus*, food.]

a•bah (sä′bä′) A region of Malaysia in NE Borneo; a British protectorate from the early 1800s until 1963.

a•bal (sä′băl) *n.* See **palmetto** 1. [NLat., genus name.]

a•ba•tier (sä-bä-tyä′), **Paul** 1854–1941. French chemist who shared a 1912 Nobel Prize.

a•ba•yon (sä′bä-yôn′) *n.* See **zabaglione.** [Fr. < Ital. *zabaglione, zabaione.*]

ab•bat (săb′ət) *n.* Witches' Sabbath. [Fr., Sabbath, sabbat < OFr., Sabbath. See SABBATH.]

ab•ba•tar•i•an (săb′ə-târ′ē-ən) *n.* **1.** One who observes Saturday as the Sabbath, as in Judaism. **2.** One who believes in strict observance of Sunday as the Sabbath. [< LLat. *sabbatārius* < Lat. *sabbatum*, Sabbath. See SABBATH.] —**Sab′ba•tar′i•an•ism** *n.*

ab•bath (săb′əth) *n.* **1.** The seventh day of the week, Saturday, observed as the day of rest and worship by Jews and some Christian groups. **2.** The first day of the week, Sunday, observed as the day of rest and worship by most Christians. [ME *sabat* < OFr. *sabbat* and OE *sabat*, both < Lat. *sabbatum* < Gk. *sabbaton* < Heb. *šabbāt* < to rest.]

ab•bat•i•cal (sə-băt′ĭ-kəl) also **sab•bat•ic** (-ĭk) *adj.* **1.** Relating to a sabbatical year. **2. Sabbatical** Relating or appropriate to the Sabbath as the day of rest. ❖ *n.* A sabbatical year. [< LLat.

sabbaticus < Gk. *sabbatikos* < *sabbaton*, Sabbath. See SABBATH.]

sabbatical year *n.* **1.** A leave of absence, often with pay, usu. granted every seventh year, as to a college professor, for travel, research, or rest. **2.** often **Sabbatical year** *Judaism* A year during which the land of ancient Israel is left fallow, observed every seven years.

Sa•bel•lic (sə-bĕl′ĭk) also **Sa•bel•li•an** (-bĕl′ē-ən) *n.* A group of extinct Italic languages that includes Oscan, Umbrian, and South Picene. [< Lat. *Sabellus*, Sabine.] —**Sa•bel′lic** *adj.*

sa•ber (sä′bər) *n.* **1.** A heavy cavalry sword with a one-edged, slightly curved blade. **2.** A light sword having an arched guard for the hand and a tapered flexible blade with a one-sided cutting edge. ❖ *tr.v.* **-bered, -ber•ing, -bers** To hit, injure, or kill with a saber. [Fr. *sabre* < obsolete Ger. *sabel* < MHGer. < Hung. *száblya* < *szabni*, to cut.]

saber rattling *n.* A display of or threat to use military power.

saber saw *n.* A portable power jigsaw used to cut straight or curved lines in wood, plastic, or soft metals.

sa•ber-toothed tiger (sä′bər-tootht′) *n.* Any of various extinct cats, esp. one of the larger members of the genus *Smilodon*, characterized by long upper canine teeth.

sa•bin (sä′bĭn) *n.* A unit of sound absorption equal to the absorption by one square foot of a surface that absorbs all incident sound. [After Wallace Clement Ware *Sabine* (1868–1919), American physicist.]

Sabin, Albert Bruce 1906–93. Amer. microbiologist who developed a live-virus vaccine against polio (1957).

Sa•bine (sä′bĭn′) *n.* **1.** A member of an ancient people of central Italy, conquered and assimilated by the Romans in 290 B.C. **2.** The Italic language of the Sabines. [ME *Sabyn* < Lat. *Sabīnus*.] —**Sa′bine′** *adj.*

Sa•bine River (sə-bēn′) A river of E TX flowing c. 925 km (575 mi) and through **Sabine Lake** to the Gulf of Mexico.

Sabin vaccine *n.* An oral poliomyelitis vaccine consisting of live attenuated polioviruses. [After Albert Bruce SABIN.]

sa•ble (sä′bəl) *n.* **1a.** A carnivorous mammal (*Martes zibellina*) of northern Europe and Asia having soft dark fur. **b.** The pelt or fur of this animal. **c.** The similar fur of other species of martens. **2a.** The color black, esp. in heraldry. **b. sables** Black garments worn in mourning. **3.** A grayish yellowish brown. **4.** A sablefish. ❖ *adj.* **1.** Of a grayish yellowish brown. **2.** Of the color black, as in heraldry or mourning. **3.** Dark; somber. **4.** Of the fur of the sable. [ME < OFr. < MLGer. *sabel* < ORuss. *sobol'*, ult. < Pers. *samōr*.]

Sable, Cape 1. A promontory of extreme S Nova Scotia, Canada, on an inlet S of **Sable Island. 2.** A cape at the SW tip of FL; the S extremity of the US mainland.

sable antelope *n.* A large African antelope (*Hippotragus niger*) having backward-curving horns and a usu. dark coat.

sa•ble•fish (sä′bəl-fĭsh′) *n., pl.* **sablefish** or **-fish•es** A dark-colored marine food fish (*Anoplopoma fimbria*) of North American Pacific waters.

sa•bot (să-bō′, săb′ō) *n.* **1.** A wooden shoe worn in some European countries. **2.** (săb′ət) A sandal or shoe having a band of leather or other material across the instep. **3.** A carrier in which a small projectile is centered so as to permit firing the projectile within a larger-caliber weapon. [Fr. < OFr. *çabot*, alteration of *savate*, old shoe, prob. of Turk. or Ar. orig.]

sab•o•tage (săb′ə-täzh′) *n.* **1.** Destruction of property or obstruction of normal operations, as by enemy agents in war. **2.** Treacherous action to defeat or hinder a cause or an endeavor; deliberate subversion. ❖ *tr.v.* **-taged, -tag•ing, -tag•es** To commit sabotage against. [Fr. < *saboter*, to walk noisily, bungle, sabotage < *sabot*, saboter, sabot. See SABOT.]

sab•o•teur (săb′ə-tûr′) *n.* One who commits sabotage. [Fr. < *saboter*, to sabotage. See SABOTAGE.]

sa•bra (sä′brə) *n.* A native-born Israeli. [NHeb. *ṣābār*, sabra, prickly pear.]

sa•bre (sä′bər) *n. & v. Chiefly British* Variant of **saber.**

sac (săk) *n.* A pouch or pouchlike structure in a plant or animal, sometimes filled with fluid. [Fr., bag < OFr. < Lat. *saccus*. See SACK¹.]

Sac (săk, sôk) *n.* Variant of **Sauk.**

SAC *abbr.* Strategic Air Command

Sac•a•ga•we•a (săk′ə-gə-wē′ə, sä-kä′gä-wē′ä) or **Sac•a•ja•we•a** (săk′ə-jə-wē′ə) 1787?–1812. Shoshone guide and interpreter who accompanied (1805–06) the Lewis and Clark expedition.

sac•a•ton (săk′ə-tōn′) *n.* A tufted perennial grass (*Sporobolus*

Albert Sabin

sabot
pair of sabots

Sacagawea

ă **pat**	oi **boy**
ā **pay**	ou **out**
âr **care**	ŏŏ **took**
ä **father**	ōō **boot**
ĕ **pet**	ŭ **cut**
ē **be**	ûr **urge**
ĭ **pit**	th **thin**
ī **pie**	th **this**
îr **pier**	hw **which**
ŏ **pot**	zh **vision**
ō **toe**	ə **about,**
ô **paw**	**item**

Stress marks:
′ (primary);
′ (secondary), as in
lexicon (lĕk′sĭ-kŏn′)

wrightii) of the southwest United States, used for pasture and hay. [Am.Sp. *zacatón* < *zacate*, coarse grass < Nahuatl *zacatl*, grass, straw.]

sac•cade (să-käd′, sə-) *n.* A rapid intermittent eye movement, as that which occurs when the eyes fix on one point after another in the visual field. [Fr., twitch < OFr. < ONFr. *saquier*, to pull < *sac*, sack. See SAC.] —**sac•cad′ic** *adj.*

sac•cate (săk′āt′) *adj.* **1.** Shaped like a pouch or sac. **2.** Having a pouch or sac. [Lat. *saccus*, bag; see SACK¹ + −ATE¹.]

sac•cha•rase (săk′ə-rās′, -rāz′) *n.* See **invertase**.

sac•cha•rate (săk′ə-rāt′) *n.* A salt or ester of saccharic acid. [SACCHAR(IC ACID) + −ATE².]

sac•char•ic acid (sə-kăr′ĭk) *n.* A white crystalline acid, COOH(CHOH)₄COOH, formed by the oxidation of glucose, sucrose, or starch.

sac•cha•ride (săk′ə-rīd′) *n.* Any of a series of carbohydrates in which the atoms of the latter two elements are in the ratio of 2:1, esp. those containing the group $C_6H_{10}O_5$.

sac•char•i•fy (sə-kăr′ə-fī′, să-) *tr.v.* -**fied**, -**fy•ing**, -**fies** To convert (starch, for example) into sugar. —**sac•char′i•fi•ca′tion** (-fĭ-kā′shən) *n.*

sac•cha•rim•e•ter (săk′ə-rĭm′ĭ-tər) *n.* A polarimeter that indicates the concentration of sugar in a solution. —**sac′cha•rim′e•try** *n.*

sac•cha•rin (săk′ər-ĭn) *n.* A white crystalline powder, C₇H₅NO₃S, having a taste about 500 times sweeter than cane sugar and used as a calorie-free sweetener.

sac•cha•rine (săk′ər-ĭn, -ə-rēn′, -ə-rīn′) *adj.* **1.** Of or characteristic of sugar or saccharin; sweet. **2.** Cloyingly sweet in attitude, tone, or character. **3.** Excessively sentimental. —**sac′cha•rine•ly** *adv.* —**sac′cha•rin′i•ty** (-ə-rĭn′ĭ-tē) *n.*

saccharo− or **sacchar−** *pref.* Sugar: *saccharide*. [< Med.Lat. *saccharum*, sugar < Lat. *saccharon* < Gk. *sakkhar* < Pali *sakkharā* < Skt. *śarkarā*.]

sac•cha•roid (săk′ə-roid′) or **sac•cha•roi•dal** (-roid′l) *adj.* Having a texture similar to that of granulated sugar. Used of rocks and minerals.

sac•cha•rom•e•ter (săk′ə-rŏm′ĭ-tər) *n.* A hydrometer that determines the amount of sugar in a solution from density measurements.

sac•cha•ro•my•ces (săk′ə-rō-mī′sēz) *n., pl.* **saccharomyces** Any of several single-celled yeasts belonging to the genus *Saccharomyces* that lack a true mycelium and many of which ferment sugar. [NLat. *Saccharomycēs*, genus name : SACCHARO− + Gk. *mukēs*, fungus.]

sac•cha•ro•my•cete (săk′ə-rō-mī′sēt′) *n.* A yeast of the family Saccharomycetaceae, including the saccharomyces. —**sac′cha•ro•my•ce′tic** (-mī-sē′tĭk), **sac′cha•ro•my•ce′tous** *adj.*

sac•cha•rose (săk′ə-rōs′) *n.* See **sucrose**.

Sac•co (săk′ō, säk′kō), **Nicola** 1891–1927. Italian-born Amer. anarchist who with Bartolomeo Vanzetti was convicted of murder and sentenced to death (1921).

sac•cu•lar (săk′yə-lər) or **sac•cu•lat•ed** (-lā′tĭd) *adj.* Formed or shaped like a sac. —**sac′cu•la′tion** (-lā′shən) *n.*

sac•cule (săk′yool) also **sac•cu•lus** (-yə-ləs) *n., pl.* **sac•cules** also **sac•cu•li** (-yə-lī′) **1.** A small sac. **2.** The smaller of two membranous sacs in the vestibule of the inner ear. [Lat. *sacculus*, dim. of *saccus*, bag. See SACK¹.]

sac•er•do•tal (săs′ər-dōt′l, săk′-) *adj.* **1.** Of or relating to priests or the priesthood; priestly. **2.** Of or relating to sacerdotalism. [ME < OFr. < Lat. *sacerdōtālis* < *sacerdōs, sacerdōt-*, priest. See **sak-** in App.] —**sac′er•do′tal•ly** *adv.*

sac•er•do•tal•ism (săs′ər-dōt′l-ĭz′əm, săk′-) *n.* The belief that priests act as mediators between God and humans.

sac fungus *n.* See **ascomycete**.

sa•chem (sā′chəm) *n.* **1a.** A chief of a Native American tribe or confederation, esp. an Algonquian chief. **b.** A member of the ruling council of the Iroquois confederacy. **2.** A high official of the Tammany Society, a political organization in New York City. [Of Massachusett orig.]

sa•cher torte (săk′ər tôrt′, zä′ĸʜər tôr′tə) *n.* A rich chocolate cake filled with apricot jam and topped with chocolate icing. [Ger. *Sachertorte* : *Sacher*, surname of a family of 19th- and 20th-cent. hoteliers + *Torte*, torte; see TORTE.]

sa•chet (să-shā′) *n.* A small packet of perfumed powder used to scent clothes, as in trunks or closets. [Fr. < OFr., dim. of *sac*, bag < Lat. *saccus*. See SACK¹.]

Sachs (zăks, săks), **Hans** 1494–1576. German writer noted for his dramas, poems, and songs.

Sachs, Nelly 1891–1970. German-born writer who shared the 1966 Nobel Prize for literature.

sack¹ (săk) *n.* **1a.** A large bag of strong coarse material for holding objects in bulk. **b.** A similar container of paper or plastic. **c.** The amount that a sack can hold. **2.** also **sacque** A short loose-fitting garment for women and children. **3.** *Slang* Dismissal from employment: *finally got the sack*. **4.** *Informal* A bed, mattress, or sleeping bag. **5.** *Baseball* A base. **6.** *Football* A successful attempt at sacking the quarterback. ❖ *tr.v.* **sacked, sack•ing, sacks 1.** To place into a sack. **2.** *Slang* To discharge from employment. **3.** *Football* To tackle (a quarterback attempting to pass the ball) behind the line of scrimmage. —**phrasal verb: sack out** *Slang* To

sleep. [ME < OE *sacc* < Lat. *saccus* < Gk. *sakkos*, of Semitic orig.; akin to Akkadian *saqqu*.] —**sack′er** *n.*

sack² (săk) *tr.v.* **sacked, sack•ing, sacks** To rob of goods or valuables, esp. after capture. ❖ *n.* **1.** The looting or pillaging of a captured city or town. **2.** Plunder; loot. [Prob. < Fr. *(mettre à) sac*, (to put in) a sack < OFr. *sac*, sack < Lat. *saccus*, sack, bag. See SACK¹.]

sack³ (săk) *n.* Any of various dry light wines from Spain and the Canary Islands, imported to England in the 16th and 17th centuries. [< Fr. *(vin) sec*, dry (wine) < OFr. < Lat. *siccus*, dry.]

sack•but (săk′bŭt′) *n.* A medieval instrument resembling the trombone. [Fr. *saquebute* < OFr. *saqueboute* : ONFr. *saquier*, to pull; see SACCADE + OFr. *bouter*, to push (of Gmc. orig.; see **bhau-** in App.).]

sack•cloth (săk′klôth′, -klŏth′) *n.* **1.** Sacking. **2a.** A rough cloth of camel's hair, goat hair, hemp, cotton, or flax. **b.** Garments made of this cloth, worn in mourning or as penance.

sack•ing (săk′ĭng) *n.* A coarse stout woven cloth, such as burlap or gunny, used for making sacks; sackcloth.

sack race *n.* A race in which the contestants compete by jumping forward with their legs enclosed in a sack.

Sack•ville (săk′vĭl′), **Thomas.** 1st Earl of Dorset and Baron Buckhurst. 1536–1608. English poet who collaborated with Thomas Norton (1532–84) on *Gorboduc* (1561).

Sack•ville-West (săk′vĭl-wĕst′), **Victoria Mary** Known as "Vita." 1892–1962. British author of *All Passion Spent* (1931).

Sa•co (sô′kō) A river rising in E-central NH and flowing c. 169 km (105 mi) SE through ME to the Atlantic Ocean.

sacr− *pref.* Variant of **sacro−**.

sa•cra (să′krə, săk′rə) *n.* Plural of **sacrum**.

sa•cral¹ (să′krəl) *adj.* Of, near, or relating to the sacrum.

sa•cral² (să′krəl) *adj.* Relating to sacred rites or observances. [< Lat. *sacer, sacr-*, sacred. See SACRED.]

sa•cral•ize (să′krə-līz′, săk′rə-) *tr.v.* -**lized**, -**liz•ing**, -**liz•es** To make sacred. —**sa′cral•i•za′tion** (-lĭ-zā′shən) *n.*

sac•ra•ment (săk′rə-mənt) *n. Christianity* **1.** A rite believed to be a means of or visible form of grace, esp.: **a.** In the Eastern, Roman Catholic, and some other Western Christian churches, any of the traditional seven rites instituted by Jesus that confer sanctifying grace. **b.** In most other Western Christian churches, the two rites, Baptism and the Eucharist, instituted by Jesus to confer sanctifying grace. **2.** often **Sacrament a.** The Eucharist. **b.** The consecrated elements of the Eucharist. [ME < OFr. *sacrement* < LLat. *sacrāmentum* < Lat., oath < *sacrāre*, to consecrate < *sacer, sacr-*, sacred. See SACRED.]

sac•ra•men•tal (săk′rə-mĕn′tl) *adj.* **1.** Of, relating to, or used in a sacrament. **2.** Consecrated or bound by or as if by a sacrament. **3.** Having the force or efficacy of a sacrament. ❖ *n.* A rite, act, or sacred object used by some Christian churches in worship. —**sac′ra•men′tal•ly** *adv.*

sac•ra•men•tal•ism (săk′rə-mĕn′tl-ĭz′əm) *n.* The doctrine that observing the sacraments is necessary for salvation and that such participation can confer grace. —**sac′ra•men′tal•ist** *n.*

Sac•ra•men•tar•i•an (săk′rə-mĕn-târ′ē-ən) *n.* One who regards the Eucharist as only the metaphorical body and blood of Jesus. —**Sac′ra•men•tar′i•an•ism** *n.*

Sac•ra•men•to (săk′rə-mĕn′tō) The cap. of CA, in the N-central part NE of Oakland. Pop. 407,018.

Sacramento Mountains A range of S-central NM extending to the TX border and rising to 3,660.9 m (12,003 ft).

Sacramento River A river of N CA rising near Mt. Shasta and flowing c. 611 km (380 mi) to San Francisco Bay.

sa•crar•i•um (sə-krâr′ē-əm, să-, sā-) *n., pl.* -**i•a** (-ē-ə) **1.** The sanctuary or sacristy of a church. **2.** Piscina. [Med.Lat. *sacrārium* < Lat., shrine < *sacer, sacr-*, sacred. See SACRED.]

sa•cred (să′krĭd) *adj.* **1.** Dedicated to or set apart for the worship of a deity. **2.** Worthy of religious veneration: *sacred teachings.* **3.** Made or declared holy: *sacred bread and wine.* **4.** Dedicated or devoted exclusively to a single use, purpose, or person. **5.** Worthy of respect; venerable. **6.** Of or relating to religious objects, rites, or practices. [ME, p. part. of *sacren*, to consecrate < OFr. *sacrer* < Lat. *sacrāre* < *sacer, sacr-*, sacred. See **sak-** in App.] —**sa′cred•ly** *adv.* —**sa′cred•ness** *n.*

sacred baboon *n.* See **hamadryas**. [< the fact that the ancient Egyptians revered it as the god Anubis.]

sacred cow *n.* One immune from criticism, often unreasonably so. [< the veneration of the cow by Hindus.]

sac•ri•fice (săk′rə-fīs′) *n.* **1a.** The act of offering something to a deity in propitiation or homage, esp. the ritual slaughter of an animal or a person. **b.** A victim offered in this way. **2a.** Forfeiture of something highly valued for the sake of one considered to have a greater value or claim. **b.** Something so forfeited. **3a.** Relinquishment of something at less than its presumed value. **b.** Something so relinquished. **c.** A loss so sustained. **4.** *Baseball* A sacrifice bunt or sacrifice fly. ❖ *v.* -**ficed**, -**fic•ing**, -**fic•es** —*tr.* **1.** To offer as a sacrifice to a deity. **2.** To forfeit (one thing) for another thing considered to be of greater value. **3.** To sell or give away at a loss. —*intr.* **1.** To make or offer a sacrifice. **2.** *Baseball* To make a sacrifice bunt or sacrifice fly. [ME < OFr. < Lat. *sacrificium* : *sacer*, sacred; see SACRED + *facere*, to make; see **dhē-** in App.] —**sac′ri•fic′er** *n.*

sacrifice bunt *n. Baseball* A bunt that allows a runner to advance a base while the batter is retired.

sacrifice fly *n. Baseball* A fly ball enabling a runner to score after it is caught by a fielder.

sac·ri·fi·cial (săk′rə-fĭsh′əl) *adj.* **1.** Of, relating to, or concerned with a sacrifice. **2.** Of or being an anode of a metal that is electrolytically decomposed while inhibiting the corrosion of another metal. —**sac′ri·fi′cial·ly** *adv.*

sac·ri·lege (săk′rə-lĭj) *n.* Desecration, profanation, misuse, or theft of something sacred. [ME < OFr. < Lat. *sacrilegium* < *sacrilegus*, one who steals sacred things : *sacer*, sacred; see SACRED + *legere*, to gather; see **leg-** in App.] —**sac′ri·le′gist** (săk′rə-lē′jĭst) *n.*

sac·ri·le·gious (săk′rə-lĭj′əs, -lē′jəs) *adj.* **1.** Grossly irreverent toward the sacred. **2.** Having committed sacrilege. —**sac′ri·le′gious·ly** *adv.* —**sac′ri·le′gious·ness** *n.*

sac·ris·tan (săk′rĭ-stən) *n.* **1.** One in charge of a sacristy. **2.** A sexton. [ME < Med.Lat. *sacristānus* < *sacrista* < Lat. *sacer*, sacred. See SACRED.]

sac·ris·ty (săk′rĭ-stē) *n., pl.* **-ties** A room in a church housing the sacred vessels and vestments; a vestry. [ME < AN < Med.Lat. *sacristia* < *sacrista*, sacristan. See SACRISTAN.]

sacro- or **sacr-** *pref.* Sacrum: sacroiliac.

sac·ro·il·i·ac (săk′rō-ĭl′ē-ăk′, să′krō-) *adj.* Of, relating to, or affecting the sacrum and ilium and their articulation or associated ligaments. ❖ *n.* The sacroiliac region or cartilage.

sac·ro·sanct (săk′rō-săngkt′) *adj.* Regarded as sacred and inviolable. [Lat. *sacrōsānctus*, consecrated with religious ceremonies : *sacrō*, ablative of *sacrum*, religious rite (< neut. of *sacer*, sacred; see SACRED) + *sānctus*, p. part. of *sancīre*, to consecrate; see **sak-** in App.] —**sac′ro·sanc′ti·ty** (-săngk′tĭ-tē) *n.*

sa·crum (să′krəm, săk′rəm) *n., pl.* **sa·cra** (să′krə, săk′rə) A triangular bone made up of five fused vertebrae and forming the posterior section of the pelvis. [NLat. < LLat. *(os) sacrum*, neut. of Lat. *sacer*, sacred (transl. of Gk. *hieron osteon*, sacred bone). See SACRED.]

sad (săd) *adj.* **sad·der, sad·dest** **1.** Affected or characterized by sorrow or unhappiness. **2.** Expressive of sorrow or unhappiness. **3.** Causing sorrow or gloom; depressing: *sad news.* **4.** Deplorable; sorry: *a sad excuse.* **5.** Dark-hued; somber. [ME, weary, sorrowful < OE *sæd*, sated, weary.] —**sad′ly** *adv.* —**sad′ness** *n.*

SYNONYMS sad, melancholy, sorrowful, doleful, woebegone These adjectives mean affected with or marked by unhappiness, as that caused by affliction. *Sad* is the most general: *"Better by far you should forget and smile/Than that you should remember and be sad"* (Christina Rossetti). *Melancholy* can refer to lingering or habitual somberness or sadness: *a melancholy poet. Sorrowful* applies to emotional pain as that resulting from loss: *sorrowful mourners at the funeral. Doleful* describes what is mournful or morose: *the doleful expression of a reprimanded child. Woebegone* suggests grief or wretchedness, especially as reflected in a person's appearance: *"His sorrow . . . made him look . . . haggard and . . . woebegone"* (George du Maurier).

Sa·dat (sə-dăt′, -dät′), **Anwar el-** 1918–81. Egyptian president (1970–81) who shared the 1978 Nobel Peace Prize.

sad·den (săd′n) *tr. & intr.v.* **-dened, -den·ing, -dens** To make or become sad.

sad·dle (săd′l) *n.* **1a.** A leather seat for a rider, secured on an animal's back by a girth. **b.** Similar tack used for attaching a pack to an animal. **c.** The padded part of a driving harness fitting over a horse's back. **d.** The seat of a bicycle, motorcycle, or similar vehicle. **e.** Something shaped like a saddle. **2a.** A cut of meat consisting of part of the backbone and both loins. **b.** The lower part of a male fowl's back. **3a.** A saddle-shaped depression in the ridge of a hill. **b.** A ridge between two peaks. ❖ *v.* **-dled, -dling, -dles** —*tr.* **1.** To put a saddle onto. **2.** To load or burden; encumber. —*intr.* **1.** To saddle a horse. **2.** To get into a saddle. —*idiom:* **in the saddle** In control; dominant. [ME *sadel* < OE *sadol*. See **sed-** in App.]

sad·dle·back (săd′l-băk′) *n.* Any of various birds, fishes, and other animals having saddle-shaped markings on the back.

sad·dle·bag (săd′l-băg′) *n.* **1.** One of a pair of pouches hanging across the back of a horse. **2.** A pouch hanging from a saddle or over the rear wheel of a motorcycle or bicycle.

sad·dle·bow (săd′l-bō′) *n.* The arched upper front part of a saddle.

sad·dle·cloth (săd′l-klôth′, -klŏth′) *n.* A cloth placed under the saddle of a racehorse and bearing its number.

saddle horse *n.* A horse bred or schooled for riding.

sad·dler (săd′lər) *n.* One that makes, repairs, or sells equipment for horses.

saddle roof *n.* A roof having a ridge and two gables.

sad·dler·y (săd′lə-rē) *n., pl.* **-ies** **1.** Equipment, such as saddles and harnesses, for horses. **2.** A shop that sells tack. **3.** The craft or business of one that makes or sells tack.

saddle shoe *n.* A flat casual shoe, usu. white, having a band of leather in a contrasting color across the instep.

saddle soap *n.* A preparation containing mild soap and neat's-

foot oil, used for cleaning and softening leather.

saddle sore *n.* **1.** A sore on a horse caused by an improperly fitted saddle. **2.** A sore on a rider caused by a chafing saddle.

saddle stitch *n.* **1.** A simple overcasting stitch, usu. of a contrasting thread. **2.** A stitch used in sewing together the leaves of a book.

sad·dle·tree (săd′l-trē′) *n.* The frame of a saddle.

Sad·du·cee (săj′ə-sē′, săd′yə-) *n.* A member of a priestly Jewish sect founded in the second century B.C. that accepted only the written Mosaic law and ceased to exist after the Temple's destruction in A.D. 70. [ME *Saducee* < OE *Sadducēas*, Sadducees < LLat. *Saddūcaeī* < Gk. *Saddoukaioi* < Mishnaic Heb. *ṣədûqî*, after *ṣādôq*, Zadok, high priest in the time of David and Solomon < *ṣādôq*, just, righteous < *ṣādaq*, to be just.] —**Sad′du·ce′an** (-sē′ən) *adj.* —**Sad′du·cee′ism** *n.*

Sade (säd, säd), **Comte Donatien Alphonse François de** Known as "Marquis de Sade." 1740–1814. French writer of works characterized by a preoccupation with sexual violence.

sa·dhe (să′də, tsä′-, -dē) also **tsa·de** (tsä′də, -dē) *n.* The 18th letter of the Hebrew alphabet. [Heb. *ṣādē, ṣādê*, of Phoenician orig.]

sa·dhu (să′dōō) *n. Hinduism* An ascetic holy man thought to have special powers. [< Skt. *sādhu-*, right, holy.]

sa·dism (să′dĭz′əm, săd′ĭz′-) *n.* **1a.** The deriving of sexual gratification from inflicting pain or emotional abuse on others. **b.** A psychological disorder in which sexual gratification is derived from inflicting pain on others. **2.** The deriving of pleasure from cruelty. **3.** Extreme cruelty. [After the Comte de SADE.] —**sa′dist** *n.* —**sa·dis′tic** (sə-dĭs′tĭk) *adj.* —**sa·dis′ti·cal·ly** *adv.*

sa·do·mas·o·chism (să′dō-măs′ə-kĭz′əm, săd′ō-) *n.* The combination of sadism and masochism, esp. the deriving of sexual gratification from inflicting or submitting to physical or emotional abuse. —**sa′do·mas′o·chist** *n.* —**sa′do·mas′o·chis′tic** *adj.*

sad sack *n. Informal* An extremely inept or clumsy person. [After a cartoon character created in 1942 by George Baker (1915–75).]

Sa·far also **Sa·phar** (sə-fär′) *n.* The second month of the year in the Islamic calendar. See table at **calendar.** [Ar. *ṣafar*, prob. < *ṣafira*, to be empty.]

sa·fa·ri (sə-fär′ē) *n., pl.* **-ris** **1.** An overland expedition, esp. one for hunting or exploring in eastern Africa. **2.** A journey or trip. [Ar. *safarīya*, journey < *safar*, departure, journey.]

safari jacket *n.* A belted shirt jacket with large patch pockets.

safe (sāf) *adj.* **saf·er, saf·est** **1.** Secure from danger, harm, or evil. **2.** Free from danger or injury; unhurt. **3.** Free from risk; sure: *a safe bet.* **4.** Affording protection: *a safe place.* **5.** *Baseball* Having reached a base without being put out. ❖ *n.* **1.** A metal container usu. having a lock, used for storing valuables. **2.** A repository for protecting stored items. **3.** *Slang* A condom. [ME *sauf* < OFr. < Lat. *salvus*, healthy. See **sol-** in App.] —**safe′ly** *adv.* —**safe′ness** *n.*

safe-con·duct (sāf′kŏn′dŭkt) *n.* **1.** An official document or an escort assuring unmolested passage, as through enemy territory. **2.** The protection afforded by such a document.

safe·crack·er (sāf′krăk′ər) *n.* One who breaks into safes in order to steal items from them. —**safe′crack′ing** *n.*

safe-de·pos·it box (sāf′dĭ-pŏz′ĭt) *n.* A fireproof metal box, usu. in a bank vault, for the secure storage of valuables.

safe·guard (sāf′gärd′) *n.* **1a.** One that serves as protection or a guard. **b.** A mechanical device designed to prevent accidents. **c.** A safe-conduct. **2a.** A protective stipulation, as in a contract. **b.** A precautionary measure. ❖ *tr.v.* **-guard·ed, -guard·ing, -guards** To ensure the safety of; protect. See Syns at **defend.**

safe house *n.* A house or apartment used as a secure refuge by the members of an organization.

safe·keep·ing (sāf′kē′pĭng) *n.* The act of keeping safe or the state of being kept safe; protection.

safe·light (sāf′līt′) *n.* A lamp allowing moderate darkroom illumination without affecting photosensitive film or paper.

safe sex *n.* Sexual activity in which safeguards, such as the use of a condom, are taken to reduce the chance of acquiring or spreading a sexually transmitted disease. —**safe′-sex′** (sāf′sĕks′) *adj.*

safe·ty (sāf′tē) *n., pl.* **-ties** **1.** The condition of being safe; freedom from danger, risk, or injury. **2.** A device designed to prevent accidents, as a lock on a firearm. **3.** *Football* **a.** A play in which a member of the team on offense downs the ball behind his own goal line, resulting in two points for the team on defense. **b.** One of two defensive backs.

safety belt *n.* **1.** A strap or belt worn as a safety precaution by a person working at great heights. **2.** See **seat belt.**

safety glass *n.* **1.** Glass that resists shattering, esp. a composite of two sheets of glass with an intermediate layer of transparent plastic. **2.** See **wire glass.** **3.** Tempered glass that breaks into rounded grains instead of jagged shards.

safety island *n.* An area marked off within a roadway from which traffic is banned, esp. to provide pedestrian safety.

safety lamp *n.* A miner's lamp with a protective wire gauze surrounding the flame to prevent ignition of flammable gases.

safety match *n.* A match that can be lighted only by being struck against a chemically prepared friction surface.

safety net *n.* **1.** A large net for catching one that falls or jumps,

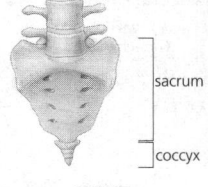

sacrum

Anwar el-Sadat
photographed in 1980

ă	pat	oi	boy
ā	pay	ou	out
âr	care	ŏŏ	took
ä	father	ōō	boot
ĕ	pet	ŭ	cut
ē	be	ûr	urge
ĭ	pit	th	thin
ī	pie	th	this
îr	pier	hw	which
ŏ	pot	zh	vision
ō	toe	ə	about,
ô	paw		item

Stress marks:
′ (primary);
′ (secondary), as in
lexicon (lĕk′sĭ-kŏn′)

as from a tightrope. **2.** A guarantee, as of physical security.

safety pin *n.* **1.** A pin in the form of a clasp, having a sheath to cover and hold the point. **2.** A pin that prevents the premature or accidental detonation of an explosive device.

safety razor *n.* See **razor** 2.

safety valve *n.* **1.** A valve in a pressure container, as in a steam boiler, that automatically opens when pressure reaches a dangerous level. **2.** An outlet for repressed energy or emotion.

saf•flow•er (săf′lou′ər) *n.* **1.** A thistlelike Eurasian plant *(Carthamus tinctorius)* of the composite family, having heads of orange flowers that yield a dyestuff and produce seeds containing an oil used in cooking, cosmetics, paints, and medicine. **2.** The dried flowers of this plant. [ME *saflour* < OFr. *safleur* < OItal. *saffiore* < Ar. *ʾaṣfar,* yellow, a yellow plant.]

safflower
Carthamus tinctorius

saf•fron (săf′rən) *n.* **1a.** A corm-producing plant *(Crocus sativus)* native to the Old World and having purple or white flowers with orange stigmas. **b.** The dried aromatic stigmas of this plant, used in cooking and dyeing. **2.** A moderate or strong orange yellow to moderate orange. [ME *safroun* < OFr. *safran* < Med.Lat. *safrānum* < Ar. *zaʿfarān.*]

Sa•fi (săf′ē) A city of W Morocco on the Atlantic Ocean WNW of Marrakesh; a former Portuguese naval base. Pop. 278,000.

S.Afr. *abbr.* South Africa

saf•ra•nine (săf′rə-nēn′, -nĭn) also **saf•ra•nin** (-nĭn) *n.* Any of a family of dyes based on phenazine, used in the textile industry and as a biological stain. [Fr. *safran,* saffron (< OFr.; see SAFFRON) + –INE[2].]

saf•role (săf′rōl′) *n.* An oily liquid, $C_{10}H_{10}O_2$, derived chiefly from oil of camphor and used in making perfume and soap. [Fr. *safran,* saffron; see SAFFRON + –OLE.]

sag (săg) *v.* **sagged, sag•ging, sags** —*intr.* **1.** To sink, droop, or settle from pressure or weight. **2.** To lose vigor, firmness, or resilience. **3.** To decline, as in value or price: *Stock prices sagged.* **4.** *Nautical* To drift to leeward. —*tr.* To cause to sag. ❖ *n.* **1a.** The act or an instance of sagging. **b.** The degree or extent to which something sags. **2.** A sagging area; a depression. **3.** A temporary decline in monetary value. **4.** *Nautical* A drift to leeward. [ME *saggen,* prob. of Scand. orig.; akin to Swed. *sacka,* to sink.] —**sag′gy** *adj.*

sagittate
sagittate leaf

sa•ga (sä′gə) *n.* **1a.** An Icelandic prose narrative of the 12th and 13th centuries, dealing with the families that settled Iceland, the kings of Norway, and Germanic gods and heroes. **b.** A modern prose narrative that resembles a saga. **2.** A long detailed report. [ON. See **sek**^{w}**-**[3] in App.]

sa•ga•cious (sə-gā′shəs) *adj.* Having or showing keen discernment, sound judgment, and farsightedness. [< Lat. *sagāx, sagāc-,* of keen perception.] —**sa•ga′cious•ly** *adv.* —**sa•ga′cious•ness** *n.*

sa•gac•i•ty (sə-găs′ĭ-tē) *n.* The quality of being discerning, sound in judgment, and farsighted; wisdom. [Fr. *sagacité* < OFr. *sagacite* < Lat. *sagācitās,* quickness of perception < *sagāx, sagāc-,* of keen perception. See SAGACIOUS.]

sag•a•more (săg′ə-môr′, -mōr′) *n.* A subordinate chief among the Algonquians. [Eastern Abenaki *sɑ̀kəmɑ.*]

Sa•gan (sā′gən), **Carl** 1934–96. Amer. astronomer noted for his research on the possibility of extraterrestrial life.

Sa•gan (sä-gäɴ′), **Françoise** Pen name Françoise Quoirez. b. 1935. French writer best known for *Bonjour Tristesse* (1954).

saga novel *n.* See **roman-fleuve.**

saguaro
Carnegiea gigantea

sage[1] (sāj) *n.* One venerated for experience, judgment, and wisdom. ❖ *adj.* **sag•er, sag•est 1.** Having or exhibiting wisdom and calm judgment. **2.** Proceeding from or marked by wisdom and calm judgment: *sage advice.* **3.** *Archaic* Serious; solemn. [ME < OFr. < VLat. **sapius* < Lat. *sapere,* to be wise.] —**sage′ly** *adv.* —**sage′ness** *n.*

sage[2] (sāj) *n.* **1a.** Any of various plants of the genus *Salvia,* esp. *S. officinalis,* having aromatic grayish-green leaves used in cooking. **b.** The leaves of this plant. **2.** Any of various similar plants in the mint family. **3.** Sagebrush. [ME *sauge* < OFr. < Lat. *salvia* < *salvus,* healthy. See **sol-** in App.]

sage•brush (sāj′brŭsh′) *n.* Any of several aromatic plants of the genus *Artemisia,* esp. *A. tridentata,* a shrub of arid regions of western North America having silver-green leaves and large clusters of small white flower heads.

sage grouse *n.* A chickenlike bird *(Centrocercus urophasianus)* of western North America having long pointed tail feathers that can be spread like a fan.

sage sparrow *n.* A small brownish-gray sparrow *(Amphispiza belli)* of dry regions of the southwest United States.

sage thrasher *n.* A light grayish-brown thrasher *(Oreoscoptes montanus)* that nests in low sage and cactus bushes in dry or desert regions of the western United States.

sag•ger also **sag•gar** (săg′ər) *n.* **1.** A protective casing of fire clay in which delicate ceramic articles are fired. **2.** Clay used to make ceramic casings. [Perh. alteration of SAFEGUARD.]

saiga
Saiga tatarica

Sa•gi•naw (săg′ə-nô′) A city of E-central MI on the **Saginaw River,** flowing c. 32 km (20 mi) into **Saginaw Bay,** a large inlet of Lake Huron. Pop. 61,799.

Sa•git•ta (sə-jĭt′ə) *n.* A constellation in the Northern Hemisphere near Aquila and Vulpecula. [Lat., *sagitta,* arrow.]

sag•it•tal (săj′ĭ-tl) *adj.* **1.** Of or relating to the suture uniting the two parietal bones of the skull. **2.** Of or relating to the sagittal plane. [NLat. *sagittālis* < Lat. *sagitta,* arrow.] —**sag′it•tal•ly** *adv.*

sagittal plane *n.* A plane that divides the body of a bilaterally symmetrical animal into right and left sections.

Sag•it•tar•i•us (săj′ĭ-târ′ē-əs) *n.* **1.** A constellation in the Southern Hemisphere near Scorpius and Capricorn. **2a.** The ninth sign of the zodiac in astrology. **b.** One born under this sign. [ME < Lat. *Sagittārius* < *sagittārius,* archer < *sagitta,* arrow.]

sag•it•tate (săj′ĭ-tāt′) *adj. Biology* Having the shape of an arrowhead: *sagittate leaves.* [Lat. *sagitta,* arrow + –ATE[1].]

sa•go (sā′gō) *n., pl.* **-gos** A starch obtained from certain sago palms and used as a food thickener and textile stiffener. [Malay *sagu,* mealy pith.]

sago palm *n.* **1.** Any of various palms of the genera *Metroxylon, Arenga,* and *Caryota* of tropical Asia. **2.** Either of two palmlike cycads *(Cycas circinalis* or *C. revoluta)* of eastern and tropical Asia.

sa•gua•ro (sə-gwär′ō, -wär′ō) also **sa•hua•ro** (sə-wär′ō) *n., pl.* **-ros 1.** A large cactus *(Carnegiea gigantea)* of the southwest United States and northern Mexico having upward-curving branches, white flowers, and edible red fruit. **2.** The fruit of this cactus. [Am.Sp., prob. of Piman orig.]

Sag•ue•nay (săg′ə-nā′) A river of S Quebec, Canada, flowing c. 201 km (125 mi) to the St. Lawrence R.

Sa•gun•to (sə-go͞on′tō, sä-) A city of E Spain NNE of Valencia. Its capture by Carthaginian forces (219–218 B.C.) precipitated the Second Punic War. Pop. 57,380.

Sa•hap•ti•an (sä-hăp′tē-ən) *n.* **1.** A North American Indian language family of Washington, Oregon, and Idaho comprising the Sahaptin and Nez Perce languages. **2.** A member of a Sahaptian-speaking people. —**Sa•hap′ti•an** *adj.*

Sa•hap•tin (sä-hăp′tĭn) *n., pl.* **Sahaptin** or **-tins 1.** A member of any of various Native American peoples of Idaho, Washington, and Oregon. **2.** The dialectally diverse Sahaptian language of the Sahaptin. [Southern Interior Salish *s′aptnx.*]

Sa•har•a (sə-hâr′ə, -hăr′ə, -hä′rə) A vast desert of N Africa extending E from the Atlantic coast to the Nile Valley and S from the Atlas Mts. to the Sudan. —**Sa•har′an** *adj. & n.*

Sa•hel (sə-hāl′, -hēl′) A semiarid region of N-central Africa S of the Sahara Desert. —**Sa•hel′i•an** *adj.*

sa•hib (sä′ĭb, -ēb, -hĭb) *n.* Used formerly as a form of respectful address for a European man in colonial India. [Hindi *sāhab,* master < Ar. *ṣāḥib,* companion, master, part. of *ṣaḥiba,* to become friends.]

said (sĕd) *v.* Past tense and past participle of **say.** ❖ *adj. Law* Aforementioned: *Said party has denied the charges.*

USAGE NOTE The adjective *said* is primarily used in legal and business writing, where it is equivalent to *aforesaid: the said tenant* (named in a lease); *said property.* Outside of these specialized contexts *said* is usually unnecessary, and *the tenant* or *the property* will suffice.

sai•ga (sī′gə) *n.* A medium-sized goat antelope *(Saiga tatarica)* of the plains of northern Eurasia having a stubby snout. [Russ. *saĭga,* of Turkic orig.]

Sai•gon (sī-gŏn′) See **Ho Chi Minh City.**

sail (sāl) *n.* **1.** *Nautical* **a.** A piece of sewn fabric fitted to the spars and rigging of a vessel so as to convert the force of the wind into forward motion of the vessel. **b.** The sails of a ship or boat. **c.** The superstructure of a submarine. **2.** *pl.* **sail** or **sails** *Nautical* A sailing vessel. **3.** *Nautical* A trip or voyage in a sailing craft. **4.** Something, such as the blade of a windmill, that resembles a sail in form or function. ❖ *v.* **sailed, sail•ing, sails** —*intr.* **1.** *Nautical* **a.** To move across the surface of water, esp. by means of a sailing vessel. **b.** To travel by water in a vessel. **c.** To start out on such a voyage or journey. **d.** To operate a sailing craft, esp. for sport. **2.** To move along or progress smoothly or effortlessly: *sailed through the exam.* —*tr. Nautical* **1.** To navigate or manage (a vessel). **2.** To voyage upon or across. ***—phrasal verb:*** **sail into** To attack or criticize vigorously. [ME *seil* < OE *segl. Sail into* < obsolete *sail,* attack < ME *sailen,* short for *assailen.* See ASSAIL.]

sail•board (sāl′bôrd′, -bōrd′) *n.* A modified surfboard having a single sail mounted on a mast that pivots on a ball joint, ridden while standing up. ❖ *intr.v.* **-board•ed, -board•ing, -boards** To sail a sailboard. —**sail′board′er** *n.*

sail•boat (sāl′bōt′) *n.* A small boat propelled by sail.

sail•cloth (sāl′klôth′, -klŏth′) *n.* **1.** A strong cotton or synthetic fabric suitable for making sails or tents. **2.** A lightweight cotton canvas used esp. for clothing and upholstery.

sail•fish (sāl′fĭsh′) *n., pl.* **sailfish** or **-fish•es** Any of various large marine fishes of the genus *Istiophorus,* having a large saillike dorsal fin and a spearlike upper jaw.

sail•ing (sā′lĭng) *n.* **1.** The skill required to operate and navigate a vessel. **2.** The sport of operating or riding in a sailboat. **3.** Departure or time of departure from a port.

sail•or (sā′lər) *n.* **1.** One who serves in a navy or works on a ship. **2.** One who travels by water. **3.** A low-crowned straw hat with a flat top and flat brim.

sail•or's-choice (sā′lərz-chois′) *n., pl.* **sailor's-choice** Any of various fishes of the North American Atlantic coast, such as the pinfish or the grunt *Haemulon parrai* of southerly waters.

sail•plane (sāl′plān′) *n.* A light glider used esp. for soaring. ❖ *intr.v.* **-planed, -plan•ing, -planes** To fly a sailplane. **—sail′-plan′er** *n.*

Sai•maa (sī′mä′), **Lake** A lake of SE Finland; largest of the **Saimaa Lakes** in the S-central and SE part of the country.

sain•foin (sān′foin′, sän′-) *n.* A Eurasian plant (*Onobrychis viciifolia*) having pinnately compound leaves and pink or white flowers, often grown as a forage crop. [Fr. < OFr. < Med.Lat. *sānum faenum* : Lat. *sānum*, neut. of *sānus*, healthy + Lat. *faenum*, hay.]

saint (sānt) *n.* **1a.** *Christianity* A person officially recognized as being entitled to public veneration and capable of interceding for people on earth. **b.** A person who has died and gone to heaven. **c.** **Saint** A member of any of various religious groups, esp. a Latter-Day Saint. **2.** *Islam & Judaism* An extraordinarily righteous person enjoying a special relationship with God. **3.** An extremely virtuous person. ❖ *tr.v.* **saint•ed, saint•ing, saints** To name, recognize, or venerate as a saint; canonize. [ME *seint* < OFr. *saint* < LLat. *sānctus* < Lat., holy, p. part. of *sancīre*, to consecrate. See **sak-** in App.]

Saint Ag•nes′ Eve (ăg′nĭs, -nĭ-sĭz) *n.* January 20th, on which young women are said to dream of their future husbands.

Saint Al•bans (ôl′bənz) A municipal borough of SE England NNW of London; founded 793. Pop. 127,657.

Saint Andrew′s cross *n.* **1.** A cross shaped like the letter X. **2.** A shrubby New World plant (*Hypericum hypericoides*) having four-petaled yellow flowers.

Saint Anthony′s cross *n.* See **tau cross.**

Saint Anthony′s fire *n.* See **erysipelas.** [< the belief that Saint Anthony′s intercession could cure it.]

Saint Au•gus•tine (ô′gə-stēn′) A city of NE FL on the Atlantic Ocean SSE of Jacksonville; founded 1565 and the oldest permanent European settlement in the US. Pop. 11,592.

Saint-Bar•thél•e•my (săn-bär-tāl-mē′) or **Saint Bar•thol•o•mew** (sănt bär-thŏl′ə-myōō′) Familiarly **Saint Barts** (bärts) An island of the French overseas department of Guadeloupe in the Leeward Is. NNW of the island of Guadeloupe.

Saint Ber•nard (sānt bər-närd′) *n.* Any of a breed of large strong dogs having a thick brown and white coat. [After the hospice at *St. Bernard* in the Swiss Alps.]

Saint Cath•a•rines (kăth′ə-rĭnz′, kăth′rĭnz) A city of SE Ontario, Canada, on the Welland Ship Canal ESE of Hamilton; founded 1790. Pop. 130,926.

Saint Charles A city of E MO on the Missouri R. NW of St. Louis; settled by French traders in 1769. Pop. 60,321.

Saint Chris•to•pher-Ne•vis (krĭs′tə-fər-nē′vĭs, -nĕv′ĭs) See **Saint Kitts and Nevis.**

Saint Clair, Lake A lake between SW Ontario, Canada, and SE MI connected with Lake Huron by the **Saint Clair River,** c. 64 km (40 mi).

Saint Croix (kroi) An island of the US Virgin Is. in the West Indies E of Puerto Rico; sold to the US by Denmark in 1917.

Saint Croix River **1.** A river rising in NW WI and flowing c. 264 km (164 mi) to the Mississippi R. SE of St. Paul MN. **2.** A river, c. 121 km (75 mi), forming part of the boundary between E ME and SW New Brunswick, Canada.

Saint Den•is (dĕn′ĭs), **Ruth** 1878–1968. Amer. choreographer who cofounded (1915) the Denishawn Dance School.

Saint-De•nis (săn-də-nē′) **1.** A city of N-central France, a suburb of Paris. Pop. 121,974. **2.** The cap. of Réunion, a port on the Indian Ocean. Pop. 121,999.

saint•dom (sānt′dəm) *n.* The condition or quality of being a saint.

Sainte-Beuve (săNt-bœv′), **Charles Augustin** 1804–69. French literary critic and historian.

saint•ed (sān′tĭd) *adj.* **1.** Having been canonized. **2.** Of saintly character; holy.

Saint E•li•as (sānt ĭ-lī′əs), **Mount** A peak, 5,492.4 m (18,008 ft), in the **Saint Elias Mountains,** a section of the Coast Ranges on the border between E AK and SW Yukon Terr., Canada.

Saint El•mo′s fire (ĕl′mōz) *n.* A visible electric discharge on a pointed object, such as the mast of a ship or the wing of an airplane, during an electrical storm. [After *St. Elmo*, 4th-cent. A.D. patron saint of sailors.]

Saint-É•tienne (săN-tā-tyĕn′) A city of SE-central France SW of Lyons. Pop. 199,528.

Saint Eu•sta•ti•us (sānt yōō-stā′shəs, -shē-əs) An island of the Netherlands Antilles in the Leeward Is. of the West Indies NW of St. Kitts; under Dutch control after 1632.

Saint-Ex•u•pé•ry (săN-tĕg-zōō-pā-rē′, -zü-), **Antoine de** 1900–44. French writer and aviator best known for his fairy tale *The Little Prince* (1943).

Saint Francis River A river rising in SE MO and flowing c. 756 km (470 mi) to the Mississippi R. in E AR.

Saint-Gau•dens (sānt-gôd′nz), **Augustus** 1848–1907. Irish-born Amer. sculptor noted for his heroic monuments.

Saint George′s (sānt jôr′jəz) The cap. of Grenada, on the SW coast of the island in the West Indies. Pop. 7,500.

Saint George′s Channel A strait between W Wales and SE Ireland connecting the Atlantic Ocean with the Irish Sea.

Saint Gott•hard (gŏt′ərd) A range of the Lepontine Alps in S-

central Switzerland; crossed by **Saint Gotthard Pass,** 2,115.2 m (6,935 ft) high.

Saint He•le•na (hə-lē′nə) A volcanic island in the S Atlantic Ocean W of Angola. With the islands of Ascension and Tristan da Cunha, it forms the British dependency of **Saint Helena.** Cap. Jamestown. Pop. 7,000.

Saint Hel•ens (hĕl′ənz) A borough of NW England ENE of Liverpool. Pop. 180,216.

Saint Helens, Mount A volcanic peak of the Cascade Range in SW WA. Before its violent eruption on May 18, 1980, it was 2,949.7 m (9,671 ft).

saint•hood (sānt′hŏŏd′) *n.* **1.** The status, character, or condition of being a saint. **2.** Saints considered as a group.

Saint John[1] An island of the US Virgin Is. E of Puerto Rico; sold to the US by Denmark in 1917.

Saint John[2] A city of S New Brunswick, Canada, at the mouth of the St. John R. on the Bay of Fundy; settled by the French in the 1630s. Pop. 72,494.

Saint John, Henry First Viscount Bolingbroke. 1678–1751. English public official who wrote *The Idea of a Patriot King* (1749).

Saint John (sānt jŏn′) or **Saint Jean** or **Saint-Jean** (săn zhän′), **Lake** A lake of S-central Quebec, Canada, connected with the Saguenay R. with the St. Lawrence R.

Saint John River (sānt) A river rising in N ME and flowing c. 673 km (418 mi) to the Bay of Fundy.

Saint John′s (jŏnz) **1.** also **Saint Johns** The cap. of Antigua and Barbuda, on the N coast of Antigua in the Leeward Is. of the West Indies. Pop. 24,359. **2.** The cap. of Newfoundland, Canada, on the SE coast of the island; first colonized by the English in 1583. Pop. 101,936.

Saint Johns River A river of NE FL flowing c. 459 km (285 mi) to the Atlantic Ocean.

Saint John′s wort also **Saint Johns•wort** (jŏnz′wûrt′, -wôrt′) *n.* Any of various herbs or shrubs of the genus *Hypericum,* having yellow flowers with five petals and numerous stamens. [< its being gathered on St. John′s Eve to ward off evil.]

Saint Joseph A city of NW MO on the Missouri R. NNW of Kansas City. Pop. 73,990.

Saint Joseph River A river of SW MI and NW IN flowing c. 338 km (210 mi) to Lake Michigan.

Saint Kitts and Ne•vis (kĭts; nē′vĭs, nĕv′ĭs) also **Saint Chris•to•pher-Ne•vis** (krĭs′tə-fər-nē′vĭs, -nĕv′ĭs) An island country in the Leeward Is. of the West Indies ESE of Puerto Rico comprising **Saint Christopher,** the largest island of the group, and the islands of Nevis and Sombrero; became independent from Great Britain in 1983. Cap. Basseterre. Pop. 41,000.

Saint Lau•rent or **Saint-Lau•rent** (sānt′ lô-rĕnt′, săn lô-rän′) A city of S Quebec, Canada, a suburb of Montreal. Pop. 74,240.

Saint Lau•rent (săn lô-rän′), **Louis Stephen** 1882–1973. Canadian politician who served as prime minister (1948–57).

Saint Lawrence (sānt), **Gulf of** An arm of the NW Atlantic Ocean off SE Canada bordered by New Brunswick, Nova Scotia, Newfoundland, and Quebec.

Saint Lawrence River A river of SE Canada flowing c. 1,207 km (750 mi) from Lake Ontario along the Ontario–NY border and through S Quebec to the Gulf of St. Lawrence.

Saint Lawrence Seaway A waterway, c. 3,781 km (2,350 mi), consisting of a system of canals, dams, and locks in the St. Lawrence R. and connecting channels through the Great Lakes; opened to navigation in 1959.

Saint Lé•o•nard or **Saint-Lé•o•nard** (sānt′ lĕn′ərd, săn lā-ō-när′) A city of S Quebec, Canada, a suburb of Montreal. Pop. 71,327.

Saint Lou•is (sānt lōō′ĭs) An independent city of E MO on the Mississippi R. just S of its confluence with the Missouri R.; settled by the French in 1763–64. Pop. 348,189.

Saint Louis encephalitis *n.* A viral encephalitis occurring in parts of North America and transmitted by a culex mosquito. [After ST. LOUIS, MO.]

Saint Lu•cia (lōō′shə, lōō-sē′ə) An island country of the West Indies S of Martinique; achieved independence from Great Britain in 1979. Cap. Castries. Pop. 141,000.

saint•ly (sānt′lē) *adj.* **-li•er, -li•est** Of, relating to, resembling, or befitting a saint. **—saint′li•ness** *n.*

Saint-Ma•lo (săn-mə-lō′) A town of NW France NNW of Nantes. Pop. 46,347.

Saint Mar•tin or **Saint Maar•ten** (sānt mär′tn) An island of the West Indies in the W Leeward Is.; administered jointly by Guadeloupe and the Netherlands Antilles.

Saint Mar•ys River (mâr′ēz) A river, c. 101 km (63 mi), rising in the E Upper Peninsula of MI and flowing to the N end of Lake Huron along part of the US-Canadian border.

Saint Mau•rice or **Saint-Mau•rice** (sānt′ môr′ĭs, -môr′, săn mô-rēs′) A river of S Quebec, Canada, flowing c. 523 km (325 mi) to the St. Lawrence R. at Trois Rivières.

Saint Mo•ritz (sānt′ mə-rĭts′, săn mô-rĭts′) A resort city of SE Switzerland on the Inn R. SSE of Chur. Pop. 5,900.

Saint Nicholas (sānt) or **Saint Nick** *n.* Santa Claus.

Saint Patrick′s Day *n.* March 17, observed in honor of Saint Patrick, the patron saint of Ireland.

Saint Paul The cap. of MN, in the SE part on the Mississippi R.

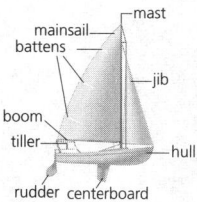

sailboat
Bermuda-rigged sailboat

St. Kitts and Nevis

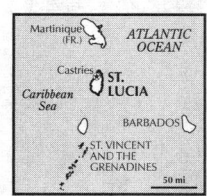

St. Lucia

adjacent to Minneapolis. Pop. 287,151.

Saint Pe·ters·burg (pēʹtərz-bûrgʹ) **1.** Formerly (1924–91) **Len·in·grad** (lĕnʹĭn-grădʹ) and **Pet·ro·grad** (pĕtʹrə-grădʹ) A city of NW Russia on the Neva R. at the head of the Gulf of Finland; founded by Peter the Great in 1703 and cap. of Russia from 1712 to 1918. Pop. 4,328,851. **2.** A city of W-central FL on Tampa Bay SSW of Tampa; settled in the mid-1800s. Pop. 248,232.

Saint Pi·erre or **Saint-Pi·erre** (săntʹ pîrʹ, pē-ârʹ, săn pyĕrʹ) The cap. of St. Pierre and Miquelon, on St. Pierre I. in the N Atlantic. Pop. 5,371.

Saint Pierre and Mi·que·lon (mĭkʹə-lŏnʹ, mē-klônʹ) A French island group and overseas department in the N Atlantic Ocean S of Newfoundland, Canada. Cap. St. Pierre, on **Saint Pierre Island.** Pop. 6,041.

Saint-Saëns (săn-sänsʹ, -sänʹ), **Charles Camille** 1835–1921. French composer noted for *Danse Macabre* (1874).

saint's day (sānts) *n., pl.* **saints' days** A day in a liturgical calendar observed in honor of a saint.

Saint-Si·mon (săn-sē-mônʹ), Comte de. Title of Claude Henri de Rouvroy. 1760–1825. French thinker who advocated a society governed by technocrats.

Saint-Simon, Duc de. Title of Louis de Rouvroy. 1675–1755. French diplomat known for his memoirs of the court of Louis XIV.

Saint Thomas (sānt) An island of the US Virgin Is. E of Puerto Rico; sold to the US by Denmark in 1917.

Saint-Tro·pez (săn-trô-pāʹ) A resort town on SE France on the Mediterranean coast of the French Riviera. Pop. 4,961.

Saint Valentine's Day (sānt) *n.* February 14, celebrated in various countries by the exchange of valentines or love tokens. [Primarily after Saint VALENTINE.]

Saint Vincent An island of St. Vincent and the Grenadines in the central Windward Is. of the West Indies; settled by the British in the mid-1700s.

Saint Vincent, Cape A promontory of SW Portugal.

Saint Vincent and the Gren·a·dines (grĕnʹə-dēnzʹ) An island country in the central Windward Is. of the West Indies comprising St. Vincent I. and the N islets of the Grenadines; part of the West Indies Federation (1958–62) and independent since 1979. Cap. Kingstown. Pop. 111,000.

Saint Vi·tus' dance also **Saint Vi·tus's dance** (vīʹtəs, -tə-sĭz) *n.* See **Sydenham's chorea.** [After *St. Vitus*, 3rd-cent. A.D. Christian martyr.]

Sai·pan (sī-pănʹ, -pänʹ, sīʹpăn) An island of the W Pacific in the S Mariana Is.; part of the US Trust Territory of the Pacific Is. —**Sai·pa·nese** (-nēzʹ, -nēsʹ) *adj. & n.*

Sa·ïs (sāʹĭs) A city of ancient Egypt in the W-central region of the Nile delta; a royal residence during the XXVI Dynasty (663–525 B.C.).

saith (sĕth, sāʹĭth) *v. Archaic* A third person singular present tense of **say.**

Sai·va (sīʹvə, shīʹ-) *n. Hinduism* One who worships Shiva. [Skt. *śaiva-*, belonging to Shiva < *Śivaḥ*, Shiva.] —**Sai·vism** *n.*

Sa·ja·ma (sə-häʹmə) A mountain, 6,574.3 m (21,555 ft), in the Andes of W Bolivia near the Chilean border.

Sa·kai (säʹkīʹ) A city of S Honshu, Japan, on Osaka Bay S of Osaka. Pop. 806,263.

Sak·a·ka·we·a (săkʹə-kə-wēʹə), **Lake** A reservoir in W-central ND; a widening of the Missouri R. created in 1956 when the Garrison Dam was completed.

sake[1] (sāk) *n.* **1.** Purpose; motive. **2.** Advantage; good: *for the sake of his health.* **3.** Personal benefit or interest; welfare. [ME, lawsuit, guilt < OE *sacu*.]

sa·ke[2] also **sa·ki** (säʹkē, -kĕ) *n.* A Japanese wine made from fermented rice. [J.]

sa·ker (säʹkər) *n.* A Eurasian falcon (*Falco cherrug*) having brown plumage. [ME *sacre* < OFr. < Ar. *ṣaqr*, prob. < Turkic **soŋqur*, falcon.]

Sa·kha·lin (săkʹə-lēnʹ, -lən, să-кнä-lyēnʹ) An island of SE Russia in the Sea of Okhotsk N of Hokkaido, Japan; colonized by Russia and Japan in the 18th and 19th cent. and under Russian control after 1875.

Sa·kha·rov (săkʹə-rôfʹ, săkʹə-rəf, säʹкнə-rəf), **Andrei Dimitrievich** 1921–89. Soviet physicist and dissident who won the 1975 Nobel Peace Prize.

Sa·ki (säʹkē) See Hector Hugh **Munro.**

Sak·ka·ra (sə-kärʹə) See **Saqqara.**

Sak·mann (zäkʹmänʹ, säkʹ-), **Bert** b. 1942. German neurobiologist who shared a 1991 Nobel Prize in medicine.

sal (săl) *n.* Salt. [ME < OFr. < Lat. *sāl*. See **sal-** in App.]

sa·laam (sə-lämʹ) *n.* **1.** A ceremonious act of deference or obeisance, esp. a low bow made with the right palm on the forehead. **2.** A respectful ceremonial greeting performed esp. in Islamic countries. [Ar. *salām*, peace, salaam < *salima*, to be safe.] —**sa·laam** *v.*

sal·a·ble also **sale·a·ble** (sāʹlə-bəl) *adj.* Offered or suitable for sale; marketable. —**sal'a·bil'i·ty** *n.* —**sal'a·bly** *adv.*

sa·la·cious (sə-lāʹshəs) *adj.* **1.** Appealing to or stimulating sexual desire. **2.** Lustful; bawdy. [< Lat. *salāx, salāc-*, fond of leaping, lustful < *salīre*, to leap.] —**sa·la'cious·ly** *adv.* —**sa·la'cious·ness, sa·lac'i·ty** (sə-lăsʹĭ-tē) *n.*

Andrei Sakharov

salamander
spotted salamander
Ambystoma maculatum

sal·ad (sălʹəd) *n.* **1a.** A dish consisting of raw green leafy vegetables, often tossed with other ingredients, served with a dressing. **b.** The course of a meal consisting of this dish. **2.** A cold dish of chopped fruit, meat, fish, eggs, or other food, usu. prepared with a dressing. **3.** A green vegetable or herb used in salad, esp. lettuce. **4.** A varied mixture. [ME *salade* < OFr., poss. < O Provençal *salada* < VLat. **salāta* < fem. p. part. of **salāre*, to salt < Lat. *sāl*, salt. See **sal-** in App.]

WORD HISTORY The word *salad* takes its origin from the fact that salt was and is an important ingredient of salad dressings. Vulgar Latin had a verb *•salāre*, "to salt," from Latin *sāl*, "salt," whose past participial form **salāta*, "having been salted," came to mean "salad." The Vulgar Latin word passed into languages descending from it, such as Portuguese (*salada*) and Old Provençal (*salada*). As in the case of so many culinary delights, the English borrowed the word and probably the dish from the French. Another Latin word for "salted," *salsus*, is the source of two other English culinary terms, *sauce* and *salsa*.

salad bar *n.* A counter in a restaurant from which customers may serve themselves salad ingredients and dressings.

salad days *pl.n.* A time of youth, innocence, and inexperience. [Coined by William Shakespeare.]

salad dressing *n.* A sauce, such as one made of mayonnaise or of oil and vinegar, that is served on salad.

Sal·a·din (sălʹə-dĭn) 1137?–93. Sultan of Egypt and Syria who captured (1187) Jerusalem and defended it during the Third Crusade (1189–92).

Sa·la·do (sə-läʹdō, sä-) **1.** also **Salado del Nor·te** (dĕl nôrʹtĕ) A river of N Argentina rising in the Andes and flowing c. 2,011 km (1,250 mi) to the Paraná R. **2.** A river, c. 1,368 km (850 mi), rising in W Argentina and flowing to the Colorado R.

sa·lal (sə-lălʹ) *n.* A small evergreen shrub (*Gaultheria shallon*) native to the Pacific coast of North America and having white or pink flowers clustered in racemes and edible purple-black berries. [Chinook Jargon *sallal* < Chinook *sálal*.]

Sal·a·man·ca (sălʹə-măngʹkə, sä'lä-mängʹkä) A city of W-central Spain WNW of Madrid; held by Moors from the 8th to the late 11th cent. Pop. 163,400.

sal·a·man·der (sălʹə-mănʹdər) *n.* **1.** Any of various small lizardlike amphibians of the order Caudata, having porous scaleless skin and four, often weak or rudimentary legs. **2a.** A mythical creature, generally resembling a lizard, believed capable of living in or withstanding fire. **b.** In the occult philosophy of Paracelsus, a being having fire as its element. **3.** An object, such as a poker, used in fire or capable of withstanding heat. **4.** *Metallurgy* A mass of solidified material, largely metallic, left in a blast-furnace hearth. **5.** A portable stove used to heat or dry buildings under construction. [ME *salamandre* < OFr. < Lat. *salamandra* < Gk.] —**sal'a·man'drine** (-drĭn) *adj.*

sa·la·mi (sə-läʹmē) *n., pl.* **-mis** Any of various highly spiced and salted sausages, made from beef or a mixture of pork and beef. [Ital., pl. of *salame*, salami < VLat. **salāmen* < **salāre*, to salt < Lat. *sāl*, salt. See **sal-** in App.]

Sal·a·mis[1] (sălʹə-mĭs, sä'lä-mēsʹ) An island of Greece in the Saronic Gulf E of Athens; site of an offshore naval battle in which the Greeks defeated the Persian fleet in 480 B.C.

Sal·a·mis[2] (sălʹə-mĭs, sä'lä-mēsʹ) An ancient city of E Cyprus; traditionally founded c. 1180 B.C.

sal ammoniac *n.* See **ammonium chloride.** [Ult. < Lat. *sāl ammōniacus*, salt of Amen : *sāl*, salt; see **sal-** in App. + *ammōniacus*, of Amen; see AMMONIA.]

sal·a·ry (sălʹə-rē, sălʹrē) *n., pl.* **-ries** Fixed compensation for services, paid on a regular basis. [ME *salarie* < AN < Lat. *salārium*, money given to Roman soldiers for salt < neut. of *salārius*, of salt < *sāl*, salt. See **sal-** in App.] —**sal'a·ried** *adj.*

salary reduction plan *n.* See **401(k).**

Sa·la·zar (sălʹə-zärʹ, sä'lə-), **Antonio de Oliveira** 1889–1970. Portuguese dictator (1932–68) who attempted to repress growing independence in Portugal's African colonies.

Sal·can·tay (sälʹkən-tīʹ, sälʹkän-) The highest peak, 6,275.4 m (20,575 ft), of the Cordillera Oriental in S Peru.

sal·chow (sălʹkouʹ) *n.* A move in figure skating in which the skater jumps from one skate, completes a full rotation, and lands on the other skate. [After Ulrich *Salchow* (1877–1949), Swedish figure skater.]

sale (sāl) *n.* **1.** The exchange of goods or services for an amount of money or its equivalent; the act of selling. **2.** An instance of selling. **3.** An opportunity for selling or being sold; demand. **4.** Availability for purchase: *pets for sale.* **5.** A selling of property to the highest bidder; an auction. **6.** A special disposal of goods at lowered prices: *coats on sale.* **7. sales a.** Activities involved in selling goods or services. **b.** Gross receipts. [ME < OE *sala* < ON.]

sale·a·ble (sāʹlə-bəl) *adj.* Variant of **salable.**

sale-lease·back (sālʹlēsʹbăkʹ) *n.* See **leaseback.**

Sa·lem (sāʹləm) **1.** A city of S India SW of Chennai (Madras). Pop. 366,712. **2.** A city of NE MA NE of Boston; founded 1626 and noted as the site of witchcraft trials (1692). Pop. 40,407. **3.** The cap. of OR, in the NW part on the Willamette R. SSW of Portland; founded c. 1840. Pop. 136,924.

sal·ep (sălʹəp) *n.* A starchy meal ground from the dried roots of various Old World orchids of the genera *Orchis* and *Eulophia*, used for food and formerly as medicine. [Fr. or Sp., both < Ottoman Turk. *sālep* < Ar. *saḥlab*, a kind of orchid, salep.]

sal·er·a·tus (săl′ə-rā′təs) *n.* Sodium or potassium bicarbonate used as a leavening agent; baking soda. [NLat. *sāl āerātus* : Lat. *sāl*, salt; see sal- in App. + NLat. *āerātus*, aerated (< Lat. *āer*, air; see AIR).]

Sa·ler·no (sə-lûr′nō, sä-lĕr′-) A city of S Italy on the **Gulf of Salerno**, an inlet of the Tyrrhenian Sea. Pop. 153,436.

sales check (sālz) *n.* A slip of paper given by a store to serve as a record or receipt of a purchase or sale.

sales·clerk (sālz′klûrk′) *n.* One who sells goods in a store.

sales·girl (sālz′gûrl′) *n.* A saleswoman.

sales·la·dy (sālz′lā′dē) *n.* A saleswoman.

sales·man (sālz′mən) *n.* A man who sells merchandise in a store or a designated territory. —**sales′man·ship′** *n.*

sales·per·son (sālz′pûr′sən) *n.* A salesman or a saleswoman.

sales·room (sālz′rōom′, -rōom′) *n.* A room in which items are displayed and offered for sale or auction.

sales tax *n.* A tax levied on the retail price of merchandise and collected by the retailer.

sales·wom·an (sālz′wŏom′ən) *n.* A woman who sells merchandise in a store or a designated territory.

Sal·ford (sôl′fərd) A borough of NW England on the Manchester Ship Canal adjacent to Manchester. Pop. 229,260.

sali– *pref.* Salt: *salimeter*. [< Lat. *sāl*, salt. See sal- in App.]

Sa·li·an (sā′lē-ən, sāl′yən) *adj.* Of or relating to a tribe of Franks who settled in the Rhine region of the Netherlands in the fourth century A.D. ❖ *n.* A Salian Frank. [< LLat. *Saliī*, the Salian Franks.]

sal·ic (săl′ĭk) *adj.* Of or relating to certain minerals, such as quartz and the feldspars, that occur in igneous rocks and are rich in silica and alumina. [S(ILICA) + AL(UMINA) + -IC.]

Sa·lic (sā′lĭk, săl′ĭk) also **Sa·lique** (sā′lĭk, săl′ĭk, sə-lēk′) *adj.* **1.** Of or relating to the Salian Franks. **2.** Of or relating to the Salic law or the legal code of the Salian Franks. [Fr. *salique* < Med.Lat. *Salicus* < LLat. *Saliī*, the Salian Franks.]

sal·i·cin (săl′ĭ-sĭn) *n.* A bitter glucoside, $C_{13}H_{18}O_7$, obtained mainly from the bark of poplar and willow trees and formerly used as an analgesic. [Fr. *salicine* < Lat. *salix, salic-*, willow.]

Salic law *n.* **1.** The legal code of the Salian Franks. **2.** A law, thought to derive from the code of laws of the Salian Franks, prohibiting a woman from succeeding to a throne.

sal·ic·y·late (sə-lĭs′ə-lāt′, -lĭt, săl′ə-sĭl′ĭt) *n.* A salt or ester of salicylic acid. [SALICYL(IC ACID) + -ATE².]

sal·i·cyl·ic acid (săl′ĭ-sĭl′ĭk) *n.* A white crystalline acid, C₆H₄(OH)(COOH), used in making aspirin, as a preservative, and in the treatment of skin conditions. [< Fr. *salicyle*, the radical of salicylic acid < *salicine*, salicin. See SALICIN.]

sa·li·ence (sā′lē-əns, sāl′yəns) also **sa·li·en·cy** (sā′lē-ən-sē, sāl′yən-) *n., pl.* **-en·ces** also **-en·cies 1.** The quality or condition of being salient. **2.** A pronounced feature or part.

sa·li·ent (sā′lē-ənt, sāl′yənt) *adj.* **1.** Projecting or jutting beyond a line or surface; protruding. **2.** Strikingly conspicuous; prominent. **3.** Springing; jumping: *salient tree toads.* ❖ *n.* **1.** A military position that projects into the position of the enemy. **2.** A projecting angle or part. [Lat. *saliēns, salient-*, pr. part. of *salīre*, to leap.] —**sa′li·ent·ly** *adv.*

sa·li·en·tian (sā′lē-ĕn′shən) *n.* An amphibian of the order Salientia (formerly Anura or Batrachia), which includes the frogs and toads. [< NLat. *Salientia*, order name < Lat. *saliēns, salient-*, pr. part. of *salīre*, to leap. See SALIENT.] —**sa′li·en′tian** *adj.*

sa·lif·er·ous (sə-lĭf′ər-əs) *adj.* Containing or yielding salt.

sa·lim·e·ter (sə-lĭm′ĭ-tər) or **sa·lom·e·ter** (-lŏm′-) *n.* A hydrometer that indicates the concentration of salt in a solution. —**sal′i·met′ric** (săl′ə-mĕt′rĭk) *adj.* —**sa·lim′e·try** *n.*

Sa·li·na (sə-lī′nə, -lē′-) *n.* **1.** A salt marsh, spring, pond, or lake. **2.** An area encrusted with salt. **3.** A saltworks. [Sp. < Lat. *salīnae*, salt pits < fem. pl. of *salīnus*, of salt. See SALINE.]

Sa·li·nas (sə-lē′nəs) A city of W CA ENE of Monterey on the Salinas River, c. 241 km (150 mi). Pop. 151,060.

sa·line (sā′lēn′, -līn′) *adj.* **1.** Of, relating to, or containing salt; salty. **2.** Of or relating to chemical salts. ❖ *n.* **1.** A salt of magnesium or of the alkalis, used as a cathartic. **2.** A saline solution, esp. one that is isotonic with blood. [Lat. *salīnus* < *sāl*, salt. See sal- in App.] —**sa·lin′i·ty** (sə-lĭn′ĭ-tē) *n.*

Sal·in·ger (săl′ĭn-jər), **J(erome) D(avid)** b. 1919. Amer. writer whose works include *The Catcher in the Rye* (1951).

sal·i·nize (săl′ə-nīz′) *tr.v.* **-nized, -niz·ing, -niz·es** To treat with salt. —**sal′i·ni·za′tion** (-nĭ-zā′shən) *n.*

sal·i·nom·e·ter (săl′ə-nŏm′ĭ-tər) *n.* An instrument that uses electrical conductivity to measure the concentration of salt in a solution. **2.** See salimeter. —**sal′i·no·met′ric** (-nə-mĕt′rĭk) *adj.* —**sal′i·nom′e·try** *n.*

Sa·lique (sā′lĭk, săl′ĭk, sə-lēk′) *adj.* Variant of **Salic.**

Salis·bur·y (sôlz′bĕr′ē, -brē) A municipal borough of S England NW of Southampton on the edge of **Salisbury Plain**, the site of Stonehenge; chartered 1220. Pop. 35,700.

Salisbury steak *n.* A patty of ground beef mixed with eggs, milk, onions, and various seasonings and broiled, fried, or baked. [After James Henry *Salisbury* (1823–1905), American physician.]

Sa·lish (sā′lĭsh) also **Sa·lish·an** (-lĭ-shən) *n., pl.* **Salish** also **-lish·ans 1.** A family of Native American languages of the northwest United States and British Columbia. **2a.** The group of Native American peoples speaking languages of the Salish family. **b.** A member of this group. [Southern Interior Salish *se′lish*, Flatheads.] —**Sa′lish·an** *adj.*

sa·li·va (sə-lī′və) *n.* The watery mixture of secretions from the salivary and oral mucous glands that lubricates chewed food, moistens the oral walls, and contains ptyalin. [Lat. *salīva.*]

sal·i·var·y (săl′ə-vĕr′ē) *adj.* **1.** Of, relating to, or producing saliva. **2.** Of or relating to a salivary gland.

salivary gland *n.* A gland that secretes saliva, esp. any of three pairs of large glands, the parotid, submaxillary, and sublingual, that secrete into the mouth.

sal·i·vate (săl′ə-vāt′) *v.* **-vat·ed, -vat·ing, -vates** —*intr.* **1.** To secrete or produce saliva. **2.** *Informal* To be full of desire or eagerness for something. —*tr.* To produce excessive salivation in. [Lat. *salīvāre, salīvāt-* < *salīva*, saliva.]

sal·i·va·tion (săl′ə-vā′shən) *n.* **1.** The act or process of secreting saliva. **2.** An abnormally abundant flow of saliva.

Salk (sôlk), **Jonas Edward** 1914–95. Amer. microbiologist who developed the first effective killed-virus polio vaccine (1954).

Salk vaccine *n.* A polio vaccine consisting of inactivated polioviruses. [After Jonas Edward SALK.]

sal·let (săl′ĭt) *n.* A light late medieval helmet with a brim flaring in the back, sometimes fitted with a visor. [ME < OFr. *sallade* < OSpan. *celada* or OItal. *celata*, both prob. < Lat. *caelāta (cassis)*, engraved (helmet), fem. p. part. of *caelāre*, to engrave < *caelum*, chisel.]

sal·low¹ (săl′ō) *adj.* **-er, -est** Of a sickly yellowish hue or complexion. ❖ *tr.v.* **-lowed, -low·ing, -lows** To make sallow. [ME *salowe* < OE *salo.*] —**sal′low·ly** *adv.* —**sal′low·ness** *n.*

sal·low² (săl′ō) *n.* A broad-leaved European willow (*Salix caprea*) having large catkins, which appear before the leaves, and tough wood used to make charcoal. [ME *salowe* < OE *sealh.*]

Sal·lust (săl′əst) Originally Gaius Sallustius Crispus 86?–34? B.C. Roman politician and historian known for his account of the conspiracy of Catiline.

sal·ly (săl′ē) *intr.v.* **-lied, -ly·ing, -lies 1.** To rush out or leap forth suddenly. **2.** To issue suddenly from a defensive or besieged position to attack an enemy. **3.** To set out on a trip or excursion. ❖ *n., pl.* **-lies 1.** A sudden rush forward; a leap. **2.** An assault from a defensive position; a sortie. **3.** A sudden emergence into action or expression; an outburst. **4.** A sudden quick witticism; a quip. **5.** A venturing forth; a jaunt. [< Fr. *saillie*, a sally < OFr. < fem. p. part. of *salir*, to rush forward < Lat. *salīre*, to leap.]

sally lunn (lŭn′) *n.* A somewhat sweet bread leavened with yeast. [After *Sally Lunn*, 18th-cent. British baker.]

sally port *n.* A gate in a fortification designed for sorties.

Sal·ma·cis (săl-mā′sĭs) *n. Greek Mythology* A nymph who loved Hermaphroditus and was united with him in one body.

sal·ma·gun·di (săl′mə-gŭn′dē) *n., pl.* **-dis 1.** A salad of chopped meat, anchovies, eggs, and onions, often arranged on lettuce and served with vinegar and oil. **2.** A mixture or assortment; a potpourri. [Fr. *salmigondis* : prob. < OFr. *salemine*, salted food (< VLat. **salāmen*; see SALAMI) + OFr. *condir*, to season (< Lat. *condīre*; see CONDIMENT).]

sal·mi (săl′mē) *n., pl.* **-mis** A highly spiced dish consisting of roasted game birds minced and stewed in wine. [Fr. *salmis*, short for *salmigondis*, salmagundi. See SALMAGUNDI.]

salm·on (săm′ən) *n., pl.* **salmon** or **-ons 1.** Any of various large food and game fishes of the genera *Salmo* and *Oncorhynchus* of northern waters, having pink flesh. **2.** A moderate, light, or strong yellowish pink to a moderate reddish orange or light orange. [ME *samoun* < OFr. *saumon* < Lat. *salmō, salmōn-*. See sel- in App.]

salm·on·ber·ry (săm′ən-bĕr′ē) *n.* **1.** Any of several prickly shrubs of the genus *Rubus*, esp. *R. spectabilis* of western North America, having trifoliate leaves and fragrant reddish flowers. **2.** The edible pink berrylike fruit of this plant.

sal·mo·nel·la (săl′mə-nĕl′ə) *n., pl.* **-nel·lae** (-nĕl′ē) or **-nel·las** or **salmonella** Any of various rod-shaped bacteria of the genus *Salmonella*, many of which are pathogenic, causing food poisoning, typhoid, and paratyphoid fever in humans. [NLat. *Salmonella*, genus name, after Daniel Elmer *Salmon* (1850–1914), American pathologist.]

sal·mo·nel·lo·sis (săl′mə-nĕ-lō′sĭs) *n., pl.* **-ses** (-sēz′) Infection with salmonellae, marked by intestinal problems and fever.

salm·o·nid (săm′ə-nĭd, săl′mə-) *adj.* Of, belonging to, or characteristic of the family Salmonidae, which includes the salmon, trout, and whitefish. [< NLat. *Salmōnidae*, family name < *Salmō*, type genus < Lat. *salmō, salmōn-*, salmon. See SALMON.] —**salm·o′nid** *n.*

salm·o·noid (săm′ə-noid′, săl′mə-) *adj.* Of, belonging to, or characteristic of the suborder Salmonoidea, which includes the salmon. —**salm·o′noid** *n.*

Salmon River A river of central ID rising in the **Salmon River Mountains** and flowing c. 684 km (425 mi) to the Snake R. The mountain range rises to 3,153.7 m (10,340 ft).

salmon trout *n.* Any of various large trouts, esp. the lake trout, the seatrout, or the steelhead.

Jonas Salk

Sa·lo·me (sə-lō′mē, săl′ə-mā′) In the Bible, the daughter of Herodias and niece of Herod Antipas, who granted her the head of John the Baptist in return for her dancing.

sa·lom·e·ter (sə-lŏm′ĭ-tər) *n.* Variant of **salimeter.**

sa·lon (sə-lŏn′, săl′ŏn′, să-lôⁿ′) *n.* **1.** A large room, such as a drawing room, used for receiving and entertaining guests. **2.** A periodic gathering of people of social or intellectual distinction. **3.** A hall or gallery for the exhibition of works of art. **4.** A commercial establishment offering a product or service related to fashion: *a beauty salon.* [Fr. < Ital. *salone,* augmentative of *sala,* hall, of Gmc. orig.]

Sa·lo·ni·ka (sə-lŏn′ĭ-kə, săl′ə-nē′kə) See **Thessaloníki.**

sa·loon (sə-lōōn′) *n.* **1.** A place where alcoholic drinks are sold and drunk; a tavern. **2.** A large room or hall for receptions, public entertainment, or exhibitions. **3.** *Nautical* **a.** The officers' dining and social room on a cargo ship. **b.** A large social lounge on a passenger ship. **4.** *Chiefly British* A sedan automobile. [Fr. *salon,* salon. See SALON.]

salp (sălp) also **sal·pa** (săl′pə) *n.* Any of various free-swimming tunicates of the genus *Salpa* of warm seas, having a translucent, somewhat flattened keglike body. [< NLat. *Salpa,* genus name < Lat., a kind of stockfish < Gk. *salpē.*] —**sal′pi·form′** (săl′pə-fôrm′) *adj.*

salping– *pref.* Salpinx: salpingitis. [< Gk. *salpinx, salping-,* trumpet.]

sal·pin·gec·to·my (săl′pĭn-jĕk′tə-mē) *n., pl.* **-mies** Surgical removal of the fallopian tube.

sal·pin·gi·tis (săl′pĭn-jī′tĭs) *n.* Inflammation of the fallopian or eustachian tube.

sal·pinx (săl′pĭngks) *n., pl.* **sal·pin·ges** (săl-pĭn′jēz) **1.** The fallopian tube. **2.** The eustachian tube. [NLat. < Gk. *salpinx,* trumpet.] —**sal·pin′gi·an** (-pĭn′jē-ən, -jən) *adj.*

sal·sa (säl′sə) *n.* **1.** A spicy sauce of chopped, usu. uncooked vegetables or fruit, esp. tomatoes, onions, and chili peppers, used as a condiment. **2.** A popular form of Latin-American dance music. [Am.Sp. < Sp., sauce < OSpan. < VLat. **salsa.* See SAUCE.]

sal·si·fy (săl′sə-fē, -fī′) *n., pl.* **-fies 1.** A European plant (*Tragopogon porrifolius*) having grasslike leaves, purple flower heads, and an edible taproot. **2.** The root of this plant, eaten as a vegetable. [Fr. *salsifis* < obsolete Ital. *(erba) salsifica.*]

sal soda *n.* A hydrated sodium carbonate used as a cleanser.

salsify
Tragopogon porrifolius

salt (sôlt) *n.* **1.** A colorless or white crystalline solid, chiefly sodium chloride, used extensively in ground or granulated form as a food seasoning and preservative. **2.** A chemical compound formed by replacing all or part of the hydrogen ions of an acid with metal ions or electropositive radicals. **3.** salts Any of various mineral salts used as laxatives or cathartics. **4.** salts Smelling salts. **5.** Epsom salts. Often used in the plural. **6.** An element that gives flavor or zest. **7.** Sharp lively wit. **8.** *Informal* A sailor, esp. when old or experienced. **9.** A saltcellar. ❖ *adj.* **1.** Containing or filled with salt. **2.** Having a salty taste or smell. **3.** Preserved in salt or a salt solution. **4a.** Flooded with seawater. **b.** Found in or near such a flooded area. ❖ *tr.v.* **salt·ed, salt·ing, salts 1.** To add, treat, season, or sprinkle with salt. **2.** To cure or preserve by treating with salt or a salt solution. **3.** To provide salt for (deer or cattle). **4.** To add zest or liveliness to: *salt a lecture with anecdotes.* **5.** To give an appearance of value to by fraudulent means, esp. to place valuable minerals in (a mine) for the purpose of deceiving. —**phrasal verbs: salt away** To put aside; save. **salt out** To separate (a dissolved substance) by adding salt to the solution. —**idioms: salt of the earth** A person or group considered the best or most worthy part of society. **worth (one's) salt** Efficient and capable. [ME < OE *sealt.* See sal- in App.]

SALT *abbr.* Strategic Arms Limitation Talks

Sal·ta (säl′tə, -tä) A city of NW Argentina NNE of Córdoba; founded 1582. Pop. 367,099.

salt-and-pep·per (sôlt′ən-pĕp′ər) *adj.* Having a close mixture of black and white: *a pepper-and-salt beard.*

sal·ta·rel·lo (säl′tə-rĕl′ō, säl′-) *n., pl.* **-rel·los** or **-rel·li** (-rĕl′ē) A lively Italian dance with a skipping step at the beginning of each measure. [Ital. < *saltare,* to leap < Lat. *saltāre.* See SALTATION.]

sal·ta·tion (săl-tā′shən, sôl-) *n.* **1.** The act of leaping, jumping, or dancing. **2.** Discontinuous movement, transition, or development. **3.** *Genetics* A single mutation that drastically alters the phenotype. [Lat. *saltātiō, saltātiōn-* < *saltātus,* p. part. of *saltāre,* to leap, freq. of *salīre,* to jump.]

sal·ta·to·ri·al (săl′tə-tôr′ē-əl, -tōr′-, sôl′-) *adj.* **1.** Of or relating to leaping or dancing. **2.** Adapted for or characterized by leaping.

sal·ta·to·ry (săl′tə-tôr′ē, -tōr′ē, sôl′-) *adj.* **1.** Of, relating to, or adapted for leaping or dancing. **2.** Proceeding by leaps rather than by smooth gradual transitions.

salt·box (sôlt′bŏks′) *n.* A frame house with two stories in front and one in back, having a pitched roof with unequal sides, being short and high in front and long and low in back.

saltbox

salt·bush (sôlt′bŏŏsh′) *n.* Any of several salt-tolerant plants of the genus *Atriplex,* esp. *A. hortensis* of Asia, grown for greens or ornament.

salt cake *n.* Impure sodium sulfate used in making paper pulp, soaps and detergents, glass, ceramic glazes, and dyes.

salt·cel·lar (sôlt′sĕl′ər) *n.* A small dish for holding and dispens-

ing salt. [Alteration of ME *salt saler* : *salt,* salt; see SALT + *saler,* saltcellar (< OFr. *saliere* < Med.Lat. *salāria* < Lat., fem. of *salārius,* of salt < *sāl,* salt; see sal- in App.).]

salt dome *n. Geology* An anticlinal fold with a columnar salt plug at its core.

salt·er (sôl′tər) *n.* **1.** One that manufactures or sells salt. **2.** One that treats meat, fish, or other foods with salt.

salt·ern (sôl′tərn) *n.* A saltworks. [OE *sealtærn* : *sealt,* salt; see SALT + *ærn,* house.]

salt gland *n.* A specialized gland in marine animals that excretes the excess salt taken into the body.

salt grass *n.* Any of various grasses, esp. North American perennial plants of the genus *Distichlis,* that grow in salt marshes and alkaline areas.

Sal·til·lo (säl-tē′yō) A city of NE Mexico SW of Monterrey; founded 1575. Pop. 284,937.

sal·tine (sôl-tēn′) *n.* A thin crisp cracker sprinkled with salt.

sal·tire (sôl′tīr′, -tîr′) *n. Heraldry* An ordinary in the shape of a Saint Andrew's cross, formed by the crossing of a bend and a bend sinister. [ME *sautour* < OFr. *saultoir,* stile < *saulter,* to jump < Lat. *saltāre.* See SALTATION.]

salt·ish (sôl′tĭsh) *adj.* Somewhat salty.

Salt Lake City The cap. of UT, in the N-central part near Great Salt Lake; settled in 1847. Pop. 181,743.

salt lick *n.* **1.** A natural deposit of exposed salt that animals lick. **2.** A block of salt or artificial medicated saline preparation set out for cattle, sheep, or deer to lick.

salt marsh *n.* Low coastal grassland frequently overflowed by the tide.

salt-marsh caterpillar (sôlt′märsh′) *n.* The larva of a common tiger moth (*Estigmene acrea*) that feeds destructively on various grasses.

Sal·ton Sea (sôl′tən) A saline lake of SE CA in the Imperial Valley, a depression known as the **Salton Sink** until 1905, when flood waters of the Colorado R. formed the lake.

salt·pe·ter (sôlt′pē′tər) *n.* **1.** See **potassium nitrate. 2.** See **sodium nitrate. 3.** See **niter.** [ME *salpetre* < OFr. < Med.Lat. *salpetrae* : Lat. *sāl,* salt; see sal- in App. + Lat. *petrae,* genitive of *petra,* rock (< Gk. *petrā;* see per-² in App.).]

salt pork *n.* Fatty pork that is cured with salt, often used as a flavoring.

Salt River 1. A river rising in E AZ and flowing c. 322 km (200 mi) to the Gila R. near Phoenix. **2.** A river rising in NE MO and flowing c. 322 km (200 mi) to the Mississippi R.

salt·shak·er (sôlt′shā′kər) *n.* A container with a perforated top for sprinkling table salt.

salt·wa·ter or **salt-wa·ter** (sôlt′wô′tər, -wŏt′ər) *adj.* **1.** Of or containing salt water. **2.** Inhabiting or occurring in seawater or salt water. **3.** Done or used in salt water.

salt·works (sôlt′wûrks′) *pl.n.* (*used with a sing. or pl. verb*) A place where salt is produced commercially.

salt·wort (sôlt′wûrt′, -wôrt′) *n.* **1.** Any of several Old World coastal plants of the genus *Salsola,* esp. *S. kali,* having awl-shaped prickly leaves. **2.** A strong-smelling succulent New World coastal shrub (*Batis maritima*) and having unisexual flowers and thick flattened leaves.

salt·y (sôl′tē) *adj.* **-i·er, -i·est 1.** Of, containing, or seasoned with salt. **2.** Suggestive of the sea or sailing life. **3.** Witty; pungent: *salty humor.* —**salt′i·ly** *adv.* —**salt′i·ness** *n.*

sa·lu·bri·ous (sə-lōō′brē-əs) *adj.* Conducive or favorable to health or well-being. [< Lat. *salūbris* < *salūs,* health. See sol- in App.] —**sa·lu·bri·ous·ly** *adv.* —**sa·lu·bri·ty** (-brĭ-tē) *n.*

sa·lu·ki (sə-lōō′kē) *n., pl.* **-kis** Any of an ancient breed of tall slender dog developed in Arabia and Egypt and having a smooth, silky, variously colored coat. [Ar. *salūqī,* of Saluq, an ancient city of S Arabia.]

sal·u·ret·ic (săl′yə-rĕt′ĭk) *n.* A saluretic drug. ❖ *adj.* Relating to or causing excretion of salt.

sal·u·tar·y (săl′yə-tĕr′ē) *adj.* **1.** Effecting or designed to effect an improvement; remedial: *salutary advice.* **2.** Favorable to health; wholesome: *a salutary climate.* [ME *saluter* < OFr. *salutaire* < Lat. *salūtāris* < *salūs, salūt-,* health. See sol- in App.] —**sal′u·tar·i·ly** (-târ′ə-lē) *adv.* —**sal′u·tar·i·ness** *n.*

sal·u·ta·tion (săl′yə-tā′shən) *n.* **1a.** A polite expression of greeting or goodwill. **b.** salutations Greetings indicating respect and affection; regards. **2.** A gesture of greeting, such as a bow. **3.** A word or phrase of greeting used to begin a letter or message. —**sal′u·ta′tion·al** *adj.*

sa·lu·ta·to·ri·an (sə-lōō′tə-tôr′ē-ən, -tōr′-) *n.* The student with the second highest academic rank in a class who delivers the salutatory at graduation exercises.

sa·lu·ta·to·ry (sə-lōō′tə-tôr′ē, -tōr′ē) *n., pl.* **-ries** An opening or welcoming statement, esp. one delivered at graduation exercises. ❖ *adj.* Of, relating to, or expressing a salutation.

sa·lute (sə-lōōt′) *v.* **-lut·ed, -lut·ing, -lutes** —*tr.* **1.** To greet or address with an expression of welcome, goodwill, or respect. **2.** To recognize (a superior) with a gesture prescribed by military regulations, as by raising the hand to the cap. **3a.** To honor formally and ceremoniously. **b.** To express warm approval of; commend. **4.** To become noticeable to. —*intr.* To make a gesture of greeting or respect. ❖ *n.* **1.** An act of greeting; a salutation. **2a.**

saluki

An act or gesture of welcome, honor, or courteous recognition. **b.** The position of the hand or rifle or the bodily posture of a person saluting a military superior. **3.** A formal military display of honor or greeting, such as the firing of cannon. [ME *saluten* < Lat. *salūtāre* < *salūs, salūt-*, health. See **sol-** in App.] —**sa•lut′er** *n.*

sal•va•ble (săl′və-bəl) *adj.* That can be salvaged or saved. [< LLat. *salvāre*, to save. See SALVAGE.]

Sal•va•dor (săl′və-dôr′, săl′və-dôr′) Formerly **Ba•hi•a** (bə-hē′ə, bä-ē′ə) A city of E Brazil on the Atlantic Ocean SSW of Recife; founded 1549. Pop. 2,072,058.

Sal•va•do•ran (săl′və-dôr′ən, -dōr′-) or **Sal•va•do•ri•an** (-dôr′ē-ən, -dōr′-) *adj.* Of or relating to El Salvador or its people or culture. ❖ *n.* A native or inhabitant of El Salvador.

sal•vage (săl′vĭj) *n.* **1a.** The rescue of a ship, its crew, or its cargo from fire or shipwreck. **b.** The ship, crew, or cargo so rescued. **c.** Compensation given to those who voluntarily aid in such a rescue. **2a.** The act of saving imperiled property from loss. **b.** The property so saved. **3.** Something saved from destruction or waste and put to further use. ❖ *tr.v.* **-vaged, -vag•ing, -vag•es 1.** To save from loss or destruction. **2.** To save (discarded or damaged material) for further use. [Obsolete Fr. < OFr. *salvaige*, right of salvage < LLat. *salvāre*, to save < Lat. *salvus*, safe. See **sol-** in App.] —**sal′vage•a•bil′i•ty** *n.* —**sal′vage•a•ble** *adj.* —**sal′vag•er** *n.*

sal•va•tion (săl-vā′shən) *n.* **1a.** Preservation or deliverance from destruction, difficulty, or evil. **b.** A source, means, or cause of such preservation or deliverance. **2.** *Christianity* **a.** Deliverance from the power or penalty of sin; redemption. **b.** The agent or means of such deliverance. [ME *savacioun* < OFr. *sauvacion* < LLat. *salvātiō, salvātiōn-* < *salvātus*, p. part. of *salvāre*, to save. See SALVAGE.] —**sal•va′tion•al** *adj.*

Salvation Army *n.* An international evangelical and charitable organization founded in 1865 by William Booth as a London revival society and renamed in 1878.

sal•va•tion•ism (săl-vā′shə-nĭz′əm) *n.* Religious doctrine stressing salvation of the soul.

Sal•va•tion•ist (săl-vā′shə-nĭst) *n.* **1.** A member of the Salvation Army. **2. salvationist** One who preaches salvation.

salve¹ (săv, säv) *n.* **1.** An analgesic or medicinal ointment. **2.** Something that soothes or heals; a balm. **3.** Flattery or commendation. ❖ *tr.v.* **salved, salv•ing, salves 1.** To soothe or heal with or as if with salve. **2.** To ease the distress or agitation of; assuage. [ME < OE *sealf*.]

salve² (sălv) *tr.v.* **salved, salv•ing, salves** To salvage. [Back-formation < SALVAGE or SALVABLE.] —**sal′vor** *n.*

sal•ver (săl′vər) *n.* A tray for serving food or drinks. [Alteration of Fr. *salve* < Sp. *salva*, salver < *salvar*, to save, taste food to detect poison < LLat. *salvāre*, to save. See SALVAGE.]

sal•ver•form (săl′vər-fôrm′) *adj. Botany* Of or relating to a gamopetalous corolla having a slender tube and an abruptly expanded limb, as in phlox.

sal•vi•a (săl′vē-ə) *n.* Any of various plants of the genus *Salvia* in the mint family, having opposite leaves, a two-lipped corolla, and two stamens. [Lat. *salvia*, sage. See SAGE².]

sal•vif•ic (săl-vĭf′ĭk) *adj.* Able or intending to bring about salvation or redemption. [LLat. *salvificus* : Lat. *salvus*, safe; see SAFE + Lat. *-ficus*, -fic.] —**sal•vif′i•cal•ly** *adv.*

sal•vo¹ (săl′vō) *n., pl.* **-vos** or **-voes 1a.** A simultaneous discharge of firearms. **b.** The simultaneous release of a rack of bombs from an aircraft. **c.** These projectiles or bombs. **2a.** A sudden outburst, as of cheers. **b.** A forceful oral or written assault. [Ital. *salva* < Fr. *salve* < Lat. *salvē*, hail, imper. of *salvēre*, to be in good health < *salvus*, safe. See **sol-** in App.]

sal•vo² (săl′vō) *n., pl.* **-vos 1.** A mental provision or reservation. **2.** An expedient for protecting one's reputation or for soothing one's conscience. [Lat. *salvō* (as in Med.Lat. *salvō iūre*, saving the right), ablative of *salvus*, safe. See SAFE.]

sal vo•la•ti•le (vō-lăt′l-ē) *n.* A solution of ammonium carbonate in alcohol or ammonia water, used in smelling salts. [NLat. *sāl volātile* : Lat. *sāl*, salt + Lat. *volātile*, neut. of *volātilis*, flying.]

sal•vor (săl′vər) *n.* **1.** One who salvages a ship or its cargo. **2.** A ship used in salvage. [SALV(AGE) + –OR¹.]

Sal•ween (săl′wēn′) A river of SE Asia rising in E Xizang (Tibet) and flowing c. 2,816 km (1,750 mi) to the Gulf of Martaban.

Salz•burg (sôlz′bûrg′, sălz′-, zälts′bo͝ork′) A city of W-central Austria SW of Linz. Pop. 143,973.

SAM *abbr.* surface-to-air missile

Sam. *abbr. Bible* Samuel

Sa•mar (sä′mär′) An island of E-central Philippines NE of Leyte in the **Samar Sea,** an arm of the Pacific Ocean.

sam•a•ra (săm′ər-ə, sə-mâr′ə, -mär′ə) *n.* A dry indehiscent winged fruit, as of the elm or maple. [Lat., elm seed.]

Sa•mar•a (sə-mâr′ə) A city of W Russia on the Volga R. ESE of Moscow; founded 1586 and known as Kuibyshev from 1935–91. Pop. 1,231,653.

Sa•mar•i•a (sə-măr′ē-ə, -mâr′-) An ancient city of central Palestine in present-day NW Jordan; founded in the 9th cent. B.C. as the cap. of the N kingdom of Israel, which was also known as **Samaria.**

Sa•mar•i•tan (sə-măr′ĭ-tn) *n.* **1.** A native or inhabitant of Samaria. **2.** often **samaritan** A Good Samaritan. ❖ *adj.* Of or relating to Samaria or to Samaritans. [ME < OE < LLat. *Samaritānus* < Gk. *Samaritēs* < *Samareia*, Samaria.]

sa•mar•i•um (sə-mâr′ē-əm, -măr′-) *n. Symbol* **Sm** A metallic rare-earth element found in monazite and bastnaesite and used in ferromagnetic alloys, in infrared absorbing glass, and as a neutron absorber in certain nuclear reactors. Atomic number 62; atomic weight 150.36; melting point 1,072°C; boiling point 1,791°C; specific gravity approx. 7.50; valence 2, 3. See table at **element.** [SAMAR(SKITE) + –IUM.]

Sam•ar•qand (săm′ər-kănd′) A city of S Uzbekistan SE of the Aral Sea; conquered by Alexander the Great in 329 B.C., destroyed by Genghis Khan c. 1220 A.D., and Tamerlane's cap. after c. 1370. Pop. 371,000.

sa•mar•skite (sə-mär′skīt′, săm′ər-) *n.* A velvet-black mineral that is a complex mixture of several rare-earth metals with niobium and tantalum oxide. [After Col. M. von *Samarski*, 19th-cent. Russian mining official.]

sam•ba (săm′bə, säm′-) *n.* **1.** A Brazilian ballroom dance of African origin. **2.** Music in duple meter for performing this dance. ❖ *intr.v.* **-baed, -ba•ing, -bas** To perform this dance. [Port., poss. of African orig.]

sam•bal (säm′bäl) *n.* A spicy condiment used esp. in Indonesia and Malaysia, made with chili peppers and other ingredients. [Malay < Tamil *sambhar* < Prakrit *saṃbhārei*, he gathers < Skt. *saṃbhārayati*, he causes to be brought together : *sam*, together; see SANSKRIT + *bharati*, he carries, brings; see **bher-¹** in App.]

sam•bar also **sam•bur** (săm′bər, säm′-) *n.* A large deer *(Cervus unicolor)* of southern Asia having three-tined antlers and a reddish-brown coat. [Hindi *sāmbar* < Skt. *śambaraḥ*.]

Sam Browne belt (săm′ broun′) *n.* A belt having a shoulder strap that runs diagonally across the chest, worn as part of a military or police uniform. [After Sir *Samuel* James *Browne* (1824–1901), British general.]

sam•bu•ca (săm-bo͞o′kə, säm-bo͞o′kä) *n.* An Italian liqueur made from elderberries and flavored with licorice. [Ital. < fem. of *sambuco*, elder < Lat. *sambūcus*.]

same (sām) *adj.* **1.** Being the very one; identical: *the same boat we rented before.* **2.** Similar in kind, quality, quantity, or degree. **3.** Conforming in every detail: *the same rules as before.* **4.** Being the one previously mentioned or indicated; aforesaid. ❖ *adv.* In the same way. ❖ *pron.* **1.** Someone or something identical with another. **2.** Someone or something previously mentioned or described. [ME < ON *samr*. See **sem-¹** in App.]

USAGE NOTE The expressions *same* and *the same* are sometimes used in place of pronouns such as *it* or *one*, as in *When you have filled out the form, please remit same to this office.* As this example suggests, the usage is associated chiefly with business and legal language. But though the usage often does sound stilted, it occurs with some frequency in informal writing, particularly in the phrase *lack of same.*

sa•mekh (sä′mĕk, -məKH) *n.* The 15th letter of the Hebrew alphabet. [Heb. *sāmek* < Phoenician **samk*, support (sense uncertain), 15th letter of the Phoenician alphabet.]

same•ness (sām′nĭs) *n.* **1.** The quality or condition of being the same. **2.** A lack of variety or change; monotony.

same-sex (sām′sĕks′) *adj.* **1.** Involving or restricted to members of the same sex: *same-sex schools.* **2.** Of or involving gay men or lesbians: *same-sex couples.*

sam hill also **Sam Hill** *n. Slang* Used as an intensive: *What in sam hill is going on?* [Ult. alteration of *hell*.]

Sa•mi (sä′mē) or **Saa•mi** (sä′-) *n., pl.* **Sami** or **-mis** or **Saami** or **-mis 1.** A member of a people of nomadic herding tradition inhabiting Lapland. **2.** Any of the Finnic languages of the Sami. [Sami < earlier *Sabme*; prob. akin to Finn. *Suomi*, Finn, Finn.]

sam•i•sen (săm′ĭ-sĕn′) *n.* Variant of **shamisen.**

sam•ite (săm′īt′, sā′mīt′) *n.* A heavy silk fabric, often interwoven with gold or silver, worn in the Middle Ages. [ME *samit* < OFr. < Med.Lat. *examitum* < Med.Gk. *hexamiton* < Gk., neut. of *hexamitos*, of six threads : *hexa-*, hexa- + *mitos*, warp thread.]

sa•miz•dat (sä′mĭz-dät′, sə-myĭz-dät′) *n.* **1a.** The secret publication and distribution of banned literature in the former Soviet Union. **b.** The literature thus produced. **2.** An underground press. [Russ. : *sam*, self; see **sem-¹** in App. + *-izdat*, short for *izdatel'stvo*, publishing house (on the model of *Gosizdat*, state publishing house < *izdat'*, to publish : *iz*, from, out of; see **eghs** in App. + *dat'*, to give; see **dō-** in App.).]

sam•let (săm′lĭt) *n.* A young salmon. [SA(L)M(ON) + –LET.]

Sam•ni•um (săm′nē-əm) An ancient country of central and S Italy; conquered by Rome in the Samnite Wars (343–290 B.C.). —**Sam′nite** (săm′nīt′) *adj. & n.*

Sa•mo•a¹ (sə-mō′ə) An island group of the S Pacific ENE of Fiji, divided between **Samoa,** a sovereign nation, and **American Samoa,** a territory of the US. The islands were populated by Polynesians perhaps as early as 1000 B.C.

Sa•mo•a² (sə-mō′ə) Formerly **Western Samoa.** An island country of the S Pacific comprising the W Samoa Is.; achieved independence in 1962. Cap. Apia, on Upolu I. Pop. 209,360.

Sa•mo•an (sə-mō′ən) *adj.* **1.** Of or relating to the islands of Samoa. **2.** Of or relating to the country of Samoa or the territory of American Samoa. ❖ *n.* **1.** A native or inhabitant of the islands

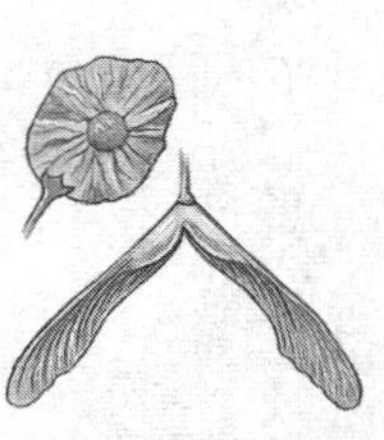

samara
top: slippery elm fruit
bottom: silver maple fruit

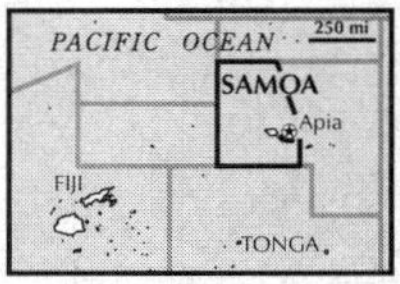

Samoa²

ă	pat	oi	boy
ā	pay	ou	out
âr	care	o͝o	took
ä	father	o͞o	boot
ĕ	pet	ŭ	cut
ē	be	ûr	urge
ĭ	pit	th	thin
ī	pie	*th*	this
îr	pier	hw	which
ŏ	pot	zh	vision
ō	toe	ə	about, item
ô	paw		

Stress marks:
′ (primary);
′ (secondary), as in
lexicon (lĕk′sĭ-kŏn′)

Samoyed

sampan

samurai

or country of Samoa. **2.** The Polynesian language of the Samoans.
Sa·mos (sā′mŏs′, săm′ŏs, sä′mŏs) An island of E Greece in the Aegean Sea off the W coast of Turkey.
sa·mo·sa (sə-mō′sə) *n.* An Indian fried turnover filled with seasoned vegetables or meat. [Hindi *samosā* < Pers. *samosa*.]
Sam·o·set (săm′ə-sĕt′) d. c. 1653. Native American leader who was the first to sell land to the Pilgrims (1625).
Sam·o·thrace (săm′ə-thrās′) or **Sam·o·thrá·ki** (sä′mô-thrä′kē) An island of NE Greece in the NE Aegean Sea off the coast of European Turkey.
sam·o·var (săm′ə-vär′) *n.* A metal urn with a spigot, used to boil water for tea and traditionally having a chimney and heated by coals. [Russ. : *samo*, self; see **sem-**¹ in App. + *varit′*, to boil.]
Sam·o·yed also **Sam·o·yede** (săm′ə-yĕd′, -oi-ĕd′, sə-moi′ĭd) *n.* **1.** See **Nenets. 2.** Any of a breed of medium-sized dog originally developed in northern Eurasia having a thick, long, white or cream-colored coat. [Obsolete Russ. *samoyed* (*samo-*, self (see SAMOVAR) + *-ed*, eater; see **ed-** in App.), by folk-ety. < Sami *sāmń emńne*, land of the Sami.] —**Sam′o·yed′, Sam′o·yed′ic** *adj.*
samp (sămp) *n. New England* Cornmeal mush. [Narragansett *nasàump*.]
sam·pan (săm′păn′) *n.* A flatbottom Asian skiff usu. propelled by two oars. [Chin. (Cantonese) *saam-páan*, equivalent to Chin. (Mandarin) *sān*, three + *băn*, board.]
sam·phire (săm′fīr′) *n.* **1.** See **glasswort. 2.** An Old World coastal plant (*Crithmum maritimum*) having fleshy compound leaves and small white flowers. [Alteration of Fr. *herbe de St. Pierre < St. Pierre*, Saint Peter.]
sam·ple (săm′pəl) *n.* **1a.** A portion, piece, or segment that is representative of a whole. **b.** An entity that is representative of a class; a specimen. **2.** *Statistics* A set of elements drawn from and analyzed to estimate the characteristics of a population. **3.** A sound that has been recorded on a sampler. ❖ *tr.v.* -**pled, -pling, -ples 1.** To take a sample of, esp. to test or examine by a sample. **2.** To use or incorporate (a segment of one audio recording) in another recording. ❖ *adj.* Serving as a representative or example. [Partly ME (< AN) and partly short for ME *ensample* (< AN), both < Lat. *exemplum*. See EXAMPLE.]
sam·pler (săm′plər) *n.* **1.** One who is employed to take and appraise samples, as of a food product. **2.** A mechanical device that is used to obtain and analyze samples. **3.** A decorative piece of cloth embroidered with various designs displaying a variety of stitches. **4a.** A representative collection or selection. **b.** A variety; an assortment. **5.** An electronic device that digitally records, stores, and manipulates sounds for later use in musical compositions. [Senses 3 and 4, partly ME, model (< AN *essamplur) and partly short for ME *ensampler* (< AN *ensamplour*), both < LLat. *exemplārium*, model, copy < Lat., copy. See EXEMPLAR.]
sam·pling (săm′plĭng) *n.* **1.** *Statistics* See **sample 2. 2a.** The act, process, or technique of selecting an appropriate sample. **b.** A small portion, piece, or segment selected as a sample.
sampling gate *n.* A circuit that produces an output only when first activated by a preliminary pulse.
sam·sa·ra (sŏm-sär′ə) *n. Hinduism & Buddhism* The eternal cycle of birth, suffering, death, and rebirth. [Skt. *saṃsāraḥ : sam*, together; see **sem-**¹ in App. + *sarati*, it flows.]
Sam·son¹ (săm′sən) In the Bible, the Israelite judge and powerful warrior who was betrayed to the Philistines by Delilah.
Sam·son² (săm′sən) *n.* A man of great physical strength. —**Sam·so′ni·an** (săm-sō′nē-ən) *adj.*
Sam·sun (săm-sōōn′) A city of N Turkey NE of Ankara on **Samsun Bay,** an inlet of the Black Sea. Pop. 326,900.
Sam·u·el¹ (săm′yōō-əl) Hebrew judge and prophet of the 11th cent. B.C. who anointed Saul as king. [Heb. *šəmû′ēl*, name of God : *šəmû*, name + *′ēl*, God.]
Sam·u·el² (săm′yōō-əl) *n.* See table at **Bible.** [After SAMUEL¹.]
Sam·u·el·son (săm′yōō-əl-sən, -yōōl-sən), **Paul Anthony** b. 1915. Amer. economist who wrote the classic textbook *Economics* (1948) and won a 1970 Nobel Prize.
sam·u·rai (săm′ə-rī′) *n., pl.* **samurai** or **-rais 1.** The Japanese feudal military aristocracy. **2.** A professional warrior belonging to this class. [J., warrior < O J. *samurafi*, : *sa-*, pref. + *morafi*, to watch, freq. of *mor-*, to guard.]
san also **-san** (sän) *n.* Used as a courtesy title in Japanese-speaking areas as a suffix to the given name, surname, or title of the person being addressed. [J. *-san*.]
San (sän) *n., pl.* **San** or **Sans 1.** A member of a traditionally nomadic hunting people of southwest Africa. **2.** Any of the Khoisan languages of the San. [Khoikhoin (Nama) : *sa*, to pick up from the ground + *-n*, common gender pl. suff.]
Sa·n′a or **Sa·na** or **Sa·naa** (sä-nä′) The cap. of Yemen, in the W part; cap. of North Yemen from 1962 to 1990. Pop. 427,000.
San An·dre·as Fault (sän ăn-drā′əs) A major zone of fractures in the earth's crust extending along the coastline of CA from the NW part to the Gulf of California.
San An·ge·lo (sän ăn′jə-lō′) A city of W-central TX SSW of Abilene. Pop. 88,439.
San An·to·ni·o (sän ăn-tō′nē-ō′) A city of S-central TX SW of Austin on the **San Antonio River,** flowing c. 322 km (200 mi) to **San Antonio Bay** on the Gulf of Mexico. Pop. 1,144,646.
san·a·tive (săn′ə-tĭv) *adj.* Having the power to cure; healing or

restorative. [ME *sanatif* < OFr. < LLat. *sānātīvus* < Lat. *sānātus*, p. part. of *sānāre*, to heal. See SANATORIUM.]
san·a·to·ri·um (săn′ə-tôr′ē-əm, -tōr′-) *n., pl.* -**to·ri·ums** or -**to·ri·a** (-tôr′ē-ə, -tōr′-) **1.** An institution for the treatment of chronic diseases or for medically supervised recuperation. **2.** A resort for improvement or maintenance of health. [< neut. of LLat. *sānātōrius*, curative < Lat. *sānātus*, p. part. of *sānāre*, to heal < *sānus*, healthy.]
san·be·ni·to (săn′bə-nē′tō) *n., pl.* -**tos** A garment of sackcloth worn at an auto-da-fé of the Spanish Inquisition by those condemned as heretics. [< Sp. *sambenito, San Benito*, Saint Benedict of Nursia (< its similarity to the scapular supposedly introduced by him).]
San Ber·nar·di·no (săn bûr′nə-dē′nō, -nər-) A city of S CA E of Los Angeles. Pop. 185,401.
San Bernardino Mountains A mountain range of S CA in the Coast Ranges S of the Mojave Desert rising to 3,507.2 m (11,499 ft).
San Bernardino Pass A pass, about 2,065 m (6,770 ft), through the Lepontine Alps in SE Switzerland.
San Blas (sän bläs′, sän bläs′), **Gulf of** An inlet of the Caribbean Sea on the N coast of Panama E of the Panama Canal.
San Cris·tó·bal (sän krĭs-tō′bəl, sän′ krē-stō′väl) A city of extreme W Venezuela near the Colombian border SSW of Maracaibo; founded 1561. Pop. 280,000.
sanc·ti·fy (săngk′tə-fī′) *tr.v.* -**fied, -fy·ing, -fies 1.** To set apart for sacred use; consecrate. **2.** To make holy; purify. **3.** To give religious sanction to, as with a vow: *sanctify a marriage.* **4.** To give social or moral sanction to. **5.** To make productive of holiness or blessing. [ME *seintefien, sanctifien* < OFr. < *saintifier* < LLat. *sānctificāre* : Lat. *sānctus*, holy < p. part. of *sancīre*, to consecrate; see **sak-** in App. + Lat. *-ficāre, -fy.*] —**sanc′ti·fi·ca′tion** (-fĭ-kā′shən) *n.* —**sanc′ti·fi′er** *n.*
sanc·ti·mo·ni·ous (săngk′tə-mō′nē-əs) *adj.* Feigning piety or righteousness. —**sanc′ti·mo′ni·ous·ly** *adv.*
sanc·ti·mo·ny (săngk′tə-mō′nē) *n.* Feigned piety or righteousness; hypocritical devoutness or high-mindedness. [Obsolete Fr. *sanctimonie* < Lat. *sānctimōnia*, sacredness < *sānctus*, holy. See SANCTIFY.]
sanc·tion (săngk′shən) *n.* **1.** Authoritative permission or approval that makes a course of action valid. **2.** Support or encouragement, as from public opinion. **3.** A consideration, influence, or principle that dictates an ethical choice. **4a.** A law or decree. **b.** The penalty for noncompliance specified in a law or decree. **5.** A penalty, specified or in the form of moral pressure, that acts to ensure compliance or conformity. **6.** A coercive measure adopted usu. by several nations acting together against a nation violating international law. ❖ *tr.v.* -**tioned, -tion·ing, -tions 1.** To give official authorization or approval to. **2.** To encourage or tolerate by indicating approval. See Syns at **approve. 3.** To penalize, esp. for violating a moral principle or international law. [ME, enactment of a law < OFr., ecclesiastical decree < Lat. *sānctiō, sānctiōn-*, binding law, penal sanction < *sānctus*, holy. See SANCTIFY.]
sanc·ti·ty (săngk′tĭ-tē) *n., pl.* -**ties 1.** Holiness of life or disposition; saintliness. **2.** The quality or condition of being considered sacred. **3.** Something considered sacred. [ME *sauncite* < OFr. *saincite* < Lat. *sānctitās < sānctus*, sacred. See SANCTIFY.]
sanc·tu·ar·y (săngk′chōō-ĕr′ē) *n., pl.* -**ies 1a.** A sacred place, such as a church, temple, or mosque. **b.** The holiest part of a sacred place. **2a.** A sacred place, such as a church, where fugitives formerly were immune to arrest. **b.** Immunity to arrest afforded by a sanctuary. **3.** A place of refuge or asylum. **4.** A reserved area in which animals, esp. wild ones, are protected from molestation. [ME < OFr. *sainctuarie* < LLat. *sānctuārium* < Lat. *sācred*. See SANCTIFY.]
sanc·tum (săngk′təm) *n., pl.* -**tums** or -**ta** (-tə) **1.** A sacred or holy place. **2.** A private place where one is free from intrusion. [LLat. *sānctum* < Lat., neut. of *sānctus*, sacred. See SANCTIFY.]
sanctum sanc·to·rum (săngk-tôr′əm, -tōr′-) *n.* **1.** *Judaism* The innermost shrine of a tabernacle and temple; the holy of holies. **2.** An inviolably private place. [LLat. *sānctum sānctōrum : sānctum*, holy place + *sānctōrum*, genitive pl. of *sānctum*, holy place.]
Sanc·tus (săngk′təs) *n., pl.* -**tus·es** A hymn of praise sung at the end of the Preface in many Eucharistic liturgies. [ME < LLat. *Sānctus* < Lat. *sānctus*, holy. See SANCTIFY.]
sand (sănd) *n.* **1a.** Small loose grains of worn or disintegrated rock. **b.** *Geology* A sedimentary material, finer than a granule and coarser than silt, with grains between 0.06 and 2.0 millimeters in diameter. **2.** A tract of land covered with sand, as a beach. Often used in the plural. **3a.** The sand in an hourglass. **b. sands** Moments of allotted time or duration. **4.** *Slang* Courage; stamina. **5.** A light grayish brown to yellowish gray. ❖ *tr.v.* **sand·ed, sand·ing, sands 1.** To sprinkle or cover with or as if with sand. **2.** To polish or scrape with sand or sandpaper. **3.** To mix with sand. **4.** To fill up (a harbor) with sand. [ME < OE.]
Sand (sănd, säɴd), **George** Pen name of Amandine Aurore Lucie Dupin. 1804–76. French writer whose works include *Lélia* (1833).
san·dal¹ (săn′dl) *n.* **1.** A shoe consisting of a sole fastened to the foot by thongs or straps. **2.** A low-cut shoe fastened to the foot by an ankle strap. **3.** A rubber overshoe cut very low and covering

little more than the sole of the shoe. **4.** A strap or band for fastening a low shoe or slipper on the foot. [ME < OFr. *sandale* < Lat. *sandalium* < Gk. *sandalion,* dim. of *sandalon,* sandal.] —**san′daled** *adj.*

san·dal² (săn′dl) *n.* Sandalwood. [ME < OFr. *sandale* (poss. via L.Gk. *santalon*) < Ar. *ṣandal* < Skt. *candanam.*]

san·dal·wood (săn′dl-wŏŏd′) *n.* **1.** Any of several tropical Asian trees of the genus *Santalum,* esp. *S. album,* having yellowish heartwood used in wood carving and yielding an oil used in perfumery. **2.** The wood of any of these trees. **3.** A light to moderate or grayish brown.

san·da·rac (săn′də-răk′) *n.* **1.** A coniferous evergreen tree (*Tetraclinis articulata*) of Spain and northern Africa having scalelike leaves and bark that yields a resin used in varnishes. **2.** The resin of this tree. [ME *sandaracha* < Lat., red pigment < Gk. *sandarakē,* realgar.]

sand·bag (sănd′băg′) *n.* A bag filled with sand and used as ballast, in the formation of protective walls, or as a weapon. ❖ *v.* **-bagged, -bag·ging, -bags** —*tr.* **1.** To put sandbags in or around. **2.** To hit with a sandbag. **3.** *Slang* **a.** To treat severely or unjustly. **b.** To force by crude means; coerce. **c.** To downplay or misrepresent one's ability in a game or activity in order to deceive (someone), esp. in gambling. —*intr. Slang* To sandbag someone, esp. in gambling. —**sand′bag′ger** *n.*

sand·bank (sănd′băngk′) *n.* A ridge of sand forming a mound, shoal, or hillside.

sand·bar (sănd′bär′) *n.* A ridge of sand formed in a river or along a shore by the action of waves or currents.

sand·blast (sănd′blăst′) *n.* **1a.** A blast of air or steam carrying sand at high velocity to etch glass or clean stone or metal surfaces. **b.** A machine used to apply such a blast. **2.** A strong wind carrying sand. ❖ *tr.v.* **-blast·ed, -blast·ing, -blasts** To apply a sandblast to. —**sand′blast′er** *n.*

sand-blind (sănd′blīnd′) *adj.* Having poor vision; partially blind. [ME < OE *sāmblind : sām-,* half + *blind,* blind.] —**sand′-blind′ness** *n.*

sand·box (sănd′bŏks′) *n.* **1.** A low box filled with sand for children to play in. **2.** A litter box, esp. for a cat.

sand·bur (sănd′bûr′) *n.* **1.** Any of several grasses of the genus *Cenchrus,* esp. *C. tribuloides,* found in eastern and tropical America and having a burlike envelope surrounding several one-grained spikelets. **2.** This burlike envelope.

Sand·burg (sănd′bûrg′, săn′-), **Carl** 1878–1967. Amer. writer known esp. for his free verse celebrating American life.

sand-cast (sănd′kăst′) *tr.v.* **-cast, -cast·ing, -casts** To make (a casting) by pouring molten metal into a sand mold.

sand·cas·tle (sănd′kăs′əl) *n.* **1.** A castlelike structure built of wet sand. **2.** Something that lacks substance or significance.

sand crack (sănd) *n.* A fissure in the side of a horse's hoof, often causing lameness.

sand dab *n.* Any of several small food fishes of the genus *Citharichthys* of Pacific waters, related to the flounders.

sand dollar *n.* **1.** Any of various thin circular echinoderms of the class Echinoidea, esp. *Echinarachnius parma,* of coastal northern Atlantic and Pacific waters, having a covering of short movable spines. **2.** The disklike internal skeleton of a sand dollar, having five radially symmetric oblong markings.

sand eel *n.* See **sand lance.**

sand·er (săn′dər) *n.* One that sands, esp.: **a.** A device that spreads sand on roads. **b.** Such a device together with the truck that carries it. **c.** A machine having a powered abrasive-covered disk or belt, used for smoothing or polishing surfaces.

sand·er·ling (săn′dər-lĭng) *n.* A small shore bird (*Crocethia alba*) related to the sandpipers and having gray and white plumage. [Perh. < SAND + −LING¹.]

sand·fish (sănd′fĭsh′) *n., pl.* **sandfish** or **-fish·es 1.** Any of various marine fishes that live or burrow in sandy or muddy bottoms. **2.** A slender fish (*Gonorhynchus gonorhynchus*) of the Pacific and Indian oceans having an annular snout.

sand flea *n.* **1.** Any of various small crustaceans that live on sandy beaches. **2.** See **chigoe** 1.

sand fly *n.* Any of various small biting flies of the genus *Phlebotomus* of tropical areas, some of which transmit diseases.

sand grouse *n.* Any of various pigeonlike birds of the genus *Pterocles* found in arid regions of arid and semiarid regions.

san·dhi (sŭn′dē, săn′-) *n.* Modification of the sound of a word or morpheme when juxtaposed with another, esp. in fluent speech, such as the change in pronunciation of *don't* in *don't you* from its pronunciation in isolation or in a phrase like *don't we.* [Skt. *saṃdhiḥ,* union, sandhi : *sam,* together; see **sem-¹** in App. + *dadhāti,* he places; see **dhē-** in App.]

sand·hill crane (sănd′hĭl′) *n.* A North American crane (*Grus canadensis*) having gray plumage and a bald red forehead.

sand·hog (sănd′hôg′, -hŏg′) *n. Slang* A laborer who works inside a caisson, as in the construction of underwater tunnels.

sand hopper *n.* See **beach flea.**

Sand·hurst (sănd′hûrst′) A village of S-central England SE of Reading; site of the Royal Military Academy.

San Di·e·go (săn dē-ā′gō) A city of S CA on **San Diego Bay,** an inlet of the Pacific Ocean. Pop. 1,223,400.

S & L *abbr.* savings and loan association

sand lance *n.* Any of several small slender marine fishes of the genus *Ammodytes* that often burrow in sand.

sand lily *n.* A low-growing plant (*Leucocrinum montanum*) of the western United States having grasslike leaves and fragrant white star-shaped flowers.

sand·lot (sănd′lŏt′) *n.* A vacant lot used esp. by children for unorganized sports and games. ❖ *adj.* Of, relating to, or played in a sandlot. —**sand′lot′ter** *n.*

S & M *abbr.* sadomasochism

sand·man (sănd′măn′) *n.* A character in fairy tales and folklore who makes children sleep by sprinkling sand in their eyes.

sand painting *n.* **1.** A ceremonial design of the Navajo and Pueblo peoples made by trickling colored sand, pollen, or powder onto a base of neutral sand. **2.** The art of making designs with colored sand.

sand·pa·per (sănd′pā′pər) *n.* Heavy paper coated on one side with sand or other abrasive material and used for smoothing surfaces. ❖ *tr.v.* **-pered, -per·ing, -pers** To rub with or as if with sandpaper. —**sand′pa′per·y** *adj.*

sand pear *n.* **1.** A Chinese tree (*Pyrus pyrifolia*) of the rose family, having edible globose fruit. **2.** The fruit of this plant.

sand·pi·per (sănd′pī′pər) *n.* Any of various small wading birds of the family Scolopacidae, usu. having a long bill with which it feeds in mud and sand.

sand shark *n.* A shark of the genus *Carcharias,* esp. *C. taurus,* of shallow temperate and tropical waters of the Atlantic.

sand·spur (sănd′spûr′) *n.* See **sandbur.**

sand·stone (sănd′stōn′) *n.* A sedimentary rock formed by the consolidation and compaction of sand and held together by a natural cement, such as silica.

sand·storm (sănd′stôrm′) *n.* A strong wind carrying clouds of sand and dust through the air.

sand table *n.* **1.** A table with raised edges, used for holding sand for children's play. **2.** A table on which a relief model of terrain is built out of sand, clay, or other material for the study of military maneuvers.

sand trap *n.* A hazard on a golf course consisting of a depression partly filled with sand.

San·dus·ky (săn-dŭs′kē, săn-) A city of N OH W of Cleveland on **Sandusky Bay,** an inlet of Lake Erie. The **Sandusky River,** c. 241 km (150 mi), flows into the bay. Pop. 27,844.

sand verbena *n.* Any of several herbs of the genus *Abronia* of western North America, having fragrant flowers grouped in long-stalked heads.

sand viper *n.* See **horned viper.**

sand·wich (sănd′wĭch, săn′-) *n.* **1a.** Two or more slices of bread with a filling such as cheese placed between them. **b.** A partly split long or round roll with a filling. **c.** One slice of bread covered with a filling. **2.** Something resembling a sandwich. ❖ *tr.v.* **-wiched, -wich·ing, -wich·es 1.** To make into or as if into a sandwich. **2.** To insert (one thing) tightly between two others esp. of differing character or quality. [After John Montagu, 4th Earl of *Sandwich* (1718–92).]

Sandwich A municipal borough of SE England N of Dover; one of the Cinque Ports. Pop. 4,227.

sandwich board *n.* Two large boards bearing placards, hinged at the top and hung over the shoulders with one board in front and the other behind, used for picketing or advertising.

sandwich generation *n.* A generation of people who give care to their children and their parents at the same time.

Sandwich Islands See **Hawaiian Islands.**

sandwich man *n.* A man who pickets or advertises by carrying a sandwich board.

sand·worm (sănd′wûrm′) *n.* Any of various segmented worms, esp. of the genera *Nereis* and *Arenicola,* generally inhabiting coastal mud or sand and often used as fishing bait.

sand·wort (sănd′wûrt′, -wôrt′) *n.* Any of numerous low-growing herbs of the genus *Arenaria,* having small, usu. white flowers often grouped in cymose clusters.

sand·y (săn′dē) *adj.* **-i·er, -i·est 1.** Covered with, full of, or consisting of sand. **2.** Having characteristics similar to sand. **3.** Of the color of sand; light yellowish brown. —**sand′i·ness** *n.*

Sandy or **Sandy City** A city of N-central Utah, a suburb of Salt Lake City. Pop. 88,418.

Sandy Hook A low peninsula of E NJ at the entrance to Lower New York Bay separating **Sandy Hook Bay** from the Atlantic.

sane (sān) *adj.* **san·er, san·est 1.** Of sound mind; mentally healthy. **2.** Having or showing sound judgment; reasonable. [Lat. *sānus,* healthy.] —**sane′ly** *adv.* —**sane′ness** *n.*

San Fer·nan·do Valley (săn fər-năn′dō) A fertile valley of S CA NW of central Los Angeles; first explored by the Spanish in 1769.

San·ford (săn′fərd), **Mount** A mountain, 4,952.3 m (16,237 ft), of S AK in the Wrangell Mts. NE of Anchorage.

San·for·ized (săn′fə-rīzd′) A trademark used for fabric preshrunk by a patented mechanical process.

San Fran·cis·co (săn frən-sĭs′kō) A city of W CA on a peninsula between the Pacific and **San Francisco Bay,** an inlet of the Pacific; founded by the Spanish as a presidio and mission in 1776. Pop. 776,733. —**San Fran·cis′can** (-kən) *n.*

San Francisco Peaks also **San Francisco Mountains** A group

George Sand

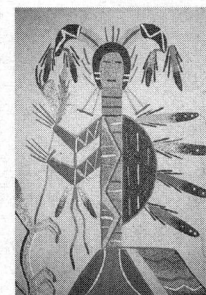

sand painting
depiction of a yei,
a Navajo deity

ă	pat	oi	boy
ā	pay	ou	out
âr	care	ŏŏ	took
ä	father	ōō	boot
ĕ	pet	ŭ	cut
ē	be	ûr	urge
ĭ	pit	th	thin
ī	pie	*th*	this
îr	pier	hw	which
ŏ	pot	zh	vision
ō	toe	ə	about,
ô	paw		item

Stress marks:
′ (primary);
′ (secondary), as in
lexicon (lĕk′sĭ-kŏn′)

Margaret Sanger
photographed in 1922

San Marino

sansevieria
Sansevieria trifasciata

of mountains rising to 3,853.1 m (12,633 ft) in N-central AZ N of Flagstaff.

sang (săng) *v.* A past tense of **sing.**

San Ga·bri·el Mountains (săn gā′brē-əl) A mountain range of S CA E and NE of Los Angeles rising to 3,074.4 m (10,080 ft).

San·ga·mon (săng′gə-mən) A river of central IL flowing c. 402 km (250 mi) SW and W to the Illinois R.

san·ga·ree (săng′gə-rē′) *n.* **1.** A sweet chilled alcoholic beverage spiced with grated nutmeg. **2.** See **sangria.** [Alteration of Sp. *sangría,* sangria. See SANGRIA.]

Sang·er (săng′ər), **Frederick** b. 1918. British biochemist who won a 1958 Nobel Prize for determining the order of amino acids in insulin and shared a 1980 Nobel Prize for developing methods for mapping DNA.

Sanger, Margaret Higgins 1879–1966. Amer. nurse who founded (1929) the organization that became the Planned Parenthood Federation (1942).

sang-froid or **sang·froid** (sän-frwä′) *n.* Coolness and composure, esp. in trying circumstances. [Fr. : *sang,* blood (< OFr. < Lat. *sanguis*) + *froid,* cold (< OFr. < VLat. **frigidus,* alteration of Lat. *frīgidus;* see FRIGID).]

San·gre de Cris·to Mountains (săng′grē dĕ krĭs′tō) A range of the S Rocky Mts. extending from S-central CO to N-central NM and rising to 4,375.2 m (14,345 ft).

san·gri·a (săng-grē′ə, săn-) *n.* A cold drink made of red or white wine mixed with brandy, sugar, fruit juice, and soda water. [Prob. < Sp. *sangría,* act of bleeding, sangria < *sangre,* blood < Lat. *sanguis, sanguin-.*]

san·guic·o·lous (săng-gwĭk′ə-ləs) *adj.* Living in the blood: *a sanguicolous parasite.* [Lat. *sanguis,* blood + –COLOUS.]

san·gui·nar·i·a (săng′gwə-nâr′ē-ə) *n.* The bloodroot. [NLat. *Sanguinaria,* genus name < Lat. *(herba) sanguinária,* a plant that stanches blood, fem. of *sanguinārius,* sanguinary. See SANGUINARY.]

san·gui·nar·y (săng′gwə-nĕr′ē) *adj.* **1.** Accompanied by bloodshed. **2.** Eager for bloodshed; bloodthirsty. **3.** Consisting of blood. [Lat. *sanguinārius < sanguis, sanguin-,* blood.] —**san′gui·nar′i·ly** (-nâr′ə-lē) *adv.*

san·guine (săng′gwĭn) *adj.* **1a.** Of the color of blood; red. **b.** Of a healthy reddish color; ruddy: *a sanguine complexion.* **2.** *Archaic* **a.** In medieval physiology, having blood as the dominant humor. **b.** Having the temperament and ruddy complexion once thought to be characteristic of this humor; passionate. **3.** Cheerfully confident; optimistic. [ME < OFr. *sanguin* < Lat. *sanguineus < sanguis, sanguin-,* blood.] —**san′guine·ly** *adv.* —**san′guine·ness, san′guin·i·ty** *n.*

san·guin·e·ous (săng-gwĭn′ē-əs) *adj.* **1.** Relating to or involving blood or bloodshed. **2.** Having the color of blood; blood-red. [< Lat. *sanguineus < sanguis, sanguin-,* blood.]

san·guin·o·lent (săng-gwĭn′ə-lənt) *adj.* Mixed or tinged with blood. [Lat. *sanguinolentus,* full of blood : *sanguis, sanguin-,* blood + *-olentus,* abounding in.]

San·hed·rin (săn-hĕd′rĭn, -hē′drĭn, săn-) *n.* The highest judicial and ecclesiastical council of the ancient Jewish nation, composed of from 70 to 72 members. [Heb. *sanhedhrîn* < Gk. *sunedrion,* council < *sunedros,* sitting in council : *sun-, syn-* + *hedra,* seat; see **sed-** in App.]

San·i·bel Island (săn′ə-bəl) An island of SW FL in the Gulf of Mexico SW of Fort Myers.

san·i·cle (săn′ĭ-kəl) *n.* Any of various plants of the genus *Sanicula,* having usu. compound leaves and formerly used as an astringent. [ME < OFr. < Med.Lat. *sānicula,* prob. < Lat. *sānus,* healthy.]

san·i·dine (săn′ĭ-dēn′, -dĭn) *n.* A glassy variety of orthoclase feldspar, known as moonstone when translucent. [Gk. *sanis, sanid-,* board (< its flat crystals) + –INE².]

sa·ni·es (sā′nē-ēz′) *n., pl.* **sanies** A thin fetid greenish fluid consisting of serum and pus discharged from a wound, ulcer, or fistula. [Lat. *saniēs.*] —**sa′ni·ous** (-əs) *adj.*

san·i·tar·i·an (săn′ĭ-târ′ē-ən) *n.* A public health or sanitation expert.

san·i·tar·i·um (săn′ĭ-târ′ē-əm) *n., pl.* **-i·ums** or **-i·a** (-ē-ə) See **sanatorium.** [NLat. *sānitārium* < Lat. *sānitās,* health. See SANITY.]

san·i·tar·y (săn′ĭ-tĕr′ē) *adj.* **1.** Of or relating to health or the protection of health. **2.** Free from elements, such as filth, that endanger health; hygienic. [Fr. *sanitaire* < Lat. *sānitās,* health. See SANITY.] —**san′i·tar′i·ly** (-târ′ə-lē) *adv.*

sanitary engineer *n.* An engineer specializing in the maintenance of urban environmental conditions conducive to the preservation of public health. —**sanitary engineering** *n.*

sanitary landfill *n.* Rehabilitated land in which garbage and trash have been buried; a landfill.

sanitary napkin *n.* A disposable pad of absorbent material worn to absorb menstrual flow.

san·i·ta·tion (săn′ĭ-tā′shən) *n.* **1.** Formulation and application of measures designed to protect public health. **2.** Disposal of sewage. [SANIT(ARY) + –ATION.]

sanitation worker *n.* A person employed, as by a municipality or private company, to collect and dispose of garbage.

san·i·tize (săn′ĭ-tīz′) *tr.v.* **-tized, -tiz·ing, -tiz·es** **1.** To make sanitary, as by disinfecting. **2.** To make more acceptable by re-

moving unpleasant or offensive features from: *sanitized language.* —**san′i·ti·za′tion** (-tĭ-zā′shən) *n.*

san·i·ty (săn′ĭ-tē) *n.* **1.** The quality or condition of being sane; soundness of mind. **2.** Soundness of judgment or reason. [ME *sanite,* health < OFr. < Lat. *sānitās < sānus,* healthy.]

San Ja·cin·to (săn jə-sĭn′tō) A river of SE TX flowing c. 209 km (130 mi) into Galveston Bay. The final battle of the Texas Revolution was fought on its banks (Apr. 21, 1836).

San Joa·quin (săn wô-kēn′, wä-) A river of central CA rising in the Sierra Nevada and flowing c. 515 km (320 mi) W and NW to form a large delta with the Sacramento R. The **San Joaquin Valley** is a fertile irrigated agricultural region.

San Jo·se (săn hō-zā′) A city of W CA SE of San Francisco; founded 1777. Pop. 894,943.

San Jo·sé (săn′ hō-sĕ′) The cap. of Costa Rica, in the central part; settled c. 1736. Pop. 315,909.

San Jose scale *n.* A destructive scale insect (*Aspidiotus perniciosus*) that damages fruit trees and fruit-bearing plants.

San Juan (săn wän′, săn hwän′) The cap. of Puerto Rico, on the NE coast; first settled (1508–09) by Ponce de León. Pop. 421,958.

San Juan Cap·is·tra·no (kăp′ĭ-strä′nō) A city of S CA SE of Santa Ana; founded as a mission in 1776. Pop. 33,826.

San Juan Hill An elevation in E Cuba near Santiago de Cuba; captured by Cuban and US forces on Jul. 1, 1898, during the Spanish-American War.

San Juan Islands An archipelago of NW WA off the SE coast of Vancouver I. N of Puget Sound.

San Juan Mountains A range of the Rocky Mts. in SW CO rising to 4,364.2 m (14,309 ft).

San Juan River A river rising in S CO and flowing c. 579 km (360 mi) to the Colorado R. in SE UT.

sank (săngk) *v.* A past tense of **sink.**

San·khya (säng′kyə) *n. Hinduism* A system of Hindu philosophy based on a dualism involving the ultimate principles of soul and potential matter. [Skt. *sāṃkhya-,* based on enumeration, Sankhya < *saṃkhyā,* enumeration : *sam,* together; see SANDHI + *khyāti,* he tells.]

San·ku·ru (säng-kōōr′ōō) A river of S and central Congo (formerly Zaire) flowing c. 1,207 km (750 mi) WNW to the Kasai R.

San Lu·cas (săn lōō′käs, săn lōō′käs), **Cape** A cape of W Mexico at the S tip of Baja California.

San Lu·is Peak (săn lōō′ĭs) A mountain, 4,274.3 m (14,014 ft), in the San Juan Mts. of SW CO.

San Lu·is Po·to·sí (săn lōō-ēs′ pō′tō-sē′) A city of central Mexico NE of León; founded in the late 1500s. Pop. 362,371.

San Ma·ri·no (săn mə-rē′nō) A country in the Apennines surrounded by Italy; traditionally founded in the 4th cent. A.D. and the world's smallest republic. The city of **San Marino** (pop. 2,797) is its cap.

San Mar·tín (săn mär-tēn′, sän), **José de** 1778–1850. Argentine revolutionary leader who played a major part in expelling the Spanish from Chile (1818) and Peru (1821).

San Ma·te·o (săn mə-tā′ō) A city of W CA SSE of San Francisco. Pop. 92,482.

San Mi·guel de Tu·cu·mán (săn′ mē-gĕl′ dĕ tōō′kōō-män′) or **Tucumán** A city of N Argentina NNW of Córdoba. Pop. 470,604.

san·nup (săn′əp) *n.* A married Native American man. [Of Massachusett orig.]

sann·ya·si (sŭn-yä′sē) or **sann·ya·sin** (-sĭn) *n., pl.* **-si** or **-sins** *Hinduism* A wandering mendicant and ascetic who has renounced all social norms and earthly obligations. [Hindi *sannyāsī* < Skt. *saṃnyāsī : saṃnyasyati,* he renounces : *sam,* together; see SANSKRIT + *ni,* down + *asyati,* he throws.]

S-A node (ĕs′ā′) *n.* The sinoatrial node.

San Pab·lo (săn păb′lō) A city of W CA NNW of Oakland near **San Pablo Bay,** a N arm of San Francisco Bay. Pop. 30,215.

San Pe·dro Channel (săn pē′drō) A strait of S CA between the mainland and Santa Catalina I. **San Pedro Bay** is an inlet of the channel.

San Pe·dro Su·la (săn pē′drō sōō′lə, sän pē′drō sōō′lä) A city of NW Honduras NW of Tegucigalpa. Pop. 397,201.

San River (sän) A river of SE Poland flowing c. 451 km (280 mi) from the Carpathian Mts. to the Vistula R.

sans (sănz, sän) *prep.* Without. [ME < OFr., blend of Lat. *sine,* without, and *absentiā,* in the absence of, ablative of *absentia,* absence < *absēns, absent-,* pr. part. of *abesse,* to be away. See AB-SENT.]

San Sal·va·dor¹ (săn săl′və-dôr′, săn săl′vä-dôr′) Formerly **Wat·lings Island** (wät′lĭngz) An island of the central Bahamas in the West Indies; generally identified as the first landfall of Christopher Columbus (Oct. 12, 1492).

San Sal·va·dor² (săn săl′və-dôr′, sän săl′vä-dôr′) The cap. of El Salvador, in the W-central part; founded in the 16th cent. Pop. 422,570.

sans-cu·lotte (sănz′kyōō-lŏt′, -kōō-, sän-kü-lôt′) *n.* **1.** A radical republican during the French Revolution. **2.** A revolutionary extremist. [Fr. : *sans,* without + *culotte,* breeches.]

San Se·bas·tián (săn sə-băs′chĭn, săn′ sĕ-väs-tyän′) A city of N Spain on the Bay of Biscay near the French border E of Bilbao. Pop. 171,540.

San•sei (săn′sā′, sän-sā′) *n., pl.* **Sansei** or **-seis** The US-born grandchild of Japanese immigrants to America. [J. : *san*, three + *sei*, generation; see ISSEI.]

san•se•vie•ri•a (săn′sə-vîr′ē-ə, -vē-ĕr′-) *n.* Any of various tropical plants of the genus *Sansevieria*, having lance-shaped leaves. [NLat. *Sansevieria*, genus name, after Raimondo di Sangro (1710–71), Prince of *San Seviero*, Italy.]

San•skrit (săn′skrĭt′) *n.* An ancient Indic language that is the language of Hinduism and the Vedas and the classical literary language of India. [Skt. *saṃskṛtam* < neut. of *saṃskṛta-*, perfected, refined : *sam*, together; see **sem-**[1] in App. + *karoti*, he makes.] —**San′skrit′ist** *n.*

San•skrit•ic (săn-skrĭt′ĭk) *n.* Indic. Not in scientific use.

sans ser•if (săn sĕr′ĭf) *n.* A typeface without serifs. —**sans-ser′if** *adj.*

San•ta (săn′tə) *n.* Santa Claus.

San•ta An•a[1] (săn′tə än′ə) **1.** (*also* sän′tä ä′nä) A city of W El Salvador NW of San Salvador. Pop. 132,200. **2.** A city of S CA E of Long Beach in the fertile valley of the **Santa Ana River,** c. 145 km (90 mi). Pop. 337,977.

San•ta An•a[2] (săn′tə än′ə) *n.* A strong dry hot wind blowing from the desert regions of southern California toward the Pacific, usu. in winter. [After the *Santa Ana* Canyon of S California.]

San•ta An•na (săn′tə än′ə), **An•to•nio López de** 1795?–1876. Mexican military leader who failed to crush the Texan revolt and in the Mexican War lost several battles (1846–47) to Gen. Zachary Taylor.

San•ta Bar•ba•ra (săn′tə bär′bər-ə, bär′brə) A city of S CA WNW of Los Angeles. Pop. 92,325.

Santa Barbara Islands A chain of islands and islets in the Pacific Ocean off S CA; separated from the mainland by **Santa Barbara Channel** in the N and San Pedro Channel in the S.

San•ta Cat•a•li•na Island (săn′tə kăt′l-ē′nə) or **Catalina Island** An island off S CA in the S Santa Barbara Is.

San•ta Cla•ra (săn′tə klăr′ə, klâr′ə) **1.** (*also* săn′tä klä′rä) A city of central Cuba ESE of Havana; founded 1689. Pop. 204,775. **2.** A city of W CA NW of San Jose. Pop. 102,361.

San•ta Claus (săn′tə klôz′) *n.* The personification of the Christmas spirit, usu. represented as a jolly fat old man with a white beard and a red suit, said to bring gifts to good children on Christmas Eve. [Prob. alteration of Du. *Sinterklaas* < MDu. *Sinterclaes*, St. Nicholas : *sint*, saint < MDu. < OFr. *saint*; see SAINT] + *heer*, lord; see MYNHEER + *claes* (short for *Niclaes*, Nicholas).]

San•ta Cruz (săn′tə krōōz′) **1.** (*also* săn′tä krōōs′) A city of central Bolivia NE of Sucre; founded c. 1560. Pop. 767,260. **2.** A city of W CA SSW of San Jose. Pop. 54,593.

San•ta Cruz de Te•ne•ri•fe (săn′tə krōōz′ də tĕn′ə-rē′fä, -rēf′, -rĭf′, săn′tä krōōth′ thĕ tĕn′ĕ-rē′fĕ) A city of the Canary Is. on the NE coast of Tenerife I. Pop. 202,112.

San•ta Cruz Island (săn′tə krōōz′) An island off S CA in the N Santa Barbara Is.

Santa Cruz Islands An island group of the SW Pacific in the SE Solomon Is.

San•ta Fe (săn′tə fā′) **1.** (*also* sän′tä fĕ′) A city of NE Argentina on the Salado R. NW of Buenos Aires; founded 1573. Pop. 342,796. **2.** The cap. of NM, in the N-central part NE of Albuquerque; est. as a Spanish settlement c. 1609 on the site of ancient Native American ruins. Pop. 62,203.

Santa Fe Trail A trade route to the SW US extending c. 1,287 km (800 mi) W from Independence MO to Santa Fe NM; first traversed in 1821.

San•ta Ger•tru•dis (săn′tə gər-trōō′dĭs) *n., pl.* **Santa Gertrudis** Any of a breed of large beef cattle that are highly resistant to heat and insects. [After the *Santa Gertrudis* section of the King Ranch in Kingsville, Texas.]

San•ta Is•a•bel (săn′tə ĭz′ə-bĕl′, săn′tä ē-sä-bĕl′) See **Malabo.**

san•ta•lol (săn′tə-lôl′, -lŏl′, -lōl′) *n.* A colorless liquid, $C_{15}H_{24}O$, obtained from sandalwood and used in perfumes. [NLat. *Santalum*, sandalwood genus (< Med.Lat. *santalum*, sandalwood; see SANDAL[2]) + -OL(E).]

San•ta Ma•ri•a (săn′tə mə-rē′ə, săn′tä mä-) A city of S Brazil W of Pôrto Alegre. Pop. 217,604.

San•ta Mar•ta (săn′tə mär′tə, săn′tä mär′tä) A city of N Colombia on the Caribbean Sea ENE of Barranquilla; founded 1525. Pop. 193,160.

San•ta Mon•i•ca (săn′tə mŏn′ĭ-kə) A city of S CA on the Pacific Ocean W of Los Angeles. Pop. 84,084.

San•tan•der (săn′tän-dĕr′) A city of N Spain on the Bay of Biscay WNW of Bilbao. Pop. 191,155.

San•ta•rém (săn′tə-rĕm′, săn′tä-rĕm′) A city of N Brazil on the Amazon R. E of Manaus; founded 1661. Pop. 264,779.

Santa Ro•sa (săn′tə rō′zə) A city of W CA NNW of San Francisco. Pop. 147,595.

Santa Rosa Island 1. An island of S CA in the NW Santa Barbara Is. separated from the mainland by the Santa Barbara Channel. **2.** A barrier island of NW FL extending c. 80 km (50 mi) along the coast of the Gulf of Mexico.

San•ta•ya•na (săn′tə-yăn′ə, săn′tä-yä′nä), **George** 1863–1952. Spanish-born Amer. philosopher primarily known for his theories of aesthetics, morality, and the spiritual life.

San•tee (săn-tē′) *n., pl.* **Santee** or **-tees** A member of a people of the eastern branch of the Sioux, comprising the Mdewakanton, Sisseton, Wahpekute, and Wahpeton peoples, presently in Nebraska, Minnesota, the Dakotas, and Canada.

Santee River A river of central SC flowing c. 230 km (143 mi) to the Atlantic Ocean.

san•te•ra (săn-tĕr′ə, sän-) *n.* A priestess of Santeria. [Am.Sp. < Sp., fem. of *santero*, cult priest. See SANTERO.]

San•te•ri•a also **san•te•ri•a** (săn′tə-rē′ə, sän′-) *n.* An African-based religion similar to voodoo, originating in Cuba and Brazil and combining the worship of traditional Yoruban deities with the worship of Roman Catholic saints. [< Am.Sp. *santería*, worship of saints < Sp. *santo*, saint < OSpan. < LLat. *sānctus*. See SAINT.]

san•te•ro (săn-tĕr′ō, sän-) *n.* A priest of Santeria. [Am.Sp. < Sp., cult priest < *santo*, saint. See SANTERIA.]

San•ti•a•go (săn′tē-ä′gō, sän′-) **1.** The cap. of Chile, in the central part ESE of Valparaiso; founded 1541. Pop. 4,385,481. **2.** also **Santiago de los Ca•bal•le•ros** (dā′ lōs kä′bəl-yĕr′ōz, dĕ′ lōs kä′vä-yĕ′rōs) A city of N Dominican Republic NW of Santo Domingo; settled c. 1500. Pop. 278,638. **3.** also **Santiago de Com•pos•te•la** (də kŏm′pɔ-stĕl′ə, kŏm′pōs-tĕ′lä) A city of NW Spain SSW of La Coruña. Pop. 62,300.

Santiago de Cu•ba (də kyōō′bə, dĕ kōō′vä) A city of SE Cuba on an islet of the Caribbean Sea; founded 1514. Pop. 432,898.

San•to Do•min•go (săn′tō də-mĭng′gō, săn′tō dō-) Formerly (1936–61) **Ci•u•dad Tru•jil•lo** (sē′ōo-däd′ trōō-hē′yō, syōō-) The cap. of the Dominican Republic, in the SE part; founded 1496. Pop. 2,100,000.

san•ton•i•ca (săn-tŏn′ĭ-kə) *n.* **1.** A perennial or shrubby Eurasian plant (*Artemisia maritima*) having numerous flower heads that yield santonin. **2.** The dried unopened flower heads of this plant. [NLat. < Lat. *(herba) santonica* < fem. of *Santonicus*, of the Santoni, a Gallic people of Aquitania.]

san•to•nin (săn′tə-nĭn) *n.* A colorless crystalline compound, $C_{15}H_{18}O_3$, obtained from species of wormwood, esp. santonica, and used as an anthelmintic. [SANTON(ICA) + -IN.]

san•toor or **san•tur** (săn′tōor′) *n.* A Persian dulcimer typically having two bridges and numerous strings, played with a pair of wooden sticks with curved ends. [Ar. *santīr* < Gk. *psaltērion*, psaltery. See PSALTERY.]

San•to•rin (săn′tə-rēn′) See **Thíra.**

San•tos (săn′təs, sän′tōōs) A city of SE Brazil on an offshore island in the Atlantic Ocean SE of São Paulo; settled in the 1540s. Pop. 428,512.

São Fran•cis•co (soun frən-sĭs′kō, frän-sĕs′kōō) A river of E Brazil flowing c. 2,896 km (1,800 mi) to the Atlantic Ocean.

São Jo•sé dos Cam•pos (zhōō-zā′ dōōs kân′pōōs) A city of SE Brazil ENE of São Paulo. Pop. 442,009.

São Lu•ís (lōō-ēs′) A city of NE Brazil on an offshore island in the Atlantic Ocean ESE of Belém; founded by the French in 1612. Pop. 695,199.

São Mi•guel (mē-gĕl′) An island of the E Azores in the Atlantic Ocean.

Saône (sōn) A river rising in the Vosges Mts. of NE France and flowing c. 431 km (268 mi) to the Rhone R. at Lyon.

São Pau•lo (pou′lō, -lō) A city of SE Brazil WSW of Rio de Janeiro; founded by Jesuits in 1554. Pop. 9,626,894.

São To•mé (tə-mā′, tōō-mĕ′) An island of São Tomé and Príncipe in the Gulf of Guinea off W Africa. The city of **São Tomé** is on the SE coast. Its pop. is 43,420.

São Tomé and Prín•ci•pe (prĭn′sə-pə, prēn′sē-pə) An island country in the Gulf of Guinea off W Africa; an overseas province of Portugal from the early 16th cent. until it achieved independence in 1975. Cap. São Tomé. Pop. 144,128.

São Vi•cen•te (vē-sĕn′tə) A city of SE Brazil on an offshore island in the Atlantic Ocean W of Santos; founded 1532. Pop. 268,732.

sap[1] (săp) *n.* **1a.** The watery fluid that circulates through a plant, carrying food and other substances to the various tissues. **b.** The fluid contents of a plant cell vacuole. **2.** An essential bodily fluid. **3.** Health and energy; vitality. **4.** *Slang* A gullible person; a dupe. **5.** A leather-covered hand weapon; a blackjack. ❖ *tr.v.* **sapped, sap•ping, saps 1.** To drain of sap. **2.** To hit or knock out with a sap. [ME < OE *sæp*.]

sap[2] (săp) *n.* A covered trench or tunnel dug to a point near or within an enemy position. ❖ *v.* **sapped, sap•ping, saps** —*tr.* **1.** To undermine the foundations of (a fortification). **2.** To deplete or weaken gradually. —*intr.* To dig a sap. [Obsolete Fr. *sappe* < Ital. *zappa*, hoe < OFr. and OItal., both < LLat. *sappa*.]

sa•pa•jou (săp′ə-jōō, -jōō) *n.* See **capuchin** 3. [Fr., of Tupian orig.]

Sa•phar (sə-fär′) *n.* Variant of **Safar.**

sap•head (săp′hĕd′) *n. Slang* A gullible or foolish person. —**sap′head′ed** *adj.*

sa•phe•nous vein (sə-fē′nəs) *n., pl.* **-nae** (-nē′) Either of two main superficial veins of the leg that begin at the foot. [*saphenous*, pertaining to the saphena (a saphenous vein) < ME < Med.Lat. *saphena*, saphenous vein < Ar. *ṣāfin*, standing with one leg slightly raised, saphena, part. of *ṣafana*, to stand with one leg slightly raised.]

sap•id (săp′ĭd) *adj.* **1a.** Perceptible to the sense of taste; having flavor. **b.** Having a strong pleasant flavor; savory. **2.** Pleasing to

santoor
detail from a painting by
Kamal-ol-Molk at Golestan
Palace, Teheran, Iran

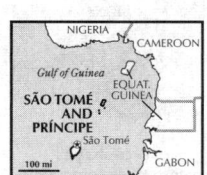

São Tomé and Príncipe

ă pat	oi boy	
ā pay	ou out	
âr care	ŏŏ took	
ä father	ōō boot	
ĕ pet	ŭ cut	
ē be	ûr urge	
ĭ pit	th thin	
ī pie	th this	
îr pier	hw which	
ŏ pot	zh vision	
ō toe	ə about,	
ô paw	item	

Stress marks:
′ (primary);
′ (secondary), as in
lexicon (lĕk′sĭ-kŏn′)

Sappho
detail from *Sappho and Phaon* by Jacques Louis David

Saqqara

sarcophagus
marble sarcophagus of Junius Bassus, c. 359 A. D.

the mind; engaging. [Lat. *sapidus* < *sapere*, to taste.] —**sa·pid′i·ty** (să-pĭd′ĭ-tē, sə-) *n.*

sa·pi·ens (sā′pē-əns, -ĕnz) *adj.* Of, relating to, or characteristic of *Homo sapiens*. [Lat. *sapiēns*, *sapient*-, pr. part. of *sapere*, to taste, be wise. See SAPIENT.]

sa·pi·ent (sā′pē-ənt) *adj.* Having great wisdom and discernment. [ME < OFr. < Lat. *sapiēns*, *sapient*-, pr. part. of *sapere*, to be wise.] —**sa′pi·ence** *n.* —**sa′pi·ent·ly** *adv.*

Sa·pir (sə-pîr′), **Edward** 1884–1939. Amer. anthropologist noted for his studies of Native American languages.

Sa·pir-Whorf hypothesis (sə-pîr′wôrf′, -hwôrf′) *n.* A hypothesis holding that the structure of a language affects its speakers' perceptions of reality and thus influences their thought patterns and worldviews. [After Edward SAPIR and Benjamin Lee WHORF.]

sap·less (săp′lĭs) *adj.* **1.** Devoid of sap; dry. **2.** Lacking spirit or energy. —**sap′less·ness** *n.*

sap·ling (săp′lĭng) *n.* **1.** A young tree. **2.** A youth.

sap·o·dil·la (săp′ə-dĭl′ə, -dē′yə) *n.* **1.** An evergreen tree (*Manilkara zapota*) of Mexico and Central America having latex that yields chicle and edible fruit with sweet yellow-brown flesh. **2.** The fruit of this plant. [Sp. *zapotillo*, dim. of *zapote*, sapodilla fruit < Nahuatl *tzapotl*.]

sap·o·na·ceous (săp′ə-nā′shəs) *adj.* Having the qualities of soap. [Lat. *sāpō*, *sāpōn*-, hair dye; see SAPONIN + –ACEOUS.]

sap·o·na·ted (săp′ə-nā′tĭd) *adj.* Combined or treated with a soap. [< Lat. *sāpō*, *sāpōn*-, hair dye. See SAPONIN.]

sa·pon·i·fi·ca·tion (sə-pŏn′ə-fĭ-kā′shən) *n.* A reaction of an ester heated with an alkali to yield an alcohol and an acid salt, esp. alkaline hydrolysis of a fat or oil to make soap.

sa·pon·i·fy (sə-pŏn′ə-fī′) *v.* **-fied**, **-fy·ing**, **-fies** —*tr.* **1.** To convert (an ester) by saponification. **2.** To convert (a fat or oil) into soap. —*intr.* To undergo saponification. [Fr. *saponifier* < Lat. *sāpō*, *sāpōn*-, hair dye. See SAPONIN.] —**sa·pon′i·fi·a·ble** *adj.* —**sa·pon′i·fi′er** *n.*

sap·o·nin (săp′ə-nĭn, sə-pō′-) *n.* Any of various plant glucosides that form soapy lathers when mixed and agitated with water, used in detergents, foaming agents, and emulsifiers. [< Lat. *sāpō*, *sāpōn*-, hair dye, of Gmc. orig.]

sa·por (sā′pər, -pôr′) *n.* A quality perceptible to the sense of taste; flavor. [ME < Lat. < *sapere*, to taste.] —**sa′po·rif′ic** (sā′pə-rĭf′ĭk, săp′ə-) *adj.* —**sa′po·rous** (sā′pər-əs, săp′ər-) *adj.*

sa·po·te (sə-pō′tē, -tā) *or* **sa·po·ta** (-tə) *n.* **1.** A Mexican and Central American tree (*Pouteria sapota*) having edible oval fruit. **2.** The fruit of this tree. [Sp. *zapota* < Nahuatl *tzapotl*.]

sap·pan·wood (sə-păn′wŏod′, săp′ăn-, -ən-) *n.* **1.** A tree (*Caesalpina sappan*) of tropical Asia having wood that yields a red dye. **2.** The wood of this tree. [Malay *sapang* + WOOD[1].]

sap·per (săp′ər) *n.* **1.** A military engineer who specializes in sapping and other field fortification activities. **2.** A military engineer who lays, detects, and disarms mines. [< SAP[2].]

Sap·phic (săf′ĭk) *adj.* **1.** Of or relating to the Greek poet Sappho. **2a.** Of, relating to, or being an Aeolic verse consisting of four syllables followed by a central choriamb and a final part of three syllables. **b.** Relating to or being a stanza of three such verses followed by a verse consisting of a dactyl followed by a spondee or trochee. **c.** Relating to or being an ode made up of such stanzas. **d.** Of, relating to, or being poetry in accentual meter composed in imitation of Sapphic quantitative verse. **3.** *often* **sapphic** Of or relating to lesbianism. ❖ *n.* A Sapphic meter, verse, stanza, or ode.

sap·phire (săf′īr′) *n.* **1.** A clear hard variety of corundum used as a gemstone that is usu. blue but may be any color except red. **2.** A corundum gem. **3.** The blue color of a gem sapphire. ❖ *adj.* **1.** Made of or resembling a gem sapphire. **2.** Having the color of a blue sapphire. [ME *saphir* < OFr. *safir* < Lat. *sapphīrus* < Gk. *sappheiros*, of Semitic orig.; akin to Heb. *sappîr*, a precious stone.]

sap·phi·rine (săf′ə-rīn′, -rēn′, sə-fīr′īn) *adj.* Of or resembling sapphire. ❖ *n.* A rare light blue or green aluminum-magnesium silicate mineral.

Sap·pho (săf′ō) fl. c. 600 B.C. Greek lyric poet whose works survive only in fragments.

Sap·po·ro (sə-pôr′ō, -pōr′ō) A city of SW Hokkaido, Japan, near the head of Ishikari Bay. Pop. 1,731,670.

sap·py (săp′ē) *adj.* **-pi·er**, **-pi·est** **1.** Full of sap; juicy. **2.** *Slang* Excessively sentimental; mawkish. **3.** *Slang* Silly or foolish. —**sap′pi·ly** *adv.* —**sap′pi·ness** *n.*

sa·pre·mi·a *also* **sa·prae·mi·a** (sə-prē′mē-ə) *n.* Blood poisoning resulting from the absorption of the products of putrefaction. —**sa·pre′mic** *adj.*

sapro– *or* **sapr–** *pref.* **1.** Decay; putrefaction; decomposition: *saprogenic*. **2.** Dead or decaying organic material: *saprophyte*. [Gk. < *sapros*, rotten.]

sap·robe (săp′rōb′) *n.* An organism that derives its nourishment from nonliving or decaying organic matter. [SAPRO– + Gk. *bios*, life; see g**w**eiə- in App.] —**sap′ro′bi·al** (să-prō′bē-əl), **sap′ro′bic** (-bĭk) *adj.* —**sap·ro′bi·cal·ly** *adv.*

sap·ro·gen·ic (săp′rə-jĕn′ĭk) *also* **sap·rog·e·nous** (sə-prŏj′ə-nəs) *adj.* Of, producing, or resulting from putrefaction. —**sap′ro·ge·nic′i·ty** (-jə-nĭs′ĭ-tē) *n.*

sap·ro·lite (săp′rə-līt′) *n.* Soft, partially decomposed rock rich in clay and remaining in its original place.

sap·ro·pel (săp′rə-pĕl′) *n.* A mud rich in organic matter formed at the bottom of a body of water. [SAPRO– + Gk. *pēlos*, mud.] —**sap′ro·pel′ic** (-pĕl′ĭk, -pē′lĭk) *adj.*

sap·roph·a·gous (să-prŏf′ə-gəs) *adj.* Feeding on decaying organic matter.

sap·ro·phyte (săp′rə-fīt′) *n.* An organism, esp. a fungus or bacterium, that feeds on dead or decaying organic matter. —**sap′ro·phyt′ic** (-fĭt′ĭk) *adj.* —**sap′ro·phyt′i·cal·ly** *adv.*

sap·ro·zo·ic (săp′rə-zō′ĭk) *adj.* **1.** Obtaining nourishment by absorption of dissolved organic and inorganic matter, as in protozoans. **2.** Feeding on dead or decaying animal matter.

sap·sa·go (săp-sā′gō, săp′sə-gō′) *n.*, *pl.* **-gos** A hard green cheese made from skim-milk curd, colored and flavored with sweet clover. [Alteration of Ger. *Schabzieger* : *schaben*, to scrape (< MHGer. < OHGer. *skaban*) + *Zieger*, whey, whey cheese (< MHGer. *ziger*, prob. of Celt. orig.).]

sap·suck·er (săp′sŭk′ər) *n.* Any of various small American woodpeckers of the genus *Sphyrapicus* that drill holes in certain trees to drink the sap and eat insects in them.

sap·wood (săp′wŏod′) *n.* The newly formed outer wood located just inside the vascular cambium of a tree trunk and active in the conduction of water.

Saq·qa·ra *also* **Sak·ka·ra** (sə-kär′ə) A village of N Egypt near Cairo; site of the oldest Egyptian pyramids.

SAR *abbr.* Sons of the American Revolution

sar·a·band *also* **sar·a·bande** (săr′ə-bănd′) *n.* **1.** A fast, erotic dance of the 16th century of Mexico and Spain. **2.** A stately court dance of the 17th and 18th centuries, in slow triple time. **3.** The music for either of these dances. [Fr. *sarabande* < Sp. *zarabanda*.]

Sar·a·cen (săr′ə-sən) *n.* **1.** A member of a pre-Islamic nomadic people of the Syrian-Arabian deserts. **2.** *Archaic* An Arab. **3.** A Muslim, esp. of the time of the Crusades. [ME < OE < LLat. *Saracēnus* < L.Gk. *Sarakēnos*, ult. < Ar. *šarq*, east.] —**Sar′a·cen′ic** (-sĕn′ĭk) *adj.*

Sar·a·gos·sa (săr′ə-gŏs′ə) *also* **Za·ra·go·za** (zär′ə-gō′zə, thä′rä-gō′thä) A city of NE Spain NE of Madrid; held by the Moors from 713 until 1118. Pop. 598,078.

Sar·ah (sâr′ə) In the Bible, the wife of Abraham and mother of Isaac. [Heb. *śârâ*, princess, fem. of *śar*, prince.]

Sa·ra·je·vo (săr′ə-yā′vō, săr′ə-yĕ-vō′) The cap. of Bosnia and Herzegovina, in the S-central part SW of Belgrade. The assassination of Archduke Francis Ferdinand and his wife here on Jun. 28, 1914, triggered the outbreak of World War I. Pop. 415,631.

Sa·ra·ma·go (sä′rə-mä′gŏo), **José** b. 1922. Portuguese writer who won the 1998 Nobel Prize for literature.

sa·ran (sə-răn′) *n.* Any of various thermoplastic resins derived from vinyl compounds and used to make packaging films, fittings, and bristles and as a fiber in various heavy fabrics. [Orig. a trademark.]

Sar·a·nac Lakes (săr′ə-năk′) A group of three lakes in the Adirondack Mts. of NE NY linked by the **Saranac River,** which flows c. 161 km (100 mi) to Lake Champlain.

Sa·ransk (sə-ränsk′) A city of W Russia W of Simbirsk; founded as a fort in the 1600s. Pop. 321,221.

sa·ra·pe (sə-rä′pē, -räp′ē) *n.* Variant of **serape.**

Sar·a·so·ta (săr′ə-sō′tə) A city of W-central FL on **Sarasota Bay,** an inlet of the Gulf of Mexico. Pop. 52,715.

Sar·a·to·ga trunk (săr′ə-tō′gə) *n.* A large traveling trunk having a rounded top. [After SARATOGA (SPRINGS).]

Sa·ra·tov (sə-rä′təf) A city of SW Russia on the Volga R. NNE of Volgorad; orig. founded 1590. Pop. 889,173.

Sa·ra·wak (sə-rä′wäk, -wäk, -wä) A region of Malaysia on NW Borneo; formerly a British protectorate (1888–1946) and a crown colony (1946–63).

sar·casm (sär′kăz′əm) *n.* **1.** A cutting, often ironic remark intended to wound. **2.** A form of wit that uses such remarks to make its victim the butt of contempt or ridicule. **3.** The use of sarcasm. [LLat. *sarcasmus* < Gk. *sarkasmos* < *sarkazein*, to bite the lips in rage < *sarx*, *sark*-, flesh.]

sar·cas·tic (sär-kăs′tĭk) *adj.* **1.** Expressing or marked by sarcasm. **2.** Given to using sarcasm. [SARC(ASM) + -*astic*, as in ENTHUSIASTIC.] —**sar·cas′ti·cal·ly** *adv.*

sarce·net (särs′nĭt) *n.* A fine soft silk cloth. [ME *sarsenet* < AN *sarzinett*, perh. < OFr. *Saracin*, Saracen < LLat. *Saracēnus*. See SARACEN.]

sarco– *or* **sarc–** *pref.* **1.** Flesh: *sarcophagic*. **2.** Striated muscle: *sarcolemma*. [Gk. *sarko-* < *sarx*, *sark*-, flesh.]

sar·co·din·i·an (sär′kə-dĭn′ē-ən) *adj.* Of or belonging to the Sarcodina, a superclass of protozoans. [NLat. *Sarcodīna*, superclass name < Gk. *sarkōdēs*, fleshy < *sarx*, *sark*-, flesh.] —**sar′co·din′i·an** *n.*

sar·coid (sär′koid′) *adj.* Relating to or resembling flesh. ❖ *n.* **1.** See **sarcoidosis. 2.** A tumor resembling a sarcoma.

sar·coid·o·sis (sär′koi-dō′sĭs) *n.*, *pl.* **-ses** (-sēz) A disease of unknown origin marked by the formation of granulomatous lesions, esp. in the liver, lungs, skin, and lymph nodes.

sar·co·lem·ma (sär′kə-lĕm′ə) *n.* A thin membrane enclosing a striated muscle fiber. [SARCO– + Gk. *lemma*, husk; see LEMMA[2].] —**sar′co·lem′mal** *adj.*

sar·co·ma (sär-kō′mə) *n.*, *pl.* **-mas** *also* **-ma·ta** (-mə-tə) A malignant tumor arising from connective tissues. [NLat. < Gk. *sar-*

kōma, sarkomat-, fleshy excrescence < *sarkoun,* to produce flesh < *sarx, sark-,* flesh.] **—sar•co′ma•toid′** (-mə-toid′), **sar•co′ma•tous** (-təs) *adj.*

sar•co•ma•to•sis (sär-kō′mə-tō′sĭs) *n.* Formation of numerous sarcomas in various parts of the body.

sar•co•mere (sär′kə-mîr′) *n.* One of the segments into which a fibril of striated muscle is divided.

sar•co•phag•ic (sär-kə-făj′ĭk, -fā′jĭk) also **sar•coph•a•gous** (sär-kŏf′ə-gəs) *adj.* Flesh-eating; carnivorous.

sar•coph•a•gus (sär-kŏf′ə-gəs) *n., pl.* **-gi** (-jī′) or **-gus•es** A stone coffin, often inscribed or decorated with sculpture. [Lat. < Gk. *sarkophagos,* coffin < *(lithos) sarkophagos,* limestone that consumed the flesh of corpses laid in it : *sarx, sark-,* flesh + *-phagos,* -phagous.]

sar•co•plasm (sär′kə-plăz′əm) *n.* The cytoplasm of a striated muscle fiber. **—sar′co•plas•mat′ic** (-plăz-măt′ĭk), **sar′co•plas′mic** (-mĭk) *adj.*

sarcoplasmic reticulum *n.* The form of endoplasmic reticulum found in striated muscle fibers.

sar•cop•tic mange (sär-kŏp′tĭk) *n.* Mange caused by the mite *Sarcoptes scabiei.* [< NLat. *Sarcoptes,* genus name : SARCO- + Gk. *koptein,* to cut.]

sar•co•some (sär′kə-sōm′) *n.* A large specialized mitrochondrion found in striated muscle. **—sar′co•so′mal** *adj.*

sar•cous (sär′kəs) *adj.* Of, relating to, or consisting of flesh or muscle tissue.

sard (särd) *n.* A clear or translucent deep orange-red to brownish-red variety of chalcedony. [ME *sarde* < OFr. < Lat. *sarda,* perh. < *Sardis,* Sardis.]

sar•dine (sär-dēn′) *n.* **1.** Any of various small or half-grown edible herrings or related fishes of the family Clupeidae, frequently canned, esp. the pilchard of European waters. **2.** Any of numerous small silvery edible freshwater or marine fishes unrelated to the sardine. ❖ *tr.v.* **-dined, -din•ing, -dines** *Slang* To pack tightly; cram. [ME *sardin* < OFr. *sardine* < Lat. *sardīna* < *sarda,* a fish, ult. < Gk. *Sardō,* Sardinia.]

Sar•din•i•a (sär-dĭn′ē-ə, -dĭn′yə) An island of Italy in the Mediterranean Sea S of Corsica; settled by Phoenicians, Greeks, and Carthaginians before the 6th cent. B.C.

Sar•din•i•an (sär-dĭn′ē-ən, -yən) *adj.* Of Sardinia or its people, language, or culture. ❖ *n.* **1.** A native or inhabitant of Sardinia. **2.** The Romance language of the Sardinians.

Sar•dis (sär′dĭs) An ancient city of W Asia Minor NE of Izmir, Turkey; destroyed by Tamerlane in 1402.

sar•di•us (sär′dē-əs) *n.* See **sard.** [ME < OE < Lat. *sarda.* See SARD.]

sar•don•ic (sär-dŏn′ĭk) *adj.* Scornfully or cynically mocking. [Fr. *sardonique,* ult. < Gk. *sardanios.*] **—sar•don′i•cal•ly** *adv.* **—sar•don′i•cism** (-ĭ-sĭz′əm) *n.*

sar•don•yx (sär-dŏn′ĭks, sär′dn-ĭks′) *n.* An onyx with alternating brown and white bands of sard and other minerals. [ME *sardonix,* prob. < Lat. *sardonyx* < Gk. *sardonux : sardion,* sard; see SARD + *onux,* onyx, nail.]

Sar•dou (sär-dōō′), **Victorien** 1831–1908. French playwright known esp. for his light comedies, including *Peril* (1861).

Sa•re•ma (sär′ə-mä′) See **Saaremaa.**

sar•gas•so (sär-găs′ō) *n., pl.* **-sos** See **gulfweed.** [Port. *sargaço.*]

Sargasso Sea A part of the N Atlantic Ocean between the West Indies and the Azores.

sar•gas•sum (sär-găs′əm) *n.* See **gulfweed.** [NLat. *Sargassum,* genus name < SARGASSO.]

sargassum fish *n.* A frogfish (*Histrio histrio*) found among the drifting gulfweed of the Atlantic and western Pacific.

sarge (särj) *n. Informal* Sergeant.

Sar•gent (sär′jənt), **John Singer** 1856–1925. Amer. painter known esp. for his portraits and watercolor landscapes.

Sar•gon II (sär′gŏn′) d. 705 B.C. Assyrian king (721–705) who completed the conquest of the N Jewish kingdom of Israel, later known as Samaria.

sa•ri (sär′ē) *n., pl.* **-ris** An outer garment worn chiefly by women of India and Pakistan, consisting of lightweight cloth with one end wrapped about the waist to form a skirt and the other draped over the shoulder or head. [Hindi *sāṛī* < Prakrit *sāḍī* < Skt. *śāṭī.*]

sar•in (sär′ĭn) *n.* A poisonous liquid, $C_4H_{10}FO_2P$, that inhibits the activity of cholinesterase and is used as a nerve gas in chemical warfare. [Ger., orig. a code name.]

Sark (särk) One of the Channel Is. in the English Channel E of Guernsey comprising **Great Sark** and **Little Sark,** joined by a natural causeway. **—Sark•ese′** (sär-kēz′, -kēs′) *adj. & n.*

Sar•ma•tia (sär-mā′shə, -shē-ə) An ancient region of E Europe NE of the Black Sea. The term is also applied to the territory between the Vistula and Volga rivers during the time of the Roman Empire. **—Sar•ma′tian** *adj. & n.*

sar•men•tose (sär-mĕn′tōs′) *adj. Botany* Having slender prostrate stolons, as in the strawberry. [Lat. *sarmentōsus,* full of twigs < *sarmentum,* twigs.]

sa•rod or **sa•rode** (sə-rōd′) *n.* A many-stringed lute of northern India that is played with a plectrum. [Urdu < Pers. *sarūd* < MPers. *srōd;* akin to Avestan *sraotəm,* hearing, sound. See **kleu-** in App.]

sa•rong (sə-rông′, -rŏng′) *n.* A garment consisting of a length of printed cloth wrapped about the waist that is worn by men and women in Malaysia, Indonesia, and the Pacific islands. [Malay *(kain) sarong,* covering (cloth), sarong.]

Sa•ron•ic Gulf (sə-rŏn′ĭk) An arm of the Aegean Sea in S Greece between Attica and the Peloponnesus E of Corinth.

Sa•ros (sär′ŏs′, sä′rôs), **Gulf of** An inlet of the NE Aegean Sea indenting NW European Turkey N of Gallipoli.

Sa•roy•an (sə-roi′ən), **William** 1908–81. Amer. writer whose works include the play *The Time of Your Life* (1939).

Sar•pe•don (sär-pēd′n, -pē′dŏn) *n. Greek Mythology* A son of Zeus and Europa who became king of Lycia and was killed by Patroclus in the Trojan War.

sar•sa•pa•ril•la (săs′pə-rĭl′ə, särs′-) *n.* **1a.** Any of several tropical American plants of the genus *Smilax.* **b.** The dried roots of any of these plants, used as a flavoring. **c.** A sweet soft drink flavored with these roots. **2.** Either of two North American plants (*Aralia hispida* or *A. nudicaulis*) having umbels of small white flowers. [Sp. *zarzaparrilla : zarza,* bramble (< Ar. *šaras,* colloquial var. of *širs,* ult. < *šarra, šarasa,* to be vicious) + *parrilla,* dim. of *parra,* vine.]

Sarthe (särt) A river of NW France flowing c. 285 km (177 mi), generally S to Angers.

sar•to•ri•al (sär-tôr′ē-əl, -tōr′-) *adj.* Of or relating to a tailor, tailoring, or tailored clothing: *sartorial elegance.* [< LLat. *sartor,* tailor. See SARTORIUS.] **—sar•to′ri•al•ly** *adv.*

sar•to•ri•us (sär-tôr′ē-əs, -tōr′-) *n., pl.* **-to•ri•i** (-tôr′ē-ī, -tōr′-) A flat narrow thigh muscle crossing the front of the thigh from the hip to the inner side of the tibia. [NLat. < LLat. *sartor,* tailor (< its producing a tailor's cross-legged position) < *sartus,* p. part. of *sarcīre,* to mend.]

Sar•tre (sär′trə, särt), **Jean Paul** 1905–80. French writer and existentialist who declined the 1964 Nobel Prize for literature.

SASE *abbr.* self-addressed stamped envelope

sash[1] (săsh) *n.* A band or ribbon worn about the waist as part of one's clothing or over the shoulder as a symbol of rank. ❖ *tr.v.* **sashed, sash•ing, sash•es** To put a band or ribbon about (the waist). [Ar. *šāš,* muslin; akin to Heb. *šēš,* byssus, fine linen, both prob. < Egypt. *šs,* linen.]

sash[2] (săsh) *n.* A frame in which window or door panes are set. ❖ *tr.v.* **sashed, sash•ing, sash•es** To furnish with a sash. [Alteration of Fr. *châssis,* frame (taken as pl.). See CHASSIS.]

sa•shay (să-shā′) *Informal intr.v.* **-shayed, -shay•ing, -shays** **1a.** To walk or proceed, esp. easily or casually. **b.** To strut or flounce in a showy manner. **2.** To perform the chassé. **3.** To move sideways. ❖ *n.* **1.** A chassé. **2.** An excursion; an outing. **3.** A figure in square dancing in which partners circle each other by taking sideways steps. [Alteration of CHASSÉ.]

sa•shi•mi (sä-shē′mē) *n.* A Japanese dish consisting of bite-size slices of fresh raw fish. [J. : *sasu,* to prick, stab + *mi,* body, meat.]

Sask. *abbr.* Saskatchewan

Sas•katch•e•wan (să-skăch′ə-wän′, -wən) A province of S-central Canada; joined the Confederation in 1905. The first permanent settlement in the area was made by the Hudson's Bay Company in 1774. Cap. Regina. Pop. 990,237.

Saskatchewan River A river of S-central Canada formed by the North and South Saskatchewan rivers and flowing c. 547 km (340 mi) to Lake Winnipeg in Manitoba.

sas•ka•toon (săs′kə-tōōn′) *n.* **1.** A shrub (*Amelanchier alnifolia*) of northwest North America having white flowers and edible dark purple fruit. **2.** The fruit of this plant. [< Cree *misaaskwatoomin,* saskatoon berry.]

Saskatoon A city of S-central Saskatchewan, Canada, on the South Saskatchewan R. NW of Regina; settled in 1883. Pop. 193,647.

Sas•quatch (săs′kwŏch, -kwăch) *n.* See **Bigfoot.** [Halkomelem (Salishan language of SW Brit. Columbia) *sē′sq′əč.*]

sass (săs) *Informal n.* Impertinent, disrespectful speech; back talk. ❖ *tr.v.* **sassed, sass•ing, sass•es** To talk impudently to. [Back-formation < SASSY[1].]

sas•sa•by (săs′ə-bē) *n., pl.* **-bies** A South African antelope (*Damaliscus lunatus*) having curved ridged horns. [Sotho (Tswana) *tshêsêbê.*]

sas•sa•fras (săs′ə-frăs′) *n.* **1.** A deciduous eastern North American tree (*Sassafras albidum*) having irregularly lobed leaves and aromatic bark, leaves, and branches. **2.** The dried root bark of this plant, used as a flavoring and a source of a volatile oil. [Sp. *sasafrás* < LLat. *saxifragia,* kind of herb, var. of (*herba*) *saxifraga,* saxifrage. See SAXIFRAGE.]

Sas•sa•ni•an or **Sa•sa•ni•an** (sə-sä′nē-ən, să-) also **Sas•sa•nid** (sə-sä′nĭd, -sän′ĭd, săs′ə-nĭd) *adj.* Of or relating to a Persian dynasty (A.D. 224–651), the last line of kings before the Arab conquest, whose rule was marked by wars against Romans, Armenians, and Huns and by the revival of Zoroastrianism. [After *Sasan,* ancestor of Ardashir I, founder of the dynasty.]

Sas•soon (sə-sōōn′, să-), **Siegfried Lorraine** 1886–1967. British writer known for his antiwar poems based on his combat experience in World War I.

sass•wood (săs′wŏŏd′) *n.* See **sassy**[2]. [Alteration of *sassywood* : SASSY[2] + WOOD[1].]

sas•sy[1] (săs′ē) *adj.* **-si•er, -si•est** **1.** Rude and disrespectful; impudent. **2.** Lively and spirited; jaunty. **3.** Stylish; chic. [Alteration

John Singer Sargent
detail from a 1907
self-portrait

sari

sarong

ă	pat	oi	boy
ā	pay	ou	out
âr	care	ŏŏ	took
ä	father	ōō	boot
ĕ	pet	ŭ	cut
ē	be	ûr	urge
ĭ	pit	th	thin
ī	pie	*th*	this
îr	pier	hw	which
ŏ	pot	zh	vision
ō	toe	ə	about,
ô	paw		item

Stress marks:
′ (primary);
′ (secondary), as in
lexicon (lĕk′sĭ-kŏn′)

of SAUCY.] —**sas′si•ly** adv. —**sas′si•ness** n.

sas•sy² (săs′ē) n., pl. **-sies** A western African tree (*Erythrophleum suaveolens*) of the pea family, having bark that yields a poison. [Of W African orig.; akin to Twi -*sésé*, plane tree, and Ewe *séséwú*, timber tree.]

sas•tru•ga (să-strōō′gə, săs′trə-, sä′strə-) also **zas•tru•ga** (ză-strōō′gə, zä-) n., pl. **-gi** (-gē) A long wavelike ridge of snow, formed by the wind and found on the polar plains. [Russ. dialectal *zastruga* : *za*, beyond + *struga*, deep place; see **sreu**- in App.]

sat (săt) v. Past tense and past participle of **sit.**

SAT (ĕs′ā-tē′) A trademark used for a set of standardized college entrance examinations.

Sat. abbr. Saturday

Sa•tan (sāt′n) n. The profoundly evil adversary of God and humanity, often identified with the leader of the fallen angels; the Devil. [ME < OE < LLat. *Satān* < Gk. *Satanas, Satān* < Heb. *śāṭān*, devil, adversary < *śāṭan*, to accuse, act as adversary.]

sa•tan•ic (sə-tăn′ĭk, sā-) or **sa•tan•i•cal** (-ĭ-kəl) adj. **1.** Relating to or suggestive of Satan or evil. **2.** Profoundly cruel or evil; fiendish. —**sa•tan′i•cal•ly** adv.

Sa•tan•ism (sāt′n-ĭz′əm) n. **1.** The worship of Satan characterized by a travesty of the Christian rites. **2. satanism** Profound wickedness. —**Sa′tan•ist** n.

sa•tay also **sa•té** or **sa•te** (sä′tā) n. A dish of southeast Asia consisting of marinated meat, poultry, or seafood grilled on skewers and dipped in peanut sauce. [Malay *saté, satai* or Indonesian *sate*, both perh. of Tamil orig.]

satch•el (săch′əl) n. A small bag, often having a shoulder strap. [ME *sachel* < OFr. < LLat. *saccellus* < Lat. *sacculus*, dim. of *saccus*, bag. See SACK¹.] —**satch′eled** adj. —**satch′el•ful′** (-fŏŏl′) n.

sate¹ (sāt) tr.v. **sat•ed, sat•ing, sates 1.** To satisfy (an appetite) fully. **2.** To satisfy to excess. [Prob. alteration of ME *saden* < OE *sadian*.]

sate² (sāt, săt) v. Archaic A past tense of **sit.**

sa•teen (să-tēn′) n. A cotton fabric with a satinlike finish. [Alteration (influenced by VELVETEEN) of SATIN.]

sat•el•lite (săt′l-īt′) n. **1.** A celestial body that orbits a planet; a moon. **2.** An object launched to orbit Earth or another celestial body. **3.** One who attends a powerful dignitary; a minion. **4.** A subservient follower; a sycophant. **5.** A nation dominated politically and economically by another. **6.** An urban or suburban community located near a big city. **7.** Genetics A short segment of a chromosome separated from the rest by a constriction, typically associated with the formation of a nucleolus. **8.** Microbiology A colony of microorganisms whose growth in culture medium is enhanced by certain substances produced by another nearby colony. [Fr., hanger-on, hireling < OFr. < Lat. *satelles, satellit*-.]

satellite cell n. **1.** Any of the cells that encapsulate the bodies of nerve cells in ganglia. **2.** A stem cell found in skeletal muscle that acts in the regeneration and repair of muscle fibers after injury.

satellite dish n. A dish antenna used to receive and transmit signals relayed by satellite.

sa•tem (sät′əm) adj. Designating those Indo-European languages, including the Indo-Iranian, Armenian, and Balto-Slavic branches, in which original palatal velar stops became fricatives (as *k′* > *s* or *š*) and labiovelar stops became plain velars (as *kʷ* > *k*). [Avestan *satəm*, hundred (a word whose initial stop illustrates the sound change). See **dekm̥** in App.]

sa•ti (sŭ-tē′, sŭt′ē′) n. Variant of **suttee.**

sa•tia•ble (sā′shə-bəl, -shē-ə-) adj. Possible to satisfy or sate: *satiable thirst.* —**sa′tia•bil′i•ty** n. —**sa′tia•bly** adv.

sa•ti•ate (sā′shē-āt′) tr.v. **-at•ed, -at•ing, -ates 1.** To satisfy (an appetite or desire) fully. **2.** To satisfy to excess. ❖ adj. (-ĭt) Filled to satisfaction. [ME *saciaten* < Lat. *satiāre, satiāt*- < *satis*, sufficient.] —**sa′ti•a′tion** n.

Sa•tie (sä-tē′), **Erik** 1866–1925. French composer whose compositions include *Socrate* (1918).

sa•ti•e•ty (sə-tī′ĭ-tē) n. The condition of being full or gratified beyond the point of satisfaction; surfeit. [Fr. *satiete* < OFr. *saciete* < Lat. *satietās* < *satis*, sufficient.]

sat•in (săt′n) n. **1.** A smooth fabric, as of silk, woven with a glossy face and a dull back. **2.** A garment made of this fabric. ❖ adj. **1.** Made of or covered with satin. **2.** Glossy, sleek, and smooth. [ME < OFr., prob. < Ar. (*'atlas*) *zaytūnī*, (satin) of Zaitun < *zaitūn*, prob. Quanzhou, China.]

sat•in•et (săt′n-ĕt′) n. A thin inferior satin or an imitation satin, esp. one containing cotton.

satin flower n. **1.** A plant (*Clarkia amoena*) of coastal California having red-blotched flowers. **2.** See **honesty** 4.

satin stitch n. An embroidery stitch worked in close parallel lines to give a solid satinlike finish.

satin weave n. A basic weave construction whereby the face of the cloth shows only warp or only weft and no twill appears.

sat•in•wood (săt′n-wŏŏd′) n. **1.** A deciduous tree (*Chloroxylon swietenia*) of India and Sri Lanka having hard yellowish close-grained wood. **2.** A West Indian tree (*Zanthoxylum flavum*) having smooth, slightly oily, lustrous wood. **3.** The wood of either of these trees.

sat•in•y (săt′n-ē) adj. Lustrous and smooth like satin.

sat•ire (săt′īr′) n. **1a.** A literary work that attacks human vice or folly through irony, derision, or wit. **b.** The branch of literature constituting such works. **2.** Irony, sarcasm, or caustic wit used to attack or expose folly or vice. [Lat. *satira*, prob. alteration (influenced by Gk. *satur*, satyr, and *satyros*, mythical burlesque) of (*lanx*) *satura*, fruit (plate) mixture < fem. of *satur*, sated, well-fitted.]

sa•tir•i•cal (sə-tĭr′ĭ-kəl) or **sa•tir′ic** (-ĭk) adj. Of, relating to, or characterized by satire. —**sa•tir′i•cal•ly** adv.

sat•i•rist (săt′ər-ĭst) n. One who is given to satire, esp. a writer of satirical works.

sat•i•rize (săt′ə-rīz′) tr.v. **-rized, -riz•ing, -riz•es** To ridicule or attack by means of satire.

sat•is•fac•tion (săt′ĭs-făk′shən) n. **1a.** The fulfillment or gratification of a desire, need, or appetite. **b.** Pleasure or contentment derived from such gratification. **c.** A source or means of gratification. **2a.** Compensation for injury or loss; reparation. **b.** The opportunity to avenge a wrong; vindication. **3.** Assurance beyond doubt; complete conviction. [ME < OFr. < Lat. *satisfactiō, satisfactiōn*-, amends < *satisfactus*, p. part. of *satisfacere*, to satisfy. See SATISFY.]

sat•is•fac•to•ry (săt′ĭs-făk′tə-rē) adj. Giving satisfaction sufficient to meet a demand or requirement; adequate. —**sat′is•fac′to•ri•ly** adv. —**sat′is•fac′to•ri•ness** n.

sat•is•fi•a•ble (săt′ĭs-fī′ə-bəl) adj. Capable of being satisfied: *satisfiable needs and desires.*

sat•is•fied (săt′ĭs-fīd′) adj. **1.** Filled with satisfaction; content: *a very satisfied customer.* **2.** Paid or discharged in full, as a debt or obligation. **3.** Convinced beyond a doubt.

sat•is•fy (săt′ĭs-fī′) v. **-fied, -fy•ing, -fies** —tr. **1.** To gratify the need, desire, or expectation of. **2.** To fulfill (a need or desire). **3a.** To free from doubt; assure. **b.** To dispel (a doubt or question). **4a.** To discharge (a debt, for example) in full. **b.** To discharge an obligation to (a creditor). **5.** To conform to the requirements of (a standard or rule); be sufficient to (an end). **6.** To make reparation for; redress. **7.** Mathematics To make the left and right sides of (an equation) equal after substituting equivalent quantities for the unknown variables in the equation. —intr. **1.** To be sufficient or adequate. **2.** To give satisfaction. [ME *satisfien* < OFr. *satisfier* < Lat. *satisfacere* : *satis*, sufficient; see **sā**- in App. + *facere*, to make.] —**sat′is•fi′er** n. —**sat′is•fy′ing•ly** adv.

SYNONYMS *satisfy, answer, fill, fulfill, meet* These verbs mean to supply fully or completely: *satisfied all requirements; answered our needs; fills a purpose; fulfilled their aspirations; met her obligations.*

Sa•to (sä′tō), **Eisaku** 1901–75. Japanese politician who won the 1974 Nobel Peace Prize.

sa•to•ri (sä-tôr′ē, -tōr′ē, sə-) n. A spiritual awakening sought in Zen Buddhism, often coming suddenly. [J.]

sa•trap (sā′trăp′, săt′răp′) n. **1.** A governor of a province in ancient Persia. **2.** A ruler. **3.** A subordinate bureaucrat or official. [ME *satrape* < OFr. < Lat. *satrapēs* < Gk. < OPers. *khshathrapāvā*, protector of the province : *khshathra*-, realm, province + *pāvā*, protector; see **pā**- in App.]

sa•tra•py (sā′trə-pē, -trăp′ē, săt′rə-pē) n., pl. **-pies 1.** The territory or sphere under the rule of a satrap. **2.** A nation, state, territory, or area controlled as if by a satrap.

sat•su•ma (săt-sōō′mə, săt′sōō-mä) n. **1.** A seedless mandarin orange native to Japan and the hardiest commercial citrus fruit. **2. Satsuma** A Japanese porcelain. [After *Satsuma*, a peninsula of southwest Kyushu, Japan.]

sat•u•rant (săch′ər-ənt) adj. Serving to saturate. ❖ n. A substance used to saturate.

sat•u•rate (săch′ə-rāt′) tr.v. **-rat•ed, -rat•ing, -rates 1.** To imbue or impregnate thoroughly. **2.** To soak, fill, or load to capacity. **3.** Chemistry To cause (a substance) to unite with the greatest possible amount of another substance. ❖ adj. (-rĭt) Saturated. [Lat. *saturāre, saturāt*-, to fill < *satur*, sated.] —**sat′u•ra•ble** (-ər-ə-bəl) adj. —**sat′u•ra′tor** n.

sat•u•rat•ed (săch′ə-rā′tĭd) adj. **1.** Unable to hold or contain more; full. **2.** Soaked with moisture; drenched. **3.** Chemistry **a.** Combined with or containing all the solute that can normally be dissolved at a given temperature. **b.** Relating to or being a fat that is predominantly composed of fatty acids having only single bonds in the carbon chain. **4.** Geology Of or relating to minerals that can crystallize from magmas even in the presence of excess silica.

saturated fat n. A fat found in animal products, dairy foods, and certain plant oils that contributes to increased cholesterol levels in the blood.

sat•u•ra•tion (săch′ə-rā′shən) n. **1a.** The act or process of saturating. **b.** The condition of being saturated. **c.** The condition of being full to or beyond satisfaction; satiety. **2.** Physics A state of a ferromagnetic substance in which an increase in applied magnetic field strength does not produce an increase in magnetization. **3.** Chemistry The state of a fully saturated compound or solution. **4.** Meteorology A condition in which air at a specific temperature contains all the water vapor it can hold. **5.** Vividness of hue; degree of difference from a gray of the same lightness or brightness. **6.** Intensive shelling or bombing of a target to destroy it. **7.** The flooding of a market with all of a commodity that consumers can purchase.

saturation point *n.* **1.** *Chemistry* The point at which a substance will receive no more of another substance in solution. **2.** The point at which no more can be absorbed or assimilated.

Sat·ur·day (săt′ər-dē, -dā′) *n.* **1.** The seventh day of the week. **2.** The Jewish Sabbath. [ME < OE *Sæternesdæg,* transl. of Lat. *Sāturnī diēs* : *Sāturnī,* genitive of *Sāturnus,* Saturn + *diēs,* day.] —**Sat′ur·days** *adv.*

Saturday night special *n. Informal* A cheap handgun easily obtained and concealed.

Sat·urn (săt′ərn) *n.* **1.** *Roman Mythology* The god of agriculture. **2.** The sixth planet from the sun and the second largest in the solar system. See table at **planet.** [ME *Saturnus* < OE < Lat. *Sāturnus,* of Etruscan orig.]

Sa·tur·ni·an (să-tûr′nē-ən, sə-) *adj.* **1.** Of or relating to the planet Saturn or its supposed astrological influence. **2.** *Archaic* Of or relating to the god Saturn or his reign.

sa·tur·ni·id (să-tûr′nē-ĭd, sə-) *n.* Any of various often large colorful moths of the family Saturniidae, such as the emperor moth. [< NLat. *Saturniidae,* family name < *Saturnia,* type genus < Lat., Saturn's daughter < fem. of *Sāturnius,* Saturnian < *Sāturnus.* See SATURN.] —**sa·tur′ni·id** *adj.*

sat·ur·nine (săt′ər-nīn′) *adj.* **1.** Having the temperament of one born under the astrological influence of Saturn. **2a.** Melancholy or sullen. **b.** Expressing bitterness or sardonicism. **3.** Produced by absorption of lead. —**sat′ur·nine′ly** *adv.*

sat·urn·ism (săt′ər-nĭz′əm) *n.* See **lead poisoning.** [< SATURN, lead (obsolete), associated by alchemists with the planet Saturn.]

Sa·tya·gra·ha (sə-tyä′grə-hə, sŭt′yə-grŭ′hə) *n.* The policy of nonviolent resistance initiated in India by Mahatma Gandhi to press for political reform. [Skt. *satyāgraha* : *satyam,* truth (< *sat-, sant-,* existing, true; see **es-** in App.) + *āgrahaḥ,* determination, insistence (*ā-,* to + *grahaḥ,* act of seizing < *gṛhṇāti,* he seizes).]

sa·tyr (sā′tər, săt′ər) *n.* **1.** often **Satyr** *Greek Mythology* A woodland creature depicted with a goat's ears, legs, and horns and a fondness for unrestrained revelry. **2.** A licentious man; a lecher. **3.** A man with satyriasis. **4.** Any of various butterflies of the family Satyridae, having brown wings with eyelike spots. [ME *satire* < OFr. < Lat. *satyrus* < Gk. *saturos.*] —**sa·tyr′ic** (sā-tîr′ĭk, sə-), **sa·tyr′i·cal** (-ĭ-kəl) *adj.*

sa·ty·ri·a·sis (sā′tə-rī′ə-sĭs, săt′ə-) *n.* Excessive sexual desire in and behavior by a male. [LLat. *satyriāsis* < Gk. *saturiāsis* < *saturos,* satyr.]

sa·tyr·id (sā′tər-ĭd, săt′ər-, sə-tī′rĭd) *n.* A butterfly of the family Satyridae, including the satyrs and wood nymphs. [< NLat. *Satyridae,* family name < *Satyrus,* type genus < Lat. *satyrus,* satyr. See SATYR.] —**sa·tyr′id** *adj.*

sauce (sôs) *n.* **1.** A flavorful seasoning or relish served as an accompaniment to food, esp. a liquid dressing or topping. **2.** Stewed fruit, usu. served with other foods. **3.** Something that adds zest, flavor, or piquancy. **4.** *Informal* Impudent speech or behavior; sauciness. **5.** *Slang* Alcoholic liquor. ❖ *tr.v.* **sauced, sauc·ing, sauc·es 1.** To flavor with sauce. **2.** To add piquancy or zest to. **3.** *Informal* To be impertinent or impudent to. [ME < OFr. < VLat. *salsa* < Lat., fem. of *salsus,* p. part. of *sallere,* to salt. See **sal-** in App.]

sauce·box (sôs′bŏks′) *n. Informal* An impertinent person.

sauce·pan (sôs′păn′) *n.* A deep cooking pan with a handle.

sauce·pot (sôs′pŏt′) *n.* A cooking pot having a close-fitting lid and a handle on either side.

sau·cer (sô′sər) *n.* **1.** A small shallow dish having a slight circular depression in the center for holding a cup. **2.** An object similar in shape to a saucer. [ME, sauce dish < OFr. *saussier* < *sauce,* sauce. See SAUCE.]

sauce suprême *n.* See **suprême** 1. [Fr. : *sauce,* sauce + *suprême,* supreme.]

sauc·y (sô′sē) *adj.* **-i·er, -i·est 1a.** Impertinent or disrespectful. **b.** Impertinent in an entertaining way; irrepressible. **2.** Piquant; pert. —**sau′ci·ly** *adv.* —**sau′ci·ness** *n.*

Sa·ud (sä-ōōd′), **Abdul Aziz ibn** 1901?–69. Saudi Arabian king (1953–64) who was unable to deal with his country's economic problems and was replaced by his brother Faisal.

Sau·di Arabia (sou′dē, sô′dē, sä-ōō′dē) A country occupying most of the Arabian Peninsula; proclaimed as a unified independent kingdom in 1932. Cap. Riyadh. Pop. 17,451,000. —**Sau′di, Sau′di A·ra′bi·an** *adj. & n.*

sau·er·bra·ten (sour′brät′n) *n.* A pot roast of beef marinated in vinegar, water, wine, and spices before being cooked. [Ger. : *sauer,* sour (< MHGer. *sūr* < OHGer.) + *Braten,* roast meat (< MHGer. *brāte,* edible flesh < OHGer. *brāto;* see **bhreu-** in App.).]

sau·er·kraut (sour′krout′) *n.* Chopped and seasoned cabbage salted and fermented in its own juice. [Ger. : *sauer,* sour; see SAUERBRATEN + *Kraut,* cabbage < MHGer. *krūt* < OHGer.).]

sau·ger (sô′gər) *n.* A small North American freshwater fish (*Sti-*

zostidion canadense) having a spotted spiny dorsal fin. [?]

Sauk (sôk) also **Sac** (săk, sôk) *n., pl.* **Sauk** or **Sauks** also **Sac** or **Sacs 1.** A member of a Native American people formerly inhabiting parts of Wisconsin, Illinois, and Iowa, with a present-day population mainly in Oklahoma. **2.** Their Algonquian language. [N.Amer.Fr. *saki* < Sauk *asaakiiha.*]

Saul (sôl) fl. 11th cent. B.C. The first king of Israel.

sault (sōō) *n.* A waterfall or rapids. [Obsolete Fr. < OFr., leap, waterfall. See SOMERSAULT.]

Sault Sainte Ma·rie (sōō′ sānt′ mə-rē′) A city of S Ontario, Canada, at the falls of the St. Marys R. opposite Michigan's Upper Peninsula. Pop. 80,054.

Sault Sainte Marie Canals Popularly called **Soo Canals** (sōō) Three ship canals bypassing the rapids on the St. Marys R. between Lakes Superior and Huron.

sau·na (sô′nə, sou′-) *n.* **1a.** A Finnish steam bath in which the steam is produced by pouring water over heated rocks. **b.** A bathhouse or room for such a bath. **2a.** A dry heat bath. **b.** A room or enclosure for such a bath. [Finn.]

saun·ter (sôn′tər) *intr.v.* **-tered, -ter·ing, -ters** To stroll. ❖ *n.* **1.** A leisurely pace. **2.** A stroll. [Prob. < ME *santren,* to muse.] —**saun′ter·er** *n.*

sau·rel (sôr′əl, sô-rĕl′) *n.* **1.** A marine fish of the genus *Trachurus,* characterized by bony lateral lines, esp. *T. trachurus* of eastern Atlantic waters. **2.** See **jack mackerel.** [Fr. < LLat. *saurus,* horse mackerel < Gk. *sauros,* lizard, horse mackerel.]

sau·ri·an (sôr′ē-ən) *n.* Any of various reptiles of the suborder Sauria, which includes the lizards. [< NLat. *Sauria,* suborder name < *saurus,* lizard < Gk. *sauros.*] —**sau′ri·an** *adj.*

saur·is·chi·an (sô-rĭs′kē-ən) *n.* A dinosaur of the order Saurischia, having a pelvic girdle similar to that of modern reptiles. [< NLat. *Saurischia,* order name : Gk. *sauros,* lizard + Gk. *iskhion,* hip joint.] —**saur·is′chi·an** *adj.*

sau·ro·pod (sôr′ə-pŏd′) *n.* Any of various large semiaquatic saurischian dinosaurs of the suborder Sauropoda, of the Jurassic and Cretaceous periods. [< NLat. *Sauropoda,* suborder name : Gk. *sauros,* lizard + NLat. *-poda,* -pod.] —**sau′ro·pod′,** sau·rop′o·dous (sô-rŏp′ə-dəs) *adj.*

sau·rop·ter·yg·i·an (sô-rŏp′tə-rĭj′ē-ən) *n.* Any of various extinct aquatic reptiles of the superorder Sauropterygia that flourished during the Mesozoic Era and included the plesiosaurs. ❖ *adj.* Of or relating to a sauropterygian. [< NLat. *Sauropterygia,* superorder name : Gk. *sauros,* lizard + Gk. *pterux, pterug-,* wing, flipper; see **pet-** in App.]

sau·ry (sôr′ē) *n., pl.* **-ries** Any of several offshore marine fishes of the family Scomberesocidae, related to the needlefishes. [< NLat. *saurus,* lizard < Gk. *sauros.*]

sau·sage (sô′sĭj) *n.* Finely chopped and seasoned meat, esp. pork, usu. stuffed into a casing and cooked or cured. [ME *sausige* < AN *sausiche* < VLat. **salsīcia* < LLat., neut. pl. of *salsīcius,* prepared by salting < *salsus,* salted. See SAUCE.]

Sau·sa·li·to (sô′sə-lē′tō) A resort city of W CA on San Francisco Bay. Pop. 7,330.

Saus·sure (sô-sōōr′, -sūr′), **Ferdinand de** 1857–1913. Swiss linguist who founded structural linguistics.

sau·té (sô-tā′, sô-) *tr.v.* **-téed, -té·ing, -tés** To fry lightly in fat in a shallow open pan. [Fr., sautéed < p. part. of *sauter,* to leap < OFr. < Lat. *saltāre.* See SALTATION.] —**sau·té′** *n.*

Sau·ternes (sô-tûrn′, sō-) *n., pl.* **-ternes** (-tûrn′, -tûrnz′) **1.** A delicate sweet white wine from the Bordeaux region of France. **2.** often **sau·terne** (-tûrn′) A sweet to moderately dry white wine from California. [Fr., after *Sauternes,* a village of southwest France.]

Sa·va (sä′və, -vä) A river rising in the Julian Alps and flowing c. 933 km (580 mi), to the Danube R.

sav·age (săv′ĭj) *adj.* **1.** Not domesticated or cultivated; wild. **2.** Not civilized; barbaric. **3.** Ferocious; fierce: *a savage temper.* **4.** Vicious or merciless; brutal. See Syns at **cruel.** **5.** Lacking polish or manners; rude. ❖ *n.* **1.** A primitive or uncivilized person. **2.** A brutal, fierce, or vicious person. **3.** A rude person; a boor. ❖ *tr.v.* **-aged, -ag·ing, -ag·es 1.** To assault ferociously. **2.** To attack without restraint or pity. [ME *sauvage* < OFr. < LLat. *salvāticus* < Lat. *silvāticus,* of the woods, wild < *silva,* forest.] —**sav′age·ly** *adv.* —**sav′age·ness** *n.*

sav·age·ry (săv′ĭj-rē) *n., pl.* **-ries 1.** The quality or condition of being savage. **2.** An act of violent cruelty. **3.** Savage behavior or nature; barbarity.

Sa·vai·i or **Sa·vai·i** (sä-vī′ē) An island of Samoa (formerly Western Samoa) in the SW Pacific Ocean.

sa·van·na also **sa·van·nah** (sə-văn′ə) *n.* A flat tropical or subtropical grassland. [Obsolete Sp. *çavana* < Taino *zabana.*]

Sa·van·nah (sə-văn′ə) A city of SE GA near the mouth of the Savannah R. Founded 1733. Pop. 131,510.

Savannah River A river, c. 505 km (314 mi), rising in NW SC and flowing along the SC–GA border to the Atlantic Ocean.

sa·vant (să-vänt′) *n.* **1.** A learned person; a scholar. **2.** An idiot savant. [Fr. < OFr., pr. part. of *savoir,* to know < VLat. **sapēre* < Lat. *sapere,* to be wise.]

sa·vate (sə-văt′, -vät′) *n.* A form of boxing in which kicking is permitted. [Fr. < OFr., old shoe.]

save¹ (sāv) *v.* **saved, sav·ing, saves** —*tr.* **1a.** To rescue from

Saturn
Voyager 2 image of Saturn

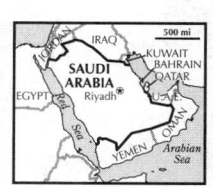

Saudi Arabia

harm, danger, or loss. **b.** To set free from the consequences of sin; redeem. **2.** To keep in a safe condition; safeguard. **3.** To prevent the waste or loss of; conserve. **4a.** To avoid spending (money) so as to keep or accumulate it. **b.** To avoid spending (money or time in an amount less than what circumstances normally require): *saved $25 at the sale; saved 15 minutes by taking a shortcut.* **5.** To set aside for future use; store. **6.** To treat with care by avoiding fatigue, wear, or damage; spare. **7.** To make unnecessary; obviate. **8a.** *Sports* To prevent (a goal by an opponent). **b.** To preserve a victory in (a game). **c.** *Baseball* To preserve (another pitcher's win) by protecting one's team's lead during a stint of relief pitching. **9.** *Computer Science* To copy (a file) from a computer's main memory to a storage medium. —*intr.* **1.** To avoid waste or expense; economize. **2.** To accumulate money: *saving for a vacation.* **3.** To preserve a person or thing from harm or loss. **4.** *Sports* An act that prevents an opponent from scoring. **2.** *Baseball* An act of saving a win. —*idiom:* **save (one's) breath** To refrain from a futile appeal or effort. [ME *saven* < OFr. *sauver* < LLat. *salvāre* < Lat. *salvus*, safe. See **sol-** in App.] —**sav′a·ble, save′a·ble** *adj.* —**sav′er** *n.*

save² (sāv) *prep.* With the exception of; except. ❖ *conj.* **1.** Were it not; except. **2.** Unless. [ME < OFr. *sauf* < Lat. *salvō*, ablative sing. of *salvus*, safe. See **sol-** in App.]

save-all (sāv′ôl′) *n.* **1.** Any of various devices for preventing waste, damage, or loss. **2.** A receptacle for catching the waste products of a process for further use in manufacture.

sav·e·loy (sāv′ə-loi′) *n.* A highly seasoned smoked pork sausage. [Alteration of obsolete Fr. *cervelat* < Ital. *cervellato*, ult. < dialectal *zervello*, brain < Lat. *cerebellum*, dim. of *cerebrum*, brain. See **ker-¹** in App.]

sav·in or **sav·ine** (sāv′ĭn) *n.* **1.** An evergreen Eurasian shrub (*Juniperus sabina*) having seed-bearing cones and yielding an oil formerly used medicinally. **2.** Any of several related plants. [ME < OE *safine* and < OFr. *savine*, both < Lat. (*herba*) *Sabīna*, Sabine (plant), savin, fem. of *Sabīnus*.]

sav·ing (sā′vĭng) *n.* **1.** Rescue from harm, danger, or loss. **2.** Avoidance of excess expenditure; economy. **3.** A reduction in expenditure or cost. **4.** Something saved. **5a. savings** Money saved. **b. savings** (*used with a sing. verb*) An amount of money saved: *a savings of $50.* **6.** *Law* An exception or reservation. ❖ *prep.* With the exception of. ❖ *conj.* Except; save.

saving grace *n.* A redeeming quality, esp. one that compensates for one's shortcomings.

sav·ings account (sā′vĭngz) *n.* A bank account with interest.

savings and loan association *n.* A financial institution that holds the funds of its members or clients in interest-bearing accounts and certificates of deposit, invests these funds esp. in home mortgage loans, and may also offer banking services.

savings bank *n.* A bank that receives and invests the savings of private depositors and pays interest on the deposits.

savings bond *n.* A nontransferable registered bond issued by the US government in denominations of $50 to $10,000.

sav·ior (sāv′yər) *n.* **1.** A person who rescues another from harm, danger, or loss. **2. Savior** *Christianity* Jesus. [ME *saviour* < OFr. *sauveour* < LLat. *salvātor* < *salvāre*, to save. See **SAVE¹.**]

sav·iour (sāv′yər) *n. Chiefly British* Variant of **savior.**

sa·voir-faire (sāv′wär-fâr′) *n.* The ability to do the right or graceful thing. [Fr. : *savoir*, to know how + *faire*, to do.]

Sa·vo·na·ro·la (sāv′ə-nə-rō′lə, sä′vō-nä-), **Girolamo** 1452–98. Italian reformer who drove the Medici family out of Florence in 1494 and was later excommunicated and executed for criticizing Pope Alexander VI.

sa·vor (sā′vər) *n.* **1.** The taste or smell of something. **2.** A specific taste or smell. **3.** A distinctive quality or sensation. ❖ *v.* **-vored, -vor·ing, -vors** —*intr.* **1.** To have a particular taste or smell: *a dish that savors of curry.* **2.** To exhibit a specified quality or characteristic; smack: *postures that savored of vanity.* —*tr.* **1.** To impart flavor or scent to; season. **2.** To taste or smell, esp. with pleasure: *savored each morsel of the feast.* **3.** To appreciate fully; enjoy or relish. [ME *savour* < OFr. < Lat. *sapor* < *sapere*, to taste.] —**sa′vor·er** *n.* —**sa′vor·ous** *adj.*

sa·vor·y¹ (sā′və-rē) *adj.* **1.** Appetizing to the taste or smell. **2.** Piquant, pungent, or salty to the taste; not sweet. **3.** Morally respectable. ❖ *n., pl.* **-ies** A dish of pungent taste. [ME *savure* < OFr. *savoure*, p. part. of *savourer*, to taste < LLat. *sapōrāre* < Lat. *sapor*, flavor. See **SAVOR.**] —**sa′vor·i·ly** *adv.* —**sa′vor·i·ness** *n.*

sa·vor·y² (sā′və-rē) *n., pl.* **-ies 1.** An annual Mediterranean aromatic herb (*Satureja hortensis*) in the mint family, having flowers with a pale lavender to white corolla. **2.** A related Mediterranean aromatic herb (*Satureja montana*) having flowers in a long white or pink corolla. **3.** The leaves of either of these plants, used as seasoning. **4.** Any of several plants of the genus *Micromeria* in the mint family. [ME *saverey*, alteration of OFr. *sarree*, alteration of Lat. *saturēia*.]

sa·vour (sā′vər) *n. & v. Chiefly British* Variant of **savor.**

sa·vour·y (sā′və-rē) *adj. & n. Chiefly British* Variant of **savory¹.**

Sa·voy¹ (sə-voi′) A ruling house of Sardinia (1720–1861) and Italy (1861–1946).

Sa·voy² (sə-voi′) A historical region and former duchy of SE France, W Switzerland, and NW Italy. —**Sa·voy′ard** (sə-voi′ärd′, sāv′oi-yärd′) *adj. & n.*

Savonarola
bronze medal by
Luca della Robbia

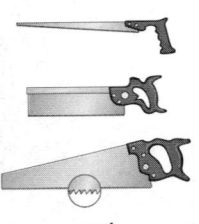

saw¹
top to bottom: compass,
backsaw, and crosscut saws

Savoy Alps A range of the W Alps in SE France rising to 4,810.2 m (15,771 ft).

sav·vy (sāv′ē) *Informal adj.* **-vi·er, -vi·est** Well informed and perceptive; shrewd. ❖ *n.* Practical understanding or shrewdness: *a banker known for financial savvy.* ❖ *tr. & intr.v.* **sav·vied** (sāv′ēd), **sav·vy·ing, sav·vies** To understand. [< Sp. *sabe* (*usted*), (you) know < *saber*, to know < OSpan. < VLat. **sapēre* < Lat. *sapere*, to be wise.] —**sav′vi·ly** *adv.*

saw¹ (sô) *n.* Any of various tools having a thin metal blade or disk with a sharp, usu. toothed edge, used for cutting hard materials. ❖ *v.* **sawed, sawed** or **sawn** (sôn), **saw·ing, saws** —*tr.* **1.** To cut or divide with a saw. **2.** To produce or shape with a saw. **3.** To make back-and-forth motions through or on. —*intr.* **1.** To use a saw. **2.** To undergo cutting with a saw: *Pine wood saws easily.* [ME *sawe* < OE *sagu.* See **sek-** in App.] —**saw′er** *n.*

saw² (sô) *n.* A familiar saying, esp. one that has become trite through repetition. [ME *sawe* < OE *sagu*, speech. See **sekʷ-³** in App.]

saw³ (sô) *v.* Past tense of **see¹.**

Sa·watch Range (sə-wôch′) A range of the Rocky Mts. in central CO rising to 4,402.1 m (14,433 ft).

saw·bones (sô′bōnz′) *n., pl.* **sawbones** or **-bones·es** (-bōn′zĭz) *Slang* A physician, esp. a surgeon.

saw·buck (sô′bŭk′) *n.* **1.** A sawhorse, esp. one having a crossed pair of legs at each end. **2.** *Slang* A ten-dollar bill.

saw·dust (sô′dŭst′) *n.* The small particles of material that fall from an object being sawed. —**saw′dust′y** *adj.*

sawed-off (sôd′ôf′, -ŏf′) *adj.* **1.** Having one end sawed off: *a sawed-off shotgun.* **2.** *Slang* Short; runty.

saw·fish (sô′fĭsh′) *n., pl.* **sawfish** or **-fish·es** Any of various marine fishes of the genus *Pristis*, related to the rays and having a bladelike snout with teeth along both sides.

saw·fly (sô′flī′) *n.* Any of various hymenopterous insects, chiefly of the family Tenthredinidae, the females of which use sawlike ovipositors to deposit their eggs in plant tissue.

saw grass *n.* A tall coastal or marshy sedge (*Cladium jamaicense*) of eastern North America, Mexico, and the West Indies, having leaves with sharp, minutely toothed margins.

saw·horse (sô′hôrs′) *n.* A frame with legs, used to support pieces of wood being sawed.

saw log *n.* A log of a size large enough to be sawed into boards.

saw·mill (sô′mĭl′) *n.* **1.** A plant where timber is sawed into boards. **2.** A large machine for sawing lumber.

sawn (sôn) *v.* A past participle of **saw¹.**

saw palmetto *n.* A small creeping palm (*Serenoa repens*) of the southeast United States having palmately divided leaves with one-ribbed segments and black one-seeded fruit.

saw set *n.* An instrument used to give set to the teeth of a saw by bending each alternate tooth slightly outward.

saw-toothed (sô′tōōtht′) *adj.* **1.** Having teeth resembling the teeth of a saw. **2.** often **saw·tooth** (-tōōth′) Having a jagged or zigzag pattern, outline, or course; serrate.

saw-whet owl (sô′hwĕt′, -wĕt′) *n.* A small brown and white owl (*Aegolius acadicus*) of North America.

saw·yer (sô′yər) *n.* **1.** One that is employed in sawing wood. **2.** Any of several beetles of the genus *Monochamus*, whose larvae bore holes in wood. **3.** See **snag** 1a. [ME *sauere, sawier* < *sawen*, to saw < *sawe*, saw. See **SAW¹.**]

sax (sāks) *n.* A saxophone.

Sax. *abbr.* Saxon

sax·a·tile (sāk′sə-tĭl′, -tīl) *adj.* Saxicolous. [Lat. *saxātilis* < *saxum*, rock. See **sek-** in App.]

Saxe-Co·burg (sāks-kō′bûrg′) A British royal house (1901–10) whose only ruler was Edward VII.

sax·horn (sāks′hôrn′) *n.* Any of a family of valved brass wind instruments that resemble the bugle and have a full even tone and wide compass. [After *Sax*, surname of 19th-cent. Belgian instrument-making family.]

sax·i·frage (sāk′sə-frĭj, -frāj′) *n.* Any of numerous herbs of the genus *Saxifraga*, with small flowers and leaves that often form a basal rosette. [Ult. < LLat. (*herba*) *saxifraga*, maidenhair fern, fem. of Lat. *saxifragus*, rock-breaking (because it grows in rock crevices) : *saxum*, rock; see **sek-** in App. + *frangere, frag-*, to break; see **bhreg-** in App.]

sax·i·tox·in (sāk′sĭ-tŏk′sĭn) *n.* A potent neurotoxin produced by certain dinoflagellates and causing food poisoning in humans who eat shellfish that have fed on these organisms. [NLat. *Saxi(domus gigantēus)*, clam species (< Lat. *saxum*, stone; see **SAXIFRAGE**) + **TOXIN.**]

Sax·o Gram·mat·i·cus (sāk′sō grə-māt′ĭ-kəs) 1150?–1220? Danish historian whose *Gesta Danorum*, a chronicle of Danish kings, contains the story of Hamlet.

Sax·on (sāk′sən) *n.* **1.** A member of a West Germanic tribal group that invaded Britain in the fifth and sixth centuries A.D. **2.** A person of English or Lowland Scots birth or descent as distinguished from one of Irish, Welsh, or Highland Scots birth or descent. **3.** A native or inhabitant of Saxony. **4.** The West Germanic language of any of the ancient Saxon peoples. **5.** The Germanic element of English as distinguished from the French and Latin elements. [ME < LLat. *Saxō, Saxon-*, of Gmc. orig. See **sek-** in App.] —**Sax′on** *adj.*

Sax·on·ism (săk′sə-nĭz′əm) *n.* An English word, phrase, or idiom of Anglo-Saxon origin.

sax·o·ny also **Sax·o·ny** (săk′sə-nē) *n., pl.* **-nies 1.** A wool fabric originally made from the wool of sheep raised in Saxony. **2.** A fine woolen yarn.

Saxony A historical region of N Germany; conquered by Charlemagne in the 8th cent. and later part of the German Empire (1871–1918).

sax·o·phone (săk′sə-fōn′) *n.* A woodwind instrument with a single-reed mouthpiece and a usu. curved conical metal tube. [After *Sax*, surname of 19th-cent. Belgian instrument-making family.] —**sax′o·phon′ist** *n.*

sax·tu·ba (săks′tōō′bə, -tyōō′-) *n.* A large bass saxhorn. [SAX(HORN) + TUBA.]

say (sā) *v.* **said** (sĕd), **say·ing, says** (sĕz) —*tr.* **1.** To utter aloud; pronounce. **2.** To express in words. **3a.** To state as one's opinion or judgment; declare. **b.** To state as a determination of fact: *say who is right.* **4.** To repeat or recite. **5.** To report or maintain; allege. **6a.** To indicate; show: *The clock says two.* **b.** To give nonverbal expression to; signify or embody. **7.** To suppose; assume. —*intr.* To make a statement; express oneself. ❖ *n.* **1.** A turn or chance to speak. **2.** The right or power to influence or make a decision. **3.** *Archaic* Something said; a statement. ❖ *adv.* **1.** Approximately. **2.** For instance. ❖ *interj.* Used to express surprise or appeal for someone's attention. —*idioms:* **I say 1.** Used preceding an utterance to call attention to it. **2.** Used as an exclamation of surprise, delight, or dismay. **that is to say** In other words. [ME *seien* < OE *secgan*. See **sek**ʷ-³ in App.] —**say′er** *n.*

Sa·yan Mountains (sä-yän′) A range of mountains in S-central Russia W of Lake Baikal.

Say·ers (sā′ərz), **Dorothy L(eigh)** 1893–1957. British writer known for her mysteries featuring Lord Peter Wimsey.

say·ing (sā′ĭng) *n.* Something, such as an adage, that is said.

sa·yo·na·ra (sī′ə-när′ə) *interj.* Goodbye. [J. *sayōnara : sayō,* thus (*sa,* that + *yō,* appearance < M Chin. *jiang*) + *nara,* if it be, indeed.]

say-so (sā′sō′) *n., pl.* **-sos** *Informal* **1.** An unsupported statement or assurance. **2.** An authoritative expression of permission or approval. **3.** The right or authority to decide.

say·yid (sä′yĭd) *n. Islam* **1.** Used as a title and form of address for a male dignitary. **2.** Used as a title for a descendant of the family of Muhammad. [Ar. < *sāda,* to become chief.]

Sb The symbol for the element **antimony.** [< Lat. *stibium.* See STIBNITE.]

SB *abbr.* **1.** *Latin Scientiae Baccalaureus* (Bachelor of Science) **2.** simultaneous broadcast **3.** Baseball (stolen base)

sb. *abbr.* substantive

SBA *abbr.* Small Business Administration

SbE *abbr.* south by east

′sblood (zblŭd) *interj. Archaic* Used as an oath. [Shortening of *God's blood.*]

SbW *abbr.* south by west

sc *abbr.* small capital

Sc The symbol for the element **scandium.**

SC *abbr.* **1.** Security Council **2.** or **S.C.** South Carolina **3.** Supreme Court

sc. *abbr.* **1.** scale **2.** scene **3.** scilicet **4.** scruple (unit of weight)

Sc. *abbr.* **1.** Scotch **2.** Scots **3.** Scottish

scab (skăb) *n.* **1.** A crust discharged from and covering a healing wound. **2.** Scabies or mange in domestic animals or livestock, esp. sheep. **3a.** Any of various plant diseases caused by fungi or bacteria and resulting in crustlike spots on fruit, leaves, or roots. **b.** The spots caused by such a disease. **4.** *Slang* A person regarded as contemptible. **5a.** A worker who refuses membership in a labor union. **b.** One who works while others are on strike. ❖ *intr.v.* **scabbed, scab·bing, scabs 1.** To become covered with scabs or a scab. **2.** To work or take a job as a scab. [ME < ON *skabb.*]

scab·bard (skăb′ərd) *n.* A sheath, as for a dagger or sword. ❖ *tr.v.* **-bard·ed, -bard·ing, -bards** To put into or furnish with such a sheath. [ME *scauberc, scabbard* < OFr. *escauberc,* poss. of Gmc. orig. See **sker-**¹ in App.]

scab·ble (skăb′əl) *tr.v.* **-bled, -bling, -bles** To work or dress (stone) roughly, preliminary to fine tooling. [ME *scaplen* < ONFr. *escapler,* to dress timber : *es-,* off (< Lat. *ex-*; see EX–) + *capler,* to cut (< VLat. **capulāre, *cappulāre*).]

scab·by (skăb′bēz) *adj.* **-bi·er, -bi·est 1.** Having, consisting of, or covered with scabs. **2.** Affected with scab or scabies. **3.** *Informal* Contemptible; vile. —**scab′bi·ness** *n.*

sca·bies (skā′bēz) *n., pl.* **scabies 1.** A contagious skin disease caused by a parasitic mite (*Sarcoptes scabiei*) and characterized by intense itching. **2.** A similar disease in animals, esp. sheep. [ME < Lat. *scabiēs* < *scabere,* to scratch.]

sca·bi·et·ic (skā′bē-ĕt′ĭk) *adj.* Of or affected with scabies.

sca·bi·o·sa (skā′bē-ō′sə, -zə, skăb′ē-) *n.* See **scabious²**. [NLat. *Scabiōsa,* genus name < Med.Lat. (*herba*) *scabiōsa,* (herb) for scabies, scabious, fem. of Lat. *scabiōsus,* mangy < *scabiēs,* itch. See SCABIES.]

sca·bi·ous¹ (skā′bē-əs, skăb′ē-) *adj.* **1.** Of or relating to scabies. **2.** Having scabs. [< Lat. *scabiōsus,* mangy. See SCABIOSA.]

sca·bi·ous² (skā′bē-əs) *n.* Any of various plants of the genus *Scabiosa,* esp. *S. atropurpurea,* having opposite leaves and vari-

ously colored flower heads. [ME *scabiose* < Med.Lat. (*herba*) *scabiōsa,* (herb) for scabies, scabious. See SCABIOSA.]

scab·land (skăb′lănd′) *n.* An elevated area of barren rocky land with little soil cover, usu. crossed by dry streambeds. Often used in the plural.

scab·rous (skăb′rəs, skā′brəs) *adj.* **1.** Having or covered with scales or small projections and rough to the touch. **2.** Difficult to handle; knotty. **3.** Dealing with scandalous or salacious material. [LLat. *scabrōsus* < *scaber, scabr-,* scurfy.] —**scab′rous·ly** *adv.*

scad¹ (skăd) *n., pl.* **scad** or **scads** Any of several carangid fishes of the genus *Decapterus,* esp. *D. punctatus* of the western Atlantic. [?]

scad² (skăd) *n. Informal* A large number or amount. Often used in the plural: *Scads of people are in the hall.* [?]

Sca·fell Pike (skô′fĕl′) A mountain, 979.1 m (3,210 ft), in the Cumbrian Mts. of NW England.

scaf·fold (skăf′əld, -ōld′) *n.* **1.** A temporary platform on which workers perform tasks at heights above the ground. **2.** A raised wooden framework or platform. **3.** A platform used in the execution of condemned prisoners, as by hanging or beheading. ❖ *tr.v.* **-fold·ed, -fold·ing, -folds 1.** To provide or support with a scaffold. **2.** To place on a scaffold. [ME < Med.Lat. *scaffaldus,* of OFr. orig.]

scaf·fold·ing (skăf′əl-dĭng, skăf′ōl′-) *n.* **1.** A scaffold or system of scaffolds. **2.** Materials used for constructing scaffolds.

scag also **skag** (skăg) *n. Slang* Heroin. [?]

scagl·io·la (skăl-yō′lə) *n.* Plasterwork in imitation of marble, consisting of ground gypsum and glue colored with marble or granite dust. [Ital., dim. of *scaglia,* chip, of Gmc. orig.]

scal·age (skā′lĭj) *n.* **1.** An assessed percentage of the total price or measured amount of goods being shipped or stored, used to figure a deduction from the price or amount to reflect normal shrinkage or depletion of the goods. **2.** The estimated amount of lumber in logs being scaled.

sca·lar (skā′lər, -lär′) *n.* **1a.** A quantity, such as mass, length, or speed, that is completely specified by its magnitude and has no direction. **b.** *Mathematics* A number, numerical quantity, or element in a field. **2.** A device that yields an output equal to the input multiplied by a constant, as in a linear amplifier. ❖ *adj.* Of or relating to a scalar. [Lat. *scālāris,* of a ladder < *scālae,* ladder. See SCALE².]

sca·la·re (skə-lâr′ē, -lär′ē) *n.* See **angelfish** 2. [Lat. *scālāre,* neut. of *scālāris,* of a ladder (< its parallel markings) < *scālae,* ladder. See SCALE².]

sca·lar·i·form (skə-lăr′ə-fôrm′) *adj. Biology* Resembling the rungs of a ladder; ladderlike. Used of certain vessels and tissues. [Lat. *scālāris,* of a ladder; see SCALARE + –FORM.]

scalar product *n.* The numerical product of the lengths of two vectors and the cosine of the angle between them.

sca·la·tion (skā-lā′shən) *n.* An arrangement of scales, as on a fish or reptile.

scal·a·wag (skăl′ə-wăg′) also **scal·ly·wag** (skăl′ē-) *n.* **1.** *Informal* A reprobate; a rascal. **2.** A white Southern supporter of the federal government during Reconstruction. [?]

scald¹ (skôld) *v.* **scald·ed, scald·ing, scalds** —*tr.* **1.** To burn with or as if with hot liquid or steam. **2.** To subject to or treat with boiling water. **3.** To heat (a liquid) almost to the boiling point. **4.** To criticize harshly; excoriate. —*intr.* To become scalded. ❖ *n.* **1.** A bodily injury caused by scalding. **2.** *Botany* **a.** A superficial discoloration on fruit, vegetables, leaves, or tree trunks caused by sudden exposure to intense sunlight or the action of gases. **b.** A disease of some cereal grasses caused by a fungus of the genus *Rhynchosporium.* [ME *scalden* < ONFr. *escalder* < LLat. *excaldāre,* to wash in hot water : Lat. *ex-,* ex- + Lat. *calidus, caldus,* warm, hot.]

scald² (skôld, skäld) *n.* Variant of **skald.**

scald³ (skôld, skäld) *n.* Variant of **scall.**

scald·ing (skôl′dĭng) *adj.* **1.** Causing a burning sensation, as from contact with hot liquid. **2.** Boiling. **3.** Scorching; searing. **4.** Harshly critical or denunciatory; scathing.

scale¹ (skāl) *n.* **1a.** One of the many small platelike dermal or epidermal structures that form the external covering of fishes, reptiles, and certain mammals. **b.** A similar part, such as one of the minute structures covering the wings of moths. **2.** *Pathology* A dry thin flake of epidermis shed from the skin. **3.** A small thin piece. **4.** *Botany* A small, thin, usu. dry plant structure, such as one that covers a tree bud. **5a.** A scale insect. **b.** A plant disease or infestation caused by scale insects. **6a.** A flaky oxide film formed on a metal, as on iron, that has been heated to high temperatures. **b.** A flake of rust. **7.** A hard mineral coating that forms on the inside surface of containers in which water is repeatedly heated. ❖ *v.* **scaled, scal·ing, scales** —*tr.* **1.** To clear or strip of scale or scales. **2.** To remove in layers or scales: *scaled off the old paint.* **3.** To cover with scales; encrust. **4.** To cause (a thin flat object) by throwing to soar through air or skip along a water surface. **5.** *Dentistry* To remove (tartar) from tooth surfaces with a pointed instrument. **6.** *Australian* **a.** To cheat; swindle. **b.** To ride on (a train, for example) without paying the fare. —*intr.* **1.** To come off in scales or layers; flake. **2.** To become encrusted. [ME < OFr. *escale,* of Gmc. orig.]

scale² (skāl) *n.* **1a.** A system of ordered marks at fixed intervals

saxophone

ă	pat	oi	boy
ā	pay	ou	out
âr	care	ŏŏ	took
ä	father	ōō	boot
ĕ	pet	ŭ	cut
ē	be	ûr	urge
ĭ	pit	th	thin
ī	pie	th	this
îr	pier	hw	which
ŏ	pot	zh	vision
ō	toe	ə	about,
ô	paw		item

Stress marks:
′ (primary);
′ (secondary), as in
lexicon (lĕk′sĭ-kŏn′)

used as a reference standard in measurement. **b.** An instrument or device bearing such marks. **c.** A standard of measurement or judgment; a criterion. **2a.** A proportion used in determining the dimensional relationship of a representation to that which it represents. **b.** A calibrated line, as on a map, indicating such a proportion. **c.** Proper proportion. **3.** A progressive classification, as of size or rank. **4.** A relative level or degree. **5.** A minimum wage fixed by contract. **6.** *Mathematics* A system of notation in which the values of numerical expressions are determined by their places relative to the chosen base of the system: *the decimal scale.* **7.** *Music* An ascending or descending collection of pitches proceeding by a specified scheme of intervals. ❖ *v.* **scaled, scal•ing, scales** —*tr.* **1.** To climb up or over; ascend: *scaled the peak.* **2.** To make in accord with a particular proportion or scale. **3.** To alter according to a standard or by degrees; adjust in calculated amounts. **4.** To estimate or measure the quantity of lumber in (logs or uncut trees). —*intr.* **1.** To climb; ascend. **2.** To rise in steps or stages. [ME < Lat. *scālae*, ladder.] —**scal′a•ble** *adj.*

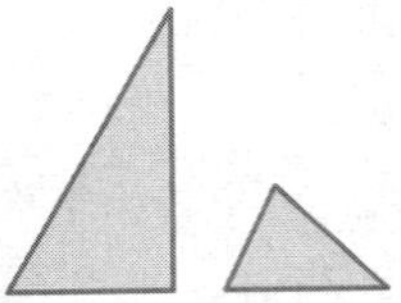

scalene
scalene triangles

scale[3] (skāl) *n.* **1.** An instrument or machine for weighing. Often used in the plural. **2.** Either of the pans, trays, or dishes of a balance. ❖ *v.* **scaled, scal•ing, scales** —*tr.* To weigh with scales. —*intr.* To have a given weight, as determined by a scale. [ME, bowl, balance < ON *skāl.*]

scale insect *n.* Any of various small homopterous insects of the superfamily Coccoidea, the females of which secrete and remain under waxy scales on plant tissue.

sca•lene (skā′lēn′, skā-lēn′) *adj.* Having three unequal sides. Used of triangles. [LLat. *scalēnus* < Gk. *skalēnos* < *skallein*, to hoe, stir up.]

scalene muscle *n.* Any of three muscles on each side of the neck that serve to bend and rotate the neck and assist breathing by raising or fixing the first two ribs.

sca•le•nus (skā-lē′nəs) *n., pl.* **-ni** (-nī, -nē) See **scalene muscle.** [LLat. *scalēnus*, scalene. See SCALENE.]

scal•er (skā′lər) *n.* An electronic circuit recording the aggregate of a specific number of signals that occur too rapidly to be recorded individually. [< SCALE[2].]

Scales (skālz) *pl.n.* (*used with a sing. verb*) See **Libra** 1, 2a.

Sca•li•a (skə-lē′ə), **Antonin** b. 1936. Amer. jurist; associate justice of the US Supreme Court (since 1986).

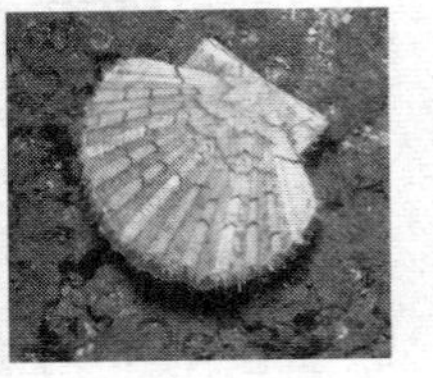

scallop
great scallop
Pecten maximus

scall (skôl, skäl) also **scald** (skôld, skäld) *n.* A scaly eruption of the skin or scalp. [ME < ON *skalli*, a bald head.]

scal•lion (skăl′yən) *n.* **1.** A young onion before it develops a bulb. **2.** Any of several onionlike plants, such as the leek. [ME *scaloun* < AN *scalun* < VLat. **escalōnia*, alteration of Lat. *(caepa) Ascalōnia*, Ascalonian (onion), shallot, fem. of *Ascalōnius*, Ascalonian < *Ascalō*, *Ascalōn-*, Ascalon (Ashkelon) < Heb. *ašqəlôn* < Canaanite **ʾaṯqalōn*, weights (sense uncertain) < **ṯaqala*, to weigh.]

scal•lop (skŏl′əp, skăl′-) also **scol•lop** (skŏl′-) or **es•cal•lop** (ĭ-skŏl′-, ĭ-skăl′-) *n.* **1a.** Any of various free-swimming marine mollusks of the family Pectinidae, having fan-shaped bivalve shells with a fluted pattern. **b.** The edible adductor muscle of this mollusk. **c.** A shell of this mollusk or a dish in a similar shape. **2.** One of a series of curved projections forming an ornamental border. **3.** A thin boneless slice of meat. ❖ *v.* **-loped, -lop•ing, -lops** —*tr.* **1.** To edge (cloth, for example) with scallops. **2.** To bake in a casserole with milk or a sauce and often with bread crumbs. **3.** To cut (meat) into thin boneless slices. —*intr.* To gather scallops for eating or sale. [ME *scalop* < OFr. *escalope*, shell, of Gmc. orig.] —**scal′lop•er** *n.*

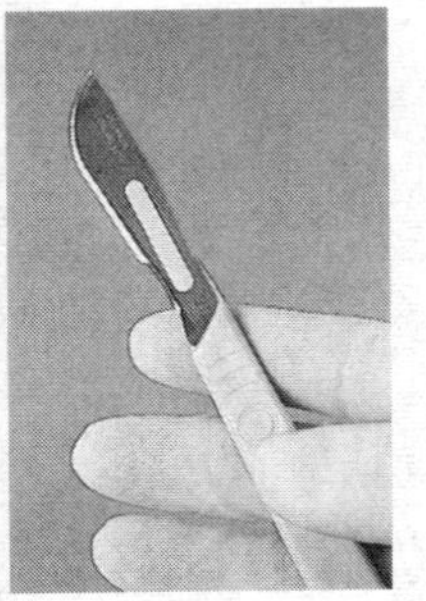

scalpel

scal•ly•wag (skăl′ē-wăg′) *n.* Variant of **scalawag.**

scal•o•gram (skā′lə-grăm′) *n.* *Psychology* A scale for measuring attitude or opinion in which agreement with a given item implies agreement with the items lower in rank.

sca•lop•pi•ne also **sca•lop•pi•ni** (skăl′ə-pē′nē, skä′lə-) *n.* Small, thinly sliced pieces of meat, esp. veal, dredged in flour, sautéed, and served in a sauce. [Ital., pl. of *scaloppina*, dim. of *scaloppa*, thin slice < Fr. *escalope* < OFr., shell (< the fillets being served curled like shells). See SCALLOP.]

scalp (skălp) *n.* **1.** The skin covering the top of the human head. **2.** A portion of this skin with its attached hair, cut from a body as a battle trophy or as proof in claiming a bounty. **3.** A piece of hide from the skull of certain animals, such as the fox, shown as proof to collect a bounty. **4.** A trophy of victory. ❖ *v.* **scalped, scalp•ing, scalps** —*tr.* **1.** To cut or tear the scalp from. **2.** To deprive of top growth or a top layer. **3.** To resell at a price higher than the established value. **4.** To buy and sell (securities or commodities) in order to make small quick profits. —*intr.* **1.** To engage in reselling something at a price higher than the established value. **2.** To buy and sell securities or commodities for small quick profits. [ME, top of the head, of Scand. orig.] —**scalp′er** *n.*

scal•pel (skăl′pəl) *n.* A small knife with a thin sharp blade used in surgery and dissection. [Lat. *scalpellum*, dim. of *scalper*, *scalprum*, knife < *scalpere*, to scratch, cut.]

scalp lock *n.* A long lock of hair left on the top of the shaven head by certain Native American men.

scal•y (skā′lē) *adj.* **-i•er, -i•est 1.** Covered or partially covered with scales. **2.** Shedding scales or flakes; flaking. —**scal′i•ness** *n.*

scaly anteater *n.* See **pangolin.**

scam (skăm) *Slang n.* A fraudulent business scheme; a swindle. ❖ *tr.v.* **scammed, scam•ming, scams** To defraud; swindle. [?] —**scam′mer** *n.*

scam•mo•ny (skăm′ə-nē) *n., pl.* **-nies 1.** An eastern Mediterranean plant *(Convolvulus scammonia)* having roots that yield a resin formerly used as a cathartic. **2.** The resin from this plant. [ME *scamonie* < OE *scammōniam* and < OFr. *scamonie*, both < Lat. *scammōnea* < Gk. *skammōniā*.]

scamp[1] (skămp) *n.* **1.** A rogue; a rascal. **2.** A mischievous youngster. [Prob. < *scamp*, to go about idly, prob. < obsolete Du. *schampen*, to decamp < MDu. *ontscampen*. See SCAMPER.]

scamp[2] (skămp) *tr.v.* **scamped, scamp•ing, scamps** To perform in a careless superficial way. [Poss. of Scand. orig.] —**scamp′er** *n.*

scam•per (skăm′pər) *intr.v.* **-pered, -per•ing, -pers** To run or go quickly and lightly. ❖ *n.* A quick light run or movement. [Prob. < Flem. *schampeeren*, freq. of obsolete Du. *schampen*, to run away < MDu. *ontscampen* < OFr. *escamper*, ult. < Lat. *ex campō*, out of the field : *ex*, away; see EX– + *campō*, ablative of *campus*, field.]

scam•pi (skăm′pē, skäm′-) *n., pl.* **scampi** Large shrimp broiled or sautéed and served in a garlic and butter sauce. [Ital., pl. of *scampo*, a kind of lobster < Gk. *kampē*, bending (< its shape), perh. < Gk. *kamptein*, to bend.]

scan (skăn) *v.* **scanned, scan•ning, scans** —*tr.* **1.** To examine closely. **2.** To look over quickly and systematically: *scanned the horizon for signs of land.* **3.** To look over or leaf through hastily. **4.** To analyze (verse) into metrical patterns. **5.** *Electronics* **a.** To move a beam of light or electrons in a systematic pattern over (a surface) in order to reproduce or sense and subsequently transmit an image. **b.** To move a radar beam in a systematic pattern over (a sector of sky) in search of a target. **6.** *Computer Science* To search (stored data) automatically for specific data. **7.** *Medicine* To examine (a body or body part) with a CAT scanner or similar scanning apparatus. **8.** To digitally encode (text, for example) with an optical scanner. —*intr.* **1.** To analyze verse into metrical patterns. **2.** To conform to a metrical pattern. **3.** *Electronics* To undergo electronic scanning. ❖ *n.* **1.** The act or an instance of scanning. **2.** Scope or field of vision. **3.** *Medicine* **a.** Examination of a body part by scanning. **b.** A picture or image produced by this means. **4.** *Electronics* A single sweep of the beam of electrons across a television screen. [ME *scannen*, to scan a verse < Lat. *scandere*, to climb, scan a verse.] —**scan′na•ble** *adj.*

Scand. *abbr.* **1.** Scandinavia **2.** Scandinavian

scan•dal (skăn′dl) *n.* **1.** A publicized incident that brings about disgrace or offends the moral sensibilities of society. **2.** A person, thing, or circumstance that causes or ought to cause disgrace or outrage. **3.** Damage to reputation or character caused by disclosure of immoral or improper behavior; disgrace. **4.** Talk that is damaging to one's character; malicious gossip. [Fr. *scandale* < OFr., cause of sin < Lat. *scandalum*, trap, temptation < Gk. *skandalon*.]

scan•dal•ize (skăn′dl-īz′) *tr.v.* **-ized, -iz•ing, -iz•es 1.** To offend the morals of. **2.** *Archaic* To dishonor; disgrace. —**scan′dal•i•za′tion** (-ĭ-zā′shən) *n.* —**scan′dal•iz′er** *n.*

scan•dal•mon•ger (skăn′dl-mŭng′gər, -mŏng′-) *n.* One who spreads malicious gossip. —**scan′dal•mon′ger•ing** *n.*

scan•dal•ous (skăn′dl-əs) *adj.* **1.** Causing scandal; shocking. **2.** Containing material damaging to reputation; defamatory. —**scan′dal•ous•ly** *adv.* —**scan′dal•ous•ness** *n.*

scandal sheet *n.* A periodical that habitually prints gossip or scandalous stories.

scan•dent (skăn′dənt) *adj.* *Botany* Climbing. [Lat. *scandēns*, *scandent-*, pr. part. of *scandere*, to climb.]

Scan•di•a (skăn′dē-ə) Scandinavia. —**Scan′di•an** *adj. & n.*

Scan•di•na•vi•a (skăn′də-nā′vē-ə, -nāv′yə) A region of N Europe comprising Norway, Sweden, and Denmark. Finland, Iceland, and the Faeroe Islands are often included in the region.

Scan•di•na•vi•an (skăn′də-nā′vē-ən, -nāv′yən) *adj.* Of or relating to Scandinavia or to its peoples, languages, or cultures. ❖ *n.* **1.** A native or inhabitant of Scandinavia. **2.** See **North Germanic.**

Scandinavian Peninsula A peninsula of N Europe including Norway and Sweden.

scan•di•um (skăn′dē-əm) *n.* *Symbol* **Sc** A highly reactive metallic element found in various rare minerals and separated as a byproduct in the processing of certain uranium ores. Atomic number 21; atomic weight 44.956; melting point 1,540°C; boiling point 2,850°C; specific gravity 2.99; valence 3. See table at **element.** [< Lat. *Scandia*, Scandinavia.] —**scan′dic** (-dĭk) *adj.*

scan•ner (skăn′ər) *n.* **1.** One that scans. **2.** A receiver that continuously broadcasts signals it detects from specified radio frequencies: *a police officer's scanner.* **3.** An optical scanner. **4.** A device, such as a CAT scanner or PET scanner, for observing internal organs, tissues, and other parts of the body.

scan•ning electron microscope (skăn′ĭng) *n.* An electron microscope that forms a three-dimensional image on a cathode-ray tube by moving a beam of focused electrons across an object and reading both the electrons scattered by the object and the secondary electrons produced by it.

scanning tunneling microscope *n.* A microscope that produces three-dimensional images of a sample's atomic topography and structure by scanning its surface with a beam of electrons.

scan·sion (skăn′shən) *n.* Analysis of verse into metrical patterns. [LLat. *scānsiō, scānsiōn-* < Lat., act of climbing < *scānsus,* p. part. of *scandere,* to climb.]

scan·so·ri·al (skăn-sôr′ē-əl, -sōr′-) *adj. Zoology* Adapted to or specialized for climbing. [< Lat. *scānsōrius* < *scānsus,* p. part. of *scandere,* to climb.]

scant (skănt) *adj.* **scant·er, scant·est 1.** Barely sufficient: *paid scant attention.* **2.** Falling short of a specific measure. **3.** Inadequately supplied; short. ❖ *tr.v.* **scant·ed, scant·ing, scants 1.** To give an inadequate portion or allowance to. **2.** To limit, as in amount or share; stint. **3.** To deal with or treat inadequately or neglectfully; slight. [ME < ON *skamt,* neut. of *skammr,* short.] —**scant′ly** *adv.* —**scant′ness** *n.*

scant·ling (skănt′lĭng, -lĭn) *n.* **1.** A very small amount; a modicum. **2.** A small timber used in construction. **3.** The dimensions of a building material, esp. the width and thickness of a timber. **4.** *Nautical* The dimensions of the structural parts of a vessel. Often used in the plural. [Alteration of ME *scantlon, scantilon,* carpenter's gauge < OFr. *escantillon,* alteration of **eschandillon* < Lat. *scandiculum,* alteration of *scandāculum,* ladder, gauge < Lat. *scandere,* to climb.]

scant·y (skăn′tē) *adj.* **-i·er, -i·est 1.** Barely sufficient or adequate. **2.** Insufficient, as in extent or degree. —**scant′i·ly** *adv.* —**scant′i·ness** *n.*

Scapa Flow (skăp′ə) A sheltered area of water in the Orkney Is. off N Scotland; site of a naval base in both World Wars.

scape¹ (skāp) *n.* **1.** *Botany* A leafless flower stalk growing directly from the ground, as in the tulip. **2.** *Biology* A stalklike part, such as a feather shaft. **3.** *Architecture* The shaft of a column. [Lat. *scāpus,* stalk, perh. < Gk. *skāpos.*]

scape² (skāp) *v. & n. Archaic* Variant of **escape.**

scape³ (skāp) *n.* A scene; a view. Often used in combination: *seascape; mindscape.* [< LANDSCAPE.]

scape·goat (skāp′gōt′) *n.* **1.** One that is made to bear the blame of others. **2.** *Bible* A live goat over whose head Aaron confessed all the sins of the children of Israel on the Day of Atonement and that was then sent into the wilderness. ❖ *tr.v.* **-goat·ed, -goat·ing, -goats** To make a scapegoat of. [SCAPE² + GOAT (transl. of Heb. *'ēz 'ōzēl,* goat that escapes, misreading of **'ăzā'zēl,* Azazel).]

scape·grace (skāp′grās′) *n.* A scoundrel; a rascal. [SCAPE² + GRACE.]

scaph·oid (skăf′oid′) *adj.* Shaped like a boat. ❖ *n.* See **navicular.** [NLat. *scaphoīdēs* < Gk. *skaphoeidēs,* like a bowl : *skaphē,* tub, boat + *-oeidēs,* -oid.]

scaph·o·pod (skăf′ə-pŏd′) *n.* See **tooth shell.** [< NLat. *Scaphopoda,* class name : Gk. *skaphē,* boat + NLat. *-poda,* -pod.]

scap·o·lite (skăp′ə-līt′) *n.* Any of a series of variously colored, often fluorescent mineral silicates of aluminum, calcium, and sodium. [Lat. *scāpus,* stalk; see SCAPE¹ + –LITE (< the prismatic shape of its crystals).]

sca·pose (skā′pōs′) *adj.* Resembling or consisting of a scape.

scap·u·la (skăp′yə-lə) *n., pl.* **-las** or **-lae** (-lē′) Either of two flat triangular bones forming the back part of the shoulder. [LLat., shoulder < Lat. *scapulae,* the shoulder blades.]

scap·u·lar (skăp′yə-lər) *n.* **1.** A monk's sleeveless outer garment that hangs from the shoulders and sometimes has a cowl. **2.** A badge worn by affiliates of certain religious orders, consisting of two pieces of cloth joined by shoulder bands and worn under the clothing on the chest and back. **3.** One of the feathers covering the shoulder of a bird. ❖ *adj.* also **scap·u·lar·y** (-lĕr′ē) *Anatomy* Of or relating to the shoulder or scapula. [ME *scapulare* < LLat. *scapulāre* < neut. of *scapulāris,* of the shoulders or scapulae < *scapula,* shoulder. See SCAPULA.]

scar¹ (skär) *n.* **1.** A mark left on the skin after a surface injury or wound has healed. **2.** A lingering sign of damage or injury, either mental or physical. **3.** *Botany* A mark indicating a former attachment, as of a leaf to a stem. **4.** A mark, such as a dent, resulting from use or contact. ❖ *v.* **scarred, scar·ring, scars** —*tr.* **1.** To mark with a scar. **2.** To leave lasting signs of damage on. —*intr.* **1.** To form a scar. **2.** To become scarred. [ME, alteration of *escare* < OFr., scab < LLat. *eschara* < Gk. *eskhara,* hearth, scab caused by burning.]

scar² (skär) *n.* **1.** A protruding isolated rock. **2.** A bare rocky place on a mountainside or other steep slope. [ME *skerre* < ON *sker,* low reef. See sker-¹ in App.]

scar·ab (skăr′əb) *n.* **1.** A scarabaeid beetle, esp. *Scarabaeus sacer,* regarded as sacred by the ancient Egyptians. **2.** A representation of this beetle, such as a cut gem, used in ancient Egypt as a talisman and a symbol of the soul. [Fr. *scarabée* < Lat. *scarabaeus* < Gk. *karabos,* crab, beetle.]

scar·a·bae·id (skăr′ə-bē′ĭd) *n.* Any of the numerous stout-bodied lamellicorn beetles of the family Scarabaeidae, which includes the June beetle and dung beetles. [< NLat. *Scarabaeidae,* family name < *Scarabaeus,* type genus < Lat. *scarabaeus,* beetle. See SCARAB.] —**scar′a·bae′id** *adj.*

scar·a·bae·us (skăr′ə-bē′əs) *n., pl.* **-bae·us·es** or **-bae·i** (-bē′ī′) See **scarab** 2. [Lat. See SCARAB.]

Scar·a·mouch also **Scar·a·mouche** (skăr′ə-mōōsh′, -mōōch′, -mouch′) *n.* A stock character in commedia dell'arte and panto-

mime, depicted as a boastful coward or buffoon. [Fr. *Scaramouche* < Ital. *Scaramuccia* < *scaramuccia,* skirmish. See sker-¹ in App.]

Scar·bor·ough (skär′bûr′ō, -bŭr′ō, -bər-ə) A municipal borough of NE England on the North Sea N of Hull; site of a Bronze Age village. Pop. 43,300.

scarce (skârs) *adj.* **scarc·er, scarc·est 1.** Insufficient to meet a demand or requirement; short in supply. **2.** Hard to find; rare or rare. ❖ *adv.* Barely or hardly; scarcely. —*idiom:* **make (oneself) scarce** *Informal* **1.** To stay away; be absent or elusive. **2.** To depart, esp. quickly or furtively; abscond. [ME *scars* < VLat. **excarpsus,* narrow, cramped < p. part. of **excarpere,* to pluck out, alteration of Lat. *excerpere,* to pick out. See EXCERPT.] —**scarce′ness** *n.*

scarce·ly (skârs′lē) *adv.* **1.** By a small margin; barely: *We scarcely made it.* **2.** Almost not; hardly: *It scarcely ever snows here.* **3.** Certainly not: *They could scarcely complain.*

> **USAGE NOTE** Because *scarcely* has the force of a negative, its use with another negative, as in *I couldn't scarcely believe it,* is incorrect. • A clause following *scarcely* is correctly introduced by *when* or *before;* the use of *than,* though common, is still unacceptable to some grammarians: *I had scarcely begun when* (or *before* but not *than*) *I was interrupted.* See Usage Notes at **double negative, hardly.**

scar·ci·ty (skâr′sĭ-tē) *n., pl.* **-ties 1.** Insufficiency of amount or supply; shortage. **2.** Rarity of appearance or occurrence.

scare (skâr) *v.* **scared, scar·ing, scares** —*tr.* To strike with sudden fear; alarm. —*intr.* To become frightened. ❖ *n.* **1.** A condition or sensation of sudden fear. **2.** A general state of alarm; a panic. ❖ *adj.* Serving or intended to frighten people. —*phrasal verb:* **scare up** *Informal* To gather or prepare with considerable effort or ingenuity. [ME *skerren, scaren* < ON *skirra* < *skjarr,* timid.] —**scar′er** *n.*

scare·crow (skâr′krō′) *n.* **1.** A crude image of a person set up to scare birds away from growing crops. **2.** Something frightening but not dangerous. **3.** A gaunt or haggard person.

scared·y-cat also **scared·y cat** (skâr′dē-kăt′) *n. Informal* One who is excessively fearful.

scare·mon·ger (skâr′mŭng′gər, -mŏng′-) *n.* One who spreads frightening rumors. —**scare′mon′ger·ing** *n.*

scare quote *n.* Either of a pair of quotation marks used to emphasize a word or phrase or to indicate its special status, esp. to express doubt about its validity or to criticize its use.

scarf¹ (skärf) *n., pl.* **scarfs** (skärfs) or **scarves** (skärvz) **1.** A long piece of cloth worn about the head, neck, or shoulders. **2.** A decorative cloth for covering the top of a piece of furniture; a runner. **3.** A sash indicating military rank. ❖ *tr.v.* **scarfed, scarf·ing, scarfs 1.** To dress, cover, or decorate with or as if with a scarf. **2.** To wrap (an outer garment) around one like a scarf. [Fr. dialectal *escarpe,* sash, sling < ONFr., var. of OFr. *escherpe,* pilgrim's neck bag < Frankish **skirpja,* small rush < Lat. *scirpus,* rush.]

scarf² (skärf) *n., pl.* **scarfs** (skärfs) **1.** A joint made by cutting or notching the ends of two pieces correspondingly and strapping or bolting them together. **2.** Either of the ends that form such a joint. ❖ *tr.v.* **scarfed, scarf·ing, scarfs 1.** To join by means of a scarf. **2.** To cut a scarf in. [ME *skarf,* prob. < ON *skarfr,* end piece of a board cut off on the bias.]

scarf³ (skärf) *tr.v.* **scarfed, scarf·ing, scarfs** *Slang* To eat or drink voraciously; devour. [Variant of SCOFF².] —**scarf′er** *n.*

scarf joint *n.* See **scarf²** 1.

scarf·skin (skärf′skĭn′) *n.* The outermost layer of skin, esp. that which forms the cuticle. [SCARF¹ + SKIN.]

scar·i·fy¹ (skăr′ə-fī′) *tr.v.* **-fied, -fy·ing, -fies 1.** To make shallow cuts in (the skin), esp. in administering a vaccine or creating decorative scarring. **2.** To break up the surface of (topsoil). **3.** To distress deeply, as with severe criticism; lacerate. **4.** *Botany* To slit or soften the outer coat of (seeds) in order to speed germination. [ME *scarifien* < OFr. *scarifier* < LLat. *scarīficāre,* alteration of Lat. *scarīfāre* < Gk. *skariphāsthai,* to sketch, scratch < *skariphos,* pencil, stylus. See skribh- in App.] —**scar′i·fi·ca′tion** (-fĭ-kā′shən) *n.* —**scar′i·fi′er** *n.*

scar·i·fy² (skăr′ə-fī′) *tr.v.* **-fied, -fy·ing, -fies** To scare.

scar·i·ous (skâr′ē-əs) also **scar·i·ose** (-ōs′) *adj.* Thin, membranous, and dry: *scarious bracts.* [NLat. *scariōsus.*]

scar·la·ti·na (skär′lə-tē′nə) *n.* See **scarlet fever.** [NLat. *(febris) scarlatina,* scarlet (fever) < Ital. *scarlattina,* fem. of *scarlattino,* scarlet, dim. of *scarlatto* < Pers. *saqirlāt.* See SCARLET.] —**scar′la·ti′nal** *adj.*

Scar·lat·ti (skär-lä′tē), Alessandro 1660–1725. Italian composer who influenced the development of opera. His son **Domenico** (1685–1757) wrote harpsichord works.

scar·let (skär′lĭt) *n.* **1.** A strong to vivid red or reddish orange. **2.** Scarlet-colored clothing or cloth. ❖ *adj.* **1.** Of the color scarlet. **2.** Flagrantly immoral or unchaste: *scarlet thoughts.* [ME, scarlet cloth, scarlet < OFr. *escarlate* < Med.Lat. *scarlata,* scarlet cloth < Pers. *saqirlāt,* rich cloth, scarlet cloth, var. of *siqillāt* < Ar., perh. < Med.Gk. **sigillatos* < Lat. *sigillātus,* decorated with raised figures < *sigilla,* little figures, pl. of *sigillum,* sigil. See SIGIL.]

scarlet fever *n.* An acute contagious disease caused by a hemolytic streptococcus, occurring predominantly in children and

scarecrow
scarecrows in a sunflower field

ă pat   oi boy
ā pay   ou out
âr care   ŏŏ took
ä father ōō boot
ĕ pet   ŭ cut
ē be   ûr urge
ĭ pit   th thin
ī pie   *th* this
îr pier   hw which
ŏ pot   zh vision
ō toe   ə about,
ô paw   item

Stress marks:
′ (primary);
′ (secondary), as in
lexicon (lĕk′sĭ-kŏn′)

marked by a scarlet skin eruption and high fever.

scarlet pimpernel *n.* The pimpernel.

scarlet runner *n.* A tropical American bean plant (*Phaseolus coccineus*) having scarlet flowers and pods with edible seeds.

scarlet sage *n.* A shrubby Brazilian plant (*Salvia splendens*) having showy scarlet flowers, red bracts, and opposite leaves.

scarlet tanager *n.* A New World bird (*Piranga olivacea*), the male of which has scarlet and black plumage.

scarp (skärp) *n.* An escarpment. ❖ *tr.v.* **scarped, scarp·ing, scarps** To cut or make into an escarpment. [Ital. *scarpa*, slope, perh. of Gmc. orig. See **sker-**[1] in App.]

scar tissue *n.* Dense fibrous connective tissue that forms over a healed wound or cut.

scarves (skärvz) *n.* A plural of **scarf**[1].

scar·y (skâr′ē) *adj.* **-i·er, -i·est** **1.** Being the cause of fright or alarm. **2.** Easily scared; very timid. —**scar′i·ly** *adv.* —**scar′i·ness** *n.*

scat[1] (skăt) *intr.v.* **scat·ted, scat·ting, scats** *Informal* To go away hastily; leave at once. [?]

scat[2] (skăt) *n.* Jazz singing in which improvised nonsense syllables are sung to a melody. ❖ *intr.v.* **scat·ted, scat·ting, scats** To sing scat. [?]

scat[3] (skăt) *n.* Excrement, esp. of an animal; dung. [?]

scathe (skāth) *tr.v.* **scathed, scath·ing, scathes** **1.** To harm or injure, esp. by fire. **2.** To criticize or denounce severely. ❖ *n.* Harm or injury. [ME *scathen* < ON *skadha*.]

scath·ing (skā′thĭng) *adj.* **1.** Bitterly denunciatory; harshly critical. **2.** Harmful or painful; injurious. —**scath′ing·ly** *adv.*

scato- *pref.* Excrement: *scatology.* [Gk. *skato-* < *skōr, skat-*, dung. See **sker-**[2] in App.]

sca·tol·o·gy (skă-tŏl′ə-jē, skə-) *n., pl.* **-gies** **1.** The study of fecal excrement, as in biology. **2.** An obsession with excrement or excretory functions. **3.** Obscene language or literature, esp. that dealing with excrement and excretory functions. —**scat′o·log′i·cal** (skăt′l-ŏj′ĭ-kəl) *adj.*

scat·ter (skăt′ər) *v.* **-tered, -ter·ing, -ters** —*tr.* **1.** To cause to separate or disperse. **2.** To distribute loosely by or as if by sprinkling; strew. **3.** *Physics* To deflect (radiation or particles). —*intr.* **1.** To separate and go in different directions; disperse. **2.** To occur or fall at widely spaced intervals. ❖ *n.* **1.** The act of scattering or the condition of being scattered. **2.** Something scattered. [ME *scateren*, perh. < dialectal alteration of OE **sceaterian*.] —**scat′ter·er** *n.*

scat·ter·brain (skăt′ər-brān′) *n.* A person regarded as flighty, thoughtless, or disorganized. —**scat′ter·brained′** *adj.*

scat·ter·good (skăt′ər-good′) *n.* A spendthrift; a wastrel.

scat·ter·ing (skăt′ər-ĭng) *n.* **1.** Something scattered, esp. a small, irregularly occurring amount or quantity. **2.** *Physics* The dispersal of a beam of particles or of radiation into a range of directions as a result of physical interactions. ❖ *adj.* Placed irregularly and far apart; scattered. —**scat′ter·ing·ly** *adv.*

scatter rug *n.* A small rug for covering a part of a floor.

scat·ter·shot (skăt′ər-shŏt′) *adj.* Covering a wide range in a random way; indiscriminate.

scat·ty (skăt′ē) *adj.* **-ti·er, -ti·est** *Chiefly British* Scatterbrained; flighty. [Prob. SCATT(ERBRAIN) + -Y[1].]

scaup (skôp) *n., pl.* **scaup** or **scaups** Either of two diving ducks (*Aythya marila* or *A. affinis*) having predominantly black and white plumage in the male. [Perh. < Sc. *scalp, scaup*, bed of mussels (< its feeding on shellfish).]

scav·enge (skăv′ənj) *v.* **-enged, -eng·ing, -eng·es** —*tr.* **1.** To search through for salvageable material: *scavenged the garbage cans for food scraps.* **2.** To collect and remove refuse from. **3.** To collect (salvageable material) by searching. **4a.** To expel (exhaust gases) from a cylinder of an internal-combustion engine. **b.** To expel exhaust gases from (such a cylinder). **5.** *Metallurgy* To clean (molten metal) by chemically removing impurities. —*intr.* **1.** To scavenge refuse. **2.** To feed on dead or decaying matter.

scav·en·ger (skăv′ən-jər) *n.* **1.** One that scavenges, as a person who looks for food in refuse. **2.** An animal that feeds on dead or decaying matter. **3.** *Chemistry* A substance added to a mixture to remove or inactivate impurities. [Alteration of ME *scauager, schavager*, street maintenance official < AN *scawager*, toll collector < *scawage*, tax on foreign merchants' goods < Flem. *scauwen*, to look at, show.]

scavenger hunt *n.* A game in which individuals or teams try to locate and bring back miscellaneous items on a list.

ScB *abbr. Latin* Scientiae Baccalaureus (Bachelor of Science)

ScD *abbr. Latin* Scientiae Doctor (Doctor of Science)

sce·na (shā′nə) *n.* **1.** A subdivision or scene of an opera. **2.** The recitative part of a larger vocal number within an opera. [Ital. < Lat. *scaena*, stage. See SCENE.]

sce·nar·i·o (sĭ-nâr′ē-ō′, -när′-, -năr′-) *n., pl.* **-os** **1.** An outline of a dramatic or literary plot. **2a.** An outline or treatment for a screenplay. **b.** A screenplay. **3.** An outline or model of an expected or supposed sequence of events. [Ital. < *scena*, scene < Lat. *scaena*. See SCENE.]

sce·nar·ist (sĭ-nâr′ĭst, -när′-, -năr′-) *n.* One who writes screenplays.

scend also **send** (sĕnd) *Nautical intr.v.* **scend·ed, scend·ing, scends** also **send·ed, send·ing, sends** To heave upward on a

wave or swell. ❖ *n.* The rising movement of a ship on a wave or swell. [Prob. alteration of SEND[1] (influenced by DESCEND or ASCEND).]

scene (sēn) *n.* **1.** Something seen by a viewer; a view or prospect. **2.** The place where an action or event occurs. **3.** The place in which the action of a play, movie, novel, or other narrative occurs; a setting. **4a.** A subdivision of an act in a dramatic presentation in which the setting is fixed and the time continuous. **b.** A shot or series of shots in a movie constituting a unit of continuous related action. **5a.** The scenery and properties for a dramatic presentation. **b.** A theater stage. **6.** A real or fictitious episode, esp. when described. **7.** A public display of passion or temper. **8a.** A sphere of activity: *the political scene.* **b.** *Slang* A situation or set of circumstances: *a bad scene.* —*idiom:* **behind the scenes 1.** Backstage. **2.** Out of public view; in secret. [Fr. *scène*, stage < OFr. < Lat. *scaena* < Gk. *skēnē*, tent, stage (via Etruscan).]

scen·er·y (sē′nə-rē) *n., pl.* **-ies** **1.** A view or views of natural features, esp. in open country. **2.** Backdrops, hangings, furnishings, and other accessories on a stage that represent the location of a scene.

scene-steal·er (sēn′stē′lər) *n.* An actor who draws attention from or overshadows other actors in the same production.

sce·nic (sē′nĭk, sĕn′ĭk) *adj.* **1.** Of or relating to the stage, stage scenery, or theatrical representation: *scenic design.* **2.** Constituting or affording pleasing views of natural features. ❖ *n.* A depiction of natural scenery. —**sce′ni·cal·ly** *adv.*

sce·nog·ra·phy (sē-nŏg′rə-fē) *n.* The art of representing objects in perspective, esp. as applied to the design of theatrical scenery. —**sce′nog′raph·er** *n.* —**sce′no·graph′ic** (-nə-grăf′ĭk) *adj.*

scent (sĕnt) *n.* **1.** A distinctive, often agreeable odor. See Syns at **smell. 2.** A perfume. **3.** An odor left by an animal. **4.** The trail of a hunted animal or fugitive. **5.** The sense of smell. **6.** A hint of something imminent; a suggestion. ❖ *v.* **scent·ed, scent·ing, scents** —*tr.* **1.** To perceive or identify by the sense of smell. **2.** To suspect or detect as if by smelling. **3.** To fill with a pleasant odor; perfume. —*intr.* To hunt prey by means of the sense of smell. Used of hounds. [ME *sent* < *senten*, to scent < OFr. *sentir* < Lat. *sentīre*, to feel.]

scent gland *n.* A specialized apocrine gland found in many mammals that produces a strong-smelling substance.

scep·ter (sĕp′tər) *n.* **1.** A staff held by a sovereign as an emblem of authority. **2.** Ruling power or authority; sovereignty. ❖ *tr.v.* **-tered, -ter·ing, -ters** To invest with royal authority. [ME *sceptre* < OFr. < Lat. *scēptrum* < Gk. *skēptron*.]

scep·tic (skĕp′tĭk) *n.* Variant of **skeptic.**

scep·ti·cal (skĕp′tĭ-kəl) *adj.* Variant of **skeptical.**

scep·ti·cism (skĕp′tĭ-sĭz′əm) *n.* Variant of **skepticism.**

scep·tre (sĕp′tər) *n. & v. Chiefly British* Variant of **scepter.**

scha·den·freu·de (shäd′n-froi′də) *n.* Pleasure derived from the misfortunes of others. [Ger. : *Schaden*, damage (< MHGer. *schade* < OHGer. *scado*) + *Freude*, joy (< MHGer. *vreude* < OHGer. *frewida* < *frō*, happy).]

sched·ule (skĕj′ool, -oo-əl, skĕj′əl) *n.* **1.** A list of times of departures and arrivals; a timetable. **2.** A plan for performing work or achieving an objective, specifying the order and allotted time for each part. **3.** A printed or written list of items in tabular form. **4a.** A program of events or appointments expected in a given time. **b.** A student's program of classes. **5.** A supplemental statement of details appended to a document. **6.** A federally regulated list of controlled substances, ranked in classes by potential for abuse. ❖ *tr.v.* **-uled, -ul·ing, -ules** **1.** To enter on a schedule. **2.** To make up a schedule for. **3.** To plan or appoint for a certain time or date. **4.** To list or rank (a controlled substance) in a schedule. [ME *sedule*, slip of parchment or paper, note < OFr. *cedule* < LLat. *schedula*, dim. of *scheda*, var. of Lat. *scida*, papyrus strip < Gk. *skhida, skhedē*; perh. akin to *skhizein*, to split. See SCHIZO–.] —**sched′u·lar** *adj.* —**sched′u·ler** *n.*

sched·uled caste (skĕj′oold, -oo-əld, skĕj′əld) *n.* Any of the historically disadvantaged Indian castes of low rank, now under government protection. [< their having been entered on a list or "schedule" during Brit. rule.]

Schee·le (shā′lə), **Karl Wilhelm** 1742–86. German-born Swedish chemist who independently discovered oxygen (c. 1772) before Joseph Priestley.

schee·lite (shā′līt′, shē′-) *n.* A variously colored mineral, CaWO₄, found in igneous rocks and used as an ore of tungsten.

schef·fler·a (shĕf-lîr′ə, -lĕr′ə, shĕf′lər-ə) *n.* Any of numerous evergreen shrubs or small trees of the genus *Schefflera*, having palmately compound leaves and unisexual flowers grouped in umbels. [NLat. *Schefflera*, genus name, after Jacob Christoph *Scheffler* (1690–1742), German botanist and physician.]

Sche·her·e·zade (shə-hĕr′ə-zäd′) *n.* A skilled woman storyteller. [After the fictional queen *Scheherezade*, skilled narrator of the tales in the anonymous *The Arabian Nights' Entertainment*.]

Scheldt (skĕlt) A river rising in N France and flowing c. 434 km (270 mi) to the North Sea.

Schel·ling (shĕl′ĭng), **Friedrich Wilhelm Joseph von** 1775–1854. German idealist philosopher whose theories of the self, nature, and art influenced romanticism.

sche·ma (skē′mə) *n., pl.* **sche·ma·ta** (skē-mä′tə, skī-mät′ə) or

sche•mas 1. A diagrammatic representation; an outline or model. **2.** *Psychology* A pattern imposed on complex reality or experience to assist in explaining it, mediate perception, or guide response. [Lat. *schēma, schēmat-,* form. See SCHEME.]

sche•mat•ic (skē-mătʹĭk, skĭ-) *adj.* Of, relating to, or in the form of a scheme or diagram. ❖ *n.* A structural or procedural diagram, esp. of an electrical or mechanical system. —**sche•matʹi•cal•ly** *adv.*

sche•ma•tism (skēʹmə-tĭzʹəm) *n.* The patterned disposition of constituents within a given system.

sche•ma•tize (skēʹmə-tīzʹ) *tr.v.* -**tized,** -**tiz•ing,** -**tiz•es** To express or reduce to a scheme: *schematized the consumption of wealth.* [Gk. *skhēmatizein,* to give form to < *skhēma, skhēmat-,* form. See SCHEME.] —**sche•ma•ti•za•tion** (-tĭ-zăʹshən) *n.*

scheme (skēm) *n.* **1.** A systematic plan of action. **2.** A secret or devious plan; a plot. See Syns at **plan. 3.** An orderly combination of related parts: *an irrigation scheme.* **4.** A chart, diagram, or outline of a system or object. ❖ *v.* **schemed, schem•ing, schemes** —*tr.* **1.** To plot: *scheming their revenge.* **2.** To contrive a plan or scheme for. —*intr.* To make plans, esp. secret or devious ones. [Lat. *schēma,* figure < Gk. *skhēma.* See **segh-** in App.] —**schemʹer** *n.*

Sche•nec•ta•dy (skə-nĕkʹtə-dē) A city of E NY on the Mohawk R. NW of Albany; first settled in 1661. Pop. 61,821.

scher•zan•do (skĕrt-sänʹdō) *Music adv. & adj.* In a light playful manner. ❖ *n., pl.* -**dos** A scherzando passage. [Ital., gerund of *scherzare,* to joke < OItal. See SCHERZO.]

scher•zo (skĕrʹtsō) *n., pl.* -**zos** or -**zi** (-tsē) *Music* A lively movement, commonly in 3/4 time. [Ital., joke, scherzo < OItal. *scherzare,* to joke, perh. of Gmc. orig.]

Schia•pa•rel•li (skē-äpʹə-rĕlʹē, skäpʹ-, shäpʹ-, skyäpʹä-rĕlʹlē), **Elsa** 1896–1973. Italian-born fashion designer noted for her use of brilliant colors and synthetic materials.

Schick test (shĭk) *n.* A test for immunity to diphtheria by injection of dilute diphtheria toxin into the skin. [After Béla *Schick* (1877–1967), American pediatrician.]

Schie•le (shēʹlə), **Egon** 1890–1918. Austrian painter and draftsman known for his aggressive, nervous style and his explicitly erotic subjects.

schil•ler (shĭlʹər) *n.* A lustrous colored reflection from certain planes in a mineral grain. [Ger., iridescence < MHGer. *schilher,* iridescent taffeta < *schilhen,* to twinkle, squint < OHGer. *scilihen,* to squint, wink.]

Schiller, Johann Christoph Friedrich von 1759–1805. German writer best known for his didactic poetry and historical plays, such as *Don Carlos* (1787).

schil•ling (shĭlʹĭng) *n.* See table at **currency.** [Ger. < MHGer. *schillinc* < OHGer. *skilling,* gold coin.]

schip•per•ke (skĭpʹər-kē, -kə) *n.* A small stocky dog of a Belgian breed, having dense long black fur and small pointed ears. [Flem., dim. of *schipper,* skipper (< the dog's use as a watchdog on a boat) < MDu. See SKIPPER¹.]

schism (skĭzʹəm, sĭzʹ-) *n.* **1.** A separation into factions. **2a.** A formal breach of union within a Christian church. **b.** The offense of attempting to produce such a breach. **3.** Disunion; discord. [ME *scisme* < OFr. < Lat. *schisma, schismat-* < Gk. *skhisma < skhizein,* to split.]

schis•mat•ic (skĭz-mătʹĭk, sĭz-) *adj.* Of, relating to, or engaging in schism. ❖ *n.* One who promotes or engages in schism. —**schis•matʹi•cal•ly** *adv.*

schist (shĭst) *n.* Any of various medium-grained to coarse-grained metamorphic rocks composed of laminated, often flaky parallel layers of chiefly micaceous minerals. [Fr. *schiste* < Lat. (*lapis*) *schistos,* fissile (stone), a kind of iron ore < Gk. *skhistos,* split, divisible < *skhizein,* to split.] —**schisʹtose** (shĭsʹtōsʹ), **schisʹtous** (-təs) *adj.*

schis•to•some (shĭsʹtə-sōmʹ) *n.* Any of several chiefly tropical trematode worms of the genus *Schistosoma,* many of which are parasitic in the blood of mammals. [NLat. *Schistosōma,* genus name : Gk. *skhistos,* split; see SCHIST + Gk. *sōma,* body; see -SOME³.] —**schisʹto•somʹal** (-sōʹməl) *adj.*

schis•to•so•mi•a•sis (shĭsʹtə-sə-mīʹə-sĭs) *n., pl.* -**ses** (-sēzʹ) Any of various diseases caused by schistosomes, widespread in rural areas of Africa, Asia, and Latin America through use of contaminated water and characterized by infection and gradual destruction of the kidneys, liver, and other organs.

schiz•o (skĭtʹsō) *n., pl.* -**os** *Offensive Slang* A schizophrenic person. —**schizʹo** *adj.*

schizo- or **schiz-** *pref.* **1.** Split; cleft: *schizocarp.* **2.** Cleavage; fission: *schizogenesis.* **3.** Schizophrenia: *schizoid.* [NLat. < Gk. *skhizo- < skhizein,* to split.]

schiz•o•carp (skĭzʹə-kärpʹ, skĭtʹsə-) *n.* A dry fruit that splits at maturity into two or more closed one-seeded parts, as in the carrot. —**schizʹo•carʹpous, schizʹo•carʹpic** *adj.*

schiz•o•gen•e•sis (skĭzʹō-jĕnʹĭ-sĭs, skĭtʹsō-) *n.* *Biology* Reproduction by fission.

schi•zog•o•ny (skĭ-zŏgʹə-nē, skĭt-sŏgʹ-) *n.* Reproduction by multiple asexual fission, characteristic of many sporozoans. —**schiʹzogʹo•nous** *adj.*

schiz•oid (skĭtʹsoidʹ) *adj.* **1.** Of, relating to, or having a personality disorder marked by extreme shyness, flat affect, reclusiveness,

and an inability to form close relationships. **2.** Schizophrenic. Not in scientific use. **3.** *Informal* Having disparate or antagonistic elements. ❖ *n.* A schizoid person.

schiz•ont (skĭzʹŏntʹ, skĭtʹsŏntʹ) *n.* A sporozoan cell produced by schizogony.

schiz•o•phre•ni•a (skĭtʹsə-frēʹnē-ə, -frĕnʹē-ə) *n.* **1.** Any of a group of psychotic disorders usu. characterized by withdrawal from reality, illogical patterns of thinking, delusions, and hallucinations and accompanied in varying degrees by other emotional, behavioral, or intellectual disturbances. **2.** A situation or condition that results from the coexistence of disparate or antagonistic qualities, identities, or activities. —**schizʹo•phrenʹic** (-frĕnʹĭk) *adj.* —**schizʹo•phrenʹi•cal•ly** *adv.*

schiz•y also **schiz•zy** (skĭtʹsē) *adj.* -**i•er,** -**i•est** *Offensive Slang* Schizophrenic or schizoid.

Schle•gel (shlāʹgəl), **August Wilhelm von** 1767–1845. German scholar and poet who edited a literary magazine with his brother **Friedrich** (1772–1829), a poet and critic whose essays formed the basis of German romanticism.

Schlei•er•ma•cher (shlīʹər-mäʹkər, -кнər), **Friedrich Ernst Daniel** 1768–1834. German philosopher who believed that the individual must develop a personal religious attitude.

schle•miel also **shle•miel** (shlə-mēlʹ) *n. Slang* A habitual bungler; a dolt. [Yiddish *shlemil,* perh. < Heb. *šəlūmîʹel,* Shelumiel, a character in the Bible (Numbers 7:36) : *šəlūmî,* my well-being (*šālôm,* well-being + -î, my) + ʹel, God.]

schlep or **schlepp** also **shlep** (shlĕp) *Slang v.* **schlepped, schlep•ping, schleps** or **schlepps** also **shlepped, shlep•ping, shleps** —*tr.* To carry clumsily or with difficulty; lug: *schlepped a shopping bag around town.* —*intr.* To move slowly or laboriously. ❖ *n.* **1.** An arduous journey. **2.** A clumsy or stupid person. [Yiddish *shlepn,* to drag, pull < MLGer. *slēpen.*]

Schles•in•ger (shlĕsʹĭn-jər), **Arthur Meier** 1888–1965. Amer. historian whose works include *The Rise of the City* (1933). His son **Arthur Meier, Jr.** (b. 1917), also a historian, was an adviser to President John F. Kennedy.

Schlesinger, John Richard b. 1926. British director whose works include the film *Far From the Madding Crowd* (1967).

Schles•wig (shlĕsʹwĭg, -wĭk, shläsʹvĭk) A historical region and former duchy of N Germany and S Denmark in S Jutland.

Schlie•mann (shlēʹmänʹ), **Heinrich** 1822–90. German archaeologist who discovered the ruins of ancient Troy (1871) and excavated Mycenae (1876).

schlie•ren (shlîrʹən) *pl.n.* **1.** *Geology* Irregular streaks in plutonic igneous rock that differ in composition from the principal mass. **2.** Regions of a transparent medium that photograph as streaks when illuminated because their densities are different from that of the bulk of the medium. [Ger., pl. of *Schliere* < dialectal *Shliere,* streaks < MHGer. *slier,* mud, slime < OHGer. *sclierrun,* pieces, bits.]

schli•ma•zel also **shli•ma•zel** (shlĭ-mäʹzəl) *n. Slang* An extremely unlucky or inept person. [Yiddish *shlimazl,* bad luck, unlucky person : MHGer. *slimp,* wrong + Yiddish *mazl,* luck (< Mishnaic Heb. *mazzāl;* see MAZEL TOV).]

schlock also **shlock** (shlŏk) *Slang n.* Something, such as merchandise, that is inferior or shoddy. ❖ *adj.* Of inferior quality; cheap or shoddy. [Poss. < Yiddish *shlak,* apoplexy, stroke, evil, nuisance < MHGer. *slag, slak,* stroke < *slahen,* to strike < OHGer. *slahan.*] —**schlockʹy, shlockʹy** *adj.*

OUR LIVING LANGUAGE A good number of English words borrowed from Yiddish (a variety of German with an admixture of Hebrew and Slavic elements) are recognizably of foreign extraction because they begin with sound combinations (shl-, shm-, shn-) not found at the beginnings of native English words. *Schlock* is such a word; it is descended from a Middle High German word for a hit or blow, and thus came to refer to damaged merchandise, and then to merchandise of poor quality. Other words beginning with this and similar sound combinations are Yiddish also: *schlep, schlemiel, schmooze, schmuck,* and *schnoz.* Of course, not all Yiddish words borrowed into English begin with the sound (sh); one need only think of *bagel, lox, blintz, nosh, meshugga,* and *kibbitz* to get a feeling for the variety of words that Yiddish-speaking Jews brought with them to America.

---

schlub also **shlub** (shlŭb) *n. Slang* A clumsy, stupid, or unattractive person. [Yiddish < Pol. *żłób,* trough, blockhead.]

schmaltz also **schmalz** (shmälts) *n.* **1.** *Informal* **a.** Excessively sentimental art or music. **b.** Maudlin sentimentality. **2.** Liquid fat, esp. chicken fat. [Yiddish *shmalts,* animal fat, sentimentality < MHGer. *smalz,* animal fat < OHGer.] —**schmaltzʹy, schmalzʹy** *adj.*

schmat•te (shmäʹtə) *n.* **1.** A rag. **2.** An old or ragged garment. [Yiddish *shmate* < Pol. *szmata.*]

schmeer also **schmear** or **shmear** (shmîr) *n. Slang* A number of things that go together; an aggregate: *bought the whole schmeer.* [Yiddish *shmir,* smear, smudge < *shmirn,* to smear, grease < MHGer. *smiren* < OHGer. *smirwen.*]

Schmidt (shmĭt), **Helmut** b. 1918. German politician who served as chancellor of West Germany (1974–82).

Schmidt system *n.* A system consisting of a concave spherical mirror with a transparent plate at its center of curvature, used in

Elsa Schiaparelli

schipperke

schnauzer
standard schnauzer

schooner
three-masted schooner

schmo or **schmoe** also **shmo** (shmō) *n., pl.* **schmoes** or **shmoes** *Slang* A stupid or obnoxious person. [< Yiddish *shmok,* penis, fool. See SCHMUCK.]

schmooze also **shmooze** (shmōōz) *Slang intr.v.* **schmoozed, schmooz•ing, schmooz•es** or **shmoozed, shmoozing, shmooz•es** To talk casually; chat. ❖ *n.* A chat. [Yiddish *shmuesn,* poss. < *shmues,* a chat, pl. of *shmue,* rumor; akin to Heb. *šәmûʿâ,* rumor, fem. passive part. of *šāmaʿ,* to hear.] —**schmooz′er** *n.*

schmuck also **shmuck** (shmŭk) *n. Slang* A clumsy or stupid person; an oaf. [Yiddish *shmok,* penis, fool, prob. < Pol. *smok,* dragon, tail.]

Schna•bel (shnä′bəl), **Artur** 1882–1951. Austrian-born Amer. pianist and composer.

schnap•per (shnäp′ər, snäp′-) *n.* A porgy (*Chrysophrys guttulatus*) of Australia, Tasmania, and New Zealand, prized as a sport fish and food fish. [Alteration of SNAPPER (influenced by Ger. *Schnapper,* snap, snapper).]

schnapps (shnäps, shnăps) *n., pl.* **schnapps** Any of various strong dry liquors, such as a strong Dutch gin. [Ger. *Schnaps,* mouthful, schnapps < LGer. *snaps* < *snappen,* to snap < MLGer., to snap at.]

schnau•zer (shnou′zər, shnou′tsər) *n.* Any of three German breeds of dog of a range of sizes, having a wiry pepper-and-salt or black coat and a blunt muzzle with wiry whiskers. [Ger. < *Schnauze,* snout, alteration of MLGer. *snūte.*]

Schnitt•ke (shnĭt′kĕ), **Alfred** 1934–98. Russian composer whose works include symphonies, chamber music, and film scores.

schnit•zel (shnĭt′səl) *n.* A thin cutlet of veal, usu. seasoned, that is dipped in batter and fried. [Ger. < MHGer. *snitzel,* dim. of *sniz,* slice < *snitzen,* to carve, freq. of *snīden,* to cut < OHGer. *snīdan.*]

Schnitz•ler (shnĭts′lər), **Arthur** 1862–1931. Austrian writer whose works include *La Ronde* (1896).

schnook also **shnook** (shnŏŏk) *n. Slang* A stupid or easily duped person. [Yiddish *shnuk,* snout, schnook < Lith. *snukis,* mug, snout.]

schnor•rer also **shnor•rer** (shnôr′ər, shnôr′-) *n. Slang* One who habitually takes advantage of the generosity of others; a parasite. [Yiddish *shnorer* < *shnorn,* to beg < MHGer. *snurren,* to hum, whir (< a beggar's musical instrument).]

schnoz (shnŏz) also **schnoz•zle** (shnŏz′əl) *n. Slang* The human nose. [Prob. alteration of Yiddish *snoyts,* snout, muzzle < Ger. *Schnauze.*]

schol•ar (skŏl′ər) *n.* **1a.** A learned person. **b.** A specialist in a given branch of knowledge: *a classical scholar.* **2.** One who attends school or studies with a teacher; a student. **3.** A student holding a particular scholarship. [ME *scoler* < OFr. *escoler* < OE *scolere,* both < Med.Lat. *scholāris* < LLat., of a school < Lat. *scola, schola,* school. See SCHOOL¹.]

schol•ar•ly (skŏl′ər-lē) *adj.* Of, relating to, or characteristic of scholars or scholarship: *scholarly pursuits.* See Syns at **learned.** —**schol′ar•li•ness** *n.*

schol•ar•ship (skŏl′ər-shĭp′) *n.* **1.** The methods, discipline, and attainments of a scholar or scholars. **2.** Knowledge resulting from study and research in a particular field. **3.** A grant of financial aid to a student.

scho•las•tic (skə-lăs′tĭk) *adj.* **1.** Of or relating to schools; academic. **2.** often **Scholastic** Of, relating to, or characteristic of Scholasticism. **3.** Adhering rigidly to scholarly methods; pedantic. ❖ *n.* **1.** often **Scholastic** A Scholastic philosopher or theologian. **2.** A dogmatist; a pedant. [Lat. *scholasticus* < Gk. *skholastikos,* learned, studious < *skholazein,* to study < *skholē,* school. See segh- in App.] —**scho•las′ti•cal•ly** *adv.*

scho•las•ti•cism (skə-lăs′tĭ-sĭz′əm) *n.* **1.** often **Scholasticism** The dominant western Christian theological and philosophical school of the Middle Ages, based on the authority of the Latin Fathers and of Aristotle and his commentators. **2.** Close adherence to traditional methods or teachings.

scho•li•ast (skō′lē-ăst′) *n.* One of the ancient commentators who annotated the classical authors. [Med.Gk. *skholiastēs* < *skholiazein,* to comment on < Gk. *skholion,* scholium. See SCHOLIUM.]

scho•li•um (skō′lē-əm) *n., pl.* **-li•ums** or **-li•a** (-lē-ə) **1.** An explanatory note or commentary, as on a Greek text. **2.** A note amplifying a proof or course of reasoning, as in mathematics. [NLat. < Gk. *skholion,* dim. of *skholē,* lecture, school. See segh- in App.]

Schön•berg (shœn′bûrg, shûrn′-, shœn′bĕrk′), **Arnold** 1874–1951. Austrian composer of *Pierrot Lunaire* (1912).

school¹ (skōōl) *n.* **1.** An institution for the instruction of children or people under college age. **2.** An institution for instruction in a skill or business. **3a.** A college or university. **b.** An institution associated with a college or university that gives instruction in a specialized field and recommends candidates for degrees. **c.** A division of an educational institution constituting several grades or classes. **d.** The student body of an educational institution. **e.** The building or buildings housing an educational institution. **4.** The process of being educated formally, esp. by a planned series of courses over a number of years. **5.** A session of instruction. **6a.** A group of people, esp. philosophers, artists, or writers, whose thought, work, or style demonstrates a common origin or influence or unifying belief. **b.** A group of people distinguished by similar manners, customs, or opinions. **7.** *Australian* A group of people gathered together for gambling. ❖ *tr.v.* **schooled, school•ing, schools 1.** To educate in or as if in a school. **2.** To train or discipline. See Syns at **teach.** ❖ *adj.* Of or relating to schools or education in schools. [ME *scole* < OE *scōl* < Lat. *schola, scola* < Gk. *skholē.* See segh- in App.]

school² (skōōl) *n.* A large group of aquatic animals, esp. fish, swimming together; a shoal. ❖ *intr.v.* **schooled, school•ing, schools** To swim in or form into a school. [ME *scole* < MDu.]

school age *n.* The age at which a child is considered old enough to attend school. —**school′-age** (skōōl′āj′) *adj.*

school board *n.* A local board that oversees public schools.

school•book (skōōl′bŏŏk′) *n.* A book for use in school.

school•boy (skōōl′boi′) *n.* A boy attending school.

school bus *n.* A vehicle used for taking schoolchildren to and from school or school-related activities.

school•child also **school child** (skōōl′chīld′) *n.* A child attending school.

school choice *n.* A public school program that allows students to choose to attend any of various participating private and public schools, usu. by means of vouchers.

school day *n.* **1.** A day on which school is in session. **2.** The part of a day during which school is in session.

school district *n.* A geographic district, the public schools of which are administered together.

school•fel•low (skōōl′fĕl′ō) *n.* A schoolmate.

school•girl (skōōl′gûrl′) *n.* A girl attending school.

school•house (skōōl′hous′) *n.* A building used as a school.

school•ing (skōōl′lĭng) *n.* **1.** Instruction or training given at school. **2.** Education from experience or exposure. **3.** The training of a horse or a horse and rider in equitation.

school•man (skōōl′mən) *n.* **1.** A man who is a professional educator or scholar. **2. Schoolman** A medieval Scholastic scholar or philosopher.

school•marm (skōōl′märm′) also **school•ma′am** (-măm′, -mäm′) *n.* A woman teacher, esp. one regarded as strict or old-fashioned. [SCHOOL¹ + dialectal *marm* (var. of MA'AM).] —**school′marm′ish** *adj.*

school•mas•ter (skōōl′măs′tər) *n.* **1.** A man who is a teacher. **2.** One who educates, guides, or instructs. **3.** A grayish-brown snapper (*Lutjanus apodus*) of the tropical Atlantic and the Gulf of Mexico. —**school′mas′ter•ly** *adj.*

school•mate (skōōl′māt′) *n.* A companion or associate in one's school.

school•mis•tress (skōōl′mĭs′trĭs) *n.* **1.** A woman who is a teacher. **2.** A headmistress of a school.

school of thought *n., pl.* **schools of thought** The point of view held by a particular group.

school•room (skōōl′rōōm′, -rŏŏm′) *n.* A classroom.

school•teach•er (skōōl′tē′chər) *n.* A person who teaches in a school below the college level.

school•work (skōōl′wûrk′) *n.* School lessons or homework.

school year *n.* The part of the year during which school is in session, typically from September to June.

schoo•ner (skōō′nər) *n.* **1.** A fore-and-aft rigged sailing vessel having at least two masts, with a foremast that is usu. smaller than the other masts. **2.** A large beer glass, generally holding a pint or more. **3.** A prairie schooner. [?]

Scho•pen•hau•er (shō′pən-hou′ər), **Arthur** 1788–1860. German philosopher whose works include *The World as Will and Representation* (1819).

schot•tische (shŏt′ĭsh, shŏ-tēsh′) *n.* **1.** A round dance in 2/4 time. **2.** A piece of music for this dance. [Ger. < *schottisch,* Scottish < MHGer. *schottesch < schotte,* a Scot < OHGer. *scotto* < LLat. *Scottus,* Irishman.]

Schou•ten Islands (skout′n) An island group of E Indonesia in the S Pacific off the N coast of New Guinea.

schrod (skrŏd) *n.* Variant of scrod.

Schrö•ding•er (shrō′dĭng-ər, shrä′-, shrœ′-), **Erwin** 1887–1961. Austrian physicist who shared a 1933 Nobel Prize.

schtick (shtĭk) *n.* Variant of **shtick.**

Schu•bert (shōō′bərt, -bĕrt′), **Franz Peter** 1797–1828. Austrian composer who perfected the form of the German art song in his more than 600 compositions for voice and piano.

Schulz (shōŏlts), **Charles Monroe** 1922–2000. Amer. cartoonist who created the *Peanuts* comic strip.

Schu•man (shōō′mən), **William Howard** 1910–92. Amer. composer whose works include *A Free Song* (1943).

Schu•mann (shōō′män′, -mən), **Robert** 1810–56. German romantic composer known particularly for his song cycles.

schuss (shōŏs, shŏŏs) *intr.v.* **schussed, schuss•ing, schuss•es** To make a schuss. ❖ *n.* **1.** A fast straight downhill run in skiing. **2.** A straight steep skiing course. [< Ger., schuss, ult. < OHGer. *scuz,* shot.]

Schuy•ler (skī′lər), **Philip John** 1733–1804. Amer. Revolutionary general who was relieved of his command after the British capture of Fort Ticonderoga (1777).

Schuyl•kill (skōōl′kĭl′, skōō′kəl) A river of SE PA flowing c. 209 km (130 mi) to the Delaware R. at Philadelphia.

schwa (shwä) *n.* **1.** A mid-central neutral vowel, typically occurring in unstressed syllables, as the final vowel of English *sofa.* **2.** The symbol (ə) used to represent this sound and also, in some systems of phonetic spelling, a stressed mid-central vowel, as in *but.* [Ger. < Heb. *šəwā'*, prob. < Syriac *(nuqzē) šwayyā*, even (points), pl. passive part. of *šwā*, to be even.]

Schwann (shvän), **Theodor** 1810–82. German physiologist who described the cell as the basic structure of animal tissue.

Schwann cell (shwän, shvän) *n.* Any of the cells that cover the nerve fibers in the peripheral nervous system and form the myelin sheath. [After Theodor SCHWANN.]

Schwarz·kopf (shwôrts′kôpf, -kôpf, shvärts′-), Dame (**Olga Maria) Elisabeth (Friederike)** b. 1915. German soprano known for her interpretations of lieder.

Schweit·zer (shwīt′sər, shvīt′-), **Albert** 1875–1965. French philosopher, physician, and missionary who won the 1952 Nobel Peace Prize.

Schwe·rin (shvä-rēn′) A city of N-central Germany on **Schwerin Lake** SW of Rostock; chartered c. 1160. Pop. 122,189.

sci·at·ic (sī-ăt′īk) *adj.* **1.** Of or relating to the ischium or the region of the hipbone in which it is located. **2.** Of or relating to sciatica. [Fr. *sciatique* < OFr. < Med.Lat. *sciaticus*, alteration of Lat. *ischiadicus* < Gk. *iskhiadikos* < *iskhias, iskhiad-*, sciatica < *iskhion*, hip.]

sci·at·i·ca (sī-ăt′ī-kə) *n.* Pain along the sciatic nerve radiating to the buttocks and the back of the thigh. [ME < Med.Lat. < fem. of *sciaticus*, of the hip. See SCIATIC.]

sciatic nerve *n.* A sensory and motor nerve originating in the sacral plexus and running through the pelvis and upper leg.

sci·ence (sī′əns) *n.* **1a.** The observation, identification, description, experimental investigation, and theoretical explanation of phenomena. **b.** Such activities restricted to a class of natural phenomena. **c.** Such activities applied to an object of inquiry or study. **2.** Methodological activity, discipline, or study: *I've got it down to a science.* **3.** An activity that appears to require study and method: *the science of purchasing.* **4.** Knowledge, esp. that gained through experience. [ME, knowledge, learning < OFr. < Lat. *scientia* < *sciēns, scient-*, pr. part. of *scīre*, to know.]

science fiction *n.* A literary or cinematic genre in which the plot is typically based on speculative scientific discoveries, environmental changes, space travel, or life on other planets. —**sci′ence·fic′tion** *adj.*

sci·en·tial (sī-ĕn′shəl) *adj.* **1.** Of or producing knowledge or science. **2.** Capable; skillful.

sci·en·tif·ic (sī′ən-tĭf′ĭk) *adj.* Of, relating to, or employing the methodology of science. [Med.Lat. *scientificus*, producing knowledge : Lat. *scientia*, knowledge; see SCIENCE + Lat. *-ficus, -fic*.] —**sci′en·tif′i·cal·ly** *adv.*

scientific method *n.* The systematic procedure for scientific investigation, generally involving the observation of phenomena, the formulation of a hypothesis concerning the phenomena, experimentation to test the hypothesis, and a conclusion that validates or modifies the hypothesis.

scientific notation *n.* A method of representing a number as a decimal number between 1 and 10 multiplied by a power of 10, as 1.0492×10^4, for example, for 10,492.

sci·en·tism (sī′ən-tĭz′əm) *n.* **1.** The collection of attitudes and practices considered typical of scientists. **2.** The belief that the investigative methods of the physical sciences are applicable in all fields of inquiry. —**sci′en·tis′tic** *adj.*

sci·en·tist (sī′ən-tĭst) *n.* A person having expert knowledge of one or more sciences, esp. a natural or physical science.

sci-fi (sī′fī′) *n., pl.* **-fis** *Informal* Science fiction.

scil·i·cet (skĭl′ĭ-sĕt′, skē′lĭ-kĕt′) *adv.* That is to say; namely. [ME < Lat. *scīlicet*, contraction of *scīre licet*, it is permitted to know : *scīre*, to know + *licet*, third pers. sing. of *licēre*, to be permitted.]

Scil·ly Islands (sĭl′ē) or **Isles of Scilly.** An archipelago comprising more than 140 small islands and islets off SW England at the entrance to the English Channel WSW of Land's End.

scim·i·tar (sĭm′ĭ-tər, -tär′) *n.* A curved Asian sword with the edge on the convex side. [Fr. *cimeterre* and Ital. *scimitarra*, both perh. ult. < Pers. *šamšīr, šimšīr* < MPers. *šafšēr, šifšēr*.]

scin·ti·gram (sĭn′tĭ-grăm′) *n.* A two-dimensional record of the distribution of a radioactive tracer in a tissue or organ, obtained by means of a scanning scintillation counter.

scin·ti·graph (sĭn′tĭ-grăf′) *n.* A device for producing a scintigram; a scintiscanner. **2.** See scintigram. —**scin′ti·graph′ic** *adj.* —**scin′ti·graph′i·cal·ly** *adv.* —**scin·tig′ra·phy** (sĭn-tĭg′rə-fē) *n.*

scin·til·la (sĭn-tĭl′ə) *n.* **1.** A minute amount; an iota or trace. **2.** A spark; a flash. [Lat., spark.] —**scin′til·lant** *adj.*

scin·til·late (sĭn′tl-āt′) *v.* **-lat·ed, -lat·ing, -lates** —*intr.* **1.** To throw off sparks; flash. **2.** To sparkle or shine. **3.** To be animated and brilliant. —*tr.* To give off (sparks or flashes). [Lat. *scintillāre, scintillāt-* < *scintilla*, spark.] —**scin′til·lant** *adj.*

scin·til·la·tion (sĭn′tl-ā′shən) *n.* **1.** The act of scintillating. **2.** A spark; a flash. **3.** *Astronomy* Rapid variation in the light of a celestial body caused by turbulence in Earth's atmosphere; a twinkling. **4.** *Physics* A flash of light produced in a phosphor by absorption of an ionizing particle or photon.

scintillation counter *n.* A device for detecting and counting scintillations produced by ionizing radiation.

scin·til·la·tor (sĭn′tl-ā′tər) *n.* A substance that glows when hit by high-energy particles or photons.

scin·ti·scan (sĭn′tĭ-skăn′) *n.* See scintigram. [SCINTI(LLATION) + SCAN.] —**scin′ti·scan′ner** *n.*

sci·o·lism (sī′ə-lĭz′əm) *n.* A pretentious attitude of scholarliness; superficial knowledgeability. [< LLat. *sciolus*, smatterer, dim. of Lat. *scius*, knowing < *scīre*, to know.] —**sci′o·list** *n.* —**sci′o·lis′tic** *adj.*

sci·on (sī′ən) *n.* **1.** A descendant or heir. **2.** also **ci·on** (sī′ən) A detached shoot or twig containing buds from a woody plant, used in grafting. [ME < OFr. *cion*, poss. of Gmc. orig.]

Sci·o·to (sī-ō′tə) A river, c. 381 km (237 mi); rising in W OH and flowing E then S to the Ohio R.

Scip·io (sĭp′ē-ō′, skĭp′-), **Publius Cornelius** Known as "Scipio the Younger." 185?–129 B.C. Roman general and politician who led the destruction of Carthage (146) in the Third Punic War.

Scipio Af·ri·ca·nus (ăf-rĭ-kä′nəs), **Publius Cornelius** Known as "Scipio the Elder." 236?–183? B.C. Roman general who invaded northern Africa, conquered Carthage, and brought the Second Punic War to an end by defeating Hannibal at Zama (202).

scir·roc·co (shə-rŏk′ō, sə-) *n.* Variant of sirocco.

scir·rhus (skĭr′əs, sĭr′-) *n., pl.* **scir·rhi** (skĭr′ī, sĭr′ī) or **scir·rhus·es** A hard dense cancerous growth usu. arising from connective tissue. [NLat. < Lat. *scirros* < Gk. *skīros, skirros* < *skīros*, hard.] —**scir′rhous, scir′rhoid′** *adj.*

scis·sile (sĭs′əl, -īl′) *adj.* Cut or split easily. [Fr. < Lat. *scissilis* < *scissus*, p. part. of *scindere*, to cut. See SCISSION.]

scis·sion (sĭzh′ən, sĭsh′-) *n.* The act of cutting or severing; division or fission. [ME < OFr. < LLat. *scissiō, scissiōn-* < Lat. *scissus*, p. part. of *scindere*, to cut, split.]

scis·sor (sĭz′ər) *tr.v.* **-sored, -sor·ing, -sors** To cut or clip with scissors or shears. ❖ *n.* **1. scissors** (*used with a sing. or pl. verb*) A cutting implement consisting of two blades joined by a swivel pin that allows the cutting edges to be opened and closed. **2. scissors** (*used with a sing. verb*) *Sports* **a.** Any of various gymnastic exercises or jumps in which the legs open and close as a scissors does. **b.** A scissors hold. [< alteration (influenced by Lat. *scissor*, cutter) of ME *sisoures*, scissors < OFr. *cisoires* < VLat. **cīsōria* < LLat., pl. of *cīsōrium*, cutting instrument < Lat. *caesus, -cīsus*, p. part. of *caedere*, to cut.]

scissors hold *n.* A wrestling hold in which the legs of one opponent are locked about another opponent.

scissors kick *n.* A swimming kick in which the legs are opened and closed like scissors, used esp. in sidestroke.

scis·sor·tail (sĭz′ər-tāl′) *n.* A scissor-tailed flycatcher.

scis·sor-tailed flycatcher (sĭz′ər-tāld′) *n.* A flycatcher (*Muscivora forficata*) of the southwest United States, Mexico, and Central America having a long forked tail.

scis·sure (sĭzh′ər, sĭsh′-) *n. Anatomy* A split or opening in an organ or part. [ME < OFr. < Lat. *scissūra* < *scissus*, p. part. of *scindere*, to split. See SCISSION.]

sclaff (sklăf) *v.* **sclaffed, sclaff·ing, sclaffs** —*intr.* To scrape or strike the ground with a golf club behind the ball before hitting it. —*tr.* **1.** To strike (the ground) with a golf club before hitting the ball. **2.** To hit (a ball) in this manner. [Sc., to strike with a flat surface.] —**sclaff** *n.* —**sclaff′er** *n.*

SCLC *abbr.* Southern Christian Leadership Conference

scle·ra (sklîr′ə) *n.* The tough white fibrous outer envelope of tissue covering all of the eyeball except the cornea. [NLat. < Gk., fem. of *sklēros*, hard.] —**scle′ral** *adj.*

scle·ren·chy·ma (sklə-rĕng′kə-mə) *n.* A supportive plant tissue that consists of thick-walled, usu. lignified cells. —**scle′ren·chym′a·tous** (sklîr′ən-kĭm′ə-təs, -kī′mə-) *adj.*

scle·rite (sklîr′īt′) *n.* A chitinous or calcareous plate, spicule, or similar part of an invertebrate, esp. one of the outer plates of an arthropod.

scle·ri·tis (sklə-rī′tĭs) *n.* Inflammation of the sclera. —**scle·rit′ic** (-rĭt′ĭk) *adj.*

sclero– or **scler–** *pref.* **1.** Hard: *sclerite.* **2.** Hardness: *sclerometer.* **3.** Sclera: *scleritis.* [Gk. *sklēro–* < *sklēros*, hard.]

scle·ro·der·ma (sklîr′ə-dûr′mə) *n.* A pathological thickening and hardening of the skin.

scle·ro·der·ma·tous (sklîr′ə-dûr′mə-təs) *adj.* **1.** Of, relating to, or affected by scleroderma. **2.** *Zoology* Having an outer covering of hard plates or bony scales.

scle·roid (sklîr′oid′) *adj. Biology* Hard or hardened.

scle·ro·ma (sklə-rō′mə) *n., pl.* **-mas** or **-ma·ta** (-mə-tə) An abnormally hard patch of body tissue. [NLat. *sclērōma* < Gk. *sklērōma*, hardening < *sklēroun*, to harden < *sklēros*, hard.]

scle·rom·e·ter (sklə-rŏm′ĭ-tər) *n.* An instrument used to determine the relative hardness of a material by measuring the pressure required to penetrate it with a diamond stylus.

scle·ro·pro·tein (sklîr′ō-prō′tēn′, -tē-ĭn) *n.* Any of a class of generally insoluble proteins, such as collagen and keratin.

scle·rosed (sklə-rōsd′, sklîr′ōst′) *adj.* **1.** Affected by sclerosis; hardened. **2.** *Botany* Lignified. [< SCLEROSIS.]

scle·ro·sis (sklə-rō′sĭs) *n., pl.* **-ses** (-sēz) **1a.** A thickening or hardening of a body part, as of an artery. **b.** A disease characterized by this thickening or hardening. **2.** *Botany* The hardening of cell walls by increased deposition of lignin. [ME *sclirosis*

Albert Schweitzer

ă	pat	oi	boy
ā	pay	ou	out
âr	care	ŏŏ	took
ä	father	ōō	boot
ĕ	pet	ŭ	cut
ē	be	ûr	urge
ĭ	pit	th	thin
ī	pie	th	this
îr	pier	hw	which
ŏ	pot	zh	vision
ō	toe	ə	about,
ô	paw		item

Stress marks:
′ (primary);
′ (secondary), as in
lexicon (lĕk′sĭ-kŏn′)

< Med.Lat. *sclīrōsis* < Gk. *sklērōsis*, hardening < *sklēroun*, to harden. See SCLEROMA.]

scle•rot•ic (sklə-rŏt′ĭk) *adj.* **1.** Affected or marked by sclerosis. **2.** *Anatomy* Of or relating to the sclera. ❖ *n.* See **sclera.**

scler•o•tin (sklîr′ə-tĭn, sklĕr′-) *n.* An insoluble protein that permeates the chitin in the cuticle of arthropods and becomes hardened and darkened by a natural tanning process. [SCLERO– + *-tin* (as in KERATIN or CHITIN).]

scle•ro•ti•um (sklə-rō′shē-əm, -shəm) *n., pl.* **-ti•a** (-shē-ə, -shə) A dense mass of branched hyphae, as in certain fungi, that are capable of remaining dormant for long periods. [NLat. < Gk. *sklērotēs*, hardness < *sklēros*, hard.]

scler•o•ti•za•tion (sklĕr′ə-tĭ-zā′shən) *n.* Hardening of the cuticle of an arthropod by substances other than chitin. [Gk. *sklērotēs*, hardness (< *sklēros*, hard) + –IZATION.]

scle•rot•o•my (sklə-rŏt′ə-mē) *n., pl.* **-mies** Surgical incision of the sclera.

scle•rous (sklîr′əs, sklĕr′-) *adj.* Hardened; toughened.

scoff[1] (skŏf, skôf) *v.* **scoffed, scoff•ing, scoffs** —*tr.* To mock at or treat with derision. —*intr.* To show or express derision or scorn. ❖ *n.* An expression of derision or scorn. [ME *scoffen* < *scof*, mockery, prob. of Scand. orig.; akin to Dan. *skof*, jest, teasing.] —**scoff′er** *n.* —**scoff′ing•ly** *adv.*

scoff[2] (skŏf, skôf) *v.* **scoffed, scoff•ing, scoffs** *Slang* —*tr.* To eat (food) quickly and greedily. —*intr.* To eat greedily. [Alteration of obsolete *scaff*.] —**scoff′er** *n.*

scoff•law (skŏf′lô′, skôf′-) *n.* One who habitually violates the law or fails to answer court summonses.

scold (skōld) *v.* **scold•ed, scold•ing, scolds** —*tr.* To reprimand or criticize harshly and usu. angrily. —*intr.* To reprove or criticize openly. ❖ *n.* One who persistently nags or criticizes. [ME *scolden*, to be abusive < *scolde*, an abusive person, prob. of Scand. orig. See **sekʷ-**[3] in App.] —**scold′er** *n.*

scold•ing (skōl′dĭng) *n.* A harsh or sharp reprimand.

sco•lex (skō′lĕks′) *n., pl.* **-li•ces** (-lĭ-sēz′) The knoblike anterior end of a tapeworm, having suckers or hooklike parts for attachment to the host. [NLat. *scōlēx* < Gk. *skōlēx*, worm.]

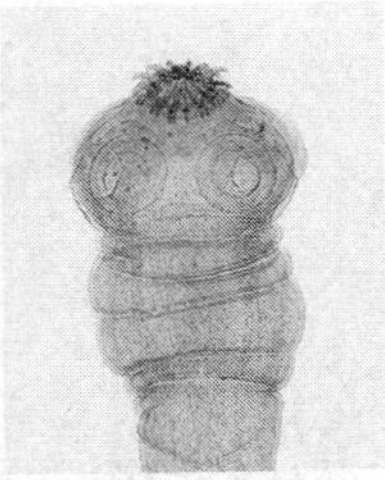

scolex

sco•li•o•sis (skō′lē-ō′sĭs, skŏl′ē-) *n.* Abnormal lateral curvature of the spine. [Gk. *skolios*, crooked + –OSIS.] —**sco′li•ot′ic** (-ŏt′ĭk) *adj.*

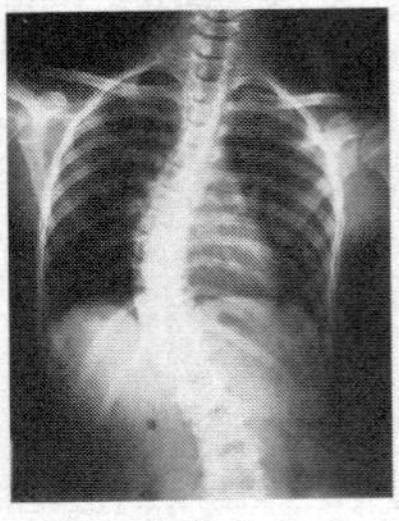

scoliosis
x-ray showing severe scoliosis of a human spine

scol•lop (skŏl′əp) *n. & v.* Variant of **scallop.**

scom•broid (skŏm′broid′) *adj.* Of or belonging to the suborder Scombroidei, which includes marine fishes such as the mackerel. [NLat. *Scombroīdeī*, suborder name < Lat. *scomber, scombr-*, mackerel < Gk. *skombros*.] —**scom′broid′** *n.*

sconce[1] (skŏns) *n.* A small defensive earthwork or fort. [Du. *schans* < Ger. *Schanze* < MHGer.]

sconce[2] (skŏns) *n.* **1.** A decorative wall bracket for holding candles or lights. **2.** A flattened candlestick that has a handle. **3.** *Slang* The human head or skull. [ME < OFr. *esconse*, lantern, hiding place < Med.Lat. *scōnsa* < Lat. *abscōnsa*, fem. p. part. of *abscondere*, to hide away : *ab-, abs-*, away; see AB–[1] + *condere*, to preserve; see **dhē-** in App.]

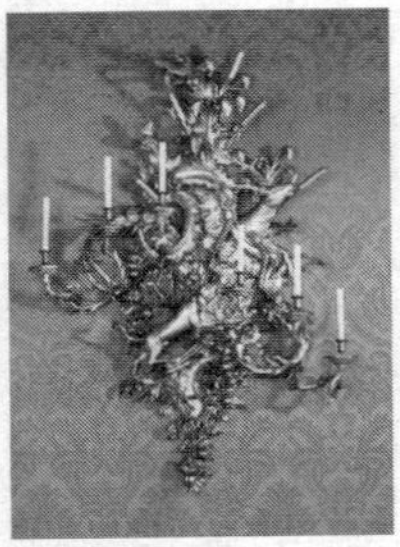

sconce[2]
18th-century gilt sconce

scone (skōn, skŏn) *n.* **1.** A small rich biscuitlike pastry or quick bread, sometimes baked on a griddle. **2.** *Utah* Yeast bread dough, deep-fried and served with honey and butter or with a savory filling. [Perh. < Du. *schoonbrood*, fine white bread < MDu. *schoonbroot* : *schoon*, bright + *broot*, bread.]

Scone (sko͞on) A village of central Scotland NE of Perth; the coronation site of Scottish kings until 1651.

scoop (sko͞op) *n.* **1a.** A shovellike utensil, usu. having a deep curved dish and a short handle. **b.** The amount that a scoop can hold. **2a.** A thick-handled cuplike utensil for dispensing balls of ice cream or other semisoft food. **b.** A portion gathered with a scoop. **3.** A ladle; a dipper. **4.** An implement for bailing water from a boat. **5.** A narrow spoon-shaped instrument for surgical extraction in cavities or cysts. **6.** The bucket or shovel, as of a dredge or backhoe. **7.** A hollow area; a cavity. **8.** An opening, as on the body of a motor vehicle, by which a fluid is directed inward. **9.** A scooping movement or action. **10.** *Informal* An exclusive news story acquired by luck or initiative before a competitor. **11.** *Informal* Current information or details. ❖ *tr.v.* **scooped, scoop•ing, scoops 1.** To take up or dip into with or as if with a scoop. **2.** To hollow out by digging. **3.** To gather or collect swiftly and unceremoniously; grab: *scooped up a handful.* **4.** *Informal* To top or outmaneuver (a competitor) in publishing an important news story. [ME *scope* < MDu. and MLGer. *schōpe*, bucket for bailing water.] —**scoop′er** *n.* —**scoop′ful′** *n.*

scoop neck *n.* A rounded, usu. low-cut neckline, as on a dress.

scoot (sko͞ot) *v.* **scoot•ed, scoot•ing, scoots** —*intr.* To go suddenly and speedily; hurry. —*tr.* *Upper Southern US* To squirt with water. —***phrasal verb:* scoot over** To move or slide to the side: *Scoot that chair over.* [Sc., to squirt, prob. of Scand. orig.] —**scoot** *n.*

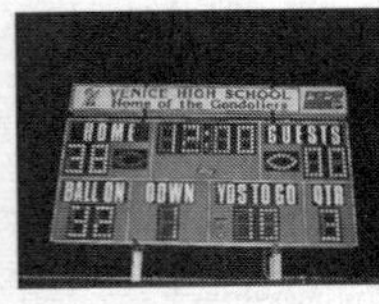

scoreboard

REGIONAL NOTE The verb *scoot,* meaning "to squirt with water," arose in the American Midlands. Two derived senses, both intransitive verbs, have become more widely known: "to slide suddenly across a surface" and "to move quickly": *The mouse scooted across the floor.* The phrasal verb *scoot over,* meaning, in its transitive sense, "to push (someone or something) to the side to make room," also arose in the Midlands but has spread throughout much of the country.

scoot•er (sko͞o′tər) *n.* **1.** A child's vehicle consisting of a long footboard between two small end wheels and an upright steering handle. **2.** A motor scooter. **3.** A flatbottom sailboat with runners that can skim over water or ice.

scop (shōp, shŏp) *n.* An Old English poet or bard. [OE.]

scope (skōp) *n.* **1.** The range of one's perceptions, thoughts, or actions. **2.** Breadth or opportunity to function. **3.** The area covered by a given activity or subject. **4.** The length or sweep of a mooring cable. **5.** *Informal* A viewing instrument such as a periscope or telescope. ❖ *tr.v.* **scoped, scop•ing, scopes** *Slang* To examine or investigate. Often used with *out.* [Ital. *scopo*, aim < Gk. *skopos*, target, aim. See **spek-** in App.]

-scope *suff.* An instrument for viewing or observing: *bronchoscope.* [NLat. *-scopium* < Gk. *-skopion* < *skopein*, to see. See **spek-** in App.]

Scopes (skōps), **John Thomas** 1900–70. Amer. teacher who was tried (Jul. 1925) for violating a state law by teaching the theory of evolution in a TN high school.

sco•pol•a•mine (skə-pŏl′ə-mēn′, -mĭn) *n.* A colorless alkaloid, $C_{17}H_{21}NO_4$, extracted from plants such as henbane, and used as a mydriatic, antinausea agent, and sedative. [NLat. *Scopolia*, plant genus (after Giovanni Antonio *Scopoli* (1723–88), Italian naturalist) + –AMINE.]

scop•u•la (skŏp′yə-lə) *n., pl.* **-lae** (-lē′) A dense brushlike tuft of hairs, as on the feet of certain insects. [Lat. *scōpula*, small brush of twigs, dim. of *scōpae*, branches, broom.] —**scop′u•late′** (-lāt′) *adj.*

-scopy *suff.* Viewing; seeing; observation: *microscopy.* [Gk. *-skopiā* < *skopein*, to see. See **spek-** in App.]

scor•bu•tic (skôr-byo͞o′tĭk) also **scor•bu•ti•cal** (-tĭ-kəl) *adj.* Of, relating to, resembling, or affected by scurvy. [NLat. *scorbūticus* < *scorbūtus*, scurvy, perh. of Gmc. orig.]

scorch (skôrch) *v.* **scorched, scorch•ing, scorch•es** —*tr.* **1.** To burn superficially so as to discolor or damage the texture of. **2.** To wither or parch with intense heat. **3.** To destroy (land and buildings) by or as if by fire so as to leave nothing salvageable to an enemy army. **4.** To subject to severe censure; excoriate. —*intr.* **1.** To become scorched or singed. **2.** To go or move at a very fast rate. ❖ *n.* **1.** A slight or surface burn. **2.** A discoloration caused by heat. **3.** Brown spotting on plant leaves caused by fungi, heat, or lack of water. [ME *scorchen*, poss. of Scand. orig.]

scorch•er (skôr′chər) *n.* **1.** One that scorches. **2.** *Informal* An extremely hot day.

score (skôr, skōr) *n.* **1.** A notch or an incision, esp. one that is made to keep a tally. **2.** *Sports & Games* **a.** A usu. numerical record of a competitive event. **b.** The total number of points made by each side in a contest, either final or at a given stage. **c.** The number of points attributed to a competitor or team. **3.** A result, usu. expressed numerically, of a test or examination. **4a.** An amount due; a debt. **b.** A grievance that requires satisfaction. **5.** A ground; a reason. **6.** A group of 20 items. **7. scores** Large numbers. **8.** *Music* **a.** The notation of a musical work. **b.** The written form of a composition for orchestral or vocal parts. **c.** The music for a film or a play. **9.** *Slang* **a.** The act of securing an advantage, esp. a surprising or significant gain. **b.** The act or an instance of buying illicit drugs. **c.** A successful robbery. **d.** A sexual conquest. ❖ *v.* **scored, scor•ing, scores** —*tr.* **1.** To mark with lines or notches, esp. for the purpose of keeping a record. **2.** To cancel or eliminate by or as if by superimposing lines. **3.** To mark the surface of (meat, for example) with usu. parallel cuts. **4.** *Sports & Games* **a.** To gain (a point) in a game or contest. **b.** To count or be worth as points. **5.** To achieve; win. **6.** To evaluate and assign a grade to. **7.** *Music* **a.** To orchestrate. **b.** To arrange for a specific instrument. **8.** To criticize cuttingly; berate. **9.** *Slang* **a.** To succeed in acquiring. **b.** To succeed in obtaining (an illicit drug). —*intr.* **1.** *Sports & Games* **a.** To make a point in a game or contest. **b.** To keep the score of a game or contest. **2.** *Slang* **a.** To achieve a purpose or advantage, esp. to make a surprising gain or coup. **b.** To seduce someone sexually. **c.** To succeed in obtaining an illicit drug. [ME < OE *scoru*, twenty < ON *skor.* See **sker-**[1] in App.] —**scor′er** *n.*

score•board (skôr′bôrd′, skōr′bōrd′) *n.* A large board that displays the score of a game or contest.

score•card (skôr′kärd′, skōr′-) *n.* **1.** A printed program or card enabling a spectator to identify players and record the progress of a game or competition. **2.** A small card used to record one's own performance in sports such as golf.

score•keep•er (skôr′kē′pər, skōr′-) *n.* An official who records the score throughout a game or competition. —**score′keep′ing** *adj. & n.*

sco•ri•a (skôr′ē-ə, skōr′-) *n., pl.* **sco•ri•ae** (skôr′ē-ē′, skōr′-) **1.** *Geology* Porous cinderlike fragments of dark lava. **2.** *Metallurgy* The refuse of a smelted metal or ore; slag. [ME, dross < Lat. *scōria* < Gk. *skōriā* < *skōr*, excrement, dung. See **sker-**[2] in App.] —**sco′ri•a′ceous** (-ā′shəs) *adj.*

sco•ri•fy (skôr′ə-fī′, skōr′-) *tr.v.* **-fied, -fy•ing, -fies** To separate (an ore) into scoria and a precious metal. —**sco′ri•fi•ca′tion** (-fĭ-kā′shən) *n.* —**sco′ri•fi′er** *n.*

scorn (skôrn) *n.* **1a.** Contempt or disdain felt toward a person or object considered despicable or unworthy. **b.** The expression of such an attitude in behavior or speech; derision. **2.** One spoken of or treated with contempt. ❖ *v.* **scorned, scorn·ing, scorns** —*tr.* **1.** To consider or treat as contemptible or unworthy. **2.** To reject or refuse with derision. See Syns at **despise.** —*intr.* To express contempt; scoff. [ME < OFr. *escarn*, of Gmc. orig.] —**scorn′er** *n.* —**scorn′ful** *adj.* —**scorn′ful·ly** *adv.*

Scor·pi·o (skôr′pē-ō′) *n.* **1.** The eighth sign of the zodiac in astrology. **2.** *pl.* **-os** One who is born under this sign. [ME < Lat. *Scorpiō* < *scorpiō*, scorpion. See SCORPION.]

scor·pi·oid (skôr′pē-oid′) *adj.* **1.** Of, relating to, or resembling a scorpion. **2.** *Botany* Like the tail of a scorpion; circinate. [Gk. *skorpioeidēs*, scorpionlike : *skorpios*, scorpion + *-oeidēs*, -oid.]

scor·pi·on (skôr′pē-ən) *n.* **1.** Any of various arachnids of the order Scorpionida of warm dry regions, having an erectile tail tipped with a venomous sting. **2.** *Scorpion* See **Scorpius.** [ME < OFr. < Lat. *scorpiō, scorpiōn-,* alteration of *scorpius* < Gk. *skorpios.*]

scorpion fish *n.* Any of numerous small, often brilliantly colored marine fishes of the family Scorpaenidae, most species of which have poisonous spines in the dorsal fin.

scorpion fly *n.* **1.** A mecopterous insect of the family Panorpidae, having in the male of most species a curved genital structure that resembles the sting of a scorpion. **2.** Any mecopterous insect; a mecopteran.

scorpion grass *n.* See **forget-me-not** 1.

Scor·pi·us (skôr′pē-əs) *also* **Scor·pi·o** (-pē-ō′) *n.* A constellation in the Southern Hemisphere near Libra and Sagittarius. [Lat. *scorpius,* scorpion, Scorpius. See SCORPION.]

Scor·se·se (skôr-sĕs′ē, skôr-), Martin b. 1942. Amer. director whose films include *Taxi Driver* (1976).

scot (skŏt) *n.* Money assessed or paid. [ME, tax, partly < ON *skot* and partly < OFr. *escot* (of Gmc. orig.).]

Scot (skŏt) *n.* **1.** A native or inhabitant of Scotland. **2.** A member of the ancient Gaelic tribe that migrated to the northern part of Britain from Ireland in about the sixth century A.D. See Usage Note at **Scottish.** [< ME *Scottes,* Sc. < OE *Scottas,* Sc., Irish < LLat. *Scottī,* Irish.]

Scot. *abbr.* **1.** Scotch **2.** Scotland **3.** Scottish

scot and lot *n.* A municipal tax formerly levied in Great Britain on the members of a community in proportion to their ability to pay. —*idiom:* **pay scot and lot** To pay in full.

scotch[1] (skŏch) *tr.v.* **scotched, scotch·ing, scotch·es 1.** To put an abrupt end to. **2.** To injure so as to render harmless. **3.** To cut or score. ❖ *n.* **1.** A surface cut or abrasion. **2.** A line drawn on the ground, as in hopscotch. [ME *scocchen,* prob. < AN *escocher,* to notch : *es-,* intensive pref. (< Lat. *ex-;* see EX-) + OFr. *coche,* notch (prob. < Lat. *coccum,* scarlet oak berry < Gk. *kokkos*).]

scotch[2] (skŏch) *tr.v.* **scotched, scotch·ing, scotch·es** To block (a wheel, for example) with a prop to prevent rolling or slipping. ❖ *n.* A block or wedge used as a prop behind or under an object likely to roll. [?]

Scotch *n.* **1.** (*used with a pl. verb*) The people of Scotland. **2.** Scots English. **3.** Scotch whisky. ❖ *adj.* **1.** Scottish. See Usage Note at **Scottish.** **2.** *Offensive* Tight with money; frugal. [Contraction of SCOTTISH.]

Scotch egg *n.* A hard-boiled egg wrapped in sausage meat, coated with bread crumbs, and deep-fried.

Scotch-I·rish (skŏch′ī′rĭsh) *n.* **1.** The people of Scotland who settled in northern Ireland or their descendants, esp. those who emigrated to North America. See Usage Note at **Scottish. 2.** The variety of Scots spoken by the Scotch-Irish. —**Scotch′-I′rish** *adj.*

Scotch·man (skŏch′mən) *n.* A Scotsman. See Usage Note at **Scottish.**

Scotch pine *n.* **1.** A Eurasian pine tree (*Pinus sylvestris*) having twisted needles arranged in fascicles of two and yellow wood that is valued as timber. **2.** The wood of this tree.

Scotch tape A trademark used for adhesive tape.

Scotch terrier *n.* See **Scottish terrier.**

Scotch verdict *n.* An inconclusive judgment or pronouncement.

Scotch whisky *n.* A whiskey distilled in Scotland from malted barley.

Scotch·wom·an (skŏch′wŏom′ən) *n.* A Scotswoman. See Usage Note at **Scottish.**

Scotch woodcock *n.* A savory dish consisting of scrambled eggs on toast with anchovies or anchovy paste.

sco·ter (skō′tər) *n.* Any of several dark-colored diving ducks of the genera *Oidemia* and *Melanitta* of northern coasts. [?]

scot-free (skŏt′frē′) *adv.* **1.** Without having to pay. **2.** Without incurring any penalty or punishment. —**scot′-free′** *adj.*

sco·tia (skō′shə) *n.* A hollow concave molding at or near the base of a column. [Lat. < Gk. *skotia* < fem. of *skotios,* shadowy (< its shadow) < *skotos,* darkness.]

Sco·tia (skō′shə) Scotland.

Scot·land (skŏt′lənd) A constituent country of the United Kingdom comprising the N part of the island of Great Britain and the Hebrides, Shetland Is., and Orkney Is. Scotland became a part of the kingdom of Great Britain by the Act of Union in 1707. Cap. Edinburgh. Pop. 5,149,500.

sco·to·ma (skə-tō′mə) *n., pl.* **-mas** or **-ma·ta** (-mə-tə) An area

of diminished vision within the visual field. [NLat. *scotōma* < LLat., dim sight < Gk. *skotōma,* dizziness < *skotoun,* to darken < *skotos,* darkness.] —**sco·to′ma·tous** *adj.*

sco·to·phil (skō′tə-fĭl′) *also* **sco·to·phil·ic** (skō′tə-fĭl′ĭk) *adj.* *Biology* Growing or functioning best in darkness. [Gk. *skotos,* darkness + -PHIL(E).]

sco·to·pi·a (skə-tō′pē-ə) *n.* The ability to see in darkness or dim light; dark-adapted vision. [Gk. *skotos,* darkness + -OPIA.] —**sco·to′pic** (-tō′pĭk, -tŏp′ĭk) *adj.*

Scots (skŏts) *adj.* Scottish. See Usage Note at **Scottish.** ❖ *n.* The English dialect used in the Scottish Lowlands. [ME *scottis,* var. of *scottisc,* Scottish < *Scotte,* sing. of *Scottes,* Sc. See SCOT.]

Scots-I·rish (skŏts′ī′rĭsh) *n.* See **Scotch-Irish.** See Usage Note at **Scottish.** ❖ *adj.* Of or relating to the Scotch-Irish or their variety of Scots.

Scots·man (skŏts′mən) *n.* A man who is a native or inhabitant of Scotland. See Usage Note at **Scottish.**

Scots·wom·an (skŏts′wŏom′ən) *n.* A woman who is a native or inhabitant of Scotland. See Usage Note at **Scottish.**

Scott (skŏt), Dred 1795?–1858. Amer. slave who sued for his liberty after spending four years with his master in a territory where slavery had been banned by the Missouri Compromise. The resulting decision by the US Supreme Court (1857) declared the Missouri Compromise unconstitutional.

Scott, Robert Falcon 1868–1912. British explorer who reached the South Pole in Jan. 1912, one month after Roald Amundsen.

Scott, Sir Walter 1771–1832. British writer of ballads and historical novels, whose works include *Ivanhoe* (1819).

Scott, Winfield 1786–1866. Amer. general who was a hero of the War of 1812 and the Mexican War (1846–48).

Scot·ti·cism (skŏt′ĭ-sĭz′əm) *n.* An idiom or other expression characteristic of Scots English.

Scot·tie *also* **Scot·ty** (skŏt′ē) *n., pl.* **-ties** A Scottish terrier.

Scot·tish (skŏt′ĭsh) *adj.* Of or relating to Scotland or its people, language, or culture. ❖ *n.* **1.** Scots English. **2.** The people of Scotland. [ME *scottisc.* See SCOTS.]

Dred Scott
detail of an 1881 painting
by Louis Schultze
(1820–1920?), after an 1858
photograph

USAGE NOTE *Scottish* is the full, original form of the adjective. *Scots* is an old Scottish variant. *Scotch* is an English contraction of *Scottish* that came into use in Scotland as well for a time but subsequently fell into disfavor there. In the interest of civility, forms involving *Scotch* are best avoided in reference to people; designations formed with *Scots* are most common (*Scot, Scotsman,* or *Scotswoman*), but those involving the full form *Scottish* are sometimes found in more formal contexts. *Scotch-Irish* is the most commonly used term for the descendants of Scots who migrated to North America, but lately *Scots-Irish* has begun to gain currency among those who know that *Scotch* is considered offensive in Scotland. There is, however, no sure rule for referring to things, since the history of variation in the use of these words has left many fixed expressions, such as *Scotch broth, Scotch whisky, Scottish rite,* and *Scots Guards.*

Scottish deerhound *n.* See **deerhound.**

Scottish Gaelic *n.* The Goidelic language of Scotland.

Scottish rite *n.* A ceremonial rite in a Masonic system.

Scottish terrier *n.* A terrier of a breed originating in Scotland, having short legs, small erect ears, and a hard wiry coat.

Scotts·dale (skŏts′dāl′) A city of S-central AZ, a suburb of Phoenix. Pop. 202,705.

scoun·drel (skoun′drəl) *n.* A villain; a rogue. [?] —**scoun′drel·ly** *adj.*

scour[1] (skour) *v.* **scoured, scour·ing, scours** —*tr.* **1a.** To clean, polish, or wash by scrubbing vigorously. **b.** To remove by scrubbing. **2.** To remove dirt or grease from (cloth or fibers) with a detergent. **3.** To clean (wheat) before milling. **4.** To clear (an area) by freeing of weeds or other vegetation. **5.** To clear (a channel or pipe) by flushing. —*intr.* **1.** To scrub something in order to clean or polish it. **2.** To have diarrhea. Used of livestock. ❖ *n.* **1.** A scouring action or effect. **2.** A place that has been scoured, as by flushing with water. **3.** A cleansing agent for wool. **4. scours** (*used with a sing. or pl. verb*) Diarrhea in livestock. [ME *scouren* < MDu. *scūren* < OFr. *escurer* < LLat. *excūrāre,* to clean out : Lat. *ex-,* ex- + LLat. *cūrāre,* to clean (< Lat., to take care of < *cūra,* care; see CURE).] —**scour′er** *n.*

scour[2] (skour) *v.* **scoured, scour·ing, scours** —*tr.* **1.** To search through or over thoroughly. **2.** To range over (an area) quickly and energetically. —*intr.* **1.** To range over or about an area, esp. in a search. **2.** To move swiftly; scurry. [ME *scouren,* to move swiftly, prob. of Scand. orig.; akin to ON *skūr,* shower.] —**scour′er** *n.*

scourge (skûrj) *n.* **1.** A source of widespread dreadful affliction and devastation such as that of war. **2.** A means of inflicting severe suffering, vengeance, or punishment. **3.** A whip used to inflict punishment. ❖ *tr.v.* **scourged, scourg·ing, scourg·es 1.** To afflict with severe suffering and devastation; ravage. **2.** To chastise severely; excoriate. **3.** To flog. [ME < AN *escorge* < OFr. *escorgier,* to whip < VLat. **excorrigiāre* : Lat. *ex-,* intensive pref.; see EX- + Lat. *corrigia,* thong (prob. of Celt. orig.).] —**scourg′er** *n.*

scour·ing rush (skour′ĭng) *n.* Any of several species of horsetail, esp. *Equisetum hyemale,* having rough-ridged stems that were

ă	pat	oi	boy
ā	pay	ou	out
âr	care	ŏŏ	took
ä	father	ōō	boot
ĕ	pet	ŭ	cut
ē	be	ûr	urge
ĭ	pit	th	thin
ī	pie	th	this
îr	pier	hw	which
ŏ	pot	zh	vision
ō	toe	ə	about,
ô	paw		item

Stress marks:
′ (primary);
′ (secondary), as in
lexicon (lĕk′sĭ-kŏn′)

formerly used for scouring utensils.

scour·ings (skour′ĭngz) *pl.n.* **1.** The refuse that remains after scouring grain. **2.** Dregs; scum.

scouse (skous) *n.* **1.** A lobscouse. **2a.** often **Scous·er** (skou′sər) A native or resident of Liverpool, England. **b.** often **Scouse** The dialect of English spoken in Liverpool.

scout¹ (skout) *v.* **scout·ed, scout·ing, scouts** —*tr.* **1.** To spy on or explore carefully in order to obtain information; reconnoiter. **2.** To observe and evaluate (a talented person), as for possible hiring. —*intr.* **1.** To search as a scout: *scout around for some gossip.* **2.** To search for talented people. ❖ *n.* **1a.** One that is dispatched from a main body to gather information, esp. in preparation for military action. **b.** The act of reconnoitering. **2.** A watcher or sentinel. **3.** One who is employed to discover and recruit talented persons, esp. in the fields of sports and entertainment. **4.** *Sports* One who is employed to observe and report on the strategies and players of rival teams. **5.** often **Scout a.** A member of the Boy Scouts. **b.** A member of the Girl Scouts. **6.** *Informal* An individual; a person: *a good scout.* **7.** *Chiefly British* A student's male servant at Oxford University. [< ME *scoute,* act of watching or spying < OFr. *escoute < escouter,* to listen, alteration of *ascouter < VLat. *ascultāre,* alteration of Lat. *auscultāre.* See **ous-** in App.] —**scout′er** *n.*

scout² (skout) *v.* **scout·ed, scout·ing, scouts** —*tr.* To reject with disdain or derision. See Syns at **despise.** —*intr.* To treat another with derision; scoff. [Of Scand. orig.]

scout·ing (skou′tĭng) *n.* **1.** The act of one that scouts. **2.** often **Scouting** The activities of the Boy Scouts or Girl Scouts.

scout·mas·ter (skout′măs′tər) *n.* The adult leader in charge of a troop of Boy Scouts.

scow (skou) *n.* A large flatbottom boat with square ends, used chiefly for transporting freight. [Du. *schouw < MDu. scouwe.*]

scowl (skoul) *v.* **scowled, scowl·ing, scowls** —*intr.* To wrinkle or contract the brow as an expression of anger or disapproval. —*tr.* To express with a frowning facial expression. ❖ *n.* A look of anger or frowning disapproval. [ME *scoulen,* prob. of Scand. orig.] —**scowl′er** *n.*

scr. *abbr.* scruple (unit of weight)

scrab·ble (skrăb′əl) *v.* **-bled, -bling, -bles** —*intr.* **1.** To scrape or grope about frenetically with the hands. **2.** To struggle by or as if by groping or scraping. **3.** To climb with scrambling, disorderly haste. **4.** To make hasty, disordered markings; scribble. —*tr.* **1.** To make or obtain by scraping together hastily. **2.** To scribble on or over. ❖ *n.* **1.** The act or an instance of scrabbling. **2.** A scribble; a doodle. [Du. *schrabbelen < MDu.,* freq. of *schrabben,* to scrape. See **sker-¹** in App.] —**scrab′bler** *n.* —**scrab′bly** *adj.*

scrab·bled (skrăb′əld) *adj.* Covered with sparse vegetation.

scrag (skrăg) *n.* **1.** A bony or scrawny person or animal. **2.** A piece of lean or bony meat, esp. a neck of mutton. **3.** *Slang* The human neck. ❖ *tr.v.* **scragged, scrag·ging, scrags** *Slang* To wring the neck of; strangle. [Perh. < dialectal *crag,* neck < ME *cragge < MDu. crāghe,* throat.]

scrag·gly (skrăg′lē) *adj.* **-gli·er, -gli·est** Ragged; unkempt.

scrag·gy (skrăg′ē) *adj.* **-gi·er, -gi·est** **1.** Jagged; rough: *scraggy cliffs.* **2.** Bony and lean: *a scraggy cat.* —**scrag′gi·ly** *adv.* —**scrag′gi·ness** *n.*

scram (skrăm) *Slang intr.v.* **scrammed, scram·ming, scrams** **1.** To leave a scene at once; go abruptly. **2.** To shut down automatically. Used of a nuclear reactor. ❖ *n.* A rapid shutting down of a nuclear reactor. [Perh. short for SCRAMBLE.]

scram·ble (skrăm′bəl) *v.* **-bled, -bling, -bles** —*intr.* **1.** To move or climb hurriedly, esp. on the hands and knees. **2.** To struggle or contend frantically in order to get something. **3.** To take off with all possible haste, as to intercept enemy aircraft. **4.** *Football* To run with the ball when there is no open receiver. Used of a quarterback. —*tr.* **1.** To mix or throw together haphazardly. **2.** To gather together in a hurried or disorderly fashion. **3.** To fry (beaten eggs) until firm but with a soft consistency. **4.** *Electronics* To distort or garble (a signal) so as to render it unintelligible without a special receiver. **5.** To cause (aircraft) to scramble. ❖ *n.* **1.** The act or an instance of scrambling. **2.** An arduous hike or climb over rough terrain. **3.** An unceremonious scuffle or struggle. **4.** See **motocross.** **5.** A swift takeoff of military aircraft in response to an alert or attack. [Perh. blend of obsolete *scamble,* to struggle for, and dialectal *cramble,* to crawl.]

scram·bled eggs (skrăm′bəld) *pl.n.* Eggs with the yolks and whites beaten together and fried.

scram·bler (skrăm′blər) *n.* **1.** An electronic device that scrambles telecommunication signals. **2.** A motorcycle designed for riding across rough terrain. **3.** *Football* A quarterback who tends to scramble.

scram·jet (skrăm′jĕt′) *n.* A ramjet airplane engine designed for hypersonic flight that burns fuel in the supersonic airstream produced by the plane. [S(UPERSONIC) + C(OMBUSTION) + RAMJET.]

Scran·ton (skrăn′tən) A city of NE PA NE of Wilkes-Barre; settled in the late 1700s. Pop. 76,415.

scrap¹ (skrăp) *n.* **1.** A small piece or bit; a fragment. **2.** **scraps** Leftover bits of food. **3.** Discarded waste material, esp. metal suitable for reprocessing. **4.** **scraps** Crisp pieces of rendered animal fat; cracklings. ❖ *tr.v.* **scrapped, scrap·ping, scraps** **1.** To break down into parts for disposal or salvage. **2.** To discard as

scree

worthless or sell to be reused as parts; junk. [ME < ON *skrap,* trifles, pieces. See **sker-¹** in App.]

scrap² (skrăp) *intr.v.* **scrapped, scrap·ping, scraps** To fight, often with the fists. ❖ *n.* A fight or a scuffle. [Perh. var. of SCRAPE.] —**scrap′per** *n.*

scrap·book (skrăp′bŏŏk′) *n.* A book with blank pages used for the mounting of pictures, clippings, or other mementos.

scrape (skrāp) *v.* **scraped, scrap·ing, scrapes** —*tr.* **1.** To remove (an outer layer, for example) from a surface by forceful strokes of an edged or rough instrument: *scraped the rust off.* **2.** To abrade or smooth by rubbing with a sharp or rough instrument. **3.** To rub (a surface) with considerable pressure, as with an edged instrument or a hard object. **4.** To draw (a hard or abrasive object) forcefully over a surface. **5.** To injure the surface of by rubbing against something rough or sharp. **6.** To amass or produce with difficulty: *scrape together some cash.* —*intr.* **1.** To come into sliding, abrasive contact. **2.** To rub or move with a harsh grating noise. **3.** To give forth a harsh grating noise. **4.** To economize by paying attention to very small amounts; scrimp. **5.** To succeed or manage with difficulty: *scraped by.* ❖ *n.* **1a.** The act of scraping. **b.** The sound of scraping. **2.** An abrasion on the skin. **3a.** An embarrassing predicament. **b.** A fight; a scuffle. [ME *scrapen < ON skrapa.* See **sker-¹** in App.]

scrap·er (skrā′pər) *n.* One that scrapes, esp. a tool for scraping off paint or other matter.

scrap·er·board (skrā′pər-bôrd′, -bōrd′) *n.* See **scratchboard.**

scrap·heap also **scrap heap** (skrăp′hēp′) *n.* **1.** A pile or heap of waste material. **2.** A place for discarding useless or worthless material.

scra·pie (skrā′pē, skrăp′ē) *n.* A usu. fatal disease of sheep and goats, marked by chronic itching and degeneration of the central nervous system. [< SCRAPE.]

scrap·ple (skrăp′əl) *n.* A boiled mush of ground pork and cornmeal set in a mold and then sliced and fried. [Dim. of SCRAP¹.]

scrap·py¹ (skrăp′ē) *adj.* **-pi·er, -pi·est** Composed of scraps; fragmentary. —**scrap′pi·ly** *adv.* —**scrap′pi·ness** *n.*

scrap·py² (skrăp′ē) *adj.* **-pi·er, -pi·est** **1.** Quarrelsome; contentious. **2.** Full of fighting spirit. See Syns at **argumentative.** —**scrap′pi·ly** *adv.* —**scrap′pi·ness** *n.*

scratch (skrăch) *v.* **scratched, scratch·ing, scratch·es** —*tr.* **1.** To make a thin shallow cut or mark on (a surface) with a sharp instrument. **2.** To use the nails or claws to dig or scrape at. **3.** To rub or scrape (the skin) to relieve itching. **4.** To scrape or strike on an abrasive surface. **5.** To write or draw by scraping a surface. **6.** To write or draw hurriedly: *scratched off a note.* **7a.** To strike out or cancel (a word, for example) by or as if by drawing lines through. **b.** *Slang* To cancel (a project, for example). **8.** To withdraw (an entry) from a contest. —*intr.* **1.** To use the nails or claws to dig, scrape, or wound. **2.** To rub or scrape the skin to relieve itching. **3.** To make a harsh scraping sound. **4.** To gather funds or produce a living with difficulty. **5a.** To withdraw from a contest. **b.** *Games* To make a shot in billiards that results in a penalty, as when the cue ball falls into a pocket. ❖ *n.* **1a.** A mark resembling a line produced by scratching. **b.** A slight wound. **2.** A hasty scribble. **3.** A sound made by scratching. **4a.** *Sports* The starting line for a race. **b.** A contestant who has been withdrawn from a competition. **5.** *Games* **a.** The act of scratching in billiards. **b.** A fluke or chance shot in billiards. **6.** Poultry feed. **7.** *Slang* Money. ❖ *adj.* **1.** Done haphazardly or by chance. **2.** Assembled hastily or at random. **3.** *Sports* Having no golf handicap. —*idioms:* **from scratch** From the very beginning. **scratch the surface** To investigate or treat something superficially. **up to scratch** *Informal* **1.** Meeting the requirements. **2.** In fit condition. [ME *scracchen,* prob. blend of *scratten,* to scratch, and *cracchen,* to scratch (poss. < MDu. *cratsen*).] —**scratch′er** *n.*

scratch·board (skrăch′bôrd′, -bōrd′) *n.* A drawing board coated with white clay and a surface layer of black ink that is scratched or scraped away to produce an effect similar to engraving.

scratch pad *n.* **1.** A pad of paper for preliminary or hasty writing, notes, or sketches. **2.** also **scratch·pad** (skrăch′păd′) *Computer Science* An internal register used for temporary storage of preliminary data.

scratch sheet *n.* A publication listing the horses withdrawn from a day's races and giving information and betting odds on the horses scheduled to race.

scratch test *n.* A test for allergy performed by scratching the skin and applying an allergen to the wound.

scratch ticket *n.* A lottery ticket on which one scratches designated areas to reveal the card's prize value.

scratch·y (skrăch′ē) *adj.* **-i·er, -i·est** **1.** Marked by or consisting of scratches. **2.** Making a harsh scratching noise. **3.** Harsh and irritating: *a scratchy fabric.* **4.** Irregular; uneven. —**scratch′i·ly** *adv.* —**scratch′i·ness** *n.*

scrawl (skrôl) *v.* **scrawled, scrawl·ing, scrawls** —*tr.* To write hastily or illegibly. —*intr.* To write in a sprawling, irregular manner. ❖ *n.* **1.** Irregular, often illegible handwriting. **2.** Something written hastily or illegibly. [Perh. < obsolete *scrawl,* to gesticulate, sprawl < ME *scrawlen,* prob. blend of *sprawlen,* to sprawl; see SPRAWL, and *craulen,* to crawl; see CRAWL¹.] —**scrawl′er** *n.* —**scrawl′y** *adj.*

scraw•ny (skrô′nē) *adj.* **-ni•er, -ni•est** Gaunt and bony. See Syns at **lean**[2]. [Alteration of dialectal *scranny*, poss. of Scand. orig.; akin to Norw. *skran*, lean.] **—scraw′ni•ness** *n.*

screak (skrēk) *intr.v.* **screaked, screak•ing, screaks 1.** To screech; shriek. **2.** To creak. ❖ *n.* **1.** A screech; a shriek. **2.** A creak. [ME *skricken* < ON *skrækja.*] **—screak′y** *adj.*

scream (skrēm) *v.* **screamed, scream•ing, screams** *—intr.* **1.** To utter a long loud piercing cry, as from pain or fear. **2.** To make a loud piercing sound. **3.** To speak or write in a heated hysterical manner. **4.** To have or produce a startling effect. *—tr.* To utter or say in or as if in a screaming voice. ❖ *n.* **1.** A long loud piercing cry or sound. **2.** *Informal* One that is hilariously or ridiculously funny. [ME *screamen*, poss. of Scand. orig.; akin to ON *scræma.*] **—scream′ing•ly** *adv.*

scream•er (skrē′mər) *n.* **1.** One that screams, esp. one that sings harshly or stridently. **2.** *Slang* A sensational headline. **3.** *Slang* One that evokes screams or laughter. **4.** *Slang* An exclamation point. **5.** Any of several large aquatic birds of the family Anhimidae of South America, having a harsh resonant call.

scream•ing mee•mies (skrē′mĭng mē′mēz) *pl.n.* (*Used with a sing. or pl. verb*) *Slang* An attack of nerves; the jitters. [Expressive of nervousness.]

scree (skrē) *n.* **1.** Loose rock debris covering a slope. **2.** A slope of loose rock debris at the base of a steep incline or cliff. [Prob. ult. < ON *skridha*, landslide < *skrīdha*, to slide.]

screech (skrēch) *n.* **1.** A high-pitched strident cry. **2.** A sound suggestive of this cry. ❖ *v.* **screeched, screech•ing, screech•es** *—tr.* To utter in or as if in a screech. *—intr.* **1.** To cry out in a high-pitched strident voice. **2.** To make a sound suggestive of a screech. [Alteration of obsolete *scrich* < ME *scrichen*, to screech, perh. of Scand. orig.] **—screech′er** *n.* **—screech′i•ness** *n.* **—screech′y** *adj.*

screech owl *n.* Any of various owls of the genus *Otus* of North America, esp. *O. asio,* having a quavering whistlelike call.

screed (skrēd) *n.* **1.** A long monotonous speech or piece of writing. **2a.** A strip of wood, plaster, or metal placed on a wall or pavement as a guide for the even application of plaster or concrete. **b.** A layer or strip of material used to level off a horizontal surface such as a floor. **c.** A smooth final surface of a substance, such as concrete, applied to a floor. [ME *screde*, fragment, strip of cloth < OE *scrēade*, shred.]

screen (skrēn) *n.* **1.** A movable device, esp. a framed construction such as a room divider or a decorative panel, designed to divide, conceal, or protect. **2.** One that serves to protect, conceal, or divide. **3.** A coarse sieve used for sifting out fine particles, as of sand, gravel, or coal. **4.** A system for preliminary appraisal and selection of personnel as to their suitability for particular jobs. **5.** A window or door insertion of framed wire or plastic mesh used to keep out insects and permit airflow. **6a.** The white or silver surface on which a picture is projected for viewing. **b.** The movie industry. **7a.** *Electronics* The phosphorescent surface on which an image is displayed, as on a television or computer monitor. **b.** *Computer Science* The information or image displayed at a given time on such a computer monitor. **8.** *Printing* A glass plate marked off with crossing lines, placed before the lens of a camera when photographing for halftone reproduction. **9.** A body of troops or ships sent to protect a larger body. **10.** *Sports* A block, set with the body, that impedes the vision or movement of an opponent. ❖ *tr.v.* **screened, screen•ing, screens 1.** To provide with a screen: *screen a porch.* **2a.** To conceal from view with or as if with a screen. See Syns at **block, hide**[1]. **b.** To protect, guard, or shield. **3.** To separate or sift out (fine particles of sand, for example) by means of a sieve or screen. **4.** To show or project (a movie, for example) on a screen. **5a.** To examine (a job applicant, for example) in order to determine suitability. **b.** To test or evaluate (a student) to determine placement in an educational system or to identify specific learning needs. **c.** To test or examine for the presence of disease or infection: *screen blood; screen a patient.* **d.** To subject to genetic screening. **6.** *Sports* To block the vision or movement of (an opponent) with the body. [ME *screne* < ONFr. *escren* < MDu. *scherm*, shield, screen. See **sker-**[1] in App.] **—screen′a•ble** *adj.* **—screen′er** *n.*

screen•ing (skrē′nĭng) *n.* **1. screenings** (*used with a sing. or pl. verb*) Refuse, such as waste coal, separated by a screen. **2.** The mesh material used to make door or window screens. **3.** A presentation of a movie. **4.** A systematic examination or assessment, as to detect an unwanted substance.

screen memory *n.* A memory that is unconsciously used to repress recollection of an associated but distressing event.

screen pass *n.* *Football* A short forward pass to a receiver in the flat who is protected by a formation of blockers.

screen•play (skrēn′plā′) *n.* The script for a movie, including descriptions of scenes and some camera directions.

screen saver *n.* A software program that constantly changes the image on a display screen to protect the screen from having an image etched onto its surface.

screen test *n.* A brief movie sequence filmed to test the ability of an aspiring performer. **—screen′-test′** (skrēn′tĕst′) *v.*

screen•writ•er (skrēn′rī′tər) *n.* One who writes screenplays. **—screen′writ′ing** *n.*

screw (skro͞o) *n.* **1a.** A cylindrical rod incised with one or more helical or advancing spiral threads, as a lead screw. **b.** The tapped collar or socket that receives this rod. **2.** A metal pin with incised threads and a slotted head that can be driven as a fastener by turning with a screwdriver. **3.** A device having a helical form, such as a corkscrew. **4.** A propeller. **5.** A twist or turn of or as if of a screw. **6.** *Slang* **a.** A prison guard. **b.** The turnkey of a jail. **7.** *Vulgar Slang* The act or an instance of having sexual intercourse. **8.** *Chiefly British Slang* **a.** Salary; wages. **b.** A small paper packet, as of tobacco. **c.** An old broken-down horse. **d.** A stingy or crafty bargainer. ❖ *v.* **screwed, screw•ing, screws** *—tr.* **1.** To drive or tighten (a screw). **2a.** To fasten, tighten, or attach by or as if by means of a screw. **b.** To attach (a tapped or threaded fitting or cap) by twisting into place. **c.** To rotate (a part) on a threaded axis. **3.** To contort (one's face). **4.** *Slang* To take advantage of; cheat. **5.** *Vulgar Slang* To have sexual intercourse with. *—intr.* **1.** To turn or twist. **2a.** To become attached by means of the threads of a screw. **b.** To be capable of such attachment. **3.** *Vulgar Slang* To have sexual intercourse. ***—phrasal verbs:*** **screw around 1.** *Slang* To act aimlessly or in a confused way and accomplish nothing. **2.** *Vulgar Slang* To be sexually promiscuous. **screw up 1.** To muster or summon up. **2.** *Slang* To make a mess of (an undertaking). **3.** *Slang* To injure; damage. **4.** *Slang* To make neurotic or anxious. ***—idiom:*** **have a screw loose** *Slang* **1.** To behave in an eccentric manner. **2.** To be insane. [ME *skrewe* < OFr. *escrove*, female screw, nut, perh. < Med.Lat. *scrōfa* < Lat., sow. See **sker-**[1] in App.] **—screw′a•ble** *adj.* **—screw′er** *n.*

screw•ball (skro͞o′bôl′) *n.* **1.** *Baseball* A pitched ball that curves in the direction opposite to that of a normal curve ball. **2.** *Slang* A person regarded as eccentric, whimsical, or irrational. ❖ *adj.* *Slang* Impulsively whimsical; eccentric.

screw bean *n.* **1.** A shrub or small tree *(Prosopis pubescens)* of southwest North America, having pinnately compound leaves and twisted pods used as fodder. **2.** The pod of this plant.

screw•driv•er (skro͞o′drī′vər) *n.* **1.** A tool used for turning screws. **2.** A cocktail made with vodka and orange juice.

screw eye *n.* A wood screw with an eyelet in place of a head.

screw jack *n.* See **jackscrew.**

screw log *n.* See **patent log.**

screw pine *n.* See **pandanus.**

screw propeller *n.* A propeller.

screw thread *n.* The continuous helical groove on a screw or the inner surface of a nut.

screw•up also **screw-up** (skro͞o′ŭp′) *n.* *Slang* **1.** One that makes a mess of an undertaking; a bungler. **2.** A blunder; a mess.

screw•worm (skro͞o′wûrm′) *n.* The screwworm fly larva.

screwworm fly *n.* A bluish fly *(Cochliomyia hominivorax)* of the New World that breeds in the living tissue of mammals, having entered usu. through open wounds or the nostrils.

screw•y (skro͞o′ē) *adj.* **-i•er, -i•est** *Slang* **1.** Eccentric; crazy. **2.** Ludicrously odd, unlikely, or inappropriate. **—screw′i•ness** *n.*

Scri•a•bin (skrē-ä′bĭn), **Alexander Nikolayevich** 1872–1915. Russian composer of orchestral and piano works.

scrib•ble (skrĭb′əl) *v.* **-bled, -bling, -bles** *—tr.* **1.** To write hurriedly without heed to legibility or style. **2.** To cover with scribbles, doodles, or meaningless marks. *—intr.* To write or draw in a hurried careless way. ❖ *n.* **1.** Careless hurried writing. **2.** Meaningless marks and lines. [ME *scriblen*, prob. < *scriben*, to write < Lat. *scrībere*, to write. See **skrībh-** in App.] **—scrib′bly** *adj.*

scrib•bler (skrĭb′lər) *n.* One who scribbles, esp. an author regarded as inferior or unimportant.

scribe (skrīb) *n.* **1.** A public clerk or secretary, esp. in ancient times. **2.** A professional copyist of manuscripts and documents. **3.** A writer or journalist. **4.** See **scriber.** ❖ *v.* **scribed, scrib•ing, scribes** *—tr.* **1.** To mark with a scriber. **2.** To write or inscribe. *—intr.* To work as a scribe. [ME < OFr. < LLat. *scrība* < Lat., keeper of accounts, secretary < *scrībere*, to write. See **skrībh-** in App.] **—scrib′al** *adj.*

Scribe (skrēb), **Augustin Eugène** 1791–1861. French playwright known for his comedies of manners.

scrib•er (skrī′bər) *n.* A sharply pointed tool used for marking lines, as on wood, metal, or ceramic.

scried (skrīd) *v.* Past tense and past participle of **scry.**

scries (skrīz) *v.* Third person singular present tense of **scry.**

scrim (skrĭm) *n.* **1.** A durable, loosely woven cotton or linen fabric used for curtains or upholstery lining or in industry. **2.** A transparent fabric used as a drop in the theater to create special effects of lights or atmosphere. [?]

scrim•mage (skrĭm′ĭj) *n.* **1.** *Football* The contest between two teams from the time the ball is snapped until it is declared dead. **2.** *Sports* A practice session or informal game, as between two units of the same team. **3a.** A rough-and-tumble struggle; a tussle. **b.** A skirmish. ❖ *intr.v.* **-maged, -mag•ing, -mag•es** *Sports* To engage in a scrimmage. [ME, alteration of *skirmisshe, scrimish.* See SKIRMISH.]

scrimp (skrĭmp) *v.* **scrimped, scrimp•ing, scrimps** *—intr.* To economize severely. *—tr.* **1.** To be excessively sparing with or of. **2.** To cut or make too small or scanty. [Perh. of Scand. orig.; akin to Swed. *skrympa*, to shrink.] **—scrimp′er** *n.* **—scrimp′y** *adj.*

scrim•shand•er (skrĭm′shăn′dər) *n.* One who carves scrimshaw. [?]

scrim•shaw (skrĭm′shô′) *n., pl.* **scrimshaw** or **-shaws 1.** The art

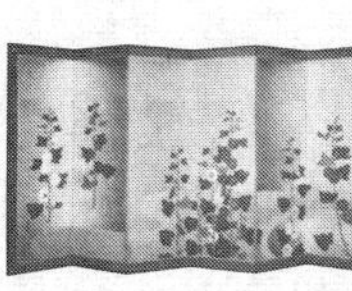

screen
Japanese decorative screen by Ogata Korin (1658–1716)

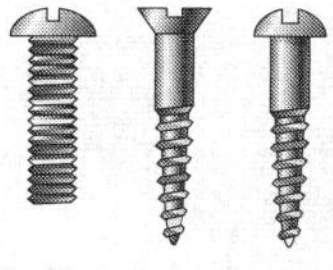

screw
left to right: round-head machine screw, flat-head wood screw, and round-head wood screw

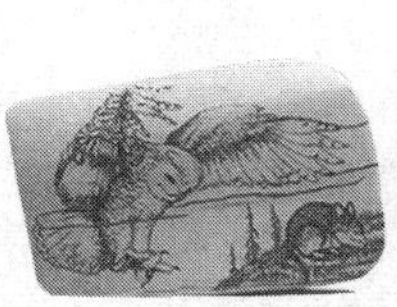

scrimshaw

ă	pat	oi	boy
ā	pay	ou	out
âr	care	o͝o	took
ä	father	o͞o	boot
ĕ	pet	ŭ	cut
ē	be	ûr	urge
ĭ	pit	th	thin
ī	pie	*th*	this
îr	pier	hw	which
ŏ	pot	zh	vision
ō	toe	ə	about, item
ô	paw		

Stress marks:
′ (primary);
′ (secondary), as in
lexicon (lĕk′sĭ-kŏn′)

of carving or incising intricate designs on whalebone or whale ivory. **2.** A decorative article made by this art. ❖ *tr. & intr.v.* **-shawed, -shaw·ing, -shaws** To decorate (whale ivory or whalebone) with intricate carvings or designs or make such designs. [Prob. < SCRIMSHANDER.]

scrip¹ (skrĭp) *n.* **1.** Paper money issued for temporary emergency use. **2.** A small scrap of paper, esp. with a short list or schedule written on it. [Perh. alteration of SCRIPT.]

scrip² (skrĭp) *n.* **1.** A provisional certificate entitling the holder to a fractional share of stock or of other jointly owned property. **2.** Such certificates considered as a group. [Short for *subscription receipt*, receipt for a portion of a loan.]

scrip³ (skrĭp) *n.* *Archaic* A wallet, small satchel, or bag. [ME *scrippe*.]

Scripps (skrĭps) Family of Amer. newspaper publishers, including **James Edmund** (1835–1906), who founded the *Detroit Evening News* (1873), and his half-brother **Edward Wyllis Scripps** (1854–1926), who formed (1907) the news agency that became United Press International.

script (skrĭpt) *n.* **1a.** Handwriting. **b.** A style of writing with cursive characters. **c.** A particular system of writing: *cuneiform script.* **2.** *Printing* **a.** A style of type that imitates handwriting. **b.** The matter set in this type. **3a.** The text of a play, broadcast, or movie. **b.** A copy of a text used by a director or performer. **4.** *Computer Science* A simple program in a utility language or an application's proprietary language. ❖ *tr.v.* **script·ed, script·ing, scripts 1.** To prepare (a text) for filming or broadcasting. **2.** To orchestrate (an event, for example) as if writing a script. [ME *skript*, a piece of writing, alteration of *scrite* < OFr. *escrit* < Lat. *scrīptum* < neut. p. part. of *scrībere*, to write. See **skrībh-** in App.]

scrip·to·ri·um (skrĭp-tôr′ē-əm, -tōr′-) *n.*, *pl.* **-to·ri·ums** or **-to·ri·a** (-tôr′ē-ə, -tōr′-) A room in a monastery for copying, writing, or illuminating manuscripts and records. [Med.Lat. *scrīptōrium* < Lat. *scrīptus*, p. part. of *scrībere*, to write. See **skrībh-** in App.]

scrip·tur·al (skrĭp′chər-əl) *adj.* **1.** Of or relating to writing; written. **2.** often **Scriptural** Of, relating to, based on, or contained in the Scriptures. **—scrip′tur·al·ly** *adv.*

Scrip·ture (skrĭp′chər) *n.* **1a.** A sacred writing or book. **b.** A passage from such a writing or book. **2.** The sacred writings of the Bible. Often used in the plural. **3. scripture** A statement regarded as authoritative. [ME < LLat. *scrīptūra* < Lat., act of writing < *scrīptus*, p. part. of *scrībere*, to write. See **skrībh-** in App.]

script·writ·er (skrĭpt′rī′tər) *n.* One who writes copy to be used in a film or broadcast. **—script′writ′ing** *n.*

scriv·en·er (skrĭv′ə-nər, skrĭv′nər) *n.* **1.** A professional copyist; a scribe. **2.** A notary. [ME *scriveiner* < *scrivein* < OFr. *escrivein* < VLat. **scrība, *scrībān-* < Lat. *scrība*, scribe. See SCRIBE.]

scro·bic·u·late (skrō-bĭk′yə-lĭt, -lāt′) *adj.* Marked with many shallow depressions, grooves, or pits. [Lat. *scrobiculus*, dim. of *scrobis*, trench; see **sker-¹** in App. + -ATE¹.]

scrod also **schrod** (skrŏd) *n.*, *pl.* **scrod** also **schrod** A young cod or haddock, esp. one split and boned for cooking. [Poss. < obsolete Du. *schrood*, slice, shred < MDu. *scrōde*.]

scrof·u·la (skrŏf′yə-lə) *n.* A form of tuberculosis affecting the lymph nodes, esp. of the neck, that is most common in children. [ME *scrophula* < LLat. *scrōfulae*, swelling of the glands, dim. of Lat. *scrōfa*, sow. See **sker-¹** in App.]

scrof·u·lous (skrŏf′yə-ləs) *adj.* **1.** Relating to, affected with, or resembling scrofula. **2.** Morally degenerate; corrupt. **—scrof′u·lous·ly** *adv.* **—scrof′u·lous·ness** *n.*

scroll (skrōl) *n.* **1a.** A roll, as of parchment or papyrus, used esp. for writing a document. **b.** An ancient book or volume written on such a roll. **2.** A list or schedule of names. **3.** An ornament or ornamental design that resembles a partially rolled scroll of paper, as the volute in Ionic capitals. **4.** *Music* The curved head above the peg box on a stringed instrument. **5.** *Heraldry* A ribbon inscribed with a motto. ❖ *v.* **scrolled, scroll·ing, scrolls —tr. 1.** To inscribe on a scroll. **2.** To roll up into a scroll. **3.** To ornament with a scroll. **4.** *Computer Science* To cause (text or graphics) to move vertically or horizontally across the screen so that a new line appears for each line that moves off the screen. **—intr.** *Computer Science* To scroll text or graphics. [ME *scrowle*, alteration of *scrowe* < OFr. *escroue, escroe*, strip of parchment, scroll, of Gmc. orig.]

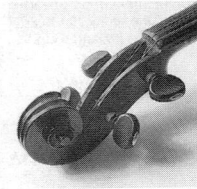

scroll
violin scroll

scroll saw *n.* A handsaw or power saw with a narrow ribbonlike blade for cutting curved or irregular shapes.

scroll·work (skrōl′wûrk′) *n.* Embellishment with a scroll motif, esp. ornamentation executed in wood with a scroll saw.

scrooch also **scrootch** (skrōōch) *intr.v.* **scrooched, scrooch·ing, scrooch·es** also **scrootched, scrootch·ing, scrootch·es** To hunch down; crouch. [Alteration (perh. influenced by CROUCH) of *scrooge, scrouge*, to squeeze, crowd.]

Scrooge also **scrooge** (skrōōj) *n.* A mean-spirited miserly person; a skinflint. [After Dickens's miser Ebenezer *Scrooge*.]

scro·tum (skrō′təm) *n.*, *pl.* **-ta** (-tə) or **-tums** The external sac of skin enclosing the testes in most mammals. [Lat. *scrōtum*.] **—scro′tal** (skrōt′l) *adj.*

scrounge (skrounj) *v.* **scrounged, scroung·ing, scroung·es** *Slang* **—tr. 1.** To obtain (something) by begging or borrowing with no intention of reparation. **2.** To obtain by salvaging or foraging. **—intr. 1.** To seek to scrounge something, as by begging. **2.** To forage about in an effort to acquire something at no cost. [Alteration of dialectal *scrunge*, to steal.] **—scroung′er** *n.*

scroung·y (skroun′jē) *adj.* **-i·er, -i·est** *Slang* Dirty or shabby: *a scroungy overcoat.*

scrub¹ (skrŭb) *v.* **scrubbed, scrub·bing, scrubs —tr. 1a.** To rub hard in order to clean. **b.** To remove (dirt or stains) by hard rubbing. **2.** To remove impurities from (a gas) chemically. **3.** *Slang* To cancel or abandon; drop. **—intr.** To clean or wash something by hard rubbing. ❖ *n.* **1.** The act or an instance of scrubbing. **2. scrubs** The articles of clothing that make up a scrub suit. **—phrasal verb: scrub up** To wash the hands and arms thoroughly, as before surgery. [ME *scrobben*, to currycomb a horse < MDu. *schrobben*, to clean by rubbing, scrape. See **sker-¹** in App.] **—scrub′ba·ble** *adj.*

scrub² (skrŭb) *n.* **1.** A straggly, stunted tree or shrub. **2.** A growth or tract of stunted vegetation. **3.** An undersized or poorly developed domestic animal. **4.** An undersized or insignificant person. **5.** *Sports* A player not on the varsity or first team. **6.** *Australian* Remote rural land; the bush. [ME, var. of *shrubbe*. See SHRUB¹.]

scrub·ber (skrŭb′ər) *n.* One that scrubs, esp.: **a.** One who cleans by scrubbing. **b.** A brush, appliance, or abrasive used in cleaning. **c.** An apparatus used for removing impurities from a gas.

scrub·by (skrŭb′ē) *adj.* **-bi·er, -bi·est 1.** Covered with or consisting of scrub or underbrush. **2.** Straggly or stunted. **3.** Paltry or shabby; wretched. **—scrub′bi·ly** *adv.* **—scrub′bi·ness** *n.*

scrub fowl *n.* See megapode.

scrub jay *n.* A crestless blue and gray jay (*Aphelocoma coerulescens*) found in dense brush or scrub, esp. in Florida.

scrub·land (skrŭb′lănd′) *n.* An area of land that is uncultivated and covered with sparse stunted vegetation.

scrub oak *n.* Either of two thicket-forming shrubs, the deciduous *Quercus ilcifolia* of the eastern United States or the evergreen *Q. dumosa* of western regions.

scrub pine *n.* **1.** A straggly pine tree (*Pinus virginiana*) of the eastern United States having prickly cones and drooping or spreading branches. **2.** See **jack pine**.

scrub suit *n.* A two-piece garment of lightweight cotton, often worn by medical personnel, esp. during surgery.

scrub typhus *n.* An infectious disease common in Asia, caused by the rickettsia *R. tsutsugamushi* and marked by fever, painful swollen lymph nodes, and skin lesions.

scrub·wom·an (skrŭb′wōōm′ən) *n.* A woman hired to clean.

scruff (skrŭf) *n.* The back of the neck; the nape. [Alteration of dialectal *scuft, scuff.*]

scruff·y (skrŭf′ē) *adj.* **-i·er, -i·est 1.** Shabby; untidy. **2.** *Chiefly British* Scaly; scabby. [< obsolete *scruff*, scurf, var. of *scurf*. See SCURF.] **—scruff′i·ly** *adv.* **—scruff′i·ness** *n.*

scrum (skrŭm) *Sports n.* A play or formation in Rugby in which the opposing forwards mass together around the ball and struggle to gain possession of the ball. ❖ *intr.v.* **scrummed, scrum·ming, scrums** To engage in a scrum. [Short for SCRUMMAGE.]

scrum·mage (skrŭm′ĭj) *Sports n.* A scrum. [Alteration of SCRIMMAGE.] **—scrum′mage** *v.* **—scrum′mag·er** *n.*

scrump·tious (skrŭmp′shəs) *adj.* Splendid; delectable. [Perh. alteration of SUMPTUOUS.] **—scrump′tious·ly** *adv.*

scrunch (skrŭnch, skrōōnch) *v.* **scrunched, scrunch·ing, scrunch·es —tr. 1.** To crush or crunch. **2.** To crumple or squeeze; hunch: *scrunched up their shoulders.* **—intr. 1.** To hunch. **2.** To move with or make a crunching sound. ❖ *n.* A crunching sound. [Prob. alteration of CRUNCH.] **—scrunch′a·ble** *adj.*

scrunch·ie also **scrunch·y** (skrŭn′chē) *n.*, *pl.* **-ies** An elasticized fabric ring used chiefly by women and girls to gather or fasten the hair. [After the company that made such rings.]

scru·ple (skrōō′pəl) *n.* **1.** An uneasy feeling arising from conscience or principle that tends to hinder action. **2.** A unit of apothecary weight equal to about 1.3 grams, or 20 grains. **3.** A minute part or amount. ❖ *intr.v.* **-pled, -pling, -ples** To hesitate as a result of conscience or principle. [ME *scrupul* < OFr. *scrupule* < Lat. *scrūpulus*, small unit of measurement, scruple, dim. of *scrūpus*, rough stone, scruple.]

scru·pu·lous (skrōō′pyə-ləs) *adj.* **1.** Conscientious and exact; painstaking. **2.** Having scruples; principled. [ME < OFr. *scrupuleux* < Lat. *scrūpulōsus* < *scrūpulus*, scruple. See SCRUPLE.] **—scru′pu·los·i·ty** (-lŏs′ĭ-tē), scru′pu·lous·ness (-ləs-nĭs) *n.* **—scru′pu·lous·ly** *adv.*

scru·ta·ble (skrōō′tə-bəl) *adj.* Capable of being understood through study and observation; comprehensible. [LLat. *scrūtābilis*, searchable < Lat. *scrūtārī*, to search. See SCRUTINY.]

scru·ti·nize (skrōōt′n-īz′) *tr.v.* **-nized, -niz·ing, -niz·es** To examine or observe with great care; inspect critically. **—scru′ti·niz′er** *n.* **—scru′ti·niz′ing·ly** *adv.*

scru·ti·ny (skrōōt′n-ē) *n.*, *pl.* **-nies 1.** A close careful examination or study. **2.** Close observation; surveillance. [ME *scrutinie*, taking of a formal vote < Lat. *scrūtinium*, inquiry, search < *scrūtārī*, to search, examine < *scrūta*, trash.]

scry (skrī) *intr.v.* **scried** (skrīd), **scry·ing, scries** (skrīz) To see or predict the future with a crystal ball. [Short for DESCRY.]

SCSI (skŭz′ē) *n.* A small computer system interface used for connecting peripheral devices. [*s*(mall) *c*(omputer) *s*(ystem) *i*(nterface).]

scu•ba (sko͞o′bə) *n.* A portable apparatus containing compressed air and used for breathing under water. [*s(elf-)c(ontained) u(nderwater) b(reathing) a(pparatus).*]

scuba diver *n.* One who uses scuba gear in underwater swimming. **—scu′ba-dive′** (sko͞o′bə-dīv′) *v.* **—scuba diving** *n.*

scud (skŭd) *intr.v.* **scud•ded, scud•ding, scuds 1.** To run or skim along swiftly and easily: *clouds scudding by.* **2.** *Nautical* To run before a gale with little or no sail set. ❖ *n.* **1.** The act of scudding. **2a.** Wind-driven clouds, mist, or rain. **b.** A gust of wind. **c.** Ragged low clouds, moving rapidly beneath another cloud layer. [Poss. < ME *scut*, rabbit, rabbit's tail. See SCUT[1].]

scu•do (sko͞o′dō) *n., pl.* **-di** (-dē) A monetary unit and coin formerly used in Italy and Sicily. [Ital., shield, scudo < Lat. *scūtum*, shield.]

scuff (skŭf) *v.* **scuffed, scuff•ing, scuffs** *—intr.* To scrape the feet while walking; shuffle. *—tr.* **1.** To scrape with the feet. **2.** To shuffle or shift (the feet), as in embarrassment. **3.** To scrape and roughen the surface of. ❖ *n.* **1.** The act or sound of scraping esp. with the feet. **2.** A worn or rough spot resulting from scraping. **3.** A flat backless house slipper. [Prob. of Scand. orig.; akin to ON *skūfa*, to push.] **—scuff′er** *n.*

scuf•fle[1] (skŭf′əl) *intr.v.* **-fled, -fling, -fles 1.** To fight or struggle confusedly at close quarters. **2.** To shuffle. ❖ *n.* A rough disorderly struggle at close quarters. [Prob. freq. of *scuff.*] **—scuf′fler** *n.*

scuf•fle[2] (skŭf′əl) *n.* A hoe that is manipulated by pushing or pulling. [Du. *schoffel*, weeding hoe < MDu., hoe, shovel.]

sculch (skŭlch) *n. New England* Variant of **culch** 3.

scull (skŭl) *n.* **1.** A long oar used at the stern of a boat and moved from side to side to propel the boat forward. **2.** One of a pair of short-handled oars used by a single rower. **3.** A small light racing boat for one, two, or four rowers, each using a pair of sculls. ❖ *v.* **sculled, scull•ing, sculls** *—tr.* To propel (a boat) with a scull or a pair of sculls. *—intr.* To use a scull or a pair of sculls to propel a boat. [ME *sculle.*] **—scull′er** *n.*

scul•ler•y (skŭl′ə-rē) *n., pl.* **-ies** A small room adjoining a kitchen, in which dishwashing and other kitchen chores are done. [ME < OFr. *escuelerie* < *escuelier*, keeper of dishes < *escuele*, dish < VLat. **scūtella*, alteration (influenced by *scūtum*, shield) of Lat. *scutella*, salver, dim. of *scutra*, platter.]

scul•lion (skŭl′yən) *n.* A servant employed to do menial tasks in a kitchen. [ME *sculyon*, prob. < OFr. *escouvillon*, dishcloth, dim. of *escouve*, broom < Lat. *scōpa.*]

scul•pin (skŭl′pĭn) *n., pl.* **-pins** or **sculpin 1.** Any of various marine and freshwater fishes of the family Cottidae, having a large flattened head and spines. **2.** A scorpion fish *(Scorpaena guttata)* of California coastal waters. [?]

sculpt (skŭlpt) *v.* **sculpt•ed, sculpt•ing, sculpts** *—tr.* **1.** To sculpture (an object). **2.** To shape, mold, or fashion esp. with artistry or precision. *—intr.* To be a sculptor. [Fr. *sculpter* < OFr. < Lat. *sculpere, sculpt-*, to carve. See SCULPTURE.]

sculp•tor (skŭlp′tər) *n.* **1.** One who produces sculptural artwork. **2.** One who shapes, molds, or fashions, esp. with artistry or precision. **3. Sculptor** A constellation in the Southern Hemisphere near Cetus and Phoenix. [Lat. < *sculpere*, to carve. See SCULPTURE.]

sculp•tress (skŭlp′trĭs) *n.* A woman who sculptures. See Usage Note at **-ess.**

sculp•ture (skŭlp′chər) *n.* **1.** The art or practice of shaping figures or designs in the round or in relief, as by chiseling marble, modeling clay, or casting in metal. **2a.** A work of art created by sculpture. **b.** Such works of art considered as a group. **3.** Ridges, indentations, or other markings, as on a shell, formed by natural processes. ❖ *v.* **-tured, -tur•ing, -tures** *—tr.* **1.** To fashion (stone, for example) into a three-dimensional figure. **2.** To represent in sculpture. **3.** To ornament with sculpture. **4.** To change the shape or contour of, as by erosion. *—intr.* To make sculptures or a sculpture. [ME < Lat. *sculptūra* < *sculptus*, p. part. of *sculpere*, to carve.] **—sculp′tur•al** *adj.* **—sculp′tur•al•ly** *adv.*

sculp•tur•esque (skŭlp′chə-rĕsk′) *adj.* Suggestive of or having the qualities of sculpture. **—sculp′tur•esque′ly** *adv.*

scultch (skŭlch) *n. New England* Variant of **culch** 3.

scum (skŭm) *n.* **1.** A filmy layer of extraneous or impure matter that forms on or rises to the surface of a liquid or body of water. **2.** The refuse or dross of molten metals. **3.** Refuse or worthless matter. **4.** *Slang* One, such as a person, that is regarded as despicable or worthless. ❖ *v.* **scummed, scum•ming, scums** *—tr.* To remove the scum from. *—intr.* To become covered with scum. [ME < MDu. *schūm.* See **(s)keu-** in App.] **—scum′mer** *n.* **—scum′mi•ly** *adv.* **—scum′mi•ness** *n.* **—scum′my** *adj.*

scum•bag (skŭm′băg′) *n. Slang* A despicable person.

scum•ble (skŭm′bəl) *tr.v.* **-bled, -bling, -bles** To soften the colors or outlines of (a painting or drawing) by covering with a film of opaque or semiopaque color or by rubbing. ❖ *n.* **1.** The effect produced by scumbling. **2.** Material used for scumbling. [Poss. < SCUM.]

scun•ner (skŭn′ər) *n.* A strong dislike; an aversion. [< ME *skunner*, to shrink back in disgust < *scurnen*, to flinch.]

scup (skŭp) *n., pl.* **scup** or **scups** A porgy *(Stenotomus chrysops)* of the northern Atlantic coastal waters, important as a food fish. [Short for Narragansett *mishcùp.*]

scup•per[1] (skŭp′ər) *n.* **1.** *Nautical* An opening in the side of a ship at deck level to allow water to run off. **2.** An opening for draining off water, as from a floor or the roof of a building. [ME *scoper-* (in *scopernail*, nail for attaching scupper-leathers to a ship), prob. < *scopen*, to scoop < *scope*, a scoop. See SCOOP.]

scup•per[2] (skŭp′ər) *tr.v.* **-pered, -per•ing, -pers 1.** *Chiefly British* To overwhelm or massacre. **2.** To ruin or destroy. [Perh. < SCUPPER[1].]

scup•per•nong (skŭp′ər-nông′, -nŏng′) *n.* **1.** See **muscadine. 2a.** A cultivated variety of the muscadine grape with sweet yellowish fruit. **b.** A wine made from this grape. [After the *Scuppernong* River in northeast North Carolina.]

scurf (skûrf) *n.* **1.** Scaly or shredded dry skin, such as dandruff. **2.** A loose scaly crust coating a surface, esp. of a plant. [ME, prob. of Scand. orig. See **sker-**[1] in App.] **—scurf′i•ness** *n.* **—scurf′y** *adj.*

scur•rile also **scur•ril** (skûr′əl, skŭr′-) *adj. Archaic* Scurrilous. [Fr. < OFr. < Lat. *scurrīlis*, jeering < *scurra*, buffoon, poss. of Etruscan orig.]

scur•ril•i•ty (skə-rĭl′ĭ-tē) *n., pl.* **-ties 1.** The quality of being vulgar, coarse, or abusive. **2.** A vulgar, coarse, or abusive remark or passage.

scur•ri•lous (skûr′ə-ləs, skŭr′-) *adj.* **1.** Given to the use of vulgar, coarse, or abusive language; foul-mouthed. **2.** Expressed in vulgar, coarse, and abusive language. **—scur′ri•lous•ly** *adv.* **—scur′ri•lous•ness** *n.*

scur•ry (skûr′ē, skŭr′ē) *intr.v.* **-ried, -ry•ing, -ries 1.** To go with light running steps; scamper. **2.** To flurry or swirl about. ❖ *n., pl.* **-ries 1.** The act of scurrying. **2.** The noise produced by scurrying. [Prob. short for HURRY-SCURRY.]

scur•vy (skûr′vē) *n.* A disease caused by deficiency of vitamin C, characterized by spongy and bleeding gums and bleeding under the skin. ❖ *adj.* **-vi•er, -vi•est** Mean; contemptible. [< ME *scurfy*, marked by scurf (influenced by Fr. *scorbut*, scurvy) < *scurf*, scurf. See SCURF.] **—scur′vi•ly** *adv.* **—scur′vi•ness** *n.*

scurvy grass *n.* **1.** Any of various plants of the genus *Cochlearia*, esp. *C. officinalis* of northern Europe, having pungent foliage and formerly used to cure scurvy. **2.** See **sea kale.**

scut[1] (skŭt) *n.* A stubby erect tail, as of a hare. [ME, hare.]

scut[2] (skŭt) *n. Informal* Routine or tedious work. [Short for SCUTWORK.]

scu•ta (skyo͞o′tə) *n.* Plural of **scutum.**

scu•tage (skyo͞o′tĭj) *n.* A tax paid in lieu of military service in feudal times. [ME < Med.Lat. *scūtāgium* < Lat. *scūtum*, shield. See SCUTUM.]

Scu•ta•ri (sko͞o′tə-rē), **Lake** A lake of SE Europe on the border between SE Montenegro and NW Albania.

scu•tate (skyo͞o′tāt) *adj.* **1.** *Zoology* Covered or protected by scutes. **2.** *Botany* Shaped like a shield or buckler: *scutate leaves.* [Lat. *scūtātus*, shield-bearing < *scūtum*, shield. See SCUTUM.]

scutch (skŭch) *tr.v.* **scutched, scutch•ing, scutch•es** To separate the valuable fibers of (flax, for example) from the woody parts by beating. ❖ *n.* An implement used for scutching. [Obsolete Fr. *escoucher* < AN *escucher* < VLat. **excuticāre*, freq. of Lat. *excutere*, to shake out : *ex-*, ex- + *quatere*, to shake.] **—scutch′er** *n.*

scutch•eon (skŭch′ən) *n.* **1.** An escutcheon. **2.** A shield-shaped object, such as a scute.

scutch grass *n.* See **Bermuda grass.**

scute (skyo͞ot) *n. Zoology* An external horny, chitinous, or bony plate or scale. [< Lat. *scūtum*, shield. See SCUTUM.]

scu•tel•late (skyo͞o-tĕl′ĭt, skyo͞ot′l-āt′) also **scu•tel•lat•ed** (skyo͞ot′l-ā′tĭd) *adj.* **1.** *Zoology* **a.** Covered with shieldlike bony plates or scales. **b.** Having a scutellum. **2.** *Botany* Shaped like a shield or platter.

scu•tel•la•tion (skyo͞ot′l-ā′shən) *n.* An arrangement or a covering of scales, as on a bird's leg.

scu•tel•lum (skyo͞o-tĕl′əm) *n., pl.* **-tel•la** (-tĕl′ə) **1.** *Zoology* A shieldlike bony plate or scale, as on the thorax of some insects. **2.** *Botany* Any of several shield-shaped structures, such as the cotyledon of a grass. [NLat. *scūtellum* < Lat., dim. of *scūtum*, shield. See SCUTUM.] **—scu•tel′lar** (-tĕl′ər) *adj.*

scu•ti•form (skyo͞o′tə-fôrm′) *adj.* Shield-shaped: *scutiform leaves.* [Lat. *scūtum*, shield; see SCUTUM + -FORM.]

scut•ter (skŭt′ər) *intr.v.* **-tered, -ter•ing, -ters** To move with a clattering, scurrying sound. [Alteration of SCUTTLE[3].]

scut•tle[1] (skŭt′l) *n.* **1.** A small opening or hatch with a movable lid in the deck or hull of a ship or in the roof, wall, or floor of a building. **2.** The lid or hatch of such an opening. ❖ *tr.v.* **-tled, -tling, -tles 1.** *Nautical* **a.** To cut or open a hole or holes in (a ship's hull). **b.** To sink (a ship) by this means. **2.** *Informal* To scrap; discard. [ME *skottell* < OFr. *escoutille*, poss. < Sp. *escotilla.*]

scut•tle[2] (skŭt′l) *n.* **1.** A metal pail for carrying coal. **2.** A shallow open basket for carrying vegetables. [ME *scutel*, basket < OE, dish < Lat. *scutella.* See SCULLERY.]

scut•tle[3] (skŭt′l) *intr.v.* **-tled, -tling, -tles** To run or move with short hurried movements; scurry. ❖ *n.* A hurried run. [ME *scottlen* poss. akin to SCUD.]

scut•tle•butt (skŭt′l-bŭt′) *n.* **1.** *Slang* Gossip; rumor. **2.** *Nautical* **a.** A drinking fountain on a ship. **b.** A cask on a ship for the day's supply of drinking water. [SCUTTLE[1] + BUTT[5].]

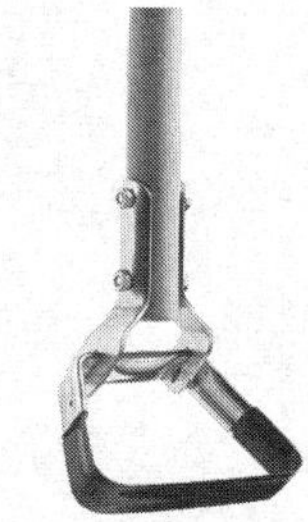

scuffle[2]
close-up of a scuffle head

ă	pat	oi	boy
ā	pay	ou	out
âr	care	o͝o	took
ä	father	o͞o	boot
ĕ	pet	ŭ	cut
ē	be	ûr	urge
ĭ	pit	th	thin
ī	pie	*th*	this
îr	pier	hw	which
ŏ	pot	zh	vision
ō	toe	ə	about, item
ô	paw		

Stress marks:
′ (primary);
′ (secondary), as in
lexicon (lĕk′sĭ-kŏn′)

scu·tum (skyōō'təm) *n., pl.* **-ta** (-tə) See **scute**. [Lat. *scūtum*, shield.]

scut·work (skŭt'wûrk') *n. Informal* Monotonous work or menial tasks. [< *scut*, worthless person, perh. < SCOUT².]

scuz·zy (skŭz'ē) *adj.* **-zi·er, -zi·est** *Slang* **1.** Dirty; grimy. **2.** Disreputable; sleazy: "*ran a scuzzy operation*" (Myra MacPherson). [Poss. < blend of SCUM and FUZZ¹.]

Scyl·la (sĭl'ə) *n. Greek Mythology* A female sea monster who lived in a cave opposite Charybdis and devoured sailors. **—idiom:** between **Scylla and Charybdis** In a position where avoidance of one danger exposes one to another danger.

scy·phis·to·ma (sī-fĭs'tə-mə) *n., pl.* **-mae** (-mē) or **-mas** A larva of a scyphozoan. [NLat. : Gk. *skuphos*, cup + Gk. *stoma*, mouth.]

scy·pho·zo·an (sī'fə-zō'ən) *n.* Any of various marine cnidarians of the class Scyphozoa, which includes the large jellyfishes, characterized by the absence of a true polyp stage. [< NLat. *Scyphozoa*, class name : Gk. *skuphos*, cup + New Lain *-zōa*, pl. of *zōon*, -zoon.] **—scy'pho·zo'an** *adj.*

Scy·ros (skī'rəs, skē'rôs) See **Skíros**.

scythe (sīth) *n.* An implement with a long curved single-edged blade and a long bent handle, used for mowing or reaping. ❖ *tr.v.* **scythed, scyth·ing, scythes** To cut with or as if with a scythe. [ME *sithe* < OE *sīthe.* See **sek-** in App.]

Scyth·i·a (sĭth'ē-ə, sĭth'-) An ancient region of Eurasia extending from the mouth of the Danube R. on the Black Sea to the territory E of the Aral Sea.

Scyth·i·an (sĭth'ē-ən, sĭth'-) *adj.* Of or relating to Scythia or its people, language, or culture. ❖ *n.* **1.** A member of the ancient nomadic people inhabiting Scythia. **2.** The Iranian language of the Scythians.

Scyth·o-Dra·vid·i·an (sĭth'ō-drə-vĭd'ē-ən, sĭth'-) *adj.* Of or relating to an ethnic group of northwest India having Iranian and Dravidian characteristics. [SCYTH(IAN) + DRAVIDIAN.]

SD *abbr.* **1.** Latin Scientiae Doctor (Doctor of Science) **2.** sight draft **3.** or **S.D.** South Dakota **4.** special delivery **5.** standard deviation

Sd. *abbr.* sound (body of water)

s.d. *abbr.* sine die

S.Dak. *abbr.* South Dakota

SDI *abbr.* Strategic Defense Initiative

SDS *abbr.* Students for a Democratic Society

Se The symbol for the element **selenium.**

SE *abbr.* **1a.** southeast **b.** southeastern **2.** stock exchange

sea (sē) *n.* **1.** The continuous body of salt water covering most of the earth's surface. **2a.** A tract of water within an ocean. **b.** A large body of salt water completely or partially enclosed by land. **c.** A large landlocked body of fresh water. **3a.** The condition of the ocean's surface in regard to its course, flow, swell, or turbulence: *a high sea.* **b.** A wave or swell, esp. a large one. **4.** Something that suggests the ocean in its overwhelming sweep or vastness: *a sea of controversy.* **5.** Seafaring as a way of life. **6.** *Astronomy* A lunar mare. **—idiom: at sea 1.** On the sea, esp. a sea voyage. **2.** In confusion or perplexity. [ME *see* < OE *sǣ.*]

sea anchor *n. Nautical* A drag, usu. a canvas-covered conical frame, trailed behind a vessel to prevent drifting or to maintain a heading into the wind.

sea anemone *n.* Any of numerous flowerlike marine cnidarians of the class Anthozoa, having a flexible cylindrical body and tentacles surrounding a central mouth.

sea bass (băs) *n.* **1.** Any of various marine food fishes of the genus *Centropristes* and related genera, esp. *C. striatus,* of coastal Atlantic waters of the United States. **2.** Any of the various similar fishes of the family Serranidea.

sea·bed (sē'bĕd') *n.* The floor of the sea or the ocean.

Sea·bee (sē'bē') *n.* A member of one of the construction battalions in the US Navy that builds naval aviation bases and shore facilities. [Alteration of *cee bee,* pronunciation of the initial letters of *construction battalion.*]

sea bird *n.* A bird, such as a petrel or albatross, that frequents the ocean, esp. far from shore.

sea biscuit *n.* See **hardtack.**

sea·board (sē'bôrd', -bōrd') *n.* **1.** A seacoast. **2.** Land near the sea.

Sea·borg (sē'bôrg'), **Glenn Theodore** 1912–99. Amer. chemist who shared a 1951 Nobel Prize.

sea·bor·gi·um (sē-bôr'gē-əm) *n. Symbol* **Sg** An artificially produced radioactive element with atomic number 106 whose most long-lived isotopes have mass numbers 259, 261, 263, 265, and 266 with half-lives of 0.9, 0.23, 0.8, 16, and 20 seconds, respectively. See table at **element.** [After Glenn Theodore SEABORG.]

sea·borne (sē'bôrn', -bōrn') *adj.* **1.** Conveyed by sea; transported by ship. **2.** Carried on or over the sea.

sea bread *n.* See **hardtack.**

sea bream *n.* Any of various marine food fishes of the family Sparidae or Bramidae, esp. *Archosargus rhomboidalis* of western Atlantic coastal waters.

Sea·bur·y (sē'bĕr'ē, -bə-rē), **Samuel** 1729–96. Amer. religious leader who was the first bishop of the Protestant Episcopal Church in America (1784–96).

sea captain *n.* The captain of a ship, esp. a merchant ship.

sea change *n.* **1.** A change caused by the sea. **2.** A marked transformation.

sea chest *n.* A box or trunk suitable for use by a sailor to store personal property.

sea·coast (sē'kōst') *n.* Land bordering the sea.

sea·cock (sē'kŏk') *n.* A valve in the hull of a boat or ship that may be opened to let water in or out.

sea cow *n.* Any of several large cylindrical herbivorous marine mammals of the order Sirenia, having a paddlelike tail and rounded front flippers and including the manatee and dugong.

sea crayfish also **sea crawfish** *n.* See **spiny lobster.**

sea cucumber *n.* Any of various cucumber-shaped echinoderms of the class Holothuroidea.

sea devil *n.* See **manta** 2.

sea dog *n.* **1.** Any of various seals or similar marine mammals. **2.** *Nautical* A very experienced sailor. **3.** **sea·dog** (sē'dôg', -dŏg') See **fogbow.**

sea duck *n.* Any of various diving ducks, such as the eider or scoter, of coastal areas.

sea eagle *n.* Any of various fish-eating eagles or similar birds.

sea elephant *n.* See **elephant seal.**

sea fan *n.* Any of various yellowish to reddish fan-shaped corals of the genus *Gorgonia,* esp. *G. flabellum,* of warm waters.

sea·far·er (sē'fâr'ər) *n.* **1.** A sailor or mariner. **2.** One who travels by sea.

sea·far·ing (sē'fâr'ĭng) *n.* A sailor's calling. ❖ *adj.* **1.** Following a life at sea. **2.** Fit to travel on the sea; seagoing.

sea feather *n.* Any of several anthozoans of the family Pennatulidae, having an elongate shaft with paired lateral pinnules.

sea fire *n.* Bioluminescence produced by marine life.

sea floor also **sea·floor** (sē'flôr', -flōr') *n.* The bottom of a sea or ocean.

sea·food (sē'fōōd') *n.* Edible fish or shellfish from the sea.

sea·fowl (sē'foul') *n.* **1.** A sea bird. **2.** Sea birds considered as a group.

sea·front (sē'frŭnt') *n.* A strip of land at the very edge of the sea, esp. land desirable for a resort.

sea·girt (sē'gûrt') *adj.* Surrounded by the sea.

sea·go·ing (sē'gō'ĭng) *adj.* Made or used for ocean voyages.

sea grape *n.* A small tropical American tree (*Coccolobis uvifera*) growing on sandy beaches and having large, glossy rounded leaves and grapelike clusters of purplish fruit.

sea green *n.* A medium green or bluish green.

sea·gull also **sea gull** (sē'gŭl') *n.* A gull, esp. one found near coastal areas.

sea holly *n.* A European seashore plant (*Eryngium maritimum*) having prickly bluish leaves and blue or purplish flowers.

sea horse *n.* **1.** A small marine fish of the genus *Hippocampus* that swims upright and has a prehensile tail, a horselike head, and a body covered with bony plates. **2.** See **walrus. 3.** *Mythology* An animal, half fish and half horse, ridden by Neptune and other sea gods. **4.** A large white-capped wave.

Sea Island cotton *n.* A tropical American species of cotton (*Gossypium barbadense*) widely cultivated for its fine long-staple fibers. [After the SEA ISLANDS.]

Sea Islands A chain of islands in the Atlantic Ocean off SC, GA, and N FL; settled by the Spanish in the 16th cent. and the English after the 17th cent.

sea kale *n.* A European seashore plant (*Crambe maritima*) of the mustard family, having edible cabbagelike leaves.

sea king *n.* A Viking pirate chief of the early Middle Ages.

seal¹ (sēl) *n.* **1a.** A die or signet having a raised or incised emblem used to stamp an impression on a receptive substance such as wax. **b.** The impression so made. **c.** The design or emblem itself, belonging exclusively to the user. **d.** A small disk or wafer of wax, lead, or paper bearing such an imprint and affixed to a document to prove authenticity or to secure it. **2.** Something, such as a commercial hallmark, that authenticates, confirms, or attests. **3.** A substance, esp. an adhesive agent such as wax, that closes or secures something or prevents seepage of moisture or air. **4.** A device that joins two systems or elements so as to prevent leakage. **5a.** An airtight closure. **b.** A closure, as on a package, proving that the contents have not been tampered with. **6.** A small decorative paper sticker. ❖ *tr.v.* **sealed, seal·ing, seals 1.** To affix a seal to in order to prove authenticity or attest to accuracy, legal weight, quality, or another standard. **2a.** To close with or as if with a seal. **b.** To close hermetically. **c.** To make fast or fill up, as with plaster or cement. **d.** To apply a waterproof coating to. **3.** To grant, certify, or designate under seal or authority. **4.** To establish or determine irrevocably. **—phrasal verb: seal off** To close tightly or surround with a barricade or cordon. [ME < OFr. *seel* < VLat. **sigellum* < Lat. *sigillum,* dim. of *signum,* sign, seal. See **sek^w-¹** in App.] **—seal'a·ble** *adj.*

seal² (sēl) *n.* **1.** Any of various aquatic carnivorous mammals of the families Phocidae and Otariidae, found chiefly in the Northern Hemisphere and having a sleek torpedo-shaped body and paddlelike flippers. **2.** The pelt or fur of one of these animals, esp. a fur seal. **3.** Leather made from the hide of one of these animals. ❖ *intr.v.* **sealed, seal·ing, seals** To hunt seals. [ME *sele* < OE *seolh.*]

sea lamprey *n.* A large marine lamprey (*Petromyzon marinus*) common in the Great Lakes and parasitic to freshwater fish.

sea-lane (sē′lān′) *n.* A permanent or commonly used sea route.

seal·ant (sē′lənt) *n.* A substance, such as sealing wax, used to seal a surface.

sea lavender *n.* Any of several salt-marsh plants of the genus *Limonium*, having small lavender or pinkish flowers.

sea legs *pl.n.* The ability to adjust one's balance to the motion of a ship, esp. in rough seas.

seal·er[1] (sē′lər) *n.* **1.** One that seals, as an undercoat of paint or varnish used to size a surface. **2.** An officer who inspects, tests, and certifies weights and measures.

seal·er[2] (sē′lər) *n.* One that is engaged in the hunting of seals.

sea lettuce *n.* Any of several green algae of the genus *Ulva*, having a leaflike thallus sometimes used in salads.

sea level *n.* The level of the ocean's surface, esp. the level halfway between mean high and low tide, used as a standard in reckoning land elevation or sea depths.

sea lily *n.* Any of various marine crinoids having a flowerlike body and a long stalk usu. anchored to the ocean floor.

seal·ing wax (sē′lĭng) *n.* A resinous preparation of shellac and turpentine, soft when heated but solidifying upon cooling, used to seal letters, batteries, or jars.

sea lion *n.* Any of several large-eared Pacific seals with a relatively long neck and limbs, esp. *Zalophus californianus*.

seal ring *n.* See **signet ring**.

seal·skin (sēl′skĭn′) *n.* **1.** The pelt or fur, esp. the underfur, of a seal. **2.** A garment made of sealskin.

Sea·ly·ham terrier (sē′lē-hăm′, -lē-əm) *n.* Any of a breed of terrier originating in Wales and having a wiry white coat, a long head, powerful jaws, and short legs. [After *Sealyham*, a town of southwest Wales.]

seam (sēm) *n.* **1a.** A line of junction formed by sewing together two pieces of material along their margins. **b.** A similar line, ridge, or groove made by fitting, joining, or lapping together two sections along their edges. **c.** A suture. **d.** A scar. **2.** A line across a surface, as a crack or wrinkle. **3.** A thin layer or stratum, as of coal or rock. ❖ *v.* **seamed, seam·ing, seams** —*tr.* **1.** To put together with or as if with a seam. **2.** To mark with a groove, wrinkle, scar, or other seamlike line. **3.** To form ridges in by purling. —*intr.* **1.** To become fissured or furrowed; crack open. **2.** To purl. [ME *seme* < OE *sēam*. See **syū-** in App.] —**seam′er** *n.*

sea-maid·en (sē′mād′n) also **sea-maid** (-mād′) *n. Mythology* A mermaid or sea nymph.

sea·man (sē′mən) *n.* **1.** A mariner or sailor. **2a.** A noncommissioned rank in the US Navy or Coast Guard that is above seaman apprentice and below petty officer. **b.** One who holds the rank of seaman, seaman apprentice, or seaman recruit.

Seaman, Elizabeth Cochrane Pen name **Nellie Bly.** 1867–1922. Amer. journalist known for her muckraking articles.

seaman apprentice *n.* A noncommissioned officer in the US Navy or Coast Guard ranking above seaman recruit and below seaman.

seaman recruit *n.* **1.** The lowest noncommissioned rank in the US Navy or Coast Guard. **2.** One who holds this rank.

sea·man·ship (sē′mən-shĭp′) *n.* Skill in navigating or handling a boat or ship.

sea mew *n.* Any of various European seagulls, esp. *Larus canus.*

seam·less (sēm′lĭs) *adj.* **1.** Having no seams. **2.** Perfectly consistent. —**seam′less·ly** *adv.* —**seam′less·ness** *n.*

sea·mount (sē′mount′) *n.* An underwater mountain rising from the ocean floor and having a submerged summit.

sea mouse *n.* Any of various large marine polychete worms of the genus *Aphrodite*, esp. *A. aculeata*, having a flattened elliptic body with overlapping scales covered by long hairs.

seam·ster (sēm′stər) *n.* A tailor. [ME *semester* < OE *sēamestre* < *sēam*, seam. See SEAM.]

seam·stress (sēm′strĭs) *n.* A woman who sews, esp. one who makes her living by sewing.

seam·y (sē′mē) *adj.* **-i·er, -i·est 1.** Sordid; base. **2.** Having, marked with, or showing a seam. —**seam′i·ness** *n.*

sé·ance (sā′äns′, -äns′) *n.* **1.** A meeting of people to receive spiritualistic messages. **2.** A meeting, session, or sitting, as of a learned or legislative body. [Fr., a sitting < OFr. *seoir*, to sit < Lat. *sedēre*. See **sed-** in App.]

sea nettle *n.* A stinging jellyfish, esp. a scyphozoan (*Dactylometra quinquecirrha*) of the tropical Atlantic.

sea oats *pl.n.* (*used with a sing. or pl. verb*) A tall coastal grass (*Uniola paniculata*) of southeast North America.

sea onion *n.* **1.** A Mediterranean plant (*Urginea maritima*) of the lily family, cultivated for its bulb that yields a powder used medicinally and as a rat poison. **2.** A small bulbous European plant (*Scilla verna*) having fragrant blue flowers.

sea otter *n.* A large marine otter (*Enhydra lutris*) of northern Pacific coastal waters, having soft, dark brown fur.

sea pen *n.* Any of various marine anthozoans of the families Stylatulidae and Funiculinidae, resembling and related to the sea feathers. [< its resemblance to a quill pen.]

sea·plane (sē′plān′) *n.* An airplane equipped with floats for landing on or taking off from a body of water.

sea·port (sē′pôrt′, -pōrt′) *n.* A harbor or town having facilities for seagoing ships.

sea power *n.* **1.** A nation having significant naval strength. **2.** Naval strength.

sea purse *n.* The egg case of skates, rays, or certain sharks.

sea·quake (sē′kwāk′) *n.* An earthquake originating under the sea floor. [SEA + (EARTH)QUAKE.]

sear[1] (sîr) *v.* **seared, sear·ing, sears** —*tr.* **1.** To char, scorch, or burn the surface of with or as if with a hot instrument. **2.** To cause to dry up and wither. —*intr.* To become withered or dried up. ❖ *n.* A condition, such as a scar, produced by searing. [ME *seren* < OE *sēarian*, to wither < *sēar*, withered.]

sear[2] (sîr) *n.* The catch in a gunlock that keeps the hammer half-cocked or fully cocked. [Prob. Fr. *serre*, something that grasps < OFr., lock < *serrer*, to grasp < VLat. *serrāre* < LLat. *serāre*, to bolt < Lat. *sera*, bar, bolt.]

sear[3] (sîr) *adj.* Variant of **sere**[1].

search (sûrch) *v.* **searched, search·ing, search·es** —*tr.* **1.** To make a thorough examination of; look over carefully in order to find something; explore. **2.** To make a careful examination or investigation of; probe. **3.** *Law* To make a thorough check of (a legal document); scrutinize. **4a.** To examine in order to find something lost or concealed: *searched my pockets for the keys.* **b.** To examine the person or personal effects of in order to find something lost or concealed: *searched the suspect.* **5.** To come to know; learn. —*intr.* To conduct a thorough investigation; seek: *searched for clues.* ❖ *n.* An act of searching. —**idiom: search me** *Slang* Used by a speaker to indicate lack of an answer to a question just asked. [ME *serchen* < AN *sercher*, var. of OFr. *cerchier* < Lat. *circāre*, to go around < Lat. *circus*, circle < Gk. *krikos, kirkos*.] —**search′a·ble** *adj.* —**search′er** *n.*

search engine *n.* **1.** A software program that that searches indexed websites and reports locations containing specified information. **2.** A website that provides a search engine for gathering information on websites.

search·ing (sûr′chĭng) *adj.* **1.** Examining closely or thoroughly; probing. **2.** Keenly observant. —**search′ing·ly** *adv.*

search·light (sûrch′līt′) *n.* **1a.** An apparatus containing a light source and a reflector for projecting a high-intensity beam of light. **b.** This beam of light. **2.** A flashlight.

search warrant *n.* A warrant giving legal authorization for a search.

sea robin *n.* Any of various marine fishes of the family Triglidae, esp. the gurnard, having a bony head and long pectoral fins with fingerlike rays that are used as feelers over the sea bottom.

sea room *n.* Unobstructed space at sea adequate for maneuvering a ship.

sea rover *n.* **1.** One that travels extensively by sea. **2.** A pirate. **3.** A pirate ship.

sea·scape (sē′skāp′) *n.* A view or picture of the sea.

sea scorpion *n.* See **sculpin** 2.

sea serpent *n.* A large snakelike marine animal often reported by mariners since antiquity but never positively identified.

sea·shell (sē′shĕl′) *n.* The calcareous shell of a marine mollusk or similar marine organism.

sea·shore (sē′shôr′, -shōr′) *n.* Land by the sea.

sea·sick·ness (sē′sĭk′nĭs) *n.* Motion sickness resulting from the pitching and rolling of a ship or boat in water, esp. at sea. —**sea′sick′** *adj.*

sea·side (sē′sīd′) *n.* The seashore.

sea slug *n.* Any of various highly colorful marine gastropods of the suborder Nudibranchia, lacking a shell and gills but having fringelike projections that serve as respiratory organs.

sea snake *n.* Any of various venomous tropical snakes of the family Hydrophidae that are adapted to living in the sea, esp. in the Pacific and Indian oceans.

sea·son (sē′zən) *n.* **1a.** One of the four natural divisions of the year, beginning astronomically at an equinox or solstice and characterized by specific meteorological or climatic conditions: spring, summer, fall, or winter in the Temperate Zones. **b.** The two divisions of the year, rainy and dry, in some tropical regions. **2.** A recurrent period characterized by certain occurrences, occupations, festivities, or crops: *the holiday season; tomato season.* **3.** A suitable, natural, or convenient time. **4.** A period of time. ❖ *v.* **-soned, -son·ing, -sons** —*tr.* **1.** To improve or enhance the flavor of (food), as by adding salt, spices, or herbs. **2.** To add zest, piquancy, or interest to. **3.** To treat or dry (lumber, for example) until ready for use; cure. **4.** To render competent through trial and experience. **5.** To accustom or inure; harden. **6.** To moderate; temper. —*intr.* To become usable, competent, or tempered. —**idioms: in season 1.** Available or ready, as for eating. **2.** Legally permitted to be caught or hunted during a specified period. **3.** At the right moment; opportunely. **4.** In heat. Used of animals. **out of season 1.** Not available, permitted, or ready to be eaten, caught, or hunted. **2.** Not at the right or proper moment; inopportunely. [ME < OFr. *seison* < Lat. *satiō, satiōn-*, sowing < *satus*, p. part. of *serere*, to plant. See **sē-** in App.]

sea·son·a·ble (sē′zə-nə-bəl) *adj.* **1.** In keeping with the time or the season. See Usage Note at **seasonal**. **2.** Occurring or performed at the proper time; timely. —**sea′son·a·bly** *adv.*

sea·son·al (sē′zə-nəl) *adj.* Of or dependent on a given season. —**sea′son·al′i·ty** (-zə-nǎl′ĭ-tē) *n.* —**sea′son·al·ly** *adv.*

sea lion

Elizabeth Seaman
photographed in 1890

ă	pat	oi	boy
ā	pay	ou	out
âr	care	ŏŏ	took
ä	father	ōō	boot
ĕ	pet	ŭ	cut
ē	be	ûr	urge
ĭ	pit	th	thin
ī	pie	th	this
îr	pier	hw	which
ŏ	pot	zh	vision
ō	toe	ə	about,
ô	paw		item

Stress marks:
′ (primary);
′ (secondary), as in
lexicon (lĕk′sĭ-kŏn′)

Seattle¹

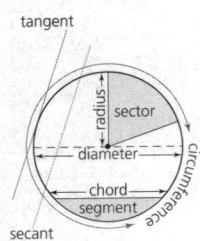

secant

tangent

radius

sector

diameter

circumference

chord

segment

secant

USAGE NOTE *Seasonal* applies to what depends on or is controlled by the season of the year: *a seasonal rise in employment.* *Seasonable* applies to what is appropriate to the season (*seasonable clothing*) or timely (*seasonable words*).

sea·son·er (sē′zə-nər) *n.* **1.** One that uses seasonings: *The cook is a heavy seasoner.* **2.** See **seasoning** 1.

sea·son·ing (sē′zə-nĭng) *n.* **1.** Something, such as a spice or herb, used to flavor food. **2.** The act or process by which something is seasoned.

season ticket *n.* A ticket valid for a specified period of time, as for a series of performances or games.

sea spider *n.* Any of various marine arthropods of the class Pycnogonida, having long legs and a relatively small body.

sea squirt *n.* Any of various sedentary tunicates of the class Ascidiacea, having a transparent sac-shaped body with two siphons. [< its squirting water when disturbed.]

sea star *n.* See **starfish**.

seat (sēt) *n.* **1.** Something, such as a chair or bench, that may be sat on. **2a.** A place in which one may sit. **b.** The right to occupy such a place or a ticket indicating this right. **3.** The part on which one rests in sitting: *a bicycle seat.* **4a.** The buttocks. **b.** The part of a garment that covers the buttocks. **5a.** A part serving as the base of something else. **b.** The surface or part on which another part sits or rests. **6a.** The place where something is located or based. **b.** A center of authority; a capital. See Syns at **center**. **7.** A place of abode or residence, esp. a large house that is part of an estate. **8.** Membership in an organization, such as a legislative body or stock exchange, that is obtained by appointment, election, or purchase. **9.** The manner of sitting on a horse. ❖ *v.* **seat·ed, seat·ing, seats** —*tr.* **1a.** To place in or on a seat. **b.** To cause or assist to sit down. **2.** To provide with a particular seat: *The usher seated me in the back row.* **3.** To have or provide seats for. **4.** To install in a position of authority or eminence. **5.** To fix firmly in place. —*intr.* To rest on or fit into another part. —*idiom.* **by the seat of (one's) pants** *Slang* **1.** In a manner based on intuition and experience rather than method. **2.** Without the use of instruments. [ME *sete*, prob. < ON *sæti*. See **sed-** in App.]

seat·back also **seat back** (sēt′băk′) *n.* The back of a chair or other type of seating.

seat belt *n.* A safety strap or harness designed to hold a person securely in a seat, as in a motor vehicle or aircraft.

seat·ing (sē′tĭng) *n.* **1a.** The act of providing or furnishing with a seat or seats. **b.** The seats so provided or furnished. **2.** The arrangement of seats in a room, auditorium, or banquet hall. **3.** The member or part on or within which another part is seated. **4.** Material for upholstering seats.

seat·mate (sēt′māt′) *n.* A person sitting next to another on a conveyance such as an airplane.

SEATO (sē′tō) *abbr.* Southeast Asia Treaty Organization

seat-of-the-pants (sēt′əv-thə-pănts′) *adj. Slang* **1.** Based on or using intuition and experience rather than a plan or method; improvised. **2.** Performed without using instruments.

sea·trout or **sea trout** (sē′trout′) *n.* **1.** Any of several marine fishes of the genus *Cynoscion*, esp. the weakfish. **2.** Any of several trouts or similar fishes that live in the sea but migrate to fresh water to spawn.

Se·at·tle¹ (sĭ-ăt′l) 1786?–1866. Native American leader of the Duwamish, Suquamish, and allied peoples, who befriended white settlers of the Pacific Northwest.

Se·at·tle² (sē-ăt′l) A city of W-central WA on Puget Sound and Lake Washington; settled in the 1850s. Pop. 563,374.

sea turtle *n.* Any of various large marine turtles of the families Cheloniidae and Dermochelyidae, including the leatherback, having large flippers and usu. living in warm waters.

seat·work (sēt′wûrk′) *n.* Lessons assigned to be done by students at their desks in the classroom.

sea urchin *n.* Any of various echinoderms of the class Echinoidea, having a soft body enclosed in a symmetrical round calcareous shell covered with long spines.

sea·wall also **sea wall** (sē′wôl′) *n.* An embankment to prevent erosion of a shoreline.

sea·ward (sē′wərd) *adv. & adj.* Toward or at the sea. ❖ *n.* A seaward place or direction. —**sea′wards** (-wərdz) *adv.*

sea·ware (sē′wâr′) *n.* Sea wrack used as fertilizer. [Poss. OE *sǣwār* : *sǣ,* sea + *wār,* seaweed.]

sea wasp *n.* Any of various jellyfishes of the class Cubozoa, having a venomous, sometimes fatal sting.

sea·wa·ter (sē′wô′tər, -wŏt′ər) *n.* The salt water in or coming from the sea or ocean.

sea·way (sē′wā′) *n.* **1.** A sea route. **2.** An inland waterway for ocean shipping. **3.** A stretch of water where waves are large enough to affect the handling of a vessel.

sea·weed (sē′wēd′) *n.* **1.** Any of numerous marine algae, such as a kelp or gulfweed. **2.** Any of various marine plants.

sea whip *n.* Any of various Atlantic gorgonian corals forming flexible colonies with few or no branches.

sea·wor·thy (sē′wûr′thē) *adj.* **-thi·er, -thi·est** Fit to traverse the seas. —**sea′wor′thi·ness** *n.*

sea wrack *n.* Material cast ashore, esp. seaweed.

se·ba·ceous (sĭ-bā′shəs) *adj.* **1.** Of, relating to, or resembling

---

fat or sebum; fatty. **2.** Secreting fat or sebum. [Lat. *sēbum,* tallow + –ACEOUS.]

se·bac·ic acid (sĭ-băs′ĭk, -bā′sĭk) *n.* A crystalline acid, COOH(CH₂)₈COOH, used in the manufacture of certain synthetic resins, fibers, and plasticizers. [< SEBACEOUS (it being orig. obtained from melted suet).]

Se·bas·to·pol (sə-băs′tə-pōl′) See Sevastopol.

SEbE *abbr.* southeast by east

sebi- or **sebo-** *pref.* Fat; sebum: *sebiferous.* [< Lat. *sēbum,* tallow.]

se·bif·er·ous (sĭ-bĭf′ər-əs) also **se·bip·a·rous** (-bĭp′-) *adj.* Producing or secreting fatty, oily, or waxy matter; sebaceous.

seb·or·rhe·a also **seb·or·rhoe·a** (sĕb′ə-rē′ə) *n.* A disease of the sebaceous glands characterized by excessive secretion of sebum or an alteration in its quality, resulting in an oily coating, crusts, or scales on the skin. —**seb′or·rhe′ic** *adj.*

SEbS *abbr.* southeast by south

se·bum (sē′bəm) *n.* The semifluid secretion of the sebaceous glands in the dermis of the skin, consisting chiefly of fat, keratin, and cellular material. [Lat. *sēbum,* tallow.]

sec¹ (sĕk) *adj.* Dry. Used of wines, esp. champagne. [Fr. < OFr. < Lat. *siccus.*]

sec² *abbr.* secant

SEC *abbr.* Securities and Exchange Commission

sec. *abbr.* **1.** second **2.** secretary **3.** section **4.** sector **5.** *Latin* secundum (according to) **6.** security

se·cant (sē′kănt′, -kənt) *n.* **1a.** A straight line intersecting a curve at two or more points. **b.** The straight line drawn from the center through one end of a circular arc and intersecting the tangent to the other end of the arc. **c.** The ratio of the length of this line to the length of the radius of the circle. **2.** The reciprocal of the cosine of an angle. [< Lat. *secāns, secant-,* pr. part. of *secāre,* to cut. See **sek-** in App.]

Sec·chi disk (sĕk′ē) *n.* A black and white disk used to gauge water clarity by measuring the depth at which it is no longer visible. [After Pietro Angelo Secchi (1818–78), Italian astronomer hired to test such a disk.]

sec·co (sĕk′ō) *n., pl.* **-cos** The art or an example of painting on dry plaster. ❖ *adj. Music* Of or being a kind of recitative in which the words are sung rapidly to minimal accompaniment, usu. just continuo. [Ital. < Lat. *siccus,* dry.]

se·cede (sĭ-sēd′) *intr.v.* **-ced·ed, -ced·ing, -cedes** To withdraw formally from membership in an organization, association, or alliance. [Lat. *sēcēdere,* to withdraw : *sē-,* apart; see **s(w)e-** in App. + *cēdere,* to go.]

se·cern (sĭ-sûrn′) *tr.v.* **-cerned, -cern·ing, -cerns** To discern as separate; discriminate. [Lat. *sēcernere,* to sever : *sē-,* apart; see **s(w)e-** in App. + *cernere,* to sever; see **krei-** in App.]

se·ces·sion (sĭ-sĕsh′ən) *n.* **1.** The act of seceding. **2.** often **Secession** The withdrawal of 11 Southern states from the Union in 1860–61, precipitating the US Civil War. [Lat. *sēcessiō, sēcessiōn-* < *sēcessus,* p. part. of *sēcēdere,* to secede. See SECEDE.] —**se·ces′sion·al** *adj.*

se·ces·sion·ism (sĭ-sĕsh′ə-nĭz′əm) *n.* The policy of those maintaining the right of secession. —**se·ces′sion·ist** *n.*

sech *abbr.* hyperbolic secant

Sech·ua·na (sĕch-wä′nə) *n.* Variant of Setswana.

Seck·el pear (sĕk′əl, sĭk′-) *n.* A variety of pear having small sweet reddish-brown fruit. [Perhaps < Seckle, a Pennsylvania farmer's name.]

se·clude (sĭ-klood′) *tr.v.* **-clud·ed, -clud·ing, -cludes 1.** To set or keep apart, as from social contact. **2.** To screen from view; make private. [ME *secluden,* to shut off < Lat. *sēclūdere : sē-,* apart; see **s(w)e-** in App. + *claudere,* to shut.]

se·clud·ed (sĭ-kloo′dĭd) *adj.* **1.** Removed or remote from others; solitary. **2.** Screened from view; sequestered. —**se·clud′ed·ly** *adv.* —**se·clud′ed·ness** *n.*

se·clu·sion (sĭ-kloo′zhən) *n.* **1a.** The act of secluding. **b.** The state of being secluded. **2.** A secluded place or abode. [Med.Lat. *sēclūsiō, sēclūsiōn-* < Lat. *sēclūsus,* p. part. of *sēclūdere,* to seclude. See SECLUDE.]

se·clu·sive (sĭ-kloo′sĭv, -zĭv) *adj.* Of, fond of, or seeking seclusion. —**se·clu′sive·ly** *adv.* —**se·clu′sive·ness** *n.*

sec·o·bar·bi·tal (sĕk′ō-bär′bĭ-tôl′, -tăl′) *n.* A white odorless barbiturate, C₁₂H₁₈N₂O₃, used in the form of its sodium salt as a sedative and hypnotic. [SECO(NDARY) + BARBITAL.]

sec·ond¹ (sĕk′ənd) *n.* **1a.** A unit of time equal to one sixtieth of a minute. **b.** The time needed for a cesium-133 atom to perform 9,192,631,770 complete oscillations. See table at **measurement**. **2.** A brief interval of time; a moment. **3.** *Mathematics* A unit of angular measure equal to one sixtieth of a minute. [ME *seconde* < OFr. < Med.Lat. (*pars minūta*) *secunda,* second (small part), fem. of Lat. *secundus,* second, following. See SECOND².]

sec·ond² (sĕk′ənd) *adj.* **1.** Coming next after the first in order, place, rank, time, or quality. **2a.** Repeating an initial instance. **b.** Reminiscent of one that is well known: *a second Waterloo.* **c.** Alternate; other: *every second year.* **3.** Inferior to another; subordinate. **4.** *Music* Being the second part, instrument, or voice in a harmonized composition. **5.** Having the second-highest ratio. Used of gears in a sequence. ❖ *n.* **1a.** The ordinal number matching the number 2 in a series. **b.** One of two equal parts. **2.** One that is next in order, place, time, or quality after the first. **3.** An article of merchandise of inferior quality. Often used in the plural. **4.** The official attendant of a contestant in a duel or boxing match. **5.** *Music* **a.** The interval between consecutive tones on the diatonic scale. **b.** A tone separated by this interval from another tone. **c.** A combination of two such tones in notation or in harmony. **d.** The second part, instrument, or voice in a harmonized composition. **6.** An utterance of endorsement, as to a parliamentary motion. **7.** The transmission gear or gear ratio used to produce forward speeds higher than those of first and lower than those of third in a motor vehicle. **8.** *Informal* A second serving of food. Often used in the plural. **9.** *Baseball* Second base. ❖ *tr.v.* **-ond•ed, -ond•ing, -onds 1.** To attend (a duelist or a boxer) as an aide or assistant. **2.** To promote or encourage; reinforce. **3.** To endorse (a motion or nomination) as a required preliminary to discussion or vote. **4.** (sĭ-kŏnd′) *Chiefly British* To transfer (a military officer, for example) temporarily. ❖ *adv.* **1.** In the second order, place, or rank. **2.** But for one other; save one: *my second worst tie.* [ME < OFr. < Lat. *secundus.* See **sek**^{w}**-**^{1} in App.]

sec•ond•ar•y (sĕk′ən-dĕr′ē) *adj.* **1a.** Of the second rank; not primary. **b.** Inferior. **c.** Minor; lesser. **2.** Derived from what is primary or original. **3.** Of, relating to, or being the shorter flight feathers projecting along the inner edge of a bird's wing. **4.** *Electricity* Having an induced current that is generated by an inductively coupled primary. Used of a circuit or coil. **5.** *Chemistry* Characterized or formed by replacement of two atoms or radicals within a molecule. Used of a compound. **6.** *Geology* Produced from another mineral by decay or alteration. **7.** Of or relating to a secondary school. **8.** Of or relating to a secondary color. **9.** *Botany* Of, relating to, or being growth or tissue caused by activity of the cambium and resulting in wider branches and stems: *secondary xylem.* ❖ *n., pl.* **-ies 1.** One that acts in an auxiliary, subordinate, or inferior capacity. **2.** One of the secondary flight feathers. **3.** *Electricity* A coil or circuit having an induced current. **4a.** *Astronomy* A celestial body that revolves around another; a satellite. **b.** The dimmer star of a binary star system. **5.** A secondary color. **6.** *Football* The defensive backfield. **—sec′ond•ar′i•ly** (-dâr′ə-lē) *adv.* **—sec′ond•ar′i•ness** *n.*

secondary accent *n.* See **secondary stress.**

secondary battery *n.* See **storage battery.**

secondary cell *n.* A rechargeable electric cell that converts chemical energy into electrical energy.

secondary color *n.* A color produced by mixing two primary colors in equal proportions.

secondary electron *n.* An electron produced in secondary emission.

secondary emission *n.* Emission of electrons from the surface of a substance due to bombardment by electrons or ions.

secondary school *n.* A school that is intermediate in level between elementary school and college and usu. offers general, technical, vocational, or college-preparatory curricula.

secondary sex characteristic *n.* Any of various anatomical, physiological, or behavioral characteristics, such as abundance of facial hair or breast development, that first appear in humans at puberty but have no direct reproductive function.

secondary stress *n.* **1.** The degree of stress weaker than a primary accent placed on a syllable in the pronunciation of a word. **2.** The mark (′) used to indicate secondary stress.

secondary wave *n.* An earthquake wave in which rock particles vibrate at right angles to the direction of wave travel.

second banana *n. Slang* **1.** One, such as an assistant or deputy, who is subordinate to another. **2.** One who serves as the straight man in a burlesque.

second base *n. Baseball* **1.** The base across the diamond from home plate, to be touched second by a runner. **2.** The position played by a second baseman.

second baseman *n. Baseball* The infielder who is positioned near and to the first-base side of second base.

second best *n.* One that is next to the best. ❖ *adv.* Next to the best. **—sec′ond-best′** (sĕk′ənd-bĕst′) *adj.*

second childhood *n.* Senility; dotage.

second class *n.* **1.** Travel accommodations ranking next below the highest or first class. **2.** Second-class mail.

sec•ond-class (sĕk′ənd-klăs′) *adj.* **1.** Of secondary status. **2.** Of or relating to travel accommodations ranking next below the highest or first class. **3.** Of a class of US and Canadian mail consisting of newspapers and periodicals. **—sec′ond class′** *adv.*

Second Coming *n. Christianity* The return of Jesus as judge for the Last Judgment.

second cousin *n.* **1.** A child of a first cousin of one's parent. **2.** A child of one's first cousin; a first cousin once removed.

sec•ond-de•gree burn (sĕk′ənd-dĭ-grē′) *n.* A burn that blisters the skin and is more severe than a first-degree burn.

Second Empire *n.* A heavily ornate style of furniture, architecture, and decoration developed in France in the mid-19th century. [After *Second Empire,* the reign of Napoleon III.]

second fiddle *n. Informal* **1.** A secondary role. **2.** One who plays a secondary role.

sec•ond-gen•er•a•tion (sĕk′ənd-jĕn′ə-rā′shən) *adj.* **1.** Of or relating to a person or persons whose parents are immigrants. **2.** Of or relating to a person or persons whose parents are citizens by birth and whose grandparents are immigrants. **3.** Of or relating to the second model or version, as of a product, in a series.

second growth *n.* Trees that cover an area after the removal of the original stand, as by cutting or fire.

sec•ond-guess (sĕk′ənd-gĕs′) *v.* **-guessed, -guess•ing, -guess•es** *—tr.* **1.** To criticize or correct after an outcome is known. **2a.** To outguess. **b.** To predict or anticipate. *—intr.* To criticize a decision after its outcome is known. **—sec′ond-guess′er** *n.*

sec•ond•hand (sĕk′ənd-hănd′) *adj.* **1.** Previously used by another; not new. **2.** Dealing in previously used merchandise. **3.** Obtained, derived, or borrowed from another; not original. ❖ *adv.* In an indirect manner; indirectly.

second hand[1] *n.* The hand on a clock or watch that marks the seconds.

second hand[2] *n.* An intermediary person or source.

second lieutenant *n.* **1.** The lowest commissioned rank in the US Army, Air Force, and Marine Corps. **2.** One who holds this rank.

sec•ond•ly (sĕk′ənd-lē) *adv.* In the second place; second.

second mortgage *n.* A mortgage taken out on property that already has one mortgage, with priority in settlement of claims given to the earlier mortgage.

second nature *n.* An acquired behavior or trait that is so long practiced as to seem innate.

se•con•do (sĭ-kōn′dō) *n., pl.* **-di** (-dē) The second part in a concert piece, esp. the lower part in a piano duet. [Ital. < Lat. *secundus,* second, following. See **sek**^{w}**-**^{1} in App.]

second person *n.* The grammatical category of forms that designate a speaker or writer referring to the person addressed. Examples of forms in the second person include English pronouns such as *you* and verb forms such as Spanish *hablas* "you speak."

sec•ond-rate (sĕk′ənd-rāt′) *adj.* Of inferior or mediocre quality or value. **—sec′ond-rate′ness** *n.* **—sec′ond-rat′er** *n.*

second sight *n.* Clairvoyance.

sec•ond-sto•ry man (sĕk′ənd-stôr′ē, -stōr′ē) *n. Informal* A burglar adept at entering through upstairs windows.

sec•ond-string (sĕk′ənd-strĭng′) *adj.* Relating to or being a substitute, as on a sports team. **—sec′ond-string′er** *n.*

second thought *n.* A reconsideration of a decision or opinion previously made.

second wind (wĭnd) *n.* **1.** The return of relative ease of breathing after the initial exhaustion that occurs during continued physical exertion. **2.** Restored energy or strength.

Second World also **second world** *n.* During the Cold War, the Communist nations of the world. **—Sec′ond-World′** *adj.*

Second World War *n.* World War II.

se•cre•cy (sē′krĭ-sē) *n., pl.* **-cies 1.** The quality or condition of being secret or hidden; concealment. **2.** The ability or habit of keeping secrets; closeness. [Alteration of ME *secretee* < *secret,* secret. See SECRET.]

se•cret (sē′krĭt) *adj.* **1.** Kept hidden from knowledge or view; concealed. **2.** Dependably discreet. **3.** Operating in a hidden or confidential manner. **4.** Not expressed; inward: *my secret thoughts.* **5.** Not frequented; secluded: *secret byways.* **6.** Known or shared only by the initiated: *secret rites.* **7.** Beyond ordinary understanding; mysterious. **8.** Containing information, the unauthorized disclosure of which poses a threat to national security. ❖ *n.* **1.** Something hidden from others or known only to oneself or to a few. **2.** Something beyond understanding or explanation; a mystery. **3.** A method or formula on which success is based. **4.** **Secret** A variable prayer formerly said after the Offertory in the Mass. [ME < OFr. < Lat. *sēcrētus* < p. part. of *sēcernere,* to set aside : *sē-,* apart; see **s(w)e-** in App. + *cernere,* to separate; see **krei-** in App.] **—se′cret•ly** *adv.*

se•cre•ta•gogue (sĭ-krē′tə-gôg′, -gŏg′) *n.* A hormone or another agent that causes or stimulates secretion.

sec•re•tar•i•at (sĕk′rĭ-târ′ē-ĭt) *n.* **1a.** The department administered by a governmental secretary, esp. for an international organization. **b.** The office occupied by such a department. **2.** The office or position of a governmental secretary. [Fr. *secrétariat* < OFr. < Med.Lat. *sēcrētāriātus* < *sēcrētārius,* secretary. See SECRETARY.]

sec•re•tar•y (sĕk′rĭ-tĕr′ē) *n., pl.* **-ies 1.** A person employed to handle correspondence, keep files, and do clerical work for another person or an organization. **2.** An officer who keeps records, takes minutes of the meetings, and answers correspondence, as for a company. **3.** An official who presides over an administrative department of state. **4.** A desk with a small bookcase on top. [ME *secretarie* < Med.Lat. *sēcrētārius,* confidential officer, clerk < Lat. *sēcrētus,* secret. See SECRET.] **—sec′re•tar′i•al** (-târ′ē-əl) *adj.*

secretary bird *n.* A large African bird of prey *(Sagittarius serpentarius)* with long legs and a crest of quills on the head.

sec•re•tar•y-gen•er•al (sĕk′rĭ-tĕr′ē-jĕn′ər-əl) *n., pl.* **sec•re•tar•ies-gen•er•al** (sĕk′rĭ-tĕr′ēz-) A principal executive officer, as in certain political parties or governmental bodies such as the United Nations.

se•crete[1] (sĭ-krēt′) *tr.v.* **-cret•ed, -cret•ing, -cret•es** To generate and separate (a substance) from cells or bodily fluids.

se•crete[2] (sĭ-krēt′) *tr.v.* **-cret•ed, -cret•ing, -cret•es 1.** To conceal in a hiding place; cache. See Syns at **hide**[1]. **2.** To steal secretly; filch. [Prob. alteration of obsolete *secret* < SECRET.]

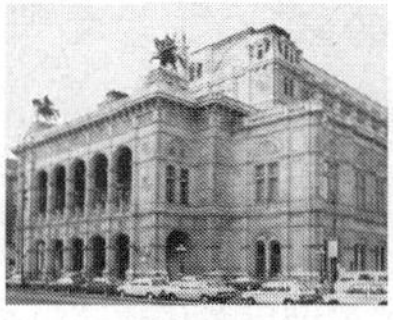

Second Empire
State Opera House, Vienna, Austria, 1861–69

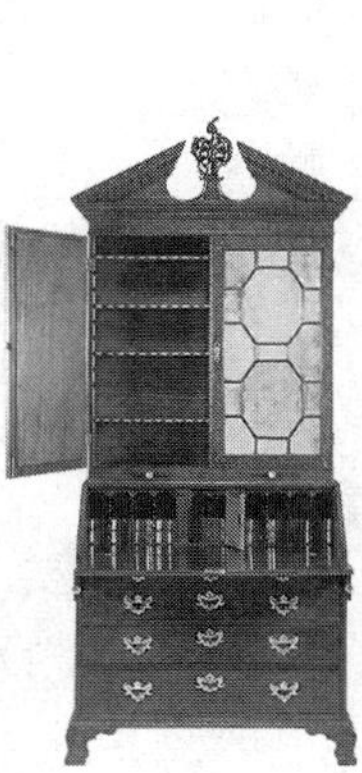

secretary
Chippendale style

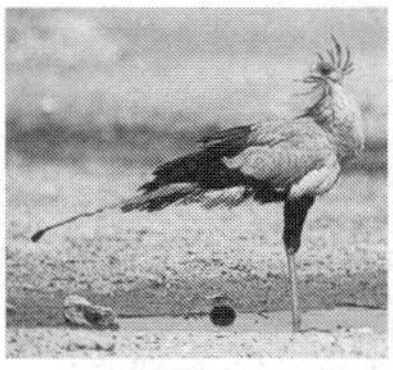

secretary bird
Sagittarius serpentarius

ă	pat	oi	boy
ā	pay	ou	out
âr	care	o͝o	took
ä	father	o͞o	boot
ĕ	pet	ŭ	cut
ē	be	ûr	urge
ĭ	pit	th	thin
ī	pie	*th*	this
îr	pier	hw	which
ŏ	pot	zh	vision
ō	toe	ə	about, item
ô	paw		

Stress marks:
′ (primary);
′ (secondary), as in
lexicon (lĕk′sĭ-kŏn′)

se•cre•tin (sĭ-krēt′n) *n.* A polypeptide hormone produced in the duodenum, esp. on contact with acid, to stimulate secretion of pancreatic juice. [SECRET(ION)¹ + –IN.]

se•cre•tion¹ (sĭ-krē′shən) *n.* **1.** The process of secreting a substance, esp. one that is not a waste, from the blood or cells. **2.** A substance, such as saliva, that is secreted. [Fr. *sécrétion* < OFr., separation < Lat. *sēcrētiō, sēcrētiōn-* < *sēcrētus*, p. part. of *sēcernere*, to set aside. See SECERN.] —**se•cre′tion•ar′y** (-shə-nĕr′ē) *adj.*

se•cre•tion² (sĭ-krē′shən) *n.* **1.** The act of concealing something in a hiding place. **2.** The act of stealing something secretly. [< SECRETE².]

se•cre•tive (sē′krĭ-tĭv, sĭ-krē′tĭv) *adj.* Having or marked by an inclination to secrecy; not open, forthright, or frank. —**se′cre•tive•ly** *adv.* —**se′cre•tive•ness** *n.*

se•cre•to•ry (sĭ-krē′tə-rē) *adj.* Relating to or performing secretion.

secret partner *n.* A partner whose participation in a business partnership is hidden from the public.

secret police *n.* A police force operating largely in secret and often using terror to suppress dissent and opposition.

secret service *n.* **1a.** Intelligence-gathering activities conducted secretly by a government agency. **b.** A government agency engaged in intelligence-gathering activities. **2. Secret Service** A branch of the US Treasury Department concerned esp. with protection of the President.

secret society *n.* An organization, such as a lodge, that requires its members to conceal certain activities, such as its rites of initiation, from outsiders.

sect (sĕkt) *n.* **1.** A group of people forming a distinct unit within a larger group by virtue of certain refinements or distinctions of belief or practice. **2.** A religious body, esp. one that has separated from a larger denomination. **3.** A faction united by common interests or beliefs. [ME *secte* < OFr. < Lat. *secta*, course, school of thought < fem. p. part. of *sequī*, to follow. See **sek^w-¹** in App.]

sect. *abbr.* **1.** section **2.** sectional

–sect *suff.* **1.** To cut; divide: *trisect.* **2.** Cut; divided: *pinnatisect.* [< Lat. *sectus*, p. part. of *secāre*, to cut. See **sek-** in App.]

sec•tar•i•an (sĕk-târ′ē-ən) *adj.* **1.** Of or characteristic of a sect. **2.** Adhering or confined to the dogmatic limits of a sect or denomination; partisan. **3.** Narrow-minded; parochial. ❖ *n.* **1.** A member of a sect. **2.** One marked by bigoted adherence to a factional viewpoint. —**sec•tar′i•an•ism** *n.*

sec•ta•ry (sĕk′tə-rē) *n., pl.* **-ries 1.** A sectarian. **2.** A dissenter from an established church, esp. a Protestant nonconformist. [Med.Lat. *sectārius* < Lat. *secta*, sect. See SECT.]

sec•tile (sĕk′təl, -tīl′) *adj.* Of or relating to a mineral that can be cut or severed smoothly by a knife but cannot withstand pulverization. [Lat. *sectilis* < *sectus*, p. part. of *secāre*, to cut. See **sek-** in App.] —**sec•til′i•ty** (-tĭl′ĭ-tē) *n.*

sec•tion (sĕk′shən) *n.* **1.** One of several components; a piece. **2.** A subdivision of a written work. **3.** *Law* A division of a statute or code. **4.** A distinct portion of a newspaper. **5.** A distinct area of a town, county, or country. **6.** A land unit equal to one square mile (2.59 square kilometers), 640 acres, or ⅟₃₆ of a township. **7.** The act or process of separating or cutting, esp. the surgical cutting or dividing of tissue. **8.** A thin slice, as of tissue, suitable for microscopic examination. **9.** A segment of a fruit, esp. a citrus fruit. **10.** Representation of a solid object as it would appear if cut by an intersecting plane, so that the internal structure is displayed. **11.** *Music* A group of instruments or voices in the same class considered as a division of a band, orchestra, or choir. **12.** A class or discussion group of students taking the same course. **13a.** A portion of railroad track maintained by a single crew. **b.** An area in a train's sleeping car containing an upper and lower berth. **14.** An army tactical unit smaller than a platoon and larger than a squad. **15.** A unit of vessels or aircraft within a division of armed forces. **16.** One of two or more vehicles, such as a bus or train, given the same route and schedule, often used to carry extra passengers. **17a.** The character (§) used in printing to mark the beginning of a section. **b.** This character used as the fourth in a series of reference marks for footnotes. ❖ *tr.v.* **-tioned, -tion•ing, -tions 1.** To separate or divide into parts. **2.** To cut or divide (tissue) surgically. **3.** To shade or crosshatch (part of a drawing) to indicate sections. [ME *seccioun* < OFr. < Lat. *sectiō, sectiōn-* < *sectus*, p. part. of *secāre*, to cut. See **sek-** in App.]

sec•tion•al (sĕk′shə-nəl) *adj.* **1.** Of or characteristic of a particular district. **2.** Composed of or divided into component sections. ❖ *n.* A piece of furniture made up of sections usable separately or together. —**sec′tion•al•ly** *adv.*

sec•tion•al•ism (sĕk′shə-nə-lĭz′əm) *n.* Excessive devotion to local interests and customs. —**sec′tion•al•ist** *n.*

sec•tion•al•ize (sĕk′shə-nə-līz′) *tr.v.* **-ized, -iz•ing, -iz•es** To divide into sections, esp. into geographic sections. —**sec′tion•al•i•za′tion** (-lĭ-zā′shən) *n.*

Section Eight *n.* **1.** A US Army discharge based on military assessment of psychological unfitness or character traits deemed undesirable. **2.** *Slang* A soldier given such a discharge. [After *Section VIII* of World War II US Army Regulation 615–360, which provided for such a discharge.]

section gang *n.* A work crew assigned to a railroad section.

section hand *n.* A laborer assigned to a section gang.

sec•tor (sĕk′tər, -tôr′) *n.* **1.** *Mathematics* **a.** The portion of a circle bounded by two radii and the included arc. **b.** A measuring instrument consisting of two graduated arms hinged together at one end. **2a.** A division of a defensive position for which one military unit is responsible. **b.** A division of an offensive military position. **3.** A part or division, as of a city. **4.** *Computer Science* A portion of a magnetic storage device making up the smallest addressable unit of information. ❖ *tr.v.* **-tored, -tor•ing, -tors** To divide (something) in sectors. [LLat. < Lat., cutter < *sectus*, p. part. of *secāre*, to cut. See **sek-** in App.] —**sec•to′ri•al** (-tôr′ē-əl, -tōr′-) *adj.*

sec•u•lar (sĕk′yə-lər) *adj.* **1.** Worldly rather than spiritual. **2.** Not specifically relating to religion or to a religious body. **3.** Relating to or advocating secularism. **4.** Not bound by monastic restrictions, esp. not belonging to a religious order. Used of the clergy. **5.** Occurring or observed once in an age or century. **6.** Lasting from century to century. ❖ *n.* **1.** A member of the secular clergy. **2.** A layperson. [ME < OFr. *seculer* < LLat. *saeculāris* < Lat., of an age < *saeculum*, generation, age.] —**sec′u•lar•ly** *adv.*

secular humanism *n.* **1.** An outlook or philosophy that advocates human rather than religious values. **2.** Secularism. —**secular humanist** *adj.* & *n.*

sec•u•lar•ism (sĕk′yə-lə-rĭz′əm) *n.* **1.** Religious skepticism or indifference. **2.** The view that religious considerations should be excluded from civil affairs or public education. —**sec′u•lar•ist** *n.* —**sec′u•lar•is′tic** *adj.*

sec•u•lar•i•ty (sĕk′yə-lăr′ĭ-tē) *n., pl.* **-ties 1.** The condition or quality of being secular. **2.** Something secular.

sec•u•lar•ize (sĕk′yə-lə-rīz′) *tr.v.* **-ized, -iz•ing, -iz•es 1.** To transfer from ecclesiastical or religious to civil or lay use or ownership. **2.** To draw away from religious orientation; make worldly. **3.** To lift the monastic restrictions from (a member of the clergy). —**sec′u•lar•i•za′tion** (-lər-ĭ-zā′shən) *n.*

se•cund (sē′kŭnd′, sĭ-kŭnd′) *adj. Biology* Arranged on or turned to one side of an axis. [Lat. *secundus*, following. See **sek^w-¹** in App.]

se•cure (sĭ-kyoŏr′) *adj.* **-cur•er, -cur•est 1.** Free from danger or attack: *a secure fortress.* **2.** Free from risk of loss; safe. **3.** Free from the risk of being intercepted or listened to by unauthorized persons. **4.** Free from fear, anxiety, or doubt. **5a.** Not likely to fail or give way; stable: *a secure stepladder.* **b.** Firmly fastened: *a secure lock.* **6.** Reliable; dependable: *secure investments.* **7.** Assured; certain. **8.** *Archaic* Careless or overconfident. ❖ *tr.v.* **-cured, -cur•ing, -cures 1.** To guard from danger or risk of loss. **2.** To make firm or tight; fasten. **3.** To make certain; ensure. **4a.** To guarantee payment of (a loan, for example). **b.** To guarantee payment to (a creditor). **5.** To get possession of; acquire. **6.** To capture or confine. **7.** To bring about; effect. **8.** To protect or ensure the privacy or secrecy of (a telephone line, for example). [Lat. *sēcūrus* : *sē-*, without; see **s(w)e-** in App. + *cūra*, care; see CURE.] —**se•cur′a•ble** *adj.* —**se•cure′ly** *adv.* —**se•cure′ment** *n.* —**se•cure′ness** *n.* —**se•cur′er** *n.*

Se•cu•ri•ties and Exchange Commission (sĭ-kyoŏr′ĭ-tēz) *n.* A US government agency that supervises the exchange of securities so as to protect investors against malpractice.

se•cu•ri•ty (sĭ-kyoŏr′ĭ-tē) *n., pl.* **-ties 1.** Freedom from risk or danger; safety. **2.** Freedom from doubt, anxiety, or fear; confidence. **3.** Something that gives or assures safety, as: **a.** A group or department of private guards. **b.** Measures adopted by a government to prevent espionage, sabotage, or attack. **c.** Measures adopted, as by a business or homeowner, to prevent a crime such as burglary or assault. **d.** Measures adopted to prevent escape. **4.** Something deposited or given as assurance of the fulfillment of an obligation; a pledge. **5.** One who undertakes to fulfill the obligation of another; a surety. **6.** A document indicating ownership or creditorship; a stock certificate or bond. [ME *securite* < OFr. < Lat. *sēcūritās* < *sēcūrus*, secure. See SECURE.]

security blanket *n.* **1.** A blanket carried by a child to reduce anxiety. **2.** *Informal* Something that dispels anxiety.

Security Council *n.* The permanent peacekeeping organ of the United Nations, composed of five permanent members and ten elected members.

security guard *n.* A person hired by a private organization to guard a physical plant and maintain order.

secy. *abbr.* secretary

se•dan (sĭ-dăn′) *n.* **1.** A closed automobile having two or four doors and a front and rear seat. **2.** A portable enclosed chair for one person, having poles in the front and rear and carried by two other people. [?]

Se•dan (sĭ-dăn′, sə-dän′) A town of NE France on the Meuse R. near the Belgian border; site of the defeat and surrender of Napoleon III (Sep. 2, 1870) in the Franco-Prussian War. Pop. 23,477.

se•date¹ (sĭ-dāt′) *adj.* Serenely deliberate, composed, and dignified. [Lat. *sēdātus*, p. part. of *sēdāre*, to settle. See **sed-** in App.] —**se•date′ly** *adv.* —**se•date′ness** *n.*

se•date² (sĭ-dāt′) *tr.v.* **-dat•ed, -dat•ing, -dates** To administer a sedative to; calm or relieve by means of sedation.

se•da•tion (sĭ-dā′shən) *n.* **1.** Reduction of anxiety, stress, irritability, or excitement by administration of a sedative agent or drug. **2.** The state or condition induced by a sedative. [ME *seda-*

cioun < OFr. *sedation* < Lat. *sēdātiō, sēdātiōn-* < *sēdātus*, p. part. of *sēdāre*, to calm. See SEDATE[1].]

sed•a•tive (sĕd′ə-tĭv) *adj.* Having a soothing, calming, or tranquilizing effect; reducing or relieving anxiety, stress, irritability, or excitement. ❖ *n.* A sedative agent or drug. [ME < OFr. *sedatif* < Med.Lat. *sēdātīvus* < Lat. *sēdātus*, p. part. of *sēdāre*, to calm. See SEDATE[1].]

sed•en•tar•y (sĕd′n-tĕr′ē) *adj.* **1.** Characterized by or requiring much sitting. **2.** Accustomed to sitting or to taking little exercise. **3.** Remaining or living in one area, as certain birds; not migratory. **4.** Attached to a surface and not moving freely, as a barnacle. [Fr. *sédentaire* < OFr. < Lat. *sedentārius* < *sedēns, sedent-*, pr. part. of *sedēre*, to sit. See **sed-** in App.] **—sed′en•tar′i•ly** (-târ′ə-lē) *adv.* **—sed′en•tar′i•ness** *n.*

Se•der (sā′dər) *n., pl.* **Se•ders** or **Se•dar•im** (sĭ-där′ĭm, sĕ-dä-rĭm′) *Judaism* The feast commemorating the exodus of the Jews from Egypt, celebrated on the first night or on the first two nights of Passover. [Heb. *sēder*, arrangement, Seder.]

sedge (sĕj) *n.* Any of numerous grasslike plants of the family Cyperaceae, having solid stems and leaves in three vertical rows. [ME *segge* < OE *secg*. See **sek-** in App.]

Sedge•moor (sĕj′mo͝or′, -môr′, -mōr′) A marshy tract in SW England where the forces of James II defeated the Duke of Monmouth (Jun. 6, 1685).

se•di•le (sĭ-dī′lē) *n., pl.* **se•di•lia** (-dĭl′yə, -dĭl′ē-ə) *Ecclesiastical* One of a set of seats, usu. three, for the use of the presiding clergy, traditionally placed on the epistle side of the choir near the altar. [Lat. *sedīle*, seat < *sedēre*, to sit. See **sed-** in App.]

sed•i•ment (sĕd′ə-mənt) *n.* **1.** Material that settles to the bottom of a liquid; lees. **2.** Solid fragments of inorganic or organic material that come from the weathering of rock and are carried and deposited by wind, water, or ice. [Lat. *sedimentum*, act of settling < *sedēre*, to sit, settle. See **sed-** in App.]

sed•i•men•ta•ry (sĕd′ə-mĕn′tə-rē, -mĕn′trē) also **sed•i•men•tal** (-mĕn′tl) *adj.* **1.** Of, containing, resembling, or derived from sediment. **2.** *Geology* Of or relating to rocks formed by the deposition of sediment.

sed•i•men•ta•tion (sĕd′ə-mən-tā′shən, -mĕn-) *n.* The act or process of depositing sediment.

sed•i•men•tol•o•gy (sĕd′ə-mən-tŏl′ə-jē, -mĕn-) *n.* The geologic study of sedimentary rock. **—sed′i•men′to•log′ic** (-mĕn′tl-ŏj′ĭk), **sed′i•men′to•log′i•cal** (-ĭ-kəl) *adj.* **—sed′i•men•tol′o•gist** *n.*

se•di•tion (sĭ-dĭsh′ən) *n.* **1.** Conduct or language inciting rebellion against the authority of a state. **2.** Insurrection; rebellion. [Ult. < Lat. *sēditiō, sēditiōn-*, party strife : *sēd-, sē-*, apart; see **s(w)e-** in App. + *itiō*, act of going (< *itus*, p. part. of *īre*, to go; see **ei-** in App.).] **—se•di′tion•ist** *n.*

se•di•tious (sĭ-dĭsh′əs) *adj.* **1.** Of or having the nature of sedition. **2.** Given to or guilty of engaging in or promoting sedition. **—se•di′tious•ly** *adv.* **—se•di′tious•ness** *n.*

se•duce (sĭ-do͞os′, -dyo͞os′) *tr.v.* **-duced, -duc•ing, -duc•es 1.** To lead away from duty, accepted principles, or proper conduct. **2.** To induce to engage in sex. **3a.** To entice or beguile into a desired state or position. **b.** To win over; attract. [ME *seduisen* < OFr. *seduire, seduis-*, alteration (influenced by Med.Lat. *sēdūcere*, to lead astray) of *suduire*, to seduce < Lat. *subdūcere*, to withdraw : *sub-*, sub- + *dūcere*, to lead; see **deuk-** in App.] **—se•duce′a•ble, se•duc′i•ble** *adj.* **—se•duc′er** *n.*

se•duce•ment (sĭ-do͞os′mənt, -dyo͞os′-) *n.* **1.** Seduction. **2.** Something that seduces.

se•duc•tion (sĭ-dŭk′shən) *n.* **1a.** The act of seducing. **b.** The condition of being seduced. **2.** Something that seduces or has the qualities to seduce; an enticement. [Lat. *sēductiō, sēductiōn-* < *sēductus*, p. part. of *sēdūcere*, to lead astray : *sē-*, apart; see **s(w)e-** in App. + *dūcere*, to lead; see **deuk-** in App.]

se•duc•tive (sĭ-dŭk′tĭv) *adj.* Tending to seduce. **—se•duc′tive•ly** *adv.* **—se•duc′tive•ness** *n.*

se•duc•tress (sĭ-dŭk′trĭs) *n.* A woman who seduces. See Usage Note at **–ess.**

sed•u•lous (sĕj′ə-ləs) *adj.* Persevering and constant in effort or application; assiduous. [< Lat. *sēdulus* < *sēdulō*, zealously : *sē*, without; see **s(w)e-** in App. + *dolō*, ablative of *dolus*, trickery (prob. < Gk. *dolos*, cunning; see **del-**[2] in App.).] **—sed′u•lous•ness, se•du′li•ty** (sĭ-do͞o′lĭ-tē, -dyo͞o′-) *n.*

se•dum (sē′dəm) *n.* Any of numerous plants of the genus *Sedum*, having thick fleshy leaves. [ME *cedum* < Lat. *sedum*, houseleek.]

see[1] (sē) *v.* **saw** (sô), **seen** (sēn), **see•ing, sees** *—tr.* **1.** To perceive with the eye. **2a.** To apprehend as if with the eye. **b.** To detect by means analogous to use of the eye. **3.** To have a mental image of; visualize. **4.** To understand; comprehend. **5.** To consider to be; regard. **6.** To believe possible; imagine. **7.** To foresee. **8.** To know through firsthand experience; undergo. **9.** To give rise to or be characterized by: *The nineties will see much change.* **10.** To find out; ascertain. **11.** To refer to; read. **12.** To take note of; recognize: *sees only the good aspects.* **13.** To meet or be in the company of. **14.** To share the companionship of often or regularly. **15a.** To visit socially; call on. **b.** To visit for consultation. **16.** To admit or receive, as for consultation or a social visit: *The doctor will see you now.* **17.** To attend; view. **18.** To escort; attend. **19.** To make sure; take care. **20.** *Games* **a.** To meet (a bet) in card games. **b.** To meet the bet of (another player). *—intr.* **1.** To have the power to perceive with or as if with the eye. **2.** To understand; comprehend. **3.** To consider. **4a.** To go and look: *She had to see for herself.* **b.** To ascertain; find out. **5.** To have foresight. **6.** To take note. ***—phrasal verbs:* see about 1.** To attend to. **2.** To investigate. **see after** To take care of. **see off** To take leave of (someone). **see out 1.** To escort (a guest) to the door. **2.** To work on (a project) until completion. **see through 1.** To understand the true character or nature of. **2.** To provide support or cooperation to (a person) throughout a period of time. **3.** To work on (a project) until completion. **see to** To attend to. ***—idioms:* see red** *Informal* To be extremely angry. **see you later** *Informal* Used to express goodbye. [ME *sen* < OE *sēon*. See **sekʷ-**[2] in App.]

SYNONYMS *see, behold, note, notice, espy, descry, observe, view, perceive, discern* These verbs refer to being or becoming visually or mentally aware of something. *See*, the most general, can mean merely to use the faculty of sight but more often implies recognition, understanding, or appreciation: *"If I have seen further (than . . . Descartes) it is by standing upon the shoulders of Giants"* (Isaac Newton). *Behold* implies gazing at or looking intently upon what is seen: *"My heart leaps up when I behold/A rainbow in the sky"* (William Wordsworth). *Note* and *notice* suggest close, detailed observation, and *note* in particular implies making a careful, systematic mental record: *Be careful to note where the road turns left. I notice that you're out of sorts. Espy* and *descry* both stress acuteness of sight that permits the detection of something distant or obscure: *"espied the misspelled Latin word in* [the] *letter"* (Los Angeles Times); *"the lighthouse, which can be descried from a distance"* (Michael Strauss). *Observe* emphasizes careful, closely directed attention: *"I saw the pots . . . and observed that they did not crack at all"* (Daniel Defoe). *View* usually suggests examination with a particular purpose in mind or in a special way: *The medical examiner viewed the victim's body. Perceive* and *discern* both imply not only visual recognition but also mental comprehension; *perceive* is especially associated with insight, and *discern*, with the ability to distinguish, discriminate, and make judgments: *"I plainly perceive* [that] *some objections remain"* (Edmund Burke). *"Your sense of humor would discern the hollowness beneath all the pomp and ceremony"* (Edna Ferber).

see[2] (sē) *n.* **1.** The official seat, center of authority, jurisdiction, or office of a bishop. **2.** *Obsolete* A cathedra. [ME < OFr. *se* < VLat. **sedem* < Lat. *sēdēs*, seat. See **sed-** in App.]

seed (sēd) *n., pl.* **seeds** or **seed 1.** A ripened plant ovule containing an embryo. **2.** A propagative part of a plant, as a tuber or spore. **3.** Seeds considered as a group. **4.** The seed-bearing stage of a plant. **5.** Something resembling a seed, as a bubble in a piece of glass. **6a.** A small amount of material used to initiate a chemical reaction. **b.** A small crystal added to a solution to initiate crystallization. **7.** A source or beginning; a germ. **8.** *Medicine* A pellet filled with a radioactive isotope that is implanted at the site of a cancerous tumor to provide localized administration of radiation. **9.** Offspring; progeny. **10.** Family stock; ancestry. **11.** Sperm; semen. **12.** A seed oyster or oysters; spat. **13.** *Sports* A player who has been seeded for a tournament, often at a given rank. ❖ *v.* **seed•ed, seed•ing, seeds** *—tr.* **1.** To plant seeds in (land, for example); sow. **2.** To plant in soil. **3.** To remove the seeds from (fruit). **4.** *Medicine* To furnish with something that grows or stimulates growth or development. **5.** *Meteorology* To sprinkle (a cloud) with particles, as of silver iodide, in order to disperse it or produce rain. **6.** *Sports* **a.** To arrange (the drawing for tournament positions) so that more skilled contestants meet in later rounds. **b.** To rank (a contestant) in this way. **7.** To help (a business, for example) in its early development. *—intr.* **1.** To sow seed. **2.** To go to seed. ❖ *adj.* **1.** Set aside for planting a new crop. **2.** Intended to help in early stages. ***—idiom:* go** (or **run**) **to seed 1.** To pass into the seed-bearing stage. **2.** To become weak or devitalized; deteriorate. [ME < OE *sǣd, sēd*. See **sē-** in App.]

seed•bed (sēd′bĕd′) *n.* **1.** A bed of soil for planting seeds. **2.** An area or source of growth or gradual manifestation.

seed cake *n.* A sweet cake or cookie containing aromatic seeds.

seed coat *n.* The often thick or hard outer coat of a seed.

seed•er (sē′dər) *n.* **1.** A machine or an implement used for planting seeds. **2.** A machine or implement used to remove the seeds from fruit. **3.** One that seeds clouds.

seed leaf *n.* See **cotyledon** 1.

seed•ling (sēd′lĭng) *n.* A young plant grown from a seed.

seed money *n.* Money used to set up a new business or enterprise.

seed oyster *n.* A young oyster, esp. one suitable for transplanting to another bed; a spat.

seed pearl *n.* A very small, often imperfect pearl.

seed plant *n.* A seed-bearing plant.

seed•pod (sēd′pŏd′) *n.* See **pod**[1] 1.

seed stock *n.* **1.** A supply of seed for planting. **2.** A source of new entities: *a seed stock of salmon in the river.*

seed•time (sēd′tīm′) *n.* **1.** A time for planting seeds. **2.** A time of new growth or development.

seed•y (sē′dē) *adj.* **-i•er, -i•est 1.** Having many seeds. **2.** Resembling seeds or a seed. **3.** Worn and shabby; unkempt. **4.** Tired or sick; unwell. **5.** Somewhat disreputable; squalid: *a seedy hotel.*

ă	pat	oi	boy
ā	pay	ou	out
âr	care	o͝o	took
ä	father	o͞o	boot
ĕ	pet	ŭ	cut
ē	be	ûr	urge
ĭ	pit	th	thin
ī	pie	*th*	this
îr	pier	hw	which
ŏ	pot	zh	vision
ō	toe	ə	about, item
ô	paw		

Stress marks:
′ (primary);
′ (secondary), as in
lexicon (lĕk′sĭ-kŏn′)

—seed′i·ly adv. —seed′i·ness n.

See·ger (sē′gər), **Peter** (**"Pete"**) b. 1919. Amer. folk singer who helped revive folk music in the 1950s and 1960s.

see·ing (sē′ĭng) conj. Inasmuch as; in view of the fact.

Seeing Eye A trademark used for a dog trained to lead a blind or visually impaired person.

seek (sēk) v. **sought** (sôt), **seek·ing, seeks** —tr. **1.** To try to locate or discover; search for. **2.** To endeavor to obtain or reach: *seek a college education.* **3.** To go to or toward: *Water seeks its own level.* **4.** To inquire for; request: *sought directions.* **5.** To try; endeavor: *seek to do good.* **6.** Obsolete To explore. —intr. To make a search or investigation. [ME *sechen, seken* < OE *sēcan.*]

seek·er (sē′kər) n. **1.** One that seeks: *a seeker of the truth.* **2.** A device used in a moving object, esp. a missile, that locates a target by detecting light, heat, or other radiation.

seel (sēl) tr.v. **seeled, seel·ing, seels** To stitch closed the eyes of (a falcon). [ME *silen* < OFr. *cillier* < Med.Lat. *ciliāre* < Lat. *cilium,* lower eyelid. See **kel-** in App.]

seem (sēm) intr.v. **seemed, seem·ing, seems 1.** To give the impression of being; appear: *The child seems healthy, but the doctor is concerned.* **2.** To appear to one's own opinion or mind: *I can't seem to get it right.* **3.** To appear to be true, probable, or evident: *It seems that it will rain.* **4.** To appear to exist: *There seems no reason to stop.* [ME *semen* < ON *sœma,* to conform to < *sœmr,* fitting. See **sem-¹** in App.]

seem·ing (sē′mĭng) adj. Apparent; ostensible. ❖ n. Outward appearance; semblance. —**seem′ing·ly** adv. —**seem′ing·ness** n.

seem·ly (sēm′lē) adj. **-li·er, -li·est 1.** Conforming to standards of conduct and good taste; suitable. **2.** Of pleasing appearance; handsome. [ME *semely* < ON *sœmiligr* < *sœmr,* fitting. See **sem-¹** in App.] —**seem′li·ness** n. —**seem′ly** adv.

seen (sēn) v. Past participle of **see¹.**

seep (sēp) intr.v. **seeped, seep·ing, seeps 1.** To pass slowly through small openings or pores; ooze. **2.** To enter, depart, or become diffused gradually. ❖ n. **1.** A spot where water or petroleum trickles out of the ground to form a pool. Seepage. [Alteration of dialectal *sipe.*]

seep·age (sē′pĭj) n. **1.** The act or process of seeping. **2.** A quantity of something that has seeped.

seer (sîr) n. **1.** (sē′ər) One that sees: *an inveterate seer of sights.* **2.** A clairvoyant. **3.** A prophet.

seer·ess (sîr′ĭs) n. A woman prophet or clairvoyant. See Usage Note at **-ess.**

seer·suck·er (sîr′sŭk′ər) n. A light thin fabric, usu. cotton or rayon, with a crinkled surface and a usu. striped pattern. [Hindi *sīrsakar* < Pers. *shīroshakar* : *shīr,* milk (< MPers.) + *o,* and (< MPers. *u* < OPers. *utā*) + *shakar,* sugar (< Skt. *śarkarā* < the resemblance of its smooth and rough stripes to the smooth surface of milk and bumpy texture of sugar).]

see·saw (sē′sô′) n. **1.** A long plank balanced on a central fulcrum so that with a person riding on each end, one end goes up as the other goes down. **2.** The act or game of riding a seesaw. **3.** A back-and-forth or up-and-down movement, as of the lead in a contest. ❖ intr.v. **-sawed, -saw·ing, -saws 1.** To play on a seesaw. **2.** To move back and forth or up and down. [Reduplication of SAW¹.]

seethe (sēth) intr.v. **seethed, seeth·ing, seethes 1.** To churn and foam as if boiling. **2a.** To be in a state of turmoil or ferment. **b.** To be violently excited or agitated. See Syns at **boil¹. 3.** Archaic To come to a boil. [ME *sethen,* to boil < OE *sēothan.*] —**seethe** n.

see-through (sē′thrōō′) adj. Transparent.

Se·fe·ri·a·des (sĕ-fĕ′rē-ä′thēs), **Giorgos Stylianou** Pen name George Seferis. 1900–71. Greek poet who won the 1963 Nobel Prize for literature.

Se·gal (sē′gəl), **George** 1924–2000. Amer. sculptor known for his realistic plaster casts of people in ordinary situations.

Se·ges·ta (sĭ-jĕs′tə, sĕ-jĕs′tä) An ancient city of NW Sicily; a Carthaginian dependency after c. 400 B.C.

seg·ment (sĕg′mənt) n. **1.** Any of the parts into which something can be divided. **2.** Mathematics **a.** The portion of a line between any two points on the line. **b.** The area bounded by a chord and the arc of a curve subtended by the chord. **c.** The portion of a sphere cut off by two parallel planes. **3.** Biology A clearly differentiated subdivision of an organism or part, such as a metamere. ❖ tr. & intr.v. **-ment·ed, -ment·ing, -ments** To divide or become divided into segments. [Lat. *segmentum < secāre,* to cut. See **sek-** in App.] —**seg′men·tar′y** (-mən-tĕr′ē) adj.

seg·men·tal (sĕg-mĕn′tl) adj. Of or relating to segments. **2.** Parted or arranged in segments. —**seg·men′tal·ly** adv.

seg·men·ta·tion (sĕg′mən-tā′shən, -mĕn-) n. **1.** Division into segments. **2.** Embryology See **cleavage** 4a.

segmentation cavity n. See **blastocoel.**

se·gno (sā′nyō) n., pl. **-gnos** Music A notational sign, esp. the sign marking the beginning or the end of a repeated section. [Ital. < Lat. *signum,* sign. See **sek^w-¹** in App.]

se·go (sē′gō) n., pl. **-gos** The succulent edible bulb of the sego lily. [Southern Paiute *sigho'o.*]

sego lily n. A western North American plant (*Calochortus nuttallii*) having showy, variously colored flowers.

Se·go·vi·a (sĭ-gō′vē-ə, sĕ-gō′vyä) A city of central Spain NNW of Madrid; site of a Roman aqueduct (1st or 2nd cent. A.D.) that is still in use. Pop. 53,005.

Pete Seeger

sego lily
Calochortus nuttallii

seine

Segovia, Andrés 1893?–1987. Spanish guitarist who spurred interest in the guitar as an instrument for classical music.

seg·re·ga·ble (sĕg′rĭ-gə-bəl) adj. **1.** That can be segregated. **2.** Genetics Able to undergo segregation.

seg·re·gant (sĕg′rĭ-gənt) Genetics adj. Differing from either parent as a result of segregation. ❖ n. A segregant type or organism.

seg·re·gate (sĕg′rĭ-gāt′) v. **-gat·ed, -gat·ing, -gates** —tr. **1.** To separate or isolate from others or from a main body or group. **2.** To impose the separation of (a race or class) from society. —intr. **1.** To become separated from a main body or mass. **2.** To practice a policy of racial segregation. **3.** Genetics To undergo genetic segregation. ❖ adj. (-gĭt, -gāt′) Separated; isolated. ❖ n. (-gĭt, -gāt′) **1.** One that is or has been segregated. **2.** Genetics See **segregant.** [Lat. *sēgregāre, sēgregāt-* : *sē-,* apart; see **s(w)e-** in App. + *grex, greg-,* flock.] —**seg′re·ga′tive** adj. —**seg′re·ga′tor** n.

seg·re·ga·tion (sĕg′rĭ-gā′shən) n. **1.** The act or process of segregating or the condition of being segregated. **2.** The policy or practice of separating people of different races, classes, or ethnic groups, as in schools or housing, esp. as a form of discrimination. **3.** Genetics The separation of paired alleles or homologous chromosomes, esp. during meiosis.

seg·re·ga·tion·ist (sĕg′rĭ-gā′shə-nĭst) n. One that advocates or practices racial segregation. —**seg′re·ga′tion·ist** adj.

se·gue (sĕg′wā′, sā′gwā′) intr.v. **-gued, -gue·ing, -gues 1.** Music To make a transition directly from one section or theme to another. **2.** To move smoothly and unhesitatingly from one state, condition, situation, or element to another. ❖ n. An act or instance of segueing. [< Ital., there follows, third-pers. sing. pr. t. of *seguire,* to follow < VLat. **sequere* < Lat. *sequī.* See **sek^w-¹** in App.]

se·gui·dil·la (sĕg′ə-dē′yə, -dēl′yə, sā′gə-, sĕ′gē-thē′lyä) n. **1.** A Spanish stanza form of four to seven lines. **2a.** A lively Spanish dance. **b.** The music for this dance, in triple meter. [Sp., dim. of *seguida,* sequence < fem. p. part. of *seguir,* to follow < VLat. **sequere* < Lat. *sequī.* See **sek^w-¹** in App.]

Se·gu·ra (sā-gŏŏr′ə, sĕ-gŏŏr′ä) A river of SE Spain flowing c. 322 km (200 mi), to the Mediterranean Sea.

sei (sā) n., pl. **seis** A sei whale. [< Norw. *seihval* : *sei,* coalfish (< ON *seidh*) + *hval,* whale (< ON *hvalr*).]

sei·cen·to (sā-chĕn′tō) n. The 17th century with reference to Italian literature and art. [Ital. < *(mille) seicento,* (one thousand) six hundred : *sei,* six (< Lat. *sex;* see **s(w)eks** in App.) + *cento,* hundred (< Lat. *centum;* see **dekm̥** in App.).]

seiche (sāsh, sĕch) n. A wave that oscillates in lakes, bays, or gulfs from a few minutes to a few hours as a result of seismic or atmospheric disturbances. [Fr. dialectal, exposed lake bottom, prob. < Fr. *sèche,* fem. of *sec,* dry. See SEC¹.]

sei·del (sīd′l, zīd′l) n. A beer mug. [Ger. < MHGer. *sīdel* < Lat. *situla,* bucket.]

seif dune (sāf, sīf) n. A sharp-crested longitudinal sand dune ranging up to 300 meters (900 feet) in height and 300 kilometers (200 miles) in length. [Ar. *sayf,* sword < Aram. *saypā* < Egypt. *sft,* knife.]

Sei·fert (sī′fərt), **Jaroslav** 1901–86. Czech poet who won the 1984 Nobel Prize for literature.

seign·eur (sān-yûr′, sĕn-yœr′) n. **1.** A man of rank, esp. a feudal lord in the ancien régime. **2.** In Canada, a man who owned a large estate originally granted by the king of France. **3.** Used as a form of address for such a man. [Fr. < OFr. *seignor* < VLat. **senior.* See SEIGNIOR.] —**seign·eur′i·al** adj.

seign·eur·y (sān′yə-rē) n., pl. **-ies** The power, rank, or estate of a seigneur.

seign·ior (sān-yôr′, sān′yôr′) n. **1.** A man of rank, esp. a feudal lord. **2.** Used as a form of address for such a man. [ME *segnour* < OFr. *seignor* < VLat. **senior* < Lat., older, comp. of *senex, sen-,* old.] —**sei·gnio′ri·al** adj.

seign·ior·age (sān′yər-ĭj) n. Revenue or a profit taken from the minting of coins, usu. the difference between the value of the bullion used and the face value of the coin. [ME *seigneurage* < OFr. < *seignor,* seignior. See SEIGNIOR.]

seign·ior·y (sān′yə-rē) n. The power, rank, or estate of a feudal lord. [ME *seigniorie* < OFr. < *seignor,* seignior. See SEIGNIOR.]

seine (sān) n. A large fishing net made to hang vertically in the water by weights at the lower edge and floats at the top. ❖ v. **seined, sein·ing, seines** —intr. To fish with such a net. —tr. To fish for or catch with such a net. [ME < OE *segne* < Gmc. **sagina* < Lat. *sagēna* < Gk. *sagēnē.*] —**sein′er** n.

Seine (sān, sĕn) A river of N France flowing c. 772 km (480 mi) generally NW to the **Bay of the Seine,** an inlet of the English Channel, near Le Havre.

seise (sēz) v. Variant of **seize** 6.

sei·sin also **sei·zin** (sē′zĭn) n. **1.** Legal possession of land, as a freehold estate. **2a.** The act or an instance of taking legal possession of land. **b.** Property thus possessed. [ME *seisine* < OFr. *saisine* < *seisir,* to seize. See SEIZE.]

seism (sī′zəm) n. See **earthquake.** [Gk. *seismos* < *seiein,* to shake.]

seis·mic (sīz′mĭk) adj. **1.** Of, subject to, or caused by an earthquake or earth vibration. **2.** Earthshaking. —**seis′mi•cal•ly** *adv.* —**seis•mic′i•ty** (-mĭs′ĭ-tē) *n.*

seis•mism (sīz′mĭz′əm) *n.* The phenomena involved in earthquakes.

seismo– or **seism**– *pref.* Earthquake: *seismograph*. [Gk. < *seismos*, seism. See SEISM.]

seis•mo•gram (sīz′mə-grăm′) *n.* The record of an earth tremor made by a seismograph.

seis•mo•graph (sīz′mə-grăf′) *n.* An instrument for detecting and recording the intensity, direction, and duration of a movement of the ground, esp. of an earthquake. —**seis•mog′ra•pher** (sīz-mŏg′rə-fər) *n.* —**seis′mo•graph′ic** (-grăf′ĭk), **seis′mo•graph′i•cal** (-ĭ-kəl) *adj.* —**seis•mog′ra•phy** *n.*

seis•mol•o•gy (sīz-mŏl′ə-jē) *n.* The geophysical science of earthquakes and the mechanical properties of the earth. —**seis′mo•log′ic** (-mə-lŏj′ĭk), **seis′mo•log′i•cal** (-ĭ-kəl) *adj.* —**seis′mo•log′i•cal•ly** *adv.* —**seis•mol′o•gist** *n.*

seis•mom•e•ter (sīz-mŏm′ĭ-tər) *n.* A detecting device that receives seismic impulses. —**seis′mo•met′ric** (-mə-mĕt′rĭk), **seis′mo•met′ri•cal** (-rĭ-kəl) *adj.*

seis•mom•e•try (sīz-mŏm′ĭ-trē) *n.* The scientific study and recording of earthquakes.

seis•mo•scope (sīz′mə-skōp′) *n.* An instrument that indicates the occurrence or time of occurrence of an earthquake. —**seis′mo•scop′ic** (-skŏp′ĭk) *adj.*

sei•tan (sā′tăn′) *n.* A chewy, protein-rich food made from wheat gluten and used as a meat substitute.

sei whale (sā) *n.* A rorqual (*Balaenoptera borealis*) that is blue-black above and white below and grows up to about 55 feet (17 meters) in length. [Partial transl. of Norw. *seihval*. See SEI.]

seize (sēz) *v.* **seized, seiz•ing, seiz•es** —*tr.* **1.** To grasp suddenly and forcibly; take or grab. **2a.** To grasp with the mind; apprehend. **b.** To possess oneself of: *seize an opportunity.* **3a.** To have a sudden overwhelming effect on. **b.** To overwhelm physically. **4.** To take into custody; capture. **5.** To take quick and forcible possession of; confiscate. **6.** also **seise** (sēz) **a.** To put (one) into possession of something. **b.** To vest ownership of a feudal property in. **7.** *Nautical* To bind with turns of small line. —*intr.* **1.** To lay sudden or forcible hold of something. **2a.** To cohere or fuse with another part as a result of high pressure or temperature and restrict or prevent further motion or flow. **b.** To come to a halt: *The talks seized up.* [ME *seisen* < OFr. *seisir*, to take possession, of Gmc. orig.] —**seiz′a•ble** *adj.* —**seiz′er** *n.*

sei•zin (sē′zĭn) *n.* Variant of **seisin**.

seiz•ing (sē′zĭng) *n. Nautical* A binding of multiple turns of thread or light line around a rope end to keep it from unlaying.

sei•zor also **sei•sor** (sē′zər, -zôr′) *n.* One that takes seisin.

sei•zure (sē′zhər) *n.* **1.** The act or an instance of seizing or the condition of being seized. **2.** A sudden attack, spasm, or convulsion, as in epilepsy. **3.** A sudden onset or sensation of feeling or emotion.

se•la•chi•an (sĭ-lā′kē-ən) *adj.* Of or belonging to the order Selachii of elasmobranch fishes that includes the sharks and in some classifications also the rays and skates. [Prob. < NLat. *Selachii*, order name < Gk. *selakhios*, cartilaginous < *selakhos*, cartilaginous fish.] —**se•la′chi•an** *n.*

se•lag•i•nel•la (sə-lăj′ə-nĕl′ə) *n.* Any of numerous fernlike, usu. prostrate plants of the genus *Selaginella*, having small scalelike leaves and bearing spores. [NLat. *Selaginella*, genus name < Lat. *selāgō, selāgin-*, a plant resembling the savin.]

se•lah (sē′lə, sĕl′ə) *interj.* Used to conclude a verse in the Psalms. [Heb. *selâ*.]

sel•dom (sĕl′dəm) *adv.* Not often; infrequently or rarely. ❖ *adj. Archaic* Infrequent; rare. [ME < OE *seldum*, alteration of *seldan*.] —**sel′dom•ness** *n.*

se•lect (sĭ-lĕkt′) *v.* **-lect•ed, -lect•ing, -lects** —*tr.* To take as a choice from among several; pick out. —*intr.* To make a choice or selection. ❖ *adj.* **1.** Singled out in preference; chosen: *a select few.* **2.** Of special quality or value; choice. **3.** Of or relating to a lean grade of beef. **4.** Careful or refined in making selections; discriminating. ❖ *n.* **1.** One that is chosen in preference to others or because of special value. **2.** (*used with a pl. verb*) Chosen or preferred items or people considered as a group. Often used with *the*. [Lat. *sēligere, sēlēct-* : *sē-*, apart; see **s(w)e-** in App. + *legere*, to choose; see **leg-** in App.] —**se•lec′ta•ble** *adj.* —**se•lect′ness** *n.* —**se•lec′tor** *n.*

se•lect•ee (sĭ-lĕk′tē′) *n.* One who is selected, esp. for military service.

se•lec•tion (sĭ-lĕk′shən) *n.* **1a.** The act or an instance of selecting or the fact of having been selected. **b.** One that is selected. **2.** A carefully chosen or representative collection of people or things. See Syns at **choice**. **3.** A literary or musical text chosen for reading or performance. **4.** *Biology* A natural or artificial process that favors or induces survival and perpetuation of one kind of organism over others.

se•lec•tion•ist (sĭ-lĕk′shə-nĭst) *adj.* also **se•lec•tion•al** (-shə-nəl) Of or relating to the view that evolution or genetic variation occurs chiefly as a result of natural selection. —**se•lec′tion•ism** *n.* —**se•lec′tion•ist** *n.*

se•lec•tive (sĭ-lĕk′tĭv) *adj.* **1.** Of or characterized by selection; discriminating. **2.** Empowered or tending to select. **3.** *Electronics*

Able to reject frequencies other than the one selected or tuned. —**se•lec′tive•ly** *adv.* —**se•lec′tive•ness** *n.*

selective service *n.* A system for calling up people for compulsory military service.

se•lec•tiv•i•ty (sĭ-lĕk′tĭv′ĭ-tē, sē′lĕk-) *n., pl.* **-ties 1.** The state or quality of being selective. **2.** The degree to which an electronic receiver is selective.

se•lect•man (sĭ-lĕkt′măn′, -mən) *n.* One of a board of town officers chosen annually in New England communities to manage local affairs.

se•lect•wom•an (sĭ-lĕkt′wŏŏm′ən) *n.* A woman who is one of a board of town officers chosen annually in New England communities to manage local affairs.

se•le•nate (sĕl′ə-nāt′) *n.* A salt or ester of selenic acid.

Se•le•ne (sə-lē′nē) *n. Greek Mythology* The goddess of the moon.

Se•len•ga (sĕl′ĕng-gä′) A river of N Mongolia and SE Russia flowing c. 1,207 km (750 mi) to Lake Baikal.

se•le•nic (sə-lē′nĭk, -lĕn′ĭk) *adj.* Of, relating to, or containing selenium.

selenic acid *n.* A highly corrosive hygroscopic white solid acid with composition H_2SeO_4.

se•le•nif•er•ous (sĕl′ə-nĭf′ər-əs) *adj.* Containing selenium.

se•le•nite (sĕl′ə-nīt′, sĭ-lē′-) *n.* Gypsum in the form of colorless clear crystals. [Lat. *selēnītēs* < Gk. *selēnītēs (lithos)*, moon (stone), selenite (so called because it was believed to wax and wane with the moon) < *selēnē*, moon. See SELENIUM.]

se•le•ni•um (sĭ-lē′nē-əm) *n. Symbol* **Se** A nonmetallic element, with red, black, and gray allotropic forms, resembling sulfur and obtained primarily as a byproduct of electrolytic copper refining; widely used in rectifiers, as a semiconductor, in xerography and in photocells. Atomic number 34; atomic weight 78.96; melting point (of gray selenium) 217°C; boiling point (gray) 684.9°C; specific gravity (gray) 4.79; (black) 4.28; valence 2, 4, or 6. See table at **element**. [Gk. *selēnē*, moon (< *selas*, light, brightness) + –IUM.]

selenium cell *n.* A photoconductive cell consisting of an insulated selenium strip between two suitable electrodes.

seleno– or **selen–** *pref.* **1.** Moon: *selenography*. **2.** Selenium: *selenosis*. [Gk. *selēno-* < *selēnē*, moon. See SELENIUM.]

sel•e•nog•ra•phy (sĕl′ə-nŏg′rə-fē) *n.* The study of the physical features of the moon. —**sel′e•nog′ra•pher, sel′e•nog′ra•phist** *n.* —**sel′e•no•graph′ic** (-nə-grăf′ĭk), **sel′e•no•graph′i•cal** (-ĭ-kəl) *adj.* —**sel′e•no•graph′i•cal•ly** *adv.*

sel•e•nol•o•gy (sĕl′ə-nŏl′ə-jē) *n.* The astronomical study of the moon. —**sel′e•no•log′i•cal** (-nə-lŏj′ĭ-kəl) *adj.* —**sel′e•nol′o•gist** *n.*

sel•e•no•sis (sĕl′ə-nō′sĭs) *n.* Poisoning, esp. of livestock, caused by ingesting selenium.

Sel•es (sĕl′əs), **Monica** b. 1973. Yugoslavian-born Amer. tennis player who between 1990 and 1993 won eight Grand Slam events.

Se•leu•ci•a (sĭ-lōō′shē-ə, -shə) An ancient city of Mesopotamia on the Tigris R. SSE of Baghdad; founded c. 300 B.C.

Se•leu•cid (sĭ-lōō′sĭd) *adj.* Of or relating to a Hellenistic dynasty founded by Seleucus I after the death of Alexander the Great. It ruled much of Asia Minor from 312 to 64 B.C. ❖ *n.* A member or subject of this dynasty.

Se•leu•cus I (sĭ-lōō′kəs) 358?–281 B.C. Macedonian general who founded and ruled (312–281) the Seleucid dynasty.

self (sĕlf) *n., pl.* **selves** (sĕlvz) **1.** The total, essential, or particular being of a person; the individual. **2.** The essential qualities distinguishing one person from another; individuality. **3.** One's consciousness of one's own being or identity; the ego. **4.** One's own interests, welfare, or advantage. **5.** *Immunology* That which the immune system identifies as belonging to the body. ❖ *pron.* Myself, yourself, himself, or herself. ❖ *adj.* **1.** Of the same character throughout. **2.** Of the same material as the article with which it is used. **3.** *Obsolete* Same or identical. [ME, selfsame < OE. See **s(w)e-** in App.]

self– *pref.* **1.** Oneself; itself: *self-control*. **2.** Automatic; automatically: *self-loading*. [ME < OE < self, self. See SELF.]

self-a•ban•doned (sĕlf′ə-băn′dənd) *adj.* Lacking self-restraint. —**self′-a•ban′don•ment** *n.*

self-ab•ne•ga•tion (sĕlf′ăb′nĭ-gā′shən) *n.* The setting aside of self-interest for the sake of others or for a belief or principle. —**self′-ab′ne•gat′ing** *adj.*

self-a•buse (sĕlf′ə-byŏŏs′) *n.* **1.** Abuse of oneself or one's abilities. **2.** Masturbation.

self-act•ing (sĕlf′ăk′tĭng) *adj.* Able to act automatically.

self-ad•dressed (sĕlf′ə-drĕst′) *adj.* Addressed to oneself.

self-ad•he•sive (sĕlf′ăd-hē′sĭv) *adj.* Having a surface coated with an adhesive and not needing any substance, such as glue, to form a bond.

self-ag•gran•dize•ment (sĕlf′ə-grăn′dĭz-mənt) *n.* The act or practice of enhancing or exaggerating one's own importance, power, or reputation. —**self′-ag•gran′diz′ing** (-ə-grăn′dī′-zĭng) *adj.*

self-a•nal•y•sis (sĕlf′ə-năl′ĭ-sĭs) *n., pl.* **-ses** (-sēz′) An independent methodical attempt to study and comprehend one's own personality, emotions, or behavior. —**self′-an′a•lyt′i•cal** (-ăn′ə-lĭt′ĭ-kəl), **self′-an′a•lyt′ic** (-ĭk) *adj.*

self-an•ni•hi•la•tion (sĕlf′ə-nī′ə-lā′shən) *n.* **1.** Self-destruc-

seismograph

tion. **2.** Loss of self-awareness, as in a mystical state.

self-as·sert·ing (sĕlf′ə-sûr′tĭng) *adj.* **1.** Asserting oneself or one's own rights or views. **2a.** Self-confident. **b.** Overbearing; arrogant.

self-as·ser·tion (sĕlf′ə-sûr′shən) *n.* Determined advancement of one's own personality, wishes, or views. —**self′-as·ser′tive** *adj.* —**self-as·ser′tive·ness** *n.*

self-as·sured (sĕlf′ə-shoŏrd′) *adj.* Having or showing confidence and poise. —**self′-as·sur′ance** (-shoŏr′əns) *n.*

self-bast·ing (sĕlf′bā′stĭng) *adj.* Prepared so as to remain moist while being cooked: *a self-basting turkey.*

self-col·ored (sĕlf′kŭl′ərd) *adj.* **1.** Being in the natural or original color. **2.** Of only one color.

self-com·mand (sĕlf′kə-mănd′) *n.* Full presence of mind; self-confidence.

self-com·pat·i·ble (sĕlf′kəm-păt′ə-bəl) *adj. Botany* Capable of self-fertilization. —**self′-com·pat′i·bil′i·ty** *n.*

self-con·cern (sĕlf′kən-sûrn′) *n.* Selfish or excessive concern for oneself. —**self′-con·cerned′** *adj.*

self-con·fessed (sĕlf′kən-fĕst′) *adj.* By one's own admission.

self-con·fi·dence (sĕlf′kŏn′fĭ-dəns) *n.* Confidence in oneself or one's own abilities. —**self′-con′fi·dent** *adj.*

self-con·scious (sĕlf′kŏn′shəs) *adj.* **1.** Aware of oneself as an individual or of one's own being, actions, or thoughts. **2.** Socially ill at ease. **3.** Excessively conscious of one's appearance or manner. **4.** Showing the effects of self-consciousness; stilted. —**self′-con′scious·ly** *adv.* —**self′-con′scious·ness** *n.*

self-con·tained (sĕlf′kən-tānd′) *adj.* **1.** Constituting a complete and independent unit in and of itself. **2a.** Not dependent on others; self-sufficient. **b.** Keeping to oneself; reserved. —**self′-con·tain′ment** *n.*

self-con·tra·dic·tion (sĕlf′kŏn′trə-dĭk′shən) *n.* **1.** The act, state, or fact of contradicting oneself. **2.** An idea or statement containing contradictions. —**self′-con′tra·dic′to·ry** (-dĭk′tə-rē) *adj.*

self-con·trol (sĕlf′kən-trōl′) *n.* Control of one's emotions, desires, or actions by one's own will. —**self′-con·trolled′** *adj.*

self-cor·rect·ing (sĕlf′kə-rĕk′tĭng) *adj.* **1.** Correcting its or one's own mistakes. **2.** Of or being a typewriter mechanism that allows for automatic correction of a typing error.

self-de·fense (sĕlf′dĭ-fĕns′) *n.* **1.** Defense of oneself when physically attacked. **2.** Defense of what belongs to oneself, as one's works. **3.** *Law* The right to protect oneself against violence or threatened violence with whatever force or means are reasonably necessary. —**self′-de·fen′sive** *adj.*

self-de·ni·al (sĕlf′dĭ-nī′əl) *n.* Sacrifice of one's own desires or interests. —**self′-de·ny′ing** (-nī′ĭng) *adj.*

self-de·pre·ci·a·tion (sĕlf′dĭ-prē′shē-ā′shən) *n.* Disparagement or undervaluation of oneself and one's abilities.

self-de·struct (sĕlf′dĭ-strŭkt′) *n.* A mechanism for causing a device to destroy itself. ❖ *intr.v.* **-struct·ed, -struct·ing, -structs** To destroy oneself or itself. [Back-formation < SELF-DESTRUCTION.]

self-de·struc·tion (sĕlf′dĭ-strŭk′shən) *n.* **1.** The act or process of destroying oneself or itself. **2.** Suicide.

self-de·struc·tive (sĕlf′dĭ-strŭk′tĭv) *adj.* **1.** Tending to do harm to oneself. **2.** Marked by an impulse or tendency to harm or kill oneself. —**self′-de·struc′tive·ness** *n.*

self-de·ter·mi·na·tion (sĕlf′dĭ-tûr′mə-nā′shən) *n.* **1.** Determination of one's own fate or course of action without compul-

sion; free will. **2.** Freedom of the people of a given area to determine their own political status; independence.

self-de·vo·tion (sĕlf′dĭ-vō′shən) *n.* Devotion or dedication of oneself, esp. to a service or ideal. —**self′-de·vot′ed·ly** (-vō′tĭd-lē) *adv.* —**self′-de·vot′ed·ness** *n.*

self-di·ges·tion (sĕlf′dĭ-jĕs′chən, -dī-) *n.* See **autolysis.**

self·dom (sĕlf′dəm) *n.* Selfhood.

self-ef·fac·ing (sĕlf′ĭ-fā′sĭng) *adj.* Not drawing attention to oneself; modest. —**self′-ef·face′ment** (-fās′mənt) *n.*

self-em·ployed (sĕlf′ĕm-ploid′) *adj.* Earning one's livelihood directly from one's own trade or business rather than as an employee of another. —**self′-em·ploy′ment** *n.*

self-en·forc·ing (sĕlf′ĕn-fôr′sĭng, -fôr′-) *adj.* Holding within itself the means or a guarantee of its enforcement.

self-es·teem (sĕlf′ĭ-stēm′) *n.* Pride in oneself; self-respect.

self-ev·i·dent (sĕlf′ĕv′ĭ-dənt) *adj.* Requiring no proof or explanation. —**self′-ev′i·dence** *n.* —**self′-ev′i·dent·ly** *adv.*

self-ex·am·i·na·tion (sĕlf′ĭg-zăm′ə-nā′shən) *n.* **1.** An introspective consideration of one's own thoughts or emotions. **2.** Examination of one's own body for medical reasons.

self-ex·plan·a·to·ry (sĕlf′ĭk-splăn′ə-tôr′ē, -tōr′ē) *adj.* Needing no explanation; obvious.

self-ex·pres·sion (sĕlf′ĭk-sprĕsh′ən) *n.* Expression of one's own personality, feelings, or ideas, as through speech or art. —**self′-ex·press′** *v.* —**self′-ex·pres′sive** (-sprĕs′ĭv) *adj.*

self-flag·el·la·tion (sĕlf′flăj′ə-lā′shən) *n.* **1.** The act of severely criticizing oneself. **2.** The act of punishing oneself.

self-ful·fill·ing (sĕlf′foŏl-fĭl′ĭng) *adj.* **1.** Achieving fulfillment as a result of having been expected or foretold: *a self-fulfilling prophecy.* **2.** Achieving self-fulfillment.

self-giv·en (sĕlf′gĭv′ən) *adj.* **1.** Originating or derived from itself. **2.** Given by oneself; self-appointed: *self-given role.*

self-giv·ing (sĕlf′gĭv′ĭng) *adj.* Characterized by self-sacrificing behavior; unselfish.

self-gov·erned (sĕlf′gŭv′ərnd) *adj.* **1.** Not controlled or swayed by others. **2.** Characterized by self-control.

self-gov·ern·ing (sĕlf′gŭv′ər-nĭng) *adj.* **1.** Exercising control or rule over oneself or itself. **2.** Having the right or power of self-government; autonomous.

self-gov·ern·ment (sĕlf′gŭv′ərn-mənt) *n.* **1.** Political independence; autonomy. **2.** Popular or representative government; democracy. **3.** Self-control.

self-hard·en·ing (sĕlf′här′dn-ĭng) *adj.* Of or relating to materials that harden without special treatment.

self-heal (sĕlf′hēl′) *n.* Any of several plants reputed to have healing powers, esp. *Prunella vulgaris,* a creeping Eurasian plant with deep violet-blue, two-lipped flowers.

self·hood (sĕlf′hoŏd′) *n.* **1.** The state of having a distinct identity; individuality. **2.** The fully developed self; an achieved personality. **3.** Self-centeredness.

self-hyp·no·sis (sĕlf′hĭp-nō′sĭs) *n.* See **autohypnosis.**

self-i·den·ti·fi·ca·tion (sĕlf′ī-dĕn′tə-fĭ-kā′shən) *n.* Identification of oneself with another person or thing.

self-im·mo·la·tion (sĕlf′ĭm′ə-lā′shən) *n.* Deliberate sacrifice of oneself, esp. by fire.

self-im·por·tance (sĕlf′ĭm-pôr′tns) *n.* Excessively high regard for one's own importance or station; conceit. —**self′-im·por′tant** *adj.* —**self′-im·por′tant·ly** *adv.*

self-in·clu·sive (sĕlf′ĭn-kloŏ′sĭv, -zĭv) *adj.* **1.** Enclosing or including itself. **2.** Whole or complete in itself.

self′-a·base′ment *n.*	**self′-de·feat′ing** *adj.*	**self′-ha′tred** *n.*	**self′-pro·tec′tive** *adj.*
self′-ab·sorbed′ *adj.*	**self′-def′i·ni′tion** *n.*	**self′-help′** *n.*	**self′-pro·tec′tive·ly** *adv.*
self′-ab·sorp′tion *n.*	**self′-dep′re·cat′ing** *adj.*	**self′-i·den′ti·ty** *n.*	**self′-pub′lished** *adj.*
self′-ac′tu·al·i·za′tion *n.*	**self′-dep′re·cat′ing·ly** *adv.*	**self′-im′age** *n.*	**self′-ref′er·ence** *n.*
self′-ac′tu·al·ize *intr.v.*	**self′-dep′re·ca′to·ry** *adj.*	**self′-im·posed′** *adj.*	**self′-ref′er·en′tial·ly** *adv.*
self′-ac′tu·al·iz′er *n.*	**self′-de·struc′tive·ly** *adv.*	**self′-im·prove′ment** *n.*	**self′-reg′u·lat′ing** *adj.*
self′-ap·point′ed *adj.*	**self′-de·vel′op·ment** *n.*	**self′-in·crim′i·nat′ing** *adj.*	**self′-reg′u·la′tion** *n.*
self′-a·ware′ *adj.*	**self′-di·rect′ed** *adj.*	**self′-in·crim′i·na′tion** *n.*	**self′-re·li′ance** *n.*
self′-a·ware′ness *n.*	**self′-di·rect′ing** *adj.*	**self′-in·crim′i·na′to·ry** *adj.*	**self′-re·li′ant** *adj.*
self′-cen′tered *adj.*	**self′-di·rec′tion** *n.*	**self′-in·dul′gence** *n.*	**self′-re·li′ant·ly** *adv.*
self′-cen′tered·ly *adv.*	**self′-dis′ci·pline** *n.*	**self′-in·dul′gent** *adj.*	**self′-rep′li·cat′ing** *adj.*
self′-cen′tered·ness *n.*	**self′-dis·cov′er·y** *n.*	**self′-in·dul′gent·ly** *adv.*	**self′-rep′li·ca′tion** *n.*
self′-clean′ing *adj.*	**self′-dis·trust′** *n.*	**self′-in·flict′ed** *adj.*	**self′-re·proach′** *n.*
self′-com·pla′cen·cy *n.*	**self′-dis·trust′ful** *adj.*	**self′-in·struc′ted** *adj.*	**self′-re·proach′ful** *adj.*
self′-com·pla′cent *adj.*	**self′-doubt′** *n.*	**self′-in·volved′** *adj.*	**self′-re·proach′ful·ly** *adv.*
self′-com·pla′cent·ly *adv.*	**self′-doubt′ing** *adj.*	**self′-in·volve′ment** *n.*	**self′-re·spect′** *n.*
self′-con′cept *n.*	**self′-ed′u·cat′ed** *adj.*	**self′-knowl′edge** *n.*	**self′-re·spect′ing** *adj.*
self′-con·cep′tion *n.*	**self′-ed′u·ca′tion** *n.*	**self′-med′i·ca′tion** *n.*	**self′-re·straint′** *n.*
self′-con·tent′ *adj. & n.*	**self′-e·lect′ed** *adj.*	**self′-ob·ser·va′tion** *n.*	**self′-re·veal′ing** *adj.*
self′-con·tent′ment *n.*	**self′-en·rich′ment** *n.*	**self′-per·pet′u·at′ing** *adj.*	**self′-rev′e·la′tion** *n.*
self′-crit′i·cal *adj.*	**self′-ex′ile** *n.*	**self′-per·pet′u·a′tion** *n.*	**self′-search′ing** *adj. & n.*
self′-crit′i·cal·ly *adv.*	**self′-ex′iled** *adj.*	**self′-pit′y** *n.*	**self′-sup·port′** *n.*
self′-crit′i·cism *n.*	**self′-fer′tile** *adj.*	**self′-pit′y·ing** *adj.*	**self′-sup·port′ed** *adj.*
self′-de·ceit′ *n.*	**self′-fer′til·i·za′tion** *n.*	**self′-pol′li·nate** *v.*	**self′-sup·port′ing** *adj.*
self′-de·ceived′ *adj.*	**self′-fer′til·ized′** *adj.*	**self′-pol′li·na′tion** *n.*	**self′-sus·tain′ing** *adj.*
self′-de·ceiv′ing *adj.*	**self′-fer′til·iz′ing** *adj.*	**self′-por′trait** *n.*	**self′-sus·tain′ing·ly** *adv.*
self′-de·cep′tion *n.*	**self′-ful·fill′ment** *n.*	**self′-pro·mot′er** *n.*	**self′-taught′** *adj.*
self′-de·cep′tive *adj.*	**self′-grat′i·fi·ca′tion** *n.*	**self′-pro·mo′tion** *n.*	**self′-un′der·stand′ing** *n.*
self′-de·cep′tive·ly *adv.*	**self′-hate′** *n.*	**self′-pro·tec′tion** *n.*	

self-in·com·pat·i·ble (sĕlf'ĭn-kəm-păt'ə-bəl) *adj. Botany* Incapable of self-fertilization. —**self'-in·com·pat'i·bil'i·ty** *n.*

self-in·duced (sĕlf'ĭn-dōōst', -dyōōst') *adj.* **1.** Induced by oneself or itself. **2.** *Electricity* Produced by self-induction.

self-in·duc·tance (sĕlf'ĭn-dŭk'təns) *n.* The ratio of the electromotive force produced in a circuit by self-induction to the rate of change of current producing it, stated in henries.

self-in·duc·tion (sĕlf'ĭn-dŭk'shən) *n.* The generation by a changing current of an electromotive force in the same circuit. —**self'-in·duc'tive** *adj.*

self-in·sur·ance (sĕlf'ĭn-shōōr'əns) *n.* Insurance of oneself or one's possessions against possible loss by regularly setting aside funds. —**self'-in·sure'** *v.* —**self'-in·sured'** *adj.*

self-in·ter·est (sĕlf'ĭn'trĭst, -ĭn'tər-ĭst) *n.* **1.** Selfish or excessive regard for one's personal advantage or interest. **2.** Personal advantage or interest. —**self'-in'ter·est·ed** *adj.*

self·ish (sĕl'fĭsh) *adj.* **1.** Concerned chiefly or only with oneself. **2.** Arising from, characterized by, or showing selfishness. —**self'ish·ly** *adv.* —**self'ish·ness** *n.*

self-jus·ti·fy·ing (sĕlf'jŭs'tə-fī'ĭng) *adj.* **1.** Making excuses for oneself or one's behavior. **2.** Justifying text margins automatically: *bought a self-justifying printer.* —**self'-jus'ti·fi·ca'tion** (-jŭs'tə-fĭ-kā'shən) *n.*

self·less (sĕlf'lĭs) *adj.* Having, exhibiting, or motivated by no concern for oneself; unselfish. —**self'less·ness** *n.*

self-lim·it·ed (sĕlf-lĭm'ĭ-tĭd) *adj.* **1.** Limited by its or one's own characteristics rather than by external influences. **2.** Running a definite course within a specific period; little modified by treatment. Used of a disease.

self-lim·it·ing (sĕlf-lĭm'ĭ-tĭng) *adj.* **1.** Limiting oneself or itself. **2.** Self-limited. —**self'-lim'i·ta'tion** (-tā'shən) *n.*

self-liq·ui·dat·ing (sĕlf'lĭk'wĭ-dā'tĭng) *adj.* **1.** Involving goods convertible into cash in a short time. Used of business transactions. **2.** Producing a return equal to the sum invested to create or maintain something. —**self'-liq'ui·da'tion** *n.*

self-load·ing (sĕlf'lō'dĭng) *adj.* Automatically ejecting a shell and loading the next round from the magazine; automatic or semiautomatic. Used of a firearm.

self-love (sĕlf'lŭv') *n.* The instinct or desire to promote one's own well-being; regard for or love of one's self. —**self'-lov'ing** *adj.*

self-made (sĕlf'mād') *adj.* **1.** Having achieved success or recognition by one's own efforts. **2.** Made by itself or oneself.

self-mail·er (sĕlf'mā'lər) *n.* A folder that can be mailed without being enclosed in an envelope. —**self'-mail'ing** *adj.*

self-mas·ter·y (sĕlf'măs'tə-rē) *n.* Self-command.

self·ness (sĕlf'nĭs) *n.* **1.** The quality or state of being self-centered; selfishness. **2.** Individuality; selfhood.

self-o·pin·ion (sĕlf'ə-pĭn'yən) *n.* An unduly high opinion of oneself.

self-o·pin·ion·at·ed (sĕlf'ə-pĭn'yə-nā'tĭd) *adj.* **1.** Obstinately insistent upon one's own opinions. **2.** Vain; conceited.

self-or·dained (sĕlf'ôr-dānd') *adj.* Ordained by oneself rather than by others; practicing one's own authority.

self-per·cep·tion (sĕlf'pər-sĕp'shən) *n.* An awareness of the characteristics that constitute one's self; self-knowledge.

self-poised (sĕlf'poizd') *adj.* **1.** In command of oneself. **2.** In a state of balance without need of support.

self-pos·ses·sion (sĕlf'pə-zĕsh'ən) *n.* Full command of one's faculties, feelings, and behavior. —**self'-pos·sessed'** *adj.*

self-pres·er·va·tion (sĕlf'prĕz'ər-vā'shən) *n.* **1.** Protection of oneself from harm or destruction. **2.** The instinct for individual preservation; the innate desire to stay alive.

self-pro·claimed (sĕlf'prō-klāmd', -prə-) *adj.* So called by oneself; self-styled.

self-pro·pelled (sĕlf'prə-pĕld') *adj.* **1.** Containing its own means of propulsion. **2.** Fired from or mounted on a moving vehicle. —**self'-pro·pul'sion** (-pŭl'shən) *n.*

self-pu·ri·fi·ca·tion (sĕlf'pyōōr'ə-fĭ-kā'shən) *n.* **1.** Naturally produced purification. **2.** Purification of oneself.

self-re·ac·tive (sĕlf'rē-ăk'tĭv) *adj.* Immunologically reactive to itself. Used of a cell or antibody.

self-re·al·i·za·tion (sĕlf'rē'ə-lĭ-zā'shən) *n.* The development or fulfillment of one's potential.

self-re·cord·ing (sĕlf'rĭ-kôr'dĭng) *adj.* Automatically recording its own functions or operations, as a machine or instrument.

self-re·crim·i·na·tion (sĕlf'rĭ-krĭm'ə-nā'shən) *n.* The act or an instance of blaming or censuring oneself.

self-ref·er·en·tial (sĕlf'rĕf'ə-rĕn'shəl) *adj.* Referring to oneself or itself: *a self-referential poem.* —**self'-ref'er·ence** *n.*

self-re·flec·tion (sĕlf'rĭ-flĕk'shən) *n.* Self-examination; introspection. —**self'-re·flec'tive** *adj.*

self-re·gard (sĕlf'rĭ-gärd') *n.* **1.** Consideration of oneself or one's interests. **2.** Self-respect.

self-right·eous (sĕlf'rī'chəs) *adj.* **1.** Piously sure of one's own righteousness; moralistic. **2.** Exhibiting pious self-assurance. —**self'-right'eous·ly** *adv.* —**self'-right'eous·ness** *n.*

self-right·ing (sĕlf'rī'tĭng) *adj.* Capable of righting itself when capsized: *a self-righting boat.*

self-ris·ing flour (sĕlf'rī'zĭng) *n.* A commercially produced mixture of flour and leavening.

self-rule (sĕlf'rōōl') *n.* Self-government.

self-sac·ri·fice (sĕlf'săk'rə-fīs') *n.* Sacrifice of one's personal interests or well-being for the sake of others or for a cause. —**self'-sac'ri·fic'ing** *adj.*

self·same (sĕlf'sām') *adj.* Being the very same; identical. —**self'same·ness** *n.*

self-sat·is·fac·tion (sĕlf'săt'ĭs-făk'shən) *n.* Satisfaction, esp. complacent satisfaction, with oneself or with one's accomplishments. —**self'-sat'is·fied'** (-fīd') *adj.*

self-seal·ing (sĕlf'sē'lĭng) *adj.* **1.** Capable of sealing itself, as after being pierced: *a self-sealing tire.* **2.** Sealable without the application of moisture: *a self-sealing envelope.*

self-seed (sĕlf'sēd') *intr.v.* **-seed·ed**, **-seed·ing**, **-seeds** To self-sow.

self-seek·ing (sĕlf'sē'kĭng) *adj.* **1.** Pursuing only one's own ends or interests. **2.** Exhibiting concern only with promoting one's own ends or interests. ❖ *n.* Determined pursuit of one's own ends or interests. —**self'-seek'er** *n.*

self-se·lec·tion (sĕlf'sĭ-lĕk'shən) *n.* Selection of or by oneself. —**self'-se·lect'ed** *adj.* —**self'-se·lec'tive** *adj.*

self-ser·vice (sĕlf'sûr'vĭs) *adj.* Being a retail commercial enterprise or a service in which the customers or users help themselves. —**self'-ser'vice** *n.*

self-serv·ing (sĕlf'sûr'vĭng) *adj.* **1.** Serving one's own interests, esp. without concern for the needs or interests of others. **2.** Exhibiting concern solely for one's own interests.

self-sow (sĕlf'sō') *intr.v.* **-sown**, **-sow·ing**, **-sows** To reproduce or spread by natural dispersion of seed.

self-start·er (sĕlf'stär'tər) *n.* **1.** See starter **2.** One who displays unusual initiative. —**self'-start'ing** *adj.*

self-stick (sĕlf'stĭk') also **self-stick·ing** (-stĭk'ĭng) *adj.* Self-adhesive: *a self-stick envelope.*

self-stor·age (sĕlf'stôr'ĭj, -stôr'-) *adj.* Of, relating to, or being a commercial facility in which customers can rent space to store possessions.

self-stud·y (sĕlf'stŭd'ē) *n.* **1.** Study or examination of oneself. **2.** A form of study in which one is to a large extent responsible for one's own instruction.

self-styled (sĕlf'stīld') *adj.* As characterized by oneself, often without right or justification: "*poets, real or self-styled*" (Constantine Fitzgibbon). See Usage Note at **so-called**.

self-suf·fi·cient (sĕlf'sə-fĭsh'ənt) *adj.* **1.** Able to provide for oneself without the help of others; independent. **2.** Having undue confidence; smug. —**self'-suf·fi'cien·cy** *n.*

self-tol·er·ance (sĕlf'tŏl'ər-əns) *n.* Tolerance by the body's immune system to its own cells and tissues.

self-treat·ment (sĕlf'trēt'mənt) *n.* Treatment of oneself without professional supervision, as to alleviate an illness.

self-trust (sĕlf'trŭst') *n.* Self-confidence.

self-will (sĕlf'wĭl') *n.* Willfulness, esp. in satisfying one's desires or adhering to one's opinions. —**self'-willed'** *adj.*

self-wind·ing (sĕlf'wīn'dĭng) *adj.* Designed in such a way that manual winding is unnecessary. Used of clocks and watches.

self-worth (sĕlf'wûrth') *n.* Self-esteem; self-respect.

Sel·juk (sĕl'jōōk', sĕl-jōōk') A Turkish dynasty ruling in central and W Asia from the 11th to the 13th cent. [< Ottoman Turk. *Seljūq,* name of the reputed ancestor of the dynasty.]

sel·kie also **sil·kie** (sĭl'kē) *n.* A creature or spirit in Scottish and Irish folklore that has the form of a seal but can also assume human form. [Dialectal dim. of SEAL².]

Sel·kirk Mountains (sĕl'kûrk') A range of the Rocky Mts. in SE British Columbia, Canada, rising to 3,524.3 m (11,555 ft).

sell (sĕl) *v.* **sold** (sōld), **sell·ing**, **sells** —*tr.* **1.** To exchange or deliver for money or its equivalent. **2.** To offer for sale, as for one's business or livelihood. **3.** To give up or surrender in exchange for a price or reward. **4.** To be purchased in (a certain quantity); achieve sales of: *a book that sold a million copies.* **5a.** To bring about or encourage sales of; promote. **b.** To cause to be accepted; advocate successfully: *We sold the proposal to the committee.* **6.** To persuade (another) to recognize the worth or desirability of something: *They sold me on the idea.* —*intr.* **1.** To exchange ownership for money or its equivalent; engage in selling. **2.** To be sold or be on sale. **3.** To attract prospective buyers; be popular on the market: *a model that doesn't sell.* **4.** To be approved of; gain acceptance. ❖ *n.* **1.** The activity or method of selling. **2.** *Slang* Something that sells or gains acceptance in a particular way: *a difficult sell.* **3.** *Slang* A deception; a hoax. —**phrasal verbs: sell off** To get rid of by selling, often at reduced prices. **sell out 1.** To put all of one's goods or possessions up for sale. **2.** *Slang* To betray one's cause or colleagues. —**idioms: sell a bill of goods** *Informal* To take unfair advantage of. **sell down the river** *Informal* To betray the true trust or faith of. **sell short 1.** To contract for the sale of securities or commodities one expects to own at a later date and at more advantageous terms. **2.** To underestimate the true value or worth of. [ME *sellen* < OE *sellan,* to give, sell.] —**sell'a·ble** *adj.*

sell·er (sĕl'ər) *n.* **1.** One that sells; a vendor. **2.** An item that sells in a certain way: *This car is an excellent seller.*

sell·er's market also **sell·ers' market** (sĕl'ərz) *n.* A market condition characterized by high prices and a supply of commodities falling short of demand.

selvage

semé

sell·ing climax (sĕl'ĭng) *n.* A sharp decline in stock prices on a heavy volume of trading followed by a rally.

selling point *n.* An aspect of a product or service that is stressed in advertising or marketing.

sell·off (sĕl'ôf', -ŏf') *n.* The sale or disposal of a relatively large number of stocks, bonds, or commodities that often causes a sharp decline in prices.

sell·out (sĕl'out') *n.* **1.** The act of selling out. **2.** An event for which all the tickets are sold. **3.** *Slang* One who has betrayed one's principles or an espoused cause.

Sel·ma (sĕl'mə) A city of S-central AL W of Montgomery; site of a voter registration drive (1965) led by Martin Luther King, Jr. Pop. 20,512.

sel·syn (sĕl'sĭn) *n.* A device by which angular movement or position in a generator is transmitted to a motor. [SEL(F) + SYN(CHRONOUS).]

selt·zer (sĕlt'sər) *n.* **1.** A natural effervescent spring water of high mineral content. **2.** See **carbonated water.** [< Ger. *Selterser (Wasser)*, (water) of Selters, in central Germany.]

sel·va (sĕl'və) *n.* A dense tropical rainforest usu. having a cloud cover, esp. in Amazonia. [Sp., forest < Lat. *silva*.]

sel·vage also **sel·vedge** (sĕl'vĭj) *n.* **1a.** The edge of a fabric that is woven so that it will not fray or ravel. **b.** An ornamental fringe at either end of an Oriental rug. **2.** The edge plate of a lock that has a slot for a bolt. [ME (influenced by MLGer. *selfegge*) : *self*, self; see SELF + *egge*, edge; see EDGE.]

selves (sĕlvz) *n.* Plural of **self.**

Selz·nick (sĕlz'nĭk), **David Oliver** 1902–65. Amer. producer whose films include *Gone With the Wind* (1939).

SEM *abbr.* scanning electron microscope

Sem. *abbr.* Semitic

se·man·teme (sĭ-măn'tēm') *n. Linguistics* An irreducible unit of meaning. [SEMANT(IC) + -EME.]

se·man·tic (sĭ-măn'tĭk) also **se·man·ti·cal** (-tĭ-kəl) *adj.* **1.** Of or relating to meaning, esp. meaning in language. **2.** Of, relating to, or according to the science of semantics. [Fr. *sémantique* < Gk. *sēmantikos*, significant < *sēmantos*, marked < *sēmainein*, *sēman-*, to signify < *sēma*, sign.] —**se·man'ti·cal·ly** *adv.*

se·man·ti·cist (sĭ-măn'tĭ-sĭst) *n.* A specialist in semantics.

se·man·tics (sĭ-măn'tĭks) *n.* (*used with a sing. or pl. verb*) **1.** *Linguistics* The study or science of meaning in language. **2.** *Linguistics* The study of relationships between signs and symbols and what they represent. **3.** The meaning or the interpretation of a word, sentence, or other language form: *We're basically agreed; let's not quibble over semantics.*

sem·a·phore (sĕm'ə-fôr', -fōr') *n.* **1.** A visual signaling apparatus with flags, lights, or mechanically moving arms, as one used on a railroad. **2.** A visual system for sending information by means of two flags that are held one in each hand, using an alphabetic code based on the position of the signaler's arms. ❖ *tr. & intr.v.* **-phored, -phor·ing, -phores** To send (a message) or to signal by semaphore. [Gk. *sēma*, sign + –PHORE.] —**sem'a·phor'ic** *adj.*

Se·ma·rang (sə-mär'äng) A city of N Java, Indonesia, on the Java Sea E of Jakarta. Pop. 1,026,671.

se·ma·si·ol·o·gy (sĭ-mā'sē-ŏl'ə-jē, -zē-) *n.* See **semantics** 2. [Gk. *sēmasiā*, meaning (< *sēmainein*, to signify; see SEMANTIC) + -LOGY.] —**se·ma'si·o·log'i·cal** (-ə-lŏj'ĭ-kəl) *adj.* —**se·ma'si·ol'o·gist** *n.*

se·mat·ic (sĭ-măt'ĭk) *adj.* Serving as a warning or signal of danger. Used esp. of the coloring of some poisonous animals. [< Gk. *sēma, sēmat-*, sign.]

sem·bla·ble (sĕm'blə-bəl) *adj.* **1.** Having a resemblance; resembling or like. **2.** Seeming; apparent. ❖ *n. Archaic* Something that closely resembles something else. [ME < OFr. < *sembler*, to resemble < Lat. *simulāre*, to simulate. See SIMULATE.] —**sem'bla·bly** *adv.*

sem·blance (sĕm'bləns) *n.* **1.** An outward or token appearance. **2.** A representation; a copy. **3.** The barest trace; a modicum. [ME < OFr. < *sembler*, to resemble. See SEMBLABLE.]

se·mé (sə-mā') *adj. Heraldry* Having a design embellished with small delicate figures, such as a lacing of stars or flowers. [Fr. < OFr., p. part. of *semer*, to sow, scatter < Lat. *sēmināre* < *sēmen, sēmin-*, seed. See **sē-** in App.]

se·meme (sē'mēm') *n.* The meaning expressed by a morpheme. [Gk. *sēma*, sign + -EME.]

se·men (sē'mən) *n.* A viscous whitish secretion of the male reproductive organs, containing and transporting spermatozoa. [ME < Lat. *sēmen*, seed, semen. See **sē-** in App.]

Se·me·nov (sə-myô'nəf), **Nikolai Nikolayevich** 1896–1986. Soviet chemist who shared a 1956 Nobel Prize.

se·mes·ter (sə-mĕs'tər) *n.* One of two divisions of 15 to 18 weeks each of an academic year. [Ger. < Lat. *(cursus) sēmēstris, (cursus)* period of six months : *sē-*, six (< *sex*; see **s(w)eks** in App.) + *mēnsis*, month; see **mē-**¹ in App.]

Se·mey (sĕ-mā') or **Sem·i·pa·la·tinsk** (sĕm'ē-pə-lä'tĭnsk) A city of NE Kazakhstan on the Irtysh R. SE of Omsk, Russia; founded 1718. Pop. 342,000.

sem·i (sĕm'ī, sĕm'ē) *n., pl.* **sem·is** *Informal* **1a.** A semitrailer. **b.** A tractor-trailer. **2.** A semifinal.

semi– *pref.* **1.** Half: *semicircle.* **2.** Partial; partially: *semiconscious.* **3.** Resembling or having some of the characteristics of: *semiofficial.* **4.** Occurring twice during: *semimonthly.* See Usage Note at **bi-**¹. [ME < Lat. *sēmi-*, half.]

sem·i·ab·stract (sĕm'ē-ăb-străkt', -ăb'străkt', sĕm'ī-) *adj.* Of or relating to an art form characterized by stylized but recognizable subject matter. —**sem'i·ab·strac'tion** *n.*

sem·i·an·nu·al (sĕm'ē-ăn'yōo-əl, sĕm'ī-) *adj.* Occurring or issued twice a year. —**sem'i·an'nu·al·ly** *adv.*

sem·i·a·quat·ic (sĕm'ē-ə-kwŏt'ĭk, -kwăt'-, sĕm'ī-) *adj.* Adapted for living or growing in or near water; not entirely aquatic.

sem·i·ar·id (sĕm'ē-ăr'ĭd) *adj.* Characterized by relatively low annual rainfall of 25 to 50 centimeters (10 to 20 inches) and having scrubby vegetation with short coarse grasses; not completely arid. —**sem'i·a·rid'i·ty** (-ə-rĭd'ĭ-tē, -ă-rĭd'-) *n.*

sem·i·au·to·mat·ic (sĕm'ē-ô'tə-măt'ĭk, sĕm'ī-) *adj.* **1.** Partially automatic. **2.** Ejecting a shell and loading the next round of ammunition automatically but requiring a trigger squeeze for each shot. ❖ *n.* A semiautomatic firearm.

sem·i·au·ton·o·mous (sĕm'ē-ô-tŏn'ə-məs, sĕm'ī-) *adj.* **1.** Partially self-governing. **2.** Having the powers of self-government within a larger organization or structure. —**sem'i·au·ton'o·my** *n.*

sem·i·breve (sĕm'ē-brēv', -brĕv', sĕm'ī-) *n. Chiefly British* A whole note in music.

sem·i·cen·ten·ni·al (sĕm'ē-sĕn-tĕn'ē-əl, sĕm'ī-) *adj.* Marking the 50th anniversary of an event. ❖ *n.* A 50th anniversary or its celebration.

sem·i·cir·cle (sĕm'ĭ-sûr'kəl) *n.* **1.** A half of a circle as divided by a diameter. **2.** An object or arrangement of objects or people in the shape of half a circle. —**sem'i·cir'cu·lar** (-kyə-lər) *adj.*

semicircular canal *n.* Any of three tubular and looped structures of the inner ear, together functioning in maintenance of the sense of balance in the body.

sem·i·clas·si·cal (sĕm'ē-klăs'ĭ-kəl, sĕm'ī-) *adj. Music* Of, relating to, or being a work that in style or form falls between the classical and popular genres.

sem·i·co·lon (sĕm'ĭ-kō'lən) *n.* A mark of punctuation (;) used to connect independent clauses and indicating a closer relationship between the clauses than a period.

sem·i·co·ma (sĕm'ē-kō'mə, sĕm'ī-) *n.* A partial or mild comatose state; a coma from which a person may be roused by stimuli. —**sem'i·co'ma·tose'** (-kō'mə-tōs', -kŏm'ə-) *adj.*

sem·i·con·duc·tor (sĕm'ē-kən-dŭk'tər, sĕm'ī-) *n.* Any of various solid crystalline substances, such as germanium or silicon, having electrical conductivity greater than insulators but less than good conductors. —**sem'i·con·duct'ing** *adj.* —**sem'i·con·duct'ive** *adj.*

semiconductor laser *n.* A solid-state device, consisting of two semiconductor layers separated by a middle layer, that generates laser radiation when charge carriers of opposite polarity meet in the middle layer.

sem·i·con·scious (sĕm'ē-kŏn'shəs, sĕm'ī-) *adj.* Partially conscious; not completely aware of sensations. —**sem'i·con'scious·ly** *adv.* —**sem'i·con'scious·ness** *n.*

sem·i·des·ert (sĕm'ē-dĕz'ərt, sĕm'ī-) *n.* A semiarid area often located between a desert and a grassland or woodland.

sem·i·de·tached (sĕm'ē-dĭ-tăcht', sĕm'ī-) *adj.* Attached to something on one side only: *a semidetached house.*

sem·i·di·am·e·ter (sĕm'ē-dī-ăm'ĭ-tər, sĕm'ī-) *n.* A celestial body's apparent radius when viewed as a disk from Earth.

sem·i·di·ur·nal (sĕm'ē-dī-ûr'nəl, sĕm'ī-) *adj.* **1.** Of, relating to, occurring, or performed during half a day. **2.** Occurring or coming approximately once every 12 hours, as the tides.

sem·i·dome (sĕm'ē-dōm', sĕm'ī-) *n.* A roof covering a semicircular space; half a dome. —**sem'i·domed'** (-dōmd') *adj.*

sem·i·el·lip·ti·cal (sĕm'ē-ĭ-lĭp'tĭ-kəl, sĕm'ī-) *adj.* Having the form or shape of half of an ellipse, esp. when divided along the major axis.

sem·i·fi·nal (sĕm'ē-fī'nəl, sĕm'ī-) *n.* **1.** A match, competition, or examination that precedes the final one. **2.** One of the two competitions of the next to the last round in an elimination tournament. —**sem'i·fi'nal** *adj.* —**sem'i·fi'nal·ist** *n.*

sem·i·fin·ished (sĕm'ē-fĭn'ĭsht, sĕm'ī-) *adj.* **1.** Made, treated, or sold to be used in a finished product. **2.** Partially finished.

sem·i·flu·id (sĕm'ē-flōō'ĭd, sĕm'ī-) *adj.* Intermediate in flow properties between solids and liquids; viscous. —**sem'i·flu'id** *n.* —**sem'i·flu·id'i·ty** *n.*

sem·i·gloss (sĕm'ē-glôs', -glŏs', sĕm'ī-) *n.* A paint that dries with a finish that is between gloss and flat. —**sem'i·gloss', sem'i·gloss'y** *adj.*

sem·i·group (sĕm'ē-grōōp', sĕm'ī-) *n. Mathematics* A set for which there is a binary operation that is closed and associative.

sem·i·in·de·pen·dent (sĕm'ē-ĭn'dĭ-pĕn'dənt, sĕm'ī-) *adj.* **1.** Partially independent. **2.** Semiautonomous.

sem·i·in·fi·nite (sĕm'ē-ĭn'fə-nīt, sĕm'ī-) *adj. Mathematics* Unbounded in one direction or dimension.

sem·i·liq·uid (sĕm'ē-lĭk'wĭd, sĕm'ī-) *adj.* Semifluid. —**sem'i·liq'uid** *n.* —**sem'i·li·quid'i·ty** *n.*

sem·i·lit·er·ate (sĕm′ē-lĭt′ər-ĭt, sĕm′ī-) *adj.* **1.** Having achieved an elementary level of ability in reading and writing. **2.** Having limited knowledge or understanding, esp. of a technical subject. —**sem′i·lit′er·a·cy** (-ər-ə-sē) *n.*

Sé·mil·lon also **Se·mil·lon** (sā′mĕl-yôN′) *n.* **1.** A variety of late-ripening grape, often blended with other grapes to produce a dry white wine. **2.** A white wine produced from this grape. [Fr. < obsolete *sémillon* < dialectal *semilhoun* < O Provençal *semilhar*, to sow < *seme*, seed < Lat. *sēmen*. See SEMEN.]

sem·i·log·a·rith·mic (sĕm′ē-lô′gə-rĭth′mĭk, -lŏg′ə-, sĕm′ī-) *adj.* Having one logarithmic and one arithmetic scale: *semilogarithmic graph paper.*

sem·i·lu·nar (sĕm′ē-lōō′nər, sĕm′ī-) also **sem·i·lu·nate** (-lōō′nāt′) *adj.* Shaped like a half-moon; crescent-shaped.

semilunar cartilage *n.* Either of the crescent-shaped wedges of fibrocartilage found in the knee joint.

semilunar valve *n.* Either of two valves, one at the opening of the aorta and the other at the opening of the pulmonary artery, each made up of three crescent-shaped cusps and serving to keep blood from flowing back into the ventricles.

sem·i·month·ly (sĕm′ē-mŭnth′lē, sĕm′ī-) *adj.* Occurring or is-sued twice a month. ❖ *n., pl.* **-lies** A semimonthly publication. ❖ *adv.* At intervals twice monthly. See Usage Note at **bi-¹**.

sem·i·nal (sĕm′ə-nəl) *adj.* **1.** Of, relating to, containing, or con-veying semen or seed. **2.** Of, relating to, or having the power to originate; creative. **3.** Highly influential in an original way; con-stituting or providing a basis for further development. [ME < OFr. < Lat. *sēminālis* < *sēmen, sēmin-*, seed. See SEMEN.] —**sem′i·nal·ly** *adv.*

seminal duct *n.* The duct of the testis that carries semen out-ward, esp. the part of the duct that runs from the epididymis to the ejaculatory duct.

seminal fluid *n.* See **semen.**

seminal vesicle *n.* Either of a pair of pouchlike glands on each side of the male urinary bladder that secrete seminal fluid.

sem·i·nar (sĕm′ə-när′) *n.* **1a.** A small group of students in a col-lege or graduate school engaged in original research or intensive study under the guidance of a professor. **b.** A course of study so pursued. **c.** A scheduled meeting of such a group. **2.** A meeting for an exchange of ideas; a conference. [Ger. < Lat. *sēminārium*, seed plot. See SEMINARY.]

sem·i·nar·i·an (sĕm′ə-nâr′ē-ən) also **sem·i·nar·ist** (-ĭst) *n.* A student at a seminary.

sem·i·nar·y (sĕm′ə-nĕr′ē) *n., pl.* **-ies 1a.** A school, esp. a theo-logical school for the training of priests, ministers, or rabbis. **b.** A school of higher education, esp. a private school for girls. **2.** A place or environment in which something is developed or nur-tured. [ME, seed plot < Lat. *sēminārium* < *sēminārius*, of seed < *sēmen, sēmin-*, seed. See **sē-** in App.]

sem·i·nif·er·ous (sĕm′ə-nĭf′ər-əs) *adj. Biology* **1.** Conveying, containing, or producing semen. **2.** Bearing seed. [Lat. *sēmen, sēmin-*, seed, semen; see SEMEN + −FEROUS.]

seminiferous tubule *n.* One of two or three twisted, curved tu-bules contained in the testis in which spermatozoa develop.

sem·i·niv·o·rous (sĕm′ə-nĭv′ər-əs) *adj.* Feeding on seeds. [Lat. *sēmen, sēmin-*, seed; see SEMEN + −VOROUS.]

Sem·i·nole (sĕm′ə-nōl′) *n., pl.* **Seminole** or **-noles 1.** A mem-ber of a Native American people made up of various primarily Creek groups who moved into Florida during the 18th and 19th centuries, with present-day populations in Oklahoma and Flor-ida. **2.** Either of their Muskogean languages. [Alteration of *Semi-nolie* < Creek *simalóoni, simanóoli*, runaway < Am.Sp. *cimarrón*. See MAROON².]

Seminole bread *n.* See **coontie.**

sem·i·no·ma (sĕm′ə-nō′mə) *n., pl.* **-mas** or **-ma·ta** (-mə-tə) A malignant tumor of the testis arising from sperm-forming tissue. [Lat. *sēmen, sēmin-*, semen; see SEMEN + −OMA.]

sem·i·no·mad (sĕm′ē-nō′mād′) *n.* One of a people whose living habits are largely nomadic but who plant some crops at a base point. —**sem′i·no·mad′ic** *adj.*

se·mi·ol·o·gy (sē′mē-ŏl′ə-jē, sĕm′ē-, sē′mī-) *n.* **1a.** The study of signs or sign language. **b.** The use of signs in signaling, as with a semaphore. **2.** Symptomatology. [Gk. *sēmeion*, sign; see SEMI-OTIC + −LOGY.]

se·mi·ot·ic (sē′mē-ŏt′ĭk, sĕm′ē-, sē′mī-) also **se·mi·ot·i·cal** (-ĭ-kəl) *adj.* **1.** Of or relating to semantics. **2.** Relating to symp-tomatology. [Gk. *sēmeiōtikos*, significant < *sēmeiōsis*, indication < *sēmeioun*, to signal, to interpret as a sign < *sēmeion*, sign < *sēma*.] —**se′mi·ot′i·cal·ly** *adv.*

se·mi·ot·ics (sē′mē-ŏt′ĭks, sĕm′ē-, sē′mī-) *n.* (*used with a sing.*

verb) The theory and study of signs and symbols, esp. as elements of language or other systems of communication. —**se′mi·o·ti′cian** (-ə-tĭsh′ən) *n.*

sem·i·o·vip·a·rous (sĕm′ē-ō-vĭp′ər-əs, sĕm′ī-) *adj.* Bearing young that are incompletely developed, as a marsupial.

Sem·i·pa·la·tinsk (sĕm′ē-pə-lä′tĭnsk) See **Semey.**

sem·i·pal·mate (sĕm′ē-păl′māt, -pä′-, -păl′māt, sĕm′ī-) also **sem·i·pal·mat·ed** (-mā′tĭd) *adj.* Having partial or reduced webbing between the toes, as some wading birds.

sem·i·par·a·site (sĕm′ē-pär′ə-sīt′, sĕm′ī-) *n.* See **hemipara-site** 1. —**sem′i·par′a·sit′ic** (-sĭt′ĭk) *adj.*

sem·i·per·me·a·ble (sĕm′ē-pûr′mē-ə-bəl, sĕm′ī-) *adj.* **1.** Par-tially permeable. **2.** Allowing passage of certain, esp. small mole-cules or ions but barring others. Used of biological and synthetic membranes. —**sem′i·per′me·a·bil′i·ty** *n.*

sem·i·por·ce·lain (sĕm′ē-pôr′sə-lĭn, -pôr′-, sĕm′ī-) *n.* Any of several glazed ceramics resembling porcelain but opaque.

sem·i·pre·cious stone (sĕm′ē-prĕsh′əs, sĕm′ī-) *n.* A gem, such as an opal, that has commercial value but is not as rare or expensive as a precious stone.

sem·i·pri·vate (sĕm′ē-prī′vĭt, sĕm′ī-) *adj.* Shared with usu. one to three other hospital patients: *a semiprivate room.*

sem·i·pro (sĕm′ē-prō′, sĕm′ī-) *adj. Informal* Semiprofessional: *a semipro baseball player.* —**sem′i·pro′** *n.*

sem·i·pro·fes·sion·al (sĕm′ē-prə-fĕsh′ə-nəl, sĕm′ī-) *adj.* **1.** Taking part in a sport for pay but not on a full-time basis. **2.** Composed of or engaged in by semiprofessional players. ❖ *n.* **1.** A semiprofessional player. **2.** One whose occupation or work has some of the characteristics of a profession or of a professional.

sem·i·pub·lic (sĕm′ē-pŭb′lĭk, sĕm′ī-) *adj.* **1.** Partially but not entirely open to the use of the public. **2.** Partially but not totally owned by the public. **3.** Open to the knowledge and judgment of only a part of the public.

sem·i·qua·ver (sĕm′ē-kwā′vər) *n. Chiefly British* A sixteenth note.

sem·i·round (sĕm′ē-round′, sĕm′ī-) *adj.* Having a round side and a flat side. ❖ *n.* (sĕm′ē-round′, sĕm′ī-) Something that has a round side and a flat side.

sem·i·skilled (sĕm′ē-skĭld′, sĕm′ī-) *adj.* **1.** Possessing some skills but not enough to do specialized work. **2.** Requiring limited skills: *a semiskilled job.*

sem·i·soft (sĕm′ē-sôft′, -sŏft′, sĕm′ī-) *adj.* **1.** Of medium soft-ness. **2.** Firm but easily sliced: *semisoft cheese.*

sem·i·sol·id (sĕm′ē-sŏl′ĭd, sĕm′ī-) *adj.* Intermediate in proper-ties, esp. in rigidity, between solids and liquids. ❖ *n.* (sĕm′ē-sŏl′ĭd, sĕm′ī-) A semisolid substance, as a stiff dough.

sem·i·sub·mers·i·ble (sĕm′ē-səb-mûr′sə-bəl, sĕm′ī-) *n.* A seagoing self-propelled barge that rides at anchor, stands on par-tially submerged vertical legs, and serves as a base of operations in offshore drilling. —**sem′i·sub·mer′si·ble** *adj.*

sem·i·sweet (sĕm′ē-swēt′, sĕm′ī-) *adj.* Having a small amount of sweetening: *semisweet chocolate.*

sem·i·syn·thet·ic (sĕm′ē-sĭn-thĕt′ĭk, sĕm′ī-) *adj.* **1.** Prepared by chemical synthesis from natural materials. **2.** Consisting of a mixture of natural and synthetic substances.

Sem·ite (sĕm′īt′) *n.* **1.** A member of a group of Semitic-speaking peoples of the Near East and northern Africa, including the Arabs, Ethiopians, Hebrews, and Phoenicians. **2.** A Jew. **3.** *Bible* A descendant of Shem.

sem·i·ter·res·tri·al (sĕm′ē-tə-rĕs′trē-əl, sĕm′ī-) *adj.* Not growing or living entirely on land; partly terrestrial.

Se·mit·ic (sə-mĭt′ĭk) *adj.* **1.** Of or relating to the Semites or their languages or cultures. **2.** Of, relating to, or being a subgroup of the Afro-Asiatic language group that includes Arabic, Hebrew, Amharic, and Aramaic. ❖ *n.* **1.** The Semitic languages. **2.** Any one of the Semitic languages. [NLat. *Sēmiticus* < *Sēmita*, Semite < LLat. *Sēm*, Shem, eponymous ancestor of the Semites < Gk. < Heb. *Šēm*.]

Se·mit·ics (sə-mĭt′ĭks) *n.* (*used with a sing. verb*) The study of the history, languages, and cultures of the Semitic peoples. —**Se·mit′i·cist** (-ĭ-sĭst), **Sem′i·tist** (sĕm′ĭ-tĭst) *n.*

Sem·i·tism (sĕm′ĭ-tĭz′əm) *n.* **1.** A Semitic word or idiom. **2.** Se-mitic traits, attributes, or customs. **3.** A policy or predisposition in favor of Jews.

sem·i·tone (sĕm′ē-tōn′, sĕm′ī-) *n. Music* An interval equal to a half tone in the standard diatonic scale. —**sem′i·to′nal** *adj.* —**sem′i·to′nal·ly** *adv.*

sem·i·trail·er (sĕm′ē-trā′lər, sĕm′ī-) *n.* A trailer having one or more sets of wheels at the rear only, with the forward portion supported by the truck tractor or towing vehicle.

semisubmersible

sem′i·at·tached′ *adj.*	**sem′i·di·vine′** *adj.*
sem′i·au·to·bi·o·graph′i·cal *adj.*	**sem′i·dry′** *adj.*
sem′i·au·to·mat′ed *adj.*	**sem′i·e·las′tic** *adj.*
sem′i·bald′ *adj.*	**sem′i·fic′tion·al** *adj.*
sem′i·bi·o·graph′i·cal *adj.*	**sem′i·fic·ti′tious** *adj.*
sem′i·civ′i·lized′ *adj.*	**sem′i·flex′i·ble** *adj.*
sem′i·col·lo·qui·al *adj.*	**sem′i·flex′i·bly** *adv.*
sem′i·dark′ness *n.*	**sem′i·for′mal** *adj.*
	sem′i·hard′ *adj.*

sem′i·mem′bra·nous *adj.*	**sem′i·o·paque′** *adj.*
sem′i·moun·tain·ous *adj.*	**sem′i·po·lit′i·cal** *adj.*
sem′i·mys′ti·cal *adj.*	**sem′i·po·lit′i·cal·ly** *adv.*
sem′i·mys′ti·cal·ly *adv.*	**sem′i·re·tired′** *adj.*
sem′i·neu′tral·i·ty *n.*	**sem′i·re·tire′ment** *n.*
sem′i·nude′ *adv. & adj.*	**sem′i·rig′id** *adj.*
sem′i·nu′di·ty *n.*	**sem′i·ru′ral** *adj.*
sem′i·of·fi′cial *adv.*	**sem′i·trans·par′ent** *adj.*
sem′i·of·fi′cial·ly *adv.*	

sem·i·trop·i·cal (sĕm′ē-trŏp′ĭ-kəl, sĕm′ī-) *adj.* Partly tropical; subtropical.

sem·i·vow·el (sĕm′ē-vou′əl) *n.* A sound with a high vowel quality, as (ē) or (ōō), functioning as a consonant before vowels, as the initial sounds of *yell* and *well.*

sem·i·week·ly (sĕm′ē-wēk′lē, sĕm′ī-) *adj.* Issued or occurring twice a week. ❖ *n., pl.* **-lies** A semiweekly event or publication. ❖ *adv.* Twice weekly. See Usage Note at **bi-**[1].

sem·i·year·ly (sĕm′ē-yîr′lē, sĕm′ī-) *adj.* Issued or occurring twice a year or once every half year. ❖ *n., pl.* **-lies** A semiyearly event or publication. ❖ *adv.* Every half year.

sem·o·li·na (sĕm′ə-lē′nə) *n.* The coarse particles of wheat left after the finer flour has passed through a bolting machine, used for pasta. [Alteration of Ital. *semolino,* dim. of *semola,* bran < Lat. *simila,* fine flour, ult. (perh. via Gk. *semidális*) of Semitic orig.; akin to Aram. *səmidā,* fine flour < Akkadian *samīdu,* type of groats < *samādu,* to grind into groats.]

sem·pi·ter·nal (sĕm′pĭ-tûr′nəl) *adj.* Enduring forever; eternal. See Syns at **infinite.** [Ult. < LLat. *sempiternālis* < Lat. *sempiternus : semper,* always; see **sem-**[1] in App. + *aeternus,* eternal; see *aiw-* in App.] —**sem′pi·ter′ni·ty** (-nĭ-tē) *n.*

sem·pli·ce (sĕm′plĭ-chā′) *adv. & adj. Music* In a simple or plain manner. [Ital. < Lat. *simplex, simplic-,* simple. See **sem-**[1] in App.]

sem·pre (sĕm′prā) *adv. Music* In the same manner throughout. [Ital., always < Lat. *semper.* See **sem-**[1] in App.]

Sem·tex (sĕm′tĕks′) *n.* A highly malleable plastic explosive. [*Semt(in),* village in the Czech Republic where the explosive is manufactured + E. EX(PLOSIVE).]

Sen. *abbr.* **1a.** senate **b.** senator **2.** or **sen.** senior

se·nar·i·us (sə-nâr′ē-əs) *n., pl.* **-i·i** (-ē-ī′, -ē-ē′) A Latin verse of six iambic feet. [Lat. *sēnārius.* See SENARY.]

sen·a·ry (sĕn′ə-rē) *adj.* **1.** Of or relating to the number six. **2.** Having six things or parts. [Lat. *sēnārius < sēnī,* six each < *sex,* six. See **s(w)eks** in App.]

sen·ate (sĕn′ĭt) *n.* **1.** An assembly or a council of citizens having the highest deliberative and legislative functions in a government, esp.: **a. Senate** The upper house of the US Congress, to which two members are elected from each state. **b.** often **Senate** The upper house in the bicameral legislature of many states in the United States. **c. Senate** The upper legislative house in Canada, France, and some other countries. **d.** The supreme council of state of the ancient Roman Republic and later of the Roman Empire. **2.** The building or hall in which a senate meets. **3.** A governing, advisory, or disciplinary body of some colleges and universities. [ME *senat* < OFr. < Lat. *senātus < senex, sen-,* old, an elder.]

sen·a·tor (sĕn′ə-tər) *n.* A member of a senate. —**sen′a·tor·ship′** *n.*

sen·a·to·ri·al (sĕn′ə-tôr′ē-əl, -tōr′-) *adj.* **1.** Of, concerning, or befitting a senator or senate. **2.** Composed of senators. —**sen′a·to′ri·al·ly** *adv.*

senatorial courtesy *n.* The custom in the US Senate of refusing to confirm a presidential appointment to office opposed by both senators from the state of the appointee or by the senior senator of the President's party.

senatorial district *n.* A territorial district from which a senator is elected.

send[1] (sĕnd) *v.* **sent** (sĕnt), **send·ing, sends** —*tr.* **1.** To cause to be conveyed by an intermediary to a destination: *send goods by plane.* **2.** To dispatch, as by a communications medium: *send a message by radio.* **3a.** To direct to go on a mission: *sent troops into the Middle East.* **b.** To require or enable to go: *sent her children to college.* **c.** To direct (a person) to a source of information; refer. **4a.** To give off (heat, for example); emit or issue. **b.** To utter or otherwise emit (sound). **5.** To hit so as to direct or propel with force; drive. **6.** To cause to take place or occur: *whatever fate may send.* **7a.** To put or drive into a given state or condition: *news that sent them into a panic.* **b.** *Slang* To transport with delight; carry away. —*intr.* **1.** To dispatch someone to do an errand or convey a message: *sent out for pizza.* **2.** To dispatch a request or an order, esp. by mail. **3.** To transmit a message or messages. —*phrasal verbs:* **send down** *Chiefly British* To suspend or dismiss from a university. **send for** To request to come by means of a message or messenger; summon. **send in 1.** To cause to arrive or to be delivered to the recipient. **2.** *Sports* To put (a player) into or back into a game or contest. **3.** To cause (someone) to arrive in or become involved in a particular place or situation: *It's time to send in the lawyers.* **send off** *Sports* To eject (a player) from a soccer game. **send up** *Informal* **1.** To send to jail. **2.** To make a parody of. —*idioms:* **send flying** *Informal* To cause to be knocked or scattered about with force. **send packing** To dismiss (someone) abruptly. [ME *senden* < OE *sendan.*] —**send′er** *n.*

send[2] (sĕnd) *v. & n.* Variant of **scend.**

Sen·dai (sĕn-dī′) A city of NE Honshu, Japan, on an inlet of the Pacific N of Tokyo. Pop. 950,893.

Sen·dak (sĕn′dăk′), **Maurice** b. 1928. American illustrator and writer of children's books, including *Where the Wild Things Are* (1963).

sen·dal (sĕn′dl) *n.* A thin light silk used in the Middle Ages for fine garments, church vestments, and banners. [ME *cendal* < OFr., ult. < Gk. *sindōn,* fine linen.]

send·off (sĕnd′ôf′, -ŏf′) *n.* **1.** A demonstration of affection and good wishes for a new undertaking. **2.** A farewell.

send-up or **send·up** (sĕnd′ŭp′) *n. Informal* An amusing imitation or parody; a takeoff.

Sen·e·ca (sĕn′ĭ-kə) *n., pl.* **Seneca** or **-cas 1.** A member of a Native American people formerly inhabiting western New York, with present-day populations in this same area and in southeast Ontario. **2.** The Iroquoian language of the Seneca. [< Du. *Sennecaas,* prob. of Mahican orig.]

Seneca, Lucius Annaeus Known as "the Younger." 4 B.C.?–A.D. 65. Roman Stoic philosopher and writer whose works include treatises on rhetoric and governance and numerous plays.

Seneca Falls A village of W-central NY on the Seneca R. ESE of Rochester; site of the first women's rights convention (1848). Pop. 6,861.

Seneca Lake A lake of W-central NY connected with Cayuga Lake by the **Seneca River,** c. 105 km (65 mi).

Seneca snakeroot *n.* An eastern North American plant (*Polygala senega*) with a terminal small white flower cluster.

se·nec·ti·tude (sĭ-nĕk′tĭ-tōōd′, -tyōōd′) *n.* Old age; elderliness. [Med.Lat. *senectitūdō* < Lat. *senectūs < senex,* old, an elder.]

sen·e·ga (sĕn′ĭ-gə) *n.* The dried roots of the Seneca snakeroot, used as an expectorant. [Alteration of SENECA.]

Sen·e·gal (sĕn′ĭ-gôl′, -gäl′) A country of W Africa on the Atlantic Ocean; achieved independence from France in 1960. Cap. Dakar. Pop. 8,102,000. —**Sen′e·ga·lese′** (-gô-lēz′, -lēs′, -gə-) *adj. & n.*

Senegal River A river of W Africa rising in W Mali and flowing c. 1,609 km (1,000 mi) to the Atlantic Ocean.

Sen·e·gam·bi·a (sĕn′ĭ-găm′bē-ə) A region of W Africa watered by the Senegal and Gambia rivers.

se·nes·cent (sĭ-nĕs′ənt) *adj.* Growing old; aging. [Lat. *senēscēns, senēscent-,* pr. part. of *senēscere,* to grow old, inchoative of *senēre,* to be old < *senex, sen-,* old.] —**se·nes′cence** *n.*

sen·e·schal (sĕn′ə-shəl) *n.* An official in a medieval noble household in charge of domestic arrangements and servants; a steward or major-domo. [ME < OFr., of Gmc. orig.]

Sen·ghor (säN-gôr′), **Léopold** 1906–2001. Senegalese poet and politician who served (1960–80) as the first president of Senegal following independence from France.

se·nile (sē′nīl′, sĕn′īl′) *adj.* **1.** Of, relating to, or characteristic of old age. **2.** Relating to or exhibiting memory loss or mental impairment associated with aging. **3.** *Geology* Eroded nearly to the base level. [Lat. *senīlis < senex, sen-,* old.] —**se′nile′ly** *adv.*

senile dementia *n.* A progressive, abnormally accelerated deterioration of mental faculties and emotional stability in old age, occurring esp. in Alzheimer's disease.

se·nil·i·ty (sĭ-nĭl′ĭ-tē) *n.* **1.** Old age. **2.** The mental and physical deterioration associated with aging.

sen·ior (sēn′yər) *adj.* **1.** Of or being the older of two, esp. the older of two persons having the same name, as father and son. **2.** Of or relating to senior citizens. **3a.** Being in a position, rank, or grade above others of the same set or class: *a senior officer.* **b.** Having precedence in making certain decisions. **4.** Of or relating to the fourth and last year of high school or college. ❖ *n.* **1a.** A person who is older than another. **b.** A senior citizen. **2a.** One that is senior, as in rank, to another. **b.** A student in the fourth year of high school or college. [ME < Lat., comp. of *senex,* old.]

senior airman *n.* A noncommissioned officer in the US Air Force ranking above airman first class and below staff sergeant.

senior chief petty officer *n.* A noncommissioned officer in the US Navy ranking above chief petty officer and below master chief petty officer.

senior citizen *n.* A person of relatively advanced age, esp. a person at or over the age of retirement. —**senior citizenry** *n.*

senior high school *n.* A high school usu. constituting grades 10, 11, and 12.

sen·ior·i·ty (sēn-yôr′ĭ-tē, -yŏr′-) *n.* **1.** The state of being older or higher in rank than others. **2.** Precedence of position, esp. over others of the same rank because of longer service.

senior lecturer *n. Chiefly British* A university teacher, esp. one ranking next below a reader.

senior master sergeant *n.* A noncommissioned officer in the US Air Force ranking above master sergeant and below chief master sergeant.

Sen·lac (sĕn′lăk′) A hill in S England near Hastings; site of the Battle of Hastings (1066), in which William the Conqueror defeated Harold II.

sen·na (sĕn′ə) *n.* **1.** Any of various plants of the genus *Cassia,* having pinnately compound leaves and showy, usu. yellow flowers. **2.** The dried leaves of *Cassia angustifolia* or *C. acutifolia,* used medicinally as a cathartic. [NLat. < Ar. *sanā;* akin to Aram. *sanyā,* a thorn-bush.]

Sen·nach·er·ib (sĭ-năk′ər-ĭb) d. 681 B.C. King of Assyria (704–681) who subjugated Babylon and rebuilt Nineveh.

sen·na·chie (sĕn′ə-kē) *n. Chiefly Scots* Variant of **shanachie.**

sen·net[1] (sĕn′ĭt) *n.* A call on a trumpet or cornet signaling the ceremonial exits and entrances of actors in Elizabethan drama. [Perh. var. of SIGNET.]

sen·net[2] (sĕn′ĭt) *n.* Any of several barracudas, esp. *Sphyraena borealis,* of the western Atlantic. [?]

Sen·nett (sĕn′ĭt), **Mack** 1880?–1960. Canadian-born Amer.

Senegal

Léopold Senghor
photographed in 1973

filmmaker known for his slapstick motion pictures.

sen·night (sĕn′īt′) *n. Archaic* A week. [ME *senight*, contraction of *seveniht* < OE *seofon nihta*, seven nights.]

sen·nit (sĕn′ĭt) *n.* **1.** Braided cordage formed by plaiting strands of rope fiber or similar material. **2.** Plaited straw, grass, or palm leaves for making hats. [?]

se·no·pi·a (sĭ-nō′pē-ə) *n.* Improvement of near vision sometimes in the aged because of swelling of the lens due to incipient cataract. [Lat. *senex, sen-,* old + −OPIA.]

se·ñor (sān-yôr′, sĕ-nyôr′) *n., pl.* **se·ño·res** (sān-yôr′ās, sĕ-nyō′rĕs) **1a.** Used as a courtesy title before the surname, full name, or professional title of a man in a Spanish-speaking area. **b.** Used as a form of polite address for a man in a Spanish-speaking area. **2.** A Spanish or Spanish-speaking man. [Sp. < OSpan. *sennor* < VLat. **senior,* lord < Lat., senior. See SENIOR.]

se·ño·ra (sān-yôr′ä, sĕ-nyō′rä) *n.* Used as a courtesy title before the surname or full name of a married woman in Spanish-speaking area. **b.** Used as a form of polite address for a woman in a Spanish-speaking area. **2.** A Spanish or Spanish-speaking woman. [Sp., fem. of *señor,* señor. See SEÑOR.]

se·ño·ri·ta (sān′yə-rē′tə, sĕ′nyō-rē′tä) *n.* **1a.** Used as a courtesy title before the surname or full name of a girl or unmarried woman in a Spanish-speaking area. **b.** Used as a form of address for a girl or young woman in a Spanish-speaking area. **2.** A Spanish or Spanish-speaking unmarried woman or girl. [Sp., dim. of *señora,* señora. See SEÑORA.]

sen·sate (sĕn′sāt′) also **sen·sat·ed** (-sā′tĭd) *adj.* **1.** Perceived by a sense or the senses. **2.** Having physical sensation. [ME *sensat* < LLat. *sēnsātus,* gifted with sense < Lat. *sēnsus,* sense. See SENSE.] —**sen′sate·ly** *adv.*

sen·sa·tion (sĕn-sā′shən) *n.* **1a.** A perception associated with stimulation of a sense organ or with a specific body condition. **b.** The faculty to feel or perceive; physical sensibility. **c.** An indefinite generalized body feeling. **2.** A state of heightened interest or emotion. **3a.** A state of intense public interest and excitement. **b.** A cause of such interest and excitement. See Syns at **wonder.** [Fr. < OFr. < Med.Lat. *sēnsātiō, sēnsātiōn-* < LLat. *sēnsātus,* gifted with sense. See SENSATE.]

sen·sa·tion·al (sĕn-sā′shə-nəl) *adj.* **1.** Of or relating to sensation. **2.** Arousing or intended to arouse strong curiosity, interest, or reaction, esp. by exaggerated or lurid details. **3.** Outstanding; spectacular. —**sen·sa′tion·al·ly** *adv.*

sen·sa·tion·al·ism (sĕn-sā′shə-nə-lĭz′əm) *n.* **1a.** The use of sensational matter or methods, esp. in writing, journalism, or politics. **b.** Sensational subject matter. **c.** Interest in or the effect of such subject matter. **2.** *Philosophy* The theory that sensation is the only source of knowledge. —**sen·sa′tion·al·ist** *n.* —**sen·sa′tion·al·is′tic** *adj.*

sen·sa·tion·al·ize (sĕn-sā′shə-nə-līz′) *tr.v.* **-ized, -iz·ing, -iz·es** To cast and present in a sensational manner. —**sen·sa′tion·al·i·za·tion** (-lĭ-zā′shən) *n.*

sense (sĕns) *n.* **1.** Any of the faculties by which stimuli are received and felt, as the faculties of hearing, sight, and equilibrium. **b.** A perception or feeling produced by a stimulus; sensation. **2. senses** The faculties of sensation as means of providing physical gratification and pleasure. **3.** Intuitive or acquired perception or ability to estimate: *a sense of timing.* **a.** A capacity to appreciate or understand: *a sense of humor.* **b.** A vague feeling or presentiment. **c.** Recognition or perception either through the senses or through the intellect; consciousness: *has no sense of shame.* **4a.** Natural understanding or intelligence, esp. in practical matters. **b.** The normal ability to think or reason soundly. Often used in the plural: *Come to your senses.* **c.** Something sound or reasonable. **5a.** A meaning that is conveyed, as in speech or writing; signification. **b.** One of the meanings of a word or phrase. See Syns at **meaning. 6a.** Judgment; consensus. **b.** Intellectual interpretation, as of the significance of an event or the conclusions reached by a group. ❖ *tr.v.* **sensed, sens·ing, sens·es 1.** To become aware of; perceive. **2.** To grasp; understand. **3.** To detect automatically: *sense radioactivity.* ❖ *adj. Genetics* Of or relating to the portion of the strand of double-stranded DNA that serves as a template for and is transcribed into RNA. [ME, meaning < OFr. *sens* < Lat. *sēnsus,* the faculty of perceiving < p. part. of *sentīre,* to feel.]

sense datum *n.* A basic unanalyzable sensation, such as a color, experienced upon stimulation of a sense organ or receptor.

sense·less (sĕns′lĭs) *adj.* **1.** Lacking sense or meaning; meaningless. **2.** Deficient in sense; foolish or stupid. **3.** Insensate; unconscious. —**sense′less·ly** *adv.* —**sense′less·ness** *n.*

sense organ *n.* A specialized organ or structure, such as the eye, ear, tongue, nose, or skin, that functions as a receptor.

sense perception *n.* Perception by or based on stimulation of the senses.

sen·si·bil·i·ty (sĕn′sə-bĭl′ĭ-tē) *n., pl.* **-ties 1.** The ability to feel or perceive. **2a.** Keen intellectual perception. **b.** Mental or emotional responsiveness toward something, such as the feelings of another. **3.** Receptiveness to impression, whether pleasant or unpleasant; acuteness of feeling. Often used in the plural. **4.** Refined awareness and appreciation in matters of feeling. **5.** The quality of being affected by changes in the environment.

sen·si·ble (sĕn′sə-bəl) *adj.* **1.** Perceptible by the senses or by the mind. **2.** Readily perceived; appreciable. **3.** Having the faculty of

sensation; able to feel or perceive. **4.** Having a perception of something. See Syns at **aware. 5.** Acting with or exhibiting good sense: *a sensible person.* [ME < OFr. < Lat. *sēnsibilis* < *sēnsus,* sense. See SENSE.] —**sen′si·ble·ness** *n.* —**sen′si·bly** *adv.*

sensible horizon *n.* The plane intersecting an observer's position perpendicular to the line formed by the observer's nadir and zenith.

sen·sil·lum (sĕn-sĭl′əm) *n., pl.* **-sil·la** (-sĭl′ə) A simple sensory receptor consisting of one cell or a few cells, esp. an epithelial cell projecting through the cuticle of arthropods. [NLat. *sēnsillum,* dim. of Lat. *sēnsus,* sense. See SENSE.]

sen·si·tive (sĕn′sĭ-tĭv) *adj.* **1.** Capable of perceiving with a sense or senses. **2.** Responsive to external conditions or stimulation. **3.** Susceptible to the attitudes, feelings, or circumstances of others. **4.** Quick to take offense; touchy. **5.** Easily irritated: *sensitive skin.* **6.** Readily altered by the action of an agent: *film that is sensitive to light.* **7.** Registering very slight differences or changes. Used of an instrument. **8.** Fluctuating or tending to fluctuate, as in price. **9.** Of or relating to classified information. ❖ *n.* **1.** A sensitive person. **2.** One held to be endowed with psychic or occult powers. [ME < OFr. *sensitif* < Med.Lat. *sēnsitīvus* < Lat. *sēnsus,* sense. See SENSE.] —**sen′si·tive·ly** *adv.* —**sen′si·tive·ness** *n.*

sensitive plant *n.* **1.** A shrubby tropical American plant (*Mimosa pudica*) having leaflets and leafstalks that fold and droop when touched. **2.** Any of various similar plants, such as *Cassia nictitans* of eastern and central North America.

sen·si·tiv·i·ty (sĕn′sĭ-tĭv′ĭ-tē) *n., pl.* **-ties 1.** The quality or condition of being sensitive. **2.** The capacity of an organ or organism to respond to stimulation. **3.** *Electronics* The degree of response of a receiver or instrument to an incoming signal or a change in the incoming signal. **4.** The degree of response of a plate or film to light, esp. to light of a specified wavelength.

sen·si·tize (sĕn′sĭ-tīz′) *v.* **-tized, -tiz·ing, -tiz·es** —*tr.* **1.** To make sensitive. **2.** To make (a film or plate) sensitive to light, esp. to light of a specific wavelength. **3.** To make hypersensitive or reactive to an antigen, such as pollen, esp. by repeated exposure. —*intr.* To become sensitive or hypersensitive. [SENSIT(IVE) + −IZE.] —**sen′si·ti·za′tion** (-tĭ-zā′shən) *n.* —**sen′si·tiz′er** *n.*

sen·si·tom·e·ter (sĕn′sĭ-tŏm′ĭ-tər) *n.* Any of various devices for measuring light sensitivity, as of photographic film. [SENSIT(IVITY) + −METER.] —**sen′si·to·met′ric** (-tə-mĕt′rĭk) *adj.* —**sen′si·tom′e·try** *n.*

sen·sor (sĕn′sər, -sôr′) *n.* **1.** A device that receives and responds to a signal or stimulus. **2.** See **sense organ.**

sen·so·ri·al (sĕn-sôr′ē-əl, -sōr′-) *adj.* Of or relating to sensations or sensory impressions. —**sen·so′ri·al·ly** *adv.*

sen·so·ri·mo·tor (sĕn′sə-rē-mō′tər) *adj.* Of, relating to, or involving both sensory and motor activity.

sen·so·ri·neu·ral (sĕn′sə-rē-nŏŏr′əl, -nyŏŏr′-) *adj.* Of, relating to, or involving the sensory nerves, esp. as they affect the hearing: *sensorineural deafness.*

sen·so·ri·um (sĕn-sôr′ē-əm, -sōr′-) *n., pl.* **-so·ri·ums** or **-so·ri·a** (-sôr′ē-ə, -sōr′-) **1.** The part of the brain that receives and coordinates all the stimuli conveyed to various sensory centers. **2.** The entire sensory system of the body. [LLat. *sēnsōrium,* organ of sensation < Lat. *sēnsus,* sense. See SENSE.]

sen·so·ry (sĕn′sə-rē) *adj.* **1.** Of or relating to the senses or sensation. **2.** Transmitting impulses from sense organs to nerve centers; afferent.

sensory deprivation *n.* Deprivation of sensory stimulation, as by prolonged isolation.

sen·su·al (sĕn′shŏŏ-əl) *adj.* **1.** Relating to or affecting any of the senses or a sense organ; sensory. **2a.** Of, relating to, given to, or providing gratification of the physical and esp. the sexual appetites. **b.** Suggesting sexuality; voluptuous. **c.** Physical rather than spiritual or intellectual. **d.** Lacking in moral or spiritual interests; worldly. —**sen′su·al·ly** *adv.* —**sen′su·al·ness** *n.*

sen·su·al·ism (sĕn′shŏŏ-ə-lĭz′əm) *n.* Excessive devotion to sensual pleasure; sensuality. —**sen′su·al·ist** *n.* —**sen′su·al·is′tic** *adj.*

sen·su·al·i·ty (sĕn′shŏŏ-ăl′ĭ-tē) *n.* **1.** The quality or state of being sensual or lascivious. **2.** Excessive devotion to sensual pleasure.

sen·su·al·ize (sĕn′shŏŏ-ə-līz′) *tr.v.* **-ized, -iz·ing, -iz·es** To make sensual. —**sen′su·al·i·za′tion** (-ə-lĭ-zā′shən) *n.*

sen·su·ous (sĕn′shŏŏ-əs) *adj.* **1.** Of, relating to, or derived from the senses. **2.** Appealing to or gratifying the senses. **3a.** Readily affected through the senses. **b.** Highly appreciative of the pleasures of sensation. —**sen′su·os′i·ty** (-ŏs′ĭ-tē), **sen′su·ous·ness** (-əs-nĭs) *n.* —**sen′su·ous·ly** *adv.*

sent (sĕnt) *v.* Past tense and past participle of **send**[1].

sen·tence (sĕn′təns) *n.* **1.** A grammatical unit that is syntactically independent and has a subject that is expressed or understood and a predicate that contains a finite verb. **2.** *Law* **a.** A court judgment, esp. a judicial decision of the punishment to be inflicted on one adjudged guilty. **b.** The penalty meted out. **3.** *Archaic* A maxim. **4.** *Obsolete* An opinion, esp. one given formally after deliberation. ❖ *tr.v.* **-tenced, -tenc·ing, -tenc·es** *Law* To pronounce sentence upon (one adjudged guilty). [ME, opinion < OFr. < Lat. *sententia < sentiēns, sentient-,* pr. part. of *sentīre,* to feel.] —**sen·ten′tial** (sĕn-tĕn′shəl) *adj.* —**sen·ten′tial·ly** *adv.*

sensitive plant
Mimosa pudica

sentence fragment *n.* A phrase or clause that is punctuated and capitalized as a sentence but does not constitute a complete grammatical sentence.

sen·tenc·er (sĕn′tən-sər) *n.* One, such as a court or judge, that pronounces sentence.

sentence stress *n.* The variation in emphasis or vocal stress on the syllables of words within a sentence.

sen·tenc·ing (sĕn′tən-sĭng) *adj.* **1.** Relating to a judicial sentence. **2.** Being or relating to the one who pronounces a judicial sentence. ❖ *n.* **1.** The act of pronouncing a judicial sentence on a defendant. **2.** This sentence.

sen·ten·tia (sĕn-tĕn′shə, -shē-ə) *n., pl.* **-ti·ae** (-shē-ē′) An adage or aphorism. [Lat. See SENTENCE.]

sen·ten·tious (sĕn-tĕn′shəs) *adj.* **1.** Terse and energetic in expression; pithy. **2.** Full of or given to using aphorisms, esp. in a pompously moralizing manner. [ME < OFr. *sententieux* < Lat. *sententiōsus,* full of meaning < *sententia,* opinion. See SENTENCE.] —**sen·ten′tious·ly** *adv.*

sen·tience (sĕn′shəns, -shē-əns) *n.* **1.** The quality or state of being sentient; consciousness. **2.** Feeling as distinguished from perception or thought.

sen·tient (sĕn′shənt, -shē-ənt) *adj.* **1.** Having sense perception; conscious. **2.** Experiencing sensation or feeling. [Lat. *sentiēns, sentient-,* pr. part. of *sentīre,* to feel.] —**sen′tient·ly** *adv.*

sen·ti·ment (sĕn′tə-mənt) *n.* **1.** A thought, view, or attitude, esp. one based mainly on emotion instead of reason: *an anti-American sentiment.* See Syns at **feeling. 2a.** Emotion; feeling: *the sentiment conveyed by the music.* **b.** Tender or romantic feeling. **c.** Maudlin emotion; sentimentality. **3.** The emotional import of a passage as distinct from its form of expression. **4.** The expression of delicate and sensitive feeling, esp. in art and literature. [ME *sentement* < OFr. < Med.Lat. *sentimentum* < Lat. *sentīre,* to feel.]

sen·ti·men·tal (sĕn′tə-mĕn′tl) *adj.* **1a.** Characterized or swayed by sentiment. **b.** Affectedly or extravagantly emotional. **2.** Resulting from or colored by emotion rather than reason or realism. **3.** Appealing to the sentiments, esp. to romantic feelings: *sentimental music.* —**sen′ti·men′tal·ly** *adv.*

sen·ti·men·tal·ism (sĕn′tə-mĕn′tl-ĭz′əm) *n.* **1.** A predilection for the sentimental. **2.** An idea or expression marked by excessive sentiment. —**sen′ti·men′tal·ist** *n.*

sen·ti·men·tal·i·ty (sĕn′tə-mĕn-tăl′ĭ-tē) *n., pl.* **-ties 1.** The quality or condition of being excessively or affectedly sentimental. **2.** A sentimental idea or an expression of it.

sen·ti·men·tal·ize (sĕn′tə-mĕn′tl-īz′) *v.* **-ized, -iz·ing, -iz·es** *—tr.* To imbue or regard with sentiment; be sentimental about. *—intr.* To behave in a sentimental manner. —**sen′ti·men′tal·i·za′tion** (-ī-zā′shən) *n.*

sen·ti·nel (sĕn′tə-nəl) *n.* One that keeps guard; a sentry. ❖ *tr.v.* **-neled, -nel·ing, -nels** *or* **-nelled, -nel·ling, -nels 1.** To watch over as a guard. **2.** To provide with a guard. **3.** To post as a guard. [Fr. *sentinelle* < Ital. *sentinella,* prob. < OItal. *sentina,* vigilance < *sentire,* to watch < Lat. *sentīre,* to feel.]

sen·try (sĕn′trē) *n., pl.* **-tries 1.** A guard, esp. a soldier posted at a given spot to prevent the passage of unauthorized persons. **2.** The duty of a sentry; watch. [Perh. alteration of obsolete *sentrinel,* var. of SENTINEL.]

sentry box *n.* A small shelter for a posted sentry.

Seoul (sōl) The cap. of South Korea, in the NW part E of Inchon; founded in the 14th cent. Pop. 10,726,862.

Sep. *abbr.* September

SEP *abbr.* simplified employee pension (plan)

se·pal (sē′pəl) *n.* One of the separate, usu. green parts forming the calyx of a flower. [NLat. *sepalum,* perh. blend of Gk. *skepē,* covering, and Lat. *petalum,* petal; see PETAL.] —**se′paled, sep′a·lous** (sĕp′ə-ləs) *adj.*

se·pal·oid (sē′pə-loid′, sĕp′ə-) *also* **se·pal·ine** (-līn′, -lĭn) *adj.* Resembling or characteristic of a sepal.

–sepalous *suff.* Having a specified kind or number of sepals: *gamosepalous.*

sep·a·ra·ble (sĕp′ər-ə-bəl, sĕp′rə-) *adj.* Possible to separate. —**sep′a·ra·bil′i·ty** *n.* —**sep′a·ra·bly** *adv.*

sep·a·rate (sĕp′ə-rāt′) *v.* **-rat·ed, -rat·ing, -rates** *—tr.* **1a.** To set or keep apart; disunite. **b.** To space apart; scatter. **c.** To sort. **2.** To differentiate or discriminate between; distinguish. **3.** To remove from a mixture or combination; isolate. **4.** To part (a couple), often by decree. **5.** To terminate a contractual relationship with; discharge. *—intr.* **1.** To come apart. **2.** To withdraw. **3.** To part company; disperse. **4.** To stop living together as spouses. **5.** To become divided into components or parts. ❖ *adj.* (sĕp′ər-ĭt, sĕp′rĭt) **1.** Set or kept apart; disunited. **2a.** Existing as an independent entity. **b.** often **Separate** Having undergone schism or estrangement from a parent body. **3.** Dissimilar from all others; distinct. **4.** Not shared; individual. **5.** *Archaic* Withdrawn from others; solitary. ❖ *n.* (sĕp′ər-ĭt, sĕp′rĭt) A garment, such as a skirt or jacket, that may be purchased separately and worn in various combinations with other garments. [ME *separaten* < Lat. *sēparātus,* p. part. of *sēparāre* : *sē-,* apart; see S(W)E- in App. + *parāre,* to prepare.] —**sep′a·rate·ly** *adv.* —**sep′a·rate·ness** *n.*

SYNONYMS *separate, divide, part, sever, sunder, divorce* These verbs mean to become or cause to become parted, disconnected, or disunited. *Separate* applies both to putting apart and to keeping apart: *"In the darkness and confusion, the bands of these commanders became separated from each other"* (Washington Irving). *Divide* implies separation by or as if by cutting or splitting into parts or shares; the term often refers to separation into opposing or hostile groups: *We divided the orange into segments.* *"'A house divided against itself cannot stand.' I believe this government cannot endure permanently half slave and half free"* (Abraham Lincoln). *Part* refers most often to the separation of closely associated persons or things: *"Because . . . nothing that God or Satan could inflict would have parted us"* (Emily Brontë). *Sever* usually implies abruptness and force: *"His head was nearly severed from his body"* (H.G. Wells). *Sunder* stresses violent tearing or wrenching apart: *The country was sundered by civil war.* *Divorce* implies complete separation: *"a priest and a soldier, two classes of men circumstantially divorced from the kind and homely ties of life"* (Robert Louis Stevenson).

sep·a·ra·tion (sĕp′ə-rā′shən) *n.* **1a.** The act or process of separating. **b.** The condition of being separated. **2.** The place at which a division or parting occurs. **3.** An interval or space that separates; a gap. **4a.** *Law* An agreement or court decree ending a spousal relationship. **b.** Discharge, as from employment.

sep·a·ra·tion·ist (sĕp′ə-rā′shə-nĭst) *n.* A separatist.

sep·a·ra·tist (sĕp′ər-ə-tĭst, sĕp′rə-, sĕp′ə-rā′-) *n.* **1.** One who secedes or advocates separation, esp. from an established church; a sectarian. **2.** One who advocates disjunction of a group from a larger group or political unit. **3.** One who advocates cultural, ethnic, or racial separation. —**sep′a·ra·tism** *n.* —**sep′a·ra·tist, sep′a·ra·tis′tic** *adj.*

sep·a·ra·tive (sĕp′ə-rā′tĭv, sĕp′ər-ə-, sĕp′rə-) *adj.* Tending to separate or to cause separation.

sep·a·ra·tor (sĕp′ə-rā′tər) *n.* One that separates, as a device for separating cream from milk.

Se·phar·di (sə-fär′dē) *n., pl.* **-dim** (-dĭm) A descendant of the Jews who lived in Spain and Portugal during the Middle Ages until persecution forced them to leave. [Med. Heb. *səpāraddî,* Spaniard < *səpārad,* Spain, adoption of Heb. *səpārad,* placename of disputed location mentioned at Obadiah 20.] —**Se·phar′dic** (-dĭk) *adj.*

se·pi·a (sē′pē-ə) *n.* **1a.** A dark brown ink or pigment originally prepared from the secretion of the cuttlefish. **b.** A drawing or picture done in sepia. **c.** A photograph in a brown tint. **2.** A dark grayish yellow brown to dark or moderate olive brown. ❖ *adj.* **1.** Of the color sepia. **2.** Done or made in sepia. [ME, cuttlefish < Lat. *sēpia,* cuttlefish, ink < Gk. *sēpiā,* cuttlefish; perh. akin to *sēpein,* to make rotten.]

Se·pik (sā′pĭk) A river, c. 1,126 km (700 mi), of N Papua New Guinea.

se·pi·o·lite (sē′pē-ə-līt′) *n.* See **meerschaum** 1. [Gk. *sēpion,* cuttlebone (< *sēpiā,* cuttlefish; see SEPIA) + -LITE.]

se·poy (sē′poi′) *n.* **1.** A regular soldier in some Middle Eastern countries, esp. an Indian soldier formerly serving under British command. **2.** The lowest enlisted rank in the British Indian army and its successors, equivalent to private. [Prob. < Port. *sipae* < Urdu *sipāhī* < Pers., cavalryman < *sipāh,* army.]

sep·pu·ku (sĕp′ōō-kōō, sĕ-pōō′-) *n.* Ritual suicide by disembowelment formerly practiced by Japanese samurai. [J. : *setsu,* to cut (< M Chin. *tshet*) + *fuku,* abdomen (< M Chin. *fuwk*).]

sep·sis (sĕp′sĭs) *n., pl.* **-ses** (-sēz) **1.** The presence of pathogenic organisms or their toxins in the blood or tissues. **2.** The poisoned condition resulting from sepsis, as in septicemia. [Gk. *sēpsis,* putrefaction < *sēpein,* to make rotten.]

sept (sĕpt) *n.* A division of a family, esp. a division of a clan. [Prob. alteration of SECT.]

Sept. *abbr.* September

sep·ta (sĕp′tə) *n.* Plural of **septum.**

sep·tage (sĕp′tĭj) *n.* The waste content found in a septic tank.

sep·tal (sĕp′təl) *adj.* Of or relating to a septum or septa.

sep·tar·i·um (sĕp-târ′ē-əm) *n., pl.* **-i·a** (-ē-ə) An irregular polygonal system of calcite-filled cracks occurring in certain rock concretions. [Lat. *saeptum,* partition; see SEPTUM + -ARIUM.] —**sep·tar′i·an** *adj.*

sep·tate (sĕp′tāt′) *adj.* Divided by a septum or septa.

Sep·tem·ber (sĕp-tĕm′bər) *n.* The ninth month of the year in the Gregorian calendar. See table at **calendar.** [ME *Septembre* < OFr. < Lat. *September,* the seventh month < *septem,* seven. See **septm** in App.]

Sep·tem·brist (sĕp-tĕm′brĭst) *n.* **1.** A bloodthirsty revolutionist or terrorist. **2.** One of the mob that massacred the imprisoned royalists in Paris, France, in September 1792.

sep·te·nar·i·us (sĕp′tə-nâr′ē-əs) *n., pl.* **-i·i** (-ē-ī′) A Latin verse used only in comedy and consisting of seven feet, esp. a catalectic iambic or trochaic tetrameter. [Lat. *septēnārius,* of seven < *septēnī,* seven each < *septem,* seven. See SEPTENNIAL.]

sep·ten·de·cil·lion (sĕp′tĕn-dĭ-sĭl′yən) *n.* **1.** The cardinal number equal to 10⁵⁴. **2.** *Chiefly British* The cardinal number equal to 10¹⁰². [Lat. *septendecim,* seventeen (*septem,* seven; see **septm** in App. + *decem,* ten; see DECI-) + (M)ILLION.] —**sep′ten·de·cil′lion** *adj.* —**sep′ten·de·cil′lionth** *adj., adv. & n.*

sep·ten·ni·al (sĕp-tĕn′ē-əl) *adj.* **1.** Occurring every seven years.

sentry box

2. Consisting of or continuing for seven years. ❖ *n.* An event that occurs every seven years. [< LLat. *septennium,* period of seven years < Lat. *septennis,* of seven years : *septem,* seven; see **septm** in App. + *annus,* year.] —**sep·ten′ni·al·ly** *adv.*

sep·ten·tri·on (sĕp-tĕn′trē-ŏn′, -ən) *n.* Obsolete Northern regions; the north. [ME < OFr. < Lat. *septentriōnēs,* seven plow oxen, the seven principal stars of Ursa Major : *septem,* seven; see **septm** in App. + *triōnēs* (pl. of *triō, trion-,* plow ox; see **tera-**[1] in App.).] —**sep·ten′tri·o·nal** (-trē-ə-nəl) *adj.*

sep·tet also **sep·tette** (sĕp-tĕt′) *n.* **1.** *Music* **a.** A composition for seven voices or seven instruments. **b.** A group of seven singers or seven instrumentalists. **2.** A group of seven. [Ger. *Septett* < Lat. *septem,* seven. See **septm** in App.]

sep·tic (sĕp′tĭk) *adj.* **1.** Of, relating to, having the nature of, or affected by sepsis. **2.** Causing sepsis; putrefactive. [Lat. *sēpticus,* putrefying < Gk. *sēptikos* < *sēptos,* rotten < *sēpein,* to make rotten.] —**sep·tic′i·ty** (-tĭs′ĭ-tē) *n.*

sep·ti·ce·mi·a (sĕp′tĭ-sē′mē-ə) *n.* A systemic disease caused by pathogenic organisms or their toxins in the bloodstream. [SEPTIC + -EMIA.] —**sep′ti·ce′mic** (-mĭk) *adj.*

sep·ti·ci·dal (sĕp′tĭ-sīd′l) *adj. Botany* Dehiscing by splitting along or through the septa. Used of a seed capsule. [SEPT(UM) + Lat. *-cīdere,* to cut (< *caedere;* see CAESURA) + -AL[1].]

septic shock *n.* A condition of physiologic shock caused by an overwhelming infection, esp. sepsis or septicemia.

septic tank *n.* A sewage-disposal tank in which a continuous flow of waste material is decomposed by anaerobic bacteria.

sep·tif·ra·gal (sĕp-tĭf′rə-gəl) *adj. Botany* Dehiscing by the breaking away of the valves from its partitions. Used of a seed capsule. [SEPT(UM) + Lat. *frangere,* to break; see **bhreg-** in App.]

sep·ti·lat·er·al (sĕp′tĭ-lăt′ər-əl) *adj.* Seven-sided. [Lat. *septem,* seven; see SEPTET + LATERAL.]

sep·til·lion (sĕp-tĭl′yən) *n.* **1.** The cardinal number equal to 10²⁴. **2.** *Chiefly British* The cardinal number equal to 10⁴². [Fr. : Lat. *septem,* seven; see SEPTET + Fr. *-illion* (as in *million,* million < OFr. *milion;* see MILLION).] —**sep·til′lion** *adj.*

sep·til·lionth (sĕp-tĭl′yənth) *n.* **1.** The ordinal number matching the number septillion in a series. **2.** One of a septillion equal parts. —**sep·til′lionth** *adv. & adj.*

sep·tu·a·ge·nar·i·an (sĕp′tōo-ə-jə-nâr′ē-ən, -tyōo-, -chōo-) *n.* A person who is 70 years old or between the ages of 70 and 80. ❖ *adj.* Of, relating to, or being a septuagenarian. [< Lat. *septuāgēnārius,* of the number seventy < *septuāgēnī,* seventy each < *septuāgintā,* seventy. See SEPTUAGINT.]

Sep·tu·a·gint (sĕp′tōo-ə-jĭnt′, sĕp-tōo′ə-jənt, -tyōo′-) *n.* A Greek version of the Hebrew Scriptures that dates from the third century B.C., [Lat. *septuāgintā,* seventy (< the traditional number of its translators) : *septem,* seven; see **septm** in App. + *-gintā,* ten; see **dekm** in App.]

sep·tum (sĕp′təm) *n., pl.* **-ta** (-tə) A thin partition or membrane that divides two cavities or soft masses of tissue in an organism: *the nasal septum.* [NLat. *septum* < Lat. *saeptum,* partition < neut. p. part. of *saepīre,* to enclose < *saepēs,* fence.]

sep·tu·ple (sĕp-tōo′pəl, -tyōo′-, -tŭp′əl) *adj.* **1.** Consisting of seven parts or members. **2.** Seven times as much in size, strength, number, or amount. ❖ *tr.v.* **-pled, -pling, -ples** To multiply by seven. ❖ *n.* A number seven times larger than another. [LLat. *septuplus,* sevenfold : Lat. *septem,* seven; see **septm** in App. + *-plus,* -fold.]

sep·tu·plet (sĕp-tŭp′lĭt, -tōo′plĭt, -tyōo′-) *n.* **1.** One of seven offspring delivered at a single birth. **2.** A group or combination of seven associated by common properties or behavior. [< SEPTUPLE, modeled on TRIPLET.]

sep·ul·cher (sĕp′əl-kər) *n.* **1.** A burial vault. **2.** A receptacle for sacred relics, esp. in an altar. ❖ *tr.v.* **-chered, -cher·ing, -chers** To place into a sepulcher; inter. [ME *sepulcre* < OFr. < Lat. *sepulcrum, sepulchrum* < *sepultus,* p. part. of *sepelīre,* to bury the dead.]

se·pul·chral (sə-pŭl′krəl, -pōol′-) *adj.* **1.** Of or relating to a sepulcher. **2.** Suggestive of the grave; funereal.

sep·ul·chre (sĕp′əl-kər) *n. & v. Chiefly British* Variant of **sepulcher.**

sep·ul·ture (sĕp′əl-chōor′, -chər) *n.* **1.** The act of interment; burial. **2.** A sepulcher. [ME < OFr. < Lat. *sepultūra < sepultus,* p. part. of *sepelīre,* to bury the dead.]

seq. *abbr.* **1.** sequel **2.** *Latin* sequens (the following)

seqq. *abbr. Latin* sequentia (the following [things])

se·qua·cious (sĭ-kwā′shəs) *adj.* **1.** Persisting in a continuous intellectual or stylistic direction. **2a.** Disposed to follow another or others. **b.** Slavishly unthinking and uncritical. [< Lat. *sequax, sequāc-,* pursuing < *sequī,* to follow. See **sek**[w]**-**[1] in App.] —**se·qua′cious·ly** *adv.* —**se·quac′i·ty** (-kwăs′ĭ-tē) *n.*

se·quel (sē′kwəl) *n.* **1.** Something that follows; a continuation. **2.** A literary, dramatic, or cinematic work whose narrative continues that of a preexisting work. **3.** A result or consequence. [ME *sequele* < OFr. *sequelle* < Lat. *sequēla < sequī,* to follow. See **sek**[w]**-**[1] in App.]

se·quel·a (sĭ-kwĕl′ə) *n., pl.* **-quel·ae** (-kwĕl′ē) **1.** A pathological condition resulting from a disease. **2.** A secondary consequence or result. [Lat. *sequēla,* sequel. See SEQUEL.]

se·que·na·tor (sē′kwə-nā′tər) *n.* See **sequencer** 2.

se·quence (sē′kwəns, -kwĕns) *n.* **1.** A following of one thing after another; succession. **2.** An order of succession; an arrangement. **3.** A related or continuous series. **4.** *Games* Three or more playing cards in consecutive order; a run. **5.** A series of related shots that constitute a complete unit of action in a movie. **6.** *Music* A melodic or harmonic pattern successively repeated at different pitches with or without a key change. **7.** *Roman Catholic Church* A hymn sung between the gradual and the Gospel. **8.** *Mathematics* An ordered set of quantities, as *x,* 2*x*², 3*x*³, 4*x*⁴. **9.** *Biochemistry* The order of constituents in a polymer, esp. the order of nucleotides in a nucleic acid or of amino acids in a protein. ❖ *tr.v.* **-quenced, -quenc·ing, -quenc·es 1.** To organize or arrange in a sequence. **2.** To determine the order of constituents in (a polymer). [ME, a type of hymn < OFr. < Med.Lat. *sequentia,* hymn, that which follows (< its following the alleluia) < LLat. < Lat. *sequēns, sequent-,* pr. part. of *sequī,* to follow. See **sek**[w]**-**[1] in App.]

se·quenc·er (sē′kwən-sər, -kwĕn′-) *n.* **1.** An electronic device or software program that can be instructed to order and modify digitally stored musical sounds for playback, as through a synthesizer. **2.** An apparatus for determining the order of constituents in a biological polymer, usu. DNA or protein.

se·quent (sē′kwənt) *adj.* **1.** Following in order or time; subsequent. **2.** Following as a result; consequent. ❖ *n.* A result; a consequence. [Lat. *sequēns, sequent-,* pr. part. of *sequī,* to follow. See SEQUENCE.]

se·quen·tial (sĭ-kwĕn′shəl) *adj.* **1.** Forming or characterized by a sequence, as of units or musical notes. **2.** Sequent. —**se·quen′ti·al′i·ty** (-shē-ăl′ĭ-tē) *n.* —**se·quen′tial·ly** *adv.*

se·ques·ter (sĭ-kwĕs′tər) *v.* **-tered, -ter·ing, -ters** —*tr.* **1.** To cause to withdraw into seclusion. **2.** To remove or set apart; segregate. **3.** *Law* **a.** To take temporary possession of (property) as security against legal claims. **b.** To requisition and confiscate (enemy property). —*intr. Chemistry* To undergo sequestration. [ME *sequestren* < OFr. < Lat. *sequestrāre* < *sequester,* depositary for safekeeping < Lat. *sequester,* depositary, trustee. See **sek**[w]**-**[1] in App.]

se·ques·trant (sĭ-kwĕs′trənt) *n.* A chemical that promotes sequestration.

se·ques·trate (sē′kwĭ-strāt′, sĕk′wĭ-, sĭ-kwĕs′trāt′) *tr.v.* **-trat·ed, -trat·ing, -trates 1.** *Chiefly British* To seize; confiscate. **2.** To seclude; sequester. [Lat. *sequestrāre, sequestrāt-,* to give up for safekeeping. See SEQUESTER.]

se·ques·tra·tion (sē′kwĭ-strā′shən, sĕk′wĭ-) *n.* **1.** The act of sequestering; segregation. **2.** *Law* **a.** Seizure of property. **b.** A writ authorizing sequestration. **3.** The inhibition or prevention of normal ion behavior by combination with added materials, esp. by formation of a coordination compound.

se·ques·trum (sĭ-kwĕs′trəm) *n., pl.* **-tra** (-trə) A fragment of dead bone separated from healthy bone as a result of injury or disease. [Lat., deposit < neut. of *sequester,* depositary, trustee. See **sek**[w]**-**[1] in App.]

se·quin (sē′kwĭn) *n.* **1.** A small shiny ornamental disk, often sewn on cloth; a spangle. **2.** A gold coin of the Venetian Republic. ❖ *tr.v.* **-quined, -quin·ing, -quins** To affix sequins to (a garment, for example). [Fr. < OFr., Venetian coin < Ital. *zecchino < zecca,* mint < Ar. *sikka,* coin die < *sakka,* to close, coin.]

se·quoi·a (sĭ-kwoi′ə) *n.* **1.** See **redwood** 1. **2.** Giant sequoia. [NLat. *Sequoia,* genus name, after SEQUOYA.]

Se·quoy·a or **Se·quoy·ah** (sĭ-kwoi′ə) Also called **George Guess.** 1770?–1843. Cherokee scholar who developed a system for transcribing the Cherokee language.

se·ra (sîr′ə) *n.* A plural of **serum.**

sé·rac also **se·rac** (sə-răk′, sā-) *n.* A large pointed mass of ice in a glacier isolated by intersecting crevasses. [Fr., cottage cheese, sérac, perh. < VLat. **serāceum,* whey < Lat. *serum.*]

se·ra·glio (sə-răl′yō, -răl′-) *n., pl.* **-glios 1.** A large harem. **2.** A sultan's palace. [Ital. *serraglio,* enclosure, seraglio, prob. partly < VLat. **serraculum,* enclosure (< **serrāre,* to lace up < Lat. *serāre < sera,* door bar), and partly < Turk. *saray,* palace (< Pers. *sarāy,* inn; see **tera-**[2] in App.).]

se·ra·i (sə-rä′ē, -rī) *n., pl.* **-is 1.** See **caravansary. 2.** See **seraglio** 2. [Turk. *saray,* palace. See SERAGLIO.]

ser·al (sîr′əl) *adj.* Of or relating to an ecological sere.

se·ra·pe (sə-rä′pē, -räp′ē) *n.* A long blanketlike shawl worn esp. by Mexican men. [Am.Sp. *sarape.*]

ser·aph (sĕr′əf) *n., pl.* **-a·phim** (-ə-fĭm) or **-aphs 1.** A celestial being having three pairs of wings. **2.** *seraphim Christianity* The first of the nine orders of angels. [Back-formation < pl. *seraphim* < ME *seraphin* < OE < LLat. *seraphīn, seraphīm* < Gk. *serapheim* < Heb. *śərāpîm,* pl. of *śārāp,* fiery serpent, seraph < *śārap,* to burn.] —**se·raph′ic** (sə-răf′ĭk), **se·raph′i·cal** (-ĭ-kəl) *adj.* —**se·raph′i·cal·ly** *adv.*

Se·ra·pis (sə-rā′pĭs) *n. Mythology* An ancient Egyptian god of the lower world, also worshiped in ancient Greece and Rome.

Serb (sûrb) *n.* **1.** A native or inhabitant of Serbia. **2.** A person of Serbian descent. [Serbian *Srb.*]

Ser·bi·a (sûr′bē-ə) A republic comprising most of Yugoslavia; a major component of the Kingdom of the Serbs, Croats, and Slovenes and a constituent republic of Yugoslavia after 1946. Serbia and Montenegro formed a new Yugoslavian state in 1992. Cap. Belgrade. Pop. 11,596,572.

Ser·bi·an (sûr′bē-ən) *n.* **1.** A native or inhabitant of Serbia; a

Sequoya

Serb. **2.** Serbo-Croatian as spoken in Serbia, written in a Cyrillic alphabet. ❖ *adj.* Of or relating to Serbia or its people, language, or culture.

Ser•bo-Cro•a•tian (sûr′bō-krō-ā′shən) *n.* **1.** The Slavic language of the Serbs and the Croats. **2.** A native speaker of Serbo-Croatian. ❖ *adj.* Of or relating to Serbo-Croatian or those who speak it.

sere[1] also **sear** (sîr) *adj.* Withered; dry. [ME < OE *sēar.*]

sere[2] (sîr) *n.* The sequence of successive ecological communities in an area from the initial stage to the climax. [< SERIES.]

ser•e•nade (sĕr′ə-nād′, sĕr′ə-nād′) *n.* **1.** *Music* A complimentary performance given to honor or express love for someone. **2.** *South Atlantic US* See **shivaree. 3.** *Music* An instrumental composition written for a small ensemble and having characteristics of the suite and the sonata. ❖ *v.* **-nad•ed, -nad•ing, -nades** *Music —tr.* To perform a serenade for. *—intr.* To perform a serenade. [Fr. *sérénade* < Ital. *serenata* < *sereno,* calm, clear, the open air < Lat. *serēnus.* See SERENE.] **—ser′e•nad′er** *n.*

ser•en•dip•i•ty (sĕr′ən-dĭp′ĭ-tē) *n., pl.* **-ties 1.** The faculty of making fortunate discoveries by accident. **2.** The fact or occurrence of such discoveries. **3.** An instance of making such a discovery. [From the characters in the Persian fairy tale *The Three Princes of Serendip,* who made such discoveries < Pers. *Sarandīp,* Sri Lanka < Ar. *Sarandīb.*] **—ser′en•dip′i•tous** *adj.* **—ser′en•dip′i•tous•ly** *adv.*

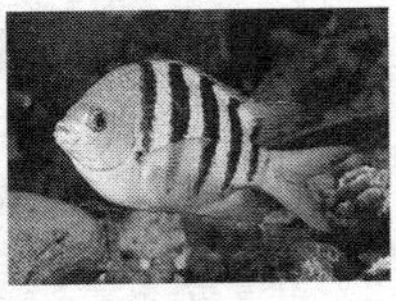

sergeant major
Abudefduf saxatilis

se•rene (sə-rēn′) *adj.* **1.** Unaffected by disturbance; calm and unruffled. See Syns at **calm. 2.** Unclouded; fair: *serene skies.* **3.** often **Serene** Used as a title and form of address for certain members of royalty: *Her Serene Highness.* [ME < Lat. *serēnus,* serene, clear.] **—se•rene′ly** *adv.* **—se•rene′ness** *n.*

Ser•en•get•i Plain (sĕr′ən-gĕt′ē) An area of N Tanzania bordering on Lake Victoria; noted for its wildlife preserve.

se•ren•i•ty (sə-rĕn′ĭ-tē) *n.* The state or quality of being serene.

serf (sûrf) *n.* **1.** A member of the lowest feudal class, attached to the land owned by a lord and required to perform labor in return for certain legal or customary rights. **2.** An agricultural laborer under various similar systems, esp. in 18th- and 19th-century Russia. **3.** A person in bondage or servitude. [ME < OFr. < Lat. *servus,* slave.] **—serf′dom** *n.*

serge (sûrj) *n.* A twilled cloth of worsted or worsted and wool, often used for suits. [ME *sarge* < OFr. < VLat. **sārica* < Lat. *sērica (vestis),* silken (clothing), fem. of *sēricus,* silken < Gk. *sērikos,* of the Seres, silken < *Sēres,* a people of E Asia, perh. China.]

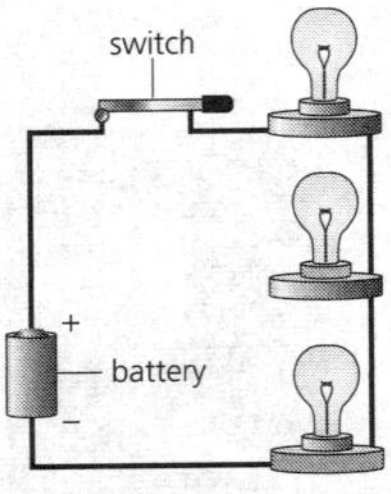

series circuit

ser•geant (sär′jənt) *n.* **1a.** A noncommissioned rank in the US Army or Marine Corps that is above corporal and below staff sergeant. **b.** Any of several ranks of noncommissioned officers in the US Army, Air Force, or Marine Corps: *master gunnery sergeant.* **2.** A police officer ranking next below a captain, lieutenant, or inspector. **3.** A sergeant at arms. [ME *sergeaunte,* a common soldier < OFr. *sergent* < Med.Lat. *serviēns, servient-,* servant, soldier < LLat., public official < Lat., pr. part. of *servīre,* to serve < *servus,* slave.] **—ser′gean•cy, ser′geant•ship′** *n.*

sergeant at arms *n., pl.* **sergeants at arms** An officer appointed to keep order within an organization, such as a legislative, judicial, or social body.

sergeant first class *n., pl.* **sergeants first class** A noncommissioned officer in the US Army ranking above staff sergeant and below master sergeant.

sergeant fish *n.* **1.** See **cobia. 2.** See **snook**[1].

sergeant major *n., pl.* **sergeants major** or **sergeant majors 1.** A noncommissioned officer serving as chief administrative assistant of a headquarters unit of the US Army or Marine Corps. **2.** *Chiefly British* A noncommissioned or warrant officer of the highest rank in a company or unit of battalion size. **3.** A small damselfish *(Abudefduf saxatilis)* of warm seas, having dark vertical stripes.

se•ri•al (sîr′ē-əl) *adj.* **1.** Of, forming, or arranged in a series. **2a.** Published or produced in installments. **b.** Relating to such publication or production. **3.** Responsible for a series of usu. criminal acts over a period of time. **4.** *Music* Relating to or based on a row of tones, esp. the 12 pitches of the chromatic scale. **5.** *Computer Science* **a.** Of or relating to the sequential transmission of the bits of a byte over one wire: *a serial port.* **b.** Of or relating to the sequential performance of multiple operations: *serial processing.* ❖ *n.* A literary or dramatic work in installments. **—se′ri•al•ly** *adv.*

se•ri•al•ism (sîr′ē-ə-lĭz′əm) *n. Music* **1.** Serial compositions. **2.** The theory or composition of such music. **—se′ri•al•ist** *n.*

se•ri•al•ize (sîr′ē-ə-līz′) *tr.v.* **-ized, -iz•ing, -iz•es** To write or publish in serial form. **—se′ri•al•i•za′tion** (-ə-lĭ-zā′shən) *n.*

serial number *n.* A number that is one of a series and is used for identification, as of a machine, weapon, or motor vehicle.

se•ri•ate (sîr′ē-āt′, -ĭt) *adj.* Arranged or occurring in a series or in rows. **—se′ri•ate′ly** *adv.*

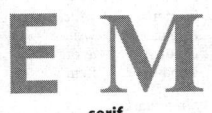

serif
sans serif typeface (*left*) and serif typeface (*right*)

se•ri•a•tim (sîr′ē-ā′tĭm, -ăt′ĭm) *adv.* One after another; in a series. [Med.Lat. *seriātim* < Lat. *seriēs,* series. See SERIES.]

se•ri•ceous (sĭ-rĭsh′əs) *adj.* **1.** Silky. **2.** *Botany* Covered with soft silky hairs. [< Lat. *sēriceus,* silken, alteration of *sēricus.* See SERGE.]

ser•i•cin (sĕr′ĭ-sĭn) *n.* A viscous gelatinous protein that forms on the surface of raw-silk fibers. [Lat. *sēricus,* silken; see SERGE + –IN.]

ser•i•e•ma (sĕr′ē-ē′mə) *n.* Either of two cranelike birds *(Cariama cristata* or *Chunga burmeisteri)* of southern South America having a tuftlike crest at the base of the bill. [Sp. < Tupi *sariema.*]

se•ries (sîr′ēz) *n., pl.* **series 1.** A number of objects or events arranged or coming one after the other in succession. **2.** A set of stamps, coins, or currency issued in a particular period. **3.** *Physics & Chemistry* A group of objects related by linearly varying successive differences in form or configuration: *a radioactive decay series.* **4.** *Mathematics* The sum of a sequentially ordered finite or infinite set of terms. **5.** *Geology* A group of rock formations closely related in time of origin and distinct as a group from other formations. **6.** *Grammar* A succession of coordinate elements in a sentence. **7a.** A succession of usu. continuously numbered issues or volumes of a publication, published with related authors or subjects and similar formats. **b.** A succession of regularly aired television programs, each one complete. **8a.** *Sports* A number of games played one after the other by the same opposing teams. **b.** *Baseball* The World Series. **9.** *Linguistics* A set of vowels or diphthongs related by ablaut. ***—idiom:* in series** In an arrangement that forms a series. [Lat. *seriēs* < *serere,* to join.]

USAGE NOTE *Series* is both a singular and a plural form. When it has the singular sense of "one set," it takes a singular verb, even when *series* is followed by *of* and a plural noun: *A series of lectures is scheduled.* When it has the plural sense of "two or more sets," it takes a plural verb: *Two series of lectures are scheduled: one for experts and one for laypeople.*

series circuit *n.* An electric circuit in which current passes through each circuit element in turn without branching.

se•ries-wound (sîr′ēz-wound′) *adj.* Of or being a motor or dynamo in which the armature circuit and the field circuit are connected in series with the external circuit.

ser•if (sĕr′ĭf) *n.* A fine line finishing off the main strokes of a letter, as at the top and bottom of *M.* [Perh. < Du. *schreef,* line < MDu. *scrēve* < *scriven,* to write < Lat. *scrībere.* See **skrībh-** in App.]

ser•i•graph (sĕr′ĭ-grăf′) *n.* A silk-screen print. [Lat. *sēricum,* silk, neut. of *sēricus,* silken; see SERGE + –GRAPH.] **—se•rig′ra•pher** (sə-rĭg′rə-fər) *n.* **—se•rig′ra•phy** (-fē) *n.*

ser•in (sĕr′ĭn) *n.* Any of several Old World finches of the genus *Serinus,* esp. a European species *(S. serinus)* closely related to the canary. [Fr. < OFr., perh. < O Provençal *serena,* a kind of bird < LLat. *sīrēna* < Lat. *sīrēn* < Gk. *seirēn.*]

ser•ine (sĕr′ēn′) *n.* An amino acid, $CH_2OHCH(NH_2)COOH$, occurring in many proteins. [SER(ICIN) + –INE[2].]

se•ri•o•com•ic (sîr′ē-ō-kŏm′ĭk) *adj.* Both serious and comic.

se•ri•ous (sîr′ē-əs) *adj.* **1.** Exhibiting or marked by careful thought or concern; somber or grave: *a face bearing a serious look.* **2a.** Requiring or carried out with much thought or consideration: *a serious effort to reform tax policy.* **b.** Designed for sophisticated tastes: *serious music.* **3.** Deeply interested or involved: *a serious golfer.* **4a.** Concerned with important rather than trivial matters: *a serious discussion.* **b.** Not joking or trifling: *He is not kidding. He is serious.* **5.** Of considerable size or scope; substantial: *a serious amount of money.* **6a.** Being of such import as to cause anxiety: *serious injuries.* **b.** Not easily answered or solved: *a serious problem.* [ME < OFr. *serieux* < LLat. *sēriōsus* < Lat. *sērius.*] **—se′ri•ous•ly** *adv.* **—se′ri•ous•ness** *n.*

SYNONYMS *serious, sober, grave, solemn, earnest* These adjectives refer to manner, appearance, disposition, or acts marked by absorption in thought, pressing concerns, or significant work. *Serious* implies a concern with responsibility and work as opposed to play: *serious students of art. Sober* emphasizes circumspection and self-restraint: *"My sober mind was no longer intoxicated by the fumes of politics"* (Edward Gibbon). *Grave* suggests the dignity and somberness associated with weighty matters: *"a quiet, grave man, busied in charts, . . . master of the art of tactics"* (Walter Bagehot). *Solemn* often adds to *grave* the suggestion of impressiveness: *the judge's solemn tone. Earnest* implies sincerity and intensity of purpose: *an earnest desire to reach an equitable solution.*

ser•jeant (sär′jənt) *n. Chiefly British* Variant of **sergeant** 2.

Ser•kin (sûr′kĭn), **Rudolf** 1903–91. Czech-born Amer. pianist known for his interpretations of the works of classical and romantic Austrian and German composers.

ser•mon (sûr′mən) *n.* **1.** A religious discourse, esp. as part of a church service. **2.** An often lengthy and tedious speech of reproof or exhortation. [ME < OFr. < Lat. *sermō, sermōn-,* discourse.] **—ser•mon′ic** (-mŏn′ĭk), **ser•mon′i•cal** (-ĭ-kəl) *adj.*

ser•mon•ette (sûr′mə-nĕt′) *n.* A short sermon.

ser•mon•ize (sûr′mə-nīz′) *v.* **-ized, -iz•ing, -iz•es** *—tr.* To deliver a sermon to (someone). *—intr.* To deliver or speak as though delivering a sermon. **—ser′mon•iz′er** *n.*

Sermon on the Mount *n.* In Matthew 5–7, a discourse of Jesus delivered on a Galilee mountainside, in which the Beatitudes are stated.

sero– *pref.* Serum: *serotherapy.* [< SERUM.]

se•ro•con•ver•sion (sîr′ō-kən-vûr′zhən, -shən) *n.* Development of antibodies in blood serum as a result of infection or immunization. **—se′ro•con•vert′** (-vûrt′) *v.*

se•ro•di•ag•no•sis (sîr′ō-dī′əg-nō′sĭs) *n., pl.* **-ses** (-sēz) Diagnosis of disease based on reactions in the blood serum of the

body. —se′ro·di·ag·nos′tic (-nŏs′tĭk) adj.
se·ro·dis·cor·dant (sîr′ō-dĭ-skôr′dnt) adj. Being a couple in which one partner has tested positive for HIV and the other has not.
se·rol·o·gy (sĭ-rŏl′ə-jē) n., pl. -gies 1. The science that deals with serums, esp. blood serum. 2. The characteristics of a disease or organism shown by study of blood serums. —se′ro·log′ic (sîr′ə-lŏj′ĭk), se′ro·log′i·cal (-ĭ-kəl) adj. —se′ro·log′i·cal·ly adv. —se·rol′o·gist n.
se·ro·neg·a·tive (sîr′ō-nĕg′ə-tĭv) adj. Showing a negative reaction to a blood serum test for a disease, such as AIDS.
se·ro·pos·i·tive (sîr′ō-pŏz′ĭ-tĭv) adj. Showing a positive reaction to a blood serum test for a disease, such as AIDS.
se·ro·pu·ru·lent (sîr′ō-pyŏŏr′ə-lənt, -pyŏŏr′yə-) adj. Consisting of serum and pus.
se·ro·sa (sĭ-rō′sə, -zə) n., pl. -sas or -sae (-sē, -zē) 1. A serous membrane, esp. one that lines the pericardial, pleural, and peritoneal cavities. 2. The chorion of a bird or reptile embryo. [NLat. serōsa, fem. of serōsus, serous < Lat. serum, serum.] —se·ro′sal (-zəl) adj.
se·ro·ther·a·py (sîr′ō-thĕr′ə-pē) n., pl. -pies Treatment of disease by administration of a serum obtained from an immunized animal. —se′ro·ther′a·pist n.
se·rot·i·nal (sĭ-rŏt′n-əl, sĕr′ə-tī′nəl) adj. Serotinous.
se·ro·tine (sĕr′ə-tīn, -tĭn′) n. Any of a genus (Eptesicus) of usu. small brown bats of Europe and Asia, esp. E. serotinus. [< NLat. sērōtinus, specific epithet < Lat., coming late (< its appearing late in the evening). See SEROTINOUS.]
se·rot·i·nous (sĭ-rŏt′n-əs, sĕr′ə-tī′nəs) adj. Botany Late in developing or blooming. [Lat. sērōtinus, coming late < sērō, at a late hour < sērus, late.]
se·ro·to·nin (sĕr′ə-tō′nĭn, sîr′-) n. An organic compound, $C_{10}H_{12}N_2O$, found esp. in the brain, blood serum, and gastric mucous membranes, and active as a neurotransmitter, in vasoconstriction, and in the stimulation of smooth muscle. [SERO– + TON(E) + –IN.]
se·ro·type (sîr′ə-tīp′, sĕr′-) n. A group of closely related microorganisms distinguished by a characteristic set of antigens. ❖ tr.v. -typed, -typ·ing, -types To classify according to serotype; assign to a particular serotype.
se·rous (sîr′əs) adj. Secreting or resembling serum.
serous fluid n. Any of various body fluids resembling serum, esp. lymph.
serous membrane n. A thin membrane lining a closed body cavity and moistened with a serous fluid.
se·row (sĕr′ō) n. Any of several goat antelopes of the genus Capricornis of mountainous regions of eastern Asia. [?]
Ser·pens (sûr′pənz, -pĕnz′) n. A constellation in the equatorial region of the northern sky near Hercules and Ophiuchus. [Lat. Serpēns < serpēns, serpent. See SERPENT.]
ser·pent (sûr′pənt) n. 1. A reptile of the order Serpentes; a snake. 2. often Serpent In the Bible, the creature that tempted Eve. b. Satan. 3. A subtle, sly, or treacherous person. 4. A firework that writhes while burning. 5. Music A wind instrument of serpentine shape, about 2.5 meters (8 feet) in length and made of brass or wood. 6. Serpent Serpens. [ME < OFr. < Lat. serpēns, serpent- < pr. part. of serpere, to creep.]
ser·pen·tar·i·um (sûr′pən-târ′ē-əm) n., pl. -i·ums or -i·a (-ē-ə) A place where snakes are kept for study or display.
ser·pen·tine (sûr′pən-tēn′, -tīn′) adj. 1. Of or resembling a serpent, as in form or movement; sinuous. 2. Subtly sly and tempting. ❖ n. (-tēn′) Any of a group of minerals, $Mg_3Si_2O_5(OH)_4$, used as a source of magnesium and asbestos and as a decorative stone. [ME < OFr. serpentin < LLat. serpentīnus < Lat. serpēns, serpent-, serpent. See SERPENT.]
serpent star n. A brittle star.
ser·pi·go (sər-pī′gō) n. Archaic A spreading skin eruption, such as ringworm. [ME < Med.Lat. serpīgō < Lat. serpere, to creep.] —ser·pig′i·nous (sər-pĭj′ə-nəs) adj.
Ser·ra (sĕr′ə, sĕr′rä), Junípero Known as "the Apostle of California." 1713–84. Spanish missionary who founded nine Franciscan missions in California (1769–82).
ser·rate (sĕr′āt′) adj. 1. Having or forming a row of small sharp projections resembling the teeth of a saw: serrate teeth. 2. Having a saw-toothed edge or margin notched with toothlike projections: serrate leaves. ❖ tr.v. -rat·ed, -rat·ing, -rates To make serrate or saw-toothed; jag the edge of. [Lat. serrātus, saw-shaped < serra, saw.]
ser·rat·ed (sĕr′ā′tĭd, sə-rā′-) adj. Saw-toothed; serrate.
ser·ra·tion (sə-rā′shən, sĕ-) n. 1. The state of being serrate. 2. A series or set of teeth or notches. 3. A single tooth or notch in a serrate edge.
ser·ried (sĕr′ēd) adj. Pressed or crowded together, esp. in rows. [P. part. of obsolete serry, to close ranks < Fr. serré, p. part. of serrer, to crowd. See SEAR².]
ser·ru·late (sĕr′yə-lĭt, -lāt′, sĕr′-) also ser·ru·lat·ed (-lā′tĭd) adj. Having a minutely serrate margin, as in a rose leaflet. [NLat. serrulātus < Lat. serrula, dim. of serra, saw.]
ser·tu·lar·i·an (sûr′chə-lâr′ē-ən, sûr′tl-âr′-) n. Any of various colonial hydroids of the genus Sertularia, having stalkless polyps arranged in pairs along a long branching stem. [< NLat. Sertulā-

ria, genus name < Lat. sertula, dim. of serta, garland < fem. p. part. of serere, to join.]
se·rum (sîr′əm) n., pl. se·rums or se·ra (sîr′ə) 1. The clear yellowish fluid obtained upon separating whole blood into its solid and liquid components. 2. Blood serum from immunized animals that contains antibodies, used to transfer immunity to another individual. 3. Watery fluid from animal tissue. 4. Whey. [Lat., whey, serum.]
serum albumin n. A protein fraction of serum, used as a substitute for plasma in the treatment of shock.
serum globulin n. A protein fraction of serum composed chiefly of antibodies.
serum hepatitis n. See hepatitis B.
serum sickness n. A hypersensitive reaction to the administration of a foreign serum, characterized by fever, swelling, skin rash, and enlargement of the lymph nodes.
ser·val (sûr′vəl, sər-văl′) n. A long-legged wildcat (Felis serval) of Africa having a tawny coat with black spots and tuftless ears. [Fr. < Port. (lobo) cerval, deerlike (wolf), lynx < LLat. cervālis < Lat. cervus, deer. See ker–¹ in App.]
ser·vant (sûr′vənt) n. 1. One who is privately employed to perform domestic services. 2. One who is publicly employed to perform services, as for a government. 3. One who expresses submission, recognizance, or debt to another: your obedient servant. [ME < OFr. < pr. part. of servir, to serve. See SERVE.]
serve (sûrv) v. served, serv·ing, serves —tr. 1a. To work for. b. To be a servant to. 2a. To prepare and offer (food, for example). b. To place food before (someone); wait on: served the guests dinner. 3a. To provide goods and services for (customers): a hotel that serves tourists. b. To supply (goods or services) to customers. 4. To assist (the celebrant) during Mass. 5a. To meet the requirements of; suffice for: This will serve the purpose. b. To be of assistance to or promote the interests of; aid: serves the national interest. 6a. To work through or complete (a period of service): served four terms in Congress. b. To be in prison for (a period or term): served 10 years for armed robbery. 7. To fight or undergo military service for: served the country in the navy. 8. To give homage and obedience to: served God. 9. To act toward (another) in a specified way: You have served me ill. 10. To copulate with. Used of male animals. 11. Law a. To deliver or present (a writ or summons). b. To present such a writ to. 12. Sports To put (a ball or shuttlecock) in play, as in tennis. 13. To bind or whip (a rope) with fine cord or wire, as a servant. 2. To do a term of duty: serve in the US Air Force. 3. To act in a particular capacity: serve as a clerk. 4. To be of service or use; function. 5. To meet requirements or needs; satisfy. 6. To wait on tables. 7. Sports To put a ball or shuttlecock into play, as in court games. 8. To assist the celebrant during Mass. ❖ n. Sports The right, manner, or act of serving in many court games. —idiom: serve (someone) right To be deserved under the circumstances. [ME serven < OFr. servir < Lat. servīre < servus, slave.]
serv·er (sûr′vər) n. 1a. One who serves food and drink. b. Something that is used in serving food and drink. 2. An altar server. 3. Law One who serves a writ or summons. 4. Sports The player who serves, as in tennis. 5. Computer Science A file server. b. A computer that processes requests for HTML and other documents that are components of webpages.
Ser·ve·tus (sər-vē′təs), Michael Originally Miguel Serveto. 1511–53. Spanish-born theologian and physician who described the circulation of blood and was executed for his denial of the Trinity.
ser·vice (sûr′vĭs) n. 1a. Employment in duties or work for another, esp. for a government. b. A government branch or department and its employees. 2a. The armed forces of a nation. b. A branch of the armed forces of a nation. 3. The performance of work or duties for a superior or as a servant. 4a. Work done for others as an occupation or business: has done service for us as a consultant. b. An act or a variety of work done for others, esp. for pay: provides full catering services. 5. A department or branch of a hospital staff that provides specified patient care. 6. Installation, maintenance, or repairs provided or guaranteed by a dealer or manufacturer. 7. A facility providing the public with the use of something, such as water. 8a. Assistance; help. b. An act of assistance or benefit; a favor. 9a. Active devotion to God, as through good works or prayer. b. A religious rite. 10a. The serving of food or the manner in which it is served. b. A set of dishes or utensils: a silver tea service. 11. Sports The act, manner, or right of serving in many court games; a serve. 12. Copulation with a female animal. Used of male animals, esp. studs. 13. Law The serving of a writ or summons. 14. The material, such as cord, used in binding or wrapping rope. 15. An answering service. ❖ tr.v. -viced, -vic·ing, -vic·es 1. To make fit for use; repair, adjust, or maintain. 2. To provide services to. 3. To make interest payments on (a debt). 4a. To copulate with (a female animal). Used of a male animal, esp. studs. b. Slang To have sex with. ❖ adj. 1. Of or relating to the armed forces of a country. 2. Intended for use in supplying or serving: a service elevator. 3. Offering repairs or maintenance: a service guarantee. 4. Offering services to the public. [ME < OFr. < Lat. servitium, slavery < servus, slave.]
Service, Robert William 1874–1958. British-born Canadian writer of poetry and novels about life in the Yukon.

serpent
early 19th-century instrument by Cramer & Key, London

Junípero Serra

serval
Felis serval

ă pat   oi boy
ā pay   ou out
âr care   ŏŏ took
ä father   ōō boot
ĕ pet   ŭ cut
ē be   ûr urge
ĭ pit   th thin
ī pie   th this
îr pier   hw which
ŏ pot   zh vision
ō toe   ə about,
ô paw   item

Stress marks:
′ (primary);
′ (secondary); as in
lexicon (lĕk′sĭ-kŏn′)

ser·vice·a·ble (sûr′vĭ-sə-bəl) *adj.* **1.** Ready for service; usable: *serviceable equipment.* **2.** Able to give long service; durable. **—ser′·vice·a·bil′i·ty, ser′vice·a·ble·ness** *n.* **—ser′vice·a·bly** *adv.*

ser·vice·ber·ry (sûr′vĭs-bĕr′ē) *n.* The shadbush or one of its fruit. [SERVICE (TREE) + BERRY.]

service break *n.* A game won on an opponent's serve.

service cap *n.* A flat-topped military cap with a visor.

service charge *n.* An additional charge for a service for which there is already a basic fee.

service dog *n.* A dog that has been specially trained to assist a disabled person with certain tasks, such as picking up an object from the floor.

service line *n. Sports* A boundary line, as in tennis or handball, that must not be overstepped in serving.

ser·vice·man (sûr′vĭs-măn′, -mən) *n.* **1.** A man who is a member of the armed forces. **2.** also **service man** A man who maintains and repairs equipment.

service mark *n.* A mark used in the sale or advertising of services to distinguish them from the services of others.

ser·vice·per·son (sûr′vĭs-pûr′sən) *n.* **1.** A member of the armed forces. **2.** also **service person** A person who maintains and repairs equipment.

service road *n.* A local road that provides access to the property bordering an expressway or interstate highway.

service station *n.* **1.** A retail establishment at which motor vehicles are refueled, serviced, and sometimes repaired. **2.** A business or branch of a business where services, esp. repairs, can be obtained.

service stripe *n.* A stripe worn on an enlisted person's sleeve to indicate a specific term of military service.

service tree *n.* Either of two Mediterranean trees (*Sorbus domestica* or *S. torminalis*) having white flowers, saw-toothed leaves, and edible fruit. [< ME *serves,* pl. of *serve,* the service tree < OE *syrfe* < VLat. **sorbea* < Lat. *sorbus.*]

ser·vice·wom·an (sûr′vĭs-wŏm′ən) *n.* **1.** A woman who is a member of the armed forces. **2.** also **service woman** A woman who maintains and repairs equipment.

ser·vi·ette (sûr′vē-ĕt′) *n. Chiefly British* A table napkin. [Fr. < OFr. *serviete,* perh. < *servir,* to serve. See SERVE.]

ser·vile (sûr′vəl, -vīl′) *adj.* **1.** Abjectly submissive; slavish. **2a.** Of or suitable to a slave or servant. **b.** Of or relating to servitude or forced labor. [ME < Lat. *servīlis < servus,* slave.] **—ser′vile·ness, ser·vil′i·ty** (sər-vĭl′ĭ-tē) *n.*

serv·ing (sûr′vĭng) *n.* **1.** The act of one that serves. **2.** An individual portion or helping of food or drink.

ser·vi·tor (sûr′vĭ-tər, -tôr′) *n.* One that performs the duties of a servant to another; an attendant. [Ult. < Lat. *servītor < servīre,* to serve. See SERVE.] **—ser′vi·tor·ship** *n.*

ser·vi·tude (sûr′vĭ-tōōd′, -tyōōd′) *n.* **1a.** A state of subjection to an owner or master. **b.** Lack of personal freedom, as to act as one chooses. **2.** Forced labor imposed as a punishment for crime. **3.** *Law* A right that grants use of another's property. [ME < OFr. < LLat. *servitūdō < Lat. servus,* slave.]

ser·vo (sûr′vō) *n., pl.* **-vos 1.** A servomechanism. **2.** A servomotor.

ser·vo·mech·a·nism (sûr′vō-mĕk′ə-nĭz′əm) *n.* **1.** A feedback mechanism that consists of a sensing element, amplifier, and servomotor, used in the automatic control of a mechanical device. **2.** A self-regulating feedback system.

ser·vo·mo·tor (sûr′vō-mō′tər) *n.* A motor that controls the action of the mechanical device in a servomechanism. [Fr. *servomoteur* : Lat. *servus,* slave + Fr. *moteur,* motor (< OFr. < Lat. *mōtor,* that which sets in motion; see MOTOR).]

ses·a·me (sĕs′ə-mē) *n.* **1.** A tropical Asian plant (*Sesamum indicum*) bearing small flat seeds used as food and as a source of oil. **2.** The seed of this plant. [ME *sisamie* < Lat. *sēsamum* < Gk. *sēsamē, sēsamon,* prob. ult. < Akkadian *šamaššammū* : *šaman,* bound form of *šamnu,* oil + *šammu,* plant.]

ses·a·moid (sĕs′ə-moid′) *adj.* Of or being any of certain small modular bones or cartilages that develop in a tendon or in the capsule of a joint. ❖ *n.* A sesamoid bone or cartilage. [Gk. *sēsamoeidēs,* shaped like a sesame seed : *sēsamon, sēsamē,* sesame; see SESAME + *-oeidēs,* -oid.] **—ses′a·moid′** *n.*

Se·so·tho (sə-sōō′tōō, -sō′tō) *n.* A Sotho language spoken in Lesotho and South Africa.

sesqui– *pref.* One and a half: *sesquicentennial.* [Lat. *sēsqui–* : *sēmis,* a half + *-que,* and.]

ses·qui·cen·ten·ni·al (sĕs′kwĭ-sĕn-tĕn′ē-əl) *adj.* Of or relating to a period of 150 years. ❖ *n.* A 150th anniversary or its celebration.

ses·quip·e·dal (sĕ-skwĭp′ĭ-dl) *adj.* Sesquipedalian. [Lat. *sēsquipedālis,* of a foot and a half in length : *sēsqui–,* sesqui- + *pēs, ped-,* foot; see ped– in App.]

ses·qui·pe·da·lian (sĕs′kwĭ-pĭ-dāl′yən) *n.* A long word. ❖ *adj.* **1.** Given to the use of long words. **2.** Long and ponderous; polysyllabic.

ses·sile (sĕs′īl′, -əl) *adj.* **1.** *Botany* Stalkless and attached directly at the base. **2.** *Zoology* Permanently attached or fixed; not free-moving. [Lat. *sessilis,* low, of sitting < *sessus,* p. part. of *sedēre,* to sit. See sed– in App.] **—ses·sil′i·ty** (sĕ-sĭl′ĭ-tē) *n.*

ses·sion (sĕsh′ən) *n.* **1a.** A meeting of a legislative or judicial body for the purpose of transacting business. **b.** A series of such meetings. **c.** The term or duration of such a series. **2.** The part of a year or of a day during which a school holds classes. **3.** An assembly of people for a common purpose or because of a common interest. **4.** *Law* A court of criminal jurisdiction in the United States. **5.** A period of time devoted to a specific activity. [ME < OFr. < Lat. *sessiō, session-,* act of sitting < *sessus,* p. part. of *sedēre,* to sit. See sed– in App.] **—ses′sion·al** *adj.* **—ses′sion·al·ly** *adv.*

Ses·sions (sĕsh′ənz), **Roger Huntington** 1896–1985. Amer. composer whose works include *Montezuma* (1962).

ses·terce (sĕs′tûrs′) *n.* A silver or bronze coin of ancient Rome equivalent to one fourth of a denarius. [Lat. *sēstertius,* a coin worth two and a half asses : *sēmis,* half + *tertius,* third; see trei– in App.]

ses·ter·tium (sĕ-stûr′shəm, -shē-əm) *n., pl.* **-tia** (-shə, -shē-ə) A monetary unit of ancient Rome equivalent to 1,000 sesterces. [Lat. *(mīlle) sēstertium,* (a thousand) sesterces, genitive pl. of *sēstertius,* sesterce. See SESTERCE.]

ses·tet (sĕ-stĕt′) *n.* **1.** A group of six lines of poetry, esp. the last six lines of a Petrarchan sonnet. **2.** A poem or stanza containing six lines. [Ital. *sestetto < sesto,* sixth < Lat. *sextus.* See s(w)eks in App.]

ses·ti·na (sĕ-stē′nə) *n.* A verse form first used by the Provençal troubadours, consisting of six six-line stanzas and a three-line envoy, with the end words of the first stanza repeated in varied order as end words in the other stanzas and also recurring in the envoy. [Ital. < *sesto,* sixth < Lat. *sextus.* See s(w)eks in App.]

Ses·tos (sĕs′təs, -tŏs) An ancient town of European Turkey at the narrowest point of the Dardanelles; site of a bridge of boats built by Xerxes I in 481 B.C. to cross the Hellespont and invade Greece.

set¹ (sĕt) *v.* **set, set·ting, sets** *—tr.* **1.** To put in a specified position; place. **2.** To put into a specified state: *set the prisoner at liberty.* **3a.** To put into a stable position: *set the post into concrete.* **b.** To fix firmly or in an immobile manner. **4.** To restore to a normal state when dislocated or broken: *set a broken arm.* **5a.** To adjust for proper functioning. **b.** To adjust (a saw) by deflecting the teeth. **c.** *Nautical* To spread open to the wind: *set the sails.* **6.** To adjust according to a standard. **7.** To adjust (an instrument or device) to a specific point or calibration. **8.** To arrange properly for use: *set a table.* **9.** To apply equipment, such as curlers, to (hair) in order to style. **10.** *Printing* **a.** To arrange (type) into words and sentences preparatory to printing; compose. **b.** To transpose into type. **11.** *Music* **a.** To compose (music) to fit a given text. **b.** To write (words) to fit a given melodic line. **12.** To arrange scenery on (a theater stage). **13.** To prescribe the unfolding of (a drama or narrative, for instance) in a specific place: *a play set in Venice.* **14.** To prescribe or establish: *set a precedent.* **15.** To prescribe as a time for: *set June 10 as the day.* **16.** To detail or assign (someone) to a particular duty, service, or station. **17.** To incite to hostile action. **18a.** To establish as the highest level of performance: *set a record.* **b.** To establish as a model. **19a.** To put in a mounting; mount. **b.** To apply jewels to; stud. **20.** To cause to sit. **21a.** To put (a hen) on eggs to hatch them. **b.** To put (eggs) beneath a hen or in an incubator. **22.** *Sports* To position (oneself) so as to be ready to start running a race. **23.** *Sports* To pass (a volleyball) in an arc so that a teammate can drive it over the net. **24a.** To value or regard something at the rate of: *She sets a great deal by good nutrition.* **b.** To fix at a given amount. **c.** To make as an estimate of worth: *We set a high value on human life.* **25.** To point to the location of (game) by holding a fixed attitude. Used of a hunting dog. **26.** *Botany* To produce, as after pollination: *set seed.* **27a.** To prepare (a trap) for catching prey. **b.** To fix (a hook) firmly into a fish's jaw. *—intr.* **1.** To disappear below the horizon. **2.** To diminish or decline; wane. **3.** To sit on eggs. Used of fowl. **4a.** To become fixed; harden. **b.** To become permanent. Used of dye. **5.** To become whole; knit. Used of a broken bone. **6.** *Botany* To mature or develop, as after pollination. **7.** *Nonstandard* To sit. **8.** To position oneself preparatory to an action, such as running a race. ❖ *adj.* **1.** Fixed or established by agreement. **2.** Established as by convention. **3.** Established deliberately; intentional. **4.** Fixed and rigid. **5.** Unwilling or very reluctant to change. **6a.** Intent and determined: *dead set against it.* **b.** Ready: *We are set to leave.* ❖ *n.* **1a.** The act or process of setting. **b.** The condition resulting from setting. **2.** The manner in which something is positioned: *the set of her cap.* **3.** A permanent firming or hardening of a substance. **4.** The deflection of the teeth of a saw. **5a.** The carriage or bearing of a part of the body. **b.** A particular psychological state, usu. that of anticipation or preparedness. **6.** A descent below the horizon. **7a.** The direction or course of wind or water. **b.** The amount that a vessel is put off its course by current. **8.** A seedling, slip, or cutting that is ready for planting. **9.** The act of arranging hair by waving and curling it. **10.** *Sports* The act of setting a volleyball for a teammate. **—phrasal verbs: set about** To begin or start. **set apart 1.** To reserve for a particular use. **2.** To make noticeable. **set aside 1.** To separate and reserve for a special purpose. **2.** To discard or reject. **3.** To declare invalid; annul or overrule. **set at** To attack or assail. **set back 1.** To slow down the progress of; hinder. **2.** *Informal* To cost. **set by** To reserve for future use. **set down 1.** To cause to sit; seat. **2.** To put in writing; record. **3a.** To regard; consider: *Just set him down as a*

sesame
Sesamum indicum

sneak. **b.** To assign to a cause; attribute. **4.** To land (an aircraft). **5.** *Baseball* To put out (a batter); retire. Used of a pitcher. **set forth 1.** To present for consideration; propose. **2.** To express in words. **set forward** To begin a journey. **set in 1.** To insert. **2.** To begin to happen or be apparent. **3.** To move toward the shore. Used of wind or water. **set off 1a.** To give rise to; cause to occur. **b.** To cause to explode. **c.** To make suddenly or demonstrably angry. **2.** To indicate as being different; distinguish. **3.** To direct attention to by contrast; accentuate. **4.** To start on a journey. **set out 1.** To begin an earnest attempt; undertake. **2.** To lay out systematically or graphically: *set out a terrace.* **3.** To display for exhibition or sale. **4.** To plant. **5.** To start a journey. **set to 1.** To begin working energetically; start in. **2.** To begin fighting. **set up 1.** To place in an upright position. **2a.** To elevate; raise. **b.** To raise in authority or power; invest with power. **c.** To put (oneself) forward as; claim to be. **d.** To assemble and erect. **3.** To establish; found. **4.** To cause. **5.** To establish in business by providing capital, equipment, or other backing. **6.** *Informal* **a.** To treat (someone) to drinks. **b.** To pay for (drinks). **7.** *Informal* To stimulate or exhilarate. **8.** To lay plans for. **9.** *Informal* To put (someone else) into a compromising situation by deceit or trickery. **10.** *Sports* To make a pass to (a teammate), creating a scoring opportunity. **set upon** To attack violently. ***—idioms:* set fire to** To cause to ignite and burn. **set foot in** To enter. **set foot on** To step on. **set in motion** To give impetus to. **set (one's) heart on** To be determined to do something. **set (one's) sights on** To have as a goal. **set on fire 1.** To cause to ignite and burn. **2.** To cause to become excited. **set sail** *Nautical* To begin a voyage on water. **set (someone) straight** To correct (someone) by providing full and accurate information. **set store by** To regard as valuable or worthwhile. **set the pace 1.** To go at a speed that other competitors attempt to match or surpass. **2.** To behave or perform in a way that others try to emulate. **set the stage for** To provide the underlying basis for. **set up housekeeping** To establish a household. **set up shop** To establish one's business operations. [ME *setten* < OE *settan.* See **sed-** in App.]

USAGE NOTE Originally *set* meant "to cause (something) to sit," so that it is now in most cases a transitive verb: *She sets the book down. He sets the table. Sit* is generally an intransitive verb: *He sits at the table.* There are some exceptions: *The sun sets* (not *sits*). *A hen sets* (or *sits*) *on her eggs.*

set² (sĕt) *n.* **1.** A group of things of the same kind that belong together and are so used. **2.** A group of persons sharing a common interest. **3.** A group of books or periodicals published as a unit. **4a.** A number of couples required for participation in a square dance. **b.** The movements constituting a square dance. **5a.** The scenery constructed for a theatrical performance. **b.** The entire enclosure in which a movie is filmed; the sound stage. **6.** *Music* **a.** A session of music, typically dance music, played before an intermission. **b.** The music so played. **7.** The collective receiving apparatus assembled to operate a radio or television. **8.** *Mathematics* A collection of distinct elements having specific common properties. **9.** *Sports* A group of games constituting one division or unit of a match, as in tennis. [ME *sette* < OFr. < Med.Lat. *secta,* retinue < Lat., faction. See SECT.]

se·ta (sē′tə) *n., pl.* **-tae** (-tē) *Biology* **1.** A stiff hair, bristle, or bristlelike process or part on an organism. **2.** The stalk of a moss capsule. [Lat. *saeta, sēta,* bristle.] **—se′tal** (sēt′l) *adj.*

se·ta·ceous (sĭ-tā′shəs) *adj.* **1.** Having or consisting of bristles; bristly. **2.** Resembling bristles or a bristle. [SET(A) + -ACEOUS.] **—se·ta′ceous·ly** *adv.*

set·back (sĕt′băk′) *n.* **1.** A check in progress; a change from better to worse. **2.** A steplike recession in a wall or a building.

set back *n. Football* An offensive back who lines up behind the quarterback.

se-ten·ant or **se ten·ant** (sə-tĕn′ənt, sĕt′n-äN′, sə-tə-näN′) *n.* A block of commemorative stamps on one sheet but varying in design, color, value, or overprint. [Fr. : *se,* reflexive pron. + *tenant,* pr. part. of *tenir,* to hold.] **—se-ten′ant** *adj.*

Seth (sĕth) In the Bible, the third son of Adam and Eve.

se·ti·form (sē′tə-fôrm′) *adj.* Shaped like a seta or bristle.

set-in (sĕt′ĭn′) *adj.* **1.** Made or placed as a part of another unit or structure: *a set-in stereo cabinet.* **2.** Made separately and stitched into the main part: *a dress with set-in sleeves.* ❖ *n.* Material, as for a book, that is inserted; an insert.

set·line (sĕt′līn′) *n.* A long fishing line towed by a boat and supporting many smaller lines bearing baited hooks.

set·off (sĕt′ôf′, -ŏf′) *n.* **1.** Something, such as a decoration, that sets off something else by contrast. **2.** Something that offsets or compensates for something else; a counterbalance. **3a.** A counterclaim. **b.** Settlement of a debt by a debtor's establishing such a claim against a creditor. **4.** *Architecture* A flat projection, as from a wall; a ledge. **5.** *Printing* See **offset** 10a.

Se·ton (sēt′n), Saint **Elizabeth Ann Bayley** Known as "Mother Seton." 1774–1821. American religious leader who founded the Sisters of Charity (1809).

se·tose (sē′tōs′) *adj.* Bristly: setaceous.

set·out (sĕt′out′) *n.* **1.** A start or beginning; an outset. **2.** An arrangement or display.

set piece *n.* **1.** A realistic piece of stage scenery constructed to stand by itself. **2.** A formally patterned artistic or literary work. **3.** Something that has been carefully planned and carried out, esp. a military operation.

set point *n.* **1.** A situation in which the set will be won by the player who scores the next point in a net game such as tennis. **2.** The point so scored.

set·screw (sĕt′skro͞o′) *n.* **1.** A screw, often without a head, used to hold two parts together. **2.** A screw used to regulate the tension of a spring.

Se·tswa·na (sĕt-swä′nə) also **Sech·ua·na** (sĕch-wä′-) *n.* See **Tswana** 2.

set·tee (sĕ-tē′) *n.* **1.** A long wood bench with a back. **2.** A sofa in small or medium size. [Perh. alteration of SETTLE.]

set·ter (sĕt′ər) *n.* **1.** One that sets. **2.** Any of several breeds of longhaired hunting dogs originally trained to indicate the presence of game by crouching in a set position.

set theory *n. Mathematics* The study of the properties of sets.

set·ting (sĕt′ĭng) *n.* **1.** The position, direction, or way in which something, such as an automatic control, is set. **2a.** The context in which a situation is set; the background. **b.** The time, place, and circumstances in which a narrative, drama, or film takes place. **3.** *Music* A composition written or arranged to fit a text, such as a poetical work. **4.** A mounting, as for a jewel. **5.** A place setting. **6.** A set of eggs in a hen's nest.

set·tle (sĕt′l) *v.* **-tled, -tling, -tles** *—tr.* **1.** To put into order; arrange or fix definitely as desired. **2.** To put firmly into a desired position or place; establish. **3a.** To establish as a resident or residents. **b.** To establish residence in; colonize. **c.** To establish in a residence, business, or profession. **4.** To restore calmness or comfort to. **5a.** To cause to sink, become compact, or come to rest. **b.** To cause (a liquid) to become clear by forming a sediment. **6.** To subdue or make orderly. **7.** To establish on a permanent basis; stabilize. **8a.** To make compensation for (a claim). **b.** To pay (a debt). **9.** To conclude (a dispute, for example) by a final decision. **10.** To decide (a lawsuit) by mutual agreement of the involved parties without court action. **11.** *Law* To secure or assign (property or title) by legal action. *—intr.* **1.** To discontinue moving and come to rest in one place. **2.** To move downward; sink or descend, esp. gradually: *Dust settled in the road.* **3a.** To become clear by the sinking of suspended particles. Used of liquids. **b.** To be separated from a solution or mixture as a sediment. **c.** To become compact by sinking, as sediment when stirred up. **4a.** To establish one's residence: *settled in Canada.* **b.** To become established or localized: *The cold settled in my chest.* **5.** To reach a decision; determine. See Syns at **decide. 6.** To come to an agreement, esp. to resolve a lawsuit out of court. **7a.** To provide compensation for a claim. **b.** To pay a debt. ❖ *n.* A long wooden bench with a high back, often including storage space beneath the seat. ***—phrasal verbs:* settle down 1.** To begin living a stable and orderly life. **2.** To become less nervous or restless. **settle for** To accept in spite of incomplete satisfaction. ***—idiom:* settle (one's) stomach** To relieve one's indigestion or nausea. [ME *setlen,* to seat < OE *setlan* < *setl,* seat. See **sed-** in App.] **—set′tle·a·ble** *adj.*

set·tle·ment (sĕt′l-mənt) *n.* **1.** The act or process of settling. **2a.** Establishment, as of a person in a business or of people in a new region. **b.** A newly colonized region. **3.** A small community. **4.** An arrangement, adjustment, or other understanding reached, as in financial or business proceedings. **5.** *Law* **a.** Transfer of property to provide for the future needs of a person. **b.** Property thus transferred. **6.** A center providing community services in an underprivileged area.

set·tler (sĕt′lər) *n.* **1.** One who settles in a new region. **2.** One who settles or decides something.

set·tlings (sĕt′lĭngz) *pl.n.* Sediment; dregs.

set·tlor (sĕt′lər) *n.* One that makes a business or financial settlement or a settlement of property.

set-to (sĕt′to͞o′) *n., pl.* **-tos** A brief, usu. heated quarrel.

Se·tú·bal (sə-to͞o′bəl) A city of SW Portugal SE of Lisbon on the **Bay of Setúbal,** an inlet of the Atlantic. Pop. 103,634.

set·up (sĕt′ŭp′) *n.* **1.** The way in which something is constituted, arranged, or planned. **2.** The gathering and organization of the equipment for an operation, procedure, or task. **3a.** Physical makeup; physique. **b.** Body posture or carriage, esp. militarily erect bearing. **4a.** *Informal* The collective ingredients, such as ice, mixers, and glasses, for serving various alcoholic drinks. Often used in the plural. **b.** A table setting, as in a restaurant. **5.** A camera position, as for a shot in a scene being filmed. **6.** *Slang* **a.** A contest arranged to result in an easy or faked victory. **b.** An endeavor intentionally made easy. **c.** A deceptive scheme, such as a fraud or hoax. **7.** A plan or strategy for a projected course of action. **8.** *Sports* A play or pass that creates a scoring opportunity.

Seu·rat (sə-rä′, sœ-), **Georges Pierre** 1859–91. French neoimpressionist painter who developed pointillism.

Seuss (so͞os), Doctor. See Theodor Seuss **Geisel.**

Se·vas·to·pol (sə-văs′tə-pōl′, sĕv′ə-stō′pəl) Formerly **Se·bas·to·pol** (sə-băs′tə-pōl′) A city of S Ukraine in the Crimea on the Black Sea W of Yalta; site of lengthy sieges during the Crimean War and World War II. Pop. 341,000.

sev·en (sĕv′ən) *n.* **1.** The cardinal number equal to 6 + 1. **2.** The seventh in a set or sequence. [ME < OE *seofon.* See **septm̥** in App.] **—sev′en** *adj. & pron.*

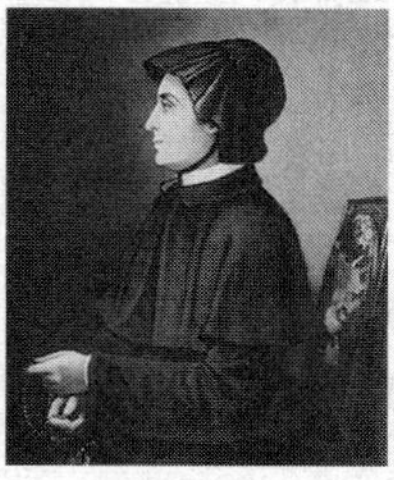

Elizabeth Seton
c. 1805 portrait by an unknown artist

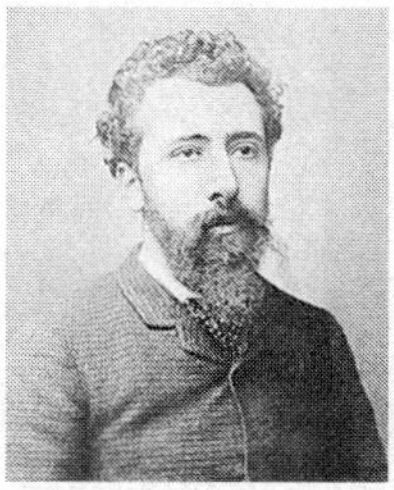

Georges Seurat

ă	pat	oi	boy
ā	pay	ou	out
âr	care	o͝o	took
ä	father	o͞o	boot
ĕ	pet	ŭ	cut
ē	be	ûr	urge
ĭ	pit	th	thin
ī	pie	*th*	this
îr	pier	hw	which
ŏ	pot	zh	vision
ō	toe	ə	about, item
ô	paw		

Stress marks:
′ (primary);
′ (secondary), as in
lexicon (lĕk′sĭ-kŏn′)

Seven Hills of Rome The hills upon which the city of Rome was built, including the Aventine, Caelian, Capitoline, Esquiline, Palatine, Quirinal, and Viminal hills.

seven seas also **Seven Seas** *pl.n.* All the oceans of the world.

sev·en·teen (sĕv′ən-tēn′) *n.* **1.** The cardinal number equal to 16 + 1. **2.** The 17th in a set or sequence. [ME *seventene* < OE *seofontīne.* See **septm** in App.] —**sev′en·teen′** *adj. & pron.*

sev·en·teenth (sĕv′ən-tēnth′) *n.* **1.** The ordinal number matching the number 17 in a series. **2.** One of 17 equal parts. —**sev′en·teenth′** *adv. & adj.*

sev·en·teen-year locust (sĕv′ən-tēn-yîr′) *n.* See **periodical cicada.**

sev·enth (sĕv′ənth) *n.* **1.** The ordinal number matching the number seven in a series. **2.** One of seven equal parts. **3.** *Music* An interval encompassing seven diatonic degrees. [ME, alteration of *sefende* < OE *seofunda* < *seofon,* seven. See **SEVEN.**] —**sev′enth** *adv. & adj.*

Sev·enth-day Adventist (sĕv′ənth-dā′) *n.* A member of a sect of Adventism distinguished chiefly for its observance of the Sabbath on Saturday.

seventh heaven *n.* **1.** A state of great joy and satisfaction. **2.** The farthest of the concentric spheres containing the stars and constituting the dwelling place of God and the angels in the Muslim and kabbalist systems.

sev·en·ti·eth (sĕv′ən-tē-ĭth) *n.* **1.** The ordinal number matching the number 70 in a series. **2.** One of 70 equal parts. —**sev′en·ti·eth** *adv. & adj.*

sev·en·ty (sĕv′ən-tē) *n.* **1.** The cardinal number equal to 7 × 10. **2. seventies a.** A decade or the numbers from 70 to 79. **b.** often **Seventies** The decade from 70 to 79 in a century. [ME < OE *-seofontig* (in *hundseofontig,* the decad seventy, seventy). See **septm** in App.] —**sev′en·ty** *adj. & pron.*

sev·en·ty-eight (sĕv′ən-tē-āt′) *n.* A phonograph record designed to be played at 78 revolutions per minute.

sev·en-up (sĕv′ən-ŭp′) *n.* A card game requiring seven points to win.

Seven Wonders of the World In ancient times, the pyramids of Egypt; the Hanging Gardens of Babylon; Phidias's statue of Zeus at Olympia; the temple of Artemis at Ephesus; the tomb, or mausoleum, of King Mausolus at Halicarnassus; the Colossus of Rhodes; and either the Pharos, or lighthouse, at Alexandria or the walls of Babylon.

sev·er (sĕv′ər) *v.* **-ered, -er·ing, -ers** —*tr.* **1.** To set or keep apart; divide or separate. **2.** To cut off (a part) from a whole. **3.** To break up (a relationship, for example); dissolve. See Syns at **separate.** —*intr.* **1.** To become cut or broken apart. **2.** To become separated or divided from each other. [ME *severen* < AN *severer* < VLat. **sēperāre* < Lat. *sēparāre.* See **SEPARATE.**]

sev·er·a·ble (sĕv′ər-ə-bəl, sĕv′rə-) *adj.* Capable of being severed or separated, as separable into legally distinct rights or obligations, as a contract. —**sev′er·a·bil′i·ty** *n.*

sev·er·al (sĕv′ər-əl, sĕv′rəl) *adj.* **1.** Being of a number more than two or three but not many. **2.** Single; distinct: "*Pshaw! said I . . . three several times*" (Laurence Sterne). **3.** Respectively different; various. **4.** *Law* Relating separately to each party of a bond or note. ❖ *pron.* (*used with a pl. verb*) An indefinite but small number; some or a few. [ME, separate < AN < Med.Lat. *sēparālis, sēperālis* < Lat. *sēpar* < *sēparāre,* to separate. See **SEPARATE.**] —**sev′er·al·ly** *adv.*

sev·er·al·fold (sĕv′ər-əl-fōld′, sĕv′rəl-) *adj.* **1.** Having several parts or members. **2.** Being several times as much or as many. —**sev′er·al·fold′** *adv.*

sev·er·al·ty (sĕv′ər-əl-tē, sĕv′rəl-) *n., pl.* **-ties 1.** The quality or condition of being separate and distinct. **2.** *Law* **a.** A separate and individual right to possession or ownership that is not shared with any other person. **b.** Land, property, or an estate owned in severalty. **c.** The quality or condition of being held or owned in severalty.

sev·er·ance (sĕv′ər-əns, sĕv′rəns) *n.* **1a.** The act or process of severing. **b.** The condition of being severed. **2.** Separation; partition. **3.** Severance pay.

severance pay *n.* A sum of money, usu. based on length of employment, for which an employee is eligible upon termination.

severance tax *n.* A tax imposed by a state on the extraction of natural resources, such as oil, that will be used in other states.

se·vere (sə-vîr′) *adj.* **-ver·er, -ver·est 1.** Unsparing or harsh, as in treatment of others: *a severe critic.* **2.** Marked by or requiring strict adherence to rigorous standards or high principles: *a severe code of behavior.* **3.** Stern or forbidding, as in manner or appearance. **4.** Extremely plain in substance or style. **5.** Causing great discomfort, damage, or distress: *a severe pain.* **6.** Very dangerous or harmful; grave or grievous: *severe mental illness.* **7.** Extremely difficult to perform or endure; trying. [Lat. *sevērus,* serious, strict. See **segh-** in App.] —**se·vere′ly** *adv.* —**se·vere′ness** *n.*

SYNONYMS *severe, stern, austere, ascetic, strict* These adjectives mean unsparing and exacting with respect to discipline or control. *Severe* implies adherence to rigorous standards or high principles and often suggests harshness: "*Praise or blame has but a momentary effect on the man whose love of beauty in the abstract makes him a severe critic on his own works*" (John Keats). *Stern*

suggests unyielding disposition, uncompromising resolution, or forbidding appearance or nature: "*a man fatally stern and implacable*" (George Meredith). *Austere* connotes aloofness or lack of feeling or sympathy and often rigid morality: *Austere officers demand meticulous conformity with military regulations.* *Ascetic* suggests self-discipline and often renunciation of worldly pleasures for spiritual improvement: "*Be systematically ascetic . . . do . . . something for no other reason than that you would rather not do it*" (William James). *Strict* means requiring or showing stringent observance of obligations, rules, or standards: "*He could not be severe nor even passably strict*" (W.H. Hudson).

se·ver·i·ty (sə-vĕr′ĭ-tē) *n., pl.* **-ties 1.** The state or quality of being severe. **2.** The act or an instance of severe behavior, esp. punishment.

Se·ver·na·ya Zem·lya (sĕv′ər-nə-yä′ zĕm′lē-ä′, -lyä′) An archipelago of N-central Russia in the Arctic Ocean N of the Taymyr Peninsula.

Sev·ern River (sĕv′ərn) **1.** A river of NW Ontario, Canada, flowing c. 676 km (420 mi) NE to Hudson Bay. **2.** A river of SW Great Britain rising in central Wales and flowing c. 338 km (210 mi) through W England to Bristol Channel.

Se·ve·rod·vinsk (sĕv′ə-rəd-vĭnsk′) A city of NW Russia on an arm of the White Sea W of Arkhangelsk. Pop. 249,071.

Se·ve·rus (sə-vîr′əs), **Lucius Septimius** A.D. 146–211. Emperor of Rome (193–211) who created a military monarchy.

se·vi·che (sə-vē′chā, sĕ-) *n.* Variant of **ceviche.**

Se·vier River (sə-vîr′) A river of W-central UT flowing c. 451 km (280 mi) through the **Sevier Desert** and emptying into **Sevier Lake,** a shrinking salt lake that is usu. dry.

Sé·vi·gné (sā-vēn-yā′), **Marquise de.** Title of Marie de Rabutin-Chantal. 1626–96. French letter writer whose correspondence depicts aristocratic life in the age of Louis XIV.

Se·ville (sə-vĭl′) A city of SW Spain on the Guadalquivir R. NNE of Cádiz. Pop. 678,902.

Sè·vres (sĕv′rə) *n.* A fine French porcelain, often elaborately decorated. [After *Sèvres,* a city of north-central France.]

sew (sō) *v.* **sewed, sewn** (sōn) or **sewed, sew·ing, sews** —*tr.* **1.** To make, repair, or fasten by stitching, as with a needle and thread. **2.** To furnish with stitches for the purpose of closing, fastening, or attaching: *sew an incision closed.* —*intr.* To work with a needle and thread or with a sewing machine. —*phrasal verb:* **sew up** *Informal* **1.** To complete successfully. **2.** To gain complete control; monopolize. **3.** To make sure of. [ME *sewen* < OE *seowian.* See **syū-** in App.] —**sew′a·ble** *adj.*

sew·age (sōō′ĭj) *n.* Liquid and solid waste carried off in sewers or drains. [Perh. *sew,* sewer (< ME, short for AN *sewere;* see SEWER[1]) + -AGE.]

Sew·all (sōō′əl), **Samuel** 1652–1730. English-born Amer. jurist who presided over the Salem witchcraft trials (1692).

Sew·ard (sōō′ərd), **William Henry** 1801–72. Amer. politician who as US secretary of state (1861–69) arranged the purchase of Alaska from Russia (1867).

Seward Peninsula A peninsula of W AK projecting into the Bering Sea just below the Arctic Circle.

Sew·ell (sōō′əl), **Anna** 1820–78. British writer of the children's classic *Black Beauty* (1877).

sew·er[1] (sōō′ər) *n.* An artificial, usu. underground conduit for carrying off sewage or rainwater. [ME < AN *sewere* < VLat. **exaquāria* : Lat. *ex-,* ex- + Lat. *aquāria,* fem. of *aquārius,* pertaining to water (< *aqua,* water; see **ak**ʷ**-ā-** in App.).]

sew·er[2] (sōō′ər) *n.* A medieval servant in charge of meal service. [ME < AN *asseour* < *asseer,* to seat guests < Lat. *assidēre,* to sit down : *ad-,* ad- + *sedēre,* to sit; see **sed-** in App.]

sew·er[3] (sō′ər) *n.* One that sews. [< *sew.*]

sew·er·age (sōō′ər-ĭj) *n.* **1.** A system of sewers. **2.** Removal of waste materials by means of a sewer system. **3.** Sewage.

sew·ing (sō′ĭng) *n.* **1.** The act, occupation, or hobby of one who sews. **2.** The article on which one is working with needle and thread; needlework.

sewing circle *n.* A group of people, esp. women, who meet regularly for the purpose of sewing, often for charity.

sewing machine *n.* A machine for sewing, often having additional attachments for special stitching.

sewn (sōn) *v.* A past participle of **sew.**

sex (sĕks) *n.* **1a.** The property or quality by which organisms are classified as female or male on the basis of their reproductive organs and functions. **b.** Either of the two divisions, designated female and male, of this classification. **2.** Females or males considered as a group. **3.** The condition or character of being female or male; the physiological, functional, and psychological differences that distinguish the female and the male. See Usage Note at **gender. 4.** The sexual urge or instinct as it manifests itself in behavior. **5.** Sexual intercourse. **6.** The genitals. ❖ *tr.v.* **sexed, sex·ing, sex·es 1.** To determine the sex of (an organism). **2.** *Slang* **a.** To arouse sexually. Often used with *up.* **b.** To increase the appeal or attractiveness of. Often used with *up.* [ME < Lat. *sexus.*]

sex- *pref.* Six: *sexpartite.* [Lat. < *sex,* six. See **s(w)eks** in App.]

sex·a·ge·nar·i·an (sĕk′sə-jə-nâr′ē-ən) *n.* A person who is 60 years old or between the ages of 60 and 70. ❖ *adj.* **1.** Being 60 years old or between the ages of 60 and 70. **2.** Of or relating to a

Sèvres
pair of 19th-century
covered urns

sex·ag·e·nar·y (sĕk-săj′ə-nĕr′ē) adj. 1. Relating to or proceeding by sixties. 2. Sexagenarian. ❖ n., pl. -ies A sexagenarian. [Lat. sexāgēnārius < sexāgēnī, sixty each < sexāgintā, sixty : sex, six; see SEX- + -gintā, ten times; see dekm̥ in App.]

sex·a·ges·i·mal (sĕk′sə-jĕs′ə-məl) adj. Of, relating to, or based on the number 60. [< Lat. sexāgēsimus, sixtieth < sexāgintā, sixty. See SEXAGENARY.]

sex cell n. A germ cell or gamete.

sex·cen·te·nar·y (sĕks-sĕn′tə-nĕr′ē, sĕk′sĕn-tĕn′ə-rē) adj. Relating to 600 or to a 600-year period. ❖ n., pl. -ies A 600th anniversary or its commemoration. [< Lat. sexcentēnī, six hundred each : sex, six; see SEX- + centēnī, a hundred each (< centum, hundred; see dekm̥ in App.).]

sex change n. The modification of a person's biological sex characteristics, by surgery and hormone treatment, to approximate those of the opposite sex.

sex chromatin n. See Barr body.

sex chromosome n. Either of a pair of chromosomes, usu. designated X or Y, in the germ cells of most animals and some plants, that combine to determine the sex and sex-linked characteristics of an individual, XX resulting in a female and XY in a male.

sex crime n. A crime, such as rape, involving illegal or coerced sexual activity. —**sex criminal** n.

sex·de·cil·lion (sĕks′dĭ-sĭl′yən) n. 1. The cardinal number equal to 10⁵¹. 2. Chiefly British The cardinal number equal to 10⁹⁶. [Lat. sexdecim, sixteen (sex, six; see SEX- in App. + decem, ten; see DECI–) + (M)ILLION.] —**sex′de·cil′lionth** adj., adv. & n.

sex·en·ni·al (sĕk-sĕn′ē-əl) adj. 1. Occurring every six years. 2. Relating to or lasting six years. ❖ n. An event that occurs every six years. [< Lat. sexennium, of six years : sex, six; see SEX- + annus, year.] —**sex·en′ni·al·ly** adv.

sex hormone n. Any of various hormones, such as estrogen and androgen, affecting the reproductive organs, development of secondary sex characteristics, and behavior patterns.

sex·ism (sĕk′sĭz′əm) n. 1. Discrimination based on gender, esp. against women. 2. Attitudes, conditions, or behaviors that promote stereotyping of social roles based on gender. —**sex′ist** adj. & n.

sex kitten n. Informal A young woman seen as sexually appealing.

sex·less (sĕks′lĭs) adj. 1. Lacking sexual characteristics; neuter. 2. Lacking in sexual interest or activity.

sex-lim·it·ed (sĕks′lĭm′ĭ-tĭd) adj. 1. Occurring or appearing only in one sex. Used of a genetic character or phenotype. 2. Having a sex-limited character or phenotype.

sex linkage n. The condition in which a gene responsible for a specific trait is located on a sex chromosome, resulting in sexually dependent inheritance of the trait.

sex-linked (sĕks′lĭngkt′) adj. 1. Carried by a sex chromosome, esp. an X chromosome. Used of genes. 2. Sexually determined. Used esp. of inherited traits.

sex object n. A person seen primarily as sexually attractive.

sex offender n. One who is convicted of a sex crime.

sex·ol·o·gy (sĕk-sŏl′ə-jē) n. The study of human sexual behavior. —**sex′o·log′ic** (sĕk′sə-lŏj′ĭk), **sex′o·log′i·cal** (-ĭ-kəl) adj. —**sex·ol′o·gist** n.

sex·par·tite (sĕks-pär′tīt′) adj. Composed of or divided into six parts, as a groined vault.

sex·pot (sĕks′pŏt′) n. Informal A woman considered to be sexually attractive.

sex symbol n. A person, esp. an entertainer or celebrity, who is widely acknowledged to have sex appeal.

sext also **Sext** (sĕkst) n. Ecclesiastical The fourth of the seven canonical hours. [ME sexte < LLat. sexta < Lat. sexta (hōra), sixth (hour), fem. of sextus, sixth. See s(w)eks in App.]

Sex·tans (sĕks′tənz) n. A constellation in the equatorial region of the sky near Leo and Hydra. [NLat. sextāns, sextant. See SEXTANT.]

sex·tant (sĕk′stənt) n. 1. A navigational instrument containing a graduated 60-degree arc, used for measuring the altitudes of celestial bodies to determine latitude and longitude. 2. Sextant See Sextans. [NLat. sextāns, sextant- < Lat., sixth part (the instrument's arc being a sixth of a circle) < sextus, sixth. See s(w)eks in App.]

sex·tet (sĕk-stĕt′) n. 1. Music a. A composition for six voices or six instruments. b. A group of six singers or six instrumentalists. 2. A group of six. [Alteration of SESTET.]

sex therapy n. The treatment of sexual dysfunction, such as impotence or frigidity, by methods involving counseling, psychotherapy, or behavior modification. —**sex therapist** n.

sex·tile (sĕk′stīl′, -stəl) adj. Of or relating to the position of two celestial bodies when they are 60° apart. [Lat. sextīlis, one sixth < sextus, sixth. See s(w)eks in App.]

sex·til·lion (sĕk-stĭl′yən) n. 1. The cardinal number equal to 10²¹. 2. Chiefly British The cardinal number equal to 10³⁶. [Fr. : Lat. sextus, sixth; see SEXTILE + Fr. -illion (as in million, million < OFr. milion; see MILLION).] —**sex·til′lion** adj.

sex·til·lionth (sĕk-stĭl′yənth) n. 1. The ordinal number matching the number sextillion in a series. 2. One of sextillion equal

parts. —**sex′til′lionth** adv. & adj.

sex·to·dec·i·mo (sĕk′stō-dĕs′ə-mō′) n., pl. -mos 1. The page size of a book composed of printer's sheets folded into 16 leaves or 32 pages. 2. A book composed of sextodecimo pages. [Lat. sextōdecimō, ablative of sextusdecimus, one sixteenth : sextus, sixth; see s(w)eks in App. + decimus, tenth (< decem, ten; see dekm̥ in App.).]

sex·ton (sĕk′stən) n. An employee or officer of a church who is responsible for the care and upkeep of church property and sometimes for ringing bells and digging graves. [ME sextein < Anglo-Lat. sextānus, prob. alteration of Med.Lat. secristānus, sacristan, var. of sacristānus. See SACRISTAN.]

Sexton, Anne 1928–74. Amer. poet whose works include the collection Live or Die (1966).

sex·tu·ple (sĕk-stōō′pəl, -styōō′-, -stŭp′əl, sĕk′stŭp′əl) tr. & intr.v. -pled, -pling, -ples To multiply or be multiplied by six. ❖ adj. 1. Consisting of six parts or members. 2. Six times as much in size, strength, number, or amount. 3. Music Having six beats to the measure. ❖ n. A number six times larger than another. [Med.Lat. sextuplus, sixfold : Lat. sextus, sixth; see SEXTILE + -plus, -fold.] —**sex·tu′ply** adv.

sex·tu·plet (sĕk-stŭp′lĭt, -stōō′plĭt, -styōō′-, sĕk′stŭp′lĭt) n. 1. One of six offspring born in a single birth. 2. A group or combination of six associated by common properties or behavior. 3. Music A group of six notes having the time value of four notes of the same kind. [< SEXTUPLE, modeled on TRIPLET.]

sex·u·al (sĕk′shōō-əl) adj. 1. Of, relating to, involving, or characteristic of sex, sexuality, the sexes, or the sex organs and their functions. 2. Implying or symbolizing erotic desires or activity. 3. Of, relating to, or involving the union of male and female gametes: sexual reproduction. [LLat. sexuālis < Lat. sexus, sex.] —**sex′u·al·ly** adv.

sexual abuse n. 1. The forcing of unwanted sexual activity by one person on another, as by the use of threats or coercion. 2. Sexual activity that is deemed improper or harmful, as between an adult and a minor.

sexual assault n. Conduct of a sexual or indecent nature toward another person that is accompanied by actual or threatened physical force or that induces fear, shame, or mental suffering.

sexual harassment n. The making of unwanted and offensive sexual advances or of sexually offensive remarks or acts, esp. by one in a superior or supervisory position.

sexual intercourse n. 1. Coitus between humans. 2. Sexual union between humans involving genital contact other than vaginal penetration by the penis.

sex·u·al·i·ty (sĕk′shōō-ăl′ĭ-tē) n. 1. The condition of being characterized and distinguished by sex. 2. Concern with or interest in sexual activity. 3. Sexual character or potency.

sex·u·al·ize (sĕk′shōō-ə-līz′) tr.v. -ized, -iz·ing, -iz·es To make sexual in character or quality. —**sex′u·al·i·za′tion** (-ə-lĭ-zā′shən) n.

sexually transmitted disease n. Any of various diseases, including chancroid, chlamydia, gonorrhea, and syphilis, that are usu. contracted through sexual intercourse or other intimate sexual contact.

sexual orientation n. The direction of one's sexual interest toward members of the same, opposite, or both sexes.

sexual relations pl.n. 1. Sexual intercourse. 2. Sexual activity between individuals.

sex work n. The performance of sex acts for hire; prostitution. —**sex worker** n.

sex·y (sĕk′sē) adj. -i·er, -i·est 1. Arousing or tending to arouse sexual desire or interest. 2. Slang Highly appealing or interesting; attractive. —**sex′i·ly** adv. —**sex′i·ness** n.

Sey·chelles (sā-shĕl′, -shĕlz′) An island country in the W Indian Ocean N of Madagascar; gained independence from Great Britain in 1976. Cap. Victoria. Pop. 74,000.

Sey·fert galaxy (sē′fərt, sī′-) n. A spiral galaxy with a small, compact, bright nucleus that exhibits variable light intensity and radio-wave emission. [After Carl Keenana Seyfert (1911–60), American astronomer.]

Sey·mour (sē′môr′, -mōr′), **Jane** 1509?–37. Queen of England (1536–37) as the third wife of Henry VIII.

sf abbr. sforzando

SF abbr. 1. sacrifice fly 2. science fiction

SFC abbr. sergeant first class

sfer·ics also **spher·ics** (sfîr′ĭks, sfĕr′-) n. (used with a sing. verb) 1. The study of atmospherics, esp. through the use of electronic detectors. 2. See atmospherics 1. [Alteration of ATMOSPHERICS.]

Sfor·za (sfôrt′sə, sfôr′tsä) Family of Milanese political leaders, including **Ludovico** (1451?–1508), duke of Milan (1481–99) and a patron of Leonardo da Vinci.

sfor·zan·do (sfôrt-sän′dō) also **for·zan·do** (fôrt-sän′dō) Music adv. & adj. Suddenly or strongly accented. ❖ n., pl. -dos or -di (-dē) A sforzando tone or chord. [Ital., gerund of sforzare, to use force : s-, intensive pref. (< Lat. ex-; see EX–) + forzare, to force (< VLat. *fortiāre < Lat. fortis, strong; see FORTIS).]

sfu·ma·to (sfōō-mä′tō) n. The blurring or the softening of sharp outlines in painting by means of subtle and gradual blending of one tone into another. [Ital. < p. part. of sfumare, to evaporate, fade out : s-, from (< Lat. ex-; see EX–) + fumare, to smoke

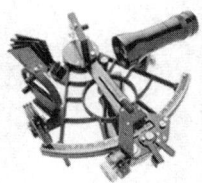

sextant

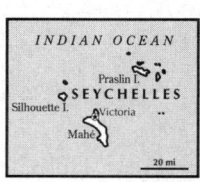

Seychelles

ă pat	oi boy
ā pay	ou out
âr care	ŏŏ took
ä father	ōō boot
ĕ pet	ŭ cut
ē be	ûr urge
ĭ pit	th thin
ī pie	th this
îr pier	hw which
ŏ pot	zh vision
ō toe	ə about,
ô paw	item

Stress marks:
′ (primary);
′ (secondary), as in
lexicon (lĕk′sĭ-kŏn′)

(< Lat. *fūmāre*; see FUMATORY).]

sfz *abbr.* sforzando

Sg¹ The symbol for the element **seaborgium.**

Sg² *abbr. Bible* Song of Songs

SG *abbr.* **1.** senior grade **2.** solicitor general **3.** Surgeon General

SGM *abbr.* sergeant major

SGML (ĕs′jē-ĕm-ĕl′) *n.* A standardized markup language for describing the logical structure of a computer document. [S(tandard) G(eneralized) M(arkup) L(anguage).]

sgraf•fi•to (skrä-fē′tō, zgrä-) *n., pl.* **-ti** (-tē) **1.** Decoration produced on pottery or ceramic by scratching through a surface of plaster or glazing to reveal a different color underneath. **2.** Ware decorated in this manner. [Ital., p. part. of *sgraffire,* to scratch < *sgraffio,* a scratch < *sgraffiare,* to scratch < OItal. : *s-,* intensive pref.; see SFORZANDO + *graffiare,* to scratch; see GRAFFITO.]

's Gra•ven•ha•ge (skrä′vən-hä′gə, sкнrä′vən-hä′кнə) See The Hague.

Sgt. or **Sgt** or **SGT** *abbr.* sergeant

SgtMaj *abbr.* sergeant major

sh (sh) *interj.* Used to urge silence.

Shaan•xi (shän′shē′) also **Shen•si** (shĕn′sē′) A province of E-central China crossed by the Wei He. Cap. Xi'an. Pop. 32,882,403.

Sha•ba (shä′bə) Formerly **Ka•tan•ga** (kə-täng′gə, -täng′-) A region of SE Congo (formerly Zaire) bordering on Zambia; site of a secessionist state from 1960 to 1963.

Sha'•ban also **Shaa•ban** (shə-bän′, shä-, shô-) *n.* The eighth month of the year in the Islamic calendar. See table at **calendar.** [Ar. *ša'bān,* perh. < *ša'aba,* to gather, disperse.]

Shab•bat (shə-bät′, shä′bəs) *n. Judaism* The Sabbath. [Heb. *šab-bāt,* sabbath. See SABBATH.]

Shab•bos (shä′bəs) *n. Judaism* The Sabbath. [Yiddish *shabes* < Heb. *šabbāt.* See SABBATH.]

shab•by (shăb′ē) *adj.* **-bi•er, -bi•est 1a.** Showing signs of wear and tear; threadbare or worn-out. **b.** Dilapidated or deteriorated in condition, esp. through neglect; seedy. **2.** Wearing threadbare clothing. **3a.** Despicable; mean. **b.** Not generous or just; unfair. **c.** Of mediocre or substandard quality. [< obsolete *shab,* scab < ME *shab* < OE *sceabb.*] —**shab′bi•ly** *adv.* —**shab′bi•ness** *n.*

Sha•bel•le (shä-bĕl′ē, shə-) or **She•be•le** (shē-bā′lĕ, shə-) A river of NE Africa rising in central Ethiopia and flowing c. 1,609 km (1,000 mi) to S Somalia.

Sha•bu•oth (shə-voo′ōt′, -əs, shä′voo-ôt′) *n.* Variant of **Sha-vuot.**

shadow play

shack (shăk) *n.* A small, crudely built cabin; a shanty. ❖ *intr.v.* **shacked, shack•ing, shacks** To live or dwell. —*idiom:* **shack up** *Slang* **1.** To sleep together or live in sexual intimacy without being married. **2.** To live, room, or stay at a place. [Poss. < Am.Sp. *jacal* < Nahuatl *xacalli,* adobe hut : *xámitl,* adobe + *calli,* house, hut.]

shack•le (shăk′əl) *n.* **1.** A metal fastening, usu. one of a pair, for encircling and confining the ankle or wrist of a prisoner or captive; a fetter or manacle. **2.** A hobble for an animal. **3.** Any of several devices, such as a clevis, used to fasten or couple. **4.** A restraint or check to action or progress. Often used in the plural. ❖ *tr.v.* **-led, -ling, -les 1.** To confine with shackles; fetter. **2.** To fasten or connect with a shackle. **3.** To restrict, confine, or hamper. [ME *schackel* < OE *sceacel,* fetter.] —**shack′ler** *n.*

shad (shăd) *n., pl.* **shad** or **shads** Any of several food fishes of the genus *Alosa,* esp. the North American species *A. sapidissima,* related to the herrings. [ME *shad* < OE *sceadd.*]

shad•ber•ry (shăd′bĕr′ē) *n.* The fruit of the shadbush. [SHAD(BUSH) + BERRY.]

shad•bush (shăd′boosh′) *n.* Any of various North American shrubs or trees of the genus *Amelanchier,* having edible blue-black or purplish fruit and smooth gray striped twigs. [< its being in bloom when shad are found in streams.]

shad•dock (shăd′ək) *n.* **1.** A tropical southeast Asian tree (*Citrus maxima*) having very large round fruit with thick rinds. **2.** The edible yellow fruit of this tree. [After Captain *Shaddock,* 17th-cent. English ship commander.]

shade (shād) *n.* **1.** Light diminished in intensity as a result of the interception of the rays; partial darkness. **2.** An area or space of partial darkness. **3.** Cover or shelter provided by interception by an object of the sun or its rays. **4.** Any of various devices used to reduce or screen light or heat. **5. shades** *Slang* Sunglasses. **6.** Relative obscurity. **7. shades a.** Dark shadows gathering at dusk. **b.** The abode of the dead; the underworld. **8.** The part of a picture or photograph depicting darkness or shadow. **9.** The degree to which a color is mixed with black or is decreasingly illuminated; gradation of darkness. **10.** A slight difference or variation; a nuance. **11.** A small amount; a trace. **12.** A disembodied spirit; a ghost. **13. shades** A present reminder of a person or situation in the past. ❖ *v.* **shad•ed, shad•ing, shades** —*tr.* **1.** To screen from light or heat. **2.** To obscure or darken. **3.** To cause shade in or on. **4a.** To represent degrees of shade or shadow in. **b.** To produce (gradations of light or color) in a drawing or picture. **5.** To change or vary by slight degrees. **6.** To make a slight reduction in. —*intr.* To pass from one quality, color, or thing to another by very slight changes or degrees. [ME < OE *sceadu.*] —**shad′er** *n.*

shade tree *n.* A tree that provides shade from sunlight.

shad•ing (shā′dĭng) *n.* **1.** A screening against light or heat. **2.** The lines or other marks used to fill in outlines of a sketch, engraving, or painting to represent gradations of color or darkness. **3.** A small variation, gradation, or difference.

sha•doof also **sha•duf** (shä-doof′) *n.* A device consisting of a long suspended pole weighted at one end and having a bucket at the other end, used in the Near East and esp. Egypt for raising water, as for the irrigation of land. [Ar. *šādūf.*]

shad•ow (shăd′ō) *n.* **1.** An area that is not or is only partially irradiated or illuminated because of the interception of radiation by an opaque object between the area and the source of radiation. **2.** The rough image cast by an object blocking rays of illumination. **3.** An imperfect imitation or copy. **4. shadows** The darkness following sunset. **5.** A feeling or cause of gloom or unhappiness. **6a.** A nearby or adjoining region; vicinity: *grew up in the shadow of the ballpark.* **b.** A dominating presence or influence: *worked in the shadow of the director.* **7a.** A darkened area of skin under the eye. **b.** An incipient growth of beard that makes the skin look darker. **8.** A shaded area in a picture or photograph. **9.** A mirrored image or reflection. **10.** A phantom; a ghost. **11a.** One, such as a detective or spy, that follows or trails another. **b.** A constant companion. **c.** *Sports* A player who guards an opponent closely. **12.** A faint indication; a foreshadowing. **13.** A vestige or inferior form: *a shadow of their past achievements.* **14.** An insignificant portion or amount; a trace. **15.** Shelter; protection. ❖ *v.* **-owed, -ow•ing, -ows** —*tr.* **1.** To cast a shadow on; shade. **2.** To make gloomy or dark; cloud. **3.** To represent vaguely, mysteriously, or prophetically. **4.** To darken in a painting or drawing; shade in. **5.** To follow, esp. in secret; trail. **6.** *Sports* To guard (an opponent) closely throughout the playing area, esp. in ice hockey. —*intr.* **1.** To change by gradual degrees. **2.** To become clouded over as if with shadows. ❖ *adj.* Not having official status. [ME < OE *sceaduwe,* oblique case of *sceadu.*] —**shad′ow•er** *n.*

shad•ow•box (shăd′ō-bŏks′) *intr.v.* **-boxed, -box•ing, -box-es** To spar with an imaginary opponent, as for exercise or training purposes. —**shad′ow•box′ing** *n.*

shadow box *n.* A shallow rectangular box usu. with a glass front that is used for holding and protecting items on display.

shad•ow•graph (shăd′ō-grăf′) *n.* **1.** An image produced by casting a shadow on a screen. **2.** See **shadow play. 3.** See **radio-graph.**

shadow play *n.* A play presented by casting shadows of puppets or actors on a screen.

shad•ow•y (shăd′ō-ē) *adj.* **-i•er, -i•est 1.** Relating to or resembling a shadow. **2.** Full of or dark with shadow. **3.** Lacking distinctness; faint. **4.** Lacking substance; unsubstantial. —**shad′ow•i•ly** *adv.* —**shad′ow•i•ness** *n.*

Shad•rach (shăd′răk) In the Bible, a young man who with Abednego and Meshach emerged unharmed from the fiery furnace of Babylon.

shad•y (shā′dē) *adj.* **-i•er, -i•est 1.** Full of shade; shaded. **2.** Casting shade: *a shady grove.* **3.** Quiet, dark, or concealed; hidden. **4.** Of dubious character or honesty; questionable. —**shad′i•ly** *adv.* —**shad′i•ness** *n.*

shaft (shăft) *n.* **1a.** The long, narrow stem or body of a spear or arrow. **b.** A spear or arrow. **2a.** A projectile suggestive of a spear or arrow in appearance or configuration. **b.** *Informal* A scornfully satirical comment; a barb. **c.** *Slang* Harsh, unfair treatment. Often used with *the.* **3.** A ray or beam of light. **4.** A long thin object or part, as: **a.** The handle or axis of various tools or implements. **b.** One of two parallel poles between which an animal is harnessed to a vehicle. **c.** A long, generally cylindrical bar that rotates and transmits power, as the drive shaft of an engine. **5.** *Zoology* The main axis of a feather, esp. its distal portion. **6.** *Anatomy* **a.** The midsection of a long bone; the diaphysis. **b.** The section of a hair projecting from the surface of the body. **7.** *Architecture* **a.** A column or obelisk. **b.** The principal portion of a column, between the capital and the base. **8.** A long, narrow, often vertical passage sunk into the earth; a tunnel. **9.** A vertical passage housing an elevator. **10.** A duct or conduit for the passage of air, as for ventilation or heating. ❖ *tr.v.* **shaft•ed, shaft•ing, shafts 1.** To equip with a shaft. **2.** *Slang* To treat in a harsh, unfair way. [ME < OE *sceaft.*]

Shaftes•bur•y (shăfts′bĕr′ē, -bə-rē), First Earl of. Title of Anthony Ashley Cooper. 1621–83. English politician considered the founder of the Whig Party.

shaft•ing (shăf′tĭng) *n.* **1.** A system of shafts, as in a machine, for transmitting motion or power. **2.** Material for making shafts. **3.** *Slang* An instance of harsh or unfair treatment.

shag¹ (shăg) *n.* **1.** A tangle or mass, esp. of rough matted hair. **2a.** A coarse long nap, as on a woolen cloth. **b.** Cloth having such a nap. **3.** A rug with a thick rough pile. **4.** Coarse shredded tobacco. ❖ *tr.v.* **shagged, shag•ging, shags** To make shaggy; roughen. [ME **shagge* < OE *sceacga,* matted hair.]

shag² (shăg) *n.* A dance step of the 1930s consisting of a hop on each foot in turn. ❖ *intr.v.* **shagged, shag•ging, shags** To perform or execute this dance. [?]

shag³ (shăg) *n.* Either of two marine birds (*Phalacrocorax aristotelis* or *P. punctatus*) of Europe and North Africa, related to the cormorant. [Perh. < its shaggy crest.]

shag⁴ (shăg) *tr.v.* **shagged, shag•ging, shags 1.** To chase and bring back; fetch. **2.** *Baseball* To chase and catch (fly balls) in practice. [Perh. < obsolete *shag*, to shake.]

shag[5] (shăg) *Chiefly British Vulgar Slang v.* **shagged, shag•ging, shags** —*tr.* To engage in sexual intercourse with. —*intr.* To engage in sexual intercourse. [Perh. < obsolete *shag*, to shake, wiggle.]

shag•bark (shăg′bärk′) *n.* An eastern North American hickory tree *(Carya ovata)* having shaggy bark.

shag•gy (shăg′ē) *adj.* **-gi•er, -gi•est 1.** Having, covered with, or resembling long rough hair or wool. **2.** Bushy or matted: *shaggy hair.* **3.** Having a rough nap or surface, as a textile. **4.** Poorly groomed; unkempt. **5.** Lacking order or clarity, as in thinking. **—shag′gi•ly** *adv.* **—shag′gi•ness** *n.*

shaggy cap *n.* See **shaggymane.**

shag•gy-dog story (shăg′ē-dôg′, -dŏg′) *n. Informal* A long anecdote with an absurd or anticlimactic punch line.

shag•gy•mane also **shag•gy mane** (shăg′ē-mān′) *n.* An edible mushroom *(Coprinus comatus)* having shaggy scales.

sha•green (shə-grēn′) *n.* **1.** The rough hide of a shark or ray, covered with numerous bony denticles and used as an abrasive and as leather. **2.** An untanned leather with a granular surface that is often dyed green. [Fr. *chagrin, sagrin* < Turk. *sağri*, crupper, leather.] **—sha•green′** *adj.*

shah (shä) *n.* Used formerly as a title for the hereditary monarch of Iran. [Pers. *shāh*, king < OPers. *khshāyathiya-*.] **—shah′dom** *n.*

Shah Ja•han (jə-hän′) 1592–1666. Mogul emperor of India (1628–58) whose reign ushered in the golden age of Mogul art and architecture.

Shahn (shän), **Benjamin ("Ben")** 1898–1969. Lithuanian-born Amer. artist whose works reflect social and political themes.

shai•tan (shī-tän′, shā-) *n.* **1.** often **Shaitan** *Islam* The Devil; Satan. **2.** An evil spirit; a fiend. [Ar. *šayṭān* < Ethiopic *śayṭān* < Aram. *sāṭānā* < Heb. *śāṭān*.]

shake (shāk) *v.* **shook** (shŏŏk), **shak•en** (shā′kən), **shak•ing, shakes** —*tr.* **1.** To cause to move to and fro with jerky movements. **2.** To cause to quiver, tremble, vibrate, or rock. **3.** To cause to lose stability or waver: *shook my beliefs.* **4.** To remove or dislodge by jerky movements. **5a.** To bring to a specified condition by or as if by shaking: *shook me out of complacency.* **b.** *Slang* To get rid of. **6.** To disturb or agitate; unnerve. **7.** To brandish or wave, esp. in anger. **8.** To clasp (hands) in greeting or leave-taking or as a sign of agreement. **9.** *Music* To trill (a note). **10.** *Games* To rattle and mix (dice) before casting. —*intr.* **1.** To move to and fro in short, irregular, often jerky movements. **2.** To tremble, as from cold or in anger. **3.** To be unsteady; totter or waver. **4.** To move something vigorously up and down or from side to side, as in mixing. **5.** *Music* To trill. **6.** To shake hands. ❖ *n.* **1.** The act of shaking. **2.** A trembling or quivering movement. **3.** *Informal* An earthquake. **4a.** A fissure in rock. **b.** A crack in timber caused by wind or frost. **5.** *Informal* A moment or instant; a trice. **6.** *Music* A trill. **7a.** See **milk shake** 1. **b.** A beverage in which the ingredients are mixed by shaking. **8.** A rough shingle used to cover rustic buildings, such as barns. **9. shakes** *Informal* Uncontrollable trembling, as in a person who is cold, frightened, feverish, or ill. **10.** *Slang* A bargain or deal. ***—phrasal verbs:*** **shake down 1.** *Slang* To extort money from. **2.** *Slang* To make a thorough search of. **3.** To subject (a new ship or aircraft) to shakedown testing. **4.** To become acclimated or accustomed. **shake off** To free oneself of; get rid of. **shake up 1.** To upset by or as if by a physical jolt or shock. **2.** To subject to a drastic rearrangement or reorganization. ***—idioms:*** **give (someone) the shake** *Slang* To escape from or get rid of. **no great shakes** *Slang* Unexceptional; ordinary. **shake a leg** *Informal* **1.** To dance. **2.** To move quickly; hurry up. **shake (another's) tree** *Slang* To arouse to action or reaction; disturb. **shake a stick at** *Slang* To point out, designate, or name. [ME *shaken* < OE *sceacan*.] **—shak′a•ble, shake′a•ble** *adj.*

shake•down (shāk′doun′) *n.* **1.** *Slang* Extortion of money, as by blackmail. **2.** *Slang* A thorough search of a place or person. **3.** A period of appraisal followed by adjustments to improve efficiency or functioning. ❖ *adj.* Serving to test a ship or aircraft and familiarize the crew with its operation.

shaken baby syndrome also **shaken infant syndrome** *n.* Brain injury in an infant caused by violent shaking, resulting in intracranial swelling and bleeding and often leading to permanent, severe brain damage or death.

shake•out (shāk′out′) *n.* **1.** The elimination of competing businesses or products in a particular field. **2.** A decline in the values of certain securities that usu. results in a depressed stock market.

shak•er (shā′kər) *n.* **1a.** One that shakes. **b.** One that impels, encourages, or supervises action. **2a.** A container used for shaking. **b.** A container used to mix or blend by shaking. **3. Shaker** A member of a Christian group originating in England in 1747, practicing communal living and observing celibacy. ❖ *adj.* also **Shaker** Relating to or constituting a style produced by Shakers that is distinctively simple, unornamented, functional, and finely crafted.

Shake•speare (shāk′spîr), **William** 1564–1616. English playwright and poet whose plays include historical works, such as *Richard II,* comedies, including *Much Ado about Nothing* and *As You Like It,* and tragedies, such as *Hamlet, Othello,* and *King Lear.* **—Shake•spear′e•an, Shake•spear′i•an** *adj. & n.*

Shakespearean sonnet *n.* The sonnet form used by Shakespeare, composed of three quatrains and a terminal couplet in iambic pentameter with the rhyme pattern *abab cdcd efef gg.*

shake•up (shāk′ŭp′) *n.* A thorough, often drastic reorganization, as of the personnel in a business or government.

shak•ing palsy (shā′kĭng) *n.* See **Parkinson's disease.**

shak•o (shăk′ō, shā′kō, shä′-) *n., pl.* **-os** or **-oes** A stiff, cylindrical military dress hat with a metal plate in front, a short visor, and a plume. [Fr. *schako* < Hung. *csákó* < *csákós (süveg)*, pointed (cap) < *csák*, peak, perh. < MHGer. *zacke*, tack, nail.]

Shak•ta (shäk′tə, säk′-) *n. Hinduism* One who worships Shakti. [Skt. *śāktaḥ* < *śaktiḥ*, Shakti. See SHAKTI.] **—Shak′tism** *n.* **—Shak′tist** *n.*

Shak•ti (shŭk′tē, shäk′-) *n., pl.* **-tis** *Hinduism* **1.** The active manifest power that creates the universe. **2.** The consort of the male expression of the divine, esp. of the god Shiva. [Skt. *śaktiḥ* < *śaknoti*, he is strong.]

shak•y (shā′kē) *adj.* **-i•er, -i•est 1.** Trembling or quivering; tremulous: *a shaky voice.* **2.** Lacking soundness or sturdiness, as of construction. **3a.** Not to be depended on; precarious: *a shaky alliance.* **b.** Wavering in firmness: *shaky confidence.* **c.** Open to question or doubt. **—shak′i•ly** *adv.* **—shak′i•ness** *n.*

shale (shāl) *n.* A fissile rock composed of layers of claylike fine-grained sediments. [Prob. < ME, shell < OE *scealu*.] **—shal′ey** *adj.*

shale oil *n.* A crude oil that is obtained from oil shale by heating and distillation.

shall (shăl) *aux.v.* Past tense **should** (shŏŏd) **1.** Used before a verb in the infinitive to show: **a.** Something that will take place or exist in the future: *We shall arrive tomorrow.* **b.** Something, such as an order, promise, requirement, or obligation: *The penalty shall not exceed two years in prison.* **c.** The will to do something or have something take place: *I shall go out if I feel like it.* **d.** Something that is inevitable: *That day shall come.* **2.** *Archaic* **a.** To be able to. **b.** To have to; must. [ME *shal* < OE *sceal*.]

USAGE NOTE The traditional rules for using *shall* and *will* prescribe a complicated pattern of use in which the meanings of the forms change according to the person of the subject. In the first person, *shall* indicates simple futurity: *I shall buy another ticket.* In the second and third persons, the same sense of futurity is expressed by *will: The comet will return in 87 years.* The use of *will* in the first person and of *shall* in the second and third may express determination, promise, obligation, or permission, depending on the context. Thus *I will leave tomorrow* indicates that the speaker is determined to leave; *You shall leave tomorrow* is likely to be interpreted as a command. The sentence *You shall have your money* expresses a promise on the part of the speaker, whereas *You will have your money* makes a simple prediction. • Such, at least, are the traditional rules, but they are followed chiefly by the English and some traditionalists, and then not with perfect consistency. Americans normally use *will* to express most of the senses reserved for *shall* in English usage. Americans use *shall* chiefly in first person invitations and questions that request an opinion or agreement, such as *Shall we go?* and in certain fixed expressions, such as *We shall overcome.* In formal style, Americans use *shall* to express an explicit obligation, as in *Applicants shall provide a proof of residence,* a sense also expressed by *must* or *should.* In speech the distinction that the English signal by the choice of *shall* or *will* may be rendered by stressing the auxiliary, as in *I* will *leave tomorrow* ("I intend to leave"); by choosing another auxiliary, such as *must* or *have to;* or by using an adverb such as *certainly.* • In addition to its sense of obligation, *shall* also can convey high moral seriousness, a usage deriving in part from the King James Bible, as in *"Righteousness shall go before him and shall set us in the way of his steps"* (Ps 85:13). The prophetic overtones that *shall* bears with it have no doubt led to its use in some of the loftiest rhetoric in English. This may be why Lincoln chose to use it instead of *will* in the Gettysburg Address: *"government of the people, by the people, for the people shall not perish from the earth."* See Usage Note at **should.**

shal•loon (shə-lo͞on′, shă-) *n.* A lightweight wool or worsted twill fabric, used chiefly for coat linings. [Fr. *chalon*, after CHÂLONS-SUR-MARNE.]

shal•lop (shăl′əp) *n.* **1.** A large heavy boat, usu. having two masts and carrying fore-and-aft or lugsails. **2.** A small open boat fitted with oars or sails, or both, and used primarily in shallow waters. [Fr. *chaloupe* < Du. *sloep*, sloop; see SLOOP, or perh. < obsolete Fr. *chaloppe*, nutshell (< OFr. *eschalope* < *escale, eschale*, shell, husk; see SCALE[1]).]

shal•lot (shăl′ət, shə-lŏt′) *n.* **1.** A type of onion with long pear-shaped aggregated bulbs. **2.** The mild-flavored bulb of this plant, used in cookery. [Obsolete Fr. *eschalotte* < OFr. *eschaloigne* < VLat. **escalōnia*. See SCALLION.]

shal•low (shăl′ō) *adj.* **-er, -est 1.** Measuring little from bottom to top or surface; lacking physical depth. **2.** Lacking depth of intellect, emotion, or knowledge. **3.** Marked by insufficient inhalation of air; weak. **4.** *Baseball* In the part of a playing area that is closer to home plate. ❖ *n.* A part of a body of water of little depth; a shoal. Often used in the plural. ❖ *tr. & intr.v.* **-lowed,**

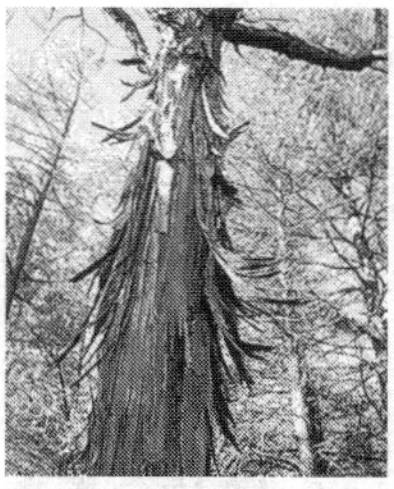

shagbark
Carya ovata

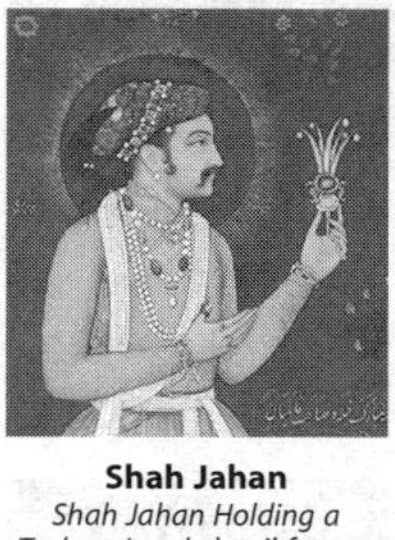

Shah Jahan
Shah Jahan Holding a Turban Jewel, detail from a 1617 miniature by Abul Hassan

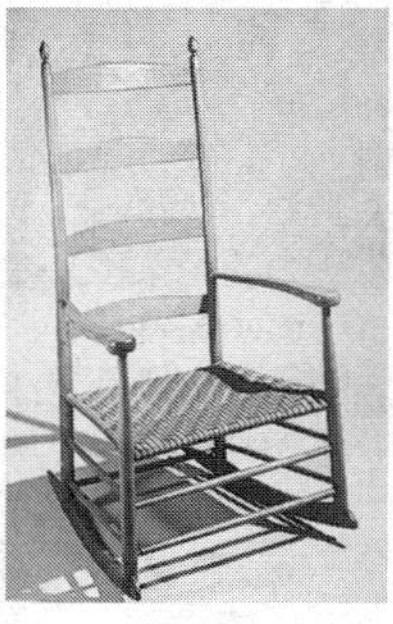

Shaker
mid- to late-19th-century rocking chair

ă	pat	oi	**boy**
ā	pay	ou	**out**
âr	**care**	ŏŏ	**took**
ä	**father**	o͞o	**boot**
ĕ	pet	ŭ	cut
ē	be	ûr	**urge**
ĭ	pit	th	**thin**
ī	pie	*th*	**this**
îr	**pier**	hw	**which**
ŏ	pot	zh	vision
ō	toe	ə	about,
ô	paw		item

Stress marks:
′ (primary);
′ (secondary), as in
lexicon (lĕk′sĭ-kŏn′)

-low·ing, -lows To make or become shallow. [ME *shalowe*.] —**shal′low·ly** *adv.* —**shal′low·ness** *n.*

sha·lom (shä-lōm′, shə-) *interj.* Used as a traditional Jewish greeting or farewell. [Heb. *šālôm*, peace.]

shalt (shălt) *aux.v. Archaic* A second person singular present tense of **shall**.

sham (shăm) *n.* **1.** Something false or empty that is purported to be genuine; a spurious imitation. **2.** The quality of deceitfulness; empty pretense. **3.** One who assumes a false character; an impostor. **4.** A decorative cover made to simulate an article of household linen and used over or in place of it. ❖ *adj.* Not genuine; fake. ❖ *v.* **shammed, sham·ming, shams** —*tr.* To put on the false appearance of; feign. —*intr.* To assume a false appearance or character. [Perh. dialectal var. of SHAME.] —**sham′mer** *n.*

sha·man (shä′mən, shā′-) *n.* A member of certain tribal societies who acts as a medium between the visible world and an invisible spirit world and practices magic or sorcery for healing, divination, and control over natural events. [Russ. < Tungus *šaman*, Buddhist monk, shaman < Tocharian B *ṣamāne*, monk < Prakrit *samana* < Skt. *śramaṇaḥ* < *śramaḥ*, religious exercise.] —**sha·man′ic** (shə-măn′ĭk) *adj.*

sha·man·ism (shä′mə-nĭz′əm, shā′-) *n.* **1.** The animistic religion of certain peoples of northern Asia in which shamans mediate between the visible and spirit worlds. **2.** A similar religion or set of beliefs, esp. among certain Native American peoples. —**sha′man·ist** *n.* —**sha′man·is′tic** *adj.*

sham·ble (shăm′bəl) *intr.v.* **-bled, -bling, -bles** To walk in an awkward, lazy, or unsteady manner, shuffling the feet. [Prob. < obsolete *shamble*, awkward, ungainly < ME *schamil*, butcher's table. See SHAMBLES.] —**sham′ble** *n.*

sham·bles (shăm′bəlz) *pl.n.* (*used with a sing. verb*) **1a.** A scene or condition of complete disorder or ruin. **b.** Great clutter or jumble; a total mess. **2a.** A place or scene of bloodshed or carnage. **b.** A scene or scene of great devastation. **3.** A slaughterhouse. **4.** *Archaic* A meat market or butcher shop. [< ME *shamel*, *shambil*, place where meat is butchered and sold < OE *sceamol*, table < Lat. *scabillum, scamillum*, dim. of *scamnum*, bench, stool.]

WORD HISTORY A place or situation referred to as a *shambles* is usually a mess, but it is no longer always the bloody mess it once was. The history of the word *shambles* begins with the Latin word *scamnum*, "a stool or bench serving as a seat, step, or support for the feet, for example." The diminutive *scamillum*, "low stool," was borrowed by speakers of Old English as *sceamol*, "stool, bench, table." Old English *sceamol* became Middle English *shamel*, which developed the specific sense in the singular and plural of "a place where meat is butchered and sold." The Middle English compound *shamelhouse* meant "slaughterhouse," a sense that the plural *shambles* developed (first recorded in 1548) along with the figurative sense "a place or scene of bloodshed" (first recorded in 1593). Our current meanings, such as "a scene or condition of disorder," are first recorded in 1926.

shame (shām) *n.* **1a.** A painful emotion caused by a strong sense of guilt, embarrassment, unworthiness, or disgrace. **b.** Capacity for such a feeling. **2.** One that brings dishonor, disgrace, or condemnation. **3.** A condition of disgrace or dishonor; ignominy. **4.** A great disappointment. ❖ *tr.v.* **shamed, sham·ing, shames 1.** To cause to feel shame; put to shame. **2.** To bring dishonor or disgrace on. **3.** To disgrace by surpassing. **4.** To force by making ashamed. —*idiom:* **put to shame 1.** To fill with shame; disgrace. **2.** To outdo thoroughly; surpass. [ME < OE *sceamu*.]

shame·faced (shām′fāst′) *adj.* **1.** Indicative of shame; ashamed. **2.** Extremely modest or shy; bashful. [By folk ety. < obsolete *shamefast*, bashful, ashamed < ME < OE *sceamfæst* : *sceamu*, shame + *fæst*, fixed; see FAST[1].] —**shame′fac′ed·ly** (-fā′sĭd-lē) *adv.* —**shame′fac′ed·ness** *n.*

shame·ful (shām′fəl) *adj.* **1a.** Causing shame; disgraceful. **b.** Giving offense; indecent. **2.** *Archaic* Full of shame; ashamed. —**shame′ful·ly** *adv.* —**shame′ful·ness** *n.*

shame·less (shām′lĭs) *adj.* **1.** Feeling no shame; impervious to disgrace. **2.** Marked by a lack of shame: *repeated a shameless lie.* —**shame′less·ly** *adv.* —**shame′less·ness** *n.*

Sha·mir (shə-mēr′), Yitzhak b. 1915. Polish-born Israeli politician who served as prime minister (1983–84 and 1986–92).

sham·i·sen (shăm′ĭ-sĕn′) also **sam·i·sen** (săm′-) *n.* A Japanese musical instrument resembling a lute, having a very long neck and three strings played with a plectrum. [J. *samisen* : *san*, three (< M Chin. *sam*) + *mi*, taste, touch (< M Chin. *mujh*) + *sen*, string (< M Chin. *sianh*).]

sham·mes (shä′məs) *n., pl.* **sham·mo·sim** (shä-mô′sĭm) *Judaism* **1.** A sexton in a synagogue. **2.** The candle used to light the other eight candles of a Hanukkah menorah. [Yiddish *shames* < Heb. *šammāš* < Aram., servant, prob. < Egypt. *šmsw*, servant < *šms*, to follow, serve.]

sham·my (shăm′ē) *n.* Variant of **chamois** 2.

sham·poo (shăm-pōō′) *n., pl.* **-poos 1.** Any of various liquid or cream preparations of soap or detergent used to wash the hair and scalp. **2.** Any of various cleaning agents for rugs, upholstery, or cars. **3.** The act or process of washing or cleaning with shampoo. ❖ *tr. & intr.v.* **-pooed, -poo·ing, -poos** To wash or undergo washing with shampoo. [< Hindi *cāmpō*, imper. of *cāmp-*,

shamisen

Ravi Shankar
playing the sitar at the
Monterey International Pop
Festival, 1967

nā, to press.] —**sham·poo′er** *n.*

sham·rock (shăm′rŏk′) *n.* Any of several plants, such as the clover, having compound leaves with three leaflets. [Ir.Gael. *seamróg*, dim. of *seamar*, clover < MIr. *semar*.]

sha·mus (shä′məs, shā′-) *n. Slang* **1.** A police officer. **2.** A private investigator. [Perh. < the Irish name *Seamus*, James Perh. < the Irish SHAMMES.]

Shan (shän, shän) *n., pl.* **Shan** or **Shans 1.** A member of any of a group of tribes inhabiting northeast Myanmar (Burma) and adjacent parts of China, Laos, and Thailand. **2.** The Tai language of the Shan.

shan·a·chie (shăn′ə-kē) also **sen·na·chie** (sĕn′-) *n. Chiefly Scots* A skilled teller of tales or legends, esp. Gaelic ones. [Sc. Gael. *seanachaidh* < OIr. *senchaid*, var. of *senchae*, historian < *sen*, old.]

Shan·dong (shän′dông′) also **Shan·tung** (shän′tŭng′, shän′tŏong′) A province of E China bordered by the Gulf of Bo Hai and the Yellow Sea. The E part of the province forms the **Shandong Peninsula.** Cap. Jinan. Pop. 84,392,827.

shan·dy (shăn′dē) *n., pl.* **-dies 1.** Shandygaff. **2.** A drink made of beer and lemonade.

shan·dy·gaff (shăn′dē-găf′) *n.* A drink made of beer or ale mixed with ginger beer, ginger ale, or lemonade. [?]

Shang (shäng) A Chinese dynasty traditionally dated 1766–1122 B.C., whose capital was present-day Anyang.

shang·hai (shăng-hī′, shăng′hī′) *tr.v.* **-haied, -hai·ing, -hais 1.** To kidnap for compulsory service aboard a ship. **2.** To induce or compel (someone) to do something, esp. by fraud or force. [After SHANGHAI[1] < the former custom of kidnapping sailors to man ships going to China.] —**shang·hai′er** *n.*

Shang·hai[1] (shăng-hī′, shăng′hī′) A city of E China at the mouth of the Chang Jiang (Yangtze R.) SE of Nanjing; opened to foreign trade by the Treaty of Nanking (1842). Pop. 6,980,000. The municipality of **Shanghai** is administered as a separate governmental unit. Pop. 8,205,598.

Shang·hai[2] (shăng-hī′) *n.* See **Cochin China[2].**

Shan·gri-la (shăng′grĭ-lä′) *n.* **1.** An imaginary remote paradise on earth; utopia. **2.** A distant and secluded hideaway, usu. of great beauty and peacefulness. [After *Shangri-La*, the imaginary land in the novel *Lost Horizon* by James Hilton.]

shank (shăngk) *n.* **1a.** The part of the human leg between the knee and ankle. **b.** A corresponding part in other vertebrates. **2a.** The whole leg of a human. **b.** A leg or leglike part. **3.** A cut of meat from the leg of a steer, calf, sheep, or lamb. **4.** The long narrow part of something, such as a nail or pin. **5.** A stem, stalk, or similar part. **6.** *Nautical* The stem of an anchor. **7.** The long shaft of a fishhook. **8.** The part of a tobacco pipe between the bowl and stem. **9.** The shaft of a key. **10.** The narrow section of the handle of a spoon. **11a.** The narrow part of the sole of a shoe under the instep. **b.** A shankpiece. **12.** A projection, such as a ring, on the back of a button by which it is sewn to cloth. **13a.** See **tang[1]** 5. **b.** The part of a tool, such as a drill, that connects the functioning head to the handle. **14a.** The latter or remaining part, esp. of a period of time. **b.** The early or primary part of a period of time. ❖ *tr.v.* **shanked, shank·ing, shanks** *Sports* To hit (a golf ball) with the heel of the club, causing the ball to veer in the wrong direction. [ME *shanke* < OE *sceanca*.] —**shanked** *adj.*

Shan·kar (shän′kär, shäng′-), **Ravi** b. 1920. Indian-born musician who popularized classical Indian music in the West.

shank·piece (shăngk′pēs′) *n.* An arch support inserted into the shank of a shoe.

Shan·non (shăn′ən) A river rising in N-central Ireland and flowing c. 386 km (240 mi) to the Atlantic Ocean.

shan't (shănt, shänt) Contraction of **shall not.**

shan·tey (shăn′tē) *n.* Variant of **chantey.**

Shan·tou (shän′tou′) also **Swa·tow** (swä′tou′) A city of SE China ENE of Hong Kong. Pop. 884,543.

shan·tung (shăn-tŭng′) *n.* **1.** A heavy fabric with a rough nubby surface, made of spun wild silk. **2.** A rayon or cotton fabric resembling shantung. [After *Shantung* (Shandong), China.]

shan·ty[1] (shăn′tē) *n., pl.* **-ties** A roughly built, often ramshackle cabin; a shack. [Prob. < Canadian Fr. *chantier*, hut in a lumber camp < Fr., timberyard < OFr., gantry < Lat. *canthērius*, rafter, nag < Gk. *kanthēlios*, pack ass.]

shan·ty[2] (shăn′tē) *n.* Variant of **chantey.**

shan·ty·town (shăn′tē-toun′) *n.* A town or a section of a town consisting chiefly of shacks.

Shan·xi (shän′shē′) also **Shan·si** (-sē′) A province of NE China bordered on the N by a section of the Great Wall. Cap. Taiyuan. Pop. 28,759,014.

shape (shāp) *n.* **1a.** The characteristic surface configuration of a thing; an outline or contour. **b.** Something distinguished from its surroundings by its outline. **2.** The contour of a person's body; the figure. **3a.** A definite distinctive form: *a new shape to my life.* **b.** A desirable form: *a fabric that holds its shape.* **4.** A form or condition in which something may exist or appear; embodiment. **5.** Assumed or false appearance; guise. **6.** A ghostly form; a phantom. **7.** Something, such as a mold or pattern, used to give or determine form. **8.** The proper condition of something necessary for action, effectiveness, or use: *in good shape.* ❖ *v.* **shaped, shap·ing, shapes** —*tr.* **1.** To give a particular form to; create. **2.** To cause to conform to a particular form or pattern; adapt to it.

3a. To plan to bring about the realization or accomplishment of; devise. **b.** To embody in a definite form. **4a.** To adapt to a particular use or purpose; adjust. **b.** To direct the course of. —*intr.* **1.** To come to pass; happen. **2.** To take on a definite shape or form. Often used with *up* or *into.* —*phrasal verb:* **shape up 1.** *Informal* To turn out; develop. **2.** To improve so as to meet a standard. [ME < OE *gesceap*, a creation.] —**shap′a·ble,** **shape′a·ble** *adj.* —**shaped** *adj.* —**shap′er** *n.*

SHAPE *abbr.* Supreme Headquarters Allied Powers, Europe
shape·less (shāp′lĭs) *adj.* **1.** Lacking a definite shape. **2.** Lacking symmetrical or attractive form; not shapely. —**shape′less·ly** *adv.* —**shape′less·ness** *n.*
shape·ly (shāp′lē) *adj.* **-li·er, -li·est 1.** Having a distinct shape. **2.** Having a pleasing shape. —**shape′li·ness** *n.*
shape-up or **shape-up** (shāp′ŭp′) *n.* An assembled group of dock workers from which the day's work crew is chosen by a representative of the union.
shape·wear (shāp′wâr′) *n.* Fitted underwear, esp. a girdle, that is designed to hold a part of the body in a particular form.
Sha·pi·ro (shə-pîr′ō), **Karl Jay** 1913–2000. Amer. poet known for his war poems and works in free verse.
Shap·ley (shăp′lē), **Harlow** 1885–1972. Amer. astronomer noted for his work in spectroscopy and photometry.
shard (shärd) also **sherd** (shûrd) *n.* **1.** A piece of broken pottery, esp. one found in an archaeological dig; a potsherd. **2a.** A fragment of a brittle substance, as of glass. **b.** A small piece or part. **3.** *Zoology* **a.** A tough sheath or covering, such as a shell. **b.** The elytron or outer wing covering of a beetle. [ME *sherd* < OE *sceard*, cut, notch. See **sker-¹** in App.]
share¹ (shâr) *n.* **1.** A part or portion belonging to, distributed to, contributed by, or owed by a person or group. **2.** An equitable portion: *do one's share of the work.* **3.** Any of the equal parts into which the capital stock of a corporation or company is divided. ❖ *v.* **shared, shar·ing, shares** —*tr.* **1.** To divide and parcel out in shares; apportion. **2.** To participate in, use, enjoy, or experience jointly or in turns. **3.** To relate (a secret or experience, for example) to another or others. **4.** To accord a share in (something) to another or others. —*intr.* **1.** To have a share or part. **2.** To allow someone to use or enjoy something that one possesses. **3.** To use or enjoy something jointly or in turns. —*idiom:* **go shares** To be concerned or partake equally or jointly, as in a business venture. [ME < OE *scearu*, division. See **sker-¹** in App.] —**share′a·ble, shar′a·ble** *adj.* —**shar′er** *n.*
share² (shâr) *n.* A plowshare. [ME < OE *scēar.* See **sker-¹** in App.]
share·crop (shâr′krŏp′) *v.* **-cropped, -crop·ping, -crops** —*intr.* To work as a sharecropper. —*tr.* To work (land) or grow (crops) as a sharecropper.
share·crop·per (shâr′krŏp′ər) *n.* A tenant farmer who gives a share of the crops raised to the landlord in lieu of rent.
share·hold·er (shâr′hōl′dər) *n.* One that owns or holds a share or shares of stock; a stockholder. —**share′hold′ing** *n.*
share·own·er (shâr′ō′nər) *n.* See **shareholder.**
share·ware (shâr′wâr′) *n.* Copyrighted software available free of charge esp. on a trial basis.
Sha·ri (shä′rē) See **Chari.**
sha·ri·'a or **sha·ri·a** (shä-rē′ä) *n. Islam* The code of law based on the Koran. [Ar. *šarī'a,* divinely ordained law < *šara'a,* to prescribe, ordain (of God).]
sha·rif (shə-rēf′) *n.* Variant of **sherif.**
shark (shärk) *n.* **1.** Any of numerous chiefly marine carnivorous fishes of the subclass Elasmobranchii, having a torpedolike body, five to seven gill openings on each side of the head, an oil-filled liver, a cartilaginous skeleton, and tough scaly skin. **2a.** A person regarded as ruthless, greedy, or dishonest. **b.** A vicious usurer. **3.** *Slang* A person unusually skilled in a particular activity. ❖ *v.* **sharked, shark·ing, sharks** —*tr. Archaic* To obtain by deceitful means. —*intr.* To practice or live by fraud and trickery. [?]
shark·skin (shärk′skĭn′) *n.* **1.** The skin of a shark. **2.** Leather made from the skin of a shark. **3.** A rayon and acetate fabric having a smooth, somewhat shiny surface.
shark sucker *n.* See **remora.**
Sha·ron (shə-rōn′), **Ariel** b. 1928. Israeli politician who was elected prime minister in 2001.
Shar·on (shăr′ən), **Plain of** A fertile plain of W Israel extending along the Mediterranean coast S of Haifa.
sharp (shärp) *adj.* **sharp·er, sharp·est 1.** Having a thin edge or fine point suitable for or capable of cutting or piercing. **2a.** Having clear form and detail: *a sharp photographic image.* **b.** Terminating in an edge or point: *sharp angular cliffs; a sharp nose.* **c.** Clearly and distinctly set forth: *sharp contrasts.* **3.** Abrupt or acute: *a sharp drop.* **4a.** Intellectually penetrating; astute. **b.** Marked by keenness and accuracy of perception: *sharp hearing.* **5.** Crafty or deceitful. **6.** Vigilant; alert. **7a.** Briskly or keenly cold and cutting: *a sharp wind.* **b.** Harsh or biting in tone or character: *sharp criticism.* **8.** Fierce or impetuous; violent: *a sharp temper.* **9.** Intense; severe: *a sharp pain.* **10a.** Sudden and shrill. **b.** Sudden and brilliant or dazzling. **11.** Strongly affecting the senses of smell and taste. **12.** Composed of hard angular particles. **13.** *Music* **a.** Raised in pitch by a semitone. **b.** Being above the proper pitch. **c.** Having the key signature in sharps. **14.** *Informal* Attractive or stylish. ❖ *adv.* **1.** In a sharp manner. **2.** Punctually; exactly.

3. *Music* Above the true or proper pitch. ❖ *n.* **1.** *Music* **a.** A sign (♯) used to indicate that a note is to be raised by a half step. **b.** A note that is raised a half step. **2.** A slender sewing needle with a very fine point. **3.** *Informal* **a.** An expert. **b.** A shrewd cheater; a sharper. ❖ *v.* **sharped, sharp·ing, sharps** *Music* —*tr.* To raise in pitch by a semitone. —*intr.* To play or sing above the proper pitch. [ME *scharp* < OE *scearp.* See **sker-¹** in App.] —**sharp′ly** *adv.* —**sharp′ness** *n.*

SYNONYMS *sharp, keen, acute* These adjectives apply literally to fine edges, points, or tips. Figuratively they indicate mental alertness and clarity of comprehension. *Sharp* suggests quickness and astuteness: "*a young man of sharp and active intellect*" (John Henry Newman). *Keen* implies clear-headedness and acuity: *a journalist with a keen mind. Acute* suggests penetrating perception or discernment: *an acute observer of politics.*

Sharp, Phillip Allen b. 1944. Amer. biologist who shared a 1993 Nobel prize in medicine.
Shar-Pei (shär′pā′) *n., pl.* **-Peis** Any of a Chinese breed of medium-sized dog having loose wrinkled skin, a short rough coat, and a blue-black mouth and tongue. [Chin. (Mandarin) *shā pí,* sand fur : *shā,* sand + *pí,* fur.]
sharp·en (shär′pən) *tr. & intr.v.* **-ened, -en·ing, -ens** To make or become sharp or sharper. —**sharp′en·er** *n.*
sharp·er (shär′pər) *n.* One that deals dishonestly with others, esp. a cheating gambler.
sharp-eyed (shärp′īd′) *adj.* **1.** Having keen eyesight. **2.** Keenly perceptive or observant; alert.
sharp·ie (shär′pē) *n., pl.* **-ies 1.** A long narrow flatbottom fishing boat having a centerboard and one or two masts, each rigged with a triangular sail. **2a.** An alert quick-witted person. **b.** A sharper. [< SHARP.]
sharp-nosed (shärp′nōzd′) *adj.* **1.** Having a thin pointed nose or snout. **2.** Having a keen sense of smell.
Sharps·burg (shärps′bûrg′) A town of extreme NW MD site of the Battle of Antietam (Sep. 16–17, 1862).
sharp-shinned hawk (shärp′shĭnd′) *n.* A small North American hawk *(Accipiter striatus)* that has short rounded wings and a long tail and preys on other birds.
sharp·shoot·er (shärp′shoō′tər) *n.* **1.** One who is highly proficient at shooting. **2a.** The second military grade of proficiency in the use of rifles and other small arms. **b.** One who holds this grade of proficiency.
sharp·shoot·ing (shärp′shoō′tĭng) *n.* **1.** High proficiency in shooting firearms. **2.** Accurate, often unexpected verbal or written attack.
sharp-sight·ed (shärp′sī′tĭd) *adj.* **1.** Having keen eyesight. **2.** Keenly perceptive or alert. —**sharp′-sight′ed·ness** *n.*
sharp-tongued (shärp′tŭngd′) *adj.* Harsh, critical, or sarcastic in speech.
sharp-wit·ted (shärp′wĭt′ĭd) *adj.* Having or exhibiting keenly perceptive intellect. —**sharp′-wit′ted·ness** *n.*
shash·lik or **shash·lick** (shäsh-lĭk′, shäsh′lĭk′) *n.* A dish consisting of marinated cubes of lamb or beef grilled or roasted on a spit, often with slices of eggplant, onion, and tomato; shish kebab. [Russ. *shashlyk,* of Turk. orig.]
Shas·ta (shăs′tə), **Mount** A volcanic peak, 4,319.4 m (14,162 ft), of the Cascade Range in N CA.
Shasta daisy *n.* A hybrid daisy derived from *Chrysanthemum maximum* and *C. lacustre,* with large white flower heads.
shat (shăt) *v. Vulgar Slang* A past tense and a past participle of **shit.**
Shatt al Ar·ab or **Shatt-al-Ar·ab** (shăt′ äl är′əb, shăt′ äl) A river channel, c. 193 km (120 mi), of SE Iraq formed by the confluence of the Tigris and Euphrates rivers and flowing to the Persian Gulf.
shat·ter (shăt′ər) *v.* **-tered, -ter·ing, -ters** —*tr.* **1.** To cause to break or burst suddenly into pieces, as with a violent blow. **2a.** To damage seriously; disable. **b.** To cause the destruction or ruin of; destroy: *shattered dreams.* —*intr.* To break into pieces; smash or burst. See Syns at **break.** ❖ *n.* **1a.** The act of shattering. **b.** The condition of being shattered. **2.** A splintered or fragmented condition. Often used in the plural. [ME *shateren* < OE **sceaterian,* to scatter.]
shatter cone *n.* A conical fragment of rock that is formed from the high pressure of volcanism or meteorite impact and has striations radiating from the apex.
shat·ter·proof (shăt′ər-proōf′) *adj.* Resistant to shattering.
Shav·a·no Peak (shăv′ə-nō) A mountain, 4,339.8 m (14,229 ft), in the Sawatch Range of the Rocky Mts. in central CO.
shave (shāv) *v.* **shaved, shaved** or **shav·en** (shā′vən), **shav·ing, shaves** —*tr.* **1a.** To remove the beard or other body hair from, with a razor or shaver. **b.** To cut (the beard, for example) at the surface of the skin with a razor or shaver. **2.** To crop, trim, or mow closely. **3a.** To remove thin slices from: *shave a board.* **b.** To cut or scrape into thin slices; shred: *shave chocolate.* **4.** To come close to or graze in passing. **5.** To limit the number of (points) scored by one's own team in an athletic contest by pointshaving. **6a.** To purchase (a note) at a reduction greater than the legal or customary rate. **b.** To cut (a price) by a slight margin. —*intr.* To remove the beard or other body hair with a razor or

Shar-Pei

shear
top: sheep shearing
bottom: pruning and
pinking shears

shaver. ❖ *n.* **1.** The act, process, or result of shaving. **2.** A thin slice or scraping; a shaving. **3.** A tool for shaving. [ME *shaven,* to scrape < OE *sceafan.*]

shav•er (shā′vər) *n.* **1a.** One who shaves. **b.** A shaving device, esp. an electric razor. **2.** *Informal* A small, esp. male child.

Sha•vi•an (shā′vē-ən) *adj.* Of, relating to, or characteristic of George Bernard Shaw or his works: *Shavian wit.* ❖ *n.* An admirer or disciple of George Bernard Shaw. [< *Shavius,* Latinization of the name *Shaw.*]

shav•ing (shā′vĭng) *n.* **1.** A thin slice or sliver, as of wood or metal, that is shaved off. **2.** The act of one that shaves.

Sha•vu•ot also **Sha•bu•oth** (shə-vōō′ōt′, -əs, shä′vōō-ôt′) *n. Judaism* A feast held on the sixth and seventh days of Sivan in commemoration of the revelation of the Law on Mount Sinai and the celebration of the wheat festival in ancient times. [Heb. *šābûʿôt,* pl. of *šābûʿa,* week < *šeba',* seven.]

Shaw (shô), **Anna Howard** 1847–1919. British-born Amer. physician who was president of the National American Woman Suffrage Association (1904–15).

Shaw, Artie b. 1910. Amer. clarinetist, band leader, and composer whose swing band exemplified the big band sound.

Shaw, George Bernard 1856–1950. Irish-born British playwright and critic who was a founder of the Fabian Society and won the 1925 Nobel Prize for literature.

Shaw, Henry Wheeler Pen name Josh Billings. 1818–85. Amer. humorist noted for his essays in the *Farmers' Allminax* (1869–80).

shawl (shôl) *n.* A square or oblong piece of cloth worn as a covering for the head, neck, and shoulders. ❖ *tr.v.* **shawled, shawl•ing, shawls** To cover with or as if with such a piece of cloth. [Ult. < Pers. *shāl,* ult. < Skt. *śāṭī,* cloth, sari.]

shawm (shôm) *n.* Any of various early double-reed wind instruments, forerunners of the modern oboe. [ME *shalmie* < OFr. *chalemie,* alteration of *chalemel* < LLat. *calamellus,* dim. of Lat. *calamus,* reed < Gk. *kalamos.*]

Shawn (shôn), **Ted** 1891–1972. Amer. dancer and choreographer noted for his partnership with Ruth Saint Denis.

Shaw•nee (shô-nē′) *n., pl.* **Shawnee** or **-nees 1.** A member of a Native American people formerly inhabiting parts of the Cumberland and central Ohio valleys, with present-day populations in Oklahoma. **2.** The Algonquian language of the Shawnee. [Backformation < obsolete *Shawnese* < Shawnee *shaawanooki,* those of the south, Shawnee.]

Shawnee cake *n. New England* See **johnnycake.** See Regional Note at **johnnycake.**

Shaw•wal (shə-wäl′) *n.* The tenth month of the year in the Islamic calendar. See table at **calendar.** [Ar. *šawwāl* < *šāla,* to rise.]

shay (shā) *n. Informal* A chaise. [Back-formation < CHAISE (taken as pl.).]

Shays (shāz), **Daniel** 1747?–1825. Amer. insurrectionist who led a raid on a government arsenal in Springfield MA to protest against the economic plight of farmers (1787).

she (shē) *pron.* **1a.** Used to refer to the woman or girl previously mentioned or implied. See Usage Note at **I¹. b.** Used to refer to a female animal. **2.** Used in place of *it* to refer to certain inanimate things, such as ships, traditionally perceived as female. ❖ *n.* A female animal or person. [ME, prob. alteration of OE *sēo,* fem. demonstrative pron. See **so-** in App.]

s/he (shē′ər-hē′, shē′hē′) *pron.* Used as a gender-neutral alternative to *he* or *she.* See Usage Note at **he¹.**

shea butter (shē, shā) *n.* A fat obtained from the seeds of the shea tree, used as food and for making soap and candles.

sheaf (shēf) *n., pl.* **sheaves** (shēvz) **1.** A bundle of cut stalks of grain or similar plants bound with straw or twine. **2.** A collection of items held or bound together. **3.** An archer's quiver. ❖ *tr.v.* **sheafed, sheaf•ing, sheafs** To gather and bind into a bundle. [ME *sheef* < OE *scēaf.*]

shear (shîr) *v.* **sheared, sheared** or **shorn** (shôrn, shōrn), **shear•ing, shears** —*tr.* **1.** To remove (fleece or hair) by cutting or clipping. **2.** To remove the hair or fleece from. **3.** To cut with or as if with shears. **4.** To divest or deprive as if by cutting: *shorn of all dignity.* —*intr.* **1.** To use a cutting tool such as shears. **2.** To move or proceed by or as if by cutting. **3.** *Physics* To become deformed by forces tending to produce a shearing strain. ❖ *n.* **1a.** A pair of scissors. Often used in the plural. **b.** Any of various implements or machines that cut with a scissorlike action. Often used in the plural. **2.** The act, process, or result of shearing. **3.** Something cut off by shearing. **4.** The act, process, or fact of shearing. Used to indicate a sheep's age: *a two-shear ram.* **5.** An apparatus used to lift heavy weights, consisting of two or more spars joined at the top and spread at the base, the tackle being suspended from the top. Often used in the plural with a singular or plural verb. **6.** *Physics* **a.** An applied force or system of forces that tends to produce a shearing strain. **b.** A shearing strain. [ME *scheren* < OE *sceran.* See **sker-¹** in App. N. < ME *shere* < OE *scēar.* See **sker-¹** in App.] —**shear′er** *n.*

sheared (shîrd) *adj.* Shaped or finished by shearing, esp. cut or trimmed to a uniform length: *a sheared fur coat.*

shear•ing strain (shîr′ĭng) *n.* A deformation of an elastic body caused by forces that produce an opposite but parallel sliding motion of the body's planes.

shearing stress *n.* See shear 6a.

shear•ling (shîr′lĭng) *n.* **1.** A year-old sheep that has been sheared once. **2.** The skin of a shearling or of a newly sheared sheep or lamb, tanned and with the wool on.

shear•wa•ter (shîr′wô′tər, -wŏt′ər) *n.* Any of various oceanic birds of the genus *Puffinus,* having slender wings that seem to shear the water as the bird flies along the surface.

sheath (shēth) *n., pl.* **sheaths** (shēthz, shēths) **1a.** A case for a blade, as of a sword. **b.** Any of various similar coverings. **2.** *Biology* An enveloping tubular structure, such as the tissue that encloses a muscle or nerve fiber. **3.** A close-fitting dress. **4.** A condom. ❖ *tr.v.* **sheathed, sheath•ing, sheaths** (shēthz, shēths) To encase or cover with or as if with a sheath; sheathe. [ME *shethe* < OE *scēath.*]

sheath•bill (shēth′bĭl′) *n.* Either of two pigeonlike shore birds (*Chionia alba* or *C. minor*) of Antarctic regions having white plumage and a horny covering on the base of the bill.

sheathe (shēth) *tr.v.* **sheathed, sheath•ing, sheathes 1.** To insert into or provide with a sheath. **2.** To retract (a claw) into a sheath. **3.** To enclose with a protective covering; encase. [ME *shethen* < *shethe,* sheath. See SHEATH.] —**sheath′er** *n.*

sheath•ing (shē′thĭng) *n.* **1.** A layer of boards or of other wood or fiber materials applied to the outer studs, joists, and rafters of a building to strengthen the structure and serve as a base for a weatherproof cladding. **2.** *Nautical* An exterior covering on the underwater part of a ship's hull that protects it against marine growths. **3.** The act of providing sheathing.

sheath knife *n.* A knife that has a fixed blade and fits into a sheath.

shea tree (shē, shā) *n.* A tropical African tree (*Butyrospermum parkii*) having oily seeds that yield shea butter. [Bambara *si.*]

sheave¹ (shēv) *tr.v.* **sheaved, sheav•ing, sheaves** To collect and bind into a sheaf. [< SHEAF.]

sheave² (shēv, shĭv) *n.* A wheel or disk with a grooved rim, esp. one used as a pulley. [ME *sheve.*]

sheaves (shēvz) *n.* Plural of **sheaf.**

She•ba (shē′bə) An ancient country of S Arabia comprising present-day Yemen. Its people colonized Ethiopia in the 10th cent. B.C. and were known for their commercial prosperity.

she•bang (shə-băng′) *n. Slang* A situation, organization, contrivance, or set of facts or things. [?]

She•bat (shə-bät′, -vät′) *n.* Variant of **Shevat.**

she•been (shə-bēn′) *n.* An unlicensed drinking establishment, esp. in Ireland, Scotland, and South Africa. [Ir.Gael. *séibín,* grain measure or tax, bad ale, dim. of *séibe,* mug, bottle.]

She•be•le (shē-bā′lĕ, shə-) See **Shabelle.**

shed¹ (shĕd) *v.* **shed, shed•ding, sheds** —*tr.* **1.** To cause to pour forth. **2.** To diffuse or radiate; send forth or impart: *shed light.* **3.** To repel without allowing penetration: *A duck's feathers shed water.* **4a.** To lose by natural process: *a snake shedding its skin.* **b.** To rid oneself of (something not wanted or needed): *shed 25 pounds by dieting.* —*intr.* **1.** To lose a natural growth or covering by natural process. **2.** To pour forth, fall off, or drop out. ❖ *n.* **1.** Something that sheds, esp. an elevation in the earth's surface from which water flows in two directions; a watershed. **2.** Something shed. —**idiom: shed blood** To take life, esp. with violence; kill. [ME *sheden,* to separate, shed < OE *scēadan,* to divide.]

shed² (shĕd) *n.* **1.** A small structure, either freestanding or attached to a larger structure, serving for storage or shelter. **2.** A large low structure often open on all sides. [Alteration of ME *shadde,* perh. var. of *shade,* shade. See SHADE.]

she'd (shēd) **1.** Contraction of *she had.* **2.** Contraction of *she would.*

shed•der (shĕd′ər) *n.* **1.** One that sheds, as a molting snake. **2.** A lobster or crab that is shedding or has just shed.

sheen (shēn) *n.* **1.** Glistening brightness; luster. **2.** Splendid attire. **3.** A glossy surface given to textiles. [< ME *shene,* beautiful < OE *scīene.*]

sheep (shēp) *n., pl.* **sheep 1.** Any of various usu. horned ruminant mammals of the genus *Ovis* in the family Bovidae, esp. the domesticated species *O. aries,* raised for wool, flesh, or skin. **2.** Leather made from the skin of one of these animals. **3a.** A person regarded as timid, weak, or submissive. **b.** One easily swayed or led. [ME < OE *scēap.*]

sheep•ber•ry (shēp′bĕr′ē) *n.* Either of two eastern North American shrubs or trees (*Viburnum lentago* or *V. prunifolium*) having white flowers and edible blue-black berries. [< the resemblance of the berries to sheep droppings.]

sheep•cote (shēp′kōt′, -kŏt′) *n. Chiefly British* A sheepfold.

sheep dip also **sheep-dip** (shēp′dĭp′) *n.* Any of various preparations of liquid disinfectant into which sheep are dipped to destroy parasites and clean their wool, esp. before shearing.

sheep•dog also **sheep dog** (shēp′dôg′, -dŏg′) *n.* A dog trained to guard and herd sheep.

sheep•fold (shēp′fōld′) *n.* A pen for sheep.

sheep•herd•er (shēp′hûr′dər) *n.* A person who herds sheep, esp. on an open range; a shepherd. —**sheep′herd′ing** *n.*

sheep•ish (shē′pĭsh) *adj.* **1.** Embarrassed, as by consciousness of a fault: *a sheepish grin.* **2.** Meek or stupid. —**sheep′ish•ly** *adv.* —**sheep′ish•ness** *n.*

sheep ked (kĕd) *n.* See **sheep tick.** [?]

sheep laurel *n.* An eastern North American evergreen shrub (*Kalmia angustifolia*) having flowers with rose-pink or crimson bell-shaped corollas and poisonous leaves.

sheep's eyes (shēps) *pl.n.* Shyly amorous glances.

sheep•shank (shēp'shăngk') *n.* A hitch made in a line to shorten it.

sheeps•head (shēps'hĕd') *n.* **1.** A food fish (*Archosargus probatocephalus*) of the Atlantic and Gulf coasts of North America having dark markings. **2.** A freshwater drum (*Aplodinotus grunniens*) of central North America. **3.** A redfish (*Semicossyphus pulcher*) of the Gulf of California.

sheep•shear•ing (shēp'shîr'ĭng) *n.* **1.** The act of shearing sheep. **2a.** The time or season when sheep are sheared. **b.** Festivities held at this time. —**sheep'shear'er** *n.*

sheep•skin (shēp'skĭn') *n.* **1.** The skin of a sheep either tanned with the fleece left on or in the form of leather or parchment. **2.** *Informal* A diploma.

sheep tick *n.* A wingless louselike fly (*Melophagus ovinus*) that is parasitic to sheep, causing loss of wool.

sheer[1] (shîr) *intr. & tr.v.* **sheered, sheer•ing, sheers** To swerve or cause to swerve from a course. ❖ *n.* **1.** A swerving or deviating course. **2.** *Nautical* The upward curve or amount of upward curve of the longitudinal lines of a ship's hull as viewed from the side. [Prob. partly < LGer. *scheren,* to move to and fro (said of boats), and partly < Du. *scheren,* to withdraw. See **sker-**[1] in App.]

sheer[2] (shîr) *adj.* **sheer•er, sheer•est 1.** Thin, fine, and transparent: *sheer curtains.* See Syns at **airy. 2a.** Completely such, without qualification or exception: *sheer happiness.* **b.** Free from admixture or adulterants; unmixed. See Syns at **pure. c.** Considered or operating apart from anything else. **3.** Almost perpendicular; steep: *sheer rock cliffs.* See Syns at **steep**[1]. ❖ *adv.* **1.** Almost perpendicularly. **2.** Completely; altogether. [Obsolete *shere,* thin, clear, partly < ME *shir,* clear (< OE *scīr*) and partly < ME *skir,* clean (< ON *skærr*).] —**sheer'ly** *adv.* —**sheer'ness** *n.*

sheesh (shēsh) *interj.* Used to express mild annoyance, surprise, or disgust. [Alteration of JESUS[1].]

sheet[1] (shēt) *n.* **1.** A broad rectangular piece of fabric serving as a basic article of bedding. **2a.** A broad, thin, usu. rectangular mass or piece of material, such as paper, metal, glass, or plywood. **b.** A flat or very shallow, usu. rectangular pan used for baking. **3.** A broad flat continuous surface or expanse. **4.** A moving expanse: *a sheet of flames.* **5.** A newspaper, esp. a tabloid. **6.** *Geology* A broad, relatively thin deposit or layer of igneous or sedimentary rock. **7.** A large block of stamps printed by a single impression of a plate before the individual stamps have been separated. ❖ *v.* **sheet•ed, sheet•ing, sheets** —*tr.* **1.** To cover with, wrap in, or provide with a sheet. **2.** To make into sheets. —*intr.* To flow or fall in a sheet. ❖ *adj.* Being in the form of a sheet. [ME *shete,* cloth < OE *scēte.*]

sheet[2] (shēt) *Nautical n.* **1.** A line attached to a boom or a clew of a sail to control its position. **2. sheets** The spaces at either end of an open boat in front of and behind the seats. —*idiom:* **three sheets to** (or **in**) **the wind** *Informal* Intoxicated; drunk. [ME *shete* < OE *scēat(line),* sheet (line) < *scēata,* corner of a sail.]

sheet anchor *n.* **1.** *Nautical* A large extra anchor intended for use in an emergency. **2.** A source of aid in emergency or danger.

sheet bend *n. Nautical* A knot in which one rope is made fast to the bight of another.

sheet glass *n.* Glass drawn from a molten bath into a thin sheet of film, commonly used to make windows.

sheet•ing (shē'tĭng) *n.* **1.** Material, such as metal or cloth, formed into or used to form sheets. **2.** The act or process of providing with or forming into sheets.

sheet lightning *n.* Lightning that appears as a broad sheetlike illumination of parts of a thundercloud, caused by the reflection of a lightning flash.

sheet metal *n.* Metal rolled into a sheet with a thickness between foil and plate. —**sheet'-met'al** (shēt'mĕt'l) *adj.*

sheet music *n.* Compositions printed on unbound sheets of paper.

Sheet•rock (shēt'rŏk') A trademark used for plasterboard.

Shef•field (shĕf'ēld') A borough of N-central England E of Manchester; long known for its cutlery. Pop. 531,928.

she•getz (shā'gĭts) *n., pl.* **shkotz•im** (shkôt'sĭm) *Offensive* A non-Jewish boy or young man. [Yiddish *sheygets* < Heb. *šeqeṣ,* blemish.]

sheik also **sheikh** (shēk, shāk) *n.* **1.** *Islam* **a.** A religious official, usu. male. **b.** A male leader of an Arab family or village. **c.** Used as a form of address for such an official or leader. **2.** *Slang* A romantically alluring man. [Ar. *šayḫ,* old man, chief < *šāḫa,* to be old.]

sheik•dom also **sheikh•dom** (shēk'dəm, shāk'-) *n.* The area ruled by a sheik.

shei•la (shē'lə) *n. Australian Slang* A girl or young woman. [< the personal name *Sheila.*]

shek•el (shĕk'əl) *n.* **1a.** Any of several ancient units of weight, esp. a Hebrew unit equal to about a half ounce. **b.** A gold or silver coin equal in weight to one of these units, esp. the chief silver coin of the ancient Hebrews. **2.** *Slang* **a.** A coin. **b. shekels** Money. [Heb. *šeqel* < *šāqal,* to weigh.]

She•khi•nah (shī-kē'nə, -кНĒ'-, -kī'-) *n. Judaism* The Divine Presence, considered female in Jewish mysticism. [Mishnaic Heb. *šəkînâ* < Heb. *šākan,* to dwell.]

shel•drake (shĕl'drāk') *n.* **1.** Any of various large Old World ducks of the genus *Tadorna,* esp. *T. tadorna,* having predominantly black and white plumage. **2.** See **merganser.** [ME *shelddrake* : *scheld,* variegated + *drake,* drake.]

shel•duck (shĕl'dŭk') *n.* See **sheldrake** 1.

shelf (shĕlf) *n., pl.* **shelves** (shĕlvz) **1a.** A flat, usu. rectangular structure composed of a rigid material, such as wood, glass, or metal, fixed at right angles to a wall or other vertical surface and used to hold or store objects. **b.** The contents or capacity of such a structure. **c.** Something, such as a projecting ledge of rock or a balcony, that resembles such a structure. **2.** A reef, sandbar, or shoal. **3.** Bedrock. —*idioms:* **off the shelf** From ready-made merchandise in stock. **on the shelf 1.** In a state of disuse. **2a.** Unemployed. **b.** Out of circulation. **c.** Retired. [ME, prob. < MLGer. *schelf.*] —**shelf'ful'** *n.*

shelf ice *n.* An extension of glacial ice into coastal waters that is in contact with the bottom only near the shore.

shelf life *n.* The length of time a product may be stored without becoming unsuitable for use or consumption.

shell (shĕl) *n.* **1a.** The usu. hard outer covering that encases certain organisms, such as mollusks, insects, and turtles; the carapace. **b.** A similar outer covering on an egg, fruit, or nut. **c.** The material that constitutes such a covering. **2.** Something resembling or having the form of a shell; esp.: **a.** An external, usu. hard protective or enclosing case or cover. **b.** A framework or exterior, as of a building. **c.** A thin layer of pastry. **d.** The external part of the ear. **3.** *Nautical* The hull of a vessel. **b.** A long narrow racing boat propelled by rowers. **4.** A small glass for beer. **5a.** An artillery projectile containing an explosive charge. **b.** A metal or cardboard case containing the charge and primer for a piece of firearms ammunition, esp. one also containing shot and fired from a shotgun. **6.** An attitude or manner masking one's true feelings or to protect one from perceived or real danger. **7.** *Physics* Any of a set of atomic energy levels occupied by electrons having the same principal quantum number. **8a.** A usu. sleeveless and collarless, typically knit blouse, often worn under another top. **b.** The outermost layer of a lined garment such as a coat. **9.** *Computer Science* A program that works with the operating system as a command processor, used to enter commands and initiate their execution. **10.** A company or corporation with few or no assets that is acquired by another company so that it can conduct business under the acquired company's legitimate legal standing. ❖ *v.* **shelled, shell•ing, shells** —*tr.* **1a.** To remove the shell of; shuck: *shell oysters.* **b.** To remove from a shell: *shell peas.* **2.** To separate the kernels of (corn) from the cob. **3.** To fire shells at; bombard. **4.** To defeat decisively. —*intr.* **1.** To shed or become free of a shell. **2.** To look for or collect shells, as on a seashore. —*phrasal verb:* **shell out** *Informal* To hand over; pay. [ME < OE *scell.*] —**shell** *adj.* —**shell'er** *n.*

she'll (shēl) Contraction of *she will.*

shel•lac also **shel•lack** (shə-lăk') *n.* **1.** A purified lac in the form of thin yellow or orange flakes, often bleached white and widely used in varnishes, paints, and inks. **2.** A thin varnish made by dissolving this substance in denatured alcohol, used to finish wood. ❖ *tr.v.* **-lacked, -lack•ing, -lacs 1.** To coat or finish with shellac. **2.** *Slang* **a.** To strike repeatedly and severely; batter. **b.** To defeat decisively. [SHEL(L) + LAC (transl. of Fr. *laque en écailles,* lac in thin plates).]

shell•back (shĕl'băk') *n.* **1.** A sailor who has crossed the equator. **2.** A veteran sailor. [< the toughness of such a sailor.]

shell bean *n.* Any of various beans cultivated for their edible seeds rather than their pods.

Shel•ley (shĕl'ē), **Mary Wollstonecraft Godwin** 1797–1851. British writer best known for the novel *Frankenstein* (1818).

Shelley, Percy Bysshe 1792–1822. British romantic poet whose works include "To a Skylark" (1820) and the lyric drama *Prometheus Unbound* (1820).

shell•fire (shĕl'fīr') *n.* The shooting or exploding of artillery shells.

shell•fish (shĕl'fĭsh') *n., pl.* **shellfish** or **-fish•es** An aquatic animal, such as a mollusk or crustacean, that has a shell or shell-like exoskeleton. —**shell'fish'ing** *n.*

shell•fish•er•y (shĕl'fĭsh'ə-rē) *n., pl.* **-ies 1.** The industry or occupation of catching, processing, or selling shellfish. **2.** A fishing ground for shellfish.

shell game *n.* **1.** A game in which a person hides a small object under one of three nutshells, thimbles, or cups, then shuffles them while spectators bet on the object's final location. **2.** A fraud or swindle.

shell jacket *n.* See **mess jacket.**

shell pink *n.* A pinkish white to strong yellowish pink.

shell•proof (shĕl'proof') *adj.* Made to withstand shellfire.

shell shock *n.* See **combat fatigue.**

shell-shocked or **shell•shocked** (shĕl'shŏkt') *adj.* **1.** Suffering from shell shock. **2.** Stunned, distressed, or exhausted from a prolonged trauma or an unexpected difficulty.

Shel•ta (shĕl'tə) *n.* A secret jargon used by traditionally itinerant people in Great Britain and Ireland, based on systematic inversion or alteration of the initial consonants of Gaelic words.

Mary Wollstonecraft Shelley
detail from a portrait by Richard Rothwell (1800–68)

ă	pat	oi	boy
ā	pay	ou	out
âr	care	ŏŏ	took
ä	father	ōō	boot
ĕ	pet	ŭ	cut
ē	be	ûr	urge
ĭ	pit	th	thin
ī	pie	th	this
îr	pier	hw	which
ŏ	pot	zh	vision
ō	toe	ə	about,
ô	paw		item

Stress marks:
ʹ (primary);
ʹ (secondary), as in
lexicon (lĕk'sĭ-kŏn')

William Tecumseh Sherman
photographed c. 1864 by
Mathew Brady

Shetland pony

Eduard Shevardnadze

[< Shelta *Sheldrū*, perh. alteration of Ir.Gael. *béarla*, language, English < OIr. *bélrae*, language < *bél*, mouth.]

shel•ter (shĕl′tər) *n.* **1a.** Something that provides cover or protection, as from the weather. **b.** A refuge; a haven. **c.** An establishment that provides temporary housing for homeless people. **2.** The state of being covered or protected. ❖ *v.* **-tered, -ter•ing, -ters** —*tr.* **1.** To provide cover or protection for. **2.** To invest (income) to protect it from taxation. —*intr.* To take cover; find refuge. [Perh. < ME *sheltron*, tight battle formation < OE *scild-truma* : *scield*, shield; see SHIELD + *truma*, troop; see deru- in App.] —**shel′ter•er** *n.*

shel•ter•belt (shĕl′tər-bĕlt′) *n.* A barrier of trees and shrubs that protects against the wind and reduces erosion.

shel•tered workshop (shĕl′tərd) *n.* A workplace that provides a supportive environment where physically or mentally disabled persons can acquire vocational skills and experience.

shelter tent *n.* A small tent usu. pitched by securing together two or more pieces of waterproof material.

shel•tie also **shel•ty** (shĕl′tē) *n., pl.* **-ties** *Informal* **1.** A Shetland pony. **2.** A Shetland sheepdog. [Prob. < ON *Hjalti*, Shetlander < *Hjaltland*, Shetland Is.]

shelve (shĕlv) *v.* **shelved, shelv•ing, shelves** —*tr.* **1.** To place or arrange on a shelf. **2.** To put away as though on a shelf; table. **3.** To cause to retire from service; dismiss. **4.** To furnish with shelves. —*intr.* To slope gradually; incline. [< SHELF (on the model of such pairs as *calf, calve*).] —**shelv′er** *n.*

shelves (shĕlvz) *n.* Plural of **shelf.**

shelv•ing (shĕl′vĭng) *n.* **1.** Shelves considered as a group. **2.** Material for shelves. **3.** An incline; a slope.

Shem (shĕm) In the Bible, the eldest son of Noah and the brother of Japheth and Ham.

She•ma (shə-mä′) *n.* A liturgical prayer consisting of three Scriptural passages (Deuteronomy 6:4-9, 11:13-21, and Numbers 15:37-41) recited twice daily by adult Jewish males to affirm their faith. [Heb. *šama‘*, hear (the first word of Deuteronomy 6:4), imper. of *šama‘*, to hear.]

Shen•an•do•ah Valley (shĕn′ən-dō′ə) A valley of N VA between the Allegheny Mts. and the Blue Ridge; drained by the **Shenandoah River**, c. 241 km (150 mi).

she•nan•i•gan (shə-nǎn′ĭ-gən) *n. Informal* **1a.** A deceitful trick; an underhand act. **b.** Remarks intended to deceive; deceit. Often used in the plural. **2a.** A playful or mischievous act; a prank. **b.** Mischief; prankishness. Often used in the plural. [?]

Shen•si (shĕn′sē′) See **Shaanxi.**

Shen•yang (shŭn′yäng′) Formerly **Muk•den** (mōōk′dən, -dĕn′, mōōk′-) A city of NE China ENE of Beijing; cap. of Liaoning province. Pop. 4,655,280.

She•ol (shē′ōl′, shē-ōl′) *n. Bible* The abode of the dead in the Bible. [Heb. *šə’ôl.*]

Shep•ard (shĕp′ərd), **Alan Bartlett, Jr.** 1923–98. Amer. naval officer who on May 5, 1961, became the first US astronaut in space.

Shepard, Sam b. 1943. Amer. playwright and actor whose plays include *Buried Child* (1978).

shep•herd (shĕp′ərd) *n.* **1.** One who herds, guards, and tends sheep. **2.** One who cares for and guides a group of people, as a minister. **3.** A German shepherd. ❖ *tr.v.* **-herd•ed, -herd•ing, -herds** To herd, guard, tend, or guide as a shepherd. [ME *shepherde* < OE *scēaphierde* : *scēap*, sheep + *hierde*, herdsman.]

shepherd dog *n.* See **sheepdog.**

shep•herd•ess (shĕp′ər-dĭs) *n.* A girl or woman who herds, guards, and tends sheep.

shepherd satellite *n.* A moon that orbits near the edge of a planetary ring, constraining the ring's extent through gravitational pull.

shep•herd's pie (shĕp′ərdz) *n.* A meat pie baked with a crust of mashed potatoes.

shepherd's purse *n.* A common Eurasian weed (*Capsella bursapastoris*) having small white flowers and flat heart-shaped or triangular fruit. [< its pouchlike pods.]

sheq•el (shĕk′əl) *n., pl.* **sheq•al•im** (shĕk′ə-lĭm) See table at **currency.** [Heb. *šeqel*. See SHEKEL.]

Sher•a•ton (shĕr′ə-tn) *adj.* Of or relating to a style of English furniture that originated about 1800, characterized by simple designs and classical ornamentation.

Sheraton, Thomas 1751–1806. British furniture designer known for his graceful neoclassical designs.

sher•bet (shûr′bĭt) *n.* **1.** also **sher•bert** (-bûrt′) A frozen dessert made of fruit juice, sugar, and water mixed with milk, egg white, or gelatin. **2.** *Chiefly British* A beverage made of sweetened diluted fruit juice. **3.** also **sherbert** *Australian* An alcoholic beverage, esp. beer. [Ottoman Turk., sweet fruit drink < Pers. *sharbat* < Ar. *šarba*, drink < *šariba*, to drink.]

Sher•brooke (shûr′brōōk′) A city of S Quebec, Canada, on the St. François R. E of Montreal. Pop. 76,786.

sherd (shûrd) *n.* Variant of **shard.**

Sher•i•dan (shĕr′ĭ-dn), **Philip Henry** 1831–88. Amer. Union general who routed Confederate forces at the Battle of Five Forks (1865).

Sheridan, Richard Brinsley 1751–1816. British playwright known for his comedies, including *The Rivals* (1775).

she•rif also **sha•rif** (shə-rēf′) *n.* **1.** A descendant of Muhammad through Fatima and her son Hussein (629?–680). **2.** The chief magistrate of Mecca in Ottoman times. **3.** A Moroccan prince or ruler. [Ar. *šarif*, noble < *šarafa*, to be highborn.]

sher•iff (shĕr′ĭf) *n.* **1.** The chief law enforcement officer for US county courts. **2.** An officer of a county or an administrative region in England, Northern Ireland, and Scotland, charged mainly with judicial duties. [ME, the representative of royal authority in a shire < OE *scīrgerēfa* : *scīr*, shire + *gerēfa*, reeve.]

Sher•man (shûr′mən), **John** 1823–1900. Amer. politician and US senator who sponsored the Sherman Antitrust Act (1890).

Sherman, Roger 1721–93. Revolutionary patriot and a signer of the Declaration of Independence (1776), the Articles of Confederation (1781), and the US Constitution (1787).

Sherman, William Tecumseh 1820–91. Amer. Union general who captured Atlanta (1864) and led the destructive March to the Sea, which effectively cut the Confederacy in two.

she•root (shə-rōōt′) *n.* Variant of **cheroot.**

Sher•pa (shûr′pə) *n., pl.* **Sherpa** or **-pas** A member of a traditionally Buddhist people of Tibetan descent living on the southern side of the Himalaya Mountains in Nepal and the region of Sikkim.

sher•ry (shĕr′ē) *n., pl.* **-ries** **1.** A fortified Spanish wine ranging from very dry to sweet and from amber to brown. **2.** A similar wine made elsewhere. [Alteration of *sherris* (taken as pl.), after *Xeres* (Jerez), Spain.]

Sher•wood (shûr′wōōd′), **Robert Emmet** 1896–1955. Amer. writer whose works include *Idiot's Delight* (1936).

Sherwood Forest A former royal forest of central England famed as the site of the legendary exploits of Robin Hood.

she's (shēz) **1.** Contraction of *she is:* She's going. **2.** Contraction of *she has:* She's been there.

Shet•land (shĕt′lənd) *n.* **1.** A fine yarn made from the wool of sheep raised in the Shetland Islands. **2.** A garment, esp. a sweater, made of this yarn. [After the SHETLAND (ISLANDS).]

Shetland Islands An archipelago of N Scotland in the Atlantic Ocean NE of the Orkney Is. —**Shet′land•er** *n.*

Shetland pony *n.* A small pony of a breed originating in the Shetland Islands and having a long thick mane and tail.

Shetland sheepdog *n.* A herding dog of a breed developed in the Shetland Islands resembling a small collie.

Shev•ard•na•dze (shĕ′vərd-näd′zə), **Eduard Amvrosiyevich** b. 1928. Georgian political leader who became head of state in 1992 and president in 1995.

She•vat (shə-vät′, shvät) also **She•bat** (shə-bät′, -vät′) *n.* The year's fifth month in the Jewish calendar. See table at **calendar.** [Heb. *šəbāṭ* < Akkadian *šabāṭu*, a month name (corresponding to parts of January and February).]

shew (shō) *v. Archaic* Variant of **show.**

shew•bread (shō′brĕd′) *n.* Variant of **showbread.**

Shey•enne (shī-ĕn′, -ăn′) A river rising in central ND and flowing c. 523 km (325 mi) to the Red R. of the North.

SHF *abbr.* superhigh frequency

Shi•ah or **Shi•a** also **Shi′•ah** or **Shi′•a** (shē′ə) *Islam* *n.* **1.** (*used with a pl. verb*) The Shiites. **2.** (*used with a sing. verb*) A Shiite. ❖ *adj.* Shiite. [Ar. *ší‘a*, a following < *šā‘a*, to become known.]

shi•at•su (shē-ät′sōō) *n.* A form of therapeutic massage in which pressure is applied with the thumbs and palms to those areas of the body used in acupuncture. [Short for J. *shiatsuryōhō* : *shi*, finger + *atsu-*, pressure + *ryōhō*, treatment.]

shib•ah (shĭv′ə) *n. Judaism* Variant of **shiva.**

shib•bo•leth (shĭb′ə-lĭth, -lĕth′) *n.* **1.** A word or pronunciation that distinguishes one group or class of people from another. **2a.** A catchword serving to identify a particular group. **b.** A commonplace saying or idea. **3.** A custom or practice that betrays one as an outsider. [Ult. < Heb. *šibbōleth*, torrent of water < the use of this word to distinguish one tribe from another that pronounced it *sibbōleth* (Judges 12:4–6).]

shied[1] (shīd) *v.* Past tense and past participle of **shy**[1].

shied[2] (shīd) *v.* Past tense and past participle of **shy**[2].

shield (shēld) *n.* **1.** A broad piece of armor made of rigid material and strapped to the arm or carried for protection. **2.** A person or thing that provides protection. **3.** A protective device or structure, as: **a.** A steel sheet attached to an artillery piece to protect gunners. **b.** *Physics* A wall or housing of concrete or lead built around a nuclear reactor to prevent the escape of radiation. **c.** *Electronics* A structure or arrangement of metal plates or mesh designed to protect a piece of electronic equipment from electrostatic or magnetic interference. **d.** A pad worn to protect a garment from perspiration. **e.** A sanitary napkin. **4.** *Zoology* A protective plate or similar hard outer covering; a scute or scutellum. **5.** Something that resembles a shield, as: **a.** An escutcheon. **b.** A decorative emblem that often serves to identify an organization or a government. **c.** A police officer's badge. **6.** *Geology* A large lowland area, the geologic nucleus of a continent, whose bedrock consists of usu. Precambrian igneous and metamorphic rocks. ❖ *v.* **shield•ed, shield•ing, shields** —*tr.* **1.** To protect or defend with or as if with a shield; guard. See Syns at **defend. 2.** To cover up; conceal. —*intr.* To act or serve as a shield or safeguard. [ME *sheld* < OE *scield*.] —**shield′er** *n.*

shield law *n.* A law that protects journalists from being compelled to reveal confidential sources of information.

Shield of David *n.* See **Magen David.**

shiel•ing (shē′lĭng, -lĭn) *n. Chiefly British* **1.** A shepherd's hut. **2.** A mountain pasture used in the summer. [< Sc. *shiel,* hut < ME *shele,* poss. < OE **scēla,* prob. of Scand. orig. See **(s)keu-** in App.]

shi•er (shī′ər) *adj.* A comparative of **shy[1]**.

shies[1] (shīz) *v.* Third person singular present tense of **shy[1]**. ❖ *n.* Plural of **shy[1]**.

shies[2] (shīz) *v.* Third person singular present tense of **shy[2]**. ❖ *n.* Plural of **shy[2]**.

shi•est (shī′ĭst) *adj.* A superlative of **shy[1]**.

shift (shĭft) *v.* **shift•ed, shift•ing, shifts** —*tr.* **1.** To exchange (one thing) for another of the same class: *shifted assignments.* **2.** To move or transfer from one place or position to another. **3.** To alter (position or place). **4.** To change (gears), as in an automobile. **5.** *Linguistics* To alter phonetically as part of a systematic historical change. —*intr.* **1.** To change position, direction, place, or form. **2a.** To provide for one's own needs; get along. **b.** To get along by tricky or evasive means. **3.** To change gears, as when driving. **4.** *Linguistics* To be altered as part of a systematic historical change. Used of speech sounds. **5.** To use a shift key. ❖ *n.* **1.** A change from one person or configuration to another; a substitution. **2a.** A group of workers that relieve another on a regular schedule. **b.** The working period of such a group. **3a.** A means to an end; an expedient. **b.** A stratagem; a trick. **4.** A change in direction. **5.** A change in attitude, judgment, or emphasis. **6.** A change in position, as: **a.** *Music* A change of the hand position in playing the violin or a similar instrument. **b.** *Football* A rearrangement of players from one formation to another just prior to the snap of the ball. **c.** *Geology* See **fault** 3. **7.** The act or an instance of using a shift key. **8.** *Physics* A change in wavelength, causing a movement of a spectral band or line. **9.** *Linguistics* **a.** A systematic change of the phonetic or phonemic structure of a language. **b.** Functional shift. **10a.** A loosely fitting dress that hangs straight from the shoulder; a chemise. **b.** A woman's undergarment; a slip or chemise. [ME *shiften* < OE *sciftan,* to arrange, divide.] —**shift′er** *n.*

shift key *n.* **1.** A key on a typewriter that, when depressed, allows uppercase letters and certain symbols to be typed. **2.** A similar key on a computer keyboard, also used to activate a function within an application when pressed concurrently with a function key, the alt key, or the control key.

shift•less (shĭft′lĭs) *adj.* **1a.** Lacking ambition or purpose; lazy. **b.** Marked by a lack of ambition or energy. **2.** Lacking resourcefulness or efficiency; incompetent. [SHIFT, expedient + –LESS.] —**shift′less•ly** *adv.* —**shift′less•ness** *n.*

shift•y (shĭf′tē) *adj.* **-i•er, -i•est 1.** Having, displaying, or suggestive of deceitful character; untrustworthy. **2.** Marked by frequent changes in direction. **3.** Able to accomplish what is needed; resourceful. —**shift′i•ness** *n.*

shi•gel•la (shĭ-gĕl′ə) *n., pl.* **-gel•lae** (-gĕl′ē) also **-gel•las** Any of various nonmotile rod-shaped bacteria of the genus *Shigella,* which includes some species that cause dysentery. [NLat. *Shigella,* genus name, after Kiyoshi *Shiga* (1870–1957), Japanese bacteriologist.]

shig•el•lo•sis (shĭg′ə-lō′sĭs) *n., pl.* **-ses** (-sēz) Dysentery caused by any of various species of shigellae.

Shih Tzu (shē′ dzo͞o′) *n.* A small dog of a breed first developed in Tibet, having a long thick coat and a square muzzle. [Chin. (Mandarin) *shīzi (gǒu),* lion (dog), Shih Tzu : *shī,* lion + *-zi,* n. suff. (< *zǐ,* son, seed).]

Shi•ism also **Shi′•ism** (shē′ĭz′əm) *n.* The religion or doctrines of the Shiites.

shi•i•ta•ke (shē-tä′kē, shē′ē-tä′kē) *n., pl.* **shiitake** An edible eastern Asian mushroom *(Lentinus edodes)* having an aromatic fleshy golden or dark brown to blackish cap and an inedible tough stipe. [J. : *shi,* oak + *take,* mushroom.]

Shi•ite also **Shi′•ite** (shē′īt′) *n.* A member of the branch of Islam that regards Ali and his descendants as the legitimate successors to Muhammad and rejects the first three caliphs. ❖ *adj.* Of or relating to the Shiites or Shiism. [Ar. *šīʿa,* partisans. See SHIAH.] —**Shi•it′ic** (-ĭt′ĭk) *adj.*

Shi•jia•zhuang (shŭ′jyä′jwäng′) also **Shih•kia•chwang** (-kyä′chwäng′) A city of NE China SW of Beijing; cap. of Hebei province. Pop. 1,372,109.

shi•ka•ri (shĭ-kär′ē, -kăr′ē) *n., pl.* **-ris 1.** A big-game hunter. **2.** A guide for big-game hunting. [Hindi *shikārī* < Pers. < *shikār,* hunting < MPers. *shkār.*]

Shi•ko•ku (shē-kô′ko͞o, shē′kô-ko͞o′) An island of S Japan between SW Honshu and E Kyushu.

shik•sa also **shik•se** (shĭk′sə) *n. Offensive* Used as a disparaging term for a non-Jewish girl or woman. [Yiddish *shikse,* fem. of *shegetz,* shegetz. See SHEGETZ.]

shill (shĭl) *Slang n.* One who poses as a satisfied customer or an enthusiastic gambler to dupe bystanders into participating in a swindle. ❖ *v.* **shilled, shill•ing, shills** —*intr.* To act as a shill. —*tr.* **1.** To act as a shill for (a deceitful enterprise). **2.** To lure (a person) into a swindle. [Perh. short for *shillaber.*]

shil•le•lagh also **shil•la•lah** (shə-lā′lē, -lə) *n.* A cudgel of oak, blackthorn, or other hardwood. [After *Shillelagh,* a village of E-central Ireland.]

shil•ling (shĭl′ĭng) *n.* **1.** A coin formerly used in the United Kingdom, worth 12 old pence prior to 1971. **2.** See table at **currency.** **3.** *Printing* A virgule. [ME < OE *scilling.*]

Shil•luk (shĭ-lo͝ok′) *n., pl.* **Shilluk** or **-luks 1.** A member of a people inhabiting the western bank of the Nile River in southern Sudan. **2.** The Nilotic language of the Shilluk.

shil•ly-shal•ly (shĭl′ē-shăl′ē) *intr.v.* **-lied** (-lēd), **-ly•ing, -lies** (-lēz) **1.** To procrastinate. **2.** To be unable to reach a decision; vacillate. **3.** To spend time on insignificant things; dawdle. ❖ *adj.* Hesitant; vacillating. ❖ *n., pl.* **-lies** Procrastination; hesitation. ❖ *adv.* Hesitantly; irresolutely. [Reduplication of the question *shall I?*] —**shil′ly-shal′li•er** *n.*

Shi•loh (shī′lō) **1.** An ancient village of central Palestine NW of the Dead Sea. In the Bible, it was a sanctuary for the Israelites and the site where the Ark of the Covenant was kept. **2.** A locality in SW TN E of Memphis; site of the Civil War Battle of Shiloh (Apr. 6–7, 1862), which ended in the withdrawal of Confederate troops.

shim (shĭm) *n.* A thin, often tapered piece of material, such as wood, stone, or metal, used to fill gaps, make something level, or adjust something to fit properly. ❖ *tr.v.* **shimmed, shim•ming, shims** To fill in, level, or adjust with a shim. [?]

shim•mer (shĭm′ər) *intr.v.* **-mered, -mer•ing, -mers 1.** To shine with a subdued flickering light. **2.** To appear as a wavering or flickering image, as in a reflection on water. ❖ *n.* A flickering or tremulous light; a glimmer. [ME *shimeren* < OE *scimerian.*] —**shim′mer•ing•ly** *adv.* —**shim′mer•y** *adj.*

shim•my (shĭm′ē) *n., pl.* **-mies 1.** Abnormal vibration or wobbling, as of car wheels. **2.** A dance popular in the 1920s, characterized by rapid shaking of the body. **3.** A chemise. ❖ *intr.v.* **-mied, -my•ing, -mies 1.** To vibrate or wobble abnormally. **2.** To shake the body in or as if in dancing the shimmy. [Perh. < alteration of CHEMISE.]

Shi•mo•no•se•ki (shĭm′ə-nō-sĕk′ē, shē′mô-nô-) A city of extreme SW Honshu, Japan; site of the signing (1895) of the treaty ending the Sino-Japanese War. Pop. 259,898.

shin[1] (shĭn) *n.* **1a.** The front part of the leg below the knee and above the ankle. **b.** The shinbone. **2.** The lower foreleg in beef cattle. Used of cuts of meat. ❖ *v.* **shinned, shin•ning, shins** —*tr.* **1.** To climb (a rope or pole, for example) by gripping and pulling alternately with the hands and legs. **2.** To kick or hit in the shins. —*intr.* **1.** To climb by shinning. **2.** To move quickly on foot. [ME *shine* < OE *scinu.*]

shin[2] (shēn, shĭn) *n.* The 22nd letter of the Hebrew alphabet. [Heb. *šîn* < Phoenician **šinn,* tooth, 21st letter of the Phoenician alphabet.]

Shi•nar (shī′nər, -när′) In the Bible, a country on the lower courses of the Tigris and Euphrates rivers.

shin•bone (shĭn′bōn′) *n.* See **tibia** 1.

shin•dig (shĭn′dĭg′) *n.* **1.** A festive party, often with dancing. **2.** See **shindy** 1. [Prob. alteration of SHINDY.]

shin•dy (shĭn′dē) *n., pl.* **-dies 1.** A commotion; an uproar. **2.** See **shindig** 1. [Perh. alteration of SHINNY[1].]

shine (shīn) *v.* **shone** (shōn) or **shined, shin•ing, shines** —*intr.* **1.** To emit light. **2.** To reflect light; glisten. **3.** To distinguish oneself in an activity or a field; excel. **4.** To be immediately apparent: *Delight shone in her eyes.* —*tr.* **1.** To aim or cast the beam or glow of (a light). **2.** *past tense and past participle* **shined** To make glossy or bright by polishing. ❖ *n.* **1.** Brightness from a source of light; radiance. **2.** Brightness from reflected light; luster. **3.** A shoeshine. **4.** Excellence in quality or appearance; splendor. **5.** Fair weather. **6. shines** *Informal* Pranks or tricks. **7.** *Offensive Slang* Used as a disparaging term for a Black person. ***—idioms:* shine up to** To try to impress or please: *shined up to the boss.* **take a shine to** *Informal* To like spontaneously. [ME *shinen* < OE *scīnan.*]

shin•er (shī′nər) *n.* **1.** One that shines, as a star or jewel. **2.** *Slang* A black eye. **3a.** Any of numerous small, often silvery North American freshwater fishes of the family Cyprinidae, esp. one of the genus *Notropis.* **b.** Any of various similar fishes.

shin•gle[1] (shĭng′gəl) *n.* **1.** A thin oblong piece of material, such as wood, that is laid in overlapping rows to cover the roof or sides of a house or other building. **2.** *Informal* A small signboard, as one indicating a professional office. **3.** A woman's close-cropped haircut. ❖ *tr.v.* **-gled, -gling, -gles 1.** To cover (a roof or building) with shingles. **2.** To cut (hair) short and close to the head. [ME < OE *scindel, scingal* < LLat. *scindula,* alteration of Lat. *scandula.*] —**shin′gler** *n.*

shin•gle[2] (shĭng′gəl) *n.* **1.** Beach gravel consisting of large smooth pebbles. **2.** A stretch of shore or beach covered with such gravel. [ME.] —**shin′gly** *adj.*

shin•gles (shĭng′gəlz) *pl.n.* (*used with a sing. or pl. verb*) An acute viral infection characterized by inflammation of the sensory ganglia of certain spinal or cranial nerves and the eruption of vesicles along the affected nerve path. [ME, alteration of Med.Lat. *cingulus,* var. of Lat. *cingulum,* girdle (the inflammation often girdling the body) < *cingere,* to gird.]

shin•leaf (shĭn′lēf′) *n.* Any of various Eurasian and North American woodland perennial herbs of the genera *Moneses* and *Pyrola,* esp. *P. elliptica,* having basal leaves.

shin•ny[1] also **shin•ney** (shĭn′ē) *n., pl.* **-nies** also **-neys 1.** Ice, street, or field hockey played informally with a ball, can, or simi-

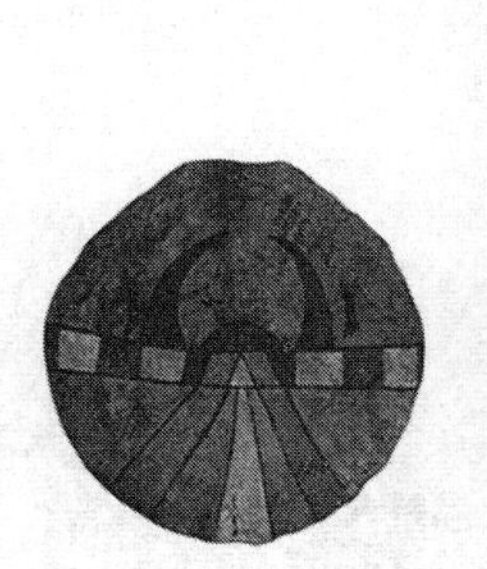

shield
early-19th-century Santa Ana Pueblo shield

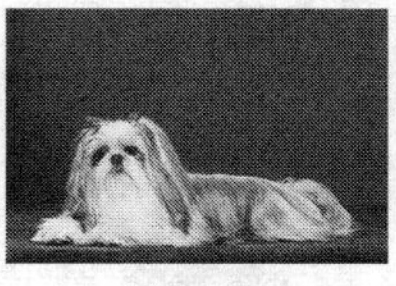

Shih Tzu

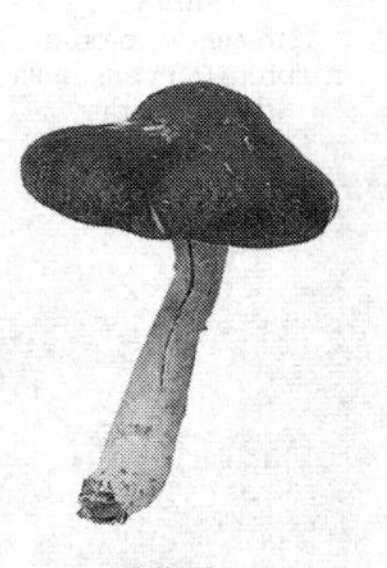

shiitake
Lentinus edodes

ă	pat	oi	boy
ā	pay	ou	out
âr	care	o͝o	took
ä	father	o͞o	boot
ĕ	pet	ŭ	cut
ē	be	ûr	urge
ĭ	pit	th	thin
ī	pie	*th*	this
îr	pier	hw	which
ŏ	pot	zh	vision
ō	toe	ə	about, item
ô	paw		

Stress marks:
′ (primary);
′ (secondary), as in
lexicon (lĕk′sĭ-kŏn′)

lar object. **2.** The curved stick used in this game. [Prob. < *shin ye,* a cry used in the game.]

shin•ny[2] (shĭn′ē) *intr.v.* **-nied** (-nēd), **-ny•ing, -nies** (-nēz) To climb by shinning. [Alteration of SHIN[1].]

shin•plas•ter (shĭn′plăs′tər) *n.* **1.** A piece of paper money issued privately and devalued by poor security or inflation. **2.** A piece of paper money of small value issued by the government, esp. by the US government from 1862 to 1878.

shin splints also **shin•splints** (shĭn′splĭnts′) *pl.n.* (*used with a sing. or pl. verb*) Any of various painful conditions of the shins caused by inflammation of the surrounding muscles, frequently occurring among runners.

Shin•to (shĭn′tō) *n.* A religion native to Japan, characterized by veneration of nature spirits and ancestors and by a lack of formal dogma. [J. *shintō* : *shin,* gods (< M Chin.) + *tō, dō,* art, way; see AIKIDO.] **—Shin′to** *adj.* **—Shin′to•ism** *n.* **—Shin′to•ist** *adj. & n.* **—Shin′to•is′tic** *adj.*

shin•y (shī′nē) *adj.* **-i•er, -i•est 1.** Radiating light; bright. **2.** Bright from reflected light; glistening. **3.** Having a sheen from being rubbed or worn smooth. **—shin′i•ness** *n.*

ship (shĭp) *n.* **1a.** A vessel of considerable size for deep-water navigation. **b.** A sailing vessel having three or more square-rigged masts. **2.** An aircraft or spacecraft. **3.** The crew of one of these vessels. **4.** One's fortune: *When my ship comes in, I'll buy a larger house.* ❖ *v.* **shipped, ship•ping, ships** *—tr.* **1.** To place or receive on board a ship: *shipped the cargo in the hold.* **2.** To cause to be transported by or as if by ship; send. **3.** To hire (a person) for work on a ship. **4.** To take in (water) over the side of a ship. *—intr.* **1.** To go aboard a ship; embark. **2.** To travel by ship. **3.** To hire oneself out or enlist for service on a ship. ***—phrasal verb:*** **ship out 1.** *Nautical* To accept a position as a crew member on a ship. **2.** To leave, as for a distant place. **3.** To send, as to a distant place. **4.** *Informal* To quit, resign from, or otherwise vacate a position. [ME < OE *scip.*] **—ship′pa•ble** *adj.*

-ship *suff.* **1a.** Quality, state, or condition: *scholarship.* **b.** Something that shows or possesses a quality, state, or condition: *courtship.* **2.** Rank, status, or office: *professorship.* **3.** Art, skill, or craft: *penmanship.* **4.** A collective body: *readership.* [ME < OE *-scipe.*]

ship biscuit *n.* See **hardtack.**

ship•board (shĭp′bôrd′, -bōrd′) *n.* **1.** The condition of being aboard a ship: *on shipboard.* **2.** *Archaic* The side of a ship. ❖ *adj.* Existing or occurring on board a ship.

ship•borne (shĭp′bôrn′, -bōrn′) *adj.* Transported by ship.

ship•build•ing (shĭp′bĭl′dĭng) *n.* The art or business of designing and constructing ships. **—ship′build′er** *n.*

ship canal *n.* A canal wide and deep enough to serve ships.

ship fitter *n.* **1.** One who positions the structural pieces of a ship for riveting and welding. **2.** A sailor in the US Navy who does sheet-metal work and plumbing on board a ship.

ship•lap (shĭp′lăp′) *n.* Wooden siding rabbeted so that the edge of one board overlaps the one next to it in a flush joint. **—ship′-lapped′** *adj.*

ship•load (shĭp′lōd′) *n.* The amount a ship can carry.

ship•man (shĭp′mən) *n.* **1.** A sailor. **2.** A shipmaster.

ship•mas•ter (shĭp′măs′tər) *n.* The officer in command of a merchant ship.

ship•mate (shĭp′māt′) *n.* A sailor serving on the same ship as another.

ship•ment (shĭp′mənt) *n.* **1.** The act or an instance of shipping goods. **2.** A quantity of cargo that is shipped together.

ship of the line *n., pl.* **ships of the line** A warship having at least two gun decks, armed powerfully enough to take a position in the line of battle.

ship•per (shĭp′ər) *n.* One that consigns or receives goods for transportation.

ship•ping (shĭp′ĭng) *n.* **1.** The act or business of transporting goods. **2.** The body of ships belonging to one port, industry, or country, often referred to in aggregate tonnage. **3.** Passage or transport on a ship.

shipping clerk *n.* One who is employed to prepare, pack, receive, or record shipments of goods.

ship-rigged (shĭp′rĭgd′) *adj.* Rigged with three or more masts and square sails.

ship•shape (shĭp′shāp′) *adj.* Orderly and neat; tidy. See Syns at **neat**[1]. [< obsolete *shipshapen,* arranged as a ship should be : SHIP + *shapen,* p. part. of SHAPE.] **—ship′shape′** *adv.*

ship•side (shĭp′sīd′) *n.* The area of a dock adjacent to a ship.

ship's papers (shĭps) *pl.n.* The documents, such as license, logbook, or bills of lading, that a ship must carry under international law and that must be shown on inspection.

ship•way (shĭp′wā′) *n.* **1.** The structure supporting a ship during construction or in dry dock. **2.** See **ship canal.**

ship•worm (shĭp′wûrm′) *n.* Any of various wormlike marine mollusks of the genera *Teredo* and *Bankia,* having rudimentary bivalve shells with which they bore into wood, esp. the submerged timbers of ships and wharves.

ship•wreck (shĭp′rĕk′) *n.* **1a.** The destruction of a ship, as by storm. **b.** The remains of a wrecked ship. **2.** A complete failure or ruin. ❖ *tr.v.* **-wrecked, -wreck•ing, -wrecks 1a.** To cause (a ship) to be destroyed. **b.** To cause (one on a ship) to suffer shipwreck. **2.** To ruin utterly.

ship•wright (shĭp′rīt′) *n.* One that builds or repairs ships.

ship•yard (shĭp′yärd′) *n.* A yard where ships are built or repaired.

Shi•raz (shē-räz′) A city of SW-central Iran SSE of Tehran; long noted for its carpets and metalwork. Pop. 1,042,801.

shire (shīr) *n.* **1.** A former administrative division of Great Britain, equivalent to a county. **2.** often **Shire** A Shire horse. [ME < OE *scīr,* official charge, administrative district.]

Shire horse *n.* A large powerful draft horse first bred in England, having long hair that grows from the knee and hock.

shire town *n. Chiefly British* See **county town.**

shirk (shûrk) *v.* **shirked, shirk•ing, shirks** *—tr.* To avoid or neglect (a duty or responsibility). *—intr.* To avoid work or duty. [Perh. < Ger. *Schurke,* scoundrel.] **—shirk′er** *n.*

Shir•ley poppy (shûr′lē) *n.* A variety of the corn poppy with pink, salmon, or scarlet flowers. [After *Shirley,* district in SE England.]

shirr (shûr) *tr.v.* **shirred, shirr•ing, shirrs 1.** To gather (cloth) into decorative rows by parallel stitching. **2.** To cook (unshelled eggs) by baking until set. [?]

shirt (shûrt) *n.* **1.** A garment for the upper part of the body, typically having a collar, sleeves, and a front opening. **2.** An undershirt. **3.** A nightshirt. ***—idioms:*** **keep (one's) shirt on** *Slang* To remain calm. **lose (one's) shirt** *Slang* To lose all one has. [ME *shirte* < OE *scyrte,* short garment. See **sker-**[1] in App.]

shirt•dress also **shirt-dress** (shûrt′drĕs′) *n.* A dress tailored like a shirt with a collar and buttons down the front.

shirt•ing (shûr′tĭng) *n.* Fabric suitable for making shirts.

shirt•sleeve (shûrt′slēv′) *n.* **1.** The sleeve of a shirt. **2. shirtsleeves** The state of wearing no outer garment over one's shirt. ❖ *adj.* **1.** also **shirt•sleeved** (-slēvd′) Dressed without a coat. **2.** also **shirtsleeves** Calling for the removal of a coat or jacket. **3.** also **shirtsleeves** Marked by informality or straightforwardness.

shirt•tail (shûrt′tāl′) *n.* **1.** The part of a shirt that extends below the waist, esp. in the back. **2.** A brief addition at the end of a newspaper article. ❖ *adj.* **1.** Very young: *shirttail kids.* **2.** Of little value; inadequate or small.

shirt•waist (shûrt′wāst′) *n.* **1.** A woman's blouse or bodice styled like a tailored shirt. **2.** See **shirtdress.**

shirt•y (shûr′tē) *adj.* **-i•er, -i•est** *Chiefly British* Ill-tempered; angry. [Prob. < *to get someone's shirt out,* to annoy, or *to keep one's shirt on,* to keep from being annoyed.]

shish ke•bab also **shish ke•bob** or **shish ka•bob** (shĭsh′ kə-bŏb′) *n.* A dish consisting of pieces of seasoned meat and sometimes vegetables roasted on skewers and served with condiments. [Armenian *shish kabab* < Turk. *şiş kebabı* : *şiş,* skewer + *kebabı,* qualifying (possessive) form of *kebap,* roasted meat, perh. ult. < Akkadian *kabābu,* to burn.]

shit (shĭt) *Vulgar Slang v.* **shit** also **shat** (shăt), **shit•ting, shits** *—intr.* To defecate. *—tr.* **1.** To defecate in. **2.** To tease or try to deceive. ❖ *n.* **1.** Excrement. **2.** The act or an instance of defecating. **3. shits** Diarrhea. Used with *the.* **4a.** Something considered disgusting, shabby, foolish, or otherwise unacceptable. **b.** A mean or contemptible person. **5.** A narcotic or intoxicant, such as heroin. **6.** Things; items. **7.** Foolish, deceitful, or boastful language. **8.** Insolent talk or behavior. **9.** Trouble or difficulty. **10.** A small or worthless amount: *He doesn't know shit.* ❖ *interj.* Used to express surprise, anger, or extreme displeasure. [ME *shitten,* prob. < OE *-sciten* (as in *besciten,* covered with excrement), p. part. of **scītan,* to defecate.]

shit•kick•er (shĭt′kĭk′ər) *n. Vulgar Slang* **1.** A coarse unsophisticated person. **2.** A big heavy shoe or boot.

shit•list also **shit list** (shĭt′lĭst′) *n. Vulgar Slang* A number of persons who are strongly disapproved of.

shit•load (shĭt′lōd′) *n. Vulgar Slang* A large amount; a lot.

shit•tah (shĭt′ə) *n.* A tree, probably a species of acacia, that is mentioned frequently in the Bible. [Heb. *šiṭṭâ*; akin to Ar. *sanṭ,* both < Egypt. *šnḏt, šnty,* acacia.]

shit•ty (shĭt′ē) *adj.* **-ti•er, -ti•est** *Vulgar Slang* **1.** Of very poor quality; highly inferior. **2.** Contemptible; despicable. **3.** Unfortunate; unpleasant. **4.** Uncomfortable; unhappy; miserable. **5.** Incompetent; inept. **6.** Trivial; insignificant.

shiv (shĭv) *n. Slang* A knife, razor, or other sharp implement, esp. one used as a weapon. [Prob. Romany *chiv,* blade.]

shiv•a also **shiv•ah** or **shib•ah** (shĭv′ə) *n. Judaism* A seven-day period of formal mourning observed after the funeral of a close relative. [Yiddish *shive* < Heb. *šib'â,* seven.]

Shi•va (shē′və) also **Si•va** (sē′və, sē′-) *n. Hinduism* One of the principal Hindu deities, worshiped as the destroyer and restorer of worlds and in numerous other forms. [Skt. *śivaḥ* < *śiva-,* auspicious, dear. See **kei-**[1] in App.] **—Shi′va•ism** *n.* **—Shi′va•ist** *n.*

shiv•a•ree (shĭv′ə-rē′, shĭv′ə-rē′) *n. Midwestern & Western US* A noisy mock serenade for newlyweds. [Alteration of CHARIVARI.]

shiv•er[1] (shĭv′ər) *v.* **-ered, -er•ing, -ers** *—intr.* **1.** To shake with or as if with cold; tremble. **2.** To quiver or vibrate, as by the force of the wind. *—tr. Nautical* To cause (a sail) to flutter by trimming it too close to the wind. ❖ *n.* **1.** An instance of shivering or trembling. **2. shivers** An attack of shivering. Used with *the.* [ME *chiveren, shiveren.*]

shiv•er[2] (shĭv′ər) *v.* **-ered, -er•ing, -ers** *—intr.* To break into

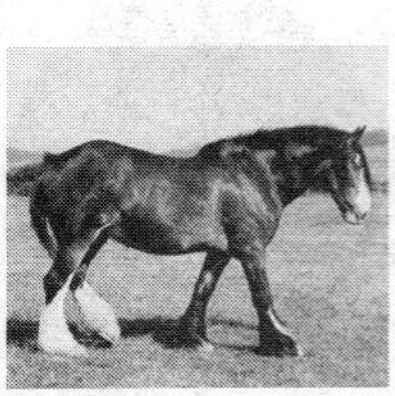

Shire horse

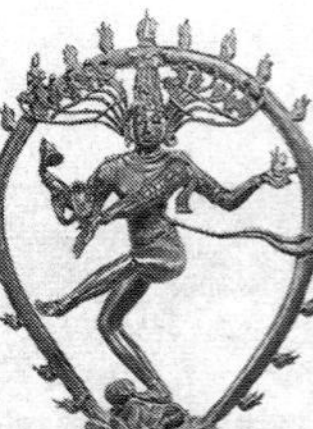

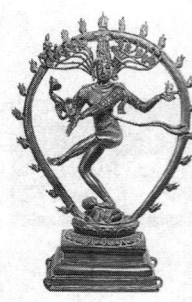

Shiva
11th-century bronze sculpture from the Chola dynasty, India

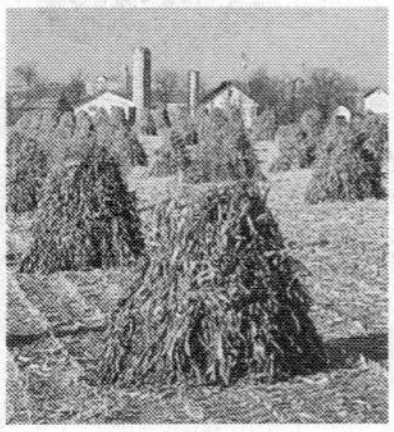

shock[2]
corn shocks

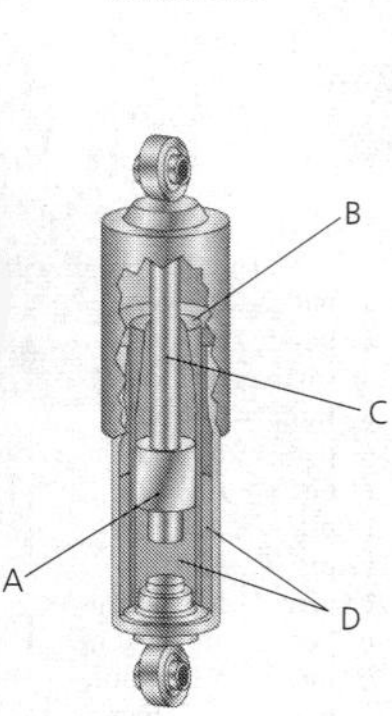

shock absorber
A. piston
B. cylinder
C. piston rod
D. oil

fragments or splinters; shatter. —*tr.* To cause to shiver. ❖ *n.* A fragment or splinter. [ME *shiveren* < *shivere*, splinter.]

shiv•er•y[1] (shĭv′ə-rē) *adj.* **1.** Trembling, as from cold or fear. **2.** Causing shivers; chilling.

shiv•er•y[2] (shĭv′ə-rē) *adj.* Easily broken; brittle.

Shi•vi•ti also **shi•vi•ti** (shə-və-tē′) *n.* A decorative plaque inscribed with the Hebrew verse "I have set the Lord always before me" (Psalms 16:8), hung in synagogues and Jewish homes as a reminder of God's presence. [Heb. *šiwwîtî*, I have set (first word of the verse) < *šiwwâ*, to set, place.]

Shi•zu•o•ka (shē′zo͞o-ô′kä) A city of E-central Honshu, Japan, on Suruga Bay SW of Yokohama. Pop. 474,219.

shkotz•im (shkôt′sĭm) *n. Offensive* Plural of **shegetz.**

shle•miel (shlə-mēl′) *n. Slang* Variant of **schlemiel.**

shlep (shlĕp) *v. & n. Slang* Variant of **schlep.**

shli•ma•zel (shlĭ-mä′zəl) *n. Slang* Variant of **schlimazel.**

shlock (shlŏk) *n. & adj. Slang* Variant of **schlock.**

shlub (shlŭb) *n. Slang* Variant of **schlub.**

shmear (shmîr) *n. Slang* Variant of **schmeer.**

shmo (shmō) *n., pl.* **shmoes** *Slang* Variant of **schmo.**

shmooze (shmo͞oz) *n. Slang* Variant of **schmooze.**

shmuck (shmŭk) *n. Slang* Variant of **schmuck.**

shnook (shno͝ok) *n. Slang* Variant of **schnook.**

shnor•rer (shnôr′ər, shnōr′-) *n. Slang* Variant of **schnorrer.**

Sho•ah (shō′ə) *n.* The mass murder of European Jews by the Nazis during World War II. [Heb. *šô'â*, calamity.]

shoal[1] (shōl) *n.* A shallow place in a body of water. ❖ *v.* **shoaled, shoal•ing, shoals** —*intr.* To become shallow. ❖ *adj.* Having little depth; shallow. [ME *shold*, shallow, shallows < OE *sceald*, shallow.]

shoal[2] (shōl) *n.* **1.** A large group; a crowd. **2.** A large school of fish or other marine animals. ❖ *intr.v.* **shoaled, shoal•ing, shoals** To come together in large numbers; throng. [Prob. MLGer. or MDu. *schōle.*]

shoat also **shote** (shōt) *n.* A young pig just after weaning. [ME *shote*, perh. of MLGer. orig.]

shock[1] (shŏk) *n.* **1a.** A violent collision or impact; a heavy blow. **b.** The effect of such a collision or blow. **2a.** Something that jars the mind or emotions as if with a violent unexpected blow. **b.** The disturbance of function, equilibrium, or mental faculties caused by such a blow; violent agitation. **3.** A severe offense to one's sense of propriety or decency; an outrage. **4.** A general physiological reaction to severe trauma or illness, usu. characterized by marked loss of blood pressure and depression of vital processes. **5.** The sensation and muscular spasm caused by an electric current passing through the body. **6.** A sudden economic disturbance, such as a rise in the price of a commodity. **7.** A shock absorber. ❖ *v.* **shocked, shock•ing, shocks** —*tr.* **1.** To strike with great surprise and emotional disturbance. **2.** To strike with disgust; offend. **3.** To induce a state of physical shock in (a person). **4.** To subject (an animal or person) to an electric shock. —*intr.* To come into contact violently, as in battle; collide. [Fr. *choc* < *choquer*, to collide with < OFr. *chuquier*, perh. of Gmc. orig.]

shock[2] (shŏk) *n.* **1.** A number of sheaves of grain stacked upright in a field for drying. **2.** A thick heavy mass: *a shock of hair.* ❖ *tr.v.* **shocked, shock•ing, shocks** To gather (grain) into shocks. [ME *shok.*]

shock absorber *n.* A device used to absorb mechanical shocks, as a hydraulic or pneumatic piston used to dampen the jarring sustained in a moving motor vehicle.

shock•er (shŏk′ər) *n.* One that startles, shocks, or horrifies.

shock•ing (shŏk′ĭng) *adj.* **1.** Highly disturbing emotionally. **2.** Highly offensive; indecent or distasteful. **3.** Very vivid or intense in tone: *shocking pink.* —**shock′ing•ly** *adv.*

shock jock *n. Informal* A host of a talk radio program given to provocative or offensive remarks and vulgar language. [*shock (radio)* + (DISC) JOCK(EY).]

Shock•ley (shŏk′lē), **William Bradford** 1910–89. British-born Amer. physicist who shared a 1956 Nobel Prize.

shock•proof (shŏk′pro͞of′) *adj.* Constructed or designed to withstand blows or jarring.

shock therapy *n.* Any of various treatments for mental disorders, such as major depression, in which a convulsion or brief coma is induced by a drug or an electric current.

shock troops *pl.n.* Soldiers specially chosen, trained, and armed to lead an attack. [Transl. of Ger. *Stosstruppen.*]

shock wave *n.* **1.** A large-amplitude compression wave, as that produced by an explosion or by supersonic motion of a body in a medium. **2.** A violent disruption, disturbance, or reaction.

shod•dy (shŏd′ē) *adj.* **-di•er, -di•est 1.** Made of or containing inferior material. **2a.** Of poor quality or craft. **b.** Rundown; shabby. **3.** Dishonest or reprehensible: *shoddy business practices.* **4.** Conspicuously and cheaply imitative. ❖ *n., pl.* **-dies 1a.** Woolen yarn made from scraps or used clothing, with some new wool added. **b.** Cloth made from or containing such yarn. **2.** Something of inferior quality; a cheap imitation. [?] —**shod′di•ly** *adv.* —**shod′di•ness** *n.*

shoe (sho͞o) *n.* **1.** A durable covering for the human foot, made of leather or similar material with a rigid sole and heel, usu. extending no higher than the ankle. **2.** A horseshoe. **3.** A part or device at the base of something or functioning as a protective covering, as: **a.** A strip of metal fitted onto the bottom of a sled runner. **b.** The base for the supports of the superstructure of a bridge. **c.** The ferrule on the end of a cane. **d.** The casing of a pneumatic tire. **4.** A device that retards or stops the motion of an object, as the part of a brake that presses against the wheel or drum. **5.** The sliding contact plate on an electric train or streetcar that conducts electricity from the third rail. **6.** A chute, as for conveying grain from a hopper. **7.** *Games* A case from which playing cards are dealt one at a time. **8. shoes** *Informal* **a.** Position: *I'd love to be in your shoes.* **b.** Plight. ❖ *tr.v.* **shod** (shŏd), **shod** or **shod•den** (shŏd′n), **shoe•ing, shoes 1.** To furnish or fit with a shoe or shoes. **2.** To cover with a wooden or metal guard to protect against wear. [ME < OE *scōh.*]

shoe•bill (sho͞o′bĭl′) *n.* A tall wading bird *(Balaeniceps rex)* native to eastern tropical Africa and having dark plumage, long black legs, and a large shoelike bill.

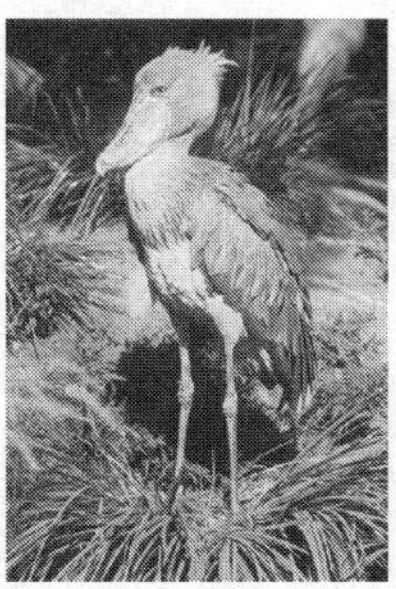

shoebill
Balaeniceps rex

shoe•box (sho͞o′bŏks′) *n.* **1.** An oblong box, usu. made of cardboard, for holding a pair of shoes. **2.** Something resembling or suggestive of such a box.

shoe•horn (sho͞o′hôrn′) *n.* A smooth curved implement, often of plastic or metal, inserted at the heel to help put on a shoe. ❖ *tr.v.* **-horned, -horn•ing, -horns** To squeeze into or as if into an insufficient space.

shoe•lace (sho͞o′lās′) *n.* A string or cord used for lacing and fastening shoes.

shoe•mak•er (sho͞o′mā′kər) *n.* One that makes or repairs shoes. —**shoe′mak′ing** *n.*

shoe•pac also **shoe•pack** (sho͞o′păk′) *n.* A heavy warm waterproof boot. [Alteration of pidgin Delaware *seppock*, shoe, shoes < Unami *chípahko*, shoes.]

shoe•shine (sho͞o′shīn′) *n.* **1.** A shiny finish put on a pair of shoes by brushing and buffing with polish. **2.** The act or an instance of putting a shiny finish on shoes.

shoe•string (sho͞o′strĭng′) *n.* **1.** See **shoelace. 2.** A small sum of money; capital that is barely adequate. ❖ *adj.* **1.** Long and slender. **2.** Marked by or consisting of a small amount of money. **3.** *Sports* At or near the feet.

shoe•tree (sho͞o′trē′) *n.* A form made of inflexible material inserted into a shoe to stretch it or preserve its shape.

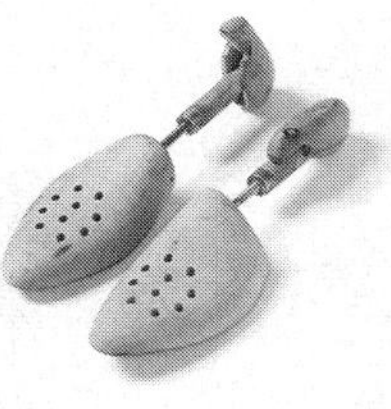

shoetree
pair of shoetrees

sho•far (shō′fär′, -fər) *n., pl.* **sho•fars** or **sho•froth** (shō-frōt′, -frōs′) *Judaism* A trumpet made of a ram's horn, blown by the ancient Hebrews on holidays and in battle, now sounded in the synagogue during Rosh Hashanah and at the end of Yom Kippur. [Heb. *šôpār*, ram's horn, shofar; akin to Akkadian *sappāru, šappāru*, fallow deer, and *sappartu*, tip of an animal's horn < Sumerian *šegbar*, fallow deer.]

sho•gi (shō′gē) *n.* A Japanese game similar to chess that is played on a board with 81 squares, each player having 20 pieces. [J. < Chin. (Mandarin) *jiàng qí* : *jiàng*, commander in chief, chief chess piece + *qí*, board game, such as chess.]

sho•gun (shō′gən) *n.* The hereditary commander of the Japanese army who until 1867 exercised absolute rule under the nominal leadership of the emperor. [J. *shōgun*, general < M Chin. *tsiang-kun* : *tsiang*, general + *kun*, army.]

sho•gun•ate (shō′gə-nĭt, -nāt′) *n.* The government, rule, or office of a shogun.

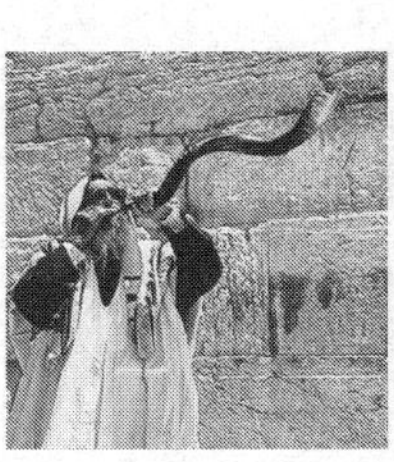

shofar

sho•ji (shō′jē) *n., pl.* **shoji** or **-jis** A translucent screen consisting of a wooden frame covered in rice paper, used as a sliding door or partition in a Japanese house. [J. *shōji* : *shō*, barrier, screen (< M Chin. *tsiang*) + *ji*, seed, n. suff. (< M Chin. *tsz*).]

Sho•la•pur (shō′lə-po͝or′) A city of W-central India on the Deccan Peninsula ESE of Mumbai (Bombay). Pop. 604,215.

Sho•lo•khov (shô′lə-kôf′, -KHəf), **Mikhail Aleksandrovich** 1905–84. Russian writer who won the 1965 Nobel Prize for literature.

shone (shōn) *v.* A past tense and a past participle of **shine.**

shoo (sho͞o) *interj.* Used to frighten away animals or birds. ❖ *tr.v.* **shooed, shoo•ing, shoos** To drive or frighten away by or as if by crying "shoo."

shoo•fly (sho͞o′flī′) *n.* A child's rocker having the seat built between two flat sides cut in the shape of an animal.

shoofly pie *n.* A pie with a filling of molasses and brown sugar. [< shooing away the flies attracted to the sweet filling.]

shoo-in (sho͞o′ĭn′) *n. Informal* **1.** A sure winner. **2.** One with a sure chance of being chosen, as for a job.

shook[1] (sho͝ok) *n.* A set of parts for assembling a barrel or packing box. [Prob. < *shook cask*, var. of *shaken cask*, cask broken down for shipment < *shaken*, dismantled and packed for transport, p. part. of SHAKE, to scatter, spread.]

shook[2] (sho͝ok) *v.* Past tense of **shake.**

shook-up (sho͝ok-ŭp′) *adj. Slang* Emotionally upset or excited; shaken.

shoon (sho͞on) *n. Archaic* A plural of **shoe.**

shoot (sho͞ot) *v.* **shot** (shŏt), **shoot•ing, shoots** —*tr.* **1a.** To hit, wound, or kill with a missile fired from a weapon. **b.** To remove or destroy with a missile: *shot out the pane.* **c.** To make (a hole, for example) by firing a weapon. **2.** To fire or let fly (a missile) from a weapon. **3a.** To discharge (a weapon). **b.** To detonate or cause to explode: *shot off a firecracker.* **4.** To inject (a drug, for example) with a hypodermic syringe. **5.** To throw out or release (a fishing line, for example). **6a.** To send forth suddenly, in-

ă	pat	oi	boy
ā	pay	ou	out
âr	care	o͝o	took
ä	father	o͞o	boot
ĕ	pet	ŭ	cut
ē	be	ûr	urge
ĭ	pit	th	thin
ī	pie	*th*	this
îr	pier	hw	which
ŏ	pot	zh	vision
ō	toe	ə	about, item
ô	paw		

Stress marks:
′ (primary);
′ (secondary), as in
lexicon (lĕk′sĭ-kŏn′)

tensely, or swiftly: *shot an angry look at me.* **b.** To emit (a form of energy). **c.** To utter (sounds or words) forcefully, rapidly, or suddenly. **7.** *Informal* To spend, use up, or waste. **8.** To pass over or through swiftly: *shooting the rapids.* **9.** To cover (country) in hunting for game. **10.** To record on film. **11.** To cause to project or protrude; extend: *shot out her arm.* **12.** To begin to grow or produce; put forth. **13.** To pour, empty out, or discharge down or as if down a chute. **14.** *Sports & Games* **a.** To throw or propel (a ball or other projectile in a game) in a specific direction. **b.** To accomplish (the objective) of a game involving a projectile; score (a point, basket, stroke, or goal). **c.** To play (a game involving projectiles, such as pool). **d.** To attain (a given score) in golf. **e.** To play (a game involving dice, esp. craps). **f.** To throw (the dice or a given score) in craps. **15.** To slide (the bolt of a lock) into or out of its fastening. **16.** To plane (the edge of a board) straight. **17.** To variegate (colored cloth) by interweaving weft threads of a different color. **18.** To measure the altitude of with an instrument: *shot the star.* —*intr.* **1.** To discharge a missile from a weapon. **2.** To discharge or fire; go off. **3a.** To gush or spurt: *Water shot out.* **b.** To appear suddenly: *The sun shot through the clouds.* **4.** To move swiftly; dart. **5.** To be felt moving or as if moving in the body. **6.** To protrude; project. **7.** To engage in hunting or the firing of weapons, esp. for sport. **8.** To put forth new growth; germinate. **9a.** To take pictures. **b.** To film a scene in a movie. **10.** *Sports & Games* To propel a ball or other object toward the goal or in a specific direction or manner. **11.** *Games* To throw dice. **12.** *Slang* To begin talking. Often used in the imperative: *I'm listening. Shoot!* **13.** To slide into or out of a fastening. Used of the bolt of a lock. ❖ *n.* **1.** The motion or movement of something that is propelled, driven, or discharged. **2a.** The young growth arising from a germinating seed; a sprout. **b.** New growth on a plant. **3.** A narrow, swift, or turbulent section of a stream. **4a.** The act of discharging a weapon or letting fly a missile. **b.** *Informal* The launching of a rocket or similar missile. **5a.** An organized shooting activity, such as a hunt. **b.** A round of shots in a contest with firearms. **6.** A session in which something is photographed, filmed, or videotaped. **7.** The distance a shot travels; the range. **8.** *Nautical* The interval between strokes in rowing. **9.** A sharp twinge or spasm of pain. **10.** An inclined channel for moving something; a chute. **11.** A body of ore in a vein. ❖ *interj.* Used to express surprise, annoyance, or disappointment. ***—phrasal verbs:* shoot down 1.** To bring down (an aircraft, for example) with gunfire or a missile. **2.** *Informal* To ruin the aspirations of; disappoint. **3.** *Informal* **a.** To put an end to; defeat. **b.** To expose as false; discredit. **shoot for (or at)** *Informal* To strive or aim for; have as a goal. **shoot up 1.** *Informal* To grow or get taller rapidly. **2.** To increase dramatically in amount. **3.** To riddle with bullets. **4.** To damage or terrorize (a town, for example) by intense or random gunfire. **5.** *Slang* To inject a drug with a hypodermic syringe. ***—idioms:* shoot from the hip** *Slang* To act or speak without forethought. **shoot off (one's) mouth (or face)** *Slang* **1.** To speak indiscreetly. **2.** To brag; boast. **shoot straight** To talk or deal honestly. **shoot the breeze (or bull)** *Slang* To spend time talking; talk idly. [ME *shoten* < OE *scēotan.*] **—shoot′er** *n.*

shoot•down (shō͞ot′doun′) *n.* Destruction or an instance of destruction of a flying aircraft with missiles or gunfire.

shoot-'em-up (shō͞ot′əm-ŭp′) *n. Informal* An entertainment, such as a movie, featuring gunfire and violence.

shoot•ing gallery (shō͞o′tĭng) *n.* An enclosed target range for practice or competition with firearms.

shooting iron *n. Slang* A firearm, esp. a handgun.

shooting script *n.* The version of a movie or television script with the scenes arranged in sequence for filming or taping.

shooting star *n.* **1.** See **meteor. 2.** Any of several North American perennial herbs of the genus *Dodecatheon,* having nodding flowers with reflexed petals.

shooting stick *n.* A stick resembling a cane, pointed at one end with a folding seat at the other, typically used by spectators at outdoor sporting events.

shoot•out also **shoot-out** (shō͞ot′out′) *n.* **1a.** A gunfight. **b.** A battle between military forces. **c.** *Slang* A dispute to settle a disagreement. **2.** *Sports* **a.** A high-scoring period or game. **b.** A means of resolving a tie after overtime, as in soccer, in which five players from each side alternately take individual shots on goal.

shoot-the-chute also **chute-the-chute** (shō͞ot′thə-shō͞ot′) *n.* An amusement ride consisting of a steep slide often with a pool of water at the end.

shoot-up (shō͞ot′ŭp′) *n. Slang* **1.** The act or an instance of shooting up a drug. **2.** A gunfight; a shootout.

shop (shŏp) *n.* **1.** also **shoppe** (shŏp) **a.** A small retail store. **b.** A specialty department in a large store. **2.** An atelier; a studio. **3.** A place for manufacturing or repairing goods or machinery. **4.** A commercial or industrial establishment: *a printing shop.* **5.** A business establishment; an office or a center of activity. **6.** A home workshop. **7a.** A schoolroom fitted with machinery and tools for instruction in industrial arts. **b.** The industrial arts as a technical science or course of study. ❖ *v.* **shopped, shop•ping, shops** —*intr.* **1.** To visit stores in search of merchandise or bargains. **2.** To look for something with the intention of acquiring it. —*tr.* To visit or buy from (a particular store). ***—phrasal verb:* shop around 1.** To shop from store to store. **2.** To look for something, such as a better job. **3.** To offer (a large block of common stock, for example) for sale to various parties. ***—idiom:* talk shop** To talk about one's work. [ME *shoppe* < OE *sceoppa,* treasure house.]

shop•keep•er (shŏp′kē′pər) *n.* One who owns or manages a shop.

shop•lift (shŏp′lĭft′) *v.* **-lift•ed, -lift•ing, -lifts** —*intr.* To shoplift merchandise. —*tr.* To steal (articles or an article) from a store that is open for business. **—shop′lift′er** *n.* **—shop′lift′ing** *n.*

shop•per (shŏp′ər) *n.* **1.** One who visits stores in search of merchandise or bargains. **2.** A commercial agent who compares the merchandise and prices of competing merchants. **3.** A commercial employee who fills mail or telephone orders. **4.** A newspaper containing advertisements and local news.

shop•ping bag (shŏp′ĭng) *n.* A strong bag with handles for carrying a shopper's purchases.

shopping center *n.* A group of stores and often restaurants and other businesses having a common parking lot.

shopping mall *n.* **1.** An urban shopping area limited to pedestrians. **2.** A shopping center with stores and businesses facing a system of enclosed walkways for pedestrians.

shop steward *n.* A union member elected to represent coworkers in dealings with management.

shop•talk (shŏp′tôk′) *n.* **1.** Talk concerning one's work or business. **2.** The jargon used in a specific business or field.

shop•worn (shŏp′wôrn′, -wōrn′) *adj.* **1.** Tarnished, frayed, faded, or otherwise defective from being on display in a store. **2.** Worn-out, as from overuse; trite: *shopworn anecdotes.*

sho•ran (shôr′ăn′, shōr′-) *n.* A short-range navigation system by which a ship or aircraft can determine its position by measuring the times required for a radar signal to reach and return from each of two ground stations. [*sho(rt)-ra(nge) n(avigation).*]

shore[1] (shôr, shōr) *n.* **1.** The land along the edge of an ocean, a sea, lake, or river; a coast. **2.** Land; country. Often used in the plural: *native shores.* **3.** Land as opposed to water. [ME *shore* < OE *scora.* See **sker-**[1] in App.]

shore[2] (shôr, shōr) *tr.v.* **shored, shor•ing, shores** To support by or as if by a prop: *shored up the sagging floors.* ❖ *n.* A beam or timber propped against a structure to provide support. [ME *shoren* < *shore,* prop, prob. < MLGer. *schōre,* barrier, or MDu. *scōre,* prop.]

shore[3] (shôr, shōr) *v. Archaic* A past tense of **shear.**

shore bird also **shore•bird** (shôr′bûrd′, shōr′-) *n.* Any of various birds that frequent coastal or inland shores.

shore dinner *n.* A meal consisting of seafood.

shore leave *n.* A sailor's leave of absence to go ashore.

shore•line (shôr′līn′, shōr′-) *n.* The edge of a body of water.

shore patrol *n.* A detail of the US Navy, Marine Corps, or Coast Guard serving as military police ashore.

shore•ward (shôr′wərd, shōr′-) *adv. & adj.* Toward, to, or on the shore. **—shore′wards** (-wərdz) *adv.*

shor•ing (shôr′ĭng, shōr′-) *n.* **1.** The act or operation of propping with shores. **2.** A system of supporting shores.

shorn (shôrn, shōrn) *v.* A past participle of **shear.**

short (shôrt) *adj.* **short•er, short•est 1.** Having little length; not long. **2.** Having little height; not tall. **3.** Extending or traveling not far or not far enough: *a short toss.* **4a.** Lasting a brief time: *a short holiday.* **b.** Appearing to pass quickly. **5.** Not lengthy; succinct: *short and to the point.* **6a.** Rudely brief; abrupt. **b.** Easily provoked; irascible. **7.** Inadequate; insufficient. **8.** Lacking in length or amount: *a board that is short two inches.* **9.** Lacking in breadth or scope. **10.** Deficient in retentiveness: *a short memory.* **11a.** Not owning the stocks or commodities one is selling in anticipation of a fall in prices. **b.** Of or relating to a short sale. **12a.** Containing a large amount of shortening; flaky. **b.** Not ductile; brittle: *short iron.* **13a.** *Linguistics* Of, relating to, or being a speech sound of relatively brief duration, as the first vowel sound in the Latin word *mălus,* "evil," as compared with the same or a similar sound of long duration, as the first vowel sound in the Latin word *mālus,* "apple tree." **b.** *Grammar* Of, relating to, or being a vowel sound in English, such as the vowel sound (ă) in *pat* or (o͝o) in *put,* that is descended from a vowel of brief duration. **14a.** Unstressed; unaccented. Used of a syllable in accentual prosody. **b.** Being of relatively brief duration. Used of a syllable in quantitative prosody. ❖ *adv.* **shorter, shortest 1.** Abruptly; quickly: *stopped short.* **2.** In a rude or curt manner. **3.** At a point before a given boundary, limit, or goal. **4.** At a disadvantage: *caught short by the storm.* **5.** Without owning what one is selling. ❖ *n.* **1.** Something short, as: **a.** A short syllable, vowel, or consonant. **b.** A brief film; a short subject. **c.** A size of clothing less long than the average for that size. **d. shorts** Short trousers extending to the knee or above. **e. shorts** Men's undershorts. **2a.** A short sale. **b.** One that sells short. **3. shorts** A byproduct of wheat processing that consists of germ, bran, and coarse meal or flour. **4. shorts** Clippings or trimmings that remain as byproducts in various manufacturing processes, often used to make an inferior variety of the product. **5a.** A short circuit. **b.** A malfunction caused by a short circuit. **6.** *Baseball* A shortstop. ❖ *v.* **short•ed, short•ing, shorts** —*tr.* **1.** To cause a short circuit in. **2.** *Informal* To give (one) less than one is entitled to; shortchange. **3a.** To sell (a stock that one does not own) in anticipation of making a profit when its price falls. **b.** To sell unowned stock in (the stock market) in anticipation of making a profit when prices fall. —*intr.* To short-circuit. —*idioms:* **for short** As an abbreviation: *He's called Ed for short.* **in short** In summary; briefly. **short for** An abbreviation of: *Ed is short for Edward.* **short of 1.** Having an inadequate supply of. **2.** Less than. **3.** Other than; without resorting to. **4.** Not quite willing to undertake or do; just this side of. **the short end of the stick** The worst side of an unequal deal. [ME < OE *sceort, scort.* See **sker-**[1] in App.] —**short′ness** *n.*

short account *n.* **1.** The account of one that sells short. **2.** The total number of open short shares in an account or in the market.

short•age (shôr′tĭj) *n.* A deficiency in amount.

short•bread (shôrt′brĕd′) *n.* A cookie made of flour, sugar, and much butter or other shortening.

short•cake (shôrt′kāk′) *n.* **1.** A dessert consisting of a biscuit or cake served with fruit and topped with cream. **2.** The biscuit or cake made for this dessert.

short•change (shôrt′chānj′) *tr.v.* **-changed, -chang•ing, -chang•es 1.** To give (someone) less change than is due in a transaction. **2.** *Informal* To treat unfairly or deceitfully; cheat. —**short′chang′er** *n.*

short circuit *n.* A low-resistance connection between two points in an electric circuit, causing the current to bypass the rest of the circuit, and often resulting in excess current flow.

short-cir•cuit (shôrt′sûr′kĭt) *v.* **-cuit•ed, -cuit•ing, -cuits** —*tr.* **1.** To cause to have a short circuit. **2.** *Informal* To hamper the progress of; impede. **3.** To bypass. —*intr.* To become affected with a short circuit.

short•com•ing (shôrt′kŭm′ĭng) *n.* A deficiency; a flaw.

short covering *n.* The buying of securities, stocks, or commodities in order to close out a short sale.

short•cut (shôrt′kŭt′) *n.* **1.** A more direct route than the customary one. **2.** A means of saving time or effort. [< CUT, direct route.] —**short′cut′** *v.*

short-day (shôrt′dā′) *adj.* Of, relating to, or being a plant that flowers only after exposure to light periods shorter than a certain critical length, as in early spring or fall.

short division *n.* The process of dividing one number by another without writing down all the steps.

short•en (shôr′tn) *v.* **-ened, -en•ing, -ens** —*tr.* **1.** To make short or shorter. **2.** *Nautical* To take in (a sail) so that less canvas is exposed to the wind, thereby reducing speed. **3.** To reduce in force, efficacy, or intensity. **4.** To add shortening to (dough) for flakiness. —*intr.* To become short or shorter. —**short′en•er** *n.*

short•en•ing (shôr′tn-ĭng, shôrt′nĭng) *n.* **1.** A fat used to make cake or pastry light or flaky. **2.** Something that has been shortened, as a word. **3.** The act or process of becoming or making shorter.

short•fall (shôrt′fôl′) *n.* **1.** A failure to attain a specified amount or level; a shortage. **2.** The amount by which a supply falls short of expectation, need, or demand.

short•hair (shôrt′hâr′) *n.* Either of two breeds of cats, characterized by short hair, a slender muscular body, large head, broad muzzle, and large round eyes.

short•haired (shôrt′hârd′) *adj.* Having a coat of short hair. Used of animals.

short•hand (shôrt′hănd′) *n.* **1.** A system of rapid handwriting using symbols for words, phrases, and letters. **2.** A system, form, or instance of abbreviated or formulaic reference.

short-hand•ed (shôrt′hăn′dĭd) *adj.* Lacking the usual or necessary number of workers, employees, players, or assistants.

short haul *n.* **1.** A short distance. **2.** A short period of time. —**short′-haul′** (shôrt′hôl′) *adj.*

short•horn (shôrt′hôrn′) *n.* Any of a breed of beef or dairy cattle that originated in northern England, having short curved horns or no horns and usu. red, white, or roan.

short-horned grasshopper (shôrt′hôrnd′) *n.* A grasshopper of the family Locustidae (or Acrididae), including the locusts that swarm over large areas destroying vegetation.

shor•ti•a (shôr′tē-ə) *n.* Any of various eastern North American and Asian evergreen stemless herbs of the genus *Shortia,* having glossy basal leaves and white, pink, or blue nodding flowers on long stalks. [NLat. *Shortia,* genus name, after Charles Wilkins *Short* (1794–1863), American physician and botanist.]

short•ie (shôr′tē) *n. & adj.* Variant of **shorty.**

short•leaf pine (shôrt′lēf′) *n.* A pine tree (*Pinus echinata*) common in the southeast United States and having dark bluish-green leaves grouped in fascicles of two.

short•list also **short-list** (shôrt′lĭst′) *n.* A list of preferable items or candidates that have been selected for final consideration, as in making an award. —**short′-list′** *v.*

short-lived (shôrt′līvd′, -lĭvd′) *adj.* Living or lasting only a short time; ephemeral. [SHORT + (LONG)-LIVED.]

USAGE NOTE The pronunciation (-līvd) is etymologically correct since the compound is derived from the noun *life,* rather than from the verb *live.* But the pronunciation (-lĭvd) is by now so common that it cannot be considered an error. In the most recent survey 43 percent of the Usage Panel preferred (-līvd), 39 percent preferred (-lĭvd), and 18 percent found both pronunciations equally acceptable.

short•ly (shôrt′lē) *adv.* **1.** In a short time; soon. **2.** In a few words; concisely. **3.** In an abrupt manner; curtly.

short order *n.* An order of food prepared and served quickly, as in a diner. —**short′-or′der** (shôrt′ôr′dər) *adj.*

short-range (shôrt′rānj′) *adj.* **1.** Designed for or limited to short distances. **2.** Of or relating to the near future.

short ribs *pl.n.* Beef rib ends between the rib roast and the plate.

short sale *n.* The sale of a security that one does not own but has borrowed in anticipation of making a profit by paying for it after its price has fallen.

short shrift *n.* **1.** Summary, careless treatment; scant attention. **2.** Quick work. **3a.** A short respite, as from death. **b.** The brief time before execution granted a condemned prisoner for confession and absolution.

short sight *n.* See **myopia** 1.

short•sight•ed (shôrt′sī′tĭd) *adj.* **1.** Nearsighted; myopic. **2.** Lacking foresight. —**short′sight′ed•ly** *adv.* —**short′sight′ed•ness** *n.*

short-spo•ken (shôrt′spō′kən) *adj.* Given to shortness or abruptness in manner or speech; curt.

short-staffed (shôrt′stăft′) *adj.* Having fewer staff members than is usual or desirable.

short•stop (shôrt′stŏp′) *n. Baseball* **1.** The field position between second and third base. **2.** The infielder in this position.

short story *n.* A short piece of prose fiction, having few characters and aiming at unity of effect.

short subject *n.* A brief film often shown before a feature-length film.

short-tem•pered (shôrt′tĕm′pərd) *adj.* Easily or quickly moved to anger; irascible.

short-term (shôrt′tûrm′) *adj.* **1.** Involving or lasting a relatively brief time. **2a.** Payable or reaching maturity within a relatively brief time, such as a year: *a short-term loan.* **b.** Acquired over a relatively brief time: *short-term capital gains.*

short ton *n.* See **ton** 1.

short-waist•ed (shôrt′wā′stĭd) *adj.* Having a distance between shoulders and waist that is shorter than average.

short•wave (shôrt′wāv′) *adj.* **1.** Having a wavelength of approx. 10 to 200 meters. **2.** Capable of receiving or transmitting at wavelengths of approx. 10 to 200 meters.

short wave *n.* An electromagnetic wave with a wavelength of approx. 200 meters or less, esp. a radio wave in the 20 to 200 meter range.

short-wind•ed (shôrt′wĭn′dĭd) *adj.* **1.** Breathing with quick labored breaths. **2.** Likely to have trouble breathing, esp. from exertion. **3.** Brief and succinct. **4.** Choppy; disconnected.

short•y also **short•ie** (shôr′tē) *Informal n., pl.* **-ies 1.** A person short in stature. **2.** A thing of less than average size, length, extension, or duration. ❖ *adj.* Of less than average size or length.

Sho•sho•ne also **Sho•sho•ni** (shō-shō′nē) *n., pl.* **Shoshone** or **-nes** also **Shoshoni** or **-nis 1.** A member of a Native American people comprising three divisions, specifically: **a.** A group inhabiting parts of Idaho, northern Utah, eastern Oregon, and western Montana, now mostly in Idaho. **b.** A group inhabiting the Great Basin area of Idaho, Utah, and Nevada south to Death Valley, California, now mostly in Nevada. **c.** A group in western Wyoming. **2.** Any of the languages of the Shoshone people. [Prob. < an Eastern Shoshone band name.] —**Sho•sho′ne•an** *adj.*

Shoshone Falls A waterfall, 64.7 m (212 ft), in the Snake R. of S ID.

Shoshone River A river, c. 193 km (120 mi), of NW WY flowing NE to the Bighorn R.

Shos•ta•ko•vich (shŏs′tə-kō′vĭch, -kô′-, shə-stə-), **Dmitri** 1906–75. Russian composer known esp. for his 15 symphonies (1925–71).

shot[1] (shŏt) *n.* **1.** The firing or discharge of a weapon. **2.** The distance over which something is shot; range. **3a.** An attempt to hit a target with a projectile. **b.** An attempt to reach a target with a rocket. **4a.** An attempt to score in a game, as in soccer. **b.** *Baseball* A home run. **5a.** The flight or path of a projectile in a game. **b.** A stroke in a game, as in golf. **6.** A pointed or critical remark. **7.** *Informal* **a.** An attempt; a try. **b.** A guess. **c.** An opportunity. **d.** A chance at odds; something to bet on: *a four-to-one shot.* **8a.** *pl.* **shot** A solid projectile designed to be discharged from a firearm or cannon. **b.** *pl.* **shot** A tiny lead or steel pellet, esp. one used in a shotgun cartridge. **9.** *Sports* The heavy metal ball that is put for distance in the shot put. **10.** One who shoots in a particular way: *a good shot.* **11a.** A charge of explosives used in blasting mine shafts. **b.** A detonation of an explosive charge. **12a.** A photographic view or exposure. **b.** A developed photographic image. **c.** A single cinematic take. **13a.** A hypodermic injection. **b.** A small amount given or applied at one time. **14.** A drink, esp. a jigger of liquor. **15.** An amount to be paid, as for drinks; a bill. **16.** *Nautical* A length of chain equal to 15 fathoms (90 feet) in the United States and 12½ fathoms (75 feet) in Great Britain. ❖ *tr.v.* **shot•ted, shot•ting, shots** To load or weight with shot. —*idioms:* **like a shot** Very quickly. **shot in the arm** *Informal* Something that boosts one's spirits. **shot in the dark** *Informal* **1.** A wild unsubstantiated guess. **2.** An attempt having little chance of success. [ME < OE *sceot.*]

shot[2] (shŏt) *v.* Past tense and past participle of **shoot.** ❖ *adj.* **1a.**

1283

short account

shot²

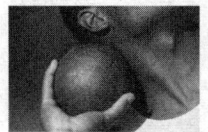

shot[1]
preparing to throw shot put

ă	pat	oi	boy
ā	pay	ou	out
âr	care	ŏŏ	took
ä	father	ōō	boot
ĕ	pet	ŭ	cut
ē	be	ûr	urge
ĭ	pit	th	thin
ī	pie	*th*	this
îr	pier	hw	which
ŏ	pot	zh	vision
ō	toe	ə	about,
ô	paw		item

Stress marks:
′ (primary);
′ (secondary), as in
lexicon (lĕk′sĭ-kŏn′)

Of changeable or variegated color; iridescent. **b.** Streaked or flecked with or as if with yarn of a different color: *a blue suit shot with purple.* **c.** Interspersed or permeated with a distinctive quality: *shot with irony.* **2.** *Informal* **a.** Worn-out; ruined. **b.** Exhausted; thoroughly tired.

shot clock *n. Basketball* A device that shows how many seconds a team has to take a shot or else lose the ball.

shote (shōt) *n.* Variant of **shoat.**

shot•gun (shŏt′gŭn′) *n.* **1.** A smoothbore gun that fires shot over short ranges. **2.** *Football* An offensive formation, used esp. for passing, in which the quarterback receives the snap several yards behind the line of scrimmage. **3.** *Southern US* A house in which several rooms join in a straight line from the front to the back. See Regional Note at **beignet.** ❖ *adj.* **1.** Obtained by or involving coercion: *a shotgun compromise.* **2.** Covering a wide range haphazardly or ineffectively: *shotgun methods of evaluation.*

shotgun marriage *n.* A marriage necessitated by pregnancy.

shot hole *n.* **1.** A drilled hole in which an explosive charge is placed before detonation. **2.** An insect hole in wood.

shot put *n.* **1.** A competition in which contestants put a heavy metal ball as far as they can. **2.** This ball. —**shot′-put′ter** (shŏt′pŏŏt′ər) *n.* —**shot′-put′ting** *n.*

shot put

shott (shŏt) *n.* Variant of **chott.**

shot•ten (shŏt′n) *adj.* Having recently spawned and thus being less desirable as food. Used of fish, esp. herring. [ME *shoten,* p. part. of *shoten,* to shoot. See SHOOT.]

should (shŏŏd) *aux.v.* Past tense of **shall. 1.** Used to express obligation or duty: *You should call her.* **2.** Used to express probability or expectation: *They should arrive soon.* **3.** Used to express conditionality or contingency: *If she should fall, then so would I.* **4.** Used to moderate the directness or bluntness of a statement: *I should think he would like to go.*

USAGE NOTE Like the rules governing the use of *shall* and *will* on which they are based, the traditional rules governing the use of *should* and *would* are largely ignored in modern American practice. Either *should* or *would* can now be used in the first person to express conditional futurity: *If I had known that, I would* (or somewhat more formally, *should*) *have answered differently.* But in the second and third persons only *would* is used: *If he had known that, he would have answered differently. Would* cannot always be substituted for *should,* however. *Should* is used in all three persons in a conditional clause: *if I* (or *you* or *he*) *should decide to go. Should* is also used in all three persons to express duty or obligation (the equivalent of *ought to*): *I* (or *you* or *he*) *should go.* On the other hand, *would* is used to express volition or promise: *I agreed that I would do it.* Either *would* or *should* is possible as an auxiliary with *like, be inclined, be glad, prefer,* and related verbs: *I would* (or *should*) *like to call your attention to an oversight.* Here *would* was acceptable on all levels to a large majority of the Usage Panel in an earlier survey and is more common in American usage than *should.* • *Should have* is sometimes incorrectly written *should of* by writers who have mistaken the source of the spoken contraction *should've.* See Usage Notes at **if,** rather, shall.

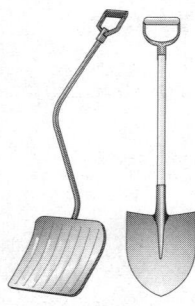

shovel
left: ergonomic snow shovel
right: D-handle round point shovel

shoul•der (shōl′dər) *n.* **1a.** The joint connecting the arm with the torso. **b.** The part of the human body between the neck and upper arm. **2a.** The joint of a vertebrate animal that connects the forelimb to the trunk. **b.** The part of an animal near this joint. **c.** The part of a bird's wing between the wrist and the trunk. **3.** The area of the back from one shoulder to the other. Often used in the plural. **4.** A cut of meat including the joint of the foreleg and adjacent parts. **5.** The portion of a garment that covers the shoulder. **6.** An angled or sloping part, as: **a.** The angle between the face and flank of a bastion in a fortification. **b.** The area between the body and neck of a bottle or vase. **7.** The area of an item or object that serves as an abutment or surrounds a projection, as the end surface of a board from which a tenon projects. **8.** The edge or border running on either side of a roadway. ❖ *v.* -**dered,** -**der•ing, -ders** —*tr.* **1.** To carry or place (a burden, for example) on the shoulders. **2.** To take on; assume: *shouldered the blame.* **3.** To push or apply force to, with or as if with the shoulder. **4.** To make (one's way) by or as if by shoving obstacles with one's shoulders. —*intr.* **1.** To push with the shoulders. **2.** To make one's way by or as if by shoving obstacles with one's shoulders. —**idioms: put (one's) shoulder to the wheel** To apply oneself vigorously; make a concentrated effort. **shoulder to shoulder 1.** In close proximity; side by side. **2.** In close cooperation. [ME *shulder* < OE *sculdor.*]

shoulder bag *n.* A handbag carried by a strap that is looped over the shoulder.

shoulder blade *n.* See **scapula.**

shoulder board *n.* One of a pair of oblong pieces of stiffened cloth worn on each shoulder of a military uniform and carrying insignia to show rank.

shoulder girdle *n.* The pectoral girdle, esp. of a human.

shoulder harness *n.* A safety belt used with a seat belt in a vehicle and worn across the chest and over the shoulder.

shoulder knot *n.* **1.** Either of two detachable braided cords worn on each shoulder of a commissioned officer's full-dress uniform. **2.** An ornamental ribbon or lace knot once worn on the shoulder.

shoulder patch *n.* A cloth patch bearing identifying markings, worn on the upper portion of the sleeve of a uniform.

shoulder strap *n.* **1.** A strap, usu. one of a pair, supporting a garment from the shoulder. **2.** A strap worn across the shoulder to support an item, such as a bag.

should•est (shŏŏd′ĭst) or **shouldst** (shŏŏdst) *aux.v. Archaic* A second person singular past tense of **shall.**

should•n't (shŏŏd′nt) Contraction of *should not.*

shout (shout) *n.* A loud cry. ❖ *tr. & intr.v.* **shout•ed, shout•ing, shouts** To say with or utter a shout. —**phrasal verb: shout down** To overwhelm or silence by shouting loudly. [ME *shoute,* perh. < ON *skúta,* a taunt.] —**shout′er** *n.*

SYNONYMS shout, bawl, bellow, holler, howl, roar, whoop, yell These verbs mean to say with or make a loud strong cry: *fans shouting their approval; bawled out orders; bellows with rage; hollered a warning; howling with pain; a crowd roaring its disapproval; children whooping at play; troops yelling as they attacked.*

shout•ing distance (shou′tĭng) *n.* A short distance: *lived within shouting distance of each other.*

shove (shŭv) *v.* **shoved, shov•ing, shoves** —*tr.* **1.** To push forward or along. **2.** To push rudely or roughly. See Syns at **push.** —*intr.* To push someone or something with force. ❖ *n.* The act of shoving; a push. —**phrasal verb: shove off 1.** To push (a boat) away from shore in leaving. **2.** *Informal* To leave. [ME *shoven* < OE *scūfan.*] —**shov′er** *n.*

shov•el (shŭv′əl) *n.* **1.** A tool with a handle and a broad scoop or blade for digging and moving material, such as snow. **2.** A large mechanical device for heavy digging or excavation. **3.** A shovelful. ❖ *v.* -**eled, -el•ing, -els** also -**elled, -el•ling, -els** —*tr.* **1.** To move or remove with a shovel. **2.** To make with a shovel. **3.** To convey or throw in a rough or hasty way, as if with a shovel. **4.** To clear or excavate with or as if with a shovel: *shoveling off the road.* —*intr.* To dig or work with a shovel. [ME < OE *scofl.*]

shov•el•er also **shov•el•ler** (shŭv′ə-lər, shŭv′lər) *n.* **1.** One that shovels: *a fast shoveler.* **2.** A duck (*Anas clypeata*) found esp. in marshes and having a long broad bill fringed with bristles, used to strain food from mud and water.

shov•el•ful (shŭv′əl-fŏŏl′) *n.* The amount that a shovel can hold.

shovel hat *n.* A stiff broad-brimmed low-crowned hat, turned up at the sides and projecting in front, worn by some English clergymen.

shov•el•nose (shŭv′əl-nōz′) *n.* A sturgeon (*Scaphirhynchus platorhynchus*) of the Mississippi River having a broad flat snout.

shov•el-nosed (shŭv′əl-nōzd′) *adj.* Having a broad flattened snout, bill, or head.

show (shō) *v.* **showed, shown** (shōn) or **showed, show•ing, shows** —*tr.* **1.** To cause or allow to be seen; display. **b.** To display for sale, in exhibition, or in competition. **2.** To conduct; guide. **3.** To direct one's attention to; point out. **4.** To manifest (an emotion, for example); reveal. **5.** To permit access to (a house, for example) when offering for sale or rent. **6.** To reveal (oneself) as in one's behavior or condition. **7.** To indicate; register. **8a.** To demonstrate by reasoning or procedure: *showed that he was wrong.* **b.** To demonstrate to by reasoning or procedure; inform or prove to. **9.** To grant; bestow: *showed no mercy.* **10.** *Law* To plead; allege: *show cause.* —*intr.* **1.** To be or become visible or evident. **2.** *Slang* To make an appearance; show up. **3a.** To be exhibited publicly. **b.** To give a performance or present an exhibition. **4.** *Sports* To finish third or better in a horserace or dog race. ❖ *n.* **1.** A display; a manifestation. **2a.** A trace or indication, as of oil in a well. **b.** The discharge of bloody mucus from the vagina indicating the start of labor. **c.** The first discharge of blood in menstruation. **3.** A false appearance; a pretense. **4a.** A striking appearance or display; a spectacle. **b.** A pompous or ostentatious display. **5.** Display or outward appearance: *a smile for show.* **6a.** A public exhibition or entertainment. **b.** An exposition for the display or demonstration of commercial products. **c.** A usu. competitive exhibition of domestic animals. **7a.** A radio or television program. **b.** A movie. **c.** A theatrical troupe or company. **8.** *Informal* An affair or undertaking: *ran the whole show.* **9.** *Sports* Third place at the finish, as in a horserace. —**phrasal verbs: show off** To display or behave ostentatiously or conspicuously. **show up 1.** To be clearly visible. **2.** To put in an appearance; arrive. **3.** To expose or reveal the true character or nature of. **4.** *Informal* To surpass, as in ability or intelligence. —**idiom: get the show on the road** *Slang* To get started. [ME *sheuen, shouen* < OE *scēawian,* to look at, display.]

show-and-tell or **show and tell** (shō′ən-tĕl′) *n.* **1.** An educational activity in which a child displays an object to the class and talks about it. **2.** A public presentation or display.

show bill *n.* An advertising poster.

show biz *n. Informal* Show business.

show•boat (shō′bōt′) *n.* **1.** A river steamboat having performers and a theater aboard for performances on the river. **2.** One who seeks attention by ostentatious behavior; a showoff. ❖ *intr.v.* -**boat•ed, -boat•ing, -boats**

show•bread or **shew•bread** (shō′brĕd′) *n.* The 12 loaves of blessed unleavened bread placed every Sabbath in the Tabernacle as an offering by the priests of ancient Israel. [Transl. of Ger. *Schaubrot* (*Schau*, sight, show + *Brot*, bread), ult. transl. of Heb. *leḥem pānîm* (*leḥem*, bread + *pānîm*, divine presence).]

show business *n.* The entertainment industry.

show•case (shō′kās′) *n.* **1.** A display case or cabinet, as in a store. **2.** A setting in which someone or something may be displayed, esp. to advantage. —**show′case′** *v.*

show•down (shō′doun′) *n.* **1.** An event, esp. a confrontation, that forces an issue to a conclusion. **2.** *Games* The showing of the players' cards to determine the winner of the pot in poker.

show•er¹ (shou′ər) *n.* **1.** A brief fall of precipitation, such as rain. **2.** A fall of a group of objects, esp. from the sky: *a meteor shower.* **3.** An abundant flow; an outpouring: *a shower of praise.* **4.** A party held to honor and present gifts to someone: *a bridal shower.* **5a.** A bath in which the water is sprayed on the bather from a showerhead, usu. secured overhead; a showerbath. **b.** The stall or tub in which such a bath is taken. ❖ *v.* **-ered, -er•ing, -ers** —*tr.* **1.** To pour down in a shower: *showered confetti on them.* **2.** To cover with or as if with a shower. **3.** To bestow abundantly or liberally. —*intr.* **1.** To fall or pour down in or as if in a shower. **2.** To wash oneself in a shower. [ME *shour* < OE *scūr.*] —**show′er•y** *adj.*

show•er² (shō′ər) *n.* One that shows: *a shower of art.*

show•er bath (shou′ər) *n.* A shower.

show•er•head (shou′ər-hĕd′) *n.* A perforated nozzle for spraying water on a bather taking a shower.

show•girl (shō′gûrl′) *n.* A woman, usu. elaborately dressed, who performs in a musical or theatrical production.

show•ing (shō′ĭng) *n.* **1.** The act of presenting or displaying. **2.** Performance, as in a competition or test of skill: *a poor showing.* **3.** A presentation of evidence, facts, or figures.

show•man (shō′mən) *n.* **1.** A theatrical producer. **2.** A dramatic or ostentatious man. —**show′man•ship′** *n.*

shown (shōn) *v.* A past participle of **show.**

show•off (shō′ôf′, -ŏf′) *n.* **1.** The act of showing off. **2.** One who shows off.

show•piece (shō′pēs′) *n.* Something exhibited, esp. as an outstanding example of its kind.

show place also **show•place** (shō′plās′) *n.* **1.** A place, such as an estate, that is viewed and frequented for its beauty or historical noteworthiness. **2.** A beautiful or ornate place.

show room *n.* A room for the display of merchandise.

show•stop•per (shō′stŏp′ər) *n. Informal* **1.** A performance or performer that evokes so much applause that the show is temporarily interrupted. **2.** A particularly arresting person or thing. —**show′stop′ping** *adj.*

show•time or **show time** (shō′tīm′) *n.* **1.** The time at which an entertainment, such as a movie, is scheduled to start. **2.** *Slang* The time at which an activity is to begin.

show•y (shō′ē) *adj.* **-i•er, -i•est 1.** Making an imposing or aesthetically pleasing display; striking: *showy flowers.* **2.** Displaying brilliance and virtuosity of ability or performance. **3.** Marked by or prone to ostentatious, often tasteless display; flashy. —**show′i•ly** *adv.* —**show′i•ness** *n.*

SYNONYMS *showy, flamboyant, ostentatious, pretentious, splashy* These adjectives mean marked by a striking, often excessively conspicuous display: *a showy rhinestone bracelet; an entertainer's flamboyant personality; an ostentatious sable coat; a pretentious scholarly edition; a splashy advertising campaign.*

---

shp or **s.hp.** *abbr.* shaft horsepower

shpt. *abbr.* shipment

shrank (shrăngk) *v.* A past tense of **shrink.**

shrap•nel (shrăp′nəl) *n., pl.* **shrapnel 1.** Fragments from an exploded artillery shell, mine, or bomb. **2a.** A 19th-century artillery shell containing metal balls, designed to explode in the air above enemy troops. **b.** The metal balls in such a weapon. [After Henry *Shrapnel* (1761–1842), British army officer.]

shred (shrĕd) *n.* **1.** A long irregular strip that is cut or torn off. **2.** A small amount; a particle: *a shred of evidence.* ❖ *tr.v.* **shred•ded** or **shred, shred•ding, shreds** To cut or tear into shreds. [ME *shrede* < OE *scrēade.*]

shred•der (shrĕd′ər) *n.* **1.** One that shreds. **2.** A device used for shredding documents, as to prevent unapproved persons from reading them.

Shreve•port (shrēv′pôrt′, -pōrt′) A city of NW LA on the Red R.; founded in the 1830s. Pop. 200,145.

shrew (shro͞o) *n.* **1.** Any of various small, chiefly insectivorous mammals of the family Soricidae, resembling a mouse but having a long pointed snout and small eyes and ears. **2.** A woman with a violent, scolding, or nagging temperament; a scold. [ME *shrewe,* villian < OE *scrēawa,* shrewmouse.]

shrewd (shro͞od) *adj.* **shrewd•er, shrewd•est 1.** Marked by keen awareness, sharp intelligence, and often practicality. See Syns at **clever. 2.** Disposed to artful and cunning practices; tricky. **3.** Sharp; penetrating: *a shrewd wind.* [ME *shrewed,* wicked < *shrewe,* rascal. See SHREW.] —**shrewd′ly** *adv.*

shrewd•ness (shro͞od′nĭs) *n.* **1.** The quality of being shrewd. **2.** An aggregation of apes.

shrew•ish (shro͞o′ĭsh) *adj.* Ill-tempered; nagging. —**shrew′ish•ly** *adv.* —**shrew′ish•ness** *n.*

shrew mole *n.* Any of several shrewlike moles of the family Talpidae, such as *Neurotrichus gibbsii* of western North America or *Uropsilus soricipes* of central Asia.

shrew•mouse (shro͞o′mous′) *n.* See **shrew 1.**

shriek (shrēk) *n.* **1.** A shrill, often frantic cry. **2.** A sound suggestive of such a cry. ❖ *v.* **shrieked, shriek•ing, shrieks** —*intr.* **1.** To utter a shriek. **2.** To make a sound like a shriek. —*tr.* To utter with a shriek. [ME *shriken,* of Scand. orig.] —**shriek′er** *n.*

shrie•val (shrē′vəl) *adj.* Of or relating to a sheriff. [< obsolete *shrieve,* var. of SHERIFF.] —**shrie′val•ty** *n.*

shrift (shrĭft) *n. Archaic* **1.** The act of shriving. **2.** Confession to a priest. **3.** Absolution given by a priest. [ME < OE *scrift* < Lat. *scrīptum,* something written < neut. p. part. of *scrībere,* to write. See SHRIVE.]

shrike (shrīk) *n.* Any of various carnivorous oscine birds of the family Laniidae, having a screeching call and a strong hooked bill. [Prob. < ME **shrik* < OE *scrīc,* thrush.]

shrill (shrĭl) *adj.* **shrill•er, shrill•est 1.** High-pitched and piercing in tone or sound: *a shrill wail.* **2.** Producing a sharp high-pitched tone or sound. **3.** Sharp or keen to the senses; harshly vivid. ❖ *v.* **shrilled, shrill•ing, shrills** —*tr.* To utter in a shrill manner; scream. —*intr.* To produce a shrill cry or sound. [ME *shrille.*] —**shrill′ness** *n.* —**shril′ly** *adv.*

shrimp (shrĭmp) *n., pl.* **shrimp** or **shrimps 1a.** Any of various small, chiefly marine decapod crustaceans of the suborder Natantia, many species of which are edible, having a compressed or elongated body with a well-developed abdomen and a long spinelike projection of the carapace. **b.** Any of various similar crustaceans. **2.** *Slang* An unimportant or small person. ❖ *intr.v.* **shrimped, shrimp•ing, shrimps** To fish for shrimp. [ME *shrimpe,* poss. of LGer. orig.] —**shrimp′er** *n.*

shrimp
Atlantic cleaner shrimp
Lysmata grabhami

shrine (shrīn) *n.* **1.** A container or receptacle for sacred relics; a reliquary. **2a.** The tomb of a venerated person, such as a saint. **b.** A place at which devotion is paid to a venerated person. **3.** A site hallowed by a venerated object or its associations. ❖ *tr.v.* **shrined, shrin•ing, shrines** To enshrine. [ME < OE *scrīn,* box < Lat. *scrīnium,* case for books or papers.]

Shrin•er (shrī′nər) *n.* A member of an international fraternal order that admits only Knights Templars and 32nd-degree Masons as members. [After the Ancient Arabic Order of Nobles of the Mystic *Shrine,* their fraternal order.]

shrink (shrĭngk) *v.* **shrank** (shrăngk) or **shrunk** (shrŭngk), **shrunk** or **shrunk•en** (shrŭng′kən), **shrink•ing, shrinks** —*intr.* **1.** To become constricted from heat, moisture, or cold. **2.** To become reduced in amount or value; dwindle. **3.** To draw back instinctively, as from something alarming; recoil. **4.** To show reluctance; hesitate. —*tr.* To cause to shrink. ❖ *n.* **1a.** The act of shrinking. **b.** The degree to which something shrinks; shrinkage. **2.** *Slang* A psychotherapist. [ME *shrinken,* to wither, shrivel up < OE *scrincan.*] —**shrink′a•ble** *adj.* —**shrink′er** *n.*

shrink•age (shrĭng′kĭj) *n.* **1.** The process of shrinking. **2.** The amount or proportion by which something shrinks. **3.** A reduction in value; depreciation. **4.** The total weight loss sustained by livestock in shipment to a market. **5.** Loss of merchandise, esp. by theft.

shrink•ing violet (shrĭng′kĭng) *n. Informal* A shy or retiring person.

shrink-wrap or **shrink•wrap** (shrĭngk′răp′) *n.* A protective wrapping consisting of a clear plastic film that is wound about an article and then shrunk by heat to form a sealed tight-fitting package. ❖ *adj.* **1.** Of or relating to shrink-wrap. **2.** Of or relating to a legal agreement, such as a software license, to which one indicates acceptance by opening the shrink-wrap that encloses a product subject to the agreement. —**shrink′-wrap′** *v.*

Shropshire²

shrive (shrīv) *v.* **shrove** (shrōv) or **shrived, shriv•en** (shrĭv′ən), **shriv•ing, shrives** —*tr.* **1.** To hear the confession of and give absolution to (a penitent). **2.** To obtain absolution for (oneself) by confessing and doing penance. —*intr. Archaic* **1.** To make or go to confession. **2.** To hear confessions. [ME *schriven* < OE *scrīfan* < Lat. *scrībere,* to write. See **skrībh-** in App.] —**shriv′er** *n.*

shriv•el (shrĭv′əl) *intr. & tr.v.* **-eled, -el•ing, -els** or **-elled, -el•ling, -els 1.** To become or make shrunken and wrinkled, often by drying: *Leaves fall and shrivel.* **2.** To lose or cause to lose vitality or intensity: *Inflation shriveled the dollar.* **3.** To become or make much less or smaller; dwindle. [?]

Shrop•shire¹ (shrŏp′shîr′, -shər) A historical region of W England on the Welsh border; part of the kingdom of Mercia during Anglo-Saxon times.

Shrop•shire² (shrŏp′shîr′, -shər, -shīr′) *n.* A large hornless dark-faced sheep of a breed developed in Shropshire.

shroud (shroud) *n.* **1.** A cloth used to wrap a body for burial; a winding sheet. **2.** Something that conceals, protects, or screens: *a shroud of fog.* **3a.** *Nautical* One of a set of ropes or wire cables stretched from a masthead to the sides of a vessel to support the mast. **b.** A similar supporting line for a smokestack or comparable structure. **c.** One of the ropes connecting the harness and canopy of a parachute. ❖ *v.* **shroud•ed, shroud•ing, shrouds** —*tr.* **1.** To wrap (a corpse) in burial clothing. **2.** To shut off from sight; screen. See Syns at **block. 3.** *Archaic* To shelter; protect. —*intr. Archaic* To take cover; find shelter. [ME *shrud,* garment < OE *scrūd.*]

ă	pat	oi	boy
ā	pay	ou	out
âr	care	o͝o	took
ä	father	o͞o	boot
ĕ	pet	ŭ	cut
ē	be	ûr	urge
ĭ	pit	th	thin
ī	pie	*th*	this
îr	pier	hw	which
ŏ	pot	zh	vision
ō	toe	ə	about, item
ô	paw		

Stress marks:
′ (primary);
′ (secondary), as in
lexicon (lĕk′sĭ-kŏn′)

Shrove·tide (shrōv′tīd′) *n.* The three days preceding Ash Wednesday. [ME *shroftide* : *shrof*-, shriving (< *shriven*, to shrive; see SHRIVE) + *tid*, time; see TIDE¹.]

Shrove Tuesday *n.* The day before Ash Wednesday. [SHROVE(TIDE) + TUESDAY.]

shrub¹ (shrŭb) *n.* A woody plant of relatively low height, having several stems arising from the base and lacking a single trunk; a bush. [ME *shrubbe* < OE *scrybb*. See sker-¹ in App.]

shrub² (shrŭb) *n.* A beverage made from fruit juice, sugar, and a liquor such as rum or brandy. [< Ar. *šurb*, a drink < *šariba*, to drink.]

shrub·ber·y (shrŭb′ə-rē) *n., pl.* **-ies** A group or planting of shrubs.

shrub·by (shrŭb′ē) *adj.* **-bi·er, -bi·est 1.** Consisting of, planted with, or covered with shrubs. **2.** Of or resembling a shrub. **—shrub′bi·ness** *n.*

shrug (shrŭg) *v.* **shrugged, shrug·ging, shrugs** —*tr.* To raise (the shoulders), esp. as a gesture of doubt, disdain, or indifference. —*intr.* To shrug the shoulders. ❖ *n.* **1.** An expressive gesture of raising the shoulders. **2.** A woman's short jacket or sweater open down the front. **—phrasal verb: shrug off 1.** To minimize the importance of. **2.** To get rid of. [ME *shruggen*.]

shrunk (shrŭngk) *v.* A past tense and a past participle of **shrink**.

shrunk·en (shrŭng′kən) *v.* A past participle of **shrink**.

shtetl (shtĕt′l, shtāt′l) *n. pl* **shtetls** or **shtet·lach** (-läкн) A small Jewish town or village formerly found throughout Eastern Europe. [Yiddish < MHGer. *stetel*, dim. of *stat*, town < OHGer., place. See stā- in App.]

shtick also **schtick** or **shtik** (shtĭk) *n. Slang* **1.** A characteristic attribute, talent, or trait that is helpful in securing recognition or attention. **2.** An entertainment routine or gimmick. [Yiddish *shtik*, piece, routine < MHGer. *stücke*, piece < OHGer. *stukki*, crust, fragment.]

shuck (shŭk) *n.* **1a.** A husk, pod, or shell, as of a pea, hickory nut, or ear of corn. **b.** The shell of an oyster or clam. **2.** *Informal* Something worthless. Often used in the plural: *didn't amount to shucks.* ❖ *tr.v.* **shucked, shuck·ing, shucks 1.** To remove the husk or shell from. **2.** *Informal* To cast off: *shucked their coats.* ❖ *interj.* **shucks** (shŭks) Used to express mild disappointment, disgust, or annoyance. [Of unknown orig. Interj., alteration of SHIT.] **—shuck′er** *n.*

shud·der (shŭd′ər) *intr.v.* **-dered, -der·ing, -ders 1.** To shiver convulsively, as from fear or revulsion. **2.** To vibrate; quiver. ❖ *n.* A convulsive shiver, as from fear or revulsion; a tremor. [ME *shodderen*, perh. of MDu. or MLGer. orig.]

shuf·fle (shŭf′əl) *v.* **-fled, -fling, -fles** —*tr.* **1.** To slide (the feet) along the floor or ground while walking. **2.** To move (something) from one place to another; transfer or shift. **3.** To put aside or under cover quickly; shunt. **4.** To mix together; jumble. **5.** *Games* To mix together (playing cards or tiles, for example) so as to make a random order of arrangement. —*intr.* **1.** To move with short sliding steps, without or barely lifting the feet. **2.** To dance with sliding and tapping steps. **3.** To move about from place to place; shift. **4.** To act in a shifty or deceitful manner; equivocate. **5.** *Games* To shuffle playing cards, tiles, or dominoes. ❖ *n.* **1.** A short sliding step or movement or a walk characterized by such steps. **2.** A dance in which the feet slide along or move close to the floor. **3.** An evasive or deceitful action; an equivocation. **4.** A confused mixture; a jumble. **5.** *Games* **a.** An act of shuffling cards, dominoes, or tiles. **b.** A player's right or turn to do this. **—phrasal verb: shuffle off 1.** To get rid of; dispose of. **2.** To evade or shirk (a responsibility, for example). **3.** *Informal* To leave; depart. [ME *shovelen*, prob. of MDu. or MLGer. orig.] **—shuf′fler** *n.*

shuf·fle·board (shŭf′əl-bôrd′, -bōrd′) *n.* **1.** A game in which disks are slid along a smooth surface toward one of two targets painted on the surface and divided into numbered scoring areas. **2.** A surface on which this game is played. [Alteration of obsolete *shove-board* < SHOVE + BOARD.]

shul (shŏŏl, shōŏl) *n. Judaism* A synagogue. [Yiddish < MHGer. *schuol*, school < OHGer. *scuola* < Lat. *scola*. See SCHOOL¹.]

Shull (shŏŏl), **Clifford Glenwood** 1915–2001. Amer. physicist who shared a 1994 Nobel Prize.

shun (shŭn) *tr.v.* **shunned, shun·ning, shuns** To avoid deliberately; keep away from. [ME *shunnen* < OE *scunian*, to abhor.] **—shun′ner** *n.*

shun·pike (shŭn′pīk′) *n.* A side road taken to avoid the tolls or traffic of a turnpike. ❖ *intr.v.* **-piked, -pik·ing, -pikes** To travel on side roads, avoiding turnpikes. [SHUN + (TURN)PIKE.] **—shun′pik′er** *n.*

shunt (shŭnt) *n.* **1.** The act or process of turning aside or moving to an alternate course. **2.** A railroad switch. **3.** *Electricity* A low-resistance connection between two points in an electric circuit that forms an alternative path for a portion of the current. **4.** *Medicine* A passage between two natural body channels, such as blood vessels, esp. one created surgically to divert or permit flow from one pathway or region to another; a bypass. ❖ *v.* **shunt·ed, shunt·ing, shunts** —*tr.* **1.** To turn or move aside or onto another course. **2.** To evade by putting aside or ignoring. **3.** To switch (a train or car) from one track to another. **4.** *Electricity* To provide or divert (current) by means of a shunt. **5.** *Medicine* To

divert flow of (a body fluid) by means of a shunt. —*intr.* **1.** To move or turn aside. **2.** *Electricity* To become diverted by means of a shunt. Used of a circuit. [ME *shunten*, to flinch.] **—shunt′er** *n.*

shush (shŭsh) *interj.* Used to express a demand for silence. ❖ *v.* **shushed, shush·ing, shush·es** To demand silence from by saying "shush."

shut (shŭt) *v.* **shut, shut·ting, shuts** —*tr.* **1.** To move (a door or lid, for example) so as to block passage through an opening. **2.** To block entrance to or exit from; close: *shut a corridor.* **3.** To fasten with a lock, catch, or latch. **4.** To confine in or as if in a closed space: *shut them in a cage.* **5.** To exclude from or as if from a closed space. **6.** To cause to stop operating: *shut down a restaurant.* —*intr.* **1.** To move or become moved so as to block passage; close. **2.** To stop operating, esp. automatically: *The electricity shuts off at midnight.* ❖ *n.* **1.** The act or time of shutting. **2.** The line of connection between welded pieces of metal. **—phrasal verbs: shut off 1.** To stop the flow or passage of; cut off. **2.** To close off; isolate. **shut out** *Sports* To prevent (an opponent) from scoring any runs or points. **shut up 1.** To cause (someone) to stop speaking; silence. **2.** To stop speaking. **—idiom: shut (one's) eyes to** To refuse to consider or acknowledge. [ME *shutten* < OE *scyttan*.]

shut·down (shŭt′doun′) *n.* A cessation of operations or activity, as at a factory.

Shute (shōŏt), **Nevil** Pen name Nevil Shute Norway. 1899–1960. British writer whose novels include *A Town Like Alice* (1950) and *On the Beach* (1957), both set in Australia.

shut·eye (shŭt′ī′) *n. Slang* Sleep.

shut-in (shŭt′ĭn′) *n.* A person confined indoors by illness or disability. ❖ *adj.* (shŭt-ĭn′) **1.** Confined to a home or hospital, as by illness. **2.** Disposed to avoid social contact.

shut·off (shŭt′ôf′, -ŏf′) *n.* **1.** A device that shuts something off. **2.** A stoppage; a cessation.

shut·out (shŭt′out′) *n.* **1.** See **lockout**. **2.** *Sports* A game in which one side does not score.

shut·ter (shŭt′ər) *n.* **1.** One that shuts, as: **a.** A hinged cover or screen for a window, usu. fitted with louvers. **b.** A mechanical device of a camera that opens and closes to control the duration of exposure of a plate or film to light. **2. shutters** *Music* The movable louvers on a pipe organ, controlled by pedals, that open and close the swell box. ❖ *tr.v.* **-tered, -ter·ing, -ters 1.** To furnish or close with shutters. **2.** To cause to cease operations.

shut·ter·bug (shŭt′ər-bŭg′) *n. Informal* An enthusiastic amateur photographer.

shut·tle (shŭt′l) *n.* **1.** A device used in weaving to carry the woof thread back and forth between the warp threads. **2.** A device for holding the thread in tatting and netting and in a sewing machine. **3a.** Regular travel back and forth over an established route by a vehicle. **b.** A vehicle used in such travel: *took the shuttle across town.* **c.** A route used in such travel. **4.** A space shuttle. ❖ *v.* **-tled, -tling, -tles** —*intr.* To go, move, or travel back and forth by or as if by a shuttle. —*tr.* **1.** To cause to move back and forth frequently. **2.** To transport by or as if by a shuttle. [ME *shutille* < OE *scytel*, dart.] **—shut′tler** *n.*

shut·tle·cock (shŭt′l-kŏk′) *n.* A small rounded piece of cork or rubber with a conical crown of feathers or plastic, used in badminton. ❖ *tr.v.* **-cocked, -cock·ing, -cocks** To throw or send back and forth like a shuttlecock.

shuttle diplomacy *n.* Diplomatic negotiations conducted by an official intermediary who travels frequently between the nations involved. **—shuttle diplomat** *n.*

shy¹ (shī) *adj.* **shi·er** (shī′ər), **shi·est** (shī′ĭst) or **shy·er, shy·est 1.** Easily startled; timid. **2a.** Drawing back from contact or familiarity with others; retiring or reserved. **b.** Marked by reserve or diffidence. **3.** Distrustful; wary. **4.** Not having paid an amount due, as in poker. **5.** Short; lacking: *Eleven is one shy of a dozen.* ❖ *intr.v.* **shied** (shīd), **shy·ing, shies** (shīz) **1.** To move suddenly, as if startled; start. **2.** To draw back, as from fear or caution; recoil. ❖ *n., pl.* **shies** (shīz) A sudden movement, as from fright; a start. [ME *shey* < OE *scēoh.*] **—shy′er** *n.* **—shy′ly** *adv.* **—shy′ness** *n.*

SYNONYMS *shy, bashful, diffident, modest, coy, demure* These adjectives mean not forward but marked by a retiring nature, reticence, or a reserve of manner. One who is *shy* draws back from others, either because of a withdrawn nature or out of timidity: *"The poor man was shy and hated society"* (George Bernard Shaw). *Bashful* suggests self-consciousness or awkwardness in the presence of others: *"I never laughed, being bashful./Lowering my head, I looked at the wall"* (Ezra Pound). *Diffident* implies lack of self-confidence: *He was too diffident to express his opinion. Modest* is associated with an unassertive nature and absence of vanity or pretension: *Despite her fame she remained a modest, unassuming person. Coy* usually implies feigned, often flirtatious shyness: *"I pictured myself as some sylvan deity, and she a coy wood nymph of whom I was in pursuit"* (Washington Irving). *Demure* often denotes an affected shyness or modesty: *assented with a demure smile.*

shy² (shī) *v.* **shied** (shīd), **shy·ing, shies** (shīz) —*tr.* To throw (something) with a swift motion; fling. —*intr.* To throw something with a swift motion. ❖ *n., pl.* **shies** (shīz) **1.** A quick throw;

shuttlecock

a fling. **2.** *Informal* A gibe; a sneer. **3.** *Informal* An attempt; a try. [Perh. < SHY[1].]

shy•lock (shī′lŏk′) *n.* *Offensive* A ruthless moneylender; a loan shark. [After *Shylock*, the ruthless Jewish usurer in *The Merchant of Venice* by William Shakespeare.]

Shym•kent (shĭm-kĕnt′) or **Chim•kent** (chĭm-) A city of S-central Kazakhstan N of Tashkent; founded in the 12th cent. Pop. 404,000.

shy•ster (shī′stər) *n.* *Slang* An unethical unscrupulous practitioner, esp. of law. [Prob. alteration of Ger. *Scheisser*, son of a bitch, bastard < *scheissen*, to defecate < MHGer. *schīzen* < OHGer. *skīzzan*.] —**shy′ster•ism** *n.*

si (sē) *n.* *Music* Ti. [Ital. < Med.Lat. See GAMUT.]

Si The symbol for the element **silicon.**

SI *abbr.* *French* Système International [d'Unités] (International System [of Units])

si•al (sī′ăl′) *n.* Rock rich in silicon and aluminum forming the upper layer of the earth's crust beneath all continental landmasses. [SI(LICON) + AL(UMINUM).]

si•al•a•gogue (sī-ăl′ə-gôg′, -gŏg′) *n.* A drug or other agent that increases the flow of saliva. [Gk. *sialon*, saliva + −AGOGUE.] —**si′al•a•gog′ic** (sī′ə-lə-gŏj′ĭk) *adj.*

si•al•ic acid (sī-ăl′ĭk) *n.* Any of a group of amino carbohydrates that are components of mucoproteins and glycoproteins, esp. in animal tissue and blood cells. [Gk. *sialon*, saliva + −IC.]

Si•al•kot (sē-ăl′kōt′) A city of NE Pakistan N of Lahore. Pop. 302,009.

Si•am (sī-ăm′) See **Thailand.**

si•a•mang (sē′ə-măng′, sē-ăm′ŏng) *n.* A large black gibbon (*Symphalangus syndactylus* or *Hylobates syndactylus*) of Sumatra and the Malay Peninsula having an inflatable throat sac. [Malay.]

Si•a•mese (sī′ə-mēz′, -mēs′) *adj.* **1.** Of or relating to Siam; Thai. **2.** Closely connected or very similar; twin. **3. siamese** Of or being a Y-shaped dual connection between two pipes or hoses and a larger pipe or hose. ❖ *n., pl.* **Siamese 1.** A native or inhabitant of Siam; a Thai. **2.** The Thai language. [After *Siam* (Thailand).]

Siamese cat *n.* A shorthaired cat of a breed developed in the Far East, having blue eyes and a pale fawn or gray coat with darker ears, face, tail, and feet.

Siamese fighting fish *n.* A small, often brightly colored aggressive freshwater fish (*Betta splendens*) native to Malaysia and Thailand and having large fins and tail.

Siamese twin *n.* Either of a pair of identical twins born with their bodies joined, a result of the incomplete division of the ovum from which they developed. [After Chang and Eng Bunker (1811–74), conjoined Chinese twins born in *Siam* (Thailand).]

Si•an (sē′än′, shē′-) See **Xi'an.**

Siang Kiang (syäng′ kyäng′, shyäng′) See **Xiang Jiang.**

Siang•tan (syäng′tän′, shyäng′-) See **Xiangtan.**

Šiau•liai (shyou′lyī′) A city of W Lithuania NW of Vilnius; under Polish rule from 1589 to 1772. Pop. 147,900.

sib (sĭb) *n.* **1a.** A blood relation; a relative. **b.** A person's relatives considered as a group; kinfolk. **2.** A brother or sister; a sibling. **3.** *Anthropology* A kinship group consisting of two or more lineages considered as being related, as by common descent from a mythic ancestor. ❖ *adj.* Related by blood; kindred. [ME *sibbe* < OE *sibb*. See s(w)e- in App.]

Sib. *abbr.* **1.** Siberia **2.** Siberian

Si•be•li•us (sĭ-bāl′ē-əs, -bāl′yəs), **Jean** 1865–1957. Finnish composer whose works include *Finlandia* (1899).

Si•be•ri•a[1] (sī-bîr′ē-ə) A region of central and E Russia stretching from the Ural Mts. to the Pacific Ocean; annexed by Russia during the 16th and 17th cent. and used as a place of exile for political prisoners. —**Si•be′ri•an** *adj. & n.*

Si•be•ri•a[2] (sī-bîr′ē-ə) *n.* A remote undesirable locale.

Siberian husky *n.* See **husky**[3] 1.

sib•i•lant (sĭb′ə-lənt) *adj.* Of, characterized by, or producing a hissing sound like that of (s) or (sh). ❖ *n.* A sibilant speech sound, such as English (s), (sh), (z), or (zh). —**sib′i•lance, sib′i•lan•cy** *n.* —**sib′i•lant•ly** *adv.*

sib•i•late (sĭb′ə-lāt′) *intr. & tr.v.* **-lat•ed, -lat•ing, -lates** To utter or pronounce with a hissing sound. [Lat. *sībilāre, sībilāt-*, to hiss.] —**sib′i•la′tion** *n.*

Si•biu (sē-byoo′) A city of central Romania NW of Bucharest; settled in the 12th cent. by German colonists. Pop. 168,619.

sib•ling (sĭb′lĭng) *n.* One of two or more individuals having one or both parents in common; a brother or sister. [ME < OE *sibb, kinsman.* See SIB.]

Si•bu•yan Sea (sē′boo-yän′) A sea in the central Philippines bordered by S Luzon, Mindoro, and the Visayan Is.

sib•yl (sĭb′əl) *n.* **1.** One of a number of women regarded as oracles or prophets by the ancient Greeks and Romans. **2.** A woman prophet. [ME *sibile* < OFr. < Lat. *Sibylla* < Gk. *Sibulla*.]

sib•yl•line (sĭb′ə-lĭn′, -lēn′) also **si•byl•ic** or **si•byl•lic** (sĭ-bĭl′ĭk) *adj.* **1.** Coming from, characteristic of, or relating to a sibyl. **2.** Prophetic; oracular.

sic[1] (sĭk) *adv.* Thus; so. Used to indicate that a quoted passage, esp. one containing an error or unconventional spelling, has been retained in its original form or written intentionally. [Lat. *sīc.* See so- in App.]

sic[2] also **sick** (sĭk) *tr.v.* **sicced, sic•cing, sics** also **sicked, sick•**

ing, sicks 1. To set upon; attack. **2.** To urge or incite to hostile action; set. [Dialectal var. of SEEK.]

Sic. *abbr.* **1.** Sicilian **2.** Sicily

sic•ca•tive (sĭk′ə-tĭv) *n.* A substance added to paints and some medicines to promote drying; a drier. [LLat. *siccatīvus,* drying < Lat. *siccātus,* p. part. of *siccāre,* to dry < *siccus,* dry.]

Si•chuan also **Sze•chwan** or **Sze•chuan** (sĕch′wän′) A province of S-central China; incorporated into the empire c. 3rd cent. A.D. Cap. Chengdu. Pop. 107,218,173.

Si•ci•ly (sĭs′ə-lē) An island of S Italy in the Mediterranean Sea W of the S end of the Italian peninsula; came under the control of the Normans in the 11th cent. A.D. and formed the nucleus of the Kingdom of the Two Sicilies, consisting of Sicily and S Italy. A later Sicilian kingdom was conquered by Garibaldi in 1860. —**Si•cil′ian** (sĭ-sĭl′yən) *adj. & n.*

sick[1] (sĭk) *adj.* **sick•er, sick•est 1a.** Suffering from or affected with a physical illness; ailing. **b.** Of or for sick persons. **c.** Nauseated. **2a.** Mentally ill or disturbed. **b.** Unwholesome, morbid, or sadistic: *a sick crime.* **3.** Defective; unsound: *a sick economy.* **4a.** Deeply distressed; upset. **b.** Disgusted; revolted. **c.** Weary; tired. **d.** Pining; longing. **5a.** In need of repairs: *a sick ship.* **b.** Constituting an unhealthy environment for those working or residing within: *a sick office building.* **6.** Unable to produce a profitable yield of crops. ❖ *n.* (*used with a pl. verb*) Sick people considered as a group. —*idiom:* **sick and tired** Thoroughly weary, discouraged, or bored. [ME < OE *sēoc.*]

sick[2] (sĭk) *v.* Variant of sic[2].

sick•bay (sĭk′bā′) *n.* **1.** The hospital and dispensary of a ship. **2.** A place where the sick or injured are treated.

sick•bed (sĭk′bĕd′) *n.* A sick person's bed.

sick building syndrome *n.* A complex of symptoms primarily affecting office workers, usu. involving skin irritation, headache, and respiratory problems, and attributed to indoor pollutants, poor ventilation, or the presence of microorganisms.

sick call *n.* **1.** A lineup of military personnel requiring medical attention. **2.** A signal announcing the time for such a lineup.

sick day *n.* A paid day off allowed an employee because of sickness.

sick•en (sĭk′ən) *tr. & intr.v.* **-ened, -en•ing, -ens** To make or become sick. See Syns at **disgust.** —**sick′en•er** *n.*

sick•en•ing (sĭk′ə-nĭng) *adj.* **1.** Revolting or disgusting; loathsome. **2.** Causing sickness. —**sick′en•ing•ly** *adv.*

sick headache *n.* **1.** A headache accompanied by nausea. **2.** A migraine.

sick•ie (sĭk′ē) *n.* *Slang* A deranged, psychotic, or morbidly obsessed person.

sick•ish (sĭk′ĭsh) *adj.* **1.** Somewhat sick. **2.** Somewhat nauseated. **3.** Somewhat revolting or nauseating. —**sick′ish•ly** *adv.*

sick•le (sĭk′əl) *n.* **1.** An implement having a semicircular blade attached to a short handle, used for cutting grain or tall grass. **2.** The cutting mechanism of a reaper or mower. ❖ *v.* **-led, -ling, -les** —*tr.* **1.** To cut with a sickle. **2.** To deform (a red blood cell) into an abnormal crescent shape. —*intr.* To assume an abnormal crescent shape. Used of red blood cells. [ME *sikel* < OE *sicol* < VLat. **sicila* < Lat. *secula.* See sek- in App.]

sick leave *n.* Paid absence from work allowed an employee because of sickness.

sick•le•bill (sĭk′əl-bĭl′) *n.* Any of several birds having long, sharply curved bills, such as *Hemignathus procerus,* a Hawaiian honeycreeper.

sickle cell *n.* An abnormal crescent-shaped red blood cell that results from a single change in the amino acid sequence of the cell's hemoglobin, which causes the cell to contort.

sickle cell anemia *n.* A hereditary form of chronic anemia in which a mutant hemoglobin gene causes red blood cells to assume a crescent shape, characterized by severe joint pain, fever, leg ulcers, and jaundice, and affecting almost exclusively Black people of Africa or of African descent.

sickle cell trait *n.* A hereditary condition, usu. harmless and without symptoms, in which an individual carries only one gene for sickle cell anemia.

sickle feather *n.* Any of the long curving feathers in the tail of a rooster.

sick•le•mi•a (sĭk′ə-lē′mē-ə) *n.* Sickle cell anemia or sickle cell trait.

sick•ly (sĭk′lē) *adj.* **-li•er, -li•est 1.** Prone to sickness. **2.** Of, caused by, or associated with sickness. **3.** Conducive to sickness. **4.** Causing nausea; nauseating. **5.** Lacking vigor or strength; feeble or weak. ❖ *tr.v.* **-lied, -ly•ing, -lies** To make sickly. —**sick′li•ness** *n.* —**sick′ly** *adv.*

sick•ness (sĭk′nĭs) *n.* **1.** The condition of being sick; illness. **2.** A disease; a malady. **3.** Nausea. **4.** A defective or unsound condition.

sick•o (sĭk′ō) *n., pl.* **-os** *Slang* A deranged, psychotic, or morbidly obsessed person. [< SICK[1].]

sick•out (sĭk′out′) *n.* An organized job action in which employees absent themselves from work on the pretext of illness.

sick pay *n.* Wages paid to an employee who is absent because of illness.

sick•room (sĭk′rōōm′, -rŏŏm′) *n.* A room occupied by a sick person.

Siamese cat

Siamese fighting fish
Betta splendens
male (top) and female
Siamese fighting fish

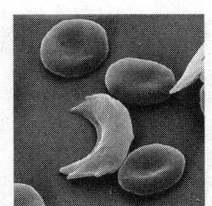

sickle cell
with three normal red
blood cells

ă	pat	oi	boy
ā	pay	ou	out
âr	care	ŏŏ	took
ä	father	ōō	boot
ĕ	pet	ŭ	cut
ē	be	ûr	urge
ĭ	pit	th	thin
ī	pie	*th*	this
îr	pier	hw	which
ŏ	pot	zh	vision
ō	toe	ə	about,
ô	paw		item

Stress marks:
′ (primary);
′ (secondary), as in
lexicon (lĕk′sĭ-kŏn′)

sic pas·sim (sĭk păs′ĭm) *adv.* Thus everywhere. Used to indicate that a term or an idea is to be found throughout a text. [Lat. *sīc passim* : *sīc*, thus + *passim*, everywhere.]

Sic·y·on (sĭsh′ē-ŏn′, sĭs′-) An ancient city of S Greece in the NE Peloponnesus near the Gulf of Corinth; at the height of its power in the 6th cent. B.C.

Sid·dons (sĭd′nz), **Sarah** 1755–1831. British actress known for her Shakespearean roles, esp. Lady Macbeth.

sid·dur (sĭd′ər, -oor′, sĕ-door′) *n.*, *pl.* **sid·du·rim** (sĭ-door′ĭm, sĭ′doo-rĭm′) *Judaism* A prayer book. [Mishnaic Heb. *siddûr*, arrangement < *siddēr*, to arrange, derived stem of *sādar*.]

side (sīd) *n.* **1.** *Mathematics* **a.** A line bounding a plane figure. **b.** A surface bounding a solid figure. **2.** A surface of an object, esp. a surface joining a top and bottom: *the four sides of a box.* **3.** A surface of an object that extends more or less perpendicularly from an observer standing in front: *the side of the ship.* **4.** Either of the two surfaces of a flat object: *the two sides of a CD.* **5a.** The part within an object or area to the left or right of the observer or of its vertical axis. **b.** The left or right half of the trunk of a human or animal body. **6a.** The space immediately next to someone. **b.** The space immediately next to something. Often used in combination: *dockside.* **7.** One of two or more contrasted parts or places within an area, identified by its location with respect to a center: *the north side of the park.* **8.** An area separated from another area by an intervening feature, such as a line or barrier: *this side of the Atlantic.* **9a.** One of two or more opposing individuals, groups, teams, or sets of opinions. **b.** One of the positions maintained in a dispute or debate. **10.** A distinct aspect: *his shy side.* **11.** Line of descent: *my aunt on my mother's side.* **12.** An incomplete script that shows the lines and cues of a single performer only. Often used in the plural. **13.** *Chiefly British* Affected superiority; arrogance. ❖ *adj.* **1.** Located on a side. **2.** From or to one side; oblique: *a side view.* **3.** Minor; incidental. **4.** In addition to the main part; supplementary. ❖ *v.* **sid·ed, sid·ing, sides** —*tr.* **1.** To provide sides or siding for. **2.** To be positioned next to. **3.** To be in agreement with; support. —*intr.* To align oneself in a disagreement. —*idioms:* **on the side 1.** In addition to the main portion. **2.** In addition to the main occupation or activity. **side by side** Next to each other; close together. **this side of** *Informal* Verging on; short of. [ME < OE *sīde*.]

side·arm (sīd′ärm′) *adj.* *Sports* Thrown with or marked by a sideways motion of the arm between shoulder and hip height and relatively parallel to the ground. —**side′arm′** *adv.*

side arm *n.* A small weapon carried at the side or waist.

side·band also **side band** (sīd′bănd′) *n.* Either of the two bands of frequencies, one just above and one just below a carrier frequency, that result from modulation of a carrier wave.

side·bar (sīd′bär′) *n.* A short, often boxed auxiliary news story that is printed alongside a longer article and typically presents additional, contrasting, or late-breaking news.

side·board (sīd′bôrd′, -bōrd′) *n.* **1.** A piece of dining room furniture having drawers and shelves for linens and tableware. **2.** A board that forms a side or part of a side.

side·burns (sīd′bûrnz′) *pl.n.* Growths of hair down the sides of a man's face in front of the ears. [Alteration of BURNSIDES.]

side·car (sīd′kär′) *n.* **1.** A one-wheeled car for a passenger, attached to the side of a motorcycle. **2.** A cocktail combining brandy, an orange-flavored liqueur, and lemon juice.

side chair *n.* A straight-backed chair without arms.

sid·ed (sī′dĭd) *adj.* Having sides usu. of a specified number or kind. Often used in combination: *many-sided; marble-sided.* —**sid′ed·ness** *n.*

side dish *n.* A dish served as an accompaniment to the main course.

side drum *n.* See snare drum.

side effect *n.* A peripheral or secondary effect, esp. an undesirable secondary effect of a drug or therapy.

side·kick (sīd′kĭk′) *n.* *Slang* A close companion or comrade.

side·light (sīd′līt′) *n.* **1.** A light coming from the side. **2.** *Nautical* Either of two lights, red to port, green to starboard, shown by ships at night. **3.** A piece of incidental information.

side·line (sīd′līn′) *n.* *Sports* **a.** A line along either of the two sides of a playing court or field, marking its limits. **b. sidelines** The space outside such limits. **2. sidelines** The position or point of view of those who observe rather than participate in an activity: *the political sidelines.* **3.** A subsidiary line of merchandise. **4.** An activity pursued in addition to one's regular occupation. ❖ *tr.v.* **-lined, -lin·ing, -lines** *Informal* To remove or keep from active participation.

side·ling (sīd′lĭng) *adj.* **1.** Directed to one side; oblique. **2.** Sloping; inclined. ❖ *adv.* Obliquely; sideways.

side·long (sīd′lông′, -lŏng′) *adj.* **1.** Directed to one side; sideways. **2.** So as to slant; sloping. ❖ *adv.* **1.** On or toward the side; sideways. **2.** In an oblique manner. [Alteration of SIDELING.]

side·man (sīd′măn′) *n.* A member of a jazz band who is not the leader or a featured soloist.

side·piece (sīd′pēs′) *n.* A part forming the side of something.

si·de·re·al (sī-dîr′ē-əl) *adj.* **1.** Of, relating to, or concerned with the stars or constellations; stellar. **2.** Measured or determined by means of the apparent daily motion of the stars. [< Lat. *sīdereus* < *sīdus, sīder-*, constellation, star.]

sidereal day *n.* The time required for a complete rotation of the earth in reference to the vernal equinox at the meridian, equal to 23 hours, 56 minutes, 4.09 seconds of mean solar time.

sidereal hour *n.* A 24th part of a sidereal day.

sidereal month *n.* The average period of revolution of the moon around the earth in reference to a fixed star, equal to 27 days, 7 hours, 43 minutes of mean solar time.

sidereal time *n.* Time based on the rotation of the earth with reference to the background of stars.

sidereal year *n.* The time required for one complete revolution of the earth about the sun, relative to the fixed stars, or 365 days, 6 hours, 9 minutes, 9.54 seconds of mean solar time.

sid·er·ite (sĭd′ə-rīt′) *n.* **1.** An ore of iron, $FeCO_3$. **2.** A meteorite consisting mainly of iron and nickel.

sidero– or **sider–** *pref.* Iron: *siderolite.* [Gk. *sīdēro-* < *sīderos.*]

sid·er·o·lite (sĭd′ər-ə-līt′) *n.* A meteorite composed of a mixed mass of iron and stone.

sid·er·o·sis (sĭd′ə-rō′sĭs) *n.* Chronic inflammation of the lungs caused by excessive inhalation of dust containing iron.

side·sad·dle (sīd′săd′l) *n.* A saddle designed so that the rider sits with both legs on one side of the horse. ❖ *adv.* On a sidesaddle.

side·show (sīd′shō′) *n.* **1.** A small show offered in addition to the main attraction. **2.** An incidental diversion or spectacle.

side·slip (sīd′slĭp′) *intr.v.* **-slipped, -slip·ping, -slips 1.** To slip or skid to one side. **2.** To slide sideways and downward in skiing. **3.** To fly sideways and downward in an airplane along the lateral axis to reduce altitude without gaining speed or from banking too deeply. —**side′slip′** *n.*

side·spin (sīd′spĭn′) *n.* A rotary motion that spins a ball horizontally.

side·split·ting (sīd′splĭt′ĭng) *adj.* **1.** Convulsively hearty; uproarious. Used of laughter. **2.** Causing convulsive laughter; extremely funny. —**side′split′ting·ly** *adv.*

side·step (sīd′stĕp′) *v.* **-stepped, -step·ping, -steps** —*intr.* **1.** To step aside: *sidestepped to make way.* **2.** To dodge an issue or a responsibility. —*tr.* **1.** To step out of the way of. **2.** To evade; skirt: *sidestep a question.* —**side′step′per** *n.*

side step *n.* A step to one side, as in boxing or dancing.

side·stroke (sīd′strōk′) *n.* A swimming stroke in which a person swims on one side and thrusts the arms forward and downward alternately while performing a scissors kick. —**side′stroke′** *v.* —**side′strok′er** *n.*

side·swipe (sīd′swīp′) *tr.v.* **-swiped, -swip·ing, -swipes** To strike along the side in passing. ❖ *n.* **1.** A glancing blow on the side. **2.** An incidental critical remark. —**side′swip′er** *n.*

side·track (sīd′trăk′) *v.* **-tracked, -track·ing, -tracks** —*tr.* **1.** To divert from a main issue or course. **2.** To delay or block the progress of deliberately. **3.** To switch from a main railroad track to a siding. —*intr.* **1.** To deviate from a main issue or course. **2.** To run into a siding. ❖ *n.* A railroad siding.

side·walk (sīd′wôk′) *n.* A paved walkway along a street.

sidewalk superintendent *n.* *Slang* A pedestrian who stops to watch construction or demolition work.

side·wall (sīd′wôl′) *n.* **1.** A wall that forms the side of something. **2.** A side surface of an automobile tire, between the edge of the tread and the wheel rim.

side·ward (sīd′wərd) *adv. & adj.* Toward or at one side. —**side′wards** (-wərdz) *adv.*

side·ways (sīd′wāz′) also **side·way** (-wā′) *adv. & adj.* **1.** Toward one side: *took a step sideways.* **2.** From one side: *sideways pressure.* **3.** With the side forward: *turned sideways.*

side-wheel (sīd′hwēl′, -wēl′) *adj.* Of, relating to, or being a steamboat with a paddle wheel on each side.

side-wheel·er (sīd′hwē′lər, -wē′-) *n.* A side-wheel steamboat.

side-whisk·ers (sīd′hwĭs′kərz, -wĭs′-) *pl.n.* Whiskers worn usu. long on the sides of a man's face.

side·wind·er (sīd′wīn′dər) *n.* **1.** A small rattlesnake (*Crotalus cerastes*) of the southwest United States and Mexico that moves by a distinctive lateral looping motion of its body. **2.** A powerful swinging punch delivered from the side.

side·wise (sīd′wīz′) *adv. & adj.* Sideways.

sid·ing (sī′dĭng) *n.* **1.** Material, such as boards, used for surfacing the outside walls of a frame building. **2.** A short section of railroad track connected by switches with a main track.

si·dle (sīd′l) *v.* **-dled, -dling, -dles** —*intr.* **1.** To move sideways. **2.** To advance in an unobtrusive, furtive, or coy way. —*tr.* To cause to move sideways. ❖ *n.* **1.** An unobtrusive, furtive, or coy advance. **2.** A sideways movement. [Back-formation < SIDELING.] —**si′dling·ly** *adv.*

Sid·ney (sĭd′nē), **Sir Philip** 1554–86. English poet, soldier, and politician whose works include the sonnet sequence *Astrophel and Stella* and the collection of pastoral idylls *Arcadia.*

Si·don (sīd′n) An ancient city of Phoenicia on the Mediterranean Sea in present-day SW Lebanon; known for its glassware and purple dyes.

Sid·ra (sĭd′rə), **Gulf of** An inlet of the Mediterranean Sea off N Libya W of Benghazi.

SIDS *abbr.* sudden infant death syndrome

siege (sēj) *n.* **1.** The surrounding and blockading of a city, town, or fortress by an army attempting to capture it. **2.** A prolonged period, as of illness: *a siege of asthma.* **3.** *Obsolete* A seat, esp. a throne. ❖ *tr.v.* **sieged, sieg•ing, sieg•es** To subject to a siege; besiege. [ME *sege* < OFr., seat < VLat. **sedicum* < **sedicāre*, to sit < Lat. *sedēre*. See **sed-** in App.]

Siege Perilous *n.* In Arthurian legend, a seat at King Arthur's Round Table kept for the knight destined to find the Holy Grail and fatal for any other occupant.

Sieg•fried (sēg′frēd′, sĭg′-) *n.* The hero of the *Nibelungenlied* and other Germanic medieval epics. [Ger. < MHGer. *Sīgfrit* < OHGer. *Sigifrith* : *sigu*, victory; see **segh-** in App. + *fridu*, peace; see **prī-** in App.]

sie•mens (sē′mənz) *n., pl.* **siemens** A unit of electrical conductance in the International System, equal to one ampere per volt. [After Ernst Werner von SIEMENS.]

Siemens (sē′mənz, zē′-), Sir **Charles William** 1823–83. German-born British engineer who invented a regenerative steam engine and designed a steamship for laying long-distance cables. His brother **Ernst Werner von Siemens** (1816–92) was a noted electrical engineer.

Si•en•a (sē-ĕn′ə, syĕ′nä) A city of W-central Italy S of Florence; founded by Etruscans. Pop. 61,888. —**Si′e•nese′** (-nēz′, -nēs′) *adj. & n.*

Sien•kie•wicz (shĕn-kyā′vĭch, -kyĕ′-), **Henryk** 1846–1916. Polish writer who won the 1905 Nobel Prize for literature.

si•en•na (sē-ĕn′ə) *n.* **1.** A special clay containing iron and manganese oxides, used as a pigment for oil and watercolor painting. **2a.** Raw sienna. **b.** Burnt sienna. [Short for *terra-sienna* < Ital. *terra di Sienna*, earth of Siena, after SIENA.]

si•er•ra (sē-ĕr′ə) *n.* **1.** A rugged range of mountains having an irregular or jagged profile. **2a.** A Spanish mackerel *(Scomberomorus sierra)* of the Pacific coast of tropical America. **b.** See **cero.** [Sp. < Lat. *serra*, saw.] —**si•er′ran** *adj.*

Sierra Le•one (lē-ōn′, -ō′nē) A country of W Africa on the Atlantic coast; a British protectorate from 1896 until it achieved independence in 1961. Cap. Freetown. Pop. 4,402,000.

Sierra Ma•dre del Sur (mä′drē dĕl so͝or′, mä′drā) A mountain range of S Mexico along the Pacific coast.

Sierra Madre Oc•ci•den•tal (ŏk′sĭ-dĕn′tl, ŏk′sē-dĕn-täl′) A mountain range of NW Mexico parallel to the Pacific coast and extending c. 1,609 km (1,000 mi) S from AZ.

Sierra Madre Or•ien•tal (ôr′ē-ĕn-täl′, ô-ryĕn-) A mountain range of NE Mexico rising as barren hills S of the Rio Grande and roughly paralleling the coast of the Gulf of Mexico.

Sierra Nevada 1. A mountain range of S Spain along the Mediterranean coast E of Granada rising to 3,480.4 m (11,411 ft). **2.** A mountain range of E CA extending c. 644 km (400 mi) between the Sacramento and San Joaquin valleys and the NV border and rising to 4,420.7 m (14,494 ft).

si•es•ta (sē-ĕs′tə) *n.* A rest or nap after the midday meal. [Sp. < Lat. *sexta (hōra)*, sixth (hour), midday, fem. of *sextus*, sixth. See SEXT.]

sieve (sĭv) *n.* A utensil of wire mesh or closely perforated metal, used for straining, sifting, ricing, or puréeing. ❖ *v.* **sieved, siev•ing, sieves** —*tr.* To pass through a sieve. —*intr.* To use a sieve; sift. [ME *sive* < OE *sife*.]

sie•vert (sē′vərt) *n.* The SI unit for the amount of ionizing radiation required to produce the same biological effect as one gray of high-penetration x-rays. [After Rolf Maximilian *Sievert* (1896–1966), Swedish radiologist.]

sieve tube *n.* A series of cells joined end to end, forming a tube through which nutrients are conducted in flowering plants and brown algae.

sift (sĭft) *v.* **sift•ed, sift•ing, sifts** —*tr.* **1.** To put (flour, for example) through a sieve or other straining device to separate out the coarse particles. **2.** To distinguish as if separating with a sieve. **3.** To apply by scattering with or as if with a sieve. **4.** To examine and sort carefully. —*intr.* **1.** To make use of a sieve. **2.** To pass through or as if through a sieve. **3.** To make a careful examination. [ME *siften* < OE *siftan*.] —**sift′er** *n.*

SIG *abbr.* special interest group

Sig. *abbr.* **1.** *Latin* signa (mark or label it) **2.** *Medicine* signature **3.** *Latin* signetur (let it be marked or labeled) **4a.** signor **b.** signore

sigh (sī) *v.* **sighed, sigh•ing, sighs** —*intr.* **1a.** To exhale audibly in a long deep breath, as in weariness or relief. **b.** To emit a similar sound: *willows sighing in the wind.* **2.** To feel longing or grief; yearn. —*tr.* **1.** To express with or as if with an audible exhalation. **2.** *Archaic* To lament. ❖ *n.* The act or sound of sighing. [ME *sighen*, prob. back-formation < *sighte*, p. t. of *siken*, to sigh < OE *sīcan*.] —**sigh′er** *n.*

sight (sīt) *n.* **1.** The ability to see. **2.** The act or fact of seeing. **3.** Field of vision. **4.** The foreseeable future; prospect: *no solution in sight.* **5.** Mental perception or consideration: *lost sight of our goals.* **6.** Something seen; a view. **7.** Something worth seeing; a spectacle. **8.** *Informal* Something unsightly. **9a.** A device used to assist aim by guiding the eye, as on a firearm or surveying instrument. **b.** An aim or observation taken with such a device. **10.** An opportunity to observe or inspect. **11.** *Upper Southern US* A large number or quantity. ❖ *v.* **sight•ed, sight•ing, sights** —*tr.* **1.** To perceive with the eyes; get sight of. **2.** To observe through a sight or an optical instrument. **3.** To adjust the sights of (a rifle, for example). **4.** To take aim with (a firearm). —*intr.* **1.** To direct one's gaze; look carefully. **2.** To take aim. —***idioms:* on sight** Immediately upon being seen. **out of sight** *Slang* Remarkable; incredible. **sight for sore eyes** *Informal* One whom it is a relief or joy to see. **sight unseen** Without seeing the object in question. [ME < OE *sihth, gesiht*, something seen. See **sek**^{w}-^{2} in App.]

sight draft *n.* A draft or bill payable on demand or upon presentation.

sight•ed (sī′tĭd) *adj.* **1.** Having the ability to see. **2.** Having eyesight of a specified kind. Often used in combination: *keen-sighted.* —**sight′ed•ness** *n.*

sight gag *n.* A comic bit or effect that depends on sight.

sight•ing (sī′tĭng) *n.* The act of catching sight of something, esp. something unusual or searched for.

sight•less (sīt′lĭs) *adj.* **1.** Unable to see with the eyes; blind. **2.** Invisible. —**sight′less•ly** *adv.* —**sight′less•ness** *n.*

sight•line also **sight line** (sīt′līn′) *n.* A line of sight, esp. one between a spectator and a performance, as in a theater.

sight•ly (sīt′lē) *adj.* **-li•er, -li•est 1.** Pleasing or appealing to see. **2.** Affording a fine view; scenic. —**sight′li•ness** *n.*

sight-read (sīt′rēd′) *v.* **-read** (-rĕd′), **-read•ing, -reads** —*tr.* To read or perform (music, for example) without preparation or prior acquaintance. —*intr.* To sight-read something. —**sight′-read′er** *n.*

sight rhyme *n.* See **eye rhyme.**

sight•see (sīt′sē′) *intr.v.* **-saw** (-sô′), **-seen** (-sēn′), **-see•ing, -sees** To tour sights of interest. —**sight′se′er** *n.*

sight•see•ing (sīt′sē′ĭng) *n.* The act or pastime of visiting sights of interest. ❖ *adj.* Used or engaged in sightseeing.

sig•il (sĭj′əl, sĭg′ĭl) *n.* **1.** A seal; a signet. **2.** A sign or an image considered magical. [Lat. *sigillum*, dim. of *signum*, sign. See **sek**^{w}-^{1} in App.]

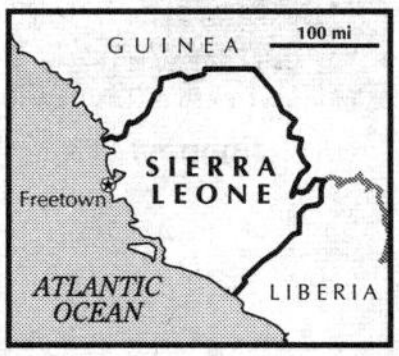

Sierra Leone

Sig•is•mund (sĭg′ĭs-mənd) 1368–1437. Holy Roman emperor (1433–37) and king of Hungary (1387–1437) and Bohemia (1419–37) who helped end the Great Schism (1378–1417) by convening the Council of Constance (1414–18).

sig•ma (sĭg′mə) *n.* **1.** The 18th letter of the Greek alphabet. **2.** A sigma baryon. [Gk. *sīgma* < Phoenician **samk*, support (sense uncertain), 15th letter of the Phoenician alphabet.] —**sig′mate′** (-māt′) *adj.*

sigma baryon *n.* Any of three unstable subatomic particles in the baryon family, having a mass 2,328 to 2,343 times that of the electron and a positive, neutral, or negative electron charge.

sig•moid (sĭg′moid′) also **sig•moi•dal** (sĭg-moid′l) *adj.* **1.** Having the shape of the letter S. **2.** Of or relating to the sigmoid colon. [Gk. *sīgmoeidēs* : *sīgma*, sigma; see SIGMA + *-oeidēs*, -oid.]

sigmoid colon *n.* An S-shaped section of the colon between the descending section and the rectum.

sig•moid•o•scope (sĭg-moi′də-skōp′) *n.* A tubular instrument for visual examination of the sigmoid colon. —**sig•moid′o•scop′ic** (-skŏp′ĭk) *adj.* —**sig′moid•os′co•py** (sĭg′moi-dŏs′kə-pē) *n.*

sign (sīn) *n.* **1.** Something that suggests the presence or existence of a fact, condition, or quality. **2a.** An act or gesture used to convey an idea, a desire, information, or a command. **b.** Sign language. **3a.** A displayed structure bearing lettering or symbols, used to identify or advertise a place of business. **b.** A posted notice bearing a designation, direction, or command. **4.** A conventional figure or device that stands for a word, phrase, or operation; a symbol, as in mathematics or in musical notation. **5.** *pl.* **sign** An indicator, such as a footprint, of the trail of an animal. **6.** A trace or vestige: *no sign of life.* **7.** A portentous incident or event; a presage. **8.** A bodily manifestation that serves to indicate the presence of malfunction or disease. **9.** One of the 12 divisions of the zodiac, each represented by a symbol. ❖ *v.* **signed, sign•ing, signs** —*tr.* **1.** To affix one's signature to. **2.** To write (one's signature). **3.** To approve or ratify (a document) by affixing a signature, seal, or other mark: *sign a bill into law.* **4.** To hire or engage by obtaining a signature on a contract. **5.** To relinquish or transfer title to (property) by signature. **6.** To provide with a sign or signs. **7.** To communicate with a sign or signs: *signed his approval with a nod.* **8.** To express by sign language: *signed her reply to the question.* **9.** To consecrate with the sign of the cross. —*intr.* **1.** To make a sign or signs; signal. **2.** To use sign language. **3.** To write one's signature. —***phrasal verbs:* sign in** To record the arrival of another or oneself by signing a register. **sign off 1.** To announce the end of a communication; conclude. **2.** To stop transmission after identifying the broadcasting station. **3.** *Informal* To express approval formally or conclusively: *got Congress to sign off on the new tax proposal.* **sign on 1.** *Informal* To enlist oneself, esp. as an employee. **2.** To start transmission with an identification of the broadcasting station. **sign out** To record the departure of another or oneself by signing a register. **sign up** To agree to be a participant or recipient by signing one's name; enlist: *sign up for military service.* [ME *signe* < OFr. < Lat. *signum*. See **sek**^{w}-^{1} in App.] —**sign′er** *n.*

Si•gnac (sēn-yăk′), **Paul** 1863–1935. French neoimpressionist painter whose works include *Port of St. Tropez* (1916).

sign•age (sī′nĭj) *n.* **1.** Signs considered as a group. **2.** The design or use of signs and symbols.

sig•nal (sĭg′nəl) *n.* **1a.** An indicator, such as a gesture or colored light, that serves as a means of communication. **b.** A message

ă	**pat**	oi	**boy**
ā	**pay**	ou	**out**
âr	**care**	o͝o	**took**
ä	**father**	o͞o	**boot**
ĕ	**pet**	ŭ	**cut**
ē	**be**	ûr	**urge**
ĭ	**pit**	th	**thin**
ī	**pie**	*th*	**this**
îr	**pier**	hw	**which**
ŏ	**pot**	zh	**vision**
ō	**toe**	ə	**about, item**
ô	**paw**		

Stress marks:
′ (primary);
′ (secondary), as in
lexicon (lĕk′sĭ-kŏn′)

signpost

silhouette
*Master James Ronnie
Swinton and Donald, 1830,
by Augustin Edouart
(1789–1861)*

communicated by such means. **2.** Something that incites action. **3.** *Electronics* An impulse or a fluctuating electric quantity, such as voltage, whose variations represent coded information. **4.** The sound, image, or message transmitted or received in telegraphy, telephony, radio, television, or radar. ❖ *adj.* Notably out of the ordinary: *a signal feat.* ❖ *v.* **-naled, -nal•ing, -nals** or **-nalled, -nal•ling, -nals** —*tr.* **1.** To make a signal to. **2.** To relate or make known by signals. —*intr.* To make a signal or signals. [ME < OFr. < Med.Lat. *signāle* < neut. of LLat. *signālis*, of a sign < Lat. *signum*, sign. See SIGN.] —**sig′nal•er, sig′nal′ler** *n.*

sig•nal•ize (sĭg′nə-līz′) *tr.v.* **-ized, -iz•ing, -iz•es 1.** To make remarkable or conspicuous. **2.** To point out particularly. —**sig′nal•i•za′tion** (-lĭ-zā′shən) *n.*

sig•nal•ly (sĭg′nə-lē) *adv.* To a conspicuous degree; notably.

sig•nal•ment (sĭg′nəl-mənt) *n.* A detailed description of a person's appearance, as for police files. [Fr. *signalement* < *signaler*, to mark out < *signal*, signal. See SIGNAL.]

sig•na•to•ry (sĭg′nə-tôr′ē, -tōr′ē) *adj.* Bound by signed agreement. ❖ *n.*, *pl.* **-ries** One that has signed a treaty or other document. [Lat. *signātōrius* < *signātus*, p. part. of *signāre*, to mark < *signum*, sign. See SIGN.]

sig•na•ture (sĭg′nə-chər) *n.* **1.** One's name as written by oneself. **2.** The act of signing one's name. **3.** A distinctive mark, characteristic, or sound indicating identity. **4.** *Medicine* The part of a physician's prescription containing directions to the patient. **5.** *Music* **a.** A sign used to indicate key. **b.** A sign used to indicate tempo. **6.** *Printing* **a.** A letter, number, or symbol at the bottom of the first page on each sheet of printed pages as a guide to the sequence of the sheets in binding. **b.** A large sheet printed with a multiple of four pages that when folded becomes a section of the book. [Fr. < OFr. < Med.Lat. *signātūra* < Lat. *signātus*, p. part. of *signāre*, to mark < *signum*, sign. See SIGN.]

sign•board (sīn′bôrd′, -bōrd′) *n.* A board bearing a sign.

signed (sīnd) *adj.* **1.** Having a signature affixed. **2.** Of, relating to, or expressed in a sign language.

sign•ee (sī-nē′) *n.* One who has signed a document, such as a contract.

sig•net (sĭg′nĭt) *n.* **1.** A seal, esp. one used officially to mark documents. **2.** The impression made with such a seal. ❖ *tr.v.* **-net•ed, -net•ing, -nets** To mark or endorse with a signet. [ME < OFr., dim. of *signe*, sign. See SIGN.]

signet ring *n.* A finger ring bearing an engraved signet.

sig•nif•i•cance (sĭg-nĭf′ĭ-kəns) also **sig•nif•i•can•cy** (-kən-sē) *n.* **1.** The state or quality of being significant. **2.** A meaning that is expressed. **3.** A covert or implied meaning. See Syns at **meaning.**

sig•nif•i•cant (sĭg-nĭf′ĭ-kənt) *adj.* **1.** Having or expressing a meaning; meaningful. **2.** Having or expressing a covert meaning; suggestive: *a significant glance.* See Syns at **expressive. 3.** Having or likely to have a major effect; important. **4.** Fairly large in amount or quantity. **5.** *Statistics* Of or relating to observations or occurrences that are too closely correlated to be attributed only to chance. [Lat. *significāns, significant-*, pr. part. of *significāre*, to signify. See SIGNIFY.] —**sig•nif′i•cant•ly** *adv.*

significant digits *pl.n.* The digits of a decimal number beginning with the leftmost nonzero digit and extending to the right to include all digits warranted by the accuracy in measurement.

significant other *n.* **1.** A person with whom one shares a long-term relationship. **2.** An important or influential person in one's life.

sig•ni•fi•ca•tion (sĭg′nə-fĭ-kā′shən) *n.* **1.** The established meaning of a word. See Syns at **meaning. 2.** The act of signifying; indication.

sig•nif•i•ca•tive (sĭg-nĭf′ĭ-kā′tĭv) *adj.* **1.** Tending to signify or indicate; indicative. **2.** Having meaning; significant. —**sig•nif′i•ca′tive•ness** *n.*

sig•ni•fied (sĭg′nə-fīd′) *n. Linguistics* The concept that a signifier denotes. [Transl. of Fr. *signifié.*]

sig•ni•fi•er (sĭg′nə-fī′ər) *n.* **1.** One that signifies. **2.** *Linguistics* A linguistic unit or pattern, such as a succession of speech sounds, written symbols, or gestures, that conveys meaning. [Transl. of Fr. *signifiant.*]

sig•ni•fy (sĭg′nə-fī′) *v.* **-fied, -fy•ing, -fies** —*tr.* **1.** To denote; mean. **2.** To make known, as with a sign or word: *signify one's intent.* —*intr.* **1.** To have meaning or importance. See Syns at **count**[1]. **2.** *Slang* To exchange humorous insults in a verbal game. [ME *signifien* < OFr. *signifier* < Lat. *significāre* : *signum*, sign; see SIGN + *-ficāre*, *-ficāre*.] —**sig′ni•fi′a•ble** *adj.* —**sig′ni•fi′er** *n.*

sign language *n.* **1.** A language that uses a system of manual, facial, and other body movements as the means of communication, esp. among deaf people. **2.** A method of communication that uses hand movements and other gestures.

sign manual *n.*, *pl.* **signs manual** A signature, esp. that of a monarch at the top of a royal decree.

sign of the cross *n.* In Christianity, a sign made by tracing the outline of a cross with the right hand as a devotional act or to invoke a blessing.

si•gnor also **si•gnior** (sēn-yôr′, -yōr′) *n.*, *pl.* **si•gno•ri** (sēn-yôr′ē, -yōr′ē) also **si•gniors** or **si•gnors** Used as a courtesy title for a man in an Italian-speaking area. [Ital., var. of *signore.* See SIGNORE.]

si•gno•ra (sēn-yôr′ə, -yōr′ə, -yō′rä) *n.*, *pl.* **si•gno•re** (sēn-

yôr′ā, -yōr′ā, -yō′rē) or **si•gno•ras** Used as a courtesy title for a married woman in an Italian-speaking area. [Ital., fem. of *signore.* See SIGNORE.]

si•gno•re (sēn-yôr′ā, -yōr′ā, -yō′rē) *n.* **1.** *pl.* **si•gno•ri** (-yôr′ē, -yō′rē) Used as a form of polite address for a man in an Italian-speaking area. **2.** A plural of **signora.** [Ital. < Med.Lat. *senior*, lord < Lat., elder; see SENIOR.]

si•gno•ri•na (sēn′yə-rē′nə, -yō-rē′nä) *n.*, *pl.* **-ne** (-nā, -ně) or **-nas** Used as a courtesy title for an unmarried woman or a girl in an Italian-speaking area. [Ital., dim. of *signora*, signora. See SIGNORA.]

si•gno•ry or **si•gnio•ry** (sēn′yə-rē) *n.*, *pl.* **-ries** See **seigniory.** [ME *signorie* < OFr. *seigneurie* < *seigneur*, seignior. See SEIGNIOR.]

sign•post (sīn′pōst′) *n.* **1.** A post supporting a sign that has information or directions. **2.** An indication, sign, or guide.

Sig•urd (sĭg′ərd) *n. Mythology* A hero in Norse myth who wins an accursed hoard of gold and is slain.

Si•ha•nouk (sē′ə-nook′), Prince **Norodom** b. 1922. Cambodian politician who served as prime minister (1955–57) and head of state (1960–70 and 1975–76).

Si•ha•sa•pa (sə-hä′sə-pə) *n.*, *pl.* **Sihasapa** or **-pas** A member of a Native American people constituting a subdivision of the Teton Sioux.

Sikh (sēk) *n.* An adherent of Sikhism. ❖ *adj.* Of or relating to the Sikhs or to Sikhism. [Hindi < Skt. *śiṣyaḥ*, disciple < *śikṣati*, he wishes to learn, desiderative of *śaknoti*, is able.]

Sikh•ism (sēk′ĭz′əm) *n.* The doctrines and practices of a monotheistic religion founded in northern India in the 16th century.

Si Kiang (sē′ kyäng′, shē′) See **Xi Jiang.**

Sik•kim (sĭk′ĭm) A region and former kingdom of NE India in the E Himalaya Mts. between Nepal and Bhutan; passed to India in 1949.

Si•kor•sky (sĭ-kôr′skē), **Igor Ivan** 1889–1972. Russian-born Amer. aviation pioneer who designed (1939) an early helicopter.

si•lage (sī′lĭj) *n.* Fodder prepared by storing and fermenting green forage plants in a silo. [Short for ENSILAGE.]

si•lane (sĭl′ān′) *n.* Any of a group of silicon hydrides having the general formula SiH that are analogous to the paraffin hydrocarbons. [SIL(ICON) + (METH)ANE.]

sild (sĭld) *n.*, *pl.* **sild** or **silds** A young herring other than a sprat that is processed as a sardine in Norway. [Norw. and Dan. < ON *sīld*, herring.]

sil•den•a•fil (sĭl-děn′ə-fĭl) *n.* A drug, $C_{22}H_{30}N_6O_4S$, used in the form of its citrate to treat sexual dysfunction by increasing the level of cyclic GMP, which increases blood flow to erectile tissues. [Perh. alter. of S(ULFON)YL + (PYRIMI)DINE + PH(EN)YL.]

si•lence (sī′ləns) *n.* **1.** The condition or quality of being or keeping still and silent. **2.** The absence of sound; stillness. **3.** A period of time without speech or noise. **4.** Refusal or failure to speak out. ❖ *tr.v.* **-lenced, -lenc•ing, -lenc•es 1.** To make silent or bring to silence: *silenced the crowd.* **2.** To curtail the expression of; suppress. [ME < OFr. < Lat. *silentium* < *silēns, silent-*, pr. part. of *silēre*, to be silent.]

si•lenc•er (sī′lən-sər) *n.* One that silences, esp. a device on the muzzle of a firearm to muffle the sound of firing.

si•lent (sī′lənt) *adj.* **1.** Marked by absence of noise or sound; still. **2.** Not inclined to speak; not talkative. **3.** Unable to speak. **4.** Refraining from speech: *Do be silent.* **5.** Not voiced or expressed; unspoken: *a silent curse.* **6.** Inactive; quiescent: *a silent volcano.* **7.** *Linguistics* Having no phonetic value; unpronounced, as the silent *b* in subtle. **8.** Having no spoken dialogue and usu. no soundtrack. Used of a film. **9.** Producing no detectable signs or symptoms: *a silent heart attack.* ❖ *n.* A silent movie. [Lat. *silēns, silent-*. See SILENCE.] —**si′lent•ly** *adv.* —**si′lent•ness** *n.*

SYNONYMS *silent, reticent, reserved, laconic* These adjectives describe people who are sparing with speech. *Silent* often implies a habitual disinclination to speak or to speak out: *"The coroner was a very silent man"* (Mary Roberts Rinehart). The term may also mean refraining from speech, as out of fear or confusion: *"The person in custody must . . . be clearly informed that he has the right to remain silent"* (Earl Warren). *Reticent* suggests a reluctance to share one's thoughts and feelings: *"She had been shy and reticent with me, and now . . . she was telling me aloud the secrets of her inmost heart"* (W.H. Hudson). *Reserved* suggests aloofness and reticence: *"a reserved man, whose inner life was intense and sufficient to him"* (Arnold Bennett). *Laconic* denotes terseness or conciseness in expression, but when applied to people it often implies an unwillingness to use words: *"Mountain dwellers and mountain lovers are a laconic tribe. They know the futility of words"* (Edna Ferber).

silent auction *n.* An auction where bids are submitted in writing.

silent butler *n.* A small receptacle with a handle and hinged cover, used for collecting ashes and crumbs.

silent partner *n.* One that makes financial investments in a business enterprise but does not share in management.

si•le•nus (sī-lē′nəs) *n.*, *pl.* **-ni** (-nī) *Greek Mythology* Any of the minor woodland deities and companions of Dionysus, depicted as men with the tails, ears, and hooves of horses. [Lat. *sīlēnus* < Gk. *sīlēnos* < *Sīlēnos*, Silenus.]

Silenus *n. Greek Mythology* A satyr, usu. depicted as drunken and jolly, in the entourage of Dionysus. [Lat. *Sīlēnus* < Gk. *Sīlēnos*.]

Si•le•sia (sī-lē′zhə, -shə, sĭ-) A region of central Europe primarily in SW Poland and N Czech Republic settled by Slavic peoples c. A.D. 500. —**Si•le′sian** *adj. & n.*

si•lex (sī′lĕks′) *n.* **1.** Silica. **2.** Finely ground tripoli used as an inert paint filler. [Lat., hard stone, flint.]

sil•hou•ette (sĭl′o͞o-ĕt′) *n.* **1.** A drawing consisting of the outline of something, esp. a human profile, filled in with a solid color. **2.** An outline that appears dark against a light background. See Syns at **outline.** ❖ *tr.v.* **-et•ted, -et•ting, -ettes** To cause to be seen as a silhouette; outline. [Fr., after Étienne de *Silhouette* (1709–67), French finance minister.]

sil•i•ca (sĭl′ĭ-kə) *n.* An abundant crystalline compound, SiO_2, occurring as quartz, sand, flint, agate, and many other minerals and used to make a variety of materials, esp. glass and concrete. [NLat. < Lat. *silex, silic-*, hard stone, flint.]

silica gel *n.* Amorphous silica that is used as a drying and dehumidifying agent, as a catalyst and catalyst carrier, as an anticaking agent in cosmetics, and in chromatography.

sil•i•cate (sĭl′ĭ-kāt′, -kĭt) *n.* **1.** Any of numerous compounds containing silicon, oxygen, and one or more metals. **2.** Any of a large group of minerals, forming over 90 percent of the earth's crust, that combine SiO_2 or SiO_4 ions with one or more metals.

si•li•ceous (sĭ-lĭsh′əs) *adj.* Containing, resembling, relating to, or consisting of silica. [< Lat. *siliceus*, of flint < *silex, silic-*, flint.]

silici– or **silic–** *pref.* **1.** Silicon: *silicate.* **2.** Silica: *silicify.* [< SILICON and SILICA.]

si•lic•ic (sĭ-lĭs′ĭk) *adj.* Relating to, resembling, containing, or derived from silica or silicon.

silicic acid *n.* A jellylike substance, H_2SiO_3, produced when sodium silicate solution is acidified.

sil•i•cide (sĭl′ĭ-sīd′) *n.* A compound of silicon with another element or radical.

si•lic•i•fy (sĭ-lĭs′ə-fī′) *v.* **-fied, -fy•ing, -fies** —*tr.* To convert into or impregnate with silica. —*intr.* To become converted into or impregnated with silica. —**si•lic′i•fi•ca′tion** (-fĭ-kā′shən) *n.*

sil•i•cle (sĭl′ĭ-kəl) *n.* A short silique usu. having a length less than three times its width. [Lat. *silicula*, dim. of *siliqua*, seed pod.]

sil•i•con (sĭl′ĭ-kən, -kŏn′) *n. Symbol* **Si** A nonmetallic element occurring extensively in the earth's crust in silica and silicates, having both an amorphous and a crystalline allotrope and used in glass, semiconducting devices, refractories, pottery, and silicones. Atomic number 14; atomic weight 28.086; melting point 1,410° C; boiling point 2,355°C; specific gravity 2.33; valence 4. See table at **element.** [< SILICA.]

silicon carbide *n.* A crystalline compound, SiC, one of the hardest known substances, used as an abrasive and heat-refractory material and in light-emitting diodes.

silicon dioxide *n.* Silica.

sil•i•cone (sĭl′ĭ-kōn′) *n.* Any of a group of semi-inorganic polymers of siloxane, characterized by high lubricity and thermal stability, extreme water repellence, and physiological inertness and used in adhesives, lubricants, paints, insulation, synthetic rubber, surgical implants, and prosthetics.

Silicon Valley A region of W CA SE of San Francisco known for its high-technology industries.

sil•i•co•sis (sĭl′ĭ-kō′sĭs) *n.* A disease of the lungs caused by continued inhalation of siliceous dust, marked by fibrosis and chronic shortness of breath. —**sil′i•cot′ic** (-kŏt′ĭk) *adj.*

si•lique (sĭ-lēk′) *n.* A dry dehiscent elongated fruit, characteristic of the mustard family, having two valves. [Fr. < OFr. < Lat. *siliqua*, seed pod.] —**sil′i•quous** (sĭl′ĭ-kwəs), **sil′i•quose′** (-kwōs′) *adj.*

silk (sĭlk) *n.* **1a.** A fiber produced by certain insect larvae to form cocoons, esp. the strong elastic fibrous secretion of silkworms used to make thread and fabric. **b.** Thread or fabric made of silk. **c.** A garment made of silk. **2. silks** The identifying garments of a jockey or harness driver. **3.** A silky filamentous material, such as the webbing spun by certain spiders or the styles forming a tuft on an ear of corn. ❖ *adj.* Composed of or similar to silk. ❖ *intr.v.* **silked, silk•ing, silks** To develop silk. Used of corn. [ME < OE *sioloc*, prob. of Slav. orig.; akin to O Church Slavonic *šelkŭ*, ult. < Gk. *sērikon*, neut. of *sērikos*, silken. See SERGE.]

silk cotton *n.* A silky fiber on the seeds of certain trees.

silk-cot•ton tree (sĭlk′kŏt′n) *n.* **1.** A spiny, deciduous, tropical tree *(Ceiba pentandra)* having palmately compound leaves and cultivated for its fruit that contain the silklike fiber kapok. **2.** Either of two trees *(Bombax ceiba* or *Cochlospermum religiosum)* having seeds surrounded by silky hairs.

silk•en (sĭl′kən) *adj.* **1.** Made of silk. **2.** Resembling silk in texture or appearance; smooth and lustrous. **3.** Delicately pleasing or caressing in effect. **4.** Luxurious.

silk hat *n.* A man's silk-covered top hat.

silk oak *n.* An Australian evergreen tree *(Grevillea robusta)* having divided fernlike leaves and showy orange flowers.

Silk Road An ancient trade route between China and the Mediterranean Sea extending some 6,440 km (4,000 mi) and linking China with the Roman Empire.

silk-screen also **silk•screen** (sĭlk′skrēn′) *n.* **1.** A stencil method of printmaking in which a design is imposed on a screen of silk or other fine mesh, with blank areas coated with an impermeable substance, and ink is forced through the mesh onto the printing surface. **2.** A print made by this method. —**silk′-screen′** *v.*

silk stocking *n.* A wealthy, aristocratic, or elegantly dressed person.

silk-stock•ing (sĭlk′stŏk′ĭng) *adj.* Wealthy; aristocratic.

silk tree *n.* An Asian tree *(Albizia julibrissin)* having pinnately compound leaves and pinkish flowers with many filaments.

silk•weed (sĭlk′wēd′) *n.* See **milkweed.**

silk•worm (sĭlk′wûrm′) *n.* Any of various caterpillars that produce silk cocoons, esp. the larva of a moth *(Bombyx mori)* native to Asia that spins a cocoon of fine strong lustrous fiber that is the source of commercial silk.

silk•y (sĭl′kē) *adj.* **-i•er, -i•est 1.** Resembling silk; lustrous. **2.** Made of silk; silken. **3.** Covered with or characterized by fine soft hairs or feathers: *a silky chick.* **4.** Ingratiating; seductive. —**silk′i•ly** *adv.* —**silk′i•ness** *n.*

silky terrier *n.* A toy terrier characterized by long silky bluish-gray hair, tan markings, and erect ears.

sill (sĭl) *n.* **1.** The horizontal member that bears the upright portion of a frame, esp. that forming the base of a window. **2.** *Geology* An approximately horizontal sheet of igneous rock intruded between older rock beds. [ME *sille* < OE *syll*, threshold.]

Sill, Mount A peak, 4,316.7 m (14,153 ft), in the Sierra Nevada range of E-central CA.

sil•la•bub (sĭl′ə-bŭb′) *n.* Variant of **syllabub.**

Sil•lan•pää (sĭl′ən-pă′), **Frans Eemil** 1888–1964. Finnish writer who won the 1939 Nobel Prize for literature.

sil•li•ma•nite (sĭl′ə-mə-nīt′) *n.* A usu. white, hard mineral, Al_2SiO_5, occurring in highly metamorphosed rock as long, slender, fibrous crystals. [After Benjamin *Silliman* (1779–1864), American chemist.]

Sills (sĭlz), **Beverly** b. 1929. Amer. soprano who was the general director of the New York City Opera (1980–89).

sil•ly (sĭl′ē) *adj.* **-li•er, -li•est 1.** Exhibiting a lack of wisdom or good sense; foolish. **2.** Lacking seriousness or responsibleness; frivolous. **3.** Semiconscious; dazed. [ME *seli, silli*, blessed, innocent, hapless < OE *gesælig*, blessed.] —**sil′li•ly** (sĭl′ə-lē) *adv.* —**sil′li•ness** *n.*

si•lo (sī′lō) *n., pl.* **-los 1a.** A tall cylindrical structure, usu. beside a barn, in which fodder is stored. **b.** A pit dug for the same purpose. **2.** An underground shelter for a missile, usu. equipped to launch the missile or raise it into a launching position. ❖ *tr.v.* **-loed, -lo•ing, -los** To store in a silo. [Sp.]

Si•lo•ne (sĭ-lō′nē, sē-lō′nĕ), **Ignazio** 1900–78. Italian novelist whose works include *Bread and Wine* (1937).

si•lox•ane (sĭ-lŏk′sān′, sī-) *n.* Any of a class of chemical compounds of silicon, oxygen, and usu. carbon and hydrogen, based on the structural unit R_2SiO, where R is an alkyl group, usu. methyl. [SIL(ICON) + OX(YGEN) + (METH)ANE.]

silt (sĭlt) *n.* A sedimentary material consisting of very fine particles intermediate in size between sand and clay. ❖ *v.* **silt•ed, silt•ing, silts** —*intr.* To become filled with silt: *The channel silted up.* —*tr.* To fill, cover, or obstruct with silt. [ME *cylte*, prob. of Scand. orig. See **sal-** in App.] —**silt•a′tion** *n.* —**silt′y** *adj.*

silt•stone (sĭlt′stōn′) *n.* A fine-grained rock of consolidated silt.

Si•lu•ri•an (sĭ-lo͝or′ē-ən, sī-) *adj.* Of or belonging to the geologic time of the third period of the Paleozoic Era, characterized by the appearance of land plants and invertebrate land animals. See table at **geologic time.** ❖ *n.* The Silurian Period or its deposits. [< Lat. *Silures*, an ancient people of SW Wales, where the rocks were first identified.]

si•lu•rid (sĭ-lo͝or′ĭd, sī-) *adj.* Of or belonging to the family Siluridae, which includes various freshwater catfishes. [< NLat. *Silūridae*, family name < Lat. *silūrus*, a large freshwater fish < Gk. *silouros*, sheatfish. See **ors-** in App.] —**si•lu′rid** *n.*

sil•va also **syl•va** (sĭl′və) *n., pl.* **-vas** or **-vae** (-vē) **1.** The trees or forests of a region. **2.** A written work on the trees or forests of a region. [Lat., forest.]

sil•van (sĭl′vən) *adj. & n.* Variant of **sylvan.**

Sil•va•nus also **Syl•va•nus** (sĭl-vā′nəs) *n. Roman Mythology* A god of forests, fields, and herding.

sil•ver (sĭl′vər) *n.* **1.** *Symbol* **Ag** A lustrous ductile malleable metallic element, occurring both uncombined and in ores such as argentite, having the highest thermal and electrical conductivity of the metals and used in jewelry, tableware, coinage, photography, dental and soldering alloys, electrical contacts, and printed circuits. Atomic number 47; atomic weight 107.868; melting point 960.8°C; boiling point 2,212°C; specific gravity 10.50; valence 1, 2. See table at **element. 2.** This metallic element as a commodity or medium of exchange. **3.** Coins made of this metallic element. **4.** A medal made of silver, awarded for second place in a competition. **5a.** Domestic articles, such as tableware, made of or plated with silver. **b.** Tableware, esp. eating and serving utensils, made of steel or another metal. **6.** A lustrous medium gray. **7.** A silver salt, esp. silver nitrate, used to sensitize paper. ❖ *adj.* **1.** Made of or containing silver. **2.** Resembling silver, esp. in having a lustrous shine; silvery. **3.** Of a lustrous medium gray. **4.** Having a soft clear resonant sound. **5.** Eloquent; persuasive. **6.** Favoring the adoption of silver as a standard of currency. **7.** Of or constituting a 25th anniversary. ❖ *v.* **-vered, -ver•ing, -vers** —*tr.* **1.** To cover, plate, or adorn with silver or a similar lustrous sub-

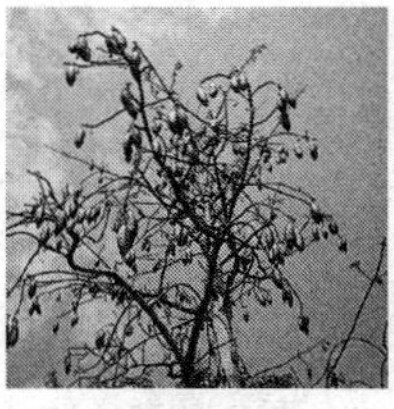

silk-cotton tree
Ceiba pentandra

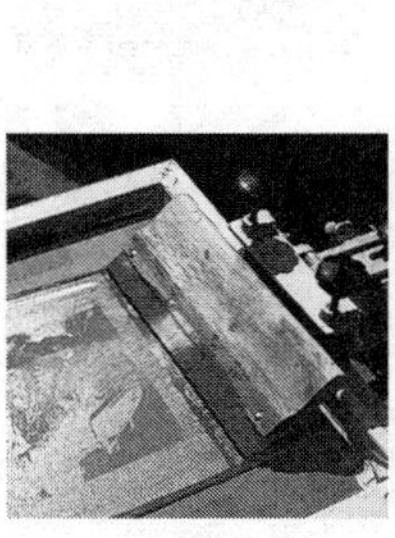

silk-screen
framed screen used for silk-screen printing

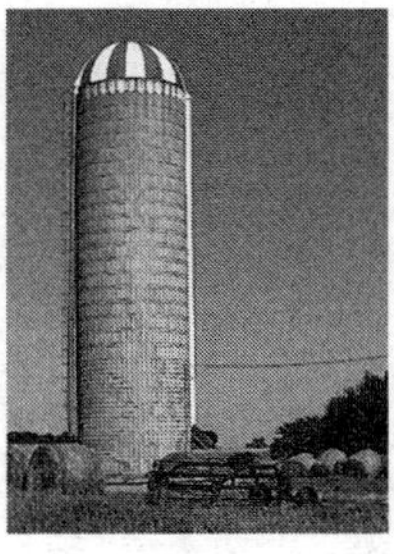

silo

ă	pat	oi	boy
ā	pay	ou	out
âr	care	o͝o	took
ä	father	o͞o	boot
ĕ	pet	ŭ	cut
ē	be	ûr	urge
ĭ	pit	th	thin
ī	pie	*th*	this
îr	pier	hw	which
ŏ	pot	zh	vision
ō	toe	ə	about, item
ô	paw		

Stress marks:
′ (primary);
′ (secondary), as in
lexicon (lĕk′sĭ-kŏn′)

stance. **2.** To give a silver color to. **3.** To coat (photographic paper) with a film of silver nitrate or other silver salt. —*intr.* To become silvery. [ME < OE *siolfor, seolfor*, prob. ult. < Akkadian *ṣarpu*, refined silver, verbal adj. of *ṣarāpu*, to smelt, refine.]

silver age *n.* A period of history secondary in achievement to that of a golden age.

sil·ver·back (sĭl′vər-băk′) *n.* A mature male gorilla having silvery white hair across the back.

sil·ver·bell tree (sĭl′vər-bĕl′) *n.* Any of several trees or shrubs of the genus *Halesia*, esp. *H. carolina* of the southeast United States, having drooping, bell-shaped white flowers.

sil·ver·ber·ry (sĭl′vər-bĕr′ē) *n.* **1.** A northeast North American shrub (*Elaeagnus commutata*) having silvery flowers, leaves, and berries. **2.** See **oleaster**.

silver bromide *n.* A pale yellow crystalline compound, AgBr, that blackens on exposure to light and is used in photographic emulsions.

silver bullet *n.* **1.** An infallible means of attack or defense. **2.** A simple remedy for a difficult or intractable problem. [< the belief that werewolves could be killed with silver bullets.]

silver certificate *n.* A bill formerly issued as legal tender by the US government in representation of deposited silver bullion.

silver chloride *n.* A white granular powder, AgCl, that turns dark on exposure to light and is used in photographic emulsions, photometry, and silver plating.

sil·ver·fish (sĭl′vər-fĭsh′) *n., pl.* **silverfish** or **-fish·es** **1.** Any of various fishes having silvery scales. **2.** A small silvery or gray bristletail (*Lepisma saccharina*) that feeds on the starchy material in bookbindings, wallpaper, clothing, and food.

silver fox *n.* **1.** A melanisitc red fox having black fur tipped with white. **2.** This fur, esp. as an article of clothing.

silver hake *n.* A marine food fish (*Merluccius bilinearis*) with silvery scales, common in American Atlantic coastal waters.

silver iodide *n.* A pale yellow odorless powder, AgI, that darkens on exposure to light and is used in photographic emulsions and medicine, esp. as an antiseptic.

silver lining *n.* A hopeful or cheerful prospect in the midst of trouble. [< the proverb "Every cloud has a silver lining."]

silver maple *n.* **1.** A North American deciduous tree (*Acer saccharinum*) having palmate leaves that are silvery below and light green above. **2.** The hard brittle wood of this tree.

sil·vern (sĭl′vərn) *adj.* **1.** Composed of silver. **2.** Resembling silver; silvery. [ME < OE *silfren* < *siolfor*. See **SILVER**.]

silver nitrate *n.* A poisonous colorless crystalline compound, AgNO₃, that turns grayish black when exposed to light in the presence of organic matter and is used in manufacturing photographic film and in medicine as a cautery.

silver perch *n.* Any of various silvery fishes resembling perch.

silver plate *n.* **1.** A coating or plating of silver. **2.** Tableware, such as flatware, made of or coated with silver.

sil·ver-plate (sĭl′vər-plāt′) *tr.v.* **-plat·ed, -plat·ing, -plates** To coat (an object) with a thin layer of silver, esp. by electroplating.

sil·ver·point (sĭl′vər-point′) *n.* **1.** A technique of drawing on specially prepared paper with a silver-tipped instrument. **2.** A drawing made by use of this technique.

silver protein *n.* A colloidal preparation of silver oxide and protein, usu. gelatin or albumin, used as an antibacterial agent.

silver screen *n.* See **screen** 6. [< a type of movie screen covered with silver-colored metallic paint.]

sil·ver·side (sĭl′vər-sīd′) *also* **sil·ver·sides** (-sīdz′) *n.* Any of various chiefly marine fishes of the family Atherinidae, characteristically having a broad silvery band along each side and including the grunion.

sil·ver·smith (sĭl′vər-smĭth′) *n.* One that makes, repairs, or replates articles of silver.

silver standard *n.* A monetary standard under which a specified quantity of silver constitutes the basic unit of currency.

Silver Star *n.* A US military decoration awarded for gallantry.

sil·ver-tongued (sĭl′vər-tŭngd′) *adj.* Having or exhibiting the power of fluent and persuasive speech; eloquent.

sil·ver·ware (sĭl′vər-wâr′) *n.* **1.** Silver or silver-plated hollowware and flatware. **2.** Metal eating and serving utensils.

sil·ver·weed (sĭl′vər-wēd′) *n.* A stoloniferous plant (*Potentilla anserina*) having pinnate leaves that are silvery beneath.

sil·ver·y (sĭl′və-rē) *adj.* **1.** Containing or coated with silver. **2.** Resembling silver in color or luster. **3.** Having a clear, softly resonant sound: *a silvery laugh.* —**sil′ver·i·ness** *n.*

sil·vex (sĭl′vĕks′) *n.* A solid toxic selective herbicide, C₉H₇O₃Cl₃, used primarily against woody plants. [Prob. Lat. *silva*, forest + EX(TERMINATOR).]

sil·vi·cul·ture (sĭl′vĭ-kŭl′chər) *n.* The care and cultivation of forest trees; forestry. [Lat. *silva*, forest + CULTURE.] —**sil′vi·cul′tur·al** *adj.* —**sil′vi·cul′tur·ist** *n.*

si·ma (sī′mə) *n.* The lower layer of the earth's outer crust that underlies the sial and is rich in silica, iron, and magnesium. [SI(LICA) + MA(GNESIUM).]

Sim·birsk (sĭm-bîrsk′, syĭm-) A city of W Russia on the Volga R. ESE of Moscow; founded 1648, known as Ulyanovsk from 1924–91. Pop. 664,025.

Sim·chat To·rah (sĕm-кнат′ tô-rä′) *also* **Sim·chas To·rah** (sĭm′кнəs tôr′ə, tôr′ə) *n. Judaism* A festival celebrating the Torah

and the completion of the year's reading cycle and its new beginning, observed on the 22nd or 23rd day of Tishri. [Heb. *śimḥat tôrâ*, rejoicing in the Torah, Simchat Torah : *śimḥat*, bound form of *śimḥâ*, joy, merriment (< *śāmēaḥ*, to rejoice) + *tôrâ*, Torah; see TORAH.]

Sim·coe (sĭm′kō), **Lake** A lake of SE Ontario, Canada, between Georgian Bay and Lake Ontario.

Si·me·non (sē-mə-nôN′), **Georges Joseph Christian** 1903–89. Belgian-born French writer known esp. for his detective novels featuring Inspector Maigret.

Sim·e·on¹ (sĭm′ē-ən) In the Bible, a son of Jacob and Leah and the forebear of one of the tribes of Israel.

Sim·e·on² In the Bible, the devout Jew who proclaimed the Nunc Dimittis while holding the infant Jesus.

Simeon Sty·li·tes (stī-lī′tēz), **Saint.** A.D. 390?–459. Syrian Christian ascetic who spent 30 years atop a column.

Sim·fer·o·pol (sĭm′fə-rō′pəl) A city of S Ukraine in the S Crimea NE of Sevastopol. Pop. 357,000.

sim·i·an (sĭm′ē-ən) *adj.* Relating to, characteristic of, or resembling an ape or monkey. ❖ *n.* An ape or monkey. [< Lat. *sīmia*, ape, prob. < *sīmus*, snub-nosed < Gk. *sīmos*.]

sim·i·lar (sĭm′ə-lər) *adj.* **1.** Related in appearance or nature; alike though not identical. **2.** *Mathematics* Having corresponding angles equal and corresponding line segments proportional. Used of geometric figures: *similar triangles.* [Fr. *similaire* < Lat. *similis*, like. See **sem-¹** in App.] —**sim′i·lar·ly** *adv.*

sim·i·lar·i·ty (sĭm′ə-lăr′ĭ-tē) *n., pl.* **-ties** **1.** The quality or condition of being similar; resemblance. **2.** A corresponding aspect or feature; an equivalence.

sim·i·le (sĭm′ə-lē) *n.* A figure of speech in which two essentially unlike things are explicitly compared, usu. by means of *like* or *as*, as in "So are you to my thoughts as food to life" (Shakespeare). [ME < Lat., likeness, comparison < neut. of *similis*, like. See SIMILAR.]

si·mil·i·tude (sĭ-mĭl′ĭ-tōōd′, -tyōōd′) *n.* **1.** Similarity; resemblance. **2a.** One closely resembling another; a counterpart. **b.** A perceptible likeness. **3.** *Archaic* A simile, allegory, or parable. [ME < OFr. < Lat. *similitūdō* < *similis*, like. See SIMILAR.]

Si·mi Valley (sē′mē, sĭm′ē) A city of S CA, a suburb of Los Angeles. Pop. 111,351.

SIMM *abbr. Computer Science* single in-line memory module

Sim·men·tal *also* **Sim·men·thal** (zĭm′ən-täl′) *n.* Any of a Swiss breed of large muscular cattle, having a reddish body and a white face and raised for meat and milk. [After *Simmental*, a valley of the Simme River in southwest-central Switzerland.]

sim·mer (sĭm′ər) *v.* **-mered, -mer·ing, -mers** —*intr.* **1.** To be cooked gently or remain just at or below the boiling point. **2a.** To be filled with pent-up emotion; seethe. **b.** To be in a state of gentle ferment. —*tr.* **1.** To cook (food) gently in a liquid just at or below the boiling point. **2.** To keep (a liquid) near or just below the boiling point. See Syns at **boil¹**. ❖ *n.* The state or process of simmering. —*phrasal verb:* **simmer down** To become calm after excitement or anger. [Alteration of ME *simpre*, to simmer, prob. of imit. orig.]

sim·nel (sĭm′nəl) *n. Chiefly British* **1.** A crisp bread made of fine wheat flour. **2.** A rich fruitcake eaten at mid-Lent, Easter, and Christmas. [ME < OFr. *siminel* < Med.Lat. *siminellus*, ult. < Lat. *simila*, fine flour. See SEMOLINA.]

si·mo·le·on (sĭ-mō′lē-ən) *n. Slang* A dollar. [?]

Si·mon (sī′mən), **Herbert Alexander** b. 1916. Amer. economist who won a 1978 Nobel Prize.

Simon, Neil b. 1927. Amer. playwright whose comedies include *The Odd Couple* (1965).

si·mo·ni·ac (sĭ-mō′nē-ăk′, sī-) *n.* One who practices simony. —**si·mo′ni·ac′, si′mo·ni′a·cal** (sī′mə-nī′ə-kəl, sĭm′ə-) *adj.* —**si′mo·ni′a·cal·ly** *adv.*

Si·mon·i·des of Ce·os (sī-mŏn′ĭ-dēz; sē′ŏs) 556?–468? B.C. Greek lyric poet known esp. for his elegies.

Simon Le·gree (lə-grē′) *n.* A brutal taskmaster. [After *Simon Legree*, a slave dealer in *Uncle Tom's Cabin*.]

si·mon-pure (sī′mən-pyōōr′) *adj.* **1.** Genuinely and thoroughly pure. **2.** Superficially or hypocritically virtuous. [< the phrase *the real Simon Pure*, after *Simon Pure*, a character in the play *A Bold Stroke for a Wife* by Susannah Centlivre (1669–1723).]

si·mo·ny (sī′mə-nē, sĭm′ə-) *n.* The buying or selling of ecclesiastical pardons, offices, or emoluments. [ME *simonie* < OFr. < LLat. *simōnia*, after *Simon Magus*, a sorcerer who tried to buy spiritual powers from the Apostle Peter (Acts 8:9–24).] —**si′mo·nist** *n.*

Simon Ze·lo·tes (zē-lō′tēz) or **Simon the Canaanite** 1st cent. A.D. In the Bible, one of the 12 Apostles; thought to have been a member of the Zealots.

si·moom (sĭ-mōōm′) *also* **si·moon** (-mōōn′) *n.* A strong hot sand-laden wind of the Sahara and Arabian deserts. [Ar. *samūm*, poisonous, simoom < *samma*, to poison < Aram. *sammā*, drug, poison.]

simp (sĭmp) *n. Slang* A simple or foolish person. [Short for SIMPLETON.]

sim·pa·ti·co (sĭm-pä′tĭ-kō′, -păt′ĭ-) *adj.* **1.** Of like mind or temperament; compatible. **2.** Having attractive qualities; pleasing. [Ital. *simpatico* (< *simpatia*, sympathy) or Sp. *simpático*

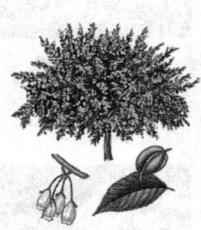

silverbell tree
Carolina silverbell
Halesia carolina

(< *simpatía*, sympathy), both < Lat. *sympathīa*. See SYMPATHY.]

sim•per (sĭm′pər) *v.* **-pered, -per•ing, -pers** —*intr.* To smile in a silly, self-conscious, often coy manner. —*tr.* To utter or express with a simper. ❖ *n.* A silly, self-conscious, often coy smile. [Perh. of Scand. orig.] —**sim′per•er** *n.*

sim•ple (sĭm′pəl) *adj.* **-pler, -plest 1.** Having or composed of only one thing, element, or part. See Syns at **pure. 2.** Not involved or complicated; easy. See Syns at **easy. 3.** Being without additions or modifications; mere: *a simple "no."* **4.** Having little or no ornamentation; not embellished or adorned. **5.** Not elaborate, elegant, or luxurious. **6.** Unassuming or unpretentious; not affected. **7a.** Having or manifesting little sense or intelligence. **b.** Uneducated; ignorant. **c.** Unworldly or unsophisticated. See Syns at **naive. 8.** Not guileful or deceitful; sincere. **9.** Humble or lowly in condition or rank. **10.** Ordinary or common. **11a.** Being a fundamental or rudimentary element; basic. **b.** Not important or significant; trivial. **12.** *Biology* Having no divisions or branches; not compound. **13.** *Music* Being without figuration or elaboration: *a simple tone.* ❖ *n.* **1.** A single component of a complex, esp. one that is unanalyzable. **2.** A fool; a simpleton. **3.** A person of humble birth or condition. **4.** A medicinal plant or the medicine obtained from it. [ME < OFr. < Lat. *simplus*; see **sem-**^{1} in App., and < *simplex*; see SIMPLEX.] —**sim′ple•ness** *n.*

simple closed curve *n.* A curve, such as a circle, that is closed and does not intersect itself.

simple fraction *n.* A fraction in which both the numerator and the denominator are whole numbers.

simple fracture *n.* A bone fracture that causes little or no damage to the surrounding soft tissues.

simple interest *n.* Interest paid only on the original principal.

simple machine *n.* A simple device, such as a lever, pulley, or inclined plane; a machine without moving parts.

sim•ple-mind•ed or **sim•ple•mind•ed** (sĭm′pəl-mīn′dĭd) *adj.* **1.** Lacking in subtlety or sophistication; naive: *a simple-minded horror movie.* **2.** Stupid or silly; foolish. **3.** Mentally impaired. —**sim′ple-mind′ed•ly** *adv.* —**sim′ple-mind′ed•ness** *n.*

simple protein *n.* A protein, such as a globulin or histone, that yields only amino acids upon hydrolysis.

simple sentence *n.* A sentence having no coordinate or subordinate clauses, as *The cat purred.*

Simple Simon *n.* A foolish fellow; a simpleton. [After *Simple Simon*, a character in a nursery rhyme.]

simple sugar *n.* See **monosaccharide.**

sim•ple•ton (sĭm′pəl-tən) *n.* A person who is felt to be deficient in judgment, good sense, or intelligence; a fool. [SIMPLE + *-ton*, as in surnames such as *Chesterton, Singleton.*]

sim•plex (sĭm′plĕks′) *adj.* **1.** Consisting of or marked by only one part or element. **2.** Of or relating to a telecommunications system in which only one message can be sent in either direction at one time. ❖ *n., pl.* **-plex•es** or **-pli•ces** (-plĭ-sēz′) **1.** *Mathematics* A Euclidean geometric spatial element having the minimum number of boundary points, such as a line segment in one-dimensional space. **2.** *Linguistics* A word that has no affixes and is not part of a compound; a simple word. [Lat., simple. See **sem-**^{1} in App.]

sim•plic•i•ty (sĭm-plĭs′ĭ-tē) *n., pl.* **-ties 1.** The property, condition, or quality of being simple or uncombined. **2.** Absence of luxury or showiness; plainness. **3.** Absence of affectation or pretense. **4a.** Lack of sophistication or subtlety; naiveté. **b.** Lack of good sense or intelligence; foolishness. **5a.** Clarity of expression. **b.** Austerity in embellishment. [ME *simplicite* < OFr. < Lat. *simplicitās* < *simplex, simplic-*, simple. See **sem-**^{1} in App.]

sim•pli•fy (sĭm′plə-fī′) *tr.v.* **-fied, -fy•ing, -fies** To make simple or simpler, as: **a.** To reduce in complexity or extent. **b.** To reduce to fundamental parts. **c.** To make easier to understand. [Fr. *simplifier* < OFr. < Med.Lat. *simplificāre* : Lat. *simplus*, simple; see SIMPLE + Lat. *-ficāre*, -fy.] —**sim′pli•fi•ca′tion** (-fĭ-kā′shən) *n.* —**sim′pli•fi′er** *n.*

sim•plism (sĭm′plĭz′əm) *n.* The tendency to oversimplify an issue or a problem by ignoring complexities or complications. —**sim•plis′tic** (sĭm-plĭs′tĭk) *adj.* —**sim•plis′ti•cal•ly** *adv.*

Sim•plon Pass (sĭm′plŏn′) A pass, 2,010 m (6,590 ft), between the Lepontine and Pennine Alps in S Switzerland.

sim•ply (sĭm′plē) *adv.* **1a.** In a plain, unadorned way: *dresses simply.* **b.** In an unambiguous way; clearly: *explained her idea simply.* **2.** Not wisely or sensibly; foolishly. **3.** Merely; only: *simply a matter of time.* **4.** Absolutely; altogether: *simply delicious.* **5.** Frankly; candidly: *You are, quite simply, the best one for the job.*

Simp•son (sĭmp′sən), **O(renthal) J(ames)** b. 1947. Amer. football player; first to rush 2,000 yards in a season.

Simpson Desert A barren uninhabited desert region of central Australia.

sim•u•la•cre (sĭm′yə-lā′kər, -lăk′ər) *n. Archaic* A simulacrum. [ME < OFr. < Lat. *simulācrum.* See SIMULACRUM.]

sim•u•la•crum (sĭm′yə-lā′krəm, -lăk′rəm) *n., pl.* **-la•cra** (-lā′krə, -lăk′rə) **1.** An image or representation. **2.** An unreal or vague semblance. [Lat. *simulācrum* < *simulāre*, to simulate. See SIMULATE.]

sim•u•lar (sĭm′yə-lər, -lär′) *Archaic n.* One that simulates; a pretender. ❖ *adj.* Simulated; sham. [< Lat. *simulāre*, to simulate. See SIMULATE.]

sim•u•late (sĭm′yə-lāt′) *tr.v.* **-lat•ed, -lat•ing, -lates 1a.** To have or take on the appearance, form, or sound of; imitate. **b.** To make in imitation of or as a substitute for. See Syns at **imitate. 2.** To make a pretense of; feign: *simulate interest.* **3.** To create a representation or model of (a physical system, for example). [Lat. *simulāre, simulāt-* < *similis*, like. See SIMILAR.] —**sim′u•la′tive** *adj.*

sim•u•lat•ed (sĭm′yə-lā′tĭd) *adj.* Made in resemblance of or as a substitute for another. See Syns at **artificial.**

sim•u•la•tion (sĭm′yə-lā′shən) *n.* **1.** The act or process of simulating. **2.** An imitation; a sham. **3.** Assumption of a false appearance. **4a.** Imitation or representation, as of a potential situation. **b.** Representation of the operation or features of one process or system through the use of another.

sim•u•la•tor (sĭm′yə-lā′tər) *n.* One that simulates, esp. an apparatus that generates test conditions approximating actual or operational conditions.

si•mul•cast (sī′məl-kăst′, sĭm′əl-) *v.* **-cast•ed, -cast•ing, -casts** —*intr.* To broadcast simultaneously by FM and AM radio or by radio and television. —*tr.* To broadcast (a program) by simulcasting. ❖ *n.* A broadcast so transmitted.

si•mul•ta•ne•ous (sī′məl-tā′nē-əs, sĭm′əl-) *adj.* **1.** Happening, existing, or done at the same time. **2.** *Mathematics* Containing variables for which there are values that can satisfy all the equations: *simultaneous equations.* [Lat. *simul*, at the same time; see **sem-**^{1} in App. + E. *-taneous*, as in INSTANTANEOUS.] —**si′mul•ta′ne•ous•ly** *adv.* —**si′mul•ta′ne•ous•ness, si′mul•ta•ne′i•ty** (-tə-nē′ĭ-tē, -nā′-) *n.*

sin^1 (sĭn) *n.* **1.** A transgression of a religious or moral law, esp. when deliberate. **2.** *Theology* **a.** Deliberate disobedience to the known will of God. **b.** A condition of estrangement from God resulting from such disobedience. **3.** Something regarded as shameful, deplorable, or utterly wrong. ❖ *intr.v.* **sinned, sin•ning, sins 1.** To violate a religious or moral law. **2.** To commit an offense or violation. [ME *sinne* < OE *synn.* See **es-** in App.]

sin^2 (sēn, sĭn) *n.* The 21st letter of the Hebrew alphabet. [Heb. *śîn*, modeled on *šîn*, shin (the following letter).]

sin^3 *abbr.* sine

Si•nai (sī′nī′), **Mount** A mountain, c. 2,288 m (7,500 ft), of the S-central Sinai Peninsula; thought to be the biblical peak on which Moses received the Ten Commandments.

Sinai Peninsula A peninsula linking SW Asia with NE Africa at the N end of the Red Sea between the Gulf of Suez and the Gulf of Aqaba; occupied by Israel in 1956 and from 1967 to 1982, when it was returned to Egyptian control.

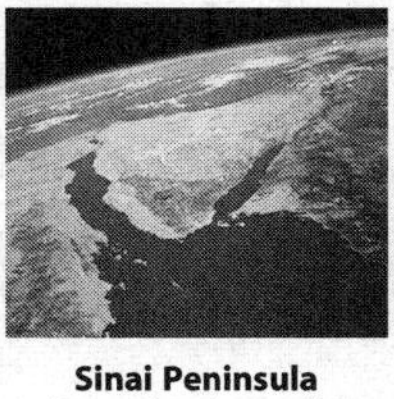

Sinai Peninsula
photo taken by *Apollo 7*

sin•an•thro•pus (sī-năn′thrə-pəs, sĭ-, sī′năn-thrō′pəs, sĭn′ăn-) *n.* See **Peking man.** [NLat. *Sīnanthrōpus*, former genus name : SINO– + Gk. *anthrōpos*, human being.]

sin•a•pism (sĭn′ə-pĭz′əm) *n.* See **mustard plaster.** [Fr. *sinapisme* < LLat. *sināpismus* < Gk. *sināpismos*, use of a mustard plaster < *sinapizein*, to apply a mustard plaster < *sināpi*, mustard.]

Si•na•tra (sə-nä′trə), **Francis Albert ("Frank")** 1915–98. Amer. singer and actor known for his mellifluous voice.

since (sĭns) *adv.* **1.** From then until now or between then and now: *They left and haven't been here since.* **2.** Before now; ago: *long since forgotten.* **3.** After some point in the past; at a subsequent time: *My friend has since moved.* ❖ *prep.* **1.** Continuously from: *friends since childhood.* **2.** Intermittently from: *She's been skiing since childhood.* ❖ *conj.* **1.** During the period subsequent to the time when: *He hasn't been home since he graduated.* **2.** Continuously from the time when: *They've been friends ever since they were in school.* **3.** Inasmuch as; because: *Since you're not interested, I won't tell you.* [ME *sinnes*, contraction of *sithenes* : *sithen*, since (< OE *siththan* : *sīth*, after + *than*, var. of *thām*, dative of *thæt*, that; see THAT) + *-es*, adv. suff.; see –S^3.]

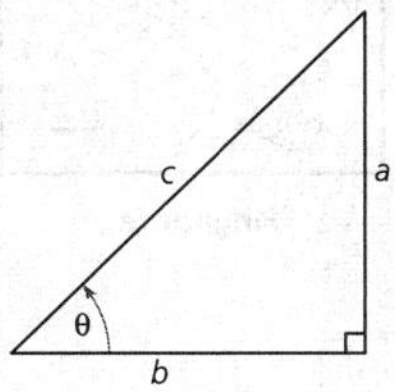

sine
$\sin\theta = \frac{a}{c}$

sin•cere (sĭn-sîr′) *adj.* **-cer•er, -cer•est 1.** Not feigned or affected; genuine: *sincere rage.* **2.** Having no hypocrisy or pretense; true. **3.** *Archaic* Pure; unadulterated. [Lat. *sincērus.* See **ker-**^{2} in App.] —**sin•cere′ly** *adv.* —**sin•cere′ness** *n.*

sin•cer•i•ty (sĭn-sĕr′ĭ-tē) *n.* The quality or condition of being sincere; genuineness, honesty, and freedom from duplicity.

sin•ci•put (sĭn′sə-pət) *n., pl.* **sin•ci•puts** or **sin•cip•i•ta** (sĭn-sĭp′ĭ-tə) **1.** The upper half of the cranium, esp. the anterior portion above and including the forehead. **2.** The forehead. [Lat. : *sēmi-*, semi- + *caput*, head; see **kaput-** in App.] —**sin•cip′i•tal** (-sĭp′ĭ-tl) *adj.*

Sin•clair (sĭn-klâr′, sĭng-), **Upton Beall** 1878–1968. Amer. writer whose novels include *The Jungle* (1906).

Sind (sĭnd) A historical region of S Pakistan along the lower Indus R.; annexed to British India in 1843, and part of Pakistan since 1947.

Sin•dhi (sĭn′dē) *n., pl.* **Sindhi** or **-dhis 1.** A member of the predominantly Muslim people of Sind. **2.** The Indic language of Sind. [Ar. *sindī* < SIND.]

sine (sīn) *n.* **1.** The ordinate of the endpoint of an arc of a unit circle centered at the origin of a Cartesian coordinate system, the arc being of length *x* and subtending a positive or negative angle. **2.** In a right triangle, the ratio of the length of the side opposite an acute angle to the length of the hypotenuse. [Med.Lat. *sinus* < Lat., curve, fold (mistranslation of Ar. *jayb*, sine, as though *jayb*, fold in a garment).]

ă	pat	oi	boy
ā	pay	ou	out
âr	care	o͝o	took
ä	father	o͞o	boot
ĕ	pet	ŭ	cut
ē	be	ûr	urge
ĭ	pit	th	thin
ī	pie	*th*	this
îr	pier	hw	which
ŏ	pot	zh	vision
ō	toe	ə	about,
ô	paw		item

Stress marks:
′ (primary);
′ (secondary), as in
lexicon (lĕk′sĭ-kŏn′)

si·ne·cure (sī′nĭ-kyŏŏr′, sĭn′ĭ-) *n.* **1.** A position or office that requires little or no work but provides a salary. **2.** *Archaic* An ecclesiastical benefice not attached to the spiritual duties of a parish. [< Med.Lat. *(beneficium) sine cūrā,* (benefice) without cure (of souls) : Lat. *sine,* without + Lat. *cūrā,* ablative of *cūra,* care; see CURE.] —**si′ne·cur·ism** *n.* —**si′ne·cur′ist** *n.*

sine curve *n.* The graph of the equation $y = \sin x$.

si·ne di·e (sī′nĭ dī′ē, sĭn′ā dē′ā′) *adv.* With no day fixed for a future meeting; indefinitely. [Med.Lat. *sine diē* : Lat. *sine,* without + Lat. *diē,* ablative of *diēs,* day.]

si·ne pro·le (sī′nĭ prō′lē, sĭn′ā) *adv. Law* Without offspring. [NLat. *sine prōle.*]

si·ne qua non (sĭn′ĭ kwä nŏn′, nōn′, sī′nĭ, kwä) *n.* An essential element or condition. [LLat. *sine quā (causā) nōn,* without which (cause) not : Lat. *sine,* without + Lat. *quā,* fem. ablative of *quī,* which + Lat. *nōn,* not.]

sin·ew (sĭn′yōō) *n.* **1.** A tendon. **2.** Vigorous strength; muscular power. **3.** The source or mainstay of vitality and strength. Often used in the plural. ❖ *tr.v.* **-ewed, -ew·ing, -ews** To strengthen with or as if with sinews. [ME *sinewe* < OE *sinewe,* oblique form of *seonu, sinu.*]

sine wave *n.* A waveform with deviation that can be graphically expressed as the sine curve.

sin·ew·y (sĭn′yōō-ē) *adj.* **1a.** Consisting of or resembling sinews. **b.** Having many sinews; stringy and tough: *a sinewy cut of beef.* **2.** Lean and muscular. See Syns at **muscular. 3.** Strong and vigorous: *sinewy prose.*

sin·fo·ni·a (sĭn-fō′nē-ə) *n.* **1.** An instrumental composition serving as an overture, as to an opera, esp. in the 18th century. **2.** A symphonic composition. [Ital. < Lat. *symphōnia,* group of musicians. See SYMPHONY.]

sin·fo·niet·ta (sĭn′fə-nyĕt′ə, -fō-) *n.* **1.** A symphony that is shorter than usual or requires fewer instruments than usual. **2.** A small symphony orchestra, esp. one consisting of stringed instruments only. [Ital., dim. of *sinfonia,* sinfonia. See SINFONIA.]

sin·ful (sĭn′fəl) *adj.* Marked by or full of sin; wicked. —**sin′ful·ly** *adv.* —**sin′ful·ness** *n.*

sing (sĭng) *v.* **sang** (săng) or **sung** (sŭng), **sung, sing·ing, sings** —*intr.* **1.** *Music* **a.** To utter words or sounds in musical tones. **b.** To vocalize songs or selections. **c.** To perform songs or selections as a trained or professional singer. **d.** To produce sounds when played. **2a.** To make melodious sounds: *birds singing.* **b.** To give or have the effect of melody; lilt. **3.** To make a high whining, humming, or whistling sound. **4.** To be filled with a buzzing or ringing sound. **5a.** To proclaim or extol something in verse. **b.** To write poetry. **6.** *Slang* To give information or evidence against someone. —*tr.* **1.** *Music* **a.** To produce the musical sound of: *sing a song.* **b.** To utter with musical inflections: *sang "hello."* **c.** To bring to a specified state by singing: *sang the baby to sleep.* **2.** To intone or chant. **3.** To proclaim or extol, esp. in verse: *sang praises.* ❖ *n. Music* A gathering of people for group singing. —*phrasal verb:* **sing out** To call out loudly. [ME *singen* < OE *singan.* See seng*h*- in App.] —**sing′a·ble** *adj.*

sing. *abbr. Grammar* singular

sing-a·long (sĭng′ə-lông′, -lŏng′) *n.* **1.** A casual gathering for group singing; a songfest. **2.** A spontaneous group singing, as by an audience at a performance.

Sin·ga·pore (sĭng′gə-pôr′, -pōr′, sĭng′ə-) A country of SE Asia comprising **Singapore Island** and numerous smaller islands; under British control from 1824 until 1965. The city of **Singapore** is the cap. Pop. 2,930,000. —**Sin′ga·por′e·an** *adj. & n.*

Singapore

WORD HISTORY *Singapore* comes from Malay *Singapora,* "Lioncity." *Pora* comes from Sanskrit *puram,* "city, fortress," and is related to Greek *polis,* "citadel, city." *Singa*– comes from Sanskrit *siṃhaḥ,* "lion," and is familiar to us in the name *Singh,* which all male Sikhs use as at least one of their personal names. Interestingly, *siṃhaḥ* is probably related to Swahili *simba,* "lion," but since lions are native to Asia as well as Africa, it is not known whether the word came into India from Africa or the other way around, or if both are from a third source.

Singapore Strait A strait off the S end of the Malay Peninsula between Singapore I. and the Riau Archipelago connecting the Strait of Malacca with the South China Sea.

singe (sĭnj) *tr.v.* **singed, singe·ing, sing·es 1.** To burn superficially; scorch. **2.** To burn off the feathers or bristles of (a carcass of a bird or animal) by subjecting briefly to flame. **3.** To burn the ends of (hair, for example). **4.** To burn the nap from (cloth) in manufacturing. ❖ *n.* A slight or surface burn; a scorch. [ME *sengen* < OE *sengan.*]

sing·er[1] (sĭng′ər) *n.* **1.** *Music* One who sings, esp. a trained or professional vocalist. **2.** A poet. **3.** A songbird.

sing·er[2] (sĭnj′ər) *n.* One that singes.

Sing·er (sĭng′ər), **Isaac Bashevis** 1904–91. Polish-born Amer. writer who won the 1978 Nobel Prize for literature.

Sing·er (sĭng′ər), **Isaac Merritt** 1811–75. Amer. inventor and manufacturer who patented (1851) a sewing machine.

Sin·gha·lese (sĭng′gə-lēz′, -lēs′) *n. & adj.* Variant of **Sinhalese.**

sin·gle (sĭng′gəl) *adj.* **1.** Not accompanied by another or others; solitary. **2a.** Consisting of one part, aspect, or section: *a single serving.* **b.** Having the same application for all; uniform. **c.** Consisting of one in number. **3.** Not divided; unbroken: *a single slab of ice.* **4a.** Separate from others; individual and distinct. **b.** Having individual opponents; involving two individuals only: *single combat.* **5a.** Honest; undisguised: *a single adoration.* **b.** Wholly attentive: *Watch with a single eye.* **6.** Designed to accommodate one person. **7a.** Unmarried. **b.** Lacking a partner: *a single parent.* **c.** Relating to the unmarried state. **d.** Of or relating to celibacy. **8.** *Botany* Having only one rank or row of petals. ❖ *n.* **1.** One that is separate and individual. **2.** An accommodation for one person, as in a hotel. **3. singles** Unmarried persons. **4.** A one-dollar bill. **5a.** A phonograph record, esp. a forty-five, with one song on each side. **b.** A song on one of these sides. **c.** A song, often from an album or compact disk, that is released for airplay. **6.** *Baseball* A hit by which a batter reaches first base safely; a one-base hit. **7.** *Sports* **a.** A hit for one run in cricket. **b.** A golf match between two players. **c.** A tennis or badminton match between two players. Often used in the plural. ❖ *v.* **-gled, -gling, -gles** —*tr.* **1.** To choose or distinguish from others. Often used with *out: singled her out.* **2.** *Baseball* **a.** To cause (a base runner) to score or advance by making a one-base hit. **b.** To cause the scoring of (a run) by a one-base hit. —*intr. Baseball* To make a single. [ME *sengle* < OFr. < Lat. *singulus.* See sem-[1] in App.] —**sin′gle·ness** *n.*

single blind *n.* A testing procedure in which the administrators do not tell the subjects if they are being given a test treatment or a control treatment in order to avoid bias in the results. —**sin′gle-blind′** (sĭng′gəl-blīnd′) *adj.*

single bond *n.* A covalent bond in which one electron pair is shared by two atoms.

sin·gle-breast·ed (sĭng′gəl-brĕs′tĭd) *adj.* Closing with a narrow overlap and fastened down the front with a single row of buttons: *a single-breasted suit.*

single cross *n. Genetics* The hybrid of two inbred lines that can be represented as AB, the product of the cross A × B, where A and B represent inbred lines.

single entry *n.* A system of bookkeeping in which a business keeps only a single account showing amounts due and amounts owed.

sin·gle-fam·i·ly (sĭng′gəl-făm′ə-lē, -făm′lē) *adj.* Relating to or being a dwelling designed for one family only.

single file *n.* A line of people, animals, or things standing or moving one behind the other. —**single file** *adv.*

sin·gle-foot (sĭng′gəl-fōŏt′) *n.* A rapid gait of a horse in which each foot strikes the ground separately; the rack. No longer in technical use. ❖ *intr.v.* **-foot·ed, -foot·ing, -foots** To go at the single-foot. —**sin′gle-foot′er** *n.*

sin·gle-hand (sĭng′gəl-hănd′) *tr.v.* **-hand·ed, -hand·ing, -hands** To sail (a boat) without the help of others. —**sin′gle-hand′er** *n.*

sin·gle-hand·ed (sĭng′gəl-hăn′dĭd) *adj.* **1.** Working or done without help; unassisted. **2.** Intended for use with one hand. **3.** Having or using only one hand. ❖ *adv.* In a single-handed manner. —**sin′gle-hand′ed·ness** *n.*

sin·gle-heart·ed (sĭng′gəl-här′tĭd) *adj.* Sincerely dedicated. —**sin′gle-heart′ed·ness** *n.*

single knot *n.* See **overhand knot.**

sin·gle-mind·ed (sĭng′gəl-mīn′dĭd) *adj.* **1.** Having one overriding purpose. **2.** Steadfast; resolute. —**sin′gle-mind′ed·ness** *n.*

sin·gle-phase (sĭng′gəl-fāz′) *adj.* Producing, carrying, or powered by a single alternating voltage.

sin·gle-sex (sĭng′gəl-sĕks′) *adj.* Same-sex.

sin·gle-space (sĭng′gəl-spās′) *v.* **-spaced, -spac·ing, -spac·es** —*tr.* To type, print, or format (copy) with no blank line between lines. —*intr.* To type, print, or format copy without line spaces.

sin·gle-stick (sĭng′gəl-stĭk′) *n.* **1.** A one-handed fencing stick fitted with a hand guard. **2.** The art, sport, or exercise of fencing with such a stick.

sin·glet (sĭng′glĭt) *n.* **1.** *Chiefly British* A man's jersey undershirt. **2.** *Physics* A multiplet with a single member.

single tax *n.* A system by which all revenue is derived from a tax on one thing, esp. land.

sin·gle·ton (sĭng′gəl-tən) *n.* **1.** *Games* A playing card that is the only one of its suit in a player's hand. **2a.** An individual separate or distinct from two or more of its group. **b.** An offspring born alone. [< the name *Singleton.*]

sin·gle-track (sĭng′gəl-trăk′) *adj.* **1.** Having just one track. **2.** Lacking mental range or flexibility; one-track.

sin·gle-tree (sĭng′gəl-trē′) *n.* See **whiffletree.** [Alteration (influenced by DOUBLETREE) of SWINGLETREE.]

sin·gly (sĭng′glē) *adv.* **1.** Without the presence of others; alone. **2.** Without help; single-handed. **3.** One by one; individually.

sing·song (sĭng′sông′, -sŏng′) *n.* **1.** Verse characterized by mechanical regularity of rhythm and rhyme. **2.** A monotonously rising and falling inflection of the voice. ❖ *adj.* Monotonous in vocal inflection or rhythm. —**sing′song′y** *adj.*

sing·spiel (sĭng′spēl′, zĭng′shpēl′) *n.* An 18th-century German musical comedy featuring songs interspersed with dialogue. [Ger. : *singen,* to sing (< MHGer. < OHGer. *singan;* see seng*h*- in App.) + *Spiel,* play; see SPIEL.]

sin·gu·lar (sĭng′gyə-lər) *adj.* **1.** Being only one; individual. **2.** Being the only one of a kind; unique. **3.** Being beyond the ordinary or usual; remarkable. **4.** Deviating from the usual or ex-

---

[marginal figure, left column:]

sine curve
a graph of the sine function
$y = \sin x$

pected; odd. **5.** *Grammar* **a.** Of, relating to, or being a noun, pronoun, or adjective denoting a single person or thing or several entities considered as a single unit. **b.** Of, relating to, or being a verb expressing the action or state of a single subject. **6.** *Logic* Of or relating to the specific as distinguished from the general; individual. ❖ *n. Grammar* **1.** The singular number or a form designating it. **2.** A word in the singular. [ME *singuler* < OFr. < Lat. *singulāris* < *singulus*, single. See SINGLE.] —**sin′gu•lar•ly** *adv.* —**sin′gu•lar•ness** *n.*

sin•gu•lar•i•ty (sĭng′gyə-lăr′ĭ-tē) *n., pl.* **-ties 1.** The quality or condition of being singular. **2.** A trait marking one as distinct from others; a peculiarity. **3.** Something uncommon or unusual. **4.** *Astrophysics* A point in space-time at which gravitational forces cause matter to have infinite density and infinitesimal volume. **5.** *Mathematics* A point at which the derivative does not exist for a given function but every neighborhood of which contains points for which the derivative exists.

sin•gu•lar•ize (sĭng′gyə-lə-rĭz′) *tr.v.* **-ized, -iz•ing, -iz•es** To make conspicuous; distinguish.

singular point *n.* See **singularity** 5.

sinh *abbr.* hyperbolic sine

Sin•ha•lese (sĭn′hə-lēz′, -lēs′) also **Sing•ha•lese** (sĭng′gə-lēz′, -lēs′) *n., pl.* **Sinhalese** also **Singhalese 1.** A member of a people constituting the majority of the population of Sri Lanka. **2.** The Indic language of the Sinhalese that is the chief language of Sri Lanka. ❖ *adj.* Of or relating to Sri Lanka, the Sinhalese, or their language or culture. [Skt. *Siṁhalam*, Sri Lanka + −ESE.]

Si•ni•cism (sĭn′ĭ-sĭz′əm, sĭn′ĭ-) *n.* A custom or trait peculiar to the Chinese. [< *Sinic*, Chinese < Med.Lat. *Sīnicus* < LLat. *Sīnae*, the Chinese. See SINO−.]

Si•ni•cize (sĭn′ĭ-sīz′, sĭn′ĭ-) *tr.v.* **-cized, -ciz•ing, -ciz•es** To make Chinese in character or to change or modify by Chinese influence. —**Si′ni•ci•za′tion** (-sĭ-zā′shən) *n.*

Si•ni•fy (sĭn′ə-fī′, sīn′ə-) *tr.v.* **-fied, -fy•ing, -fies** To Sinicize. [LLat. *Sīnae*, the Chinese; see SINO− + −FY.] —**Si′ni•fi•ca′tion** (-fĭ-kā′shən) *n.*

sin•is•ter (sĭn′ĭ-stər) *adj.* **1.** Suggesting or threatening evil. **2.** Presaging trouble; ominous: *sinister clouds.* **3.** Attended by or causing disaster or inauspicious circumstances. **4.** On the left side; left. **5.** *Heraldry* Located on or being the side of a shield on the wearer's left. [ME *sinistre*, unfavorable < OFr. < Lat. *sinister*, on the left, unlucky.] —**sin′is•ter•ly** *adv.* —**sin′is•ter•ness** *n.*

sin•is•tral (sĭn′ĭ-strəl, sĭ-nĭs′trəl) *adj.* **1.** Of or facing the left. **2.** Left-handed. **3.** *Zoology* Relating to or being a gastropod shell that has its aperture to the left when facing the observer with the apex upward. —**sin′is•tral•ly** *adv.*

sin•is•trorse (sĭn′ĭ-strôrs′) *adj.* Growing upward in a spiral that turns from right to left: *a sinistrorse vine.* [Lat. *sinistrōrsus*, turned toward the left, contraction of *sinistrōversus* : *sinistrō*, toward the left (< ablative of *sinister*, left) + *versus*, p. part. of *vertere*, to turn; see **wer-²** in App.] —**sin′is•trorse′ly** *adv.*

sin•is•trous (sĭn′ĭ-strəs, sĭ-nĭs′trəs) *adj. Archaic* Sinister; inauspicious. —**sin′is•trous•ly** *adv.*

Si•nit•ic (sĭ-nĭt′ĭk, sī-) *n.* The branch of Sino-Tibetan that comprises Chinese. [SIN(O)− + *-itic* (as in SEMITIC).] —**Si•nit′ic** *adj.*

sink (sĭngk) *v.* **sank** (săngk) or **sunk** (sŭngk), **sunk, sink•ing, sinks** —*intr.* **1.** To descend to the bottom; submerge. **2a.** To fall or drop to a lower level, esp. slowly or in stages. **b.** To subside or settle gradually, as a massive structure. **3.** To appear to move downward, as the setting sun. **4.** To slope downward; incline. **5.** To pass into a specified condition: *sank into sleep.* **6a.** To deteriorate in quality or condition. **b.** To diminish, as in value. **7.** To become weaker, quieter, or less forceful. **8a.** To drop or fall slowly, as from weakness or fatigue. **b.** To feel great disappointment or discouragement. **9.** To seep or soak; penetrate. **10.** To make an impression; become felt or understood: *Her words sank in.* —*tr.* **1.** To cause to descend beneath a surface. **2.** To cause to drop or lower. **3.** To force into the ground. **4.** To dig or drill (a mine or well) in the earth. **5.** To occupy the full attention of; engross. **6a.** To make weaker, quieter, or less forceful. **b.** To reduce in quantity or worth. **7.** To debase the nature of; degrade. **8.** To bring to a low or ruined state; defeat or destroy. **9.** To suppress or hide. **10.** *Informal* To defeat, as in a game. **11a.** To invest. **b.** To invest with no prospect of return. **12.** To pay off (a debt). **13.** *Sports* To get (a ball) into a hole or basket. ❖ *n.* **1.** A water basin with a drainpipe and generally a piped supply of water. **2.** A cesspool. **3.** A sinkhole. **4.** A means of absorbing or removing a substance or a form of energy from a system. **5.** A place regarded as wicked and corrupt. —**idiom: sink or swim** *Informal* To fail or succeed without alternative. [ME *sinken* < OE *sincan.*] —**sink′a•ble** *adj.*

sink•age (sĭng′kĭj) *n.* **1.** The process, amount, or degree of sinking. **2.** A sunken area; a depression.

sink•er (sĭng′kər) *n.* **1.** One that sinks, as a weight used for sinking fishing lines or nets. **2.** *Slang* A doughnut.

sink•hole (sĭngk′hōl′) *n.* A surface depression communicating with a cave system, occurring in limestone regions and formed by collapse of a cavern roof or by solution.

Sin•kiang Ui•ghur or **Sin•kiang Ui•gur** (sĭn′kyäng′ wē′gər, shĭn′jyäng′) See **Xinjiang Uygur.**

sink•ing fund (sĭng′kĭng) *n.* A fund accumulated to pay off a corporate or public debt.

sin•ner (sĭn′ər) *n.* **1.** One that sins. **2.** A scamp.

Sinn Fein (shĭn fān′, fĕ′ĭn) *n.* An Irish society founded about 1905 to promote political and economic independence from England, unification of Ireland, and Irish cultural renewal, now the political branch of the Irish Republican Army. [Ir.Gael. *sinn féin* : *sinn*, we (< MIr. < OIr.) + *féin*, self (< MIr. < OIr.; see **s(w)e-** in App.).] —**Sinn Fein′er** *n.* —**Sinn′ Fein′ism** *n.*

Sino− *pref.* Chinese: *Sinology.* [< LLat. *Sīnae*, the Chinese < Gk. *Sīnai* < Ar. *Sīn*, China, prob. < Chin. *Qín*, Qin. See QIN.]

si•no•a•tri•al node (sī′nō-ā′trē-əl) *n.* A small mass of specialized cardiac muscle fibers in the right atrium of the heart that acts as a pacemaker by generating the regular electric impulses of the heartbeat.

Si•no•logue also **Sin•o•log** (sī′nə-lôg′, -lŏg′, sĭn′ə-) *n.* A student of or specialist in Sinology.

Si•nol•o•gy (sī-nŏl′ə-jē, sĭ-) *n.* The study of Chinese language, literature, or civilization. —**Si′no•log′i•cal** (sī′nə-lŏj′ĭ-kəl, sĭn′ə-) *adj.* —**Si•nol′o•gist** *n.*

Si•no•pe (sə-nō′pē) *n.* A satellite of Jupiter. [Lat. *Sinōpē*, woman unsuccessfully courted by Zeus < Gk.]

Si•no•phile (sī′nə-fīl′, sĭn′ə-) *n.* One who admires China, its people, or its culture. —**Si′no•phil′i•a** (-fĭl′ē-ə) *n.*

Si•no•phobe (sī′nə-fōb′, sĭn′-) *n.* One who fears or dislikes China, its people, or its culture. —**Si′no•pho′bi•a** *n.* —**Si′no•pho′bic** *adj.*

Si•no-Ti•bet•an (sī′nō-tĭ-bĕt′n, sĭn′ō-) *n.* A language family that includes the Sinitic and Tibeto-Burman branches. —**Si′no-Ti•bet′an** *adj.*

sin•se•mil•la (sĭn′sə-mē′yə, -mĭl′ə) *n.* A highly potent form of marijuana obtained from unpollinated female plants. [Sp. : *sin*, without (< Lat. *sine*) + *semilla*, seed (< OSpan. dialectal *semilla* < LLat. *sēminia*, neut. pl. of *sēminium* < *sēmen*; see SEMEN.)]

sin tax *n. Informal* A tax on certain items, such as cigarettes and alcohol, regarded as neither necessities nor luxuries.

sin•ter (sĭn′tər) *n.* **1.** *Geology* A chemical sediment or crust deposited by a mineral spring. **2.** A mass formed by sintering. ❖ *v.* **-tered, -ter•ing, -ters** —*tr.* To cause (metallic powder, for example) to sinter. —*intr.* To form a coherent mass by heating without melting. [Ger. < MHGer., dross, metal slag < OHGer.] —**sin′ter•a•bil′i•ty** *n.*

sin•u•ate (sĭn′yōō-ĭt, -āt′) *intr.v.* **-at•ed, -at•ing, -ates** To bend or curve; wind: *a road that sinuates through the Alps.* ❖ *adj.* also **sin•u•at•ed** (-ā′tĭd) Having a wavy indented margin. [Lat. *sinuāre, sinuāt-*, to bend < *sinus*, curve.] —**sin′u•ate•ly** *adv.* —**sin′u•a′tion** *n.*

Sin•ui•ju (shĭn′wē-jōō′) A city of W North Korea on Korea Bay at the mouth of the Yalu Jiang. Pop. 300,000.

sin•u•os•i•ty (sĭn′yōō-ŏs′ĭ-tē) *n., pl.* **-ties 1.** The quality or condition of being sinuous. **2.** A bending or curving shape or movement.

sin•u•ous (sĭn′yōō-əs) *adj.* **1.** Characterized by many curves or turns; winding. **2.** Characterized by supple and lithe movements. **3.** Not direct; devious. **4.** Sinuate: *a sinuous leaf.* [< Lat. *sinuōsus* < *sinus*, curve.] —**sin′u•ous•ly** *adv.* —**sin′u•ous•ness** *n.*

si•nus (sī′nəs) *n.* **1.** A depression or cavity formed by a bending or curving. **2.** *Anatomy* **a.** A dilated channel or receptacle containing chiefly venous blood. **b.** Any of various air-filled cavities in the bones of the skull, esp. one communicating with the nostrils. **3.** *Pathology* A fistula leading from a pus-filled cavity. **4.** *Botany* A recess or indentation between lobes of a leaf or corolla. [ME, hollow in the body < Med.Lat. < Lat., curve, hollow.]

si•nus•i•tis (sī′nə-sī′tĭs) *n.* Inflammation of the sinuses or a sinus, esp. in the nasal region.

sinus node *n.* See **sinoatrial node.**

si•nu•soid (sī′nə-soid′, -nyə-) *n.* **1.** *Mathematics* See **sine curve. 2.** *Anatomy* Any of the venous cavities through which blood passes in various glands and organs. [Med.Lat. *sinus*, sine; see SINE + −OID.] —**si′nu•soi′dal** (-soid′l) *adj.*

sinusoidal projection *n.* A map projection in which areas are equal to corresponding areas on a globe, the parallels and the prime meridian being straight lines and the other meridians being increasingly curved outward from the prime meridian.

Si•on (sī′ən) *n.* Variant of **Zion.**

Siou•an (sōō′ən) *n.* **1.** A large North American Indian family of languages spoken from Lake Michigan to the Rocky Mountains and southward to Arkansas as well as in South Carolina. **2.** A member of a Siouan-speaking people. —**Siou′an** *adj.*

Sioux (sōō) *n., pl.* **Sioux** (sōō, sōōz) **1.** A member of a group of Native American peoples, also known as the Dakota, inhabiting the northern Great Plains from Minnesota to eastern Montana and from southern Saskatchewan to Nebraska, with present-day populations mainly in North and South Dakota. **2.** Any of the Siouan languages of the Sioux peoples. [N.Amer.Fr., short for *nadouéssioux* < Ottawa *naadowessiwag.*]

Sioux City A city of NW IA on the Missouri R. near the SD–NE border. Pop. 85,013.

Sioux Falls A city of SE SD near the MN border; first settled c. 1856. Pop. 123,975.

sip (sĭp) *v.* **sipped, sip•ping, sips** —*tr.* **1.** To drink in small quantities. **2.** To sip from. —*intr.* To drink something in sips. ❖ *n.* **1.** The act of sipping. **2.** A small quantity of liquid sipped. [ME *sip-*

ă	pat	oi	boy
ā	pay	ou	out
âr	care	ŏŏ	took
ä	father	ōō	boot
ĕ	pet	ŭ	cut
ē	be	ûr	urge
ĭ	pit	th	thin
ī	pie	th	this
îr	pier	hw	which
ŏ	pot	zh	vision
ō	toe	ə	about,
ô	paw		item

Stress marks:
′ (primary);
′ (secondary), as in
lexicon (lĕk′sĭ-kŏn′)

pen; prob. akin to LGer. *sippen.*] **—sip′per** *n.*

si•phon also **sy•phon** (sī′fən) *n.* **1.** A pipe or tube fashioned or deployed in an inverted U shape and filled until atmospheric pressure is sufficient to force a liquid from a reservoir at one end of the tube over a barrier higher than the reservoir and out the other end. **2.** *Zoology* A tubular organ, esp. of aquatic invertebrates such as squids, by which water is taken in or expelled. ❖ *v.* **-phoned, -phon•ing, -phons** *—tr.* To draw off or convey through or as if through a siphon. *—intr.* To pass through a siphon. [ME < Lat. *sīphō, sīphōn-* < Gk. *sīphōn.*] **—si′phon•al, si•phon′ic** (sī-fŏn′ĭk) *adj.*

si•phon•o•phore (sī-fŏn′ə-fôr′, -fōr′, sī′fə-nə-) *n.* Any of various transparent marine hydrozoans of the order Siphonophora, including the Portuguese man-of-war. [< NLat. *Sīphōnophora,* order name : Gk. *sīphōn,* tube + Gk. *-phora,* neut. pl. of *-phoros,* -phore.]

si•phon•o•stele (sī-fŏn′ə-stēl′, sī′fə-nə-stē′lē) *n. Botany* A type of stele in which the vascular cylinder surrounds a pith.

Sip•par (sĭ-pär′) An ancient city of N Babylonia on the Euphrates R. SSW of present-day Baghdad.

sip•pet (sĭp′ĭt) *n.* A small piece of toast or bread soaked in gravy or other liquid or used as a garnish. [< *sip,* alteration of SOP.]

Si•quei•ros (sĭ-kā′rōs), **David Alfaro** 1896?–1974. Mexican painter known for his murals.

sir (sûr) *n.* **1. Sir** Used as an honorific before the given name or the full name of baronets and knights. **2.** Used as a form of polite address for a man: *Don't forget your hat, sir.* **3.** Used as a salutation in a letter: *Dear Sir or Madam.* [ME, var. of *sire,* sire. See SIRE.]

sir•dar (sûr′där′, sər-där′) *n.* A person of high rank, esp. in India. [Hindi *sardār* < Pers. : *sar,* head; see **ker-**[1] in App. + *-dār,* holder.]

sire (sīr) *n.* **1.** A father. **2.** The father of an animal, esp. a domesticated mammal. **3.** *Archaic* A male ancestor; a forefather. **4.** *Archaic* A gentleman of rank. **5.** *Archaic* Used as a form of address for a superior, esp. a king. ❖ *tr.v.* **sired, sir•ing, sires** To father; beget. [ME < OFr. < VLat. **seior* < Lat. *senior,* older, comp. of *senex,* old.]

si•ren (sī′rən) *n.* **1a.** A device in which compressed air or steam is driven against a rotating perforated disk to create a loud, often wailing sound as a signal or warning. **b.** An electronic device producing a similar sound as a signal or warning: *a fire siren.* **2.** Any of several salamanders of the family Sirenidae having an eellike body, external gills, and no hind limbs. [Fr. *sirène* < OFr. *sereine,* Siren < LLat. *Sīrēna* < Lat. *Sīrēn* < Gk. *Seirēn.*]

Siren *n.* **1.** *Greek Mythology* One of a group of sea nymphs whose sweet singing lured mariners to destruction on the rocks around their island. **2. siren** A woman regarded as seductive and beautiful. [ME *serein* < OFr. *sereine.* See SIREN.]

si•re•ni•an (sī-rē′nē-ən) *n.* See **sea cow.** ❖ *adj.* Of or belonging to the order of sea cows. [< NLat. *Sīrēnia,* order name < Lat. *Sīrēn,* Siren. See SIREN.]

Sir•i•us (sĭr′ē-əs) *n.* A star in the constellation Canis Major, the brightest star in the sky. [Lat. *Sīrius* < Gk. *Seirios* < *seirios,* burning.]

sir•loin (sûr′loin′) *n.* A cut of meat, esp. of beef, from the upper part of the loin just in front of the round. [ME *surloine* < OFr. *surlonge,* **surloigne* : *sur,* above (< Lat. *super;* see **uper** in App.) + *longe, loigne,* loin; see LOIN.]

si•roc•co (sə-rŏk′ō) also **sci•roc•co** (shə-, sə-) *n., pl.* **-cos 1.** A hot humid south or southeast wind blowing over the Mediterranean Sea from North Africa to southern Europe. **2.** A hot or warm southerly wind, esp. one moving toward a low barometric pressure center. [Ital. *scirocco* < Ar. *šarq,* east.]

Sí•ros (sē′rôs′) See **Syros.**

sir•rah (sĭr′ə) *n. Obsolete* Mister; fellow. Used as a contemptuous form of address. [Alteration of SIR.]

sir•ree also **sir•ee** (sə-rē′) *n. Informal* Sir. Used for emphasis after *yes* or *no.*

sir•up (sĭr′əp, sûr′-) *n.* Variant of **syrup.**

sir•up•y (sĭr′ə-pē, sûr-) *adj.* Variant of **syrupy.**

sir•vente (sîr-väɴt′, sər-vĕnt′) also **sir•ven•tes** (sər-vĕn′tĭs, -vĕnts′) *n., pl.* **-ventes** (-väɴt′, -vĕnts′) also **-vent•es** (-vĕn′təs) A satirical form of lyric verse of the Provençal troubadours. [Fr. < Provençal *sirventes* < O Provençal < *sirvent,* servant (the position of a lover towards his mistress) < Lat. *serviēns, servient-,* pr. part. of *servīre,* to serve < *servus,* servant.]

sis (sĭs) *n. Informal* Sister.

si•sal (sī′səl) *n.* **1.** A Mexican and Central American plant *(Agave sisalana)* widely cultivated for its large sword-shaped leaves that yield stiff fibers used for cordage and rope. **2.** The fiber of this plant or of other members of the genus *Agave.* [Am.Sp., after *Sisal,* a town of SE Mexico in the Yucatán.]

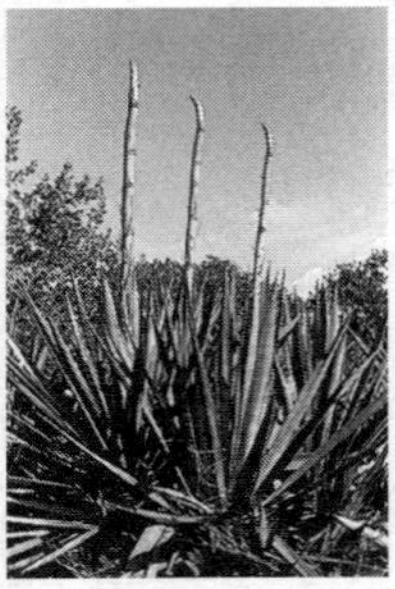

sisal
Agave sisalana

sis•kin (sĭs′kĭn) *n.* Any of several small finches, such as the pine siskin of North America. [Obsolete Du. *sīsken* < MDu., dim. of *sīs* < MLGer. *csītze,* prob. < Czech *číž,* of imit. orig.]

Sis•ley (sĭs′lē, sĭz′-, sēs-lā′), **Alfred** 1839–99. British-born French impressionist painter noted for his outdoor scenes.

Sis•se•ton (sĭs′ĭ-tən) *n., pl.* **Sisseton** or **-tons** A member of a Native American people of the Santee branch of the Sioux.

sis•si•fied (sĭs′ə-fīd′) *adj.* Of, relating to, or having the characteristics of a sissy; timid, cowardly, or effeminate.

sis•sy (sĭs′ē) *n., pl.* **-sies 1.** A boy or man regarded as effeminate. **2.** A person regarded as timid or cowardly. **3.** *Informal* Sister. [Dim. of SIS.] **—sis′si•ness, sis′sy•ness** *n.* **—sis′sy** *adj.* **—sis′sy•ish** *adj.*

sis•ter (sĭs′tər) *n.* **1.** A female having the same parents as another or one parent in common with another. **2.** A girl or woman who shares a common ancestry, allegiance, character, or purpose with another or others, specifically: **a.** A kinswoman. **b.** A woman fellow member, as of a sorority. **c.** A close woman friend or companion. **d.** A fellow African-American woman or girl. **e.** A woman who advocates, fosters, or takes part in the feminist movement. **3.** *Informal* Used as a form of address for a woman or girl. **4. Sister** *Ecclesiastical* **a.** A member of a religious order of women; a nun. **b.** Used as a form of address for such a woman, alone or followed by the woman's name. **5.** *Chiefly British* A nurse, esp. the head nurse in a ward. ❖ *adj.* **1.** Related by or as if by sisterhood; closely related: *sister ships; sister cities.* **2.** *Genetics* Of or being one of an identical pair: *sister chromatids.* [ME < ON *systir.* See **swesor-** in App.] **—sis′ter•ly** *adj. & adv.*

sis•ter•hood (sĭs′tər-ho͝od′) *n.* **1.** The state or relationship of being a sister or sisters. **2.** The quality of being sisterly. **3.** A society, esp. a religious society, of women. **4.** Association or unification of women in a common cause.

sis•ter-in-law (sĭs′tər-ĭn-lô′) *n., pl.* **sis•ters-in-law** (-tərz-) **1.** The sister of one's spouse. **2.** The wife of one's brother. **3.** The wife of the brother of one's spouse.

Sis•tine (sĭs′tēn′, sĭ-stēn′) also **Six•tine** (sĭk′stēn′, -stīn′) *adj.* **1.** Of or relating to one of the popes named Sixtus, esp. Sixtus IV (reigned 1471–84). **2.** Of or relating to the Sistine Chapel in the Vatican. [Ital. *sistino* < NLat. *sixtīnus* < Med.Lat. *Sixtus,* the name of several popes < Lat. *Sextus,* Roman praenomen < *sextus,* sixth. See SEXT.]

sis•trum (sĭs′trəm) *n., pl.* **-trums** or **-tra** (-trə) A percussion instrument of ancient Egypt, Sumeria, and Rome consisting of metal rods or loops attached to a metal frame. [ME < Lat. *sīstrum* < Gk. *seistron* < *seiein,* to shake.]

Sis•y•phe•an (sĭs′ə-fē′ən) *adj.* **1.** *Greek Mythology* Of or relating to Sisyphus. **2.** Endlessly laborious or futile. [< Lat. *Sisyphēius* < Gk. *Sisupheios* < *Sisuphos,* Sisyphus.]

Sis•y•phus (sĭs′ə-fəs) *n. Greek Mythology* A cruel king of Corinth doomed forever to roll a huge stone to a hilltop in Hades only to have it roll back. [Lat. *Sisyphus* < Gk. *Sisuphos.*]

sit (sĭt) *v.* **sat** (săt), **sit•ting, sits** *—intr.* **1.** To rest with the torso vertical and the body supported on the buttocks. **2a.** To rest with the hindquarters lowered onto a supporting surface. Used of animals. **b.** To perch. Used of birds. **3.** To cover eggs for hatching; brood. **4.** To be situated or located: *a house that sits on a hill.* **5.** To lie or rest: *dishes sitting on a shelf.* See Usage Note at **set**[1]. **6.** To pose for an artist or photographer. **7a.** To occupy a seat as a member of a body of officials: *sit in Congress.* **b.** To be in session. **8.** To remain inactive or unused. **9.** To affect one with or as if with a burden; weigh. **10.** To fit, fall, or drape in a specified manner: *The jacket sits well on you.* **11.** To be agreeable to one; please: *The idea sat well with us.* **12.** *Chiefly British* To take an examination, as for a degree. **13.** To blow from a particular direction. Used of the wind. **14.** To keep watch or take care of a child. *—tr.* **1.** To cause to sit; seat: *Sit yourself over there.* **2.** To keep one's seat on (an animal). **3.** To sit on (eggs) for the purpose of hatching. **4.** To provide seating accommodation for: *a theater that sits 1,000 people.* ❖ *n.* **1a.** The act of sitting. **b.** A period of time spent sitting. **2.** The way in which an article of clothing fits. ***—phrasal verbs:*** **sit down** To take a seat. **sit in 1.** To be present or participate as a visitor at a discussion or music session. **2.** To act as a substitute: *sat in for the vacationing news anchor.* **3.** To take part in a sit-in. **sit on** (or **upon**) *Informal* **1.** To confer about. **2.** To suppress or repress. **3.** To postpone action or resolution regarding. **sit out 1.** To stay until the end of. **2.** To refrain from taking part in. **sit up 1.** To rise from lying down to a sitting position. **2.** To sit with the spine erect. **3.** To stay up past the customary bedtime. **4.** To become suddenly alert. ***—idiom:*** **sit tight** *Informal* To be patient and await the next move. [ME *sitten* < OE *sittan.* See **sed-** in App.]

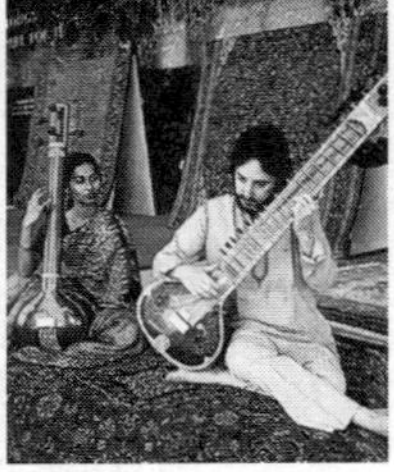

sitar

si•tar (sĭ-tär′) *n.* A stringed instrument of India made of seasoned gourds and teak and having a track of 20 movable frets with 6 or 7 metal playing strings above and usu. 13 sympathetic resonating strings below. [Hindi *sitār* < Pers. : *si,* three; see **trei-** in App. + *tār,* string; see **ten-** in App.] **—si•tar′ist** *n.*

sit•com (sĭt′kŏm′) *n. Informal* A situation comedy.

sit-down (sĭt′doun′) *n.* **1.** A work stoppage in which the workers refuse to leave their place of employment until their demands are considered or met. **2.** An obstruction of normal activity by the act of a large group sitting down in public to express a grievance or protest. **3.** *Informal* An act, instance, or period of sitting. **4.** *Informal* A meal for people seated at a table. ❖ *adj.* **1.** Performed or accomplished while sitting down. **2.** Intended for people seated at a table.

site (sīt) *n.* **1.** The place where a structure or group of structures was, is, or is to be located. **2.** The place or setting of something. **3.** A website. ❖ *tr.v.* **sit•ed, sit•ing, sites** To situate on a site. [ME < OFr. < Lat. *situs.* See SITUS.]

sith (sĭth) *conj. Archaic* Since. [ME *sithe* < OE *siththa*, var. of *sith-than.* See SINCE.] —**sith** *adv. & prep.*

sit-in (sĭt′ĭn′) *n.* **1.** An organized protest in which participants seat themselves and refuse to move. **2.** The act of occupying the seats or an area of a segregated establishment to protest racial discrimination.

Sit•ka (sĭt′kə) A town of SE AK on the W coast of Baranof I.; founded 1799 and cap. of the territory from 1867 to 1906. Pop. 8,835.

Sitka spruce *n.* **1.** A large spruce (*Picea sitchensis*) of coastal Pacific regions from southern Alaska to northern California, having flattened needles and drooping twigs and branchlets. **2.** The light strong wood of this tree.

si•tos•ter•ol (sĭ-tŏs′tə-rôl′, -rōl′, sĭ-) *n.* Any of a group of sterols that occur in high concentrations in certain plants, such as yams, and are used in the synthesis of steroid hormones. [Gk. *sītos*, food, grain + STEROL.]

sit•ter (sĭt′ər) *n.* **1.** One that sits, esp.: **a.** A person who cares for young children when the parents are not home; a babysitter. **b.** One who poses for artists. **2.** A brooding hen.

Sitter, Willem de 1872–1934. Dutch astronomer noted for his work on cosmology and relativity.

sit•ting (sĭt′ĭng) *n.* **1.** The act or position of one that sits. **2.** A period during which one is seated and occupied with a single activity, such as reading a book. **3.** A session, as of a court. **4a.** An act, condition, or period of brooding on eggs by a bird; incubation. **b.** The number of eggs under a brooding bird; a clutch. ❖ *adj.* **1.** Incubating a nest of eggs. **2.** Occupying an official position; incumbent. **3a.** Of or for sitting. **b.** Done or executed while sitting.

Sitting Bull Originally Tantanka Iyotanka. 1834?–90. Hunkpapa Sioux leader who guided his people to victory against Gen. George A. Custer's cavalry at the Battle of Little Bighorn (1876).

sitting duck *n. Informal* An easy target or victim.

sitting room *n.* A living room.

sit•u•ate (sĭch′ōō-āt′) *tr.v.* **-at•ed, -at•ing, -ates** **1.** To place in a certain spot or position; locate. **2.** To place under particular circumstances or in a given condition. ❖ *adj.* (-ĭt, -āt′) *Archaic* Situated. [ME < Med.Lat. *situāre, situāt-*, to place < Lat. *situs*, location. See tkei- in App.]

sit•u•at•ed (sĭch′ōō-ā′tĭd) *adj.* **1.** Having a place or location; located. **2.** Supplied with money.

sit•u•a•tion (sĭch′ōō-ā′shən) *n.* **1a.** The way in which something is positioned with respect to its surroundings. **b.** The place in which something is situated; a location. **2.** Position or status with regard to conditions and circumstances. **3.** The combination of circumstances at a given moment; a state of affairs. **4.** A critical, problematic, or striking set of circumstances. **5.** A position of employment. —**sit′u•a′tion•al** *adj.* —**sit′u•a′tion•al•ly** *adv.*

situation comedy *n.* A humorous radio or television series featuring the reactions of a regular cast of characters to unusual situations, such as misunderstandings.

situation ethics *n.* (*used with a sing. or pl. verb*) A system of ethics that evaluates acts in light of their situational context rather than by the application of moral absolutes.

sit-up (sĭt′ŭp′) *n.* A physical exercise in which one raises the torso from a supine to a sitting position and then lies back down again without moving the legs.

si•tus (sī′təs) *n., pl.* **situs** Position, esp. normal or original position, as of a body organ or part. [Lat. See tkei- in App.]

Sit•well (sĭt′wĕl′, -wəl) Family of British writers, including Dame **Edith Sitwell** (1887–1964) and her brothers Sir **Osbert** (1892–1969) and **Sacheverell** (1897–1988).

sitz bath (sĭts, zĭts) *n.* **1.** A bathtub shaped like a chair in which one bathes in a sitting position, immersing only the hips and buttocks. **2.** A bath taken in such a tub esp. for therapeutic reasons. [Partial transl. of Ger. *Sitzbad* : *Sitz*, act of sitting (< *sitzen*, to sit, ult. < OHGer. *sizzen*; see sed- in App.) + *Bad*, bath.]

sitz•mark (sĭts′smärk′, zĭts′-) *n.* A hollow made in the snow by a skier who has fallen backward. [Partial transl. of Ger. *Sitzmarke* : *Sitz*, act of sitting; see SITZ BATH + *Marke*, mark.]

Si•va (shē′və, sē′-) *n. Hinduism* Variant of **Shiva.**

Si•van (sĭv′ən) *n.* The ninth month of the year in the Jewish calendar. See table at **calendar.** [Heb. *sîwān* < Akkadian *sīmānu*, season, time, a month name.]

Si•wa•lik Hills (sĭ-wä′lĭk) A range of the S Himalaya Mts. extending c. 1,689 km (1,050 mi) from SW Kashmir through N India into S Nepal.

six (sĭks) *n.* **1.** The cardinal number equal to 5 + 1. **2.** The sixth in a set or sequence. **3.** Something having six parts, units, or members, esp. a motor vehicle having six cylinders. —*idiom:* **at sixes and sevens** In a state of confusion or disorder. [ME < OE. See s(w)eks in App.] —**six** *adj. & pron.*

six-gun (sĭks′gŭn′) *n.* A six-chambered revolver.

Six Nations *pl.n.* The Iroquois confederacy after it was joined by the Tuscarora in 1722.

six-pack (sĭks′păk′) *n.* **1.** Six units of a commodity, as six cans of beer, sold in a package. **2.** The contents of a six-pack.

six•pence (sĭks′pəns) *n.* **1.** A coin formerly used in Britain and worth six pennies. **2.** The sum of six pennies.

six•pen•ny (sĭks′pĕn′ē, -pə-nē) *adj.* **1.** Valued at, selling for, or worth sixpence. **2.** Of little worth; paltry.

sixpenny nail *n.* A nail 2 inches (5.1 centimeters) long. [< its original price per hundred.]

six-shoot•er (sĭks′shōō′tər) *n. Informal* A six-chambered revolver; a six-gun.

six•teen (sĭk-stēn′) *n.* **1.** The cardinal number equal to the sum of 15 + 1. **2.** The 16th in a set or sequence. [ME *sixtene* < OE *sixtȳne.* See s(w)eks in App.] —**six•teen′** *adj. & pron.*

six•teen•mo (sĭk-stēn′mō) *n., pl.* **-mos** See **sextodecimo.**

six•teenth (sĭk-stēnth′) *n.* **1.** The ordinal number matching the number 16 in a series. **2.** One of 16 equal parts. —**six•teenth′** *adv. & adj.*

sixteenth note *n. Music* A note having one sixteenth the time value of a whole note.

sixth (sĭksth) *n.* **1.** The ordinal number matching the number six in a series. **2.** One of six equal parts. **3.** *Music* **a.** An interval of six degrees in a diatonic scale. **b.** A tone separated by this interval from a given tone. **c.** The harmonic combination of two tones separated by this interval. **d.** The sixth tone of a scale; the submediant. —**sixth** *adv. & adj.*

sixth sense *n.* A power of perception seemingly independent of the five senses; keen intuition.

six•ti•eth (sĭk′stē-ĭth) *n.* **1.** The ordinal number matching the number 60 in a series. **2.** One of 60 equal parts. —**six′ti•eth** *adv. & adj.*

Six•tine (sĭk′stēn′, -stīn′) *adj.* Variant of **Sistine.**

six•ty (sĭks′tē) *n., pl.* **-ties** **1.** The cardinal number equal to 6 × 10. **2. sixties** A decade or the numbers from 60 to 69. **b.** often **Sixties** The decade from 60 to 69 in a century. [ME < OE *sixtig.* See s(w)eks in App.] —**six′ty** *adj. & pron.*

six•ty-fourth note (sĭks′tē-fôrth′, -fōrth′) *n. Music* A note having one sixty-fourth the time value of a whole note.

six•ty-nine (sĭks′tē-nīn′) *n. Vulgar Slang* Oral-genital sex between two people at the same time. [< the resemblance of the figure 69 to the position assumed by the two people.]

siz•a•ble also **size•a•ble** (sī′zə-bəl) *adj.* Of considerable size; fairly large. —**siz′a•ble•ness** *n.* —**siz′a•bly** *adv.*

size¹ (sīz) *n.* **1.** The physical dimensions, proportions, magnitude, or extent of an object. **2.** Any of a series of graduated categories of dimension whereby manufactured articles, such as shoes, are classified. **3a.** Considerable extent, amount, or dimensions. **b.** Relative amount or number, as of population. **4.** Character, value, or status with reference to importance or the capacity to meet given requirements: *Try this on for size.* **5.** The actual state of affairs: *about the size of it.* ❖ *tr.v.* **sized, siz•ing, siz•es** **1.** To arrange, classify, or distribute according to size. **2.** To make, cut, or shape to a required size. ❖ *adj.* Sized. Often used in combination: *bite-size appetizers.* —*phrasal verb:* **size up** To make an estimate, opinion, or judgment of. [ME *sise* < OFr., court session, law, short for *assise.* See ASSIZE.] —**siz′er** *n.*

size² (sīz) *n.* Any of several gelatinous or glutinous substances usu. made from glue, wax, or clay and used as a glaze or filler for porous materials such as paper, cloth, or wall surfaces. ❖ *tr.v.* **sized, siz•ing, siz•es** To treat or coat with size or a similar substance. [ME *sise*, prob. < OFr., a setting. See SIZE¹.]

sized (sīzd) *adj.* Having a particular or specified size. Often used in combination: *a medium-sized car.*

siz•ing (sī′zĭng) *n.* **1.** A glaze or filler; size. **2.** Treatment of a fabric or other surface with size.

siz•zle (sĭz′əl) *intr.v.* **-zled, -zling, -zles** **1.** To make the hissing sound characteristic of frying fat. **2.** To seethe with anger or indignation. **3.** To be very hot. ❖ *n.* A hissing sound. [Perh. freq. of ME *sissen*, to hiss, of imit. orig.]

siz•zler (sĭz′lər) *n.* **1.** One that sizzles. **2.** *Informal* A very hot day.

SJ *abbr.* Society of Jesus

Sjael•land (shĕl′än′) also **Zea•land** (zē′lənd) An island of E Denmark bounded by the Kattegat and the Baltic Sea and separated from Sweden by the Oresund.

SJD *abbr. Latin* Scientiae Juridicae Doctor (Doctor of Juridical Science)

SK *abbr.* Saskatchewan

sk. *abbr.* sack

ska (skä) *n.* Popular music originating in Jamaica in the 1960s, having elements of rhythm and blues, jazz, and calypso, a fast tempo, and a strong accent placed on the offbeat. [< the phrase (*Love*) *Ska(voovie)*, greeting used by Jamaican bassist Cluet Johnson, one of the early creators of ska, or, imit. of the sound of a guitar in tandem with a rim click on a snare drum.]

skag (skăg) *n. Slang* Variant of **scag.**

Skag•er•rak also **Skag•er•ak** (skăg′ə-răk′, skä′gə-räk′) A broad strait between SE Norway and NW Denmark linking the North Sea and the Kattegat.

Skag•way (skăg′wā′) A town of SE AK at the head of the Lynn Canal NNW of Juneau; a boom town during the Alaskan gold rush (1897–98). Pop. 862.

skald also **scald** (skôld, skäld) *n.* A medieval Scandinavian poet. [ON *skāld.* See sekʷ-³ in App.] —**skald′ic** *adj.*

skank (skăngk) *n.* **1.** Disgusting or indecent matter; filth. **2.** One who is considered disgusting or indecent, often for being sexually promiscuous. [Of Jamaican orig.] —**skank′y** *adj.*

skat (skăt) *n.* **1.** A trick-taking card game for three active players

Sitting Bull
photographed in 1885

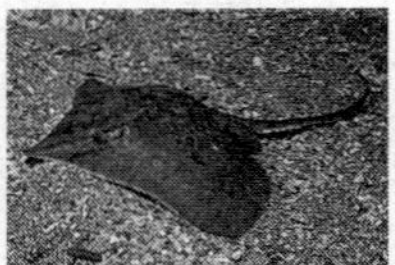

skate[2]
longnose skate
Raja rhina

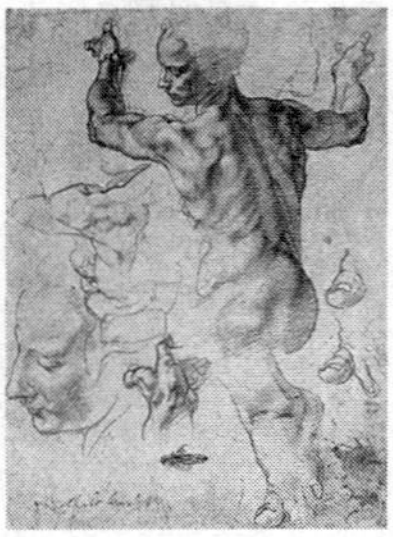

sketch
sketch by Michelangelo for the *Libyan Sibyl* at the Sistine Chapel

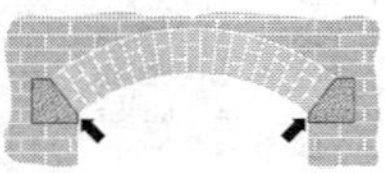

skewback

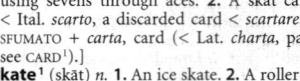

using sevens through aces. **2.** A skat card combination. [Ger. < Ital. *scarto*, a discarded card < *scartare*, to reject : *s-*, out; see SFUMATO + *carta*, card (< Lat. *charta*, paper made of papyrus; see CARD¹).]

skate¹ (skāt) *n.* **1.** An ice skate. **2.** A roller skate. **3.** A skateboard. **4.** The act or a period of skating. ❖ *intr.v.* **skat•ed, skat•ing, skates 1.** To glide or move along on or as if on skates. **2.** To ride or perform stunts on a skateboard. **3.** *Informal* To act in an irresponsible or superficial manner. [< Du. *schaats*, stilt, skate (taken as pl.) < MDu. *schaetse* < ONFr. *escache*, stilt, perh. of Gmc. orig.]

skate² (skāt) *n.* Any of various rays of the genus *Raja*, having a flattened body and greatly expanded pectoral fins that extend around the head. [ME *scate* < ON *skata*.]

skate³ (skāt) *n.* **1.** A person. **2.** A decrepit horse; a nag. [Perh. alteration of dialectal *skite*, contemptible person. See BLATHERSKITE.]

skate•board (skāt′bôrd′, -bōrd′) *n.* A short narrow board having a set of four wheels mounted under it, ridden mainly as a sport in a standing or crouching position. **—skate′board′** *v.* **—skate′board′er** *n.*

skat•er (skā′tər) *n.* **1.** One who skates, as on ice. **2.** One who skateboards. **3.** See **water strider.**

skat•ole (skăt′ōl, -ôl) also **skat•ol** (-ôl, -ōl, -ŏl) *n.* A crystalline organic compound, C_9H_9N, having a strong fecal odor, found in feces, beets, and coal tar and used as a fixative in perfumery. [Gk. *skōr*, *skat-*, dung; see **sker-²** in App. + –OLE.]

Skaw (skô) A cape on the N extremity of Jutland, Denmark, extending into the Skagerrak and the Kattegat.

skean (skēn) *n.* A double-edged dagger once used in Ireland and Scotland. [ME *skene* < Ir.Gael. *scian* < OIr. *scían*.]

Skeat (skēt), **Walter William** 1835–1912. English philologist who wrote *An Etymological Dictionary of the English Language* (1879–82).

ske•dad•dle (skĭ-dăd′l) *intr.v.* **-dled, -dling, -dles** *Informal* To leave hastily; flee. [?]

Skee•na (skē′nə) A river rising in W British Columbia, Canada, and flowing c. 579 km (360 mi) to the Pacific Ocean.

skeet (skēt) *n.* A form of trapshooting in which thrown clay targets are shot at from different stations. [Alteration of SHOOT.]

skee•ter (skē′tər) *n. Chiefly Southern US* See **mosquito.** See Regional Note at **possum.**

skeeter hawk *n. South Atlantic US* See **dragonfly.** See Regional Note at **dragonfly.**

skeg (skĕg) *n.* **1.** A structure that connects the keel and sternpost of a ship. **2.** A vertical structure at the stern of a vessel that supports the rudder and protects the propeller. **3.** A small finlike structure at the stern of a small boat or surfboard, serving as a keel to keep the boat on course. [Du. *scheg*, perh. < ON *skegg*, beard, beak of a ship.]

skein (skān) *n.* **1a.** A length of thread or yarn wound in a long loose coil. **b.** Something suggesting the coil of a skein; a complex tangle: *a twisted skein of lies.* **2.** A flock of geese or similar birds in flight. [ME *skeine* < OFr. *escaigne*.]

skel•e•tal (skĕl′ĭ-tl) *adj.* **1.** Of or relating to a skeleton, esp. a vertebrate skeleton. **2.** Consisting of basic or essential elements: *a skeletal narrative of the incident.* **—skel′e•tal•ly** *adv.*

skeletal muscle *n.* A usu. voluntary muscle made up of elongated, multinucleated, transversely striated muscle fibers, having principally bony attachments.

skel•e•ton (skĕl′ĭ-tn) *n.* **1a.** The internal structure composed of bone and cartilage that protects and supports a vertebrate organism; endoskeleton. **b.** The hard external supporting and protecting structure in many invertebrates, such as mollusks, and certain vertebrates, such as turtles; exoskeleton. **2.** A supporting structure or framework, as of a building. **3.** An outline or sketch. **4.** Something reduced to its basic or minimal parts. **5.** One that is very thin or emaciated. ❖ *adj.* **1.** Of, relating to, or resembling a skeleton. **2.** Reduced to the basic or minimal parts or members: *a skeleton crew.* ***—idiom:* skeleton in (one's) closet** A source of shame that is kept secret. [Gk. *skeleton (sōma)*, dried-up (body), neut. of *skeletos* < *skellesthai*, to dry up.]

skel•e•ton•ize (skĕl′ĭ-tn-īz′) *tr.v.* **-ized, -iz•ing, -iz•es 1.** To reduce to skeleton form. **2.** To outline or sketch briefly. **3.** To reduce in size or number.

skeleton key *n.* A key with a large portion of the bit filed away so that it can open different locks.

skel•lum (skĕl′əm) *n. Scots* A rascal; a rogue. [Du. *schelm* < LGer. < MLGer.]

Skel•ton (skĕl′tən), **John** 1460?–1529. English poet and scholar whose satires include *Speke Parrot* (1521).

skep (skĕp) *n.* A beehive, esp. one of straw. [ME, basket < ON *skeppa*, a dry measure, and < OE *sceppe* (< ON *skeppa*).]

skep•tic also **scep•tic** (skĕp′tĭk) *n.* **1.** One who doubts, questions, or disagrees with assertions or generally accepted conclusions. **2.** One skeptical in religious matters. **3.** *Philosophy* **a.** often **Skeptic** An adherent of a school of skepticism. **b. Skeptic** A member of an ancient Greek school of skepticism, esp. that of Pyrrho of Elis (360?–272? B.C.). [Lat. *Scepticus*, disciple of Pyrrho of Elis < Gk. *Skeptikos* < *skeptesthai*, to examine. See **spek-** in App.]

skep•ti•cal also **scep•ti•cal** (skĕp′tĭ-kəl) *adj.* **1.** Marked by or given to doubt; questioning. **2.** Relating to or characteristic of skeptics or skepticism. **—skep′ti•cal•ly** *adv.*

skep•ti•cism also **scep•ti•cism** (skĕp′tĭ-sĭz′əm) *n.* **1.** A doubting or questioning attitude or state of mind; dubiety. See Syns at **uncertainty. 2.** *Philosophy* **a.** The doctrine that absolute knowledge is impossible, either in a particular domain or in general. **b.** A methodology based on an assumption of doubt with the aim of acquiring approximate or relative certainty. **3.** Doubt or disbelief of religious tenets.

sker•ry (skĕr′ē) *n., pl.* **-ries** A small rocky reef or island. [Sc., dim. of ON *sker*. See **sker-¹** in App.]

sketch (skĕch) *n.* **1.** A hasty or undetailed drawing or painting often made as a preliminary study. **2.** A brief general account or presentation; an outline. **3a.** A brief, light, or informal literary composition. **b.** *Music* A brief composition, esp. for the piano. **c.** A short, often satirical scene or play in a revue or variety show; a skit. **4.** *Informal* An amusing person. ❖ *v.* **sketched, sketch•ing, sketch•es** *—tr.* To make a sketch of; outline. *—intr.* To make a sketch. [Du. *schets* < Ital. *schizzo* < *schizzare*, to splash, of imit. orig.] **—sketch′er** *n.*

sketch•book (skĕch′bo͝ok′) *n.* **1.** A pad of paper used for sketching. **2.** A book of literary sketches.

sketch•pad (skĕch′păd′) *n.* See **sketchbook** 1.

sketch•y (skĕch′ē) *adj.* **-i•er, -i•est 1.** Resembling a sketch; giving only major points or parts. **2a.** Lacking in substance or completeness; incomplete. **b.** Slight; superficial. **—sketch′i•ly** *adv.* **—sketch′i•ness** *n.*

skew (skyo͞o) *v.* **skewed, skew•ing, skews** *—intr.* **1.** To take an oblique course or direction. **2.** To look obliquely or sideways. *—tr.* **1.** To turn or place at an angle. **2.** To give a bias to; distort. ❖ *adj.* **1.** Placed or turned to one side; asymmetrical. **2.** Distorted or biased in meaning or effect. **3.** Having a part that diverges, as in gearing. **4a.** *Mathematics* Neither parallel nor intersecting. Used of straight lines in space. **b.** *Statistics* Not symmetrical about the mean. Used of distributions. ❖ *n.* An oblique or slanting movement, position, or direction. [ME *skewen*, to escape, run sideways < ONFr. *eskiuer*, of Gmc. orig.] **—skew′ness** *n.*

skew arch *n.* An arch having sides not at right angles to the face of its abutments.

skew•back (skyo͞o′băk′) *n.* Either of two inset abutments sloped to support an arch.

skew•bald (skyo͞o′bôld′) *adj.* Having spots or patches of white on a coat that is not black. ❖ *n.* A skewbald animal, esp. a horse. [ME *skeued*, of mixed colors (prob. < *skeu*, sky, cloud, of Scand. orig.; see **(s)keu-** in App.) + BALD.]

skew•er (skyo͞o′ər) *n.* **1.** A long metal or wooden pin used to secure or suspend food during cooking; a spit. **2.** Any of various picks or rods like a skewer in shape or function. ❖ *tr.v.* **-ered, -er•ing, -ers** To hold together or pierce with or as if with a skewer. [ME *skuer*, perh. of Scand. orig.]

skew lines *pl.n.* Straight lines that are not in the same plane and do not intersect.

ski (skē) *n., pl.* **skis 1a.** One of a pair of long flat runners of plastic, metal, or wood that curve upward in front and may be attached to a boot for gliding or traveling over snow. **b.** A water ski. **2.** Something used as a runner on a vehicle. ❖ *v.* **skied, ski•ing, skis** *—intr.* To travel or glide on skis, esp. as a sport. *—tr.* To travel or glide over on skis. [Norw. < ON *skīdh*, stick, snowshoe.] **—ski′a•ble** *adj.* **—ski′er** *n.*

ski•a•gram (skī′ə-grăm′) *n.* **1.** A picture or photograph made up of shadows or outlines. **2.** See **radiograph.** [Gk. *skiā*, shadow + –GRAM.]

ski boot *n.* A stiff padded boot that is fastened to the foot and locked into place in a ski binding.

skid (skĭd) *n.* **1.** The act of sliding or slipping over a surface, often sideways. **2a.** A plank, log, or timber, usu. one of a pair, used as a support or track for sliding or rolling heavy objects. **b.** A pallet for loading or handling goods. **c.** One of several logs or timbers forming a skid road. **3. skids** *Nautical* A wooden framework attached to the side of a ship to prevent damage, as when unloading. **4.** A shoe or drag applying pressure to a wheel to brake a vehicle. **5.** A runner in the landing gear of certain aircraft. **6. skids** *Slang* A path to ruin or failure. ❖ *v.* **skid•ded, skid•ding, skids** *—intr.* **1.** To slide sideways while moving because of loss of traction. See Syns at **slide. 2.** To slide without revolving. **3.** To move sideways in a turn because of insufficient banking. Used of an airplane. *—tr.* **1.** To brake (a wheel) with a skid. **2.** To haul on a skid or skids. [Perh. of Scand. orig.]

skid•der (skĭd′ər) *n.* **1a.** One that skids. **b.** One that uses a skid. **2.** A heavy four-wheel tractor used to haul logs, esp. over rugged terrain.

skid•dy (skĭd′ē) *adj.* **-di•er, -di•est** Liable to skid or cause skidding: *skiddy roads.*

skid road *n.* **1.** A track made of logs laid transversely about five feet apart and used to haul logs to a loading platform or a mill. **2.** *Slang* Skid row.

skid row (rō) *n. Slang* A squalid district inhabited chiefly by derelicts and vagrants. [Alteration of SKID ROAD (once a downtown area frequented by loggers).]

skied¹ (skēd) *v.* Past tense and past participle of **ski.**

skied² (skīd) *v.* Past tense and past participle of **sky.**

skies (skīz) *n.* Plural of **sky.** ❖ *v.* Third person singular present tense of **sky.**

skiff (skĭf) *n.* A flatbottom open boat of shallow draft, having a pointed bow and a square stern and propelled by oars, sail, or motor. [ME *skif* < OFr. *esquif* < OItal. *schifo,* of Gmc. orig.]

skif•fle (skĭf′əl) *n.* Jazz, folk, or country music played on unconventional instruments such as kazoos, washboards, or jugs. [?]

ski•jor•ing (skē′jôr′ĭng, -jōr′-) *n.* A sport in which a skier is drawn over ice or snow by a horse or vehicle. [Norw. *skikjøring* : *ski,* ski; see SKI + *kjøring,* driving (< *kjøre,* to drive < ON *keyra*).]

ski jump *n.* **1.** A jump or leap made by a skier, esp. in a competition. **2.** A course or chute prepared for a ski jump. **—ski jump** *v.* **—ski jumper** *n.*

skil•ful (skĭl′fəl) *adj. Chiefly British* Variant of **skillful.**

ski lift *n.* A power-driven conveyor, usu. with attached tow bars, suspended chairs, or gondolas, used to carry skiers to the top of a trail or slope.

skill (skĭl) *n.* **1.** Proficiency, facility, or dexterity that is acquired or developed through training or experience. **2a.** An art, trade, or technique, particularly one requiring use of the hands or body. **b.** A developed talent or ability: *writing skills.* **3.** *Obsolete* A reason; a cause. [ME *skil* < ON, discernment.]

skilled (skĭld) *adj.* **1.** Having or showing skill; expert. See Syns at **proficient. 2.** Requiring specialized ability or training.

skil•let (skĭl′ĭt) *n.* **1.** See **frying pan.** See Regional Notes at **andiron, frying pan. 2.** *Chiefly British* A long-handled stewing pan or saucepan sometimes having legs. [ME *skelet* < OFr. *escuelete,* dim. of *escuele,* plate < Lat. *scutella,* dim. of *scutra,* platter.]

skill•ful (skĭl′fəl) *adj.* **1.** Possessing or exercising skill; expert. See Syns at **proficient. 2.** Marked by, exhibiting, or requiring skill. **—skill′ful•ly** *adv.* **—skill′ful•ness** *n.*

skim (skĭm) *v.* **skimmed, skim•ming, skims** *—tr.* **1a.** To remove floating matter from (a liquid). **b.** To remove (floating matter) from a liquid. **c.** To take away the choicest or most readily attainable contents or parts from. **2.** To coat or cover with or as if with a thin layer, as of scum. **3a.** To throw so as to bounce or slide: *skimmed stones across the pond.* **b.** To glide or pass quickly and lightly over or along (a surface). **4.** To read or glance through (a book, for example) quickly or superficially. **5.** *Slang* To fail to declare part of (certain income) to avoid tax payment. *—intr.* **1.** To move or pass swiftly and lightly over or near a surface; glide. **2.** To give a quick and superficial reading, scrutiny, or consideration; glance. **3.** To become coated with a thin layer. **4.** *Slang* To fail to declare certain income to avoid tax payment. ❖ *n.* **1.** The act of skimming. **2.** Something that has been skimmed. **3.** A thin layer or film. **4.** *Slang* The profit gained by skimming. [ME *skimmen,* perh. < OFr. *escumer,* to remove scum < *escume,* scum, of Gmc. orig. See **(s)keu-** in App.]

ski mask *n.* A knitted covering for the head and face, worn esp. by skiers for protection from the cold.

skim•board (skĭm′bôrd′, -bōrd′) *n.* A thin, flat, round or rectangular board used in skimboarding.

skim•board•ing (skĭm′bôr′dĭng, -bōr′-) *n.* The sport of riding a skimboard over shallow water on a beach and into oncoming waves close to shore.

skim•mer (skĭm′ər) *n.* **1.** One that skims, such as a large perforated spoon used in skimming liquids. **2.** A light, usu. straw hat with a wide brim and a flat shallow crown. **3a.** Any of several chiefly coastal birds of the genus *Rynchops,* having a long bill with a longer lower mandible for skimming the water's surface for food. **b.** A black skimmer.

skim milk *n.* Milk from which the cream has been removed.

ski•mo•bile (skē′mō-bēl′, -mə-) *n.* See **snowmobile.**

skimp (skĭmp) *v.* **skimped, skimp•ing, skimps** *—tr.* **1.** To deal with hastily, carelessly, or with poor material. **2.** To provide for or supply inadequately; be stingy with. *—intr.* To be stingy or very thrifty. ❖ *adj.* Scanty; skimpy. [Obsolete *skimp,* scanty, perh. < alteration of SCRIMP.]

skimp•y (skĭm′pē) *adj.* **-i•er, -i•est 1.** Inadequate, as in size or fullness, esp. through economizing or stinting: *a skimpy meal.* **2.** Unduly thrifty; niggardly. **—skimp′i•ly** *adv.* **—skimp′i•ness** *n.*

skin (skĭn) *n.* **1.** The membranous tissue forming the external covering or integument of an animal and consisting in vertebrates of the epidermis and dermis. **2.** An animal pelt, esp. of a small or young animal. **3.** A usu. thin, closely adhering outer layer. **4.** A container for liquids that is made of animal skin. **5.** *Music* A drumhead. **6.** *Informal* One's life or physical survival: *lied to save his skin.* ❖ *v.* **skinned, skin•ning, skins** *—tr.* **1.** To remove skin from. **2.** To bruise, cut, or injure the skin or surface of. **3.** To remove (an outer covering); peel off: *skin off the bark.* **4.** To cover with or as if with skin. **5.** *Slang* To fleece; swindle. *—intr.* **1.** To become covered with or as if with skin: *The pond skins over with ice.* **2.** To pass with little room to spare: *barely skinned by.* ❖ *adj. Slang* Of, relating to, or depicting pornography. ***—idioms:*** **by the skin of (one's) teeth** By the smallest margin. **get under (someone's) skin 1.** To irritate or stimulate; provoke. **2.** To preoccupy someone; become an obsession. **under the skin** Beneath the surface; fundamentally. [ME < ON *skinn.* See **sek-** in App.] **—skin′less** *adj.*

skin-deep (skĭn′dēp′) *adj.* Superficial; shallow: *a skin-deep acquaintanceship.* ❖ *adv.* In a shallow manner; superficially.

skin-dive (skĭn′dīv′) *intr.v.* **-dived, -div•ing, -dives** To engage in skin diving.

skin diving *n.* The sport of swimming under water with flippers and a face mask and usu. with a snorkel rather than a portable air supply. **—skin diver** *n.*

skin effect *n.* The tendency of alternating current to flow near the surface of a conductor.

skin flick *n. Slang* A pornographic film.

skin•flint (skĭn′flĭnt′) *n.* One who is very reluctant to spend money; a miser.

skin game *n. Slang* **1.** A fraudulent gambling game. **2.** A swindle.

skin graft *n.* A surgical graft of healthy skin from one part of the body to another or from one individual to another in order to replace damaged or lost skin. **—skin grafting** *n.*

skin•head (skĭn′hĕd′) *n.* **1.** A person with a shaven head. **2.** A member of any of various groups of people who shave their heads and sometimes participate in white-supremacist and anti-immigrant activities.

skink (skĭngk) *n.* Any of numerous smooth shiny lizards of the family Scincidae, having small or rudimentary legs. [Lat. *scincus* < Gk. *skinkos.*]

skinned (skĭnd) *adj.* Having skin of a specified kind. Often used in combination: *fair-skinned; dark-skinned.*

skin•ner (skĭn′ər) *n.* **1.** One that flays, dresses, or sells animal skins. **2.** *Western US* A mule driver.

Skinner, B(urrhus) F(rederick) 1904–90. Amer. behavioristic psychologist noted for his theories of stimulus-response behavior. **—Skin•ner′i•an** (skĭ-nîr′ē-ən) *adj. & n.* **—Skin′ner•ism** *n.*

Skinner, Cornelia Otis 1901–79. Amer. actress and writer known for her one-woman shows.

Skinner box *n.* A soundproof light-resistant box or cage used in laboratories to isolate an animal for experiments in operant conditioning. [After Burrhus Frederick SKINNER.]

skin•ny (skĭn′ē) *adj.* **-ni•er, -ni•est 1.** Very thin. See Syns at **lean**[2]. **2.** Of, relating to, or resembling skin. ❖ *n. Slang* Inside information; the real facts. **—skin′ni•ness** *n.*

skin•ny-dip (skĭn′ē-dĭp′) *intr.v.* **-dipped, -dip•ping, -dips** *Informal* To swim in the nude. **—skin′ny-dip′per** *n.*

skin patch *n.* See **transdermal patch.**

skin test *n.* A test for detecting an allergy or infectious disease, performed using a patch test, scratch test, or intracutaneous injection of an allergen or extract of the disease-causing organism.

skin•tight (skĭn′tīt′) *adj.* Fitting closely to the skin.

skip (skĭp) *v.* **skipped, skip•ping, skips** *—intr.* **1a.** To move by hopping on one foot and then the other. **b.** To leap lightly about. **2.** To bounce over or be deflected from a surface; skim or ricochet. **3.** To pass from point to point, omitting or disregarding what intervenes. **4.** To be promoted in school beyond the next regular class or grade. **5.** *Informal* To leave hastily; abscond: *skipped out of town.* **6.** To misfire. Used of an engine. *—tr.* **1.** To leap or jump lightly over: *skip rope.* **2a.** To pass over without mentioning; omit. **b.** To miss or omit as one in a series: *My heart skipped a beat.* **3.** To cause to bounce lightly over a surface; skim. **4.** To be promoted beyond (the next grade or level). **5.** *Informal* To leave hastily. **6.** *Informal* To fail to attend. ❖ *n.* **1.** A leaping or jumping movement, esp. a gait in which hops and steps alternate. **2.** An act of passing over something; an omission. [ME *skippen,* perh. of Scand. orig.] **—skip′pa•ble** *adj.*

skimmer

skip•jack (skĭp′jăk′) *n., pl.* **skipjack** or **-jacks 1.** Any of several marine food fishes of the genus *Euthynnus,* related to and resembling the tuna, esp. an economically important striped species *(E. pelamis)* occurring in all tropical areas. **2.** Any of various fishes, such as the bluefish, that habitually leap out of the water. **3.** *pl.* **-jacks** *Nautical* A small sailboat having a bottom shaped like a flat V and vertical sides.

ski plane also **ski•plane** (skē′plăn′) *n.* An airplane equipped with skis for landing on or taking off from a snow-covered surface.

ski pole *n.* A lightweight pole with a handgrip, sometimes a wrist strap, and a sharp point encircled slightly above by a disk, used in pairs by snow skiers.

skip•per[1] (skĭp′ər) *n.* **1.** The master of a ship. **2.** A coach, director, or other leader. [ME < MDu. < *scip,* ship.] **—skip′per** *v.*

skip•per[2] (skĭp′ər) *n.* **1.** One that skips. **2.** Any of numerous butterflies of the families Hesperiidae and Megathymidae, having a hairy mothlike body, hooked tips on the antennae, and a darting flight pattern. **3.** Any of several marine fishes that often leap above water, esp. the saury *Cololabis saira* of Pacific waters.

skirl (skûrl) *v.* **skirled, skirl•ing, skirls** *—intr.* To produce a high shrill wailing tone. Used of bagpipes. *—tr.* To play (a piece) on bagpipes. ❖ *n.* **1.** The shrill sound made by the chanter pipe of bagpipes. **2.** A shrill wailing sound. [ME *skrillen, skirlen,* prob. of Scand. orig.]

skir•mish (skûr′mĭsh) *n.* **1.** A minor battle in war, as one between small forces or between large forces avoiding direct conflict. **2.** A minor or preliminary conflict or dispute. ❖ *intr.v.* **-mished, -mish•ing, -mish•es** To engage in a minor battle or dispute. [ME *skirmisshe,* alteration (influenced by ME *skirmisshen,* to brandish a weapon) of *skarmush* < OFr. *eskarmouch* < OItal. *scaramuccia,* of Gmc. orig. See **sker-**[1] in App.]

Skí•ros also **Sky•ros** or **Scy•ros** (skī′rəs, skē′rôs) An island of E

ă	**pat**	oi	**boy**
ā	**pay**	ou	**out**
âr	**care**	o͝o	**took**
ä	**father**	o͞o	**boot**
ĕ	**pet**	ŭ	**cut**
ē	**be**	ûr	**urge**
ĭ	**pit**	th	**thin**
ī	**pie**	*th*	**this**
îr	**pier**	hw	**which**
ŏ	**pot**	zh	**vision**
ō	**toe**	ə	**about, item**
ô	**paw**		

Stress marks:
′ (primary);
′ (secondary), as in
lexicon (lĕk′sĭ-kŏn′)

skort

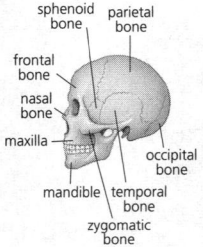

sphenoid bone
parietal bone
frontal bone
nasal bone
maxilla
mandible
temporal bone
zygomatic bone
occipital bone

skull
lateral view of an adult
human skull

skunk
striped skunk
Mephitis mephitis

Greece in the Aegean Sea NE of Euboea; occupied by Athenians in the 5th cent. B.C.

skir·ret (skŭr′ĭt) *n.* An eastern Asian plant (*Sium sisarum*) having sweet tuberous edible roots. [ME *skirwhit*, alteration of OFr. *eschervi*, prob. < Ar. *karawyā*, caraway < Gk. *karō*.]

skirt (skûrt) *n.* **1.** The part of a garment, such as a dress, that hangs freely from the waist down. **2.** A garment hanging from the waist and worn esp. by women and girls. **3.** A part or attachment resembling the skirt of a garment, esp.: **a.** One of the leather flaps hanging from the side of a saddle. **b.** The lower outer section of a rocket vehicle. **4.** An outer edge; a border. **5. skirts** The edge, as of a town; the outskirts. **6.** *Offensive Slang* A woman. ❖ *v.* **skirt·ed, skirt·ing, skirts** —*tr.* **1.** To lie along or form the edge of; border. **2.** To pass around rather than across or through. **3.** To pass close to; miss narrowly. **4.** To evade, as by circumlocution: *skirted the issue.* —*intr.* To lie along, move along, or be an edge or border. [ME < ON *skyrta*, shirt. See **sker-¹** in App.]

skirt steak *n.* A cut of beef from the lower part of the brisket.

skit (skĭt) *n.* **1.** A short, usu. comic dramatic performance or work; a sketch. **2.** A short humorous or satirical piece of writing. [?]

ski tow *n.* **1.** A ski lift in which skiers cling to a continuous rope as they are pulled up a slope. **2.** See **ski lift.**

skit·ter (skĭt′ər) *v.* **-tered, -ter·ing, -ters** —*intr.* **1.** To move rapidly along a surface, usu. with frequent light contacts or changes of direction; skip or glide quickly. **2.** To fish by drawing a lure or baited hook over the surface of the water with a skipping movement. —*tr.* To cause to skitter. [Prob. freq. of dialectal *skite*, to run rapidly, perh. of Scand. orig.; akin to ON *skjóta*, to shoot. See SHOOT.]

skit·ter·y (skĭt′ə-rē) *adj.* Moving quickly, restlessly, or irregularly; skittish.

skit·tish (skĭt′ĭsh) *adj.* **1.** Moving quickly and lightly; lively. **2.** Restlessly active or nervous; restive. **3.** Undependably variable; mercurial or fickle. **4.** Shy; bashful. [ME, perh. of Scand. orig.; akin to ON *skjóta*, to shoot. See SHOOT.] —**skit′tish·ly** *adv.* —**skit′tish·ness** *n.*

skit·tle (skĭt′l) *n.* **1. skittles** (*used with a sing. verb*) A British form of ninepins, in which a wooden disk or ball is thrown to knock down the pins. **2.** One of the pins used in skittles. [Perh. of Scand. orig.]

skive (skīv) *tr.v.* **skived, skiv·ing, skives** To cut thin layers off (leather, for example); pare. [Of Scand. orig.]

skiv·er (skī′vər) *n.* **1.** One, such as a cutting tool, that skives. **2.** A soft thin leather split off the outside of sheepskin and used for bookbinding.

Skiv·vies (skĭv′ēz) A trademark used for underwear.

skoal (skōl) *interj.* Used as a drinking toast. [Dan. and Norw. *skaal*, cup, skoal < ON *skāl*, bowl, drinking vessel.]

Skop·je (skôp′yə′, -yĕ) or **Skop·lje** (-lə′, -lyĕ) The cap. of Macedonia, in the N-central part on the Vardar R.; under Turkish control from 1392 to 1913. Pop. 448,229.

skort (skôrt) *n.* A pair of shorts having a flap or panel across the front and sometimes the back to resemble a skirt. [SK(IRT) + (SH)ORT.]

skosh (skōsh) *n. Slang* A small amount; a bit. [J. *sukoshi*.]

Skr. or **Skt.** *abbr.* Sanskrit

sku·a (skyōō′ə) *n.* **1.** Any of several large predatory sea birds of the genus *Catharacta* related to the jaeger, esp. the great skua. **2.** *Chiefly British* See **jaeger 1.** [NLat., alteration of Faroese *skúvur* < ON *skúfr*, tassel, seagull.]

skulk (skŭlk) *intr.v.* **skulked, skulk·ing, skulks** **1.** To lie in hiding, as out of cowardice or bad conscience; lurk. **2.** To move about stealthily. **3.** To evade work or obligation; shirk. ❖ *n.* **1.** One who hides, lurks, or practices evasion. **2.** A congregation of vermin, esp. foxes, or of thieves. [ME *skulken*, of Scand. orig.]

skull (skŭl) *n.* **1.** The bony or cartilaginous framework of the head of vertebrates, made up of the bones of the braincase and face; cranium. **2.** *Informal* The head, regarded as the seat of thought or intelligence. **3.** A death's-head. [ME *skulle*, prob. of Scand. orig.]

skull·cap (skŭl′kăp′) *n.* **1a.** A light close-fitting brimless cap. **b.** A yarmulke. **2.** Any of various plants of the genus *Scutellaria*, having clusters of two-lipped flowers.

skull·dug·ger·y or **skul·dug·ger·y** (skŭl-dŭg′ə-rē) *n.*, *pl.* **-ger·ies** Crafty deception or trickery or an instance of it. [Prob. alteration of Sc. *sculduddery*, obscenity, fornication.]

skulled (skŭld) *adj.* Having a skull, esp. of a specified type. Often used in combination: *broad-skulled.*

skunk (skŭngk) *n.* **1a.** Any of several small, mostly carnivorous New World mammals of the genus *Mephitis* and related genera, having a bushy tail and glossy black fur with white markings, and ejecting a foul-smelling oily liquid from glands near the anus when frightened or in danger. **b.** The fur of this mammal. **2.** *Slang* **a.** A person regarded as obnoxious or despicable. **b.** A person whose company is avoided. ❖ *tr.v.* **skunked, skunk·ing, skunks** *Slang* **1.** To defeat overwhelmingly, esp. by keeping from scoring. **2a.** To cheat (someone). **b.** To fail to pay (an amount due). [Of Massachusett orig.]

skunk bear *n.* See **wolverine.**

skunk cabbage *n.* **1.** An ill-smelling eastern North American swamp plant (*Symplocarpus foetidus*) having minute flowers en-

closed in a mottled greenish or purplish spathe. **2.** A western North American plant (*Lysichitum americanum*) having a bright yellow spathe with an inflated upper part.

skunk grape *n.* See **fox grape.**

Skunk River A river rising in central IA and flowing c. 425 km (264 mi) to the Mississippi R.

skunk·weed (skŭngk′wēd′) *n.* A dioecious, ill-smelling, dichotomously branched annual plant (*Croton texensis*) of the central and southwest United States.

sky (skī) *n.*, *pl.* **skies** (skīz) **1.** The expanse of air over a given point on the earth; the upper atmosphere as seen from the earth's surface. **2.** The appearance of the upper atmosphere, esp. with reference to weather. Often used in the plural. **3.** The celestial regions; the heavens. **4.** The highest level or degree: *reaching for the sky.* ❖ *tr.v.* **skied** (skīd), **sky·ing, skies** (skīz) **1.** To hit or throw (a ball, for example) high in the air. **2.** To hang (a painting, for example) on a wall above the line of vision. [ME < ON *skȳ*, cloud. See **(s)keu-** in App.]

sky blue *n.* A light to pale blue.

sky·board (skī′bôrd′, -bōrd′) *n.* A lightweight board similar to a snowboard, usu. equipped with foot bindings and a recovery parachute, used for skysurfing. —**sky′board′ing** *n.*

sky burial *n.* A traditional Tibetan funeral practice in which the body of a dead person is exposed to the open air to be eaten by vultures.

sky·dive (skī′dīv′) *intr.v.* **-dived, -div·ing, -dives** To jump and fall freely from an airplane, performing various maneuvers before pulling the ripcord of a parachute. —**sky′div′er** *n.* —**sky′div′ing** *n.*

Skye (skī), **Isle of** An island of NW Scotland in the Inner Hebrides.

Skye terrier *n.* A small terrier of a breed native to the Isle of Skye, having a long low body, short legs, and shaggy hair.

sky·ey (skī′ē) *adj.* Of, from, or resembling the sky.

sky-high (skī′hī′) *adv.* **1.** To a very high level: *garbage piled sky-high.* **2.** In a lavish or enthusiastic manner. **3.** In pieces or to pieces; apart: *blew the bridge sky-high.* ❖ *adj.* **1.** High up in the air. **2.** Exorbitantly high in cost or value.

sky·hook or **sky-hook** (skī′hŏŏk′) *n.* A helicopter whose fuselage is configured so as to be mounted with a steel line and hook used to lift and transport heavy objects.

sky·jack (skī′jăk′) *tr.v.* **-jacked, -jack·ing, -jacks** To subject (an aircraft) to air piracy. [SKY + (HI)JACK.] —**sky′jack′er** *n.* —**sky′jack′ing** *n.*

sky·lark (skī′lärk′) *n.* An Old World lark (*Alauda arvensis*) with brown plumage, noted for singing while flying. ❖ *intr.v.* **-larked, -lark·ing, -larks** To play actively and boisterously.

sky·light (skī′līt′) *n.* **1.** An overhead window, as in a roof, admitting daylight. **2.** Light from the sky.

sky·line (skī′līn′) *n.* **1.** The line along which the earth and the sky appear to meet; the horizon. **2.** The outline of a group of buildings or a mountain range seen against the sky.

sky·rock·et (skī′rŏk′ĭt) *n.* A firework that ascends high into the air where it explodes in a brilliant cascade of flares and starlike sparks. ❖ *intr. & tr.v.* **-et·ed, -et·ing, -ets** To rise or cause to rise rapidly and suddenly.

Sky·ros (skī′rəs, skē′rôs) See **Skíros.**

sky·sail (skī′səl, -sāl′) *n.* A small square sail above the royal in a square-rigged vessel.

sky·scrap·er (skī′skrā′pər) *n.* A very tall building.

sky·surf·ing (skī′sûr′fĭng) *n.* The sport of performing maneuvers or stunts during free fall while riding a skyboard. —**sky′surf′** *v.* —**sky′surf′er** *n.*

sky·walk (skī′wôk′) *n.* An elevated, usu. enclosed walkway between two buildings.

sky·ward (skī′wərd) *adv. & adj.* At or toward the sky. —**sky′wards** *adv.*

sky wave *n.* A radio wave that travels upward.

sky·way (skī′wā′) *n.* **1.** A route regularly used by airplanes; an air lane. **2.** An elevated highway.

sky·writ·ing (skī′rī′tĭng) *n.* **1.** The process of writing in the sky by releasing a visible vapor from an airplane. **2.** The letters or words so formed. —**sky′write′** *v.* —**sky′writ′er** *n.*

SL *abbr.* **1.** salvage loss **2.** sea level **3.** source language

s.l. *abbr. Latin* sine loco (without place of publication)

slab¹ (slăb) *n.* **1.** A broad, flat, thick piece, as of stone or cheese. **2.** An outside piece cut from a log when squaring it for lumber. **3.** *Baseball* The pitcher's rubber. ❖ *tr.v.* **slabbed, slab·bing, slabs** **1.** To make or shape into slabs or a slab. **2.** To cover or pave with slabs. **3.** To dress (a log) by cutting slabs. [ME.]

slab² (slăb) *adj. Archaic* Viscid. [Prob. of Scand. orig.]

slab-sid·ed (slăb′sī′dĭd) *adj.* **1.** Having flat sides. **2.** *Informal* Tall and slim; lanky.

slack¹ (slăk) *adj.* **slack·er, slack·est** **1.** Moving slowly; sluggish. **2.** Lacking in activity; not busy: *a slack season for hotels.* **3.** Not tense or taut; loose: *a slack rope.* See Syns at **loose.** **4.** Lacking firmness; flaccid: *a slack grip.* **5.** Lacking in diligence or care; negligent: *a slack worker.* **6.** Flowing or blowing with little speed: *a slack current.* **7.** *Linguistics* Pronounced with the muscles of the tongue and jaw relatively relaxed; lax. ❖ *v.* **slacked, slack·ing, slacks** —*tr.* **1.** To make slower or looser; slacken. **2.** To be careless or remiss in doing: *slack one's duty.* **3.** To slake (lime). *—intr.* **1.** To be or become slack. **2.** To evade work; shirk. ❖ *n.* **1.** A loose part, as of a rope or sail. **2.** A lack of tension; looseness. **3.** A period of little activity; a lull. **4a.** A cessation of movement in a current of air or water. **b.** An area of still water. **5.** Unused capacity. **6. slacks** Casual trousers that are not part of a suit. ❖ *adv.* In a slack manner: *a banner hanging slack.* ***—phrasal verb:*** **slack off** To decrease in activity or intensity. [ME *slak* < OE *slæc.*] **—slack′ly** *adv.* **—slack′ness** *n.*

slack^{2} (slăk) *n.* A mixture of coal fragments, coal dust, and dirt that remains after screening coal. [ME *sleck.*]

slack^{3} (slăk) *n. Chiefly British* **1.** A small dell or hollow. **2.** A bog; a morass. [ME *slak* < ON *slakki.*]

slack-baked (slăk′bākt′) *adj.* Not fully baked or done; half-baked: *slack-baked bread.*

slack•en (slăk′ən) *tr. & intr.v.* **-ened, -en•ing, -ens 1.** To make or become slower; slow down: *Air speed slackened.* **2.** To make or become less tense, taut, or firm; loosen: *The tension in the room slackened.* **3.** To make or become less vigorous, intense, or severe; ease: *slacken discipline.*

slack•er (slăk′ər) *n.* **1.** One who shirks work or responsibility. **2.** One who tries to evade military service in wartime; a draft dodger.

slack water *n.* **1.** A period of cessation in the strong flow of a current of water, esp. at high or low tide. **2.** An area in a sea or river unaffected by currents; still water.

slag (slăg) *n.* **1.** The vitreous mass left as a residue by the smelting of metallic ore. **2.** See **scoria** 1. ❖ *tr. & intr.v.* **slagged, slag•ging, slags** To change into or form slag. [LGer. *slagge* < MLGer.] **—slag′gy** *adj.*

slain (slān) *v.* Past participle of **slay.**

slake (slāk) *v.* **slaked, slak•ing, slakes** *—tr.* **1.** To satisfy (a craving); quench: *slaked her thirst.* **2.** To lessen the force or activity of; moderate: *slaking his anger.* **3.** To cool or refresh by wetting or moistening. **4.** To combine (lime) chemically with water or moist air. *—intr.* To undergo a slaking process; crumble or disintegrate, as lime. [ME *slaken,* to abate < OE *slacian* < *slæc,* slack, sluggish. See SLACK^{1}.]

slaked lime (slākt) *n.* See **calcium hydroxide.**

sla•lom (slä′ləm) *n.* **1.** The act or sport of skiing in a zigzag course. **2.** A race on skis or in vehicles along such a course, laid out with markers such as flags. ❖ *intr.v.* **-lomed, -lom•ing, -loms** To move or race in a slalom. [Norw. *slalåm* : *slad,* sloping + *låm,* path.] **—sla′lom•er, sla′lom•ist** *n.*

slam^{1} (slăm) *v.* **slammed, slam•ming, slams** *—tr.* **1.** To shut with force and loud noise: *slammed the door.* **2.** To put, throw, or otherwise forcefully move so as to produce a loud noise: *slammed the book on the desk.* **3.** To hit or strike with great force. **4.** *Slang* To criticize harshly; censure forcefully. *—intr.* **1.** To close or swing into place with force so as to produce a loud noise. **2.** To hit something with force; crash: *slammed into a truck.* ❖ *n.* **1a.** A forceful impact that makes a loud noise. **b.** A noise so produced. **2.** An act of shutting forcefully and loudly. **3.** *Slang* A harsh or devastating criticism. **4.** A poetry slam. [Perh. of Scand. orig.]

slam^{2} (slăm) *n.* **1.** The winning of all the tricks or all but one during the play of one hand in bridge and other whist-derived card games. **2.** A contract to make a slam. [?]

slam-bang (slăm′băng′) *adv. & adj. Slang* **1.** With force and much noise. **2.** With heedless speed; slapdash. **3.** With vigorous, relentless action and pace.

slam dunk *n.* **1.** *Basketball* A dramatic, forceful dunk shot. **2.** A dramatically successful action.

slam-dunk (slăm′dŭngk′) *v.* **-dunked, -dunk•ing, -dunks** *—intr. Basketball* To make a slam dunk. *—tr.* **1.** *Basketball* To shoot (the ball) in a slam dunk. **2.** To make a forceful dramatic move against (another). **—slam′-dunk′er** *n.*

slam•mer (slăm′ər) *n.* **1.** One that slams. **2.** *Slang* A jail. [< SLAM^{1}.]

slan•der (slăn′dər) *n.* **1.** *Law* Oral communication of false statements injurious to a person's reputation. **2.** A false and malicious statement or report about someone. ❖ *v.* **-dered, -der•ing, -ders** *—tr.* To utter a slander about. *—intr.* To utter or spread slander. [ME *slaundre* < OFr. *esclandre,* alteration of *escandle* < Lat. *scandalum,* cause of offense. See SCANDAL.] **—slan′der•er** *n.* **—slan′der•ous** *adj.* **—slan′der•ous•ly** *adv.*

slang (slăng) *n.* **1.** A kind of language esp. occurring in casual and playful speech, usu. made up of short-lived coinages and figures of speech deliberately used in place of standard terms for effects such as raciness, humor, or irreverence. **2.** Language peculiar to a group; argot or jargon: *thieves' slang.* ❖ *v.* **slanged, slang•ing, slangs** *—intr.* **1.** To use slang. **2.** To use angry and abusive language. *—tr.* To attack with abusive language; vituperate. [?] **—slang′i•ly** *adv.* **—slang′i•ness** *n.* **—slang′y** *adj.*

slant (slănt) *v.* **slant•ed, slant•ing, slants** *—tr.* **1.** To give a direction other than perpendicular or horizontal to; make diagonal; cause to slope. **2.** To present so as to conform to a particular bias or appeal to a certain audience. *—intr.* To have or go in a direction other than perpendicular or horizontal; slope. ❖ *n.* **1a.** A line, plane, course, or direction other than perpendicular or horizontal; a slope. **b.** A sloping thing or piece of ground. **2.** *Printing* A virgule. **3a.** A personal point of view or opinion. **b.** A bias. [Alteration of obsolete *slent* < ME *slenten,* to fall aslant, perh. of Scand. orig.]

SYNONYMS *slant, incline, lean, slope, tilt, tip* These verbs mean to depart or cause to depart from true vertical or horizontal: *rays of light slanting through the window; inclined her head toward the speaker; leaned against the railing; a driveway that slopes downhill; tilted his hat at a rakish angle; tipped her chair against the wall.*

slant rhyme *n.* See **off rhyme.**

slant•ways (slănt′wāz′) *adv.* Slantwise.

slant•wise (slănt′wīz′) *adv.* At a slant or slope; obliquely. ❖ *adj.* Slanting; oblique.

slap (slăp) *n.* **1a.** A sharp blow made with the open hand or with a flat object; a smack. **b.** The sound of such a blow. **2.** A sharp insult. ❖ *v.* **slapped, slap•ping, slaps** *—tr.* **1.** To strike with a flat object, such as the palm of the hand. **2.** To cause to strike sharply and loudly: *slapped the book against the desk.* **3.** To put or place quickly or carelessly: *slapped butter on a bagel.* **4.** To criticize or insult sharply. **5.** To subject to a legal obligation, such as a fine: *slapped him with a lawsuit.* *—intr.* To strike or beat with the force and sound of a slap. ❖ *adv. Informal* Directly and with force. ***—phrasal verb:*** **slap down 1.** To restrain or correct by a sharp blow or emphatic censure. **2.** To put a sudden end to; suppress. ***—idiom:*** **slap on the wrist** A nominal or token punishment. [ME *slappe.*] **—slap′per** *n.*

slap•dash (slăp′dăsh′) *adj.* Hasty and careless, as in execution. ❖ *adv.* In a reckless haphazard manner.

slap•hap•py (slăp′hăp′ē) *adj.* **-pi•er, -pi•est** *Slang* **1.** Dazed, silly, or incoherent from or as if from blows to the head; punch-drunk. **2.** Happy-go-lucky.

slap•jack (slăp′jăk′) *n.* A pancake; a flapjack.

slap shot *n.* A fast-moving shot made in hockey with a full swinging stroke.

slap•stick (slăp′stĭk′) *n.* **1.** A form of comedy marked by chases, collisions, and crude practical jokes. **2.** A paddle designed to make a loud whacking sound, once used in farces.

slash (slăsh) *v.* **slashed, slash•ing, slash•es** *—tr.* **1.** To cut or form by cutting with forceful sweeping strokes. **2.** To lash with sweeping strokes. **3.** To make a gash or gashes in. **4.** *Sports* To swing a stick at (an opponent) in ice hockey or lacrosse, in violation of the rules. **5.** To cut a slit or slits in, esp. to reveal an underlying color: *slash a sleeve.* **6.** To criticize sharply. **7.** To reduce or curtail greatly. *—intr.* **1.** To make forceful sweeping strokes with or as if with a sharp instrument. **2.** To cut one's way with such strokes. ❖ *n.* **1.** A forceful sweeping stroke made with a sharp instrument. **2.** A long cut or other opening made by such a stroke; a gash or slit. **3.** A decorative slit in a fabric or garment. **4.** Branches and other residue left on a forest floor after the cutting of timber. **5.** Wet or swampy ground overgrown with bushes and trees. Often used in the plural. **6.** *Printing* A virgule. ❖ *conj. Informal* As well as; and. Used in combination and often rendered as a virgule in print: *an actor-slash-writer; a waiter/dancer.* [Perh. < obsolete Fr. *esclachier,* to break, var. of *esclater* < OFr. < *esclat,* splinter. See SLAT.] **—slash′er** *n.*

slash-and-burn (slăsh′ənd-bûrn′) *adj.* **1.** Of or being a form of agriculture in which an area of forest is cleared by cutting and burning and is then planted, usu. for several seasons, before being left to return to forest. **2.** Drastic or destructive.

slash•ing (slăsh′ĭng) *adj.* **1.** Bitingly critical or satiric: *slashing wit.* **2.** Dashing; pelting: *a slashing hailstorm.* **3.** Brilliant; intense: *slashing colors.* **—slash′ing•ly** *adv.*

slash pine *n.* A pine tree *(Pinus elliotti)* of swampy coastal areas of the southeast United States that yields pulp, rosin, timber, and turpentine.

slat (slăt) *n.* **1.** A narrow strip of metal or wood, as in a Venetian blind. **2.** A movable auxiliary airfoil running along the leading edge of the wing of an airplane. **3. slats** *Slang* The ribs. ❖ *tr.v.* **slat•ted, slat•ting, slats** To provide or make with slats. [ME *sclat* < OFr. *esclat,* splinter, prob. of Gmc. orig.]

slatch (slăch) *n. New England* **1.** A momentary lull between breaking waves, favorable for launching a boat. **2.** A lull in a high windstorm. [Variant of SLACK^{1}.]

slate (slāt) *n.* **1.** A fine-grained metamorphic rock that splits into thin smooth-surfaced layers. **2a.** A piece of this rock cut for use as roofing or surfacing material or as a writing surface. **b.** A writing tablet made of a similar material. **3.** A record of past performance or activity: *start over with a clean slate.* **4.** A list of the candidates of a political party running for various offices. **5.** A dark or bluish gray to dark bluish or dark purplish gray. ❖ *adj.* **1.** Made of slate. **2.** Of the color slate. ❖ *tr.v.* **slat•ed, slat•ing, slates 1.** To cover (a roof, for example) with slate. **2.** To put on a list of candidates. **3.** To schedule or designate. [ME *sclate* < OFr. *esclate,* splinter, fem. of *esclat.* See SLAT.]

slate black *n.* A purplish black.

slate blue *n.* A grayish blue to dark bluish gray.

slate-col•ored junco (slāt′kŭl′ərd) *n.* A junco *(Junco hyemalis)* of eastern North America having dark gray upper parts and a white abdomen.

slat•er (slā′tər) *n.* **1.** One who lays slate surfaces, as on roofs. **2.** See **pill bug. 3.** See **sow bug.**

Slater, Samuel 1768–1835. British-born textile pioneer in Amer-

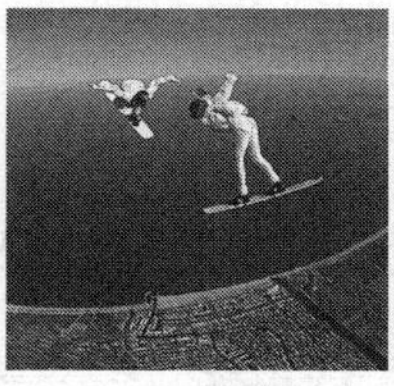

skysurfing

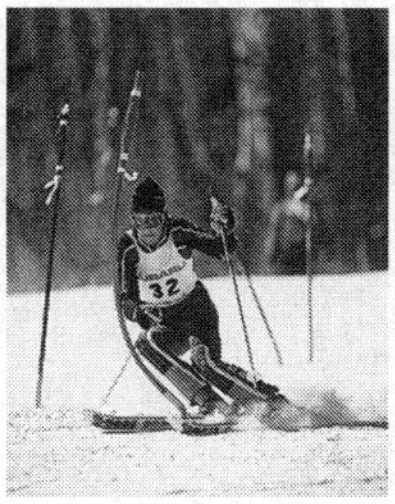

slalom

ă	pat	oi	boy
ā	pay	ou	out
âr	care	o͝o	took
ä	father	o͞o	boot
ĕ	pet	ŭ	cut
ē	be	ûr	urge
ĭ	pit	th	thin
ī	pie	*th*	this
îr	pier	hw	which
ŏ	pot	zh	vision
ō	toe	ə	about, item
ô	paw		

Stress marks:
′ (primary);
′ (secondary), as in
lexicon (lĕk′sĭ-kŏn′)

ica who oversaw construction of the nation's first successful water-powered cotton mill (1790–93).

slath·er (slăth′ər) *tr.v.* **-ered, -er·ing, -ers** *Informal* **1.** To use or give great amounts of; lavish. **2a.** To spread thickly. **b.** To spread thickly with something. ❖ *n. Slang* A great amount. Often used in the plural: *slathers of jewels.* [?]

slat·ing (slā′tĭng) *n.* Slates for covering roofs, walls, or other surfaces.

slat·tern (slăt′ərn) *n.* An untidy dirty woman. [Perh. < dialectal *slattering,* slovenly, pr. part. of dialectal *slatter,* to slop.]

slat·tern·ly (slăt′ərn-lē) *adj.* **1.** Characteristic of or befitting a slattern. **2.** Slovenly; untidy. —**slat′tern·li·ness** *n.*

slat·y (slā′tē) *adj.* **-i·er, -i·est 1.** Composed of or resembling slate. **2.** Having the color of slate.

slaugh·ter (slô′tər) *n.* **1.** The killing of animals esp. for food. **2.** The killing of a large number of people; a massacre. ❖ *tr.v.* **-tered, -ter·ing, -ters 1.** To kill (animals) esp. for food; butcher. **2a.** To kill (people) in large numbers; massacre. **b.** To kill in a violent or brutal manner. [ME, of Scand. orig.] —**slaugh′ter·er** *n.* —**slaugh′ter·ous** *adj.*

slaugh·ter·house (slô′tər-hous′) *n.* **1.** A place where animals are butchered. **2.** A scene of massacre or carnage.

Slav (släv) *n.* A member of one of the Slavic-speaking peoples of eastern Europe. [ME *Sclave* < Med.Lat. *Sclāvus* < L.Gk. *Sklabos,* alteration of O Slav. *Slověninŭ.*]

Slav. *abbr.* Slavic

sledge

slave (slāv) *n.* **1.** One bound in servitude as the property of a person or household. **2.** One who is abjectly subservient to a specified person or influence. **3.** One who works extremely hard. **4.** A machine or component controlled by another machine or component. ❖ *intr.v.* **slaved, slav·ing, slaves 1.** To work very hard or doggedly; toil. **2.** To trade in or transport slaves. [ME *sclave* < OFr. *esclave* < Med.Lat. *sclāvus* < *Sclāvus,* Slav (< the widespread enslavement of captured Slavs in the early M Ages). See SLAV.]

slave ant *n.* An ant captured and raised as a worker by slave-making ants.

Slave Coast A region of W Africa along the Bight of Benin on the Gulf of Guinea; an exportation base for slaves from the 16th to the early 19th cent.

slave driver *n.* **1.** An overseer of slaves at work. **2.** A severely exacting employer or supervisor.

slave·hold·er (slāv′hōl′dər) *n.* One who owns or holds slaves. —**slave′hold′ing** *adj. & n.*

slave-mak·ing ant (slāv′mā′kĭng) *n.* Any of various species of ant, such as *Formica sanguinea* of Europe, that raid the nests of other ants and carry off the pupae in order to provide workers for their own colonies.

sledgehammer

slav·er¹ (slăv′ər) *intr.v.* **-ered, -er·ing, -ers 1.** To slobber; drool. **2.** To behave in an obsequious manner; fawn. ❖ *n.* **1.** Saliva drooling from the mouth. **2.** Senseless and effusive talk; drivel. [ME *slaveren,* prob. < ON *slafra.*]

slav·er² (slā′vər) *n.* One, such as a person or ship, that is engaged in the trafficking of slaves.

Slave River A river, c. 499 km (310 mi), of W-central Canada flowing between Lake Athabasca in NE Alberta and Great Slave Lake in the S Northwest Terrs.

slav·er·y (slā′və-rē, slāv′rē) *n., pl.* **-ies 1.** The state of one bound in servitude as the property of a slaveholder or household. **2a.** The practice of owning slaves. **b.** A mode of production in which slaves constitute the principal labor force. **3.** The condition of being subject or addicted to a specified influence. **4.** A condition of hard work and subjection.

slave state *n.* **1. Slave State** Any of the 15 states of the Union in which slavery was legal before the Civil War. **2.** A nation under totalitarian rule.

slave trade *n.* Traffic in slaves.

slav·ey (slā′vē) *n., pl.* **-eys** A household servant, esp. an overworked one.

Slav·ic (slä′vĭk) *adj.* **1.** Of or relating to the Slavs or their languages. **2.** Of or relating to the branch of the Indo-European language family that includes such languages as Russian, Serbo-Croatian, and Polish, and is composed of the East Slavic, South Slavic, and West Slavic subdivisions. ❖ *n.* The Slavic branch of Indo-European.

slav·ish (slā′vĭsh) *adj.* **1.** Of or characteristic of a slave or slavery; servile. **2.** Showing no originality; blindly imitative. —**slav′ish·ly** *adv.* —**slav′ish·ness** *n.*

slav·oc·ra·cy (slā-vŏk′rə-sē) *n., pl.* **-cies** A ruling group of slaveholders or advocates of slavery, as in the southern United States before 1865. —**slav′o·crat′** (slā′və-krăt′) *n.*

Sla·vo·ni·a (slə-vō′nē-ə, -vōn′yə) A historical region of N Croatia between the Drava and Sava rivers. —**Sla·vo′ni·an** *adj. & n.*

Sla·von·ic (slə-vŏn′ĭk) *n.* Slavic. [< Med.Lat. *Sclāvōnia,* Slav. lands < *Sclāvus,* Slav. See SLAV.] —**Sla·von′ic** *adj.*

Slav·o·phile (slä′və-fīl′) also **Slav·o·phil** (-fĭl′) *n.* **1.** An admirer of Slavic peoples or their culture. **2.** A person advocating the supremacy of Slavic culture, esp. over western European influences, as in 19th-century Russia. —**Sla·voph′i·lism** (slə-vŏf′ə-lĭz′əm) *n.*

slaw (slô) *n. Chiefly Southern US* Coleslaw.

slay (slā) *tr.v.* **slew** (slōō), **slain** (slān), **slay·ing, slays 1.** To kill violently. **2.** *past tense and past participle often* **slayed** *Slang* To overwhelm, as with laughter or love. [ME *slen, slayen* < OE *slēan.*] —**slay′er** *n.*

SLE *abbr.* systemic lupus erythematosus

sleave (slēv) *n. Archaic* A fine thread or skein of thread. [< ME *sleven,* to disentangle < OE *slæfan,* to cut < *slāf,* p. t. of *slīfan,* to split.]

sleaze (slēz) *n.* A sleazy condition, quality, or appearance.

sleaze·bag (slēz′băg′) *n. Slang* A sleazy person.

slea·zy (slē′zē) *adj.* **-zi·er, -zi·est 1a.** Shabby, dirty, and vulgar; tawdry. **b.** Dishonest or corrupt; disreputable. **2.** Made of low-quality materials; cheap or shoddy. **3.** Thin and loosely woven; flimsy. [?] —**slea′zi·ly** *adv.* —**slea′zi·ness** *n.*

sled (slĕd) *n.* **1.** A vehicle on runners, used for carrying people or loads over ice and snow; a sledge. **2.** A light wooden frame on runners, used for coasting over snow or ice. ❖ *v.* **sled·ded, sled·ding, sleds** —*tr.* To carry on a sled. —*intr.* To ride or use a sled. [ME *sledde* < MDu.] —**sled′der** *n.*

sled·ding (slĕd′ĭng) *n.* **1.** The act of using a sled. **2.** Conditions conducive to the use of a sled. **3.** *Informal* A specific kind of progress toward a goal; the going: *The plan faces tough sledding.*

sled dog *n.* A dog, such as a husky, used to pull a dogsled, esp. in Arctic regions.

sledge (slĕj) *n.* A vehicle on low runners drawn by work animals, such as horses, and used to transport loads across ice, snow, and rough ground. ❖ *tr. & intr.v.* **sledged, sledg·ing, sledg·es** To convey or travel on a sledge. [Du. dialectal *sleedse,* perh. dim. of Du. *slede,* sled < MDu. *sledde.*]

sledge·ham·mer (slĕj′hăm′ər) *n.* A long heavy hammer, often wielded with both hands, used for driving wedges and for other heavy work. ❖ *tr.v.* **-mered, -mer·ing, -mers** To strike with or as if with a sledgehammer. ❖ *adj.* Ruthlessly severe; crushing. [ME *slegge* (< OE *slecg*) + HAMMER.]

sleek (slēk) *adj.* **sleek·er, sleek·est 1.** Smooth and lustrous as if polished; glossy. **2.** Well-groomed and neatly tailored. **3.** Healthy or well-fed; thriving. **4.** Polished or smooth in manner, esp. in an unctuous way; slick. ❖ *tr.v.* **sleeked, sleek·ing, sleeks 1.** To make sleek; slick. **2.** To gloss over; conceal. [Variant of SLICK.] —**sleek′ly** *adv.* —**sleek′ness** *n.*

sleep (slēp) *n.* **1a.** A natural periodic state of rest for the mind and body, in which the eyes usu. close and consciousness is completely or partly lost, so that there is a decrease in body movement and responsiveness to external stimuli. **b.** A period of this form of rest. **c.** A state of inactivity resembling or suggesting sleep; unconsciousness, dormancy, hibernation, or death. **2.** *Botany* The folding together of leaflets or petals at night or in the absence of light. **3.** A crust of dried tears or mucus around the eye. ❖ *v.* **slept** (slĕpt), **sleep·ing, sleeps** —*intr.* **1.** To be in the state of sleep or to fall asleep. **2.** To be in a condition resembling sleep. —*tr.* **1.** To pass or get rid of by sleeping: *slept away the day.* **2.** To provide sleeping accommodations for: *This tent sleeps three.* —***phrasal verbs:* sleep around** *Informal* To be sexually active with more than one partner. **sleep in 1.** To sleep at one's place of employment: *a cook who sleeps in.* **2a.** To oversleep. **b.** To sleep late on purpose. **sleep on** To think about (something) overnight before deciding. **sleep over** To spend the night as a guest in another's home. **sleep together** To have sexual relations. **sleep with** To have sexual relations with. [ME *slepe* < OE *slǣp.*]

sleep apnea *n.* A temporary suspension of breathing occurring repeatedly during sleep that often affects overweight people or those having a neurological disorder.

sleep·er (slē′pər) *n.* **1.** One that sleeps. **2.** A sleeping car. **3.** Children's pajamas, usu. with legs that cover the feet. Often used in the plural. **4a.** One that achieves unexpected recognition or success, as a racehorse or movie. **b.** A spy or saboteur who is planted in an enemy country and who lives unobtrusively as a citizen of that country until activated into clandestine operations by a prearranged signal. **5.** A horizontal structural member on or near the ground that supports weight. **6.** *Chiefly British* A railroad crosstie. **7.** Any of various usu. small fishes of the family Eleotridae, noted for their habit of lying immobile.

sleep-in (slēp′ĭn′) *adj.* Living at one's place of employment.

sleep·ing bag (slē′pĭng) *n.* A large, warmly lined, usu. zippered bag for sleeping, esp. outdoors.

sleeping car *n.* A railroad car having accommodations for sleeping.

sleeping pill *n.* A sedative or hypnotic drug, esp. a barbiturate, in the form of a pill or capsule used to relieve insomnia.

sleeping porch *n.* A well-ventilated, usu. screened porch or gallery used as an occasional sleeping quarters.

sleeping sickness *n.* An often fatal, endemic infectious disease in tropical Africa, caused by either of two trypanosomes (*Trypanosoma rhodesiense* or *T. gambiense*) transmitted by the tsetse fly and characterized by fever, headache, and lymph node swelling, followed by weakness, sleepiness, and coma.

sleep-learn·ing (slēp′lûr′nĭng) *n.* Attempted instruction in a subject, such as a foreign language, during sleep, usu. by means of recordings.

sleep·less (slēp′lĭs) *adj.* **1a.** Marked by a lack of sleep: *a sleepless night.* **b.** Unable to sleep. **2.** Always alert or active; never resting.

—**sleep′less•ly** *adv.* —**sleep′less•ness** *n.*
sleep•o•ver (slēp′ō′vər) *n.* **1.** An instance of spending the night as a guest at another's home. **2.** An overnight guest.
sleep•walk•ing (slēp′wô′kĭng) *n.* The act or an instance of walking or performing another activity associated with wakefulness while asleep or in a sleeplike state. —**sleep′walk′** *v.* —**sleep′walk′er** *n.*
sleep•wear (slēp′wâr′) *n.* See **nightclothes.**
sleep•y (slē′pē) *adj.* **-i•er, -i•est 1a.** Ready for or needing sleep. **b.** Sluggish from sleep. **2.** Inducing sleep. **3.** Inactive; quiet: *a sleepy town.* —**sleep′i•ly** *adv.* —**sleep′i•ness** *n.*
sleep•y•head (slē′pē-hĕd′) *n. Informal* One who is in need of or groggy from sleep.
sleet (slēt) *n.* **1.** Precipitation consisting of usu. transparent frozen or partially frozen raindrops. **2.** A mixture of rain and snow or hail. **3.** A thin icy coating that forms when rain or sleet freezes, as on trees or streets. ❖ *intr.v.* **sleet•ed, sleet•ing, sleets** To shower sleet. [ME *slete* < OE **slēte.*] —**sleet′y** *adj.*
sleeve (slēv) *n.* **1.** A part of a garment that covers all or part of an arm. **2.** A case into which an object or device fits: *a record sleeve.* ❖ *tr.v.* **sleeved, sleev•ing, sleeves** To furnish or fit with sleeves or a sleeve. ***—idiom:*** **up (one's) sleeve** Hidden but ready to be used. [ME *sleve* < OE *slēf.*] —**sleeve′less** *adj.*
sleeve coupling *n.* A thin steel cylinder joining the ends of two lengths of shafting or pipe.
sleeve dog *n.* A very small Pekingese, usu. 15 centimeters (6 inches) or less in height.
sleigh (slā) *n.* A light vehicle mounted on low runners for use on snow or ice, having one or more seats and usu. drawn by a horse. ❖ *intr.v.* **sleighed, sleigh•ing, sleighs** To ride in or drive a sleigh. [Du. *slee*, var. of *slede* < MDu. *slēde.*] —**sleigh′er** *n.*
sleight (slīt) *n.* **1.** Deftness; dexterity. **2.** A clever or skillful trick or deception; an artifice or stratagem. [ME, alteration of *sleahthe* < ON *slœgdh* < *slœgr*, sly.]
sleight of hand *n., pl.* **sleights of hand 1.** A trick or set of tricks performed by a juggler or magician so quickly and deftly that the manner of execution cannot be observed; legerdemain. **2.** Performance of conjuring tricks. **3.** Skill in such performance.
slen•der (slĕn′dər) *adj.* **-er, -est 1a.** Having little width in proportion to height or length; long and thin. **b.** Thin and delicate in build; gracefully slim. **2.** Small in amount or extent; meager: *slender wages.* [ME *sclendre, slendre.*] —**slen′der•ize′** *v.* —**slen′der•ly** *adv.* —**slen′der•ness** *n.*
slender loris *n.* A very small tailless loris *(Loris gracilis)* of southern India and Sri Lanka having large eyes with dark circles around them and very short fingers and toes.
slept (slĕpt) *v.* Past tense and past participle of **sleep.**
sleuth (slo͞oth) *n.* **1.** A detective. **2.** See **sleuthhound** 1. ❖ *v.* **sleuthed, sleuth•ing, sleuths** *—tr.* To track or follow. *—intr.* To act as a detective. [Short for SLEUTHHOUND.]
sleuth•hound (slo͞oth′hound′) *n.* **1.** A dog used for tracking or pursuing, such as a bloodhound. **2.** A detective. [ME *sleuth*, animal track (< ON *slōdh*) + HOUND.]
slew[1] also **slue** (slo͞o) *n. Informal* A large amount or number; a lot: *a slew of bills.* [Ir.Gael. *sluagh*, multitude < OIr. *slúag.*]
slew[2] (slo͞o) *v.* Past tense of **slay.**
slew[3] (slo͞o) *n.* Variant of **slough**[1].
slew[4] (slo͞o) *v. & n.* Variant of **slue**[1].
slice (slīs) *n.* **1.** A thin broad piece cut from a larger object: *ate a slice of cheese.* **2.** A portion or share: *a slice of the profits.* **3a.** A knife with a broad thin flexible blade, used for cutting and serving food. **b.** A similar implement for spreading printing ink. **4.** *Sports* **a.** The course of a ball that curves in the direction of the dominant hand of the player propelling it, as to the right of a right-handed player. **b.** A stroke that sends a ball on such a course. ❖ *v.* **sliced, slic•ing, slic•es** *—tr.* **1.** To cut or divide into slices. **2.** To cut from a larger piece: *slice off a piece.* **3.** To cut through or across with or as if with a knife. **4.** To divide into portions or shares; parcel out. **5.** To spread, work at, or clear away with a bladed tool such as a slice bar. **6.** *Sports* To hit (a ball) in a slice. *—intr.* **1.** To move like a knife. **2.** *Sports* To hit a ball in a slice. [ME, splinter < OFr. *esclice* < *esclicier*, to splinter, of Gmc. orig.] —**slice′a•ble** *adj.* —**slic′er** *n.*
slice bar *n.* An iron tool with a broad flat end, used to loosen and clear out clinkers from furnace grates.
slice of life *n., pl.* **slices of life** An episode of actual experience represented realistically in a dramatic, fictional, or journalistic work. —**slice′-of-life′** (slīs′əv-līf′) *adj.*
slick (slĭk) *adj.* **slick•er, slick•est 1.** Smooth, glossy, and slippery. **2.** Deftly executed; adroit. **3.** Shrewd; wily. **4.** Superficially attractive or plausible but lacking depth or soundness; glib. ❖ *n.* **1.** A smooth or slippery surface or area. **2a.** A floating film of oil. **b.** A trail of floating material: *a garbage slick.* **3.** An implement that makes a surface slick, esp. a chisel for smoothing and polishing. **4.** *Informal* A magazine, usu. of large popular readership, printed on high-quality glossy paper. **5.** A smooth or treadless tire, often used for racing. ❖ *tr.v.* **slicked, slick•ing, slicks 1.** To make smooth, glossy, or oily. **2.** *Informal* To make neat, trim, or tidy: *slicked themselves up.* [ME *slike* < OE **slice.* V., ME *sliken* < Late OE *-slīcian, -slȳcian* (in *nīgslȳcod*, freshly smoothed).] —**slick′ly** *adv.* —**slick′ness** *n.*
slick•en (slĭk′ən) *tr. & intr.v.* **-ened, -en•ing, -ens** To make or become slick. —**slick′en•er** *n.*
slick•en•side (slĭk′ən-sīd′) *n.* A polished striated rock surface caused by one rock mass sliding over another in a fault plane. [Dialectal *slicken*, glossy (alteration of SLICK) + SIDE.]
slick•er (slĭk′ər) *n.* **1a.** A long water-repellant coat usu. made of oilskin. **b.** A raincoat made of a glossy or shiny material, such as plastic or rubber. **2.** A tool for dressing hides. **3.** *Informal* A cheat; a swindler. **4.** *Informal* A person with stylish clothing and manners.
slid•den (slĭd′n) *v. Archaic* A past participle of **slide.**
slide (slīd) *v.* **slid** (slĭd), **slid•ing, slides** *—intr.* **1.** To move over a surface while maintaining smooth continuous contact. **2.** To coast on a slippery surface, such as ice or snow. **3.** To pass smoothly and quietly; glide. **4.** To go unattended or unacted upon: *Let the matter slide.* **5.** To lose a secure footing or position; shift out of place; slip. **6a.** To move downward. **b.** To return to a less favorable or less worthy condition. **7.** *Baseball* To drop down and skid into a base to avoid being put out. *—tr.* **1.** To cause to slide or slip. **2.** To place covertly or deftly: *slid the stolen goods into his pocket.* ❖ *n.* **1.** A sliding movement or action. **2.** A smooth surface or track for sliding, usu. inclined: *a water slide.* **3.** A playground apparatus for children to slide on, typically consisting of a smooth chute mounted by a ladder. **4.** A part that operates by sliding, as the U-shaped section of tube on a trombone that is moved to change the pitch. **5.** An image on a transparent base for projection on a screen. **6.** A small glass plate for mounting specimens to be examined under a microscope. **7.** A fall of a mass of rock, earth, or snow down a slope; an avalanche or landslide. **8.** *Music* **a.** A slight portamento used in violin playing, passing quickly from one note to another. **b.** An ornamentation consisting of two grace notes approaching the main note. **c.** A small metal or glass tube worn over a finger or held in the hand, used in playing bottleneck-style guitar. **d.** The bottleneck style of guitar playing. [ME *sliden* < OE *slīdan.*]

SYNONYMS *slide, slip, glide, coast, skid, slither* These verbs mean to move smoothly and continuously over or as if over a slippery surface. *Slide* usually implies rapid easy movement without loss of contact with the surface: *The coal slid down a chute to the cellar. Slip* is often applied to accidental sliding resulting in loss of balance or foothold: *slipped on a patch of ice. Glide* refers to smooth, free-flowing, seemingly effortless movement: *"four snakes gliding up and down a hollow"* (Ralph Waldo Emerson). *Coast* applies especially to downward movement resulting from the effects of gravity or momentum: *The driver let the truck coast down the incline. Skid* implies an uncontrolled, often sideways sliding caused by a lack of traction: *The bus skidded on wet pavement. Slither* can mean to slip and slide, as on an uneven surface, often with friction and noise: *"The detached crystals slithered down the rock face"* (H.G. Wells). The word can also suggest the sinuous gliding motion of a reptile: *An iguana slithered across the path.*

slid•er (slī′dər) *n.* **1.** One that slides. **2.** *Baseball* A fast pitch that breaks in the same direction as a curve ball at the last moment.
slide rule *n.* A device consisting of logarithmically scaled rules mounted to slide along each other so that multiplication, division, and other more complex computations are reduced to the mechanical equivalent of addition or subtraction.
slide valve *n.* A valve that slides back and forth over ports, esp. one in the cylinder wall of a steam engine that permits the intake and outflow of steam to move the piston.
slid•ing scale (slī′dĭng) *n.* A scale in which indicated prices, taxes, or wages vary in accordance with another factor, as medical charges with a patient's income.
sliding tackle *n.* A tackle in soccer in which the defender leaps forward or slides and extends a leg in order to disrupt the play or get possession of the ball.
sli•er (slī′ər) *adj.* A comparative of **sly.**
sli•est (slī′ĭst) *adj.* A superlative of **sly.**
slieve (slēv) *n. Irish* A mountain. [Ir.Gael. *sliabh* < OIr. *slíab.*]
slight (slīt) *adj.* **slight•er, slight•est 1.** Small in size, degree, or amount. **2.** Lacking strength, substance, or solidity; frail: *slight evidence.* **3.** Of small importance or consideration; trifling. **4.** Small and slender in build or construction; delicate. ❖ *tr.v.* **slight•ed, slight•ing, slights 1.** To treat as of small importance; make light of. **2.** To treat with discourteous reserve or inattention. **3.** To do negligently or thoughtlessly; scant. ❖ *n.* **1.** The act or an instance of slighting. **2.** A deliberate discourtesy; a snub. [ME, slender, smooth, poss. of Scand. orig.] —**slight′ness** *n.*
slight•ing (slī′tĭng) *adj.* Conveying or constituting a slight; belittling: *a slighting look.* —**slight′ing•ly** *adv.*
slight•ly (slīt′lē) *adv.* **1.** To a small degree or extent; somewhat. **2.** Slenderly; delicately: *slightly built.*
Sli•go (slī′gō) A municipal borough of N Ireland on **Sligo Bay**, an inlet of the Atlantic Ocean. Pop. 17,232.
slim (slĭm) *adj.* **slim•mer, slim•mest 1.** Small in girth or thickness in proportion to height or length; slender. **2.** Small in quantity or amount; meager: *slim hopes.* ❖ *intr. & tr.v.* **slimmed, slim•ming, slims 1.** To become or make slim. **2.** To lose or cause to lose weight, as by dieting or exercise. [Du., bad, sly < MDu. *slimp*, slim, bad, crooked.] —**slim′ly** *adv.* —**slim′mer** *n.* —**slim′ness** *n.*

ă	pat	oi	boy
ā	pay	ou	out
âr	care	o͝o	took
ä	father	o͞o	boot
ĕ	pet	ŭ	cut
ē	be	ûr	urge
ĭ	pit	th	thin
ī	pie	*th*	this
îr	pier	hw	which
ŏ	pot	zh	vision
ō	toe	ə	about, item
ô	paw		

Stress marks:
′ (primary);
′ (secondary), as in
lexicon (lĕk′sĭ-kŏn′)

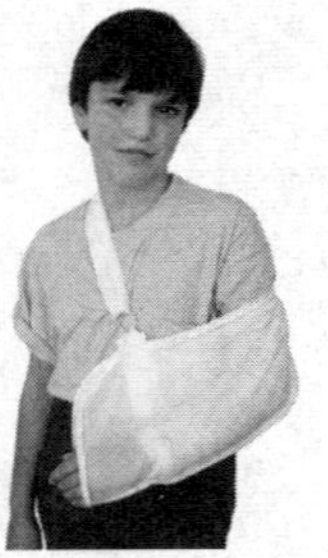

sling[1]

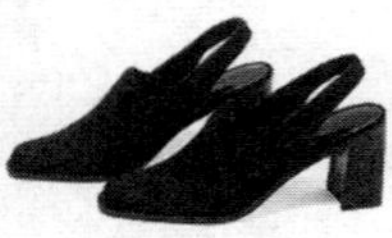

slingback
pair of slingbacks

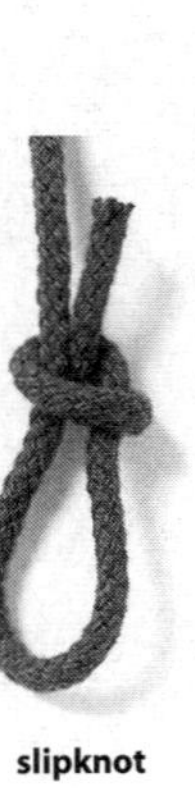

slipknot

slime (slīm) *n.* **1.** A thick, sticky, slippery substance. **2.** A mucous substance secreted by certain animals, such as fish or slugs. **3.** Soft moist earth; mud. **4.** Vile or disgusting matter. **5.** *Slang* A despicable or repulsive person. ❖ *tr.v.* **slimed, slim•ing, slimes 1.** To smear with slime. **2.** To remove slime from (fish to be canned, for example). [ME < OE *slīm.*]

slime•ball (slīm′bôl′) *n. Slang* A despicable or disgusting person. [SLIME + *-ball* (prob. as in ODDBALL).]

slime mold *n.* **1.** Any of various primitive organisms of the phylum Acrasiomycota, esp. of the genus *Dictyostelium*, that grow on dung and decaying vegetation and have a life cycle characterized by a slimelike amoeboid stage and a multicellular reproductive stage. **2.** Any of various organisms of the phylum Myxomycota that grow on decaying vegetation and in moist soil and have a similar but more advanced life cycle.

slim•sy (slĭm′zē) also **slimp•sy** (slĭmp′sē) *adj.* **-si•er, -si•est** *Informal* Frail; flimsy. [Blend of SLIM and FLIMSY.]

slim•y (slī′mē) *adj.* **-i•er, -i•est 1.** Consisting of or resembling slime; viscous. **2.** Covered with or exuding slime. **3.** Vile; foul. **—slim′i•ly** *adv.* **—slim′i•ness** *n.*

sling[1] (slĭng) *n.* **1a.** A weapon consisting of a looped strap in which a stone is whirled and then let fly. **b.** A slingshot. **2.** A loop for supporting, cradling, or hoisting something, esp.: **a.** A strap of a shoe that fits over the heel. **b.** A strap used to carry a rifle over the shoulder. **c.** *Nautical* A rope or chain that attaches to the mast and supports a yard. **d.** A band suspended from the neck to support an injured arm or hand. **3.** The act of hurling a missile. ❖ *tr.v.* **slung** (slŭng), **sling•ing, slings 1.** To hurl with or as if with a sling. **2.** To place or carry in a sling. **3.** To move with a sling: *sling cargo.* **4.** To hang loosely or freely; let swing. [ME *slinge.*] **—sling′er** *n.*

sling[2] (slĭng) *n.* A drink consisting of brandy, whiskey, or gin, sweetened and usu. lemon-flavored. [?]

sling•back or **sling-back** (slĭng′băk′) *n.* A shoe with a strap that wraps around the back of the heel.

sling•shot (slĭng′shŏt′) *n.* A Y-shaped stick having an elastic strap attached to the prongs, used for flinging small stones.

slink (slĭngk) *v.* **slunk** (slŭngk) also **slinked, slink•ing, slinks** *—intr.* To move in a quiet, furtive manner; sneak: *slunk away.* *—tr.* To give birth to prematurely. ❖ *n.* An animal, esp. a calf, born prematurely. ❖ *adj.* Born prematurely. [ME *slinken* < OE *slincan.*] **—slink′ing•ly** *adv.*

slink•y (slĭng′kē) *adj.* **-i•er, -i•est 1.** Stealthy, furtive, and sneaking. **2.** *Informal* Graceful, sinuous, and sleek: *wore a slinky outfit to the party.* **—slink′i•ly** *adv.* **—slink′i•ness** *n.*

slip[1] (slĭp) *v.* **slipped, slip•ping, slips** *—intr.* **1a.** To move smoothly, easily, and quietly. **b.** To move stealthily; steal. **2.** To pass gradually, easily, or imperceptibly: *The time slipped by.* **3a.** To slide involuntarily and lose one's balance or foothold. See Syns at **slide. b.** To slide out of place; shift position: *The gear slipped.* **4.** To escape, as from a grasp, fastening, or restraint: *slipped away.* **5.** To decline from a former or standard level; fall off. **6.** To fall behind a scheduled production rate. **7.** To fall into fault or error. Often used with *up.* *—tr.* **1.** To cause to move in a smooth, easy, or sliding motion. **2.** To place or insert smoothly and quietly. **3.** To put on or remove (clothing) easily or quickly: *slip on a sweater.* **4.** To get loose or free from; elude. **5.** To give birth to prematurely. Used of animals. **6.** To unleash or free (a dog or hawk) to pursue game. **7.** To release, loose, or unfasten: *slip a knot.* **8.** To dislocate (a bone). **9.** To pass (a knitting stitch) from one needle to another without knitting it. ❖ *n.* **1.** The act or an instance of slipping or sliding. **2.** An accident or mishap, esp. a falling down. **3a.** An error in conduct or thinking; a mistake. **b.** A slight error or oversight, as in speech or writing: *a slip of the tongue.* **4.** *Nautical* **a.** A docking place for a ship between two piers. **b.** A slipway. **5.** *Nautical* The difference between a vessel's actual speed through water and the speed at which the vessel would move if the screw were propelling against a solid. **6a.** A woman's undergarment of dress length with shoulder straps. **b.** A half-slip. **7.** A pillowcase. **8.** *Geology* The relative displacement of formerly adjacent points on opposite sides of a fault. **9.** The difference between optimal and actual output in a mechanical device. **10.** Movement between two parts where none should exist, as between a pulley and a belt. **11.** A sideways movement of an airplane when banked too far. ***—idioms:* give (someone) the slip** *Slang* To escape the pursuit of. **let slip** To say inadvertently. **slip one over on** *Informal* To hoodwink; trick. [ME *slippen*, prob. of MLGer. or MDu. orig.]

slip[2] (slĭp) *n.* **1.** A part of a plant cut or broken off for grafting or planting; a scion or cutting. **2.** A long narrow piece; a strip. **3.** A slender youthful person. **4.** A small piece of paper, esp. a small form, document, or receipt: *a deposit slip; a sales slip.* **5.** A narrow pew in a church. ❖ *tr.v.* **slipped, slip•ping, slips** To make a slip from (a plant or plant part). [Prob. < MLGer. or MDu. *slippe.*]

slip[3] (slĭp) *n.* Thinned potter's clay used for decorating or coating ceramics. [ME, slime < OE *slypa.*]

SLIP *abbr.* Serial Line Internet Protocol

slip•case (slĭp′kās′) *n.* A protective box with one open end or more, used for storing a book. **—slip′cased′** *adj.*

slip•cov•er (slĭp′kŭv′ər) *n.* A fitted removable cover, usu. of cloth, for a piece of upholstered furniture. **—slip′cov′er** *v.*

slip•dress or **slip dress** (slĭp′drĕs′) *n.* A sleeveless dress with narrow shoulder straps, usu. made from thin silky material.

slip•knot (slĭp′nŏt′) *n.* **1.** A knot made with a loop so that it slips easily along the rope or cord around which it is tied. **2.** A knot that can readily be untied by pulling one free end.

slip-on (slĭp′ŏn′, -ôn′) *n.* A garment easily donned or removed. **—slip′-on′** *adj.*

slip•o•ver (slĭp′ō′vər) *n.* A garment, such as a sweater, designed to be put on or taken off over the head.

slip•page (slĭp′ĭj) *n.* **1.** The act or an instance of slipping, esp. movement away from an original or secure place. **2.** The amount or extent of slipping. **3.** A decline in level, performance, or achievement. **4.** Loss of motion or power due to slipping.

slipped disk (slĭpt) *n.* Protrusion of a part of an intervertebral disk through the fibrocartilage, occurring usu. in the lower lumbar region and often causing back pain or sciatica.

slip•per (slĭp′ər) *n.* A low shoe that can be slipped on and off easily and usu. worn indoors. **—slip′pered** *adj.*

slipper flower *n.* See **calceolaria.**

slip•per•wort (slĭp′ər-wûrt′, -wôrt′) *n.* See **calceolaria.**

slip•per•y (slĭp′ə-rē) *adj.* **-i•er, -i•est 1.** Causing or tending to cause sliding or slipping: *a slippery sidewalk.* **2.** Tending to slip, as from one's grasp: *a slippery bar of soap.* **3.** Not trustworthy; elusive or tricky. [Alteration of obsolete *slipper* < ME < OE *slipor.*] **—slip′per•i•ness** *n.*

slippery elm *n.* **1.** A deciduous eastern North American tree *(Ulmus rubra)* having hard wood and mucilaginous inner bark formerly used medicinally. **2.** Its wood.

slip•py (slĭp′ē) *adj.* Slippery. **—slip′pi•ly** *adv.*

slip ring *n.* A metal ring mounted on a rotating part of a machine to provide a continuous electrical connection through brushes on stationary contacts.

slip-sheet (slĭp′shēt′) *n.* A blank sheet of paper slipped between newly printed sheets to prevent offsetting. **—slip′-sheet′** *v.*

slip•shod (slĭp′shŏd′) *adj.* **1.** Marked by carelessness; sloppy or slovenly. See Syns at **sloppy. 2.** Slovenly in appearance; shabby or seedy. **—slip′shod′di•ness** *n.*

slip•slop (slĭp′slŏp′) *n.* **1.** Trivial conversation or writing; twaddle. **2.** *Archaic* Unappetizing liquid or watery food; slops. [Reduplication of SLOP[1].]

slip•stitch (slĭp′stĭch′) *n.* A concealed stitch used for sewing together two layers of fabric, as with hems and facings.

slip•stream (slĭp′strēm′) *n.* **1.** The turbulent flow of air driven backward by the propeller or propellers of an aircraft. **2.** The area of reduced pressure or forward suction produced by and immediately behind a fast-moving object as it moves through air or water. ❖ *intr.v.* **-streamed, -stream•ing, -streams** To drive or cycle in the slipstream of a vehicle ahead.

slip-up (slĭp′ŭp′) *n.* An error; an oversight.

slip•ware (slĭp′wâr′) *n.* Pottery coated or decorated with slip.

slip•way (slĭp′wā′) *n.* A sloping surface leading down to the water, on which ships are built or repaired.

slit (slĭt) *n.* A long, straight, narrow cut or opening. ❖ *tr.v.* **slit, slit•ting, slits 1.** To make a slit or slits in. **2.** To cut lengthwise into strips; split. [ME *slitte* < *slitten*, to split < OE *slītan*, to cut up.] **—slit′ter** *n.* **—slit′ty** *adj.*

slith•er (slĭth′ər) *v.* **-ered, -er•ing, -ers** *—intr.* **1.** To glide or slide like a reptile. **2.** To walk with a sliding or shuffling gait. **3.** To slip and slide, as on a loose or uneven surface. See Syns at **slide.** *—tr.* To cause to slither. ❖ *n.* A slithering movement or gait. [ME *slethren*, var. of *sliddren* < OE *slidrian*, freq. of *slīdan*, to slide.] **—slith′er•y** *adj.*

sliv•er (slĭv′ər) *n.* **1.** A slender piece cut, split, or broken off; a splinter. **2.** A small narrow piece, portion, or plot: *a sliver of land.* **3.** (*also* slī′vər) A continuous strand of loose wool, flax, or cotton, ready for drawing and twisting. ❖ *tr. & intr.v.* **-ered, -er•ing, -ers** To split or become split into slivers. [ME *slivere* < *sliven*, to split < OE *slīfan.*]

sliv•o•vitz (slĭv′ə-vĭts) *n.* A dry colorless plum brandy. [Serbo-Croatian *šljivovica* < *šljiva*, plum. See **sleiə-** in App.]

Sloan (slōn), **John French** 1871–1951. Amer. painter whose works include *Sunday, Women Drying Their Hair* (1912).

slob (slŏb) *n. Informal* A person regarded as slovenly, crude, or obnoxious. [Ir.Gael. *slab*, mud < OIr., prob. of Scand. orig.; akin to Swed. dialectal *slabb*, mud.] **—slob′bish, slob′by** *adj.*

slob•ber (slŏb′ər) *v.* **-bered, -ber•ing, -bers** *—intr.* **1.** To let saliva or liquid spill out from the mouth; drool. **2.** To express sentiment or enthusiasm effusively or incoherently; gush. *—tr.* To wet or smear with or as if with slobber. ❖ *n.* **1.** Saliva or liquid running from the mouth; drool. **2.** Effusive or incoherent expression; drivel. [ME *sloberen*, perh. of LGer. orig.] **—slob′ber•er** *n.* **—slob′ber•y** *adj.*

slob ice *n. Canadian* Slushy or broken ice floating as a mass at sea. [< dialectal *slob*, muddy land < Ir.Gael. *slab*, mud. See SLOB.]

sloe (slō) *n.* **1.** See **blackthorn. 2.** Either of two eastern North American plum trees or shrubs, *Prunus alleghaniensis* having dark purple fruit or *P. americana* having yellow or red fruit. **3.** The tart plumlike fruit of either of these plants. [ME *slo* < OE *slā.* See **sleiə-** in App.]

sloe-eyed (slō′īd′) *adj.* Having slanted dark eyes.

sloe gin *n.* A gin-based liqueur flavored with fresh sloes.

slog (slŏg) *v.* **slogged, slog•ging, slogs** —*intr.* **1.** To walk or progress with a slow heavy pace; plod: *slog across the swamp.* **2.** To work diligently for long hours: *slogged away at Latin.* —*tr.* **1.** To make (one's way) with a slow heavy pace against resistance. **2.** To strike with heavy blows. ❖ *n.* **1.** A long exhausting march or hike. **2.** A long session of hard work. [Perh. alteration of SLUG[3].] —**slog′ger** *n.*

slo•gan (slō′gən) *n.* **1.** A phrase expressing the aims or nature of an enterprise, organization, or candidate; a motto. **2.** A phrase used repeatedly, as in promotion. **3.** A battle cry of a Scottish clan. [Alteration of Sc. *slogorne,* battle cry < Gael. *sluagh-ghairm* : *sluagh,* host; see SLEW[1] + *gairm,* shout.]

slo•gan•eer (slō′gə-nîr′) *n.* A person who invents or uses slogans. —**slo′gan•eer′** *v.*

slo•gan•ize (slō′gə-nīz′) *tr.v.* **-ized, -iz•ing, -iz•es** To express as or in slogans or a slogan. —**slo′gan•iz•er** *n.*

sloop (slo͞op) *n.* A single-masted, fore-and-aft-rigged sailing boat with a short standing bowsprit or none at all and a single headsail set from the forestay. [Du. *sloep* < MDu. *slūpen,* to glide.]

sloop of war *n., pl.* **sloops of war** A small warship carrying guns on one deck only.

slop[1] (slŏp) *n.* **1.** Spilled or splashed liquid. **2.** Soft mud or slush. **3.** Unappetizing watery food or soup. **4.** Waste food used to feed pigs or other animals; swill. Often used in the plural. **5.** Mash remaining after alcohol distillation. Often used in the plural. **6.** Human excrement. Often used in the plural. **7.** Repulsively effusive writing or speech; drivel. ❖ *v.* **slopped, slop•ping, slops** —*intr.* **1.** To be spilled or splashed. **2.** To spill over; overflow. **3.** To walk heavily or messily in or as if in mud; plod. **4.** To express oneself effusively; gush. —*tr.* **1.** To spill (liquid). **2.** To spill liquid on. **3.** To serve unappetizingly or clumsily; dish out. **4.** To feed slops to (animals): *slopped the hogs.* [ME *sloppe,* a muddy place, perh. < OE **sloppe,* dung, slime.]

slop[2] (slŏp) *n.* **1. slops** Articles of clothing and bedding issued or sold to sailors. **2. slops** Short full trousers worn in the 16th century. **3.** A loose outer garment, such as a smock or overalls. **4. slops** *Chiefly British* Cheap ready-made garments. [ME *sloppe,* a kind of garment < OE *-slop* (in *oferslop,* surplice).]

slope (slōp) *v.* **sloped, slop•ing, slopes** —*intr.* **1.** To diverge from the vertical or horizontal; incline. See Syns at **slant. 2.** To move on a slant; ascend or descend. —*tr.* To cause to slope. ❖ *n.* **1.** An inclined line, surface, plane, position, or direction. **2.** A stretch of ground forming a natural or artificial incline: *ski slopes.* **3a.** A deviation from the horizontal. **b.** The amount or degree of such deviation. **4.** *Mathematics* **a.** The rate at which an ordinate of a point of a line on a coordinate plane changes with respect to a change in the abscissa. **b.** The tangent of the angle of inclination of a line or the slope of the tangent line for a curve or surface. [Prob. < ME *aslope,* sloping.] —**slop′er** *n.* —**slop′ing•ly** *adv.*

slo-pitch (slō′pĭch′) *n.* Variant of **slow-pitch.**

slop•py (slŏp′ē) *adj.* **-pi•er, -pi•est 1.** Lacking neatness or order; untidy: *a sloppy room.* **2.** Lacking care or precision; slipshod: *sloppy language.* **3.** *Informal* Oversentimental; gushy. **4.** Of, resembling, or covered with slop; muddy or slushy. **5.** Watery and unappetizing. **6.** Spotted or splashed with liquid. —**slop′pi•ly** *adv.* —**slop′pi•ness** *n.*

SYNONYMS *sloppy, slovenly, unkempt, slipshod* These adjectives mean marked by an absence of due or proper care or attention. *Sloppy* evokes the idea of careless spilling, spotting, or splashing; it suggests slackness, untidiness, or diffuseness: *"I do not see how the sloppiest reasoner can evade that"* (H.G. Wells). *Slovenly* implies habitual negligence and a lack of system or thoroughness: *a slovenly appearance. Unkempt* stresses dishevelment resulting from a neglectful lack of proper maintenance: *"an unwashed brow, an unkempt head of hair"* (Sir Walter Scott). *Slipshod* suggests inattention to detail and a general absence of meticulousness: *"the new owners' camp . . . a slipshod and slovenly affair, tent half stretched, dishes unwashed"* (Jack London).

slosh (slŏsh) *v.* **sloshed, slosh•ing, slosh•es** —*tr.* **1.** To spill or splash (a liquid) copiously or clumsily. **2.** To agitate in a liquid. —*intr.* To splash, wade, or flounder in water or another liquid. ❖ *n.* **1.** Slush. **2.** The sound of splashing liquid. [Perh. blend of SLOP[1] and SLUSH.] —**slosh′y** *adj.*

sloshed (slŏsht) *adj. Slang* Intoxicated; drunk.

slot[1] (slŏt) *n.* **1.** A narrow opening; a groove or slit: *a mail slot.* **2.** A gap between a main and auxiliary airfoil to provide space for airflow and facilitate the passage of air over the wing. **3a.** An assigned place in a sequence or schedule: *a new time slot for the show.* **b.** A position of employment in an organization or hierarchy. **4.** *Computer Science* A long narrow socket in a computer into which an expansion card can be inserted. **5.** *Informal* A slot machine designed for gambling. **6a.** *Football* A gap between an end and a tackle in an offensive line. **b.** *Sports* The area in front of the goal between the face-off circles on an ice hockey rink. ❖ *tr.v.* **slot•ted, slot•ting, slots 1.** To cut or make a slot or slots in. **2.** To put into or assign to a slot. [ME, hollow of the breastbone < OFr. *esclot.*]

slot[2] (slŏt) *n.* The track or trail of an animal, esp. a deer. [Obsolete Fr. *esclot,* horse's hoofprint < OFr., perh. < ON *slōdh,* track.]

sloth (slôth, slōth, slŏth) *n.* **1.** Aversion to work or exertion; laziness; indolence. **2.** Any of various slow-moving arboreal edentate mammals of the family Bradypodidae of South and Central America, having long hooklike claws by which they hang upside down from tree branches. **3.** A company of bears. [ME *slowth* < *slow,* slow. See SLOW.]

sloth bear *n.* A bear *(Melursus ursinus)* of India and Sri Lanka having a long snout, long sticky tongue, and dark shaggy hair.

sloth•ful (slôth′fəl, slōth′-, slŏth′-) *adj.* Disinclined to exertion or work. —**sloth′ful•ly** *adv.* —**sloth′ful•ness** *n.*

slot machine *n.* A vending or gambling machine operated by the insertion of coins into a slot.

slouch (slouch) *v.* **slouched, slouch•ing, slouch•es** —*intr.* **1.** To sit, stand, or walk with an awkward, drooping, excessively relaxed posture. **2.** To droop or hang carelessly, as a hat. —*tr.* To cause to droop; stoop. ❖ *n.* **1.** An awkward, drooping, excessively relaxed posture or gait. **2.** *Slang* An awkward, lazy, or inept person: *no slouch at bridge.* [?] —**slouch′i•ly** *adv.* —**slouch′i•ness** *n.* —**slouch′y** *adj.*

slouch hat *n.* A soft hat with a broad flexible brim.

slough[1] (slo͞o, slou) also **slew** (slo͞o) *n.* **1.** A depression or hollow, usu. filled with deep mud or mire. **2.** also **slue** A stagnant swamp, marsh, bog, or pond, esp. as part of a bayou, inlet, or backwater. **3.** A state of deep despair or moral degradation. [ME < OE *slōh.*] —**slough′y** *adj.*

slough[2] (slŭf) *n.* **1.** The dead outer skin shed by a reptile or amphibian. **2.** *Medicine* A layer or mass of dead tissue separated from surrounding living tissue, as in a wound. **3.** An outer layer or covering that is shed. ❖ *v.* **sloughed, slough•ing, sloughs** —*intr.* **1.** To be cast off or shed; come off. **2.** To shed a slough. **3.** *Medicine* To separate from surrounding living tissue. Used of dead tissue. —*tr.* To discard as undesirable or unfavorable; get rid of. [ME *slughe.*]

Slough (slou) A municipal borough of SE England, a suburb of London. Pop. 96,900.

Slo•vak (slō′väk′, -văk′) also **Slo•va•ki•an** (slō-vä′kē-ən, -văk′ē-ən) *n.* **1a.** A native or inhabitant of Slovakia. **b.** A person of Slovak descent. **2.** The Slavic language of the Slovaks. ❖ *adj.* Of or relating to Slovakia or its people, language, or culture. [Slovak *Slovák;* akin to O Church Slavonic *Slověne,* Slav.]

Slo•va•ki•a (slō-vä′kē-ə, -văk′ē-ə) A country of central Europe; part of Czechoslovakia from 1918–93. Cap. Bratislava. Pop. 5,347,000.

slov•en (slŭv′ən) *n.* One who is habitually careless in personal appearance or work. [ME *slovein,* perh. < MFlem. *sloovin,* a scold, gossip < MLGer. *slôven,* to dress carelessly; akin to Du. *sloof,* untidy woman.]

Slo•vene (slō′vēn′) also **Slo•ve•ni•an** (slō-vē′nē-ən, -vēn′yən) *n.* **1a.** A native or inhabitant of Slovenia. **b.** A person of Slovenian descent. **2.** The Slavic language of the Slovenes. ❖ *adj.* Of or relating to Slovenia or its people, language, or culture. [Ger. *Slowene* < Slovene *Slovȇnec,* ult. < O Church Slavonic *Slověne,* Slav.]

Slo•ve•ni•a (slō-vē′nē-ə, -vēn′yə) A country of the NW Balkan Peninsula. It came under Austrian control after 1335; former constituent republic of Yugoslavia 1918–91. Cap. Ljubljana. Pop. 1,942,000.

slov•en•ly (slŭv′ən-lē) *adj.* **1.** Untidy, as in dress or appearance. **2.** Marked by negligence; slipshod. See Syns at **sloppy.** —**slov′en•li•ness** *n.* —**slov′en•ly** *adv.*

slow (slō) *adj.* **slow•er, slow•est 1a.** Not moving or able to move quickly; proceeding at a low speed. **b.** Marked by a retarded tempo: *a slow waltz.* **2a.** Taking or requiring a long time: *the slow job of making bread.* **b.** Taking more time than is usual: *a slow worker.* **3.** Allowing movement or action only at a low speed: *a slow track.* **4.** Registering a time or rate behind or below the correct one: *a slow clock.* **5.** Lacking in promptness or willingness; not precipitate: *They were slow to accept our invitation.* **6.** Characterized by a low volume of sales or transactions. **7.** Lacking liveliness or interest; boring: *a slow party.* **8.** Not having or exhibiting intellectual or mental quickness. **9.** Only moderately warm; low: *a slow oven.* ❖ *adv.* **slower, slowest 1.** So as to fall behind the correct time or rate. **2.** At a low speed. ❖ *v.* **slowed, slow•ing, slows** —*tr.* **1.** To make slow or slower. **2.** To delay; retard. —*intr.* To become slow or slower. [ME < OE *slāw.*] —**slow′ly** *adv.* —**slow′ness** *n.*

USAGE NOTE *Slow* may sometimes be used instead of *slowly* after a verb: *We drove the car slow.* In formal writing *slowly* is generally preferred. *Slow* is often used in speech and informal writing, especially when brevity and forcefulness are sought: *Drive slow! Slow* is also the established idiomatic form with certain senses of common verbs: *The watch runs slow. Take it slow.*

slow•down (slō′doun′) *n.* The act or process of slowing down; a slackening of pace: *a production slowdown.*

slow-foot•ed (slō′fo͝ot′ĭd) *adj.* Proceeding at a tediously slow pace: *a slow-footed story.* —**slow′-foot′ed•ness** *n.*

slow infection *n.* An infection having a long incubation period, as that caused by a slow virus or by a prion.

slow loris *n.* A large loris *(Nycticebus coucang)* of Indonesia, having a corpulent, almost tailless body and noted for its very slow cautious movements.

slow match *n.* A match or fuse that burns slowly at a known rate,

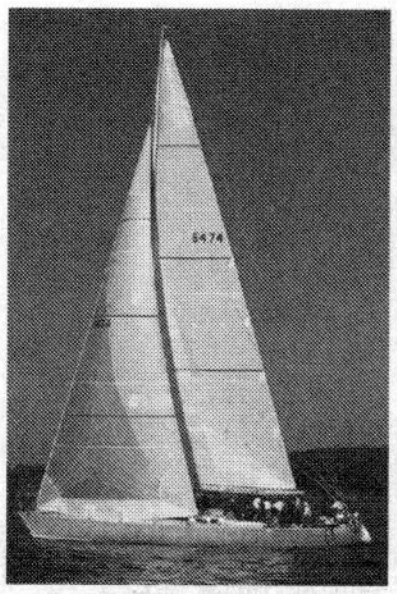

sloop

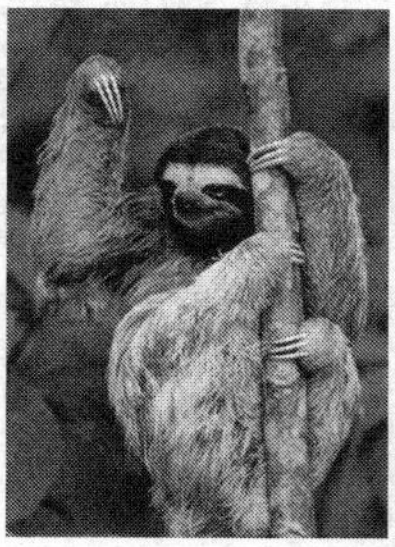

sloth
brown-throated three-toed sloth
Bradypus variegatus

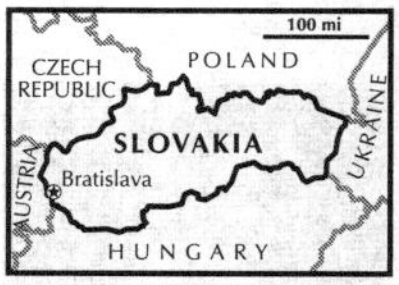

Slovakia

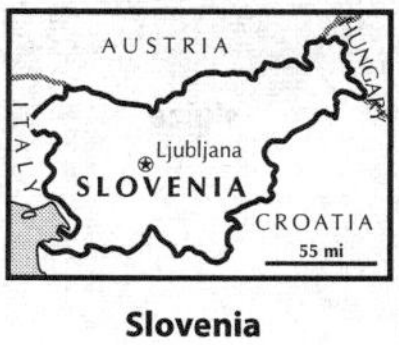

Slovenia

ă	pat	oi	boy
ā	pay	ou	out
âr	care	o͝o	took
ä	father	o͞o	boot
ĕ	pet	ŭ	cut
ē	be	ûr	urge
ĭ	pit	th	thin
ī	pie	*th*	this
îr	pier	hw	which
ŏ	pot	zh	vision
ō	toe	ə	about, item
ô	paw		

Stress marks:
′ (primary);
′ (secondary), as in
lexicon (lĕk′sĭ-kŏn′)

used to set off explosives or fire cannons and muzzle-loading firearms.

slow motion *n.* A filmmaking technique in which the action on screen is slower than normal. —**slow′-mo′tion** (slō′mō′shən) *adj.*

slow-pitch also **slo-pitch** (slō′pĭch′) *n.* Softball in which there are ten players to a team and legal pitches must travel in an arc from three to ten feet high.

slow•poke (slō′pōk′) *n. Informal* One that moves, works, or acts slowly.

slow virus *n.* Any of a group of animal viruses that cause diseases having an unusually long incubation period, as Creutzfeldt-Jakob disease.

slow-wit•ted or **slow-wit•ted** (slō′wĭt′ĭd) *adj.* Slow to comprehend. —**slow′-wit′ted•ly** *adv.* —**slow′-wit′ted•ness** *n.*

slow•worm (slō′wûrm′) *n.* A limbless lizard (*Anguis fragilis*) of Europe, western Asia, and northern Africa having a smooth snakelike body and feeding chiefly on slugs. [Alteration (influenced by SLOW) of ME *slowurm* < OE *slāwyrm : slā-*, earthworm, slowworm + *wyrm*, worm; see WORM.]

slub (slŭb) *tr.v.* **slubbed, slub•bing, slubs** To draw out and twist (a strand of textile fiber) for spinning. ❖ *n.* **1.** A soft thick nub in yarn that is an imperfection or purposely set for effect. **2.** A slightly twisted roll of fiber, as of silk. [?]

sludge (slŭj) *n.* **1.** Semisolid material such as the type precipitated by sewage treatment. **2.** Mud, mire, or ooze covering the ground or forming a deposit, as on a riverbed. **3.** Finely broken or half-formed ice on a body of water, esp. the sea. **4.** An agglutination of blood cells forming a semisolid mass that can impede circulation. ❖ *intr.v.* **sludged, sludg•ing, sludg•es** To agglutinate into a semisolid mass. Used of blood cells. [Perh. alteration of dialectal *slutch*, mire.] —**sludg′y** *adj.*

slue¹ also **slew** (slōō) *v.* **slued, slu•ing, slues** also **slewed, slew•ing, slews** —*tr.* **1.** To turn (something) on an axis; rotate: *slued the chair around.* **2.** To turn sharply; veer: *slued the car around.* —*intr.* **1.** To turn about an axis; pivot. **2.** To turn or slide sideways or off course; skid. ❖ *n.* **1.** The act of sluing. **2.** The position to which something has slued. [?]

slue² (slōō) *n.* Variant of **slew¹**.

slue³ (slōō) *n.* Variant of **slough¹** 2.

slug¹ (slŭg) *n.* **1.** A round bullet larger than buckshot. **2.** *Informal* A shot or gulp of liquor. **3.** A small metal disk for use in a vending or gambling machine, esp. one used illegally. **4.** A lump of metal or glass prepared for further processing. **5.** *Printing* **a.** A strip of type metal, less than type-high and thicker than a lead, used for spacing. **b.** A line of cast type in a strip of metal. **c.** A compositor's type line of identifying marks or instructions, inserted temporarily in copy. **6.** *Physics* The unit of mass accelerated at one foot per second per second when acted on by a force of one pound. ❖ *tr.v.* **slugged, slug•ging, slugs** **1.** *Printing* To add slugs to. **2.** To drink rapidly or in large gulps. [Perh. < SLUG² (< its shape).]

slug² (slŭg) *n.* **1.** Any of various small, chiefly terrestrial gastropod mollusks of the genus *Limax* and related genera, having a slow-moving elongated body with no shell or only a flat rudimentary shell on or under the skin. **2.** The smooth soft larva of certain insects, such as the sawfly. **3.** A slimy mass of aggregated amoeboid cells from which the sporophore of a cellular slime mold develops. **4.** *Informal* A sluggard. [ME *slugge*, sluggard, prob. of Scand. orig.]

slug²
spotted garden slug
Limax maximus

slug³ (slŭg) *tr.v.* **slugged, slug•ging, slugs** To strike heavily, esp. with the fist or a bat. ❖ *n.* A blow with the fist or a bat. [Poss. < SLUG¹.] —**slug** *n.*

slug•a•bed (slŭg′ə-bĕd′) *n.* One inclined to stay in bed out of laziness.

slug•fest (slŭg′fĕst′) *n.* **1.** *Slang* A fight marked by an extended exchange of heavy blows. **2.** *Baseball* A game in which there are many hits and runs scored.

slug•gard (slŭg′ərd) *n.* A slothful person; an idler. ❖ *adj.* Lazy. [ME *sluggart*, prob. < *sluggi*, lazy, prob. of Scand. orig.] —**slug′gard•ly** *adj.*

slug•ger (slŭg′ər) *n.* **1.** One that slugs, as a fighter who delivers hard swinging punches. **2.** *Baseball* A batter who hits many extra-base hits.

slug•gish (slŭg′ĭsh) *adj.* **1.** Displaying little movement or activity; slow; inactive. **2.** Lacking alertness, vigor, or energy; indolent. **3.** Slow to perform or respond to stimulation. [ME, prob. < *slugge*, lazy person. See SLUG².] —**slug′gish•ly** *adv.* —**slug′gish•ness** *n.*

sluice (slōōs) *n.* **1a.** An artificial channel for conducting water, with a valve or gate to regulate the flow. **b.** A valve or gate used in such a channel; a floodgate. **2.** A body of water impounded behind a floodgate. **3.** An artificial channel, esp. for carrying excess water. **4.** A long inclined trough, as for carrying logs or separating gold ore. ❖ *v.* **sluiced, sluic•ing, sluic•es** —*tr.* **1.** To flood or drench with or as if with a flow of released water. **2.** To wash with water flowing in a sluice. **3.** To draw off or let out by a sluice. **4.** To send (logs, for example) down a sluice. —*intr.* To flow out from or as if from a sluice. [ME *scluse* < OFr. *escluse* < LLat. *exclūsa* < Lat., fem. p. part. of *exclūdere*, to shut out. See EXCLUDE.]

sluice

slum (slŭm) *n.* A heavily populated urban area characterized by substandard housing and squalor. Often used in the plural. ❖

intr.v. **slummed, slum•ming, slums** To visit impoverished areas or squalid locales, esp. out of curiosity or for amusement. —**idiom: slum it** To endure conditions or accommodations that are worse than what one is accustomed to. [?] —**slum′mer** *n.* —**slum′my** *adj.*

slum•ber (slŭm′bər) *v.* **-bered, -ber•ing, -bers** —*intr.* **1.** To sleep. **2.** To be dormant or quiescent. —*tr.* To pass (time) in sleep: *slumbered the night away.* ❖ *n.* **1.** Sleep. **2.** A state of inactivity or dormancy. [ME *slumeren, slumberen,* freq. of *slumen,* to doze, prob. < *slume,* light sleep < OE *slūma.*] —**slum′ber•er** *n.*

slum•ber•ous (slŭm′bər-əs) or **slum•brous** (-brəs) *adj.* **1.** Sleepy; drowsy. **2a.** Suggestive of or resembling sleep. **b.** Quiet; tranquil. **3.** Causing or inducing sleep; soporific. —**slum′ber•ous•ly** *adv.* —**slum′ber•ous•ness** *n.*

slum•ber•y (slŭm′bə-rē) *adj.* Slumberous.

slum•gul•lion (slŭm-gŭl′yən) *n.* A watery meat stew. [Perh. *slum,* muddy deposit in a mining sluice + dialectal *gullion,* mud (perh. < Ir.Gael. *goilín,* pit).]

slum•lord (slŭm′lôrd′) *n.* An owner of slum property, esp. one that overcharges tenants and allows deterioration.

slump (slŭmp) *intr.v.* **slumped, slump•ing, slumps** **1.** To fall or sink heavily; collapse. **2.** To droop, as in sitting; slouch. **3a.** To decline suddenly; fall off. **b.** To perform poorly or inadequately: *The team has been slumping for a month.* **4a.** To sink or settle, as into mud. **b.** To slide down or spread out thickly, as mud. ❖ *n.* **1.** The act or an instance of slumping. **2.** A drooping or slouching posture. **3.** A sudden falling off or decline, as in activity or prices. **4.** An extended period of poor performance, as in a sport. **5.** See **grunt** 1. [Prob. of Scand. orig.]

slung (slŭng) *v.* Past tense and past participle of **sling¹**.

slunk (slŭngk) *v.* A past tense and a past participle of **slink**.

slur (slûr) *tr.v.* **slurred, slur•ring, slurs** **1.** To pronounce indistinctly. **2.** To talk about disparagingly or insultingly. **3.** To pass over lightly or carelessly; treat without due consideration. **4.** *Music* **a.** To glide over (a series of notes) smoothly without a break. **b.** To mark with a slur. **5.** *Printing* To blur or smear. ❖ *n.* **1.** A disparaging remark; an aspersion. **2.** A slurred utterance or sound. **3.** *Music* **a.** A curved line connecting notes on a score to indicate that they are to be played or sung legato. **b.** A passage played or sung in this manner. **4.** *Printing* A smeared or blurred impression. [Prob. < ME *sloor,* mud.]

slurp (slûrp) *v.* **slurped, slurp•ing, slurps** —*tr.* To eat or drink noisily. —*intr.* To slurp something. ❖ *n.* **1.** A loud sucking noise made in eating or drinking. **2.** *Slang* A mouthful of a liquid. [Du. *slurpen.*]

slur•ry (slûr′ē) *n., pl.* **-ries** A thin mixture of a liquid, esp. water, and any of several finely divided substances, such as cement or clay particles. [ME *slori,* perh. < *sloor,* mud.]

slush (slŭsh) *n.* **1.** Partially melted snow or ice. **2.** Soft mud; slop; mire. **3.** *Nautical* Grease or fat discarded from a ship's galley. **4.** A greasy compound used as a lubricant for machinery. **5.** Maudlin speech or writing. **6.** A drink made of flavored syrup poured over crushed ice. ❖ *v.* **slushed, slush•ing, slush•es** —*tr.* **1.** To daub (machinery) with slush. **2.** To fill (joints in masonry) with mortar. **3.** *Nautical* To wash down (a deck) by splashing with water. **4.** To splash or soak with slush or mud. —*intr.* **1.** To walk or proceed through slush. **2.** To make a splashing or slushy sound. [Perh. of Scand. orig.; akin to Norw. *slask,* sloppy weather.]

slush fund *n.* **1.** A fund reserved for undesignated purposes, esp. one raised by a group for corrupt practices. **2.** Money formerly raised by the sale of garbage from a warship to buy small items of luxury for the crew.

slush•y (slŭsh′ē) *adj.* **-i•er, -i•est** **1.** Consisting of, covered with, or full of slush. **2.** Resembling slush, as in consistency. **3.** Revoltingly sentimental; maudlin. —**slush′i•ly** *adv.* —**slush′i•ness** *n.*

slut (slŭt) *n.* **1a.** A person, esp. a woman, considered sexually promiscuous. **b.** A woman prostitute. **2.** A slovenly woman; a slattern. [ME *slutte.*] —**slut′tish, slut′ty** *adj.*

sly (slī) *adj.* **sli•er** (slī′ər), **sli•est** (slī′ĕst) also **sly•er, sly•est** **1.** Adept in craft or cunning. **2.** Lacking or marked by a lack of candor. **3.** Playfully mischievous; roguish. —**idiom: on the sly** In a way intended to escape notice: *took payments on the sly.* [ME *sleigh* < ON *slœgr.*] —**sly′ly** *adv.* —**sly′ness** *n.*

sly•boots (slī′bōōts′) *pl.n.* (*used with a sing. verb*) *Informal* A sly person.

Sm¹ The symbol for the element **samarium**.

Sm² *abbr. Bible* Samuel

SM *abbr.* **1.** *Latin* Scientiae Magister (Master of Science) **2.** service mark **3.** stage manager

S-M or **S/M** *abbr.* sadomasochism

smack¹ (smăk) *v.* **smacked, smack•ing, smacks** —*tr.* **1.** To press together and open (the lips) quickly and noisily, as in eating. **2.** To kiss noisily. **3.** To strike sharply and with a loud noise. —*intr.* **1.** To make or give a smack. **2.** To collide sharply and noisily. ❖ *n.* **1.** The loud sharp sound of smacking. **2.** A noisy kiss. **3.** A sharp blow or slap. ❖ *adv.* **1.** With a smack: *fell smack on her head.* **2.** Directly. [Perh. of MFlem. orig. or imit.]

smack² (smăk) *n.* **1a.** A distinctive flavor or taste. **b.** A suggestion or trace. **2.** A small amount; a smattering. ❖ *intr.v.* **smacked, smack•ing, smacks** **1.** To have a distinctive flavor or taste. Used with *of.* **2.** To give an indication; be suggestive. Often used with *of: statements that smacked of arrogance.* [ME < OE *smæc.*]

smack³ (smăk) *n.* A fishing boat sailing under various rigs, often having a well used to transport the catch to market. [Du. or LGer. *smak < smakken,* to fling, dash.]

smack⁴ (smăk) *n. Slang* Heroin. [Prob. var. of *smeck < Yiddish shmek,* a sniff, smell < *shmekn,* to sniff, smell < MHGer. *smecken, smacken,* to smell, taste < OHGer. *smac,* smell, taste.]

smack-dab (smăk′dăb′) *adv. Slang* Squarely; directly. [SMACK¹ + DAB¹, with a sudden impact.]

smack·er (smăk′ər) *n.* **1.** One that smacks, as a loud kiss. **2.** *Slang* A dollar.

smack·ing (smăk′ĭng) *adj.* Brisk; vigorous; spanking.

s-mail (ĕs′māl′) *n. Informal* Snail mail.

small (smôl) *adj.* **small·er, small·est 1.** Being below the average in size or magnitude. **2.** Limited in importance or significance; trivial. **3.** Limited in degree or scope: *small farm operations.* **4.** Lacking position, influence, or status; minor. **5.** Unpretentious; modest: *made a small living.* **6.** Not fully grown; young. **7.** Narrow in outlook; petty: *a small mind.* **8.** Having been belittled; humiliated: *felt small.* **9.** Diluted; weak. Used of alcoholic beverages. **10.** Lacking force or volume: *a small voice.* ❖ *adv.* **1.** In small pieces. **2.** Without loudness or forcefulness; softly. **3.** In a small manner. ❖ *n.* **1.** A part that is smaller or narrower than the rest: *the small of the back.* **2. smalls a.** Small things considered as a group. **b.** *Chiefly British* Small items of clothing. [ME *smal* < OE *smæl.*] —**small′ish** *adj.* —**small′ness** *n.*

SYNONYMS *small, diminutive, little, miniature, minuscule, minute, petite, tiny* These adjectives mean being notably below the average in size or magnitude: *a small house; diminutive in stature; little hands; a miniature camera; a minuscule amount of rain; minute errors; a petite figure; tiny feet.* **ANTONYM** *large*

small arm *n.* A firearm that can be carried in the hand.

small beer *n.* **1.** Weak or inferior beer. **2.** Unimportant things; trivia. ❖ *adj.* Trivial; unimportant.

small-bore (smôl′bôr′, -bōr′) *adj.* **1.** Of, relating to, or being a firearm of small caliber. **2.** Trivial or parochial in character.

small calorie *n.* See **calorie** 1.

small cap *adj.* **1.** Of or relating to companies whose retained earnings are small and whose outstanding shares of common stock have a small market value. **2.** Of or relating to mutual funds that invest in the stock of such companies. [SMALL + CAP³.]

small capital *n.* A letter having the form of a capital letter but smaller; for example: SMALL CAPITALS.

small change *n.* **1.** Coins of low denomination. **2.** Something of little value or significance.

small-claims court (smôl′klāmz′) *n.* A special court for simplified and efficient handling of small claims on debts.

small·clothes (smôl′klōthz′, -klōz′) *pl.n.* **1.** Men's close-fitting knee breeches worn in the 18th century. **2.** *Chiefly British* Small items of clothing, such as underwear.

Smal·ley (smô′lē), **Richard Errett** b. 1943. Amer. chemist who shared a 1996 Nobel Prize.

small fry *n.* **1.** Small children. **2.** Young or small fish. **3.** Persons or things regarded as unimportant.

small hours *pl.n.* The early hours after midnight.

small intestine *n.* The upper part of the intestine, consisting of the duodenum, jejunum, and ileum, where digestion is completed and nutrients are absorbed by the blood.

small-mind·ed (smôl′mīn′dĭd) *adj.* **1.** Having a narrow or selfish attitude. **2.** Characterized by pettiness or selfishness. —**small′-mind′ed·ly** *adv.* —**small′-mind′ed·ness** *n.*

small·mouth bass (smôl′mouth′ băs) *n.* A North American freshwater food and game fish (*Micropterus dolomieui*) having a shorter upper jaw than the similar largemouth bass.

small potatoes *pl.n. Informal* **1.** A person or thing regarded as unimportant. **2.** An insignificant amount or sum.

small·pox (smôl′pŏks′) *n.* An acute, highly infectious, often fatal disease caused by a poxvirus and marked by high fever, aches, and widespread skin eruptions that form pockmarks. [Late ME *small pockes,* small sacs (as opposed to *great pockes,* syphilis).]

small print *n.* See **fine print.**

small-scale (smôl′skāl′) *adj.* **1.** Limited in scope or extent; modest. **2.** Created on a small scale: *a small-scale model.*

small talk *n.* Casual or trivial conversation.

small·time or **small-time** (smôl′tīm′) *adj. Informal* Insignificant or unimportant; minor. —**small′-tim′er** *n.*

small time *n. Informal* A modest or minor level of attainment in a competitive field.

smalt (smôlt) *n.* A deep blue paint and ceramic pigment produced by pulverizing a glass made of silica, potash, and cobalt oxide. [Fr. < Ital. *smalto,* enamel, glaze, of Gmc. orig.]

smalt·ite (smôl′tīt′) also **smalt·ine** (smôl′tĭn, -tēn′) *n.* A white to silver-gray mineral, (Co,Ni)As₃, that is an ore of cobalt.

sma·rag·dine (smə-răg′dĕn′) *adj.* **1.** Of or relating to emeralds. **2.** Having the color of emeralds. ❖ *n.* also **sma·ragd** (smə-răgd′, smär′ăgd′) Emerald. [ME < Lat. *smaragdinus,* emerald-green < Gk. *smaragdinos < smaragdos,* emerald.]

sma·rag·dite (smə-răg′dīt′) *n.* A fibrous green amphibole mineral occurring in rocks such as eclogite. [Fr. < Lat. *smaragdus,* emerald < Gk. *smaragdos.*]

smarm (smärm) *n.* Smarmy speech or behavior. [Back-formation < SMARMY.]

smarm·y (smär′mē) *adj.* **-i·er, -i·est 1.** Hypocritically, complacently, or effusively earnest; unctuous. **2.** Sleek. [< *smarm,* to smear.] —**smarm′i·ness** *n.*

smart (smärt) *adj.* **smart·er, smart·est 1a.** Characterized by sharp quick thought; bright. See Syns at **intelligent. b.** Amusingly clever; witty: *a smart quip.* **c.** Impertinent; insolent. **2.** Energetic or quick in movement: *a smart pace.* **3.** Canny and shrewd in dealings with others: *a smart negotiator.* **4.** Fashionable; elegant. **5a.** Of, relating to, or being a highly automated device, esp. one that imitates human intelligence: *smart missiles.* **b.** *Computer Science* Having a processor and thus capable of processing data independently of a host computer: *a smart terminal.* ❖ *intr.v.* **smart·ed, smart·ing, smarts 1a.** To cause a sharp, usu. superficial stinging pain. **b.** To be the location of such a pain: *My leg smarts.* **c.** To feel such a pain. **2.** To suffer acutely, as from mental distress or remorse. **3.** To suffer or pay a heavy penalty. ❖ *n.* **1.** Sharp mental or physical pain. **2. smarts** *Slang* Intelligence; expertise. —**phrasal verb: smart off** *Informal* To speak or act impertinently. —**idiom: right smart** *New England & Southern US* A lot; a considerable amount: *He did right smart of the work himself.* [ME, stinging, keen, alert < OE *smeart,* causing pain.] —**smart′ly** *adv.* —**smart′ness** *n.*

smart al·eck (ăl′ĭk) *n. Informal* **1.** A person regarded as obnoxiously self-assertive. **2.** An impudent person. [Perhaps after *Aleck* Hoag, 19th-cent. American confidence man and thief.] —**smart′-al·eck** (smärt′ăl′ĭk), **smart′-al·eck·y** (-ĭ-kē) *adj.*

smart-ass (smärt′ăs′) *n. Vulgar Slang* A smart aleck. —**smart′-ass′** *adj.*

smart bomb *n.* A bomb that can be guided by radio waves, television, or a laser beam directly to its target.

smart card *n.* A plastic card containing a computer chip that enables the holder to make purchases, enter restricted areas, or perform other operations requiring data stored on the chip.

smart drug *n.* Any of various substances reputed to enhance memory and other cognitive processes.

smart·en (smär′tn) *v.* **-ened, -en·ing, -ens** —*tr.* **1.** To improve in appearance or stylishness; spruce up. **2.** To make quicker: *smarten the pace.* —*intr.* To make oneself smart or smarter.

smart money *n.* **1.** *Games* Bets or a bet placed by experienced gamblers or those having privileged information. **2.** *Informal* **a.** Experienced, well-informed investors. **b.** Investments made by experienced and well-informed people.

smart·weed (smärt′wēd′) *n.* Any of various marsh plants of the genus *Polygonum,* having sheathlike stipules and small, densely clustered pink, white, or green flowers.

smart·y (smär′tē) *n., pl.* **-ies** *Informal* **1.** A smart aleck. **2.** A quick-witted person.

smar·ty-pants (smär′tē-pănts′) *pl.n. (used with a sing. verb) Informal* A smart aleck.

smash (smăsh) *v.* **smashed, smash·ing, smash·es** —*tr.* **1.** To break (something) into pieces suddenly, noisily, and violently; shatter. See Syns at **break. 2a.** To throw or dash (something) violently so as to shatter or crush. **b.** To strike with a heavy blow; batter. **3.** *Sports* To hit or strike (a ball, for example) forcefully: *smashed the ball into the bleachers.* **4.** To crush or destroy completely. —*intr.* **1.** To strike or collide suddenly, noisily, and violently: *The car smashed into a tree.* **2.** To break suddenly into pieces, as from a violent blow or collision. **3.** *Sports* To smash a ball, puck, or shuttlecock. **4.** To be crushed or destroyed. **5.** To go bankrupt. ❖ *n.* **1a.** The act or sound of smashing. **b.** The condition of having been smashed. **2a.** Total defeat or destruction; ruin. **b.** Financial failure; bankruptcy. **3.** A collision or crash. **4a.** A drink made of mint, sugar, soda water, and alcoholic liquor, usu. brandy. **b.** A soft drink made of crushed fruit. **5.** *Sports* A forceful overhand stroke, as in tennis. **6.** *Informal* A resounding success. ❖ *adj. Informal* Of, relating to, or being a resounding success. ❖ *adv.* With a sudden violent crash. [Prob. of imit. orig.] —**smash′er** *n.*

smashed (smăsht) *adj. Slang* Intoxicated; drunk.

smash·ing (smăsh′ĭng) *adj.* **1.** Serving to smash: *a smashing blow to the head.* **2.** *Informal* Extraordinarily impressive or fine; wonderful: *a smashing success.* —**smash′ing·ly** *adv.*

smash·up (smăsh′ŭp′) *n.* **1.** A total collapse or defeat. **2.** A serious collision between vehicles; a wreck.

smat·ter (smăt′ər) *v.* **-tered, -ter·ing, -ters** —*tr.* **1.** To speak (a language) without fluency. **2.** To study or approach superficially; dabble in. —*intr.* To prattle. ❖ *n.* A smattering. [ME *smateren,* to make dirty, speak foolishly, chatter.] —**smat′ter·er** *n.*

smat·ter·ing (smăt′ər-ĭng) *n.* **1.** Superficial or piecemeal knowledge. **2.** A small scattered amount or number.

smear (smîr) *v.* **smeared, smear·ing, smears** —*tr.* **1a.** To spread or daub with a sticky, greasy, or dirty substance. **b.** To apply by spreading or daubing: *smeared lotion on my face.* **2.** To stain by or as if by spreading or daubing with a sticky, greasy, or dirty substance. **3.** To stain or attempt to destroy the reputation of; vilify. **4.** *Slang* To defeat utterly; smash. —*intr.* To be or become stained or dirtied. ❖ *n.* **1.** A mark made by smearing; a spot or blot. **2.** A substance to be spread on a surface. **3.** *Biology* A sample, as of blood, spread on a slide for microscopic examina-

ă	pat	oi	boy
ā	pay	ou	out
âr	care	ŏŏ	took
ä	father	ōō	boot
ĕ	pet	ŭ	cut
ē	be	ûr	urge
ĭ	pit	th	thin
ī	pie	*th*	this
îr	pier	hw	which
ŏ	pot	zh	vision
ō	toe	ə	about,
ô	paw		item

Stress marks:
′ (primary);
′ (secondary), as in
lexicon (lĕk′sĭ-kŏn′)

smelter
copper smelter

tion or on the surface of a culture medium. **4a.** Vilification or slander. **b.** A vilifying or slanderous remark. [ME *smeren,* to anoint < OE *smerian.*]

smear·case (smîr′kās′) *n. Pennsylvania* See **cottage cheese.** See Regional Note at **gum band.** [Penn. Dutch *Schmierkees* < Ger. *Schmierkäse,* a kind of spreadable cheese : *schmieren,* to smear (< MHGer. *smirwen* < OHGer.) + *Käse,* cheese (< MHGer. *kaese* < OHGer. *kāsi* < Lat. *cāseus.*)]

smear·y (smîr′ē) *adj.* **-i·er, -i·est 1.** Having been smeared. **2.** Tending to smear or soil. —**smear′i·ness** *n.*

smec·tic (smĕk′tĭk) *adj.* Of or relating to a phase of a liquid crystal in which molecules are aligned in distinct layers, with their axes perpendicular to the plane of the layers. [< Gk. *smēktos,* smeared < *smēkhein,* to wash off.]

smeg·ma (smĕg′mə) *n.* A sebaceous secretion, esp. the cheesy one that collects under the prepuce or around the clitoris. [Lat. *smēgma,* detergent < Gk. < *smēkhein,* to wash off.]

smell (smĕl) *v.* **smelled** or **smelt** (smĕlt), **smell·ing, smells** —*tr.* **1.** To perceive the scent of (something) by means of the olfactory nerves. **2.** To sense the presence of by or as if by the olfactory nerves; detect or discover. —*intr.* **1.** To use the sense of smell; perceive the scent of something. **2.** To have or emit an odor. **3.** To be suggestive; have a touch of something. **4.** To have or emit an unpleasant odor; stink. **5.** To appear to be dishonest; suggest evil or corruption. ❖ *n.* **1.** The sense by which odors are perceived; the olfactory sense. **2.** That quality of something that may be perceived by the olfactory sense. **3.** The act or an instance of smelling. **4.** A distinctive enveloping or characterizing quality; an aura or trace: *the smell of success.* —*idiom:* **smell a rat** *Slang* To suspect that something is wrong. [ME *smellen.*]

SYNONYMS *smell, aroma, odor, scent* These nouns denote a quality that can be perceived by the olfactory sense: *the smell of gas; the aroma of frying onions; hospital odors; the scent of pine needles.*

smell·ing salts (smĕl′ĭng) *pl.n. (used with a sing. or pl. verb)* Any of various preparations of ammonium carbonate and perfume, sniffed as a restorative or stimulant.

smell·y (smĕl′ē) *adj.* **-i·er, -i·est** *Informal* Having a noticeable, usu. unpleasant or offensive odor.

smelt¹ (smĕlt) *v.* **smelt·ed, smelt·ing, smelts** —*tr.* To melt or fuse (ores) in order to separate the metallic constituents. —*intr.* To melt or fuse. Used of ores. [Du. or LGer. *smelten* < MDu. or MLGer.]

smelt² (smĕlt) *n., pl.* **smelts** or **smelt** Any of various small silvery marine and freshwater food fishes of the family Osmeridae found in cold waters of the Northern Hemisphere, esp. *Osmerus mordax* of North America and *O. eperlanus* of Europe. [ME < OE.]

smelt³ (smĕlt) *v.* A past tense and a past participle of **smell.**

smelt·er (smĕl′tər) *n.* **1a.** An apparatus for smelting. **b.** also **smelt·er·y** (smĕl′tə-rē) *pl.* **-ies** An establishment for smelting. **2.** One who is engaged in the smelting industry.

Sme·ta·na (smĕt′n-ə, smĕt′tä-nä), **Bedřich** 1824–84. Czech composer of *The Bartered Bride* (1866).

smew (smyōō) *n.* A small Old World merganser (*Mergus albellus*), the male of which has white and black plumage. [?]

smid·gen also **smid·geon** or **smid·gin** (smĭj′ən) *n.* A very small quantity or portion; a bit or mite. [Prob. alteration of dialectal *smitch,* particle, perh. ult. < ME *smite,* perh. < p. part. of *smiten,* to smite. See SMITE.]

smi·lax (smī′lāks′) *n.* **1.** See **catbrier. 2.** A slender vine (*Asparagus asparagoides*) that has glossy foliage and is popular as a floral decoration. [Lat. *smīlax,* bindweed < Gk.]

smile (smīl) *n.* **1.** A facial expression characterized by an upward curving of the corners of the mouth and indicating pleasure, amusement, or derision. **2.** A pleasant or favorable disposition or aspect. ❖ *v.* **smiled, smil·ing, smiles** —*intr.* **1.** To have or form a smile. **2a.** To look with favor or approval. **b.** To express cheerful acceptance or equanimity. —*tr.* **1.** To express with a smile. **2.** To effect or accomplish with or as if with a smile. [< ME *smilen,* to smile, prob. of Scand. orig.] —**smil′er** *n.* —**smil′ing·ly** *adv.*

smil·ey (smī′lē) *n., pl.* **-eys** An emoticon, esp. one depicting a smiling face [:-)]. ❖ *adj.* Having a cheerful and happy disposition; smiling.

smirch (smûrch) *tr.v.* **smirched, smirch·ing, smirch·es 1.** To soil, stain, or dirty with or as if with a smearing agent. **2.** To dishonor; defame. ❖ *n.* Something, such as a blot, smear, or stain, that smirches. [ME *smorchen.*]

smirk (smûrk) *intr.v.* **smirked, smirk·ing, smirks** To smile in an affected, often offensively self-satisfied manner. ❖ *n.* An affected, often offensively self-satisfied smile. [ME *smirken* < OE *smercian,* to smile.] —**smirk′er** *n.* —**smirk′ing·ly, smirk′i·ly** *adv.* —**smirk′y** *adj.*

smite (smīt) *v.* **smote** (smōt), **smit·ten** (smĭt′n) or **smote, smit·ing, smites** —*tr.* **1a.** To inflict a heavy blow on, with or as if with the hand, a tool, or a weapon. **b.** To drive or strike (a weapon, for example) forcefully onto or into something else. **2.** To attack, damage, or destroy by or as if by blows. **3a.** To afflict: *smitten by the plague.* **b.** To afflict retributively; chasten or chastise. **4.** To affect sharply with great feeling: *was smitten by remorse.* —*intr.* To deal a blow with or as if with the hand or a

Bessie Smith
photographed in 1936 by
Carl Van Vechten
(1880–1964)

Joseph Smith

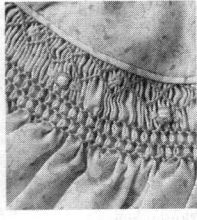

smocking

hand-held weapon. [ME *smiten* < OE *smītan,* to smear.] —**smit′er** *n.*

smith (smĭth) *n.* **1.** A metalworker. Often used in combination: *a silversmith.* **2.** A blacksmith. **3.** One who makes or works at something specified. Often used in combination: *a locksmith.* [ME < OE.]

Smith, Adam 1723–90. Scottish political economist and philosopher whose *Wealth of Nations* (1776) laid the foundations of classical free-market economic theory.

Smith, Alfred Emanuel 1873–1944. Amer. politician who was defeated in the 1928 presidential election by Herbert Hoover.

Smith, Bessie 1894?–1937. Amer. singer and songwriter who became a leading jazz and blues singer in the 1920s.

Smith, David 1906–65. Amer. sculptor known for his use of scrap and welded metal, as in *Medals of Dishonor* (1938).

Smith, Hannah Whitall 1832–1911. Amer. evangelist who was a founder of the Woman's Christian Temperance Union (1874).

Smith, Ian b. 1919. Zimbabwean politician who unilaterally declared the independence of Rhodesia in 1965.

Smith, Jedediah Strong 1799–1831. Amer. trader and explorer who opened a number of frontier trade routes.

Smith, John 1580?–1631. English colonist, explorer, and writer noted for his invaluable maps and accounts of explorations in Virginia and New England.

Smith, Joseph 1805–44. Amer. religious leader who founded (1830) the Church of Jesus Christ of Latter-day Saints and led his congregation from NY to W IL, where he was murdered.

Smith, Julia Evelina 1792–1886. Amer. suffragist who with her sister **Abby Hadassah Smith** (1797–1878) refused to pay taxes until she could vote.

Smith, Kathryn Elizabeth ("Kate") 1909–86. Amer. singer noted esp. for her rendition of "God Bless America."

Smith, Margaret Chase 1897–1995. Amer. politician who served as a US representative (1940–49) and senator (1949–73) from ME.

Smith, Michael 1932–2000. British-born Canadian biochemist who shared a 1993 Nobel Prize in chemistry.

smith·er·eens (smĭth′ə-rēnz′) *pl.n. Informal* Fragments or splintered pieces; bits. [< Ir.Gael. *smidirīn,* dim. of *smiodar,* small fragment.]

smith·er·y (smĭth′ə-rē) *n., pl.* **-ies 1.** The occupation or craft of a smith. **2.** See **smithy.**

Smith·son (smĭth′sən), **James** 1765–1829. British chemist, mineralogist, and philanthropist whose bequest to the US helped establish (1846) the Smithsonian Institution.

smith·son·ite (smĭth′sə-nīt′) *n.* A mineral, ZnCO₃, sometimes used as a source of zinc. [After James SMITHSON.]

smith·y (smĭth′ē, smĭth′ē) *n., pl.* **-ies** A blacksmith's shop; a forge. [ME < ON *smidhja.*]

smit·ten (smĭt′n) *v.* A past participle of **smite.**

smock (smŏk) *n.* A loose coatlike outer garment, often worn to protect the clothes. ❖ *tr.v.* **smocked, smock·ing, smocks 1.** To clothe in a smock. **2.** To decorate (fabric) with smocking. [ME, woman's undergarment < OE *smoc.*]

smock·ing (smŏk′ĭng) *n.* Needlework decoration of small, regularly spaced gathers stitched into a honeycomb pattern.

smog (smŏg, smôg) *n.* **1.** Fog that has become mixed and polluted with smoke. **2.** A form of air pollution produced by the photochemical reaction of sunlight with hydrocarbons and nitrogen oxides released into the atmosphere, esp. by automotive emissions. [SM(OKE) + (F)OG¹.] —**smog′gy** *adj.* —**smog′less** *adj.*

smoke (smōk) *n.* **1.** The vaporous system made up of small particles of carbonaceous matter in the air, resulting mainly from the burning of organic material. **2.** A suspension of fine solid or liquid particles in a gaseous medium. **3.** A cloud of fine particles. **4.** Something insubstantial, unreal, or transitory. **5a.** The act of smoking tobacco. **b.** The duration of this act. **6.** *Informal* Tobacco in a form that can be smoked, esp. a cigarette. **7.** A substance used in warfare to produce a smoke screen. **8.** Something used to conceal or obscure. **9.** A pale to grayish blue to bluish or dark gray. ❖ *v.* **smoked, smok·ing, smokes** —*intr.* **1a.** To draw in and exhale smoke from a cigarette, cigar, or pipe. **b.** To engage in smoking regularly or habitually. **2.** To emit smoke or a smokelike substance. **3.** To emit smoke excessively. **4.** *Slang* **a.** To go or proceed at high speed. **b.** To play or perform energetically. —*tr.* **1a.** To draw in and exhale the smoke of (tobacco, for example). **b.** To do so regularly or habitually. **2.** To preserve (meat or fish) by exposure to the aromatic smoke of burning hardwood, usu. after pickling. **3a.** To fumigate (a house, for example). **b.** To expose (animals, esp. insects) to smoke in order to immobilize or drive away. **4.** To expose (glass) to smoke in order to darken or change its color. **5.** *Slang* To kill; murder. —*phrasal verb:* **smoke out 1.** To force out of a place of hiding or concealment by or as if by the use of smoke. **2.** To detect and bring to public view; expose or reveal. —*idiom:* **smoke and mirrors** Something that deceives or distorts the truth. [ME < OE *smoca.*] —**smok′a·ble, smoke′a·ble** *adj.*

smoke bomb *n.* A bomb that gives out thick smoke upon exploding, used esp. to mark a target or create a smoke screen.

smoke detector *n.* An alarm device that automatically detects the presence of smoke.

smoke-filled room (smōk′fĭld′) *n.* A place, esp. a hotel room, where people gather to negotiate or make deals in private.

smoke·house (smōk′hous′) *n.* A structure in which meat or fish is cured with smoke.

smoke·jump·er (smōk′jŭm′pər) *n.* A firefighter who drops by parachute into a forest fire.

smoke·less (smōk′lĭs) *adj.* **1.** Emitting or containing little or no smoke. **2.** Free from the use of smoking tobacco or from the smoke generated by such use: *a smokeless office.*

smokeless powder *n.* A relatively smoke-free propellant charge composed mainly of nitrocellulose, used in ammunition.

smokeless tobacco *n.* **1.** Tobacco cut for chewing. **2.** See **snuff³** 1a.

smok·er (smō′kər) *n.* **1.** One who smokes tobacco. **2.** A device, such as a stove, that emits smoke. **3.** A smoking car. **4.** An informal social gathering for men.

smoke screen or **smoke·screen** (smōk′skrēn′) *n.* **1.** Artificial smoke used to conceal military areas or operations. **2.** An action or statement used to conceal or deceive.

smoke·stack (smōk′stăk′) *n.* A large chimney or vertical pipe through which combustion vapors, gases, and smoke are discharged. ❖ *adj.* Of, relating to, or involved in heavy manufacturing or the processing of materials.

smoke tree *n.* Either of two deciduous plants, *Cotinus obovatus,* a tree of the southern United States, or *C. coggygria,* a shrub of Eurasia, having plumelike clusters of small yellowish flowers.

smok·ing car (smō′kĭng) *n.* A railroad car in which smoking is allowed.

smoking gun *n. Informal* Something that serves as indisputable evidence or proof, esp. of a crime.

smoking jacket *n.* A man's evening jacket, often made of a fine fabric, elaborately trimmed, and usu. worn at home.

smoking room *n.* A room set aside for smokers.

smok·y (smō′kē) *adj.* **-i·er, -i·est** **1.** Emitting smoke in profuse volume. **2.** Mixed or filled with smoke. **3.** Resembling smoke: *a smoky haze.* **4.** Discolored or soiled with or as if with smoke. **5.** Tasting of smoke. —**smok′i·ly** *adv.* —**smok′i·ness** *n.*

Smoky Hill River A river rising in E CO and flowing c. 901 km (560 mi) E across central KS to join the Republican R. and form the Kansas R.

smoky quartz *n.* A transparent or semitransparent brown or gray to nearly black variety of quartz, used as a gemstone.

Smoky River A river of W-central Alberta, Canada, flowing c. 402 km (250 mi) to the Peace R.

smol·der also **smoul·der** (smōl′dər) *intr.v.* **-dered, -der·ing, -ders** **1.** To burn with little smoke and no flame. **2.** To exist in a suppressed state. **3.** To show signs of repressed anger or hatred. ❖ *n.* Thick smoke resulting from a slow fire. [ME *smolderen,* to suffocate < *smolder,* smoke, prob. alteration of *smorther* < OE *smorian,* to smoke.]

Smo·lensk (smō-lĕnsk′, smə-) A city of W Russia on the Dnieper R. WSW of Moscow. Pop. 349,342.

Smol·lett (smŏl′ĭt), **Tobias George** 1721–71. British writer whose adventure novels include *Roderick Random* (1748).

smolt (smōlt) *n.* A young salmon at the stage when it becomes covered with silvery scales and first migrates from fresh water to the sea. [ME < Med.Lat. *smoltus,* prob. of OE orig.]

smooch (smōōch) *Slang* *v.* A kiss. ❖ *intr.v.* **smooched, smooch·ing, smooch·es** To kiss. [Alteration of E. dialectal *smouch,* perh. imit. of the sound of a kiss.]

smoosh (smōōsh) *tr.v.* **smooshed, smoosh·ing, smoosh·es** *Informal* To squash or mash. [Imit.]

smooth (smōōth) *adj.* **smooth·er, smooth·est** **1.** Having a surface free from irregularities, roughness, or projections; even. **2.** Having a fine texture. **3.** Free from hair, whiskers, or stubble. **4.** Having an even consistency. **5.** Having an even or gentle motion or movement. **6.** Having no obstructions or difficulties. **7.** Serene: *a smooth temperament.* **8.** Bland: *a smooth wine.* **9.** Ingratiatingly polite and agreeable. **10.** Having no grossness or coarseness in dress or manner. ❖ *v.* **smoothed, smooth·ing, smoothes** —*tr.* **1.** To make (something) even, level, or unwrinkled. **2.** To rid of obstructions, hindrances, or difficulties. **3.** To soothe or tranquilize; make calm. **4.** To make less harsh or crude; refine. —*intr.* To become smooth. ❖ *n.* **1.** The act of smoothing. **2.** A smooth surface or part. [ME *smothe* < OE *smōth.*] —**smooth′er** *n.* —**smooth′ly** *adv.* —**smooth′ness** *n.*

smooth·bore also **smooth bore** (smōōth′bôr′, -bōr′) *adj.* Having no rifling within the barrel. Used of a firearm. ❖ *n.* A firearm having no rifling.

smooth breathing *n.* **1.** The symbol (ʼ) written over some initial vowels and diphthongs in ancient Greek to indicate that a word does not begin with the sound (h). **2.** In ancient Greek, an initial vowel or diphthong not preceded by the sound (h).

smooth dogfish *n.* Any of several dogfishes lacking a spine in front of the dorsal fin, esp. a species (*Mustelus canis*) found abundantly on the American Atlantic coast.

smooth·en (smōō′thən) *tr.* & *intr.v.* **-ened, -en·ing, -ens** To make or become smooth.

smooth hound *n.* Any dogfish of the genus *Mustelus,* esp. a smooth dogfish (*M. mustelus*) of southern Europe.

smooth·ie also **smooth·y** (smōō′thē) *n., pl.* **-ies** *Slang* **1.** A per-

son regarded as being assured and artfully ingratiating in manner. **2.** A smooth-tongued person.

smooth muscle *n.* Muscle tissue that contracts without conscious control, made up of spindle-shaped unstriated cells with single nuclei and found in the walls of the internal organs, excluding the heart.

smooth-tongued (smōōth′tŭngd′) *adj.* Speaking or spoken in an artfully suave manner; ingratiating.

smor·gas·bord (smôr′gəs-bôrd′, -bōrd′) *n.* **1.** A buffet meal featuring a varied number of dishes. **2.** A varied collection. [Swed. *smörgåsbord : smörgås,* bread and butter (*smör,* butter < ON + Swed. dialectal *gås,* lump of butter < ON *gās,* goose; see GOSLING) + *bord,* table (< ON *bordh*).]

smote (smōt) *v.* Past tense and a past participle of **smite.**

smoth·er (smŭth′ər) *v.* **-ered, -er·ing, -ers** —*tr.* **1a.** To suffocate (another). **b.** To deprive (a fire) of the oxygen necessary for combustion. **2.** To conceal, suppress, or hide. **3.** To cover thickly: *smother chicken in sauce.* **4.** To lavish a surfeit of a given emotion on (someone). —*intr.* **1a.** To suffocate. **b.** To be extinguished. **2.** To be concealed or suppressed. **3.** To be surfeited with an emotion. ❖ *n.* Something, such as a dense cloud of smoke, that smothers or tends to smother. [ME *smotheren < smorther,* dense smoke. See SMOLDER.]

smoth·er·y (smŭth′ə-rē) *adj. Upper Southern US* Confined. Used of a place: *"Other places do seem so cramped up and smothery, but a raft don't"* (Mark Twain).

smoul·der (smōl′dər) *v.* & *n.* Variant of **smolder.**

SMTP *abbr.* Simple Mail Transfer Protocol

smudge (smŭj) *v.* **smudged, smudg·ing, smudg·es** —*tr.* **1.** To make dirty, esp. in one small area. **2.** To smear or blur (something). **3.** To fill (an orchard, for example) with smoke from a smudge pot to prevent damage from insects or frost. —*intr.* **1.** To smear something as with dirt, soot, or ink. **2.** To become smudged. ❖ *n.* **1.** A blotch or smear. **2.** A smoky fire used as a protection against insects or frost. [ME *smogen.*] —**smudg′i·ly** *adv.* —**smudg′i·ness** *n.* —**smudg′y** *adj.*

smudge pot *n.* A receptacle in which oil or another smoky fuel is burned to protect an orchard from insects or frost.

smudge pot

smudge stick *n.* A wand made of various dried leaves or herbs that produces fragrant smoke when burned, used originally among certain Native American peoples to cleanse places, persons, or objects of negative spiritual energies.

smug (smŭg) *adj.* **smug·ger, smug·gest** Exhibiting or feeling great or offensive satisfaction with oneself or with one's situation; self-righteously complacent. [Perh. akin to LGer. *smuck,* neat < MLGer. < *smucken,* to adorn.] —**smug′ly** *adv.* —**smug′ness** *n.*

smug·gle (smŭg′əl) *v.* **-gled, -gling, -gles** —*tr.* **1.** To import or export without paying lawful customs charges or duties. **2.** To bring in or take out illicitly or by stealth. —*intr.* To engage in smuggling. [Prob. LGer. *smukkeln, smuggeln* or MDu. *smokkelen.*] —**smug′gler** *n.*

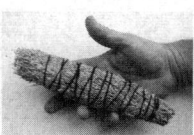

smudge stick
desert sage bundle

smut (smŭt) *n.* **1a.** A particle of dirt. **b.** A smudge made by soot, smoke, or dirt. **2a.** Obscenity in speech or writing. **b.** Pornography. **3a.** Any of various plant diseases, esp. of cereal grasses, caused by parasitic fungi of the order Ustilaginales that form black powdery masses of spores on the affected parts. **b.** A fungus causing such a disease. ❖ *v.* **smut·ted, smut·ting, smut·es** —*tr.* **1.** To blacken or smudge, as with smoke. **2.** To affect (a plant) with smut. **3.** To free (grain, for example) from smut. **4.** To make obscene. —*intr.* **1.** To emit smut. **2.** To be or become blackened or smudged. **3.** To become affected with smut, as a plant. [< ME *smotten, smutten,* to defile.] —**smut′ti·ly** *adv.* —**smut′ti·ness** *n.* —**smut′ty** *adj.*

smutch (smŭch) *tr.v.* **smutched, smutch·ing, smutch·es** To soil or stain. ❖ *n.* A stain or spot of dirt. [Perh. alteration of SMUDGE.] —**smutch′y** *adj.*

Smuts (smŭts, smœts), **Jan Christiaan** 1870–1950. South African soldier and prime minister (1919–24 and 1939–48).

Smyr·na (smûr′nə) See **Izmir.**

Sn The symbol for the element **tin** 1. [< LLat. *stannum,* tin. See STANNIC.]

SN *abbr.* seaman

snack (snăk) *n.* **1.** A hurried or light meal. **2.** Food eaten between meals. ❖ *intr.v.* **snacked, snack·ing, snacks** To eat a hurried or light meal. [ME *snak,* var. of *snacche,* trap, bite < *snacchen,* to snap. See SNATCH.] —**snack′er** *n.*

snack bar *n.* A lunch counter or small restaurant where light meals are served.

snaf·fle (snăf′əl) *n.* A bit for a horse, consisting of two bars joined at the center, as by a joint. ❖ *tr.v.* **-fled, -fling, -fles** To put on or control with a snaffle. [?]

sna·fu (snă-fōō′) *Slang* *n., pl.* **-fus** A chaotic or confused situation. ❖ *adj.* In a state of confusion or chaos. ❖ *tr.v.* **-fued, -fu·ing, -fus** To make confused or chaotic. [*s(ituation) n(ormal,) a(ll) f(ucked) u(p).*]

snag (snăg) *n.* **1.** A rough, sharp, or jagged protuberance, as: **a.** A tree or a part of a tree that protrudes above the surface in a body of water. **b.** A snaggletooth. **2.** A break, pull, or tear in fabric. **3.** An unforeseen or hidden obstacle. **4.** A short or imperfectly developed branch of a deer's antler. ❖ *v.* **snagged, snag·ging,**

snaffle
loose ring French training
snaffle bit

ă pat   oi boy
ā pay   ou out
âr care   ŏŏ took
ä father   ōō boot
ĕ pet   ŭ cut
ē be   ûr urge
ĭ pit   th thin
ī pie   th this
îr pier   hw which
ŏ pot   zh vision
ō toe   ə about,
ô paw   item

Stress marks:
′ (primary);
′ (secondary), as in
lexicon (lĕk′sĭ-kŏn′)

snapdragon

snapping turtle
alligator snapping turtle
Macroclemys temmincki

snare drum

snags —*tr.* **1.** To tear, break, hinder, or destroy by or as if by a snag. **2.** *Informal* To catch unexpectedly and quickly. **3.** To free of snags: *snagged the river.* **4.** To catch (a fish), esp. by hooking in a place other than its mouth. —*intr.* To be damaged by a snag. [Of Scand. orig.] **—snag′gy** *adj.*

snag•gle•tooth (snăg′əl-to͞oth′) *n.* A tooth that is broken or not in alignment with the others. [< SNAG + TOOTH.]

snail (snāl) *n.* **1.** Any of numerous aquatic or terrestrial mollusks of the class Gastropoda, typically having a spirally coiled shell, a broad retractile foot, and a distinct head. **2.** A slow-moving, lazy, or sluggish person. [ME < OE *snægl.*]

snail darter *n.* A small snail-eating darter *(Percina tanasi)* that formerly was found only in the Little Tennessee River of the southeast United States.

snail fever *n.* See **schistosomiasis.**

snail mail *n. Informal* Mail delivered by a postal system, as distinct from e-mail. [< the purported slowness of some postal systems.]

snail-paced (snāl′pāst′) *adj.* Moving with extreme slowness.

snake (snāk) *n.* **1.** Any of numerous scaly, legless, sometimes venomous reptiles of the suborder Serpentes or Ophidia (order Squamata), having a long tapering cylindrical body and found in most tropical and temperate regions. **2.** A treacherous person. **3.** A long, highly flexible metal wire or coil used for cleaning drains. **4. Snake** See **Hydra** 2. ❖ *v.* **snaked, snak•ing, snakes** —*tr.* **1.** To drag or pull lengthwise, esp. to drag with a rope or chain. **2.** To pull with quick jerks. **3.** To move in a sinuous or gliding manner. —*intr.* To move with a sinuous motion. [ME < OE *snaca.*]

Snake *n., pl.* **Snake** or **Snakes** See **Shoshone** 1a.

snake•bird (snāk′bûrd′) *n.* See **anhinga.**

snake•bit (snāk′bĭt′) also **snake•bit•ten** (-bĭt′n) *adj.* Experiencing a period of misfortune or inability to succeed.

snake•bite (snāk′bīt′) *n.* **1.** The bite of a snake. **2.** Poisoning resulting from the bite of a venomous snake.

snake charmer *n.* One who uses rhythmic music and body movements to control snakes.

snake dance *n.* **1.** A ceremonial dance of the Hopi in which the dancers traditionally carry live snakes in their mouths. **2.** A procession of people who move forward in a zigzag line.

snake doctor *n.* **1.** *Chiefly Southern US* See **dragonfly.** See Regional Note at **dragonfly. 2.** See **hellgrammite.**

snake eyes *pl.n.* (*used with a sing. verb*) A throw of two dice that turns up one spot on each.

snake feeder *n. Midland US* See **dragonfly.** See Regional Note at **dragonfly.**

snake fence *n.* See **worm fence.**

snake•fish (snāk′fĭsh′) *n., pl.* **snakefish** or **-fish•es** Any of several fishes resembling a snake, esp. the lizardfish *Trachinocephalus myops* of the eastern Atlantic and western Pacific oceans.

snake•head (snāk′hĕd′) *n.* See **turtlehead.**

snake in the grass *n., pl.* **snakes in the grass** See **snake** 2.

snake•mouth (snāk′mouth′) *n.* A North American orchid *(Pogonia ophioglossoides)* having a solitary rose-purple flower with a fringed lip.

snake oil *n.* **1.** A preparation fraudulently peddled as a cure for many ills. **2.** Speech or writing intended to deceive; humbug.

snake pit *n. Slang* **1.** A place of disorder and chaos. **2.** A mental health facility.

snake plant *n.* A stemless plant *(Sansevieria trifasciata)* having narrow, often mottled leaves and cultivated as a houseplant.

Snake River A river of the NW US rising in NW WY and flowing c. 1,670 km (1,038 mi) to the Columbia R. in SE WA.

snake•root (snāk′ro͞ot′, -ro͝ot′) *n.* Any of various plants, such as sanicle, having roots reputed to cure snakebite.

snake•skin (snāk′skĭn′) *n.* The skin of a snake, esp. when prepared as leather.

snake•weed (snāk′wēd′) *n.* Any of various plants, such as bistort, reputed to have the power to cure snakebite.

snak•y (snā′kē) *adj.* **-i•er, -i•est 1.** Relating to or characteristic of snakes. **2.** Having the form or movement of a snake; serpentine. **3.** Overrun with snakes. **4.** Treacherous; sly. **—snak′i•ly** *adv.* **—snak′i•ness** *n.*

snap (snăp) *v.* **snapped, snap•ping, snaps** —*intr.* **1.** To make a brisk sharp cracking sound. **2.** To break suddenly with a brisk sharp cracking sound. **3a.** To give way abruptly under pressure or tension. **b.** To suffer a physical or mental breakdown, esp. while under stress. **4.** To bring the jaws briskly together, often with a clicking sound; bite. **5.** To snatch or grasp suddenly and with eagerness. **6.** To speak abruptly or sharply. **7.** To move swiftly and smartly. **8.** To flash or appear to flash light; sparkle. **9.** To open, close, or fit together with a click. —*tr.* **1.** To snatch at with or as if with the teeth; bite. **2.** To pull apart or break with a snapping sound. **3.** To utter abruptly or sharply: *snapped out a command.* **4a.** To cause to emit a snapping sound. **b.** To close or latch with a snapping sound. **5.** To cause to move abruptly and smartly. **6a.** To take (a photograph). **b.** To photograph. **7.** *Football* To center (a football); hike. ❖ *n.* **1.** A sudden sharp cracking sound or the action producing such a sound. **2.** A sudden breaking. **3.** A clasp, catch, or other fastening device that operates with a snapping sound. **4.** A sudden attempt to bite, snatch, or grasp. **5a.** The sound produced by rapid movement of a finger from the thumb tip to the base of the thumb. **b.** The act of producing this sound. **6.** The sudden release of something held under pressure or tension. **7.** A thin, crisp, usu. circular cookie. **8a.** Capacity to make a snapping sound; elasticity. **b.** *Informal* Briskness, liveliness, or energy. **9.** A brief spell of brisk cold weather. **10.** Something accomplished without effort. **11a.** A snapshot. **b.** The taking of a snapshot. **12.** A snap bean. **13.** *Football* The passing of a football from the center to a back that initiates each play. ❖ *adj.* **1.** Made or done suddenly, with little or no preparation. **2.** Fastening with a snap. **3.** *Informal* Simple; easy. ❖ *adv.* With a snap. ***—phrasal verbs:*** **snap back** To recover quickly. **snap to** To pay attention or begin complying abruptly. **snap up** To acquire quickly. ***—idiom:*** **snap out of it** *Informal* To move quickly back to one's normal condition from an undesirable condition, such as depression. [Prob. < ME *snappe,* a quick bite, prob. < MLGer. or MDu. *snappen,* to seize, snap.]

snap bean *n.* See **string bean** 1.

snap-brim (snăp′brĭm′) *n.* A hat having a flexible brim, usu. turned down in front and up at the back.

snap•drag•on (snăp′drăg′ən) *n.* Any of several plants of the genus *Antirrhinum,* esp. the Mediterranean herb *A. majus,* having two-lipped, variously colored flowers. [< the imagined resemblance of the flowers to the mouth of a dragon.]

snap pea *n.* A variety of snow pea cultivated for its plump crisp edible pod.

snap•per (snăp′ər) *n.* **1.** One that snaps. **2.** *pl.* **snapper** or **-pers** Any of numerous widely distributed marine fishes of the family Lutjanidae (or Lutianidae), found chiefly in warm coastal waters of the Pacific and Atlantic. **3.** A snapping turtle. **4.** See **schnapper.**

snap•ping beetle (snăp′ĭng) *n.* See **click beetle.**

snapping turtle *n.* Any of several large freshwater turtles of the family Chelydridae of North, Central, and northern South America, having a rough shell and powerful hooked jaws that close with a snap.

snap•pish (snăp′ĭsh) *adj.* **1.** Likely to snap or bite, as a dog. **2.** Irritable and curt. **—snap′pish•ly** *adv.* **—snap′pish•ness** *n.*

snap•py (snăp′ē) *adj.* **-pi•er, -pi•est 1.** *Informal* Lively or energetic; brisk. **2.** *Informal* Smart or chic. **3.** Snappish: *a snappy retort.* **—snap′pi•ly** *adv.* **—snap′pi•ness** *n.*

snap roll *n.* An aerial maneuver in which an aircraft is put through a sharp roll of 360° about its longitudinal axis.

snap•shot (snăp′shŏt′) *n.* **1.** A photograph taken with a small hand-held camera. **2.** An isolated observation.

snare[1] (snâr) *n.* **1.** A trapping device, often consisting of a noose, used for capturing birds and small mammals. **2.** Something that serves to entangle the unwary. **3.** A surgical instrument with a wire loop controlled by a mechanism in the handle, used to remove growths. ❖ *tr.v.* **snared, snar•ing, snares** To trap with or as if with a snare. See Syns at **catch.** [ME < OE *sneara* and < ON *snara.*] **—snar′er** *n.*

snare[2] (snâr) *n.* **1.** Any of the wires or cords stretched across the lower drumhead of a snare drum so as to vibrate against it. **2.** A snare drum. [Prob. < Du. *snaar,* string < MDu. *snāre.*]

snare drum *n.* A small double-headed drum having one or more wires or cords stretched across the bottom head.

snarf (snärf) *tr.v.* **snarfed, snarf•ing, snarfs** *Slang* To eat or drink rapidly or eagerly; devour. [Prob. SN(ORT) + (SC)ARF[3].]

snark•y (snär′kē) *adj.* **-i•er, -i•est** *Slang* Irritable or short-tempered; irascible. [< dialectal *snark,* to nag < *snark, snork,* to snore, snort < Du. and LGer. *snorken,* of imit. orig.] **—snark′i•ly** *adv.*

snarl[1] (snärl) *v.* **snarled, snarl•ing, snarls** —*intr.* **1.** To growl viciously while baring the teeth. **2.** To speak angrily or threateningly. —*tr.* To utter with anger or hostility. ❖ *n.* **1.** A vicious growl. **2.** A vicious, hostile utterance. [Frequentative of obsolete *snar,* perh. < Du. or LGer. *snarren,* to rattle, prob. of imit. orig.] **—snarl′er** *n.* **—snarl′ing•ly** *adv.* **—snarl′y** *adj.*

snarl[2] (snärl) *n.* **1.** A tangled mass, as of hair or yarn. **2.** A confused, complicated, or tangled situation; a predicament. ❖ *v.* **snarled, snarl•ing, snarls** —*intr.* To become tangled or confused. —*tr.* **1.** To tangle or knot (hair, for example). **2.** To confuse; complicate. [ME *snarle,* trap, prob. dim. of *snare.* See SNARE[1].] **—snarl′er** *n.* **—snarl′y** *adj.*

snatch (snăch) *v.* **snatched, snatch•ing, snatch•es** —*tr.* **1a.** To grasp or seize hastily, eagerly, or suddenly. **b.** *Sports* To raise (a weight) using a snatch. **2.** To grasp or seize illicitly. —*intr.* To make grasping or seizing motions. ❖ *n.* **1.** The act of snatching; a quick grasp or grab. **2.** A brief period of time. **3.** A small amount; a bit or fragment. **4.** *Slang* A kidnapping. **5.** *Sports* A lift in weightlifting in which the weight is raised in one motion from the floor to an overhead position. **6.** *Vulgar Slang* The vulva. [ME *snacchen.*] **—snatch′er** *n.*

snatch block *n. Nautical* A block that can be opened on one side to receive the looped part of a line without unreeving it.

snatch•y (snăch′ē) *adj.* **-i•er, -i•est** Occurring in snatches; intermittent.

snaz•zy (snăz′ē) *adj.* **-zi•er, -zi•est** *Slang* Fashionable or flashy. [?] **—snaz′zi•ness** *n.*

SNCC *abbr.* Student Nonviolent Coordinating Committee

sneak (snēk) *v.* **sneaked** also **snuck** (snŭk), **sneak•ing, sneaks** —*intr.* **1.** To go or move in a quiet, stealthy way. **2.** To behave in a cowardly or servile manner. —*tr.* To move, give, take, or put in a quiet, stealthy manner. ❖ *n.* **1.** A person regarded as stealthy, cowardly, or underhand. **2.** An instance of sneaking; a quiet, stealthy movement. **3.** *Informal* A sneaker. ❖ *adj.* **1.** Carried out in a clandestine manner. **2.** Perpetrated without warning. [Prob. akin to ME *sniken*, to creep < OE *snīcan*.]

USAGE NOTE *Snuck* is an Americanism first introduced in the 19th century as a nonstandard regional variant of *sneaked.* The use of *snuck* has become more common with every generation, and is now used by educated speakers in all regions. But in formal written English, many writers and editors have a lingering unease about the form; 67 percent of the Usage Panel disapproved of *snuck* in our 1988 survey. Nevertheless, an examination of recent sources shows that its use is also increasing in written English: *snuck* was almost 20 percent more common in newspaper articles published in 1995 than in 1985.

sneak•er (snēʹkər) *n.* **1.** One who sneaks. **2.** A sports shoe usu. made of canvas and having soft rubber soles.

sneak•ing (snēʹkĭng) *adj.* **1.** Acting in a stealthy furtive way. **2.** Unavowed; secret. **3.** Gradually growing or persistent.

sneak preview *n.* A single public showing of a movie before its general release.

sneak thief *n.* One who steals without breaking into buildings or using violence.

sneak•y (snēʹkē) *adj.* **-i•er, -i•est** Furtive; surreptitious. **—sneakʹi•ly** *adv.* **—sneakʹi•ness** *n.*

sneer (snîr) *n.* **1.** A scornful facial expression characterized by a slight raising of one corner of the upper lip. **2.** A contemptuous facial expression, sound, or statement. ❖ *v.* **sneered, sneer•ing, sneers** —*tr.* To utter with a sneer or in a sneering manner. —*intr.* **1.** To assume a scornful, contemptuous, or derisive facial expression. **2.** To speak in a scornful, contemptuous, or derisive manner. [< ME *sneren*, to mock < OE *fnǣran*, to breathe heavily.] **—sneerʹer** *n.* **—sneerʹful, sneerʹy** *adj.* **—sneerʹing•ly** *adv.*

sneeze (snēz) *intr.v.* **sneezed, sneez•ing, sneez•es** To expel air forcibly from the mouth and nose in an explosive, spasmodic involuntary action resulting chiefly from irritation of the nasal mucous membrane. ❖ *n.* An instance or the sound of sneezing. ***—phrasal verb:* sneeze at** *Informal* To treat as unimportant. [ME *snesen* < *fnesen* < OE *fnēosan*.] **—sneezʹer** *n.* **—sneezʹy** *adj.*

sneeze•guard (snēzʹgärdʹ) *n.* A transparent panel or canopy mounted above a salad bar or food counter as a sanitary barrier.

sneeze•weed (snēzʹwēdʹ) *n.* Any of several New World herbs of the genus *Helenium* of the composite family, having yellow to red-purple rayed flower heads.

Snef•fels (snĕfʹəlz), **Mount** A peak, 4,315.8 m (14,150 ft), in the San Juan Mts. of SW CO.

snell (snĕl) *n.* A length of fine material, such as gut, that connects a fishhook to a heavier line; a length of leader. [?]

Snel•len chart (snĕlʹən) *n.* A chart for testing visual acuity, usu. with letters printed in lines of decreasing size, that a patient is asked to read or identify at a fixed distance. [After Herman *Snellen* (1834–1908), Dutch ophthalmologist.]

Snellen test *n.* A test for visual acuity using a Snellen chart.

SNG *abbr.* **1.** substitute natural gas **2.** synthetic natural gas

snick (snĭk) *v.* **snicked, snick•ing, snicks** —*tr.* **1.** To cut with short strokes; snip. **2.** To make a small cut in; nick. **3.** To cause to click. —*intr.* **1.** To snip. **2.** To make a nick or nicks. **3.** To click. ❖ *n.* **1.** A cut made by snicking. **2.** A clicking sound. [?]

snick•er (snĭkʹər) *intr.v.* **-ered, -er•ing, -ers** To utter a snicker. ❖ *n.* A slightly stifled laugh. [Perh. imit.]

snick•er•snee (snĭkʹər-snēʹ) *n.* **1.** A knife resembling a sword. **2.** *Archaic* The act of fighting with knives. [Alteration of obsolete *stick or snee*, to cut and thrust (in knife fighting) < Du. *steken of snijden* : *steken*, to stab (< MDu.) + *of*, or + *snijden*, to cut (< MDu. *sniden*).]

snide (snīd) *adj.* **snid•er, snid•est** Derogatory in a malicious, superior way; sarcastic. [?] **—snideʹly** *adv.* **—snideʹness** *n.*

sniff (snĭf) *v.* **sniffed, sniff•ing, sniffs** —*intr.* **1a.** To inhale a short audible breath through the nose, as in smelling something. **b.** To sniffle. **2.** To use the sense of smell, as in savoring or investigating. **3.** To regard something in a contemptuous or dismissive manner. **4.** *Informal* To pry; snoop. —*tr.* **1.** To inhale forcibly through the nose. **2.** To smell, as in savoring or investigating. **3.** To perceive or detect by or as if by sniffing. **4.** To utter in a contemptuous or haughty manner. ❖ *n.* **1.** An instance or the sound of sniffing. **2.** Something sniffed or perceived by or as if by sniffing; a whiff. [ME *sniffen*, prob. of Scand. orig.] **—sniffʹa•ble** *adj.* **—sniffʹer** *n.*

snif•fle (snĭfʹəl) *intr.v.* **-fled, -fling, -fles 1.** To breathe audibly through a runny or congested nose. **2.** To weep or whimper lightly with spasmodic congestion of the nose. ❖ *n.* **1.** The act or sound of sniffling. **2. sniffles** A condition, such as a cold, accompanied by congestion of the nose. [Frequentative of SNIFF.] **—snifʹfler** *n.* **—snifʹfly** (snĭfʹə-lē, snĭfʹlē) *adj.*

sniff•y (snĭfʹē) *adj.* **-i•er, -i•est** *Informal* Disposed to show arrogance or contempt. **—sniffʹi•ly** *adv.* **—sniffʹi•ness** *n.*

snif•ter (snĭfʹtər) *n.* **1.** A pear-shaped goblet with a narrow top, used esp. in serving brandy. **2.** *Slang* A small portion of liquor. [< ME *snifteren*, to sniff, perh. of Scand. orig.]

snig•ger (snĭgʹər) *n.* A snicker. ❖ *intr.v.* **-gered, -ger•ing, -gers** To snicker. [Perh. alteration of SNICKER.]

snig•gle (snĭgʹəl) *v.* **-gled, -gling, -gles** —*intr.* To fish for eels by thrusting a baited hook into their hiding places. —*tr.* To catch (an eel) in this manner. [< dialectal *snig*, a small eel < ME *snigge*; prob. akin to OE *snægl*, snail.]

snip (snĭp) *v.* **snipped, snip•ping, snips** —*tr.* To cut, clip, or separate with short quick strokes. —*intr.* To cut or clip with short quick strokes. ❖ *n.* **1.** An instance of snipping or the sound produced by snipping. **2a.** A small cut made with scissors or shears. **b.** A small piece cut or clipped off. **c.** A bit or scrap. **3.** *Informal* **a.** One that is small or slight in size or stature. **b.** A person regarded as impertinent or mischievous. **4. snips** (*used with a sing. or pl. verb*) Hand shears used in cutting sheet metal. [Du. or LGer. *snippen*.] **—snipʹper** *n.*

snipe (snīp) *n.* **1.** *pl.* **snipe** or **snipes a.** Any of various long-billed shore birds of the genus *Gallinago* or *Capella*, esp. the common, widely distributed species *G. gallinago* or *C. gallinago*. **b.** Any of various similar or related birds. **2.** A shot, esp. a gunshot, from a concealed place. ❖ *intr.v.* **sniped, snip•ing, snipes 1.** To shoot at individuals from a concealed place. **2.** To shoot snipe. **3.** To make malicious underhand remarks or attacks. [ME, prob. < ON *-snīpa* (as in *mȳrisnīpa*, marsh snipe).]

snipe hunt *n.* **1.** An elaborate practical joke in which an unsuspecting person takes part in a bogus hunt for a snipe, typically being left alone in the dark with instructions not to move until the snipe appears. **2.** A futile search or endeavor.

snip•er (snīʹpər) *n.* **1.** A skilled military shooter detailed to spot and pick off enemy soldiers from a concealed place. **2.** One who shoots at other people from a concealed place.

snip•pet (snĭpʹĭt) *n.* **1.** A bit, scrap, or morsel. **2.** *Informal* A small or mischievous person.

snip•pet•y (snĭpʹĭ-tē) *adj.* **-i•er, -i•est 1.** Made up of snippets. **2.** *Informal* Snippy; impertinent.

snip•py (snĭpʹē) *adj.* **-pi•er, -pi•est** *Informal* **1.** Sharp-tongued; impertinent: *a snippy retort.* **2.** Occurring in pieces; fragmentary.

snit (snĭt) *n.* *Informal* A state of agitation or irritation. [?]

snitch (snĭch) *Slang v.* **snitched, snitch•ing, snitch•es** —*tr.* To steal (something, usu. something of little value); pilfer. —*intr.* To turn informer. ❖ *n.* **1.** A thief. **2.** An informer. [?] **—snitchʹer** *n.*

sniv•el (snĭvʹəl) *intr.v.* **-eled, -el•ing, -els** or **-elled, -el•ling, -els 1.** To sniffle. **2.** To complain or whine tearfully. **3.** To run at the nose. ❖ *n.* **1.** The act of sniffling or sniveling. **2.** Nasal mucus. [ME *snivelen*.] **—snivʹel•er** *n.*

snob (snŏb) *n.* **1.** One who tends to patronize, rebuff, or ignore people regarded as social inferiors and to imitate, admire, or seek association with people regarded as social superiors. **2.** One who affects an offensive air of self-satisfied superiority in matters of taste or intellect. [Earlier *snob*, cobbler, lower-class person, person who aspires to social prominence.] **—snobʹby** *adj.*

snob•ber•y (snŏbʹə-rē) *n., pl.* **-ies** Snobbish behavior or an instance of it.

snob•bish (snŏbʹĭsh) *adj.* Of, befitting, or resembling a snob; pretentious. **—snobʹbish•ly** *adv.* **—snobʹbish•ness** *n.*

snob•bism (snŏbʹĭzʹəm) *n.* Snobbery.

snood (sno͞od) *n.* **1.** A small netlike cap worn by women to keep the hair in place. **2.** A headband or fillet. **3.** A fleshy wrinkled fold of skin that hangs down over a turkey's beak. ❖ *tr.v.* **snood•ed, snood•ing, snoods** To hold (the hair) in place with a snood. [ME *snod*, headband < OE *snōd*. See **(s)nē-** in App.]

snook[1] (sno͝ok, sno͞ok) *n., pl.* **snook** or **snooks** Any of several chiefly marine percoid fishes of the family Centropomidae, esp. *Centropomus undecimalis*, a food and game fish of warm Atlantic waters. [Du. *snoek*, pike < MDu. *snoec*.]

snook[2] (sno͝ok, sno͞ok) *n.* A derisive or defiant gesture. [?]

snook•er (sno͝okʹər) *n.* Pocket billiards played with 15 red balls and 6 balls of other colors. ❖ *tr.v.* **-ered, -er•ing, -ers 1.** *Slang* **a.** To lead (another) into a situation in which all possible choices are undesirable; trap. **b.** To fool; dupe. **2.** To leave one's opponent in the game of snooker unable to take a direct shot without striking a ball out of the required order. [?]

snoop (sno͞op) *intr.v.* **snooped, snoop•ing, snoops** To pry into others' private affairs, esp. by prowling about. ❖ *n.* One who snoops. [Du. *snoepen*, to eat on the sly.] **—snoopʹer** *n.*

snoop•y (sno͞oʹpē) *adj.* **-i•er, -i•est** *Informal* Likely to snoop. See Syns at **curious. —snoopʹi•ly** *adv.* **—snoopʹi•ness** *n.*

snoot (sno͞ot) *Informal n.* **1.** A snout or nose. **2.** A snob. ❖ *tr.v.* **snoot•ed, snoot•ing, snoots** To treat haughtily. [Dialectal var. of SNOUT.]

snoot•y (sno͞oʹtē) *adj.* **-i•er, -i•est** *Informal* **1.** Snobbishly aloof; haughty. **2.** High-class; exclusive. **—snootʹi•ly** *adv.* **—snootʹi•ness** *n.*

snooze (sno͞oz) *intr.v.* **snoozed, snooz•ing, snooz•es** To take a light nap; doze. ❖ *n.* A brief light sleep. [?]

Sno•qual•mie Falls (snō-kwŏlʹmē) A waterfall, 82.4 m (270 ft) high, in the **Snoqualmie River**, c. 113 km (70 mi), of W-central WA.

snore (snôr, snōr) *intr.v.* **snored, snor•ing, snores** To breathe during sleep with harsh snorting noises caused by vibration of the soft palate. ❖ *n.* **1.** The act or an instance of snoring. **2.** The noise

ă	pat	oi	boy
ā	pay	ou	out
âr	care	o͝o	took
ä	father	o͞o	boot
ĕ	pet	ŭ	cut
ē	be	ûr	urge
ĭ	pit	th	thin
ī	pie	*th*	this
îr	pier	hw	which
ŏ	pot	zh	vision
ō	toe	ə	about, item
ô	paw		

Stress marks:
ʹ (primary);
ʹ (secondary), as in
lexicon (lĕkʹsĭ-kŏnʹ)

so produced. [ME *snoren,* to snort < *fnoren* < OE *fnora,* sneezing.] —**snor′er** *n.*

snor•kel (snôr′kəl) *n.* **1.** A breathing apparatus used by swimmers and skin divers, consisting of a long tube held in the mouth. **2.** A retractable vertical tube in a submarine that contains air-intake and exhaust pipes permitting extended periods of submergence at periscope depth. ❖ *intr.v.* **-keled, -kel•ing, -kels** To dive using a snorkel. [Ger. *Schnorchel* < dialectal, nose (< its resemblance in shape to a nose).] —**snor′kel•er** *n.*

Snor•ri Stur•lu•son (snôr′ē stûr′lə-sən, snôr′ē stœr′lə-sŏn) 1179–1241. Icelandic historian and chieftain whose works include *Heimskringla,* a series of sagas.

snort (snôrt) *n.* **1a.** A rough noisy sound made by breathing forcefully through the nostrils, as a horse or pig does. **b.** A similar sound. **2.** *Slang* **a.** A drink of liquor, esp. when swallowed in one gulp. **b.** A small amount of cocaine or heroin sniffed at one time. ❖ *v.* **snort•ed, snort•ing, snorts** —*intr.* **1a.** To breathe noisily and forcefully through the nostrils. **b.** To make a sound resembling noisy breathing. **2.** To make an abrupt noise expressive of scorn, ridicule, or contempt. **3.** *Slang* To ingest a drug, such as cocaine, by sniffing. —*tr.* **1.** To express by snorting: *snorted his disapproval.* **2.** *Slang* To ingest by sniffing. [< ME *snorten,* to snort < *fnorten,* var. of *fnoren.* See SNORE.] —**snort′er** *n.*

snot (snŏt) *n.* *Slang* **1.** Nasal mucus; phlegm. **2.** An annoying, arrogant, or impertinent person. [ME < OE *gesnot.*]

snot•ty (snŏt′ē) *adj.* **-ti•er, -ti•est** *Slang* **1.** Dirtied with nasal mucus. **2.** Impertinent; arrogant: *ignored his snotty comments.* —**snot′ti•ly** *adv.* —**snot′ti•ness** *n.*

snout (snout) *n.* **1a.** The projecting nose, jaws, or anterior facial part of an animal's head. **b.** A similar prolongation of the anterior portion of the head in certain insects, such as weevils; a rostrum. **c.** A spout or nozzle shaped like such a projection. **2.** *Slang* The human nose. [ME, prob. of OE orig.]

snout beetle *n.* A weevil of the family Curculionidae, having the front of the head elongated to form a snout.

snow (snō) *n.* **1.** Frozen precipitation in the form of white or translucent hexagonal ice crystals that fall in soft white flakes. **2.** A falling of snow; a snowstorm. **3.** Something resembling snow, as: **a.** The white specks on a television screen resulting from weak reception. **b.** *Slang* Cocaine. **c.** *Slang* Heroin. ❖ *v.* **snowed, snow•ing, snows** —*intr.* To fall as or in snow. —*tr.* **1.** To cover, shut off, or close off with snow: *snowed in.* **2.** *Slang* To overwhelm with insincere talk, esp. flattery. —**phrasal verb: snow under 1.** To overwhelm. **2.** To defeat by a great margin. [ME < OE *snāw.*]

Snow, C(harles) P(ercy) 1905–80. British writer known esp. for his series *Strangers and Brothers* (1940–70).

snowboard

snow•ball (snō′bôl′) *n.* **1a.** A mass of soft wet snow packed into a ball that can be thrown, as in play. **b.** *Chiefly Southern US* A cup of crushed or shaved ice flavored with colored syrup. **2.** Any of several plants having rounded clusters of white flowers, as the guelder rose. ❖ *v.* **-balled, -ball•ing, -balls** —*intr.* **1.** To grow rapidly in significance, importance, or size. **2.** To throw snowballs. —*tr.* **1.** To cause to grow or increase rapidly. **2.** To throw snowballs at.

snow•bank (snō′băngk′) *n.* A pile or heap of snow.

snow•bell (snō′bĕl′) *n.* Any of various shrubs or trees of the genus *Styrax,* esp. *S. japonicus* and *S. obassia* of eastern Asia, having bell-shaped white flowers.

Snow•belt also **Snow Belt** (snō′bĕlt′) The N and NE US.

snow•ber•ry (snō′bĕr′ē) *n.* **1.** Any of various shrubs of the genus *Symphoricarpos,* esp. *S. albus* of North America, having small pinkish flowers and white berries. **2.** Any of various tropical American shrubs or vines of the genus *Chiococca,* having white globular fruit and small yellow or white flowers.

snow•bird (snō′bûrd′) *n.* **1.** Any of several birds, such as the junco and the snow bunting, common in snowy regions. **2.** *Slang* One who moves to a warm place in winter.

snow blindness *n.* A usu. temporary loss of vision and inflammation of the eye, caused by exposure to bright sunlight and ultraviolet rays reflected from snow or ice. —**snow′-blind′** (snō′blīnd′), **snow′-blind′ed** (-blīn′dĭd) *adj.*

snow•blink (snō′blĭngk′) *n.* A white sky glow reflected from snow fields.

snow•blow•er or **snow blower** (snō′blō′ər) *n.* A machine that clears snow from a surface by collecting a swath of snow and projecting it forcefully through a chute.

snow•board (snō′bôrd′, -bōrd′) *n.* A board resembling a small surfboard and equipped with bindings, used to descend snow-covered slopes on one's feet without ski poles. —**snow′board′** *v.* —**snow′board′er** *n.*

snow•bound (snō′bound′) *adj.* Confined in one place by heavy snow.

snow bunting *n.* A finch (*Plectrophenax nivalis*) of northern regions having predominantly white winter plumage.

snow•bush (snō′bŏŏsh′) also **snow•brush** (-brŭsh′) *n.* A spiny shrub (*Ceanothus cordulatus*) of California and Oregon having large clusters of small white flowers.

snow•cap (snō′kăp′) *n.* Snow covering a mountain peak, esp. such snow existing year-round. —**snow′capped′** *adj.*

snow cone *n.* A confection made of crushed ice and flavored

snowmobile

syrup inserted into a paper cone and mounded on top.

Snow•don (snōd′n) A massif of NW Wales rising to 1,085.8 m (3,560 ft).

snow•drift (snō′drĭft′) *n.* A mass or bank of snow piled up by the wind.

snow•drop (snō′drŏp′) *n.* Any of several bulbous Eurasian plants of the genus *Galanthus,* having solitary nodding white flowers that bloom in early spring.

snow•fall (snō′fôl′) *n.* **1.** A fall of snow. **2.** The amount of snow that falls during a given period or in a specified area.

snow fence *n.* Temporary fencing made of slats wired together, used to prevent snow from drifting onto walks or roads.

snow•field (snō′fēld′) *n.* A large expanse of snow, esp. at the head of a glacier.

snow•flake (snō′flāk′) *n.* **1.** A single flake or crystal of snow. **2.** Any of several bulbous European herbs of the genus *Leucojum,* having white flowers and fleshy fruit. **3.** See **snow bunting.**

snow goose *n.* A North American wild goose (*Chen caerulescens* or *Anser caerulescens)* that breeds in Arctic regions and has white plumage with black wingtips as an adult.

snow-in-sum•mer (snō′ĭn-sŭm′ər) *n.* A woolly mat-forming perennial herb (*Cerastium tomentosum)* native to Italy and cultivated in rock gardens for its white flowers.

snow job *n.* *Slang* An effort to deceive, overwhelm, or persuade with insincere talk, esp. flattery.

snow leopard *n.* A large feline mammal (*Panthera uncia*) of the highlands of central Asia having long thick whitish-gray fur with dark markings like those of a leopard.

snow line *n.* **1.** The lower altitudinal boundary of a snow-covered area, esp. of one that is perennially covered, such as the snowcap of a mountain. **2.** The fluctuating latitudinal boundaries around the polar regions marking the extent of snow cover.

snow•mak•ing (snō′mā′kĭng) *n.* Production of artificial snow in the form of granular ice particles for ski slopes.

snow•man (snō′măn′) *n.* A human figure made from packed snow, usu. by piling large snowballs on top of each other.

Snow•mass Mountain (snō′măs) A peak, 4,298.1 m (14,092 ft), in the Elk Mts. of W-central CO.

snow•melt (snō′mĕlt′) *n.* **1.** The runoff from melting snow. **2.** A period or season when such runoff occurs.

snow•mo•bile (snō′mō-bēl′, -mə-) *n.* A small vehicle with ski-like runners in front and tanklike treads, ridden by straddling a seat and used for traveling on snow. [SNOW + (AUTO)MOBILE.] —**snow′mo•bil′er** *n.* —**snow′mo•bil′ing** *n.*

snow-on-the-moun•tain (snō′ŏn-thə-moun′tən, -ôn-) *n.* A widely cultivated plant (*Euphorbia marginata)* of the central United States having white-margined leaves and showy white bracts.

snow•pack (snō′păk′) *n.* An area of naturally formed, packed snow that usu. melts during the warmer months.

snow pea *n.* **1.** A variety of the common pea having a soft thick pod. **2.** The edible young pod of this plant.

snow pellet *n.* A small white ice particle that falls as precipitation and typically breaks apart upon hitting a surface. Often used in the plural.

snow plant *n.* A fleshy saprophytic plant (*Sarcodes sanguinea*) of the mountains of western North America having a scaly reddish stalk and scarlet flowers.

snow•plow (snō′plou′) *n.* **1.** A plowlike device or vehicle used to remove snow, esp. from roads and railroad tracks. **2.** A maneuver in snow skiing in which the tips of the skis are brought together to slow or stop progress. ❖ *intr.v.* **-plowed, -plow•ing, -plows** To perform a snowplow in skiing.

snow•shoe (snō′shōō′) *n.* An oblong or racket-shaped frame containing interlaced strips that is attached to the foot for walking on deep snow. ❖ *intr.v.* **-shoed, -shoe•ing, -shoes** To travel on snowshoes. —**snow′sho′er** *n.*

snowshoe hare *n.* A medium-sized hare (*Lepus americanus*) of northern North America having large, heavily furred feet and fur that is white in winter and brown in summer.

snow•storm (snō′stôrm′) *n.* A storm with heavy snow.

snow•suit (snō′sōōt′) *n.* A child's zippered winter coverall.

snow thrower *n.* See **snowblower.**

snow tire *n.* A tire with a deep tread or studs to give added traction on snow-covered surfaces.

snow-white (snō′hwīt′, -wīt′) *adj.* White as snow.

snow•y (snō′ē) *adj.* **-i•er, -i•est 1a.** Abounding in or covered with snow. **b.** Subject to snow. **2.** Resembling snow, esp. in whiteness. —**snow′i•ly** *adv.* —**snow′i•ness** *n.*

snowy egret *n.* A medium-sized egret (*Egretta thula*) with white plumage, black legs, and yellow feet, found in warm parts of the Western Hemisphere.

snowy owl *n.* A large diurnal owl (*Nyctea scandiaca*) of Arctic and subarctic regions having snow-white plumage with dark markings.

snub (snŭb) *tr.v.* **snubbed, snub•bing, snubs 1.** To ignore or behave coldly toward; slight. **2.** To dismiss, turn down, or frustrate the expectations of. **3.** *Nautical* **a.** To check the movement of (a rope or cable running out) by turning it quickly around a cleat or post. **b.** To secure (a vessel, for example) in this manner. **4.** To stub out (a cigarette, for example). ❖ *n.* **1.** A deliberate slight or affront. **2.** *Nautical* A sudden checking, as of a rope or cable running out. ❖ *adj.* Unusually short: *a snub nose.* [ME *snubben,* to rebuke.] **—snub′ber** *n.*

snub-nosed (snŭb′nōzd′) *adj.* **1.** Having a short turned-up nose. **2.** Having a very short barrel: *a snub-nosed pistol.*

snuck (snŭk) *v. Usage Problem* A past tense and a past participle of *sneak.* See Usage Note at **sneak.**

snuff¹ (snŭf) *v.* **snuffed, snuff•ing, snuffs** *—tr.* **1.** To inhale audibly through the nose; sniff. **2.** To sense or examine by smelling; sniff at. *—intr.* To sniff; inhale. ❖ *n.* The act of snuffing or the sound produced by it. [ME *snoffen,* to snuff a candle, sniffle, prob. < *snoffe,* SNUFF².]

snuff² (snŭf) *n.* The charred portion of a candlewick. ❖ *tr.v.* **snuffed, snuff•ing, snuffs 1.** To extinguish: *snuffed out the candles.* **2.** To put a sudden end to; destroy: *lives snuffed out by war.* **3.** *Slang* To kill; murder. **4.** To cut off the charred portion of (a candlewick). [ME *snoffe,* poss. of LGer. orig.]

snuff³ (snŭf) *n.* **1.** A preparation of finely pulverized tobacco that can be drawn up into the nostrils by inhaling. **b.** The quantity of this tobacco that is sniffed at a single time; a pinch. **2.** A powdery substance, such as a medicine, taken by sniffing. ❖ *intr.v.* **snuffed, snuff•ing, snuffs** To use or sniff snuff. **—idiom: up to snuff** *Informal* **1.** Normal in health. **2.** Up to standard; adequate. [Du. *snuf,* short for *snuftabak* : Du. *snuffen,* to sniff; see SNUFFLE + *tabak,* tobacco.]

snuff•box (snŭf′bŏks′) *n.* A small, often decorated box with a hinged lid, used for carrying snuff.

snuff•er¹ (snŭf′ər) *n.* One who uses snuff.

snuff•er² (snŭf′ər) *n.* **1a.** A candlesnuffer. **b.** One who snuffs out candles. **2. snuffers** An instrument resembling shears, used for cutting the snuff from or extinguishing candles.

snuff film *n. Slang* A movie in a purported genre of explicit pornography culminating in the actual violent death of a participant in a sex act.

snuf•fle (snŭf′əl) *v.* **-fled, -fling, -fles** *—intr.* **1.** To breathe noisily, as through a blocked nose. **2.** To sniff. **3.** To talk or sing nasally; whine. *—tr.* To utter in a snuffling tone. ❖ *n.* **1.** The act of snuffling or the sound produced by it. **2. snuffles** The sniffles. [Prob. < Du. *snuffelen,* to sniff about, prob. freq. of *snuffen,* to sniff < MDu. *snuiven.*] **—snuf′fler** *n.* **—snuf′fly** *adj.*

snug¹ (snŭg) *adj.* **snug•ger, snug•gest 1.** Comfortably sheltered; cozy. **2.** Small but well arranged. **3a.** Closely secured and well built; compact. **b.** Close-fitting. **c.** *Nautical* Seaworthy. **4a.** Offering freedom from financial worry. **b.** Safe; secure. ❖ *v.* **snugged, snug•ging, snugs** *—tr.* To make snug or secure. *—intr.* To nestle; snuggle. **—phrasal verb: snug down** *Nautical* To prepare (a vessel) to weather a storm, as by taking in sail. [Of Scand. orig.] **—snug, snug′ly** *adv.* **—snug′ness** *n.*

snug² (snŭg) *n. Chiefly British* A very small private room in a pub. [Short for SNUGGERY.]

snug•ger•y (snŭg′ə-rē) *n., pl.* **-ies** *Chiefly British* A snug position or place.

snug•gle (snŭg′əl) *v.* **-gled, -gling, -gles** *—intr.* **1.** To lie or press close together; cuddle. **2.** To curl up closely or comfortably; nestle. *—tr.* To draw close or hold closely, as for comfort or in affection; hug. [Frequentative of SNUG¹.]

so¹ (sō) *adv.* **1.** In the condition or manner expressed or indicated; thus: *Hold the brush so.* **2.** To the amount or degree expressed or understood; to such an extent: *She was so weary that she fell.* **3.** To a great extent; to such an evident degree: *The idea is so obvious.* **4.** Because of the reason given; consequently: *She was weary and so fell.* **5.** Afterward; then: *to the gas station and so home.* **6.** In the same way; likewise: *You were on time and so was I.* **7.** Apparently; well, then. Used in expressing astonishment, disapproval, or sarcasm: *So you think you've got troubles?* **8.** In truth; indeed: *"You aren't right." "I am so!"* ❖ *adj.* **1.** True; factual: *It isn't so.* **2.** In good order: *Everything must be exactly so.* ❖ *conj. Usage Problem* **1.** With the result or consequence that: *He failed to appear, so we went on without him.* **2.** In order that: *I stayed so I could see you.* ❖ *pron.* Such as has already been suggested or specified; the same: *She became a loyal friend and remained so.* ❖ *interj.* Used to express surprise or comprehension: *So! You've finished at last.* **—idioms: so as to** In order to. **so many 1.** Forming an unspecified number: *so many memos each week.* **2.** Forming a group: *fought like so many tigers.* **so much 1.** In that degree; to that extent: *so much the better.* **2.** In such a degree; to such an extent: *so much alike in ideas.* **3.** So great in quantity, degree, or extent: *so much rain.* **4.** Equivalent to in quantity, degree, or extent: *so much nonsense.* **5.** An unspecified amount or degree: *so much a yard.* **6.** Everything that can be said or done. Used to summarize or dismiss: *so much for that.* **so much as** Used as an intensive to indicate something unexpected; even: *wouldn't so much as smile.* **so that 1.** In order that. **2.** With the result or consequence that. **so what** Used to express contempt or lack of interest. [ME < OE *swā.* See **swo-** in App.]

contexts, as in *They will double up so* (or *so that*) *room can be found for the guests.* • Both *so* and *so that* are acceptably used to introduce clauses that state a result or consequence: *The bridge was closed, so* (or *so that*) *we went back.* • *So* is frequently used in informal speech to string together the elements of a narrative. This practice should not be carried over into formal writing, which generally requires that connections be made more explicit. See Usage Note at **as¹.**

so² (sō) *n. Music* Variant of **sol¹.**

SO *abbr.* **1.** seller's option **2.** significant other **3.** strikeout

so. or **So.** *abbr.* **1.** south **2.** southern

soak (sōk) *v.* **soaked, soak•ing, soaks** *—tr.* **1a.** To make thoroughly wet or saturated by or as if by placing in liquid. **b.** To immerse in liquid for a period of time. **2.** To absorb (liquid, for example) through or as if through pores or interstices: *soaked up the milk.* **3.** To remove (a stain, for example) by continued immersion: *soaked out the grease spots.* **4.** *Informal* To take in or accept mentally, esp. eagerly and easily: *soaked up the gossip.* **5.** *Informal* **a.** To drink (alcoholic liquor), esp. to excess. **b.** To make (a person) drunk. **6.** *Slang* To overcharge (a person). *—intr.* **1.** To be immersed until thoroughly saturated. **2.** To penetrate or permeate; seep: *Let their words soak in.* **3.** *Slang* To drink to excess. ❖ *n.* **1a.** The act or process of soaking. **b.** The condition of being soaked. **2.** Liquid for soaking something. **3.** *Slang* A drunkard. [ME *soken* < OE *socian.*] **—soak′er** *n.*

soak•age (sō′kĭj) *n.* **1a.** The process of soaking. **b.** The condition of being soaked. **2.** The amount of liquid that soaks into, through, or out of an object.

so-and-so (sō′ən-sō′) *n., pl.* **-sos 1.** An unnamed or unspecified person or thing. **2.** *Informal* A son of a gun.

soap (sōp) *n.* **1.** A cleansing agent made from a mixture of the sodium salts of various fatty acids of natural oils and fats. **2.** A metallic salt of a fatty acid. **3.** *Slang* Money, esp. that which is used for bribery. **4.** A soap opera. ❖ *tr.v.* **soaped, soap•ing, soaps 1.** To treat or cover with or as if with soap. **2a.** *Informal* To soft-soap; cajole. **b.** *Slang* To bribe. **—idiom: no soap** *Slang* **1.** Not possible or permissible. **2.** Unsuccessful; futile. [ME *sope* < OE *sāpe.*]

soap•bark (sōp′bärk′) *n.* **1.** A Chilean evergreen tree (*Quillaja saponaria*) of the rose family, having bark used as soap and as a source of saponin. **2.** The bark of this tree.

soap•ber•ry (sōp′bĕr′ē) *n.* **1a.** Any of various chiefly tropical trees of the genus *Sapindus,* having pulpy fruit that lathers like soap. **b.** This fruit. **2.** The buffalo berry.

soap•box (sōp′bŏks′) *n.* **1.** A carton in which soap is packed. **2.** A temporary platform used while making an impromptu or nonofficial public speech. ❖ *intr.v.* **-boxed, -box•ing, -box•es** *Informal* To engage in impromptu or nonofficial public speaking, often flamboyantly. **—idiom: on (one's) soapbox** Speaking one's views passionately or self-importantly.

soap bubble *n.* **1.** A bubble formed from soapy water. **2.** Something beautiful but transient or illusory.

soap opera *n.* **1.** A drama, typically performed as a serial on daytime television or radio, characterized by stock characters and situations, sentimentality, and melodrama. **2.** A series of experiences characterized by dramatic displays of emotion. [< its orig. having been sponsored by soap companies.]

soap plant *n.* **1.** Any of several bulbous plants of the genus *Chlorogalum,* esp. *C. pomeridianum,* of western North America, having small white flowers and bulbs that produce a soapy lather when crushed. **2.** Any of various plants having parts used as soap.

soap•stone (sōp′stōn′) *n.* A soft metamorphic rock composed mostly of the mineral talc. [< its smooth soapy feel.]

soap•suds (sōp′sŭdz′) *pl.n.* Suds from soapy water.

soap•wort (sōp′wûrt′, -wôrt′) *n.* See **bouncing Bet.** [< its yielding a soapy substance when the leaves are bruised.]

soap•y (sō′pē) *adj.* **-i•er, -i•est 1.** Consisting of or containing soap. **2.** Covered with soap. **3.** Resembling soap. **4.** *Slang* Unctuous; oily. **—soap′i•ly** *adv.* **—soap′i•ness** *n.*

soar (sôr, sōr) *intr.v.* **soared, soar•ing, soars 1.** To rise, fly, or glide high and with little apparent effort. **2.** To climb swiftly or powerfully. **3.** To glide in an aircraft while maintaining altitude. **4.** To ascend suddenly above the normal or usual level: *Our spirits soared.* ❖ *n.* **1.** The act of soaring. **2.** The altitude or scope attained in soaring. [ME *soren* < OFr. *essorer* < VLat. **exaurāre* : Lat. *ex-,* ex- + Lat. *aura,* air (< Gk. *aurā,* breeze; see AURA).] **—soar′er** *n.* **—soar′ing•ly** *adv.*

soar•ing (sôr′ĭng, sōr′-) *n.* The act of gliding while maintaining altitude, esp. the sport of flying a heavier-than-air craft by using ascending currents of air.

so•a•ve (sō-ä′vā) *n.* A dry white Italian table wine. [Ital. < Lat. *suāvis,* sweet, delightful. See **swād-** in App.]

sob (sŏb) *v.* **sobbed, sob•bing, sobs** *—intr.* **1.** To weep aloud with convulsive gasping; cry uncontrollably. See Syns at **cry. 2.** To make a sound resembling that of loud weeping. *—tr.* **1.** To utter

snowshoe

with sobs. **2.** To put or bring (oneself) into a specified condition by sobbing: *sob oneself to sleep.* ❖ *n.* The act or sound of sobbing. [ME *sobben,* perh. of LGer. orig.]

SOB (ĕs′ō-bē′) *n. Vulgar* A son of a bitch.

so·ba (sō′bə) *n.* A Japanese noodle made with buckwheat flour. [J., buckwheat, buckwheat noodle.]

so·ber (sō′bər) *adj.* **-er, -est 1.** Habitually abstemious in the use of alcoholic liquors or drugs; temperate. **2.** Not intoxicated or affected by the use of drugs. **3.** Plain or subdued: *sober attire.* **4.** Devoid of frivolity, excess, exaggeration, or speculative imagination; straightforward: *a sober assessment.* **5.** Marked by seriousness, gravity, or solemnity of conduct or character. See Syns at **serious. 6.** Marked by circumspection and self-restraint. ❖ *tr. & intr.v.* **-bered, -ber·ing, -bers** To make or become sober. [ME < OFr. *sobre* < Lat. *sōbrius.* See **s(w)e-** in App.] **—so′ber·ly** *adv.* **—so′ber·ness** *n.*

so·ber·sid·ed (sō′bər-sī′dĭd) *adj.* Devoid of extreme qualities, such as exaggeration; sober. **—so′ber·sid′ed·ness** *n.*

so·ber·sides (sō′bər-sīdz′) *pl.n.* (*used with a sing. verb*) A sober-sided person.

so·bri·e·ty (sə-brī′ĭ-tē, sō-) *n.* **1.** Gravity in bearing, manner, or treatment. **2.** Moderation in or abstinence from consumption of alcoholic liquor or use of drugs. [ME *sobriete* < OFr. < Lat. *sōbrietās* < *sōbrius,* sober. See SOBER.]

so·bri·quet (sō′brĭ-kā′, -kĕt′, sō′brĭ-kā′, kĕt′) also **sou·bri·quet** (soō′brĭ-kā′, -kĕt′, soō′brĭ-kā′, kĕt′) *n.* **1.** An affectionate or humorous nickname. **2.** An assumed name. [Fr. < OFr. *soubri-quet,* chuck under the chin.]

sob sister *n.* **1.** A journalist, esp. a woman, employed as a writer or an editor of sob stories. **2.** A sentimental, ineffective person who seeks to do good.

sob story *n.* **1.** A tale of personal hardship or misfortune intended to arouse pity. **2.** A maudlin plea given as an explanation or rationalization.

Soc. *abbr.* Socialist

so·ca (sō′kə) *n.* A style of music, originating in the West Indies, that is a blend of soul and calypso. [SO(UL) + CA(LYPSO).]

soc·age (sŏk′ĭj, sō′kĭj) *n.* Feudal tenure of land by a tenant in return for agricultural or other nonmilitary services or for payment of rent in money. [ME *sokage* < *soke,* soke. See SOKE.] **—soc′ag·er** *n.*

so-called (sō′kôld′) *adj.* **1.** Commonly called. **2.** Incorrectly or falsely termed.

USAGE NOTE In most editorial practice, quotation marks are not used to set off descriptions that follow expressions such as *so-called* and *self-styled*: *his so-called foolproof method* (not *"fool-proof method"*).

soc·cer (sŏk′ər) *n.* A game played on a rectangular field with net goals at either end in which two teams of 11 players each try to drive a ball into the other's goal by kicking, heading, or using any part of the body except the arms and hands. [Alteration of *assoc.,* abbr. of *association football.*]

soccer mom *n.* An American mother living in the suburbs whose time is often spent transporting her children from one athletic activity or event to another.

So·chi (sō′chē, sô′chĭ) A city of extreme SW Russia on the NE shore of the Black Sea. Pop. 327,739.

so·cia·bil·i·ty (sō′shə-bĭl′ĭ-tē) *n., pl.* **-ties 1.** The disposition or quality of being sociable. **2.** An instance of being sociable.

so·cia·ble (sō′shə-bəl) *adj.* **1.** Fond of the company of others; gregarious. **2.** Marked by or affording occasion for agreeable conversation and conviviality. **3.** Pleasant, friendly, and affable. ❖ *n.* A social. [Fr. < Lat. *sociābilis* < *sociāre,* to share, join < *socius,* companion. See sekʷ-¹ in App.] **—so′cia·ble·ness** *n.* **—so′cia·bly** *adv.*

so·cial (sō′shəl) *adj.* **1a.** Living together in communities. **b.** Of or relating to communal living. **c.** Of or relating to society. **2.** Living together in organized groups or similar close aggregates: *social insects.* **3.** Involving allies or members of a confederacy. **4.** Of or relating to the upper classes. **5a.** Inclined to seek out or enjoy the company of others; sociable. **b.** Spent in or marked by friendly relations or companionship. **c.** Intended for convivial activities. **6.** Of, relating to, or occupied with matters affecting human welfare. ❖ *n.* An informal social gathering, as of the members of a church congregation. [ME *sociale,* domestic < OFr. *social* < Lat. *sociālis,* of companionship < *socius,* companion. See sekʷ-¹ in App.] **—so′cial·ly** *adv.*

social anthropology *n. Chiefly British* Cultural anthropology.

social contract *n.* An agreement among the members of an organized society or between the governed and the government defining and limiting the rights and duties of each.

social Darwinism *n.* The application of Darwinism to the study of human society, specifically a theory in sociology that individuals or groups achieve advantage over others as the result of genetic or biological superiority.

social democracy *n.* A political theory advocating the use of democratic means to move gradually from capitalism to socialism. **—social democrat** *n.* **—social democratic** *adj.*

social disease *n.* **1.** A sexually transmitted disease; venereal disease. **2.** A disease having its highest incidence among socioeco-

nomic groups predisposed to it by a given set of adverse living or working conditions.

social drinker *n.* A person who drinks alcoholic beverages in moderation and chiefly when socializing.

social engineering *n.* The practical application of sociological principles to social problems. **—social engineer** *n.*

social insurance *n.* An insurance program carried out or mandated by a government to provide economic assistance to the unemployed, the elderly, or the disabled.

so·cial·ism (sō′shə-lĭz′əm) *n.* **1.** Any of various theories or systems of social organization in which the means of producing and distributing goods is owned collectively or by a centralized government that often plans and controls the economy. **2.** The stage in Marxist-Leninist theory intermediate between capitalism and communism, in which collective ownership of the economy under the dictatorship of the proletariat has not yet been successfully achieved.

so·cial·ist (sō′shə-lĭst) *n.* **1.** An advocate of socialism. **2.** often **Socialist** A member of a political party or group that advocates socialism. ❖ *adj.* **1.** Of, promoting, or practicing socialism. **2.** often **Socialist** Of, belonging to, or constituting a socialist party or political group.

so·cial·is·tic (sō′shə-lĭs′tĭk) *adj.* Of, advocating, or tending toward socialism. **—so′cial·is′ti·cal·ly** *adv.*

socialist realism *n.* A Marxist aesthetic doctrine that seeks to promote the development of socialism through didactic use of literature, art, and music.

so·cial·ite (sō′shə-līt′) *n.* One prominent in fashionable society.

so·ci·al·i·ty (sō′shē-ăl′ĭ-tē) *n., pl.* **-ties 1a.** The state or quality of being sociable; sociability. **b.** An instance of sociableness. **2.** The tendency to form communities and societies.

so·cial·ize (sō′shə-līz′) *v.* **-ized, -iz·ing, -iz·es** —*tr.* **1.** To place under government or group ownership or control. **2.** To make fit for companionship with others; make sociable. **3.** To convert or adapt to the needs of society. —*intr.* To take part in social activities. **—so′cial·i·za′tion** (-shə-lĭ-zā′shən) *n.* **—so′cial·iz′er** *n.*

so·cial·ized medicine (sō′shə-līzd′) *n.* A government-regulated system for providing health care for all by means of subsidies derived from taxation.

so·cial-mind·ed (sō′shəl-mīn′dĭd) *adj.* Interested in social service or the welfare of society in general.

social psychiatry *n.* The branch of psychiatry that deals with the relationship between social environment and mental illness. **—social psychiatrist** *n.*

social psychology *n.* The branch of psychology that deals with the behavior of groups and the influence of social factors on the individual. **—social psychologist** *n.*

social register *n.* A directory listing persons of social prominence in a community.

social science *n.* **1.** The study of human society and of individual relationships in and to society. **2.** Any of a group of disciplines that deal with such study, generally regarded as including sociology, psychology, anthropology, economics, political science, and history. **—social scientist** *n.*

social secretary *n.* A personal secretary who handles social correspondence and appointments.

social security *n.* **1.** often **Social Security** A US government program financed by employer and employee payments that provides retirement insurance, disability benefits, and unemployment compensation. **2.** The economic assistance provided by social security.

social service *n.* **1.** Organized efforts to advance human welfare; social work. **2.** A service, such as free school lunches, provided by a government for its disadvantaged citizens. Often used in the plural.

social studies *pl.n.* (*used with a sing. or pl. verb*) A course of study including geography, history, government, and sociology, taught in secondary and elementary schools.

social work *n.* Organized work intended to advance the social conditions of a community, esp. of the disadvantaged, by providing psychological counseling, guidance, and assistance, esp. in the form of social services. **—social worker** *n.*

so·ci·e·tal (sə-sī′ĭ-tl) *adj.* Of or relating to the structure, organization, or functioning of society. **—so·ci′e·tal·ly** *adv.*

so·ci·e·ty (sə-sī′ĭ-tē) *n., pl.* **-ties 1a.** The totality of social relationships among humans. **b.** A group of humans broadly distinguished from other groups by mutual interests, participation in characteristic relationships, shared institutions, and a common culture. **c.** The institutions and culture of a distinct self-perpetuating group. **2.** An organization or association of persons engaged in a common profession, activity, or interest. **3a.** The rich, privileged, and fashionable social class. **b.** The socially dominant members of a community. **4.** Companionship; company. **5.** *Biology* A colony or community of organisms, usu. of the same species: *an insect society.* [Fr. *société* < OFr. < Lat. *societās,* fellowship < *socius,* companion. See sekʷ-¹ in App.]

Society Islands An island group of W French Polynesia in the S Pacific E of Samoa; a French protectorate since 1843.

Society of Friends *n.* A Christian denomination, founded in the mid-17th century in England, that rejects formal sacraments and creed, a priesthood, and violence; the Quakers.

Society of Jesus *n. Roman Catholic Church* An order of regular clergy, founded by Saint Ignatius of Loyola in 1534, that is strongly committed to education, theological scholarship, and missionary work.

So•cin•i•an (sō-sĭn′ē-ən) *n.* An adherent of a 16th-century Italian sect holding unitarian views, including denial of the divinity of Jesus. [NLat. *Sociniānus*, after Laelius SOCINUS and Faustus SOCINUS.] —**So•cin′i•an** *adj.* —**So•cin′i•an•ism** *n.*

So•ci•nus (sō-sī′nəs), **Faustus** 1539–1604. Italian theologian who based his anti-Trinitarian teachings on the doctrine formulated by his uncle **Laelius Socinus** (1525–62).

socio– *pref.* **1.** Society: *sociometry.* **2.** Social: *socioeconomic.* [Fr. < Lat. *socius,* companion. See **sek**^w–¹ in App.]

so•ci•o•bi•ol•o•gy (sō′sē-ō-bī-ŏl′ə-jē, -shē-) *n.* The study of the biological determinants of social behavior, based on the theory that such behavior is often genetically transmitted and subject to evolutionary processes. —**so′ci•o•bi′o•log′i•cal** (-bī′ə-lŏj′ĭ-kəl) *adj.* —**so′ci•o•bi•ol′o•gist** *n.*

so•ci•o•cul•tur•al (sō′sē-ō-kŭl′chər-əl, -shē-) *adj.* Of or involving both social and cultural factors.

so•ci•o•ec•o•nom•ic (sō′sē-ō-ĕk′ə-nŏm′ĭk, -ē′kə-, -shē-) *adj.* Of or involving both social and economic factors.

so•ci•o•lin•guis•tics (sō′sē-ō-lĭng-gwĭs′tĭks, -shē-) *n.* (*used with a sing. verb*) The study of language and linguistic behavior as influenced by social and cultural factors. —**so′ci•o•lin′guist** *n.* —**so′ci•o•lin•guis′tic** *adj.*

so•ci•ol•o•gy (sō′sē-ŏl′ə-jē, -shē-) *n.* **1.** The study of human social behavior, esp. the study of the origins, organization, institutions, and development of human society. **2.** Analysis of a social institution or societal segment as a self-contained entity or in relation to society as a whole. [Fr. *sociologie* : *socio-,* socio- + *-logie,* study (< Gk. *-logiā*; see –LOGY).] —**so′ci•o•log′ic** (-ə-lŏj′ĭk), **so′ci•o•log′i•cal** (-ĭ-kəl) *adj.* —**so′ci•o•log′i•cal•ly** *adv.* —**so′ci•ol′o•gist** *n.*

so•ci•om•e•try (sō′sē-ŏm′ĭ-trē, -shē-) *n.* The quantitative study of interpersonal relationships in populations, esp. the study and measurement of preferences.

so•ci•o•path (sō′sē-ə-păth′, -shē-) *n.* One who is affected with a personality disorder marked by antisocial behavior. —**so′ci•o•path′ic** *adj.*

so•ci•o•po•lit•i•cal (sō′sē-ō-pə-lĭt′ĭ-kəl, -shē-) *adj.* Involving both social and political factors.

so•ci•o•psy•cho•log•i•cal (sō′sē-ō-sī′kə-lŏj′ĭ-kəl, -shē-) *adj.* **1.** Of or relating to social psychology. **2.** Of, relating to, or combining social and psychological factors.

so•ci•o•re•li•gious (sō′sē-ō-rĭ-lĭj′əs, -shē-) *adj.* Involving social and religious factors.

sock¹ (sŏk) *n.* **1.** *pl.* **socks** or **sox** (sŏks) A short stocking reaching a point between the ankle and the knee. **2.** *Meteorology* A windsock. **3a.** A light shoe worn by comic actors in ancient Greek and Roman plays. **b.** Comic drama; comedy. ❖ *tr.v.* **socked, sock•ing, socks** To provide with socks. —*phrasal verbs:* **sock away** *Informal* To put (money) away in a safe place for future use. **sock in** To close to air traffic. [ME *socke* < OE *socc,* a kind of light shoe < Lat. *soccus,* poss. < Gk. *sunkhis, sukkhos,* Phrygian shoe.]

sock² (sŏk) *v.* **socked, sock•ing, socks** —*tr.* To hit or strike forcefully; punch. —*intr.* To deliver a blow. —*idiom:* **sock it to (someone)** *Slang* To deliver a forceful comment or physical blow to someone else. [?] —**sock** *n.*

sock•dol•a•ger also **sock•dol•o•ger** (sŏk-dŏl′ə-jər) *n. Slang* **1.** A final blow or remark. **2.** Something outstanding. [Ult. < SOCK².]

sock•et (sŏk′ĭt) *n.* **1.** An opening or cavity into which an inserted part is designed to fit: *a light bulb socket.* **2.** *Anatomy* **a.** The concave part of a joint that receives the end of a bone. **b.** A hollow or concavity into which a part, such as the eye, fits. ❖ *tr.v.* **-et•ed, -et•ing, -ets** To furnish with or insert into a socket. [ME *soket* < AN, spearhead, dim. of *soc,* plowshare, prob. of Celt. orig. See **sū–** in App.]

socket wrench *n.* A wrench with a usu. interchangeable socket to fit over a nut or bolt.

sock•eye salmon (sŏk′ī′) *n.* A salmon (*Oncorhynchus nerka*) of northern Pacific coastal waters that is a commercially valuable food fish. [By folk ety. < Halkomelem (Salishan language of SW Brit. Columbia) *sthǝqǝ′y.*]

so•cle (sŏk′əl) *n.* **1.** A plain square block higher than a plinth, serving as a pedestal for sculpture, a vase, or a column. **2.** A plain plinth supporting a column. [Fr. < Ital. *zoccolo,* wooden shoe < Lat. *socculus,* dim. of *soccus,* a kind of light shoe. See SOCK¹.]

So•co•tra (sə-kō′trə) An island of Yemen in the Indian Ocean at the mouth of the Gulf of Aden; joined Southern Yemen (now Yemen) in 1967.

Soc•ra•tes (sŏk′rə-tēz′) 470?–399 B.C. Greek philosopher who initiated a question-and-answer method of teaching as a means of achieving self-knowledge.

So•crat•ic (sə-krăt′ĭk, sō-) *adj.* Of or relating to Socrates or his philosophizing.

Socratic irony *n.* Profession of ignorance while questioning another in order to arrive at the truth.

sod¹ (sŏd) *n.* **1.** A section of grass-covered surface soil held together by matted roots; turf. **2.** The ground, esp. when covered with grass. ❖ *tr.v.* **sod•ded, sod•ding, sods** To cover with sod.

[ME < MLGer. or MDu. *sode.*]

sod² (sŏd) *Chiefly British Vulgar Slang n.* **1.** A sodomite. **2.** A person regarded as obnoxious or contemptible. **3.** A fellow; a guy. ❖ *tr.v.* **sod•ded, sod•ding, sods** To damn. —*phrasal verb:* **sod off** Used in the imperative to dismiss someone angrily. [Short for SODOMITE.]

so•da (sō′də) *n.* **1a.** Any of various forms of sodium carbonate. **b.** Chemically combined sodium. **2a.** See **carbonated water. b.** *Chiefly Northeastern US, Eastern Missouri, & Southwestern Illinois* See **soft drink.** See Regional Note at **tonic. 3.** A refreshment made from carbonated water, ice cream, and usu. a flavoring. **4.** *Games* The card turned face up at the beginning of faro. [ME *sode,* soda, saltwort, soda < OItal. *soda,* perh. < Ar. *suwayd,* soda, soda plant, or *suwayda,* type of saltwort.]

soda ash *n.* Sodium carbonate in powdery white form, used esp. as an industrial chemical.

soda biscuit *n.* **1.** A breadlike biscuit leavened with baking soda. **2.** See **soda cracker.**

soda bread *n.* A quick bread leavened with baking soda and buttermilk or sour milk.

soda cracker *n.* A thin, usu. square cracker leavened slightly with baking soda.

soda fountain *n.* **1.** An apparatus with faucets for dispensing soda water. **2.** A counter equipped for preparing and serving soft drinks, ice-cream dishes, or sandwiches.

soda lime *n.* A mixture of calcium oxide and sodium or potassium hydroxide, used as a drying agent and carbon dioxide absorbent.

so•da•lite (sōd′l-īt′) *n.* A blue-white mineral, Na$_4$Al$_3$Si$_3$O$_{12}$Cl, found in igneous rocks.

so•dal•i•ty (sō-dăl′ĭ-tē) *n., pl.* **-ties 1.** A society or an association, esp. a devotional or charitable society for the laity in the Roman Catholic Church. **2.** Fellowship. [Fr. *sodalité* < OFr. < Lat. *sodālitās,* fellowship < *sodālis,* companion. See **s(w)e-** in App.] —**so′da•list** (sōd′l-ĭst, sō-dăl′ĭst) *n.*

soda niter *n.* See **sodium nitrate.**

soda pop *n.* See **soft drink.**

soda water *n.* **1a.** See **carbonated water. b.** See **soft drink. 2.** A solution of water, sodium bicarbonate, and acid.

sod•den (sŏd′n) *adj.* **1.** Thoroughly soaked; saturated. **2.** Soggy and heavy from improper cooking; doughy. **3.** Expressionless, stupid, or dull, esp. from drink. **4.** Unimaginative; torpid. [ME *soden,* boiled, p. part. of *sethen,* to boil. See SEETHE.] —**sod′den•ly** *adv.* —**sod′den•ness** *n.*

Sod•dy (sŏd′ē), **Frederick** 1877–1956. British chemist who won a 1921 Nobel Prize.

so•dic (sō′dĭk) *adj.* Relating to or containing sodium. [SOD(IUM) + –IC.]

so•di•um (sō′dē-əm) *n. Symbol* **Na** A soft, light, highly reactive metallic element that is naturally abundant in combined forms, esp. in common salt, and is used in a wide variety of industrially important compounds. Atomic number 11; atomic weight 22.99; melting point 97.8°C; boiling point 892°C; specific gravity 0.971; valence 1. See table at **element.** [SOD(A) + –IUM.]

sodium alginate *n.* A powdery or crystalline compound, C$_6$H$_7$O$_6$Na, used as a food thickener and stabilizer.

sodium barbital *n.* A powder, C$_8$H$_{11}$N$_2$NaO$_3$, the soluble sodium salt of barbital, used as a hypnotic and sedative.

sodium benzoate *n.* The sodium salt of benzoic acid, NaC$_7$H$_5$O$_2$, used as a food preservative and an intermediate in dye manufacture and in the production of pharmaceuticals.

sodium bicarbonate *n.* See **baking soda.**

sodium borate *n.* A crystalline compound, Na$_2$B$_4$O$_7$·10H$_2$O, used in making glass, detergents, and pharmaceuticals.

sodium carbonate *n.* A powdery compound, Na$_2$CO$_3$, used in making baking soda, glass, ceramics, detergents, and soap.

sodium chlorate *n.* A crystalline compound, NaClO$_3$, used as a bleaching and oxidizing agent and in explosives.

sodium chloride *n.* A colorless or white crystalline compound, NaCl, used in the manufacture of chemicals and as a food preservative and seasoning; common salt.

sodium citrate *n.* A crystalline or granular compound, C$_6$H$_5$Na$_3$O$_7$, used in photography and in medicine esp. as an anticoagulant of blood stored for transfusion.

sodium cyanide *n.* A poisonous crystalline compound, NaCN, used in extracting gold and silver from ores.

sodium cyclamate *n.* An artificially prepared salt of cyclamic acid, C$_6$H$_{12}$NO$_3$SNa, once used as a low-calorie sweetener.

sodium dichromate *n.* A poisonous red-orange crystalline compound, Na$_2$Cr$_2$O$_7$·2H$_2$O, used as an oxidizing agent.

sodium fluoride *n.* A crystalline salt, NaF, used in fluoridation of water, in treatment of tooth decay, and as a pesticide.

sodium fluor•o•ac•e•tate (floor′ō-ăs′ĭ-tāt′, -flôr′-, -flōr′-) *n.* A poisonous white powdery compound, C$_2$H$_2$FNaO$_2$, used in wildlife control.

sodium glu•ta•mate (gloo′tə-māt′) *n.* Monosodium glutamate.

sodium hydroxide *n.* A strongly alkaline compound, NaOH, used in making chemicals and soaps.

sodium hypochlorite *n.* An unstable salt, NaOCl, usu. stored in solution and used as a fungicide and an oxidizing bleach.

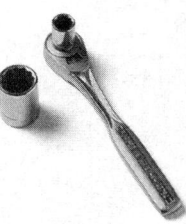

socket wrench

sockeye salmon
Oncorhynchus nerka

ă	pat	oi	boy
ā	pay	ou	out
âr	care	ŏŏ	took
ä	father	ōō	boot
ĕ	pet	ŭ	cut
ē	be	ûr	urge
ĭ	pit	th	thin
ī	pie	th	this
îr	pier	hw	which
ŏ	pot	zh	vision
ō	toe	ə	about,
ô	paw		item

Stress marks:
′ (primary);
′ (secondary), as in
lexicon (lĕk′sĭ-kŏn′)

sodium nitrate *n.* A crystalline compound, $NaNO_3$, used in the manufacture of explosives, in glass and pottery enamel, and as fertilizer.

sodium pentothal *n.* Thiopental sodium.

sodium perborate *n.* A crystalline compound, $NaBO_3 \cdot 4H_2O$, used as a mild alkaline oxidizing agent in dentifrices, a topical antiseptic and deodorant, and an industrial reagent.

sodium peroxide *n.* A powder, Na_2O_2, used industrially as an oxidizing and bleaching agent.

sodium phosphate *n.* Any of various sodium salts of phosphoric acid, esp. NaH_2PO_4, Na_2HPO_4, and Na_3PO_4, used in pharmaceutical manufacture, medicine, and chemistry.

so·di·um-po·tas·si·um pump (sō′dē-əm-pə-tăs′ē-əm) *n.* A mechanism of active transport that moves potassium ions into and sodium ions out of a cell.

sodium propionate *n.* A crystalline compound, $C_3H_5O_2Na$, used as a fungicide.

sodium silicate *n.* Any of various water-soluble silicate glass compounds used as a preservative for eggs, in plaster and cement, and in various purification and refining processes.

sodium sulfate *n.* A crystalline compound, Na_2SO_4, used to manufacture paper, glass, dyes, and pharmaceuticals.

sodium sulfide *n.* A hygroscopic compound, Na_2S, used as a metal ore reagent and in photography and printing.

sodium sulfite *n.* A crystalline or powdered compound, Na_2SO_3, used in preserving foods, developing photographs, and making paper.

sodium thiosulfate *n.* A translucent crystalline compound, $Na_2S_2O_3 \cdot 5H_2O$, used as a photographic fixing agent and a bleach.

sodium tri·pol·y·phos·phate (trī-pŏl′ē-fŏs′fāt′) *n.* A white powder, $Na_5O_{10}P_3$, used as a water softener and as a food preservative and texturizer.

so·di·um-va·por lamp (sō′dē-əm-vā′pər) *n.* An electric lamp containing a small amount of sodium and neon gas, used in generating yellow light for streetlights.

Sod·om[1] (sŏd′əm) A city of ancient Palestine possibly located S of the Dead Sea. In the Bible, it was destroyed along with Gomorrah because of its wickedness and depravity.

Sod·om[2] or **sod·om** (sŏd′əm) *n.* A place known for vice and corruption. [After SODOM[1].]

sod·om·y (sŏd′ə-mē) *n.* Any of various forms of sexual intercourse held to be unnatural or abnormal, esp. anal intercourse or bestiality. [ME *sodomie* < OFr. < *Sodome*, Sodom < Lat. *Sodoma* < Gk. < Heb. *sədôm*.] —**sod′om·ite′** *n.* —**sod′om·ize′** *v.*

so·ev·er (sō-ĕv′ər) *adv.* At all; in any way.

so·fa (sō′fə) *n.* A long upholstered seat typically with a back and arms. [Turk. < Ar. *ṣuffa*, carpet, divan < Aram. *ṣippətā*, mat.]

so·far (sō′fär′) *n.* A system for determining the position of survivors lost at sea by which an explosion is set off underwater, the time needed for the waves to reach three different locations is calculated, and the position of the explosion is found by triangulation. [*so(und) f(ixing) a(nd) r(anging)*.]

so far as *conj.* Insofar as: *So far as I am concerned, it is over.*

sof·fit (sŏf′ĭt) *n.* The underside of an architectural element, such as a cantilever, arch, staircase, or cornice. [Fr. *soffite* < Ital. *soffitto* < VLat. *suffīctus*, p. part. of *suffīgere*, to fasten beneath. See SUFF.]

So·fi·a (sō′fē-ə, sō-fē′ə) The cap. of Bulgaria, in the W-central part; became the cap. in 1879. Pop. 1,114,476.

S. of Sol. *abbr.* Bible Song of Solomon

soft (sôft, sŏft) *adj.* **soft·er, soft·est 1a.** Easily molded, cut, or worked. **b.** Yielding readily to pressure or weight. **2.** Out of condition; flabby. **3.** Smooth or fine to the touch: *a soft fabric.* **4a.** Not loud, harsh, or irritating: *a soft voice.* **b.** Not brilliant or glaring; subdued: *soft colors.* **5.** Not sharply drawn or delineated: *soft charcoal shading.* **6.** Mild; balmy: *a soft breeze.* **7a.** Of a gentle disposition; tender. **b.** Affectionate: *a soft glance.* **c.** Attracted or emotionally involved: *soft on her.* **d.** Not stern; lenient. **e.** Lacking strength of character; weak. **f.** *Informal* Simple-minded; foolish: *soft in the head.* **8a.** *Informal* Easy: *a soft job.* **b.** Based on conciliation or negotiation rather than on threats or power plays. **c.** Gradually declining in trend; not firm: *a soft economy.* **d.** *Sports* Scored on a shot that the goalie should have blocked: *a soft goal.* **9.** Informal and entertaining without confronting difficult issues or hard facts: *a discussion of soft topics.* **10.** Using or based on data not readily quantifiable or amenable to experimental verification or refutation: *The lawyer downplayed the soft evidence.* **11.** Softcore. **12.** Being a turn in a specific direction at an angle less acute than other possible routes: *a soft right.* **13.** Of or relating to a paper currency as distinct from a hard currency backed by gold. **14.** Having low dissolved mineral content. **15.** Having a low or lower power of penetration: *soft x-rays.* **16.** *Linguistics* **a.** Being the sound of *c* in *certain* or *g* in *gem.* **b.** Voiced and weakly articulated: *a soft consonant.* **c.** Palatalized, as certain consonants in Slavic languages. **17.** Unprotected against nuclear attack. ❖ *n.* A soft object or part. ❖ *adv.* In a soft manner; gently. [ME, pleasant, calm < OE *sōfte*.] —**soft′ly** *adv.* —**soft′ness** *n.*

soft·ball (sôft′bôl′, sŏft′-) *n.* **1.** A variation of baseball played on a smaller diamond with a larger, softer ball that is pitched underhand. **2.** The ball used in this game.

soft-boil (sôft′boil′, sŏft′-) *tr.v.* **-boiled, -boil·ing, -boils** To boil (an egg) in the shell to a soft consistency.

soft-boiled (sôft′boild′, sŏft′-) *adj.* **1.** Boiled in the shell to a soft consistency. Used of an egg. **2.** *Informal* **a.** Softhearted; lenient. **b.** Sentimental.

soft·bound (sôft′bound′, sŏft′-) *adj.* Not bound between hard covers: *softbound books.*

soft chancre *n.* See chancroid.

soft clam *n.* See soft-shell clam.

soft coal *n.* See bituminous coal.

soft·core or **soft-core** (sôft′kôr′, -kōr′, sŏft′-) *adj.* **1.** Being less explicit than hard-core material in depicting or describing sexual activity. **2.** Moderate: *a softcore sports fan.*

soft·cov·er (sôft′kŭv′ər, sŏft′-) *adj.* Not bound between hard covers: *softcover books; a softcover edition.*

soft drink *n.* A nonalcoholic flavored carbonated beverage, usu. commercially prepared and sold in bottles or cans. See Regional Note at **tonic.**

soft drug *n.* A drug that is believed to be nonaddictive and less damaging to the health than a hard drug.

soft·en (sô′fən, sŏf′ən) *v.* **-ened, -en·ing, -ens** —*tr.* **1.** To make soft or softer. **2.** To undermine or reduce the strength, morale, or resistance of. **3.** To make less harsh, strident, or critical. —*intr.* To become soft or softer. —**soft′en·er** *n.*

soft-finned (sôft′fĭnd′, sŏft′-) *adj.* Having fins supported by flexible cartilaginous rays. Used of bony fishes.

soft goods *pl.n.* See dry goods.

soft hail *n.* See snow pellet.

soft·head (sôft′hĕd′, sŏft′-) *n.* A foolish person.

soft·head·ed (sôft′hĕd′ĭd, sŏft′-) *adj.* Lacking judgment, realism, or firmness. —**soft′head′·ed·ness** *n.*

soft·heart·ed (sôft′här′tĭd, sŏft′-) *adj.* Easily moved; tender. —**soft′heart′ed·ness** *n.*

soft·ie (sôf′tē, sŏf′-) *n.* Variant of softy.

soft landing *n.* The landing of a space vehicle on a celestial body or on Earth so as to prevent damage to the vehicle.

soft line *n.* A moderate or flexible policy or position, as on a political issue. [SOFT + (HARD) LINE.] —**soft′-line′** *adj.* —**soft′-lin′er** *n.*

soft money *n.* Political donations made in such a way as to avoid federal regulations or limits, as by donating to a party organization rather than to a particular candidate or campaign.

soft palate *n.* The movable fold that is suspended from the rear of the hard palate and closes off the nasal cavity from the oral cavity during swallowing or sucking.

soft paste also **soft-paste** (sôft′pāst′, sŏft′-) *n.* Any of various ceramics containing frit and refined clay.

soft pedal *n.* A pedal used to mute tone, as on a piano.

soft-ped·al (sôft′pĕd′l, sŏft′-) *tr.v.* **-aled, -al·ing, -als** or **-alled, -al·ling, -als 1.** *Music* To soften or mute the tone of by depressing the soft pedal. **2.** *Informal* To make less emphatic or obvious; play down.

soft rock *n.* A form of rock 'n' roll that is restrained in style and is characterized by the predominance of melody.

soft roe *n.* The spermatozoa or testes of a fish; milt.

soft-shell (sôft′shĕl′, sŏft′-) *adj.* also **soft-shelled** (-shĕld′) Having a soft, brittle, or unhardened shell. ❖ *n.* A soft-shelled aquatic animal.

soft-shell clam *n.* A common edible North American clam (*Mya arenaria*) having a thin elongated shell, found esp. along the Atlantic coast.

soft-shell crab *n.* A marine crab before its shell has hardened after molting, esp. the edible species *Callinectes sapidus* of eastern North America in this stage.

soft-shelled turtle *n.* Any of various freshwater turtles of the family Trionychidae, having a flat carapace covered with leathery skin and a fleshy elongated snout.

soft-shoe (sôft′shōō′, sŏft′-) *n.* Tap dancing performed while wearing shoes without metal taps.

soft shoulder *n.* A border of soft earth running along the edge of a road.

soft soap *n.* **1.** A fluid or semifluid soap. **2.** *Informal* Flattery; cajolery.

soft-soap (sôft′sōp′, sŏft′-) *tr.v.* **-soaped, -soap·ing, -soaps** *Informal* To flatter in order to gain something; cajole. —**soft′-soap′er** *n.*

soft-spo·ken (sôft′spō′kən, sŏft′-) *adj.* **1.** Speaking with a soft or gentle voice. **2.** Smooth; ingratiating.

soft spot *n.* **1.** A tender or sentimental feeling. **2.** A weak or vulnerable point: *a soft spot in his defenses.* **3.** See fontanel.

soft-top (sôft′tŏp′) *n.* A car having a top constructed of cloth or a combination of metal and cloth. —**soft′-top′** *adj.*

soft touch *n.* One easily persuaded or taken advantage of.

soft·ware (sôft′wâr′, sŏft′-) *n.* *Computer Science* The programs, routines, and symbolic languages that control the functioning of hardware and direct its operation.

soft water *n.* Water containing little or no dissolved salts of calcium or magnesium, esp. water containing less than 85.5 parts per million of calcium carbonate.

soft·wood (sôft′wŏŏd′, sŏft′-) *n.* **1.** The wood of a coniferous tree. **2.** A coniferous tree.

soft·y or **soft·ie** (sôf′tē, sŏf′-) *n., pl.* **-ies** *Informal* **1.** A person regarded as weak or sentimental. **2.** A person who finds it difficult to punish or be strict.

Sog·di·an (sŏg′dē-ən) *n.* **1.** A member of an ancient Iranian people who lived in the area around Samarkand and Chinese Turkistan. **2.** Their extinct Middle Iranian language. [Lat. *Sogdiānus* < Gk. *Sogdoi,* Sogdians < OPers. *Sug(u)da-.*] —**Sog′di·an** *adj.*

sog·gy (sŏg′ē, sô′gē) *adj.* **-gi·er, -gi·est 1.** Saturated or sodden with moisture; soaked: *soggy clothes.* **2.** Lacking spirit; dull: *a soggy bit of dialogue.* **3.** Humid; sultry: *a soggy afternoon in August.* [< dialectal *sog,* to be soaked (< ME *soggon,* soaked, prob. of Scand. orig.) or < dialectal *sog,* swamp.] —**sog′gi·ly** *adv.* —**sog′gi·ness** *n.*

Sog·na·fjord or **Sog·ne Fjord** (sông′nə-fyôr′) A long narrow inlet of the Norwegian Sea in SW Norway.

So·ho (sō′hō′) **1.** A district of central London, England, known for its restaurants, theaters, and nightclubs. **2.** also **So·Ho** A district of New York City in SW Manhattan noted for its galleries, shops, restaurants, and artists' lofts.

soi-di·sant (swä′dē-zän′) *adj.* Self-styled; so-called. [Fr. : *soi,* oneself + *disant,* saying.]

soi·gné also **soi·gnée** (swän-yā′) *adj.* **1.** Showing sophisticated elegance; fashionable. **2.** Well-groomed; polished. [Fr. < OFr., p. part. of *soigner,* to take care of, of Gmc. orig.]

soil¹ (soil) *n.* **1.** The top layer of the earth's surface, consisting of rock and mineral particles mixed with organic matter. **2.** A particular kind of earth or ground: *sandy soil.* **3.** Country; land: *native soil.* **4.** The agricultural life. **5.** A place or condition favorable to growth; a breeding ground. [ME < AN, a piece of ground (influenced in meaning by Lat. *solium,* soil) < Lat. *solium,* seat. See **sed-** in App.]

soil² (soil) *v.* **soiled, soil·ing, soils** —*tr.* **1.** To make dirty, particularly on the surface. **2.** To disgrace; tarnish. **3.** To corrupt; defile. **4.** To dirty with excrement. —*intr.* To become dirty, stained, or tarnished. ❖ *n.* **1a.** The state of being soiled. **b.** A stain. **2.** Filth, sewage, or refuse. **3.** Manure, esp. human excrement, used as fertilizer. [ME *soilen* < OFr. *souiller* (< VLat. **suculāre* < LLat. *suculus,* dim. of Lat. *sūs,* pig; see **sū-** in App.) or < *souil,* pigsty, wallow (< Lat. *solium,* seat; see **soil¹**).]

soil³ (soil) *tr.v.* **soiled, soil·ing, soils 1.** To feed (livestock) soilage. **2.** To purge (livestock) by feeding with soilage. [?]

soil·age (soi′lĭj) *n.* Green crops cut to feed livestock.

soil pipe *n.* A drainpipe that carries off wastes from a plumbing fixture, esp. from a toilet.

soil·ure (soi′lyər) *n.* **1.** Soiling or the condition of being soiled. **2.** A blot, stain, or smudge.

soi·ree also **soi·rée** (swä-rā′) *n.* An evening party or reception. [Fr. *soirée* < OFr. *seree* < *seir,* evening < Lat. *sērō,* at a late hour < *sērus,* late.]

so·journ (sō′jûrn′, sō-jûrn′) *intr.v.* **-journed, -journ·ing, -journs** To reside temporarily. ❖ *n.* A temporary stay; a brief period of residence. [ME *sojournen* < OFr. *sojorner* < VLat. **subdiurnāre* : Lat. *sub-,* sub- + LLat. *diurnum,* day (< Lat., daily ration < neut. of *diurnus,* daily < *diēs,* day; see **dyeu-** in App.).] —**so′journ′er** *n.*

soke (sōk) *n.* **1.** In early English law, the right of local jurisdiction, generally one of the feudal rights of lordship. **2.** The district over which soke jurisdiction was exercised. [ME < Med.Lat. *sōca* < OE *sōcn,* act of seeking.]

So·khu·mi or **Su·khu·mi** (sōōk′ə-mē, sōōкн′-) A city of W Georgia on the Black Sea NW of Tbilisi; the administrative cap. of the republic of Abkhazia. Pop. 122,000.

sol¹ (sōl) also **so** (sō) *n. Music* The fifth tone of the diatonic scale in solfeggio. [ME < Med.Lat. See GAMUT.]

sol² (sōl) *n.* An old French coin worth 12 deniers. [Fr. < OFr. < LLat. *solidus,* solidus. See SOLIDUS.]

sol³ (sōl) *n., pl.* **so·les** (sō′lās) See table at **currency.** [Sp., sun (< the drawing on the coin) < Lat. *sōl,* sun. See **sāwel-** in App.]

sol⁴ (sŏl, sōl) *n.* A colloidal solution. [< SOLUTION.]

Sol (sōl, sŏl) *n.* The sun. [ME < Lat. *sōl.* See **sāwel-** in App.]

sol. *abbr.* **1.** soluble **2.** solution

so·la¹ (sō′lə) *n.* A plural of **solum.**

so·la² (sō′lə) *adv.* By oneself; alone. Used as a stage direction to a female character. [Ital., fem. of *solo,* solo. See SOLO.]

sol·ace (sŏl′ĭs) *n.* **1.** Comfort in sorrow, misfortune, or distress; consolation. **2.** A source of comfort or consolation. ❖ *tr.v.* **-aced, -ac·ing, -ac·es 1.** To comfort, cheer, or console, as in trouble or sorrow. **2.** To allay or assuage. [ME *solas* < OFr. < Lat. *sōlācium* < *sōlārī,* to console.] —**sol′ac·er** *n.*

so·lan (sō′lən) *n.* See **gannet.** [ME *soland* : ON *sūla,* pillar, gannet + ON *önd,* duck.]

so·la·na·ceous (sō′lə-nā′shəs) *adj.* Of or belonging to the nightshade family. [< NLat. *Solānāceae,* family name < *Solānum,* type genus < Lat. *sōlānum,* nightshade. See SOLANINE.]

so·la·nine (sō′lə-nēn′, -nĭn) also **so·la·nin** (-nĭn) *n.* A poisonous alkaloid, $C_{45}H_{73}NO_{15}$, found in potato sprouts, tomatoes, and nightshade. [Fr. < Lat. *sōlānum,* nightshade < *sōl,* sun. See **sāwel-** in App.]

so·lar (sō′lər) *adj.* **1.** Of, relating to, or proceeding from the sun: *solar rays.* **2.** Using or operated by energy derived from the sun. **3.** Determined or measured in reference to the sun: *the solar year.*

[ME < Lat. *sōlāris* < *sōl,* sun. See **sāwel-** in App.]

solar battery *n.* A system consisting of a large number of connected solar cells.

solar cell *n.* A semiconductor device that converts the energy of sunlight into electric energy.

solar collector *n.* Any of several devices that absorb and accumulate solar radiation for use as a source of energy.

solar constant *n.* The average density of solar radiation measured outside Earth's atmosphere and at Earth's mean distance from the sun, equal to 1.4 kilowatts per square meter.

solar day *n.* A mean solar day.

solar flare *n.* A sudden eruption of hydrogen gas on the surface of the sun, associated with sunspots and often followed by disturbances in Earth's magnetic field.

solar furnace *n.* A parabolic reflector that focuses solar radiation to obtain temperatures as high as 4,000°C (7,200°F).

so·lar·im·e·ter (sō′lə-rĭm′ĭ-tər) *n.* An instrument used to measure the flux of solar radiation through a surface.

so·lar·i·um (sō-lâr′ē-əm, sə-) *n., pl.* **-i·a** (-ē-ə) or **-i·ums** A room, gallery, or glassed-in porch exposed to the sun. [Lat. *sōlārium,* terrace, flat housetop < *sōl,* sun. See **sāwel-** in App.]

so·lar·ize (sō′lə-rīz′) *v.* **-ized, -iz·ing, -iz·es** —*tr.* To affect by exposing to sunlight. —*intr.* To be overexposed. Used of photographic film. —**so′lar·i·za′tion** (-lər-ĭ-zā′shən) *n.*

solar month *n.* One twelfth of a solar year, totaling 30 days, 10 hours, 29 minutes, 3.8 seconds.

solar panel *n.* A group of connected solar cells.

solar plexus *n.* **1.** The large network of sympathetic nerves and ganglia located in the peritoneal cavity behind the stomach and having branching tracts that supply nerves to the abdominal viscera. **2.** The pit of the stomach. [< its radially branching ganglia.]

solar system *n.* **1.** often **Solar System** The sun together with the nine planets and all other celestial bodies that orbit the sun. **2.** A system of planets or other bodies orbiting another star.

solar wind (wĭnd) *n.* A stream of high-speed, ionized particles ejected primarily from the sun's corona.

solar year *n.* The period of time required for the earth to make one complete revolution around the sun, measured from one vernal equinox to the next and equal to 365 days, 5 hours, 48 minutes, 45.51 seconds.

sold (sōld) *v.* Past tense and past participle of **sell.**

sol·dan (sōl′dən, sōl′-) also **sou·dan** (sōōd′n) *n.* A sultan in Egypt. [ME < OFr. < Ar. *sultān.* See SULTAN.]

sol·der (sŏd′ər) *n.* **1.** Any of various fusible alloys, usu. tin and lead, used to join metallic parts. **2.** Something that joins or cements. ❖ *v.* **-dered, -der·ing, -ders** —*tr.* **1.** To unite or repair (parts, for example) with solder. **2.** To join or unite: *The agreement soldered their alliance.* —*intr.* **1.** To unite or repair something with solder. **2.** To be joined or united. [ME *soudur* < OFr. *soldure* < *soulder,* to solder < Lat. *solidāre,* to make solid < *solidus,* solid. See SOLID.] —**sol′der·a·ble** *adj.* —**sol′der·er** *n.*

sol·der·ing iron (sŏd′ər-ĭng) *n.* An implement with a pointed or wedge-shaped metal tip that heats up for use in soldering.

sol·dier (sōl′jər) *n.* **1.** One who serves in an army. **2.** An enlisted person or a noncommissioned officer. **3a.** An active, loyal, and militant follower. **b.** A trusted follower of an organized crime leader. **4a.** A sexually undeveloped form of certain ants and termites, having large heads and powerful jaws specialized to serve as fighting weapons. **b.** One of a group of honeybees that swarm in defense of a hive. ❖ *intr.v.* **-diered, -dier·ing, -diers 1.** To be or serve as a soldier. **2.** To make a show of working. [ME *soudier,* mercenary < AN *soldeier* and OFr. *soudier,* both < OFr. *sol, soud, sou* < LLat. *solidum, soldum,* pay < *solidus,* solidus. See SOLIDUS.]

WORD HISTORY Our word *soldier* comes from the word *soldeier* in a variety of Old French spoken by the Normans in England. This word derives from *sol* or *sou,* the name for a coin and also meaning "pay." (This became modern French *sou,* still the name of a coin.) Thus a *soldeier* was one who fought for pay. This was a concept worth expressing in an era when others were not paid for fighting but did it in service to a feudal superior. Semantically, then, *soldier* is parallel to the word *mercenary,* which goes back to Latin *mercēnārius,* "working for pay."

sol·dier·ly (sōl′jər-lē) *adj.* Of or befitting a soldier.

soldier of fortune *n., pl.* **soldiers of fortune** One who will serve in any army or undertake risky tasks for personal gain or love of adventure.

sol·dier·y (sōl′jə-rē) *n.* **1.** Soldiers considered as a group. **2.** The profession of soldiering.

sold-out (sōld′out′) *adj.* Having all tickets or accommodations completely sold, esp. ahead of time.

sole¹ (sōl) *n.* **1.** The underside of the foot. **2.** The underside of a shoe or boot, often excluding the heel. **3.** The part on which something else rests while in a vertical position, esp.: **a.** The bottom surface of a plow. **b.** The bottom surface of the head of a golf club. ❖ *tr.v.* **soled, sol·ing, soles 1.** To furnish (a shoe or boot) with a sole. **2.** To put the sole of (a golf club) on the ground, as in preparing to make a stroke. [ME < OFr. *solea, solea* < *solum,* bottom, sole of the foot.]

sole² (sōl) *adj.* **1.** Being the only one: *the sole survivor of the crash.* **2.** Of or relating to only one individual or group; exclusive: *The*

solar panel
solar panels on the roof
of a home

court has the sole right to decide. **3.** *Law* Single; unmarried. [ME, alone < OFr. *sol* < Lat. *sōlus.* See **s(w)e-** in App.]

sole[3] (sōl) *n., pl.* **sole** or **soles 1.** Any of various chiefly marine flatfish of the family Soleidae, related to and resembling the flounders, esp. any of several European species, such as *Solea solea,* valued as food fishes. **2.** Any of various other flatfish, esp. certain coastal flounders. [ME < OFr. < Lat. *solea,* sandal, flatfish (< its shape). See SOLE[1].]

sol•e•cism (sŏl′ĭ-sĭz′əm, sō′lĭ-) *n.* **1.** A nonstandard usage or grammatical construction. **2.** A violation of etiquette. **3.** An impropriety, mistake, or incongruity. [Lat. *soloecismus* < Gk. *soloikismos* < *soloikizein,* to speak incorrectly < *soloikos,* speaking incorrectly, after *Soloi* (Soli), an Athenian colony in Cilicia where a dialect regarded as substandard was spoken.] **—sol′e•cist** *n.* **—sol′e•cis′tic** *adj.*

sole•ly (sōl′lē, sō′lē) *adv.* **1.** Alone; singly: *solely responsible.* **2.** Entirely; exclusively: *did it solely for love.*

sol•emn (sŏl′əm) *adj.* **1.** Deeply earnest, serious, and sober. **2.** Somberly or gravely impressive. See Syns at **serious. 3.** Performed with full ceremony. **4.** Invoking the force of religion; sacred: *a solemn vow.* **5.** Gloomy; somber. [ME *solemne* < OFr. < Lat. *sollemnis,* established, customary. See **sol-** in App.] **—sol′emn•ly** *adv.* **—sol′emn•ness** *n.*

so•lem•ni•ty (sə-lĕm′nĭ-tē) *n., pl.* **-ties 1.** The quality or condition of being solemn. **2.** A solemn observance or proceeding.

sol•em•nize (sŏl′əm-nīz′) *tr.v.* **-nized, -niz•ing, -niz•es 1.** To celebrate or observe with dignity and gravity. **2.** To perform with formal ceremony: *solemnize a marriage.* **3.** To make serious or grave. **—sol′em•ni•za′tion** (-nĭ-zā′shən) *n.*

so•le•noid (sō′lə-noid′) *n.* **1.** A coil of wire that acts like a magnet when a current passes through it. **2.** An assembly used as a switch, consisting of a coil and a metal core free to slide along the coil axis under the influence of the magnetic field. [Fr. *solénoïde* < Gk. *sōlēnoeidēs,* pipe-shaped : *sōlēn,* pipe + *-oeidēs,* -oid.] **—so′le•noi′dal** (-noid′l) *adj.* **—so′le•noi′dal•ly** *adv.*

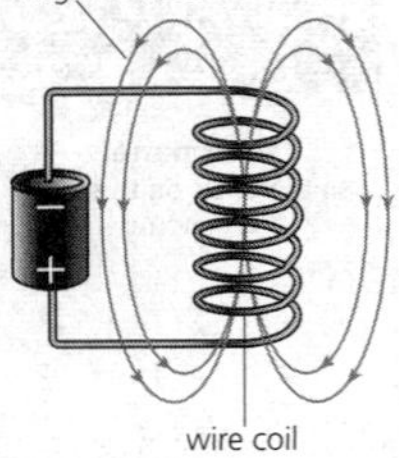

solenoid

So•lent (sō′lənt) A narrow channel between the Isle of Wight and the S mainland of England.

sole•plate (sōl′plāt′) *n.* The underside of a clothes iron.

sole•print (sōl′prĭnt′) *n.* **1.** A print of the sole of the foot. **2.** A print of the sole of the foot made for identification.

so•les (sō′lās) *n.* Plural of **sol[3]**.

so•le•us (sō′lē-əs) *n., pl.* **-le•i** (-lē-ī′) A broad flat muscle of the calf of the leg, situated under the gastrocnemius. [NLat. < Lat. *solea,* sandal. See SOLE[1].]

sol-fa (sōl-fä′) *Music n.* **1.** The set of syllables *do, re, mi, fa, sol, la,* and *ti,* used to represent the tones of the scale. **2.** Use of these syllables. ❖ *intr. & tr.v.* **-faed, -fa•ing, -fas** To use the sol-fa syllables or sing using these syllables. [Ital. *solfa* < Med.Lat. : *sol,* note of the scale; see GAMUT + *fa,* note of the scale; see GAMUT.]

sol•fa•ta•ra (sōl′fə-tär′ə) *n.* A volcanic area that gives off sulfurous gases and steam. [Ital. < *solfo,* sulfur < Lat. *sulfur.*]

sol•fège (sŏl-fĕzh′, sōl-) *n.* Solfeggio. [Fr. < Ital. *solfeggio.* See SOLFEGGIO.]

sol•feg•gio (sōl-fĕj′ē-ō′, -fĕj′ō) *n., pl.* **-feg•gi** (-fĕj′ē) or **-gios 1.** Use of the sol-fa syllables to note the tones of the scale; solmization. **2.** A singing exercise in which the sol-fa syllables are used instead of text. [Ital. < *solfa,* sol-fa. See SOL-FA.]

sol•fe•ri•no (sōl′fə-rē′nō) *n.* A moderate purplish red. [After *Solferino,* a village of N Italy.]

so•lic•it (sə-lĭs′ĭt) *v.* **-it•ed, -it•ing, -its** *—tr.* **1.** To seek to obtain by persuasion, entreaty, or formal application. **2.** To petition persistently; importune. **3.** To entice or incite to evil or illegal action. **4.** To approach or accost (a person) with an offer of sexual services. *—intr.* **1.** To make solicitation or petition for something desired. **2.** To solicit someone sexually. [ME *soliciten,* to disturb < OFr. *solliciter* < Lat. *sollicitāre* < *sollicitus,* troubled. See SOLICITOUS.] **—so•lic′i•ta′tion** *n.*

so•lic•i•tor (sə-lĭs′ĭ-tər) *n.* **1.** One that solicits, esp. one that seeks trade or contributions. **2.** The chief law officer of a city, town, or government department. **3.** *Chiefly British* An attorney who represents clients in certain lower courts and prepares cases for barristers to present in the higher courts.

solicitor general *n., pl.* **solicitors general 1.** A law officer assisting an attorney general. **2.** The chief law officer in a state not having an attorney general.

so•lic•i•tous (sə-lĭs′ĭ-təs) *adj.* **1a.** Anxious or concerned: *a solicitous parent.* **b.** Expressing care or concern: *solicitous inquiries.* See Syns at **thoughtful. 2.** Full of desire; eager. **3.** Marked by anxious care and often hovering attentiveness. **4.** Extremely careful; meticulous. [Lat. *sollicitus* : *sollus,* entire; see **sol-** in App. + *citus,* p. part. of *ciēre,* to set in motion; see **kei-**[2] in App.] **—so•lic′i•tous•ly** *adv.* **—so•lic′i•tous•ness** *n.*

so•lic•i•tude (sə-lĭs′ĭ-to͞od′, -tyo͞od′) *n.* **1.** The state of being solicitous; care or concern, as for the well-being of another. See Syns at **anxiety. 2.** A cause of anxiety or concern. Often used in the plural.

sol•id (sŏl′ĭd) *adj.* **-er, -est 1a.** Of definite shape and volume; not liquid or gaseous. **b.** Firm or compact in substance. **2.** Not hollowed out: *a solid block of wood.* **3.** Being the same substance or color throughout: *solid gold.* **4.** *Mathematics* Of, relating to, or being a three-dimensional geometric figure or body. **5.** Having no gaps or breaks; continuous: *a solid line of people.* **6.** Of good quality and substance: *a solid foundation.* **7.** Substantial; hearty: *a solid meal.* **8.** Sound; reliable: *solid facts.* **9.** Financially sound. **10.** Upstanding and dependable: *a solid citizen.* **11.** Written without a hyphen or space. For example, the word *software* is a solid compound. **12.** *Printing* Having no leads between the lines. **13.** Acting together; unanimous: *a solid voting bloc.* **14.** *Slang* Excellent; first-rate. ❖ *n.* **1.** A substance having a definite shape and volume; one that is neither liquid nor gaseous. **2.** *Mathematics* A geometric figure having three dimensions. ❖ *adv.* **1.** As a whole; unanimously. **2.** Without a break or opening; completely or continuously: *The hotel was booked solid all weekend.* [ME *solide* < OFr. < Lat. *solidus.* See **sol-** in App.] **—sol′id•ly** *adv.* **—sol′id•ness** *n.*

solid angle *n.* An angle formed by all rays from a common point that pass through a closed curve.

sol•i•dar•i•ty (sŏl′ĭ-dăr′ĭ-tē) *n.* A union of interests, purposes, or sympathies among members of a group; fellowship of responsibilities and interests. [Fr. *solidarité* < *solidaire,* interdependent < OFr., in common < Lat. *solidus,* solid, whole. See SOLID.]

solid geometry *n.* The branch of mathematics that deals with three-dimensional figures and surfaces.

so•lid•i•fy (sə-lĭd′ə-fī′) *v.* **-fied, -fy•ing, -fies** *—tr.* **1.** To make solid, compact, or hard. **2.** To make strong or united. *—intr.* To become solid or united. **—so•lid′i•fi•ca′tion** (-fĭ-kā′shən) *n.*

so•lid•i•ty (sə-lĭd′ĭ-tē) *n.* **1.** The condition or property of being solid. **2.** Soundness of mind, moral character, or finances.

solid of revolution *n.* A volume generated by the rotation of a plane figure about an axis in its plane.

solid propellant *n.* A rocket propellant in solid form, combining fuel and oxidizer to form a compact cohesive grain.

solid solution *n.* A homogeneous crystalline structure in which two or more types of atoms or molecules share a common lattice, as in certain alloys.

sol•id-state (sŏl′ĭd-stāt′) *adj.* Of or relating to a device, such as a semiconductor, in which electric, magnetic, and optical phenomena interact through crystalline materials, rather than through heated filaments, moving parts, or vacuum gaps.

solid-state physics *n.* The branch of physics that deals with the physical properties of solid materials, esp. the electromagnetic, thermodynamic, and structural properties of crystalline solids.

sol•i•dus (sŏl′ĭ-dəs) *n., pl.* **-di** (-dī′) **1.** A gold coin of the Roman Empire used in Europe until the 15th century. **2.** *Printing* A virgule; a slash. [ME < LLat. *(nummus) solidus,* a solid (sesterce) < Lat. *solidus,* solid. See SOLID.]

so•li•fluc•tion (sō′lə-flŭk′shən, sŏl′ə-) *n.* The slow, downhill movement of soil or other material in areas typically underlain by frozen ground. [Lat. *solum,* soil + Lat. *flūctiō, flūctiōn-,* a flowing (< *flūctus,* p. part. of *fluere,* to flow; see **bhleu-** in App.).]

so•lil•o•quy (sə-lĭl′ə-kwē) *n., pl.* **-quies 1a.** A dramatic or literary form of discourse in which a character reveals his or her thoughts when alone or unaware of the presence of other characters. **b.** A specific speech or piece of writing in this form of discourse. **2.** The act of speaking to oneself. [LLat. *sōliloquium* : Lat. *sōlus,* alone; see **s(w)e-** in App. + Lat. *loquī,* to speak.] **—so•lil′o•quist** (-kwĭst), **so•lil′o•quiz′er** (-kwī′zər) *n.* **—so•lil′o•quize′** (-kwīz′) *v.*

So•ling•en (zō′lĭng-ən) A city of W-central Germany ESE of Düsseldorf; chartered 1374. Pop. 166,064.

sol•ip•sism (sŏl′ĭp-sĭz′əm, sō′lĭp-) *n. Philosophy* The theory that the self is the only thing that has reality or can be known and verified. [Lat. *sōlus,* alone; see **s(w)e-** in App. + Lat. *ipse,* self + -ISM.] **—sol′ip•sist** *n.* **—sol′ip•sis′tic** *adj.*

sol•i•taire (sŏl′ĭ-târ′) *n.* **1.** A gem, such as a diamond, that is set alone. **2.** *Games* Any of a number of card games played by one person. **3.** Any of several thrushes of the genus *Myadestes,* found in North and Central America and noted for their beautiful song. **4.** Either of two large, flightless, extinct birds *(Raphus solitarius* and *Pezophaps solitaria)* native to the Mascarene Islands. [Fr., solitary < OFr. See SOLITARY.]

sol•i•tar•y (sŏl′ĭ-tĕr′ē) *adj.* **1.** Existing, living, or going without others; alone: *a solitary traveler.* See Syns at **alone. 2.** Happening, done, or made alone: *a solitary evening.* **3.** Remote from civilization; secluded. **4.** Having no companions; lonesome or lonely. **5.** *Zoology* Living alone or in pairs only. **6.** Single and set apart from others. ❖ *n., pl.* **-ies 1.** A person who lives alone; a recluse. **2.** The confinement of a prisoner in isolation from all other prisoners. [ME < OFr. *solitaire* < Lat. *sōlitārius* < *sōlitās,* solitude < *sōlus,* alone. See **s(w)e-** in App.] **—sol′i•tar′i•ly** (-târ′ə-lē) *adv.* **—sol′i•tar′i•ness** *n.*

sol•i•ton (sŏl′ĭ-tŏn′) *n.* A pulselike wave that can exist in nonlinear systems, does not obey the superposition principle, and does not disperse. [SOLIT(ARY) + -ON[1].]

sol•i•tude (sŏl′ĭ-to͞od′, -tyo͞od′) *n.* **1.** The state or quality of being alone or remote from others. **2.** A lonely or secluded place. [ME < OFr. < Lat. *sōlitūdō* < *sōlus,* alone. See **s(w)e-** in App.]

sol•i•tud•i•nar•i•an (sŏl′ĭ-to͞od′n-âr′ē-ən, -tyo͞od′-) *n.* One leading a solitary or secluded life. [Lat. *sōlitūdō, sōlitūdin-,* solitude; see SOLITUDE + -ARIAN.]

sol•ler•et (sŏl′ə-rĕt′) *n.* A steel shoe made of overlapping plates, forming a part of a medieval suit of armor. [Fr. < OFr., dim. of *soller,* shoe < LLat. *subtēlāris (calceus),* (shoe gear) for the sole of the foot < *subtēl,* the hollow of the foot : Lat. *sub-,* sub- + Lat. *tālus,* ankle; see TALUS[1].]

sol•mi•za•tion (sŏl′mĭ-zā′shən) *n. Music* The act or a system of using syllables, esp. sol-fa syllables, to represent the tones of the scale. [Fr. *solmisation* < *solmiser,* to sol-fa : *sol,* note of the scale (< Med.Lat.; see GAMUT) + *mi,* note of the scale (< Med.Lat.; see GAMUT).]

so•lo (sō′lō) *n., pl.* **-los 1.** *Music* A composition or passage for an individual voice or instrument, with or without accompaniment. **2.** A performance by a single singer or instrumentalist. **3.** *Games* Any of various card games in which one player singly opposes others. ❖ *adj.* **1.** *Music* Composed, arranged for, or performed by a single voice or instrument. **2.** Made or done by a single individual. ❖ *adv.* Unaccompanied; alone. ❖ *intr.v.* **-loed, -lo•ing, -los 1.** To perform a solo. **2.** To fly an airplane without a companion or an instructor, esp. for the first time. [Ital. < Lat. *sōlus,* alone. See **s(w)e-** in App.]

so•lo•ist (sō′lō-ĭst) *n.* One who performs a solo.

so•lo•is•tic (sō′lō-ĭs′tĭk) *adj.* **1.** Of, relating to, or containing a solo or soloist. **2.** Having elements or qualities of or appropriate to a solo or a soloist.

Solo man *n.* A fossil hominid specimen previously classed as a distinct species but now generally regarded as an archaic example of *Homo sapiens.* [After the *Solo* River of central Java.]

Sol•o•mon (sŏl′ə-mən) fl. 10th cent. B.C. King of Israel famous for his wisdom. [Heb. *šəlōmōh,* his peace : *šālōm,* peace + *-ōh,* his.]

Sol•o•mon•ic (sŏl′ə-mŏn′ĭk) *adj.* Exhibiting or requiring the exercise of great wisdom, esp. in making difficult decisions.

Solomon Islands[1] An island group of the W Pacific E of New Guinea. The N Solomons are part of Papua New Guinea; the S islands are an independent country.

Solomon Islands[2] A country comprising the Solomon Is. SE of Bougainville; a British protectorate after 1893 and independent since 1978. Cap. Honiara. Pop. 366,000.

Sol•o•mon's plume (sŏl′ə-mənz) *n.* See **false Solomon's seal.**

Solomon's seal *n.* **1.** A six-pointed star or hexagram supposed to possess mystical powers. **2.** Any of several plants of the genus *Polygonatum,* having paired drooping flowers.

so•lon (sō′lən, -lŏn′) *n.* **1.** A wise lawgiver. **2.** A legislator. [After SOLON.]

Solon 638?–559? B.C. Athenian lawgiver and poet whose reforms ended class privilege by birth.

so long *interj. Informal* Used to express goodbye.

so long as *conj.* **1.** During the time that; while: *We'll stay so long as you need us.* **2.** Inasmuch as; since. **3.** Provided that.

sol•stice (sŏl′stĭs, sōl′-, sôl′-) *n.* **1.** Either of two times of the year, the summer solstice or the winter solstice, when the sun is at its greatest distance from the celestial equator. **2.** A highest point or culmination. [ME < OFr. < Lat. *sōlstitium* : *sōl,* sun; see **sāwel-** in App. + *-stitium,* a stoppage; see **stā-** in App.] **—sol•sti′tial** (-stĭsh′əl) *adj.*

sol•u•bil•i•ty (sŏl′yə-bĭl′ĭ-tē) *n., pl.* **-ties 1.** The quality or condition of being soluble. **2.** The amount of a substance that can be dissolved in a given amount of solvent.

sol•u•bi•lize (sŏl′yə-bə-līz′) *tr.v.* **-lized, -liz•ing, -liz•es** To make (a substance such as a fat or lipid) soluble or more soluble, esp. in water, by the action of a detergent or other agent.

sol•u•ble (sŏl′yə-bəl) *adj.* **1.** That can be dissolved, esp. easily dissolved: *soluble fats.* **2.** Possible to solve or explain: *soluble mysteries.* [ME < OFr. < LLat. *solūbilis* < Lat. *solvere,* to loosen. See **leu-** in App.] **—sol′u•ble•ness** *n.* **—sol′u•bly** *adv.*

soluble glass *n.* See **sodium silicate.**

soluble RNA *n.* Transfer RNA.

so•lum (sō′ləm) *n., pl.* **-la** (-lə) or **-lums** The upper layers of a soil profile in which topsoil formation occurs. [Lat., base, ground.]

so•lus (sō′ləs) *adv. & adj.* By oneself; alone. Used as a stage direction to a male character. [Lat. *sōlus,* alone. See SOLO.]

sol•ute (sŏl′yo͞ot, sō′lo͞ot) *n.* A substance dissolved in another substance. ❖ *adj.* Being in solution; dissolved. [< ME, loose, porous < Lat. *solūtus,* p. part. of *solvere,* to loosen. See **leu-** in App.]

so•lu•tion (sə-lo͞o′shən) *n.* **1a.** A homogeneous mixture of two or more substances, which may be solids, liquids, gases, or a combination of these. **b.** The process of forming such a mixture. **2.** The state of being dissolved. **3a.** The method or process of solving a problem. **b.** The answer to or disposition of a problem. **4.** *Law* Payment or satisfaction of a claim or debt. **5.** The act of separating or breaking up; dissolution. [ME < OFr. < Lat. *solūtiō, solūtiōn-* < *solūtus,* p. part. of *solvere,* to loosen. See SOLUTE.]

So•lu•tre•an also **So•lu•tri•an** (sə-lo͞o′trē-ən) *adj.* Of or relating to the Old World Upper Paleolithic culture that succeeded the Aurignacian and was characterized by new stone implements and stylized symbolic forms of art. [Fr. *solutréen,* after *Solutré-Pouilly,* a village of east-central France.]

solv•a•ble (sŏl′və-bəl, sôl′-) *adj.* Possible to solve: *solvable problems.* **—solv′a•bil′i•ty, solv′a•ble•ness** *n.*

sol•va•tion (sŏl-vā′shən, sôl-) *n.* Any of a class of chemical reactions in which solute and solvent molecules combine with relatively weak covalent bonds. [SOLV(ENT) + –ATION.]

Sol•vay process (sŏl′vā, sôl-vā′) *n.* A process used to produce large quantities of sodium carbonate from sodium chloride, ammonia, and carbon dioxide. [After Ernest *Solvay* (1838–1922), Belgian chemist.]

solve (sŏlv, sôlv) *v.* **solved, solv•ing, solves** *—tr.* **1.** To find a solution to. **2.** To work out a correct solution to (a problem). *—intr.* To solve an equation: *solved for x.* [ME *solven,* to loosen < Lat. *solvere.* See **leu-** in App.] **—solv′er** *n.*

SYNONYMS *solve, decipher, resolve, unravel* These verbs mean to clear up or explain something puzzling or unintelligible: *solve a riddle; decipher a code; resolve a problem; unravel a mystery.*

sol•vent (sŏl′vənt, sôl′-) *adj.* **1.** Capable of meeting financial obligations. **2.** *Chemistry* Capable of dissolving another substance. ❖ *n.* **1.** *Chemistry* **a.** A substance in which another substance is dissolved, forming a solution. **b.** A substance, usu. a liquid, capable of dissolving another substance. **2.** Something that solves or explains. [Fr. < Lat. *solvēns, solvent-,* pr. part. of *solvere,* to loosen. See SOLVE.] **—sol′ven•cy** *n.*

sol•vol•y•sis (sŏl-vŏl′ĭ-sĭs, sôl-) *n.* A chemical reaction in which the solute and solvent react to form a new compound. [SOLV(ENT) + –LYSIS.] **—sol′vo•lyt′ic** (-və-lĭt′ĭk) *adj.*

Sol•way Firth (sŏl′wā′) An arm of the Irish Sea separating NW England from SW Scotland.

Sol•zhe•ni•tsyn (sōl′zhə-nēt′sĭn, səl-zhə-nyē′tsĭn), **Aleksandr Isayevich** b. 1918. Soviet writer and dissident who won the 1970 Nobel Prize for literature.

so•ma[1] (sō′mə) *n., pl.* **-ma•ta** (-mə-tə) or **-mas 1.** The entire body of an organism, exclusive of the germ cells. **2.** See **cell body. 3.** The body of an individual as contrasted with the mind or psyche. [NLat. *sōma* < Gk., body.]

so•ma[2] (sō′mə) *n.* An intoxicating or hallucinogenic beverage, used as an offering to the Hindu gods and consumed in Vedic ritual sacrifices. [Skt. *somaḥ*; akin to *sunoti,* he presses.]

So•ma•li (sō-mä′lē) *n., pl.* **Somali** or **-lis 1.** A member of a Muslim people of Somalia and parts of adjacent nations. **2.** The Cushitic language of the Somali and an official language of Somalia.

So•ma•li•a (sō-mä′lē-ə, -mäl′yə) A country of extreme E Africa on the Gulf of Aden and the Indian Ocean; formed in 1960 from colonies previously held by Italy and Great Britain. Cap. Mogadishu. Pop. 9,077,000. **—So•ma′li•an** *adj. & n.*

So•ma•li•land (sō-mä′lē-lănd′, sə-) A region of E Africa comprising Somalia, Djibouti, and SE Ethiopia.

so•mat•ic (sō-măt′ĭk) *adj.* **1.** Of, relating to, or affecting the body, esp. as distinguished from a body part, the mind, or the environment; corporeal or physical. See Syns at **bodily. 2.** Of or relating to the wall of the body cavity, esp. as distinguished from the head, limbs, or viscera. **3.** Of or relating to a somatic cell or the somatoplasm. [Fr. *somatique* < Gk. *sōmatikos* < *sōma, sōmat-,* body. See SOMA[1].] **—so•mat′i•cal•ly** *adv.*

somatic cell *n.* Any cell of a plant or animal other than a germ cell.

somato– *pref.* **1.** Body: *somatology.* **2.** Soma: *somatoplasm.* [Gk. *sōmato-* < *sōma, sōmat-,* body.]

so•ma•tol•o•gy (sō′mə-tŏl′ə-jē) *n.* **1.** The physiological and anatomical study of the body. **2.** See **physical anthropology. —so′ma•to•log′ic** (sō′mə-tl-ŏj′ĭk, sō-măt′l-), **so′ma•to•log′i•cal** (-ĭ-kəl) *adj.* **—so′ma•tol′o•gist** *n.*

so•mat•o•me•din (sō-măt′ə-mēd′n, sō′mə-tə-) *n.* Any of a group of peptides produced by the liver upon stimulation by somatotropin that act directly on cartilage cells to stimulate skeletal growth. [Perh. SOMATO(TROPIN) + (INTER)MED(IARY) + –IN.]

so•mat•o•plasm (sō-măt′ə-plăz′əm, sō′mə-tə-) *n.* **1.** The entirety of specialized protoplasm, other than germ plasm, constituting the body. **2.** The protoplasm of a somatic cell. **—so′ma•to•plas′tic** (sō′mə-tə-plăs′tĭk) *adj.*

so•mat•o•pleure (sō-măt′ə-plo͝or′, sō′mə-tə-) *n.* A complex sheet of embryonic cells in craniate vertebrates, formed by association of part of the mesoderm with the ectoderm and developing as the internal body wall. [NLat. *sōmatopleura* : SOMATO– + Gk. *pleura,* side.]

so•mat•o•stat•in (sō-măt′ə-stăt′n, sō′mə-tə-) *n.* A polypeptide hormone produced chiefly by the hypothalamus that inhibits the secretion of various other hormones, such as somatotropin and insulin. [SOMATO(TROPIN) + –STAT + –IN.]

so•mat•o•tro•pin (sə-măt′ə-trō′pĭn, sō′mə-tə-) also **so•mat•o•tro•phin** (-trō′fĭn) *n.* See **human growth hormone.** [SOMATO– + –TROP(IC) + –IN.]

so•mat•o•type (sō-măt′ə-tīp′, sō′mə-tə-) *n.* Body type; physique. **—so•mat′o•typ′ic** (-tĭp′ĭk) *adj.*

som•ber (sŏm′bər) *adj.* **1a.** Dark; gloomy. **b.** Dull or dark in color. **2a.** Melancholy; dismal. **b.** Serious; grave. [Fr. *sombre* < OFr. < **sombrer,* to cast a shadow < LLat. *subumbrāre* < Lat. *sub umbrā,* in shadow : *sub,* under; see SUB– + *umbrā,* ablative of *umbra,* shadow.] **—som′ber•ly** *adv.* **—som′ber•ness** *n.*

som•bre (sŏm′bər) *adj. Chiefly British* Variant of **somber.**

som•bre•ro (sŏm-brâr′ō, səm-) *n., pl.* **-ros** A large straw or felt hat with a broad brim and tall crown, worn esp. in Mexico and the American Southwest. [Sp., perh. < *sombra,* shade, prob. < *sombrar,* to shade < LLat. *subumbrāre,* to cast a shadow. See SOMBER.]

Sombrero An island of St. Kitts and Nevis in the Leeward Is. of the West Indies.

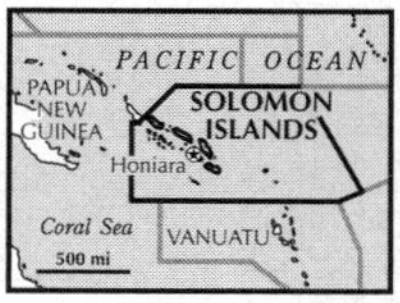

Solomon Islands[2]

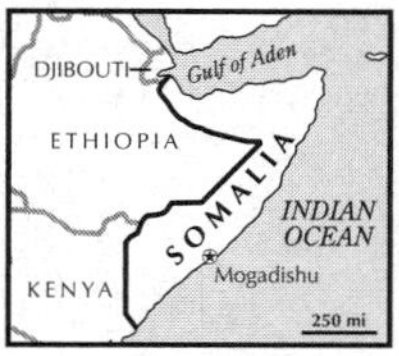

Somalia

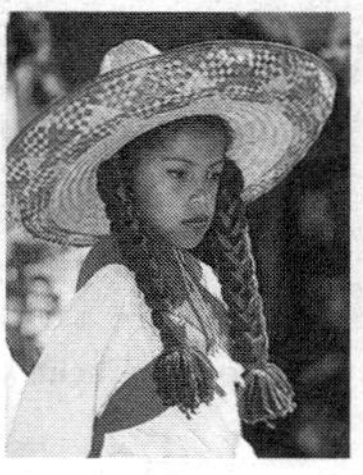
sombrero
young girl in traditional dance costume for Cinco de Mayo

ă pat	oi boy
ā pay	ou out
âr care	o͝o took
ä father	o͞o boot
ĕ pet	ŭ cut
ē be	ûr urge
ĭ pit	th thin
ī pie	*th* this
îr pier	hw which
ŏ pot	zh vision
ō toe	ə about, item
ô paw	

Stress marks:
′ (primary);
′ (secondary), as in **lexicon** (lĕk′sĭ-kŏn′)

som·brous (sŏm′brəs) *adj. Archaic* Somber in aspect or in character.

some (sŭm) *adj.* **1.** Being an unspecified number or quantity: *Some people came into the room. Would you like some sugar?* **2.** Being a portion or an unspecified number or quantity of a whole or group: *He likes some modern art but not all.* **3.** Being a considerable number or quantity: *She has been directing films for some years now.* **4.** Unknown or unspecified by name: *Some man called.* **5.** *Logic* Being part and perhaps all of a class. **6.** *Informal* Remarkable: *She is some skier.* ❖ *pron.* **1.** An indefinite or unspecified number or portion: *We took some of the books.* See Usage Note at **every. 2.** An indefinite additional quantity: *did the assigned work and then some.* ❖ *adv.* **1.** Approximately; about: *Some 400 people attended the rally.* **2.** *Informal* Somewhat: *some tired.* [ME < OE *sum,* a certain one. See **sem-**[1] in App.]

–some[1] *suff.* Characterized by a specified quality, condition, or action: *bothersome.* [ME *-some* < OE *-sum.* See **sem-**[1] in App.]

–some[2] *suff.* A group of a specified number of members: *three-some.* [ME *-sum* < OE *sum,* some. See **SOME.**]

–some[3] *suff.* **1.** Body: *centrosome.* **2.** Chromosome: *monosome.* [< Gk. *sōma,* body.]

some·bod·y (sŭm′bŏd′ē, -bŭd′ē, -bə-dē) *pron.* An unspecified or unknown person; someone. See Usage Note at **he**[1]. ❖ *n., pl.* **-ies** A person of importance.

some·day (sŭm′dā′) *adv.* At an indefinite time in the future.

some·how (sŭm′hou′) *adv.* In a way not specified, understood, or known.

some·one (sŭm′wŭn′, -wən) *pron.* An unspecified or unknown person; somebody. ❖ *n.* A person of importance.

some·place (sŭm′plās′) *adv. & n.* Somewhere.

som·er·sault also **sum·mer·sault** (sŭm′ər-sôlt′) *n.* **1.** An acrobatic stunt in which the body rolls forward or backward in a complete revolution with the knees bent and the feet coming over the head. **2.** A complete reversal, as of sympathies or opinions. ❖ *intr.v.* **-sault·ed, -sault·ing, -saults** To perform a somersault. [Obsolete Fr. *sombresault,* var. of *sobresault* < O Provençal *sobresaut : sobre-,* above (< Lat. *suprā;* see **uper** in App.) + *saut,* leap (< Lat. *saltus* < p. part. of *salīre,* to leap).]

som·er·set also **sum·mer·set** (sŭm′ər-sĕt′) *n.* See **somersault 1.** ❖ *intr.v.* **-set·ted, -set·ting, -sets** To perform a somersault. [Alteration of SOMERSAULT.]

Som·er·ville (sŭm′ər-vĭl′) A city of E MA, a suburb of Boston. Pop. 77,478.

Somerville, Mary Fairfax Greig 1780–1872. British mathematician and astronomer. The first women's college at Oxford University was funded by and named after her.

so·mes·thet·ic (sō′mĕs-thĕt′ĭk) *adj.* Somatosensory. [Gk. *sōma,* body; see SOMA[1] + Gk. *aisthētikos,* of sense perception; see AESTHETIC.]

some·thing (sŭm′thĭng) *pron.* **1.** An undetermined or unspecified thing: *"We're all recalling something, furtively seeking something"* (Virginia Woolf). **2.** An unspecified or undetermined amount or extent: *We know something about the early settlers in this area.* **3.** One having some or many of the same attributes, character, or essence as another: *Trying to fix the computer myself was something of a mistake.* ❖ *n.* **1.** A remarkable or important thing or person: *He thinks he is something in that uniform.* **2.** One who falls into a specified age range. Often used in combination: *fortysomethings who attended their class reunion.* ❖ *adj.* Of, relating to, or being a member of a specified age range. Often used in combination: *a party for twentysomething singles.* ❖ *adv.* **1.** A little; somewhat: *She looks something like her mother.* **2.** *Informal* To an extreme degree: *drinks something fierce.* **—idiom: something else** *Informal* One that is very special or quite remarkable.

some·time (sŭm′tīm′) *adv.* **1.** At an indefinite or unstated time: *Let's meet sometime today.* **2.** At an indefinite time in the future: *Let's get together sometime.* **3.** *Obsolete* Sometimes. **4.** *Archaic* Formerly. ❖ *adj.* **1.** Having been at some prior time; former. **2.** *Usage Problem* Occasional.

some·times (sŭm′tīmz′) *adv.* **1.** At times; now and then. **2.** *Obsolete* At some previous time; formerly.

some·way (sŭm′wā′) also **some·ways** (-wāz′) *adv.* In some way or another; somehow.

some·what (sŭm′hwŏt′, -wŏt′, -hwŭt′, -wŭt′, -hwət, -wət) *adv.* To some extent or degree; rather. ❖ *pron.* Something: *The news was somewhat of a surprise.*

some·where (sŭm′hwâr′, -wâr′) *adv.* **1.** At, in, or to a place not specified or known: *found it somewhere at home.* **2.** To a place or

Stephen Sondheim

state of further development or progress: *finally got somewhere.* **3.** Approximately; roughly. ❖ *n.* An unknown or unspecified place.

some·wheres (sŭm′hwârz′, -wârz′) *adv. Informal* Somewhere.

so·mite (sō′mīt′) *n.* **1.** See **metamere. 2.** A segmental mass of mesoderm in the vertebrate embryo that develops into muscles and vertebrae. [Gk. *sōma,* body; see SOMA[1] + -ITE[1].] **—so·mit′ic** (sō-mĭt′ĭk) *adj.*

Somme (sŭm, sôm) A river of N France flowing c. 241 km (150 mi) W and NW to the English Channel.

som·me·lier (sŭm′əl-yā′, sŏ′mə-lyā′) *n.* One who is employed to serve wine, as at a restaurant. [Fr. < OFr., officer in charge of provisions, pack-animal driver, alteration of *sommerier < *sommier,* beast of burden < VLat. **saumārius.* See SUMMER[2].]

som·nam·bu·late (sŏm-năm′byə-lāt′) *intr.v.* **-lat·ed, -lat·ing, -lates** To walk or perform another act while asleep or in a sleeplike condition. **—som·nam′bu·lar** (-lər) *adj.* **—som′nam·bu·la′tion** *n.*

som·nam·bu·lism (sŏm-năm′byə-lĭz′əm) *n.* See **sleepwalking. —som·nam′bu·list** *n.* **—som·nam′bu·lis′tic** *adj.*

somni– or **somn–** *pref.* Sleep: *somnambulate.* [< Lat. *somnus,* sleep. See **swep-** in App.]

som·ni·fa·cient (sŏm′nə-fā′shənt) *adj.* Tending to produce sleep; hypnotic. **—som′ni·fa′cient** *n.*

som·nif·er·ous (sŏm-nĭf′ər-əs) also **som·nif·ic** (-nĭf′ĭk) *adj.* Inducing sleep; soporific. **—som·nif′er·ous·ly** *adv.*

som·nil·o·quy (sŏm-nĭl′ə-kwē) *n., pl.* **-quies** The act or habit of talking in one's sleep. [SOMNI– + Lat. *loquī,* to speak; see SOLILOQUY.] **—som·nil′o·quist** *n.*

som·no·lent (sŏm′nə-lənt) *adj.* **1.** Drowsy; sleepy. **2.** Inducing or tending to induce sleep; soporific. [ME *sompnolent* < OFr. < Lat. *somnolentus : somnus,* sleep; see **swep-** in App. + *-olentus,* abounding in.] **—som′no·lence** *n.* **—som′no·lent·ly** *adv.*

so·mo·ni (sō-mô-nē′) *n.* See table at **currency.** [Tajik *somonī,* after Ismoil *Somoni* (Ismail Samanid) (died 907), founder of the Persian dynasty that is considered to be the first Tajik state.]

So·mo·za De·bay·le (sə-mō′zə də-bī′lä, sō-mō′sä dĕ-bī′lĕ), **Anastasio** 1925–80. Nicaraguan president (1963–79) who was overthrown by the Sandinista National Liberation Front and later assassinated.

son (sŭn) *n.* **1.** One's male child. **2.** A male descendant. **3.** A man considered as if in a relationship of child to parent: *a son of the soil.* **4.** One personified or regarded as a male descendant. **5.** Used as a familiar form of address for a young man. **6. Son** *Christianity* The second person of the Trinity. [ME < OE *sunu.* See **seuə-** in App.] **—son′ly** *adj.*

so·nance (sō′nəns) *n.* Sound.

so·nant (sō′nənt) *adj.* Voiced, as a speech sound. ❖ *n.* **1.** A voiced speech sound. **2.** A syllabic consonant in Indo-European. [Lat. *sonāns, sonant-,* pr. part. of *sonāre,* to sound.]

so·nar (sō′när′) *n.* **1.** A system using transmitted and reflected underwater sound waves to detect and locate submerged objects or measure the distance to the floor of a body of water. **2.** An apparatus, as one in a submarine, using sonar. **3.** Echolocation. [*so*(*und*) *na*(*vigation and*) *r*(*anging*).]

so·na·ta (sə-nä′tə) *n.* A composition for one or more solo instruments, one of which is usu. a keyboard instrument, usu. consisting of three or four independent movements varying in key, mood, and tempo. [Ital. < fem. p. part. of *sonare,* to sound < Lat. *sonāre.*]

sonata form *n. Music* A form of a movement having three sections, the exposition, development, and recapitulation, often with a coda.

son·a·ti·na (sŏn′ə-tē′nə) *n.* A sonata having shorter movements than the typical sonata. [Ital., dim. of *sonata,* sonata. See SONATA.]

Sond·heim (sŏnd′hīm′), **Stephen** b. 1930. Amer. composer and lyricist whose musicals include *Gypsy* (1959).

sone (sōn) *n.* A subjective unit of loudness, equal to the loudness of a pure tone having a frequency of 1,000 hertz at 40 decibels as perceived by a person with normal hearing. [Lat. *sonus,* a sound.]

son et lu·mière (sôn′ ā lüm-yâr′) *n.* A historical theatrical entertainment using recorded sound, lighting, and other effects and presented at night in a historic, usu. outdoor setting. [Fr. : *son,* sound + *et,* and + *lumière,* light.]

song (sông, sŏng) *n.* **1.** *Music* **a.** A brief composition written or adapted for singing. **b.** The act or art of singing. **2.** A distinctive or characteristic sound made by an animal, such as a bird or an insect. **3a.** Poetry; verse. **b.** A lyric poem or ballad. **—idiom: for a song** *Informal* At a low price. [ME < OE *sang.* See **sengʷh-** in App.]

Song also **Sung** (sŏong) A Chinese dynasty (960–1279) marked by cultural advance and prosperity. [Chin. (Mandarin) *Sòng,* after *Sòng* prefecture, where its founder was crowned emperor.]

song and dance (sông, sŏng) *n., pl.* **song and dances** or **songs and dances 1.** A theatrical performance that combines singing and dancing. **2.** *Slang* An excessively elaborate story or explanation, sometimes intended to deceive or mislead.

song·bird (sông′bûrd′, sŏng′-) *n.* A bird, esp. of the suborder Oscines of passerines, with a melodious song or call.

Song Da (sông′ dä′) See **Black River** 1.

song·fest (sông′fĕst′, sŏng′-) *n.* A casual group sing.

song•ful (sông′fəl, sŏng′-) *adj.* Melodious; tuneful. —**song′ful•ly** *adv.* —**song′ful•ness** *n.*

Song•hai also **Song•hay** (sông′hī′, sŏng-gī′) An ancient empire of W Africa in present-day Mali; founded c. 700 by Berbers and at the height of its power around 1500.

Song Hong (sông′ hông′) See **Red River** 1.

Song•hua (sông′hwä′) also **Sun•ga•ri** (sŏŏng′gə-rē′) A river of NE China rising near the North Korean border and flowing c. 1,850 km (1,150 mi) to the Amur R.

Song of Solomon (sông, sŏng) *n.* See table at **Bible.**

Song of Songs (sông, sŏng) *n.* See table at **Bible.**

song•smith (sông′smĭth′, sŏng′-) *n.* See **songwriter.**

song sparrow (sông, sŏng) *n.* A common North American sparrow (*Melospiza melodia*) having streaked brownish plumage and noted for its melodious song.

song•ster (sông′stər, sŏng′-) *n.* **1a.** One who sings. **b.** See **songwriter.** **2.** A songbird.

song•stress (sông′strĭs, sŏng′-) *n.* **1.** A woman who performs songs. **2.** A woman who writes songs.

song thrush (sông, sŏng) *n.* An Old World songbird (*Turdus philomelos*) having brown upper plumage and a spotted breast.

song•writ•er (sông′rī′tər, sŏng′-) *n.* One who writes lyrics or tunes, or both, for songs.

son•ic (sŏn′ĭk) *adj.* **1.** Of or relating to audible sound. **2.** Having a speed approaching or being that of sound in air, about 1,220 kilometers (760 miles) per hour at sea level. [< Lat. *sonus,* a sound.] —**son′ic•al•ly** *adv.*

sonic barrier *n.* The sudden sharp increase in aerodynamic drag experienced by aircraft approaching the speed of sound.

sonic boom *n.* An explosive sound due to the shock wave radiating from aircraft traveling at or above the speed of sound.

son-in-law (sŭn′ĭn-lô′) *n., pl.* **sons-in-law** (sŭnz′-) The husband of one's daughter.

son•net (sŏn′ĭt) *n.* **1.** A 14-line verse form usu. having one of several conventional rhyme schemes. **2.** A poem in this form. [Fr. or Ital. *sonetto* (Fr. < Ital.) < O Provençal *sonet,* dim. of *son,* song < Lat. *sonus,* a sound.]

son•net•eer (sŏn′ĭ-tîr′) *n.* **1.** A composer of sonnets. **2.** An inferior poet.

son•ny (sŭn′ē) *n., pl.* **-nies** Used as a familiar form of address for a boy or young man. [Dim. of SON.]

sono– *pref.* Sound: *sonobuoy.* [< Lat. *sonus,* sound. See SONIC.]

so•no•buoy (sŏn′ə-bōō′ē, -boi′) *n.* A buoy equipped with an acoustic receiver and a radio transmitter that emits radio signals when it detects underwater sounds.

son of a bitch *Vulgar n., pl.* **sons of bitches** A person regarded as thoroughly mean or disagreeable. ❖ *interj.* Used in annoyance, disgust, disappointment, or amazement.

son of a gun *Informal n., pl.* **sons of guns 1.** A person; a fellow. **2.** A rascal; a scamp. ❖ *interj.* Used to express annoyance, disappointment, or surprise.

Son of God *n. Christianity* Jesus.

Son of Man *n.* **1.** *Christianity* Jesus. **2. son of man** A human.

son•o•gram (sŏn′ə-grăm′, sō′nə-) *n.* An image, as of an unborn fetus, produced by ultrasonography.

So•no•ma (sə-nō′mə) A district of W CA N of San Francisco; famous for its numerous vineyards.

son•o•lu•mi•nes•cence (sŏn′ə-lōō′mə-nĕs′əns) *n.* The emission of light caused by the collapse of bubbles formed when sound waves pass through a liquid.

son•o•rant (sŏn′ər-ənt, sō-nôr′-, sə-nôr′-, -nōr′-) *n.* A usu. voiced speech sound characterized by relatively free air flow through the vocal tract and capable of being syllabic, as a vowel, liquid, or nasal. [SONOR(OUS) + -ANT.]

so•nor•i•ty (sə-nôr′ĭ-tē, -nŏr′-) *n., pl.* **-ties 1.** The quality or state of being sonorous; resonance. **2.** A sound. **3.** *Linguistics* The degree to which a speech sound is like a vowel.

son•o•rous (sŏn′ər-əs, sə-nôr′-, -nŏr′-) *adj.* **1.** Having or producing sound. **2.** Having or producing a full, deep, or rich sound. **3.** Impressive in style of speech: *a sonorous oration.* **4.** (*also* sō′nər-əs) Produced in the manner of a sonorant. [< Lat. *sonōrus* < *sonor,* sound < *sonāre,* to sound.] —**so•no′rous•ly** *adv.* —**so•no′rous•ness** *n.*

Son•tag (sŏn′tăg′), **Susan** b. 1933. Amer. writer noted esp. for her essays in *Against Interpretation* (1966).

Soo Canals (sōō) See **Sault Sainte Marie Canals.**

Soo•chow (sōō′chou′, -jō′) See **Suzhou.**

soon (sōōn) *adv.* **soon•er, soon•est 1.** In the near future; shortly. **2.** Without hesitation; promptly: *as soon as possible.* **3.** Before the usual or appointed time; early. **4.** With willingness; readily: *I'd as soon leave right now.* **5.** *Obsolete* Immediately. —**idioms: no sooner than** As soon as. **sooner or later** At some time; eventually. [ME *sone* < OE *sōna,* immediately.]

soon•er (sōō′nər) *n. Slang* **1.** A person who settled homestead land in the western United States before it was officially made available, in order to have first choice of location. **2. Sooner** A native or resident of Oklahoma. [< SOON.]

soot (sŏŏt, sōōt) *n.* The fine black particles, chiefly composed of carbon, produced by incomplete combustion of coal, oil, wood, or other fuels. [ME < OE *sōt.* See sed- in App.] —**soot** *v.*

sooth (sōōth) *Archaic adj.* **1.** Real; true. **2.** Soft; smooth. ❖ *n.* Truth; reality. [ME < OE *sōth.* See es- in App.]

soothe (sōōth) *v.* **soothed, sooth•ing, soothes** —*tr.* **1.** To calm or placate. **2.** To ease or relieve (pain, for example). —*intr.* To bring comfort, composure, or relief. [ME *sothen* < OE *sōthian* < *sōth,* true. See es- in App.] —**sooth′er** *n.*

sooth•fast (sōōth′fäst′) *adj. Archaic* **1.** Truthful; honest. **2.** True; real. [ME *sothfast* < OE *sōthfæst* : *sōth,* truth; see SOOTH + *fæst,* fixed, fast; see FAST[1].]

sooth•ing (sōō′thĭng) *adj.* Tending to soothe. —**sooth′ing•ly** *adv.* —**sooth′ing•ness** *n.*

sooth•say (sōōth′sā′) *intr.v.* **-said** (-sĕd′), **-say•ing, -says** (-sĕz′) To foretell future events; predict.

sooth•say•er (sōōth′sā′ər) *n.* One who claims to be able to foretell events or predict the future; a seer.

sooth•say•ing (sōōth′sā′ĭng) *n.* **1.** The art or practice of foretelling events. **2.** A prediction; a prophecy.

soot•y (sŏŏt′ē, sōō′tē) *adj.* **-i•er, -i•est 1.** Covered with or as if with soot. **2.** Of or producing soot. **3.** Blackish or dusky in color. —**soot′i•ness** *n.*

sooty mold *n.* **1.** A blackish growth produced by fungi of the genus *Capnodium,* which grows in the droppings of aphids on plants. **2.** Any of the fungi that produce such growth.

sooty tern *n.* A tern (*Sterna fuscata*) found along most tropical coasts, having black plumage above and white below.

sop (sŏp) *tr.v.* **sopped, sop•ping, sops 1.** To dip, soak, or drench in a liquid; saturate. **2.** To take up by absorption: *sop up water.* ❖ *n.* **1.** A piece of food soaked or dipped in a liquid. **2a.** Something yielded to placate or soothe. **b.** A bribe. [< ME *soppe,* bread dipped in liquid < OE *sopp-* (in *soppcuppe,* cup for dipping bread in).]

SOP *abbr.* standard operating procedure

sop. *abbr.* soprano

so•pai•pil•la (sō′pī-pē′yə) or **so•pa•pil•la** (-pə-) *n.* A crisp, puffy, deep-fried pastry often served with honey or syrup. [Am.Sp., dim. of Sp. *sopaipa,* fried dough sweetened with honey < earlier *xopaipa* < Mozarabic *xupaipa,* dim. of *šúppa, súppa,* bread soaked in oil < OSpan. *sopa,* food soaked in liquid, of Gmc. orig.]

soph. *abbr.* sophomore

soph•ism (sŏf′ĭz′əm) *n.* **1.** A plausible but fallacious argument. **2.** Deceptive or fallacious argumentation. [ME *sophime, sophisme* < OFr. *sophime* < Lat. *sophisma* < Gk. < *sophizesthai,* to be subtle < *sophos,* clever, wise.]

soph•ist (sŏf′ĭst) *n.* **1a.** One skilled in elaborate and devious argumentation. **b.** A scholar or thinker. **2. Sophist** Any of a group of professional fifth-century B.C. Greek philosophers and teachers who speculated on theology, metaphysics, and the sciences. [ME *sophiste* < Lat. *sophista* < Gk. *sophistēs* < *sophizesthai,* to become wise < *sophos,* clever.]

so•phis•tic (sə-fĭs′tĭk) or **so•phis•ti•cal** (-tĭ-kəl) *adj.* **1.** Of, relating to, or characteristic of sophists. **2.** Apparently sound but really fallacious; specious. —**so•phis′ti•cal•ly** *adv.*

so•phis•ti•cate (sə-fĭs′tĭ-kāt′) *v.* **-cat•ed, -cat•ing, -cates** —*tr.* **1.** To cause to become less natural, esp. to make less naive and more worldly. **2.** To make impure; adulterate. **3.** To make more complex or inclusive; refine. —*intr.* To use sophistry. ❖ *n.* (-kĭt) A sophisticated person. [ME *sophisticaten,* to adulterate < Med.Lat. *sophisticāre, sophisticāt-* < Lat. *sophisticus,* sophistic < Gk. *sophistikos < sophistēs,* sophist. See SOPHIST.] —**so•phis′ti•ca′tion** *n.* —**so•phis′ti•ca′tor** *n.*

so•phis•ti•cat•ed (sə-fĭs′tĭ-kā′tĭd) *adj.* **1.** Having acquired worldly knowledge or refinement; lacking natural simplicity or naiveté. **2.** Very complex or complicated. **3.** Suitable for or appealing to the tastes of sophisticates.

soph•is•try (sŏf′ĭ-strē) *n., pl.* **-tries 1.** Plausible but fallacious argumentation. **2.** A plausible but misleading or fallacious argument.

Soph•o•cles (sŏf′ə-klēz′) 496?–406 B.C. Greek dramatist whose plays include *Oedipus Rex.* —**Soph′o•cle′an** *adj.*

Sophocles

soph•o•more (sŏf′ə-môr′, -mōr′, sŏf′môr′, -mōr′) *n.* **1a.** A second-year student in a US college. **b.** A tenth-grade student in a US high school. **2.** A person in the second year of carrying out an endeavor. ❖ *adj.* **1.** Of or relating to the second year of an endeavor, esp. of attending a school or college. **2.** Being the second in a series: *a singer's sophomore album.* [Alteration (prob. influenced by Gk. *sophos,* wise, and *mōros,* stupid) of *sophumer* < obsolete *sophom,* sophism, dialectic exercise, var. of SOPHISM.]

soph•o•mor•ic (sŏf′ə-môr′ĭk, -mōr′-, sŏf′môr′-, -mōr′-) *adj.* **1.** Of or characteristic of a sophomore. **2.** Exhibiting great immaturity and lack of judgment. —**soph′o•mor′i•cal•ly** *adv.*

so•por (sō′pôr′) *n.* A deep, lethargic, or unnatural sleep. [Lat. See swep- in App.]

sop•o•rif•er•ous (sŏp′ə-rĭf′ər-əs, sō′pə-) *adj.* Inducing or tending to induce sleep; soporific. —**sop′o•rif′er•ous•ly** *adv.* —**sop′o•rif′er•ous•ness** *n.*

sop•o•rif•ic (sŏp′ə-rĭf′ĭk, sō′pə-) *adj.* **1.** Inducing or tending to induce sleep. **2.** Drowsy; sleepy. ❖ *n.* A drug or other substance

ă	pat	oi	boy
ā	pay	ou	out
âr	care	ŏŏ	took
ä	father	ōō	boot
ĕ	pet	ŭ	cut
ē	be	ûr	urge
ĭ	pit	th	thin
ī	pie	th	this
îr	pier	hw	which
ŏ	pot	zh	vision
ō	toe	ə	about,
ô	paw		item

Stress marks: ′ (primary); ′ (secondary), as in **lexicon** (lĕk′sĭ-kŏn′)

that induces sleep; a hypnotic.

sop•ping (sŏp′ĭng) *adj.* Thoroughly soaked; drenched. ❖ *adv.* Extremely; very: *sopping wet.*

sop•py (sŏp′ē) *adj.* **-pi•er, -pi•est 1.** Soaked; sopping. **2.** Rainy. **3.** Sentimental; maudlin.

so•pra•ni•no (sō′prə-nē′nō, sŏp′rə-) *n., pl.* **-nos** A musical instrument, such as a recorder, that is higher in pitch than the soprano of its family. [Ital., dim. of *soprano*, soprano. See SOPRANO.]

so•pran•o (sə-prăn′ō, -prä′nō) *n., pl.* **-os 1.** The highest singing voice of a woman or young boy. **2.** A singer having such a voice. **3.** The tonal range characteristic of a soprano. **4.** An instrument that sounds within this range. **5.** A vocal or instrumental part written within this range. [Ital. < *sopra*, above < Lat. *suprā*. See **uper** in App.]

soprano clef *n.* The C clef positioned to indicate that the bottom line of a staff represents the pitch of middle C.

so•ra (sôr′ə, sōr′ə) *n.* A North American rail (*Porzana carolina*) having grayish-brown plumage and a short stout bill, commonly found in freshwater bogs or swamps. [?]

sorb¹ (sôrb) *tr.v.* **sorbed, sorb•ing, sorbs** To take up and hold, as by absorption or adsorption. [Back-formation < ABSORB and ADSORB.] **—sorb′a•bil′i•ty** *n.* **—sorb′a•ble** *adj.* **—sorb′ent** *adj. & n.*

sorb² (sôrb) *n.* **1.** Any of several Old World trees of the genus *Sorbus* in the rose family, as the service tree or the rowan. **2.** The fruit of any of these plants. [Fr. *sorbe*, sorb fruit < OFr. *sourbe* < VLat. **sorba* < Lat. *sorbum*.]

Sorb *n.* A member of a Slavic people inhabiting the region of Lusatia in eastern Germany and southwest Poland. [Ger. *Sorbe*, perh. var. of *Serbe*, Serb < Serbian *Srb, Serb.*]

sor•bet (sôr′bĭt, sôr-bā′) *n.* A frozen dessert similar to a frappé, usu. made from fruit juice and mushy in consistency. [Fr. < Ottoman Turk. *sherbet*, sweet fruit drink. See SHERBET.]

Sor•bi•an (sôr′bē-ən) *n.* **1.** A Sorb. **2.** The Slavic language of the Sorbs. **—Sor′bi•an** *adj.*

sor•bic acid (sôr′bĭk) *n.* A white crystalline solid, $C_6H_8O_2$, found in the berries of the mountain ash or prepared synthetically and used as a food preservative and fungicide. [< SORB².]

sor•bi•tol (sôr′bĭ-tôl′, -tōl′, -tŏl′) *n.* A white sweetish crystalline alcohol, $C_6H_{14}O_6$, found in various berries and fruits or prepared synthetically and used as a flavoring agent, a sugar substitute for people with diabetes, and as a moisturizer in cosmetics and other products. [SORB² + -IT(E)² + -OL¹.]

sor•cer•er (sôr′sər-ər) *n.* One who practices sorcery; a wizard. [ME *sorser, sorcerer* < OFr. *sorcier* < VLat. **sortiārius* < Lat. *sors, sort-*, lot, fortune.]

sor•cer•ess (sôr′sər-ĭs) *n.* A woman who practices sorcery.

sor•cer•y (sôr′sə-rē) *n.* Use of supernatural power over others through the assistance of spirits; witchcraft. [ME *sorcerie* < OFr. < *sorcier*, sorcerer. See SORCERER.] **—sor′cer•ous** *adj.* **—sor′cer•ous•ly** *adv.*

sor•did (sôr′dĭd) *adj.* **1.** Filthy or dirty; foul. **2.** Depressingly squalid; wretched. **3.** Morally degraded. **4.** Exceedingly mercenary; grasping. [ME *sordide*, festering, purulent < Lat. *sordidus*, dirty < *sordēre*, to be dirty.] **—sor′did•ly** *adv.* **—sor′did•ness** *n.*

sor•di•no (sôr-dē′nō) *n., pl.* **-ni** (-nē) *Music* A mute for an instrument. [Ital., dim. of *sordo*, deaf, mute < Lat. *surdus*.]

sore (sôr, sōr) *adj.* **sor•er, sor•est 1.** Painful to the touch; tender. **2.** Feeling physical pain; hurting. **3.** Causing misery, sorrow, or distress; grievous: *in sore need.* **4.** Causing embarrassment or irritation: *a sore subject.* **5.** Full of distress; sorrowful. **6.** *Informal* Angry; offended. ❖ *n.* **1.** An open skin lesion, wound, or ulcer. **2.** A source of pain, distress, or irritation. ❖ *tr.v.* **sored, sor•ing, sores** To mutilate the legs or feet of (a horse) to induce a particular gait in the animal. ❖ *adv. Archaic* Sorely. [ME < OE *sār.*] **—sore′ness** *n.*

sore•head (sôr′hĕd′, sōr′-) *n. Slang* One who is easily offended, annoyed, or angered.

sore•ly (sôr′lē, sōr′-) *adv.* **1.** Painfully; grievously. **2.** Extremely; greatly: *Their skills were sorely needed.*

sore throat *n.* Any of various inflammations of the tonsils, pharynx, or larynx characterized by pain in swallowing.

sor•ghum (sôr′gəm) *n.* **1.** An Old World grass (*Sorghum bicolor*), several varieties of which are widely cultivated as grain and forage or as a source of syrup. **2.** Syrup made from the juice of this plant. [NLat. *Sorghum*, genus name < Ital. *sorgo*, a tall cereal grass, prob. < Med.Lat. *surgum*, perh. var. of VLat. **syricum* < neut. of Lat. *Syricus*, Syrian < *Syria*, Syria.]

sor•go also **sor•gho** (sôr′gō) *n., pl.* **-gos** also **-ghos** Any of various sorghums that are cultivated as a source of syrup. [Ital. See SORGHUM.]

so•ri (sôr′ī, sōr′ī) *n.* Plural of **sorus.**

so•ri•tes (sə-rī′tēz, sô-) *n., pl.* **sorites** *Logic* A form of argument in which a series of incomplete syllogisms is so arranged that the predicate of each premise forms the subject of the next until the subject of the first is joined with the predicate of the last in the conclusion. [Lat. < Gk. *sōreitēs* < *sōros*, heap.]

So•ro•ca•ba (sôr′ōō-kä′bä) A city of S Brazil W of São Paulo. Pop. 378,366.

so•ro•ral (sə-rôr′əl, -rōr′-) *adj.* Of, relating to, or resembling a sister; sisterly. [< Lat. *soror*, sister. See **swesor-** in App.]

so•ror•ate (sə-rôr′ĭt, -rōr′-) *n.* The custom of marriage of a man to his wife's sister or sisters, usu. after the wife has died or proved sterile. [< Lat. *soror*, sister. See SORORAL.]

so•ror•i•cide (sə-rôr′ĭ-sīd′, -rōr′-) *n.* **1.** The killing of one's sister. **2.** One who kills one's own sister. [Lat. *soror*, sister; see **swesor-** in App. + -CIDE.] **—so•ror′i•cid′al** (-sīd′l) *adj.*

so•ror•i•ty (sə-rôr′ĭ-tē, -rōr′-) *n., pl.* **-ties 1.** A chiefly social organization of women students at a college or university. **2.** An association or society of women. [Med.Lat. *sorōritās* < Lat. *soror*, sister. See **swesor-** in App.]

sorp•tion (sôrp′shən) *n.* **1.** The process of sorbing. **2.** The state of being sorbed. **—sorp′tive** *adj.*

sor•rel¹ (sôr′əl, sŏr′-) *n.* **1.** Any of several plants of the genus *Rumex*, having acid-flavored leaves sometimes used as salad greens, esp. *R. acetosella*, a widely naturalized Eurasian species. **2.** Any of various plants of the genus *Oxalis*, having usu. compound leaves with three leaflets. [ME *sorel* < OFr. *surele* < *sur*, sour, of Gmc. orig.]

sor•rel² (sôr′əl, sŏr′-) *n.* **1.** A brownish orange to light brown. **2.** A sorrel-colored horse or other animal. [< ME *sorel*, sorrel-colored < OFr. < *sor*, red-brown, of Gmc. orig.]

sorrel tree *n.* See **sourwood.**

Sor•ren•to (sə-rĕn′tō, sôr-) A resort town of S Italy on the **Sorrento Peninsula**, separating the Bay of Naples from the Gulf of Salerno. Pop. 17,301.

sor•row (sŏr′ō, sôr′ō) *n.* **1.** Mental suffering or pain caused by injury, loss, or despair. **2.** A source or cause of sorrow; a misfortune. **3.** Expression of sorrow; grieving. ❖ *intr.v.* **-rowed, -row•ing, -rows** To feel or express sorrow. See Syns at **grieve.** [ME *sorwe* < OE *sorg.*] **—sor′row•er** *n.*

sor•row•ful (sŏr′ō-fəl, -ə-fəl, sôr′-) *adj.* Affected with, marked by, causing, or expressing sorrow. See Syns at **sad. —sor′row•ful•ly** *adv.* **—sor′row•ful•ness** *n.*

sor•ry (sŏr′ē, sôr′ē) *adj.* **-ri•er, -ri•est 1.** Feeling or expressing sympathy, pity, or regret. **2.** Worthless or inferior; paltry: *a sorry excuse.* **3.** Causing sorrow, grief, or misfortune; grievous: *a sorry development.* [ME *sori* < OE *sārig*, sad < *sār*, sore.] **—sor′ri•ly** *adv.* **—sor′ri•ness** *n.*

sort (sôrt) *n.* **1.** A group of persons or things of the same general character; a kind. **2.** Character or nature: *books of a subversive sort.* **3.** One that typifies a group or exemplifies a characteristic: *His talk was a sort of primer on the subject.* **4.** A person; an individual: *The clerk is a decent sort.* **5.** *Printing* One of the characters in a font of type. Often used in the plural. **6.** An act or instance of sorting. ❖ *tr.v.* **sort•ed, sort•ing, sorts 1.** To arrange according to class, kind, or size; classify. See Syns at **arrange. 2.** To separate from others: *sort out the wheat from the chaff.* **3.** To clarify by going over mentally: *sorting out her problems.* **—idioms: after a sort** In a haphazard or imperfect way. **of sorts** (or **a sort**) **1.** Of a mediocre or inferior kind. **2.** Of one kind or another. **out of sorts 1.** Slightly ill. **2.** Irritable; cross. **sort of** *Informal* Somewhat; rather. [ME < OFr. < Lat. *sors, sort-*, lot.] **—sort′a•ble** *adj.* **—sort′er** *n.*

sor•tie (sôr′tē, sôr-tē′) *n.* **1.** An armed attack, esp. one made from a place surrounded by enemy forces. **2.** A flight of a combat aircraft on a mission. ❖ *intr.v.* **-tied, -tie•ing, -ties** To go on a sortie. [Fr. < fem. p. part. of *sortir*, to go out < OFr.]

sor•ti•lege (sôr′tl-ĭj) *n.* **1.** The act or practice of foretelling the future by drawing lots. **2.** Sorcery; witchcraft. [ME < OFr. < Med.Lat. *sortilegium*, diviner : Lat. *sors, sort-*, lot + Lat. *legere*, to read; see **leg-** in App.]

so•rus (sôr′əs, sōr′-) *n., pl.* **so•ri** (sôr′ī, sōr′ī) **1.** A cluster of sporangia borne on the underside of a fern frond. **2.** A reproductive structure in certain fungi and lichens. [NLat. *sōrus* < Gk. *sōros*, heap.]

SOS (ĕs′ō-ĕs′) *n.* **1.** The letters represented by the Morse code signal · · · — — — · · · , used as an international distress signal, esp. by ships and aircraft. **2.** A call or signal for help.

So•sno•wiec (sôs-nô′vyĕts) A city of S Poland, a suburb of Katowice. Pop. 259,481.

so-so (sō′sō′) *adj.* Neither very good nor very bad; passable. ❖ *adv.* Neither very well nor very poorly; passably.

so•ste•nu•to (sō′stə-nōō′tō, sô′-) *Music adv. & adj.* In a manner that is sustained as long as or beyond a note's full value. ❖ *n., pl.* **-tos** or **-ti** (-tē) A sostenuto passage or movement. [Ital., p. part. of *sostenere*, to sustain < Lat. *sustinēre*. See SUSTAIN.]

sot (sŏt) *n.* A drunkard. [ME, fool < OE *sott* < OFr. *sot.*]

so•te•ri•ol•o•gy (sō-tîr′ē-ŏl′ə-jē) *n.* The theological doctrine of salvation as effected by Jesus. [Gk. *sōtērion*, deliverance (< *sōtēr*, savior < *saos, sōs*, safe) + -LOGY.] **—so•te′ri•o•log′ic** (-ə-lŏj′ĭk), **so•te′ri•o•log′i•cal** (-ĭ-kəl) *adj.*

So•thic (sō′thĭk, sŏth′ĭk) *adj.* **1.** Of, relating to, or deriving from the name of Sothis. **2.** Being the ancient Egyptian calendar year, consisting of 365¼ days. **3.** Being a cycle consisting of 1,460 years of 365 days in the ancient Egyptian calendar. [< Gk. *Sōthis*, the star Sirius. See SOTHIS.]

So•this (sō′thĭs) *n.* See **Sirius.** [Gk. *Sōthis* < Egypt. *spdt.*]

So•tho (sō′tō) *n.* **1a.** A group of closely related Bantu languages, including Tswana, spoken in southern Africa. **b.** Any of these languages. **2.** A member of a Sotho-speaking people.

so·tol (sō′tŏl′) *n.* **1.** Any of several tall woody plants of the genus *Dasylirion* of southwest North America having prickly leaves and whitish flowers. **2.** An alcoholic beverage produced from the trunks of these plants. [Perh. < Sp. *soto*, thicket, woods < Lat. *saltus*, narrow pass, woodland.]

sot·ted (sŏt′ĭd) *adj.* Muddled or stupefied, esp. with liquor; besotted. —**sot′ted·ly** *adv.* —**sot′ted·ness** *n.*

sot·tish (sŏt′ĭsh) *adj.* **1.** Stupefied from or as if from drink. **2.** Tending to drink excessively. —**sot′tish·ly** *adv.*

sot·to vo·ce (sŏt′ō vō′chē, sŏt′tō vō′chĕ) *adv. & adj.* **1.** In soft tones, so as not to be overheard; in an undertone. **2.** *Music* In very soft tones. [Ital. : *sotto*, under + *voce*, voice.]

sou (soo) *n.* One of several coins formerly used in France, worth a small amount. [Fr. < OFr. *sol* < LLat. *solidus*, solidus. See SOLIDUS.]

sou. or **Sou.** *abbr.* **1.** south **2.** southern

sou·a·ri nut (soo-är′ē) *n.* **1.** A South American evergreen tree (*Caryocar nuciferum*) having drupes with nutlike stones containing seeds used as food and as a source of cooking oil. **2.** The nut of this tree. [Fr. *saouari* < Galibi *sawarra*.]

sou·bise (soo-bēz′) *n.* A sauce of onions or onion purée. [Fr., after Charles de Rohan, Prince de *Soubise* (1715–87), French soldier.]

sou·brette (soo-brĕt′) *n.* **1a.** A saucy coquettish maidservant in comedies or comic opera. **b.** An actress or a singer taking such a part. **2.** A young woman regarded as flirtatious or frivolous. [Fr. < Provençal *soubreto*, fem. of *soubret*, conceited < *soubra*, to leave aside < O Provençal *sobrar*, to be excessive < Lat. *superāre* < *super*, above. See **super** in App.]

sou·bri·quet (soo′brĭ-kā′, -kĕt′, soo′brĭ-kā′, -kĕt′) *n.* Variant of **sobriquet**.

sou·chong (soo′chŏng′, -shŏng′) *n.* Any of several varieties of black tea native to China and adjacent regions. [Chin. (Cantonese) *siú-chúng* (ch′à), souchong (tea), equivalent to Chin. (Mandarin) *xiǎo*, small + *zhǒng*, kind.]

sou·dan (sood′n) *n.* Variant of **soldan**.

souf·flé (soo-flā′) *n.* A light fluffy baked dish made with egg yolks and beaten egg whites combined with various other ingredients. [Fr. < p. part. of *souffler*, to puff up < OFr. *soffler* < Lat. *sufflāre* : *sub-*, sub- + *flāre*, to blow.] —**souf·flé′** *adj.* —**souf·fléed′** *adj.*

sough (sou, sŭf) *intr.v.* **soughed**, **sough·ing**, **soughs** To make a soft murmuring or rustling sound. ❖ *n.* A soft murmuring or rustling sound. [ME *swowen*, *soughen* < OE *swōgan*.]

sought (sôt) *v.* Past tense and past participle of **seek**.

souk (sook, shook) *n.* A market, or part of a market, in an Arab city. [Ar. *sūq* < Aram. *šuqā*, street, market < Akkadian *sūqu*, street < *sâqu*, to be narrow.]

soul (sōl) *n.* **1.** The animating and vital principle in human beings, credited with the faculties of thought, action, and emotion and often conceived as an immaterial entity. **2.** The spiritual nature of humans, regarded as immortal, separable from the body at death, and susceptible to happiness or misery in a future state. **3.** The disembodied spirit of a dead human. **4.** A human: *"the homes of some nine hundred souls"* (Garrison Keillor). **5.** The central or integral part; the vital core. **6.** A person considered as the perfect embodiment of an intangible quality; a personification: *I am the very soul of discretion.* **7.** A person's emotional or moral nature. **8.** A sense of emotional strength or spiritual vitality held to derive from Black and esp. African-American cultural experience, as expressed in language and music. **9.** A strong, deeply felt emotion conveyed by a speaker, performer, or artist. **10.** Soul music. [ME < OE *sāwol*.]

soul brother *n. Slang* An African-American man or boy.

soul food *n.* Food, such as ham hocks and collard greens, traditionally eaten by southern African Americans.

soul·ful (sōl′fəl) *adj.* Full of or expressing deep feeling; profoundly emotional. —**soul′ful·ly** *adv.* —**soul′ful·ness** *n.*

soul kiss *n.* A kiss in which the tongue enters the partner's mouth; a French kiss.

soul·less (sōl′lĭs) *adj.* Lacking sensitivity or the capacity for deep feeling. —**soul′less·ly** *adv.* —**soul′less·ness** *n.*

soul mate *n.* One of two persons compatible with each other in disposition, point of view, or sensitivity.

soul music *n.* Popular music developed by African Americans, combining elements of gospel music and rhythm and blues.

soul-search·ing (sōl′sûr′chĭng) *n.* A penetrating examination of one's motives, convictions, and attitudes.

soul sister *n. Slang* An African-American woman or girl.

sound¹ (sound) *n.* **1a.** Vibrations transmitted through an elastic solid or a liquid or gas, with frequencies from approx. 20 to 20,000 hertz, capable of being detected by the human ear. **b.** Transmitted vibrations of any frequency including those outside the range of human hearing. **c.** The sensation stimulated in the organs of hearing by such vibrations in the air or other medium. **d.** Such sensations considered as a group. **2.** A distinctive noise. **3.** The distance over which something can be heard. **4.** *Linguistics* **a.** An articulation made by the vocal apparatus. **b.** The distinctive character of such an articulation: *The words bear and bare have the same sound.* **5.** A mental impression; an implication: *didn't like the sound of it.* **6.** Auditory material that is recorded, as for a

movie. **7.** Meaningless noise. **8.** *Music* A distinctive style, as of an orchestra or a singer. **9.** *Archaic* Rumor; report. ❖ *v.* **sound·ed**, **sound·ing**, **sounds** —*intr.* **1a.** To make or give forth a sound. **b.** To be given forth as a sound. **2.** To present a particular impression: *That sounds reasonable.* —*tr.* **1.** To cause to give forth or produce a sound. **2.** To summon, announce, or signal by a sound. **3.** *Linguistics* To articulate; pronounce. **4.** To make known; celebrate. **5.** To examine (a body organ or part) by causing to emit sound; auscultate. —*phrasal verb:* **sound off 1.** To express one's views vigorously. **2.** To count cadence when marching in military formation. [ME *soun* < OFr. *son* < Lat. *sonus*.]

sound² (sound) *adj.* **sound·er**, **sound·est 1.** Free from defect, decay, or damage; in good condition. **2.** Free from disease or injury. See Syns at **healthy. 3.** Having a firm basis; unshakable. **4.** Financially secure or safe. **5a.** Based on valid reasoning. See Syns at **valid. b.** Free from logical flaws. **6.** Thorough; complete: *a sound flogging.* **7.** Deep and unbroken; undisturbed. **8.** Free from moral defect; upright. **9.** Worthy of confidence; trustworthy. **10.** Marked by or showing common sense and good judgment; levelheaded. **11.** Compatible with an accepted point of view; conservative. **12.** *Law* Legally valid. ❖ *adv.* Thoroughly; deeply. [ME < OE *gesund*.] —**sound′ly** *adv.* —**sound′ness** *n.*

sound³ (sound) *n.* **1a.** A long, relatively wide body of water, larger than a strait or a channel, connecting larger bodies of water. **b.** A long wide ocean inlet. **2.** The air bladder of a fish. [ME < OE *sund*, swimming, sea.]

sound⁴ (sound) *v.* **sound·ed**, **sound·ing**, **sounds** —*tr.* **1.** To measure the depth of (water), esp. by means of a weighted line; fathom. **2.** To try to learn the attitudes or opinions of. **3.** To probe (a body cavity) with a sound. —*intr.* **1.** To measure depth. **2.** To dive swiftly downward. Used of a whale or fish. **3.** To look into a possibility; investigate. ❖ *n.* An instrument used to examine or explore body cavities or dilate strictures in them. [ME *sounden* < OFr. *sonder* < *sonde*, sounding line, prob. of Gmc. orig.] —**sound′a·ble** *adj.*

sound-a·like (sound′ə-līk′) *n.* One that closely resembles another in sound, esp. by imitation.

sound barrier *n.* **1.** See **sonic barrier. 2.** A set of tall wooden, plastic, or concrete barriers placed along a road or highway to muffle the sound of traffic.

sound bite *n.* A brief statement, as by a politician, taken from an audiotape or videotape and broadcast esp. during a news report.

sound·board (sound′bôrd′, -bōrd′) *n.* See **sounding board** 1.

sound box *n. Music* A chamber in the body of an instrument, such as a cello, that intensifies the resonance of the tone.

sound effect *n.* An imitative sound, as of thunder or an explosion, produced artificially, as for a film. Often used in the plural.

sound·er¹ (soun′dər) *n.* One that makes a sound.

sound·er² (soun′dər) *n.* One that sounds, esp. a device for making soundings of the sea.

sound·er³ (soun′dər) *n.* A herd of wild boar. [ME < OFr. *sondre*, of Gmc. orig.]

sound·ing¹ (soun′dĭng) *n.* **1.** The act of one that sounds. **2.** A probe of the environment for scientific observation. **3a.** A measured depth of water. **b.** Water shallow enough for depth measurements to be taken by a hand line. Often used in the plural.

sound·ing² (soun′dĭng) *adj.* **1.** Emitting a full sound; resonant. **2.** Noisy but with little significance.

sounding board *n.* **1.** *Music* **a.** A thin board forming the upper portion of the resonant chamber in an instrument, such as a piano, and serving to increase resonance. **b.** A structure placed behind or over a podium or platform to reflect music or a speaker's voice to an audience. **2.** A person or group whose reactions to an idea or a point of view serve as a measure of its effectiveness or acceptability. **3.** A device or means serving to spread or popularize an idea or a point of view.

sounding lead (lĕd) *n.* The metal weight at the end of a sounding line.

sounding line *n.* A line marked at intervals of fathoms and weighted at one end, used to determine water depth.

sounding rocket *n.* A rocket used to make observations anywhere within the earth's atmosphere.

sound·man (sound′măn′) *n.* One in charge of recording, transmitting, or amplifying sound or producing sound effects.

sound·proof (sound′proof′) *adj.* Not penetrable by audible sound. —**sound′proof′** *v.*

sound·scape (sound′skāp′) *n.* An atmosphere or environment created by or with sound: *the raucous soundscape of a city street.* [SOUND¹ + (LAND)SCAPE.]

sound stage also **sound·stage** (sound′stāj′) *n.* A usu. soundproof room or studio used in the production of movies.

sound·track also **sound track** (sound′trăk′) *n.* **1.** The narrow strip at one side of a movie film that carries the sound recording. **2a.** The music that accompanies a movie. **b.** A commercial recording of such music.

sound truck *n.* A truck or other vehicle having one or more loudspeakers used for broadcasting messages.

sound wave *n.* A longitudinal pressure wave of audible or inaudible sound.

soup (soop) *n.* **1.** A liquid food prepared from meat, fish, or vegetable stock and often containing solid ingredients. **2.** *Slang* Some-

souk
Beirut, Lebanon

thing having the appearance or a consistency suggestive of soup, esp.: **a.** Dense fog. **b.** Nitroglycerine. **3.** A chaotic or unfortunate situation. —*phrasal verb:* soup up *Slang* To modify (something) so as to increase its capacity to perform or satisfy, esp. to add horsepower to (a vehicle). —*idiom:* in the soup *Slang* Having difficulties; in trouble. [ME *soupe* < OFr., of Gmc. orig. Soup up < SOUP, material injected into a horse to make it run faster (influenced by SUPERCHARGE).]

soup·çon (soop-sôn′, soop′sôn′) *n.* A very small amount; a trace. [Fr. < OFr. *sospeçon*, suspicion < Lat. *suspectiō, suspection-*, fear < *suspectus*, p. part. of *suspicere*, to suspect. See SUSPECT.]

soup du jour (soop′ də zhoor′) *n., pl.* **soups du jour** A soup featured by a restaurant on a given day. [Fr. *soupe du jour* : *soupe*, soup + *du*, of the + *jour*, day.]

soup kitchen *n.* A place where food is offered free or at very low cost to the needy.

soup·spoon (soop′spoon′) *n.* A spoon somewhat larger than a teaspoon, used for eating soup.

soup·y (soo′pē) *adj.* **-i·er, -i·est 1.** Having the appearance or consistency of soup. **2.** *Informal* Foggy: *soupy weather.* **3.** *Informal* Sentimental.

sour (sour) *adj.* **sour·er, sour·est 1.** Having a taste characteristic of that produced by acids; sharp, tart, or tangy. **2.** Made acid or rancid by fermentation. **3.** Having the characteristics of fermentation or rancidity; tasting or smelling of decay. **4a.** Bad-tempered and morose; peevish: *a sour temper.* **b.** Displeased with something one formerly admired or liked; disenchanted. **5a.** Not measuring up to the expected or usual ability or quality; bad. **b.** Not having the correct or properly produced pitch: *a sour note.* **6.** Of, relating to, or being excessively acid soil that is damaging to crops. **7.** Containing excessive sulfur compounds. Used of gasoline. ❖ *n.* **1.** The sensation of sour taste, one of the four primary tastes. **2.** Something sour. **3.** A mixed drink made esp. with whiskey, lemon or lime juice, and sugar. ❖ *tr. & intr.v.* **soured, sour·ing, sours 1.** To make or become sour. **2.** To make or become disagreeable, disillusioned, or disenchanted. [ME < OE *sūr.*] —**sour′ish** *adj.* —**sour′ly** *adv.* —**sour′ness** *n.*

sour·ball (sour′bôl′) *n.* A round piece of hard tart candy.

source (sôrs, sōrs) *n.* **1.** The point at which something springs into being or from which it derives or is obtained. **2.** The point of origin, such as a spring, of a stream or river. See Syns at **origin.** **3.** One that causes, creates, or initiates; a maker. **4.** One, such as a person or document, that supplies information. **5.** *Physics* The point or part of a system where energy or mass is added to the system. ❖ *v.* **sourced, sourc·ing, sourc·es** —*tr.* **1.** To specify the origin of (a communication); document. **2.** To obtain (parts or materials) from another business, country, or locale for manufacture. —*intr.* To source parts or materials. [ME < OFr. *sourse* < fem. p. part. of *sourdre*, to rise < Lat. *surgere.* See SURGE.]

source book *n.* **1.** A primary document, as of history, literature, or religion, on which secondary writings are based. **2.** A collection of such documents.

source code *n.* Code that is written by a programmer in a high-level language and can be read by people but not computers.

source language *n.* The language from which a translation is to be made or from which a word is borrowed.

sour cherry *n.* **1.** A deciduous shrub or small tree (*Prunus cerasus*) having white flowers and tart red fruit. **2.** This fruit.

sour cream *n.* Cream that has been soured artificially or naturally by the action of lactic-acid bacteria, widely used in cooking and as a garnish.

sour·dine (soor-dēn′) *n.* **1.** An obsolete double-reed instrument with a soft tone. **2.** A mute, esp. one for a violin. [Fr. < Ital. *sordina*, fem. of *sordino*, a mute. SEE SORDINO.]

sour·dough (sour′dō′) *n.* **1.** Sour fermented dough used as leaven in making bread. **2.** An early settler or prospector, esp. in Alaska and northwest Canada. [Sense 2 < an association with using pieces of sourdough to leaven bread in the winter.]

sour grapes *pl.n.* Denial of the desirability of something after finding that it cannot be reached or acquired.

sour gum *n.* A deciduous tree (*Nyssa sylvatica*) of eastern North America having glossy, somewhat leathery leaves and soft wood.

Sou·ris (soor′is) A river, c. 724 km (450 mi), rising in S Saskatchewan, Canada, and flowing SE in a great loop into N ND then NE to the Assiniboine R. in SW Manitoba.

sour mash *n.* **1.** A mixture of new mash and mash from a preceding run used to distill certain malt whiskeys. **2.** Whiskey so distilled.

sour orange *n.* **1.** A spiny evergreen tree (*Citrus aurantium*) native to southern Vietnam and widely cultivated in warmer regions, having globose, reddish-orange, highly acidic fruit. **2.** This fruit.

sour·puss (sour′poos′) *n. Slang* A habitually gloomy or sullen person. [SOUR + PUSS².]

sour salt *n.* Crystals of citric acid used in cooking.

sour·sop (sour′sŏp′) *n.* **1.** A tropical American evergreen tree (*Annona muricata*) bearing spiny fruit with tart edible pulp. **2.** The fruit of this tree.

sour·wood (sour′wood′) *n.* A deciduous tree (*Oxydendrum arboreum*) of eastern North America having small white urn-shaped flowers. [So called < its sour-tasting leaves.]

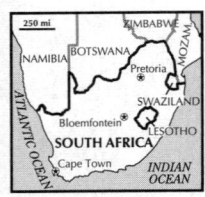

South Africa

Sou·sa (soo′zə, -sə), **John Philip** Known as "the March King." 1854–1932. Amer. composer of *Stars and Stripes Forever* (1897).

sou·sa·phone (soo′zə-fōn′, -sə-) *n.* A large brass wind instrument, similar in range to the tuba, having a flared bell and a shape adapted to being carried in marching bands. [After John Philip SOUSA.]

sous-chef (soo′shĕf′, soo-shĕf′) *n., pl.* **sous-chefs** (-shĕfs′, -shĕf′) The chef who is second in authority in a restaurant or kitchen, ranking below the head chef. [Fr. : *sous*, under + *chef*, chef.]

souse¹ (sous) *v.* **soused, sous·ing, sous·es** —*tr.* **1.** To plunge into a liquid. **2.** To make soaking wet; drench. **3.** To steep in a mixture, as in pickling. **4.** *Slang* To make intoxicated. —*intr.* To become immersed or soaking wet. ❖ *n.* **1.** The act or process of sousing. **2a.** Food steeped in pickle, esp. pork trimmings. **b.** The liquid used in pickling; brine. **3.** *Slang* **a.** A drunkard. **b.** A period of heavy drinking; a binge. [ME *sousen*, prob. < OFr. **souser*, to pickle < *souz, sous*, pickled meat, of Gmc. orig. See **sal-** in App.]

souse² (sous) *v.* **soused, sous·ing, sous·es** *Archaic* —*tr.* To pounce on; attack. —*intr.* To swoop down, as an attacking hawk does. ❖ *n. Obsolete* A swooping motion of attack. [< ME *souse*, swooping motion, alteration of *sours*, source, a rising. See SOURCE.]

Sousse (soos) also **Su·sah** or **Su·sa** (soo′sə, -zə) A city of NE Tunisia on an inlet of the Mediterranean Sea; founded in ancient times by the Phoenicians. Pop. 69,530.

sous vide (soo vēd′) *n.* The cooking of various ingredients in a plastic pouch. [Fr., in a vacuum, vacuum-packed : *sous*, under + *vide*, vacuum.] —**sous-vide′** *adj.*

sou·tache (soo-tăsh′) *n.* A narrow flat braid in a herringbone pattern. [Fr. < Hung. *sujtás*.]

sou·tane (soo-tän′, -tăn′) *n.* A cassock, esp. one that buttons up and down the front. [Fr., alteration (influenced by Fr. *sous*, under) of obsolete *sottane* < Ital. *sottana* < *sotto*, under < Lat. *subtus* < *sub.* See **upo** in App.]

Sou·ter (soo′tər), **David Hackett** b. 1939. Amer. jurist; appointed associate justice of the Supreme Court in 1990.

south (south) *n.* **1a.** The direction along a meridian 90° clockwise from east; the direction to the right of sunrise. **b.** The cardinal point on the compass 180° clockwise from due north and directly opposite north. **2.** An area or region lying in the south. **3.** often **South a.** The southern part of the earth. **b.** The southern part of a region or country. **4. South** The southern part of the United States, esp. the states that fought for the Confederacy in the Civil War. ❖ *adj.* **1.** To, toward, of, facing, or in the south. **2.** Originating in or coming from the south. ❖ *adv.* **1.** In, from, or toward the south. **2.** *Slang* Into a worse or inferior condition, as of decreased value: *stocks that headed south.* [ME < OE *sūth.* See **sāwel-** in App.]

South Africa A country of S Africa on the Atlantic and Indian oceans. Orig. inhabited by Khoikhoin, San, and Bantu-speaking peoples, it was administered by a union of British and Boer colonies after 1910, operating under a policy of apartheid. An interim constitution ending white rule was adopted in 1993; multiracial elections were first held in 1994. Caps. Pretoria, Cape Town, and Bloemfontein. Pop. 40,436,000. —**South African** *adj. & n.*

South America A continent of the S Western Hemisphere SE of North America between the Atlantic and Pacific oceans extending from the Caribbean Sea S to Cape Horn. —**South American** *adj. & n.*

South·amp·ton (south-hămp′tən, sou-thămp′-) A borough of S-central England on an inlet of the English Channel opposite the Isle of Wight. Pop. 209,192.

Southampton Island An island of E Nunavut, Canada, at the entrance to Hudson Bay.

South Atlantic Ocean The S part of the Atlantic Ocean, extending S from the equator to Antarctica.

South Bend A city of N IN NW of Fort Wayne; built on the site of a fur-trading post est. 1820. Pop. 107,789.

south·bound (south′bound′) *adj.* Going toward the south.

south by east *n.* The direction or compass point halfway between due south and south-southeast, or 168°45′ east of due north. ❖ *adv. & adj.* Toward or from south by east.

south by west *n.* The direction or compass point halfway between due south and south-southwest, or 168°45′ west of due north. ❖ *adv. & adj.* Toward or from south by west.

South Car·o·li·na (kăr′ə-lī′nə) A state of the SE US bordering on the Atlantic Ocean; admitted as one of the original Thirteen Colonies in 1788. It seceded from the Union in 1860, precipitating the Civil War. Cap. Columbia. Pop. 4,012,012. —**South Car′o·lin′i·an** (-lĭn′ē-ən) *adj. & n.*

South Central Niger-Congo *n.* A branch of the Niger-Congo language family.

South China Sea An arm of the W Pacific bounded by SE China, Taiwan, the Philippines, Borneo, and Vietnam.

South Dakota A state of the N-central US; admitted as the 40th state in 1889. The region was split off from ND at the time it achieved statehood. Cap. Pierre. Pop. 754,844. —**South Dakotan** *adj. & n.*

South·down (south′doun′) *n.* Any of a breed of small hornless sheep of English origin, having short dense wool that is finely textured. [After the SOUTH DOWNS.]

South Downs See **Downs**.

south·east (south-ēst′, sou-ēst′) n. **1.** The direction or compass point halfway between due south and due east, or 135° east of due north. **2.** An area or region lying in the southeast. **3.** Southeast A region of the southeast United States generally including Alabama, Georgia, South Carolina, and Florida. ❖ adj. **1.** To, toward, of, facing, or in the southeast. **2.** Originating in or coming from the southeast. ❖ adv. In, from, or toward the southeast. —**south·east′ern** adj.

Southeast Asia A region of Asia bounded by the Indian subcontinent, China, and the Pacific Ocean and including Indochina, the Malay Peninsula, and the Malay Archipelago. —**Southeast Asian** adj. & n.

southeast by east n. The direction or compass point halfway between southeast and east-southeast, or 123°45′ east of due north. ❖ adv. & adj. Toward or from southeast by east.

southeast by south n. The direction or compass point halfway between southeast and south-southeast, or 146°15′ east of due north. ❖ adv. & adj. Toward or from southeast by south.

south·east·er (south-ē′stər, sou-ē′-) n. A storm or gale blowing from the southeast.

south·east·er·ly (south-ē′stər-lē, sou-ē′-) adj. **1.** Situated toward the southeast. **2.** Coming or being from the southeast. —**south·east′er·ly** adv.

south·east·ward (south-ēst′wərd, sou-ēst′-) adv. & adj. Toward, to, or in the southeast. ❖ n. A southeastward direction, point, or region. —**south·east′ward·ly** adv. & adj. —**south·east′wards** adv.

South-end-on-Sea (sou′thĕnd-ŏn-sē′, -ôn-) A borough of SE England at the mouth of the Thames R. Pop. 167,023.

south·er (sou′thər) n. A strong wind coming from the south.

south·er·ly (sŭth′ər-lē) adj. **1.** Situated toward the south. **2.** Coming or being from the south. ❖ n., pl. **-lies** A storm or wind coming from the south. —**south′er·ly** adv.

south·ern (sŭth′ərn) adj. **1.** Situated in, toward, or facing the south. **2.** Coming from the south. **3.** Native to or growing in the south. **4.** often **Southern** Of, relating to, or characteristic of southern regions or the South. **5.** Being south of the equator. [ME southerne < OE sūtherne. See **sāwel-** in App.] —**south′ern·ness′** n.

Southern Alps A mountain range of South I., New Zealand, rising to 3,766.4 m (12,349 ft).

Southern Bug (boog, book) See **Bug** 2.

Southern Cross n. A constellation in the Southern Hemisphere near Centaurus and Musca.

Southern Crown n. See **Corona Australis**.

south·ern·er also **South·ern·er** (sŭth′ər-nər) n. A native or inhabitant of the south, esp. the southern United States.

Southern Hemisphere n. **1.** The half of the earth south of the equator. **2.** Astronomy The half of the celestial sphere south of the celestial equator.

South·ern·ism (sŭth′ər-nĭz′əm) n. **1.** An expression or pronunciation characteristic of the southern United States or southern England. **2.** A trait, attitude, or practice typical of the South or southerners, esp. in the United States.

southern lights pl.n. See **aurora australis**.

south·ern·most (sŭth′ərn-mōst′) adj. Farthest south.

southern oscillation n. The cyclic variation of atmospheric pressure at sea level in the eastern and central regions of the southern Pacific Ocean, as a result of the periodic warming and cooling of surface water known as El Niño and La Niña.

Southern Paiute n. **1.** See **Paiute** 2. **2.** The Uto-Aztecan language of the Southern Paiute.

south·ern·wood (sŭth′ərn-wood′) n. An aromatic southern European shrubby plant (Artemisia abrotanum) having finely divided grayish foliage and globose white flower heads.

Southern Yemen A former country of SW Asia on the Arabian Peninsula. A British protectorate from 1882 to 1914, it became independent in 1967 and united with North Yemen in 1990.

Sou·they (sou′thē, sŭth′ē), **Robert** 1774–1843. British writer noted for his poetry, criticism, and biographical works.

South·field (south′fēld′) A city of SE MI, a suburb of Detroit on the Rouge R. Pop. 78,296.

South Frigid Zone See **Frigid Zone**.

South Gate A city of S CA, a suburb of Los Angeles. Pop. 96,375.

South Georgia A British-administered island in the S Atlantic Ocean E of Cape Horn, a dependency of the Falkland Is.

south·ing (sou′thĭng) n. **1.** The difference in latitude between two positions as a result of a movement to the south. **2.** Progress toward the south.

South Island An island of New Zealand SW of North I., from which it is separated by Cook Strait.

South Korea A country of E Asia at the S end of the Korean peninsula. Part of the ancient country of Korea, its present border with North Korea was set in 1953 at the end of the Korean War. Cap. Seoul. Pop. 44,453,000. —**South Korean** adj. & n.

south·land or **South·land** (south′lănd′, -lənd) n. A region in the south of a country or area. —**south′land·er** n.

South Na·han·ni (nə-hăn′ē) A river of SW Northwest Terrs., Canada, flowing c. 563 km (350 mi) to the Liard R.

South Orkney Islands A group of British-administered islands in the S Atlantic Ocean SE of Cape Horn.

South Pacific Ocean The S part of the Pacific Ocean, extending S from the equator to Antarctica.

south·paw (south′pô′) n. Slang A left-handed person, esp. a left-handed baseball pitcher. [< the batter facing east.]

South Pi·cene (pī′sēn′) n. An extinct Sabellic language spoken in east central Italy from the seventh to the third centuries B.C. [< Lat. Pīcēnum, ancient region of E-central Italy.]

South Platte River A river of central and NE CO and W-central NE flowing c. 724 km (450 mi) E to the North Platte R. to form the Platte R.

South Polar Region See **Polar Regions**.

South Pole n. **1a.** The southern end of Earth's axis of rotation, a point in Antarctica. **b.** The celestial zenith of this terrestrial point. **c.** south pole The southern end of the axis of rotation of a planet or other celestial body. **2.** south pole The south-seeking magnetic pole of a straight magnet.

south·ron (sŭth′rən) n. **1.** often **Southron** A person who lives in the south, esp. an Englishman as called by a Scot. **2.** A native or inhabitant of the American South. Used by the Confederates in the Civil War. ❖ adj. Scots Southern. [ME, var. of southerne, southern. See SOUTHERN.]

South Sandwich Islands A group of British-administered volcanic islands in the S Atlantic Ocean ESE of Cape Horn; now included in the British Antarctic Terr.

South Saskatchewan River A river of Canada flowing c. 885 km (550 mi) from S Alberta to central Saskatchewan to form the Saskatchewan R.

South Sea Islands The islands of the S Pacific, roughly coextensive with Oceania. —**South Sea Is′land·er** n.

South Seas The oceans S of the equator, esp. the S Pacific. The name **South Sea**, or El Mar del Sur, was first used by Balboa for the entire Pacific Ocean.

South Shetland Islands An archipelago in the S Atlantic Ocean off Antarctica, part of the British Antarctic Terr.

South Slavic n. A subdivision of the Slavic languages that includes Bulgarian, Macedonian, Serbo-Croatian, Slovene, and the extinct Old Church Slavonic.

south-south·east (south′south-ēst′, sou′sou-ēst′) n. The direction or compass point halfway between south and southeast, or 157°30′ of due north. ❖ adj. To, toward, of, facing, or in the south-southeast. ❖ adv. In, from, or toward the south-southeast.

south-south·west (south′south-wĕst′, sou′sou-wĕst′) n. The direction or compass point halfway between due south and southwest, or 157°30′ west of due north. ❖ adj. To, toward, of, facing, or in the south-southwest. ❖ adv. In, from, or toward the south-southwest.

South Temperate Zone See **Temperate Zone**.

South Vietnam A former country of SE Asia (1954–75) that became part of Vietnam after the Vietnam War. —**South Vietnamese** adj. & n.

south·ward (south′wərd, sŭth′ərd) adv. & adj. Toward, to, or in the south. ❖ n. A southward direction, point, or region. —**south′ward·ly** adv. & adj. —**south′wards** adv.

south·west (south-wĕst′, sou-wĕst′) n. **1.** The direction or compass point halfway between due south and due west, or 135° west of due north. **2.** An area or region lying in the southwest. **3.** Southwest A region of the southwest United States generally including New Mexico, Texas, Arizona, California, and Nevada and sometimes Utah and Colorado. ❖ adj. **1.** To, toward, of, facing, or in the southwest. **2.** Originating in or coming from the southwest. ❖ adv. In, from, or toward the southwest. —**south·west′ern** adj.

South-West Africa See **Namibia**.

southwest by south n. The direction or compass point halfway between southwest and south-southwest, or 146°15′ west of due north. ❖ adv. & adj. Toward or from southwest by south.

southwest by west n. The direction or compass point halfway between southwest and west-southwest, or 123°45′ west of due north. ❖ adv. & adj. Toward or from southwest by west.

south·west·er (south-wĕs′tər, sou-wĕs′-) also **sou′·west·er** (sou-wĕs′-) n. **1.** A storm or gale from the southwest. **2.** A waterproof hat with a broad brim for the neck.

south·west·er·ly (south-wĕs′tər-lē, sou-wĕs′-) adj. **1.** Situated toward the southwest. **2.** Coming or being from the southwest. —**south·west′er·ly** adv.

south·west·ward (south-wĕst′wərd, sou-wĕst′-) adv. & adj. Toward, to, or in the southwest. ❖ n. A southwestward direction, point, or region. —**south·west′ward·ly** adv. & adj. —**south·west′wards** adv.

Sou·tine (soo-tēn′), **Chaim** 1893–1943. Lithuanian-born French expressionist painter known for his distorted figures.

sou·ve·nir (soo′və-nîr′, soo′və-nîr′) n. A token of remembrance. [Fr. < OFr., memory < Lat. subvenīre, to come to mind : sub-, sub- + venīre, to come; see g**w**ā- in App.]

sov·er·eign (sŏv′ər-ĭn, sŏv′rĭn) n. **1.** One that exercises supreme, permanent authority, esp. in a nation or other governmental unit, as: **a.** A king, queen, or other noble person who serves as chief of state; a ruler or monarch. **b.** A national governing council or committee. **2.** A nation that governs territory out-

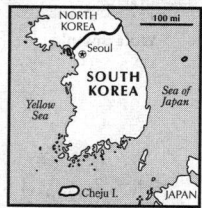

South Korea

ă	pat	oi	boy
ā	pay	ou	out
âr	care	oo	took
ä	father	oo	boot
ĕ	pet	ŭ	cut
ē	be	ûr	urge
ĭ	pit	th	thin
ī	pie	th	this
îr	pier	hw	which
ŏ	pot	zh	vision
ō	toe	ə	about,
ô	paw		item

Stress marks:
′ (primary);
′ (secondary), as in
lexicon (lĕk′sĭ-kŏn′)

Wole Soyinka

spathe

spadix

spadix

Spain

side its borders. **3.** A gold coin formerly used in Great Britain. ❖ *adj.* **1.** Self-governing; independent. **2.** Having supreme rank or power. **3.** Paramount; supreme. **4a.** Of superlative strength or efficacy. **b.** Unmitigated: *sovereign contempt.* [ME *soverain* < OFr. < VLat. **superānus* < Lat. *super,* above. See **uper** in App.] —**sov′er•eign•ly** *adv.*

sov•er•eign•ty (sŏv′ər-ĭn-tē, sŏv′rĭn-) *n., pl.* -**ties 1.** Supremacy of authority or rule as exercised by a sovereign or sovereign state. **2.** Royal rank, authority, or power. **3.** Complete independence and self-government. **4.** A territory existing as an independent state.

so•vi•et (sō′vē-ĕt′, -ĭt, sŏv′ē-, sō′vē-ĕt′) *n.* **1.** One of the popularly elected legislative assemblies that existed at local, regional, and national levels in the former Soviet Union. **2a. Soviet** A native or inhabitant of the former Soviet Union. **b. Soviets** The government of the former Soviet Union. Used with *the.* ❖ *adj.* **1.** often **Soviet** Of or relating to the Union of Soviet Socialist Republics. **2.** Of or relating to a soviet. [Russ. *sovet,* council, soviet < ORuss. *sŭvětŭ.* See **ksun-** in App.]

so•vi•et•ize also **So•vi•et•ize** (sō′vē-ĭ-tīz′, sŏv′ē-) *tr.v.* -**ized,** -**iz•ing,** -**iz•es 1.** To cause to come under Soviet control. **2.** To cause to conform to Soviet political, social, and cultural policy. —**so′vi•et•i•za′tion** (-ĭ-tĭ-zā′shən) *n.*

So•vi•et•ol•o•gy (sō′vē-ĭ-tŏl′ə-jē, sŏv′ē-) *n.* Study of the former Soviet Union. —**So′vi•et•ol′o•gist** *n.*

Soviet Union See **Union of Soviet Socialist Republics.**

sow[1] (sō) *v.* **sowed, sown** (sōn) or **sowed, sow•ing, sows** —*tr.* **1.** To scatter (seed) over the ground for growing. **2.** To impregnate (a growing medium) with seed. **3.** To propagate; disseminate: *sow rumors.* **4.** To strew or cover with something; spread thickly. —*intr.* To scatter seed for growing. [ME *sowen* < OE *sāwan.* See **sē-** in App.] —**sow′er** *n.*

sow[2] (sou) *n.* **1a.** An adult female hog. **b.** The adult female of several other animals, such as the bear. **2a.** A channel that conducts molten iron to the molds in a pig bed. **b.** The mass of metal solidified in such a mold. [ME < OE *sugu* and OE *sū;* see **sū-** in App.]

sow•bel•ly (sou′bĕl′ē) *n. Informal* Salt pork.

sow bug (sou) *n.* **1.** Any of various small terrestrial isopod crustaceans, chiefly of the genera *Oniscus* and *Porcellio,* having an oval segmented body. **2.** A pill bug. [< its piglike shape.]

So•we•to (sə-wĕt′ō, -wā′tō) A city of NE South Africa SW of Johannesburg. Comprised of a number of townships inhabited by Black South Africans, violent rioting took place in 1976, when a student protest led to clashes with police. Pop. 596,632.

sow thistle (sou) *n.* Any of various plants of the genus *Sonchus,* esp. *S. oberaceus* of Eurasia, having prickly leaves and rayed yellow flower heads.

sox (sŏks) *n.* A plural of **sock**[1] 1.

soy (soi) *n.* **1.** The soybean. **2.** Soy sauce. [Du. *soja, soya* < J. *shōyu* < Chin. (Mandarin) *jiàngyóu,* soy sauce : *jiàng,* soy paste + *yóu,* sauce.]

soy•a (soi′ə) *n.* The soybean. [Du. See SOY.]

soy•bean (soi′bēn′) *n.* **1.** A southeast Asian leguminous plant (*Glycine max*), widely cultivated for forage and soil improvement and for its nutritious seeds. **2.** The seed of this plant.

So•yin•ka (shô-yĭng′kə), **Wole** b. 1934. Nigerian writer who won the 1986 Nobel Prize for literature.

soy•milk (soi′mĭlk′) *n.* A milk substitute made from soybeans.

soy sauce *n.* A salty brown liquid condiment made by fermenting soybeans and roasted wheat or barley in brine.

SP *abbr.* **1.** self-propelled **2.** shore patrol **3.** single pole **4.** specialist **5.** submarine patrol

sp. *abbr.* **1.** species **2.** specimen **3.** spelling

Sp. *abbr.* Spanish

s.p. *abbr.* sine prole

spa (spä) *n.* **1.** A resort providing therapeutic baths. **2.** A resort area having mineral springs. **3.** A fashionable hotel or resort. **4.** A health spa. **5.** A tub for relaxation or invigoration, usu. including a device for raising whirlpools. **6.** *Eastern New England* See **soda fountain** 2. [After *Spa,* resort town in eastern Belgium.]

space (spās) *n.* **1a.** *Mathematics* A set of elements or points satisfying specified geometric postulates: *non-Euclidean space.* **b.** The infinite extension of the three-dimensional region in which all matter exists. **2a.** The expanse in which the solar system, stars, and galaxies exist; the universe. **b.** The region of this expanse beyond Earth's atmosphere. **3a.** An extent or expanse of a surface or three-dimensional area. **b.** A blank or empty area: *the spaces between words.* **c.** An area provided for a particular purpose: *a parking space.* **4.** Reserved or available accommodation on a public transportation vehicle. **5a.** A period or interval of time. **b.** A little while. **6.** Sufficient freedom from external pressure for oneself and one's needs. **7.** *Music* One of the intervals between the lines of a staff. **8.** *Printing* One of the blank pieces of type or other means used for separating words or characters. **9.** One of the intervals during the telegraphic transmission of a message when the key is open or not in contact. **10.** Blank sections in printed material or broadcast time available for use by advertisers. ❖ *v.* **spaced, spac•ing, spac•es** —*tr.* **1.** To organize or arrange with spaces between. **2.** To separate or keep apart. **3.** *Slang* To stupefy or disorient from or as if from a drug. Often used with *out.* —*intr. Slang* To be or become stupefied or disoriented.

Often used with *out.* [ME, area < OFr. *espace* < Lat. *spatium.*] —**spac′er** *n.*

space age also **Space Age** *n.* The period from 1957 through the present, in which spacecraft have orbited Earth and explored celestial bodies. —**space′-age′** *adj.*

space bar *n.* A bar at the bottom of the keyboard of a typewriter or computer that when pressed down introduces a horizontal space into text, as between words.

space cadet *n. Slang* One who shows difficulty in grasping reality or in responding appropriately to it; a spacy person.

space capsule *n.* A vehicle or compartment for transporting, protecting, and supporting humans or animals in outer space or at very high atmospheric altitudes.

space charge *n.* The excess of electrons or ions in a given volume.

space•craft (spās′krăft′) *n., pl.* **spacecraft** A vehicle intended to be launched into space.

spaced (spāst) *adj. Slang* Spaced-out.

spaced-out (spāst′out′) *adj. Slang* Stupefied or disoriented from or as if from a drug.

space flight *n.* Flight beyond the atmosphere of Earth.

space heater *n.* An appliance that warms a small area, such as one room, typically by radiant electric heat.

space lattice *n.* See **crystal lattice.**

space•less (spās′lĭs) *adj.* Having no limits or boundaries.

space medicine *n.* The medical science concerned with the biological, physiological, and psychological effects of space flight on humans.

space•port (spās′pôrt′, -pōrt′) *n.* An installation for sheltering, testing, maintaining, and launching spacecraft.

space probe *n.* A spacecraft carrying instruments intended for use in exploration of the physical properties of outer space or celestial bodies other than Earth.

space•ship or **space ship** (spās′shĭp′) *n.* See **spacecraft.**

space shuttle *n.* A reusable spacecraft with wings for controlled descent in the atmosphere, designed to transport astronauts between Earth and an orbiting space station.

space station *n.* A large satellite that can support a human crew and remain in orbit around Earth for an extended period and serve as a base for activities, such as scientific research.

space suit *n.* A protective pressure suit designed to permit the wearer relatively free movement in space.

space-time (spās′tīm′) *n. Physics* The four-dimensional continuum of one temporal and three spatial coordinates in which any event or physical object is located.

space walk *n.* An excursion by an astronaut outside a spacecraft in space. —**space walk** *v.* —**space walker** *n.*

space writer *n.* A writer who is paid according to the amount of space his or her material occupies in print.

spa•cial (spā′shəl) *adj.* Variant of **spatial.**

spac•ing (spā′sĭng) *n.* **1a.** The act of arranging with intervening spaces. **b.** The result of so arranging. **c.** A system of or allowance for intervals. **2.** Spaces or a space, as in print.

spa•cious (spā′shəs) *adj.* **1.** Generous or large in area or extent; roomy. **2.** Vast in range or scope: *a spacious view.* —**spa′cious•ly** *adv.* —**spa′cious•ness** *n.*

Spack•le (spăk′əl) A trademark used for a powder to be mixed with water or a ready-to-use plastic paste designed to fill cracks and holes in plaster before painting or papering.

spac•y or **spac•ey** (spā′sē) *adj.* -**i•er, -i•est** *Slang* **1.** Stupefied or disoriented from or as if from drug use. **2.** Eccentric.

spade[1] (spād) *n.* **1.** A sturdy digging tool having a thick handle and a heavy flat blade that can be pressed into the ground with the foot. **2.** Any of various similar digging or cutting tools. ❖ *tr.v.* **spad•ed, spad•ing, spades** To dig or cut with a spade. [ME < OE *spadu.*] —**spad′er** *n.*

spade[2] (spād) *n.* **1.** *Games* **a.** A black leaf-shaped figure on certain playing cards. **b.** A playing card with this figure. **c. spades** (*used with a sing. or pl. verb*) The suit of cards represented by this figure. **2.** *Offensive Slang* Used as a disparaging term for a Black person. —**idiom: in spades** To a considerable degree; in the extreme. [Ital. *spade,* pl. of *spada,* card suit < Lat. *spatha,* sword, broad-bladed stirrer < Gk. *spathē,* broad blade.]

spade•fish (spād′fĭsh′) *n., pl.* **spadefish** or **-fish•es** Any of several marine food fishes of the family Ephippidae, esp. *Chaetodipterus faber,* of Atlantic coastal waters. [< its shape.]

spade•work (spād′wûrk′) *n.* **1.** Work requiring a spade. **2.** Preparatory work necessary for a project or an activity.

spa•dix (spā′dĭks) *n., pl.* -**di•ces** (-dĭ-sēz′) A fleshy clublike spike bearing minute flowers, usu. enclosed within a sheathlike spathe, as in the jack-in-the-pulpit. [Lat. *spādīx,* broken-off palm branch < Gk. < *spān,* to stretch.]

spa•ghet•ti (spə-gĕt′ē) *n.* **1.** Pasta in long, often thick strands. **2.** *Electricity* A slender tube of insulating material that covers bare wire. [Ital., pl. dim. of *spago,* cord.]

spa•ghet•ti•ni (spăg′ĭ-tē′nē) *n.* Pasta in long fine strands. [Ital., dim. of *spaghetti,* spaghetti. See SPAGHETTI.]

spaghetti Western *n.* A low-budget Western film made by a European, esp. an Italian, film company.

Spain (spān) A country of SW Europe comprising most of the Iberian Peninsula and the Balearic and Canary Is.; first colonized by Phoenicians and Greeks and unified as a kingdom in 1479. Cap. Madrid. Pop. 39,143,000.

spake (spāk) *v. Archaic* A past tense of **speak.**

spall (spôl) *n.* A chip, fragment, or flake from a piece of stone or ore. ❖ *v.* **spalled, spall•ing, spalls** —*tr.* To break up into chips or fragments. —*intr.* To chip or crumble. [ME *spalle.*]

spal•la•tion (spô-lā′shən) *n.* A nuclear reaction in which many particles are ejected from an atomic nucleus by incident particles of sufficiently high energy.

spam (spăm) *n.* Unsolicited, usu. commercial, e-mail sent indiscriminately to multiple individuals or newsgroups; junk e-mail. [< SPAM (prob. inspired by a comedy routine on the Brit. television series *Monty Python's Flying Circus,* in which the word is repeated incessantly).] —**spam** *v.*

Spam A trademark used for a canned meat product consisting primarily of chopped pork pressed into a loaf.

spam•bot (spăm′bŏt′) *n.* A bot that sends out junk e-mail.

span[1] (spăn) *n.* **1.** The extent or measure of space between two points or extremities, as of a bridge; the breadth. **2.** The distance between the tips of the wings of an airplane. **3.** The section between two intermediate supports of a bridge. **4.** Something, such as a bridge, that extends from one point to another. **5.** The distance from the tip of the thumb to the tip of the little finger when the hand is fully extended, formerly used as a unit of measure equal to about nine inches (23 centimeters). **6.** A period of time. ❖ *tr.v.* **spanned, span•ning, spans 1.** To measure by or as if by the fully extended hand. **2.** To encircle with the hand or hands in or as if in measuring. **3.** To extend across in space or time. [ME, unit of measurement < OE *spann.*]

span[2] (spăn) *tr.v.* **spanned, span•ning, spans** To bind or fetter. ❖ *n.* A pair of animals, such as oxen, matched in size, strength, or color and driven as a team. [Du. *spannen,* to harness < MDu.]

span[3] (spăn) *v. Archaic* A past tense of **spin.**

Span. *abbr.* Spanish

span•cel (spăn′səl) *n.* A rope used to hobble an animal, as a sheep. ❖ *tr.v.* **-celed, -cel•ing, -cels** or **-celled, -cel•ling, -cels** To hobble with a spancel. [Du. *spansel* < *spannen,* to bind, harness. See SPAN².]

Span•dau (spăn′dou′, shpän′-) A district of Berlin, Germany; site of a fortress used to imprison Nazi war criminals after the Nuremburg trials of 1945 to 1946.

span•dex (spăn′dĕks) *n.* A synthetic fiber or fabric made from a polymer containing polyurethane, used in the manufacture of elastic clothing. ❖ *adj.* Of or relating to spandex or its elastic qualities. [Alteration of EXPAND.]

span•drel also **span•dril** (spăn′drəl) *n.* **1.** The roughly triangular space between the left or right exterior curve of an arch and the rectangular framework surrounding it. **2.** The space between two arches and a horizontal molding or cornice above them. [ME *spaundrell,* prob. < *spandre,* space between supporting timbers < AN *spaundre* < *spandre,* to spread out < Lat. *expandere.* See EXPAND.]

spang (spăng) *adv. Informal* Precisely; squarely. [Prob. < dialectal *spang,* to leap, jerk, bang, prob. of imit. orig.]

span•gle (spăng′gəl) *n.* **1.** A small, often circular piece of sparkling metal or plastic sewn esp. on garments for decoration. **2.** A small sparkling object, drop, or spot: *spangles of sunlight.* ❖ *v.* **-gled, -gling, -gles** —*tr.* To adorn or cause to sparkle by covering with or as if with spangles. —*intr.* To sparkle in the manner of spangles. [ME *spangel,* dim. of *spange* < MDu., clasp.] —**span′gly** *adj.*

Spang•lish (spăng′glĭsh) *n.* Spanish characterized by numerous borrowings from English. [Blend of SPANISH and ENGLISH.]

Span•iard (spăn′yərd) *n.* A native or inhabitant of Spain. [ME < OFr. *Espaniard* < *Espaigne,* Spain < Lat. *Hispānia.*]

span•iel (spăn′yəl) *n.* **1.** Any of several breeds of small-sized to medium-sized dogs, usu. having drooping ears and a wavy silky coat. **2.** A docile or servile person. [ME *spainol* < OFr. *espaignol,* Spaniard, Sp. dog < VLat. **Hispāniōlus,* Sp. < *Hispānia,* Spain.]

Span•ish (spăn′ĭsh) *adj.* **1.** Of or relating to Spain or its people or culture. **2.** Of or relating to the Spanish language. ❖ *n.* **1.** The Romance language of the largest part of Spain and most of Central and South America. **2.** (*used with a pl. verb*) The people of Spain. [Alteration (influenced by Lat. *Hispānia,* Spain) of ME *Spainish* < *Spaine,* Spain < OFr. *Espaigne.* See SPANIARD.]

Spanish America The former Spanish possessions in the New World, including most of South and Central America, Mexico, Cuba, Puerto Rico, the Dominican Republic, and other small islands in the Caribbean.

Spanish American also **Span•ish-A•mer•i•can** (spăn′ĭsh-ə-mĕr′ĭ-kən) *n.* **1.** A native or inhabitant of Spanish America. **2.** A US citizen or resident of Hispanic descent. ❖ *adj.* **Spanish-American 1.** Of or relating to Spanish America or its peoples or cultures. **2.** Of or relating to Spain and America, esp. the United States.

Spanish-American War *n.* A war between Spain and the United States in 1898, as a result of which Spain ceded Puerto Rico, the Philippine Islands, and Guam to the United States and abandoned all claim to Cuba, which became independent in 1902.

Spanish bayonet *n.* Any of several New World plants of the genus *Yucca,* esp. *Y. aloifolia* or *Y. baccata,* having a tall woody stem, stiff swordlike pointed leaves, and white flowers.

Spanish cedar *n.* **1.** Any of several tropical American trees of the genus *Cedrela,* esp. *C. odorata,* having reddish aromatic wood used for cabinetwork and cigar boxes. **2.** This wood.

Spanish chestnut *n.* **1.** A deciduous Mediterranean tree (*Castanea sativa*) with edible nuts in a spiny bur. **2.** The nut of this tree.

Spanish fly *n.* See **cantharis.**

Spanish lime *n.* See **genip** 1.

Spanish mackerel *n.* Any of various marine food fishes of the genus *Scomberomorus,* esp. a commercially important species, *S. maculatus,* of American Atlantic coastal waters.

Spanish Main 1. The coastal region of mainland Spanish America in the 16th and 17th cent., from the Isthmus of Panama to the mouth of the Orinoco R. **2.** The section of the Caribbean crossed by Spanish ships in colonial times.

Spanish moss *n.* An epiphytic bromeliad plant (*Tillandsia usneoides*) of the southeast United States and tropical America having gray threadlike stems drooping in long matted clusters.

Spanish needles *pl.n.* (*used with a sing. or pl. verb*) See **beggar ticks** 1a.

Spanish omelet *n.* An omelet served with an often spicy sauce of tomatoes, onions, and peppers.

Spanish onion *n.* A mild-flavored yellow-skinned onion (*Allium fistulosum*) having yellowish-white flowers.

Spanish paprika *n.* A mild seasoning made from pimientos.

Spanish rice *n.* A dish consisting of rice cooked with tomatoes, spices, chopped onions, and green peppers.

Spanish Sahara See **Western Sahara.**

spank (spăngk) *v.* **spanked, spank•ing, spanks** —*tr.* To slap on the buttocks with a flat object or with the open hand, as for punishment. —*intr.* To move briskly or spiritedly. ❖ *n.* A slap on the buttocks. [Perh. of imit. orig.]

spank•er (spăng′kər) *n. Nautical* A usu. gaff-headed sail set from the aftermost lower mast of a sailing ship.

spank•ing (spăng′kĭng) *adj.* **1.** *Informal* Exceptional of its kind; remarkable. **2.** Swift and vigorous. **3.** Brisk and fresh: *a spanking breeze.* ❖ *adv.* Used as an intensive: *a spanking clean shirt.* ❖ *n.* A number of spanks delivered in rapid succession, as for punishment. [Perh. of Scand. orig.]

span•ner (spăn′ər) *n.* **1.** A wrench having a hook, hole, or pin at the end for meshing with a related device on another object. **2.** *Chiefly British* A wrench. [Ger., winding tool < *spannen,* to stretch < MHGer. < OHGer. *spannan.*]

span-new (spăn′no͞o′, -nyo͞o′) *adj.* Entirely new. [ME *spannewe,* partial transl. of ON *spānnȳr* : *spānn,* shingle, chip + *nȳr,* new; see **newo-** in App.]

span•worm (spăn′wûrm′) *n.* See **measuring worm.** [< SPAN¹.]

spar[1] (spär) *n.* **1.** *Nautical* A wooden or metal pole, such as a boom, yard, or bowsprit, used to support sails and rigging. **2.** A usu. metal pole used as part of a crane or derrick. **3.** A main structural member in an airplane wing or a tail assembly that runs from tip to tip or from root to tip. ❖ *tr.v.* **sparred, spar•ring, spars 1.** To supply with spars. **2.** *Archaic* To fasten with a bolt. [ME *sparre,* rafter.]

spar[2] (spär) *intr.v.* **sparred, spar•ring, spars 1a.** To fight with an opponent in a short bout or practice session, as in boxing or the martial arts. **b.** To make boxing or fighting motions without hitting one's opponent. **2.** To bandy words about in argument; dispute. **3.** To fight by striking with the feet and spurs. Used of gamecocks. ❖ *n.* **1.** A motion of attack or defense in boxing. **2.** A sparring match. [ME *sparren,* to thrust or strike rapidly, perh. < obsolete Fr. *esparer,* to kick < OItal. *sparare,* to fling : *s-,* intensive pref.; see SFORZANDO + *parare,* to ward off; see PARRY.]

spar[3] (spär) *n.* A nonmetallic, readily cleavable translucent or transparent light-colored mineral with a shiny luster, such as feldspar. [LGer. < MLGer.]

spare (spâr) *v.* **spared, spar•ing, spares** —*tr.* **1.** To refrain from treating harshly; treat mercifully or leniently. **2.** To refrain from harming or destroying. **3.** To save or relieve from experiencing or doing (something): *spared herself the trouble.* **4.** To hold back from; withhold or avoid. **5.** To use with restraint. **6.** To give or grant out of one's resources; afford. —*intr.* **1.** To be frugal. **2.** To refrain from inflicting harm; be merciful or lenient. ❖ *adj.* **spar•er, spar•est 1a.** Kept in reserve. **b.** Being in excess of what is needed; extra. See Syns at **superfluous. c.** Free for other use; unoccupied. **2a.** Not lavish, abundant, or excessive. **b.** Lean and trim. See Syns at **lean**². **3.** Not profuse or copious. ❖ *n.* **1.** A replacement, esp. a tire, reserved for future need. **2.** *Sports* **a.** The act of knocking down all ten pins with two successive rolls of a bowling ball. **b.** The score so made. —***idiom:* to spare** In addition to what is needed. [ME *sparen* < OE *sparian.*] —**spare′ly** *adv.* —**spare′ness** *n.* —**spar′er** *n.*

spare•ribs (spâr′rĭbz′) *pl.n.* Pork ribs with most of the meat trimmed off. [Alteration of obsolete *ribspare* < LGer. *ribbesper,* pickled pork ribs roasted on a spit < MLGer. *ribbespēr* : *ribbe,* rib + *spēr,* spear, spit.]

spare tire *n.* **1.** An additional tire carried in a vehicle as a replacement for one that goes flat. **2.** *Slang* A paunch; a potbelly.

sparge (spärj) *tr.v.* **sparged, sparg•ing, sparg•es 1.** To spray or sprinkle. **2.** To introduce air or gas into (a liquid). ❖ *n.* A sprinkle. [Obsolete Fr. *espargier* < OFr. < Lat. *spargere.*] —**sparg′er** *n.*

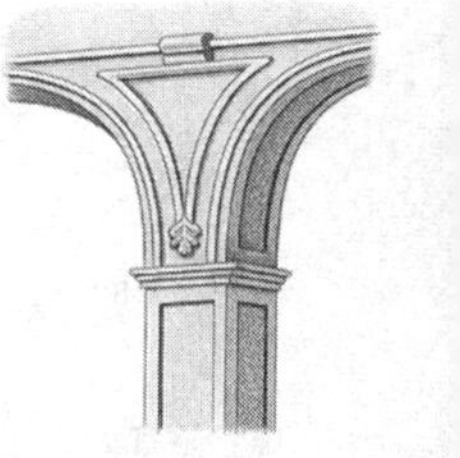

spandrel

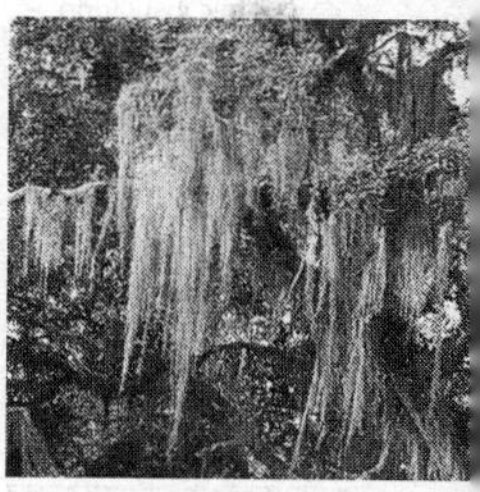

Spanish moss
Tillandsia usneoides

ă	pat	oi	boy
ā	pay	ou	out
âr	care	o͝o	took
ä	father	o͞o	boot
ĕ	pet	ŭ	cut
ē	be	ûr	urge
ĭ	pit	th	thin
ī	pie	*th*	this
îr	pier	hw	which
ŏ	pot	zh	vision
ō	toe	ə	about, item
ô	paw		

Stress marks:
′ (primary);
′ (secondary), as in
lexicon (lĕk′sĭ-kŏn′)

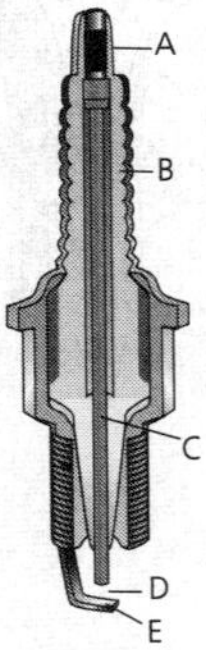

spark plug
cutaway view
A. terminal
B. ceramic insulation
C. center electrode
D. gap
E. ground electrode

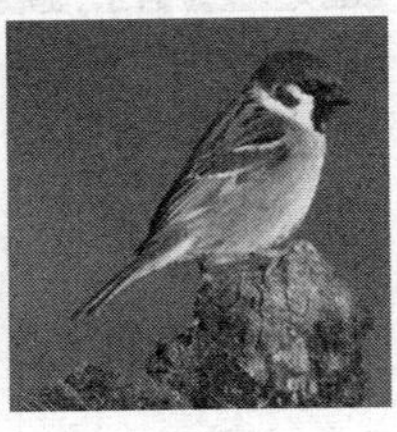

sparrow
tree sparrow
Passer montanus

spar•ing (spâr′ĭng) *adj.* **1.** Given to or marked by prudence and restraint in the use of material resources. **2.** Deficient or limited in quantity, fullness, or extent. **3.** Forbearing; lenient. **—spar′ing•ly** *adv.* **—spar′ing•ness** *n.*

SYNONYMS *sparing, frugal, thrifty, economical* These adjectives mean exercising or reflecting care in the use of resources, such as money. *Sparing* stresses restraint, as in expenditure: *sparing of words. Frugal* implies self-denial and abstention from luxury: *a frugal diet. Thrifty* suggests industry, care, and diligence in conserving means: *grew up impoverished and learned to be thrifty. Economical* emphasizes prudence, skillful management, and the avoidance of waste: *an economical use of energy.*

spark[1] (spärk) *n.* **1.** An incandescent particle, esp.: **a.** One thrown off from a burning substance. **b.** One resulting from friction. **c.** One remaining in an otherwise extinguished fire; an ember. **2.** A glistening particle, as of metal. **3.** A flash of light. **4.** A trace or suggestion, as: **a.** A quality or feeling with latent potential; a seed or germ. **b.** A vital, animating, or activating factor. **5. sparks** (*used with a sing. verb*) *Informal* A radio operator aboard a ship. **6.** *Electricity* **a.** The flash of light resulting from a disruptive discharge through an insulating material. **b.** The discharge itself. ❖ *v.* **sparked, spark•ing, sparks** *—intr.* **1.** To give off sparks. **2.** To give an enthusiastic response. **3.** To operate correctly. Used of the ignition system of an internal-combustion engine. *—tr.* **1.** To set in motion; activate. **2.** To rouse to action; spur. [ME *sparke* < OE *spearca.*] **—spark′er** *n.*

spark[2] (spärk) *n.* **1.** An elegantly dressed, self-conscious young man. **2.** A male suitor; a beau. ❖ *v.* **sparked, spark•ing, sparks** *—tr.* To court or woo. *—intr.* To play the suitor. [Perh. of Scand. orig., or < SPARK[1].] **—spark′er** *n.*

Spark, Dame **Muriel Sarah** b. 1918. Scottish writer known for her satirical novels, including *Memento Mori* (1958).

spark arrester *n.* A device designed to keep sparks from escaping, as at a chimney opening.

spark chamber *n.* A device consisting of electrically charged parallel metal plates in a chamber filled with inert gas, used to detect a charged subatomic particle as it passes through the chamber, leaving a trail of sparks.

spark coil *n.* An induction coil used to produce a spark, as in an internal-combustion engine.

spark gap *n.* A gap in an otherwise complete electric circuit across which a discharge occurs at a prescribed voltage.

spark•ing plug (spär′kĭng) *n. Chiefly British* A spark plug.

spar•kle (spär′kəl) *v.* **-kled, -kling, -kles** *—intr.* **1.** To give off sparks. **2.** To give off or reflect flashes of light; glitter. **3.** To be brilliant in performance. **4a.** To shine with animation. **b.** To flash with wit. **5.** To release gas bubbles; effervesce. *—tr.* To cause to flash and glitter. ❖ *n.* **1.** A small spark or gleaming particle. **2.** A glittering quality. **3.** Brilliant animation; vivacity. **4.** Emission of gas bubbles; effervescence. [ME *sparklen,* freq. of *sparken,* to spark. See SPARK[1].]

spar•kler (spär′klər) *n.* **1.** One, such as a highly polished metallic surface, that sparkles. **2.** *Informal* A diamond. **3.** A firework that burns slowly and gives off a shower of sparks.

spar•kling water (spär′klĭng) *n.* Water charged with carbon dioxide.

sparkling wine *n.* Any of various effervescent wines produced by a process involving fermentation in the bottle.

spark•ly (spär′klē) *adj.* **-li•er, -li•est 1a.** Giving off tiny flashes of light; glittery. **b.** Lively; vivacious. **2.** Effervescent.

spark plug *n.* **1.** A device inserted in the head of an internal-combustion engine cylinder that ignites the fuel mixture by means of an electric spark. **2.** *Informal* One who gives life or energy to an endeavor.

spark transmitter *n.* A now obsolete radio transmitter that derives its output from the oscillating discharge of a capacitor to an inductor and across a spark gap.

spark•y (spär′kē) *adj.* **-i•er, -i•est** Animated; lively.

spar•ling (spär′lĭng) *n.* **1.** The common European smelt *(Osperus eperlanus).* **2.** A young or immature herring. [ME *sperlinge* < OFr. *esperlinge,* of Gmc. orig.]

spar•row (spăr′ō) *n.* **1.** Any of various small New World finches of the family Emberizidae, having brownish or grayish plumage and including the song sparrow and other closely related species. **2.** Any of several similar or related birds, such as the house sparrow. [ME *sparowe* < OE *spearwa.*]

spar•row•grass (spăr′ə-grăs′, spăr′ō-) *n. Eastern US* Asparagus. [By folk ety. < ASPARAGUS.]

sparrow hawk *n.* **1.** A small hawk *(Accipter nisus)* of Europe, Africa, and central Asia that has short broad wings and preys on small birds. **2.** A small North American falcon *(Falco sparverius)* that feeds chiefly on insects and mice.

sparse (spärs) *adj.* **spars•er, spars•est** Occurring, growing, or settled at widely spaced intervals; not thick or dense. [Lat. *sparsus,* p. part. of *spargere,* to scatter.] **—sparse′ly** *adv.* **—sparse′ness, spar′si•ty** (spär′sĭ-tē) *n.*

Spar•ta (spär′tə) also **Lac•e•dae•mon** (lăs′ĭ-dē′mən) A city-state of ancient Greece in the SE Peloponnesus; noted for its militarism. The Peloponnesian Wars (460–404 B.C.) with Athens led to Sparta's hegemony over all of Greece.

Spar•ta•cus (spär′tə-kəs) Died 71 B.C. Thracian gladiator who led a slave revolt in Italy (73–71) that was ultimately crushed at Lucania (71), where he was killed.

Spar•tan (spär′tn) *adj.* **1.** Of or relating to Sparta or its people. **2.** also **spartan a.** Rigorously self-disciplined or self-restrained. **b.** Simple, frugal, or austere: *a spartan diet.* **c.** Marked by brevity of speech; laconic. **d.** Courageous in the face of pain, danger, or adversity. ❖ *n.* **1.** A citizen of Sparta. **2.** One of Spartan character. **—Spar′tan•ism** *n.* **—Spar′tan•ly** *adv.*

spar•te•ine (spär′tē-ēn′, -ĭn) *n.* A bitter poisonous liquid alkaloid, $C_{15}H_{26}N_2$, obtained from the broom *Cytisus scoparius* or the lupin *Lupinus luteus.* [NLat. *Spartium,* broom genus (< Lat. *spartum,* a kind of broom < Gk. *sparton*) + -INE[2].]

spar varnish *n.* A waterproof varnish.

spasm (spăz′əm) *n.* **1.** A sudden involuntary contraction of a muscle or group of muscles. **2.** A sudden burst of energy, activity, or emotion. [ME *spasme* < OFr. < Lat. *spasmus* < Gk. *spasmos* < *spān,* to pull.]

spas•mod•ic (spăz-mŏd′ĭk) *adj.* **1.** Relating to, affected by, or having the character of a spasm; convulsive. **2.** Happening intermittently; fitful. **3.** Given to sudden outbursts of energy or feeling; excitable. [NLat. *spasmōdicus* < Gk. *spasmōdēs* < *spasmos,* spasm. See SPASM.] **—spas•mod′i•cal•ly** *adv.*

spas•tic (spăs′tĭk) *adj.* **1.** Of, relating to, or characterized by spasms: *a spastic colon.* **2.** Affected by spastic paralysis. **3.** *Offensive Slang* Clumsy or inept. ❖ *n.* A person affected with spastic paralysis. [Lat. *spasticus* < Gk. *spastikos* < *spān,* to pull.] **—spas′ti•cal•ly** *adv.* **—spas•tic′i•ty** (spă-stĭs′ĭ-tē) *n.*

spastic colon *n.* See **irritable bowel syndrome.**

spastic paralysis *n.* A chronic pathological condition marked by persistent muscle spasms and exaggerated tendon reflexes due to damage to motor nerves of the central nervous system.

spat[1] (spăt) *v.* A past tense and a past participle of **spit**[1].

spat[2] (spăt) *n., pl.* **spat** or **spats 1.** An oyster or similar bivalve mollusk in the larval stage, esp. when it settles to the bottom and begins to develop a shell. **2.** The spawn of an oyster or a similar mollusk. ❖ *intr.v.* **spat•ted, spat•ting, spats** To spawn. Used of oysters and similar mollusks. [ME.]

spat[3] (spăt) *n.* A cloth or leather gaiter covering the shoe upper and the ankle and fastening under the shoe with a strap. Often used in the plural. [Short for *spatterdash* : SPATTER + DASH[1].]

spat[4] (spăt) *n.* **1.** A brief quarrel. **2.** *Informal* A slap or smack. **3.** A spattering sound, as of raindrops. ❖ *v.* **spat•ted, spat•ting, spats** *—intr.* **1.** To engage in a brief quarrel. **2.** To strike with a light spattering sound; slap. *—tr. Informal* To slap. [?]

spatch•cock (spăch′kŏk) *n.* A dressed and split chicken for roasting or broiling on a spit. ❖ *tr.v.* **-cocked, -cock•ing, -cocks 1.** To prepare (a dressed chicken) for grilling by splitting open. **2.** To introduce or interpose, esp. in a labored or unsuitable manner. [Perh. alteration of *spitchcock,* a way of cooking an eel.]

spate (spāt) *n.* **1.** A sudden flood, rush, or outpouring. **2.** *Chiefly British* **a.** A flash flood. **b.** A freshet resulting from rain or melting snow. **c.** A sudden heavy fall of rain. [ME.]

spathe (spāth) *n.* A leaflike bract that encloses or subtends a flower cluster or spadix, as in the jack-in-the-pulpit. [Lat. *spatha,* broadsword < Gk. *spathē,* broad blade.]

spath•ic (spăth′ĭk) *adj.* Having good cleavage. Used of minerals. [Ger. *Spath, Spat,* spar (< MHGer. *spāt*) + -IC.]

spa•tial also **spa•cial** (spā′shəl) *adj.* Of, relating to, involving, or having the nature of space. [< Lat. *spatium,* space.] **—spa′ti•al′i•ty** (spā′shē-ăl′ĭ-tē) *n.* **—spa′tial•ly** *adv.*

spa•ti•o•tem•po•ral (spā′shē-ō-tĕm′pər-əl) *adj.* **1.** Of, relating to, or existing in both space and time. **2.** Of or relating to space-time. [Lat. *spatium,* space + TEMPORAL[1].]

spat•ter (spăt′ər) *v.* **-tered, -ter•ing, -ters** *—tr.* **1.** To scatter (a liquid) in drops or small splashes. **2.** To spot, splash, or soil. **3.** To sully the reputation of; defame. *—intr.* **1.** To come forth in drops or small splashes: *Grease spattered everywhere.* **2.** To fall in or as if in a shower, as rain. ❖ *n.* **1a.** The act of spattering. **b.** The condition of being spattered. **2.** A spattering sound. **3a.** A drop or splash of something spattered. **b.** A small amount; a smattering. [Perh. of LGer. orig.]

spat•ter•dock (spăt′ər-dŏk′) *n.* An aquatic plant *(Nuphar advena)* of eastern Mexico and the eastern and central United States, having emergent broad leaves and globe-shaped yellow flowers. [SPATTER + DOCK[4].]

spat•u•la (spăch′ə-lə) *n.* **1.** A small implement having a broad flat flexible blade that is used to mix, spread, or lift material. **2.** A device used to press down the tongue while examining the mouth or throat. [Lat., flat piece of wood, splint, dim. of *spatha,* broadsword. See SPATHE.] **—spat′u•lar** *adj.*

spat•u•late (spăch′ə-lĭt) *adj.* Shaped like a spatula.

spav•in (spăv′ĭn) *n.* A disease affecting horses in which the accumulation of new bone or lymph enlarges the hock joint. [ME *spaven* < OFr. *espavain,* swelling, perh. of Gmc. orig.]

spav•ined (spăv′ĭnd) *adj.* **1.** Afflicted with spavin: *a spavined horse.* **2.** Marked by damage, deterioration, or ruin.

spawn (spôn) *n.* **1.** The eggs of aquatic animals such as bivalve mollusks, fishes, and amphibians. **2.** Offspring occurring in numbers; brood. **3.** A person who is the issue of a parent or family. **4.** The source of something; a germ or seed. **5.** A product or an outcome. **6.** Mycelia of mushrooms or other fungi grown in specially prepared organic matter for planting in beds. ❖ *v.* **spawned, spawn•ing, spawns** —*intr.* **1.** To deposit eggs; produce spawn. **2.** To produce offspring in large numbers. —*tr.* **1.** To produce or deposit (spawn). **2.** To produce in large numbers. **3.** To give rise to; engender: *tyranny that spawned revolt.* **4.** To cause to spawn; bring forth; produce. **5.** To plant with mycelia grown in specially prepared organic matter. [ME *spawne* < *spawnen*, to spawn < AN *espaundre* < Lat. *expandere*. See EX-PAND.] —**spawn'er** *n.*

spay (spā) *tr.v.* **spayed, spay•ing, spays** To remove surgically the ovaries of (an animal). [ME *spaien* < AN *espeier*, to cut with a sword < *espee*, sword < Lat. *spatha*. See SPATHE.]

spaz or **spazz** (spăz) *n., pl.* **spazz•es** *Offensive Slang* A clumsy or inept person. [Short for SPASTIC and SPASM.]

SPCA *abbr.* Society for the Prevention of Cruelty to Animals

SPCC *abbr.* Society for the Prevention of Cruelty to Children

speak (spēk) *v.* **spoke** (spōk), **spo•ken** (spō'kən), **speak•ing, speaks** —*intr.* **1.** To utter words or articulate sounds with ordinary speech modulation; talk. **2a.** To convey thoughts, opinions, or emotions orally. **b.** To express oneself. **c.** To be on speaking terms. **3.** To deliver an address or a lecture. **4a.** To make a statement in writing: *The biography speaks of loneliness.* **b.** To act as spokesperson. **5a.** To convey a message by nonverbal means. **b.** To be expressive. **c.** To be appealing. **6.** To make a reservation or request. Often used with *for: Is this dance spoken for?* **7a.** To produce a characteristic sound: *The drums spoke.* **b.** To give off a sound on firing. Used of guns or cannon. **8.** To make communicative sounds. **9.** To give an indication or a suggestion. —*tr.* **1.** To articulate in a speaking voice. **2.** To converse in or be able to converse in (a language). **3a.** To express aloud; tell: *speak the truth.* **b.** To express in writing. **4.** *Nautical* To hail and communicate with (another vessel) at sea. **5.** To convey by nonverbal means. —*phrasal verbs:* **speak out** To talk freely and fearlessly, as about a public issue. **speak up 1.** To speak loud enough to be audible. **2.** To speak without fear or hesitation. —*idioms:* **so to speak** In a manner of speaking. **speak down to** To speak condescendingly to. **to speak of** Worthy of mention. [ME *speken* < OE *sprecan, specan.*] —**speak'a•ble** *adj.*

-speak *suff.* Language characteristic of: *doctorspeak; cop-speak.* [< NEWSPEAK.]

speak•eas•y (spēk'ē'zē) *n., pl.* **-ies** A place for the illegal sale and consumption of alcoholic drinks, as during Prohibition.

speak•er (spē'kər) *n.* **1a.** One who speaks. **b.** A spokesperson. **2.** One who delivers a public speech. **3.** often **Speaker** The presiding officer of a legislative assembly. **4.** A loudspeaker. —**speak'er•ship'** *n.*

speak•er•phone (spē'kər-fōn') *n.* A telephone or telephone attachment that contains both a loudspeaker and a microphone, allowing several persons to participate in a call at the same time.

speak•ing (spē'kĭng) *adj.* **1a.** Capable of speech. **b.** Involving speaking or talking: *a speaking part in the play.* **2.** Expressive or telling; eloquent. **3.** True to life; lifelike: *a speaking likeness.* —*idiom:* **on speaking terms 1.** Friendly enough to exchange superficial remarks. **2.** Ready and willing to communicate; not alienated or estranged.

speaking in tongues *n.* See **gift of tongues.**

speaking tube *n.* A tube used to convey the voice over a short distance, as from one part of a ship to another.

spear[1] (spîr) *n.* **1.** A weapon consisting of a long shaft with a sharply pointed end. **2.** A shaft with a sharp point and barbs for spearing fish. **3.** A soldier armed with a spear. ❖ *v.* **speared, spear•ing, spears** —*tr.* **1.** To pierce with or as if with a spear. **2.** To catch with a thrust of the arm. **3a.** *Football* To block (an opponent) by ramming with the helmet, in violation of the rules. **b.** *Sports* To jab (an opponent) with the blade of a hockey stick, in violation of the rules. —*intr.* To stab at something with or as if with a spear. [ME *spere* < OE.] —**spear'er** *n.* —**spear'like'** *adj.*

spear[2] (spîr) *n.* A slender stalk, as of asparagus. ❖ *intr.v.* **speared, spear•ing, spears** To sprout like a spear. [Alteration of SPIRE[2].]

spear-car•ri•er (spîr'kăr'ē-ər) *n.* **1.** A minor member of an operatic or dramatic cast, usu. having no speaking part. **2.** One whose presence or performance has little effect.

spear•fish[1] (spîr'fĭsh') *n., pl.* **spearfish** or **-fish•es** Either of two large marine game fishes (*Tetrapturus angustirostris* or *T. belone*) related to the sailfish and marlin, having the upper jaw elongated into a spearlike projection.

spear•fish[2] (spîr'fĭsh') *intr.v.* **-fished, -fish•ing, -fish•es** To fish with a spear, spearlike implement, or spear gun. —**spear'-fish'er** *n.*

spear gun *n.* A device for mechanically shooting a spearlike missile under water, as in spearfishing.

spear•head (spîr'hĕd') *n.* **1.** The sharp head of a spear. **2a.** The leading forces in a military thrust. **b.** The driving force in a given action, endeavor, or movement. ❖ *tr.v.* **-head•ed, -head•ing, -heads** To be the leader of (a movement, for example).

spear•man (spîr'mən) *n.* A man armed with a spear.

spear•mint (spîr'mĭnt') *n.* An aromatic Eurasian plant (*Mentha spicata*) having clusters of small purplish flowers and yielding an oil used widely as a flavoring.

spear•wort (spîr'wûrt', -wôrt') *n.* Any of several plants related to the buttercups, esp. *Ranunculus flammula* of Eurasia, having lance-shaped leaves and yellow flowers.

spec (spĕk) *Informal n.* **1. specs** The specifications, as for a building to be constructed. **2.** Speculation. ❖ *tr.v.* **spec'd, spec'ing, specs** or **specced** (spĕkt), **spec•cing** (spĕk'ĭng), **specs** To write or supply specifications for. ❖ *adj.* **1.** Of or relating to specifications. **2.** Done, constructed, produced, or purchased as a speculation. —*idiom:* **on spec** On a speculation basis; with no assurance of profit. —**spec'er** *n.*

spe•cial (spĕsh'əl) *adj.* **1.** Surpassing what is common or usual; exceptional. **2a.** Distinct among others of a kind: *a special medication.* **b.** Primary; chief. **3.** Peculiar to a specific person or thing; particular. **4a.** Having a limited or specific function, application, or scope: *a special role.* **b.** Arranged for a particular occasion or purpose. **5.** Regarded with particular affection and admiration. **6.** Additional; extra. ❖ *n.* **1.** Something arranged, issued, or appropriated to a particular service or occasion: *the commuter special.* **2.** A featured attraction, such as a reduced price. **3.** A television production that features a specific work, given topic, or particular performer. [ME < OFr. *especial* < Lat. *specialis* < *speciēs*, kind. See SPECIES.] —**spe'cial•ly** *adv.*

special delivery *n.* The delivery of a piece of mail, for an additional charge, by a special messenger.

special education *n.* Instruction for students whose learning needs cannot be met by a standard school curriculum.

special effect *n.* A visual effect added to a film, for example, to create an illusion. Often used in the plural.

Special Forces *pl.n.* A branch of the US Army composed of soldiers specially trained in guerrilla fighting.

special handling *n.* The handling of fourth-class or parcel-post mail as first-class mail for an extra charge.

special interest *n.* A person, group, or organization attempting to influence legislators in favor of one particular interest or issue. —**spe'cial-in'ter-est** (spĕsh'əl-ĭn'trĭst, -tər-ĭst, -trĕst') *adj.*

spe•cial•ism (spĕsh'ə-lĭz'əm) *n.* **1.** Concentration of one's efforts in a given occupation or field of study. **2.** A field of specialization.

spe•cial•ist (spĕsh'ə-lĭst) *n.* **1.** A person who is devoted to a particular occupation or branch of study or research. **2.** A physician whose practice is limited to a particular branch of medicine or surgery, esp. one who is certified by a board of physicians. **3.** Any of several noncommissioned ranks in the US Army that correspond to that of corporal through sergeant first class. —**spe'cial•ist, spe'cial•is'tic** *adj.*

spe•ci•al•i•ty (spĕsh'ē-ăl'ĭ-tē) *n., pl.* **-ties 1.** A distinguishing mark or feature. **2. specialities** Special points of consideration; particulars. **3.** *Chiefly British* A specialty.

spe•cial•i•za•tion (spĕsh'ə-lĭ-zā'shən) *n.* **1.** The act of specializing or the process of becoming specialized. **2.** *Biology* **a.** Adaptation, as of an organ, to a specific function or environment. **b.** A character, feature, or organism resulting from such adaptation.

spe•cial•ize (spĕsh'ə-līz') *v.* **-ized, -iz•ing, -iz•es** —*intr.* **1.** To pursue a special activity, occupation, or field of study. **2.** *Biology* To develop so as to become adapted to a specific function or environment. **3.** To concentrate on a particular activity or product. —*tr.* **1.** To make specific mention of; particularize. **2.** To give a particular character or function to. **3.** *Biology* To adapt to a particular function or environment. **4.** To specify the payee in endorsing (a check).

special jury *n.* See **blue-ribbon jury.**

spe•cial-needs or **special needs** (spĕsh'əl-nēdz') *adj.* Of or relating to people who have specific needs, as those associated with a disability.

Special Olympics *pl.n.* A program of competitive sports for physically or mentally disabled athletes.

special pleading *n.* **1.** *Law* Assertion of new or special matter to offset the opposing party's allegations, as an alternative to direct denial. **2.** A presentation of an argument that emphasizes only a favorable or single aspect of the question at issue.

special relativity *n.* The physical theory of space and time developed by Albert Einstein, based on the postulates that the laws of physics are identical in all frames of reference moving at a uniform velocity and that the speed of light from a uniformly moving source is always the same, regardless of how fast or slow the source or its observer is moving.

spe•cial•ty (spĕsh'əl-tē) *n., pl.* **-ties 1.** A special pursuit, occupation, aptitude, or skill. **2.** A branch of medicine or surgery, such as cardiology, in which a physician specializes. **3.** A special feature or characteristic; a peculiarity. **4.** The state or quality of being special or distinctive. **5.** An item or a product of a distinctive kind or of particular superiority: *Pastry is the chef's specialty.* **6.** *Law* A special contract or agreement, esp. a deed kept under seal.

spe•ci•a•tion (spē'shē-ā'shən, -sē-) *n.* The evolutionary formation of new biological species, usu. by the division of a single species into two or more genetically distinct ones. [SPECI(ES) + -ATION.] —**spe'ci•a'tion•al** *adj.*

spe•cie (spē'shē, -sē) *n.* Coined money; coin. —*idiom:* **in specie 1.** In coin. **2.** In a similar manner; in kind: *He repaid the offense in specie.* **3.** *Law* In the same kind or shape; as specified. [< (*in*) *specie*, (in) the actual form < Lat. (*in*) *speciē*, (in) kind,

Special Olympics
relay runner

ablative of *speciēs*. See SPECIES.]

spe·cies (spē′shēz, -sēz) *n., pl.* **species 1.** *Biology* **a.** A fundamental category of taxonomic classification, ranking below a genus and consisting of related organisms capable of interbreeding. See table at **taxonomy. b.** An organism belonging to such a category, represented in binomial nomenclature by an uncapitalized Latin adjective or noun following a capitalized genus name, as in *Equus caballus,* the horse. **2.** *Logic* A class of individuals or objects grouped by virtue of their common attributes; a division subordinate to a genus. **3a.** A kind, variety, or type. **b.** The human race; humankind. **4.** *Roman Catholic Church* **a.** The outward appearance or form of the Eucharistic elements that is retained after their consecration. **b.** Either of the consecrated elements of the Eucharist. **5.** *Obsolete* **a.** An outward form or appearance. **b.** Specie. **6.** *Chemistry* A chemical entity, as an atom. [ME, logical classification < Lat. *speciēs,* a seeing, kind. See **spek-** in App.]

spe·cies·ism (spē′shē-zĭz′əm, -sē-) *n.* Human intolerance or discrimination on the basis of species.

spec·i·fi·a·ble (spĕs′ə-fī′ə-bəl) *adj.* Possible to specify.

spe·cif·ic (spĭ-sĭf′ĭk) *adj.* **1.** Explicitly set forth; definite. **2.** Relating to, characterizing, or distinguishing a species. **3.** Special, distinctive, or unique. **4a.** Intended for, applying to, or acting on a particular thing. **b.** Concerned particularly with the subject specified. Often used in combination: *"age-specific voting patterns"* (A. Dianne Schmidley). **5a.** Being a disease produced by a particular microorganism or condition. **b.** Having a remedial influence or effect on a particular disease. **6.** *Immunology* Having an affinity limited to a particular antibody or antigen. **7a.** Being a customs charge levied on merchandise by unit or weight rather than according to value. **b.** Being a commodity rate applicable to the transportation of a single commodity between named points. ❖ *n.* **1a.** Something particularly fitted to a use or purpose. **b.** A remedy intended for a particular ailment or disorder. **2a.** A distinguishing quality or attribute. **b. specifics** Distinct items or details; particulars. [LLat. *specificus* : Lat. *speciēs,* kind, species; see SPECIES + Lat. *-ficus,* -fic.] —**spe·cif′i·cal·ly** *adv.* —**spec′i·fic′i·ty** (spĕs′ə-fĭs′ĭ-tē) *n.*

spec·i·fi·ca·tion (spĕs′ə-fĭ-kā′shən) *n.* **1.** The act of specifying. **2a. specifications** A detailed exact statement of particulars, esp. a statement prescribing materials, dimensions, and quality of work for something to be built, installed, or manufactured. **b.** A single item specified. **3.** An exact written description of an invention to a patent applicant.

specific epithet *n.* The uncapitalized Latin adjective or noun that follows a capitalized genus name in binomial nomenclature and serves to distinguish a species from others in the same genus, as *saccharum* in *Acer saccharum* (sugar maple).

specific gravity *n.* The ratio of the mass of a solid or liquid to the mass of an equal volume of distilled water at 4°C (39°F) or of a gas to an equal volume of air or hydrogen under prescribed conditions of temperature and pressure.

specific heat *n.* **1.** The ratio of the amount of heat required to raise the temperature of a unit mass of a substance by one unit of temperature to that required to raise the temperature of a unit mass of a reference material, usu. water, by the same amount. **2.** The amount of heat, in calories, required to raise the temperature of one gram of a substance by one Celsius degree.

specific impulse *n.* A performance measure for rocket propellants that is equal to units of thrust per unit weight of propellant consumed per unit time.

specific performance *n.* *Law* The performance of a contract as specified in its terms.

specific resistance *n.* Electrical resistivity.

spec·i·fy (spĕs′ə-fī′) *tr.v.* **-fied, -fy·ing, -fies 1.** To state explicitly or in detail: *specified the amount needed; specified that they would come.* **2.** To include in a specification. **3.** To determine or bring about (a specific result): *a gene that specifies the synthesis of a protein.* [ME *specifien* < OFr. *specifier* < LLat. *specificāre* < *specificus,* specific. See SPECIFIC.] —**spec′i·fi′er** *n.*

spec·i·men (spĕs′ə-mən) *n.* **1.** An individual, item, or part representative of a class, genus, or whole. **2.** A sample, as of tissue, blood, or urine, used for analysis and diagnosis. **3.** *Informal* An individual; a person: *a disagreeable specimen.* [Lat., example < *specere,* to look at. See **spek-** in App.]

spe·cious (spē′shəs) *adj.* **1.** Having the ring of truth or plausibility but actually fallacious: *a specious argument.* **2.** Deceptively attractive. [ME, attractive < Lat. *speciōsus* < *speciēs,* appearance. See **spek-** in App.] —**spe′cious·ly** *adv.* —**spe′ci·os′i·ty** (-shē-ŏs′ĭ-tē), **spe′cious·ness** (-shəs-nĭs) *n.*

speck (spĕk) *n.* **1.** A small spot, mark, or discoloration. **2.** A tiny amount; a bit. ❖ *tr.v.* **specked, speck·ing, specks** To mark with specks. [ME *specke* < OE *specca*.]

speck·le (spĕk′əl) *n.* A speck or small spot, as a natural dot of color on skin, plumage, or foliage. [ME *spakle*.] —**speck′le** *v.*

speck·led (spĕk′əld) *adj.* **1.** Dotted or covered with speckles, esp. flecked with small spots of contrasting color. **2.** Of a mixed character; motley.

speckled trout *n.* See brook trout.

specs also **specks** (spĕks) *pl.n. Informal* Eyeglasses; spectacles.

spec·ta·cle (spĕk′tə-kəl) *n.* **1a.** Something that can be seen or viewed, esp. something of a remarkable or impressive nature. **b.**

A public performance or display, esp. one on a large or lavish scale. **c.** A regrettable public display, as of bad behavior: *made a spectacle of himself.* **2. spectacles a.** A pair of eyeglasses. **b.** Something resembling eyeglasses in shape or suggesting them in function. [ME < OFr. < Lat. *spectāculum* < *spectāre,* to watch, freq. of *specere,* to look at. See **spek-** in App.]

spec·ta·cled (spĕk′tə-kəld) *adj.* **1.** Wearing spectacles. **2.** Having markings suggesting spectacles. Used of animals.

spec·tac·u·lar (spĕk-tăk′yə-lər) *adj.* Of the nature of a spectacle; impressive or sensational. ❖ *n.* Something that is spectacular, as: **a.** A single dramatic production of unusual length or lavishness. **b.** An elaborate display. —**spec·tac′u·lar′i·ty** (-lăr′ĭ-tē) *n.* —**spec·tac′u·lar·ly** *adv.*

spec·tate (spĕk′tāt) *intr.v.* **-tat·ed, -tat·ing, -tates** To attend (a horserace or other sporting event, for example) as a spectator. [Back-formation < SPECTATOR.]

spec·ta·tor (spĕk′tā′tər) *n.* An observer of an event. [Lat. *spectātor* < *spectāre,* to watch. See SPECTACLE.] —**spec′ta·to′ri·al** (-tə-tôr′ē-əl, -tôr′-) *adj.* —**spec′ta·tor·ship′** *n.*

spec·ter (spĕk′tər) *n.* **1.** A ghostly apparition; a phantom. **2.** A haunting or disturbing image or prospect. [Fr. *spectre* < Lat. *spectrum,* appearance, apparition. See SPECTRUM.]

spec·ti·no·my·cin (spĕk′tə-nō-mī′sĭn) *n.* A broad-spectrum antibiotic, $C_{14}H_{24}N_2O_7$, obtained from a species of gram-negative bacteria (*Streptomyces spectabilis*) or produced synthetically and used esp. in the treatment of penicillin-resistant gonorrhea. [NLat. *spect(ābilis)*, specific epithet (< Lat., visible < *spectāre,* to watch; see SPECTACLE) + (ACT)INOMYCIN.]

spec·tra (spĕk′trə) *n.* A plural of **spectrum.**

spec·tral (spĕk′trəl) *adj.* **1.** Of or resembling a specter. **2.** Of, relating to, or produced by a spectrum. —**spec·tral′i·ty** (-trăl′ĭ-tē), **spec′tral·ness** (-trəl-nĭs) *n.* —**spec′tral·ly** *adv.*

spectral line *n.* A bright or dark line in a spectrum produced by emission or absorption of light of a single wavelength.

spec·tre (spĕk′tər) *n.* Chiefly British Variant of **specter.**

spectro– *pref.* Spectrum: *spectrograph.* [< SPECTRUM.]

spec·tro·gram (spĕk′trə-grăm′) *n.* A graphic or photographic representation of a spectrum.

spec·tro·graph (spĕk′trə-grăf′) *n.* **1.** A spectroscope equipped to photograph or otherwise record spectra. **2.** A spectrogram. —**spec′tro·graph′ic** *adj.* —**spec′tro·graph′i·cal·ly** *adv.* —**spec·trog′ra·phy** (-trŏg′rə-fē) *n.*

spec·tro·he·li·o·gram (spĕk′trō-hē′lē-ə-grăm′) *n.* A photograph of the sun taken in a narrow wavelength band centered on a selected wavelength.

spec·tro·he·li·o·graph (spĕk′trō-hē′lē-ə-grăf′) *n.* An instrument used to make spectroheliograms. —**spec′tro·he·li·og′ra·phy** (-ŏg′rə-fē) *n.*

spec·tro·he·li·o·scope (spĕk′trō-hē′lē-ə-skōp′) *n.* An instrument used to observe solar radiation directly.

spec·trom·e·ter (spĕk-trŏm′ĭ-tər) *n.* A spectroscope equipped with scales for measuring wavelengths or indexes of refraction. —**spec′tro·met′ric** (-trə-mĕt′rĭk) *adj.* —**spec·trom′e·try** *n.*

spec·tro·pho·tom·e·ter (spĕk′trō-fō-tŏm′ĭ-tər) *n.* An instrument used to determine the intensity of various wavelengths in a spectrum of light. —**spec′tro·pho′to·met′ric** (-fō′tə-mĕt′rĭk) *adj.* —**spec′tro·pho·tom′e·try** *n.*

spec·tro·scope (spĕk′trə-skōp′) *n.* An instrument for the production and observation of spectra. —**spec′tro·scop′ic** (-skōp′ĭk), **spec′tro·scop′i·cal** (-ĭ-kəl) *adj.*

spec·tros·co·py (spĕk-trŏs′kə-pē) *n., pl.* **-pies** Study of spectra, esp. experimental observation of optical spectra. —**spec·tros′co·pist** *n.*

spec·trum (spĕk′trəm) *n., pl.* **-tra** (-trə) or **-trums 1.** *Physics* The distribution of a characteristic of a physical system, esp.: **a.** A distribution of electromagnetic energies arranged in order of wavelengths. **b.** A distribution of charged atomic or subatomic particles arranged in order of masses. **2.** A graphic or photographic representation of such a distribution. **3a.** A range of values of a quantity or set of related quantities. **b.** A broad sequence or range of related qualities, ideas, or activities. [Lat., appearance < *specere,* to look at. See **spek-** in App.]

spec·u·lar (spĕk′yə-lər) *adj.* Of, resembling, or produced by a mirror or speculum. —**spec′u·lar·ly** *adv.*

spec·u·late (spĕk′yə-lāt′) *v.* **-lat·ed, -lat·ing, -lates** —*intr.* **1.** To meditate on a subject; reflect. **2.** To engage in a course of reasoning often based on inconclusive evidence. **3.** To engage in the buying or selling of a commodity with an element of risk on the chance of profit. —*tr.* To assume to be true without conclusive evidence. [Lat. *speculārī, speculāt-,* to observe < *specula,* watchtower < *specere,* to look at. See **spek-** in App.]

spec·u·la·tion (spĕk′yə-lā′shən) *n.* **1a.** Contemplation or consideration of a subject; meditation. **b.** A conclusion, opinion, or theory reached by conjecture. **c.** Reasoning based on inconclusive evidence; conjecture; supposition. **2a.** Engagement in risky business transactions on the chance of quick or considerable profit. **b.** A commercial or financial transaction involving speculation.

spec·u·la·tive (spĕk′yə-lə-tĭv, -lā′-) *adj.* **1.** Of, marked by, or based upon contemplative speculation. **2a.** Given to conjecture or speculation. **b.** Marked by inquisitive interest. **3a.** Engaging in, given to, or involving financial speculation. **b.** Spent in speculation. **c.** Involving chance; risky. —**spec′u·la·tive·ly** *adv.* —**spec′u·la·tive·ness** *n.*

spec·u·la·tor (spĕk′yə-lā′tər) *n.* One that speculates.

spec·u·lum (spĕk′yə-ləm) *n., pl.* **-la** (-lə) or **-lums** **1.** A mirror or polished metal plate used as a reflector in optical instruments. **2.** An instrument for dilating the opening of a body cavity for medical examination. **3.** *Zoology* **a.** A bright, often iridescent patch of color on the wings of certain birds, esp. ducks. **b.** A transparent spot in the wings of some butterflies or moths. [ME, surgical speculum < Lat., mirror < *specere*, to look at. See **spek-** in App.]

speech (spēch) *n.* **1a.** The faculty or act of speaking. **b.** The faculty or act of expressing or describing thoughts, feelings, or perceptions by the articulation of words. **2.** Something spoken; an utterance. **3.** Vocal communication; conversation. **4.** A talk or public address. **5.** One's habitual manner or style of speaking. **6.** The language or dialect of a nation or region: *American speech.* **7.** The study of oral communication, speech sounds, and vocal physiology. **8.** *Archaic* Rumor. [ME *speche* < OE *sprǣc, spǣc.*]

speech act *n.* See **performative.**

speech community *n.* A group of speakers who recognize the same language or dialect of a language as a standard.

speech·i·fy (spē′chə-fī′) *intr.v.* **-fied, -fy·ing, -fies** To give a speech. —**speech′i·fi′er** *n.*

speech·less (spēch′lĭs) *adj.* **1.** Lacking the faculty of speech. **2.** Temporarily unable to speak, as through wonder. **3.** Refraining from speech; silent. **4.** Unexpressed or inexpressible in words. —**speech′less·ness** *n.*

speech·mak·er (spēch′mā′kər) *n.* One who makes a speech. —**speech′mak′ing** *n.*

speech pathology *n.* The study of speech defects and disorders such as stuttering and dysphasia. —**speech pathologist** *n.*

speech therapy *n.* Treatment of speech defects and disorders, esp. through use of exercises and audio-visual aids that develop new speech habits. —**speech therapist** *n.*

speech·writ·er (spēch′rī′tər) *n.* One who writes speeches for others, esp. as a profession. —**speech′writ′ing** *n.*

speed (spēd) *n.* **1.** *Physics* The rate or a measure of the rate of motion, esp.: **a.** Distance traveled divided by the time of travel. **b.** The first derivative of distance with respect to time. **c.** The magnitude of a velocity. **2.** Swiftness of action. **3a.** The act of moving rapidly. **b.** The state of being in rapid motion; rapidity. See Syns at **haste. 4.** A transmission gear or set of gears in a vehicle. **5a.** A numerical expression of the sensitivity of a photographic film, plate, or paper to light. **b.** The capacity of a lens to accumulate light at an appropriate aperture. **c.** The length of time required or permitted for a camera shutter to open and admit light. **6.** *Slang* A stimulant drug, esp. amphetamine or methamphetamine. **7.** *Slang* One that suits or appeals to a person's inclinations, skills, or character. **8.** *Archaic* Prosperity; luck. ❖ *v.* **sped** (spĕd) or **speed·ed, speed·ing, speeds** —*tr.* **1.** To cause to go, move, or proceed quickly; hasten. **2.** To increase the speed or rate of; accelerate: *speed up a car.* **3.** To wish Godspeed to. **4.** To further, promote, or expedite (a legal action, for example). **5.** *Archaic* To help to succeed or prosper; aid. —*intr.* **1.** To go, move, or proceed quickly: *sped to the rescue.* **b.** To drive at a speed exceeding a legal limit. **2.** To pass quickly: *The days sped by.* **3.** To move, work, or happen at a faster rate; accelerate: *His pulse sped up.* **4.** *Archaic* **a.** To prove successful; prosper. **b.** To get along in a specified manner; fare. —*idiom:* **up to speed 1a.** Operating at maximum speed. **b.** Producing something or performing at an acceptable rate or level. **2.** *Informal* Fully informed or conversant with. [ME *spede* < OE *spēd*, success, swiftness.]

speed·ball (spēd′bôl′) *n. Slang* An intravenous dose of cocaine mixed with heroin or an amphetamine.

speed·boat (spēd′bōt′) *n.* A fast motorboat.

speed brake *n.* A flap on an aircraft for decreasing speed while in flight in preparation for landing.

speed bump *n.* A ridge set crosswise into a paved surface or a dirt road to make the operators of vehicles slow down.

speed·er (spē′dər) *n.* One that speeds, esp. a driver who exceeds a legal or safe speed.

speed·ing (spē′dĭng) *adj.* Moving with speed. ❖ *n.* The act or an instance of driving esp. a motor vehicle faster than is allowed by law.

speed limit *n.* The maximum speed legally permitted on a given stretch of road.

speed metal *n.* Heavy metal music that is exceptionally harsh and fast.

speed·om·e·ter (spĭ-dŏm′ĭ-tər, spē-) *n.* **1.** An instrument for indicating speed. **2a.** An instrument for indicating distance traveled as well as rate of speed. **b.** An odometer.

speed-read·ing (spēd′rē′dĭng) *n.* A method of reading rapidly by assimilating several words or phrases at a glance or by skimming. —**speed′-read′** *v.*

speed skate *n.* An ice skate for racing, fitted with a long blade that extends beyond the heel and toe of the boot. —**speed skater** *n.* —**speed skating** *n.*

speed·ster (spēd′stər) *n.* **1.** A fast driver. **2.** A fast car.

speed trap *n.* A deployment of concealed police officers or electronic devices on a stretch of road to catch speeders.

speed·up (spēd′ŭp′) *n.* **1.** An increase in speed; acceleration. **2.** A required increase of production with no pay increase.

speed·way (spēd′wā′) *n.* **1.** A course for automobile or motorcycle racing. **2.** A road for fast-moving traffic.

speed·well (spēd′wĕl′) *n.* Any of various plants of the genus *Veronica*, having opposite leaves and small, usu. blue flowers.

speed·writ·ing (spēd′rī′tĭng) *n.* A form of shorthand that uses letters of the alphabet. —**speed′writ′er** *n.*

speed·y (spē′dē) *adj.* **-i·er, -i·est 1.** Characterized by rapid motion. **2.** Accomplished or arrived at without delay; prompt. See Syns at **fast¹.** —**speed′i·ly** *adv.* —**speed′i·ness** *n.*

Speer (spîr, shpâr), **Albert** 1905–81. German Nazi politician who was Hitler's official architect (1934–45).

speiss (spīs) *n.* An arsenic compound or a mixture of arsenic compounds resulting from the smelting of iron, cobalt, nickel, and copper ores. [Ger. *Speise*, food, speiss < MHGer. *spīse*, food < OHGer. *spīsa*, prob. < Med.Lat. *spēnsa*, storehouse, or *spēsa*, provisions, both < Lat. *expēnsa (pecūnia)*, (money) paid out. See EXPENSE.]

Speke (spēk), **John Hanning** 1827–64. British explorer in Africa who was one of the first Europeans to explore Lake Tanganyika (1858).

spe·le·ol·o·gy (spē′lē-ŏl′ə-jē) *n.* **1.** The scientific study of caves. **2.** Exploration of caves. [Fr. *spéléologie* < Lat. *spēlēum*, cave (< Gk. *spēlaion*) + *-logie*, -logy.] —**spe′le·o·log′i·cal** (-ə-lŏj′ĭ-kəl) *adj.* —**spe′le·ol′o·gist** *n.*

spell¹ (spĕl) *v.* **spelled** or **spelt** (spĕlt), **spell·ing, spells** —*tr.* **1.** To name or write in order the letters constituting (a word or part of a word). **2.** To constitute the letters of (a word). **3.** To add up to; signify. —*intr.* To form words by means of letters. —*phrasal verbs:* **spell down** To defeat in a spelling bee. **spell out 1.** To make perfectly clear and understandable. **2.** To read slowly and laboriously. **3.** To puzzle out; comprehend by study. [ME *spellen*, to read letter by letter < OFr. *espeller* (of Gmc. orig.).]

spell² (spĕl) *n.* **1a.** A word or formula believed to have magic power. **b.** A bewitched state; a trance. **2.** A compelling attraction; charm or fascination. ❖ *tr.v.* **spelled, spell·ing, spells** To put (someone) under a spell. [ME, discourse < OE.]

spell³ (spĕl) *n.* **1.** A short indefinite period of time. **2.** *Informal* A period of weather of a particular kind: *a dry spell.* **3a.** One's turn at work. **b.** A period of work; a shift. **4.** *Australian* A period of rest. **5.** *Informal* A period of physical or mental disorder or distress: *a dizzy spell.* **6.** *Informal* A short distance. ❖ *v.* **spelled, spell·ing, spells** —*tr.* **1.** To relieve (someone) from work temporarily by taking a turn. **2.** To allow to rest a while. —*intr.* **1.** To take turns working. **2.** *Australian* To rest for a time from an activity. [< ME *spelen*, to spare < OE *spelian*, substitute for.]

spell·bind (spĕl′bīnd′) *tr.v.* **-bound** (-bound′), **-bind·ing, -binds** To hold under or as if under a spell; enchant or fascinate. [Back-formation < SPELLBOUND.]

spell·bind·er (spĕl′bīn′dər) *n.* One that holds others spellbound, esp. an enthralling speaker or an interesting book.

spell·bound (spĕl′bound′) *adj.* Entranced by or as if by a spell; fascinated.

spell checker or **spell·check·er** (spĕl′chĕk′ər) *n.* An application within most word processing programs that checks for spelling errors in documents. —**spell check** *v.*

spell·down (spĕl′doun′) *n.* See **spelling bee.**

spell·er (spĕl′ər) *n.* **1.** One who spells words. **2.** An elementary textbook containing exercises that teach spelling.

spell·ing (spĕl′ĭng) *n.* **1a.** The forming of words with letters in an accepted order; orthography. **b.** The art or study of orthography. **2.** The way in which a word is spelled.

spelling bee *n.* A contest in which competitors are eliminated as they fail to spell a given word correctly.

spelling pronunciation *n.* A pronunciation of a word that differs from the historically established one, arising from the word's spelling, as when *often* is pronounced with a (t).

spelt¹ (spĕlt) *n.* A hardy wheat grown mostly in Europe. [ME < OE < LLat. *spelta*, prob. of Gmc. orig.]

spelt² (spĕlt) *v.* A past tense and a past participle of **spell¹.**

spel·ter (spĕl′tər) *n.* Zinc, esp. in the form of ingots, slabs, or plates. [Prob. of Du. or LGer. orig.]

spe·lunk·er (spĭ-lŭng′kər, spē′lŭng′-) *n.* One who explores caves chiefly as a hobby; a caver. [< obsolete *spelunk*, cave < ME < OFr. *spelunque* < Lat. *spēlunca* < Gk. *spēlunx.*] —**spe′lunk′ing** *n.*

spen·cer¹ (spĕn′sər) *n. Nautical* A trysail. [Perh. < the name *Spencer*.]

spen·cer² (spĕn′sər) *n.* **1.** A short double-breasted overcoat worn by men in the early 19th century. **2.** A close-fitting waist-length jacket worn by women. [After George John *Spencer*, 2nd Earl Spencer (1758–1834).]

Spencer, Herbert 1820–1903. British philosopher who applied the theory of evolution to philosophy and ethics.

Spencer Gulf An inlet of the Indian Ocean off S-central Australia.

Spen·ce·ri·an¹ (spĕn-sîr′ē-ən) *adj.* Of or relating to Herbert Spencer or his philosophy. ❖ *n.* A follower of Herbert Spencer.

Spen·ce·ri·an² (spĕn-sîr′ē-ən) *adj.* Of or relating to an ornate style of writing using rounded letters slanted to the right. [After

ă	pat	oi	boy
ā	pay	ou	out
âr	care	oo	took
ä	father	oo	boot
ĕ	pet	ŭ	cut
ē	be	ûr	urge
ĭ	pit	th	thin
ī	pie	th	this
îr	pier	hw	which
ŏ	pot	zh	vision
ō	toe	ə	about,
ô	paw		item

Stress marks:
′ (primary);
′ (secondary); as in
lexicon (lĕk′sĭ-kŏn′)

Platt Rogers *Spencer* (1800–64), American handwriting expert.]

spend (spĕnd) *v.* **spent** (spĕnt), **spend·ing, spends** —*tr.* **1.** To use up or put out; expend: *spent an hour exercising.* **2.** To pay out (money). **3.** To wear out; exhaust: *The storm finally spent itself.* **4.** To pass (time) in a specified manner or place. **5a.** To throw away; squander. **b.** To give up (one's time or efforts, for example) to a cause; sacrifice. —*intr.* **1.** To pay out or expend money. **2.** To be exhausted or consumed. [ME *spenden,* partly < OE *-spendan* (< Lat. *expendēre,* to expend; see EXPEND) and partly < OFr. *despendre,* to weigh out; see DISPENSE.] —**spend′a·ble** *adj.* —**spend′er** *n.*

SYNONYMS *spend, disburse, expend* These verbs mean to pay or give out money or an equivalent: *spent ten dollars for a ticket; disbursed funds from the account; expended energy on a project.*

Spen·der (spĕn′dər), Sir **Stephen Harold** 1909–95. British writer whose works include *Poems of Dedication* (1947).

spend·ing money (spĕn′dĭng) *n.* Cash for small personal needs.

spend·thrift (spĕnd′thrĭft′) *n.* One who spends money recklessly or wastefully. ✣ *adj.* Wasteful or extravagant. [SPEND + THRIFT, accumulated wealth (obsolete).]

spend·y (spĕn′dē) *adj. Pacific Northwest* Expensive; costly.

Speng·ler (spĕng′lər, -glər, shpĕng′-), **Oswald** 1880–1936. German philosopher who argued that civilizations are subject to the same cycle of growth and decay as humans.

Spen·ser (spĕn′sər), **Edmund** 1552?–99. English poet known chiefly for his allegorical epic romance *The Faerie Queene* (1590–96). —**Spen·se′ri·an** (spĕn-sîr′ē-ən) *adj.*

Spenserian sonnet *n.* A sonnet form composed of three quatrains and a couplet in iambic pentameter with the rhyme scheme *abab bcbc cdcd ee.*

Spenserian stanza *n.* A stanza consisting of eight lines of iambic pentameter and a final alexandrine, rhymed *ababbcbcc.*

spent (spĕnt) *adj.* **1.** Used up; consumed: *a spent youth.* **2.** Having come to an end; passed. **3.** Depleted of energy, force, or strength; exhausted: *spent workers.* **4.** *Nautical* Of or relating to a vessel at the end of a voyage, with fuel, stores, and water consumed and cargo discharged.

sperm[1] (spûrm) *n., pl.* **sperm** or **sperms 1.** A male gamete or reproductive cell; a spermatozoon. **2.** Semen. [ME *sperme,* semen < OFr. *esperme* < LLat. *sperma* < Gk.] —**sperm′ous** *adj.*

sperm[2] (spûrm) *n.* A substance, such as spermaceti, associated with the sperm whale. [Short for SPERMACETI.]

sperm– or **sperma–** *pref.* Variants of **spermi–.**

–sperm *suff.* Seed: *endosperm.* [Gk. *-spermos < sperma,* seed.]

sper·ma·ce·ti (spûr′mə-sĕt′ē, -sĕt′ē) *n., pl.* **-tis** A waxy white substance from the head of the sperm whale or another cetacean and used for making candles, ointments, and cosmetics. [ME < Med.Lat. *spermacētī* : LLat. *sperma,* semen; see SPERM[1] + Lat. *cētī,* genitive of *cētus,* whale; see CETUS.]

sper·ma·go·ni·um also **sper·mo·go·ni·um** (spûr′mə-gō′nē-əm) *n., pl.* **-ni·a** (-nē-ə) A cup-shaped cavity or receptacle in which the spermatia of certain lichens and fungi are produced. [NLat. : *sperma,* sperm; see SPERM[1] + *-gonium,* seed, cell (< Gk. *gonos,* seed; see GONO–).]

sper·ma·ry (spûr′mə-rē) *n., pl.* **-ries** An organ or a gland in which male gametes are formed, esp. in invertebrate animals. [NLat. *spermārium* < LLat. *sperma,* semen. See SPERM[1].]

sper·ma·the·ca (spûr′mə-thē′kə) *n.* A receptacle in the reproductive tracts of certain female invertebrates, esp. insects, in which spermatozoa are stored.

sper·mat·ic (spər-măt′ĭk) *adj.* **1.** Of, relating to, or resembling sperm. **2.** Containing, conveying, or producing sperm. **3.** Of or relating to a spermary.

spermatic cord *n.* A cordlike structure that includes the vas deferens and passes from the abdominal cavity via the inguinal canal into the scrotum to the back of the testicle.

sper·ma·tid (spûr′mə-tĭd) *n.* Any of the four haploid cells formed by meiosis in a male organism that develop into spermatozoa without further division.

sper·ma·ti·um (spər-mā′shē-əm, -shəm) *n., pl.* **-ti·a** (-shē-ə, -shə) A nonmotile cell in red algae and certain lichens and fungi that functions as a male gamete. [NLat. < Gk. *spermation,* dim. of *sperma, spermat-,* semen.] —**sper·ma′tial** (-shəl) *adj.*

spermato– or **spermat–** *pref.* **1.** Seed: *spermatophyte.* **2a.** Sperm: *spermatic.* **b.** Spermatozoon: *spermatophore.* [Gk. < *sperma, spermat-,* seed. See SPERM[1].]

sper·mat·o·cyte (spər-măt′ə-sīt′, spûr′mə-tə-) *n.* A diploid cell that undergoes meiosis to form four spermatids.

sper·mat·o·gen·e·sis (spər-măt′ə-jĕn′ĭ-sĭs, spûr′mə-tə-) *n.* Formation and development of spermatozoa by meiosis and spermiogenesis.

sper·mat·o·go·ni·um (spər-măt′ə-gō′nē-əm, spûr′mə-tə-) *n., pl.* **-ni·a** (-nē-ə) Any of the cells of the gonads in male organisms that are the progenitors of spermatocytes. [NLat. : SPERMATO– + *-gonium,* seed; see SPERMAGONIUM.] —**sper·mat′o·go′ni·al** (-nē-əl) *adj.*

sper·mat·o·phore (spər-măt′ə-fôr′, -fōr′, spûr′mə-tə-) *n.* A capsule or compact mass of spermatozoa extruded by the males of certain invertebrates and primitive vertebrates and directly transferred to the reproductive parts of the female. —**sper·ma·**

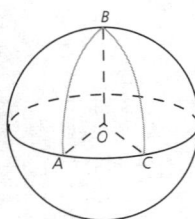

spherical angle
The spherical angle *ABC* is equal to the plane angle *AOC.*

sphinx
the Great Sphinx of Giza, Egypt

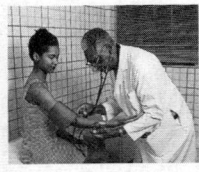

sphygmomanometer

toph′o·ral (spûr′mə-tŏf′ər-əl) *adj.*

sper·mat·o·phyte (spər-măt′ə-fīt′, spûr′mə-tə-) *n.* A seed-bearing plant, such as a conifer or a flowering plant. —**sper·mat′o·phyt′ic** (-fĭt′ĭk) *adj.*

sper·mat·or·rhe·a (spər-măt′ə-rē′ə, spûr′mə-tə-) *n.* Involuntary discharge of semen without orgasm.

sper·mat·o·zo·id (spər-măt′ə-zō′ĭd, spûr′mə-tə-) *n.* A ciliated male gamete produced in an antheridium.

sper·mat·o·zo·on (spər-măt′ə-zō′ŏn′, -ən, spûr′mə-tə-) *n., pl.* **-zo·a** (-zō′ə) The mature fertilizing gamete of a male organism, usu. consisting of a round or cylindrical nucleated cell, a short neck, and a thin motile tail. —**sper·mat′o·zo′al** (-zō′əl), **sper·mat′o·zo′an** (-zō′ən), **sper·mat′o·zo′ic** (-zō′ĭk) *adj.*

spermi– or **sperma–** or **spermo–** or **sperm–** *pref.* **1.** Seed: *spermophile.* **2.** Sperm: *spermicide.* [Gk. *spermo-, sperm- < sperma,* seed.]

sper·mi·cide (spûr′mĭ-sīd′) *n.* An agent that kills spermatozoa, esp. a contraceptive. —**sper′mi·cid′al** (-sīd′l) *adj.*

sper·mi·o·gen·e·sis (spûr′mē-ō-jĕn′ĭ-sĭs) *n.* Transformation of a spermatid into a spermatozoon. [NLat. *spermium,* spermatozoon (prob. < LLat. *sperma, semen;* see SPERM[1]) + –GENESIS.] —**sper′mi·o·ge·net′ic** (-jə-nĕt′ĭk) *adj.*

sper·mo·go·ni·um (spûr′mə-gō′nē-əm) *n.* Variant of **spermagonium.**

sperm oil *n.* A waxy yellow oil obtained from the head of the sperm whale and used as an industrial lubricant.

sperm·o·phile (spûr′mə-fīl′) *n.* The ground squirrel.

sperm whale *n.* Any of several large, toothed whales of the family Physeteridae, esp. *Physeter catodon* or *P. macrocephalus,* of tropical and temperate oceans, whose massive head has a cavity containing sperm oil and spermaceti and whose long intestines often contain ambergris.

Sper·ry (spĕr′ē), **Elmer Ambrose** 1860–1930. Amer. engineer and inventor of the gyrocompass (1910).

sper·ry·lite (spĕr′ĭ-līt′) *n.* A white crystalline platinum mineral, essentially PtAs$_2$. [After Francis Louis *Sperry* (died 1906), Canadian chemist.]

spes·sar·tite (spĕs′ər-tīt′) also **spes·sar·tine** (-tēn′) *n.* A red to brownish-red mineral of the garnet group, Mn$_3$Al$_2$(SiO$_4$)$_3$. [Fr., after *Spessart,* a hilly area of central Germany.]

spew (spyōō) *v.* **spewed, spew·ing, spews** —*tr.* **1.** To send or force out in or as if in a stream; eject forcefully or in large amounts. **2.** To vomit or otherwise cast out through the mouth. —*intr.* **1.** To flow or gush forth. **2.** To vomit. ✣ *n.* Something spewed. [ME *spewen* < OE *spīwan.*] —**spew′er** *n.*

SPF *abbr.* sun protection factor

sphag·num (sfăg′nəm) *n.* Any of various pale or ashy mosses of the genus *Sphagnum,* the decomposed remains of which form peat. [NLat. < Lat. *sphagnos,* a kind of moss < Gk., a kind of shrub.] —**sphag′nous** *adj.*

sphal·er·ite (sfăl′ə-rīt′) *n.* The primary ore of zinc, ZnS, occurring in usu. yellow-brown or brownish-black crystals or cleavage masses. [Gk. *sphaleros,* deceitful (< *sphallein,* to trip, it being easily mistaken for galena) + –ITE[1].]

sphene (sfēn) *n.* A titanium mineral in some granite and metamorphic rocks, CaTiSiO$_5$, occurring in usu. small brown or yellow crystals. [Fr. *sphène* < Gk. *sphēn,* wedge.]

sphen·ic (sfĕn′ĭk) *adj.* Shaped like a wedge.

spheno– or **sphen–** *pref.* Wedge; wedge-shaped: *sphenodon.* [Gk. *sphēno- < sphēn,* wedge.]

sphe·no·don (sfē′nə-dŏn′, sfĕn′ə-) *n.* See **tuatara.** [NLat. *Sphēnodon,* genus name : SPHENO– + –ODON.]

sphe·no·gram (sfē′nə-grăm′, sfĕn′ə-) *n.* A cuneiform character.

sphe·noid (sfē′noid′) *n.* The sphenoid bone. ✣ *adj.* **1.** Wedge-shaped. **2.** Of or relating to the sphenoid bone. —**sphe·noi′dal** (-noid′l) *adj.*

sphenoid bone *n.* A compound bone with winglike processes, situated at the base of the skull.

spher– *pref.* Variant of **sphero–.**

spher·al (sfîr′əl) *adj.* **1.** Of, relating to, or having the shape of a sphere; spherical. **2.** Symmetrical.

sphere (sfîr) *n.* **1.** *Mathematics* A three-dimensional surface, all points of which are equidistant from a fixed point. **2.** A spherical object or figure. **3.** A celestial body, such as a planet or star. **4.** The sky, appearing as a hemisphere to an observer. **5.** Any of a series of postulated concentric, transparent revolving globes that together contained the moon, sun, planets, and stars. **6.** The extent of a person's knowledge, interests, or social position. **7.** An area of power, control, or influence; domain. ✣ *tr.v.* **sphered, spher·ing, spheres 1.** To form into a sphere. **2.** To put in or within a sphere. **3.** To surround or encompass. [ME *spere* < OFr. *espere* < Lat. *sphaera* < Gk. *sphaira.*] —**sphe·ric′i·ty** (sfĭ-rĭs′ĭ-tē) *n.*

sphere of influence *n., pl.* **spheres of influence** A territorial area over which influence is wielded by one nation.

spher·i·cal (sfîr′ĭ-kəl, sfĕr′-) also **spher·ic** (-ĭk) *adj.* **1a.** Having the shape of a sphere; globular. **b.** Having a shape approximating that of a sphere. **2.** Of or relating to a sphere. **3.** Of or relating to celestial bodies. —**spher′i·cal·ly** *adv.* —**spher′i·cal·ness** *n.*

spherical aberration *n.* The blurring of an image that occurs when light from the margin of a lens or mirror with a spherical surface comes to a shorter focus than light from the central portion.

spherical angle *n.* The angle formed at the intersection of the arcs of two great circles.

spherical coordinate *n.* Any of a set of coordinates in a three-dimensional system for locating points in space by means of a radius vector and two angles measured from the center of a sphere with respect to two arbitrary, fixed, perpendicular directions.

spherical geometry *n.* The geometry of circles, angles, and figures on the surface of a sphere.

spherical polygon *n.* A part of a spherical surface that is bounded by arcs of three or more great circles.

spherical triangle *n.* A triangle the three sides of which are arcs of great circles.

spherical trigonometry *n.* The modified form of trigonometry applied to spherical triangles.

spher•ics[1] (sfîr′ĭks, sfĕr′-) *n.* (*used with a sing. verb*) **1.** Spherical geometry. **2.** Spherical trigonometry.

spher•ics[2] (sfîr′ĭks, sfĕr′-) *n.* Variant of **sferics.**

sphero– or **spher–** *pref.* Sphere: *spherometer.* [Lat. *sphaero-* < Gk. *sphairo-* < *sphaira,* sphere.]

spher•oid (sfîr′oid′, sfĕr′-) *n.* A body that is shaped like a sphere but is not perfectly round, esp. an ellipsoid that is generated by revolving an ellipse around one of its axes. **—sphe•roi′dal** (sfĭ-roid′l), **sphe•roi′dic** (-roi′dĭk) *adj.* **—sphe•roi′dal•ly** *adv.* **—sphe′roi•dic′i•ty** (-dĭs′ĭ-tē) *n.*

sphe•rom•e•ter (sfĭ-rŏm′ĭ-tər) *n.* An instrument for measuring the curvature of a surface, as of a sphere or cylinder.

spher•o•plast (sfîr′ə-plăst′, sfĕr′-) *n.* A bacterial cell whose cell wall is absent or deficient, giving it a spherical form.

spher•ule (sfîr′o͞ol, -yo͞ol, sfĕr′-) *n.* A miniature sphere; a globule. [LLat. *sphaerula,* dim. of Lat. *sphaera,* ball. See SPHERE.] **—spher′u•lar** (sfîr′yə-lər, sfĕr′-) *adj.*

spher•u•lite (sfîr′yə-līt′, -ə-līt′, sfĕr′-) *n.* A small, usu. spheroidal body consisting of radiating crystals, found in obsidian and other glassy lava rocks. **—spher′u•lit′ic** (-lĭt′ĭk) *adj.*

spher•y (sfîr′ē) *adj.* **-i•er, -i•est 1.** Of or relating to the celestial spheres. **2.** Resembling a celestial body.

sphinc•ter (sfĭngk′tər) *n.* A ringlike muscle that constricts a body passage or orifice and relaxes as required by normal physiological functioning. [LLat. *sphincter* < Gk. *sphinktēr* < *sphingein,* to bind tight.] **—sphinc′ter•al** *adj.*

sphin•gid (sfĭn′jĭd) *n.* A moth of the family Sphingidae; a hawk moth. [< NLat. *Sphingidae,* family name < *Sphinx,* type genus < Lat., sphinx. See SPHINX.] **—sphin′gid** *adj.*

sphinx (sfĭngks) *n., pl.* **sphinx•es** or **sphin•ges** (sfĭn′jēz′) **1.** *Mythology* A figure in Egyptian myth having the body of a lion and the head of a man, ram, or hawk. **2.** often **Sphinx** *Greek Mythology* A winged creature having the head of a woman and the body of a lion, who killed those unable to answer its riddle. **3.** A puzzling or mysterious person. [ME *Spynx* < Lat. *Sphinx* < Gk.]

sphinx moth *n.* See **hawkmoth.**

sphyg•mic (sfĭg′mĭk) *adj. Physiology* Of or relating to the pulse.

sphygmo– or **sphygm–** *pref.* Pulse: *sphygmograph.* [Gk. *sphugmo-* < *sphugmos,* pulsation < *sphuzein, sphug-,* to throb.]

sphyg•mo•gram (sfĭg′mə-grăm′) *n.* The record or tracing produced by a sphygmograph.

sphyg•mo•graph (sfĭg′mə-grăf′) *n.* An instrument for graphically recording the form, strength, and variations of the arterial pulse. **—sphyg′mo•graph′ic** *adj.* **—sphyg•mog′ra•phy** (-mŏg′rə-fē) *n.*

sphyg•mo•ma•nom•e•ter (sfĭg′mō-mə-nŏm′ĭ-tər) also **sphyg•mom•e•ter** (sfĭg-mŏm′ĭ-tər) *n.* An instrument for measuring blood pressure in the arteries, esp. one consisting of a pressure gauge and a rubber cuff that wraps around the upper arm. **—sphyg′mo•ma•nom′e•try** *n.*

spic also **spick** (spĭk) *n. Offensive Slang* Used as a disparaging term for a Hispanic person. [Alteration of obsolete *spig,* a Mexican, short for *spiggoty,* perh. < an accented pronunciation of *(No) speak the (English).*]

spi•ca (spī′kə) *n.* **1.** *pl.* **-cae** (-kē, -sē) or **-cas** A bandage applied in overlapping opposite spirals to immobilize a digit or limb. **2.** A binary star in the constellation Virgo. [Lat. *spīca,* ear of grain. Sense 2 < its shape.]

spi•cate (spī′kāt′) *adj.* Borne in or forming a spike. [Lat. *spīcātus* < *spīca,* ear of grain.]

spic•ca•to (spĭ-kä′tō) *Music n., pl.* **-tos** A technique of bowing in which the bow is made to bounce slightly from the string. ❖ *adj.* Of or employing spiccato. [Ital., p. part. of *spiccare,* to separate : *s-,* from; see SFUMATO + *piccare,* to pierce, impale (< VLat. **piccāre;* see PICK[1]).]

spice (spīs) *n.* **1a.** Any of various pungent aromatic plant substances, such as nutmeg, used to flavor foods or beverages. **b.** These substances considered as a group. **2.** Something adding zest or flavor. **3.** A pungent aroma; a perfume. ❖ *tr.v.* **spiced, spic•ing, spic•es 1.** To season with spices. **2.** To add zest or flavor to: *spiced up their lives.* [ME < OFr. *espice* < LLat. *speciēs,* wares, spices < Lat., kind. See SPECIES.]

spice•bush (spīs′bo͝osh′) *n.* An aromatic deciduous shrub *(Lindera benzoin)* of eastern North America having clusters of early-blooming small yellow flowers.

spicebush swallowtail *n.* A large swallowtail *(Papilio troilus)* of eastern North America that feeds on spicebushes, having dark forewings and bluish-green hindwings.

Spice Islands See **Moluccas.**

spic•er•y (spī′sə-rē) *n., pl.* **-ies 1.** Spices considered as a group. **2.** The aromatic or pungent quality of spices. **3.** *Archaic* A place where spices are stored.

spick-and-span also **spic-and-span** (spĭk′ən-spăn′) *adj.* **1.** Immaculately clean; spotless. **2.** Brand-new; fresh. [Short for obsolete *spick and span-new* : *spick,* spike (var. of SPIKE[1]) + SPAN-NEW.]

spic•ule (spĭk′yo͞ol) also **spic•u•la** (-yə-lə) *n., pl.* **-ules** also **-u•lae** (-yə-lē) A small needlelike structure or part, such as one of the silicate or calcium carbonate processes supporting the soft tissue of certain invertebrates. [Lat. *spīculum.* See SPICULUM.] **—spic′u•lar** (-yə-lər), **spic′u•late** (-yə-lĭt, -lāt′) *adj.*

spic•u•lum (spĭk′yə-ləm) *n., pl.* **-la** (-lə) A spicule or similar needlelike structure, such as a spine of an echinoderm. [Lat. *spīculum,* dim. of *spīca,* point, ear of grain.]

spic•y (spī′sē) *adj.* **-i•er, -i•est 1.** Having the flavor, aroma, or quality of spice. **2.** Piquant; zesty: *a spicy tomato sauce.* **3.** Producing or abounding in spices. **4.** High-spirited; lively. **5.** Slightly scandalous; risqué. **—spic′i•ly** *adv.* **—spic′i•ness** *n.*

spi•der (spī′dər) *n.* **1.** Any of numerous arachnids of the order Araneae, having a body divided into a cephalothorax bearing eight legs and an unsegmented abdomen bearing spinnerets that produce silk used esp. to make webs for trapping insects. **2.** One that resembles a spider, as in appearance, character, or movement. **3.** *New England, Upper Northern, & South Atlantic US* See **frying pan.** See Regional Note at **frying pan. 4.** A trivet. [ME *spither* < OE *spīthra.*]

spider crab *n.* Any of various crabs, such as those of the genera *Libinia* and *Macrocheira,* having long legs and a relatively small triangular body.

spider flower *n.* See **cleome.**

spider mite *n.* See **red spider.**

spider monkey *n.* Any of several tropical American monkeys of the genus *Ateles,* having long legs and a long prehensile tail and lacking a thumb.

spi•der•wort (spī′dər-wûrt′, -wôrt′) *n.* Any of various New World herbs of the genus *Tradescantia,* having blue or purple flowers with six hairy stamens. [Prob. < its thin, hairy stamens.]

spi•der•y (spī′də-rē) *adj.* **1a.** Resembling a spider in form, characteristics, or behavior. **b.** Resembling a spider's web; very fine: *spidery handwriting.* **2.** Infested with spiders.

spied (spīd) *v.* Past tense and past participle of **spy.**

spie•gel•ei•sen (spē′gə-lī′zən) *n.* An alloy of iron containing approx. 15 percent manganese and small quantities of carbon and silicon, used in the Bessemer process. [Ger. : *Spiegel,* mirror (ult. < Lat. *speculum;* see SPECULUM) + *Eisen,* iron (< MHGer. *īsen* < OHGer. *īsan;* see **eis-** in App.).]

spiel (spēl, shpēl) *Informal n.* A lengthy or extravagant speech or argument usu. intended to persuade. ❖ *intr. & tr.v.* **spieled, spiel•ing, spiels** To talk or say (something) at length or extravagantly. [Ger., play, or Yiddish *shpil,* both < MHGer. *spil* < OHGer.] **—spiel′er** *n.*

Spiel•berg (spēl′bûrg′), **Steven** b. 1946. Amer. film director whose works include *Schindler's List* (1993).

spies (spīz) *n.* Plural of **spy.** ❖ *v.* Third person singular present tense of **spy.**

spiff (spĭf) *Informal tr.v.* **spiffed, spiff•ing, spiffs** To make attractive, stylish, or up-to-date: *spiffed up the the old storefront.* ❖ *n.* Attractiveness or charm in appearance, dress, or manners. [Poss. < dialectal *spiff,* well-dressed.]

spiff•y (spĭf′ē) *Informal adj.* **-i•er, -i•est** Smart in appearance or dress; stylish. ❖ *tr.v.* **-ied, -y•ing, -ies** To make attractive, stylish, or up-to-date: *spiffying up my wardrobe.* [Poss. < dialectal *spiff,* dandified.] **—spiff′i•ly** *adv.* **—spiff′i•ness** *n.*

spig•ot (spĭg′ət) *n.* **1.** A faucet. See Regional Note at **andiron. 2.** A wooden faucet placed in the bunghole of a cask. **3.** The vent plug of a cask. [ME, perh. < OFr. **espigot,* dim. of O Provençal *espiga,* ear of grain < Lat. *spīca.*]

spike[1] (spīk) *n.* **1a.** A long thick sharp-pointed piece of wood or metal. **b.** A heavy nail. **2.** A spikelike part or projection, as: **a.** A pointed projection on the top of a fence or wall. **b.** A pointed rod for impaling papers; a spindle. **c.** A tuft of hair that is stiffened, as with hair spray or soap, into a point. **d. 3a.** One of several sharp metal projections set in the sole and often the heel of an athletic shoe for grip. **b. spikes** A pair of athletic shoes with such spikes. **4. spikes** A pair of spike heels. **5.** An unbranched antler of a young deer. **6.** A young mackerel usu. 15 centimeters (6 inches) or less in length. **7a.** A sharp rise followed by a sharp decline in a graph or in the tracing of a scientific instrument. **b.** A sharp momentary increase in voltage or electric current. **c.** A sudden steep increase in prices. **8.** *Sports* The act of driving a volleyball at a sharp angle into the opponent's court. **9.** *Football* The act of throwing the ball down against the ground after a successful play. ❖ *tr.v.* **spiked, spik•ing, spikes 1a.** To secure or provide with a spike. **b.** To shape into spikes. **2.** To impale, pierce, or injure with a spike. **3.** *Sports* To injure with spiked shoes. **4.** *Infor-*

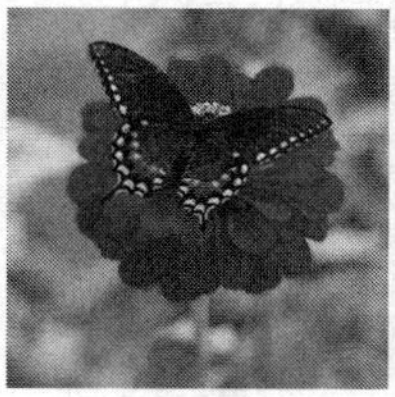

spicebush swallowtail
Papilio troilus

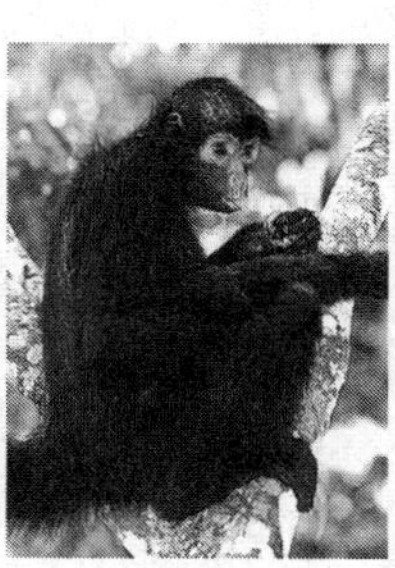

spider monkey

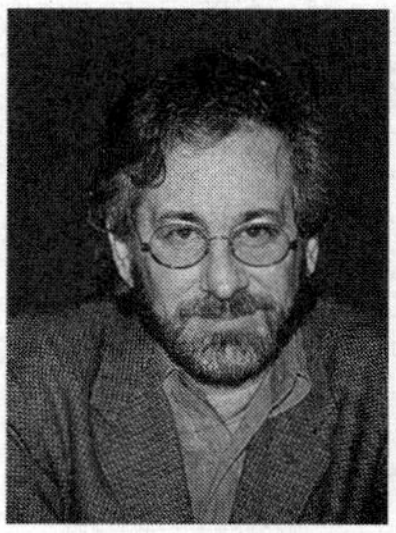

Steven Spielberg

ă	pat	oi	boy
ā	pay	ou	out
âr	care	o͝o	took
ä	father	o͞o	boot
ĕ	pet	ŭ	cut
ē	be	ûr	urge
ĭ	pit	th	thin
ī	pie	*th*	this
îr	pier	hw	which
ŏ	pot	zh	vision
ō	toe	ə	about, item
ô	paw		

Stress marks:
′ (primary);
′ (secondary), as in
lexicon (lĕk′sĭ-kŏn′)

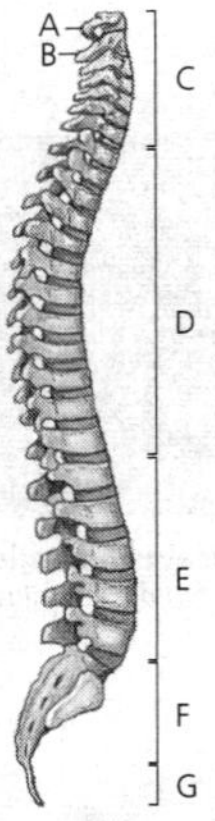

spinal column
right lateral view of an adult human spinal column
A. atlas
B. axis
C. cervical vertebrae
D. thoracic vertebrae
E. lumbar vertebrae
F. sacrum
G. coccyx

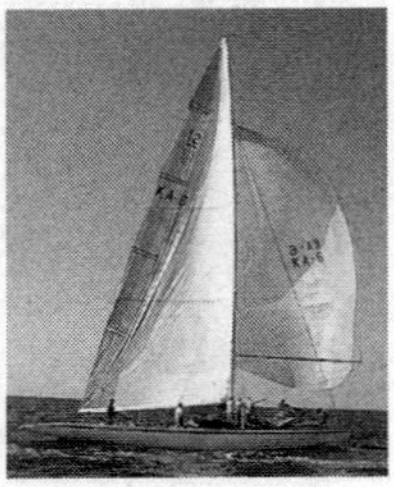

spinnaker

mal To put an end to; terminate: *spiked the rumor.* **5.** *Informal* **a.** To add alcoholic liquor to: *spiked the punch with rum.* **b.** To add a poison or other chemical to. **c.** To add flavor or spice to. **6a.** *Sports* To hit (a volleyball) in a spike. **b.** *Football* To throw (the ball) down in a spike. **7.** To render (a muzzleloading gun) useless by driving a spike into the vent. **8.** To manifest (a sharp increase in body temperature): *spike a fever.* [ME < ON *spīk.*] **—spiked** *adj.*

spike² (spīk) *n.* **1.** An ear of grain, as of wheat. **2.** *Botany* A usu. elongated unbranched inflorescence with stalkless flowers arranged along an axis. [ME < Lat. *spīca.*]

spike heel *n.* **1.** A very thin high heel used on a woman's shoe. **2.** A woman's shoe with a very thin high heel.

spike lavender *n.* An aromatic Mediterranean plant *(Lavandula latifolia)* of the mint family, yielding an oil similar to that of true lavender.

spike•let (spīk′lĭt) *n.* A small or secondary spike, characteristic of grasses and sedges.

spike•nard (spīk′närd′) *n.* **1.** An aromatic perennial herb *(Nardostachys jatamansi)* of the Himalaya Mountains having rose-purple flowers. **2.** An ointment of antiquity, probably prepared from this herb. **3.** A North American plant *(Aralia racemosa)* having aromatic roots and bipinnately compound leaves. [ME < AN < Med.Lat. *spīca nardī* : Lat. *spīca*, spike, ear + Lat. *nardī*, genitive of *nardus*, nard.]

spik•y (spī′kē) *adj.* **-i•er, -i•est 1.** Having one or more projecting sharp points. **2.** Grouchy or cross in temperament. **—spik′i•ly** *adv.* **—spik′i•ness** *n.*

spile (spīl) *n.* **1.** A post used as a foundation; a pile. **2.** A wooden plug; a bung. **3.** A spigot used in taking sap from a tree. ❖ *tr.v.* **spiled, spil•ing, spiles 1.** To support with a spile. **2.** To plug or tap with a spile. [Du. *spijl*, wooden pin < MDu. *spīle.*]

spill¹ (spĭl) *v.* **spilled** or **spilt** (spĭlt), **spill•ing, spills** —*tr.* **1.** To cause or allow (a substance) to run or fall out of a container. **2.** To scatter (objects) from containment. **3.** To shed (blood). **4.** *Nautical* **a.** To relieve the pressure of wind on (a sail). **b.** To cause or allow (wind) to be lost from a sail. **5.** To cause to fall. **6.** *Informal* To disclose (something previously unknown); divulge. —*intr.* **1.** To run or fall out of a container or containment. **2.** To come to the ground suddenly and involuntarily. **3.** To pour out or spread beyond limits. ❖ *n.* **1.** The act of spilling. **2.** An amount spilled. **3.** A fall, as from a horse. **4.** A spillway. [ME *spillen*, to shed blood, to spill < OE *spillan*, to kill.] **—spill′er** *n.*

spill² (spĭl) *n.* **1.** A piece of wood or rolled paper used to light a fire. **2.** A small peg or rod, esp. one used as a plug. [ME *spille.*]

spill•age (spĭl′ĭj) *n.* **1.** The act of spilling. **2.** An amount spilled.

spil•li•kin (spĭl′ĭ-kĭn) *n.* **1. spillikins** (*used with a sing. verb*) The game of jackstraws. **2.** A jackstraw. [Prob. alteration of Flem. *spelleken*, dim. of *spelle*, pin < MFlem., ult. < Med.Lat. *spīnula*, dim. of Lat. *spīna*, thorn.]

spill•o•ver (spĭl′ō′vər) *n.* **1.** The act or an instance of spilling over. **2.** An amount or quantity spilled over.

spill•way (spĭl′wā′) *n.* A channel for an overflow of water, as from a reservoir.

spilth (spĭlth) *n.* **1.** The act of spilling. **2.** An amount spilled.

spin (spĭn) *v.* **spun** (spŭn), **spin•ning, spins** —*tr.* **1a.** To draw out and twist (fibers) into thread. **b.** To form (thread or yarn) in this manner. **2.** To form (a web or cocoon, for example) by extruding viscous filaments. **3.** To make or produce by or as if by drawing out and twisting. **4a.** To relate or create: *spun tales for the children.* **b.** To prolong or extend: *spin out a visit.* **5.** To cause to rotate swiftly; twirl. **6.** To shape or make by a twirling or rotating process. **7.** To provide an interpretation of (a statement or event, for example), esp. to sway public opinion. **8.** *Slang* To play (a recording), esp. as a disc jockey. —*intr.* **1.** To make thread or yarn by drawing out and twisting fibers. **2.** To extrude viscous filaments, forming a web or cocoon. **3.** To rotate rapidly; whirl. **4.** To seem to be whirling, as from dizziness; reel. **5.** To ride or drive rapidly. **6.** To fish with a light rod, lure, and line and a reel with a stationary spool. ❖ *n.* **1.** The act of spinning. **2.** A swift whirling motion. **3.** A state of mental confusion. **4.** *Informal* A short drive in a vehicle. **5.** The flight condition of an aircraft in a nose-down, spiraling, stalled descent. **6a.** A distinctive point of view, emphasis, or interpretation. **b.** A distinctive character or style. **7.** *Physics* **a.** The intrinsic angular momentum of a subatomic particle. **b.** The total intrinsic angular momentum of an atomic nucleus. **c.** A quantum number expressing spin. ***—phrasal verb:* spin off** To derive (a product, for example) from something larger. ***—idiom:* spin (one's) wheels** *Informal* To expend effort with no result. [ME *spinnen* < OE *spinnan.*]

spi•na bif•i•da (spī′nə bĭf′ĭ-də) *n.* A congenital defect in which the spinal column is imperfectly closed so that part of the meninges or spinal cord protrudes, often resulting in hydrocephalus and other neurological disorders. [NLat. *spīna bifida* : Lat. *spīna*, spine + Lat. *bifida*, split in two.]

spin•ach (spĭn′ĭch) *n.* **1.** A widely cultivated southwest Asian plant *(Spinacia oleracea)* having succulent edible leaves. **2.** The leaves of this plant, eaten as a vegetable. [ME < OFr. *espinache* < Med.Lat. *spinăchium* < Ar. *'isfānāḥ* < Pers. *espanāj, espenākh.*]

spi•nal (spī′nəl) *adj.* **1.** Of, relating to, or situated near the spine or spinal cord; vertebral: *spinal injury.* **2.** Resembling a spine or spinous part. ❖ *n.* An anesthetic injected into the spinal cord to induce anesthesia. **—spi′nal•ly** *adv.*

spinal anesthesia *n.* Partial or complete anesthesia produced by injecting an anesthetic into the spinal canal.

spinal canal *n.* The passage formed by successive openings in the articulated vertebrae in the spinal column.

spinal column *n.* The series of articulated vertebrae that extends from the cranium to the coccyx or the end of the tail, encasing the spinal cord and forming the supporting axis of the body.

spinal cord *n.* The cord of nerve tissue that extends from the medulla oblongata down through the spinal column and from which the spinal nerves branch off to various body parts.

spinal nerve *n.* Any of the nerves that arise in pairs from the spinal cord, of which there are 31 pairs in the human body.

spin casting *n.* See **spinning** 2. **—spin caster** *n.*

spin•dle (spĭn′dl) *n.* **1a.** A rod or pin, tapered at one end and usu. weighted at the other, on which fibers are spun into thread. **b.** A pin or rod holding a bobbin or spool on which thread is wound on an automated spinning machine. **2.** Any of various mechanical parts that revolve or serve as axes for larger revolving parts, as in a lock or a lathe. **3.** Any of various long thin stationary rods, as: **a.** A spike on which papers may be impaled. **b.** A baluster. **4.** *Biology* The spindle-shaped achromatic structure, composed of microtubules, along which the chromosomes are distributed in mitosis and meiosis. **5.** *Coastal New Jersey* See **dragonfly.** See Regional Note at **dragonfly.** ❖ *v.* **-dled, -dling, -dles** —*tr.* **1.** To furnish or equip with a spindle or spindles. **2.** To impale or perforate on a spindle. —*intr.* To grow into a thin, elongated, or weak form. [ME *spindel*, alteration of OE *spinel.*]

spindle fiber *n.* One of a network of achromatic filaments that extend inward from the poles of a dividing cell, forming a spindle-shaped figure.

spindle tree *n.* See **euonymus.**

spin•dling (spĭnd′lĭng) *adj.* Spindly.

spin•dly (spĭnd′lē) *adj.* **-dli•er, -dli•est** Slender and elongated, esp. in a way that suggests weakness.

spin doctor *n. Slang* A person who publicizes favorable interpretations of the words and actions of a public figure, esp. a politician.

spin•drift (spĭn′drĭft′) *n.* Windblown sea spray. [Variant of Sc. *spenedrift* : *spene* (var. of obsolete *spoon*, to run before the wind) + DRIFT.]

spine (spīn) *n.* **1.** The spinal column of a vertebrate. **2.** *Zoology* Any of various pointed projections, processes, or appendages of animals. **3.** *Botany* A strong, sharp-pointed, usu. woody outgrowth from a stem or leaf; a thorn. **4.** Something that resembles or suggests a backbone, as: **a.** The hinged back of a book. **b.** The crest of a ridge. **5.** Strength of character; courage or willpower. [ME < OFr. *espine* < Lat. *spīna.*]

spine-chill•ing (spīn′chĭl′ĭng) *adj.* Extremely frightening, esp. in an eerie way: *a spine-chilling novel.*

spi•nel also **spi•nelle** (spĭ-nĕl′) *n.* **1.** A hard, variously colored mineral, $MgAl_2O_4$, having usu. octahedral crystals, of which the red variety is valued as a gem and is sometimes confused with ruby. **2.** Any of a series of minerals that are oxides of magnesium, iron, zinc, manganese, or aluminum. [Ital. *spinella*, dim. of *spina*, thorn (< its sharply pointed crystals) < Lat. *spīna.*]

spine•less (spīn′lĭs) *adj.* **1.** Lacking courage or willpower. **2.** *Biology* **a.** Having no spiny processes. **b.** Lacking a spinal column; invertebrate. **—spine′less•ness** *n.*

spi•nes•cent (spī-nĕs′ənt) *adj.* **1.** *Botany* Having a spine or spines. **2.** Terminating in a spine. [LLat. *spīnēscēns, spīnēscent-*, pr. part. of *spīnēscere*, to become thorny < Lat. *spīna*, thorn.] **—spi•nes′cence** *n.*

spin•et (spĭn′ĭt) *n.* **1a.** A small compact upright piano. **b.** A small compact upright electronic organ. **2.** A small harpsichord with a single keyboard. [< obsolete Fr. *espinette*, small harpsichord < Ital. *spinetta*, perh. dim. of *spīna*, thorn (presumably so called because the strings of the original instrument were plucked with quills). See SPINEL.]

Spin•garn (spĭn′gärn′), **Joel Elias** 1875–1939. Amer. poet and critic who was a founder (1909) and president (1930–39) of the NAACP.

spi•ni•fex (spī′nə-fĕks′) *n.* Any of various clump-forming perennial Australian grasses, chiefly of the genus *Triodia*, growing in arid regions and having awl-shaped pointed leaves. [NLat. *Spīnifex*, former genus name : Lat. *spīna*, thorn + Lat. *-fex*; see **dhē-** in App.]

spin•meis•ter (spĭn′mī′stər) *n. Slang* A spin doctor.

spin•na•ker (spĭn′ə-kər) *n.* A large triangular sail set on a spar that swings out opposite the mainsail, used on yachts when running before the wind. [Perh. ult. < *Sphinx*, name of the first yacht to use such a sail, or *spin*, to move rapidly (var. of Sc. *spene*, to run before the wind; see SPINDRIFT).]

spin•ner (spĭn′ər) *n.* **1.** One that spins. **2.** A fishing lure that rotates rapidly. **3.** A fairing fitted over the hub of the propeller in some aircraft. **4.** *Games* An arrow that is spun on a dial to indicate the next move in some board games.

spin•ner•et (spĭn′ə-rĕt′) *n.* **1.** Any of various tubular structures from which spiders and certain insect larvae, such as silkworms, secrete the silk threads from which they form webs or cocoons.

2. A device for making nylon and other synthetic fibers, consisting of a plate pierced with holes through which plastic material is extruded in filaments.

spin•ney (spĭn′ē) *n., pl.* **-neys** *Chiefly British* A small grove; a copse. [Obsolete Fr. *espinoi* < OFr. *espinei*, thorny place < VLat. **spīnēta*, pl. of Lat. *spīnētum*, thorn hedge < *spīna*, thorn.]

spin•ning (spĭn′ĭng) *n.* **1.** The process of making fibrous material into yarn or thread. **2.** The act of fishing with a light rod and a reel having a bail or similar device that guides the line around a stationary spool and that can be disengaged to let the line run freely.

spinning frame *n.* A machine that draws and twists fibers into yarn and winds it on spindles.

spinning jenny *n.* An early form of spinning machine having several spindles.

spinning mule *n.* See **mule**[1] 4.

spinning wheel *n.* A device for making yarn or thread, having a foot-driven or hand-driven wheel and a single spindle.

spin•off or **spin-off** (spĭn′ôf′, -ŏf′) *n.* **1a.** A divestiture by a corporation of a division or subsidiary by issuing to stockholders shares in a new company set up to continue operating the division or subsidiary. **b.** This new company. **2.** Something, such as a product, derived from something larger and more or less unrelated; a byproduct. **3.** Something derived from an earlier work, such as a television show starring a character with a minor role in another show.

spi•nose (spī′nōs′) *adj.* Bearing spines; spiny: *a spinose plant.* [Lat. *spīnōsus* < *spīna*, thorn.] —**spi′nose′ly** *adv.* —**spi•nos′i•ty** (-nŏs′ĭ-tē) *n.*

spi•nous (spī′nəs) *adj.* **1.** Resembling a spine or thorn. **2.** Having spines or similar projections; spiny.

Spi•no•za (spĭ-nō′zə), **Baruch** or **Benedict** 1632–77. Dutch philosopher and theologian whose pantheistic doctrine advocated an intellectual love of God.

Spi•no•zism (spĭ-nō′zĭz′əm) *n.* A monistic approach to philosophy in which all reality is held to consist of one substance, usu. termed God or Nature, of which minds and bodies are both attributes. [After Baruch SPINOZA.] —**Spi•no′zist** *adj. & n.* —**Spi•no•zis′tic** *adj.*

spin•ster (spĭn′stər) *n.* **1.** A woman who has remained single beyond the conventional age for marrying. **2.** A single woman. **3.** A person whose occupation is spinning. [ME *spinnestere*, female spinner : *spinnen*, to spin; see SPIN + *-estere*, *-ster*, -ster.] —**spin′ster•hood′** *n.* —**spin′ster•ish** *adj.*

spin-the-bot•tle (spĭn′thə-bŏt′l) *n.* A game in which players take turns spinning a bottle and kissing the person it points toward when it comes to rest.

spin•to (spĭn′tō) *adj.* Of, relating to, or being a lyric operatic voice with some attributes of the dramatic voice: *a spinto soprano.* [Ital., p. part. of *spingere*, to push < VLat. **expingere* : Lat. *ex-*, ex- + Lat. *pangere*, to fasten.] —**spin′to** *n.*

spi•nule (spĭn′yo͞ol) *n.* A small spine or thorn. [Lat. *spīnula*, dim. of *spīna*, thorn.]

spin•y (spī′nē) *adj.* **-i•er, -i•est 1.** Bearing or covered with spines, thorns, or similar stiff projections. **2.** Shaped like a spine. **3.** Difficult; troublesome. —**spin′i•ness** *n.*

spiny anteater *n.* See **echidna.**

spin•y-finned (spī′nē-fĭnd′) *adj.* Having fins supported by sharp spiny inflexible rays. Used of a fish.

spin•y-head•ed worm (spī′nē-hĕd′ĭd) *n.* Any of various worms of the phylum Acanthocephala that live parasitically in the intestines of vertebrates and have a cylindrical retractile proboscis with many rows of hooked spines.

spiny lobster *n.* Any of various edible marine decapod crustaceans of the family Palinuridae, having a spiny carapace and lacking the large pincers characteristic of true lobsters.

spin•y-rayed (spī′nē-rād′) *adj.* Spiny-finned.

spir•a•cle (spĭr′ə-kəl, spī′rə-) *n.* **1.** *Zoology* A respiratory aperture, esp.: **a.** Any of several tracheal openings in the exoskeleton of an insect or a spider. **b.** A small respiratory opening behind the eye of certain fishes, such as sharks, rays, and skates. **c.** The blowhole of a cetacean. **2.** An aperture or opening through which air is admitted and expelled. [ME < Lat. *spīrāculum* < *spīrāre*, to breathe.] —**spi•rac′u•lar** (spī-răk′yə-lər, spĭ-) *adj.*

spi•ral (spī′rəl) *n.* **1a.** A curve on a plane that winds around a fixed center point at a continuously increasing or decreasing distance from the point. **b.** A three-dimensional curve that turns around an axis at a constant or continuously varying distance while moving parallel to the axis; a helix. **c.** Something with the form of such a curve: *a spiral of smoke.* **2.** *Printing* A spiral binding. **3.** The course of an object rotating on its longitudinal axis. **4.** A continuously accelerating increase or decrease: *the wage-price spiral.* ❖ *adj.* **1.** Of or resembling a spiral. **2.** Circling around a center at a continuously increasing or decreasing distance. **3.** Coiling around an axis in a constantly changing series of planes; helical. **4.** *Printing* Relating to or having a spiral binding. ❖ *v.* **-raled, -ral•ing, -rals** also **-ralled, -ral•ling, -rals** —*intr.* **1.** To take a spiral form or course. **2.** To rise or fall with steady acceleration. —*tr.* To cause to take a spiral form or course. [Med.Lat. *spīrālis*, of a spiral < Lat. *spīra*, coil. See SPIRE[2].] —**spi•ral′i•ty** (spī-răl′ĭ-tē) *n.* —**spi′ral•ly** *adv.*

spiral binding *n.* A binding for notebooks and booklets in which a cylindrical spiral of wire or plastic is passed through a row of punched holes at the edge of a tablet. —**spi′ral-bound′** (spī′rəl-bound′) *adj.*

spiral galaxy *n.* A galaxy having a spiral structure.

spi•rant (spī′rənt) *n.* See **fricative.** ❖ *adj.* Fricative. [Lat. *spīrāns*, *spīrant-*, pr. part. of *spīrāre*, to breathe.]

spire[1] (spīr) *n.* **1.** A top part or point that tapers upward; a pinnacle. **2.** A structure or formation that tapers to a point at the top. **3.** A slender tapering part, such as a newly sprouting blade of grass. ❖ *v.* **spired, spir•ing, spires** —*tr.* To furnish with a spire. —*intr.* To rise and taper steeply. [ME < OE *spīr.*]

spire[2] (spīr) *n.* **1a.** A spiral. **b.** A single turn of a spiral. **2.** The area farthest from the aperture and nearest the apex on a coiled gastropod shell. [Lat. *spīra*, coil < Gk. *speira.*]

spi•re•a also **spi•rae•a** (spī-rē′ə) *n.* Any of various shrubs of the genus *Spiraea* of the rose family, having clusters of small white or pink flowers and including the meadowsweet. [Lat. *spīraea*, meadowsweet < Gk. *speiraia*, privet < *speira*, coil.]

spi•reme (spī′rēm′) also **spi•rem** (-rĕm′) *n.* The tangle of filaments that appears at the beginning of the prophase portion of meiosis or mitosis. [Ger. *Spirem* < Gk. *speirēma*, coil < *speirāsthai*, to be coiled around < *speira*, coil.]

spi•rif•er•ous (spī-rĭf′ər-əs) *adj.* Having a spiral structure or spiral parts. [Prob. < NLat. *spīrifer* : Lat. *spīra*, coil; see SPIRE[2] + Lat. *-fer*, -fer.]

spi•ril•lum (spī-rĭl′əm) *n., pl.* **-ril•la** (-rĭl′ə) **1.** Any of various aerobic bacteria of the genus *Spirillum*, having an elongated spiral form and bearing a tuft of flagella. **2.** Any of various other spiral-shaped microorganisms. [NLat. *Spīrillum*, genus name, dim. of Lat. *spīra*, coil. See SPIRE[2].]

spir•it (spĭr′ĭt) *n.* **1a.** The vital principle or animating force within living beings. **b.** Incorporeal consciousness. **2.** The soul, considered as departing from a person's body at death. **3. Spirit** The Holy Spirit. **4.** A supernatural being, as: **a.** An angel or demon. **b.** A being inhabiting or embodying a particular place, object, or natural phenomenon. **c.** A fairy or sprite. **5a.** The part of a human associated with the mind, will, and feelings: *with us in spirit.* **b.** The essential nature of a person or group. **6.** A person as characterized by a stated quality: *a proud spirit.* **7a.** An inclination or tendency of a specified kind: *a generous spirit.* **b.** A causative, activating, or essential principle: *The party was announced in a joyous spirit.* **8. spirits** A mood or emotional state. **9.** A particular mood or emotional state characterized by vigor and animation: *sang with spirit.* **10.** Strong loyalty or dedication. **11.** The predominant mood of an occasion or period. **12.** The actual though unstated sense or significance of something: *the spirit of the law.* **13.** An alcohol solution of an essential or volatile substance. Often used in the plural with a singular verb. **14. spirits** An alcoholic beverage, esp. distilled liquor. ❖ *tr.v.* **-it•ed, -it•ing, -its 1.** To carry off mysteriously or secretly: *spirited away the papers.* **2.** To impart courage, animation, or determination to; inspirit. [ME < OFr. *espirit* < Lat. *spīritus*, breath < *spīrāre*, to breathe.]

spir•it•ed (spĭr′ĭ-tĭd) *adj.* **1.** Animated, vigorous, or courageous. **2.** Having a given mood or nature. Used in combination: *high-spirited.* —**spir′it•ed•ness** *n.*

spir•it•ism (spĭr′ĭ-tĭz′əm) *n.* Spiritualism. —**spir′it•ist** *n.* —**spir′it•is′tic** *adj.*

spir•it•less (spĭr′ĭt-lĭs) *adj.* Lacking energy or enthusiasm; listless. —**spir′it•less•ly** *adv.* —**spir′it•less•ness** *n.*

spirit level *n.* See **level** 7a.

spirit of turpentine *n.* See **turpentine** 1.

spirit of wine *n.* Rectified ethyl alcohol.

spir•it•ous (spĭr′ĭ-təs) *adj.* **1.** Spirituous. **2.** *Archaic* Highly refined; pure.

spir•i•tu•al (spĭr′ĭ-cho͞o-əl) *adj.* **1.** Of, relating to, consisting of, or having the nature of spirit; not tangible or material. **2.** Of, concerned with, or affecting the soul. **3.** Of, from, or relating to God; deific. **4.** Of or belonging to a church or religion; sacred. **5.** Relating to or having the nature of spirits or a spirit; supernatural. ❖ *n.* **1.** *Music* **a.** A religious folk song of African-American origin. **b.** A work composed in imitation of such a song. **2.** Religious, spiritual, or ecclesiastical matters. Often used in the plural. [ME < OFr. *spirituel* < Lat. *spīrituālis*, of breathing, spiritual < *spīritus*, breath. See SPIRIT.] —**spir′i•tu•al•ly** *adv.* —**spir′i•tu•al•ness** *n.*

spir•i•tu•al•ism (spĭr′ĭ-cho͞o-ə-lĭz′əm) *n.* **1a.** The belief that the dead communicate with the living, as through a medium; spiritism. **b.** The practices or doctrines of those holding such a belief; spiritism. **2.** A philosophy, doctrine, or religion emphasizing the spiritual aspect of being. —**spir′i•tu•al•ist** *n.* —**spir′i•tu•al•is′tic** *adj.*

spir•i•tu•al•i•ty (spĭr′ĭ-cho͞o-ăl′ĭ-tē) *n., pl.* **-ties 1.** The state, quality, manner, or fact of being spiritual. **2.** The clergy. **3.** Something, such as property or revenue, that belongs to the church or to a cleric. Often used in the plural.

spir•i•tu•al•ize (spĭr′ĭ-cho͞o-ə-līz′) *tr.v.* **-ized, -iz•ing, -iz•es 1.** To impart a spiritual nature to. **2.** To invest with or treat as having a spiritual sense or meaning. —**spir′i•tu•al•i•za′tion** (-ə-lĭ-zā′shən) *n.* —**spir′i•tu•al•iz′er** *n.*

spir•i•tu•al•ty (spĭr′ĭ-cho͞o-əl-tē) *n., pl.* **-ties** Property or reve-

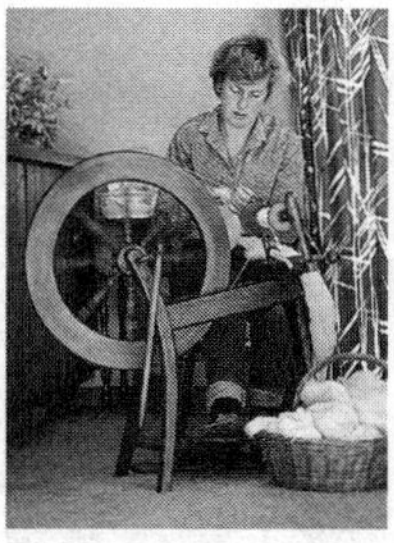

spinning wheel

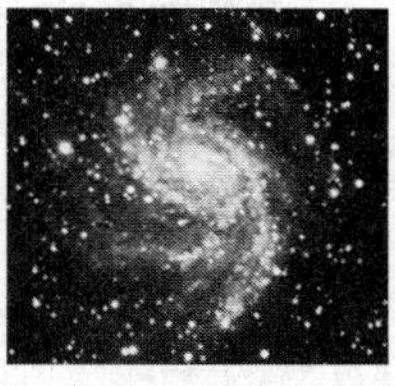

spiral galaxy
spiral galaxy NGC 6946 in Cepheus

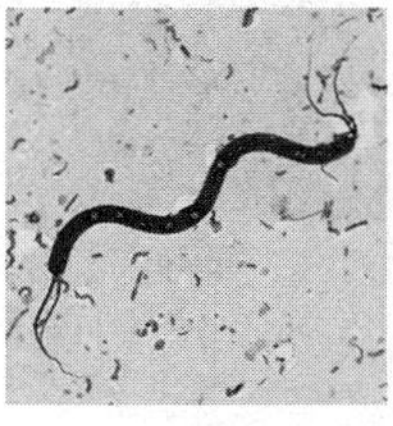

spirillum

ă	pat	oi	boy
ā	pay	ou	out
âr	care	o͝o	took
ä	father	o͞o	boot
ĕ	pet	ŭ	cut
ē	be	ûr	urge
ĭ	pit	th	thin
ī	pie	*th*	this
îr	pier	hw	which
ŏ	pot	zh	vision
ō	toe	ə	about, item
ô	paw		

Stress marks:
′ (primary);
′ (secondary), as in
lexicon (lĕk′sĭ-kŏn′)

nue belonging to the church or to a cleric; spirituality. Often used in the plural.

spir•i•tu•el also **spir•i•tu•elle** (spĭr′ĭ-cho͞o-ĕl′, spē′rē-to͞o-ĕl′, -tü-) *adj.* Having or evidencing a refined mind and wit. [Fr. < OFr., spiritual. See SPIRITUAL.]

spir•i•tu•ous (spĭr′ĭ-cho͞o-əs) *adj.* **1.** Having the nature of or containing alcohol; alcoholic. **2.** Distilled. Used of an alcoholic beverage. **—spir′i•tu•os′i•ty** (-ŏs′ĭ-tē) *n.*

spiro– *pref.* Respiration: *spirometer.* [< Lat. *spīrāre,* to breathe.]

spi•ro•chete (spī′rə-kēt′) *n.* Any of various slender spiral motile bacteria of the order Spirochaetales, many of which are pathogenic, causing syphilis and other diseases. [NLat. *Spīrochaeta,* genus name : Lat. *spīra,* coil; see SPIRE² + NLat. *chaeta,* bristle, hair; see CHAETA.] **—spi′ro•chet′al** (-kēt′l) *adj.*

spi•ro•che•to•sis (spī′rə-kē-tō′sĭs) *n., pl.* **-ses** (-sēz) Any of various diseases, such as syphilis, caused by spirochetes.

spi•ro•graph (spī′rə-grăf′) *n.* An instrument for registering the depth and rapidity of respiratory movements. **—spi′ro•graph′ic** *adj.* **—spi•rog′ra•phy** (spī-rŏg′rə-fē) *n.*

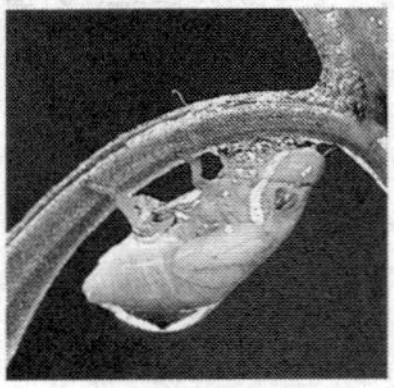

spittlebug

spi•ro•gy•ra (spī′rə-jī′rə) *n.* Any of various filamentous freshwater green algae of the genus *Spirogyra,* having chloroplasts in spirally twisted bands. [NLat. *Spīrogȳra,* genus name : Lat. *spīra,* coil; see SPIRE² + Gk. *gūros,* ring.]

spi•roid (spī′roid′) *adj.* Resembling a spiral.

spi•rom•e•ter (spī-rŏm′ĭ-tər) *n.* An instrument for measuring the volume of air entering and leaving the lungs. **—spi′ro•met′ric** (-rə-mĕt′rĭk) *adj.* **—spi•rom′e•try** *n.*

spirt (spûrt) *n. & v. Chiefly British* Variant of **spurt.**

spir•u•la (spĭr′yə-lə, spĭr′ə-) *n., pl.* **-lae** (-lē′) A small cephalopod mollusk of the genus *Spirula,* having a spirally coiled, partitioned internal shell. [LLat. *spīrula,* twisted cake, dim. of Lat. *spīra,* coil. See SPIRE².]

spi•ru•li•na (spī′rə-lē′nə, spîr′ə-) *n.* A cyanobacterium of the genus *Spirulina,* valued as a food or nutritional supplement for its high protein content. [NLat. *Spīrulīna,* genus name < LLat. *spīrula,* twisted cake. See SPIRULA.]

spit¹ (spĭt) *n.* **1.** Saliva, esp. when expectorated; spittle. **2.** The act of expectorating. **3.** Something, such as the frothy secretion of spittle bugs, that resembles spit. **4.** A brief scattered fall of rain or snow. **5.** *Informal* The perfect likeness: *He's the spit and image of his father.* ❖ *v.* **spat** (spăt) or **spit, spit•ting, spits** *—tr.* **1.** To eject from the mouth: *spat out grape seeds.* **2.** To eject as if from the mouth: *a fire spitting sparks.* **3.** To emit suddenly and forcefully: *spat out an insult.* *—intr.* **1.** To eject matter from the mouth; expectorate. **2.** To express contempt or animosity by or as if by ejecting matter from the mouth. **3.** To make a hissing or sputtering noise. **4.** To rain or snow in light scattered drops or flakes. ***—phrasal verb:* spit up** To vomit. [ME < *spitten,* to spit < OE *spittan,* ult. of imit. orig.]

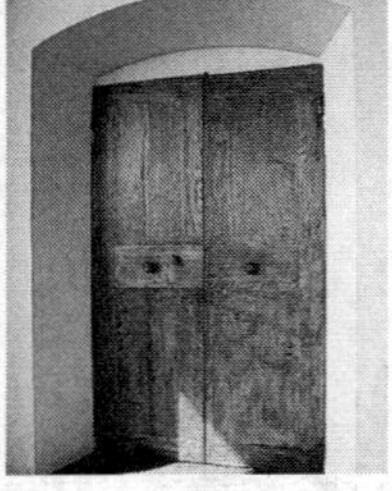

splay

spit² (spĭt) *n.* **1.** A slender pointed rod on which meat is impaled for roasting. **2.** A narrow point of land extending into a body of water. ❖ *tr.v.* **spit•ted, spit•ting, spits** To impale on or as if on a spit. [ME < OE *spitu.*]

spit•al (spĭt′l) *n. Archaic* A hospital, esp. one for contagious patients. [ME *spitel,* short for *hospital.* See HOSPITAL.]

spit and polish *n.* Attention to appearance and order, as in a military unit. **—spit′-and-pol′ish** (spĭt′n-pŏl′ĭsh) *adj.*

spit•ball (spĭt′bôl′) *n.* **1.** A piece of paper chewed, crumpled, and used as a projectile. **2.** *Baseball* An illegal pitch in which a foreign substance, such as saliva, is applied to the ball.

spit curl *n.* A spiral curl of hair pressed flat against the cheek, temple, or forehead. [< the use of saliva to fix the curl.]

spite (spīt) *n.* **1.** Malicious ill will prompting an urge to hurt or humiliate. **2.** An instance of malicious feeling. ❖ *tr.v.* **spit•ed, spit•ing, spites 1a.** To show spite toward. **b.** To vent spite on. **2a.** To fill with spite. **b.** To annoy. ***—idiom:* in spite of** Not stopped by; regardless of: *They kept going in spite of their fears.* [ME, short for *despit.* See DESPITE.]

spite•ful (spīt′fəl) *adj.* Filled with, prompted by, or showing spite; malicious. **—spite′ful•ly** *adv.* **—spite′ful•ness** *n.*

spit•fire (spĭt′fīr′) *n.* A quick-tempered or highly excitable person.

Spits•ber•gen (spĭts′bûr′gən) An island of Norway in Svalbard in the Arctic Ocean E of N Greenland.

spit•ter (spĭt′ər) *n.* **1.** One that spits: *a spitter of invective.* **2.** *Baseball* See **spitball** 2.

spit•ting cobra (spĭt′ĭng) *n.* See **ringhals.**

spitting image *n.* A perfect likeness or counterpart. [Prob. < alteration of *spitten,* dialectal p. part. of SPIT¹ (the close resemblance of one person to another being likened in folk sayings to the former person having been spat out of the latter's mouth).]

spit•tle (spĭt′l) *n.* **1.** Spit; saliva. **2.** The frothy liquid secreted by spittlebugs. [ME *spitel,* alteration of *spatel* < OE *spātl.*]

spit•tle•bug (spĭt′l-bŭg′) *n.* Any of various leaping homopterous insects of the family Cercopidae, the nymphs of which form frothy masses of liquid on plant stems.

spit•toon (spĭ-to͞on′) *n.* A bowl-shaped, usu. metal vessel, often with a funnel-shaped cover, into which tobacco chewers periodically spit. [SPIT¹ + *-oon,* as in BALLOON.]

spitz (spĭts) *n.* A dog of any of several northern breeds, such as the Samoyed, having a long, thick, usu. white coat, pointed muzzle and ears, and a tail curled over the back. [Ger. *Spitz* < *spitz,* pointed < MHGer. *spiz* < OHGer. *spizzi.*]

spiv (spĭv) *n. Chiefly British Slang* **1.** One, usu. unemployed, who lives by one's wits. **2.** One who shirks work or responsibility; a slacker. [Dialectal *spif,* dandified, dandy.]

splanch•nic (splăngk′nĭk) *adj.* Of or relating to the viscera; visceral: *a splanchnic nerve.* [NLat. *splanchnicus* < Gk. *splankhnikos* < *splankhna,* inward parts.]

splash (splăsh) *v.* **splashed, splash•ing, splash•es** *—tr.* **1.** To propel or scatter (a fluid) about in flying masses. **2.** To scatter fluid onto in flying masses; wet, stain, or soil with flying fluid. **3.** To cause (something) to scatter fluid in flying masses: *splashed their hands in the water.* **4.** To make (one's way) with or by scattering of fluid. **5.** To apply patches or spots of a contrasting, usu. bright color to. **6.** To display or publicize very noticeably. *—intr.* **1a.** To cause a fluid to scatter in flying masses: *splashed about in the pool.* **b.** To fall into or move through fluid with this effect: *We splashed through the waves.* **2a.** To move, spill, or fly about in scattered masses. **b.** To produce a sound or sight associated with this effect. ❖ *n.* **1.** The act or sound of splashing. **2a.** A flying mass of fluid. **b.** A small amount, esp. of a fluid. **3.** A marking produced by or as if by scattered fluid. **4.** A great though often short-lived impression; a stir. [Prob. alteration of PLASH.] **—splash′er** *n.*

splash•board (splăsh′bôrd′, -bōrd′) *n.* **1.** A structure that protects the upper part of a vehicle from splashes of mud. **2.** *Nautical* A screen on a boat to keep water from splashing onto the deck. **3.** A board for closing a spillway or sluice.

splash•down (splăsh′doun′) *n.* The landing of a spacecraft or missile in water.

splash•guard (splăsh′gärd′) *n.* See **mudguard.**

splash•y (splăsh′ē) *adj.* **-i•er, -i•est 1.** Making or likely to make splashes. **2.** Covered with splashes of color. **3.** Showy; ostentatious. See Syns at **showy. —splash′i•ly** *adv.* **—splash′i•ness** *n.*

splat¹ (splăt) *n.* A slat of wood, as one in the middle of a chair back. [Perh. < ME *splatten,* to split open, perh. < Med.Lat. *splattāre,* of LGer. orig.]

splat² (splăt) *n.* A smacking or splashing noise. ❖ *adv.* With a smacking or splashing noise: *fell splat on the floor.* [Imit.]

splat•ter (splăt′ər) *v.* **-tered, -ter•ing, -ters** *—tr.* To spatter (something), esp. to soil with splashes of liquid. *—intr.* To spatter, esp. to move or fall so as to cause splashes. ❖ *n.* A splash of liquid. [Perh. blend of SPLASH and SPATTER.]

splay (splā) *adj.* **1.** Spread or turned out. **2.** Clumsy or clumsily formed; awkward. ❖ *n. Architecture* An oblique angle or bevel given to the sides of an opening in a wall so that the opening is wider on one side of the wall than on the other. ❖ *v.* **splayed, splay•ing, splays** *—tr.* **1.** To spread (the limbs, for example) out or apart, esp. clumsily. **2.** To make slanting or sloping; bevel. **3.** To dislocate (a bone). Used of an animal. *—intr.* **1.** To be spread out or apart. **2.** To slant or slope. [< ME *splayen,* to spread out, short for *displayen.* See DISPLAY.]

splay•foot (splā′fo͝ot′) *n.* **1.** A physical deformity characterized by abnormally flat and turned-out feet. **2.** A foot so affected. **—splay′foot′ed** *adj.*

spleen (splēn) *n.* **1a.** A large, highly vascular lymphoid organ, lying in the human body to the left of the stomach below the diaphragm, serving to filter and store blood and produce lymphocytes. **b.** A homologous organ or tissue in other vertebrates. **2.** *Obsolete* This organ conceived as the seat of emotions or passions. **3.** Ill temper: *vent one's spleen.* **4.** *Archaic* Melancholy. **5.** *Obsolete* A whim; a caprice. [ME *splen* < OFr. *esplen* < Lat. *splēn* < Gk.] **—spleen′y** *adj.*

spleen•ful (splēn′fəl) *adj.* Affected by or filled with spleen.

spleen•wort (splēn′wûrt′, -wôrt′) *n.* Any of numerous widely distributed evergreen ferns of the genus *Asplenium,* having undivided to featherlike fronds and oblong to linear sori.

splen•dent (splĕn′dənt) *adj.* **1.** Shining or lustrous; brilliant. **2.** Admired by many; illustrious. [ME < OFr. *esplendent* < Lat. *splendēns, splendent-,* pr. part. of *splendēre,* to shine.]

splen•did (splĕn′dĭd) *adj.* **1.** Brilliant with light or color; radiant: *a splendid field of poppies.* **2.** Magnificent; grand; sumptuous: *splendid costumes.* **3.** Outstanding; surpassing: *a splendid character.* **4.** Very good or satisfying: *a splendid day.* [Lat. *splendidus* < *splendēre,* to shine.] **—splen′did•ly** *adv.* **—splen′did•ness** *n.*

splen•dif•er•ous (splĕn-dĭf′ər-əs) *adj.* Splendid. [ME < Med.Lat. *splendiferus* < LLat. *splendōrifer* : Lat. *splendor,* splendor; see SPLENDOR + Lat. *-fer,* -fer.]

splen•dor (splĕn′dər) *n.* **1.** Great light or luster; brilliance. **2a.** Magnificent appearance or display; grandeur. **b.** Something grand or magnificent. **3.** Great fame; glory. [ME *splendoure* < OFr. *splendour* < Lat. *splendor* < *splendēre,* to shine.] **—splen′dor•ous, splen′drous** (splĕn′drəs) *adj.*

splen•dour (splĕn′dər) *n. Chiefly British* Variant of **splendor.**

sple•nec•to•my (splĭ-nĕk′tə-mē) *n., pl.* **-mies** Surgical removal of the spleen. **—sple•nec′to•mize′** (-mīz′) *v.*

sple•net•ic (splĭ-nĕt′ĭk) also **sple•net•i•cal** (-ĭ-kəl) *adj.* **1.** Of or relating to the spleen. **2.** Ill-humored or irritable. ❖ *n.* A person regarded as irritable. [LLat. *splēnēticus* < Lat. *splēn,* spleen. See SPLEEN.] **—sple•net′i•cal•ly** *adv.*

splen•ic (splĕn′ĭk) *adj.* Of, in, near, or relating to the spleen.

sple•ni•us (splē′nē-əs) *n., pl.* **-ni•i** (-nē-ī′) Either of two muscles of the back of the neck that rotate and extend the head and neck. [NLat. *splēnius* < Lat. *splēnium*, patch, plaster (< its shape) < Gk. *splēnion* < *splēn*, spleen.]

spleno– or **splen–** *pref.* Spleen: *splenomegaly.* [Gk. *splēno–* < *splēn*, spleen.]

sple•no•meg•a•ly (splē′nō-měg′ə-lē, splěn′ō-) *n., pl.* **-lies** Enlargement of the spleen.

splice (splīs) *tr.v.* **spliced, splic•ing, splic•es 1a.** To join (two pieces of film, for example) at the ends. **b.** To join (ropes, for example) by interweaving strands. **2.** To join (pieces of wood) by overlapping and binding at the ends. **3.** To join together or insert (segments of DNA or RNA) so as to form new genetic combinations or alter a genetic structure. **4.** *Slang* To marry. ❖ *n.* **1.** A joining by splicing. **2.** A place where parts have been spliced. [Obsolete Du. *splissen* < MDu.] **—splic′er** *n.*

spliff (splĭf) *n. Slang* A marijuana cigarette. [Jamaican E.]

spline (splīn) *n.* **1a.** Any of a series of projections on a shaft that fit into slots on a corresponding shaft, enabling both to rotate together. **b.** The groove or slot for such a projection. **2.** A flexible piece of wood, hard rubber, or metal used in drawing curves. **3.** A wooden or metal strip; a slat. [?]

splint (splĭnt) *n.* **1.** A thin piece split off from a larger one; a splinter. **2a.** A rigid device used to prevent motion of a joint or of the ends of a fractured bone. **b.** A dental appliance to protect teeth from grinding or moving out of place. **3.** A thin flexible wooden strip, such as one used in basketry. **4.** A plate or strip of metal. **5.** A bony enlargement of a horse's cannon bone or splint bone. ❖ *tr.v.* **splint•ed, splint•ing, splints** To support or restrict with or as if with a splint. [ME < MDu. or MLGer. *splinte*.]

splint bone *n.* Either of two small metacarpal or metatarsal bones in horses or related animals.

splin•ter (splĭn′tər) *n.* **1.** A sharp slender piece, as of wood or metal, split or broken off from a main body. **2.** A splinter group. ❖ *v.* **-tered, -ter•ing, -ters** *—intr.* To split or break into sharp slender pieces. See Syns at **break.** *—tr.* To cause to splinter. [ME < MDu.] **—splin′ter•y** *adj.*

splinter group *n.* A group, such as a religious sect or political faction, that has broken away from a parent group.

split (splĭt) *v.* **split, split•ting, splits** *—tr.* **1.** To divide from end to end or along the grain by or as if by a sharp blow. See Syns at **tear**[1]. **2a.** To break, burst, or rip apart with force; rend. See Syns at **break. b.** To affect with force in a way that suggests tearing apart: *A lightning bolt split the night sky.* **3.** To separate (people or groups, for example); disunite. **4.** To divide and share: *split a dessert.* **5.** To divide, as for convenience or proper ordering: *split the project up.* **6.** To separate (leather, for example) into layers. **7.** To mark (a vote or ballot) in favor of candidates from different parties. **8.** To divide (stock) by issuing multiples of the existing stock with a corresponding reduction in the price of each share, so that the total value of the stock is unchanged. **9.** *Sports* To win half the games of (a series or double-header). **10.** *Slang* To depart from; leave. *—intr.* **1.** To become separated into parts, esp. to undergo lengthwise division. **2.** To become broken or ripped apart, esp. from internal pressure. **3.** To become or admit of being divided: *split up into teams.* **4.** *Informal* To become divided or part company as a result of discord or disagreement. **5.** To divide or share something with others. **6.** *Slang* To depart; leave. ❖ *n.* **1.** The act of splitting or the result of it. **2.** A breach or rupture in a group. **3.** A splinter. **4.** Something broken and portioned out; a share. **5.** *Sports* The recorded time for an interval or segment of a race. **6.** A strip of flexible wood used for making baskets. **7a.** A bottle of an alcoholic or carbonated beverage half the usual size. **b.** A drink of half the usual quantity. **c.** A half pint. **8.** A dessert of sliced fruit, ice cream, and toppings. **9.** An acrobatic feat in which the legs are stretched out straight in opposite directions at right angles to the trunk. Often used in the plural. **10.** An arrangement of bowling pins left standing, in which two or more pins remain standing with one or more pins between them knocked down. **11.** A single thickness of a split hide. ❖ *adj.* **1.** Having been divided or separated. **2.** Fissured longitudinally; cleft. **3a.** Quoted in 16ths rather than in 8ths. Used of stocks. **b.** Having been split. Used of stocks. **—idiom: split hairs** To see or make trivial distinctions; quibble. [Du. *splitten* < MDu.] **—split′ter** *n.*

Split (splĭt) A city of SW Croatia on the Dalmatian coast of the Adriatic Sea; founded as a Roman colony. Pop. 200,459.

split-brain (splĭt′brān′) *adj.* Of, relating to, or subjected to surgical separation of the hemispheres of the brain by severing the corpus callosum: *split-brain operations.*

split decision *n.* A decision declaring the winner of a boxing match in which the judges and referee are not unanimous in their opinions.

split end *n.* **1.** *Football* A pass receiver who lines up apart from the rest of the formation. **2.** The end of a hair that has split into strands.

split-fin•gered fastball (splĭt′fĭng′gərd) *n. Baseball* A fastball thrown with the ball held between the index and middle finger, dropping sharply as it nears home plate.

split infinitive *n.* An infinitive verb form with an element, usu. an adverb, interposed between *to* and the verb form, as in *to boldly go.*

split-lev•el (splĭt′lěv′əl) *adj.* Having the floors of adjoining rooms separated by about half a story: *a split-level ranch house.* **—split′-lev′el** *n.*

split personality *n.* **1.** Multiple personality. Not in scientific use. **2.** Schizophrenia. Not in scientific use.

split rail *n.* A fence rail split lengthwise from a log. **—split′-rail′** (splĭt′rāl′) *adj.*

split second *n.* An instant; a flash. [Short for *split second hands,* a stopwatch with two independent second hands.]

splits•ville (splĭts′vĭl′) *Slang adv. & adj.* In or into a state of separation or breakup. ❖ *n.* A state of separation or breakup.

split ticket *n.* A ballot cast for candidates of two or more political parties.

split•ting (splĭt′ĭng) *adj.* Very severe: *a splitting headache.*

splotch (splŏch) *n.* An irregularly shaped spot, stain, or colored or discolored area. ❖ *tr.v.* **splotched, splotch•ing, splotch•es** To mark with splotches or a splotch. [Perh. blend of SPOT, BLOT[1] and BOTCH.] **—splotch′i•ness** *n.* **—splotch′y** *adj.*

splurge (splûrj) *v.* **splurged, splurg•ing, splurg•es** *—intr.* **1.** To indulge in an extravagant expense or luxury. **2.** To be showy or ostentatious. *—tr.* To spend extravagantly or wastefully. ❖ *n.* **1.** An extravagant display. **2.** An expensive indulgence; a spree. [Perh. blend of SPLASH and SURGE.] **—splurg′y** *adj.*

splut•ter (splŭt′ər) *v.* **-tered, -ter•ing, -ters** *—intr.* **1.** To make repeated or sporadic spitting sounds. **2.** To speak incoherently, as when confused or angry. *—tr.* To utter or express hastily and incoherently. ❖ *n.* A spluttering noise. [Perh. alteration of SPUTTER.] **—splut′ter•er** *n.* **—splut′ter•y** *adj.*

Spock (spŏk), **Benjamin McLane** 1903–98. Amer. pediatrician who wrote *Baby and Child Care* (orig. published 1946).

Spode (spōd) A trademark used for a brand of fine china and earthenware.

spod•u•mene (spŏj′ə-mēn′) *n.* A greenish to pinkish mineral, LiAlSi₂O₆, used as a lithium ore and in transparent varieties as a gemstone. [Fr. *spodumène* < Ger. *Spodumen* < Gk. *spodoumenos,* pr. part. of *spodousthai,* to be burned to ashes < *spodos,* wood ashes (the mineral becoming gray in air).]

spoil (spoil) *v.* **spoiled** or **spoilt** (spoilt), **spoil•ing, spoils** *—tr.* **1a.** To impair the value or quality of. **b.** To damage irreparably; ruin. **2.** To impair the completeness, perfection, or unity of; flaw grievously. **3.** To harm the character, nature, or attitude of by oversolicitude, overindulgence, or excessive praise. **4.** *Archaic* **a.** To plunder; despoil. **b.** To take by force. *—intr.* **1.** To become unfit for use or consumption, as from decay. Used esp. of perishables, such as food. **2.** To pillage. ❖ *n.* **1. spoils a.** Goods or property seized from a victim after a conflict. **b.** Incidental benefits reaped by a winner, esp. political patronage enjoyed by a party or candidate. **2.** An object of plunder; prey. **3.** Refuse material removed from an excavation. **4.** *Archaic* The act of plundering; spoliation. **—phrasal verb: spoil for** To be eager for. [ME *spoilen,* to plunder < OFr. *espoillier* < Lat. *spoliāre* < *spolium,* booty.]

spoil•age (spoi′lĭj) *n.* **1a.** The process of becoming spoiled. **b.** The condition of being spoiled. **2a.** Something spoiled. **b.** The degree to which something has been spoiled.

spoil•er (spoi′lər) *n.* **1.** One who seizes spoils or booty. **2.** Something that causes spoilage. **3a.** A long narrow hinged plate on the upper surface of an airplane wing that reduces lift and increases drag when raised. **b.** An air deflector mounted usu. at the rear of an automobile to reduce lift at high speeds. **4.** A candidate for office who has little chance of winning but may prevent another candidate from winning. **5.** A published piece of information that divulges a surprise, such as a plot twist in a movie.

spoil•sport (spoil′spôrt′, -spōrt′) *n.* One who mars the pleasure of others.

spoils system *n.* The postelection practice of rewarding the winner's loyal supporters with public offices.

Spo•kane (spō-kăn′) A city of E WA near the ID border on the falls of the **Spokane River**, c. 193 km (120 mi). Pop. 195,629.

spoke¹ (spōk) *n.* **1.** One of the rods or braces connecting the hub and rim of a wheel. **2.** *Nautical* One of the handles projecting from the rim of a ship's wheel. **3.** A rod or stick that may be inserted into a wheel to prevent it from turning. **4.** A rung of a ladder. ❖ *tr.v.* **spoked, spok·ing, spokes 1.** To equip with spokes. **2.** To impede (a wheel) by inserting a rod. [ME < OE *spāca.*]

spoke² (spōk) *v.* Past tense of **speak. 2.** *Archaic* A past participle of **speak.**

spo·ken (spō′kən) *v.* Past participle of **speak.** ❖ *adj.* **1.** Expressed orally; uttered. **2.** Speaking or using speech in a certain way or voice. Often used in combination: *plainspoken.*

spoke·shave (spōk′shāv′) *n.* A drawknife of a design originally used for shaping spokes, now used for making rounded edges.

spokes·man (spōks′mən) *n.* A man who speaks on behalf of another or others. See Usage Note at **man.** [Prob. *spoke,* p. part. of SPEAK + MAN.]

spokes·per·son (spōks′pûr′sən) *n.* A spokesman or a spokeswoman. See Usage Note at **man.**

spokes·wom·an (spōks′wŏŏm′ən) *n.* A woman who speaks on behalf of another or others. See Usage Note at **man.**

spo·li·a·tion (spō′lē-ā′shən) *n.* **1.** The act of despoiling or plundering. **2.** Seizure of neutral vessels at sea by a belligerent power in time of war. **3.** *Law* Intentional alteration or destruction of a document. [ME *spoliacioun* < AN < Lat. *spoliātiō, spoliātiōn-* < *spoliātus,* p. part. of *spoliāre,* to despoil. See SPOIL.] —**spo′li·a′tor** *n.*

spon·da·ic (spŏn-dā′ĭk) *adj.* Of or written in spondees. [Fr. *spondaïque* < LLat. *spondaicus,* alteration of *spondīacus* < Gk. *spondeiakos* < *spondeios,* spondee. See SPONDEE.]

spon·dee (spŏn′dē′) *n.* A metrical foot consisting of two long or stressed syllables. [ME *sponde* < OFr. *spondee* < Lat. *spondēum* < neut. of *spondēus,* of libations, spondaic < Gk. *spondeios* < *spondē,* libation. See spend- in App.]

spon·dy·li·tis (spŏn′dl-ī′tĭs) *n.* Inflammation of the vertebrae. [Gk. *spondulos,* vertebra + -ITIS.]

sponge (spŭnj) *n.* **1a.** Any of numerous sessile, chiefly marine invertebrate animals of the phylum Porifera, having a porous fibrous skeleton and often forming irregularly shaped colonies attached to an underwater surface. **b.** The light fibrous flexible absorbent skeleton of certain of these organisms, used for bathing and cleaning. **2a.** A porous piece of plastic, rubber, or other material, similar in absorbency to this skeleton and used for the same purposes. **b.** Metal in a porous, brittle form, as after the removal of other metals in processing, used as a raw material in manufacturing. **3.** A gauze pad used to absorb blood and other fluids, as in surgery. **4.** A small contraceptive pad that contains a spermicide and is placed against the cervix. **5.** Dough that has been or is being leavened. **6.** A light cake, such as sponge cake. **7.** A sponge bath. **8.** One who habitually depends on others for one's own maintenance. **9a.** *Informal* A glutton. **b.** *Slang* A drunkard. ❖ *v.* **sponged, spong·ing, spong·es** —*tr.* **1.** To moisten, wipe, or clean with or as if with a sponge: *sponge off the table.* **2.** To wipe out; erase. **3.** To absorb with or as if with a sponge: *sponge up the mess.* **4.** *Informal* To obtain free: *sponge a meal.* —*intr.* **1.** To fish for sponges. **2.** *Informal* To live by relying on the generosity of others: *sponged off her parents.* [ME < OE < Lat. *spongia* < Gk. *spongiā* < *spongos.*]

sponge bath *n.* A bath in which the bather washes with a wet sponge or washcloth without immersing.

sponge cake *n.* A very light porous cake made of flour, sugar, beaten eggs, and flavoring and containing no shortening.

spong·er (spŭn′jər) *n.* **1.** One that gathers sponges. **2.** *Informal* A person who sponges on others; a parasite.

sponge rubber *n.* A soft porous rubber used in toys, cushions, gaskets, and weather stripping and as a vibration dampener.

spon·gi·form (spŭn′jī-fôrm′) *adj.* **1.** Resembling a sponge; spongy. **2.** Of or being one of a group of transmissible degenerative encephalopathies characterized by the spongelike appearance of brain tissue. [Lat. *spongia,* sponge; see SPONGE + –FORM.]

spon·gin (spŭn′jĭn) *n.* A horny sulfur-containing protein related to keratin that forms the skeletal structure of certain classes of sponges.

spong·y (spŭn′jē) *adj.* **-i·er, -i·est** Resembling a sponge in elasticity, absorbency, or porousness. —**spong′i·ness** *n.*

spongy mesophyll *n.* A leaf tissue consisting of loosely arranged, chloroplast-bearing, usu. lobed cells.

spon·son (spŏn′sən) *n.* **1.** Any of several structures that project from the side of a boat or ship, esp. a gun platform. **2.** A short curved air-filled projection on the hull of a seaplane, imparting stability in the water. [Perh. alteration of EXPANSION.]

spon·sor (spŏn′sər) *n.* **1.** One who assumes responsibility for another person or a group during a period of instruction, apprenticeship, or probation. **2.** One who vouches for the suitability of a candidate for admission. **3.** A legislator who proposes and urges adoption of a bill. **4.** One who presents a candidate for baptism or confirmation; a godparent. **5.** One that finances a project or an event carried out by another, esp. a business enterprise that pays for radio or television programming in return for advertising time. ❖ *tr.v.* **-sored, -sor·ing, -sors** To act as a sponsor for. [LLat. *spōnsor,* sponsor in baptism < Lat., surety < *spōnsus,* p.

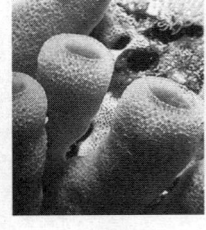

sponge
pink tube sponge

part. of *spondēre,* to pledge. See spend- in App.] —**spon·so′ri·al** (-sôr′ē-əl, -sōr′-) *adj.* —**spon′sor·ship′** *n.*

spon·ta·ne·i·ty (spŏn′tə-nē′ĭ-tē, -nā′-) *n., pl.* **-ties 1.** The quality or condition of being spontaneous. **2.** Spontaneous behavior, impulse, or movement.

spon·ta·ne·ous (spŏn-tā′nē-əs) *adj.* **1.** Happening or arising without apparent external cause; self-generated. **2.** Arising from a natural inclination or impulse and not from external incitement or constraint. **3.** Unconstrained and unstudied in manner or behavior. **4.** Growing without cultivation or human labor. [< LLat. *spontāneus,* of one's own accord < Lat. *sponte.*] —**spon·ta′ne·ous·ly** *adv.* —**spon·ta′ne·ous·ness** *n.*

spontaneous abortion *n.* See **miscarriage** 1.

spontaneous combustion *n.* Ignition of a substance caused by a localized heat-increasing reaction between the oxidant and the fuel and not involving an outside source of heat.

spontaneous generation *n.* See **abiogenesis.**

spon·toon (spŏn-tōōn′) *n.* A short pike carried by infantry officers and sergeants in the 18th century. [Fr. *sponton* < Ital. *spuntone* : s-, intensive pref.; see SFORZANDO + *puntone,* kind of weapon, augmentative of *punto,* point (< Lat. *pūnctum* < neut. p. part. of *pungere,* to pierce, prick).]

spoof (spōōf) *n.* **1.** Nonsense; tomfoolery. **2.** A hoax. **3.** A gentle satirical imitation; a light parody. ❖ *tr.v.* **spoofed, spoof·ing, spoofs 1.** To deceive. **2.** To satirize gently. [After *Spoof,* game invented by Arthur Roberts (1852–1933), British comedian.]

spook (spōōk) *n.* **1.** *Informal* A ghost; a specter. **2.** *Slang* A secret agent. ❖ *v.* **spooked, spook·ing, spooks** *Informal* —*tr.* **1.** To haunt. **2.** To startle and cause nervous activity in; frighten. —*intr.* To become frightened and nervous. [Du. < MDu. *spooc.*]

spook·y (spōō′kē) *adj.* **-i·er, -i·est** *Informal* **1.** Suggestive of ghosts or a ghost; eerie. **2.** Easily startled; skittish. —**spook′i·ly** *adv.* —**spook′i·ness** *n.*

spool¹ (spōōl) *n.* **1a.** A cylinder on which wire, thread, or string is wound. **b.** The amount of wire, thread, or string wound on a spool. **c.** Something like a spool in shape or function. **2.** A reel for magnetic tape. ❖ *tr. & intr.v.* **spooled, spool·ing, spools** To wind or be wound on or off a spool. [ME *spole* < ONFr. *espole* and < MDu. and MLGer. *spoele* (ONFr. < MDu.).]

spool² (spōōl) *tr.v.* **spooled, spool·ing, spools** To store (data sent to a printer) in a spooler. [*s(imultaneous) p(eripheral) o(perations) o(n) l(ine).*]

spool·er (spōō′lər) *n.* A computer program that sequences print jobs by temporarily storing them in a buffer and sending each to the printer when the printer is able to process it.

spoon (spōōn) *n.* **1.** A utensil consisting of a small, shallow bowl on a handle, used in preparing, serving, or eating food. **2.** Something similar to this utensil or its bowl, as: **a.** A shiny curved metallic fishing lure. **b.** A paddle or an oar with a curved blade. **3.** *Sports* The three wood golf club. ❖ *v.* **spooned, spoon·ing, spoons** —*tr.* **1.** To lift, scoop up, or carry with or as if with a spoon. **2.** *Sports & Games* To shove or scoop (a ball) into the air. —*intr.* **1.** To fish with a spoon lure. **2.** *Sports & Games* To give a ball an upward scoop. **3.** *Informal* To engage in amorous behavior, such as caressing. [ME < OE *spōn,* chip of wood.]

spoon·bill (spōōn′bĭl′) *n.* **1a.** Any of several long-legged wading birds similar to the ibis but having a long flat bill with a broadly spatulate tip. **b.** Any of various broad-billed ducks, such as the shoveler. **2.** See **paddlefish.**

spoon bread *n.* *Chiefly Southern US* A soft light bread made with cornmeal, eggs, butter, and milk, baked in a bowl.

spoon·drift (spōōn′drĭft′) *n.* See **spindrift.** [Obsolete *spoon,* to run before the wind + DRIFT.]

spoon·er·ism (spōō′nə-rĭz′əm) *n.* A transposition of sounds of two or more words, esp. a ludicrous one, such as *Let me sew you to your sheet* for *Let me show you to your seat.* [After William Archibald *Spooner* (1844–1930), British cleric.]

spoon-feed (spōōn′fēd′) *tr.v.* **-fed** (-fĕd′), **-feed·ing, -feeds 1.** To feed (another) with a spoon. **2.** To treat (another) so as to discourage independence, as by overindulgence. **3a.** To inform or teach (another) in an oversimplified way. **b.** To provide (knowledge or information) in an oversimplified way.

spoon·ful (spōōn′fŏŏl′) *n., pl.* **-fuls** The amount that a spoon holds.

spoon·y also **spoon·ey** (spōō′nē) *adj.* **-i·er, -i·est 1.** Enamored in a silly or sentimental way. **2.** Feebly sentimental.

spoor (spōōr) *n.* The track or trail of an animal, esp. a wild animal. ❖ *tr. & intr.v.* **spoored, spoor·ing, spoors** To track (an animal) by following its spoor or engage in such tracking. [Afr. < MDu. See **spera-** in App.]

Spor·a·des (spôr′ə-dēz′, spô-rä′thēs) Two island groups of Greece in the Aegean Sea, consisting of the **Northern Sporades** off the central mainland and the **Southern Sporades** off the coast of Turkey.

spo·rad·ic (spə-răd′ĭk, spô-) also **spo·rad·i·cal** (-ĭ-kəl) *adj.* **1.** Occurring irregularly; having no pattern or order in time. See Syns at **periodic. 2.** Appearing singly or at widely scattered localities. **3.** Isolated; unique. [Med.Lat. *sporadicus,* scattered < Gk. *sporadikos* < *sporas, sporad-*.] —**spo·rad′i·cal·ly** *adv.*

spo·ran·gi·o·phore (spə-răn′jē-ə-fôr′, -fōr′) *n.* **1.** A specialized branch bearing one or more sporangia. **2.** A stalk of a sporangium. [SPORANGI(UM) + –PHORE.]

spo•ran•gi•um (spə-răn′jē-əm) *n., pl.* **-gi•a** (-jē-ə) A single-celled or many-celled structure in which spores are produced, as in fungi and ferns. [NLat. *sporangium* : SPOR(O)– + Gk. *angeion*, vessel; see ANGIO–.] —**spo•ran′gi•al** (-jē-əl) *adj.*

spore (spôr, spōr) *n.* **1.** A small, usu. single-celled reproductive body that is capable of growing into a new organism, produced esp. by certain bacteria and algae, and by all nonseedbearing plants. **2.** Either of the similar reproductive bodies in angiosperms and gymnosperms that give rise to the plant structures that produce male or female gametes. **3.** A dormant nonreproductive body formed by certain bacteria in response to adverse environmental conditions. ❖ *intr.v.* **spored, spor•ing, spores** To produce spores. [Gk. *sporā*, seed.]

spore case *n.* See **sporangium.**

spo•ri•cide (spôr′ĭ-sīd′, spōr′-) *n.* A substance used to kill spores. —**spo′ri•cid′al** (-sīd′l) *adj.*

spo•rif•er•ous (spə-rĭf′ər-əs, spô-, spō-) *adj.* Producing spores.

sporo– or **spor–** *pref.* Spore: *sporocyst.* [Gk. < *sporā*, seed.]

spo•ro•carp (spôr′ə-kärp′, spōr′-) *n.* **1.** A multicellular structure in which spores are formed, esp. in red algae and certain fungi and slime molds. **2.** A receptacle containing sporangia.

spo•ro•cyst (spôr′ə-sĭst′, spōr′-) *n.* **1.** A resting cell that produces asexual plant spores. **2a.** A protective case or cyst in which sporozoites develop and from which they are transferred to different hosts. **b.** A sporozoite enclosed in such a case. **3.** A saclike larval stage in many trematode worms.

spo•ro•gen•e•sis (spôr′ə-jĕn′ĭ-sĭs, spōr′-) *n.* **1.** Production or formation of spores. **2.** Reproduction by means of spores. —**spo′ro•gen′ic** (-jĕn′ĭk), **spo•rog′e•nous** (spə-rŏj′ə-nəs, spô-, spō-) *adj.*

spo•rog•o•ny (spə-rŏg′ə-nē, spô-, spō-) *n.* Reproduction by multiple fission of a spore or zygote, characteristic of many sporozoans.

spo•ro•phore (spôr′ə-fôr′, spōr′ə-fōr′) *n.* A spore-bearing structure, esp. in fungi.

spo•ro•phyll (spôr′ə-fĭl′, spōr′-) *n.* A leaf or leaflike organ that bears spores.

spo•ro•phyte (spôr′ə-fīt′, spōr′-) *n.* The spore-producing phase in the life cycle of a plant that exhibits alternation of generations. —**spo′ro•phyt′ic** (-fĭt′ĭk) *adj.*

–sporous *suff.* Having a specified number or kind of spores: *heterosporous.*

spo•ro•zo•an (spôr′ə-zō′ən, spōr′-) *n.* Any of numerous parasitic protozoans of the class Sporozoa, most of which reproduce sexually and asexually in alternate generations by means of spores. [< NLat. *Sporozōa*, class name : SPORO– + *-zōa*, pl. of *-zōon*, -zoon.] —**spo′ro•zo′an** *adj.*

spo•ro•zo•ite (spôr′ə-zō′īt′, spōr′-) *n.* Any of the minute undeveloped sporozoans produced by sporogony.

spor•ran (spôr′ən, spŏr′-) *n.* A leather or fur pouch traditionally worn at the front of the kilt. [Sc. Gael. *sporan* < MIr. *sparán*, poss. < LLat. *bursa*, bag. See BURSA.]

sport (spôrt, spōrt) *n.* **1a.** Physical activity that is governed by a set of rules or customs and often engaged in competitively. **b.** A particular form of this activity. **2.** An active pastime; a form of recreation. **3a.** Mockery; jest. **b.** An object of mockery, jest, or play. **c.** A joking mood or attitude. **4a.** One known for the manner of one's acceptance of rules, esp. of a game, or of a difficult situation. **b.** *Informal* One who accepts rules or difficult situations well. **c.** *Informal* A pleasant companion. **5.** *Informal* **a.** A person who lives a jolly, extravagant life. **b.** A gambler at sporting events. **6.** *Biology* An organism that shows a marked change from the normal type or parent stock, typically as a result of mutation. **7.** *Obsolete* Amorous dalliance; lovemaking. ❖ *v.* **sport•ed, sport•ing, sports** —*intr.* **1.** To play or frolic. **2.** To joke or trifle. **3.** *Biology* To mutate. —*tr.* To display or show off. ❖ *adj.* or **sports 1.** Of, relating to, or appropriate for sports. **2.** Designed or appropriate for outdoor or informal wear. [ME *sporte*, short for *disporte* < OFr. *desport*, pleasure < *desporter*, to divert. See DISPORT.] —**sport′ful** *adj.* —**sport′ful•ly** *adv.* —**sport′ful•ness** *n.*

sport fish *n.* A fish prized for the sport involved in catching it.

sport•fish•ing (spôrt′fĭsh′ĭng, spōrt′-) *n.* The sport of catching fish using a rod and reel.

sport•ing (spôr′tĭng, spōr′-) *adj.* **1.** Used in or appropriate for sports: *sporting goods.* **2.** Characterized by sportsmanship. **3.** Of or associated with gambling. —**sport′ing•ly** *adv.*

sporting chance *n. Informal* A fair chance for success.

spor•tive (spôr′tĭv, spōr′-) *adj.* **1.** Playful; frolicsome. **2.** Relating to or interested in sports. **3.** *Archaic* Amorous or wanton. —**spor′tive•ly** *adv.* —**spor′tive•ness** *n.*

sports bra *n.* A garment providing support and protection for the breasts, worn esp. during athletic activity.

sports car *n.* An automobile equipped for racing, esp. an aerodynamically shaped one-passenger or two-passenger vehicle having a low center of gravity and steering and suspension designed for precise control at high speeds.

sports•cast (spôrts′kăst′, spōrts′-) *n.* A broadcast of a sports event or of sports news. [*sports*, pl. of SPORT + (BROAD)CAST.] —**sports′cast′er** *n.*

sports•man (spôrts′mən, spōrts′-) *n.* **1.** A man who is active in sports. **2.** A person whose conduct and attitude exhibit sportsmanship. —**sports′man•like′**, **sports′man•ly** *adj.*

sports•man•ship (spôrts′mən-shĭp′, spōrts′-) *n.* **1.** The fact or practice of participating in sports or a sport. **2.** Conduct and attitude viewed as befitting athletes, as fair play.

sports medicine *n.* The branch of medicine that deals with injuries or illnesses resulting from sports and athletics.

sports•wear (spôrts′wâr′, spōrts′-) *n.* Clothes designed for comfort and casual wear.

sports•wom•an (spôrts′wo͝om′ən, spōrts′-) *n.* **1.** A woman who is active in sports. **2.** A woman whose conduct and attitude exhibit sportsmanship.

sports•writ•er (spôrts′rī′tər, spōrts′-) *n.* A person who writes about sports, esp. for a newspaper or magazine. —**sports′-writ′ing** *n.*

sport-u•til•i•ty vehicle (spôrt′yo͞o-tĭl′ĭ-tē, spōrt′-) *n.* A roomy four-wheel-drive vehicle, designed for off-road use.

sport•y (spôr′tē, spōr′-) *adj.* **-i•er, -i•est 1.** Appropriate for sport or participation in sports. **2.** Exhibiting sportsmanship. **3.** Flashy; jazzy. —**sport′i•ly** *adv.* —**sport′i•ness** *n.*

spor•u•late (spôr′yə-lāt′, spōr′-) *intr.v.* **-lat•ed, -lat•ing, -lates** To produce or release spores. [< NLat. *sporula*, small spore, dim. of *spora*, spore < Gk. *sporā*, seed. See SPORE.] —**spor′u•la′tion** *n.*

spot (spŏt) *n.* **1.** A place of relatively small and definite limits. **2a.** A mark on a surface contrasting in color to its surroundings. **b.** A blemish, mark, or pimple on the skin. **c.** A stain or blot. **3.** *Games* **a.** A mark or pip on a playing card; a spade, club, diamond, or heart. **b.** A playing card with a specified number of such spots indicating its value. **4.** *Informal* A piece of paper money worth a specified number of dollars. **5a.** A location; a locale. **b.** A point of interest. **c.** A position or an item in an ordered arrangement. **6.** *Informal* A situation, esp. a troublesome one. **7.** A flaw in one's reputation or character. **8.** A short presentation or commercial on television or radio. **9.** *Informal* A spotlight. **10.** *pl.* **spot** or **spots** A small edible croaker (*Leiostomus xanthurus*) of North American Atlantic waters having a dark mark above each pectoral fin. **11.** *Chiefly British* A small amount; a bit. ❖ *v.* **spot•ted, spot•ting, spots** —*tr.* **1.** To cause a spot or spots to appear on, esp.: **a.** To soil with spots. **b.** To decorate with spots; dot. **2.** To harm; besmirch. **3.** To place in a particular location; situate precisely. **4.** To detect or discern, esp. visually; spy. **5.** To remove spots from, as in a laundry. **6.** *Sports* To yield a favorable scoring margin to. **7.** *Sports* To act as a spotter for (a gymnast, for example). **8.** *Informal* To lend: *Can you spot me $25 until payday?* —*intr.* **1.** To become marked with spots. **2.** To cause a discoloration or make a stain. **3.** To locate targets from the air during combat or training missions. ❖ *adj.* **1.** Made, paid, or delivered immediately: *a spot sale.* **2.** Of, relating to, or being a market in which payment or delivery is immediate. **3.** Involving random or selective instances or actions. **4.** Presented between major radio or television programs. —***idiom:* on the spot 1.** Without delay; at once. **2.** At the scene of action. **3.** Under pressure or attention; in a pressed position. [ME < OE.] —**spot′ta•ble** *adj.*

spot check *n.* A random or selective inspection or investigation. —**spot′-check′** (spŏt′chĕk′) *v.*

spot•less (spŏt′lĭs) *adj.* **1.** Perfectly clean. See Syns at **clean. 2.** Unblemished; impeccable. —**spot′less•ness** *n.*

spot•light (spŏt′līt′) *n.* **1.** A strong beam of light that illuminates a small area, used esp. to center attention on a stage performer. **2.** Public notoriety or prominence. **3.** An artificial source of light with a strongly focused beam, esp. a lamp that produces a spotlight. ❖ *tr.v.* **-light•ed** or **-lit** (-lĭt), **-light•ing, -lights 1.** To light with a spotlight. **2.** To focus attention on.

spot price *n.* The market price of a commodity.

Spot•syl•va•nia (spŏt′səl-vān′yə) A village of NE VA SW of Fredericksburg; site of a Civil War battle (May 8–21, 1864).

spot•ted (spŏt′ĭd) *adj.* Marked or stained with or as if with spots: *a spotted fabric.*

spotted fever *n.* **1.** Any of various often fatal infectious diseases, such as typhus, characterized by skin eruptions and caused by rickettsia that are transmitted by ticks and mites. **2.** An epidemic form of cerebrospinal meningitis.

spotted owl *n.* A large North American owl (*Strix occidentalis*) of old-growth forests from southwest British Columbia to central Mexico, having dark brown plumage with a heavily spotted chest and barred belly.

spot•ter (spŏt′ər) *n.* **1.** One that applies spots. **2.** One that looks for, locates, and reports something, as: **a.** A military lookout. **b.** *Informal* A person hired to detect dishonest acts by employees. **3.** *Sports* **a.** One who identifies players on the field, as for an announcer. **b.** One who is responsible for watching and guarding a performer during practice to prevent injury, as in weightlifting. **4.** One employed by a dry cleaner to remove spots.

spot•ty (spŏt′ē) *adj.* **-ti•er, -ti•est 1.** Lacking consistency; uneven. **2.** Having or marked with spots; spotted. —**spot′ti•ly** *adv.* —**spot′ti•ness** *n.*

spot welding *n.* Welding of overlapping pieces of metal at circular areas by application of great pressure and electric current. —**spot′-weld′** (spŏt′wĕld′) *v.* —**spot′-weld′er** *n.*

spou•sal (spou′zəl, -səl) *adj.* **1.** Of or concerning marriage; nuptial. **2.** Of or concerning a spouse. ❖ *n.* Marriage; nuptials. Often

sporran

spotted owl
Strix occidentalis

ă **pat**	oi **boy**
ā **pay**	ou **out**
âr **care**	o͝o **took**
ä **father**	o͞o **boot**
ĕ **pet**	ŭ **cut**
ē **be**	ûr **urge**
ĭ **pit**	th **thin**
ī **pie**	*th* **this**
îr **pier**	hw **which**
ŏ **pot**	zh **vision**
ō **toe**	ə **about, item**
ô **paw**	

Stress marks:
′ (primary);
′ (secondary), as in
lexicon (lĕk′sĭ-kŏn′)

springer spaniel
Welsh springer spaniel

used in the plural. [< ME *spousaille*, marriage < OFr. *espousaille* < Lat. *spōnsālia*, betrothal < neut. pl. of *spōnsālis*, of marriage < *spōnsus*, p. part. of *spondēre*, to pledge. See SPOUSE.]

spousal equivalent *n.* A domestic partner.

spouse (spous, spouz) *n.* A marriage partner; a husband or wife. ❖ *tr.v.* (spouz, spous) **spoused, spous·ing, spous·es** *Archaic* To marry; wed. [ME < OFr. *spous* < Lat. *spōnsus* < p. part. of *spondēre*, to pledge. See **spend-** in App.]

spout (spout) *v.* **spout·ed, spout·ing, spouts** —*intr.* 1. To gush forth in a rapid stream or in spurts. 2. To discharge a liquid or other substance continuously or in spurts. 3. *Informal* To speak volubly and tediously. —*tr.* 1. To cause to flow or spurt out. 2. To utter volubly and tediously. 3. *Chiefly British* To pawn. ❖ *n.* 1. A tube, mouth, or pipe through which liquid is released or discharged. 2. A continuous stream of liquid. 3. The burst of spray from the blowhole of a whale. 4. *Chiefly British* A pawnshop. [ME *spouten*, ult. of imit. orig.] —**spout′er** *n.*

spout·ing (spou′tĭng) *n. Chiefly Pennsylvania & New Jersey* See **gutter.** 2. See Regional Note at **gutter.**

spp. *abbr.* species (plural)

SPQR *abbr. Latin* Senatus Populusque Romanus (the Senate and the people of Rome)

sprach·ge·fühl (shprä╦н′gə-fül′) *n.* An ear for idiomatically correct or appropriate language. [Ger. : *Sprache*, language (ult. < OHGer. *sprāhha*) + *Gefühl*, feeling (< *fühlen*, to feel < MHGer. *vuelen* < OHGer. *vuolen*).]

sprag (sprăg) *n.* **1a.** A piece of wood or metal wedged under a wheel or between spokes to prevent rolling. **b.** A pointed stake angled into the ground from a vehicle to prevent motion. 2. A prop for a mine roof. [Perh. of Scand. orig.]

sprain (sprān) *n.* 1. A painful wrenching or laceration of the ligaments of a joint. 2. The condition resulting from a sprain. ❖ *tr.v.* **sprained, sprain·ing, sprains** To cause a sprain to (a joint or ligament). [?]

sprang (sprăng) *v.* A past tense of **spring.**

sprat (sprăt) *n.* 1. A small marine food fish (*Clupea sprattus*) of northeast Atlantic waters. 2. Any of various other similar fishes, such as a young herring. [ME *sprot, spratte* < OE *sprot.*]

sprawl (sprôl) *v.* **sprawled, sprawl·ing, sprawls** —*intr.* 1. To sit or lie with the body and limbs spread out awkwardly. 2. To spread out in a straggling or disordered fashion. —*tr.* To cause to spread out in a straggling or disordered fashion. ❖ *n.* 1. A sprawling position or posture. 2. Haphazard growth or extension outward, esp. that due to real estate development on the outskirts of a city: *urban sprawl.* [ME *sprawlen* < OE *sprēawlian*, to writhe.]

spray¹ (sprā) *n.* 1. Water or other liquid moving in a mass of dispersed droplets. **2a.** A fine jet of liquid discharged from a pressurized container. **b.** Such a pressurized container or an atomizer. **c.** Any of numerous commercial products, including paints, that are dispensed from containers in this manner. ❖ *v.* **sprayed, spray·ing, sprays** —*tr.* 1. To disperse (a liquid) in a mass or jet of droplets. 2. To apply a spray to (a surface). —*intr.* 1. To discharge sprays of liquid. 2. To move in the form of a spray. [< obsolete *spray*, to sprinkle < MDu. *sprayen.*] —**spray′er** *n.*

spray² (sprā) *n.* 1. A small branch bearing buds, flowers, or berries. 2. Something, such as a decorative motif, that resembles a floral spray. [ME < OE **spræg.*]

spray paint *n.* Paint in an aerosol container for spraying onto surfaces. —**spray′-paint′** (sprā′pānt′) *v.*

spread (sprĕd) *v.* **spread, spread·ing, spreads** —*tr.* 1. To open to a fuller extent or width; stretch: *spread a tablecloth.* 2. To widen the gap between; move farther apart: *spread one's fingers.* **3a.** To distribute over a surface in a layer. **b.** To cover with a layer: *spread bread with butter.* **4a.** To distribute widely: *The storm spread destruction.* **b.** To make a wide or extensive arrangement of: *spread the parts out on the floor.* **c.** To exhibit or display the full extent of: *the scene that was spread before us.* 5. To cause to become widely seen or known; scatter or disseminate. **6a.** To prepare (a table) for eating; set. **b.** To arrange (a food or a meal) on a table. 7. To flatten (a rivet end, for example) by pounding. —*intr.* 1. To be extended or enlarged. 2. To become distributed or widely dispersed. 3. To increase in range of occurrence; become known or prevalent over a wide area. 4. To be displayed or visible in broad or full extent. 5. To become or admit of being distributed in a layer. 6. To become separated; be forced farther apart. ❖ *n.* **1a.** The act of spreading. **b.** Dissemination, as of news; diffusion. **2a.** An open area of land; an expanse. **b.** A ranch, a farm, or an estate. 3. The extent or limit to which something is or can be spread; range. 4. A cloth covering for a bed, table, or other piece of furniture. 5. *Informal* An abundant meal laid out on a table. 6. A food to be spread on bread or crackers. **7a.** Two facing pages of a magazine or newspaper, often with related matter extending across the fold. **b.** A story or advertisement running across two or more columns of a magazine or newspaper. 8. A difference, as between two figures. **9a.** A position taken in two or more options or futures contracts in order to profit from a change in their relative prices. **b.** The difference between the price asked and bid for a particular security. 10. A number of points offered to equalize the chances of winning in a wager on a competition, usu. between sports teams. 11. Wingspread. [ME *spreden* < OE *-sprǣdan* (as in *tōsprǣdan*, to spread out).] —**spread′a·bil′i·ty** *n.* —**spread′a·**

ble *adj.* —**spread′a·bly** *adv.*

spread eagle *n.* **1a.** The figure of an eagle with wings and legs spread. **b.** The emblem on the obverse of the Great Seal of the United States. 2. A posture or design resembling such an emblem or figure.

spread-ea·gle (sprĕd′ē′gəl) *adj.* 1. Having the arms and legs stretched out. 2. *Informal* Full of patriotic or jingoistic rhetoric. ❖ *v.* **-gled, -gling, -gles** —*tr.* To place in a spread-eagle position, esp. as a punishment. —*intr.* 1. To assume a spread-eagle position. 2. To make a grandiloquent patriotic speech.

spread·er (sprĕd′ər) *n.* One that spreads, as: **a.** A butter knife. **b.** An implement for distributing fertilizer or seed. **c.** A device, such as a bar, for keeping wires or stays apart. **d.** *Nautical* A horizontal support used to spread shrouds on a mast.

spread·sheet (sprĕd′shēt′) *n.* 1. A piece of paper with rows and columns for recording financial data for use in comparative analysis. 2. *Computer Science* An accounting or bookkeeping program for displaying data in rows and columns.

sprech·stim·me (shprĕ╦н′shtĭm′ə) *n.* A form of dramatic declamation, in which the speaker uses lilt and rhythm but not precise pitches. [Ger. : *sprechen*, to speak (< MHGer. *sprēchen* < OHGer. *sprehhan*) + *Stimme*, voice (< MHGer. *stimme* < OHGer. *stimma*).]

spree (sprē) *n.* 1. A carefree, lively outing. 2. A drinking bout. A sudden indulgence in or outburst of an activity. See Syns at **binge.** [Perh. alteration of Sc. *spreath*, cattle raid < Ir. and Sc. Gael. *spréidh, spré*, cattle, wealth < MIr. *preit, preid*, booty, ult. < Lat. *praeda.* See **ghend-** in App.]

Spree (sprā, shprā) A river of E Germany flowing c. 402 km (250 mi) N to the Havel R. at Berlin.

spri·er (sprī′ər) *adj.* A comparative of **spry.**

spri·est (sprī′ĭst) *adj.* A superlative of **spry.**

sprig (sprĭg) *n.* **1a.** A small shoot or twig of a plant. **b.** An ornament in this shape. 2. A small brad without a head. 3. A young, immature person. ❖ *tr.v.* **sprigged, sprig·ging, sprigs** 1. To decorate with a design of sprigs. 2. To remove a sprig or sprigs from (a bush or tree). 3. To fasten with a small headless brad. [ME *sprigge*, alteration of *spring* < OE, source of water.]

spright (sprīt) *n.* Variant of **sprite.**

spright·ly (sprīt′lē) *adj.* **-li·er, -li·est** Full of spirit and vitality; lively; brisk. ❖ *adv.* In a lively, animated manner. —**spright′li·ness** *n.*

sprig·tail (sprĭg′tāl′) *n.* 1. See **pintail.** 2. See **ruddy duck.**

spring (sprĭng) *v.* **sprang** (sprăng) or **sprung** (sprŭng), **sprung, spring·ing, springs** —*intr.* 1. To move upward or forward in a single quick motion or a series of such motions; leap. 2. To move suddenly on or as if on a spring: *The door sprang shut.* 3. To appear or come into being quickly: *New businesses sprang up.* 4. To issue or emerge suddenly: *A cry sprang from her lips.* 5. To extend or curve upward, as an arch. 6. To arise from a source; develop. 7. To become warped, split, or cracked. Used of wood. 8. To move out of place; come loose, as parts of a mechanism. 9. *Slang* To pay another's expenses: *He sprang for lunch.* —*tr.* 1. To cause to leap, dart, or come forth suddenly. 2. To jump over. 3. To release from a checked or inoperative position; actuate: *spring a trap.* **4a.** To cause to warp, split, or crack. **b.** To bend by force. 5. To present or disclose unexpectedly or suddenly. 6. *Slang* To release from prison or other confinement. ❖ *n.* 1. An elastic device, such as a coil of wire, that regains its original shape after compression or extension. 2. An actuating force or factor; a motive. **3a.** Elasticity; resilience. **b.** Energetic bounce. 4. The act or an instance of jumping or leaping. 5. A usu. rapid return to normal shape after removal of stress; recoil. 6. A small stream of water flowing naturally from the earth. 7. A source, origin, or beginning. **8a.** The season of the year between winter and summer, comprising March, April, and May in the Northern Hemisphere or, as calculated astronomically, extending from the vernal equinox to the summer solstice. **b.** A time of growth and renewal. 9. A warping, bending, or cracking, as that caused by excessive force. 10. *Architecture* The point at which an arch or vault rises from its support. ❖ *adj.* 1. Of or acting like a spring; resilient. 2. Having or supported by springs. **3a.** Of, relating to, occurring in, or appropriate to the season of spring. **b.** Grown during the season of spring. [ME *springen* < OE *springan.* N., ME *springe* < OE *spring*, wellspring.]

spring beauty *n.* Any of various spring-flowering plants of the genus *Claytonia*, esp. *C. virginica* of eastern North America, having narrow leaves and white or pinkish flowers.

spring·board (sprĭng′bôrd′, -bōrd′) *n.* 1. *Sports* **a.** A flexible board mounted on a fulcrum with one end secured, used by gymnasts in vaulting. **b.** See **diving board.** 2. Something that helps to launch a career or activity.

spring·bok (sprĭng′bŏk′) also **spring·buck** (-bŭk′) *n., pl.* **springbok** or **-boks** also **springbuck** or **-bucks** A small brown and white gazelle (*Antidorcas marsupialis*) of southern Africa noted for its habit of repeatedly leaping high into the air when startled. [Afr. : *spring*, to leap up (< MDu. *springhen*) + *bok*, male deer (< MDu. *boc*).]

spring chicken *n.* 1. A young chicken, esp. one from two to ten months old. 2. *Slang* A young person.

spring-clean·ing (sprĭng′klē′nĭng) *n.* A thorough cleaning, esp. of a residence when winter is over.

springe (sprĭnj) *n.* **1.** A device for snaring small game, made by attaching a noose to a branch under tension. **2.** A trap or snare. [ME. *branch*, *spring*. See SPRING.]

spring·er (sprĭng′ər) *n.* **1.** A springer spaniel. **2.** *Western US* A cow about to give birth. **3.** *Architecture* **a.** The bottom stone of an arch resting on the support. **b.** The point or place where the curve of an arch or vault begins.

springer spaniel *n.* A dog of either of two breeds of spaniels, the English springer spaniel or the Welsh springer spaniel.

spring fever *n.* A feeling of languor or yearning brought on by the coming of spring.

Spring·field (sprĭng′fēld′) **1.** The cap. of IL, in the central part; became state cap. in 1837. Pop. 111,454. **2.** A city of SW MA on the Connecticut R. near the CT border; settled 1636. Pop. 152,082. **3.** A city of SW MO SSW of Kansas City. Pop. 151,580.

Springfield rifle *n.* A magazine-fed breechloading bolt-action .30-caliber rifle used by the US Army esp. in World War I. [After SPRINGFIELD, MA.]

spring·form pan (sprĭng′fôrm′) *n.* A cake pan having an upright rim that can be detached from the bottom.

spring·halt (sprĭng′hôlt′) *n.* See **stringhalt.** [Alteration of STRINGHALT.]

spring·head (sprĭng′hĕd′) *n.* A fountainhead; a source.

spring·house (sprĭng′hous′) *n.* A small storehouse constructed over a spring and used to keep food cool.

spring·let (sprĭng′lĭt) *n.* A small spring of water; a rill.

spring-load·ed (sprĭng′lō′dĭd) *adj.* Secured or loaded by means of a spring.

spring lock *n.* A lock in which the bolt shoots automatically by means of a spring.

spring peeper *n.* A small brown tree frog (*Hyla crucifer*) of eastern North America having a shrill high-pitched call.

spring roll *n.* See **egg roll.** [Transl. of Chin. (Mandarin) *chūn juǎn* : *chūn*, spring + *juǎn*, roll.]

spring·tail (sprĭng′tāl′) *n.* Any of various small wingless insects of the order Collembola, having abdominal appendages that act as springs to catapult them through the air.

spring·tide (sprĭng′tīd′) *n.* Springtime.

spring tide *n.* **1.** The exceptionally high and low tides that occur when the moon is new or full and the sun, moon, and earth are aligned. **2.** A great flood or rush, as of emotion.

spring·time (sprĭng′tīm′) *n.* The season of spring.

spring·wood (sprĭng′wŏŏd′) *n.* Young, usu. soft wood that lies directly beneath the bark and develops in early spring.

spring·y (sprĭng′ē) *adj.* **-i·er, -i·est 1.** Marked by resilience; elastic. **2.** Abounding in freshwater springs. **—spring′i·ly** *adv.* **—spring′i·ness** *n.*

sprin·kle (sprĭng′kəl) *v.* **-kled, -kling, -kles** *—tr.* **1.** To scatter in drops or particles. **2.** To scatter drops or particles on. **3.** To intersperse with something as if by scattering. **4.** To distribute or intersperse at random. *—intr.* **1.** To scatter something in drops or particles. **2.** To fall or rain in small or infrequent drops. ❖ *n.* **1.** The act of sprinkling. **2.** A light rainfall. **3.** A small amount; a sprinkling. **4.** A small particle of candy sprinkled on ice cream as a topping. Often used in the plural. [ME *sprenklen*, perh. of MDu. or MLGer. orig.]

sprin·kler (sprĭng′klər) *n.* **1.** One that sprinkles, esp.: **a.** An outlet on a sprinkler system. **b.** A device with perforations through which water issues from a hose to sprinkle a lawn. **2.** A sprinkler system. ❖ *tr.v.* **-klered, -kler·ing, -klers** To equip with a sprinkler system.

sprinkler system *n.* A fire-extinguishing system consisting of a network of overhead pipes that release water automatically when a predetermined temperature has been reached.

sprin·kling (sprĭng′klĭng) *n.* **1.** A small amount or quantity; a modicum. **2.** A small quantity sparsely distributed.

sprint (sprĭnt) *n.* **1.** The act or an instance of sprinting, esp. a short race at top speed. **2.** A burst of speed or activity. ❖ *v.* **sprint·ed, sprint·ing, sprints** *—intr.* To move rapidly or at top speed for a brief period, as in running or swimming. *—tr.* To move over (a distance) rapidly or at top speed for a brief period. [Poss. alteration of ME *sprenten*, to spring up, of Scand. orig.; akin to Swed. dialectal *sprinta* and ON *spretta*, to jump.] **—sprint′er** *n.*

sprit (sprĭt) *n. Nautical* **1.** A spar extending diagonally across a fore-and-aft sail from the lower part of the mast to the peak of the sail. **2.** A bowsprit. [ME < OE *sprēot*, pole.]

sprite also **spright** (sprīt) *n.* **1.** A small or elusive supernatural being; an elf or pixy. **2.** An elflike person. **3.** A specter or ghost. **4.** *Archaic* A soul. **5.** *Meteorology* A large, dim, red flash that appears above active thunderstorms in conjunction with lightning. [ME *spreit* < OFr. *espirit* < Lat. *spīritus*. See SPIRIT.]

sprit·sail (sprĭt′səl, -sāl′) *n.* A quadrilateral sail extended by a spar running diagonally along the sail's peak.

spritz (sprĭts, shprĭts) *tr.v.* **spritzed, spritz·ing, spritz·es** To squirt or spray (something) quickly. ❖ *n.* A quick squirt or spray, as of carbonated water. [Penn. Dutch *schpritze* < MHGer. *sprützen*, to spray.]

spritz·er (sprĭt′sər, shprĭt′-) *n.* A drink made of wine and carbonated water. [Ger. < *spritzen*, to spray < MHGer. *sprützen.*]

sprock·et (sprŏk′ĭt) *n.* **1.** Any of various toothlike projections arranged on a wheel rim to engage the links of a chain. **2.** A cylinder with a toothed rim that engages in the perforations of photographic or movie film to pull it through a camera or projector. [?]

sprocket wheel *n.* A wheel rimmed with toothlike projections, used to engage the links of a chain in a pulley or drive system.

sprout (sprout) *v.* **sprout·ed, sprout·ing, sprouts** *—intr.* **1.** To begin to grow; give off shoots or buds. **2.** To emerge and develop rapidly. *—tr.* To cause to emerge and grow. ❖ *n.* **1.** A young plant growth, such as a bud or shoot. **2.** Something resembling a sprout, as in rapid growth. **3. sprouts a.** The young shoots of plants such as alfalfa and soybean, usu. eaten raw. **b.** Brussels sprouts. [ME *spruten* < OE *-sprūtan* (as in *āsprūtan*, to sprout forth).]

spruce¹ (sprōōs) *n.* **1a.** Any of various coniferous evergreen trees of the genus *Picea*, having needlelike foliage, drooping cones, and soft wood often used for paper pulp. **b.** Any of various similar or related trees. **c.** The wood of any of these trees. **2.** A grayish green to dark greenish black. [Short for obsolete *Spruce fir*, Prussian fir < ME *Spruce*, Prussia, alteration of *Pruce* < AN *Pruz* < Med.Lat. *Prussia.*]

spruce¹
blue spruce
Picea pungens

spruce² (sprōōs) *adj.* **spruc·er, spruc·est** Neat, trim, and smart in appearance. ❖ *v.* **spruced, spruc·ing, spruc·es** *—tr.* To make neat and trim: *spruce up the house.* *—intr.* To make oneself neat and smart in appearance. [Perh. < obsolete *spruce leather*, Prussian leather < ME *Spruce*, Prussia. See SPRUCE¹.] **—spruce′ly** *adv.* **—spruce′ness** *n.*

spruce budworm *n.* The highly destructive larva of a tortricid moth (*Choristoneura fumiferana*) of the northern United States and southern Canada that feeds on forest conifers.

spruce grouse *n.* A grouse (*Canachites canadensis*) that is dark gray barred with black, found in swampy forests of northern North America and popular as a game bird.

spruce pine *n.* See **scrub pine 1.**

sprue¹ (sprōō) *n.* A chronic, chiefly tropical disease marked by diarrhea, emaciation, and anemia, caused by malabsorption of nutrients from the intestinal tract. [Du. *spruw* < MDu. *sprouwe.*]

sprue² (sprōō) *n.* **1.** The hole through which molten material is channelled into a mold. **2.** The waste material filling or protruding from this hole after hardening. **3.** The usu. plastic rod or framework that secures molded objects such as game pieces before their first use. [Perh. of Sc. orig.]

sprung (sprŭng) *v.* A past tense and the past participle of **spring.**

sprung rhythm *n.* A poetic rhythm designed to imitate the rhythm of speech, in which each foot has one stressed syllable, either standing alone or followed by a varying number of unstressed syllables. [Coined by Gerard Manley Hopkins.]

spry (sprī) *adj.* **spri·er** (sprī′ər), **spri·est** (sprī′ĭst) or **spry·er, spry·est** Lively, active, and brisk; vigorous. [Perh. of Scand. orig.] **—spry′ly** *adv.* **—spry′ness** *n.*

spt. *abbr.* seaport.

spud (spŭd) *n.* **1.** *Slang* A potato. **2.** A sharp spadelike tool for rooting or digging out weeds. **3.** A short section of pipe or a threaded fitting that completes a connection. ❖ *v.* **spud·ded, spud·ding, spuds 1.** To remove with a sharp spadelike tool. **2.** To begin drilling operations on. [ME *spudde*, short knife.]

spue (spyōō) *v. & n. Obsolete* Variant of **spew.**

spume (spyōōm) *n.* Foam or froth on a liquid, as on the sea. ❖ *intr.v.* **spumed, spum·ing, spumes** To froth or foam. [ME < OFr. *espume* < Lat. *spūma.*] **—spu′mous, spum′y** *adj.*

spu·mo·ni or **spu·mo·ne** (spōō-mō′nē) *n.* An Italian ice cream with layers of different colors or flavors and often fruits and nuts. [Ital., augmentative of *spuma*, foam < Lat. *spūma.*]

spun (spŭn) *v.* Past tense and past participle of **spin.**

spun glass *n.* **1.** See **fiberglass. 2.** Fine blown glass having delicate threading or filigree.

spunk (spŭngk) *n.* **1.** *Informal* Spirit; pluck. **2.** Punk, touchwood, or other tinder. [Sc. Gael. *spong*, tinder < Lat. *spongia*, sponge. See SPONGE.]

spunk·y (spŭng′kē) *adj.* **-i·er, -i·est** *Informal* Spirited; plucky. **—spunk′i·ly** *adv.* **—spunk′i·ness** *n.*

spun silk *n.* A yarn made from short-fibered silk and silk waste.

spun sugar *n.* See **cotton candy.**

spur (spûr) *n.* **1.** A short spike or spiked wheel that attaches to the heel of a rider's boot and is used to urge a horse forward. **2.** Something that serves as a goad or incentive. **3.** A spurlike attachment or projection, as: **a.** A spinelike process on the leg of some birds. **b.** A climbing iron; a crampon. **c.** A gaff attached to the leg of a gamecock. **d.** A short or stunted branch of a tree. **e.** A bony outgrowth or protuberance. **4.** A lateral ridge projecting from a mountain or mountain range. **5.** An oblique reinforcing prop or stay of timber or masonry. **6.** *Botany* A tubular or saclike extension of the corolla or calyx of a flower, as in a columbine or larkspur. **7.** An ergot growing on rye. **8.** A spur track. ❖ *v.* **spurred, spur·ring, spurs** *—tr.* **1.** To urge (a horse) on by the use of spurs. **2.** To incite or stimulate. *—intr.* **1.** To ride quickly by spurring a horse. **2.** To proceed in haste. [ME *spure* < OE *spura.* See **spera-** in App.]

spur
top: metal spurs
bottom: long-spurred columbine

spurge (spûrj) *n.* Any of various plants of the genus *Euphorbia*, having milky juice and small unisexual flowers surrounded by a cuplike structure of fused bracts. [ME < OFr. *espurge* < *espurgier*, to purge (< its use as a purgative) < Lat. *expūrgāre*. See EXPUR-GATE.]

spur gear *n.* A gear with teeth radially arrayed on the rim parallel to its axis.

spu·ri·ous (spyŏor′ē-əs) *adj.* **1.** Lacking authenticity or validity in essence or origin; not genuine; false. **2.** Of illegitimate birth. **3.** *Botany* Similar in appearance but unlike in structure or function. Used of plant parts. [< LLat. *spurius* < Lat., illegitimate, prob. of Etruscan orig.] —**spu′ri·ous·ly** *adv.* —**spu′ri·ous·ness** *n.*

spurious wing *n.* See alula.

spurn (spûrn) *v.* **spurned, spurn·ing, spurns** —*tr.* **1.** To reject disdainfully or contemptuously; scorn. See Syns at refuse[1]. **2.** To kick at or tread on disdainfully. —*intr.* To reject something contemptuously. ❖ *n.* **1.** A contemptuous rejection. **2.** *Archaic* A kick. [ME *spurnen* < OE *spurnan*. See spere- in App.] —**spurn′er** *n.*

spur-of-the-mo·ment (spûr′əv-thə-mō′mənt) *adj.* Occurring or made hastily on impulse: *a spur-of-the-moment choice.*

spurred (spûrd) *adj.* **1.** Wearing spurs. **2.** Having spurs or a spur: *spurred flowers; spurred boots.*

spur·ry also **spur·rey** (spûr′ē, spŭr′ē) *n., pl.* **-ries** also **-reys** Any of several weedy low-growing herbs of the genera *Spergula* or *Spergularia,* esp. *Spergula arvensis* of Europe, having linear whorled leaves and small white flowers. [Du. *spurrie* < MDu. *speurie,* prob. < Med.Lat. *spergula,* prob. < Lat. *spargere,* to scatter.]

spurt (spûrt) *n.* **1.** A sudden forcible gush or jet. **2.** A sudden short burst, as of activity or growth. ❖ *v.* **spurt·ed, spurt·ing, spurts** —*intr.* **1.** To gush forth suddenly in a jet. **2.** To make a brief intense effort or show a sudden increase in activity or speed. —*tr.* To force out in a spurt. [?]

spur track *n.* A short side track that connects with the main track of a railroad system.

sput·nik (spoot′nĭk, spŭt′-, spoot′nyĭk) *n.* Any of a series of Soviet satellites sent into Earth orbit, esp. the first, launched October 4, 1957. [Russ. *sputnik (zemli),* fellow traveler (of Earth) : *so-, s-,* together; see ksun in App. + *put′,* path, way; see pent- in App. + *-nik,* n. suff.]

sput·ter (spŭt′ər) *v.* **-tered, -ter·ing, -ters** —*intr.* **1.** To spit out or spray particles of saliva or food from the mouth in noisy bursts. **2.** To spit out words or sounds in an excited or confused manner. **3.** To make sporadic spitting or popping sounds. **4.** *Physics* To cause the atoms of a solid to be removed from the surface by bombardment with atoms in a discharge tube. —*tr.* **1.** To eject in short bursts with spitting or popping sounds. **2.** To utter in an excited or confused manner. **3.** *Physics* To coat (a solid surface) with metal atoms by sputtering. ❖ *n.* **1.** The act or sound of sputtering. **2.** Matter emitted in sputtering. **3.** Excited or confused utterance. [Prob. of LGer. orig.; akin to Du. *sputteren.*] —**sput′ter·er** *n.* —**sput′ter·y** *adj.*

spu·tum (spyoo′təm) *n., pl.* **-ta** (-tə) Matter coughed up and usu. ejected from the mouth, including saliva, foreign material, and substances such as mucus or phlegm, from the respiratory tract. [Lat. *spūtum* < neut. p. part. of *spuere,* to spit.]

Spuy·ten Duy·vil Creek (spīt′n dī′vəl) A narrow channel in SE NY separating N Manhattan I. from the mainland and linking the Harlem and Hudson rivers.

spy (spī) *n., pl.* **spies** (spīz) **1.** An agent employed by a state to obtain secret information concerning its potential or actual enemies. **2.** One employed by a company to obtain confidential information about its competitors. **3.** One who secretly keeps watch on another or others. **4.** An act of spying. ❖ *v.* **spied** (spīd), **spy·ing, spies** (spīz) —*tr.* **1.** To observe secretly with hostile intent. **2.** To discover by close observation. **3.** To catch sight of. **4.** To investigate intensively. —*intr.* **1.** To engage in espionage. **2.** To seek or observe something secretly and closely. **3.** To make a careful investigation. [ME *spie* < OFr. *espie* < *espier,* to watch, of Gmc. orig. See spek- in App.]

spy·glass (spī′glăs′) *n.* **1.** A small telescope. **2.** A pair of binoculars. Often used in the plural.

spy·mas·ter (spī′măs′tər) *n.* One who directs clandestine intelligence activities.

sq. *abbr.* **1.** squadron **2.** or **Sq.** square

squab (skwŏb) *n.* **1.** A newly hatched or unfledged pigeon. **2a.** A soft thick cushion, as for a couch. **b.** A couch. ❖ *adj.* Young and undeveloped; newly hatched or unfledged. [Prob. of Scand. orig.; akin to Swed. dialectal *squabb,* fat flesh.]

squab·ble (skwŏb′əl) *intr.v.* **-bled, -bling, -bles** To engage in a disagreeable argument, usu. over a trivial matter; wrangle. ❖ *n.* A noisy quarrel, usu. about a trivial matter. [Prob. of Scand. orig.] —**squab′bler** *n.*

squad (skwŏd) *n.* **1.** A small group of people organized in an endeavor or activity. **2.** The smallest tactical unit of military personnel. **3.** A small unit of police or traffic officers. **4.** *Sports* An athletic team. [Obsolete Fr. *esquade* < OFr. *escadre* < OSpan. *escuadra* and OItal. *squadra,* both < VLat. **exquadra,* square. See SQUARE.]

squad car *n.* A police automobile connected by radio with headquarters.

squad·ron (skwŏd′rən) *n.* **1.** A naval unit consisting of two or more divisions of a fleet. **2.** An armored cavalry unit subordinate

to a regiment and consisting of two or more troops. **3.** A cavalry or armored unit of a European army, corresponding to a company. **4.** A basic tactical air force unit, subordinate to a group and consisting of two or more flights. **5.** A multitude or horde. [Ital. *squadrone,* augmentative of *squadra,* squad. See SQUAD.]

squa·lene (skwā′lēn′) *n.* An unsaturated aliphatic hydrocarbon, $C_{30}H_{50}$, found esp. in human sebum and in the liver oil of sharks, that is an intermediate in the biosynthesis of cholesterol. [NLat. *Squalus,* shark genus (< Lat. *squalus,* a sea fish) + -ENE.]

squal·id (skwŏl′ĭd) *adj.* **1.** Dirty and wretched, as from poverty or lack of care. **2.** Morally repulsive; sordid. [Lat. *squālidus* < *squālēre,* to be filthy < *squālus,* filthy.] —**squal′id·ly** *adv.* —**squal′id·ness, squa·lid′i·ty** (skwŏ-lĭd′ĭ-tē) *n.*

squall[1] (skwôl) *n.* A loud, harsh cry. ❖ *intr.v.* **squalled, squall·ing, squalls** To scream or cry loudly and harshly. [Prob. of Scand. orig.; akin to ON *skvala,* to squeal.] —**squall′er** *n.*

squall[2] (skwôl) *n.* **1.** A brief sudden violent windstorm, often accompanied by rain or snow. **2.** *Informal* A brief commotion. ❖ *intr.v.* **squalled, squall·ing, squalls** To blow strongly for a brief period. [Prob. of Scand. orig.]

squall line *n.* A line of thunderstorms preceding a cold front.

squall·y (skwô′lē) *adj.* **-i·er, -i·est 1.** Characterized by gusts of wind. **2.** *Informal* Marked by commotion or disturbance.

squal·or (skwŏl′ər) *n.* A filthy and wretched condition or quality. [Lat. *squālor* < *squālēre,* to be filthy. See SQUALID.]

squa·ma (skwā′mə, skwä′-) *n., pl.* **-mae** (-mē′) **1.** A scale or scalelike structure. **2.** A thin platelike mass, as of bone. [Lat. *squāma.*] —**squa′mate** (-māt′) *adj.*

squa·ma·tion (skwə-mā′shən) *n.* **1.** The condition of being scaly. **2.** An arrangement of scales, as on a fish.

squa·mo·sal (skwə-mō′səl, -zəl) *adj.* Of or relating to the thin platelike part of the human temporal bone or to a corresponding part in other vertebrates. ❖ *n.* A squamosal bone. [< Lat. *squāmōsus,* squamous. See SQUAMOUS.]

squa·mous (skwā′məs, skwä′-) also **squa·mose** (-mōs′) *adj.* **1.** Covered with or formed of scales; scaly. **2.** Resembling a scale or scales; thin and flat like a scale. **3.** Of or relating to the thin platelike part of the temporal bone. [Lat. *squāmōsus* < *squāma,* scale.] —**squa′mous·ness** *n.*

squamous cell carcinoma *n.* A carcinoma that arises from squamous epithelium and is the most common form of skin cancer.

squamous epithelium *n.* Epithelium consisting of one or more cell layers, the most superficial of which is composed of flat scalelike or platelike cells.

squa·mu·lose (skwā′myə-lōs′, skwä′-) *adj.* Having or consisting of minute scales. [Lat. *squāmula,* dim. of *squāma,* scale + -OSE[1].]

squan·der (skwŏn′dər) *tr.v.* **-dered, -der·ing, -ders 1.** To spend wastefully or extravagantly; dissipate. **2.** To fail to take advantage of; lose a chance for. **3.** *Obsolete* To scatter. ❖ *n.* Extravagant expenditure; prodigality. [?] —**squan′der·er** *n.* —**squan′der·ing·ly** *adv.*

Squan·to (skwŏn′tō) d. 1622. Native American who helped the colonists in Massachusetts develop agricultural techniques and served as an interpreter with the Wampanoag.

square (skwâr) *n.* **1.** A plane figure having four equal sides. **2.** Something having an equal-sided rectangular form. **3.** A T-shaped or L-shaped instrument for drawing or testing right angles. **4.** *Mathematics* The product obtained when a number or quantity is multiplied by itself: *49 is the square of 7.* **5.** *Games* Any of the quadrilateral spaces on a board, as in chess. **6a.** An open, usu. four-sided area at the intersection of two or more streets, often planted with grass and trees for use as a park. **b.** A rectangular space enclosed by streets and occupied by buildings; a block. **7.** *Slang* A person who is regarded as dull, rigidly conventional, and out of touch with current trends. **8.** *Slang* A square meal. Often used in the plural: *three squares a day.* ❖ *adj.* **squar·er, squar·est 1.** Having four equal sides and four right angles. **2.** Forming a right angle. **3a.** Expressed in units measuring area: *square feet.* **b.** Having a specified length in each of two equal dimensions: *a room that is 12 feet square.* **4.** Having a base that is a square: *a square pyramid.* **5.** *Nautical* Set at right angles to the mast and keel. Used of the yards of a square-rigged ship. **6.** Approximately rectangular and equilateral in cross section. **7.** Characterized by blocklike solidity or sturdiness. **8.** Honest; direct: *a square answer.* **9.** Just; equitable: *a square deal.* **10.** Having all accounts settled; even. **11.** *Sports* Even; tied. **12.** *Slang* Rigidly conventional; dull. ❖ *v.* **squared, squar·ing, squares** —*tr.* **1.** To cut to a square or rectangular shape. **2.** To test for conformity to a desired plane, straight line, or right angle. **3.** To mark into squares. Often used with *off.* **4a.** To bring into conformity or agreement. **b.** To bring (oneself) into a better position or relation. **5.** To set straight or at approximate right angles: *square one's cap.* **6.** To bring into balance; settle. **7.** *Sports* To even the score of. **8.** *Mathematics* **a.** To raise (a number or quantity) to the second power. **b.** To find a square equal in area to (the area of a given figure). **9.** *Informal* To bribe or fix. —*intr.* **1.** *Mathematics* To be at right angles. **2.** To agree or conform. ❖ *adv.* **1.** *Mathematics* At right angles. **2.** In a square shape. **3.** In a solid manner; firmly. **4.** Directly; straight: *ran square into it.* **5.** In an honest,

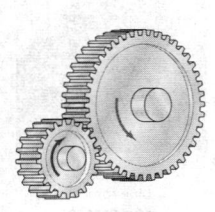

spur gear

straightforward manner. ***—phrasal verbs:*** **square away 1.** *Nautical* To square the yards of a sailing vessel. **2.** To put away or in order. **square off** To assume a fighting stance; prepare to fight. **square up** To settle a bill or debt. ***—idioms:*** **on the square 1.** *Mathematics* At right angles. **2.** Honestly and openly. **out of square 1.** *Mathematics* Not at exact right angles. **2.** Not in agreement. **square peg in a round hole** *Informal* A misfit. [ME < OFr. *esquarre* < VLat. **exquadra* < **exquadrāre*, to square : Lat. *ex-*, ex- + *quadrāre*, to give a square shape to (< *quadrum*, a square; see **kʷetwer-** in App.).] **—square′ness** *n.* **—squar′er** *n.*

square bracket *n.* One of a pair of marks, [ ], used to enclose written or printed material or to indicate a mathematical expression considered as a single quantity.

square dance *n.* **1.** A dance in which sets of four couples form squares. **2.** Any of various similar group dances of rural origin. **—square′-dance′** (skwâr′dăns′) *v.* **—square dancer** *n.*

square knot *n.* A common double knot in which the loose ends are parallel to the standing parts, most often used to join the ends of two cords or lines.

square•ly (skwâr′lē) *adv.* **1.** *Mathematics* At right angles: *sawed the beam squarely.* **2.** In a square shape. **3.** So as to make solid contact; firmly: *struck the ball squarely.* **4.** Directly; straight: *aimed squarely at the target.* **5.** In an honest, straightforward manner: *spoke squarely about drug abuse.*

square matrix *n.* *Mathematics* A matrix with equal numbers of rows and columns.

square meal *n.* A substantial nourishing meal.

square measure *n.* A system of units used in measuring area.

square one *n.* *Informal* The starting point. [Alluding to board games with numbered squares.]

square-rigged (skwâr′rĭgd′) *adj.* Fitted with square sails as the principal sails.

square-rig•ger (skwâr′rĭg′ər) *n.* A square-rigged vessel.

square root *n.* A divisor of a quantity that when squared gives the quantity.

square sail *n.* *Nautical* A four-sided sail extended by a yard suspended horizontally across the mast.

square•tail (skwâr′tāl′) *n.* See **brook trout.**

squar•ish (skwâr′ĭsh) *adj.* Somewhat or almost square: *a squarish room.* **—squar′ish•ly** *adv.* **—squar′ish•ness** *n.*

squar•rose (skwăr′ōs′, skwär′-) *adj.* *Botany* **1.** Having rough or spreading scalelike processes. **2.** Spreading or recurved at the tip: *squarrose bracts.* [Lat. *squarrōsus*, scabby.]

squash[1] (skwŏsh, skwôsh) *n.* **1.** Any of various tendril-bearing plants of the genus *Cucurbita*, having fleshy edible fruit with a leathery rind. **2.** The fruit of any of these plants. [< alteration of Narragansett *askútasquash.*]

squash[2] (skwŏsh, skwôsh) *v.* **squashed, squash•ing, squash•es** *—tr.* **1.** To beat, squeeze, or press into a pulp or a flattened mass; crush. **2.** To put down or suppress; quash. **3.** To silence or fluster, as with crushing words. *—intr.* **1.** To become crushed, flattened, or pulpy, as by pressure or impact. **2.** To move with a splashing or sucking sound. ❖ *n.* **1a.** The act or sound of squashing. **b.** The fact or condition of being squashed. **2.** A crushed or crowded mass. **3.** *Sports* A racket game played in a closed, walled court with a rubber ball. **4.** *Chiefly British* A citrus-based soft drink. ❖ *adv.* With a squashing sound. [ME *squachen* < OFr. *esquasser* < VLat. **exquassāre* : Lat. *ex-*, intensive pref.; see EX– + Lat. *quassāre*, to shatter, freq. of *quatere*, to shake.] **—squash′er** *n.*

squash•y (skwŏsh′ē, skwô′shē) *adj.* **-i•er, -i•est 1.** Easily squashed. **2.** Overripe and soft; pulpy. **3.** Boggy; marshy: *squashy ground.* **—squash′i•ly** *adv.* **—squash′i•ness** *n.*

squat (skwŏt) *v.* **squat•ted, squat•ting, squats** *—intr.* **1.** To sit in a crouching position with knees bent and the buttocks on or near the heels. **2.** To crouch down, as an animal does. **3.** To settle on unoccupied land without legal claim. **4.** To occupy a given piece of public land in order to acquire title to it. *—tr.* **1.** To put (oneself) into a squat. **2.** To occupy as a squatter. ❖ *adj.* **squat•ter, squat•test 1.** Short and thick; low and broad. **2.** Crouched in a squat. ❖ *n.* **1.** The act of squatting. **2.** A squatting or crouching posture. **3.** *Sports* A lift or a weightlifting exercise in which one squats and stands while holding a weighted barbell supported by the back of the shoulders. **4.** The place occupied by a squatter. **5.** The lair of an animal such as a hare. **6.** A small or worthless amount; diddly-squat. [ME *squatten* < OFr. *esquatir*, to crush : *es-*, intensive pref. (< Lat. *ex-*; see EX–) + *quatir*, to press flat (< VLat. **coāctīre* < Lat. *coāctus*, p. part. of *cōgere*, to compress : *co-*, co- + *agere*, to drive; see **ag-** in App.).] **—squat′ter** *n.*

squaw (skwô) *n.* *Offensive* **1.** A Native American woman, esp. a wife. **2.** *Offensive Slang* A woman or wife. [Massachusett *squa*, younger woman.]

squaw•fish (skwô′fĭsh′) *n., pl.* **squawfish** or **-fish•es** Any of several large cyprinid freshwater fishes of the genus *Ptychocheilus* of western North America.

squawk (skwôk) *v.* **squawked, squawk•ing, squawks** *—intr.* **1.** To utter a harsh scream; screech. **2.** *Informal* To complain or protest noisily or peevishly. *—tr.* To utter with or as if with a squawk. [Imit.] **—squawk** *n.* **—squawk′er** *n.*

squaw•root (skwô′ro͞ot′, -ro͝ot′) *n.* **1.** A parasitic eastern North American plant *(Conopholis americana)* having yellowish flowers and a brown scaly stem. **2.** An eastern North American plant *(Trillium erectum)* having ill-smelling purple to yellow flowers and dark red fruit.

squeak (skwēk) *v.* **squeaked, squeak•ing, squeaks** *—intr.* **1.** To give forth a squeak. **2.** *Slang* To turn informer. *—tr.* To utter in a thin shrill voice. ❖ *n.* **1.** A short shrill cry or sound. **2.** An escape. ***—phrasal verb:*** **squeak through** (or **by**) To manage barely to pass, win, or survive. [ME *squeken*, perh. of Scand. orig.]

squeak•er (skwē′kər) *n.* **1.** One that squeaks. **2.** *Informal* Something, such as an election, that is won, passed, or achieved by the narrowest of margins or time periods.

squeak•y (skwē′kē) *adj.* **-i•er, -i•est 1.** Characterized by squeaking tones: *a squeaky voice.* **2.** Tending to squeak: *squeaky shoes.* **—squeak′i•ly** *adv.* **—squeak′i•ness** *n.*

squeal (skwēl) *v.* **squealed, squeal•ing, squeals** *—intr.* **1.** To give forth a squeal. **2.** *Slang* To turn informer; betray an accomplice or secret. *—tr.* To utter or produce with a squeal. ❖ *n.* A loud shrill cry or sound: *a squeal of surprise.* [ME *squelen*, prob. of imit. orig.] **—squeal′er** *n.*

squea•mish (skwē′mĭsh) *adj.* **1a.** Easily nauseated or sickened. **b.** Nauseated. **2.** Easily shocked or disgusted. **3.** Excessively fastidious or scrupulous. [ME *squeimous*, alteration of AN *escoymous.*] **—squea′mish•ly** *adv.* **—squea′mish•ness** *n.*

squee•gee (skwē′jē) *n.* **1.** A T-shaped implement having a crosspiece edged with rubber or leather that is drawn across a surface to remove water, as in washing windows. **2.** A similar implement or a rubber roller used in printing and photography. [Perh. < obsolete *squeege*, to press, alteration of SQUEEZE.] **—squee′gee** *v.*

squeeze (skwēz) *v.* **squeezed, squeez•ing, squeez•es** *—tr.* **1.** To press hard on or together; compress. **2.** To press gently, as in affection. **3.** To exert pressure on, as by way of extracting liquid: *squeeze an orange.* **4.** To extract by or as if by applying pressure: *squeeze juice from a lemon.* **5.** To extract by dishonest means; extort. **6.** To pressure or intimidate (someone) to comply with a demand. **7.** To obtain room for by pressure; cram. **8.** To manage to find time or space for. **9.** *Games* To force (an opponent) to discard a potentially winning card in bridge. *—intr.* **1.** To give way under pressure. **2.** To exert pressure. **3.** To force one's way. ❖ *n.* **1.** The act or an instance of squeezing. **2.** An amount squeezed out. **3.** A handclasp or brief embrace. **4.** A group crowded together; a crush. **5.** *Informal* A squeeze play. **6.** Financial pressure caused by shortages or narrowing economic margins. **7.** Pressure or intimidation to comply with a demand. **8.** *Games* A forced discard of a potentially winning card in bridge. **9.** *Slang* One's primary romantic partner or sweetheart. ***—phrasal verbs:*** **squeeze off** To fire (a round of bullets) by squeezing the trigger. **squeeze through** (or **by**) To manage narrowly to pass, win, or survive. [Prob. alteration of obsolete *quease*, to press < ME *queisen* < OE *cwȳsan.*] **—squeez′a•ble** *adj.* **—squeez′er** *n.*

squeeze play *n.* **1.** *Baseball* A play in which the batter attempts to bunt so that a runner on third base may score. **2.** *Informal* Pressure exerted, as to achieve a goal.

squelch (skwĕlch) *v.* **squelched, squelch•ing, squelch•es** *—tr.* **1.** To crush by or as if by trampling; squash. **2.** To put down or silence, as with a crushing retort. **3.** To suppress or inhibit. *—intr.* To produce a splashing, squishing, or sucking sound, as when walking through ooze. ❖ *n.* **1.** A squishing sound. **2.** A crushing reply. **3.** An electric circuit that cuts off a radio receiver when the signal is too weak for reception of anything but noise. [Prob. imit.] **—squelch′er** *n.*

sque•teague (skwĭ-tēg′) *n., pl.* **squeteague 1.** See **weakfish. 2.** Any of several related fishes. [Of Algonquian orig.]

squib (skwĭb) *n.* **1a.** A small firecracker. **b.** A broken firecracker that burns but does not explode. **2a.** A brief satirical or witty writing or speech, such as a lampoon. **b.** A short, sometimes humorous piece in a newspaper or magazine, usu. used as a filler. ❖ *v.* **squibbed, squib•bing, squibs** *—intr.* To write or utter squibs. *—tr.* **1.** To write or utter squibs against; lampoon. **2.** *Football* To kick (the ball) low on a kickoff so that it bounces along the ground. [Prob. imit.]

squid (skwĭd) *n., pl.* **squids** or **squid** Any of various marine cephalopod mollusks of the genus *Loligo* and related genera, having an elongated body, ten arms surrounding the mouth, and a vestigial internal shell. [?]

SQUID (skwĭd) *n.* A device that measures minute changes in magnetic flux by means of a pair of Josephson junctions, often used to detect extremely small changes in magnetic fields, electric currents, and voltages. [*s(uperconducting) qu(antum) i(nterference) d(evice).*]

squig•gle (skwĭg′əl) *n.* A small wiggly mark or scrawl. ❖ *intr.v.* **-gled, -gling, -gles 1.** To squirm and wriggle. **2.** To make squiggles. [Perh. blend of SQUIRM and WIGGLE.] **—squig′gly** *adj.*

squill (skwĭl) *n.* **1.** Any of several bulbous Eurasian and African plants of the genus *Scilla*, having narrow leaves and bell-shaped blue, white, or pink flowers. **2.** See **sea onion** 1. **3.** The dried inner scales of the bulbs of any of these plants, used as rat poison and formerly as a cardiac stimulant, expectorant, and diuretic. [ME < Lat. *scilla*, *squilla*, shrimp, squill < Gk. *skilla.*]

squil•la (skwĭl′ə) *n., pl.* **squil•las** or **squil•lae** (skwĭl′ē′) Any of various burrowing predatory marine crustaceans of the order

square knot

squash[1]
butternut squash
Cucurbita moschata

ă	pat	oi	boy
ā	pay	ou	out
âr	care	o͝o	took
ä	father	o͞o	boot
ĕ	pet	ŭ	cut
ē	be	ûr	urge
ĭ	pit	th	thin
ī	pie	*th*	this
îr	pier	hw	which
ŏ	pot	zh	vision
ō	toe	ə	about, item
ô	paw		

Stress marks:
′ (primary);
′ (secondary), as in
lexicon (lĕk′sĭ-kŏn′)

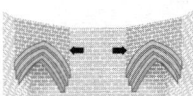

squinch¹

Stomatopoda, having movable stalked eyes and a pair of jointed grasping appendages. [NLat. *Squilla*, genus name < Lat. *squilla*, shrimp. See SQUILL.]

squinch¹ (skwĭnch) *n.* A section of masonry vaulting or corbeling set diagonally across the interior angle between two walls to provide a transition from a square to a polygonal or circular base on which to construct a dome. [Alteration of *scuncheon* < ME *sconchon* < OFr. *escoinson* : *es-*, out of (< Lat. *ex-*; see EX-) + *coin*, angle, wedge; see COIN.]

squinch² (skwĭnch) *tr.v.* **squinched, squinch·ing, squinch·es** To squeeze, twist, or draw together. [Alteration of SQUINT.]

squint (skwĭnt) *v.* **squint·ed, squint·ing, squints** —*intr.* **1.** To look with the eyes partly closed, as in bright sunlight. **2a.** To look or glance sideways. **b.** To look askance, as in disapproval. **3.** To have an indirect reference or inclination. **4.** To be affected with strabismus. —*tr.* **1.** To cause to squint. **2.** To close (the eyes) partly while looking. ❖ *n.* **1.** The act or an instance of squinting. **2a.** A sideways glance. **b.** A quick look or glance. **3.** An oblique reference or inclination. **4.** See strabismus. **5.** A hagioscope. ❖ *adj.* **1.** Looking obliquely or askance. **2.** Squint-eyed. [Short for ASQUINT.] —**squint′er** *n.* —**squint′y** *adj.*

squint-eyed (skwĭnt′īd′) *adj.* **1.** Affected with strabismus. **2.** Looking with narrowed or squinting eyes. **3.** Looking askance, as in envy.

squire (skwīr) *n.* **1.** A man who attends or escorts a woman; a gallant. **2.** An English country gentleman, esp. the chief landowner in a district. **3.** A judge or other local dignitary. **4.** A young nobleman attendant upon a knight and ranked next below a knight in feudal hierarchy. ❖ *tr.v.* **squired, squir·ing, squires** To attend as a squire; escort. [ME *squier* < OFr. *esquier*. See ESQUIRE.]

squire·ar·chy or **squir·ar·chy** (skwīr′är′kē) *n., pl.* **-chies** The landed gentry considered as a group or class.

squirm (skwûrm) *intr.v.* **squirmed, squirm·ing, squirms 1.** To twist about in a wriggling snakelike motion; writhe. **2.** To feel or exhibit signs of humiliation or embarrassment. ❖ *n.* **1.** The act of squirming. **2.** A squirming movement. [?] —**squirm′er** *n.* —**squirm′y** *adj.*

squir·rel (skwûr′əl, skwŭr′-) *n.* **1.** Any of various arboreal rodents of the genus *Sciurus* and related genera of the family Sciuridae, having a long flexible bushy tail and including the gray squirrel. **2.** Any of various other rodents of the family Sciuridae, as the flying squirrel. **3.** The fur of one of these rodents. ❖ *tr.v.* **-reled, -rel·ing, -rels** or **-relled, -rel·ling, -rels** To hide or store: *squirreled it away.* [ME *squirel* < AN *esquirel* < VLat. *scūriolus*, dim. of *scūrius*, alteration of Lat. *sciūrus* < Gk. *skiouros* : *skiā*, shadow + *ourā*, tail; see ors- in App.]

squirrel monkey
Saimiri sciureus

squir·rel·ly (skwûr′ə-lē, skwŭr′-) *adj. Slang* **1.** Eccentric. **2.** Cunningly unforthcoming or reticent.

squirrel monkey *n.* Any of several small, brightly colored arboreal monkeys of the genus *Saimiri*, widely distributed in South and Central American jungles and having a white face, a black nose and mouth, and a long nonprehensile tail.

squirt (skwûrt) *v.* **squirt·ed, squirt·ing, squirts** —*intr.* **1.** To issue forth in a thin forceful stream or jet; spurt. **2.** To eject liquid in a jet. —*tr.* **1.** To eject (liquid) forcibly in a thin stream from a narrow opening. **2.** To wet with a spurt of liquid. ❖ *n.* **1.** The act of squirting. **2.** An instrument used for squirting. **3.** A squirted jet of liquid. **4a.** A small or young person. **b.** An insignificant or contemptible person. [ME *squirten*, poss. of MDu. or MLGer. orig.] —**squirt′er** *n.*

squirt gun *n.* A toy gun designed to squirt a stream of water.

squirt·ing cucumber (skwûr′tĭng) *n.* A hairy Mediterranean vine (*Ecballium elaterium*) having fruit that when ripe discharges its seeds and juice explosively.

squish (skwĭsh) *v.* **squished, squish·ing, squish·es** —*tr.* To squeeze or crush together or into a flat mass; squash. —*intr.* To emit the gurgling or sucking sound of soft mud being walked on. ❖ *n.* **1.** A squishing sound. **2.** *Slang* A weak and ineffective person. [Prob. alteration of SQUASH².]

squish·y (skwĭsh′ē) *adj.* **-i·er, -i·est 1.** Soft and wet; spongy. **2.** Sloppily sentimental.

sr *abbr.* steradian

Sr The symbol for the element strontium.

Sr. *abbr.* **1.** or **sr.** senior **2.** señor **3.** *Ecclesiastical* sister (title)

Sra. *abbr.* señora

SRAM (ĕs′răm′) *n.* Static RAM.

Sra·nan·ton·go (srä′nən-tŏng′gō) *n.* A creole based on English, spoken in coastal Suriname and widely used as a lingua franca. [Sranantongo : *Sranan*, Suriname + *tongo*, tongue (< E. TONGUE).]

Sri (srē, shrē) *n.* **1.** Used in India as a title of respect for a man. **2.** *Hinduism* Used as a title for a deity or holy man. [Hindi *śrī* < Skt., splendor, majesty, honorific pref.]

Sri Lan·ka (srē lăng′kə, shrē) Formerly **Cey·lon** (sĭ-lŏn′, sā-) An island country in the Indian Ocean off SE India; became a British colony in 1798 and achieved independence in 1948. Cap. Colombo. Pop. 17,865,000. —**Sri Lan′kan** *adj. & n.*

Sri·na·gar (srē-nŭg′ər) A city of N India on the Jhelum R. N of Amritsar; founded in the 6th cent. A.D. Pop. 586,038.

sRNA *abbr.* soluble RNA

SRO *abbr.* **1.** single room occupancy **2.** standing room only

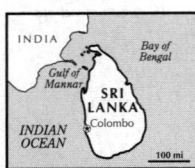

Sri Lanka

Srta. *abbr.* señorita

SS¹ (ĕs′ĕs′) *n.* An elite quasi-military unit of the Nazi party that served as Hitler's personal guard and as a special security force in Germany and the occupied countries. [Ger., abbr. for *Schutzstaffel* : *Schutz*, defense + *Staffel*, echelon.]

SS² *abbr.* **1.** saints **2.** shortstop **3.** Social Security **4.** *Bible* Song of Solomon **5.** steamship **6.** Sunday school

ss. *abbr.* **1.** scilicet **2.** sections **3.** *Latin semis* (one half)

SSA *abbr.* Social Security Administration

SSE *abbr.* south-southeast

SSG or **SSgt** *abbr.* staff sergeant

SSI *abbr.* Supplemental Security Income

SSN *abbr.* Social Security number

ssp. *abbr.* subspecies

SSR *abbr.* Soviet Socialist Republic

SSRI (ĕs′ĕs-är-ī′) *n.* A class of drugs that inhibit the uptake of serotonin by the central nervous system, often used in the treatment of depression. [*s(elective) s(erotonin) r(euptake) i(nhibitor)*.]

SSS *abbr.* Selective Service System

SST *abbr.* supersonic transport

SSW *abbr.* south-southwest

ST *abbr.* **1.** short ton **2.** standard time

st. *abbr.* **1.** stanza **2.** statute **3.** stet **4.** stone (weight) **5.** strophe

St. *abbr.* **1.** saint **2.** state **3.** strait **4.** street

–st *suff.* Variant of **–est²**.

stab (stăb) *v.* **stabbed, stab·bing, stabs** —*tr.* **1.** To pierce or wound with or as if with a pointed weapon. **2.** To plunge (a pointed weapon or instrument) into something. **3.** To make a thrusting or poking motion at or into. —*intr.* **1.** To thrust with or as if with a pointed weapon: *stabbed at the food with her fork.* **2.** To inflict a wound with or as if with a pointed weapon. ❖ *n.* **1.** A thrust with a pointed weapon or instrument. **2.** A wound inflicted with or as if with a pointed weapon. **3.** A sudden piercing pain. **4.** An attempt; a try: *made a stab at the answer.* —**idiom: stab (someone) in the back** To harm (someone) by treachery or betrayal of trust. [ME *stabben*.] —**stab′ber** *n.*

Sta·bat Ma·ter (stä′bät mä′tər, stăb′ät mä′tər) *n.* A medieval Latin hymn on the sorrows of the Virgin Mary at the Crucifixion or a musical setting of this hymn. [< Med.Lat. *Stābat Māter (dolōrōsa)*, the Mother was standing (full of sorrow), the first words of the hymn : Lat. *stābat*, third pers. sing. imperfect t. of *stāre*, to stand + Med.Lat. *Māter*, Mother (of God).]

sta·bile (stā′bĭl, -bəl, -bĭl′, -bēl′) *adj.* Immobile; unchangeable; stable. ❖ *n.* An abstract sculpture, usu. of sheet metal, resembling a mobile but having no moving parts. [Lat. *stabilis*, stable. See STABLE¹.]

sta·bil·i·ty (stə-bĭl′ĭ-tē) *n., pl.* **-ties 1.** The state or quality of being stable, esp.: **a.** Resistance to change, deterioration, or displacement. **b.** Constancy of character or purpose; steadfastness. **c.** Reliability; dependability. **2.** The ability of an object, such as a ship, to maintain equilibrium or resume its original, upright position after displacement, as by the sea.

sta·bi·lize (stā′bə-līz′) *v.* **-lized, -liz·ing, -liz·es** —*tr.* **1.** To make stable or steadfast. **2.** To maintain the stability of (an airplane, for example) by means of a stabilizer. **3.** To keep from fluctuating; fix the level of. —*intr.* To become stable, steadfast, or fixed. —**sta′bi·li·za′tion** (-lĭ-zā′shən) *n.*

sta·bi·liz·er (stā′bə-lī′zər) *n.* **1.** One that makes or keeps something stable. **2.** A device, such as a gyroscopically controlled fin, that prevents excessive rolling of a ship in heavy seas. **3.** An airfoil that stabilizes an aircraft or missile in flight. **4.** *Chemistry* A substance that renders a solution, mixture, suspension, or state resistant to chemical change.

stabilizer bar *n.* See anti-sway bar.

sta·ble¹ (stā′bəl) *adj.* **-bler, -blest 1a.** Resistant to change of position or condition; not easily moved or disturbed: *a stable platform.* **b.** Not subject to sudden or extreme change or fluctuation: *a stable economy.* **c.** Maintaining equilibrium; self-restoring: *a stable aircraft.* **2.** Enduring or permanent: *a stable peace.* **3a.** Consistently dependable. **b.** Not subject to mental illness or irrationality. **4.** *Physics* Having no known mode of decay; indefinitely long-lived. Used of atomic particles. **5.** *Chemistry* Not easily decomposed or otherwise modified chemically. [ME < OFr. *estable* < Lat. *stabilis*. See stā- in App.] —**sta′ble·ness** *n.* —**sta′bly** *adv.*

sta·ble² (stā′bəl) *n.* **1a.** A building for the shelter and feeding of domestic animals, esp. horses and cattle. **b.** A group of animals lodged in such a building. **2a.** All the racehorses of an owner or racing establishment. **b.** The personnel employed to keep and train a stable. **3.** A group, as of athletes or entertainers, under common management. ❖ *v.* **-bled, -bling, -bles** —*tr.* To put or keep in or as if in a stable. —*intr.* To live in or as if in a stable. [ME < OFr. *estable* < Lat. *stabulum*, stable, standing place. See stā- in App.]

stab·lish (stăb′lĭsh) *tr.v.* **-lished, -lish·ing, -lish·es** *Archaic* To establish.

stac·ca·to (stə-kä′tō) *adj.* **1.** *Music* Cut short crisply; detached: *staccato octaves.* **2.** Marked by or composed of abrupt disconnected parts or sounds: *staccato applause from the audience.* ❖ *n., pl.* **-tos** or **-ti** (-tē) A staccato manner or sound. [Ital., p. part. of *staccare*, to detach, short for *distaccare* < obsolete Fr. *destacher*

< OFr. *destachier*. See DETACH.] **—stac•ca′to** *adv.*

stack (stăk) *n.* **1.** A large, usu. conical pile of straw or fodder arranged for outdoor storage. **2.** An orderly pile, esp. one arranged in layers. **3.** *Computer Science* A section of memory and its associated registers used for temporary storage of information in which the item most recently stored is the first to be retrieved. **4.** A group of three rifles supporting each other, butt downward and forming a cone. **5a.** A chimney or flue. **b.** A group of chimneys arranged together. **6.** A vertical exhaust pipe, as on a ship. **7.** An extensive arrangement of bookshelves. Often used in the plural. **8. stacks** The area of a library in which most of the books are shelved. **9.** A stackup. **10.** An English measure of coal or cut wood, equal to 108 cubic feet (3.06 cubic meters). **11.** *Informal* A large quantity: *a stack of work to do.* ❖ *v.* **stacked, stack•ing, stacks** *—tr.* **1.** To arrange in a stack; pile. **2.** To load or cover with stacks or piles. **3a.** *Games* To prearrange the order of (a deck of cards) so as to increase the chance of winning. **b.** To prearrange or fix unfairly so as to favor a particular outcome. **4.** To direct (aircraft) to circle at different altitudes while waiting to land. *—intr.* To form a stack. ***—phrasal verb:* stack up** *Informal* **1.** To measure up or equal. **2.** To make sense; add up. [ME *stac* < ON *stakkr.*] **—stack′a•ble** *adj.* **—stack′er** *n.*

stacked (stăkt) *adj. Vulgar Slang* Large-breasted.

stack•up (stăk′ŭp′) *n.* A deployment of aircraft circling an airport at designated altitudes while waiting to land.

stad•dle (stăd′l) *n.* A base or support, esp. a platform on which hay or straw is stacked. [ME *stathel* < OE *stathol.* See **stā-** in App.]

stad•hold•er (stăd′hōl′dər) also **stadt•hold•er** (stăt′-) *n.* **1.** A governor or viceroy formerly stationed in a province of the Netherlands. **2.** The chief magistrate of the former Netherlands republic. [Partial transl. of Du. *stadhouder* : *stad*, place; see **stā-** in App. + *houder*, holder.]

sta•di•a¹ (stā′dē-ə) *n.* **1a.** A telescopic instrument having two parallel lines through which intervals on a calibrated rod are observed, used to measure distances. **b.** The parallel lines in this instrument. **c.** The calibrated rod so used. **2.** The technique of measuring distances with this instrument. [Ital., prob. < Lat., pl. of *stadium*, a unit of length. See STADIUM.]

sta•di•a² (stā′dē-ə) *n.* A plural of **stadium.**

sta•di•um (stā′dē-əm) *n., pl.* **-di•ums** or **-di•a** (-dē-ə) **1.** A large, usu. open structure for sports events with tiered seating for spectators. **2.** A course on which foot races were held in ancient Greece, having tiers of seats for spectators. **3.** An ancient Greek measure of distance, based on the length of such a course and equal to about 185 meters (607 feet). **4.** *Medicine* A stage or period in the course of a disease. **5.** *Biology* A stage in the development or life history of an organism. [ME, unit of length < Lat. < Gk. *stadion*, perh. alteration (influenced by *stadios*, firm) of *spadion*, racetrack < *spān*, to pull.]

Staël (stäl), Madame de. Title of Baronne Anne Louise Germaine Necker de Staël-Holstein. 1766–1817. French writer and literary patron who introduced romanticism to French literature.

staff¹ (stăf) *n., pl.* **staffs** or **staves** (stāvz) **1a.** A stick or cane carried as an aid in walking or climbing. **b.** A stout stick used as a weapon; a cudgel. **c.** A pole on which a flag is displayed; a flagstaff. **d.** A rod or baton carried as a symbol of authority. **2.** *pl.* **staffs** A rule or similar graduated stick used for testing or measuring, as in surveying. **3.** *pl.* **staffs a.** A group of assistants to a manager, executive, or other person in authority. **b.** A group of military officers assigned to assist a commanding officer in an executive or advisory capacity. **c.** The personnel who carry out a specific enterprise. **4.** Something that serves as a staple or support. **5.** *Music* A set of five horizontal lines and four intermediate spaces used in notation to represent a sequence of pitches. ❖ *tr.v.* **staffed, staff•ing, staffs 1.** To provide with a staff of workers or assistants. **2.** To serve on the staff of. [ME *staf* < OE *stæf.*]

staff² (stăf) *n.* A building material of plaster and fiber used as an exterior wall covering of temporary buildings, as at expositions. [Perh. < Ger. *Stoff*, stuff.]

Staf•fa (stăf′ə) An island of W Scotland in the Inner Hebrides W of Mull.

staff•er (stăf′ər) *n. Informal* A member of a staff.

Staf•ford•shire terrier (stăf′ərd-shîr′, -shər) *n.* See **American Staffordshire terrier.** [After *Staffordshire*, a county of W-central England.]

staff sergeant *n.* **1.** A noncommissioned officer in the US Army ranking above sergeant and below sergeant first class. **2.** A noncommissioned officer in the US Air Force ranking above senior airman and below technical sergeant. **3.** A noncommissioned officer in the US Marine Corps ranking above sergeant and below gunnery sergeant.

staff tree *n.* See **bittersweet** 1.

stag (stăg) *n.* **1.** The adult male of various deer, esp. the red deer. **2.** A male animal, esp. a pig, castrated after reaching sexual maturity. **3.** A person who attends a social gathering unaccompanied by a partner, esp. a man unaccompanied by a woman. **4.** A social gathering for men only. ❖ *adj.* **1.** Of or for men only. **2.** Pornographic. ❖ *adv.* Unaccompanied. ❖ *intr.v.* **stagged, stag•ging, stags** To attend a social gathering unaccompanied by a partner. Used esp. of men. [ME *stagge* < OE *stagga.*]

stag beetle *n.* Any of numerous large beetles of the family Lucanidae, having large branched mandibles in the male.

stage (stāj) *n.* **1.** A raised and level floor or platform. **2a.** A raised platform on which theatrical performances are presented. **b.** An area in which actors perform. **c.** The acting profession, or the world of theater. Used with *the.* **3.** The scene of an event or of a series of events. **4.** A platform on a microscope that supports a slide for viewing. **5.** A scaffold for workers. **6.** A resting place on a journey, esp. one providing overnight accommodations. **7.** The distance between stopping places on a journey; a leg. **8.** A stagecoach. **9.** A level or story of a building. **10.** The height of the surface of a river or other fluctuating body of water above a set point. **11a.** A level, degree, or period of time in the course of a process, esp. a step in development. **b.** A point in the course of an action or series of events. **12.** One of two or more successive propulsion units of a rocket vehicle, each of which fires after the preceding one has been jettisoned. **13.** *Geology* A subdivision in the classification of stratified rocks, ranking just below a series and representing rock formed during a chronological age. **14.** *Electronics* An element or a group of elements in a complex arrangement of parts, esp. a single tube or transistor and its accessory components in an amplifier. ❖ *v.* **staged, stag•ing, stag•es** *—tr.* **1.** To exhibit or present on or as if on a stage. **2.** To produce or direct (a theatrical performance). **3.** To arrange and carry out. **4.** *Medicine* To determine the extent or progression of (a cancer, for example). *—intr.* **1.** To be adaptable to or suitable for theatrical presentation. **2.** To stop at a designated place in the course of a journey. [ME < OFr. *estage* < VLat. **staticum* < Lat. *status*, p. part. of *stāre*, to stand. See **stā-** in App.] **—stage′ful′** *n.*

stage•coach (stāj′kōch′) *n.* A four-wheeled horse-drawn vehicle formerly used to transport mail and passengers over a regular route.

stage•craft (stāj′krăft′) *n.* Skill in the techniques and devices of the theater.

stage fright *n.* Acute nervousness associated with performing or speaking before an audience.

stage•hand (stāj′hănd′) *n.* A worker who shifts scenery, adjusts lighting, and performs other tasks required in a theatrical production.

stage left *n.* The area of the stage to the left of the center of the stage when facing the audience.

stage-man•age (stāj′măn′ĭj) *tr.v.* **-aged, -ag•ing, -ag•es 1.** To serve as overall supervisor of the stage and actors for (a theatrical production). **2.** To direct or manipulate from behind the scenes, as to achieve a desired effect; orchestrate. **—stage management** *n.* **—stage manager** *n.*

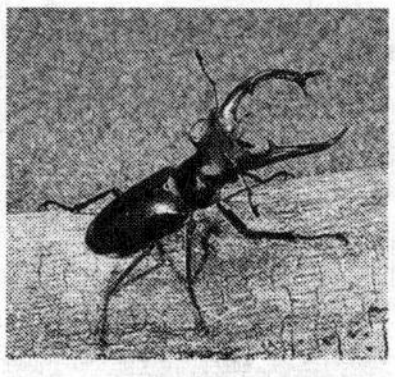

stag beetle

stag•er (stā′jər) *n.* One who possesses the wisdom of long experience.

stage right *n.* The area of the stage to the right of the center of the stage when facing the audience.

stage-struck (stāj′strŭk′) *adj.* Enthralled by the theater or intensely eager for a career in acting.

stage whisper *n.* **1.** The conventional whisper of an actor, intended to be heard by the audience but supposedly inaudible to others on stage. **2.** A whisper that can be or is intended to be overheard.

stag•ey (stā′jē) *adj.* Variant of **stagy.**

stag•gard (stăg′ərd) *n.* A male red deer in its fourth year. [ME < *stagge*, stag. See STAG.]

stag•ger (stăg′ər) *v.* **-gered, -ger•ing, -gers** *—intr.* **1.** To move or stand unsteadily, as if under a great weight; totter. **2.** To begin to lose confidence or strength of purpose; waver. *—tr.* **1.** To cause to totter, sway, or reel. **2a.** To overwhelm with emotion or astonishment. **b.** To cause to waver or lose confidence. **3.** To place on or as if on alternating sides of a center line; set in a zigzag row or rows. **4.** To arrange in alternating or overlapping time periods. **5.** To arrange (the wings of a biplane) so that the leading edge of one wing is either ahead of or behind the leading edge of the other wing. **6.** *Sports* To arrange (the start of a running race) with the starting point in the outside lanes progressively closer to the finish line so as to neutralize the advantage of competing in the shorter inside lanes. ❖ *n.* **1.** A tottering, swaying, or reeling motion. **2.** A staggered pattern, arrangement, or order. **3. staggers** (*used with a sing. verb*) Any of various diseases of the nervous system in animals, esp. horses, cattle, or other domestic animals, marked by a staggering gait and frequent falling. [Alteration of ME *stakeren* < ON *stakra*, freq. of *staka*, to push.] **—stag′ger•er** *n.* **—stag′ger•y** *adj.*

stag•ger•bush (stăg′ər-bo͝osh′) *n.* A deciduous shrub *(Lyonia mariana)* of the eastern United States having poisonous foliage and white or pink flowers clustered in racemes.

stag•ger•ing (stăg′ər-ĭng) *adj.* Causing great astonishment, amazement, or dismay; overwhelming: *a staggering defeat.*

stag•horn fern (stăg′hôrn′) *n.* Any of several tropical epiphytic ferns of the genus *Platycerium*, having large, dichotomously divided fertile fronds that resemble antlers.

staghorn sumac *n.* An eastern North American deciduous shrub or tree *(Rhus typhina)* having pinnately compound leaves, small greenish flowers, and hairy crimson fruit.

stag•hound (stăg′hound′) *n.* Any of several dogs formerly used in hunting stags and other large game.

stag•ing (stā′jĭng) *n.* **1.** A temporary platform or system of plat-

ă	pat	oi	boy
ā	pay	ou	out
âr	care	o͝o	took
ä	father	o͞o	boot
ĕ	pet	ŭ	cut
ē	be	ûr	urge
ĭ	pit	th	thin
ī	pie	*th*	this
îr	pier	hw	which
ŏ	pot	zh	vision
ō	toe	ə	about, item
ô	paw		

Stress marks:
′ (primary);
′ (secondary), as in
lexicon (lĕk′sĭ-kŏn′)

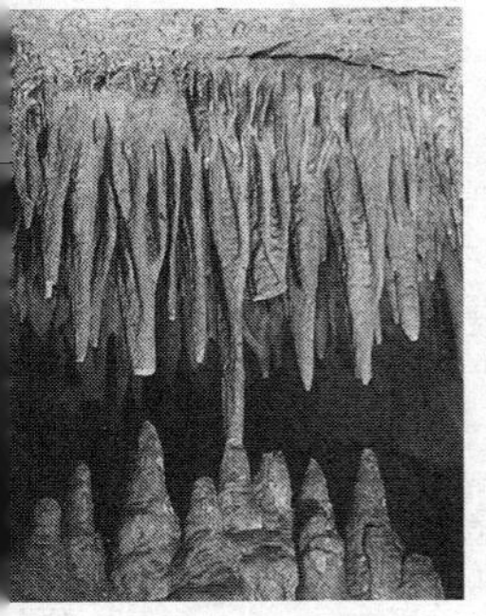

stalactite
stalactites (*top*) and stalagmites (*bottom*) in the Luray Caverns, Virginia

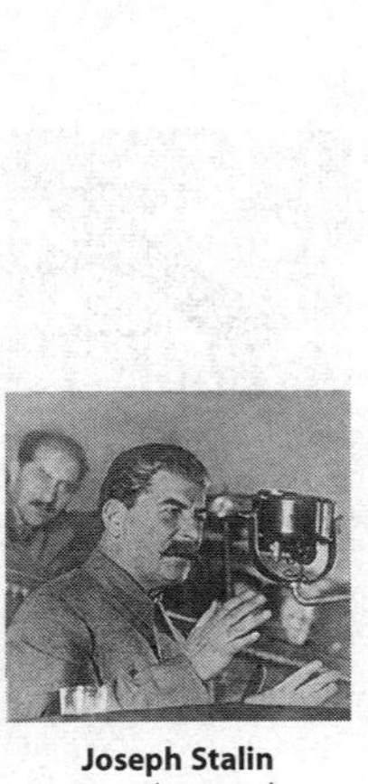

Joseph Stalin
1936 photograph

forms used for support; scaffolding. **2.** The process or manner of staging a play. **3.** The act of jettisoning a stage of a multistage rocket. **4a.** The operation of stagecoaches as an enterprise. **b.** Travel by stagecoach.

staging area *n.* A place where troops or equipment in transit are assembled and processed, as before a military operation.

Sta•gi•ra (stə-jī′rə) or **Sta•gi•rus** (-rəs) An ancient city of Macedonia in NE Greece; birthplace of Aristotle.

stag•nant (stăg′nənt) *adj.* **1.** Not moving or flowing; motionless. **2.** Foul or stale from standing. **3a.** Showing little or no sign of activity or advancement; not developing or progressing; inactive. **b.** Lacking vitality or briskness; sluggish or dull. [Lat. *stāgnāns, stāgnant-*, pr. part. of *stāgnāre*, to be stagnant. See STAGNATE.] **—stag′nan•cy** *n.* **—stag′nant•ly** *adv.*

stag•nate (stăg′nāt′) *intr.v.* **-nat•ed, -nat•ing, -nates** To be or become stagnant. [Lat. *stāgnāre, stāgnāt-* < *stāgnum*, swamp.] **—stag•na′tion** *n.*

stag•y also **stag•ey** (stā′jē) *adj.* **-i•er, -i•est** Having a theatrical, esp. an artificial or affected, character or quality. **—stag′i•ly** *adv.*

staid (stād) *adj.* **1.** Characterized by sedate dignity and often a strait-laced sense of propriety; sober. **2.** Fixed; permanent. [< obsolete *staid*, p. part. of STAY¹.] **—staid′ly** *adv.* **—staid′ness** *n.*

stain (stān) *v.* **stained, stain•ing, stains** *—tr.* **1.** To discolor, soil, or spot. **2.** To bring into disrepute; taint. **3.** To color (glass, for example) with a coat of penetrating liquid dye or tint. **4.** To treat (specimens for the microscope) with a reagent or dye that makes visible certain structures without affecting others. *—intr.* To produce or receive discolorations. ❖ *n.* **1.** A discolored or soiled spot or smudge. **2.** A blemish on one's character or reputation. **3.** A liquid applied esp. to wood that penetrates the surface and imparts a rich color. **4.** A reagent or dye used for staining microscopic specimens. [ME *steinen*, partly < OFr. *desteindre, desteign-*, to deprive of color (*des-*, dis- + *teindre*, to dye < Lat. *tingere*), and partly < ON *steina*, to paint.] **—stain′a•ble** *adj.* **—stain′er** *n.*

stained glass (stānd) *n.* Glass colored by mixing pigments into the glass, fusing colored metallic oxides onto the glass, or painting and baking transparent colors on the glass surface.

stain•less (stān′lĭs) *adj.* **1.** Without stain or blemish. **2.** Resistant to stain or corrosion: *stainless metal.* **3.** Made of a stainless material: *a stainless teapot.* **—stain′less•ly** *adv.*

stainless steel *n.* Any of various steels that are alloyed with at least 10 percent chromium and sometimes contain other elements and are resistant to corrosion or rusting.

stair (stâr) *n.* **1.** A series or flight of steps; a staircase. Often used in the plural. **2.** One of a flight of steps. [ME < OE *stǣger*. See **steigh-** in App.]

stair•case (stâr′kās′) *n.* A flight or series of flights of steps and a supporting structure connecting separate levels.

stair•way (stâr′wā′) *n.* See **staircase.**

stair•well (stâr′wĕl′) *n.* A vertical shaft around which a staircase has been built.

stake (stāk) *n.* **1.** A piece of wood or metal pointed at one end for driving into the ground as a marker, fence pole, or tent peg. **2a.** A vertical post to which an offender is bound for execution by burning. **b.** Execution by burning. Used with *the.* **3.** A vertical post secured in a socket at the edge of a platform, as on a truck bed, to help retain the load. **4.** *Mormon Church* A territorial division consisting of a group of wards under the jurisdiction of a president. **5.** *Sports & Games* **a.** Money or property risked in a wager or gambling game. See Syns at **bet. b.** The prize awarded the winner of a contest or race. **c.** A race offering a prize to the winner, esp. a horserace in which the prize consists of money contributed equally by the horse owners. In all three senses, often used in the plural. **6a.** A share or an interest in an enterprise, esp. a financial share. **b.** Personal interest or involvement. **7.** A grubstake. ❖ *tr.v.* **staked, stak•ing, stakes 1a.** To mark the location or limits of with or as if with stakes: *staked out a claim.* **b.** To claim as one's own. **2.** To fasten, secure, or support with a stake or stakes. **3.** To tether or tie to a stake. **4.** To gamble or risk; hazard. **5.** To provide working capital for; finance. ***—phrasal verb:*** **stake out 1.** To assign (a police officer, for example) to an area to conduct surveillance. **2.** To keep under surveillance. ***—idiom:*** **at stake** At risk; in question. [ME < OE *staca.*]

stake•hold•er (stāk′hōl′dər) *n.* **1.** One who holds the bets in a game or contest. **2.** One who has a share or interest, as in an enterprise.

stake•out (stāk′out′) *n.* Surveillance of an area, building, or person, esp. by the police.

sta•lac•tite (stə-lăk′tīt′, stăl′ək-) *n.* An icicle-shaped mineral deposit, usu. calcite or aragonite, hanging from the roof of a cavern, formed from the dripping of mineral-rich water. [NLat. *stalactītēs* < Gk. *stalaktos*, dripping < *stalassein, stalak-*, to drip.] **—sta•lac′ti•form′** *adj.* **—stal′ac•tit′ic** (stăl′ăk-tĭt′ĭk, stə-lăk′-) *adj.*

sta•lag (stä′läg′, stăl′ăg′) *n.* A German prisoner-of-war camp. [Ger., short for *Stammlager*, base camp : *Stamm*, base, stem (< MHGer. *stam* < OHGer.; see **stā-** in App.) + *Lager*, camp, bed (< MHGer. *leger* < OHGer. *legar*, bed, lair; see LAGER).]

sta•lag•mite (stə-lăg′mīt′, stăl′əg-) *n.* A conical mineral deposit, usu. calcite or aragonite, built up on the floor of a cavern, formed from the dripping of mineral-rich water. [NLat. *stalagmītēs*, a drop < Gk. *stalagma*, a drop, or *stalagmos*, dropping, both < *stalassein, stalak-*, to drip.] **—stal′ag•mit′ic** (stăl′əg-mĭt′ĭk, stə-lăg′-) *adj.*

stale¹ (stāl) *adj.* **stal•er, stal•est 1.** Having lost freshness, effervescence, or palatability: *stale bread; stale air.* **2.** Lacking originality or spontaneity: *a stale joke.* **3.** Impaired in efficacy, vigor, or spirit, as from inactivity. ❖ *tr. & intr.v.* **staled, stal•ing, stales** To make or become stale. [ME, settled, clear (used of beer or wine), prob. < OFr. *estale*, slack, settled, clear < *estaler*, to come to a halt < *estal*, standing place, stand, of Gmc. orig. See **stel-** in App.] **—stale′ly** *adv.* **—stale′ness** *n.*

stale² (stāl) *intr.v.* **staled, stal•ing, stales** To urinate. Used esp. of horses and camels. ❖ *n.* The urine of these animals. [ME *stalen*, poss. of LGer. orig.; akin to MLGer. *stallen.*]

stale•mate (stāl′māt′) *n.* **1.** A situation in which further action is blocked; a deadlock. **2.** A drawing position in chess in which the king, although not in check, can move only into check and no other piece can move. [Obsolete *stale* (< ME, prob. < AN *estale*, fixed position < OFr. *estal*; see STALE¹) + MATE².] **—stale′mate′** *v.*

Sta•lin (stä′lĭn, stăl′ĭn), **Joseph** 1879–1953. Soviet politician who was general secretary of the Communist Party (1922–53) and premier (1941–53) of the USSR.

Sta•lin•grad (stä′lĭn-grăd′, stə-lyĭn-grät′) See **Volgograd.**

Sta•lin•ism (stä′lə-nĭz′əm) *n.* The bureaucratic, authoritarian exercise of state power and mechanistic application of Marxist-Leninist principles associated with Stalin. **—Sta′lin•ist** *adj. & n.* **—Sta′lin•ize′** *v.*

stalk¹ (stôk) *n.* **1a.** A stem or main axis of a herbaceous plant. **b.** A stem or similar structure that supports a plant part such as a flower, flower cluster, or leaf. **2.** A slender or elongated support or structure, as one that holds up an organ or another body part. [ME, prob. dim. of *stale*, upright of a ladder, post, handle < OE *stalu.* See **stel-** in App.] **—stalk′y** *adj.*

stalk² (stôk) *v.* **stalked, stalk•ing, stalks** *—intr.* **1.** To walk with a stiff, haughty, or angry gait. **2.** To move threateningly or menacingly. **3.** To track prey or quarry. *—tr.* **1.** To pursue by tracking stealthily. **2.** To follow or observe (a person) persistently, esp. out of obsession or derangement. **3.** To go through (an area) in pursuit of prey or quarry. [ME *stalken* < OE *-stealcian*, to move stealthily (in *bestealcian*, to move stealthily).] **—stalk′er** *n.*

stalked (stôkt) *adj.* Having a stalk or stem. Often used in combination: *long-stalked.*

stalk•ing-horse (stô′kĭng-hôrs′) *n.* **1.** Something used to cover one's true purpose; a decoy. **2.** A sham candidate put forward, as to divide the opposition. **3a.** A horse trained to conceal the hunter while stalking. **b.** A canvas screen made in the figure of a horse, used for similar concealment.

stall¹ (stôl) *n.* **1.** A compartment for one domestic animal in a barn or shed. **2a.** A booth, cubicle, or stand used by a vendor, as at a market. **b.** A small compartment: *a shower stall.* **3a.** An enclosed seat in the chancel of a church. **b.** A pew in a church. **4.** *Chiefly British* A seat in the front part of a theater. **5.** A space marked off, as in a garage, for parking a motor vehicle. **6.** A protective sheath for a finger or toe. **7.** The sudden unintended loss of power in an engine. **8.** A condition in which an aircraft or airfoil experiences an interruption of airflow resulting in loss of lift and a tendency to drop. ❖ *v.* **stalled, stall•ing, stalls** *—tr.* **1.** To put or lodge in a stall. **2.** To maintain in a stall for fattening: *to stall cattle.* **3.** To halt the motion or progress of; bring to a standstill. **4.** To cause (a motor or motor vehicle) accidentally to stop running. **5.** To cause (an aircraft) to go into a stall. *—intr.* **1.** To live or be lodged in a stall. Used of an animal. **2.** To stick fast in mud or snow. **3.** To come to a standstill: *Negotiations stalled.* **4.** To stop running as a result of mechanical failure. **5.** To lose forward flying speed, causing a stall. Used of an aircraft. [ME *stalle* < OE *steall*, standing place, stable. See **stel-** in App.]

stall² (stôl) *n.* A ruse or tactic used to mislead or delay. ❖ *v.* **stalled, stall•ing, stalls** *—tr.* To employ delaying tactics against: *stall off creditors.* *—intr.* To employ delaying tactics. [Alteration (influenced by STALL¹) of obsolete *stale*, pickpocket's accomplice < ME, decoy < AN *estale*, of Gmc. orig.; poss. akin to OE *stǣl, stathol*, place, position. See STADDLE.]

stall-feed (stôl′fēd′) *tr.v.* **-fed** (-fĕd′), **-feed•ing, -feeds** To lodge and feed (an animal) in a stall for fattening.

stal•lion (stăl′yən) *n.* An adult male horse that has not been castrated, esp. one kept for breeding. [ME *stalione*, alteration of *staloun* < AN *estaloun*, of Gmc. orig. See **stel-** in App.]

stal•wart (stôl′wərt) *adj.* **1.** Having or marked by imposing physical strength. **2.** Firm and resolute; stout. ❖ *n.* **1.** One who is physically and morally strong. **2.** One who steadfastly supports an organization or a cause. [ME, alteration of *stalworth* < OE *stǣlwierthe*, serviceable, prob. alteration of **statholwierthe*, steadfast : *stathol*, foundation; see STADDLE + *weorth*, valuable; see **wer-²** in App.] **—stal′wart•ly** *adv.* **—stal′wart•ness** *n.*

sta•men (stā′mən) *n., pl.* **sta•mens** or **sta•mi•na** (stā′mə-nə, stăm′ə-) The pollen-producing reproductive organ of a flower, usu. consisting of a filament and an anther. [Lat. *stāmen*, thread. See **stā-** in App.]

Stam·ford (stăm′fərd) A city of SW CT on Long Island Sound and the NY border; settled in 1641. Pop. 117,083.

stamin– *pref.* Stamen: *staminate.* [Lat. *stāmen, stāmin-,* thread, warp. See STAMEN.]

stam·i·na[1] (stăm′ə-nə) *n.* Physical or moral strength to resist or withstand illness, fatigue, or hardship; endurance. [Lat. *stāmina,* pl. of *stāmen,* thread, thread of life spun by the Fates. See STA·MEN.]

sta·mi·na[2] (stā′mə-nə, stăm′ə-) *n.* A plural of **stamen.**

stam·i·nal[1] (stăm′ə-nəl) *adj.* Of or relating to stamina or endurance.

sta·mi·nal[2] (stā′mə-nəl, stăm′ə-) *adj.* Of or relating to stamens or a stamen.

sta·mi·nate (stā′mə-nĭt, -nāt′, stăm′ə-) *adj.* Having stamens but lacking pistils: *staminate flowers.*

stam·i·node (stā′mə-nōd′, stăm′ə-) also **stam·i·no·di·um** (stā′mə-nō′dē-əm, stăm′ə-) *n., pl.* **-nodes** also **-no·di·a** (-nō′dē-ə) A sterile stamen, sometimes resembling a petal, as in the canna. [NLat. *stāminōdium* < Lat. *stāmen, stāmin-,* thread. See STAMEN.]

stam·mel (stăm′əl) *n.* **1.** *Obsolete* A coarse woolen cloth for undergarments. **2.** *Archaic* The red color of stammel. [Prob. alteration of *stamin* < ME *stamyn* < OFr. *estamine* < VLat. **stāmina* < Lat., fem. of *stāmineus,* consisting of threads < *stāmen, stāmin-,* thread. See **stā-** in App.]

stam·mer (stăm′ər) *v.* **-mered, -mer·ing, -mers** —*intr.* To speak with a stammer. —*tr.* To utter with a stammer. ❖ *n.* A way of speaking marked by involuntary pauses or repetitions. [ME *stameren* < OE *stamerian.*] —**stam′mer·er** *n.*

stamp (stămp) *v.* **stamped, stamp·ing, stamps** —*tr.* **1.** To bring down (the foot) forcibly. **2.** To bring the foot down onto (an object or surface) forcibly. **3.** To extinguish or destroy by or as if by trampling underfoot: *stamp out a fire.* **4.** To crush or grind with a heavy instrument: *stamp ore.* **5.** To form or cut out by application of a mold, form, or die. **6.** To imprint or impress with a mark, design, or seal. **7.** To impress forcibly or permanently. **8.** To affix an adhesive stamp to. **9.** To identify, characterize, or reveal. —*intr.* **1.** To thrust the foot forcibly downward. **2.** To walk with forcible heavy steps. See Usage Note at **stomp.** ❖ *n.* **1.** The act of stamping. **2a.** An implement or device used to impress, cut out, or shape something to which it is applied. **b.** An impression or shape formed by such an implement or device. **3.** An official mark, design, or seal that indicates ownership, approval, completion, or the payment of a tax. **4a.** A small piece of gummed paper sold by a government for attachment to an article that is to be mailed; a postage stamp. **b.** A similar piece of gummed paper issued for a specific purpose. **5.** An identifying or characterizing mark or impression. **6.** Characteristic nature or quality: *a person of her stamp.* [ME *stampen,* poss. alteration of OE *stempan,* to pound in a mortar.]

stam·pede (stăm-pēd′) *n.* **1.** A sudden frenzied rush of panic-stricken animals. **2.** A sudden headlong rush or flight of a crowd of people. **3.** A mass impulsive action. ❖ *v.* **-ped·ed, -ped·ing, -pedes** —*tr.* **1.** To cause (a herd of animals) to flee in panic. **2.** To cause (a crowd of people) to act on mass impulse. —*intr.* **1.** To flee in a headlong rush. **2.** To act on mass impulse. [Sp. *estampida,* uproar, stampede < Provençal < *estampir,* to stamp, of Gmc. orig.] —**stam·ped′er** *n.*

WORD HISTORY The Spanish word *estampida,* meaning "explosion, bang, crash, uproar," seems a vivid term to describe a sudden rush of animals, such as buffaloes or cattle, and was first so used in American Spanish. From this use came our word *stampede* (actually from the Spanish *estampido,* a masculine noun corresponding to the feminine *estampida,* first recorded in 1828). Thus *stampede,* now a general English word, is an Americanism, a word or expression that originated in the United States. The United States was later to see stampedes of miners rushing westward to find gold. Not surprisingly, an early instance of the application of this word to humans is found in the *San Francisco Herald* in 1851.

stamp·er (stăm′pər) *n.* One that stamps: *a metal stamper.*

stamp mill *n.* **1.** A machine that crushes ore. **2.** A building in which ore is crushed.

stance (stăns) *n.* **1.** The attitude or position of a standing person or animal, esp. the position assumed by an athlete preparatory to action. **2.** Mental posture; point of view. [Fr., position < Ital. *stanza* < VLat. **stantia* < Lat. *stāns, stant-,* pr. part. of *stāre,* to stand. See **stā-** in App.]

stanch[1] (stônch, stänch, stănch) also **staunch** (stônch, stänch) *tr.v.* **stanched, stanch·ing, stanch·es** also **staunched, staunch·ing, staunch·es 1.** To stop or check the flow of (blood or tears, for example). **2.** To stop the flow of blood from (a wound). **3.** To stop, check or allay. See Usage Note at **staunch**[1]. [ME *stanchen* < OFr. *estanchier* < VLat. **stanticāre,* to stop, prob. < Lat. *stāns, stant-,* pr. part. of *stāre,* to stand. See **stā-** in App.] —**stanch′er** *n.*

stanch[2] (stônch, stänch, stănch) *adj.* Variant of **staunch**[1]. See Usage Note at **staunch**[1].

stan·chion (stăn′chən, -shən) *n.* **1.** An upright pole, post, or support. **2.** A framework consisting of two or more vertical bars, used to secure cattle in a stall or at a feed trough. ❖ *tr.v.* **-chioned, -chion·ing, -chions 1.** To equip with stanchions. **2.** To confine (cattle) by means of stanchions. [ME *stanchon* < OFr. *estanchon,* prob. < *estance,* act of standing upright, prop < *estans,* pr. part. of *ester,* to stand < Lat. *stāre.* See **stā-** in App.]

stand (stănd) *v.* **stood** (stŏŏd), **stand·ing, stands** —*intr.* **1a.** To rise to an upright position on the feet. **b.** To assume or maintain an upright position as specified: *stand to one side.* **2a.** To maintain an upright position on the feet. **b.** To maintain an upright or vertical position on a base or support. **c.** To be placed or situated: *The building stands at the corner.* **3a.** To remain stable, upright, or intact. **b.** To remain valid, effective, or unaltered. **4.** To be or show a specified figure or amount: *The balance stands at $500.* **5.** To measure a specified height when in an upright position: *stands six feet tall.* **6.** To take up or maintain a specified position, altitude, or course. **7.** To be in a position of possible gain or loss. **8a.** To be in a specified state or condition. **b.** To exist in a particular form. **9.** To be at a specified level on or as if on a scale: *stands third in her class.* **10a.** To come to a stop; remain motionless. **b.** To remain stationary or inactive. **11.** To remain without flowing or being disturbed; be or become stagnant. **12.** *Nautical* To take or hold a particular course or direction: *a ship standing in toward shore.* **13.** To be available as a sire. Used of horses. **14.** *Chiefly British* To be a candidate for public office. —*tr.* **1.** To cause to stand; place upright. **2.** To engage in or encounter. **3a.** To resist successfully; withstand. **b.** To put up with patiently or resolutely; bear. See Syns at **bear**[1]. **4.** To submit to or undergo: *stand trial.* **5.** To tolerate and benefit from: *I could stand some sleep.* **6.** To perform the duty of: *stand guard.* **7.** *Informal* To treat (someone) or pay the cost of (food or drink): *We'll stand dinner.* ❖ *n.* **1.** The act of standing. **2.** A ceasing of work or activity; a standstill or halt. **3.** A stop on a performance tour. **4.** The place or station where a person stands. **5.** A booth, stall, or counter for the display of goods for sale. **6.** A parking space reserved for taxis. **7.** A desperate or decisive effort at defense or resistance, as in a battle. **8.** A position or opinion one is prepared to uphold. **9. stands** The bleachers at a playing field or stadium. **10.** *Law* A witness stand. **11.** A small rack, prop, or table for holding any of various articles. **12.** A group or growth of tall plants or trees. —*phrasal verbs:* **stand by 1.** To be ready or available to act. **2.** To wait for something, such as a broadcast, to resume. **3.** To remain uninvolved; refrain from acting. **4.** To remain loyal to; aid or support. **5.** To keep or maintain: *stood by her decision.* **stand down 1.** *Law* To leave a witness stand. **2.** To withdraw, as from a political contest. **3.** To end a state of readiness or alert. **4.** To go off duty. **stand for 1.** To represent; symbolize. **2.** To advocate or support. **3.** To put up with; tolerate. **stand in** To act as a stand-in. **stand off 1.** To stay at a distance; remain apart or aloof. **2.** To put off; evade. **3.** *Nautical* To maintain a course away from shore. **stand on 1.** To be based on; depend on. **2.** To insist on observance of. **stand out 1.** To protrude; project. **2.** To be conspicuous, distinctive, or prominent. **3.** To refuse compliance or maintain opposition; hold out. **4.** *Nautical* To maintain a course away from shore. **stand over 1.** To watch or supervise closely. **2.** To hold over; postpone. **stand to** To take up positions for action. **stand up 1.** To remain valid, sound, or durable: *His claim stood up in court.* **2.** *Informal* To fail to keep a date with. —*idioms:* **stand a chance** To have a chance, as of gaining or accomplishing something. **stand (one's) ground 1.** To maintain one's position against an attack. **2.** To refuse to compromise; be unyielding. **stand on (one's) own (or two) feet** To be independent and responsible for oneself. **stand pat 1.** To refuse to change one's position or opinion. **2.** *Games* To play one's poker hand without drawing more cards. **stand to reason** To be consistent with reason. **stand up for 1.** To side with; defend. **2.** To stand up with. **stand up to** To confront fearlessly; face up to. **stand up with** To act as best man or maid of honor for (the groom or bride) at a wedding. [ME *standen* < OE *standan.* See **stā-** in App.] —**stand′er** *n.*

stand·a·lone (stănd′ə-lōn′) *adj.* Self-contained and usu. independently operating: *a stand-alone computer terminal.*

stan·dard (stăn′dərd) *n.* **1.** A flag, banner, or ensign, esp.: **a.** The ensign of a chief of state, nation, or city. **b.** A long tapering flag bearing heraldic devices distinctive of a person or corporation. **c.** An emblem or flag of an army, raised on a pole to indicate the rallying point in battle. **d.** The colors of a mounted or motorized military unit. **2a.** An acknowledged measure of comparison for quantitative or qualitative value; a criterion. **b.** An object that under specified conditions defines, represents, or records the magnitude of a unit. **3.** The set proportion by weight of gold or silver to alloy metal for use in coinage. **4.** The commodity or commodities backing a monetary system. **5.** Something, such as a product, that is widely recognized or employed. **6a.** A degree or level of requirement, excellence, or attainment. **b.** A requirement of moral conduct. Often used in the plural. **7.** *Chiefly British* A grade level in elementary schools. **8.** A pedestal, stand, or base. **9.** *Botany* **a.** The large upper petal of the flower of a pea or related plant. **b.** One of the narrow upright petals of an iris. **10.** A shrub or small tree that through grafting or training has a single stem of limited height with a crown of leaves and flowers at its apex. **11.** *Music* A composition continually used in repertoires. ❖ *adj.* **1.** Serving as or conforming to a standard of measurement or value. **2.** Widely recognized as a model of authority or excellence. **3.** Acceptable but of less than top quality. **4.** Normal, familiar, or usual. **5.** Commonly used or supplied. **6.** *Linguistics* Conforming to established educated usage in speech or writing. [ME < OFr. *estandard*, rallying place, prob. < Frankish **standhard : *standan*, to stand; see **stā-** in App. + **hard*, fast, hard.] —**stan′dard•ly** *adv.*

stan•dard-bear•er (stăn′dərd-bâr′ər) *n.* **1.** One who carries a standard or banner, esp. of a military unit. **2.** An outstanding leader or representative, as of a political party.

stan•dard•bred (stăn′dərd-brĕd′) *n.* Any of an American breed of trotting and pacing horses developed esp. for harness racing by crossing esp. Thoroughbreds with Morgans.

standard candle *n.* A candela.

standard deviation *n.* A statistic used as a measure of the dispersion or variation in a distribution, equal to the square root of the mean of the squares of the deviations from the mean of the distribution.

Standard English *n.* The variety of English that is generally acknowledged as the model for the speech and writing of educated speakers.

standing stone

> **USAGE NOTE** The term *Standard English* is sometimes used to denote the variety of English prescribed by traditional prescriptive norms, including rules and usages that many educated speakers do not systematically conform to in their speech or writing. Recently, however, the term has more often been used to distinguish the speech and writing of middle-class educated speakers from the speech of other groups and classes, which are termed *nonstandard*. This is the sense in which the word is used in the usage labels in this Dictionary. In this sense, though, the term is highly elastic and variable, since what counts as Standard English will depend on both the locality and the particular varieties that Standard English is being contrasted with. No matter how it is interpreted, however, Standard English in this sense should not be regarded as being necessarily correct or unexceptionable, since it will include many kinds of language that could be faulted on various grounds, such as the language of corporate memos and television advertisements.

standard gauge *n.* **1.** A railroad track having a width of 56½ inches (143.5 centimeters). **2.** A railroad or railroad car built to standard gauge specification.

stan•dard•ize (stăn′dər-dīz′) *tr.v.* **-ized, -iz•ing, -iz•es 1.** To cause to conform to a standard. **2.** To evaluate by comparing with a standard. —**stan′dard•i•za′tion** (-dər-dĭ-zā′shən) *n.*

standard model *n.* A model of fundamental forces and particles that explains their behavior and interactions in terms of symmetries and the destruction of symmetries.

standard time *n.* The time in any of 24 time zones, usu. the mean solar time at the central meridian of each zone.

stand•by (stănd′bī′) *n., pl.* **-bys 1.** One that can always be relied on, as in an emergency. **2.** A favorite or frequent choice. **3.** One kept in readiness to serve as a substitute. ❖ *adj.* **1.** Kept in reserve for use when needed. **2.** Of, relating to, or waiting for unreserved travel space that is made available by an airline only shortly before departure. ❖ *adv.* On a standby basis. —**idiom: on standby** Ready and waiting.

Elizabeth Cady Stanton
detail of an 1889 portrait by
Anna Elizabeth Klumpke
(1856–1942)

stand-down or **stand•down** (stănd′doun′) *n.* A relaxation from a state of readiness or alert.

stand•ee (stăn-dē′) *n.* One using standing room. See Usage Note at **-ee¹**.

stand-in (stănd′ĭn′) *n.* **1.** One who substitutes for an actor while the lights and camera are adjusted or during hazardous action. **2.** A substitute.

stand•ing (stăn′dĭng) *n.* **1a.** Status with respect to rank, reputation, or position in society or a profession. **b.** High reputation; esteem. **2.** Continuance in time; duration. **3.** *Law* The right or capacity to initiate a suit. **4.** The act of one that stands. **5.** A place where a person or thing stands. **6. standings** *Sports* A listing of individual competitors or of teams in a league according to their record of performance. ❖ *adj.* **1a.** Remaining upright; erect. **b.** Not cut down: *standing timber.* **2.** Performed or done from a standing position. **3.** Permanent and unchanging; fixed. **4.** Remaining in force or use indefinitely: *a standing invitation.* **5.** Not movable; stationary. **6.** Not flowing or circulating; stagnant.

standing crop *n.* The total amount of living organisms, as of plankton, in a specific area at a given time.

standing order *n.* An order or rule held to be in force until specifically changed or withdrawn, esp. a regulation relating to military or parliamentary procedure.

standing room *n.* Space in which to stand, as in a public place where all seats are filled. —**stand′ing-room′** (stăn′dĭng-rōōm′, -rōōm′) *adj.*

standing stone *n.* A prehistoric monument of a class found chiefly in the British Isles and northern France, consisting of a single tall, upright megalith.

standing wave *n.* A wave having points of periodic maximum vibration in between fixed points of zero vibration, produced whenever a wave is confined within boundaries.

Stan•dish (stăn′dĭsh′), **Miles** or **Myles** 1584?–1656. English colonial leader in America hired by the Pilgrims to accompany

them to the New World (1620).

stand•off (stănd′ôf′, -ŏf′) *n.* **1.** A tie or draw, as in a contest. **2.** A situation in which one force neutralizes or counterbalances the other. ❖ *adj.* Standoffish.

stand•off•ish (stănd-ô′fĭsh, -ŏf′ĭsh) *adj.* Aloof or reserved. —**stand•off′ish•ness** *n.*

stand•out (stănd′out′) *n.* One that is conspicuous by virtue of excellence or superiority.

stand•pat (stănd′păt′) *adj.* Opposed or resistant to change; stubbornly conservative. —**stand′pat′ter** *n.*

stand•pipe (stănd′pīp′) *n.* A large vertical pipe into which water is pumped in order to produce a desired pressure.

stand•point (stănd′point′) *n.* A position from which things are considered or judged; a point of view.

stand•still (stănd′stĭl′) *n.* Total cessation, as of activity.

stand-up or **stand-up** (stănd′ŭp′) *adj.* **1.** Standing erect; upright. **2.** Taken, done, or used while standing. **3.** Of or being a performer who stands alone on a stage and delivers a comic monologue. **4.** *Slang* Courageous and steadfast. ❖ *n.* Standup comedy.

Stan•ford-Bi•net test (stăn′fərd-bĭ-nā′) *n.* A standard intelligence test adapted from the Binet-Simon scale for use in the United States, esp. in the assessment of children. [After *Stanford* University in western California near Palo Alto.]

stang (stăng) *v. Obsolete* A past tense of **sting.**

stan•hope (stăn′hōp′, stăn′əp) *n.* A light open horse-drawn carriage with one seat and two or four wheels. [After the Reverend Fitzroy *Stanhope* (1787–1864), British clergyman.]

Stan•is•las I Lesz•czyń•ski (stăn′ĭ-slôs lĕsh-chĭn′skē) 1677–1766. King of Poland (1704–09 and 1733–36) who ruled during the War of the Polish Succession (1733–35).

Stan•i•slav•sky (stăn′ĭ-slăv′skē, -släf′-), **Konstantin** 1863–1938. Russian director who developed a method of acting emphasizing psychological motivation.

stank (stăngk) *v.* A past tense of **stink.**

Stan•ley or **Port Stan•ley** (stăn′lē) A town in the E Falkland Is., administrative cap. of the British dependency. Pop. 1,557.

Stanley, Edward George Geoffrey Smith. 14th Earl of Derby. 1799–1869. British politician who served as prime minister (1852, 1858–59, and 1866–68).

Stanley, Sir Henry Morton 1841–1904. British journalist known esp. for his expedition into Africa in search of David Livingstone.

Stanley, Wendell Meredith 1904–71. Amer. biochemist who shared a 1946 Nobel Prize.

Stanley Pool An expansion of the Congo R. in W-central Africa on the border of the Democratic Republic of the Congo (formerly Zaire) and the Republic of the Congo.

Stan•ley•ville (stăn′lē-vĭl′) See **Kisangani.**

stan•nic (stăn′ĭk) *adj.* Of, relating to, or containing tin, esp. with valence 4. [LLat. *stannum*, tin (< Lat., an alloy of silver and lead, alteration of *stagnum*, prob. of Celt. orig.) + –IC.]

stannic chloride *n.* A caustic liquid, SnCl₄, used as a conductive coating and in ceramics.

stan•nite (stăn′īt′) *n.* A gray to black mineral, Cu₂FeSnS₄, with a metallic luster. [< LLat. *stannum*, tin. See STANNIC.]

stan•nous (stăn′əs) *adj.* Of, relating to, or containing tin, esp. with valence 2. [LLat. *stannum*, tin; see STANNIC + –OUS.]

stannous fluoride *n.* A powder, SnF₂, used to fluoridate toothpaste.

Stan•o•voi Range or **Stan•o•voi Range** (stăn′ə-voi′, stə-nə-voi′) A mountain range of SE Russia N of the Amur R.

Stan•ton (stăn′tən), **Edwin McMasters** 1814–69. Amer. public official who served as US secretary of war (1862–68). His dismissal by President Andrew Johnson and his subsequent refusal to leave office precipitated the impeachment of Johnson.

Stanton, Elizabeth Cady 1815–1902. 7Amer. feminist and social reformer who helped organize the first women's rights convention, held in Seneca Falls NY (1848).

stan•za (stăn′zə) *n.* One of the divisions of a poem or song, composed of two or more lines and usu. characterized by a common pattern of meter, rhyme, and number of lines. [Ital. See STANCE.] —**stan•za′ic** (-zā′ĭk) *adj.*

sta•pe•dec•to•my (stā′pĭ-dĕk′tə-mē, -pē-) *n., pl.* **-mies** Surgical removal of the stapes. [NLat. *stapēs, stapēd-*, stapes; see STAPES + –ECTOMY.]

sta•pe•li•a (stə-pē′lē-ə) *n.* Any of various plants of the genus *Stapelia*, including the starfish flower. [NLat. *Stapelia*, genus name, after Jan Bode van *Stapel* (died 1636), Dutch botanist.]

sta•pes (stā′pēz) *n., pl.* **stapes** or **sta•pe•des** (stā′pĭ-dēz′) The innermost of the three small bones of the middle ear, shaped somewhat like a stirrup. [NLat. *stapēs, stapēd-* < Med.Lat. stirrup.] —**sta•pe′di•al** (stā-pē′dē-əl) *adj.*

staph (stăf) *n. Informal* Staphylococcus. —**staph** *adj.*

staphylo– *pref.* Cluster; resembling a cluster: *staphylococcus.* [NLat. < Gk. *staphulē*, bunch of grapes.]

staph•y•lo•coc•cus (stăf′ə-lō-kŏk′əs) *n., pl.* **-coc•ci** (-kŏk′sī, -kŏk′ī) A spherical gram-positive bacterium of the genus *Staphylococcus*, usu. occurring in clusters and causing boils, septicemia, and other infections. —**staph′y•lo•coc′cal** (-kŏk′əl), **staph′y•lo•coc′cic** (-kŏk′sĭk, -kŏk′ĭk) *adj.*

sta•ple¹ (stā′pəl) *n.* **1.** A principal raw material or commodity grown or produced in a region. **2.** A major item of trade in steady demand. **3.** A basic dietary item, such as flour. **4.** A principal element or feature. **5.** The fiber of cotton, wool, or flax, graded as to length and fineness. ❖ *adj.* **1.** Produced or stocked in large quantities to meet steady demand. **2.** Principal; main. ❖ *tr.v.* **-pled, -pling, -ples** To grade (fibers) according to length and fineness. [ME, official export market < AN *estaple,* perh. < MDu. *stāpel,* heap, emporium.]

sta·ple² (stā′pəl) *n.* **1.** A thin piece of wire in the shape of a square bracket that is driven by a device through sheets of paper or similar material and flattened to serve as a fastening. **2.** A U-shaped metal loop with pointed ends, driven into a surface to hold a bolt, hook, or hasp or to hold wiring in place. ❖ *tr.v.* **-pled, -pling, -ples** To secure or fasten by means of a staple or staples. [ME < OE *stapol,* post, pillar.]

sta·pler¹ (stā′plər) *n.* A dealer in staple goods or fibers.

sta·pler² (stā′plər) *n.* A device used to bind material together by means of staples.

star (stär) *n.* **1a.** A self-luminous celestial body that consists of a mass of gas held together by its own gravity and generates energy by nuclear reactions in its interior. **b.** Any of the celestial bodies visible at night from Earth as relatively stationary, usu. twinkling points of light. **c.** Something regarded as resembling a star. **2.** A graphic design having five or more radiating points, often used as a symbol of rank or merit. **3a.** An artistic performer or athlete whose leading role or superior performance is acknowledged. **b.** One who is highly celebrated in a field or profession. **4a.** An asterisk (*). **b.** The star key on a telephone. **5.** A white spot on the forehead of a horse. **6.** A planet or constellation of the zodiac believed in astrology to influence personal destiny. **7. stars** The future; destiny. ❖ *adj.* **1.** Outstanding or famous, esp. in performing something: *a star figure skater.* **2.** Of or relating to a star or stars. ❖ *v.* **starred, star·ring, stars** —*tr.* **1a.** To ornament with stars. **b.** To award or mark with a star for excellence. **2.** To mark with an asterisk. **3.** To present or feature (a performer) in a leading role. —*intr.* **1.** To play the leading role in a theatrical or film production. **2.** To do an outstanding job; perform excellently. —*idioms:* **have stars in (one's) eyes** To be dazzled or enraptured. **see stars** To experience bright flashing sensations, as from a blow to the head. [ME *sterre* < OE *steorra.* See **ster-** in App.]

star anise *n.* **1.** An aromatic eastern Asian evergreen tree (*Illicium verum*) having purple-red flowers and starlike clusters of anise-scented fruit. **2.** The fruit of this plant.

star apple *n.* **1.** A tropical American evergreen tree (*Chrysophyllum cainito*) having smooth-skinned green or purple fruit and purplish flowers. **2.** The edible fruit of this tree.

Sta·ra Za·go·ra (stä′rə zə-gôr′ə) A city of central Bulgaria ENE of Plovdiv. Pop. 150,451.

star·board (stär′bərd) *n.* The right-hand side of a ship or aircraft as one faces forward. ❖ *adj.* On the right-hand side as one faces forward. ❖ *adv.* To or toward the right-hand side as one faces forward. [ME *sterbord* < OE *stēorbord* : *stēor-,* a steering; see **stā-** in App. + *bord,* side of a ship.]

star·burst (stär′bûrst′) *n.* A shape or design with emanating rays that resembles the flash produced by an exploding star.

starch (stärch) *n.* **1.** A naturally abundant nutrient carbohydrate, $(C_6H_{10}O_5)_n$, found chiefly in the seeds, fruits, tubers, roots, and stem pith of plants, notably in corn, potatoes, wheat, and rice, and commonly prepared as a white amorphous tasteless powder. **2.** Any of various substances, such as natural starch, used to stiffen cloth, as in laundering. **3. starches** Foods having a high content of starch, as breads and potatoes. **4a.** Stiff behavior. **b.** Vigor; mettle. ❖ *tr.v.* **starched, starch·ing, starch·es** To stiffen with starch. [ME *starche,* substance used to stiffen cloth (sense uncertain) < *sterchen,* to stiffen < OE **stercan.*]

Star Chamber *n.* **1.** A 15th- to 17th-century English court consisting of judges who were appointed by the Crown and sat in closed session on cases involving state security. **2. star chamber** A court or group that engages in secret, harsh, or arbitrary procedures. [So called because the ceiling of the original courtroom was decorated with stars.]

starch syrup *n.* See **glucose** 2.

starch wheat *n.* See **emmer.**

starch·y (stär′chē) *adj.* **-i·er, -i·est 1a.** Containing starch. **b.** Stiffened with starch. **2.** Of or resembling starch. **3.** Stiff; formal. —**starch′i·ly** *adv.* —**starch′i·ness** *n.*

star-crossed (stär′krôst′, -krŏst′) *adj.* Ill-fated.

star·dom (stär′dəm) *n.* **1.** The status of a performer acknowledged as a star. **2.** Star performers considered as a group.

star·dust (stär′dŭst′) *n.* **1.** A dreamlike, romantic, or uncritical sense of well-being. **2.** A cluster of stars too distant to be seen individually, resembling a dimly luminous cloud of dust. Not in scientific use. **3.** Minute particles of matter that are supposed to fall to Earth from the stars. Not in scientific use.

stare (stâr) *v.* **stared, star·ing, stares** —*intr.* **1.** To look directly and fixedly, often with a wide-eyed gaze. **2.** To be conspicuous; stand out. **3.** To stand on end; bristle, as hair or feathers. —*tr.* To look at directly and fixedly. ❖ *n.* An intent gaze. —*phrasal verb:* **stare down** To cause to waver or give in by or as if by staring. —*idiom:* **stare (one) in the face 1.** To be plainly visible or obvious; force itself on (one's) attention. **2.** To be imminent or

---

unavoidable. [ME *staren* < OE *starian.*] —**star′er** *n.*

sta·rets (stär′yĭts) *n., pl.* **star·tsy** (stär′tsē) A male spiritual adviser, often a monk or hermit, in the Russian Orthodox Church. [Russ., elder, starets < O Church Slavonic *starĭtsĭ,* elder < *starŭ,* old. See **stā-** in App.]

star facet *n.* One of the eight small triangular facets in the crown of a brilliant-cut gem.

star·fish (stär′fĭsh′) *n., pl.* **starfish** or **-fish·es** Any of various marine echinoderms of the class Asteroidea, having a thick, often spiny body with five arms extending from a central disk.

star·flow·er (stär′flou′ər) *n.* **1.** Any of several small plants of the genus *Trientalis,* esp. *T. borealis* of northeast North America, having white starlike flowers. **2.** Any of several plants having star-like flowers.

star fruit *n.* See **carambola** 2. [< its cross section.]

star·gaze (stär′gāz′) *intr.v.* **-gazed, -gaz·ing, -gaz·es 1.** To gaze at the stars. **2.** To daydream.

star·gaz·er (stär′gā′zər) *n.* **1a.** *Informal* An astronomer. **b.** An astrologer. **2.** A daydreamer. **3.** Any of various bottom-dwelling marine percoid fishes of the families Uranoscopidae and Dactyloscopidae, having eyes on the top of the head.

star grass *n.* **1.** Any of various plants of the genus *Hypoxis,* having grasslike leaves and star-shaped white or yellow flowers. **2.** See **colicroot** 1.

stark (stärk) *adj.* **stark·er, stark·est 1.** Bare or blunt: *stark language.* **2.** Complete or utter; extreme: *a stark contrast.* **3.** Harsh; grim: *the stark reality of an epidemic.* ❖ *adv.* Utterly; entirely: *stark raving mad.* [ME, stiff, severe, strong < OE *stearc.*] —**stark′ly** *adv.* —**stark′ness** *n.*

stark·ers (stär′kərz) *adj. Chiefly British Slang* Stark naked. [Alteration of *stark naked.*]

star key *n.* The pushbutton in the lower left corner of a telephone dialing pad, marked with an asterisk.

star·let (stär′lĭt) *n.* **1.** A small star. **2.** A young film actress publicized as a future star.

star·light (stär′līt′) *n.* The light from the stars.

star·ling¹ (stär′lĭng) *n.* Any of various Old World passerine birds of the family Sturnidae, having a short tail, pointed wings, and dark, often iridescent plumage, esp. *Sturnus vulgaris,* widely naturalized in North America. [ME < OE *stærlinc* : *stær,* starling + *-linc,* n. suff.; see **-LING¹**.]

star·ling² (stär′lĭng) *n.* A protective structure of pilings surrounding a pier of a bridge. [Perh. alteration of ME *stadelinge* < *stathel,* foundation < OE *stathol.* See **stā-** in App.]

star·lit (stär′lĭt′) *adj.* Illuminated by starlight.

star-nosed mole (stär′nōzd′) *n.* A mole (*Condylura cristata*) of North America having 22 small fleshy tentacles encircling the end of its nose in a starlike pattern.

star-of-Beth·le·hem (stär′əv-bĕth′lĭ-hĕm′) *n., pl.* **star-of-Bethlehem** or **stars-of-Bethlehem** (stärz′-) **1.** Any of numerous bulbous perennial herbs of the genus *Ornithogalum* in the lily family, esp. *O. arabicum* or *O. umbellatum* of the Mediterranean region, having narrow leaves and a cluster of star-shaped white flowers. **2.** Any of several similar or related plants. [After the star that guided the Magi to Bethlehem.]

Star of David *n., pl.* **Stars of David** or **Star of Davids** See **Magen David.**

Starr (stär), **Ringo** b. 1940. British musician who was the drummer of The Beatles (1962–70).

star·ry (stär′ē) *adj.* **-ri·er, -ri·est 1.** Marked or set with stars or starlike objects. **2.** Shining or glittering like stars. **3.** Shaped like a star. **4.** Illuminated by stars; starlit. **5.** Of or coming from the stars; stellar. —**star′ri·ness** *n.*

star·ry-eyed (stär′ē-īd′) *adj.* Having a naively enthusiastic, overoptimistic, or romantic view; unrealistic.

Stars and Bars (stärz) *n.* (used with a sing. or pl. verb) The first Confederate flag.

Stars and Stripes *n.* (used with a sing. or pl. verb) The flag of the United States.

star sapphire *n.* A sapphire with a polished convex surface exhibiting asterism.

star shell *n.* An artillery shell that explodes in midair with a shower of lights, used for illumination and signaling.

star·ship (stär′shĭp′) *n.* A spacecraft designed for human interstellar travel.

Star-Span·gled Banner (stär′spăng′gəld) *n.* The flag of the United States.

star·struck or **star-struck** (stär′strŭk′) *adj.* Fascinated by or exhibiting a fascination with fame or famous people.

start (stärt) *v.* **start·ed, start·ing, starts** —*intr.* **1.** To begin an activity or movement; set out. **2.** To have a beginning; commence. **3.** To move suddenly or involuntarily. **4.** To come quickly into view, life, or activity; spring forth. **5.** *Sports* To be in the initial lineup of a game or race. **6.** To protrude or bulge. **7.** To become loosened or disengaged. —*tr.* **1.** To commence; begin. **2.** To set into motion, operation, or activity. **3.** To introduce; originate. **4.** *Sports* **a.** To play in the initial lineup of (a game). **b.** To put (a player) into the initial lineup of a game. **c.** To enter (a participant) into a race or game. **5.** To found; establish. **6.** To tend in an early stage of development. **7.** To rouse (game) from its hiding place or lair; flush. **8.** To cause to become displaced or

---

star-nosed mole
Condylura cristata

ă	pat	oi	boy
ā	pay	ou	out
âr	care	ŏŏ	took
ä	father	ōō	boot
ĕ	pet	ŭ	cut
ē	be	ûr	urge
ĭ	pit	th	thin
ī	pie	*th*	this
îr	pier	hw	which
ŏ	pot	zh	vision
ō	toe	ə	about,
ô	paw		item

Stress marks:
′ (primary);
′ (secondary), as in
lexicon (lĕk′sĭ-kŏn′)

loosened. ❖ *n.* **1a.** A beginning; a commencement. **b.** The beginning of a new construction project. **2.** A place or time of beginning. **3.** *Sports* **a.** A starting line for a race. **b.** A signal to begin a race. **c.** An instance of beginning a game or race. **4.** A startled reaction or movement. **5.** A part that has become dislocated or loosened. **6.** A position of advantage over others, as in a race; a lead. **7.** An opportunity granted to pursue a career or course of action. —*idioms:* **start something** *Informal* To cause trouble. **to start with 1.** At the beginning; initially. **2.** In any case. [ME *sterten*, to move or leap suddenly < OE **styrtan.*]

start•er (stär′tər) *n.* **1.** One that starts. **2.** An attachment for starting an internal-combustion engine without hand cranking. **3.** A device that initiates a flow of high voltage across the electrodes of a fluorescent lamp. **4.** *Sports* **a.** One who signals the start of a race. **b.** A participant that starts in a game or race. **5.** *Baseball* **a.** The first pitcher for a team in a game. **b.** A pitcher who regularly begins games for a team. **6.** The first in a series, esp. the first course of a meal; an appetizer. —*idiom:* **for starters** *Informal* To begin with; initially.

star thistle *n.* Any of several Eurasian plants of the genus *Centaurea*, esp. *C. calcitrapa*, having spiny purplish flower heads.

start•ing block (stär′tĭng) *n.* **1.** An apparatus that braces a runner's feet at the start of a race, consisting of two angled supports adjustably mounted on a rigid frame that is usu. anchored to the track. **2.** One of the raised platforms mounted at one end of a pool from which swimmers begin a race.

starting gate *n. Sports* **1.** A series of stalls with interconnected doors that open simultaneously at the beginning of a race. **2.** A movable barrier that starts an automatic timer when pushed aside by a competitor, such as a skier.

star•tle (stär′tl) *v.* **-tled, -tling, -tles** —*tr.* **1.** To cause to make a quick involuntary movement or start. **2.** To alarm, frighten, or surprise suddenly. —*intr.* To become alarmed, frightened, or surprised. ❖ *n.* A sudden mild shock; a start. [ME *stertlen*, to run about < OE *steartlian*, to kick.] —**star′tling•ness** *n.*

star topology *n. Computer Science* A topology for a LAN in which all nodes are connected to one central node.

star•tsy (stär′tsē) *n.* Plural of **starets.**

start-up or **start•up** (stärt′ŭp′) *n.* The act or process of setting into operation or motion.

star•va•tion (stär-vä′shən) *n.* **1.** The act or process of starving. **2.** The condition of being starved.

starve (stärv) *v.* **starved, starv•ing, starves** —*intr.* **1.** To suffer or die from extreme or prolonged lack of food. **2.** *Informal* To be hungry. **3.** To suffer from deprivation. **4.** *Archaic* To suffer or die from cold. —*tr.* **1.** To cause to starve. **2.** To force to a specified state by starving. [ME *sterven*, to die < OE *steorfan.*]

starve•ling (stärv′lĭng) *n.* One that is starving or being starved. ❖ *adj.* **1.** Starving. **2.** Poor in quality; inadequate.

star•wort (stär′wûrt′, -wôrt′) *n.* Any of various plants having star-shaped flowers or flower heads, as the aster.

stash (stăsh) *Slang tr.v.* **stashed, stash•ing, stash•es** To hide or store away in a secret place. ❖ *n.* **1.** A secret place where something is hidden or stored. **2.** An amount of something, such as money or an illegal drug, that has been hidden or stored. [?]

sta•sis (stā′sĭs, stăs′ĭs) *n., pl.* **sta•ses** (stā′sēz, stăs′ēz) **1.** A condition of balance among various forces; motionlessness. **2.** *Pathology* Stoppage of the normal flow of a body substance, as of blood through an artery. [Gk., stationariness. See **stā-** in App.]

–stasis *suff.* **1.** Slowing; stoppage: *bacteriostasis.* **2.** Stable state: *homeostasis.* [< Gk. *stasis*, standstill. See STASIS.]

stat¹ (stăt) *n.* A statistic.

stat² (stăt) *adv.* With no delay; at once. ❖ *adj.* Immediate. [Short for Lat. *statim.* See **stā-** in App.]

stat. *abbr.* **1.** statistic **2.** statistics **3.** statuary **4.** statute

–stat *suff.* **1.** Something that stabilizes: *rheostat.* **2.** A device for reflecting something specified in a constant direction: *heliostat.* **3.** Something that inhibits: *fungistat.* [NLat. *-stata* < Gk. *-statēs*, one that causes to stand, or < *statos*, standing. See **stā-** in App.]

state (stāt) *n.* **1.** A condition or mode of being, as with regard to circumstances: *a state of confusion.* **2.** A condition of being in a stage or form, as of structure, growth, or development: *the larval state.* **3.** A mental or emotional condition: *in a manic state.* **4.** *Informal* A condition of excitement or distress. **5.** *Physics* The condition of a physical system with regard to phase, form, composition, or structure. **6.** Social position or rank. **7.** Ceremony; pomp. **8a.** The supreme public power within a sovereign political entity. **b.** The sphere of supreme civil power within a given polity: *matters of state.* **9.** A specific mode of government. **10.** A body politic, esp. one constituting a nation. **11.** One of the more or less internally autonomous territorial and political units composing a federation under a sovereign government. ❖ *adj.* **1.** Of or relating to a body politic or to an internally autonomous territorial or political unit constituting a federation under one government. **2.** Owned and operated by a state. ❖ *tr.v.* **stat•ed, stat•ing, states** To set forth in words; declare. [ME < OFr. *estat* < Lat. *status.* See **stā-** in App.] —**stat′a•ble, state′a•ble** *adj.*

state attorney *n.* A prosecuting attorney for a state.

state•craft (stāt′krăft′) *n.* The art of leading a country.

state•hood (stāt′hood′) *n.* The status of being a state, esp. of the United States.

state•house also **state house** (stāt′hous′) *n.* A building in which a state legislature holds sessions; a state capitol.

state•less (stāt′lĭs) *adj.* **1.** Having no state. **2.** Having no recognized citizenship in a state or nation. —**state′less•ness** *n.*

state•ly (stāt′lē) *adj.* **-li•er, -li•est 1.** Dignified and impressive, as in size or proportions. See Syns at **grand. 2.** Majestic; lofty. ❖ *adv.* In a ceremonious or imposing manner. [ME *statly* < *state*, state, rank. See STATE.] —**state′li•ness** *n.*

state•ment (stāt′mənt) *n.* **1.** The act of stating or declaring. **2.** Something stated; a declaration. **3.** *Law* A formal pleading. **4.** An abstract of a commercial or financial account showing an amount due; a bill. **5.** A monthly report sent to a debtor or bank depositor. **6.** *Computer Science* An elementary instruction in a programming language. **7.** An overall impression or mood created esp. by means other than words: *The curtains made a strong decorative statement.*

Stat•en Island (stăt′n) A borough of New York City coextensive with **Staten Island** in New York Bay SW of Manhattan I. The island was permanently settled in the mid-1600s and became part of New York City in 1898. Pop. 443,728.

state of the art *n.* The highest level of development, as of a device, technique, or scientific field, achieved at a particular time. —**state′-of-the-art′** (stāt′əv-thē-ärt′) *adj.*

stat•er¹ (stā′tər) *n.* A resident of a particular state or type of state. Often used in combination: *Lone Star staters.*

sta•ter² (stā′tər) *n.* Any of various gold, silver, or electrum coins of ancient Greece. [ME < LLat. *statēr* < Gk. < *histanai*, *sta-*, to set on a scale, weigh. See SYSTEM.]

state•room (stāt′room′, -room′) *n.* A private cabin or compartment with sleeping accommodations on a ship or train.

state's evidence (stāts) *n.* **1.** Evidence for the prosecution in US state or federal trials. **2.** One that gives evidence for the state in criminal proceedings.

States-Gen•er•al (stāts′jĕn′ər-əl) *pl.n.* **1.** A legislative assembly of representatives from the estates of a nation, as opposed to a provincial assembly. **2.** The legislative assembly in France before the Revolution.

state•side (stāt′sīd′) *adj.* **1.** Of or in the continental United States. **2.** *Alaska* Of or in the 48 contiguous states of the United States. ❖ *adv. Informal* **1.** To, toward, or in the continental United States. **2.** *Alaska* To, toward, or in the 48 contiguous states of the United States.

REGIONAL NOTE After World War II the term *stateside* gained currency among Alaskans, as in *"Most of the owners live in Anchorage; some 14% live stateside"* (Alaska Magazine). It may or may not be capitalized. *Stateside, the lower states, the South,* and *(the) Outside* are all used in Alaska to denote "the 48 contiguous states." All these terms, however, are losing out to the *Lower 48.*

states•man (stāts′mən) *n.* **1.** A man who is a leader in national or international affairs. **2.** A male political leader seen as disinterestedly promoting the public good. —**states′man•like′, states′man•ly** *adj.* —**states′man•ship** *n.*

states' rights also **States' rights** (stāts) *pl.n.* **1.** All rights not delegated to the federal government by the Constitution nor denied by it to the states. **2.** The political position advocating strict interpretation of the Constitution with regard to the limitation of federal powers and the extension of the autonomy of the individual state to the greatest possible degree. —**states' righter** *n.*

States' Rights Party *n.* A former political party founded in 1948 by Southern Democrats to consolidate opposition to civil rights policies of the regular Democratic Party.

states•wom•an (stāts′woŏm′ən) *n.* **1.** A woman who is a leader in national or international affairs. **2.** A woman political leader seen as disinterestedly promoting the public good.

state•wide (stāt′wīd′) *adj.* Occurring or extending throughout a state. ❖ *adv.* Throughout a state.

stat•ic (stăt′ĭk) *adj.* **1a.** Having no motion; being at rest; quiescent. **b.** Fixed; stationary. **2.** *Physics* Of or relating to bodies at rest or forces that balance each other. **3.** *Electricity* Of, relating to, or producing stationary charges; electrostatic. ❖ *n.* **1.** Interference or noise, such as crackling in a receiver, produced when static or atmospheric electricity disturbs signal reception. **2.** *Informal* **a.** Back talk. **b.** Interference; obstruction. **c.** Angry or heated criticism. [NLat. *staticus*, relating to weight < Gk. *statikos*, causing to stand < *statos*, standing. See **stā-** in App.] —**stat′i•cal, stat•ick′y** *adj.* —**stat′i•cal•ly** *adv.*

stat•i•ce (stăt′ī-sē′, stăt′ĭs) *n.* See **sea lavender.** [Lat. *staticē*, an astringent plant < Gk. *statikē* < fem. of *statikos*, causing to stand, astringent < *statos*, standing. See **stā-** in App.]

static electricity *n.* **1.** An accumulation of electric charge on an insulated body. **2.** Electric discharge resulting from the accumulation of electric charge on an insulated body.

static pressure *n.* The pressure exerted by a still liquid or gas.

static RAM *n.* A type of RAM that is quicker than dynamic RAM, does not need to be refreshed, and is used primarily for cache memory.

stat•ics (stăt′ĭks) *n.* (used with a sing. or pl. verb) The equilibrium mechanics of stationary bodies.

static tube *n.* A specialized tube used to measure the static pressure in a stream of fluid.

stat•in (stăt′n) *n.* Any of a class of drugs that reduce serum cholesterol levels by inhibiting the synthesis of cholesterol by the liver. [< the names of such drugs (such as *fluvastatin, pravastatin*), ult. < −STAT + −IN.]

sta•tion (stā′shən) *n.* **1a.** A place or position where a person or thing stands or is assigned to stand; a post. **b.** An area where a person is assigned to work. **2.** The place, building, or establishment from which a service is provided or operations are directed: *a police station.* **3.** A stopping place along a route, esp. a stop for refueling or for taking on passengers; a depot. **4.** Social position; rank. **5.** An establishment equipped for observation and study. **6a.** An establishment equipped for radio or television transmission. **b.** One that broadcasts radio or television transmissions. **c.** A frequency assigned to a broadcaster. **7.** An input or output point along a communications system. **8.** *Ecology* **a.** The normal habitat of a particular plant or animal community. **b.** The exact place of occurrence of a species or individual within a given habitat. **9. Station** *Roman Catholic Church* Any of the 14 Stations of the Cross. ❖ *tr.v.* **-tioned, -tion•ing, -tions** To assign to a position; post. [ME *stacioun* < OFr. *station* < Lat. *statiō, statiōn-.* See **stā-** in App.]

sta•tion•ar•y (stā′shə-nĕr′ē) *adj.* **1a.** Not moving. **b.** Not capable of being moved; fixed. **2.** Unchanging: *a stationary sound.* ❖ *n., pl.* **-ar•ies** One that is stationary. [ME *stacionarie* < OFr. *stationnaire* < Med.Lat. *statiōnārius* < Lat., of a military station < *statiō, statiōn-,* station. See STATION.]

stationary front *n.* A transition zone between two nearly stationary air masses of different density.

stationary orbit *n.* A geostationary orbit.

stationary wave *n.* See **standing wave.**

station break *n.* An intermission in a radio or television program for identification of the network or station.

sta•tion•er (stā′shə-nər) *n.* **1.** One that sells stationery. **2.** *Archaic* **a.** A publisher. **b.** A bookseller. [ME *stacioner,* a bookseller < Med.Lat. *statiōnārius,* shopkeeper (as against a peddler), prob. < Lat. *statiō, statiōn-,* place of business. See STATION.]

sta•tion•er•y (stā′shə-nĕr′ē) *n.* **1.** Writing paper and envelopes. **2.** Writing materials and office supplies.

station house also **sta•tion•house** (stā′shən-hous′) *n.* **1.** A police station. **2.** A fire station.

sta•tion•mas•ter (stā′shən-măs′tər) *n.* An official in charge of a railroad or bus station.

Sta•tions of the Cross (stā′shənz) *pl.n.* **1.** A devotion in some Christian churches consisting of prayers before representations of the Passion of Jesus. **2.** The 14 crucifixes or images representing the sufferings of Jesus.

sta•tion-to-sta•tion (stā′shən-tə-stā′shən) *adj.* Of, relating to, or designating a long-distance telephone call in which the caller is charged upon reaching anyone at the receiving number. ❖ *adv.* By station-to-station long-distance telephone.

station wagon *n.* An automobile having an extended interior with a third seat or luggage platform and a tailgate. [Orig. a covered wagon traveling from a train station to a hotel.]

stat•ism (stā′tĭz′əm) *n.* The practice or doctrine of giving a centralized government control over economic planning and policy. —**stat′ist** *adj. & n.*

sta•tis•tic (stə-tĭs′tĭk) *n.* **1.** A numerical datum. **2.** A numerical value, such as standard deviation or mean, that characterizes the sample or population from which it was derived. **3.** One viewed as a nameless item of statistical information. [Ult. < NLat. *statisticus,* of statecraft. See STATISTICS.]

stat•is•ti•cian (stăt′ĭ-stĭsh′ən) *n.* **1.** A mathematician specializing in statistics. **2.** A compiler of statistical data.

sta•tis•tics (stə-tĭs′tĭks) *n.* **1.** (*used with a sing. verb*) The mathematics of the collection, organization, and interpretation of numerical data, esp. the analysis of population characteristics by inference from sampling. **2.** (*used with a pl. verb*) Numerical data. [< Ger. *Statistik,* political science < NLat. *statisticus,* of state affairs < Ital. *statista,* person skilled in statecraft < *stato,* state < OItal. < Lat. *status,* position, form of government. See **stā-** in App.] —**sta•tis′ti•cal** (-tĭ-kəl) *adj.* —**sta•tis′ti•cal•ly** *adv.*

sta•tive (stā′tĭv) *adj.* Belonging to or designating a class of verbs that express a state or condition. ❖ *n.* A verb of the stative class. [Lat. *statīvus,* stationary < *stāre, stat-,* to stand. See **stā-** in App.]

stato– *pref.* **1.** Resting; remaining: *statoblast.* **2.** Equilibrium; balance: *statocyst.* [Lat. *status,* standing, placed. See **stā-** in App.]

stat•o•blast (stăt′ə-blăst′) *n.* An asexually produced encapsulated bud of a freshwater bryozoan that remains inactive through winter and develops into a new organism in spring.

stat•o•cyst (stăt′ə-sĭst′) *n.* A small organ of balance in many invertebrates, consisting of a fluid-filled sac containing statoliths that stimulate sensory cells when the animal moves.

stat•o•lith (stăt′l-ĭth′) *n.* A small movable concretion of calcium carbonate found in statocysts; an otolith.

sta•tor (stā′tər) *n.* The stationary part of a motor, dynamo, or turbine, or other working machine about which a rotor turns. [Lat., one that stands < *stāre,* to stand. See **stā-** in App.]

stat•u•ar•y (stăch′ōō-ĕr′ē) *n., pl.* **-ies** **1.** Statues considered as a group. **2.** The art of making statues. **3.** A sculptor. ❖ *adj.* Of, relating to, or suitable for a statue. [< Lat. *statuārius,* of a statue < *statua,* statue. See STATUE.]

stat•ue (stăch′ōō) *n.* A three-dimensional form sculpted, modeled, carved, or cast in material such as clay or bronze. [ME < OFr. < Lat. *statua < statuere,* to set up. See STATUTE.]

stat•u•esque (stăch′ōō-ĕsk′) *adj.* Suggestive of a statue, as in proportion, grace, or dignity; stately. —**stat′u•esque′ly** *adv.*

stat•u•ette (stăch′ōō-ĕt′) *n.* A small statue.

stat•ure (stăch′ər) *n.* **1.** The natural height of a human or animal in an upright position. **2.** An achieved level; status. [ME < OFr. < Lat. *statūra.* See **stā-** in App.]

stat•us (stăt′əs, stā′təs) *n.* **1.** Position relative to that of others; standing. **2.** High standing; prestige. **3.** *Law* The legal character or condition of a person or thing. **4.** A state of affairs; situation. [Lat. See **stā-** in App.]

status Indian *n. Canadian* A federally registered member of a band or First Nation, having special status under Canadian law. See Usage Note at **First Nation.**

status quo (kwō) *n.* The existing condition or state of affairs. [Lat. *status quō,* state in which : *status,* state + *quō,* ablative of *quī,* which.]

status symbol *n.* Something, such as a possession or an activity, by which one's social or economic prestige is measured.

stat•u•ta•ble (stăch′ə-tə-bəl) *adj.* **1.** Enacted, regulated, or authorized by statute; statutory. **2.** *Law* Legally punishable; recognized by statute: *a statutable offense.*

stat•ute (stăch′ōōt) *n.* **1.** A law enacted by a legislature. **2.** A decree or edict, as of a ruler. **3.** An established law or rule, as of a corporation. [ME < OFr. *estatut* < LLat. *statūtum* < neut. of Lat. *statūtus,* p. part. of *statuere,* to set up < *status,* position. See **stā-** in App.]

statute law *n.* A law established by legislative enactment.

statute mile *n.* See **mile** 1.

statute of limitations *n., pl.* **statutes of limitations** A statute setting a time limit on legal action in certain cases.

stat•u•to•ry (stăch′ə-tôr′ē, -tōr′ē) *adj.* **1.** Of or relating to a statute. **2.** Enacted, regulated, or authorized by statute. —**stat′u•to′ri•ly** *adv.*

statutory offense *n.* A legal offense declared by statute.

statutory rape *n.* Sexual relations with a person under the statutory age of consent.

staunch[1] (stônch, stänch) also **stanch** (stônch, stänch, stănch) *adj.* **staunch•er, staunch•est** also **stanch•er, stanch•est** **1.** Firm and steadfast; true. See Syns at **faithful. 2.** Strong or substantial in construction or constitution. [ME *staunche* < AN *estaunche < estaunchier,* to stanch, var. of OFr. *estanchier.* See STANCH[1].] —**staunch′ly** *adv.* —**staunch′ness** *n.*

staunch[2] (stônch, stänch) *v.* Variant of **stanch**[1]. See Usage Note at **staunch**[1].

stau•ro•lite (stôr′ə-līt′) *n.* A brownish to black mineral, chiefly (FeMg)$_2$Al$_9$Si$_4$O$_{23}$(OH), often having crossed intergrown crystals and sometimes used as a gem. [Gk. *stauros,* cross; see **stā-** in App. + −LITE.] —**stau′ro•lit′ic** (-lĭt′ĭk) *adj.*

stave (stāv) *n.* **1.** A narrow strip of wood forming part of the sides of a barrel, tub, or similar structure. **2.** A rung of a ladder or chair. **3.** A staff or cudgel. **4.** *Music* See **staff**[1] 5. **5.** A set of verses; a stanza. ❖ *v.* **staved** or **stove** (stōv), **stav•ing, staves** —*tr.* **1.** To break in or puncture the staves of. **2.** To break or smash a hole in. **3.** To crush or smash inward. **4.** To furnish with staves. —*intr.* To be or become crushed in. —*phrasal verb:* **stave off** To keep or hold off; repel. [Back-formation < *staves,* pl. of STAFF[1].]

staves (stāvz) *n.* A plural of **staff**[1].

staves•a•cre (stāvz′ā′kər) *n.* **1.** A larkspur, *Delphinium staphisagria,* of southern Europe with greenish-white flowers. **2.** The seeds of this plant, formerly used medicinally. [By folk ety. < ME *staphisagre* < Lat. *staphis agria* < Gk. *staphis agriā : staphis,* stavesacre + *agria,* fem. of *agrios,* wild; see **agro-** in App.]

Stav•ro•pol (stăv-rō′pəl, stăv′rə-pəl) A city of SW Russia SE of Rostov; founded 1777. Pop. 333,347.

stay[1] (stā) *v.* **stayed, stay•ing, stays** —*intr.* **1.** To continue to be in a place or condition: *stay home; stay calm.* **2.** To remain or sojourn as a guest or lodger: *stay at a hotel.* **3.** To stop moving; halt. **4.** To wait; pause. **5.** To endure or persist. **6.** To keep up in a race or contest. **7.** *Games* To meet a bet in poker without raising it. **8.** To stand one's ground; remain firm. **9.** *Archaic* To cease from a specified activity. —*tr.* **1.** To stop or halt; check. **2.** To postpone; delay. **3.** To delay or stop the effect of (an order, for example) by legal action or mandate. **4.** To satisfy or appease temporarily. **5.** To remain during. **6.** To wait for; await. ❖ *n.* **1.** The act of halting; check. **2.** The act of coming to a halt. **3.** A brief period of residence or visiting. **4.** A suspension or postponement of a legal action or an execution. —*idioms:* **stay put** To remain in a fixed

ă	pat	oi	boy
ā	pay	ou	out
âr	care	ōō	took
ä	father	ōō	boot
ĕ	pet	ŭ	cut
ē	be	ûr	urge
ĭ	pit	th	thin
ī	pie	th	this
îr	pier	hw	which
ŏ	pot	zh	vision
ō	toe	ə	about,
ô	paw		item

Stress marks:
′ (primary);
′ (secondary), as in
lexicon (lĕk′sĭ-kŏn′)

or established position. **stay the course** To hold out or persevere to the end of a race or challenge. [ME *steien* < OFr. *ester, esteir* < Lat. *stāre.* See **stā–** in App.]

SYNONYMS *stay, remain, wait, abide, tarry, linger* These verbs mean to continue to be in a given place. *Stay* is the least specific, though it can also suggest that the person involved is a guest or visitor: *"Must you go? Can't you stay?"* (Charles J. Vaughan). *Remain* often implies continuing or being left after others have gone: *remained at the end of the meeting. Wait* suggests remaining in readiness, anticipation, or expectation: *"Your father is waiting for me to take a walk with him"* (Booth Tarkington). *Abide* implies continuing for a lengthy period: *"Abide with me"* (Henry Francis Lyte). *Tarry* and *linger* both imply a delayed departure, but *linger* more strongly suggests reluctance to leave: *"She was not anxious but puzzled that her husband tarried"* (Eden Phillpotts). *"I alone sit lingering here"* (Henry Vaughan).

stay² (stā) *tr.v.* **stayed, stay•ing, stays** **1.** To brace, support, or prop up. **2.** To strengthen or sustain mentally or spiritually. **3.** To rest or fix on for support. ❖ *n.* **1.** A support or brace. **2.** A strip of bone, plastic, or metal, used to stiffen a garment or part, such as a corset or shirt collar. **3. stays** A corset. [ME *staien* < OFr. *estaiier* < *estaie,* a support, of Gmc. orig.]

stay³ (stā) *n.* **1.** *Nautical* A heavy rope or cable, usu. of wire, that provides fore-and-aft support for a mast or spar. **2.** A rope used to steady, guide, or brace. [ME < OE *stæg.*]

stay-at-home (stā′ăt-hōm′) *adj.* **1.** Inclined to remain in one's home, locality, or country. **2.** *Sports* Not engaging much in the offensive play: *a stay-at-home defenseman.* ❖ *n.* A person who stays at or works from home.

stay•ing power (stā′ĭng) *n.* The ability to endure or last.

stay•sail (stā′səl, -sāl′) *n. Nautical* A triangular sail hoisted on a stay.

STD *abbr.* sexually transmitted disease

std. *abbr.* standard

Ste. *abbr. French* sainte (feminine form of saint)

stead (stĕd) *n.* **1.** The place, position, or function properly or customarily occupied by another. **2.** Advantage; service; purpose. ❖ *tr.v.* **stead•ed, stead•ing, steads** To be of advantage or service to; benefit. [ME *stede* < OE. See **stā–** in App.]

stead•fast also **sted•fast** (stĕd′făst′, -fəst) *adj.* **1.** Fixed or unchanging; steady. **2.** Firmly loyal or constant. See Syns at **faithful.** [ME *stedefast* < OE *stedefæst* : *stede,* place; see STEAD + *fæst,* fixed, fast.] —**stead′fast′ly** *adv.* —**stead′fast′ness** *n.*

stead•y (stĕd′ē) *adj.* **-i•er, -i•est** **1.** Firm in position or place; fixed. **2.** Direct and unfaltering; sure. **3.** Free or almost free from change, variation, or fluctuation; uniform. **4.** Not easily excited or upset. **5.** Unwavering, as in purpose; steadfast. **6.** Reliable; dependable. **7.** Temperate; sober. ❖ *tr. & intr.v.* **stead•ied, stead•y•ing, stead•ies** To make or become steady. ❖ *interj. Nautical* Used to direct a helmsman to keep a ship's head in the same direction. ❖ *n., pl.* **-ies** The person whom one dates regularly, usu. exclusively. —**stead′i•er** *n.* —**stead′i•ly** *adv.* —**stead′i•ness** *n.*

steady state *n. Physics* A stable condition that does not change over time or in which any one change is continually balanced by another.

steady state theory *n.* The theory describing a steady state universe.

steady state universe *n.* A model universe in which the density of matter is constant over space and time, and the expansion of the universe, required on other grounds, is compensated for by the continuous creation of matter. The model is generally believed to be discredited by the discovery of the background radiation of the big bang.

steak (stāk) *n.* **1.** A slice of meat, typically beef, usu. cut across the muscle grain and served broiled or fried. **2.** A thick slice of a large fish cut across the body. **3.** A patty of ground meat broiled or fried. [ME *steike* < ON *steik.*]

steak house or **steak•house** (stāk′hous′) *n.* A restaurant that specializes in beefsteak dishes.

steak knife *n.* A table knife with a sharp, usu. serrated blade.

steak tartare *n.* Raw finely chopped or ground beef served with onion, seasonings, and raw egg. [STEAK + Fr. *tartare,* Tartar.]

steal (stēl) *v.* **stole** (stōl), **sto•len** (stō′lən), **steal•ing, steals** —*tr.* **1.** To take (the property of another) without right or permission. **2.** To get or effect surreptitiously or artfully: *stole the ball.* **3.** To move, carry, or place surreptitiously. **4.** To draw attention unexpectedly in (an entertainment), esp. by being the outstanding performer. **5.** *Baseball* To advance safely to (another base) during the delivery of a pitch, without the aid of a base hit, walk, passed ball, or wild pitch. —*intr.* **1.** To commit theft. **2.** To move, happen, or elapse stealthily or unobtrusively. **3.** *Baseball* To steal a base. ❖ *n.* **1.** The act of stealing. **2.** *Slang* A bargain. **3.** *Baseball* A stolen base. **4.** *Basketball* An act of gaining possession of the ball from an opponent. —**idiom: steal (someone's) thunder** To use, appropriate, or preempt the use of another's idea. [ME *stelen* < OE *stelan.*] —**steal′er** *n.*

stealth (stĕlth) *n.* **1.** The act of moving, proceeding, or acting in a covert way. **2.** The quality or characteristic of being furtive or covert. **3.** *Archaic* The act of stealing. ❖ *adj.* **1.** Having or providing the ability to prevent detection by radar. **2.** Not disclosing one's true ideology, affiliations, or positions: *a stealth candidate.* [ME *stelth,* prob. < OE **stælth.*]

stealth•y (stĕl′thē) *adj.* **-i•er, -i•est** Marked by or acting with quiet, caution, and secrecy intended to avoid notice. —**stealth′i•ly** *adv.* —**stealth′i•ness** *n.*

steam (stēm) *n.* **1a.** The vapor phase of water. **b.** A mist of cooling water vapor. **2a.** Pressurized water vapor used for heating, cooking, or to provide mechanical power. **b.** The power produced by using steam. **c.** Steam heating. **3.** Power; energy. ❖ *v.* **steamed, steam•ing, steams** —*intr.* **1.** To produce or emit steam. **2.** To become or rise up as steam. **3.** To become misted or covered with steam. **4.** To move by means of steam power. **5.** *Informal* To become very angry; fume. —*tr.* To expose to steam. [ME *steme* < OE *stēam.*]

steam bath *n.* **1.** Bathing by exposure to steam. **2.** A room or building that provides bathing with steam.

steam•boat (stēm′bōt′) *n.* A steamship, esp. one used on rivers and other inland waterways.

steam boiler *n.* A closed tank in which water is converted into steam under pressure.

steam chest *n.* A compartment in a steam engine through which steam is delivered from the boiler to a cylinder.

steam engine *n.* An engine that converts the heat energy of pressurized steam into mechanical energy, esp. one in which steam drives a piston in a closed cylinder.

steam•er (stē′mər) *n.* **1.** One that steams. **2.** A steamship. **3.** A vehicle, machine, or engine driven by steam. **4.** A container in which something is steamed. **5.** See **soft-shell clam.**

steamer rug *n.* A warm blanket used esp. by shipboard passengers while sitting in deck chairs.

steamer trunk *n.* A small trunk originally designed to fit under the bunk of a steamship cabin.

steam•fit•ter (stēm′fĭt′ər) *n.* One who installs and repairs heating, ventilating, refrigerating, and air-conditioning systems. —**steam′fit′ting** *n.*

steam heating *n.* A heating system in which steam is generated in a boiler and piped to radiators.

steam iron *n.* A pressing iron that holds and heats water to be emitted as steam on the cloth being pressed.

steam•roll•er (stēm′rō′lər) *n.* **1a.** A steam-driven machine equipped with a heavy roller for smoothing road surfaces. **b.** A similar machine with an internal-combustion engine. **2.** A ruthless or irresistible force or power. ❖ *v.* also **steam•roll** (-rōl′) **-roll•ered, -roll•er•ing, -roll•ers** also **-rolled, -roll•ing, -rolls** —*tr.* **1.** To smooth or level (a road) with a steamroller. **2.** To overwhelm or suppress ruthlessly; crush. —*intr.* To move or proceed with overwhelming force.

steam•ship (stēm′shĭp′) *n.* A large vessel propelled by one or more steam-driven screws, propellers, or paddles.

steam shovel *n.* **1.** A large steam-driven machine for digging. **2.** See **power shovel.**

steam table *n.* A table in which containers of cooked food are kept warm by hot water or steam circulating below.

steam turbine *n.* A turbine operated by highly pressurized steam directed against vanes on a rotor.

steam•y (stē′mē) *adj.* **-i•er, -i•est** **1.** Filled with or emitting steam. **2.** Erotic. —**steam′i•ly** *adv.* —**steam′i•ness** *n.*

ste•ap•sin (stē-ăp′sĭn) *n.* A digestive enzyme of pancreatic juice that catalyzes the hydrolysis of fats to fatty acids and glycerol. [Gk. *stear,* tallow + (PE)PSIN.]

ste•a•rate (stē′ə-rāt′, stîr′āt′) *n.* A salt or ester of stearic acid. [STEAR(IC) + –ATE².]

ste•ar•ic (stē-ăr′ĭk, stîr′ĭk) *adj.* **1.** Of, relating to, or similar to stearin or fat. **2.** Of or relating to stearic acid. [Fr. *stéarique* < Gk. *stear,* tallow.]

stearic acid *n.* A colorless waxlike fatty acid, $CH_3(CH_2)_{16}COOH$, occurring in natural and vegetable fats and used in making soaps, candles, and lubricants.

ste•a•rin (stē′ər-ĭn, stîr′ĭn) also **ste•a•rine** (stē′ər-ĭn, -ə-rēn′, stîr′ĭn) *n.* **1.** A colorless ester of glycerol and stearic acid, $C_3H_5(C_{18}H_{35}O_2)_3$, found in most animal and vegetable fats and used in the manufacture of soaps, candles, and adhesives and for textile sizing. **2.** The solid form of fat. [Fr. *stéarine* : Gk. *stear,* tallow + Fr. *-ine,* -in.]

ste•a•tite (stē′ə-tīt′) *n.* See **soapstone.** [Lat. *steatītis,* a precious stone < Gk. < *stear, steat-,* tallow.]

steato– or **steat–** *pref.* Fat: *steatopygia.* [Gk. < *stear, steat-,* tallow.]

ste•at•o•pyg•i•a (stē-ăt′ə-pĭj′ē-ə, -pī′jē-ə) *n.* An extreme accumulation of fat on the buttocks. [STEATO– + Gk. *pugē,* rump + –IA¹.] —**ste′at•o•pyg′ic** (stē′ə-tə-pĭj′ĭk, -pī′jĭk) , **ste′a•to•py′gous** (-pī′gəs) *adj.*

ste•a•tor•rhe•a also **ste•a•tor•rhoe•a** (stē′ə-tə-rē′ə, stē-ăt′ə-) *n.* **1.** Overaction of the sebaceous glands. **2.** Excessive discharge of fat in the feces.

sted•fast (stĕd′făst′, -fəst) *adj.* Variant of **steadfast.**

steed (stēd) *n.* A horse, esp. a spirited one. [ME *stede* < OE *stēda,* stallion. See **stā–** in App.]

steel (stēl) *n.* **1.** A generally hard, strong durable malleable alloy of iron and carbon, usu. containing between 0.2 and 1.5 percent carbon, often with other constituents such as manganese, chro-

steamboat

steel drum

mium, nickel, or silicon, depending on the desired alloy properties, and widely used as a structural material. **2.** Something made of steel. **3.** A quality suggestive of this alloy, esp. a hard, unflinching character. **4.** Steel gray. ❖ *adj.* **1a.** Made with, relating to, or consisting of steel: *steel beams.* **b.** Very firm or strong: *a steel grip.* **2.** Of a steel gray. ❖ *tr.v.* **steeled, steel·ing, steels 1.** To cover, plate, edge, or point with steel. **2.** To make hard, strong, or obdurate; strengthen. [ME *stel* < OE *style, stēl.*]

steel band *n. Music* A steel drum band.

steel blue *n.* **1.** A medium grayish blue. **2.** One of several blue colors taken on by steel while being tempered.

steel drum *n.* A metal percussion instrument of Trinidadian origin, fashioned from an oil barrel and having a concave array of flattened areas that produce different tones when struck. —**steel drummer** *n.*

Steele (stēl), **Mount** A mountain, 5,076.4 m (16,644 ft), in the St. Elias Mts. of SW Yukon Terr., Canada.

Steele, Sir Richard 1672–1729. English writer of plays and essays who founded and edited *The Tatler* (1709–11) and with Joseph Addison *The Spectator* (1711–12).

steel engraving *n.* **1.** The art or process of engraving on a steel plate. **2.** An impression produced with such a plate.

steel gray *n.* A dark to purplish gray.

steel guitar *n.* **1.** An acoustic guitar with a metal resonator built into the body, often played with a slide and producing a twangy variable tone. **2.** See **Hawaiian guitar.**

steel·head (stēl′hĕd′) *n.* The anadromous variety of the rainbow trout, having silvery, unstriped sides.

steel-trap (stēl′trăp′) *adj.* Very quick and keen; trenchant.

steel wool *n.* Fine fibers of steel, matted or woven together to form an abrasive for cleaning, smoothing, or polishing.

steel·work (stēl′wûrk′) *n.* **1.** Something made of steel. **2. steelworks** (*used with a sing. verb*) A plant where steel is made; a foundry. —**steel′work′er** *n.*

steel·y (stē′lē) *adj.* **-i·er, -i·est 1.** Made of steel. **2.** Resembling steel, as in color or hardness. —**steel′i·ness** *n.*

steel·yard (stēl′yärd′) *n.* A balance consisting of a scaled arm suspended off center, a hook at the shorter end on which to hang the object being weighed, and a counterbalance at the longer end that can be moved to find the weight. [STEEL + YARD¹, rod.]

Steen (stān), **Jan** 1626?–79. Dutch genre painter whose depictions of domestic life include *Village Wedding* (1635).

steen·bok (stēn′bŏk′, stān′-) also **stein·bok** (stīn′-) *n.* A small antelope (*Raphicerus campestris*) of southern and eastern Africa having a brownish coat and short pointed horns in the male. [Afr. < MDu. *steenboc*, ibex : *steen*, stone + *boc*, buck.]

steep¹ (stēp) *adj.* **steep·er, steep·est 1.** Having a sharp inclination; precipitous. **2.** At a rapid or precipitous rate: *a steep rise in salaries.* **3a.** Excessive; stiff: *a steep price.* **b.** Ambitious; difficult. ❖ *n.* A precipitous slope. [ME *stepe* < OE *stēap.*] —**steep′ly** *adv.* —**steep′ness** *n.*

SYNONYMS *steep, abrupt, precipitous, sheer* These adjectives mean so sharply inclined as to be almost perpendicular: *steep cliffs; an abrupt drop-off; precipitous hills; a sheer descent.*

---

steep² (stēp) *v.* **steeped, steep·ing, steeps** —*tr.* **1.** To soak in liquid in order to cleanse, soften, or extract a given property from. **2.** To infuse or subject thoroughly to. **3.** To make thoroughly wet; saturate. —*intr.* To undergo a soaking in liquid. ❖ *n.* **1a.** The act or process of steeping. **b.** The state of being steeped. **2.** A liquid, bath, or solution into which something is steeped. [ME *stepen*, perh. of OE orig.] —**steep′er** *n.*

steep·en (stē′pən) *tr. & intr.v.* **-ened, -en·ing, -ens** To make or become steep or steeper.

stee·ple (stē′pəl) *n.* **1.** A tall tower forming the superstructure of a building, such as a church or temple, and usu. surmounted by a spire. **2.** A steeple's spire. [ME *stepel* < OE *stēpel.*]

stee·ple·bush (stē′pəl-boŏsh′) *n.* See **hardhack.**

stee·ple·chase (stē′pəl-chās′) *n. Sports* **1.** A horserace across open country or over an obstacle course. **2.** A footrace over a closed track with four hurdles and a water obstacle. [Church steeples being landmarks.] —**stee′ple·chas′er** *n.*

stee·pled (stē′pəld) *adj.* **1.** Having steeples or a steeple: *a tiny, steepled church.* **2.** Steeply inclined: *steepled roofs.*

stee·ple·jack (stē′pəl-jăk′) *n.* One who builds or maintains very high structures, such as steeples.

steer¹ (stîr) *v.* **steered, steer·ing, steers** —*tr.* **1.** To guide by means of a device such as a rudder, paddle, or wheel. **2a.** To direct the course of. **b.** To maneuver (a person) into a place or course of action. —*intr.* **1.** To guide a vessel or vehicle. **2.** To follow or move in a set course. **3.** To admit of being steered or guided. ❖ *n.* A piece of advice. —**idiom: steer clear of** To stay away from; avoid. [ME *steren* < OE *stēran.* See **stā-** in App.] —**steer′a·ble** *adj.* —**steer′er** *n.*

steer² (stîr) *n.* A male bovine animal castrated before reaching sexual maturity. [ME < OE *stēor.* See **stā-** in App.]

steer·age (stîr′ĭj) *n.* **1.** The act or practice of steering. **2.** *Nautical* **a.** The effect of the helm on a ship. **b.** The section of a passenger ship, originally near the rudder, providing the cheapest travel accommodations.

steer·age·way (stîr′ĭj-wā′) *n.* The minimum rate of motion re-

quired for a ship or boat to be maneuvered by the helm.

steer·ing committee (stîr′ĭng) *n.* A committee that sets agendas and schedules of business, as for a legislative body.

steering gear *n.* The mechanism by which dispositions of the steering controls of a vehicle are transferred to a rudder, wheel, or other part that directs the vehicle's course.

steering wheel *n.* A wheel that controls steering, as on a boat.

steers·man (stîrz′mən) *n.* One who steers a ship.

steeve¹ (stēv) *Nautical n.* A spar or derrick with a block at one end, used for stowing cargo. ❖ *tr.v.* **steeved, steev·ing, steeves** To stow or pack (cargo) in the hold of a ship. [< ME *steven*, to stow, prob. < OSpan. *estibar*, to steeve, or < O Catalan *stivar*, both < Lat. *stīpāre.*]

steeve² (stēv) *Nautical n.* The angle formed by the bowsprit and the horizon or the keel. ❖ *v.* **steeved, steev·ing, steeves** —*tr.* To incline (a bowsprit) upward at an angle with the horizon or the keel. —*intr.* To have an upward inclination. Used of a bowsprit. [?]

Ste·fáns·son (stĕf′ən-sən), **Vilhjálmur** 1879–1962. Canadian-born explorer and ethnologist who studied the language and culture of the Inuit and Eskimo.

Stef·fens (stĕf′ənz), **(Joseph) Lincoln** 1866–1936. Amer. journalist considered a pioneer of muckraking journalism.

Steg·ner (stĕg′nər), **Wallace Earle** 1909–93. Amer. writer whose novels include *Angle of Repose* (1971).

steg·o·don (stĕg′ə-dŏn′) *n.* Any of various extinct elephantlike mammals of the genus *Stegodon* and related genera of the Pliocene to the Pleistocene epochs. [NLat. *Stegodon*, genus name : Gk. *stegos*, roof (< *stegein*, to cover; see **(s)teg-** in App.) + -ODON (so called because of the distinctive ridges on its molars).]

steg·o·saur (stĕg′ə-sôr′) also **steg·o·sau·rus** (stĕg′ə-sôr′əs) *n.* Any of several herbivorous dinosaurs of the suborder Stegosauria of the Jurassic to the Cretaceous periods, having a double row of upright bony plates along the back and a relatively small head. [NLat. *Stegosaurus*, genus name : Gk. *stegos*, roof; see **STEGODON** + Gk. *sauros*, lizard.]

Stei·chen (stī′kən), **Edward Jean** 1879–1973. Amer. photographer who was a pioneer of photography as a fine art.

stein (stīn) *n.* A mug, esp. one for beer, usu. holding about a pint. [Ger., prob. short for *Steinkrug*, stone jug : *Stein*, stone (< MHGer. < OHGer.) + *Krug*, jug.]

Stein, Gertrude 1874–1946. Amer. writer whose works include *The Autobiography of Alice B. Toklas* (1933).

Stein·beck (stīn′bĕk′), **John Ernst** 1902–68. Amer. writer of short stories and novels, most notably *The Grapes of Wrath* (1939). He won the 1962 Nobel Prize for literature.

stein·bok (stīn′bŏk′) *n.* Variant of **steenbok.**

Stein·em (stī′nəm), **Gloria** b. 1934. Amer. feminist who was a founding editor (1972) of *Ms.* magazine.

Stein·er (stī′nər, shtī′-), **Rudolf** 1861–1925. Austrian social philosopher who founded a Christianized school of theosophy, called anthroposophy.

Stein·heim man (stīn′hīm′, shtīn′-) *n.* A fossil hominid specimen previously classed as a distinct species but now generally regarded as an archaic example of *Homo sapiens.* [After *Steinheim*, in SW Germany.]

Stein·metz (stīn′mĕts′, shtīn′-), **Charles Proteus** 1865–1923. German-born Amer. electrical engineer and inventor known for his theoretical studies of alternating current.

Stein·way (stīn′wā′), **Henry Engelhard** 1797–1871. German-born Amer. piano maker who founded the Steinway & Sons piano company in New York City (1853).

ste·le (stē′lē, stēl) *n.* **1.** also **ste·la** (stē′lə), *pl.* **steles** also **-lae** (-lē) An upright stone or slab with an inscribed or sculptured surface, used as a monument or as a commemorative tablet in the face of a building. **2. stele** (stēl, stē′lē) The central core of tissue in the stem or root of a vascular plant, consisting of xylem, phloem and supporting tissues. [Gk. *stēlē*, pillar. See **stel-** in App.] —**ste′lar** (-lər) *adj.*

Stel·la (stĕl′ə), **Frank Philip** b. 1936. Amer. painter known for his geometric abstract works.

stel·lar (stĕl′ər) *adj.* **1.** Of, relating to, or consisting of stars. **2a.** Of or relating to a star performer. **b.** Outstanding; principal. [LLat. *stēllāris* < Lat. *stēlla*, star. See **ster-** in App.]

stellar wind (wĭnd) *n.* The varying flow of plasma ejected from the surface of a star into interstellar space.

stel·late (stĕl′āt′) also **stel·lat·ed** (-ā′tĭd) *adj.* Arranged or shaped like a star; radiating from a center. [Lat. *stēllātus* < *stēlla*, star. See **ster-** in App.] —**stel′late·ly** *adv.*

stel·li·form (stĕl′ə-fôrm′) *adj.* Shaped like a star. [NLat. *stelliformis* : Lat. *stēlla*, star; see **STELLAR** + Lat. *-fōrmis*, form (< *fōrma*; see FORM).]

stel·lu·lar (stĕl′yə-lər) *adj.* **1.** Having the form of a small star. **2.** Bespangled with small stars. [< LLat. *stēllula*, dim. of Lat. *stēlla*, star. See STELLAR.]

stem¹ (stĕm) *n.* **1a.** The main ascending axis of a plant; a stalk or trunk. **b.** A slender stalk supporting or connecting another plant part, such as a leaf or flower. **2.** A banana stalk bearing several bunches of bananas. **3.** A connecting or supporting part, esp.: **a.** The tube of a tobacco pipe. **b.** The slender upright support of a wineglass or goblet. **c.** The small projecting shaft with an ex-

steeple
Sharon Congregational
Church, Vermont

stele
Assyrian relief carving

panded crown by which a watch is wound. **d.** The rounded rod in the center of certain locks about which the key fits and is turned. **e.** The shaft of a feather or hair. **f.** The upright stroke of a typeface or letter. **g.** *Music* The vertical line extending from the head of a note. **4.** The main line of descent of a family. **5.** *Linguistics* The main part of a word to which affixes are added. **6.** *Nautical* The curved upright beam at the fore of a vessel into which the hull timbers are scarfed to form the prow. **7.** The tubular glass structure mounting the filament or electrodes in an incandescent bulb or vacuum tube. ❖ *v.* **stemmed, stem•ming, stems** —*intr.* To have or take origin or descent. —*tr.* **1.** To remove the stem of. **2.** To provide with a stem. **3.** To make headway against: *stemmed the rebellion.* —**idiom: from stem to stern** From one end to another. [ME < OE *stefn, stemn.* See **stā-** in App.]

SYNONYMS *stem, arise, derive, emanate, flow, issue, originate, proceed, rise* These verbs mean to come forth or come into being: *customs that stem from the past; misery that arose from war; rights that derive from citizenship; approval that emanated from them; joy that flows from friendship; hate that issues from fear; a bill that originated in Congress; a mistake that proceeded from haste; rebellion that rises in the towns.*

stem² (stĕm) *v.* **stemmed, stem•ming, stems** —*tr.* **1.** To stop or hold back by or as if by damming; stanch. **2.** To plug or tamp (a blast hole, for example). **3.** *Sports* To point (skis) inward. —*intr.* *Sports* To point skis inward in order to slow down or turn. [ME *stemmen* < ON *stemma.*]

stem cell *n.* An unspecialized cell that gives rise to a specific specialized cell, such as a blood cell.

stem•ma (stĕm′ə) *n., pl.* **stem•ma•ta** (stĕm′ə-tə) or **stem•mas 1.** A scroll recording the genealogy of an ancient Roman family; a family tree. **2.** The genealogy of the manuscripts of a literary work. **3.** A small circular simple eye present in various insect larvae. [Lat. *stemma, stemmat-* < Gk., garland < *stephein,* to encircle.]

stemmed (stĕmd) *adj.* **1.** Having the stems removed. **2.** Provided with a stem or a specific type of stem. Often used in combination: *long-stemmed roses.*

stem rust *n.* A rust disease affecting the stem of a plant.

stem•son (stĕm′sən) *n. Nautical* A piece of supporting timber bolted to the stem and keelson at their junction near the bow of a wooden vessel. [STEM¹ + (KEEL)SON.]

stem turn *n.* A turn in skiing made by stemming the uphill ski, transferring weight to its inside edge, and bringing the other ski into a parallel position after making the turn.

stem•ware (stĕm′wâr′) *n.* Glassware mounted on a stem with a broad base.

stem-wind•er (stĕm′wīn′dər) *n.* **1.** A stem-winding watch. **2.** A rousing oration, esp. a political one.

stem-wind•ing (stĕm′wīn′dĭng) *adj.* Wound by turning an expanded crown on the stem.

stench (stĕnch) *n.* **1.** A strong foul odor; a stink. **2.** A foul quality: *the stench of corrupt government.* [ME < OE *stenc,* odor.]

sten•cil (stĕn′səl) *n.* **1.** A sheet, as of plastic, in which lettering or a design has been cut so that ink or paint applied to the sheet will reproduce the pattern on the surface beneath. **2.** The lettering or design so produced. **3.** The process of printing with such a sheet. ❖ *tr.v.* **-ciled, -cil•ing, -cils** or **-cilled, -cil•ling, -cils 1.** To mark with a stencil. **2.** To produce by stencil. [< ME *stencelled,* adorned brightly < OFr. *estenceler,* to adorn brightly < *estencele,* spark < VLat. **stincilla,* alteration of Lat. *scintilla,* spark.] —**sten′cil•er** *n.*

stencil
stencil *(left)* and painted motif

Sten•dhal (stĕn-däl′, stän-, stäN-) Pen name of Marie Henri Beyle. 1783–1842. French writer who influenced the development of the modern novel with his psychological romances.

Sten•gel (stĕng′gəl), **Charles Dillon** Known as "Casey." 1890?–1975. Amer. baseball player and manager, most notably of the New York Yankees (1948–60).

sten•o (stĕn′ō) *n., pl.* **-os 1.** A stenographer. **2.** Stenography.

steno– *pref.* Narrow; small: *stenotopic.* [Gk. < *stenos.*]

sten•o•bath•ic (stĕn′ə-băth′ĭk) *adj.* Limited to or able to live only within a narrow range of water depths. [STENO– + Gk. *bathos,* depth + –IC.] —**sten′o•bath′ic** *n.*

sten•o•graph (stĕn′ə-grăf′) *n.* **1.** A keyboard machine for reproducing letters in a shorthand system. **2.** A character in shorthand.

ste•nog•ra•pher (stə-nŏg′rə-fər) *n.* One skilled in stenography, esp. one employed to take and transcribe dictation or testimony.

ste•nog•ra•phy (stə-nŏg′rə-fē) *n.* **1.** The art or process of writing in shorthand. **2.** The art or practice of transcribing speech with a stenograph. **3.** Material transcribed in shorthand. —**sten′o•graph′ic** (stĕn′ə-grăf′ĭk), **sten′o•graph′i•cal** (-ĭ-kəl) *adj.* —**sten′o•graph′i•cal•ly** *adv.*

sten•o•ha•line (stĕn′ə-hā′līn, -hăl′īn) *adj.* Limited to or able to live only within a narrow range of saltwater concentrations. [STENO– + Gk. *halinos,* of salt (< *hals, hal-,* salt; see HALO–).]

ste•nosed (stə-nōzd′, -nōst′) *adj.* Characterized by stenosis.

ste•no•sis (stə-nō′sĭs) *n., pl.* **-ses** (-sēz) A constriction or narrowing of a duct or passage. [Gk. *stenōsis,* a narrowing < *stenoun,* to narrow < *stenos,* narrow.] —**ste•not′ic** (-nŏt′ĭk) *adj.*

sten•o•ther•mal (stĕn′ə-thûr′məl) also **sten•o•ther•mic**

(-mĭk) or **sten•o•ther•mous** (-məs) *adj.* Capable of living or growing only within a limited range of temperature. —**sten′o•therm′** *n.*

sten•o•top•ic (stĕn′ə-tŏp′ĭk) *adj.* Able to adapt only to a narrow range of environmental conditions. Used of a plant or an animal. [STENO– + Gk. *topos,* place + –IC.]

sten•o•type (stĕn′ə-tīp′) *n.* **1.** A keyboard machine used to record dictation in shorthand by a series of phonetic symbols. **2.** A phonetic symbol or combination of symbols produced by such a machine. ❖ *tr.v.* **-typed, -typ•ing, -types** To record or transcribe (matter) with a stenotype machine. [STENO(GRAPHY) + TYPE.] —**sten′o•typ′ist** *n.*

sten•o•typ•y (stĕn′ə-tī′pē) *n., pl.* **-ies** The art or process of transcribing with a stenotype machine.

stent (stĕnt) *n.* A tubular surgical device inserted into a blood vessel or other passage to prevent closure, as during anastomosis. [After Charles R. *Stent* (1845–1901), English dentist.]

sten•tor (stĕn′tôr′) *n.* Any of several trumpet-shaped ciliate protozoans of the genus *Stentor,* living in dark freshwater pools and feeding chiefly on smaller microorganisms. [After *Stentor,* a Greek herald.]

sten•to•ri•an (stĕn-tôr′ē-ən, -tōr′-) *adj.* Extremely loud. [After *Stentor,* a loud-voiced Greek herald in the *Iliad.*]

step (stĕp) *n.* **1a.** The single complete movement of raising one foot and putting it down in another spot, as in walking. **b.** A manner of walking; a particular gait. **c.** A fixed rhythm or pace, as in marching: *keep step.* **d.** The sound of a footstep. **e.** A footprint. **2a.** The distance traversed by moving one foot ahead of the other. **b.** A very short distance: *just a step away.* **c. steps** Course; path. **3.** One of a series of movements of the feet used in a dance. **4a.** A rest for the foot in ascending or descending. **b. steps** Stairs. **c.** Something, such as a ledge, that resembles a step of a stairway. **5a.** One of a series of actions, processes, or measures taken to achieve a goal. **b.** A stage in a process. **6.** A degree in progress or a grade or rank in a scale. **7.** *Music* **a.** The interval that separates two successive tones of a scale. **b.** A degree of a scale. **8.** *Nautical* The frame or support in which the heel of a mast is fixed. ❖ *v.* **stepped, step•ping, steps** —*intr.* **1.** To put or press the foot: *step on the brake.* **2.** To shift or move slightly by taking a step or two: *step back.* **3.** To walk a short distance to a given place or in a given direction. **4.** To move with the feet in a given manner: *step lively.* **5.** To move into a new situation by or as if by taking a single step. **6.** To treat with arrogant indifference: *stepped on them.* —*tr.* **1.** To put or set (the foot) down: *step foot on land.* **2.** To measure by pacing: *step off ten yards.* **3.** To furnish with steps; make steps in. **4.** *Computer Science* To cause (a computer) to execute a single instruction. **5.** *Nautical* To place (a mast) in its step. —**phrasal verbs: step aside** To resign from a post, esp. when being replaced. **step down 1.** To resign from a high post. **2.** To reduce, esp. in stages. **step in 1.** To enter into an activity or situation. **2.** To intervene. **step out 1.** To walk briskly. **2.** To go outside for a short time. **3.** *Informal* To go out for a special evening of entertainment. **4.** To withdraw; quit. **step up 1.** To increase, esp. in stages. **2.** To come forward. —**idioms: in step 1.** Moving in rhythm. **2.** In conformity with one's environment. **out of step 1.** Not moving in rhythm. **2.** Not in conformity with one's environment. **step by step** By degrees. **step on it** *Informal* To go faster; hurry. [ME < OE *stæpe, stepe.*]

step– *pref.* Related by means of a remarriage rather than by blood: *stepparent.* [ME < OE *stēop-.*]

step•broth•er (stĕp′brŭth′ər) *n.* A son of one's stepparent.

step•child (stĕp′chīld′) *n.* **1.** A child of one's spouse by a previous union. **2.** Something that does not receive appropriate care, respect, or attention.

step dance *n.* A dance focusing mainly on steps.

step•daugh•ter (stĕp′dô′tər) *n.* A spouse's daughter by a previous union.

step-down (stĕp′doun′) *adj.* **1.** Decreasing in stages: *a step-down gear.* **2.** *Electricity* Serving to reduce voltage: *a step-down transformer.* ❖ *n.* A reduction in amount or size.

step•fam•i•ly (stĕp′făm′ə-lē, -făm′lē) *n., pl.* **-lies** A family with one or more stepchildren.

step•fa•ther (stĕp′fä′thər) *n.* The husband of one's mother and not one's natural father.

steph•a•no•tis (stĕf′ə-nō′tĭs) *n., pl.* **-tis•es** Any of various woody climbing plants of the genus *Stephanotis,* esp. *S. floribunda* of Madagascar, cultivated for its showy fragrant white flowers. [Gk. *stephanōtis,* deserving a crown < *stephanos,* crown, wreath < *stephein,* to crown.]

Ste•phen (stē′vən), Saint. d. c. A.D. 36. Christian protomartyr who, according to the New Testament, was stoned to death.

Stephen I Often called Saint Stephen. 975?–1038. King of Hungary (997?–1038) considered the founder of the Hungarian state.

Stephen, Sir Leslie 1832–1904. British writer and editor whose works include *The History of English Thought in the Eighteenth Century* (1876).

Stephen of Blois (blwä) 1097?–1154. King of England (1135–54) who was the last Norman king of the realm.

Ste•phens (stē′vənz), **Alexander Hamilton** 1812–83. Amer. politician and vice president of the Confederacy (1861–65).

Ste•phen•son (stē′vən-sən), **George** 1781–1848. British railway

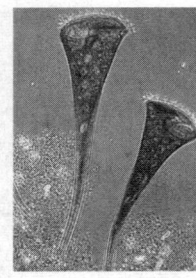

stentor

pioneer who built the first passenger railway (1825). His son **Robert** (1803–59) built railroads and bridges.

step-in (stĕp′ĭn′) *adj.* Put on by stepping into. ❖ *n.* **1. step-ins** Panties with wide legs. **2.** A step-in garment.

step·lad·der (stĕp′lăd′ər) *n.* A portable ladder with a hinged supporting frame and usu. topped with a small platform.

step·moth·er (stĕp′mŭth′ər) *n.* The wife of one's father and not one's natural mother.

step·par·ent (stĕp′pâr′ənt, -păr′-) *n.* A stepfather or stepmother.

steppe (stĕp) *n.* A vast semiarid grass-covered plain, as found in southeast Europe, Siberia, and central North America. [Ger. < Russ. *step*'.]

stepped-up (stĕpt′ŭp′) *adj.* Increased in pace or intensity; heightened: *a stepped-up political campaign.*

step·per (stĕp′ər) *n.* **1.** One that steps, esp. in a fast or spirited manner. **2.** *Informal* A dancer.

step·ping·stone (stĕp′ĭng-stōn′) *n.* **1.** A stone that provides a place to step, as in crossing a stream. **2.** An advantageous position for advancement toward a goal.

step·sis·ter (stĕp′sĭs′tər) *n.* A daughter of one's stepparent.

step·son (stĕp′sŭn′) *n.* A spouse's son by a previous union.

step stool *n.* A stool, often with folding steps attached, on which one stands to reach high objects.

step-up (stĕp′ŭp′) *adj.* **1.** Increasing in steps or by stages. **2.** *Electricity* Serving to increase voltage: *a step-up transformer.* ❖ *n.* An increase in size, amount, or activity.

step·wise (stĕp′wīz′) *adj.* **1.** Marked by a gradual progression as if step by step. **2.** *Music* Moving from one tone to an adjacent one. —**step′wise′** *adv.*

ster. *abbr.* sterling

–ster *suff.* **1.** One that is associated with, participates in, makes, or does: *songster.* **2.** One that is: *youngster.* [ME < OE *-estre*, female agent suff.]

ste·ra·di·an (stī-rā′dē-ən) *n.* A unit of measure equal to the solid angle subtended at the center of a sphere by an area on the surface of the sphere that is equal to the radius squared. See table at **measurement.** [STE(REO)– + RADIAN.]

ster·co·ra·ceous (stûr′kə-rā′shəs) also **ster·co·rous** (stûr′kər-əs) *adj.* Consisting of or relating to excrement. [Lat. *stercus, stercor-,* dung; see **sker-**[2] in App. + –ACEOUS.]

stere (stîr) *n.* A unit of volume equal to one cubic meter. [Fr. *stère* < Gk. *stereos,* solid, hard.]

ster·e·o (stĕr′ē-ō′, stîr′-) *n., pl.* **-os 1a.** A stereophonic sound-reproduction system. **b.** Stereophonic sound. **2.** A stereotype. **3.** A stereoscopic system or photograph. ❖ *adj.* **1.** Stereophonic. **2.** Stereoscopic.

stereo– *pref.* **1.** Solid; solid body: *stereotropism.* **2.** Three-dimensional: *stereoscope.* [Gk. < *stereos,* solid.]

ster·e·o·bate (stĕr′ē-ō-bāt′, stîr′-) *n.* **1.** See **stylobate. 2.** The foundation of a stone building, its top course sometimes being a stylobate. [Lat. *stereobatēs* < Gk. **stereobatēs : stereos,* solid; see STEREO– + *-batēs,* walker (< *bainein,* to go; see gʷā- in App.).]

ster·e·o·chem·is·try (stĕr′ē-ō-kĕm′ĭ-strē, stîr′-) *n.* The branch of chemistry that deals with spatial arrangements of atoms in molecules and the chemical and physical effects of these arrangements. —**ster′e·o·chem′i·cal** (-ĭ-kəl) *adj.*

ster·e·o·chro·my (stĕr′ē-ə-krō′mē, stîr′-) *n., pl.* **-mies** The art or process of mural painting with pigments mixed with water glass. —**ster′e·o·chrome′** *n.* —**ster′e·o·chro′mic** *adj.*

ster·e·o·gram (stĕr′ē-ə-grăm′, stîr′-) *n.* **1.** A picture or diagram that gives the impression of solidity. **2.** A stereograph.

ster·e·o·graph (stĕr′ē-ə-grăf′, stîr′-) *n.* Two stereoscopic pictures or one picture with two superposed stereoscopic images, designed to give a three-dimensional effect when viewed through a stereoscope or special glasses. ❖ *tr.v.* **-graphed, -graph·ing, -graphs** To make a stereographic picture of.

ster·e·og·ra·phy (stĕr′ē-ŏg′rə-fē, stîr′-) *n.* **1.** The art or technique of depicting solid bodies on a plane surface. **2.** Photography that involves the use of stereoscopic equipment. —**ster′e·o·graph′ic** (-ə-grăf′ĭk), **ster′e·o·graph′i·cal** (-ĭ-kəl) *adj.* —**ster′e·o·graph′i·cal·ly** *adv.*

ster·e·o·i·so·mer (stĕr′ē-ō-ī′sə-mər, stîr′-) *n.* One of a set of isomers whose molecules have the same atoms bonded to each other but differ in the way these atoms are arranged in space.

ster·e·o·i·som·er·ism (stĕr′ē-ō-ī-sŏm′ə-rĭz′əm, stîr′-) *n.* Isomerism due to differences in the spatial arrangement of atoms in a molecule. —**ster′e·o·i′so·mer′ic** (-ī′sə-mĕr′ĭk) *adj.*

ster·e·o·li·thog·ra·phy (stĕr′ē-ō-lĭ-thŏg′rə-fē, stîr′-) *n.* A three-dimensional printing process that makes a solid object from a computer image by using a computer-controlled laser to draw the shape of the object onto the surface of liquid plastic.

ster·e·ol·o·gy (stĕr′ē-ŏl′ə-jē, stîr′-) *n.* The study of three-dimensional properties of objects or matter usu. observed two-dimensionally. —**ster′e·o·log′ic** (-ə-lŏj′ĭk), **ster′e·o·log′i·cal** (-ĭ-kəl) *adj.* —**ster′e·ol′o·gist** *n.*

ster·e·o·phon·ic (stĕr′ē-ə-fŏn′ĭk, stîr′-) *adj.* Of or used in a sound-reproduction system that uses two or more separate channels to give a more natural distribution of sound. —**ster′e·o·phon′i·cal·ly** (-ĭ-kəl-lē) *adv.* —**ster′e·oph′o·ny** (-ē-ŏf′ə-nē) *n.*

ster·e·op·sis (stĕr′ē-ŏp′sĭs, stîr′-) *n.* Stereoscopic vision.

ster·e·op·ti·con (stĕr′ē-ŏp′tĭ-kŏn′, stîr′-) *n.* A magic lantern, esp. one with two projectors arranged so as to produce dissolving views. [New Latin : STEREO– + Gk. *optikon,* neut. of *optikos,* optic; see OPTIC.]

ster·e·o·scope (stĕr′ē-ə-skōp′, stîr′-) *n.* An instrument with two eyepieces used to impart a three-dimensional effect to two photographs of the same scene from slightly different angles.

ster·e·o·scop·ic (stĕr′ē-ə-skŏp′ĭk, stîr′-) *adj.* **1.** Of or relating to stereoscopy. **2.** Of or relating to a stereoscope. —**ster′e·o·scop′i·cal·ly** *adv.*

ster·e·os·co·py (stĕr′ē-ŏs′kə-pē, stîr′-) *n.* **1.** The viewing of objects as three-dimensional. **2.** The technique of making or using stereoscopes and stereoscopic slides.

ster·e·o·tax·is (stĕr′ē-ə-tăk′sĭs, stîr′-) *n.* **1.** A method in neurosurgery and neurological research for locating points within the brain using an external three-dimensional frame of reference usu. based on the Cartesian coordinate system. **2.** Movement of an organism in response to contact with a solid body. —**ster′e·o·tac′tic** (-tăk′tĭk) *adj.*

ster·e·o·trop·ism (stĕr′ē-ŏt′rə-pĭz′əm, stîr′-) *n.* See **thigmotropism.** —**ster′e·o·trop′ic** (-ē-ə-trŏp′ĭk) *adj.*

ster·e·o·type (stĕr′ē-ə-tīp′, stîr′-) *n.* **1.** A conventional, formulaic, and oversimplified conception or image. **2.** One seen as embodying or conforming to a stereotype. **3.** *Printing* A metal printing plate cast from a matrix molded from a raised printing surface. ❖ *tr.v.* **-typed, -typ·ing, -types 1.** To make a stereotype of. **2.** To characterize by a stereotype. **3.** To give a fixed, unvarying form to. **4.** To print from a stereotype. [Fr. *stéréotype,* stereotype printing : *stéréo–,* solid (< Gk. *stereo–*; see STEREO–) + *type,* printing type (< OFr., symbol < LLat. *typus*; see TYPE).] —**ster′e·o·typ′er** *n.* —**ster′e·o·typ′ic** (-tĭp′ĭk), **ster′e·o·typ′i·cal** (-ĭ-kəl) *adj.* —**ster′e·o·typ′i·cal·ly** *adv.*

ster·e·o·typed (stĕr′ē-ə-tīpt′, stîr′-) *adj.* **1.** Lacking originality or creativity. **2.** *Printing* Made from stereotype plates. **3.** Of or relating to stereotypy.

ster·e·o·ty·py (stĕr′ē-ə-tī′pē, stîr′-) *n., pl.* **-pies 1.** Excessive repetition or lack of variation in movements, ideas, or patterns of speech, esp. as a symptom of a developmental or psychiatric disorder. **2.** *Printing* The process or art of making stereotype plates.

ster·ic (stĕr′ĭk, stîr′-) also **ster·i·cal** (-ĭ-kəl) *adj.* Of or relating to the spatial arrangement of atoms in a molecule. [STER(EO)– + –IC.] —**ster′i·cal·ly** *adv.*

ste·rig·ma (stə-rĭg′mə) *n., pl.* **-ma·ta** (-mə-tə) A slender projection of the basidium of some fungi that bears a basidiospore. [NLat. < Gk. *stērigma,* support < *stērizein, stērig-,* to support.]

ster·il·ant (stĕr′ə-lənt) *n.* A sterilizing agent.

ster·ile (stĕr′əl, -īl′) *adj.* **1.** Not producing or incapable of producing offspring. **2a.** Not producing or incapable of producing seed, fruit spores, or other reproductive structures. Used of plants or their parts. **b.** Producing little or no vegetation; unfruitful: *sterile land.* **3.** Free from live bacteria or other microorganisms: *a sterile operating area.* **4.** Lacking imagination, creativity, or vitality. **5.** Lacking the power to function; not productive or effective; fruitless. [ME < OFr. < Lat. *sterilis.*] —**ster′ile·ly** *adv.* —**ster′ile·ness,** **ste·ril′i·ty** (stə-rĭl′ĭ-tē) *n.*

ster·il·i·za·tion (stĕr′ə-lĭ-zā′shən) *n.* **1.** The act or procedure of sterilizing. **2.** The condition of being sterile or sterilized.

ster·il·ize (stĕr′ə-līz′) *tr.v.* **-ized, -iz·ing, -iz·es 1.** To remove live bacteria or other microorganisms from. **2.** To make (a person or an animal) unable to produce offspring. **3a.** To make incapable of bearing fruit or germinating. **b.** To render (land) unfruitful. **4.** *Economics* To place (gold) in safekeeping so as not to affect the supply of money or credit. **5.** To make inoffensive or innocuous. —**ster′il·iz′er** *n.*

ster·let (stûr′lĭt) *n.* A sturgeon (*Acipenser ruthenus*) of the Black and Caspian seas, used as a source of caviar. [Russ. *sterlyad'* < ORuss. *sterlyagi,* of Gmc. orig.]

ster·ling (stûr′lĭng) *n.* **1.** British money, esp. the pound as the basic monetary unit of the United Kingdom. **2.** British coinage of silver or gold, having as a standard of fineness 0.500 for silver and 0.91666 for gold. **3a.** Sterling silver. **b.** Articles made of sterling silver. ❖ *adj.* **1.** Consisting of or relating to sterling or British money. **2.** Made of sterling silver: *a sterling teaspoon.* **3.** Of the highest quality: *a sterling character.* [ME, silver penny : poss. *sterre,* star; see STAR + *-ling,* diminutive suff. (< the small star stamped on the coin); see –LING[1].]

Sterling Heights A city of SE MI, a suburb of Detroit. Pop. 124,471.

sterling silver *n.* **1.** An alloy of 92.5 percent silver with copper or another metal. **2.** Objects made of this alloy.

stern[1] (stûrn) *adj.* **stern·er, stern·est 1.** Hard, harsh, or severe in manner or character: *a stern teacher.* See Syns at **severe. 2.** Grim, gloomy, or forbidding in appearance or outlook. **3.** Firm or unyielding; uncompromising. **4.** Inexorable; relentless: *stern necessity.* [ME *sterne* < OE *styrne.*] —**stern′ly** *adv.* —**stern′ness** *n.*

stern[2] (stûrn) *n.* **1.** *Nautical* The rear part of a ship or boat. **2.** A rear part or section. [ME *sterne,* perh. of Scand. orig.; akin to ON *stjörn,* rudder. See **stā-** in App.]

Stern, Isaac 1920–2001. Russian-born Amer. violinist considered

stereoscope

among the great virtuosos of the 20th cent.

ster•na (stûr′nə) *n.* A plural of **sternum.**

ster•nal (stûr′nəl) *adj.* Of, relating to, or near the sternum.

stern chaser *n.* A gun or cannon mounted on the stern of a ship for firing at a pursuing vessel.

Sterne (stûrn), **Laurence** 1713–68. British writer whose works include *Tristram Shandy* (1761–67).

stern•fore•most (stûrn′fôr′mōst′, -fôr′-) *adv.* With the stern foremost; backward.

stern•most (stûrn′mōst′) *adj.* Closest to the stern.

stern•post (stûrn′pōst′) *n. Nautical* The principal upright post at the stern of a vessel, usu. serving to support the rudder.

stern sheets *pl.n.* The stern area of an open boat.

stern•son (stûrn′sən) *n. Nautical* A bar of metal or wood set between the keelson and the sternpost to fortify the joint. [STERN² + (KEEL)SON.]

ster•num (stûr′nəm) *n., pl.* **-nums** or **-na** (-nə) A long flat bone in most vertebrates that is situated along the ventral midline of the thorax and articulates with the ribs. [NLat. < Gk. *sternon,* breast, breastbone.]

ster•nu•ta•tion (stûr′nyə-tā′shən) *n.* **1.** The act of sneezing. **2.** A sneeze. [ME *sternutacioun* < Lat. *sternūtātiō, sternūtātiōn-* < *sternūtāre,* freq. of *sternuere,* to sneeze.]

ster•nu•ta•tor (stûr′nyə-tā′tər) *n.* A substance that irritates the nasal and respiratory passages and causes coughing, sneezing, lacrimation, and sometimes vomiting.

ster•nu•ta•to•ry (stûr-nyōo′tə-tôr′ē, -tōr′ē, -nōo′-) *adj.* Causing or tending to cause sneezing. —**ster•nu′ta•to′ry** *n.*

stern•ward (stûrn′wərd) *adv. & adj.* Toward, to, or in the stern. —**stern′wards** *adv.*

stern•way (stûrn′wā′) *n. Nautical* The backward movement of a vessel.

stern-wheel•er (stûrn′hwē′lər, -wē′lər) *n.* A steamboat propelled by a paddle wheel at the stern.

ster•oid (stîr′oid′, stĕr′-) *n.* Any of numerous fat-soluble organic compounds having as a basis 17 carbon atoms arranged in four rings and including sterols, adrenal and sex hormones, and the precursors of certain vitamins. [STER(OL) + -OID.] —**ster′oid, ste•roi′dal** (stĭ-roid′l, stĕ-) *adj.*

ste•roid•o•gen•e•sis (stĭ-roi′də-jĕn′ĭ-sĭs, stĕr′oi-, stîr′-) *n.* Production of steroids by living organisms. —**ste•roid′o•gen′ic** (-jĕn′ĭk) *adj.*

ster•ol (stîr′ôl′, -ōl′, stĕr′-) *n.* Any of a group of predominantly unsaturated solid alcohols of the steroid group, such as cholesterol and ergosterol, present in the fatty tissues of plants and animals. [Short for CHOLESTEROL.]

ster•tor (stûr′tər) *n.* A heavy snoring sound in respiration. [NLat. < Lat. *stertere,* to snore.] —**ster′to•rous** *adj.*

stet (stĕt) *v.* **stet•ted, stet•ting, stets** —*intr.* To direct that a letter, word, or other matter marked for omission or correction be retained. Used in the imperative. —*tr.* To nullify (a correction or deletion) in printed matter. [Lat., third pers. sing. pr. subjunctive of *stāre,* to stand. See **stā-** in App.]

steth•o•scope (stĕth′ə-skōp′) *n.* Any of various instruments used for listening to sounds produced within the body. [Fr. *stéthoscope* : Gk. *stēthos,* chest + Fr. *-scope,* an instrument for viewing (< Lat. *-scopium;* see –SCOPE).] —**steth′o•scop′ic** (-skŏp′ĭk) *adj.* —**ste•thos′co•py** (stĕ-thŏs′kə-pē) *n.*

Stet•son (stĕt′sən) A trademark used for a hat having a high crown and wide brim.

Stet•tin (stə-tēn′, shtĕ-) See **Szczecin.**

Steu•ben (stōo′bən, styōo′-, stōo-bĕn′, styōo-, shtoi′bən), Baron **Friedrich Wilhelm Ludolf Gerhard Augustin von** 1730–94. Prussian-born Amer. Revolutionary military leader who trained the troops under Gen. George Washington.

ste•ve•dore (stē′vĭ-dôr′, -dōr′) *n.* One who is employed in the loading or unloading of ships. ❖ *tr. & intr.v.* **-dored, -dor•ing, -dores** To load or unload the cargo of (a ship) or engage in the process of loading or unloading such a vessel. [Sp. *estibador* < *estibar,* to stow < Lat. *stīpāre,* to pack.]

ste•ve•dore's knot (stē′vĭ-dôrz′, -dōrz′) also **stevedore knot** *n. Nautical* A knot tied in the end of a line to prevent it from unreeving.

Ste•vens (stē′vənz), **John Paul** b. 1920. Amer. jurist; associate justice of the US Supreme Court (since 1975).

Stevens, Nettie Marie 1861–1912. Amer. cytogeneticist whose studies led to the discovery of the chromosomal determination of sex.

Stevens, Thaddeus 1792–1868. Amer. politician who led the impeachment proceedings against Andrew Johnson (1868).

Stevens, Wallace 1879–1955. Amer. poet whose works include "Sunday Morning" (1923).

Ste•ven•son (stē′vən-sən), **Adlai Ewing** 1835–1914. Vice President of the US (1893–97). His grandson **Adlai Ewing Stevenson** (1900–65) ran unsuccessfully for President in 1952 and 1956.

Stevenson, Robert Louis Balfour 1850–94. British writer of essays, poetry, and novels, including *Treasure Island* (1883) and *The Strange Case of Dr. Jekyll and Mr. Hyde* (1886).

stew (stōo, styōo) *v.* **stewed, stew•ing, stews** —*tr.* To cook (food) by boiling slowly. —*intr.* **1.** To undergo cooking by boiling slowly. See Syns at **boil¹. 2.** *Informal* To suffer with oppres-

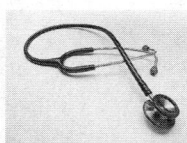

stethoscope

stevedore's knot

sive heat or stuffy confinement; swelter. **3.** *Informal* To be anxious or agitated. See Syns at **brood.** ❖ *n.* **1a.** A dish cooked by stewing, esp. a mixture of meat or fish and vegetables with stock. **b.** A mixture like this. **2.** *Informal* Mental agitation. **3.** *Archaic* A brothel. Often used in the plural. [ME *stewen,* to bathe in a steam bath, stew < OFr. *estuver,* poss. < VLat. **extūpāre, *extūfāre,* to bathe, evaporate < Lat. *ex-,* ex- + VLat. **tūfus,* hot vapor (< Gk. *tūphos,* fever; see TYPHUS).] —**stew′y** *adj.*

stew•ard (stōo′ərd, styōo′-) *n.* **1.** One who manages another's property, finances, or other affairs. **2.** One who is in charge of the household affairs of a large estate, club, hotel, or resort. **3.** A ship's officer in charge of provisions and dining arrangements. **4.** An attendant on a ship or airplane. **5.** An official who supervises or helps to manage an event. **6.** A shop steward. **7.** A wine steward. ❖ *intr. & tr.v.* **-ard•ed, -ard•ing, -ards** To serve as a steward or as the steward of. [ME < OE *stīward* : *stig, stī,* hall + *weard,* keeper.] —**stew′ard•ship′** *n.*

stew•ard•ess (stōo′ər-dĭs, styōo′-) *n.* A woman flight attendant. See Usage Note at **-ess.**

Stew•art (stōo′ərt, styōo′-), **Henry** See Lord **Darnley.**

Stewart, James ("Jimmy") 1908–97. Amer. actor whose motion pictures include *It's a Wonderful Life* (1946).

Stewart, Potter 1915–85. Amer. jurist; associate justice of the US Supreme Court (1958–81).

Stewart Island A volcanic island of S New Zealand off the S coast of South I.

Stewart River A river of central Yukon Terr., Canada, flowing c. 533 km (331 mi) to the Yukon R.

stewed (stōod, styōod) *adj.* **1.** Cooked by stewing: *stewed prunes.* **2.** *Informal* Intoxicated; drunk.

stge. *abbr.* storage

sthe•ni•a (sthə-nī′ə, sthē′nē-ə) *n.* A condition of bodily strength, vigor, or vitality. [NLat. < Gk. *sthenos,* strength. See **segh-** in App.] —**sthen′ic** (sthĕn′ĭk) *adj.*

stib•ine (stĭb′ēn) *n.* A colorless flammable poisonous gas, SbH₃, often used as a fumigant. [< ME *stibium,* antimony < Lat., var. of *stimi* < Gk. *stibi, stimmi,* of Coptic orig.; akin to Egypt. *stm.*]

stib•nite (stĭb′nīt′) *n.* A lead-gray mineral, Sb₂S₃, that is the chief source of antimony. [Fr. *stibine,* stibnite (< Lat. *stibium,* antimony; see STIBINE) + -ITE¹.]

stich (stĭk) *n.* A line of verse. [Gk. *stikhos.* See **steigh-** in App.]

stich•ic (stĭk′ĭk) *adj.* Composed of verses in the same meter.

sti•chom•e•try (stĭ-kŏm′ĭ-trē) *n.* The division of prose into lines of fixed length or into lines whose lengths correspond to the natural divisions of sense, as in manuscripts preceding the adoption of punctuation. [Gk. *stikhos,* stich; see **steigh-** in App. + -METRY.] —**stich′o•met′ric** (stĭk′ə-mĕt′rĭk) *adj.*

stich•o•myth•i•a (stĭk′ə-mĭth′ē-ə) also **sti•chom•y•thy** (stĭ-kŏm′ə-thē) *n.* Alteration between speakers of lines or parts of lines of verse in Greek drama. [Gk. *stikhomūthiā* < *stikhomūthein,* to speak in alternating lines : *stikhos,* stich; see **steigh-** in App. + *mūthos,* speech.] —**stich′o•myth′ic** *adj.*

stick (stĭk) *n.* **1.** A long slender piece of wood, esp.: **a.** A branch or stem cut from a tree or shrub. **b.** A piece of wood, such as a tree branch, that is used for fuel, lumber, or another specific purpose. **c.** A wand, staff, baton, or rod. **d.** *Sports & Games* Any of various implements shaped like a rod and used in play. **2.** A walking stick; a cane. **3.** Something slender and often cylindrical in form. **4.** *Slang* A marijuana cigarette. **5a.** The control device of an aircraft that operates the elevators and ailerons. **b.** *Informal* A stick shift. **6.** *Nautical* A mast or a part of a mast. **7.** *Printing* **a.** A composing stick. **b.** A stickful. **8.** A timber tree. **9.** *Informal* A piece of furniture. **10.** A poke, thrust, or stab with a stick or similar object. **11.** A threatened penalty. **12.** The condition or power of adhering. **13. sticks** *Informal* **a.** A remote area; backwoods. **b.** A city or town regarded as dull or unsophisticated. **14.** *Informal* A person regarded as stiff, boring, or spiritless. **15.** *Archaic* A difficulty or obstacle; a delay. ❖ *v.* **stuck** (stŭk), **stick•ing, sticks** —*tr.* **1.** To pierce, puncture, or penetrate with a pointed instrument. **2.** To kill by piercing. **3.** To thrust or push (a pointed instrument) into or through another object. **4.** To fasten into place by forcing an end or point into something. **5.** To fasten or attach with or as if with pins, nails, or similar devices. **6.** To fasten or attach with an adhesive material, such as glue. **7.** To cover or decorate with objects piercing the surface. **8.** To fix, impale, or transfix on a pointed object. **9.** To put, thrust, or push: *stuck a flower in his buttonhole.* **10.** To detain or delay. **11.** *past tense and past participle* **sticked** (stĭkt) To prop (a plant) with sticks or brush on which to grow. **12.** *past tense and past participle* **sticked** *Printing* To set (type) in a composing stick. **13.** *Informal* To confuse, baffle, or puzzle. **14.** To cover or smear with something sticky. **15.** *Informal* To put blame or responsibility on; burden. **16.** *Slang* To defraud or cheat. —*intr.* **1.** To be or become fixed or embedded in place by having the point thrust in. **2.** To become or remain attached or in close association by or as if by adhesion; cling: *stick together in a crowd.* **3a.** To remain firm, determined, or resolute. **b.** To remain loyal or faithful. **c.** To persist or endure. **4.** To scruple or hesitate. **5.** To become fixed, blocked, checked, or obstructed: *The drawer stuck and would not open.* **6.** To project or protrude: *hair sticking out.* **7.** *Sports* To throw a jab in boxing.

—*phrasal verbs:* **stick around** *Informal* To remain; linger.

stick out 1. To be prominent. **2.** *Informal* To put up with. **stick up** To rob, esp. at gunpoint. **—idioms: be stuck on** *Informal* To be very fond of. **stick (one's) neck out** *Informal* To make oneself vulnerable; take a risk. **stick to (or by) one's guns** To hold fast to an opinion or a set course of action. **stick up for** To defend or support. [ME *stikke* < OE *sticca.*]

stick·ball (stĭk′bôl′) *n.* A form of baseball played with a rubber ball and a stick, such as one made from the handle of a broom, for a bat. **—stick′ball′er** *n.*

stick·er (stĭk′ər) *n.* **1.** One that sticks, as an adhesive label. **2.** A tenacious or diligent person. **3.** A thorn, prickle, or barb. **4.** Something puzzling or bewildering, as a riddle.

sticker price *n.* The list price for an automobile or other motor vehicle.

stick figure *n.* A picture of a human or animal figure showing the head as a circle and the other body parts as straight lines.

stick·ful (stĭk′fŭl′) *n. Printing* The amount of type a composing stick will hold.

stick·han·dle (stĭk′hăn′dl) *intr.v.* **-dled, -dling, -dles** To move, maneuver, and have control over the puck in ice hockey or the ball in lacrosse and field hockey. **—stick′han′dler** *n.*

sticking plaster (stĭk′ĭng) *n.* See **plaster** 3.

sticking point *n.* A point, issue, or situation that causes or is likely to cause an impasse.

stick insect *n.* Any of several insects of the family Phasmidae, such as the walking stick, that resemble sticks or twigs.

stick-in-the-mud (stĭk′ĭn-thə-mŭd′) *n., pl.* **stick-in-the-muds** *Informal* One without initiative, imagination, or enthusiasm.

stick·le (stĭk′əl) *intr.v.* **-led, -ling, -les 1.** To argue or contend stubbornly, esp. about trivial points. **2.** To have or raise objections; scruple. [Variant of ME *stightlen,* to contend, freq. of *stighten,* to arrange < OE *stihtian, stihtan.* See **steigh-** in App.]

stick·le·back (stĭk′əl-băk′) *n.* Any of various small freshwater and marine fishes of the family Gasterosteidae, having erectile spines along the back. [ME *stikelbak* : OE *sticel,* prick + ME *bak,* back; see BACK¹.]

stick·ler (stĭk′lər) *n.* **1.** One who insists on something unyieldingly. **2.** Something puzzling or difficult.

Stick·ley (stĭk′lē), **Gustav** 1857–1942. Amer. designer credited with creating the Mission furniture style.

stick·pin (stĭk′pĭn′) *n.* A decorative pin worn on a necktie.

stick·seed (stĭk′sēd′) *n.* Any of various plants of the genera *Hackelia* or *Lappula,* with clinging barbed fruits.

stick shift *n.* An automotive transmission with a shift lever operated by hand.

stick·tight (stĭk′tīt′) *n.* **1.** See **beggar ticks** 1a. **2.** See **bur marigold.**

stick-to-it·ive·ness (stĭk-tōō′ĭ-tĭv-nĭs) *n. Informal* Unwavering pertinacity; perseverance.

stick·um (stĭk′əm) *n.* An adhesive substance. [STICK + *-um* (var. of 'EM).]

stick·up (stĭk′ŭp′) *n. Slang* A robbery, esp. at gunpoint. [< the expression *"Stick up your hands!"*]

stick·weed (stĭk′wēd′) *n.* Any of various plants having clinging seeds or fruit, esp. ragweed.

stick·y (stĭk′ē) *adj.* **-i·er, -i·est 1.** Having the property of adhering or sticking to a surface; adhesive. **2.** Covered with an adhesive agent. **3.** Warm and humid; muggy: *a sticky day.* **4.** *Informal* Painful or difficult: *a sticky situation.* **5.** *Economics* Tending to remain the same despite changes in the economy. Used of prices or wages. **—stick′i·ly** *adv.* **—stick′i·ness** *n.*

sticky fingers *pl.n. Informal* A tendency to steal. **—stick′y-fin′gered** (stĭk′ē-fĭng′gərd) *adj.*

sticky wicket *n. Informal* A difficult or embarrassing problem or situation.

stied (stīd) *v.* Past tense and past participle of **sty¹.**

Stieg·litz (stēg′lĭts), **Alfred** 1864–1946. Amer. photographer known for his stark black-and-white images.

sties¹ (stīz) *n.* Plural of **sty¹.** ❖ *v.* Third person singular present tense of **sty¹.**

sties² (stīz) *n.* Plural of **sty².**

stiff (stĭf) *adj.* **stiff·er, stiff·est 1.** Difficult to bend; rigid. **2a.** Not moving or operating easily or freely; resistant: *a stiff hinge.* **b.** Lacking ease or comfort of movement; not limber: *a stiff neck.* **3.** Drawn tightly; taut. **4a.** Rigidly formal. **b.** Lacking ease or grace. **5.** Not liquid, loose, or fluid; thick. **6.** Firm, as in purpose; resolute. **7.** Having a strong, swift, steady force or movement: *a stiff breeze.* **8.** Potent or strong: *a stiff drink.* **9.** Difficult, laborious, or arduous. **10.** Difficult to comprehend or accept; harsh or severe: *a stiff penalty.* **11.** Excessively high: *a stiff price.* **12.** *Nautical* Not likely to heel excessively under sail. ❖ *adv.* **1.** In a stiff manner: *frozen stiff.* **2.** To a complete extent; totally. ❖ *n. Slang* **1.** A corpse. **2.** A person seen as constrained, priggish, or overformal. **3.** A drunk. **4.** A person: *a lucky stiff.* **5.** A hobo; a tramp. **6.** A person who tips poorly. ❖ *tr.v.* **stiffed, stiff·ing, stiffs** *Slang* **1.** To tip (someone) inadequately or not at all, as for a service rendered. **2a.** To cheat (someone) of something owed. **b.** To fail to give or supply (something expected or promised). [ME < OE *stīf.*] **—stiff′ish** *adj.* **—stiff′ly** *adv.* **—stiff′ness** *n.*

describe what is very firm and does not easily bend or give way. *Stiff,* the least specific, refers to what can be flexed only with difficulty (*a brush with stiff bristles*); with reference to persons it often suggests a lack of ease, cold formality, or fixity, as of purpose: *"stiff in opinions"* (John Dryden). *Rigid* and *inflexible* apply to what cannot be bent without damage or deformation (*a table of rigid plastic; an inflexible knife blade*); figuratively they describe what does not relent or yield: *"under the dictates of a rigid disciplinarian"* (Thomas B. Aldrich). *"In religion the law is written, and inflexible, never to do evil"* (Oliver Goldsmith). *Inelastic* refers to what will not stretch and spring back without marked physical change: *inelastic construction materials. Tense* means stretched tight and figuratively applies to what is marked by tautness or strain: *"that tense moment of expectation"* (Arnold Bennett).

stiff-arm (stĭf′ärm′) *Football tr.v.* **-armed, -arm·ing, -arms** To straight-arm. ❖ *n.* A straight-arm.

stiff·en (stĭf′ən) *tr. & intr.v.* **-ened, -en·ing, -ens** To make or become stiff or stiffer. **—stiff′en·er** *n.*

stiff·ie (stĭf′ē) *n. Vulgar Slang* An erection of the penis.

stiff-necked (stĭf′někt′) *adj.* Stubborn and arrogant or aloof. See Syns at **obstinate.**

sti·fle¹ (stī′fəl) *v.* **-fled, -fling, -fles** **—tr. 1.** To interrupt or cut off (the voice, for example). **2.** To keep in or hold back; repress. **3.** To kill by preventing respiration; smother or suffocate. **—intr. 1.** To feel smothered or suffocated by or as if by close confinement in a stuffy room. **2.** To die of suffocation. [ME *stiflen,* alteration (influenced by ON *stȳfla,* to stop up) of *stuffen, stuflen,* to stifle, choke, drown < OFr. *estoufer,* of Gmc. orig.] **—sti′fler** *n.*

sti·fle² (stī′fəl) *n.* The joint of the hind leg analogous to the human knee in certain quadrupeds, as the horse. [ME, poss. < OFr. *estivel,* pipe, leg, tibia < Lat. *stīpes,* stick.]

sti·fling (stī′flĭng) *adj.* **1.** Very hot or stuffy almost to the point of being suffocating. **2.** Engendering a feeling of stultification, repression, or suffocation. **—sti′fling·ly** *adv.*

stig·ma (stĭg′mə) *n., pl.* **stig·ma·ta** (stĭg-mä′tə, -măt′ə, stĭg′mə-) or **stig·mas 1.** A mark or token of infamy, disgrace, or reproach. **2.** A small mark; a scar or birthmark. **3.** *Medicine* A mark or characteristic indicative of a history of a disease or abnormality. **4.** *Psychology* A mark or spot on the skin that bleeds as a symptom of hysteria. **5. stigmata** Marks or sores corresponding to the wounds of Jesus on the Cross. **6.** *Biology* A small mark, spot, or pore, such as an eyespot in certain algae. **7.** *Botany* The receptive apex of the pistil of a flower, on which pollen is deposited. **8.** *Archaic* A mark burned into the skin of a criminal or slave; a brand. [ME *stigme,* brand < Lat. *stigma, stigmat-,* tattoo indicating slave or criminal status < Gk., tattoo mark < *stizein, stig-,* to prick.] **—stig′mal** *adj.*

stig·mat·ic (stĭg-măt′ĭk) *adj.* **1.** Relating to, resembling, or having stigmata or a stigma. **2.** Anastigmatic. ❖ *n.* A person marked with religious stigmata. **—stig·mat′i·cal·ly** *adv.*

stig·ma·tism (stĭg′mə-tĭz′əm) *n.* **1.** The condition of being affected by stigmata. **2.** The state of a refracting or reflecting system in which light rays from a single point are accurately focused at another point. **3.** Normal eyesight.

stig·ma·tist (stĭg′mə-tĭst) *n.* A stigmatic.

stig·ma·tize (stĭg′mə-tīz′) *tr.v.* **-tized, -tiz·ing, -tiz·es 1.** To characterize or brand as disgraceful or ignominious. **2.** To mark with stigmata or a stigma. **3.** To cause stigmata to appear on. [Med.Lat. *stigmatizāre,* to brand < Gk. *stigmatizein,* to mark < *stigma, stigmat-,* tattoo mark. See STIGMA.] **—stig′ma·ti·za′tion** (-tĭ-zā′shən) *n.* **—stig′ma·tiz′er** *n.*

Sti·kine (stī-kēn′) A river rising in the **Stikine Mountains** of NW British Columbia, Canada, and flowing c. 539 km (335 mi) through SE AK to the Pacific Ocean.

stil·bene (stĭl′bēn′) *n.* A crystalline compound, $C_{14}H_{12}$, used in dyes and optical bleaches and as a phosphor. [Gk. *stilbos,* shining (< *stilbein,* to shimmer) + -ENE.]

stil·bes·trol (stĭl-bĕs′trôl′, -trōl′) *n.* DES. [STILB(ENE) + ESTR(US) + -OL.]

stil·bite (stĭl′bīt′) *n.* A white or yellow zeolite mineral, $(Ca,Na)_2Al_2Si_2O_{18} \cdot 7H_2O$. [Fr. < Gk. *stilbos,* shining. See STILBENE.]

stile¹ (stīl) *n.* **1.** A set or series of steps for crossing a fence or wall. **2.** A turnstile. [ME < OE *stigel.* See **steigh-** in App.]

stile² (stīl) *n.* A vertical part of a panel or frame, as in a door. [Prob. < Du. *stijl,* doorpost < MDu., poss. < Lat. *stilus,* pole, post.]

sti·let·to (stĭ-lĕt′ō) *n., pl.* **-tos** or **-toes 1a.** A small dagger with a slender tapering blade. **b.** Something shaped like such a dagger. **2.** A small sharp-pointed instrument that makes eyelet holes in needlework. [Ital., dim. of *stilo,* dagger < Lat. *stilus,* stylus, spike.]

stiletto heel *n.* A high heel on women's shoes that is thinner than a spike heel.

still¹ (stĭl) *adj.* **still·er, still·est 1.** Free of sound. **2.** Low in sound; hushed or subdued. **3.** Not moving or in motion. **4.** Free from disturbance, agitation, or commotion. **5.** Free from a noticeable current: *still waters.* **6.** Not carbonated; lacking effervescence. **7.** Of or relating to a single or static photograph as opposed to a movie. ❖ *n.* **1.** Silence; quiet. **2.** A still photograph, esp. one taken

stile¹

ă pat	oi boy
ā pay	ou out
âr care	ŏŏ took
ä father	ōō boot
ĕ pet	ŭ cut
ē be	ûr urge
ĭ pit	th thin
ī pie	*th* this
îr pier	hw which
ŏ pot	zh vision
ō toe	ə about,
ô paw	item

Stress marks:
′ (primary),
′ (secondary), as in
lexicon (lĕk′sĭ-kŏn′)

still²

stipulate¹

stingray
blue-spotted stingray
Taeniura lymma

from and used to promote a movie. **3.** A still-life picture. ❖ *adv.* **1.** Without movement; motionlessly. **2.** Up to or at the time indicated; yet: *still had not made up her mind; is still waiting.* **3.** In increasing amount or degree: *and still further complaints.* **4.** In addition; besides: *had still another helping.* **5.** All the same; nevertheless. ❖ *v.* **stilled, still·ing, stills** —*tr.* **1.** To make still or tranquil. **2.** To make quiet; silence. **3.** To make motionless. **4.** To allay; calm. —*intr.* To become still. —*idiom:* **still and all** *Informal* After taking everything into consideration; nevertheless: *Still and all, we may win.* [ME < OE *stille.* See **stel-** in App.]

still² (stĭl) *n.* **1.** An apparatus for distilling liquids consisting of a vessel in which the substance is vaporized by heat and a cooling device in which the vapor is condensed. **2.** A distillery. [< ME *stillen,* to distill < *distillen.* See DISTILL.]

still alarm *n.* A fire alarm transmitted silently, as by telephone, rather than by sounding the conventional signal apparatus.

still·birth (stĭl′bûrth′) *n.* The birth of a dead child or fetus. **2.** A child or fetus dead at birth.

still·born (stĭl′bôrn′) *adj.* **1.** Dead at birth. **2.** Failing before or at the very beginning or inception; abortive.

still hunt *n.* The hunting of game by stalking or ambushing. —**still′-hunt′** (stĭl′hŭnt′) *v.* —**still′-hunt′er** *n.*

still life *n., pl.* **still lifes 1.** Representation of inanimate objects, such as fruit, in painting or photography. **2.** Such a representation. —**still′-life′** (stĭl′līf′) *adj.*

still·ness (stĭl′nĭs) *n.* The state or an instance of being quiet.

Still·son (stĭl′sən) A trademark used for a monkey wrench having serrated jaws that tighten as pressure is applied to the handle.

still water A flat or level section of a stream without discernible water motion or current. —**still′-wa′ter** *adj.*

still·y (stĭl′ē) *adj.* **-i·er, -i·est** Quiet; calm. —**still′ly** *adv.*

stilt (stĭlt) *n.* **1.** Either of a pair of long slender poles each equipped with a raised footrest to enable the user to walk above the ground. **2.** Any of various tall posts or pillars used as support, as for a dock or building. **3a.** A wide-ranging American wading bird (*Himantopus mexicanus*) with long pink legs, black and white plumage, and a long slender bill. **b.** A related bird (*Cladorhyncus leucocephala*) of Australia. ❖ *tr.v.* **stilt·ed, stilt·ing, stilts** To place or raise on stilts. [ME *stilte.* See **stel-** in App.]

stilt·ed (stĭl′tĭd) *adj.* **1.** Stiffly or artificially formal; stiff. **2.** *Architecture* Having some vertical length between the impost and the beginning of the curve. Used of an arch. —**stilt′ed·ly** *adv.* —**stilt′ed·ness** *n.*

Stil·ton (stĭl′tən) *n.* A rich waxy cheese with a blue-green mold. [After *Stilton,* a village of E-central England.]

Stil·well (stĭl′wĕl′, -wəl), **Joseph Warren** Known as "Vinegar Joe." 1883–1946. Amer. army officer who commanded Allied forces in China, Burma, and India during World War II.

Stim·son (stĭm′sən), **Henry Lewis** 1867–1950. Amer. public official who served as US secretary of state (1929–33) and as secretary of war (1940–45).

stim·u·lant (stĭm′yə-lənt) *n.* **1.** An agent, esp. a chemical agent such as caffeine, that temporarily arouses or accelerates physiological or organic activity. **2.** A stimulus or an incentive. **3.** A food or drink believed to have a stimulating effect. ❖ *adj.* Serving as a stimulus; stimulating.

stim·u·late (stĭm′yə-lāt′) *v.* **-lat·ed, -lat·ing, -lates** —*tr.* **1.** To rouse to activity or heightened action, as by spurring or goading; excite. **2.** To increase temporarily the activity of (a body part). **3.** To excite or invigorate (a person, for example) with a stimulant. —*intr.* To act as a stimulant or stimulus. [Lat. *stimulāre, stimulāt-,* to goad on < *stimulus,* goad.] —**stim′u·lat′er, stim′u·la′tor** *n.* —**stim′u·la′tion** *n.* —**stim′u·la′tive, stim′u·la·to′ry** (-lə-tôr′ē, -tōr′ē) *adj.*

stim·u·lus (stĭm′yə-ləs) *n., pl.* **-li** (-lī′) **1.** Something causing or regarded as causing a response. **2.** An agent, action, or condition that elicits or accelerates a physiological or psychological activity or response. **3.** Something that incites or rouses to action; an incentive. [Lat., goad.]

sting (stĭng) *v.* **stung** (stŭng), **sting·ing, stings** —*tr.* **1.** To pierce or wound painfully with or as if with a sharp-pointed structure or organ, as that of certain insects. **2.** To cause to feel a sharp smarting pain by or as if by pricking with a sharp point. **3.** To cause to suffer keenly in the mind or feelings. **4.** To spur on by or as if by sharp irritation. **5.** *Slang* To cheat or overcharge. —*intr.* **1.** To have, use, or wound with or as if with a sharp-pointed structure or organ, as that of certain insects. **2.** To cause or feel a sharp smarting pain. ❖ *n.* **1.** The act of stinging. **2.** The wound or pain caused by or as if by stinging. **3.** A sharp piercing organ or part, often ejecting a venomous secretion, as the modified ovipositor of a bee. **4.** A stinging power, quality, or capacity. **5.** A keen stimulus or incitement; a goad or spur. **6.** *Slang* A complicated confidence game planned and executed with great care, esp. an operation organized and implemented by undercover agents to apprehend criminals. [ME *stingen* < OE *stingan.*]

sting·er (stĭng′ər) *n.* **1.** One that stings, esp. an insult, that stings or wounds emotionally. **2.** A stinging organ or part. **3.** A sharp blow. **4.** *Slang* One who participates in or organizes the operation of a sting. **5.** A cocktail of crème de menthe and brandy.

sting·ing hair (stĭng′ĭng) *n.* A glandular plant hair that expels an irritating fluid.

sting·ray (stĭng′rā′) *n.* Any of various rays of the family Dasyatidae, having a whiplike tail armed with one or more venomous spines capable of inflicting severe injury.

stin·gy (stĭn′jē) *adj.* **-gi·er, -gi·est 1.** Giving or spending reluctantly. **2.** Scanty or meager: *a stingy meal.* [Perh. alteration of dialectal *stingy,* stinging < STING.] —**stin′gi·ly** *adv.* —**stin′gi·ness** *n.*

stink (stĭngk) *v.* **stank** (stăngk) or **stunk** (stŭngk), **stunk, stink·ing, stinks** —*intr.* **1.** To emit a strong foul odor. **2.** To be offensive or abhorrent. **3.** *Slang* To have something to an extreme or offensive degree. **4.** *Slang* **a.** To be of an extremely low or bad quality. **b.** To have the appearance of dishonesty or corruption: *Something about his testimony stinks.* —*tr.* To cause to stink: *garbage that stinks up the yard.* ❖ *n.* **1.** A strong offensive odor; a stench. **2.** *Slang* A scandal or controversy. —*idiom:* **make (or raise) a stink** *Slang* To make a great fuss. [ME *stinken* < OE *stincan,* to emit a smell.] —**stink′y** *adj.*

stink bomb *n.* A small bomb, often in the form of a capsule, that emits a foul odor on detonation.

stink·bug (stĭngk′bŭg′) *n.* Any of numerous hemipterous insects of the family Pentatomidae, having a broad flattened body and emitting a foul odor.

stink·er (stĭng′kər) *n.* **1.** One that stinks. **2.** *Slang* **a.** An irritating, disgusting, or contemptible person. **b.** Something very difficult. **c.** One that is of poor quality or is shoddy.

stink·er·oo (stĭng′kə-rōō′) *n., pl.* **-er·oos** *Slang* One that is contemptible, disgusting, irritating, or very bad. [< STINKER.]

stink·horn (stĭngk′hôrn′) *n.* Any of several foul-smelling fungi of the order Phallales, such as *Phallus impudicus* or *P. ravenelii,* having a thick cylindrical stalk and a narrow cap.

stink·ing (stĭng′kĭng) *adj.* **1.** Having a foul smell; fetid. **2.** *Slang* Drunk; intoxicated. ❖ *adv. Slang* Used as an intensive: *stinking rich.* —**stink′ing·ly** *adv.* —**stink′ing·ness** *n.*

stink·o (stĭng′kō) *adj. Slang* **1.** Intoxicated; drunk. **2.** Of poor or inferior quality. [< STINK.]

stink·pot (stĭngk′pŏt′) *n.* **1.** *Slang* One who is despised. **2.** A small musk turtle (*Sternotherus odoratus*) of the eastern and southern United States. **3.** *Slang* A motorboat. **4.** An earthenware jar with combustibles emitting a suffocating smoke, once used in naval warfare.

stink stone also **stink·stone** (stĭngk′stōn′) *n.* A variety of limestone that emits a disagreeable odor when struck or rubbed.

stink·weed (stĭngk′wēd′) *n.* Any of various plants that have flowers or foliage with an unpleasant odor.

stink·wood (stĭngk′wŏŏd′) *n.* **1a.** A southern African deciduous tree (*Ocotea bullata*) having wood with an unpleasant odor. **b.** The hard heavy wood of this tree. **2.** Any of several trees having wood with an unpleasant odor.

stint¹ (stĭnt) *v.* **stint·ed, stint·ing, stints** —*tr.* **1.** To restrict or limit, as in amount; be sparing with. **2.** *Archaic* To stop. —*intr.* **1.** To subsist on a meager allowance; be frugal. **2.** *Archaic* To stop or desist. ❖ *n.* **1.** A length of time spent in a particular way: *a two-year stint in the military.* **2.** A fixed amount of work allotted. See Syns at **task. 3.** A limit or restriction. [ME *stinten,* to cease < OE *styntan,* to blunt.] —**stint′er** *n.*

stint² (stĭnt) *n.* Any of several small sandpipers of the genera *Erolia* or *Calidris* of northern regions. [ME *stint* < OE.]

stipe (stīp) *n.* A supporting stalk or stemlike structure, esp. the stalk of a pistil, the petiole of a fern frond, or the stalk that supports the cap of a mushroom. [Fr. < Lat. *stīpes,* post.]

sti·pel (stī′pəl, stī-pĕl′) *n.* A minute stipule at the base of a leaflet. [NLat. *stipella,* dim. of *stipula,* stipule. See STIPULE.] —**sti·pel′late** (stī-pĕl′īt, stī′pə-lāt′) *adj.*

sti·pend (stī′pĕnd′, -pənd) *n.* A fixed and regular payment, such as a salary for services rendered. [ME *stipendie* < OFr. < Lat. *stīpendium,* soldier's pay < *stipendium* : *stips, stip-,* a small payment + *pendere,* to weigh, pay.]

sti·pen·di·ar·y (stī-pĕn′dē-ĕr′ē) *adj.* **1.** Receiving a stipend. **2.** Compensated by stipend: *stipendiary services.* ❖ *n., pl.* **-ies** A recipient of a stipend.

sti·pes (stī′pēz) *n., pl.* **stip·i·tes** (stĭp′ĭ-tēz′) **1.** The basal segment of the maxilla of an insect or a crustacean. **2.** *Botany* A stalklike support or structure; a stipe. [NLat. *stīpes, stīpit-* < Lat., post.] —**sti′pi·form′** (stī′pə-fôrm′), **stip′i·ti·form′** (stĭp′ĭ-tə-) *adj.*

stip·ple (stĭp′əl) *tr.v.* **-pled, -pling, -ples 1.** To draw, engrave, or paint in dots or short strokes. **2.** To apply (paint, for example) in dots or short strokes. **3.** To dot, fleck, or speckle. ❖ *n.* **1.** A method of drawing, engraving, or painting using dots or short strokes. **2.** The effect thus produced or a similar appearance. [Du. *stippelen,* freq. of *stippen,* to speckle < *stip,* dot < MDu.] —**stip′pler** *n.*

stip·u·lar (stĭp′yə-lər) *adj.* Of, relating to, or resembling a stipule.

stip·u·late¹ (stĭp′yə-lāt′) *v.* **-lat·ed, -lat·ing, -lates** —*tr.* **1a.** To lay down as a condition of an agreement; require by contract. **b.** To specify or arrange in an agreement: *stipulate a fair price.* **2.** To guarantee or promise (something) in an agreement. —*intr.* **1.** To make an express demand or provision in an agreement. **2.** To form an agreement. [Lat. *stipulārī, stipulāt-,* to bargain.] —**stip′u·la′tor** *n.*

stip·u·late² (stĭp′yə-lĭt) *adj.* Having stipules.

stip·u·la·tion (stĭp′yə-lā′shən) *n.* **1.** The act of stipulating. **2.** Something stipulated, esp. a term or condition in an agreement. **—stip′u·la·to′ry** (-lə-tôr′ē, -tōr′ē) *adj.*

stip·ule (stĭp′yōol) *n.* One of the usu. small paired appendages at the base of a leafstalk in certain plants, such as roses. [NLat. *stipula* < Lat., stalk.]

stir¹ (stûr) *v.* **stirred, stir·ring, stirs** *—tr.* **1a.** To pass an implement through (a liquid, for example) in circular motions so as to mix or cool the contents. **b.** To introduce (an ingredient, for example) into a liquid or mixture. **c.** To mix together the ingredients of before cooking or use. **2.** To cause to move or shift, esp. slightly or with irregular motion: *A breeze stirred the branches.* **3.** To prod into brisk or vigorous action; bestir. **4a.** To rouse, as from indifference, and prompt to action. **b.** To provoke deliberately. **5.** To excite strong feelings in. *—intr.* **1.** To change position slightly. **2a.** To move about actively; bestir oneself. **b.** To move away from a customary or usual place or position. **3.** To take place; happen. **4.** To be capable of being moved. **5.** To be roused or affected by strong feelings. ❖ *n.* **1.** A stirring, mixing, or poking movement. **2.** A slight movement. **3.** A disturbance or commotion. **4.** An excited reaction. [ME *stiren* < OE *styrian*, to excite, agitate.] **—stir′rer** *n.*

stir² (stûr) *n. Slang* Prison. [?]

stir·cra·zy (stûr′krā′zē) *adj. Informal* Distraught or restless from long confinement in or as if in prison.

stir-fry (stûr′frī′) *tr.v.* **-fried, -fry·ing, -fries** To fry quickly in a small amount of oil all over high heat while stirring continuously. ❖ *n.* Stir-fried food.

stirk (stûrk) *n. Chiefly British* A heifer or bullock, esp. between one and two years old. [ME < OE *stīrc*. See **stā-** in App.]

stirps (stûrps) *n., pl.* **stir·pes** (stûr′pēz) **1.** A line of descendants of common ancestry; stock. **2.** *Law* A person from whom a family is descended. [Lat., stem, lineage.]

stir·ring (stûr′ĭng) *adj.* **1.** Exciting strong feelings, as of inspiration; rousing. **2.** Active; lively. ❖ *n.* A slight motion or moving about. **—stir′ring·ly** *adv.*

stir·rup (stûr′əp, stĭr′-) *n.* **1.** A flat-based loop or ring hung from either side of a horse's saddle to support the rider's foot. **2.** A part or device shaped like an inverted U in which something is supported, held, or fixed. **3.** *Nautical* A rope on a ship that hangs from a yard and has an eye at the end through which a footrope is passed for support. **4.** *Anatomy* See **stapes**. [ME *stirope* < OE *stīgrāp* : *stīgan*, to mount; see **steigh-** in App. + *rāp*, rope.]

stir·rup-cup (stûr′əp-kŭp′, stĭr′-) *n.* A farewell drink, esp. for a rider who is mounted to depart.

stirrup leather *n.* The strap fastening a stirrup to a saddle.

stitch (stĭch) *n.* **1.** A single complete movement of a threaded needle in sewing or surgical suturing. **2a.** A single loop of yarn around an implement such as a knitting needle. **b.** The link, loop, or knot made in this way. **3.** A mode of arranging the threads in sewing, knitting, or crocheting: *a purl stitch.* **4.** A sudden sharp pain, esp. in the side. **5.** *Informal* An article of clothing. **6.** *Informal* The least part; a bit. **7.** A ridge between two furrows. ❖ *v.* **stitched, stitch·ing, stitch·es** *—tr.* **1a.** To fasten or join with or as if with stitches. **b.** To mend or repair with stitches: *stitched up the tear.* **2.** To decorate or ornament with or as if with stitches. **3.** To fasten together with staples or thread. *—intr.* To make stitches; sew. *—idiom:* **in stitches** *Informal* Laughing uncontrollably. [ME *stiche* < OE *stice*, sting.] **—stitch′er** *n.*

stitch·er·y (stĭch′ə-rē) *n.* Needlework; sewing.

stitch·wort (stĭch′wûrt′, -wôrt′) *n.* Any of several low-growing plants of the genus *Stellaria*, having opposite leaves and star-shaped flowers. [ME < OE *sticwyrt*, agrimony : *stice*, side pain; see STITCH + *wyrt*, plant; see WORT¹.]

stith·y (stĭth′ē, stĭth′ē) *n., pl.* **-ies** **1.** An anvil. **2.** A forge or smithy. [ME *stethi* < ON *stethi*. See **stā-** in App.]

sti·ver (stī′vər) *n.* **1.** A nickel coin used in the Netherlands and worth ¹⁄₂₀ of a guilder. **2.** Something of small value. [Du. *stuiver* < MDu. *stuyver*.]

stk. *abbr.* stock

STM *abbr. Latin* Sacrae Theologiae Magister (Master of Sacred Theology)

sto·a (stō′ə) *n., pl.* **sto·as** or **sto·ae** (stō′ē′) An ancient Greek covered walk or colonnade, usu. having columns on one side and a wall on the other. [Gk., porch. See **stā-** in App.]

stoat (stōt) *n., pl.* **stoat** or **stoats** *Chiefly British* The ermine, esp. when in its brown color phase. [ME.]

stob (stŏb) *n. Chiefly Southern US* A short straight piece of wood. [ME, stump, var. of *stubbe*, *stub*. See STUB.]

sto·chas·tic (stō-kăs′tĭk) *adj.* **1.** Of, relating to, or marked by conjecture. **2.** *Statistics* **a.** Involving or containing a random variable or variables: *stochastic calculus.* **b.** Involving chance or probability. [Gk. *stokhastikos* < *stokhastēs*, diviner < *stokhazesthai*, to guess at < *stokhos*, aim, goal.] **—sto·chas′ti·cal·ly** *adv.*

stock (stŏk) *n.* **1.** A supply accumulated for future use; a store. **2.** The total merchandise kept on hand, as by a commercial establishment or warehouse. **3.** All the animals kept or raised on a farm; livestock. **4a.** The capital or fund that a corporation raises by selling shares entitling the stockholder to dividends and other rights of ownership. **b.** The number of shares that each stock-

holder possesses. **c.** A stock certificate. **d.** The part of a tally or record of account formerly given to a creditor. **e.** A debt symbolized by a tally. **5.** The trunk or main stem of a tree or another plant. **6a.** A plant or stem onto which a graft is made. **b.** A plant or tree from which cuttings and slips are taken. **7a.** The original progenitor of a family line. **b.** The descendants of a common ancestor; a family line, esp. of a specified character: *comes from farming stock.* **c.** Ancestry or lineage; antecedents. **d.** The type from which a group of animals or plants has descended. **e.** A race, family, or other related group of animals or plants. **f.** An ethnic group or other major division of the human race. **g.** A group of related languages or families of languages. **8.** The raw material out of which something is made. **9.** The broth in which meat, fish, bones, or vegetables are simmered, used as a base for soup, gravy, or sauces. **10a.** A main upright part, esp. a supporting structure or block. **b. stocks** *Nautical* The timber frame that supports a ship during construction. **c.** A frame in which an animal is held for shoeing or for veterinary treatment. Often used in the plural. **11. stocks** A former punitive device consisting of a heavy timber frame with holes for confining the ankles and sometimes the wrists. **12.** *Nautical* A crosspiece at the end of the shank of an anchor. **13.** The wooden block from which a bell is suspended. **14a.** The rear handle or support of a rifle, pistol, or automatic weapon, to which the barrel and mechanism are attached. **b.** The long supporting structure and mooring beam of field-gun carriages that trails along the ground to provide stability and support. **15.** A handle, such as that of various carpentry tools. **16.** The frame of a plow, to which the share, coulter, and other parts are fastened. **17a.** A theatrical stock company. **b.** The repertoire of such a company. **c.** A theater or theatrical activity, esp. outside of a main theatrical center. **18.** *Botany* Any of several Eurasian and Mediterranean plants of the genus *Matthiola* in the mustard family, esp. *M. incana*, having variously colored flower clusters. **19.** *Games* The portion of a card deck or of a domino set that is not dealt out but is drawn from during a game. **20.** *Geology* A body of intrusive igneous rock of which less than 100 square kilometers (40 square miles) is exposed. **21.** *Zoology* A compound organism. **22a.** Personal reputation or status. **b.** Confidence or credence. **23a.** A long white neckcloth worn as part of a formal riding habit. **b.** A broad scarf worn around the neck, esp. by certain clerics. **24.** Rolling stock. ❖ *v.* **stocked, stock·ing, stocks** *—tr.* **1.** To provide or furnish with a stock of something, esp.: **a.** To supply (a shop) with merchandise. **b.** To supply (a farm) with livestock. **c.** To fill (a stream, for example) with fish. **2.** To keep for future sale or use. **3.** *Obsolete* To put (someone) in the stocks as a punishment. *—intr.* **1.** To gather and lay in a supply of something: *stock up on paper.* **2.** To put forth new shoots. Used of a plant. ❖ *adj.* **1.** Kept regularly in stock. **2.** Repeated often without any thought or originality. **3.** Employed in dealing with stock or merchandise. **4a.** Of or relating to the raising of livestock. **b.** Used for breeding. **5a.** Of or relating to a stock company or its repertoire. **b.** Of or being a conventional character or situation in literary or cinematic works. *—idioms:* **in stock** Available for sale or use. **out of stock** Not available for sale or use. [ME *stok* < OE *stocc*, tree trunk.] **—stock′age** *n.* **—stock′er** *n.*

stock·ade (stō-kād′) *n.* **1.** A defensive barrier made of strong posts or timbers driven upright side by side into the ground. **2a.** A similar fenced or enclosed area, esp. one for protection. **b.** A jail on a military base. ❖ *tr.v.* **-ad·ed, -ad·ing, -ades** To fortify, protect, or surround with a stockade. [Obsolete Fr. *estocade* < Sp. *estacada* < *estaca*, stake, of Gmc. orig.]

stock·breed·ing (stŏk′brē′dĭng) *n.* The breeding and raising of livestock. **—stock′breed′er** *n.*

Stock·bridge (stŏk′brĭj′) *n.* A subtribe of the Mahican confederacy formerly inhabiting southwest Massachusetts, with a present-day population in central Wisconsin.

stock·bro·ker (stŏk′brō′kər) *n.* One that acts as an agent in the buying and selling of stocks or other securities; a broker. **—stock′bro·ker·age** *n.* **—stock′brok′ing** *n.*

stock car *n.* **1.** An automobile of a standard make modified for racing. **2.** A railroad car for carrying livestock.

stock certificate *n.* A certificate establishing ownership of a stated number of shares in a corporation's stock.

stock company *n.* **1.** A company or corporation whose capital is divided into shares. **2.** A permanent company that performs a repertoire of plays, usu. at a single theater.

stock dividend *n.* A dividend paid to stockholders in shares of stock rather than cash.

stock dove (dŭv) *n.* An Old World bird (*Columba oenas*) having grayish plumage. [Prob. < living in tree trunks.]

stock exchange *n.* **1.** A place where stocks, bonds, or other securities are bought and sold. **2.** An association of stockbrokers who meet to trade stocks and bonds according to fixed regulations.

stock·fish (stŏk′fĭsh′) *n., pl.* **stockfish** or **-fish·es** A fish, such as a cod, cured by being split and air-dried without salt. [ME *stokfish*, transl. of MDu. *stocvisch* : *stoc*, tree limb (perh. < its being dried on wooden racks) + *vische*, fish.]

stock·hold·er (stŏk′hōl′dər) *n.* One who owns a share or shares of stock in a company. **—stock′hold′ing** *n.*

Stock·holm (stŏk′hōlm′, -hōm′) The cap. of Sweden, in the E part on the Baltic Sea. Pop. 684,576.

stirrup
left: Western stirrup
right: English stirrup

stockinette stitch

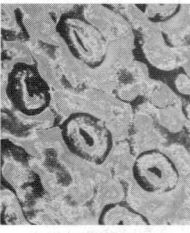

stoma
scanning electron
micrograph showing
stomata of a ginkgo leaf

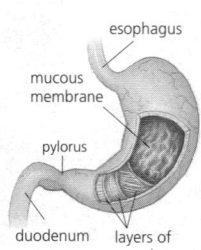

stomach
cutaway of an adult human
stomach

esophagus

mucous
membrane

pylorus

duodenum

layers of
muscle

stock·i·nette also **stock·i·net** (stŏk′ə-nĕt′) n. An elastic knitted fabric used esp. in making undergarments, bandages, and babies' clothes. [Alteration of *stocking net.*]

stockinette stitch n. A knitting pattern made by alternating rows of plain stitches and purl stitches.

stock·ing (stŏk′ĭng) n. **1.** A close-fitting, usu. knitted covering for the foot and leg. **2.** An item resembling this covering. [< dialectal *stock* < ME *stokke*, leg covering, prob. < *stok*, stock. See STOCK.] —**stock′inged** adj.

stocking cap n. A close-fitting knitted cap that resembles a stocking and often has a long tapering tail with a tassel.

stock-in-trade also **stock in trade** (stŏk′ĭn-trād′, stŏk′ĭn-trād′) n. **1.** All the merchandise and equipment kept on hand and used in carrying on a business. **2.** The resources available to and habitually used by a person in a given situation.

stock·job·ber (stŏk′jŏb′ər) n. *Chiefly British* A stock-exchange operator who deals only with brokers. **2.** A stockbroker, esp. an unscrupulous one. —**stock′job′ber·y** n.

stock·man (stŏk′mən) n. **1.** A man who owns or raises livestock. **2.** A man who is in charge of livestock or works on a stock farm. **3.** A man who is employed in a stockroom or warehouse.

stock market n. **1.** See **stock exchange. 2.** The business transacted at a stock exchange. **3.** The prices offered for stocks and bonds in general. —**stock′-mar′ket** (stŏk′mär′kĭt) adj.

stock option n. A right to buy or sell specific securities or commodities at a stated price within a specified time.

stock·own·er (stŏk′ō′nər) n. See **stockholder.** —**stock′own′er·ship′** n.

stock·pile (stŏk′pīl′) n. A supply stored for future use, usu. carefully accrued and maintained. ❖ *tr.v.* **-piled, -pil·ing, -piles** To stock a supply for future use. —**stock′pil′er** n.

Stock·port (stŏk′pôrt′, -pōrt′) A borough of NW England S of Manchester; chartered 1220. Pop. 291,447.

stock·pot (stŏk′pŏt′) n. **1.** A pot used for preparing soup stock. **2.** A rich supply or resource.

stock·room also **stock room** (stŏk′rōōm′, -rŏŏm′) n. A room in which a store of goods or materials is kept.

stock saddle n. A large, heavy, often ornamented saddle with a raised curved pommel originally used on cattle ranches in the West and Southwest.

stock-still (stŏk′stĭl′) adj. Completely still; motionless. —**stock′still′** adv.

stock·tak·ing (stŏk′tā′kĭng) n. **1.** A reappraisal of a situation, a person, or one's own position or prospects. **2.** The act or process of inventorying stock.

Stock·ton (stŏk′tən) A city of central CA on the San Joaquin R. S of Sacramento; settled in 1848. Pop. 243,771.

Stock·ton-on-Tees (stŏk′tən-ŏn-tēz′, -ŏn-) A borough of NE England WNW of Middlesbrough. Pop. 177,794.

stock·y (stŏk′ē) adj. **-i·er, -i·est 1.** Solidly built; sturdy. **2.** Chubby; plump. —**stock′i·ly** adv. —**stock′i·ness** n.

stock·yard (stŏk′yärd′) n. A large enclosed yard, usu. with pens or stables, in which livestock, such as cattle or pigs, are temporarily kept until slaughtered, sold, or shipped elsewhere.

stodg·y (stŏj′ē) adj. **-i·er, -i·est 1a.** Dull, unimaginative, and commonplace. **b.** Prim or pompous; stuffy. **2.** Indigestible and starchy; heavy; *stodgy food.* **3.** Solidly built; stocky. [< *stodge*, thick filling food < *stodge*, to cram.] —**stodg′i·ly** adv. —**stodg′i·ness** n.

sto·gy or **sto·gie** (stō′gē) n., pl. **-gies 1.** A cheap cigar. **2.** A rough heavy shoe or boot. [After *Conestoga* in southeast Pennsylvania.]

sto·ic (stō′ĭk) n. **1.** One who is seemingly indifferent to or unaffected by joy, grief, pleasure, or pain. **2. Stoic** A member of an originally Greek school of philosophy, founded by Zeno about 308 B.C., believing that God determined everything for the best and that virtue is sufficient for happiness, and in its later Roman form advocating the calm acceptance of all occurrences. ❖ *adj.* also **sto·i·cal** (-ĭ-kəl) Seemingly indifferent to or unaffected by pleasure or pain; impassive. [ME *Stoic*, a Stoic < Lat. *Stōicus* < Gk. *Stōikos* < *stoā* (*poikilē*), (Painted) Porch, where Zeno taught. See **stā-** in App.] —**sto′i·cal·ly** adv. —**sto′i·cal·ness** n.

stoi·chi·om·e·try (stoi′kē-ŏm′ĭ-trē) n. **1.** Calculation of the quantities of reactants and products in a chemical reaction. **2.** The quantitative relationship between reactants and products in a chemical reaction. [Gk. *stoikheion*, element; see **steigh-** in App. + **-METRY**.] —**stoi′chi·o·met′ric** (-ə-mĕt′rĭk) adj. —**stoi′chi·o·met′ri·cal·ly** adv.

sto·i·cism (stō′ĭ-sĭz′əm) n. **1.** Indifference to pleasure or pain; impassiveness. **2. Stoicism** The doctrines or philosophy of the Stoics.

stoke (stōk) v. **stoked, stok·ing, stokes** —*tr.* **1.** To stir up and feed (a fire or furnace). **2.** To feed fuel to and tend the fire of (a furnace). —*intr.* **1.** To stoke a furnace or fire. **2.** *Informal* To eat steadily and in large quantities.

stoke·hold (stōk′hōld′) n. The area or compartment into which a ship's furnaces or boilers open.

stoke·hole (stōk′hōl′) n. **1.** The space about the opening in a furnace or boiler. **2.** *Nautical* A stokehold.

Stoke-on-Trent (stōk′ŏn-trĕnt′, -ŏn-) A borough of W-central England S of Manchester. Pop. 252,914.

stok·er (stō′kər) n. **1.** One who is employed to feed fuel to and tend a furnace, as on a steam locomotive or a steamship. **2.** A mechanical device for feeding coal to a furnace. [Du. < *stoken*, to stoke < MDu. *stōken*, to poke.]

Stoker, Abraham Known as "Bram." 1847–1912. British writer of the gothic horror novel *Dracula* (1897).

Sto·kow·ski (stə-kôv′skē, -kôf′-, -kou′-), **Leopold Antoni Stanislaw** 1882–1977. British-born Amer. conductor of the Philadelphia Orchestra (1914–36).

STOL abbr. short takeoff and landing

stole[1] (stōl) n. **1.** *Ecclesiastical* A long scarf, usu. of embroidered silk or linen, worn over the left shoulder by deacons and over both shoulders by priests and bishops while officiating. **2.** A woman's long scarf worn about the shoulders. **3.** A long robe or outer garment worn by matrons in ancient Rome. [ME < OE < Lat. *stola*, garment, robe < Gk. *stolē*. See **stel-** in App.]

stole[2] (stōl) v. Past tense of **steal.**

sto·len (stō′lən) v. Past participle of **steal.**

stol·id (stŏl′ĭd) adj. **-er, -est** Having or revealing little emotion or sensibility; impassive. [Lat. *stolidus*, unmoving, stupid. See **stel-** in App.] —**sto·lid′i·ty** (stō-lĭd′ĭ-tē, stə-), **stol′id·ness** (stŏl′ĭd-nĭs) n. —**stol′id·ly** adv.

stol·len (stō′lən) n., pl. **stollen** or **-lens** A rich yeast bread containing raisins, citron, and chopped nutmeats. [Ger., prop. support, stollen, support.]

sto·lon (stō′lŏn′, -lən) n. **1.** *Botany* A shoot that bends to the ground or grows horizontally above the ground and produces roots and shoots at the nodes. **2.** *Zoology* A stemlike structure of certain colonial organisms from which new individuals arise by budding. [Lat. *stolō, stolōn-*, shoot. See **stel-** in App.] —**sto′lon·ate′** (-lə-nāt′) adj.

sto·lon·if·er·ous (stō′lə-nĭf′ər-əs) adj. Bearing or forming stolons. —**sto′lon·if′er·ous·ly** adv.

sto·ma (stō′mə) n., pl. **-ma·ta** (-mə-tə) or **-mas 1.** *Botany* One of the minute pores in the epidermis of a leaf or stem through which gases and water vapor pass. **2.** *Anatomy* A small aperture in the surface of a membrane. **3.** A surgically constructed opening, esp. one in the abdominal wall that permits the passage of waste after a colostomy or ileostomy. **4.** *Zoology* A mouthlike opening, such as the oral cavity of a nematode. [NLat. < Gk., mouth.] —**sto′mal, sto′ma·tal** adj.

stom·ach (stŭm′ək) n. **1a.** The enlarged saclike portion of the alimentary canal, one of the principal organs of digestion, located in vertebrates between the esophagus and the small intestine. **b.** A similar digestive structure of many invertebrates. **c.** Any of the four compartments into which the stomach of a ruminant is divided. **2.** The abdomen or belly. **3.** An appetite for food. **4.** A desire or inclination, esp. for something difficult or unpleasant. **5.** Courage; spirit. **6.** *Obsolete* Pride. ❖ *tr.v.* **-ached, -ach·ing, -achs 1.** To bear; tolerate. **2.** *Obsolete* To resent. [ME < OFr. *stomaque, estomac* < Lat. *stomachus* < Gk. *stomakhos*, gullet < *stoma*, mouth.]

stom·ach·ache (stŭm′ək-āk′) n. Pain in the stomach or abdomen.

stom·ach·er (stŭm′ə-kər) n. A heavily embroidered or jeweled garment formerly worn over the chest and stomach.

sto·mach·ic (stə-măk′ĭk) adj. **1.** Of or relating to the stomach; gastric. **2.** Beneficial to or stimulating digestion in the stomach. ❖ *n.* An agent, such as a medicine, that strengthens or stimulates the stomach. —**sto·mach′i·cal·ly** adv.

stomach pump n. A suction pump with a flexible tube inserted into the stomach through the mouth and esophagus to empty the stomach in an emergency, as in a case of poisoning.

sto·mate (stō′māt′) n. *Botany* See **stoma** 1. [Perh. back-formation < STOMATA.]

sto·mat·ic (stō-măt′ĭk) adj. **1.** Of or relating to the mouth. **2.** Of, having, or resembling a stoma.

sto·ma·ti·tis (stō′mə-tī′tĭs) n. Inflammation of the mucous tissue of the mouth.

stomato– or **stomat–** pref. Mouth; stoma: *stomatitis.* [< Gk. *stoma, stomat-*, mouth.]

sto·mat·o·pod (stō-măt′ə-pŏd′) n. Any of various marine crustaceans of the order Stomatopoda, which includes the squilla. [< NLat. *Stomatopoda*, order name : STOMATO– + –POD.]

sto·ma·tous (stō′mə-təs) adj. Of, having, or resembling a stoma.

–stome suff. Mouth; stoma: *peristome.* [< Gk. *stoma*, mouth.]

sto·mo·de·um also **sto·mo·dae·um** (stō′mə-dē′əm) n., pl. **-de·a** also **-dae·a** (-dē′ə) The anterior or oral portion of the alimentary canal of an embryo. [NLat. : Gk. *stoma*, mouth + Gk. *hodaios*, on the way (< *hodos*, road).]

stomp (stŏmp, stômp) v. **stomped, stomp·ing, stomps** —*tr.* To tread or trample heavily or violently on. —*intr.* To tread or trample heavily or violently. ❖ *n.* **1.** A dance involving a rhythmic heavy step. **2.** The jazz music for this dance. [Variant of STAMP.] —**stomp′er** n. —**stomp′ing·ly** adv.

USAGE NOTE *Stomp* and *stamp* are interchangeable in the sense "to trample" or "to tread on violently": *stomped* (or *stamped*) to *death; stomping* (or *stamping*) *horses.* Only *stamp* is used with *out* in the sense "to eliminate": *stamp out a fire. Stamp* is also standard in the sense "to strike the ground with the foot, as in anger or frustration," as in *He stamped his foot and began to cry.*

stomp•ing ground (stŏm′pĭng, stôm′-) *n.* A customary territory or favorite gathering place.

–stomy *suff.* A surgical operation in which an artificial opening is made into a specified organ or part: *colostomy.* [Gk. *stoma,* opening, mouth + –Y².]

stone (stōn) *n.* **1a.** Concreted earthy or mineral matter; rock. **b.** Such concreted matter of a particular type. Often used in combination: *sandstone.* **2.** A small piece of rock. **3.** Rock or a piece of rock shaped or finished for a particular purpose, esp.: **a.** A piece of rock that is used in construction: *a coping stone.* **b.** A gravestone or tombstone. **c.** A grindstone, millstone, or whetstone. **d.** A milestone or boundary. **4.** A gem or precious stone. **5.** Something resembling a stone in shape or hardness. **6.** *Botany* The hard covering enclosing the seed in certain fruits, such as the plum. **7.** *Pathology* A mineral concretion in a body part or organ, such as the kidney; a calculus. **8.** *pl.* **stone** A unit of weight in Great Britain, 14 pounds (6.4 kilograms). **9.** *Printing* A table with a smooth surface on which page forms are composed. ❖ *adj.* **1.** Relating to or made of stone: *a stone wall.* **2.** Made of stoneware or earthenware. **3.** Complete; utter: *a stone liar.* ❖ *adv.* Completely; utterly: *stone cold; standing stone still.* ❖ *tr.v.* **stoned, ston•ing, stones** **1.** To hurl or throw stones at, esp. to kill with stones. **2.** To remove the stones or pits from. **3.** To furnish, fit, pave, or line with stones. **4.** To rub on or with a stone in order to polish or sharpen. **5.** *Obsolete* To make hard or indifferent. [ME < OE *stān.*]

Stone, Edward Durell 1902–78. Amer. architect who was an exponent of the International Style.

Stone, Harlan Fiske 1872–1946. Amer. jurist; associate justice (1925–41) and chief justice (1941–46) of the US Supreme Court.

Stone, Lucy 1818–93. Amer. feminist who organized the first national women's rights convention (1850).

Stone Age *n.* **1.** The earliest known period of human culture, characterized by the use of stone tools. **2.** *Slang* An extremely backward or primitive condition or era.

stone-blind (stōn′blīnd′) *adj.* Completely blind. —**stone′-blind′ness** *n.*

stone-broke (stōn′brōk′) *adj. Informal* Completely broke; having no money.

stone•chat (stōn′chăt′) *n.* A small Old World thrush (*Saxicola torquata*) of open grassy regions, the male of which has dark plumage and chestnut underparts. [< the resemblance of its call to the sound of falling pebbles.]

stone crab *n.* A large edible crab (*Menippe mercenaria*) found along the Atlantic coast of the southern United States.

stone•crop (stōn′krŏp′) *n.* **1.** Any of various plants of the genus *Sedum,* having fleshy leaves and variously colored flowers. **2.** Any of various related plants. [ME < OE *stāncropp* : *stān,* stone; see STONE + *cropp,* cluster, sprout.]

stone•cut•ter (stōn′kŭt′ər) *n.* **1.** One that cuts or carves stone. **2.** A machine for dressing stone. —**stone′cut′ting** *n.*

stoned (stōnd) *adj. Slang* Drunk or intoxicated. [Earlier *stone,* shortening of *stone-drunk,* drunk senseless.]

stone-deaf (stōn′dĕf′) *adj.* Completely deaf.

stone•fish (stōn′fĭsh′) *n., pl.* **stonefish** or **-fish•es** Any of several tropical scorpion fishes of the genus *Synanceja,* esp. *S. verrucosa,* resembling a rock and ejecting a deadly venom.

stone•fly (stōn′flī′) *n.* Any of numerous weak-flying insects of the order Plecoptera, whose flat elongated nymphs live under stones along the banks of streams.

stone fruit *n.* See **drupe.**

stone-ground (stōn′ground′) *adj.* Ground between millstones, esp. buhrstones: *stone-ground flour.*

stone•heart•ed (stōn′här′tĭd) *adj.* Variant of **stonyhearted.**

Stone•henge (stōn′hĕnj′) A group of standing stones on Salisbury Plain in S England. Dating to c. 2000–1800 B.C., Stonehenge was probably a religious center and astronomical observatory.

stone marten *n.* **1.** A Eurasian marten (*Martes foina*) having brown fur with lighter underfur and often inhabiting rocky inlets and crevices. **2.** The fur of this animal.

stone•ma•son (stōn′mā′sən) *n.* One that prepares and lays stones in building. —**stone′ma′son•ry** *n.*

Stone Mountain A massive granite monadnock, 514.2 m (1,686 ft), in NW-central GA E of Atlanta; site of a huge Confederate memorial (carved 1917–67).

ston•er (stō′nər) *n.* **1.** One that stones. **2.** *Slang* **a.** One who is habitually intoxicated by alcohol or drugs. **b.** One who is a delinquent or failure. [STON(E) + –ER¹.]

stone•roll•er (stōn′rō′lər) *n.* **1.** A minnow (*Campostoma anomalum*) of the central and southern United States, having a horny ridge near the edge of the lower lip used for scraping food from the bottom of a body of water. **2.** A sucker (*Hypentelium nigricans*) of the central and southern United States, common in swift or rocky streams.

stone's throw (stōnz) *n.* A short distance.

stone•wall (stōn′wôl′) *v.* **-walled, -wall•ing, -walls** —*intr.* **1.** *Informal* **a.** To engage in delaying tactics; stall. **b.** To refuse to answer or cooperate. **2.** *Sports* To play defensively rather than trying

to score in cricket. —*tr. Informal* To refuse to answer or cooperate with; resist or rebuff.

stone•ware (stōn′wâr′) *n.* A heavy nonporous nontranslucent pottery, such as jasper ware, that is fired at a high temperature.

stone•work (stōn′wûrk′) *n.* **1.** The technique or process of working in stone. **2.** Work that is made of stone; stonemasonry. —**stone′work′er** *n.*

stone•wort (stōn′wûrt′, -wôrt′) *n.* Any of various submerged aquatic algae of the genus *Chara* that are frequently encrusted with calcium carbonate deposits.

ston•y also **ston•ey** (stō′nē) *adj.* **-i•er, -i•est** **1.** Covered with or full of stones. **2.** Resembling stone, as in hardness. **3a.** Hard-hearted and unfeeling; unemotional. **b.** Exhibiting no feeling or warmth; impassive. **4.** Emotionally numbing or paralyzing. —**ston′i•ly** *adv.* —**ston′i•ness** *n.*

ston•y•heart•ed (stō′nē-här′tĭd) also **stone•heart•ed** (stōn′-) *adj.* Devoid of kindness or sympathy; hardhearted.

stony meteorite *n.* Any of various meteorites consisting largely of silicate minerals and classified as chondrites or achondrites.

Stony Tunguska See **Tunguska.**

stood (stŏŏd) *v.* Past tense and past participle of **stand.**

stooge (stŏŏj) *n.* **1.** The partner in a comedy team who feeds lines to the other comedian. **2.** One who allows oneself to be used for another's advantage; a puppet. **3.** *Slang* A stool pigeon. ❖ *intr.v.* **stooged, stoog•ing, stoog•es** To be a stooge or behave like one. [?]

stool (stŏŏl) *n.* **1.** A backless and armless single seat supported on legs or a pedestal. **2.** A low bench or support for the feet or knees in sitting or kneeling, as a footrest. **3.** A toilet seat; a commode. **4.** Fecal matter from a single bowel movement. **5.** *Botany* **a.** A stump or rootstock that produces shoots or suckers. **b.** A shoot or growth from a stool. ❖ *intr.v.* **stooled, stool•ing, stools** **1.** *Botany* To send up shoots or suckers. **2.** To evacuate the bowels; defecate. **3.** *Slang* To act as a stool pigeon. [ME < OE *stōl.* See **stā-** in App.]

stool•ie (stŏŏ′lē) *n. Slang* A stool pigeon.

stool pigeon *n.* **1.** *Slang* A person acting as a decoy or as an informer, esp. one who is a spy for the police. **2.** A pigeon used as a decoy. [< the practice of tying decoy pigeons to a stool to attract other pigeons.]

stoop¹ (stŏŏp) *v.* **stooped, stoop•ing, stoops** —*intr.* **1.** To bend forward and down from the waist or the middle of the back. **2.** To walk or stand, esp. habitually, with the head and upper back bent forward. **3.** To bend or sag downward. **4a.** To lower or debase oneself. **b.** To descend from a superior position; condescend. **5.** To yield; submit. **6.** To swoop down, as a bird in pursuing its prey. —*tr.* **1.** To bend (the head or body) forward and down. **2.** To debase; humble. ❖ *n.* **1.** The act of stooping. **2.** A forward bending of the head and upper back, esp. when habitual. **3.** An act of self-abasement or condescension. **4.** A descent, as of a bird of prey. [ME *stoupen* < OE *stūpian.*] —**stoop′er** *n.*

stoop² (stŏŏp) *n. Chiefly Northeastern US* A small porch, platform, or staircase leading to the entrance of a house or building. [Du. *stoep,* front veranda < MDu.]

REGIONAL NOTE Originally brought to the Hudson Valley of New York by settlers from the Netherlands, a few items of Dutch vocabulary have survived there from colonial times until the present. *Stoop,* "a small porch," comes from Dutch *stoep;* this word is now in general use in the Northeast and is probably spreading. The word *olicook,* which appears to be dying out, means "doughnut," and comes from Dutch *oliekoek*—literally, "oil cake." And the Dutch word *kill* for a small running stream is used throughout New York State.

stoop³ (stŏŏp) *n.* Variant of **stoup.**

stoop•ball (stŏŏp′bôl′) *n.* A game patterned on baseball in which a player throws a ball against a stoop or wall and the number of bounces indicates the bases reached.

stop (stŏp) *v.* **stopped, stop•ping, stops** —*tr.* **1.** To close (an opening) by covering, filling in, or plugging up: *The tea leaves stopped the drain.* **2.** To constrict (an opening): *My nose is stopped up.* **3.** To obstruct or block passage on (a road, for example). **4.** To prevent the flow or passage of. **5a.** To halt the motion or progress of: *stopped me and asked directions.* **b.** To block or deflect (a blow, for example). **c.** To be or get in the way of (a bullet or other missile); be killed or wounded by. **6a.** To cause to desist or to change a course of action. **b.** To prevent or restrain: *stopped him from complaining.* **7.** To discontinue or cease: *He stopped his complaining.* **8a.** To defeat (an opponent or opposing team). **b.** To defeat in boxing by a knockout or technical knockout. **9.** To order a bank to withhold payment of: *stopped the check.* **10.** *Music* **a.** To press down (a string on a stringed instrument) on the fingerboard to produce a desired pitch. **b.** To close (a hole on a wind instrument) with the finger in sounding a desired pitch. —*intr.* **1.** To cease moving, progressing, acting, or operating; come to a halt: *My watch stopped.* **2.** To put an end to what one is doing; cease. **3.** To interrupt one's course or journey for a brief visit or stay. Often used with *by, in,* or *off.* ❖ *n.* **1.** The act of stopping or the condition of being stopped; cessation. **2.** A finish; an end. **3.** A stay or visit, as one taken during a trip. **4.** A place at which someone or something stops. **5.** A device or means that obstructs,

Lucy Stone

stopwatch

stork
saddle-billed stork
Ephippiorhyncus
senegalensis

blocks, or plugs up. **6.** An order given to a bank to withhold payment on a check. **7.** A part in a mechanism that stops or regulates movement. **8.** The effective aperture of a lens, controlled by a diaphragm. **9.** A mark of punctuation, esp. a period. **10.** *Music* **a.** The act of stopping a string or hole on an instrument. **b.** A fret on a stringed instrument. **c.** A hole on a wind instrument. **d.** A device used as a key for closing the hole on a wind instrument. **e.** A tuned set of pipes. **f.** A knob, key, or pull that regulates such a set of pipes. **11.** *Nautical* A line used for securing something temporarily: *a sail stop.* **12.** *Linguistics* **a.** One of a set of speech sounds that is a plosive or a nasal. **b.** A plosive. **13.** The depression between the muzzle and top of the skull of an animal, esp. a dog. **14.** *Games* A stopper. **15.** *Architecture* A projecting stone, often carved, at the end of a molding. ❖ *adj.* Of, relating to, or being of use at the end of an operation or activity: *a stop code.* [ME *stoppen* < OE *-stoppian*, prob. < VLat. **stuppāre*, to caulk < Lat. *stuppa*, tow, broken flax < Gk. *stuppē*.] —**stop′pa·ble** *adj.*

SYNONYMS stop, cease, desist, discontinue, halt, quit These verbs mean to bring or come to an end: *stop arguing; ceased crying; desist from complaining; discontinued the treatment; halting the convoy; quit laughing.* **ANTONYM** start

stop-and-go (stŏp′ənd-gō′) *adj.* Alternately proceeding and halting: *stop-and-go traffic.*

stop bath *n.* An acid solution used to check the developing process of a photographic negative or print.

stop·cock (stŏp′kŏk′) *n.* A valve that regulates the flow of fluid through a pipe; a faucet.

stope (stōp) *n.* An excavation in the form of steps made by the mining of ore from steeply inclined or vertical veins. ❖ *tr.v.* **stoped, stop·ing, stopes** To remove (ore) from or mine by means of a stope. [Perh. < LGer., step < MLGer. *stōpe.*] —**stop′er** *n.*

stop·gap (stŏp′găp′) *n.* An improvised substitute for something lacking; a temporary expedient. ❖ *adj.* Serving as a stopgap: *a stopgap budget bill.*

stop·light (stŏp′līt′) *n.* **1.** A light on the rear of a vehicle that is activated when the brakes are applied. **2.** See **traffic light.**

stop order *n.* An order to a broker to buy or sell a stock when it reaches a specified level of decline or gain in price.

stop·o·ver (stŏp′ō′vər) *n.* **1.** An interruption of a trip for stopping somewhere. **2.** A place visited briefly during a trip.

stop·page (stŏp′ĭj) *n.* The act of stopping or the condition of being stopped; a halt: *called for a work stoppage.*

stop payment *n.* An order to one's bank not to honor a check one has drawn.

stop·per (stŏp′ər) *n.* **1.** A device, such as a plug, that is inserted to close an opening. **2.** One that stops something: *a conversation stopper.* ❖ *tr.v.* **-pered, -per·ing, -pers** To close with or as if with a stopper.

stop·ple (stŏp′əl) *n.* A stopper; a plug. ❖ *tr.v.* **-pled, -pling, -ples** To close with a stopper or plug. [ME *stoppell* < ME *stoppen*, to stop. See STOP.]

stop street *n.* A street intersection at which a vehicle must come to a complete stop before entering a through street.

stop·watch (stŏp′wŏch′) *n.* A watch that can be instantly started and stopped by pushing a button, used to measure an exact duration of time.

stop·word (stŏp′wûrd′) *n.* A frequently used word, such as *a* or *the,* that is not indexed in webpages and thus is not used in search engine queries.

stor·age (stôr′ĭj, stōr′-) *n.* **1a.** The act of storing goods or the state of being stored. **b.** A space for storing goods. **c.** The price charged for storing goods. **2.** The charging or regenerating of a storage battery. **3.** *Computer Science* The part of a computer that stores information for subsequent use or retrieval.

storage battery *n. Electricity* A group of reversible or rechargeable secondary cells acting as a unit.

storage cell *n.* See **secondary cell.**

storage device *n.* A hardware device, such as a hard disk, used to record and store data.

sto·rax (stôr′ăks′, stōr′-) *n.* **1.** See **snowbell. 2.** An aromatic resin obtained from the snowbell. **3.** A brownish aromatic resin used in perfume and medicine and obtained from any of several trees of the genus *Liquidambar,* esp. *L. orientalis,* of Turkey. [ME < Lat., alteration of *styrax* < Gk. *sturax,* perh. of Semitic orig.; akin to Ugaritic *ẕurwu* and Heb. *ṣŏrî,* aromatic resin.]

store (stôr, stōr) *n.* **1.** A place where merchandise is sold; a shop. **2.** A stock or supply reserved for future use. **3. stores** Supplies, esp. of food, clothing, or arms. **4.** A place where commodities are kept; a warehouse or storehouse. **5.** A great quantity or number; an abundance. ❖ *tr.v.* **stored, stor·ing, stores 1.** To reserve for future use. **2.** To fill, supply, or stock. **3.** To deposit or receive in a storehouse or warehouse for safekeeping. **4.** *Computer Science* To copy (data) into memory or onto a storage device. **—idiom: in store 1.** Forthcoming. **2.** In reserve; stored. [ME *stor,* supply < OFr. *estor < estorer,* to build < Lat. *īnstaurāre,* to restore. See *stā-* in App.] —**stor′a·ble** *adj.* —**stor′er** *n.*

store-bought (stôr′bôt′, stōr′-) *adj.* Manufactured and bought at retail; not homemade: *store-bought pie.*

store·front (stôr′frŭnt′, stōr′-) *n.* **1.** The side of a store or shop

facing a street. **2.** A room or suite of rooms in a commercial building at street level. —**store′front′** *adj.*

store·house (stôr′hous′, stōr′-) *n.* **1.** A place or building in which goods are stored; a warehouse. **2.** An abundant source or supply: *a storehouse of knowledge.*

store·keep·er (stôr′kē′pər, stōr′-) *n.* **1.** One who keeps a retail store or shop. **2.** One in charge of receiving or distributing stores or supplies. —**store′keep′ing** *n.*

store·own·er (stôr′ō′nər) *n.* One who owns or operates a store or shop.

store·room (stôr′rōōm′, -rŏŏm′, stōr′-) *n.* A room in which things are stored.

store·wide (stôr′wīd′, stōr′-) *adj.* Involving, applying to, or occurring throughout a whole store: *a storewide sale.*

sto·rey (stôr′ē, stōr′ē) *n. Chiefly British* Variant of **story**[2].

sto·reyed (stôr′ēd, stōr′-) *adj. Chiefly British* Variant of **storied**[2].

sto·ried[1] (stôr′ēd, stōr′-) *adj.* **1.** Celebrated or famous in history or story. **2.** Ornamented with designs representing scenes from history, legend, or story: *storied tapestry.*

sto·ried[2] (stôr′ēd, stōr′-) *adj.* Having or consisting of a given number of stories. Often used in combination: *a two-storied house.*

stork (stôrk) *n.* Any of various large wading birds of the family Ciconiidae, chiefly of the Eastern Hemisphere, having long legs and a long straight bill. [ME < OE *storc.*]

storks·bill (stôrks′bĭl′) *n.* **1.** Any of various plants of the genus *Erodium,* having fruit with a narrow beaklike tip. **2.** See **geranium** 2.

storm (stôrm) *n.* **1.** An atmospheric disturbance manifested in strong winds accompanied by rain, snow, hail, or sleet and often by thunder and lightning. **2.** A wind with a speed from 64 to 73 miles (from 103 to 117 kilometers) per hour, according to the Beaufort scale. **3.** A heavy shower of objects, such as missiles. **4.** A strong or violent outburst, as of emotion or excitement. **5.** A violent disturbance or upheaval, as in political, social, or domestic affairs. **6.** A sudden violent attack on a fortified place. **7.** A storm window. ❖ *v.* **stormed, storm·ing, storms** —*intr.* **1a.** To blow forcefully. **b.** To precipitate rain, snow, hail, or sleet. **2.** To be extremely angry; rant and rage. **3.** To move or rush tumultuously, violently, or angrily. —*tr.* To assault, capture, or captivate by storm. [ME < OE.]

storm·bound (stôrm′bound′) *adj.* Delayed, confined, or cut off from communication by a storm.

storm cell *n.* An air mass that contains up and down drafts in convective loops and functions as the smallest unit of a storm-producing system.

storm cellar *n.* See **cyclone cellar.**

storm center *n.* **1.** The central area of a storm, esp. the point of lowest barometric pressure within a storm. **2.** A center of trouble, disturbance, or argument.

storm door *n.* An outer or additional door added for protection against inclement weather.

storm petrel *n.* Any of various small sea birds of the family Hydrobatidae, esp. *Hydrobates pelagicus* of the North Atlantic Ocean and the Mediterranean Sea, having sooty plumage.

storm trooper *n.* **1a.** A member of the Nazi militia noted for brutality and violence. **b.** One who resembles a member of the Nazi militia. **2.** A member of a force of shock troops. [< *storm troops,* transl. of Ger. *Sturmtruppen : Sturm(abteilung),* Storm (Division) + *Truppen,* troops.]

storm window *n.* A secondary window attached over the usual window to protect against the wind and cold.

storm·y (stôr′mē) *adj.* **-i·er, -i·est 1.** Subject to, marked by, or affected by storms; tempestuous. **2.** Marked by violent emotions, speech, or actions. —**storm′i·ly** *adv.* —**storm′i·ness** *n.*

stormy petrel *n.* **1.** See **storm petrel. 2.** One who brings discord or appears at the onset of trouble; a rebel.

sto·ry[1] (stôr′ē, stōr′ē) *n., pl.* **-ries 1.** An account or recital of an event or a series of events, either true or fictitious, as: **a.** An account or report regarding the facts of an event or group of events. **b.** An anecdote. **c.** A lie. **2a.** A usu. fictional prose or verse narrative intended to interest or amuse the hearer or reader; a tale. **b.** A short story. **3.** The plot of a narrative or dramatic work. **4.** A news article or broadcast. **5.** Something viewed as or providing material for a literary or journalistic treatment. **6.** The background information regarding something: *What's the story on this case?* **7.** Romantic legend or tradition. ❖ *tr.v.* **-ried, -ry·ing, -ries 1.** To decorate with scenes representing historical or legendary events. **2.** *Archaic* To tell as a story. [ME *storie* < OFr. *estorie, estoire* < Lat. *historia.*]

sto·ry[2] (stôr′ē, stōr′ē) *n., pl.* **-ries 1.** A complete horizontal division of a building, constituting the area between two adjacent levels. **2.** The set of rooms on the same level of a building. [ME *storie, story* < Med.Lat. *historia,* picture, story (prob. < painted windows or sculpture on the front of buildings) < Lat. *historia,* history. See HISTORY.]

sto·ry·board (stôr′ē-bôrd′, stōr′ē-bōrd′) *n.* A panel or series of panels of rough sketches outlining the scene sequence and major changes of action or plot in a production to be shot on film or video. —**sto′ry·board′** *v.*

sto•ry•book (stôr′ē-bŏŏk′, stōr′-) n. A book containing a collection of stories, usu. for children. —**sto′ry•book′** adj.

story line n. The plot of a story or dramatic work.

sto•ry•tell•er (stôr′ē-tĕl′ər, stōr′-) n. **1a.** One who tells or writes stories. **b.** One who relates anecdotes. **2.** Informal One who tells lies. —**sto′ry•tell′ing** n.

sto•ry•writ•er (stôr′ē-rī′tər, stōr′-) n. **1.** One who writes stories. **2.** One who writes news stories, as for the media.

stoss (stôs, shtôs, shtōs) adj. Facing the direction from which a glacier moves. Used of a rock or slope in its path. [< Ger. Stoss-, push, blow (as in Stosseite, stoss side) < stossen, to push < MHGer. stōzen < OHGer. stōzan.]

stound (stound) n. Archaic A short time; a while. [ME < OE stund. See stā- in App.]

stoup also **stoop** (stōōp) n. **1.** Ecclesiastical A basin or font for holy water at the entrance of a church. **2.** A drinking vessel, such as a cup or tankard. **3.** Scots A bucket or pail. [ME stoup, bucket, jar < ON staup, cup.]

Stour (stour, stōōr) A river, c. 64 km (40 mi), of SE England emptying into the North Sea in two channels.

stout (stout) adj. **stout•er, stout•est 1.** Bold, brave, or determined; firm and resolute. **2.** Strong in body; sturdy. **3.** Strong in structure or substance; solid or substantial. **4.** Bulky in figure; thickset or corpulent. See Syns at **fat. 5.** Powerful; forceful. **6.** Stubborn or uncompromising. ❖ n. **1a.** A thickset or corpulent person. **b.** A garment size for a large or heavy figure. **2.** A strong, very dark beer or ale. [ME < OFr. estout, of Gmc. orig. See **stel-** in App.] —**stout′ish** adj. —**stout′ly** adv. —**stout′ness** n.

stout•en (stout′n) tr. & intr.v. **-ened, -en•ing, -ens** To make or become stout or stouter.

stout•heart•ed (stout′här′tĭd) adj. Brave; valiant. —**stout′-heart′ed•ly** adv. —**stout′heart′ed•ness** n.

stove[1] (stōv) n. **1.** An apparatus in which electricity or a fuel is used to furnish heat, as for cooking or warmth. **2.** A device that produces heat for specialized, esp. industrial purposes. **3.** A kiln. **4.** Chiefly British A hothouse. [ME, heated room, prob. < MLGer. or MDu., both prob. < VLat. *extūfa < *extūfāre, to heat with steam. See STEW.]

stove[2] (stōv) v. A past tense and a past participle of **stave.**

stove•pipe (stōv′pīp′) n. **1.** A pipe, usu. of thin sheet iron, used to conduct smoke or fumes from a stove into a chimney flue. **2.** A man's tall silk hat.

sto•ver (stō′vər) n. The dried stalks and leaves of a cereal crop, used as fodder after the grain has been harvested. [ME, provisions < Norman Fr. estovers < OFr. estovier, to be necessary < Lat. est opus, it is necessary : est, third pers. sing. pr. t. of esse, to be; see ESSENCE + opus, need, work.]

stow (stō) tr.v. **stowed, stow•ing, stows 1a.** To place or arrange, esp. in a neat, compact way. **b.** To fill (a place or container) by packing tightly. **2.** To store for future use. **3.** Slang To refrain from; stop. **4.** To provide lodging for; quarter. —**phrasal verb: stow away 1.** To hide oneself aboard a conveyance to obtain free transportation. **2.** Informal To consume (food or drink) greedily. [ME stowen, place < OE stōw. See **stā-** in App.]

stow•age (stō′ĭj) n. **1a.** The act, manner, or process of stowing. **b.** The state of being stored. **2a.** Space or room for storage. **b.** A place or container for storage. **3.** Goods in storage or to be stowed. **4.** A charge for storing goods.

stow•a•way (stō′ə-wā′) n. A person who hides aboard a ship or other conveyance in order to obtain free passage.

Stowe (stō), **Harriet (Elizabeth) Beecher** 1811–96. Amer. writer noted esp. for her novel Uncle Tom's Cabin (1852).

STP abbr. standard temperature and pressure

str. abbr. **1.** steamer **2. Str.** strait **3.** Music stringed **4.** strophe

stra•bis•mus (strə-bĭz′məs) n. A visual defect in which one eye cannot focus with the other because of imbalance of the eye muscles. [NLat. < Gk. strabismos, condition of squinting < strabizein, to squint < strabos, squinting.] —**stra•bis′mal** (-məl), **stra•bis′mic** (-mĭk) adj.

Stra•bo (strā′bō) 63? B.C.–A.D. 24? Greek geographer and historian whose work describes the people and countries known to the Greeks during the reign of Augustus.

Stra•chey (strā′kē), **(Giles) Lytton** 1880–1932. British historian best known for Eminent Victorians (1918).

strad•dle (străd′l) v. **-dled, -dling, -dles** —tr. **1a.** To stand or sit with a leg on each side of; bestride. **b.** To be on both sides of; extend over or across. **2.** To appear to favor both sides of (an issue). **3.** To fire shots behind and in front of (a target) to determine the range. —intr. **1.** To walk, stand, or sit with the legs wide apart, esp. to sit astride. **2.** To spread out in a disorderly way; sprawl. **3.** To appear to favor both sides of an issue. ❖ n. **1.** The act or posture of sitting astride. **2.** An equivocal or noncommittal position. **3.** The option to buy or sell a specific asset, such as a block of stock, at a set price before a certain date. —idiom: straddle the fence Informal To be undecided or uncommitted. [Akin to STRIDE.] —**strad′dler** n.

Stra•di•va•ri (străd′ə-vär′ē, -vâr′ē), **Antonio** Often called Antonius Stradivarius. 1644?–1737. Italian violinmaker who developed the proportions of the modern violin.

strafe (strāf) tr.v. **strafed, straf•ing, strafes** To attack (ground troops, for example) with a machine gun or cannon from a low-flying aircraft. [< Ger. (Gott) strafe (England), (God) punish (England), World War I slogan < strafen, to punish < MHGer. strāfen, to admonish.] —**strafe** n. —**straf′er** n.

Straf•ford (străf′ərd), 1st Earl of. Title of Thomas Wentworth. 1593–1641. English politician and principal minister to Charles I who was convicted of treason by Parliament and executed.

strag•gle (străg′əl) intr.v. **-gled, -gling, -gles 1.** To stray or fall behind. **2.** To proceed or spread out in a scattered or irregular group. ❖ n. A scattered or disorderly group, as of people or things. [ME straglen, to wander.] —**strag′gler** n.

strag•gly (străg′lē) adj. **-gli•er, -gli•est** Growing or spread out in a disorderly or aimless way: straggly ivy.

straight (strāt) adj. **straight•er, straight•est 1.** Extending continuously in the same direction without curving: a straight line. **2.** Having no waves or bends: straight hair. **3a.** Not bent or bowed; rigid or erect. **b.** Sports Of or relating to a midair position, as in diving, in which the body is held rigid without bending at the hips or knees. **4.** Perfectly horizontal or vertical; level or even. **5a.** Direct and candid. **b.** Following a direct or correct method or approach; systematic: straight reasoning. **c.** Coming from a reliable source; factual. **6a.** Showing or marked by honesty or fair-mindedness. **b.** Right; correct. **7.** Neatly arranged; orderly. **8a.** Uninterrupted; consecutive: their fourth straight victory. **b.** Having the parts or details in correct sequence. **c.** Games Constituting a straight in poker. **9.** Undeviatingly supportive, as of a principle or a political party. **10a.** Not deviating from the socially normal, usual, or acceptable; conventional. **b.** Conventional to an extreme degree. **11.** Heterosexual. **12.** Slang Not being under the influence of alcohol or drugs. **13a.** Not deviating from the normal or strict form. **b.** Not altered, embellished, or modified. **14a.** Concerned with serious or important matters: a straight drama. **b.** Of or relating to a straight man. **15.** Not mixed with anything else; undiluted: straight bourbon. **16.** Sold without discount regardless of the amount purchased. ❖ adv. **1.** In a straight line; directly. **2.** In an erect posture; upright. **3.** Sports In the straight position, as in diving. **4.** Without detour or delay: went straight home. **5.** Without circumlocution; candidly. **6.** In a neat and orderly condition. **7.** In an honest, law-abiding, or virtuous manner. **8.** Without stopping; continuously: walked six hours straight. **9.** Without embellishment or modification. **10.** Without ice, water, or a mixer. ❖ n. **1a.** The straight part, as of a road. **b.** The straight part of a racecourse between the winning post and the last turn. **2.** A straight line. **3.** A straight form or position. **4.** Games A poker hand containing five cards of various suits in numerical sequence, ranked above three of a kind and below a flush. **5.** A conventional person, esp. a member of established society. **6.** A heterosexual person. —idiom: straight up Served without ice. [ME < p. part. of strecchen, to stretch. See STRETCH.] —**straight′ly** adv. —**straight′ness** n.

straight-a•head (strāt′ə-hĕd′) adj. Conforming to a conventional style or mode; standard.

straight and narrow n. The way of proper conduct and moral integrity. Used with the. [Alteration (by misunderstanding) of strait and narrow < "Strait is the gate, and narrow is the way, which leadeth unto life" (Matthew 7:14) (< STRAIT, narrow).]

straight angle n. An angle of 180°.

straight-arm (strāt′ärm′) tr.v. **-armed, -arm•ing, -arms 1.** Football To ward off (a tackler) by holding the arm out straight with the elbow locked and the palm of the hand placed against the opponent's body; stiff-arm. **2.** To force or ward off by or as if by holding the arm out straight. —**straight′-arm′** n.

straight•a•way (strāt′ə-wā′) adj. **1.** Extending in a straight line or course without a curve or turn. **2.** Unhesitating; immediate: a straightaway denial. ❖ n. A straight course, stretch, or track. ❖ adv. (strāt′ə-wā′) At once; immediately.

straight chain n. An organic molecular structure in the form of an unbranched open chain.

straight•edge (strāt′ĕj′) n. A rigid flat rectangular bar, as of wood or metal, with a straight edge for testing or drawing straight lines. —**straight′edged′** adj.

straight•en (strāt′n) tr. & intr.v. **-ened, -en•ing, -ens** To make or become straight or straighter. —**straight′en•er** n.

straight face n. A face that betrays no sign of emotion. —**straight′-faced′** (strāt′fāst′) adj.

straight flush n. Games A hand in which all five cards are of the same suit and in numerical sequence, ranked above four of a kind in poker.

straight•for•ward (strāt-fôr′wərd) adj. **1.** Proceeding in a straight course; direct. **2a.** Not circuitous or evasive; honest and frank. See Syns at **frank**[1]. **b.** Free from ambiguity or pretense; plain and open. ❖ adv. In a direct course or an honest manner. —**straight•for′ward•ly** adv. —**straight•for′ward•ness** n. —**straight•for′wards** adv.

straight•jack•et (strāt′jăk′ĭt) n. & v. Variant of **straitjacket.**

straight-laced (strāt′lāst′) adj. Variant of **strait-laced.**

straight-line (strāt′līn′) adj. **1.** Lying in a straight line. **2.** Relating to or being a device whose linkage produces or copies motion in straight lines. **3.** Accounting Of or being a mode of amortization by equal payments at stated intervals over a given period of time.

straight man n. The partner in a comedy team who feeds lines

ă	pat	oi	boy
ā	pay	ou	out
âr	care	ŏŏ	took
ä	father	ōō	boot
ĕ	pet	ŭ	cut
ē	be	ûr	urge
ĭ	pit	th	thin
ī	pie	th	this
îr	pier	hw	which
ŏ	pot	zh	vision
ō	toe	ə	about,
ô	paw		item

Stress marks:
′ (primary);
′ (secondary), as in
lexicon (lĕk′sĭ-kŏn′)

to the other comedian, who then makes witty replies.
straight off *adv.* At once; immediately.

straight-out (strāt′out′) *adj.* **1.** Straightforward; blunt. **2.** Complete; unmitigated.

straight poker *n.* Poker in which each player is dealt five cards face down, bets are made, and the showdown takes place without any new cards being drawn.

straight razor *n.* A razor consisting of a blade hinged to a handle into which it slips when not in use.

straight ticket *n.* A ballot cast for one party's candidates.

straight•way (strāt′wā′, -wā′) *adv.* **1.** In a direct course. **2.** Without delay; at once.

strain¹ (strān) *v.* **strained, strain•ing, strains** —*tr.* **1.** To pull, draw, or stretch tight. **2.** To exert or tax to the utmost. **3.** To injure or impair by overuse or overexertion; wrench. **4.** To stretch or force beyond the proper or legitimate limit. **5.** *Physics* To alter (the relations between the parts of a structure or shape) by applying an external force; deform. **6a.** To pass (gravy, for example) through a filter such as a strainer. **b.** To draw off or remove by filtration. **7.** To embrace or clasp tightly; hug. —*intr.* **1.** To make violent or steady efforts; strive hard. **2.** To be or become wrenched or twisted. **3.** To be subjected to great stress. **4.** To pull forcibly or violently. **5.** To stretch or exert one's muscles or nerves to the utmost. **6.** To filter, trickle, or ooze. **7.** To be extremely hesitant; balk. ❖ *n.* **1a.** The act of straining. **b.** The state of being strained. **2a.** Extreme or laborious effort, exertion, or work. **b.** A great or excessive pressure, demand, or stress on one's body, mind, or resources. **3.** A wrench, twist, or other physical injury due to excessive tension, effort, or use. **4.** *Physics* A deformation caused by stress. **5.** An exceptional degree or pitch. [ME *streinen* < OFr. *estreindre, estrein-*, to bind tightly < Lat. *stringere*.]

strain² (strān) *n.* **1.** The collective descendants of a common ancestor; a race, stock, line, or breed. **2.** Any of the various lines of ancestry united in an individual or a family; ancestry or lineage. **3.** *Biology* A group of organisms of the same species, having distinctive characteristics but not usu. considered a separate breed or variety. **4.** An artificial variety of a domestic animal or cultivated plant. **5.** A kind or sort. **6a.** An inborn or inherited tendency or character. **b.** An inherent quality; a streak. **7a.** The tone, tenor, or substance of an utterance or of an action. **b.** A prevailing quality, as of attitude or behavior. **8.** *Music* A passage of musical expression; a tune or an air. Often used in the plural. **9a.** A passage of poetic and esp. lyrical expression. **b.** An outburst or flow of eloquent or impassioned language. [ME *strene* < OE *strēon*, something gained, offspring.]

strained (strānd) *adj.* **1.** Having been passed through a strainer. **2.** Done with or marked by excessive effort; forced: *strained humor.* **3.** Extended beyond proper limits: *a strained meaning.* **4.** Antagonized to the verge of open conflict: *strained relations.* **5.** Twisted; wrenched: *a strained ankle.*

strain•er (strā′nər) *n.* **1.** One that strains, as a device used to separate liquids from solids. **2.** An apparatus for tightening, stretching, or strengthening.

strain gauge *n.* An extensometer.

strain•ing beam (strā′nĭng) *n.* A horizontal tie beam connecting two queen posts in a roof truss.

strain•om•e•ter (strā-nŏm′ĭ-tər) *n.* An extensometer.

strait (strāt) *n.* **1.** A narrow channel joining two larger bodies of water. Often used in the plural with a singular verb. **2.** A position of difficulty, perplexity, distress, or need. Often used in the plural: *in desperate straits.* ❖ *adj.* **1a.** Difficult; stressful. **b.** Having or marked by limited funds or resources. **2.** *Archaic* **a.** Narrow. **b.** Affording little space or room; confined. **c.** Fitting tightly; constricted. **3.** *Archaic* Strict, rigid, or righteous. [ME *streit*, narrow, a strait < OFr. *estreit*, tight, narrow < Lat. *strictus*, p. part. of *stringere*, to draw tight.] —**strait′ly** *adv.* —**strait′ness** *n.*

strait•en (strāt′n) *tr.v.* **-ened, -en•ing, -ens 1a.** To make narrow. **b.** To enclose in a limited area; confine. **2.** To put or bring into difficulties or distress, esp. financial hardship. **3.** *Archaic* To restrict in latitude or scope.

strait•jack•et also **straight•jack•et** (strāt′jăk′ĭt) *n.* **1.** A long-sleeved jacketlike garment used to bind the arms tightly against the body as a means of restraining a violent patient or prisoner. **2.** Something that restricts, hinders, or confines. —**strait′jack′et** *v.*

strait-laced or **straight-laced** (strāt′lāst′) *adj.* **1.** Excessively strict in behavior, morality, or opinions. **2.** Having or wearing a tightly laced garment. [STRAIT, tightly (obsolete) + *-laced* (< LACE).] —**strait′-lac′ed•ly** (-lā′sĭd-lē, -lāst′lē) *adv.* —**strait′-lac′ed•ness** *n.*

Straits Settlements (strāts) A former British crown colony comprising parts of the S and W Malay Peninsula and adjacent islands, including Singapore.

strake (strāk) *n. Nautical* A single continuous line of planking or metal plating extending on a vessel's hull from stem to stern. [ME, prob. < OE *straca.*]

stra•mo•ni•um (strə-mō′nē-əm) *n.* **1.** See **jimsonweed. 2.** The dried poisonous leaves of the jimsonweed, used in the treatment of asthma. [NLat., specific epithet, perh. ult. < Tatar *turman*, a medicine for horses.]

strand¹ (strănd) *n.* The land bordering a body of water; a beach. ❖ *v.* **strand•ed, strand•ing, strands** —*tr.* **1.** To drive or run

strainer
tea ball strainer

ashore or aground. **2.** To bring into or leave in a difficult or helpless position. **3.** *Baseball* To leave (a base runner) on base at the end of an inning. —*intr.* **1.** To be driven or run ashore or aground. **2.** To be brought into or left in a difficult or helpless position. [ME < OE.]

strand² (strănd) *n.* **1.** A complex of fibers or filaments twisted together into a cable, rope, thread, or yarn. **2a.** A single filament, such as a fiber or thread, of a woven or braided material. **b.** A wisp or a tress of hair. **3.** Something plaited or twisted into a ropelike length: *a strand of pearls; a strand of DNA.* **4.** One of the elements woven into an intricate whole. ❖ *tr.v.* **strand•ed, strand•ing, strands 1.** To make or form (a rope, for example) by twisting strands together. **2.** To break a strand of (a rope, for example). [ME *strond.*]

strand line also **strand•line** (strănd′līn′) *n.* A shoreline, esp. one marking an earlier and higher water level.

strange (strānj) *adj.* **strang•er, strang•est 1.** Not previously known; unfamiliar. **2a.** Out of the ordinary; unusual or striking. **b.** Differing from the normal. **3.** Not of one's own or a particular locality, environment, or kind; exotic. **4a.** Reserved in manner; distant. **b.** Not comfortable or at ease; constrained. **5.** Not accustomed or conditioned. **6.** *Archaic* Of, relating to, or characteristic of another place or part of the world; foreign. ❖ *adv.* In a strange manner. [ME < OFr. *estrange*, extraordinary, foreign < Lat. *extrāneus*, adventitious, foreign < *extrā*, outside < fem. ablative of *exter*, outward. See **eghs** in App.] —**strange′ly** *adv.*

SYNONYMS *strange, peculiar, odd, queer, outlandish, eccentric, curious* These adjectives describe what deviates from the usual or customary. *Strange* refers especially to what is unfamiliar, unknown, or inexplicable: *traveling through strange lands. Peculiar* particularly describes what is distinct from all others: *the peculiar odor of cloves.* Something that is *odd* or *queer* fails to accord with what is ordinary, usual, or expected; both terms can suggest strangeness or peculiarity: *It's odd that his name is never mentioned. "Now, my suspicion is that the universe is not only queerer than we suppose, but queerer than we can suppose"* (J.B.S. Haldane). *Outlandish* suggests alien or bizarre strangeness: *outlandish clothes. Eccentric* refers particularly to what is strange and departs strikingly from the conventional: *innovative but eccentric compositions. Curious* suggests strangeness that excites interest: *Americans abroad often acquire a curious accent.*

strange attractor *n. Physics* An attractor for which the approach to the final set of physical properties is chaotic.

strange•ness (strānj′nĭs) *n.* **1.** The quality or condition of being strange. **2.** *Physics* A quantum property of the strange quark whose conservation accounts for the absence of certain strong-interaction decay modes among hadrons.

strange particle *n.* An unstable elementary particle with non-zero total strangeness.

strange quark *n.* A quark with a charge of $-\frac{1}{3}$, a mass about 400 times that of the electron, and a strangeness of −1.

strang•er (strān′jər) *n.* **1.** One who is neither a friend nor an acquaintance. **2.** A foreigner, newcomer, or outsider. **3.** One who is unaccustomed to or unacquainted with something specified; a novice. **4.** A visitor or guest. **5.** *Law* One that is neither privy nor party to a title, act, or contract. [ME < OFr. *estrangier* < *estrange*, strange. See STRANGE.]

strange star *n.* See **quark star.**

stran•gle (străng′gəl) *v.* **-gled, -gling, -gles** —*tr.* **1a.** To kill by squeezing the throat so as to choke or suffocate; throttle. **b.** To cut off the oxygen supply of; smother. **2.** To suppress, repress, or stifle. **3.** To inhibit the growth or action of; restrict. —*intr.* **1.** To become strangled. **2.** To die from suffocation or strangulation; choke. [ME *stranglen* < OFr. *estrangler* < Lat. *strangulāre* < Gk. *strangalan* < *strangalē*, halter.] —**stran′gler** *n.*

stran•gle•hold (străng′gəl-hōld′) *n.* **1.** *Sports* An illegal wrestling hold used to choke an opponent. **2.** A force or action that restricts or suppresses freedom or progress.

stran•gles (străng′gəlz) *pl.n. (used with a sing. verb)* An infectious disease of horses, caused by the bacterium *Streptococcus equi* and marked by inflammation of the mucous membranes that causes a strangling or choking sensation. [< ME *strangle*, strangulation < *stranglen*, to strangle. See STRANGLE.]

stran•gu•late (străng′gyə-lāt′) *v.* **-lat•ed, -lat•ing, -lates** —*tr.* **1.** To strangle. **2.** *Pathology* To compress, constrict, or obstruct (an organ, duct, or other body part) so as to cut off the flow of blood or other fluid. —*intr.* To be or become strangled, compressed, constricted, or obstructed. [Lat. *strangulāre, strangulāt-*. See STRANGLE.] —**stran′gu•la′tion** *n.*

stran•gu•ry (străng′gyə-rē) *n., pl.* **-ries** Slow painful urination. [ME < Lat. *strangūria* < Gk. *strangouriā* : *stranx, strang-*, drop, trickle + *-ouriā, -uria.*]

strap (străp) *n.* **1a.** A long narrow strip of pliant material such as leather. **b.** Such a strip equipped with a buckle or similar fastener to bind or secure objects. **2.** A thin flat metal or plastic band used to fasten or clamp objects together or into position. **3.** A narrow band formed into a loop for grasping with the hand. **4.** A razor strop. **5.** A strip of leather used in flogging. ❖ *tr.v.* **strapped, strap•ping, straps 1.** To fasten or secure with a strap: *strapped a kayak to the car's roof.* **2.** To beat with a strap. **3.** To sharpen (a razor, for example). [Alteration of STROP.] —**strap′py** *adj.*

strap·hang·er (străp′hăng′ər) *n.* **1.** One who grips a hanging strap or similar device for support while riding as a passenger on a bus or subway. **2.** One who uses public transportation.

strap·less (străp′lĭs) *adj.* Having no strap or straps, as a dress or an undergarment. —**strap′less** *n.*

strap·pa·do (stră-pā′dō, -pä′-) *n., pl.* **-does 1.** A form of torture in which the victim is first lifted off the ground by a rope attached to the wrists and tied behind the back and then dropped partway to the ground with a jerk. **2.** The apparatus used in this torture. [Alteration of Fr. *strapade* < OFr. < OItal. *strappata* < *strappare*, to stretch tight, of Gmc. orig.]

strapped (străpt) *adj. Informal* In financial need.

strap·per (străp′ər) *n.* A powerfully built, robust person.

strap·ping (străp′ĭng) *adj.* Having a sturdy muscular physique; robust. ❖ *n.* **1.** Straps considered as a group. **2.** Material for making straps.

Stras·bourg (străs′bŏŏrg′, sträz′-, sträz-bŏŏr′) A city of NE France near the German border E of Nancy; under German control from 1871 to 1919. Pop. 252,274.

strass (străs) *n.* See **paste**¹ 2. [Ger. *Strass* or Fr. *stras*, both perhaps after Josef *Strasser*, 18th-cent. German jeweler.]

stra·ta (strā′tə, străt′ə) *n.* A plural of **stratum.**

strat·a·gem (străt′ə-jəm) *n.* **1.** A military maneuver to deceive or surprise an enemy. **2.** A clever, often underhand scheme to achieve an objective. [ME < OFr. *stratageme* < OItal. *stratagemma* < Lat. *stratēgēma* < Gk. < *stratēgein*, to be a general < *stratēgos*, general : *stratos*, army + *agein*, to lead. See **ag**- in App.]

stra·te·gic (strə-tē′jĭk) also **stra·te·gi·cal** (-jĭ-kəl) *adj.* **1.** Of or relating to strategy. **2a.** Important or essential to a plan of action. **b.** Essential to the conduct of war. **c.** Highly important to an objective. **3.** Intended to destroy the military potential of an enemy: *strategic bombing.* —**stra·te′gi·cal·ly** *adv.*

stra·te·gics (strə-tē′jĭks) *n. (used with a sing. verb)* The art of strategy.

strat·e·gist (străt′ə-jĭst) *n.* One who is skilled in strategy.

strat·e·gize (străt′ə-jīz′) *v.* **-gized, -giz·ing, -giz·es** —*tr.* To plan a strategy for (a business or financial venture, for example). —*intr.* To determine strategies; plan.

strat·e·gy (străt′ə-jē) *n., pl.* **-gies 1a.** The science and art of using a nation's forces to execute approved plans as effectively as possible. **b.** The science and art of military command in the planning and conduct of war. **2.** A plan of action resulting from strategy or intended to accomplish a specific goal. See Syns at **plan. 3.** The art or skill of using stratagems in endeavors such as politics. [Fr. *stratégie* < Gk. *stratēgiā*, office of a general < *stratēgos*, general. See STRATAGEM.]

Strat·ford-on-Av·on (străt′fərd-ŏn-ā′vŏn, -ŏn-) also **Strat·ford-up·on-Av·on** (-ə-pŏn, -pŏn-) A municipal borough of central England SSE of Birmingham; birthplace and home of William Shakespeare. Pop. 20,100.

strath (străth) *n. Scots* A wide flat river valley. [Sc. Gael. *srath* < OIr.]

strath·spey (străth′spā′, străth′spā′) *n.* **1.** A Scottish dance, slower than a reel, for two dancers. **2.** The music for this dance. [After *Strath Spey*, valley of the river Spey in Scotland.]

strat·i (străt′ī, strā′tī) *n.* Plural of **stratus.**

strati- *pref.* Stratum: *stratiform.* [< STRATUM.]

stra·tic·u·late (strə-tĭk′yə-lĭt) *adj. Geology* Having thin layers. [< STRATUM.] —**stra·tic′u·la′tion** (-lā′shən) *n.*

strat·i·fi·ca·tion (străt′ə-fĭ-kā′shən) *n.* **1a.** Formation or deposition of layers, as of rock or sediments. **b.** The condition of being stratified. **2.** A layered configuration.

strat·i·fied charge engine (străt′ə-fīd′) *n.* An internal-combustion engine with a divided ignition cylinder that burns rich fuel in a chamber near the spark plug to improve the combustion of a very lean mixture throughout the rest of the cylinder.

strat·i·form (străt′ə-fôrm′) *adj.* Forming a layer or arranged in layers.

strat·i·fy (străt′ə-fī′) *v.* **-fied, -fy·ing, -fies** —*tr.* **1.** To form, arrange, or deposit in layers. **2.** To preserve (seeds) by placing them between layers of moist sand or similar material. **3a.** To arrange or separate into castes, classes, or social levels. **b.** To separate into a sequence of graded status levels. —*intr.* **1.** To become layered; form strata. **2.** To develop different levels of caste, class, privilege, or status.

stra·tig·ra·phy (strə-tĭg′rə-fē) *n.* The study of rock strata, esp. the distribution, deposition, and age of sedimentary rocks. —**strat′i·graph′ic** (străt′ĭ-grăf′ĭk), **strat′i·graph′i·cal** (-ĭ-kəl) *adj.* —**strat′i·graph′i·cal·ly** *adv.*

stra·toc·ra·cy (strə-tŏk′rə-sē) *n., pl.* **-cies** Government by the armed forces. [Gk. *stratos*, army + -CRACY.] —**strat′o·crat′ic** (străt′ə-krăt′ĭk) *adj.*

strat·o·cu·mu·lus (străt′ō-kyōōm′yə-ləs, strā′tō-) *n., pl.* **-li** (-lī′) A low-lying cloud formation occurring in extensive horizontal layers with rounded summits. [STRAT(US) + CUMULUS.]

strat·o·pause (străt′ə-pôz′) *n.* The boundary between the stratosphere and the mesosphere located about 50 kilometers (31 miles) above the earth's surface. [STRATO(SPHERE) + PAUSE.]

strat·o·sphere (străt′ə-sfîr′) *n.* **1.** The region of the atmosphere above the troposphere and below the mesosphere. **2.** An extremely high or the highest point or degree on a ranked scale. [Fr. *stratosphère* : Lat. *strātus*, a spreading out; see STRATUS + *-sphère*, sphere (< OFr. *espere*; see SPHERE).]

strat·o·spher·ic (străt′ə-sfîr′ĭk, -sfĕr′-) *adj.* **1.** Of, relating to, or characteristic of the stratosphere. **2.** Extremely or unreasonably high. —**strat′o·spher′i·cal·ly** *adv.*

strat·o·vol·ca·no (străt′ō-vŏl-kā′nō, strā′tō-) *n., pl.* **-nos** A volcano composed of alternating layers of lava and ash.

stra·tum (strā′təm, străt′əm) *n., pl.* **-ta** (-tə) or **-tums 1.** A horizontal layer of material, esp. one of several stacked parallel layers. **2.** *Geology* A bed or layer of sedimentary rock that is visually distinguishable from adjacent layers. **3.** Any of the regions of the atmosphere, such as the troposphere, that occur as layers. **4.** *Biology* A layer of tissue, as of the skin. **5.** A level of society of people with similar social, cultural, or economic status. **6.** One of a number of layers, levels, or divisions in an organized system. [Lat. *strātum*, a covering < neut. p. part. of *sternere*, to spread. See STRATUS.] —**stra′tal** (strāt′l) *adj.*

> **USAGE NOTE** The standard singular form is *stratum*; the standard plural is *strata* (sometimes *stratums*), not *stratas*.

stra·tus (strā′təs, strā′təs) *n., pl.* **strat·i** (-ī) A low-altitude cloud formation consisting of a horizontal layer of gray clouds. [< Lat. *strātus*, p. part. of *sternere*, to stretch, extend.]

Strauss (strous, shtrous), **Johann** 1804–49. Austrian violinist and composer of waltzes and other works, notably *Redetzky March* (1848). His son **Johann** (1825–99) is remembered for his waltzes, such as "The Blue Danube" (1867).

Strauss, Richard 1864–1949. German composer known chiefly for his symphonic poems, such as *Don Quixote* (1897), and his operas, including *Salome* (1905).

Stra·vin·sky (strə-vĭn′skē), **Igor Fyodorovich** 1882–1971. Russian-born composer whose ballets include *The Rite of Spring* (1913).

straw (strô) *n.* **1a.** Stalks of threshed grain, used as bedding and fodder, for thatching, and for weaving or braiding. **b.** A single stalk of threshed grain. **2.** Something, such as a basket, made of straw. **3.** A slender tube used for sucking up a liquid. **4a.** Something of minimal value or importance. **b.** Something with too little substance to provide support in a crisis. ❖ *adj.* **1.** Of, relating to, or made of straw. **2.** Containing or used for straw, as a barn. **3.** Of the color of straw; yellowish. **4.** Having little or no value or substance; unimportant. **5.** Of or constituting a straw man. —*idiom:* **straw in the wind** A slight hint of something to come. [ME < OE *strēaw.*] —**straw′y** *adj.*

straw·ber·ry (strô′bĕr′ē) *n.* **1.** Any of various low-growing plants of the genus *Fragaria,* having white flowers and an aggregate fruit consisting of a red fleshy edible receptacle and numerous seedlike fruitlets. **2.** The fruit of this plant. ❖ *adj.* Containing or having the flavor of strawberries. [ME < OE *strēawberige* : *strēaw,* straw; see STRAW + *berige, berie,* berry.]

strawberry blond also **strawberry blonde** *adj.* Reddish blond.

strawberry bush *n.* A shrub (*Euonymus americanus*) of the eastern United States having showy pinkish fruit.

strawberry mark *n.* A red nevus or birthmark, occurring usu. on the face or scalp and resembling a strawberry.

strawberry roan *n.* A horse having reddish and white hair.

strawberry shrub *n.* See **Carolina allspice.**

strawberry tomato *n.* **1.** Any of several plants of the genus *Physalis,* such as *P. pubescens* and *P. pruinosa* of eastern North America, having yellow flowers and edible yellowish fruit. **2.** The fruit of this plant.

strawberry tree *n.* Any of several evergreen shrubs of the genus *Arbutus,* esp. *A. unedo,* native to southern Europe and having scarlet strawberrylike fruit.

straw·board (strô′bôrd′, -bōrd′) *n.* A coarse yellow cardboard made of straw pulp.

straw boss *n. Informal* A worker who acts as a boss or crew leader in addition to performing regular duties.

straw·flow·er (strô′flou′ər) *n.* A stout Australian plant (*Helichrysum bracteatum*) having flower heads with showy, variously colored bracts that retain their color when dried.

straw-hat (strô′hăt′) *adj.* Of or relating to summer theater that operates in suburban or resort areas.

straw man *n.* **1.** A person who is set up as a cover or front for a questionable enterprise. **2.** An argument or opponent set up so as to be easily defeated. **3.** A bundle of straw made into the likeness of a man and often used as a scarecrow.

straw mushroom *n.* A tropical and subtropical edible mushroom (*Volvariella volvacea*) having a white cap and a long stipe with a swollen base.

straw vote *n.* An unofficial vote or poll indicating the trend of opinion on a candidate or issue.

straw wine *n.* A sweet dessert wine made from grapes that have been dried on straw.

straw·worm (strô′wûrm′) *n.* The larva of the wasp *Harmolita grandis* of western North America that damages grain.

straw yellow *n.* A pale yellow.

stray (strā) *intr.v.* **strayed, stray·ing, strays 1a.** To move away from a group, deviate from the correct course, or go beyond established limits. **b.** To become lost. **2.** To wander about without

stratiform
Ernst Tinaja, a layered formation of limestone, Big Bend National Park, Texas

ă	pat	oi	boy
ā	pay	ou	out
âr	care	ŏŏ	took
ä	father	ōō	boot
ĕ	pet	ŭ	cut
ē	be	ûr	urge
ĭ	pit	th	thin
ī	pie	th	this
îr	pier	hw	which
ŏ	pot	zh	vision
ō	toe	ə	about,
ô	paw		item

Stress marks:
′ (primary);
′ (secondary), as in
lexicon (lĕk′sĭ-kŏn′)

a goal; roam. See Syns at **wander. 3.** To follow a winding course; meander. **4.** To deviate from a moral, proper, or right course; err. **5.** To become diverted from a subject or train of thought; digress. See Syns at **swerve. ❖** *n.* One that has strayed, esp. a domestic animal wandering about. **❖** *adj.* **1.** Straying or having strayed; wandering or lost. **2.** Scattered or separate. [ME *straien* < OFr. *estraier* < *estree*, highway < Lat. *strāta*. See STREET.] **—stray′er** *n.*

Stray•horn (strā′hôrn′), **William ("Billy")** 1915–67. Amer. jazz pianist and composer whose works include "Take the A Train."

streak (strēk) *n.* **1.** A line, mark, smear, or band differentiated by color or texture from its surroundings. **2.** An inherent, often contrasting quality: *a stubborn streak.* **3.** *Informal* **a.** A brief run or stretch, as of luck. **b.** An unbroken series, as of wins or losses. **4.** A ray or flash of light: *a streak of lightning.* **5.** *Mineralogy* The color of the fine powder produced when a mineral is rubbed against a hard surface. Used as a distinguishing characteristic. **6.** *Microbiology* A bacterial culture inoculated by drawing a bacteria-laden needle across the surface of a solid culture medium. **❖** *v.* **streaked, streak•ing, streaks** *—tr.* **1.** To mark with streaks: *rain streaking the pavement.* **2.** To lighten (strands of hair) with a chemical preparation. **3.** *Microbiology* To inoculate in order to produce a streak. *—intr.* **1.** To form streaks. **2.** To be or become streaked. **3.** To move at high speed; rush. **4.** To run naked in public, esp. as a prank. [ME *streke*, line < OE *strica*.] **—streak′er** *n.*

streak•y (strē′kē) *adj.* **-i•er, -i•est 1.** Marked with, characterized by, or occurring in streaks. **2.** Variable or uneven in character or quality. **—streak′i•ly** *adv.* **—streak′i•ness** *n.*

stream (strēm) *n.* **1a.** A flow of water in a channel or bed, as a brook or small river. **b.** A steady current in such a flow of water. **2.** A steady current of a fluid. **3.** A steady flow or succession. **4.** A trend, course, or drift, as of opinion. **5.** A beam or ray of light. **❖** *v.* **streamed, stream•ing, streams** *—intr.* **1.** To flow in or as if in a stream. **2.** To pour forth or give off a stream; flow. **3.** To come or go in large numbers; pour. **4.** To extend, wave, or float outward. **5a.** To leave a continuous trail of light. **b.** To give forth a continuous stream of light rays or beams; shine. *—tr.* **1.** To emit, discharge, or exude (a body fluid, for example). **2.** *Computer Science* To transmit (data) in real time, esp. over the Internet. **—idiom: on stream** In or into operation or production. [ME *streme* < OE *strēam*. See **sreu-** in App.] **—stream′y** *adj.*

stream•bed (strēm′bĕd′) *n.* The channel through which a natural stream of water runs or used to run.

stream•er (strē′mər) *n.* **1a.** A long narrow flag, banner, or pennant. **b.** A long narrow strip of material used for ornament or decoration. **2.** A column of light shooting across the sky in the aurora borealis. **3.** An extension of rays from the sun's corona. **4.** A newspaper headline across a full page.

stream•let (strēm′lĭt) *n.* A small stream.

stream•line (strēm′līn′) *tr.v.* **-lined, -lin•ing, -lines 1.** To construct or design in a form that offers the least resistance to fluid flow. **2.** To improve the appearance or efficiency of; modernize. **3a.** To organize. **b.** To simplify. **❖** *n.* **1.** A line parallel to the direction of flow of a fluid at a given instant. **2.** The path of one particle in a flowing fluid. **3.** A contour that offers minimum resistance to fluid flow.

stream•lined (strēm′līnd′) *adj.* **1a.** Designed or arranged to offer the least resistance to fluid flow. **b.** Reduced to essentials; lacking anything extra. **c.** Effectively organized or simplified. **2.** Having flowing, graceful lines; sleek. **3.** Improved in appearance or efficiency; modernized.

stream of consciousness *n., pl.* **streams of consciousness 1.** A literary technique that presents the thoughts and feelings of a character as they occur. **2.** *Psychology* The conscious experience of an individual regarded as a continuous flowing series of images and ideas running through the mind.

stream•side (strēm′sīd′) *n.* The land adjacent to a stream.

street (strēt) *n.* **1a.** A public way or thoroughfare in a city or town, usu. with a sidewalk or sidewalks. **b.** Such a public way considered apart from the sidewalks. **c.** A public way or road along with the houses or buildings abutting it. **2.** The people living, working, or habitually gathering in or along a street. **3. Street** A district identified with a specific profession. **4.** The streets of a city viewed as the scene of crime, poverty, or dereliction. **❖** *adj.* **1.** Near or giving passage to a street. **2a.** Taking place in the street. **b.** Living or making a living on the streets. **c.** Performing on the street. **d.** Crude; vulgar. **3.** Appropriate for wear or use in public. **—idiom: on** (or **in**) **the street 1.** Without a job; idle. **2.** Without a home; homeless. **3.** Out of prison; at liberty. [ME *strete* < OE *strǣt, strēt* < LLat. *strāta*, paved road < Lat., fem. p. part. of *sternere*, to stretch, extend, pave.]

street•car (strēt′kär′) *n.* A public vehicle operated on rails along a regular route, usu. through the streets of a city.

street hockey *n.* A variation of ice hockey played on pavement usu. with a ball instead of a puck.

street•lamp (strēt′lămp′) *n.* See **streetlight.**

street•light (strēt′līt′) *n.* One of a series of lights that are usu. attached to tall poles, spaced at intervals along a public street or roadway, and illuminated from dusk to dawn.

street name *n.* **1.** The name of a street. **2.** The name of a broker or brokerage firm as used when registering a security owned by a customer in order to simplify trading. **3.** An alternative or slang

streetcar
Brussels, Belgium

term for something, esp. an illegal drug. **4.** An alternative name that a person chooses or is given, esp. as used in inner city neighborhoods.

street-smart (strēt′smärt′) *adj.* Having or displaying street smarts.

street smarts *pl.n.* Shrewd awareness of how to survive in an often hostile urban environment.

street theater *n.* Dramatization of social and political issues, usu. enacted outside, as on the street or in a park.

street•walk•er (strēt′wô′kər) *n.* A prostitute, esp. one who solicits in the streets. **—street′walk′ing** *n.*

street•wise (strēt′wīz′) *adj.* Having street smarts.

strength (strĕngkth, strĕngth, strĕnth) *n.* **1.** The state, property, or quality of being strong. **2.** The power to resist attack; impregnability. **3.** The power to resist strain or stress; durability. **4.** The ability to maintain a moral or intellectual position firmly. **5.** Capacity or potential for effective action. **6a.** The number of people constituting a normal or ideal organization. **b.** Military capability in terms of personnel and materiel. **7a.** A source of power or force. **b.** One regarded as the embodiment of protective or supportive power; a support or mainstay. **c.** An attribute or quality of particular worth or utility; an asset. **8.** Degree of intensity, force, effectiveness, or potency in terms of a particular property, as: **a.** Degree of concentration, distillation, or saturation; potency. **b.** Operative effectiveness or power. **c.** Intensity, as of sound or light. **d.** Intensity or vehemence, as of emotion or language. **9.** Effective or binding force; efficacy: *the strength of an argument.* **10.** Firmness of or a continuous rising tendency in prices, as on the stock market. **11.** *Games* Power to take tricks derived from the value of cards held. **—idiom: on the strength of** On the basis of. [ME < OE *strengthu.*]

SYNONYMS *strength, power, might, energy, force* These nouns denote the capacity to act or work effectively. *Strength* refers especially to physical, mental, or moral robustness or vigor: "*enough work to do, and strength enough to do the work*" (Rudyard Kipling). *Power* is the ability to do something and especially to produce an effect: "*I do not think the United States would come to an end if we lost our power to declare an Act of Congress void*" (Oliver Wendell Holmes, Jr.). *Might* often implies abundant or extraordinary power: "*He could defend the island against the whole might of the German Air Force*" (Winston S. Churchill). *Energy* refers especially to a latent source of power: "*The same energy of character which renders a man a daring villain would have rendered him useful to society*" (Mary Wollstonecraft). *Force* is the application of power or strength: "*the overthrow of our institutions by force and violence*" (Charles Evans Hughes).

strength•en (strĕngk′thən, strĕng′-, strĕn′-) *v.* **-ened, -en•ing, -ens** *—tr.* To make strong or increase the strength of. *—intr.* To become strong or stronger. **—strength′en•er** *n.*

stren•u•ous (strĕn′yōō-əs) *adj.* **1.** Requiring great effort, energy, or exertion. **2.** Vigorously active; energetic or zealous. [< Lat. *strēnuus.*] **—stren′u•ous•ly** *adv.* **—stren′u•ous•ness** *n.*

strep (strĕp) *adj.* Streptococcal. **❖** *n.* Streptococcus.

strep throat *n.* A throat infection, often epidemic, caused by hemolytic streptococci and characterized by fever and inflammation of the tonsils.

strepto– *pref.* **1.** Twisted; twisted chain: *streptococcus.* **2.** Streptococcus: *streptokinase.* [< Gk. *streptos* < *strephein*, to turn.]

strep•to•ba•cil•lus (strĕp′tō-bə-sĭl′əs) *n., pl.* **-cil•li** (-sĭl′ī) Any of various gram-negative, rod-shaped, often pathogenic bacteria of the genus *Streptobacillus*, occurring in chains, esp. *S. moniliformis*, which causes a type of rat-bite fever.

strep•to•coc•cus (strĕp′tə-kŏk′əs) *n., pl.* **-coc•ci** (-kŏk′sī, -kŏk′ī) A round to ovoid, gram-positive, often pathogenic bacterium of the genus *Streptococcus* that occurs in pairs or chains and causes various diseases in humans, including scarlet fever and strep throat. **—strep′to•coc′cal, strep′to•coc′cic** (-kŏk′sĭk, -kŏk′ĭk) *adj.*

strep•to•kin•ase (strĕp′tō-kĭn′ās, -āz, -kī′nās, -nāz) *n.* A proteolytic enzyme produced by streptococci that is used medically to dissolve blood clots.

strep•to•my•ces (strĕp′tə-mī′sēz) *n., pl.* **streptomyces** Any of various actinomycetes of the genus *Streptomyces*, including several strains that produce antibiotics. [NLat. *Streptomycēs*, genus name : STREPTO– + Gk. *mukēs*, fungus.]

strep•to•my•cin (strĕp′tə-mī′sĭn) *n.* An antibiotic, $C_{21}H_{39}O_{12}N_7$, obtained from the actinomycete *Streptomyces griseus*, and used against bacterial infections such as tuberculosis. [STREPTOMYC(ES) + –IN.]

strep•to•thri•cin (strĕp′tə-thrī′sĭn, -thrĭs′ĭn) *n.* Any of a group of antibiotics obtained from the actinomycete *Streptomyces lavendulae* and active against bacteria and some fungi. [NLat. *Streptothrix, Streptothric-*, genus of bacteria (STREPTO– + Gk. *thrix, trikh-*, hair) + –IN.]

stress (strĕs) *n.* **1.** Importance, significance, or emphasis placed on something. See Syns at **emphasis. 2.** *Linguistics* **a.** The relative force with which a sound or syllable is spoken. **b.** The emphasis placed on the sound or syllable spoken most forcefully in a word or phrase. **3a.** The relative force of sound or emphasis given a syllable or word in accordance with a metrical pattern. **b.** A syllable having strong relative emphasis in a metrical pattern. **4.** Accent or a mark representing such emphasis or force. **5.** *Physics* **a.** An applied force or system of forces that tends to strain or deform a body. **b.** The internal resistance of a body to such an applied force or system of forces. **6a.** A mentally or emotionally disruptive or upsetting condition occurring in response to adverse external influences and usu. characterized by increased heart rate, a rise in blood pressure, muscular tension, irritability, and depression. **b.** A stimulus or circumstance causing such a condition. **7.** A state of extreme difficulty, pressure, or strain. ❖ *tr.v.* **stressed, stress•ing, stress•es 1.** To place emphasis on: *stressed safety.* **2.** To give prominence to (a syllable or word) in pronouncing or in accordance with a metrical pattern. **3.** To subject to physical or mental pressure, tension, or strain. **4.** To subject to mechanical pressure or force. **5.** To construct so as to withstand a specified stress. ***—phrasal verb:* stress out** *Informal* To subject to or undergo extreme stress, as from working too much. [ME *stresse,* hardship, partly < *destresse* (< OFr.; see DISTRESS) and partly < OFr. *estrece,* narrowness, oppression (< VLat. **strictia* < Lat. *strictus,* p. part. of *stringere,* to draw tight).]

stressed-out (strĕsd′out′) *adj. Informal* Undergoing or suffering the effects of extreme stress.

stress fracture *n.* A fracture of bone caused by repeated application of a heavy load, such as the constant pounding on a surface by runners, gymnasts, and dancers.

stress•ful (strĕs′fəl) *adj.* Full of or tending to cause stress. **—stress′ful•ly** *adv.* **—stress′ful•ness** *n.*

stres•sor (strĕs′ər) *n.* An agent, condition, or other stimulus that causes stress to an organism.

stress test *n.* A graded test to measure an individual's heart rate and oxygen intake during strenuous physical exercise.

stretch (strĕch) *v.* **stretched, stretch•ing, stretch•es** *—tr.* **1.** To lengthen, widen, or distend. **2.** To cause to extend from one place to another or across a given space. **3.** To make taut; tighten. **4.** To reach or put forth; extend: *stretched out his hand.* **5a.** To extend (oneself or one's limbs, for example) to full length. **b.** To extend (oneself) when lying down. **c.** To put to torture on the rack. **6.** To wrench or strain (a muscle, for example). **7a.** To extend or enlarge beyond the usual or proper limits. **b.** To subject to undue strain. **8a.** To expand in order to fulfill a larger function: *stretch a paycheck.* **b.** To increase the quantity of by admixture or dilution. **9.** To prolong: *stretch out an argument.* **10.** *Informal* To fell by a blow. *—intr.* **1.** To become lengthened, widened, or distended. **2.** To extend or reach over a distance or area or in a given direction. **3.** To lie down at full length: *stretched out for a nap.* **4.** To extend one's muscles or limbs, as on awakening. **5.** To extend over a given period of time. ❖ *n.* **1.** The act of stretching or the state of being stretched. **2.** The extent or scope to which something can be stretched; elasticity. **3.** A continuous or unbroken length, area, or expanse. **4.** A straight section of a racecourse or track, esp. the section leading to the finish line. **5a.** A continuous period of time. **b.** *Slang* A term of imprisonment. **c.** *Informal* The last stage of an event, period, or process. **6.** *Baseball* The movement in which a pitcher raises both hands to the height of the head and then lowers them to the waist for a short pause before pitching the ball, used esp. when runners are on base. ❖ *adj.* **1.** Made of an elastic material that stretches easily. **2.** Of, relating to, or being a vehicle, such as a limousine, having an extended seating area. ***—idiom:* stretch (one's) legs** To go for a walk, esp. after a lengthy period of sitting. [ME *strecchen* < OE *streccan.*] **—stretch′a•bil′i•ty** *n.* **—stretch′a•ble** *adj.*

stretch•er (strĕch′ər) *n.* **1.** A litter, usu. of canvas stretched over a frame, for the sick, wounded, or dead. **2.** One that stretches, such as the wooden framework on which canvas is stretched for an oil painting. **3.** A usu. horizontal tie beam or brace serving to support or extend a framework. **4.** A brick or stone laid parallel to the face of a wall so that only its long side is showing.

stretch mark *n.* A shiny line on the skin of the abdomen, breasts, thighs, or buttocks caused by the stretching and weakening of elastic tissues, as during pregnancy.

stretch-out (strĕch′out′) *n.* **1a.** The act of stretching out. **b.** The condition of being stretched out. **c.** An extension or prolongation. **2.** An increase in the work required of industrial workers without a commensurate pay increase.

stretch receptor *n.* A sensory receptor in a muscle that responds to the stretching of tissue.

stretch runner *n.* A runner or racehorse that makes a strong effort in the last stretch of a race.

stretch•y (strĕch′ē) *adj.* **-i•er, -i•est 1.** Capable of being stretched: *a stretchy fabric.* **2.** Tending to stretch excessively.

stret•ta (strĕt′ə) *n., pl.* **stret•te** (strĕt′ā) or **stret•tas** See **stretto** 2. [Ital., fem. of *stretto,* stretto. See STRETTO.]

stret•to (strĕt′ō) *n., pl.* **stret•ti** (strĕt′ē) or **stret•tos** *Music* **1.** A close succession or overlapping of statements of the subject in a fugue, esp. in the final section. **2.** A final section, as of an opera, having an acceleration in tempo to produce a climax. [Ital., narrow, stretto < Lat. *strictus,* strict. See STRICT.]

streu•sel (stro͞o′zəl) *n.* A crumblike topping for coffee cakes and rich breads, made of flour, sugar, butter, cinnamon, and sometimes chopped nutmeats. [Ger., streusel < MHGer. *ströusel,* something strewn < *ströuwen,* to sprinkle < OHGer. *strowwen.*]

strew (stro͞o) *tr.v.* **strewed, strewn** (stro͞on) or **strewed, strew•ing, strews 1.** To spread here and there; scatter: *strewed flowers down the aisle.* **2.** To cover (an area) with things scattered or sprinkled. **3.** To be or become dispersed over (a surface). **4.** To spread (something) over a wide area; disseminate. [ME *strewen* < OE *strēowian.*]

stri•a (strī′ə) *n., pl.* **stri•ae** (strī′ē) **1.** A thin narrow groove or channel. **2.** A thin line or band, esp. one of several that are parallel or close together. [Lat.]

stri•ate (strī′āt′) *tr.v.* **-at•ed, -at•ing, -ates** To mark with striae or striations. ❖ *adj.* also **stri•at•ed** (-ā′tĭd) **1.** Marked with striae; striped, grooved, or ridged. **2.** Consisting of a stria or striae. [< Lat. *striātus,* furrowed < *stria,* furrow. See STRIA.]

stri•a•tion (strī-ā′shən) *n.* **1.** The state of being striated or having striae. **2.** One of a number of parallel lines or scratches on the surface of a rock that were inscribed by rock fragments embedded in the base of a glacier as it moved across the rock. **3.** The form taken by striae. **4.** A stria.

strick•en (strĭk′ən) *v.* A past participle of **strike.** ❖ *adj.* **1.** Struck or wounded, as by a projectile. **2a.** Overwhelmingly afflicted, as by disease, trouble, or painful emotion. **b.** Incapacitated; disabled. **3.** Having the contents made even with the top of a measuring device or container; level.

strick•le (strĭk′əl) *n.* **1.** An instrument used to level off grain or other material in a measure. **2.** A foundry tool used to shape a mold in sand or loam. **3.** A tool for sharpening scythes. [ME *strikelle,* perh. < OE *stricel,* teat, strickle.] **—strick′le** *v.*

strict (strĭkt) *adj.* **strict•er, strict•est 1.** Precise; exact: *a strict definition.* **2.** Complete; absolute: *strict loyalty.* **3.** Kept within narrowly specific limits. **4.** Rigorous in discipline. **5.** Exacting in enforcement, observance, or requirement: *strict standards.* See Syns at **severe. 6.** Conforming completely to rule, principle, or condition: *a strict vegetarian.* **7.** *Botany* Stiff, narrow, and upright. [ME *stricte,* narrow, small < Lat. *strictus,* tight, strict, p. part. of *stringere,* to draw tight. See **streig-** in App.] **—strict′ly** *adv.* **—strict′ness** *n.*

stric•ture (strĭk′chər) *n.* **1.** A restraint, limit, or restriction. **2.** An adverse remark or criticism; censure. **3.** *Pathology* An abnormal narrowing of a duct or passage. [ME, an abnormal narrowing of a bodily part < LLat. *strictūra,* contraction < Lat. *strictus,* p. part. of *stringere,* to draw tight. See STRICT.]

stride (strīd) *v.* **strode** (strōd), **strid•den** (strĭd′n), **strid•ing, strides** *—intr.* **1.** To walk with long steps, esp. in a hasty or vigorous way. **2.** To take a single long step, as in passing over an obstruction. **3.** To stand or sit astride; straddle. *—tr.* **1.** To walk with long steps on, along, or over. **2.** To step over or across. **3.** To be astride of; straddle. ❖ *n.* **1.** The act of striding. **2a.** A single long step. **b.** The distance traveled in such a step. **3a.** A single coordinated movement of the four legs of a horse or other animal, completed when the legs return to their initial relative position. **b.** The distance traveled in such a movement. **4.** A step of progress; an advance. Often used in the plural. ***—idioms:* hit (one's) stride 1.** To achieve a steady effective pace. **2.** To attain a maximum level of competence. **take in stride** To cope with calmly, without a break in routine. [ME *striden* < OE *strīdan.*] **—strid′er** *n.*

stri•dent (strīd′nt) *adj.* Loud, harsh, grating, or shrill; discordant. [Lat. *strīdēns, strīdent-,* pr. part. of *strīdere,* to make harsh sounds, ult. of imit. orig.] **—stri′dence, stri′den•cy** *n.* **—stri′dent•ly** *adv.*

stride piano *n.* A style of jazz piano playing in which the right hand plays the melody and the left hand alternates between the bass notes on the strong beats and chords on the weak ones. [< *stride bass.*] **—stride pianist** *n.*

stri•dor (strī′dər, -dôr′) *n.* **1.** A harsh, shrill, grating, or creaking sound. **2.** *Pathology* A harsh high-pitched sound in inhalation or exhalation. [Lat. *strīdor* < *strīdere,* to make harsh sounds, ult. of imit. orig.]

strid•u•late (strĭj′ə-lāt′) *v.* **-lat•ed, -lat•ing, -lates** *—intr.* To produce a shrill grating, chirping, or hissing sound by rubbing body parts together, as certain insects do. *—tr.* To produce by rubbing body parts together. **—strid′u•la′tion** *n.* **—strid′u•la•to′ry** (-lə-tôr′ē, -tōr′ē) *adj.*

strid•u•lous (strĭj′ə-ləs) *adj.* **1.** Characterized by or making a shrill grating sound or noise. **2.** Relating to or characterized by stridor. [< Lat. *strīdulus* < *strīdere,* to make harsh sounds, ult. of imit. orig.] **—strid′u•lous•ly** *adv.*

strife (strīf) *n.* **1.** Heated, often violent dissension; bitter conflict. **2.** A struggle, fight, or quarrel. **3.** Contention or competition between rivals. **4.** *Archaic* Earnest endeavor or striving. [ME *strif* < OFr. *estrit, estrif* < Frankish **strīd.*]

strig•il (strĭj′əl) *n.* An instrument used in ancient Greece and Rome for scraping the skin after a bath. [Lat. *strigilis.*]

stri•gose (strī′gōs′) *adj.* **1.** *Zoology* Marked with fine close-set grooves, ridges, or streaks. **2.** *Botany* Having stiff, straight, closely appressed hair: *strigose leaves.* [NLat. *strigōsus* < *striga,* bristle < Lat., windrow, furrow.]

strike (strīk) *v.* **struck** (strŭk), **struck** or **strick•en** (strĭk′ən), **strik•ing, strikes** *—tr.* **1a.** To hit sharply, as with the hand, the fist, or a weapon. **b.** To inflict (a blow). **2.** To penetrate or pierce. **3a.** To collide with or crash into. **b.** To cause to come into violent or forceful contact: *She struck her knee against the desk.* **c.** To

ă	pat	oi	boy
ā	pay	ou	out
âr	care	o͝o	took
ä	father	o͞o	boot
ĕ	pet	ŭ	cut
ē	be	ûr	urge
ĭ	pit	th	thin
ī	pie	*th*	this
îr	pier	hw	which
ŏ	pot	zh	vision
ō	toe	ə	about, item
ô	paw		

Stress marks:
′ (primary);
′ (secondary), as in
lexicon (lĕk′sĭ-kŏn′)

thrust (a weapon, for example) in or into someone or something. **d.** To damage or destroy, as by forceful contact. **4.** To make a military attack on; assault. **5.** To afflict suddenly, as with a disease or impairment. **6.** To cause to become by or as if by a blow: *struck him dead.* **7a.** To snap at or seize (a bait). **b.** To hook (a fish that has taken the bait) by a pull on the line. **8.** To wound by biting. Used esp. of a snake. **9.** To form by stamping, printing, or punching. **10.** To produce or play by manipulating strings or keys. **11.** To indicate by a percussive or chiming sound: *The clock struck nine.* **12.** To produce as if by playing a musical instrument: *The report struck a positive note.* **13a.** To produce by friction or a blow: *struck fire from the flints.* **b.** To produce flame, light, or a spark from by friction: *strike a match.* **14.** To remove or separate with or as if with a blow. **15.** To eliminate or expunge. **16a.** To come upon; discover: *struck gold.* **b.** To come to; attain: *finally struck the main trail.* **17a.** To fall upon; shine on. **b.** To become audible to. **18.** To affect keenly or forcibly; impress. **19.** To enter the mind of: *an idea struck me suddenly.* **20a.** To cause (a strong emotion) to penetrate deeply. **b.** To affect or overcome with strong emotion. **21a.** To make and confirm the terms of (a bargain). **b.** To achieve (a balance, for example) by careful weighing or reckoning. **22.** To take on or assume (a pose, for example). **23.** *Nautical* **a.** To haul down (a mast or sail). **b.** To lower (a flag or sail) in salute or surrender. **c.** To lower (cargo) into a hold. **24.** To remove (theatrical properties, a set, or technical equipment) from a stage. **25.** To dismantle and pack up for departure. **26.** To undertake a strike against (an employer). **27a.** To level or even (a measure, as of grain). **b.** To smooth or shape with a strickle. **28a.** To send (plant roots) out or down. **b.** To cause (a plant cutting) to take root. —*intr.* **1.** To deal a blow or blows with or as if with the fist or a weapon; hit. **2.** To aim a stroke or blow. **3.** To make contact suddenly or violently; collide. **4.** To begin a military attack. **5.** To penetrate or pierce. **6.** To take bait. **7.** To dart or shoot suddenly forward in an attempt to inflict a bite or wound. Used of snakes and wild animals. **8.** To set out or proceed, esp. in a new direction: *struck off into the woods.* **9.** To begin to move: *The horse struck into a gallop.* **10a.** To send out roots. **b.** To sprout. **11a.** To indicate the time by making a percussive or chiming sound. **b.** To become indicated by percussive or chiming sounds: *The hour has struck.* **12.** To become ignited. **13.** To discover something suddenly or unexpectedly. **14.** To fall, as light or sound. **15.** To have an effect; make an impression. **16.** To engage in a strike against an employer. **17.** To interrupt by pushing oneself forward. **18.** To strive diligently for a specific technical rating in the US Navy. ❖ *n.* **1.** An act or a gesture of striking. **2.** An attack, esp. a military air attack on a cluster of targets. **3a.** A cessation of work by employees in support of demands made on their employer, as for higher pay or improved conditions. **b.** A temporary stoppage of normal activity undertaken as a protest. **4.** A sudden achievement or valuable discovery, as of a precious mineral. **5a.** The taking of bait by a fish. **b.** A pull on a fishing line indicating this. **6.** A quantity of coins or medals struck at the same time. **7.** *Baseball* **a.** A pitched ball that is counted against the batter, typically one that is swung at and missed, fouled off, or judged to have passed through the strike zone. **b.** A perfectly thrown ball. **8.** An unfavorable condition, circumstance, or characteristic; a disadvantage. **9.** An unlawful act, esp. one that results in a conviction. **10.** *Sports* The knocking down of all the pins in bowling with the first bowl of a frame. **11.** The taking root and growing of a plant cutting. **12.** *Geology* The course or bearing of a structural surface, such as an inclined bed, as it intersects a horizontal plane. **13.** The removal of all properties, sets, and technical equipment following a final performance, as of a play or concert. **14.** A strickle. ***—phrasal verbs:* strike down 1.** To cause to fall by a blow. **2.** To incapacitate or kill. **3.** To render ineffective; cancel. **strike out 1.** To begin a course of action. **2.** To set out energetically. **3.** *Baseball* **a.** To pitch three strikes to (a batter), putting the batter out. **b.** To be struck out. **4.** To fail in an endeavor. **strike up 1a.** To start to play music or sing. **b.** To start to play or sing (something). **c.** To cause to start to play or sing. **2.** To initiate or begin. ***—idioms:* on strike** Engaged in a work stoppage. **strike hands** To conclude a bargain or reach an agreement. **strike it rich** *Informal* To have sudden financial success. [ME *striken* < OE *strīcan*, to stroke.]

strike•bound (strīkʹbound′) *adj.* Closed, immobilized, or slowed down by a strike: *a strikebound airline.*

strike•break•er (strīkʹbrā′kər) *n.* One who works or provides an employer with workers during a strike. **—strikeʹbreak′ing** *n.*

strike•out (strīkʹout′) *n. Baseball* An out made by a batter charged with three strikes and credited to the pitcher.

strike•o•ver (strīkʹō′vər) *n.* The act or an instance of typing a character over one already typed.

strike price *n.* The fixed price at which the owner of an option can purchase, in the case of a call, or sell, in the case of a put, the underlying security or commodity.

strik•er (strīʹkər) *n.* **1.** One who strikes, as an employee on strike. **2.** One that strikes, as the clapper in a bell. **3a.** A harpoon. **b.** One who uses a harpoon; a harpooner. **4.** An enlisted person in usu. intensive training for a naval technical rating. **5.** *Sports* A forward on a soccer team.

strike-slip fault (strīkʹslĭp′) *n. Geology* A fault in which surfaces on opposite sides of the fault plane have moved horizontally and parallel to the strike of the fault.

strike zone *n. Baseball* The area over home plate through which a pitch must pass to be called a strike, roughly between the batter's armpits and knees.

strik•ing (strīʹkĭng) *adj.* Arresting the attention and producing a vivid impression on the sight or the mind. **—strikʹing•ly** *adv.* **—strikʹing•ness** *n.*

striking price *n.* The price at which a put or call option may be exercised.

Strind•berg (strĭndʹbûrg, strĭnʹ-), **(Johan) August** 1849–1912. Swedish writer whose plays include *Miss Julie* (1888). **—Strind•bergʹi•an** *adj.*

string (strĭng) *n.* **1.** A cord usu. made of fiber, used for fastening, tying, or lacing. **2.** Something configured as a long, thin line. **3.** A plant fiber. **4.** A set of objects threaded together. **5.** A series of similar or related acts, events, or items arranged or falling in or as if in a line. **6.** *Computer Science* A set of consecutive characters. **7.** *Informal* **a.** A set of animals, esp. racehorses, belonging to one owner; a stable. **b.** A scattered group of businesses under one ownership or management. **8.** *Sports* A group of players ranked according to ability on a team. **9.** *Music* **a.** A cord stretched on an instrument and struck, plucked, or bowed to produce tones. **b. strings** The section of a band or orchestra composed of stringed instruments. **c. strings** Stringed instruments or their players considered as a group. **10.** *Architecture* **a.** A stringboard. **b.** A stringcourse. **11.** *Games* The balk line in billiards. **12.** *Sports* A complete game consisting of ten frames in bowling. **13.** *Informal* A limiting or hidden condition. Often used in the plural: *a gift with no strings attached.* ❖ *v.* **strung** (strŭng), **string•ing, strings** —*tr.* **1.** To fit or furnish with strings or a string: *string a guitar.* **2.** To thread on a string. **3.** To arrange in a string or series. Often used with *out.* **4.** To fasten, tie, or hang with a string or strings. **5.** To stretch out or extend. **6.** To strip (vegetables) of fibers. —*intr.* **1.** To form strings or become stringlike. **2.** To extend or progress in a string, line, or succession. ***—phrasal verbs:* string along** *Informal* **1.** To go along with something; agree. **2.** To keep (someone) waiting or in uncertainty. **3.** To fool, cheat, or deceive. **string out** To draw out; prolong. **string up** *Informal* To kill (someone) by hanging. ***—idiom:* on a** (or **the**) **string** Under one's control or influence. [ME < OE *streng.*]

string bass (bās) *n.* See **double bass.**

string bean *n.* **1a.** A bushy or climbing tropical American plant *(Phaseolus vulgaris)* having narrow green edible pods. **b.** The pod of this plant. **2.** *Slang* A tall thin person.

string•board (strĭngʹbôrd′, -bōrd′) *n.* A board along the side of a staircase supporting or covering the ends of the steps.

string•course (strĭngʹkôrs′, -kōrs′) *n.* A horizontal band or molding set in the face of a building as a design element.

stringed (strĭngd) *adj. Music* **1.** Having strings. Often used in combination: *a six-stringed lute.* **2.** Produced by stringed instruments: *stringed chamber music.*

stringed instrument *n.* An instrument, such as a violin, viola, cello, or double bass, in which sound is produced by plucking, striking, or bowing taut strings.

strin•gen•do (strĭn-jĕnʹdō) *adj. Music* Played with an accelerating tempo. [Ital., gerund of *stringere*, to draw tight < Lat.] **—strin•genʹdo** *adv.*

strin•gent (strĭnʹjənt) *adj.* **1.** Imposing rigorous standards of performance; severe: *stringent safety measures.* **2.** Constricted; tight: *a stringent time limit.* **3.** Characterized by scarcity of money, credit restrictions, or other financial strain. [Lat. *stringēns, stringent-*, pr. part. of *stringere*, to draw tight. See **streig-** in App.] **—strinʹgen•cy** *n.* **—strinʹgent•ly** *adv.*

string•er (strĭngʹər) *n.* **1.** One that strings: *a stringer of beads.* **2.** *Architecture* **a.** A long heavy horizontal timber used as a support or connector. **b.** A stringboard. **3.** A horizontal timber supporting upright posts. **4.** *Sports* A member of a string or squad on a team. Often used in combination: *a first-stringer.* **5.** A part-time or freelance correspondent for the news media.

string•halt (strĭngʹhôlt′) *n.* A nervous disorder in horses marked by spasmodic movements in the hind legs that cause the feet to rise abnormally high. [STRING, tendon + HALT[2].]

string quartet *n.* **1.** An ensemble of four musicians playing stringed instruments, usu. two violins, a viola, and a cello. **2.** A composition for such a group.

string•y (strĭngʹē) *adj.* **-i•er, -i•est 1.** Consisting of, resembling, or containing strings or a string. **2.** Slender and sinewy; wiry. **3.** Forming strings, as a viscous liquid; ropy. **—stringʹi•ly** *adv.* **—stringʹi•ness** *n.*

strip[1] (strĭp) *v.* **stripped, strip•ping, strips** —*tr.* **1a.** To remove clothing or covering from. **b.** To deprive of (clothing or covering). **2.** To deprive of honors, rank, office, privileges, or possessions; divest. **3a.** To remove all excess detail from; reduce to essentials. **b.** To remove equipment, furnishings, or supplementary parts or attachments from. **4.** To clear of a natural covering or growth; make bare. **5.** To remove an exterior coating, as of paint, from. **6.** To remove the leaves from the stalks of. **7.** To dismantle (a firearm, for example) piece by piece. **8.** To damage or break the threads of (a screw, for example) or the teeth of (a gear). **9.** To press the last drops of milk from (a cow, for example). **10.** To rob of wealth or property; despoil. **11.** To mount (a photographic positive or negative) on paper to be used in making a printing plate. —*intr.* **1a.** To undress completely. **b.** To perform a striptease. **2.** To fall away or be removed; peel. ❖ *n.* A striptease. [ME *stripen* < OE *-strȳpan*, to plunder (in *bestrȳpan*, to plunder).] **—strip′pa•ble** *adj.*

strip² (strĭp) *n.* **1a.** A long narrow piece, usu. of uniform width: *a strip of paper.* **b.** A long narrow region of land or body of water. **2.** A comic strip. **3.** An airstrip. **4.** An area, as along a busy street or highway, lined with a great number and variety of commercial establishments. ❖ *tr.v.* **stripped, strip•ping, strips** To cut or tear into strips. [ME, perh. < MLGer. *strippe*, strap, thong.]

strip-crop•ping (strĭp′krŏp′ĭng) *n.* The growing of a cultivated crop, such as cotton, and a sod-forming crop, such as alfalfa, in alternating strips following the contour of the land, in order to minimize erosion.

stripe¹ (strīp) *n.* **1a.** A long narrow band distinguished, as by color or texture, from the surrounding material or surface. **b.** A textile pattern of parallel bands or lines on a contrasting background. **c.** A fabric having such a pattern. **2.** A strip of cloth or braid worn on a uniform to indicate rank, awards received, or length of service; a chevron. **3.** Sort; kind. ❖ *tr.v.* **striped, strip•ing, stripes** To mark with stripes or a stripe. [ME, poss. < MDu. or MLGer. *strīpe.*]

stripe² (strīp) *n.* A stroke or blow, as with a whip. [ME.]

striped (strīpt, strī′pĭd) *adj.* Having lines or bands of different color or texture.

striped bass (băs) *n.* A North American food and game fish *(Morone saxatilis)* chiefly of coastal waters, having dark longitudinal stripes along its sides.

strip•er (strī′pər) *n.* **1.** *Slang* A member of the armed forces, a cadet corps, or a commercial flight crew who wears stripes designating rank or length of service. Often used in combination: *a four-striper.* **2.** See **striped bass.**

strip•ing (strī′pĭng) *n.* **1.** The act or process of marking or decorating with stripes. **2a.** The stripes placed on something. **b.** A pattern of stripes.

strip•ling (strĭp′lĭng) *n.* An adolescent youth. [ME, poss. < *strip*, strip. See STRIP².]

strip mall *n.* A shopping complex containing a row of stores and restaurants that usu. open onto a common parking lot.

strip mine *n.* An open mine, esp. a coal mine, whose seams or outcrops run close to ground level and are exposed by the removal of topsoil and overburden.

strip-mine (strĭp′mīn′) *v.* **-mined, -min•ing, -mines** —*tr.* **1.** To mine (ore) from a strip mine. **2.** To subject to strip mining: *strip-mined the land.* —*intr.* To engage in strip mining. **—strip miner** *n.*

stripped-down (strĭpt′doun′) *adj.* Having only essential or minimal features; lacking anything extra.

strip•per (strĭp′ər) *n.* **1.** One that strips, as one that strips photographic negatives or positives. **2.** A chemical product for removing a surface covering, such as paint or varnish, from furniture or floors. **3.** One who performs a striptease. **4.** An oil well that produces ten barrels or fewer per day.

strip-search (strĭp′sûrch′) *tr.v.* **-searched, -search•ing, -search•es** To search (a person) for illegal articles by first requiring the removal of all clothing. **—strip search** *n.*

strip•tease (strĭp′tēz′) *n.* A performance, as in a burlesque act, in which a person slowly removes clothing, usu. to musical accompaniment. **—strip′teas′er** *n.*

strip•y (strī′pē) *adj.* **-i•er, -i•est** Marked with or suggestive of stripes; striped.

strive (strīv) *intr.v.* **strove** (strōv), **striv•en** (strĭv′ən) or **strived, striv•ing, strives 1.** To exert much effort or energy; endeavor. **2.** To struggle or fight forcefully; contend: *strive for justice.* [ME *striven* < OFr. *estriver* < *estrit, estrif*, quarrel. See STRIFE.] **—striv′er** *n.* **—striv′ing•ly** *adv.*

strobe (strōb) *n.* **1.** A strobe light. **2.** A stroboscope. **3.** A spot of higher than normal intensity in the sweep of an indicator, as on a radar screen, used as a reference mark.

strobe light *n.* A flash lamp that produces high-intensity short-duration light pulses by electric discharge in a gas.

stro•bi•la (strō-bī′lə) *n., pl.* **-lae** (-lē) A part or structure that buds to form a series of segments, as the main body part of a tapeworm. [NLat. < Gk. *strobilē*, twisted plug of lint < *strobilos*, pine cone. See STROBILUS.] **—stro•bi′lar** *adj.*

stro•bi•lus (strō-bī′ləs) also **stro•bile** (strō′bīl′, -bəl) *n., pl.* **-bi•li** (-bī′lī) or **-biles** A conelike structure, such as a pine cone, that consists of overlapping sporophylls spirally arranged along a central axis. [LLat., pine cone < Gk. *strobilos* < *strobos*, a whirling.]

stro•bo•scope (strō′bə-skōp′) *n.* Any of various instruments used to observe moving objects by making them appear stationary, esp. with pulsed illumination or mechanical devices that intermittently interrupt observation. [Gk. *strobos*, a whirling + -SCOPE.] **—stro′bo•scop′ic** (-skŏp′ĭk) *adj.* **—stro′bo•scop′i•cal•ly** *adv.*

stro•bo•tron (strō′bə-trŏn′) *n.* A gas-filled cathode-ray tube that produces bright flashes of light for a stroboscope.

strode (strōd) *v.* Past tense of **stride.**

Stro•heim (strō′hīm′), **Erich von** 1885–1957. Austrian-born Amer. actor and director who is best known for his roles in *La Grande Illusion* (1937) and *Sunset Boulevard* (1950).

stroke¹ (strōk) *n.* **1.** The act or an instance of striking, as with the hand; a blow or impact. **2a.** The striking of a bell or gong. **b.** The sound so produced. **c.** The time so indicated. **3.** A sudden action or process having a strong impact or effect. **4.** A sudden occurrence or result. **5.** A sudden severe attack, as of paralysis or sunstroke. **6.** A sudden loss of brain function caused by a blockage or rupture of a blood vessel to the brain, characterized by loss of muscular control, diminution or loss of sensation or consciousness, dizziness, or slurred speech. **7.** An inspired or effective idea or act. **8a.** A single uninterrupted movement, esp. when repeated or in a back-and-forth motion. **b.** Any of a series of movements of a piston from one end of the limit of its motion to another. **9a.** A single completed movement of the limbs and body, as in swimming. **b.** The manner or rate of executing such a movement. **10a.** The rower who sits nearest the coxswain or the stern and sets the tempo for the other rowers. **b.** The position occupied by this person. **11.** *Sports* **a.** A movement of the upper torso and arms for the purpose of striking a ball, as in golf. **b.** The manner of executing such a movement. **c.** A scoring unit in golf counted for such a movement. **12a.** A mark made by a writing or marking implement. **b.** The act of making such a mark. **c.** A printed line in a graphic character that resembles such a mark. **13.** A distinctive effect or deft touch. ❖ *v.* **stroked, strok•ing, strokes** —*tr.* **1a.** To mark with a single short line. **b.** To draw a line through; cancel: *stroked out the words.* **2.** To set the pace for (a rowing crew). **3.** To hit or propel (a ball, for example) with a smooth swing. —*intr.* **1.** To make or perform a stroke. **2.** To row at a particular rate per minute. [ME, prob. < OE **strāc.*]

stroke² (strōk) *tr.v.* **stroked, strok•ing, strokes 1.** To rub lightly, with or as if with the hand or something in it; caress. **2.** *Informal* To behave attentively or flatteringly toward, as to win over. ❖ *n.* A light caressing movement. [ME *stroken* < OE *strācian* < **strāc*, stroke.] **—strok′er** *n.*

stroke play *n.* See **medal play.**

stroll (strōl) *v.* **strolled, stroll•ing, strolls** —*intr.* **1.** To go for a leisurely walk. **2.** To travel from place to place seeking work or gain. —*tr.* To walk along or through at a leisurely pace. ❖ *n.* A leisurely walk. [Prob. Ger. dialectal *strollen*, var. of *strolchen* < *Strolch*, fortuneteller, vagabond, perh. < Ital. dialectal *strolegh* < Ital. *astròlogo*, astrologer, fortuneteller, ult. < Gk. *astrologos*, astronomer, astrologer. See ASTROLOGY.]

stroll•er (strō′lər) *n.* **1.** One who strolls. **2.** A light chairlike carriage with three of four wheels for transporting small children. **3.** An itinerant actor or performer. **4.** A vagabond.

stro•ma (strō′mə) *n., pl.* **-ma•ta** (-mə-tə) **1.** The connective tissue framework of an organ, gland, or other structure. **2.** The spongy colorless framework of a red blood cell or other cell. [LLat. *strōma*, mattress, covering < Gk., bed.] **—stro′mal** *adj.* **—stro•mat′ic** (-măt′ĭk) *adj.*

stro•mat•o•lite (strō-măt′l-īt′) *n.* A sedimentary structure of laminated carbonate or silicate rocks, produced over geologic time by the trapping of sediment by groups of microorganisms, esp. cyanobacteria. [LLat. *strōma*, *strōmat-*, covering; see STROMA + -LITE.] **—stro•mat′o•lit′ic** (-măt′l-ĭt′ĭk) *adj.*

Strom•bo•li (strŏm′bə-lē, strōm′bō-) An island of S Italy in the Lipari Is. off NE Sicily in the Tyrrhenian Sea. Its volcano, 926.6 m (3,038 ft), erupted violently in 1930 and 1966.

strong (strông) *adj.* **strong•er, strong•est 1a.** Physically powerful; capable of exerting great physical force. **b.** Marked by great physical power. **2.** In good or sound health; robust. **3.** Economically or financially sound or thriving. **4.** Having force of character, will, morality, or intelligence. **5.** Having or showing ability or achievement in a specified field. **6.** Capable of the effective exercise of authority. **7a.** Capable of withstanding force or wear; solid, tough, or firm. **b.** Having great binding strength. **8.** Not easily captured or defeated. **9.** Not easily upset; resistant to harmful or unpleasant influences. **10.** Having force or rapidity of motion. **11a.** Persuasive, effective, and cogent. **b.** Forceful and pointed; emphatic. **c.** Forthright and explicit, often offensively so. **12.** Extreme; drastic. **13.** Having force of conviction or feeling; uncompromising. **14.** Intense in degree or quality. **15a.** Having an intense or offensive effect on the senses: *strong light.* **b.** Clear and loud. **c.** Readily noticeable; remarkable. **d.** Readily detected or received: *a strong signal.* **16a.** Having a high concentration of an essential or active ingredient. **b.** Containing a considerable percentage of alcohol. **c.** Powerfully effective. **17.** Of or relating to a color having a high degree of saturation. **18.** Having a specified number of units or members: *100,000 strong.* **19.** Marked by steady or rising prices. **20.** *Linguistics* **a.** Of or relating to verbs in Germanic languages that form their past tense and their past participle by a change in stem vowel, sometimes adding the suffix *-(e)n*, to the participle, as *take, took, taken.* **b.** Of or relating to the inflection of nouns or adjectives in Germanic languages with endings that historically did not contain a suffix with an *n.* **21.** Stressed or accented in pronunciation or poetic meter. Used of a word or syllable. ❖ *adv.* In a strong, powerful, or vigorous manner; forcefully. [ME < OE *strang.*] **—strong′ish** *adj.* **—strong′ly** *adv.*

strong-arm (strông′ärm′) *Informal adj.* Using physical force or

strip-cropping

stroller

ă	pat	oi	boy
ā	pay	ou	out
âr	care	ŏŏ	took
ä	father	ōō	boot
ĕ	pet	ŭ	cut
ē	be	ûr	urge
ĭ	pit	th	thin
ī	pie	*th*	this
îr	pier	hw	which
ŏ	pot	zh	vision
ō	toe	ə	about, item
ô	paw		

Stress marks:
′ (primary);
′ (secondary), as in
lexicon (lĕk′sĭ-kŏn′)

coercion. ❖ *tr.v.* **-armed, -arm·ing, -arms** **1.** To use physical force or coercion against. **2.** To rob by force.

strong·box (strông′bŏks′) *n.* A stoutly made box or safe in which valuables are deposited.

strong force *n.* See **strong interaction.**

strong·hold (strông′hōld′) *n.* **1.** A fortified place or a fortress. **2a.** A place of survival or refuge. **b.** An area specially dominated or occupied by a group or marked by a quality.

strong interaction *n.* A fundamental interaction between elementary particles that causes protons and neutrons to bind together in the atomic nucleus.

strong·man (strông′măn′) *n.* **1.** A powerful influential political figure who exercises leadership and control by force. **2.** One who performs feats of strength, as at a circus.

strong-mind·ed (strông′mīn′dĭd) *adj.* **1.** Having a determined will. **2.** Having a vigorous, independent mind. **—strong′-mind′ed·ly** *adv.* **—strong′-mind′ed·ness** *n.*

strong·point (strông′point′) *n.* A military stronghold.

strong room *n.* A strongly built fireproof room designed for the safekeeping of money or valuables.

strong side *n.* *Football* The side of a formation having more players; the side on which the tight end is positioned.

strong suit *n.* **1.** A quality, activity, or skill in which a person excels. **2.** *Games* A long suit in a card game such as bridge that contains high cards.

stron·gyle also **stron·gyl** (strŏn′jĭl′, -jəl) *n.* Any of various nematode worms of the family Strongylidae, often parasitic in the gastrointestinal tract of mammals, esp. horses. [NLat. *Strongylus*, type genus < Gk. *strongulos*, round.]

stron·gy·lo·sis (strŏn′jə-lō′sĭs) *n.* Infestation with strongyles.

stron·ti·an·ite (strŏn′chē-ə-nīt′, -shə-nīt′) *n.* A gray to yellowish-green ore of strontium, SrCO₃. [< *strontian*, strontianite, ultimately after *Strontian* in west-central Scotland.]

stron·ti·um (strŏn′chē-əm, -tē-əm, -shəm) *n. Symbol* **Sr** A soft, easily oxidized metallic element that ignites spontaneously in air when finely divided and is used in pyrotechnic compounds and various alloys. Atomic number 38; atomic weight 87.62; melting point 769°C; boiling point 1,384°C; specific gravity 2.54; valence 2. See table at **element.** [< NLat. *strontia*, strontium oxide < E. *strontian*. See STRONTIANITE.] **—stron′tic** (-tĭk) *adj.*

strontium 90 *n.* The strontium isotope with mass 90, having a half-life of 28 years, that is a high-energy beta emitter and constitutes a radiation hazard in fallout.

strop (strŏp) *n.* **1.** A strap, esp. a short rope whose ends are spliced together to make a ring. **2.** A flexible strip of leather or canvas used for sharpening a razor. ❖ *tr.v.* **stropped, strop·ping, strops** To sharpen (a razor) on a strop. [ME *strope*, band of leather, prob. < OE, thong for an oar < Lat. *stroppus*, twisted cord < Gk. *strophos* < *strephein*, to turn.]

stro·phan·thin (strō-făn′thĭn) *n.* A toxic glycoside or mixture of glycosides obtained from the seeds of certain plants of the genus *Strophanthus*, esp. *S. kombé*, used medicinally as a cardiac stimulant. [NLat. *Strophanthus*, genus name (Gk. *strophos*, twisted cord; see STROP + Gk. *anthos*, flower) + –IN.]

stro·phe (strō′fē) *n.* **1a.** The first of a pair of stanzas of alternating form on which the structure of a given poem is based. **b.** A stanza containing irregular lines. **2.** The first division of the triad constituting a section of a Pindaric ode. **3a.** The first movement of the chorus in classical Greek drama while turning from one side of the orchestra to the other. **b.** The part of a choral ode sung while this movement is executed. [Gk. *strophē*, a turning, stanza < *strephein*, to turn.] **—stro′phic** (strō′fĭk, strŏf′ĭk) *adj.*

stro·phoid (strō′foid′) *n.* The curve traced out by points P and P′ which lie on lines through a fixed point A where the midpoint M of PP′ is on a fixed line and the absolute value |PM| = the absolute value |P′M| = the absolute value |MO|, where O is the projection of A onto that fixed line. [Gk. *strophos*, twisted cord (< *strephein*, to turn) + –OID.]

stroph·u·lus (strŏf′yə-ləs) *n., pl.* **-li** (-lē) A disease, common esp. among children, sometimes associated with intestinal disturbances and characterized by a papular eruption of the skin. [NLat. < Gk. *strophos*, twisted cord < *strephein*, to turn.]

strop·py (strŏp′ē) *adj.* **-pi·er, -pi·est** *Chiefly British* Easily offended or annoyed; ill-tempered or belligerent. [Perh. alteration of OBSTREPEROUS.]

stroud (stroud) *n.* A coarse woolen cloth or blanket. [After *Stroud*, an urban district of SW-central England.]

strove (strōv) *v.* Past tense of **strive.**

struck (strŭk) *v.* Past tense and a past participle of **strike.** ❖ *adj.* Affected or shut down by a labor strike.

struc·tur·al (strŭk′chər-əl) *adj.* **1a.** Of, relating to, having, or characterized by structure. **b.** Affecting structure. **2.** Used in or necessary to building. **3.** Concerned with or resulting from political or esp. economic structure. **4.** *Geology* Of or relating to the structure of rocks and other aspects of the earth's crust. **5.** *Biology* Of or relating to organic structure; morphological. **6.** Relating to or concerned with systematic structure in a field of study, such as linguistics or the behavioral sciences. ❖ *n.* A part of a structure that bears a weight or the structural piece used for such a part. **—struc′tur·al·ly** *adv.*

structural formula *n.* A chemical formula that shows how the

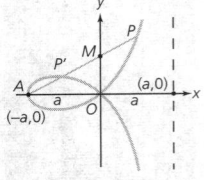

atoms and bonds in a molecule are arranged.

structural gene *n.* A gene that determines the amino acid sequence of a protein.

struc·tur·al·ism (strŭk′chər-ə-lĭz′əm) *n.* **1.** A method of analyzing phenomena, as in linguistics or psychology, marked by contrasting the elemental structures of the phenomena in a system of binary opposition. **2.** A school that advocates and employs such a method. **—struc′tur·al·ist** *adj. & n.*

struc·tur·al·ize (strŭk′chər-ə-līz′) *tr.v.* **-ized, -iz·ing, -iz·es** To form, organize, or incorporate into a structure. **—struc′tur·al·i·za′tion** (-ə-lĭ-zā′shən) *n.*

structural linguistics *n.* (*used with a sing. verb*) **1.** A method of synchronic linguistic analysis employing structuralism, esp. in contrasting those formal structures, such as phonemes or sentences, that make up systems, such as phonology or syntax. **2.** A school of such a method of linguistics, developed in the United States from the 1930s to the 1950s.

structural steel *n.* Steel shaped for use in construction.

struc·ture (strŭk′chər) *n.* **1.** Something made up of a number of parts that are held or put together in a particular way. **2.** The way in which parts are arranged or put together to form a whole; makeup. **3.** The interrelation or arrangement of parts in a complex entity. **4.** Something constructed, such as a building. **5.** *Biology* **a.** The arrangement or formation of the tissues, organs, or other parts of an organism. **b.** An organ or other part of an organism. ❖ *tr.v.* **-tured, -tur·ing, -tures** To give form or arrangement to. [ME, the process of building < Lat. *strūctūra* < *strūctus*, p. part. of *struere*, to construct.]

struc·tured (strŭk′chərd) *adj.* **1.** Having a well-defined structure or organization. **2.** *Psychology* Having a limited number of correct or nearly correct answers. Used of a test.

stru·del (strōōd′l, shtrōōd′l) *n.* A pastry made with fruit or cheese rolled up in layers of thin sheets of dough and then baked. [Ger. < MHGer., whirlpool.]

strug·gle (strŭg′əl) *v.* **-gled, -gling, -gles** *—intr.* **1.** To exert muscular energy, as against a material force or mass: *struggled with the heavy load.* **2.** To be strenuously engaged with a problem, task, or undertaking. **3.** To make a strenuous effort; strive. **4.** To contend or compete. **5.** To progress with difficulty. *—tr.* To move or place (something) with an effort. ❖ *n.* **1.** The act of struggling. **2.** Strenuous effort; striving. **3.** Combat; strife. [ME *struglen*.] **—strug′gler** *n.* **—strug′gling·ly** *adv.*

strum (strŭm) *v.* **strummed, strum·ming, strums** *—tr.* **1.** To play (a stringed musical instrument) by stroking or brushing the strings. **2.** To play (music) in this way. *—intr.* To strum a stringed instrument. ❖ *n.* The act or sound of strumming. [Perh. imit.] **—strum′mer** *n.*

stru·ma (strōō′mə) *n., pl.* **-mae** (-mē) or **-mas** **1a.** See **scrofula.** **b.** See goiter. **2.** *Botany* A cushionlike swelling at a moss capsule base. [Lat. *strūma*, scrofulous tumor.] **—stru·mat′ic** (-măt′ĭk), **stru′mose′** (-mōs′), **stru′mous** (-məs) *adj.*

Struma A river of W Bulgaria and NE Greece flowing c. 348 km (216 mi) to the Aegean Sea.

strum·pet (strŭm′pĭt) *n.* A woman prostitute. [ME.]

strung (strŭng) *v.* Past tense and past participle of **string.** ❖ *adj.* Tense or exhausted.

strung-out (strŭng′out′) *adj. Slang* **1a.** Stupefied from ingestion of or withdrawal from a drug. **b.** Addicted to a drug. **2a.** Debilitated from long drug use. **b.** Physically or emotionally exhausted.

strut (strŭt) *v.* **strut·ted, strut·ting, struts** *—intr.* To walk with pompous bearing; swagger. *—tr.* **1.** To display in order to impress others. **2a.** To provide (a structure) with a strut or struts. **b.** To brace or separate with or as if with a strut. ❖ *n.* **1.** A pompous self-important gait. **2.** A structural element used to brace or strengthen a framework by resisting longitudinal compression. **—idiom: strut (one's) stuff** *Slang* To behave or perform ostentatiously; show off. [ME *strouten*, to stand out < OE *strūtian*, to stand out stiffly.] **—strut′ter** *n.*

stru·thi·ous (strōō′thē-əs, -thē-) *adj.* Of, relating to, or resembling an ostrich or a related bird; ratite. [< LLat. *strūthiō*, ostrich < L.Gk. *strouthiōn* < Gk. *strouthos*.]

strych·nine (strĭk′nīn′, -nĭn, -nēn′) *n.* An extremely poisonous crystalline alkaloid, $C_{21}H_{22}O_2N_2$, derived from nux vomica and related plants and used as a poison for rodents and other pests and topically in medicine as a stimulant for the central nervous system. [Fr. < NLat. *Strychnos*, genus name < Lat. *strychnon*, a kind of nightshade < Gk. *strukhnon*.]

strych·nin·ism (strĭk′nĭ-nĭz′əm, -nĭ-, -nē-) *n.* A pathological condition induced by strychnine poisoning.

Stu·art (stōō′ərt, styōō′-) Ruling house of Scotland (1371–1603) and of England and Scotland (1603–49 and 1660–1714).

Stuart, Charles Edward Known as "the Young Pretender." 1720–88. Pretender to the British throne who led the last Jacobite rising (1745–46) but was defeated in battle and fled to France.

Stuart, Gilbert Charles 1755–1828. Amer. painter particularly known for his portraits of George Washington.

Stuart, Henry See Lord **Darnley.**

Stuart, James Ewell Brown Known as "Jeb." 1833–64. Amer. Confederate general who was mortally wounded during the Wilderness Campaign (1864).

Stuart, James (Francis) Edward Known as "the Old Pretender."

1688–1766. Pretender to the British throne who made two unsuccessful attempts to take the throne (1708–15).

stub (stŭb) *n.* **1.** The usu. short end remaining after something bigger has been used up. **2.** Something cut short or arrested in development. **3a.** The part of a check or receipt retained as a record. **b.** The part of a ticket returned as a voucher of payment. ❖ *tr.v.* **stubbed, stub•bing, stubs 1a.** To pull up (weeds) by the roots. **b.** To clear (a field) of weeds. **2.** To strike (one's toe or foot) against something accidentally. **3.** To snuff out (a cigarette butt) by crushing. [ME *stubbe,* tree stump < OE *stybb.*]

stub•ble (stŭb′əl) *n.* **1.** The short stiff stalks of grain or hay left after harvest. **2.** Something similar, esp. the short growth of hair that eventually protrudes from the skin after shaving. [ME *stuble* < OFr. *estuble* < Lat. *stupula, stupla,* var. of *stipula,* straw.] **—stub′bled** *adj.* **—stub′bly** *adj.*

stub•born (stŭb′ərn) *adj.* **-er, -est 1a.** Unreasonably, often perversely unyielding; bullheaded. **b.** Firmly resolved or determined; resolute. See Syns at **obstinate. 2.** Characterized by perseverance; persistent. **3.** Difficult to treat or deal with. [ME *stuborn.*] **—stub′born•ly** *adv.* **—stub′born•ness** *n.*

Stubbs (stŭbz), **William** 1825–1901. British historian and prelate known for his study of the constitutional history of medieval England.

stub•by (stŭb′ē) *adj.* **-bi•er, -bi•est 1a.** Having the nature of or suggesting a stub, as in shortness or thickness. **b.** Having a short, stocky build; thickset. **2.** Short and blunt, as from much use. **3.** Covered with or made of stubs. **4.** Short and bristly. **—stub′bi•ly** *adv.* **—stub′bi•ness** *n.*

stub nail *n.* A short thick nail.

stuc•co (stŭk′ō) *n., pl.* **-coes** or **-cos 1.** A durable finish for exterior walls, usu. composed of cement, sand, and lime, and applied while wet. **2.** A fine plaster for interior wall ornamentation, such as moldings. **3.** A plaster or cement finish for interior walls. **4.** Stuccowork. ❖ *tr.v.* **-coed, -co•ing, -coes** or **-cos** To finish or decorate with stucco. [Ital., of Gmc. orig.]

stuc•co•work (stŭk′ō-wûrk′) *n.* Ornamental work or moldings or a finish done in stucco. **—stuc′co•work′er** *n.*

stuck (stŭk) *v.* Past tense and past participle of **stick.**

stuck-up (stŭk′ŭp′) *adj. Informal* Snobbish; conceited.

stud¹ (stŭd) *n.* **1.** An upright post in the framework of a wall for supporting sheets of lath, wallboard, or similar material. **2.** A small knob, nail head, or rivet fixed in and slightly projecting from a surface. **3a.** A small ornamental button mounted on a short post for insertion through an eyelet, as on a dress shirt. **b.** A buttonlike earring mounted on a slender post, as of gold or steel, for wearing in a pierced earlobe. **4a.** Any of various protruding pins or pegs in machinery, used mainly as a support or pivot. **b.** One of a number of small metal cleats embedded in a snow tire to increase traction on slippery or snowy roads. **5.** A metal crosspiece used as a brace in a link, as in a chain cable. ❖ *tr.v.* **stud•ded, stud•ding, studs 1.** To provide with or construct with studs or a stud. **2.** To set with studs or a stud. **3.** To be scattered over. [ME *stode* < OE *studu.* See **stā-** in App.]

stud² (stŭd) *n.* **1a.** A group of animals, esp. horses, kept for breeding. **b.** A male animal, such as a stallion, kept for breeding. **c.** A stable or farm where these animals are kept. **2.** *Slang* **a.** A man regarded as virile and sexually active. **b.** A man regarded as attractive **3.** *Games* Stud poker. ***—idiom:* at stud** Available or offered for breeding. Used of animals. [ME *stod,* establishment for breeding horses < OE *stōd.* See **stā-** in App.]

stud•book (stŭd′bo͝ok′) *n.* A book registering the pedigrees of thoroughbred animals, esp. horses.

stud•ding (stŭd′ĭng) *n.* **1a.** The wood framework of a wall or partition. **b.** Lumber cut for studs. **2.** Something with which a surface is studded.

stud•ding•sail (stŭn′səl, stŭd′ĭng-sāl′) *n.* A narrow rectangular sail set from an extension of a yard of a square-rigged ship. [?]

stu•dent (sto͞od′nt, styo͞od′-) *n.* **1.** One who is enrolled or attends classes at a school, college, or university. **2a.** One who makes a study of something. **b.** An attentive observer. [ME, alteration (influenced by Lat. *studēre,* to study) of *studient, studiant* < OFr. *estudiant,* one who studies < pr. part. of *estudier,* to study < Med.Lat. *studiāre* < Lat. *studium,* study. See STUDY.]

student lamp *n.* A reading lamp having a flexible adjustable neck and intended for use on a desk.

student teacher *n.* A college student pursuing a degree in education who teaches in a classroom under the supervision of an experienced, certified teacher. **—student teaching** *n.*

student union *n.* A building on a college campus with facilities for social and organizational activities.

stud•fish (stŭd′fĭsh′) *n., pl.* **studfish** or **-fish•es** Either of two small, brightly colored topminnows *(Fundulus catenatus* or *F. stellifer)* of the southeast United States. [STUD¹ + FISH.]

stud•horse also **stud horse** (stŭd′hôrs′) *n.* A stallion kept for breeding.

stud•ied (stŭd′ēd) *adj.* **1.** Resulting from deliberation and careful thought. **2.** Lacking spontaneity; contrived. **3.** Learned; knowledgeable. **—stud′ied•ly** *adv.* **—stud′ied•ness** *n.*

stu•di•o (sto͞o′dē-ō, styo͞o′-) *n., pl.* **-os 1.** An artist's workroom. **2.** A photographer's establishment. **3.** An establishment where an art is taught or studied. **4a.** A room, building, or group of buildings where movies, television shows, or radio programs are produced. **b.** A room or building where tapes and records are produced. **5.** A company that produces films. **6.** A studio apartment. [Ital. < Lat. *studium,* eagerness, application. See STUDY.]

studio apartment *n.* A small apartment usu. consisting of one main living space, a small kitchen, and a bathroom.

studio couch *n.* A couch that can be made to serve as a double bed by sliding the frame of a cot from beneath it.

stu•di•ous (sto͞o′dē-əs, styo͞o′-) *adj.* **1a.** Given to diligent study. **b.** Conducive to study. **2.** Marked by steady attention and effort; assiduous. **3.** Giving or evincing careful regard; heedful. **4.** Deliberate; contrived. [ME < Lat. *studiōsus* < *studium,* eagerness. See STUDY.] **—stu′di•ous•ly** *adv.* **—stu′di•ous•ness** *n.*

stud poker *n.* Poker in which the first round of cards, and often the last, is dealt face down and the others face up. [Prob. short for *studhorse poker.*]

stud•work (stŭd′wûrk′) *n.* **1.** Work ornamented or covered with studs. **2.** The supportive framework, as of a wall.

stud•y (stŭd′ē) *n., pl.* **-ies 1a.** The act or process of studying. **b.** The pursuit of knowledge, as by observation or research. **2.** Attentive scrutiny. **3.** A branch of knowledge. **4. studies** A branch or department of learning: *African studies.* **5a.** A work, such as a thesis, that results from studious endeavor. **b.** A literary work on a given subject. **c.** A preliminary sketch, as for a work of art. **6.** *Music* A composition intended as a technical exercise. **7.** A state of mental absorption. **8.** A room intended or equipped for studying or writing. **9.** One who memorizes something, esp. a performer who memorizes a part: *a quick study.* ❖ *v.* **-ied, -y•ing, -ies** *—tr.* **1.** To apply one's mind purposefully to the acquisition of knowledge or understanding of (a subject). **2.** To read carefully. **3.** To memorize. **4.** To take (a course) at a school. **5.** To inquire into; investigate. **6.** To examine closely; scrutinize. **7.** To give careful thought to; contemplate: *study the next move.* *—intr.* **1.** To apply oneself to learning, esp. by reading. **2.** To pursue a course of study. **3.** To ponder; reflect. [ME *studie* < OFr. *estudie* < Lat. *studium* < *studēre,* to study.]

study hall *n.* **1.** A schoolroom reserved for study. **2.** A period set aside for study.

stuff (stŭf) *n.* **1.** The material out of which something is made or formed; substance. **2.** The essential substance or elements; essence. **3.** *Informal* **a.** Unspecified material. **b.** Household or personal articles considered as a group. **c.** Worthless objects. **4.** *Slang* Specific talk or actions. **5.** *Sports* **a.** The control a player has over a ball, esp. to give it spin, english, curve, or speed. **b.** The result of such control. **6.** Special capability. **7.** *Chiefly British* Woven material, esp. woolens. **8.** *Slang* Money; cash. **9.** *Slang* A drug, esp. one that is illegal or habit-forming. ❖ *v.* **stuffed, stuff•ing, stuffs** *—tr.* **1a.** To pack tightly; cram. **b.** To block (a passage); plug. **c.** *Basketball* To block (a shot or an opponent who is shooting), esp. before the ball is released. **2.** To place forcefully into a container or space; thrust. **3a.** To fill with an appropriate stuffing. **b.** To fill (an animal skin) for mounting or display. **4.** To cram with food. **5.** To fill (the mind). **6.** To put fraudulent votes into (a ballot box). **7.** To apply a preservative and softening agent to (leather). *—intr.* To overeat; gorge. ***—idiom:* stuff (one's) face** *Slang* To eat greedily. [ME < OFr. *estoffe* < *estoffer,* to equip, of Gmc. orig.]

stuffed shirt (stŭft) *n. Informal* A person regarded as pompous or stiff.

stuff•er (stŭf′ər) *n.* **1.** One that stuffs. **2.** A flier, insert, or enclosure that is mailed with a bill or other item.

stuff•ing (stŭf′ĭng) *n.* **1.** Padding put in cushions and upholstered furniture. **2.** Food put into the cavity of a piece of meat or a vegetable that has been hollowed out.

stuffing box *n.* An enclosure containing packing to prevent leakage around a moving machine part.

stuff•y (stŭf′ē) *adj.* **-i•er, -i•est 1.** Insufficiently ventilated; close. **2.** Having the respiratory passages blocked. **3a.** Dull; boring. **b.** Rigidly adhering to standards of conduct; strait-laced. **—stuff′i•ly** *adv.* **—stuff′i•ness** *n.*

stull (stŭl) *n.* **1.** A supporting prop in a mine. **2.** A platform braced against the sides of a work area in a mine. [Prob. < Ger. *Stollen* < MHGer. *stolle,* prop, support < OHGer. *stollo.* See **stel-** in App.]

stul•ti•fy (stŭl′tə-fī′) *tr.v.* **-fied, -fy•ing, -fies 1.** To render useless or ineffectual; cripple. **2.** To cause to appear stupid, inconsistent, or ridiculous. [LLat. *stultificāre,* to make foolish : Lat. *stultus,* foolish; see **stel-** in App. + Lat. *-ficāre,* -fy.] **—stul′ti•fi•ca′tion** (-fĭ-kā′shən) *n.* **—stul′ti•fi′er** *n.*

stum (stŭm) *n.* **1.** Unfermented or partly fermented grape juice; must. **2.** Vapid wine renewed by an admixture of stum. ❖ *tr.v.* **stummed, stum•ming, stums** To ferment (vapid wine) by adding stum. [Du. *stom,* dumb, stum < MDu.]

stum•ble (stŭm′bəl) *v.* **-bled, -bling, -bles** *—intr.* **1a.** To miss one's step; trip and almost fall. **b.** To proceed unsteadily or falteringly; flounder. See Syns at **blunder. c.** To act or speak falteringly or clumsily. **2.** To make a mistake; blunder. **3.** To fall into evil ways. **4.** To come upon accidentally or unexpectedly. *—tr.* To cause to stumble. ❖ *n.* **1.** The act of stumbling. **2.** A mistake or blunder. [ME *stumblen,* prob. of Scand. orig.] **—stum′bler** *n.* **—stum′bling•ly** *adv.*

stuccowork

ă	pat	oi	boy
ā	pay	ou	out
âr	care	o͝o	took
ä	father	o͞o	boot
ĕ	pet	ŭ	cut
ē	be	ûr	urge
ĭ	pit	th	thin
ī	pie	*th*	this
îr	pier	hw	which
ŏ	pot	zh	vision
ō	toe	ə	about, item
ô	paw		

Stress marks:
′ (primary);
′ (secondary), as in
lexicon (lĕk′sĭ-kŏn′)

stum·ble·bum (stŭm′bəl-bŭm′) *n. Slang* **1.** A person regarded as blundering or inept. **2.** A punch-drunk or second-rate prize-fighter.

stum·bling block (stŭm′blĭng) *n.* An obstacle or impediment.

stump (stŭmp) *n.* **1.** The part of a tree trunk left protruding from the ground after the tree has come down. **2.** A part, as of a tooth, remaining after the main part has been cut away, broken off, or worn down. **3a. stumps** *Informal* The legs. **b.** An artificial leg. **4.** A short thickset person. **5.** A heavy footfall. **6.** A place or occasion used for political oratory. **7.** A roll or piece of soft leather, paper, or similar material that is rubbed on the surface of a charcoal or pencil drawing to shade or soften it. **8.** *Sports* Any one of the three upright sticks in a cricket wicket. ❖ *v.* **stumped, stump·ing, stumps** —*tr.* **1.** To reduce to a stump. **2.** To clear stumps from. **3.** To stub (a toe or foot). **4.** To walk over heavily or clumsily. **5.** To traverse (a district) making political speeches. **6.** To shade (a drawing) with a stump. **7.** To challenge (someone); baffle. **8.** *Informal* To bring to a halt; baffle. —*intr.* **1.** To walk heavily or clumsily. **2.** To go about making political speeches. [ME *stumpe,* poss. < MLGer. *stump.*] —**stump′er** *n.* —**stump′i·ness** *n.* —**stump′y** *adj.*

stump·age (stŭm′pĭj) *n.* **1.** Standing timber regarded as a commodity. **2.** The value of standing timber. **3.** The right to cut standing timber.

stun (stŭn) *tr.v.* **stunned, stun·ning, stuns** **1.** To daze or render senseless, by or as if by a blow. **2.** To overwhelm or daze with a loud noise. **3.** To stupefy, as with the emotional impact of an experience; astound. ❖ *n.* A blow or shock that stupefies. [ME *stonen* < OFr. *estoner* < VLat. **extonāre* : Lat. *ex-,* ex- + Lat. *tonāre,* to thunder; see **(s)tenə-** in App.]

stung (stŭng) *v.* Past tense and past participle of **sting.**

stun gun *n.* A weapon designed to stun or temporarily immobilize a victim, esp. by delivering a high-voltage electric shock.

stunk (stŭngk) *v.* A past tense and the past participle of **stink.**

stun·ner (stŭn′ər) *n.* **1.** One that stuns, as **a.** An astounding, unexpected event. **b.** An exceptionally good-looking person.

stun·ning (stŭn′ĭng) *adj.* **1.** Causing or capable of causing emotional shock or loss of consciousness. **2.** Of a strikingly attractive appearance. **3a.** Impressive. **b.** Surprising.

stunt¹ (stŭnt) *tr.v.* **stunt·ed, stunt·ing, stunts** To check the growth or development of. ❖ *n.* **1.** One that stunts. **2.** One that is stunted. **3.** A plant disease that causes dwarfing. [< ME *stunnt,* foolish, short-witted, short (influenced by ON *stuttr,* short, dwarfish) < OE *stunt.*] —**stunt′ed·ness** *n.*

stunt² (stŭnt) *n.* **1.** A feat displaying unusual strength, skill, or daring. **2.** Something done to attract attention or publicity. ❖ *intr.v.* **stunt·ed, stunt·ing, stunts** To perform stunts or a stunt. [?]

stunt·man (stŭnt′măn′) *n.* A man who substitutes for a performer in scenes involving physical risk.

stunt·wom·an (stŭnt′wŏŏm′ən) *n.* A woman who substitutes for a performer in scenes involving physical risk.

stu·pa (stōō′pə) *n.* A dome-shaped monument, used to house Buddhist relics or to commemorate significant facts of Buddhism or Jainism. [Skt. *stūpaḥ,* tuft of hair, crown of head, summit, stupa.]

stupe (stōōp, styōōp) *n.* A hot, wet, often medicated cloth used as a compress. [ME < Lat. *stuppa, stūpa,* tow < Gk. *stuppē, stupeion,* course fiber of hemp or flax.]

stu·pe·fa·cient (stōō′pə-fā′shənt, styōō′-) *adj.* Inducing stupor. ❖ *n.* A drug that induces stupor. [Lat. *stupefaciēns, stupefacient-,* pr. part. of *stupefacere,* to stupefy. See STUPEFY.]

stu·pe·fac·tion (stōō′pə-făk′shən, styōō′-) *n.* **1a.** The act or an instance of stupefying. **b.** The state of being stupefied. **2.** Great astonishment or consternation. —**stu′pe·fac′tive** (-făk′tĭv) *adj.* & *n.*

stu·pe·fy (stōō′pə-fī′, styōō′-) *tr.v.* **-fied, -fy·ing, -fies** **1.** To dull the senses or faculties of. **2.** To amaze. [ME *stupefien* < OFr. *stupefier* < Lat. *stupefacere* : *stupēre,* to be stunned + *facere,* to make; see FACT.] —**stu′pe·fi′er** *n.*

stu·pen·dous (stōō-pĕn′dəs, styōō-) *adj.* **1.** Of astounding force, volume, degree, or excellence; marvelous. **2.** Amazingly large or great; huge. [< LLat. *stupendus,* stunning, gerundive of Lat. *stupēre,* to be stunned.] —**stu·pen′dous·ly** *adv.* —**stu·pen′dous·ness** *n.*

stu·pid (stōō′pĭd, styōō′-) *adj.* **-er, -est** **1.** Slow to learn or understand; obtuse. **2.** Tending to make poor decisions or careless mistakes. **3.** Marked by a lack of intelligence or care; foolish or careless: *a stupid mistake.* **4.** Dazed, stunned, or stupefied. **5.** Pointless; worthless: *quit the stupid job.* ❖ *n.* A stupid or foolish person. [Lat. *stupidus* < *stupēre,* to be stunned.] —**stu′pid·ly** *adv.* —**stu′pid·ness** *n.*

stu·pid·i·ty (stōō-pĭd′ĭ-tē, styōō-) *n., pl.* **-ties** **1.** The quality or condition of being stupid. **2.** A stupid act, remark, or idea.

stu·por (stōō′pər, styōō′-) *n.* **1.** A state of reduced or suspended sensibility. **2.** A state of mental numbness, as from shock; a daze. [ME < Lat. < *stupēre,* to be stunned.] —**stu′por·ous** *adj.*

stur·dy (stûr′dē) *adj.* **-di·er, -di·est** **1.** Having or showing rugged physical strength. **2.** Substantially made or built; stout: *sturdy canvas.* **3.** Marked by resoluteness or determination; firm. **4.** Vigorous or robust. ❖ *n.* See **gid.** [ME, stubborn, reckless, sturdy

< OFr. *estourdi,* p. part. of *estourdir,* to stun, perh. < VLat. **exturdīre,* to be giddy as a thrush : Lat. *ex-,* intensive pref.; see EX- + Lat. *turdus,* thrush.] —**stur′di·ly** *adv.* —**stur′di·ness** *n.*

stur·geon (stûr′jən) *n.* Any of various large freshwater and marine fishes of the family Acipenseridae of the Northern Hemisphere, having edible flesh and valued as a source of caviar. [ME < AN < OFr. *estourgeon,* of Gmc. orig.]

Sturm und Drang (shtōōrm′ ŏŏnt dräng′) *n.* **1.** Turmoil; ferment. **2.** A late-18th-century German romantic literary movement whose works typically depicted the struggles of a highly emotional individual against conventional society. [Ger., storm and stress, after *Sturm und Drang,* a drama by Friedrich Maximilian von Klinger (1752–1831).]

stut·ter (stŭt′ər) *intr. & tr.v.* **-tered, -ter·ing, -ters** To speak or utter with a spasmodic repetition or prolongation of sounds. ❖ *n.* The act or habit of stuttering. [Frequentative of dialectal *stut* < ME *stutten.*] —**stut′ter·er** *n.* —**stut′ter·ing·ly** *adv.*

Stutt·gart (stŭt′gärt′, stŏŏt′-, shtŏŏt′-) A city of SW Germany on the Neckar R. SSE of Heidelberg. Pop. 594,406.

Stuy·ve·sant (stī′vĭ-sənt), **Peter** *or* **Petrus** 1592?–1672. Dutch colonial governor of New Netherland (1646–64), who was forced to surrender the colony to England.

sty¹ (stī) *n., pl.* **sties** (stīz) **1.** An enclosure for swine. **2.** A filthy place. ❖ *tr. & intr.v.* **stied** (stīd), **sty·ing, sties** (stīz) To shut up in or live in a sty. [ME < OE *stig.*]

sty² *also* **stye** (stī) *n., pl.* **sties** *also* **styes** (stīz) An inflammation of one or more sebaceous glands of an eyelid. [Alteration of ME *styanye* : *styan,* sty (< OE *stīgend* < pr. part. of *stīgan,* to rise; see **steigh-** in App.) + *eye, ye,* eye; see EYE.]

styg·i·an *also* **Styg·i·an** (stĭj′ē-ən) *adj.* **1a.** Gloomy and dark. **b.** Infernal; hellish. **2.** Of or relating to the river Styx. [< Lat. *Stygius* < Gk. *Stugios* < *Stux, Stug-,* Styx.]

styl– *pref.* Variant of **stylo-.**

sty·lar (stī′lər, -lär′) *adj.* **1.** Of, relating to, or resembling a stylus. **2.** *Biology* Of or relating to a style.

sty·late (stī′lāt′) *adj.* Having a style or styles.

style (stīl) *n.* **1.** The way in which something is said, done, expressed, or performed. **2.** The combination of distinctive features of literary or artistic expression, execution, or performance characterizing a particular person, group, school, or era. **3.** Sort; type. **4.** A quality of imagination and individuality expressed in one's actions and tastes. **5a.** A comfortable and elegant mode of existence. **b.** A mode of living. **6a.** The fashion of the moment, esp. of dress; vogue. **b.** A particular fashion. **7.** A customary manner of presenting printed material, including punctuation, spelling, and typography. **8.** A form of address; a title. **9a.** An implement used for etching or engraving. **b.** A slender pointed writing instrument used by the ancients on wax tablets. **10.** The needle of a phonograph. **11.** The gnomon of a sundial. **12.** *Botany* The usu. slender part of a pistil, situated between the ovary and the stigma. **13.** *Zoology* A slender, tubular, or bristlelike process. **14.** *Medicine* A surgical probing instrument; a stylet. **15.** *Obsolete* A pen. ❖ *tr.v.* **styled, styl·ing, styles** **1.** To call or name; designate. **2.** To make consistent with rules of style. **3.** To give style to: *style hair.* [ME < OFr. < Lat. *stylus, stilus,* spike, pointed instrument used for writing, style. See STYLUS.] —**styl′er** *n.* —**styl′ing** *n.*

style·book (stīl′bŏŏk′) *n.* A book giving rules and examples, as of usage, punctuation, and typography, used esp. in preparation of copy for publication.

sty·let (stī-lĕt′, stī′lĭt) *n.* **1.** A slender pointed instrument or weapon. **2a.** A surgical probe. **b.** A fine wire that is run through a catheter, cannula, or hollow needle to keep it stiff or clear of debris. **3.** *Zoology* A small stiff needlelike organ or appendage. [Fr. < Ital. *stiletto,* stiletto. See STILETTO.]

sty·li (stī′lī) *n.* A plural of **stylus.**

sty·li·form (stī′lə-fôrm′) *adj.* Having the shape of a style; slender and pointed: *a styliform bone or appendage.*

styl·ish (stī′lĭsh) *adj.* Conforming to the current fashion: *stylish clothes.* —**styl′ish·ly** *adv.* —**styl′ish·ness** *n.*

styl·ist (stī′lĭst) *n.* **1.** One with an artful literary style. **2.** One who designs or consults on decorating, dress, or beauty styles. **3.** A hairdresser.

sty·lis·tic (stī-lĭs′tĭk) *adj.* Of or relating to style, esp. literary style. —**sty·lis′ti·cal·ly** *adv.*

sty·lis·tics (stī-lĭs′tĭks) *n.* (*used with a sing. verb*) The study of the use of elements of language style in particular contexts.

sty·lite (stī′līt′) *n.* One of a number of early Christian ascetics who lived unsheltered on the tops of high pillars. [LGk. *stūlītēs* < Gk. *stūlos,* pillar. See **stā-** in App.] —**sty·lit′ic** (-lĭt′ĭk) *adj.* —**styl′lit·ism** (stī′lĭ-tĭz-əm) *n.*

sty·lize (stī′līz′) *tr.v.* **-ized, -iz·ing, -iz·es** **1.** To restrict or make conform to a particular style. **2.** To represent conventionally. —**styl′i·za′tion** (stī′lĭ-zā′shən) *n.* —**styl′iz′er** *n.*

stylo– *or* **styli–** *or* **styl–** *pref.* Style: *stylopodium.* [< Lat. *stilus, stylus,* stake, stem, style. See STYLUS.]

sty·lo·bate (stī′lə-bāt′) *n. Architecture* The immediate foundation of a row of classical columns. [Lat. *stylobata* < Gk. *stūlobatēs* : *stūlos,* pillar; see **stā-** in App. + *bainein,* to walk; see **gʷā-** in App.]

sty·loid (stī′loid′) *adj.* **1.** Resembling a style in shape; slender and pointed: *styloid muscles.* **2.** *Anatomy* Of, relating to, or being

stupa
Shwedagon Stupa, Yangon, Myanmar

any of several slender pointed bone processes.

sty·lo·lite (stī′lə-līt′) *n.* A contact zone found along adjacent calcareous rock layers, appearing in cross section as a series of jagged interlocking up-and-down projections that resemble a suture. [Gk. *stūlos*, pillar; see STYLITE + −LITE.]

sty·lo·po·di·um (stī′lə-pō′dē-əm) *n., pl.* **-di·a** (-dē-ə) An enlargement at the base of the style of flowers in certain plants of the parsley family.

sty·lus (stī′ləs) *n., pl.* **-lus·es** or **-li** (-lī) **1.** A sharp pointed instrument used for writing, marking, or engraving. **2.** *Computer Science* A pointed instrument used as an input device on a pressure-sensitive screen. **3.** A phonograph needle. **4.** A sharp pointed tool used for cutting record grooves. [Lat., alteration of *stilus*.]

sty·mie also **sty·my** (stī′mē) *tr.v.* **-mied** (-mēd), **-mie·ing** also **-my·ing** (-mē-ĭng), **-mies** (-mēz) To thwart; stump. ❖ *n.* **1.** An obstacle or obstruction. **2.** *Sports* A situation in golf in which an opponent's ball obstructs the line of play of one's own ball on the putting green. [?]

styp·sis (stĭp′sĭs) *n.* The action or application of a styptic. [LLat. *stȳpsis* < Gk. *stūpsis* < *stūphein*, to contract.]

styp·tic (stĭp′tĭk) *adj.* **1.** Contracting the tissues or blood vessels; astringent. **2.** Tending to check bleeding by contracting the tissues or blood vessels; hemostatic. ❖ *n.* A styptic drug or substance. [ME *stiptik* < OFr. *stiptique* < Lat. *stȳpticus* < Gk. *stūptikos* < *stūphein*, to contract.]

styptic pencil *n.* A short medicated stick, often of alum, applied to a cut to check bleeding.

Styr (stîr) A river of NW Ukraine flowing c. 436 km (271 mi) N to the Pripet R.

sty·rene (stī′rēn′) *n.* A colorless oily liquid, $C_6H_5CH:CH_2$, the monomer for polystyrene. [Lat. *styrax*, storax; see STORAX + −ENE.]

Sty·ro·foam (stī′rə-fōm′) A trademark used for a light resilient polystyrene plastic.

Sty·ron (stī′rən), **William** b. 1925. Amer. writer whose novels include *Lie Down in Darkness* (1951).

Styx (stĭks) *n. Greek Mythology* The river in Hades across which the souls of the dead are ferried. [Lat. < Gk. *Stux.*]

su·a·ble (sōō′ə-bəl) *adj.* Subject to suit in a court of law. —**su′a·bil′i·ty** *n.*

sua·sion (swā′zhən) *n.* Persuasion. [Ult. < Lat. *suāsiō, suāsiōn-* < *suāsus*, p. part. of *suādēre*, to advise. See **swād-** in App.]

sua·sive (swā′sĭv) *adj.* Having the power to persuade or convince; persuasive. [Lat. *suāsus*, p. part. of *suādēre*, to advise; see SUASION + −IVE.] —**sua′sive·ly** *adv.* —**sua′sive·ness** *n.*

suave (swäv) *adj.* **suav·er, suav·est** Smoothly agreeable and courteous. [Fr., agreeable < OFr. < Lat. *suāvis*, delightful, sweet. See **swād-** in App.] —**suave′ly** *adv.* —**suave′ness, suav′i·ty** (swä′vĭ-tē) *n.*

sub¹ (sŭb) *n. Informal* **1.** See submarine 1. **2.** See submarine 2. See Regional Note at **submarine.**

sub² (sŭb) *Informal n.* A substitute. ❖ *intr.v.* **subbed, sub·bing, subs** To act as a substitute.

sub. *abbr.* **1.** subaltern **2a.** suburb **b.** suburban

sub− *pref.* **1.** Below; under; beneath: *subsoil.* **2a.** Subordinate; secondary: *subplot.* **b.** Subdivision: *subregion.* **3.** Less than completely or normally; nearly; almost: *subhuman.* [ME < Lat. < *sub*, under. See **upo** in App.]

sub·ac·id (sŭb-ăs′ĭd) *adj.* Somewhat sharp or acid in character: *subacid remarks.*

sub·a·cute (sŭb′ə-kyōōt′) *adj.* **1.** Somewhat or moderately acute: *subacute petals.* **2.** Between acute and chronic.

subacute scle·ros·ing panencephalitis (sklə-rō′sĭng) *n.* An often fatal degenerative disease of the brain occurring chiefly in young people and caused by a measles virus several years after the original infection. [*sclerosing* < *sclerose*, to harden, back-formation < SCLEROSED.]

sub·aer·i·al (sŭb-âr′ē-əl) *adj.* Located or occurring on or near the surface of the earth.

sub·al·pine (sŭb-ăl′pīn′) *adj.* **1.** Of or relating to regions at or near the foot of the Alps. **2.** Of, relating to, inhabiting, or growing in mountainous regions just below the timberline.

sub·al·tern (sŭb-ôl′tərn, sŭb′əl-tûrn′) *adj.* **1.** Lower in position or rank; secondary. **2.** *Chiefly British* Holding a military rank just below that of captain. **3.** *Logic* In the relation of a particular proposition to a universal with the same subject, predicate, and quality. [Fr. *subalterne* < OFr. < LLat. *subalternus* : Lat. *sub-, sub-* + Lat. *alternus*, alternate (< *alter*, other; see **al-** in App.).] —**sub·al′tern** *n.*

sub·al·ter·nate (sŭb-ôl′tər-nĭt) *adj.* **1.** Subordinate. **2.** *Botany*

Arranged in an alternating pattern but tending to become opposite. Used of leaves. —**sub·al′ter·na′tion** (-nā′shən) *n.*

sub·ant·arc·tic (sŭb′ănt-ärk′tĭk, -är′tĭk) *adj.* Of or resembling regions just north of the Antarctic Circle.

sub·a·que·ous (sŭb-ă′kwē-əs, -ăk′wē-) *adj.* **1.** Formed or adapted for underwater use or operation; submarine. **2.** Found or occurring underwater: *subaqueous organisms.*

sub·a·rach·noid (sŭb′ə-răk′noid) *adj.* Situated or occurring beneath the arachnoid membrane or between the arachnoid and the pia mater: *subarachnoid space.*

sub·arc·tic (sŭb-ärk′tĭk, -är′tĭk) *adj.* Of or resembling regions just south of the Arctic Circle.

sub·as·sem·bly (sŭb′ə-sĕm′blē) *n., pl.* **-blies** An assembled unit designed to be incorporated into a larger unit.

sub·a·tom·ic (sŭb′ə-tŏm′ĭk) *adj.* **1.** Of or relating to particles that are smaller than an atom. **2.** Having dimensions or participating in reactions characteristic of the constituents of the atom.

subatomic particle *n.* Any of various units of matter smaller than an atom, as an elementary particle or a hadron.

sub·au·di·tion (sŭb′ô-dĭsh′ən) *n.* **1.** The act of understanding and mentally supplying a word or thought that has been implied but not expressed. **2.** A word or thought supplied by subaudition. [LLat. *subaudītiō, subaudītiōn-* < *subaudītus*, p. part. of *subaudīre*, to supply an omitted word : Lat. *sub-, sub-* + Lat. *audīre*, to hear.]

sub·base (sŭb′bās′) *n.* The lowermost strip or molding of a baseboard.

sub·cab·i·net (sŭb′kăb′ə-nĭt) *adj.* Of, relating to, or being an administrative position below cabinet level.

sub·ce·les·tial (sŭb′sĭ-lĕs′chəl) *adj.* **1.** Lower than celestial; terrestrial. **2.** Mundane.

sub·cel·lu·lar (sŭb-sĕl′yə-lər) *adj.* **1.** Situated or occurring within a cell. **2.** Smaller in size than ordinary cells: *subcellular organisms.* **3.** Below the cellular level: *subcellular research.*

sub·cen·ter (sŭb′sĕn′tər) *n.* A secondary center, esp. a commercial or shopping area located away from the main business sector of a city. —**sub·cen′tral** (-trəl) *adj.*

sub·chas·er (sŭb′chā′sər) *n. Informal* A submarine chaser.

sub·class (sŭb′klăs′) *n.* **1.** A subdivision of a set or class. **2.** *Biology* A taxonomic category of related organisms ranking between a class and an order.

sub·cla·vi·an (sŭb-klā′vē-ən) *adj. Anatomy* **1.** Situated beneath the clavicle. **2.** Of or relating to a subclavian part. **3.** Of or relating to the subclavian artery or vein. [< NLat. *subclāvius* : SUB- + Lat. *clāvis*, key; see CLAVICLE.] —**sub·cla′vi·an** *n.*

subclavian artery *n.* A part of a major artery of the upper extremities or forelimbs that passes beneath the clavicle and is continuous with the axillary artery.

subclavian vein *n.* A part of a major vein of the upper extremities or forelimbs that passes beneath the clavicle and is continuous with the axillary vein.

sub·cli·max (sŭb-klī′măks′) *n.* A stage in the ecological succession of a plant or animal community immediately preceding a climax and often persisting because of the effects of fire, flood, or other conditions.

sub·clin·i·cal (sŭb-klĭn′ĭ-kəl) *adj.* Not manifesting characteristic clinical symptoms. Used of a disease or condition.

sub·com·pact (sŭb-kŏm′păkt′) *n.* An automobile smaller than a compact.

sub·com·po·nent (sŭb′kəm-pō′nənt) *n.* A portion of a component, esp. an electronic component; a subassembly.

sub·con·scious (sŭb-kŏn′shəs) *adj.* Not wholly conscious; partially or imperfectly conscious. ❖ *n.* The part of the mind below the level of conscious perception. —**sub·con′scious·ly** *adv.* —**sub·con′scious·ness** *n.*

sub·con·ti·nent (sŭb′kŏn′tə-nənt, sŭb-kŏn′-) *n.* **1.** A large landmass, such as India, that is part of a continent but is considered either geographically or politically as an independent entity. **2.** A large landmass, such as Greenland, smaller than a continent. —**sub′con·ti·nen′tal** (-nĕn′tl) *adj.*

sub·con·tract (sŭb-kŏn′trăkt′, sŭb′kŏn′trăkt) *n.* A contract that assigns some obligations of a prior contract to another party. ❖ *intr. & tr.v.* (sŭb-kŏn′trăkt′, sŭb′kən-trăkt′) **-tract·ed, -tract·ing, -tracts** To make a subcontract or a subcontract for.

sub·con·trac·tor (sŭb-kŏn′trăk′tər, sŭb′kən-trăk′tər) *n.* One that enters into a subcontract and assumes some of the obligations of the primary contractor.

sub·con·trar·y (sŭb-kŏn′trĕr′ē) *n., pl.* **-ries** *Logic* A proposition related to another in such a way that both may be true, but both cannot be false.

sub·cor·tex (sŭb-kôr′tĕks) *n., pl.* **-ti·ces** (-tĭ-sēz′) The portion

sub′ab·dom′i·nal *adj.*	**sub·cat′e·go·ry** *n.*	**sub·le′thal·ly** *adv.*	**sub·sam′ple** *n. & tr.v.*
sub′ap′i·cal *adj.*	**sub·com·mit′tee** *n.*	**sub·lim′it** *n.*	**sub·spe′cial·ist** *n.*
sub′ap′i·cal·ly *adv.*	**sub·cu′ta·ne·ous** *adj.*	**sub′mar′ket** *adj. & n.*	**sub·spe′cial·i·za′tion** *n.*
sub·a′que·ous *adj.*	**sub·di·rec′to·ry** *n.*	**sub·nu′cle·ar** *adj.*	**sub·spe′cial·ize** *intr.v.*
sub·ar′id *adj.*	**sub·dur′al** *adj.*	**sub′o·ce·an′ic** *adj.*	**sub·spe′cial·ty** *n.*
sub·ax′il·lar′y *adj.*	**sub′field′** *n.*	**sub′per·i·os′te·al** *adj.*	**sub·strat′o·sphere′** *n.*
sub′base′ment *n.*	**sub·freez′ing** *adj.*	**sub′pop·u·la′tion** *n.*	**sub′strat·o·spher′ic** *adj.*
sub′branch′ *n.*	**sub·gen′re** *n.*	**sub′re′gion** *n.*	**sub·top′ic** *n.*
sub·cal′i·ber *adj.*	**sub·le′thal** *adj.*	**sub′re′gion·al** *adj.*	**sub′tribe′** *n.*

of the brain immediately below the cerebral cortex. —**sub‧cor′ti‧cal** (-tĭ-kəl) *adj.* —**sub‧cor′ti‧cal‧ly** *adv.*

sub‧cul‧ture (sŭb′kŭl′chər) *n.* **1.** A subdivision of a cultural group differentiated by status, ethnicity, residence, religion, or other factors that unify the group and act on each member. **2.** One culture of microorganisms derived from another. —**sub‧cul′tur‧al** *adj.*

sub‧dea‧con (sŭb-dē′kən) *n.* **1.** A cleric ranking just below a deacon. **2.** A cleric who assists the deacon at High Mass.

sub‧deb (sŭb′dĕb′) *n. Informal* A subdebutante.

sub‧deb‧u‧tante (sŭb-dĕb′yə-tänt′) *n.* A teenage girl approaching her debut.

sub‧der‧mal (sŭb′dûr′məl) *adj.* Located or placed beneath the skin; subcutaneous. —**sub‧der′mal‧ly** *adv.*

sub‧di‧ac‧o‧nate (sŭb′dī-ăk′ə-nĭt) *n.* The office, order, or rank of subdeacon. [LLat. *subdiāconātus* < *subdiāconus*, subdeacon (partial transl. of L.Gk. *hupodiākonos*) : Lat. *sub-*, sub- + LLat. *diāconus*, deacon; see DEACON.] —**sub′di‧ac′o‧nal** *adj.*

sub‧di‧vide (sŭb′dĭ-vīd′, sŭb′dĭ-vīd′) *v.* **-vid‧ed, -vid‧ing, -vides** —*tr.* **1.** To divide a part or parts of into smaller parts. **2.** To divide into a number of parts, esp. to divide (land) into lots. —*intr.* To form into subdivisions. —**sub′di‧vid′er** *n.*

sub‧di‧vi‧sion (sŭb′dĭ-vĭzh′ən, sŭb′dĭ-vĭzh′ən) *n.* **1a.** The act or process of subdividing. **b.** A subdivided part. **2.** An area of real estate composed of subdivided lots. —**sub′di‧vi′sion‧al** *adj.*

sub‧dom‧i‧nant (sŭb-dŏm′ə-nənt) *n. Music* The fourth tone of a diatonic scale, next below the dominant. ❖ *adj.* **1.** *Zoology* Less than dominant; ranking below one that is dominant. **2.** *Ecology* Prevalent in a community but below the dominant in importance. Used of a species.

sub‧duc‧tion (səb-dŭk′shən) *n.* A geologic process in which one edge of one lithospheric plate is forced below the edge of another. [Fr. < Lat. *subductus*, p. part. of *subdūcere*, to draw away from below : *sub-*, sub- + *dūcere*, to lead; see **deuk-** in App.] —**sub‧duct′** *v.*

sub‧due (səb-dōō′, -dyōō′) *tr.v.* **-dued, -du‧ing, -dues 1.** To conquer and subjugate; vanquish. See Syns at **defeat. 2.** To quiet or bring under control by physical force or persuasion; make tractable. **3.** To make less intense or prominent; tone down. **4.** To bring (land) under cultivation. [ME *subduen,* alteration (influenced by Lat. *subdere,* to subject) of OFr. *suduire,* to seduce < Lat. *subdūcere,* to withdraw : *sub-*, away; see SUB- + *dūcere,* to lead; see **deuk-** in App.] —**sub‧du′a‧ble** *adj.* —**sub‧du′er** *n.*

sub‧em‧ployed (sŭb′ĕm-ploid′) *adj.* Of or relating to workers or segments of the paid labor force that are unemployed, underemployed, or underpaid. —**sub‧em‧ploy′ment** *n.*

sub‧en‧try (sŭb′ĕn′trē) *n., pl.* **-tries** An entry, such as one in a reference work, that is included within a main entry.

sub‧e‧qua‧to‧ri‧al (sŭb′ē-kwə-tôr′ē-əl, -tôr′-, -ĕk‧wə-) *adj.* Belonging to a region adjacent to an equatorial region.

su‧ber‧ic acid (sōō-bĕr′ĭk) *n.* A crystalline dibasic acid, HOOC(CH₂)₆COOH, used in the manufacture of plastics. [Fr. *subérique* < Lat. *sūber,* cork.]

su‧ber‧in (sōō′bər-ĭn) *n.* A waxy waterproof substance present in the cell walls of cork tissue in plants. [Fr. *subérine* : Lat. *sūber,* cork + Fr. *-ine,* adj. suff.; see -INE².]

su‧ber‧i‧za‧tion (sōō′bər-ĭ-zā′shən) *n.* Deposition of suberin on plant cell walls, converting them into cork tissue.

su‧ber‧ize (sōō′bə-rīz′) *tr.v.* **-ized, -iz‧ing, -iz‧es** To cause to undergo suberization. [< Lat. *sūber,* cork.]

sub‧fam‧i‧ly (sŭb′făm′ə-lē) *n., pl.* **-lies 1.** *Biology* A taxonomic category of related organisms ranking between a family and a genus. **2.** *Linguistics* A division of languages below a family and above a branch.

sub‧floor‧ing (sŭb′flôr′ĭng, -flôr′-) or **sub‧floor** (-flôr′, -flōr′) *n.* A rough floor over which a finished floor, flooring material, or carpet is laid.

sub‧fusc (sŭb-fŭsk′) *adj.* Of a dark, dull, or somber color. ❖ *n.* Dark, dull clothing. [Lat. *subfuscus,* brownish : *sub-*, sub- + *fuscus,* dark.]

sub‧ge‧nus (sŭb′jē′nəs) *n., pl.* **-gen‧e‧ra** (-jĕn′ər-ə) An occasionally used taxonomic category ranking between a genus and a species. —**sub‧ge‧ner′ic** (-jə-nĕr′ĭk) *adj.*

sub‧gla‧cial (sŭb-glā′shəl) *adj.* Formed or deposited beneath a glacier. —**sub‧gla′cial‧ly** *adv.*

sub‧grade (sŭb′grād′) *n.* The level layer of rock or earth upon which the foundation of a road or railway is laid.

sub‧group (sŭb′grōōp′) *n.* **1.** A distinct group within a group; a subdivision of a group. **2.** A subordinate group. **3.** *Mathematics* A group that is a subset of a group. ❖ *tr.v.* **-grouped, -group‧ing, -groups** To divide into subgroups.

sub‧gum (sŭb′gŭm′) *n.* A dish of Chinese origin made with mixed vegetables. [Chin. (Cantonese) *shap kam.*]

sub‧head (sŭb′hĕd′) or **sub‧head‧ing** (-ĭng) *n.* **1.** The heading or title of a subdivision of a printed subject. **2.** A subordinate heading or title.

sub‧hu‧man (sŭb-hyōō′mən) *adj.* **1.** Below the human race in evolutionary development. **2.** Regarded as not being fully human. —**sub‧hu′man** *n.*

Su‧bic Bay (sōō′bĭk) An inlet of the South China Sea off W-central Luzon, Philippines, W of Manila Bay.

sub‧in‧dex (sŭb-ĭn′dĕks) *n., pl.* **-di‧ces** (-dĭ-sēz′) **1.** *Mathematics* A subscript. **2.** *pl.* **-dic‧es** or **-dex‧es** An index of measurement based on relatively few variables, esp. a trade index based on the performance of a particular group or type of stocks.

sub‧in‧feu‧date (sŭb-ĭn-fyōō′dāt′) also **sub‧in‧feud** (-fyōōd′) *tr.v.* **-dat‧ed, -dat‧ing, -dates** also **-feud‧ed, -feud‧ing, -feuds** To lease (lands) by subinfeudation.

sub‧in‧feu‧da‧tion (sŭb′ĭn-fyōō-dā′shən) *n.* **1.** The sublease of a portion of a feudal estate by a vassal to a subtenant who pays fealty to the vassal. **2.** The lands so leased. —**sub‧in‧feu′da‧to′ry** (-fyōō′də-tôr′ē, -tōr′ē) *adj.*

sub‧ir‧ri‧gate (sŭb-ĭr′ĭ-gāt′) *tr.v.* **-gat‧ed, -gat‧ing, -gates** To irrigate from beneath, as by underground pipes. —**sub‧ir′ri‧ga′tion** *n.*

su‧bi‧to (sōō′bē-tō′) *adv. Music* Quickly; suddenly. [Ital. < Lat. *subitō* < neut. ablative sing. of *subitus,* sudden < p. part. of *subīre,* to come secretly. See SUDDEN.]

subj. *abbr.* **1.** subject **2.** subjective **3.** subjunctive

sub‧ja‧cent (sŭb-jā′sənt) *adj.* **1.** Located beneath or below; underlying. **2.** Lying lower but not directly beneath. [Lat. *subiacēns, subiacent-,* pr. part. of *subiacēre,* to lie below : *sub-*, sub- + *iacēre,* to lie.] —**sub‧ja′cen‧cy** *n.*

sub‧ject (sŭb′jĭkt) *adj.* **1.** Being under the power or authority of another or others. **2.** Prone; disposed: *subject to getting sick.* **3.** Likely to incur or receive; exposed: *subject to misinterpretation.* **4.** Contingent or dependent: *a vacation subject to the weather.* ❖ *n.* **1.** One who is under the rule of another or others, esp. one who owes allegiance to a government or ruler. **2a.** One concerning which something is said or done. **b.** Something treated or indicated in a work of art. **c.** *Music* A theme of a composition, esp. of a fugue. **3.** A course or area of study. **4.** A basis for action; a cause. **5a.** One that experiences or is subjected to something. **b.** One that is the object of medical or scientific study. **c.** One who is under surveillance. **6.** *Grammar* The noun, noun phrase, or pronoun in a sentence or clause that denotes the doer of the action or what is described by the predicate and that in some languages can be identified by its position in simple sentences and in other languages by inflectional endings. **7.** *Logic* The term of a proposition about which something is affirmed or denied. **8.** *Philosophy* **a.** The essential nature or substance of something as distinguished from its attributes. **b.** The mind or thinking part as distinguished from the object of thought. ❖ *tr.v.* (səb-jĕkt′) **-ject‧ed, -ject‧ing, -jects 1.** To submit for consideration. **2.** To submit to the authority of someone or something. **3.** To expose to something: *subjected to infection.* **4.** To cause to experience something: *subjected to cold.* **5.** To subjugate; subdue. [ME < OFr. < Lat. *subiectus* < p. part. of *subicere,* to subject : *sub-*, sub- + *iacere,* to throw.] —**sub‧jec′tion** (səb-jĕk′shən) *n.*

SYNONYMS subject, matter, topic, theme These nouns denote the principal idea or point of a speech, a piece of writing, or an artistic work. *Subject* is the most general: "*Well, honor is the subject of my story*" (Shakespeare). *Matter* refers to the material that is the object of thought or discourse: "*This distinction seems to me to go to the root of the matter*" (William James). A *topic* is a subject of discussion or argument: "*They would talk of . . . other fashionable topics, such as pictures, taste, Shakespeare*" (Oliver Goldsmith). *Theme* refers especially to an idea, point of view, or perception that is developed in a work of art: "*To produce a mighty book, you must choose a mighty theme*" (Herman Melville).

sub‧jec‧tive (səb-jĕk′tĭv) *adj.* **1a.** Proceeding from or taking place in a person's mind rather than the external world: *a subjective decision.* **b.** Particular to a given person; personal: *subjective experience* **2.** Moodily introspective. **3.** Existing only in the mind; illusory. **4.** *Psychology* Existing only within the experiencer's mind. **5.** *Medicine* Of, relating to, or being a symptom or condition perceived by the patient and not by the examiner. **6.** Expressing or bringing into prominence the individuality of the artist or author. **7.** *Grammar* Relating to or being the nominative case. **8.** Relating to the real nature of something; essential. —**sub‧jec′tive‧ly** *adv.* —**sub‧jec′tive‧ness, sub‧jec‧tiv′i‧ty** (sŭb′jĕk‧tĭv′ĭ-tē) *n.*

subjective idealism *n. Philosophy* The theory that nature has no objective existence independent of the minds that perceive it.

sub‧jec‧tiv‧ism (səb-jĕk′tə-vĭz′əm) *n.* **1.** The quality of being subjective. **2a.** The doctrine that all knowledge is restricted to the conscious self and its sensory states. **b.** A theory or doctrine that emphasizes the subjective elements in experience. **3.** Any of various theories holding that the only valid standard of judgment is that of the individual. —**sub‧jec′tiv‧ist** *n.* —**sub‧jec‧tiv‧is′tic** *adj.*

subject matter *n.* Matter under consideration in a written work or speech; a theme.

sub‧join (səb-join′) *tr.v.* **-joined, -join‧ing, -joins** To add at the end; append. [Obsolete Fr. *subjoindre* < Lat. *subiungere* : *sub-*, sub- + *iungere,* to join; see **yeug-** in App.]

sub‧join‧der (səb-join′dər) *n.* Something subjoined. [< SUBJOIN (on the model of REJOINDER).]

sub ju‧di‧ce (sŭb jōō′dĭ-sē′, sōōb yōō′dĭ-kā′) *adv.* Under judicial deliberation; before a judge or court of law. [Lat. *sub iūdice* : *sub,* beneath, before + *iūdice,* ablative of *iūdex,* judge.]

sub·ju·gate (sŭb′jə-gāt′) *tr.v.* **-gat·ed, -gat·ing, -gates 1.** To bring under control; conquer. See Syns at **defeat. 2.** To make subservient; enslave. [ME *subjugaten* < Lat. *subiugāre, subiugāt-* : *sub-*, sub- + *iugum*, yoke; see **yeug-** in App.] —**sub′ju·ga′tion** *n.* —**sub′ju·ga′tor** *n.*

sub·junc·tion (səb-jŭngk′shən) *n.* **1.** The act of subjoining or the condition of being subjoined. **2.** Something subjoined. [LLat. *subiūnctiō, subiūnctiōn-* < Lat. *subiūnctus*, p. part. of *subiungere*, to subjoin. See SUBJOIN.]

sub·junc·tive (səb-jŭngk′tĭv) *adj.* Of, relating to, or being a mood of a verb used in some languages for contingent or hypothetical action, action viewed subjectively, or grammatically subordinate statements. ❖ *n.* **1.** The subjunctive mood. **2.** A subjunctive construction. See Usage Note at **if.** [LLat. *subiūnctīvus* < Lat. *subiūnctus*, p. part. of *subiungere*, to subjoin, subordinate (transl. of Gk. *hupotaktikos*, subordinate, subjunctive). See SUBJOIN.]

sub·king·dom (sŭb′kĭng′dəm) *n.* A taxonomic category of related organisms that is a major division of a kingdom.

sub·late (sŭb′lāt′) *tr.v.* **-lat·ed, -lat·ing, -lates** *Logic* To negate, deny, or contradict. [< Lat. *sublātus*, p. part. of *tollere*, to take away : *sub-*, sub- + *lātus*, taken; see **telə-** in App.]

sub·lease (sŭb′lēs′) *tr.v.* **-leased, -leas·ing, -leas·es 1.** To sublet (property). **2.** To rent (property) under a sublease. ❖ *n.* (sŭb′lēs′) A lease of property granted by a lessee.

sub·let (sŭb′lĕt′) *tr.v.* **-let, -let·ting, -lets 1.** To rent (property one holds by lease) to another. **2.** To subcontract (work). ❖ *n.* (sŭb′lĕt′) Sublet property, esp. an apartment.

sub·li·mate (sŭb′lə-māt′) *v.* **-mat·ed, -mat·ing, -mates** —*tr.* **1.** *Chemistry* To cause (a solid or gas) to change state without becoming a liquid. **2.** *Psychology* To modify the natural expression of (an instinctual impulse, esp. a sexual one) in a socially acceptable manner. —*intr. Chemistry* To be sublimated. Used of a solid or gas. [Lat. *sublīmāre, sublīmāt-*, to elevate < *sublīmis*, uplifted.]

sub·li·ma·tion (sŭb′lə-mā′shən) *n.* **1.** The act or process of sublimating. **2.** Something that has been sublimated.

sub·lime (sə-blīm′) *adj.* **1.** Characterized by nobility; majestic. **2a.** Of high spiritual, moral, or intellectual worth. **b.** Not to be excelled; supreme. **3.** Inspiring awe; impressive. **4.** *Archaic* Raised aloft; set high. **5.** *Obsolete* Of lofty appearance or bearing; haughty. ❖ *n.* **1.** Something sublime. **2.** An ultimate example. ❖ *v.* **-limed, -lim·ing, -limes** —*tr.* **1.** To render sublime. *Chemistry* To cause to sublimate. —*intr. Chemistry* To sublimate. [Fr. < OFr., sublimated < Lat. *sublīmis*, uplifted.] —**sub·lime′ly** *adv.* —**sub·lime′ness, sub·lim′i·ty** (sə-blĭm′ĭ-tē) *n.*

sub·lim·i·nal (sŭb-lĭm′ə-nəl) *adj. Psychology* **1.** Below the threshold of conscious perception. Used of stimuli. **2.** Inadequate to produce conscious awareness but able to evoke a response: *subliminal propaganda.* [SUB– + Lat. *līmen, līmin-*, threshold.] —**sub·lim′i·nal·ly** *adv.*

sub·lin·gual (sŭb-lĭng′gwəl) *adj.* Situated beneath or on the underside of the tongue. ❖ *n.* A sublingual part, such as a gland, artery, or duct. —**sub·lin′gual·ly** *adv.*

sub·lit·to·ral (sŭb-lĭt′ər-əl) *adj.* **1a.** Of or situated near the seashore. **b.** Of or relating to an organism living near or just below the low tide level of a shore. **2.** Of or relating to the portion of the littoral zone that extends from the low-tide line out to a depth of about 200 meters. **3.** Of or relating to the deeper part of a lake below the area in which rooted plants grow.

sub·lu·na·ry (sŭb-loo′nə-rē, sŭb′loo-nĕr′ē) *also* **sub·lu·nar** (-loo′nər) *adj.* **1.** Situated beneath the moon. **2.** Of this world; earthly. [LLat. *sublūnāris* : Lat. *sub-*, sub- + Lat. *lūna*, moon; see **leuk-** in App.]

sub·lux·a·tion (sŭb′lŭk-sā′shən) *n.* Incomplete or partial dislocation of a bone in a joint.

sub·ma·chine gun (sŭb′mə-shēn′) *n.* A lightweight automatic gun that shoots pistol ammunition, is usu. fired from the shoulder or hip, and often has the capacity for single rounds.

sub·man·dib·u·lar (sŭb′măn-dĭb′yə-lər) *adj.* Submaxillary.

sub·mar·gin·al (sŭb-mär′jə-nəl) *adj.* **1.** Near the margin of a body, organ, or part. **2.** Of low productivity; infertile.

sub·ma·rine (sŭb′mə-rēn′, sŭb′mə-rēn′) *n.* **1.** *Nautical* A vessel that is capable of operating submerged. **2.** A large sandwich on a long split roll filled with layers of meat, cheese, tomatoes, lettuce, and condiments. ❖ *adj.* Beneath the surface of the water; undersea. ❖ *v.* **-rined, -rin·ing, -rines** —*tr.* **1.** To attack by submarine, esp. with torpedoes. **2.** *Sports* To knock down with a blow to the legs. **3.** *Baseball* To pitch (a ball) with an underhand motion. —*intr.* To slide, drive, or throw under something.

REGIONAL NOTE The long sandwich featuring layers of meat and cheese on a crusty Italian roll or French bread goes by a variety of names. *Submarine* and *sub* are widespread. In Maine, it is called an *Italian sandwich.* Elsewhere in New England and in Sacramento, California, it is often called a *grinder.* New York City knows it as a *hero.* In the Delaware Valley, including Philadelphia and southern New Jersey, the sandwich is called a *hoagie.* Speakers in Miami use the name *Cuban sandwich.* Along the Gulf Coast the same sandwich is often called a *poor boy.* In New Orleans, a *poor boy* is likely to be offered in a version featuring fried oysters.

submarine chaser *n.* A small fast ship equipped to pursue and attack submarines.

sub·ma·rin·er (sŭb-mə-rē′nər, sŭb′mär′ə-nər) *n.* A member of the crew of a submarine.

sub·max·il·la (sŭb′măk-sĭl′ə) *n., pl.* **-max·il·lae** (-măk-sĭl′ē) The lower jaw or mandible, esp. in humans.

sub·max·il·lar·y (sŭb-măk′sə-lĕr′ē) *adj.* **1.** Of or relating to the lower jaw: *a submaxillary fracture.* **2.** Situated beneath the maxilla. ❖ *n., pl.* **-ies** An anatomical part, such as a gland, situated beneath the maxilla.

sub·me·di·ant (sŭb-mē′dē-ənt) *n. Music* The sixth tone of a diatonic scale.

sub·merge (səb-mûrj′) *v.* **-merged, -merg·ing, -merg·es** —*tr.* **1.** To place under water. **2.** To cover with water; inundate. **3.** To hide from view; obscure. —*intr.* To go under or as if under water. [Lat. *submergere* : *sub-*, sub- + *mergere*, to plunge.] —**sub·mer′gence** *n.*

sub·merged (səb-mûrjd′) *adj.* **1.** *Botany* Growing or remaining under water: *submerged leaves.* **2.** Living in poverty or misery. **3.** Having been hidden.

sub·merg·i·ble (səb-mûr′jə-bəl) *adj.* That can be immersed in or can remain under water. —**sub·merg′i·bil′i·ty** *n.*

sub·merse (səb-mûrs′) *tr.v.* **-mersed, -mers·ing, -mers·es** To submerge. [Prob. back-formation < SUBMERSION < LLat. *submersiō, submersiōn-* < Lat. *submersus*, p. part. of *submergere*, to submerge. See SUBMERGE.] —**sub·mer′sion** (-mûr′zhən, -shən) *n.*

sub·mersed (səb-mûrst′) *adj. Botany* Growing or remaining under water.

sub·mers·i·ble (səb-mûr′sə-bəl) *adj.* Submergible. ❖ *n.* A vessel capable of operating or remaining under water.

sub·mi·cro·scop·ic (sŭb′mī-krə-skŏp′ĭk) *adj.* Too small to be resolved by an optical microscope.

sub·min·i·a·ture (sŭb-mĭn′ē-ə-choor′, -chər) *adj.* Smaller than miniature; exceedingly small.

sub·min·i·a·tur·ize (sŭb-mĭn′ē-ə-chə-rīz′) *tr.v.* **-ized, -iz·ing, -iz·es** To make subminiature, esp. to manufacture or design (electronic equipment) in subminiature size. —**sub·min′i·a·tur·i·za′tion** (-chər-ĭ-zā′shən) *n.*

sub·miss (səb-mĭs′) *adj. Archaic* Submissive. [Lat. *submissus*, p. part. of *submittere*, to set under. See SUBMIT.]

sub·mis·sion (səb-mĭsh′ən) *n.* **1a.** The act of submitting to the power of another. **b.** The state of having submitted. **2.** The state of being submissive or compliant. **3a.** The act of submitting something, such as a manuscript, for consideration. **b.** Something so submitted. [Ult. < Lat. *submissiō, submissiōn-*, a lowering < *submissus*, p. part. of *submittere*, to set under. See SUBMIT.]

sub·mis·sive (səb-mĭs′ĭv) *adj.* Inclined or willing to submit. —**sub·mis′sive·ly** *adv.* —**sub·mis′sive·ness** *n.*

sub·mit (səb-mĭt′) *v.* **-mit·ted, -mit·ting, -mits** —*tr.* **1.** To yield or surrender (oneself) to the will or authority of another. **2.** To subject to a condition or process. **3.** To commit (something) to the consideration or judgment of another. **4.** To offer as a proposition or contention. —*intr.* **1.** To give in to the authority, power, or desires of another. See Syns at **yield. 2.** To allow oneself to be subjected to something. [ME *submitten* < Lat. *submittere*, to set under : *sub-*, sub- + *mittere*, to cause to go.] —**sub·mit′tal** (-mĭt′l) *n.* —**sub·mit′ter** *n.*

sub·mon·tane (sŭb′mŏn′tān′, -mŏn-tān′) *adj.* Located under or at the base of a mountain or mountain range.

sub·nor·mal (sŭb-nôr′məl) *adj.* Less than normal; below the average. ❖ *n.* One viewed as subnormal in some respect, such as in coordination. —**sub′nor·mal′i·ty** (-nôr-măl′ĭ-tē) *n.*

sub·note·book (sŭb′nōt′book′) *n.* A portable computer that is smaller than a notebook computer.

sub·or·bit·al (sŭb-ôr′bĭ-tl) *adj.* **1.** Having or following a trajectory of less than one orbit. Used of a rocket or spacecraft. **2.** *Anatomy* Situated on or below the floor of the orbit of the eye. ❖ *n.* A suborbital part, such as a bone, nerve, or cartilage.

sub·or·der (sŭb′ôr′dər) *n.* **1.** *Biology* A taxonomic category of related organisms ranking between an order and a family. **2.** A subdivision of a category termed an order.

sub·or·di·nate (sə-bôr′dn-ĭt) *adj.* **1.** Belonging to a lower or inferior class or rank; secondary. **2.** Subject to the authority or control of another. ❖ *n.* One that is subordinate. ❖ *tr.v.* (sə-bôr′dn-āt′) **-nat·ed, -nat·ing, -nates 1.** To put in a lower or inferior rank or class. **2.** To make subservient; subdue. [ME *subordinat* < Med.Lat. *subōrdinātus*, p. part. of *subōrdināre*, to subordinate : Lat. *sub-*, sub- + Lat. *ōrdināre*, to set in order (< *ōrdō, ōrdin-*, order; see **ar-** in App.).] —**sub·or′di·nate·ly** *adv.* —**sub·or′di·nate·ness, sub·or′di·na′tion** (-nā′shən) *n.* —**sub·or′di·na′tive** (-nə′tĭv) *adj.*

subordinate clause *n.* See **dependent clause.**

subordinate conjunction *n.* A conjunction, such as *after, because, if,* or *where,* that introduces a dependent clause.

sub·orn (sə-bôrn′) *tr.v.* **-orned, -orn·ing, -orns 1.** To induce (a person) to commit an unlawful or evil act. **2.** *Law* **a.** To induce (a person) to commit perjury. **b.** To procure (perjured testimony). [Lat. *subōrnāre* : *sub-*, secretly; see SUB– + *ōrnāre*, to equip.] —**sub′or·na′tion** (sŭb′ôr-nā′shən) *n.* —**sub·orn′er** *n.*

sub·ox·ide (sŭb-ŏk′sīd′) *n.* An oxide containing a relatively small amount of oxygen.

submarine

ă	pat	oi	boy
ā	pay	ou	out
âr	care	ŏŏ	took
ä	father	ōō	boot
ĕ	pet	ŭ	cut
ē	be	ûr	urge
ĭ	pit	th	thin
ī	pie	*th*	this
îr	pier	hw	which
ŏ	pot	zh	vision
ō	toe	ə	about,
ô	paw		item

Stress marks:
′ (primary);
′ (secondary), as in
lexicon (lĕk′sĭ-kŏn′)

sub•phy•lum (sŭb'fī'ləm) *n.*, *pl.* **-la** (-lə) *Biology* A taxonomic category of related organisms ranking between a phylum and a class.

sub•plot (sŭb'plŏt') *n.* **1.** A plot subordinate to the main plot of a literary work or film. **2.** A subdivision of a plot of land, esp. a plot used for experimental purposes.

sub•poe•na (sə-pē'nə) *n.* A writ summoning a person to court to give testimony. ❖ *tr.v.* **-naed, -na•ing, -nas** To serve with such a writ. [ME *suppena* < Med.Lat. *sub poenā*, under a penalty : Lat. *sub*, under; see SUB– + Lat. *poenā*, ablative of *poena*, penalty (< Gk. *poinē*); see kʷei- in App.]

sub•prin•ci•pal (sŭb-prĭn'sə-pəl) *n.* **1.** An assistant school principal. **2.** An auxiliary or bracing rafter in a frame.

sub•pro•fes•sion•al (sŭb'prə-fĕsh'ə-nəl) *n.* A paraprofessional. —**sub'pro•fes'sion•al** *adj.*

sub•rep•tion (sŭb-rĕp'shən) *n.* **1.** A calculated misrepresentation through concealment of the facts. **2.** An inference drawn from a subreption. [LLat. *subreptiō, subreptiōn-* < Lat., theft < *subreptus*, p. part. of *surripere*, to take away secretly. See SURREPTITIOUS.] —**sub'rep•ti'tious** (-tĭsh'əs) *adj.*

sub•ro•gate (sŭb'rō-gāt') *tr.v.* **-gat•ed, -gat•ing, -gates** To substitute (one person) for another. [ME *subrogaten* < Lat. *subrogāre, subrogāt-* : *sub-*, instead of; see SUB– + *rogāre*, to ask; see reg- in App.]

sub•ro•ga•tion (sŭb'rō-gā'shən) *n.* The substitution of one person for another, esp. the legal doctrine of substituting one creditor for another.

sub ro•sa (sŭb rō'zə) *adv.* In secret; privately or confidentially. [Lat. *sub rosā*, under the rose (< hanging a rose over a meeting as a symbol of confidentiality).]

sub•rou•tine (sŭb'rōō-tēn') *n. Computer Science* A set of instructions that performs a specific task for a main routine, requiring direction back to the main routine when finished.

sub-Sa•har•an (sŭb'sə-hâr'ən, -hăr'-, -hăr'-) *adj.* Of, relating to, or situated in the region of Africa south of the Sahara.

sub•scribe (səb-scrīb') *v.* **-scribed, -scrib•ing, -scribes** —*tr.* **1.** To pledge or contribute (a sum of money). **2.** To sign (one's name) at the end of a document. **3.** To sign one's name to in attestation, testimony, or consent: *subscribe a will.* **4.** To authorize (someone) to receive or access electronic texts or services, esp. over the Internet. —*intr.* **1a.** To contract to purchase a certain number of issues of a publication, tickets to a series of events or performances, or a utility service, for example. **b.** To receive or be allowed to access electronic texts or services by subscription. **2.** To promise to pay or contribute money. **3.** To feel or express hearty approval. See Syns at **assent. 4.** To sign one's name. **5.** To affix one's signature to a document as a witness or to show consent. [ME *subscriben* < Lat. *subscrībere* : *sub-*, sub- + *scrībere*, to write; see skribh- in App.] —**sub•scrib'er** *n.*

sub•script (sŭb'skrĭpt') *n.* A character set, printed, or written below and immediately to one side of another. [< Lat. *subscrīptus*, p. part. of *subscrībere*, to subscribe. See SUBSCRIBE.] —**sub'script'** *adj.*

sub•scrip•tion (səb-skrĭp'shən) *n.* **1a.** A purchase made by signed order, as for a periodical for a given time period or for a series of performances. **b.** An agreement to receive or be given access to electronic texts or services, esp. over the Internet. **2.** Acceptance, as of a doctrine, demonstrated by signing one's name. **3a.** The raising of money from subscribers. **b.** A sum of money so raised. **4.** The signing of one's name. **5.** Something subscribed. [Ult. < Lat. *subscrīptiō, subscrīptiōn-*, something written underneath < *subscrīptus*, p. part. of *subscrībere*, to subscribe. See SUBSCRIBE.] —**sub•scrip'tive** *adj.* —**sub•scrip'tive•ly** *adv.*

sub•se•quence (sŭb'sĭ-kwĕns', -kwəns) *n.* **1.** Something subsequent; a sequel. **2.** The fact or quality of being subsequent. **3.** (-sē'kwəns) *Mathematics* A sequence contained in another sequence.

sub•se•quent (sŭb'sĭ-kwĕnt', -kwənt) *adj.* Following in time or order; succeeding. [ME < OFr. < Lat. *subsequēns, subsequent-*, pr. part. of *subsequī*, to follow close after : *sub-*, close after; see SUB– + *sequī*, to follow; see sekʷ-¹ in App.] —**sub'se•quent'ly** *adv.* —**sub'se•quent'ness** *n.*

sub•serve (səb-sûrv') *tr.v.* **-served, -serv•ing, -serves** To serve to promote (an end); be useful to. [Lat. *subservīre* : *sub-*, sub- + *servīre*, to serve; see SERVE.]

sub•ser•vi•ent (səb-sûr'vē-ənt) *adj.* **1.** Subordinate in capacity or function. **2.** Obsequious; servile. **3.** Useful as a means or a tool; promoting an end. [Lat. *subserviēns, subservient-*, pr. part. of *subservīre*, to subserve. See SUBSERVE.] —**sub•ser'vi•ence, sub•ser'vi•en•cy** *n.* —**sub•ser'vi•ent•ly** *adv.*

sub•set (sŭb'sĕt') *n.* A set contained within a set.

sub•shell (sŭb'shĕl') *n.* One of the energy levels in the electron shell of an atom.

sub•shrub (sŭb'shrŭb') *n.* **1.** An herb having a woody lower stem. **2.** A low shrub; an undershrub.

sub•side (səb-sīd') *intr.v.* **-sid•ed, -sid•ing, -sides 1.** To sink to a lower or normal level. **2.** To sink or settle down, as into a sofa. **3.** To sink to the bottom, as a sediment. **4.** To become less agitated or active; abate. See Syns at **decrease.** [Lat. *subsīdere* : *sub-*, sub- + *sīdere*, to settle; see sed- in App.] —**sub•si'dence** (səb-sīd'ns, sŭb'sĭ-dns) *n.*

sub•sid•i•ar•y (səb-sĭd'ē-ĕr'ē) *adj.* **1.** Serving to assist or supplement; auxiliary. **2.** Secondary in importance; subordinate. **3.** Of, relating to, or of the nature of a subsidy. ❖ *n., pl.* **-ar•ies 1.** One that is subsidiary to another. **2.** A subsidiary company. **3.** *Music* A theme subordinate to a main theme or subject. [Lat. *subsidiārius* < *subsidium*, support. See SUBSIDY.] —**sub•sid'i•ar'i•ly** (-âr'ə-lē) *adv.*

subsidiary cell *n.* A plant epidermal cell associated with guard cells and morphologically different from other epidermal cells.

subsidiary company *n.* A company having more than half of its stock owned by another company.

sub•si•dize (sŭb'sĭ-dīz') *tr.v.* **-dized, -diz•ing, -diz•es 1.** To assist or support with a subsidy. **2.** To secure the assistance of by granting a subsidy. —**sub'si•di•za'tion** (-dĭ-zā'shən) *n.* —**sub'si•diz'er** *n.*

sub•si•dy (sŭb'sĭ-dē) *n., pl.* **-dies 1.** Monetary assistance granted by a government to a person or group in support of an enterprise regarded as being in the public interest. **2.** Financial assistance given by one person or government to another. **3.** Money formerly granted to the British Crown by Parliament. [ME *subsidie* < AN < Lat. *subsidium*, support : *sub-*, behind, beneath; see SUB– + *sedēre*, to sit; see sed- in App.]

sub•sist (səb-sĭst') *v.* **-sist•ed, -sist•ing, -sists** —*intr.* **1a.** To exist; be. **b.** To stay in existence. **2.** To maintain life; live: *subsisted on oats.* **3.** To be logically conceivable. —*tr.* To maintain with provisions. [Lat. *subsistere*, to support : *sub-*, sub- + *sistere*, to stand; see stā- in App.] —**sub•sist'er** *n.*

sub•sis•tence (səb-sĭs'təns) *n.* **1.** The act or state of subsisting. **2.** A means of subsisting, esp. one barely sufficient to maintain life. **3.** Something with real or substantial existence. **4.** *Christianity* Hypostasis. —**sub•sis'tent** *adj.*

sub•soil (sŭb'soil') *n.* The layer or bed of earth beneath the topsoil. ❖ *tr.v.* **-soiled, -soil•ing, -soils** To plow or turn up the subsoil of. —**sub'soil'er** *n.*

sub•so•lar (sŭb-sō'lər) *adj.* **1.** Situated directly beneath the sun. **2.** Located between the tropics; equatorial.

sub•son•ic (sŭb-sŏn'ĭk) *adj.* **1.** Of less than audible frequency. **2.** Having a speed less than that of sound in a designated medium.

subsp. *abbr.* subspecies

sub•spe•cies (sŭb'spē'shēz, -sēz) *n., pl.* **subspecies** *Biology* A taxonomic subdivision of a species, usu. based on geographic distribution. —**sub'spe•cif'ic** (-spĭ-sĭf'ĭk) *adj.*

subst. *abbr.* **1.** substantive **2.** substitute

sub•stage (sŭb'stāj') *n.* The part of a microscope located below the stage, on which accessories are held in place.

sub•stance (sŭb'stəns) *n.* **1a.** That which has mass and occupies space; matter. **b.** A material of a particular kind or constitution. **2a.** Essential nature; essence. **b.** Gist; heart. **3.** That which is solid and practical in character, quality, or importance. **4.** Density; body: *Air has little substance.* **5.** Material possessions; goods; wealth. [ME < OFr. < Lat. *substantia* < *substāns, substant-*, pr. part. of *substāre*, to be present : *sub-*, sub- + *stāre*, to stand; see stā- in App.]

substance abuse *n.* Excessive use of addictive substances, esp. alcohol or narcotic drugs. —**substance abuser** *n.*

substance P *n.* A short-chain polypeptide that functions as a neurotransmitter esp. in the transmission of pain impulses. [< P(AIN).]

sub•stan•dard (sŭb-stăn'dərd) *adj.* **1.** Failing to meet a standard; below standard. **2.** *Linguistics* **a.** Of, relating to, or indicating a speech pattern that does not conform to that of the prestige group in a speech community or to that of the standard language. **b.** Not in accord with notions of good English; nonstandard.

sub•stan•tial (səb-stăn'shəl) *adj.* **1.** Of, relating to, or having substance; material. **2.** True or real; not imaginary. **3.** Solidly built; strong. **4.** Ample; sustaining: *ate a substantial breakfast.* **5.** Considerable in importance, value, degree, amount, or extent: *won the election by a substantial margin.* **6.** Possessing wealth or property; well-to-do. ❖ *n.* **1.** An essential. Often used in the plural. **2.** A solid thing. Often used in the plural. [ME *substancial* < OFr. *substantiel* < Lat. *substantialis* < *substantia*, substance. See SUBSTANCE.] —**sub•stan'ti•al'i•ty** (-shē-ăl'ĭ-tē) *n.* —**sub•stan'tial•ly** *adv.*

sub•stan•ti•a ni•gra (səb-stăn'shē-ə nī'grə, nĭg'rə) *n.* A layer of large pigmented nerve cells in the midbrain that produce dopamine and whose destruction is associated with Parkinson's disease. [NLat. : Lat. *substantia*, substance + Lat. *nigra*, fem. of *niger*, black.]

sub•stan•ti•ate (səb-stăn'shē-āt') *tr.v.* **-at•ed, -at•ing, -ates 1.** To support with proof or evidence; verify. **2a.** To give material form to; embody. **b.** To make firm or solid. **3.** To give substance to; make real or actual. [NLat. *substantiāre, substantiāt-* < Lat. *substantia*, substance. See SUBSTANCE.] —**sub•stan'ti•a'tion** *n.*

sub•stan•ti•val (sŭb'stən-tī'vəl) *adj. Grammar* Of or relating to a substantive. —**sub•stan'ti•val•ly** *adv.*

sub•stan•tive (sŭb'stən-tĭv) *adj.* **1.** Substantial; considerable. **2.** Independent in existence or function; not subordinate. **3.** Not imaginary; real. **4.** Of or relating to the essence or substance; essential. **5.** Having a solid basis; firm. **6.** *Grammar* Expressing or designating existence; for example, the verb *to be.* **7.** *Grammar*

Being a noun or noun equivalent. ❖ *n.* *Grammar* A word or group of words functioning as a noun. [ME *substantif,* self-sufficient, independent < OFr., substantive < LLat. *substantīvus* < Lat. *substantia,* substance. See SUBSTANCE.] —**sub′stan·tive·ly** *adv.* —**sub′stan·tive·ness** *n.*

substantive right *n.* A basic right seen as part of the order of society and independent of, not subordinate to, human law.

sub·sta·tion (sŭb′stā′shən) *n.* A subsidiary or branch station, as of a post office or an electric utility.

sub·stit·u·ent (səb-stĭch′ōō-ənt) *n.* An atom, radical, or group substituted for another in a molecule. [Lat. *substituēns, substituent-,* pr. part. of *substituere,* to substitute. See SUBSTITUTE.] —**sub′stit′u·ent** *adj.*

sub·sti·tute (sŭb′stĭ-tōōt′, -tyōōt′) *n.* **1.** One that takes the place of another; a replacement. **2.** *Grammar* A word or construction used in place of another. ❖ *v.* **-tut·ed, -tut·ing, -tutes** —*tr.* **1.** To put or use (a person or thing) in place of another. **2.** *Chemistry* To replace (one or more elements or radicals in a compound) by other elements or radicals. —*intr.* To take the place of another. [ME < OFr. *substitut* < Lat. *substitūtus,* p. part. of *substituere,* to substitute : *sub-,* in place of; see SUB– + *statuere,* to cause to stand; see **stā-** in App.] —**sub′sti·tut′a·bil′i·ty** *n.* —**sub′sti·tut′a·ble** *adj.*

sub·sti·tu·tion (sŭb′stĭ-tōō′shən, -tyōō′-) *n.* **1a.** The act or an instance of substituting. **b.** The state of being substituted. **2.** One substituted; a replacement. —**sub′sti·tu′tion·al, sub′sti·tu′tion·ar·y** *adj.* —**sub′sti·tu′tion·al·ly** *adv.*

sub·sti·tu·tive (sŭb′stĭ-tōō′tĭv, -tyōō′-) *adj.* Serving or capable of serving as a substitute.

sub·strate (sŭb′strāt′) *n.* **1.** The material or substance on which an enzyme acts. **2.** *Biology* A surface on which an organism grows or is attached. **3.** An underlying layer; a substratum. **4.** *Linguistics* An indigenous language that contributes features to the language of an invading people who impose their language on the indigenous population. [< SUBSTRATUM.]

sub·stra·tum (sŭb′strā′təm, -străt′əm) *n.,* *pl.* **-stra·ta** (-strā′tə, -străt′ə) or **-stra·tums 1a.** An underlying layer. **b.** Subsoil. **2.** A foundation or groundwork. **3.** The material on which another material is coated or fabricated. **4.** *Philosophy* The characterless substance that supports attributes of reality. **5.** *Biology* A substrate. **6.** *Linguistics* A substrate. [NLat. *substrātum* < neut. of Lat. *substrātus,* p. part. of *substernere,* to lay under : *sub-,* sub- + *sternere,* to stretch, spread.] —**sub·stra′tive** *adj.*

sub·struc·tion (sŭb-strŭk′shən) *n.* A foundation; a substructure. [Lat. *substrūctiō, substrūctiōn-* < *substrūctus,* p. part. of *substruere,* to build beneath : *sub-,* sub- + *struere,* to build, pile up.] —**sub·struc′tion·al** *adj.*

sub·struc·ture (sŭb′strŭk′chər) *n.* **1.** The supporting part of a structure; the foundation. **2.** The earth bank or bed supporting railroad tracks. —**sub·struc′tur·al** *adj.*

sub·sume (səb-sōōm′) *tr.v.* **-sumed, -sum·ing, -sumes** To classify, include, or incorporate in a more comprehensive category or under a general principle. [Med.Lat. *subsūmere* : Lat. *sub-,* sub- + Lat. *sūmere,* to take.] —**sub·sum′a·ble** *adj.*

sub·sump·tion (səb-sŭmp′shən) *n.* **1a.** The act of subsuming. **b.** Something subsumed. **2.** *Logic* The minor premise of a syllogism. [Lat. *subsūmptiō, subsūmptiōn-,* a subsuming < *subsūmptus,* p. part. of *subsūmere,* to subsume. See SUBSUME.] —**sub·sump′tive** *adj.*

sub·sur·face (sŭb′sûr′fəs, sŭb-sûr′-) *adj.* Of, relating to, or situated in an area beneath a surface, esp. the surface of the earth or a body of water.

sub·teen (sŭb′tēn′) *adj.* Relating to, intended for, or being a preadolescent child or children; preteen: *a subteen dance.* ❖ *n.* **1.** See **preteen. 2. subteens** The preadolescent years.

sub·tem·per·ate (sŭb-tĕm′pər-ĭt, -tĕm′prĭt) *adj.* Of or occurring within the colder regions of the Temperate Zones.

sub·ten·ant (sŭb-tĕn′ənt) *n.* One that rents property, such as land or a house, from a tenant. —**sub·ten′an·cy** *n.*

sub·tend (səb-tĕnd′) *tr.v.* **-tend·ed, -tend·ing, -tends 1.** *Mathematics* To be opposite to and delimit: *The side of a triangle subtends the opposite angle.* **2.** To underlie so as to enclose or surround. [Lat. *subtendere,* to extend underneath : *sub-,* sub- + *ten-dere,* to extend; see **ten-** in App.]

sub·ter·fuge (sŭb′tər-fyōōj′) *n.* A deceptive stratagem or device. [Fr. < OFr. *suterfuge* < LLat. *subterfugium* < Lat. *subter-fugere,* to escape : *subter,* secretly, beneath; see **upo** in App. + *fugere,* to flee.]

sub·ter·mi·nal (sŭb-tûr′mə-nəl) *adj.* Located or occurring near an end.

sub·ter·ra·ne·an (sŭb′tə-rā′nē-ən) *adj.* **1.** Situated or operating beneath the earth's surface; underground. **2.** Hidden; secret. [Lat. *subterrāneus* : *sub-,* sub- + *terra,* earth; see **ters-** in App.] —**sub′ter·ra′ne·an·ly** *adv.*

sub·ter·res·tri·al (sŭb′tə-rĕs′trē-əl) *adj.* Subterranean; underground.

sub·text (sŭb′tĕkst′) *n.* **1.** The implicit meaning or theme of a literary text. **2.** The underlying personality of a dramatic character as implied by a script or text and interpreted by an actor in performance. —**sub·tex′tu·al** (-tĕks′chōō-əl) *adj.*

sub·tile (sŭt′l, sŭb′təl) *adj.* Subtle. [ME < OFr. *subtil* < Lat.

subtīlis, fine, delicate. See SUBTLE.] —**sub′tile·ly** *adv.* —**sub·til′i·ty** (səb-tĭl′ĭ-tē), **sub′tile·ness** (sŭt′l-nĭs, sŭb′təl-), **sub′til·ty** (sŭt′l-tē, sŭb′təl-) *n.*

sub·til·ize (sŭt′l-īz′, sŭb′tə-līz′) *v.* **-ized, -iz·ing, -iz·es** —*tr.* To render subtle. —*intr.* To argue or discuss with fine subtlety. —**sub′til·i·za′tion** (-ĭ-zā′shən) *n.*

sub·ti·tle (sŭb′tīt′l) *n.* **1.** A secondary, usu. explanatory title, as of a book. **2.** A printed translation of the dialogue of a foreign-language film shown at the bottom of the screen. ❖ *tr.v.* **-tled, -tling, -tles 1.** To give a subtitle to. **2.** To provide with subtitles.

sub·tle (sŭt′l) *adj.* **sub·tler, sub·tlest 1a.** So slight as to be difficult to detect or analyze; elusive: *a subtle smile.* **b.** Difficult to understand; abstruse. **2.** Able to make fine distinctions: *a subtle mind.* **3a.** Characterized by skill or ingenuity; clever. **b.** Crafty or sly; devious. **c.** Operating in a hidden, usu. injurious way; insidious: *a subtle poison.* [ME *sotil* < OFr. < Lat. *subtīlis.*] —**sub′tle·ness** *n.* —**sub′tly** *adv.*

sub·tle·ty (sŭt′l-tē) *n., pl.* **-ties 1.** The quality or state of being subtle. **2.** Something subtle, as a nicety of thought.

sub·ton·ic (sŭb-tŏn′ĭk) *n.* *Music* The seventh tone of a diatonic scale, immediately below the tonic.

sub·tor·rid (sŭb-tôr′ĭd, -tŏr′-) *adj.* Subtropical.

sub·to·tal (sŭb-tōt′l) *adj.* Less than total; incomplete. ❖ *n.* (sŭb′tōt′l) The total of part of a series of numbers. ❖ *v.* (sŭb′tōt′l) **-taled, -tal·ing, -tals** also **-talled, -tal·ling, -tals** —*tr.* To total part of (a series of numbers). —*intr.* To arrive at a subtotal.

sub·tract (səb-trăkt′) *v.* **-tract·ed, -tract·ing, -tracts** —*tr.* To take away; deduct. —*intr.* To perform the arithmetic operation of subtraction. [Lat. *subtrahere, subtract-* : *sub-,* sub- + *trahere,* to draw.] —**sub·tract′er** *n.*

sub·trac·tion (səb-trăk′shən) *n.* **1.** The act or process of subtracting; deduction. **2.** *Mathematics* The arithmetic operation of finding the difference between two quantities or numbers.

sub·trac·tive (səb-trăk′tĭv) *adj.* **1.** Producing or involving subtraction. **2a.** Of or being a color produced by light passing through or reflecting off a colorant, such as a filter or pigment, that absorbs certain wavelengths and transmits or reflects others. **b.** Of or being any of the primary colors cyan, magenta, or yellow. **3.** Of or being a photographic process that produces a positive image by superposing or mixing substances that selectively absorb colored light.

sub·tra·hend (sŭb′trə-hĕnd′) *n.* A quantity or number to be subtracted from another. [< Lat. *subtrahendum,* neut. gerundive of *subtrahere,* to subtract. See SUBTRACT.]

sub·trop·i·cal (sŭb-trŏp′ĭ-kəl) *adj.* Of, relating to, or being the geographic areas adjacent to the Tropics.

sub·trop·ics (sŭb-trŏp′ĭks) *pl.n.* Subtropical regions.

sub·type (sŭb′tīp′) *n.* A group forming a type within a larger type.

su·bu·late (sōō′byə-lĭt, -lāt′, sŭb′yə-) *adj.* *Biology* Tapering to a point; awl-shaped: *a subulate leaf.* [NLat. *sābulātus* < Lat. *sūbula,* awl. See **syū-** in App.]

sub·um·brel·la (sŭb′ŭm-brĕl′ə) *n.* The concave underside of the body of a jellyfish.

sub·u·nit (sŭb′yōō′nĭt) *n.* A subdivision of a larger unit.

sub·urb (sŭb′ûrb′) *n.* **1.** A usu. residential area or community outlying a city. **2. suburbs** The usu. residential region around a major city; the environs. [ME *suburbe* < OFr. < Lat. *suburbium* : *sub-,* sub- + *urbs, urb-,* city.]

sub·ur·ban (sə-bûr′bən) *adj.* **1.** Of, relating to, or characteristic of a suburb. **2.** Located or residing in a suburb. **3.** Of, relating to, or characteristic of the culture, customs, and manners typical of life in the suburbs. ❖ *n.* A suburbanite.

sub·ur·ban·ite (sə-bûr′bə-nīt′) *n.* One living in a suburb.

sub·ur·ban·ize (sə-bûr′bə-nīz′) *tr.v.* **-ized, -iz·ing, -izes** To render suburban; impart a suburban character to. —**sub·ur′ban·i·za′tion** (-bə-nĭ-zā′shən) *n.*

sub·ur·bi·a (sə-bûr′bē-ə) *n.* **1.** The suburbs. **2.** Suburbanites considered as a group.

sub·ven·tion (səb-vĕn′shən) *n.* **1.** Provision of help or support. **2.** An endowment or a subsidy, as one from a government to a research institution; a financial aid grant. [Ult. < LLat. *subventiō, subventiōn-,* assistance < Lat. *subventus,* p. part. of *subvenīre,* to come to help : *sub-,* beneath, behind; see SUB– + *venīre,* to come; see **g**ʷ**ā-** in App.] —**sub·ven′tion·ar′y** *adj.*

sub·ver·sion (səb-vûr′zhən, -shən) *n.* **1a.** The act or an instance of subverting. **b.** The condition of being subverted. **2.** *Obsolete* A cause of overthrow or ruin. [Ult. < LLat. *subversiō, subversiōn-* < Lat. *subversus,* p. part. of *subvertere,* to subvert. See SUBVERT.] —**sub·ver′sion·ar′y** *adj.*

sub·ver·sive (səb-vûr′sĭv, -zĭv) *adj.* Intended or serving to subvert, esp. intended to overthrow or undermine an established government. —**sub·ver′sive** *n.* —**sub·ver′sive·ly** *adv.* —**sub·ver′sive·ness** *n.*

sub·vert (səb-vûrt′) *tr.v.* **-vert·ed, -vert·ing, -verts 1.** To destroy completely; ruin. **2.** To undermine the character, morals, or allegiance of; corrupt. **3.** To overthrow completely. See Syns at **overthrow.** [ME *subverten* < OFr. *subvertir* < Lat. *subvertere* : *sub-,* sub- + *vertere,* to turn; see **wer-²** in App.] —**sub·vert′er** *n.*

sub·vi·rus (sŭb-vī′rəs) *n., pl.* **-rus·es** A viral protein or other

ă	pat	oi	boy
ā	pay	ou	out
âr	care	ŏŏ	took
ä	father	ōō	boot
ĕ	pet	ŭ	cut
ē	be	ûr	urge
ĭ	pit	th	thin
ī	pie	*th*	this
îr	pier	hw	which
ŏ	pot	zh	vision
ō	toe	ə	about,
ô	paw		item

Stress marks:
′ (primary);
′ (secondary), as in
lexicon (lĕk′sĭ-kŏn′)

substance smaller than a virus and having some of the properties of a virus. —**sub•vi′ral** (-rəl) *adj.*

sub•vo•cal (sŭb-vō′kəl) *adj.* Characterized by movement of the lips or other speech organs without audible sounds. —**sub•vo′cal•ly** *adv.*

sub•vo•cal•ize (sŭb-vō′kə-līz′) *tr. & intr.v.* **-ized, -iz•ing, -iz•es** To articulate subvocally or engage in subvocal articulation. —**sub•vo′cal•i•za′tion** (-kə-lĭ-zā′shən) *n.* —**sub•vo′cal•iz′er** *n.*

sub•way (sŭb′wā′) *n.* **1a.** An underground urban railroad, usu. operated by electricity. **b.** A passage for such a railroad. **2.** An underground tunnel or passage, as for pedestrians.

suc•ce•da•ne•um (sŭk′sĭ-dā′nē-əm) *n., pl.* **-ne•a** (-nē-ə) A substitute. [NLat. *succēdāneum* < Lat., neut. sing. of *succēdāneus*, substituted < *succēdere*, to succeed. See SUCCEED.]

suc•ceed (sək-sēd′) *v.* **-ceed•ed, -ceed•ing, -ceeds** —*intr.* **1.** To come next in time or succession; follow after another; replace another in an office or a position. **2.** To accomplish something desired or intended. **3.** *Obsolete* To devolve upon a person by way of inheritance. —*tr.* **1.** To follow in time or order. **2.** To come after and take the place of. See Syns at **follow.** [ME *succeden* < OFr. *succeder* < Lat. *succēdere* : *sub-*, near; see SUB- + *cēdere*, to go.] —**suc•ce′dent** (sək-sēd′nt) *adj.* —**suc•ceed′er** *n.*

suc•cès d′es•time (sük-sĕ′ dĕs-tēm′) *n.* An important but unpopular success or achievement. [Fr. : *succès*, success + *de*, of + *estime*, esteem.]

suc•cès fou (sük-sĕ′ fōō′) *n.* A wild success. [Fr. : *succès*, success + *fou*, mad.]

suc•cess (sək-sĕs′) *n.* **1.** The achievement of something desired, planned, or attempted. **2a.** The gaining of fame or prosperity. **b.** The extent of such gain. **3.** One that is successful. **4.** *Obsolete* A result or an outcome. [Lat. *successus* < p. part. of *succēdere*, to succeed. See SUCCEED.]

suc•cess•ful (sək-sĕs′fəl) *adj.* **1.** Having a favorable outcome. **2.** Having obtained something desired or intended: *was successful in stopping the leak.* **3.** Having achieved wealth or eminence. —**suc•cess′ful•ly** *adv.* —**suc•cess′ful•ness** *n.*

suc•ces•sion (sək-sĕsh′ən) *n.* **1.** The act or process of following in order or sequence. **2.** A group of people or things arranged or following in order; a sequence. **3a.** The sequence in which one person after another succeeds to a title, throne, dignity, or estate. **b.** The right of a person or line of persons to so succeed. **c.** The person or line having such a right. **4a.** The act or process of succeeding to the rights or duties of another. **b.** The act or process of becoming entitled as a legal beneficiary to the property of a deceased person. **5.** *Ecology* The gradual and orderly evolution of an ecosystem until a climax is reached. [ME < OFr. < Lat. *successiō, successiōn-* < *successus*, p. part. of *succēdere*, to succeed. See SUCCEED.] —**suc•ces′sion•al** *adj.* —**suc•ces′sion•al•ly** *adv.*

suc•ces•sive (sək-sĕs′ĭv) *adj.* **1.** Following in uninterrupted order; consecutive. **2.** Of, characterized by, or involving succession. —**suc•ces′sive•ly** *adv.* —**suc•ces′sive•ness** *n.*

successive approximation *n.* A method for estimating the value of an unknown quantity by repeated comparison to a sequence of known quantities.

suc•ces•sor (sək-sĕs′ər) *n.* One that succeeds another.

suc•ci•nate (sŭk′sə-nāt′) *n.* A salt or ester of succinic acid.

suc•cinct (sək-sĭngkt′) *adj.* **-er, -est** Concise and terse: *a succinct reply.* **2.** *Archaic* Encircled as if by a girdle; girded. [ME *succincte*, girt < OFr. < Lat. *succīnctus*, p. part. of *succingere*, to gird from below : *sub-*, sub- + *cingere*, to gird.] —**suc•cinct′ly** *adv.* —**suc•cinct′ness** *n.*

suc•cin•ic acid (sək-sĭn′ĭk) *n.* A crystalline dicarboxylic acid, $C_4H_6O_4$, occurring naturally as an intermediate in the Krebs cycle and synthesized for use in pharmaceuticals and perfumes. [Fr. *succinique* < Lat. *succinum*, amber.]

suc•cin•yl•cho•line (sŭk′sə-nĭl-kō′lēn) *n.* A crystalline compound, $C_{14}H_{30}O_4$, formed by esterification of succinic acid with choline and used medically to produce brief but complete muscular relaxation. [SUCCIN(IC ACID) + −YL + CHOLINE.]

suc•cor (sŭk′ər) *n.* **1.** Assistance in time of want, difficulty, or distress; relief. **2.** One that affords succor. ❖ *tr.v.* **-cored, -cor•ing, -cors** To give succor to. [ME *sucur*, back-formation < *sucurs* (taken as pl.) < OFr. *secors* < Med.Lat. *succursus* < p. part of Lat. *succurrere*, to run to the aid of : *sub-*, sub- + *currere*, to run.] —**suc′cor•a•ble** *adj.* —**suc′cor•er** *n.*

suc•co•ry (sŭk′ə-rē) *n., pl.* **-ries** See **chicory** 1. [Perh. alteration of ME *cicoree.* See CHICORY.]

suc•co•tash (sŭk′ə-tăsh′) *n.* A stew consisting of kernels of corn, lima beans, and sometimes tomatoes. [Narragansett *msíckquatash*, boiled whole-kernel corn.]

Suc•coth also **Suk•koth** (sook′əs, soo-kōs′, soo-kôt′) *n. Judaism* A harvest festival lasting for 7 days beginning on the 15th of Tishri that commemorates the open huts in which the Israelites resided during their 40 years in the wilderness. [Heb. *sukkôt*, (feast) of booths (commemorating the temporary shelters of the Jews in the wilderness), pl. of *sukkâ*, booth < *sākak*, to weave together, screen.]

suc•cour (sŭk′ər) *n. & v. Chiefly British* Variant of **succor.**

suc•cu•bus (sŭk′yə-bəs) also **suc•cu•ba** (-bə) *n., pl.* **-bus•es** or **-bi** (-bī′, -bē′) also **-bae** (-bē′, -bī′) **1.** A female demon supposed

subway
Paris Metro station

Antonio José de Sucre

to descend upon and have sexual intercourse with a man while he sleeps. **2.** An evil spirit; a demon. [ME < Med.Lat., alteration of Lat. *succuba*, paramour < *succubāre*, to lie under : *sub-*, sub- + *cubāre*, to lie down.]

suc•cu•lent (sŭk′yə-lənt) *adj.* **1.** Full of juice or sap. **2.** *Botany* Having thick fleshy water-storing leaves or stems. **3.** Highly interesting or enjoyable; delectable. ❖ *n. Botany* A succulent plant. [Lat. *succulentus* < *succus*, juice.] —**suc′cu•lence, suc′cu•len•cy** *n.* —**suc′cu•lent•ly** *adv.*

suc•cumb (sə-kŭm′) *intr.v.* **-cumbed, -cumb•ing, -cumbs 1.** To submit to an overpowering force or yield to an overwhelming desire; give up or give in. See Syns at **yield.** **2.** To die. [ME *succomben*, to bring down < OFr. *succomber* < Lat. *succumbere*, to lie under, yield : *sub-*, sub- + *-cumbere*, to lie down, as in *accumbere*, to lie down.]

suc•cus•sion (sə-kŭsh′ən) *n.* **1.** The act or process of shaking violently, esp. as a method of diagnosis to detect the presence of fluid and air in a body cavity. **2.** The condition of being shaken violently. [Lat. *succussiō, succussiōn-* < *succussus*, p. part. of *succutere*, to toss up : *sub-*, up from below; see SUB- + *quatere*, to shake.] —**suc•cus′sa•to′ry** (s-kŭs′ə-tôr′ē, -tôr′ē) *adj.*

such (sŭch) *adj.* **1a.** Of this kind: *a single parent, one of many such people in town.* **b.** Of a kind specified or implied: *a boy such as yourself.* **2a.** Of a degree or quality indicated: *His anxiety was such that he twitched.* **b.** Of so extreme a degree or quality: *never dreamed of such wealth.* ❖ *adv.* **1.** To so extreme a degree; so: *such beautiful flowers.* **2.** Very; especially: *has been in such poor health.* ❖ *pron.* **1a.** Such a person or persons or thing or things: *was the mayor and as such presided.* **b.** Itself alone or within itself: *Money as such is seldom enough.* **2.** Someone or something implied or indicated: *Such are the fortunes of war.* **3.** Similar things or people; the like: *pins, needles, and such.* —**idiom: such as** For example. [ME < OE *swylc.* See **swo-** in App.]

such and such *adj.* Not specified; unnamed or undetermined: *They agreed to meet at such and such a place.* ❖ *pron.* Something unspecified or undetermined.

such•like (sŭch′līk′) *adj.* Of the same kind; similar. ❖ *pron.* Persons or things of such a kind.

Sü•chow (soo′chou′, sü′jō′) See **Xuzhou.**

suck (sŭk) *v.* **sucked, suck•ing, sucks** —*tr.* **1.** To draw (liquid) into the mouth by movements of the tongue and lips that create suction. **2a.** To draw in by establishing a partial vacuum: *This device sucks up dirt.* **b.** To draw in by or as if by a current in a fluid. **c.** To draw or pull as if by suction. **3.** To draw nourishment through or from. **4.** To hold, moisten, or maneuver (a sweet, for example) in the mouth. **5.** *Vulgar Slang* To perform fellatio on. —*intr.* **1.** To draw something in by or as if by suction. **2.** To draw nourishment; suckle. **3.** To make a sound caused by suction. **4.** *Vulgar Slang* To be disgustingly disagreeable or offensive. ❖ *n.* **1.** The act or sound of sucking. **2.** Suction. **3.** Something drawn in by sucking. —*phrasal verbs:* **suck in** To take advantage of; cheat. **suck up** *Slang* To behave obsequiously; fawn. [ME *suken* < OE *sūcan.*]

suck•er (sŭk′ər) *n.* **1.** One that sucks, esp. an unweaned domestic animal. **2.** *Informal* **a.** One who is easily deceived; a dupe. **b.** One that is indiscriminately attracted to something specified: *a sucker for pizza.* **3.** *Slang* **a.** An unspecified thing. Used as a generalized term of reference, often as an intensive. **b.** A person. Used as a generalized term of reference, often as an intensive: *He's a mean sucker.* **4.** A lollipop. **5a.** A piston or piston valve, as in a syringe. **b.** A tube or pipe, such as a siphon, through which something is sucked. **6.** Any of numerous chiefly North American freshwater fishes of the family Catostomidae, having a thick-lipped mouth adapted for feeding by suction. **7.** *Zoology* An organ or other structure adapted for sucking nourishment or for clinging to objects by suction. **8.** *Botany* A secondary shoot produced from the base or roots of a woody plant that gives rise to a new plant. ❖ *v.* **-ered, -er•ing, -ers** —*tr.* **1.** To strip suckers or shoots from (plants). **2.** *Informal* To trick; dupe. —*intr. Botany* To send out suckers or shoots.

suck•er•fish (sŭk′ər-fĭsh′) *n., pl.* **suckerfish** or **-fish•es** See **remora.**

sucker punch *n. Slang* An unexpected punch or blow. —**suck′er-punch′** *v.*

suck•ing (sŭk′ĭng) *adj.* Not yet weaned.

sucking louse *n.* Any of various small insects of the order Anoplura with mouthparts for piercing and sucking.

suck•le (sŭk′əl) *v.* **-led, -ling, -les** —*tr.* **1a.** To cause or allow to take milk at the breast or udder; nurse. **b.** To take milk at the breast or udder of. **2.** To take in as sustenance; have as nourishment. **3.** To nourish as if with the milk of the breast; nurture. —*intr.* To suck at the breast or udder. [ME *suclen*, perh. < *suklinge*, suckling. See SUCKLING.]

suck•ler (sŭk′lər) *n.* **1.** An unweaned mammal, esp. a suckling calf. **2.** An animal that suckles its young; a mammal.

suck•ling (sŭk′lĭng) *n.* A young mammal that has not been weaned. ❖ *adj.* Unweaned. [ME *sukling* : *souken, suken*, to suck; see SUCK + *-ling*, one that is young; see −LING[1].]

Suckling, Sir John 1609–42. English poet and courtier whose works include *Aglaura* (1637).

su•crase (soo′krās′, -krāz′) *n.* See **invertase.** [Fr. *sucre*, sugar

(< OFr. *sukere*; see SUGAR) + –ASE².]

Su·cre (sōō′krä, -krĕ) The constitutional cap. of Bolivia, in the S-central part SE of La Paz; founded in 1538 as Chuquisaca and renamed in 1840. Pop. 144,944.

Sucre, Antonio José de 1795–1830. South American military leader who helped secure independence from Spain and served as the first president of Bolivia (1826–28).

su·crose (sōō′krōs′) *n.* A crystalline disaccharide carbohydrate, $C_{12}H_{22}O_{11}$, found in many plants but extracted as ordinary sugar mainly from sugar cane and sugar beets, widely used as a sweetener or preservative and in the manufacture of plastics and soaps. [Fr. *sucre*, sugar; see SUCRASE + –OSE².]

suc·tion (sŭk′shən) *n.* **1.** The act or process of sucking. **2.** A force that causes a fluid or solid to be drawn into an interior space or to adhere to a surface because of the difference between the external and internal pressures. ❖ *tr.v.* **-tioned, -tion·ing, -tions** **1.** To draw away or remove by the force of suction. **2.** To clean or evacuate (a body cavity, for example) by the force of suction. ❖ *adj.* **1.** Creating suction. **2.** Operating or operated by suction. [LLat. *sūctiō, sūctiōn*- < Lat. *sūctus*, p. part. of *sūgere*, to suck.]

suction cup *n.* A cup-shaped device, usu. of plastic or rubber, designed to adhere to a flat surface by means of suction.

suction pump *n.* A pump for drawing up a liquid by means of suction produced by a piston drawn through a cylinder.

suction stop *n. Linguistics* See click 4.

suc·to·ri·al (sŭk-tôr′ē-əl, -tōr′-) *adj.* **1.** Adapted for sucking or clinging by suction: *a suctorial organ.* **2.** Having organs or parts adapted for sucking or clinging. [< NLat. *sūctōrius* < Lat. *sūctus*, p. part. of *sūgere*, to suck.]

suc·to·ri·an (sŭk-tôr′ē-ən, -tōr′-) *n.* A protozoan of the class Suctoria, in its adult form being sessile and feeding by means of suctorial tentacles. [< NLat. *Suctōria*, class name < neut. pl. of *sūctōrius*, suctorial. See SUCTORIAL.]

Su·dan (sōō-dăn′) **1.** A region of N Africa S of the Sahara and N of the equator extending from the Atlantic coast to the mountains of Ethiopia. **2.** A country of NE Africa S of Egypt; jointly administered by Great Britain and Egypt from 1899 to 1956. Cap. Khartoum. Pop. 28,947,000. —**Su′da·nese′** (sōōd′n-ēz′, -ēs′) *adj.* & *n.*

su·da·to·ri·um (sōō′də-tôr′ē-əm, -tōr′-) *n., pl.* **-to·ri·a** (-tôr′ē-ə, -tōr′ē-ə) A hot-air room used for sweat baths. [Lat. *sūdātōrium* < neut. of *sūdātōrius*, for sweating < *sūdātus*, p. part. of *sūdāre*, to sweat. See sweid- in App.]

su·da·to·ry (sōō′də-tôr′ē, -tōr′ē) *adj.* Sudorific. ❖ *n., pl.* **-ries** **1.** See sudatorium. **2.** See sudorific. [Lat. *sūdātōrius*, inducing sweat, and *sūdātōrium*, sudatorium. See SUDATORIUM.]

Sud·bur·y (sŭd′bĕr′ē, -bə-rē) A city of SE Ontario, Canada, N of Georgian Bay. Pop. 92,059.

sudd (sŭd) *n.* A floating mass of vegetation that often obstructs navigation in tropical rivers. [Ar., obstruction, sudd < *sadda*, to obstruct.]

sud·den (sŭd′n) *adj.* **1.** Happening without warning; unforeseen. **2.** Characterized by hastiness; abrupt or rash. **3.** Characterized by rapidity; quick and swift. —**idiom: all of a sudden** Very quickly and unexpectedly; suddenly. [ME *sodain* < OFr. < VLat. *subitānus* < Lat. *subitāneus* < *subitus* < p. part. of *subīre*, to approach stealthily : *sub-*, secretly; see SUB- + *īre*, to go; see ei- in App.] —**sud′den·ly** *adv.* —**sud′den·ness** *n.*

sudden death *n.* Extra play added to determine the winner of a tied game, often with the victory awarded to the first to score. —**sud′den-death′** (sŭd′n-dĕth′) *adj.*

sudden infant death syndrome *n.* A fatal syndrome that affects sleeping infants under a year old, characterized by a sudden cessation of breathing.

Su·de·ten (sōō-dāt′n, zōō-) also **Su·de·tes** (sōō-dē′tēz) A series of mountain ranges along the Czech-Polish border between the Elbe and Oder rivers extending for c. 298 km (185 mi) and rising to 1,603 m (5,256 ft).

Su·de·ten·land (sōō-dāt′n-länd′, -länt′, zōō-) A historical region of N Czech Republic along the Polish border; occupied by Germany from 1938 to 1945.

su·do·rif·er·ous (sōō′də-rĭf′ər-əs) *adj.* Producing or secreting sweat: *sudoriferous glands.* [< LLat. *sūdōrifer* : Lat. *sūdor*, sweat; see sweid- in App. + Lat. *-fer*, -fer.]

su·do·rif·ic (sōō′də-rĭf′ĭk) *adj.* Causing or increasing sweat. ❖ *n.* A sudorific medicine. [NLat. *sūdōrificus* : Lat. *sūdor*, sweat; see sweid- in App. + Lat. *-ficus*, -fic.]

Su·dra (sōō′drə) *n.* A member of the lowest of the four major castes of traditional Indian society, comprising artisans, laborers, and menials. [Skt. *śūdraḥ*.]

suds (sŭdz) *pl.n.* **1.** Soapy water. **2.** Foam; lather. **3.** *Slang* Beer. [Perh. < obsolete Du. *zudse*, marsh < MDu. *sudse*.]

suds·y (sŭd′zē) *adj.* **-i·er, -i·est** Full of or resembling suds.

sue (sōō) *v.* **sued, su·ing, sues** —*tr.* **1.** *Law* **a.** To petition (a court) for redress of grievances or recovery of a right. **b.** To institute proceedings against (a person) for redress of grievances: *sued them for breach of contract.* **c.** To carry (an action) through to a final decision. **2.** To court; woo. **3.** *Obsolete* To make a petition to; appeal to; beseech. —*intr.* **1.** *Law* To institute legal proceedings; bring suit. **2.** To make an appeal or entreaty. **3.** To pay court; woo. [ME *sewen* < AN *suer* < VLat. **sequere*, to follow

< Lat. *sequī*. See sekʷ-¹ in App.] —**su′er** *n.*

Sue (sōō, sü), **Eugène** 1804–57. French writer whose novels include *The Mysteries of Paris* (1842–43).

suede also **suède** (swād) *n.* **1.** Leather with a soft napped surface. **2.** Fabric made to resemble suede. [Short for *Suède gloves*, partial transl. of Fr. *gants de Suède*, gloves of Sweden < *Suède*, Sweden.]

su·et (sōō′ĭt) *n.* The hard fat around the kidneys of cattle and sheep, used in cooking and for making tallow. [ME < AN **suet*, accusative of *sue*, tallow, var. of OFr. *sieu* < Lat. *sēbum*.]

Sue·to·ni·us (swē-tō′nē-əs) fl. 2nd cent. A.D. Roman historian whose major work, *Lives of the Caesars*, is an account of the first 12 Roman emperors.

Su·ez (sōō-ĕz′, sōō′ĕz′) A city of NE Egypt on the Gulf of Suez at the S terminus of the Suez Canal. Pop. 388,000.

Suez, Gulf of An arm of the Red Sea off NE Egypt W of the Sinai Peninsula.

Suez, Isthmus of An isthmus of NE Egypt connecting Africa and Asia and bordered by the Mediterranean Sea on the N and the Gulf of Suez on the S.

Suez Canal A ship canal, c. 166 km (103 mi), traversing the Isthmus of Suez and linking the Red Sea and the Gulf of Suez with the Mediterranean Sea; built under the supervision of Ferdinand de Lesseps and opened in 1869.

suf. or **suff.** *abbr.* suffix

Suff. *abbr.* suffragan

suf·fer (sŭf′ər) *v.* **-fered, -fer·ing, -fers** —*intr.* **1.** To feel pain or distress; sustain loss, injury, harm, or punishment. **2.** To tolerate or endure evil, injury, pain, or death. See Syns at bear¹. **3.** To appear at a disadvantage: *His singing suffers by comparison with yours.* —*tr.* **1.** To undergo or sustain (something painful, injurious, or unpleasant). **2.** To experience; undergo: *suffer a change in staff.* **3.** To endure or bear; stand: *She does not suffer fools.* **4.** To permit; allow: *"They were not suffered to aspire to so exalted a position as that of streetcar conductor"* (Edmund S. Morgan). [ME *suffren* < OFr. *sufrir* < VLat. **sufferīre* < Lat. *sufferre* : *sub-*, sub- + *ferre*, to carry; see bher-¹ in App.] —**suf′fer·er** *n.* —**suf′fer·ing·ly** *adv.*

suf·fer·a·ble (sŭf′ər-ə-bəl, sŭf′rə-) *adj.* Possible to suffer, endure, or permit; tolerable. —**suf′fer·a·ble·ness** *n.* —**suf′fer·a·bly** *adv.*

suf·fer·ance (sŭf′ər-əns, sŭf′rəns) *n.* **1.** Patient endurance, esp. of pain or distress. **2.** Suffering; misery. **3.** Sanction or permission implied or given by failure to prohibit; tacit consent. [ME *suffrance* < OFr. *sufrance* < Lat. *sufferentia* < *sufferēns, sufferent-*, pr. part. of *sufferre*, to suffer.]

suf·fer·ing (sŭf′ər-ĭng, sŭf′rĭng) *n.* **1.** The condition of one who suffers; the bearing of pain or distress. **2.** An instance of pain or distress.

suf·fice (sə-fīs′) *v.* **-ficed, -fic·ing, -fic·es** —*intr.* **1.** To meet present needs or requirements; be sufficient. **2.** To be equal to a specified task; be capable. —*tr.* To satisfy the needs or requirements of; be enough for. [ME *suffisen* < OFr. *suffire, suffis*- < Lat. *sufficere* : *sub-*, sub- + *facere*, to make; see dhē- in App.] —**suf·fic′er** *n.*

suf·fi·cien·cy (sə-fĭsh′ən-sē) *n., pl.* **-cies** **1.** The condition or quality of being sufficient. **2.** An adequate amount or quantity. **3.** Adequate means to live in modest comfort.

suf·fi·cient (sə-fĭsh′ənt) *adj.* **1.** Being as much as is needed. **2.** *Archaic* Competent; qualified. [ME < OFr. < Lat. *sufficiēns, sufficient*-, pr. part. of *sufficere*, to suffice. See SUFFICE.] —**suf·fi′cient·ly** *adv.*

suf·fix (sŭf′ĭks) *n.* An affix added to the end of a word or stem, serving to form a new word or functioning as an inflectional ending, such as *-ness* in *gentleness* or *-s* in *sits.* ❖ *tr.v.* **-fixed, -fix·ing, -fix·es** To add as a suffix. [NLat. *suffīxum* < Lat., neut. of *suffīxus*, p. part. of *suffīgere*, to fasten underneath, affix : *sub-*, sub- + *fīgere*, to fix, fasten.] —**suf′fix·al** *adj.* —**suf′fix·a′tion, suf·fix′ion** (sə-fĭk′shən) *n.*

suf·fo·cate (sŭf′ə-kāt′) *v.* **-cat·ed, -cat·ing, -cates** —*tr.* **1.** To kill or destroy by preventing access to air or oxygen. **2.** To impair the respiration of; asphyxiate. **3.** To cause discomfort to by or as if by cutting off the supply of fresh air. **4.** To suppress the development, imagination, or creativity of; stifle. —*intr.* **1.** To die from lack of air or oxygen; be asphyxiated. **2.** To feel discomfort from lack of fresh air. **3.** To become or feel suppressed; be stifled. [Lat. *suffōcāre, suffōcāt*- : *sub-*, sub- + *faucēs*, throat.] —**suf′fo·cat′ing·ly** *adv.* —**suf′fo·ca′tion** *n.* —**suf′fo·ca′tive** *adj.*

Suf·folk¹ (sŭf′ək) A historical region of E England bordering the North Sea; formerly part of the Anglo-Saxon kingdom of East Anglia.

Suf·folk² (sŭf′ək) *n.* **1.** Any of an English breed of hornless sheep with black face and black legs. **2.** Any of a breed of English draft horses of a chestnut color, having short legs and a thickset heavy body. [After *Suffolk*, a county of E England.]

suf·fra·gan (sŭf′rə-gən) *n.* **1.** A bishop elected or appointed as an assistant to the bishop or ordinary of a diocese. **2.** A bishop regarded in position as subordinate to an archbishop or a metropolitan. [ME < OFr. < Med.Lat. *suffrāgāneus*, voting, supporting < Lat. *suffrāgium*, support, right to vote < *suffrāgārī*, to express support. See bhreg- in App.] —**suf′fra·gan** *adj.* —**suf′fra·gan·ship′** *n.*

Sudan

Suez Canal

Suffolk²

suf·frage (sŭf′rĭj) *n.* **1a.** The right or privilege of voting; franchise. **b.** The exercise of such a right. **2.** A vote cast in deciding a disputed question or in electing a person to office. **3.** A short intercessory prayer. [ME, intercessory prayer < OFr. < Med.Lat. *suffrāgium* < Lat., the right to vote < *suffrāgārī*, to express support. See **bhreg-** in App.]

suf·fra·gette (sŭf′rə-jĕt′) *n.* An advocate of women's suffrage, esp. in the United Kingdom. **—suf′fra·get′tism** *n.*

suf·fra·gist (sŭf′rə-jĭst) *n.* An advocate of the extension of political voting rights, esp. to women. **—suf′fra·gism** *n.*

suf·fru·tes·cent (sŭf′rōō-tĕs′ənt) also **suf·fru·ti·cose** (sŭf-rōō′tĭ-kōs′) *adj.* Having a stem that is woody at the base; somewhat shrubby. [NLat. *suffrutēscēns, suffrutēscent-* : Lat. *sub-*, sub- + NLat. *frutēscēns,* frutescent (< Lat. *frutex,* shrub).]

suf·fuse (sə-fyōōz′) *tr.v.* **-fused, -fus·ing, -fus·es** To spread through or over, as with liquid or light. [Lat. *suffundere, suffūs-* : *sub-,* sub- + *fundere,* to pour; see **gheu-** in App.] **—suf·fu′sion** *n.* **—suf·fu′sive** (-fyōō′sĭv, -zĭv) *adj.*

Su·fi (sōō′fē) *Islam n., pl.* **-fis** A Muslim mystic. ❖ *adj.* Of or relating to the Sufis. [Ar. *ṣūfī,* (man) of wool, Sufi < *ṣūf,* wool (prob. < their woolen garments), perh. < Aram. *ṣippā, ṣuppā,* carded wool.] **—Su′fic** (-fĭk), **Su·fis′tic** (-fĭs′tĭk) *adj.* **—Su′fism** (-fĭz′əm) *n.*

sug·ar (shŏŏg′ər) *n.* **1.** A sweet crystalline or powdered substance, consisting of sucrose obtained mainly from sugar cane and sugar beets and used esp. in foods to improve taste. **2.** Any of a class of water-soluble crystalline carbohydrates, including sucrose and lactose, having a sweet taste and classified as monosaccharides, disaccharides, and trisaccharides. **3.** A unit, such as a lump or cube, in which sugar is dispensed or taken. **4.** *Slang* Sweetheart. Used as a term of endearment. ❖ *v.* **-ared, -ar·ing, -ars** **—tr. 1.** To coat, cover, or sweeten with sugar. **2.** To make less distasteful or more appealing. **—intr. 1.** To form sugar. **2.** To form granules; granulate. **3.** To make sugar or syrup from sugar maple sap. Often used with *off.* [ME *sugre* < OFr. *sukere* < Med.Lat. *succārum* < OItal. *zucchero* < Ar. *sukkar* < Pers. *shakar* < Skt. *śarkarā,* grit, ground sugar.] **—sug′ar·er** *n.*

suffragist
members of the National
American Woman Suffrage
Association, photographed
in 1913

sugar apple *n.* See **sweetsop.**

sugar beet *n.* A form of the common beet (*Beta vulgaris*) having fleshy white roots from which sugar is obtained.

sug·ar·ber·ry (shŏŏg′ər-bĕr′ē) *n.* See **hackberry.**

sugar bush *n.* A grove of sugar maples.

sugar cane or **sug·ar·cane** (shŏŏg′ər-kān′) *n.* A tall tropical southeast Asian grass (*Saccharum officinarum*) having thick tough stems that are a chief source of sugar.

sug·ar·coat (shŏŏg′ər-kōt′) *tr.v.* **-coat·ed, -coat·ing, -coats 1.** To cause to seem more appealing or pleasant. **2.** To coat with sugar: *sugarcoat a pill.*

sug·ar·cured (shŏŏg′ər-kyŏŏrd′) *adj.* Cured with a preparation of sugar, salt, and nitrate: *a sugar-cured ham.*

sugar daddy *n. Slang* A wealthy, usu. older man who gives expensive gifts to a young person in return for sexual favors or companionship.

sug·ared (shŏŏg′ərd) *adj.* **1.** Sweetened with sugar. **2.** Made more appealing or pleasant.

sug·ar·house (shŏŏg′ər-hous′) *n.* A sugar refinery or processing plant, esp. a building in which maple sap is boiled down to yield maple syrup and maple sugar.

sug·ar·less (shŏŏg′ər-lĭs) *adj.* **1.** Containing no sugar. **2.** Sweetened with a substance other than sucrose.

sugar loaf *n.* **1.** A large conical loaf of pure concentrated sugar. **2.** Something, such as a mountain, that resembles a loaf of sugar in shape. **—sug′ar-loaf′** (shŏŏg′ər-lōf′) *adj.*

Sug·ar·loaf Mountain (shŏŏg′ər-lōf′) A peak, 395.3 m (1,296 ft), in Rio de Janeiro, Brazil, at the entrance to Guanabara Bay.

sugar maple *n.* **1.** An eastern North American maple tree (*Acer saccharum*) having sap that is the source of maple syrup and maple sugar and hard wood used in cabinetmaking. **2.** The wood of this tree.

sugar maple
Acer saccharum

sugar of lead (lĕd) *n.* See **lead acetate.**

sugar of milk *n.* Lactose.

sugar orchard *n.* See **sugar bush.**

sugar pea *n.* A variety of snow pea having a sweet, crisp, edible pod.

sugar pine *n.* A tall evergreen timber tree (*Pinus lambertiana*) of the Pacific coast of North America having needles with white lines on the back that are grouped in fascicles of five.

sug·ar·plum (shŏŏg′ər-plŭm′) *n.* A small round piece of sugary candy.

sug·ar·y (shŏŏg′ə-rē) *adj.* **-i·er, -i·est 1.** Characterized by or containing sugar. **2.** Tasting or looking like sugar. **3.** Excessively or cloyingly sweet: *a sugary smile.* **—sug′ar·i·ness** *n.*

sug·gest (sag-jĕst′, sə-jĕst′) *tr.v.* **-gest·ed, -gest·ing, -gests 1.** To offer for consideration or action; propose. **2.** To bring or call to mind by logic or association; evoke. **3.** To make evident indirectly; intimate or imply. **4.** To serve as or provide a motive for; prompt or demand. [Lat. *suggerere, suggest-* : *sub-,* up; see **SUB-** + *gerere,* to carry.] **—sug·gest′er** *n.*

SYNONYMS *suggest, imply, hint, intimate, insinuate* These verbs mean to convey thoughts or ideas by indirection. *Suggest* refers to the calling of something to mind as the result of an association of ideas: "*his erect and careless attitude suggesting assurance and power*" (Joseph Conrad). To *imply* is to suggest a thought or idea by letting it be inferred from something else, such as a statement, that is more explicit: *The effusive praise the professor heaped on one of the students seemed to imply disapproval of the rest. Hint* refers to an oblique or covert suggestion that often contains clues: *My imagination supplied the explanation you only hinted at. Intimate* applies to indirect, subtle expression that often reflects discretion, tact, or reserve: *intimated that the couple were having marital problems.* To *insinuate* is to suggest something, usually something unpleasant, in a sly manner: *insinuated that the candidate raised money unethically.*

sug·gest·i·bil·i·ty (sag-jĕs′tə-bĭl′ĭ-tē, sə-jĕs′-) *n.* Responsiveness or susceptibility to suggestion.

sug·gest·i·ble (sag-jĕs′tə-bəl, sə-jĕs′-) *adj.* Readily influenced by suggestion: *suggestible young minds.*

sug·ges·tion (sag-jĕs′chən, sə-jĕs′-) *n.* **1.** The act of suggesting. **2.** Something suggested. **3.** The process by which one thought or mental image leads to another. **4a.** A psychological process by which an idea is induced in or adopted by another without argument, command, or coercion. **b.** An idea or response so induced. **5.** A hint or trace.

sug·ges·tive (sag-jĕs′tĭv, sə-jĕs′-) *adj.* **1a.** Tending to suggest; evocative. **b.** Stimulating further thought. **c.** Conveying a hint or suggestion. **2.** Tending to suggest something improper or indecent. **—sug·ges′tive·ly** *adv.* **—sug·ges′tive·ness** *n.*

Su·har·to (sə-här′tō, sōō-) b. 1921. Indonesian military and political leader who seized power from Sukarno (1967) and became president in 1968.

Sui (swā) A Chinese dynasty (581–618) that reunified China after a period of declining centralized government. [Chin. (Mandarin) *Suí.*]

su·i·cid·al (sōō′ĭ-sīd′l) *adj.* **1.** Causing, intending, or relating to suicide. **2.** Dangerous to oneself or to one's interests; self-destructive or ruinous. **—su′i·cid′al·ly** *adv.*

su·i·cide (sōō′ĭ-sīd′) *n.* **1.** The act or an instance of intentionally killing oneself. **2.** The destruction or ruin of one's own interests. **3.** One who commits suicide. [Lat. *suī,* of oneself; see **s(w)e-** in App. + -CIDE.]

su·i ge·ne·ris (sōō′ī jĕn′ər-ĭs, sōō′ē) *adj.* Being the only example of its kind; unique. [Lat. *suī generis* : *suī,* of its own + *generis,* genitive of *genus,* kind.]

su·int (sōō′ĭnt, swĭnt) *n.* A grease formed from dried perspiration found in the fleece of sheep, used as a source of potash. [Fr. < OFr. < *suer,* to sweat < Lat. *sūdāre.* See **sweid-** in App.]

suit (sōōt) *n.* **1a.** A set of matching outer garments, esp. one consisting of a coat with trousers or a skirt. **b.** A costume for a special activity: *a diving suit.* **2.** A group of things used together; a set or collection. **3.** *Games* Any of the four sets of 13 playing cards (clubs, diamonds, hearts, and spades) in a standard deck. **4.** Attendance required of a vassal at his feudal lord's court or manor. **5.** *Law* A court proceeding to recover a right or claim. **6.** The act or an instance of courting a woman; courtship. **7.** *Slang* One who wears a business suit, esp. an executive. ❖ *v.* **suit·ed, suit·ing, suits** **—tr. 1.** To meet the requirements of; fit. **2.** To make appropriate or suitable; adapt. **3.** To be appropriate for; befit. **4.** To please; satisfy. **5.** To provide with clothing; dress. **—intr. 1.** To be suitable or acceptable. **2.** To be in accord; agree or match. **—phrasal verb: suit up** To put on clothing designed for a special activity. [ME *sute* < AN < VLat. **sequita,* act of following, fem. of **sequitus,* p. part. of **sequere,* to follow < Lat. *sequī.* See **SUITOR**.]

suit·a·ble (sōō′tə-bəl) *adj.* Appropriate to a purpose or occasion. **—suit′a·bil′i·ty, suit′a·ble·ness** *n.* **—suit′a·bly** *adv.*

suit·case (sōōt′kās′) *n.* A usu. rectangular piece of luggage for carrying clothing.

suite (swēt) *n.* **1.** A staff of attendants or followers; a retinue. **2a.** A group of related things intended to be used together; a set. **b.** (*also* sōōt) A set of matching furniture. **3.** A series of connected rooms used as a living unit. **4.** *Music* An instrumental composition consisting of a succession of dances in the same or related keys or of a series of varying movements. **5.** *Computer Science* **a.** A group of software products packaged and sold together. **b.** A group of procedures that work cooperatively: *the TCP/IP suite of protocols.* [Fr. < OFr. See **SUIT**.]

suit·ing (sōō′tĭng) *n.* Fabric from which suits are made.

suit·or (sōō′tər) *n.* **1.** A man who is courting a woman. **2.** A person who makes a petition or request. **3.** *Law* A person who sues in court; a plaintiff; a petitioner. **4.** A person or group seeking to purchase controlling interest in a company. [ME, plaintiff < AN < Lat. *secūtor,* follower < *secūtus,* p. part. of *sequī,* to follow. See **sekʷ-¹** in App.]

Su·kar·no (sōō-kär′nō) 1901–70. Indonesian politician who served as Indonesia's first president (1949–67) and was ousted from office by a coup d'état.

Su·khu·mi (sōōk′ə-mē, sōōKH′-) See **Sokhumi.**

su·ki·ya·ki (sōō′kē-yä′kē) *n.* A Japanese dish of thinly sliced meat, bean curd, and vegetables. [J. : *suki,* strip (< *suku,* to be thin) + *yaku,* to roast.]

Suk·koth (sŏok′əs, sŏo-kōs′, sŏo-kôt′) *n. Judaism* Variant of Succoth.

Su·la·we·si (sŏo′lä-wä′sē) also **Cel·e·bes** (sĕl′ə-bēz′, sĕ-lē′bēz′, sĕ-lä′bēs) An island of central Indonesia E of Borneo.

sul·cate (sŭl′kāt′) *adj. Biology* Having narrow, deep furrows or grooves, as a stem or tissue. [Lat. *sulcātus,* p. part. of *sulcāre,* to furrow < *sulcus,* furrow.]

sul·cus (sŭl′kəs) *n., pl.* **-ci** (-kī, -sī) **1.** A deep narrow furrow or groove, as in an organ or tissue. **2.** Any of the narrow fissures separating adjacent convolutions of the brain. [Lat.] —**sul′cal** *adj.*

Su·lei·man I (sŏo′lā-män′, -lə-) Known as "Suleiman the Magnificent." 1494?–1566. Sultan of Turkey (1520–66) under whose governance the Ottoman Empire reached the height of its power.

sul·fa (sŭl′fə) *adj.* Of, relating to, or containing sulfanilamide or any sulfa drug. [Short for SULFA(NILAMIDE).]

sul·fa·di·a·zine (sŭl′fə-dī′ə-zēn′) *n.* A sulfa drug, $C_{10}H_{10}N_4O_2S$, used esp. in the treatment of toxoplasmosis.

sulfa drug *n.* Any of a group of synthetic organic compounds, derived chiefly from sulfanilamide and capable of inhibiting bacterial growth and activity.

sul·fa·nil·a·mide (sŭl′fə-nĭl′ə-mīd′, -mĭd) *n.* A white crystalline sulfonamide, $C_6H_8N_2SO_2$, used in the treatment of various bacterial infections. [SULF(O)– + ANIL(INE) + AMIDE.]

sul·fate (sŭl′fāt′) *n.* A chemical compound containing the bivalent group SO_4. ❖ *v.* **-fat·ed, -fat·ing, -fates** —*tr.* **1.** To treat or react with sulfuric acid or a sulfate. **2.** *Electricity* To cause lead sulfate to accumulate on (the plates of a lead-acid battery). —*intr.* To become sulfated. [Fr. < Lat. *sulfur,* sulfur.]

sul·fide (sŭl′fīd′) *n.* A compound of bivalent sulfur with an electropositive element or group, esp. a binary compound of sulfur with a metal.

sul·fi·nyl (sŭl′fə-nĭl′) *n.* The bivalent group SO. [SULF(O)– + –IN + –YL.]

sul·fite (sŭl′fīt′) *n.* A salt or ester of sulfurous acid. —**sul·fit′ic** (-fĭt′ĭk) *adj.*

sulfo– or **sulf–** *pref.* Sulfur: *sulfate.* [< SULFUR.]

sulfon– *pref.* Sulfonic: *sulfonamide.* [< SULFONE.]

sul·fon·a·mide (sŭl-fŏn′ə-mīd′, -mĭd) *n.* **1.** Any of a group of organic sulfur compounds containing the radical O_2NH_2 and including the sulfa drugs. **2.** See **sulfa drug.**

sul·fo·nate (sŭl′fə-nāt′) *n.* A salt or ester of sulfonic acid. ❖ *tr.v.* **-nat·ed, -nat·ing, -nates** **1.** To introduce into (an organic compound) one or more sulfonic acid groups. **2.** To treat with sulfonic acid. —**sul′fo·na′tion** *n.*

sul·fone (sŭl′fōn′) *n.* Any of various organic sulfur compounds having a sulfonyl group that is attached to two carbon atoms.

sul·fon·ic (sŭl-fŏn′ĭk) *adj.* Of or relating to the chemical group SO_2OH.

sulfonic acid *n.* Any of several organic acids containing one or more sulfonic groups.

sul·fo·ni·um (sŭl-fō′nē-əm) *n.* A positive ion or univalent radical containing trivalent sulfur, such as H_3S. [SULF(O)– + (AMM)ONIUM.]

sul·fo·nyl (sŭl′fə-nĭl′) *n.* The bivalent radical SO_2.

sulf·ox·ide (sŭl-fŏk′sīd′) *n.* Any of various organic compounds that contain a sulfinyl group.

sul·fur also **sul·phur** (sŭl′fər) *n.* *Symbol* **S** A yellow nonmetallic element occurring widely in nature in several free and combined allotropic forms and used in rubber vulcanization and in the manufacture of insecticides, pharmaceuticals, and many sulfur compounds, esp. sulfuric acid. Atomic number 16; atomic weight 32.066; melting point 112.8°C; (monoclinic) 119.0°C; boiling point 444.6°C; specific gravity (rhombic) 2.07; (monoclinic) 1.957; valence 2, 4, 6. See table at **element.** ❖ *tr.v.* **-fured, -fur·ing, -furs** also **-phured, -phur·ing, -phurs** To treat with sulfur or a compound of sulfur. [ME < AN *sulfre* < Lat. *sulfur.*]

sul·fu·rate (sŭl′fə-rāt′, -fyə-) *tr.v.* **-rat·ed, -rat·ing, -rates** To treat or combine with sulfur. —**sul′fu·ra′tion** *n.*

sulfur bacterium *n.* Any of several bacteria that oxidize inorganic sulfur compounds, esp. a rod-shaped gram-negative bacterium of the genus *Thiobacillus.*

sulfur dioxide *n.* A colorless, extremely irritating gas or liquid, SO_2, used in many industrial processes.

sul·fu·re·ous (sŭl-fyŏor′ē-əs) *adj.* Of or relating to sulfur; sulfurous.

sul·fu·ret (sŭl′fə-rĕt′, -fyə-) *tr.v.* **-ret·ed, -ret·ing, -rets** or **-ret·ted, -ret·ting, -rets** To sulfurize. ❖ *n.* A sulfide. [< NLat. *sulfurētum,* sulfide : *sulf-,* sulfur (< Lat. *sulfur*) + *-urētum,* obsolete chemical salt.]

sul·fu·ric (sŭl-fyŏor′ĭk) *adj.* Of, relating to, or containing sulfur, esp. with valence 6.

sulfuric acid *n.* A highly corrosive, dense, oily liquid, H_2SO_4, used to manufacture a wide variety of chemicals and materials including fertilizers, paints, detergents, and explosives.

sul·fur·ize (sŭl′fə-rīz′, -fyə-) *tr.v.* **-ized, -iz·ing, -iz·es** **1.** To treat or impregnate with sulfur; sulfuret. **2.** To bleach or fumigate with sulfur or sulfur dioxide. —**sul′fur·i·za′tion** (-fər-ĭ-zā′shən, -fyər-) *n.*

sul·fur·ous (sŭl′fər-əs, -fyər-, sŭl-fyŏor′əs) *adj.* **1.** Of, relating to, derived from, or containing sulfur, esp. with valence 4. **2.** Characteristic of or emanating from burning sulfur. **3.** also **sul·phur·ous** Fiery; hellish.

sulfurous acid *n.* A colorless solution of sulfur dioxide in water, H_2SO_3, characterized by a suffocating sulfurous odor, used as a bleaching agent, preservative, and disinfectant.

sul·fur·yl (sŭl′fə-rĭl′, -fyə-) *n.* See **sulfonyl.**

sulk (sŭlk) *intr.v.* **sulked, sulk·ing, sulks** To be sullenly aloof or withdrawn, as in silent resentment or protest. ❖ *n.* A mood or display of sullen aloofness or withdrawal.

sulk·y¹ (sŭl′kē) *adj.* **-i·er, -i·est** **1.** Sullenly aloof or withdrawn. **2.** Gloomy; dismal. [Perh. alteration of obsolete *sulke,* sluggish, perh. ult. < OE *āsolcen* < p. part. of *āseolcan,* to become sluggish.] —**sulk′i·ly** *adv.* —**sulk′i·ness** *n.*

sulk·y² (sŭl′kē) *n., pl.* **-ies** An open two-wheeled vehicle accommodating only the driver and drawn by one horse, used esp. in harness racing. [< SULKY¹ < its having only one seat).]

Sul·la (sŭl′ə), **Lucius Cornelius** 138–78 B.C. Roman general and dictator (82–79) who marched on Rome and seized power from his political rival Marius (88).

sul·lage (sŭl′ĭj) *n.* **1.** Silt deposited by a current of water. **2.** Waste materials or sewage; refuse. [Perh. < Fr. *souiller,* to soil. See SULLY.]

sul·len (sŭl′ən) *adj.* **-er, -est** **1.** Showing a brooding ill humor or silent resentment; morose or sulky. **2.** Gloomy or somber in tone, color, or portent. **3.** Sluggish; slow. [ME *solein* < AN *solein,* alone < *sol,* single < Lat. *sōlus,* by oneself alone. See **s(w)e–** in App.] —**sul′len·ly** *adv.* —**sul′len·ness** *n.*

Sul·li·van (sŭl′ə-vən), **Anne Mansfield** 1866–1936. Amer. educator who was the teacher of Helen Keller.

Sullivan, Sir **Arthur Seymour** 1842–1900. British composer known for a series of comic operas, including *H.M.S. Pinafore* (1878), written with the lyricist W.S. Gilbert.

Sullivan, Louis Henry or **Henri** 1856–1924. Amer. architect known for his early steel-frame designs for skyscrapers.

sul·ly (sŭl′ē) *tr.v.* **-lied, -ly·ing, -lies** **1.** To mar the cleanness or luster of; soil or stain. **2.** To defile; taint. ❖ *n., pl.* **-lies** *Archaic* Something that stains or spots. [Prob. < Fr. *souiller* < OFr. See SOIL².]

Sul·ly (sŭl′ē, sŏo-lē′, sü-), Duc de. Title of Maximilien de Béthune. 1560–1641. French politician and chief minister to Henry IV who replenished the treasury and encouraged industry.

Sul·ly (sŭl′ē), **Thomas** 1783–1872. British-born Amer. painter of *Washington's Passage of the Delaware* (c. 1818).

Sul·ly-Prud·homme (sŭl′ē-prŏo′dəm, sü-lē′prü-dôm′), **René François Armand** 1839–1907. French poet who won the 1901 Nobel Prize for literature.

sul·phur¹ (sŭl′fər) *n.* Any of various butterflies of the genus *Colias* and related genera of the family Pieridae, having yellow or orange wings marked with black. [Short for *sulphur butterfly.*]

sul·phur² (sŭl′fər) *n. & v.* Variant of **sulfur.**

sul·phur-bot·tom (sŭl′fər-bŏt′əm) *n.* See **blue whale.**

sul·phur·ous (sŭl′fər-əs, -fyər-, sŭl-fyŏor′əs) *adj.* Variant of **sulfurous** 3.

sul·tan (sŭl′tən) *n.* **1.** A ruler of a Muslim country, esp. of the former Ottoman Empire. **2.** A powerful person. [Fr. < OFr., ruler of Turkey < Turk. < Ar. *sulṭān* < Aram. *šulṭānā,* ruler < *šəlaṭ,* to rule.]

sul·tan·a (sŭl-tăn′ə, -tä′nə) *n.* **1a.** The wife, mother, sister, or daughter of a sultan. **b.** The mistress of a sultan, king, or prince. **2.** An often yellow seedless raisin of a kind originally produced in Asia Minor. [Ital., fem. of *sultano,* sultan < Ar. *sulṭān.* See SULTAN.]

sul·tan·ate (sŭl′tə-nāt′) *n.* **1.** The office, power, or reign of a sultan. **2.** A country ruled by a sultan.

sul·try (sŭl′trē) *adj.* **-tri·er, -tri·est** **1a.** Very humid and hot. **b.** Extremely hot; torrid. **2.** Expressing or arousing desire. [< obsolete *sulter,* to swelter, poss. alteration of SWELTER.] —**sul′tri·ly** *adv.* —**sul′tri·ness** *n.*

Su·lu (sŏo′lŏo) *n., pl.* **Su·lu** or **-lus** A member of a Muslim people inhabiting the Sulu Archipelago. [Sama (Austronesian language of the Philippines) *sulu,* current.]

Sulu Sea An arm of the W Pacific between the Philippines and N Borneo. The **Sulu Archipelago,** a chain of small islands belonging to the Philippines, separates the Sulu Sea from the Celebes Sea SW of Mindanao.

sum (sŭm) *n.* **1.** *Mathematics* **a.** An amount obtained as a result of adding numbers. **b.** An arithmetic problem. **2.** The whole amount, quantity, or number; an aggregate. **3.** An amount of money. **4.** A summary. **5.** The central idea or point; the gist. ❖ *tr.v.* **summed, sum·ming, sums 1.** *Mathematics* To add. **2.** To give a summary of; summarize. —*phrasal verb:* **sum up 1.** To present the substance of (material) in a condensed form; summarize. **2.** To describe or assess concisely. [ME *summe* < OFr. < Lat. *summa* < fem. of *summus,* highest. See **uper** in App.]

su·mac also **su·mach** (sŏo′măk, shŏo′-) *n.* Any of various shrubs and small trees of the genus *Rhus,* having compound leaves and usu. red hairy fruit and including poison ivy and poison oak. [ME, preparation made from sumac < OFr. (poss. via Med.Lat. *sumach*) < Ar. *summāq,* sumac tree < Aram. dark red < *səmaq,* to be red.]

Su·ma·tra (sŏo-mä′trə) An island of W Indonesia in the Indian

Suleiman I

sulky²

Ocean S of the Malay Peninsula; under Dutch control from the 17th cent. until it joined newly independent Indonesia in 1949. —Su•ma′tran *adj. & n.*

Sum•ba (sŏŏm′bə, -bä) An island of S-central Indonesia in the Lesser Sunda Is. S of Flores.

Sum•ba•wa (sŏŏm-bä′wə, -wä) A volcanic island of S-central Indonesia in the Lesser Sunda Is. W of Flores.

Su•mer (sŏŏ′mər) An ancient country of S Mesopotamia in present-day S Iraq; reached the height of its power under the Akkadian dynasty founded (c. 2340 B.C.) by Sargon I.

Su•me•ri•an (sŏŏ-mîr′ē-ən, -mĕr′-) *adj.* Of or relating to ancient Sumer or its people, language, or culture. ❖ *n.* **1.** A member of an ancient people, probably of non-Semitic origin, who established a nation of city-states in Sumer in the fourth millennium B.C. **2.** The language of the Sumerians.

sum•ma (sŏŏm′ə, sŭm′ə) *n., pl.* **-mas** or **sum•mae** (sŏŏm′ī, sŭm′ē) A comprehensive treatise, esp. in philosophy or theology. [Med.Lat. < Lat., the whole. See SUM.]

sum•ma cum lau•de (sŏŏm′ə kŏŏm lou′də, -dā, -dē, sŭm′ə kŭm lô′dē) *adv. & adj.* With the greatest honor. Used to express the highest academic distinction. [Lat. *summā cum laude,* with highest praise : *summā,* fem. ablative of *summus,* highest + *cum,* with + *laude,* ablative of *laus,* praise.]

sum•ma•rize (sŭm′ə-rīz′) *intr. & tr.v.* **-rized, -riz•ing, -riz•es** To make a summary or make a summary of. —**sum′ma•ri•za′tion** (sŭm′ər-ĭ-zā′shən) *n.* —**sum′ma•ri′zer** *n.*

sum•ma•ry (sŭm′ə-rē) *adj.* **1.** Presenting the substance in a condensed form; concise. **2.** Performed speedily and without ceremony: *a summary rejection.* ❖ *n., pl.* **-ries** A presentation of a body of material in condensed form or by reducing it to its main points; an abstract. [ME < Med.Lat. *summārius,* of or concerning the sum < Lat. *summa,* sum. See SUM.] —**sum•mar′i•ly** (sə-mĕr′ə-lē) *adv.* —**sum′ma•ri•ness** *n.*

sum•mate (sə-māt′) *v.* **-ma•ted, -ma•ting, -mates** —*tr.* To sum up. —*intr.* To form or constitute a cumulative effect.

sum•ma•tion (sə-mā′shən) *n.* **1.** The act or process of adding; addition. **2.** A sum or aggregate. **3.** A concluding part of a speech or argument containing a summary of principal points, esp. of a case before a court of law. [NLat. *summātiō, summātiōn-* < LLat. *summātus,* p. part. of *summāre,* to sum up < Lat. *summa,* sum. See SUM.]

sum•mer¹ (sŭm′ər) *n.* **1.** The usu. warmest season of the year, occurring between spring and autumn and constituting June, July, and August in the Northern Hemisphere or, as calculated astronomically, extending from the summer solstice to the autumnal equinox. **2.** A period of fruition, fulfillment, happiness, or beauty. **3.** A year. ❖ *v.* **-mered, -mer•ing, -mers** —*tr.* To lodge or keep during the summer. —*intr.* To pass the summer. ❖ *adj.* **1.** Of, having to do with, occurring in, or appropriate to the season of summer. **2.** Grown during the season of summer. [ME *sumer* < OE *sumor.* See **sem-²** in App.] —**sum′mer•ly** *adv. & adj.*

sum•mer² (sŭm′ər) *n.* **1.** A heavy horizontal timber that serves as a supporting beam, esp. for a floor. **2.** A lintel. **3.** A large stone usu. set on top of a column or pilaster to support an arch or lintel. [ME, beam, pack animal < AN *sumer* < VLat. **saumārius* < LLat. *sagmārius,* pertaining to a packsaddle, packhorse < *sagma,* packsaddle. See SUMPTER.]

sum•mer•ca•ter (sŭm′ər-kā′tər) *n.* Maine A summer resident of Maine. [Prob. SUMMER¹ + (VA)CAT(ION) + -ER¹.]

summer cypress *n.* A Eurasian annual plant (*Kochia scoparia*) having narrow dense foliage that turns bright red.

summer flounder *n.* A fluke (*Paralichthys dentatus*) of the Atlantic coast of the United States.

sum•mer•house (sŭm′ər-hous′) *n.* A small roofed structure in a park or garden affording shade and rest; a gazebo.

sum•mer•sault (sŭm′ər-sôlt′) *n. & v.* Variant of **somersault.**

summer savory *n.* See **savory²** 1.

summer school *n.* An academic session held during the summer, chiefly for supplementary and remedial study.

sum•mer•set (sŭm′ər-sĕt′) *n. & v.* Variant of **somerset.**

summer solstice *n.* In the Northern Hemisphere, the solstice that occurs on or about June 21.

summer squash *n.* Any of several varieties of squash, such as the crookneck or the cymling, that are eaten shortly after being picked rather than kept in storage.

summer stock *n.* Theatrical productions of stock companies presented during the summer.

sum•mer•time (sŭm′ər-tīm′) *n.* The summer season.

sum•mer•wood (sŭm′ər-wŏŏd′) *n.* Wood that is produced during the latter part of the growing season and is harder and less porous than springwood.

sum•mer•y (sŭm′ə-rē) *adj.* Of, intended for, or suggesting summer.

sum•ming-up (sŭm′ĭng-ŭp′) *n., pl.* **sum•mings-up** (sŭm′ĭngz-) A summary, often including an assessment.

sum•mit (sŭm′ĭt) *n.* **1.** The highest point or part; the top. **2.** The highest level or degree that can be attained. **3a.** The highest level, as of government officials. **b.** A conference or meeting of high-level leaders, usu. intended to shape a program of action. ❖ *v.* **-mit•ed, -mit•ing, -mits** —*tr.* To climb to the summit of (a mountain). —*intr.* To climb to the summit of a mountain. [ME

somet < OFr. *sommette,* dim. of *som,* top < Lat. *summum* < neut. of *summus,* highest. See **uper** in App.]

sum•mit•eer (sŭm′ĭ-tîr′) *n.* An official who takes part in a summit conference.

sum•mit•ry (sŭm′ĭ-trē) *n.* **1.** The holding of a summit conference. **2.** Participation in summit conferences.

sum•mon (sŭm′ən) *tr.v.* **-moned, -mon•ing, -mons** **1.** To call together; convene. **2.** To request to appear; send for. **3.** *Law* To order to appear in court by the issuance of a summons. **4.** To order to take a specified action; bid. **5.** To call forth; evoke: *Summon up your courage.* [ME *somonen* < OFr. *somondre* < VLat. **summonere* < Lat. *summonēre,* to remind privately, hint to : *sub-,* secretly; see SUB- + *monēre,* to warn; see **men-¹** in App.] —**sum′mon•er** *n.*

sum•mons (sŭm′ənz) *n., pl.* **-mons•es** **1.** A call by an authority to appear, come, or do something. **2.** *Law* **a.** A notice summoning a defendant to appear in court. **b.** A notice summoning a person to report to court as a juror or witness. ❖ *tr.v.* **-monsed, -mons•ing, -mons•es** *Law* To serve a court summons to. [ME *somons* < OFr. *somonse* < fem. p. part. of *somondre,* to summon. See SUMMON.]

sum•mum bo•num (sŏŏm′əm bō′nəm) *n.* The greatest or supreme good. [Lat. : *summum,* neut. of *summus,* highest + *bonum,* good.]

Sum•ner (sŭm′nər), **Charles** 1811–74. Amer. politician who was an outspoken opponent of slavery.

su•mo (sŏŏ′mō) *n.* A Japanese form of men's wrestling in which a fighter loses if forced from the ring or if he touches the ground other than with the soles of his feet. [J. *sumō* : *su,* mutually + *mō,* to rush at.]

sump (sŭmp) *n.* **1a.** A low-lying place, such as a pit, that receives drainage. **b.** A cesspool. **2.** A hole at the lowest point of a mine shaft into which water is drained in order to be pumped out. **3.** The crankcase or oil reservoir of an internal-combustion engine. [ME *sompe,* marsh < MLGer. *sump* or < MDu. *somp.* Sense 2 < Ger. *Sumpf,* swamp, sump < MHGer., swamp.]

sump pump *n.* A pump that removes liquid from a sump.

sump•ter (sŭmp′tər) *n.* A pack animal, such as a horse or mule. [ME, driver of a packhorse < OFr. *sometier* < VLat. **saumatārius* < LLat. *sagma, sagmat-,* packsaddle < Gk. < *sattein,* to pack.]

sump•tu•ar•y (sŭmp′chŏŏ-ĕr′ē) *adj.* **1.** Regulating or limiting personal expenditures. **2a.** Regulating commercial or real-estate activities. **b.** Regulating personal behavior on moral or religious grounds. [Lat. *sūmptuārius* < *sūmptus,* expense < p. part. of *sūmere,* to take, buy.]

sump•tu•ous (sŭmp′chŏŏ-əs) *adj.* Of a size or splendor suggesting great expense; lavish. [ME < OFr. *sumptueux* < Lat. *sūmptuōsus* < *sūmptus,* expense. See SUMPTUARY.] —**sump′tu•ous•ly** *adv.* —**sump′tu•ous•ness** *n.*

Su•my (sŏŏ′mē) A city of N Ukraine NW of Kharkiv. Pop. 305,000.

sun (sŭn) *n.* **1.** often **Sun** A star that is the basis of the solar system and sustains life on Earth as the source of heat and light, having a mean distance from Earth of about 150 million kilometers (93 million miles) and a diameter of approx. 1,390,000 kilometers (864,000 miles). **2.** A star that is the center of a planetary system. **3.** The radiant energy, esp. heat and visible light, emitted by the sun; sunshine. ❖ *v.* **sunned, sun•ning, suns** —*tr.* To expose to the sun's rays, as for warming, drying, or tanning. —*intr.* To expose oneself or itself to the sun. —*idiom:* **under the sun** On the earth; in the world. [ME < OE *sunne.* See **sāwel-** in App.]

Sun. *abbr.* Sunday

sun•baked (sŭn′bākt′) *adj.* Baked, dried, or hardened by exposure to sunlight: *sunbaked bricks.*

sun•bath (sŭn′băth′, -bäth′) *n.* An exposure of the body to the sun.

sun•bathe (sŭn′bāth′) *intr.v.* **-bathed, -bath•ing, -bathes** To expose the body to the sun. —**sun′bath′er** (-bā′thər) *n.*

sun•beam (sŭn′bēm′) *n.* A ray of sunlight. [ME *sunnebem* < OE *sunnebēam* (transl. of LLat. *columna lūcis,* pillar of light) : *sunne,* sun; see SUN + *bēam,* tree, building post; see BEAM.]

WORD HISTORY The word *sunbeam* is believed to have entered English in the ninth century through the work of the English king Alfred the Great, who undertook a number of translations of great Latin writings. In one of these works appears several times the Latin phrase *columna lūcis,* which we would today translate as "a column of light." Since the Old English translator did not have the word *column* in his vocabulary, he substituted *beam,* which meant "a tree" or "a wood building post." *Columna lūcis* was thus rendered as *sunnebēam,* or "sun post," which survives as our *sunbeam.*

Sun•belt also **Sun Belt** (sŭn′bĕlt′) The S and SW US.

sun•bird (sŭn′bûrd′) *n.* Any of various tropical Old World passerine birds of the family Nectariniidae, having a curved bill and often brightly colored plumage in the male.

sun bittern *n.* A cranelike tropical American bird (*Eurypyga helias*) having mottled brownish plumage and often spreading its wings and tail in a showy display.

sun•block also **sun block** (sŭn′blŏk′) *n.* A preparation that prevents sunburn by filtering out the sun's ultraviolet rays, often

sumo

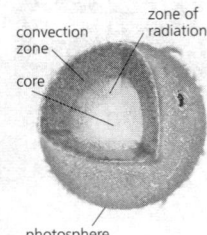
sun
cutaway of the sun

zone of radiation

convection zone

core

photosphere

purported to offer more protection than sunscreen.

sun·bon·net (sŭn′bŏn′ĭt) *n.* A woman's wide-brimmed bonnet with a flap at the back to protect the neck from the sun.

sun·bow (sŭn′bō′) *n.* A rainbow resulting from refraction of sunlight through a spray of water.

sun·burn (sŭn′bûrn′) *n.* Inflammation or blistering of the skin caused by overexposure to direct sunlight. ❖ *tr. & intr.v.* **-burned** or **-burnt** (-bûrnt′), **-burn·ing, -burns** To affect or be affected with sunburn.

sun·burst (sŭn′bûrst′) *n.* **1.** A sudden burst of sunlight, as through clouds. **2a.** A pattern or design consisting of a central disk with radiating spires. **b.** A brooch with such a design.

sun·choke (sŭn′chōk′) *n.* See **Jerusalem artichoke** 2. [SUN + (ARTI)CHOKE .]

sun·dae (sŭn′dē, -dā′) *n.* A dish of ice cream with a topping such as syrup, fruits, nuts, or whipped cream. [Perh. alteration of SUN-DAY.]

Sun·da Islands (sŭn′də, soon′-) A group of islands of the W Malay Archipelago between the South China Sea and the Indian Ocean. The **Greater Sunda Islands** include Sumatra, Borneo, Java, and Sulawesi; the **Lesser Sunda Islands** lie E of Java and extend from Bali to Timor.

sun dance *n.* A religious ceremony practiced among Native American peoples of the Great Plains, marked by several days of fasting and group dancing.

Sun·day (sŭn′dē, -dā′) *n.* **1.** The first day of the week. **2.** The Sabbath for many Christians. [ME < OE *sunnandæg*. See **sāwel-** in App.] —**Sun′days** *adv.*

Sunday, William Ashley ("Billy") 1862–1935. Amer. evangelist who was a professional baseball player (1883–91) before he became a Presbyterian minister in 1903.

Sunday punch *n. Slang* **1.** A knockout blow. **2.** Something capable of destroying an opponent or opposing force.

Sunday school *n.* **1.** A school, generally affiliated with a church or synagogue, that offers religious instruction for children on Sundays. **2.** The teachers and pupils of such a school.

sun deck *n.* A roof, balcony, or terrace used for sunbathing.

sun·der (sŭn′dər) *tr.* **-dered, -der·ing, -ders** —*tr.* To break or wrench apart; sever. See Syns at **separate**. —*intr.* To break into parts. ❖ *n.* A division or separation. [ME *sundren* < OE *sundrian*.] —**sun′der·ance** *n.*

Sun·der·land (sŭn′dər-lənd) A borough of NE England on the North Sea ESE of Newcastle; est. as a shipbuilding center in the 14th cent. Pop. 297,806.

sun·dew (sŭn′doo′, -dyoo′) *n.* Any of several insectivorous plants of the genus *Drosera*, growing in wet ground and having leaves covered with sticky hairs. [Obsolete Du. *sondauw* : *son*, sun (< MDu. *sonne*; see **sāwel-** in App.) + *dauw*, dew (< MDu. *dau*.)]

sun·di·al (sŭn′dī′əl) *n.* An instrument that indicates local apparent solar time by the shadow cast by a central projecting pointer on a surrounding calibrated dial.

sun disk *n.* An ancient Middle Eastern symbol consisting of a disk set between outspread wings, representing the sun god.

sun·dog (sŭn′dôg′, -dŏg′) *n.* **1.** A parhelion. **2.** A small halo or rainbow near the horizon just off the parhelic circle.

sun·down (sŭn′doun′) *n.* The time of sunset.

sun·down·er (sŭn′dou′nər) *n.* **1.** *Australian* A vagrant; a tramp. **2.** *Chiefly British* A drink taken at sundown.

sun·dress (sŭn′drĕs′) *n.* A light summer dress with a bodice that exposes the arms and shoulders.

sun·dries (sŭn′drēz) *pl.n.* Articles too small or numerous to be specified; miscellaneous items. [< SUNDRY.]

sun·drops (sŭn′drŏps′) *pl.n.* (*used with a sing. or pl. verb*) See **evening primrose**.

sun·dry (sŭn′drē) *adj.* Various; miscellaneous. [ME *sundri* < OE *syndrig*, separate.]

sun·fish (sŭn′fĭsh′) *n., pl.* **sunfish** or **-fish·es** **1.** Any of various small North American percoid freshwater fishes of the family Centrarchidae, having laterally compressed, often brightly colored bodies. **2.** Any of several large marine fishes of the family Molidae, esp. the ocean sunfish.

sun·flow·er (sŭn′flou′ər) *n.* **1.** Any of several plants of the genus *Helianthus*, esp. *H. annuus*, having tall coarse stems and large yellow-rayed flower heads that produce edible seeds rich in oil. **2.** The seeds of this plant.

sung (sŭng) *v.* A past tense and the past participle of **sing**.

Sung (soong) See **Song**.

Sun·ga·ri (soong′gə-rē) See **Songhua**.

sun·glass (sŭn′glăs′) *n.* **1.** A convex lens used to focus the sun's rays and produce heat. **2. sunglasses** Eyeglasses with tinted or polarizing lenses to protect the eyes from the sun.

sun·glow (sŭn′glō′) *n.* A rose or yellow glow in the sky preceding sunrise or following sunset.

sun god *n. Mythology* A god that personifies the sun.

sunk (sŭngk) *v.* A past tense and the past participle of **sink**.

sunk·en (sŭng′kən) *v. Obsolete* A past participle of **sink**. ❖ *adj.* **1.** Depressed, fallen in, or hollowed: *sunken cheeks.* **2.** Situated beneath the surface of the water or ground; submerged. **3.** Below a surrounding level: *a sunken meadow.*

sunk fence *n.* A walled ditch or hedge sunk in the ground to serve as a fence without impairing the view or scenic appeal.

sun·lamp or **sun lamp** (sŭn′lămp′) *n.* **1.** A lamp that radiates ultraviolet rays used in therapeutic and cosmetic treatments. **2.** A high-intensity lamp with parabolic mirrors, used in photography.

sun·less (sŭn′lĭs) *adj.* **1.** Being without sunlight; dark or overcast. **2.** Gloomy; cheerless. —**sun′less·ness** *n.*

sun·light (sŭn′lĭt′) *n.* The light of the sun; sunshine.

Sunlight Peak A mountain, 4,288 m (14,059 ft), in the San Juan Mts. of SW CO.

sun·lit (sŭn′lĭt′) *adj.* Illuminated by the sun.

sunn (sŭn) *n.* **1.** A tropical Asian plant (*Crotalaria juncea*) having yellow flowers. **2.** A tough fiber obtained from the stems of this plant. [Hindi *san* < Skt. *śaṇa-*, hempen < *śaṇaḥ*, hemp.]

Sun·na also **Sun·nah** (soon′ə) *n. Islam* **1.** The way of life prescribed as normative in Islam, based on the teachings and practices of Muhammad and on exegesis of the Koran. **2.** Muhammad's way of life viewed as a model for Muslims. [Ar. *sunna*, customary practice, tradition < *sanna*, to sharpen, shape, enact.]

Sun·ni (soon′ē) *n.* **1.** The branch of Islam that accepts the first four caliphs as rightful successors of Muhammad. **2.** *pl.* **Sunni** or **-nis** A Muslim belonging to this branch; a Sunnite. [Ar. *sunnī*, adherent of the Sunna < *sunna*, customary practice, tradition. See SUNNA.] —**Sun′ni** *adj.*

Sun·nite (soon′īt′) *n.* A Sunni Muslim. [< SUNNI.]

sun·ny (sŭn′ē) *adj.* **-ni·er, -ni·est** **1.** Exposed to or abounding in sunshine: *a sunny room.* **2.** Cheerful; genial: *a sunny smile.* —**sun′ni·ly** *adv.* —**sun′ni·ness** *n.*

sun·ny-side up (sŭn′ē-sīd′) *adj.* Fried only on one side. Used of eggs.

Sun·ny·vale (sŭn′ē-vāl′) A city of W CA WNW of San Jose. Pop. 131,760.

sun porch also **sun·porch** (sŭn′pôrch′, -pōrch′) *n.* An enclosed porch designed as a sunroom.

sun protection factor *n.* The degree to which a sunscreen or similar preparation protects the skin from ultraviolet rays, usu. expressed numerically.

sun·rise (sŭn′rīz′) *n.* **1.** The event or time of the daily first appearance of the sun above the eastern horizon. **2.** A beginning or an emergence: *the sunrise of classical art.*

Sunrise Manor A community of SE NV, a suburb of Las Vegas. Pop. 156,120.

sun·roof (sŭn′roof′, -roof′) *n.* A roof on a motor vehicle having a panel that can be slid back or raised.

sun·room (sŭn′room′, -room′) *n.* A room or an enclosed porch with large windows designed to admit much sunlight.

sun·scald (sŭn′skôld′) *n.* Localized injury or death of the tissues of a woody plant caused by excessive sun in summer and by the combined effects of sun and cold in winter.

sun·screen (sŭn′skrēn′) *n.* A preparation, often in the form of a cream or lotion, used to protect the skin from the ultraviolet rays of the sun. —**sun′screen′ing** *adj.*

sun·set (sŭn′sĕt′) *n.* **1.** The event or time of the daily disappearance of the sun below the western horizon. **2.** A decline or final phase: *the sunset of an empire.* ❖ *adj.* Providing for the automatic termination of a government program or agency unless deliberately reauthorized by law.

sun·shade (sŭn′shād′) *n.* Something, such as an awning or a billed cap, used or worn as a protection from the sun's rays.

sun·shine (sŭn′shīn′) *n.* **1a.** The light or the direct rays from the sun. **b.** The warmth given by the sun's rays. **c.** A location or surface on which the sun's rays fall. **2a.** Radiant cheerfulness; geniality. **b.** A source of cheerfulness. ❖ *adj.* Requiring governmental bodies to hold open meetings and sometimes to permit public access to records. —**sun′shin′y** *adj.*

sun·spot (sŭn′spŏt′) *n.* Any of the relatively cool dark spots that appear periodically in groups on the surface of the sun and are associated with strong magnetic fields.

sun·stroke (sŭn′strōk′) *n.* Heat stroke caused by exposure to the sun and characterized by a rise in temperature, convulsions, and coma.

sun·tan (sŭn′tăn′) *n.* A tan color on the skin resulting from exposure to the sun. —**sun′tanned′** *adj.*

sun·up (sŭn′ŭp′) *n.* The time of sunrise.

Sun Valley A resort area of S-central ID E of Boise; first promoted by the Union Pacific Railroad in the 1930s.

sun·ward (sŭn′wərd) *adv. & adj.* Toward or at the sun: *bathers facing sunward.* —**sun′wards** *adv.*

Sun Yat-sen (soon′ yät′sĕn′) 1866–1925. Chinese politician who served as provisional president of the republic after the fall of the Manchu (1911–12).

sup¹ (sŭp) *tr. & intr.v.* **supped, sup·ping, sups** To eat or drink (something) or engage in eating or drinking by taking small swallows or mouthfuls. ❖ *n.* A sip. [ME *soupen* < OE *sūpan.*]

sup² (sŭp) *intr.v.* **supped, sup·ping, sups** To eat an evening meal; have supper. [ME *soupen* < OFr. *souper* < *soupe*, soup. See SOUP.]

sup. *abbr.* **1.** superior **2.** superlative **3.** supine **4a.** supplement **b.** supplementary **5.** supply **6.** *Latin* supra (above)

Sup.Ct. *abbr.* **1.** superior court **2.** Supreme Court

su·per (soo′pər) *n.* **1.** *Informal* An article or product of superior size, quality, or grade. **2.** *Informal* **a.** A superintendent in an apartment or office building. **b.** A supernumerary. **3.** *Printing* A

sunburst
on a 1775 blanket chest

sunflower

Sun Yat-sen

ă	pat	oi	boy
ā	pay	ou	out
âr	care	oo	took
ä	father	oo	boot
ĕ	pet	ŭ	cut
ē	be	ûr	urge
ĭ	pit	th	thin
ī	pie	th	this
îr	pier	hw	which
ŏ	pot	zh	vision
ō	toe	ə	about,
ô	paw		item

Stress marks:
′ (primary);
′ (secondary), as in
lexicon (lĕk′sĭ-kŏn′)

thin starched cotton mesh used to super spines and covers of books. ❖ *adj. Informal* **1.** Very large, great, or extreme. **2.** Excellent; first-rate. ❖ *adv. Informal* Especially; extremely. ❖ *tr.v.* **-pered, -per•ing, -pers** *Printing* To reinforce (a book spine or cover) with super. [< SUPER–.]

super– *pref.* **1.** Above; over; upon: *superimpose.* **2.** Superior in size, quality, number, or degree: *superfine.* **3a.** Exceeding a norm: *supersaturate.* **b.** Excessive in degree or intensity: *supersubtle.* **c.** Containing a specified ingredient in an unusually high proportion: *superphosphate.* **4.** More inclusive than a specified category: *superorder.* [Lat. < *super,* over, above. See **uper** in App.]

su•per•a•ble (s○̄○′pər-ə-bəl) *adj.* Possible to overcome; surmountable: *superable problems.* [Lat. *superābilis* < *superāre,* to overcome < *super,* over. See **uper** in App.] —**su′per•a•ble•ness** *n.* —**su′per•a•bly** *adv.*

su•per•a•bound (s○̄○′pər-ə-bound′) *intr.v.* **-bound•ed, -bound•ing, -bounds** To be unusually or excessively abundant.

su•per•a•bun•dant (s○̄○′pər-ə-bŭn′dənt) *adj.* Abundant to excess. —**su′per•a•bun′dance** *n.* —**su′per•a•bun′dant•ly** *adv.*

su•per•al•loy (s○̄○′pər-ăl′oi) *n.* Any of several complex temperature-resistant alloys.

su•per•an•nu•ate (s○̄○′pər-ăn′y○̄○-āt′) *tr.v.* **-at•ed, -at•ing, -ates 1.** To allow to retire on a pension because of age or infirmity. **2.** To set aside or discard as old-fashioned or obsolete. [Back-formation < SUPERANNUATED.]

su•per•an•nu•at•ed (s○̄○′pər-ăn′y○̄○-ā′tĭd) *adj.* **1.** Retired or ineffective because of advanced age. **2.** Outmoded; obsolete. [< Med.Lat. *superannuātus,* over one year old : Lat. *super-,* super- + Lat. *annus,* year.]

su•per•at•om (s○̄○′pər-ăt′əm) *n.* See **Bose-Einstein condensate.**

su•perb (s○̄○-pûrb′) *adj.* **1.** Of unusually high quality; excellent. **2.** Majestic; imposing: *The cheetah is a superb animal.* **3.** Rich; luxurious. [Lat. *superbus,* arrogant, superior. See **uper** in App.] —**su•perb′ly** *adv.* —**su•perb′ness** *n.*

Super Bowl *n.* A football game played each year to determine the championship of the National Football League.

su•per•bug (s○̄○′pər-bŭg′) *n.* A strain of bacteria that is resistant to all antibiotics.

su•per•cal•en•der (s○̄○′pər-kăl′ən-dər) *n.* A calender with a number of rollers for giving a high finish or gloss to paper. ❖ *tr.v.* **-dered, -der•ing, -ders** To process (paper) in a supercalender.

su•per•car•go (s○̄○′pər-kär′gō) *n., pl.* **-goes** or **-gos** An officer on a merchant ship who has charge of the cargo and its sale and purchase. [Alteration of *supracargo,* alteration of Sp. *sobrecargo* : *sobre-,* over (< Lat. *super-;* see SUPER–) + *cargo,* cargo; see CARGO.]

su•per•charge (s○̄○′pər-chärj′) *tr.v.* **-charged, -charg•ing, -charg•es 1.** To increase the power of (an engine, for example), as by fitting with a supercharger. **2.** To charge heavily or excessively: *an atmosphere that was supercharged with tension.*

su•per•charg•er (s○̄○′pər-chär′jər) *n.* A blower or compressor, usu. driven by the engine, for supplying air under high pressure to the cylinders of an internal-combustion engine.

su•per•cil•i•ar•y (s○̄○′pər-sĭl′ē-ĕr′ē) *adj.* **1.** Of, relating to, or being in the area of the eyebrow. **2.** Located over the eyebrow or the eye. [NLat. *superciliāris* < Lat. *supercilium,* eyebrow. See SUPERCILIOUS.]

su•per•cil•i•ous (s○̄○′pər-sĭl′ē-əs) *adj.* Feeling or showing haughty disdain. See Syns at **proud.** [Lat. *superciliōsus* < *supercilium,* eyebrow, pride : *super-,* super- + *cilium,* lower eyelid; see **kel–** in App.] —**su′per•cil′i•ous•ly** *adv.* —**su′per•cil′i•ous•ness** *n.*

su•per•class (s○̄○′pər-klăs′) *n.* A taxonomic category ranking below a phylum and above a class.

su•per•clus•ter (s○̄○′pər-klŭs′tər) *n.* A group of neighboring clusters of galaxies.

su•per•col•lid•er (s○̄○′pər-kə-līd′ər) *n.* A high-energy particle accelerator.

su•per•com•put•er (s○̄○′pər-kəm-py○̄○′tər) *n.* A mainframe computer that is among the largest, fastest, or most powerful of those available at a given time.

su•per•con•duc•tiv•i•ty (s○̄○′pər-kŏn′dŭk-tĭv′ĭ-tē) *n.* The vanishing of electrical resistance in certain metals, alloys, and ceramics at temperatures near absolute zero and in some compounds at much higher temperatures. —**su′per•con•duc′tive** (-kən-dŭk′tĭv) *adj.* —**su′per•con•duc′tor** (-dŭk′tər) *n.*

su•per•con•ti•nent (s○̄○′pər-kŏn′tə-nənt) *n.* A large hypothetical continent, esp. Pangaea, that is thought to have split into smaller ones in the geologic past.

su•per•cool (s○̄○′pər-k○̄○l′) *v.* **-cooled, -cool•ing, -cools** —*tr.* To cool (a liquid) below a transition temperature without the transition occurring, esp. to cool below the freezing point without solidification. —*intr.* To become supercooled.

su•per•dense (s○̄○′pər-dĕns′) *adj.* Of or relating to an extreme condition in which matter is forced into nonclassical states, as when electrons are forced into protons, leaving only neutrons, or the matter is compressed beyond this point into a singularity.

su•per•dom•i•nant (s○̄○′pər-dŏm′ə-nənt) *n.* See **submediant.**

su•per•du•per (s○̄○′pər-d○̄○′pər) *adj. Slang* Great; marvelous. [Reduplication of SUPER.]

su•per•e•go (s○̄○′pər-ē′gō, -ĕg′ō) *n., pl.* **-gos** In Freudian theory, the division of the unconscious formed through the internalization of moral standards of parents and society, which censors and restrains the ego. [NLat. (transl. of Ger. *Überich* : *über-,* over, above + *Ich,* ego, a special use of *ich,* I, as a psychoanalytic term): Lat. *super-,* super- + NLat. *ego,* ego; see EGO.]

su•per•em•i•nent (s○̄○′pər-ĕm′ə-nənt) *adj.* Preeminent. —**su′per•em′i•nence** *n.* —**su′per•em′i•nent•ly** *adv.*

su•per•er•o•gate (s○̄○′pər-ĕr′ə-gāt′) *intr.v.* **-gat•ed, -gat•ing, -gates** To do more than is required, ordered, or expected. [LLat. *superērogāre, superērogāt-,* to spend over and above : Lat. *super-,* super- + Lat. *ērogāre,* to spend (*ē-, ex-,* ex- + *rogāre,* to ask; see **reg–** in App.).] —**su′per•er′o•ga′tion** (-gā′shən) *n.*

su•per•e•rog•a•to•ry (s○̄○′pər-ĭ-rŏg′ə-tôr′ē, -tōr′ē) also **su•per•e•rog•a•tive** (-tĭv) *adj.* **1.** Performed or observed beyond the required or expected degree. **2.** Superfluous; unnecessary.

su•per•fam•i•ly (s○̄○′pər-făm′ə-lē) *n., pl.* **-lies** A taxonomic category ranking below an order or its subdivisions and above a family.

su•per•fec•ta (s○̄○′pər-fĕk′tə) *n.* A method of betting in which the bettor, in order to win, must pick the first four finishers of a race in the correct sequence. [SUPER– + (PER)FECTA.]

su•per•fe•cun•da•tion (s○̄○′pər-fē′kən-dā′shən, -fĕk′ən-) *n.* Fertilization of more than one ovum within a single menstrual cycle by separate acts of coitus, esp. by different males.

su•per•fe•tate (s○̄○′pər-fē′tāt′) *intr.v.* **-tat•ed, -tat•ing, -tates** To conceive when a fetus is already present in the uterus. [Lat. *superfētāre, superfētāt-* : *super-,* super- + *fētāre,* to breed (< *fētus,* offspring; see **dhē(i)–** in App.).] —**su′per•fe•ta′tion** *n.*

su•per•fi•cial (s○̄○′pər-fĭsh′əl) *adj.* **1.** Of, affecting, or being on or near the surface: *a superficial wound.* **2.** Concerned with or comprehending only what is apparent or obvious; shallow. **3.** Apparent rather than actual or substantial: *a superficial resemblance.* **4.** Trivial; insignificant. [ME < OFr. *superficiel* < Lat. *superficiālis* < *superficiēs,* surface. See SUPERFICIES.] —**su′per•fi′ci•al′i•ty** (-fĭsh′ē-ăl′ĭ-tē), **su′per•fi′cial•ness** (-fĭsh′əl-nĭs) *n.* —**su′per•fi′cial•ly** *adv.*

su•per•fi•cies (s○̄○′pər-fĭsh′ēz, -fĭsh′ē-ēz′) *n., pl.* **superficies 1.** The outer surface of an area or a body. **2.** External appearance or aspect. [Lat. *superficiēs* : *super-,* super- + *faciēs,* face; see FACE.]

su•per•fine (s○̄○′pər-fīn′) *adj.* **1.** Of exceptional quality or refinement. **2.** Excessively delicate or refined. **3.** Of extra fine texture: *superfine sandpaper.* —**su′per•fine′ness** *n.*

su•per•flu•id (s○̄○′pər-fl○̄○′ĭd) *n.* A fluid, such as a liquid form of helium, exhibiting a frictionless flow at temperatures close to absolute zero. —**su′per•flu•id′i•ty** (-fl○̄○-ĭd′ĭ-tē) *n.*

su•per•flu•i•ty (s○̄○′pər-fl○̄○′ĭ-tē) *n., pl.* **-ties 1.** The quality or condition of being superfluous. **2.** Something superfluous. **3.** Overabundance; excess.

su•per•flu•ous (s○̄○-pûr′fl○̄○-əs) *adj.* Being beyond what is required or sufficient. [ME < OFr. *superflueux* < Lat. *superfluus* < *superfluere,* to overflow : *super-,* super- + *fluere,* to flow.] —**su•per′flu•ous•ly** *adv.* —**su•per′flu•ous•ness** *n.*

SYNONYMS *superfluous, excess, extra, spare, supernumerary, surplus* These adjectives mean being more than is needed, desired, required, or appropriate: *delete superfluous words; trying to lose excess weight; found some extra change on the dresser; sleeping in the spare room; supernumerary ornamentation; distributed surplus food.*

super G *n.* A downhill skiing race that has fewer gates set farther apart than those in a giant slalom. [*super g(iant slalom)*.]

su•per•gene (s○̄○′pər-jēn′) *n.* A group of closely linked genes occupying a large chromosomal segment and frequently functioning as a genetic unit.

su•per•gi•ant (s○̄○′pər-jī′ənt) *n.* Any of various very large bright stars, such as Betelgeuse or Rigel, having a luminosity that is thousands of times greater than that of the sun.

su•per•graph•ics (s○̄○′pər-grăf′ĭks) *n.* (*used with a sing. or pl. verb*) Brightly colored and simply designed graphic shapes of billboard proportions.

su•per•grav•i•ty (s○̄○′pər-grăv′ĭ-tē) *n.* The part of supersymmetry theory that attempts to merge the theory of gravity with the other fundamental forces by postulating the graviton's supersymmetric counterpart, the gravitino.

su•per•heat (s○̄○′pər-hēt′) *tr.v.* **-heat•ed, -heat•ing, -heats 1.** To heat excessively; overheat. **2.** To heat (steam or other vapor not in contact with its own liquid) beyond its saturation point at a given pressure. **3.** To heat (a liquid) above its boiling point without causing vaporization. ❖ *n.* (s○̄○′pər-hēt′) **1.** The amount by which a vapor is superheated. **2.** The heat imparted during the process of superheating. —**su′per•heat′er** *n.*

su•per•he•lix (s○̄○′pər-hē′lĭks) *n., pl.* **-he•lix•es** or **-hel•i•ces** (hĕl′ĭ-sēz′, hē′lĭ-) A molecular structure in which a helix is itself coiled into a helix, as of overwound circular DNA. —**su′per•hel′i•cal** (-hĕl′ĭ-kəl, -hē′lĭ-) *adj.*

su•per•he•ro (s○̄○′pər-hîr′ō) *n., pl.* **-roes** A figure, esp. in a comic strip or cartoon, endowed with superhuman powers and usu. portrayed as fighting evil or crime.

su·per·het·er·o·dyne (sōō′pər-hĕt′ər-ə-dīn′) *adj.* Of, relating to, or being a form of radio reception in which the frequency of an incoming radio signal is mixed with a locally generated signal and converted to an intermediate frequency in order to facilitate amplification. ❖ *n.* A superheterodyne radio receiver. [SUPER(SONIC) + HETERODYNE.]

su·per·high frequency (sōō′pər-hī′) *n.* A radio frequency between 3,000 and 30,000 megahertz.

su·per·high·way (sōō′pər-hī′wā′) *n.* **1.** A broad highway, often with six or more lanes, used for high-speed traffic. **2.** See **expressway.**

su·per·hu·man (sōō′pər-hyōō′mən) *adj.* **1.** Above or beyond the human; preternatural or supernatural. **2.** Beyond ordinary or normal human ability, power, or experience. —**su′per·hu·man′i·ty** (-măn′ĭ-tē) *n.* —**su′per·hu′man·ly** *adv.*

su·per·im·pose (sōō′pər-ĭm-pōz′) *tr.v.* **-posed, -pos·ing, -pos·es 1.** To lay or place (something) on or over something else. **2.** To add as a distinct feature, element, or quality. —**su′per·im·pos′a·ble** *adj.* —**su′per·im′po·si′tion** (-ĭm′pə-zĭsh′ən) *n.*

su·per·in·cum·bent (sōō′pər-ĭn-kŭm′bənt) *adj.* Lying or resting on or above something. —**su′per·in·cum′bence, su′per·in·cum′ben·cy** *n.*

su·per·in·duce (sōō′pər-ĭn-dōōs′, -dyōōs′) *tr.v.* **-duced, -duc·ing, -duc·es** To introduce as an addition. [Lat. *superindūcere* : *super-,* super- + *indūcere,* to lead in; see INDUCE.] —**su′per·in·duc′tion** (-dŭk′shən) *n.*

su·per·in·fect (sōō′pər-ĭn-fĕkt′) *tr.v.* **-fect·ed, -fect·ing, -fects** To cause (a cell, for example) to be further infected with a microorganism; infect a second time or more.

su·per·in·fec·tion (sōō′pər-ĭn-fĕk′shən) *n.* **1.** The act or process of superinfecting a cell or organism. **2.** An infection following a previous one, esp. when caused by microorganisms that have become resistant to antibiotics used earlier.

su·per·in·tend (sōō′pər-ĭn-tĕnd′, sōō′prĭn-) *tr.v.* **-tend·ed, -tend·ing, -tends** To oversee and direct; supervise. [LLat. *superintendere* : Lat. *super-,* super- + Lat. *intendere,* to direct one's attention to; see INTEND.] —**su′per·in·ten′dence** *n.*

su·per·in·ten·dent (sōō′pər-ĭn-tĕn′dənt, sōō′prĭn-) *n.* **1.** A person who has the authority to supervise or direct. **2.** A janitor or custodian in a building, esp. in an apartment house. —**su′per·in·ten′dent** *adj.*

su·pe·ri·or (sōō-pîr′ē-ər) *adj.* **1.** Higher than another in rank, station, or authority. **2.** Of a higher nature or kind. **3.** Of great value or excellence; extraordinary. **4.** Greater in number or amount than another. **5.** Affecting an attitude of disdain or conceit; haughty and supercilious. **6.** Above being affected or influenced; indifferent or immune. **7.** Located higher than another; upper. **8.** *Botany* Inserted or situated above the perianth. Used of an ovary. **9.** *Printing* Set above the main line of type. **10.** *Logic* Of wider or more comprehensive application; generic. Used of a term or proposition. ❖ *n.* **1.** One that surpasses another in rank or quality. **2.** *Ecclesiastical* The head of a religious community, such as a monastery or convent. **3.** *Printing* A superior character, as the number 2 in x². [ME < OFr. < Lat., comp. of *superus,* upper < *super,* over. See **uper** in App.] —**su′pe′ri·or′i·ty** (-ôr′ĭ-tē, -ŏr′-) *n.* —**su·pe′ri·or·ly** *adv.*

Superior, Lake The largest and westernmost of the Great Lakes, between the N-central US and S Ontario, Canada.

superior conjunction *n.* The position of a celestial body when it is on the opposite side of the sun from Earth.

superior court *n.* A court of general jurisdiction, above the inferior courts and below the higher courts of appeal.

superiority complex *n.* **1.** An exaggerated feeling of being superior to others. **2.** A psychological defense mechanism in which feelings of superiority counter or conceal feelings of inferiority.

superior planet *n.* A planet whose mean distance from the sun is greater than that of Earth's.

su·per·ja·cent (sōō′pər-jā′sənt) *adj.* Resting or lying immediately above or on something else. [Lat. *superiacēns, superiacent-,* pr. part. of *superiacēre,* to lie over : *super-,* super- + *iacēre,* to lie down.]

su·per·la·tive (sōō-pûr′lə-tĭv) *adj.* **1.** Of the highest order, quality, or degree; surpassing or superior to all others. **2.** Excessive or exaggerated. **3.** *Grammar* Of, relating to, or being the extreme degree of comparison of an adjective or adverb, as in *best* or *most brightly.* ❖ *n.* **1.** Something of the highest possible excellence. **2.** The highest degree; the acme. **3.** *Grammar* **a.** The superlative degree. **b.** An adjective or adverb expressing the superlative degree. [ME *superlatif* < OFr. < LLat. *superlātīvus* < Lat. *superlātus,* p. part. of *superferre,* to carry over a person or thing, exaggerate : *super-,* super- + *lātus,* p. part. of *ferre,* to carry; see **telə-** in App.] —**su·per′la·tive·ly** *adv.*

su·per·lin·er (sōō′pər-lī′nər) *n.* **1.** A very large luxurious oceangoing passenger ship. **2a.** A railway car fitted with more capacious, comfortable, or luxurious accommodations than usual. **b.** A railway train with such cars.

su·per·lu·na·ry (sōō′pər-lōō′nə-rē) also **su·per·lu·nar** (-nər) *adj.* Situated beyond the moon. [SUPER- + (SUB)LUNARY.]

su·per·man (sōō′pər-măn′) *n.* **1.** A man with more than human powers. **2.** An ideal superior man who, according to Nietzsche, forgoes transient pleasure, exercises creative power, and is the goal of human evolution. [Transl. of Ger. *Übermensch* : *über-,* super- + *Mensch,* man.]

su·per·mar·ket (sōō′pər-mär′kĭt) *n.* A large self-service retail market that sells food and household goods.

su·per·mod·el (sōō′pər-mŏd′l) *n.* A successful, internationally famous fashion model.

su·per·mol·e·cule (sōō′pər-mŏl′ĭ-kyōōl′) *n.* See **macromolecule.**

su·per·nal (sōō-pûr′nəl) *adj.* **1.** Celestial; heavenly. **2.** Of, coming from, or being in the sky or high above. [ME < OFr. < Lat. *supernus.* See **uper** in App.] —**su·per′nal·ly** *adv.*

su·per·na·tant (sōō′pər-nāt′nt) *adj.* Floating on the surface. ❖ *n.* also **su·per·nate** (sōō′pər-nāt′) The clear fluid above a sediment or precipitate. [Lat. *supernatāns, supernatant-,* pr. part. of *supernatāre,* to float : *super-,* super- + *natāre,* to swim, freq. of *nāre;* see **snā-** in App.]

su·per·nat·u·ral (sōō′pər-năch′ər-əl) *adj.* **1.** Of or relating to existence outside the natural world. **2.** Attributed to a power that seems to violate or go beyond natural forces. **3.** Of or relating to a deity. **4.** Of or relating to the immediate exercise of divine power; miraculous. **5.** Of or relating to the miraculous. ❖ *n.* That which is supernatural. —**su′per·nat′u·ral·ly** *adv.* —**su′per·nat′u·ral·ness** *n.*

su·per·nat·u·ral·ism (sōō′pər-năch′ər-ə-lĭz′əm) *n.* **1.** The quality of being supernatural. **2.** Belief in a supernatural agency that intervenes in the course of natural laws. —**su′per·nat′u·ral·ist** *n.* —**su′per·nat′u·ral·is′tic** *adj.*

su·per·nor·mal (sōō′pər-nôr′məl) *adj.* **1.** Greatly exceeding the normal but still obeying natural laws. **2.** Paranormal.

su·per·no·va (sōō′pər-nō′və) *n., pl.* **-vae** (-vē) or **-vas** A rare celestial phenomenon involving the explosion of most of the material in a star, resulting in an extremely bright short-lived object that emits vast amounts of energy.

su·per·nu·mer·ar·y (sōō′pər-nōō′mə-rĕr′ē, -nyōō′-) *adj.* **1.** Exceeding a fixed, prescribed, or standard number; extra. **2.** Exceeding the required or desired number or amount; superfluous. See Syns at **superfluous.** ❖ *n., pl.* **-ies 1.** One that is in excess of the regular, necessary, or usual number. **2.** An actor without a speaking part, as one who appears in a crowd scene. [Lat. *supernumerārius* : *super,* above; see SUPER- + *numerum,* accusative of *numerus,* number; see **nem-** in App.]

su·per·or·der (sōō′pər-ôr′dər) *n.* A taxonomic category ranking below a class or subclass and above an order.

su·per·or·di·nate (sōō′pər-ôr′dn-ĭt) *adj.* **1.** Of higher rank, status, or value. **2.** *Logic* Of or being the relation of a universal proposition to a particular proposition in which the terms are the same and occur in the same order. [SUPER- + (SUB)ORDINATE.] —**su′per·or′di·nate** *n.* —**su′per·or′di·nate′** (-ôr′dn-āt′) *v.* —**su′per·or′di·na′tion** (-ôr′dn-ā′shən) *n.*

su·per·or·gan·ism (sōō′pər-ôr′gə-nĭz′əm) *n.* A group of organisms, such as an insect colony, that functions as a unit.

su·per·o·vu·late (sōō′pər-ō′vyə-lāt′, -ŏv′yə-) *v.* **-lat·ed, -lat·ing, -lates** —*intr.* To produce mature ova at an accelerated rate or in a large number at one time. —*tr.* To cause (an animal) to superovulate. —**su′per·o·vu·la′tion** *n.*

su·per·par·a·sit·ism (sōō′pər-păr′ə-sī-tĭz′əm, -sī-) *n.* Infestation of parasites by other parasites.

su·per·phos·phate (sōō′pər-fŏs′fāt′) *n.* **1.** An acid phosphate. **2.** A mixture of gypsum and monobasic calcium phosphate resulting from the action of sulfuric acid on phosphate rock, used as a fertilizer.

su·per·phys·i·cal (sōō′pər-fĭz′ĭ-kəl) *adj.* **1.** Exceeding or going beyond the purely physical. **2.** Not explained by known physical laws; preternatural or supernatural.

su·per·pose (sōō′pər-pōz′) *tr.v.* **-posed, -pos·ing, -pos·es 1.** To set or place (one thing) over or above something else. **2.** *Mathematics* To place (one geometric figure) over another so that all like parts coincide. [Prob. Fr. *superposer,* back-formation < *superposition,* superposition < LLat. *superpositiō, superpositiōn-* < Lat. *superpositus,* p. part. of *superpōnere,* to place over : *super-,* super- + *pōnere,* to place; see POSITION.]

su·per·po·si·tion (sōō′pər-pə-zĭsh′ən) *n.* **1.** The act of superposing or the state of being superposed. **2.** *Geology* The principle that in a group of stratified sedimentary rocks the lowest were the earliest to be deposited.

superposition principle *n.* A principle holding that two or more solutions to a linear equation or set of linear equations can be added together so that their sum is also a solution.

su·per·pow·er (sōō′pər-pou′ər) *n.* A powerful and influential nation, esp. a nuclear power that dominates its allies or client states in an international power bloc.

su·per·re·al·ism (sōō′pər-rē′ə-lĭz′əm) *n.* An artistic and literary movement characterized by extreme realism. —**su′per·re·al,** **su′per·re·al·is′tic** *adj.* —**su′per·re·al·ist** *n.*

su·per·sat·u·rate (sōō′pər-săch′ə-rāt′) *tr.v.* **-rat·ed, -rat·ing, -rates 1.** To cause (a chemical solution) to be more highly concentrated than is normally possible under given conditions of temperature and pressure. **2.** To cause (a vapor) to exceed the normal saturation vapor pressure at a given temperature. —**su′per·sat′u·ra′tion** *n.*

su·per·sav·er (sōō′pər-sā′vər) *n.* An airline ticket, purchased

ă	pat	oi	boy
ā	pay	ou	out
âr	care	ŏŏ	took
ä	father	ōō	boot
ĕ	pet	ŭ	cut
ē	be	ûr	urge
ĭ	pit	th	thin
ī	pie	*th*	this
îr	pier	hw	which
ŏ	pot	zh	vision
ō	toe	ə	about,
ô	paw		item

Stress marks:
′ (primary);
′ (secondary), as in
lexicon (lĕk′sĭ-kŏn′)

typically well ahead of the departure date, that affords the purchaser considerable savings over regular fare.

su·per·scribe (sōō′pər-skrīb′) *tr.v.* **-scribed, -scrib·ing, -scribes** **1.** To write on the outside or upper part of (a letter, for example). **2.** To write (a name or address, for example) on the top or outside. [Lat. *superscrībere,* to write over : *super-,* super- + *scrībere,* to write; see **skrībh-** in App.]

su·per·script (sōō′pər-skrĭpt′) *n.* A character set, printed, or written above and immediately to one side of another. [Lat. *superscrīptus,* p. part. of *superscrībere,* to write over. See SUPER-SCRIBE.] **—su′per·script** *adj.*

su·per·scrip·tion (sōō′pər-skrĭp′shən) *n.* **1.** Something written above or outside something else. **2.** The act of superscribing. **3.** The part of a prescription that bears the Latin word *recipe,* represented by the symbol R.

su·per·sede (sōō′pər-sēd′) *tr.v.* **-sed·ed, -sed·ing, -sedes** **1.** To take the place of; replace. **2.** To cause to be set aside, esp. to displace as inferior or antiquated. See Syns at **replace.** [ME *superceden,* to postpone < OFr. *superceder* < Lat. *supersedēre,* to refrain from : *super-,* super- + *sedēre,* to sit; see **sed-** in App.] **—su′per·ses′sion** (-sĕsh′ən) *n.*

su·per·se·de·as (sōō′pər-sē′dē-əs) *n.* A writ containing a command to stay legal proceedings, as in the halting or delaying of the execution of a sentence. [ME < Med.Lat. *supersedeas,* you must desist (< the writ) < Lat., second pers. sing. pr. subjunctive of *supersedēre,* to desist from. See SUPERSEDE.]

su·per·se·dure (sōō′pər-sē′jər) *n.* **1.** The act or process of superseding. **2.** Replacement of a queen bee that has grown old or weak by one that is younger or more vigorous.

su·per·sen·si·ble (sōō′pər-sĕn′sə-bəl) *adj.* Beyond or above perception by the senses. **—su′per·sen′si·bly** *adv.*

su·per·son·ic (sōō′pər-sŏn′ĭk) *adj.* **1.** Having, caused by, or relating to a speed greater than the speed of sound in a given medium, esp. air. **2.** Of or relating to sound waves beyond human audibility. **—su′per·son′i·cal·ly** *adv.*

su·per·son·ics (sōō′pər-sŏn′ĭks) *n.* (used with a sing. verb) The study of phenomena produced by the motion of a body through a medium at velocities greater than that of sound.

supersonic transport *n.* A large transport airplane engineered to operate at supersonic speeds.

su·per·star (sōō′pər-stär′) *n.* **1.** A widely acclaimed star, as in movies or sports, who has great popular appeal. **2.** One that is extremely popular or prominent or is a major attraction. **—su′per·star′dom** (sōō′pər-stär′dəm) *n.*

su·per·sta·tion (sōō′pər-stā′shən) *n.* A television or radio station that broadcasts to a nationwide audience by satellite, cable, or both.

su·per·sti·tion (sōō′pər-stĭsh′ən) *n.* **1.** An irrational belief that something unrelated to an event influences its outcome. **2a.** A belief, practice, or rite maintained by ignorance of the laws of nature or by faith in magic or chance. **b.** A fearful or abject state of mind due to such ignorance or irrationality. **c.** Idolatry. [Ult. < Lat. *superstitiō, superstitiōn-* < *superstes, superstit-,* standing over. See **stā-** in App.]

su·per·sti·tious (sōō′pər-stĭsh′əs) *adj.* **1.** Inclined to believe in superstition. **2.** Of, characterized by, or due to superstition. **—su′per·sti′tious·ly** *adv.* **—su′per·sti′tious·ness** *n.*

su·per·store (sōō′pər-stôr′, -stōr′) *n.* A very large retail store that stocks diversified merchandise.

su·per·stra·tum (sōō′pər-strā′təm, -străt′əm) *n., pl.* **-stra·ta** (-strā′tə, -străt′ə) **1.** One layer or stratum superimposed on another. **2.** *Linguistics* The language of a later invading people imposed on and leaving features in an indigenous language.

su·per·string (sōō′pər-strĭng′) *n. Physics* The elementary particle in a theory of space-time incorporating supersymmetry. [SUPER(SYMMETRY) + STRING.]

su·per·struc·ture (sōō′pər-strŭk′chər) *n.* **1.** A physical or conceptual structure extended or developed from a basic form. **2.** The part of a building or other structure above the foundation. **3.** The parts of a ship's structure above the main deck. **4.** The rails, sleepers, and other parts of a railway. **5.** In Marxism, the ideologies or institutions of a society as distinct from the basic processes and direct social relations of material production and economics.

su·per·sym·me·try (sōō′pər-sĭm′ĭ-trē) *n.* A grand unified field theory that attempts to unify the fundamental forces by postulating a symmetry relating the known fermions to hypothetical bosons and the known bosons to hypothetical fermions.

su·per·tank·er (sōō′pər-tăng′kər) *n.* A very large ship, usu. between 100,000 and 400,000 displacement tons, used for transporting oil and other liquids in large quantities.

supertanker

su·per·ti·tle (sōō′pər-tīt′l) *n.* A written record or translation of the dialogue or lyrics of an opera or a choral work, for example, shown on a screen above the performers.

su·per·ton·ic (sōō′pər-tŏn′ĭk) *n. Music* The second tone of a diatonic scale.

su·per·vene (sōō′pər-vēn′) *intr.v.* **-vened, -ven·ing, -venes** **1.** To come or occur as something extraneous, additional, or unexpected. See Syns at **follow.** **2.** To follow immediately after; ensue. **3.** *Philosophy* To be dependent on a set of facts or properties in such a way that change can occur only after change has occurred

in those facts or properties. [Lat. *supervenīre* : *super-,* super- + *venīre,* to come; see *gʷā-* in App.] **—su′per·ven′ient** (-vēn′yənt) *adj.* **—su′per·ven′tion** (-vĕn′shən) *n.*

su·per·vise (sōō′pər-vīz′) *tr.v.* **-vised, -vis·ing, -vis·es** To have the charge and direction of; superintend. [ME *supervisen* < Med.Lat. *supervidēre, supervīs-* : Lat. *super-,* super- + Lat. *vidēre,* to see; see **weid-** in App.]

su·per·vi·sion (sōō′pər-vĭzh′ən) *n.* The act, process, or function of supervising. See Syns at **care.**

su·per·vi·sor (sōō′pər-vī′zər) *n.* **1.** One who supervises. **2.** One who is in charge of a particular department or unit, as in a governmental agency or school system. **3.** One who is an elected administrative officer in certain US counties and townships. **—su′per·vi′so·ry** (-vī′zə-rē) *adj.*

su·per·wom·an (sōō′pər-wōōm′ən) *n.* **1.** A woman who performs all the duties typically associated with several different full-time roles, such as wage earner, mother, and wife. **2.** A woman with more than human powers.

su·pi·nate (sōō′pə-nāt′) *v.* **-nat·ed, -nat·ing, -nates** **—tr.** **1.** To turn (the hand and forearm) so that the palm is upward or forward. **2.** To turn (the foot) so that the outer edge of the sole bears the body's weight. **—intr.** To be supinated; undergo supination. [Lat. *supīnāre, supīnāt-* < *supīnus,* backward. See SUPINE.] **—su′pi·na′tion** *n.*

su·pi·na·tor (sōō′pə-nā′tər) *n.* A muscle, esp. in the forearm, that effects or assists supination.

su·pine (sōō-pīn′, sōō′pīn′) *adj.* **1.** Lying on the back or having the face upward. **2.** Having the palm upward. **3.** Marked by or showing lethargy, passivity, or blameworthy indifference. **4.** Inclined; sloping. **❖** *n. Grammar* A defective Latin verbal noun of the fourth declension, having very limited syntax and only two cases. [ME *supin,* Latin verbal noun < LLat. *supīnum (verbum),* (verb) lying on its back, (verb) going back, neut. of Lat. *supīnus.* See **upo** in App.] **—su·pine′ly** *adv.* **—su·pine′ness** *n.*

sup·per (sŭp′ər) *n.* **1a.** A light evening meal when dinner is taken at midday. **b.** A light meal eaten before going to bed. **2.** A dance or social affair where supper is served. [ME < OFr. *souper,* to sup, supper. See SUP².]

sup·plant (sə-plănt′) *tr.v.* **-plant·ed, -plant·ing, -plants** **1.** To usurp the place of, esp. through intrigue or underhanded tactics. **2.** To displace and substitute for (another). See Syns at **replace.** [ME *supplanten* < OFr. *supplanter* < Lat. *supplantāre,* to trip up : *sub-,* sub- + *planta,* sole.]

sup·ple (sŭp′əl) *adj.* **-pler, -plest** **1.** Readily bent; pliant. **2.** Moving and bending with agility; limber. **3.** Yielding or changing readily; compliant or adaptable. [ME *souple* < OFr. < Lat. *supplex, suppliant-.*] **—sup′ple** *v.* **—sup′ple·ness** *n.* **—sup′ply, sup′ple·ly** *adv.*

sup·ple·ment (sŭp′lə-mənt) *n.* **1.** Something added to complete a thing, make up for a deficiency, or extend or strengthen the whole. **2.** A section added to a book or document to give further information or correct errors. **3.** A separate section devoted to a special subject inserted into a newspaper, for example. **4.** *Mathematics* The angle or arc that when added to a given angle or arc makes 180° or a semicircle. **❖** *tr.v.* (-mĕnt′) **-ment·ed, -ment·ing, -ments** To provide or form a supplement to. [ME < OFr. < Lat. *supplēmentum* < *supplēre,* to complete. See SUPPLY.] **—sup′ple·men·tar′i·ty** (-târ′ĭ-tē) *n.* **—sup′ple·men′ta·ry** (-mĕn′tl) *adj.* **—sup′ple·men·ta′tion** (-mĕn-tā′shən) *n.*

supplementary angle *n.* See **supplement** 4.

sup·ple·tion (sə-plē′shən) *n. Linguistics* The use of an unrelated form to complete a paradigm, as the past tense *went* of the verb *go, goes, going, gone.* [< Lat. *supplētus,* p. part. of *supplēre,* to supply. See SUPPLY.] **—sup′ple′tive** *adj.*

sup·pli·ant (sŭp′lē-ənt) *adj.* Asking humbly and earnestly; beseeching. **❖** *n.* A supplicant. [< ME, one who supplicates < OFr., pr. part. of *supplier,* to entreat < Lat. *supplicāre.* See SUPPLICATE.] **—sup′pli·ance** *n.* **—sup′pli·ant·ly** *adv.*

sup·pli·cant (sŭp′lĭ-kənt) *n.* One who supplicates; a suppliant. [< Lat. *supplicāns, supplicant-,* pr. part. of *supplicāre,* to kneel down. See SUPPLICATE.] **—sup′pli·cant** *adj.*

sup·pli·cate (sŭp′lĭ-kāt′) *v.* **-cat·ed, -cat·ing, -cates** **—tr.** **1.** To ask for humbly or earnestly, as by praying. **2.** To make a humble entreaty to; beseech. **—intr.** To make a humble, earnest petition; beg. [ME *supplicaten* < Lat. *supplicāre, supplicāt-* < *supplex, supplic-,* suppliant.] **—sup′pli·ca′tion** *n.* **—sup′pli·ca·to′ry** (-kə-tôr′ē, -tōr′ē) *adj.*

sup·ply (sə-plī′) *v.* **-plied, -ply·ing, -plies** **—tr.** **1.** To make available for use; provide: *supplied sheets for every bed.* **2.** To furnish or equip with. **3.** To fill sufficiently; satisfy. **4.** To make up for (a deficiency, for example); compensate for. **5.** To serve temporarily as a substitute in (a church, for example). **—intr.** To fill a position as a substitute. **❖** *n., pl.* **-plies** **1.** The act of supplying. **2.** Something that is or can be supplied. **3.** An amount available or sufficient for a given use; stock. **4.** Materials or provisions stored and used as needed. Often used in the plural. **5.** *Economics* The amount of a commodity available for meeting a demand or for purchase at a given price. **6.** A cleric serving as a substitute or temporary pastor. [ME *supplien,* to help, complete < OFr. *soupleer,* to fill up < Lat. *supplēre* : *sub-,* from below; see SUB– +

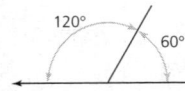

supplement
supplementary angles

120°   60°

plēre, to fill; see **pelə-¹** in App.] —**sup•pli′er** *n.*

sup•ply-side (sə-plī′sīd′) *adj.* Of, relating to, or being an economic theory stating that reduction of taxes, esp. in the higher tax brackets, will increase investment, productivity, and income throughout an economic system. —**supply side** *n.*

sup•port (sə-pôrt′, -pōrt′) *tr.v.* **-port•ed, -port•ing, -ports 1.** To bear the weight of, esp. from below. **2.** To hold in position so as to keep from falling, sinking, or slipping. **3.** To be capable of bearing; withstand. **4.** To keep from weakening or failing; strengthen. **5.** To provide for or maintain by supplying with money or necessities. **6.** To furnish corroborating evidence for. **7a.** To aid the cause, policy, or interests of. **b.** To argue in favor of; advocate. **8.** To endure; tolerate. **9.** To act in a secondary or subordinate role to (a leading performer). ❖ *n.* **1a.** The act of supporting. **b.** The state of being supported. **2.** One that supports. **3.** Maintenance, as of a family, with the necessities of life. [ME *supporten* < OFr. *supporter* < Lat. *supportāre*, to carry : *sub-*, from below; see SUB– + *portāre*, to carry; see **per-²** in App.]

SYNONYMS *support, uphold, back, advocate, champion* These verbs mean to give aid or encouragement to a person or cause. *Support* is the most general: *supported the policies that the mayor proposed.* To *uphold* is to maintain or affirm in the face of a challenge or strong opposition: *"The Declaration of Right upheld the principle of hereditary monarchy"* (Edmund Burke). *Back* suggests material or moral support intended to contribute to or assure success: *research backed by the government. Advocate* implies verbal support, often in the form of pleading or arguing: *Scientists advocate reducing saturated fats in the diet.* To *champion* is to fight for one that is under attack or is unable to act in its own behalf: *"championed the government and defended the system of taxation"* (Samuel Chew).

sup•port•a•ble (sə-pôr′tə-bəl, -pōr′-) *adj.* Bearable; endurable. —**sup•port′a•bil′i•ty** *n.* —**sup•port′a•bly** *adv.*

sup•port•er (sə-pôr′tər, -pōr′-) *n.* **1.** One that supports, as a structural member of a building. **2.** One who promotes or advocates; an adherent. **3.** An athletic supporter. **4.** *Heraldry* An animal or figure that supports a shield in a coat of arms.

support group *n.* A group of people, sometimes led by a therapist, who provide each other moral support, information, and advice on problems relating to some shared characteristic or experience: *a support group for cancer survivors.*

support hose *pl.n.* Elasticized stockings designed to reduce stress on the blood vessels in the legs.

sup•por•tive (sə-pôr′tĭv, -pōr′-) *adj.* Furnishing support or assistance. —**sup•por′tive•ly** *adv.* —**sup•por′tive•ness** *n.*

support level *n.* A price at which a security or the market becomes attractive to investors.

sup•pos•a•ble (sə-pō′zə-bəl) *adj.* That can be supposed or conjectured. —**sup•pos′a•bly** *adv.*

sup•pose (sə-pōz′) *v.* **-posed, -pos•ing, -pos•es** —*tr.* **1.** To assume to be true or real for the sake of argument or explanation. **2a.** To believe, esp. on uncertain or tentative grounds. **b.** To consider to be probable or likely. **3.** To imply as an antecedent condition; presuppose. **4.** To consider as a suggestion. —*intr.* To imagine; conjecture. [ME *supposen* < OFr. *supposer*, alteration (influenced by *poser*, to place) of Med.Lat. *suppōnere* < Lat., to put under : *sub-*, sub- + *pōnere*, to place; see **apo-** in App.]

sup•posed (sə-pōzd′, -pō′zĭd) *adj.* **1.** Presumed to be true or real without conclusive evidence. **2.** Intended. **3a.** Required. **b.** Permitted. **c.** Firmly believed; expected. —**sup•pos′ed•ly** (-pō′zĭd-lē) *adv.*

sup•pos•ing (sə-pō′zĭng) *conj.* Assuming that.

sup•po•si•tion (sŭp′ə-zĭsh′ən) *n.* **1.** The act of supposing. **2.** Something supposed; an assumption. —**sup′po•si′tion•al** *adj.* —**sup′po•si′tion•al•ly** *adv.*

sup•po•si•tious (sŭp′ə-zĭsh′əs) *adj.* Suppositious.

sup•pos•i•ti•tious (sə-pŏz′ĭ-tĭsh′əs) *adj.* **1.** Substituted with fraudulent intent; spurious. **2.** Hypothetical; supposed. [< Lat. *suppositīcius < suppositus*, p. part. of *suppōnere*, to substitute. See SUPPOSE.] —**sup•pos′i•ti′tious•ly** *adv.*

sup•pos•i•tive (sə-pŏz′ĭ-tĭv) *adj.* Of the nature of, including, or involving supposition. ❖ *n. Grammar* A conjunction, such as *if*, that introduces a supposition. —**sup•pos′i•tive•ly** *adv.*

sup•pos•i•to•ry (sə-pŏz′ĭ-tôr′ē, -tōr′ē) *n., pl.* **-ries** A plug of medication designed to melt at body temperature within a body cavity other than the mouth, esp. the rectum. [ME < OFr. *suppositorie* < Med.Lat. *suppositōrium* < LLat., neut. of *suppositōrius*, placed under < Lat. *suppositus*, p. part. of *suppōnere*, to put under. See SUPPOSE.]

sup•press (sə-prĕs′) *tr.v.* **-pressed, -press•ing, -press•es 1.** To put an end to forcibly; subdue. **2.** To curtail or prohibit the activities of. **3.** To keep from being revealed, published, or circulated. **4.** To deliberately exclude (unacceptable desires or thoughts) from the mind. **5.** To inhibit the expression of (an impulse, for example); check. **6.** To reduce the incidence or severity of (a cough, for example); arrest. [ME *suppressen* < Lat. *supprimere, suppress-* : *sub-*, sub- + *premere*, to press.] —**sup•press′ant** *n.* —**sup•press′i•ble** *adj.*

sup•pres•sion (sə-prĕsh′ən) *n.* **1.** The act of suppressing. **2.** The state of being suppressed. **3.** *Psychology* Conscious exclusion of

unacceptable desires, thoughts, or memories from the mind.

sup•pres•sive (sə-prĕs′ĭv) *adj.* Tending or serving to suppress.

sup•pres•sor (sə-prĕs′ər) *n.* **1.** or **sup•press•er** One that suppresses. **2.** A gene that suppresses the phenotypic expression of another gene, esp. of a mutant gene. **3.** A device, such as a resistor or grid, that is used in an electrical or electronic system to reduce unwanted currents.

sup•pu•rate (sŭp′yə-rāt′) *intr.v.* **-rat•ed, -rat•ing, -rates** To form or discharge pus. [ME *suppuraten* < Lat. *suppūrāre, suppūrāt-* : *sub-*, sub- + *pūs, pūr-*, pus; see **pŭ-** in App.]

sup•pu•ra•tion (sŭp′yə-rā′shən) *n.* **1.** The formation or discharge of pus. **2.** Pus. —**sup′pu•ra′tive** *adj.*

supra– *pref.* **1.** Above; over; on top of: *suprarenal.* **2.** Greater than; transcending: *supramolecular.* [Lat. < *suprā*, above, beyond. See **uper** in App.]

su•pra•lim•i•nal (sōō′prə-lĭm′ə-nəl) *adj.* Being above the threshold of consciousness or of sensation. Used of stimuli.

su•pra•mo•lec•u•lar (sōō′prə-mə-lĕk′yə-lər) *adj.* **1.** Consisting of more than one molecule. **2.** Of greater complexity than a molecule.

su•pra•or•bi•tal (sōō′prə-ôr′bĭ-tl) *adj.* Located above the orbit of the eye: *the supraorbital ridge.*

su•pra•re•nal (sōō′prə-rē′nəl) *adj.* Located on or above the kidney. ❖ *n.* A suprarenal part, esp. an adrenal gland.

suprarenal gland *n.* See **adrenal gland.**

su•pra•vi•tal (sōō′prə-vīt′l) *adj.* Relating to or capable of staining living cells after their removal from a living or recently dead organism: *a supravital stain.*

su•prem•a•cist (sōō-prĕm′ə-sĭst) *n.* One who believes that a certain group is or should be supreme.

su•prem•a•cy (sōō-prĕm′ə-sē) *n., pl.* **-cies 1.** The quality or condition of being supreme. **2.** Supreme power or authority.

su•prem•a•tism (sōō-prĕm′ə-tĭz′ən) *n.* A school and theory of geometric abstract art that originated in Russia in the early 20th century and influenced constructivism. [Russ. *suprematizm* < Fr. *suprématie*, supremacy < SUPREMACY.] —**su•prem′a•tist** *adj. & n.*

su•preme (sōō-prēm′) *adj.* **1.** Greatest in power, authority, or rank; paramount or dominant. **2.** Greatest in importance, degree, significance, character, or achievement. **3.** Ultimate; final. [Lat. *suprēmus*, superl. of *superus*, upper < *super*, over. See **uper** in App.] —**su•preme′ly** *adv.* —**su•preme′ness** *n.*

su•prême (sōō-prĕm′, -prēm′) *n.* **1.** A velouté made with chicken stock, cream, and egg yolks. **2.** A dish made or served with this sauce, esp. chicken. [Fr., supreme, suprême < Lat. *suprēmus*, supreme. See SUPREME.]

Supreme Being *n.* God.

Supreme Court *n.* **1.** The highest federal court in the United States, consisting of nine justices and having jurisdiction over all other courts in the nation. **2. supreme court** The highest court in most states within the United States.

Supreme Soviet *n.* The legislature of the former Soviet Union. [Transl. of Russ. *Verkhovnyĭ Sovet.*]

su•pre•mo (sōō-prē′mō′, sə-) *n., pl.* **-mos** *Chiefly British* One who is highest in authority or command. [Sp. and Ital., supreme, supremo < Lat. *suprēmus.* See SUPREME.]

Supt. *abbr.* superintendent

suq (sōōk, shook) *n.* Variant of **souk.**

Su•qua•mish (sə-kwä′mĭsh) *n., pl.* **Suquamish** or **-mish•es 1.** A member of a Native American people formerly inhabiting an area of the eastern shore of Puget Sound. **2.** The Coast Salish language of the Suquamish.

sur– *pref.* **1.** Over; above; upon: *surprint.* **2.** Additional: *surtax.* [ME < OFr. < Lat. *super-.* See **uper** in App.]

su•ra (sōōr′ə) *n. Islam* Any of the 114 chapters of the Koran. [Ar. *sūra < sūra <* Aram. *šūrā*, absolute form of *šurātā*, row, line.]

Su•ra•ba•ya also **Su•ra•ba•ja** (sōōr′ə-bä′yə) A city of NE Java, Indonesia, on the Java Sea. Pop. 2,027,913.

su•rah (sōōr′ə) *n.* A soft twilled fabric of silk or of a blend of silk and rayon. [Fr. *surat*, after SURAT.]

Su•ra•kar•ta (sōōr′ə-kär′tə) A city of S-central Java, Indonesia, E of Bandung. Pop. 469,888.

su•ral (sōōr′əl) *adj.* Of or relating to the calf of the leg. [NLat. *sūrālis* < Lat. *sūra*, calf of the leg.]

Su•rat (sōōr′ət, sə-rät′) A city of W-central India on the Gulf of Khambhat N of Mumbai (Bombay). Pop. 1,498,817.

sur•base (sûr′bās′) *n.* A molding or border above the base of a structure such as a baseboard.

sur•cease (sûr′sēs′, sər-sēs′) *tr. & intr.v.* **-ceased, -ceas•ing, -ceas•es** To bring or come to an end; stop. ❖ *n.* Cessation. [ME *surcesen*, var. (influenced by *cesen*, to cease) of *sursesen < surseser* < OFr. *surseoir, sursis-*, to refrain < Lat. *supersedēre.* See SUPERSEDE.]

sur•charge (sûr′chärj′) *n.* **1.** A sum added to the usual amount or cost. **2.** An overcharge, esp. when unlawful. **3.** An additional or excessive burden; an overload. **4a.** A new value or denomination overprinted on a postage or revenue stamp. **b.** The stamp to which a new value has been applied. **5.** *Law* The act of surcharging. ❖ *tr.v.* **-charged, -charg•ing, -charg•es 1.** To charge (a person) an additional sum. **2.** To overcharge (a person). **3.** To place an excessive burden on; overload. **4.** To fill beyond capac-

supporter
coat of arms of the
Peracchio family, Piedmont,
Italy

ă	pat	oi	boy
ā	pay	ou	out
âr	care	ŏŏ	took
ä	father	ōō	boot
ĕ	pet	ŭ	cut
ē	be	ûr	urge
ĭ	pit	th	thin
ī	pie	th	this
îr	pier	hw	which
ŏ	pot	zh	vision
ō	toe	ə	about,
ô	paw		item

Stress marks:
′ (primary);
′ (secondary), as in
lexicon (lĕk′sĭ-kŏn′)

ity; overfill. **5.** To print a surcharge on (a postage or revenue stamp). **6.** *Law* To show an omission of a credit in (an account). **7.** To require (a person) to reimburse funds spent without authorization. [ME < *surchargen*, to overtax < OFr. *surcharger* : *sur-*, sur- + *chargier*, to charge; see CHARGE.]

sur•cin•gle (sûr′sĭng′gəl) *n.* **1.** A girth that binds a saddle, pack, or blanket to the body of a horse. **2.** *Archaic* The fastening belt on a clerical cassock; a cincture. [ME *sursengle* < OFr. *surcengle* : *sur-*, sur- + *cengle*, belt (< Lat. *cingula* < *cingere*, to gird; see CINGULUM).] —**sur′cin′gle** *v.*

sur•coat (sûr′kōt′) *n.* **1.** A loose outer coat or gown. **2.** A tunic worn in the Middle Ages by a knight over his armor. [ME *surcote* < OFr. : *sur-*, sur- + *cote*, coat; see COAT.]

surd (sûrd) *n.* **1.** *Mathematics* An irrational number, such as $\sqrt{2}$. **2.** *Linguistics* A voiceless sound in speech. ❖ *adj. Linguistics* Voiceless, as a sound. [Med.Lat. *surdus*, speechless, surd (transl. of Ar. *(jaḏr) 'aṣamm*, deaf (root), surd, transl. of Gk. *alogos*, speechless, surd) < Lat., deaf, speechless.]

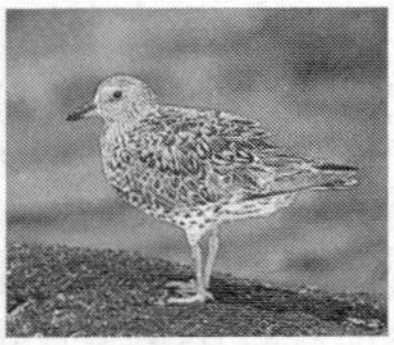

surfbird
Aphriza virgata

sure (sho͝or, shûr) *adj.* **sur•er, sur•est 1.** Impossible to doubt or dispute; certain. **2.** Not hesitating or wavering; firm. **3.** Confident, as of something awaited or expected. **4a.** Bound to come about or happen; inevitable. **b.** Having one's course directed; destined or bound. **5.** Certain not to miss or err; steady. **6a.** Worthy of being trusted or depended on; reliable. **b.** Free from or marked by freedom from doubt. **7.** Careful to do something. **8.** *Obsolete* Free from harm or danger; safe. ❖ *adv. Informal* Surely; certainly. ***—idioms:* for sure** *Informal* Certainly; unquestionably. **make sure** To establish something without doubt; make certain. **sure enough** As one might have expected; certainly. **to be sure** Indeed; certainly. [ME < OFr., safe < Lat. *sēcūrus*. See SECURE.] —**sure′ness** *n.*

sure-fire or **sure•fire** (sho͝or′fīr′) *adj. Informal* Bound to be successful or perform as expected: *a sure-fire solution to the problem.*

sure-foot•ed or **sure•foot•ed** (sho͝or′fo͝ot′ĭd) *adj.* **1.** Not liable to stumble or fall. **2.** Confident and capable. —**sure′-foot′ed•ly** *adv.* —**sure′-foot′ed•ness** *n.*

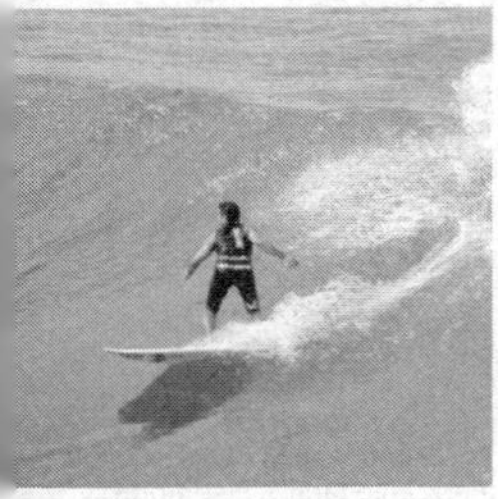

surfing

sure•ly (sho͝or′lē) *adv.* **1.** With confidence; unhesitatingly. **2.** Undoubtedly; certainly. **3.** Without fail.

sure thing *n.* An outcome that is assured; a certainty. ❖ *interj.* Of course; certainly.

sur•e•ty (sho͝or′ĭ-tē) *n., pl.* **-ties 1.** The condition of being sure, esp. of oneself; self-assurance. **2.** Something beyond doubt; a certainty. **3.** A pledge or promise made to secure against loss, damage, or default; a security. **4.** One contracted to be responsible for another, esp. one who assumes responsibilities or debts in the event of default. [ME *surte* < OFr. < Lat. *sēcūritās* < *sēcūrus*, sure. See SECURE.] —**sur′e•ty•ship′** *n.*

surf (sûrf) *n.* The waves of the sea as they break upon a shore or reef. ❖ *v.* **surfed, surf•ing, surfs** —*intr.* **1.** To engage in surfing. **2.** *Informal* To look at a variety of things casually, esp. while browsing the Internet or television channels. —*tr.* **1a.** To ride on or along (a wave) on a surfboard. **b.** To engage in surfing at: *surfed Malibu Beach.* **2.** *Informal* To browse (the Internet or television channels, for example). [?] —**surf′y** *adj.*

sur•face (sûr′fəs) *n.* **1a.** The outer or the topmost boundary of an object. **b.** A material layer constituting such a boundary. **2.** *Mathematics* **a.** The boundary of a three-dimensional figure. **b.** The two-dimensional locus of points located in three-dimensional space. **c.** A portion of space having length and breadth but no thickness. **3.** The superficial or external aspect. **4.** An airfoil. ❖ *adj.* **1.** Relating to, on, or at a surface. **2.** Relating to or occurring on or near the surface of the earth. **3a.** Superficial. **b.** Apparent as opposed to real. ❖ *v.* **-faced, -fac•ing, -fac•es** —*tr.* To provide with a surface or apply a surface to. —*intr.* **1.** To rise to the surface. **2.** To emerge after concealment. **3.** To work or dig a mine at or near the surface of the ground. ***—idiom:* on the surface** To all intents and purposes; to all outward appearances. [Fr. : *sur-*, above (< OFr.; see SUR–) + *face*, face (< OFr.; see FACE).]

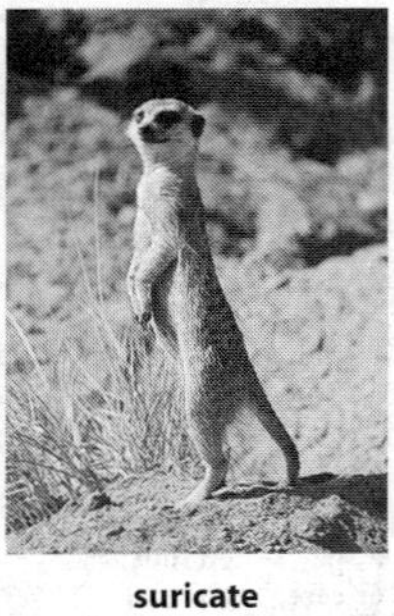

suricate
Suricata suricatta

sur•face-ac•tive (sûr′fəs-ăk′tĭv) *adj.* Of, relating to, or being a substance capable of reducing the surface tension of a liquid in which it is dissolved. Used esp. of detergents.

surface mail *n.* **1.** Mail transported over land and sea rather than by air. **2.** The system of transporting surface mail.

surface of revolution *n., pl.* **surfaces of revolution** A surface generated by revolving a plane curve about an axis in its plane.

surface plate *n.* See **planometer.**

surface structure *n.* In generative grammar, the structure that corresponds with the actual form of a sentence.

surface tension *n.* **1.** A property of liquids arising from unbalanced molecular cohesive forces at or near the surface, as a result of which the surface tends to contract. **2.** A measure of this property.

sur•face-to-air missile (sûr′fəs-tə-âr′) *n.* A guided missile launched from land or sea against an airborne target.

sur•face-to-sur•face missile (sûr′fəs-tə-sûr′fəs) *n.* A missile launched from land or sea at a target that is also on the earth's surface.

sur•fac•tant (sər-făk′tənt, sûr′făk′-) *n.* **1.** A surface-active substance. **2.** A substance that is secreted by the alveolar cells of the lung and serves to maintain the stability of pulmonary tissue by reducing the surface tension of fluids that coat the lung. [SURF(ACE)-ACT(IVE) + A(GE)NT.]

surf•bird (sûrf′bûrd′) *n.* A shore bird *(Aphriza virgata)* of the Pacific coast of North and South America having dark, heavily spotted plumage and a black tail with a broad white base.

surf•board (sûrf′bôrd′, -bōrd′) *n.* A long, narrow, somewhat rounded board, usu. having one or two fins, used for surfing. —**surf′board′** *v.*

surf•board•er (sûrf′bôr′dər, -bōr′-) *n.* See **surfer** 1.

surf•board•ing (sûrf′bôr′dĭng, -bōr′-) *n.* See **surfing** 1.

surf•boat (sûrf′bōt′) *n.* A strong seaworthy boat that can be launched or landed in heavy surf.

surf•cast•ing (sûrf′kăs′tĭng) *n.* The activity of fishing from shore, esp. by casting a line into the surf. —**surf′cast′er** *n.*

surf clam *n.* Any of various usu. large edible clams of the family Mactridae, commonly living in the surf of coastal waters.

surf duck *n.* A scoter, esp. the surf scoter.

sur•feit (sûr′fĭt) *v.* **-feit•ed, -feit•ing, -feits** —*tr.* To feed or supply to excess, satiety, or disgust. —*intr. Archaic* To overindulge. ❖ *n.* **1a.** Overindulgence in food or drink. **b.** The result of such overindulgence; satiety or disgust. **2.** An excessive amount. [ME *surfeten* < *surfait*, excess < OFr. < p. part. of *surfaire*, to overdo : *sur-*, sur- + *faire*, to do (< Lat. *facere*; see **dhē-** in App.).] —**sur′feit•er** *n.*

surf•er (sûr′fər) *n.* **1.** One who engages in the sport of surfing. **2.** *Informal* One who casually looks at something offering numerous options, esp. the Internet or television.

surf fish *n.* See **surfperch.**

sur•fi•cial (sər-fĭsh′əl) *adj.* Of, relating to, or occurring on or near the surface of the earth. [SURF(ACE) + (SUPERF)ICIAL.]

surf•ing (sûr′fĭng) *n.* **1.** The sport of riding on the crest or along the tunnel of a wave, esp. on a surfboard. **2.** The activity of casually looking at something that offers numerous options, such as the Internet or television.

surf•perch (sûrf′pûrch′) *n., pl.* **surfperch** or **-perch•es** Any of various viviparous marine fishes of the family Embiotocidae, found along the North American Pacific coast.

surf scoter *n.* A North American sea duck *(Melanitta perspicillata)*, the male of which is black with a white forehead.

surf•side (sûrf′sīd′) *adj.* Situated at or near the seashore.

surf zone *n.* See **breaker zone.**

surge (sûrj) *v.* **surged, surg•ing, surg•es** —*intr.* **1.** To rise and move in a billowing or swelling manner. **2.** To roll or be tossed about on waves, as a boat. **3.** To move like advancing waves: *The crowd surged toward the gate.* **4.** To increase suddenly. **5.** To improve one's performance suddenly, esp. in bettering one's standing in a competition. **6.** *Nautical* To slip around a windlass. Used of a rope. —*tr. Nautical* To loosen or slacken (a cable) gradually. ❖ *n.* **1.** A heavy billowing or swelling motion like that of great waves. **2a.** Wave motion with low height and a shorter period than a swell. **b.** A coastal rise in water level caused by wind. **3.** The forward and backward motion of a ship subjected to wave action. **4.** A sudden onrush: *a surge of joy.* **5.** A period of intense effort that improves a competitor's standing, as in a race. **6.** A sudden transient increase or oscillation in electric current or voltage. **7.** An instability in the power output of an engine. **8.** *Astronomy* A brief violent disturbance occurring during the eruption of a solar flare. **9.** *Nautical* **a.** The part of a windlass into which the cable surges. **b.** A temporary release or slackening of a cable. [Prob. Fr. *sourdre, sourge-* (< OFr.) and Fr. *surgir*, to rise (< OFr., to cast anchor < O Catalan), both < Lat. *surgere*, to rise : *sub-*, from below; see SUB– + *regere*, to lead straight; see **reg-** in App.]

sur•geon (sûr′jən) *n.* A physician specializing in surgery. [ME *surgien* < AN, short for OFr. *cirurgien* < *cirurgie*, surgery. See SURGERY.]

sur•geon•fish (sûr′jən-fĭsh′) *n., pl.* **surgeonfish** or **-fish•es** Any of various bright-colored tropical marine fishes of the family Acanthuridae, having one or more sharp erectile spines near the base of the tail.

Surgeon General *n., pl.* **Surgeons General 1.** The chief general officer in the medical departments of the US Army, Navy, or Air Force. **2.** The chief medical officer in the US Public Health Service or in a state public health service.

sur•geon's knot (sûr′jənz) *n., pl.* **surgeons' knots** Any of several knots, esp. one similar to a square knot, used in surgery for tying ligatures or stitching incisions.

surge protector *n.* A device containing electrical outlets that protects equipment plugged into it from a surge in current.

sur•ger•y (sûr′jə-rē) *n., pl.* **-ies 1.** The branch of medicine that deals with the diagnosis and treatment of injury, deformity, and disease by manual and instrumental means. **2.** A surgical operation or procedure, esp. one involving the removal or replacement of a diseased organ or tissue. **3.** An operating room or a laboratory of a surgeon or of a hospital's surgical staff. **4.** The skill or work of a surgeon. **5.** *Chiefly British* **a.** A physician's, dentist's, or veterinarian's office. **b.** The period during which a physician, dentist, or veterinarian consults with or treats patients in the office. [ME *surgerie* < OFr., alteration of *cirurgerie* < *cirurgie* < Lat. *chīrūrgia* < Gk. *kheirourgiā* < *kheirourgos*, working by hand : *kheir*, hand; see **ghes-** in App. + *ergon*, work; see **werg-** in App.]

sur•gi•cal (sûr′jĭ-kəl) *adj.* **1.** Of, relating to, or characteristic of surgeons or surgery. **2.** Used in surgery. **3.** Resulting from or occurring after surgery. **4.** Extremely accurate; precise: *surgical air strikes.* [< SURGEON.] **—sur′gi•cal•ly** *adv.*

Su•ri•ba•chi (so͝or′ə-bä′chē), **Mount** A volcanic hill on Iwo Jima in the W Pacific; captured by US Marines in 1945 during World War II.

su•ri•cate (so͝or′ĭ-kāt′) *n.* A small burrowing carnivorous mammal *(Suricata suricatta)* of southern Africa, related to the mongoose. [Fr. < obsolete Du. *surikat,* macaque, prob. of S African orig.]

su•ri•mi (sə-rē′mē, so͞o-) *n.* Minced processed fish used in the preparation of imitation seafood, esp. imitation shellfish. [J. : *suru,* to process, mash + *mi,* meat.]

Su•ri•na•me (so͞o′rə-nä′mə) also **Su•ri•nam** (so͝or′ə-năm′, -näm′) Formerly **Dutch Guiana.** A country of NE South America on the Atlantic Ocean; ceded to the Dutch in 1667 and gained full independence in 1975. Cap. Paramaribo. Pop. 418,000. **—Su′ri•na•mese′** (-nä-mēz′, -mēs′) *adj. & n.*

Suriname River also **Surinam River** A river of Suriname flowing c. 644 km (400 mi) to the Atlantic Ocean.

sur•ly (sûr′lē) *adj.* **-li•er, -li•est 1.** Sullenly ill-humored; gruff. **2.** *Obsolete* Arrogant; domineering. [ME *sirly,* masterful, lordly < *sir,* lord. See SIR.] **—sur′li•ly** *adv.* **—sur′li•ness** *n.*

sur•mise (sər-mīz′) *v.* **-mised, -mis•ing, -mis•es** *—tr.* To infer (something) without sufficient evidence. *—intr.* To make a conjecture; guess. ❖ *n.* A guess; a conjecture. [ME *surmisen,* to accuse < OFr. *surmise,* fem. p. part. of *surmettre* : *sur-,* sur- + *mettre,* to put (< Lat. *mittere*).]

sur•mount (sər-mount′) *tr.v.* **-mount•ed, -mount•ing, -mounts 1.** To overcome (an obstacle, for example); conquer. **2.** To ascend to the top of; climb. **3a.** To place something above; top. **b.** To be above or on top of. **4.** *Obsolete* To surpass or exceed in amount. [ME *surmonten* < OFr. *surmonter* : *sur-,* sur- + *monter,* to mount; see MOUNT[1].] **—sur•mount′a•ble** *adj.* **—sur•mount′er** *n.*

sur•mul•let (sər-mŭl′ĭt, sûr′mŭl′-) *n., pl.* **surmullet** or **-lets** See **goatfish.** [Fr. *surmulet* < OFr. *sormulet* : prob. *sor,* reddish brown (of Gmc. orig.) + *mulet,* mullet; see MULLET.]

sur•name (sûr′nām′) *n.* **1.** A name shared in common to identify the members of a family, as distinguished from each member's given name. **2.** A nickname or epithet added to a person's name. ❖ *tr.v.* **-named, -nam•ing, -names** To give a surname to. [ME, partial transl. of OFr. *surnom* : *sur-,* sur- + *nom,* name.]

sur•pass (sər-păs′) *tr.v.* **-passed, -pass•ing, -pass•es 1.** To be beyond the limit, powers, or capacity of; transcend. **2.** To be or go beyond, as in degree; exceed. [Fr. *surpasser* < OFr., to transgress : *sur-,* sur- + *passer,* pass; see PASS.]

sur•pass•ing (sər-păs′ĭng) *adj.* Exceptional; exceeding.

sur•plice (sûr′plĭs) *n.* A loose-fitting white ecclesiastical gown with wide sleeves, worn over a cassock. [ME *surplis* < AN *surpliz,* var. of OFr. *sourpeliz* < Med.Lat. *superpellīcium* : Lat. *super-,* super- + Med.Lat. *pellīcium,* fur coat (< Lat., neut. of *pellīcius,* made of skin < *pellis,* skin; see **pel-**[1] in App.).]

sur•plus (sûr′pləs, -plŭs′) *adj.* Being more than or in excess of what is needed or required. See Syns at **superfluous.** ❖ *n.* **1.** An amount or a quantity in excess of what is needed. **2.** *Accounting* **a.** Total assets minus the sum of all liabilities. **b.** Excess of a corporation's net assets over the face value of its capital stock. **c.** Excess of receipts over expenditures. [ME, an excess, surplus < OFr., an excess < Med.Lat. *superplūs* : Lat. *super-,* super- + Lat. *plūs,* more; see **pelə-**[1] in App.]

sur•plus•age (sûr′plə-sĭj) *n.* **1.** Surplus; excess. **2.** An excess of words; verbiage. **3.** *Law* Irrelevant matter in a pleading.

surplus value *n.* The difference between the value of the product produced by labor and the actual price of labor as paid out in wages in Marxian analysis of capitalism.

sur•print (sûr′prĭnt′) *tr.v.* **-print•ed, -print•ing, -prints 1.** To overprint. **2.** To superimpose (a second negative) on a previously printed image of the first negative. **—sur′print′** *n.*

sur•pris•al (sər-prī′zəl) *n.* The act of surprising or the state of being surprised.

sur•prise (sər-prīz′) *tr.v.* **-prised, -pris•ing, -pris•es 1.** To encounter suddenly or unexpectedly; take or catch unawares. **2.** To attack or capture suddenly and without warning. **3.** To cause to feel wonder, astonishment, or amazement, as at something unanticipated. **4a.** To cause (someone) to do or say something unintended. **b.** To elicit or detect through surprise. ❖ *n.* **1.** The act of surprising or the condition of being surprised. **2.** Something, such as an unexpected gift, that surprises. [ME *surprisen,* to overcome < OFr. *surprise,* fem. p. part. of *surprendre,* to surprise : *sur-,* sur- + *prendre,* to take (< Lat. *prehendere, prēndere,* to seize; see **ghend-** in App.).] **—sur•pris′er** *n.* **—sur•pris′ing•ly** *adv.*

SYNONYMS *surprise, astonish, amaze, astound* These verbs mean to affect a person strongly as being unexpected or unusual. To *surprise* is to fill with often sudden wonder or disbelief as being unanticipated or out of the ordinary: *I surprised my friend with an unexpected party. Astonish* suggests overwhelming surprise: *The sight of such an enormous crowd astonished us. Amaze* implies astonishment and often bewilderment: *The violinist's virtuosity amazed the audience. Astound* connotes shock, as from something unprecedented in one's experience: *We were astounded at the beauty of the mountains.*

sur•re•al (sə-rē′əl) *adj.* **1.** Having qualities attributed to or associated with surrealism. **2.** Having an oddly dreamlike quality. [Back-formation < SURREALISM.] **—sur•re′al•ly** *adv.*

sur•re•al•ism (sə-rē′ə-lĭz′əm) *n.* **1.** A 20th-century literary and artistic movement that attempts to express the workings of the subconscious and is characterized by fantastic imagery and incongruous juxtaposition of subject matter. **2.** Literature or art produced in this style. [Fr. *surréalisme* : *sur-,* beyond (< OFr.; see SUR–) + *réalisme,* realism (< *réalité,* reality < Med.Lat. *reālitās* < *reālis,* real; see REAL[1]).] **—sur•re′al•ist** *n.*

sur•re•al•is•tic (sə-rē′ə-lĭs′tĭk) *adj.* **1.** Of or relating to surrealism. **2.** Having an oddly dreamlike or unreal quality.

sur•re•but•ter (sûr′rĭ-bŭt′ər) also **sur•re•but•tal** (-bŭt′l) *n.* A plaintiff's reply to a defendant's rebuttal.

sur•re•join•der (sûr′rĭ-join′dər) *n.* A plaintiff's reply to a defendant's rejoinder.

sur•ren•der (sə-rĕn′dər) *v.* **-dered, -der•ing, -ders** *—tr.* **1.** To relinquish possession or control of to another because of demand or compulsion. See Syns at **relinquish. 2.** To give up in favor of another. **3.** To give up or give back (something granted). **4.** To give up or abandon: *surrender all hope.* **5.** To give over or resign (oneself) to something, as to an emotion. **6.** *Law* To restore (an estate, for example), esp. to give up (a lease) before expiration of the term. *—intr.* To give oneself up, as to an enemy. ❖ *n.* **1.** The act or an instance of surrendering. **2.** *Law* **a.** The delivery of a prisoner, fugitive from justice, or other principal in a suit into legal custody. **b.** The act of surrendering or of being surrendered to bail. **c.** Restoration of an estate. [ME *surrenderen* < OFr. *surrendre* : *sur-,* sur- + *rendre,* to deliver; see RENDER.]

sur•rep•ti•tious (sûr′əp-tĭsh′əs) *adj.* **1.** Obtained, done, or made by clandestine or stealthy means. **2.** Acting with or marked by stealth. [ME < Lat. *surreptīcius* < *surreptus,* p. part. of *surripere,* to take away secretly : *sub-,* secretly; see SUB– + *rapere,* to seize.] **—sur′rep•ti′tious•ly** *adv.* **—sur′rep•ti′tious•ness** *n.*

sur•rey (sûr′ē, sŭr′ē) *n., pl.* **-reys** A four-wheeled horse-drawn pleasure carriage having two or four seats. [Short for *Surrey cart,* after *Surrey,* a county of SE England.]

Surrey A historical region of SE England; dominated by Mercia and Wessex in Anglo-Saxon times and overrun by the Danes in the 9th cent.

sur•ro•ga•cy (sûr′ə-gə-sē, sŭr′-) *n., pl.* **-cies 1.** The condition of being a surrogate, esp. a surrogate mother. **2.** *Law* The office of a surrogate.

sur•ro•gate (sûr′ə-gĭt, -gāt′, sŭr′-) *n.* **1.** One that takes the place of another; a substitute. **2a.** A person or animal that functions as a substitute for another, as in a social or family role. **b.** A surrogate mother. **3.** *Psychology* A figure of authority who takes the place of the father or mother in a person's unconscious or emotional life. **4.** *Law* A judge in New York and some other states having jurisdiction over the probate of wills and the settlement of estates. ❖ *adj.* Substitute. ❖ *tr.v.* (-gāt′) **-gat•ed, -gat•ing, -gates 1.** To put in the place of another, esp. as a successor; replace. **2.** To appoint (another) as a replacement for oneself. [ME < Lat. *surrogātus,* p. part. of *surrogāre,* to substitute, var. of *subrogāre.* See SUBROGATE.]

surrogate mother *n.* **1.** A woman who bears a child for another person or for a couple, often for pay, as after surgical implantation of a fertilized egg. **2.** One that acts as, serves as, or is a mother substitute. **—surrogate motherhood** *n.*

sur•round (sə-round′) *tr.v.* **-round•ed, -round•ing, -rounds 1.** To extend on all sides of simultaneously; encircle. **2.** To enclose or confine on all sides so as to bar escape or outside communication. ❖ *n.* **1.** Something, such as fencing or a border, that surrounds. **2a.** The area around a thing or place. **b.** Surroundings; environment. **3.** A method of hunting wild animals by surrounding them and driving them to a place from which they cannot escape. [ME *surrounden,* to inundate < OFr. *suronder* < LLat. *superundāre* : Lat. *super-,* super- + Lat. *undāre,* to rise in waves (< *unda,* wave; see **wed-** in App.).]

sur•round•ings (sə-roun′dĭngz) *pl.n.* The external circumstances, conditions, and objects that affect existence and development; the environment.

sur•tax (sûr′tăks′) *n.* **1.** An additional tax. **2.** A tax levied on corporations or individuals after net income has exceeded a certain level. ❖ *tr.v.* **-taxed, -tax•ing, -tax•es** To levy a surtax on.

sur•ti•tle (sûr′tīt′l) *n.* See **supertitle.**

sur•veil (sər-vāl′) *tr.v.* **-veilled, -veil•ling, -veils** To keep under surveillance. [Back-formation < SURVEILLANCE.]

sur•veil•lance (sər-vā′ləns) *n.* **1.** Close observation of a person or group, esp. one under suspicion. **2.** The act of observing or the condition of being observed.

sur•veil•lant (sər-vā′lənt) *adj.* Exercising surveillance. ❖ *n.* One that exercises surveillance. [Fr., pr. part. of *surveiller,* to watch over : *sur-,* over (< OFr.; see SUR–) + *veiller,* to watch (< OFr. *veillier* < Lat. *vigilāre* < *vigil,* watchful).]

sur•vey (sər-vā′, sûr′vā′) *v.* **-veyed, -vey•ing, -veys** *—tr.* **1.** To examine or look at comprehensively. **2.** To inspect carefully; scrutinize. **3.** To determine the boundaries, area, or elevations of

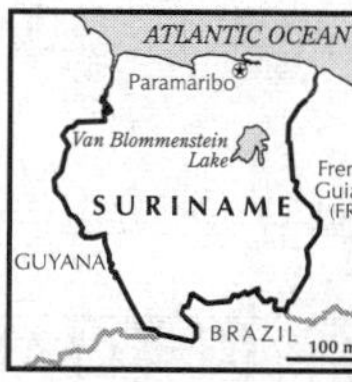

Suriname

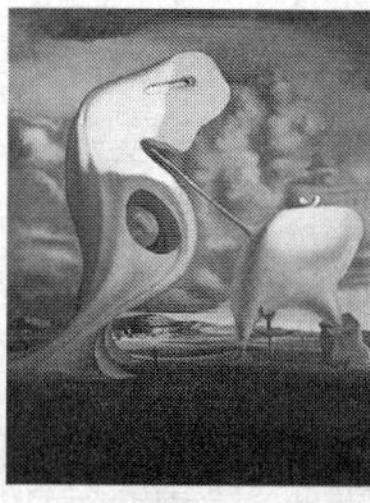

surrealism
Architectonic Angelus of Millet, 1933, by Salvador Dalí

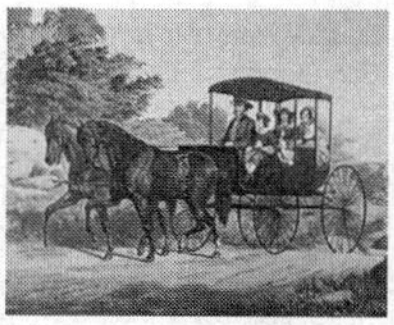

surrey
Life in the Country: The Morning Ride, 1859 lithograph by Currier and Ives

ă	pat	oi	boy
ā	pay	ou	out
âr	care	o͝o	took
ä	father	o͞o	boot
ĕ	pet	ŭ	cut
ē	be	ûr	urge
ĭ	pit	th	thin
ī	pie	*th*	this
îr	pier	hw	which
ŏ	pot	zh	vision
ō	toe	ə	about, item
ô	paw		

Stress marks:
′ (primary);
′ (secondary), as in
lexicon (lĕk′sĭ-kŏn′)

(land or structures on the earth's surface) by surveying. **4.** *Chiefly British* To inspect and determine the structural condition of (a building). **5.** To conduct a statistical survey on. **6.** To range one's gaze leisurely over. —*intr.* To make a survey. ❖ *n.* (sûr′vā′) *pl.* **-veys 1.** A detailed inspection or investigation. **2.** A general or comprehensive view. **3.** A gathering of a representative data sample. **4a.** The process of surveying. **b.** A report on or map of what has been surveyed. [ME *surveien* < OFr. *surveeir* < Med.Lat. *supervidēre* : Lat. *super-*, super- + Lat. *vidēre*, to look; see **weid-** in App.] —**sur•vey′or** *n.*

survey course *n.* An academic course consisting of an overview of a broad topic or field of knowledge.

sur•vey•ing (sər-vā′ĭng) *n.* The measurement of dimensional relationships, as of horizontal distances, elevations, directions, and angles, on the earth's surface esp. for locating property boundaries, construction layout, and mapmaking.

sur•vey•or's level (sər-vā′ərz) *n., pl.* **surveyors' levels** An instrument having a telescope and attached spirit level mounted on a tripod and rotating around a vertical axis.

sur•viv•a•ble (sər-vī′və-bəl) *adj.* **1.** Capable of surviving. **2.** That can be survived. —**sur•viv′a•bil′i•ty** *n.*

sur•viv•al (sər-vī′vəl) *n.* **1a.** The act or process of surviving. **b.** The fact of having survived. **2.** Something, such as an ancient custom or belief, that has survived.

survival of the fittest *n.* Natural selection conceived of as a struggle for life in which only those organisms best adapted to existing conditions are able to survive and reproduce.

sur•viv•al•ist (sər-vī′və-lĭst) *n.* One whose primary goal is personal or group survival, as after nuclear war.

sur•vive (sər-vīv′) *v.* **-vived, -viv•ing, -vives** —*intr.* **1.** To remain alive or in existence. **2.** To carry on despite hardships or trauma; persevere. **3.** To remain functional or usable. —*tr.* **1.** To live longer than; outlive. **2.** To live or persist through. **3.** To cope with (a trauma or setback); persevere after. [ME *surviven* < OFr. *sourvivre* < Lat. *supervīvere* : super-, super- + *vīvere*, to live; see **gʷeiə-** in App.] —**sur•vi′vor** *n.*

sur•vi•vor•ship (sər-vī′vər-shĭp′) *n.* **1.** *Law* The right of a person who survives a partner or joint owner to the entire ownership of something that was previously owned jointly. **2.** The condition of being a survivor.

Su•sa (sōō′sə, -zə) A ruined city of SW Iran S of Hamaden; cap. of the kingdom of Elam.

Su•sah or **Su•sa** (sōō′sə, -zə) See **Sousse**.

Su•san B. Anthony Day (sōō′zən) *n.* February 15, observed in the United States in commemoration of the birth in 1820 of Susan B. Anthony.

Su•san•na (sōō-zăn′ə) In the Apocrypha, a captive in Babylon who was falsely accused of adultery.

sus•cep•tance (sə-sĕp′təns) *n.* *Electronics* The imaginary part of the complex admittance. [(*electric*) *suscept*(*ibility*), a measure of the ease of polarization of a dielectric + −ANCE.]

sus•cep•ti•bil•i•ty (sə-sĕp′tə-bĭl′ĭ-tē) *n., pl.* **-ties 1.** The quality or condition of being susceptible. **2.** The capacity to be affected by deep emotions or strong feelings; sensitivity. **3. susceptibilities** Sensibilities; feelings.

sus•cep•ti•ble (sə-sĕp′tə-bəl) *adj.* **1.** Easily influenced or affected. **2.** Likely to be affected: *susceptible to colds.* **3.** Especially sensitive; highly impressionable. **4.** Permitting an action to be performed; capable of undergoing: *a statement susceptible of proof.* [LLat. *susceptibilis* < Lat. *susceptus*, p. part. of *suscipere*, to receive : *sub-*, from below; see SUB- + *capere*, to take; see **kap-** in App.] —**sus•cep′ti•bly** *adv.*

sus•cep•tive (sə-sĕp′tĭv) *adj.* **1.** Receptive. **2.** Susceptible. —**sus•cep′tive•ness, sus•cep′tiv′i•ty** *n.*

su•shi (sōō′shē) *n.* Cold cooked rice dressed with vinegar that is shaped into bite-sized pieces and topped with raw or cooked fish, or formed into a roll with fish, egg, or vegetables and wrapped in seaweed. [J.]

Su•si•a•na (sōō′zē-ä′nə, -ăn′ə) See **Elam**.

sus•lik (sŭs′lĭk, sōōs′-) *n.* **1.** Any of several ground squirrels of Europe and Asia, esp. the small grayish European species *Citellus citellus.* **2.** The pelt or fur of this animal. [Russ. < ORuss. *susolŭ.*]

sus•pect (sə-spĕkt′) *v.* **-pect•ed, -pect•ing, -pects** —*tr.* **1.** To surmise to be true or probable; imagine. **2.** To have doubts about; distrust. **3.** To think (a person) guilty without proof. —*intr.* To have suspicion. ❖ *n.* (sŭs′pĕkt′) One who is suspected, esp. of having committed a crime. ❖ *adj.* (sŭs′pĕkt′, sə-spĕkt′) Open to or viewed with suspicion. [ME *suspecten* < OFr. *suspecter* < Lat. *suspectāre*, freq. of *suspicere*, to look up at, suspect : *su-*, *sub-*, from below; see SUB- + *specere*, to look at; see **spek-** in App.]

sus•pend (sə-spĕnd′) *v.* **-pend•ed, -pend•ing, -pends** —*tr.* **1.** To bar for a period from a privilege, office, or position, usu. as a punishment. **2.** To cause to stop for a period; interrupt. **3a.** To hold in abeyance; defer. **b.** To render temporarily ineffective. **4.** To hang so as to allow free movement. **5.** To support or keep from falling without apparent attachment, as by buoyancy. —*intr.* **1.** To cease for a period; delay. **2.** To fail to make payments or meet obligations. [ME *suspenden* < OFr. *suspendre* < Lat. *suspendere* : *sub-*, from below; see SUB- + *pendere*, to hang.]

sus•pend•ed animation (sə-spĕn′dĭd) *n.* A temporary interruption of the vital functions resembling death.

suspension
Fugue No. 4 from J.S. Bach's *Well-Tempered Clavier*, Book I

suspension bridge
San Francisco–Oakland Bay Bridge

sus•pend•er (sə-spĕn′dər) *n.* **1.** One, such as a hook, that suspends something else. **2.** An often elastic strap worn over the shoulders to support trousers. Often used in the plural. **3.** *Chiefly British* A garter.

sus•pense (sə-spĕns′) *n.* **1.** The condition of being physically suspended. **2a.** The state or quality of being undecided, uncertain, or doubtful. **b.** Pleasurable excitement and anticipation regarding an outcome. **3.** Anxiety or apprehension due to an uncertain, undecided, or mysterious situation. [ME < OFr. *suspens* < Lat. *suspēnsus*, p. part. of *suspendere*, to suspend. See SUSPEND.] —**sus•pense′ful** *adj.*

suspense account *n.* A temporary account in which entries of credits or charges are made until their proper disposition can be determined.

sus•pen•sion (sə-spĕn′shən) *n.* **1.** The act of suspending or the condition of being suspended, esp.: **a.** A temporary abrogation or deferment, as of a law. **b.** A temporary ban that prohibits someone from fulfilling a particular task or duty, such as attending school. **c.** A postponement, as of judgment or decision. See Syns at **pause**. *Music* **a.** The prolongation of one or more tones of a chord into a following chord to create a temporary dissonance. **b.** The tone so prolonged. **3.** A device from which a mechanical part is suspended. **4.** The system of springs and other devices that insulates the chassis of a vehicle from shocks transmitted through the wheels. **5.** *Chemistry* A system in which minute particles are dispersed throughout a fluid out of which they are likely to settle if left undisturbed.

suspension bridge *n.* A bridge having the roadway suspended from cables that are anchored at either end and usu. supported at intervals by towers.

suspension point *n.* One of a series of dots, usu. three, used to indicate an incomplete statement or the omission of a word or words from a written text.

sus•pen•sive (sə-spĕn′sĭv) *adj.* **1.** Serving or tending to suspend or temporarily stop something. **2.** Marked by or causing suspense. —**sus•pen′sive•ly** *adv.* —**sus•pen′sive•ness** *n.*

sus•pen•sor (sə-spĕn′sər) *n.* **1.** *Botany* A multicellular filamentous structure in seed-bearing plants that connects the embryo to the endosperm. **2.** An athletic supporter. [NLat. *suspēnsor*, one that suspends < Lat. *suspēnsus*, p. part. of *suspendere*, to suspend. See SUSPEND.]

sus•pen•so•ry (sə-spĕn′sə-rē) *adj.* **1.** Supporting or suspending. **2.** Delaying completion. ❖ *n., pl.* **-ries 1.** A support or truss. **2.** An athletic supporter.

suspensory ligament *n.* A ligament that supports an organ or body part, esp. a fibrous membrane that holds the lens of the eye in place.

sus•pi•cion (sə-spĭsh′ən) *n.* **1.** The act of suspecting something, esp. something wrong, on little evidence or without proof. **2.** The condition of being suspected, esp. of wrongdoing. **3.** A state of uncertainty; doubt. See Syns at **uncertainty**. **4.** A minute amount or slight indication; a trace. ❖ *tr.v.* **-cioned, -cion•ing, -cions** *Nonstandard* To suspect. [ME, alteration of *suspicioun* < AN, var. of OFr. *sospeçon* < Lat. *suspiciō*, *suspectiōn-* < *suspectus*, p. part. of *suspicere*, to watch. See SUSPECT.] —**sus•pi′cion•al** *adj.*

sus•pi•cious (sə-spĭsh′əs) *adj.* **1.** Arousing or apt to arouse suspicion; questionable: *suspicious behavior.* **2.** Tending to suspect; distrustful. **3.** Expressing suspicion. —**sus•pi′cious•ly** *adv.* —**sus•pi′cious•ness** *n.*

sus•pire (sə-spīr′) *intr.v.* **-pired, -pir•ing, -pires 1.** To breathe. **2.** To sigh. [ME *suspiren*, to sigh < Lat. *suspīrāre* : *sub-*, from below; see SUB- + *spīrāre*, to breathe.] —**sus′pi•ra′tion** (sŭs′pə-rā′shən) *n.*

Sus•que•han•na (sŭs′kwə-hăn′ə) *n., pl.* **Susquehanna** or **-nas** See **Susquehannock** 1.

Susquehanna River A river of the NE US rising in central NY and flowing c. 714 km (444 mi) to Chesapeake Bay.

Sus•que•han•nock (sŭs′kwə-hăn′ək) *n., pl.* **Susquehannock** or **-nocks 1.** A member of an extinct Native American people living along the Susquehanna River in New York, Pennsylvania, and Maryland. **2.** Their Iroquoian language.

Sus•sex (sŭs′ĭks) An Anglo-Saxon kingdom of S England bordering on the English Channel; founded in the 5th cent. A.D. and captured by the kingdom of Wessex in 825.

Sussex spaniel *n.* A strong stocky dog of a breed developed in Sussex, a county of southeast England, having long ears, short legs, and a silky golden-brown coat.

sus•tain (sə-stān′) *tr.v.* **-tained, -tain•ing, -tains 1.** To keep in existence; maintain. **2.** To supply with necessities or nourishment; provide for. **3.** To support from below; keep from falling or sinking; prop. **4.** To support the spirits, vitality, or resolution of; encourage. **5.** To bear up under; withstand. **6.** To experience or suffer. **7.** To affirm the validity of. **8.** To prove or corroborate; confirm. **9.** To keep up (a joke or assumed role, for example) competently. [ME *sustenen* < OFr. *sustenir* < Lat. *sustinēre* : *sub-*, from below; see SUB- + *tenēre*, to hold; see **ten-** in App.] —**sus•tain′er** *n.* —**sus•tain′ment** *n.*

sus•tain•a•ble (sə-stā′nə-bəl) *adj.* **1.** Capable of being sustained. **2.** Capable of being continued with minimal long-term effect on the environment: *sustainable agriculture.* —**sus•tain′a•bil′i•ty** *n.*

sus·tained yield (sə-stānd′) *n.* **1.** The continuing yield of a biological resource, such as timber, by controlled periodic harvesting. **2.** The quantity of a resource so harvested.

sus·tain·ing pedal (sə-stā′nĭng) *n.* The right pedal of a piano, which stops the action of the dampers and allows the strings to vibrate freely.

sus·te·nance (sŭs′tə-nəns) *n.* **1a.** The act of sustaining. **b.** The condition of being sustained. **2.** The supporting of life or health; maintenance. **3.** Something, esp. food, that sustains life or health. **4.** Means of livelihood. [ME < OFr. < *sustenir*, to sustain. See SUSTAIN.]

sus·ten·tac·u·lar (sŭs′tən-tăk′yə-lər, -tĕn-) *adj. Anatomy* Serving to support. [< LLat. *sustentāculum*, support < Lat. *sustentāre*, to support, freq. of *sustinēre*, to sustain. See SUSTAIN.]

sus·ten·ta·tion (sŭs′tən-tā′shən, -tĕn-) *n.* **1.** Something that sustains; a support. **2.** Sustenance. [ME < OFr. < Lat. *sustentātiō, sustentātiōn-* < *sustentātus*, p. part. of *sustentāre*, to support. See SUSTENTACULAR.] —**sus′ten·ta′tive** (-tā′tĭv) *adj.*

Su·su (sōō′sōō) *n., pl.* **Susu** or **Su·sus 1.** A member of a West African people inhabiting parts of Guinea and Sierra Leone. **2.** The Mande language of the Susu.

su·sur·ra·tion (sōō′sə-rā′shən) *also* **su·sur·rus** (sōō-sûr′əs, -sûr′-) *n.* A soft whispering or rustling sound; a murmur. [ME *susurracioun* < LLat. *susurrātiō, susurrātiōn-* < Lat. *susurrātus*, p. part. of *susurrāre*, to whisper < *susurrus*, whisper, ult. of imit. orig.] —**su·sur′rant** (sōō-sûr′ənt, -sûr′-), **su·sur′rous** (-sûr′əs, -sûr′-) *adj.*

Suth·er·land (sŭth′ər-lənd), **George** 1862–1942. Amer. jurist; associate justice of the US Supreme Court (1922–38).

Sutherland, Joan b. 1926. Australian soprano noted for her interpretations of the works of Bellini and Donizetti.

Sutherland Falls A waterfall, 581 m (1,904 ft), of SW South I., New Zealand.

Sut·lej (sŭt′lĕj′) A river, c. 1,448 km (900 mi), flowing from SW Xizang (Tibet) through N India and E Pakistan to join the Chenab R.; one of the five rivers of the Punjab.

sut·ler (sŭt′lər) *n.* An army camp follower who peddles provisions to the soldiers. [Obsolete Du. *soeteler* < LGer. *sudeler, suteler* < Ger. *sudeln*, to dirty < MHGer. *sudelen*.]

su·tra (sōō′trə) *n.* **1.** *Hinduism* Any of various aphoristic doctrinal summaries produced generally between 500 and 200 B.C. and later incorporated into Hindu literature. **2.** *also* **sut·ta** (sōōt′ə) *Buddhism* A scriptural narrative, esp. one regarded as by the Buddha. [Skt. *sūtram*. See syū- in App.]

sut·tee *also* **sa·ti** (sŭ-tē′, sŭt′ē′) *n.* **1.** The now illegal act or practice by a Hindu widow of cremating herself on her husband's funeral pyre to fulfill her true role as wife. **2.** *pl.* **-tees** *also* **-tis** A widow who commits such an act. [Skt. *satī*, virtuous woman, suttee < fem. pr. part. of *asti*, s-, she is, is true. See **es-** in App.]

Sut·ter (sŭt′ər), **John Augustus** 1803–80. Amer. pioneer who emigrated from Switzerland. The discovery of gold on his land led to the California gold rush (1848–49).

Sutt·ner (zōōt′nər, sōōt′-), **Bertha von** 1843–1914. Austrian pacifist who won the 1905 Nobel Peace Prize.

su·ture (sōō′chər) *n.* **1a.** The joining of two surfaces or edges together along a line by or as if by sewing. **b.** The material, such as thread, gut, or wire, used in this procedure. **c.** The line or stitch so formed. **2.** *Medicine* **a.** The fine thread or other material used surgically to close a wound or join tissues. **b.** The stitch so formed. **3.** *Anatomy* The line of junction or an immovable joint between two bones, esp. of the skull. **4.** *Biology* A seamline joint or line of articulation, such as the line of dehiscence in a dry fruit. ❖ *tr.v.* **-tured, -tur·ing, -tures** To join by sutures or a suture. [ME < Lat. *sūtūra*, p. part. of *suere*, to sew. See syū- in App.] —**su′tur·al** *adj.*

SUV *abbr.* sport-utility vehicle

Su·va (sōō′və, -vä) The cap. of Fiji, on the SE coast of Viti Levu. Pop. 74,000.

Su·vo·rov (sōō-vôr′əf), **Count Aleksandr Vasilevich** 1729–1800. Russian field marshal famous for his campaigns in the Russo-Turkish War (1787–92).

Su·wan·nee (sə-wä′nē, swä′-) A river, c. 386 km (240 mi), flowing from SE GA across N FL to the Gulf of Mexico.

Su·won (sōō′wŭn′) A city of NW South Korea S of Seoul. Pop. 644,805.

su·ze·rain (sōō′zər-ən, -zə-rān′) *n.* **1.** A nation that controls another nation in international affairs but allows it domestic sovereignty. **2.** A feudal lord to whom fealty was due. [Fr. < OFr. *suserain* : prob. *sus*, up (< Lat. *sūrsum, sūsum*, upward < *subvorsum*, turned upward : *subs-, sub-*, from under; see SUB- + *vorsum*, neut. of *vorsus*, var. of *versus*, p. part. of *vertere*, to turn; see VERSUS) + *souverain*, sovereign; see SOVEREIGN.] —**su′ze·rain·ty** (sōō′zər-ən-tē, -zə-rān′tē) *n., pl.* **su·ze·rain·ties** The power or domain of a suzerain.

Su·zhou (sōō′jō′) *also* **Soo·chow** (-chou′, -jō′) A city of E China WNW of Shanghai; probably founded before the 5th cent. B.C. Pop. 706,500.

Sval·bard (svãl′bär′) A Norwegian archipelago comprising Spitsbergen and other islands in the Arctic Ocean.

svc. *abbr.* service

svelte (svĕlt) *adj.* **svelt·er, svelt·est** Slender or graceful in figure

or outline; slim. [Fr. < Ital. *svelto* < p. part. of *svellere*, to stretch out < VLat. **exvellere* < Lat. *ēvellere* : *ē-, ex-, ex- + vellere*, to pull.] —**svelte′ly** *adv.* —**svelte′ness** *n.*

Sven·ga·li (svĕn-gä′lē, sfĕn-) *n., pl.* **-lis** A person who evilly tempts another to do what is desired. [After *Svengali*, the hypnotist villain in the novel *Trilby* by George du Maurier.]

Sverd·lovsk (sfĕrd-lôfsk′) See **Yekaterinburg.**

Sver·drup Islands (svĕr′drəp, sfĕr′-) A group of islands of N Canada, in the Arctic Ocean W of Ellesmere I.

svgs. *abbr.* savings

sw *abbr.* short wave

SW *abbr.* **1.** southwest **2.** southwestern

Sw. *abbr.* Swedish

swab *also* **swob** (swŏb) *n.* **1a.** A small piece of absorbent material on the end of a stick or wire, used for cleansing or applying medicine. **b.** A specimen of mucus or other material removed with a swab. **2.** A sponge or patch of absorbent material used to clean the bore of a firearm or cannon. **3.** A mop used for cleaning floors or decks. **4.** *Slang* A sailor. **5.** *Slang* A lout. ❖ *tr.v.* **swabbed, swab·bing, swabs** *also* **swobbed, swob·bing, swobs 1.** To use a swab on. **2.** To clean with a swab. [Back-formation < *swabber*, mop for a ship's deck (< obsolete Du. *zwabber < zwabben*, to mop) or < obsolete Du. *swabbe*, mop (< MDu.).]

swab·bie *also* **swab·by** (swŏb′ē) *n., pl.* **-bies** *Slang* A sailor. [SWAB + -Y³.]

Swa·bi·a (swã′bē-ə) A historical region of SW Germany with parts of present-day France and Switzerland; center of the **Swabian League** from 1488 to 1534. —**Swa′bi·an** *adj. & n.*

swad·dle (swŏd′l) *tr.v.* **-dled, -dling, -dles 1.** To wrap or bind in bandages; swathe. **2.** To wrap (a baby) in swaddling clothes. **3.** To restrain or restrict. ❖ *n.* A band or cloth used for swaddling. [ME *swadlen*, prob. back-formation < *swadling (band), swathel(bonde)*, swaddling (cloth) < **swathelen*, prob. freq. of OE *swathian*, to swathe.]

swad·dling clothes (swŏd′lĭng) *pl.n.* **1.** Strips of cloth wrapped around a newborn infant to hold its legs and arms still. **2.** Restrictions imposed on the immature.

swag (swăg) *n.* **1a.** An ornamental drapery or curtain draped in a curve between two points. **b.** An ornamental festoon of flowers or fruit. **c.** A carving or plaster molding of such an ornament. **2.** A promotional item, esp. one given for free. **3.** *Slang* Stolen property; loot. **4.** *Australian* The pack or bundle containing the personal belongings of a swagman. ❖ *intr.v.* **swagged, swag·ging, swags 1.** *Chiefly British* To lurch or sway. **2.** *Australian* To travel about with a pack or swag. [Prob. of Scand. orig.]

swage (swāj) *n.* **1.** A tool used to bend or shape cold metal. **2.** A stamp or die for marking or shaping metal. **3.** A swage block. ❖ *tr.v.* **swaged, swag·ing, swag·es** To bend or shape by or as if by using a swage. [ME, ornamental border < OFr. *souage*.]

swage block *n.* A metal block with holes or grooves for shaping metal objects.

swag·ger (swăg′ər) *v.* **-gered, -ger·ing, -gers** —*intr.* **1.** To walk or conduct oneself insolently or arrogantly; strut. **2.** To brag; boast. —*tr.* To browbeat or bully (someone). ❖ *n.* **1.** A swaggering movement or gait. **2.** Boastful or conceited expression. [Prob. freq. of SWAG.] —**swag′ger·er** *n.*

swagger stick *n.* A short metal-tipped cane carried esp. by officers in the armed forces.

swag·man (swăg′măn′) *n. Australian* A man who seeks casual work while traveling about carrying his swag.

Swa·hi·li (swä-hē′lē) *n., pl.* **Swahili** or **-lis 1.** A Bantu language of the coast and islands of eastern Africa from Somalia to Mozambique. It is an official language of Tanzania and is widely used as a lingua franca in eastern and east-central Africa. **2.** An inhabitant of coastal eastern Africa for whom Swahili is the mother tongue. [Swahili < Ar. *sawāḥilī*, of the coasts < *sawāḥil*, pl. of *sāḥil*, coast, active part. of *sahala*, to scrape off, smooth.] —**Swa·hi′li·an** *adj.*

swain (swān) *n.* **1.** A country lad, esp. a young shepherd. **2.** A beau. [ME, young man, servant < ON *sveinn*. See **s(w)e-** in App.]

swale (swāl) *n.* **1.** A low tract of land, esp. when moist or marshy. **2.** A long, narrow, usu. shallow trough between ridges on a beach, running parallel to the coastline. **3.** A shallow troughlike depression that carries water mainly during rainstorms or snow melts. [Perh. < ME, shade, perh. of Scand. orig.]

swal·low¹ (swŏl′ō) *v.* **-lowed, -low·ing, -lows** —*tr.* **1.** To cause (food or drink, for example) to pass through the mouth and throat into the stomach. **2.** To put up with (something unpleasant). **3.** To refrain from expressing; suppress: *swallow one's feelings.* **4.** To consume or destroy as if by ingestion; devour. **5.** *Slang* To believe without question. **6.** To take back; retract. **7.** To say inarticulately; mumble: *The actor swallowed his lines.* —*intr.* To perform the act of swallowing. ❖ *n.* **1.** The act of swallowing. **2.** An amount swallowed. [ME *swalowen* < OE *swelgan*.] —**swal′low·er** *n.*

swal·low² (swŏl′ō) *n.* **1.** Any of various small graceful swift-flying passerine birds of the family Hirundinidae, having long pointed wings, a usu. notched or forked tail, and a large mouth for catching flying insects. **2.** Any of various similar birds, such as a swift. [ME *swalowe* < OE *swealwe*.]

ă	pat	oi	boy
ā	pay	ou	out
âr	care	ŏŏ	took
ä	father	ōō	boot
ĕ	pet	ŭ	cut
ē	be	ûr	urge
ĭ	pit	th	thin
ī	pie	th	this
îr	pier	hw	which
ŏ	pot	zh	vision
ō	toe	ə	about,
ô	paw		item

Stress marks:
′ (primary);
′ (secondary), as in
lexicon (lĕk′sĭ-kŏn′)

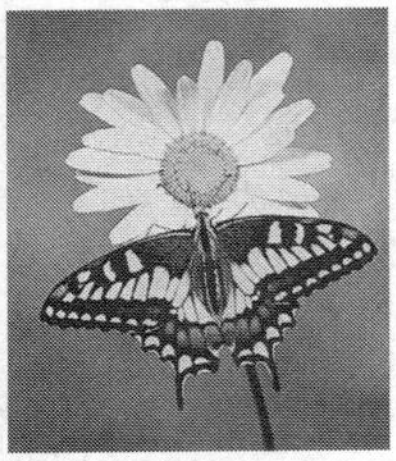

swallowtail
Oregon swallowtail
Papilio oregonius

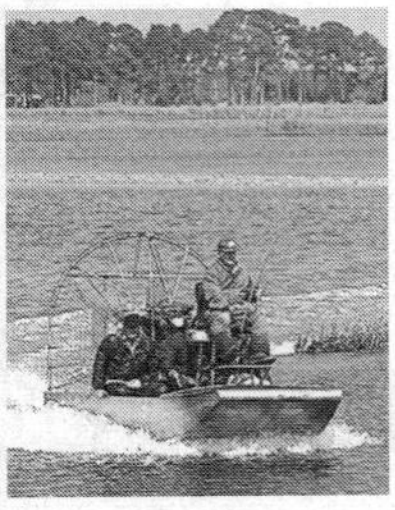

swamp boat

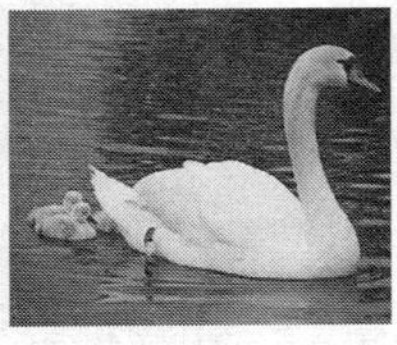

swan
mute swan
Cygnus olor

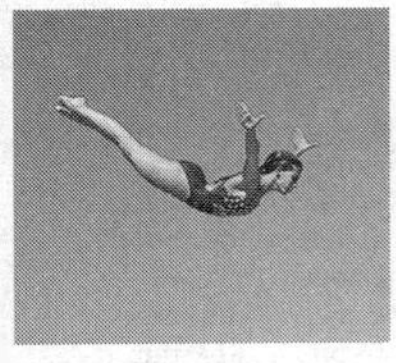

swan dive

swal•low•tail (swŏl′ō-tāl′) *n.* **1a.** The deeply forked tail of a swallow. **b.** Something similar to the tail of a swallow. **2.** See **tailcoat. 3.** Any of various colorful, widely distributed butterflies of the family Papilionidae, usu. having an extension at the end of each hind wing that resembles the tails of certain swallows. **—swal′low-tailed′** *adj.*

swal•low•wort (swŏl′ō-wûrt′, -wôrt′) *n.* **1.** See **celandine** 1. **2.** Any of several vines of the genus *Cynanchum,* esp. *C. nigrum,* of Europe having small brownish-purple flowers. [< the shape of its pod.]

swam (swăm) *v.* Past tense of **swim.**

swa•mi (swä′mē) *n., pl.* **swa•mis 1a.** *Hinduism* A religious teacher. **b.** A mystic; a yogi. **2.** Used as a form of address for such a person. [Hindi *svāmī,* master, swami < Skt., being one's own master, possessing proprietary rights. See **s(w)e-** in App.]

Swam•mer•dam (svä′mər-däm′), **Jan** 1637–80. Dutch naturalist known for his pioneering microscopic research.

swamp (swŏmp, swômp) *n.* **1a.** A seasonally flooded bottomland with more woody plants than a marsh and better drainage than a bog. **b.** A lowland region saturated with water. **2.** A situation or place fraught with difficulties and imponderables. ❖ *v.* **swamped, swamp•ing, swamps** *—tr.* **1.** To drench in or cover with or as if in or with water. **2.** To inundate or burden; overwhelm. **3.** To fill (a ship or boat) with water to the point of sinking it. *—intr.* To become full of water or sink. [Perh. of Low German orig.] **—swamp′i•ness** *n.* **—swamp′y** *adj.*

swamp boat *n.* A flatbottom boat propelled by an airplane propeller projecting above the stern and used in swamps or shallow waters.

swamp•er (swŏm′pər, swôm′-) *n.* **1.** One who lives in or close to a swamp. **2.** One who clears a swamp or forest. **3a.** A helper, as in a restaurant. **b.** A truck driver's assistant.

swamp fever *n.* **1.** Malaria. **2.** Equine infectious anemia. **3.** Leptospirosis.

swamp pink *n.* An orchid *(Arethusa bulbosa)* of northeast North America having a usu. rose-colored flower.

swamp potato *n. Botany* Arrowhead.

swan (swŏn) *n.* **1.** Any of various large aquatic birds of the family Anatidae chiefly of the genera *Cygnus* and *Olor,* having webbed feet, a long slender neck, and usu. white plumage. **2.** See **Cygnus.** ❖ *intr.v.* **swanned, swan•ning, swans** *Chiefly British* To travel around from place to place. [ME < OE.]

swan dive *n.* A forward dive performed with the legs straight together and the arms stretched out from the sides and then brought together over the head as the diver enters the water.

swank (swăngk) *adj.* **swank•er, swank•est 1.** Imposingly fashionable or elegant; grand. **2.** Ostentatious; pretentious. ❖ *n.* **1.** Smartness in style or bearing; elegance. **2.** Swagger. ❖ *intr.v.* **swanked, swank•ing, swanks** To act ostentatiously or pretentiously; swagger. [Perh. akin to MHGer. *swanken,* to swing.]

swank•y (swăng′kē) *adj.* **-i•er, -i•est** Swank. **—swank′i•ly** *adv.* **—swank′i•ness** *n.*

swan•ny (swŏn′ē) *intr.v. Chiefly Southern US* To declare; swear. Used in the phrase *I swanny* as an interjection. [Prob. alteration of dialectal *(I) s' wan ye,* (I) shall warrant ye.]

swan's-down also **swans•down** (swŏnz′doun′) *n.* **1.** The soft down of a swan. **2.** A soft woolen fabric used esp. for baby clothes. **3.** Flannelette.

Swan•sea (swän′zē, -sē) A borough of S Wales on **Swansea Bay,** an inlet of the Bristol Channel. Pop. 189,329.

swan•skin (swŏn′skĭn′) *n.* **1.** The skin of a swan with the feathers attached. **2.** Any of several flannel or cotton fabrics with a soft nap.

swan song *n.* **1.** A farewell or final appearance, action, or work. **2.** The beautiful legendary song sung by a swan only once in its lifetime, as it is dying.

swap (swŏp) *v.* **swapped, swap•ping, swaps** *—intr.* To trade one thing for another. *—tr.* To exchange (one thing) for another. ❖ *n.* An exchange of one thing for another. [ME *swappen,* to strike, strike hands in a bargain.] **—swap′per** *n.*

sward (swôrd) also **swarth** (swôrth) *n.* **1.** Land covered with grassy turf. **2.** A lawn or meadow. [ME < OE *sweard,* skin.]

sware (swâr) *v. Archaic* A past tense of **swear.**

swarf (swôrf) *n.* Fine metallic filings or shavings removed by a cutting tool. [Of Scand. orig.; akin to ON *svarf.*]

swarm¹ (swôrm) *n.* **1.** A large number of insects or other small organisms, esp. when in motion. **2.** A group of bees with a queen bee in migration to establish a new colony. **3.** An aggregation of persons or animals, esp. when in turmoil or moving in mass. ❖ *v.* **swarmed, swarm•ing, swarms** *—intr.* **1a.** To move or emerge in a swarm. **b.** To leave a hive as a swarm. Used of bees. **2.** To move or gather in large numbers. **3.** To be overrun; teem. See Syns at **teem¹**. *—tr.* To fill with a crowd. [ME, group of bees < OE *swearm.*] **—swarm′er** *n.*

swarm² (swôrm) *v.* **swarmed, swarm•ing, swarms** *—intr.* To climb by gripping with the arms and legs. *—tr.* To climb (something) in this manner. [?]

swarm spore *n.* See **zoospore.**

swart (swôrt) *adj. Archaic* Swarthy. [ME *swarte* < OE *sweart.*]

swarth•y (swôr′thē) *adj.* **-i•er, -i•est** Having a dark complexion or color: *a swarthy sailor.* [Alteration of *swarty* < SWART.] **—swarth′i•ly** *adv.* **—swarth′i•ness** *n.*

swash (swŏsh, swôsh) *n.* **1a.** A splash of water or other liquid hitting a solid surface. **b.** The sound of such a splash. **2a.** A narrow channel through which tides flow. **b.** A bar over which waves wash freely. **3.** See **uprush. 4a.** Swagger or bluster. **b.** A swaggering or blustering person. ❖ *v.* **swashed, swash•ing, swash•es** *—intr.* **1.** To strike, move, or wash with a splashing sound. **2.** To swagger. *—tr.* **1.** To splash (a liquid). **2.** To splash a liquid against. [Prob. imit.]

swash•buck•ler (swŏsh′bŭk′lər, swôsh′-) *n.* **1.** A flamboyant swordsman or adventurer. **2.** A sword-wielding ruffian or bully. **3.** A dramatic or literary work dealing with a swashbuckler. [Prob. < the striking of bucklers in fighting.] **—swash′buck′ling** *adj.*

swash letter *n.* An ornamental italic letter with elaborate flowing flourishes and tails. [?]

swas•ti•ka (swŏs′tĭ-kə) *n.* **1.** An ancient cosmic or religious symbol formed by a cross with the ends of the arms bent at right angles in either a clockwise or a counterclockwise direction. **2.** Such a symbol with a clockwise bend to the arms, used as the emblem of the Nazi party and of the German state under Adolf Hitler. [Skt. *svastikaḥ,* sign of good luck, swastika < *svasti,* well-being : *su-,* well + *asti,* being; see **es-** in App.]

swat (swŏt) *tr.v.* **swat•ted, swat•ting, swats** To deal a sharp blow to; slap. ❖ *n.* A sharp blow; a slap. [Alteration of SQUAT, to squash (obsolete and dialectal).]

SWAT *abbr.* special weapons and tactics

swatch (swŏch) *n.* **1.** A sample strip or piece of material. **2.** A representative portion; a sample. **3.** A strip or swath of land. [?]

swath (swŏth, swôth) also **swathe** (swŏ*th,* swô*th,* swā*th*) *n.* **1a.** The width of a scythe stroke or a mowing-machine blade. **b.** A path of this width made in mowing. **c.** The mown grass or grain lying on such a path. **2.** Something likened to a swath; a strip. ***—idiom:* cut a swath 1.** To create a great stir, impression, or display. **2.** To extend in distinctive physical length and width. [ME *swathe* < OE *swæth,* track.]

swathe¹ (swŏ*th,* swô*th,* swā*th*) *tr.v.* **swathed, swath•ing, swathes 1.** To wrap or bind with or as if with bandages. **2.** To enfold or constrict. ❖ *n.* A wrapping, binding, or bandage. [ME *swathen* < OE *swathian.*] **—swath′er** *n.*

swathe² (swŏ*th,* swô*th,* swā*th*) *n.* Variant of **swath.**

Swa•tow (swä′tou′) See **Shantou.**

swat•ter (swŏt′ər) *n.* **1.** A fly swatter. **2.** *Baseball* A hard-hitting batter.

sway (swā) *v.* **swayed, sway•ing, sways** *—intr.* **1.** To swing back and forth or to and fro. **2.** To incline or bend to one side; veer. **3a.** To incline toward change, as in opinion. **b.** To fluctuate, as in outlook. *—tr.* **1.** To cause to swing back and forth or to and fro. **2.** To cause to incline or bend to one side. **3.** *Nautical* To hoist (a mast or yard) into position. **4a.** To divert; deflect. **b.** To exert influence on or control over. **5.** *Archaic* **a.** To rule or govern. **b.** To wield, as a scepter. ❖ *n.* **1.** The act of moving from side to side with a swinging motion. **2.** Power; influence. **3.** Dominion or control. [ME *sweien,* prob. of Scand. orig.] **—sway′er** *n.*

sway•back (swā′băk′) *n.* Excessive inward or downward curvature of the spine, esp. in a horse. **—sway′backed′** *adj.*

Swa•zi (swä′zē) *n., pl.* **Swazi** or **-zis 1.** A member of a southeast African people of Swaziland and adjacent parts of South Africa. **2.** The Nguni language of this people.

Swa•zi•land (swä′zē-lănd′) A country of SE Africa between South Africa and Mozambique; gained independence from Great Britain in 1968. Cap. Mbabane. Pop. 832,000.

SWbS *abbr.* southwest by south

SWbW *abbr.* southwest by west

swear (swâr) *v.* **swore** (swôr, swōr), **sworn** (swôrn, swōrn), **swear•ing, swears** *—intr.* **1.** To make a solemn declaration, invoking a deity or a sacred person or thing. **2.** To make a solemn promise; vow. **3.** To use profane oaths; curse. **4.** *Law* To give evidence or testimony under oath. *—tr.* **1.** To declare or affirm solemnly by invoking a deity or a sacred person or thing. **2.** To promise or pledge with a solemn oath; vow. **3.** To utter or bind oneself to (an oath). **4.** *Law* To administer a legal oath to. **5.** To say or affirm earnestly and with great conviction. ❖ *n.* A swearword. ***—phrasal verbs:* swear at** To use abusive, violent, or blasphemous language against; curse. **swear by 1.** To have great reliance on or confidence in. **2.** To have reliable knowledge of; be sure of. **3.** To take an oath by. **swear in** To administer a legal or official oath to. **swear off** *Informal* To pledge to renounce or give up. **swear out** *Law* To obtain (an arrest warrant) by making a charge under oath. [ME *sweren* < OE *swerian.*] **—swear′er** *n.*

swear•word (swâr′wûrd′) *n.* An obscene or blasphemous word.

sweat (swĕt) *v.* **sweat•ed** or **sweat, sweat•ing, sweats** *—intr.* **1.** To excrete perspiration through the pores in the skin; perspire. **2.** To exude in droplets. **3.** To condense atmospheric moisture. **4a.** To release moisture, as hay in the swath. **b.** To ferment, as tobacco during curing. **5.** *Informal* **a.** To work long and hard. **b.** To suffer much, as for a misdeed. **6.** *Informal* To fret or worry. *—tr.* **1.** To excrete (moisture) through a porous surface. **2.** To gather and condense (moisture) on a surface. **3.** To cause to perspire, as by exercise. **4.** To make damp or wet with perspiration.

5. To cause to work excessively; overwork. **6.** To overwork and underpay (employees). **7.** *Slang* **a.** To interrogate (someone) under duress. **b.** To extract (information) from someone under duress. **8.** *Metallurgy* To join (metal parts) by interposing cold solder and then heating. **9.** To steam (vegetables or other food). ❖ *n.* **1.** The colorless saline moisture excreted by the sweat glands; perspiration. **2.** Condensation of moisture in the form of droplets on a surface. **3a.** The process of sweating. **b.** A condition or period of sweating: *work up a sweat.* **4.** Strenuous, exhaustive labor; drudgery. **5.** A run given to a horse as exercise before a race. **6.** *Informal* An anxious, fretful condition. **7.** *Informal* A sweatsuit. —**phrasal verb: sweat out** *Slang* **1.** To endure anxiously. **2.** To await (something) anxiously. —**idioms: no sweat** *Slang* Easily done or handled. **sweat blood** *Informal* **1.** To work diligently or strenuously. **2.** To worry intensely. **sweat bullets** *Slang* To sweat profusely. **sweat of (one's) brow** Hard work. [ME *sweten* < OE *swǣtan.* See **sweid-** in App.]

sweat·band (swĕt′bănd′) *n.* **1.** A band of fabric or leather sewn inside the crown of a hat as protection against sweat. **2.** A band of material worn around the head or wrist to absorb sweat.

sweat·box (swĕt′bŏks′) *n.* **1.** A box in which something, such as hides or fruit, is fermented by sweating. **2.** *Slang* A confined place where a person sweats, esp.: **a.** An interrogation room. **b.** A prison cell used for special punishment.

sweat equity *n.* Work, esp. in repairing or refurbishing, performed to increase the value of a home.

sweat·er (swĕt′ər) *n.* **1.** A jacket or pullover made esp. of knit, crocheted, or woven wool, cotton, or synthetic yarn. **2.** One that sweats, esp. profusely. **3.** Something that induces sweating; a sudorific.

sweat gland *n.* Any of the numerous small, tubular glands found in human skin that secrete perspiration externally through pores to help regulate body temperature.

sweat·house (swĕt′hous′) *n.* Any of various structures often heated by fire or by pouring water over hot stones and used by some Native American peoples to induce sweating, as for medicinal or spiritual purposes.

sweat·pants (swĕt′pănts′) *pl.n.* Pants made traditionally of cotton jersey usu. having a drawstring or elasticized waist and elasticized cuffs and worn esp. for exercising.

sweat·shirt (swĕt′shûrt′) *n.* A usu. long-sleeved collarless oversize pullover made traditionally of heavy cotton jersey that has a fleeced backing.

sweat·shop (swĕt′shŏp′) *n.* A shop or factory in which employees work long hours at low wages under poor conditions.

sweat·suit or **sweat suit** (swĕt′sōōt′) *n.* A two-piece outfit consisting of a sweatshirt and sweat pants, usu. worn for exercise.

sweat·y (swĕt′ē) *adj.* **-i·er, -i·est 1.** Covered with or smelling of sweat. **2.** Causing sweat: *a sweaty job.* —**sweat′i·ly** *adv.* —**sweat′i·ness** *n.*

swede (swēd) *n.* See **rutabaga.** [Introduced from Sweden.]

Swede *n.* **1.** A native or inhabitant of Sweden. **2.** A person of Swedish ancestry. [LGer. (< MLGer. *Swēde*) or Du. *Zweed* (< MDu. *Swēde*).]

Swe·den (swēd′n) A country of N Europe on the E Scandinavian Peninsula. Cap. Stockholm. Pop. 8,780,000.

Swe·den·borg (swēd′n-bôrg′, sväd′n-bôr′ē), **Emanuel** 1688–1772. Swedish scientist and theologian whose visions and writings inspired his followers to establish the Church of the New Jerusalem. —**Swe′den·bor′gi·an** *adj. & n.*

Swed·ish (swē′dĭsh) *adj.* Of or relating to Sweden, the Swedes, or their culture or language. ❖ *n.* The North Germanic language of Sweden and parts of Finland.

Swedish massage *n.* A system of massage for the muscles and joints, developed in Sweden in the 19th century.

Swedish turnip *n.* See **rutabaga.**

sweep (swēp) *v.* **swept** (swĕpt), **sweep·ing, sweeps** —*tr.* **1.** To clean or clear, as of dirt, with or as if with a broom or brush. **2.** To clear away with or as if with a broom or brush. **3.** To clear (a path or space) with or as if with a broom. **4a.** To search thoroughly. **b.** *Electronics* To search for and remove (eavesdropping devices) from a place. **5.** To touch or brush lightly, as with a trailing garment. **6.** To pass over or through a surface or medium with a continuous movement. **7.** To clear, drive, or convey with relentless force: *The floods swept away everything.* **8.** To wipe out at a single stroke. Often used with *away.* **9.** To remove or carry off with a swift brushing motion. **10.** To move across or through swiftly and with great intensity. **11.** To pass quickly across, as when searching. **12.** To drag the bottom of (a body of water). **13a.** To win all the stages of (a game or contest). **b.** To win overwhelmingly in. —*intr.* **1.** To clean or clear a surface with or as if with a broom or brush. **2.** *Electronics* To search for and remove eavesdropping devices. **3.** To move swiftly with strong, steady force. **4.** To move swiftly in a lofty manner, as if in a trailing robe: *She swept by in silence.* **5.** To trail, as a long garment. **6.** To extend gracefully, esp. in a long curve: *The hills sweep down to the sea.* **7.** To extend in a wide range. ❖ *n.* **1.** A clearing out or removal with or as if with a broom or brush. **2.** *Electronics* The act or an instance of sweeping. **3a.** A wide curving motion. **b.** The range or scope encompassed by sweeping. **4.** A broad reach or extent. **5.** A curve or contour. **6.** *Football* An end run in which a lineman

leaves the line of scrimmage and blocks for the ball carrier. **7.** One who sweeps, as a chimney sweep. **8.** Sweepings. Often used in the plural. **9a.** The winning of all stages of a game or contest. **b.** An overwhelming victory or success. **10.** *Nautical* A long oar used to propel a boat. **11.** A long pole attached to a pivot and used to raise or lower a bucket in a well. **12. sweeps** (used with a sing. or pl. verb) *Informal* Sweepstakes. **13a. sweeps** The period every fall, winter, and spring when television ratings are accrued and studied and advertising rates are reset. **b.** The survey conducted to determine these ratings. **14.** *Electronics* The steady motion of an electron beam across a cathode-ray tube. —**idiom: sweep (one) off (one's) feet** To cause an immediate and strongly positive response in (a person); impress deeply. [ME *swepen,* perh. < *swepe,* p. t. of *swopen,* to sweep along. See SWOOP.]

sweep·back (swēp′băk′) *n.* The backward slant of the leading edge of an airfoil.

sweep·er (swē′pər) *n.* **1.** One that sweeps. **2.** A carpet sweeper. **3.** *Sports* A defender who plays between the last line of defenders and the goal in some configurations in soccer.

sweep·ing (swē′pĭng) *adj.* **1.** Having wide-ranging influence or effect. **2.** Moving in or as if in a wide curve. **3.** Indiscriminate; wholesale. **4.** Overwhelming; complete. ❖ *n.* **1.** The action of one that sweeps. **2. sweepings** Things swept up; refuse. —**sweep′ing·ly** *adv.*

sweep·stakes (swēp′stāks′) *pl.n.* (used with a sing. or pl. verb) **1.** A lottery in which the participants' stakes form a fund awarded as a prize to one or several winners. **2.** An event or contest, esp. a horserace, the result of which determines the winner of such a lottery. **3.** The prize won in such a lottery.

sweet (swēt) *adj.* **sweet·er, sweet·est 1.** Having the taste of sugar or a substance containing or resembling sugar, as honey. **2a.** Containing or derived from sugar. **b.** Retaining some natural sugar; not dry: *a sweet wine.* **3a.** Pleasing to the senses; agreeable. **b.** Pleasing to the mind or feelings; gratifying. **4.** Having a pleasing disposition; lovable. **5.** Kind; gracious. **6.** Fragrant; perfumed. **7.** Not saline or salted. **8.** Not spoiled, sour, or decaying; fresh. **9.** Free of acid or acidity: *sweet soil.* **10.** Low in sulfur content: *sweet fuel oil.* **11.** *Music* Of, relating to, or being a form of jazz characterized by adherence to a melodic line and a time signature. **12.** *Slang* **a.** Remarkable; outstanding. **b.** Used as an intensive: *won a sweet million dollars.* ❖ *adv.* In a sweet manner; sweetly. ❖ *n.* **1.** Sweet taste or quality; sweetness. **2.** Something sweet to the taste. **3. sweets** Foods, such as candy or pastries, that are high in sugar content. **b.** *Informal* Sweet potatoes. **4.** *Chiefly British* **a.** A sweet dish, such as pudding, served as dessert. **b.** A sweetmeat or confection. **5.** A dear or beloved person. **6.** Something pleasing to the mind or feelings. —**idiom: sweet on** *Informal* Enamored of; in love with. [ME *swete* < OE *swēte.* See **swād-** in App.] —**sweet′ly** *adv.* —**sweet′ness** *n.*

Sweet, Henry 1845–1912. British phonetician known esp. for his *History of English Sounds* (1874).

sweet alyssum *n.* An annual or perennial Mediterranean herb (*Lobularia maritima*) of the mustard family, having long-lasting flowers varying in size and color.

sweet-and-sour (swēt′n-sour′) *adj.* Flavored with a sauce containing sugar and vinegar: *sweet-and-sour pork.*

sweet basil *n.* See **basil** 1a.

sweet bay *n.* **1.** A shrub or small tree (*Magnolia virginiana*) of the southeast United States and eastern coastal areas, having large fragrant white flowers and red fruit. **2.** See **laurel** 1.

sweet birch *n.* **1.** An eastern North American birch (*Betula lenta*) having aromatic stems with brownish bark that does not peel into papery flakes. **2.** The wood of this tree.

sweet·bread (swēt′brĕd′) *n.* The thymus gland or pancreas of a young animal, esp. a calf or lamb, used for food.

sweet·bri·er also **sweet·bri·ar** (swēt′brī′ər) *n.* A Eurasian rose (*Rosa eglanteria*) having prickly stems, fragrant leaves, bright pink flowers, and scarlet hips.

sweet cherry *n.* **1.** A large deciduous Eurasian tree (*Prunus avium*) of the rose family, having red-brown birchlike bark and sweet edible fruit. **2.** The fruit of this tree.

sweet cic·e·ly (sĭs′ə-lē) *n.* **1.** Any of various perennial New World herbs of the genus *Osmorhiza,* having fleshy aromatic roots, compound leaves, and white flowers. **2.** An aromatic European perennial herb (*Myrrhis odorata*) having compound leaves and white flowers. [ME *seseli* < Lat. *seselis* < Gk.]

sweet cider *n.* Unfermented cider.

sweet clover *n.* See **melilot.**

sweet corn *n.* The common table and canning variety of corn (*Zea mays* var. *rugosa*), having sweet kernels when young.

sweet·en (swēt′n) *v.* **-ened, -en·ing, -ens** —*tr.* **1.** To make sweet or sweeter by adding sugar, honey, or another sweet substance. **2.** To make more pleasant or agreeable. **3.** To soften or soothe. **4.** To make bearable; alleviate. **5.** *Informal* **a.** To increase the value of (collateral for a loan) by adding more securities. **b.** To enhance the attractiveness or financial desirability of (an offer, for example). **6.** *Games* To increase the value of (an unwon poker pot) by making stakes before reopening. **7.** To make less acidic. **8.** To remove sulfur compounds from (fuel oil or gas). —*intr.* To become sweet.

sweet·en·er (swēt′n-ər) *n.* **1.** Something that sweetens. **2.** *Infor-*

Swaziland

Sweden

mal An added inducement or incentive.

sweet·en·ing (swēt′n-ĭng) *n.* **1.** The act or process of making sweet. **2.** Something that sweetens; a sweetener.

sweet fern *n.* An aromatic deciduous shrub (*Comptonia peregrina*) of eastern North America having narrow, deeply lobed fernlike leaves and clusters of minute flowers.

sweet flag *n.* A hardy perennial herb (*Acorus calamus*) of the Northern Hemisphere growing in marshy places and having grasslike leaves and aromatic rhizomes.

sweet gale *n.* A deciduous swamp shrub (*Myrica gale*) of northern Eurasia and North America having aromatic resinous leaves used in medicine and tiny yellowish fruits.

sweet gum *n.* **1.** Any of several trees of the genus *Liquidambar,* esp. *L. styraciflua* of North America and Central America, having prickly fruit clusters and wood used to make furniture. **2.** The aromatic resin obtained from this tree.

sweet·heart (swēt′härt′) *n.* **1.** One who is loved. **2.** Used as a familiar term of endearment. **3.** *Informal* **a.** A person regarded as generous or lovable. **b.** Something cherished for its excellent qualities. ❖ *adj.* Involving privileged treatment of a favored party; illegally or unethically favorable.

sweet·ie (swē′tē) *n. Informal* Sweetheart; dear.

sweet·ing (swē′tĭng) *n.* **1.** A sweet apple. **2.** *Archaic* Sweetheart.

sweet marjoram *n.* See marjoram.

sweet·meat (swēt′mēt′) *n.* A sweet delicacy.

sweet pea *n.* An annual climbing herb (*Lathyrus odoratus*) of the pea family, native to Italy and having variously colored fragrant flowers.

sweet pepper *n.* Any of numerous varieties of the *Capsicum annuum* pepper having mild nonpungent fruits.

sweet potato *n.* **1a.** A tropical American vine (*Ipomoea batatas*), having funnel-shaped flowers and cultivated for its fleshy tuberous orange root. **b.** The root of this vine, eaten cooked as a vegetable. **2.** *Informal* An ocarina.

sweet·shop (swēt′shŏp′) *n. Chiefly British* A candy store.

sweet·sop (swēt′sŏp′) *n.* **1.** A tropical American evergreen tree (*Annona squamosa*) cultivated for its yellowish-green fruit with sweet edible pulp. **2.** The fruit of this tree.

sweet sorghum *n.* See sorgo.

sweet spot *n.* The place on a bat, club, racket, or paddle, where it is most effective to hit a ball.

sweet talk *n. Informal* Flattery; cajolery. —**sweet-talk** (swēt′tôk′) *v.*

sweet tooth *n. Informal* A fondness or craving for sweets.

sweet William *n.* An annual, biennial, or perennial herb (*Dianthus barbatus*) native to Eurasia and having flat-topped dense clusters of varicolored flowers.

swell (swĕl) *v.* **swelled, swelled** or **swol·len** (swō′lən), **swell·ing, swells** —*intr.* **1.** To increase in size or volume as a result of internal pressure; expand. **2a.** To increase in force, size, number, or degree. **b.** To grow in loudness or intensity. **3.** To bulge out, as a sail. **4a.** To rise or extend above the surrounding level, as clouds. **b.** To rise in swells, as the sea. **5a.** To be or become filled or puffed up, as with pride. **b.** To rise from within. —*tr.* **1.** To cause to increase in volume, size, number, degree, or intensity. **2.** To fill with emotion. ❖ *n.* **1a.** The act or process of swelling. **b.** The condition of being swollen. **2.** A swollen part; a bulge or protuberance. **3.** A long deep wave on water that travels a long distance at sea. **4.** A rise in the land; a rounded elevation. **5.** *Informal* One who is fashionably dressed or socially prominent. **6.** *Music* **a.** A crescendo followed by a gradual diminuendo. **b.** The sign indicating this. **c.** A device on an instrument, such as an organ, for regulating volume. ❖ *adj.* **swell·er, swell·est** *Informal* **1.** Fashionably elegant; stylish. **2.** Excellent; wonderful. [ME *swellen* < OE *swellan*.]

swell box *n. Music* A chamber of an organ that houses a pipe or pipes and has shutters for controlling volume.

swelled head (swĕld) *n. Informal* An unduly high opinion of oneself.

swell·fish (swĕl′fĭsh′) *n., pl.* **swellfish** or **-fish·es** See puffer.

swell·head (swĕl′hĕd′) *n. Informal* An arrogant or conceited person. —**swell′head′ed** *adj.*

swell·ing (swĕl′ĭng) *n.* **1.** The state of being swollen. **2.** Something swollen, esp. an abnormally swollen body part or area.

swel·ter (swĕl′tər) *v.* **-tered, -ter·ing, -ters** —*intr.* To suffer from oppressive heat. —*tr.* **1.** To affect with oppressive heat. **2.** *Archaic* To exude (venom, for example). ❖ *n.* A condition of oppressive heat. [ME *swelteren,* freq. of *swelten,* to faint from heat < OE *sweltan,* to perish.]

swel·ter·ing (swĕl′tər-ĭng) *adj.* **1.** Oppressively hot and humid; sultry. **2.** Suffering from heat. —**swel′ter·ing·ly** *adv.*

swel·try (swĕl′trē) *adj.* **-tri·er, -tri·est** Sweltering.

swept (swĕpt) *v.* Past tense and past participle of sweep.

swept·back (swĕpt′băk′) *adj.* **1.** Angled rearward from the points of attachment. Used esp. of aircraft wings. **2.** Having wings of this type. Used of an aircraft.

swept·wing (swĕpt′wĭng′) *adj.* Having sweptback wings. Used of an aircraft. ❖ *n.* A sweptback wing.

swerve (swûrv) *tr. & intr.v.* **swerved, swerv·ing, swerves** To turn aside or be turned aside from a straight course. ❖ *n.* The act of swerving. [ME *swerven* < OE *sweorfan,* to rub, scour.]

sweet gum
Liquidambar styraciflua

SWG *abbr.* standard wire gauge

swid·den (swĭd′n) *n.* An area cleared for temporary cultivation by cutting and burning the vegetation. [Dialectal alteration of obsolete *swithen* < ON *svidhna,* to be burned.]

swift (swĭft) *adj.* **swift·er, swift·est** **1.** Moving or capable of moving with great speed; fast. See Syns at fast¹. **2.** Coming, occurring, or done quickly; instant. **3.** Quick to act or react; prompt: *swift to act.* ❖ *adv.* Swiftly. Often used in combination: *swift-running.* ❖ *n.* **1a.** A cylinder on a carding machine. **b.** A reel that holds yarn as it is being wound. **2.** Any of various small dark insect-eating birds of the family Apodidae, related to the hummingbirds and noted for their swift flight. **3.** Any of various small fast-moving North American lizards of the genera *Sceloporus* and *Uta.* [ME < OE.] —**swift′ly** *adv.* —**swift′ness** *n.*

Swift, Jonathan 1667–1745. Irish-born English writer whose satirical works include *Gulliver's Travels* (1726).

swig (swĭg) *Informal n.* A deep draft, esp. of liquor; a gulp. [?] —**swig** *v.* —**swig′ger** *n.*

swill (swĭl) *v.* **swilled, swill·ing, swills** —*tr.* **1.** To drink greedily or grossly. **2.** To flood with water, as for washing. **3.** To feed (animals) with swill. —*intr.* To drink or eat greedily or to excess. ❖ *n.* **1.** A mixture of liquid and solid food fed to animals, esp. pigs; slop. **2.** Kitchen waste; garbage. **3.** A deep draft of liquor. **4.** Nonsense; rubbish. [ME *swilen,* to wash out < OE *swilian.*] —**swill′er** *n.*

swim (swĭm) *v.* **swam** (swăm), **swum** (swŭm), **swim·ming, swims** —*intr.* **1.** To move through water by means of the limbs, fins, or tail. **2.** To move as though gliding through water. **3.** To float on water or another liquid. **4a.** To be covered or flooded with or as if with a liquid. **b.** To possess a superfluity; abound. **5.** To experience a floating or giddy sensation; be dizzy. **6.** To appear to spin or reel lazily. —*tr.* **1.** To move through or across (a body of water) by swimming. **2.** To execute (a given stroke) in swimming. **3.** To cause to swim or float. ❖ *n.* **1a.** The act of swimming. **b.** A period of time spent swimming. **2.** A gliding motion. **3.** A state of dizziness. **4.** An area, as of a river, abounding in fish. ❖ *adj.* Of, relating to, or used for swimming. —**idioms: in the swim** Active in the general current of affairs. **swim against the stream** To move counter to a prevailing trend. [ME *swimmen* < OE *swimman.*] —**swim′ma·ble** *adj.* —**swim′mer** *n.*

swim bladder *n.* See air bladder 1.

swim·mer·et (swĭm′ə-rĕt′, swĭm′ə-rĕt′) *n.* One of the paired abdominal appendages of certain aquatic crustaceans, such as shrimp, lobsters, and isopods, that function primarily for carrying the eggs in females and are usu. adapted for swimming.

swim·ming (swĭm′ĭng) *n.* The act, sport, or technique of one that swims. ❖ *adj.* **1.** Relating to or used in swimming. **2.** Capable of swimming: *swimming insects.*

swim·ming·ly (swĭm′ĭng-lē) *adv.* Very easily and successfully.

swimming pool *n.* A structure, often a rectangular concrete-lined excavation, filled with water and used for swimming.

swim·suit (swĭm′sōot′) *n.* A garment worn while swimming.

swim·wear (swĭm′wâr′) *n.* Clothing designed to be worn for swimming or with swimsuits.

Swin·burne (swĭn′bûrn′), **Algernon Charles** 1837–1909. British poet and critic whose verse attacked the conventions of Victorian morality.

swin·dle (swĭn′dl) *v.* **-dled, -dling, -dles** —*tr.* **1.** To cheat or defraud, as of money. **2.** To obtain by fraud. —*intr.* To use fraud to obtain money or property. ❖ *n.* The act or an instance of swindling. [Back-formation < *swindler,* one who swindles < Ger. *Schwindler,* giddy person, cheat < *schwindeln,* to be dizzy, swindle < MHGer. < OHGer. *swintilōn,* freq. of *swintan,* to disappear.] —**swin′dler** *n.*

Swin·don (swĭn′dən) A municipal borough of S-central England ENE of Bristol. Pop. 151,600.

swine (swīn) *n., pl.* **swine** **1.** Any of various omnivorous ungulates of the family Suidae, including pigs, having a stout body, a thick skin, and a short neck. **2.** A person regarded as brutish or contemptible. [ME < OE *swīn.* See sū- in App.]

swine·herd (swīn′hûrd′) *n.* One who tends swine.

swine·pox (swīn′pŏks′) *n.* An infectious viral disease of domesticated swine marked by skin lesions.

swing (swĭng) *v.* **swung** (swŭng), **swing·ing, swings** —*intr.* **1.** To move back and forth suspended or as if suspended from above. **2.** To hit at something with a sweeping motion of the arm: *swung at the ball.* **3.** To move laterally or in a curve. **4.** To turn in place on or as if on a hinge or pivot. **5.** To move along with an easy swaying gait. **6.** To propel oneself from one place or position to another by grasping a fixed support. **7.** To ride on a swing. **8.** To shift from one attitude, opinion, or condition to another; vacillate. **9.** *Slang* To be put to death by hanging. **10.** *Music* **a.** To have a subtle, intuitively felt rhythm or sense of rhythm. **b.** To play with such a sense of rhythm. **11.** *Slang* **a.** To be lively, trendy, and exciting. **b.** To engage in promiscuous sex. **c.** To exchange sex partners. Used esp. of married couples. **d.** To have a sexual orientation toward one or both sexes. —*tr.* **1.** To cause to move back and forth, as on a swing. **2.** To cause to move in a broad arc or curve. **3a.** To cause to move with a sweeping motion. **b.** To lift and convey with a sweeping motion. **4.** To suspend so as to sway or turn freely. **5a.** To suspend on hinges. **b.** To cause to turn on hinges. **6.** To cause to shift from one attitude, opinion, or condition to another. **7.** *Informal* **a.** To manage or arrange successfully. **b.** To bring around to the desired result. **8.** *Music* To play (music) with a subtle, intuitively felt sense of rhythm. ❖ *n.* **1.** The act or an instance of swinging; movement back and forth or in one particular direction. **2.** The sweep or scope of something that swings. **3.** A blow or stroke executed with a sweeping motion of the arm. **4.** The manner in which one swings something, such as a bat. **5.** A shift from one attitude, opinion, or condition to another. **6.** Freedom of action. **7a.** A swaying graceful motion. **b.** A sweep back and forth. **8.** A course or tour that returns to the starting point. **9.** A seat suspended from above, as by ropes, on which one can ride back and forth for recreation. **10.** The normal rhythm of life or pace of activities. **11.** A steady vigorous rhythm or movement, as in verse. **12.** A regular movement up or down, as in stock prices. **13.** *Music* **a.** A type of popular dance music developed about 1935 and based on jazz but employing less improvisation and simpler harmonic patterns. **b.** A ballroom dance performed to this music. **c.** A subtle, intuitively felt rhythmic quality or sense of rhythm. ❖ *adj.* **1.** *Music* Relating to or performing swing. **2.** Determining an outcome; decisive. ***—idiom:* in full swing** At the highest level of activity or operation. [ME *swingen,* to beat, brandish < OE *swingan,* to flog, strike, swing.] **—swing′y** *adj.*

swing-by (swĭng′bī′) *n., pl.* **-bys** An interplanetary mission in which a space vehicle uses planetary gravitation for changes in course.

swinge (swĭnj) *tr.v.* **swinged, swinge•ing** also **swing•ing, swing•es** *Archaic* To punish with blows; thrash. [ME *swengen* < OE *swengan,* to shake.] **—swing′er** (swĭn′jər) *n.*

swing•er (swĭng′ər) *n.* **1.** One that swings. **2.** *Slang* **a.** One who actively seeks excitement and follows the latest trends. **b.** One who engages in promiscuous sex. **c.** A member of a couple, esp. a married couple, who exchanges sexual partners.

swing•ing (swĭng′ĭng) *Slang adj.* **1.** Spirited; up-to-date. **2.** Attracting a lively, trendy crowd. **3a.** Sexually promiscuous. **b.** Exchanging sexual partners, esp. spouses.

swin•gle•tree (swĭng′gəl-trē) *n.* See **whiffletree.** [< E. *swingle,* wooden instrument used for beating flax < ME < MDu. *swinghel.*]

swing•man (swĭng′mən) *n. Basketball* A player who plays well in two different positions, esp. forward and guard.

swing shift *n.* The work shift between the day and the night shifts, usu. 4 P.M. to midnight.

swing-wing (swĭng′wĭng′) *adj.* Of or being an airplane with wings constructed to allow the outer portion to fold back along the fuselage to produce streamlining at high speeds.

swin•ish (swī′nĭsh) *adj.* **1.** Resembling or befitting swine. **2.** Bestial or brutish.

swipe (swīp) *n.* **1.** A sweeping blow or stroke. **2.** *Informal* A critical remark. **3.** A lever, esp. one that raises the bucket in a well. ❖ *v.* **swiped, swip•ing, swipes** —*tr.* **1.** To hit with a sweeping motion. **2.** To pass (a swipe card) through an electronic reader. **3.** *Informal* To steal; filch. —*intr.* To make a sweeping stroke. [Perh. var. of SWEEP.]

swipe card *n.* A plastic card with a magnetic strip containing encoded data that is read by passing the card through an electronic device, used esp. to make electronic transactions and to provide access to restricted areas.

swirl (swûrl) *v.* **swirled, swirl•ing, swirls** —*intr.* **1.** To move with a twisting or whirling motion; eddy. **2.** To be dizzy or disoriented. **3.** To be arranged in a spiral, whorl, or twist. —*tr.* **1.** To cause to move in a swirl. **2.** To form into or arrange in a spiral, whorl, or twist. ❖ *n.* **1.** A whirling or eddying motion or mass. **2.** Something that coils, twists, or whirls. **3.** Whirling confusion or disorder. [ME *swyrl,* eddy, prob. of LGer. or Scand. orig.] **—swirl′y** *adj.*

swish (swĭsh) *v.* **swished, swish•ing, swish•es** —*intr.* **1.** To move with a hissing or whistling sound. **2.** To rustle, as silk. —*tr.* **1.** To cause to make a swishing sound. **2.** To strike or cut with a swishing sound. **3.** To whip with a rod. ❖ *n.* **1a.** A sharp whistling or rustling sound. **b.** A movement making such a sound. **2a.** A rod used for flogging. **b.** A stroke made with such a rod. **3.** *Offensive Slang* Used as a disparaging term for a homosexual man. ❖ *adj.* **1.** *Informal* Fashionable; posh. **2.** *Slang* Effeminate. [Imit.]

swish•y (swĭsh′ē) *adj.* **-i•er, -i•est 1.** Producing a swishing sound. **2.** *Slang* Effeminate.

Swiss (swĭs) *adj.* Of or relating to Switzerland or its people or culture. ❖ *n.* **1.** *pl.* **Swiss a.** A native or inhabitant of Switzerland. **b.** A person of Swiss descent. **2.** also **swiss** A crisp sheer cotton fabric used for curtains or light garments. **3.** A firm white or pale yellow cheese with holes, originally produced in Switzerland. [Fr. *Suisse* < MHGer. *Swīzer* < *Swīz,* Switzerland.]

Swiss chard *n.* A variety of beet *(Beta vulgaris* var. *cicla)* having large succulent leaves used as a vegetable.

Swiss Guard *n.* A member of a corps of soldiers of Swiss birth employed at the Vatican as bodyguards to the pope.

Swiss steak *n.* A round steak pounded with flour and braised in stock with vegetables.

switch (swĭch) *n.* **1.** A thin flexible rod, stick, or twig, esp. one used for whipping. **2.** The bushy tip of the tail of certain animals. **3.** A thick strand of real or synthetic hair used as part of a coiffure. **4.** A flailing or lashing, as with a switch. **5.** A device used to break or open an electric circuit or divert current from one conductor to another. **6.** A device consisting of two sections of railroad track and accompanying apparatus used to transfer rolling stock from one track to another. **7a.** The operating of a switching device. **b.** The result of such an act. **8.** An exchange or swap, esp. a secret one. **9.** A transference or shift, as of opinion. ❖ *v.* **switched, switch•ing, switch•es** —*tr.* **1.** *Chiefly Southern US* To whip with or as if with a switch, esp. in punishing a child. **2.** To jerk or swish abruptly or sharply. **3.** To shift, transfer, or divert. **4.** To exchange. **5.** To connect, disconnect, or divert (an electric current) by operating a switch. **6.** To cause (an electric current or appliance) to begin or cease operation: *switched the lights on.* **7.** *Informal* To produce as if by operating a control. Often used with *on.* **8.** To move (rolling stock) from one track to another; shunt. —*intr.* **1.** To make or undergo a shift or exchange. **2.** To swish sharply from side to side. [Prob. of LGer. or Flem. orig.] **—switch′a•ble** *adj.* **—switch′er** *n.*

switch•back (swĭch′băk′) *n.* **1.** A road, trail, or railroad track that ascends a steep incline in a zigzag course. **2.** A sharp bend in a road or trail ascending a steep incline. **3.** *Chiefly British* A roller coaster. ❖ *intr.v.* **-backed, -back•ing, -backs** To proceed in sharp turns in alternating directions on a steep incline.

switch•blade (swĭch′blād′) *n.* A pocketknife with a spring-operated blade that opens when a release on the handle is pressed.

switch•board (swĭch′bôrd′, -bōrd′) *n.* **1.** One or more panels accommodating control switches and other apparatus for operating electric circuits. **2.** See **telephone exchange.**

switch•er•oo (swĭch′ə-ro͞o′) *n., pl.* **-oos** *Slang* An unexpected variation or reversal. [Alteration of SWITCH.]

switch hitter *n. Baseball* A player who can bat either right-handed or left-handed. **—switch′-hit′** (swĭch′hĭt′) *v.*

switch knife *n.* See **switchblade.**

switch•man (swĭch′mən) *n.* A man who operates railroad switches.

switch•o•ver (swĭch′ō′vər) *n.* A complete shift, as from one system to another.

switch•yard (swĭch′yärd′) *n.* An area where railroad cars are switched and trains assembled.

Switz. *abbr.* Switzerland

Swit•zer (swĭt′sər) *n.* A Swiss. [Ult. < MHGer. *Swīzer.* See SWISS.]

Swit•zer•land (swĭt′sər-lənd) A country of W-central Europe; became part of the Holy Roman Empire in the 10th cent.; by 1499 achieved independence as a confederation of cantons. Cap. Bern. Pop. 6,995,000.

swiv•el (swĭv′əl) *n.* **1.** A link, pivot, or other fastening that permits the free turning of attached parts. **2.** A pivoted support that allows an attached object, such as a chair, to turn in a horizontal plane. **3.** A gun that turns on a pivot. ❖ *v.* **-eled, -el•ing, -els** or **-elled, -el•ling, -els** —*tr.* **1.** To turn or rotate on or as if on a swivel. **2.** To secure, fit, or support with a swivel. —*intr.* To turn on or as if on a swivel. [ME *swyvel.*]

swivel chair *n.* A chair that swivels on its base.

swiv•el-hipped (swĭv′əl-hĭpt′) *adj.* Characterized by an exaggerated swinging movement of the hips.

swiv•et (swĭv′ĭt) *n. Informal* Extreme distress or discomposure. [?]

swiz•zle (swĭz′əl) *n.* Any of various tall mixed drinks usu. made with rum. [?]

swizzle stick *n.* A small thin rod for stirring mixed drinks.

swob (swŏb) *n. & v.* Variant of **swab.**

swol•len (swō′lən) *v.* A past participle of **swell.** ❖ *adj.* **1.** Expanded by or as if by internal pressure; distended: *a swollen toe.* **2.** Overblown; bombastic: *swollen rhetoric.*

swoon (swo͞on) *intr.v.* **swooned, swoon•ing, swoons 1.** To faint. **2.** To be overwhelmed by ecstatic joy. ❖ *n.* **1.** A fainting spell; syncope. **2.** A state of ecstasy or rapture. [ME *swounen,* prob. < *iswowen,* in a swoon < OE *geswōgen,* p. part. of **swōgan,* to suffocate.]

swoop (swo͞op) *v.* **swooped, swoop•ing, swoops** —*intr.* **1.** To move in a sudden sweep. **2.** To make a rush or an attack with or as if with a sudden sweeping movement. Often used with *down.* —*tr.* To seize or snatch in or as if in a sudden sweeping movement. ❖ *n.* The act or an instance of swooping. [ME *swopen,* to sweep along < OE *swāpan,* to sweep, swing.]

swoosh (swo͞osh, swo͝osh) *v.* **swooshed, swoosh•ing, swoosh•es** —*intr.* **1.** To move with or make a rushing sound. **2.** To flow or swirl copiously. —*tr.* To cause to move with or make a rushing or swirling sound. [Imit.]

swop (swŏp) *v. & n. Chiefly British* Variant of **swap.**

sword (sôrd) *n.* **1.** A weapon consisting typically of a long straight or slightly curved pointed blade having one or two cutting edges and set into a hilt. **2.** An instrument of death or destruction. **3a.**

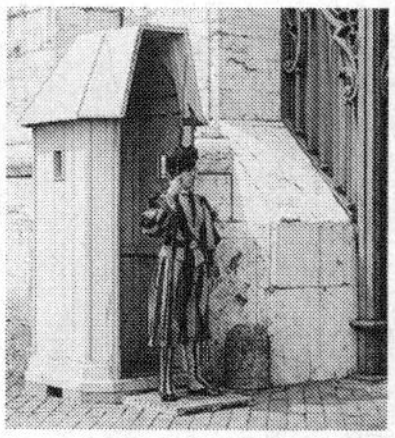

Swiss Guard

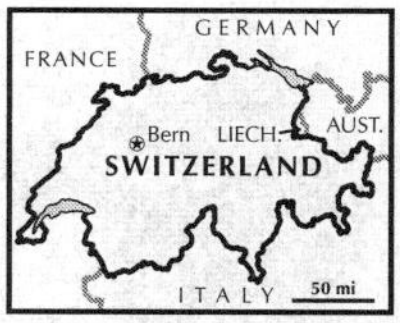

Switzerland

ă pat
ā pay
âr care
ä father
ĕ pet
ē be
ĭ pit
ī pie
îr pier
ŏ pot
ō toe
ô paw
oi boy
ou out
o͝o took
o͞o boot
ŭ cut
ûr urge
th thin
th this
hw which
zh vision
ə about, item

Stress marks:
′ (primary);
′ (secondary), as in
lexicon (lĕk′sĭ-kŏn′)

The use of force, as in war. **b.** Military power or jurisdiction. **—idioms: at swords' points** Ready for a fight. **put to the sword** To kill; slay. [ME < OE *sweord.*]

sword cane *n.* A cane with a hollow shaft in which a sword can be concealed.

sword dance *n.* A dance performed with swords, esp. one performed around swords laid on the ground.

sword fern *n.* Any of various ferns of the genus *Nephrolepis,* including the Boston fern, having bipinnately compound fronds and sori at the vein tips.

sword·fish (sôrd′fĭsh′) *n., pl.* **swordfish** or **-fish·es** A large marine fish (*Xiphias gladius*) with a long swordlike extension of the upper jaw that serves as a weapon.

sword grass *n.* Any of various grasses or grasslike plants having pointed swordlike leaves.

sword knot *n.* A decorative loop or tassel on a sword hilt.

sword lily *n. Botany* See **gladiolus** 1.

sword of Damocles *n.* Constant threat; imminent peril.

sword·play (sôrd′plā′) *n.* The act or art of using a sword.

swords·man (sôrdz′mən) *n.* **1.** A man who is skilled in the use of swords. **2.** A fencer. **—swords′man·ship′** *n.*

sword·tail (sôrd′tāl′) *n.* A small, brightly colored live-bearing freshwater fish (*Xiphophorus helleri*) of Central America having a long tapering extension of the caudal fin in the male.

swore (swôr, swōr) *v.* Past tense of **swear.**

sworn (swôrn, swōrn) *v.* Past participle of **swear.** ❖ *adj.* **1.** Having been asserted as true under oath: *sworn statements.* **2.** Bound or empowered by an oath. **3.** Avowed: *a sworn friend.*

swum (swŭm) *v.* Past participle of **swim.**

swung (swŭng) *v.* Past tense and past participle of **swing.**

swung dash *n.* A character (~) used to stand for all or part of a word that has previously been spelled out.

Syb·a·ris (sĭb′ər-ĭs) An ancient Greek city of S Italy on the Gulf of Taranto; noted for its wealth and luxury.

Syb·a·rite (sĭb′ə-rīt′) *n.* **1.** often **sybarite** A person devoted to pleasure and luxury; a voluptuary. **2.** A native or inhabitant of Sybaris. [Lat. *Sybarīta,* native of Sybaris < Gk. *Subarītēs* < *Subaris,* Sybaris (< the notorious luxury of its inhabitants).] **—syb′a·rit·ism** (-rī-tĭz′əm) *n.*

syb·a·rit·ic (sĭb′ə-rĭt′ĭk) *adj.* **1.** Devoted to or marked by pleasure and luxury. **2. Sybaritic** Of or relating to Sybaris or its people. **—syb′a·rit′i·cal·ly** *adv.*

syc·a·mine (sĭk′ə-mīn′, -mĭn) *n.* A tree mentioned in the Bible, thought to be a species of mulberry. [Lat. *sȳcamīnus* < Gk. *sūkamīnos,* mulberry tree, of Semitic orig.; akin to Aram. *šiqmin,* pl. of *šiqmā,* mulberry.]

syc·a·more (sĭk′ə-môr′, -mōr′) *n.* **1.** Any of various deciduous trees of the genus *Platanus,* esp. *P. occidentalis* of eastern North America, having palmately lobed leaves, ball-like, hairy fruit clusters, and bark that flakes off in large colorful patches. **2.** A Eurasian deciduous maple tree (*Acer pseudoplatanus*) having palmately lobed leaves, winged fruits, and greenish flowers. **3.** A fig tree (*Ficus sycomorus*) of Africa and adjacent southwest Asia, having clusters of figs borne on short leafless twigs. [ME *sicamour,* a kind of fig tree < OFr. *sicamor* < Lat. *sȳcomorus* < Gk. *sūkomoros,* perh. alteration (influenced by *sūkon,* fig, and *moron,* black mulberry) of a Semitic source akin to Heb. **šiqmâ,* eastern sycamore-fig (*Ficus sycomorus*).]

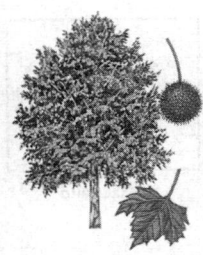

sycamore
American sycamore
Platanus occidentalis

syce (sīs) *n.* A stableman or groom, esp. in India. [Hindi *sā'is* < Ar., active part. of *sāsa,* to tend, manage, perh. denominative < **sūs,* horse; akin to Heb. *sûs.*]

sy·cee (sī-sē′) *n.* Lumps of pure silver stamped by a banker or an assayer and formerly used in China as money. [Chin. (Cantonese) *saisz,* fine silk (so called because the pure silver can be spun into fine threads), equivalent to Chin. (Mandarin) *xì,* thin, fine + *sī,* silk, thread.]

sy·co·ni·um (sī-kō′nē-əm) *n., pl.* **-ni·a** (-nē-ə) The fleshy multiple fruit of the fig, having an enlarged, hollow globose floral receptacle open at the apex. [NLat. *sȳcōnium* < Gk. *sukon,* fig.]

syc·o·phan·cy (sĭk′ə-fən-sē, sĭk′kə-) *n., pl.* **-cies** The fawning behavior of a sycophant; servile flattery.

syc·o·phant (sĭk′ə-fənt, sĭk′kə-) *n.* A servile self-seeker who seeks favor by flattering influential people. [Lat. *sȳcophanta,* informer, slanderer < Gk. *sūkophantēs,* informer < *sūkon phainein,* to show a fig (prob. orig. said of denouncers of theft or exportation of figs) : *sūkon,* fig + *phainein,* to show; see **bhā-**[1] in App.] **—syc′o·phan′tic** (-făn′tĭk), **syc′o·phan′ti·cal** (-tĭ-kəl) *adj.* **—syc′o·phan·tism** *n.*

Syc·o·rax (sĭk′ə-răks′) *n.* The satellite of Uranus that is 17th in distance from the planet. [After *Sycorax,* witch and mother of Caliban in *The Tempest* by William Shakespeare.]

sy·co·sis (sī-kō′sĭs) *n.* A chronic inflammation of the hair follicles, esp. of the beard, marked by eruption of pimples and nodules. [Lat. *sȳcōsis,* sore resembling a fig < Gk. *sūkōsis* < *sūkon,* fig.]

Syd·en·ham's chorea (sĭd′n-əmz) *n.* A nervous disorder occurring chiefly in childhood or during pregnancy, closely associated with rheumatic fever and characterized by rapid jerky involuntary movements of the body. [After Thomas *Sydenham* (1624–89), English physician.]

Syd·ney (sĭd′nē) A city of SE Australia on an inlet of the Tasman Sea. Met. area pop. 3,713,500.

sy·e·nite (sī′ə-nīt′) *n.* An igneous rock composed primarily of alkali feldspar. [Lat. *Syēnītēs (lapis),* (stone) of Syene < *Syēnē,* Syene, an ancient city of S Egypt < Gk. *Suēnē.*] **—sy′e·nit′ic** (-nĭt′ĭk) *adj.*

syl·la·bar·y (sĭl′ə-bĕr′ē) *n., pl.* **-ies** **1.** A list of syllables. **2.** A set of written characters for a language, each character representing a syllable. [NLat. *syllabārium* < Lat. *syllaba,* syllable. See SYLLABLE.]

syl·lab·ic (sĭ-lăb′ĭk) *adj.* **1a.** Of or consisting of a syllable or syllables. **b.** Pronounced with every syllable distinct. **2.** *Linguistics* Designating a sound that is or can be the most sonorant segment of a syllable, as a vowel or a resonant. In the word *riddle* (rĭd′l), the two syllabic sounds are the (ĭ) and the (l). **3.** Of or being a form of verse based on the number of syllables in a line rather than the arrangement of accents or quantities. ❖ *n. Linguistics* A syllabic sound. [Med.Lat. *syllabicus* < Gk. *sullabikos* < *sullabē,* syllable. See SYLLABLE.] **—syl·lab′i·cal·ly** *adv.*

syl·lab·i·fy (sĭ-lăb′ə-fī′) or **syl·lab·i·cate** (-kāt′) *tr.v.* **-fied, -fy·ing, -fies** or **-cat·ed, -cat·ing, -cates** To form or divide into syllables. **—syl·lab′i·fi·ca′tion** (-fĭ-kā′shən), **syl·lab′i·ca′tion** (-kā′shən) *n.*

syl·la·bism (sĭl′ə-bĭz′əm) *n.* **1.** Division of a word or phrase into syllables. **2.** Use of syllabic characters in writing. [Lat. *syllaba,* syllable; see SYLLABLE + -ISM.]

syl·la·bize (sĭl′ə-bīz′) *tr.v.* **-bized, -biz·ing, -biz·es** To syllabify. [Med.Lat. *syllabizāre,* to quibble < Gk. *sullabizein,* to syllabify < *sullabē,* syllable. See SYLLABLE.]

syl·la·ble (sĭl′ə-bəl) *n.* **1a.** A unit of spoken language consisting of an uninterrupted sound formed by a vowel, diphthong, or syllabic consonant alone or by any of these sounds with one or more consonants. **b.** One or more written letters or phonetic symbols that approximate a spoken syllable. **2.** The slightest bit of spoken or written expression. ❖ *tr.v.* **-bled, -bling, -bles** To pronounce in syllables. [ME *sillable* < AN, alteration of OFr. *sillabe* < Lat. *syllaba* < Gk. *sullabē* < *sullambanein,* to combine in pronunciation : *sun-,* syn- + *lambanein, lab-,* to take.]

syl·la·bub also **sil·la·bub** (sĭl′ə-bŭb′) *n.* **1.** A drink made of sweetened milk or cream curdled with wine or spirits. **2.** A cold dessert made with sweetened cream thickened with gelatin and beaten with wine, spirits, or fruit juice. [?]

syl·la·bus (sĭl′ə-bəs) *n., pl.* **-bus·es** or **-bi** (-bī′) **1.** An outline or summary of the main points of a text, lecture, or course of study. **2.** *Law* A short statement preceding a report on an adjudged case and summarizing the court's rulings. [Med.Lat., prob. alteration (influenced by Gk. *sullambanein,* to put together) of Lat. *sillybus,* parchment label < Gk. *sillubos.*]

syl·lep·sis (sĭ-lĕp′sĭs) *n., pl.* **-ses** (-sēz) A construction in which a word governs two or more other words but agrees in number, gender, or case with only one or has a different meaning when applied to each, as in *He lost his coat and his temper.* [LLat. *syllēpsis* < Gk. *sullēpsis* : *sun-,* syn- + *lēpsis,* a taking (< *lambanein, lēp-,* to take).] **—syl·lep′tic** (-tĭk) *adj.*

syl·lo·gism (sĭl′ə-jĭz′əm) *n.* **1.** *Logic* A form of deductive reasoning consisting of a major premise, a minor premise, and a conclusion; for example, *All humans are mortal,* the major premise, *I am a human,* the minor premise, *therefore, I am mortal,* the conclusion. **2.** Reasoning from the general to the specific; deduction. **3.** A subtle or specious piece of reasoning. [ME *silogisme* < OFr. < Lat. *syllogismus* < Gk. *sullogismos* < *sullogizesthai,* to infer : *sun-,* syn- + *logizesthai,* to count, reckon (< *logos,* reason; see leg- in App.).] **—syl′lo·gist** *n.* **—syl′lo·gis′tic, syl′lo·gis′ti·cal** *adj.*

syl·lo·gize (sĭl′ə-jīz′) *v.* **-gized, -giz·ing, -giz·es** *—intr.* To reason or argue by syllogisms. *—tr.* To deduce by syllogism. **—syl′lo·gi·za′tion** (-jĭ-zā′shən) *n.* **—syl′lo·giz′er** *n.*

sylph (sĭlf) *n.* **1.** A slim graceful woman or girl. **2.** In the occult philosophy of Paracelsus, a being that has air as its element. [NLat. *sylpha,* perh. blend of Lat. *sylvestris,* of the forest (< *silva, sylva,* forest) and Lat. *nympha,* nymph; see NYMPH.]

sylph·id (sĭl′fĭd) *n.* A young or diminutive sylph. ❖ *adj.* Relating to or resembling a sylph. [Fr. *sylphide* < *sylphe,* sylph < NLat. *sylpha.* See SYLPH.]

syl·va (sĭl′və) *n.* Variant of **silva.**

syl·van also **sil·van** (sĭl′vən) *adj.* **1.** Relating to or characteristic of woods or forest regions. **2.** Located in or inhabiting a wood or forest. **3.** Abounding in trees; wooded. ❖ *n.* One that lives in or frequents the woods. [Med.Lat. *sylvānus* < Lat. *Silvānus,* god of the woods < *silva,* forest.]

syl·van·ite (sĭl′və-nīt′) *n.* A pale yellow to silver-white ore of gold and silver, (Au,Ag)Te₂. [Fr., after TRANSYLVANIA.]

Syl·va·nus (sĭl-vā′nəs) *n. Roman Mythology* Variant of **Silvanus.**

syl·vat·ic (sĭl-văt′ĭk) *adj.* **1.** Affecting only wild animals. **2.** Sylvan. [Lat. *sylvāticus,* wild < *silva, sylva,* forest.]

syl·vite (sĭl′vīt′) also **syl·vine** (sĭl′vēn′) or **syl·vin·ite** (-vĭ-nīt′) *n.* A colorless vitreous mineral, KCl, the major ore of potassium. [Alteration of *sylvine* < Fr. < NLat. *(sāl dīgestīvus) Sylviī,* (digestive salt) of Sylvius, probably after Franz de la Boë, or Franciscus Sylvius (1614–72), Dutch physician.]

sym. *abbr.* **1.** symbol **2.** symmetrical **3.** symphony

sym– *pref.* Variant of **syn–.**

sym•bi•ont (sĭm′bē-ŏnt′, -bī-) *n.* An organism in a symbiotic relationship. [Gk. *sumbiōn, sumbiount-,* pr. part. of *sumbioun,* to live together. See SYMBIOSIS.] —**sym′bi•on′tic** *adj.*

sym•bi•o•sis (sĭm′bē-ō′sĭs, -bī-) *n., pl.* **-ses** (-sēz) **1.** *Biology* A close prolonged association between two or more different organisms of different species. **2.** A relationship of mutual benefit or dependence. [Gk. *sumbiōsis, companionship < sumbioun,* to live together < *sumbios,* living together < *sun-, syn- + bios,* life; see gʷeiə- in App.] —**sym′bi•ot′ic** (-ŏt′ĭk), **sym′bi•ot′i•cal** (-ĭ-kəl) *adj.* —**sym′bi•ot′i•cal•ly** *adv.*

sym•bol (sĭm′bəl) *n.* **1.** One that represents something else by association, resemblance, or convention, esp. a material object representing something invisible. **2.** A printed or written sign used to represent an operation, element, quantity, quality, or relation, as in mathematics or music. **3.** *Psychology* An object or image that an individual unconsciously uses to represent repressed thoughts, feelings, or impulses: *a phallic symbol.* ❖ *tr.v.* **-boled, -bol•ing, -bols** To symbolize. [ME *symbole,* creed < OFr. < Lat. *symbolum,* token, mark < Gk. *sumbolon,* token for identification (by comparison with a counterpart) : *sun-, syn- + ballein,* to throw; see gʷelə- in App.]

sym•bol•ic (sĭm-bŏl′ĭk) also **sym•bol•i•cal** (-ĭ-kəl) *adj.* **1.** Of, relating to, or expressed by means of symbols or a symbol. **2.** Serving as a symbol. **3.** Using symbolism: *symbolic art.* —**sym•bol′i•cal•ly** *adv.* —**sym•bol′i•cal•ness** *n.*

symbolic language *n.* A high-level programming language.

symbolic logic *n.* A treatment of formal logic in which a system of symbols is used to represent quantities and relationships.

sym•bol•ism (sĭm′bə-lĭz′əm) *n.* **1.** The practice of representing things by means of symbols or of attributing symbolic meanings or significance to objects, events, or relationships. **2.** A system of symbols or representations. **3.** A symbolic meaning or representation. **4.** Revelation or suggestion of intangible conditions or truths by artistic invention. **5. Symbolism** The movement, theory, or practice of the late 19th-century Symbolists.

sym•bol•ist (sĭm′bə-lĭst) *n.* **1.** One who uses symbols or symbolism. **2a.** One who interprets or represents conditions or truths with symbols or symbolism. **b.** often **Symbolist** Any of a group of chiefly French writers and artists of the late 19th century who rejected realism and used symbols to evoke ideas and emotions. ❖ *adj.* **1.** Of or relating to symbolism. **2.** often **Symbolist** Of or relating to the Symbolists. —**sym′bol•is′tic** *adj.* —**sym′bol•is′ti•cal•ly** *adv.*

sym•bol•ize (sĭm′bə-līz′) *v.* **-ized, -iz•ing, -iz•es** —*tr.* **1.** To serve as a symbol of. **2.** To represent or identify by a symbol. —*intr.* To use symbols. —**sym′bol•i•za′tion** (-bə-lĭ-zā′shən) *n.* —**sym′bol•iz′er** *n.*

sym•bol•o•gy (sĭm-bŏl′ə-jē) *n.* **1.** The study or interpretation of symbols or symbolism. **2.** The use of symbols.

sym•met•al•lism (sĭm-mĕt′l-ĭz′əm) *n.* A system of coinage in which a unit of currency is pegged to a combination of two or more metals in fixed proportions.

sym•met•ri•cal (sĭ-mĕt′rĭ-kəl) also **sym•met•ric** (-rĭk) *adj.* Of or exhibiting symmetry. —**sym•met′ri•cal•ly** *adv.*

symmetric matrix *n. Mathematics* A matrix that is its own transpose.

sym•me•trize (sĭm′ĭ-trīz′) *tr.v.* **-trized, -triz•ing, -triz•es** To give symmetry to; make symmetrical or proportional. —**sym′me•tri•za′tion** (-trĭ-zā′shən) *n.*

sym•me•try (sĭm′ĭ-trē) *n., pl.* **-tries 1.** Exact correspondence of form and constituent configuration on opposite sides of a dividing line or plane or about a center or an axis. See Syns at **proportion. 2.** A relationship of characteristic correspondence, equivalence, or identity among constituents of an entity or between different entities. **3.** Beauty as a result of balance or harmonious arrangement. [Lat. *symmetria* < Gk. *summetriā* < *summetros,* of like measure : *sun-, syn- + metron,* measure; see mē-¹ in App.]

Sym•onds (sĭm′əndz, sī′məndz), **John Addington** 1840–93. British writer of *The Renaissance in Italy* (1875–86).

Sy•mons (sī′mənz), **Arthur** 1865–1945. British writer whose works include *The Symbolist Movement in Literature* (1899).

sym•pa•thec•to•my (sĭm′pə-thĕk′tə-mē) *n., pl.* **-mies** Surgical removal of a part of the sympathetic nervous system.

sym•pa•thet•ic (sĭm′pə-thĕt′ĭk) *adj.* **1.** Of, expressing, feeling, or resulting from sympathy. **2.** Favorably inclined. **3.** Agreeably suited to one's disposition or mood; congenial. **4.** Of, relating to, or acting on the sympathetic nervous system. **5a.** Relating to or being vibrations, esp. musical tones, produced in one body by and at the same frequency as vibrations from a nearby body. **b.** Emitting such vibrations. [Gk. *sumpathētikos < sumpatheia,* sympathy. See SYMPATHY.] —**sym′pa•thet′i•cal•ly** *adv.*

sympathetic ink *n.* See **invisible ink.**

sympathetic nervous system *n.* The part of the autonomic nervous system originating in the thoracic and lumbar regions of the spinal cord that inhibits or opposes the physiological effects of the parasympathetic nervous system, as in speeding up the heart and contracting blood vessels.

sym•pa•thize (sĭm′pə-thīz′) *intr.v.* **-thized, -thiz•ing, -thiz•es 1.** To feel or express compassion, as for another's suffering; commiserate. **2.** To share or understand the feelings or ideas of another. **3.** To be in accord; correspond. —**sym′pa•thiz′er** *n.*

sym•pa•tho•lyt•ic (sĭm′pə-thō-lĭt′ĭk) *adj.* Opposing the physiological effects caused by stimulation of the sympathetic nervous system. [SYMPATH(ETIC) + −LYTIC.]

sym•pa•tho•mi•met•ic (sĭm′pə-thō-mĭ-mĕt′ĭk, -mī-) *adj.* Producing physiological effects resembling those caused by the sympathetic nervous system. ❖ *n.* A sympathomimetic drug or agent. [SYMPATH(ETIC) + MIMETIC.]

sym•pa•thy (sĭm′pə-thē) *n., pl.* **-thies 1a.** A relationship or affinity between people or things in which whatever affects one correspondingly affects the other. **b.** Mutual understanding or affection arising from this relationship or affinity. **2a.** The act or power of sharing the feelings of another. **b.** A feeling or expression of pity or sorrow for the distress of another; compassion or commiseration. Often used in the plural. **3.** Harmonious agreement; accord: *He is in sympathy with their beliefs.* **4.** A feeling of loyalty; allegiance. Often used in the plural. **5.** *Physiology* A relation between parts or organs by which a disease or disorder in one induces an effect in the other. [Lat. *sympathīa* < Gk. *sumpatheia* < *sumpathēs,* affected by like feelings : *sun-, syn- + pathos,* emotion.]

sympathy strike *n.* A strike by a body of workers for the purpose of supporting a cause or another group of strikers.

sym•pat•ric (sĭm-păt′rĭk) *adj. Ecology* Occupying the same or overlapping geographic areas without interbreeding. Used of populations of closely related species. [SYN− + Gk. *patriā,* fatherland (< *patēr, patr-,* father; see pəter- in App.) + −IC.] —**sym•pat′ri•cal•ly** *adv.* —**sym′pat′ry** (sĭm′păt′rē, -pə-trē) *n.*

sym•pet•al•ous (sĭm-pĕt′l-əs) *adj.* Having united petals; gamopetalous.

sym•phon•ic (sĭm-fŏn′ĭk) *adj.* **1.** Relating to, being, or similar to a symphony. **2.** Harmonious in sound.

symphonic poem *n.* A piece of music, popular in the late 19th century, based on an extramusical theme and usu. consisting of a single extended movement for a symphony orchestra.

sym•pho•ni•ous (sĭm-fō′nē-əs) *adj.* Being in a state of accord; harmonious. —**sym•pho′ni•ous•ly** *adv.*

sym•pho•nist (sĭm′fə-nĭst) *n.* One who composes symphonies.

sym•pho•ny (sĭm′fə-nē) *n., pl.* **-nies 1.** *Music* **a.** An extended piece in three or more movements for symphony orchestra. **b.** An instrumental passage in a vocal or choral composition. **c.** An instrumental overture or interlude, as in early opera. **2.** *Music* **a.** A symphony orchestra. **b.** An orchestral concert. **3.** Harmony, esp. of sound or color. **4.** Something marked by a harmonious combination of elements. [ME *symphonye,* harmony < OFr. *symphonie* < Lat. *symphōnia* < Gk. *sumphōniā* < *sumphōnos,* harmonious : *sun-, syn- + phōnē,* sound; see bhā- in App.]

symphony orchestra *n.* A large orchestra composed of string, wind, and percussion sections.

sym•phy•sis (sĭm′fĭ-sĭs) *n., pl.* **-ses** (-sēz) **1a.** A growing together of bones originally separate, as of the two pubic bones. **b.** A line or junction thus formed. **c.** An articulation in which bones are united by cartilage without a synovial membrane. **2.** The coalescence of similar parts or organs. [Gk. *sumphusis < sumphuein,* to cause to grow together : *sun-, syn- + phuein,* to cause to grow; see bheua- in App.] —**sym′phy•se′al** (sĭm′fĭ-sē′əl), **sym•phys′i•al** (sĭm-fĭz′ē-əl) *adj.*

sym•po•di•um (sĭm-pō′dē-əm) *n., pl.* **-di•a** (-dē-ə) *Botany* A primary axis that develops from a series of short lateral branches, as in the grapevine. [NLat. : SYN− + Gk. *podion,* base (< *pous, pod-,* foot; see ped- in App.).]

sym•po•si•ac (sĭm-pō′zē-ăk′) *adj.* Of, relating to, or appropriate to a symposium. ❖ *n. Archaic* A symposium.

sym•po•si•arch (sĭm-pō′zē-ärk′) *n.* **1.** The master or director of a symposium, esp. one in ancient Greece. **2.** A toastmaster. [Gk. *sumposiarkhos : sumposion,* symposium; see SYMPOSIUM + *arkhos,* ruler; see −ARCH.]

sym•po•si•ast (sĭm-pō′zē-ăst′, -əst) *n.* A participant in a symposium.

sym•po•si•um (sĭm-pō′zē-əm) *n., pl.* **-si•ums** or **-si•a** (-zē-ə) **1.** A meeting or conference for discussion of a topic, esp. one in which the participants form an audience and make presentations. **2.** A collection of writings on a particular topic, as in a magazine. **3.** A convivial meeting for drinking, music, and intellectual discussion among the ancient Greeks. [Lat., drinking party < Gk. *sumposion : sun-, syn- + posis,* drinking; see pō(i)- in App.]

symp•tom (sĭm′təm, sĭmp′-) *n.* **1.** A characteristic sign or indication of the existence of something else. **2.** A sign or an indication of disorder or disease, esp. when experienced by an individual as a change from normal function, sensation, or appearance. [ME *sinthoma,* symptom of a disease < Med.Lat. *sinthōma* < LLat. *symptōma* < Gk. *sumptōma, sumptōmat-,* a happening, symptom of a disease < *sumpiptein,* to coincide : *sun-, syn- + piptein, ptō-,* to fall; see pet- in App.]

symp•to•mat•ic (sĭm′tə-măt′ĭk, sĭmp′-) *adj.* **1.** Of, relating to, or based on symptoms. **2.** Being a symptom, as of a disease. —**symp′to•mat′i•cal•ly** *adv.*

symp•to•ma•tol•o•gy (sĭm′tə-mə-tŏl′ə-jē, sĭmp′-) *n.* **1.** The medical science of symptoms. **2.** The combined symptoms of a disease. [NLat. *symptōmatologia* : Gk. *sumptōma, sumptōmat-,* symptom; see SYMPTOM + Lat. *-logia,* -logy.] —**symp′to•mat′o•log′i•cal** (-măt′l-ŏj′ĭ-kəl) *adj.*

symp·tom·ize (sĭm′tə-mīz′, sĭmp′-) or **symp·tom·a·tize** (-tə-mə-tīz′) tr.v. **-ized, -iz·ing, -iz·es** or **-tized, -tiz·ing, -tiz·es** To be a symptom of (a disease, for example).

syn. abbr. synonym

syn– or **sym–** pref. **1a.** Together; with: synecology. **b.** United: syncarp. **2a.** Same; similar: sympatric. **b.** At the same time: synesthesia. [Gk. sun- < sun. See **ksun** in App.]

syn·aer·e·sis (sĭ-nĕr′ĭ-sĭs) n. Variant of **syneresis.**

syn·aes·the·sia (sĭn′ĭs-thē′zhə) n. Variant of **synesthesia.**

syn·a·gogue also **syn·a·gog** (sĭn′ə-gŏg′, -gôg′) n. **1.** A place of meeting for worship and religious instruction in the Jewish faith. **2.** A congregation of Jews for the purpose of worship or religious study. **3.** Judaism as organized or typified in local congregations. [ME < OFr. sinagoge < LLat. synagōga < Gk. sunagōgē, assembly, synagogue < sunagein, to bring together : sun-, syn- + agein, to lead; see **ag–** in App.] —**syn′a·gog′i·cal** (-gŏj′ĭ-kəl), **syn′a·gog′al** (-gŏg′əl, -gôg′-) adj.

syn·a·le·pha also **syn·a·loe·pha** (sĭn′ə-lē′fə) n. The blending into one syllable of two successive vowels of adjacent syllables, esp. to fit a poetic meter; for example, th' elite for the elite. [NLat. < Gk. sunaloiphē < sunaleiphein, to unite two syllables : sun-, syn- + aleiphein, to smear.]

syn·apse (sĭn′ăps′, sĭ-năps′) n. The junction across which a nerve impulse passes from an axon terminal to a neuron, muscle cell, or gland cell. ❖ intr.v. **-apsed, -aps·ing, -aps·es 1.** To form a synapse. **2.** To undergo synapsis. [Gk. sunapsis, point of contact < sunaptein, to join together : sun-, syn- + haptein, to fasten.]

syn·ap·sis (sĭ-năp′sĭs) n., pl. **-ses** (-sēz) The side-by-side association of homologous paternal and maternal chromosomes during the first prophase of meiosis. [NLat. < Gk. sunapsis, point of contact. See SYNAPSE.]

syn·ap·tic (sĭ-năp′tĭk) adj. Of or relating to synapsis or a synapse. [< Gk. sunaptos, joined together < sunaptein, to join together. See SYNAPSE.] —**syn·ap′ti·cal·ly** adv.

syn·ap·to·some (sĭ-năp′tə-sōm′) n. A saclike structure formed by nerve endings at a synapse that remains intact after homogenization of nerve tissue. —**syn·ap′to·so′mal** adj.

syn·ar·thro·sis (sĭn′är-thrō′sĭs) n., pl. **-ses** (-sēz) Anatomy A form of articulation in which the bones are rigidly joined by fibrous tissue. [Gk. < sunarthrousthai, to be joined by articulation : sun-, syn- + arthron, a joint.]

sync or **synch** (sĭngk) Informal n. **1.** Synchronization. **2.** Harmony; accord. ❖ intr. & tr.v. **synced, sync·ing, syncs** or **synched, synch·ing, synchs** To synchronize.

syn·car·pous (sĭn-kär′pəs) adj. Having or consisting of united carpels. Used of a pistil. —**syn′car·py** n.

syn·chro (sĭng′krō, sĭn′-) n., pl. **-chros** A selsyn.

synchro– pref. Synchronized; synchronous: synchrotron.

syn·chro·cy·clo·tron (sĭng′krō-sī′klə-trŏn′, sĭn′-) n. A cyclotron that accelerates protons and positive ions by synchronizing the frequency of the accelerating potential with the frequency of the accelerated particles to compensate for increases in particle mass at relativistic speeds.

syn·chro·flash (sĭng′krō-flăsh′, sĭn′-) n. A device used in photography to synchronize the peak of a flash with the opening of the camera shutter. —**syn′chro·flash′** adj.

syn·chro·mesh (sĭng′krə-mĕsh′, sĭn′-) n. **1.** An automotive gear-shifting system in which the gears are synchronized at the same speeds before engaging to effect a smooth shift. **2.** A gear in such a system.

syn·chro·nal (sĭng′krə-nəl, sĭn′-) adj. Synchronous.

syn·chron·ic (sĭn-krŏn′ĭk, sĭng-) adj. **1.** Synchronous. **2.** Of or relating to the study of phenomena, such as linguistic features, or of events of a particular time, without reference to their historical context. —**syn·chron′i·cal·ly** adv.

syn·chro·nic·i·ty (sĭng′krə-nĭs′ĭ-tē, sĭn′-) n., pl. **-ties 1.** The state or fact of being synchronous or simultaneous; synchronism. **2.** Coincidence of events that seem to be meaningfully related, conceived in Jungian theory as an explanatory principle on the same order as causality.

syn·chro·nism (sĭng′krə-nĭz′əm, sĭn′-) n. **1.** Coincidence in time; simultaneousness. **2.** A chronological listing of historical personages or events so as to indicate parallel existence or occurrence. **3.** Representation in the same artwork of events that occurred at different times. —**syn′chro·nis′tic, syn′chro·nis′ti·cal** (-tĭ-kəl) adj. —**syn′chro·nis′ti·cal·ly** adv.

syn·chro·nize (sĭng′krə-nīz′, sĭn′-) v. **-nized, -niz·ing, -niz·es** —intr. **1.** To be simultaneous. **2.** To operate in unison. —tr. **1a.** To cause to occur or operate with exact coincidence in time or rate. **b.** To cause to occur or operate at the same time as something else. **2.** To arrange (historical events) in a synchronism so as to indicate parallel occurrence. **3.** To cause (soundtrack and action) to match exactly in a film. [Gk. sunkhronizein, to be contemporary < sunkhronos, contemporaneous. See SYNCHRONOUS.] —**syn′chro·ni·za′tion** (-nĭ-zā′shən) n. —**syn′chro·niz′er** n.

syn·chro·nized swimming (sĭng′krə-nīzd′, sĭn′-) n. A sport in which swimmers, singly or in groups, perform dancelike movements often to music.

syn·chro·nous (sĭng′krə-nəs, sĭn′-) adj. **1.** Occurring or existing at the same time. **2.** Moving or operating at the same rate. **3a.** Having identical periods. **b.** Having identical period and phase. [< LLat. synchronus < Gk. sunkhronos : sun-, syn- + khronos, time.] —**syn′chro·nous·ly** adv. —**syn′chro·nous·ness** n.

synchronous motor n. A motor with a speed directly proportional to the frequency of its alternating current power.

synchronous orbit n. A geostationary orbit.

syn·chro·ny (sĭng′krə-nē, sĭn′-) n., pl. **-nies** Simultaneous occurrence; synchronism. [< SYNCHRONOUS.]

syn·chro·tron (sĭng′krə-trŏn′, sĭn′-) n. An accelerator in which charged particles are accelerated around a fixed circular path by an electric field and held to the path by an increasing magnetic field.

synchrotron radiation n. Electromagnetic radiation emitted by high-energy particles when accelerated to relativistic speeds in a magnetic field.

syn·cli·nal (sĭn-klī′nəl) adj. **1.** Sloping downward from opposite directions to meet in a common point or line. **2.** Geology Relating to, formed by, or forming a syncline.

syn·cline (sĭn′klīn′) n. Geology A fold in rocks in which the rock layers dip inward from both sides toward the axis.

syn·co·pate (sĭng′kə-pāt′, sĭn′-) tr.v. **-pat·ed, -pat·ing, -pates 1.** Grammar To shorten (a word) by syncope. **2.** Music To modify (rhythm) by syncopation. [LLat. syncopāre, syncopāt- < syncopē, syncope. See SYNCOPE.] —**syn′co·pa′tor** n.

syn·co·pa·tion (sĭng′kə-pā′shən, sĭn′-) n. **1.** Music A shift of accent in a passage or composition that occurs when a normally weak beat is stressed. **2.** Something, such as rhythm, that is syncopated. **3.** Grammar Syncope.

syn·co·pe (sĭng′kə-pē, sĭn′-) n. **1.** Grammar The shortening of a word by omission of a sound, letter, or syllable from the middle of the word; for example, bos'n for boatswain. **2.** Pathology A brief loss of consciousness due to a temporary deficiency of oxygen in the brain. [Ult. < LLat. syncopē < Gk. sunkopē < sunkoptein, to cut short : sun-, syn- + koptein, to strike.] —**syn′co·pal** (sĭng′kə-pəl, sĭn′-), **syn·cop′ic** (sĭn-kŏp′ĭk) adj.

syn·cre·tism (sĭng′krĭ-tĭz′əm, sĭn′-) n. **1.** Reconciliation or fusion of differing systems of belief, esp. with partial success or a heterogeneous result. **2.** Linguistics The merging of two or more originally different inflectional forms. [Gk. sunkrētismos, union < sunkrētizein, to unite (in the manner of the Cretan cities) : sun-, syn- + Krēs, Krēt-, Cretan.] —**syn′cret′ic** (-krĕt′ĭk), **syn′cre·tis′tic** (-krī-tĭs′tĭk) adj. —**syn′cre·tist** n.

syn·cre·tize (sĭng′krĭ-tīz′, sĭn′-) v. **-tized, -tiz·ing, -tiz·es** —tr. To reconcile and unite (differing religious beliefs, for example), esp. with partial success or a heterogeneous result. —intr. To syncretize differing elements or beliefs. [Gk. sunkrētizein, to unite against a common enemy. See SYNCRETISM.]

syn·cy·ti·um (sĭn-sĭsh′ē-əm) n., pl. **-cy·ti·a** (-sĭsh′ē-ə) A multinucleated mass of cytoplasm that is not separated into individual cells. [NLat. : SYN– + CYT(O)– + –IUM.] —**syn·cy′ti·al** (-sĭsh′ē-əl) adj.

syn·dac·tyl (sĭn-dăk′təl) n. An animal, esp. a bird or mammal, that has two or more fused digits. [Fr. syndactyle : Gk. sun-, syn- + Gk. daktulos, finger.] —**syn·dac′tyl, syn·dac′ty·lous** (-tə-ləs) adj.

syn·dac·ty·ly (sĭn-dăk′tə-lē) or **syn·dac·tyl·ism** (-tə-lĭz′əm) n. Biology **1.** The condition of having two or more fused digits, as occurs normally in certain mammals and birds. **2.** A congenital anomaly in humans characterized by two or more fused fingers or toes.

syn·des·mo·sis (sĭn′dĕz-mō′sĭs, -dĕs-) n., pl. **-ses** (-sēz) An articulation in which the bones are joined by a ligament. [NLat. < Gk. sundesmos, bond, ligament < sundein, to bind together. See SYNDETIC.] —**syn′des·mot′ic** (-mŏt′ĭk) adj.

syn·det·ic (sĭn-dĕt′ĭk) adj. **1.** Serving to connect, as a conjunction; copulative or conjunctive. **2.** Connected by a conjunction. [Gk. sundetikos < sundetos, bound together < sundein, to bind together : sun-, syn- + dein, to bind.]

syn·dic (sĭn′dĭk) n. **1.** One appointed to represent an organization in business transactions; a business agent. **2.** A civil magistrate or similar government official in some European countries. [Fr. < OFr. sindiz < LLat. syndicus < Gk. sundikos, public advocate : sun-, syn- + dikē, justice; see **deik–** in App.] —**syn′di·cal** adj.

syn·di·cal·ism (sĭn′dĭ-kə-lĭz′əm) n. A radical political movement that advocates bringing industry and government under the control of federations of labor unions by the use of direct action, such as general strikes and sabotage. [Fr. syndicalisme < (chambre) syndicale, trade union, fem. of syndical, of a labor union < syndic, delegate. See SYNDIC.] —**syn′di·cal·ist** adj. & n. —**syn′di·cal·is′tic** adj.

syn·di·cate (sĭn′dĭ-kĭt) n. **1.** An association of people or firms authorized to undertake a duty or transact specific business. **2.** An association of people or firms formed to engage in an enterprise or promote a common interest. **3.** A loose affiliation of gangsters in control of organized criminal activities. **4.** An agency that sells articles, features, or photographs for publication in a number of newspapers or periodicals simultaneously. **5.** A company consisting of a number of separate newspapers; a newspaper chain. **6.** The office, position, or jurisdiction of a syndic or body of syndics. ❖ v. (-kāt′) **-cat·ed, -cat·ing, -cates** —tr. **1a.** To or-

syncopation
from Mozart's Symphony
no. 25

ganize into or manage as a syndicate. **b.** To sell shares in. **2.** To sell (an article, feature, or photograph) through a syndicate. **3.** To sell (a television series, for example) directly to independent stations. —*intr.* To join together in a syndicate. [Fr. *syndicat* < OFr., office of syndic < Med.Lat. *syndicātus* < LLat. *syndicus*, syndic. See SYNDIC.] —**syn'di•ca'tion** *n.* —**syn'di•ca'tor** *n.*

syn•drome (sĭn'drōm') *n.* **1.** A group of symptoms that collectively indicate or characterize a disease or other abnormal condition. **2a.** A complex of symptoms indicating the existence of an undesirable condition or quality. **b.** A distinctive or characteristic pattern of behavior. [Gk. *sundromē*, concurrence of symptoms < *sundromos*, running together : *sun-*, syn- + *dromos*, a running.] —**syn•drom'ic** (-drŏm'ĭk, -drōm'ĭk) *adj.*

syne (sīn) *Scots adv.* **1.** Before now; ago. **2.** Afterward; since then; since. **3.** Thereupon; next. ❖ *conj.* Since. ❖ *prep.* Since. [Sc. < ME *sithen* < OE *siththan.*]

syn•ec•do•che (sĭ-nĕk'də-kē) *n.* A figure of speech in which a part is used for the whole (as *hand* for *sailor*), the whole for a part (as *the law* for *police officer*), the specific for the general (as *cutthroat* for *assassin*), the general for the specific (as *thief* for *pickpocket*), or the material for the thing made from it (as *steel* for *sword*). [Ult. < Lat. *synecdochē* < Gk. *sunekdokhē* < *sunekdekhesthai*, to take on a share of : *sun-*, syn- + *ekdekhesthai*, to understand (*ek-*, out of; see **eghs** in App. + *dekhesthai*, to take; see **dek-** in App.).] —**syn•ec•doch'ic** (sĭn'ĕk-dŏk'ĭk), **syn'ec•doch'i•cal** (-ĭ-kəl) *adj.*

syn•e•col•o•gy (sĭn'ĭ-kŏl'ə-jē) *n.* The study of the ecological interrelationships among communities of organisms. —**syn'e•co•log'ic** (-kə-lŏj'ĭk), **syn'e•co•log'i•cal** (-ĭ-kəl) *adj.*

syn•aer•e•sis also **syn•aer•e•sis** (sĭ-nĕr'ĭ-sĭs) *n., pl.* **-ses** (-sēz') **1.** *Linguistics* The combining into one syllable of two consecutive vowels or syllables, as in a diphthong. **2.** *Chemistry* Exudation of the liquid component of a gel. [LLat. *synaeresis* < Gk. *sunairesis* < *sunairein*, to contract : *sun-*, syn- + *hairein*, to take, grasp.]

syn•er•get•ic (sĭn'ər-jĕt'ĭk) also **syn•er•gic** (sĭ-nûr'jĭk) *adj.* Synergistic.

syn•er•gid (sĭ-nûr'jĭd, sĭn'ər-) *n.* One of two small cells lying near the egg in the embryo sac of a flowering plant. [NLat. *synergida* < Gk. *sunergos*, working together. See SYNERGISM.]

syn•er•gism (sĭn'ər-jĭz'əm) *n.* **1.** Synergy. **2.** *Christianity* The doctrine that individual salvation is achieved through a combination of human will and divine grace. [NLat. *synergismus* < Gk. *sunergos*, working together : *sun-*, syn- + *ergon*, work; see **werg-** in App.]

syn•er•gist (sĭn'ər-jĭst) *n.* **1.** A synergistic organ, drug, or agent. **2.** *Christianity* An adherent of synergism.

syn•er•gis•tic (sĭn'ər-jĭs'tĭk) *adj.* **1.** Of or relating to synergy. **2.** Producing or capable of producing synergy. **3.** *Christianity* Of or relating to synergism. —**syn'er•gis'ti•cal•ly** *adv.*

syn•er•gy (sĭn'ər-jē) *n., pl.* **-gies 1.** The interaction of two or more agents or forces so that their combined effect is greater than the sum of their individual effects. **2.** Cooperative interaction among groups, such as corporate subsidiaries, that creates an enhanced combined effect. [< Gk. *sunergiā*, cooperation < *sunergos*, working together. See SYNERGISM.]

syn•e•sis (sĭn'ĭ-sĭs) *n.* A construction in which a form, such as a pronoun, differs in number but agrees in meaning with the word governing it, as in *If the group is too large, split them in two.* [Gk. *sunesis*, union, understanding < *suniēnai*, to bring together : *sun-*, syn- + *hīenai*, to send, hurl.]

syn•es•the•sia also **syn•aes•the•sia** (sĭn'ĭs-thē'zhə) *n.* **1.** A condition in which one type of stimulation evokes the sensation of another, as when the hearing of a sound produces the visualization of a color. **2.** A sensation felt in one part of the body as a result of a stimulus applied to another, as in referred pain. **3.** The description of one kind of sense impression by using words that normally describe another. —**syn'es•thet'ic** (-thĕt'ĭk) *adj.*

syn•es•thete (sĭn'ĭs-thēt') *n.* A person who experiences synesthesia, as by having a secondary sensation of sound as color.

syn•fu•el (sĭn'fyoo'əl) *n.* A liquid or gaseous fuel derived from coal, shale, or tar sand or obtained by fermentation of certain substances, such as grain. [SYN(THETIC) + FUEL.]

syn•ga•my (sĭng'gə-mē) *n.* The fusion of two gametes in fertilization. —**syn•gam'ic** (sĭn-găm'ĭk), **syn'ga•mous** (sĭng'gə-məs) *adj.*

Synge (sĭng), **John Millington** 1871–1909. Irish playwright whose works, based on rural Irish life, include *The Playboy of the Western World* (1907).

syn•i•ze•sis (sĭn'ĭ-zē'sĭs) *n., pl.* **-ses** (-sēz) *Linguistics* The union in pronunciation of two adjacent vowels into one syllable without forming a diphthong. [LLat. *synizēsis* < Gk. *sunizēsis* < *sunizein*, to collapse : *sun-*, syn- + *hizein*, to settle down; see **sed-** in App.]

syn•kar•y•on (sĭn-kăr'ē-ŏn', -ē-ən) *n.* The nucleus of a fertilized egg immediately after the male and female nuclei have fused. [SYN- + Gk. *karuon*, nut, seed.]

syn•od (sĭn'əd) *n.* **1.** An ecclesiastical council or assembly. **2.** A council or an assembly. [ME < Lat. *synodus* < Gk. *sunodos*, meeting, assembly : *sun-*, syn- + *hodos*, way, course.] —**syn'od•al** (sĭn'ə-dl) *adj.*

syn•od•ic (sĭ-nŏd'ĭk) or **syn•od•i•cal** (-nŏd'ĭ-kəl) *adj.* **1.** Of or relating to a synod; synodal. **2.** Relating to the conjunction of ce-

lestial bodies, esp. the interval between two successive conjunctions of a planet or the moon with the sun.

synodic month *n.* See lunar month.

syn•o•nym (sĭn'ə-nĭm') *n.* **1.** A word having the same or nearly the same meaning as another word or other words in a language. **2.** A word or an expression that serves as a figurative or symbolic substitute for another. **3.** *Biology* An obsolete taxonomic name. [ME *sinonyme* < OFr. *synonyme* < Lat. *synōnymum* < Gk. *sunōnumon* < neut. of *sunōnumos*, synonymous. See SYNONYMOUS.] —**syn'o•nym'ic, syn'o•nym'i•cal** *adj.* —**syn'o•nym'i•ty** *n.*

syn•on•y•mize (sĭ-nŏn'ə-mīz') *tr.v.* **-mized, -miz•ing, -miz•es** To analyze or provide the synonyms of (words or a word).

syn•on•y•mous (sĭ-nŏn'ə-məs) *adj.* **1.** Having the same or a similar meaning. **2.** Equivalent in connotation. [< Med.Lat. *synōnymus* < Gk. *sunōnumos* : *sun-*, syn- + *onoma, onuma,* name; see **nō-men-** in App.] —**syn•on'y•mous•ly** *adv.*

syn•on•y•my (sĭ-nŏn'ə-mē) *n., pl.* **-mies 1.** The quality of being synonymous; equivalence of meaning. **2.** Study and classification of synonyms. **3.** A list, book, or system of synonyms. **4.** *Biology* A list or record of the scientific names that have been applied to a taxonomic group.

syn•op•sis (sĭ-nŏp'sĭs) *n., pl.* **-ses** (-sēz) A brief outline or general view; an abstract; a summary. [LLat. < Gk. *sunopsis*, general view : *sun-*, syn- + *opsis*, view; see **ok**ʷ- in App.]

syn•op•size (sĭ-nŏp'sīz') *tr.v.* **-sized, -siz•ing, -siz•es** To make a synopsis of; summarize. [Gk. *sunopsizein*, to sum up < *sunopsis*, general view. See SYNOPSIS.]

syn•op•tic (sĭ-nŏp'tĭk) also **syn•op•ti•cal** (-tĭ-kəl) *adj.* **1.** Of or constituting a synopsis; presenting a summary of the principal parts or a general view of the whole. **2a.** Taking the same point of view. **b.** often **Synoptic** Relating to or being the first three gospels of the New Testament, which correspond closely and differ largely from John. **3.** Of or relating to weather data obtained nearly simultaneously over a large area of the atmosphere. [Gk. *sunoptikos* < *sunopsis*, general view. See SYNOPSIS.] —**syn•op'ti•cal•ly** *adv.*

syn•os•to•sis (sĭn'ŏs-tō'sĭs) *n., pl.* **-ses** (-sēz) The fusion of normally separate skeletal bones. [SYN- + Gk. *osteon*, bone; see **ost-** in App. + −OSIS.] —**syn'os•tot'ic** (-tŏt'ĭk) *adj.*

syn•o•vi•a (sĭ-nō'vē-ə) *n.* A clear viscid lubricating fluid secreted by membranes in joint cavities, sheaths of tendons, and bursae. [NLat., coined by Paracelsus.] —**syn•o'vi•al** *adj.*

sy•no•vi•tis (sī'nə-vī'tĭs) *n.* Inflammation of a synovial membrane. [NLat. *synovium,* synovia-secreting membrane (< SYNOVIA) + −ITIS.]

syn•sep•al•ous (sĭn-sĕp'ə-ləs) *adj.* Having united sepals; gamosepalous.

syn•tac•tic (sĭn-tăk'tĭk) or **syn•tac•ti•cal** (-tĭ-kəl) *adj.* Of, relating to, or conforming to the rules of syntax. [Gk. *suntaktikos,* putting together < *suntaktos,* constructed < *suntassein,* to construct. See SYNTAX.] —**syn•tac'ti•cal•ly** *adv.*

syn•tac•tics (sĭn-tăk'tĭks) *n. (used with a sing. verb)* The branch of semiotics that deals with the formal properties of signs and symbols. [< SYNTACTIC.]

syn•tag•ma (sĭn-tăg'mə) also **syn•tagm** (sĭn'tăm) *n., pl.* **-tag•mas** or **-tag•ma•ta** (-tăg'mə-tə) also **-tagms** A sequence of words in a particular syntactic relationship to one another; a construction. [NLat. < Fr. *syntagme* < Gk. *suntagma, suntagmat-,* arrangement, syntactic unit < *suntassein,* to put in order. See SYNTAX.]

syn•tax (sĭn'tăks') *n.* **1a.** The study of the rules for forming grammatical sentences. **b.** A publication, such as a book, that presents such rules. **c.** The pattern of formation of sentences or phrases in a language. **d.** Such a pattern in a particular sentence or discourse. **2.** *Computer Science* The rules governing the formation of statements in a programming language. **3.** A systematic orderly arrangement. [Fr. *syntaxe* < LLat. *syntaxis* < Gk. *suntaxis* < *suntassein,* put in order : *sun-*, syn- + *tassein, tag-,* to arrange.]

synth (sĭnth) *n.* **1.** A synthesizer. **2.** A style of light popular music made with synthesizers.

syn•the•sis (sĭn'thĭ-sĭs) *n., pl.* **-ses** (-sēz') **1a.** The combining of separate elements or substances to form a coherent whole. **b.** The complex whole so formed. **2.** *Chemistry* Formation of a compound from simpler compounds or elements. **3.** *Philosophy* **a.** Reasoning from the general to the particular; logical deduction. **b.** The combination of thesis and antithesis in the Hegelian dialectical process whereby a new and higher level of truth is produced. [Lat., collection < Gk. *sunthesis* < *suntithenai,* to put together : *sun-*, syn- + *tithenai, the-,* to put; see **dhē-** in App.] —**syn'the•sist** *n.*

synthesis gas *n.* A mixture of gases made as feedstock, esp. a fuel produced by controlled combustion of coal in the presence of water vapor.

syn•the•size (sĭn'thĭ-sīz') *v.* **-sized, -siz•ing, -siz•es** —*tr.* **1.** To combine so as to form a new, complex product. **2.** To form or produce by chemical synthesis. —*intr.* To form a synthesis.

syn•the•sized (sĭn'thĭ-sīzd') *adj.* **1.** Relating to or being an instrument whose sound is modified or augmented by a synthesizer. **2.** Relating to or being compositions performed on synthesizers or synthesized instruments.

syn•the•siz•er (sĭn'thĭ-sī'zər) *n.* **1.** One that synthesizes. **2.**

Music An electronic instrument, often played with a keyboard, that combines simple waveforms to produce more complex sounds, such as those of various other instruments.

syn·the·tase (sĭn′thĭ-tās′, -tāz′) *n.* See **ligase.**

syn·thet·ic (sĭn-thĕt′ĭk) *adj.* **1.** Relating to, involving, or of the nature of synthesis. **2.** *Chemistry* Produced by synthesis, esp. not of natural origin. **3a.** Not natural or genuine; artificial or contrived. **b.** Prepared or made artificially: *synthetic leather.* See Syns at **artificial. 4.** *Linguistics* Relating to or being a language, such as Russian, that uses inflectional affixes to express syntactic relationships. **5.** *Logic & Philosophy* Relating to or being a proposition that attributes to a subject a predicate not inherent in the subject and that does not result in a contradiction if negated. ❖ *n.* A synthetic chemical compound or material. [Gk. *sunthetikos,* skilled in putting together, component < *sunthetos,* combined < *suntithenai,* to put together. See SYNTHESIS.] **—syn·thet′i·cal·ly** *adv.*

synthetic division *n.* A method of dividing polynomials when the divisor is a polynomial of the first degree, by using only the coefficients of the terms.

syph·i·lis (sĭf′ə-lĭs) *n.* A chronic infectious disease caused by a spirochete (*Treponema pallidum*), either transmitted by direct contact, usu. in sexual intercourse, or passed from mother to child in utero and characterized by local formation of chancres and systemic infection leading to general paresis. [NLat., from "*Syphilis, sive Morbus Gallicus,*" "Syphilis, or the French Disease," title of a poem by Girolamo Fracastoro (1478?–1553) < *Syphilus,* the poem's protagonist.]

syph·i·lit·ic (sĭf′ə-lĭt′ĭk) *adj.* Of, relating to, or affected with syphilis. ❖ *n.* A person affected with syphilis. [NLat. *syphiliticus* < *syphilis.* See SYPHILIS.]

sy·phon (sī′fən) *n. & v.* Variant of **siphon.**

Syr. *abbr.* Syria

Syr·a·cuse (sĭr′ə-kyōōs′, -kyōōz′) **1.** A city of SE Sicily, Italy, on the Ionian Sea SSE of Catania; founded by colonists from Corinth in the 8th cent. B.C. Pop. 126,136. **2.** A city of central NY ESE of Rochester. Pop. 147,306.

Syr Dar·ya (sĭr där′yə, dər-yä′) A river of S Kyrgyzstan, E Uzbekistan, N Tajikistan, and S Kazakhstan, rising in the Tian Shan and flowing c. 2,220 km (1,380 mi) to the Aral Sea.

Sy·ri·a (sĭr′ē-ə) A country of SW Asia on the E Mediterranean coast; a province of the Ottoman Empire (1516–1918) and a French territory from 1920 to 1944. Cap. Damascus. Pop. 13,844,000. **—Syr′i·an** *adj. & n.*

Syr·i·ac (sĭr′ē-ăk′) *n.* An ancient Aramaic language spoken in Syria from the 3rd to the 13th century that survives as the liturgical language of several Eastern Christian churches.

Syrian Desert A desert region of N Arabia in N Saudi Arabia, W Iraq, SE Syria, and E Jordan.

sy·rin·ga (sə-rĭng′gə) *n.* The mock orange. [NLat. < Gk. *surinx, suring-,* shepherd's pipe (its hollow stems making pipes).]

sy·ringe (sə-rĭnj′, sĭr′ĭnj) *n.* **1.** A medical instrument used to inject fluids into the body or draw them from it. **2.** A hypodermic syringe. [ME *syryng* < Med.Lat. *syringa* < LLat., injection < Gk. *sūrinx, sūring-,* shepherd's pipe.]

sy·rin·go·my·e·li·a (sə-rĭng′gō-mī-ē′lē-ə) *n.* A chronic disease of the spinal cord characterized by the presence of fluid-filled cavities. [NLat. *syringomyelia* : Gk. *sūrinx, sūring-,* spinal cavity + Gk. *muelos,* marrow (< *mūs,* mouse, muscle; see MŪS- in App.).]

syr·inx (sĭr′ĭngks) *n., pl.* **sy·rin·ges** (sə-rĭn′jēz, -rĭng′gēz) or **syr·inx·es 1.** *Music* See **panpipe. 2.** *Zoology* The vocal organ of a bird, located at or close to the division of the trachea into the bronchi. [Lat. *syrinx* < Gk. *sūrinx.*]

Sy·ros (sī′rŏs′) also **Sí·ros** (sē′rôs′) An island of Greece in the N-central Cyclades.

syr·phid (sûr′fĭd) *n.* Any of numerous flies of the family Syrphidae, many of which have a form or coloration mimicking that of bees or wasps. [< NLat. Syrphidae, family name < *Syrphus,* type genus < Gk. *surphos,* gnat.] **—syr′phid** *adj.*

syr·phus fly (sûr′fəs) *n.* See **syrphid.** [NLat. *Syrphus,* fly genus. See SYRPHID.]

syr·up also **sir·up** (sĭr′əp, sûr′-) *n.* **1.** A thick sweet sticky liquid, consisting of a sugar base, natural or artificial flavorings, and water. **2.** The juice of a fruit or plant boiled with sugar until thick and sticky. **3.** A concentrated solution of sugar in water, often used as a vehicle for medicine. [ME *sirup* < OFr. *sirop* < Med.Lat. *siropus* < Ar. *šarāb* < *šariba,* to drink.]

syr·up·y also **sir·up·y** (sĭr′ə-pē, sûr′-) *adj.* **1.** Resembling syrup in taste or consistency. **2.** Cloyingly sweet or sentimental.

sys·ad·min (sĭs′əd-mĭn′) *n.* A system administrator.

sys·op (sĭs′ŏp′) *n.* A system operator.

sys·tal·tic (sĭ-stôl′tĭk, -stäl′-) *adj.* Alternately contracting and dilating, as the heart; pulsating. [LLat. *systalticus* < Gk. *sustaltikos* < *sustellein,* to contract : *sun-, syn-* + *stellein,* to send; see stel- in App.]

sys·tem (sĭs′təm) *n.* **1.** A group of interacting, interrelated, or interdependent elements forming a complex whole. **2.** A functionally related group of elements, esp.: **a.** The human body regarded as a functional physiological unit. **b.** An organism as a whole, esp. with regard to its vital processes or functions. **c.** A group of physiologically or anatomically complementary organs or parts: *the nervous system.* **d.** A group of interacting mechanical or electrical components. **e.** A network of structures and channels, as for communication, travel, or distribution. **f.** A network of related computer software, hardware, and data transmission devices. **3.** An organized set of interrelated ideas or principles. **4.** A social, economic, or political organizational form. **5.** A naturally occurring group of objects or phenomena: *the solar system.* **6.** A set of objects or phenomena grouped together for classification or analysis. **7.** A condition of harmonious, orderly interaction. **8.** An organized and coordinated method; a procedure. See Syns at **method. 9.** The prevailing social order; the establishment. Used with *the.* [LLat. *systēma, systēmat-* < Gk. *sustēma* < *sunistanai,* to combine : *sun-, syn-* + *histanai, stē-,* set up, establish; see stā- in App.]

system administrator *n.* One who manages and maintains computer systems and software, as for a business.

sys·tem·at·ic (sĭs′tə-măt′ĭk) also **sys·tem·at·i·cal** (-ĭ-kəl) *adj.* **1.** Of, characterized by, based on, or constituting a system. **2.** Carried on using step-by-step procedures. **3.** Purposefully regular; methodical. **4.** Of classification or taxonomy. **—sys′tem·at′i·cal·ly** *adv.*

sys·tem·at·ics (sĭs′tə-măt′ĭks) *n. (used with a sing. verb)* **1.** The science of systematic classification. **2.** A system of classification. **3.** *Biology* The systematic classification of organisms and their evolutionary relationships; taxonomy.

sys·tem·a·tism (sĭs′tə-mə-tĭz′əm, sĭ-stĕm′ə-) *n.* **1.** The practice of classifying or systematizing. **2.** Adherence to a system or systems.

sys·tem·a·tist (sĭs′tə-mə-tĭst, sĭ-stĕm′ə-) *n.* **1.** One who adheres to or formulates a system or systems. **2.** A taxonomist.

sys·tem·a·tize (sĭs′tə-mə-tīz′) *tr.v.* **-tized, -tiz·ing, -tiz·es** To form into a system. See Syns at **arrange. —sys′tem·a·ti·za′tion** (-tĭ-zā′shən) *n.* **—sys′tem·a·tiz′er** *n.*

sys·tem·ic (sĭ-stĕm′ĭk, -stē′mĭk) *adj.* **1.** Of or relating to systems or a system. **2a.** Of, relating to, or affecting the entire body or an entire organism. **b.** Relating to or affecting a given body system. **—sys·tem′i·cal·ly** *adv.*

systemic lupus er·y·the·ma·to·sus (ĕr′ə-thē′mə-tō′sĭs) *n.* An inflammatory autoimmune disease of the connective tissue, characterized by fever, skin lesions, joint pain, and anemia, and often affecting multiple organ systems.

sys·tem·ize (sĭs′tə-mīz′) *tr.v.* **-ized, -iz·ing, -iz·es** To systematize. **—sys′tem·i·za′tion** (-tə-mĭ-zā′shən) *n.* **—sys′tem·iz′er** *n.*

system operator *n.* One who operates a bulletin board system.

sys·tems analysis (sĭs′təmz) *n.* **1.** The study of an activity or procedure to determine the desired end and the most efficient method of obtaining this end. **2.** The act, process, or profession of systems analysis. **—systems analyst** *n.*

sys·to·le (sĭs′tə-lē) *n.* The rhythmic contraction of the heart, esp. of the ventricles, by which blood is pumped. [Gk. *sustolē,* contraction < *sustellein,* to contract. See SYSTALTIC.] **—sys·tol′ic** (sĭ-stŏl′ĭk) *adj.*

syz·y·gy (sĭz′ə-jē) *n., pl.* **-gies 1.** *Astronomy* **a.** Either of two points in the orbit of a celestial body, esp. the moon, where the body is in opposition to or in conjunction with the sun. **b.** The configuration of the sun, the moon, and Earth lying in a straight line. **2.** The combining of two feet into a single metrical unit in classical prosody. [LLat. *syzygia* < Gk. *suzugiā,* union < *suzugos,* paired : *sun-, su-, syn-* + *zugon,* yoke; see yeug- in App.] **—sy·zyg′i·al** (sĭ-zĭj′ē-əl) *adj.*

Szcze·cin (shchĕ′chēn′) also **Stet·tin** (stə-tēn′, shtĕ-) A city of NW Poland near the mouth of the Oder R.; ruled by Sweden from 1648 to 1720. Pop. 413,561.

Sze·chuan (sĕch′wän′) or **Sze·chwan** (sĕch′wän′) See Sichuan.

Sze·ged (sĕg′ĕd′) A city of S Hungary on the Tisza R. near the Serbian border. Pop. 178,690.

Szé·kes·fe·hér·vár (sā′kĕsh-fĕ′hâr-vär′) A city of central Hungary on the Danube R. SSW of Budapest. Pop. 109,714.

Szell (sĕl, zĕl), **George** 1897–1970. Hungarian-born Amer. conductor of the Cleveland Orchestra (1946–70).

Szent-Györ·gyi (sänt-jôr′jē, sĕnt-dyœr′dyĭ), **Albert** 1893–1986. Hungarian-born Amer. biochemist who isolated vitamin C and won a 1937 Nobel Prize.

Szi·lard (zĭl′ərd, zə-lärd′), **Leo** 1898–1964. Hungarian-born Amer. physicist who helped develop the first atomic bomb but later opposed the construction of nuclear weapons.

Szold (zōld), **Henrietta** 1860–1945. Amer. Zionist leader who was a founder of Hadassah (1912).

Szym·bor·ska (shĭm-bôr′skə), **Wislawa** b. 1923. Polish poet who won the 1996 Nobel Prize for literature.

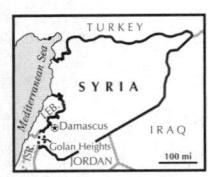

Syria

Tt

t¹ or **T** (tē) *n., pl.* **t's** or **T's** also **ts** or **Ts 1.** The 20th letter of the modern English alphabet. **2.** Any of the speech sounds represented by the letter *t.* **3.** The 20th in a series. **4.** Something shaped like the letter T. **—idiom: to a T** Perfectly; precisely.

t² *abbr.* top quark

T¹ The symbol for the isotope tritium.

T² *abbr.* **1.** temperature **2.** tenor **3.** tesla **4.** Thursday **5.** thymine **6.** time reversal **7.** township **8.** Tuesday

t. *abbr.* **1.** tare **2a.** teaspoon **b.** teaspoonful **3.** *Latin* tempore (in the time of) **4.** time **5.** ton **6.** transitive **7.** troy (system of weights)

T. *abbr.* **1.** tablespoon **2.** tablespoonful

ta (tä) *interj. Chiefly British* Used to express thanks.

Ta The symbol for the element **tantalum.**

TA *abbr.* teaching assistant

Taal¹ (tä-äl′) A lake of SW Luzon, Philippines, S of Manila. It contains Volcano I., site of the active volcano **Mount Taal.**

Taal² (täl) *n.* See **Afrikaans.** [Afr. < MDu. *tāle,* speech.]

tab¹ (tăb) *n.* **1.** A projection, flap, or short strip attached to an object to facilitate opening, handling, or identification. **2.** A small, usu. decorative flap or tongue on a garment. **3.** A small auxiliary airfoil that is attached to a larger one and helps stabilize an aircraft. ❖ *tr.v.* **tabbed, tab·bing, tabs** To supply with a tab or tabs. [?]

tab² (tăb) *n.* **1.** *Informal* **a.** A bill or check, such as one for a meal in a restaurant. **b.** Cost; price: *The tab for maintenance is high.* **2a.** A tabulator on a typewriter. **b.** A key on a computer keyboard for formatting, esp. indenting, text. ❖ *intr.v.* **tabbed, tab·bing, tabs** To press the tab on a typewriter or computer keyboard. **—idiom: keep tabs on** *Informal* To observe carefully. [Short for TABLET or TABULATION. Sense 2, short for TABULATOR.]

tab. *abbr.* table

ta·ba·nid (tə-bā′nĭd, -băn′ĭd) *n.* Any of various bloodsucking dipterous flies of the family Tabanidae, which includes the horse-flies. [NLat. *Tabānidae,* family name < Lat. *tabānus,* horsefly.]

tab·ard (tăb′ərd) *n.* **1.** A short heavy cape of coarse cloth, formerly worn outdoors. **2a.** A tunic or capelike garment worn by a knight over his armor and emblazoned with his coat of arms. **b.** A similar garment worn by a herald and bearing his lord's coat of arms. **3.** An embroidered pennant attached to a trumpet. [ME < OFr. *tabart* or OSpan. *tabardo.*]

Ta·bas·co (tə-băs′kō) A trademark used for a spicy sauce made from a strong-flavored red pepper.

tabasco pepper *n.* A very pungent pepper (*Capsicum frutescens*) grown principally in the Gulf Coast states for commercial production of hot sauces.

tab·bou·leh or **ta·bou·leh** (tə-boō′lē) *n.* A Lebanese salad of bulgur wheat, scallions, tomatoes, mint, and parsley. [Ar. *tabbūla,* prob. < *tābal,* coriander, seasoning.]

tab·by (tăb′ē) *n., pl.* **-bies 1.** A rich watered silk. **2.** A fabric of plain weave. **3a.** A domestic cat with a striped or brindled coat of a gray or tawny color. **b.** A domestic cat, esp. a female. **4.** *South Atlantic US* A mixture of oyster shells, lime, sand, and water used as a building material. ❖ *adj.* **1.** Having light and dark striped markings. **2.** Made of or resembling watered silk. [Fr. *tabis* < OFr. *atabis* < Med.Lat. *attabī* < Ar. *ʿattābī,* after al-ʿAttābīya, a suburb of Baghdad, Iraq.]

tab·er·na·cle (tăb′ər-năk′əl) *n.* **1.** often **Tabernacle** The portable sanctuary in which the Jews carried the Ark of the Covenant through the desert. **2.** often **Tabernacle** A case or box on a church altar containing the consecrated host and wine of the Eucharist. **3.** A place of worship. **4.** A niche for a statue or relic. **5.** *Nautical* A boxlike support in which the heel of a mast is stepped. [ME < OFr. < LLat. *tabernāculum* < Lat., tent, dim. of *taberna,* hut. See TAVERN.] **—tab′er·nac′u·lar** *adj.*

ta·bes dor·sa·lis (tā′bēz dôr-sā′lĭs, -săl′ĭs) *n.* An advanced form of syphilis in which there is progressive deterioration of the spinal cord, resulting in shooting pain, gradual loss of muscle coordination, and disturbances of sensation and movement. [NLat. *tābēs dorsālis* : Lat. *tābēs,* wasting away + Med.Lat. *dorsālis,* of the back, dorsal.]

tab·la (tä′blə, tŭb′lə) *n.* A small hand drum of northern India. [Hindi *tablā* < Ar. *ṭabla* < Aram. *ṭabl,* drum, perh. of Pers. orig.; akin to MPers. *tumbag,* drum.]

tab·la·ture (tăb′lə-choŏr′, -chər) *n.* **1.** An engraved tablet or surface. **2.** *Music* A system of notation using letters, symbols, or other visual cues instead of standard notation to indicate how a musical piece is to be played. [Fr., alteration of Ital. *intavolatura* < *intavolare,* to put on a board : *in-,* in + *tavola,* table, board (< Lat. *tabula*).]

ta·ble (tā′bəl) *n.* **1a.** An article of furniture supported by one or more vertical legs and having a flat horizontal surface. **b.** The objects laid out for a meal on such a table. **2.** The food and drink served at meals; fare. **3.** The company of people assembled around a table, as for a meal. **4.** *Games* A piece of furniture serving as a playing surface, as for faro, roulette, or dice. Often used in the plural. **5.** *Games* **a.** Either of the leaves of a backgammon board. **b. tables** *Obsolete* The game of backgammon. **6.** A plateau or tableland. **7a.** A flat facet cut across the top of a precious stone. **b.** A stone or gem cut in this fashion. **8.** *Architecture* **a.** A raised or sunken rectangular panel on a wall. **b.** A raised horizontal surface or continuous band on an exterior wall; a stringcourse. **9.** An orderly arrangement of data, esp. one in columns and rows. **10.** An abbreviated list, as of contents; a synopsis. **11.** An engraved slab bearing an inscription or a device. **12. tables** A system of laws or decrees; a code. ❖ *tr.v.* **-bled, -bling, -bles 1.** To put or place on a table. **2.** To postpone consideration of; shelve. **3.** To enter in a list or table; tabulate. **—idioms: on the table 1.** Up for discussion. **2.** Postponed or put aside for consideration at a later date. **under the table 1.** In secret. **2.** Into a completely intoxicated state. [ME < OFr. < Lat. *tabula,* board.]

tab·leau (tăb′lō′, tă-blō′) *n., pl.* **tab·leaux** or **tab·leaus** (tăb′lōz′, tă-blōz′) **1.** A vivid or graphic description. **2.** A striking incidental scene. **3.** An interlude during a scene when all the performers on stage freeze in position and then resume action. **4.** A tableau vivant. [Fr. < OFr. *tablel,* dim. of *table,* surface prepared for painting. See TABLE.]

tableau vi·vant (vē-vän′) *n., pl.* **tab·leaux vi·vants** (tă-blō′ vē-vän′) A scene presented on stage by costumed actors who remain silent and motionless as if in a picture. [Fr. : *tableau,* picture + *vivant,* living.]

ta·ble·cloth (tā′bəl-klôth′, -klŏth′) *n.* A cloth to cover a table, esp. during a meal.

ta·ble d'hôte (tā′bəl dōt′, tä′blə) *n., pl.* **ta·bles d'hôte** (tā′bəl dōt′, tä′blə) A full-course meal offering a limited number of choices and served at a fixed price in a restaurant or hotel. [Fr. : *table,* table + *de,* of + *hôte,* host.]

ta·ble-hop (tā′bəl-hŏp′) *intr.v.* **-hopped, -hop·ping, -hops** *Informal* To move around from table to table greeting friends, as in a restaurant or nightclub. **—ta′ble-hop′per** *n.*

ta·ble·land (tā′bəl-lănd′) *n.* A flat elevated region; a plateau or mesa.

table linen (tā′bəl) *n.* Tablecloths and napkins.

table salt *n.* See **salt 1.**

ta·ble·spoon (tā′bəl-spoōn′) *n.* **1.** A large spoon used for serving food. **2.** A cooking measure equal to 3 teaspoons, or ½ fluid ounce (15 milliliters).

ta·ble·spoon·ful (tā′bəl-spoōn-foōl′) *n., pl.* **-fuls** The amount that a tablespoon can hold.

tab·let (tăb′lĭt) *n.* **1.** A slab or plaque, as of stone or ivory, with a surface that is intended for or bears an inscription. **2a.** A thin sheet or leaf, used as a writing surface. **b.** A set of such leaves fastened together, as in a book. **c.** A pad of writing paper glued together along one edge. **3.** A small flat pellet of medication to be taken orally. **4.** A small flat cake of a prepared substance, such as soap. ❖ *tr.v.* **-let·ed, -let·ing, -lets 1.** To inscribe on a tablet. **2.** To form into a tablet. [ME *tablette* < OFr. *tablete,* dim. of *table,* table. See TABLE.]

table talk *n.* Casual mealtime conversation.

table tennis *n.* A game similar to lawn tennis, played on a table with wooden bats and a small hollow plastic ball.

ta·ble·top (tā′bəl-tŏp′) *n.* The flat surface of a table. ❖ *adj.* Made or designed for use on the top of a table.

ta·ble·ware (tā′bəl-wâr′) *n.* The dishes, glassware, and silverware used in setting a table for a meal.

table wine *n.* A wine suitable for serving with a meal.

tab·loid (tăb′loid′) *n.* A newspaper of small format giving the news in condensed form, usu. with illustrated, often sensational material. ❖ *adj.* **1.** In summary form; condensed. **2.** Lurid or sensational. [< *tabloid journalism* < Tabloid, trademark for a drug or chemical in condensed form.]

tabloid TV *n.* Television news presented in a fast-paced, condensed form, usu. with sensational material.

ta·boo also **ta·bu** (tə-boō′, tă-) *n., pl.* **-boos** also **-bus 1.** A ban or inhibition resulting from social custom or emotional aversion. **2a.** A prohibition, esp. in Polynesia and other South Pacific islands, excluding something from use, approach, or mention because of its sacred and inviolable nature. **b.** An object, word, or act protected by such a prohibition. ❖ *adj.* Excluded or forbid-

Tabriz²

tadpole
tadpole in four stages of
development

den from use, approach, or mention. ❖ *tr.v.* **-booed, -boo·ing,
-boos** also **-bued, -bu·ing, -bus** To exclude from use, approach,
or mention. [Tongan *tabu*, under prohibition.]

ta·bor also **ta·bour** (tā′bər) *n.* A small drum, often having a
snare, played by a fifer to accompany the fife. [ME *tabur* < OFr.,
alteration of *tambur*. See TAMBOUR.]

tab·o·ret also **tab·ou·ret** (tăb′ə-rĕt′, -rā′) *n.* **1.** A low stool
without a back or arms. **2.** A low stand or cabinet. **3.** An embroidery frame. [Fr. *tabouret* < OFr. *taburet*, dim. of *tabur*, tabor.
See TABOR.]

ta·bou·leh (tə-bōō′lə) *n.* Variant of **tabbouleh.**

Ta·briz¹ (tə-brēz′, tä-) A city of NW Iran E of Lake Urmia.
Pop. 1,166,203.

Ta·briz² (tä-brēz′) *n.* A cotton and wool Persian rug with designs
of stylized animals, hunting scenes, and floral motifs.

tab·u·lar (tăb′yə-lər) *adj.* **1.** Having a plane surface; flat. **2.** *Geology* Tending to split into thin flat pieces. **3.** Organized as a table
or list. **4.** Calculated by means of a table. [Lat. *tabulāris*, of boards
< *tabula*, board.] **—tab′u·lar·ly** *adv.*

tab·u·la ra·sa (tăb′yə-lə rä′sə, -zə) *n., pl.* **tab·u·lae ra·sae**
(tăb′yə-lē′ rä′sē, -zē) **1a.** The mind before it receives the impressions gained from experience. **b.** The unformed featureless mind
in the philosophy of John Locke. **2.** A need or an opportunity to
start from the beginning. [Med.Lat. *tabula rāsa* : Lat. *tabula*, tablet + Lat. *rāsa*, fem. of *rāsus*, erased.]

tab·u·lar·ize (tăb′yə-lə-rīz′) *tr.v.* **-ized, -iz·ing, -iz·es** To put
into tabular form. **—tab′u·lar·i·za′tion** (-lər-ĭ-zā′shən) *n.*

tab·u·late (tăb′yə-lāt′) *tr.v.* **-lat·ed, -lat·ing, -lates 1.** To arrange in tabular form; condense and list. **2.** To cut or form with
a plane surface. ❖ *adj.* (tăb′yə-lĭt, -lāt′) Having a plane surface.
[Lat. *tabula*, writing + –ATE¹.] **—tab′u·la′tion** *n.*

tab·u·la·tor (tăb′yə-lā′tər) *n.* **1.** One that tabulates. **2.** A machine that reads, sorts, and prints out data from punch cards. **3.**
A typewriter mechanism for setting automatic stops or margins.

ta·bun (tä′bōōn′) *n.* A poisonous combustible liquid that is soluble in organic solvents, C₅H₁₁N₂O₂P, used as a nerve gas in chemical warfare. [Ger., orig. a code name.]

tac·a·ma·hac (tăk′ə-mə-hăk′) *n.* **1.** Any of several aromatic
resinous substances used in ointments and incense. **2.** See **balsam poplar.** [Sp. *tacamahaca* < Nahuatl *tecamaca.*]

ta·cet (tā′sĭt, täs′ĭt, tä′kĕt′) *v. Music* Be silent. [Lat., third pers.
sing. pr. t. of *tacēre*, to be silent.]

tach (tăk) *n. Informal* A tachometer.

tach·i·na fly (tăk′ə-nə) *n.* Any of several bristly, usu. grayish
dipterous flies of the family Tachinidae, the larvae of which are
parasitic on other insects. [NLat. *Tachina*, type genus < Gk. *ta-
khīnē*, fem. of *takhinos*, swift < *takhos*, speed.]

tach·i·nid (tăk′ə-nĭd′) *n.* See **tachina fly.** ❖ *adj.* Of or belonging to the family Tachinidae. [NLat. *Tachinidae*, family name
< *Tachina*, type genus. See TACHINA FLY.]

tach·isme or **tach·ism** (tăsh′ĭz′əm) *n.* A French school of art
that originated in the 1950s and is characterized by irregular
splotches of color applied haphazardly to the canvas. [Fr. *tachisme* < *tache*, stain < OFr. *teche*, mark, of Gmc. origin. See
deik- in App.] **—tach′iste, tach′ist** *n.*

ta·chis·to·scope (tə-kĭs′tə-skōp′, tə-) *n.* An apparatus that
projects a series of images onto a screen at rapid speed to test visual perception, memory, and learning. [Gk. *takhistos*, superl. of
takhus, swift + –SCOPE.]

ta·chom·e·ter (tă-kŏm′ĭ-tər, tə-) *n.* An instrument used to
measure the rotations per minute of a rotating shaft. [Gk. *takhos*,
speed + –METER.] **—tach′o·met′ric** (tăk′ə-mĕt′rĭk) *adj.* **—ta·
chom′e·try** *n.*

tachy– *pref.* Rapid; accelerated: *tachymeter.* [Gk. *takhu-
< takhus*, swift.]

tach·y·car·di·a (tăk′ĭ-kär′dē-ə) *n.* A rapid heart rate, esp. one
above 100 beats per minute in an adult. [TACHY– + Gk. *kardiā*,
heart; see CARDIA.]

ta·chyg·ra·phy (tə-kĭg′rə-fē, tə-) *n.* The art or practice of rapid
writing or shorthand, esp. the stenography of the ancient Greeks
and Romans.

tach·y·lyte also **tach·y·lite** (tăk′ə-līt′) *n.* A glassy black basalt
of volcanic origin. [Ger. *Tachylyt* : Gk. *takhu-*, tachy– + Gk. *lutos*,
soluble (< *lūein*, to loosen; see leu- in App.).]

ta·chym·e·ter (tă-kĭm′ĭ-tər, tə-) *n.* A surveying instrument
used for the rapid determination of distances, elevations, and
bearings. **—ta·chym′e·try** *n.*

tach·y·on (tăk′ē-ŏn′) *n.* A hypothetical subatomic particle that
always travels faster than the speed of light. **—tach′y·on′ic** *adj.*

tac·it (tăs′ĭt) *adj.* **1.** Not spoken. **2.** Implied by or inferred from
actions or statements. **3.** *Archaic* Not speaking; silent. [Lat. *taci-
tus*, silent, p. part. of *tacēre*, to be silent.] **—tac′it·ly** *adv.*
—tac′it·ness *n.*

tac·i·turn (tăs′ĭ-tûrn′) *adj.* Habitually untalkative. [Fr. *taciturne*
< OFr. < Lat. *taciturnus* < *tacitus*, silent. See TACIT.] **—tac′i·
tur′ni·ty** (-tûr′nĭ-tē) *n.* **—tac′i·turn·ly** *adv.*

Tac·i·tus (tăs′ĭ-təs), **Publius Cornelius** A.D. 55?–120? Roman
historian whose works concern Rome in the 1st cent. A.D.

tack¹ (tăk) *n.* **1.** A short light nail with a sharp point and a flat
head. **2.** *Nautical* **a.** A line for holding down the weather clew of
a course. **b.** A line for hauling the outer lower corner of a stud-

dingsail to the boom. **c.** The part of a sail, such as the weather
clew of a course, to which this line is fastened. **d.** The lower forward corner of a fore-and-aft sail. **3.** *Nautical* **a.** The position of
a vessel relative to the side from which the wind is blowing. **b.**
The act of changing a sailing vessel's course by bringing the bow
across the wind. **c.** The distance or leg sailed between changes of
position or direction. **4a.** A course of action meant to minimize
opposition to the attainment of a goal. **b.** An approach, esp. one
of a series of changing approaches. **5.** A large loose stitch made
as a temporary binding or as a marker. **6.** Stickiness, as that of a
newly painted surface. ❖ *v.* **tacked, tack·ing, tacks** —*tr.* **1.** To
fasten or attach with or as if with a tack. **2.** To fasten or mark
(cloth or a seam, for example) with a loose basting stitch. **3.** To
put together loosely and arbitrarily. **4.** To add as an extra item;
append. **5.** *Nautical* To bring (a vessel) into the wind in order to
change course or direction. —*intr.* **1.** *Nautical* **a.** To change the
direction or course of a vessel by bringing the bow across the
wind. **b.** To change tack: *The ship tacked to starboard.* **2.** To
change one's course of action. [ME *tak*, fastener < ONFr. *taque*,
prob. of Gmc. orig.] **—tack′er** *n.*

tack² (tăk) *n.* Food, esp. coarse or inferior foodstuffs. [?]

tack³ (tăk) *n.* The harness for a horse, including the bridle and
saddle. [Short for TACKLE.]

tack·le (tăk′əl) *n.* **1.** The equipment used in a particular activity,
esp. in fishing; gear. **2.** (*often* tā′kəl) *Nautical* **a.** A system of ropes
and blocks for raising and lowering weights of rigging and pulleys
for applying tension. **b.** A rope and its pulley. **3.** *Sports* **a.** The act
of stopping an opposing player carrying the ball, esp. by forcing
the opponent to the ground, as in football or Rugby. **b.** The act
of obstructing a player in order to cause loss of possession of the
ball, as in soccer. **4.** *Football* **a.** Either of the two line players on a
team positioned between the guard and the end. **b.** This position.
❖ *v.* **-led, -ling, -les** —*tr.* **1.** To grab hold of and wrestle with (an
opponent). **2.** *Sports* **a.** To stop (an opponent carrying the ball),
esp. by forcing the opponent to the ground. **b.** To obstruct (a
player with the ball) in order to cause loss of possession of the
ball. **3.** To engage or deal with: *tackle a problem.* **4.** To harness (a
horse). —*intr. Sports* To tackle an opponent in possession of the
ball. [ME *takel* < MDu. or MLGer.] **—tack′ler** *n.*

tack·ling (tăk′lĭng) *n.* Gear; tackle.

tack·y¹ (tăk′ē) *adj.* **-i·er, -i·est** Slightly adhesive or gummy to
the touch; sticky. [< TACK¹.] **—tack′i·ness** *n.*

tack·y² (tăk′ē) *adj.* **-i·er, -i·est** *Informal* **1.** Neglected and in a
state of disrepair. **2a.** Lacking style or good taste; tawdry. **b.** Distasteful or offensive; tasteless: *a tacky remark.* [< *tackey*, an inferior horse.] **—tack′i·ly** *adv.* **—tack′i·ness** *n.*

ta·co (tä′kō) *n., pl.* **-cos** A dish consisting of a corn tortilla folded
around a filling such as ground meat or cheese. [Am.Sp. < Sp.,
plug, wad of bank notes.]

Ta·co·ma (tə-kō′mə) A city of W-central WA on an arm of
Puget Sound S of Seattle. Pop. 193,556.

Ta·con·ic Mountains (tə-kŏn′ĭk) A range of the Appalachian
Mts. rising to 1,163.9 m (3,816 ft).

tac·o·nite (tăk′ə-nīt′) *n.* A variety of chert containing magnetite
and hematite, mined as an iron ore. [After the TACONIC
(MOUNTAINS).]

tact (tăkt) *n.* **1.** Acute sensitivity to what is proper and appropriate
in dealing with others, including the ability to speak or act without offending. **2.** *Archaic* The sense of touch. [Fr. < OFr., sense
of touch < Lat. *tāctus* < p. part. of *tangere*, to touch. See **tag-** in
App.]

tact·ful (tăkt′fəl) *adj.* Possessing or exhibiting tact; considerate
and discreet. **—tact′ful·ly** *adv.* **—tact′ful·ness** *n.*

tac·tic (tăk′tĭk) *n.* An expedient for achieving a goal; a maneuver.
[Fr. *tactique*, tactics < Gk. *taktika.* See TACTICS.]

tac·ti·cal (tăk′tĭ-kəl) *adj.* **1.** Of, relating to, or using tactics. **2a.**
Of, relating to, used in, or involving military or naval operations
that are smaller, closer to base, and less significant than strategic
operations. **b.** Carried out in support of military or naval operations. **3.** Marked by adroitness, ingenuity, or skill. **—tac′ti·cal·
ly** *adv.*

tac·ti·cian (tăk-tĭsh′ən) *n.* **1.** One who is skilled in the planning
and execution of military tactics. **2.** A clever maneuverer.

tac·tics (tăk′tĭks) *n.* **1a.** (*used with a sing. verb*) The military art
that deals with securing objectives set by strategy, esp. the technique of deploying and directing troops, ships, and aircraft in effective maneuvers against an enemy. **b.** (*used with a pl. verb*) Maneuvers used against an enemy. **2.** (*used with a sing. or pl. verb*) A
procedure or set of maneuvers engaged in to achieve an end, an
aim, or a goal. [NLat. *tactica* < Gk. *taktika*, matters pertaining to
arrangement, or < *taktikē* (*tekhnē*), (art) of deploying forces in
war, both < *taktikos*, of order < *taktos*, arranged < *tassein*, *tag-*,
to arrange.]

tac·tile (tăk′təl, -tīl′) *adj.* **1a.** Perceptible to the sense of touch;
tangible. **b.** Characterized by or conveying an illusion of tangibil-
ity. **2.** Used for feeling: *a tactile organ.* **3.** Of, relating to, or proceeding from the sense of touch; tactual. [< Lat. *tāctilis* < *tāctus*,
p. part. of *tangere*, to touch. See TACT.] **—tac′tile·ly** *adv.* **—tac·
til′i·ty** (-tĭl′ĭ-tē) *n.*

tactile corpuscle *n.* An end organ of touch in sensitive skin, as
in the fingertips.

tac•tion (tăk′shən) *n.* The act of touching; contact. [Lat. *tāctiō, tāctiōn-* < *tāctus*, p. part. of *tangere*, to touch. See TACT.]

tact•less (tăkt′lĭs) *adj.* Lacking or exhibiting a lack of tact; bluntly inconsiderate or indiscreet. **—tact′less•ly** *adv.*

tac•tu•al (tăk′cho͞o-əl) *adj.* Tactile. [Lat. *tāctus*, touch; see TACT + -AL[1].] **—tac′tu•al•ly** *adv.*

tad (tăd) *n. Informal* **1.** A small amount or degree; a bit. **2.** A small boy. ***—idiom:* a tad** To a small degree; somewhat: *acting a tad silly.* [Perh. short for TADPOLE.]

tad•pole (tăd′pōl′) *n.* The limbless aquatic larva of a frog or toad, having gills and a long flat tail. [ME *taddepol* : *tadde, tode*, toad; see TOAD + *pol*, head; see POLL.]

Ta•dzhik (tä-jĭk′, tə-) *n. & adj.* Variant of **Tajik.**

Ta•dzhik•i•stan (tä-jĭk′ĭ-stăn′, -stän′) See **Tajikistan.**

Tae•gu (tī-go͞o′) A city of SE South Korea NNW of Pusan. Pop. 2,031,000.

Tae•jon (tī-jôn′, -jŏn′) A city of central South Korea SSE of Seoul. Pop. 866,148.

tae kwon do (tī′ kwŏn′ dō′) *n.* A Korean art of self-defense; a style of karate. [Korean *t'aekwŏndo* : *t'ae-*, to trample + *kwŏn*, fist + *-do*, way.]

tael (tāl) *n.* **1.** Any of various units of weight used in eastern Asia, roughly equivalent to 38 grams (1⅓ ounces). **2.** A monetary unit formerly used in China, equivalent in value to this weight of standard silver. [Port. < Malay *tahil, tael.*]

tae•ni•a also **te•ni•a** (tē′nē-ə) *n., pl.* **-ni•ae** (-nē-ē′) or **-ni•as 1.** A narrow band or ribbon for the hair that was worn in ancient Greece. **2.** *Architecture* A band in the Doric order that separates the frieze from the architrave. **3.** *Anatomy* A ribbonlike band of tissue or muscle. **4.** A flatworm of the genus *Taenia*, which includes many tapeworms. [Lat., ribbon, tapeworm < Gk. *tainiā*. See **ten-** in App.]

tae•ni•a•sis also **te•ni•a•sis** (tē-nī′ə-sĭs) *n.* Infestation with tapeworms.

taf•fe•ta (tăf′ĭ-tə) *n.* A crisp smooth plain-woven fabric with a slight sheen, made of various fibers, such as silk, rayon, or nylon, and used esp. for women's garments. [ME < OFr. *taffetas* < OItal. *taffetà* < Turk. *tafta* < Pers. *tāftah*, silk or linen cloth < p. part. of *tāftan*, to twist, spin.] **—taf′fe•ta** *adj.*

taff•rail (tăf′rāl′, -rəl) *n. Nautical* **1.** The rail around the stern of a vessel. **2.** The flat upper part of the stern of a vessel, made of wood and often richly carved. [Alteration of *tafferel*, carved panel < Du. *tafereel*, panel for carving or painting < MDu. *tafeleel, tafereel* < OFr. *tablel.* See TABLEAU.]

taffrail log *n.* See **patent log.**

taf•fy (tăf′ē) *n., pl.* **-fies** A sweet chewy candy of molasses or brown sugar boiled until very thick and then pulled until the candy is glossy and holds its shape. [?]

taf•i•a also **taf•fi•a** (tăf′ē-ə) *n.* A cheap rum distilled from molasses and refuse sugar in the West Indies. [Fr., perh. of West Indian Creole orig.]

Taft (tăft), **Helen** 1861–1943. First Lady of the US (1909–13).

Taft, William Howard 1857–1930. The 27th President of the US (1909–13), who later served as chief justice of the US Supreme Court (1921–30).

tag[1] (tăg) *n.* **1.** A strip of leather, paper, metal, or plastic attached to something or hung from a wearer's neck to identify, classify, or label. **2.** The plastic or metal tip at the end of a shoelace. **3.** The contrastingly colored tip of an animal's tail. **4.** A bright piece of feather, floss, or tinsel surrounding the shank of the hook on a fishing fly. **5a.** A dirty matted lock of wool. **b.** A loose lock of hair. **6.** A rag; a tatter. **7.** A fragment. **8.** An ornamental flourish, esp. at the end of a signature. **9.** A designation or epithet, esp. an unwelcome one. **10a.** A brief quotation used in a discourse to give it an air of erudition or authority. **b.** A cliché or similar short conventional idea used to embellish a discourse. **c.** The refrain or last lines of a song or poem. **d.** The closing lines of a speech in a play; a cue. **11.** *Computer Science* **a.** A label assigned to identify data in memory. **b.** A sequence of characters in a markup language used to provide information, such as formatting specifications, about a document. ❖ *v.* **tagged, tag•ging, tags** *—tr.* **1.** To label, identify, or recognize with or as if with a tag. **2.** To put a ticket on (a motor vehicle) for a traffic or parking violation. **3.** To charge with a crime. **4.** To add as an appendage. **5.** To follow closely. **6.** To cut the tags from (sheep). **7.** To add a taggant to. **8.** To mark or vandalize (a surface) with graffiti. *—intr.* To follow after; accompany: *I tagged along with them.* [ME *tagge*, dangling piece of cloth on a garment, poss. of Scand. orig.] **—tag′ger** *n.*

tag[2] (tăg) *n.* **1.** *Games* A children's game in which one player pursues the others in order to tag one of them, who then pursues in turn. **2.** *Baseball* The act of tagging a base runner. **3.** *Sports* The act of tagging a ball carrier in touch football. ❖ *tr.v.* **tagged, tag•ging, tags 1.** To touch (another player) in the game of tag. **2.** *Baseball* To touch (a base runner) with the ball in order to make a putout. **3.** *Sports* To touch (a ball carrier) instead of tackling in touch football. ***—phrasal verb:* tag up** *Baseball* To return to and touch a base with one foot before running to the next base after a fielder catches a fly. [Perh. var. of Sc. *tig*, touch, tap, prob. alteration of ME *tek.*]

Ta•ga•log (tə-gä′lôg, -ləg) *n., pl.* **Tagalog** or **-logs 1.** A member of a people native to the Philippines and inhabiting Manila and its adjacent provinces. **2.** The Austronesian language of the Tagalog. [Perh. Tagalog, river people : *taga-*, native of + *ilog*, river.]

tag•a•long also **tag-a•long** (tăg′ə-lông′, -lŏng′) *n.* One that persistently follows another.

Tag•an•rog (tăg′ən-rŏg′, tə-gən-rôk′) A city of SW Russia on the **Gulf of Taganrog,** an arm of the Sea of Azov; annexed by Russia in 1769. Pop. 290,457.

tag day *n.* A day on which collectors for a charitable fund solicit contributions, giving each contributor a tag.

tag end *n.* **1.** The very end. **2.** Something left over; a remnant.

tag•gant (tăg′ənt) *n.* Any of various substances, such as microscopic pieces of multilayered colored plastic, added to a product to indicate its source of manufacture. [Short for *Microtaggant*, trademark for tags identifying explosives.]

tag•ger (tăg′ər) *n.* **1.** One that tags, esp. in the game of tag. **2. taggers** Very thin sheet iron, usu. plated with tin.

tag line also **tag•line** (tăg′līn′) *n.* **1.** An ending line, as in a play or joke, that makes a point. **2.** An often repeated phrase associated with an individual, organization, or commercial product.

Ta•gore (tə-gôr′, -gōr′, tä-), Sir **Rabindranath** 1861–1941. Bengali writer who won the 1913 Nobel Prize for literature.

tag question *n.* A question used after a statement when seeking or expecting confirmation of that statement, as *wasn't he* in *He was here, wasn't he?*

tag sale *n.* A sale of used household items usu. affixed with labels marked with the price.

tag team *n.* A team of two or more wrestlers who take turns competing against one of the wrestlers on another team.

Ta•gus (tā′gəs) also **Ta•jo** (tä′hō) A river of the Iberian Peninsula flowing c. 941 km (585 mi) to the Atlantic Ocean.

ta•hi•ni (tə-hē′nē) *n.* A thick paste made from ground sesame seeds. [Turk. *tāhin*, sesame flour or oil < Ar. *ṭaḥīna* < *ṭaḥanīn*, flour < *ṭaḥana*, to grind.]

Ta•hi•ti (tə-hē′tē) An island of the S Pacific in the Windward group of the Society Is. in French Polynesia; first settled by Polynesians in the 14th cent.

Ta•hi•tian (tə-hē′shən) *adj.* Of or relating to Tahiti or its people, language, or culture. ❖ *n.* **1.** A native or inhabitant of Tahiti. **2.** The Polynesian language of Tahiti.

Ta•hoe (tä′hō), **Lake** A lake on the CA-NV border W of Carson City, NV.

tah•sil•dar also **tah•seel•dar** (tə-sēl′där′) *n.* A district official in India in charge of revenues and taxation. [Urdu *taḥsīldār* < Pers. : *taḥṣīl*, collection, revenue (< Ar., infinitive of *ḥaṣṣala*, to collect, derived stem of *ḥaṣala*, to obtain) + *-dār*, having.]

Tai (tī) *n., pl.* **Tai** or **Tais 1.** A family of languages spoken in southeast Asia and southern China that includes Thai, Lao, and Shan. **2.** A member of any of the Tai-speaking peoples of Thailand, Myanmar (Burma), Laos, China, and Vietnam. **3.** Thai. ❖ *adj.* **1.** Of or relating to Tai, its speakers, or their culture. **2.** Thai.

tai chi or **Tai Chi** (tī′ chē′, jē′) also **tai chi chuan** or **Tai Chi Chuan** (chwän′) *n.* A Chinese system of physical exercises esp. for self-defense and meditation. [Chin. (Mandarin) *taìjíquán* : *taì*, highest + *jí*, reach + *quán*, boxing.]

Tai•chung (tī′cho͝ong′, -jo͝ong′) A city of W-central Taiwan SW of Taipei. Pop. 621,566.

tai•ga (tī′gə) *n.* A subarctic evergreen coniferous forest of northern Eurasia located just south of the tundra and dominated by firs and spruces. [Russ. *taĭga*, of Altaic orig.]

tail[1] (tāl) *n.* **1.** The posterior part of an animal, esp. when elongated and extending beyond the trunk or main part of the body. **2.** The bottom, rear, or hindmost part. **3.** The rear end of a wagon or other vehicle. **4a.** The rear portion of the fuselage of an aircraft. **b.** An assembly of stabilizing planes and control surfaces in this rear portion. **5.** The vaned rear portion of a bomb or missile. **6.** An appendage to the rear or bottom of a thing. **7.** The long luminous stream of gas and dust forced from the head of a comet when it is close to the sun. **8.** A braid of hair; a pigtail. **9.** Something that follows or takes the last place: *the tail of a journey.* **10.** A train of followers; a retinue. **11.** The end of a line of persons or things. **12.** The short closing line of certain stanzas of verse. **13.** The refuse or dross remaining from processes such as distilling or milling. **14.** *Printing* The bottom of a page; the bottom margin. **15.** The side of a coin not having the principal design and the date. Often used in the plural with a singular verb. **16.** *Informal* The trail of a person or an animal in flight. **17.** *Informal* A person assigned or employed to follow and report on someone else's movements and actions. **18. tails a.** A formal evening costume typically worn by men. **b.** A tailcoat. **19a.** *Slang* The buttocks. **b.** *Vulgar Slang* A sexual partner, esp. a woman. ❖ *adj.* **1.** Of or relating to a tail or tails. **2.** Situated in the tail, as of an airplane. ❖ *v.* **tailed, tail•ing, tails** *—tr.* **1.** To provide with a tail. **2.** To deprive of a tail; dock. **3.** To serve as the tail of. **4.** To connect (often dissimilar or incongruous objects) by or as if by the tail or end. **5.** To set one end of (a beam, board, or brick) into a wall. **6.** *Informal* To follow and keep under surveillance. *—intr.* **1.** To become lengthened or spaced when moving in a line: *The patrol tailed out in pairs.* **2.** To be inserted at one end into a wall, as a floor timber or beam. **3.** *Informal* To follow. **4.** *Nautical* **a.** To go aground with the stern foremost. **b.** To lie or swing with

William Howard Taft
detail from a portrait by William Valentine Schevill (1864–1951)

Sir Rabindranath Tagore

ă	pat	oi	boy
ā	pay	ou	out
âr	care	o͝o	took
ä	father	o͞o	boot
ĕ	pet	ŭ	cut
ē	be	ûr	urge
ĭ	pit	th	thin
ī	pie	*th*	this
îr	pier	hw	which
ŏ	pot	zh	vision
ō	toe	ə	about, item
ô	paw		

Stress marks:
′ (primary);
′ (secondary), as in
lexicon (lĕk′sĭ-kŏn′)

tail fin
tail fins on a 1959 Cadillac
convertible

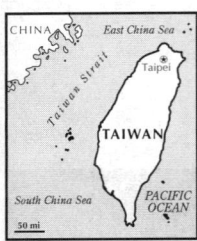

Taiwan

Tajikistan

the stern in a named direction, as when riding at anchor or on a mooring. **5.** *Sports* To veer from a straight course in the direction of the dominant hand of the player propelling the ball: *a pitch that tails away.* —*phrasal verbs:* **tail down** To ease a heavy load down a steep slope. **tail off (or away)** To diminish gradually; dwindle or subside. [ME < OE *tægel.*]

tail² (tāl) *n. Law* Limitation of the inheritance of an estate to a particular party. [ME *taille* < OFr., division < *taillier,* to cut. See TAILOR.]

tail·back (tāl′băk′) *n. Football* The back on an offensive team who lines up farthest from the line of scrimmage.

tail beam *n.* See **tailpiece** 3.

tail·board (tāl′bôrd′, -bōrd′) *n.* See **tailgate** 1.

tail·bone (tāl′bōn′) *n.* See **coccyx.**

tail·coat (tāl′kōt′) *n.* A man's black coat worn for formal daytime occasions and having a long rounded and split tail.

tail end *n.* **1.** The hindmost part. **2.** The very end.

tail fan *n.* The fanlike posterior structure of a lobster, shrimp, or other crustacean, formed from the telson and the last pair of uropods and used for backward locomotion.

tail fin also **tail·fin** (tāl′fĭn′) *n.* **1.** A fin at the posterior part of the body of a fish, crustacean, whale, or other aquatic animal. **2.** An ornamental projection shaped like a fin on the rear fender of an automobile.

tail·gate (tāl′gāt′) *n.* **1.** A hinged board or closure at the rear of a vehicle, such as a truck, that can be lowered during loading and unloading. **2.** One of the pair of gates downstream in a canal lock. ❖ *v.* **-gat·ed, -gat·ing, -gates** —*tr.* To drive so closely behind (another vehicle) that one risks collision in an emergency. —*intr.* **1.** To follow another vehicle too closely. **2.** To participate in a picnic that is served from the tailgate of a vehicle. —**tail′gat′er** *n.*

tail·ing (tā′lĭng) *n.* **1. tailings** Refuse or dross remaining after ore has been processed. **2.** *Architecture* The portion of a tailed beam, brick, or board inside a wall.

tail lamp *n.* See **taillight.**

taille (tāl, tä′yə) *n.* A form of direct royal taxation that was levied in France before 1789 on nonprivileged subjects and lands. [Fr. < OFr., division. See TAIL².]

tail·light (tāl′līt′) *n.* A red light or one of a pair mounted on the rear end of a vehicle.

tai·lor (tā′lər) *n.* One that makes, repairs, and alters garments such as suits, coats, and dresses. ❖ *v.* **-lored, -lor·ing, -lors** —*tr.* **1.** To make (a garment), esp. to specific requirements or measurements. **2.** To fit or provide (a person) with clothes made to that person's measurements. **3.** To make, alter, or adapt for a particular end or purpose. —*intr.* To pursue the trade of a tailor. [ME < AN *taillour* < OFr. *tailleor* < *taillier,* to cut < LLat. *tāliāre* < Lat. *tālea,* a cutting.]

tai·lor·bird (tā′lər-bûrd′) *n.* Any of several Old World tropical passerine birds of the genus *Orthotomus* that characteristically stitch leaves together with plant fibers to make nests.

tai·lored (tā′lərd) *adj.* **1.** Made by a tailor; custom-made. **2.** Simple, trim, or severe in line or design.

tai·lor-made (tā′lər-mād′) *adj.* **1.** Made by a tailor. **2.** Perfectly fitted to a condition, preference, or purpose; made or as if made to order. ❖ *n.* A garment made by a tailor.

tail·piece (tāl′pēs′) *n.* **1.** A piece forming an end; an appendage. **2.** *Printing* An ornamental engraving or a design at the end of a chapter or the bottom of a page. **3.** *Architecture* A beam tailed into a wall. **4.** *Music* A triangular piece of ebony to which the lower ends of the strings of a violin or other related instruments are attached.

tail·pipe (tāl′pīp′) *n.* The pipe through which exhaust gases from an engine are discharged.

tail·race (tāl′rās′) *n.* **1.** The part of a millrace below the water wheel through which the spent water flows. **2.** A channel for floating away mine tailings and refuse.

tail·spin (tāl′spĭn′) *n.* **1.** The rapid descent of an aircraft in a steep, spiral spin. **2.** *Informal* A loss of emotional control sometimes resulting in emotional collapse.

tail·stock (tāl′stŏk′) *n.* The movable part of a lathe that supports the dead center.

tail wind or **tail·wind** (tāl′wĭnd′) *n.* A wind blowing in the same direction as that of a ship or another vehicle.

Tai·myr Peninsula (tī-mîr′) See **Taymyr Peninsula.**

Tai·nan (tī′nän′) A city of SW Taiwan on the South China Sea; settled in 1590. Pop. 609,934.

Taí·na·ron (tā′nə-rôn′, tĕ′nä-), **Cape** Formerly **Cape Mat·a·pan** (măt′ə-păn′) A cape of S mainland Greece.

Taine (tān, tĕn), **Hippolyte Adolphe** 1828–93. French philosopher and historian who was an exponent of positivism.

Tai·no (tī′nō) *n., pl.* **Taino** or **-nos 1.** A member of an Arawak people of the Greater Antilles and the Bahamas who became extinct under Spanish colonization during the 16th century. **2.** Their language. [Sp., of American Indian orig.]

taint (tānt) *v.* **taint·ed, taint·ing, taints** —*tr.* **1.** To affect with or as if with a disease. **2.** To affect with decay or putrefaction; spoil. **3.** To corrupt morally. **4.** To affect with a tinge of something reprehensible. —*intr.* To become affected with decay or putrefaction; spoil. ❖ *n.* **1.** A moral defect considered as a stain or spot. **2.** An infecting touch, influence, or tinge. [Partly

< obsolete *taynt,* to color, dye (< AN *teint* < p. part. of *teindre* < Lat. *tingere*), and partly < ME *tainten,* to convict (short for *atteinten* < OFr. *ataint,* p. part. of *ataindre,* to attain, touch upon; see ATTAIN).]

tai·pan¹ (tī′păn′) *n.* **1.** A foreign businessman or a trader in China. **2.** A foreigner who is a chief executive of a business or company operating in China; a tycoon. [Chin. (Cantonese) *taaî-paan,* equivalent to Chin. (Mandarin) *tái,* big + *bān,* class.]

tai·pan² (tī′păn) *n.* A large, extremely venomous elapid snake (*Oxyuranus scutellatus*) of Australia and New Guinea having long fangs and large venom glands. [Wik-Mungan (Aboriginal language of NE Australia) *dhayban.*]

Tai·pei also **Tai·peh** (tī′pā′, -bā′) The cap. of Taiwan, in the N part; headquarters of Chiang Kai-shek and the Chinese Nationalists after 1949. Pop. 2,327,641.

Tai·wan (tī′wän′) Officially **Republic of Chi·na** (chī′nə) Formerly **For·mo·sa** (fôr-mō′sə) A country off the SE coast of China comprising the island of **Taiwan,** the Pescadores, and other smaller islands. Cap. Taipei. Pop. 18,457,923.

Tai·wan·ese (tī′wä-nēz′, -nēs′) *adj.* Of or relating to Taiwan or its peoples, languages, or cultures. ❖ *n., pl.* **Taiwanese 1.** A native or inhabitant of Taiwan. **2.** The variety of Chinese spoken on Taiwan.

Taiwan Strait An arm of the Pacific Ocean between Taiwan and China linking the East China Sea with the South China Sea.

Tai·yu·an also **Tai·yü·an** (tī′yōō-än′, -yüän′) A city of NE China SW of Beijing. Pop. 1,390,000.

Ta·jik also **Ta·dzhik** (tä-jĭk′, tə-) *n., pl.* **Tajik** or **-jiks** also **Ta·dzhik** or **-dzhiks 1.** A member of a people inhabiting Tajikistan and neighboring areas in Uzbekistan, Afghanistan, and China. **2.** The Iranian language of the Tajik people, closely related to Persian. ❖ *adj.* Of or relating to the Tajik people or their language or culture.

Ta·jik·i·stan also **Ta·dzhik·i·stan** (tä-jĭk′ĭ-stän′, -stän′) A region and republic of W-central Asia bordering on Afghanistan and China; settled by the Tajik by the 10th cent. and a constituent republic of the USSR from 1929–91. Cap. Dushanbe. Pop. 5,993,000.

Ta·jo (tä′hō) See **Tagus.**

ta·ka (tä′kə) *n.* See table at **currency.** [Bengali *ṭākā* < Skt. *ṭaṅkaḥ,* stamped coin.]

Tak·ak·kaw (tăk′ə-kô′) A waterfall, 503.3 m (1,650 ft), in SE British Columbia, Canada.

Ta·ka·mat·su (tä′kä-mät′sōō) A city of NE Shikoku, Japan, on the Inland Sea. Pop. 331,031.

Ta·ka·tsu·ki (tä-kät′sōō-kē, tä′kä-tsōō′kē) A city of SW Honshu, Japan, between Osaka and Kyoto. Pop. 361,283.

take (tāk) *v.* **took** (tōōk), **tak·en** (tā′kən), **tak·ing, takes** —*tr.* **1.** To get into one's possession by force, skill, or artifice, esp.: **a.** To capture physically; seize: *take an enemy fortress.* **b.** To seize with authority; confiscate. **c.** To kill, snare, or trap (fish or game, for example). **d.** *Sports & Games* To acquire in a game or competition; win. **e.** *Sports & Games* To defeat. **f.** *Sports* To catch (a ball in play), esp. in baseball. **2.** To grasp with the hands; grip: *Take your partner's hand.* **3.** To encounter or catch in a particular situation; come upon; discover. **4.** To deal a blow to; strike or hit. **5.** To affect favorably or winsomely; charm or captivate. **6a.** To put (food or drink, for example) into the body; eat or drink. **b.** To draw in; inhale: *took a deep breath.* **7.** To expose one's body to (healthful or pleasurable treatment, for example). **8.** To bring or receive into a particular relation, association, or other connection: *take a new partner into the firm.* **9.** To engage in sex with. **10.** To accept and place under one's care or keeping. **11.** To appropriate for one's own or another's use or benefit; obtain by purchase; secure or buy. **12.** To assume for oneself: *took all the credit.* **13a.** To charge or oblige oneself with the fulfillment of (a task or duty, for example); commit oneself to. **b.** To pledge one's obedience to; impose (a vow or promise) upon oneself. **c.** To impose upon oneself; subject oneself to. **d.** To accept or adopt for one's own. **e.** To put forth or adopt as a point of argument, defense, or discussion. **f.** To require or have as a fitting or proper accompaniment: *Intransitive verbs take no direct object.* **14.** To pick out; select or choose: *take any card.* **15a.** To choose for one's own use; avail oneself of the use of. **b.** To use (something) as when in operation: *This camera takes 35mm film.* **c.** To use (something) as a means of conveyance or transportation: *take a train to Boston.* **d.** To use (something) as a means of safety or refuge. **e.** To choose and then adopt (a particular route or direction) while on foot or while operating a vehicle: *Take a right at the next corner.* **16.** To assume occupancy of: *take a seat.* **17.** To require (something) as a basic necessity. **18.** To obtain from a source; derive or draw. **19.** To obtain, as through measurement or a specified procedure. **20.** To write or make a record of, esp. in shorthand or cursive writing. **21.** To create (an image, likeness, or representation), as by drawing, painting, or photography. **22.** To include or distribute (a charge) in a financial record. **23a.** To accept (something owed, offered, or given) either reluctantly or willingly: *take criticism.* **b.** To include or distribute (a charge) in a financial record. **c.** To put up with; endure or tolerate. **d.** *Baseball* To refrain from swinging at (a pitched ball). **e.** To be affected with; catch. **f.** To be hit or penetrated by. **g.** To withstand.

24a. To accept or believe (something put forth) as true. **b.** To follow (advice or a lead, for example). **c.** To accept, handle, or deal with in a particular way: *took it in stride.* **d.** To consider in a particular relation or from a particular viewpoint: *take the bitter with the sweet.* **25.** To undertake, make, or perform: *take a walk; take a decision.* **26a.** To allow to come in; give access or admission to; admit. **b.** To provide room for; accommodate. **c.** To become saturated or impregnated with (dye, for example). **27a.** To understand or interpret. **b.** To consider; assume: *Take the matter as settled.* **c.** To consider to be equal to; reckon: *We take their number at 1,000.* **d.** To perceive or feel; experience. **28.** To carry, convey, lead, or cause to go along to another place. **29.** To remove from a place: *take the dishes from the sink.* **30.** To secure by removing: *The dentist took two molars.* **31.** To cause to die; kill or destroy. **32.** To subtract: *take 15 from 30.* **33.** To exact: *The storm took its toll.* **34a.** To commit and apply oneself to the study of. **b.** To study for with success. **35.** *Informal* To swindle, defraud, or cheat. —*intr.* **1.** To acquire possession. **2.** To engage or mesh; catch, as gears or other mechanical parts. **3.** To start growing; root or germinate. **4.** To have the intended effect; operate or work: *The skin graft took.* **5.** To gain popularity or favor. **6.** To become: *He took sick.* ❖ *n.* **1a.** The act or process of taking. **b.** That which is taken. **2a.** A quantity collected at one time, esp. the amount of profit or receipts taken on a business arrangement or venture. **b.** The number of fish, game birds, or other animals killed or captured at one time. **3.** *Sports* The amount of money collected as admission to a sporting event; the gate. **4.** The uninterrupted running of a movie or television camera or a set of recording equipment in filming a movie or television program or cutting a record. **5a.** A scene filmed or televised without interrupting the run of the camera. **b.** A recording made in a single session. **6a.** A physical reaction, such as a rash, indicating a successful vaccination. **b.** A successful graft. **7.** *Slang* An attempt or a try. **8.** *Informal* ***—phrasal verbs:*** **take after 1.** To follow as an example. **2.** To resemble in appearance, temperament, or character. **take apart 1.** To divide into parts after disassembling. **2.** To dissect or analyze (a theory, for example), usu. in an effort to discover flaws. **3.** *Slang* To beat up; thrash. **take back** To retract (something stated or written). **take down 1.** To bring to a lower position from a higher one. **2.** To take apart; dismantle. **3.** To lower the arrogance or the self-esteem of (a person). **4.** To put down in writing. **take for 1.** To regard as: *Do you take me for a fool?* **2.** To consider mistakenly. **take in 1.** To grant admittance to; receive as a guest or employee. **2.** To reduce in size; make smaller or shorter. **3.** To include or constitute. **4.** To understand. **5.** To deceive or swindle. **6.** To look at thoroughly; view: *took in the sights.* **7.** To accept (work) to be done in one's house for pay. **8.** To convey (a prisoner) to a police station. **take off 1.** To remove, as clothing. **2.** To release: *took the brake off.* **3.** To deduct as a discount. **4.** To carry off or away. **5.** *Slang* **a.** To go off; leave. **b.** To achieve wide use or popularity. **6.** To rise into the air or begin flight. **7.** To discontinue. **8.** To withhold service due, as from one's work. **take on 1.** To undertake or begin to handle. **2.** To hire; engage. **3.** To oppose in competition. **4.** *Informal* To display violent or passionate emotion. **5.** To acquire (an appearance, for example) as or as if one's own. **take out 1.** To extract; remove: *took the splinter out.* **2.** To secure (a license, for example) by application to an authority. **3.** *Informal* To escort, as a date. **4.** To give vent to. **5.** To obtain as an equivalent in a different form. **6.** *Informal* To begin a course; set out. **7.** *Slang* **a.** To kill; murder. **b.** To search for and destroy in an armed attack or other such encounter. **take over 1.** To assume control, management, or responsibility. **2.** To assume the control or management of or the responsibility for. **3.** To become dominant. **take to 1.** To have recourse to; go to, as for safety. **2.** To develop as a habit or a steady practice. **3.** To become fond of or attached to. **take up 1.** To raise; lift. **2.** To reduce in size; shorten or tighten. **3.** To pay off (an outstanding debt, mortgage, or note). **4.** To accept (an option, a bet, or a challenge) as offered. **5.** To begin again; resume. **6.** To use up, consume, or occupy. **7.** To develop an interest in or devotion to. **8.** To deal with. **9.** To assume: *took up a friendly attitude.* **10.** To absorb or adsorb. **11.** To enter into (a profession or business). ***—idioms:*** **on the take** *Informal* Taking or seeking to take bribes or illegal income. **take a bath** *Informal* To experience serious financial loss. **take account of** To take into consideration. **take away from** To detract. **take care** To be careful. **take care of** To assume responsibility for the maintenance, support, or treatment of. **take charge** To assume control or command. **take effect 1.** To become operative, as under law or regulation. **2.** To produce the desired reaction. **take exception** To express opposition by argument; object to. **take five (or ten)** *Slang* To take a short rest or break, as of five or ten minutes. **take for granted 1.** To consider as true, real, or forthcoming; anticipate correctly. **2.** To underestimate the value of. **take heart** To be confident or courageous. **take hold 1.** To seize, as by grasping. **2.** To become established. **take it 1.** To understand; assume. **2.** *Informal* To endure abuse, criticism, or other harsh treatment. **take it on the chin** *Slang* To endure punishment, suffering, or defeat. **take it or leave it** To accept or reject unconditionally. **take it out on** *Informal* To abuse (someone) in venting one's own anger. **take notice of** To pay attention to. **take (one's) breath away** To put into a state of awe or shock. **take (one's) time** To act slowly or at one's leisure. **take place** To happen; occur. **take root 1.** To become established or fixed. **2.** To become rooted. **take shape** To take on a distinctive form. **take sick** *Chiefly Southern US* To become ill. **take sides** To associate with and support a particular faction, group, cause, or person. **take stock 1.** To take an inventory. **2.** To make an estimate or appraisal, as of resources or of oneself. **take stock in** To trust, believe in, or attach importance to. **take the cake 1.** To be the most outrageous or disappointing. **2.** To win the prize; be outstanding. **take the fall (or hit)** *Slang* To incur blame or censure, either willingly or unwillingly. **take the heat** *Slang* To incur and endure heavy censure or criticism. **take to the cleaners** *Slang* To take all the money or possessions of, esp. by outsmarting or swindling. **take up with** *Informal* To begin to associate with; consort with. [ME *taken* < OE *tacan* < ON *taka.*]

take•a•way also **take-a•way** (tāk′ə-wā′) *adj. Chiefly British* Takeout.

take•down (tāk′doun′) *adj.* Having the capability of being taken down or apart. ❖ *n.* **1a.** A takedown article or apparatus. **b.** The mechanism that makes this procedure easy. **2.** *Sports* A move in wrestling or the martial arts in which a standing opponent is forced to the floor. **3.** *Informal* **a.** The act of humiliating a person. **b.** An instance of such humiliation.

take-home pay (tāk′hōm′) *n.* The amount of one's salary remaining after taxes and other deductions have been withheld.

take-in (tāk′ĭn′) *n. Informal* The act or an instance of swindling or cheating; a deception.

take-no-pris•on•ers (tĕk′nō-prĭz′ə-nərz, -prĭz′nərz) *adj.* Extremely ardent or aggressive: *a take-no-prisoners stance against fraud.*

take•off (tāk′ôf′, -ŏf′) *n.* **1.** The act of rising in flight. Used of an aircraft or rocket. **2.** The point or place of takeoff. **3.** *Informal* An amusing imitative caricature, parody, or burlesque.

take•out also **take-out** (tāk′out′) *adj.* **1.** Intended to be eaten off the premises. **2.** Selling or intended for the sale of takeout food products. **—take′-out′** *n.*

take•o•ver also **take-o•ver** (tāk′ō′vər) *n.* The act or an instance of assuming control or management of or responsibility for something, such as a nation. **—take′o′ver** *adj.*

tak•er (tā′kər) *n.* One that takes or takes up something, such as a wager or purchase: *There were no takers on the bets.*

take-up (tāk′ŭp′) *n.* **1.** The act of taking or tightening up. **2.** A device for reducing slack or taking up lost motion.

ta•kin (tä′kēn′) *n.* A large ruminant mammal *(Budorcas taxicolor)* of the mountains of China, Myanmar (Burma), and the Himalayas, having backward-pointing horns and a shaggy coat. [Prob. < Digaro (Tibeto-Burman language of NE India).]

tak•ing (tā′kĭng) *adj.* **1.** Capturing interest; fetching. **2.** Contagious; catching. Used of an infectious disease. ❖ *n.* **1.** The act of one that takes. **2.** Something taken, as a catch of fish. **3.** A government action assuming ownership of real property by eminent domain. **4. takings** *Informal* Receipts, esp. of money.

Ta•ki-Ta•ki (tä′kē-tä′kē) *n.* See **Sranantongo.** [Sranantongo, prob. alteration and redup. of E. TALK.]

Ta•kli•ma•kan also **Ta•kla•ma•kan** (tä′klə-mə-kän′) A desert of W China between the Tian Shan and the Kunlun Mts.

ta•la (tä′lə) *n., pl.* **tala** See table at **currency.** [Samoan < E. DOLLAR.]

Ta•la•ud Islands (tə-lout′, tä-lä′o͞od) or **Ta•laur Islands** (-lour′, -lä′o͞or) An island group of NE Indonesia.

Tal•bot (tôl′bət, tăl′-) *n.* A large white or light-colored English hound, having long ears and heavy jaws, formerly used for tracking and hunting. [ME, personal name < OFr.]

talc (tălk) *n.* A fine-grained white, greenish, or gray mineral, $Mg_3Si_4O_{10}(OH)_2$, having a soft soapy feel and used in talcum and face powder and as a filler in paper and plastics. ❖ *tr.v.* **talcked, talck•ing, talcs** or **talced, talc•ing, talcs** To apply this substance to (a photographic plate, for example). [Fr. < Med.Lat. *talcum* and OSpan. *talco,* both < Ar. *ṭalq* < Pers. *talk.*] **—talc′ose′** (tăl′kōs′), **talc′ous, talck′y** *adj.*

Tal•ca•hua•no (täl′kə-wä′nō, -hwä′-, täl′kä-) A city of central Chile on the Pacific near Concepción. Pop. 246,853.

tal•cum (tăl′kəm) *n.* **1.** Talc. **2.** Talcum powder. [Med.Lat. See TALC.]

talcum powder *n.* A fine, often perfumed powder made from purified talc for use on the skin.

tale (tāl) *n.* **1.** A recital of events or happenings; a report or revelation. **2.** A malicious story, piece of gossip, or petty complaint. **3.** A deliberate lie. **4.** A narrative of real or imaginary events; a story. **5.** *Archaic* A tally or reckoning; a total. [ME < OE *talu.*]

tale•bear•er (tāl′bâr′ər) *n.* One who spreads malicious stories or gossip. **—tale′bear′ing** *adj. & n.*

tal•ent (tăl′ənt) *n.* **1.** A marked innate ability, as for artistic accomplishment. **2a.** Natural endowment or ability of a superior quality. **b.** A person or group of people having such ability. **3.** A variable unit of weight and money used in ancient Greece, Rome, and the Middle East. [ME, inclination, disposition < OFr. < Med.Lat. < Lat., balance, sum of money < Gk. *talanton.* See **telə-** in App.] **—tal′ent•ed** *adj.*

talent scout *n.* An agent who goes in search of talented people

ă	pat	oi	boy
ā	pay	ou	out
âr	care	o͝o	took
ä	father	o͞o	boot
ĕ	pet	ŭ	cut
ē	be	ûr	urge
ĭ	pit	th	thin
ī	pie	*th*	this
îr	pier	hw	which
ŏ	pot	zh	vision
ō	toe	ə	about, item
ô	paw		

Stress marks:
′ (primary);
′ (secondary), as in
lexicon (lĕk′sĭ-kŏn′)

for acting, sports, or business.
talent show *n.* A show that features amateur performers whose talents may win them recognition or awards.
ta•ler also **tha•ler** (tä′lər) *n., pl.* **taler** or **-lers** also **thaler** or **-lers** Any of numerous silver coins that once served as a currency unit in certain Germanic countries. [Ger. See DOLLAR.]
tales (tālz, tā′lēz) *n., pl.* **tales** A writ allowing for a summons of jurors. [ME < Med.Lat. *tālēs dē circumstantibus,* such (persons) from those standing about (a phrase used in the writ) < Lat., pl. of *tālis,* such. See **to-** in App.]
tale•tell•er (tāl′tĕl′ər) *n.* **1.** One who tells stories; a storyteller. **2.** A talebearer; a tattletale. —**tale′tell′ing** *adj. & n.*
ta•li (tā′lī′) *n.* Plural of **talus[1]**.
Tal•i•ban (tăl′ə-băn′) *n.* A fundamentalist Muslim group that controlled much of Afghanistan from 1995 until US military intervention in 2001. [Pashto *tālibān,* pl. of *tālib,* student < Ar. *ṭālib* < *ṭalaba,* to seek.]
Ta•lien (tä′lyĕn′) See **Dalian.**
tal•i•on (tăl′ē-ən) *n.* A punishment identical to the offense. [ME *talioun* < AN < Lat. *tāliō, tāliōn-.* See **telə-** in App.]
tal•i•ped (tăl′ə-pĕd′) *adj.* Having a clubfoot; clubfooted. ❖ *n.* A person with a clubfoot. [< NLat. *tālipēs, tāliped-,* clubfoot. See TALIPES.]
tal•i•pes (tăl′ə-pēz′) *n.* See **clubfoot** 1. [NLat. *tālipēs, tāliped-* : Lat. *tālus,* ankle + Lat. *pēs, ped-,* foot; see –PED.]
tal•i•pot (tăl′ə-pŏt′) *n.* A tall palm tree *(Corypha umbraculifera)* of India and Sri Lanka having a spreading crown of very large fanlike leaves and a giant inflorescence. [Ult. < Skt. *tālapattram,* palm leaf used for writing : *tālaḥ,* fan palm; see TODDY + *pattram,* leaf; see **pet-** in App.]
tal•is•man (tăl′ĭs-mən, -ĭz-) *n., pl.* **-mans 1.** An object marked with magic signs, believed to confer on its bearer supernatural powers or protection. **2.** Something that seems magical in power. [Ult. < Ar. *ṭilasm* < L.Gk. *telesma* < Gk., consecration ceremony < *telein,* to consecrate, fulfill < *telos,* result. See **kʷel-** in App.] —**tal′is•man′ic** (-ĭs-măn′ĭk, -ĭz-), **tal′is•man′i•cal** (-ĭ-kəl) *adj.*
talk (tôk) *v.* **talked, talk•ing, talks** —*tr.* **1.** To articulate (words). **2.** To give expression to in words: *talk treason.* **3.** To speak of or discuss (something): *talk business.* **4.** To speak or know how to speak in (an idiom or language). **5.** To gain, influence, or bring into a specified state by talking: *talked me into coming.* **6.** To spend (a period of time) by or as if by talking. —*intr.* **1.** To converse by means of spoken language: *We talked for hours.* **2.** To articulate words: *The baby can't talk yet.* **3.** To imitate the sounds of human speech. **4.** To express one's thoughts or emotions by means of spoken language. **5.** To convey one's thoughts in a way other than by spoken words: *talk with one's hands.* **6.** To express one's thoughts in writing. **7.** To parley or negotiate with someone. **8.** To spread rumors; gossip. **9.** To allude to something. **10.** To consult or confer with someone. **11.** To reveal information concerning oneself or others, esp. under pressure. **12.** *Informal* To be efficacious: *Money talks.* ❖ *n.* **1.** An exchange of ideas or opinions; a conversation. **2.** A speech or lecture. **3.** Hearsay, rumor, or speculation. **4.** A subject of conversation. **5.** A conference or negotiation. Often used in the plural. **6.** Jargon; slang. **7.** Empty speech or unnecessary discussion. **8.** A particular manner of speech. **9.** Something, such as the sounds of animals, felt to resemble human talk. ***—phrasal verbs:*** **talk around 1.** To persuade. **2.** To speak indirectly about. **talk at** To address orally with no regard for or interest in a reaction or response. **talk back 1.** To make an impertinent reply. **2.** To make a belligerent response. **talk down 1.** To depreciate. **2.** To speak with insulting condescension. **3.** To silence (a person), esp. by speaking in a loud and domineering manner. **4.** To direct and control (an aircraft during an approach for landing) by radioed instructions. **talk out 1.** To discuss (a matter) exhaustively. **2.** To resolve or settle by discussion. **3.** *Chiefly British* To block (proposed legislation) by filibustering. **talk over 1.** To consider thoroughly in conversation; discuss. **2.** To win (someone) over by persuasion. **talk up 1.** To speak in favor of; promote. **2.** To speak up in a frank, often insolent manner. ***—idioms:*** **talk big** *Informal* To brag. **talk sense** To speak rationally and coherently. [ME *talken.*] —**talk′er** *n.*
talk•a•thon (tôk′ə-thŏn′) *n.* A lengthy session of discussions, speeches, or debate.
talk•a•tive (tô′kə-tĭv) *adj.* Marked by or having a disposition to talk. —**talk′a•tive•ly** *adv.* —**talk′a•tive•ness** *n.*
talk•back (tôk′băk′) *n.* A one-way communications link from a control booth to a recording or broadcasting studio.
talk•ie (tô′kē) *n. Informal* A movie with a soundtrack.
talk•ing book (tô′kĭng) *n.* A recorded reading of a book, designed for use by the visually impaired.
talking head *n. Slang* The image of a person, as on a television news show, who talks at length directly to the camera.
talking point *n.* Something, such as a persuasive point, that helps support an argument or discussion.
talk•ing-to (tô′kĭng-to͞o′) *n., pl.* **-tos** *Informal* A scolding.
talk radio *n.* Broadcast radio programming consisting of talk shows, often including telephone conversations with members of the audience.
talk show *n.* A television or radio show featuring talk, as among hosts, guests, and listeners.

tallith

tandem bicycle

talk•y (tô′kē) *adj.* **-i•er, -i•est 1.** Talkative; loquacious. **2.** Containing or given to too much talk. —**talk′i•ness** *n.*
tall (tôl) *adj.* **tall•er, tall•est 1a.** Having greater than ordinary height. **b.** Having considerable height, esp. in relation to width; lofty. **2.** Having a specified height. **3.** *Informal* Fanciful or exaggerated; boastful. **4.** Impressively great or difficult: *a tall order.* **5.** *Archaic* Excellent; fine. ❖ *adv.* With proud bearing; straight. [ME, brave, quick < OE *getæl,* swift.] —**tall′ness** *n.*
tal•lage (tăl′ĭj) *n.* An occasional tax levied by the Anglo-Norman kings on crown lands and royal towns. ❖ *tr.v.* **-laged, -lag•ing, -lag•es** To levy a tax on. [ME *taillage* < OFr. < *taillier,* to cut, tax. See TAILOR.]
Tal•la•has•see (tăl′ə-hăs′ē) The cap. of FL, in the NW part; founded as cap. of the Florida Terr. in 1824. Pop. 150,624.
Tal•la•hatch•ie (tăl′ə-hăch′ē) A river rising in N MS and flowing c. 371 km (230 mi) generally SW to the Yazoo R.
Tal•la•poo•sa (tăl′ə-po͞o′sə) A river rising in NW GA and flowing c. 431 km (268 mi) to the Coosa R.
tall•boy (tôl′boi′) *n. Chiefly British* A highboy.
Tal•ley•rand-Pé•ri•gord (tăl′ē-rănd′pĕr′ĭ-gôr′, tä-lĕ-räɴ-pā-rē-gôr′), **Charles Maurice de** 1754–1838. French public official during the French Revolution, Napoleon's reign, the Bourbon restoration, and the reign of Louis Philippe.
Tal•linn also **Tal•lin** (tăl′ĭn, tä′lĭn) The cap. of Estonia, in the NW part on the Gulf of Finland. Pop. 447,672.
tal•lith also **tal•lis** (tä′lĭs, tä-lēt′) *n., pl.* **tal•lith•im** (tä-lē′sĭm, -lā′-, tä′lē-tēm′) or **tal•liths** also **tal•li•sim** (tä-lē′sĭm, -lā′-) *Judaism* A shawl with zizith traditionally worn by Jewish males, esp. during morning prayer. [Mishnaic Heb. *ṭallît,* cover < Heb. *ṭillēl,* to cover < Aram. *ṭallel* < *ṭālal,* shade.]
tall oil (täl, tôl) *n.* A resinous liquid mixture of rosin acids and fatty acids obtained as a byproduct in the treatment of pine pulp and used in soaps, emulsions, and lubricants. [Partial transl. of Ger. *Tallöl* < partial transl. of Swed. *tallolja* : *tall,* pine (< ON *thöll,* young pine tree) + *olja,* oil.]
tal•low (tăl′ō) *n.* **1.** Hard fat obtained from cattle, sheep, or horses and used in foodstuffs or to make candles, leather dressing, soap, and lubricants. **2.** Any of various similar fats, such as those obtained from plants. ❖ *tr.v.* **-lowed, -low•ing, -lows 1.** To smear or cover with tallow. **2.** To fatten (animals) to obtain tallow. [ME *talow.*] —**tal′low•y** *adj.*
tal•ly (tăl′ē) *n., pl.* **-lies 1.** A reckoning or score. **2a.** A stick on which notches keep a count or score. **b.** A tally once used to keep a record of amounts paid or owed. **3.** A mark used in recording a number of acts or objects, most often in series of five, consisting of four vertical lines canceled diagonally or horizontally by a fifth line. **4.** An identifying or classifying label, ticket, or piece of metal or wood, esp. in gardens and greenhouses. **5.** Something that is very similar or corresponds to something else; a double or counterpart. ❖ *v.* **-lied, -ly•ing, -lies** —*tr.* **1.** To reckon or count. **2.** To record by making a mark. **3.** *Sports & Games* To score (a point or goal) in a game or contest. **4.** To label, as with a tally, for identification or classification. **5.** To cause to correspond or agree. —*intr.* **1.** To be alike; correspond or agree. **2.** To keep score. **3.** *Sports & Games* To score a point or goal. [ME *taly* < AN *tallie* < Med.Lat. *tallia* < Lat. *tālea,* stick.]
tal•ly•ho (tăl′ē-hō′) *interj.* Used to urge hounds on during a fox hunt. ❖ *v.* **-hoed, -ho•ing, -hos** —*tr.* To urge (hounds) on during a fox hunt by shouting "tallyho" when the fox is sighted. —*intr.* To shout "tallyho" as a hunting cry. ❖ *n., pl.* **-hos 1.** The cry of "tallyho." **2.** A fast coach drawn by four horses. [Prob. alteration of Fr. *taïaut* < OFr. *thialau, taho.*]
Tal•mud (täl′mo͝od, tăl′məd) *n. Judaism* The collection of ancient Rabbinic writings consisting of the Mishnah and the Gemara, constituting the basis for much of Jewish law. [Mishnaic Heb. *talmûd,* learning, instruction < Heb. *lāmad,* to learn.] —**Tal•mu′dic** (täl-mo͞o′dĭk, -myo͞o′-, tăl-), **Tal•mu′di•cal** (-dĭ-kəl) *adj.* —**Tal′mud•ist** (täl′mo͝o-dĭst, tăl′mə-) *n.*
tal•on (tăl′ən) *n.* **1a.** The claw of a bird of prey. **b.** The similar claw of a predatory animal. **2.** Something similar to or suggestive of an animal's claw. **3.** The part of a lock that the key presses in order to shoot the bolt. **4.** *Games* The part of the deck of cards in certain card games left on the table after the deal. **5.** *Architecture* An ogee molding. [ME *taloun* < OFr. *talon,* heel < VLat. **tālō, tālōn-* < Lat. *tālus,* ankle.]
ta•lus[1] (tā′ləs) *n., pl.* **-li** (-lī′) **1.** The bone of the ankle that articulates with the tibia and fibula to form the ankle joint. **2.** The ankle. [Lat. *tālus,* ankle.]
ta•lus[2] (tā′ləs) *n., pl.* **-lus•es** A sloping mass of rock debris at a cliff base. [Fr. *talus* < OFr. *talu,* earthwork slope < Lat. *talūtium,* gold-bearing outcrop, perh. of Celt. orig.]
tam (tăm) *n.* A tam-o'-shanter.
ta•ma•le (tə-mä′lē) *n.* A Mexican dish made of fried chopped meat and crushed peppers wrapped in cornhusks spread with masa, and steamed. [< Am.Sp. *tamales,* pl. of *tamal,* tamale < Nahuatl *tamalli.*]
tam•a•rack (tăm′ə-răk′) *n.* A deciduous North American larch tree *(Larix laricina)* having short needles borne on spur shoots. [Canadian Fr. *tamarac,* prob. of Algonquian orig.]
tam•a•rau also **tam•a•rao** (tăm′ə-rou′) *n., pl.* **-raus** also **-raos** A small grayish-black short-horned buffalo *(Bubalus*

mindorensis) of the island of Mindoro. [Tagalog *tamaráw.*]

ta·ma·ri (tə-mä′rē) *n.* Soy sauce made with little or no wheat. [J.]

tam·a·rin (tăm′ə-rĭn, -răn′) *n.* Any of various small long-tailed arboreal monkeys of the genera *Leontideus* and *Saguinus* of Central and South America. [Fr. < Galibi.]

tam·a·rind (tăm′ə-rĭnd′) *n.* **1.** A tropical Asian evergreen tree (*Tamarindus indica*) having pinnately compound leaves, pale yellow flowers, and long pods containing small seeds embedded in an edible pulp. **2.** The fruit of this tree. [ME < OFr. *tamarinde* < Ar. *tamr hindī* : *tamr*, dates + *hindī*, of India (< Pers. *Hind*, India; see HINDI).]

tam·a·risk (tăm′ə-rĭsk′) *n.* Any of numerous African and Eurasian shrubs or small trees of the genus *Tamarix*, having small scalelike leaves. [ME *tamarisc* < LLat. *tamariscus*, var. of Lat. *tamarīx, tamaric-*.]

Ta·ma·yo (tä-mä′yō), **Rufino** 1899–1991. Mexican artist whose works were influenced by pre-Columbian symbols.

tam·bour (tăm′bŏŏr′, tăm-bŏŏr′) *n.* **1.** A drum or drummer. **2a.** A small wooden embroidery frame consisting of two concentric hoops between which fabric is stretched. **b.** Embroidery made on such a frame. **3.** A rolling front or top for a desk or table, consisting of narrow strips of wood glued to canvas. **4.** *Architecture* See **drum** 3a. ❖ *v.* **-boured, -bour·ing, -bours** —*tr.* To do (embroidery) on a tambour. —*intr.* To embroider at or on a tambour. [ME < OFr., ult. < Ar. *ṭanbūr*, stringed musical instrument; prob. akin to Pers. *tambūr*, lute < MPers.]

tam·bou·ra or **tam·bu·ra** (tăm-bŏŏr′ə) *n.* An unfretted lute of India and Turkey, used as a drone. [Urdu *ṭambūra* < Pers. *ṭanbūra* < Ar. *ṭanbūr*. See TAMBOUR.]

tam·bou·rin (tăm′bŏŏ-rĭn, tän-bŏŏ-răN′) *n.* **1a.** A long, narrow, two-headed drum used in Provence. **b.** One who plays this drum. **2.** A style of dance in lively two-beat rhythm, accompanied by this drum. [Provençal *tambourin* < OFr., dim. of *tambour*, tambour. See TAMBOUR.]

tam·bou·rine (tăm′bə-rēn′) *n.* **1.** A percussion instrument made up of a small drumhead with jingling disks fitted into the rim. **2.** A similar instrument without a drumhead. [Fr. *tambourin*, small drum < OFr. See TAMBOURIN.]

Tam·bov (täm-bôf′, -bôv′) A city of W Russia SE of Moscow; founded as a fortress in 1636. Pop. 311,303.

tam·bu·rit·za (tăm-bŏŏr′ĭt-sə, täm′bə-rĭt′sə) *n.* A Balkan mandolinlike stringed instrument. [Serbo-Croatian *tamburica*, dim. of *tambura*, stringed instrument < Ottoman Turk. *ṭambūra* < Pers. *ṭanbūra*. See TAMBOURA.]

tame (tām) *adj.* **tam·er, tam·est 1.** Brought from wildness into a domesticated or tractable state. **2.** Naturally unafraid; not timid. **3.** Submissive; docile; fawning. **4.** Insipid; flat: *a tame party.* **5.** Sluggish; languid; inactive. ❖ *tr.v.* **tamed, tam·ing, tames 1.** To make tractable; domesticate. **2.** To subdue or curb. **3.** To tone down; soften. [ME < OE *tam.*] —**tam′a·ble, tame′a·ble** *adj.* —**tame′ly** *adv.* —**tame′ness** *n.* —**tam′er** *n.*

Tam·er·lane (tăm′ər-lān′) or **Tam·bur·laine** (-bər-) 1336–1405. Mongolian conqueror of Persia, Turkey, and India.

Tam·il (tăm′əl, tŭm′-, tä′məl) *n., pl.* **Tamil** or **-ils 1.** A member of a Dravidian people of southern India and northern Sri Lanka. **2.** The Dravidian language of the Tamil. ❖ *adj.* Of or relating to the Tamil or their language or culture. [Tamil.]

Tamm (täm), **Igor Yevgeneevich** 1895–1971. Russian physicist who shared a 1958 Nobel Prize.

Tam·muz also **Tham·muz** (tä′mŏŏz) *n.* The tenth month of the year in the Jewish calendar. See table at **calendar.** [Heb. *tammūz*; akin to Iraqi Ar. *tabbūz*, July, both ult. < Sumerian *dumu-zi*, Dumuzi, a dying and rising shepherd god : *dumu*, son + *zi*, true, effective.]

tam-o′-shan·ter (tăm′ə-shăn′tər) *n.* A Scottish cap or braided bonnet, sometimes having a pompon, tassel, or feather in the center. [After the hero of *"Tam o' Shanter,"* a poem by Robert Burns.]

ta·mox·i·fen (tə-mŏk′sə-fĕn) *n.* A nonsteroidal estrogen antagonist used in the treatment and prevention of breast cancer. [T(RANS)- + AM(INO)- + alter. of OXY- + alter. of PHEN(OL).]

tamp (tămp) *tr.v.* **tamped, tamp·ing, tamps 1.** To pack down tightly by a succession of blows or taps. **2.** To pack clay, sand, or dirt into (a drill hole) above an explosive. [Perh. back-formation < *tampin*, var. of TAMPION.]

Tam·pa (tăm′pə) A city of W-central FL on **Tampa Bay,** an inlet of the Gulf of Mexico. Pop. 303,447.

tam·per¹ (tăm′pər) *v.* **-pered, -per·ing, -pers** —*intr.* **1.** To interfere in a harmful manner. **2.** To tinker with something foolishly. **3.** To engage in improper or secret dealings, as in an effort to influence. See Syns at **interfere.** —*tr.* To alter improperly. [Prob. alteration of TEMPER.] —**tam′per·er** *n.*

tamp·er² (tăm′pər) *n.* A neutron reflector in an atomic bomb that delays the expansion of the exploding material, making possible a longer-lasting and more energetic explosion.

Tam·pe·re (tăm′pə-rā′, täm′-) A city of SW Finland NNW of Helsinki. Pop. 175,504.

tam·per·proof (tăm′pər-prŏŏf′) *adj.* Designed to prevent tampering or provide evidence of tampering.

Tam·pi·co (tăm-pē′kō, täm-) A city of E-central Mexico near

the Gulf of Mexico NNE of Mexico City. Pop. 267,957.

tam·pi·on (tăm′pē-ən) also **tom·pi·on** (tŏm′-) *n.* A plug or cover for the muzzle of a cannon or gun to keep out dust and moisture. [ME < OFr. *tampon*, var. of *tapon*, rag for stopping a hole, of Gmc. orig.]

tam·pon (tăm′pŏn′) *n.* A plug of absorbent material inserted into a body cavity or wound to check a flow of blood or to absorb secretions, esp. one for the vagina during menstruation. [Fr. < OFr. See TAMPION.] —**tam′pon′** *v.*

tam-tam¹ (tŭm′tŭm′, tăm′tăm′) *n.* A gong having a metal disk struck with a felt-covered hammer or stick, used in a gamelan orchestra. [Ult. of imit. orig.]

tam-tam² (tŭm′tŭm′, tăm′tăm′) *n.* Variant of **tom-tom.**

tan¹ (tăn) *v.* **tanned, tan·ning, tans** —*tr.* **1.** To convert (hide) into leather, as by treating with tannin. **2.** To make brown by exposure to the sun. **3.** *Informal* To thrash; beat. —*intr.* To become suntanned. ❖ *n.* **1.** A light or moderate yellowish brown to brownish orange. **2.** The brown color that sun rays impart to light skin. **3.** Tanbark. **4a.** Tannin. **b.** A solution derived from tannin. ❖ *adj.* **tan·ner, tan·nest 1.** Of the color tan. **2.** Having a suntan. **3.** Used in or relating to tanning. [ME *tannen* < OE **tannian* < Med.Lat. *tannāre* < *tannum*, tanbark, prob. of Celt. orig.]

tan² *abbr. Mathematics* tangent

Ta·na (tä′nə, -nä) also **Lake Tsa·na** (tsä′-) A lake of NW Ethiopia; source of the Blue Nile.

tan·a·ger (tăn′ĭ-jər) *n.* Any of various small New World passerine birds of the family Thraupidae, often having brightly colored plumage in the males and usu. living in forests. [NLat. *tanagra*, alteration of Port. *tangará* < Tupi *tangará.*]

Tan·a·gra (tăn′ə-grə, tə-năg′rə) An ancient city of E-central Greece in E Boeotia; site of a Spartan defeat of Athenian forces in 457 B.C.

Ta·nakh (tä-näKH′) *n.* The sacred book of Judaism, consisting of the Torah, the Prophets, and the Writings; the Hebrew Scriptures. [Acronym < the initial letters of the Heb. names for the Torah, the Prophets, and the Writings : *t(ôrâ)* + *n(əḏî'îm)* + *k(əṯûḇôt).*]

Tan·a·na (tăn′ə-nô′) A river of E and S AK flowing c. 764 km (475 mi) from the Wrangell Mts. to the Yukon R.

Ta·na·na·rive (tə-năn′ə-rēv′, tä-nä-nä-rēv′) See **Antananarivo.**

Tana River 1. A river of central Kenya flowing c. 805 km (500 mi) to the Indian Ocean. **2.** A river, c. 322 km (200 mi), of NE Norway emptying into an inlet of the Arctic Ocean.

tan·bark (tăn′bärk′) *n.* **1.** The bark of various trees used as a source of tannin. **2.** Shredded bark from which the tannin has been extracted, used to cover circus arenas and other surfaces.

Tan·cred (tăng′krĭd) 1078?–1112. Norman soldier who was a leader of the First Crusade (1096–99).

tan·dem (tăn′dəm) *n.* **1.** A two-wheeled carriage drawn by horses harnessed one before the other. **2.** A team of carriage horses harnessed in single file. **3.** A tandem bicycle. **4.** An arrangement of two or more persons or objects placed one behind the other. ❖ *adj.* Having two identical components arranged one behind the other. [Lat., at last, at length. See **to-** in App.]

tandem bicycle *n.* A bicycle built for two or more people sitting one behind the other.

tan·door (tăn-dŏŏr′) *n., pl.* **-doors** or **-door·i** (-dŏŏr′ē) A cylindrical oven made of clay, heated to a high heat over charcoal or wood and used in India. [Hindi and Urdu *tandūr* < Pers., var. of *tanūr* < MPers. < Ar. < Akkadian *tinūru*, oven.]

tan·door·i (tăn-dŏŏr′ē) *adj.* Cooked in a tandoor. [Hindi *tandūri* < *tandūr*, tandoor. See TANDOOR.]

Ta·ney (tô′nē), **Roger Brooke** 1777–1864. Amer. jurist; chief justice of the US Supreme Court (1836–64).

tang¹ (tăng) *n.* **1.** A distinctively sharp taste, flavor, or odor. **2.** A distinctive quality that adds piquancy. **3.** A trace, hint, or smattering. **4.** A sharp point, tongue, or prong. **5.** A projection by which a tool, such as a knife, is attached to its handle or stock. **6.** A surgeonfish. ❖ *tr.v.* **tanged, tang·ing, tangs 1.** To furnish with a tang. **2.** To give a tang to. [ME *tange*, of Scand. orig.] —**tang′i·ness** *n.* —**tang′y** *adj.*

tang² (tăng) *n.* A loud ringing sound; a twang. [Imit.] —**tang** *v.*

Tang (täng) A Chinese dynasty (618–907) known for its wealth and its encouragement of the arts and literature.

Tan·gan·yi·ka (tăn′gən-yē′kə, tăng′-) A former country of E-central Africa; gained independence from Great Britain in 1961 and joined with Zanzibar to form Tanzania in 1964. —**Tan′gan·yi′kan** *adj. & n.*

Tanganyika, Lake A lake of E-central Africa between Congo (formerly Zaire) and Tanzania.

Tan·ge (tän′gē), **Kenzo** b. 1913. Japanese architect who designed the Peace Center and Park (1949–56) as part of the rebuilding of Hiroshima after World War II.

tan·ge·lo (tăn′jə-lō′) *n., pl.* **-los 1.** A hybrid citrus tree derived from grapefruit and tangerine. **2.** The aromatic fruit of this tree. [Blend of TANGERINE and POMELO.]

tan·gen·cy (tăn′jən-sē) also **tan·gence** (-jəns) *n.* The condition of being tangent.

tan·gent (tăn′jənt) *adj.* **1.** Making contact at a single point or along a line; touching but not intersecting. **2.** Irrelevant. ❖ *n.* **1.**

tandoor

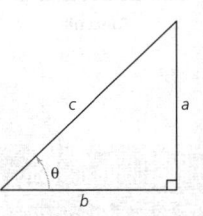

tangent
tan θ = ³⁄b

A line, curve, or surface meeting another line, curve, or surface at a common point and sharing a common tangent line or tangent plane at that point. **2.** The trigonometric function of an acute angle in a right triangle that is the ratio of the length of the side opposite the angle to the length of the side adjacent to the angle. **3.** A sudden digression or change of course. **4.** *Music* An upright pin in a keyboard instrument, esp. in a clavichord, that rises to sound a string when a key is depressed and stops the string at a preset length to set the pitch. [Lat. *(līnea) tangēns, tangent-,* touching (line), pr. part. of *tangere,* to touch. See **tag-** in App.]

tan·gen·tial (tăn-jĕn′shəl) also **tan·gen·tal** (-jĕn′tl) *adj.* **1.** Of, relating to, or moving along or in the direction of a tangent. **2.** Merely touching or slightly connected. **3.** Only superficially relevant; divergent: *a tangential remark.* —**tan·gen′ti·al·i·ty** (-shē-ăl′ĭ-tē) *n.* —**tan·gen′tial·ly** *adv.*

tan·ger·ine (tăn′jə-rēn′, tăn′jə-rēn′) *n.* **1.** A widely cultivated variety of mandarin orange having deep red-orange fruit with easily separated segments. **2.** A strong reddish orange to strong or vivid orange. [Short for *tangerine orange,* after *Tanger* (Tangier), Morocco.]

tan·gi·ble (tăn′jə-bəl) *adj.* **1a.** Discernible by the touch; palpable. **b.** Possible to touch. **c.** Possible to be treated as fact; real or concrete. **2.** Possible to understand or realize. **3.** *Law* That can be valued monetarily. ❖ *n.* **1.** Something palpable or concrete. **2. tangibles** Material assets. [LLat. *tangibilis* < Lat. *tangere,* to touch. See **tag-** in App.] —**tan′gi·bil′i·ty** *n.* —**tan′gi·bly** *adv.*

Tan·gier (tăn-jîr′) also **Tan·giers** (-jîrz′) A city of N Morocco at the W end of the Strait of Gibraltar. Pop. 307,000.

tan·gle[1] (tăng′gəl) *v.* **-gled, -gling, -gles** —*tr.* **1.** To mix together or intertwine in a confused mass; snarl. **2.** To involve in hampering or awkward complications; entangle. **3.** To catch and hold in or as if in a net; entrap. See Syns at **catch**. —*intr.* **1.** To be or become entangled. **2.** *Informal* To enter into argument, dispute, or conflict. ❖ *n.* **1.** A confused, intertwined mass. **2.** A jumbled or confused state. **3.** A state of bewilderment. **4.** *Informal* An argument or altercation. [ME *tangilen,* to involve in an embarrassing situation, var. of *tagilen,* prob. of Scand. orig.] —**tan′gly** *adj.*

tan·gle[2] (tăng′gəl) *n.* A large seaweed of the genus *Laminaria.* [Of Scand. orig.; akin to ON *thöngull,* seaweed.]

tan·gled (tăng′gəld) *adj.* Complicated and difficult to unravel. See Syns at **complex.**

tan·go (tăng′gō) *n., pl.* **-gos 1.** A Latin American ballroom dance in 2/4 or 4/4 time. **2.** The music for this dance. ❖ *intr.v.* **-goed, -go·ing, -gos** To perform this dance. [Am.Sp., poss. of Niger-Congo orig.; akin to Ibibio *tamgu,* to dance.] —**tan′go·like′** *adj.*

tan·gram (tăng′grəm) *n.* A Chinese puzzle consisting of a square cut into five triangles, a square, and a rhomboid, to be reassembled into different figures. [Perh. partial transl. of Chin. (Mandarin) *táng tú* : *táng,* Tang + *tú,* picture, diagram.]

Tang·shan (tăng′shän′, däng′-) A city of NE China ESE of Beijing. Pop. 1,484,515.

Tan·guy (tän-gē′), **Yves** 1900–55. French-born Amer. painter whose works include *Indefinite Divisibility* (1942).

tanh *abbr.* hyperbolic tangent

Ta·nis (tā′nĭs) An ancient city of Egypt in the E delta of the Nile R.; important during the XIX and XXI Dynasties.

tan·ist (tăn′ĭst, thô′nĭst) *n.* In ancient Ireland, the heir apparent to a Celtic chief, elected during the chief's lifetime. [Ir.Gael. *tánaiste,* second, tanist < OIr. *tánaise.* See **sed-** in App.] —**tan′ist·ry** *n.*

tank (tăngk) *n.* **1a.** A large, often metallic container for holding or storing liquids or gases. **b.** The amount that a tank can hold: *She bought a tank of gas.* **2.** A usu. artificial pond or cistern, used to hold water for drinking or irrigation. **3.** An enclosed, heavily armored combat vehicle that is armed with cannon and machine guns and moves on continuous tracks. **4.** A tank top. **5.** *Slang* A jail or jail cell. ❖ *v.* **tanked, tank·ing, tanks** —*tr.* To place, store, or process in a tank. —*intr. Slang* To suffer a sudden decline or failure. —**phrasal verb: tank up 1.** *Slang* To drink to the point of intoxication. **2.** To fill the tank of a motor vehicle with gasoline. [Partly < Gujarati *tānkh,* cistern (< Skt. *taḍāgaḥ,* pond, perh. of Dravidian orig.) and partly < Port. *tanque,* reservoir (var. of *estanque* < *estancar,* to dam up < VLat. **stanticāre;* see STANCH[1].] —**tank′ful** (-fŏŏl′) *n.*

tan·ka[1] (täng′kə) *n.* A Japanese verse form in five lines, the first and third of five syllables and the rest of seven. [J.]

tan·ka[2] (täng′kə) *n.* A Tibetan religious painting on fabric, usu. portraying the Buddha or lamas in stereotyped aspects. [Tibetan *thaṅka,* something rolled up.]

tank·age (tăng′kĭj) *n.* **1a.** The act or process of putting or storing in a tank. **b.** The amount that a tank can hold. **c.** A fee for tank storage. **2.** Animal residues that remain after rendering fat in a slaughterhouse, used for fertilizer or feed.

tank·ard (tăng′kərd) *n.* A large drinking cup having a single handle and often a hinged cover. [ME.]

tank destroyer *n.* A high-speed armored vehicle equipped with antitank guns.

tanked (tăngkt) *adj. Slang* Intoxicated; drunk.

tank·er (tăng′kər) *n.* **1.** A ship, plane, or truck for transporting liquids in bulk. **2.** A member of a military tank crew.

tanka[2]

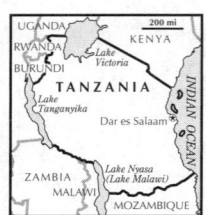

Tanzania

tapa[1]
detail of a Fijian tapa

tank farm *n.* A group of tanks, as for the commercial storage of oil.

tank suit *n.* **1.** A tight-fitting one-piece women's swimsuit with shoulder straps. **2.** A brief, tight-fitting men's swimsuit.

tank top *n.* A sleeveless, tight-fitting, usu. knit shirt with no front opening. [< its resemblance to a TANK SUIT.]

tank town *n.* A small town. [So called because trains would stop there only to replenish water.]

tan·nate (tăn′āt′) *n.* A salt or ester of tannic acid. [TANN(IN) + -ATE[2].]

tan·ner[1] (tăn′ər) *n.* One that tans hides.

tan·ner[2] (tăn′ər) *n. Chiefly British* A sixpenny coin formerly used in Britain; a sixpence. [?]

tan·ner·y (tăn′ə-rē) *n., pl.* **-ies** An establishment where hides are tanned.

tan·nic (tăn′ĭk) *adj.* Of, relating to, or obtained from tannin.

tannic acid *n.* Any of various yellowish complex organic compounds, esp. $C_{14}H_{10}O_9$, derived from nutgalls and certain plants and used in tanning and in dyeing as a mordant.

tan·nif·er·ous (tă-nĭf′ər-əs) *adj.* Having or yielding tannin.

tan·nin (tăn′ĭn) *n.* **1.** Tannic acid. **2.** Any of various chemically different substances capable of promoting tanning. [Fr. < *tan,* crushed oak bark < OFr. < Med.Lat. *tannum.* See TAN[1].]

tan·ning (tăn′ĭng) *n.* **1.** The art or process of making leather from rawhides. **2.** Browning of the skin by exposure to sun and weather. **3.** *Informal* A beating; a whipping.

tanning bed *n.* A structure lined with sunlamps used to give a suntan to the skin.

Ta·no·an (tä′nō-ən) *n.* An American Indian language family of New Mexico and Arizona. [< Sp. *Tano,* name for the Southern Tewas of NM < Tewa.] —**Ta′no·an** *adj.*

tan·sy (tăn′zē) *n., pl.* **-sies** Any of several Eurasian plants of the genus *Tanacetum,* esp. *T. vulgare,* having buttonlike yellow flower heads and aromatic leaves. [ME < OFr. *tanesie* < VLat. **tanacēta* < LLat. *tanacētum,* wormwood.]

Tan·ta (tän′tä) A city of N Egypt in the Nile R. delta N of Cairo. Pop. 380,000.

tan·tal·ic (tăn-tăl′ĭk) *adj.* Of or containing tantalum.

tan·ta·lite (tăn′tə-līt′) *n.* A black to red-brown mineral, $(Fe,Mn)(Ta,Nb)_2O_6$, distinguished from columbite by the predominance of tantalum over niobium and used as an ore of both elements. [TANTAL(UM) + -ITE[1].]

tan·ta·lize (tăn′tə-līz′) *tr.v.* **-lized, -liz·ing, -liz·es** To excite (another) by exposing something desirable while keeping it out of reach. [< Lat. *Tantalus,* Tantalus. See TANTALUS.] —**tan′ta·li·za′tion** (-lĭ-zā′shən) *n.* —**tan′ta·liz′er** *n.*

tan·ta·lum (tăn′tə-ləm) *n. Symbol* **Ta** A hard heavy metallic element that is exceptionally resistant to chemical attack below 150° C and is used to make electronic components, nuclear reactor parts, and surgical instruments. Atomic number 73; atomic weight 180.948; melting point 2,996°C; boiling point 5,425°C; specific gravity 16.6; valence 2, 3, 4, 5. See table at **element.** [NLat. < Lat. *Tantalus,* Tantalus (< its high resistance to absorbing acids even when immersed in them). See TANTALUS.]

Tan·ta·lus (tăn′tə-ləs) *n. Greek Mythology* A king who was condemned in Hades to stand in water that receded when he tried to drink and under fruit that receded when he reached for it. [Lat. < Gk. *Tantalos.* See **telə-** in App.]

tan·ta·mount (tăn′tə-mount′) *adj.* Equivalent in effect or value: *a request tantamount to a demand.* [< obsolete *tantamount,* an equivalent < AN *tant amunter,* to amount to as much : *tant,* so much, so great (< Lat. *tantum,* neut. of *tantus < tam,* so; see **to-** in App.) + *amunter,* to amount to, var. of OFr. *amonter;* see AMOUNT.]

tan·ta·ra (tăn-tär′ə, -tär′ə) *n.* **1a.** A trumpet or horn fanfare. **b.** A sound like a tantara. **2.** A hunting cry. [Imit.]

tan·tiv·y (tăn-tĭv′ē) *adv.* At full gallop; at top speed. ❖ *n., pl.* **-ies 1.** A hunting cry. **2.** A fast furious gallop; top speed. [?]

tan·tra (tŭn′trə, tăn′-) *n.* Any of a class of Hindu, Buddhist, or Jainist religious literature concerned with powerful ritual acts of body, speech, and mind. [Skt. *tantram,* loom, doctrine. See **ten-** in App.] —**tan′tric** (-trĭk) *adj.* —**tan′trism** (-trĭz′əm) *n.*

tan·trum (tăn′trəm) *n.* A fit of bad temper. [?]

Tan·tung (tän′tŏŏng′) See **Dandong.**

Tan·za·ni·a (tăn′zə-nē′ə) A country of E-central Africa on the Indian Ocean; formed by Tanganyika and Zanzibar in 1964. Official cap. Dodoma; de facto cap. Dar es Salaam. Pop. 28,846,000. —**Tan·za′ni·an** *adj. & n.*

tan·zan·ite (tăn′zə-nīt′) *n.* A transparent variety of zoisite, used as a gem. [After TANZANIA.]

Tao (dou, tou) *n.* **1.** In Taoism, the basic, eternal principle of the universe that transcends reality and is the source of being, nonbeing, and change. **2.** In Confucianism, the right manner of human activity and virtuous conduct. [Chin. (Mandarin) *dào,* way.]

Tao·ism (tou′ĭz′əm, dou′-) *n.* A principal philosophy and system of religion of China based on the teachings of Lao-tzu in the sixth century B.C. that advocates preserving and restoring the Tao in the body and the cosmos. —**Tao′ist** *n.* —**Tao·is′tic** *adj.*

Taos[1] (tous, tä′ōs) *n., pl.* **Taos 1.** A member of a Pueblo people located north-northeast of Santa Fe, New Mexico. **2.** The Tanoan language of the Taos people.

Taos[2] (tous, tä′ōs) A resort town of N NM NNE of Santa Fe. Pop. 4,700.

tap[1] (tăp) *v.* **tapped, tap•ping, taps** —*tr.* **1.** To strike gently with a light blow or blows. **2.** To give a light rap with. **3.** To produce with a succession of light blows: *tap out a rhythm.* **4.** To select, as for membership in an organization. **5a.** To repair (shoe heels or toes) by applying a thin layer of leather or a substitute material. **b.** To attach metal plates to (shoe toes or heels). —*intr.* **1.** To deliver a gentle light blow or blows. **2.** To walk making light clicks. ❖ *n.* **1a.** A gentle blow. **b.** The sound of such a blow. **2a.** A thin layer of leather or a substitute applied to a worn-down shoe heel or toe. **b.** A metal plate attached to the toe or heel of a shoe. **3.** *Linguistics* See **flap** 8. [ME *tappen*, poss. < OFr. *taper.*]

tap[2] (tăp) *n.* **1.** A valve and spout used to regulate delivery of a fluid at the end of a pipe. **2.** A plug for a bunghole; a spigot. **3a.** Liquor drawn from a spigot. **b.** Liquor of a particular brew, cask, or quality. **4.** *Medicine* The removal of fluid from a body cavity. **5.** A tool for cutting an internal screw thread. **6.** A makeshift terminal in an electric circuit. **7.** A wiretap. ❖ *tr.v.* **tapped, tap•ping, taps 1.** To furnish with a spigot or tap. **2.** To pierce in order to draw off liquid. **3.** To draw (liquid) from a vessel or container. **4.** *Medicine* To withdraw fluid from (a body cavity). **5.** To make a connection with or open outlets from. **6a.** To wiretap (a telephone). **b.** To establish an electric connection in (a power line), as to divert current secretly. **7.** To establish access to or a connection with: *tapped a new market for reference books.* **8.** To take advantage of; make use of. **9.** To cut screw threads in (a collar, socket, or other fitting). **10.** *Informal* To ask (a person) for money. ***—phrasal verb:* tap into 1.** To establish a connection with; have access to. **2.** To take advantage of: *tapped into their enthusiasm to improve the school.* ***—idiom:* on tap 1.** Ready to be drawn; in a tapped cask. **2.** Available for immediate use; ready. [ME *tappe* < OE *tæppa.*]

ta•pa[1] (tä′pə, tăp′ə) *n.* **1.** The inner bark of the paper mulberry. **2.** A paperlike cloth made in the South Pacific islands from this bark or similar bark. [Marquesan and Tahitian.]

ta•pa[2] (tä′pä) *n.* Any of various small, often spicy dishes served as appetizers. [Sp., lid, appetizer, of Gmc. orig.]

Ta•pa•jós also **Ta•pa•joz** (tăp′ə-zhôs′, tä′pä-) A river of N Brazil flowing c. 965 km (600 mi) NE to the Amazon R.

tap•as (tŭp′əs) *n.* *Hinduism* Religious austerity. [Skt. *tapaḥ, tapas-*, heat, austerity.]

tap dance *n.* A dance in which the rhythm is sounded out by the clicking taps on the heels and toes of a dancer's shoes. **—tap′-dance′** (tăp′dăns′) *v.* **—tap dancer** *n.*

tape (tāp) *n.* **1.** A narrow strip of strong woven fabric, as that used in sewing or bookbinding. **2.** A continuous narrow, flexible strip of cloth, metal, paper, or plastic, such as adhesive tape or magnetic tape. **3.** A string stretched across the finish line of a racetrack to be broken by the winner. **4a.** A length, reel, or cassette of magnetic tape. **b.** A recording made on magnetic tape. **5.** A tape measure. ❖ *v.* **taped, tap•ing, tapes** —*tr.* **1a.** To fasten, secure, strengthen, or wrap with a tape. **b.** To bind together (book sections) by applying strips of tape to. **2.** To measure with a tape measure. **3.** To record (sounds or pictures) on magnetic tape. —*intr.* To make a recording on magnetic tape. [ME < OE *tæppe.*] **—tape′a•ble** *adj.*

tape deck *n.* A tape recorder and player having no built-in amplifiers or speakers, used as an audio system component.

tape grass *n.* See **eelgrass.**

tape•line (tāp′līn′) *n.* See **tape measure.**

tape measure *n.* A tape of cloth, paper, or steel marked off in a linear scale, as of inches, for taking measurements.

ta•pe•nade (tä′pə-näd′) *n.* A spread of Provençal origin made of puréed black olives, capers, and anchovies. [Fr. < Provençal *tapéno*, capers.]

ta•per (tā′pər) *n.* **1.** A small or very slender candle. **2.** A long waxcoated wick used to light candles or gas lamps. **3.** A source of feeble light. **4a.** A gradual decrease in thickness or width of an elongated object. **b.** A gradual decrease, as in action or force. ❖ *v.* **-pered, -per•ing, -pers** —*intr.* **1.** To become gradually narrower or thinner toward one end. **2.** To diminish or lessen gradually. Often used with *off.* —*tr.* **1.** To make thinner or narrower at one end. **2.** To make smaller gradually. ❖ *adj.* Gradually decreasing in size toward a point. [ME < OE *tapor*, poss. ult. < Lat. *papyrus*, papyrus (sometimes used for candlewicks). See PAPER.]

tape-re•cord (tāp′rĭ-kôrd′) *tr.v.* **-cord•ed, -cord•ing, -cords** To record on magnetic tape.

tape recorder *n.* A mechanical device for recording on magnetic tape and usu. for playing back the recorded material.

tape recording *n.* **1a.** A magnetic tape on which sound or visual images have been recorded. **b.** The material recorded on a magnetic tape. **2.** The act of recording on magnetic tape.

tap•es•try (tăp′ĭ-strē) *n., pl.* **-tries 1.** A heavy cloth woven with rich, often varicolored designs or scenes, usu. hung on walls for decoration and sometimes used to cover furniture. **2.** Something felt to resemble a tapestry. ❖ *tr.v.* **-es•tried** (-ĭ-strēd), **-es•try•ing, -es•tries** (-ĭ-strēz) **1.** To hang or decorate with tapestry. **2.** To make, weave, or depict in a tapestry. [ME *tapiceri, tapstri* < OFr. *tapisserie* < *tapisser*, to cover with carpet < *tapis*, carpet < Gk. *tapētion*, dim. of *tapēs*, perh. of Iran. orig.]

ta•pe•tum (tə-pē′təm) *n., pl.* **-ta** (-tə) **1.** *Botany* A nutritive tissue within the sporangium, particularly within an anther. **2.** *Anatomy* **a.** A membranous layer or region, esp. the iridescent membrane of the choroid of certain mammals. **b.** A layer of fibers of the corpus callosum. [Med.Lat. *tapētum*, coverlet < Lat. *tapēte*, **tapētum* < Gk. *tapēs, tapēt-*. See TAPESTRY.]

tape•worm (tāp′wûrm′) *n.* Any of various ribbonlike, often very long flatworms of the class Cestoda, parasitic in the intestines of vertebrates, including humans.

ta•phon•o•my (tə-fŏn′ə-mē) *n.* **1.** The study of the conditions and processes of fossilization. **2.** The conditions and processes of fossilization. [Gk. *taphē*, grave + -NOMY.]

tap house *n.* A tavern or bar.

tap•i•o•ca (tăp′ē-ō′kə) *n.* A beady starch obtained from the root of the cassava, used for puddings and as a thickener in cooking. [Port. < Tupi *typióca* : *ty*, juice + *pyá*, heart + *oca*, to remove.]

ta•pir (tā′pər, tə-pîr′) *n.* Any of several large, chiefly nocturnal ungulates of the genus *Tapirus* of tropical areas, having a heavy body, short legs, and a long fleshy flexible upper lip. [Perh. Fr., ult. < Tupi *tapiira*, tapir.]

tapir
Baird's tapir
Tapirus bairdii

tap•is (tăp′ē, tăp′ĭs, tă-pē′) *n.* *Obsolete* Tapestry or comparable material used for draperies, carpeting, and furniture covering. ***—idiom:* on the tapis** Under consideration. [ME < OFr. See TAPESTRY.]

tap•per (tăp′ər) *n.* One that taps.

tap•pet (tăp′ĭt) *n.* A lever or projecting arm that moves or is moved by contact with another part, usu. to transmit a certain motion. [Prob. < TAP[1].]

tap•ping (tăp′ĭng) *n.* **1a.** The act of one that taps. **b.** The process or means by which something is tapped. **2.** Something that is taken or drawn by tapping.

tap•pit-hen (tăp′ĭt-hĕn′) *n.* *Scots* **1.** A crested hen. **2.** A large mug with a knobbed lid. [Sc. *tappit*, crested (var. of *topped*, p. part. of TOP[1]) + HEN.]

tap•room (tăp′ro͞om′, -ro͝om′) *n.* A bar or barroom.

tap•root (tăp′ro͞ot′, -ro͝ot′) *n.* The main root of a plant, usu. growing straight downward from the stem.

taps (tăps) *pl.n.* *(used with a sing. or pl. verb)* A bugle call or drum signal sounded at night as an order to put out lights, as at a military camp, and also sounded at military funerals. [Perh. alteration of *taptoo*, tattoo, var. of TATTOO[1].]

tarantula

tap•ster (tăp′stər) *n.* One who draws and serves liquor for customers; a bartender.

ta•que•ri•a (tä′kə-rē′ə) *n.* A place where tacos, burritos, and other Mexican dishes are made and sold. [Am.Sp. *taquería* < *taco*, taco. See TACO.]

tar[1] (tär) *n.* **1.** A dark oily viscous material, consisting mainly of hydrocarbons, produced by the destructive distillation of organic substances such as wood, coal, or peat. **2.** Coal tar. **3.** A solid residue of tobacco smoke containing byproducts of combustion. ❖ *tr.v.* **tarred, tar•ring, tars** To coat with or as if with tar. ***—idiom:* tar and feather 1.** To punish (a person) by covering with tar and feathers. **2.** To criticize severely and devastatingly; excoriate. [ME < OE *teru.* See **deru-** in App.]

tar[2] (tär) *n.* *Informal* A sailor. [Poss. short for TARPAULIN.]

tar•a•did•dle (tăr′ə-dĭd′l) *n.* Variant of **tarradiddle.**

Ta•ra•hu•ma•ra (tär′ə-ho͞o-mär′ə, tăr′-) *n., pl.* **Tarahumara** or **-ras 1.** A member of a Native American people of north-central Mexico. **2.** Their Uto-Aztecan language. [Am.Sp. < alteration of Tarahumara *Rarámuri*, the people, Tarahumara.]

Ida Tarbell

tar•an•tel•la (tăr′ən-tĕl′ə) *n.* **1.** A lively whirling Italian dance. **2.** Its music, in 6/8 time. [Ital., after TARANTO.]

tar•an•tism (tăr′ən-tĭz′əm) *n.* A disorder marked by an uncontrollable urge to dance, esp. prevalent in Italy from the 15th to the 17th century. [NLat. *tarantismus*, after TARANTO.]

Ta•ran•to (tär′ən-tō′, tə-răn′tō, tä′rän-tō′) A city of SE Italy ESE of Naples on the **Gulf of Taranto,** an arm of the Ionian Sea; founded in the 8th cent. B.C. Pop. 232,200.

ta•ran•tu•la (tə-răn′chə-lə) *n., pl.* **-las** or **-lae** (-lē′) **1.** Any of various large, hairy, chiefly tropical spiders of the family Theraphosidae, capable of inflicting a painful but not seriously poisonous bite. **2.** A large wolf spider *(Lycosa tarentula)* of southern Europe, once thought to cause tarantism. [Med.Lat. < OItal. *tarantola*, after TARANTO.]

Ta•ras•can (tə-răs′kən) also **Ta•ras•co** (-răs′kō) *n., pl.* **-cans** also **Tarasco** or **-cos 1a.** A member of a Mesoamerican Indian people of southwest Mexico whose civilization was at its height from the 14th century until the Spanish conquest. **b.** A descendant of this people. **2.** The language of the Tarascans, of no known linguistic affiliation.

Ta•ra•wa (tə-rä′wə, tăr′ə-wä′, tä′rä-) The cap. of Kiribati, an island group of the W Pacific Ocean.

tar baby *n.* A situation or problem from which it is virtually impossible to disentangle oneself. [After "Bre'r Rabbit and the *Tar Baby*," an Uncle Remus story by Joel Chandler Harris.]

Tar•bell (tär′bəl), **Ida Minerva** 1857–1944. Amer. writer and editor noted for her muckraking investigations of industry.

tar•boosh also **tar•bush** (tär-bo͞osh′) *n.* A brimless, usu. red felt cap with a silk tassel, worn by some Middle Eastern Muslim men either by itself or as the base of a turban. [Egypt. Ar. *ṭarbūš*

ă	pat	oi	boy
ā	pay	ou	out
âr	care	o͝o	took
ä	father	o͞o	boot
ĕ	pet	ŭ	cut
ē	be	ûr	urge
ĭ	pit	th	thin
ī	pie	*th*	this
îr	pier	hw	which
ŏ	pot	zh	vision
ō	toe	ə	about, item
ô	paw		

Stress marks:
′ (primary);
′ (secondary), as in
lexicon (lĕk′sĭ-kŏn′)

< Turk. *terposh*, prob. < Pers. *sarpūsh*, headdress : *sar*, head; see *ker-*[1] in App. + *pūsh*, to don.]

tar camphor *n.* See **naphthalene.**

tar·di·grade (tär′dĭ-grād′) *n.* Any of various slow-moving microscopic invertebrates of the phylum Tardigrada related to the arthropods and living in water or damp moss. ❖ *adj.* **1.** Of or belonging to the Tardigrada. **2.** Slow in action; slow-moving. [NLat. *Tardigrada*, phylum name < neut. pl. of Lat. *tardigradus*, slow-moving : *tardus*, slow + *-gradus*, walking (< *gradī*, to go; see TRANSGRESS). Sense 2 < Lat. *tardigradus.*]

tar·dive (tär′dĭv) *adj.* Having symptoms that develop slowly or appear long after inception. Used of a disease. [Fr., fem. of *tardif* < OFr., slow. See TARDY.]

tardive dyskinesia *n.* A chronic disorder of the nervous system characterized by involuntary jerky movements, usu. caused by prolonged treatment with antipsychotic drugs.

tar·dy (tär′dē) *adj.* **-di·er, -di·est 1.** Occurring, arriving, acting, or done after the scheduled, expected, or usual time; late. **2.** Moving slowly; sluggish. [Alteration of ME *tardive*, slow, ult. < Lat. *tardus.*] —**tar′di·ly** *adv.* —**tar′di·ness** *n.*

tare[1] (târ) *n.* **1.** Any of various weedy plants of the genus *Vicia*, esp. the common vetch. **2.** Any of several weedy plants that grow in grain fields. **3. tares** An unwelcome or objectionable element. [ME.]

tare[2] (târ) *n.* **1.** The weight of a container or wrapper deducted from the gross weight to obtain net weight. **2.** A deduction from gross weight to allow for the weight of a container. **3.** *Chemistry* A counterbalance, esp. an empty vessel counterbalancing the weight of a similar container. ❖ *tr.v.* **tared, tar·ing, tares** To determine or indicate the tare of. [ME < OFr., ult. < Ar. *ṭarḥ*, rejection, subtraction < *ṭaraḥa*, to throw away.]

targe (tärj) *n. Archaic* A light shield or buckler. [ME < OFr. See TARGET.]

tar·get (tär′gĭt) *n.* **1a.** An object that is shot at to test accuracy in rifle or archery practice. **b.** Something aimed or fired at. **2.** An object of criticism or attack. **3.** One to be influenced or changed by an action or event. **4.** A desired goal. **5.** A railroad signal that indicates the position of a switch by its color, position, and shape. **6.** The sliding sight on a surveyor's leveling rod. **7.** A small round shield. **8a.** A structure in a television camera tube with a storage surface that is scanned by an electron beam to generate a signal output current similar to the charge-density pattern stored on the surface. **b.** A usu. metal part in an x-ray tube on which a beam of electrons is focused and from which x-rays are emitted. ❖ *tr.v.* **-get·ed, -get·ing, -gets 1.** To make a target of. **2.** To aim at or for. **3.** To establish as a target or goal. —*idiom:* **on target** Completely accurate, precise, or valid: *observations that were right on target.* [ME, small targe < OFr. *targuete*, var. of *targete*, dim. of *targe*, light shield, of Gmc. orig.] —**tar′get·a·ble** *adj.*

target date *n.* A date established as a target or goal.

target language *n.* **1.** The language into which a text written in another language is to be translated. **2.** A language that a nonnative speaker is in the process of learning.

Tar·gum (tär′gŏŏm′, -gŏŏm′) *n.* Any of several Aramaic explanatory translations or paraphrasings of the Hebrew Scriptures. [Mishnaic Heb. *targûm* < Aram. *targamā*, back-formation < *tarǝmānā*, interpreter. See DRAGOMAN.]

Tar Heel or **Tar·heel** (tär′hēl′) *n.* A native or resident of North Carolina. [Perh. from tar once being a major product.]

tar·iff (tăr′ĭf) *n.* **1a.** A list or system of duties imposed by a government on imported or exported goods. **b.** A duty or duties so imposed. **2.** A schedule of prices or fees. ❖ *tr.v.* **-iffed, -iff·ing, -iffs** To fix a duty or price on. [Ital. *tariffa* < OItal. < Ar. *ta'rīf*, notification, infinitive of *'arrafa*, to announce, derived stem of *'arafa*, to know.]

Ta·rim He (tä′rĕm′ hŭ′) A river of W China flowing c. 2,092 km (1,300 mi) E to Lop Nur.

Tarim Pen·di (pŭn′dē′) An arid basin of W China S of the Tian Shan and traversed by the Tarim He.

Tar·king·ton (tär′kĭng′tǝn), **(Newton) Booth** 1869–1946. Amer. writer whose novels include *Alice Adams* (1921).

tar·la·tan also **tar·le·tan** (tär′lǝ-tǝn, -lǝ-tn) *n.* A thin, stiffly starched muslin in open plain weave. [Fr. *tarlatane*, alteration of earlier *tarnatane.*]

tar·mac (tär′măk′) *n.* A tarmacadam road or surface, esp. an airport runway. ❖ *v.* **-macked, -mack·ing, -macs** —*tr.* To cause (an aircraft) to sit on a taxiway. —*intr.* To sit on a taxiway. Used of an aircraft. [Orig. a trademark.]

tar·mac·ad·am (tär′mǝ-kăd′ǝm) *n.* A pavement consisting of layers of crushed stone with a tar binder pressed to a smooth surface.

tarn (tärn) *n.* A small mountain lake, esp. one formed by glaciers. [ME *tarne*, of Scand. orig.]

Tarn A river of S France flowing c. 378 km (235 mi) generally W and SW to the Garonne R.

tar·nal (tär′nǝl) *adj. & adv. Chiefly New England & Upper Southern US* Damned. See Regional Note at **tarnation.** [Alteration of ETERNAL.] —**tar′nal·ly** *adv.*

tar·na·tion (tär-nā′shǝn) *New England & Southern US n.* The act of damning or the condition of being damned. ❖ *interj.* Used to express anger or annoyance. [TARN(AL) + (DAMN)ATION.]

The noun and interjection *tarnation* illustrate the addition of a suffix to a word. *Tarnation* and *darnation* are both euphemistic forms of *damnation*. *Tarnation* seems to have been influenced by *tarnal*, another mild oath derived from *(e)ternal!*

tar·nish (tär′nĭsh) *v.* **-nished, -nish·ing, -nish·es** —*tr.* **1.** To dull the luster of; discolor, esp. by exposure to air or dirt. **2a.** To detract from or spoil; taint. **b.** To cast aspersions on; sully. —*intr.* **1.** To lose luster; become discolored. **2.** To diminish or become tainted. ❖ *n.* **1.** The condition of being tarnished. **2.** Discoloration of a metal surface caused by corrosion or oxidation. **3.** The condition of being sullied or tainted. [ME *ternisshen* < OFr. *ternir, ternis-*, to dull < *terne*, dull, of Gmc. orig.] —**tar′nish·a·ble** *adj.*

Tar·nów (tär′nŏŏf′) A city of SE Poland E of Cracow; a cultural center in the 15th and 16th cent. Pop. 121,582.

ta·ro (tä′rō, tăr′ō) *n., pl.* **-ros 1a.** A widely cultivated tropical Asian plant (*Colocasia esculenta*) having broad peltate leaves and a large, starchy edible tuber. **b.** The tuber of this plant. **2a.** A similar plant of the genus *Xanthosoma*. **b.** The large starchy tuber of this plant. [Prob. Tahitian.]

tar·ok also **tar·oc** (tär′ǝk) *n.* A card game developed in Italy in the 14th century, played with a 78-card pack consisting of four suits plus the 22 tarot cards as trumps. [Ital. *tarocchi*, pl. of *tarocco*, tarot.]

tar·ot (tăr′ō, tǝ-rō′) *n.* **1a.** Any of a set of usu. 78 playing cards including 22 cards depicting vices, virtues, and elemental forces, used in fortunetelling. **b.** Any of these 22 pictorial cards used as trump in tarok. **2. tarots** Tarok. [Fr. < Ital. *tarocco.*]

tarp (tärp) *n. Informal* A tarpaulin.

tar·pa·per (tär′pā′pǝr) *n.* Heavy paper impregnated or coated with tar, used as a waterproof material in building.

tar·pau·lin (tär-pô′lĭn, tär′pǝ-) *n.* **1.** Material, such as waterproofed canvas, used to cover and protect things from moisture. **2.** A sheet of this material. [Prob. alteration of TAR[1] + PALL[1] + —ING[2].]

tar pit *n.* An accumulation of natural tar or asphalt at the earth's surface, esp. one that traps animals and preserves their bones.

tar·pon (tär′pǝn) *n., pl.* **tarpon** or **-pons** Any of several fishes of the family Elopidae or Megalopidae, esp. a large silvery game fish (*Megalops atlanticus*) of Atlantic coastal waters. [?]

tar·ra·did·dle also **tar·a·did·dle** (tär′ǝ-dĭd′l) *n.* **1.** A petty falsehood; a fib. **2.** Silly pretentious language; twaddle. [?]

tar·ra·gon (tăr′ǝ-gŏn′, -gǝn) *n.* An aromatic Eurasian herb (*Artemisia dracunculus*) having linear to lance-shaped leaves and small whitish-green flower heads arranged in loose, spreading panicles. [NLat. *tarchon* < Med.Gk. *tarkhōn* < Ar. *ṭarḥūn*, perh. < Gk. *drakōn*, dragon, tarragon.]

Tar·ra·sa (tǝ-rä′sǝ, tä-rä′sä) A city of NE Spain NNW of Barcelona; founded in Roman times. Pop. 158,063.

tar·ri·ance (tăr′ē-ǝns) *n. Archaic* **1.** The act of tarrying. **2.** A temporary stay; a sojourn.

Tar River A river of NE NC flowing c. 346 km (215 mi) to an estuary of Pamlico Sound.

tar·ry[1] (tăr′ē) *v.* **-ried, -ry·ing, -ries** —*intr.* **1.** To delay or be late in going, coming, or doing. See Syns at **stay**[1]. **2.** To wait. **3.** To remain or stay temporarily, as in a place; sojourn. —*tr. Archaic* To wait for. ❖ *n.* A temporary stay. [ME *tarien.*] —**tar′ri·er** *n.*

tar·ry[2] (tär′ē) *adj.* **-ri·er, -ri·est** Of, resembling, or covered with tar.

tar·sal (tär′sǝl) *adj.* **1.** Of, relating to, or situated near the tarsus of the foot or eyelid. **2.** Of or relating to the tarsus of the eyelid. [NLat. *tarsālis* < *tarsus*, tarsus. See TARSUS.]

tarsal plate *n.* See **tarsus** 2.

tar·si·er (tär′sē-ǝr, -sē-ā′) *n.* Any of several small nocturnal arboreal primates of the genus *Tarsius* of the East Indies and the Philippines, having large round eyes, a long tail, and long digits tipped with soft disklike pads. [Fr. < *tarse*, tarsus (< its elongated ankles) < NLat. *tarsus.* See TARSUS.]

tar·so·met·a·tar·sus (tär′sō-mĕt′ǝ-tär′sǝs) *n., pl.* **-si** (-sī, -sē) A compound bone between the tibia and the toes of a bird's leg. —**tar′so·met′a·tar′sal** (-sǝl) *adj.*

tar·sus (tär′sǝs) *n., pl.* **-si** (-sī, -sē) **1a.** The section of the vertebrate foot between the leg and the metatarsus. **b.** The bones making up this section, esp. the seven small bones of the human ankle. **2.** A fibrous plate that supports and shapes the edge of the eyelid. **3.** *Zoology* **a.** The tarsometatarsus. **b.** The distal part of the leg of an arthropod. [NLat. < Gk. *tarsos*, ankle. See *ters-* in App.]

Tarsus A city of S Turkey near the Mediterranean Sea W of Adana. Pop. 225,000.

tart[1] (tärt) *adj.* **tart·er, tart·est 1.** Having a sharp pungent taste; sour. **2.** Sharp or bitter in tone or meaning; cutting. [ME < OE *teart*, severe.] —**tart′ly** *adv.* —**tart′ness** *n.*

tart[2] (tärt) *n.* **1a.** A pastry shell with shallow sides, no top crust, and any of various fillings. **b.** *Chiefly British* A pie. **2a.** A prostitute. **b.** A woman considered sexually promiscuous. ❖ *tr.v.* **tart·ed, tart·ing, tarts** *Chiefly British* To dress up or make fancy in a tawdry, garish way. Often used with *up.* [ME *tarte* < OFr., perh. alteration of *tartane* < LLat. *torta*, a bread.]

tar·tan[1] (tär′tn) *n.* **1a.** Any of numerous textile patterns consist-

---

tarot
selection of tarot cards

tarsier
Philippine tarsier
Tarsius syrichta

ing of stripes of varying widths and colors crossed at right angles against a solid background, each forming a distinctive design worn by the members of a Scottish clan. **b.** A twilled wool fabric or garment having such a pattern. **2.** A plaid fabric. [ME *tartane*, poss. < OFr. *tiretaine*, linsey-woolsey, prob. < *tire*, a kind of cloth < *tire*, silk cloth < Lat. *Tyrius*, Tyrian (cloth) < *Tyrus*, Tyre.] —**tar′tan** *adj.*

tar•tan² (tär′tn, tär-tăn′) *n.* A small single-masted Mediterranean ship with a large lateen sail. [Fr. *tartane* < Provençal *tartano* < O Provençal *tartana*, buzzard, of imit. orig.]

tar•tar (tär′tər) *n.* **1.** *Dentistry* A hard yellowish deposit on the teeth, consisting of organic secretions and food particles deposited in various salts. **2.** A reddish acid compound, chiefly potassium bitartrate, in the juice of grapes, deposited on casks during winemaking. [ME *tartre*, potassium bitartrate < OFr. < Med.Lat. *tartarum*, argol < Med.Gk. *tartaron*.]

Tar•tar (tär′tər) *n.* **1.** also **Ta•tar** (tä′tər) A member of any of the Turkic and Mongolian peoples of central Asia who invaded western Asia and eastern Europe in the Middle Ages. **2.** Variant of **Tatar** 1, 2. **3.** often **tartar** A ferocious or violent person. [ME *Tartre* < OFr. *Tartare* < Med.Lat. *Tartarus*, alteration (influenced by Lat. *Tartarus*, Tartarus) of Pers. *Tātār*, Tatar, of Turkic orig.]

tartar emetic *n.* A poisonous crystalline compound, $K(SbO)C_4H_4O_6 \cdot \frac{1}{2}H_2O$, used in medicine as an expectorant and in the treatment of parasitic infections, such as schistosomiasis.

tar•tare steak (tär-tär′, tär′tär′) *n.* See **steak tartare**.

tar•tar•ic (tär-tăr′ĭk) *adj.* Of, relating to, or derived from tartar or tartaric acid.

tartaric acid *n.* Any of four isomeric crystalline organic compounds, $C_4H_6O_6$, used to make cream of tartar and baking powder, as a sequestrant, and in effervescent beverages and photographic chemicals.

tar•tar•ous (tär′tər-əs) *adj.* Consisting of, derived from, or containing tartar.

tartar sauce *n.* Mayonnaise mixed with chopped onion, olives, pickles, and capers and served as a sauce with fish. [Transl. of Fr. *sauce tartare* : *sauce*, sauce + *tartare*, Tartar.]

Tar•ta•rus (tär′tər-əs) *n.* **1.** *Greek Mythology* The regions below Hades where the Titans were confined. **2.** An infernal region. [Lat. < Gk. *Tartaros*.] —**Tar•tar′e•an** (-tär′ē-ən) *adj.*

Tar•ta•ry (tär′tə-rē) or **Ta•ta•ry** (tä′-) A vast region of E Europe and W Asia controlled by the Mongols in the 13th and 14th cent.

tart•let (tärt′lĭt) *n.* A small pastry tart.

tar•trate (tär′trāt′) *n.* A salt or ester of tartaric acid.

tar•trat•ed (tär′trā′tĭd) *adj.* Containing, combined with, or derived from tartaric acid.

tar•tuffe also **tar•tufe** (tär-tŏŏf′, -tŏŏf′) *n.* A hypocrite, esp. one who affects religious piety. [After the protagonist of *Tartuffe*, a play by Molière.] —**tar•tuff′fe•ry** *n.*

tart•y (tär′tē) *adj.* -**i•er**, -**i•est** Of, relating to, or suggestive of a prostitute. —**tart′i•ly** *adv.* —**tart′i•ness** *n.*

tar•weed (tär′wēd′) *n.* **1.** Any of several resinous western American and Chilean plants of the genus *Madia*, having rayed yellow flower heads. **2.** Any of several similar plants.

Ta•ser (tā′zər) A trademark used for a high-voltage stun gun.

Tash•kent (täsh-kĕnt′, täsh-) The cap. of Uzbekistan, in the NE part near the Kazakhstan border. Pop. 2,094,000.

task (tăsk) *n.* **1.** A piece of work assigned or done as part of one's duties. **2.** A difficult or tedious undertaking. **3.** A function to be performed; an objective. ❖ *tr.v.* **tasked, task•ing, tasks 1.** To assign a task to or impose a task on. **2.** To overburden with labor; tax. —*idiom:* **take** (or **call** or **bring**) **to task** To reprimand or censure. [ME *taske*, imposed work, tax < ONFr. *tasque* < VLat. *tasca*, alteration of *taxa* < Lat. *taxāre*, to feel, reproach, reckon. See TAX.]

task•bar (tăsk′bär′) *n.* A row of buttons or graphical controls on a computer screen that allow the user to select any of a number of open programs by clicking on the appropriate one.

task force *n.* **1.** A temporary grouping of military units or forces under one commander for a specific operation or assignment. **2.** A temporary grouping of individuals and resources for a specific objective.

task•mas•ter (tăsk′măs′tər) *n.* **1.** One who imposes tasks, esp. burdensome or laborious ones. **2.** A source of burden or responsibility.

task•mis•tress (tăsk′mĭs′trĭs) *n.* A woman who imposes tasks, esp. burdensome or laborious ones.

Tas•man (tăz′mən), Abel Janszoon 1603?–59. Dutch navigator who was the first European to sight Tasmania and New Zealand (1642).

Tas•ma•ni•a (tăz-mā′nē-ə, -mān′yə) Formerly **Van Die•men's**

Land (văn dē′mənz, văn) An island state of SE Australia separated from the mainland by Bass Strait. —**Tas•ma′ni•an** *adj.* & *n.*

Tasmanian devil *n.* A burrowing nocturnal carnivorous marsupial (*Sarcophilus harrisii*) of Tasmania having a predominantly blackish coat and a long, almost hairless tail.

Tasmanian tiger *n.* See **Tasmanian wolf**.

Tasmanian wolf *n.* A large wolflike carnivorous marsupial (*Thylacinus cynocephalus*) of Tasmania, believed to be extinct, having a pointed head and dark stripes across its back.

Tasman Sea An arm of the S Pacific between SE Australia and W New Zealand.

tasse (tăs) also **tas•set** (tăs′ĭt) *n.* One of a series of jointed overlapping metal splints hanging from a corselet, used as armor for the lower trunk and thighs. [Poss. Fr., pouch < OFr., perh. ult. < VLat. *tasca*, task, money pouch. See TASK.]

tas•sel (tăs′əl) *n.* **1.** A bunch of loose threads or cords bound at one end and hanging free at the other, used as an ornament. **2.** Something that resembles such an ornament, esp. the pollen-bearing inflorescence of a corn plant. ❖ *v.* -**seled, -sel•ing, -sels** or -**selled, -sel•ling, -sels** —*tr.* To fringe or decorate with tassels. —*intr.* To put forth a tassellike inflorescence. Used esp. of corn. [ME < OFr., fastening, clasp < VLat. *tassellus*, blend of Lat. *tessella*, small die; see TESSELLATE, and *taxillus*, dim. of *tālus*, knucklebone, ankle.]

Tas•so (tăs′ō, tä′sō), **Torquato** 1544–95. Italian poet known for the epic *Jerusalem Delivered* (1581).

taste (tāst) *v.* **tast•ed, tast•ing, tastes** —*tr.* **1.** To distinguish the flavor of by taking into the mouth. **2.** To eat or drink a small quantity of. **3.** To partake of, esp. for the first time; experience. **4.** To perceive as if by the sense of taste. **5.** *Archaic* To appreciate or enjoy. —*intr.* **1.** To distinguish flavors in the mouth. **2.** To have a distinct flavor. **3.** To eat or drink a small amount. **4.** To have experience or enjoyment; partake. ❖ *n.* **1a.** The sense that distinguishes the sweet, sour, salty, and bitter qualities of dissolved substances in contact with the taste buds on the tongue. **b.** This sense in combination with the senses of smell and touch, which together receive a sensation of a substance in the mouth. **2a.** The sensation of sweet, sour, salty, or bitter qualities produced by or as if by a substance placed in the mouth. **b.** The unified sensation produced by any of these qualities plus a distinct smell and texture; flavor. **c.** A distinctive perception as if by the sense of taste. **3.** The act of tasting. **4.** A small quantity eaten or tasted. **5.** A limited or first experience; a sample. **6.** A personal preference or liking. **7a.** The faculty of discerning what is aesthetically excellent or appropriate. **b.** A manner indicative of the quality of such discernment. **8a.** The sense of what is proper, seemly, or least likely to give offense in a given social situation. **b.** A manner indicative of the quality of this sense. **9.** *Obsolete* The act of testing; trial. [ME *tasten*, to touch, taste < OFr. *taster* < VLat. *tastāre*, prob. alteration of Lat. *taxāre*, prob. freq. of *tangere*, to touch. See tag- in App.] —**tast′a•ble** *adj.*

taste bud *n.* Any of numerous spherical or ovoid clusters of receptor cells found mainly in the epithelium of the tongue and constituting the end organs of the sense of taste.

taste•ful (tāst′fəl) *adj.* **1.** Having, showing, or being in keeping with good taste. **2.** Pleasing in flavor; tasty. —**taste′ful•ly** *adv.* —**taste′ful•ness** *n.*

taste•less (tāst′lĭs) *adj.* **1.** Lacking flavor; insipid. **2.** Not having or showing good taste. —**taste′less•ly** *adv.* —**taste′less•ness** *n.*

taste•mak•er (tāst′mā′kər) *n.* One that determines or strongly influences current trends or styles, as in fashion.

tast•er (tā′stər) *n.* **1.** One that tastes, esp. one who samples a food or beverage for quality. **2.** Any of several devices or implements used in tasting.

tast•y (tā′stē) *adj.* -**i•er**, -**i•est** **1.** Having a pleasing flavor; savory. **2.** Having or showing good taste; tasteful. —**tast′i•ly** *adv.* —**tast′i•ness** *n.*

tat¹ (tăt) *intr. & tr.v.* **tat•ted, tat•ting, tats** To do tatting or make (lace) by tatting. [Prob. back-formation < TATTING.]

tat² also **TAT** (tăt) *n.* A gene in the HIV virus that stimulates the host cell to replicate genetic components of the virus. [*t*(*rans*)*a*(*c*)*t*(*ivator*) (*gene*).]

TAT *abbr.* Thematic Apperception Test

ta•ta•mi (tä-tä′mē, tə-) *n., pl.* **tatami** or -**mis** Straw matting used as a floor covering esp. in a Japanese house. [J.]

Ta•tar (tä′tər) *n.* **1.** also **Tar•tar** (tär′tər) A member of a group of Turkic peoples primarily inhabiting Tatarstan in west-central Russia and parts of Siberia and Central Asia. **2.** Any of their Turkic languages. **3.** Variant of **Tartar** 1. **4.** tatar A ferocious or violent person; a tartar.

Ta•tar•stan (tä′tər-stăn′) An autonomous republic of west-central Russia; a constituent republic of the USSR from 1920 to 1991.

Ta•ta•ry (tä′tə-rē) See **Tartary**.

Tate (tāt), **Allen** 1899–1979. Amer. writer and leading exponent of New Criticism known esp. for his poetry.

Tate, Nahum 1652–1715. English poet and playwright who was appointed poet laureate in 1692.

ta•ter (tā′tər) *n. Upper Southern US* Variant of **potato**. See Regional Notes at **holler²**, **possum**.

Tasmanian devil
Sarcophilus harrisii

tatami

ă pat	oi	boy
ā pay	ou	out
âr care	ŏŏ	took
ä father	ŏŏ	boot
ĕ pet	ŭ	cut
ē be	ûr	urge
ĭ pit	th	thin
ī pie	th	this
îr pier	hw	which
ŏ pot	zh	vision
ō toe	ə	about,
ô paw		item

Stress marks:
′ (primary);
′ (secondary), as in
lexicon (lĕk′sĭ-kŏn′)

Ta·tra Mountains (tä′trə) A range of the Carpathian Mts. in E-central Europe along the Slovak-Polish border.

tat·ter[1] (tăt′ər) n. **1.** A torn and hanging piece of cloth; a shred. **2. tatters** Torn and ragged clothing; rags. ❖ tr. & intr.v. **-tered, -ter·ing, -ters** To make or become ragged. [ME tater, of Scand. orig.]

tat·ter[2] (tăt′ər) n. One that makes tatting.

tat·ter·de·mal·ion (tăt′ər-dĭ-māl′yən, -mā′lē-ən) n. A person wearing ragged or tattered clothing; a ragamuffin. ❖ adj. Ragged; tattered. [Prob. TATTERED + -demalion, of unknown meaning.]

tat·tered (tăt′ərd) adj. **1.** Torn into shreds; ragged. **2.** Having ragged clothes; dressed in tatters. **3a.** Shabby or dilapidated. **b.** Disordered or disrupted.

tat·ter·sall also **Tat·ter·sall** (tăt′ər-sôl′, -səl) n. **1.** A pattern of dark lines forming squares on a light background. **2.** Cloth having this pattern. ❖ adj. Having such a pattern. [After Tattersall's horse market in London, England, after Richard Tattersall (1724–95), British auctioneer.]

tat·ting (tăt′ĭng) n. **1.** Handmade lace fashioned by looping and knotting a single strand of heavy-duty thread on a small hand shuttle. **2.** The act or art of making such lace. [?]

tat·tle (tăt′l) v. **-tled, -tling, -tles** —intr. **1.** To reveal the plans or activities of another; gossip. **2.** To chatter aimlessly; prate. —tr. To reveal through gossiping. ❖ n. **1.** Aimless chatter; prattle. **2.** Gossip; talebearing. **3.** A tattletale. [ME tatelen, to stammer, prob. < MDu., of imit. orig.]

tat·tler (tăt′lər) n. **1.** One who tattles. **2.** Any of several shore birds related to and resembling the sandpipers, esp. one of the genus Heteroscelus that is noted for its loud cry.

tat·tle·tale (tăt′l-tāl′) n. One who tattles on others; an informer or talebearer. ❖ adj. Revealing; telltale.

tattletale gray n. Grayish white.

tat·too[1] (tă-tōō′) n., pl. **-toos 1.** A signal sounded on a drum or bugle to summon soldiers or sailors to their quarters at night. **2.** A display of military exercises offered as evening entertainment. **3.** A continuous even drumming or rapping. ❖ v. **-tooed, -too·ing, -toos** —intr. To beat out an even rhythm, as with the fingers. —tr. To beat or tap rhythmically on. [Alteration of Du. taptoe, tap-shut (closing time for taverns), tattoo : tap, spigot, tap (< MDu. tappe) + toe, shut (< MDu.; see **de-** in App.).]

tat·too[2] (tă-tōō′) n., pl. **-toos 1.** A permanent mark made on the skin by pricking and ingraining an indelible pigment or by raising scars. **2.** A design made on the skin with a temporary dye such as henna or ink. ❖ tr.v. **-tooed, -too·ing, -toos 1.** To mark (the skin) thus. **2.** To form (a tattoo) on the skin. [Of Polynesian orig.] —tat·too′er n. —tat·too′ist n.

tat·ty (tăt′ē) adj. **-ti·er, -ti·est** Somewhat worn, shabby, or dilapidated. [Prob. < tat, a rag, shabby person.]

Ta·tum (tā′təm) **Arthur ("Art")** 1910–56. Amer. jazz pianist noted for his harmonic and rhythmic innovations.

Tatum, Edward Lawrie 1909–75. Amer. biochemist who shared a 1958 Nobel Prize.

Ta·tung (tä′tŏŏng′) See **Datong.**

tau (tou, tô) n. **1.** The 19th letter of the Greek alphabet. **2.** A negatively charged elementary particle of the lepton family, having a mass about 3,550 times that of the electron. [Gk. < Phoenician *taww, mark, 22nd letter of the Phoenician alphabet.]

tau cross n. A figure or structure in the shape of a T.

taught (tôt) v. Past tense and past participle of **teach.**

tau neutrino n. A probably stable, electrically neutral, elementary particle in the lepton family having a mass less than 60 times that of the electron.

taunt[1] (tônt) tr.v. **taunt·ed, taunt·ing, taunts 1.** To reproach in a mocking, insulting, or contemptuous manner. See Syns at **ridicule. 2.** To drive or incite (a person) by taunting. ❖ n. A scornful remark or tirade; a jeer. [?] —taunt′er n.

taunt[2] (tônt) adj. Nautical Unusually tall. Used of masts. [?]

Tau·nus Mountains (tou′nəs, -nŏŏs′) A range of W Germany extending NE from the Rhine R.

taupe (tōp) n. A brownish gray. [Fr. < OFr., mole < Lat. talpa.] —taupe adj.

tau·rine[1] (tôr′īn′) adj. Of, relating to, or resembling a bull. [Lat. taurīnus < taurus, bull. See **tauro-** in App.]

tau·rine[2] (tôr′ēn′) n. A colorless crystalline substance, $C_2H_7NO_3S$, formed by the hydrolysis of taurocholic acid and found in the fluids of the muscles and lungs of many animals. [Gk. tauros, bull; see **tauro-** in App. + -INE[2].]

tau·ro·cho·lic acid (tôr′ō-kôl′ĭk, -kŏl′ĭk) n. A crystalline acid, $C_{26}H_{45}NO_7S$, involved in the emulsification of fats and occurring as a sodium salt in the bile of humans, oxen, and other mammals. [< Gk. tauros, bull. See **tauro-** in App.]

Tau·rus (tôr′əs) n. **1.** A constellation in the Northern Hemisphere near Orion and Aries. **2a.** The second sign of the zodiac. **b.** One who is born under this sign. [ME < Lat., bull, the constellation Taurus. See **tauro-** in App.]

Taurus Mountains A range of S Turkey parallel to the Mediterranean coast that rises to 3,736.6 m (12,251 ft).

Tau·sug (tou′sŏŏg′) n. An Austronesian language spoken in the Sulu Archipelago. [Tausug : ta'u, people + sūg, current.]

taut (tôt) adj. **taut·er, taut·est 1.** Pulled or drawn tight; not slack. See Syns at **tight. 2.** Strained; tense. **3a.** Kept in trim shape;

neat and tidy. **b.** Marked by the efficient, sparing, or concise use of something, such as language. [ME tohte, distended, perh. ult. < OE togian, to drag. See TOW[1].] —taut′ly adv. —taut′ness n.

taut·en (tôt′n) tr. & intr.v. **-ened, -en·ing, -ens** To make or become taut.

tauto- or **taut-** pref. Same; identical: tautomerism. [Gk. < tauto, the same, contraction of to auto : to, the; see **to-** in App. + auto, neut. of autos, same, self.]

tau·tog also **tau·taug** (tô′tôg′, -tŏg′, tô-tôg′, -tŏg′) n. A dark-colored edible marine fish (Tautoga onitis) found along the North American Atlantic coast. [Narragansett tautaũg.]

tau·tol·o·gize (tô-tŏl′ə-jīz′) intr.v. **-gized, -giz·ing, -giz·es** To use tautology. —tau·tol′o·gist (-jĭst) n.

tau·tol·o·gy (tô-tŏl′ə-jē) n., pl. **-gies 1a.** Needless repetition of the same sense in different words; redundancy. **b.** An instance of such repetition. **2.** Logic An empty statement composed of simpler statements in a fashion that makes it logically true whether the simpler statements are factually true or false; for example, Either we'll go or we'll stay. [LLat. tautologia < Gk. tautologiā < tautologos, redundant : tauto-, tauto- + logos, saying; see –LOGY.] —tau′to·log′i·cal (tôt′l-ŏj′ĭ-kəl), tau′to·log′ic (-ĭk) adj. —tau′to·log′i·cal·ly adv.

tau·tom·er·ism (tô-tŏm′ə-rĭz′əm) n. Chemical isomerism characterized by relatively easy interconversion of isomeric forms in equilibrium. [TAUTO- + (ISO)MERISM.] —tau′to·mer (tô′tə-mər) n. —tau′to·mer′ic (tô′tə-mĕr′ĭk) adj.

tau·to·nym (tô′tə-nĭm′) n. A taxonomic designation, such as Gorilla gorilla, in which the genus and species names are the same, commonly used in zoology. —tau′to·nym′ic, tau·ton′y·mous (tô-tŏn′ə-məs) adj. —tau·ton′y·my n.

tav also **taw** (täf, tôf) n. The 23rd letter of the Hebrew alphabet. [Heb. tāw < Phoenician *taww, mark, 22nd letter of the Phoenician alphabet.]

tav·ern (tăv′ərn) n. **1.** An establishment licensed to sell alcoholic beverages to be consumed on the premises. **2.** An inn for travelers. [ME taverne < OFr. < Lat. taberna, hut, tavern, prob. < *traberna < trabs, trab-, beam. See TRAVE.]

ta·ver·na (tə-vûr′nə, tä-vĕr′nä) n. A café or small restaurant in Greece. [Mod.Gk., ult. < Lat. taberna. See TAVERN.]

Tav·er·ner (tăv′ər-nər), **John** 1490?–1545. British composer and organist best known for his Masses and motets.

taw[1] (tô) tr.v. **tawed, taw·ing, taws** To convert (skin) into white leather by mineral tanning, as with alum and salt. [ME tawen < OE tawian, to prepare.] —taw′er n.

taw[2] (tô) n. **1.** Chiefly Southern US A large fancy marble used for shooting. **2.** The line from which a player shoots in marbles. **3.** A game of marbles. ❖ intr.v. **tawed, taw·ing, taws** To shoot a marble. [?]

taw[3] (täf, tôf) n. Variant of **tav.**

taw·dry (tô′drē) adj. **-dri·er, -dri·est 1.** Gaudy and cheap in nature or appearance. **2.** Shameful or indecent: tawdry secrets. ❖ n. Cheap and gaudy finery. [< tawdry lace, lace necktie, alteration of St. Audrey's lace, after St. Audrey (St. Etheldreda), queen of Northumbria, who died in 679 of a throat tumor, supposedly because when young she liked fancy necklaces.] —taw′dri·ly adv. —taw′dri·ness n.

taw·ny (tô′nē) n. A light brown to brownish orange. [ME < AN taune, var. of OFr. tane < p. part. of taner, to tan. See TAN[1].] —taw′ni·ness n. —taw′ny adj.

tax (tăks) n. **1.** A contribution for the support of a government required of persons, groups, or businesses within the domain of that government. **2.** A fee or dues levied on the members of an organization to meet its expenses. **3.** A burdensome or excessive demand; a strain. ❖ tr.v. **taxed, tax·ing, tax·es 1.** To place a tax on (income, property, or goods). **2.** To exact a tax from. **3.** Law To assess (court costs, for example). **4.** To make difficult or excessive demands upon: taxed my patience. **5.** To make a charge against; accuse. [ME < taxen, to tax < OFr. taxer < Med.Lat. taxāre < Lat., to touch, reproach, reckon, freq. of tangere, to touch. See **tag-** in App.] —tax′er n.

tax- pref. Variant of **taxo-.**

tax·a (tăk′sə) n. Plural of **taxon.**

tax·a·ble (tăk′sə-bəl) adj. Subject to taxation. ❖ n. One that is subject to taxation. —tax′a·bil′i·ty n. —tax′a·bly adv.

tax·a·tion (tăk-sā′shən) n. **1a.** The act or practice of imposing taxes. **b.** The fact of being taxed. **2.** An assessed amount of tax. **3.** Revenue gained from taxes.

tax-de·duct·i·ble (tăks′dĭ-dŭk′tə-bəl) adj. Exempt from inclusion in one's taxable income.

tax-de·ferred (tăks′dĭ-fûrd′) adj. Of or relating to an investment or its income that is not liable to taxation until the income is withdrawn or an appointed date is reached.

tax·eme (tăk′sēm′) n. A grammatical feature that cannot be analyzed or has no meaning by itself, as the order of phonemes or the stress of syllables in a word. [Gk. taxis, order, arrangement; see TAXIS + -EME.] —tax·e′mic adj.

tax-ex·empt (tăks′ĭg-zĕmpt′) adj. **1.** Not subject to taxation. **2.** Producing interest that is exempt from income tax. ❖ n. A tax-exempt security.

tax-free (tăks′frē′) adj. Not subject to taxation; tax-exempt.

tax·i (tăk′sē) n., pl. **tax·is** or **tax·ies** A taxicab. ❖ v. **tax·ied**

The taxonomic organization of species is hierarchical. Each species belongs to a genus, each genus belongs to a family, and so on through order, class, phylum, and kingdom. Associations within the hierarchy reflect evolutionary relationships, which are deduced typically from morphological and physiological similarities between species. So, for example, species in the same genus are more closely related and more alike than species that are in different genera within the same family.

Carolus Linnaeus, an 18th-century Swedish botanist, devised the system of binomial nomenclature used for naming species. In this system, each species is given a two-part Latin name, formed by appending a specific epithet to the genus name. By convention, the genus name is capitalized, and both the genus name and specific epithet are italicized; for example, *Canis familiaris* or simply *C. familiaris.*

Modern taxonomy recognizes five kingdoms, into which the estimated five million species of the world are divided. This table presents a familiar organism from each kingdom and the names of the taxonomic groups to which it belongs.

COMMON NAME	KINGDOM	PHYLUM*	CLASS	ORDER	FAMILY	GENUS	SPECIES
Domesticated Dog	Animalia (animals)	Chordata	Mammalia	Carnivora	Canidae	*Canis*	*C. familiaris*
Sugar Maple	Plantae (plants)	Magnoliophyta	Rosidae	Sapindales	Aceraceae	*Acer*	*A. saccharum*
Bread Mold	Fungi (fungi)	Zygomycota	Zygomycetes	Mucorales	Mucoraceae	*Rhizopus*	*R. stolonifer*
Tuberculosis Bacterium	Prokaryotae (bacteria)	Firmicutes	Actinobacteria	Actinomycetales	Mycobacteriaceae	*Mycobacterium*	*M. tuberculosis*
Pond Alga	Protoctista (algae, molds, protozoans)	Chlorophyta	Euconjugatae	Zygnematales	Zygnemataceae	*Spirogyra*	*S. crassa*

*In botanical nomenclature, "division" is used instead of "phylum."

(tăk′sēd), **tax•i•ing** or **tax•y•ing, tax•ies** or **tax•is** (tăk′sēz) —*intr.* **1.** To be transported by taxi. **2.** To move slowly on the ground or on the surface of the water before takeoff or after landing. Used of an aircraft. —*tr.* **1.** To transport by or as if by taxi. **2.** To cause (an aircraft) to taxi. [Short for TAXIMETER or TAXICAB.]

taxi– *pref.* Variant of taxo–.

tax•i•cab (tăk′sē-kăb′) *n.* An automobile that carries passengers for a fare, usu. calculated by a taximeter.

taxi dancer *n.* A woman employed, as by a dance hall or nightclub, to dance with the patrons for a fee.

tax•i•der•my (tăk′sĭ-dûr′mē) *n.* The art or operation of preparing, stuffing, and mounting the skins of dead animals for exhibition in a lifelike state. —**tax′i•der′mal, tax′i•der′mic** *adj.* —**tax′i•der′mist** *n.*

tax•i•me•ter (tăk′sē-mē′tər) *n.* An instrument installed in a taxicab to compute and indicate the fare. [Fr. *taximètre,* alteration of *taxamètre* < Ger. *Taxameter* : Med.Lat. *taxa,* tax (< *taxāre,* to tax; see TAX) + *-meter,* meter (< Gk. *metron,* measure; see –METER).]

tax•ing (tăk′sĭng) *adj.* Burdensome; wearing.

tax•is (tăk′sĭs) *n., pl.* **tax•es** (tăk′sēz) **1.** *Biology* The movement of a free-moving organism or cell toward or away from an external stimulus, such as light. **2.** *Medicine* The moving of a body part by manipulation into normal position, as after a dislocation. [Gk., arrangement < *tassein, tag-,* to arrange.]

–taxis *suff.* **1.** Arrangement: *homotaxis.* **2.** Responsive movement; taxis: *chemotaxis.* [Gk. < *taxis.* See TAXIS.]

taxi squad *n. Football* **1.** A group of professional players who are under contract to and practice with a team but are ineligible to play in official games. **2.** The four extra players of a professional team who are prepared to play on short notice.

taxi stand *n.* An area reserved for waiting taxicabs.

tax•i•way (tăk′sē-wā′) *n.* A usu. paved strip at an airport for use by aircraft in taxiing to and from a runway.

tax•man (tăks′măn′) *n.* One that is responsible for the collection of federal, state, or local taxes.

taxo– or **taxi–** or **tax–** *pref.* Order; arrangement: *taxidermy.* [< Gk. *taxis.* See TAXIS.]

Tax•ol (tăk′sôl, -sōl) A trademark used for the drug paclitaxel.

tax•on (tăk′sŏn′) *n., pl.* **tax•a** (tăk′sə) A taxonomic category or group, such as a phylum, order, family, genus, or species. [NLat., back-formation < TAXONOMY.]

tax•o•nom•ic (tăk′sə-nŏm′ĭk) also **tax•o•nom•i•cal** (-ĭ-kəl) *adj.* Of or relating to taxonomy. —**tax′o•nom′i•cal•ly** *adv.*

tax•on•o•my (tăk-sŏn′ə-mē) *n., pl.* **-mies 1.** The classification of organisms in an ordered system that indicates natural relationships. **2.** The science, laws, or principles of classification; systematics. **3.** Division into ordered groups or categories. [Fr. *taxonomie* : Gk. *taxis,* arrangement; see TAXIS + *-nomie,* method (< Gk. *-nomiā;* see –NOMY).] —**tax•on′o•mist** *n.*

tax•pay•er (tăks′pā′ər) *n.* One that pays taxes or is subject to taxation. —**tax′pay′ing** *adj.*

tax return *n.* See **return** 16.

tax shelter *n.* A financial arrangement, such as the use of special depletion allowances, that reduces taxes on current earnings. —**tax′-shel′tered** (tăks′shĕl′tərd) *adj.*

–taxy *suff.* Order; arrangement: *phyllotaxy.* [Gk. *-taxiā* < *taktos,* arranged. See TAXIS.]

Tay (tā) A river of central Scotland rising in the Grampian Mts. and flowing c. 190 km (118 mi) through **Loch Tay** to the **Firth of Tay,** an inlet of the North Sea.

Tay•lor (tā′lər), **Cecil Percival** b. 1929. Amer. jazz pianist and composer who was a leader of the free jazz movement of the 1960s.

Taylor, Elizabeth b. 1932. British-born Amer. actress whose film credits include *National Velvet* (1944).

Taylor, Joseph Hooton, Jr. b. 1941. Amer. physicist who shared a 1993 Nobel Prize.

Taylor, Paul b. 1930. Amer. choreographer whose avant-garde works include *Three Epitaphs* (1956) and *Orbs* (1966).

Taylor, Zachary Known as "Old Rough and Ready." 1784–1850. The 12th President of the US (1849–50), who became a national hero during the Mexican War (1846–48).

Tay•myr Peninsula or **Tai•myr Peninsula** (tī-mîr′) A peninsula of N-central Russia extending N between the Laptev and Kara seas.

Tay-Sachs disease (tā′săks′) *n.* A fatal hereditary disease that affects young children almost exclusively of eastern European Jewish descent, in which an enzyme deficiency leads to the accumulation of gangliosides in nervous tissue. [After Warren *Tay* (1843–1927), British physician, and Bernard *Sachs* (1858–1944), American neurologist.]

taz•za (tät′sə, -tsä) *n.* A shallow ornamental vessel usu. on a pedestal. [Ital., cup, tazza < Ar. *ṭašt,* basin. See DEMITASSE.]

Tb¹ The symbol for the element **terbium.**

Tb² *abbr. Bible* Tobit

TB *abbr.* tuberculosis

t.b. *abbr.* **1.** trial balance **2.** tubercle bacillus

TBA *abbr.* to be announced

T-ball also **tee-ball** (tē′bôl′) *n.* A form of baseball played by young children in which the ball is hit from a stationary position on top of a tee.

T-bar (tē′bär′) *n.* A ski lift consisting of a bar suspended like an inverted T against which skiers lean.

TBD *abbr.* to be determined

Tbi•li•si (tə-bə-lē′sē, -byĭ-lē′syĭ) also **Tif•lis** (tĭf′lĭs, tyə-flēs′) The cap. of Georgia, in the SE part on the Kura R.; came under Russian control in 1801. Pop. 1,268,000.

T-bill (tē′bĭl′) *n.* A US Treasury note.

T-bone (tē′bōn′) *n.* A thick porterhouse steak taken from the small end of the loin and containing a T-shaped bone.

tbs. or **tbsp.** *abbr.* **1.** tablespoon **2.** tablespoonful

Tc The symbol for the element **technetium.**

T cell *n.* Any of the lymphocytes that mature in the thymus and have the ability to recognize specific peptide antigens through receptors on the cell surface. [*t(hymus-derived) cell.*]

Tchai•kov•sky (chī-kôf′skē), **Peter Ilich** 1840–93. Russian

Zachary Taylor
detail from a 1848 portrait attributed to James Reid Lambdin (1807–89)

composer whose works include the ballet *Swan Lake* (1877). —**Tchai•kov′sky•an, Tchai•kov′ski•an** *adj.*

tchotch•ke (chŏch′kə) *n.* Variant of **chachka.**

TCP/IP *n.* A protocol for communication between computers, used as a standard for transmitting data over networks and as the basis for standard Internet protocols. [*T(ransmission) C(ontrol) P(rotocol)/I(nternet) P(rotocol).*]

TD *abbr.* **1.** tank destroyer **2.** touchdown **3.** Treasury Department

TDD *abbr.* telecommunications device for the deaf

TDY *abbr.* temporary duty

Te¹ (dĕ) *n.* **1.** In Taoism, the power through which the Tao is actualized. **2.** In Confucianism, the virtuous moral strength embodied in wise people. [Chin. (Mandarin) *dé,* virtue, moral character.]

Te² The symbol for the element **tellurium.**

tea (tē) *n.* **1a.** An eastern Asian evergreen shrub or small tree (*Camellia sinensis*) having fragrant nodding cup-shaped white flowers and glossy leaves. **b.** The young dried leaves of this plant, used to make a hot beverage. **2.** An aromatic, slightly bitter beverage made by steeping tea leaves in boiling water. **3.** Any of various beverages, made as by steeping the leaves of certain plants or by extracting an infusion esp. from beef. **4.** Any of various plants having leaves used to make a tealike beverage. **5.** A tea rose. **6.** *Chiefly British* **a.** An afternoon refreshment consisting esp. of sandwiches and cakes served with tea. **b.** High tea. **7.** An afternoon reception or social gathering at which tea is served. **8.** *Slang* Marijuana. [Prob. Du. *thee* < Malay *teh* < Chin. (Amoy) *te* (equivalent to Chin. (Mandarin) *chá*).]

WORD HISTORY "*Here thou, great Anna! whom three realms obey,/Dost sometimes counsel take—and sometimes tea.*" When Alexander Pope wrote these lines from *The Rape of the Lock* in 1714, *tea* still rhymed with *obey.* This was true of many words spelled with *ea,* and it was just about in Pope's time that nearly all these words started changing their pronunciation from (ā) to (ē), as in our modern pronunciation of *tea* (tē). Most modern English words whose main vowel sound is spelled *ea* were pronounced with long vowels in Middle and Old English. Many of these vowels were shortened in the 16th and 17th centuries to their modern pronunciations, as in our words *dead* and *sweat.* But those words that were pronounced with an (ā) sound in Middle English did not undergo this sound change and kept their long vowels, undergoing the further change in Pope's time to the modern "long e" sound. There were several exceptions to this last sound change, most notably the words *break, great,* and *steak.* Interestingly, the old pronunciation is also retained in Irish family names, such as *Reagan, Shea, Beatty,* and *Yeats* (in contrast to British family names such as *Keats*).

tea bag *n.* A small porous sack holding enough tea leaves to make an individual serving of tea.

tea ball *n.* A small perforated metal ball for holding tea leaves that are to be steeped in hot water.

tea•ber•ry (tē′bĕr′ē) *n.* **1.** See **wintergreen** 1a. **2.** See **witherod.** [< the use of its leaves as a tea substitute.]

tea biscuit *n.* Any of various plain cookies or biscuits often served with tea.

tea caddy *n.* A small box or container for holding loose tea.

tea•cake (tē′kāk′) *n.* See **tea biscuit.**

tea•cart (tē′kärt′) *n.* See **tea wagon.**

teach (tēch) *v.* **taught** (tôt), **teach•ing, teach•es** —*tr.* **1.** To impart knowledge or skill to. **2.** To provide knowledge of; instruct in. **3.** To condition to a certain action or frame of mind. **4.** To cause to learn by example or experience. **5.** To advocate or preach. **6.** To carry on instruction on a regular basis in. —*intr.* To give instruction, esp. as an occupation. [ME *techen* < OE *tǣcan.* See **deik-** in App.]

SYNONYMS *teach, instruct, educate, train, school* These verbs mean to impart knowledge or skill. *Teach* is the most widely applicable: *taught the child to draw; taught literature at the college.* *Instruct* usually suggests methodical teaching: *instructed them in music theory.* *Educate* often implies formal instruction but especially stresses the development of innate capacities: "*We are educated by others . . . and this cultivation . . . is the soil in which our desires, passions, and motives grow*" (Mary Shelley). *Train* suggests concentration on particular skills intended to fit a person for a desired role: *trained the vocational students to be computer technicians.* *School* often implies an arduous learning process: *schooled the youngster to play the viola.*

Teach (tēch) also **Thatch** (thăch), **Edward** Known as "Blackbeard." d. 1718. English pirate in the Caribbean.

teach•a•ble (tē′chə-bəl) *adj.* **1.** That can be taught: *teachable skills.* **2.** Able and willing to learn. —**teach′a•bil′i•ty, teach′a•ble•ness** *n.* —**teach′a•bly** *adv.*

teach•er (tē′chər) *n.* One who teaches, esp. one hired to teach.

teacher bird *n.* See **ovenbird** 1. [Imit. of the bird's song.]

teach•ers college also **teach•ers' college** (tē′chərz) *n.* A college with a special curriculum for training teachers.

teacher's pet *n.* **1.** A student in special favor with a teacher. **2.** One who has gained favor with an authority.

teach-in (tēch′ĭn′) *n.* An extended session, as at a college, for lectures and discussions on a usu. controversial issue.

teach•ing (tē′chĭng) *n.* **1.** The act, practice, occupation, or profession of a teacher. **2a.** Something taught. **b.** A precept or doctrine. Often used in the plural. ❖ *adj.* **1.** Of, involving, or used for teaching. **2.** Working as a teacher.

teaching assistant *n.* A graduate student awarded a fellowship that provides financial aid in exchange for teaching duties. —**teaching assistantship** *n.*

teaching fellow *n.* See **teaching assistant.**

teaching hospital *n.* A hospital associated with a medical school and serving as a practical educational site for medical students, interns, residents, and other health workers.

tea•cup (tē′kŭp′) *n.* A small cup used with a saucer for serving tea. —**tea′cup•ful′** *n.*

tea dance *n.* A late-afternoon dance.

tea garden *n.* **1.** A garden open to the public where tea and light refreshments are served. **2.** A tea plantation.

tea•house (tē′hous′) *n.* A public establishment serving tea and light refreshments.

teak (tēk) *n.* **1a.** A tall evergreen tree (*Tectona grandis*) of southeast Asia having hard heavy durable yellowish-brown wood. **b.** The wood of this tree, used esp. for furniture and in shipbuilding. **2.** A grayish yellowish brown or grayish to moderate brown. [Port. *teca* < Malayalam *tēkka.*]

tea•ket•tle (tē′kĕt′l) *n.* A covered kettle with a spout and handle, used for boiling water, as for tea.

teak•wood (tēk′wood′) *n.* Teak.

teal (tēl) *n., pl.* **teal** or **teals** **1.** Any of several small short-necked freshwater ducks, esp. of the genus *Anas,* that feed on the surface of the water and often have brightly marked plumage. **2.** A moderate or dark bluish green to greenish blue. [ME *tele.*] —**teal** *adj.*

team (tēm) *n.* **1.** *Sports & Games* A group on the same side. **2.** A group organized to work together. **3a.** Two or more draft animals used to pull a vehicle or farm implement. **b.** A vehicle along with the animal or animals harnessed to it. **4.** A group of animals exhibited or performing together. **5.** A brood or flock. **6.** *Obsolete* Offspring; lineage. See Usage Note at **collective noun.** ❖ *v.* **teamed, team•ing, teams** —*tr.* **1.** To harness or join together to form a team. **2.** To transport or haul with a draft team. —*intr.* **1.** To form a team or association. Often used with *up.* **2.** To drive a team or truck. [ME, draft team < OE *tēam.* See **deuk-** in App.]

team foul *n. Basketball* One of a stipulated number of personal fouls allowed for a team in a given period of play before the opposing team is granted a bonus free throw for each personal foul.

team•mate (tēm′māt′) *n.* A fellow member of a team.

team play *n.* **1.** Collective play participated in by team members. **2.** Collective effort and cooperation. —**team player** *n.*

team•ster (tēm′stər) *n.* **1.** One who drives a truck for hauling loads, esp. as an occupation. **2.** One who drives a team.

team-teach (tēm′tēch′) *tr. & intr.v.* **-taught** (-tôt′), **-teach•ing, -teach•es** To teach cooperatively with other teachers or engage in such teaching.

team teaching *n.* A method of classroom instruction in which several teachers combine their individual subjects into one course that they teach as a team to a group of students.

team•work (tēm′wûrk′) *n.* Cooperative effort by the members of a group or team to achieve a common goal.

tea party *n.* An afternoon social gathering at which tea and light refreshments are served.

tea•pot (tē′pŏt′) *n.* A covered pot with a spout in which tea is steeped and from which it is served.

tea•poy (tē′poi′) *n.* **1.** A small table for holding a tea service. **2.** A small decorative three-legged table. [Hindi *tipāī,* alteration (influenced by *tir,* three) of Pers. *si-pāya,* three : *si,* three; see **trei-** in App. + MPers. *pāī,* foot; see **ped-** in App.]

tear¹ (târ) *v.* **tore** (tôr, tōr), **torn** (tôrn, tōrn), **tear•ing, tears** —*tr.* **1.** To pull apart or into pieces by force; rend. **2.** To make (an opening) by ripping: *tore a hole in my sock.* **3.** To lacerate (the skin, for example). **4.** To separate forcefully; wrench. **5.** To divide or disrupt. —*intr.* **1.** To become torn. **2.** To move with heedless speed; rush headlong. ❖ *n.* **1.** The act of tearing. **2.** The result of tearing; a rip or rent. **3.** A great rush; a hurry. **4.** *Slang* A carousal; a spree. —*phrasal verbs:* **tear around** *Informal* **1.** To move about in excited, often angry haste. **2.** To lead a wild life. **tear at** **1.** To pull at or attack violently. **2.** To distress greatly. **tear away** To remove (oneself, for example) unwillingly or reluctantly. **tear down** **1.** To demolish. **2.** To take apart; disassemble. **3.** To vilify or denigrate. **tear into** To attack with great vigor or violence. **tear up** **1.** To tear to pieces. **2.** To make an opening in. [ME *teren* < OE *teran.*] —**tear′er** *n.*

SYNONYMS *tear, rip, rend, split, cleave* These verbs mean to separate or pull apart by force. *Tear* involves pulling something apart or into pieces: "*She tore the letter in shreds*" (Edith Wharton). *Rip* implies rough or forcible tearing: *ripped up the old floorboards.* *Rend* usually refers to violent tearing or wrenching apart: "*Come as the winds come, when/Forests are rended*" (Sir Walter Scott). To *split* is to cut or break something into parts or layers, especially along its entire length or along a natural line of division: "*They* [wood stumps] *warmed me twice—once while I was splitting them, and again when they were on the fire*" (Henry David Thoreau).

Cleave most often refers to splitting with or as if with a sharp instrument: *The butcher cleft the side of beef into smaller portions.*

tear^2 (tîr) *n.* **1a.** A drop of the clear salty liquid that is secreted by the lacrimal gland of the eye to lubricate the surface between the eyeball and eyelid and to wash away irritants. **b. tears** A profusion of this liquid spilling from the eyes and wetting the cheeks, esp. as an expression of emotion. **c. tears** The act of weeping: *criticism that left me in tears.* **2.** A drop of a liquid or hardened fluid. ❖ *intr.v.* **teared, tear•ing, tears** To fill with tears. [ME < OE *tēar.* See **dakru-** in App.]

tear•drop (tîr′drŏp′) *n.* **1.** A single tear. **2.** A tear-shaped object.

tear•ful (tîr′fəl) *adj.* **1.** Filled with or accompanied by tears. **2.** So piteous as to excite tears. **—tear′ful•ness** *n.*

tear gas (tîr) *n.* Any of various agents that on dispersal, usu. from grenades or projectiles, irritate the eyes and cause blinding tears. **—tear′-gas′** (tîr′găs′) *v.*

tear•ing (târ′ĭng) *adj.* Marked by great or violent haste.

tear•jerk•er (tîr′jûr′kər) *n. Slang* A grossly sentimental story, drama, or performance. **—tear′-jerk′ing** *adj.*

tea•room (tē′ro͞om′, -ro͝om′) *n.* A restaurant or shop serving tea and other refreshments.

tea rose *n.* **1.** Any of several cultivated roses derived from *Rosa odorata,* native to China and having fragrant yellowish or pink flowers. **2.** Any of a group of cultivated roses having open, cup-shaped flowers that bloom nearly year-round. **3.** A pale to strong yellowish pink.

tear•stain (tîr′stān′) *n.* A track or mark left by tears.

tear•y (tîr′ē) *adj.* **-i•er, -i•est 1a.** Filled or wet with tears. **b.** Of or resembling tears. **2.** Causing weeping: *a teary goodbye.* **3.** Inclined to weep. **—tear′i•ly** *adv.* **—tear′i•ness** *n.*

tear•y-eyed (tîr′ē-īd′) *adj.* **1.** Having tears in the eyes, as from emotion. **2.** Marked by tears or weeping.

Teas•dale (tēz′dāl′), **Sara** 1884–1933. Amer. poet whose collections include *Love Songs* (1917).

tease (tēz) *v.* **teased, teas•ing, teas•es** *—tr.* **1.** To annoy or pester; vex. **2.** To make fun of; mock playfully. **3.** To arouse hope, desire, or curiosity in without affording satisfaction. **4a.** To urge persistently; coax. **b.** To gain by persistent coaxing. **c.** To deal with or have an effect on as if by teasing. **5.** To cut (tissue, for example) into pieces for examination. **6.** To disentangle and dress the fibers of (wool, for example). **7.** To raise the nap of (cloth) by dressing, as with a fuller's teasel. **8.** To ruffle (the hair) by combing from the ends toward the scalp for an airy effect. *—intr.* To annoy or make fun of someone persistently. ❖ *n.* **1a.** The act of teasing. **b.** The state of being teased. **2.** One that teases, as: **a.** One given to playful mocking. **b.** A flirt. **c.** A preliminary remark or act intended to whet the curiosity. ***—phrasal verb:* tease out** To get by or as if by untangling or releasing with a pointed tool or device. [ME *tesen,* to comb apart < OE *tǣsan.*]

tea•sel (tē′zəl) *n.* **1.** Any of several plants of the genus *Dipsacus,* native to the Old World and having flower heads surrounded by spiny bracts. **2a.** The bristly flower head of *D. sativus,* used to make a napped surface, as on wool. **b.** A wire device used to make a napped surface. ❖ *tr.v.* **-seled, -sel•ing, -sels** or **-selled, -sel•ling, -sels** To make a napped surface on (a fabric). [ME *tesel* < OE *tǣsel.*]

teas•er (tē′zər) *n.* **1a.** One that teases, as a device for teasing wool. **b.** One who engages in teasing; a tease. **2.** A puzzling problem. **3.** An advertisement that attracts customers by offering something extra or free. **4.** *Slang* An attention-getting vignette or highlight presented before a television show.

tea service *n.* A set of articles, such as matching cups and a teapot, used in serving tea.

tea•shop (tē′shŏp′) *n.* **1.** See **tearoom. 2.** *Chiefly British* A luncheonette or small restaurant.

tea•spoon (tē′spo͞on′) *n.* **1.** The common small spoon used esp. in serving and consuming tea, coffee, and desserts. **2.** A household cooking measure equal to ⅓ tablespoon (about 5 milliliters).

tea•spoon•ful (tē′spo͞on-fo͝ol′) *n., pl.* **-fuls** The amount that a teaspoon can hold.

teat (tēt, tĭt) *n.* A nipple of the mammary gland; a mamilla. [ME *tete* < OFr., of Gmc. orig.] **—teat′ed** *adj.*

tea table *n.* A small table used for serving tea.

tea•time (tē′tīm′) *n.* The usual or traditional time for serving tea, as late afternoon.

tea towel *n.* A cloth for drying dishes; a dishtowel.

tea tray *n.* A tray for holding a tea service.

tea tree *n.* **1.** Any of various evergreen shrubs or small trees of the genus *Leptospermum,* native to Australia and New Zealand, having small needlelike leaves and white, pink, or red flowers. **2.** Any of several Australian trees of the genus *Melaleuca,* whose leaves yield an oil used in various herbal preparations.

tea wagon *n.* A small table on wheels for serving tea or holding dishes.

Te•bal•di (tə-bäl′dē, tē-), **Renata** b. 1922. Italian-born operatic soprano known for her portrayal of dramatic heroines.

Te•bet or **Te•beth** (tā′vās, tĕ-vĕt′) *n.* Variants of **Tevet.**

tech (tĕk) *Informal n.* **1.** A technician. **2.** Technology. **3.** Technical work. ❖ *adj.* Technical.

tech. *abbr.* **1.** technical **2.** technician

teched (tĕcht) *adj.* Variant of **tetched.**

tech•ie also **tek•kie** (tĕk′ē) *n. Informal* One who studies or is interested or proficient in a technical field, esp. electronics.

tech•ne•ti•um (tĕk-nē′shē-əm, -shəm) *n. Symbol* **Tc** A radioactive metal, the first synthetically produced element, used as a tracer and to inhibit corrosion in steel; its longest-lived isotope is Tc 98 with a half-life of 4.2×10^6 years. Atomic number 43; melting point 2,200°C; specific gravity 11.50; valence 0, 2, 4, 5, 6, 7. See table at **element.** [< Gk. *tekhnētos,* artificial < *tekhnāsthai,* to make by art < *tekhnē,* art. See TECHNICAL.]

tech•ne•tron•ic (tĕk′nĭ-trŏn′ĭk) *adj.* Of or marked by the changes effected by modern technology and electronics.

tech•nic (tĕk′nĭk) *n.* **1. technics** (*used with a sing. or pl. verb*) The theory, principles, or study of an art or a process. **2. technics** (*used with a pl. verb*) Technical details, rules, or methods. ❖ *adj.* Technical. [< Gk. *tekhnikos,* of art < *tekhnē,* art. See TECHNICAL.]

tech•ni•cal (tĕk′nĭ-kəl) *adj.* **1.** Of or derived from technique. **2a.** Having special skill or practical knowledge esp. in a mechanical or scientific field. **b.** Used in or peculiar to a given field or profession; specialized. **3a.** Belonging or relating to a given subject. **b.** Of, relating to, or involving the practical, mechanical, or industrial arts or the applied sciences. **4a.** Abstract or theoretical. **b.** Of or employing the methodology of science; scientific. **5.** According to principle; formal rather than practical: *a technical advantage.* **6.** Industrial and mechanical; technological. **7.** Relating to or based on analysis of market indicators, such as trading volume and price fluctuations, rather than underlying economic conditions such as inflation and unemployment. ❖ *n. Sports* A technical foul. [< Gk. *tekhnikos,* of art < *tekhnē,* art.] **—tech′ni•cal•ly** *adv.* **—tech′ni•cal•ness** *n.*

technical foul *n. Sports* A foul, esp. in basketball, that is called, as for unsportsmanlike conduct, and does not usu. involve physical contact with an opponent during play.

tech•ni•cal•i•ty (tĕk′nĭ-kăl′ĭ-tē) *n., pl.* **-ties 1.** The quality or condition of being technical. **2.** Something meaningful or relevant only to a specialist: *a legal technicality.*

technical knockout *n.* A victory in boxing awarded by the referee when it appears that one fighter is too badly injured to continue.

technical school *n.* **1.** A vocational school at the secondary-school level. **2.** A post-secondary vocational school that trains students in a variety of skills, esp. in the manual trades, health care, and computer technology.

technical sergeant *n.* A noncommissioned officer in the US Air Force ranking above staff sergeant and below master sergeant.

tech•ni•cian (tĕk-nĭsh′ən) *n.* An expert in a technique, as: **a.** One whose occupation requires training in a specific technical process: *an electronics technician.* **b.** One who is known for skill in an intellectual or artistic technique.

Tech•ni•col•or (tĕk′nĭ-kŭl′ər) A trademark used for a method of making color motion pictures in which films sensitive to different primary colors are exposed simultaneously and are later superimposed to produce the full-color print.

tech•nique (tĕk-nēk′) *n.* **1.** The systematic procedure by which a complex or scientific task is accomplished. **2.** also **tech•nic** (tĕk′nĭk) **a.** The way in which the fundamentals, as of an artistic work, are handled. **b.** Skill or command in handling such fundamentals. [Fr., technical, technique < Gk. *tekhnikos,* technical. See TECHNICAL.]

tech•no (tĕk′nō) *n.* Any of various styles of dance music characterized by electronic sounds and a high-energy, rhythmic beat.

techno– *pref.* Technology: *technophobia.* [< TECHNO(LOGY).]

tech•no•bab•ble (tĕk′nō-băb′əl) *n.* Technical jargon.

tech•noc•ra•cy (tĕk-nŏk′rə-sē) *n., pl.* **-cies** A government or social system controlled by technicians, esp. technical experts. [Gk. *tekhnē,* skill; see TECHNICAL + –CRACY.] **—tech′no•crat′** *n.* **—tech′no•crat′ic** *adj.*

tech•no•log•i•cal (tĕk′nə-lŏj′ĭ-kəl) also **tech•no•log•ic** (-lŏj′ĭk) *adj.* **1.** Relating to or involving technology, esp. scientific technology. **2.** Affected by or resulting from scientific and industrial progress. **—tech′no•log′i•cal•ly** *adv.*

tech•nol•o•gist (tĕk-nŏl′ə-jĭst) *n.* A specialist in technology.

tech•nol•o•gize (tĕk-nŏl′ə-jīz′) *tr.v.* **-gized, -giz•ing, -giz•es** To modify or affect by technology; make technological.

tech•nol•o•gy (tĕk-nŏl′ə-jē) *n., pl.* **-gies 1a.** The application of science, esp. to industrial or commercial objectives. **b.** The scientific method and material used to achieve a commercial or industrial objective. **2.** Electronic or digital products and systems considered as a group: *office technology.* **3.** *Anthropology* The body of knowledge available to a society that is of use in fashioning implements, practicing manual arts and skills, and extracting or collecting materials. [Gk. *tekhnologiā,* systematic treatment of an art or craft : *tekhnē,* skill + *-logiā,* -logy.]

tech•no•pho•bi•a (tĕk′nə-fō′bē-ə) *n.* Fear of or aversion to technology, esp. computers and high technology. **—tech′no•phobe′** *n.* **—tech′no•pho′bic** (-fō′bĭk) *adj.*

tech•no•struc•ture (tĕk′nō-strŭk′chər) *n.* **1.** A large-scale corporate system. **2.** A network of skilled professionals who control such a corporate system. [TECHNO(LOGY) + STRUCTURE.]

teasel
common teasel
Dipsacus sylvestris

Renata Tebaldi
photographed in
costume c. 1955

ă	pat	oi	boy
ā	pay	ou	out
âr	care	o͝o	took
ä	father	o͞o	boot
ĕ	pet	ŭ	cut
ē	be	ûr	urge
ĭ	pit	th	thin
ī	pie	*th*	this
îr	pier	hw	which
ŏ	pot	zh	vision
ō	toe	ə	about, item
ô	paw		

Stress marks:
′ (primary);
′ (secondary), as in
lexicon (lĕk′sĭ-kŏn′)

tech·y (tĕch′ē) adj. Variant of **tetchy**.

tec·ton·ic (tĕk-tŏn′ĭk) adj. **1.** Geology Relating to, causing, or resulting from structural deformation of the earth's crust. **2a.** Relating to construction or building. **b.** Architectural. [LLat. tectonicus < Gk. tektonikos < tektōn, builder.] —**tec·ton′i·cal·ly** adv.

tec·ton·ics (tĕk-tŏn′ĭks) n. (used with a sing. verb) **1.** The study of the earth's structural features. **2.** The art or science of construction, esp. of large buildings.

tec·ton·ism (tĕk′tə-nĭz′əm) n. **1.** The structural behavior of an element of the earth's crust. **2.** Crustal instability.

tec·trix (tĕk′trĭks) n., pl. **-tri·ces** (-trī-sēz′) One of the coverts of a bird's wing. Often used in the plural. [Lat. tēctrīx, fem. of tēctor, plasterer < tēctus, p. part. of tegere, to cover. See **(s)teg-** in App.]

tec·tum (tĕk′təm) n., pl. **-ta** (-tə) A rooflike structure of the body, esp. the dorsal part of the midbrain. [Lat. tēctum, roof < neut. p. part. of tegere, to cover. See **(s)teg-** in App.]

Te·cum·seh (tĭ-kŭm′sə) or **Te·cum·tha** (-thə) 1768–1813. Shawnee leader who attempted to establish a confederacy to unify Native Americans against white encroachment.

ted (tĕd) tr.v. **ted·ded, ted·ding, teds** Chiefly New England To strew or spread (newly mown grass, for example) for drying. [ME tedden.]

ted·der (tĕd′ər) n. Chiefly New England A machine that spreads newly mown hay for drying. —**ted′der** v.

ted·dy (tĕd′ē) n., pl. **-dies** **1.** A woman's undergarment combining a camisole top and panties. **2.** A teddy bear.

teddy bear also **Teddy bear** n. A child's toy bear, usu. stuffed with soft material and covered with furlike plush. [After Teddy, nickname of Theodore Roosevelt, depicted in a cartoon sparing the life of a bear cub.]

Teddy boy n. In Britain, esp. during the 1950s, a tough youth wearing a modified style of Edwardian clothes. [< the name Teddy, nickname for Edward, after EDWARD VII.]

Te De·um (tā′ dā′əm, -ōōm, tē′ dē′əm) n. A hymn of praise to God sung as part of a liturgy. [< LLat. Tē Deum (laudāmus), You, God, (we praise).]

te·di·ous (tē′dē-əs) adj. **1.** Tiresome by reason of length, slowness, or dullness; boring. See Syns at **boring**. **2.** Obsolete Moving or progressing very slowly. [ME < LLat. taediōsus < Lat. taedium, tedium. See TEDIUM.] —**te′di·ous·ly** adv. —**te′di·ous·ness** n.

te·di·um (tē′dē-əm) n. The quality or condition of being tedious; boredom. [Lat. taedium < taedēre, to weary.]

tee¹ (tē) n. **1.** The letter t. **2.** Something shaped like a T. **3.** A mark aimed at in certain games, such as curling or quoits. —**idiom: to a tee** Perfectly; exactly.

tee² (tē) n. **1.** A small peg with a concave top for holding a golf ball for an initial drive. **2.** The designated area of each golf hole from which a player makes the first stroke. **3.** A device used to stand a football on end for a kickoff. **4.** A shaft with a concave top attached to a flat base, used to hold the ball in T-ball. ❖ tr.v. **teed, tee·ing, tees** To place (a golf ball) on a tee. Often used with up. —**phrasal verb: tee off** **1.** To drive a golf ball from the tee. **2.** Slang To start or begin. **3.** Slang To make or become angry or disgusted. [Back-formation < obsolete Sc. teaz (taken as a pl.).]

tee-ball (tē′bôl′) n. Variant of **T-ball**.

teem¹ (tēm) v. **teemed, teem·ing, teems** —intr. **1.** To be full of things; abound or swarm. **2.** Obsolete To be or become pregnant; bear young. —tr. Archaic To give birth to. [ME temen, to beget, bear < OE tīeman, tēman. See **deuk-** in App.] —**teem′er** n. —**teem′ing·ly** adv.

teem² (tēm) tr.v. **teemed, teem·ing, teems** To pour out or empty. [ME temen < ON tōma.]

teen¹ (tēn) n. **1. teens a.** The numbers 13 through 19. **b.** The 13th through 19th items in a series or scale, as years of a century. **2.** A teenager. ❖ adj. Teenage.

teen² (tēn) n. Archaic Misery; grief. [ME tene < OE tēona.]

teen·age (tēn′āj′) also **teen·aged** (-ājd′) adj. Of, relating to, or applicable to teenagers.

teen·ag·er (tēn′ā′jər) n. A person between the ages of 13 and 19; an adolescent.

teen·er (tē′nər) n. Informal A teenager.

tee·ny (tē′nē) also **teen·sy** (tēn′sē) adj. **-ni·er, -ni·est** also **-si·er, -si·est** Informal Tiny. [Alteration of TINY.]

teen·y·bop·per (tē′nē-bŏp′ər) n. Slang **1.** A young teenage girl. **2.** A teenager who follows the latest fad or craze.

teen·y-ween·y (tē′nē-wē′nē) or **teen·sy-ween·sy** (tēn′sē-wēn′sē) adj. Informal Tiny. [Reduplication of TEENY.]

tee·pee (tē′pē) n. Variant of **tepee**.

Tees (tēz) A river of NE England flowing c. 113 km (70 mi) to the North Sea.

tee shirt n. Variant of **T-shirt**.

tee·ter (tē′tər) v. **-tered, -ter·ing, -ters** —intr. **1.** To walk or move unsteadily or unsurely; totter. **2.** To alternate, as between opposing positions; vacillate. **3.** To seesaw. —tr. To cause to tee-

teething ring

Kiri Te Kanawa
photographed c. 1970

ter or seesaw. ❖ n. Northeastern US **1.** See **seesaw** 1. **2.** A teetering motion. [ME titeren, prob. < ON titra, to shake.]

tee·ter·board (tē′tər-bôrd′, -bōrd′) n. Northeastern US **1.** See **seesaw** 1. **2.** A board with one end raised so that when an acrobat or tumbler jumps onto it, another performer standing on the opposite end is tossed into the air.

tee·ter-tot·ter (tē′tər-tŏt′ər) n. Upper Northern & Western US See **seesaw** 1.

teeth (tēth) n. Plural of **tooth**.

teethe (tēth) intr.v. **teethed, teeth·ing, teethes** To grow teeth; cut one's teeth. [ME tethen < teth, pl. of tooth, tooth. See TOOTH.]

teeth·er (tē′thər) n. An object or device, such as a teething ring, for a baby to bite on during teething.

teeth·ing (tē′thĭng) n. The eruption and cutting of teeth, esp. the milk teeth; dentition.

teething ring n. A ring of hard plastic or rubber upon which a teething baby can bite.

teeth·ridge (tēth′rĭj′) n. The ridge of gum behind the upper front teeth.

tee·to·tal (tē-tōt′l) adj. **1.** Of, relating to, or practicing complete abstinence from alcoholic beverages. **2.** Total; absolute. [Prob. partly TEE¹ (pronunciation of the first letter in TOTAL) + total (abstinence), and partly redup. of TOTAL.]

tee·to·tal·er or **tee·to·tal·ler** (tē-tōt′l-ər) also **tee·to·tal·ist** (-ĭst) n. One who abstains completely from alcoholic beverages. —**tee′to′tal·ism** n.

tee·to·tum (tē-tō′təm) n. A top, usu. having four lettered sides, used to play various games of chance. [< earlier T totum (< the letter tee) < totum, teetotum < Lat. tōtum, neut. sing. of tōtus, all. See **teutā-** in App.]

teff (tĕf) n. A perennial grass (Eragrostis tef) native to northeastern Africa and southwestern Arabia, used as a cereal crop and livestock forage. [Amharic ṭef.]

te·fil·lin (tə-fĭl′ĭn, -fē-lēn′) pl.n. Judaism The phylacteries. [Mishnaic Heb. tapillîn, pl. of tapillâ, prayer < Heb. hitpallēl, to pray.]

TEFL abbr. teaching English as a foreign language

Tef·lon (tĕf′lŏn′) A trademark for a waxy opaque material, polytetrafluoroethylene, as a coating on cooking utensils and in industry to prevent sticking.

teg also **tegg** (tĕg) n. A sheep in its second year or before its first shearing. [?]

teg·men (tĕg′mən) n., pl. **-mi·na** (-mə-nə) A covering or integument, such as the inner coat of a seed. [Lat. tegimen, tegmen, covering < tegere, to cover. See **(s)teg-** in App.]

teg·men·tum (tĕg-mĕn′təm) n. **1.** See **tegmen**. **2.** A part of the midbrain consisting of white fibers running lengthwise through gray matter. [Lat. tegumentum, tegmentum, covering < tegere, to cover. See **(s)teg-** in App.] —**teg·men′tal** (-təl) adj.

Te·gu·ci·gal·pa (tə-gōō′sə-gäl′pə, tĕ-gōō′sĕ-gäl′pä) The cap. of Honduras, in the S-central part. Pop. 597,512.

teg·u·lar (tĕg′yə-lər) also **teg·u·lat·ed** (-lā′tĭd) adj. Of or resembling a tile. [< Lat. tēgula, tile < tegere, to cover. See **(s)teg-** in App.] —**teg′u·lar·ly** adv.

teg·u·ment (tĕg′yə-mənt) n. A natural outer covering; an integument. [ME < Lat. tegumentum < tegere, to cover. See **(s)teg-** in App.] —**teg·u·men·ta·ry** (-mĕn′tə-rē, -mĕn′trē), **teg′u·men′tal** (-mĕn′tl) adj.

Teh·ran or **Te·he·ran** (tē′ə-rän′, -răn′, tĕ-răn′, -rän′) The cap. of Iran, in the N-central part. Pop. 6,750,043.

Te·huan·te·pec (tə-wän′tə-pĕk′, tĕ-wän′tĕ-), **Isthmus of** An isthmus of S Mexico between the Bay of Campeche and the **Gulf of Tehuantepec**, a wide inlet of the Pacific Ocean.

Te·huel·che (tə-wĕl′chē, tā-wĕl′chä) n., pl. **Tehuelche** or **-ches** **1.** A member of a South American Indian people formerly inhabiting most of Patagonia, with a small present-day population in southern Argentina. **2.** Their language. —**Te·huel′che·an** (-chē-ən) adj.

Teil·hard de Char·din (tā-yär′ də shär-dăn′), **Pierre** 1881–1955. French philosopher who maintained that the universe and humankind are evolving toward a perfect state.

Te·ja·no (tā-hä′nō, tĕ-) n. A style of conjunto music originating in southern Texas and combining influences from country music, rhythm and blues, and popular Latin styles. [Am.Sp., Texan < Tejas, Texas.]

Te Ka·na·wa (tĭ kä′nə-wə), **Dame Kiri** b. 1944. New Zealand operatic soprano noted for her rich lyric voice.

tek·kie (tĕk′ē) n. Informal Variant of **techie**.

tek·tite (tĕk′tīt′) n. Any of numerous generally small rounded dark brown to green glassy objects composed of silicate glass, thought to have been formed by the impact of a meteorite with the earth's surface. [Gk. tēktos, molten (< tēkein, to melt) + -ITE¹.] —**tek·tit′ic** (-tĭt′ĭk) adj.

tel. abbr. **1.** telegram **2.** telegraph **3.** telephone

tel-¹ pref. Variant of **tele-**.

tel-² pref. Variant of **telo-**.

tel·aes·the·sia (tĕl′ĭs-thē′zhə) n. Variant of **telesthesia**.

tel·a·mon (tĕl′ə-mŏn′) n., pl. **-mon·es** (-mō′nēz) Architecture A figure of a man used as a supporting pillar. [Lat. telamōn < Gk., bearer. See **telə-** in App.]

Tel·a·mon (tĕl′ə-mən, -mŏn′) n. Greek Mythology One of the

Argonauts and the father of Ajax.

tel·an·gi·ec·ta·sia (tĕl-ăn′jē-ĕk-tā′zhə) also **tel·an·gi·ec·ta·sis** (-ĕk′tə-sĭs) *n.* Chronic dilation of groups of capillaries causing elevated dark red blotches on the skin. [NLat. : TEL(O)- + Gk. ANGEION, vessel; see angeion + Gk. *ektasis,* expansion (< *ekteinein,* to stretch out : *ek-,* *ex-,* ex- + *teinein,* to stretch; see ten- in App.).] —**tel′an·gi·ec·tat′ic** (-tăt′ĭk) *adj.*

Tel A·viv–Ya·fo (tĕl′ ə-vēv′yä′fō, ä-vēv′-) or **Tel A·viv–Jaf·fa** (-jăf′ə, -yä′fə) A city of W-central Israel WNW of Jerusalem. Tel Aviv was founded in 1909 by settlers from the ancient city of Jaffa; the communities merged in 1950. Pop. 357,100.

tele- or **tel-** *pref.* **1.** Distance; distant: *telesthesia.* **2a.** Telegraph; telephone: *telegram.* **b.** Television: *telecast.* [Gk. *tēle-* < *tēle,* far off.]

tel·e·cast (tĕl′ĭ-kăst′) *v.* **-cast** or **-cast·ed, -cast·ing, -casts** —*intr.* To broadcast a television program. —*tr.* To broadcast (a program) by television. ❖ *n.* A television broadcast. —**tel′e·cast′er** *n.*

tel·e·com (tĕl′ĭ-kŏm′) *n. Informal* Telecommunications.

tel·e·com·mu·ni·cate (tĕl′ĭ-kə-myōō′nĭ-kāt′) *v.* **-cat·ed, -cat·ing, -cates** —*tr.* To transmit (data, for example) by telecommunication. —*intr.* To communicate by means of telecommunication. —**tel′e·com·mu′ni·ca′tor** *n.*

tel·e·com·mu·ni·ca·tion (tĕl′ĭ-kə-myōō′nĭ-kā′shən) *n.* **1.** The science and technology of communication at a distance by electronic transmission of impulses, as by telegraph, telephone, radio, or television. Often used in the plural with a singular verb. **2.** The electronic systems used in such transmission. Often used in the plural. **3.** A message so transmitted.

tel·e·com·mute (tĕl′ĭ-kə-myōōt′) *intr.v.* **-mut·ed, -mut·ing, -mutes** To work at home using a computer connected to the network of one's employer. —**tel′e·com·mut′er** *n.*

tel·e·con·fer·ence (tĕl′ĭ-kŏn′fər-əns, -frəns) *n.* A conference held among people in different locations by means of telecommunications equipment, such as closed-circuit television. —**tel′e·con′fer·ence** *v.* —**tel′e·con′fer·enc·ing** *n.*

tel·e·course (tĕl′ĭ-kôrs′, -kōrs′) *n.* A course of televised lectures, as one offered by a university.

tel·e·fac·sim·i·le (tĕl′ə-făk-sĭm′ə-lē) *n.* A fax machine.

tel·e·film (tĕl′ə-fĭlm′) *n.* A film made for television.

tel·e·gen·ic (tĕl′ə-jĕn′ĭk) *adj.* Having physical and personal qualities deemed appealing on television.

tel·e·gram (tĕl′ĭ-grăm′) *n.* A message transmitted by telegraph. ❖ *tr. & intr.v.* **-grammed, -gram·ming, -grams** To telegraph (something) or be telegraphed.

tel·e·graph (tĕl′ĭ-grăf′) *n.* **1.** A communications system that transmits and receives simple unmodulated electric impulses, esp. one in which the transmission and reception stations are directly connected by wires. **2.** A message transmitted by telegraph; a telegram. ❖ *v.* **-graphed, -graph·ing, -graphs** —*tr.* **1.** To transmit (a message) by telegraph. **2.** To send or convey a message to (a recipient) by telegraph. **3a.** To make known (a feeling, for example) by nonverbal means. **b.** To make known (an intended action, for example) in advance or unintentionally. —*intr.* To send or transmit a telegram. —**te·leg′ra·pher** (tə-lĕg′rə-fər) *n.* —**te·leg′ra·phist** (-fĭst) *n.*

tel·e·graph·ic (tĕl′ĭ-grăf′ĭk) also **tel·e·graph·i·cal** (-ĭ-kəl) *adj.* **1.** Of or transmitted by telegraph. **2.** Brief or concise.

telegraph plant *n.* A tropical Asian plant (*Desmodium motorium*) having trifoliolate compound leaves, whose very small lateral leaflets move by jerks under the sun's influence.

te·leg·ra·phy (tə-lĕg′rə-fē) *n.* Communication by means of the telegraph.

Tel·e·gu (tĕl′ə-gōō′) *n. & adj.* Variant of **Telugu.**

tel·e·ki·ne·sis (tĕl′ĭ-kə-nē′sĭs, -kī-) *n.* The movement of objects by scientifically inexplicable means, as by the exercise of an occult power. —**tel′e·ki·net′ic** (-nĕt′ĭk) *adj.*

Te·lem·a·chus (tə-lĕm′ə-kəs) *n. Greek Mythology* The son of Odysseus and Penelope, who helped kill Penelope's suitors.

Te·le·mann (tā′lə-män′), **Georg Philipp** 1681–1767. German composer of the late baroque period.

tel·e·mark (tĕl′ə-märk′) *n.* A downhill turn performed on cross-country skis in which the outside ski is advanced ahead of the other and angled inward until the turn is complete. [Norw., after *Telemark,* a region of S Norway.]

tel·e·mar·ket·ing (tĕl′ə-mär′kĭ-tĭng) *n.* The marketing of goods or services by telephone. —**tel′e·mar′ket·er** *n.*

tel·e·med·i·cine (tĕl′ə-mĕd′ĭ-sĭn) *n.* The use of telecommunications to deliver or expedite the delivery of health care services. —**tel′e·med′i·cal** (-ĭ-kəl) *adj.*

tel·e·me·ter (tĕl′ə-mē′tər, tə-lĕm′ĭ-tər) *n.* Any of various measuring, transmitting, and receiving systems used in telemetry. ❖ *tr.v.* (tĕl′ə-mē′tər) **-tered, -ter·ing, -ters** To measure and transmit (data) using telemetry.

te·lem·e·try (tə-lĕm′ĭ-trē) *n.* The science or process of transmitting, as by wire or radio, data measured at a remote location to a distant receiving station for recording and analysis. —**tel′e·met′ric** (tĕl′ə-mĕt′rĭk), **tel′e·met′ri·cal** (-rĭ-kəl) *adj.*

tel·en·ceph·a·lon (tĕl′ĕn-sĕf′ə-lŏn′, -lən) *n.* The anterior portion of the forebrain, constituting the cerebral hemispheres and related parts. —**tel′en·ce·phal′ic** (-sə-făl′ĭk) *adj.*

tel·e·ol·o·gy (tĕl′ē-ŏl′ə-jē, tē′lē-) *n., pl.* **-gies 1.** The study of design or purpose in natural phenomena. **2.** The use of ultimate purpose or design as a means of explaining phenomena. **3.** Belief in or the perception of purposeful development toward an end, as in nature or history. [Gk. *teleios, teleos,* perfect, complete (< *telos,* end, result; see kʷel- in App.) + -LOGY.] —**tel′e·o·log′i·cal** (-ə-lŏj′ĭ-kəl), **tel′e·o·log′ic** (-ĭk) *adj.* —**tel′e·o·log′i·cal·ly** *adv.* —**tel′e·ol′o·gist** *n.*

tel·e·ost (tĕl′ē-ŏst′, tēl′ē-) also **tel·e·os·te·an** (-ŏs′tē-ən) *adj.* Of or belonging to the Teleostei or Teleostomi, a large group of fishes with bony skeletons, including most common fishes. [< NLat. *Teleosteī,* group name (Gk. *teleos,* complete; see TELEOLOGY + *osteon,* bone; see ost- in App.) and < NLat. *Teleostomi,* group name (Gk. *teleos,* complete + Gk. *stoma,* mouth).] —**tel′e·ost′** *n.*

te·lep·a·thy (tə-lĕp′ə-thē) *n.* Communication through means other than the senses, as by the exercise of an occult power. —**tel′e·path′ic** (tĕl′ə-păth′ĭk) *adj.* —**tel′e·path′i·cal·ly** *adv.* —**te·lep′a·thist** *n.*

tel·e·phone (tĕl′ə-fōn′) *n.* An instrument that converts voice and other sound signals into a form that can be transmitted to remote locations and receives and reconverts waves into sound signals. ❖ *v.* **-phoned, -phon·ing, -phones** —*tr.* **1.** To speak with (a person) by telephone. **2.** To initiate or make a telephone connection with; place a call to. **3.** To transmit (a message, for example) by telephone. —*intr.* To engage in communication by telephone. —**tel′e·phon′er** *n.*

telephone book *n.* A directory of telephone subscribers with their telephone numbers and often their addresses.

telephone booth *n.* A small enclosure for a public telephone.

telephone exchange *n.* A central system of equipment that establishes connections between individual telephones.

telephone tag *n.* A series of unsuccessful calls exchanged by two people attempting to contact each other by telephone.

tel·e·phon·ic (tĕl′ə-fŏn′ĭk) *adj.* **1.** Of or relating to telephones. **2.** Transmitted or conveyed by telephone. —**tel′e·phon′i·cal·ly** *adv.*

te·leph·o·ny (tə-lĕf′ə-nē) *n.* **1.** The transmission of sound between distant stations, esp. by radio or telephone. **2.** The technology and manufacture of telephone equipment. —**te·leph′o·nist** *n.*

tel·e·pho·to (tĕl′ə-fō′tō) *adj.* **1.** Of, relating to, or being a photographic lens or lens system used to produce a large image of a distant object. **2.** Of or relating to an instrument that electrically transmits photographs. ❖ *n., pl.* **-tos 1.** A telephoto lens. **2.** A photograph made with a telephoto lens.

tel·e·pho·to·graph (tĕl′ə-fō′tə-grăf′) *n.* **1.** A telephoto. **2.** A photograph transmitted and reproduced by telephotography. —**tel′e·pho′to·graph′** *v.*

tel·e·pho·tog·ra·phy (tĕl′ə-fə-tŏg′rə-fē) *n.* **1.** The process or technique of photographing distant objects, using a telephoto lens on a camera. **2.** The technique or process of transmitting photographs over a distance. —**tel′e·pho′to·graph′ic** (-fō′tə-grăf′ĭk) *adj.*

tel·e·play (tĕl′ə-plā′) *n.* A play written or adapted for television.

tel·e·por·ta·tion (tĕl′ə-pôr-tā′shən, -pōr-) *n.* A hypothetical method of transportation in which matter or information is dematerialized, usu. instantaneously, at one point and recreated at another. [TELE- + (TRANS)PORTATION.]

tel·e·print·er (tĕl′ə-prĭn′tər) *n.* A teletypewriter.

tel·e·proc·ess·ing (tĕl′ə-prŏs′ĕs′ĭng, -prō′sĕs′-) *n.* Data processing by means of remote terminals.

Tel·e·Promp·Ter (tĕl′ə-prŏmp′tər) A trademark for a device used in television to show an actor or speaker an enlarged line-by-line reproduction of a script, unseen by the audience.

tel·e·ran (tĕl′ə-răn′) *n.* An air-traffic control system in which the image of a ground-based radar unit is televised to aircraft in the vicinity as a navigational aid. [Orig. a trademark.]

tel·e·scope (tĕl′ĭ-skōp′) *n.* **1.** An arrangement of lenses or mirrors or both that gathers visible light, permitting observation or photographic recording of distant objects. **2.** Any of various devices, such as a radio telescope, used to observe distant objects by detecting and collecting invisible radiation. ❖ *v.* **-scoped, -scop·ing, -scopes** —*tr.* **1.** To cause to slide inward or outward in overlapping sections, as the cylindrical sections of a small hand telescope do. **2.** To make more compact or concise; condense. —*intr.* To slide inward or outward in or as if in overlapping cylindrical sections. [NLat. *telescopium* or Ital. *telescopio,* both < Gk. *tēleskopos,* far-seeing : *tēle-,* tele- + *skopos,* watcher; see **spek-** in App.]

tel·e·scop·ic (tĕl′ĭ-skŏp′ĭk) *adj.* **1.** Of or relating to a telescope. **2.** Seen or obtained by means of a telescope. **3.** Visible only by means of a telescope. **4.** Capable of discerning distant objects. **5.** Extensible or compressible by or as if by the sliding of overlapping sections. —**tel′e·scop′i·cal·ly** *adv.*

Tel·e·sco·pi·um (tĕl′ĭ-skō′pē-əm) *n.* A constellation in the Southern Hemisphere between Pavo and Sagittarius. [NLat. < *telescopium,* telescope. See TELESCOPE.]

te·les·co·py (tə-lĕs′kə-pē) *n.* The art or study of making and operating telescopes. —**te·les′co·pist** *n.*

tel·e·shop·ping (tĕl′ə-shŏp′ĭng) *n.* The buying and selling of consumer products by way of television and telephone. —**tel•e•shop′** v.

Te•les Pi•res (tĕl′ĭs pîr′ĭs) A river of central Brazil flowing c. 965 km (600 mi) NW as a tributary of the Tapajós R.

tel•es•the•sia also **tel•aes•the•sia** (tĕl′ĭs-thē′zhə) n. Response to or perception of distant stimuli by extrasensory means. —**tel′es•thet′ic** (-thĕt′ĭk) adj.

Te•les•to (tə-lĕs′tō) n. A satellite of Saturn. [< Gk. Telestō, daughter of Oceanus and Tethys.]

tel•e•text (tĕl′ĭ-tĕkst′) n. An electronic communications system in which printed information is broadcast by television signal to sets equipped with decoders.

tel•e•thon (tĕl′ə-thŏn′) n. A lengthy television program to raise funds for a charity. [TELE- + (MARA)THON.]

Tel•e•type (tĕl′ĭ-tīp′) A trademark used for a teletypewriter.

tel•e•type•writ•er (tĕl′ĭ-tīp′rī′tər) n. An electromechanical typewriter that either transmits or receives messages coded in electrical signals carried by telegraph or telephone wires.

te•leu•to•spore (tə-lōō′tə-spôr′, -spōr′) n. See **teliospore**. [Gk. teleutē, termination (< telos, end; see kʷel- in App.) + SPORE.]

tel•e•van•gel•ist (tĕl′ĭ-văn′jə-lĭst) n. An evangelist who conducts religious telecasts. —**tel′e•van′gel•ism** n.

tel•e•vise (tĕl′ə-vīz′) tr. & intr v. -vised, -vis•ing, -vis•es To broadcast or be broadcast by television. —**tel′e•vi′sor** n.

tel•e•vi•sion (tĕl′ə-vĭzh′ən) n. **1.** The transmission of successive visual images, generally with accompanying sound, as electromagnetic waves and the reconversion of received waves into visual images. **2a.** An electronic apparatus that receives electromagnetic waves and displays the reconverted images on a screen. **b.** The integrated audible and visible content of the electromagnetic waves received and converted by such an apparatus. **3.** The industry of producing and broadcasting television programs. [Fr. télévision : télé-, far (< Gk. tēle-, tele–) + vision, vision; see VISION.]

tel•ex (tĕl′ĕks′) n. **1.** A communications system consisting of teletypewriters connected to a telephonic network to send and receive signals. **2.** A message sent or received by such a system. [TEL(ETYPEWRITER) + EX(CHANGE).] —**tel′ex′** v.

tel•ic (tĕl′ĭk, tē′lĭk) adj. Directed or tending toward a goal or purpose; purposeful. [Gk. telikos < telos, end. See kʷel- in App.]

te•li•o•spore (tē′lē-ə-spôr′, -spōr′) n. A thick-walled, usu. blackish resting spore of some rusts and smuts, from which the basidium arises. [TELI(UM) + SPORE.]

te•li•um (tē′lē-əm) n., pl. **-li•a** (-lē-ə) A pustulelike sorus formed on the tissue of a plant infected by a rust fungus and producing teliospores. [NLat. < Gk. teleios, complete. See TELEOLOGY.] —**te′li•al** (-lē-əl) adj.

tell¹ (tĕl) v. **told** (tōld), **tell•ing, tells** —tr. **1.** To give a detailed account of; narrate: told us a story. **2.** To communicate by speech or writing; express with words: tell the truth. **3.** To make known; reveal: tell a secret. **4.** To notify; inform. **5.** To inform positively; assure. **6.** To give instructions to; direct: told them to sit down. **7.** To discover by observation; discern. **8.** To name or number one by one; count: There are 16 windows, all told. —intr. **1.** To give an account or revelation. **2.** To give evidence; inform. **3.** To have an effect or impact. —**phrasal verb: tell off** Informal To rebuke severely; reprimand. [ME tellen < OE tellan.] —**tell′a•ble** adj.

tell² (tĕl) n. A mound, esp. in the Middle East, made up of the remains of a succession of previous settlements. [Ar. tall.]

tell-all (tĕl′ôl′) Informal adj. Revealing intimate or scandalous details: a tell-all memoir. ❖ n. A publication, esp. a memoir, that reveals intimate or scandalous information.

tell•er (tĕl′ər) n. **1.** One who tells. **2a.** A bank employee who receives and pays out money. **b.** An automated teller machine. **3.** One who counts votes in a legislative assembly. —**tell′er•ship′** n.

Teller, Edward b. 1908. Hungarian-born Amer. physicist who helped develop the atomic bomb.

tell•ing (tĕl′ĭng) adj. **1.** Having force and producing a striking effect. **2.** Revealing previously unknown information. —**tell′ing•ly** adv.

tell•tale (tĕl′tāl′) n. **1.** One who informs on another; a talebearer. **2.** Something that indicates or reveals information; a sign. **3.** Any of various devices that indicate or register information, esp.: **a.** A time clock. **b.** Nautical One of the brightly colored lengths of yarn or ribbon attached to the shrouds, stays, or sails of a sailboat, indicating wind direction relative to the boat's motion. **c.** A row of strips hung above a railroad track to warn a passing train of low clearance ahead. **4.** Sports A resonant metal strip across the bottom of the front wall of a racquets or squash court above which the ball must be hit.

tel•lu•ri•an (tĕ-lōōr′ē-ən) adj. Of, relating to, or inhabiting the earth. ❖ n. An inhabitant of the earth; a terrestrial.

tel•lu•ric (tĕ-lōōr′ĭk) adj. **1.** Of or relating to Earth. **2.** Derived from or containing tellurium, esp. with valence 6.

telluric acid n. A white crystalline inorganic acid, H_6TeO_6, used as a chemical reagent.

tel•lu•ride (tĕl′yə-rīd′) n. A binary compound of tellurium.

tel•lu•ri•on (tĕ-lōōr′ē-ŏn′) also **tel•lu•ri•an** (-ən) n. An apparatus that shows how the movement of the earth on its axis and around the sun causes day and night and the seasons. [NLat. : TELLURO- + Gk. -ion, diminutive suff.]

tel•lu•ri•um (tĕ-lōōr′ē-əm) n. Symbol **Te** A brittle metallic element usu. found in combination with gold and other metals, produced commercially as a byproduct of copper refining and used to alloy stainless steel and lead, in ceramics, and, as bismuth telluride, in thermoelectric devices. Atomic number 52; atomic weight 127.60; melting point 449.5°C; boiling point 989.8°C; specific gravity 6.24; valence 2, 4, 6. See table at **element**.

telluro– or **tellur–** pref. **1.** Earth: tellurian. **2.** Tellurium: tellurous. [< Lat. tellūs, tellūr-, earth.]

tel•lu•rom•e•ter (tĕl′yə-rŏm′ĭ-tər) n. A surveying instrument that measures distance by timing reflected microwaves.

tel•lu•rous (tĕl′yər-əs, tĕ-lōōr′əs) adj. Of, relating to, or derived from tellurium, esp. with valence 4.

tel•ly (tĕl′ē) n., pl. **-lies** Chiefly British A television set.

tel•net (tĕl′nĕt′) n. **1.** often **Telnet** An Internet communications protocol that enables a computer to function as a terminal working from a remote computer. **2.** A program that implements this protocol. ❖ intr.v. **-net•ted, -net•ting, -nets** or **-net•ed, -net•ing, -nets** To access an account over the Internet using this protocol.

telo– or **tel–** pref. End: telophase. [< Gk. telos, end. See kʷel- in App.]

tel•o•cen•tric (tĕl′ə-sĕn′trĭk, tē′lə-) adj. Having the centromere in a terminal position. Used of a chromosome.

te•lom•er•ase (tə-lŏm′ə-rās′, -rāz′) n. An enzyme found in the telomeres of certain chromosomes that is active in cell division and may have a role in the proliferation of cancer cells.

tel•o•mere (tĕl′ə-mîr′, tē′lə-) n. Either of the sections of DNA occurring at the ends of a chromosome.

tel•o•phase (tĕl′ə-fāz′, tē′lə-) n. The final stage of mitosis or meiosis during which the chromosomes of daughter cells are grouped in new nuclei. —**tel′o•phas′ic** adj.

tel•os (tĕl′ŏs, tē′lŏs) n. The end of a goal-oriented process. [Gk. See kʷel- in App.]

tel•o•tax•is (tĕl′ə-tăk′sĭs) n. Movement or orientation of an organism toward or away from a particular stimulus.

tel•pher (tĕl′fər) n. **1.** A small traveling car, usu. driven by electricity, suspended from or moving on an overhead rail or cable. **2.** A transportation system using telphers. ❖ tr.v. **-phered, -pher•ing, -phers** To transport by telpher. [Alteration of tel-epher : TELE- + Gk. pherein, to carry; see bher-¹ in App.]

tel•son (tĕl′sən) n. **1.** The rearmost segment of the body of certain arthropods. **2.** An extension of this segment, such as the middle lobe of the tail fan of a lobster. [Gk., limit.]

Tel•u•gu also **Tel•e•gu** (tĕl′ə-gōō′) n., pl. **Telugu** or **-gus** also **Telegu** or **-gus 1.** A Dravidian language spoken in central India. **2.** A member of the Dravidian people who speak Telugu. ❖ adj. Of Telugu, its speakers, or their culture.

tem•blor (tĕm′blər, -blôr′) n. See **earthquake**. [Sp., a trembling, earthquake < temblar, to shake < VLat. *tremulāre < Lat. tremulus, shaking. See TREMULOUS.]

tem•er•ar•i•ous (tĕm′ə-râr′ē-əs) adj. Presumptuously or recklessly daring. [< Lat. temerārius < temere, rashly.] —**tem′er•ar′i•ous•ly** adv.

te•mer•i•ty (tə-mĕr′ĭ-tē) n. Foolhardy disregard of danger. [ME temerite < OFr. < Lat. temeritās < temere, rashly.]

Tem•ne (tĕm′nē) n., pl. **Temne** or **-nes 1.** A member of a people living in Sierra Leone. **2.** Their West Atlantic language.

temp (tĕmp) Informal n. A temporary worker, as in an office. ❖ intr.v. **temped, temp•ing, temps** To work as a temporary worker.

temp. abbr. **1.** temperature **2.** template **3.** temporary **4.** Latin tempore (in the time of)

Tem•pe (tĕm′pē′) A city of S-central AZ E of Phoenix; seat of Arizona State University (est. 1885). Pop. 158,625.

Tempe, Vale of A valley of NE Greece between Mt. Olympus and Mt. Ossa.

tem•per (tĕm′pər) v. **-pered, -per•ing, -pers** —tr. **1.** To modify by the addition of a moderating element; moderate. **2.** To bring to a desired consistency, texture, hardness, or other physical condition by or as if by blending, admixing, or kneading: temper clay. **3.** To harden or strengthen (metal or glass) by application of heat or by heating and cooling. **4.** To strengthen through experience or hardship; toughen. **5a.** To attune. **b.** Music To adjust (the pitch of an instrument) to a temperament. —intr. To be or become tempered. ❖ n. **1.** A state of mind or emotions; disposition. See Syns at **mood¹**. **2.** Calmness of mind or emotions; composure. **3a.** A tendency to become easily angry or irritable. **b.** An outburst of rage. **4.** A characteristic general quality; tone. **5a.** The condition of being tempered. **b.** The degree of hardness and elasticity of a metal, chiefly steel, achieved by tempering. **6.** A modifying substance or agent added to something else. **7.** Archaic A middle course between extremes; a mean. [ME temperen < OE temprian < Lat. temperāre, prob. < var. of tempus, tempor-, time, season.] —**tem′per•a•bil′i•ty** n. —**tem′per•a•ble** adj. —**tem′per•er** n.

tem•per•a (tĕm′pər-ə) n. **1.** A painting medium in which pigment is mixed with water-soluble glutinous materials such as size or egg yolk. **2.** Painting done in this medium. [Ital. < temperare, to mingle < Lat. temperāre. See TEMPER.]

tem•per•a•ment (tĕm′prə-mənt, tĕm′pər-ə-) n. **1a.** The manner of thinking, behaving, or reacting typical of a specific person. **b.** One's distinguishing mental and physical characteristics according to medieval physiology, resulting from dominance of one of the four humors. **2.** Excessive irritability or sensitiveness. [ME < Lat. *temperāmentum* < *temperāre*, to temper. See TEMPER.]

tem•per•a•men•tal (tĕm′prə-mĕn′tl, tĕm′pər-ə-) *adj.* **1.** Relating to or caused by temperament. **2.** Excessively sensitive or irritable; moody. **3.** Likely to perform unpredictably; undependable. **—tem′per•a•men′tal•ly** *adv.*

tem•per•ance (tĕm′pər-əns, tĕm′prəns) *n.* **1.** Moderation and self-restraint, as in behavior. **2.** Restraint in the use of or abstinence from alcoholic liquors.

tem•per•ate (tĕm′pər-ĭt, tĕm′prĭt) *adj.* **1.** Exercising moderation and self-restraint. **2.** Moderate in degree or quality; restrained. **3.** Marked by moderate temperatures, weather, or climate; neither hot nor cold. **4.** *Biology* Of or relating to a virus that infects bacterial cells but rarely causes lysis. [ME *temperat* < Lat. *temperātus* < p. part. of *temperāre*, to temper. See TEMPER.] **—tem′per•ate•ly** *adv.* **—tem′per•ate•ness** *n.*

Temperate Zone Either of two intermediate latitude zones of the earth, the **North Temperate Zone,** between the Arctic Circle and the Tropic of Cancer, or the **South Temperate Zone,** between the Antarctic Circle and the Tropic of Capricorn.

tem•per•a•ture (tĕm′pər-ə-cho͝or′, -chər, tĕm′prə-) *n.* **1a.** The degree of hotness or coldness of a body or environment. **b.** A measure of the average kinetic energy of the particles in a sample of matter, expressed in terms of units or degrees designated on a standard scale. **2a.** The degree of heat in the body of a living organism, usu. about 37.0°C (98.6°F) in humans. **b.** An abnormally high condition of body heat caused by illness; a fever. [ME, temperate weather < Lat. *temperātūra*, due measure < *temperātus*, p. part. of *temperāre*, to mix. See TEMPER.]

temperature gradient *n.* The rate of change of temperature with displacement in a given direction from a given point.

tem•pered (tĕm′pərd) *adj.* **1.** Having a specified temper or disposition. Often used in combination: *sweet-tempered.* **2.** Adjusted or attuned by the addition of a counterbalancing element; moderated or measured. **3.** Made appropriately hard or flexible by tempering: *tempered steel.* **4.** Having the requisite degree of hardness or elasticity. Used of glass or a metal. **5.** *Music* Tuned to temperament. Used of a scale, an interval, a semitone, or intonation.

tem•pest (tĕm′pĭst) *n.* **1.** A violent windstorm, frequently accompanied by rain, snow, or hail. **2.** Furious agitation, commotion, or tumult; an uproar. ❖ *tr.v.* **-pest•ed, -pest•ing, -pests** To cause a tempest around or in. ***—idiom:* tempest in a teacup (or teapot)** A great disturbance or uproar over a matter of little or no importance. [ME < OFr. *tempeste* < VLat. **tempesta*, var. of Lat. *tempestās* < *tempus*, time.]

tem•pes•tu•ous (tĕm-pĕs′cho͞o-əs) *adj.* **1.** Of, relating to, or resembling a tempest. **2.** Tumultuous; stormy: *a tempestuous relationship.* [ME < LLat. *tempestuōsus* < *tempestūs*, tempest, var. of *tempestās.* See TEMPEST.] **—tem•pes′tu•ous•ly** *adv.*

Tem•plar (tĕm′plər) *n.* **1.** A Knight Templar. **2. templar** A lawyer or student of law having chambers in the Temple in London. [ME *templer* < AN < Med.Lat. *templārius* < Lat. *templum*, temple. See TEMPLE[1].]

tem•plate also **tem•plet** (tĕm′plĭt) *n.* **1.** A pattern or gauge, such as a thin metal plate with a cut pattern, used as a guide in making something accurately, as in woodworking. **2.** *Computer Science* **a.** A document or file with a preset format, used as a starting point for a particular application. **b.** An overlay that fits over a keyboard and has labels describing the functions of each key. **3.** A horizontal piece of stone or timber used to distribute weight or pressure, as over a door frame. **4.** *Biochemistry* A molecule of a nucleic acid, such as DNA, that serves as a pattern for the synthesis of a macromolecule, as of RNA. [Prob. < Fr. *templet*, dim. of *temple*, temple of a loom. See TEMPLE[3].]

tem•ple[1] (tĕm′pəl) *n.* **1a.** A building dedicated to religious ceremonies or worship. **b. Temple** Either of two successive buildings in ancient Jerusalem serving as the primary center for Jewish worship. **c.** *Judaism* A synagogue, esp. of a Reform congregation. **2.** Something regarded as having within it a divine presence. **3.** A building used for meetings by a fraternal order. **4.** A building reserved for a highly valued function. **5. Temple** Either of two groups of buildings in London, the Inner Temple and the Middle Temple, that house two of the four Inns of Court and occupy the site of the medieval Knights Templars establishment. [ME < OE *tempel* < Lat. *templum.*]

tem•ple[2] (tĕm′pəl) *n.* **1.** The flat region on either side of the forehead. **2.** Either of the sidepieces of an eyeglasses frame that extends along the temple and over the ear. [ME < OFr. < VLat. **tempula* < Lat. *tempora*, pl. of *tempus*, temple of the head.]

tem•ple[3] (tĕm′pəl) *n.* A device in a loom that keeps the cloth stretched to the correct width. [ME *tempille* < OFr. *temple*, poss. < Lat. *templum*, small piece of timber.]

Temple, Shirley See Shirley Temple **Black.**

temple tree *n.* See **frangipani** 1.

tem•po (tĕm′pō) *n., pl.* **-pos** or **-pi** (-pē) **1.** *Music* The speed at which music is or ought to be played. **2.** A characteristic rate or rhythm of activity. [Ital. < Lat. *tempus*, time.]

tem•po•ral[1] (tĕm′pər-əl, tĕm′prəl) *adj.* **1.** Of, relating to, or limited by time. **2.** Of or relating to the material world; worldly. **3.** Lasting only for a time; not eternal; passing. **4.** Secular or lay; civil. **5.** *Grammar* Expressing time: *a temporal adverb.* [ME < OFr. < Lat. *temporālis* < *tempus, tempor-*, time.] **—tem′po•ral•ly** *adv.*

tem•po•ral[2] (tĕm′pər-əl, tĕm′prəl) *adj.* Of, relating to, or near the temples of the skull. [LLat. *temporālis* < Lat. *tempora*, pl. of *tempus*, temple.]

temporal bone *n.* Either of a pair of compound bones forming the sides and base of the skull.

temporal lobe *n.* The lower lateral lobe of either cerebral hemisphere, located in front of the occipital lobe and containing the sensory center of hearing in the brain.

tem•po•ral•i•ty (tĕm′pə-răl′ĭ-tē) *n., pl.* **-ties 1.** The condition of being temporal or bounded in time. **2. temporalities** Temporal possessions, esp. of the Church or clergy.

tem•po•rar•y (tĕm′pə-rĕr′ē) *adj.* Lasting, used, serving, or enjoyed for a limited time: *a temporary job.* ❖ *n., pl.* **-ies** *Informal* One that serves for a limited time: *an office staffed by temporaries.* [Lat. *temporārius* < *tempus, tempor-*, time.] **—tem′po•rar′i•ly** *adv.* **—tem′po•rar′i•ness** *n.*

tem•po•rize (tĕm′pə-rīz′) *intr.v.* **-rized, -riz•ing, -riz•es 1.** To act evasively to gain time, avoid argument, or postpone a decision. **2.** To engage in discussions or negotiations, esp. to achieve a compromise or gain time. **3.** To yield to current circumstances or necessities; act to suit the time. [Fr. *temporiser* < OFr. < Med.Lat. *temporizāre*, to pass one's time < Lat. *tempus, tempor-*, time.] **—tem′po•ri•za′tion** (-pər-ĭ-zā′shən) *n.* **—tem′po•riz′er** *n.*

tem•po•ro•man•dib•u•lar (tĕm′pə-rō-măn-dĭb′yə-lər) *adj.* Of or formed by the temporal bone and the mandible.

temporomandibular joint syndrome *n.* A disorder caused by faulty articulation of the temporomandibular joint and marked by pain in the head and neck, tinnitus, and dizziness.

tempt (tĕmpt) *v.* **tempt•ed, tempt•ing, tempts** *—tr.* **1.** To try to get (someone) to do wrong, esp. by a promise of reward. **2.** To be inviting or attractive to. **3.** To provoke or to risk provoking. **4.** To cause to be strongly disposed. *—intr.* To be attractive or inviting. [ME *tempten* < OFr. *tempter* < Lat. *temptāre*, to feel, try.] **—tempt′a•ble** *adj.* **—tempt′er** *n.*

temp•ta•tion (tĕmp-tā′shən) *n.* **1.** The act of tempting or the state of being tempted. **2.** Something tempting or enticing.

tempt•ing (tĕmp′tĭng) *adj.* Having strong appeal; enticing: *a tempting repast.* **—tempt′ing•ly** *adv.* **—tempt′ing•ness** *n.*

tempt•ress (tĕmp′trĭs) *n.* A woman who tempts or allures. See Usage Note at **–ess.**

tem•pu•ra (tĕm′po͞o-rə, tĕm-po͝or′ə) *n.* A dish of vegetables and seafood dipped in batter and deep-fried. [J.]

Te•mu•co (tĕ-mo͞o′kō) A city of central Chile SSW of Concepción; founded 1881. Pop. 211,693.

ten (tĕn) *n.* **1.** The cardinal number equal to 9 + 1. **2.** The tenth in a set or sequence. **3.** Something having ten parts, units, or members. **4.** *Games* A playing card marked with ten spots. **5.** A ten-dollar bill. [ME < OE *tīen.* See **dekm̥** in App.] **—ten** *adj. & pron.*

ten. *abbr.* **1.** tenor **2.** tenuto

ten•a•ble (tĕn′ə-bəl) *adj.* **1.** Capable of being maintained in argument; rationally defensible: *a tenable theory.* **2.** Capable of being held against assault; defensible: *a tenable outpost.* [Fr. < OFr. < *tenir*, to hold < Lat. *tenēre.* See **ten-** in App.] **—ten′a•bil′i•ty, ten′a•ble•ness** *n.* **—ten′a•bly** *adv.*

ten•ace (tĕn′ās′, tĕ-nās′, tĕn′ĭs) *n. Games* A combination of two nonsequential high cards of the same suit, esp. in a bridge or whist hand. [Fr. < Sp. *tenaza*, tongs, tenace < *tenaces*, pl. of *tenaz*, tenacious < Lat. *tenāx, tenāc-.* See TENACIOUS.]

te•na•cious (tə-nā′shəs) *adj.* **1.** Holding or tending to hold persistently to something, such as a point of view. **2.** Holding together firmly; cohesive. **3.** Clinging to another object or surface; adhesive: *tenacious lint.* **4.** Tending to retain; retentive. [< Lat. *tenāx, tenāc-*, holding fast < *tenēre*, to hold. See **ten-** in App.] **—te•na′cious•ly** *adv.* **—te•na′cious•ness** *n.*

te•nac•i•ty (tə-năs′ĭ-tē) *n.* The state or quality of being tenacious.

te•nac•u•lum (tə-năk′yə-ləm) *n., pl.* **-la** (-lə) A slender hooked surgical instrument for lifting parts. [LLat. *tenāculum*, holder < Lat. *tenēre*, to hold. See **ten-** in App.]

ten•an•cy (tĕn′ən-sē) *n., pl.* **-cies 1.** Possession or occupancy of a property by title, under a lease, or on payment of rent. **2.** The period of a tenant's occupancy or possession. **3.** A habitation held or occupied by a tenant.

ten•ant (tĕn′ənt) *n.* **1.** One that pays rent to use or occupy property owned by another. **2.** A dweller in a place; an occupant. **3.** *Law* One who holds or possesses lands, tenements, or sometimes personal property by any kind of title. ❖ *tr. & intr.v.* **-ant•ed, -ant•ing, -ants** To hold as a tenant or be a tenant. [ME < OFr. < pr. part. of *tenir*, to hold < Lat. *tenēre.* See **ten-** in App.]

tenant farmer *n.* One who farms land owned by another and pays rent in cash or in kind.

ten•ant•ry (tĕn′ən-trē) *n.* **1.** Tenants considered as a group. **2.** The condition of being a tenant; tenancy.

ten-cent store (tĕn′sĕnt′) *n.* See **five-and-ten.**

tench (tĕnch) *n., pl.* **tench** or **tench•es** An edible Eurasian fresh-

temple[1]
Temple of Hadrian, Ephesus, Turkey, A.D. 117–138

ă	pat	oi	boy
ā	pay	ou	out
âr	care	o͝o	took
ä	father	o͞o	boot
ĕ	pet	ŭ	cut
ē	be	ûr	urge
ĭ	pit	th	thin
ī	pie	*th*	this
îr	pier	hw	which
ŏ	pot	zh	vision
ō	toe	ə	about, item
ô	paw		

Stress marks:
′ (primary);
′ (secondary), as in
lexicon (lĕk′sĭ-kŏn′)

water fish (*Tinca tinca*) having small scales and two barbels near the mouth. [ME *tenche* < OFr. < LLat. *tinca*, prob. of Celt. orig.]

Ten Commandments *pl.n. Bible* The ten injunctions given by God to Moses on Mount Sinai.

tend[1] (tĕnd) *intr.v.* **tend·ed, tend·ing, tends 1.** To have a tendency. **2.** To be disposed or inclined: *tends toward exaggeration.* **3.** To move or extend in a certain direction. [ME *tenden* < OFr. *tendre* < Lat. *tendere*. See **ten-** in App.]

tend[2] (tĕnd) *v.* **tend·ed, tend·ing, tends** —*tr.* **1.** To have the care of; watch over; look after: *tend a child.* **2.** To manage the activities and transactions of; run: *tend bar.* —*intr.* **1.** To be an attendant or servant. **2.** To apply one's attention; attend. [ME *tenden*, short for *attenden*, to wait on. See ATTEND.]

> **SYNONYMS** *tend, attend, mind, minister, watch* These verbs mean to have the care or supervision of: *tended her plants; attends the sick; minded the furnace; ministered to flood victims; watched the house for the owners.*

ten·den·cy (tĕn′dən-sē) *n., pl.* **-cies 1.** Movement or prevailing movement in a given direction. **2.** A characteristic likelihood. **3.** A predisposition to think, act, behave, or proceed in a particular way. **4a.** An implicit direction or purpose. **b.** An implicit point of view in written or spoken matter; a bias. [Med.Lat. *tendentia* < Lat. *tendēns, tendent-*, pr. part. of *tendere*, to tend. See TEND[1].]

ten·den·tious also **ten·den·cious** (tĕn-dĕn′shəs) *adj.* Marked by a strong implicit point of view; partisan: *a tendentious account.* [< Med.Lat. *tendentia*, a cause. See TENDENCY.] —**ten·den′tious·ly** *adv.* —**ten·den′tious·ness** *n.*

ten·der[1] (tĕn′dər) *adj.* **-er, -est 1a.** Easily crushed or bruised; fragile: *a tender petal.* **b.** Easily chewed or cut: *tender beef.* **2.** Young and vulnerable. **3.** Frail; delicate. **4.** Sensitive to frost or severe cold; not hardy. **5a.** Easily hurt; sensitive. **b.** Painful; sore. **6a.** Considerate and protective; solicitous. **b.** Marked by or expressing gentle emotions; loving. **c.** Given to sympathy or sentimentality; soft. **7.** *Nautical* Likely to heel easily under sail; crank. ❖ *tr.v.* **-dered, -der·ing, -ders 1.** To make tender. **2.** *Archaic* To treat with tender regard. [ME < OFr. *tendre* < Lat. *tener.* See **ten-** in App.] —**ten′der·ly** *adv.* —**ten′der·ness** *n.*

ten·der[2] (tĕn′dər) *n.* **1.** A formal offer, as: **a.** *Law* An offer of money or service in payment of an obligation. **b.** A written offer to contract goods or services at a specified cost or rate; a bid. **2.** Something, esp. money, offered in payment. ❖ *tr.v.* **-dered, -der·ing, -ders** To offer formally. See Syns at **offer.** [< Fr. *tendre*, to offer < OFr. < Lat. *tendere*, to hold forth, extend. See **ten-** in App.] —**ten′der·er** *n.*

tend·er[3] (tĕn′dər) *n.* **1.** One who tends something. **2.** *Nautical* A vessel attendant on other vessels, esp. one that ferries supplies between ship and shore. **3.** A railroad car attached to the rear of a locomotive and designed to carry fuel and water.

ten·der·foot (tĕn′dər-fŏŏt′) *n., pl.* **-foots** or **-feet** (-fēt′) **1.** A newcomer not yet hardened to rough outdoor life; a greenhorn. **2.** An inexperienced person; a novice. **3.** often **Tenderfoot** A Boy Scout of the lowest rank.

ten·der·heart·ed (tĕn′dər-här′tĭd) *adj.* Easily moved by another's distress; compassionate. —**ten′der·heart′ed·ly** *adv.* —**ten′der·heart′ed·ness** *n.*

ten·der·ize (tĕn′də-rīz′) *tr.v.* **-ized, -iz·ing, -iz·es** To make (meat) tender, as by marinating, pounding, or applying a tenderizer. —**ten′der·i·za′tion** (-dər-ĭ-zā′shən) *n.*

ten·der·iz·er (tĕn′də-rī′zər) *n.* A substance, such as a plant enzyme, applied to meat to make it tender.

ten·der·loin (tĕn′dər-loin′) *n.* **1.** The tenderest part of a loin of beef or pork or a similar cut of meat. **2.** A city district known for vice and graft. [Sense 2, after the *Tenderloin*, an area of New York City (< the easy income it once afforded corrupt policemen).]

ten·di·ni·tis also **ten·do·ni·tis** (tĕn′də-nī′tĭs) *n.* Inflammation of a tendon. [NLat. *tendō, tendin-*, tendon; see TENDINOUS + –ITIS.]

ten·di·nous (tĕn′də-nəs) *adj.* **1.** Of, having, or resembling a tendon. **2.** Sinewy. [NLat. *tendō, tendin-*, tendon (alteration of Med. Lat. *tendō, tendōn-*; see TENDON) + –OUS.]

ten·don (tĕn′dən) *n.* A band of tough inelastic fibrous tissue that connects a muscle with its bony attachment. [Med.Lat. *tendō, tendōn-*, alteration (influenced by Lat. *tendere*, to stretch) of Gk. *tenōn.* See **ten-** in App.]

ten·dril (tĕn′drəl) *n.* **1.** A twisting threadlike structure by which a twining plant, such as a grape, grasps an object or a plant for support. **2.** Something, such as a ringlet of hair, that is long, slender, and curling. [Fr. *tendrillon* < OFr., dim. of *tendron*, young shoot < *tendre*, tender. See TENDER[1].]

ten·du (tän′dōō) *n.* Any of several Asian ebony trees. [Hindi *tendū* < Skt. *tainduka-*, pertaining to *tindukaḥ*, the evergreen tree *Diospyros embryopteris.*]

Ten·e·brae (tĕn′ə-brā′, -brē′) *pl.n.* (*used with a sing. or pl. verb*) *Roman Catholic Church* The office of matins and lauds sung on the last three days of Holy Week, with a ceremony of candles. [Med.Lat. < Lat. *tenebrae*, darkness.]

ten·e·brif·ic (tĕn′ə-brĭf′ĭk) *adj.* **1.** Serving to obscure or darken. **2.** Gloomy; dark. [Lat. *tenebrae*, darkness + -FIC.]

te·neb·ri·o·nid (tə-nĕb′rē-ə-nĭd′, tĕn′ə-brī′-) *n.* See **darkling beetle.** [< NLat. *Tenebriōnidae*, family name < *Tenebriō*, type

Alfred, Lord Tennyson

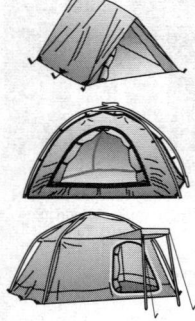

tent[1]
top to bottom: A-frame, pop, and umbrella tents

genus < Lat. *tenebriō, tenebriōn-*, one who avoids light < *tenebrae*, darkness.] —**te·neb′ri·o·nid′** *adj.*

ten·e·brous (tĕn′ə-brəs) also **te·neb·ri·ous** (tə-nĕb′rē-əs) *adj.* Dark and gloomy. [Ult. < Lat. *tenebrōsus* < *tenebrae*, darkness.] —**ten′e·bros′i·ty** (-brŏs′ĭ-tē) *n.*

ten·e·ment (tĕn′ə-mənt) *n.* **1.** A building for human habitation, esp. one rented to tenants. **2.** A rundown low-rental apartment building that just meets minimum standards. **3.** *Chiefly British* An apartment or room leased to a tenant. **4.** *Law* Property, such as land or franchises, held by one person leasing it from another. [ME, house < OFr. < Med.Lat. *tenēmentum* < Lat. *tenēre*, to hold. See **ten-** in App.] —**ten·e·men′tal** (-mĕn′tl) *adj.*

Ten·er·ife (tĕn′ə-rĭf′, -rēf′, tĕ′nĕ-rē′fĕ) A Spanish island of the Canary Is. in the Atlantic Ocean.

te·nes·mus (tə-nĕz′məs) *n.* A painfully urgent but ineffectual attempt to urinate or defecate. [Med.Lat. *tēnesmus*, var. of Lat. *tēnesmos* < Gk. *teinesmos* < *teinein*, to strain, stretch. See **ten-** in App.]

ten·et (tĕn′ĭt) *n.* An opinion, doctrine, or principle held as truth by a person or esp. by an organization. [Prob. < Med.Lat. < Lat., third pers. sing. pr. indic. of *tenēre*, to hold. See **ten-** in App.]

ten-gal·lon hat (tĕn′găl′ən) *n.* See **cowboy hat.** [Perh. < Sp. *galón*, braid, galloon (wrapped in rows above the brim) < Fr. *galon.* See GALLOON.]

ten·ge (tĕn-gĕ′) *n., pl.* **tenge** See table at **currency.** [Kazakh; akin to Skt. *ṭaṅkaḥ*, stamped coin.]

Teng Hsiao-ping (tŭng′ shyou′pĭng′, dŭng′) See **Deng Xiao-ping.**

te·ni·a (tē′nē-ə) *n.* Variant of **taenia.**

te·ni·a·sis (tē-nī′ə-sĭs) *n.* Variant of **taeniasis.**

ten·ner (tĕn′ər) *n. Informal* **1.** A ten-dollar bill. **2.** *Chiefly British* A ten-pound note.

Tenn. *abbr.* Tennessee

Ten·nes·see (tĕn′ĭ-sē′, tĕn′ĭ-sē′) A state of the SE US S of KY; admitted as the 16th state in 1796. Cap. Nashville. Pop. 5,689,283. —**Ten′nes·se′an** *adj. & n.*

Tennessee River A river of the SE US rising in E TN and flowing c. 1,049 km (652 mi) to the Ohio R.

Tennessee walking horse *n.* Any of a breed of lightly built saddle horses developed in Tennessee from Morgan and standard-bred stock and having an easy gait.

Tennessee warbler *n.* A small warbler (*Vermivora peregrina*) of North America having green and white plumage.

Ten·niel (tĕn′yəl), Sir **John** 1820–1914. British cartoonist and illustrator of *Alice's Adventures in Wonderland* (1865).

ten·nis (tĕn′ĭs) *n.* **1.** A game played with rackets and a light ball by two players or two pairs of players on a rectangular court, as of grass or clay, divided by a net. **2.** Court tennis. [ME *tenetz, tenyes*, court tennis < AN *tenetz* and OFr. *tenez*, pl. imper. of *tenir*, to hold < Lat. *tenēre.* See DETAIN.]

tennis bracelet *n.* A bracelet containing many small gemstones set and linked one after the other into a narrow chain.

tennis elbow *n.* A painful inflammation of the tissue surrounding the elbow, caused by strain from sports such as tennis.

tennis shoe *n.* See **sneaker** 2.

Ten·ny·son (tĕn′ĭ-sən), **Alfred.** 1st Baron Tennyson. 1809–92. British poet whose works include *In Memoriam* (1850). —**Ten′ny·so′ni·an** (-sō′nē-ən) *adj.*

teno– or **tenon–** *pref.* Tendon: *tenotomy.* [< Gk. *tenōn*, tendon. See **ten-** in App.]

Te·noch·ti·tlán (tĕ-nôch′tē-tlän′) An ancient Aztec cap. on the site of present-day Mexico City; founded c. 1325 and destroyed by the Spanish in 1521.

ten·on (tĕn′ən) *n.* A projection on the end of a piece of wood shaped for insertion into a mortise to make a joint. ❖ *tr.v.* **-oned, -on·ing, -ons** To provide with or join with a tenon. [ME < OFr. < *tenir*, to hold < Lat. *tenēre.* See **ten-** in App.]

ten·or (tĕn′ər) *n.* **1.** A continuous unwavering course. **2.** The word, phrase, or subject with which the vehicle of a metaphor is identified, as *life* in "*Life's but a walking shadow*" (Shakespeare). **3a.** The course of thought or argument running through something written or spoken. **b.** General sense; purport. **4.** *Law* **a.** The exact meaning or actual wording of a document as distinct from its effect. **b.** An exact copy of a document. **5.** *Music* **a.** The highest natural adult male voice. **b.** One who sings this part. **c.** An instrument that sounds within this range. **d.** A vocal or instrumental part written within this range. [ME < AN < Lat., uninterrupted course < *tenēre*, to hold, continue. See **ten-** in App.]

tenor clef *n.* The C clef positioned to indicate that the fourth line from the bottom of a staff represents the pitch of middle C.

te·nor·rha·phy (tĕ-nôr′ə-fē) *n., pl.* **-phies** The surgical uniting of divided tendons with sutures. [TENO– + Gk. *raphē*, suture (< *raptein*, to sew; see **wer-**[2] in App.) + -Y[3].]

ten·o·syn·o·vi·tis (tĕn′ō-sĭn′ə-vī′tĭs) *n.* Inflammation of a tendon sheath.

te·not·o·my (tĕ-nŏt′ə-mē) *n., pl.* **-mies** Surgical cutting or division of a tendon.

ten·pen·ny nail (tĕn′pĕn′ē, -pə-nē) *n.* A nail 3.0 inches (7.6 centimeters) long. [< its original price per hundred.]

ten·pin (tĕn′pĭn′) *n.* **1.** One of the bottle-shaped pins used in bowling. **2. tenpins** (*used with a sing. verb*) See **bowling** 1a.

ten·pound·er (tĕn'poun'dər) *n.* See **ladyfish**.

ten·rec (tĕn'rĕk') also **tan·rec** (tăn'-) *n.* Any of various insectivorous mammals of the family Tenrecidae of Madagascar and adjacent islands, similar to the hedgehog but having a long snout and often no tail. [Fr. < Malagasy *tandraka*.]

TENS (tĕnz) *n.* A technique used to relieve pain in a body part in which electrodes on the skin intermittently stimulate surface nerves, blocking the transmission of pain signals. [*t(ranscutaneous) e(lectrical) n(erve) s(timulation)*.]

Ten·sas (tĕn'sô') A river of NE LA flowing c. 402 km (250 mi) S to the Ouachita R.

tense[1] (tĕns) *adj.* **tens·er, tens·est 1.** Tightly stretched; taut. See Syns at **stiff, tight. 2.** In a state of mental or nervous tension. **3.** Characterized by nervous tension or suspense. **4.** *Linguistics* Enunciated with taut muscles, as the sound (ē) in *keen*. ❖ *tr. & intr.v.* **tensed, tens·ing, tens·es** To make or become tense. [Lat. *tēnsus*, p. part. of *tendere*, to stretch. See **ten-** in App.] —**tense'ly** *adv.* —**tense'ness** *n.*

tense[2] (tĕns) *n.* **1.** Any one of the inflected forms in the conjugation of a verb that indicates the time, such as past, present, or future, as well as the continuance or completion of the action or state. **2.** A set of tense forms indicating a particular time. [ME *tens* < OFr., time < Lat. *tempus*.]

ten·sile (tĕn'səl, -sīl') *adj.* **1.** Of or relating to tension. **2.** Capable of being stretched or extended; ductile. [NLat. *tēnsilis* < Lat. *tēnsus*, stretched out. See TENSE[1].] —**ten·sil'i·ty** (tĕn-sĭl'ĭ-tē) *n.*

tensile strength *n.* The maximum tension a material can withstand without tearing.

ten·sim·e·ter (tĕn-sĭm'ĭ-tər) *n.* An apparatus for measuring differences in vapor pressure. [TENSI(ON) + −METER.]

ten·si·om·e·ter (tĕn'sē-ŏm'ĭ-tər) *n.* **1.** An instrument for measuring tensile strength. **2.** An instrument used to measure the surface tension of a liquid. [TENSIO(N) + −METER.] —**ten'si·o·met'ric** (-ə-mĕt'rĭk) *adj.* —**ten'si·om'e·try** *n.*

ten·sion (tĕn'shən) *n.* **1a.** The act or process of stretching something tight. **b.** The condition of so being stretched; tautness. **2a.** A force tending to stretch or elongate something. **b.** A measure of such a force. **3a.** Mental, emotional, or nervous strain. **b.** Barely controlled hostility or a strained relationship between people or groups. **4.** A balanced relation between strongly opposing elements. **5.** The interplay of conflicting elements in a piece of literature, esp. a poem. **6.** A device for regulating tautness, esp. that of thread on a sewing machine or loom. **7.** *Electricity* Voltage or potential; electromotive force. ❖ *tr.v.* **-sioned, -sion·ing, -sions** To subject to tension; tighten. [Lat. *tēnsiō, tēnsiōn-*, a stretching out < *tēnsus*, p. part. of *tendere*, to stretch. See TENSE[1].] —**ten'sion·al** *adj.*

ten·si·ty (tĕn'sĭ-tē) *n., pl.* **-ties** The state of being tense.

ten·sive (tĕn'sĭv) *adj.* **1.** Of or causing tension. **2.** *Physiology* Giving or causing the sensation of stretching or tension.

ten·sor (tĕn'sər, -sôr') *n.* **1.** *Anatomy* A muscle that stretches or tightens a body part. **2.** *Mathematics* A set of quantities that obey certain transformation laws relating the bases in one generalized coordinate system to those of another and involving partial derivative sums. [NLat. *tēnsor* < Lat. *tēnsus*, p. part. of *tendere*, to stretch. See TENSE[1].] —**ten·so'ri·al** (-sôr'ē-əl, -sōr'-) *adj.*

ten-speed (tĕn'spēd') *n.* A bicycle having ten different gears.

ten-strike (tĕn'strīk') *n.* **1.** *Sports* A strike in bowling. **2.** *Informal* A remarkably successful stroke or act.

tent[1] (tĕnt) *n.* **1.** A portable shelter, as of canvas, stretched over a supporting framework of poles with ropes and pegs. **2.** Something resembling such a portable shelter. ❖ *v.* **tent·ed, tent·ing, tents** —*intr.* To camp in a tent. —*tr.* **1.** To cover with a tent. **2.** To supply with or put up in tents. [ME < OFr. *tente* < VLat. *tenta* < fem. p. part. of Lat. *tendere*, to stretch out. See **ten-** in App.]

tent[2] (tĕnt) *n.* A small cylindrical plug of lint or gauze used to keep open or probe a wound or orifice. ❖ *tr.v.* **tent·ed, tent·ing, tents** To keep (a wound or orifice) open with such a plug. [ME *tente* < OFr. < *tenter*, to probe < Lat. *tentāre*, to feel, try. See TENTATIVE.]

tent[3] (tĕnt) *tr.v.* **tent·ed, tent·ing, tents** *Scots* **1.** To pay heed to. **2.** To attend; wait on. [ME *tenten* < *tent*, attention, short for *attent* < OFr. *attente* < VLat. **attendita* < fem. p. part. of Lat. *attendere*, to wait on. See ATTEND.]

ten·ta·cle (tĕn'tə-kəl) *n.* **1.** *Zoology* An elongated flexible unsegmented extension, used for feeling, grasping, or locomotion. **2.** *Botany* One of the sensitive hairs on the leaves of insectivorous plants, such as the sundew. **3.** A similar part or extension. [NLat. *tentāculum* < Lat. *tentāre*, to feel, try. See TENTATIVE.] —**ten·tac'u·lar** (-tăk'yə-lər) *adj.*

ten·ta·cled (tĕn'tə-kəld) *adj.* Having tentacles.

tent·age (tĕn'tĭj) *n.* A group or supply of tents.

ten·ta·tive (tĕn'tə-tĭv) *adj.* **1.** Not fully worked out, concluded, or agreed on; provisional. **2.** Uncertain; hesitant. [Med.Lat. *tentātīvus* < Lat. *tentātus*, p. part. of *tentāre*, to try, var. of *temptāre*.] —**ten'ta·tive·ly** *adv.* —**ten'ta·tive·ness** *n.*

tent caterpillar *n.* Any of several destructive caterpillars of the family Lasiocampidae, esp. of the genus *Malacosoma*, whose colonies construct silken tentlike webs in tree branches.

tent·ed (tĕn'tĭd) *adj.* **1.** Covered with tents. **2.** Sheltered in a tent

or in tents. **3.** Resembling a tent.

ten·ter (tĕn'tər) *n.* **1.** A framework on which milled cloth is stretched for drying without shrinkage. **2.** *Archaic* A tenterhook. ❖ *tr.v.* **-tered, -ter·ing, -ters** To stretch (cloth) on a tenter. [ME *teyntur, tentour*, prob. ult. < Lat. *tentōrium*, shelter made of stretched skins < *tendere*, to stretch. See TENT[1].]

ten·ter·hook (tĕn'tər-hŏŏk') *n.* A hooked nail for securing cloth on a tenter. —*idiom:* **on tenterhooks** In a state of uneasiness, suspense, or anxiety.

tenth (tĕnth) *n.* **1.** The ordinal number matching the number ten in a series. **2.** One of ten equal parts. [ME *tenthe*, alteration of *tethe* < OE *tēotha*. See TITHE.] —**tenth** *adv. & adj.*

tent stitch *n.* A short diagonal embroidery stitch that forms close, even, parallel rows to fill in a pattern or background.

ten·u·is (tĕn'yŏŏ-ĭs) *n., pl.* **-u·es** (-yŏŏ-ēz') *Linguistics* **1.** A voiceless stop. **2.** A voiceless unaspirated stop in ancient Greek. [NLat. (transl. of Gk. *psīlos*) < Lat., thin. See TENUOUS.]

te·nu·i·ty (tĕ-nŏŏ'ĭ-tē, -nyŏŏ'-) *n.* The quality or condition of being tenuous. [ME *tenuite* < OFr. < Lat. *tenuitās*, thinness < *tenuis*, thin. See TENUOUS.]

ten·u·ous (tĕn'yŏŏ-əs) *adj.* **1.** Long and thin; slender: *tenuous strands*. **2.** Having a thin consistency; dilute. **3.** Having little substance; flimsy: *a tenuous argument*. [Lat. *tenuis*. See **ten-** in App.] —**ten'u·ous·ly** *adv.* —**ten'u·ous·ness** *n.*

ten·ure (tĕn'yər, -yŏŏr') *n.* **1a.** The act, fact, or condition of holding something in one's possession, as real estate or an office; occupation. **b.** A period during which something is held. **2.** The status of holding one's position on a permanent basis without periodic contract renewals. [ME < OFr. *teneure* < *tenir*, to hold < Lat. *tenēre*, to hold. See **ten-** in App.] —**ten·u'ri·al** (-yŏŏr'ē-əl) *adj.* —**ten·u'ri·al·ly** *adv.*

ten·ured (tĕn'yərd, -yŏŏrd') *adj.* Having tenure.

ten·ure-track (tĕn'yər-trăk', -yŏŏr'-) *adj.* Of or relating to a teaching or research position, as at a college, that can lead to tenure.

te·nu·to (tə-nŏŏ'tō) *adv. & adj. Music* So as to be held for the full time value; sustained. [Ital.< p. part. of *tenere*, to hold < Lat. *tenēre*. See **ten-** in App.]

te·o·cal·li (tē'ə-kăl'ē, tē'ō-kä'lē) *n., pl.* **-lis** A temple of ancient Mexico, usu. built on a pyramidal mound. [Nahuatl : *teōtl*, god + *calli*, house.]

te·o·sin·te (tē'ə-sĭn'tē, tē'ō-) *n.* A tall Mexican and Central American annual plant *(Zea mexicana)* related to corn and cultivated for fodder. [Am.Sp. < Nahuatl *teocintli* : *teōtl*, sacred + *cintli*, dried ear of corn.]

Te·o·ti·hua·cán (tā'ə-tē'wä-kän', tĕ'ō-) An ancient city of central Mexico NE of present-day Mexico City.

te·pal (tē'pəl, tĕp'əl) *n.* A division of the perianth of a flower having a virtually indistinguishable calyx and corolla, as in tulips and lilies. [Fr. *tépale*, alteration of *pétale*, petal < NLat. *petalum*. See PETAL.]

tep·a·ry bean (tĕp'ə-rē) *n.* **1.** An annual twining plant *(Phaseolus acutifolius* var. *latifolius)* of southwest North America. **2.** The edible bean of this plant. [?]

te·pee also **tee·pee** or **ti·pi** (tē'pē) *n., pl.* **-pees** or **-pis** A portable dwelling of certain Native American peoples, esp. on the Great Plains, consisting of a conical framework of poles covered with skins or bark. [Sioux *t^hípi*, dwelling.]

teph·ra (tĕf'rə) *n.* Solid matter that is ejected into the air by an erupting volcano. [Gk. *tephrā*, ash. See dheg^wh- in App.]

Te·pic (tĕ-pēk') A city of W Mexico NW of Guadalajara. Pop. 145,741.

tep·id (tĕp'ĭd) *adj.* **1.** Moderately warm; lukewarm. **2.** Lacking in emotional warmth or enthusiasm; halfhearted. [ME < Lat. *tepidus* < *tepēre*, to be lukewarm.] —**te·pid'i·ty, tep'id·ness** *n.* —**tep'id·ly** *adv.*

TEPP (tĕp) *n.* A crystalline organophosphorus compound, $C_8H_{20}O_7P_2$, that inhibits the action of acetylcholinesterase and is used as an insecticide and in medicine as a stimulant. [T(ETRA)− + E(THYL) + P(YRO)− + P(HOSPHATE).]

te·qui·la (tə-kē'lə) *n.* An alcoholic liquor distilled from the fermented juice of the Central American century plant *Agave tequilana*. [Am.Sp., after *Tequila*, in W-central Mexico.]

Ter. *abbr.* **1.** terrace **2.** territory

tera− *pref.* **1.** One trillion (10^{12}): terahertz. **2.** 1,099,511,627,776 (2^{40}): terabyte. [< Gk. *teras*, monster.]

ter·a·byte (tĕr'ə-bīt') *n.* **1.** A unit of computer memory or data storage capacity equal to 1,024 gigabytes (2^{40} bytes). **2.** One trillion bytes. See Usage Note at **megabyte**.

ter·a·flop (tĕr'ə-flŏp') *n.* A measure of computing speed equal to one trillion floating-point operations per second. [TERA− + FLOP.]

ter·a·hertz (tĕr'ə-hûrts') *n.* One trillion (10^{12}) hertz.

ter·aph (tĕr'əf) *n., pl.* **ter·a·phim** (-ə-fĭm') A small image or idol of an ancient Semitic household god. [Back-formation < *teraphim*, teraphim < Heb. *tərāpîm*, household gods.]

terato− or **terat−** *pref.* **1.** Congenital malformation: *teratogenic.* **2.** Malignancy: *teratoma.* [Gk. < *teras, terat-*, portent, monster.]

te·rat·o·gen (tə-răt'ə-jən, tĕr'ə-tə-) *n.* An agent, such as a virus or drug, that causes malformation of an embryo or fetus.

ter·a·to·gen·ic (tĕr'ə-tə-jĕn'ĭk) *adj.* Of, relating to, or causing

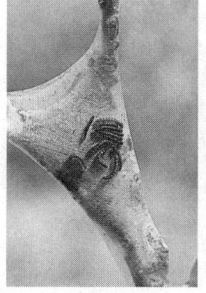
tent caterpillar
tent caterpillar colony

tepee
Washita Battlefield National Historic Site, Cheyenne, Oklahoma

malformations of an embryo or fetus. —**ter′a·to·ge·nic′i·ty** (-jə-nĭs′ĭ-tē) n. —**ter′a·to·gen′e·sis** (-ĭ-sĭs) n.

ter·a·toid (tĕr′ə-toid′) adj. Abnormal in form or development; malformed.

ter·a·tol·o·gy (tĕr′ə-tŏl′ə-jē) n. The biological study of birth defects. —**ter′a·to·log′i·cal** (-ə-tl-ŏj′ĭ-kəl) adj.

ter·a·to·ma (tĕr′ə-tō′mə) n., pl. **-mas** or **-ma·ta** (-mə-tə) A tumor consisting of different types of tissue, as of skin, hair, and muscle, caused by the development of independent germ cells.

ter·bi·um (tûr′bē-əm) n. Symbol **Tb** A soft metallic rare-earth element used in x-ray and color television tubes. Atomic number 65; atomic weight 158.925; melting point 1,356°C; boiling point 3,123°C; specific gravity 8.229; valence 3, 4. See table at **element**. [After *Ytterby*, a town in Sweden.]

terbium metal n. Any of several rare-earth metals separable from other metals as a group and including europium, terbium, and gadolinium.

Ter·borch or **Ter Borch** (tər-bôrk′, -bôrкн′), **Gerard** 1617–81. Dutch painter of portraits and genre scenes.

terce (tûrs) n. Variant of **tierce** 1.

Ter·cei·ra (tər-sîr′ə, tĕr-sā′rə) A Portuguese island of the central Azores in the N Atlantic.

ter·cel (tûr′səl) also **tier·cel** (tûr′səl) n. A male hawk used in falconry. [ME < OFr. *terçuel* < VLat. **tertiōlus*, dim. of Lat. *tertius*, third. See **trei-** in App.]

ter·cen·ten·a·ry (tûr′sĕn-tĕn′ə-rē, tər-sĕn′tə-nĕr′ē) n., pl. **-ries** A 300th anniversary or its celebration. ❖ adj. Of or relating to a span of 300 years or to a 300th anniversary. [Lat. *ter*, thrice; see TERN² + CENTENARY.]

ter·cen·ten·ni·al (tûr′sĕn-tĕn′ē-əl) n. A tercentenary. —**ter′cen·ten′ni·al** adj.

ter·cet (tûr′sĭt) n. 1. A group of three lines of verse, often rhyming together or with another triplet. 2. *Music* See **triplet** 4. [Fr. < Ital. *terzetto* < dim. of *terzo*, third < Lat. *tertius*. See **trei-** in App.]

ter·e·bene (tĕr′ə-bēn′) n. A mixture of terpenes prepared from oil of turpentine, used as an expectorant and antiseptic. [Fr. *térébène* < *térébinthe*, terebinth < OFr. *terebinte*. See TEREBINTH.]

ter·e·binth (tĕr′ə-bĭnth′) n. A small Mediterranean tree (*Pistacia terebinthus*) that is a source of tanning material and turpentine. [ME *terebinthe* < OFr. *terebinte* < Lat. *terebinthus* < Gk. *terebinthos*.]

ter·e·bin·thine (tĕr′ə-bĭn′thĭn, -thĭn′) also **ter·e·bin·thic** (-thĭk) adj. 1. Of or relating to the terebinth. 2. Relating to, consisting of, or resembling turpentine.

te·re·do (tĕr′ē-dō, -rā′dō) n., pl. **-dos** A shipworm of the genus *Teredo*. [NLat. *Terēdō*, genus name < Lat. *terēdō*, a kind of worm < Gk. *terēdōn*. See **tera-¹** in App.]

Ter·ence (tĕr′əns) 185?–159? B.C. African-born Roman playwright whose comedies include *Phormio* and *Adelphi*.

Te·re·sa (tə-rē′sə, -zə, -rā′-), **Mother** 1910–97. Albanian-born Indian nun who won the 1979 Nobel Peace Prize.

Te·resh·ko·va (tĕr′ĕ-shkō′və, tyĭ-ryĭ′-), **Valentina Vladmirovna** b. 1937. Soviet cosmonaut who was the first woman in space (Jun. 1963).

Te·re·si·na (tĕr′ĭ-zē′nə) A city of NE Brazil on the Parnaíba R. ESE of Belém; founded 1852. Pop. 598,411.

te·rete (tĕ-rēt′) adj. Cylindrical but usu. slightly tapering at both ends, circular in cross section, and smooth-surfaced. [< Lat. *teres*, *teret-*, rounded. See **tera-¹** in App.]

Te·reus (tîr′ē-əs, tîr′yōōs′) n. Greek Mythology A king of Thrace who raped Philomela and who was changed into a hoopoe.

ter·giv·er·sate (tər-jĭv′ər-sāt′, tûr′jĭ-vər-) intr.v. **-sat·ed, -sat·ing, -sates** 1. To use evasions or ambiguities; equivocate. 2. To change sides; apostatize. [Lat. *tergiversārī, tergiversāt-*: *tergum*, the back + *versāre*, to turn; see **wer-²** in App.] —**ter′gi·ver·sa′tion** n. —**ter′gi·ver·sa′tor** (-sā′tər) n.

ter·gum (tûr′gəm) n., pl. **-ga** (-gə) The upper or dorsal surface, esp. of a body segment of an insect or other arthropod. [Lat., back.] —**ter′gal** (-gəl) adj.

ter·i·ya·ki (tĕr′ē-yä′kē) n. A Japanese dish consisting of grilled or broiled slices of marinated meat or shellfish. [J. : *teri*, glaze + *yaki*, to broil.]

term (tûrm) n. 1a. A limited period of time. b. A period of time assigned to a person to serve: *a six-year term as senator.* c. A period when a school or court is in session. 2a. A point in time at which something ends; termination. b. The end of a normal gestation period. c. A deadline, as for making a payment. 3. *Law* a. A fixed period of time for which an estate is granted. b. An estate granted for a fixed period. 4a. A word or group of words having a particular meaning: *explained the term gridlock.* b. **terms** Language of a certain kind; chosen words. 5. One of the elements of a proposed or concluded agreement; a condition. Often used in the plural. 6. **terms** The relationship between two people or groups; personal footing. 7. *Mathematics* a. One of the quantities composing a ratio or fraction or forming a series. b. One of the quantities connected by addition or subtraction signs in an equation; a member. 8. *Logic* Each of the two concepts being compared or related in a proposition. 9. A stone or post marking a boundary, esp. a pillar adorned with a head and upper torso. ❖ tr.v. **termed, term·ing, terms** To designate; call. —*idiom:* in

terms of 1. As measured or indicated by; in units of. **2.** In relation to; with reference to. [ME *terme* < OFr. < Lat. *terminus*, boundary. N., senses 4–8 < ME *terme* < Med.Lat. *terminus* < LLat., mathematical or logical term < Lat., boundary, limit.]

ter·ma·gant (tûr′mə-gənt) n. A quarrelsome scolding woman. ❖ adj. Shrewish; scolding. [< ME *Termagaunt*, imaginary Muslim deity portrayed as a violent character in medieval mystery plays, alteration of *Tervagant* < OFr.]

term·er (tûr′mər) n. One serving a specified term.

ter·mi·na·ble (tûr′mə-nə-bəl) adj. 1. Possible to terminate. 2. Terminating after a designated date. —**ter′mi·na·bil′i·ty, ter′mi·na·ble·ness** n. —**ter′mi·na·bly** adv.

ter·mi·nal (tûr′mə-nəl) adj. 1. Of, relating to, situated at, or forming a limit, boundary, extremity, or end. 2. *Botany* Growing or appearing at the end of a stem, branch, stalk, or similar part. 3. Of, relating to, occurring at, or being the end of a section or series; final. See Syns at **last¹**. 4. Relating to or occurring in a term or each term: *terminal inventories.* 5. Causing, ending in, or approaching death; fatal. ❖ n. 1. A point or part that forms the end. 2. An ornamental figure or object placed at the end of a larger structure; a finial. 3. *Electricity* a. A position in a circuit or device at which a connection is normally established or broken. b. A passive conductor at such a position used to facilitate the connection. 4a. Either end of a railroad or other transportation line; a terminus. b. A station at the end of a transportation line or at a major junction on a transportation line. c. A town at the end of a transportation line. 5. *Computer Science* A device, often equipped with a keyboard and a video display, by which one can read, enter, or manipulate information in a computer system. [ME < Lat. *terminālis* < *terminus*, boundary.] —**ter′mi·nal·ly** adv.

ter·mi·nate (tûr′mə-nāt′) v. **-nat·ed, -nat·ing, -nates** —tr. 1. To bring to an end or halt. 2. To occur at or form the end of; conclude or finish. 3. To discontinue the employment of; dismiss. —intr. 1. To come to an end: *Negotiations terminated yesterday.* 2. To have as an end or result. [Lat. *termināre, termināt-* < *terminus*, end.]

ter·mi·na·tion (tûr′mə-nā′shən) n. 1. The act of terminating or the condition of being terminated. 2a. The end of something in time; the conclusion. b. An end of something in space; a limit or an edge. 3. A result; an outcome. 4. *Linguistics* The end of a word, as a suffix, inflectional ending, or final morpheme. —**ter′mi·na′tion·al** adj.

ter·mi·na·tive (tûr′mə-nā′tĭv) adj. Serving, designed, or tending to terminate; conclusive. —**ter′mi·na′tive·ly** adv.

ter·mi·na·tor (tûr′mə-nā′tər) n. 1. One that terminates. 2. The dividing line between the bright and shaded regions of the disk of the moon or an inner planet.

ter·mi·nol·o·gy (tûr′mə-nŏl′ə-jē) n., pl. **-gies** 1. The technical terms used in a particular field, subject, science, or art; nomenclature. 2. The study of nomenclature. [Ger. *Terminologie* < Med.Lat. *terminus*, expression. See TERM.] —**ter′mi·no·log′i·cal** (-nə-lŏj′ĭ-kəl) adj. —**ter′mi·nol′o·gist** n.

term insurance n. Insurance providing coverage for losses during a stated period but becoming void upon its expiration.

ter·mi·nus (tûr′mə-nəs) n., pl. **-nus·es** or **-ni** (-nī′) 1. The final point; the end. 2. An end point on a transportation line or the town in which it is located. 3a. A boundary or border. b. A stone or post marking a border. [Lat.]

ter·mi·nus ad quem (tĕr′mĭ-nōōs′ ăd kwĕm′, tûr′mə-nəs ăd) n. 1. A goal or finishing point. 2. A final limiting point in time. [Lat., limit to which.]

ter·mi·nus a quo (tĕr′mĭ-nōōs′ ä kwō′, tûr′mə-nəs ä) n. 1. A starting point or origin. 2. The first point in a specified period of time. [Lat. *terminus ā quō*, limit from which.]

ter·mi·tar·i·um (tûr′mĭ-târ′ē-əm) n., pl. **-i·a** (-ē-ə) A nest built by a colony of termites.

ter·mi·tar·y (tûr′mĭ-tĕr′ē) n., pl. **-ies** See **termitarium**.

ter·mite (tûr′mīt′) n. Any of numerous pale-colored, usu. soft-bodied social insects of the order Isoptera, many species of which feed on wood, often destroying trees and wooden structures. [NLat. *Termes*, genus name < LLat. *termes, termit-*, woodworm, alteration of Lat. *tarmes.*]

ter·mit·ic (tər-mĭt′ĭk) adj. Of or formed by termites.

term·less (tûrm′lĭs) adj. 1. Having no bounds or limits; unending. 2. Unconditional: *termless surrender.*

term limit n. A statutory restriction on the number of terms an official or officeholder may serve. Often used in the plural.

term paper n. A lengthy written work required of a student on a topic drawn from the subject matter of a course of study.

tern¹ (tûrn) n. Any of various sea birds of the genus *Sterna* and related genera, related to and resembling the gulls but smaller and having a forked tail. [Of Scand. orig.]

tern² (tûrn) n. 1. *Games* A set of three, esp. a combination of three numbers that wins a lottery prize. 2. A three-masted schooner. [ME *terne* < OFr. < *ternes* < Lat. *ternās*, accusative pl. of *ternī*, three each < *ter*, thrice. See **trei-** in App.]

ter·na·ry (tûr′nə-rē) adj. 1. Composed of three or arranged in threes. 2. *Mathematics* a. Having the base three. b. Involving three variables. ❖ n., pl. **-ries** A group of three. [ME < Lat. *ternārius* < *ternī*, three each. See TERN².]

ter·nate (tûr′nāt′, -nĭt) adj. Arranged in or consisting of sets or

Mother Teresa

Valentina Tereshkova

termitarium
Kakadu National Park,
Australia

groups of three, as a compound leaf with three leaflets. [NLat. *ternātus* < Med.Lat., p. part. of *ternāre*, treble < Lat. *ternī*, three each. See TERN².] —**ter′nate·ly** *adv.*

Ter·na·te (tər-nä′tä, tĕr-nä′tĕ) An island of E Indonesia in the N Moluccas E of NE Sulawesi; settled by the Portuguese (1521–74) and subjugated by the Dutch in 1683.

terne·plate (tûrn′plāt′) *n.* Sheet iron or steel plated with an alloy of three or four parts of lead to one part of tin, used as roofing. [Prob. Fr. *terne*, dull (< OFr.; see TARNISH) + PLATE.]

ter·pene (tûr′pēn′) *n.* Any of various unsaturated hydrocarbons, $C_{10}H_{16}$, found in essential oils and oleoresins of plants such as conifers and used in organic syntheses. [Obsolete *terp(entine)*, var. of TURPENTINE + –ENE.] —**ter·pe′nic** *adj.* —**ter′pe·noid′** *adj. & n.*

ter·pin·e·ol (tər-pĭn′ē-ôl′, -ōl′, -ŏl′) *n.* Any of three isomeric alcohols, $C_{10}H_{17}OH$, occurring naturally in the essential oils of certain plants and used as solvents in perfumes, soaps, and medicine. [TERP(ENE) + –INE² + –OL¹.]

ter·pol·y·mer (tər-pŏl′ə-mər) *n.* A polymer that consists of three distinct monomers. [< Lat. *ter*, thrice. See *trei*- in App.]

Terp·sich·o·re (tûrp-sĭk′ə-rē) *n.* 1. *Greek Mythology* The Muse of dancing and choral singing. 2. **terpsichore** The art of dancing. [Lat. *Terpsichorē* < Gk. *Terpsikhorē* < fem. of *terpsikhoros*, danceloving : *terpein*, to delight + *khoros*, dance; see **gher**- in App.]

terp·si·cho·re·an (tûrp′sĭ-kə-rē′ən, tûrp′sĭ-kôr′ē-ən, -kōr′-) *adj.* Of or relating to dancing. ❖ *n.* A dancer.

Terr. *abbr.* 1. terrace 2. territory

ter·ra (tĕr′ə) *n., pl.* **ter·rae** (tĕr′ē) A rough upland or mountainous region of the moon with a relatively high albedo. [Lat., earth, land. See TERRACE.]

terra al·ba (ăl′bə, ôl′bə) *n.* 1. Finely pulverized gypsum used in making paper and paints and as a nutrient for growing yeast. 2. Kaolin. [NLat. : Lat. *terra*, earth + Lat. *alba*, fem. of *albus*, white.]

ter·race (tĕr′ĭs) *n.* 1a. A porch or walkway bordered by colonnades. b. A platform extending outdoors from a floor of a house or apartment building. 2. An open, often paved area adjacent to a house serving as an outdoor living space; a patio. 3. A raised bank of earth having vertical or sloping sides and a flat top. 4. A flat narrow stretch of ground, often having a steep slope facing a river, lake, or sea. 5a. A row of buildings erected on raised ground or on a sloping site. b. A section of row houses. c. A residential street, esp. along the top or slope of a hill. 6. A narrow strip of landscaped earth in the middle of a street. 7. *Chiefly Upper Northern & Midwestern US* See **parking** 3. See Regional Note at **parking.** ❖ *tr.v.* **-raced, -rac·ing, -rac·es** 1. To provide (a house, for example) with a terrace or terraces. 2. To form (a hillside or sloping lawn, for example) into terraces. [Fr. < OFr. < O Provençal *terrassa* < VLat. *terrācea*, fem. of *terrāceus*, earthen < Lat. *terra*, earth. See **ters**- in App.]

ter·ra cot·ta or **ter·ra-cot·ta** or **ter·ra-cot·ta** (tĕr′ə-kŏt′ə) *n.* 1a. A hard semifired waterproof ceramic clay used in pottery and building construction. b. Ceramic wares made of this material. 2. A brownish orange. [Ital. : *terra*, earth (< Lat.; see TERRACE) + *cotta*, baked, cooked (< Lat. *cocta*, fem. p. part. of *coquere*, to cook; see **pekʷ**- in App.]

terra fir·ma (fûr′mə) *n.* Solid ground; dry land. [NLat. : Lat. *terra*, earth + Lat. *firma*, fem. of *firmus*, solid.]

ter·rain (tə-rān′) *n.* 1a. A tract of ground. b. A particular geographic area; a region: *knows this terrain well.* 2. The surface features of an area of land; topography. [Fr. < OFr. < VLat. *terrānum*, alteration of Lat. *terrēnum* < neut. of *terrēnus*, of earth. See TERRENE.]

terra in·cog·ni·ta (ĭn′kŏg-nē′tə, -kŏg′nĭ-tə) *n., pl.* **terrae in·cog·ni·tae** (ĭn′kŏg-nē′tē, -kŏg′nĭ-tē′) 1. An unknown land; an unexplored region. 2. A new or unexplored field of knowledge. [NLat. : Lat. *terra*, land + Lat. *incognita*, fem. of *incognitus*, unknown.]

ter·rane also **ter·rain** (tə-rān′, tĕr′ān) *n.* 1. A series of related rock formations. 2. An area having a preponderance of a particular rock or rock groups. [Alteration of TERRAIN.]

ter·ra·pin (tĕr′ə-pĭn) *n.* Any of various North American aquatic turtles of the family Emydiolae, esp. of the genus *Malaclemys.* [Alteration of *torope* < Virginia Algonquian.]

ter·ra·que·ous (tĕr-ā′kwē-əs, -ăk′wē-) *adj.* Composed of land and water. [Lat. *terra*, earth; see **ters**- in App. + AQUEOUS.]

ter·rar·i·um (tə-râr′ē-əm) *n., pl.* **-i·ums** or **-i·a** (-ē-ə) A small enclosure or closed container in which selected living plants and sometimes small land animals, such as turtles, are kept. [NLat. *terrārium* : Lat. *terra*, earth; see **ter**- + –ARIUM.]

ter·raz·zo (tə-răz′ō, tĕ-rät′sō) *n.* A flooring material of marble or stone chips set in mortar and polished when dry. [Ital., perh. < O Provençal *terrassa*, terrace. See TERRACE.]

Ter·re Haute (tĕr′ə hōt′, hŭt′) A city of W IN on the Wabash R. WSW of Indianapolis. Pop. 59,614.

ter·rene (tĕ-rēn′, tĕr′ēn′) *adj.* Of or relating to the earth; earthly. [ME < Lat. *terrēnus* < *terra*, earth. See **ters**- in App.]

ter·re·plein (tĕr′ə-plān′) *n.* A platform or level ground surface on which heavy guns are mounted. [Fr. *terreplein* < Ital. *terrapieno* < *terrapienare*, to fill with earth : *terra* (< Lat.; see **ters**- in App.) + *pieno*, full (< Lat. *plēnus*; see **pelə-¹** in App.).]

ter·res·tri·al (tə-rĕs′trē-əl) *adj.* 1. Of or relating to the earth or

its inhabitants. 2. Having a worldly, mundane character or quality. 3. Of, relating to, or composed of land. 4. *Biology* Living on land; not aquatic: *a terrestrial animal.* ❖ *n.* An inhabitant of the earth. [ME < Lat. *terrestris* < *terra*, earth. See **ters**- in App.] —**ter·res′tri·al·ly** *adv.* —**ter·res′tri·al·ness** *n.*

terrestrial planet *n.* Any of the four planets, Mercury, Venus, Earth, or Mars, nearest the sun and similar in size and density.

ter·ret (tĕr′ĭt) *n.* 1. One of the metal rings on a harness through which the reins pass. 2. A ring on an animal's collar, used for attaching a leash. [ME *teret*, var. of *toret* < OFr., dim. of *tour, tor*, a round. See TOUR.]

terre-verte (tĕr′vĕrt′) *n.* An olive-green pigment commonly made from glauconite, used by artists. [Fr. : *terre*, earth (< Lat. *terra*; see **ters**- in App.) + *verte*, fem. of *vert*, green (< OFr. *verd*; see VERDANT).]

ter·ri·ble (tĕr′ə-bəl) *adj.* 1. Causing great fear or alarm; dreadful: *a terrible curse.* 2. Extremely formidable. 3. Extreme in extent or degree; intense. 4a. Unpleasant; disagreeable: *terrible food.* b. Very bad: *a terrible movie.* [ME < OFr. < Lat. *terribilis* < *terrēre*, to frighten.] —**ter′ri·ble·ness** *n.*

ter·ri·bly (tĕr′ə-blē) *adv.* 1. In a terrible manner: *terribly wounded.* 2. Extremely; very: *I'm terribly sorry.* 3. To a great extent; very much: *Would you mind terribly if I left?*

ter·ric·o·lous (tĕ-rĭk′ə-ləs) *adj.* Living on or in the ground: *terricolous worms.* [< Lat. *terricola*, earth-dweller : *terra*, earth; see **ters**- in App. + *-cola*, -colous.]

ter·ri·er (tĕr′ē-ər) *n.* Any of several breeds of hunting dog originally developed for driving game from burrows. [ME < OFr. *(chien) terrier*, ground (dog), terrier < Med.Lat. *terrārius*, of the earth < Lat. *terra*. See **ters**- in App.]

ter·rif·ic (tə-rĭf′ĭk) *adj.* 1. Very good or fine; splendid: *a terrific fiddler.* 2. Awesome; astounding: *terrific speed.* 3. Causing terror or great fear; terrifying. 4. Very bad or unpleasant; frightful: *a terrific headache.* [Lat. *terrificus* : *terrēre*, to frighten + *-ficus*, -fic.] —**ter·rif′i·cal·ly** *adv.*

ter·ri·fy (tĕr′ə-fī′) *tr.v.* **-fied, -fy·ing, -fies** 1. To fill with terror; make deeply afraid. 2. To menace or threaten; intimidate. [Lat. *terrificāre* < *terrificus*, terrific. See TERRIFIC.]

ter·rig·e·nous (tĕ-rĭj′ə-nəs) *adj.* Derived from the land, esp. by erosive action. Used primarily of sediments. [< Lat. *terrigena*, earth-born : *terra*, earth; see **ters**- in App. + –GENOUS.]

ter·rine (tĕ-rēn′) *n.* 1. An earthenware container for cooking and serving food. 2. Any of various dishes prepared or cooked in a terrine. [Fr. See TUREEN.]

terrace
terraced rice fields in
Indonesia

ter·ri·to·ri·al (tĕr′ĭ-tôr′ē-əl, -tōr′-) *adj.* 1. Of or relating to the geographic area under a given jurisdiction. 2. Relating or restricted to a particular territory; regional. 3. often **Territorial** Of or relating to an administrative territory. 4. often **Territorial** Organized for national or home defense. 5. *Biology* Displaying territoriality; defending a territory from intruders. ❖ *n.* also **Territorial** A member of a territorial army. —**ter′ri·to′ri·al·ly** *adv.*

ter·ri·to·ri·al·ism (tĕr′ĭ-tôr′ē-ə-lĭz′əm, -tōr′-) *n.* 1. A social system that gives authority and influence in a state to the landowners. 2. A system of church government based on primacy of civil power. —**ter′ri·to′ri·al·ist** *n.*

ter·ri·to·ri·al·i·ty (tĕr′ĭ-tôr′ē-ăl′ĭ-tē, -tōr′-) *n., pl.* **-ties** 1. The status of a territory. 2. A behavior pattern in animals consisting of the occupation and defense of a territory.

ter·ri·to·ri·al·ize (tĕr′ĭ-tôr′ē-ə-līz′, -tōr′-) *tr.v.* **-ized, -iz·ing, -iz·es** 1. To make a territory of; organize as a territory. 2. To extend by adding territory. —**ter′ri·to′ri·al·i·za′tion** (-ə-lĭ-zā′shən) *n.*

territorial waters *pl.n.* Inland and coastal waters under the jurisdiction of a nation or state, esp. the ocean waters within 3 or 12 miles (4.8 or 19.3 kilometers) of the shoreline.

ter·ri·to·ry (tĕr′ĭ-tôr′ē, -tōr′ē) *n., pl.* **-ries** 1. An area of land; a region. 2. The land and waters under the jurisdiction of a government. 3a. A political subdivision of a country. b. A geographic region, such as a colonial possession, dependent on an external government. 4. often **Territory a.** A subdivision of the United States that is administered by an appointed or elected governor and elected legislature. b. A similarly organized political subdivision of Canada or Australia. 5. An area for which a person is responsible as a representative or agent. 6. *Sports* The area of a field defended by a specified team. 7. *Biology* An area occupied by a single animal, mating pair, or group and often vigorously defended against intruders. 8. A sphere of action or interest; a province. [ME < Lat. *territōrium* < *terra*, earth. See **ters**- in App.]

ter·ror (tĕr′ər) *n.* 1. Intense, overpowering fear. See Syns at **fear.** 2. One that instills intense fear. 3. The ability to instill intense fear. 4. Violence committed or threatened to intimidate or coerce, as for military or political purposes. 5. *Informal* An annoying or intolerable pest. [ME *terrour* < OFr. *terreur* < Lat. *terror* < *terrēre*, to frighten.]

ter·ror·ism (tĕr′ə-rĭz′əm) *n.* The unlawful use or threatened use of force or violence to intimidate or coerce societies or governments, often for ideological or political reasons.

ter·ror·ist (tĕr′ər-ĭst) *n.* One that engages in acts or an act of terrorism. —**ter′ror·ist, ter′ror·is′tic** *adj.*

ter·ror·ize (tĕr′ə-rīz′) *tr.v.* **-ized, -iz·ing, -iz·es** 1. To fill or overpower with terror; terrify. 2. To coerce by intimidation or fear. —**ter′ror•i•za′tion** (-ər-ĭ-zā′shən) n. —**ter′ror•iz′er** n.

ter•ry (tĕr′ē) n., pl. **-ries** 1. One of the uncut loops that form the pile of a fabric. 2. A pile fabric, usu. of cotton, with uncut loops on both sides, used for bath towels and robes. [?]

Terry, Dame **Ellen Alice** or **Alicia** 1847–1928. British actress known for her Shakespearean roles.

terse (tûrs) adj. **ters•er, ters•est** Brief and to the point; effectively concise: a terse one-word answer. [Lat. tersus, p. part. of tergēre, to cleanse.] —**terse′ly** adv. —**terse′ness** n.

ter•tial (tûr′shəl) adj. Of, relating to, or being the third row of flight feathers on the basal section of a bird's wing. ❖ n. A tertial feather. [Lat. tertius, third; see TERTIARY + -AL¹.]

ter•tian (tûr′shən) adj. Recurring every other day or, when considered inclusively, every third day: tertian malaria. ❖ n. Pathology A tertian fever, such as vivax malaria. [ME terciana, tertian fever < Lat. (febris) tertiāna, (fever) of the third (day) < tertius, third. See trei- in App.]

ter•ti•ar•y (tûr′shē-ĕr′ē) adj. 1. Third in place, order, degree, or rank. 2. Of, relating to, or being the short flight feathers nearest the body on the rear edge of a bird's wing. 3. Chemistry a. Of or relating to salts of acids containing three replaceable hydrogen atoms. b. Of or being an organic compound in which a group, such as an amine, is bound to three nonelementary radicals. 4. **Tertiary** Of or belonging to the geologic time of the first period of the Cenozoic Era, characterized by the appearance of modern flora and of apes and other large mammals. See table at **geologic time.** ❖ n., pl. **-ies** 1. A tertiary feather. 2. **Tertiary** The Tertiary Period or its deposits. 3. Roman Catholic Church A member of a religious Third Order. [Lat. tertiārius < tertius, third. See trei- in App.]

tertiary color n. 1. A color resulting from the mixture of two secondary colors. 2. A color resulting from the equal mixture of a primary color with either of the secondary colors adjacent to it on a color wheel.

ter•ti•um quid (tûr′shē-əm kwĭd′, tĕr′tē-ŏŏm′) n. 1. Something that cannot be classified into either of two groups considered exhaustive; an intermediate thing or factor. 2. A third person or thing of indeterminate character. [LLat. : Lat. tertium, neut. of tertius, third + quid, something.]

Ter•tul•lian (tər-tŭl′yən, -tŭl′ē-ən) A.D. 160?–230? Carthaginian theologian who formed his own schismatic sect.

ter•va•lent (tər-vā′lənt, tûr′vā′-) adj. Trivalent.

ter•za ri•ma (tĕr′tsə rē′mə) n., pl. **ter•ze ri•me** (tĕr′tsĕ rē′mĕ) A verse form of Italian origin consisting of tercets of 10 or 11 syllables with the middle line rhyming with the first and third lines of the following tercet. [Ital. : terza, fem. of terzo, third + rima, rhyme.]

TESL abbr. teaching English as a second language

tes•la (tĕs′lə) n. The International System unit of magnetic flux density equal to one weber per square meter. [After Nikola TESLA.]

Tesla, Nikola 1856–1943. Serbian-born physicist who discovered the principles of alternating current (1881).

tesla coil n. An air-core transformer used as a source of high-frequency power, as for x-ray tubes. [After Nikola TESLA.]

TESOL abbr. 1. Teachers of English to Speakers of Other Languages 2. teaching English to speakers of other languages

tes•sel•late (tĕs′ə-lāt′) tr.v. **-lat•ed, -lat•ing, -lates** To form into a mosaic pattern, as with tesserae. [< Lat. tessellātus, of small square stones < tessella, small cube, dim. of tessera, a square. See TESSERA.] —**tes′sel•la′tion** n.

tes•ser•a (tĕs′ər-ə) n., pl. **tes•ser•ae** (tĕs′ə-rē′) One of the small glass or stone squares used to make mosaic patterns. [Lat. < Gk., neut. of tesseres, var. of tessares, four. See kʷetwer- in App.]

tes•ser•act (tĕs′ə-răkt′) n. The four-dimensional equivalent of a cube. [Gk. tessera, neut. pl. of tesseres, four; see TESSERA + aktīs, ray of light; see ACTINO-.]

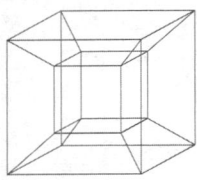

tesseract

tes•si•tu•ra (tĕs′ĭ-tŏŏr′ə) n. The prevailing range of a vocal or instrumental part, within which most of the tones lie. [Ital. < Lat. textūra, web, structure. See TEXTURE.]

test¹ (tĕst) n. 1. A procedure for critical evaluation; a means of determining the presence, quality, or truth of something; a trial. 2. A series of questions, problems, or physical responses designed to determine knowledge, intelligence, or ability. 3. A basis for evaluation or judgment. 4. Chemistry a. A physical or chemical change by which a substance may be detected or its properties ascertained. b. A reagent used to cause or promote such a change. c. A positive result obtained. 5. A cupel. ❖ v. **test•ed, test•ing, tests** —tr. 1. To subject to a test; try. 2a. To determine the presence or properties of (a substance). b. To assay (metal) in a cupel. —intr. 1. To undergo a test. 2. To administer a test. 3. To achieve a score or rating on tests. 4. To exhibit a given characteristic when subjected to a test. [ME, cupel < OFr., pot < Lat. testū, testum.] —**test′a•bil′i•ty** n. —**test′a•ble** adj.

test² (tĕst) n. A hard external covering, as that of certain amoebas, dinoflagellates, and sea urchins. [Lat. testa, shell.]

tes•ta (tĕs′tə) n., pl. **-tae** (-tē′) See seed coat. [Lat., shell.]

tes•ta•cean (tĕ-stā′shən) n. Any of various rhizopods of the order Testacea, characterized by the presence of a shell. [< NLat. Testācea, order name < Lat., neut. pl. of testāceus, covered with a

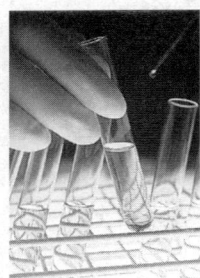

test tube

shell < testa, shell.] —**tes•ta′cean** adj.

tes•ta•ceous (tĕ-stā′shəs) adj. 1. Biology a. Having a hard shell or shell-like outer covering. b. Composed of a shell or shell-like material. 2. Having the reddish-brown or brownish-yellow hue of bricks. [< Lat. testāceus < testa, shell.]

tes•ta•cy (tĕs′tə-sē) n. The condition of being testate.

tes•ta•ment (tĕs′tə-mənt) n. 1. Something that serves as tangible proof. 2. A statement of belief; a credo. 3. Law A written document providing for the disposition of a person's property after death; a will. 4. **Testament** Bible Either of the two main divisions of the Christian Bible. 5. Archaic A covenant between humans and God. [ME, a will < Lat. testāmentum < testārī, to make a will < testis, witness. See trei- in App.] —**tes′ta•men′tar•y** (-mĕn′tə-rē, -mĕn′trē) adj.

tes•tate (tĕs′tāt′) adj. Having made a legally valid will before death. [ME < Lat. testātus, p. part. of testārī, to make one's will. See TESTAMENT.]

tes•ta•tor (tĕs′tā′tər, tĕ-stā′tər) n. One who has made a legally valid will before death. [ME testatour < AN < Lat. testātor < testārī, to make one's will. See TESTAMENT.]

tes•ta•trix (tĕ-stā′trĭks) n., pl. **-tri•ces** (-trī-sēz′) A woman who has made a legally valid will before death. [Lat., fem. of testātor, testator. See TESTATOR.]

test ban n. A mutual and voluntary agreement between nations to forgo testing of nuclear weapons, esp. under specified conditions, as in the atmosphere or under water.

test case n. A legal action whose outcome is likely to set a precedent or test the constitutionality of a statute.

test•cross (tĕst′krôs′, -krŏs′) n. A cross between an individual exhibiting the dominant phenotype of a trait and an individual that is homozygous recessive for that trait in order to determine the genotype of the dominant individual. —**test′cross′** v.

test-drive (tĕst′drīv′) tr.v. **-drove** (-drōv′), **-driv•en** (-drĭv′ən), **-driv•ing, -drives** To drive (a motor vehicle) to evaluate it. —**test′ drive′** n.

test•ee (tĕs-tē′) n. One who takes or has taken a test.

test•er¹ (tĕs′tər) n. One that tests: a battery tester.

tes•ter² (tĕs′tər, tē′stər) n. A canopy, as over a bed or pulpit. [ME < Med.Lat. testrum < LLat. testa, skull < Lat., shell.]

tes•ter³ (tĕs′tər) n. See teston 2. [Alteration of TESTON.]

tes•ti•cle (tĕs′tĭ-kəl) n. A testis, esp. within a scrotum. [ME testicule < Lat. testiculus, dim. of testis, testis. See TESTIS.]

tes•tic•u•lar (tĕ-stĭk′yə-lər) adj. Of or relating to a testis.

tes•tic•u•late (tĕ-stĭk′yə-lĭt) adj. 1. Having the shape of a testicle; ovoid. 2. Botany Having two oblong tubes, as some orchids. 3. Testicular.

tes•ti•fy (tĕs′tə-fī′) v. **-fied, -fy•ing, -fies** —intr. 1. To make a declaration of truth or fact under oath; submit testimony. 2. To express or declare a strong belief, esp. to make a declaration of faith. 3. To make a statement based on personal knowledge in support of an asserted fact; bear witness. 4. To serve as evidence. —tr. 1. To declare publicly; make known. 2. To state or affirm under oath. 3. To bear witness to; provide evidence for. [ME testifien < Lat. testificārī : testis, witness; see trei- in App. + -ficārī, -fy.] —**tes′ti•fi•ca′tion** (-fĭ-kā′shən) n. —**tes′ti•fi′er** n.

tes•ti•mo•ni•al (tĕs′tə-mō′nē-əl) n. 1. A statement in support of a particular truth, fact, or claim. 2. A written affirmation of another's character or worth; a personal recommendation. 3. Something given in appreciation of a person's service or achievement; a tribute. ❖ adj. Relating to or constituting a testimony or testimonial. [ME < OFr., of evidence < LLat. testimōniālis < Lat. testimōnium, testimony. See TESTIMONY.]

tes•ti•mo•ny (tĕs′tə-mō′nē) n., pl. **-nies** 1a. A declaration by a witness under oath, as that given before a court. b. All such declarations, spoken or written, offered in a legal case or deliberative hearing. 2. Evidence in support of a fact or assertion; proof. 3. A public declaration regarding a religious experience. 4a. The stone tablets inscribed with the Law of Moses. b. The ark containing these tablets. [ME < OFr. testimonie < Lat. testimōnium < testis, witness. See TESTIFY.]

tes•tis (tĕs′tĭs) n., pl. **-tes** (-tēz) 1. The reproductive gland in a male vertebrate, the source of spermatozoa and the androgens. 2. An analogous gland in an invertebrate animal, such as a hydra. [Lat., witness, testis. See TESTIFY.]

test match n. A match in cricket or Rugby played by all-star teams from different countries.

tes•ton (tĕs′tŏn′) also **tes•toon** (tĕ-stōōn′) n. 1. A 16th-century French silver coin. 2. An English coin stamped with the image of Henry VIII's head. [Fr. < Ital. testone, augmentative of testa, head < LLat., skull < Lat., shell.]

tes•tos•ter•one (tĕs-tŏs′tə-rōn′) n. A crystalline steroid hormone, $C_{19}H_{28}O_2$, produced in the testes or synthetically and responsible for male secondary sex characteristics. [TEST(IS) + STER(OL) + -ONE.]

test paper n. 1. A paper bearing a student's work for an examination. 2. Paper saturated with a reagent, such as litmus, used in making chemical tests.

test pattern n. A geometric chart transmitted by a television station to assist viewers in adjusting reception.

test pilot n. A pilot who tests new or experimental aircraft.

test tube n. A clear cylindrical glass tube usu. open at one end

test-tube (tĕst′tōōb′, -tyōōb′) *adj.* Produced or cultivated in a test tube.

test-tube baby *n.* A baby developed from an egg fertilized outside the body and implanted in the uterus.

tes·tu·di·nal (tĕs-tōōd′n-əl, -tyōōd′-) *adj.* Testudinate.

tes·tu·di·nate (tĕs-tōōd′n-ĭt, -āt′, -tyōōd′-) *adj.* Of, relating to, or resembling a turtle or tortoise. ❖ *n.* A turtle or tortoise. [< NLat. *Testūdināta*, order name < *Testūdō*, type genus < Lat. *testūdō, testūdin-*, tortoise. See TESTUDO.]

tes·tu·do (tĕ-stōō′dō, -styōō′-) *n., pl.* **-dos 1.** A Roman siege device consisting of a movable screen protecting the besiegers' approach to a wall. **2.** An overhead cover formed by the overlapping shields of besiegers. [Lat. *testūdō* < *testa*, shell.]

tes·ty (tĕs′tē) *adj.* **-ti·er, -ti·est** Irritated, impatient, or exasperated; peevish: *a testy refusal to help.* [Alteration of ME *testif*, headstrong < OFr. *testu* < *teste*, head < LLat. *testa*, skull. See TESTON.] **—tes′ti·ly** *adv.* **—tes′ti·ness** *n.*

WORD HISTORY To the casual eye *testy* and *heady* seem to have no connection; a more thoughtful examination reveals that both words refer to the head. The *head* in *heady* is easy to see in both the form and meanings of the word. The earliest sense, first recorded in a work composed before 1382, is "headlong, headstrong," which is clearly a "head" sense; but so is the better-known current sense "apt to go to the head, intoxicating." To see the *head* in *testy*, we must look back to the Old French word *testu*, the source of our word. *Testu* is derived from the Old French word *teste*, "head" (Modern French *tête*), itself from a colloquial Late Latin word for "skull," *testa*. In English *testy* developed another sense, "aggressive, contentious," which passed into the sense we are familiar with, "irritable."

Tet (tĕt) *n.* The lunar New Year as celebrated in Vietnam. [Vietnamese *tết.*]

te·tan·ic (tĭ-tăn′ĭk) *adj.* **1.** Of, relating to, or causing tetanus. **2.** Of, relating to, or causing tetany. **—te·tan′i·cal·ly** *adv.*

tet·a·nize (tĕt′n-īz′) *tr.v.* **-nized, -niz·ing, -niz·es** To affect with tetanic convulsions; produce or induce tetanus in. **—tet′a·ni·za′tion** (-nī-zā′shən) *n.*

tet·a·nus (tĕt′n-əs) *n.* **1.** An acute, often fatal disease marked by spasmodic contraction of voluntary muscles, esp. those of the neck and jaw, and caused by the toxin of the bacillus *Clostridium tetani*, which typically infects the body through a deep wound. **2.** A state of continuous muscular contraction, esp. when induced artificially by rapidly repeated stimuli. [ME < Lat. < Gk. *tetanos*, rigid, tetanus. See ten- in App.] **—tet′a·nal** (tĕt′n-əl) *adj.*

tet·a·ny (tĕt′n-ē) *n., pl.* **-nies** An abnormal condition characterized by periodic painful muscular spasms and tremors, caused by faulty calcium metabolism and associated with diminished function of the parathyroid glands. [< TETANUS.]

tetch·y also **tech·y** (tĕch′ē) *adj.* **-i·er, -i·est** Peevish; testy. [Prob. < ME *tache, teche*, blemish < OFr. *tache, teche* < VLat. **tacca* < Goth. *taikns*, sign. See deik- in App.] **—tetch′i·ly** *adv.* **—tetch′i·ness** *n.*

tête-à-tête (tāt′ə-tāt′, tĕt′ə-tĕt′) *adv. & adj.* Without the intrusion of a third person; in intimate privacy: *talk tête-à-tête.* ❖ *n.* **1.** A private conversation between two persons. **2.** A sofa for two, esp. an S-shaped one allowing the two occupants to face each other. [Fr. : *tête*, head + *à*, to + *tête*, head.]

tête-bêche (tĕt′bĕsh′) *adj.* Of, relating to, or being a pair of postage stamps printed with one upside down in relation to the other. [Fr. : *tête*, head + *bêche* (short for obsolete *béchevet*, double head of a bed).]

teth (tĕt, tĕs) *n.* The ninth letter of the Hebrew alphabet. [Heb. *ṭêt*, of Phoenician orig.]

teth·er (tĕth′ər) *n.* **1a.** A rope, chain, or similar restraint for holding an animal in place, allowing a short radius in which it can move about. **b.** A similar ropelike restraint used as a safety measure, esp. for young children and astronauts. **2.** The extent or limit of one's resources, abilities, or endurance. ❖ *tr.v.* **-ered, -er·ing, -ers** To fasten or restrict with or as if with a tether. [ME *tedir, tethir* < ON *tjothr.*]

teth·er·ball (tĕth′ər-bôl′) *n.* A game in which two people hit a ball hung by a cord from an upright post until one has wound the cord around the post.

Te·thys (tē′thĭs) *n.* **1.** *Greek Mythology* A Titan and sea goddess who was sister and wife of Oceanus. **2.** *Astronomy* A satellite of Saturn. [Gk. *Tēthys* < Gk. *Tēthus.*]

Te·ton (tē′tŏn′) *n., pl.* **Teton** or **-tons** A member of the largest and westernmost of the Sioux peoples, including the Oglala, Hunkpapa, Brulé, and Miniconjou.

Te·ton Range (tē′tŏn′, tĕt′n) A range of the Rocky Mts. in NW WY and SE ID rising to 4,198.6 m (13,766 ft).

tet·ra (tĕt′rə) *n.* Any of numerous small colorful tropical freshwater fish of the family Characidae, such as the neon tetra, often kept in home aquariums. [Short for NLat. *Tetragonopterīnī*, group name : LLat. *tetragōnum*, tetragon; see TETRAGON + Gk. *pteron*, wing.]

tetra- or **tetr-** *pref.* **1.** Four: *tetrode.* **2.** Containing four of a specified kind of atom, radical, or group: *tetrachloride.* [Gk. See kʷetwer- in App.]

tet·ra·ba·sic (tĕt′rə-bā′sĭk) *adj.* **1.** Containing four replaceable hydrogen atoms in a molecule. Used of acids. **2.** Containing four univalent basic atoms or radicals. Used of bases or salts. **—tet′ra·ba·sic′i·ty** (-sĭs′ĭ-tē) *n.*

tet·ra·caine (tĕt′rə-kān′) *n.* A crystalline compound, $C_{15}H_{24}N_2O_2$, related to procaine and used as a local anesthetic.

tet·ra·chlo·ride (tĕt′rə-klôr′īd′, -klōr′-) *n.* A chemical compound containing four chlorine atoms per molecule.

tet·ra·chlo·ro·eth·yl·ene (tĕt′rə-klôr′ō-ĕth′ə-lēn′, -klōr′-) also **tet·ra·chlor·eth·yl·ene** (-klôr-ĕth′-, -klōr-) *n.* Perchloroethylene.

tet·ra·chord (tĕt′rə-kôrd′) *n. Music* A series of four diatonic tones encompassing the interval of a perfect fourth. [Gk. *tetrakhordon* < neut. of *tetrakhordos*, four-stringed : *tetra-*, tetra- + *khordē*, string.] **—tet′ra·chor′dal** (-kôr′dl) *adj.*

tet·ra·cy·cline (tĕt′rə-sī′klēn′, -klĭn) *n.* An antibiotic, $C_{22}H_{24}N_2O_8$, derived from certain microorganisms of the genus *Streptomyces* and used to treat a variety of infections. [TETRA- + CYCL(IC) + -INE².]

tet·rad (tĕt′răd′) *n.* **1.** A group or set of four. **2.** A tetravalent atom, radical, or element. **3.** *Biology* **a.** A four-part structure that forms during the prophase of meiosis and consists of two homologous chromosomes, each composed of two sister chromatids. **b.** *Botany* A group of four cells, as of spores, formed by division of one mother cell. [Gk. *tetras, tetrad-.* See kʷetwer- in App.] **—te·trad′ic** *adj.*

tet·ra·dy·na·mous (tĕt′rə-dĭ′nə-məs) *adj.* Having six stamens, two of which are shorter than the others. [TETRA- + Gk. *dunamis*, strength; see DYNAMIC + -OUS.]

tet·ra·eth·yl lead also **tet·ra·eth·yl·lead** (tĕt′rə-ĕth′əl-lĕd′) *n.* A poisonous oily liquid, $Pb(C_2H_5)_4$, used in gasoline for internal-combustion engines as an antiknock agent.

tetraethyl pyrophosphate *n.* TEPP.

tet·ra·gon (tĕt′rə-gŏn′) *n.* A four-sided polygon; a quadrilateral. [LLat. *tetragōnum* < Gk. *tetragōnon* : *tetra-*, tetra- + *-gōnon*, -gon.] **—te·trag′o·nal** (tĕ-trăg′ə-nəl) *adj.* **—te·trag′o·nal·ly** *adv.*

Tet·ra·gram·ma·ton (tĕt′rə-grăm′ə-tŏn′) *n.* The four Hebrew letters usu. transliterated as YHWH or JHVH, used as a biblical proper name for God. [ME *Tetragramaton* < Gk. *tetragrammaton*, four-letter word < neut. of *tetragrammatos*, four-lettered : *tetra-*, tetra- + *gramma, grammat-*, letter; see gerbh- in App.]

tet·ra·he·dral (tĕt′rə-hē′drəl) *adj.* **1.** Of or relating to a tetrahedron. **2.** Having four faces. **—tet′ra·he′dral·ly** *adv.*

tet·ra·he·drite (tĕt′rə-hē′drīt′) *n.* A grayish-black mineral, $(CuFe)_{12}Sb_4S_{13}$, often containing other elements and used as an ore of copper. [Ger. *Tetraëdrit* < Gk. *tetraedros*, four-faced (< its four-faced crystals). See TETRAHEDRON.]

tet·ra·he·dron (tĕt′rə-hē′drən) *n., pl.* **-drons** or **-dra** (-drə) A polyhedron with four faces. [L.Gk. *tetraedron* < Gk., neut. of *tetraedros*, four-faced : *tetra-*, tetra- + *hedrā*, face of a geometric solid; see sed- in App.]

tet·ra·hy·dro·can·nab·i·nol (tĕt′rə-hī′drə-kə-năb′ə-nôl′, -nōl′, -nŏl′) *n.* THC.

te·tral·o·gy (tĕ-trăl′ə-jē, -trŏl′-) *n., pl.* **-gies 1.** A series of four related dramatic, operatic, or literary works. **2.** *Medicine* A complex of four symptoms. [Gk. *tetralogia* : *tetra-*, tetra- + *-logos*, word, saying; see -LOGY.]

tet·ra·mer (tĕt′rə-mər) *n.* A polymer consisting of four identical monomers. [TETRA- + (POLY)MER.] **—tet′ra·mer′ic** (-mĕr′ĭk) *adj.*

te·tram·er·ous (tĕ-trăm′ər-əs) *adj.* **1.** Having or consisting of four similar parts. **2.** *Botany* Having flower parts, such as petals, in sets of four. **—te·tram′er·ism** *n.*

te·tram·e·ter (tĕ-trăm′ĭ-tər) *n.* **1.** A line of verse consisting of four metrical feet. **2.** A line of verse consisting of four measures of two feet each. [LLat. *tetrametrus* < Gk. *tetrametron* < neut. of *tetrametros*, having four measures : *tetra-*, tetra- + *-metron*, measure; see -METER.] **—te·tram′e·ter** *adj.*

tet·ra·ploid (tĕt′rə-ploid′) *adj.* Having four times the haploid number of chromosomes in the cell nucleus. ❖ *n.* A tetraploid individual. **—tet′ra·ploi′dy** *n.*

tet·ra·pod (tĕt′rə-pŏd′) *adj.* Having four feet, legs, or leglike appendages. ❖ *n.* A tetrapod vertebrate. **—tet′ra·pod′** *n.*

te·trap·ter·ous (tĕ-trăp′tər-əs) *adj.* Having four wings.

tet·rarch (tĕt′rärk′, tē′trärk′) *n.* **1a.** A subordinate ruler. **b.** One of four joint rulers. **2.** A governor of one of four divisions of a country or province, esp. in the ancient Roman Empire. **3.** The commander of a subdivision of a phalanx in ancient Greece. [ME *tetrarche*, a Roman tetrarch < OFr. < LLat. *tetrarcha* < Lat. *tetrarchēs* < Gk. *tetrarkhēs* : *tetra-*, tetra- + *-arkhēs*, -arch.] **—te·trar′chic** (tĕ-trär′kĭk, tē-) *adj.*

tet·rar·chy (tĕt′rär′kē, tē′trär′kē) also **tet·rar·chate** (-kāt′, -kĭt) *n., pl.* **-chies** also **-chates 1.** The area ruled by a tetrarch. **2a.** Joint rule by four governors. **b.** The four governors so ruling.

tet·ra·spore (tĕt′rə-spôr′, -spōr′) *n.* One of four spores produced by meiosis in certain red algae.

tet·ra·va·lent (tĕt′rə-vā′lənt) *adj.* Having valence 4.

tet·raz·zi·ni also **Tet·raz·zi·ni** (tĕt′rə-zē′nē) *adj.* Made with noodles, mushrooms, and almonds in a cream sauce topped with

tetrahedron

cheese: *turkey tetrazzini.* [After Luisa *Tetrazzini* (1871–1940), Italian operatic soprano.]

tet·rode (tĕt′rōd′) *n.* A four-element electron tube with an anode, cathode, control grid, and additional electrode.

te·tro·do·tox·in (tĕ-trō′də-tŏk′sĭn) *n.* A potent neurotoxin, $C_{11}H_{17}N_3O_8$, found in many puffers and certain newts. [NLat. *Tetrodōn,* genus name (Gk. *tetra-,* tetra- + NLat. *-odōn,* -odon) + TOXIN.]

te·trox·ide (tĕ-trŏk′sīd′) *n.* A chemical compound containing four oxygen atoms per molecule.

tet·ryl (tĕt′rəl) *n.* A yellow crystalline compound, $C_7H_5N_5O_8$, used as a detonator. [< its four nitrite groups.]

tet·ter (tĕt′ər) *n. Chiefly Southern US* Any of various skin diseases, such as eczema, psoriasis, or herpes, characterized by eruptions and itching. [ME *teter* < OE.]

Teut. *abbr.* **1.** Teuton **2.** Teutonic

Teu·to·bur·ger Wald (tōō′tə-bûr′gər wôld′, toi′tō-bŏŏr′gər vält′) A range of wooded hills in NW Germany between the upper Ems and the Weser rivers.

Teu·ton (tōōt′n, tyōōt′n) *n.* **1.** A member of an ancient people, probably of Germanic or Celtic origin, who lived in Jutland until about 100 B.C. **2.** A member of any of the peoples speaking a Germanic language, esp. a German. [Lat. *Teutonī,* Teutons < *teutā-* in App.]

Teu·ton·ic (tōō-tŏn′ĭk, tyōō-) *adj.* **1.** Of or relating to the ancient Teutons. **2.** Of or relating to the Germanic languages or their speakers. ❖ *n.* Germanic. [Lat. *Teutonicus* < *Teutonī,* Teutons. See TEUTON.]

Teu·ton·ism (tōōt′n-ĭz′əm, tyōōt′-) also **Teu·ton·i·cism** (tōō-tŏn′ĭ-sĭz′əm, tyōō-) *n.* **1.** A Germanism. **2.** German character or civilization. —**Teu′ton·ist** *n.*

Teu·ton·ize (tōōt′n-īz′, tyōōt′-) *tr.v.* **-ized, -iz·ing, -iz·es** To Germanize. —**Teu′ton·i·za′tion** (-ĭ-zā′shən) *n.*

Te·vet also **Te·bet** or **Te·beth** (tā′vās, tĕ-vĕt′) *n.* The fourth month of the year in the Jewish calendar. See table at **calendar.** [Heb. *ṭēbēt* < Akkadian *ṭebētu,* a month name (December/January).]

Te·wa (tā′wə, tĕ′wə) *n., pl.* **Tewa** or **-was** **1.** A member of a group of Pueblo peoples of northern New Mexico. **2.** The group of Tanoan languages spoken by the Tewa.

Tewkes·bur·y (tōōks′bĕr′ē, -bə-rē, -brē, tyōōks′-) A municipal borough of W-central England on the Severn R.; site of the last battle of the Wars of the Roses (1471). Pop. 9,554.

Tex. *abbr.* Texas

Tex·ar·kan·a (tĕk′sär-kăn′ə) A city of SW AR on the TX border SW of Little Rock. Pop. 26,448. It is adjacent to **Texarkana** TX, in the NE part of that state. Pop. 34,782.

tex·as (tĕk′səs) *n.* A structure on a river steamboat containing the pilothouse and the officers' quarters. [After TEXAS (because steamboat cabins were named after states and the officers' quarters were the largest).]

Texas A state of the S-central US; admitted as the 28th state in 1845. The region won its independence from Mexico in 1836 and was a self-governing republic until 1845. Cap. Austin. Pop. 20,851,820. —**Tex′an** *adj. & n.*

Texas fever *n.* An infectious disease of cattle first identified in Texas, characterized by high fever, anemia, and emaciation and caused by a parasitic protozoan *(Babesia bigemina).*

Texas leaguer *n. Baseball* A fly ball that drops between an infielder and an outfielder for a hit. [After the *Texas League,* a baseball minor league.]

Texas Ranger *n.* **1.** A member of a division of the Texas state highway patrol. **2.** A member of a former mounted force of Texans organized in 1835 to maintain order on the frontier.

Tex-Mex (tĕks′mĕks′) *adj.* Of or marked by a blend of Mexican and southwest US cultural elements. [TEX(AS) + MEX(ICAN).]

text (tĕkst) *n.* **1a.** The original words of something written or printed, as opposed to a paraphrase, translation, revision, or condensation. **b.** The printed version of a speech. **c.** Words, as of a libretto, that are set to music in a composition. **d.** Words treated as data by a computer. **2.** The body of a printed work as distinct from headings, illustrative matter, or front and back matter in a book. **3.** One of the editions or forms of a written work. **4.** Something, such as a literary work, regarded as an object of critical analysis. **5.** A passage from the Scriptures or another authoritative source used as the basis for a discourse or an argument. **6.** A passage from a written work used as the starting point of a discussion. **7.** A subject; a topic. **8.** A textbook. [ME *texte* < OFr. < LLat. *textus,* written account < Lat. *textus,* structure, context, body of a passage < p. part. of *texere,* to weave, fabricate.]

text·book (tĕkst′bŏŏk′) *n.* A book used for the formal study of a subject. ❖ *adj.* Being a typical example of its kind; classic: *a textbook case of schizophrenia.* —**text′book′ish** *adj.*

text edition *n.* An edition of a book designed esp. for use in schools or colleges.

tex·tile (tĕks′tīl′, -təl) *n.* **1.** A cloth, esp. one manufactured by weaving or knitting; a fabric. **2.** Fiber or yarn for weaving or knitting into cloth. [Lat. < neut. of *textilis,* woven < *textus,* p. part. of *texere,* to weave. See TEXT.]

tex·tu·al (tĕks′chōō-əl) *adj.* Of, relating to, or conforming to a text. —**tex′tu·al·ly** *adv.*

textual criticism *n.* **1.** The study of manuscripts or printings to determine the original or most authoritative form of a text, esp. of a piece of literature. **2.** Literary criticism stressing close reading and detailed analysis of a particular text.

tex·tu·al·ism (tĕks′chōō-ə-lĭz′əm) *n.* **1.** Strict adherence to a text, esp. of the Scriptures. **2.** Textual criticism, esp. of the Scriptures. —**tex′tu·al·ist** *n.*

tex·tu·ar·y (tĕks′chōō-ĕr′ē) *adj.* Of or contained in a text; textual. ❖ *n., pl.* **-ies** A specialist in the Scriptures.

tex·ture (tĕks′chər) *n.* **1.** A structure of interwoven fibers or other elements. **2.** The distinctive physical composition or structure of something, esp. with respect to the size, shape, and arrangment of its parts. **3a.** The appearance and feel of a surface: *the smooth texture of soap.* **b.** A rough or grainy surface quality. **4.** Distinctive or identifying quality or character. **5.** The quality given to a piece of art, literature, or music by the interrelationship of its elements. ❖ *tr.v.* **-tured, -tur·ing, -tures** To give texture to, esp. to impart desirable surface characteristics to. [ME < OFr. < Lat. *textūra* < *textus,* p. part. of *texere,* to weave. See TEXT.] —**tex′tur·al** *adj.* —**tex′tur·al·ly** *adv.* —**tex′tured** *adj.*

tex·tur·ize (tĕks′chə-rīz′) *tr.v.* **-ized, -iz·ing, -iz·es** To give a desired texture to by a special process. —**tex′tur·iz′er** *n.*

tex·tus re·cep·tus (tĕk′təs rĭ-sĕp′təs) *n.* **1. Textus Receptus** The Greek text of the New Testament that became standard in printed editions from the 16th to the end of the 19th century. **2.** The text of a written work that is generally considered genuine or original. [Lat., received text : *textus,* text + *receptus,* p. part. of *recipere,* to receive.]

tfr. *abbr.* transfer

TG *abbr.* transformational grammar

t.g. *abbr.* type genus

TGIF *abbr.* thank God it's Friday

Th¹ The symbol for the element **thorium.**

Th² *abbr.* **1.** *Bible* Thessalonians **2.** Thursday

–th¹ *suff.* Variant of **-eth¹.**

–th² *suff.* **1.** Act; process: *spilth.* **2.** State; quality: *dearth.* [ME < OE *-thu,* n. suff.]

–th³ also **-eth** *suff.* Used to form ordinal numbers: *millionth.* [ME *-the* < OE *-tha, -the.*]

Thack·er·ay (thăk′ə-rē, thăk′rē), **William Makepeace** 1811–63. British writer whose novels include *Vanity Fair* (1847–48). —**Thack′er·ay·an** *adj.*

Thai (tī) *n., pl.* **Thai** or **Thais 1a.** A native or inhabitant of Thailand. **b.** A member of a Tai-speaking people who constitute the predominant ethnic group of Thailand. **2.** The language of the Tai family that is the official language of Thailand. **3.** Tai. ❖ *adj.* **1.** Of or relating to Thailand or its peoples, languages, or cultures. **2.** Tai.

Thai·land (tī′lănd′, -lənd) A country of SE Asia on the **Gulf of Thailand,** an arm of the South China Sea; became a constitutional monarchy in 1932. Prior to 1939, the country was known as Siam. Cap. Bangkok. Pop. 59,396,000.

Thailand

thal·a·men·ceph·a·lon (thăl′ə-mĕn-sĕf′ə-lŏn′) *n.* See diencephalon. [THALAM(US) + ENCEPHALON.]

thal·a·mus (thăl′ə-məs) *n., pl.* **-mi** (-mī′) **1.** *Anatomy* A large ovoid mass of gray matter situated in the posterior part of the forebrain that relays sensory impulses to the cerebral cortex. **2.** *Botany* The receptacle of a flower. [Lat., inner chamber < Gk. *thalamos.*] —**tha·lam′ic** (thə-lăm′ĭk) *adj.*

thal·as·se·mi·a (thăl′ə-sē′mē-ə) *n.* An inherited form of anemia occurring chiefly among people of Mediterranean descent, caused by faulty synthesis of part of the hemoglobin molecule. [Gk. *thalassa,* sea + -EMIA.] —**thal′as·se′mic** *adj.*

tha·las·sic (thə-lăs′ĭk) *adj.* Of or relating to seas or oceans, esp. smaller seas. [Fr. *thalassique* < Gk. *thalassa,* sea.]

thal·as·soc·ra·cy (thăl′ə-sŏk′rə-sē) *n., pl.* **-cies** Naval or commercial supremacy on the seas. [Gk. *thalassokratiā :* thalassa, sea + -kratiā, -cracy.]

Thal·berg (thôl′bûrg′, thôl′-), **Irving Grant** 1899–1936. Amer. film producer and vice president of Metro-Goldwyn-Mayer.

tha·ler (tä′lər) *n.* Variant of **taler.**

Tha·les (thā′lēz) 624?–546? B.C. Greek philosopher who was a founder of geometry and abstract astronomy. —**Tha·le′sian** (thā-lē′zhən) *adj.*

Tha·li·a (thə-lī′ə, thā′lē-ə, thăl′yə) *n. Greek Mythology* **1.** The Muse of comedy and pastoral poetry. **2.** One of the three Graces.

tha·lid·o·mide (thə-lĭd′ə-mīd′) *n.* A sedative and hypnotic drug, $C_{13}H_{10}N_2O_4$, withdrawn from sale after it was found to cause severe birth defects, esp. of the limbs, when taken during pregnancy. [(PH)THAL(IC ACID) + (IM)ID(E) + (I)MIDE.]

thal·lic (thăl′ĭk) *adj.* Of, relating to, or containing thallium, esp. with valence 3.

thal·li·um (thăl′ē-əm) *n. Symbol* **Tl** A soft, malleable, highly toxic metallic element, used in photocells, infrared detectors, and low-melting glass. Atomic number 81; atomic weight 204.38; melting point 303.5°C; boiling point 1,457°C; specific gravity 11.85; valence 1, 3. See table at **element.** [THALL(O)- (< its green spectral line) + -IUM.]

thallo– or **thall–** *pref.* **1a.** Young, green shoot: *thallium.* **b.** Thallus: *thalloid.* **2.** Thallium: *thallous.* [Gk. < *thallos.* See THALLUS.]

thal·loid (thăl′oid′) also **thal·loi·dal** (thə-loid′l) *adj.* Of, resembling, or constituting a thallus.

thal•lo•phyte (thăl′ə-fīt′) *n.* Any of a group of plantlike organisms showing no differentiation into stem, root, or leaf, such as algae. **—thal′lo•phyt′ic** (-fĭt′ĭk) *adj.*

thal•lous (thăl′əs) *adj.* Of, relating to, or containing thallium, esp. with valence 1.

thal•lus (thăl′əs) *n., pl.* **thal•li** (thăl′ī) or **-lus•es** A plant body undifferentiated into stem, root, or leaf. [Lat., green stalk < Gk. *thallos* < *thallein*, to sprout.]

thal•weg (täl′vĕg′) *n. Geology* **1.** The line defining the lowest points along the length of a river bed or valley. **2.** A subterranean stream. [Ger. : *Tal, Thal*, valley (< MHGer. *tal* < OHGer.) + *Weg*, way (< MHGer. *wec, weg* < OHGer. *weg*; see **wegh-** in App.).]

Thames (tĕmz) **1.** A river of SE Ontario, Canada, flowing c. 257 km (160 mi) SW to Lake St. Clair. **2.** A river of S England flowing c. 338 km (210 mi) E to a wide estuary on the North Sea. **3.** (thāmz, tāmz) A tidal estuary of SE CT flowing c. 24 km (15 mi) to Long Island Sound.

Tham•muz (tä′mo͝oz′) *n.* Variant of **Tammuz.**

than (*th*ăn, *th*ən) *conj.* **1.** Used to introduce the second element or clause of an unequal comparison: *She is a better athlete than I.* **2.** Used to introduce the second element after certain words indicating difference: *He draws differently than she does.* **3.** *Usage Problem* When. Used esp. after *hardly* and *scarcely*: *I had scarcely walked in the door than the commotion started.* ❖ *prep. Usage Problem* In comparison with: *disliked no one more than her.* [ME < OE *thanne, than.* See **to-** in App.]

USAGE NOTE According to the traditional view, the case of a pronoun following *than* is determined by whether the pronoun serves as the subject or object of the verb that is "understood." Thus, the standard rule requires *Pat is taller than I* on the assumption that this sentence is elliptical for *Pat is taller than I am* but allows *The news surprised Pat more than me*, since this sentence is taken as elliptical for *The news surprised Pat more than it surprised me.* However, *than* is quite commonly treated as a preposition when followed by an isolated noun phrase, and as such occurs with a pronoun in the objective case: *John is taller than me.* Though this usage is predominant in speech and has reputable literary precedent, it is still widely regarded as incorrect. • Comparatives using *as . . . as* can be analyzed in a parallel way to those using *than.* Traditional grammarians insist that *I am not as tall as he* is the only correct form, and though both literary precedent and syntactic arguments can be marshaled in support of the analysis of the second *as* as a preposition, one should treat this use of *as* as a conjunction in formal writing. See Usage Notes at **as¹, different, scarcely.**

than•age (thā′nĭj) *n.* **1.** The rank, jurisdiction, or office of a thane. **2.** The land held by a thane.

than•a•tol•o•gy (thăn′ə-tŏl′ə-jē) *n.* The study of death and dying, esp. in their psychological and social aspects. [Gk. *thanatos*, death + –LOGY.] **—than′a•to•log′i•cal** (-tl-ŏj′ĭ-kəl) *adj.* **—than′a•tol′o•gist** *n.*

than•a•top•sis (thăn′ə-tŏp′sĭs) *n.* A meditation upon death. [Gk. *thanatos*, death + –OPSIS.]

Than•a•tos (thăn′ə-tōs′) *n.* **1.** Death as a personification or as a philosophical notion. **2.** See **death instinct** 1. [Gk.] **—than′a•tot′ic** (-tŏt′ĭk) *adj.*

thane (thān) *n.* **1.** A freeman granted land by the king in return for military service in Anglo-Saxon England and ranking above an ordinary freeman and below a nobleman. **2.** A feudal lord or baron in Scotland. [ME < OE *thegn.* See **tek-** in App.] **—thane′ship′** *n.*

thank (thăngk) *tr.v.* **thanked, thank•ing, thanks 1.** To express gratitude to; give thanks to: *He thanked her for the gift.* **2.** To hold responsible; credit. [ME *thanken* < OE *thancian.*]

thank•ful (thăngk′fəl) *adj.* **1.** Aware and appreciative of a benefit; grateful. **2.** Expressive of gratitude: *responded with a thankful smile.* **—thank′ful•ly** *adv.* **—thank′ful•ness** *n.*

thank•less (thăngk′lĭs) *adj.* **1.** Not feeling or showing gratitude; ungrateful. **2.** Not likely to be appreciated: *a thankless job.* **—thank′less•ly** *adv.* **—thank′less•ness** *n.*

thanks (thăngks) *pl.n.* **1.** Grateful feelings or thoughts; gratitude. **2.** An expression of gratitude. ❖ *interj.* Used to express thanks. ***—idioms:* no thanks to** Without the benefit of help from. **thanks to** On account of; because of.

thanks•giv•ing (thăngks-gĭv′ĭng) *n.* **1.** An act of giving thanks; an expression of gratitude, esp. to God: *a hymn of thanksgiving.* **2. Thanksgiving** Thanksgiving Day.

Thanksgiving Day *n.* **1.** The fourth Thursday of November, observed as a legal holiday in the United States to commemorate the feast held at Plymouth in 1621 by the colonists and the Wampanoag people and marked by the giving of thanks to God for harvest and health. **2.** The second Monday of October, celebrated in Canada by the giving of thanks to God for harvest and health.

thank•wor•thy (thăngk′wûr′*th*ē) *adj.* **-thi•er, -thi•est** Worthy of or deserving thanks.

thank-you (thăngk′yo͞o′) *n.* An expression of gratitude.

Thant (thänt, thănt), **U** 1909–74. Burmese diplomat who served as secretary-general of the United Nations (1961–71).

Thap•sus (thăp′səs) An ancient city of N Africa on the Mediterranean Sea in present-day Tunisia.

Thar Desert (tär) also **Great Indian Desert** A sandy region of NW India and SE Pakistan between the Indus and Sutlej river valleys.

Tharp (thärp), **Twyla** b. 1941. Amer. dancer and choreographer whose works include *Deuce Coupe* (1973).

Thá•sos (thā′sŏs′, thä′sôs) An island of NE Greece in the N Aegean Sea; ceded to Greece in 1913.

that (*th*ăt, *th*ət) *pron., pl.* **those** (*th*ōz) **1a.** Used to refer to the one designated, implied, mentioned, or understood: *Whose soup is that?* **b.** Used to refer to the one, thing, or type specified as follows: *The relics found were those of an earlier time.* **c.** Used to refer to the event, action, or time just mentioned: *After that, he fled.* **2.** Used to indicate the farther or less immediate one: *That is for sale; this is not.* **3.** Used to emphasize the idea of a previously expressed word or phrase: *He was fed up, and that to a great degree.* **4.** The one, kind, or thing; something: *She followed the calling of that she loved.* **5. those** Used to indicate an unspecified number of people. **6.** Used as a relative pronoun to introduce a clause, esp. a restrictive clause: *the car that has the flat tire.* **7a.** In, on, by, or with which: *each summer that the concerts are performed.* **b.** According to what; insofar as: *not that I know of.* ❖ *adj., pl.* **those 1.** Being the one singled out, implied, or understood: *that place.* **2.** Being the one farther removed or less obvious: *That route is shorter than this one.* ❖ *adv.* **1.** To such an extent or degree: *Is your problem that complicated?* **2.** To a high degree; very: *didn't take him that seriously.* ❖ *conj.* **1.** Used to introduce a noun clause that is usu. the subject or object of a verb or a predicate nominative: *That your dogs bark is inevitable.* **2.** Used to introduce a subordinate clause stating a result, wish, purpose, reason, or cause: *hoped that he would stop.* **3a.** Used to introduce an anticipated subordinate clause following the expletive *it* occurring as subject of the verb: *It is true that I want to stop.* **b.** Used to introduce a subordinate clause modifying an adverb or adverbial expression: *will go anywhere that they can.* **c.** Used to introduce a subordinate clause that is joined to an adjective or noun as a complement: *was sure that she was right.* **4.** Used to introduce an elliptical exclamation of desire: *Oh, that I were rich!* ***—idioms:* at that 1.** In addition; besides. **2.** Regardless of what has been said or implied. **that is** To explain more clearly; in other words: *the first floor, that is, the floor at street level.* [ME < OE *thæt.* See **to-** in App.]

USAGE NOTE The standard rule requires that *that* should be used only to introduce a restrictive (or defining) relative clause, which identifies the entity being talked about; in this use it should never be preceded by a comma. Thus, in the sentence *The house that Jack built has been torn down*, the clause *that Jack built* is a restrictive clause identifying the specific house that was torn down. A related rule stipulates that *which* should be used with nonrestrictive (or nondefining) clauses, which give additional information about an entity that has already been identified in the context; in this use, *which* is always preceded by a comma. Thus, we say *The students in Chemistry 101 have been complaining about the textbook, which* (not *that*) *is hard to follow.* The clause *which is hard to follow* is nonrestrictive in that it does not indicate which text is being complained about; even if the clause were omitted, we would know that the phrase *the textbook* refers to the text in Chemistry 101. • Some grammarians extend the rule and insist that, just as *that* should be used only in restrictive clauses, *which* should be used only in nonrestrictive clauses. Thus, they suggest that we should avoid sentences such as *I need a book which will tell me all about gardening*, where the restrictive clause *which will tell me all about gardening* indicates which sort of book is needed. But this extension of the rule is far from universally accepted, and the use of *which* with restrictive clauses is common. Furthermore, since *that* cannot be used with clauses introduced by a preposition (whether or not restrictive), *which* is used with both clauses when such a clause is joined by *and* or *or* to another that does not begin with a preposition, as in *It is a philosophy in which ordinary people may find solace and which many have found reason to praise.* Such constructions are often considered cumbersome, however, and it may be best to recast the sentence completely to avoid the problem. • *That* is often omitted in a relative clause when the subject of the clause is different from the word that the clause refers to. Thus, we may say either *the book that I was reading* or *the book I was reading.* In addition, *that* is commonly omitted before other kinds of subordinate clauses, as in *I think we should try again* where *that* would precede *we.* These constructions omitting *that* are entirely idiomatic, even in more formal contexts. See Usage Notes at **doubt, this, whatever, which, who.**

that•a•way (*th*ăt′ə-wā′) *adv. Southern & Midland US* That way. [Alteration of *that way.*]

thatch (thăch) *n.* **1.** Plant stalks or foliage, such as reeds, used for roofing. **2.** Something that resembles thatch. **3.** Dead turf. ❖ *tr.v.* **thatched, thatch•ing, thatch•es** To cover with or as if with thatch. [ME *thacche*, alteration of *thak* < OE *thæc.* See **(s)teg-** in App.] **—thatch′er** *n.* **—thatch′y** *adj.*

Thatch, Edward See Edward **Teach.**

Thatch•er (thăch′ər), **Margaret Hilda** b. 1925. British politician who served as prime minister (1979–90).

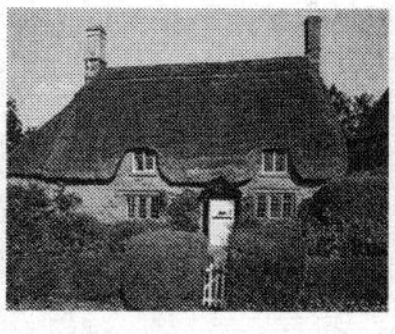

thatch
thatched roof on an English cottage

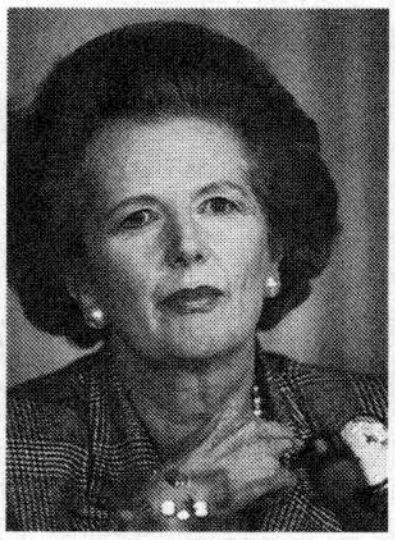

Margaret Thatcher
photographed in 1991

ă	pat	oi	boy
ā	pay	ou	out
âr	care	o͝o	took
ä	father	o͞o	boot
ĕ	pet	ŭ	cut
ē	be	ûr	urge
ĭ	pit	th	thin
ī	pie	*th*	this
îr	pier	hw	which
ŏ	pot	zh	vision
ō	toe	ə	about, item
ô	paw		

Stress marks:
′ (primary);
′ (secondary), as in
lexicon (lĕk′sĭ-kŏn′)

thau•ma•tol•o•gy (thô′mə-tŏl′ə-jē) n., pl. **-gies 1.** The study of miracles. **2.** A discourse on miracles. [Gk. *thauma, thaumat-,* wonder + –LOGY.]

thau•ma•turge (thô′mə-tûrj′) also **thau•ma•tur•gist** (-tûr′jĭst) n. A performer of miracles or magic feats. [Gk. *thaumatourgos : thauma, thaumat-,* wonder + *ergon,* work; see werg- in App.]

thau•ma•tur•gy (thô′mə-tûr′jē) n. The working of miracles or magic. **—thau′ma•tur′gic, thau′ma•tur′gi•cal** adj.

thaw (thô) v. **thawed, thaw•ing, thaws** —intr. **1.** To change from a frozen solid to a liquid by gradual warming. **2.** To lose stiffness, numbness, or impermeability by being warmed: *thawed out by the stove.* **3.** To become warm enough for snow and ice to melt. **4.** To become less formal, aloof, or reserved. —tr. To cause to thaw. ❖ n. **1.** The process of thawing. **2.** A warm period in the cold season when ice and snow melt. **3.** A relaxation of reserve, restraints, or tensions. [ME *thawen* < OE *thawian.*]

ThB abbr. Latin Theologiae Baccalaureus (Bachelor of Theology)

THC (tē′ăch-sē′) n. A compound, $C_{21}H_{30}O_2$, obtained from cannabis or made synthetically, that is the primary intoxicant in marijuana and hashish. [T(ETRA)H(YDRO)C(ANNABINOL).]

ThD abbr. Latin Theologiae Doctor (Doctor of Theology)

the[1] (thē before a vowel and for emphasis; thə before a consonant) def.art. **1a.** Used before singular or plural nouns and noun phrases that denote particular, specified persons or things: *the dress I wore.* **b.** Used before a noun, and generally stressed, to emphasize one of a group or type as the most outstanding or prominent: *considered it the neighborhood.* **c.** Used to indicate uniqueness: *the moon.* **d.** Used before nouns that designate natural phenomena or points of the compass: *the weather.* **e.** Used as the equivalent of a possessive adjective before names of some parts of the body: *a wave of the hand.* **f.** Used before a noun specifying a field of endeavor: *the law.* **g.** Used before a proper name, as of a monument or ship: *the Alamo.* **h.** Used before the plural form of a numeral denoting a specific decade of a century or of a life span: *the Thirties.* **2.** Used before a singular noun indicating that the noun is generic: *The wolf is endangered.* **3a.** Used before an adjective extending it to signify a class and giving it the function of a noun: *the rich.* **b.** Used before an absolute adjective: *the best we have.* **4.** Used before a present participle, signifying the action in the abstract: *the weaving of rugs.* **5.** Used before a noun with the force of *per: $1.50 the box.* [ME < OE, alteration (influenced by *th*-, oblique case stem of demonstrative pron.) of *se,* masc. demonstrative pron.; see so- in App.]

the[2] (thē before a vowel; thə before a consonant) adv. **1.** Because of that. Used before a comparative: *thinks the worse of you.* **2.** To that extent; by that much: *the sooner the better.* **3.** Beyond any other: *enjoyed reading the most.* [ME < OE *thȳ, thē,* instrumental of *thæt,* neut. demonstrative pron. See to- in App.]

the- pref. Variant of theo-.

the•an•throp•ic (thē′ăn-thrŏp′ĭk) also **the•an•throp•i•cal** (-ĭ-kəl) adj. Having both divine and human natures. [< L.Gk. *theanthrōpos,* god-man : Gk. *theo-,* theo- + Gk. *anthrōpos,* man.]

the•an•thro•pism (thē-ăn′thrə-pĭz′əm) n. **1.** Attribution of human traits to God; anthropomorphism. **2.** Christianity The doctrine of the theanthropic nature of Jesus.

the•ar•chy (thē′är′kē) n., pl. **-chies 1.** Government or rule by a god or by priests; theocracy. **2.** A hierarchy of gods.

the•a•ter or **the•a•tre** (thē′ə-tər) n. **1.** A building, room, or outdoor structure for plays, films, or other dramatic performances. **2.** A room with tiers of seats used for lectures or demonstrations. **3a.** Dramatic literature or its performance; drama. **b.** The milieu of actors and playwrights. **4a.** The quality or effectiveness of a theatrical production. **b.** Dramatic material or the use of such material. **5.** The audience assembled for a dramatic performance. **6.** A place that is the setting for dramatic events. **7.** A large geographic area in which military operations are coordinated. [ME *theatre* < OFr. < Lat. *theātrum* < Gk. *theātron* < *theāsthai,* to watch < *theā,* a viewing.]

the•a•ter•go•er (thē′ə-tər-gō′ər) n. One who attends the theater. **—the′a•ter•go′ing** adj. & n.

the•a•ter-in-the-round (thē′ə-tər-ĭn-thə-round′) n., pl. **the•a•ters-in-the-round** (thē′ə-tərz-) See **arena theater.**

theater of the absurd n. A form of drama that emphasizes the absurdity of human existence, as by illogical plots.

the•at•ri•cal (thē-ăt′rĭ-kəl) also **the•at•ric** (-rĭk) adj. **1.** Of, relating to, or suitable for dramatic performance or the theater. **2.** Marked by exaggerated self-display and unnatural behavior; affectedly dramatic. ❖ n. **1.** Stage performances or a stage performance, esp. by amateurs. Often used in the plural. **2.** **theatricals** Affectedly dramatic gestures or behavior; histrionics. **—the•at′ri•cal′i•ty** (-kăl′ĭ-tē), **the•at′ri•cal•ness** (-kəl-nĭs). **—the•at′ri•cal•ly** adv.

the•at•ri•cal•ism (thē-ăt′rĭ-kə-lĭz′əm) n. Theatrical manner or style; showiness.

the•at•ri•cal•ize (thē-ăt′rĭ-kə-līz′) tr.v. **-ized, -iz•ing, -iz•es 1.** To adapt to performance on the stage; dramatize. **2.** To make a spectacle of; display showily. **—the•at′ri•cal•i•za′tion** (-kə-lĭ-zā′shən) n. **—the•at′ri•cal•iz′er** n.

the•at•rics (thē-ăt′rĭks) n. **1.** (used with a sing. verb) The art of the theater. **2.** (used with a pl. verb) Theatrical effects or mannerisms; histrionics: *ignored their childish theatrics.*

the•ba•ine (thē′bə-ēn′, thĭ-bā′ĭn) n. A poisonous alkaloid, $C_{19}H_{21}NO_3$, obtained from opium. [< NLat. *(herba) thēbaia,* (herb of) Thebes, Egypt. opium < Lat. *thebaea,* fem. of *Thēbaeus,* Theban < *Thēbae,* Thebes < Gk. *Thēbai.*]

The•be (thē′bē) n. A satellite of Jupiter. [Lat. *Thēbē,* a nymph, daughter of the river god Asopus < Gk.]

Thebes (thēbz) **1.** An ancient city of Upper Egypt on the Nile R.; flourished from the mid-22nd to the 18th cent. B.C. **2.** An ancient city of Boeotia in E-central Greece NW of Athens. **—The′ban** (thē′bən) adj. & n.

the•ca (thē′kə) n., pl. **-cae** (-sē′, -kē′) A case, covering, or sheath, such as the pollen sac of an anther. [Lat. *thēca,* case, receptacle < Gk. *thēkē.* See dhē- in App.] **—the′cal** (-kəl) adj.

the•cate (thē′kāt′) adj. Having a theca; encased or sheathed.

the•co•dont (thē′kə-dŏnt′) n. Any of various extinct primitive archosaurs of the order Thecodontia of the late Permian and Triassic periods, having teeth in sockets and probably ancestral to the dinosaurs. [NLat. *Thēcodontia,* order name : Gk. *thēkē,* chest, sheath; see dhē- in App. + Gk. *-odōn, -odont-,* -odont.]

thee (thē) pron. The objective case of **thou**[1]. **1a.** Used as the direct object of a verb. **b.** Used as the indirect object of a verb. **2.** Used as the object of a preposition. **3.** Used in the nominative as well as the objective case, esp. by members of the Society of Friends.

thee•lin (thē′lĭn) n. See **estrone.** [Gk. *thēlus,* female + -IN.]

thee•lol (thē′lôl′, -lŏl′, -lōl′) n. See **estriol.** [THEEL(IN) + -OL[2].]

theft (thĕft) n. **1.** The act or an instance of stealing; larceny. **2.** Obsolete Something stolen. [ME < OE *thīefth.*]

their (thâr) adj. The possessive form of **they. 1.** Used as a modifier before a noun: *their home.* **2.** Usage Problem His, her, or its: *"It is fatal for anyone who writes to think of their sex"* (Virginia Woolf). See Usage Notes at **he**[1], **they.** [ME < ON *theira,* theirs. See to- in App.]

theirs (thârz) pron. (used with a sing. or pl. verb) **1.** Used to indicate the one or ones belonging to them: *The red house is theirs.* **2.** Usage Problem His or hers. See Usage Notes at **he**[1], **they.** [ME < *their,* these. See THEIR.]

their•selves (thâr-sĕlvz′) also **their•self** (-sĕlf′) pron. Chiefly Southern & South Midland US Themselves. See Note at **hisself.**

the•ism (thē′ĭz′əm) n. Belief in a god or gods, esp. belief in a personal God as creator and ruler of the world. **—the′ist** n. **—the•is′tic, the•is′ti•cal** adj. **—the•is′ti•cal•ly** adv.

The•lon (thē′lŏn′) A river, c. 885 km (550 mi), of N Canada rising E of Great Slave Lake and flowing E to Hudson Bay.

T-help•er cell or **T helper cell** (tē′hĕl′pər) n. See **helper T cell.**

them (thĕm, thəm) pron. **1.** Used as the direct object of a verb: *We saw them at camp.* **2.** Used as the indirect object of a verb: *We gave them cake.* **3.** Used as the object of a preposition: *This is for them.* **4.** Informal Used as a predicate nominative: *It's them.* See Usage Notes at **be, I**[1]. **5.** Nonstandard They: *"Them's the kind I like"* (American Dialect Dictionary). **6.** Nonstandard Used reflexively as the indirect object of a verb: *They ought to get them a new place to live.* ❖ adj. Nonstandard Those: *"Them dogs will find the end of them footprints before ten o'clock"* (William Faulkner). [ME < ON *theim* and OE *thǣm;* see to- in App.]

the•mat•ic (thĭ-măt′ĭk) adj. **1.** Of, relating to, or being a theme. **2.** Linguistics Of, constituting, or relating to the theme of a word: *a thematic vowel.* [Gk. *thematikos < thema, themat-,* theme. See THEME.] **—the•mat′i•cal•ly** adv.

Thematic Apperception Test n. A projective test in which the subject interprets a series of drawings of relatively ambiguous life situations.

theme (thēm) n. **1.** A topic of discourse or discussion. See Syns at **subject. 2.** A subject of artistic representation. **3.** An implicit or recurrent idea; a motif. **4.** A short composition assigned to a student as a writing exercise. **5.** Music A principal melodic phrase in a composition, esp. a melody forming the basis of a set of variations. **6.** Linguistics A stem. **7.** See **topic** 4. [ME *teme,* theme < OFr. *tesme* < Lat. *thema* < Gk. See dhē- in App.]

theme park n. An amusement park in which all the settings and attractions have a central theme, such as the future.

theme song n. **1.** An often repeated song in a musical play that is identified with the work or a character. **2.** A song identified with a performer or radio or television program.

The•mis•to•cles (thə-mĭs′tə-klēz′) 527?–460? B.C. Athenian official who directed the naval victory over Persia (480).

them•selves (thĕm-sĕlvz′, thəm-) pron. **1.** Those ones identical with them: **a.** Used reflexively as the direct or indirect object of a verb or as the object of a preposition: *They prepared themselves.* **b.** Used for emphasis: *The cooks themselves eat later.* **c.** Used in an absolute construction: *Newcomers themselves, they knew few people.* **2.** Their normal or healthy condition: *They're fully recovered and quite themselves again.*

then (thĕn) adv. **1.** At that time: *I was still in school then.* **2.** Next in time, space, or order; immediately afterward: *watched the movie and then went to bed.* **3.** In addition; moreover; besides: *It costs $20, and then there's the sales tax.* **4.** Used after but to qualify or balance a preceding statement: *The star was nervous, but then who isn't on the first night.* **5.** In that case; accordingly: *If traffic is heavy, then allow extra time.* **6.** As a consequence; therefore: *The*

case, then, is closed. ❖ *n.* That time or moment: *The plane leaves at four; until then let's shop.* ❖ *adj.* Being so at that time: *the then president.* —**idiom: then again** From another standpoint; on the other hand: *I need a vacation. Then again, so do my coworkers.* [ME < OE *thenne*. See **to-** in App.]

then and there *adv.* At that precise time and place; on the spot: *resigned then and there.*

the·nar (thē′när′) *n.* The fleshy mass on the palm of the hand at the base of the thumb. ❖ *adj.* Of or relating to the thenar. [Gk., palm of the hand.]

thence (thĕns, thĕns) *adv.* **1.** From that place; from there: *flew to Helsinki and thence to Moscow.* **2.** From that circumstance or source; therefrom. **3.** *Archaic* From that time; thenceforth. See Usage Note at **whence.** [ME *thennes* : *thenne*, from there (< OE *thanon*; see **to-** in App.) + *-es*, genitive sing. suff.; see –s³.]

thence·forth (thĕns-fôrth′, -fōrth′, thĕns-) *adv.* From that time forward; thereafter.

thence·for·ward (thĕns-fôr′wərd, thĕns-) also **thence·for·wards** (-wərdz) *adv.* **1.** Thenceforth. **2.** From that time or place onward.

theo- or **the–** *pref.* God: *theomorphism.* [Gk. < *theos.* See **dhēs-** in App.]

the·o·bro·mine (thē′ō-brō′mēn′) *n.* A bitter alkaloid, $C_7H_8N_4O_2$, derived from the cacao bean and used as a diuretic, vasodilator, and myocardial stimulant. [NLat. *Theobrōma*, genus of trees (Gk. *theo-*, theo- + *brōma*, food) + –INE².]

the·o·cen·tric (thē′ō-sĕn′trĭk) *adj.* Centering on God as the prime concern: *a theocentric cosmology.*

the·oc·ra·cy (thē-ŏk′rə-sē) *n.*, *pl.* **-cies 1.** A government ruled by or subject to religious authority. **2.** A state so governed.

the·o·crat (thē′ə-krăt′) *n.* **1.** A ruler of a theocracy. **2.** A believer in theocracy. —**the′o·crat′ic, the′o·crat′i·cal** *adj.*

The·oc·ri·tus (thē-ŏk′rĭ-təs) 3rd cent. B.C. Greek poet who composed the earliest known pastoral poems.

the·od·i·cy (thē-ŏd′ĭ-sē) *n.*, *pl.* **-cies** A vindication of God's goodness and justice in the face of the existence of evil. [After *Essai de téodicée,* a work by Baron Gottfried Wilhelm von Leibniz : Gk. *theo-*, theo- + Gk. *dikē,* order, right; see **deik-** in App.]

the·od·o·lite (thē-ŏd′l-īt′) *n.* An optical instrument consisting of a small mounted telescope rotatable in horizontal and vertical planes, used in surveying and meteorology. [NLat. *theodolitus, theodelitus.*] —**the′o·do·lit′ic** (-lĭt′ĭk) *adj.*

The·o·do·ra (thē′ə-dôr′ə, -dōr′-) 508?–548. Byzantine empress (525–548) as the wife and adviser of Justinian I.

The·od·o·ric (thē-ŏd′ə-rĭk) A.D. 454?–526. King of the Ostrogoths (474–526) who founded a kingdom in Italy (493).

The·o·do·sius I (thē′ə-dō′shəs, -shē-əs) A.D. 346?–395. Emperor of Rome who ruled jointly (379–392) with Gratian and Valentinian II and independently (392–395).

the·og·o·ny (thē-ŏg′ə-nē) *n.*, *pl.* **-nies** An account of the gods' origin and genealogy. —**the′o·gon′ic** (-ə-gŏn′ĭk) *adj.*

the·o·lo·gi·an (thē′ə-lō′jən) *n.* One learned in theology.

the·o·log·i·cal (thē′ə-lŏj′ĭ-kəl) also **the·o·log·ic** (-lŏj′ĭk) *adj.* Of or relating to theology or to specialized religious study. —**the′o·log′i·cal·ly** *adv.*

the·ol·o·gize (thē-ŏl′ə-jīz′) *v.* **-gized, -giz·ing, -giz·es** —*tr.* To make theological in form or significance. —*intr.* To speculate about theology. —**the·ol′o·giz′er** *n.*

the·ol·o·gy (thē-ŏl′ə-jē) *n.*, *pl.* **-gies 1.** The study of the nature of God and religious truth. **2.** A system or school of opinions concerning God and religious questions. **3.** A course of specialized religious study usu. at a college or seminary. [ME *theologie* < OFr. < Lat. *theologia* < Gk. *theologiā* : *theo-*, theo- + *-logiā*, -logy.]

the·om·a·chy (thē-ŏm′ə-kē) *n.*, *pl.* **-chies** Strife or battle among gods, as in the Homeric poems. [Gk. *theomakhiā* : *theo-* + *makhē,* battle.]

the·o·mor·phism (thē′ō-môr′fĭz′əm) *n.* Depiction or conception of humans as having the form of a god. —**the′o·mor′phic** *adj.*

the·oph·a·ny (thē-ŏf′ə-nē) *n.*, *pl.* **-nies** An appearance of a god to a human; a divine manifestation. [Med.Lat. *theophania* < L.Gk. *theophaneia* : Gk. *theo-*, theo- + Gk. *phainein, phan-*, to show.]

The·o·phras·tus (thē′ə-frăs′təs) 371?–287? B.C. Greek philosopher who succeeded Aristotle as leader of the Peripatetics.

the·oph·yl·line (thē-ŏf′ə-lĭn) *n.* A colorless crystalline alkaloid, $C_7H_8N_4O_2$, derived from tea leaves or made synthetically, used in medicine esp. as a bronchial dilator. [THEO(BROMINE) + PHYLL(O)- + –INE².]

the·o·rem (thē′ər-əm, thîr′əm) *n.* **1.** An idea that has been demonstrated as true or is assumed to be so demonstrable. **2.** *Mathematics* A proposition that has been or is to be proved on the basis of explicit assumptions. [LLat. *theōrēma* < Gk. *theōrein*, to look at < *theōros,* spectator. See THEORY.]

the·o·ret·i·cal (thē′ə-rĕt′ĭ-kəl) also **the·o·ret·ic** (-rĕt′ĭk) *adj.* **1.** Of, relating to, or based on theory. **2.** Restricted to theory; not practical: *theoretical physics.* **3.** Given to theorizing; speculative. [LLat. *theōrēticus* < Gk. *theōrētikos* < *theōrētos,* observable < *theōrein,* to look at. See THEOREM.] —**the′o·ret′i·cal·ly** *adv.*

the·o·re·ti·cian (thē′ər-ĭ-tĭsh′ən, thîr′ĭ-) *n.* One who formu-

lates, studies, or is expert in the theory of a science or an art.

the·o·rist (thē′ər-ĭst, thîr′ĭst) *n.* One who theorizes; a theoretician.

the·o·rize (thē′ə-rīz′, thîr′īz) *v.* **-rized, -riz·ing, -riz·es** —*intr.* To formulate theories or a theory; speculate. —*tr.* To propose a theory about. —**the′o·ri·za′tion** (-ər-ĭ-zā′shən) *n.* —**the′o·riz′er** *n.*

the·o·ry (thē′ə-rē, thîr′ē) *n.*, *pl.* **-ries 1.** A set of statements or principles devised to explain a group of facts or phenomena, esp. one that has been repeatedly tested or is widely accepted and can be used to make predictions about natural phenomena. **2.** The branch of a science or art consisting of its explanatory statements, accepted principles, and methods of analysis, as opposed to practice. **3.** A set of theorems that constitute a systematic view of a branch of mathematics. **4.** Abstract reasoning; speculation. **5.** A belief that guides action or assists comprehension or judgment: *the theory that less is more.* **6.** An assumption based on limited information or knowledge; a conjecture. [LLat. *theōria* < Gk. *theōriā* < *theōros,* spectator : prob. *thea,* a viewing + *-oros,* seeing (< *horān,* to see).]

theory of games *n.* See **game theory.**

the·os·o·phy (thē-ŏs′ə-fē) *n.*, *pl.* **-phies 1.** Religious philosophy or speculation about the nature of the soul based on mystical insight into the nature of God. **2.** often **Theosophy** The system of beliefs of the Theosophical Society, founded in New York City in 1875, incorporating aspects of Buddhism and Brahmanism, esp. the belief in reincarnation and spiritual evolution. [Med.Lat. *theosophia* < L.Gk. *theosophiā* : Gk. *theo-*, theo- + Gk. *sophiā,* wisdom.] —**the′o·soph′ic** (-ə-sŏf′ĭk), **the′o·soph′i·cal** (-ĭ-kəl) *adj.* —**the·os′o·phist** *n.*

ther·a·peu·tic (thĕr′ə-pyōō′tĭk) also **ther·a·peu·ti·cal** (-tĭ-kəl) *adj.* **1.** Having or exhibiting healing powers: *a therapeutic agent.* **2.** Of or relating to therapeutics. [NLat. *therapeuticus* < Gk. *therapeutikos* < *therapeutēs,* one who administers < *therapeuein,* to serve, administer < *theraps, therap-*, attendant. See THERAPY.] —**ther′a·peu′ti·cal·ly** *adv.*

therapeutic abortion *n.* Abortion induced to save the life of the mother.

therapeutic index *n.* The ratio between the toxic dose and the therapeutic dose of a drug, used as a measure of the relative safety of the drug for a particular treatment.

ther·a·peu·tics (thĕr′ə-pyōō′tĭks) *n.* (*used with a sing. verb*) Medical treatment of disease; the art or science of healing. —**ther′a·peu′tist** *n.*

ther·a·pist (thĕr′ə-pĭst) *n.* One who specializes in the provision of a particular therapy.

the·rap·sid (thə-răp′sĭd) *n.* Any of various reptiles of the order Therapsida of the Permian and Triassic periods, many of which are considered direct ancestors of mammals. [< NLat. *Therapsida,* order name : Gk. *thēr,* wild animal; see THEROPOD + Gk. *hapsis, hapsid-,* arch, vault (< their enlarged lower temporal opening); see APSIS.] —**the·rap′sid** *adj.*

ther·a·py (thĕr′ə-pē) *n.*, *pl.* **-pies 1.** Treatment of illness or disability. **2.** Psychotherapy. **3.** Healing power or quality: *the therapy of fresh air and sun.* [NLat. *therapia* < Gk. *therapeia* < *therapeuein,* to treat medically. See THERAPEUTIC.]

Ther·a·va·da (thĕr′ə-vä′də) *n.* *Buddhism* A conservative branch of Buddhism that adheres to Pali scriptures and the nontheistic ideal of self-purification to nirvana and is dominant in Sri Lanka, Myanmar (Burma), Thailand, Laos, and Cambodia. [Pali *theravāda* : *thera,* an elder < Skt. *sthavirah,* old man < *sthavira-,* old, venerable; see **stā-** in App.) + *vāda,* doctrine (< Skt. *vādah,* statement, doctrine).]

there (thâr) *adv.* **1.** At or in that place: *sit over there.* **2.** To, into, or toward that place: *wouldn't go there.* **3.** At that stage, moment, or point: *Stop there!* **4.** In that matter: *I can't agree with him there.* ❖ *pron.* **1.** Used to introduce a clause or sentence: *There must be another exit.* **2.** Used to indicate an unspecified person in direct address: *Hello there.* ❖ *adj.* **1.** Used for emphasis after the demonstrative pronoun *that* or after a noun modified by the demonstrative adjective *that* or *those*: *that there; those people there.* **2.** *Nonstandard* Used for emphasis between a demonstrative adjective meaning "that" or "those" and a noun: *There's gold in them there hills.* ❖ *n.* That place or point: *went on from there.* ❖ *interj.* Used to express feelings such as relief, sympathy, or anger: *There, now I can have some peace!* [ME < OE *thǣr, ther.* See **to-** in App.]

theodolite

ă	pat	oi	boy
ā	pay	ou	out
âr	care	ŏŏ	took
ä	father	ōō	boot
ĕ	pet	ŭ	cut
ē	be	ûr	urge
ĭ	pit	th	thin
ī	pie	*th*	this
îr	pier	hw	which
ŏ	pot	zh	vision
ō	toe	ə	about,
ô	paw		item

Stress marks:
′ (primary);
′ (secondary), as in
lexicon (lĕk′sĭ-kŏn′)

there·a·bouts (thâr′ə-bouts′) also **there·a·bout** (-bout′) *adv.*
1. Near that place, about there: *somewhere in New York or there-
abouts.* **2.** About that number, amount, or time.

there·af·ter (thâr-ăf′tər) *adv.* From a specified time onward;
from then on.

there·a·gainst (thâr′ə-gĕnst′) *adv.* Against or in opposition to
that.

there·at (thâr-ăt′) *adv.* **1.** At that place; there. **2.** At that event;
on account of that.

there·by (thâr-bī′) *adv.* **1.** By that means; because of that. **2.** In
connection with that.

there·for (thâr-fôr′) *adv.* For that.

there·fore (thâr′fôr′, -fōr′) *adv.* For that reason or cause; consequently or hence. [ME : *there, there*; see THERE + *for, fore, for*;
see FOR.]

there·from (thâr-frŭm′, -frŏm′) *adv.* From that place, time, or
thing.

there·in (thâr-ĭn′) *adv.* **1.** In that place, time, or thing. **2.** In that
circumstance or respect.

there·in·af·ter (thâr′ĭn-ăf′tər) *adv.* In a later part, as of a
speech or book.

ther·e·min (thĕr′ə-mĭn) *n.* An electronic instrument played by
moving the hands near its two antennas, often used for high
tremolo effects. [After Leo *Theremin* (1896–1993), Russian engineer and inventor.]

there·of (thâr-ŭv′, -ŏv′) *adv.* **1.** Of or concerning this, that, or
it. **2.** From that cause or origin; therefrom.

there·on (thâr-ŏn′, -ôn′) *adv.* **1.** On or upon this, that, or it. **2.**
Archaic Following that immediately; thereupon.

The·re·sa (tə-rē′sə, -zə, -rā′-), Saint. Known as "Theresa of
Ávila." 1515–82. Spanish nun who founded the reformed order
of Carmelites (1562).

there·to (thâr-tōō′) *adv.* **1.** To that, this, or it. **2.** *Archaic* In addition to that; furthermore.

there·to·fore (thâr′tə-fôr′, -fōr′) *adv.* Until that time; before
that.

there·un·der (thâr-ŭn′dər) *adv.* Under this, that, or it.

there·un·to (thâr′ŭn-tōō′) *adv.* *Archaic* To that, this, or it;
thereto.

there·up·on (thâr′ə-pŏn′, -pôn′) *adv.* **1.** Concerning that matter; upon that. **2.** Directly following that; forthwith. **3.** In consequence of that; therefore.

there·with (thâr-wĭth′, -wĭth′) *adv.* **1.** With that, this, or it. **2.** In
addition to that. **3.** *Archaic* Immediately thereafter.

there·with·al (thâr′wĭth-ôl′, -wĭth-) *adv.* With all that, this, or
it; besides.

the·ri·o·mor·phic (thîr′ē-ə-môr′fĭk) also **the·ri·o·mor·
phous** (-fəs) *adj.* Thought of as having the form of a beast. Used
of a deity. [Gk. *thērion*, dim. of *thēr*, wild beast; see THEROPOD +
–MORPHIC.]

therm (thûrm) *n.* A unit of heat equal to 100,000 British thermal
units (1.054 × 10^8 joules). [Gk. *thermē*, heat < *thermos*, warm,
hot. See gʷher- in App.]

–therm *suff.* An animal having a specified kind of body temperature: *poikilotherm.* [< Gk. *thermē*, heat < *thermos*, warm, hot. See
gʷher- in App.]

ther·mal (thûr′məl) *adj.* **1.** Of, relating to, using, producing, or
caused by heat. **2.** Intended or designed to help retain body heat.
❖ *n.* A rising current of warm air. **—ther′mal·ly** *adv.*

thermal noise *n.* Unwanted currents or voltages in an electronic
component resulting from the agitation of electrons by heat.

thermal pollution *n.* Industrial discharge of heated water into a
river, lake, or other body of water, causing a rise in temperature
that endangers aquatic life.

ther·mic (thûr′mĭk) *adj.* Thermal.

therm·i·on (thûr′mī′ən) *n.* An electrically charged particle, esp.
an electron, emitted by a conducting material at high temperatures. **—therm′i·on′ic** (-mī-ŏn′ĭk) *adj.*

thermionic current *n.* A flow of thermions.

therm·i·on·ics (thûr′mī-ŏn′ĭks) *n.* (*used with a sing. or pl. verb*)
The physics of thermionic phenomena.

thermionic tube *n.* An electron tube in which the source of electrons is a heated electrode.

therm·is·tor (thûr′mĭs′tər) *n.* A resistor made of semiconductors having resistance that varies rapidly and predictably with
temperature. [THERM(AL) + (RES)ISTOR.]

Ther·mit (thûr′mĭt, -mīt′) A trademark used for a welding and
incendiary mixture of fine aluminum powder with a metallic
oxide that when ignited yields an intense heat.

thermo– or **therm–** *pref.* **1.** Heat: *thermochemistry.* **2.** Thermoelectric: *thermojunction.* [< Gk. *thermē*, heat < *thermos*, warm,
hot. See gʷher- in App.]

ther·mo·chem·is·try (thûr′mō-kĕm′ĭ-strē) *n.* The chemistry
of heat and heat-associated chemical phenomena. **—ther′mo·
chem′i·cal** (-ĭ-kəl) *adj.* **—ther′mo·chem′ist** *n.*

ther·mo·cline (thûr′mə-klīn′) *n.* A layer in a large body of

Theresa of Ávila
detail from a c. 1826
portrait by François Gérard
(1770–1837)

water that sharply separates regions differing in temperature, so
that the temperature gradient across the layer is abrupt.

ther·mo·cou·ple (thûr′mə-kŭp′əl) *n.* A thermoelectric device
used to measure temperatures accurately, esp. one consisting of
two dissimilar metals joined so that a potential difference generated between the points of contact is a measure of the temperature difference between the points.

ther·mo·dur·ic (thûr′mō-dŏŏr′ĭk, -dyŏŏr′-) *adj.* Capable of
surviving high temperatures, esp. those of pasteurization. Used
of a microorganism. [THERMO– + Lat. *dūrāre*, to last + –IC.]

ther·mo·dy·nam·ic (thûr′mō-dī-năm′ĭk) *adj.* **1.** Characteristic of or resulting from the conversion of heat into other forms
of energy. **2.** Of or relating to thermodynamics. **—ther′mo·dy·
nam′i·cal·ly** *adv.*

ther·mo·dy·nam·ics (thûr′mō-dī-năm′ĭks) *n.* **1.** (*used with a
sing. verb*) The branch of physics that deals with the relationships
and conversions between heat and other forms of energy. **2.** (*used
with a pl. verb*) Thermodynamic phenomena and processes.

ther·mo·e·lec·tric (thûr′mō-ĭ-lĕk′trĭk) also **ther·mo·e·lec·
tri·cal** (-trĭ-kəl) *adj.* Characteristic of, resulting from, or using
electrical phenomena occurring in conjunction with a flow of
heat. **—ther′mo·e·lec′tri·cal·ly** *adv.*

ther·mo·e·lec·tric·i·ty (thûr′mō-ĭ-lĕk-trĭs′ĭ-tē, -ē′lĕk-) *n.*
Electricity generated by a flow of heat, as in a thermocouple.

ther·mo·e·lec·tron (thûr′mō-ĭ-lĕk′trŏn′) *n.* An electron
emitted by a material at high temperatures.

ther·mo·gram (thûr′mə-grăm′) *n.* A record made by a thermo-
graph.

ther·mo·graph (thûr′mə-grăf′) *n.* **1.** A thermometer that records the temperature it indicates. **2.** The apparatus used in diagnostic thermography.

ther·mog·ra·phy (thər-mŏg′rə-fē) *n., pl.* **-phies 1.** A process
for producing raised lettering, as on stationery, by application of
a powder fused by heat to the fresh ink. **2.** A diagnostic technique
in which an infrared camera produces images that reveal sites of
abnormal tissue growth by measuring temperature variations on
the surface of the body. **—ther′mo·graph′ic** (-mə-grăf′ĭk) *adj.*
—ther′mo·graph′i·cal·ly *adv.*

ther·mo·junc·tion (thûr′mō-jŭngk′shən) *n.* The point of contact between two dissimilar metals in a thermocouple.

ther·mo·la·bile (thûr′mō-lā′bīl, -bĭl′) *adj.* Subject to destruction, decomposition, or great change by heating. Used esp. of biochemical substances.

ther·mo·lu·mi·nes·cence (thûr′mō-lōō′mə-nĕs′əns) *n.* A
phenomenon in which certain minerals release previously absorbed radiation upon being moderately heated.

ther·mol·y·sis (thər-mŏl′ĭ-sĭs) *n., pl.* **-ses** (-sēz′) **1.** *Physiology*
Dissipation of heat from the body, as by evaporation. **2.** *Chemistry* Dissociation or decomposition of compounds by heat.
—ther′mo·lyt′ic (thûr′mə-lĭt′ĭk) *adj.*

ther·mom·e·ter (thər-mŏm′ĭ-tər) *n.* An instrument for measuring temperature, esp. one having a graduated glass tube with a
bulb containing a liquid, such as mercury, that expands and rises
in the tube as the temperature increases.

ther·mom·e·try (thər-mŏm′ĭ-trē) *n.* **1.** Measurement of temperature. **2.** The technology of temperature measurement.
—ther′mo·met′ric (thûr′mō-mĕt′rĭk) *adj.*

ther·mo·nu·cle·ar (thûr′mō-nōō′klē-ər, -nyōō′-) *adj.* **1.** Of,
relating to, or derived from the fusion of atomic nuclei at high
temperatures: *thermonuclear reactions.* **2.** Of, relating to, or
characterized by the use of atomic weapons based on fusion, esp.
as distinguished from those based on fission.

ther·mo·pe·ri·od·ism (thûr′mō-pîr′ē-ə-dĭz′əm) also **ther·
mo·pe·ri·o·dic·i·ty** (-dĭs′ĭ-tē) *n.* The effect on an organism of
the rhythmic fluctuation of temperature, as that accompanying
the alternation of day and night.

ther·mo·phil·ic (thûr′mō-fĭl′ĭk) *adj.* Requiring high temperatures for normal development, as certain bacteria. **—ther′mo·
phile′** (-fīl′) *n.*

ther·mo·pile (thûr′mə-pīl′) *n.* A device consisting of a number
of connected thermocouples, used for measuring temperature or
generating current. [THERMO– + PILE¹.]

ther·mo·plas·tic (thûr′mə-plăs′tĭk) *adj.* Becoming soft when
heated and hard when cooled. ❖ *n.* A thermoplastic resin.
—ther′mo·plas·tic′i·ty (-plă-stĭs′ĭ-tē) *n.*

Ther·mop·y·lae (thər-mŏp′ə-lē) A narrow pass of E-central
Greece; site of an unsuccessful Spartan stand against the Persians
in 480 B.C.

ther·mo·re·cep·tor (thûr′mō-rĭ-sĕp′tər) *n.* A sensory receptor that responds to heat and cold.

ther·mo·reg·u·late (thûr′mō-rĕg′yə-lāt′) *intr.v.* **-lat·ed,
-lat·ing, -lates 1.** To regulate body temperature. **2.** To undergo
thermoregulation.

ther·mo·reg·u·la·tion (thûr′mō-rĕg′yə-lā′shən) *n.* Maintenance of a constant internal body temperature independent from
the environmental temperature. **—ther′mo·reg′u·la·to′ry**
(-rĕg′yə-lə-tôr′ē, -tōr′ē) *adj.*

ther·mos (thûr′məs) *n., pl.* **-mos·es** A vacuum bottle used to
keep beverages hot or cold. [Orig. a trademark.]

ther·mo·set·ting (thûr′mō-sĕt′ĭng) *adj.* Permanently solidifying on being heated. Used of certain synthetic resins.

ther·mo·sphere (thûr′mə-sfîr′) n. The outermost shell of the atmosphere, between the mesosphere and outer space, where temperatures increase steadily with altitude. —**ther′mo·spher′ic** (-sfîr′ĭk, -sfĕr′ĭk) adj.

ther·mo·sta·ble (thûr′mō-stā′bəl) also **ther·mo·sta·bile** (-bəl, -bīl′) adj. Unaffected by relatively high temperatures, as certain ferments. —**ther′mo·sta·bil′i·ty** (-stə-bĭl′ĭ-tē) n.

ther·mo·stat (thûr′mə-stăt′) n. A device, as in a home heating system, that automatically responds to temperature changes and activates switches controlling the equipment. —**ther′mo·stat′ic** adj. —**ther′mo·stat′i·cal·ly** adv.

ther·mo·tax·is (thûr′mə-tăk′sĭs) n., pl. **-tax·es** (-tăk′sēz) **1.** Movement of a living organism in response to temperature changes. **2.** Normal regulation or adjustment of body temperature. —**ther′mo·tac′tic** (-tăk′tĭk), **ther′mo·tax′ic** (-sĭk) adj.

ther·mot·ro·pism (thər-mŏt′rə-pĭz′əm) n. The tendency of plants or other organisms to bend toward or away from heat. —**ther′mo·trop′ic** (thûr′mə-trŏp′ĭk) adj.

–thermy suff. Heat: diathermy. [NLat. -thermia < Gk. thermē, heat < thermos, warm, hot. See **gʷher-** in App.]

the·ro·pod (thîr′ə-pŏd′) n. Any of various large carnivorous bipedal saurischian dinosaurs of the suborder Theropoda of the Jurassic and Cretaceous periods, characterized by large jaws and short forelimbs. [< NLat. Thēropoda, suborder name : Gk. thēr, wild beast; see **ghwer-** in App. + NLat. -poda, -pod.] —**the·rop′o·dan** (thĭ-rŏp′ə-dən) adj. & n.

Thes. abbr. Bible Thessalonians

the·sau·rus (thĭ-sôr′əs) n., pl. **-sau·ri** (-sôr′ī′) or **-sau·rus·es 1.** A book of synonyms, often including related and contrasting words and antonyms. **2.** A book of selected words or concepts, such as a specialized vocabulary of a particular field. [Lat. thēsaurus, treasury < Gk. thēsauros.]

these (thēz) pron. & adj. Plural of **this**. [ME < OE thæs, var. of thās, pl. of thes, this, this. See to- in App.]

The·se·us (thē′sē-əs, -syōōs′) n. Greek Mythology A hero and king of Athens who slew the Minotaur and united Attica.

the·sis (thē′sĭs) n., pl. **-ses** (-sēz) **1.** A proposition maintained by argument. **2.** A dissertation advancing an original point of view based on research, esp. as required for an academic degree. **3.** A hypothetical proposition, esp. one not proved. **4.** The first stage of the Hegelian dialectic process. **5a.** The long or accented part of a metrical foot, esp. in quantitative verse. **b.** The unaccented or short part of a metrical foot, esp. in accentual verse. **6.** Music The accented section of a measure. [Lat. < Gk. < tithenai, the-, to put. See **dhē-** in App. Senses 5 and 6, ME < LLat., lowering of the voice < Gk., downbeat < tithenai.]

thes·pi·an (thĕs′pē-ən) adj. **1.** Of or relating to drama; dramatic. **2. Thespian** Of Thespis. ❖ n. An actor or actress.

Thes·pis (thĕs′pĭs) 6th cent. B.C. Greek poet who reputedly originated Greek tragedy.

Thes·sa·lo·ni·ans (thĕs′ə-lō′nē-ənz) pl.n. (used with a sing. verb) See table at **Bible**.

Thes·sa·lo·ní·ki (thĕ′sä-lô-nē′kē) also **Thes·sa·lo·ni·ca** (-lô-nī′kə, -lŏn′ĭ-kə) or **Sa·lo·ni·ka** (sə-lŏn′ĭ-kə, săl′ə-nē′kə) A city of NE Greece on an inlet of the Aegean Sea; flourished after c. 146 as the cap. of Macedon. Pop. 406,413.

Thes·sa·ly (thĕs′ə-lē) A region of E-central Greece between the Pindus Mts. and the Aegean Sea. —**Thes·sa′lian** (thĕ-sā′lē-ən, -sāl′yən), **Thes′sa·lo′ni·an** (-lō′nē-ən) adj. & n.

the·ta (thā′tə, thē′-) n. The eighth letter of the Greek alphabet. [Gk. thēta, of Phoenician orig.; akin to Heb. têt, teth.]

theta rhythm n. A waveform on an electroencephalogram with a frequency of 4 to 8 hertz, recorded chiefly in the hippocampus of carnivorous mammals when alert or aroused.

thet·ic (thĕt′ĭk, thē′tĭk) also **thet·i·cal** (thĕt′ĭ-kəl, thē′tĭ-) adj. **1.** Beginning with, constituting, or relating to the thesis in prosody. **2.** Presented dogmatically; arbitrarily prescribed. [Gk. thetikos < thetos, placed < tithenai, the-, to put. See **dhē-** in App.]

The·tis (thē′tĭs) n. Greek Mythology One of the Nereids, the wife of Peleus and mother of Achilles.

the·ur·gy (thē′ûr-jē) n., pl. **-gies 1.** Divine or supernatural intervention in human affairs. **2.** The performance of miracles with supernatural assistance. **3.** Magic performed with the aid of beneficent spirits, as formerly practiced by the Neo-Platonists. [LLat. theūrgia < Gk. theourgia, sacramental rite, mystery : theo-, theo- + -ourgia, -urgy.] —**the·ur′gic, the·ur′gi·cal** adj. —**the·ur′gi·cal·ly** adv. —**the′ur·gist** n.

thew (thyōō) n. **1.** A well-developed sinew or muscle. **2.** Muscular power or strength. Often used in the plural. [ME, habit, virtue, strength (sense influenced by SINEW) < OE thēaw, a custom, habit.] —**thew′y** adj.

they (thā) pron. **1.** Used to refer to the ones previously mentioned or implied. **2.** Usage Problem Used to refer to the one previously mentioned or implied, esp. as a substitute for generic he. See Usage Note at **he¹. 3a.** Used to refer to people in general. **b.** Used to refer to people in general as seen in a position of authority. [ME < ON their, masc. pl. demonstrative and personal pron. See to- in App.]

USAGE NOTE The use of the third-person plural pronoun they to refer to a singular noun or pronoun is attested as early as 1300.

The practice is found in the works of many admired writers, is widespread in mainstream publications, and is so common in speech that it generally passes unnoticed. However, despite its convenience as a substitute for phrases such as he or she, many people avoid using they to refer to a singular antecedent out of respect for the traditional grammatical rule concerning pronoun agreement, and the usage is rejected by most of the Usage Panel. Eighty-two percent find the sentence The typical student in the program takes about six years to complete their course work unacceptable. Thus, writers should exercise caution in using they in similar contexts in writing. See Usage Notes at **any, anyone, he¹.**

they'd (thād) **1.** Contraction of they had. **2.** Contraction of they would.

they'll (thāl) Contraction of they will.

they're (thâr) Contraction of they are.

they've (thāv) Contraction of they have.

thi– pref. Variant of **thio–**.

thi·a·mine (thī′ə-mĭn, -mēn′) also **thi·a·min** (-mĭn) n. A vitamin, $C_{12}H_{17}ClN_4OS$, of the vitamin B complex, found in meat, yeast, and the bran coat of grains and necessary for carbohydrate metabolism. [Alteration of thiamin : THI(O)– + (VIT)AMIN.]

thi·a·zide (thī′ə-zīd′, -zĭd) n. Any of a group of drugs that block reabsorption of sodium in the distal tubules of the kidneys, used as diuretics. [THI(O)– + AZ(O)– + –IDE.]

thi·a·zine (thī′ə-zēn′) n. Any of a class of organic chemical compounds with a ring composed of one sulfur atom, one nitrogen atom, and four carbon atoms, used in making dyes.

thi·a·zole (thī′ə-zōl′) n. **1.** A colorless or pale yellow liquid, C_3H_3NS, with a five-member ring composed of a nitrogen atom, a sulfur atom, and three carbon atoms, used in making dyes and fungicides. **2.** Any of its various derivatives.

thick (thĭk) adj. **thick·er, thick·est 1a.** Relatively great in extent from one surface to the opposite, usu. in the smallest solid dimension; not thin. **b.** Measuring a specified number of units in this dimension: two inches thick. **2.** Heavy in form, build, or stature; thickset: a thick neck. **3.** Having component parts in a close, crowded state or arrangement; dense: a thick forest. **4.** Having or suggesting a heavy or viscous consistency: thick tomato sauce. **5.** Having a great number; abounding. **6.** Impenetrable by the eyes: a thick fog. **7a.** Not easy to hear or understand; indistinctly articulated. **b.** Producing indistinctly articulated sounds. **8.** Strongly apparent; conspicuous: a thick brogue. **9.** Informal Lacking mental agility; stupid. **10.** Informal Very friendly; intimate. **11.** Informal Going beyond what is tolerable; excessive. ❖ adv. **1.** In a thick manner; deeply or heavily. **2.** In a close, compact state or arrangement; densely. **3.** So as to be thick; thickly: Slice the bread thick. ❖ n. **1.** The thickest part. **2.** The most active or intense part. —**idiom: thick and thin** Good and bad times. [ME thicke < OE thicce.] —**thick′ish** adj. —**thick′ly** adv.

thick·en (thĭk′ən) tr. & intr.v. **-ened, -en·ing, -ens 1.** To make or become thick or thicker. **2.** To make or become more intense, intricate, or complex. —**thick′en·er** n.

thick·en·ing (thĭk′ə-nĭng) n. **1.** The act or process of making or becoming thick. **2.** Material used to thicken. **3.** A thickened part.

thick·et (thĭk′ĭt) n. **1.** A dense growth of shrubs or underbrush; a copse. **2.** Something suggestive of a dense growth of plants, as in thickness. [OE thiccet < thicce, thick. See THICK.]

thick·head (thĭk′hĕd′) n. A person regarded as stupid; a blockhead. —**thick′head′ed** adj.

thick milk n. Pennsylvania See **clabber**. [Transl. of Ger. Dickmilch.]

thick·ness (thĭk′nĭs) n. **1.** The quality or condition of being thick. **2.** The dimension between two surfaces of an object, usu. the dimension of smallest measure. **3.** A layer, sheet, stratum, or ply: Each floor is a single thickness of concrete.

thick·set (thĭk′sĕt′) adj. **1.** Having a solid stocky form or body; stout. **2.** Positioned or placed closely together.

thick-skinned (thĭk′skĭnd′) adj. **1.** Having a thick skin or rind. **2.** Not easily offended. **3.** Largely unaffected by the needs and feelings of other people; insensitive.

thick-wit·ted (thĭk′wĭt′ĭd) adj. Stupid; dull.

thief (thēf) n., pl. **thieves** (thēvz) One who steals, esp. by stealth. [ME < OE thēof.]

thieve (thēv) tr. & intr.v. **thieved, thiev·ing, thieves** To take (something) by theft or commit theft. [Perh. < OE thēofian < thēof, thief.]

thiev·er·y (thē′və-rē) n., pl. **-ies** Thieving.

thiev·ish (thē′vĭsh) adj. **1.** Given to thieving. **2.** Of, similar to, or characteristic of a thief; furtive.

thigh (thī) n. **1a.** The portion of the human leg between the hip and the knee. **b.** The corresponding part in the hind leg of a quadruped or other vertebrate animal. **2.** The second segment of a bird's leg, containing the tibia and fibula. **3.** The femur of an insect's leg. [ME < OE thēoh.]

thigh·bone (thī′bōn′) n. See **femur** 1.

thig·mo·tax·is (thĭg′mə-tăk′sĭs) n. See **stereotaxis** 2. [Gk. thigma, touch (< thiganein, to touch; see **dheigh-** in App.) + –TAXIS.] —**thig′mo·tac′tic** (-tăk′tĭk) adj.

thig·mot·ro·pism (thĭg-mŏt′rə-pĭz′əm) n. The turning or bending response of an organism upon direct contact with a solid

ă pat	oi boy
ā pay	ou out
âr care	ŏŏ took
ä father	ōō boot
ĕ pet	ŭ cut
ē be	ûr urge
ĭ pit	th thin
ī pie	th this
îr pier	hw which
ŏ pot	zh vision
ō toe	ə about,
ô paw	item

Stress marks:
′ (primary);
′ (secondary), as in
lexicon (lĕk′sĭ-kŏn′)

surface or object. [Gk. *thigma*, touch; see THIGMOTAXIS + –TROPISM.] —**thig′mo·trop′ic** (thĭg′mə-trŏp′ĭk, -trō′pĭk) *adj.*

thill (thĭl) *n.* Either of the two long shafts between which an animal is fastened when pulling a wagon. [ME *thille,* perh. < OE, plank.]

thim·ble (thĭm′bəl) *n.* **1.** A hard pitted cup worn for protection on the finger that pushes the needle in sewing. **2.** Any of various tubular sockets or sleeves in machinery. **3.** *Nautical* **a.** A metal ring fitted in an eye of a sail to prevent chafing. **b.** A metal ring around which a rope splice is passed. [ME *thimbil,* alteration of OE *thȳmel,* leather finger covering < *thūma,* thumb.]

thim·ble·ber·ry (thĭm′bəl-bĕr′ē) *n.* **1.** Any of several North American raspberries, esp. *Rubus parviflorus, R. occidentalis,* or *R. odoratus* of the rose family, having thimble-shaped aggregate fruit. **2.** The fruit of any of these plants.

thim·ble·ful (thĭm′bəl-fo͝ol′) *n.* **1.** A very small quantity. **2.** The amount that a thimble can hold.

thim·ble·rig (thĭm′bəl-rĭg′) *n.* **1.** See **shell game** 1. **2.** One who operates a thimblerig. ❖ *tr.v.* **-rigged, -rig·ging, -rigs** To swindle with or as if with a thimblerig.

thim·ble·weed (thĭm′bəl-wēd′) *n.* Any of several North American plants of the genus *Anemone,* having cylindrical thimblelike fruit clusters.

thi·mer·o·sal (thī-mĕr′ə-săl′) *n.* A cream-colored crystalline powder, $C_9H_9HgNaO_2S$, used as a local antiseptic. [THI(O)– + MER(CURY) + –O– + SAL(ICYLATE).]

Thim·phu (thĭm′po͞o′, tĭm′-) also **Thim·bu** (-bo͞o′) The cap. of Bhutan, in the W part in the E Himalaya Mts. Pop. 30,340.

thin (thĭn) *adj.* **thin·ner, thin·nest 1a.** Relatively small in extent from one surface to the opposite, usu. in the smallest solid dimension. **b.** Not great in diameter or cross section; fine: *thin wire.* **2.** Lean or slender in form, build, or stature. **3a.** Not dense or concentrated; sparse. **b.** More rarefied than normal: *thin air.* **4a.** Flowing with relative ease; not viscous. **b.** Watery. **5a.** Sparsely supplied or provided; scanty: *a thin menu.* **b.** Having a low number of transactions: *thin trading in the stock market.* **6.** Lacking force or substance; flimsy. **7.** Lacking resonance or fullness; tinny. **8.** Lacking radiance or intensity. **9.** Not having enough photographic density or contrast to make satisfactory prints. Used of a negative. ❖ *adv.* **1.** In a thin manner. **2.** So as to be thin: *Cut the cheese thin.* ❖ *tr. & intr.v.* **thinned, thin·ning, thins** To make or become thin or thinner. [ME < OE *thynne.* See **ten-** in App.] —**thin′ly** *adv.* —**thin′ness** *n.* —**thin′nish** *adj.*

thine (thīn) *pron.* (*used with a sing. or pl. verb*) Used to indicate the one or ones belonging to thee. ❖ *adj.* A possessive form of **thou**[1]. Used instead of *thy* before an initial vowel or *h: thine orchard.* [ME *thin.* See THY.]

thing (thĭng) *n.* **1.** An entity, idea, or quality perceived, known, or thought to have its own existence. **2a.** The real or concrete substance of an entity. **b.** An entity existing in space and time. **c.** An inanimate object. **3.** Something referred to by a word, symbol, sign, or idea; a referent. **4.** A creature: *poor thing.* **5.** An individual object: *There wasn't a thing in sight.* **6a.** *Law* That which can be possessed or owned. Often used in the plural: *things personal.* **b.** **things** Possessions; belongings: *packed her things.* **c.** An article of clothing: *Put on your things.* **7. things** The equipment needed for an activity or special purpose: *cleaning things.* **8.** An object or entity that is not or cannot be named specifically. **9a.** An act, deed, or work. **b.** The result of work or activity: *always building things.* **10.** A thought, notion, or utterance. **11.** A piece of information. **12.** A means to an end: *just the thing to increase sales.* **13.** An end or objective. **14.** A matter of concern. **15.** A turn of events; a circumstance. **16a. things** The general state of affairs; conditions. **b.** A particular state of affairs; a situation. **17.** *Informal* A persistent illogical feeling, as a desire or aversion; an obsession: *has a thing about seafood.* **18.** *Informal* The latest fad or fashion; the rage. **19.** *Slang* An activity uniquely suitable and satisfying to one: *do your own thing.* —*idioms:* **first thing** *Informal* Right away; before anything else. **see** (or **hear**) **things** To have hallucinations. [ME < OE.]

thing·a·ma·bob or **thing·u·ma·bob** (thĭng′ə-mə-bŏb′) also **thing·um·bob** (thĭng′əm-bŏb′) *n. Informal* A thingamajig. [Alteration of *thingumbob :* obsolete *thingum* (< THING) + BOB[2].]

thing·a·ma·jig also **thing·um·a·jig** (thĭng′ə-mə-jĭg′) *n. Informal* Something difficult to classify or whose name has been forgotten or is not known. [Alteration of obsolete *thingum* (< THING) + JIG.]

thing-in-it·self (thĭng′ĭn-ĭt-sĕlf′) *n., pl.* **things-in-them·selves** (thĭngz′ĭn-thĕm-sĕlvz′) See **noumenon.**

think (thĭngk) *v.* **thought** (thôt), **think·ing, thinks** —*tr.* **1.** To have or formulate in the mind. **2a.** To reason about or reflect on; ponder: *Think it through.* **b.** To decide by reasoning, reflection, or pondering. **3.** To judge or regard; look upon: *I think it fair.* **4.** To believe; suppose: *I think you are correct.* **5a.** To expect; hope. **b.** To intend. **6.** To call to mind; remember. **7.** To visualize; imagine. **8.** To devise or evolve; invent: *thought up a plan.* **9.** To bring into a given condition by mental preoccupation. **10.** To concentrate one's thoughts on. —*intr.* **1.** To exercise the power of reason, as by conceiving ideas, drawing inferences, and using judgment. **2.** To weigh or consider an idea: *thinking about moving.* **3a.** To bring a thought to mind by imagination or invention. **b.** To

recall a thought or an image to mind. **4.** To believe; suppose: *He thinks of himself as a wit.* **5.** To have care or consideration. **6.** To dispose the mind in a given way: *Do you think so?* ❖ *adj. Informal* Requiring much thought to create or assimilate. ❖ *n.* The act or an instance of deliberate or extended thinking; a meditation. —*idioms:* **come to think of it** *Informal* When one considers the matter; on reflection. **think aloud** (or **out loud**) To speak one's thoughts audibly. **think better of** To change one's mind about; reconsider. **think little of** To regard as inferior; have a poor opinion of. **think nothing of** To give little consideration to; regard as routine or usual. **think twice** To weigh something carefully. [ME *thenken* < OE *thencan.*]

think·a·ble (thĭng′kə-bəl) *adj.* Possible to consider or be considered; conceivable. —**think′a·bly** *adv.*

think·er (thĭng′kər) *n.* **1.** One who devotes much time to thought or meditation. **2.** One who thinks or reasons in a certain way: *a careful thinker.*

think·ing (thĭng′kĭng) *n.* **1.** The act or practice of one that thinks; thought. **2.** A way of reasoning; judgment. ❖ *adj.* Marked by thought or thoughtfulness; rational.

thinking cap *n.* A state in which one thinks, esp. carefully.

think piece *n.* A newspaper article consisting of news analysis, background material, and personal opinions.

think tank *n.* A group or institution for intensive research and problem solving, esp. in technology, social or political strategy, or armament.

thin·ner (thĭn′ər) *n.* A liquid, such as turpentine, mixed with paint or varnish to reduce its viscosity.

thin-skinned (thĭn′skĭnd′) *adj.* **1.** Having a thin rind or skin. **2.** Oversensitive, esp. to criticism or insult.

thio– or **thi–** *pref.* Containing sulfur, used esp. of a compound in which oxygen has been replaced by a divalent sulfur: *thiourea.* [Gk. *theio-* < *theion,* sulfur.]

thi·o·car·ba·mide (thī′ə-kär′bə-mīd′) *n.* See **thiourea.**

thi·o·cy·a·nate (thī′ō-sī′ə-nāt′) *n.* A salt or ester of thiocyanic acid.

thi·o·cy·an·ic acid (thī′ō-sī-ăn′ĭk) *n.* An unstable colorless liquid, HSCN, used in the form of esters as an insecticide.

Thi·o·kol (thī′ə-kôl′, -kōl′, -kŏl′) A trademark used for any of various polysulfide polymers in the form of liquids, water dispersions, and rubbers used in seals and sealants.

thi·ol (thī′ôl′, -ōl′, -ŏl′) *n.* See **mercaptan.**

thion– *pref.* Sulfur: *thionic.* [< Gk. *theion,* sulfur.]

thi·on·ic (thī-ŏn′ĭk) *adj.* Of, relating to, containing, or derived from sulfur.

thi·o·nyl (thī′ə-nĭl′) *n.* See **sulfinyl.**

thi·o·pen·tal sodium (thī′ō-pĕn′tăl′, -tôl′) *n.* A yellowish-white hygroscopic powder, $C_{11}H_{17}N_2O_2SNa$, injected intravenously as a general anesthetic and psychotherapy to induce a relaxed state. [THIO– + PENT(OBARBIT)AL SODIUM.]

thi·o·phene (thī′ə-fēn′) *n.* A colorless liquid, C_4H_4S, used as a solvent. [THIO– + PH(ENO)– + –ENE.]

thi·o·sul·fate (thī′ō-sŭl′fāt′) *n.* A salt or ester of thiosulfuric acid.

thi·o·sul·fu·ric acid (thī′ō-sŭl-fyo͝or′ĭk) *n.* An unstable acid, $H_2S_2O_3$, formed by replacement of an oxygen atom by a sulfur atom in sulfuric acid.

thi·o·u·ra·cil (thī′ō-yo͝or′ə-sĭl′) *n.* A crystalline compound, $C_4H_4N_2OS$, that interferes with the synthesis of thyroxine, used to reduce the action of the thyroid gland.

thi·o·u·re·a (thī′ō-yo͝o-rē′ə) *n.* A lustrous crystalline compound, $(NH_2)_2CS$, used as a developer in photography and photocopying and in various organic syntheses.

Thí·ra (thîr′ə, thē′rä) Formerly **San·to·rin** (săn′tə-rēn′) A volcanic island of SE Greece in the S Cyclades Is. N of Crete.

third (thûrd) *n.* **1.** The ordinal number matching the number three in a series. **2.** One of three equal parts. **3.** *Music* **a.** An interval of three degrees in a diatonic scale. **b.** A tone separated by three degrees from a given tone, esp. the third tone of a scale. **4.** The transmission gear or gear ratio for forward speeds next higher to those of second in a motor vehicle. **5.** *Baseball* Third base. **6. thirds** Merchandise whose quality is below the standard set for seconds. [ME *thridde, thardde,* third < OE *thridda.* See **trei-** in App.] —**third** *adv. & adj.*

third base *n. Baseball* **1.** The third of the bases on the diamond counterclockwise from home plate. **2.** The position played by the third baseman.

third baseman *n. Baseball* The infielder near third base.

third class *n.* **1.** A class of mail in the US postal system including all printed matter, except newspapers and magazines, that weighs less than 16 ounces and is unsealed. **2.** Accommodations, as on a ship or train, of the third and usu. lowest order of luxury and price. —**third′-class′** *adj.* —**third′ class′** *adv.*

third degree *n.* Mental or physical torture used to obtain information or a confession from a prisoner.

third-de·gree burn (thûrd′dĭ-grē′) *n.* A severe burn in which the skin and underlying tissues are destroyed.

third dimension *n.* **1.** The quality of depth or thickness in an object or a space. **2.** The quality of seeming real or lifelike. —**third′-di·men′sion·al** (thûrd′dĭ-mĕn′shə-nəl) *adj.*

third eyelid *n.* See **nictitating membrane.**

third force *n.* A group of people or nations that mediates between two opposed groups, such as hostile nations.

third·hand (thûrd′hănd′) *adj.* **1.** Acquired from or through two intermediate sources: *a thirdhand report.* **2a.** Previously used by two other owners. **b.** Dealing in merchandise previously used by two other owners. —**third′hand′** *adv.*

third·ly (thûrd′lē) *adv.* In the third place, rank, or order.

third market *n.* The market in stocks that are listed on an organized exchange but are traded outside of the exchange by brokers representing institutional investors.

Third Order *n. Roman Catholic Church* A confraternity of laypersons associated with a religious order.

third party *n.* **1.** A political party organized as opposition to the existing parties in a two-party system. **2.** One other than the principals involved in a transaction.

third person *n.* **1.** The grammatical category of forms that designate a person or thing other than the speaker or the one spoken to. Examples of forms in the third person include English pronouns such as *she* and *they* and verb forms such as Spanish *hablan* "they speak." **2.** A discourse or literary style in which the narrator recounts his or her own experiences or impressions using such forms.

third rail *n.* **1.** The rail that supplies the high voltage to power a train on an electric railway. **2.** A subject that tends to be avoided because of its offensive or controversial nature.

third-rate (thûrd′rāt′) *adj.* Of third quality or value, esp. of less quality or value than second-rate.

Third Reich *n.* The German state from 1933 to 1945 under Adolf Hitler. [Partial transl. of Ger. *(das) Dritte Reich,* (the) Third Empire : *dritte,* third + *Reich,* empire; see REICH.]

third-stream (thûrd′strēm′) *adj.* Of, relating to, or being music that blends classical music with jazz.

Third World also **third world** *n.* **1.** The developing nations of Africa, Asia, and Latin America. **2.** Minority groups as a whole within a larger prevailing culture. —**Third′-World′** *adj.* —**Third World′er** *n.*

thirst (thûrst) *n.* **1a.** A sensation of dryness in the mouth and throat related to a need or desire to drink. **b.** The desire to drink. **2.** An insistent desire; a craving: *a thirst for knowledge.* ❖ *intr.v.* **thirst·ed, thirst·ing, thirsts** **1.** To feel a need to drink. **2.** To have a strong craving; yearn. [ME < OE *thurst.* See **ters-** in App.] —**thirst′er** *n.*

thirst·y (thûr′stē) *adj.* **-i·er, -i·est** **1.** Desiring to drink. **2.** Arid; parched. **3.** Craving something. **4.** Very absorbent: *a thirsty sponge.* —**thirst′i·ly** *adv.* —**thirst′i·ness** *n.*

thir·teen (thûr-tēn′) *n.* **1.** The cardinal number that is equal to the sum of 12 + 1. **2.** The 13th in a set or sequence. **3.** Something having 13 parts, units, or members. [ME *thyrtene,* alteration of *thrittene* < OE *thrēotīne.* See **trei-** in App.] —**thir′teen′** *adj. & pron.*

thir·teenth (thûr-tēnth′) *n.* **1.** The ordinal number matching the number 13 in a series. **2.** One of 13 equal parts. —**thir′teenth′** *adv. & adj.*

thir·ti·eth (thûr′tē-ĭth) *n.* **1.** The ordinal number matching the number 30 in a series. **2.** One of 30 equal parts. —**thir′ti·eth** *adv. & adj.*

thir·ty (thûr′tē) *n., pl.* **-ties** **1.** The cardinal number equal to 3 × 10. **2. thirties a.** A decade or the numbers from 30 to 39: *They settled down in their thirties.* **b.** often **Thirties** The decade from 30 to 39 in a century. **3.** An indication of the end of a news story, usu. written 30. [ME *thritty, thirty* < OE *thrītig.* See **trei-** in App.] —**thir′ty** *adj. & pron.*

thir·ty-eight (thûr′tē-āt′) *n.* A .38-caliber revolver.

thir·ty-sec·ond note (thûr′tē-sĕk′ənd) *n.* A musical note with a time value equivalent to ¹⁄₃₂ of a whole note.

thir·ty-thir·ty (thûr′tē-thûr′tē) *n.* A rifle that fires a .30-caliber cartridge with a 30-grain powder charge.

thir·ty-three (thûr′tē-thrē′) *n.* A phonograph record designed to be played at 33⅓ revolutions per minute.

thir·ty-two·mo (thûr′tē-tōō′mō) *n., pl.* **-mos** **1.** The page size (3½ by 5½ inches) that results when a printer's sheet is folded into 32 equal sections. **2.** A book composed of pages of this size.

Thirty Years' War *n.* A series of wars in central Europe (1618–48) that stemmed from conflict between Protestants and Catholics and from political struggles between the Holy Roman Empire and other powers.

this (thĭs) *pron., pl.* **these** (thēz) **1a.** Used to refer to the person or thing present, nearby, or just mentioned: *This is my cat.* **b.** Used to refer to what is about to be said: *Listen to this.* **c.** Used to refer to the present event, action, or time: *said he'd be back before this.* **2.** Used to indicate the nearer or the more immediate one: *This is mine and that is yours.* ❖ *adj., pl.* **these** **1.** Being just mentioned or present in space, time, or thought: *early this morning.* **2.** Being nearer or more immediate: *this side and that side.* **3.** Being about to be stated or described: *Wait for this story.* **4.** *Informal* Used as an indefinite article: *lost this book.* ❖ *adv.* To this extent; so: *this late.* [ME < OE. See **to-** in App.]

USAGE NOTE *This* and *that* are both used as demonstrative pronouns to refer to a thought expressed earlier: *The letter was unopened; that* (or *this*) *in itself casts doubt on the inspector's theory.*

That is sometimes prescribed as the better choice in referring to what has gone before (as in the preceding example). When the referent is yet to be mentioned, only *this* is used: *This* (not *that*) *is what bothers me: we have no time to consider late applications.* • *This* is often used in speech and informal writing as a substitute for the use of the indefinite article to refer to a specific thing or person: *I have this feeling that I forgot it.* This informal usage is best avoided in formal writing except where conversational tone is deliberately being sought. See Usage Note at **that.**

this·a·way (thĭs′ə-wā′) *adv. Southern & Midland US* This way.

This·be (thĭz′bē) *n. Greek & Roman Mythology* A young woman who killed herself after the suicide of her lover, Pyramus.

this·tle (thĭs′əl) *n.* **1.** Any of numerous weedy plants, chiefly of the genera *Cirsium, Carduus,* or *Onopordum* of the composite family, having prickly leaves and variously colored flower heads surrounded by prickly bracts. **2.** Any of various similar or related plants. [ME < OE *thistel.*]

this·tle·down (thĭs′əl-doun′) *n.* The silky down attached to the seedlike fruit of a thistle; pappus.

thith·er (thĭth′ər, thĭth′-) *adv.* To or toward that place; in that direction; there. ❖ *adj.* Located or being on the more distant side; farther. [ME < OE *thider.* See **to-** in App.]

thith·er·to (thĭth′ər-tōō′, thĭth′-) *adv.* Up to that time.

thith·er·ward (thĭth′ər-wərd, thĭth′-) *adv.* Thither.

thix·ot·ro·py (thĭk-sŏt′rə-pē) *n.* The property exhibited by certain gels of becoming fluid when stirred or shaken and returning to the semisolid state upon standing. [< Gk. *thixis,* touch < *thinganein, thig-,* to touch. See **dheigh-** in App.]

ThM *abbr. Latin* Theologiae Magister (Master of Theology)

tho also **tho'** (thō) *conj. & adv. Informal* Though.

thole (thōl) *n.* A thole pin. [ME *tholle* < OE *thol.*]

thole pin *n.* A wooden peg set in pairs in the gunwales of a boat as an oarlock.

Thom·as (tŏm′əs), Saint. One of the 12 Apostles, who doubted that Jesus had risen from the dead until he saw the wounds.

Thomas, Clarence b. 1948. Amer. jurist who was appointed an associate justice of the US Supreme Court in 1991.

Thomas, Dylan Marlais 1914–53. Welsh poet known for his bardic voice experiments with syllabic verse.

Thomas, George Henry 1816–70. Amer. Union general who fought at Shiloh (1862) and Chickamauga (1863).

Thomas, Norman Mattoon 1884–1968. Amer. socialist who was a founder of the American Civil Liberties Union (1920).

Thomas, Seth 1785–1859. Amer. clockmaker and a pioneer in the mass production of clocks.

Thomas à Kem·pis (ə kĕm′pĭs, ä) 1380?–1471. German ecclesiastic and writer of devotional literature, probably including *The Imitation of Christ* (1426).

Tho·mism (tō′mĭz′əm) *n.* The theological and philosophical system of Saint Thomas Aquinas, a system that dominated scholasticism. —**Tho′mist** *n.* —**Tho·mis′tic** *adj.*

Thomp·son (tŏmp′sən, tŏm′-), **Benjamin.** Count Rumford. 1753–1814. Amer.-born British public official and physicist who concluded that heat is produced by moving particles.

Thompson, Dorothy 1894–1961. Amer. journalist noted for her radio broadcasts and syndicated column "On the Record" (1936–41).

Thompson, Sir John Sparrow David 1844–94. Canadian politician who served as prime minister (1892–94).

Thompson River A river, c. 489 km (304 mi), of S British Columbia, Canada, flowing W and SW to the Fraser R.

Thompson submachine gun *n.* A .45-caliber submachine gun. [After John *Thompson* (1860–1940), American army officer.]

Thom·sen (tŏm′sən), **Christian Jürgensen** 1788–1865. Danish archaeologist who proposed a three-part system for the chronological classification of prehistoric artifacts, divided into the Stone, Bronze, and Iron ages.

Thom·son (tŏm′sən), **James** 1700–48. Scottish-born British poet whose works presaged romanticism.

Thomson, Sir Joseph John 1856–1940. British physicist who won a 1906 Nobel Prize.

Thomson, Virgil Garnett 1896–1989. Amer. composer best known for the opera *Four Saints in Three Acts* (1927).

thong (thông, thŏng) *n.* **1.** A narrow strip, as of leather, used for binding or lashing. **2.** A whip of plaited leather or cord. **3.** A sandal held on the foot by a strip that fits between the first and second toes and a strap. **4.** A garment for the lower body that exposes the buttocks, consisting of a narrow strip of fabric that passes between the thighs supported by a waistband. [ME < OE *thwong.*]

Thor (thôr) *n. Mythology* The Norse god of thunder. [ON *Thôrr.* See **(s)tenə-** in App.]

tho·rac·ic (thə-răs′ĭk) *adj.* Of, relating to, or located in or near the thorax; of the thoracic cavity. —**tho·rac′i·cal·ly** *adv.*

thoracic duct *n.* The main duct of the lymphatic system, ascending through the thoracic cavity along the spinal column and discharging lymph and chyle into the left subclavian vein.

tho·ra·cot·o·my (thôr′ə-kŏt′ə-mē, thōr′-) *n., pl.* **-mies** Surgical incision of the chest wall. [Lat. *thôrax, thôrâc-,* thorax + –TOMY.]

thistle
bull (or common) thistle
Cirsium vulgare

ă pat | oi boy
ā pay | ou out
âr care | ŏŏ took
ä father | ōō boot
ĕ pet | ŭ cut
ē be | ûr urge
ĭ pit | th thin
ī pie | th this
îr pier | hw which
ŏ pot | zh vision
ō toe | ə about,
ô paw | item

Stress marks:
′ (primary);
′ (secondary), as in
lexicon (lĕk′sĭ-kŏn′)

Henry David Thoreau
1856 daguerreotype

tho·rax (thôr′ăks′, thōr′-) n., pl. **tho·rax·es** or **tho·ra·ces** (thôr′ə-sēz′, thōr′-) **1.** The part of the human body between the neck and the diaphragm, partially encased by the ribs and containing the heart and lungs; the chest. **2.** A part in other vertebrates that corresponds to the human thorax. **3.** The second or middle region of the body of an arthropod, between the head and the abdomen. [ME < Lat. *thōrāx,* breastplate, chest < Gk.]

Tho·ra·zine (thôr′ə-zēn′, thōr′-) A trademark used for chlorpromazine.

Tho·reau (thə-rō′, thôr′ō), **Henry David** 1817–62. Amer. writer whose works include "Civil Disobedience" (1849) and *Walden* (1854). **—Tho·reau′vi·an** (-vē-ən) *adj.*

tho·ri·a (thôr′ē-ə, thōr′-) n. See **thorium dioxide.**

tho·ri·a·nite (thôr′ē-ə-nīt′, thōr′-) n. A highly radioactive blackish or yellowish mineral, ThO₂, isomorphous with uraninite. [THORIA + -AN² + -ITE¹.]

tho·rite (thôr′īt′, thōr′-) n. A vitreous brownish-yellow to black radioactive mineral, ThSiO₄, an ore of thorium.

tho·ri·um (thôr′ē-əm, thōr′-) n. *Symbol* **Th** A radioactive metallic element that is recovered commercially from monazite and used in magnesium alloys; its longest-lived isotope, Th 232, has a half-life of 1.41×10^{10} years and is used as a source of nuclear energy. Atomic number 90; atomic weight 232.038; approx. melting point 1,750°C; approx. boiling point 4,500°C; approx. specific gravity 11.7; valence 4. See table at **element.** [After THOR.] **—tho′ric** (thôr′-, thōr′-) *adj.*

thorium dioxide n. A heavy powder, ThO₂, obtained from monazite and used in gas mantles and as a catalyst.

thorn (thôrn) n. **1.** *Botany* **a.** A modified branch in the form of a sharp, woody spine. **b.** Any of various plants bearing thorns. **2.** Any of various sharp spiny protuberances; a prickle. **3.** One that causes sharp pain, irritation, or discomfort. **4.** The runic letter þ originally representing either sound of the Modern English *th,* as in *the* and *thin,* used in Old English and Middle English manuscripts. [ME < OE.]

thorn apple n. See **datura.**

thorn·back (thôrn′băk′) n. **1.** A European ray (*Raja clavata*) having spines along the back. **2.** A fish (*Platyrhinoidis triseriata*) of Pacific waters, related to the guitarfish.

thorn·bush (thôrn′bŏŏsh′) n. Any of various shrubs or bushes having thorns or spines.

Thorn·dike (thôrn′dīk′), **Edward Lee** 1874–1949. Amer. psychologist noted for his study of animal intelligence.

thorn·y (thôr′nē) adj. **-i·er, -i·est 1.** Full of or covered with thorns. **2.** Spiny. **3.** Painfully controversial; vexatious: *thorny issues.* **—thorn′i·ly** adv. **—thorn′i·ness** n.

tho·ron (thôr′ŏn′, thōr′-) n. A radioactive isotope of radon, Rn 220, having a half-life of 54.5 seconds and produced by the disintegration of thorium. [THOR(IUM) + -ON².]

thor·ough (thûr′ō, thŭr′ō) adj. **1.** Exhaustively complete. **2.** Painstakingly accurate or careful. **3.** Absolute; utter. ❖ *prep.* & *adv. Archaic* Variant of **through.** [ME *thorow,* through, thorough < OE *thuruh,* from end to end, through. See **terə-²** in App.] **—thor′ough·ly** adv. **—thor′ough·ness** n.

thor·ough·bass or **thor·ough bass** (thûr′ō-bās′, thûr′ə-, thŭr′-) n. See **continuo.** [THOROUGH, through and through + BASS².]

thorough brace n. One of several leather bands passed from front to back of a carriage, supporting it and serving as a spring. **—thor′ough-braced′** (thûr′ō-brāst′, thŭr′-) adj.

thor·ough·bred (thûr′ō-brĕd′, thûr′ə-, thŭr′-) n. **1.** A purebred or pedigreed animal, esp. a horse. **2. Thoroughbred** Any of a breed of horses, bred chiefly for racing, originating from a cross between Arabian stallions and English mares. **3.** A well-bred person. **—thor′ough·bred′** adj.

thor·ough·fare (thûr′ō-fâr′, thûr′ə-, thŭr′-) n. **1.** A main road or public highway. **2a.** A place of passage from one location to another. **b.** Right to such passage. **3.** A heavily traveled passage, such as a strait. [ME *thurghfare : thurgh, thorow,* through; see THOROUGH + *fare,* road (< OE *faru, fær < faran,* to go; see FARE).]

thor·ough·go·ing (thûr′ō-gō′ĭng, thûr′ə-, thŭr′-) adj. **1.** Very thorough; complete. **2.** Unmitigated; unqualified.

thor·ough·paced (thûr′ō-pāst′, thûr′ə-, thŭr′-) adj. **1.** Trained in all paces or gaits, as a horse. **2.** Thoroughgoing; complete.

thor·ough·pin (thûr′ō-pĭn′, thûr′ə-, thŭr′-) n. An abnormal swelling of the hock joint in horses and related animals. [< its resemblance to a pin passing through the hock.]

thor·ough·wort (thûr′ō-wûrt′, -wôrt′, thûr′ə-, thŭr′-) n. See **boneset.** [THOROUGH, through + WORT¹.]

thorp (thôrp) n. *Archaic* A hamlet. [ME < OE.]

Thorpe (thôrp), **James Francis ("Jim")** 1888–1953. Amer. athlete who won the decathlon and pentathlon in the 1912 Olympics.

Thor·vald·sen or **Thor·wald·sen** (tôr′wôl′sən, thôr′-, tŏŏr′väl′-), **(Albert) Bertel** 1768?–1844. Danish sculptor whose neoclassical works include *Lion of Lucerne* (1819).

those (thōz) pron. & adj. Plural of **that.** [ME *thos* < OE *thās,* these. See THESE.]

Thoth (thōth, tōt) n. *Mythology* The Egyptian god of the moon and of wisdom and learning, usu. represented as having the head of an ibis.

thou¹ (thou) pron. Used to address a single person, esp. as a fa-

Jim Thorpe

miliar form in a literary or devotional context. [ME < OE *thū,* second person nominative sing. personal pron. See **tu-** in App.]

thou² (thou) n. *Slang* A thousand, esp. of dollars.

though (thō) conj. **1.** Despite the fact that; although: *He still loves her, though he's wrong.* **2.** Conceding or supposing that; even if: *Though I may fail, I will still try.* See Usage Note at **although.** ❖ *adv.* **1.** However; nevertheless. **2.** *Informal* Used as an intensive: *Wouldn't that beat all, though?* [ME, of Scand. orig. See **to-** in App.]

thought (thôt) v. Past tense and past participle of **think.** ❖ n. **1.** The act or process of thinking; cogitation. **2.** A product of thinking. See Syns at **idea.** **3.** The faculty of thinking or reasoning. **4.** The intellectual activity or production of a particular time or group: *feminist thought.* **5.** Consideration; attention. **6a.** Intention; purpose. **b.** Expectation or conception: *no thought of being wrong.* **—idiom: a thought** To a small degree; somewhat: *You could be a thought more considerate.* [ME < OE *gethōht, thōht.*]

thought·ful (thôt′fəl) adj. **1.** Engrossed in thought; contemplative. **2.** Exhibiting or marked by careful thought. **3.** Having or showing heed for the happiness of others and a propensity for anticipating their needs or wishes. **—thought′ful·ly** adv. **—thought′ful·ness** n.

SYNONYMS *thoughtful, considerate, attentive, solicitous* These adjectives mean having or showing concern for the well-being of others. Although *thoughtful* and *considerate* are often used interchangeably, *thoughtful* implies a tendency to anticipate needs or wishes, whereas *considerate* stresses sensitivity to another's feelings: *It was thoughtful of you to bring flowers. I wish I had more considerate neighbors. Attentive* suggests devoted, assiduous attention: *an editor who is attentive to detail. Solicitous* implies deep concern that often verges on anxiety or expresses itself in exaggerated and sometimes cloying attentiveness: *a solicitous and meddlesome cousin.* See also Syns at **pensive.**

thought·less (thôt′lĭs) adj. **1.** Marked by or showing lack of due thought or care; careless. **2.** Inconsiderate; inattentive: *a thoughtless remark.* **3.** Lacking thought: *The debate turned into thoughtless bickering.* **—thought′less·ly** adv. **—thought′less·ness** n.

thou·sand (thou′zənd) n. The cardinal number equal to 10 × 100 or 10³. [ME < OE *thūsend.*] **—thou′sand** adj. & pron.

Thousand Island dressing n. A salad dressing made with mayonnaise, chili sauce, and seasonings. [Perh. after the THOUSAND ISLANDS.]

Thousand Islands A group of more than 1,800 islands of N NY and SE Ontario, Canada, in the St. Lawrence R.

Thousand Oaks A city of S CA W of Los Angeles. Pop. 117,005.

thou·sandth (thou′zəndth, -zənth) n. **1.** The ordinal number matching the number 1,000 in a series. **2.** One of 1,000 equal parts. **—thou′sandth** adj. & adv.

thp also **t.hp.** abbr. thrust horsepower

Thrace (thrās) A region and ancient country of the SE Balkan Peninsula N of the Aegean Sea; colonized by Greeks in the 7th cent. B.C.

Thra·cian (thrā′shən) adj. Of or relating to Thrace or its people. ❖ n. **1.** A native or inhabitant of Thrace. **2.** The Indo-European language of the ancient Thracians.

Thrale (thrāl), **Mrs.** See Hester Lynch **Piozzi.**

thrall (thrôl) n. **1.** One, such as a slave, held in bondage. **2.** One intellectually or morally enslaved. **3.** Servitude; bondage. ❖ *tr.v.* **thralled, thrall·ing, thralls** *Archaic* To enslave. [ME < OE *thrǣl* < ON *thrǣll.*] **—thrall′dom, thral′dom** n.

thrash (thrăsh) v. **thrashed, thrash·ing, thrash·es** —*tr.* **1.** To beat with or as if with a flail, esp. as a punishment. **2.** To flail. **3.** To defeat utterly. **4.** To thresh. **5.** To sail (a boat) against opposing winds or tides. —*intr.* **1.** To move wildly or violently. **2.** To strike or flail. **3.** To thresh. **4.** To sail against opposing tides or winds. ❖ n. **1.** The act or an instance of thrashing. **2.** *Music* See **speed metal. —phrasal verb: thrash out** To discuss fully. [Variant of THRESH.] **—thrash′er** n.

thrash·er (thrăsh′ər) n. Any of various New World songbirds of the genus *Toxostoma,* having a long curved beak and usu. a brown head and back. [Perh. alteration of THRUSH¹.]

thrash·ing (thrăsh′ĭng) n. A severe beating.

thra·son·i·cal (thrā-sŏn′ĭ-kəl, thrə-) adj. Boastful. [After *Thrasō,* a character in the play *Eunuchus* by Terence.]

thread (thrĕd) n. **1a.** Fine cord of a fibrous material, such as flax, made of two or more filaments twisted together and used in needlework and weaving. **b.** A piece of such cord. **2a.** A thin strand, cord, or filament of natural or manufactured material. **b.** Something that suggests the fineness or thinness of such a strand, cord, or filament: *a thread of smoke.* **c.** Something that suggests the continuousness of such a thread: *the thread of his argument.* **3.** A helical or spiral ridge on a screw, nut, or bolt. **4a.** A portion of a program that can run independently of and concurrently with other portions. **b.** A set of posts on a newsgroup, composed of an initial post about a topic and all responses to it. **5. threads** *Slang* Clothes. ❖ v. **thread·ed, thread·ing, threads** —*tr.* **1a.** To pass one end of a thread through the eye of (a needle, for example). **b.** To pass (something) through in the manner of a thread. **c.** To pass a tape or film into or through (a device). **d.** To pass (a tape or film) into or through a device. **2.** To connect by running a thread through; string: *thread beads.* **3a.** To make one's way cautiously through: *threading dark alleys.* **b.** To make (one's way) cautiously through something. **4.** To occur here and there throughout; pervade. **5.** To machine a thread on (a screw, nut, or bolt). *—intr.* **1.** To make one's way cautiously. **2.** To proceed by a winding course. **3.** To form a thread when dropped from a spoon, as boiling sugar syrup. [ME < OE *thrǣd.* See **terə-**[1] in App.] **—thread′er** *n.*

thread•bare (thrĕd′bâr′) *adj.* **1.** Having the nap worn down so that the filling or warp shows through; frayed or shabby: *threadbare rugs.* **2.** Wearing old, shabby clothing. **3.** Overused and worn out; hackneyed: *threadbare excuses.*

thread•fin (thrĕd′fĭn′) *n., pl.* **threadfin** or **-fins** Any of various chiefly tropical marine fishes of the family Polynemidae, having threadlike rays extending from the pectoral fin.

thread•worm (thrĕd′wûrm′) *n.* See **pinworm.**

thread•y (thrĕd′ē) *adj.* **-i•er, -i•est 1.** Consisting of or resembling thread; filamentous. **2.** Capable of forming or tending to form threads; viscid. **3.** *Medicine* Weak and shallow. Used of a pulse. **4.** Lacking fullness of tone; thin: *a thready voice.* **—thread′i•ness** *n.*

threat (thrĕt) *n.* **1.** An expression of an intention to inflict pain, injury, evil, or punishment. **2.** An indication of impending danger or harm. **3.** One that is regarded as a possible danger; a menace. ❖ *tr.v.* **threat•ed, threat•ing, threats** *Archaic* To threaten. [ME < OE *thrēat,* oppression.]

threat•en (thrĕt′n) *v.* **-ened, -en•ing, -ens** *—tr.* **1.** To express a threat against. **2.** To be a source of danger to; menace. **3.** To give signs or warning of; portend. **4.** To announce the possibility of in a threat. *—intr.* **1.** To express or use threats. **2.** To indicate danger or harm. **—threat′en•er** *n.*

threat•ened (thrĕt′nd) *adj. Ecology* At risk of becoming endangered. Used of a plant or animal.

three (thrē) *n.* **1.** The cardinal number equal to 2 + 1. **2.** The third in a set or sequence. **3.** Something having three parts, units, or members. [ME < OE *thrī.* See **trei-** in App.] **—three** *adj. & pron.*

three-bag•ger (thrē′băg′ər) *n.* See **three-base hit.**

three-base hit (thrē′bās′) *n. Baseball* A base hit that allows the batter to reach third base without being put out.

three-card monte (thrē′kärd) *n.* A gambling game in which the dealer shows a player three cards, then turns them face down and moves them around, and the player must guess the position of a particular card.

three-col•or (thrē′kŭl′ər) *adj.* Of, relating to, or being a color printing or photographic process in which three primary colors are transferred by three different plates or filters to a surface, reproducing all the colors of the subject matter.

3-D or **3D** also **three-D** (thrē′dē′) *adj.* Three-dimensional. ❖ *n.* A three-dimensional medium, display, or performance, esp. a cinematic or graphic medium in three dimensions.

three-deck•er (thrē′dĕk′ər) *n.* **1.** A ship having three decks, esp. one of a class of sail-powered warships with guns on three decks. **2.** Something with three levels or layers, as: **a.** A three-story apartment building. **b.** A sandwich having three slices of bread.

three-di•men•sion•al (thrē′dĭ-mĕn′shə-nəl, -dī-) *adj.* **1.** Of, relating to, having, or existing in three dimensions. **2.** Having or appearing to have extension in depth. **3.** Treating many aspects of a subject; lifelike.

three-gait•ed (thrē′gā′tĭd) *adj.* Trained in the walk, trot, and canter. Used of a horse.

three-leg•ged race (thrē′lĕg′ĭd, -lĕgd′) *n.* A race in which runners are in pairs with their near legs tied together.

Three Mile Island An island in the Susquehanna R. in SE PA; site of a major nuclear accident in Mar. 1979.

three•pence (thrĕp′əns, thrĭp′-, thrŭp′-) *n., pl.* **threepence** or **-penc•es 1.** A coin worth three pennies, formerly used in Great Britain. **2.** The sum of three pennies.

three•pen•ny (thrĕp′ə-nē, thrĭp′-, thrŭp′-) *adj.* **1.** Worth or priced at threepence. **2.** Very small; trifling.

three-piece (thrē′pēs′) *adj.* Made in or consisting of three parts or pieces, as a suit with a jacket, trousers, and a vest.

three-ply (thrē′plī′) *adj.* Consisting of three layers or strands.

three-point landing (thrē′point′) *n.* An airplane landing in which the two main wheels and the nose wheel, tail wheel, or rear skid all touch the ground simultaneously.

three-quar•ter (thrē′kwôr′tər) *adj.* **1.** Of or extending to three fourths of the usual full length. **2.** Depicting the subject turned slightly from a full frontal view.

three-ring circus (thrē′rĭng′) *n.* **1.** A circus having simultaneous performances in three separate rings. **2.** *Informal* A confusing, engrossing, or amusing situation.

three R's *pl.n.* Reading, writing, and arithmetic, considered as the fundamentals of elementary education. [< the phrase *reading, 'riting, and 'rithmetic.*]

three•score (thrē′skôr′, -skōr′) *adj.* Being three times twenty; sixty. **—three′score′** *n. & pron.*

three•some (thrē′səm) *n.* **1.** A group of three persons or things. **2.** An activity involving three people, esp. a golf match in which one player competes against two others who alternate their play. ❖ *adj.* Consisting of or performed by three.

three-square (thrē′skwâr′) *adj.* Having an equilateral triangular cross section: *a three-square file.*

three-wheel•er (thrē′hwē′lər, -wē′-) *n.* A vehicle having three wheels, as a small all-terrain motor vehicle.

thren•o•dy (thrĕn′ə-dē) *n., pl.* **-dies** A poem or song of mourning or lamentation. [Gk. *thrēnōidiā* : *thrēnos,* lament + *aoidē, ōidē,* song; see ODE.] **—thre•no′di•al** (thrə-nō′dē-əl), **thre•nod′ic** (-nŏd′ĭk) *adj.* **—thren′o•dist** *n.*

thre•o•nine (thrē′ə-nēn′, -nĭn) *n.* A crystalline essential amino acid, $C_4H_9NO_3$, that is obtained from the hydrolysis of protein. [Prob. < *threose,* a kind of sugar (alteration of *erythrose* : ERYTHRO– + –OSE[2]) + –INE[2].]

thresh (thrĕsh) *v.* **threshed, thresh•ing, thresh•es** *—tr.* **1a.** To beat the stems and husks of (grain or cereal plants) with a machine or flail to separate the grains or seeds from the straw. **b.** To separate (grains or seeds) in this manner. **2.** To discuss or examine (an issue, for example) repeatedly. **3.** To beat severely; thrash. *—intr.* **1.** To thresh grain or seeds. **2.** To thrash about; toss. [ME *thresshen* < OE *therscan.* See **terə-**[1] in App.]

thresh•er (thrĕsh′ər) *n.* **1.** One that threshes: *a thresher of grain.* **2.** A threshing machine. **3.** Any of various large sharks of the genus *Alopias,* having a tail with a long whiplike upper lobe with which it strikes the surface of the water.

thresh•ing machine (thrĕsh′ĭng) *n.* A farm machine used in threshing grain or seed plants.

thresh•old (thrĕsh′ōld′, -hōld′) *n.* **1.** A piece of wood or stone beneath a door; a doorsill. **2.** An entrance or doorway. **3.** The place or point of beginning; the outset. **4.** The point that must be exceeded to begin producing a given effect or result or to elicit a response. [ME *thresshold* < OE *therscold.* See **terə-**[1] in App.]

threw (thrōō) *v.* Past tense of **throw.**

thrice (thrīs) *adv.* **1.** Three times. **2.** In a threefold quantity or degree. **3.** *Archaic* Extremely; greatly. [ME *thries,* adverbial genitive of *thrie* < OE *thrīga.* See **trei-** in App.]

thrift (thrĭft) *n.* **1.** Wise economy in the management of money and other resources; frugality. **2.** Vigorous growth of living things, such as plants. **3.** Any of several densely tufted plants of the genus *Armeria,* esp. *A. maritima,* having white to pink flower heads with a funnel-shaped scarious calyx. **4.** A savings and loan association, credit union, or savings bank. [ME, prosperity, perh. < ON < *thrīfask,* to thrive. See THRIVE.]

thrift•less (thrĭft′lĭs) *adj.* **1.** Careless in handling money; wasteful. **2.** *Archaic* Lacking usefulness or value. **—thrift′less•ly** *adv.* **—thrift′less•ness** *n.*

thrift shop *n.* A shop that sells used articles, esp. clothing, as to benefit a charitable organization.

thrift•y (thrĭf′tē) *adj.* **-i•er, -i•est 1.** Practicing or marked by the practice of thrift; wisely economical. See Syns at **sparing. 2.** Industrious and thriving; prosperous. **3.** Growing vigorously, as a plant. **—thrift′i•ly** *adv.* **—thrift′i•ness** *n.*

thrill (thrĭl) *v.* **thrilled, thrill•ing, thrills** *—tr.* **1.** To cause a sudden intense sensation; excite greatly. **2.** To give great pleasure to; delight. **3.** To cause to quiver, tremble, or vibrate. *—intr.* **1.** To feel a sudden quiver of excitement or emotion. **2.** To quiver, tremble, or vibrate. ❖ *n.* **1.** A quivering or trembling caused by sudden excitement or emotion. **2.** A source or cause of excitement or emotion. **3.** *Pathology* A slight palpable vibration accompanying certain cardiac and circulatory abnormalities. [ME *thrillen,* alteration of *thirlen,* to pierce < OE *thyrlian* < *thyrel,* hole. See **terə-**[2] in App.]

thrill•er (thrĭl′ər) *n.* One that thrills, esp. a sensational or suspenseful book, story, play, or movie.

thrips (thrĭps) *n., pl.* **thrips** Any of various minute insects of the order Thysanoptera, many of which are major pests of cereals and fruit trees. [Lat. *thrīps,* woodworm < Gk.]

thrive (thrīv) *intr.v.* **thrived** or **throve** (thrōv), **thrived** or **thriv•en** (thrĭv′ən), **thriv•ing, thrives 1.** To make steady progress; prosper. **2.** To grow vigorously; flourish. [ME *thriven* < ON *thrīfask,* reflexive of *thrīfa,* to seize.] **—thriv′er** *n.*

throat (thrōt) *n.* **1.** The anterior portion of the neck. **2.** *Anatomy* The portion of the digestive tract that lies between the rear of the mouth and the esophagus and includes the fauces and the pharynx. **3.** A narrow passage or part suggestive of the human throat. ❖ *tr.v.* **throat•ed, throat•ing, throats** To pronounce with a harsh or guttural voice. ***—idiom:* ram** (or **shove**) **down (someone's) throat** *Informal* To compel to accept or consider. [ME *throte* < OE.]

throat•latch (thrōt′lăch′) *n.* A strap passing under the neck of a horse for holding a bridle or halter in place.

throat•y (thrō′tē) *adj.* **-i•er, -i•est** Uttered or sounding as if uttered deep in the throat; guttural, hoarse, or husky. **—throat′i•ly** *adv.* **—throat′i•ness** *n.*

throb (thrŏb) *intr.v.* **throbbed, throb•bing, throbs 1.** To beat rapidly or violently, as the heart; pound. **2.** To vibrate, pulsate, or sound with a steady pronounced rhythm: *boat engines throbbing.* ❖ *n.* The act of throbbing; a beating, palpitation, or vibration. [ME *throbben,* of imit. orig.]

throe (thrō) *n.* **1.** A severe pang or spasm of pain, as in childbirth. **2. throes** A condition of agonizing struggle or trouble: *the throes of poverty.* [ME *throwe,* perh. alteration of *thrawe* < OE *thrawu,* genitive of *thrēah,* pain, affliction.]

throm•bin (thrŏm′bĭn) *n.* A protease in blood that facilitates

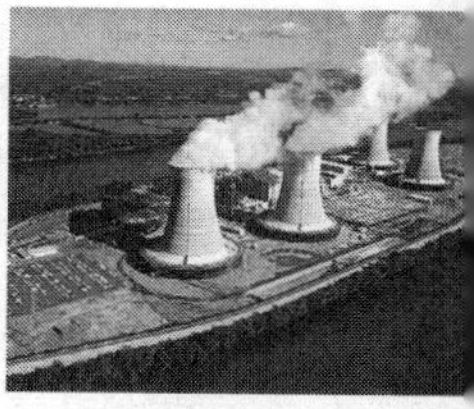

Three Mile Island
aerial view of Three Mile Island nuclear power plant

ă	pat	oi	boy
ā	pay	ou	out
âr	care	ŏŏ	took
ä	father	ōō	boot
ĕ	pet	ŭ	cut
ē	be	ûr	urge
ĭ	pit	th	thin
ī	pie	*th*	this
îr	pier	hw	which
ŏ	pot	zh	vision
ō	toe	ə	about, item
ô	paw		

Stress marks:
′ (primary);
′ (secondary), as in
lexicon (lĕk′sĭ-kŏn′)

blood clotting by converting fibrinogen to fibrin.

thrombo– or **thromb–** *pref.* Blood clot; blood clotting: *thromboplastic.* [Gk. < *thrombos,* clot.]

throm·bo·cyte (thrŏm′bə-sīt′) *n.* **1.** See **blood platelet. 2.** A nucleated, spindle-shaped cell of nonmammalian vertebrates that promotes blood clotting. —**throm′bo·cyt′ic** (-sĭt′ĭk) *adj.*

throm·bo·cy·to·pe·ni·a (thrŏm′bə-sī′tə-pē′nē-ə) *n.* An abnormal decrease in the number of platelets in circulatory blood. —**throm′bo·cy′to·pe′nic** *adj.*

throm·bo·em·bo·lism (thrŏm′bō-ĕm′bə-lĭz′əm) *n.* The blocking of a blood vessel by a blood clot dislodged from its site of origin. —**throm′bo·em·bol′ic** (-ĕm-bŏl′ĭk) *adj.*

throm·bo·ki·nase (thrŏm′bō-kī′nās, -nāz) *n.* See **thromboplastin.**

throm·bo·phle·bi·tis (thrŏm′bō-flĭ-bī′tĭs) *n.* Inflammation of a vein associated with the formation of a blood clot.

throm·bo·plas·tic (thrŏm′bō-plăs′tĭk) *adj.* **1.** Causing or promoting blood clotting: *a thromboplastic protein.* **2.** Of or relating to thromboplastin. —**throm′bo·plas′ti·cal·ly** *adv.*

throm·bo·sis (thrŏm-bō′sĭs) *n., pl.* **-ses** (-sēz) The formation, presence, or development of a thrombus. [NLat. *thrombōsis* < Gk., a clotting < *thrombousthai,* to clot < *thrombos,* clot.]

throm·box·ane (thrŏm-bŏk′sān) *n.* Any of several compounds, derived from platelets or synthesized, that stimulate clotting and constriction of blood vessels.

throm·bus (thrŏm′bəs) *n., pl.* **-bi** (-bī) A fibrinous clot formed in a blood vessel or in a chamber of the heart. [NLat. < Gk. *thrombos,* clot.]

throne (thrōn) *n.* **1.** A chair occupied by an exalted personage on state or ceremonial occasions, often situated on a dais and sometimes having ornate decoration. **2a.** A personage who occupies a throne. **b.** The power, dignity, or rank of such a personage; sovereignty. **3. thrones** *Christianity* The third of the nine orders of angels. ❖ *tr. & intr.v.* **throned, thron·ing, thrones** To install in or occupy a throne. [ME, alteration of *trone* < OFr. < Lat. *thronus* < Gk. *thronos.*]

throng (thrông, thrŏng) *n.* **1.** A large group of people close together; a multitude. **2.** A large group of things; a host. ❖ *v.* **thronged, throng·ing, throngs** —*tr.* **1.** To crowd into; fill. **2.** To press in on. —*intr.* To gather, press, or move in a throng. [ME < OE *gethrang.*]

thros·tle (thrŏs′əl) *n.* **1.** Any of various Old World thrushes, esp. a song thrush. **2.** A machine formerly used for spinning fibers such as cotton or wool. [ME < OE.]

throt·tle (thrŏt′l) *n.* **1.** A valve that regulates the flow of a fluid, as in an internal-combustion engine. **2.** A lever or pedal controlling such a valve. ❖ *tr.v.* **-tled, -tling, -tles 1a.** To regulate the flow of (fuel) in an engine. **b.** To regulate the speed of (an engine) with a throttle. **2.** To suppress: *throttled the press.* **3.** To strangle; choke. [Short for *throttle valve* < *throttle,* to strangle, choke < ME *throtelen,* prob. < *throte,* throat. See THROAT.] —**throt′tler** *n.*

throt·tle·hold (thrŏt′l-hōld′) *n.* See **stranglehold** 2.

through (thrōō) *prep.* **1.** In one side and out the opposite or another side of: *through the tunnel.* **2.** Among or between; in the midst of: *a walk through the flowers.* **3.** By way of: *climbed in through the window.* **4a.** By the means or agency of: *bought through a dealer.* **b.** Into and out of the handling, care, processing, modification, or consideration of: *The report went through our office.* **5.** Here and there in; around: *a tour through France.* **6.** From the beginning to the end of: *through the night.* **7.** At or to the end of; done or finished with, esp. successfully: *through the initial period.* **8.** Up to and including: *The play runs through May.* **9.** Past and without stopping for: *drove through a red light.* **10.** Because of; on account of: *succeeded through hard work.* ❖ *adv.* **1.** From one end or side to another or an opposite end or side: *opened it and went through.* **2.** From beginning to end; completely: *read it through.* **3.** Throughout the whole extent or thickness; thoroughly: *got soaked through.* **4.** Over the total distance; all the way: *drove through.* **5.** To a conclusion or an accomplishment: *see it through.* ❖ *adj.* **1.** Allowing continuous passage; unobstructed. **2a.** Affording transportation to a destination with few or no stops and no transfers. **b.** Continuing on a highway without exiting. **3.** Passing or extending from one end, side, or surface to another. **4.** Having finished; at completion: *through with the job.* **5.** Having no further concern, dealings, or connection: *I'm through with him.* **6a.** Having no more use, value, or potential; washed-up: *He's through as an athlete.* **b.** Doomed to death or destruction. —*idiom:* **through and through 1.** In every part; throughout. **2.** In every aspect; completely. [ME *thurh, through* < OE *thurh.* See **terə-²** in App.]

through·ly (thrōō′lē) *adv. Archaic* Thoroughly.

through·out (thrōō-out′) *prep.* **1.** In, to, through, or during every part of; all through. ❖ *adv.* **1.** In or through all parts; everywhere. **2.** During the entire time or extent.

through·put (thrōō′pŏŏt′) *n.* Output or production, as of a computer program, over a period of time.

through·way (thrōō′wā′) *n.* Variant of **thruway.**

throve (thrōv) *v.* A past tense of **thrive.**

throw (thrō) *v.* **threw** (thrōō), **thrown** (thrōn), **throw·ing, throws** —*tr.* **1.** To propel through the air with a motion of the

hand or arm. **2.** To discharge into the air by any means: *a machine that throws tennis balls.* **3.** To hurl or fling with great force or speed: *threw themselves on the food.* **4a.** To force (an opponent) to the ground or floor, as in wrestling or the martial arts. **b.** To cause to fall off. **5.** *Informal* To cause confusion or perplexity in; disconcert or nonplus. **6.** To put on or off hastily or carelessly. **7a.** To put (suddenly or forcefully) into a given condition, position, or activity: *threw some supper together.* **b.** To devote, apply, or direct. **8.** To form on a potter's wheel. **9.** To twist (fibers) into thread. **10.** *Games* **a.** To roll (dice). **b.** To roll (a particular combination) with dice. **c.** To discard or play (a card). **11.** To send forth; project: *threw me a look of pity.* **12.** To cause (one's voice) to seem to come from a source other than oneself. **13.** To cause to fall on or over something; cast. **14.** To bear (young). Used of cows or horses, for example. **15.** To arrange or give (a party, for example). **16.** To move (a lever or switch) in order to activate, deactivate, or control a device. **17.** *Informal* To lose or give up (a contest, for example) purposely. **18.** To abandon oneself to; have: *threw a fit.* **19.** To commit (oneself), esp. for leniency or support. **20.** To deliver (a punch), as in boxing. —*intr.* To cast, fling, or hurl something. ❖ *n.* **1.** The act or an instance of throwing. **2.** The distance to which something is or can be thrown: *a stone's throw away.* **3.** *Games* **a.** A roll or cast of dice. **b.** The combination of numbers so obtained. **4.** *Informal* A single chance, venture, or instance. **5.** *Sports* The act of throwing or a technique used to throw an opponent, as in wrestling. **6a.** A light coverlet, such as an afghan. **b.** A scarf or shawl. **7a.** The radius of a circle described by a crank, cam, or similar machine part. **b.** The maximum displacement of a machine part moved by another part, such as a cam. **8.** *Geology* The amount of vertical displacement of a fault. —*phrasal verbs:* **throw away 1a.** To get rid of as useless. **b.** *Games* To discard. **2a.** To fail to take advantage of. **b.** To waste or use foolishly. **3.** To utter or perform in an offhand, seemingly careless way: *threw the best line away.* **throw back 1.** To hinder the progress of; check. **2.** To revert to an earlier type or stage in one's past. **3.** To cause to depend; make reliant. **throw in 1.** To insert or introduce into the course of something. **2.** To add (an extra thing or amount) with no additional charge. **3.** To engage (a clutch, for example). **throw off 1.** To cast out; rid oneself of. **2.** To give off; emit. **3.** To distract, divert, or mislead. **4.** To do, finish, or accomplish in a casual or offhand way; toss off. **throw open** To make more accessible, esp. suddenly or dramatically. **throw out 1.** To give off; emit. **2.** To reject or discard. **3.** To get rid of as useless. **4.** *Informal* To offer, as a suggestion or plan. **5.** To force to leave a place or position, esp. in an abrupt or unexpected manner. **6a.** To disengage (a clutch, for example). **b.** To put out of alignment. **7.** *Baseball* To put out (a base runner) by throwing the ball to the player guarding the base to which the base runner is moving. **throw over 1.** To overturn. **2.** To abandon. **3.** To reject. **throw up 1.** To vomit. **2.** To abandon; relinquish. **3.** To construct hurriedly. **4.** To refer to something repeatedly. **5.** To project, play, or otherwise display (a slide, videotape, or other recorded image). —*idioms:* **throw cold water on** To express misgivings about or disapproval of; discourage. **throw in the towel** (or **sponge**) To admit defeat; give up. **throw oneself at** To make strong or aggressive efforts to attract the interest or affection of (another). **throw (one's) weight around** *Slang* To use power or authority, esp. in an excessive or heavy-handed way. **throw the baby out with the bath water** *Slang* To discard something valuable along with something not desired, usu. unintentionally. **throw up (one's) hands** To indicate or express utter hopelessness. [ME *throwen,* to turn, twist, hurl < OE *thrāwan.* See **terə-¹** in App.] —**throw′er** *n.*

SYNONYMS throw, cast, hurl, fling, pitch, toss These verbs mean to propel something through the air with a motion of the hand or arm. *Throw* is the least specific: *throw a ball.* *Cast* usually refers to throwing something light: *cast her line into the stream.* *Hurl* and *fling* mean to throw with great force: "*Him the Almighty Power/Hurl'd headlong flaming from th' Ethereal Sky*" (John Milton). *He flung the tarpaulin over the boat.* *Pitch* often means to throw with careful aim: "*a special basket in my study . . . into which I pitch letters, circulars, pamphlets and so forth*" (H.G. Wells). *Toss* usually means to throw lightly or casually: "*Campton tossed the card away*" (Edith Wharton). See also Syns at **confuse.**

throw·a·way (thrō′ə-wā′) *n.* **1a.** Designed or intended to be discarded after use. **b.** Readily discarding things. **c.** Having been rejected by parents or guardians. **2.** Written or delivered in a low-key or offhand manner. —**throw′a·way′** *n.*

throw·back (thrō′băk′) *n.* **1.** A reversion to a former type or ancestral characteristic. **2.** See **atavism** 2.

throw-in (thrō′ĭn′) *n.* A play used to restart play in soccer after the ball has gone over the touchline, in which a player flings the ball with both hands over the head back onto the field.

throw pillow *n.* A pillow used esp. for decoration, as on a sofa.

throw rug *n.* See **scatter rug.**

throw·ster (thrō′stər) *n.* One that twists fibers into thread.

throw-weight or **throw weight** (thrō′wāt′) *n.* The total weight of a missile's explosive and nonexplosive payload.

thru (thrōō) *prep., adv., & adj. Informal* Through.

thrum¹ (thrŭm) *v.* **thrummed, thrum·ming, thrums** —*tr.* **1.**

Music To play (a stringed instrument) idly or monotonously. **2.** To speak, repeat, or recite in a monotonous tone of voice; drone. —*intr.* **1.** *Music* To thrum a stringed instrument. **2.** To drone. ❖ *n.* A thrumming sound. [Imit.]

thrum² (thrŭm) *n.* **1a.** The fringe of warp threads left on a loom after the cloth has been cut off. **b.** One of these threads. **2.** A loose end, fringe, or tuft of thread. **3. thrums** *Nautical* Short bits of rope yarn inserted into canvas to roughen the surface. ❖ *tr.v.* **thrummed, thrum·ming, thrums 1.** To cover or trim with thrums; fringe. **2.** *Nautical* To sew thrums in (canvas). [ME < OE *-thrum,* ligament (in *tungethrum,* ligament of the tongue).]

thrush¹ (thrŭsh) *n.* **1.** Any of numerous migratory songbirds of the family Turdidae, usu. having brownish upper plumage and a spotted breast. **2.** Any of various similar or related birds, as a water thrush. [ME *thrushe* < OE *thrysce.*]

thrush² (thrŭsh) *n.* **1.** A contagious disease caused by the fungus *Candida albicans,* marked by small whitish eruptions on the mouth, throat, and tongue. **2.** An infection of the frog of a horse's foot, often resulting from unhygienic stall conditions. [Prob. of Scand. orig.]

thrust (thrŭst) *v.* **thrust, thrust·ing, thrusts** —*tr.* **1.** To push or drive quickly and forcibly. See Syns at **push. 2.** To issue or extend. **3.** To force into a given condition or situation. **4.** To include or interpolate improperly. **5.** To force on an unwilling or improper recipient. **6.** *Archaic* To stab; pierce. —*intr.* **1.** To shove something into or at something else; push. **2.** To pierce or stab with or as if with a pointed weapon. **3.** To force one's way. ❖ *n.* **1.** A forceful shove or push. **2a.** A driving force or pressure. **b.** The forward-directed force developed in a jet or rocket engine as a reaction to the rearward ejection of exhaust gases. **3.** A piercing movement made with or as if with a pointed weapon; a stab. **4.** The essence, the point. **5.** *Architecture* Outward or lateral stress in a structure, as that exerted by an arch or vault. **6.** An attack or assault, esp. by an armed force. [ME *thrusten* < ON *thrȳsta.*] —**thrust'er** *n.* —**thrust'ful** *adj.*

thrust fault *n.* *Geology* A reverse fault in which the fault plane is inclined at an angle equal to or less than 45°.

thrust stage *n.* A stage that extends into the audience's portion of a theater beyond the usual location of the proscenium and often has seats facing it on three sides.

thru·way also **through·way** (thrōō'wā') *n.* See **expressway.**

Thu. *abbr.* Thursday

Thu·cyd·i·des (thōō-sĭd'ĭ-dēz') 460?–400? B.C. Greek historian noted for his account of the Peloponnesian War.

thud (thŭd) *n.* **1.** A dull sound, as of a heavy object falling. **2.** A blow or fall causing a thud. ❖ *intr.v.* **thud·ded, thud·ding, thuds** To make a heavy dull sound. [Perh. < ME *thudden,* to strike with a weapon < OE *thyddan,* of imit. orig.]

thug (thŭg) *n.* **1.** A person given to violence, esp. for criminal ends. **2.** One of a band of professional assassins formerly active in northern India. [Hindi *thag,* perh. < Skt. *sthagah,* a cheat < *sthagati, sthagayati,* he conceals. See **(s)teg-** in App.] —**thug'ger·y** *n.* —**thug'gish** *adj.*

Thug·gee (thŭg'ē) *n.* Robbery and assassination as practiced by the Thugs. [Hindi *thagī* < *thag,* Thug. See THUG.]

thu·ja (thōō'jə, thyōō'-) *n.* See **arborvitae** 1. [NLat. *Thuja,* arborvitae genus < Med.Lat. *thuia,* cedar < Gk. *thuiā.*]

Thu·le¹ (thōō'lē) The most northerly region of the habitable world to ancient Greek geographers, variously identified as Iceland, Norway, and the Shetland Is.

Thu·le² (tōō'lē) A Native American culture that spread eastward across coastal Arctic regions to eastern Canada and Greenland from its beginnings in the Bering Strait region, flourishing from about 1000 to 1600. [After THULE¹.]

thu·li·um (thōō'lē-əm) *n.* *Symbol* **Tm** A rare-earth element obtained commercially from monazite, having an x-ray emitting isotope that is used in small portable medical x-ray units. Atomic number 69; atomic weight 168.934; melting point 1,545°C; boiling point 1,727°C; specific gravity 9.3; valence 2, 3. See table at **element.** [After THULE¹.]

thumb (thŭm) *n.* **1a.** The short thick digit of the human hand, next to the index finger and opposable to each of the other four digits. **b.** A corresponding digit in other animals, esp. primates. **2.** The part of a glove or mitten that covers the thumb. ❖ *v.* **thumbed, thumb·ing, thumbs** —*tr.* **1.** To scan (written matter) by turning over pages with or as if with the thumb. **2.** To disarrange, soil, or wear by careless or frequent handling. **3.** *Informal* To solicit (a ride) from a vehicle by signaling with the thumb. —*intr.* **1.** To thumb written matter. **2.** *Informal* To hitchhike. —**idioms: all thumbs** Lacking physical coordination, skill, or grace; clumsy. **thumb (one's) nose** To express scorn or ridicule by or as if by placing the thumb on the nose and wiggling the fingers. **thumbs down** An expression of rejection, refusal, or disapproval. **thumbs up** An expression of approval, success, or hope. **under (one's) thumb** Under the control of or subordinate to someone. [ME < OE *thūma.*]

thumb·hole (thŭm'hōl') *n.* **1.** An opening made to fit a thumb, as in a bowling ball. **2.** *Music* The hole on a wind instrument that is opened or closed with the thumb.

thumb index *n.* A series of rounded indentations in the front edge of a book, each labeled, as with a letter, to indicate a section

of the book. —**thumb'-in'dex** (thŭm'ĭn'dĕks') *v.*

thumb·nail (thŭm'nāl') *n.* **1.** The nail of the thumb. **2.** A reduced image of a graphic or document page, used in order to view multiple images on a screen simultaneously or to download such images more rapidly. ❖ *adj.* **1.** Of or of the size of a thumbnail. **2.** Brief; cursory.

thumb piano *n.* An African musical instrument, such as the kalimba or mbira, that has a small sound box fitted with a row of tuned tabs that are plucked with the thumbs.

thumb·print (thŭm'prĭnt') *n.* A print made by the thumb, esp. by the pad of the thumb.

thumb·screw (thŭm'skrōō') *n.* **1.** A screw designed so that it can be turned with the thumb and fingers. **2.** An instrument of torture formerly used to compress the thumb.

thumbs-down (thŭmz'doun') *n.* An act, instance, or sign of disapproval.

thumbs-up (thŭmz'ŭp') *n.* An act, instance, or sign of approval.

thumb·tack (thŭm'tăk') *n.* A tack with a smooth rounded head that can be pressed into place with the thumb. ❖ *tr.v.* **-tacked, -tack·ing, -tacks** To affix with a thumbtack.

thump (thŭmp) *n.* **1.** A blow with a blunt object. **2.** The muffled sound produced by or as if by a thud. ❖ *v.* **thumped, thump·ing, thumps** —*tr.* **1.** To beat with or as if with a blunt object so as to produce a thud. **2.** *Informal* To beat soundly or thoroughly; drub. —*intr.* **1.** To hit or fall in such a way as to produce a thump; pound. **2.** To walk with heavy steps; stump. **3.** To throb audibly. [Prob. of imit. orig.] —**thump'er** *n.*

thump·ing (thŭm'pĭng) *adj. Informal* Outstanding.

Thun (tōōn), **Lake of** A lake of central Switzerland SE of Bern at the foot of the Bernese Alps.

thun·der (thŭn'dər) *n.* **1.** The crashing or booming sound produced by rapidly expanding air along the path of the electrical discharge of lightning. **2.** A sound that resembles or suggests thunder. ❖ *v.* **-dered, -der·ing, -ders** —*intr.* **1.** To produce thunder. **2.** To produce sounds like thunder. **3.** To utter loud vociferous remarks or threats. —*tr.* To express violently, commandingly, or angrily; roar. [ME < OE *thunor.* See **(s)tenə-** in App.] —**thun'der·er** *n.*

Thunder Bay A city of SW Ontario, Canada, on **Thunder Bay,** an inlet of Lake Superior. Pop. 113,662.

thun·der·bird (thŭn'dər-bûrd') *n.* A spirit of thunder, lightning, and rain in the form of a huge bird in the mythology of certain Native American peoples.

thun·der·bolt (thŭn'dər-bōlt') *n.* **1.** A discharge of lightning accompanied by thunder. **2.** A flash of lightning conceived as a bolt or dart from the heavens. **3a.** One that acts with sudden destructive fury. **b.** A startling, forceful action.

thun·der·clap (thŭn'dər-klăp') *n.* **1.** A single sharp crash of thunder. **2.** Something, such as a startling piece of news, that is similar to a crash of thunder in suddenness or violence.

thun·der·cloud (thŭn'dər-kloud') *n.* **1.** A large dark cloud charged with electricity and producing thunder and lightning; a cumulonimbus cloud. **2.** Something menacing or dreadful.

thun·der·head (thŭn'dər-hĕd') *n.* The swollen upper portion of a thundercloud, usu. associated with a thunderstorm.

thun·der·ous (thŭn'dər-əs) *adj.* **1.** Producing thunder or a similar sound. **2.** Loud and unrestrained like thunder.

thun·der·show·er (thŭn'dər-shou'ər) *n.* A brief rainstorm accompanied by thunder and lightning.

thun·der·stone (thŭn'dər-stōn') *n.* **1.** Any of various mineral concretions, such as a belemnite, formerly supposed to be thunderbolts. **2.** *Archaic* A flash of lightning conceived as a stone; a thunderbolt.

thun·der·storm (thŭn'dər-stôrm') *n.* A transient, sometimes violent storm of thunder and lightning, often accompanied by rain and sometimes hail.

thun·der·struck (thŭn'dər-strŭk') *adj.* Affected with sudden astonishment or amazement.

thunk¹ (thŭngk) *n.* A dull, hollow sound. ❖ *intr.v.* **thunked, thunk·ing, thunks** To make a dull, hollow sound. [Imit.]

thunk² (thŭngk) *v. Nonstandard* A past tense and a past participle of **think.**

Thur. *abbr.* Thursday

Thur·ber (thûr'bər), **James Grover** 1894–1961. Amer. writer and cartoonist known for his humorous essays and drawings.

thu·ri·ble (thōōr'ə-bəl) *n.* A censer used in certain ecclesiastical ceremonies or liturgies. [ME *thorible* < OFr. *thurible* < Lat. *thūribulum* < *thūs, thūr-,* incense < alteration of Gk. *thuos < thūein,* to sacrifice.]

thu·ri·fer (thōōr'ə-fər) *n.* An acolyte who carries a thurible. [Lat. *thūrifer,* incense-bearing : *thūs, thūr-,* incense; see THURIBLE + *-fer, -fer.*]

Thu·rin·gi·a (thōō-rĭn'jē-ə, -jə) A historical region of central Germany crossed by the **Thuringian Forest.**

Thu·rin·gi·an (thōō-rĭn'jē-ən, -jən) *n.* **1.** A member of an ancient tribe inhabiting central Germany until the sixth century A.D. **2.** A native or inhabitant of Thuringia. —**Thu·rin'gi·an** *adj.*

Thur·mond (thûr'mənd), **Strom** b. 1902. Amer. politician who entered the US Senate in 1956 and in 1998 became the longest-serving senator in US history.

thunderbird
summit of a totem pole in Thunderbird Park, Vancouver Island, British Columbia

ă	pat	oi	boy
ā	pay	ou	out
âr	care	ŏŏ	took
ä	father	ōō	boot
ĕ	pet	ŭ	cut
ē	be	ûr	urge
ĭ	pie	th	thin
ī	pie	th	this
îr	pier	hw	which
ŏ	pot	zh	vision
ō	toe	ə	about,
ô	paw		item

Stress marks:
' (primary);
' (secondary), as in
lexicon (lĕk'sĭ-kŏn')

Thurs·day (thûrz′dē, -dā′) *n.* The fifth day of the week. [ME < OE *thūres dæg*, alteration (influenced by ON *thōrsdagr*, Thor's day) of *thunres dæg*, Thor's day (transl. of Lat. *Iovis diēs*, Jupiter's day) : *thunres*, genitive of *thunor*, thunder; see **(s)tena-** in App. + *dæg*, day.] **—Thurs′days** *adv.*

Thursday Island An island of NE Australia in Torres Strait NW of Cape York; noted for its pearl fishing beds.

Thurs·ton Island (thûr′stən) An island off Antarctica between the Bellinghausen and Amundsen seas.

thus (thŭs) *adv.* **1.** In this manner: *Lay the pieces out thus.* See Usage Note at **thusly. 2.** To a stated degree or extent; so. **3.** Therefore; consequently: *Thus I had to resign.* **4.** For example: *Few large US cities are state capitals; thus New York is not the seat of its state's government.* [ME < OE. See **to-** in App.]

thus·ly (thŭs′lē) *adv.* Usage Problem Thus.

> **USAGE NOTE** Although the word *thusly* has gained some currency in educated usage, it is widely regarded as incorrect. In an earlier survey a large majority of the Usage Panel deemed its use incorrect. In formal writing *thus* can still be used in such sentences as *Hold it thus.* In other styles, expressions such as *this way* and *like this* are more natural.

Thutmose III
c. 1479–25 B.C. painted
limestone relief

Thut·mo·se III (thoōt-mō′sə) d. 1450 B.C. King of Egypt (1504?–1450) who conquered Syria.

thwack (thwăk) *tr.v.* **thwacked, thwack·ing, thwacks** To strike or hit with a flat object; whack. ❖ *n.* A hard blow with a flat object; a whack. [Imit.]

thwart (thwôrt) *tr.v.* **thwart·ed, thwart·ing, thwarts 1.** To prevent the occurrence, realization, or attainment of. **2.** To oppose and defeat the efforts, plans, or ambitions of. ❖ *n.* A seat across a boat on which a rower may sit. ❖ *adj.* **1.** Extending, lying, or passing across; transverse. **2.** Eager to oppose, esp. wrongly; perverse. ❖ *adv. & prep. Archaic* Athwart; across. [ME *thwerten* < *thwert*, across < ON *thvert*, neut. of *thverr*, transverse.] **—thwart′er** *n.*

thy (thī) *adj.* The possessive form of **thou¹.** Used as a modifier before a noun. [ME, var. of *thin*, thine < OE *thīn*. See **tu-** in App.]

Thy·es·te·an (thī-ĕs′tē-ən, thī-ĭ-stē′ən) *adj.* Cannibalistic.

Thy·es·tes (thī-ĕs′tēz) *n. Greek Mythology* A king of Mycenae who unknowingly ate the flesh of his own sons, served to him by his brother Atreus as revenge for seducing his wife and usurping the throne. [Gk. *Thuestēs.*]

thy·la·cine (thī′lə-sīn′) *n.* See **Tasmanian wolf.** [< NLat. *Thȳlacīnus*, genus name < Gk. *thūlakos*, sack.]

thy·la·koid (thī′lə-koid′) *n.* A saclike membrane that is the structural unit of the grana in the chloroplasts of plant cells. [Gk. *thūlakos*, sack + –OID.]

thyme

thyme (tīm) *n.* Any of several aromatic Eurasian herbs or low shrubs of the genus *Thymus*, esp. *T. vulgaris* of southern Europe, having leaves used as a seasoning. [ME < OFr. *thym* < Lat. *thymum* < Gk. *thumon.*]

thy·mec·to·my (thī-mĕk′tə-mē) *n., pl.* **-mies** Surgical removal of the thymus. [THYM(US) + –ECTOMY.]

–thymia *suff.* State or condition of mind: *schizothymia.* [NLat. *-thȳmia* < Gk. *-thūmiā* < *thūmos*, mind, soul.]

thy·mic¹ (tī′mĭk, thī′-) *adj.* Of or relating to thyme.

thy·mic² (thī′mĭk) *adj.* Of or relating to the thymus.

thy·mi·dine (thī′mĭ-dēn′) *n.* A nucleoside, $C_{10}H_{14}N_2O_5$, composed of thymine and deoxyribose, that is a constituent of DNA. [THYM(INE) + –ID(E) + –INE².]

thy·mine (thī′mēn′) *n.* A pyrimidine base, $C_5H_6N_2O_2$, that is an essential constituent of DNA. [*thym(ic acid)*, acid obtained from the thymus + –INE².]

thy·mo·cyte (thī′mə-sīt′) *n.* A lymphocyte that derives from the thymus and is the precursor of a T cell.

thy·mol (thī′môl′, -mŏl′) *n.* A white crystalline aromatic compound, $C_{10}H_{14}O$, derived from thyme oil and other oils or synthesized and used as an antiseptic and a preservative.

thy·mo·sin (thī′mə-sĭn) *n.* A hormone secreted by the thymus that stimulates development of T cells.

thy·mus (thī′məs) *n., pl.* **-mus·es** A small gland situated behind the breastbone, consisting mainly of lymphatic tissue and serving as the site of T cell differentiation. [NLat. < Gk. *thumos*, warty excrescence, thymus.]

thyro- or **thyr-** *pref.* Thyroid: *thyroxine.* [< THYROID.]

thy·ro·cal·ci·to·nin (thī′rō-kăl′sĭ-tō′nĭn) *n.* See **calcitonin.**

thy·roid (thī′roid′) *n.* **1.** The thyroid gland. **2.** The thyroid cartilage. **3.** A preparation of the thyroid gland of certain animals, used to treat hypothyroid conditions. **4.** An artery, vein, nerve, or other part in the thyroid region. [Gk. *thureoeidēs* : *thureos*, oblong shield (< *thurā*, door; see **dhwer-** in App.) + *-oeidēs*, -oid.] **—thy′roi′dal** *adj.*

thyroid cartilage *n.* The largest cartilage of the larynx, forming the Adam's apple.

thy·roid·ec·to·my (thī′roi-dĕk′tə-mē) *n., pl.* **-mies** Surgical removal of the thyroid gland.

thyroid gland *n.* A two-lobed endocrine gland found in all vertebrates, located at the base of the neck and producing various hormones, such as triiodothyronine and calcitonin.

thy·roid·i·tis (thī′roi-dī′tĭs) *n.* Inflammation of the thyroid gland.

---

thy·roid-stim·u·lat·ing hormone (thī′roid-stĭm′yə-lā′tĭng) *n.* See **thyrotropin.**

thy·ro·tox·i·co·sis (thī′rō-tŏk′sĭ-kō′sĭs) *n.* A condition resulting from excessive concentrations of thyroid hormones in the body, as in hyperthyroidism.

thy·ro·tro·pin (thī′rə-trō′pĭn, thī-rŏt′rə-) also **thy·ro·tro·phin** (-fĭn) *n.* A hormone secreted by the anterior lobe of the pituitary gland that stimulates and regulates the activity of the thyroid gland. [THYRO- + –TROP(HIC) + –IN.]

thy·ro·tro·pin-re·leas·ing hormone (thī′rə-trō′pĭn-rĭ-lē′sĭng, thī-rŏt′rə-) *n.* A hormone secreted by the hypothalamus that stimulates release of thyrotropin.

thy·rox·ine (thī-rŏk′sēn′, -sĭn) also **thy·rox·in** (-rŏk′sĭn) *n.* An iodine-containing hormone, $C_{15}H_{11}I_4NO_4$, produced by the thyroid gland, that increases the rate of cell metabolism and regulates growth and is made synthetically for treatment of thyroid disorders. [THYR(O)- + OX(Y)- + IN(DOLE).]

thyrse (thûrs) *n.* A dense paniclelike flower cluster, as of the lilac, in which the lateral branches terminate in cymes. [Lat. *thyrsus*, thyrsus. See THYRSUS.]

thyr·sus (thûr′səs) *n., pl.* **-si** (-sī) **1.** *Mythology* A staff tipped with a pine cone and twined with ivy, carried by Dionysus and Dionysian revelers. **2.** *Botany* A thyrse. [Lat. < Gk. *thursos.*]

thy·sa·nu·ran (thī′sə-noōr′ən, -nyoōr′-) *n.* A wingless insect of the order Thysanura, constituting the bristletails. [< NLat. *Thysanūra*, order name : Gk. *thusanos*, tassel + Gk. *-oura*, neut. pl. of *-ouros*, tailed (< *ourā*, tail; see –UROUS).] **—thy′sa·nu′ran** *adj.*

thy·self (thī-sĕlf′) *pron. Archaic* Yourself. Used as the reflexive or emphatic form of *thee* or *thou.*

THz *abbr.* terahertz

ti (tē) *n. Music* The seventh tone in the diatonic scale in solfeggio. [Alteration of SI.]

ti² (tē) *n., pl.* **tis** An eastern Asian tropical shrub (*Cordyline terminalis*) having a terminal tuft of long narrow leaves and edible roots. [Tahitian and Maori *tī.*]

Ti The symbol for the element **titanium.**

Ti·a·hua·na·co (tē′ə-wə-nä′kō) A site of pre-Incan ruins in W Bolivia near the S end of Lake Titicaca.

Tian·an·men Square (tyän′än′mĕn′) An extensive open area in central Beijing, China, adjacent to the Forbidden City.

Tian·jin (tyän′jĭn′) also **Tien·tsin** (tyĕn′tsĭn′) A city of NE China near the Bo Hai SE of Beijing. Pop. 5,804,023.

Tian Shan (tyän′ shän′) A mountain range of W Kyrgyzstan, SW Kazakhstan, and NW China rising to 7,443.8 m (24,406 ft).

ti·ar·a (tē-ăr′ə, -âr′ə, -är′ə) *n.* **1.** An ornamental, often jeweled crownlike semicircle worn on the head by women on formal occasions. **2.** The triple crown worn by the pope. [Lat. *tiāra*, turban, headband < Gk. *tiārā.*]

Ti·ber (tī′bər) A river of central Italy flowing c. 406 km (252 mi) through Rome to the Tyrrhenian Sea.

Ti·be·ri·as (tī-bîr′ē-əs), **Lake** Sea of **Galilee.**

Ti·be·ri·us (tī-bîr′ē-əs) 42 B.C.–A.D. 37. Emperor of Rome (A.D. 14–37) who was chosen by Augustus as his heir. **—Ti·be′ri·an** (-ən) *adj.*

Ti·bet (tə-bĕt′) **1.** A historical region of central Asia between the Himalaya and Kunlun mountains; under Chinese control after 1720. **2.** See **Xizang.**

Ti·bet·an (tĭ-bĕt′n) *adj.* Of or relating to Tibet, the Tibetans, or their language or culture. ❖ *n.* **1a.** A native or inhabitant of Tibet. **b.** A member of a Buddhist people constituting the main ethnic population of Tibet and neighboring regions. **2.** The Tibeto-Burman language of the Tibetans.

Tibetan Buddhism *n.* A form of Buddhism with an admixture of indigenous animism that is practiced in Tibet, Mongolia, Bhutan, and neighboring areas.

Ti·bet·o-Bur·man (tĭ-bĕt′ō-bûr′mən) *n.* A branch of the Sino-Tibetan language family that includes Tibetan and Burmese. **—Ti·bet′o-Bur′man** *adj.*

tib·i·a (tĭb′ē-ə) *n., pl.* **-i·ae** (-ē-ē′) or **-i·as 1a.** The inner and larger of the two bones of the lower human leg, extending from the knee to the ankle. **b.** A corresponding bone in other vertebrates. **2.** The fourth division of an insect's leg, between the femur and the tarsi. **3.** *Music* An ancient flute. [Lat. *tībia*, pipe, shinbone.] **—tib′i·al** *adj.*

tic (tĭk) *n.* A habitual spasmodic muscular movement or contraction, usu. of the face or extremities. ❖ *intr.v.* **ticced, tic·cing, tics** To have a tic; produce tics. [Fr.]

tic dou·lou·reux (dōō′lə-roō′) *n.* See **trigeminal neuralgia.** [Fr. : *tic*, tic + *douloureux*, painful.]

Ti·ci·no (tĭ-chē′nō) A river of S Switzerland and N Italy flowing c. 248 km (154 mi) generally S to the Po R.

tiara

tick¹ (tĭk) *n.* **1.** A light sharp clicking sound made repeatedly by a machine, such as a clock. **2.** *Chiefly British* A moment. **3.** A light mark used to check off or call attention to an item. **4.** *Informal* A unit on a scale; a degree. ❖ *v.* **ticked, tick·ing, ticks** *—intr.* **1.** To emit recurring clicking sounds. **2.** To function characteristically or well: *what makes people tick.* *—tr.* **1.** To count or record with or as if with the sound of ticks. **2.** To mark or check off (a listed item) with a tick: *ticked off each name.* **—phrasal verb: tick off** *Informal* To make angry or annoyed. [ME *tek*, light tap.]

tick[2] (tĭk) *n.* **1.** Any of numerous small bloodsucking parasitic arachnids of the family Ixodidae, many of which transmit febrile diseases, such as Lyme disease. **2.** Any of various usu. wingless louselike insects of the family Hippoboscidae that are parasitic, as on sheep. [ME *tik*, perh. < OE **ticca*.]

tick[3] (tĭk) *n.* **1a.** A cloth case for a mattress or pillow. **b.** A light mattress without inner springs. **2.** Ticking. [ME *tikke*, prob. < MDu. *tīke*, ult. < Lat. *thēca*, receptacle < Gk. *thēkē*. See **dhē-** in App.]

tick[4] (tĭk) *n.* *Chiefly British* Credit or an amount of credit. [Short for TICKET.]

tick-borne (tĭk**′**bôrn′, -bōrn′) *adj.* Carried or transmitted by ticks: *a tick-borne disease.*

tick•er (tĭk**′**ər) *n.* **1a.** A telegraphic instrument that receives news reports and prints them on paper tape. **b.** Any of various devices that receive and display similar information electronically. **2.** *Slang* A watch. **3.** *Slang* The heart.

ticker tape *n.* The paper strip used by a telegraphic ticker.

tick•et (tĭk**′**ĭt) *n.* **1a.** A paper slip or card indicating that its holder has paid for or is entitled to a specified service, right, or consideration. **b.** An e-ticket. **2.** A certifying document, esp. a captain's or pilot's license. **3.** An identifying or descriptive tag attached to merchandise; a label. **4.** A list of candidates proposed or endorsed by a political party; a slate. **5.** A legal summons, esp. for a traffic violation. **6.** The proper or desirable thing. **7.** *Informal* A means to an end. ❖ *tr.v.* **-et•ed, -et•ing, -ets 1.** To provide with a ticket for passage or admission. **2.** To attach a ticket to; tag. **3.** To designate for a specified use or end; destine: *funds that are ticketed for research.* **4.** To serve (an offender) with a legal summons: *ticket a speeding motorist.* [Obsolete Fr. *etiquet*, label, note < OFr. *estiquet*, post serving as a target in certain sports, notice, label < *estiquier*, to stick, of Gmc. orig.]

tick fever *n.* Any of various febrile diseases transmitted by ticks, such as Rocky Mountain spotted fever and Texas fever.

tick•ing (tĭk**′**ĭng) *n.* A strong, tightly woven fabric of cotton or linen used to make pillow and mattress coverings.

tick•le (tĭk**′**əl) *v.* **-led, -ling, -les** —*tr.* **1.** To touch (the body) lightly so as to cause laughter or twitching movements. **2a.** To tease or excite pleasurably; titillate: *suspense that tickles one's curiosity.* **b.** To fill with mirth or pleasure; delight. —*intr.* To feel or cause a tingling sensation. ❖ *n.* **1.** The act of tickling. **2.** A tickling sensation. ***—idiom:*** **tickled pink** *Informal* Very pleased; delighted. [ME *tikelen*, perh. freq. of *ticken*, to touch lightly.]

tick•ler (tĭk**′**lər) *n.* **1.** One that tickles. **2.** A memorandum, book, or file to aid the memory.

tick•lish (tĭk**′**lĭsh) *adj.* **1.** Sensitive to tickling. **2.** Easily offended or upset; touchy. **3.** Requiring skillful or tactful handling; delicate. **—tick′lish•ly** *adv.* **—tick′lish•ness** *n.*

tick•seed (tĭk**′**sēd′) *n.* **1.** See **coreopsis. 2.** The tickseed sunflower. [< TICK[2] (< its seed's shape).]

tickseed sunflower *n.* Any of several weeds of the genus *Bidens* of the composite family, having yellow ray flowers and barbed achenes that cling to clothing and fur.

tick•tack also **tic-tac** (tĭk**′**tăk′) *n.* **1.** A steady ticking sound, as of a clock. **2.** A prankster's device for tapping on a door or window from a distance. [Imit.]

tick•tack•toe also **tick-tack-toe** or **tic-tac-toe** (tĭk′tăk′tō**′**) *n.* A game played by two people, each trying to make a line of three X's or three O's in a boxlike figure with nine spaces. [Prob. imit. of the sounds of the original children's game, played with a pencil and a slate.]

tick•tock (tĭk**′**tŏk′) *n.* A clock's ticking sound. [Imit.]

tick trefoil *n.* Any of various plants of the genus *Desmodium*, usu. having trifoliolate compound leaves and jointed seedpods. [< TICK[2] (< the way its pods adhere to animals).]

tick•y-tack•y (tĭk**′**ē-tăk′ē) *n.* Shoddy material, as for building standardized housing. ❖ *adj.* **1.** Made of shoddy material; cheaply built. **2a.** Marked by mediocre uniformity of look or style. **b.** Tawdry; tacky. [Reduplication of TACKY[2].]

Ti•con•der•o•ga (tī′kŏn-də-rō**′**gə) A village of NE NY between Lake George and Lake Champlain; orig. a French fortress.

t.i.d. *abbr. Latin* ter in die (three times a day)

tid•al (tīd**′**l) *adj.* **1.** Relating to or affected by tides. **2.** Dependent on or scheduled by the time of high tide. **—tid′al•ly** *adv.*

tidal basin *n.* A body of water in an area subject to tides whose water level is maintained at a desired level by artificial means.

tidal flat *n.* A nearly flat coastal area, alternately covered and exposed by the tides, and consisting of unconsolidated sediments.

tidal pool *n.* A pool of water remaining after a tide has retreated.

tidal wave *n.* **1.** The swell or crest of surface ocean water created by the tides. **2a.** An unusual, often destructive rise of water along the seashore, as from a storm. **b.** A tsunami. **3.** An overwhelming manifestation; a flood.

tid•bit (tĭd**′**bĭt′) also **tit•bit** (tĭt**′**-) *n.* A choice morsel, as of gossip or food. [Perh. obsolete and dialectal *tid*, tender + BIT[1].]

tid•dly•winks (tĭd**′**lē-wĭngks′) also **tid•dle•dy•winks** (tĭd**′**l-dē-) *pl.n.* (*used with a sing. verb*) A game in which players try to snap small disks into a cup by pressing them on the edge with a larger disk. [Poss. dialectal *tiddly*, little + WINK.]

tide[1] (tīd) *n.* **1a.** The periodic variation in the surface level of the oceans and of bays, gulfs, inlets, and estuaries, caused by gravitational attraction of the moon and sun. **b.** A specific occurrence of such a variation. **c.** Flood tide. **2.** Stress exerted on a body or part of a body by gravitational attraction of another. **3.** Something that fluctuates like the waters of the tide. **4.** A time or season. Often used in combination: *eventide.* **5.** A favorable occasion; an opportunity. ❖ *v.* **tid•ed, tid•ing, tides** —*intr.* **1.** To rise and fall like the tide. **2.** *Nautical* To drift or ride with the tide: *tided off the reef.* —*tr.* To carry along with or as if with the tide. ***—phrasal verb:*** **tide over** To support through a difficult period. [ME < OE *tīd*, division of time. See **dā-** in App.]

tide[2] (tīd) *intr.v.* **tid•ed, tid•ing, tides** *Archaic* To betide; befall. [ME *tiden* < OE *tīdan*. See **dā-** in App.]

tide chart *n.* A chart listing the predicted times and heights of the high and low tides for a given location, throughout one year.

tide•land (tīd**′**lănd′) *n.* Coastal land submerged during high tide.

tide•mark (tīd**′**märk′) *n.* **1.** A line or mark on a shore indicating the highest or lowest level reached by the tide. **2.** A trace or indication of past activity.

tide pool *n.* See **tidal pool.**

tide•rip (tīd**′**rĭp′) *n.* See **rip current.**

tide•wa•ter (tīd**′**wô′tər, -wŏt′ər) *n.* **1.** Water that inundates land at flood tide. **2.** Water affected by the tides, esp. tidal streams. **3.** Low coastal land drained by tidal streams.

tide•way (tīd**′**wā′) *n.* A channel in which a tidal current runs.

tid•ing (tī**′**dĭng) *n.* A piece of information or news. Often used in the plural: *sad tidings.* [ME *tiding*, perh. < ON *tīdhendi*, events < *tīdhr*, occurring. See **dā-** in App.]

ti•dy (tī**′**dē) *adj.* **-di•er, -di•est 1.** Orderly and neat in appearance or procedure. See Syns at **neat**[1]. **2.** *Informal* Adequate; satisfactory. **3.** *Informal* Substantial; considerable. ❖ *v.* **-died, -dy•ing, -dies** —*tr.* To put in order: *tidied up the house.* —*intr.* To make things tidy: *tidied up after dinner.* ❖ *n., pl.* **-dies** A decorative protective covering for the arms or headrest of a chair. [ME *tidi*, in season, healthy < *tide*, time. See TIDE[1].] **—ti′di•ly** *adv.* **—ti′di•ness** *n.*

ti•dy•tips (tī**′**dē-tĭps′) *pl.n.* (*used with a sing. or pl. verb*) A Californian herb (*Layia platyglossa*) with daisylike flowers.

tie (tī) *v.* **tied, ty•ing** (tī**′**ĭng), **ties** —*tr.* **1.** To fasten or secure with or as if with a cord, rope, or strap. **2.** To fasten by drawing together the parts or sides and knotting with strings or laces: *tied her shoes.* **3a.** To make by fastening ends or parts: *tie a knot.* **b.** To put a knot or bow in: *tie a scarf.* **4.** To confine or restrict as if with cord. **5.** To bring together in relationship; connect or unite. **6a.** To equal (an opponent or an opponent's score) in a contest. **b.** To equal an opponent's score in (a contest). **7.** *Music* To join (notes) by a tie. —*intr.* **1.** To be fastened or attached. **2.** To achieve equal scores in a contest. ❖ *n.* **1.** A cord, string, or other means by which something is tied. **2.** Something that connects or unites; a link: *marital ties.* **3.** A necktie. **4.** A beam or rod that joins parts and gives support. **5.** One of the beams, usu. made of wood, laid across a railroad bed to secure the rails. **6a.** An equality of scores, votes, or performance in a contest. **b.** A contest so resulting; a draw. **7.** *Music* A curved line above or below two notes of the same pitch, indicating that the tone is to be sustained for their combined duration. ***—phrasal verbs:*** **tie in** To bring into or have a close or effective relation; connect or coordinate. **tie into** To attack energetically. **tie up 1.** *Nautical* To secure or be secured to a shore or pier; dock. **2.** To impede the progress of; block. **3.** To keep occupied; engage. **4.** To place (funds) so as to make inaccessible for other uses. ***—idioms:*** **tie one on** *Slang* To become intoxicated; go on a drinking spree. **tie the knot** *Slang* **1.** To get married. **2.** To perform a marriage ceremony. [ME *tien* < OE *tīgan*. See **deuk-** in App.]

tie•back (tī**′**băk′) *n.* **1.** A decorative loop of fabric, cord, or metal for parting and draping a curtain to the side. **2. tiebacks** A pair of curtains intended to be tied back.

tie beam *n.* A horizontal beam forming the base of a triangular truss for a pitched roof, connecting the two side walls and supporting a pair of principals.

tie•break•er (tī**′**brā′kər) also **tie•break** (-brāk′) *n.* An additional contest or period of play designed to establish a winner among tied contestants. **—tie′break′ing** *adj.*

tie-dye (tī**′**dī′) *tr.v.* **-dyed, -dye•ing, -dyes** To dye (fabric) after tying parts of the fabric so that they will not absorb dye, giving the fabric a streaked or mottled look. ❖ *n.* **1.** The process of tie-dyeing. **2.** A tie-dyed fabric or garment.

tie-in (tī**′**ĭn′) *n.* A thing related to or connected with another.

tie line *n.* **1.** A communications link between extensions of a private telephone system. **2.** A connection between systems, such as electrical power or communications systems.

Tien•tsin (tyĕn**′**tsĭn**′**) See **Tianjin.**

Tie•po•lo (tē-ĕp**′**ə-lō′, tyĕ**′**pō-), **Giovanni Battista** 1696–1770. Italian painter noted for his command of perspective.

tier[1] (tîr) *n.* **1.** One of a series of rows placed one above another. **2.** A rank or class. ❖ *tr. & intr.v.* **tiered, tier•ing, tiers** To arrange (something) into or rise in tiers. [ME *tire*, row, rank < OFr. < *tirer*, to draw out. See TIRADE.]

ti•er[2] (tī**′**ər) *n.* One that ties: *a tier of knots.*

tierce (tîrs) *n.* **1.** also **Tierce** (tîrs) or **terce** or **Terce** (tûrs) *Ecclesiastical* The third of the seven canonical hours. No longer in litur-

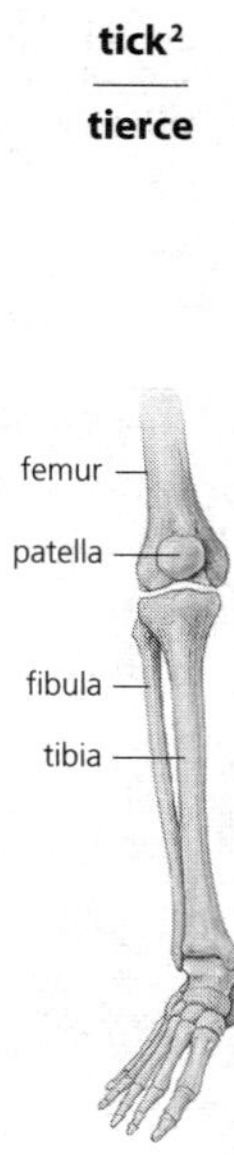
femur
patella
fibula
tibia

tibia

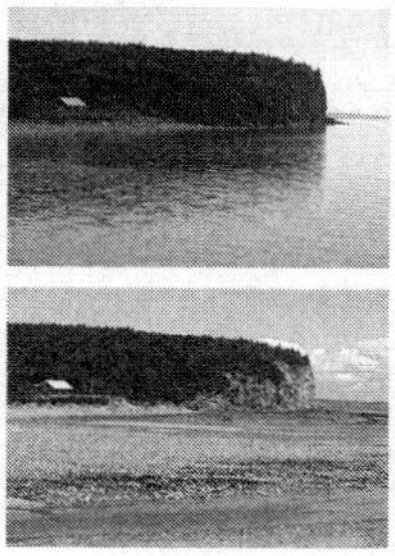

tide[1]
top: high tide in the Bay of Fundy
bottom: low tide from the same perspective

ă pat	oi boy
ā pay	ou out
âr care	o͝o took
ä father	o͞o boot
ĕ pet	ŭ cut
ē be	ûr urge
ĭ pit	th thin
ī pie	*th* this
îr pier	hw which
ŏ pot	zh vision
ō toe	ə about, item
ô paw	

Stress marks:
′ (primary);
′ (secondary), as in
lexicon (lĕk**′**sĭ-kŏn′)

gical use. **2.** A measure of liquid capacity, equal to a third of a pipe, or 42 gallons (159 liters). **3.** *Games* A sequence of 3 cards of the same suit. **4.** *Sports* The third position from which a parry or thrust can be made in fencing. **5.** *Music* An interval of a third. [ME < OFr. < fem. of *tiers*, third < Lat. *tertius*. See **trei-** in App.]

tier·cel (tîr′səl) *n.* Variant of **tercel.**

tier·ce·ron (tîr′sə-rŏn) *n.* A secondary or intermediate rib in a rib vault that rises from one of the main springers and connects to a point on the ridge rib. [Fr. < *tierce*, tierce. See TIERCE.]

tie rod *n.* **1.** A metal rod that joins and reinforces parts in a structure. **2.** Either of two metal rods or arms that transmit motion to the front axle in certain vehicular steering systems.

Ti·er·ra del Fue·go (tē-ĕr′ə dĕl fwā′gō, tyĕr′rä dĕl fwĕ′gō) An archipelago off S South America separated from the mainland by the Strait of Magellan. The main island, also called **Tierra del Fuego,** is divided between Chile and Argentina.

tier table *n.* A table having several shelflike tops, one above the other.

tie tack *n.* A short pin with a decorative head, used to attach a tie to a shirt front by means of a snap or chain.

Tie·tê (tyə-tā′, tyĭ-tĕ′) A river of SE Brazil flowing c. 805 km (500 mi) to the Paraná R.

tie-up (tī′ŭp′) *n.* A temporary immobilization, as of traffic.

tie vine *n. Lower Southern US* The bindweed.

tiff (tĭf) *n.* **1.** A fit of irritation. **2.** A petty quarrel. ❖ *intr.v.* **tiffed, tiff·ing, tiffs** To quarrel. [?]

tif·fa·ny (tĭf′ə-nē) *n., pl.* **-nies** A thin transparent gauze of silk or cotton muslin. [Prob. < obsolete Fr. *tiphanie,* Epiphany < OFr. < LLat. *theophania.* See THEOPHANY.]

Tiffany, Louis Comfort 1848–1933. Amer. artist who developed an opalescent colored glass.

Tiffany glass *n.* Stained or iridescent glass of a kind popular in the early 1900s for vases and lampshades.

tif·fin (tĭf′ĭn) *n. Chiefly British* A meal at midday; a luncheon. [Short for *tiffing,* gerund of *tiff,* to sip.]

Tif·lis (tĭf′lĭs, tyä-flēs′) See **Tbilisi.**

ti·ger (tī′gər) *n.* **1a.** A large carnivorous feline mammal (*Panthera tigris*) of Asia having a tawny coat with transverse black stripes. **b.** Any of various similar wild felines, such as the jaguar, mountain lion, or lynx. **2.** A person regarded as aggressive, audacious, or fierce. [ME *tigre* < OE *tigras,* tigers, and < OFr. *tigre,* both < Lat. *tigris* < Gk., of Iran. orig.] —**ti′ger·ish** *adj.*

tiger beetle *n.* Any of numerous brightly colored predatory beetles of the family Cicindelidae, chiefly of warm sandy regions, having larvae that live in vertical burrows.

tiger cat *n.* **1.** Any of various small wild felines, such as the ocelot, margay, or jaguarundi, that resemble the tiger in appearance or behavior. **2.** A domestic cat, esp. a tabby, having markings like those of a tiger.

ti·ger-eye (tī′gər-ī′) also **ti·ger's-eye** (tī′gərz-ī′) *n.* A yellowbrown semiprecious chatoyant gemstone consisting of quartz with parallel veins of silicified altered crocidolite.

tiger lily *n.* An eastern Asian perennial (*Lilium lancifolium*) having large black-spotted reddish-orange flowers.

tiger moth *n.* Any of numerous often brightly colored moths of the family Arctiidae, having spotted or striped wings.

tiger salamander *n.* A large terrestrial salamander (*Ambystoma tigrinum*) found in most parts of North America and having distinctive light olive bars or spots.

tiger shark *n.* A large voracious shark (*Galeocerdo cuvieri*) of tropical waters, grayish brown in color with vertical bars.

tiger swallowtail *n.* A large swallowtail butterfly (*Papilio glaucus*) of eastern North America, mostly yellow with narrow black bands across the wings.

tight (tīt) *adj.* **tight·er, tight·est** **1.** Fixed or fastened firmly in place. **2.** Stretched or drawn out fully. **3.** Of such close construction as to be impermeable. **4a.** Leaving little empty space through compression; compact: *a tight weave.* **b.** Affording little spare time; full. **5.** Closely reasoned or concise: *a tight argument.* **6.** Fitting close or too close to the skin; snug. **7.** *Slang* Personally close; intimate. **8.** Constricted. **9.** Reluctant to spend or give; stingy. **10a.** Obtainable with difficulty or only at a high price. **b.** Affected by scarcity: *a tight market.* **11.** Difficult to deal with or get out of: *a tight spot.* **12.** Barely profitable: *a tight bargain.* **13.** Closely contested; close. **14.** *Chiefly British* Neat and trim in appearance or arrangement. **15.** Marked by full control over elements or subordinates; firm: *tight management.* **16.** *Slang* Intoxicated; drunk. **17.** *Baseball* Inside. ❖ *adv.* **tight·er, tight·est** **1.** Firmly; securely. **2.** Soundly: *sleep tight.* **3.** Snugly or with constriction: *shoes laced too tight.* [ME, dense, of Scand. orig.] —**tight′ly** *adv.* —**tight′ness** *n.*

SYNONYMS *tight, taut, tense* These adjectives mean not slack or loose on account of being pulled or drawn out fully: *a tight skirt; taut sails; tense piano strings.*

tight·en (tīt′n) *tr. & intr.v.* **-ened, -en·ing, -ens** To make or become tight or tighter. —**tight′en·er** *n.*

tight end *n. Football* An offensive end who lines up close to a tackle.

tight·fist·ed (tīt′fĭs′tĭd) *adj.* Close-fisted; stingy. —**tight′fist′ed·ness** *n.*

tight·lipped also **tight-lipped** (tīt′lĭpt′) *adj.* **1.** Having the lips pressed together. **2.** Loath to speak; close-mouthed. —**tight′lipped′ness** *n.*

tight·rope (tīt′rōp′) *n.* **1.** A tightly stretched rope or wire on which acrobats perform high above the ground. **2.** An extremely precarious course or situation.

tights (tīts) *pl.n.* **1.** A snug stretchable garment for the lower body and the legs, generally worn by women and girls. **2.** A similar, often full-length garment designed for athletic use, worn esp. by acrobats and dancers.

tight·wad (tīt′wŏd′) *n. Slang* A miser.

tig·lic acid (tĭg′lĭk) *n.* A syrupy poisonous liquid, $C_5H_8O_2$, derived from croton oil and used in making perfumes and flavoring agents. [< NLat. (*Croton*) *tiglium,* croton species, perh. < Gk. *tîlos,* diarrhea (< the use of croton oil as a purgative).]

ti·glon (tī′glən) also **ti·gon** (-gən) *n.* The hybrid offspring of a male tiger and a female lion. [TIG(ER) + L(I)ON.]

Ti·gré (tē-grā′) *n.* A Semitic language of Eritrea.

ti·gress (tī′grĭs) *n.* **1.** A female tiger. **2.** A woman regarded as daring or fierce.

Ti·gri·nya (tə-grēn′yə) *n.* A Semitic language of Eritrea, where it is the official language, and of northern Ethiopia.

Ti·gris (tī′grĭs) A river rising in E Turkey and flowing c. 1,850 km (1,150 mi) through Iraq to the Euphrates R.

Ti·jua·na (tē′ə-wä′nə, tē-hwä′nə) A city of extreme NW Mexico on the US border S of San Diego. Pop. 429,500.

Ti·kal (tē-käl′) A ruined Mayan city of N Guatemala; the largest and possibly the oldest of the Mayan cities.

tike (tīk) *n.* Variant of **tyke.**

ti·ki (tē′kē) *n., pl.* **-kis** **1.** *Tiki Mythology* A male figure in Polynesian myth, sometimes identified as the first man. **2.** A wooden or stone image of a Polynesian god. **3.** A Maori figurine representing an ancestor. [Maori.]

til¹ (tĭl) *n.* See **sesame.** [Hindi < Skt. *tilaḥ.*]

til² (tĭl) *prep.* Until. ❖ *conj.* Until. See Usage Note at **till².**

ti·la·pi·a (tə-lä′pē-ə, -lä′-) *n.* Any of various African cichlid food fishes of the genus *Tilapia.* [NLat. *Tilapia,* genus name.]

Til·burg (tĭl′bûrg′, -bœrн′) A city of S Netherlands near the Belgian border SE of Rotterdam. Pop. 162,891.

til·bur·y (tĭl′bĕr′ē, -bə-rē) *n., pl.* **-ies** A light two-wheeled open carriage with two seats, used in the 19th century. [After *Tilbury,* a 19th-cent. London coach builder.]

til·de (tĭl′də) *n.* A diacritical mark (˜) placed over an *n* in Spanish to indicate the palatal nasal sound (ny), as in *cañon,* or over a vowel in Portuguese to indicate nasalization, as in *lã, pão.* [Sp., alteration of obsolete Catalan *title* < Lat. *titulus,* superscription.]

Til·den (tĭl′dən), **Samuel Jones** 1814–86. Amer. politician who ran unsuccessfully for President in 1876. Although he won the popular vote, he lost the electoral vote.

tile (tīl) *n.* **1.** A thin flat or convex slab of hard material, such as baked clay or plastic, laid in rows to cover walls, floors, and roofs. **2.** A short length of pipe made of clay or concrete, used in sewers and drains. **3.** A hollow fired clay or concrete block used for building walls. **4.** Tiles considered as a group. **5.** *Games* A marked playing piece, as in mahjong. ❖ *tr.v.* **tiled, til·ing, tiles** To cover or provide with tiles. [ME < OE *tigele* < Lat. *tēgula < tegere,* to cover. See **(s)teg-** in App.] —**til′er** *n.*

tile·fish (tīl′fĭsh′) *n., pl.* **tilefish** or **-fish·es** A reddish-blue percoid marine food fish (*Lopholatilus chamaeleonticeps*) of deep Atlantic waters having a fleshy flap on the nape and small yellow spots on the upper sides and fins. [*tile-* (short for NLat. *Lopholatilus,* genus name : Gk. *lophos,* crest, fin + NLat. *latilus,* dim. of *latus,* a kind of perch < Gk. *latos*) + FISH.]

til·ing (tī′lĭng) *n.* **1.** Tile laying. **2.** Tiles. **3.** A tiled surface.

till¹ (tĭl) *tr.v.* **tilled, till·ing, tills** To prepare (land) for the raising of crops, as by plowing and harrowing; cultivate. [ME *tilen* < OE *tilian.*] —**till′a·ble** *adj.*

till² (tĭl) *prep.* Until. ❖ *conj.* Until. [ME < OE *til* < ON.]

USAGE NOTE *Till* and *until* are generally interchangeable in both writing and speech, though as the first word in a sentence *until* is usually preferred. In the 18th century the spelling *'till* became fashionable, as if *till* were a shortened form of *until.* Although *'till* is now nonstandard, *'til* is sometimes used in this way and is considered acceptable.

till³ (tĭl) *n.* **1.** A drawer, small chest, or compartment for money, as in a store. **2.** A supply of money; a purse. [ME *tille.*]

till⁴ (tĭl) *n.* Glacial drift made up of an unconsolidated mixture of clay, sand, pebbles, cobbles, and boulders. [?]

till·age (tĭl′ĭj) *n.* **1.** Cultivation of land. **2.** Tilled land.

til·land·si·a (tĭ-lănd′zē-ə) *n.* Any of various usu. epiphytic bromeliad plants of the genus *Tillandsia,* such as Spanish moss, of tropical and subtropical America. [NLat. *Tillandsia,* genus name, after Elias *Tillands* (1640–93), Finno-Swedish botanist.]

till·er¹ (tĭl′ər) *n.* One that tills land; a tiller of soil.

til·ler² (tĭl′ər) *n.* A lever used to turn a rudder and steer a boat. [ME *tiler,* stock of a crossbow < OFr. *telier* < Med.Lat. *tēlārium,* weaver's beam < Lat. *tēla,* web, weaver's beam.]

til·ler³ (tĭl′ər) *n.* A shoot, esp. from the base of a grass. ❖ *intr.v.* **-lered, -ler·ing, -lers** To send forth shoots from the base. Used of a grass. [ME **tiller* < OE *telgor.*]

Til·lich (tĭl′ĭk, -ĬKH), **Paul Johannes** 1886–1965. German-born Amer. theologian and philosopher.

Til·ly (tĭl′ē), **Count of.** Title of Johann Tserclaas. 1559–1632. Flemish field marshal during the Thirty Years' War.

tilt[1] (tĭlt) *v.* **tilt·ed, tilt·ing, tilts** —*tr.* **1.** To cause to slope, as by raising one end; incline: *tilted the chair backward.* **2a.** To aim or thrust (a lance) in a joust. **b.** To charge (an opponent); attack. **3.** To forge with a tilt hammer. —*intr.* **1.** To slope; incline. See Syns at **slant. 2.** To favor one side over another in a dispute; lean. **3a.** To fight with lances; joust. **b.** To engage in a combat or struggle; fight. ❖ *n.* **1.** The act of tilting or the condition of being tilted. **2a.** An inclination from the horizontal or vertical; a slant. **b.** A sloping surface, as of the ground. **3a.** A tendency to favor one side in a dispute. **b.** An implicit preference; a bias. **4a.** A medieval sport in which two mounted knights with lances charged together and attempted to unhorse one another. **b.** A thrust or blow with a lance. **5.** A combat, esp. a verbal one; a debate. **6.** A tilt hammer. —*idiom:* **at full tilt** *Informal* At full speed. [ME *tilten*, to cause to fall, perh. of Scand. orig.] —**tilt′er** *n.*

tilt[2] (tĭlt) *n.* A canopy or an awning for a boat, wagon, or cart. ❖ *tr.v.* **tilt·ed, tilt·ing, tilts** To cover (a vehicle) with a tilt. [ME *telte, tent* < OE *teld.*]

tilth (tĭlth) *n.* **1.** Cultivation of land; tillage. **2.** Tilled earth. [ME < OE < *tilian,* to labor.]

tilt hammer *n.* A heavy forge hammer having a pivoted lever by which it is tilted up and then allowed to drop.

tilt·yard (tĭlt′yärd′) *n.* An enclosed yard for tilting contests.

Tim. *abbr. Bible* Timothy

tim·bal also **tym·bal** (tĭm′bəl) *n.* A kettledrum. [Fr. *timbale* < OFr., alteration of *tamballe,* alteration of OSpan. *atabal,* small drum < *aṭ-ṭabl,* the drum : *al-, the* + *ṭabl,* drum; see TABLA.]

tim·bale (tĭm′bəl, tĭm-bäl′, tăm-) *n.* **1.** A custardlike dish of cheese, chicken, fish, or vegetables baked in a drum-shaped pastry mold. **2.** The pastry mold in which this food is baked. [Fr., timbal, mold. See TIMBAL.]

tim·ber (tĭm′bər) *n.* **1a.** Trees or wooded land considered as a source of wood. **b.** Wood used as a building material; lumber. **2a.** A dressed piece of wood, esp. a beam in a structure. **b.** *Nautical* A rib in a ship's frame. **3.** A person considered to have qualities suited for a particular activity. ❖ *tr.v.* **-bered, -ber·ing, -bers** To support or frame with timbers. [ME < OE, building, trees for building. See dem- in App.]

tim·bered (tĭm′bərd) *adj.* **1.** Covered with trees; wooded. **2.** Made of or framed by timbers, esp. exposed timbers.

tim·ber·head (tĭm′bər-hĕd′) *n. Nautical* An upper end of a timber that projects above a deck and is used as a bolster.

timber hitch *n.* A knot used for fastening a rope around a spar or log to be hoisted or towed.

tim·ber·ing (tĭm′bər-ĭng) *n.* Timber or objects made of it.

tim·ber·land (tĭm′bər-lănd′) *n.* Forested land, esp. land containing timber of commercial value.

tim·ber·line (tĭm′bər-lĭn′) *n.* **1.** The elevation in a mountainous region above which trees do not grow. **2.** The northern or southern latitude beyond which trees do not grow.

timber rattlesnake *n.* A venomous snake (*Crotalus horridus* subsp. *horridus*) of the United States having a yellowish-brown color and wide transverse bands on the back.

timber right *n.* A claim to the trees on property belonging to another. Often used in the plural.

timber wolf *n.* See **gray wolf.**

tim·ber·work (tĭm′bər-wûrk′) *n.* A structure made with timbers, as the framework of a boat or house.

tim·bre (tăm′bər, tĭm′-) *n.* The combination of qualities of a sound that distinguishes it from other sounds of the same pitch and volume. [Fr. < OFr., drum, clapperless bell, prob. < Med.Gk. *timbanon,* drum < Gk. *tumpanon,* kettledrum.]

tim·brel (tĭm′brəl) *n.* An ancient tambourinelike instrument. [Dim. of ME *timbre,* drum < OFr. See TIMBRE.]

Tim·buk·tu (tĭm′bŭk-tōō′, tĭm-bŭk′tōō) A city of central Mali near the Niger R. NE of Bamako; founded in the 11th cent. Pop. 19,166.

time (tīm) *n.* **1a.** A nonspatial continuum in which events occur in apparently irreversible succession from the past through the present to the future. **b.** An interval separating two points on this continuum; a duration: *passed the time reading.* **c.** A number, as of years, days, or minutes, representing such an interval. **d.** A similar number representing a specific point on this continuum, reckoned in hours and minutes: *The time is 6:17 A.M.* **e.** A system by which such intervals are measured or such numbers are reckoned: *solar time.* **2a.** An interval, esp. a span of years, marked by similar events, conditions, or phenomena; an era. Often used in the plural: *hard times.* **b. times** The present with respect to prevailing conditions and trends: *change with the times.* **3.** A suitable or opportune moment or season. **4a.** Periods or a period designated for a given activity: *time for bed.* **b.** Periods or a period necessary or available for a given activity. **c.** A period at one's disposal. **5.** An appointed or fated moment, esp. of death or giving birth. **6a.** One of several instances. **b. times** Used to indicate the number of instances by which something is multiplied or divided: *many times smaller.* **7a.** One's lifetime. **b.** One's period of greatest activity or engagement. **c.** A person's experience during a specific period or on a certain occasion: *had a good time.* **8a.** A period of military service. **b.** A period of apprenticeship. **c.** *Informal* A prison sentence. **9a.** The customary period of work: *full time.* **b.** The period spent working. **c.** The hourly pay rate. **10.** The period during which a radio or television program or commercial is broadcast. **11.** The rate of speed of a measured activity: *double time.* **12.** *Music* **a.** The meter of a musical pattern: *three-quarter time.* **b.** The rate of speed at which a piece of music is played; the tempo. **13.** *Chiefly British* The hour at which a pub closes. **14.** *Sports* A time-out. ❖ *adj.* **1.** Of, relating to, or measuring time. **2.** Constructed so as to operate at a particular moment: *a time release.* **3.** Payable on a future date or dates. **4.** Of or relating to installment buying: *time payments.* ❖ *tr.v.* **timed, tim·ing, times 1.** To set the time for (an event or occasion). **2.** To adjust to keep accurate time. **3.** To adjust so that a force is applied or an action occurs at the desired time. **4.** To record the speed or duration of: *time a runner.* **5.** To set or maintain the tempo, speed, or duration of. —*idioms:* **against time** With a quickly approaching time limit. **at one time 1.** Simultaneously. **2.** At a period or moment in the past. **at the same time** However; nonetheless. **at times** On occasion; sometimes. **behind the times** Out-of-date; old-fashioned. **for the time being** Temporarily. **from time to time** Once in a while; at intervals. **high time** The appropriate or urgent time: *It's high time you start working.* **in good time 1.** In a reasonable length of time. **2.** When or before due. **3.** Quickly. **in no time** Almost instantly; immediately. **in time 1.** Before a time limit expires. **2.** Within an indefinite time; eventually. **3.** *Music* **a.** In the proper tempo. **b.** Played with a meter. **on time 1.** According to schedule; punctual or punctually. **2.** By paying in installments. **time after time** Again and again; repeatedly. **time and again** Again and again; repeatedly. **time of (one's) life** A highly pleasurable experience. **time on (one's) hands** An interval with nothing to do. **time out of mind** Time long past; time immemorial. **time was** There was once a time. [ME < OE *tīma.* See **dā-** in App.]

time and a half *n.* A rate of pay that is one and a half times the regular rate, as for overtime work.

time and motion study *n.* An analysis of the efficiency with which an industrial operation is performed.

time bill *n.* A bill of exchange payable at an indicated future time.

time bomb *n.* **1.** A bomb with a detonating mechanism that can be set for a particular time. **2.** Something that threatens to have an abruptly disastrous outcome in the future.

time capsule *n.* A sealed container preserving contemporary articles and records for future scientists and scholars.

time·card (tīm′kärd′) *n.* A card, either filled out by an employee or stamped by a time clock, recording the employee's starting and quitting times or work hours each workday.

time clock *n.* A clock that records the starting and quitting times of employees, usu. by punching timecards.

time deposit *n.* A bank deposit that cannot be withdrawn before a date specified at the time of deposit.

time dilatation *n.* See **time dilation.**

time dilation *n.* The relativistic slowing of a clock that moves with respect to a stationary observer.

timed-re·lease (tīmd′rĭ-lēs′) or **time-re·lease** (tīm′-) *adj.* Releasing ingredients gradually to produce a sustained effect.

time exposure *n.* **1.** A photographic exposure made by leaving the shutter open a relatively long time, generally a second or more. **2.** An image so made.

time frame *n.* A period in which something occurs or is to occur.

time-hon·ored (tīm′ŏn′ərd) *adj.* Respected or adhered to because of age or age-old observance.

time immemorial *n., pl.* **times immemorial 1.** Time long past, beyond memory or record. **2.** *Law* Time antedating legal records.

time·keep·er (tīm′kē′pər) *n.* **1.** One who records time, as: **a.** *Sports* One who keeps track of elapsed time in a sporting event. **b.** One who keeps records of the hours worked by employees. **2.** A device for keeping time; a timepiece. —**time′keep′ing** *adj.*

time-lapse (tīm′lăps′) *adj.* Of, using, or being a technique that photographs a naturally slow process, such as plant growth, on movie film at intervals, so that continuous projection of the frames gives an accelerated view of the process.

time·less (tīm′lĭs) *adj.* **1.** Independent of time; eternal. **2.** Unaffected by time; ageless. **3.** *Archaic* Untimely or premature. —**time′less·ly** *adv.* —**time′less·ness** *n.*

time·line (tīm′lĭn′) *n.* **1.** A schedule of activities or events; a timetable. **2a.** A chronology. **b.** A representation or exhibit of key events within a particular historical period.

time loan *n.* A loan to be paid within or by a specified time.

time lock *n.* A lock, as for a bank vault, containing a mechanism that prevents its being opened before a fixed time.

time·ly (tīm′lē) *adj.* **-li·er, -li·est 1.** Occurring at a suitable or opportune time; well-timed: *a timely remark.* **2.** *Archaic* Coming too early; premature. ❖ *adv.* **1.** In time; opportunely. **2.** *Archaic* Early; soon. —**time′li·ness** *n.*

time machine *n.* A fictional or hypothetical device by means of which one may travel into the future and the past.

time note *n.* An instrument, such as a promissory note, that specifies dates or a date of payment.

time·ous (tī′məs) *adj.* Timely. —**time′ous·ly** *adv.*

ă pat	oi	boy
ā pay	ou	out
âr care	ŏŏ	took
ä father	ōō	boot
ĕ pet	ŭ	cut
ē be	ûr	urge
ĭ pit	th	thin
ī pie	th	this
îr pier	hw	which
ŏ pot	zh	vision
ō toe	ə	about,
ô paw		item

Stress marks:
′ (primary);
′ (secondary), as in
lexicon (lĕk′sĭ-kŏn′)

time-out or **time out** (tīm′out′) n. **1.** *Sports* A brief cessation of play at the request of a team or official for rest, consultation, or substitution. **2.** A short break. **3.** A corrective measure or punishment for young children in which they are separated from others for a brief period.

time·piece (tīm′pēs′) n. An instrument, such as a clock or watch, that measures, registers, or records time.

tim·er (tī′mər) n. **1.** One who keeps track of time; a timekeeper. **2.** A timepiece, esp. one used for measuring and signaling the end of time intervals, as on a stove. **3.** A switch or regulator that controls or activates and deactivates another mechanism at set times. **4.** A device that times the sparks igniting the fuel in an internal-combustion engine.

time-re·lease (tīm′rĭ-lēs′) adj. Variant of **timed-release.**

time reversal n. *Mathematics* An operation representing a transformation from a given physical system undergoing a given sequence of events to a system in which the exact reverse sequence of events takes place.

times (tīmz) prep. Multiplied by: *Five times two is ten.*

time·sav·ing (tīm′sā′vĭng) adj. Serving to save time through an efficient method or a shorter route. **—time′sav′er** n.

time·serv·er (tīm′sûr′vər) n. One who conforms to the prevailing ways and opinions of one's time or condition for personal advantage; an opportunist. **—time′serv′ing** adj. & n.

time-shar·ing (tīm′shâr′ĭng) n. **1.** A technique permitting many users simultaneous access to a central computer through remote terminals. **2.** also **time-share** (-shâr′) Joint ownership or lease of vacation property by several people who take turns occupying the premises for fixed periods. **—time′-share′** v.

time sheet n. A sheet that records the number of hours worked by employees during a pay period.

time signature n. *Music* A sign placed on a staff to indicate the meter, commonly a numerical fraction of which the numerator is the number of beats per measure and the denominator represents the kind of note getting one beat.

times sign n. The symbol × for multiplication.

Times Square An intersection in New York City at the juncture of Broadway, Seventh Avenue, and 42nd Street.

time study n. See **time and motion study.**

time·ta·ble (tīm′tā′bəl) n. A schedule listing the times at which certain events are expected to take place.

time-test·ed (tīm′tĕs′tĭd) adj. Proved effective over time.

time trial n. A competitive event in which participants are timed, as in covering a set distance, often used to select qualifiers for another event.

time warp n. A hypothetical discontinuity or distortion occurring in the flow of time that would move events from one time period to another or suspend the passage of time.

time·work (tīm′wûrk′) n. Work paid for at a rate per unit of time, as by the hour. **—time′work′er** n.

time·worn (tīm′wôrn′, -wōrn′) adj. **1.** Showing the effects of long use or wear: *timeworn lanes.* **2.** Used too often; trite.

time zone n. Any of the 24 longitudinal divisions of the earth's surface in which a standard time is kept, each being about 15° of longitude in width and observing a clock time one hour earlier than the zone immediately to the east.

tim·id (tĭm′ĭd) adj. **-er, -est 1.** Lacking self-confidence; shy. **2.** Fearful and hesitant: *This problem calls for a bold, not timid, response.* [Lat. *timidus* < *timēre,* to fear.] **—ti·mid′i·ty, tim′id·ness** n. **—tim′id·ly** adv.

tim·ing (tī′mĭng) n. **1.** The art or operation of regulating occurrence, pace, or coordination to achieve the most desirable effects, as in music, the theater, athletics, or mechanics. **2.** The synchronization of the sparking of the plugs with the movement of the pistons in an internal-combustion engine.

timing belt n. A cogged belt, usu. of reinforced rubber, that drives the camshaft in an internal-combustion engine.

timing chain n. A metal chain that functions as a timing belt.

Ti·mi·șoa·ra (tē′mē-shwär′ə) A city of W Romania near the Yugoslavian border WNW of Bucharest. Pop. 325,349.

ti·moc·ra·cy (tī-mŏk′rə-sē) n., pl. **-cies 1.** A state described by Plato as being governed on principles of honor and military glory. **2.** An Aristotelian state in which civic honor or political power increases with the amount of property one owns. [Ult. < Gk. *tīmokratiā* : *tīmē,* honor, value + *-kratiā,* -cracy.] **—ti′mo·crat′ic** (tī′mə-krăt′ĭk) adj.

Ti·mor (tē′môr′, tē-môr′) An island of SE Indonesia in the E Lesser Sundas. West Timor, formerly Netherlands Timor, became part of Indonesia in 1949. East Timor was an overseas province of Portugal from 1914 until 1975. Annexed by Indonesia in 1976, East Timor declared independence in 1999 and held its first elections in 2001.

tim·or·ous (tĭm′ər-əs) adj. Full of apprehensiveness; timid. [ME < OFr. *timoureux* < Med.Lat. *timōrōsus* < Lat. *timor, timōr-,* fear < *timēre,* to fear.] **—tim′or·ous·ly** adv. **—tim′or·ous·ness** n.

Timor Sea An arm of the Indian Ocean between Timor and Australia.

tim·o·thy (tĭm′ə-thē) n., pl. **-thies** Any of several grasses of the genus *Phleum,* esp. *P. pratense* of Eurasia and *P. alpinum* of North America, widely cultivated for hay. [Probably after *Timothy* Hanson, an 18th-cent. American farmer.]

Timothy n. See table at **Bible.**

Timothy, Saint. 1st cent. A.D. Christian leader and companion of Saint Paul. Two epistles of the Bible are addressed to him.

tim·pa·ni also **tym·pa·ni** (tĭm′pə-nē) pl.n. (*used with a sing. or pl. verb*) A set of *timpano* (Ital., of *timpano,* kettledrum < Lat. *tympanum,* drum. See TYMPANUM.]

tim·pa·nist also **tym·pa·nist** (tĭm′pə-nĭst) n. One who plays the kettledrums and other percussion instruments in an orchestra.

tim·pa·num (tĭm′pə-nəm) n. Variant of **tympanum.**

Tim·u·cu·a (tĭm′ə-kōō′ə) n., pl. **Timucua** or **-cu·as 1.** A member of an extinct Native American people formerly inhabiting northern Florida. **2.** Their language.

tin (tĭn) n. **1.** *Symbol* **Sn** A malleable metallic element obtained chiefly from cassiterite and used to coat other metals to prevent corrosion and in numerous alloys, such as soft solder, pewter, type metal, and bronze. Atomic number 50; atomic weight 118.71; melting point 231.89°C; boiling point 2,270°C; specific gravity 7.31; valence 2, 4. See table at **element. 2.** Tin plate. **3.** A container or box made of tin plate. **4.** *Chiefly British* **a.** A container for preserved foodstuffs; a can. **b.** Its contents. ❖ *tr.v.* **tinned, tin·ning, tins 1.** To plate or coat with tin. **2.** *Chiefly British* To preserve or pack in tins; can. ❖ adj. **1.** Of or made of tin. **2a.** Constructed of inferior material. **b.** Spurious. [ME < OE.]

tin·a·mou (tĭn′ə-mōō′) n. Any of various chickenlike or quaillike birds of the family Tinamidae of Central and South America. [Fr., perh. of Galibi orig.]

Tin·ber·gen (tĭn′bər-gən, -bĕr′кнən), **Jan** 1903–94. Dutch economist who shared a 1969 Nobel Prize. His brother **Nikolaas** (1907–88), a Dutch-born British ethologist, shared a 1973 Nobel Prize.

tin·cal (tĭng′kəl) n. Crude borax. [Malay *tingkal.*]

tin can n. **1.** A container of tin-coated sheet metal used esp. for preserving food. **2.** *Informal* A naval destroyer.

tinct (tĭngkt) n. A color or tint. ❖ adj. Colored lightly or faintly; tinged. [ME, a transforming elixir < Lat. *tīnctus,* a dyeing < p. part. of *tingere,* to dye.]

tinc·to·ri·al (tĭngk-tôr′ē-əl, -tōr′-) adj. Relating to the processes of dyeing or coloring. [< Lat. *tīnctōrius* < *tīnctus,* p. part. of *tingere,* to dye.] **—tinc·to′ri·al·ly** adv.

tinc·ture (tĭngk′chər) n. **1.** A coloring or dyeing substance; a pigment. **2.** An imparted color; a tint. **3.** A quality that colors, pervades, or distinguishes. **4.** A trace or vestige. **5.** An alcohol solution of a nonvolatile medicine: *tincture of iodine.* **6.** *Heraldry* A metal, color, or fur. ❖ *tr.v.* **-tured, -tur·ing, -tures 1.** To stain or tint with a color. **2.** To infuse, as with a quality; impregnate. [ME < Lat. *tīnctūra,* a dyeing < *tīnctus,* p. part. of *tingere,* to dye.]

Tin·dal or **Tin·dale** (tĭn′dl), **William** See William **Tyndale.**

tin·der (tĭn′dər) n. Readily combustible material, such as dry twigs, used to kindle fires. [ME < OE *tynder.*]

tin·der·box (tĭn′dər-bŏks′) n. **1.** A metal box for holding tinder. **2.** A potentially explosive place or situation.

tine (tīn) n. **1.** A branch of a deer's antlers. **2.** A prong on an implement such as a fork or pitchfork. [ME < OE *tind.*] **—tined** (tīnd) adj.

tin·e·a (tĭn′ē-ə) n. See **ringworm.** [ME < Med.Lat. < Lat., a gnawing worm.] **—tin′e·al** adj.

tin ear n. *Informal* An insensitivity to music or to sounds of a given kind: *a writer with a tin ear for dialogue.*

tin·foil also **tin foil** (tĭn′foil′) n. A thin pliable sheet of aluminum or tin-lead alloy, used as a protective wrapping.

ting (tĭng) n. A single light metallic sound, as of a small bell. ❖ *intr.v.* **tinged** (tĭngd), **ting·ing, tings** To give forth a light metallic sound. [< ME *tingen,* to cause to ring, of imit. orig.]

tinge (tĭnj) *tr.v.* **tinged** (tĭnjd), **tinge·ing** or **ting·ing** (tĭn′jĭng), **ting·es 1.** To apply a trace of color to; tint. **2.** To affect slightly, as with a contrasting quality. ❖ n. **1.** A small amount of a color incorporated or added. **2.** A slight added element, property, or influence. [ME *tingen* < Lat. *tingere.*]

tin·gle (tĭng′gəl) v. **-gled, -gling, -gles** —*intr.* **1.** To have a prickly stinging sensation, as from cold. **2.** To cause a prickly stinging sensation or feeling. —*tr.* To cause to tingle. ❖ n. A prickly stinging sensation. [ME *tinglen,* alteration of *tinklen.* See TINKLE.] **—tin′gler** n. **—tin′gly** adj.

tin·horn (tĭn′hôrn′) n. *Slang* A petty braggart pretending to be rich and important. [< the horn-shaped metal can used in chuck-a-luck for shaking the dice.] **—tin′horn′** adj.

Ti·ni·an (tĭn′ē-ăn′, tē′nē-än′) An island of the W Pacific in the S Mariana Is.; departure point for the planes that dropped atomic bombs on Hiroshima and Nagasaki (1945).

tin·ker (tĭng′kər) n. **1.** A traveling mender of metal household utensils. **2.** *Chiefly British* A member of any of various traditionally itinerant groups of people living esp. in Scotland and Ireland; a traveler. **3.** One who enjoys experimenting with and repairing machine parts. **4.** A clumsy repairer or worker; a meddler. ❖ v. **-kered, -ker·ing, -kers** —*intr.* **1.** To work as a tinker. **2.** To make unskilled or experimental efforts at repair; fiddle: *tinkering with the economy.* —*tr.* **1.** To mend as a tinker. **2.** To manipulate unskillfully or experimentally. [ME *tinkere.*] **—tin′ker·er** n.

tin·ker's damn also **tin·ker's dam** (tĭng′kərz) n. *Slang* The smallest degree or amount.

Tin·ker·toy (tĭng′kər-toi′) A trademark used for a construction toy consisting of pieces that fit together.

tin·kle (tĭng′kəl) v. **-kled, -kling, -kles** —intr. **1.** To make light metallic sounds, as those of a small bell. **2.** Informal To urinate. —tr. **1.** To cause to tinkle. **2.** To signal or call by tinkling. ❖ n. **1.** A light clear metallic sound or a sound suggestive of it. **2.** An act or instance of tinkling. [ME tinklen, freq. of tinken, to emit a brief metallic sound, perh. of imit. orig.] —**tin′kly** adj.

tin liz·zie (lĭz′ē) n. Slang A dilapidated or cheap car. [After Tin Lizzie, nickname for the Ford Model T automobile, perh. < Lizzie, nickname for Elizabeth and commonly given to horses.]

tin·ner (tĭn′ər) n. **1.** A tin miner. **2.** One that makes or deals in tinware; a tinsmith.

tin·ni·tus (tĭ-nī′təs, tĭn′ĭ-) n., pl. **-tus·es** A chronic ringing or buzzing sound in one or both ears usu. caused by a specific condition, such as an ear infection. [Lat. tinnītus < p. part. of tinnīre, to ring, of imit. orig.]

tin·ny (tĭn′ē) adj. **-ni·er, -ni·est 1.** Of, containing, or yielding tin. **2.** Tasting or smelling of tin: tinny canned food. **3.** Having a thin metallic sound: a high tinny voice. **4.** Weak or thin; flimsy. —**tin′ni·ly** adv. —**tin′ni·ness** n.

Tin Pan Alley n. **1.** A district associated with musicians, composers, and publishers of popular music. **2.** The publishers and composers of popular music considered as a group. [Prob. < tin pan, tinny piano + ALLEY¹.]

tin parachute n. Slang An employment agreement that guarantees a severance payment to employees who are dismissed after a company has had a change in ownership. [On the model of GOLDEN PARACHUTE.]

tin plate n. Thin sheet iron or steel coated with tin to prevent rusting, used esp. to make cans and pots.

tin-plate (tĭn′plāt′) tr.v. **-plat·ed, -plat·ing, -plates** To coat with tin by dipping or electroplating. —**tin′-plat′er** n.

tin pyrites n. See **stannite**.

tin·sel (tĭn′səl) n. **1.** Very thin sheets, strips, or threads of a glittering material used as a decoration. **2.** Something sparkling or showy but basically valueless. ❖ adj. **1.** Made of or decorated with tinsel. **2.** Gaudy, showy, and valueless. ❖ tr.v. **-seled, -sel·ing, -sels** or **-selled, -sel·ling, -sels 1.** To decorate with or as if with tinsel. **2.** To give a false sparkle to. [ME tineseile < OFr. estincelle, spangle. See STENCIL.]

tin·smith (tĭn′smĭth′) n. One that makes and repairs things made of light metal.

tin·stone (tĭn′stōn′) n. See **cassiterite**.

tint (tĭnt) n. **1.** A shade of a color, esp. a pale or delicate variation. **2.** A gradation of a color made by adding white to it to lessen its saturation. **3.** A slight coloration; a tinge. **4.** A barely detectable amount or degree; a trace. **5.** A shaded effect in engraving produced by fine, close, parallel lines. **6.** Printing A panel of light color on which matter in another color is to be printed, as in an illustration. **7.** A dye for the hair. ❖ tr. & intr.v. **tint·ed, tint·ing, tints** To give a tint to or take on a tint. [Alteration of TINCT.] —**tint′er** n.

Tin·tag·el Head (tĭn-tăj′əl) A promontory in SW England NE of Plymouth; reputed birthplace of King Arthur.

tin·tin·nab·u·lar (tĭn′tĭ-năb′yə-lər) also **tin·tin·nab·u·lar·y** (-lĕr′ē) or **tin·tin·nab·u·lous** (-ləs) adj. Of or relating to bells or the ringing of bells. [< TINTINNABULUM.]

tin·tin·nab·u·la·tion (tĭn′tĭ-năb′yə-lā′shən) n. The ringing or sounding of bells. [< TINTINNABULUM.]

tin·tin·nab·u·lum (tĭn′tĭ-năb′yə-ləm) n., pl. **-la** (-lə) A small tinkling bell. [ME < Lat. tintinnābulum < tintinnāre, to jingle, redup. of tinnīre, to ring, of imit. orig.]

Tin·to·ret·to (tĭn′tə-rĕt′ō, tēn′tō-rĕt′tō) 1518–94. Italian painter of Saint George and the Dragon (c. 1550).

tin·type (tĭn′tīp′) n. See **ferrotype** 1.

tin·work (tĭn′wûrk′) n. **1.** Articles made of tin or tin plate. **2.** **tinworks** (used with a sing. verb) A place where tin is worked.

ti·ny (tī′nē) adj. **-ni·er, -ni·est** Extremely small; minute. See Syns at **small**. [Alteration of ME tine.] —**ti′ni·ness** n.

tip¹ (tĭp) n. **1.** The end of a pointed or projecting object. **2.** A piece or an attachment, such as a cap or ferrule, to be fitted to the end of something else. ❖ tr.v. **tipped, tip·ping, tips 1.** To furnish with a tip. **2.** To cover or decorate the tip of. **3.** To remove the tip of. **4.** To dye the ends of (hair or fur) in order to blend or improve appearance. —**phrasal verb: tip in** Printing To attach (an insert) in a book by gluing along the binding edge. [ME.]

tip² (tĭp) v. **tipped, tip·ping, tips** —tr. **1.** To push or knock over; overturn or topple: bumped the table and tipped a vase. **2.** To move to a slanting position; tilt. **3.** To touch or raise (one's hat) in greeting. **4.** Chiefly British **a.** To empty (something) by overturning; dump. **b.** To dump (rubbish, for example). —intr. **1.** To topple over; overturn. **2.** To become tilted; slant. See Syns at **slant.** ❖ n. **1.** The act of tipping. **2.** A tilt or slant; an incline. **3.** Chiefly British A place for dumping something, such as rubbish, as from a mine. —**idioms: tip (one's) hand** To reveal one's resources or intentions. **tip the scales 1.** To register weight at a certain amount. **2.** To offset the balance of a situation. [ME tipen.]

tip³ (tĭp) v. **tipped, tip·ping, tips** —tr. **1.** To strike gently; tap. **2a.** Baseball To hit (a pitched ball) with the side of the bat so that it glances off. **b.** Sports To tap or deflect (a ball, for example), esp. in scoring. —intr. **1.** Sports To deflect or glance off. Used of a ball or puck. **2.** Baseball A tipped pitched ball. [< ME tippe, a tap, perh. of LGer. orig.]

tip⁴ (tĭp) n. **1.** A small sum of money given to someone for performing a service; a gratuity. **2a.** A piece of confidential, advance, or inside information. **b.** A helpful hint. ❖ v. **tipped, tip·ping, tips** —tr. **1a.** To give a tip to: tipped the waiter. **b.** To give as a tip: tipped a dollar. **2.** To provide with an informational tip. —intr. To give tips or a tip: tips lavishly. [?] —**tip′per** n.

tip·cart (tĭp′kärt′) n. A cart having a body that can be tilted to dump the contents.

tip·i (tē′pē) n. Variant of **tepee**.

tip-in (tĭp′ĭn′) n. **1.** Basketball A field goal scored by tapping the ball into the basket with the fingertips. **2.** Sports A goal in hockey scored at close range by a short stroke of a stick.

tip-off¹ (tĭp′ôf′, -ŏf′) n. Informal **1.** An informational tip. **2.** An indication of an otherwise unknown fact or probability.

tip-off² (tĭp′ôf′, -ŏf′) n. Basketball An act of starting play at the beginning of a period with a jump ball. [TIP³ + (KICK)OFF.]

tip of the iceberg n., pl. **tips of the iceberg** A small evident part or aspect of something largely hidden.

Tip·pe·ca·noe (tĭp′ē-kə-nōō′) A river, c. 274 km (170 mi), rising in NE IN and flowing to the Wabash R.; site of Gen. William Henry Harrison's defeat of the Shawnee (1811).

Tip·per·ar·y (tĭp′ə-râr′ē) A town of S-central Ireland SW of Dublin. The song "It's a Long Way to Tipperary" was used as a march by the British in World War I. Pop. 4,984.

tip·pet (tĭp′ĭt) n. **1.** A covering for the shoulders, as of fur, with long ends that hang in front. **2.** A long stole worn by members of the Anglican clergy. **3.** A long hanging part, as of a sleeve. [ME tipet, perh. < tip, tip of an object.]

tip·ple¹ (tĭp′əl) tr. & intr.v. **-pled, -pling, -ples** To drink (alcoholic liquor) or engage in such drinking, esp. habitually or to excess. ❖ n. Alcoholic liquor. [Perh. back-formation < ME tipeler, bartender.] —**tip′pler** n.

tip·ple² (tĭp′əl) n. **1a.** An apparatus for unloading freight cars by tipping them. **b.** The place where this is done. **2.** A place for screening coal and loading it into trucks or railroad cars. [< dialectal tipple, to overturn, freq. of TIP².]

tip·py (tĭp′ē) adj. **-pi·er, -pi·est** Likely to tip or tilt.

tip·staff (tĭp′stăf′) n., pl. **-staves** (-stāvz′, -stăvz′) or **-staffs 1.** A staff with a metal tip, carried as a sign of office. **2.** An officer, such as a bailiff or constable, who carries a tipstaff.

tip·ster (tĭp′stər) n. Informal One who sells tips or information, as to bettors or speculators.

tip·sy (tĭp′sē) adj. **-si·er, -si·est 1.** Slightly intoxicated. **2.** Unsteady or crooked. [< TIP².] —**tip′si·ly** adv. —**tip′si·ness** n.

tip·toe (tĭp′tō′) intr.v. **-toed, -toe·ing, -toes** To walk or move quietly on one's toes. ❖ n. The tip of a toe. ❖ adj. **1.** Standing or walking on one's toes. **2.** Stealthy; wary. ❖ adv. **1.** On one's toes. **2.** Stealthily; warily. —**idiom: on tiptoe** Full of anticipation.

tip·top (tĭp′tŏp′) n. **1.** The highest point; the summit. **2.** The highest degree of quality or excellence. ❖ adj. Excellent; first-rate: in tiptop condition. ❖ adv. Very well; excellently.

ti·rade (tī′rād′, tī-rād′) n. A long angry or violent speech, usu. censorious or denunciatory; a diatribe. [Fr. < OFr., act of firing < tirer, to draw out, endure, prob. back-formation < martirant, pr. part. of martirer, to torture (influenced by mar, to one's misfortune, and tiranz, executioner, tyrant) < martir, martyr < LLat. martyr. See MARTYR.]

tir·a·mi·su (tĭr′ə-mē′sōō, -mē-sōō′) n. A dessert of cake infused with a liquid such as coffee or rum and layered with a rich cheese filling. [Ital. tira mi sù, pick me up : tira, pick, imper. of tirare, to pick, draw + mi, me + su, up.]

Ti·ran (tə-rän′) A strait off the S tip of the Sinai Peninsula in NE Egypt connecting the Red Sea with the Gulf of Aqaba.

Ti·ra·në also **Ti·ra·na** (tə-rä′nə, tē-) The cap. of Albania, in the W-central part; became cap. in 1920. Pop. 244,153.

tire¹ (tīr) v. **tired, tir·ing, tires** —intr. **1.** To grow weary. **2.** To grow bored or impatient. —tr. **1.** To diminish the strength or energy of; fatigue. **2.** To exhaust the interest or patience of; bore. [ME tiren < OE tēorian, tyrian.]

tire² (tīr) n. **1.** A covering for a wheel, usu. made of rubber reinforced with cords of nylon, fiberglass, or other material and filled with compressed air. **2.** A hoop of metal or rubber fitted around a wheel. [ME, iron rim of a wheel, prob. < tir, attire, short for tire < attire, to attire. See ATTIRE.]

tire³ (tīr) Archaic tr.v. **tired, tir·ing, tires** To adorn or attire. ❖ n. **1.** Attire. **2.** A headband or headdress. [ME tiren, short for attiren, to attire. See ATTIRE.]

tired (tīrd) adj. **1a.** Exhausted; fatigued. **b.** Impatient; bored. **2.** Overused; hackneyed. —**tired′ly** adv. —**tired′ness** n.

tire iron n. A tool consisting of a metal bar having one end shaped like a chisel and often the other in the form of a socket wrench, used for changing tires on metal rims.

tire·less (tīr′lĭs) adj. Not yielding to fatigue; untiring or indefatigable. —**tire′less·ly** adv. —**tire′less·ness** n.

Ti·re·si·as (tī-rē′sē-əs) n. Greek Mythology A blind soothsayer of Thebes.

titmouse
tufted titmouse
Parus bicolor

Tito
photographed c. 1949

toad
Fowler's toad
Bufo woodhousei fowleri

tire·some (tīr′səm) *adj.* Causing fatigue or boredom; wearisome. See Syns at **boring. —tire′some·ness** *n.*

Ti·rich Mir (tĭr′ĭch mîr′) A mountain, 7,695.2 m (25,230 ft), of the Hindu Kush in N Pakistan.

ti·ro (tī′rō) *n.* Variant of **tyro.**

Ti·rol (tə-rōl′, tī-, tĭ-, tī′rōl′) See **Tyrol.**

Tir·so de Mo·li·na (tĭr′sō dä mə-lē′nə, thĕ mō-lē′nä) 1584?–1648. Spanish playwright who introduced the character Don Juan in *The Seducer of Seville* (1630).

Ti·ruch·chi·rap·pal·li (tĭr′ə-chə-rä′pə-lē) A city of SE India SSW of Chennai (Madras). Pop. 387,223.

Tir·yns (tĭr′ĭnz, tī′rĭnz) An ancient city of S Greece in the E Peloponnesus; site of ruined Mycenaean palaces.

'tis (tĭz) Contraction of *it is.*

ti·sane (tĭ-zăn′, -zän′) *n.* An herbal infusion or similar preparation drunk as a beverage or for its mildly medicinal effect. [Fr., barley water < OFr. < Lat. *ptisana.* See PTISAN.]

Tish·ri (tĭsh′rē, -rä) *n.* The first month of the year in the Jewish calendar. See table at **calendar.** [Heb. *tišrî* < Akkadian *tašrītu,* beginning, name of a month < *šurrû,* to begin.]

Ti·siph·o·ne (tĭ-sĭf′ə-nē) *n. Greek & Roman Mythology* One of the three Furies.

tis·sue (tĭsh′ōō, -yōō) *n.* 1. A fine, very thin fabric, such as gauze. 2. Tissue paper. 3. A soft absorbent piece of paper used as toilet paper, a handkerchief, or a towel. 4. An interwoven or interrelated number of things; a web; a network. 5. *Biology* An aggregation of morphologically similar cells and intercellular matter performing one or more functions in the body. [ME *tissu,* a rich kind of cloth < OFr. < p. part. of *tistre,* to weave < Lat. *texere.*] **—tis′su·ey** *adj.* **—tis′su·lar** *adj.*

tissue culture *n.* 1. The technique or process of keeping tissue alive and growing in a culture medium. 2. A culture of tissue grown by this technique or process.

tissue paper *n.* Thin translucent paper used for packing, wrapping, or protecting delicate articles.

tissue plasminogen activator *n.* An enzyme that converts plasminogen to plasmin, used to dissolve blood clots rapidly and selectively, esp. in the treatment of heart attacks and certain kinds of stroke.

Ti·sza (tĭs′ô) also **Ti·sa** (tē′sə) A river of central Europe rising in the Carpathian Mts. in W Ukraine and flowing c. 965 km (600 mi) to the Danube R.

tit¹ (tĭt) *n.* 1. A titmouse. 2. Any of various small similar or related birds. ❖ *adj. New England & Upstate New York* Small; undersized. [Short for TITMOUSE. Adj., ME *tit-,* as in *titmose,* titmouse. See TITMOUSE.]

tit² (tĭt) *n.* 1. *Vulgar Slang* A woman's breast. 2. A teat. [ME < OE *titt.*]

Tit. *abbr. Bible* Titus

Ti·tan (tīt′n) *n.* 1. *Greek Mythology* One of a family of giants, the children of Uranus and Gaea, who sought to rule heaven and were overthrown in turn by the family of Zeus. 2. **titan** A person of colossal size, strength, or achievement. 3. The largest satellite of Saturn. [Ult. < Lat. *Tītān* < Gk.]

ti·tan·ate (tīt′n-āt′) *n.* A salt or ester of titanic acid.

Ti·tan·ess (tīt′n-ĭs) *n. Greek Mythology* One of the daughters of Gaea and Uranus.

Ti·ta·ni·a (tĭ-tā′nē-ə, -tān′yə, tī-) *n.* 1. The queen of the fairies and wife of Oberon in medieval folklore. 2. A satellite of Uranus. [< Lat. *Tītānia,* the goddess Diana, sister to the sun < fem. of *Tītānius,* of the Titans < *Tītān.* See TITAN.]

ti·tan·ic¹ (tī-tăn′ĭk) *adj.* Of or relating to the Titans. **2a.** Having great stature or enormous strength; huge or colossal: *titanic creatures of the deep.* **b.** Of enormous scope, power, or influence. **—ti·tan′i·cal·ly** *adv.*

ti·tan·ic² (tī-tăn′ĭk, -tā′nĭk, tĭ-) *adj.* Relating to or containing titanium, esp. with valence 4.

titanic acid (tī-tăn′ĭk, -tā′nĭk, tĭ-) *n.* A powdered inorganic acid, H_2TiO_3, used as a mordant.

ti·tan·if·er·ous (tīt′n-ĭf′ər-əs) *adj.* Containing or yielding titanium.

Ti·tan·ism (tīt′n-ĭz′əm) *n.* The spirit of revolt against an established order; rebelliousness.

ti·tan·ite (tīt′n-īt′) *n.* See **sphene.**

ti·ta·ni·um (tī-tā′nē-əm, tĭ-) *n. Symbol* **Ti** A strong, low-density, highly corrosion-resistant metallic element that occurs widely in igneous rocks and is used to alloy aircraft metals for low weight, strength, and high-temperature stability. Atomic number 22; atomic weight 47.87; melting point 1,660°C; boiling point 3,287°C; specific gravity 4.54; valence 2, 3, 4. See table at **element.** [< Lat. *Tītān,* Titan. See TITAN.]

titanium dioxide *n.* A white powder, TiO_2, used as an exceptionally opaque white pigment.

titanium white *n.* Titanium dioxide.

ti·tan·ous (tī-tăn′əs, -tā′nəs, tĭ-) *adj.* Relating to or containing titanium, esp. with valence 3.

tit·bit (tĭt′bĭt′) *n.* Variant of **tidbit.**

ti·ter also **ti·tre** (tī′tər) *n.* 1. Concentration of a substance in solution determined by titration. 2. The minimum volume needed to cause a particular result in titration. [Fr. *titre* < OFr. *title,* title. See TITLE.]

tit for tat *n.* Repayment in kind, as for an injury; retaliation. [Prob. alteration of *tip for tap.*]

tithe (tīth) *n.* **1a.** A tenth part of one's annual income contributed voluntarily or due as a tax, esp. for the support of the clergy or church. **b.** The institution or obligation of paying tithes. **2.** A tax or assessment of one tenth. **3a.** A tenth part. **b.** A very small part. ❖ *v.* **tithed, tith·ing, tithes** *—tr.* **1.** To contribute or pay a tenth part of (one's annual income). **2.** To levy a tithe on. *—intr.* To pay a tithe. [ME < OE *teotha.* See dekm̥ in App.] **—tith′a·ble** (tī′thə-bəl) *adj.* **—tith′er** *n.*

tith·ing (tī′thĭng) *n.* An administrative division consisting of ten householders in the old English system of frankpledge.

ti·ti¹ (tĭt′ī′, tē′tē′) *n., pl.* **-tis** **1.** A New World shrub or small tree (*Cyrilla racemiflora*) of warm swampy areas having leathery leaves and yellow fruit. **2.** An evergreen shrub or small tree (*Cliftonia monophylla*) of the southeast United States having glossy leathery leaves and winged fruit. [?]

ti·ti² (tē-tē′) *n., pl.* **-tis** Any of various small long-tailed arboreal monkeys of the genus *Callicebus,* living in tropical regions of South America. [Sp. *titi* < Aymara *titi.*]

ti·tian (tĭsh′ən) *n.* A brownish orange. [After TITIAN.]

Titian 1488?–1576. Italian painter known esp. for his vigorous colors and his compositional use of backgrounds. **—Ti′tian·esque′** *adj.*

Ti·ti·ca·ca (tĭt′ĭ-kä′kə, tē′tē-kä′kä), **Lake** A freshwater lake of South America in the Andes on the Bolivia-Peru border.

tit·il·late (tĭt′l-āt′) *v.* **-lat·ed, -lat·ing, -lates** *—tr.* **1.** To stimulate by touching lightly; tickle. **2.** To excite (another) pleasurably, superficially, or erotically. *—intr.* To excite another, esp. in a superficial pleasurable manner. [Lat. *tītillāre, tītillāt-,* to tickle.] **—tit′il·lat′er** *n.* **—tit′il·la′tion** *n.* **—tit′il·la′tive** *adj.*

tit·i·vate (tĭt′ə-vāt′) *tr.v.* **-vat·ed, -vat·ing, -vates** To make decorative additions to; spruce up. [Alteration of earlier *tidivate :* perh. TIDY + (ELE)VATE.] **—tit′i·va′tion** *n.*

tit·lark (tĭt′lärk′) *n.* See **pipit.** [*tit-,* as in TIT(MOUSE) + LARK¹.]

ti·tle (tīt′l) *n.* **1.** An identifying name given to a book, play, film, musical composition, or other work. **2.** A general or descriptive heading, as of a book chapter. **3a.** Written material in a film or television show, typically presenting credits, narration, or dialogue. Often used in the plural. **b.** A written piece of translated dialogue superimposed at the bottom of the frame during a film; a subtitle. **4.** *Law* A heading that names a document, statute, or proceeding. **5.** A division of a law book, declaration, or bill, generally larger than a section or an article. **6.** A written work that is published or about to be published. **7.** *Law* **a.** The coincidence of all the elements that constitute the fullest legal right to control and dispose of property or a claim. **b.** The aggregate evidence that gives rise to a legal right of possession or control. **c.** The instrument, such as a deed, that constitutes this evidence. **8a.** Something that provides a basis for or justifies a claim. **b.** A legitimate or alleged right. **9.** A formal appellation attached to the name of a person or family by virtue of office, rank, hereditary privilege, noble birth, or attainment or used as a mark of respect. **10.** A descriptive name; an epithet. **11.** *Sports* A championship. **12.** *Ecclesiastical* **a.** A source of income or area of work required of a candidate for ordination in the Church of England. **b.** A Roman Catholic church in or near Rome having a cardinal for its nominal head. ❖ *tr.v.* **-tled, -tling, -tles** **1.** To give a title to; entitle. **2.** To call by a name; style. [ME < OE *titul,* superscription, and < OFr. *title,* title, both < Lat. *titulus.*]

ti·tled (tīt′ld) *adj.* Having a title, esp. a noble title.

ti·tle·hold·er (tīt′l-hōl′dər) *n.* **1.** One, esp. a champion, who holds a title. **2.** One that holds legal title to something.

title page *n.* A front page of a book with its title, author and publisher names, and place of publication.

ti·tlist (tīt′lĭst, -l-ĭst) *n.* The holder of a competitive title; a champion: *a chess titlist.*

tit·man (tĭt′mən) *n. New England & Upstate New York* **1.** A runt, esp. a piglet. **2.** A small person. [TIT¹ + MAN.]

tit·mouse (tĭt′mous′) *n., pl.* **-mice** (-mīs′) Any of numerous small insect-eating passerine birds of the family Paridae, including esp. members of the genus *Parus,* such as the chickadee. [Alteration of ME *titmose :* tit- (prob. < ON *tittr,* titmouse) + *mose,* titmouse (< OE *māse*).]

Ti·to (tē′tō), Marshal. Orig. Josip Broz. 1892–1980. Yugoslavian politician who served as president (1953–80). **—Ti′to·ism** *n.*

ti·trant (tī′trənt) *n.* A substance, such as a solution, of known concentration used in titration.

ti·trate (tī′trāt′) *tr. & intr.v.* **-trat·ed, -trat·ing, -trates** To determine the concentration of (a solution) by titration or perform the act of titration. [< Fr. *titrer* < *titre,* titer. See TITER.] **—ti′trat·a·ble** *adj.* **—ti′tra′tor** *n.*

ti·tra·tion (tī-trā′shən) *n.* The process, act, or method of determining the concentration of a substance in solution by adding to it a standard reagent of known concentration in measured amounts until a reaction of definite and known proportion is completed and then calculating the unknown concentration.

ti·tre (tī′tər) *n.* Variant of **titer.**

ti·tri·met·ric (tī′trə-mĕt′rĭk) *adj.* Of or relating to measurement by titration. **—ti′tri·met′ri·cal·ly** *adv.*

tit·ter (tĭt′ər) *intr.v.* **-tered, -ter·ing, -ters** To laugh in a restrained nervous way; giggle. ❖ *n.* A nervous giggle. [Prob. imit.] —**tit′ter•er** *n.* —**tit′ter•ing•ly** *adv.*

tit•tle (tĭt′l) *n.* **1.** A small diacritic mark, such as an accent, vowel mark, or dot over an *i*. **2.** The tiniest bit; an iota. [ME *titil* < Med.Lat. *titulus*, diacritical mark < Lat., title, superscription.]

tit•tle-tat•tle (tĭt′l-tăt′l) *n.* Petty gossip; trivial talk. [Reduplication of TATTLE.] —**tit′tle-tat′tle** *v.*

tit•tup (tĭt′əp) *intr.v.* -**tuped,** -**tup•ing,** -**tups** or -**tupped,** -**tup•ping,** -**tups** To move in a lively capering manner; prance. ❖ *n.* A lively capering manner of moving or walking; a prance. [Perh. imit. of the sound of a horse's hooves.]

tit•u•ba•tion (tĭch′ə-bā′shən) *n.* The staggering or stumbling gait characteristic of certain nervous disorders. [Lat. *titubātiō, titubātiōn-,* a staggering < *titubātus,* p. part. of *titubāre,* to stagger.]

tit•u•lar (tĭch′ə-lər) *adj.* **1.** Relating to, having the nature of, or constituting a title. **2a.** Existing in name only; nominal. **b.** Bearing the title of a church or monastery no longer active. **3.** Bearing a title. **4.** Derived from a title: *the titular role in a play.* ❖ *n.* One holding a title. [< Lat. *titulus,* title.]

tit•u•lar•y (tĭch′ə-lĕr′ē) *n., pl.* -**ies** A titleholder; a titular.

Ti•tus[1] (tī′təs) A.D. 39–81. Emperor of Rome (79–81) who was instrumental in the capture of Jerusalem (70).

Ti•tus[2] (tī′təs) *n.* See table at **Bible.**

Titus, Saint. 1st cent. A.D. Christian leader and companion of Saint Paul. An epistle of the Bible is addressed to him.

Ti•u (tē′oō) *n. Mythology* The Germanic god of war and the sky. [OE *Tīw.* See **dyeu-** in App.]

Ti•wa (tē′wä) *n., pl.* **Tiwa** or -**was 1.** A member of a group of Pueblo peoples of northern New Mexico. **2.** The group of Tanoan languages spoken by the Tiwa.

tiz•zy (tĭz′ē) *n., pl.* -**zies** *Slang* A state of nervous excitement or confusion; a dither. [?]

TKO *abbr.* technical knockout

Tl The symbol for the element **thallium.**

Tlal•ne•pan•tla (tläl′nə-pänt′lä, -nĕ-) A city of S-central Mexico N of Mexico City. Pop. 778,173.

Tla•loc (tlä-lôk′) *n. Mythology* The rain god of the Aztecs.

TLC *abbr.* tender loving care

Tlin•git (tlĭng′gĭt, -kĭt, klĭng′kĭt) *n., pl.* **Tlingit** or -**gits 1.** A member of a Native American people inhabiting the coastal and island areas of southeast Alaska. **2.** The language of the Tlingit.

T lymphocyte *n.* See **T cell.**

Tm[1] The symbol for the element **thulium.**

Tm[2] *abbr.* Timothy

TM *abbr.* **1.** trademark **2.** transcendental meditation

tme•sis (tmē′sĭs, mē′-) *n., pl.* -**ses** (-sēz) Separation of the parts of a compound word by one or more intervening words; for example, *where I go ever* instead of *wherever I go.* [LLat. *tmēsis* < Gk., a cutting < *temnein,* to cut.]

TN *abbr.* Tennessee

tn. *abbr.* ton

Tnpk. *abbr.* turnpike

TNT (tē′ĕn-tē′) *n.* A crystalline compound, $CH_3C_6H_2(NO_2)_3$, used as a high explosive. [T(RI)N(ITRO)T(OLUENE).]

to (toō; tə *when unstressed*) *prep.* **1a.** In a direction toward so as to reach: *went to the city.* **b.** Toward: *turned to me.* **2a.** Reaching as far as: *The water was clear to the bottom.* **b.** To the extent or degree of: *loved him to distraction.* **c.** With the resultant condition of: *nursed her back to health.* **3.** Toward a given state: *helping women to equality.* **4.** In contact with; against: *faces pressed to the windows.* **5.** In front of: *face to face.* **6.** Used to indicate appropriation or possession: *the top to the jar.* **7.** Concerning; regarding: *an answer to my letter.* **8.** In a particular relationship with: *parallel to the road.* **9.** As an accompaniment or a complement of: *danced to the tune.* **10.** Composing; constituting: *two cups to a pint.* **11.** In accord with: *suited to her abilities.* **12.** As compared with: *superior to the others.* **13a.** Before: *The time is ten to five.* **b.** Up till; until: *worked from nine to five.* **14a.** For the purpose of: *out to lunch.* **b.** In honor of: *a toast to the queen.* **15a.** Used before a verb to indicate the infinitive: *I'd like to go.* **b.** Used alone when the infinitive is understood: *Go if you want to.* **16a.** Used to indicate the relationship of a verb with its complement: *refer to a dictionary.* **b.** Used with a reflexive pronoun to indicate exclusivity or separateness: *had it to ourselves.* ❖ *adv.* **1.** In one direction; toward a person or thing. **2.** Into a shut or closed position: *pushed the door to.* **3.** Into a state of consciousness: *The patient came to.* **4.** Into a state of action or attentiveness: *sat down for lunch and fell to.* **5.** *Nautical* Into the wind. [ME < OE *tō.*]

toad (tōd) *n.* **1.** Any of numerous tailless amphibians chiefly of the family Bufonidae, related to the frogs but more terrestrial and with a broader body and rougher drier skin. **2.** The horned lizard. **3.** A repulsive person. [ME *tode* < OE *tādige.*]

toad•eat•er (tōd′ē′tər) *n.* A toady. [Orig. an eater or pretend eater of poisonous toads who was part of a scam.]

toad•fish (tōd′fĭsh′) *n., pl.* **toadfish** or -**fish•es** Any of various scaleless fishes of the family Batrachoididae of warm waters, having a broad flattened head and a wide mouth.

toad•flax (tōd′flăks′) *n.* **1.** Any of various plants of the genus *Linaria,* having narrow leaves and spurred two-lipped flowers. **2.** See **butter-and-eggs.**

toad•stone (tōd′stōn′) *n.* A stone once worn as a charm and believed to have been formed in the body of a toad.

toad•stool (tōd′stoōl′) *n.* An inedible or poisonous fungus with an umbrella-shaped fruiting body.

toad•y (tō′dē) *n., pl.* -**ies** A person who flatters or defers to others for self-serving reasons; a sycophant. ❖ *tr. & intr.v.* -**ied,** -**y•ing,** -**ies** To be a toady to or behave like a toady. [< TOAD.]

to and fro *adv.* Back and forth.

to-and-fro (toō′ən-frō′) *n.* **1.** Movement back and forth; reciprocating movement. **2.** Debate over an issue; vacillation.

toast[1] (tōst) *v.* **toast•ed, toast•ing, toasts** —*tr.* **1.** To heat and brown (bread, for example) by placing in a toaster or an oven or close to a fire. **2.** To warm thoroughly, as before a fire. —*intr.* To become toasted. ❖ *n.* **1.** Sliced bread heated and browned. **2.** *Slang* One that is doomed, in trouble, or unworthy of further consideration. [ME *tosten* < OFr. *toster* < VLat. **tostāre,* freq. of Lat. *torrēre,* to parch, burn. See **ters-** in App.]

toast[2] (tōst) *n.* **1a.** The act of raising a glass and drinking in honor of a person or thing. **b.** A proposal to drink to someone or something or a speech given before such a drink. **c.** One honored by a toast. **2.** A person receiving much attention or acclaim. ❖ *v.* **toast•ed, toast•ing, toasts** —*tr.* To drink to the honor of. —*intr.* To propose or drink a toast. [Perh. < TOAST[1], from using spiced toast to flavor drinks.]

toast•er (tō′stər) *n.* A mechanical device used to toast bread, esp. by exposure to electrically heated wire coils.

toaster oven *n.* An electrical appliance that can be used as either a toaster or an oven.

toast•mas•ter (tōst′măs′tər) *n.* A man who proposes the toasts and introduces the speakers at a banquet.

toast•mis•tress (tōst′mĭs′trĭs) *n.* A woman who proposes the toasts and introduces the speakers at a banquet.

toast•y (tō′stē) *adj.* -**i•er,** -**i•est** Pleasantly warm.

to•bac•co (tə-băk′ō) *n., pl.* -**cos** or -**coes 1.** Any of various plants of the genus *Nicotiana,* esp. *N. tabacum,* native to tropical America and widely cultivated for their leaves, which are dried and processed chiefly for use in snuff or for smoking. **2.** The leaves of these plants. **3.** Products made from these plants. **4.** The habit of smoking tobacco. **5.** A crop of tobacco. [Sp. *tabaco,* poss. of Caribbean orig.]

tobacco budworm *n.* The destructive larva of a noctuid moth (*Heliothis virescens*) that feeds on tobacco plants.

tobacco hornworm *n.* The destructive larva of a hawk moth (*Manduca sexta*) of the southern United States and the West Indies that feeds on the leaves of tobacco plants.

tobacco mosaic virus *n.* A retrovirus that causes mosaic in tobacco and some other plants.

to•bac•co•nist (tə-băk′ə-nĭst) *n.* A dealer in tobacco and smoking supplies.

tobacco worm *n.* See **tobacco hornworm.**

To•ba•go (tə-bā′gō) An island of Trinidad and Tobago in the SE West Indies NE of Trinidad; became a British colony in 1899 and gained independence with Trinidad in 1962.

to-be (toō-bē′) *adj.* That is to be; future. Often used postpositively and in combination: *a graduate-to-be.*

To•bit[1] (tō′bĭt) In the Bible, a Hebrew captive in Nineveh. [Gk. *Tōbit* < Heb. *ṭôbīyāh,* Yahweh (is) my good : *ṭôb,* good + -*î,* my + *yāh,* Yahweh.]

To•bit[2] (tō′bĭt) *n.* See table at **Bible.** [After TOBIT[1].]

to•bog•gan (tə-bŏg′ən) *n.* A long narrow runnerless sled made of thin boards curled upward in front. ❖ *intr.v.* -**ganed,** -**gan•ing,** -**gans 1.** To coast or ride on a toboggan. **2.** *Slang* To decline or fall rapidly. [Canadian Fr. *tobagan* < Micmac *topaghan.*] —**to•bog′gan•er, to•bog′gan•ist** *n.*

To•bol (tə-bôl′) A river rising in the SE Ural Mts. and flowing c. 1,690 km (1,050 mi) to the Irtysh R.

to•by also **To•by** (tō′bē) *n., pl.* -**bies** A drinking mug, usu. in the shape of a stout man wearing a large three-cornered hat. [After *Toby,* a nickname for *Tobias.*]

To•can•tins (tō′kăn-tēns′) A river, c. 2,639 km (1,640 mi), flowing from central Brazil near Brasília N to the Pará R.

toc•ca•ta (tə-kä′tə) *n.* A virtuoso composition, usu. for the organ or another keyboard instrument, in free style with brilliant passagework. [Ital. < fem. p. part. of *toccare,* to touch < VLat. **toccāre.*]

To•char•i•an (tō-kâr′ē-ən, -kär′-, -kär′-) *n.* **1.** A member of a people living in Chinese Turkistan until about the tenth century. **2.** Either of the two Indo-European languages of this people, Tocharian A and Tocharian B, recorded from the seventh to the ninth century. **3.** A branch of the Indo-European language family consisting of these two languages. [< Lat. *Tocharī,* the Tocharians < Gk. *Tokharoi.*]

to•col•o•gy also **to•kol•o•gy** (tō-kŏl′ə-jē) *n.* The science of childbirth; midwifery or obstetrics. [Gk. *tokos,* childbirth; see **tek-** in App.]

to•coph•er•ol (tō-kŏf′ə-rôl′, -rōl′) *n.* Any of a group of closely related, fat-soluble alcohols constituting vitamin E and similar compounds. [Gk. *tokos,* offspring. See TOCOLOGY + Gk. *pherein,* to carry; see **bher-**[1] in App.]

Tocque•ville (tōk′vĭl, tôk′-, tôk-vēl′), **Alexis Charles Henri Clérel de** 1805–59. French politician, traveler, and historian who

tobacco mosaic virus
top side of a tobacco leaf

toboggan

toby

toggle bolt

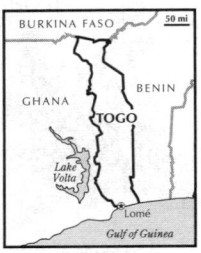

Togo

wrote *Democracy in America* (1835).

toc·sin (tŏk′sĭn) *n.* **1a.** An alarm sounded on a bell. **b.** A bell used to sound an alarm. **2.** A warning; an omen. [Fr., alteration of *toquassen* < OFr. *touque-sain* < O Provençal *tocasenh* : *tocar*, to strike (< VLat. **toccāre*) + *senh*, bell (< LLat. *signum* < Lat., signal; see SIGN).]

tod (tŏd) *n. Chiefly British* **1.** A unit of weight for wool, esp. one equivalent to about 28 pounds (12.7 kilograms). **2.** A bushy clump, as of ivy. [ME *todde*.]

to·day (tə-dā′) *n.* The present day, time, or age. ❖ *adv.* **1.** During or on the present day. **2.** During or at the present time. ❖ *adj.* Of the present time. [ME *to dai* < OE *tō dæge* : *tō*, to + *dæge*, dative of *dæg*, day.]

tod·dle (tŏd′l) *intr.v.* **-dled, -dling, -dles** **1.** To walk with short, unsteady steps. **2.** To walk leisurely; stroll. ❖ *n.* An unsteady gait. [?]

tod·dler (tŏd′lər) *n.* **1.** One who toddles, esp. a young child learning to walk. **2.** A size of clothing for children between the ages of about one and three.

tod·dy (tŏd′ē) *n., pl.* **-dies** **1.** A hot toddy. **2a.** The sweet sap of several tropical Asian palm trees, esp. palmyra and *Caryota urens*, used as a beverage. **b.** A liquor fermented from this sap. [Hindi *tāṛī*, sap of palm < *tāṛ*, palm < Skt. *tālaḥ*, perh. of Dravidian orig.]

to-do (tə-dōō′) *n., pl.* **-dos** (-dōōz′) *Informal* A commotion or stir.

to·dy (tō′dē) *n., pl.* **-dies** Any of various small birds of the family Todidae of the West Indies, having colorful, predominantly green plumage and a red throat. [Prob. < Fr. *todier* < NLat. *Todus*, genus name < Lat. *todus*, a small bird.]

toe (tō) *n.* **1a.** One of the digits of a vertebrate. **b.** The forepart of a foot or hoof. **c.** The terminal segment of an invertebrate's limb. **2.** The part of a sock, shoe, or boot that covers the digits of the foot. **3.** The lowest, outermost, or endmost part, as: **a.** The part of the head of a golf club farthest from the shaft. **b.** The part of a vertical shaft that turns in a bearing. **c.** The lowest part of an embankment or dam. **4.** The lowest part, as of an embankment or a dam. ❖ *v.* **toed, toe·ing, toes** **-tr.** **1.** To touch, kick, or reach with the toe. **2.** To drive (a golf ball) with the toe of the club. **3.** To set or adjust at an oblique angle. Used with *in* or *out.* **4a.** To drive (a nail or spike) at an oblique angle. **b.** To fasten or secure with obliquely driven nails or spikes. **-intr.** To stand, walk, move, or be formed with the toes pointed in a specified direction: *He toes out.* **—idioms: on (one's) toes** Ready to act; alert. **step (or tread) on (someone's) toes** To hurt, offend, or encroach on the feelings, actions, or province of. **toe the line (or mark) 1.** To adhere to doctrines or rules conscientiously; conform. **2.** *Sports & Games* To touch a mark or line with the toe or hands in readiness for the start of a race or competition. [ME < OE *tā.* See **deik-** in App.]

toe·cap (tō′kăp′) *n.* A reinforced covering of leather or metal for the toe of a shoe or boot.

toe crack *n.* A sand crack in the front part of a horse's hoof.

toed (tōd) *adj.* **1.** Having a toe, esp. of a specified number or kind. Often used in combination: *even-toed.* **2a.** Driven obliquely: *a toed nail.* **b.** Secured by toed nails.

toe dance *n.* A dance that is performed on the toes, esp. in ballet. **—toe dancer** *n.*

TOEFL (tō′fəl) A trademark for a standardized examination for proficiency in English as a foreign language.

toe·hold (tō′hōld′) *n.* **1.** A small indentation or ledge on which the foot can find support in climbing. **2.** A slight or initial advantage useful for future progress. **3.** *Sports* A wrestling hold in which one competitor wrenches the other's foot.

toe loop *n.* A jump in figure skating in which the skater, moving backward, takes off from the back outer edge of one skate, makes a full spin in the air, and lands on the back outer edge of the same skate.

toe·nail (tō′nāl′) *n.* **1.** The nail on a toe. **2.** A nail driven obliquely, as to join vertical and horizontal beams. **—toe′nail′** *v.*

toe shoe *n.* A ballet slipper with a hardened, reinforced toe that enables a dancer to perform or dance on the toes.

toff (tŏf) *n. Chiefly British Slang* A member of the upper classes, esp. one who is elegantly dressed. [Prob. var. of TUFT, a gold tassel worn by titled students at Oxford and Cambridge.]

tof·fee (tŏ′fē, tôf′ē) *n.* A hard chewy candy made of brown sugar or molasses and butter. [Alteration of TAFFY.]

toft (tŏft, tôft) *n. Chiefly British* **1.** A homestead. **2.** A hillock. [ME < OE < ON *topt.* See **dem-** in App.]

to·fu (tō′fōō) *n.* A protein-rich food coagulated from an extract of soybeans. [J. *tōfu* < Chin. *dòufu* : *dòu*, bean + *fú*, curdled.]

tog (tŏg, tôg) *Informal n.* **1. togs** Clothes: *gardening togs.* **2.** A coat or cloak. ❖ *tr.v.* **togged, tog·ging, togs** To dress or clothe. [Short for obsolete *togeman* < obsolete Fr. *togue*, cloak < Lat. *toga*, garment. See TOGA.]

to·ga (tō′gə) *n.* **1.** A loose one-piece outer garment worn in public by male citizens in ancient Rome. **2.** A robe of office; a professional or ceremonial gown. [Lat. See **(s)teg-** in App.] **—to′gaed** (tō′gəd) *adj.*

to·geth·er (tə-gĕth′ər) *adv.* **1.** In or into a single group, mass, or place: *gather together.* **2.** In or into contact: *mixed together.* **3a.** In

association with or in relationship to one another; mutually or reciprocally: *getting along together.* **b.** By joint or cooperative effort: *ironed together.* **4.** Regarded collectively; in total: *worth more than all of us together.* **5.** In or into a unified structure or arrangement: *put it together.* **6.** Simultaneously: *rang out together.* **7.** In harmony or accord: *stand together.* **8.** *Informal* Into an effective, coherent condition: *Get yourself together.* ❖ *adj. Slang* **1.** Emotionally stable and effective in performance: *She's really together.* **2.** In tune with what is going on; hip. [ME < OE *tōgædere.*] **—to·geth′er·ness** *n.*

tog·gle (tŏg′əl) *n.* **1.** A pin, rod, or crosspiece fitted or inserted into a loop in a rope, chain, or strap to tighten, prevent slipping, or hold an attached object. **2.** A device or apparatus with a toggle joint. ❖ *v.* **-gled, -gling, -gles** **-tr.** To furnish or fasten with a toggle. **-intr.** To alternate between two or more electronic, mechanical, or computer-related options, usu. by the operation of a single switch or keystroke. [?]

toggle bolt *n.* A fastener consisting of a threaded bolt and a spring-loaded toggle, used to secure objects to thin or hollow walls.

toggle joint *n.* A joint made of two arms attached by a pivot shaped like an elbow, allowing force to be exerted at the ends of the arms as the joint is expanded.

toggle switch *n.* A switch that uses a toggle joint with a spring to open or close an electric circuit as an attached lever is pushed through a small arc.

To·gliat·ti also **Tol·yat·ti** (tōl-yä′tē, tô-lyät′tē) A city of W Russia on the Volga R. NW of Samara. Pop. 594,000.

To·go (tō′gō′) A country of W Africa on the Gulf of Guinea; gained independence in 1960. Cap. Lomé. Pop. 3,928,000.

togue (tōg) *n.* See **lake trout**. [Canadian Fr. < Micmac *atogh-waasu.*]

To·ho·no O'o·dham (tō-hō′nō ō′ə-däm) *n., pl.* **Tohono O'o·dham** or **Tohono O'o·dhams** See **Papago**.

toil¹ (toil) *intr.v.* **toiled, toil·ing, toils** **1.** To labor continuously; work strenuously. **2.** To proceed with difficulty: *toiling over the mountains.* ❖ *n.* **1.** Exhausting labor or effort. **2.** *Archaic* Strife; contention. [ME *toilen* < AN *toiler*, to stir about < Lat. *tudiculāre* < *tudicula*, a machine for bruising olives, dim. of *tudes*, hammer.] **—toil′er** *n.*

toil² (toil) *n.* **1.** Something that binds, snares, or entangles; an entrapment. Often used in the plural: *caught in the toils of despair.* **2.** *Archaic* A net for trapping game. [Fr. *toile*, cloth < OFr. *teile* < Lat. *tēla*, web.]

toile (twäl) *n.* A sheer fabric, such as linen. [Fr. See TOIL².]

toi·let (toi′lĭt) *n.* **1a.** A fixture for defecation and urination, consisting of a bowl fitted with a hinged seat and connected to a waste pipe and a flushing apparatus; a privy. **b.** A room or booth containing such a fixture. **2.** The act or process of dressing or grooming oneself. **3.** Dress; attire; costume. **4.** The cleansing of a body area as part of a surgical or medical procedure. **5.** *Archaic* A dressing table. [Fr. *toilette*, clothes bag < OFr. *tellette*, dim. of *teile*, cloth. See TOIL².]

toilet paper *n.* Thin absorbent paper, usu. in rolls, used to clean oneself after defecation or urination.

toi·let·ry (toi′lĭ-trē) *n., pl.* **-ries** An article, such as toothpaste or a hairbrush, used in personal grooming or dressing.

toi·lette (twä-lĕt′) *n.* **1.** The act or process of dressing or grooming oneself; toilet. **2.** A person's dress or style of dress. **3.** A gown or costume. [Fr. See TOILET.]

toilet tissue *n.* See **toilet paper**.

toilet training *n.* The training of a child to use a toilet.

toilet water *n.* A scented liquid with a high alcohol content used in bathing or applied as a skin freshener.

toil·some (toil′səm) *adj.* Characterized by or requiring toil. **—toil′some·ly** *adv.* **—toil′some·ness** *n.*

To·jo Hi·de·ki (tō′jō′ hē′dĕ-kē) 1884–1948. Japanese army officer who ruled as dictator (1941–44).

to·ka·mak (tō′kə-mäk′, tŏk′ə-) *n.* A doughnut-shaped chamber used in fusion research in which a plasma is heated and confined by magnetic fields. [Russ. < *to(roidal'naya) kam(era s) ak(sial'nym magnitnym polem)*, toroidal chamber with axial magnetic field.]

To·ka·ra Islands (tō-kär′ə, -kä′rä) A group of islands of Japan in the N Ryukyu group S of Kyushu.

To·kay (tō-kā′) *n.* **1.** A variety of white grape originally grown near Tokaj (formerly Tokay), a town of eastern Hungary. **2.** A wine made from this grape.

toke (tōk) *Slang n.* A puff on a cigarette, a marijuana cigarette, or a pipe of hashish or another mind-altering substance. [Perh. < Sp. *toque*, a hit < *tocar*, to touch < VLat. *toccāre.*] **—toke** *v.*

To·ke·lau Islands (tō′kə-lou′) An island group of New Zealand in the central Pacific in the N Ryukyu Is. N of Samoa.

to·ken (tō′kən) *n.* **1.** Something serving as an indication, proof, or expression of something else; a sign. **2.** Something that signifies or evidences authority, validity, or identity: *The scepter is a token of regal status.* **3.** A distinguishing feature or characteristic. **4.** One that represents a group, as an employee whose presence is used to prevent the employer from being accused of discrimination. **5.** A keepsake or souvenir. **6.** A piece of stamped metal used as a substitute for currency. ❖ *tr.v.* **-kened, -ken·ing, -kens** To betoken or symbolize; portend. ❖ *adj.* **1.** Done as an indication or pledge. **2a.** Perfunctory; minimal: *token resistance.* **b.** Merely symbolic: *refused to be the token woman on the committee.* ***—idioms:*** **by the same token** In like manner; similarly. **in token of** As an indication of. [ME < OE *tācen.* See **deik-** in App.]

to·ken·ism (tō′kə-nĭz′əm) *n.* **1.** The policy of making only a symbolic gesture, as toward racial integration. **2.** The practice of hiring or appointing a token number of people from underrepresented groups, as to deflect criticism.

To·klas (tō′kləs), **Alice B.** 1877–1967. Amer. writer who was the longtime companion of Gertrude Stein.

to·kol·o·gy (tō-kŏl′ə-jē) *n.* Variant of **tocology.**

to·ko·no·ma (tō′kə-nō′mə) *n.* A niche or an alcove in a Japanese home for displaying a piece of art. [J. : *toko,* alcove + *no,* of + *ma,* room.]

Tok Pis·in (tŏk′ pĭs′ĭn) *n.* A pidgin based on English and spoken in Papua New Guinea. [Pidgin E. : E. TALK + E. PIDGIN.]

To·ku·ga·wa (tō′ko͝o-gä′wä) *adj.* Of or relating to a family of shoguns that ruled Japan from 1603 to 1867, a period marked by centralized feudalism and exclusionary policies against the West.

To·ku·shi·ma (tō′kə-shē′mä) A city of E Shikoku, Japan, on the Inland Sea. Pop. 265,243.

To·ky·o (tō′kē-ō′, -kyō) Formerly **E·do** (ĕd′ō) The cap. of Japan, in E-central Honshu on **Tokyo Bay,** an inlet of the Pacific; founded in the 12th cent. Pop. 8,080,286.

to·la (tō′lə, tō-lä′) *n.* A unit of weight used in India, equal to the weight of one silver rupee (11.7 grams or 180 troy grains). [Hindi *tolā* < Skt. *tulā,* weight. See **telə-** in App.]

tol·booth also **toll·booth** (tōl′bo͞oth′) *n. Scots* A prison; a jail. [ME *tolbothe,* town hall containing customs offices and prison cells : *tol,* toll; see TOLL[1] + *bothe,* booth; see BOOTH.]

tol·bu·ta·mide (tŏl-byo͞o′tə-mīd′) *n.* A white powder, $C_{12}H_{18}N_2O_3S$, that lowers the level of sugar in the blood and is used in the treatment of diabetes. [TOL(U) + BUT– + AMIDE.]

told (tōld) *v.* Past tense and past participle of **tell[1].**

tole also **tôle** (tōl) *n.* A lacquered or enameled metalware, usu. gilded and elaborately painted. [Fr. *tôle,* sheet metal, var. of *table,* table, slab < OFr. < Lat. *tabula,* board.]

To·le·do[1] (tə-lē′dō) **1.** (*also* tō-lĕ′thō) A city of central Spain near the Tagus R. SSW of Madrid; a provincial cap. (712–1031) of Moorish Spain. Pop. 57,778. **2.** A city of NW OH on Lake Erie; incorp. 1837. Pop. 313,619.

To·le·do[2] also **to·le·do** (tə-lē′dō) *n., pl.* **-dos** A fine-tempered sword or steel sword blade made in Toledo, Spain.

tol·er·a·ble (tŏl′ər-ə-bəl) *adj.* **1.** Capable of being tolerated; endurable. **2.** Fairly good. See Syns at **average.** **—tol′er·a·bil′i·ty, tol′er·a·ble·ness** *n.* **—tol′er·a·bly** *adv.*

tol·er·ance (tŏl′ər-əns) *n.* **1.** The capacity for or the practice of recognizing and respecting the beliefs or practices of others. **2a.** Leeway for variation from a standard. **b.** The permissible deviation from a specified value of a structural dimension, often expressed as a percent. **3.** The capacity to endure hardship or pain. **4.** *Medicine* **a.** Physiological resistance to a poison. **b.** The capacity to absorb a drug continuously or in large doses without adverse effect. **5a.** Acceptance of a tissue graft or transplant without immunological rejection. **b.** Unresponsiveness to an antigen that normally produces an immunological reaction.

tol·er·ant (tŏl′ər-ənt) *adj.* **1.** Inclined to tolerate the beliefs, practices, or traits of others; forbearing. See Syns at **broad-minded.** **2.** Able to withstand or endure an adverse environmental condition. **—tol′er·ant·ly** *adv.*

tol·er·ate (tŏl′ə-rāt′) *tr.v.* **-at·ed, -at·ing, -ates** **1.** To allow without prohibiting or opposing; permit. **2.** To recognize and respect (the rights, beliefs, or practices of others). **3.** To put up with; endure. See Syns at **bear[1].** **4.** *Medicine* To have tolerance for (a substance or pathogen). [Lat. *tolerāre, tolerāt-,* to bear. See **telə-** in App.] **—tol′er·a′tive** *adj.* **—tol′er·a′tor** *n.*

tol·er·a·tion (tŏl′ə-rā′shən) *n.* **1.** Tolerance with respect to the actions and beliefs of others. **2.** Official recognition of the right to hold dissenting opinions, esp. on religion.

tol·i·dine (tŏl′ĭ-dēn′) *n.* Any of several isomeric bases, $C_{14}H_{16}N_2$, derived from toluene, one of which is used as an analytical reagent. [TOL(UENE) + –ID(E) + –INE[2].]

Tol·kien (tōl′kēn′, tŏl′-), **J(ohn) R(onald) R(euel)** 1892–1973. British philologist and writer of the fantasies *The Hobbit* (1937) and *The Lord of the Rings* (1954–55).

toll[1] (tōl) *n.* **1.** A fixed charge or tax for a privilege, esp. for passage across a bridge or along a road. **2.** A charge for a service, such as a long-distance telephone call. **3.** An amount or extent of loss or destruction, as of life, health, or property. ❖ *tr.v.* **tolled, toll·ing, tolls** **1.** To exact as a toll. **2.** To charge a fee for using (a structure, such as a bridge). [ME < OE, var. of *toln* < Med.Lat. *tolōnīum* < Lat. *telōnēum,* tollbooth < Gk. *telōneion* < *telōnēs,* tax collector < *telos,* tax. See **telə-** in App.]

toll[2] (tōl) *v.* **tolled, toll·ing, tolls** *—tr.* **1.** To sound (a large bell) slowly at regular intervals. **2.** To announce or summon by tolling. *—intr.* To sound in slowly repeated single tones. ❖ *n.* **1.** The act of tolling. **2.** The sound of a bell being struck. [ME *tollen,* to ring an alarm, perh. < *tollen,* to entice, pull, var. of *tillen* < OE *-tyllan.*]

toll·booth[1] (tōl′bo͞oth′) *n.* A booth where a toll is collected.

toll·booth[2] (tōl′bo͞oth′) *n.* Variant of **tolbooth.**

toll bridge *n.* A bridge at which a toll is charged for crossing.

toll call *n.* A telephone call for which a higher rate is charged than that standard for a local call.

toll·gate (tōl′gāt′) *n.* **1.** A gate barring passage, as to a road, until a toll is collected. **2.** A tollbooth equipped with a gate.

toll·house (tōl′hous′) *n.* **1.** A house adjoining a tollgate and occupied by a toll collector. **2.** See **tollbooth[1].**

Toll House cookie *n.* A trademark used for a cookie made with flour, butter, brown sugar, semisweet chocolate chips, and often chopped nuts.

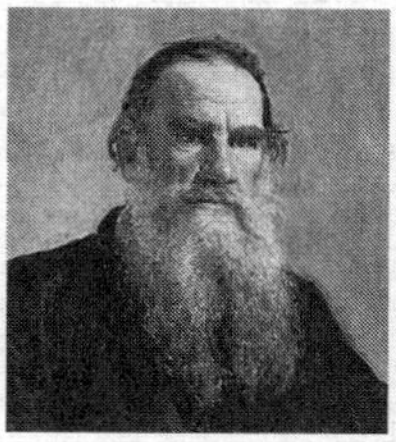

Leo Tolstoy
detail from an 1887 portrait by Ilja Repin (1844–1930)

Tol·stoy or **Tol·stoi** (tōl′stoi, tŏl′-, təl-stoi′), Count **Leo** or **Lev Nikolayevich** 1828–1910. Russian writer whose works include *War and Peace* (1864–69) and *Anna Karenina* (1873–76). **—Tol·stoy′an, Tol·stoi′an** *adj.*

Tol·tec (tŏl′tĕk′, tŏl′-) *n., pl.* **Toltec** or **-tecs** A member of a Nahuatl-speaking people of central and southern Mexico whose empire flourished from the 10th to the 12th century. [Sp. *tolteca* < Nahuatl *toltecatl,* artisan, mechanic.] **—Tol·tec′an** *adj.*

tol·u·ate (tŏl′yo͞o-āt′) *n.* A salt or ester of toluic acid.

To·lu·ca (tə-lo͞o′kə, tō-lo͞o′kä) A city of S-central Mexico W of Mexico City; founded 1530. Pop. 487,612.

tol·u·ene (tŏl′yo͞o-ēn′) also **tol·u·ol** (-ôl′, -ōl′, -ŏl′) *n.* A flammable liquid, $CH_3C_6H_5$, obtained from coal tar or petroleum and used in aviation fuel and other high-octane fuels, in dyestuffs and explosives, and as a solvent. [*tolu,* a resin < which it was orig. obtained (< Sp., after *Tolú,* seaport in NW Colombia) + –ENE.]

to·lu·ic acid (tə-lo͞o′ĭk) *n.* Any of three isomeric acids, $C_8H_8O_2$, derived from toluene. [TOLU(ENE) + –IC.]

to·lu·i·dine (tə-lo͞o′ĭ-dēn′) *n.* Any of three isomers, C_7H_9N, used to make dyes. [TOLU(ENE) + –ID(E) + –INE[2].]

Tol·yat·ti (tōl-yät′ē, tô-lyät′tē) See **Togliatti.**

tol·yl (tŏl′əl) *n.* The group C_7H_7, derived from toluene.

tom (tŏm) *n.* The male of various animals, esp. a male cat or turkey. [*Tom,* nickname for *Thomas.*]

Tom *n. Offensive* An Uncle Tom.

tom·a·hawk (tŏm′ə-hôk′) *n.* **1.** A light ax formerly used as a tool or weapon by certain Native American peoples. See Regional Note at **pone.** **2.** A similar implement or weapon. [Virginia Algonquian *tamahaac.*] **—tom′a·hawk′** *v.*

to·mal·ley (tə-măl′ē, tŏm′ăl′ē) *n., pl.* **-leys** The soft green liver of cooked lobster, considered a delicacy. [Galibi *tamali.*]

to·man (tō-män′) *n.* A gold coin formerly used in Persia worth 10,000 dinars. [Pers. *tūmān* < Turkic *tümen,* unit of 10,000.]

Tom and Jerry *n.* A hot drink consisting usu. of rum, a beaten egg, milk or water, sugar, and spices. [After Corinthian *Tom* and *Jerry* Hawthorn, characters in *Life in London,* a novel by Pierce Egan (1772–1849).]

to·ma·til·lo (tō′mə-tē′yō, -tēl′yō) *n., pl.* **-los** **1.** A species of ground cherry *(Physalis ixocarpa)* native to Mexico and having an edible yellow to purple viscid fruit. **2.** The fruit of this plant. [Am.Sp., dim. of *tomate,* tomato. See TOMATO.]

to·ma·to (tə-mā′tō, -mä′-) *n., pl.* **-toes** **1.** A widely cultivated South American plant *(Lycopersicon esculentum)* having edible, fleshy, usu. red fruit. **2.** The fruit of this plant. [Alteration of Sp. *tomate* < Nahuatl *tomatl.*] **—to·ma′to·ey** (-tō-ē) *adj.*

tomato fruit·worm (fro͞ot′wûrm′) *n.* The destructive larva of a noctuid moth *(Heliothis zea)* of the United States that burrows into the fruit of tomato plants.

tomato hornworm *n.* The destructive larva of a North American hawk moth *(Manduca quinquemaculata)* that feeds on the leaves of tomato plants.

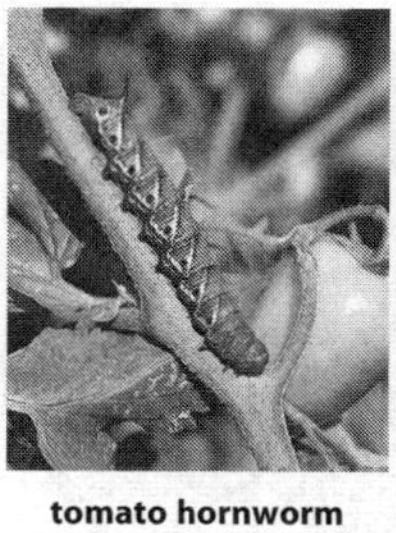

tomato hornworm
Manduca quinquemaculata

tomb (to͞om) *n.* **1.** A grave or other place of burial. **2.** A vault or chamber for burial of the dead. **3.** A monument commemorating the dead. [ME < OFr. *tombe* < LLat. *tumba* < Gk. *tumbos.*]

tom·bac (tŏm′băk) *n.* An alloy of copper with zinc and sometimes other metals, used in making inexpensive jewelry. [Fr. < Du. *tombak* < Malay *tembaga.*]

Tom·baugh (tŏm′bô′), **Clyde William** 1906–97. Amer. astronomer who discovered the planet Pluto (1930).

Tom·big·bee (tŏm-bĭg′bē) A river, c. 644 km (400 mi), rising in NE MS and flowing through W AL to join the Alabama R.

tom·bo·lo (tŏm′bə-lō′) *n., pl.* **-los** A sandbar that connects an island to the mainland or to another island. [Ital. < Lat. *tumulus,* mound. See TUMULUS.]

tom·boy (tŏm′boi′) *n.* A girl considered boyish or masculine.

tomb·stone (to͞om′stōn′) *n.* A stone placed over a grave as a marker; a gravestone.

tom·cat (tŏm′kăt′) *n.* A male cat. ❖ *intr.v.* **-cat·ted, -cat·ting, -cats** *Slang* To pursue women sexually. Used of men.

tom·cod (tŏm′kŏd′) *n., pl.* **tomcod** or **-cods** Either of two edible marine fishes, *Microgadus tomcod* of northern Atlantic waters or *M. proximus* of northern Pacific waters.

Tom Collins *n.* A drink consisting of gin, lemon or lime juice,

ă	pat	oi	boy
ā	pay	ou	out
âr	care	o͝o	took
ä	father	o͞o	boot
ĕ	pet	ŭ	cut
ē	be	ûr	urge
ĭ	pit	th	thin
ī	pie	*th*	this
îr	pier	hw	which
ŏ	pot	zh	vision
ō	toe	ə	about, item
ô	paw		

Stress marks:
′ (primary);
′ (secondary), as in
lexicon (lĕk′sĭ-kŏn′)

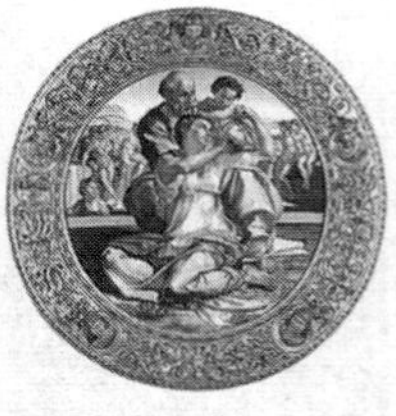

tondo
Holy Family, the "Doni tondo," c. 1504 by Michelangelo

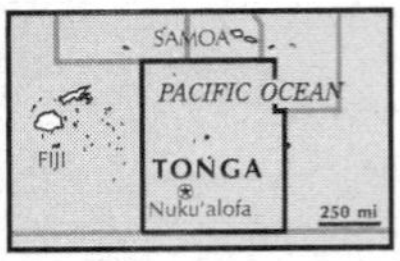
SAMOA
PACIFIC OCEAN
FIJI
TONGA
Nuku'alofa
250 mi

Tonga

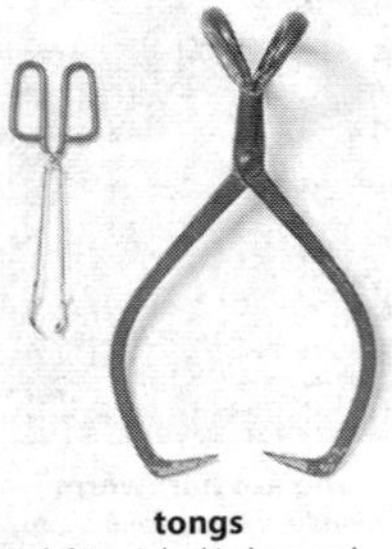

tongs
left to right: kitchen and block-ice tongs

carbonated water, and sugar. [< the name *Tom Collins.*]

Tom, Dick, and Harry *n. Informal* Anybody at all; a member of the public at large.

tome (tōm) *n.* **1.** One of the books in a work of several volumes. **2.** A book, esp. a large or scholarly one. [Fr. < Lat. *tomus* < Gk. *tomos*, section < *temnein*, to cut.]

–tome *suff.* **1.** Part; area; segment: *dermatome.* **2.** Cutting instrument: *microtome.* [NLat. *-tomus* < Gk. *-tomos*, a cutting < *tomos.* See TOME.]

to•men•tose (tō-mĕn′tōs′, tō′mən-) *adj. Biology* Covered with short dense matted hairs. [NLat. *tōmentōsus* < Lat. *tōmentum*, cushion stuffing.]

to•men•tum (tō-mĕn′təm) *n., pl.* **-ta** (-tə) **1.** *Anatomy* A network of extremely small blood vessels passing between the pia mater and the cerebral cortex. **2.** *Biology* A covering of closely matted woolly hairs. [Lat. *tōmentum*, cushion stuffing.]

tom•fool (tŏm′fo͞ol′) *n.* A stupid or foolish person. ❖ *adj.* Extremely foolish or stupid. [*Tom*, nickname for Thomas + FOOL.]

tom•fool•er•y (tŏm-fo͞o′lə-rē) *n., pl.* **-ies 1.** Foolish behavior. **2.** Something trivial or foolish; nonsense.

tom•my also **Tom•my** (tŏm′ē) *n., pl.* **-mies** *Chiefly British* A British soldier. [Short for *Tommy Atkins* < *Thomas Atkins*, a name often used on sample forms.]

Tommy gun *n. Informal* A Thompson submachine gun.

tom•my•rot (tŏm′ē-rŏt′) *n. Informal* Utter foolishness; nonsense. [Dialectal *tommy*, fool (< *Tommy*, nickname for Thomas) + ROT.]

to•mog•ra•phy (tō-mŏg′rə-fē) *n.* Any of several techniques for making detailed x-rays of a plane section of a solid object while blurring out the images of other planes. [Gk. *tomos*, section; see TOME + –GRAPHY.] **—to′mo•gram′** (tō′mə-grăm′) *n.* **—to′mo•graph′** (-grăf′) *n.*

to•mor•row (tə-môr′ō, -mŏr′ō) *n.* **1.** The day following today. **2.** The future. ❖ *adv.* On or for the day following today. [ME *to morow* < OE *tō morgenne*, in the morning : *tō*, at, on + *morgenne*, dative of *morgen*, morning.]

tom•pi•on (tŏm′pē-ən) *n.* Variant of **tampion.**

Tomsk (tŏmsk, tômsk) A city of central Russia NE of Novosibirsk. Pop. 497,662.

Tom Thumb *n.* **1.** A hero of English folklore, who was no bigger than his father's thumb. **2.** A very small person.

tom•tit (tŏm′tĭt′) *n.* A small bird, such as a titmouse.

tom-tom (tŏm′tŏm′) also **tam-tam** (tŭm′tŭm′, tăm′tăm′) *n.* **1.** Any of various small-headed drums, usu. long and narrow, beaten with the hands. **2.** A monotonous rhythmic drumbeat or similar sound. [Hindi *ṭamṭam*, prob. of imit. orig.]

–tomy *suff.* Act of cutting; incision: *gastrotomy.* [NLat. *-tomia* < Gk. *-tomiā* < *tomos*, a cutting < *temnein*, to cut.]

ton (tŭn) *n.* **1.** A unit of weight equal to 2,000 pounds (0.907 metric ton or 907.18 kilograms). **2.** A unit of weight equal to 2,240 pounds (1.016 metric tons or 1,016.05 kilograms). **3.** A metric ton. See table at **measurement. 4.** A unit of capacity for cargo in maritime shipping, normally estimated at 40 cubic feet. **5.** A unit of internal capacity of a ship equal to 100 cubic feet. **6.** A unit for measuring the displacement of ships, equal to 35 cubic feet, and supposed to equal the volume taken by a long ton of seawater. **7.** *Informal* **a.** A large extent, amount, or number. Often used in the plural: *has a ton of work; gets tons of fan mail.* **b.** Used adverbially with *a* or in the plural to mean "to a great degree or extent" or "frequently": *felt a ton better; has seen her tons lately.* [ME *tonne*, a measure of weight. See TUN.]

ton•al (tō′nəl) *adj.* Of or relating to tones, a tone, or tonality. **—ton′al•ly** *adv.*

to•nal•i•ty (tō-năl′ĭ-tē) *n., pl.* **-ties 1.** *Music* **a.** A system or arrangement of seven tones built on a tonic key. **b.** The arrangement of all the tones and chords of a composition in relation to a tonic. **2.** The scheme of the tones in a painting.

ton•do (tŏn′dō, tôn′-) *n., pl.* **-dos** also **-di** (-dē) A round painting, relief, or similar work of art. [Ital., short for *rotondo*, round < Lat. *rotundus*. See ROTUND.]

tone (tōn) *n.* **1.** *Music* **a.** A sound of distinct pitch, quality, and duration; a note. **b.** The interval of a major second in the diatonic scale; a whole step. **c.** A recitational melody in a Gregorian chant. **2a.** The quality or character of sound. **b.** The characteristic quality or timbre of a particular instrument or voice. **3a.** The pitch of a word used to determine its meaning or to distinguish differences in meaning. **b.** The particular or relative pitch of a word, phrase, or sentence. **4.** Manner of expression in speech or writing: *took an angry tone with the reporters.* **5.** A general quality, effect, or atmosphere: *a room with an elegant tone.* **6a.** A color or shade of color: *light tones of blue.* **b.** Quality of color. **7.** The general effect in painting of light, color, and shade. **8.** *Physiology* **a.** The normal state of elastic tension or partial contraction in resting muscles. **b.** Normal firmness of a tissue or organ. ❖ *v.* **toned, ton•ing, tones** *—tr.* **1.** To give a particular tone or inflection to. **2.** To soften or change the color of (a photographic negative, for example). **3.** To sound monotonously; intone. **4.** To make firmer or stronger. Often used with *up: exercises that tone up the body.* *—intr.* **1.** To assume a particular color quality. **2.** To harmonize in color. ***—phrasal verb:* tone down** To make less vivid, harsh, or violent; moderate. [ME *ton* < OFr. < Lat. *tonus* < Gk. *tonos*, a stretching, string. See **ten-** in App.]

tone arm *n.* The arm of a phonograph turntable that holds the cartridge.

tone cluster *n. Music* A dissonant group of closely spaced notes played at the same time.

tone color *n.* The timbre of a singing voice or an instrument.

tone-deaf (tōn′dĕf′) *adj.* Unable to distinguish differences in musical pitch.

tone language *n.* A language, such as Mandarin, in which pitch or the pitch contour distinguishes the meanings of words that are otherwise the same phonologically.

tone•less (tōn′lĭs) *adj.* **1.** Lacking tone. **2.** Lacking vitality; listless. **—tone′less•ly** *adv.* **—tone′less•ness** *n.*

ton•eme (tō′nēm) *n.* A type of phoneme that occurs in languages that use tone to convey differences in lexical meaning.

tone poem *n.* See **symphonic poem.**

ton•er (tō′nər) *n.* One that tones, as: **a.** A chemical bath used to change the color of a photographic print or preserve black-and-white prints or movie film. **b.** A powdery ink used dry or suspended in a liquid to produce a photocopy. **c.** A lotion used to refresh the skin.

tone row (rō) *n. Music* An ordering of notes employing all 12 pitches of the chromatic scale.

ton•ey (tō′nē) *adj.* Variant of **tony.**

tong¹ (tông, tŏng) *tr.v.* **tonged, tong•ing, tongs** To seize, hold, or manipulate with tongs. [Back-formation < TONGS.]

tong² (tông, tŏng) *n.* **1.** A Chinese association or political party. **2.** An association of Chinese in the United States, believed to be involved in organized crime. [Chin. (Cantonese) *t'ông*, assembly hall, familial relationship between cousins, equivalent to Chin. (Mandarin) *táng*.]

Ton•ga (tŏng′gə) A country in the SW Pacific E of Fiji comprising c. 150 islands; gained independence in 1970. Cap. Nukuʻalofa. Pop. 98,000.

Ton•gan (tŏng′gən, tŏng′ən) *adj.* Of or relating to Tonga or its people, language, or culture. ❖ *n.* **1.** A native or inhabitant of Tonga. **2.** The Polynesian language of Tonga.

tongs (tôngz, tŏngz) *pl.n.* (*used with a sing. or pl. verb*) A grasping device consisting of two arms that are joined, often at one end, as by a pivot or a scissorlike hinge. [ME *tonges*, pl. of *tonge* < OE *tong*.]

tongue (tŭng) *n.* **1a.** The fleshy movable muscular organ, attached in most vertebrates to the floor of the mouth, that is the principal organ of taste, an aid in chewing and swallowing, and an important organ of speech in humans. **b.** An analogous organ or part in invertebrate animals, as in certain insects or mollusks. **2.** The tongue of an animal, such as a cow, used as food. **3.** A spoken language or dialect. **4a.** Speech; talk. **b.** The act or power of speaking: *had no tongue to answer.* **c. tongues** Speech or vocal sounds produced in a state of religious ecstasy. **d.** Style or quality of utterance: *a sharp tongue.* **5.** The bark or baying of a hunting dog that sees game. **6.** Something resembling a tongue in shape or function, as: **a.** The vibrating end of a reed in a wind instrument. **b.** A flame. **c.** The flap of material under the laces or buckles of a shoe. **d.** A spit of land; a promontory. **e.** A bell clapper. **f.** The harnessing pole attached to the front axle of a horse-drawn vehicle. **7.** A protruding strip along the edge of a board that fits into a groove on the edge of another board. ❖ *v.* **tongued, tongu•ing, tongues** *—tr.* **1.** *Music* To separate or articulate (notes played on a brass or wind instrument) by shutting off the stream of air with the tongue. **2.** To touch or lick with the tongue. **3a.** To provide (a board) with a tongue. **b.** To join by means of a tongue and groove. **4.** *Archaic* To scold. *—intr.* **1.** *Music* To articulate notes on a brass or wind instrument. **2.** To project. ***—idioms:* have** (or **speak with**) **a forked tongue** To speak deceitfully; prevaricate or lie. **hold (one's) tongue** To be or keep silent. **lose (one's) tongue** To lose the capacity to speak, as from shock. **on the tip of (one's) tongue** On the verge of being recalled or expressed. [ME < OE *tunge*. See **dn̥ghū-** in App.]

tongue and groove *n.* A joint made by fitting a tongue on the edge of a board into a matching groove on another board.

tongue depressor *n.* A thin blade for pressing down the tongue during a medical examination of the mouth and throat; a spatula.

tongue•fish (tŭng′fĭsh′) *n., pl.* **tonguefish** or **-fish•es** Any of various marine flatfishes of the family Cynoglossidae, having the posterior part of the body tapering to a point.

tongue-in-cheek (tŭng′ĭn-chēk′) *adj.* Meant or expressed ironically or facetiously.

tongue-lash•ing (tŭng′lăsh′ĭng) *n. Informal* A scolding.

tongue•less (tŭng′lĭs) *adj.* **1.** Having no tongue. **2.** Lacking the faculty of speech; mute. **3.** Speechless; silent.

tongue-tie (tŭng′tī′) *n.* Restricted mobility of the tongue resulting from abnormal shortness of the frenum. ❖ *tr.v.* **-tied, -ty•ing, -ties** To make tongue-tied.

tongue-tied (tŭng′tīd′) *adj.* **1.** Speechless or confused in expression, as from shyness. **2.** Affected with tongue-tie.

tongue twister *n.* **1.** A word or group of words difficult to articulate rapidly, as *Shall she sell seashells?* **2.** Something difficult to pronounce.

tongu•ing (tŭng′ĭng) *n.* Movement of the tongue in order to articulate notes on a brass or wind instrument.

–tonia *suff.* Degree or state of tonicity: *myotonia.* [NLat. < Lat. *tonus.* See TONE.]

ton·ic (tŏn′ĭk) *n.* **1.** An agent, such as a medication, that restores or increases bodily tone. **2.** An invigorating, refreshing, or restorative agent or influence. **3.** See **tonic water. 4.** *Boston* See **soft drink. 5.** *Music* The first note of a diatonic scale; the keynote. **6.** *Linguistics* A tonic accent. ❖ *adj.* **1.** Producing or stimulating physical, mental, or emotional vigor. **2a.** *Physiology* Of, relating to, or producing tone or tonicity in muscles or tissue. **b.** *Medicine* Marked by continuous tension or contraction of muscles: *a tonic spasm.* **3.** *Music* Of or based on the keynote. **4.** Stressed, as a syllable; accented. [NLat. *tonicus,* of tension or tone < Gk. *tonikos,* capable of extension < *tonos,* a stretching, tone. See TONE.] **—ton′i·cal·ly** *adv.*

REGIONAL NOTE Generic terms for carbonated soft drinks vary widely in the United States. Probably the two most common words competing for precedence are *soda,* used in the northeast United States as well as St. Louis and vicinity, and *pop,* used from the Midwest westward. In the South any soft drink, regardless of flavor or brand name, is referred to as a *Coke, cold drink,* or just plain *drink.* Speakers in Western Maryland and Boston and its environs have a term of their own: *tonic.* See Note at **dope.**

tonic accent *n. Linguistics* A stress produced by a change, esp. a rise, in pitch as distinguished from increased volume.

to·nic·i·ty (tō-nĭs′ĭ-tē) *n., pl.* **-ties 1.** Normal firmness or functional readiness in body tissues or organs. **2.** The sustained partial contraction of resting or relaxed muscles.

tonic sol-fa *n. Music* A system of notation based on relationships between tones in a key and replacing the usual staff notation with solmization syllables or their abbreviations.

tonic water *n.* A carbonated beverage flavored with quinine.

to·night (tə-nīt′) *adv.* On or during the present or coming night. ❖ *n.* This night or this day's night. [ME *to night* < OE *tō niht,* at night : *tō,* at, on + *niht,* night; see NIGHT.]

ton·ka bean (tŏng′kə) *n.* **1.** A tropical South American tree (*Dipteryx odorata*) having pulpy egg-shaped one-seeded pods and fragrant seeds used as a flavoring. **2.** The seed of this tree. [Perh. < Galibi *tonka.*]

Ton·kin (tŏn′kĭn′, tŏng′-) A historical region of SE Asia in present-day N Vietnam on the **Gulf of Tonkin,** an arm of the South China Sea. **—Ton′kin·ese′** (-ēz′, -ēs′) *adj. & n.*

Ton·le Sap (tŏn′lā săp′, săp′) A lake of central Cambodia; an outlet for the floodwaters of the Mekong R.

ton-mile (tŭn′mīl′) *n.* A unit of freight transportation equivalent to a ton of freight moved one mile.

ton·nage (tŭn′ĭj) *n.* **1.** The number of tons of water that a ship displaces when afloat. **2.** The capacity of a merchant ship in units of 100 cubic feet. **3.** A duty or charge per ton on cargo, as at a port or canal. **4.** The total shipping of a country or port, figured in tons, with reference to carrying capacity. **5.** Weight measured in tons. [TON + –AGE. Sense 3, ME < OFr. < *tonne,* tun. See TONNE.]

tonne (tŭn) *n.* A metric ton. [Fr. < OFr., tun < LLat. *tunna,* prob. of Celt. orig.]

ton·neau (tə-nō′, tŏn′ō′) *n., pl.* **-neaus** The rear seating compartment of an early type of automobile. [Fr. < OFr. *tonnel,* cask. See TUNNEL.]

to·nom·e·ter (tō-nŏm′ĭ-tər) *n.* **1.** Any of various instruments for measuring pressure or tension. **2.** An instrument for measuring hydrostatic pressure within the eyeball, used to detect glaucoma. **3.** *Music* An instrument used to determine the pitch or vibration rate of tones. [Gk. *tonos,* tension; see TONE + –METER.] **—to′no·met′ric** (tō′nə-mĕt′rĭk) *adj.* **—to·nom′e·try** *n.*

to·no·plast (tō′nə-plăst′) *n.* The cytoplasmic membrane that surrounds a vacuole of a plant cell. [Gk. *tonos,* string, tension; see ten– in App.] + –PLAST.]

ton·sil (tŏn′səl) *n.* A small oral mass of lymphoid tissue, esp. either of two such masses embedded in the lateral walls of the opening between the mouth and the pharynx, of uncertain function but believed to help protect the body from respiratory infections. [< Lat. *tōnsillae,* tonsils, dim. of *tōlēs,* swollen tonsils.] **—ton′sil·lar** *adj.*

ton·sil·lec·to·my (tŏn′sə-lĕk′tə-mē) *n., pl.* **-mies** Surgical removal of tonsils or a tonsil.

ton·sil·li·tis (tŏn′sə-lī′tĭs) *n.* Inflammation of the tonsils.

tonsillo– or **tonsill–** *pref.* Tonsil: *tonsillectomy.* [< Lat. *tōnsillae,* tonsils. See TONSIL.]

ton·sil·lot·o·my (tŏn′sə-lŏt′ə-mē) *n., pl.* **-mies** Surgical incision of a tonsil.

ton·so·ri·al (tŏn-sôr′ē-əl, -sōr-) *adj.* Of or relating to barbering or a barber. [< Lat. *tōnsōrius* < *tōnsor,* barber < *tōnsus,* p. part. of *tondēre,* to shear.]

ton·sure (tŏn′shər) *n.* **1.** The act of shaving the head or part of the head, esp. as a preliminary to becoming a priest or a member of a monastic order. **2.** The shaved part of a monk's or priest's head. ❖ *tr.v.* **-sured, -sur·ing, -sures** To shave the head of. [ME < OFr. < Med.Lat. *tōnsūra* < Lat., a shearing < *tōnsus,* p. part. of *tondēre,* to shear.]

ton·tine (tŏn′tēn′, tŏn-tēn′) *n.* An investment plan in which participants buy shares in a common fund and receive an annu-

ity, with the entire fund going to the final survivor or to those who survive after a specified time. [Fr., after Lorenzo *Tonti* (1635–90?), Italian-born French banker.]

to·nus (tō′nəs) *n., pl.* **-nus·es** Bodily or muscular tone; tonicity. [Lat., tone. See TONE.]

ton·y also **ton·ey** (tō′nē) *adj.* **-i·er, -i·est** *Informal* Marked by an elegant or exclusive manner or quality. [< TONE.]

Tony, *pl.* **-nys** A trademark for an award for excellence in the production and creation of Broadway shows. [After *Tony,* nickname of Antoinette Perry (1888–1946), American actress and director.]

too (tōō) *adv.* **1.** In addition; also: *He's coming too.* **2.** More than enough; excessively: *worries too much.* **3.** To a regrettable degree: *an error all too apparent.* **4.** Very; extremely; immensely: *only too willing.* **5.** *Informal* Indeed; so: *You will too!* [ME < OE *tō,* to, furthermore.]

took (tōok) *v.* Past tense of **take.**

tool (tōol) *n.* **1.** A device, such as a saw, used to perform or facilitate manual or mechanical work. **2a.** A machine, such as a lathe, used to cut and shape machine parts or other objects. **b.** The cutting part of such a machine. **3.** Something regarded as needed for carrying out an occupation or profession. **4.** Something used in the performance of an operation; an instrument. **5.** *Vulgar Slang* A penis. **6.** A person used to carry out the designs of another; a dupe. **7a.** A bookbinder's hand stamp. **b.** A design impressed on a book cover by such a stamp. **8.** An application program, often one that creates, manipulates, modifies, or analyzes other programs. ❖ *v.* **tooled, tool·ing, tools** *—tr.* **1.** To form, work, or decorate with a tool. **2.** To ornament (a book cover) with a bookbinder's tool. **3.** *Slang* To drive (a vehicle). *—intr.* **1.** To work with a tool. **2.** *Slang* To drive or ride in a vehicle. *—phrasal verb:* **tool up** To provide an industry or a factory with machinery and tools suitable for a job. [ME < OE *tōl,* poss. < ON.]

tool·bar (tōol′bär′) *n.* A row of icons on a computer screen that activate commands or functions when clicked.

tool·box (tōol′bŏks′) *n.* A case for carrying or storing tools.

tool·ing (tōol′ĭng) *n.* **1.** Work or ornamentation done with tools, esp. on leather. **2.** The process of providing a factory with machinery in preparation for production.

tool·mak·er (tōol′mā′kər) *n.* One that makes tools, esp. a skilled machinist trained in making and repairing tools and parts. **—tool′mak′ing** *n.*

tool·shed (tōol′shĕd′) *n.* A small building in which tools are kept.

toon[1] (tōon) *n.* **1.** A tall tree (*Cedrela toona*) of tropical Asia and Australia having dark red aromatic wood. **2.** The wood of this tree. [Hindi *tūn* < Skt. *tunnaḥ,* var. *tuṇiḥ.*]

toon[2] (tōon) *n. Informal* **1.** A cartoon, esp. an animated cartoon. **2.** A character in an animated cartoon.

too·nie also **twoo·nie** (tōo′nē) *n. Informal* A Canadian coin worth two dollars. [TWO + –IE (modeled on LOONIE).]

toot (tōot) *v.* **toot·ed, toot·ing, toots** *—intr.* **1.** To sound a horn or whistle in short blasts. **2.** To make this or a similar sound. **3.** *Slang* To snort cocaine. *—tr.* **1.** To blow or sound (a horn or whistle). **2.** To sound (a blast, for example) on a horn or whistle. **3.** *Slang* To snort cocaine. ❖ *n.* **1.** A blast, as of a horn. **2.** *Slang* A drinking binge. **3.** *Slang* Cocaine, esp. a small amount snorted at one time. [Ult. of imit. orig.] **—toot′er** *n.*

tooth (tōoth) *n., pl.* **teeth** (tēth) **1a.** One of a set of hard bonelike structures rooted in sockets in the jaws of vertebrates, typically composed of a core of soft pulp surrounded by a layer of hard dentin coated with cementum or enamel at the crown and used for biting or chewing food or as a means of attack or defense. **b.** A similar structure in invertebrates, such as one of the pointed ridges on the shell of a mollusk. **2.** A projecting part resembling a tooth in shape or function, as on a comb, gear, or saw. **3.** A small notched projection along a margin, esp. of a leaf. **4.** A rough surface, as of metal. **5a.** Something that injures or destroys with force. Often used in the plural. **b.** **teeth** Effective means of enforcement; muscle. **6.** Taste or appetite. ❖ *v.* **toothed, tooth·ing, tooths** *—tr.* **1.** To furnish (a tool, for example) with teeth. **2.** To make a jagged edge on. *—intr.* To become interlocked; mesh. **—idioms:** **get** (or **sink**) **(one's) teeth into** *Slang* To be actively involved in; get a firm grasp of. **show** (or **bare**) **(one's) teeth** To express a readiness to fight; threaten defiantly. **to the teeth** Lacking nothing; completely. [ME < OE *tōth.* See **dent**– in App.]

tooth·ache (tōoth′āk′) *n.* An aching pain in or near a tooth.

tooth and nail *adv.* With every available resource; with unrelenting effort.

tooth·brush (tōoth′brŭsh′) *n.* A brush for cleaning teeth.

toothed (tōotht, tōothd) *adj.* Having teeth, esp. of a certain number or type. Often used in combination: *saw-toothed.*

toothed whale *n.* Any of various whales of the suborder Odontoceti, having numerous conical teeth.

tooth fairy *n.* A fairy supposed to leave money under a child's pillow in place of a baby tooth that has just fallen out.

tooth·less (tōoth′lĭs) *adj.* **1.** Lacking teeth. **2.** Lacking force; ineffectual. **—tooth′less·ly** *adv.* **—tooth′less·ness** *n.*

tooth·paste (tōoth′pāst′) *n.* A paste for cleaning teeth.

tooth·pick (tōoth′pĭk′) *n.* A small piece of wood or other material for removing food particles from between the teeth.

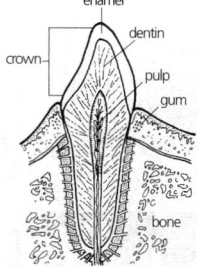

tooth
cross section of an incisor

tooth•pow•der (to͞oth′pou′dər) *n.* Powder for cleaning teeth.

tooth shell *n.* Any of various burrowing marine mollusks of the class Scaphopoda, having a long tapering curved shell.

tooth•some (to͞oth′səm) *adj.* **1.** Delicious; luscious. **2.** Pleasant; attractive. **3.** Sexually attractive or exciting. **—tooth′some•ly** *adv.* **—tooth′some•ness** *n.*

tooth•wort (to͞oth′wûrt′, -wôrt′) *n.* **1.** Any of several eastern North American plants of the genus *Cardamine,* such as the crinkleroot, having fleshy rhizomes and palmately divided leaves. **2.** A parasitic European plant *(Lathraea squamaria)* having scaly stems and pinkish flowers.

tooth•y (to͞o′thē) *adj.* **-i•er, -i•est** Having or showing prominent teeth. **—tooth′i•ly** *adv.*

too•tle (to͞ot′l) *intr.v.* **-tled, -tling, -tles 1.** To toot softly and repeatedly, as on a flute. **2.** *Informal* To walk or drive in a leisurely manner; amble. ❖ *n.* The act or sound of tootling, as on a flute. [Frequentative of TOOT.]

toots (to͝ots) *n. Slang* Babe; sweetie. [Perh. short for TOOTSIE.]

toot•sie (to͝ot′sē) *n. Slang* **1.** Toots. **2.** A girl or young woman. **3.** or **toot•sy** (-sē) A person's foot. [Of unknown orig. Sense 3, alteration of *footsie,* dim. of FOOT.]

toot•sy (to͝ot′sē) *n., pl.* **-sies** *Slang* Variant of **tootsie** 3.

top¹ (tŏp) *n.* **1.** The uppermost part, point, surface, or end. **2.** The part farthest from a given reference point: *took a jump shot from the top of the key.* **3.** The crown of the head. **4.** The part of a plant, such as a rutabaga, above the ground. **5.** Something, such as a lid, that covers or forms an uppermost part. **6.** A garment covering the upper part of the body, esp. the upper half of a two-piece garment. **7.** *Nautical* A platform enclosing the head of each mast of a sailing ship, to which the topmast rigging is attached. **8.** The highest degree, pitch, or point; the peak, acme, or zenith. **9a.** The highest position or rank. **b.** A person in this position. **10.** *Games* The highest card or cards in a suit or hand. **11.** The best part. **12.** The earliest part or beginning. **13.** *Baseball* The first half of an inning. **14.** *Sports* **a.** A stroke that lands above the center of a ball, as in golf or tennis, giving it a forward spin. **b.** This forward spin. ❖ *adj.* **1.** Situated at the top. **2.** Of the highest degree, quality, rank, or amount. **3.** In a position of preeminence. ❖ *v.* **topped, top•ping, tops** *—tr.* **1.** To form, furnish with, or serve as a top. **2.** To reach the top of. **3.** To go over the top of. **4.** To exceed or surpass. **5.** To be at the head of. **6.** To remove the top or uppermost part from; crop: *topped the trees.* **7.** *Sports* **a.** To strike the upper part of (a ball), giving it forward spin. **b.** To make (a stroke) in this way. *—intr.* To make a finish, an end, or a conclusion. ***—phrasal verbs:*** **top off 1.** To fill up (a container), esp. when it is almost full to begin with. **2.** To finish up. **top out 1.** To put the framework for the top story on (a building). **2.** To fill up (a ship, for example). **3.** To cease rising. ***—idioms:*** **off the top of (one's) head** *Informal* In an impromptu way. **on top 1.** At the highest point or peak. **2.** In a dominant, controlling, or successful position. **on top of** *Informal* **1.** In control of. **2.** Fully informed about. **3.** In addition to; besides. **4.** Following closely on; coming immediately after. **on top of the world** *Informal* In a position of great happiness or success. **over the top 1.** Surpassing a goal or quota. **2.** Over the breastwork, as an attack in trench warfare. [ME < OE.]

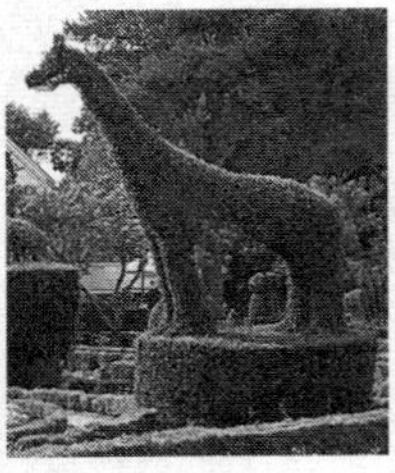

topiary
Green Animals, Portsmouth, Rhode Island

top² (tŏp) *n.* A toy having one end tapered to a point, allowing it to be spun, as by suddenly pulling a string wound around it. [ME < OE.]

top– *pref.* Variant of **topo–.**

to•paz (tō′păz′) *n.* **1a.** A colorless, blue, yellow, brown, or pink aluminum silicate mineral, often found in association with granitic rocks and valued as a gemstone, esp. in the brown and pink varieties. **b.** Any of various yellow gemstones, esp. a yellow variety of sapphire or corundum. **2.** A light yellow variety of quartz. **3.** Either of two colorful South American hummingbirds *(Topaza pyra* or *T. pella).* [ME *topace* < OFr. < Lat. *topazus* < Gk. *topazos.*]

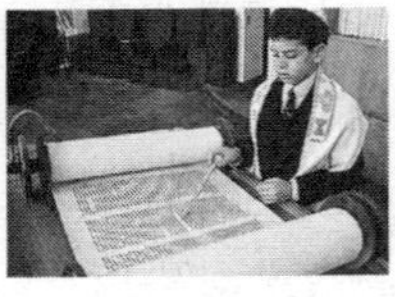

Torah

to•paz•o•lite (tə-păz′ə-līt′) *n.* A green-yellow to yellow-brown variety of andradite, $Ca_3Fe_2Si_3O_{12}$, similar in color and transparency to topaz. [*topazo-,* topaz + –LITE.]

top banana *n. Slang* **1.** The main comic in a burlesque show. **2.** The head person, as of a group or project. [So called < the presentation of a banana to the comedian who has the punch line in a three-person burlesque routine.]

top boot *n.* A high boot usu. having its upper part made of a different material or with leather of a contrasting color or texture.

top•coat (tŏp′kōt′) *n.* A lightweight overcoat.

top dog *n. Slang* One seen to have the dominant position or highest authority. **—top′-dog′** (tŏp′dôg′, -dŏg′) *adj.*

top dollar *n.* The highest amount being paid for a commodity or service: *paid top dollar for the tickets.*

top-drawer (tŏp′drôr′) *adj.* Of the highest importance, rank, privilege, or merit.

top-dress (tŏp′drĕs′) *tr.v.* **-dressed, -dress•ing, -dress•es 1.** To cover (a road surface) with loose material that is not worked in. **2.** To cover (farmland) with fertilizer.

top dressing *n.* **1.** A covering of loose gravel on a road. **2.** A fertilizer covering put on soil without being plowed under.

tope¹ (tōp) *tr. & intr.v.* **toped, top•ing, topes** To drink (liquor) habitually and excessively or engage in such drinking. [Poss. < obsolete *tope,* interj. used in proposing a toast.] **—top′er** *n.*

tope² (tōp) *n.* A small, rough-skinned, widely distributed shark *(Galeorhinus galeus)* having an elongated conical snout. [?]

tope³ (tōp) *n.* See **stupa.** [Hindi *top,* prob. < Prakrit *thūpo* < Skt. *stūpaḥ.*]

To•pe•ka (tə-pē′kə) The cap. of KS, in the NE part W of Kansas City; founded 1854. Pop. 122,377.

top•flight (tŏp′flīt′) *adj. Informal* First-rate; excellent.

Top 40 *pl.n.* The forty most popular musical recordings or songs of a given time period. ❖ *adj.* Relating to, made up of, or broadcasting the Top 40.

top•gal•lant (tə-găl′ənt, tŏp-) *adj.* **1.** *Nautical* Of, relating to, or being the mast above the topmast, its sails, or its rigging. **2.** Raised above adjacent parts or structures.

top-ham•per also **top ham•per** (tŏp′hăm′pər) *n.* **1.** *Nautical* Weight or materials, such as spars, stored either aloft or on the upper decks. **2.** Cumbersome unnecessary matter.

top hat *n.* A man's hat having a narrow brim and a tall cylindrical crown, usu. made of silk.

top-heav•y (tŏp′hĕv′ē) *adj.* **-i•er, -i•est 1.** Likely to topple because of too much weight at the top. **2.** *Accounting* Overcapitalized. **3.** Having an excessive number of managers. **—top′-heav′i•ness** *n.*

To•phet (tō′fĕt′, -fĭt) *n.* **1.** An extremely unpleasant or painful condition or place. **2.** Hell. [ME < Heb. *tōpet,* a place where children were burned.]

top-hole (tŏp′hōl′) *adj. Chiefly British* First-rate; excellent.

to•phus (tō′fəs) *n., pl.* **-phi** (-fī) **1.** A deposit of urates in the skin and tissue around a joint or in the external ear, occurring in gout. **2.** A concretion of mineral salts and organic matter on the teeth. [Lat. *tōphus,* tufa.]

to•pi¹ also **to•pee** (tō-pē′, tō′pē) *n., pl.* **-pis** also **-pees** A pith helmet worn to protect against sun and heat. [Hindi *topī,* hat.]

to•pi² (tō′pē) *n., pl.* **topi** or **-pis** A sassaby *(Damaliscus lunatus* subsp. *topi)* of eastern Africa having a glossy dark brown coat. [Prob. of Swahili orig.]

to•pi•ar•y (tō′pē-ĕr′ē) *adj.* Of or characterized by the clipping or trimming of live shrubs or trees into decorative shapes, as of animals. ❖ *n., pl.* **-ies 1.** Topiary work or art. **2.** A topiary garden. [Lat. *topiārius* < *topia,* ornamental gardening < Gk. *topia,* pl. of *topion,* field, dim. of *topos,* place.]

top•ic (tŏp′ĭk) *n.* **1.** The subject of a speech, essay, thesis, or discourse. **2.** A subject of discussion or conversation. **3.** A subdivision of a theme, thesis, or outline. See Syns at **subject. 4.** *Linguistics* A word or phrase in a sentence, usu. providing information from previous discourse or shared knowledge, that the rest of the sentence elaborates or comments on. [Obsolete *topic,* rhetorical argument, sing. of *Topics,* work by Aristotle < Lat. *Topica* < Gk. *Topika,* commonplaces < neut. pl. of *topikos,* of a place < *topos,* place.]

top•i•cal (tŏp′ĭ-kəl) *adj.* **1.** Of or belonging to a particular location or place; local. **2.** Currently of interest; contemporary. **3.** *Medicine* Of or applied to an isolated or localized area of the body: *a topical anesthetic.* **4.** Of, arranged by, or relating to a particular topic or topics. [< Gk. *topikos* < *topos,* place.] **—top′i•cal′i•ty** (-kăl′ĭ-tē) *n.* **—top′i•cal•ly** *adv.*

topic sentence *n.* The sentence within a paragraph or discourse that states the main thought, usu. at the beginning.

top•knot (tŏp′nŏt′) *n.* **1.** A crest or knot of hair or feathers on the crown of the head. **2.** A ribbon or bow worn as a headdress.

top•less (tŏp′lĭs) *adj.* **1.** Having no top: *topless jars.* **2a.** Having no part covering the breasts: *a topless bathing suit.* **b.** Wearing no top: *topless dancers.* **c.** Permitting or featuring exposure of the breasts: *a topless beach.* **3.** So high as to appear to extend out of sight: *the topless Alps.*

top-lev•el (tŏp′lĕv′əl) *adj.* **1.** Of or relating to the highest office or rank. **2.** Of or relating to top-level people.

top•loft•y (tŏp′lôf′tē, -lŏf′-) *adj.* **-i•er, -i•est** Haughty; pretentious. **—top′loft′i•ness** *n.*

top•mast (tŏp′məst, -măst′) *n.* A mast extending upward from the top of a lower mast of a sailing ship.

top•min•now (tŏp′mĭn′ō) *n.* **1.** Any of several small New World freshwater fishes of the genus *Fundulus,* related to the killifishes. **2.** Any of various small viviparous New World fishes of the family Poeciliidae of fresh or brackish waters.

top•most (tŏp′mōst′) *adj.* Highest; uppermost.

top-notch or **top•notch** (tŏp′nŏch′) *adj. Informal* First-rate; excellent.

topo– or **top–** *pref.* Place; region: *toponymy.* [Gk. < *topos,* place.]

to•pog•ra•phy (tə-pŏg′rə-fē) *n., pl.* **-phies 1.** Detailed precise description of a place or region. **2.** Graphic representation of the surface features of a place or region on a map, indicating their relative positions and elevations. **3.** A description or an analysis of a structured entity. **4a.** The surface features of a place or region. **b.** The surface features of an object: *The topography of a crystal.* **5.** The surveying of the features of a place or region. **6.** The study or description of an anatomical region or part. **—top′o•graph′** (tŏp′ə-grăf′) *n.* **—to•pog′ra•pher** (tə-pŏg′rə-fər) *n.* **—top′o•graph′ic** (tŏp′ə-grăf′ĭk), **top′o•graph′i•cal** (-ĭ-kəl) *adj.* **—top′o•graph′i•cal•ly** *adv.*

to•pol•o•gy (tə-pŏl′ə-jē) *n., pl.* **-gies 1.** Topographic study of a given place, esp. the history of a region as indicated by topogra-

phy. **2.** *Medicine* The anatomical structure of a specific area or part of the body. **3.** *Mathematics* The study of the properties of geometric figures or solids that are not affected by changes in size or shape, such as stretching or bending. **4.** *Computer Science* The arrangement in which the nodes of a LAN are connected to each other. **—top′o•log′ic** (tŏp′ə-lŏj′ĭk), **top′o•log′i•cal** (-ĭ-kəl) *adj.* **—top′o•log′i•cal•ly** *adv.* **—to•pol′o•gist** *n.*

top•o•nym (tŏp′ə-nĭm′) *n.* **1.** A place name. **2.** A name derived from a place or region. [Back-formation < TOPONYMY.] **—top′o•nym′ic, top′o•nym′i•cal** *adj.*

to•pon•y•my (tə-pŏn′ə-mē) *n., pl.* **-mies 1a.** The place names of a region or language. **b.** The study of such place names. **2.** *Anatomy* Nomenclature with respect to a region of the body rather than to organs or structures.

to•pos (tō′pōs, -pŏs) *n., pl.* **-poi** (-poi) A traditional theme or motif. [Gk., short for *(koinos) topos,* (common)place.]

top•per (tŏp′ər) *n.* **1.** One that removes tops or puts tops on. **2a.** One that is exceedingly good of its kind. **b.** *Slang* Something, such as a witticism, that surpasses all before it. **3.** A woman's short lightweight coat. **4.** *Slang* A top hat.

top•ping (tŏp′ĭng) *n.* **1.** A sauce, frosting, or garnish for food. **2.** A part or layer that forms the top. **3. toppings** The cropped parts of plants or trees after pruning. ❖ *adj.* **1.** Highest in rank or eminence. **2.** *Chiefly British* First-rate.

top•ple (tŏp′əl) *v.* **-pled, -pling, -ples** *—tr.* To push or throw over; overturn. See Syns at **overthrow.** *—intr.* **1.** To totter and fall. **2.** To lean over as if about to fall. [Frequentative of TOP[1].]

top quark *n.* A hypothetical quark with a charge of +⅔ and a mass about 360,000 times that of the electron.

top round *n.* A cut of meat, such as a steak or roast, taken from the inner section of a round of beef.

tops (tŏps) *adj. Slang* First-rate; excellent.

top•sail (tŏp′səl, -sāl′) *n.* **1.** A square sail set above the lowest sail on the mast of a square-rigged ship. **2.** A triangular or square sail set above the gaff of a lower sail on a fore-and-aft-rigged ship.

topsail schooner *n.* A schooner carrying two or more square topsails on its foremast.

top-se•cret (tŏp′sē′krĭt) *adj.* **1.** Containing information whose unauthorized disclosure would pose the gravest threat to national security: *top-secret reports.* **2.** Of or relating to top-secret information: *top-secret clearance.* **3.** Accessible or known to authorized personnel only: *a top-secret mission.*

top•side (tŏp′sīd′) *n.* **1.** The surface of a ship's hull above the water line. Often used in the plural. **2.** The highest position of authority. ❖ *adv. & adj.* **1.** On or to the upper parts of a ship; on deck. **2.** In a position of authority.

top•soil (tŏp′soil′) *n.* The upper part of the soil. ❖ *tr.v.* **-soiled, -soil•ing, -soils** To remove topsoil from (land).

top•spin (tŏp′spĭn′) *n.* Forward rotation imparted to a ball by a stroke, as in tennis.

top•stitch (tŏp′stĭch′) *tr.v.* **-stitched, -stitch•ing, -stitch•es** To sew a row of stitching close to the seam or edge of (a garment) on the outer side of the fabric.

top•sy-tur•vy (tŏp′sē-tûr′vē) *adv.* **1.** With the top downward and the bottom up; upside-down. **2.** In or into a state of utter disorder or confusion. ❖ *adj.* **-vi•er, -vi•est 1.** Turned or positioned upside down; inverted. **2.** Confused or disordered. ❖ *n., pl.* **-vies** The quality or condition of being topsy-turvy. [Prob. < TOP[1] + obsolete *terve,* to overturn (< ME *terven*).] **—top′sy-tur′vi•ly** *adv.* **—top′sy-tur′vi•ness** *n.*

toque (tōk) *n.* **1.** A woman's small, brimless, close-fitting hat. **2.** A plumed velvet cap with a full crown and small rolled brim, worn in 16th-century France. [Fr. < Sp. *toca.*]

tor (tôr) *n.* **1.** A high rock or pile of rocks on the top of a hill. **2.** A rocky peak or hill. [ME < OE *torr,* prob. of Celt. orig.]

To•rah also **to•rah** (tôr′ə, tōr′ə, toir′ə, tô-rä′) *n. Judaism* **1.** The first five books of the Hebrew Scriptures. See table at **Bible. 2.** A scroll of parchment containing the first five books of the Hebrew Scriptures, used in a synagogue during services. **3.** The entire body of Jewish religious law and learning including both sacred literature and oral tradition. [Heb. *tôrâ,* law, instruction < *hôrâ,* to throw, direct, teach, derived stem of *yārâ,* to throw, shoot.]

torch (tôrch) *n.* **1a.** A portable light produced by a burning stick of resinous wood or burning material wound about the end of a stick of wood; a flambeau. **b.** *Chiefly British* A flashlight. **2.** Something that serves to illuminate, enlighten, or guide. **3.** *Slang* An arsonist. **4.** A portable apparatus that produces a very hot flame by the combustion of gases, used in welding and construction. ❖ *tr.v.* **torched, torch•ing, torch•es** *Slang* To cause to burn or undergo combustion. [ME *torche* < OFr. < VLat. **torca,* alteration of Lat. *torqua,* var. of *torquēs,* torque < Lat. *torquēre,* to twist.]

torch•bear•er (tôrch′bâr′ər) *n.* **1.** One that carries a torch. **2.** One who imparts knowledge or inspiration to others.

tor•chère (tôr-shâr′) also **tor•chier** or **tor•chiere** (-chîr′) *n.* A usu. tall floor lamp with a bowl-shaped part that diffuses the light or directs it upward. [Fr. < *torche,* torch. See TORCH.]

tor•chon lace (tôr′shŏn′) *n.* Lace made of coarse linen or cotton thread twisted in geometric patterns. [Fr. *torchon,* duster < OFr. < *torche,* twisted straw, torch. See TORCH.]

torch song *n.* A sentimental love song, typically one in which the singer laments an unrequited love. **—torch singer** *n.*

torch•wood (tôrch′wo͝od′) *n.* **1.** Any of several tropical American trees of the genus *Amyris,* esp. *A. balsamifera,* having resinous wood that burns with a torchlike flame. **2.** The wood of any of these trees.

torch•y (tôr′chē) *adj.* **-i•er, -i•est** Of or relating to a torch song or torch singer.

tore[1] (tôr, tōr) *v.* Past tense of **tear[1].**

tore[2] (tôr, tōr) *n.* See **torus** 4. [Fr. < Lat. *torus.*]

tor•e•a•dor (tôr′ē-ə-dôr′) *n.* A matador; a bullfighter. [Sp. < *torear,* to fight bulls < *toro,* bull < Lat. *taurus.* See **tauro-** in App.]

to•re•ro (tə-râr′ō, tō-rĕ′rō) *n., pl.* **-ros** A matador or one of the supporting team. [Sp. < LLat. *taurārius* < Lat. *taurus,* bull. See **tauro-** in App.]

to•reu•tics (tə-ro͞o′tĭks) *n.* *(used with a sing. verb)* The art of working metal or other materials by the use of embossing and chasing to form minute detailed reliefs. [< Gk. *toreutikos,* of metal work < *toreutos,* worked in relief < *toreuein,* to work thus < *toreus,* a boring tool. See **terə-[1]** in App.] **—to•reu′tic** *adj.*

to•ri (tôr′ī, tōr′ī) *n.* Plural of **torus.**

to•ri•i (tôr′ē-ē′, tōr′-) *n., pl.* **torii** The gateway of a Shinto temple, consisting of two uprights supporting a concave crosspiece with projecting ends and a straight crosspiece beneath it. [J. : *tori,* bird + *i-* (< *iru,* to dwell).]

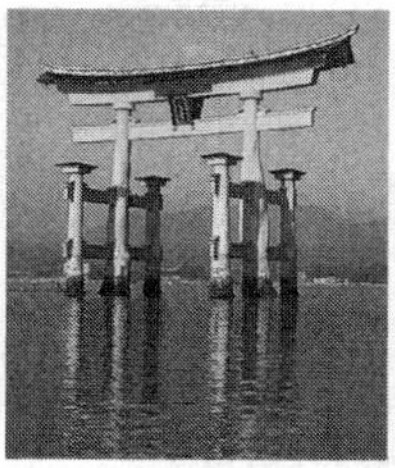

torii
Itsukushima Shrine, Miyajima Island, Japan

To•ri•no (tō-rē′nō) See **Turin.**

Tor•mé (tôr-mā′), **Melvin Howard ("Mel")** 1925–99. Amer. jazz singer and songwriter whose recordings include *Lulu's Back in Town* (1956).

tor•ment (tôr′mĕnt′) *n.* **1.** Great physical pain or mental anguish. **2.** A source of harassment, annoyance, or pain. **3.** The torture inflicted on prisoners under interrogation. ❖ *tr.v.* (tôr-mĕnt′, tôr′mĕnt′) **-ment•ed, -ment•ing, -ments 1.** To cause to undergo physical or mental torture. **2.** To agitate or upset greatly. **3.** To annoy, pester, or harass. [ME < OFr. < Lat. *tormentum* < *torquēre,* to twist.]

tor•men•til (tôr′mən-tĭl′) *n.* A perennial Eurasian plant *(Potentilla erecta)* having yellow flowers and astringent roots. [ME *tormentille* < Med.Lat. *tormentilla,* fem. dim. of Lat. *tormentum,* torment (used as an analgesic). See TORMENT.]

tor•men•tor also **tor•ment•er** (tôr-mĕn′tər, tôr′mĕn′-) *n.* **1.** One that torments. **2.** A hanging at each side of a stage directly behind the proscenium that blocks the wing area and sidelights from the audience. **3.** A sound-absorbent screen used on a movie set to prevent echo.

torn (tôrn, tōrn) *v.* Past participle of **tear[1].**

tor•na•do (tôr-nā′dō) *n., pl.* **-does** or **-dos 1.** A rotating column of air ranging in width from a few yards to more than a mile and whirling at destructively high speeds, usu. accompanied by a funnel-shaped downward extension of a cumulonimbus cloud. **2.** A violent thunderstorm in western Africa or nearby Atlantic waters. **3.** A whirlwind or hurricane. [Alteration of Sp. *tronada,* thunderstorm < *tronar,* to thunder < Lat. *tonāre.* See **(s)tenə-** in App.] **—tor•na′dic** (-nā′dĭk, -năd′ĭk) *adj.*

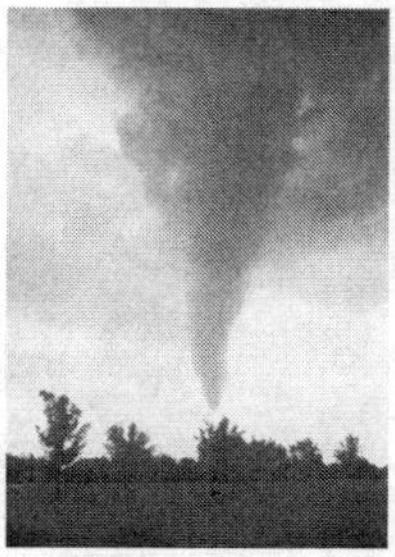

tornado

Tor•ne (tôr′nə) also **Tor•ni•o** (tôr′nē-ō′) A river of N Sweden rising near the Norwegian border in **Lake Torne** and flowing c. 402 km (250 mi) to the Gulf of Bothnia.

tor•nil•lo (tôr-nĭl′ō, -nē′ō) *n., pl.* **-los** See **screw bean.** [Am.Sp. < Sp., screw, dim. of *torno,* lathe < Lat. *tornus.* See TURN.]

to•roid (tôr′oid′, tōr′-) *n.* **1.** *Mathematics* **a.** A surface generated by a closed curve rotating about but not intersecting or containing an axis in its own plane. **b.** A solid having such a surface. **2.** A body having the shape of a toroid. [TOR(US) + -OID.] **—to•roi′dal** (tô-roid′l) *adj.*

To•ron•to (tə-rŏn′tō) The cap. of Ontario, Canada, in the S part of the province on Lake Ontario. Pop. 653,734.

to•rose (tôr′ōs′, tōr′-) *adj.* Cylindrical and having ridges or swellings. [Lat. *torōsus* < *torus,* knot, bulge.]

tor•pe•do (tôr-pē′dō) *n., pl.* **-does 1.** A cigar-shaped self-propelled underwater projectile launched from a submarine, aircraft, or ship and designed to detonate on contact with or in the vicinity of a target. **2.** Any of various submarine explosive devices, esp. a submarine mine. **3.** A small explosive warning device placed on a railroad track and fired by the weight of the train. **4.** An explosive fired in an oil or gas well to begin or increase the flow. **5.** A small firework consisting of gravel wrapped in tissue paper with a percussion cap. **6.** See **electric ray. 7.** *Slang* A professional assassin or thug. **8.** *Chiefly New Jersey* See **submarine** 2. See Regional Note at **submarine.** ❖ *tr.v.* **-doed, -do•ing, -does 1.** To attack, strike, or sink with a torpedo. **2.** To destroy decisively; wreck. [Lat. *torpēdō,* numbness, electric ray < *torpēre,* to be stiff.]

torpedo boat *n.* A small fast warship equipped for firing torpedoes.

tor•pid (tôr′pĭd) *adj.* **1.** Deprived of the power of motion or feeling; benumbed. **2.** Dormant; hibernating. **3.** Lethargic; apathetic. [Lat. *torpidus* < *torpēre,* to be stiff.] **—tor′pid•ly** *adv.*

tor•pid•i•ty (tôr-pĭd′ĭ-tē) *n.* Torpor.

tor•por (tôr′pər) *n.* **1.** A state of mental or physical inactivity or insensibility. **2.** Lethargy; apathy. **3.** The dormant, inactive state of a hibernating or estivating animal. [Lat. < *torpēre,* to be stiff.]

ă	**pat**	oi	**boy**
ā	**pay**	ou	**out**
âr	**care**	o͝o	**took**
ä	**father**	o͞o	**boot**
ĕ	**pet**	ŭ	**cut**
ē	**be**	ûr	**urge**
ĭ	**pit**	th	**thin**
ī	**pie**	*th*	**this**
îr	**pier**	hw	**which**
ŏ	**pot**	zh	**vision**
ō	**toe**	ə	**about,**
ô	**paw**		**item**

Stress marks:
′ (primary);
′ (secondary), as in
lexicon (lĕk′sĭ-kŏn′)

—**tor′po·rif′ic** (-pə-rĭf′ĭk) *adj.*

torque¹ (tôrk) *n.* **1.** The moment of a force; the measure of a force's tendency to produce torsion and rotation about an axis, equal to the vector product of the radius vector from the axis of rotation to the point of application of the force and the force vector. **2.** A turning or twisting force. ❖ *tr.v.* **torqued, torqu·ing, torques** To impart torque to. [< Lat. *torquēre,* to twist.]

torque² (tôrk) *n.* A collar, a necklace, or an armband made of a strip of twisted metal, worn by the ancient Gauls, Germans, and Britons. [Fr. < OFr. < Lat. *torquēs* < *torquēre,* to twist.]

torque converter *n.* A mechanical or hydraulic device for changing the ratio of torque to speed between the input and output shafts of a mechanism.

Tor·que·ma·da (tôr′kə-mä′də, tôr′kĕ-mä′thä), **Tomás de** 1420–98. Spanish Dominican friar who was appointed grand inquisitor in 1487.

torr (tôr) *n., pl.* **torr** A unit of pressure that is equal to approx. 1.316 × 10⁻³ atmospheres or 133.3 pascals. [After Evangelista TORRICELLI.]

Tor·rance (tôr′əns, tŏr′-) A city of S CA S of Los Angeles; founded c. 1912. Pop. 137,946.

Tor·rens (tôr′ənz, tŏr′-) A salt lake of S-central Australia NNW of Adelaide.

tor·rent (tôr′ənt, tŏr′-) *n.* **1.** A turbulent swift-flowing stream. **2.** A heavy downpour; a deluge. **3.** A heavy uncontrolled outpouring: *a torrent of insults.* [Lat. *torrēns, torrent-* < pr. part. of *torrēre,* to burn. See ters- in App.]

tor·ren·tial (tô-rĕn′shəl, tə-) *adj.* **1.** Resembling, flowing in, or forming torrents. **2.** Resulting from the action of fast-flowing streams: *torrential erosion.* **3.** Flowing or surging abundantly; wild: *torrential applause.* —**tor·ren′tial·ly** *adv.*

Tor·re·ón (tôr′ē-ōn′, -rĕ-) A city of N Mexico W of Monterrey; founded 1893. Pop. 328,086.

Tor·res Strait (tôr′ĭs) A strait between New Guinea and NE Australia connecting the Arafura Sea with the Coral Sea.

Tor·reys Peak (tôr′ēz, tŏr′-) A mountain, 4,351.4 m (14,267 ft) in the Front Range of the Rocky Mts. in central CO.

Tor·ri·cel·li (tôr′ə-chĕl′ē, tŏr′ē-), **Evangelista** 1608–47. Italian physicist who invented the mercury barometer.

tor·rid (tôr′ĭd, tŏr′-) *adj.* **-er, -est 1.** Parched with the heat of the sun; intensely hot. **2.** Scorching; burning: *the torrid noonday sun.* **3.** Passionate; ardent: *a torrid love scene.* **4.** Hurried; rapid: *a torrid pace.* [Lat. *torridus* < *torrēre,* to parch. See ters- in App.] —**tor·rid′i·ty, tor′rid·ness** *n.* —**tor′rid·ly** *adv.*

Torrid Zone The central latitude zone of the earth, between the Tropics of Cancer and Capricorn.

Tor·ri·jos Her·re·ra (tôr-rē′hōs ĕr-rĕ′rä), **Omar** 1929–81. Panamanian military and political leader who seized power in a coup d'état and ruled as a virtual dictator (1968–81).

tor·sade (tôr-säd′, -säd′) *n.* A trimming of twisted ribbon or cord, used esp. on hats. [Fr. < *tors* < VLat. **torsus,* alteration of Lat. *tortus,* p. part. of *torquēre,* to twist.]

Tór·shavn (tôr′shoun′) The cap. of the Faeroe Is., on SE Straymoy I. Pop. 14,671.

tor·sion (tôr′shən) *n.* **1a.** The act of twisting or turning. **b.** The condition of being twisted or turned. **2.** The stress or deformation caused when one end of an object is twisted in one direction and the other is held motionless or twisted oppositely. [Ult. < LLat. *torsiō, torsiōn-,* a wringing pain, var. of Lat. *tortiō* < *tortus,* p. part. of *torquēre,* to twist.] —**tor′sion·al** *adj.*

torsion balance *n.* An instrument with which small forces, as of electricity or magnetism, are measured by means of the torsion they produce in a wire or slender rod.

torsion bar *n.* A part of an automotive suspension consisting of a bar that twists to maintain stability.

tor·so (tôr′sō) *n., pl.* **-sos** or **-si** (-sē) **1.** The human body excluding the head and limbs; trunk. **2.** A statue of the human body with the head and limbs omitted or removed. **3.** A truncated or unfinished thing. [Ital., trunk of a statue < OItal., stalk, stem < VLat. **tursus* < Lat. *thyrsus,* stalk. See THYRSUS.]

tort (tôrt) *n. Law* Damage, injury, or a wrongful act done willfully, negligently, or in circumstances involving strict liability but not involving breach of contract, for which a civil suit can be brought. [ME, injury < OFr. < Med.Lat. *tortum* < Lat., neut. p. part. of *torquēre,* to twist.]

torte (tôrt, tôr′tə) *n.* A rich cake made with many eggs and little flour and usu. containing chopped nuts. [Ger., perh. < Ital. *torta,* cake, tart < LLat., a kind of bread.]

tor·tel·li·ni (tôr′tl-ē′nē) *n.* Pasta in small rings stuffed usu. with meat or cheese and served in soup or with a sauce. [Ital., dim. of *tortelli,* a kind of pasta, pl. dim. of *torta,* cake < LLat. *torta,* a kind of bread.]

tor·ti·col·lis (tôr′tĭ-kŏl′ĭs) *n.* A contracted state of the neck muscles that causes the head to rotate and tilt sideways, forwards, or backwards. [NLat. : Lat. *tortus,* twisted, p. part. of *torquēre,* to twist + *collum,* neck; see kʷel- in App.]

tor·til·la (tôr-tē′yə) *n.* A thin disk of unleavened bread made from masa or wheat flour and baked on a hot surface. [Am.Sp., dim. of Sp. *torta,* cake < LLat., a kind of bread.]

tor·toise (tôr′tĭs) *n.* **1a.** Any of various terrestrial turtles, esp. one of the family Testudinidae, having thick clublike hind limbs

tortoise
desert tortoise
Gopherus agassizii

torus

and a high rounded carapace. **b.** *Chiefly British* A terrestrial or freshwater chelonian. **2.** One that moves slowly; a laggard. [Alteration (influenced by PORPOISE) of ME *tortuce* < Med.Lat. *tortūca,* alteration of LLat. *tartarūcha,* fem. of *tartarūchus,* of the underworld. See TURTLE¹.]

tortoise beetle *n.* Any of several small, brightly colored beetles of the subfamily Cassidinae, shaped like a tortoise.

tor·toise·shell also **tor·toise shell** (tôr′tĭs-shĕl′) *n.* **1a.** The mottled, horny, translucent brownish covering of the carapace of certain tortoises or turtles, esp. the hawksbill, used to make combs, jewelry, and other articles. **b.** A synthetic imitation of natural tortoiseshell. **2.** See hawksbill. **3.** A domestic cat having fur with brown, black, and yellowish markings. **4.** Any of several butterflies, chiefly of the genus *Nymphalis,* having wings with orange, black, and brown markings. —**tor′toise-shell′** *adj.*

Tor·to·la (tôr-tō′lə) An island of the British Virgin Is. in the West Indies E of Puerto Rico.

tor·tri·cid (tôr′trĭ-sĭd) *n.* Any of various small thick-bodied moths of the family Tortricidae, having larvae that feed on the leaves of trees. [< NLat. *Tortrīcidae,* family name < *Tortrīx, Tortrīc-,* type genus. See TORTRIX.] —**tor′tri·cid** *adj.*

tor·trix (tôr′trĭks) *n.* A moth of the family Tortricidae; a tortricid. [New Latin *Tortrīx,* genus name < Lat. **tortrīx,* one that twists < *tortus,* p. part. of *torquēre,* to twist. See TORTUOUS.]

Tor·tu·ga (tôr-tōō′gə) An island in the West Indies off N Haiti; a pirate refuge in the 17th cent.

tor·tu·os·i·ty (tôr′chōō-ŏs′ĭ-tē) *n., pl.* **-ties 1.** The quality or condition of being tortuous; twistedness or crookedness. **2.** A bent or twisted part, passage, or thing.

tor·tu·ous (tôr′chōō-əs) *adj.* **1.** Having or marked by repeated turns or bends; winding or twisting. **2.** Not straightforward; circuitous; devious. **3.** Highly involved; complex. [ME < AN < Lat. *tortuōsus* < *tortus,* a twisting < p. part. of *torquēre,* to twist.] —**tor′tu·ous·ly** *adv.* —**tor′tu·ous·ness** *n.*

USAGE NOTE Traditionally, *tortuous* and *torturous* have had distinct primary meanings. *Tortuous* means "twisting" (*a tortuous road*) or by extension "complex" or "devious." *Torturous* refers primarily to torture and its pain. However, *torturous* has also come to be used in the sense of "twisted" or "strained," for which the related adjective *tortured* is an even stronger synonym: *tortured reasoning.*

---

tor·ture (tôr′chər) *n.* **1a.** Infliction of severe physical pain as a means of punishment or coercion. **b.** An instrument or a method for inflicting such pain. **2.** Excruciating physical or mental pain; agony. **3.** Something causing severe pain or anguish. ❖ *tr.v.* **-tured, -tur·ing, -tures 1.** To subject (a person or an animal) to torture. **2.** To bring great physical or mental pain upon (another). **3.** To twist or turn abnormally; distort. [ME < OFr. < LLat. *tortūra* < Lat. *tortus,* p. part. of *torquēre,* to twist.] —**tor′tur·er** *n.*

tor·tur·ous (tôr′chər-əs) *adj.* **1.** Of, relating to, or causing torture. **2.** Twisted; strained. See Usage Note at **tortuous.** —**tor′tur·ous·ly** *adv.*

tor·u·la (tôr′yə-lə, -ə-lə, tŏr′-) *n., pl.* **-lae** (-lē′, -lī′) or **-las** Any of a group of fungi similar to the yeasts but lacking asci, many of which ferment sugars. [NLat. *Torula,* fungus genus, fem. dim. of *torus,* bulge.]

To·ruń (tôr′ōōn′, -ōōn′yə) A city of N-central Poland on the Vistula R. NW of Warsaw; founded 1231. Pop. 202,360.

to·rus (tôr′əs, tŏr′-) *n., pl.* **to·ri** (tôr′ī, tŏr′ī) **1.** *Architecture* A large convex molding, semicircular in cross section, at the base of a classical column. **2.** *Anatomy* A bulging or rounded projection or swelling. **3.** *Botany* The receptacle of a flower. **4.** *Mathematics* A toroid generated by a circle; a surface having the shape of a doughnut. [Lat., bulge, knot, torus.] —**tor′ic** *adj.*

To·ry (tôr′ē, tŏr′ē) *n., pl.* **-ries 1a.** A member of a British political party, founded in 1689, that was the opposition party to the Whigs and has been known as the Conservative Party since about 1832. **b.** A member of a Conservative Party, as in Canada. **2.** An American who favored the British side during the American Revolution. **3.** often **tory** A supporter of traditional political and social institutions; a political conservative. [Ir.Gael. *tóraidhe,* robber < OIr. *tóir,* pursuit.] —**To′ry** *adj.* —**To′ry·ism** *n.*

Tos·ca·ni·ni (tŏs′kə-nē′nē, tōs′kä-), **Arturo** 1867–1957. Italian conductor of the Metropolitan Opera (1908–21) and the New York Philharmonic (1928–36).

toss (tôs, tŏs) *v.* **tossed, toss·ing, toss·es** —*tr.* **1.** To throw lightly or casually or with a sudden slight jerk: *tossed the shirt on the floor.* See Syns at **throw. 2.** To throw, fling, or heave continuously about; pitch to and fro: *boats tossed about.* **3.** To throw upward: *The bull tossed him over the fence.* **4.** To mix (a salad) lightly so as to cover with dressing. **5.** To discuss informally; bandy. **6.** To move or lift (the head) with a sudden motion. **7.** To disturb or agitate; upset. **8.** To throw to the ground. **9a.** To flip (coins) in order to decide an issue. **b.** To flip coins with: *I'll toss you to see who goes first.* **10.** To put in a given position, condition, or situation: *tossed the criminal in jail.* **11.** To throw away; discard. **12.** To disqualify or eject. —*intr.* **1.** To be thrown here and there; be flung to and fro. **2.** To move about restlessly; twist and turn. **3.** To flip a coin to decide an issue. ❖ *n.* **1.** The act of tossing or the condition of being tossed. **2.** The distance that something is or can be tossed. **3.** An abrupt upward movement, as of the head. **4.** A flipping of a coin to decide an issue. ***—phrasal verbs:* toss down** *Informal* To drink in one draft by suddenly tilting. **toss off** *Informal* **1.** To drink up in one draft. **2.** To do or finish effortlessly or casually. [ME *tossen*, poss. of Scand. orig.] **—toss′er** *n.*

toss•pot (tôs′pŏt′, tŏs′-) *n.* A drunkard.

toss•up (tôs′ŭp′, tŏs′-) *n. Informal* **1.** An even chance or choice. **2.** The flipping of a coin to decide an issue.

tos•ta•da (tō-stä′də) or **tos•ta•do** (-dō) *n., pl.* **-das** or **-dos** A tortilla or tortilla chip deep-fried until crisp. [Am.Sp. < Sp., fem. p. part. of *tostar*, to toast < VLat. **tostāre*. See TOAST[1].]

tot[1] (tŏt) *n.* **1.** A small child. **2.** A small amount. [?]

tot[2] (tŏt) *tr.v.* **tot•ted, tot•ting, tots** To total: *totted it up.*

to•tal (tōt′l) *n.* **1.** An amount obtained by addition; a sum. **2.** A whole quantity; an entirety. ❖ *adj.* **1.** Of, relating to, or constituting the whole; entire. See Syns at **whole. 2.** Complete; utter; absolute: *total concentration; a total effort.* ❖ *v.* **-taled, -tal•ing, -tals** or **-talled, -tal•ling, -tals** —*tr.* **1.** To determine the total of; add up. **2.** To equal a total of; amount to. **3.** To wreck completely; demolish. —*intr.* To add up; amount. [ME, whole < OFr. < Med.Lat. *tōtālis* < Lat. *tōtus*. See **teutā-** in App.]

total eclipse *n.* An eclipse in which the entire surface of a celestial body is obscured.

to•tal•i•tar•i•an (tō-tăl′ĭ-târ′ē-ən) *adj.* Of, being, or imposing a form of government in which the political authority exercises absolute and centralized control over all aspects of life. ❖ *n.* A practitioner or supporter of such a government. [TOTAL + (AUTHOR)ITARIAN.] **—to•tal′i•tar′i•an•ism** *n.*

to•tal•i•ty (tō-tăl′ĭ-tē) *n., pl.* **-ties 1.** The quality or state of being total. **2.** An aggregate amount; a sum. **3.** The phase of an eclipse when it is total.

to•tal•i•za•tor (tōt′l-ĭ-zā′tər) *n.* A machine for computing and showing totals, esp. a pari-mutuel machine showing the total number and amounts of bets at a racetrack.

to•tal•ize (tōt′l-īz′) *tr.v.* **-ized, -iz•ing, -iz•es** To make or combine into a total. **—to′tal•i•za′tion** (-ĭ-zā′shən) *n.*

to•tal•iz•er (tōt′l-ī′zər) *n.* A pari-mutuel machine.

to•tal•ly (tōt′l-ē) *adv.* Entirely; wholly; completely.

tote[1] (tōt) *tr.v.* **tot•ed, tot•ing, totes** *Informal* **1.** To haul; lug. **2.** To have on one's person; pack: *toting guns.* ❖ *n.* **1.** *Informal* A load; a burden. **2.** A tote bag. [Perh. (via Black West African E.) of Bantu orig.; akin to Kongo *-tota*, to pick up.] **—tot′er** *n.*

tote[2] (tōt) *tr.v.* **tot•ed, tot•ing, totes** *Informal* **1.** To determine the total of; add up. **2.** To sum up; summarize.

tote[3] (tōt) *n. Informal* A pari-mutuel machine.

tote bag *n.* A large handbag or shopping bag.

tote board *n.* A large, usu. electrically operated board that displays changing numerical information.

to•tem (tō′təm) *n.* **1a.** An animal, plant, or natural object serving among certain tribal or traditional peoples as the emblem of a clan or family and sometimes revered as its founder, ancestor, or guardian. **b.** A representation of such an object. **c.** A social group having a common affiliation to such an object. **2.** A venerated emblem or symbol. [Ojibwa *nindoodem*, my totem.] **—to•tem′ic** (-tĕm′ĭk) *adj.*

to•tem•ism (tō′tə-mĭz′əm) *n.* **1.** A belief in totems or in kinship through common affiliation to a totem. **2.** The practice of establishing affiliation through totems. **—to′tem•ist** *n.* **—to′tem•is′tic** *adj.*

totem pole *n.* **1.** A post carved and painted with a series of family or clan crests or with figures representing mythic beings and erected usu. before a dwelling, as among certain Native American peoples of the northwest coast of North America. **2.** *Slang* A hierarchy: *low on the totem pole.*

toth•er or **t'oth•er** (tŭth′ər) *pron. & adj. Informal* The other. [< ME *the tother*, alteration of *thet other*, that other : *thet*, the (< OE *thæt*; see THAT) + *other*, other; see OTHER.]

to•ti•pal•mate (tō′tĭ-păl′māt′) *adj.* Having webbing that connects each of the four anterior toes, as in water birds. [Lat. *tōtus*, whole; see TOTAL + PALMATE.] **—to′ti•pal•ma′tion** *n.*

to•tip•o•ten•cy (tō-tĭp′ə-tən-sē, tō′tĭ-pōt′n-sē) also **to•tip•o•tence** (tō-tĭp′ə-təns, tō′tĭ-pōt′ns) *n., pl.* **-cies** also **-ten•ces** The ability of a cell, such as an egg, to give rise to unlike cells and thus develop into a new organism or part. [Lat. *tōtus*, whole; see TOTAL + POTENCY.] **—to•tip′o•tent** *adj.*

tot•ter (tŏt′ər) *intr.v.* **-tered, -ter•ing, -ters 1a.** To sway as if about to fall. **b.** To appear about to collapse. **2.** To walk unsteadily or feebly; stagger. ❖ *n.* The act or condition of tottering. [ME *toteren*, perh. of Scand. orig.] **—tot′ter•er** *n.* **—tot′ter•y** *adj.*

tou•can (to͞o′kăn′, -kän′, to͞o-kăn′, -kän′) *n.* Any of various tropical American birds of the family Ramphastidae, having brightly colored plumage and a very large bill. [Fr. < Port. *tucano* or Sp. *tucán*, both < Tupi *tucano*, type of bird.]

touch (tŭch) *v.* **touched, touch•ing, touch•es** —*tr.* **1.** To cause or permit a part of the body, esp. the hand or fingers, to come in contact with so as to feel: *touched the smooth stone.* **2a.** To bring something into light contact with: *touched the sore spot with a probe.* **b.** To bring (one thing) into light contact with something else. **3.** To press or push lightly; tap. **4.** To lay hands on in violence. **5.** To eat or drink; taste: *didn't touch her food.* **6.** To disturb or move by handling. **7a.** To meet without going beyond; adjoin. **b.** *Mathematics* To be tangent to. **c.** To come up to; reach. **d.** To match in quality; equal. **8.** To deal with, esp. in passing; treat briefly or allusively. **9.** To be pertinent to; concern. **10.** To affect the emotions of; move to tender response. **11.** To injure slightly: *plants touched by frost.* **12.** To color slightly; tinge. **13a.** To draw with light strokes. **b.** To change or improve by adding fine lines or strokes. **14.** To stamp (tested metal). **15.** *Slang* To wheedle a loan or handout from. **16a.** *Archaic* To strike or pluck the keys or strings of (a musical instrument). **b.** To play (a musical piece). —*intr.* **1.** To touch someone or something. **2.** To be or come into contact: *Don't let the live wires touch.* ❖ *n.* **1.** The act or an instance of touching. **2.** The physiological sense by which external objects or forces are perceived through contact with the body. **3.** A sensation experienced in touching something with a characteristic texture: *felt the touch of snowflakes on her face.* **4.** A light push; a tap. **5.** A discernible mark or effect left by contact with something. **6.** A small change or addition, or the effect achieved by it. **7.** A suggestion, hint, or tinge: *a touch of jealousy.* **8.** A mild attack: *a touch of the flu.* **9.** A small amount; a dash: *a touch of salt.* **10a.** A manner or technique of striking the keys of a keyboard instrument. **b.** The resistance to pressure characteristic of the keys of a keyboard. **11.** A characteristic way of doing things. **12.** A facility; a knack: *lose one's touch.* **13.** The state of being in contact or communication: *out of touch.* **14.** An official stamp indicating the quality of a metal product. **15.** *Slang* **a.** The act of approaching someone for a loan or handout. **b.** A prospect for a loan or handout. **16.** *Sports* The area just outside the sidelines in soccer or just outside and including the sidelines in Rugby. ***—phrasal verbs:* touch down** To make contact with the ground; land. **touch off 1.** To cause to explode; fire. **2.** To initiate; trigger. **3.** To describe or portray with deft precision. **touch on** (or **upon**) **1.** To deal with (a topic) in passing. **2.** To pertain to; concern. **3.** To approach being; verge on. **touch up** To improve by making minor corrections, changes, or additions. ***—idiom:* touch base** (or **bases**) *Informal* To renew a line of communication. [ME *touchen* < OFr. *touchier*, ult. < VLat. **toccāre*.] **—touch′a•ble** *adj.* **—touch′er** *n.*

touch-and-go (tŭch′ən-gō′) *adj.* Dangerous and uncertain in nature or outcome; precarious; delicate.

touch•back (tŭch′băk′) *n. Football* A play in which the defensive team recovers and downs the ball behind its own goal line after the offense has kicked or passed it there.

touch•down (tŭch′doun′) *n.* **1.** *Football* An act of carrying, receiving, or gaining possession of the ball across the opponent's goal line for a score of six points. **2.** The contact, or moment of contact, of a landing aircraft or spacecraft with the landing surface. [< the earlier practice of touching the ball to the ground behind the goal line.]

tou•ché (to͞o-shā′) *interj.* Used to acknowledge a hit in fencing or a successful criticism or an effective point in argument. [Fr. < p. part. of *toucher*, to hit or wound in fencing < OFr. *touchier*, to touch. See TOUCH.]

touched (tŭcht) *adj.* **1.** Emotionally affected; moved. **2.** Somewhat demented or mentally unbalanced.

touch football *n.* A variety of football in which the ball carrier is downed by touching rather than tackling.

touch•hole (tŭch′hōl′) *n.* The opening in early firearms and cannons through which the powder was ignited.

touch•ing (tŭch′ĭng) *adj.* Eliciting or capable of eliciting sympathy or tenderness. ❖ *prep.* Concerning; about. **—touch′ing•ly** *adv.* **—touch′ing•ness** *n.*

touch•line (tŭch′līn′) *n.* Either of the sidelines bordering the playing field in soccer and Rugby.

touch-me-not (tŭch′mē-nŏt′) *n.* **1.** See **jewelweed. 2.** See **sensitive plant** 1. [< ripe seedpods bursting when touched.]

touch•pad or **touch pad** (tŭch′păd′) *n.* A pointing device consisting of a soft pad sensitized to finger movement or pressure and used esp. on laptop computers as an alternative to a mouse.

touch•screen or **touch screen** (tŭch′skrēn′) *n.* A monitor screen that can detect and respond to something, such as a finger or stylus, pressing on it.

touch•stone (tŭch′stōn′) *n.* **1.** A hard black stone, such as jasper or basalt, formerly used to test the quality of gold and silver by comparing the streak left on the stone by one of these metals with that of a standard alloy. **2.** A quality or example used to test the excellence or genuineness of others.

touch-tone also **touch•tone** (tŭch′tōn′) *adj.* Of or being a telephone with a dialing system that has pushbuttons that generate tones of differing pitch corresponding to the digits of the number being called. ❖ *n.* A touch-tone telephone.

touch-type (tŭch′tīp′) *tr. & intr.v.* **-typed, -typ•ing, -types** To type (a document, for example) or engage in typing without having to look at the keyboard, the fingers having been trained to locate the keys by position. **—touch′-typ′ist** *n.*

touch•up (tŭch′ŭp′) *n.* The act or an instance of finishing or improving by small changes, corrections, or additions.

touch•wood (tŭch′wo͝od′) *n.* Material, such as decayed wood, that is used as tinder; punk. [< its being easy to ignite.]

touch•y (tŭch′ē) *adj.* **-i•er, -i•est 1.** Tending to take offense with slight cause; oversensitive. **2.** Requiring special tact or skill in handling; delicate: *a touchy situation.* **3.** Highly sensitive to touch.

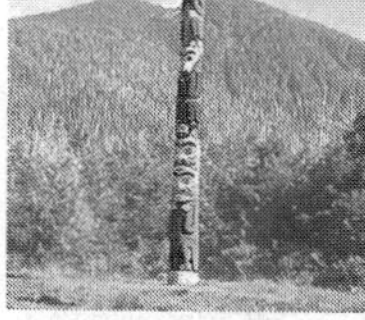

totem pole
Saxman Totem Park,
Ketchikan, Alaska

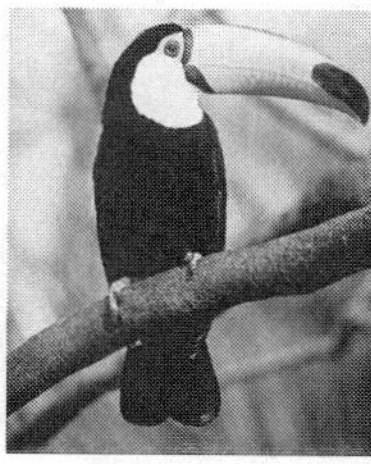

toucan
toco toucan
Ramphastos toco

ă	**pat**	oi	**boy**
ā	**pay**	ou	**out**
âr	**care**	o͝o	**took**
ä	**father**	o͞o	**boot**
ĕ	**pet**	ŭ	**cut**
ē	**be**	ûr	**urge**
ĭ	**pit**	th	**thin**
ī	**pie**	*th*	**this**
îr	**pier**	hw	**which**
ŏ	**pot**	zh	**vision**
ō	**toe**	ə	**about,**
ô	**paw**		**item**

Stress marks:
′ (primary);
′ (secondary), as in
lexicon (lĕk′sĭ-kŏn′)

Used of a body part. **4.** Easily ignited; flammable. —**touch′i·ly** *adv.* —**touch′i·ness** *n.*

touch·y-feel·y (tŭch′ē-fē′lē) *adj. Informal* **1.** Marked by or emphasizing physical closeness and emotional openness: *a touchy-feely motivational meeting.* **2.** Based on sentiment or intuition, esp. to the exclusion of critical judgment.

tough (tŭf) *adj.* **tough·er, tough·est 1.** Able to withstand great strain without tearing or breaking; strong and resilient. **2.** Hard to cut or chew. **3.** Physically hardy; rugged. **4.** Severe; harsh: *a tough winter.* **5a.** Aggressive; pugnacious. **b.** Inclined to violent or disruptive behavior; rowdy or rough. **6.** Demanding or troubling; difficult: *tough questions.* **7.** Strong-minded; resolute. **8.** *Slang* Unfortunate; too bad: *a tough break.* **9.** *Slang* Fine; great. ❖ *n.* A violent or rowdy person; a hoodlum or thug. —**idiom: tough it out** *Slang* To get through despite hardship; endure. [ME *tōh.*] —**tough′ly** *adv.* —**tough′ness** *n.*

tough·en (tŭf′ən) *tr. & intr.v.* **-ened, -en·ing, -ens** To make or become tough. —**tough′en·er** *n.*

tough·ie (tŭf′ē) *n. Informal* **1.** A thug; a tough. **2.** A difficult problem.

tough love *n.* The use of strict disciplinary measures and limitations on freedoms or privileges as a means of fostering responsibility and expressing care or concern.

tough-mind·ed (tŭf′mīn′dĭd) *adj.* Facing facts and difficulties with strength and determination; realistic and resolute. —**tough′-mind′ed·ly** *adv.* —**tough′-mind′ed·ness** *n.*

Tou·lon (tōō-lōn′) A city of SE France on the Mediterranean Sea ESE of Marseille. Pop. 167,788.

Tou·louse (tōō-lōōz′) A city of S France on the Garonne R. SE of Bordeaux; cap. of the Visigoths (419–507) and the Carolingian kingdom of Aquitaine (781–843). Pop. 358,598.

Tou·louse-Lau·trec (tōō-lōōs′lō-trĕk′, tōō-lōōz′-), **Henri de** 1864–1901. French artist known for his images of the music halls and cafés of Montmartre.

tou·pee (tōō-pā′) *n.* **1.** A partial wig or hairpiece worn to cover a bald spot. **2.** A curl or lock of hair worn during the 18th century as a topknot on a periwig. [Fr. *toupet,* dim. of OFr. *toupe,* tuft of hair < Frankish *top.*]

tour (tōōr) *n.* **1.** A trip with visits to various places of interest for business, pleasure, or instruction. **2.** A group organized for such a trip or for a shorter sightseeing excursion. **3.** A brief trip to or through a place for the purpose of seeing it. **4.** A journey to fulfill a round of engagements in several places: *a concert tour.* **5.** A shift, as in a factory. **6.** A period of duty at a single place or job. ❖ *v.* **toured, tour·ing, tours** *—intr.* **1.** To travel from place to place, esp. for pleasure. **2.** To travel among various places while fulfilling engagements. *—tr.* **1.** To make a tour of. **2.** To present (a play, for example) on a tour. [ME, a turn < OFr. < Lat. *tornus,* lathe. See TURN.] —**tour′er** *n.*

tou·ra·co also **tu·ra·co** (tōōr′ə-kō′) *n., pl.* **-cos** Any of various weak-flying cuckoolike African birds of the family Musophagidae, many of which have brightly colored plumage and long tails. [Fr., perh. of W African orig.]

Tou·raine (tōō-rān′, -rĕn′) A historical region and former province of W-central France; taken by the English in 1152 and recaptured by the French in 1204.

Tou·rane (tōō-rän′) See **Da Nang.**

tour·bil·lion (tōōr-bĭl′yən) *n.* **1a.** A whirlwind. **b.** A vortex, as of a whirlwind or whirlpool. **2.** A skyrocket that has a spiral flight. [ME *turbilloun* < OFr. *torbeillon,* ult. < Lat. *turbō* < Gk. *turbē,* noise, confusion. See TURBID.]

tour de force (tōōr′ də fôrs′, fôrs′) *n., pl.* **tours de force** (tōōr′) A feat requiring great virtuosity or strength. [Fr. : *tour,* turn, feat + *de,* of + *force,* strength.]

Tou·ret·ter (tōō-rĕt′ər) *n.* One who has Tourette's syndrome.

Tou·rette's syndrome (tōō-rĕts′) or **Tou·rette syndrome** (-rĕt′) *n.* A severe neurological disorder characterized by facial and body tics, often accompanied by grunts and compulsive utterances, as of obscenities. [After Georges Gilles de la *Tourette* (1857–1904), French physician.]

tour·ism (tōōr′ĭz′əm) *n.* **1.** The practice of traveling for pleasure. **2.** The business of providing tours and tourist services.

tour·ist (tōōr′ĭst) *n.* One who travels for pleasure. —**tour′is·tic** *adj.* —**tour′ist·y** *adj.*

tourist class *n.* The lowest class of accommodations on some passenger ships and airplanes.

tourist trap *n.* A place, such as a shop or resort area, that offers overpriced goods and services to tourists.

tour·ma·line (tōōr′mə-lĭn, -lēn′) *n.* A complex crystalline silicate containing aluminum, boron, and other elements, used esp. in its green, clear, and blue varieties as a gemstone. [Fr. < Sinhalese *toramalli,* carnelian.]

tour·na·ment (tōōr′nə-mənt, tûr′-) *n.* **1.** A series of contests in which a number of contestants compete and the one that prevails through the final round or that finishes with the best record is declared the winner. **2.** A medieval martial sport in which two groups of mounted and armored combatants fought against each other with blunted lances or swords. [ME *tournement,* a medieval sport < OFr. *torneiement < torneier,* to tourney. See TOURNEY.]

tour·ne·dos (tōōr′nə-dō′) *n., pl.* **tour·ne·dos** (-dō′, -dōz′) A fillet of beef cut from the tenderloin, often bound in bacon or

Toussaint L'Ouverture
French engraving c. 1800

suet for cooking. [Fr. : *tourner,* to turn (< OFr.; see TURN) + *dos,* the back (< Lat. *dorsum*).]

tour·ney (tōōr′nē, tûr′-) *intr.v.* **-neyed, -ney·ing, -neys** To compete in a tournament. ❖ *n., pl.* **-neys** A tournament. [ME *torneien* < OFr. *torneier < *tornizāre,* to turn around < Lat. *tornāre,* to turn in a lathe. See TURN.]

tour·ni·quet (tōōr′nĭ-kĭt, tûr′-) *n.* A device, typically a tightly encircling bandage, used to check bleeding by temporarily stopping the flow of blood through a limb. [Fr. : *tourner,* to turn (< OFr.; see TURN) + *-iquet,* diminutive suff. (< OFr.).]

Tours (tōōr) A city of W-central France on the Loire R.; a Huguenot stronghold before 1685. Pop. 129,506.

tou·sle (tou′zəl, -səl) *tr.v.* **-sled, -sling, -sles** To disarrange or rumple; dishevel. ❖ *n.* A disheveled mass, as of hair. [ME *touselen,* freq. of *tousen,* to pull roughly.]

Tous·saint L'Ou·ver·ture (tōō-săn′ lōō-vĕr-tür′), **François Dominique** 1743?–1803. Haitian military and political leader who led a successful slave insurrection (1791–93) and helped the French expel the British from Haiti (1798).

tout (tout) *v.* **tout·ed, tout·ing, touts** *—intr.* **1.** To solicit customers, votes, or patronage, esp. in a brazen way. **2.** *Chiefly British* To tout information on racehorses. *—tr.* **1.** To solicit or importune. **2.** *Chiefly British* To obtain or sell information on (a racehorse or stable) for the guidance of bettors. **3.** To promote or praise energetically; publicize. ❖ *n.* **1.** *Chiefly British* One who touts information on racehorses. **2.** One who solicits customers brazenly or persistently. [ME *tuten,* to peer.] —**tout′er** *n.*

to·va·rich (tə-vär′ĭch, -ĭsh) or **to·va·rish** (-ĭsh) *n.* A comrade. [Russ. *tovarishch* < ORuss. *tovarishchǐ,* sing. of *tovarishchi,* business associates < O Turkic *tavar ishchi,* merchant : *tavar,* wealth, trade + *ishchi,* one who works (< *ish,* work, business).]

tow¹ (tō) *tr.v.* **towed, tow·ing, tows** To draw or pull behind by a chain or line. See Syns at **pull.** ❖ *n.* **1a.** The act or an instance of towing. **b.** The condition of being towed. **2.** Something that tows. **3.** Something, such as a barge, that is towed. **4.** A rope or cable used in towing. —**idiom: in tow 1.** Under close guidance; in one's charge. **2.** As a companion or follower. [ME *towen* < OE *togian.* See **deuk-** in App.] —**tow′a·ble** *adj.* —**tow′er** *n.*

tow² (tō) *n.* Coarse broken flax or hemp fiber prepared for spinning. [ME, poss. < OE *tow-,* spinning (in *towcræft,* spinning craft, spinning).]

tow·age (tō′ĭj) *n.* **1.** The act or service of towing. **2.** A charge for towing.

to·ward (tôrd, tōrd, tə-wôrd′) *prep.* also **to·wards** (tôrdz, tōrdz, tə-wôrdz′) **1.** In the direction of: *toward home.* **2.** In a position facing: *his back toward me.* **3.** Somewhat before in time: *toward morning.* **4.** With regard to; in relation to: *turned toward the future.* **5.** In furtherance or partial fulfillment of: *five dollars toward the bill.* **6.** By way of achieving; with a view to: *efforts toward peace.* ❖ *adj.* (tôrd, tōrd) **1.** Favoring success or a good outcome; propitious. **2.** often **towards** Happening soon; imminent. **3.** *Obsolete* Being quick to understand or learn. [ME < OE *tōweard* : *tō,* to + *-weard,* -ward.]

to·ward·ly (tôrd′lē, tōrd′-) *adj. Archaic* **1.** Appearing likely to succeed; promising. **2.** Advantageous; favorable.

tow·a·way zone (tō′ə-wā′) A no-parking zone from which motor vehicles may be towed away.

tow·boat (tō′bōt′) *n.* **1.** See **tugboat. 2.** A powerful shallow-draft boat with a broad bow, intended to push barges on rivers and canals.

tow·el (tou′əl) *n.* A piece of absorbent cloth or paper for wiping or drying. ❖ *v.* **-eled, -el·ing, -els** or **-elled, -el·ling, -els** *—tr.* To wipe or rub dry with a towel. *—intr.* To towel oneself. [ME *towaille* < OFr. *toaille,* of Gmc. orig.]

tow·el·ette (tou′ə-lĕt′) *n.* A small, usu. moistened piece of paper or cloth used for cleansing.

tow·el·ing also **tow·el·ling** (tou′ə-lĭng, tou′lĭng) *n.* Any of various fabrics of cotton or linen used for making towels.

tow·er (tou′ər) *n.* **1.** A building or part of a building that is exceptionally high in proportion to its width and length. **2.** A tall slender structure used for observation, signaling, or pumping. **3.** One that conspicuously embodies strength, firmness, or another virtue. **4.** A computer system whose components are arranged in a vertical stack and housed in a tall narrow cabinet. ❖ *intr.v.* **-ered, -er·ing, -ers** **1.** To appear at or rise to a conspicuous height; loom. **2.** To fly directly upward before swooping or falling. Used of certain birds. **3.** To demonstrate great superiority; be preeminent. [ME *tur, tour, towr* < OE *torr* and < OFr. *tur,* both < Lat. *turris,* prob. < Gk. *tursis, turris.*]

tow·er·ing (tou′ər-ĭng) *adj.* **1.** Of imposing height. **2.** Outstanding; preeminent. **3.** Very great or intense.

tow·head (tō′hĕd′) *n.* **1.** A head of white-blond hair resembling tow. **2.** A person having such hair. —**tow′head′ed** *adj.*

tow·hee (tō′hē, tō-hē′) *n.* **1.** A North American bird (*Pipilo erythrophthalmus*) that has black, white, and rust-colored plumage in the male. **2.** Any of several finches of the genera *Pipilo* or

Chlorura, found in the western United States. [Imit. of the song of some of these birds.]

tow·line (tō′lĭn′) *n.* A line used in towing a vessel or vehicle.

town (toun) *n.* **1a.** A population center that is larger than a village and smaller than a city. **b.** A territorial and political unit governed by a town meeting, esp. in New England. **c.** *Informal* A city: *New York is a big town.* **d.** *Chiefly British* A rural village that has a market or fair periodically. **e.** The residents of a town: *The whole town attended the parade.* **2.** An area that is more densely populated or developed than the surrounding area: *went into town to shop.* **3.** The residents of a community in which a university or college is located, as opposed to the students and faculty. **4.** A group of prairie dog burrows. —*idiom:* **on the town** *Informal* In spirited pursuit of the entertainment offered by a city or town. [ME < OE *tūn*, enclosed place, village. See **dheuə-** in App.]

town crier *n.* **1.** A person formerly employed by a town to proclaim announcements in the streets. **2.** *Informal* A gossip.

town hall *n.* A building containing the offices of the public officials of a town and housing the town council and courts.

town·house or **town house** (toun′hous′) *n.* **1.** A residence in a city. **2.** A row house, esp. a fashionable one.

town·ie also **town·y** (tou′nē) *n., pl.* **-ies** *Informal* A permanent resident of a town, esp. one in a college town who is academically unaffiliated with the local college or university.

town manager *n.* An administrator appointed to manage the government of a town.

town meeting *n.* A legislative assembly of inhabitants of a town.

towns·folk (tounz′fōk′) *pl.n.* The people of a town.

Town·shend (toun′zənd), **Charles** 1725–67. British politician who sponsored the Townshend Acts (1767), which levied duties on imports to the American colonies.

town·ship (toun′shĭp′) *n.* **1.** A subdivision of a county in most northeast and Midwest US states, having the status of a unit of local government with varying governmental powers. **2.** A public land surveying unit of 36 sections or 36 square miles. **3.** An ancient administrative division of a large parish in England. **4.** A suburb or city in South Africa formerly designated by the government as a predominantly Black residential area.

towns·man (tounz′mən) *n.* **1.** A man who resides in a town. **2.** A male fellow resident of one's town.

towns·peo·ple (tounz′pē′pəl) *pl.n.* The inhabitants or citizens of a town or city.

towns·wom·an (tounz′wŏŏm′ən) *n.* **1.** A woman who resides in a town. **2.** A female fellow resident of one's town.

tow·path (tō′păth′, -päth′) *n.* A path along a canal or river used by animals towing boats.

tox·a·phene (tŏk′sə-fēn′) *n.* A toxic solid compound, $C_{10}H_{10}Cl_8$, used as an insecticide. [TOX(I)– + (C)A(M)PHENE.]

tox·e·mi·a (tŏk-sē′mē-ə) *n.* A condition in which the blood contains toxins, as from the growth of microorganisms. —**tox·e′mic** *adj.*

toxi– or **toxo–** or **tox–** *pref.* Poison; poisonous: *toxaphene.* [< Lat. *toxicum.* See TOXIC.]

tox·ic (tŏk′sĭk) *adj.* **1.** Of or caused by a toxin or other poison. **2.** Capable of causing injury or death, esp. by chemical means; poisonous. ❖ *n.* A toxic chemical or other substance. [LLat. *toxicus* < Lat. *toxicum*, poison < Gk. *toxikon*, poison for arrows, poison < neut. of *toxikos*, of a bow < *toxon*, bow < OPers. **taxša-*, an arrow.] —**tox′i·cal·ly** *adv.*

tox·i·cant (tŏk′sĭ-kənt) *n.* A poison or poisonous agent. ❖ *adj.* Poisonous; toxic.

tox·ic·i·ty (tŏk-sĭs′ĭ-tē) *n., pl.* **-ties 1.** The quality or condition of being toxic. **2.** The degree of toxicity.

toxico– or **toxic–** *pref.* Poison: *toxicosis.* [< Lat. *toxicum.* See TOXIC.]

tox·i·co·gen·ic (tŏk′sĭ-kō-jĕn′ĭk) *adj.* **1.** Producing poison or toxic substances. **2.** Derived from or having toxic matter.

tox·i·col·o·gy (tŏk′sĭ-kŏl′ə-jē) *n.* The study of the nature, effects, and detection of poisons and the treatment of poisoning. —**tox′i·co·log′i·cal** (-kə-lŏj′ĭ-kəl), **tox′i·co·log′ic** (-ĭk) *adj.* —**tox′i·co·log′i·cal·ly** *adv.* —**tox′i·col′o·gist** *n.*

tox·i·co·sis (tŏk′sĭ-kō′sĭs) *n., pl.* **-ses** (-sēz) A diseased condition resulting from poisoning.

toxic shock syndrome *n.* An acute infection marked by high fever, a sunburnlike rash, vomiting, and diarrhea, followed in severe cases by shock, caused by a toxin-producing strain of the bacterium *Staphylococcus aureus* and occurring chiefly among menstruating women who use tampons.

tox·i·gen·ic (tŏk′sə-jĕn′ĭk) *adj.* Producing poison; toxicogenic. —**tox′i·ge·nic′i·ty** (-jə-nĭs′ĭ-tē) *n.*

tox·in (tŏk′sĭn) *n.* A poisonous substance, esp. a protein, that is produced by living cells or organisms and is capable of causing disease but is often also capable of inducing neutralizing antibodies or antitoxins.

tox·in-an·ti·tox·in (tŏk′sĭn-ăn′tĭ-tŏk′sĭn) *n.* A mixture of a toxin and its antitoxin with a slight excess of toxin, formerly used as a vaccine.

tox·oid (tŏk′soid′) *n.* A substance that has been treated to destroy its toxic properties but retains the capacity to stimulate production of antitoxins, used in immunization.

tox·o·plas·ma (tŏk′sə-plăz′mə) *n.* Any of various parasitic

---

sporozoans of the genus *Toxoplasma.*

tox·o·plas·mo·sis (tŏk′sō-plăz-mō′sĭs) *n., pl.* **-mo·ses** (-mō′sēz) A disease caused by the sporozoan *Toxoplasma gondii*, esp.: **a.** A congenital disease marked by lesions of the central nervous system that can cause blindness and brain damage. **b.** An acquired disease marked by fever, swollen lymph nodes, and lesions in the liver, heart, lungs, and brain.

toy (toi) *n.* **1.** An object for children to play with. **2.** Something of little importance; a trifle. **3.** An amusement; a pastime. **4.** A small ornament; a bauble. **5.** A diminutive thing or person. **6.** A dog of a very small breed or of a variety smaller than the standard variety of its breed. **7.** *Scots* A loose covering for the head, formerly worn by women. **8.** *Chiefly Southern US* A shooter marble. ❖ *intr.v.* **toyed, toy·ing, toys 1.** To amuse oneself idly; trifle. **2.** To treat something casually or without seriousness. [ME *toye*, amorous play, some fun.]

To·ya·ma (tō-yä′mä) A city of W-central Honshu, Japan, on **Toyama Bay**, an inlet of the Sea of Japan. Pop. 324,073.

toy line *n. Chiefly Southern US* The line used in a game of marbles.

Toyn·bee (toin′bē), **Arnold Joseph** 1889–1975. British historian who studied cyclical patterns in civilizations.

To·yo·ha·shi (tō′yō-hä′shē) A city of S-central Honshu, Japan, on the Pacific Ocean SE of Nagoya. Pop. 349,590.

toy·on (toi′ŏn′) *n.* An evergreen Californian shrub (*Heteromeles arbutifolia*) having leathery leaves, small white flowers, and red fleshy berrylike fruit. [Sp. *tollon* < Gk. *tolon.*]

To·yo·na·ka (tō′yō-nä′kä) A city of S Honshu, Japan, a suburb of Osaka. Pop. 403,224.

To·yo·ta (toi-ō′tə, tō-yō′tä) A city of S-central Honshu, Japan, ESE of Nagoya. Pop. 341,453.

Tp. *abbr.* township

TPA or **tPA** *abbr.* tissue plasminogen activator

Tpk. *abbr.* turnpike

TR or **T-R** *abbr.* transmit-receive

tr. *abbr.* **1.** transitive **2a.** translated **b.** translation **c.** translator **3a.** transpose **b.** transposition **4.** treasurer **5a.** trust **b.** trustee

tra·be·at·ed (trā′bē-ā′tĭd) also **tra·be·ate** (-bē-ĭt, -āt′) *adj. Architecture* Having horizontal beams or lintels. [< Lat. *trabs*, beam (influenced by *trabeātus*, clothes in the trabea, a ritual garment).] —**tra′be·a′tion** *n.*

tra·bec·u·la (trə-bĕk′yə-lə) *n., pl.* **-lae** (-lē′) **1.** A small supporting beam or bar. **2.** *Anatomy* Any of the supporting strands of connective tissue projecting into an organ and constituting part of the framework of that organ. [Lat. *trabēcula*, dim. of *trabs*, beam-, beam.] —**tra·bec′u·lar** *adj.*

Trab·zon (träb-zŏn′, träb-zôn′) or **Treb·i·zond** (trĕb′ĭ-zŏnd′) A city of NE Turkey on the Black Sea. Pop. 145,400.

trace[1] (trās) *n.* **1a.** A visible mark, such as a footprint, made or left by the passage of a person, animal, or thing. **b.** Evidence or an indication of the former presence or existence of something; a vestige. **2.** A barely perceivable indication; a touch: *a trace of sarcasm.* **3a.** An extremely small amount. **b.** A constituent, such as a chemical element, present in quantities less than a standard limit. **4.** A path or trail beaten out by the passage of animals or people. **5.** A way or route followed. **6.** A line drawn by a recording instrument, such as a cardiograph. **7.** *Mathematics* **a.** The point at which a line or the curve in which a surface intersects a coordinate plane. **b.** The sum of the elements of the principal diagonal of a matrix. **8.** An engram. ❖ *v.* **traced, trac·ing, trac·es** —*tr.* **1.** To follow the course or trail of. **2.** To ascertain the successive stages in the development or progress of. **3.** To locate or discover by searching or researching evidence. **4.** To draw (a line or figure); sketch; delineate. **5.** To form (letters) with special concentration or care. **6a.** To copy by following lines seen through a sheet of transparent paper. **b.** To follow closely (a prescribed pattern): *The skater traced a figure eight.* **7a.** To imprint (a design) by pressure with an instrument on a superimposed pattern. **b.** To make a design or series of markings on (a surface) by such pressure with a pattern. **8.** To record (a variable), as on a graph. —*intr.* **1.** To make one's way along a trail or course. **2.** To have origins; be traceable. ❖ *adj.* Occurring in extremely small amounts or in quantities less than a standard limit. [ME, track < OFr. < *tracier*, to make one's way < VLat. **tractiāre* < Lat. *tractus*, a dragging, course < p. part. of *trahere*, to draw.] —**trace′a·bil′i·ty** *n.* —**trace′a·ble** *adj.* —**trace′a·bly** *adv.*

trace[2] (trās) *n.* **1.** One of two side straps or chains connecting a harnessed draft animal to a vehicle or whiffletree. **2.** A bar or rod, hinged at either end to another part, that transfers movement from one part of a machine to another. [ME *trais* < OFr., pl. of *trait*, a hauling, harness strap < Lat. *tractus*, a hauling < p. part. of *trahere*, to haul.]

trace element *n.* **1.** A chemical element required in minute quantities by an organism to maintain proper physical functioning. **2.** A minute quantity or amount.

trac·er (trā′sər) *n.* **1a.** One who is employed to locate missing goods or persons. **b.** An investigation or inquiry organized to trace missing goods or persons. **2.** Any of several instruments used in making tracings or in imprinting designs by tracing. **3.** A tracer bullet. **4.** An identifiable substance, such as a radioactive isotope, that is introduced into a biological or mechanical system

---

ă pat oi boy
ā pay ou out
âr care ŏŏ took
ä father ōō boot
ĕ pet ŭ cut
ē be ûr urge
ĭ pit th thin
ī pie *th* this
îr pier hw which
ŏ pot zh vision
ō toe ə about,
ô paw item

Stress marks:
′ (primary);
′ (secondary), as in
lexicon (lĕk′sĭ-kŏn′)

and can be followed through the course of a process.

tracer bullet *n.* A bullet that leaves a luminous or smoky trail.

trac·er·y (trā′sə-rē) *n., pl.* **-ies** Ornamental work of interlaced and branching lines, esp. the lacy openwork in a Gothic window. [< TRACE¹.] **—trac′er·ied** *adj.*

tra·che·a (trā′kē-ə) *n., pl.* **-che·ae** (-kē-ē′) or **-che·as 1.** *Anatomy* A thin-walled, cartilaginous tube descending from the larynx to the bronchi and carrying air to the lungs. **2.** *Zoology* One of the internal respiratory tubes of insects and some other terrestrial arthropods. **3.** *Botany* One of the tubular conductive vessels in the xylem of vascular plants. [ME *trache* < Med.Lat. *trāchēa* < LLat. *trāchīa* < Gk. *(artēria) trākheia,* rough (artery), trachea (as opposed to the smooth vessels that carry blood and not air), fem. of *trākhus.*] **—tra′che·al** *adj.*

tra·che·ate (trā′kē-āt′, -ĭt) *adj.* Having tracheae. Used of arthropods. ❖ *n.* A tracheate arthropod.

tra·che·id (trā′kē-ĭd, -kēd′) *n.* A xylem cell in vascular plants. **—tra·che′i·dal** (trā-kē′ĭ-dl, -kēd′l) *adj.*

tra·che·i·tis (trā′kē-ī′tĭs) *n.* Inflammation of the trachea.

tracheo– or **trache–** *pref.* Trachea: *tracheid.* [NLat. *trāchēo–* < Med.Lat. *trāchēa.* See TRACHEA.]

tra·che·o·bron·chi·al (trā′kē-ō-brŏng′kē-əl) *adj.* Of or relating to the trachea and the bronchi.

tra·che·ole (trā′kē-ōl′) *n.* One of the fine branching tubes of the trachea of an insect. [NLat. *trāchēola,* dim. of Med.Lat. *trāchēa,* trachea. See TRACHEA.]

tra·che·o·phyte (trā′kē-ə-fīt′) *n.* Any of various vascular plants having a conducting system of xylem and phloem. [< NLat. *Trāchēophyta,* division name : TRACHEO– + Gk. *phuta,* pl. of *phuton,* plant; see bheuə- in App.]

tra·che·os·to·my (trā′kē-ŏs′tə-mē) *n., pl.* **-mies 1.** Surgical construction of an opening in the trachea to facilitate breathing. **2.** The opening so made.

tra·che·ot·o·my (trā′kē-ŏt′ə-mē) *n., pl.* **-mies** Surgical incision of the trachea through the neck, as to make an artificial opening for breathing.

tra·cho·ma (trə-kō′mə) *n.* A contagious disease of the conjunctiva and cornea, caused by the gram-negative bacterium *Chlamydia trachomatis* and characterized by inflammation, hypertrophy, and formation of granules of adenoid tissue. [NLat. *trāchōma* < Gk. *trākhōma* < *trākhus,* rough.]

tra·chyte (trā′kīt′, trăk′īt′) *n.* A light-colored igneous rock consisting essentially of alkali feldspar. [Fr. < Gk. *trākhus,* rough.] **—tra·chyt′ic** (trə-kĭt′ĭk) *adj.*

trac·ing (trā′sĭng) *n.* **1.** A reproduction made by superimposing a transparent sheet and copying the lines of the original on it. **2.** A graphic record made by a recording instrument, such as a cardiograph or seismograph.

track (trăk) *n.* **1a.** A mark or succession of marks left by something that has passed. **b.** A path, route, or course indicated by such marks. **2.** A path along which something moves; a course. **3a.** A course of action; a method of proceeding. **b.** An intended or proper course. **4.** A succession of ideas; a train of thought. Awareness of something occurring or passing: *lost track of time.* **6.** *Sports* **a.** A course laid out for running or racing. **b.** Athletic competition on such a course; track events. **c.** Track and field. **7.** A rail or set of parallel rails upon which railroad cars or other vehicles run. **8. tracks** The boundary, formerly often delineated by train tracks, that separates two neighborhoods of different social class: *grew up on the wrong side of the tracks.* **9.** Either of the continuous metal belts with which vehicles such as bulldozers and tanks move over the ground. **10.** A metal groove or ridge that holds, guides, and reduces friction for a moving device or apparatus. **11.** Any of several courses of study to which students are assigned according to ability, achievement, or needs. **12a.** A distinct path, as along a length of film or magnetic tape, on which sound, images, or other information is recorded. **b.** A distinct selection from a sound recording, usu. containing an individual work or part of a larger work. **c.** One of the separate sound recordings that are combined so as to be heard simultaneously, as in stereophonic sound reproduction. **13.** *Computer Science* One of the concentric magnetic rings that form the separate data storage areas on a disk. **14. tracks** *Slang* Needle marks on the skin from multiple intravenous injections, as from habitual drug use. ❖ *v.* **tracked, track·ing, tracks** *—tr.* **1.** To follow the tracks of; trail. **2.** To move over or along; traverse. **3.** To carry on the shoes and deposit. **4.** To observe or monitor the course of (aircraft, for example), as by radar. **5.** To observe the progress of; follow. **6.** To equip with a track. **7.** To assign (a student) to a curricular track. *—intr.* **1.** To move along a track. **2.** To follow a course; travel. **3.** To keep a constant distance apart. Used of a pair of wheels. **4.** To be in alignment. **5a.** To follow the undulations in the groove of a phonograph record. Used of a needle. **b.** To move across magnetic heads. Used of magnetic tape. **—phrasal verb: track down** To pursue until found or captured. **—idiom: in one's tracks** Exactly where one is standing. [ME *trak* < OFr. *trac,* perh. of Gmc. orig.] **—track′a·ble** *adj.* **—track′er** *n.*

track·age (trăk′ĭj) *n.* **1.** Railway tracks. **2a.** The right of one railroad company to use the track system of another. **b.** The charge for this right.

track and field *n.* Athletic events performed on a running track

and the field associated with it. **—track′-and-field′** (trăk′ən-fēld′) *adj.*

track·ball (trăk′bôl′) *n.* A ball mounted in a stationary housing, rotated to control a pointer on a computer screen.

track·ing (trăk′ĭng) *n.* **1.** The placing of students in any of several courses of study according to ability, achievement, or needs. **2.** The position of a magnetic tape as it moves across magnetic heads, as in a VCR.

tracking shot *n.* A movie shot made by a camera moving steadily on a track or dolly.

tracking station *n.* A station for observing the path of and maintaining contact with an object in the atmosphere or in space esp. by means of radar or radio.

track·less (trăk′lĭs) *adj.* **1.** Not running on tracks or rails. **2.** Unmarked by trails or paths.

trackless trolley *n.* A trolley bus.

track light *n.* A light mounted on and movable along an electrified metal track. **—track lighting** *n.*

track·man (trăk′mən) *n.* A worker employed to maintain or inspect railroad tracks.

track record *n. Informal* A record of actual performance or accomplishment.

track·suit (trăk′soōt′) *n.* A loose-fitting jacket and pants worn by athletes and exercisers usu. preceding and following workouts.

track·walk·er (trăk′wô′kər) *n.* A worker employed to inspect a section of railroad track.

tract¹ (trăkt) *n.* **1a.** An expanse of land or water. **b.** A specified or limited area of land. **2.** *Anatomy* **a.** A system of organs and tissues that together perform a specialized function: *the alimentary tract.* **b.** A bundle of nerve fibers having a common origin, termination, and function. **3.** *Archaic* A stretch or lapse of time. [ME, period of time < Lat. *tractus,* course, space, period of time < p. part. of *trahere,* to draw.]

tract² (trăkt) *n.* A leaflet or pamphlet containing a declaration or appeal, esp. one put out by a religious or political group. [ME *tracte,* treatise, prob. short for Lat. *tractātus* < p. part. of *tractāre,* to discuss, freq. of *trahere,* to draw.]

tract³ (trăkt) *n.* The verses from Scripture sung during Lent or on Ember Days after the gradual in the Roman Catholic Mass. [ME *tracte* < Med.Lat. *tractus* < Lat., a drawing out (< its being an uninterrupted solo). See TRACT¹.]

trac·ta·ble (trăk′tə-bəl) *adj.* **1.** Easily managed or controlled; governable. **2.** Easily handled or worked; malleable. [Lat. *tractabilis* < *tractāre,* to manage, freq. of *trahere,* to draw.] **—trac′ta·bil′i·ty, trac′ta·ble·ness** *n.* **—trac′ta·bly** *adv.*

Trac·tar·i·an·ism (trăk-târ′ē-ə-nĭz′əm) *n.* The religious opinions and principles of the founders of the Oxford movement, put forth in a series of pamphlets entitled *Tracts for the Times.* **—Trac·tar′i·an** *adj. & n.*

trac·tate (trăk′tāt′) *n.* A treatise; an essay. [Lat. *tractātus.* See TRACT².]

tract house *n.* One of numerous houses of similar or complementary design built on a tract of land. **—tract housing** *n.*

trac·tile (trăk′təl, -tīl′) *adj.* Capable of being drawn out in length; ductile: *a tractile metal.* [< Lat. *tractus,* p. part. of *trahere,* to draw.] **—trac·til′i·ty** (-tĭl′ĭ-tē) *n.*

trac·tion (trăk′shən) *n.* **1a.** The act of drawing or pulling. the drawing of a vehicle or load over a surface by motor power. **b.** The condition of being drawn or pulled. **2.** Pulling power, as of a draft animal. **3.** Adhesive friction, as of a tire on a road. **4.** *Medicine* A sustained pull applied mechanically, as to the neck, so as to correct fractured or dislocated bones, overcome muscle spasms, or relieve pressure. [Med.Lat. *tractiō, tractiōn-* < Lat. *tractus,* p. part. of *trahere,* to pull.] **—trac′tion·al** *adj.*

trac·tive (trăk′tĭv) *adj.* Serving to pull or draw; exerting traction. [< Lat. *tractus,* p. part. of *trahere,* to draw.]

trac·tor (trăk′tər) *n.* **1.** A vehicle having a powerful gasoline or diesel motor and usu. large, heavily treaded rear tires, used esp. for pulling farm implements or machinery. **2.** A truck having a cab and no body, used for pulling large vehicles such as vans or trailers. **3.** Something that pulls or draws. **4a.** An airplane propeller mounted in front of the supporting surfaces. **b.** An airplane having such a propeller. **5.** A toothed mechanism that automatically advances perforated continuous-form paper through a computer printer.

trac·tor-trail·er (trăk′tər-trā′lər) *n.* A truck consisting of a tractor attached to a semitrailer or trailer.

Tra·cy (trā′sē), **Spencer** 1900–67. Amer. actor whose motion pictures include *Captains Courageous* (1937) and *Boys Town* (1938).

trade (trād) *n.* **1.** The business of buying and selling commodities; commerce. See Syns at **business. 2.** The people working in or associated with a business or industry. **3.** The customers of a specified business or industry; clientele. **4.** The act or an instance of buying or selling; transaction. **5.** An exchange of one thing for another. **6.** An occupation, esp. one requiring skilled labor; craft. **7.** The trade winds. Often used in the plural. ❖ *v.* **trad·ed, trad·ing, trades** *—intr.* **1.** To engage in buying and selling for profit. **2.** To make an exchange of one thing for another. **3.** To be offered for sale: *Stocks traded at lower prices this morning.* **4.** To shop or buy regularly. *—tr.* **1.** To give in exchange for something else.

2. To buy and sell (stock, for example). **3.** To pass back and forth. ❖ *adj.* **1.** Relating to trade or commerce. **2.** Relating to or serving a particular trade. **3.** Relating to books that are primarily published to be sold commercially. —*phrasal verbs:* **trade down** To trade something in for something else of lower value or price. **trade in** To trade or sell (an old or used item), using the proceeds as partial payment on a new purchase. **trade on** To put to calculated and often unscrupulous advantage; exploit. **trade up** To trade something in for something else of greater value or price. [ME, course < MLGer.] —**trad•a•ble, trade•a•ble** *adj.*

trade acceptance *n.* A bill of exchange for the amount of a purchase drawn by the seller on the purchaser, with the purchaser's signature and time and place of payment.

trade book *n.* A book published for distribution to the general public through booksellers.

trade discount *n.* A discount on the list price granted by a manufacturer or wholesaler to buyers in the same trade.

trade edition *n.* A book edition published as a trade book.

trade-in (trād′ĭn′) *n.* **1.** Merchandise accepted as partial payment for a new purchase. **2.** A transaction involving such merchandise.

trade language *n.* A language, esp. a pidgin, used by speakers of different native languages for communication in commercial trade.

trade-last (trād′lăst′) *n. Informal* A compliment overheard about someone else that one offers to repeat to that person in return for a similar remark overheard about oneself.

trade•mark (trād′märk′) *n.* **1.** A name, symbol, or other device identifying a product, officially registered and legally restricted to the use of the owner or manufacturer. **2.** A distinctive characteristic by which a person or thing comes to be known. ❖ *tr.v.* **-marked, -mark•ing, -marks 1.** To label (a product) with proprietary identification. **-2.** To register (something) as a trademark.

trade name *n.* **1.** A name identifying a commercial product or service, which may or may not be a registered trademark. **2.** The name by which the trade knows a commodity, service, or process. **3.** The name under which a business firm operates.

trade•off or **trade-off** (trād′ôf′, -ŏf′) *n.* An exchange of one thing in return for another, esp. relinquishment of one benefit or advantage for another regarded as more desirable.

trad•er (trā′dər) *n.* **1.** One that trades; a dealer: *a gold trader; a trader in bonds.* **2.** *Nautical* A ship employed in foreign trade.

trade route *n.* A route used by traveling traders or merchant ships.

trade school *n.* A secondary school that offers instruction in skilled trades; a vocational school.

trade secret *n.* A secret formula, method, or device that gives one an advantage over competitors.

trades•man (trādz′mən) *n.* **1.** A man engaged in retail trade. **2.** A craftsman.

trades•peo•ple (trādz′pē′pəl) *pl.n.* **1.** People engaged in retail trade. **2.** Skilled workers.

trade union *n.* A labor union, esp. one limited to people in the same trade. —**trade unionism** *n.* —**trade unionist** *n.*

trade wind (wĭnd) *n.* Any of a consistent system of prevailing winds occupying most of the Tropics and blowing northeasterly in the Northern Hemisphere and southeasterly in the Southern Hemisphere. Often used in the plural. [< obsolete *to blow trade,* to blow in a regular course < TRADE, regular course (obsolete).]

trad•ing card (trā′dĭng) *n.* A card with a picture or design printed on it, often one of a set collected and traded.

trading post *n.* A station or store in a sparsely settled area established by traders to barter supplies for local products.

trading stamp *n.* A stamp given by a retailer to a buyer for a purchase of a specified amount and intended to be redeemed in quantity for merchandise.

tra•di•tion (trə-dĭsh′ən) *n.* **1.** The passing down of elements of a culture from generation to generation, esp. by oral communication. **2a.** A mode of thought or behavior followed by a people continuously from generation to generation; a custom or usage. **b.** A set of such customs and usages viewed as a coherent body of precedents influencing the present. **3.** A body of unwritten religious precepts. **4.** A time-honored practice or set of such practices. [Ult. < Lat. *trāditiō, trāditiōn-* < *trāditus,* p. part. of *trādere,* to hand over, deliver, entrust : *trā-, trāns-, trans-* + *dare,* to give; see **dō-** in App.]

tra•di•tion•al (trə-dĭsh′ə-nəl) *adj.* Of, relating to, or in accord with tradition. —**tra•di′tion•al•ly** *adv.*

tra•di•tion•al•ism (trə-dĭsh′ə-nə-lĭz′əm) *n.* **1.** Adherence to tradition, esp. in cultural or religious practice. **2.** A system holding that all knowledge is derived from original divine revelation and is transmitted by tradition. —**tra•di′tion•al•ist** *adj. & n.* —**tra•di′tion•al•is′tic** *adj.*

tra•di•tion•al•ize (trə-dĭsh′ə-nə-līz′) *tr.v.* **-ized, -iz•ing, -iz•es** To make traditional.

tra•duce (trə-dōōs′, -dyōōs′) *tr.v.* **-duced, -duc•ing, -duc•es** To cause humiliation or disgrace to by making malicious and false statements. [Lat. *trādūcere,* to lead as a spectacle, dishonor : *trā-, trāns-, trans-* + *dūcere,* to lead; see **deuk-** in App.] —**tra•duce′ment** *n.* —**tra•duc′er** *n.*

tra•du•cian•ism (trə-dōō′shə-nĭz′əm, -dyōō′-) *n. Theology* The belief that the soul is inherited from the parents along with the body. [< LLat. *trādūciānus,* believer in traducianism < *trādux, trāduc-,* inheritance < Lat., vine-branch trained for propagation < *trādūcere,* to lead across. See TRADUCE.]

Tra•fal•gar (trə-făl′gər), **Cape** A cape on the SW coast of Spain NW of the Strait of Gibraltar. The British navy defeated the French and Spanish fleets off Cape Trafalgar in 1805.

traf•fic (trăf′ĭk) *n.* **1a.** The passage of people or vehicles along routes of transportation. **b.** Vehicles or pedestrians in transit. **2a.** The commercial exchange of goods; trade. **b.** Illegal or improper commercial activity. **3a.** The business of moving passengers and cargo through a transportation system. See Syns at **business. b.** The amount of cargo or number of passengers conveyed. **4a.** The conveyance of messages or data through a system of communication: *routers that manage Internet traffic.* **b.** Messages or data conveyed through such a system. **5.** Social or verbal exchange; communication. ❖ *intr.v.* **-ficked, -fick•ing, -fics** To carry on trade or other dealings. [Fr. *trafic* < OFr. *trafique* < OItal. *traffico* < *trafficare,* to trade, perh. < Catalan *trafegar,* to decant < VLat. **trānsfaecāre : trāns-,* trans- + *faex, faec-,* dregs; see FECES.] —**traf′fick•er** *n.*

traffic circle *n.* A circular one-way road at a junction of thoroughfares, facilitating an uninterrupted flow of traffic.

traffic island *n.* A raised area over which cars may not pass at a junction of thoroughfares or between opposing traffic lanes.

traffic light *n.* A road signal for directing vehicular traffic by means of colored lights, typically red for stop, green for go, and yellow for proceed with caution.

trag•a•canth (trăg′ə-kănth′, trăj′-) *n.* **1.** Any of various thorny Middle Eastern shrubs of the genus *Astragalus,* esp. *A. gummifer,* yielding a gum used in pharmaceuticals, adhesives, and textile printing. **2.** The gum of this plant. [Lat. *tragacantha* < Gk. *tragakantha : tragos,* goat + *akantha,* thorn.]

tra•ge•di•an (trə-jē′dē-ən) *n.* **1.** A writer of tragedies. **2.** One who performs tragic roles in the theater.

tra•ge•di•enne (trə-jē′dē-ĕn′) *n.* A woman who performs tragic roles in the theater. [Fr., fem. of *tragédien,* tragedian < OFr. *tragedian* < *tragedie,* tragedy. See TRAGEDY.]

trag•e•dy (trăj′ĭ-dē) *n., pl.* **-dies 1a.** A drama or literary work in which the main character is brought to ruin or suffers extreme sorrow, esp. as a consequence of a tragic flaw, moral weakness, or inability to cope with unfavorable circumstances. **b.** The genre made up of such works. **c.** The art or theory of writing or producing these works. **2.** A play, film, television program, or other narrative work that portrays or depicts calamitous events and has an unhappy ending. **3.** A disastrous event, esp. one involving distressing loss or injury to life. **4.** A tragic aspect or element. [ME *tragedie* < OFr. < Lat. *tragoedia* < Gk. *tragōidiā : tragos,* goat + *aoidē, ōidē,* song.]

trag•ic (trăj′ĭk) also **trag•i•cal** (-ĭ-kəl) *adj.* **1.** Relating to or characteristic of dramatic tragedy or tragedies. **2.** Writing or performing in tragedy. **3.** Having the elements of tragedy; involving death, grief, or destruction. [Lat. *tragicus* < Gk. *tragikos* < *tragos,* goat.] —**trag′i•cal•ly** *n.*

tragic flaw *n.* A flaw in the character of the protagonist of a tragedy that brings the protagonist to ruin or sorrow.

tragic irony *n.* Dramatic irony in a tragedy.

trag•i•com•e•dy (trăj′ĭ-kŏm′ĭ-dē) *n., pl.* **-dies 1.** A drama combining elements of tragedy and comedy. **2.** The genre made up of such works. **3.** An incident or situation having both comic and tragic elements. [Fr. *tragicomédie* < Ital. *tragicommedia* < LLat. *tragicōmoedia,* short for Lat. *tragicocōmoedia : tragicus,* tragic; see TRAGIC + *cōmoedia,* comedy; see COMEDY.] —**trag′i•com′ic** (-kŏm′ĭk), **trag′i•com′i•cal** (-ĭ-kəl) *adj.* —**trag′i•com′i•cal•ly** *adv.*

trag•o•pan (trăg′ə-păn′) *n.* Any of several Asian pheasants of the genus *Tragopan,* the male of which has two blue hornlike appendages on the head. [NLat. *Tragopān,* genus name < Lat. *tragopān,* fabulous bird < Gk. : *tragos,* goat + *Pān,* Pan; see PAN.]

tra•gus (trā′gəs) *n., pl.* **-gi** (-gī, -jī) **1.** The projection of skin-covered cartilage in front of the meatus of the external ear. **2.** Any of the hairs growing in the meatus of the external ear. [NLat. < Gk. *tragos,* goat, hairy part of the ear.]

trail (trāl) *v.* **trailed, trail•ing, trails** —*tr.* **1.** To allow to drag or stream behind, as along the ground. **2.** To drag (the body, for example) wearily or heavily. **3a.** To follow the traces or scent of, as in hunting; track. **b.** To follow the course taken by; pursue: *trail a fugitive.* **4.** To follow behind. **5.** To lag behind (an opponent). —*intr.* **1.** To drag or be dragged along, brushing the ground. **2.** To extend, grow, or droop loosely over a surface. **3.** To drift in a thin stream: *smoke trailing from a dying fire.* **4.** To become gradually fainter; dwindle: *His voice trailed off.* **5.** To walk or proceed with dragging steps; trudge. **6.** To be behind in competition; lag. ❖ *n.* **1a.** A marked or beaten path, as through woods or wilderness. **b.** An overland route. **2a.** A mark, trace, course, or path left by a moving body. **b.** The scent of a person or animal: *The dogs lost the trail of the fox.* **3.** Something that is drawn along or follows behind; a train. **4.** A succession of things that come afterward or are left behind. **5.** Something that hangs loose and long. **6.** The part of a gun carriage that rests or slides on the ground. **7.** The act of trailing. [ME *trailen,* prob. < OFr. *trailler,* to hunt without a foreknown course < VLat. **trāgulāre,* to make a deer double back and forth, perh. alteration of Lat. *trahere*, to pull, draw.]

trail bike *n.* **1.** See **dirt bike** 1. **2.** See **mountain bike**.

trail·blaz·er (trāl′blā′zər) *n.* **1.** One that blazes a trail. **2.** An innovative leader in a field; a pioneer. —**trail′blaz′ing** *adj.*

trail·er (trā′lər) *n.* **1.** A large transport vehicle designed to be hauled by a truck or tractor. **2.** A furnished vehicle drawn by a truck or automobile and used when parked as a dwelling or office. **3a.** A short filmed advertisement for a movie; a preview. **b.** A short blank strip of film at the end of a reel. ❖ *v.* **-ered, -er·ing, -ers** —*tr.* To transport by a trailer. —*intr.* To travel or live in a trailer.

trailer park *n.* An area in which parking space for house trailers is rented, usu. providing utilities and services.

trail·ing arbutus (trā′lǐng) *n.* A low-growing evergreen shrub (*Epigaea repens*) of eastern North America having leathery leaves and clusters of fragrant pink or white flowers.

trailing edge *n.* The rearmost edge of a moving structure, such as an airfoil.

trail mix *n.* A mixture of high-energy foods, such as dried fruit, nuts, chocolate, and seeds, eaten as a snack esp. by hikers.

train (trān) *n.* **1.** A series of connected railroad cars pulled or pushed by one or more locomotives. **2.** A long line of moving people, animals, or vehicles. **3.** The personnel, vehicles, and equipment following and providing supplies and services to a combat unit. **4.** A part of a gown that trails behind the wearer. **5.** A staff of people following in attendance; a retinue. **6a.** An orderly succession of related events or thoughts; a sequence. **b.** A series of consequences wrought by an event; aftermath. **7.** A set of linked mechanical parts: *a train of gears.* **8.** A string of gunpowder that acts as a fuse for exploding a charge. ❖ *v.* **trained, train·ing, trains** —*tr.* **1.** To coach or accustom to a mode of behavior or performance. **2.** To make proficient with specialized instruction and practice. See Syns at **teach. 3.** To prepare physically, as with a regimen. **4.** To cause (a plant or one's hair) to take a desired course or shape, as by manipulating. **5.** To focus on or aim at (a goal, mark, or target); direct. **6.** To let drag behind; trail. —*intr.* To give or undergo a course of training. **2.** To travel by railroad train. [ME, trailing part of a gown < OFr. < *trainer,* to drag < VLat. **tragīnāre* < **tragere,* to pull, back-formation < *tractus,* p. part. of Lat. *trahere.*] —**train′a·bil′i·ty** *n.* —**train′a·ble** *adj.*

train·band (trān′bǎnd′) *n.* A company of trained militia in England or America from the 16th to the 18th century. [Contraction of *trained band.*]

train·ee (trā-nē′) *n.* One who is being trained. —**train·ee′ship′** *n.*

train·er (trā′nər) *n.* **1.** One who trains, esp. one who coaches athletes, racehorses, or show animals. **2.** A contrivance or apparatus used in training.

train·ing (trā′nǐng) *n.* **1.** The process or routine of one who trains. **2.** The state of being trained.

training school *n.* **1.** A school that gives practical vocational and technical instruction. **2.** A detention home that offers vocational training to juvenile offenders.

training wheels *pl.n.* A pair of small wheels attached to the rear axle of a bicycle so that beginning riders can ride without falling over.

train·load (trān′lōd′) *n.* The number of occupants or the amount of material that a passenger or freight train can hold.

train·man (trān′mən) *n.* A member of the operating crew on a railroad train, esp. the brakeman.

train oil *n.* Oil obtained from the blubber of a whale or other marine animal. [ME *trane* < MDu. See **dakru-** in App.]

traipse (trāps) *v.* **traipsed, traips·ing, traips·es** —*intr.* To walk or tramp about; gad. —*tr.* To walk or tramp over or about. [Perh. ult. < OFr. *trespasser,* to trespass. See TRESPASS.]

trait (trāt) *n.* **1.** A distinguishing feature, as of a person's character. **2.** A genetically determined characteristic or condition. **3a.** A stroke or line as if with a pencil. **b.** A slight degree or amount, as of a quality; a touch or trace. [ME, shot < OFr. < Lat. *tractus,* a drawing out, line. See TRACT¹.]

trai·tor (trā′tər) *n.* One who betrays one's country, a cause, or a trust, esp. one who commits treason. [ME < OFr. < Lat. *trāditor* < *trāditus,* p. part. of *trādere,* to betray. See TRADITION.]

trai·tor·ous (trā′tər-əs) *adj.* **1.** Having the character of a traitor; disloyal. **2.** Constituting treason. —**trai′tor·ous·ly** *adv.*

Tra·jan (trā′jən) Originally Marcus Ulpius Trajanus A.D. 53–117. Roman emperor (98–117) whose reign was marked by an extensive building program.

tra·ject (trə-jěkt′) *tr.v.* **-ject·ed, -ject·ing, -jects** To transmit. [Lat. *trāicere, trāiect-,* to throw across : *trā-, trāns-,* trans- + *iacere,* to throw.] —**tra·jec′tion** *n.*

tra·jec·to·ry (trə-jěk′tə-rē) *n., pl.* **-ries 1a.** The path of a projectile or other moving body through space. **b.** A chosen or taken course. **2.** *Mathematics* A curve that cuts all of a given family of curves or surfaces at the same angle. [NLat. *trāiectōria* < Lat. *trāiectus,* p. part. of *trāicere,* to throw across. See TRAJECT.]

tram¹ (trăm) *n.* **1.** *Chiefly British* **a.** A streetcar. **b.** A streetcar line. **2.** A cable car, esp. one suspended from an overhead cable. **3.** A four-wheeled open box-shaped wagon or iron car run on tracks

Trajan

in a coal mine. ❖ *tr.v.* **trammed, tram·ming, trams** To move or convey in a tram. [Sc., shaft of a barrow, prob. < MFlem.]

tram² (trăm) *n.* **1.** An instrument for gauging and adjusting machine parts; a trammel. **2.** Accurate mechanical adjustment. ❖ *tr.v.* **trammed, tram·ming, trams** To adjust or align (mechanical parts) with a trammel. [Short for TRAMMEL.]

tram³ (trăm) *n.* A heavy silk thread used for the weft in fine velvet or silk. [ME, contrivance < OFr. *traime,* contrivance, weft < Lat. *trāma,* weft, woof.]

tram·line (trăm′līn′) *n. Chiefly British* A streetcar line.

tram·mel (trăm′əl) *n.* **1.** A shackle used to teach a horse to amble. **2.** Something that restricts activity, expression, or progress; a restraint. **3.** A vertically set fishing net of three layers, consisting of a finely meshed net between two nets of coarse mesh. **4.** An instrument for describing ellipses. **5.** An instrument for gauging and adjusting parts of a machine; a tram. **6.** An arrangement of links and a hook in a fireplace for raising and lowering a kettle. ❖ *tr.v.* **-meled, -mel·ing, -mels** or **-melled, -mel·ling, -mels 1.** To enmesh in or as if in a fishing net. **2.** To hinder the activity or free movement of. [ME *tramale,* a kind of net < OFr. *tramail* < LLat. *trēmaculum* : Lat. *trēs,* three; see **trei-** in App. + Lat. *macula,* mesh.] —**tram′mel·er** *n.*

tra·mon·tane (trə-mŏn′tān′, trăm′ən-tān′) *adj.* **1.** Dwelling beyond or coming from the far side of the mountains, esp. the Alps as viewed from Italy. **2.** From another country; foreign. ❖ *n.* **1.** A person who lives beyond the mountains. **2.** A foreigner; a stranger. **3.** A cold north wind in Italy. [Ital. *tramontano* < Lat. *trānsmontānus* : *trāns-,* trans- + *montānus,* of a mountain; see MOUNTAIN.]

tramp (trămp) *v.* **tramped, tramp·ing, tramps** —*intr.* **1.** To walk with a firm heavy step; trudge. **2a.** To travel on foot; hike. **b.** To wander about aimlessly. —*tr.* **1.** To traverse on foot: *tramp the fields.* **2.** To tread down; trample. ❖ *n.* **1a.** A heavy footfall. **b.** The sound produced by heavy walking or marching. **2.** A walking trip; a hike. **3.** One who travels aimlessly about on foot, doing odd jobs or begging for a living; a vagrant. **4a.** A prostitute. **b.** A person regarded as promiscuous. **5.** *Nautical* A tramp steamer. **6.** A metal plate attached to the sole of a shoe for protection, as when spading ground. [ME *trampen,* to walk heavily < MLGer.] —**tramp′er** *n.* —**tramp′ish** *adj.* —**tramp′y** *adj.*

tram·ple (trăm′pəl) *v.* **-pled, -pling, -ples** —*tr.* **1.** To beat down with the feet so as to crush, bruise, or destroy; tramp on. **2.** To treat harshly or ruthlessly. —*intr.* **1.** To tread heavily or destructively. **2.** To inflict injury as if by treading heavily. ❖ *n.* The action or sound of trampling. [ME *tramplen,* freq. of *trampen,* to tramp. See TRAMP.] —**tram′pler** *n.*

tram·po·line (trăm′pə-lēn′, -lǐn) *n.* A strong taut sheet, usu. of canvas, attached with springs to a metal frame and used for gymnastic springing and tumbling. [Sp. *trampolín* and Ital. *trampolino* (Ital. < Sp.) < *tràmpoli,* stilts, of Gmc. orig.] —**tram′po·lin′er, tram′po·lin′ist** *n.*

tramp steamer *n. Nautical* A commercial vessel with no regular schedule that takes on and discharges cargo as hired.

tram·way (trăm′wā′) *n.* **1.** A track or way for trams, as in a mine. **2.** *Chiefly British* A streetcar line. **3.** A cable or system of cables for a cable car.

trance (trăns) *n.* **1.** A hypnotic, cataleptic, or ecstatic state. **2.** Detachment from one's physical surroundings, as in contemplation or daydreaming. **3.** A semiconscious state, as between sleeping and waking; a daze. ❖ *tr.v.* **tranced, tranc·ing, tranc·es** To put into a trance; entrance. [ME *traunce* < OFr. *transe,* passage, fear, vision < *transir,* to die, be numb with fear < Lat. *trānsīre,* to go over or across. See TRANSIENT.]

tran·quil (trăng′kwəl, trăn′-) *adj.* **1.** Free from commotion or disturbance. See Syns at **calm. 2.** Free from anxiety, tension, or restlessness; composed. **3.** Steady; even: *a tranquil flame.* [ME *tranquil* < Lat. *tranquillus.*] —**tran′quil·ly** *adv.*

tran·quil·ize also **tran·quil·lize** (trăng′kwə-līz′, trăn′-) *v.* **-ized, -iz·ing, -iz·es** also **-lized, -liz·ing, -liz·es** —*tr.* **1.** To make tranquil; pacify. **2.** To sedate or relieve of anxiety or tension by the administration of a drug. —*intr.* **1.** To become tranquil; relax. **2.** To have a calming or soothing effect. —**tran′quil·i·za′tion** (-kwə-lǐ-zā′shən) *n.*

tran·quil·iz·er (trăng′kwə-līz′ər, trăn′-) *n.* **1.** One that serves to tranquilize. **2.** Any of various drugs used to reduce tension or anxiety. **3.** An antipsychotic drug. Not in scientific use.

tran·quil·li·ty or **tran·quil·i·ty** (trăng-kwĭl′ĭ-tē, trăn-) *n.* The quality or state of being tranquil; serenity.

trans– *pref.* **1.** Across; on the other side; beyond: *transpolar.* **2.** Through: *transcontinental.* **3.** Change; transfer: *transliterate.* **4.** A prefix used to denote a geometric isomer in which a pair of identical atoms or groups are located on opposite sides of a double bond or ring: *trans-butene.* [< Lat. *trāns-* < *trāns,* across, beyond, through. See **terə-²** in App.]

trans·act (trăn-săkt′, -zăkt′) *v.* **-act·ed, -act·ing, -acts** —*tr.* To do, carry on, or conduct: *transact business.* —*intr.* To conduct business. [Lat. *trānsigere, trānsāct-* : *trāns-,* trans- + *agere,* to drive, do; see **ag-** in App.] —**trans·ac′tor** *n.*

trans·ac·ti·nide (trăn-săk′tə-nīd′, -zăk′-) *adj.* Of or belonging to the series of elements whose atomic numbers are greater than 103.

trans·ac·tion (trăn-săk′shən, -zăk′-) *n.* **1.** The act of transacting or the fact of being transacted. **2.** Something transacted, esp. a business agreement or exchange. **3.** Communication involving two or more people that affects all those involved; personal interaction. **4. transactions** A record of business at a meeting; proceedings. —**trans·ac′tion·al** *adj.*

transactional analysis *n.* A system of psychotherapy that analyzes personal relationships and interactions in terms of conflicting or complementary ego states that correspond to the roles of parent, child, and adult.

Trans A·lai (trăns′ ə-lī′, trănz′) A range of the Pamir Mts. in E Tajikistan and S Kyrgyzstan rising to 7,138.5 m (23,405 ft).

trans·al·pine (trăns-ăl′pīn′, trănz-) *adj.* Of, living on, or coming from the other side of the Alps, esp. as seen from Italy.

Transalpine Gaul The part of ancient Gaul NW of the Alps, including France and Belgium.

trans·am·i·nase (trăns-ăm′ə-nās′, -nāz′, trănz-) *n.* Any of a group of enzymes that catalyze transamination.

trans·am·i·na·tion (trăns-ăm′ə-nā′shən, trănz-) *n.* **1.** Transfer of an amino group from one chemical compound to another. **2.** Transposition of an amino group within a chemical compound.

trans·at·lan·tic (trăns′ət-lăn′tĭk, trănz′-) *adj.* **1.** Situated on or coming from the other side of the Atlantic Ocean. **2.** Spanning or crossing the Atlantic Ocean.

trans·ax·le (trăns-ăk′səl, trănz-) *n.* An automotive part that combines the transmission and the differential and is used on vehicles with front-wheel drive. [TRANS(MISSION) + AXLE.]

Trans·cau·ca·sia (trăns′kô-kā′zhə, trănz′-) A region of Georgia, Armenia, and Azerbaijan between the Caucasus Mts. and Turkey and Iran. —**Trans′cau·ca′sian** *adj. & n.*

trans·ceiv·er (trăn-sē′vər) *n.* A transmitter and receiver in a single unit sharing some circuits.

tran·scend (trăn-sĕnd′) *v.* **-scend·ed, -scend·ing, -scends** —*tr.* **1.** To pass beyond the limits of. **2.** To be greater than, as in intensity or power; surpass. **3.** To exist above and independent of (material experience or the universe). —*intr.* To be transcendent; excel. [Ult. < Lat. *trānscendere* : *trāns-*, trans- + *scandere*, to climb.]

tran·scen·dent (trăn-sĕn′dənt) *adj.* **1.** Surpassing others; preeminent or supreme. **2.** Lying beyond ordinary perception. **3.** *Philosophy* **a.** Transcending the Aristotelian categories. **b.** In Kant's theory of knowledge, being beyond the limits of experience and hence unknowable. **4.** Being above and independent of the material universe. Used of the Deity. —**tran·scen′dence, tran·scen′den·cy** *n.* —**tran·scen′dent·ly** *adv.*

tran·scen·den·tal (trăn′sĕn-dĕn′tl) *adj.* **1.** *Philosophy* **a.** Concerned with the a priori or intuitive basis of knowledge as independent of experience. **b.** Asserting a fundamental irrationality or supernatural element in experience. **2.** Surpassing all others; superior. **3.** Beyond common thought or experience; mystical or supernatural. **4.** *Mathematics* Of or relating to a real or complex number that is not the root of any polynomial that has positive degree and rational coefficients. —**tran′scen·den′tal·ly** *adv.*

tran·scen·den·tal·ism (trăn′sĕn-dĕn′tl-ĭz′əm) *n.* **1.** A literary and philosophical movement asserting the existence of an ideal spiritual reality transcending the empirical and knowable through intuition. **2.** The quality or state of being transcendental. —**tran′scen·den′tal·ist** *n.*

transcendental meditation *n.* A technique of meditation derived from Hindu traditions that promotes deep relaxation through the use of a mantra.

trans·con·ti·nen·tal (trăns′kŏn-tə-nĕn′tl) *adj.* Spanning or crossing a continent.

tran·scribe (trăn-skrīb′) *tr.v.* **-scribed, -scrib·ing, -scribes 1.** To make a full written or typewritten copy of (dictated material, for example). **2.** *Computer Science* To transfer (information) from one recording and storing system to another. **3.** *Music* To adapt or arrange (a composition) for a voice or an instrument other than the original. **4.** To record, usu. on tape, for later broadcast. **5.** *Linguistics* To represent (speech sounds) by phonetic symbols. **6.** To translate or transliterate. **7.** *Biology* To cause (DNA) to undergo transcription. [Lat. *trānscrībere* : *trāns-*, trans- + *scrībere*, to write; see **skrībh-** in App.] —**tran·scrib′a·ble** *adj.* —**tran·scrib′er** *n.*

tran·script (trăn′skrĭpt′) *n.* **1.** Something transcribed, esp. a written or typewritten copy. **2.** *Biology* A sequence of RNA produced by transcription. [ME < Med.Lat. *trānscrīptum* < Lat., neut. p. part. of *trānscrībere*, to transcribe. See TRANSCRIBE.]

tran·scrip·tase (trăn-skrĭp′tās, -tāz) *n.* A polymerase that catalyzes the formation of RNA from a DNA template in the process of transcription. **2.** Reverse transcriptase.

tran·scrip·tion (trăn-skrĭp′shən) *n.* **1.** The act or process of transcribing. **2.** Something that has been transcribed, esp.: **a.** *Music* An adaptation of a composition. **b.** A recorded radio or television program. **c.** *Linguistics* A representation of speech sounds in phonetic symbols. **3.** *Biology* The process by which messenger RNA is synthesized from a DNA template. —**tran·scrip′tion·al** *adj.* —**tran·scrip′tion·ist** *n.*

trans·cur·rent (trăns-kûr′ənt, -kŭr′-) *adj.* Extending or running transversely.

trans·cu·ta·ne·ous (trăns′kyoō-tā′nē-əs) *adj.* Transdermal.

trans·der·mal (trăns-dûr′məl, trănz-) *adj.* Through or by way of the skin.

transdermal patch *n.* An adhesive pad that delivers a time-release dose of medication through the skin into the bloodstream.

trans·duce (trăns-doōs′, -dyoōs′, trănz-) *tr.v.* **-duced, -duc·ing, -duc·es 1.** To convert (energy) from one form to another. **2.** To transfer (genetic material or characteristics) from one bacterial cell to another. Used of a bacteriophage or plasmid. [Back-formation < TRANSDUCER.]

trans·duc·er (trăns-doō′sər, -dyoō′-, trănz-) *n.* A substance or device that converts input energy of one form into output energy of another. [< Lat. *trānsdūcere*, to transfer : *trāns-*, trans- + *dū-cere*, to lead; see **deuk-** in App.]

trans·duc·tion (trăns-dŭk′shən, trănz-) *n.* Transfer of genetic material from one bacterial cell to another by the incorporation of bacterial DNA into a bacteriophage. [< Lat. *transductus*, p. part. of *trānsdūcere*, to transfer. See TRANSDUCER.] —**trans·duc′tion·al** *adj.*

tran·sect (trăn-sĕkt′) *tr.v.* **-sect·ed, -sect·ing, -sects** To divide by cutting transversely. —**tran·sec′tion** *n.*

tran·sept (trăn′sĕpt′) *n.* **1.** The transverse part of a cruciform church, crossing the nave at right angles. **2.** Either of the two lateral arms of such a part. [NLat. *trānsēptum* : Lat. *trāns-*, trans- + Lat. *saeptum*, partition; see SEPTUM.] —**tran·sep′tal** (-sĕp′təl) *adj.*

tran·se·unt (trăn′sē-ənt) *adj. Philosophy* Productive of effects outside the mind. [Lat. *trānsiēns, trānseunt-*, pr. part. of *trānsīre*, to go over. See TRANSIENT.]

trans fatty acid (trăns) *n.* An unsaturated fatty acid produced by the partial hydrogenation of vegetable oils that is found in many fried and commercially prepared foods and may contribute to increased blood cholesterol levels.

trans·fec·tion (trăns-fĕk′shən) *n.* Infection of a cell with purified viral nucleic acid, resulting in subsequent replication of the virus in the cell. [TRANS– + (IN)FECTION.] —**trans·fect′** *v.*

trans·fer (trăns-fûr′, trăns′fər) *v.* **-ferred, -fer·ring, -fers** —*tr.* **1.** To convey or cause to pass from one place, person, or thing to another. **2.** *Law* To make over the possession or legal title of; convey. **3.** To convey (a design, for example) from one surface to another, as by impression. —*intr.* **1.** To move oneself from one location or job to another. **2.** To withdraw from one educational institution or course of study and enroll in another. **3.** To change from one public conveyance to another: *transferred to another bus.* ❖ *n.* (trăns′fər) **1.** also **trans·fer·al** (trăns-fûr′əl) The conveyance or removal of something from one place, person, or thing to another. **2.** One who transfers or is transferred. **3.** A design conveyed by contact from one surface to another. **4a.** A ticket entitling a passenger to transfer as part of one trip. **b.** A place where such a change is made. **5.** also **transferal** *Law* A conveyance of title or property from one person to another. [ME *transferren* < OFr. *transferer* < Lat. *trānsferre* : *trāns-*, trans- + *ferre*, to carry; see **bher-¹** in App.] —**trans·fer′a·bil·i·ty** *n.* —**trans·fer′a·ble, trans·fer′ra·ble** *adj.* —**trans·fer′rer** *n.*

trans·fer·ase (trăns′fə-rās′, -rāz′) *n.* Any of various enzymes that catalyze the transfer of a chemical group, such as a phosphate or amine, from one molecule to another.

trans·fer·ee (trăns′fə-rē′) *n.* **1.** *Law* To whom a conveyance of title or property is made. **2.** One who is transferred.

trans·fer·ence (trăns-fûr′əns, trăns′fər-əns) *n.* **1a.** The act or process of transferring. **b.** The fact of being transferred. **2.** In psychoanalysis, the process by which emotions associated with one person, such as a parent, unconsciously shift to another, esp. to the analyst. —**trans′fer·en′tial** (trăns′fə-rĕn′shəl) *adj.*

transfer factor *n.* A polypeptide secreted by lymphocytes that can transfer immunity from one cell or individual to another.

trans·fer·mi·um (trăns-fûr′mē-əm, -fĕr′-) *adj.* Having an atomic number greater than 100 (fermium).

trans·fer·or (trăns′fə-rôr′) *n. Law* One who conveys a title or property.

transfer payment *n.* A noncompensatory government payment to individuals, as for welfare or social security benefits.

trans·fer·rin (trăns-fĕr′ĭn) *n.* A beta globulin in blood serum that transports iron. [TRANS– + FERR(O)– + –IN.]

transfer RNA *n.* One of a class of RNA molecules that transport amino acids to ribosomes for incorporation into a polypeptide undergoing synthesis.

transfer station *n.* **1.** A station, as on a rail line, where a passenger can transfer from one public conveyance to another. **2.** A facility where solid waste materials, such as yard waste and demolition materials, are transferred from small vehicles to large trucks for efficient transport to landfills and other disposal sites.

trans·fig·u·ra·tion (trăns-fĭg′yə-rā′shən) *n.* **1a.** A marked change in form or appearance; a metamorphosis. **b.** A change that glorifies or exalts. **2. Transfiguration a.** *Bible* The emanation of radiance from Jesus on the mountain. **b.** The Christian feast marking this event, observed on August 6 or 19.

trans·fig·ure (trăns-fĭg′yər) *tr.v.* **-ured, -ur·ing, -ures 1.** To alter the outward appearance of; transform. **2.** To exalt or glorify. [Ult. < Lat. *trānsfigūrāre* : *trāns-*, trans- + *figūra*, form; see **dheigh-** in App.] —**trans·fig′ure·ment** *n.*

trans•fi•nite (trăns-fī′nīt′) *adj.* Going beyond the finite.

transfinite number *n.* A number that is greater than any finite number.

trans•fix (trăns-fĭks′) *tr.v.* **-fixed, -fix•ing, -fix•es 1.** To pierce with or as if with a pointed weapon. **2.** To fix fast; impale. **3.** To render motionless, as with terror, amazement, or awe. [Lat. *trānsfīgere, trānsfīx-* : *trāns-*, trans- + *fīgere*, to pierce, fasten.] **—trans•fix′ion** (-fĭk′shən) *n.*

trans•form (trăns-fôrm′) *v.* **-formed, -form•ing, -forms** *—tr.* **1.** To change markedly the appearance or form of. **2.** To change the nature, function, or condition of; convert. **3.** *Mathematics* To subject to a transformation. **4.** *Electricity* To subject to the action of a transformer. **5.** *Genetics* To subject (a cell) to transformation. *—intr.* To undergo a transformation. ❖ *n.* (trăns′fôrm′) The result, as a mathematical quantity, of a transformation. [Ult. < Lat. *trānsfōrmāre* : *trāns-*, trans- + *fōrma*, form.] **—trans•form′a•ble** *adj.*

trans•for•ma•tion (trăns′fər-mā′shən, -fôr-) *n.* **1a.** The act or an instance of transforming. **b.** The state of being transformed. **2.** A marked change, as in appearance, usu. for the better. **3.** *Mathematics* **a.** Replacement of the variables in an algebraic expression by their values in terms of another set of variables. **b.** A mapping of one space onto another or onto itself. **4.** *Linguistics* **a.** A rule that systematically converts one syntactic form or form of a sentence into another. **b.** A construction or sentence derived by such a rule. **5.** *Genetics* **a.** The change in an animal cell that occurs upon infection by a cancer-causing virus. **b.** Alteration of a bacterial cell by introduction of DNA from another bacterial cell, esp. a pathogen. **—trans′for•ma′tion•al, trans•form′a•tive** (-fôr′mə-tĭv) *adj.*

transformational grammar *n.* A grammar that accounts for the constructions of a language by linguistic transformations and phrase structures, esp. generative grammar.

trans•form•er (trăns-fôr′mər) *n.* **1.** One that transforms. **2.** A device used to transfer electric energy from one circuit to another, esp. a pair of inductively coupled wire coils that effect such a transfer with a change in voltage, current, phase, or impedance.

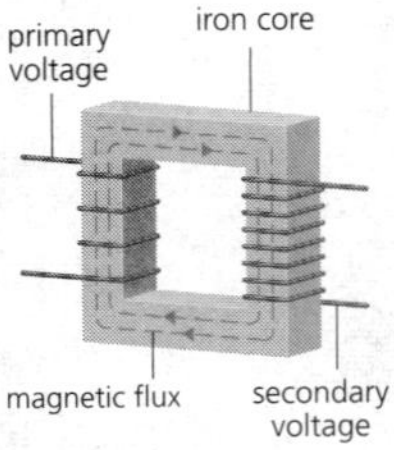

transformer
iron core transformer

trans•form fault (trăns′fôrm′) *n. Geology* A strike-slip fault common in mid-ocean ridge regions.

trans•fuse (trăns-fyo͞oz′) *tr.v.* **-fused, -fus•ing, -fus•es 1.** To pour (something) out of one vessel into another. **2.** To instill or impart. **3.** To diffuse through; permeate. **4.** *Medicine* To administer a transfusion of or to. [ME *transfusen*, to transmit < Lat. *trānsfundere, trānsfūs-*, to transfuse : *trāns-*, trans- + *fundere*, to pour; see **gheu-** in App.] **—trans•fus′er** *n.* **—trans•fus′i•ble, trans•fus′a•ble** *adj.* **—trans•fu′sive** (-fyo͞o′sĭv, -zĭv) *adj.*

trans•fu•sion (trăns-fyo͞o′zhən) *n.* **1.** The act or process of transfusing. **2.** *Medicine* The transfer of blood or blood products from one person to another. **—trans•fu′sion•al** *adj.*

trans•gen•dered (trăns-jĕn′dərd, trănz-) also **trans•gen•der** (-dər) *adj.* **1.** Appearing as, wishing to be considered as, or having undergone surgery to become a member of the opposite sex. **2.** Of or relating to a transgendered person or transgendered people.

trans•gen•e•sis (trăns-jĕn′ĭ-sĭs, trănz-) *n.* The transfer of cloned genetic material from one species or breed to another.

trans•gen•ic (trăns-jĕn′ĭk, trănz-) *adj.* **1.** Carrying genes transferred from another species or breed. **2.** Of or relating to the study of transgenic organisms.

trans•gen•ics (trăns-jĕn′ĭks, trănz-) *n.* (*used with a sing. or pl. verb*) The study of or methodology used to create transgenic animals or plants.

trans•gress (trăns-grĕs′, trănz-) *v.* **-gressed, -gress•ing, -gress•es** *—tr.* **1.** To go beyond or over (a limit or boundary); exceed or overstep. **2.** To act in violation of (the law, for example). *—intr.* **1.** To commit an offense by violating a law or command; sin. **2.** To spread over land. Used of the sea. [Ult. < Lat. *trānsgredī, trānsgress-*, to step across : *trāns-*, trans- + *gradī*, to go; see **ghredh-** in App.] **—trans•gress′i•ble** *adj.* **—trans•gres′sive** *adj.* **—trans•gres′sor** *n.*

trans•gres•sion (trăns-grĕsh′ən, trănz-) *n.* **1.** A violation of a law, command, or duty. See Syns at **breach. 2.** The exceeding of due bounds. **3.** A relative rise in sea level resulting in deposition of marine strata over terrestrial strata.

trans•gres•sive (trăns-grĕs′ĭv, trănz-) *adj.* **1.** Exceeding a limit or boundary, esp. of social acceptability. **2.** Of or relating to a genre of fiction, filmmaking, or art characterized by graphic depictions of behavior that violates socially acceptable norms, often involving violence, drug use, and sexual deviancy. **3.** Of or relating to geological transgression. **—trans•gres′sive•ly** *adv.*

tran•ship (trăn-shĭp′) *v.* Variant of **transship.**

trans•hu•mance (trăns-hyo͞o′məns, trănz-) *n.* Transfer of livestock from one grazing ground to another with the changing of seasons. [Fr. < *transhumer*, to move livestock seasonally < Sp. *trashumar* : Lat. *trāns-*, trans- + Lat. *humus*, ground; see **dhghem-** in App.] **—trans•hu′mant** *adj. & n.*

tran•si•ent (trăn′zē-ənt, -zhənt, -shənt) *adj.* **1.** Passing with time; transitory. **2.** Remaining in a place only a brief time. **3.** *Physics* Decaying with time, esp. as a simple exponential function of time. ❖ *n.* **1.** One that is transient, esp. a hotel guest or boarder of brief duration. **2.** *Physics* A transient disturbance or oscillation, esp. in an electric current. [Alteration of Lat. *trānsiēns, trānseunt-*, pr. part. of *trānsīre*, to go over : *trāns-*, over; see TRANS– + *īre*, to go; see **ei-** in App.] **—tran′si•ent•ly** *adv.* **—tran′si•ence, tran′si•en•cy** *n.*

trans•il•lu•mi•na•tion (trăns′ĭ-lo͞o′mə-nā′shən, trănz′-) *n.* The passing of a light through the walls of a body part or organ to facilitate medical inspection. **—trans′il•lu′mi•nate′** (-lo͞o′mə-nāt′) *v.* **—trans′il•lu′mi•na′tor** *n.*

tran•sis•tor (trăn-zĭs′tər, -sĭs′-) *n.* **1.** A small electronic device containing a semiconductor and having at least three electrical contacts, used in a circuit as an amplifier, detector, or switch. **2.** A transistor radio. [TRANS(FER) + (RES)ISTOR.]

tran•sis•tor•ize (trăn-zĭs′tə-rīz′, -sĭs′-) *tr.v.* **-ized, -iz•ing, -iz•es** To equip (an electronic device) with transistors.

transistor radio *n.* A small portable radio using transistors.

tran•sit (trăn′sĭt, -zĭt) *n.* **1.** The act of passing over, across, or through; passage. **2a.** Conveyance of people or goods from one place to another, esp. on a local public transportation system. **b.** The system or vehicles used for such conveyance. **3.** A transition or change, as to a spiritual existence at death. **4.** *Astronomy* **a.** The passage of a celestial body across the observer's meridian. **b.** The passage of a smaller celestial body or its shadow across the disk of a larger celestial body. **5.** A surveying instrument similar to a theodolite that measures horizontal and vertical angles. ❖ *v.* **-sit•ed, -sit•ing, -sits** *—tr.* **1.** To pass over, across, or through. **2.** To revolve (the telescope of a surveying transit) about its horizontal transverse axis in order to reverse its direction. *—intr. Astronomy* To make a transit. [ME *transite* < Lat. *trānsitus* < p. part. of *trānsīre*, to go across. See TRANSIENT.]

tran•si•tion (trăn-zĭsh′ən, -sĭsh′-) *n.* **1.** Passage from one form, state, style, or place to another. **2a.** Passage from one subject to another in discourse. **b.** A word, phrase, sentence, or series of sentences connecting one part of a discourse to another. **3.** *Music* **a.** A modulation, esp. a brief one. **b.** A passage connecting two themes. **4.** A period during childbirth that precedes the expulsive phase of labor, characterized by strong uterine contractions. **5.** *Sports* The process of changing from defense to offense, or from offense to defense. ❖ *intr.v.* **-tioned, -tion•ing, -tions** To make a transition. **—tran•si′tion•al, tran•si′tion•ar′y** (-zĭsh′ə-nĕr′ē) *adj.* **—tran•si′tion•al•ly** *adv.*

transition element *n.* Any of the metallic elements having an incomplete inner electron shell, marked by multiple valences, colored compounds, and the formation of stable complex ions.

transition metal *n.* A transition element.

tran•si•tive (trăn′sĭ-tĭv, -zĭ-) *adj.* **1.** *Grammar* Expressing an action carried from the subject to the object; requiring a direct object to complete meaning. Used of a verb or verb construction. **2.** Marked by or involving transition. **3.** *Logic & Mathematics* Of or relating to a relationship between three elements such that if the relationship holds between the first and second elements and between the second and third elements, it necessarily holds between the first and third elements. ❖ *n. Grammar* A transitive verb. **—tran′si•tive•ly** *adv.* **—tran′si•tive•ness, tran′si•tiv′i•ty** *n.*

tran•si•to•ry (trăn′sĭ-tôr′ē, -tōr′ē, trăn′zĭ-) *adj.* Existing or lasting only a short time; short-lived or temporary. **—tran′si•to′ri•ly** *adv.* **—tran′si•to′ri•ness** *n.*

Trans•jor•dan (trăns′jôr′dn, trănz′-) See **Jordan. —Trans′jor•da′ni•an** (-jôr-dā′nē-ən) *adj. & n.*

Trans•kei (trăns-kā′, -kī′) A former internally self-governing Black African homeland in SE South Africa on the Indian Ocean coast; dissolved and reintegrated into South Africa by the 1993 interim constitution. **—Trans•kei′an** *adj. & n.*

trans•late (trăns′lāt′, trănz′-, trăns-lāt′, trănz-) *v.* **-lat•ed, -lat•ing, -lates** *—tr.* **1.** To render in another language. **2a.** To put into simpler terms; explain. **b.** To express in different words; paraphrase. **3a.** To change from one form, function, or state to another; transform: *translate ideas into reality.* **b.** To express in another medium. **4.** To transfer from one place or condition to another. **5.** To forward or retransmit (a telegraphic message). **6a.** *Ecclesiastical* To transfer (a bishop) to another see. **b.** To convey to heaven without death. **7.** *Physics* To subject (a body) to translation. **8.** *Biology* To subject (messenger RNA) to translation. **9.** *Archaic* To enrapture. *—intr.* **1a.** To make a translation. **b.** To work as a translator. **2.** To admit of translation. **3.** To be changed or transformed in effect. Often used with *into* or *to.* [ME *translaten* < OFr. *translater* < Lat. *trānslātus*, p. part. of *trānsferre*, to transfer : *trāns-*, trans- + *lātus*, brought; see **telə-** in App.] **—trans•lat′a•bil′i•ty** *n.* **—trans•lat′a•ble** *adj.*

trans•la•tion (trăns-lā′shən, trănz-) *n.* **1a.** The act or process of translating, esp. from one language into another. **b.** The state of being translated. **2.** A translated version of a text. **3.** *Physics* Motion of a body in which every point of the body moves parallel to and the same distance as every other point of the body. **4.** *Biology* The process by which messenger RNA directs the amino acid sequence of a growing polypeptide during protein synthesis. **—trans•la′tion•al, trans′la•to′ry** (-lə-tôr′ē, -tōr′ē) *adj.*

trans•la•tor (trăns′lā′tər, trănz′-, trăns-lā′tər, trănz-) *n.* **1.** One that translates, esp.: **a.** One employed to render written works into another language. **b.** A computer program that renders one language or data format into another. **2.** An interpreter. **—trans′la•to′ri•al** (-lə-tôr′ē-əl, -tōr′-) *adj.*

trans•lit•er•ate (trăns-lĭt′ə-rāt′, trănz-) *tr.v.* **-at•ed, -at•ing,**

-ates To represent (letters or words) in the corresponding characters of another alphabet. [TRANS– + Lat. *littera, lītera,* letter + –ATE¹.] —**trans·lit′er·a′tion** (-ə-rā′shən) *n.*

trans·lo·cate (trăns-lō′kāt′, trănz-) *tr.v.* **-cat·ed, -cat·ing, -cates** 1. To cause to change from one place or position to another; displace. 2. *Genetics* To cause (a chromosomal segment) to undergo translocation.

trans·lo·ca·tion (trăns′lō-kā′shən, trănz′-) *n.* 1. A change of location. 2. *Genetics* **a.** A transfer of a chromosomal segment to a new position. **b.** A translocated chromosomal segment.

trans·lu·cent (trăns-lōō′sənt, trănz-) *adj.* 1. Transmitting light but causing sufficient diffusion to prevent perception of distinct images. 2. Clear; lucid. [Lat. *trānslūcēns, trānslūcent-,* pr. part. of *trānslūcēre,* to shine through : *trāns-, trans-* + *lūcēre,* to shine; see **leuk-** in App.] —**trans′lu′cence, trans·lu′cen·cy** *n.* —**trans·lu′cent·ly** *adv.*

trans·lu·mi·nal (trăns-lōō′mə-nəl, trănz-) *adj.* Passing or occurring across a lumen, as of a blood vessel.

trans·lu·nar (trăns-lōō′nər, trănz-, trăns-lōō′-, trănz-lōō′-) *adj.* Extending beyond the moon or its orbit around the earth.

trans·ma·rine (trăns′mə-rēn′, trănz′-) *adj.* 1. Crossing the sea. 2. Beyond or coming from across the sea.

trans·mem·brane (trăns-mĕm′brān, trănz-) *adj.* Passing or occurring across a membrane.

trans·mi·grant (trăns-mī′grənt, trănz-) *n.* 1. One that transmigrates. 2. One in transit through a country on the way to the country in which one intends to settle.

trans·mi·grate (trăns-mī′grāt′, trănz-) *intr.v.* **-grat·ed, -grat·ing, -grates** 1. To migrate. 2. To pass into another body after death. Used of the soul. —**trans′mi·gra′tion** *n.* —**trans′mi·gra′tion·ism** *n.* —**trans′mi·gra′tor** *n.* —**trans·mi′gra·to·ry** (-mī′grə-tôr′ē, -tōr′ē) *adj.*

trans·mis·si·ble (trăns-mĭs′ə-bəl, trănz-) *adj.* That can be transmitted. —**trans′mis′si·bil′i·ty** *n.*

trans·mis·sion (trăns-mĭsh′ən, trănz-) *n.* **1a.** The act or process of transmitting. **b.** The fact of being transmitted. 2. Something, such as a message, that is transmitted. 3. An automotive assembly including gears that transmit power from the engine to a driving axle. 4. The sending of information from a transmitter. [Lat. *trānsmissiō, trānsmissiōn-,* a sending across < *trānsmissus,* p. part. of *trānsmittere,* to transmit. See TRANSMIT.] —**trans·mis′sive** (-mĭs′ĭv) *adj.*

trans·mis·som·e·ter (trăns′mĭ-sŏm′ĭ-tər, trănz′-) *n.* A device used to measure transmission of light through a medium. [TRANSMISS(ION) + –METER.] —**trans′mis·som′e·try** *n.*

trans·mit (trăns-mĭt′, trănz-) *v.* **-mit·ted, -mit·ting, -mits** *—tr.* 1. To send from one person, thing, or place to another; convey. 2. To cause to spread; pass on. 3. To impart or convey to others by heredity or inheritance; hand down. 4. To pass along (information); communicate. **5a.** *Electronics* To send (a signal), as by wire or radio. **b.** *Physics* To cause (a disturbance) to propagate through a medium. 6. To convey (force or energy) from one part of a mechanism to another. *—intr.* To send out a signal. [Ult. < Lat. *trānsmittere* : *trāns-, trans-* + *mittere,* to send.] —**trans·mit′ta·ble** *adj.* —**trans·mit′tal** (-mĭt′l) *n.*

trans·mit·tance (trăns-mĭt′ns, trănz-) *n.* 1. A transmission. 2. *Physics* The ratio of the radiant energy transmitted to the total radiant energy incident on a given body.

trans·mit·ter (trăns-mĭt′ər, trănz-) *n.* 1. One that transmits. **2a.** An electronic device that generates a carrier wave, modulates it with a signal to be broadcast, and radiates the resulting wave from an antenna. **b.** The portion of a telephone that converts the incident sounds into electrical impulses that are conveyed to a remote receiver. **c.** A telegraphic sending instrument. 3. A neurotransmitter.

trans·mog·ri·fy (trăns-mŏg′rə-fī′, trănz-) *tr.v.* **-fied, -fy·ing, -fies** To change into a different shape or form, esp. one that is fantastic or bizarre. [?] —**trans·mog′ri·fi·ca′tion** (-fĭ-kā′shən) *n.*

trans·mon·tane (trăns-mŏn′tān′, trănz-, trăns′mŏn-tān′, trănz′-) *adj.* Tramontane. [Lat. *trānsmontānus.* See TRAMONTANE.]

trans·mun·dane (trăns′mŭn-dān′, trănz′-, trăns-mŭn′dān′, trănz-) *adj.* Existing or extending beyond the physical world.

trans·mu·ta·tion (trăns′myōō-tā′shən, trănz′-) *n.* **1a.** The act or an instance of transmuting; transformation. **b.** The state of being transmuted. 2. *Physics* Transformation of one element into another by one or a series of nuclear reactions. 3. The supposed conversion of base metals into gold or silver in alchemy. —**trans′mu·ta′tion·al, trans·mu′ta·tive** (-myōō′tə-tĭv) *adj.*

trans·mute (trăns-myōōt′, trănz-) *v.* **-mut·ed, -mut·ing, -mutes** *—tr.* To change from one form, nature, substance, or state into another; transform. *—intr.* To undergo transmutation. [ME *transmuten* < Lat. *trānsmūtāre* : *trāns-, trans-* + *mūtāre,* to change.] —**trans·mut′a·bil′i·ty** *n.* —**trans·mut′a·ble** *adj.* —**trans·mut′a·bly** *adv.* —**trans·mut′er** *n.*

trans·na·tion·al (trăns-năsh′ə-nəl, trănz-) *adj.* 1. Reaching beyond or transcending national boundaries. 2. Relating to or involving several nations or nationalities.

trans·o·ce·an·ic (trăns′ō-shē-ăn′ĭk, trănz′-) *adj.* 1. Situated beyond or on the other side of the ocean. 2. Spanning or crossing

the ocean: *laid transoceanic telephone cables.*

tran·som (trăn′səm) *n.* **1a.** A crosspiece over a door or between a door and a window above it. **b.** A small hinged window above a door or window. 2. A horizontal dividing bar of wood or stone in a window. 3. A lintel. 4. *Nautical* A flat or nearly flat surface at the stern of a vessel. 5. The horizontal beam on a cross or gallows. [ME *traunsom,* prob. alteration of Lat. *trānstrum,* crossbeam < *trāns,* across. See TRANS–.]

tran·son·ic (trăn-sŏn′ĭk) *adj.* Of or relating to aerodynamic flow or flight conditions at speeds near the speed of sound. [TRAN(S)– + SONIC.]

trans·pa·cif·ic (trăns′pə-sĭf′ĭk, trănz′-) *adj.* 1. Situated on or coming from the other side of the Pacific Ocean. 2. Spanning or crossing the Pacific Ocean.

trans·par·en·cy (trăns-pâr′ən-sē, -păr′-) *n., pl.* **-cies** 1. A transparent object, esp. a photographic slide that is viewed by light shining through it from behind or by projection. 2. also **trans·par·ence** (-pâr′əns, -păr′-) The quality or state of being transparent.

trans·par·ent (trăns-pâr′ənt, -păr′-) *adj.* 1. Capable of transmitting light so that objects or images can be seen as if there were no intervening material. 2. Permeable to electromagnetic radiation of specified frequencies, as to visible light waves. 3. So fine in texture that it can be seen through; sheer. See Syns at **airy. 4a.** Easily seen through or detected; obvious. **b.** Free from guile; candid or open. 5. *Obsolete* Shining through; luminous. [ME < OFr. < Med.Lat. *trānspārēns, trānspārent-,* pr. part. of *trānspārēre,* to show through : Lat. *trāns-, trans-* + Lat. *pārēre,* to show.] —**trans·par′ent·ly** *adv.*

trans·per·son·al (trăns-pûr′sə-nəl, trănz-) *adj.* Transcending or reaching beyond the personal or individual.

tran·spic·u·ous (trăn-spĭk′yōō-əs) *adj.* Easily understood or seen through. [< NLat. *trānspicuus* < Lat. *trānspicere,* to see through : *trāns-, trans-* + *specere,* to look at; see **spek-** in App.]

tran·spi·ra·tion (trăn′spə-rā′shən) *n.* The act or process of transpiring, esp. through the stomata of plant tissue or the pores of the skin. —**tran′spi·ra′tion·al** *adj.*

tran·spire (trăn-spīr′) *v.* **-spired, -spir·ing, -spires** *—tr.* To give off (vapor containing waste products) through the pores of the skin or the stomata of plant tissue. *—intr.* 1. To become known; come to light. 2. *Usage Problem* To come about; happen or occur. 3. To give off vapor containing waste products, as through pores. [Fr. *transpirer* < Med.Lat. *trānspīrāre* : Lat. *trāns-, trans-* + Lat. *spīrāre,* to breathe.]

USAGE NOTE The usage of *transpire* to mean "to happen" has been the butt of critics for over a century, but resistance to it may be waning. In a 1969 survey, this usage was acceptable only to 38 percent of the Usage Panel in the sentence *All of these events transpired after last week's announcement.* In 1988, 58 percent of the Panel found it acceptable; in 2001, 66 percent.

trans·pla·cen·tal (trăns′plə-sĕn′tl) *adj.* Passing through or occurring across the placenta. —**trans′pla·cen′tal·ly** *adv.*

trans·plant (trăns-plănt′) *v.* **-plant·ed, -plant·ing, -plants** *—tr.* 1. To uproot and replant (a growing plant). 2. To transfer from one place or residence to another; relocate. 3. *Medicine* To transfer (tissue or an organ) from one body or body part to another. *—intr.* To be capable of undergoing transplantation. ❖ *n.* (trăns′plănt′) 1. The act or process of transplanting. 2. Something transplanted. 3. *Medicine* An operation for transplanting: *surgical transplant of a cornea.* [Ult. < LLat. *trānsplantāre* : Lat. *trāns, trans-* + Lat. *plantāre,* to plant.] —**trans·plant′a·ble** *adj.* —**trans′plan·ta′tion** *n.* —**trans·plant′er** *n.*

trans·po·lar (trăns-pō′lər) *adj.* Extending across or crossing either of the Polar Regions.

tran·spond·er (trăn-spŏn′dər) *n.* A radio or radar transceiver activated for transmission by reception of a predetermined signal. [TRAN(SMITTER) + (RE)SPONDER.]

trans·pon·tine (trăns-pŏn′tīn′) *adj.* 1. Situated on the other side of a bridge. 2. Similar to or characteristic of melodramas once performed in London theaters south of the Thames.

trans·port (trăns-pôrt′, -pōrt′) *tr.v.* **-port·ed, -port·ing, -ports** 1. To carry from one place to another; convey. 2. To move to strong emotion; carry away; enrapture. 3. To send abroad to a penal colony; deport. See Syns at **banish.** ❖ *n.* (trăns′pôrt′, -pōrt′) 1. The act of transporting; conveyance. 2. The condition of being transported by emotion; rapture. 3. A vehicle used to transport passengers, mail, freight, or military equipment. **4a.** The system of transporting passengers or goods in a particular country or area. **b.** The vehicles, such as buses and trains, used in such a system. 5. A device that moves magnetic tape beyond the recording head, as of a tape recorder. 6. A deported convict. [Ult. < Lat. *trānsportāre* : *trāns-, trans-* + *portāre,* to carry; see **per-²** in App.] —**trans·port′a·bil′i·ty** *n.* —**trans·port′a·ble** *adj.* —**trans·port′er** *n.* —**trans·por′tive** *adj.*

trans·por·ta·tion (trăns′pər-tā′shən) *n.* **1a.** The act or an instance of transporting. **b.** The state of being transported. 2. A means of conveyance. 3. The business of conveying passengers or goods. 4. A charge for public conveyance; a fare. 5. Deportation to a penal colony.

trans·pose (trăns-pōz′) *v.* **-posed, -pos·ing, -pos·es** *—tr.* 1.

transom

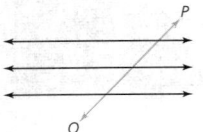

transversal
Line *PQ* is a transversal.

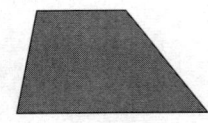

trapezoid

To reverse or transfer the order or place of; interchange. **2.** To put into a different place or order. **3.** *Mathematics* To move (a term) from one side of an algebraic equation to the other side, reversing its sign to maintain equality. **4.** *Music* To write or perform (a composition) in a key other than the original or given key. **5.** To render into another language. **6.** To alter in form or nature; transform. —*intr.* **1.** *Music* To write or perform music in a different key. **2.** To admit of being transposed. ❖ *n.* (trăns′pōz′) *Mathematics* A matrix formed by interchanging the rows and columns of a given matrix. [ME *transposen,* to transform < OFr. *transposer,* alteration (influenced by *poser,* to put, place) of Lat. *trānspōnere,* to transfer : *trāns-,* trans- + *pōnere,* to place; see **apo-** in App.] —**trans·pos′a·ble** *adj.*

trans·po·si·tion (trăns′pə-zĭsh′ən) *n.* **1a.** The act or an instance of transposing. **b.** The state of being transposed. **2.** Something transposed. **3.** *Genetics* Transfer of a segment of DNA to a new position on the same or another chromosome or plasmid. —**trans′po·si′tion·al** *adj.*

trans·po·son (trăns-pō′zŏn) *n.* A segment of DNA that can replicate itself and insert the copy into a new position within the same or another chromosome or plasmid. [TRANSPOS(ITION) + −ON¹.]

trans·ra·cial (trăns-rā′shəl, trănz-) *adj.* Involving two or more races: *a transracial adoption.*

trans·sex·u·al (trăns-sĕk′shōō-əl) *n.* **1.** One who wishes to be considered by society as a member of the opposite sex. **2.** One who has undergone a sex change. —**trans·sex′u·al** *adj.* —**trans·sex′u·al·ism, trans·sex′u·al′i·ty** (-ăl′ĭ-tē) *n.*

trans·ship (trăns-shĭp′) also **tran·ship** (trăn-shĭp′) *tr. & intr.v.* **-shipped, -ship·ping, -ships** To transfer or be transferred from one conveyance to another for reshipment. —**trans·ship′ment** *n.*

tran·sub·stan·ti·ate (trăn′səb-stăn′shē-āt′) *tr.v.* **-at·ed, -at·ing, -ates 1.** To change (one substance) into another; transmute. **2.** *Christianity* To change the substance of (the Eucharistic bread and wine) into the body and blood of Jesus. [Med.Lat. *trānsubstantiāre, trānsubstantiāt-* : Lat. *trāns-,* trans- + Lat. *substantia,* substance; see SUBSTANCE.]

tran·sub·stan·ti·a·tion (trăn′səb-stăn′shē-ā′shən) *n.* **1.** Conversion of one substance into another. **2.** In many Christian churches, the doctrine that the Eucharistic bread and wine become the body and blood of Jesus. —**tran′sub·stan′ti·a′tion·al·ist** *n.*

tran·su·date (trăn-sōō′dāt′, -syōō′-, trăn′sōō-dāt′, -syōō-) also **tran·su·da·tion** (trăn′sōō-dā′shən, -syōō-) *n.* **1.** A product of the process of transuding. **2.** A substance that transudes.

tran·sude (trăn-sōōd′, -syōōd′, -zōōd′, -zyōōd′) *intr.v.* **-sud·ed, -sud·ing, -sudes** To pass through pores or interstices in the manner of perspiration. [NLat. *trānsūdāre* : Lat. *trāns-,* trans- + Lat. *sūdāre,* to sweat; see **sweid-** in App.] —**tran·su′da·to′ry** (trăn-sōō′də-tôr′ē, -tôr′ē, -syōō′-) *adj.*

trans·u·ran·ic (trăns′yōō-răn′ĭk, trănz′-) also **trans·u·ra·ni·um** (-rā′nē-əm) *adj.* Having an atomic number greater than 92. [TRANS- + URAN(IUM) + −IC.]

Trans·vaal (trăns-väl′, trănz-) A region of NE South Africa. An independent Boer state after the 1850s, then a British territory (1877) and crown colony (1900), Transvaal became a part of South Africa in 1910.

trans·val·ue (trăns-văl′yōō, trănz-) *tr.v.* **-ued, -u·ing, -ues** To evaluate by a new standard or principle, esp. by one that varies from conventional standards. —**trans·val′u·a′tion** *n.*

trans·ver·sal (trăns-vûr′səl, trănz-) *adj.* Transverse. ❖ *n. Mathematics* A line that intersects a system of other lines.

trans·verse (trăns-vûrs′, trănz-, trăns′vûrs′, trănz′-) *adj.* Situated or lying across; crosswise. ❖ *n.* Something that is transverse. [Lat. *trānsversus* < p. part. of *trānsvertere,* to turn across : *trāns-,* trans- + *vertere,* to turn; see **wer-²** in App.] —**trans·verse′ly** *adv.*

transverse colon *n.* The part of the colon that lies across the upper part of the abdominal cavity.

transverse flute *n.* See **flute** 1a.

transverse process *n.* A process projecting outward from the side of a vertebra.

trans·ves·tite (trăns-vĕs′tīt′, trănz-) *n.* A person who dresses and acts in a style or manner traditionally associated with the opposite sex. [Ger. *Transvestit* : Lat. *trāns-,* trans- + Lat. *vestīre,* to dress; see TRAVESTY.] —**trans·ves′tism** (-tĭz′əm), **trans·ves′ti·tism** (-tĭ-tĭz′əm) *n.*

Tran·syl·va·nia (trăn′sĭl-vān′yə, -vā′nē-ə) A historical region of W Romania bounded by the Transylvanian Alps and the Carpathian Mts. —**Tran′syl·va′ni·an** *adj. & n.*

Transylvanian Alps A range of the S Carpathian Mts. extending across central Romania and rising to 2,544 m (8,343 ft).

trap¹ (trăp) *n.* **1.** A contrivance for catching and holding animals, as a concealed pit or a clamplike device that springs shut suddenly. **2.** A stratagem for catching or tricking an unwary person. **3.** A confining or undesirable circumstance from which escape or relief is difficult: *the trap of poverty.* **4.** A device for sealing a passage against the escape of gases, esp. a bend in a drainpipe that prevents the return flow of sewer gas by means of a water barrier. **5.** *Sports* **a.** A device that hurls clay pigeons into the air in trapshooting. **b.** A land hazard or bunker on a golf course; a sand

trap. **c. traps** A measured length of roadway over which electronic timers register the speed of a racing vehicle. **6.** *Baseball* See web 10. **7.** *Sports* **a.** A defensive strategy or play in which two or more defenders converge on an offensive player shortly after the player gains possession of the ball or puck. **b.** The act of trapping a soccer ball. **8.** *Football* A running play in which the ball carrier advances through a hole in the defensive line created by allowing a defensive lineman to penetrate the backfield. **9.** A light two-wheeled carriage with springs. **10.** A trapdoor. **11. traps** *Music* Percussion instruments, esp. in a jazz band. **12.** *Slang* The human mouth. ❖ *v.* **trapped, trap·ping, traps** —*tr.* **1.** To catch in or as if in a trap; ensnare. See Syns at **catch. 2.** To place in a confining or embarrassing position. **3.** To seal off (gases) by a trap. **4.** To furnish with traps or a trap. **5.** *Sports* **a.** To catch (a ball) immediately after it has hit the ground. **b.** To gain control of (a moving soccer ball) by allowing it to hit and bounce off a part of the body other than the arm or hand. —*intr.* **1.** To set traps for game. **2.** To engage in trapping furbearing animals. [ME < OE *træppe.*]

trap² (trăp) *Informal n.* Personal belongings or household goods. Often used in the plural. ❖ *tr.v.* **trapped, trap·ping, traps** To furnish with trappings. [ME *trap,* trapping, perh. alteration of OFr. *drap,* cloth < LLat. *drappus.*]

trap³ (trăp) *n.* Any of several dark fine-grained igneous rocks often used in making roads. [Swed. *trapp* < *trappa,* step < MLGer. *trappe.*]

tra·pan (trə-păn′) *v.* Variant of **trepan²**.

trap·door (trăp′dôr′, -dōr′) *n.* A hinged or sliding door in a floor, roof, or ceiling.

trap·door spider (trăp′dôr′, -dōr′) *n.* Any of various spiders of the family Ctenizidae, found in warm climates, that construct a silk-lined burrow with a hinged lid.

tra·peze (tră-pēz′, trə-) *n.* **1.** A short horizontal bar suspended from two parallel ropes, used for gymnastics exercises or acrobatic stunts. **2.** An article of women's clothing that hangs down from the shoulders and swings out around the hips and legs. [Fr. *trapèze* < LLat. *trapezium,* trapezoid. See TRAPEZIUM.]

tra·pe·zi·um (trə-pē′zē-əm) *n., pl.* **-zi·ums** or **-zi·a** (-zē-ə) **1.** A quadrilateral having no parallel sides. **2.** *Chiefly British* A trapezoid. **3.** A bone in the wrist at the base of the thumb. [LLat. *trapezium,* trapezoid < Gk. *trapezion,* dim. of *trapeza,* table : *tra-,* four; see kʷetwer- in App. + *peza,* foot; see **ped-** in App.]

tra·pe·zi·us (trə-pē′zē-əs) *n., pl.* **-us·es** Either of two large flat triangular muscles running from the base of the occiput to the middle of the back. [NLat. < LLat. *trapezium,* trapezium (< the shape of the muscles paired). See TRAPEZIUM.]

tra·pe·zo·he·dron (trə-pē′zō-hē′drən, trăp′ĭ-zō-) *n., pl.* **-drons** or **-dra** (-drə) Any of several forms of crystal with trapeziums as faces. [TRAPEZ(IUM) + −HEDRON.]

trap·e·zoid (trăp′ĭ-zoid′) *n.* **1.** A quadrilateral having two parallel sides. **2.** A small bone in the wrist, situated near the base of the index finger. [NLat. *trapezoīdēs* < Gk. *trapezoeidēs,* trapeziumshaped : *trapeza,* table (see TRAPEZIUM + −oeidēs, -oid.] —**trap′e·zoid′, trap′e·zoi′dal** (-zoid′l) *adj.*

trap·line (trăp′līn′) *n.* **1.** A route or circuit along which a series of animal traps is set. **2.** The traps so set.

trap·per (trăp′ər) *n.* One who traps animals for their fur.

trap·ping (trăp′ĭng) *n.* **1.** An ornamental covering or harness for a horse; a caparison. Often used in the plural. **2. trappings a.** Articles of dress or adornment, esp. accessories. **b.** Characteristic or symbolic signs: *all the trappings of power.*

Trap·pist (trăp′ĭst) *n.* A member of the main branch of Cistercian monks, established in 1664 at La Trappe Monastery in northwest France. —**Trap′pist** *adj.*

trap·shoot·ing (trăp′shōō′tĭng) *n. Sports* Shooting at clay pigeons hurled up from spring traps. —**trap′shoot′er** *n.*

tra·pun·to (trə-pōōn′tō) *n., pl.* **-tos** Quilting in which the design is outlined with running stitches and then padded from underneath. [Ital. < p. part. of *trapungere,* to embroider : Lat. *trāns-,* trans- + Lat. *pungere,* to prick.]

trash (trăsh) *n.* **1a.** Worthless or discarded material or objects; refuse or rubbish. **b.** Something broken off or removed to be discarded, esp. plant trimmings. **c.** The refuse of sugar cane after extraction of the juice. **2.** A place or receptacle where rubbish is discarded: *threw the peel in the trash.* **3a.** Empty words or ideas. **b.** Worthless or offensive literary or artistic material. **c.** Disparaging, often abusive speech about a person or group. **4.** A person or group regarded as worthless or contemptible. ❖ *tr.v.* **trashed, trash·ing, trash·es 1.** *Slang* **a.** To throw away; discard: *trashed the broken toaster.* **b.** To wreck or destroy by or as if by vandalism; reduce to trash or ruins. **c.** To beat up; assault. **d.** To subject to scathing criticism or abuse. **2a.** To remove twigs or branches from. **b.** To cut off the outer leaves of (growing sugar cane). [Prob. of Scand. orig.]

trashed (trăsht) *adj. Slang* Drunk or intoxicated.

OUR LIVING LANGUAGE Expressions for intoxication are among those that best showcase the creativity of slang. The boundless inventiveness in expressing the ordinary in not-so-ordinary ways led Walt Whitman to describe slang as "*an attempt of common humanity to escape from bald literalism, and express itself illimitably.*" Colloquial and slang expressions meaning "intoxicated" can fill several pages in slang thesauruses. Most fall into a few general groups. Common are expressions that originally meant "damaged, badly affected by something," such as *trashed, smashed, crocked, blitzed, hammered, wasted, messed up,* and *blasted.* Cooking terms are also common, such as *baked, fried,* and *boiled.* Terms relating to liquids or being filled are a natural source of metaphors for filling oneself up with drink: *sloshed, oiled, tanked,* and *loaded* are but a few. Some terms are not easily classified, such as *plastered, blotto,* and *stoned.*

trash talk *n.* Disparaging, often insulting or vulgar speech about another person or group. [African American Vernacular E.] —**trash′-talk′** (trăsh′tôk′) *v.*

trash•y (trăsh′ē) *adj.* **-i•er, -i•est 1.** Resembling or containing trash; cheap or worthless. **2.** In very poor taste or of very poor quality. —**trash′i•ly** *adv.* —**trash′i•ness** *n.*

Tra•si•me•no (trä′zə-mā′nō, -zē-mĕ′-), **Lake** A lake in central Italy W of Perugia; site of Hannibal's defeat of a Roman force in 217 B.C.

trass (trăs) *n.* A light-colored tuff used in hydraulic cement. [Du. *tras,* short for obsolete *terras, tiras,* poss. < Ital. *terrazzo,* stone chips. See TERRAZZO.]

trat•to•ri•a (trä′tə-rē′ə) *n.* An informal restaurant or tavern serving simple Italian dishes. [Ital. < *trattore,* host < *trattare,* to treat < Lat. *tractāre.* See TREAT.]

trau•ma (trô′mə, trou′-) *n., pl.* **-mas** or **-ma•ta** (-mə-tə) **1.** A serious injury or shock to the body, as from violence or an accident. **2.** An emotional wound or shock that creates substantial lasting damage to the psychological development of a person. **3.** A product of the process of transuding. [Gk. See **terə-**[1] in App.] —**trau•mat′ic** (-măt′ĭk) *adj.* —**trau•mat′i•cal•ly** *adv.*

trau•ma•tism (trô′mə-tĭz′əm, trou′-) *n.* **1.** The condition produced by a trauma. **2.** A wound or injury.

trau•ma•tize (trô′mə-tīz′, trou′-) *tr.v.* **-tized, -tiz•ing, -tiz•es 1.** To wound or injure (a tissue), as in a surgical operation. **2.** To subject to psychological trauma.

trau•ma•tol•o•gy (trô′mə-tŏl′ə-jē, trou′-) *n.* The branch of medicine that deals with serious wounds and injuries. —**trau′ma•to•log′i•cal** *adj.* —**trau′ma•tol′o•gist** *n.*

tra•vail (trə-vāl′, trăv′āl′) *n.* **1.** Work, esp. when arduous; toil. **2.** Tribulation or agony; anguish. **3.** The labor of childbirth. ❖ *intr.v.* **-vailed, -vail•ing, -vails 1.** To work strenuously; toil. **2.** To be in the labor of childbirth. [ME < OFr. < *travailler,* to work hard < VLat. **tripāliāre,* to torture with a tripalium < LLat. *tripālium,* instrument of torture, prob. < Lat. *tripālis,* having three stakes : *tri-,* tri- + *pālus,* stake.]

trave (trāv) *n.* **1.** *Architecture* **a.** A crossbeam. **b.** A section, as of a ceiling, formed by crossbeams. **2.** A wooden frame that confines a horse being shod. [ME < OFr. < Lat. *trabs, trab-.*]

trav•el (trăv′əl) *v.* **-eled, -el•ing, -els** or **-elled, -el•ling, -els** —*intr.* **1.** To go from one place to another, as on a trip; journey. **2.** To go from place to place as a salesperson or agent. **3.** To be transmitted, as light; move or pass. **4.** To advance or proceed. **5.** To go about in the company of a particular group; associate: *travels in wealthy circles.* **6.** To move along a course, as in a groove. **7.** To admit of being transported without loss of quality. **8.** *Informal* To move swiftly. **9.** *Basketball* To walk or run illegally while holding the ball. —*tr.* To pass or journey over or through; traverse. ❖ *n.* **1.** The act or process of traveling; movement or passage from one place to another. **2. travels a.** A series of journeys. **b.** An account of one's journeys. **3.** Activity or traffic along a route or through a given point. **4.** The business of arranging trips for travelers. **5a.** The motion of a piece of machinery, esp. of a reciprocating part. **b.** The length of such motion. [ME *travelen,* alteration of *travailen,* to toil < OFr. *travailler.* See TRAVAIL.]

travel agency *n.* A business attending to travelers' transportation, itinerary, and accommodations. —**travel agent** *n.*

travel bureau *n.* See **travel agency.**

trav•eled or **trav•elled** (trăv′əld) *adj.* **1.** Having made journeys; experienced in travel. **2.** Frequented by travelers.

trav•el•er or **trav•el•ler** (trăv′əl-ər, trăv′lər) *n.* **1.** One who travels or has traveled. **2.** *Chiefly British* **a.** A traveling salesperson. **b.** A member of any of various groups of traditionally itinerate people living esp. in Scotland and Ireland. **3.** *Nautical* **a.** A metal ring that moves freely back and forth on a rope, rod, or spar. **b.** This rope, rod, or spar.

trav•el•er's check (trăv′əl-ərz, trăv′lərz) *n., pl.* **traveler's checks** or **travelers' checks** An internationally redeemable draft valid only with the purchaser's endorsement against his or her original signature on the draft.

trav•el•ing salesman (trăv′ə-lĭng, trăv′lĭng) *n.* A salesman who travels in a given territory.

trav•e•logue also **trav•e•log** (trăv′ə-lôg′, -lŏg′) *n.* **1.** A lecture about travel, often accompanied by a film, a video, or slides. **2.** A narrated film or video about travel.

Tra•ven (trā′vən), **B.** Originally Berick Traven Torsvan? 1890–1969. Amer.-born writer best known for his novel *The Treasure of the Sierra Madre* (1935).

Trav•ers (trăv′ərz), **P(amela) L.** 1906–96. Australian-born British writer whose works include *Mary Poppins* (1934).

tra•verse (trə-vûrs′, trăv′ərs) *v.* **-versed, -vers•ing, -vers•es** —*tr.* **1.** To travel or pass across, over, or through. **2.** To move to and fro over; cross and recross. **3.** To go up, down, or across (a slope) diagonally or in a zigzag manner, as in skiing. **4.** To cause to move laterally on a pivot; swivel. **5.** To extend across; cross. **6.** To look over carefully; examine. **7.** To go counter to; thwart. **8.** *Law* **a.** To deny formally (an allegation of fact by the opposing party) in a suit. **b.** To join issue upon (an indictment). **9.** To survey by traverse. —*intr.* **1.** To move to the side or back and forth. **2.** To turn laterally; swivel. **3a.** To traverse a slope, as in skiing. **b.** To slide one's blade with pressure toward the hilt of the opponent's foil in fencing. ❖ *n.* **trav•erse** (trăv′ərs, trə-vûrs′) **1.** A passing across, over, or through. **2.** A route or path across or over. **3.** Something that lies across, esp.: **a.** An intersecting line; a transversal. **b.** *Architecture* A structural crosspiece; a transom. **c.** A gallery, deck, or loft crossing from one side of a building to the other. **d.** A railing, curtain, screen, or similar barrier. **e.** A defensive barrier across a rampart or trench. **4.** Something that obstructs and thwarts; an obstacle. **5.** *Nautical* The zigzag route of a vessel forced by contrary winds to sail on different courses. **6.** A zigzag or diagonal course on a steep slope, as in skiing. **7a.** A lateral movement, as of a lathe tool across a piece of wood. **b.** A part of a mechanism that moves in this manner. **c.** The lateral swivel of a mounted gun. **8.** A line established by sighting in surveying a tract of land. **9.** *Law* A formal denial of the opposing party's allegation of fact in a suit. ❖ *adj.* **trav•erse** (trăv′ərs, trə-vûrs′) Lying or extending across; transverse. [ME *traversen* < OFr. *traverser* < VLat. **trāversāre* < LLat. *trānsversāre* < Lat. *trānsversus,* transverse. See TRANSVERSE.] —**tra•vers′a•ble** *adj.* —**tra•vers′al** *n.* —**tra•vers′er** *n.*

trav•erse rod (trăv′ərs) *n.* A horizontal rod having a mechanism for drawing attached draperies with a pull cord.

trav•er•tine (trăv′ər-tēn′, -tĭn) *n.* **1.** A light-colored porous calcite, $CaCO_3$, deposited from solution in ground or surface waters. **2.** A compact calcium carbonate used as a facing material in construction. [Fr. < Ital. *travertino,* alteration of *tivertino* < Lat. *(lapis) tīburtīnus,* (stone) of Tibur (Tivoli), an ancient city of central Italy.]

trav•es•ty (trăv′ĭ-stē) *n., pl.* **-ties 1.** An exaggerated or grotesque imitation. **2.** A debased or grotesque likeness: *a travesty of justice.* ❖ *tr.v.* **-tied, -ty•ing, -ties** To make a travesty of; parody or ridicule. [< obsolete, disguised, burlesqued < Fr. *travesti,* p. part. of *travestir,* to disguise, parody < Ital. *travestire* : Lat. *trāns-,* trans- + Lat. *vestīre,* to dress (< *vestis,* garment; see **wes-**[2] in App.).]

Trav•is (trăv′ĭs), **William Barret** 1809–36. Amer. military leader who commanded the defense of the Alamo (1836).

tra•vois (trə-voi′, trăv′oi′) *n., pl.* **tra•vois** (trə-voiz′, trăv′oiz′) A conveyance formerly used by Plains Indians consisting of a frame slung between poles and pulled by a dog or horse. [Canadian Fr., alteration of obsolete *travoy* < *travail,* cart-shaft < Fr., horse restraining frame, alteration of LLat. *tripālium,* device with three stakes, prob. < Lat. *tripālis,* having three stakes. See TRAVAIL.]

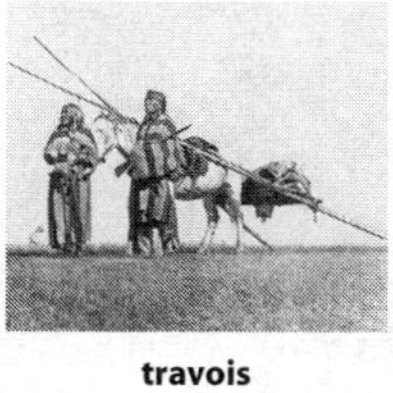

travois
photogravure from a photograph by Edward Sheriff Curtis (1868–1952)

trawl (trôl) *n.* **1.** A trawl net. **2.** See **setline.** ❖ *v.* **trawled, trawl•ing, trawls** —*tr.* To catch (fish) with a trawl. —*intr.* **1.** To fish with a trawl. **2.** To troll. [Poss. ME *trawelle,* perh. < MDu. *tragel,* dragnet, poss. < Lat. *trāgula* < *trahere,* to drag.]

trawl•er (trô′lər) *n.* **1.** A vessel used for trawling. **2.** One who trawls.

trawl line *n.* See **setline.**

trawl net *n.* A large tapered fishing net that is towed along the sea bottom.

tray (trā) *n.* **1.** A shallow flat receptacle with a raised edge or rim, used for carrying, holding, or displaying articles. **2.** A tray with its contents. [ME < OE *trēg.* See **deru-** in App.]

treach•er•ous (trĕch′ər-əs) *adj.* **1.** Marked by betrayal of fidelity, confidence, or trust; perfidious. **2.** Not to be relied on; not dependable or trustworthy. **3.** Marked by unforeseen hazards; dangerous or deceptive. —**treach′er•ous•ly** *adv.* —**treach′er•ous•ness** *n.*

treach•er•y (trĕch′ə-rē) *n., pl.* **-ies 1.** Willful betrayal of fidelity, confidence, or trust; perfidy. **2.** The act or an instance of such betrayal. [ME *trecherie* < OFr. < *trichier,* to trick, prob. < VLat. **triccāre.* See TRICK.]

trea•cle (trē′kəl) *n.* **1.** Cloying speech or sentiment. **2.** *Chiefly British* Molasses. **3.** A medicinal compound formerly used as an antidote for poison. [ME *triacle,* antidote for poison < OFr. < Lat. *thēriaca* < Gk. *thēriakē (antidotos),* (antidote against) wild animals, fem. of *thēriakos,* of wild animals < *thērion,* dim. of *thēr,* beast. See **ghwer-** in App.]

trea•cly (trē′klē) *adj.* Cloyingly sweet or sentimental.

tread (trĕd) *v.* **trod** (trŏd), **trod•den** (trŏd′n) or **trod, tread•ing, treads** —*tr.* **1.** To walk on, over, or along. **2.** To press beneath the feet; trample. **3.** To subdue harshly or cruelly; crush. **4.** To form by walking or trampling: *tread a path.* **5.** To execute by walking or dancing: *tread a measure.* **6.** To copulate with. Used of a male bird. —*intr.* **1a.** To go on foot; walk. **b.** To set down the foot; step. **2.** To press, crush, or injure something by or as if by trampling. Often used with *on* or *upon.* **3.** To copulate. Used of birds. ❖ *n.* **1a.** The act, manner, or sound of treading. **b.** An instance of treading; a step. **c.** A mark made by treading, as in snow. **2.** The upper horizontal part of a step in a staircase. **3a.** The part

ă pat	oi boy
ā pay	ou out
âr care	o͝o took
ä father	o͞o boot
ĕ pet	ŭ cut
ē be	ûr urge
ĭ pit	th thin
ī pie	*th* this
îr pier	hw which
ŏ pot	zh vision
ō toe	ə about, item
ô paw	

Stress marks:
′ (primary);
′ (secondary), as in
lexicon (lĕk′sĭ-kŏn′)

of a wheel or tire that makes contact with the road or rails. **b.** The grooved face of a tire. **4.** The part of a shoe sole that touches the ground. **5.** Either of the continuous metal belts with which bulldozers, tanks, and certain other vehicles move over the ground. **—idiom: tread water 1.** To keep the head above water while in an upright position by pumping the legs. **2.** To expend effort but make little or no progress. [ME *treden* < OE *tredan*.] **—tread′less** *adj.*

tread·le (trĕd′l) *n.* A pedal or lever operated by the foot for circular drive, as in a sewing machine. ❖ *intr.v.* **-led, -ling, -les** To work a treadle. [ME *tredel* < OE, step of a stair < *tredan*, to tread.] **—tread′ler** *n.*

tread·mill (trĕd′mĭl′) *n.* **1a.** A mechanism rotated by people treading on the moving steps of a wheel. **b.** A similar device operated by an animal treading a continuous sloping belt. **2.** An exercise device consisting of a continuous endless moving belt on which a person can walk or jog while remaining in one place. **3.** A monotonous task or set of tasks seeming to have no end.

treas. *abbr.* **1.** treasurer **2.** treasury

trea·son (trē′zən) *n.* **1.** Violation of allegiance toward one's country or sovereign, esp. the betrayal of one's country by waging war against it or by purposely aiding its enemies. **2.** A betrayal of trust or confidence. [ME < AN *treson* < Lat. *trāditiō, trāditiōn-*, a handing over. See TRADITION.]

trea·son·a·ble (trē′zə-nə-bəl) *adj.* Relating to, constituting, or involving treason. **—trea′son·a·bly** *adv.*

trea·son·ous (trē′zə-nəs) *adj.* Treasonable. **—trea′son·ous·ly** *adv.*

treas·ure (trĕzh′ər) *n.* **1.** Accumulated or stored wealth such as jewels or other valuables. **2.** Valuable or precious possessions of any kind. **3.** One considered esp. precious or valuable. ❖ *tr.v.* **-ured, -ur·ing, -ures 1.** To keep or regard as precious; value highly. See Syns at **appreciate. 2.** To accumulate and store away. [ME *tresure* < OFr. *tresor* < Lat. *thēsaurus* < Gk. *thēsauros*.] **—treas′ur·a·ble** *adj.*

treasure hunt *n.* A game in which the players attempt to find hidden articles by means of a series of clues.

treas·ur·er (trĕzh′ər-ər) *n.* One who has charge of funds or revenues, esp. the chief financial officer of a government, corporation, or association. [ME *tresurer* < AN *tresorer* < LLat. *thēsaurārius* < Lat., of treasure < *thēsaurus*, treasure. See TREASURE.]

treas·ure-trove (trĕzh′ər-trōv′) *n.* **1.** Treasure found hidden. **2.** *Law* Silver or gold in the form of bullion, plate, or money that is found hidden and has no known owner. **3.** A discovery of great value. [AN *tresor trove* : OFr. *tresor*, treasure; see TREASURE + OFr. *trove*, p. part. of *trover*, to find; see TROVER.]

treas·ur·y (trĕzh′ə-rē) *n., pl.* **-ies 1.** A place in which treasure is kept. **2a.** A place in which private or public funds are received, kept, and managed. **b.** Such funds or revenues. **3.** A collection of literary or artistic treasures. **4. Treasury a.** The department of a government in charge of the collection, management, and expenditure of the public revenue. **b.** A security, such as a note, issued by the US Treasury.

Treasury bill *n.* A short-term obligation of the US Treasury having a maturity period of one year or less and sold at a discount from face value.

Treasury bond *n.* A long-term obligation of the US Treasury having a maturity period of more than ten years and paying interest semiannually.

Treasury note *n.* An intermediate-term obligation of the US Treasury having a maturity period of one to ten years and paying interest semiannually.

treat (trēt) *v.* **treat·ed, treat·ing, treats** **—tr. 1.** To act or behave in a specified manner toward. **2.** To regard and handle in a certain way. Often used with *as: treated the matter as a joke.* **3.** To deal with in writing or speech; discuss. **4.** To deal with or represent artistically in a specified manner or style. **5a.** To provide with food, entertainment, or gifts at one's own expense. **b.** To give (someone or oneself) something pleasurable. **6.** To subject to a process, action, or change, esp. to a chemical or physical process or application. **7a.** To give medical aid to (someone). **b.** To give medical aid to counteract (a disease or condition). **—intr. 1.** To deal with a subject or topic in writing or speech. Often used with *of.* **2.** To pay for another's entertainment, food, or drink. **3.** To engage in negotiations, as to reach a settlement or agree on terms. ❖ *n.* **1.** Something, such as one's food or entertainment, that is paid for by someone else. **2.** A source of special delight or pleasure. [ME *tretien* < OFr. *traitier* < Lat. *tractāre*, freq. of *trahere*, to draw.] **—treat′er** *n.*

SYNONYMS *treat, deal, handle* These verbs mean to act in a specified way with regard to someone or something: *treats his guests with courtesy; dealt rationally with the problem; handling a case with discretion.*

treat·a·ble (trē′tə-bəl) *adj.* Possible to treat; responsive to treatment.

trea·tise (trē′tĭs) *n.* **1.** A systematic, usu. extensive written discourse on a topic. **2.** *Obsolete* A tale or narrative. [ME *treatis* < AN *tretiz*, alteration of *treteiz* < VLat. *tractāticius* < Lat. *tractātus*, p. part. of *tractāre*, to drag about, deal with. See TREAT.]

treat·ment (trēt′mənt) *n.* **1a.** The act, manner, or method of

treble clef

tree frog
red-eyed tree frog
Agalychnis callidryas

handling or dealing with someone or something. **b.** *Informal* The usual methods of dealing with a given situation: *gave the opposing team the treatment.* **2a.** Administration or application of remedies to a patient or for a disease or injury; therapy. **b.** The substance or remedy so applied. **3a.** An outline of the plot, characters, and action for a screenplay. **b.** An adaptation of a literary work that serves as the basis for a screenplay.

trea·ty (trē′tē) *n., pl.* **-ties 1a.** A formal agreement between two or more states, as to terms of peace or trade. **b.** The document in which such an agreement is set down. **2.** A contract or agreement. **3.** *Obsolete* **a.** Negotiation for the purpose of reaching an agreement. **b.** An entreaty. [ME *tretee* < OFr. *traite* < Lat. *tractātus*, discussion < p. part. of *tractāre*, to drag about, deal with. See TREAT.]

treaty Indian *n. Canadian* A status Indian belonging to a band that has signed a treaty with the federal government.

treaty port *n.* A port kept open for foreign trade according to a treaty, esp. formerly in China, Korea, and Japan.

Treb·bia (trĕb′yä) A river of NW Italy flowing c. 113 km (70 mi) N to the Po R.

Treb·bia·no (trĕb-byä′nō, trĕ′bē-ä′-) *n., pl.* **-nos** A white grape used extensively in the production of Italian wines and balsamic vinegar. [Ital.]

Treb·i·zond (trĕb′ĭ-zŏnd′) **1.** A former Greek empire bordering the S coast of the Black Sea; founded in 1204 and conquered by Ottoman Turks in 1461. **2.** See Trabzon.

treb·le (trĕb′əl) *adj.* **1.** Triple. **2.** *Music* Relating to or having the highest part, voice, or range. **3.** High-pitched; shrill. ❖ *n.* **1.** *Music* **a.** The highest part, voice, instrument, or range. **b.** A singer or player of this part. **2.** A high shrill sound or voice. ❖ *tr. & intr.v.* **-led, -ling, -les** To make or become triple. [ME < OFr. < Med.Lat. *triplum* < Lat., neut. of *triplus*, triple. See TRIPLE.] **—treb′le·ness** *n.* **—treb′ly** *adv.*

treble clef *n.* A symbol indicating the second line from the bottom of a staff as the pitch of G above middle C.

treb·u·chet (trĕb′yə-shĕt′) also **treb·uc·ket** (-ə-kĕt′) *n.* A medieval catapult for hurling heavy stones. [ME < OFr. < *trebucher*, to overthrow : *tre-*, over (< Lat. *trāns-*; see TRANS−) + *but*, trunk of the body (of Gmc. orig.).]

tre·cen·to (trā-chĕn′tō) *n.* The 14th century, esp. with reference to Italian art and literature. [Ital. < *(mil) trecento*, (one thousand) three hundred : *tre*, three (< Lat. *trēs*; see **trei-** in App.) + *cento*, hundred (< Lat. *centum*; see **dekm̥** in App.).]

tre·de·cil·lion (trē′dĭ-sĭl′yən) *n.* **1.** The cardinal number equal to 10^{42}. **2.** *Chiefly British* The cardinal number equal to 10^{78}. [Lat. *tredecim*, thirteen (*trēs*, three; see **trei-** in App. + *decem*, ten; see DECI−) + (M)ILLION.] **—tre′de·cil′lion** *adj.* **—tre′de·cil′lionth** *adj., adv. & n.*

tree (trē) *n.* **1a.** A perennial woody plant having a main trunk and usu. a distinct crown. **b.** A plant or shrub resembling a tree in form or size. **2.** Something, such as a clothes tree, that resembles a tree in form. **3.** A wooden beam, post, stake, or bar used as part of a framework or structure. **4.** A saddletree. **5a.** A diagram that has branches in descending lines showing relationships, as of hierarchy or lineage: *a telephone tree; a family tree.* **b.** The structure or arrangement illustrated by such a diagram. **6.** *Archaic* **a.** Gallows. **b.** The cross on which Jesus was crucified. ❖ *tr.v.* **treed, tree·ing, trees 1.** To force up a tree. **2.** *Informal* To force into a difficult position; corner. **3.** To supply with trees. **4.** To stretch (a shoe or boot) onto a shoetree. **—idiom: up a tree** *Informal* In a situation of great difficulty or perplexity; helpless. [ME < OE *trēow.* See **deru-** in App.]

Tree, Sir **Herbert Beerbohm** 1853–1917. British actor who founded the Royal Academy of Dramatic Art (1904).

tree belt *n. Massachusetts* See **parking** 3. See Regional Note at **parking.**

treed (trēd) *adj.* Planted or covered with trees; wooded.

tree farm *n.* An area of forest land for commercial use.

tree fern *n.* Any of various tropical treelike ferns with a terminal crown of large, pinnately divided fronds.

tree frog *n.* Any of various small arboreal frogs of the family Hylidae, having long toes terminating in adhesive disks.

tree·hop·per (trē′hŏp′ər) *n.* Any of numerous, generally small tropical homopterous insects of the family Membracidae, having mouthparts for sucking the sap from trees.

tree house *n.* A structure built among the limbs of a tree.

tree·hug·ger (trē′hŭg′ər) *n. Informal* An environmentalist, esp. a supporter of forest preservation and logging restrictions.

tree lawn *n. Chiefly Upper Northern US* See **parking** 3. See Regional Note at **parking.**

tree line *n.* See **timberline.**

tre·en (trē′ən) *n.* Wooden cookware, tableware, or eating utensils. [< ME, made of wood < OE *trēowen* < *trēow*, tree. See TREE.]

tree·nail or **tre·nail** (trē′nāl′, trĕn′əl, trŭn′əl) also **trun·nel** (trŭn′əl) *n.* A wooden peg that swells when wet and is used to fasten timbers, esp. in shipbuilding.

tree-of-heav·en (trē′əv-hĕv′ən) *n.* A deciduous, rapidly growing tree (*Ailanthus altissima*) native to China and having sweetish fetid male flowers.

tree of knowledge *n.* The tree in the Garden of Eden whose forbidden fruit Adam and Eve tasted.

tree of life *n., pl.* **trees of life 1.** A tall palm (*Mauritia flexuosa*) of South America having fan-shaped leaves. **2.** A tree in the Garden of Eden whose fruit, if eaten, gave eternal life.

tree shrew *n.* Any of various small squirrellike arboreal mammals of the family Tupaiidae, found in southern Asia and thought to be related to both insectivores and primates.

tree squirrel *n.* See **squirrel** 1.

tree surgery *n.* Treatment of diseased or damaged trees by filling cavities and pruning and bracing branches. **—tree surgeon** *n.*

tree toad *n.* See **tree frog.**

tree•top (trē′tŏp′) *n.* The uppermost part of a tree.

tref (trāf) *adj. Judaism* Not kosher according to dietary law. [Yiddish *treyf* < Heb. *ṭərēpâ*, carrion < *ṭārap*, to tear.]

tre•foil (trē′foil′, trĕf′oil′) *n.* **1.** Any of various plants of the genera *Trifolium, Lotus,* and related genera of the pea family, having compound trifoliate leaves. **2.** An ornament, symbol, or architectural form having the appearance of a trifoliate leaf. [ME < AN *trifoil* < Lat. *trifolium* : *tri-*, tri- + *folium*, leaf; see **bhel-** in App.]

tre•ha•la (trĭ-hä′lə) *n.* A sugarlike edible substance obtained from the pupal case of an Old World beetle of the genus *Larinus.* [NLat. *trehala* < Turk. *tīqāla* < Pers. *tīghāl.*]

tre•ha•lose (trĭ-hä′lōs′, -lōz′) *n.* A sweet-tasting crystalline disaccharide, $C_{12}H_{22}O_{11}$, found in trehala and in many fungi.

treil•lage (trē-yäzh′, trā′lĭj) *n.* Latticework, esp. a trellis for a vine. [Fr. < OFr. *treille*, bower supported by trelliswork < Lat. *trichila*, bower, arbor.]

trek (trĕk) *intr.v.* **trekked, trek•king, treks 1.** To make a slow or arduous journey. **2.** To journey on foot, esp. through mountainous areas. **3.** *South African* To travel by ox wagon. ❖ *n.* **1.** A journey or leg of a journey, esp. when slow or difficult. **2.** *South African* A journey by ox wagon, esp. a migration such as that of the Boers from 1835 to 1837. [Afr., to travel by ox wagon < Du. *trekken*, to travel < MDu. *trecken*, to pull.] **—trek′ker** *n.*

trel•lis (trĕl′ĭs) *n.* **1.** A structure of open latticework, esp. one used as a support for creeping plants. **2.** An arbor or arch made of latticework. ❖ *tr.v.* **-lised, -lis•ing, -lis•es 1.** To provide with a trellis, esp. to train (a vine) on a trellis. **2.** To make (something) in the form of a trellis. [ME *trelis* < OFr. < VLat. **trilīcius* < Lat. *trilīx, trilīc-*, woven with three threads : *tri-*, tri- + *līcium*, thread.]

trel•lis•work (trĕl′ĭs-wûrk′) *n.* Latticework.

trem•a•tode (trĕm′ə-tōd′) *n.* Any of numerous parasitic flatworms of the class Trematoda, having a thick outer cuticle and one or more suckers or hooks for attaching to host tissue. [< NLat. *Trēmatōda*, class name < Gk. *trēmatōdēs*, having holes < *trēma, trēmat-*, perforation. See **terə-**[1] in App.]

trem•ble (trĕm′bəl) *intr.v.* **-bled, -bling, -bles 1.** To shake involuntarily, as from excitement or anger; quake. **2.** To feel fear or anxiety. **3.** To vibrate or quiver. ❖ *n.* **1.** The act or state of trembling. **2.** A convulsive fit of shaking. Often used in the plural. **3. trembles** (*used with a sing. verb*) **a.** An infectious viral disease of sheep that affects the nervous system, often causing prolonged trembling. **b.** Poisoning of domestic animals, esp. cattle and sheep, caused by eating white snakeroot or rayless goldenrod and marked by muscular tremors and weakening. [ME *tremblen* < OFr. *trembler* < VLat. **tremulāre* < Lat. *tremulus*, trembling. See TREMULOUS.] **—trem′bler** *n.* **—trem′bly** *adj.*

tre•men•dous (trĭ-mĕn′dəs) *adj.* **1a.** Extremely large in amount, extent, or degree; enormous: *a tremendous task.* **b.** *Informal* Marvelous; wonderful. **2.** Capable of making one tremble; terrible. [< Lat. *tremendus*, gerundive of *tremere*, to tremble.] **—tre•men′dous•ly** *adv.* **—tre•men′dous•ness** *n.*

trem•o•lite (trĕm′ə-līt′) *n.* A white to gray amphibole mineral, $Ca_2Mg_5Si_8O_{22}(OH)_2$, typically occurring in aggregates. [Fr. *trémolite*, after *Tremola*, a valley in the Swiss Alps.]

trem•o•lo (trĕm′ə-lō′) *n., pl.* **-los 1a.** A tremulous effect produced by rapid repetition of a single tone. **b.** A similar effect produced by rapid alternation of two tones. **2.** A device on an organ for producing a tremulous effect. **3.** A vibrato in singing, often excessive or poorly controlled. [Ital. < Lat. *tremulus*, tremulous. See TREMULOUS.]

trem•or (trĕm′ər) *n.* **1.** A shaking or vibrating movement, as of the earth. **2.** A trembling or quivering effect. **3.** An involuntary trembling or quivering, as from nervous agitation. **4.** A nervous quiver or thrill. **5.** A state or feeling of nervous agitation or tension. **6.** A tremulous sound; a quaver. [ME, terror < OFr. < Lat., a trembling < *tremere*, to tremble.]

trem•u•lant (trĕm′yə-lənt) *adj.* Tremulous; trembling.

trem•u•lous (trĕm′yə-ləs) *adj.* **1.** Marked by trembling, quivering, or shaking. **2.** Timid or fearful; timorous. [< Lat. *tremulus* < *tremere*, to tremble.] **—trem′u•lous•ly** *adv.*

tre•nail (trē′nāl′, trĕn′əl, trŭn′əl) *n.* Variant of **treenail.**

trench (trĕnch) *n.* **1.** A deep furrow or ditch. **2.** A long narrow ditch embanked with its own soil and used for concealment and protection in warfare. **3.** A long steep-sided valley on the ocean floor. ❖ *v.* **trenched, trench•ing, trench•es** —*tr.* **1.** To cut a trench in. **2.** To fortify with trenches. **3.** To place in a trench. **4.** To make a cut in; carve. —*intr.* **1.** To dig trenches or a trench. **2.** To verge or encroach. Often used with *on* or *upon.* [ME *trenche* < OFr. < *trenchier*, to cut, perh. < VLat. **trincāre*, var. of Lat. *truncāre* < *truncus*, trunk. See **terə-**[2] in App.]

trench•ant (trĕn′chənt) *adj.* **1.** Forceful, effective, and vigorous: *a trenchant argument.* **2.** Caustic; cutting: *trenchant criticism.* **3.** Distinct; clear-cut. [ME < OFr., cutting < pr. part. of *trenchier*, to cut. See TRENCH.] **—trench′an•cy** *n.* **—trench′ant•ly** *adv.*

trench coat *n.* A belted raincoat in a military style, having straps on the shoulders and deep pockets.

trench•er[1] (trĕn′chər) *n.* **1.** A wooden board or platter on which food is carved or served. **2.** *Archaic* The pleasure of the table; food. [ME *trenchur* < AN *trenchour* < *trencher*, to cut, perh. < VLat. **trincāre.* See TRENCH.]

trench•er[2] (trĕn′chər) *n.* One that digs trenches.

trench•er•man (trĕn′chər-mən) *n.* **1.** A hearty eater. **2.** *Archaic* One who frequents another's table; a parasite.

trench fever *n.* An acute infectious disease characterized by chills and fever, caused by the microorganism *Rickettsia quintana* and transmitted by the louse *Pediculus humanus.*

trench foot *n.* A condition of the foot resembling frostbite, caused by prolonged exposure to cold and dampness.

trench mortar *n.* A mortar designed for use in forward positions, esp. in trenches.

trench mouth *n.* A painful infection of the mouth and throat caused by the bacterium *Fusobacterium fusiforme* in combination with the spirochete *Treponema vincentii* and marked by ulcerations of the mucous membranes, bleeding, and foul breath.

trend (trĕnd) *n.* **1.** The general direction in which something tends to move. **2.** A general tendency or inclination. **3.** Current style; vogue. ❖ *intr.v.* **trend•ed, trend•ing, trends 1.** To extend, incline, or veer in a specified direction. **2.** To show a general tendency; tend. [< ME *trenden*, to revolve < OE *trendan.*]

trend•set•ter (trĕnd′sĕt′ər) *n.* One that initiates or popularizes a trend. **—trend′set′ting** *adj.*

trend•y (trĕn′dē) *Informal adj.* **-i•er, -i•est** Of or in accord with the latest fad or fashion: *trendy clothes.* **—trend′i•ly** *adv.* **—trend′i•ness** *n.* **—trend′y** *n.*

Trent (trĕnt) also **Tren•to** (trĕn′tō) A city of N Italy NW of Venice; site of the Council of Trent (1545–63). Pop. 98,833.

Tren•ti•no-Al•to-A•di•ge (trĕn-tē′nō-äl′tō-ä′dē-jĕ′) A region of NE Italy bordering on Switzerland and Austria.

Tren•ton (trĕn′tən) The cap. of NJ, in the W-central part on the Delaware R.; settled c. 1679 by Quakers. Pop. 85,403.

Trent River A river of central England flowing c. 274 km (170 mi) NE to join the Ouse R. and form the Humber estuary.

tre•pan[1] (trĭ-păn′) *n.* **1.** A rock-boring tool used in mining for sinking shafts. **2.** *Medicine* A trephine. ❖ *tr.v.* **-panned, -pan•ning, -pans 1.** To bore (a shaft) with a trepan. **2.** *Medicine* To trephine. [ME *trepane*, surgical crown saw < Med.Lat. *trepanum* < Gk. *trūpanon*, borer < *trūpān*, to pierce < *trūpē*, hole. See **terə-**[1] in App.] **—trep′a•na′tion** (trĕp′ə-nā′shən) *n.*

tre•pan[2] (trĭ-păn′) also **tra•pan** (trə-) *Archaic tr.v.* **-panned, -pan•ning, -pans** To trap; ensnare. ❖ *n.* **1.** A trickster. **2.** A trick or snare. [?]

tre•pang (trĭ-păng′) *n.* A sea cucumber of the genus *Holothuria* of the southern Pacific and Indian oceans, used in soup, esp. in China and Indonesia. [Malay *teripang.*]

tre•phine (trĭ-fīn′) *n.* A surgical instrument having circular sawlike edges, used to cut out disks of bone, usu. from the skull. ❖ *tr.v.* **-phined, -phin•ing, -phines** To operate on with a trephine. [Fr. *tréphine* < obsolete E. *trefine* < Lat. *trēs fīnēs*, three ends : *trēs*, three; see **trei-** in App. + *fīnēs*, pl. of *fīnis*, end.] **—treph′i•na′tion** (trĕf′ə-nā′shən) *n.*

trep•id (trĕp′ĭd) *adj.* Timid; timorous. [Lat. *trepidus*, anxious.]

trep•i•da•tion (trĕp′ĭ-dā′shən) *n.* **1.** A state of alarm or dread; apprehension. See Syns at **fear. 2.** An involuntary trembling. [Lat. *trepidātiō, trepidātiōn-* < *trepidātus*, p. part. of *trepidāre*, to be in a state of confusion < *trepidus*, anxious.]

trep•o•ne•ma (trĕp′ə-nē′mə) *n., pl.* **-ma•ta** (-mə-tə) or **-mas** Any of a group of spirochetes of the genus *Treponema*, including those that cause syphilis. [NLat. *Treponēma*, genus name : Gk. *trepein*, to turn + Gk. *nēma*, thread; see **(s)nē-** in App.] **—trep′o•ne′mal, trep′o•nem′a•tous** (-nĕm′ə-təs) *adj.*

trep•o•ne•ma•to•sis (trĕp′ə-nē′mə-tō′sĭs) *n., pl.* **-ses** (-sēz) An infection or disease caused by a treponema.

trep•o•neme (trĕp′ə-nēm′) *n.* A treponema.

tres•pass (trĕs′pəs, -păs′) *intr.v.* **-passed, -pass•ing, -pass•es 1.** To commit an offense or a sin; transgress or err. **2.** *Law* To commit an unlawful injury to the person, property, or rights of another, with actual or implied force or violence, esp. to enter onto another's land wrongfully. **3.** To infringe on the privacy, time, or attention of another. ❖ *n.* (trĕs′păs′, -pəs) **1.** Transgression of a moral or social law, code, or duty. **2.** *Law* **a.** The act of trespassing. **b.** A suit brought for trespassing. **3.** An intrusion or infringement on another. See Syns at **breach.** [ME *trespassen* < OFr. *trespasser* : *tres-*, over (< Lat. *trāns-*; see TRANS–) + *passer*, to pass; see PASS.] **—tres′pass•er** *n.*

tress (trĕs) *n.* **1.** A long lock or ringlet of hair. **2.** *Archaic* A plait of hair. [ME *tresse* < OFr., perh. < VLat. **tricia*, rope, braid < Gk. *trikhiā*, rope < *thrix, trikh-*, hair.]

tres•tle (trĕs′əl) *n.* **1.** A horizontal beam or bar held up by two pairs of divergent legs and used as a support. **2.** A framework consisting of vertical slanted supports and horizontal crosspieces supporting a bridge. [ME *trestel* < OFr., alteration of VLat. **trāstellum, trānstellum*, dim. of Lat. *trānstrum*, beam. See TRANSOM.]

trestle table *n.* A table having a top supported by trestles.

trefoil

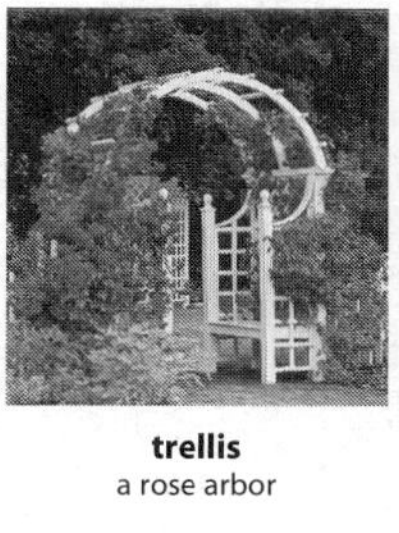

trellis
a rose arbor

ă	pat	oi	boy
ā	pay	ou	out
âr	care	ŏŏ	took
ä	father	ōō	boot
ĕ	pet	ŭ	cut
ē	be	ûr	urge
ĭ	pit	th	thin
ī	pie	*th*	this
îr	pier	hw	which
ŏ	pot	zh	vision
ō	toe	ə	about, item
ô	paw		

Stress marks:
′ (primary);
′ (secondary), as in
lexicon (lĕk′sĭ-kŏn′)

tres·tle·tree (trĕs′əl-trē′) *n. Nautical* One of a pair of horizontal beams set into a masthead to support the crosstrees.

tres·tle·work (trĕs′əl-wûrk′) *n.* A trestle or system of trestles, as that supporting a bridge.

tret·i·noin (trĕt′ĭ-noin′) *n.* See **retinoic acid.** [T(RANS–) + RETINO(IC ACID) + –IN.]

tre·val·ly (trə-văl′ē) *n., pl.* **-lies** An Australian food fish of the genus *Caranx.* [Perh. alteration of CAVALLA.]

Tre·vel·yan (trə-vĕl′yən, -vĭl′-), Sir **George Otto** 1838–1928. British historian whose works include *The American Revolution* (1899–1907). His son **George Macaulay Trevelyan** (1876–1962) wrote three books (1907–11) on Garibaldi.

Trèves (trĕv) See **Trier.**

trews (trōōz) *pl.n.* Close-fitting trousers, usu. of tartan. [Variant of obsolete *trouse.* See TROUSER.]

trey (trā) *n., pl.* **treys** A card, die, or domino with three pips. [ME *treye* < OFr. *treie* < Lat. *tria,* neut. of *trēs,* three. See **trei-** in App.]

tri– *pref.* **1.** Three: *trilobate.* **2a.** Occurring at intervals of three: *trimonthly.* **b.** Occurring three times during: *triweekly.* [ME < Lat. and Gk.; see **trei-** in App.]

tri·a·ble (trī′ə-bəl) *adj.* **1.** Capable of being tried or tested. **2.** *Law* Subject to judicial examination. —**tri′a·ble·ness** *n.*

tri·ad (trī′ăd′, -əd) *n.* **1.** A group of three. **2.** *Music* A chord of three tones, esp. one built on a given root tone plus a major or minor third and a perfect fifth. **3.** A section of a Pindaric ode consisting of the strophe, antistrophe, and epode. [LLat. *trias, triad-* < Gk., three. See **trei-** in App.] —**tri·ad′ic** *adj.*

tri·age (trē-äzh′, trē′äzh′) *n.* **1.** A process for sorting injured people into groups based on their need for immediate medical treatment. **2.** A system used to allocate a scarce commodity, such as food, only to those capable of deriving the greatest benefit from it. **3.** A process in which things are ranked in terms of importance or priority. ❖ *tr.v.* **-aged, -ag·ing, -ag·es** To sort or allocate by triage. [Fr. < *trier,* to sort < OFr.]

tri·al (trī′əl, trīl) *n.* **1.** *Law* Examination of evidence and applicable law by a competent tribunal to determine the issue of specified charges or claims. **2a.** The act or process of testing, trying, or putting to the proof. **b.** An instance of such testing, esp. as part of a series of tests or experiments: *a clinical trial of a drug.* **3.** An effort or attempt. **4.** A state of pain or anguish that tests patience, endurance, or belief. **5.** A trying, troublesome, or annoying person or thing. See Syns at **burden**¹. **6.** A preliminary competition or test to determine qualifications, as in a sport. ❖ *adj.* **1.** Of, relating to, or used in a trial. **2.** Attempted or advanced on a provisional or experimental basis: *a trial separation.* **3.** Made or done in the course of a trial or test. —*idioms:* **on trial** In the process of being tried, as in a court of law. **trial by fire** A test of one's abilities, esp. the ability to perform well under pressure. [ME *trial,* a testing < AN *trial* < *trier,* to sort, try.]

trial and error *n.* A method of reaching a correct solution or satisfactory result by trying out various means or theories until error is sufficiently reduced or eliminated. —**tri′al-and-er′ror** (trī′əl-ăn-ĕr′ər, trīl′-) *adj.*

trial balance *n.* A statement of all the open debit and credit items in a double-entry ledger, made to test their equality.

trial balloon *n.* An idea or a plan advanced tentatively to test reaction. [< testing weather conditions with balloons.]

trial jury *n.* See **petit jury.**

tri·a·logue (trī′ə-lôg′, -lŏg′) *n.* A conversation or discussion involving three people or groups.

trial run *n.* A test, as of performance.

tri·am·cin·o·lone (trī′ăm-sĭn′ə-lōn′) *n.* A synthetic glucocorticoid, C₂₁H₂₇FO₆, used in the treatment of allergic and respiratory disorders. [Perh. < TRI– + AM(YL) + *cin(ene),* a terpene (< CINEOLE) + (PREDNIS)OLONE.]

tri·an·gle (trī′ăng′gəl) *n.* **1a.** The plane figure formed by connecting three points not in a straight line by straight line segments; a three-sided polygon. **b.** Something shaped like such a figure. **2.** Any of various flat three-sided drawing and drafting guides, used esp. to draw straight lines at specific angles. **3.** *Music* A percussion instrument consisting of a piece of metal in the shape of a triangle open at one angle. **4.** A relationship involving three people, esp. a ménage à trois. [ME < OFr. < Lat. *triangulum* < neut. of *triangulus,* three-angled : *tri-, tri-* + *angulus,* angle.]

tri·an·gu·lar (trī-ăng′gyə-lər) *adj.* **1.** Of, relating to, or shaped like a triangle. **2.** Having a triangle for a base: *a triangular pyramid.* **3.** Relating to or involving three entities, such as three people, objects, or ideas. —**tri·an′gu·lar′i·ty** (-lăr′ĭ-tē) *n.* —**tri·an′gu·lar·ly** *adv.*

tri·an·gu·late (trī-ăng′gyə-lāt′) *tr.v.* **-lat·ed, -lat·ing, -lates 1.** To divide into triangles. **2.** To survey by triangulation. **3.** To make triangular. **4.** To measure by using trigonometry. ❖ *adj.* (trī-ăng′gyə-lĭt) **1.** Of or relating to triangles; triangular. **2.** Made up of or marked with triangles.

tri·an·gu·la·tion (trī-ăng′gyə-lā′shən) *n.* **1a.** A surveying technique in which a region is divided into triangular elements based on a line of known length so that measurements may be made by the application of trigonometry. **b.** The network of triangles so laid out. **2.** The location of an unknown point by the formation of a triangle with the unknown point and two known points as the vertices.

Tri·an·gu·lum (trī-ăng′gyə-ləm) *n.* A northern constellation near Aries. [Lat. *triangulum,* triangle. See TRIANGLE.]

Triangulum Aus·tra·le (ô-strā′lē) A southern constellation near Apus. [NLat. *Triangulum Austrāle* : Lat. *triangulum,* triangle + Lat. *austrāle,* neut. of *austrālis,* southern.]

tri·ar·chy (trī′är′kē) *n., pl.* **-chies 1.** Government by three people; a triumvirate. **2.** A country governed by three rulers.

Tri·as·sic (trī-ăs′ĭk) *adj.* Of or belonging to the geologic time of the first period of the Mesozoic Era, characterized by the diversification of land life, the rise of dinosaurs, and the appearance of the earliest mammals. See table at **geologic time.** ❖ *n.* The Triassic Period or its deposits. [LLat. *trias,* triad < the subdivision of this period into three parts); see TRIAD + –IC.]

tri·ath·lete (trī-ăth′lēt) *n.* One who competes in a triathlon.

tri·ath·lon (trī-ăth′lən, -lŏn′) *n.* An athletic contest consisting of three successive events, usu. long-distance swimming, bicycling, and running. [TRI– + (DEC)ATHLON.]

tri·a·tom·ic (trī′ə-tŏm′ĭk) *adj.* **1.** Containing three atoms per molecule. **2.** Containing three replaceable atoms or radicals.

tri·ax·i·al (trī-ăk′sē-əl) *adj.* Having three axes. —**tri·ax′i·al′i·ty** (-ăl′ĭ-tē) *n.*

tri·a·zine (trī′ə-zēn′, trī-ăz′ēn′) *n.* A compound having three carbon and three nitrogen atoms in a six-membered ring, esp. any of three isomers of C₃H₃N₃.

tri·a·zole (trī′ə-zōl′, trī-ăz′ōl′) *n.* Any of several compounds with composition C₂H₃N₃, having a five-membered ring of two carbon atoms and three nitrogen atoms.

trib. *abbr.* tributary

trib·ade (trĭb′əd) *n.* A lesbian. [Fr. < Lat. *tribas, tribad-* < Gk. < *tribein,* to rub. See TRIBOLOGY.] —**trib′a·dism** *n.*

trib·al (trī′bəl) *adj.* Of, relating to, or characteristic of a tribe. —**trib′al·ly** *adv.*

trib·al·ism (trī′bə-lĭz′əm) *n.* **1.** The organization, culture, or beliefs of a tribe. **2.** A strong feeling of identity with and loyalty to one's tribe or group. —**trib′al·ist** *n.* —**trib′al·is′tic** *adj.*

tri·ba·sic (trī-bā′sĭk) *adj.* **1.** Containing three replaceable hydrogen atoms or radicals. Used of an acid. **2.** Containing three univalent basic atoms or radicals. Used of a base or salt.

tribe (trīb) *n.* **1.** A unit of sociopolitical organization consisting of a number of families, clans, or other groups who share a common ancestry and culture and among whom leadership is typically neither formalized nor permanent. **2.** An ancient political, ethnic, or ancestral division, esp.: **a.** Any of the three divisions of the ancient Romans, namely, the Latin, Sabine, and Etruscan. **b.** Any of the 12 divisions of ancient Israel. **c.** A phyle of ancient Greece. **3.** A group of people sharing an occupation, interest, or habit. **4.** *Informal* A large family. **5.** *Biology* A taxonomic category placed between a subfamily and a genus or between a suborder and a family. [ME < OFr. *tribu* < Lat. *tribus,* division of the Roman people, perh. of Etruscan orig., or poss. < *tri-,* three; see **trei-** in App.]

tribes·man (trībz′mən) *n.* **1.** A man who is a member of one's own tribe. **2.** A member of a tribal people.

tribes·peo·ple (trībz′pē′pəl) *pl.n.* **1.** The people of one's own tribe. **2.** An aboriginal people living in tribes.

tribes·wom·an (trībz′wŏŏm′ən) *n.* **1.** A woman who is a member of one's own tribe. **2.** A woman who is a member of a tribal aboriginal people.

tri·bo·e·lec·tric·i·ty (trī′bō-ĭ-lĕk-trĭs′ĭ-tē, -ē′lĕk-, trī′bō-) *n., pl.* **-ties** An electrical charge produced by friction between two objects. [Gk. *tribos,* a rubbing < *tribein,* to rub. See **terə-**¹ in App. + ELECTRICITY.] —**tri′bo·e·lec′tric** *adj.*

tri·bol·o·gy (trī-bŏl′ə-jē, trĭb-) *n.* The science of the mechanisms of friction, lubrication, and wear of interacting surfaces that are in relative motion. [Gk. *tribos,* a rubbing (< Gk. *tribein,* to rub; see TRIBOELECTRICITY) + –LOGY.] —**tri′bo·log′i·cal** (trī′bə-lŏj′ĭ-kəl, trĭb′ə-) *adj.* —**tri·bol′o·gist** *n.*

tri·brach (trī′brăk′) *n.* A metrical foot having three short or unstressed syllables. [Lat. *tribrachys* < Gk. *tribrakhus* : *tri-, tri-* + *brakhus,* short.]

trib·u·la·tion (trĭb′yə-lā′shən) *n.* **1.** Great affliction, trial, or distress; suffering. **2.** An experience that tests one's endurance, patience, or faith. See Syns at **burden**¹. [Ult. < Lat. *trībulātiō, trībulātiōn-* < *trībulātus,* p. part. of *trībulāre,* to oppress < Lat. *trībulum,* threshing-sledge. See **terə-**¹ in App.]

tri·bu·nal (trī-byōō′nəl, trĭ-) *n.* **1.** *Law* **a.** A seat or court of justice. **b.** The bench on which a judge or other presiding officer sits in court. **2.** A committee or board appointed to adjudicate in a particular matter. **3.** Something that has the power to determine or judge. [ME < OFr. < Lat. *tribūnal,* judge's platform < *tribūnus,* tribune. See TRIBUNE¹.]

trib·u·nate (trĭb′yə-nāt′, trī-byōō′nĭt) *n.* The rank, office, dignity, or authority of a tribune.

trib·une¹ (trĭb′yōōn′, trī-byōōn′) *n.* **1.** An officer of ancient Rome elected by the plebeians to protect their rights from arbitrary acts of the patrician magistrates. **2.** A protector or champion of the people. [ME < OFr. *tribun* < Lat. *tribūnus* < *tribus,* tribe. See TRIBE.] —**trib′u·nar′y** (trĭb′yə-nĕr′ē) *adj.*

trib·une² (trĭb′yōōn′, trī-byōōn′) *n.* **1.** A raised platform or dais from which a speaker addresses an assembly. **2.** See **gallery** 3c. [Fr. < OFr., part of a church, speaking platform < OItal. *tribuna*

< Med.Lat. *tribūna*, alteration of Lat. *tribūnal*. See TRIBUNAL.]

trib·u·tar·y (trĭb′yə-tĕr′ē) *adj.* **1.** Making additions or yielding supplies; contributory. **2.** Paid in tribute. **3.** Paying tribute: *a tributary colony.* ❖ *n., pl.* **-ies 1.** A stream that flows into a larger stream or other body of water. **2.** A ruler or nation that pays tribute. [ME *tributarie*, paying tribute < Lat. *tribūtārius* < *tribūtum*, tribute. See TRIBUTE.]

trib·ute (trĭb′yōōt) *n.* **1.** A gift, payment, declaration, or other acknowledgment of gratitude, respect, or admiration. **2.** Evidence attesting to some praiseworthy quality or characteristic. **3a.** A payment made by one ruler or nation to another in acknowledgment of submission or as the price of security. **b.** A tax imposed for such payment. **4.** Any payment exacted for protection. **5a.** A payment or tax given by a feudal vassal to an overlord. **b.** The obligation to make such a payment. [ME *tribut* < OFr. < Lat. *tribūtum* < neut. p. part. of *tribuere*, to pay, distribute < *tribus*, tribe. See TRIBE.]

tri·cam·er·al (trī-kăm′ər-əl) *adj.* Of or being a legislature composed of three chambers. [TRI– + Lat. *camera*, chamber; see CAMERA + –AL¹.]

tri·car·box·yl·ic (trī′kär-bŏk-sĭl′ĭk) *adj.* Having three carboxyl groups.

tricarboxylic acid cycle *n.* See **Krebs cycle**.

trice (trīs) *n.* A very short period of time; an instant. ❖ *tr.v.* **triced, tric·ing, tric·es** *Nautical* To hoist and secure with a rope: *trice up a sail.* [< ME (at a) *trise*, at one pull < *trisen*, to hoist < MDu. *trīsen* < *trīse*, pulley. V. < ME *trisen*.]

tri·cen·ten·ni·al (trī′sĕn-tĕn′ē-əl) *adj.* Tercentenary. ❖ *n.* A tercentenary event or celebration.

tri·ceps (trī′sĕps′) *n., pl.* **-ceps·es** (-sĕp′sĭz) also **triceps** A large three-headed extensor muscle of the upper arm. [< Lat., three-headed : *tri-*, tri- + *caput*, head; see **kaput-** in App.]

tri·cer·a·tops (trī-sĕr′ə-tŏps′) *n.* A herbivorous Cretaceous dinosaur of the genus *Triceratops*, having a large horn above either eye and a smaller horn on the nose. [NLat. *Tricerātops*, genus name : Gk. *tri-*, tri- + Gk. *keras, kerāt-*, horn; see **ker-¹** in App. + Gk. *ōps*, eye, face; see **okʷ-** in App.]

tri·chi·a·sis (trī-kī′ə-sĭs) *n.* A condition of ingrowing hairs about an orifice, esp. ingrowing eyelashes.

tri·chi·na (trī-kī′nə) *n., pl.* **-nae** (-nē) or **-nas** A small slender parasitic nematode worm (*Trichinella spiralis*) that infests the intestines of various mammals and those larvae become encysted in muscles. [NLat. < Gk. *trikhinē*, fem. of *trikhinos*, hairy < *thrix, trikh-*, hair.]

trich·i·nize (trĭk′ə-nīz′) *tr.v.* **-nized, -niz·ing, -niz·es** To infect with trichinae. —**trich′i·ni·za′tion** (-nĭ-zā′shən) *n.*

trich·i·no·sis (trĭk′ə-nō′sĭs) *n.* A disease caused by eating undercooked trichinous meat, usu. pork, and characterized by fever, nausea, muscular pain, and edema of the face.

tri·chi·nous (trī-kī′nəs, trĭk′ə-nəs) *adj.* **1.** Containing trichinae. **2.** Of or relating to trichinae or trichinosis.

trich·ite (trĭk′īt′) *n.* A small dark needle-shaped crystal.

tri·chlo·ride (trī-klôr′īd′, -klôr′-) also **tri·chlo·rid** (-klôr′ĭd, -klôr′-) *n.* A compound containing three chlorine atoms per molecule.

tri·chlo·ro·a·ce·tic acid (trī-klôr′ō-ə-sē′tĭk, -klôr′-) *n.* A deliquescent corrosive crystalline compound, CCl_3COOH, used as a herbicide, an astringent, and an antiseptic.

tri·chlo·ro·eth·ane (trī-klôr′ō-ĕth′ān′, -klôr′-) *n.* Either of two colorless, nonflammable, isomeric compounds, $C_2H_3Cl_3$, having a sweet odor, used as solvents for adhesives, pesticides, and lubricants, and in industrial cleaning solutions.

tri·chlo·ro·eth·yl·ene (trī′klôr′ō-ĕth′ə-lēn′, -klôr′-) also **tri·chlor·eth·yl·ene** (trī′klôr-, -klôr′-) *n.* A heavy toxic liquid, C_2HCl_3, used as a solvent for oils and waxes.

tricho– or **trich–** *pref.* Hair; thread; filament: *trichocyst.* [Gk. *trikho-* < *thrix, trikh-*, hair.]

trich·o·cyst (trĭk′ə-sĭst′) *n.* A hairlike stinging or grasping organ in the outer cytoplasm of certain protozoans. —**trich′o·cys′tic** *adj.*

trich·o·gyne (trĭk′ə-jīn′, -gĭn′) *n.* A hairlike terminal process forming the receptive part of the female reproductive structure in certain fungi or algae.

trich·oid (trĭk′oid′, trī′koid′) *adj.* Resembling hair.

trich·ome (trĭk′ōm′, trī′kōm′) *n.* A hairlike or bristlelike outgrowth, as from the epidermis of a plant. [Gk. *trikhōma*, growth of hair < *trikhoun*, to cover with hair < *thrix, trikh-*, hair.] —**tri·chom′ic** (trĭ-kŏm′ĭk, -kō′mĭk) *adj.*

trich·o·mo·nad (trĭk′ə-mō′năd′) *n.* Any of various flagellate protozoans of the genus *Trichomonas*, occurring as parasites in the digestive and urogenital tracts of vertebrates. [NLat. *Trichomonas, monad-*, genus name : TRICHO– + LLat. *monas, monad-*, unit; see MONAD.] —**trich′o·mo·nad′al** (-năd′l), **trich′o·mon′al** (-mō′nəl) *adj.*

trich·o·mo·ni·a·sis (trĭk′ə-mə-nī′ə-sĭs) *n., pl.* **-ses** (-sēz′) **1.** A vaginal inflammation caused by a trichomonad (*Trichomonas vaginalis*) and resulting in a persistent discharge and itching. **2.** An infection caused by trichomonads, as a disease of cattle that commonly results in infertility or abortion. [NLat. *Trichomonas*, genus name; see TRICHOMONAD + –IASIS.]

tri·chop·ter·an (trī-kŏp′tər-ən) *n.* An insect of the order Tri-

choptera, constituting the caddis flies. [< NLat. *Trichoptera*, order name : Gk. *trikho-*, tricho- + Gk. *-pteron*, wing; see –PTER.]

tri·cho·sis (trī-kō′sĭs) *n., pl.* **-ses** (-sēz) Any hair disease.

trich·o·til·lo·ma·ni·a (trĭk′ō-tĭl′ō-mā′nē-ə, -măn′yə) *n.* The compulsion to tear or pluck out the hair on one's head and face and often to ingest it. [TRICHO– + Gk. *tillein*, to pluck hair + –MANIA.]

tri·chot·o·my (trī-kŏt′ə-mē) *n., pl.* **-mies 1.** Division into three parts or elements. **2.** A system based on three parts or elements. [NLat. *trichotomia* : Gk. *trikha*, in three parts; see **trei-** in App. + NLat. *-tomia, -tomy*.] —**tri·chot′o·mous** *adj.*

–trichous *suff.* Having a specified kind of hair or hairlike part: *peritrichous.* [< Gk. *-trikhos* < *thrix, trikh-*, hair.]

tri·chro·ism (trī′krō-ĭz′əm) *n.* The property possessed by certain minerals of exhibiting three different colors when viewed from three different directions under white lights. [< Gk. *trikhroos*, three-colored : *tri-*, tri- + *khrōs*, color.] —**tri·chro′ic** *adj.*

tri·chro·mat (trī′krō-măt′) *n.* A trichromatic person.

tri·chro·mat·ic (trī′krō-măt′ĭk) also **tri·chrome** (trī′krōm′) or **tri·chro·mic** (trī-krō′mĭk) *adj.* **1.** Of, relating to, or having three colors, as in photography. **2.** Having perception of the three primary colors, as in normal vision. —**tri·chro′ma·tism** (trī-krō′mə-tĭz′əm) *n.*

trick (trĭk) *n.* **1.** An act or procedure intended to achieve an end by deceptive or fraudulent means. **2.** A mischievous action; a prank. **3.** A stupid, disgraceful, or childish act or performance. **4a.** A peculiar trait or characteristic; a mannerism. **b.** A peculiar event with unexpected, often deceptive results. **c.** A deceptive or illusive appearance; an illusion. **5a.** A special skill; a knack. **b.** A convention or specialized skill peculiar to a particular field. **6.** A feat of magic or legerdemain. **7.** A difficult, dexterous, or clever act designed to amuse. **8.** *Games* **a.** All the cards played in a single round, one from each player. **b.** One such round. **9a.** A period or turn of duty, as at the helm of a ship. **b.** *Slang* A prison term. **10.** *Slang* **a.** An act of prostitution. **b.** A prostitute's customer. **11.** *Slang* A robbery or theft. ❖ *tr. & intr.v.* **tricked, trick·ing, tricks** To cheat or deceive or to practice trickery or deception. ❖ *adj.* **1.** Of, relating to, or involving tricks. **2.** Capable of performing tricks: *a trick dog.* **3.** Designed or made for doing a trick or tricks: *trick dice.* **4.** Weak, defective, or liable to fail: *a trick knee.* —*phrasal verb:* **trick out** (or **up**) *Informal* To ornament or adorn, often garishly. —*idioms:* **how's tricks** *Informal* Used to make a friendly inquiry about a person or that person's affairs. **not miss a trick** To be extremely alert. [ME *trik* < ONFr. *trique* < *trikier*, to deceive, prob. < VLat. *triccāre < Lat. *trīcārī*, to play tricks < *trīcae*, tricks.] —**trick′er** *n.*

trick·er·y (trĭk′ə-rē) *n., pl.* **-ies** The practice or use of tricks; deception by stratagem.

trick·ish (trĭk′ĭsh) *adj.* Characterized by or tending to use tricks or trickery. —**trick′ish·ly** *adv.* —**trick′ish·ness** *n.*

trick·le (trĭk′əl) *v.* **-led, -ling, -les** —*intr.* **1.** To flow or fall in drops or in a thin stream. **2.** To move or proceed slowly or bit by bit: *People trickled in.* —*tr.* To cause to trickle. ❖ *n.* **1.** The act or condition of trickling. **2.** A slow, small, or irregular quantity that moves, proceeds, or occurs intermittently. [ME *triklen*, perh. var. of *striklen*, freq. of *striken*, to flow. See STRIKE.]

trickle charge *n.* An electric charge supplied to a storage battery at a continuous low rate to keep it fully charged.

trick·le-down (trĭk′əl-doun′) *adj.* Of or relating to the economic theory that financial benefits accorded to big businesses and wealthy investors will pass down to profit smaller businesses and consumers.

trick or treat *interj.* Used as a greeting by children when trick-or-treating.

trick-or-treat (trĭk′ər-trēt′) *intr.v.* **-treat·ed, -treat·ing, -treats** To engage in the practice of asking for treats on Halloween and threatening to play tricks on those who refuse.

trick·ster (trĭk′stər) *n.* **1.** One that swindles or plays tricks. **2.** often **Trickster** A mischievous or roguish figure in myth or folklore, often an animal, who typically makes up for physical weakness with cunning and subversive humor.

trick·sy (trĭk′sē) *adj.* **-si·er, -si·est 1.** Smartly attired; dapper. **2.** Sportive; mischievous. **3.** Crafty; cunning; devious. **4.** Likely to cause trouble and therefore requiring special care.

trick·y (trĭk′ē) *adj.* **-i·er, -i·est 1.** Given to or characterized by trickery. **2.** Requiring caution or skill: *a tricky recipe.* —**trick′i·ly** *adv.* —**trick′i·ness** *n.*

tri·clin·ic (trī-klĭn′ĭk) *adj.* Having three unequal axes intersecting at oblique angles. Used of certain crystals.

tri·clin·i·um (trī-klĭn′ē-əm) *n., pl.* **-i·a** (-ē-ə) **1.** A couch facing three sides of a rectangular table, used by the ancient Greeks and Romans for reclining at meals. **2.** A room with such a couch or couches; a dining room. [Lat. *trīclīnium* < Gk. *triklīnion*, dim. of *triklīnos*, room with three couches : *tri-*, three; see **trei-** in App. + *klīnē*, couch; see **klei-** in App.]

tri·col·or (trī′kŭl′ər) *n.* **1.** A flag having three colors. **2.** also **Tricolor** The French flag. ❖ *adj.* also **tri·col·ored** (-ərd) Having three colors.

tri·corn also **tri·corne** (trī′kôrn′) *n.* A hat having the brim turned up on three sides. ❖ *adj.* Having three corners, horns, or projections. [Fr. *tricorne* < Lat. *tricornis*, three-horned : *tri-*, tri-

tricorn

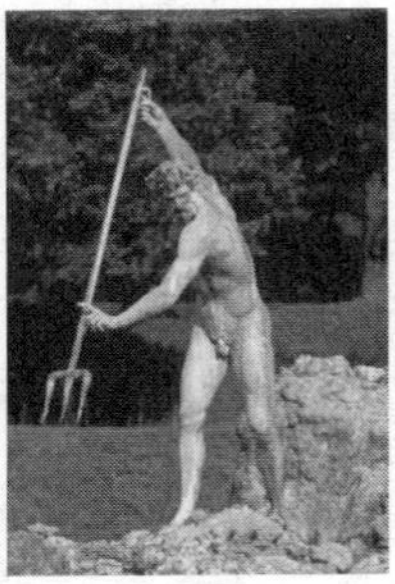

trident
statue of Neptune wielding a trident

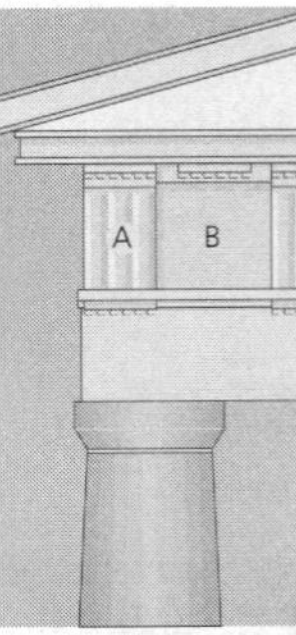

triglyph
entablature of a Doric order building
A. triglyph
B. metope

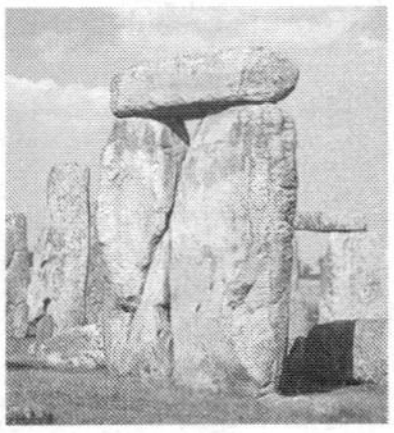

trilithon
Stonehenge, Salisbury Plain, England

+ *cornū*, horn; see **ker-**[1] in App.]

tri•cor•nered (trī′kôr′nərd) *adj.* Having three corners.

tri•cos•tate (trī-kŏs′tāt′) *adj.* Having three costae.

tri•cot (trē′kō) *n.* **1.** A plain knitted cloth of any of various yarns. **2.** A soft ribbed cloth of wool or a wool blend, usu. used for dresses. [Fr. < *tricoter*, to knit < OFr., to beat, run < *tricote*, short thick stick, dim. of *estrique, trique*, stick for leveling measures of grain < *estriquier*, to strike off, of Gmc. orig.]

tric•o•tine (trĭk′ə-tēn′, trē′kə-) *n.* A sturdy worsted fabric with a double twill. [Fr. < *tricot*, tricot. See TRICOT.]

tri•crot•ic (trī-krŏt′ĭk) *adj. Medicine* Having three waves or elevations to one beat of the pulse. [< Gk. *trikrotos*, having a triple beat : *tri-*, three; see **trei-** in App. + *krotein*, to beat.]

tri•cus•pid (trī-kŭs′pĭd) *n.* An organ or part, esp. a tooth, having three cusps. ❖ *adj.* also **tri•cus•pi•dal** (-pĭ-dəl) or **tri•cus•pi•date** (-pĭ-dāt′) **1.** Having three cusps. **2.** Of or relating to the tricuspid valve. [< Lat. *tricuspis, tricuspid-*, having three points : *tri-*, tri- + *cuspis*, point.]

tricuspid valve *n.* The three-segmented valve of the heart that keeps blood in the right ventricle from flowing back into the right atrium.

tri•cy•cle (trī′sĭk′əl, -sĭ-kəl) *n.* A three-wheeled vehicle, used esp. by small children and usu. propelled by pedals. [Fr. : *tri-*, three (< Gk. *tri-*; see TRI–) + Gk. *kuklos*, wheel; see CYCLE.]

tri•cy•clic (trī-sī′klĭk, -sĭk′lĭk) *adj.* Having or being a molecular structure that contains three closed rings: *a tricyclic molecule.* ❖ *n.* A tricyclic antidepressant drug.

tricyclic antidepressant *n.* Any of a group of antidepressant drugs that block the reuptake of norepinephrine and serotonin in the central nervous system.

tri•dac•tyl (trī-dăk′təl) also **tri•dac•ty•lous** (-tə-ləs) *adj.* Having three digits or claws on each limb. [Gk. *tridaktulos*, three-fingered : *tri-*, tri-; see **trei-** in App. + *daktulos*, finger.]

tri•dent (trīd′nt) *n.* **1.** A long three-pronged fork or weapon, esp. a three-pronged spear used for fishing. **2.** *Greek & Roman Mythology* The three-pronged spear carried by Neptune or Poseidon. ❖ *adj.* also **tri•den•tate** (trī-dĕn′tāt) Having three protrusions, such as teeth or prongs. [ME < OFr. < Lat. *tridēns, trident-* : *tri-*, tri- + *dēns*, tooth; see **dent-** in App.]

Tri•den•tine (trī-dĕn′tīn′, -tēn′) *adj.* Of or relating to a council held by the Roman Catholic Church in Trent, Italy, from 1545 to 1563, as a response to calls for reform and the spread of Protestantism. ❖ *n.* A Roman Catholic who conforms to the Tridentine Creed formulated at that council. [Med.Lat. *Tridentīnus* < Lat., area around Tridentum < *Tridentum* (Trent).]

tri•di•men•sion•al (trī′dĭ-mĕn′shə-nəl, -dī-) *adj.* Of, relating to, or having three dimensions.

tried (trīd) *v.* Past tense and past participle of **try.** ❖ *adj.* **1.** Thoroughly tested and proved to be good or trustworthy. **2.** Made to undergo trials or distress. Often used in combination: *a much-tried teacher.*

tried-and-true (trīd′ən-tro͞o′) *adj.* Tested and proved to be worthy or good.

tri•en•ni•al (trī-ĕn′ē-əl) *adj.* **1.** Occurring every third year. **2.** Lasting three years. ❖ *n.* **1.** A third anniversary. **2.** An event occurring every three years. [< Lat. *triennis* < *triennium*, triennium. See TRIENNIUM.] **—tri•en′ni•al•ly** *adv.*

tri•en•ni•um (trī-ĕn′ē-əm) *n., pl.* **-en•ni•ums** or **-en•ni•a** (-ĕn′ē-ə) A period of three years. [Lat. : *tri-*, tri- + *annus*, year.]

tri•er (trī′ər) *n.* **1a.** One that tries; a test or tester. **b.** One who keeps attempting something despite failure. **2.** *Law* One who examines and settles a case; a judge or juror. **3a.** An instrument or a device that sifts, filters, or separates grain, for example, from impurities. **b.** An instrument or a device, such as a tube, for taking samples, as of wine.

Trier (trîr) also **Trèves** (trĕv) A city of SW Germany on the Moselle R. near the Luxembourg border; under French control from 1797 until 1815. Pop. 94,190.

tri•er•arch (trī′ə-rärk′) *n.* **1.** The captain of a Greek trireme. **2.** An Athenian who outfitted and maintained a trireme as a part of his civic duties. [Lat. *triērarchus* < Gk. *triērarkhos* : *triērēs*, trireme; see **trei-** in App. + *arkhos*, ruler; see –ARCH.]

tri•er•ar•chy (trī′ə-rär′kē) *n., pl.* **-chies 1.** The authority or office of a trierarch. **2.** The system whereby an Athenian furnished and maintained a trireme for the polis.

tries (trīz) *v.* Third person singular present tense of **try.** ❖ *n.* Plural of **try.**

Tri•este (trē-ĕst′, -ĕs′tē) A city of extreme NE Italy on the **Gulf of Trieste,** an inlet of the Gulf of Venice at the head of the Adriatic Sea. From 1947 to 1954 it was the center of the **Free Territory of Trieste** administered by the United Nations. Pop. 229,216.

tri•fa•cial (trī-fā′shəl) *adj.* Trigeminal.

tri•fec•ta (trī-fĕk′tə) *n.* A system of betting in which the bettor must pick the first three winners in the correct sequence. [TRI– + (PER)FECTA.]

tri•fid (trī′fĭd′) *adj.* Divided or cleft into three narrow parts or lobes. [Lat. *trifidus* : *tri-*, tri- + *findere, fid-*, to split.]

tri•fle (trī′fəl) *n.* **1.** Something of little importance or value. **2.** A small amount; a jot. **3.** A dessert typically consisting of plain or sponge cake soaked in sherry, rum, or brandy and topped with jam or jelly, custard, and whipped cream. **4a.** A moderately hard variety of pewter. **b. trifles** Utensils made from this variety of pewter. ❖ *v.* **-fled, -fling, -fles** —*intr.* **1.** To deal with something as if it were of little significance or value. **2.** To act, perform, or speak with little seriousness or purpose; jest. **3.** To play or toy with something. —*tr.* To waste (time, for example). ***—idiom:* a trifle** Very little; somewhat. [ME *trufle, trifle* < OFr. *trufle*, mockery, dim. of *truffe*, deception.] **—tri′fler** (trī′flər) *n.*

tri•fling (trī′flĭng) *adj.* **1.** Of slight worth or importance. **2.** Frivolous or idle. **—tri′fling•ly** *adv.*

tri•fo•cal (trī-fō′kəl, trī′fō′-) *adj.* **1.** Having three focal lengths. **2.** Having one section that corrects for distant vision, a second section that corrects for medium vision, and a third that corrects for near vision, as an eyeglass lens. ❖ *n.* **1.** A trifocal lens. **2. trifocals** Eyeglasses having trifocal lenses.

tri•fo•li•ate (trī-fō′lē-ĭt) also **tri•fo•li•at•ed** (-ā′tĭd) *adj.* Having three leaves or leaflike parts, as in the trillium.

tri•fo•li•o•late (trī-fō′lē-ə-lāt′) *adj.* Having three leaflets.

tri•fo•ri•um (trī-fôr′ē-əm, -fōr′-) *n., pl.* **-fo•ri•a** (-fôr′ē-ə, -fōr′-) *Architecture* A gallery of arches above the side-aisle vaulting in the nave of a church. [Med.Lat., a gallery in Canterbury Cathedral (later taken to mean "with three openings").]

tri•formed (trī′fôrmd′) also **tri•form** (-fôrm′) *adj.* Having three different forms or parts.

tri•fur•cate (trī-fûr′kĭt, -kāt′, trī′fər-kāt′) also **tri•fur•cat•ed** (trī′fər-kā′tĭd) *adj.* Having three forks or branches: *trifurcate antennae.* **—tri′fur•ca′tion** *n.*

trig[1] (trĭg) *adj.* **1.** Smart and trim, as in looks. **2.** Being in good condition. ❖ *tr.v.* **trigged, trig•ging, trigs** To make trim or neat, esp. in dress. [ME, true < ON *tryggr*, loyal, true. See **deru-** in App.] **—trig′ly** *adv.* **—trig′ness** *n.*

trig[2] (trĭg) *tr.v.* **trigged, trig•ging, trigs 1.** To stop (a wheel) from rolling, as with a wedge. **2.** To prop up; support. ❖ *n.* A wedge or other braking device. [Perh. of Scand. orig.; akin to ON *tryggr*, firm. See TRIG[1].]

trig[3] (trĭg) *n. Informal* Trigonometry.

tri•gem•i•nal (trī-jĕm′ə-nəl) *adj.* Of or relating to the trigeminal nerves; trifacial.

trigeminal nerve *n.* Either of the fifth pair of cranial nerves, having sensory and motor functions in the face, teeth, mouth, and nasal cavity.

trigeminal neuralgia *n.* Paroxysmal shooting pains of the facial area around one or more branches of the trigeminal nerve, often precipitated by irritation of the affected area.

trig•ger (trĭg′ər) *n.* **1a.** The lever pressed by the finger to discharge a firearm. **b.** A similar device used to release or activate a mechanism. **2.** An event that precipitates other events. **3.** *Electronics* A pulse or circuit that initiates the action of another component. ❖ *tr.v.* **-gered, -ger•ing, -gers 1.** To set off; initiate. **2.** To fire or explode (a weapon or explosive charge). [Du. *trekker* < MDu. *trecker* < *trecken*, to pull.]

trig•ger•fish (trĭg′ər-fĭsh′) *n., pl.* **triggerfish** or **-fish•es** Any of various brightly colored fishes of the family Balistidae of warm coastal waters, having an erectile spine.

trig•ger-hap•py (trĭg′ər-hăp′ē) *adj. Slang* **1.** Tending or desiring to shoot a firearm before adequately identifying the target. **2.** Inclined to react violently at slight provocation.

trig•ger•man (trĭg′ər-mən) *n.* **1.** An underworld gunman who in premeditation shoots a victim. **2.** A gunman; a shooter.

tri•glyc•er•ide (trī-glĭs′ə-rīd′) *n.* An ester of three fatty acids and glycerol that is the chief constituent of fats and oils.

tri•glyph (trī′glĭf′) *adj. Architecture* An ornament in a Doric frieze, consisting of a projecting block having on its face two parallel vertical glyphs or grooves and two half grooves or chamfers on either vertical end, that separates the metopes. [Lat. *trīglyphus* < Gk. *trigluphos* : *tri-*, three; see **trei-** in App. + *gluphē*, carving; see GLYPH.] **—tri•glyph′ic** *adj.*

tri•gon (trī′gŏn′) *n.* **1.** A triangular lyre or harp of Roman and Greek antiquity. **2.** See **triplicity** 3. **3.** *Archaic* A triangle. [Lat. *trigōnum* < Gk. *trigōnon* < neut. of *trigōnos*, triangular : *tri-*, tri- + *gōniā*, angle; see –GON.]

trigonometric function *n.* A function of an angle expressed as the ratio of two of the sides of a right triangle that contains that angle; the sine, cosine, tangent, cotangent, secant, and cosecant.

trig•o•nom•e•try (trĭg′ə-nŏm′ĭ-trē) *n.* The branch of mathematics that deals with the relationships between the sides and the angles of triangles and the calculations based on them, particularly the trigonometric functions. [NLat. *trigōnometria* : Gk. *trigōnon*, triangle; see TRIGON + Gk. *-metriā*, -metry.] **—trig′o•no•met′ric** (-nə-mĕt′rĭk), **trig′o•no•met′ri•cal** (-rĭ-kəl) *adj.* **—trig′o•no•met′ri•cal•ly** *adv.*

tri•gram (trī′grăm′) *n.* **1.** A figure composed of three solid or interrupted parallel lines, esp. as used in Chinese philosophy or divination according to the I Ching. **2.** See **trigraph** 3. **—tri′gram•mat′ic** (-grə-măt′ĭk) *adj.*

tri•graph (trī′grăf′) *n.* **1.** Three letters spelling one consonant, vowel, or diphthong, such as *igh* in *high.* **2.** A group of three letters, esp. of frequent occurrence in a given language, as *ing* in English. **3.** Any combination of three letters of an alphabet. **—tri•graph′ic** *adj.* **—tri•graph′i•cal•ly** *adv.*

tri•hal•o•meth•ane (trī′hăl-ə-mĕth′ān′) *n.* A chemical compound, sometimes occurring in chlorinated water, containing three halogen atoms in place of the three hydrogen atoms normally present in a methane molecule.

tri•he•dral (trī-hē′drəl) *adj.* Having or formed by three planes meeting at a point. ❖ *n.* See **trihedron.**

tri•he•dron (trī-hē′drən) *n., pl.* **-drons** or **-dra** (-drə) A figure formed by three planes meeting at a point.

tri•hy•brid (trī-hī′brĭd) *n.* The hybrid of parents that differ at only three gene loci, for which each parent is homozygous.

tri•i•o•do•thy•ro•nine (trī′ī-ō′dō-thī′rə-nēn′, -ī-ŏd′ō-) *n.* A thyroid hormone, $C_{15}H_{12}I_3NO_4$, similar to thyroxine but more potent, used in the treatment of hypothyroidism. [TRI– + IODO– + *thyronine,* an amino acid (THYR(O)– + –ON(E) + –INE[2]).]

trike (trīk) *n. Informal* A tricycle.

tri•lat•er•al (trī-lăt′ər-əl) *adj.* Having or involving three sides, countries, or parties. [< Lat. *trilaterus* : *tri-,* tri- + *latus, later-,* side.] **—tri•lat′er•al•ly** *adv.*

tril•by (trĭl′bē) *n., pl.* **tril•bies** A soft felt hat with a deeply creased crown. [After *Trilby,* the novel by George du Maurier (because such a hat was worn in the original stage production based on the novel).]

tri•lin•e•ar (trī-lĭn′ē-ər) *adj.* Relating to, having, or bounded by three lines.

tri•lin•gual (trī-lĭng′gwəl) *adj.* **1.** Using or able to use three languages, esp. with equal fluency. **2.** Of, relating to, or expressed in three languages. ❖ *n.* One who can use three languages, esp. with equal fluency. **—tri•lin′gual•ism** *n.*

tri•lit•er•al (trī-lĭt′ər-əl) *adj.* Consisting of three letters, esp. of three consonants. Used chiefly of roots in Semitic languages. ❖ *n.* **1.** A three-letter word or word element. **2.** A triliteral root or word.

tri•lith•on (trī-lĭth′ŏn, trī′lĭ-thŏn′) also **tri•lith** (trī′lĭth) *n.* A prehistoric structure consisting of two large stones set upright to support a third on their tops, found esp. in Europe. [Gk., neut. of *trilithos,* having three stones : *tri-,* tri- + *lithos,* stone.]

trill (trĭl) *n.* **1.** A fluttering or tremulous sound, as that made by certain birds; a warble. **2.** *Music* **a.** The rapid alternation of two tones either a whole or a half tone apart. **b.** A vibrato. **3.** *Linguistics* **a.** A rapid vibration of one speech organ against another, as of the tongue against the alveolar ridge in Spanish *rr.* **b.** A speech sound pronounced with such a vibration. ❖ *v.* **trilled, trill•ing, trills** *—tr.* **1.** To sound, sing, or play with a trill. **2.** To articulate (a sound) with a trill. *—intr.* To produce or give forth a trill. [Ital. *trillo* < *trillare,* to trill, prob. ult. of imit. orig.]

Tril•ling (trĭl′ĭng), **Lionel** 1905–75. Amer. literary critic whose works include *Beyond Culture* (1965).

tril•lion (trĭl′yən) *n.* **1.** The cardinal number equal to 10^{12}. **2.** *Chiefly British* The cardinal number equal to 10^{18}. [Fr. : *tri-,* third power (< Lat. *tri-,* tri-) + *(m)illion,* million (< OFr. *milion;* see MILLION).] **—tril′lion** *adj.*

tril•lionth (trĭl′yənth) *n.* **1.** The ordinal number matching the number one trillion in a series. **2.** One of a trillion equal parts. **—tril′lionth** *adv. & adj.*

tril•li•um (trĭl′ē-əm) *n.* Any of various plants of the genus *Trillium,* usu. having a cluster of three leaves and a three-petaled flower. [NLat. *Trillium,* genus name, prob. < Swed. *trilling,* triplet (< its three leaves) < obsolete Swed. *tri,* three < OSwed. *thrīr.* See **trei-** in App.]

tri•lo•bate (trī-lō′bāt′) or **tri•lo•bat•ed** (-bā′tĭd) also **tri•lobed** (trī′lōbd′) *adj.* Having three lobes, as certain leaves.

tri•lo•bite (trī′lə-bīt′) *n.* Any of numerous extinct marine arthropods of the class Trilobita of the Paleozoic Era, having a segmented body divided into three vertical lobes. [NLat. *Trilobītēs,* former class name < Gk. *trilobos,* three-lobed : *tri-,* tri- + *lobos,* lobe.] **—tri′lo•bit′ic** (-bĭt′ĭk) *adj.*

tri•loc•u•lar (trī-lŏk′yə-lər) *adj.* Having three chamberlike divisions or cavities, as the capsule of a plant.

tril•o•gy (trĭl′ə-jē) *n., pl.* **-gies** A group of three dramatic or literary works related in subject or theme. [Gk. *trilogiā,* series of three related tragedies : *tri-,* tri- + *logos,* word, saying; see –LOGY.]

trim (trĭm) *v.* **trimmed, trim•ming, trims** *—tr.* **1.** To make neat or tidy by clipping, pruning, or smoothing: *trimmed his beard.* **2a.** To remove (excess) by cutting: *trim a budget.* **b.** To remove the excess from by or as if by cutting. **3.** To ornament; decorate. **4.** *Informal* **a.** To thrash; beat. **b.** To defeat soundly. **c.** To cheat. **d.** To rebuke; scold. **5.** *Nautical* **a.** To adjust (the sails and yards) so that they receive the wind properly. **b.** To balance (a ship) by shifting its cargo or ballast. **6.** To balance (an aircraft) in flight by regulating the control surfaces and tabs. **7.** To furnish or equip. *—intr.* **1.** *Nautical* **a.** To be in or retain equilibrium. **b.** To make sails and yards ready for sailing. **2a.** To affect or maintain cautious neutrality. **b.** To fashion one's views for momentary popularity or advantage. ❖ *n.* **1a.** State of order, arrangement, or appearance; condition: *in good trim.* **b.** A condition of good health or fitness. **2a.** Exterior ornamentation on a building or vehicle. **b.** Decoration or ornament, as for clothing. **3.** Material used in commercial window displays. **4.** Dress or equipment. **5.** Excised or rejected material, such as film cut in editing. Often used in the plural. **6.** Personal quality; character. **7.** A cutting or clipping to make neat. **8.** *Nautical* **a.** The readiness of a vessel for sailing with regard to ballast, sails, and yards. **b.** The balance of a ship. **c.** The difference between the draft at the bow and at the stern. **9.** The position of an aircraft relative to its horizontal axis. ❖ *adj.* **trim•mer, trim•mest 1a.** In good or neat order. **b.** In good physical condition; fit; slim. **2.** Having lines, edges, or forms of neat and pleasing simplicity. See Syns at **neat**[1]. ❖ *adv.* In a trim manner. [ME *trimmen,* to make firm < OE *trymman* < *trum,* strong. See **deru-** in App.] **—trim′ly** *adv.* **—trim′ness** *n.*

tri•ma•ran (trī′mə-răn′) *n.* A fast sailboat with three parallel hulls. [TRI– + (CATA)MARAN.]

Trim•ble (trĭm′bəl), **David** b. 1944. Politician of Northern Ireland who shared the 1998 Nobel Peace Prize.

tri•mer (trī′mər) *n.* A molecule formed by combining three identical smaller molecules. [TRI– + (POLY)MER.] **—tri•mer′ic** (-mĕr′ĭk) *adj.*

trim•er•ous (trĭm′ər-əs) *adj.* **1.** Having three similar segments or parts. **2.** *Botany* Having flower parts, such as petals, sepals, and stamens, in sets of three. **—trim′er•ism** *n.*

tri•mes•ter (trī-mĕs′tər, trī′mĕs′-) *n.* **1.** A period or term of three months. **2.** One of three terms into which an academic year is divided in some universities and colleges. [Fr. *trimestre* < Lat. *trimēstris, trimēnstris,* of three months : *tri-,* tri- + *mēnsis,* month; see **mē-**[1] in App.] **—tri•mes′tral** (-trəl), **tri•mes′tri•al** *adj.*

trim•e•ter (trĭm′ĭ-tər) *n.* **1.** A line of verse consisting of three metrical feet. **2.** A line of verse consisting of three measures of two feet each. [LLat. < Lat. *trimetrus* < Gk. *trimetros* : *tri-,* tri- + *metron,* measure; see METER[1].] **—tri•met′ric** (trī-mĕt′rĭk), **tri•met′ri•cal** (-rĭ-kəl) *adj.*

tri•met•ro•gon (trī-mĕt′rə-gŏn′) *n.* A system of aerial photography in which one vertical and two oblique photographs are simultaneously taken for use in topographic mapping. [TRI– + *Metrogon,* trademark for a kind of camera lens.]

trim•mer (trĭm′ər) *n.* **1.** One that trims: *a hedge trimmer.* **2.** One who changes one's opinions, esp. political opinions, to suit the needs of the moment. **3.** *Electronics* A variable component used to make fine adjustments to capacity or resistance. **4.** *Architecture* A beam across an opening, such as a hearth, into which the ends of joists can be fitted.

trim•ming (trĭm′ĭng) *n.* **1.** The act of one that trims. **2.** Something added as ornament, esp. a band of lace or embroidery on clothing. **3. trimmings** Accessories; extras. **4. trimmings** Scraps or material removed when something is trimmed. **5.** *Informal* A sound defeat, beating, or punishment.

tri•month•ly (trī-mŭnth′lē) *adj.* Done, occurring, or appearing every three months. **—tri•month′ly** *adv.*

tri•morph (trī′môrf′) *n.* **1.** A substance that occurs in three distinct crystalline forms. **2.** One of the crystalline forms in which a trimorphic substance occurs.

tri•mor•phic (trī-môr′fĭk) also **tri•mor•phous** (-fəs) *adj.* **1.** *Biology* Having or occurring in three differing forms. **2.** *Chemistry* Crystallizing in three distinct forms. **—tri•mor′phi•cal•ly** *adv.* **—tri•mor′phism** *n.*

Tri•mur•ti (trĭ-mo͝or′tē) *n. Hinduism* The triad of Brahma the creator, Vishnu the preserver, and Shiva the destroyer. [Skt. *trimūrtiḥ* : *tri-,* three; see **trei-** in App. + *mūrtiḥ,* form.]

tri•nal (trī′nəl) *adj.* Having three parts; threefold.

tri•na•ry (trī′nə-rē) *adj.* Consisting of three parts or proceeding by threes; ternary.

trine (trīn) *adj.* **1.** Threefold; triple. **2a.** Of or relating to an astrologically favorable positioning of two celestial bodies 120° apart. **b.** In astrology, situated 120° apart. ❖ *n.* **1.** A group of three. **2.** In astrology, the aspect of two planets when 120° apart. **3. Trine** *Christianity* See **Trinity** 2. [ME < OFr. < Lat. *trīnus,* sing. of *trīnī,* three each. See **trei-** in App.]

Trin•i•dad (trĭn′ĭ-dăd′) An island of Trinidad and Tobago in the Atlantic Ocean off NE Venezuela; ceded to Great Britain in 1802 and joined with Tobago in 1888 to form the colony of Trinidad and Tobago (1898). **—Trin′i•dad′i•an** *adj. & n.*

Trinidad and Tobago An island country of the SE West Indies off NE Venezuela; gained independence from Great Britain in 1962. Cap. Port of Spain. Pop. 1,257,000.

Trin•i•tar•i•an (trĭn′ĭ-târ′ē-ən) *adj.* **1.** Of, relating to, or believing in the Christian Trinity or the doctrine of the Trinity. **2. trinitarian** Having three members, parts, or facets. ❖ *n.* One who believes in the Christian doctrine of the Trinity. **—Trin′i•tar′i•an•ism** *n.*

tri•ni•tro•ben•zene (trī-nī′trō-bĕn′zēn′, -bĕn-zēn′) *n.* A crystalline compound, $C_6H_3(NO_2)_3$, derived from trinitrotoluene and used as an explosive.

tri•ni•tro•phe•nol (trī-nī′trō-fē′nôl′, -nŏl′) *n.* Picric acid.

tri•ni•tro•tol•u•ene (trī-nī′trō-tŏl′yo͞o-ēn′) also **tri•ni•tro•tol•u•ol** (-ôl′, -ōl′, -ŏl′) *n.* TNT.

trin•i•ty (trĭn′ĭ-tē) *n., pl.* **-ties 1.** A group consisting of three closely related members. **2. Trinity** *Theology* In most Christian faiths, the union of three divine persons, the Father, Son, and Holy Spirit, in one God. **3. Trinity** Trinity Sunday. [ME *trinite* < OFr. < Lat. *trīnitās* < *trīnus,* trine. See TRINE.]

Trinity River A river, c. 821 km (510 mi), of E TX formed near Dallas and flowing to **Trinity Bay,** an arm of Galveston Bay.

Trinity Sunday *n.* The first Sunday after Pentecost, celebrated by a feast in honor of the Trinity.

trin•ket (trĭng′kĭt) *n.* **1.** A small ornament, such as a piece of jew-

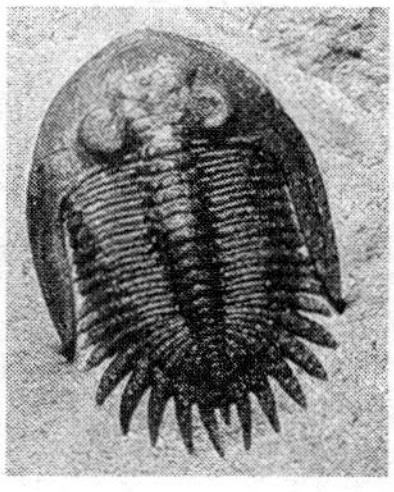

trilobite

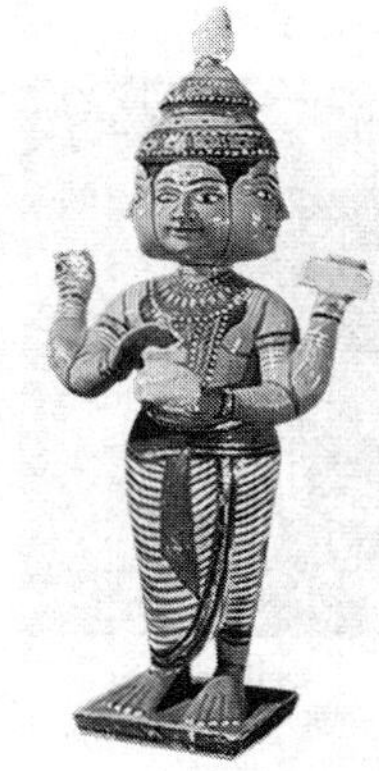

Trimurti
c. 18th-century Indian statue of Trimurti

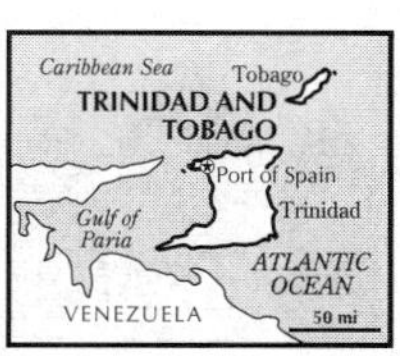

Trinidad and Tobago

ă	pat	oi	boy
ā	pay	ou	out
âr	care	o͝o	took
ä	father	o͞o	boot
ĕ	pet	ŭ	cut
ē	be	ûr	urge
ĭ	pit	th	thin
ī	pie	*th*	this
îr	pier	hw	which
ŏ	pot	zh	vision
ō	toe	ə	about, item
ô	paw		

Stress marks:
′ (primary);
′ (secondary), as in
lexicon (lĕk′sĭ-kŏn′)

elry. **2.** A trivial thing; a trifle. [?]

tri•no•mi•al (trī-nō′mē-əl) *adj.* Consisting of three names or terms, as a taxonomic designation. ❖ *n.* **1.** A three-part taxonomic designation indicating genus, species, and subspecies or variety, such as *Brassica oleracea botrytis,* the cauliflower. **2.** *Mathematics* A polynomial with three terms, such as $x^2 + 4x - 3$. [TRI– + (BI)NOMIAL.] **—tri•no′mi•al•ism** *n.*

tri•nu•cle•o•tide (trī-no͞o′klē-ə-tīd′, -nyo͞o′-) *n.* A triplet of nucleotides; a codon.

tri•o (trē′ō) *n., pl.* **-os 1.** *Music* **a.** A composition for three voices or three instruments. **b.** A group of three singers or three instrumentalists. **c.** The middle, contrasting section of a minuet, scherzo, march, or various other forms. **2.** A group of three. [Fr., composition for three voices < Ital. : *tri-,* three (< Lat.; see **trei-** in App.) + *(du)o,* duet; see DUO.]

tri•ode (trī′ōd′) *n.* A highly evacuated electron tube containing an anode, a cathode, and a control grid.

tri•ol (trī′ôl′, -ōl′, -ŏl′) *n.* A chemical compound containing three hydroxyl groups.

tri•o•let (trē′ə-lĭt, trī′-, trē′ə-lā′) *n.* A poem or stanza of eight lines with a rhyme scheme *abaaabab,* in which the fourth and seventh lines duplicate the first and the eighth line the second. [Fr., dim. of *trio,* trio. See TRIO.]

tri•ose (trī′ōs′) *n.* One of a group of monosaccharides that contain three carbon atoms.

tri•ox•ide (trī-ŏk′sīd′) also **tri•ox•id** (-ŏk′sĭd) *n.* An oxide containing three oxygen atoms per molecule.

trip (trĭp) *n.* **1.** A going from one place to another; a journey. **2.** A stumble or fall. **3.** A maneuver causing someone to stumble or fall. **4.** A mistake. **5.** *Slang* **a.** A hallucinatory experience induced by a psychedelic drug. **b.** An intense, stimulating, or exciting experience: *a power trip.* **6.** *Slang* **a.** A usu. temporary but absorbing interest or preoccupation. **b.** A certain way of life or situation. **7.** A light or nimble tread. **8a.** A device, such as a pawl, for triggering a mechanism. **b.** The action of such a device. ❖ *v.* **tripped, trip•ping, trips** *—intr.* **1.** To stumble. **2.** To make a mistake: *I tripped up on the question.* **3.** To move nimbly with light rapid steps; skip. **4.** To be released, as a tooth on an escapement wheel in a watch. **5.** To make a trip. **6.** *Slang* To have a drug-induced hallucination. *—tr.* **1.** To cause to stumble or fall. **2.** To trap or catch in an error or inconsistency. **3.** To release (a catch, trigger, or switch), thereby setting something in operation. **4.** *Nautical* **a.** To raise (an anchor) from the bottom. **b.** To tip or turn (a yardarm) into a position for lowering. **c.** To lift (an upper mast) in order to remove the fid before lowering. ***—idiom:* trip the light fantastic** To dance. [ME, act of tripping < *trippen,* to trip < OFr. *tripper,* to stamp the foot, of Gmc. orig.]

tri•pal•mi•tin (trī-păl′mĭ-tĭn) *n.* See **palmitin.**

tri•par•tite (trī-pär′tīt) *adj.* **1.** Composed of or divided into three parts. **2.** Relating to or executed by three parties. **—tri′part•ti′tion** (-tĭsh′ən) *n.*

tripe (trīp) *n.* **1.** The light-colored rubbery lining of the stomach of cattle or other ruminants, used as food. **2.** *Informal* Something of no value. [ME < OFr. *tripes,* intestines, tripe.]

tri•ped•al (trī-pĕd′l) *adj.* Having three feet or legs; tripodal.

tri•pet•al•ous (trī-pĕt′l-əs) *adj.* Having three petals.

trip ham•mer also **trip•ham•mer** or **trip-ham•mer** (trĭp′hăm′ər) *n.* A heavy power-operated hammer that is lifted by a cam or lever and then dropped.

tri•phen•yl•meth•ane (trī-fĕn′əl-mĕth′ān′, -fē′nəl-) *n.* A colorless crystalline hydrocarbon, $(C_6H_5)_3CH$, from which a large number of synthetic dyes are derived by substitution.

tri•phib•i•an (trī-fĭb′ē-ən) *adj.* Operating on land, on water, or in air. ❖ *n.* A triphibian aircraft. [TRI– + (AM)PHIBIAN.]

tri•phos•phate (trī-fŏs′fāt′) *n.* A salt or ester containing three phosphate groups.

tri•phos•pho•py•ri•dine nucleotide (trī-fŏs′fō-pĭr′ĭ-dēn′) *n.* NADP.

triph•thong (trĭf′thông′, -thŏng′, trĭp′-) *n.* A compound vowel sound resulting from the succession of three simple ones and functioning as a unit. [TRI– + (DI)PHTHONG.] **—triph•thon′gal** (-thông′əl, -thŏng′əl) *adj.*

tri•pin•nate (trī-pĭn′āt′) *adj.* Divided into pinnae that are subdivided into smaller, further subdivided leaflets or lobes, as in many ferns. **—tri•pin′nate′ly** *adv.*

tri•plane (trī′plān′) *n.* An airplane with wings placed above each other in three levels.

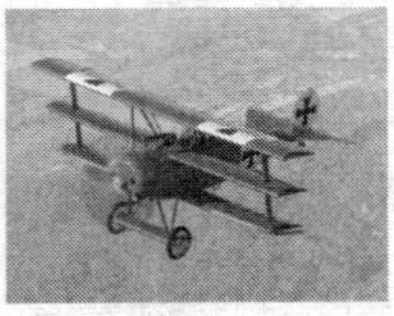
triplane

tri•ple (trĭp′əl) *adj.* **1.** Consisting of three parts or members. **2.** Three times as much in size, strength, number, or amount. **3.** *Music* Having three beats to a measure. ❖ *n.* **1.** A number or quantity three times as great as another. **2.** A group of three. **3.** *Baseball* See **three-base hit. 4.** See **trifecta.** ❖ *v.* **-pled, -pling, -ples** *—tr.* To make three times as great in number or amount. *—intr.* **1.** To be or become tripled. **2.** *Baseball* To make a three-base hit. [ME < OFr. < Lat. *triplus* (on the model of Gk. *triploos*) : Lat. *tri-,* three; see **trei-** in App. + *-plus,* -fold.]

triple bond *n.* A covalent bond in which three electron pairs are shared between two atoms.

Triple Crown *n.* **1.** *Sports* An unofficial championship title attained by a horse that wins the three traditional races for a specified category. **2.** *Baseball* An unofficial championship title achieved by a player who leads the league in batting average, home runs, and runs batted in.

tri•ple-deck•er (trĭp′əl-dĕk′ər) *n. Informal* Something, such as a structure, that has three decks, floors, or layers.

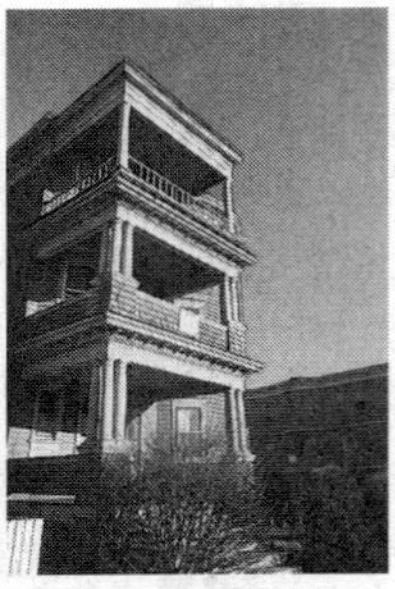
triple-decker
triple-decker house

tri•ple-head•er also **tri•ple•head•er** (trĭp′əl-hĕd′ər) *n. Sports* A contest consisting of three games or events in a row.

triple jump *n.* A distance jump in track and field consisting of a hop landing on the takeoff foot, a stride landing on the other foot, and a jump landing on both feet.

triple measure *n.* See **triple time.**

triple play *n. Baseball* A defensive play that suddenly ends an inning by executing three consecutive putouts.

triple point *n.* The temperature and pressure at which the gaseous, liquid, and solid phases of a substance coexist in equilibrium.

trip•let (trĭp′lĭt) *n.* **1.** A group or set of three of one kind. **2.** One of three children born at one birth. **3.** A group of three lines of verse. **4.** *Music* A group of three notes having the time value of two notes of the same kind. **5.** *Physics* A multiplet with three components. **6.** *Genetics* A unit of three successive nucleotides in a molecule of DNA or RNA that codes for a specific amino acid; a codon or anticodon. [TRIPL(E) + (DOUBL)ET.]

tri•ple•tail (trĭp′əl-tāl′) *n.* Any of several chiefly marine percoid fishes of the family Lobotidae of warm waters, having dorsal and anal fins that resemble extra tails.

triple time *n. Music* A time or rhythm having three beats to the measure. **—tri′ple-time′** (trĭp′əl-tīm′) *adj.*

tri•plex (trĭp′lĕks′, trī′plĕks′) *adj.* **1.** Composed of three parts; threefold; triple. **2.** Having three apartments, divisions, or floors. ❖ *n.* Something, such as an apartment building, that is triplex. [Lat. See **trei-** in App.]

trip•li•cate (trĭp′lĭ-kĭt) *n.* One of three identical objects or copies. ❖ *tr.v.* (-kāt′) **-cat•ed, -cat•ing, -cates 1.** To triple. **2.** To make three identical copies of. [< ME, triple < Lat. *triplicātus,* p. part. of *triplicāre,* to triple < *triplex, triplic-,* threefold. See TRIPLEX.] **—trip′li•cate•ly** *adv.* **—trip′li•ca′tion** *n.*

tri•plic•i•ty (trĭ-plĭs′ĭ-tē, trī-) *n., pl.* **-ties 1.** The quality or condition of being triple. **2.** A group of three. **3.** In astrology, one of four zodiac groups consisting of three signs separated from each other by 120°. [ME, three signs of the zodiac < LLat. *triplicitās,* triplicity < Lat. *triplex, triplic-,* triplex. See TRIPLEX.]

trip•lo•blas•tic (trĭp′lō-blăs′tĭk) *adj.* Having three germ layers. Used of the vertebrate embryo. [Gk. *triploos,* triple + –BLASTIC.]

trip•loid (trĭp′loid′) *adj.* Having three times the haploid number of chromosomes in the cell nucleus. ❖ *n.* A triploid organism or cell. **—trip′loi•dy** *n.*

trip•ly (trĭp′lē) *adv.* **1.** In three ways. **2.** To a triple degree. **3.** Three times.

tri•pod (trī′pŏd′) *n.* **1.** A three-legged object, such as a stool. **2.** An adjustable three-legged stand, as for a camera. [Lat. *tripūs, tripod-* < Gk. *tripous,* three-footed : *tri-,* tri- + *pous,* foot; see –POD.] **—trip′o•dal** (trĭp′ə-dl, trī′pŏd′l) *adj.*

trip•o•li (trĭp′ə-lē) *n., pl.* **-lis** A porous lightweight siliceous sedimentary rock composed of the shells of diatoms or radiolarians or of finely weathered chert, used as an abrasive and a polish. [Fr., prob. after TRIPOLI, Lebanon.]

Tripoli 1. A historical region of N Africa roughly coextensive with Tripolitania; became part of the Barbary States in the 16th cent. **2.** A city of NW Lebanon on the Mediterranean NNE of Beirut; probably founded after the 7th cent. B.C. Pop. 198,000. **3.** The cap. of Libya, in the NW part on the Mediterranean; settled by Phoenicians from Tyre. Pop. 858,500. **—Tri•pol′i•tan** (trĭ-pŏl′ĭ-tn) *adj. & n.*

Tri•pol•i•ta•ni•a (trĭ-pŏl′ĭ-tā′nē-ə, -tān′yə, trĭp′ə-lĭ-) A historical region of N Africa bordering on the Mediterranean Sea; orig. a Phoenician colony and later held by Carthage and Rome (after 46 B.C.). **—Tri•pol′i•ta′ni•an** *adj. & n.*

tri•pos (trī′pŏs′) *n., pl.* **-pos•es** Any of the examinations for the B.A. degree with honors at Cambridge University in England. [Alteration of Lat. *tripūs, tripod-,* tripod (< the stool upon which a degree holder was appointed to sit and dispute humorously with candidates for that degree). See TRIPOD.]

trip•per (trĭp′ər) *n.* **1.** *Slang* One who is hallucinating from a psychedelic drug. **2.** A tripping or triggering device on a mechanism. **3.** *Chiefly British* One on a short pleasure trip.

trip•pet (trĭp′ĭt) *n.* A cam or projection in a mechanism designed to strike another part at regular intervals. [ME *tripet,* piece of wood used in a game < *trippen,* to trip. See TRIP.]

trip•ping (trĭp′ĭng) *adj.* **1.** Moving quickly and lightly; nimble. **2.** Speaking or flowing easily; fluent. **—trip′ping•ly** *adv.*

trip•tane (trĭp′tān′) *n.* A colorless liquid antiknock additive, C_7H_{16}, used in aviation fuels. [Shortening and alteration of *trimethylbutane* : TRI– + METHYL + BUTANE.]

trip•tych (trĭp′tĭk) *n.* **1.** A work consisting of three painted or carved panels that are hinged together. **2.** A hinged writing tablet consisting of three leaves, used in ancient Rome. [< Gk. *triptukhos,* threefold : *tri-,* tri- + *ptux, ptukh-,* fold.]

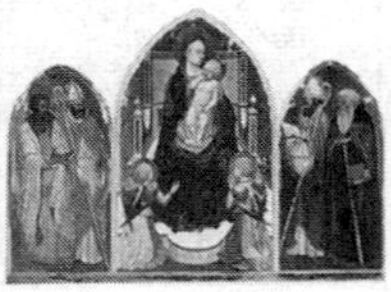
triptych
San Giovenale Triptych, 1422, by Masaccio

trip•wire (trĭp′wīr′) *n.* **1.** A wire set near ground level to trip or trap an enemy. **2.** A wire or line that activates a trap, for example, when pulled. **3.** A small frontline military force whose involvement in hostilities will engage a larger force.

tri·que·trous (trī-kwē′trəs, -kwĕt′rəs) *adj.* Three-edged; having three salient angles. [< Lat. *triquetrus*, three-cornered : *tri-*, tri- + *-quetrus*, -cornered.]

tri·reme (trī′rēm′) *n.* An ancient Greek or Roman galley or warship, having three tiers of oars on each side. [Lat. *trirēmis* : *tri-*, tri- + *rēmus*, oar.]

tri·sac·cha·ride (trī-săk′ə-rīd′, -rĭd) *n.* A carbohydrate that yields three monosaccharides upon hydrolysis.

tri·sect (trī-sĕkt′, trī′sĕkt′) *tr.v.* **-sect·ed, -sect·ing, -sects** To divide into three equal parts. —**tri·sec′tion** (trī′sĕk′shən, trī-sĕk′-) *n.* —**tri·sec′tor** (trī′sĕk′tər, trī-sĕk′-) *n.*

tri·sep·al·ous (trī-sĕp′ə-ləs) *adj.* Having three sepals. Used of the calyx of a flower.

tris·kai·dek·a·pho·bi·a (trĭs′kī-dĕk′ə-fō′bē-ə, trĭs′kī-) *n.* An abnormal fear of the number 13. [Gk. *triskaideka*, thirteen (*treis*, three; see **trei-** in App. + *kai*, and + *deka*, ten; see DECA–) + –PHOBIA.]

tri·skel·i·on (trī-skĕl′ē-ən, trī-) also **tri·skele** (trī′skēl′, trĭs′kēl′) *n., pl.* **-skel·i·a** (-skĕl′ē-ə) also **-skeles** A figure consisting of three curved lines or branches or three stylized human arms or legs radiating from a common center. [NLat. < Gk. *triskelēs*, three-legged : *tri-*, tri- + *skelos*, leg.]

tris·mus (trĭz′məs) *n.* See **lockjaw** 2. [NLat. < Gk. *trismos*, a grinding, var. of *trigmos*, a scream.] —**tris′mic** (-mĭk) *adj.*

tris·oc·ta·he·dron (trĭs-ŏk′tə-hē′drən) *n., pl.* **-drons** or **-dra** (-drə) A solid figure having 24 equal faces, every three of which correspond to one face of an octahedron. [Gk. *tris*, thrice; see **trei-** in App. + OCTAHEDRON.] —**tris·oc′ta·he′dral** *adj.*

tri·so·di·um (trī-sō′dē-əm) *adj.* Having three sodium atoms.

tri·so·my (trī-sō′mē, trī′sō′-) *n., pl.* **-mies** The condition of having three copies of a given chromosome in each somatic cell rather than the normal number of two. [TRI– + –SOM(E)[3] + –Y[2].] —**tri′some** *n.* —**tri·so′mic** *adj.*

trisomy 21 *n.* See **Down syndrome.**

Tris·tan (trĭs′tən, -tän′, -tän′) or **Tris·tram** (-trəm) *n.* In Arthurian legend, a knight who loved the Irish princess Iseult, the betrothed of his uncle King Mark of Cornwall.

Tris·tan da Cun·ha (trĭs′tən də kōō′nə) An island and volcanic island group of the S Atlantic Ocean between S Africa and S South America; administered as a dependency of St. Helena.

triste (trēst) *adj.* Sad; wistful. [ME < OFr. < Lat. *tristis*.]

trist·ful (trĭst′fəl) *adj.* Sorrowful; gloomy. [ME : *triste*, sad; see TRISTE + *-ful*, -ful.] —**trist′ful·ness** *n.*

tris·tich (trĭs′tĭk) *n.* A strophe, stanza, or poem consisting of three lines. [TRI– + (DI)STICH.]

tri·sul·fide (trī-sŭl′fīd′) *n.* A sulfide containing three sulfur atoms per molecule.

tri·syl·la·ble (trī′sĭl′ə-bəl) *n.* A three-syllable word. —**tri′syl·lab′ic** (-sĭ-lăb′ĭk), **tri′syl·lab′i·cal** (-ĭ-kəl) *adj.*

trite (trīt) *adj.* **trit·er, trit·est** 1. Lacking power to evoke interest from overuse or repetition; hackneyed. 2. *Archaic* Frayed or worn out by use. [Lat. *trītus* < p. part. of *terere*, to wear out. See **terə-**[1] in App.] —**trite′ly** *adv.* —**trite′ness** *n.*

tri·the·ism (trī′thē-ĭz′əm) *n. Christianity* The belief that God the Father, God the Son, and God the Holy Spirit are three gods. —**tri′the·ist** *n.* —**tri′the·is′tic, tri′the·is′ti·cal** *adj.*

trit·i·ca·le (trĭt′ĭ-kä′lē) *n.* 1. A hardy hybrid of wheat and rye having a high yield. 2. The grain of this hybrid. [Lat. *trīticum*, wheat (< *trītus*, p. part. of *terere*, to rub, thresh; see TRITE) + *sēcale*, rye.]

trit·i·um (trĭt′ē-əm, trĭsh′ē-) *n.* A rare radioactive hydrogen isotope with atomic mass 3 and half-life 12.5 years, prepared artificially for use as a tracer and a constituent of hydrogen bombs. [< Gk. *tritos*, third. See **trei-** in App.]

tri·ton[1] (trīt′n) *n.* Any of various chiefly tropical marine gastropod mollusks of the family Cymatiidae, having a pointed spiral shell. [Lat. *Trītōn*, Triton. See TRITON.]

tri·ton[2] (trī′tŏn′) *n.* The nucleus of tritium, consisting of two neutrons and one proton. [TRIT(IUM) + –ON[1].]

Tri·ton (trīt′n) *n.* 1. *Greek Mythology* A god of the sea, son of Poseidon and Amphitrite, portrayed as having the head and trunk of a man and the tail of a fish. 2. *Astronomy* A satellite of Neptune. [Lat. *Trītōn* < Gk.]

tri·tone (trī′tōn′) *n. Music* An interval composed of three whole tones. [Med.Lat. *tritonus* < Gk. *tritonos*, having three tones : *tri-*, three; see **trei-** in App. + *tonos*, tone; see TONE.]

trit·u·rate (trĭch′ə-rāt′) *tr.v.* **-rat·ed, -rat·ing, -rates** To pulverize. ❖ *n.* (-ər-ĭt) A triturated substance, esp. a powdered drug. [LLat. *trītūrāre, trītūrāt-*, to thresh < Lat. *trītūra*, a threshing < *trītus*, p. part. of *terere*, to thresh. See **terə-**[1] in App.] —**trit′u·ra·ble** *adj.* —**trit′u·ra′tor** *n.*

trit·u·ra·tion (trĭch′ə-rā′shən) *n.* 1. The act or process of triturating. 2. The composing of a dental amalgam by mortar and pestle.

tri·umph (trī′əmf) *intr.v.* **-umphed, -umph·ing, -umphs** 1. To be victorious or successful; win. 2. To rejoice over a success or victory; exult. 3. To receive honors upon return from a victory in ancient Rome. Used of a general. ❖ *n.* 1. The fact of being victorious; victory or conquest. 2. A noteworthy or spectacular success. 3. Exultation or rejoicing over victory or success. 4. A public celebration in ancient Rome for a victorious commander and his army. 5. *Obsolete* A public celebration or spectacular pageant. [Ult. < Lat. *triumphāre* < *triumphus*, triumph < earlier *triumpus*, ult. (prob. via Etruscan) < Gk. *thriambos*, hymn to Dionysus.]

tri·um·phal (trī-ŭm′fəl) *adj.* 1. Relating or similar to a triumph. 2. Celebrating a triumph: *a triumphal ode.*

tri·um·phal·ism (trī-ŭm′fə-lĭz′əm) *n.* The attitude or belief that a particular doctrine, esp. a religion or political theory, is superior to all others. —**tri·um′phal·ist** *n.*

tri·um·phant (trī-ŭm′fənt) *adj.* 1. Exulting in success or victory. 2. Victorious; conquering. 3. *Archaic* Triumphal. 4. *Obsolete* Magnificent; splendid. —**tri·um′phant·ly** *adv.*

tri·um·vir (trī-ŭm′vər) *n., pl.* **-virs** or **-vi·ri** (-və-rī′) 1. One of three men sharing public administration or civil authority in ancient Rome. 2. One of three people sharing public administration or civil authority. [ME < Lat., back-formation < *triumvirī*, board of three < *trium virum*, of three men : *trium*, genitive pl. of *trēs*, three; see **trei-** in App. + *virum*, archaic genitive pl. of *vir*, man; see **wī-ro-** in App.] —**tri·um′vi·ral** *adj.*

tri·um·vi·rate (trī-ŭm′vər-ĭt) *n.* 1. Government by triumvirs. 2. The office or term of a triumvir. 3. A body or group of triumvirs. 4. An association or a group of three. [Lat. *triumvirātus* < *triumvirī*, board of three. See TRIUMVIR.]

tri·une (trī′yōōn′) *adj.* Being three in one. Used esp. of the Christian Trinity. ❖ *n.* A trinity. [TRI– + Lat. *ūnus*, one; see **oi-no-** in App.] —**tri·u′ni·ty** (trī-yōō′nĭ-tē) *n.*

tri·va·lent (trī-vā′lənt) *adj.* Having valence 3. —**tri·va′lence, tri·va′len·cy** *n.*

tri·valve (trī′vălv′) *adj.* Having three valves.

Tri·van·drum (trī-văn′drəm) A city of SW India on the Arabian Sea SSW of Bangalore. Pop. 524,000.

triv·et (trĭv′ĭt) *n.* 1. A metal stand with short feet, used under a hot dish on a table. 2. A three-legged metal stand for cooking vessels in a hearth. [ME *trevet*, stand for cooking vessels < OE *trefet*, prob. alteration of Lat. *tripēs, triped-* : *tri-*, tri- + *pēs*, foot; see **ped-** in App.]

triv·i·a[1] (trĭv′ē-ə) *pl.n.* (*used with a sing. or pl. verb*) Insignificant or inessential matters; trifles. [Lat., neut. pl. of *trivium*, crossroads, gutter (influenced by TRIVIAL). See TRIVIUM.]

triv·i·a[2] (trĭv′ē-ə) *n.* Plural of **trivium.**

triv·i·al (trĭv′ē-əl) *adj.* 1. Of little significance or value. 2. Ordinary; commonplace: *a trivial occurrence.* 3. Concerned with or involving trivia. 4. *Biology* Relating to or designating a species; specific. 5. *Mathematics* **a.** Of, relating to, or being the solution of an equation in which every variable is equal to zero. **b.** Of, relating to, or being the simplest possible case; self-evident. [ME *trivialle*, of the trivium (< Med.Lat. *triviālis* < *trivium*, trivium; see TRIVIUM) and Lat. *triviālis*, ordinary (< *trivium*, crossroads).] —**triv′i·al·ly** *adv.*

WORD HISTORY The history of *trivial* goes back to the Latin word *trivium*, formed from the prefix *tri-*, "three," and *via*, "road." *Trivium* thus meant "the meeting place of three roads, especially as a place of public resort." The publicness of such a place also gave the word a pejorative sense, and the Latin adjective *triviālis*, derived from *trivium*, meant "appropriate to the street corner, commonplace, vulgar." *Trivial* is first recorded in English with a sense identical to that of *triviālis* in 1589. Shortly after that *trivial* is recorded in the sense most familiar to us, "of little importance or significance," making it a word now used of things less weighty than grammar, rhetoric, and logic.

triv·i·al·i·ty (trĭv′ē-ăl′ĭ-tē) *n., pl.* **-ties** 1. The quality or condition of being trivial. 2. Something trivial.

triv·i·al·ize (trĭv′ē-ə-līz′) *tr.v.* **-ized, -iz·ing, -iz·es** To reduce to triviality. —**triv′i·al·i·za′tion** (-ə-lĭ-zā′shən) *n.*

trivial name *n.* 1. A common or vernacular name as distinguished from a specific name, as *chimpanzee* for *Pan troglodytes.* 2. See **specific epithet.** 3. *Chemistry* A common or historic name for a substance, not used in official nomenclature, as *sucrose* for β-D-fructofuranosyl-α-D-glucopyranoside.

triv·i·um (trĭv′ē-əm) *n., pl.* **-i·a** (-ē-ə) The lower division of the seven liberal arts in medieval schools, consisting of grammar, logic, and rhetoric. [Med.Lat. < Lat., crossroads : *tri-*, tri- + *via*, road; see **wegh-** in App.]

tri·week·ly (trī-wēk′lē) *adj.* 1. Happening, done, or appearing three times a week. 2. Happening, done, or appearing every three weeks. ❖ *adv.* 1. Three times a week. 2. Every three weeks. ❖ *n., pl.* **-lies** A periodical published triweekly.

–trix *suff.* 1. A female that is connected with a specified thing: *testatrix.* 2. A geometric point, line, or surface: *directrix.* [ME < Lat. *-trix*, fem. of *-tor*, n. suff.]

tRNA *abbr.* transfer RNA

Tro·as (trō′ăs′) also **Tro·ad** (-ăd′) An ancient region of NW Asia Minor surrounding the city of Troy.

Tro·bri·and Islands (trō′brē-ănd′, - änd′) An island group of Papua New Guinea in the Solomon Sea off E New Guinea.

tro·car (trō′kär′) *n.* A sharp-pointed surgical instrument used with a cannula to puncture a body cavity for fluid aspiration. [Fr. *trocart : trois*, three (< OFr. < Lat. *trēs*; see **trei-** in App.) + *carre*, side of an instrument (< *carrer*, to square < Lat. *quadrāre* < *quadrum*, square; see **kʷetwer-** in App.).]

tro·cha·ic (trō-kā′ĭk) *adj.* Of, relating to, or consisting of tro-

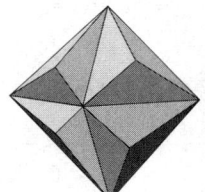

trisoctahedron

Triton
*Triton Fountain, Rome,
by Bernini*

trombone

chees. [Lat. *trochāicus* < Gk. *trokhaikos* < *trokhaios*, trochee. See TROCHEE.] —**tro•cha′ic** *n.*

tro•chan•ter (trō-kăn′tər) *n.* **1.** Any of several bony processes on the upper part of the femur of many vertebrates. **2.** The second proximal segment of the leg of an insect. [NLat. < Gk. *trokhantēr*, ball of the hip joint < *trekhein*, to run.] —**tro•chan′ter•al, tro′chan•ter′ic** (trō′kən-tĕr′ĭk, -kăn-) *adj.*

tro•che (trō′kē) *n.* A small circular medicinal lozenge; a pastille. [Back-formation < ME *trocis, troches* (taken as pl.) < OFr. *trocisse* < LLat. *trochiscus* < Gk. *trokhiskos*, dim. of *trokhos*, wheel < *trekhein*, to run.]

tro•chee (trō′kē) *n.* A metrical foot consisting of a stressed syllable followed by an unstressed one, as in *season*, or of a long syllable followed by a short. [Fr. *trochée* < Lat. *trochaeus* < Gk. *trokhaios*, a running < *trekhein*, to run.]

troch•le•a (trŏk′lē-ə) *n.*, pl. **-le•ae** (-lē-ē′) An anatomical structure that resembles a pulley, esp. the part of the distal end of the humerus that articulates with the ulna. [Lat., system of pulleys < Gk. *trokhileia*; akin to *trekhein*, to run.]

troch•le•ar (trŏk′lē-ər) *adj.* **1.** Of, resembling, or situated near a trochlea. **2.** Of or relating to the trochlear nerve. **3.** *Botany* Shaped like a pulley.

trochlear nerve *n.* Either of the fourth pair of cranial nerves that innervate the superior oblique muscles of the eyeballs.

tro•choid (trō′koid′, trŏk′oid′) *n.* A curve traced by a point on or connected with a circle as the circle rolls along a fixed straight line. ❖ *adj.* also **tro•choi•dal** (trō-koid′l, trŏk-oid′l) **1.** Capable of or exhibiting rotation about a central axis. **2.** Permitting rotation, as a pivot. [Gk. *trokhoeidēs*, wheellike : *trokhos*, wheel; see TROCHEE + *-oeidēs*, -oid.]

troch•o•phore (trŏk′ə-fôr′, -fōr′) *n.* The small free-swimming ciliated aquatic larva of various invertebrates, including certain mollusks and annelids. [Gk. *trokhos*, wheel (< *trekhein*, to run) + –PHORE.]

trod (trŏd) *v.* Past tense and a past participle of **tread.**

trod•den (trŏd′n) *v.* A past participle of **tread.**

trof•fer (trŏf′ər, trô′fər) *n.* An inverted, usu. metal trough suspended from a ceiling as a fixture for fluorescent lighting tubes. [Alteration of TROUGH.]

trog•lo•dyte (trŏg′lə-dīt′) *n.* **1a.** A member of a fabulous or prehistoric race of people that lived in caves, dens, or holes. **b.** A person considered to be reclusive, reactionary, out of date, or brutish. **2.** An anthropoid ape, such as a gorilla. **3.** An animal that lives underground. [< Lat. *Trōglodytae*, a people said to be cave dwellers < Gk. *Trōglodutai*, alteration (influenced by *trōglē*, hole, and *-dutai*, those who enter) of *Trōgodutai*.] —**trog′lo•dyt′ic** (-dĭt′ĭk), **trog′lo•dyt′i•cal** (-ĭ-kəl) *adj.*

tro•gon (trō′gŏn′) *n.* Any of various colorful tropical or subtropical birds of the family Trogonidae. [Gk. *trōgōn*, pr. part. of *trōgein*, to gnaw. See **tera–**[1] in App.]

troi•ka (troi′kə) *n.* **1a.** A Russian carriage drawn by a team of three horses abreast. **b.** A team of three horses abreast. **2.** See **triumvirate** 4. [Russ. *troĭka* < *troje*, group of three. See **trei–** in App.]

tro•i•lite (trō′ə-līt′, troi′līt′) *n.* A nonmagnetic variety of the mineral pyrrhotite, found in meteorites and having almost no ferrous iron deficiency. [After D. *Troili*, 18th-cent. Italian scientist.]

Troi•lus (troi′ləs, trō′ə-ləs) *n.* A son of King Priam of Troy, depicted as Cressida's lover in medieval romance.

Trois Ri•vières or **Trois-Ri•vières** (trwä rē-vyĕr′) A city of S Quebec, Canada, at the confluence of the St. Lawrence and St. Maurice rivers; founded 1634. Pop. 48,419.

Tro•jan[1] (trō′jən) *n.* **1.** A native or inhabitant of ancient Troy. **2.** A person of courageous determination or energy. [ME < Lat. *Trōiānus* < *Trōia*, Troy < Gk. *Troiā, Trōiā* < *Trōs*, the mythical founder of Troy.] —**Tro′jan** *adj.*

Tro•jan[2] (trō′jən) *adj.* Of or relating to a celestial body, esp. an asteroid, that is in a Lagrangian point and orbits at Jupiter's distance from the sun. [< the names of heroes of the Trojan War used for these asteroids.]

Trojan horse *n.* **1.** A subversive group or device placed within enemy ranks. **2.** The wooden horse in which, according to legend, Greeks hid and gained access to Troy. **3.** *Computer Science* A program that appears to be legitimate but is designed to have destructive effects, as to data residing in the computer onto which the program was loaded.

Trojan War *n. Greek Mythology* The ten-year war waged against Troy by the Greeks, caused by the abduction of Helen by Paris and resulting in the burning and destruction of Troy.

troll[1] (trōl) *v.* **trolled, troll•ing, trolls** —*tr.* **1a.** To fish for by trailing a baited line from behind a slowly moving boat. **b.** To fish in by trailing a baited line. **c.** To trail (a baited line) in fishing. **2.** *Slang* To patrol (an area) in search for someone or something. **3.** *Music* **a.** To sing in succession the parts of (a round, for example). **b.** To sing heartily: *troll a carol.* **4.** To roll or revolve. —*intr.* **1.** To fish by trailing a line, as from a moving boat. **2a.** To wander about. **b.** *Slang* To troll an area. **3.** *Music* To sing heartily. **4.** To roll or spin around. ❖ *n.* **1a.** The act of trolling for fish. **b.** A lure, such as a spoon, used for trolling. **2.** *Music* A vocal composition in successive parts; a round. [ME *trollen*, to wander

about < OFr. *troller*, of Gmc. orig.] —**troll′er** *n.*

troll[2] (trōl) *n.* A supernatural creature of Scandinavian folklore, variously portrayed as a friendly or mischievous dwarf or as a giant, that lives in caves or under bridges. [ON.]

trol•ley also **trol•ly** (trŏl′ē) *n.*, pl. **-leys** also **-lies 1.** A streetcar. **2.** A device that conducts current, as from a third rail, to the motor of an electric vehicle. **3.** A small truck or car on a track used, as in a mine, for conveying materials. **4.** A wheeled carriage, cage, or basket that travels on an overhead track. **5.** *Chiefly British* A cart. ❖ *tr. & intr.v.* **-leyed, -ley•ing, -leys** also **-lied** (-lēd), **-ly•ing, -lies** (-lēz) To convey (passengers) or travel by trolley. [Prob. < TROLL[1].]

trolley bus *n.* An electric bus that does not run on tracks and is powered by electricity from an overhead wire.

trolley car *n.* A streetcar.

trol•lop (trŏl′əp) *n.* **1.** A slovenly or untidy woman; a slattern. **2.** A prostitute. [Perh. < TROLL[1], to roll about, wallow.]

Trol•lope (trŏl′əp), **Anthony** 1815–82. British writer whose works include *Barchester Towers* (1857). —**Trol•lo•pi•an** (trə-lōp′ē-ən, -lō′pē-, trŏl′ə-pē′-) *adj.*

trom•bone (trŏm-bōn′, trăm-, trŏm′bōn′) *n.* A brass instrument consisting of a long cylindrical tube bent upon itself twice, ending in a bell-shaped mouth, and having a movable U-shaped slide for producing different pitches. [Fr. < Ital., augmentative of *tromba*, trumpet, of Gmc. orig.] —**trom•bon′ist** *n.*

trom•mel (trŏm′əl) *n.* A revolving cylindrical sieve used for screening or sizing rock and ore. [Ger. < MHGer. *trummel*, dim. of *trumme*, drum, prob. of imit. orig.]

tromp (trŏmp) *v.* **tromped, tromp•ing, tromps** *Informal* —*intr.* **1.** To walk heavily and noisily; tramp. **2.** To apply heavy foot pressure on something. —*tr.* **1.** To trample underfoot. **2.** To defeat soundly; trounce. [Variant of TRAMP.]

trompe (trŏmp) *n.* A device in which water falling through a perforated pipe entrains air through the pipe to produce an air blast for a furnace or forge. [Fr. < OFr., trumpet. See TRUMP[2].]

trompe l'oeil (trômp′ loi′) *n.*, pl. **trompe l'oeils** (loi′) **1.** A style of painting that gives an illusion of photographic reality. **2.** A painting or effect created in this style. [Fr. *trompe l'œil : trompe*, third pers. sing. pr. t. of *tromper*, to deceive + *le*, the + *œil*, eye.]

–tron *suff.* **1.** Vacuum tube: *dynatron.* **2.** Device for manipulating subatomic particles: *betatron.* [Gk., instrumental n. suff.]

tro•na (trō′nə) *n.* A vitreous gray or white mineral, $Na_2CO_3 \cdot NaHCO_3 \cdot 2H_2O$, used as a source of sodium carbonate. [Swed., prob. < Ar. dialectal *trōn*, var. of Ar. *naṭrūn*, natron. See NATRON.]

Trond•heim (trŏn′hām′, trôn′-) A city of central Norway on **Trondheim Fjord,** an inlet of the Norwegian Sea; founded in 997 the cap. of Norway until 1380. Pop. 140,646.

troop (trōōp) *n.* **1.** A group or company. **2a.** A group of soldiers. **b. troops** Military units; soldiers. **c.** A unit of cavalry, armored vehicles, or artillery in a European army, corresponding to a platoon in the US army. **3.** A unit of Boy Scouts or Girl Scouts with an adult leader. **4.** A great many; a lot. ❖ *intr.v.* **trooped, troop•ing, troops 1.** To move or go as a throng. **2.** To assemble or move in crowds. **3.** To consort; associate. [Fr. *troupe* < OFr. *trope*, prob. < VLat. **troppu-.*]

troop•er (trōō′pər) *n.* **1a.** A member of a cavalry unit. **b.** A cavalry horse. **2a.** A mounted police officer. **b.** A state police officer.

troop•ship (trōōp′shĭp′) *n.* A ship for transporting troops.

trop– *pref.* Variant of **tropo–.**

trope (trōp) *n.* **1.** A figure of speech using words in nonliteral ways, such as a metaphor. **2.** A word or phrase interpolated as an embellishment in the sung parts of certain medieval liturgies. [Lat. *tropus* < Gk. *tropos*, turn, figure of speech.] —**trop′i•cal** (trŏp′ĭ-kəl) *adj.*

troph•al•lax•is (trŏf′ə-lăk′sĭs, trō′fə-) *n.*, pl. **-lax•es** (-lăk′sēz) Mutual exchange of food between adults and larvae of certain social insects such as bees. [TROPH(O)– + Gk. *allaxis*, exchange (< *allassein*, to exchange < *allos*, other; see **al–** in App.).]

troph•ic (trŏf′ĭk, trō′fĭk) *adj.* **1.** Of or relating to nutrition. **2.** *Ecology* Of or involving the feeding habits or food relationship of different organisms in a food chain.

–trophic *suff.* **1.** Of, relating to, or characterized by a specified kind of nutrition: *polytrophic.* **2.** Acting on something specified: *gonadotrophic.* [< TROPHIC.]

trophic level *n.* A group of organisms that occupy the same position in a food chain.

tropho– or **troph–** *pref.* Nutrition; nutritive: *trophoblast.* [Gk. < *trophē* < *trephein*, to nourish.]

tro•pho•blast (trō′fə-blăst′) *n.* The outermost layer of cells of the blastocyst that functions in the implantation and nutrition of the embryo. —**tro′pho•blas′tic** *adj.*

tro•pho•zo•ite (trō′fə-zō′īt′) *n.* A protozoan, esp. of the class Sporozoa, in the active stage of its life cycle.

tro•phy (trō′fē) *n.*, pl. **-phies 1a.** A prize or memento received as a symbol of victory, esp. in sports. **b.** A specimen or part, such as a lion's head, preserved as a token of a successful hunt. **c.** A memento, as of one's personal achievements. **d.** The spoils of war, dedicated in classical antiquity with an inscription to a deity. **2.** *Architecture* A painted or sculpted representation of a group of weapons or armor. [Fr. *trophée* < OFr. *trophee* < Lat. *trophaeum*, monument to victory, var. of *tropaeum* < Gk. *tropaion* < neut. of

tropaios, of defeat < *tropē*, a turning, rout.]
–trophy *suff.* Nutrition; growth: *hypertrophy.* [Gk. *-trophiā* < *trophē* < *trephein*, to nourish.]
trophy wife *n.* An attractive, young wife married to a usu. older, affluent man.
trop·ic (trŏp′ĭk) *n.* **1a.** Either of two parallels of latitude, the Tropic of Cancer or the Tropic of Capricorn, representing the points farthest north and south at which the sun can shine directly overhead. **b. Tropics** or **tropics** The region of the earth's surface lying between these latitudes. **2.** *Astronomy* Either of two corresponding parallels of celestial latitude that are the limits of the apparent northern and southern passages of the sun. ❖ *adj.* Of or relating to the Tropics; tropical. [ME *tropik* < OFr. *tropique* < LLat. *tropicus* < Lat., of a turn < Gk. *tropikos* < *tropē*, a turning.]
–tropic *suff.* **1.** Turning or changing in a specified way or in response to a specified stimulus: *heliotropic.* **2.** Affecting or attracted to something specified: *gonadotropic.* [< Gk. *tropē*, a turning. See TROPIC.]
trop·i·cal (trŏp′ĭ-kəl) *adj.* **1.** Of, occurring in, or characteristic of the Tropics. **2.** Hot and humid; torrid. ❖ *n.* A tropical plant. **—trop′i·cal·ly** *adv.*
tropical cyclone *n.* A violent storm originating over tropical or subtropical waters, characterized by violent rainstorms and high-velocity cyclonic winds.
tropical fish *n.* Any of various small brightly colored fishes native to tropical waters and often kept in home aquariums.
tropical storm *n.* A cyclonic storm having winds ranging from approx. 48 to 121 kilometers (30 to 75 miles) per hour.
tropical year *n.* See **solar year.**
trop·ic·bird (trŏp′ĭk-bûrd′) *n.* Any of several predominantly white, swift-flying sea birds of the genus *Phaethon* of warm regions, having a pair of long central tail feathers.
Tropic of Cancer *n.* The parallel of latitude 23°27′ north of the equator, the northern limit of the Torrid Zone.
Tropic of Capricorn *n.* The parallel of latitude 23°27′ south of the equator, the southern limit of the Torrid Zone.
tro·pine (trō′pēn′, -pĭn) also **tro·pin** (-pĭn) *n.* A white crystalline poisonous alkaloid, $C_8H_{15}NO$, obtained chiefly by hydrolysis of atropine. [< ATROPINE.]
tro·pism (trō′pĭz′əm) *n.* The movement of an organism or a part toward or away from an external stimulus, such as light, heat, or gravity. [< –TROPISM.] **—tro·pis′tic** *adj.*
–tropism *suff.* Tropism: *phototropism.* [< Gk. *tropē*, a turning. See –TROPIC.]
tropo– or **trop–** *pref.* **1.** Turning; change: *troposphere.* **2.** Tropism: *tropotaxis.* [Gk. < *tropē*, turn.]
tro·po·col·la·gen (trō′pə-kŏl′ə-jən, trŏp′ə-) *n.* The molecular component of a collagen fiber, consisting of three polypeptide chains coiled around each other.
tro·pol·o·gy (trō-pŏl′ə-jē) *n., pl.* **-gies 1.** The use of tropes in speech or writing. **2.** A mode of biblical interpretation that finds moral meanings in the tropes of the Bible. [LLat. *tropologia* < L.Gk. *tropologiā* < Gk. *tropos*, type; see TROPE + Gk. *-logiā*, -logy.] **—tro′po·log′i·cal** (trō′pə-lŏj′ĭk, trŏp′ə-) **tro′po·log′i·cal·ly** *adv.*
tro·po·my·o·sin (trō′pə-mī′ə-sĭn, trŏp′ə-) *n.* Any of a group of muscle proteins that bind to molecules of actin and troponin to regulate the interaction of actin and myosin during muscle contraction.
tro·po·nin (trō′pə-nĭn, trŏp′ə-) *n.* A protein of muscle tissue that binds with calcium and acts together with tropomyosin in the regulation of muscle contraction. [TROPO(MYOSIN) + -IN.]
tro·po·pause (trō′pə-pôz′, trŏp′ə-) *n.* The boundary between the troposphere and the stratosphere varying in altitude from approx. 8 kilometers (5 miles) at the poles to approx. 18 kilometers (11 miles) at the equator.
tro·po·phyte (trō′pə-fīt′, trŏp′ə-) *n.* A plant adapted to climatic conditions in which periods of heavy rainfall alternate with periods of drought. **—tro′po·phyt′ic** (-fĭt′ĭk) *adj.*
tro·po·sphere (trō′pə-sfîr′, trŏp′ə-) *n.* The lowest region of the atmosphere between the earth's surface and the tropopause, characterized by decreasing temperature with increasing altitude. **—tro′po·spher′ic** (-sfîr′ĭk, -sfĕr′-) *adj.*
tro·po·tax·is (trō′pə-tăk′sĭs, trŏp′ə-) *n.* The movement or orientation of an organism in response to two stimuli, esp. lights, by means of different sense organs.
–tropous *suff.* Turning in a specified way or from a specified stimulus: *amphitropous.* [< Gk. *-tropos*, of turning < *tropos*, changeable < *trepein*, to turn.]
–tropy *suff.* The state of turning in a specified way or from a specified stimulus: *thixotropy.* [Gk. *-tropiā* < *-tropos*, -tropous.]
trot (trŏt) *n.* **1a.** The gait of a horse or other four-footed animal, between a walk and a canter in speed, in which diagonal pairs of legs move forward together. **b.** A ride on a horse at this pace. **2.** A gait of a person, faster than a walk; a jog. **3.** *Sports* A race for trotters. **4.** See **pony 4. 5. trots** *Informal* Diarrhea. Used with *the.* **6.** A toddler. **7.** *Archaic* An old woman; a crone. ❖ *v.* **trot·ted, trot·ting, trots —intr.** **1.** To go or move at a trot. **2.** To proceed rapidly; hurry. **—tr.** To cause to move at a trot. **—phrasal verb: trot out** *Informal* To present for inspection or admiration. [ME < OFr. < *troter*, to trot < of Gmc. orig.]

troth (trôth, trŏth, trōth) *n.* **1a.** Betrothal. **b.** One's pledged fidelity. **2.** Good faith; fidelity. ❖ *tr.v.* **trothed, troth·ing, troths** To pledge or betroth. [ME *trouthe, trothe*, var. of *treuthe* < OE *trēowth*, truth. See deru- in App.]
troth·plight (trôth′plīt′, trŏth′-, trōth′-) *Archaic n.* A betrothal. ❖ *tr.v.* **-plight·ed, -plight·ing, -plights** To betroth.
trot·line (trŏt′lĭn′) *n.* See **setline.** [Perh. < TROT.]
Trot·sky or **Trot·ski** (trŏt′skē, trôt′-), **Leon** 1879–1940. Russian revolutionary theoretician who was a leader of the Bolshevik Revolution (1917) but was banished (1929) for his opposition to Stalin.
Trot·sky·ism (trŏt′skē-ĭz′əm) *n.* The Communist theories advocated by Leon Trotsky, including the principle of worldwide revolution. **—Trot′sky·ist, Trot′sky·ite′** (-īt′) *n.*
trot·ter (trŏt′ər) *n.* **1.** A horse that trots, esp. one trained for harness racing. **2.** *Informal* A foot, esp. the foot of a pig or sheep prepared as food.
trou·ba·dour (trōo′bə-dôr′, -dōr′, -dōor′) *n.* **1.** One of a class of 12th- and 13th-century lyric poets in southern France, northern Italy, and northern Spain, who wrote songs in langue d'oc often about courtly love. **2.** A strolling minstrel. [Fr. < Provençal *trobador* < O Provençal < *trobar*, to compose, perh. < VLat. **tropāre* < LLat. *tropus*, trope, song < Lat., trope. See TROPE.]
trou·ble (trŭb′əl) *n.* **1.** A state of distress, affliction, danger, or need. **2.** A distressing or difficult circumstance or situation. **3.** A cause or source of distress, disturbance, or difficulty. **4.** Effort, especially when inconvenient or bothersome. **5.** A condition of pain, disease, or malfunction. **6a.** Public unrest or disorder. **b.** An instance of this; a disturbance. ❖ *v.* **-led, -ling, -les —tr.** **1.** To agitate; stir up. **2.** To afflict with pain or discomfort. **3.** To cause emotional strain or anxiety to; worry or distress. **4.** To inconvenience; bother. **—intr.** To take pains: *They trouble over every detail.* [ME < OFr. < *troubler*, to trouble < VLat. **turbulare*, alteration of LLat. *turbidāre* < Lat. *turbidus*, confused. See TURBID.] **—trou′bler** *n.*

SYNONYMS *trouble, ail, distress, worry* These verbs mean to cause anxious uneasiness in: *questions that trouble all parents; asked what's ailing him; events that distress us; a fever that worries the doctor.*

trou·ble·mak·er (trŭb′əl-mā′kər) *n.* One that stirs up trouble or strife.
trou·ble·shoot also **trou·ble-shoot** (trŭb′əl-shōot′) *v.* **-shot** (-shŏt′), **-shoot·ing, -shoots —intr.** To work or serve as a troubleshooter. **—tr.** To investigate as a troubleshooter; determine and settle problems with.
trou·ble·shoot·er also **trou·ble-shoot·er** (trŭb′əl-shōo′tər) *n.* **1.** A worker whose job is to locate and eliminate sources of trouble, as in mechanical operations. **2.** A mediator skilled in settling disputes esp. of a diplomatic or industrial nature.
trou·ble·some (trŭb′əl-səm) *adj.* **1.** Causing trouble or anxiety; worrisome. **2.** Difficult; trying. **—trou′ble·some·ly** *adv.*
trouble spot *n.* A location or site of possible difficulty.
trou·blous (trŭb′ləs) *adj.* **1a.** Full of trouble. **b.** Uneasy; troubled. **2.** Causing trouble; troublesome.
trough (trôf, trŏf) *n.* **1a.** A long, narrow, generally shallow receptacle for holding water or feed for animals. **b.** Any of various similar containers for domestic or industrial use, such as washing. **2.** A gutter under the eaves of a roof. **3.** A long narrow depression, as between waves. **4.** A low point in a business cycle or on a statistical graph. **5.** *Meteorology* An elongated region of relatively low atmospheric pressure, often associated with a front. **6.** *Physics* A minimum point in a wave or an alternating signal. [ME < OE *trog*. See deru- in App.]
trounce (trouns) *v.* **trounced, trounc·ing, trounc·es —tr.** **1.** To thrash; beat. **2.** To defeat decisively. **—intr.** To censure something or someone forcefully. [?]
troupe (trōop) *n.* A company or group, esp. of touring actors, singers, or dancers. ❖ *intr.v.* **trouped, troup·ing, troupes** To tour with a theatrical company. [Fr., troop. See TROOP.]
troup·er (trōo′pər) *n.* **1.** A member of a theatrical company. **2.** A veteran actor or performer. **3.** A reliable, uncomplaining, often hard-working person.
trou·pi·al (trōo′pē-əl) *n.* Any of several tropical American birds of the genus *Icterus*, related to the orioles and New World blackbirds, esp. *I. icterus*, having orange and black plumage. [Fr. *troupiale* < *troupe*, flock. See TROOP.]
trou·ser (trou′zər) *n.* An outer garment for covering the body from the waist to the ankles, divided into sections to fit each leg separately. Often used in the plural. ❖ *adj.* Of, designed for, or found on trousers: *trouser legs.* [Back-formation < *trousers*, alteration of obsolete *trouse* < Sc. Gael. *triubhas.*]
trous·seau (trōo′sō, trōo-sō′) *n., pl.* **-seaux** (-sōz, -sōz′) or **-seaus** The possessions, such as clothing and linens, that a bride assembles for her marriage. [Fr. < OFr., dim. of *trousse*, bundle. See TRUSS.]
trout (trout) *n., pl.* **trout** or **trouts** **1.** Any of various freshwater or anadromous food and game fishes of the family Salmonidae, esp. of the genera *Salmo* and *Salvelinus*, usu. having a speckled body with small scales. **2.** Any of various similar but unrelated fishes, such as the troutperch. [ME *troute* < OE *trūht* < LLat.

Leon Trotsky

trūcta, perh. < Gk. *trōktēs*, a sea fish with sharp teeth < *trōgein*, to gnaw. See **terə-¹** in App.]

trout lily *n.* See **dogtooth violet.**

trout·perch (trout′pûrch′) *n., pl.* **troutperch** or **-perch·es** A small North American freshwater fish (*Percopsis omiscomaycus*) having a translucent body and an adipose fin.

trou·vère (troo-vâr′) also **trou·veur** (-vûr′, -vœr′) *n.* One of a class of poet-musicians flourishing in northern France in the 12th and 13th centuries, who composed chiefly narrative works, such as the chansons de geste, in langue d'oïl. [Fr. < OFr. *trovere* < *trover*, to compose < VLat. **tropāre*. See TROUBADOUR.]

trove (trōv) *n.* A collection of valuable items discovered or found; a treasure-trove. [Short for (TREASURE-)TROVE.]

tro·ver (trō′vər) *n.* A common-law action to recover damages for property illegally withheld or wrongfully converted to use by another. [< AN, to compose, invent, find, prob. < VLat. **tropāre*. See TROUBADOUR.]

trow (trō) *intr.v.* **trowed, trow·ing, trows 1.** *Archaic* To think. **2.** *Obsolete* To suppose. [ME *trowen* < OE *trēowian*, to trust. See **deru-** in App.]

trow·el (trou′əl) *n.* **1.** A flat-bladed hand tool for leveling, spreading, or shaping substances such as cement or mortar. **2.** A small implement with a pointed scoop-shaped blade used for digging, as in setting plants. ❖ *tr.v.* **-eled, -el·ing, -els** or **-elled, -el·ling, -els** To spread, smooth, form, or scoop with a trowel. [ME *trowell* < OFr. *truele* < LLat. *truella*, dim. of Lat. *trua*, ladle.] —**trow′el·er, trow′el·ler** *n.*

troy (troi) *adj.* Of or expressed in troy weight. [ME *troye*, after TROYES.]

Troy 1. also **Il·i·on** (ĭl′ē-ən, -ŏn′) or **Il·i·um** (-ē-əm) An ancient city of NW Asia Minor; legendary site of the Trojan War. **2.** A city of SE MI, a suburb of Detroit. Pop. 80,959.

Troyes (trwä) A city of NE France on the Seine ESE of Paris; noted in medieval times for its annual fairs, which set standards of weights and measures for Europe. Pop. 125,000.

troy weight *n.* A system of units of weight in which the grain is the same as in the avoirdupois system and the pound contains 12 ounces, 240 pennyweights, or 5,760 grains.

tru·an·cy (troo′ən-sē) also **tru·ant·ry** (-ən-trē) *n., pl.* **-cies** also **-ries** The act or condition of being absent without permission.

tru·ant (troo′ənt) *n.* **1.** One who is absent without permission, esp. from school. **2.** One who shirks work or duty. ❖ *adj.* **1.** Absent without permission, esp. from school. **2.** Idle, lazy, or neglectful. ❖ *intr.v.* **-ant·ed, -ant·ing, -ants** To be truant. [ME, beggar < OFr. See **terə-¹** in App.]

truant officer *n.* An official who investigates school truancy.

truce (troos) *n.* **1.** A temporary cessation or suspension of hostilities by agreement of the opposing sides; an armistice. **2.** A respite from a disagreeable state of affairs. ❖ *tr. & intr.v.* **truced, truc·ing, truc·es** To end or be ended with a truce. [ME *trewes*, pl. of *trewe*, treaty, pledge < OE *trēow*. See **deru-** in App.]

Tru·cial Oman (troo′shəl) See **United Arab Emirates.**

truck¹ (trŭk) *n.* **1.** Any of various heavy motor vehicles designed for carrying or pulling loads. **2.** A hand truck. **3.** A wheeled platform, sometimes equipped with a motor, for conveying loads in a warehouse or freight yard. **4.** One of the swiveling frames of wheels under each end of a railroad car or trolley car. **5.** A set of bookshelves mounted on four wheels or casters, used in libraries. **6.** *Nautical* A small piece of wood placed at the top of a mast or flagpole, usu. having holes or sheaves through which halyards can be passed. **7.** *Chiefly British* A railroad freight car without a top. ❖ *v.* **trucked, truck·ing, trucks** —*tr.* To transport by truck. —*intr.* **1.** To carry goods by truck. **2.** To drive a truck. **3.** *Slang* To move or travel in a steady but easy manner. [Short for TRUCKLE or < Lat. *trochus*, iron hoop (< Gk. *trochos*, wheel).]

truck² (trŭk) *v.* **trucked, truck·ing, trucks** —*tr.* **1.** To exchange; barter. **2.** To peddle. —*intr.* To have dealings or commerce; traffic. ❖ *n.* **1.** Articles of commerce; trade goods. **2.** Garden produce raised for the market. **3.** *Informal* Worthless goods; stuff or rubbish. **4.** Barter; exchange. **5.** *Informal* Dealings; business. [ME *trukien* < ONFr. *troquer*.]

truck·age (trŭk′ĭj) *n.* **1.** Transportation of goods by truck. **2.** A charge for transportation by truck.

Truck·ee (trŭk′ē) A river, c. 193 km (120 mi), rising in E CA and flowing E and NE into NW NV.

truck·er (trŭk′ər) *n.* **1.** One who drives a truck. **2.** One engaged in trucking goods.

truck farm *n.* A farm producing vegetables for the market. [< TRUCK².] —**truck farmer** *n.* —**truck farming** *n.*

truck·le (trŭk′əl) *n.* A small wheel or roller; a caster. ❖ *intr.v.* **-led, -ling, -les** To be servile or submissive. [ME *trocle*, pulley < AN < Lat. *trochlea*, system of pulleys. See TROCHLEA.] —**truck′ler** *n.*

truckle bed *n.* A trundle bed.

truck·load (trŭk′lōd′) *n.* The quantity that a truck can hold.

truck stop *n.* An establishment that sells fuel for trucks and usu. maintains a restaurant for truck drivers.

truc·u·lence (trŭk′yə-ləns) also **truc·u·len·cy** (-lən-sē) *n.* **1.** A disposition or apparent disposition to fight, esp. fiercely. **2.** Ferociously cruel actions or behavior.

truc·u·lent (trŭk′yə-lənt) *adj.* **1.** Disposed to fight; pugnacious.

trowel
top to bottom: inside corner, pointing, and finishing trowels

trug

[no additional image]

Bess Truman
1967 portrait by Greta Kempton (1903–91)

2. Expressing bitter opposition; scathing. **3.** Disposed to or exhibiting violence or destructiveness; fierce. [Lat. *truculentus* < *trux*, *truc*-, fierce. See **terə-²** in App.]

Tru·deau (troo-dō′, troo′dō′), Pierre Elliott 1919–2000. Canadian prime minister (1968–79 and 1980–84).

trudge (trŭj) *intr.v.* **trudged, trudg·ing, trudg·es** To walk in a laborious heavy-footed way; plod. ❖ *n.* A long tedious walk. [?] —**trudg′er** *n.*

trudg·en also **trudg·eon** (trŭj′ən) *n.* A swimming stroke in which an alternating overarm movement is combined with a scissors kick. [After John *Trudgen* (1852–1902), British swimmer.]

true (troo) *adj.* **tru·er, tru·est 1a.** Consistent with fact or reality; not false or erroneous. See Usage Note at **fact. b.** Truthful. **2.** Real; genuine. See Syns at **authentic. 3.** Reliable; accurate: *a true prophecy.* **4.** Faithful, as to a friend, vow, or cause; loyal. See Syns at **faithful. 5.** Sincerely felt or expressed; unfeigned. **6.** Fundamental; essential: *his true motive.* **7.** Rightful; legitimate. **8.** Exactly conforming to a rule, standard, or pattern. **9.** Accurately shaped or fitted. **10.** Accurately placed, delivered, or thrown. **11.** Quick and exact in sensing and responding. **12.** Determined with reference to the earth's axis, not the magnetic poles: *true north.* **13.** Conforming to the definitive criteria of a natural group; typical: *a true crab.* **14.** Narrowly particularized; highly specific: *the truest sense of the word.* ❖ *adv.* **1.** In accord with reality, fact, or truthfulness. **2.** Unswervingly; exactly. **3.** So as to conform to a type, standard, or pattern. ❖ *tr.v.* **trued, tru·ing** or **true·ing, trues** To position (something) so as to make it balanced, level, or square. ❖ *n.* **1.** Truth or reality. Used with *the.* **2.** Proper alignment or adjustment: *out of true.* [ME *trewe* < OE *trēowe*, firm, trustworthy. See **deru-** in App.] —**true′ness** *n.*

true bill *n. Law* A bill of indictment endorsed by a grand jury.

true-blue (troo′bloo′) *adj.* Loyal or faithful; staunch. [< the adoption of the color blue by 17th-cent. Scottish Presbyterians in opposition to the Royalists' red.]

true·born (troo′bôrn′) *adj.* Being authentically such by birth.

true bug *n.* A wingless or four-winged insect of the order Hemiptera, esp. of the suborder Heteroptera, including the bedbug and louse, having mouthparts adapted for sucking.

true-false test (troo′fôls′) *n.* A test in which statements are to be marked either true or false.

true-life (troo′līf′) *adj.* Presenting conditions and esp. human relationships accurately; true to life: *a true-life romance.*

true·love (troo′lŭv′) *n.* One's beloved; a sweetheart.

true lovers' knot *n.* See **love knot.**

true·pen·ny (troo′pĕn′ē) *n., pl.* **-nies** An honest, trustworthy person.

true rib *n.* Any of the ribs attached to the sternum by a costal cartilage, esp. any of the seven upper ribs on either side of the thorax in humans.

true seal *n.* See **earless seal.**

Truf·faut (troo-fō′), François 1932–84. French new wave filmmaker whose works include *The 400 Blows* (1959).

truf·fle (trŭf′əl) *n.* **1.** Any of various fleshy ascomycetous edible fungi, chiefly of the genus *Tuber*, that grow underground on or near the roots of trees and are valued as a delicacy. **2.** Any of various chocolate confections, esp. one made of a mixture including chopped nuts, rolled into balls and covered with cocoa powder. [Alteration of Fr. *trufe* < OFr. < O Provençal *trufa* < VLat. **tūfera*, truffles < dialectal var. of Lat. *tūber*, lump.]

trug (trŭg) *n. Chiefly British* A shallow, usu. oval gardening basket made with wide strips of wood. [ME, a shallow wooden tray, measure of corn, perh. < ON *trog*, trough. See **deru-** in App.]

tru·ism (troo′ĭz′əm) *n.* A self-evident truth. —**tru·is′tic** (troo-ĭs′tĭk) *adj.*

Tru·ji·llo (troo-hē′ō, -yō) A city of NW Peru NW of Lima; founded 1534. Pop. 521,200.

Trujillo Mo·li·na (mō-lē′nə, -nä), Rafael Leónidas 1891–1961. Dominican soldier and dictator (1930–61).

Truk Islands (trŭk, trook) See **Chuuk.**

trull (trŭl) *n.* A woman prostitute. [Perh. < Ger. *Trulle* < MHGer. *trulle*; akin to ON *trulle*, creature, troll.]

tru·ly (troo′lē) *adv.* **1.** Sincerely; genuinely. **2.** Truthfully; accurately. **3.** Indeed: *truly ugly.* **4.** Properly: *not truly civilized.*

Tru·man (troo′mən), Elizabeth ("Bess") 1885–1982. First Lady of the US (1945–53).

Truman, Harry S. 1884–1972. The 33rd President of the US (1945–53), who authorized the use of the atomic bomb against Japan (1945).

Trum·bo (trŭm′bō), Dalton 1905–76. Amer. screenwriter who was blacklisted and imprisoned for his refusal to testify before the House Un-American Activities Committee.

Trum·bull (trŭm′bəl), John 1756–1843. Amer. painter of historical scenes, such as *The Battle of Bunker's Hill* (1786).

Trumbull, Jonathan 1710–85. Amer. politician who as governor of Connecticut (1769–84) provided support for the Continental Army during the American Revolution.

trump¹ (trŭmp) *n. Games* **a.** A suit in card games that outranks all others for the duration of a hand. Often used in the plural. **b.** A card of such a suit. **c.** A trump card. **2.** A key resource to be used at an opportune moment. **3.** *Informal* A reliable or admirable person. ❖ *v.* **trumped, trump·ing, trumps** —*tr.* **1.** *Games*

To take (a card or trick) with a trump. **2.** To get the better of (an adversary or competitor, for example) by using a crucial, often hidden resource. —*intr. Games* To play a trump. ***—phrasal verb:* trump up** To devise fraudulently. [Alteration of TRIUMPH.]

trump[2] (trŭmp) *n.* A trumpet. [ME *trompe* < OFr. See TRUMPET.]

trump card *n.* **1.** *Games* A card in the trump suit, held in reserve for winning a trick. **2.** A key resource to be used at an opportune moment; a trump.

trump•er•y (trŭm′pə-rē) *n., pl.* **-ies 1.** Showy but worthless finery; bric-a-brac. **2.** Nonsense; rubbish. **3.** Deception; trickery; fraud. [ME *trompery*, deceit < OFr. *tromperie* < *tromper*, to deceive.]

trum•pet (trŭm′pĭt) *n.* **1a.** *Music* A soprano brass wind instrument consisting of a long metal tube looped once and ending in a flared bell, the modern type having three valves for producing variations in pitch. **b.** Something like this instrument in shape or sound. **2.** A resounding call, as that of the elephant. ❖ *v.* **-pet•ed, -pet•ing, -pets** —*intr.* **1.** *Music* To play a trumpet. **2.** To give forth a resounding call. —*tr.* To sound or proclaim loudly. [ME *trumpette* < OFr. *trompette*, dim. of *trompe*, horn < OHGer. *trumpa*.]

trumpet creeper *n.* A deciduous woody vine *(Campsis radicans)* of the eastern United States having opposite compound leaves and trumpet-shaped reddish-orange flowers.

trum•pet•er (trŭm′pĭ-tər) *n.* **1.** *Music* One who plays the trumpet. **2.** One who announces something, as a herald. **3.** Any of several large cranelike birds of the genus *Psophia* of tropical South America, having a loud resonant call. **4a.** The trumpeter swan. **b.** A variety of domestic pigeon having a shell-shaped crest and heavily feathered feet.

trumpeter swan *n.* A large white swan *(Olor buccinator)* of western North America having a loud buglelike call.

trumpet honeysuckle *n.* A vine *(Lonicera sempervirens)* of the eastern United States having tubular reddish flowers.

trumpet vine *n.* See **trumpet creeper.**

trun•cate (trŭng′kāt′) *tr.v.* **-cat•ed, -cat•ing, -cates 1.** To shorten by or as if by cutting off. **2.** To shorten (a number) by dropping one or more digits after the decimal point. **3.** To replace (the edge of a crystal) with a plane face. ❖ *adj.* **1.** Appearing to terminate abruptly, as a leaf of a tulip tree. **2.** Truncated. [Lat. *truncāre, truncāt-* < *truncus*, trunk. See **terə-[2]** in App.] **—trun′cate′ly** *adv.* **—trun•ca′tion** *n.*

trun•ca•ted (trŭng′kā′tĭd) *adj.* **1.** Having the apex cut off and replaced by a plane, esp. one parallel to the base. Used of a cone or pyramid. **2a.** Lacking one or more syllables, esp. in the final foot; catalectic. **b.** Lacking an initial or final syllable. Used of a line of verse. **3.** Truncate.

trun•cheon (trŭn′chən) *n.* **1.** A short stick carried by police; a billy club. **2.** A staff carried as a symbol of office or authority; a baton. **3.** *Obsolete* **a.** A heavy club; a cudgel. **b.** A thick cutting from a plant, as for grafting. [ME *tronchon*, piece broken off, club < ONFr. < VLat. **trunciō, trunciōn-* < Lat. *truncus*, trunk. See TRUNK.] **—trun′cheon** *v.*

trun•dle (trŭn′dl) *n.* **1.** A small wheel or roller. **2.** The motion or noise of rolling. **3.** A trundle bed. **4.** A low-wheeled cart; a dolly. ❖ *v.* **-dled, -dling, -dles** —*tr.* **1.** To push or propel on wheels or rollers. **2.** To spin; twirl. —*intr.* To move along by or as if by rolling or spinning. [Variant of dialectal *trendle*, wheel < ME < OE *trendel*, circle.] **—trun′dler** *n.*

trundle bed *n.* A low bed on casters that can be rolled under another bed for storage.

trunk (trŭngk) *n.* **1a.** The main woody axis of a tree. **b.** *Architecture* The shaft of a column. **2a.** The body of a human or animal excluding the head and limbs. **b.** The thorax of an insect. **3.** A proboscis, esp. that of an elephant. **4a.** A main body, apart from tributaries or appendages. **b.** The main stem of a blood vessel or nerve apart from the branches. **5.** A trunk line. **6.** A chute or conduit. **7.** *Nautical* **a.** A watertight shaft connecting two or more decks. **b.** The housing for the centerboard of a vessel. **8.** *Nautical* Any of certain structures projecting above part of a main deck, as: **a.** A covering over the hatches of a ship. **b.** An expansion chamber on a tanker. **c.** A cabin on a small boat. **9a.** A covered compartment for storage, generally at the rear of an automobile. **b.** A large packing case or box that clasps shut, used as luggage or for storage. **10. trunks** Shorts worn for swimming or other athletics. [ME *trunke* < OFr. *tronc* < Lat. *truncus*. See **terə-[2]** in App.]

trunk•fish (trŭngk′fĭsh′) *n., pl.* **trunkfish** or **-fish•es** Any of various colorful tropical marine fishes of the family Ostraciidae, having a body enclosed in bony armorlike plates.

trunk hose *pl.n.* Short ballooning breeches worn by men in Europe in the 16th and 17th centuries. [Perh. < obsolete *trunk*, to cut off < Lat. *truncāre*. See TRUNCATE.]

trunk line *n.* **1.** A direct line between two telephone switchboards. **2.** The main line of a communications or transportation system.

trun•nel (trŭn′əl) *n.* Variant of **treenail.**

trun•nion (trŭn′yən) *n.* A pin or gudgeon, esp. either of two small cylindrical projections on a cannon forming an axis on which it pivots. [Fr. *trognon*, stump.]

truss (trŭs) *n.* **1.** *Medicine* A supportive device, usu. a pad with a belt, worn to prevent enlargement of a hernia or the return of a reduced hernia. **2a.** A rigid framework, as of wooden beams or metal bars, designed to support a structure, such as a roof. **b.** *Architecture* A bracket. **3.** Something gathered into a bundle; a pack. **4.** *Nautical* An iron fitting by which a lower yard is secured to a mast. **5.** *Botany* A compact cluster of flowers at the end of a stalk. ❖ *tr.v.* **trussed, truss•ing, truss•es 1.** To tie up or bind tightly. **2.** To bind or skewer the wings or legs of (a fowl) before cooking. **3.** To support or brace with a truss. [ME *trusse*, bundle < OFr. *trousse* < *torser, trousser*, to truss, poss. < VLat. **torsāre* < **torsus*, var. of Lat. *tortus*, p. part. of *torquēre*, to twist.]

truss bridge *n.* A bridge supported by trusses.

trust (trŭst) *n.* **1.** Firm reliance on the integrity, ability, or character of a person or thing. **2.** Custody; care. See Syns at **care. 3.** Something committed into the care of another; a charge. **4a.** The condition and resulting obligation of having confidence placed in one: *a public trust.* **b.** One in which confidence is placed. **5.** Reliance on something in the future; hope. **6.** Reliance on the intention and ability of a purchaser to pay in the future; credit. **7.** *Law* **a.** A legal title to property held by one party for the benefit of another. **b.** The confidence reposed in a trustee when giving the trustee legal title to property to administer for another, together with the trustee's obligation regarding that property and the beneficiary. **c.** The property so held. **8.** A combination of firms or corporations for the purpose of reducing competition and controlling prices throughout a business or an industry. ❖ *v.* **trust•ed, trust•ing, trusts** —*intr.* **1.** To have or place reliance; depend: *Trust to destiny.* **2.** To be confident; hope. **3.** To sell on credit. —*tr.* **1.** To have or place confidence in; depend on. **2.** To expect with assurance; assume. **3.** To believe. **4.** To place in the care of another; entrust. **5.** To grant discretion to confidently. **6.** To extend credit to. ***—idiom:* in trust** In the possession or care of a trustee. [ME *truste*, perh. < ON *traust*, confidence. See **deru-** in App.] **—trust′er** *n.*

trust•bust•er (trŭst′bŭs′tər) *n.* One that seeks to prosecute or dissolve business trusts. **—trust′bust′ing** *adj. & n.*

trust company *n.* A commercial bank or other corporation that manages trusts.

trus•tee (trŭ-stē′) *n.* **1.** *Law* One, such as a bank, that holds legal title to property to administer it for a beneficiary. **2.** A member of a board elected or appointed to direct the funds and policy of an institution. **3.** A country responsible for supervising a trust territory. See Usage Note at **–ee[1]**. ❖ *v.* **-teed, -tee•ing, -tees** —*tr.* To place (property) in the care of a trustee. —*intr.* To function or serve as a trustee.

trus•tee•ship (trŭ-stē′shĭp′) *n.* **1.** The position or function of a trustee. **2a.** Administration of a territory by a country or countries so commissioned by the United Nations. **b.** See **trust territory.**

trust•ful (trŭst′fəl) *adj.* Inclined to believe or confide readily; full of trust. **—trust′ful•ly** *adv.* **—trust′ful•ness** *n.*

trust fund *n.* Property, esp. money and securities, held or settled in trust.

trust territory *n.* A colony or territory placed under the administration of one or more countries by the United Nations.

trust•wor•thy (trŭst′wûr′*th*ē) *adj.* **-thi•er, -thi•est** Warranting trust; reliable. **—trust′wor′thi•ness** *n.*

trust•y (trŭs′tē) *adj.* **-i•er, -i•est** Meriting trust; trustworthy. ❖ *n., pl.* **-ies 1.** A convict regarded as worthy of trust and therefore granted special privileges. **2.** A trusted person. **—trust′i•ly** *adv.* **—trust′i•ness** *n.*

truth (tro͞oth) *n., pl.* **truths** (tro͞o*th*z, tro͞oths) **1.** Conformity to fact or actuality. **2.** A statement proven to be or accepted as true. **3.** Sincerity; integrity. **4.** Fidelity to an original or standard. **5a.** Reality; actuality. **b.** That which is considered to be the supreme reality and to have the ultimate meaning and value of existence. [ME *trewthe*, loyalty < OE *trēowth*. See **deru-** in App.]

Truth, Sojourner 1797?–1883. Amer. abolitionist and feminist who escaped from slavery in 1827.

truth•ful (tro͞oth′fəl) *adj.* **1.** Consistently telling the truth; honest. **2.** Corresponding to reality; true. **—truth′ful•ly** *adv.* **—truth′ful•ness** *n.*

truth serum *n.* Any of various hypnotic or anesthetic drugs, such as scopolamine or thiopental sodium, used to induce a subject under questioning to talk without inhibition.

truth table *n. Logic* A table listing the truth-values of a proposition that result from all the possible combinations of the truth-values of its components.

truth-val•ue (tro͞oth′văl′yo͞o) *n. Logic* The truth or falsity of a proposition.

try (trī) *v.* **tried** (trīd), **try•ing, tries** (trīz) —*tr.* **1.** To make an effort to do or accomplish (something); attempt. **2.** To taste, sample, or otherwise test in order to determine strength, effect, worth, or desirability. **3.** *Law* **a.** To examine or hear (evidence or a case) by judicial process. **b.** To put (an accused person) on trial. **4.** To subject to great strain or hardship; tax. **5.** To melt (lard, for example) to separate out impurities; render. **6.** To smooth, fit, or align accurately. —*intr.* To make an effort; strive. ❖ *n., pl.* **tries** (trīz) **1.** An attempt; an effort. **2.** *Sports* In Rugby, an act of advancing the ball past the opponent's goal line and grounding it there for a score of three points. ***—phrasal verbs:* try on 1.** To don (a garment) to test its fit. **2.** To test or use experimentally.

Harry S. Truman
detail from a 1948 portrait
by Greta Kempton
(1903–91)

truss bridge

Sojourner Truth
photographed c. 1864

ă	pat	oi	boy
ā	pay	ou	out
âr	care	o͝o	took
ä	father	o͞o	boot
ĕ	pet	ŭ	cut
ē	be	ûr	urge
ĭ	pit	th	thin
ī	pie	*th*	this
îr	pier	hw	which
ŏ	pot	zh	vision
ō	toe	ə	about, item
ô	paw		

Stress marks:
′ (primary);
′ (secondary), as in
lexicon (lĕk′sĭ-kŏn′)

try out 1. To undergo a competitive qualifying test, as for a job or an athletic team. **2.** To test or use experimentally. —*idiom:* **try (one's) hand** To attempt to do something for the first time. [ME *trien* < OFr. *trier*, to pick out < VLat. **triāre*.]

try·ing (trī′ĭng) *adj.* Causing strain, hardship, or distress.

try·out (trī′out′) *n.* **1.** A test to ascertain the qualifications of applicants, as for an athletic team. **2.** An experimental performance of a play before its official opening.

try·pan·o·some (trĭ-păn′ə-sōm′) *n.* Any of various parasitic flagellate protozoans of the genus *Trypanosoma*, transmitted to vertebrates by certain insects and often causing diseases such as sleeping sickness and nagana. [< NLat. *Trypanosōma*, genus name : Gk. *trūpanon*, auger (< *trūpān*, to bore < *trūpē*, hole; see **tera-**[1] in App.) + Gk. *sōma*, body; see —SOME[3].]

try·pan·o·so·mi·a·sis (trĭ-păn′ə-sō-mī′ə-sĭs) *n., pl.* **-ses** (-sēz′) A disease or infection caused by a trypanosome.

tryp·sin (trĭp′sĭn) *n.* A pancreatic enzyme that catalyzes the hydrolysis of proteins to form smaller polypeptide units. [Perh. Gk. *trīpsis*, a rubbing (< its having been first obtained by rubbing a pancreas with glycerin) < *trībein*, to rub. See **tera-**[1] in App. + —IN.] —**tryp′tic** (-tĭk) *adj.*

tryp·sin·o·gen (trĭp-sĭn′ə-jən) *n.* The inactive precursor of trypsin, produced by the pancreas and converted to trypsin in the small intestine by enterokinase.

tryp·ta·mine (trĭp′tə-mēn′) *n.* A crystalline substance, $C_{10}H_{12}N_2$, formed from tryptophan that is an intermediate in various metabolic processes. [TRYPT(OPHAN) + AMINE.]

tryp·to·phan (trĭp′tə-făn′) also **tryp·to·phane** (-fān′) *n.* An essential amino acid, $C_{11}H_{12}N_2O_2$, formed from proteins during digestion by the action of proteolytic enzymes. [*trypt(ic)*, of trypsin (formed on the model of *pepsin, peptic*); see TRYPSIN + —PHAN(E).]

try·sail (trī′səl, -sāl′) *n.* A small fore-and-aft sail hoisted abaft the foremast and mainmast in a storm to keep a ship's bow to the wind. [< TRY, a lying to (obsolete).]

try square *n.* A carpenter's measuring tool consisting of a ruled metal straightedge at right angles to a straight piece.

tryst (trĭst) *n.* **1.** An agreement, as between lovers, to meet at a certain time and place. **2.** A meeting or meeting place that has been agreed on. See Syns at **engagement**. ❖ *intr.v.* **tryst·ed, tryst·ing, trysts** To keep a tryst. [ME *trist* < OFr. *triste*, a waiting place (in hunting). See **deru-** in App.] —**tryst′er** *n.*

TS *abbr.* tensile strength

tsa·de (tsä′də, -dē) *n.* Variant of **sadhe.**

Tsa·na (tsä′nə, -nä), Lake See Lake **Tana.**

tsar (zär, tsär) *n.* Variant of **czar** 1. See Usage Note at **czar.**

tsats·ke (tsäts′kə) *n.* Variant of **chachka.**

tset·se disease (tsĕ′tsē, tsĕ′-) *n.* See **nagana.**

tsetse fly *n.* Any of several two-winged bloodsucking African flies of the genus *Glossina,* often carrying and transmitting pathogenic trypanosomes to humans and livestock. [Afr. < Sotho (Tswana) *tsêtsê.*]

TSgt *abbr.* technical sergeant

TSH *abbr.* thyroid-stimulating hormone

Tshi·lu·ba (chĭ-lōō′bə) *n.* See **Luba** 2.

T-shirt also **tee shirt** (tē′shûrt′) *n.* **1.** A short-sleeved collarless undershirt. **2.** An outer shirt of a design similar to the T-shirt. [Perh. < its being shaped like a T when spread out.]

tsim·mes or **tzim·mes** (tsĭm′ĭs) *n.* **1.** A stew of vegetables or fruits cooked slowly over very low heat. **2.** *Informal* A state of confusion. [Yiddish *tsimes* : MHGer. *ze, zuo,* to, for (< OHGer.; see **de-** in App.) + MHGer. *imbiz,* light meal (< OHGer. < *enbizzan,* to eat : *in,* in; see **en** in App. + *bīzan, bizzan,* to bite; see **bheid-** in App.).]

Tsi·mshi·an (chĭm′shē-ən, tsĭm′-) *n., pl.* **Tsimshian** or **-ans 1.** A member of a Native American people inhabiting a coastal area of western British Columbia and extreme southeast Alaska. **2.** The family of languages spoken by the Tsimshian and related peoples.

Tsi·nan (jē′nän′) See **Jinan.**

Tsing·hai (tsĭng′hī′) See **Qinghai.**

Tsing·tao (tsĭng′dou′) See **Qingdao.**

Tsin·kiang (tsĭn′kyäng′, chĭn′jyäng′) See **Quanzhou.**

Tsi·tsi·har (tsē′tsē′här′) See **Qiqihar.**

tsk (a *t*-like sound made by suction rather than plosion; *conventional spelling pronunciation;* tĭsk) *interj.* Used to express disappointment or sympathy. ❖ *n.* A sucking noise made by suddenly releasing the tongue from the hard palate, used to express disappointment or sympathy. —**tsk** *v.*

tsp. *abbr.* **1.** teaspoon **2.** teaspoonful

T-square (tē′skwâr′) *n.* A rule having a short, sometimes sliding perpendicular crosspiece at one end, used by drafters for establishing and drawing parallel lines.

TSR (tē′ĕs-är′) *n.* In systems without multitasking capabilities, a

program, such as a spell checker, that resides in memory so it may be quickly recalled while another program runs. [*t(erminate and) s(tay) r(esident).*]

TSS *abbr.* toxic shock syndrome

Tsu·ga·ru Strait (tsōō-gä′rōō) A channel between Honshu and Hokkaido in N Japan.

tsu·na·mi (tsōō-nä′mē) *n., pl.* **-mis** A very large ocean wave caused by an underwater earthquake or volcanic eruption. [J. : *tsu,* port + *nami,* wave.] —**tsu·na′mic** *adj.*

tsu·ris also **tzu·ris** (tsōōr′ĭs, tsûr′-) *n. Informal* Trouble; aggravation. [Yiddish *tsores,* pl. of *tsure* < Heb. *ṣārâ* < *ṣārar,* to become narrow.]

Tsu·shi·ma (tsōō-shē′mə, tsōō′shē-mä′) Two islands of SW Japan separated from Kyushu by **Tsushima Strait.**

tsu·tsu·ga·mu·shi disease (tsōō′tsōō-gə-mōō′shē) *n.* See **scrub typhus.** [J. *tsutsugamushi,* typhus mite : *tsutsuga,* illness + *mushi,* tick.]

Tsve·ta·e·va (tsvyĭ-tä′yə-və), Marina Ivanovna 1892–1941. Russian poet whose works include the collection *Evening Album* (1910).

Tswa·na (tswä′nə, swä′-) *n., pl.* **Tswana** or **-nas 1.** A member of a Bantu people inhabiting Botswana and western South Africa. **2.** The Sotho language of the Tswana.

Tt *abbr. Bible* Titus

TT *abbr.* **1.** or **TTY** teletypewriter **2.** trust territory

Tu *abbr.* Tuesday

TU *abbr.* **1.** trade union **2.** transmission unit

Tu·a·mo·tu Archipelago (tōō′ä-ə-mō′tōō) An island group of French Polynesia in the S Pacific E of Tahiti.

Tuan (twän) *n.* Used in Malay as a form of respectful address for a man. [Malay, perh. < *tua,* old.]

Tua·reg (twä′rĕg′) *n., pl.* **Tuareg** or **-regs** A member of a Muslim Berber-speaking people inhabiting the western and central Sahara and western Sahel. [Ar. *tawāriq.*]

tu·a·ta·ra (tōō′ə-tär′ə) *n., pl.* **tuatara** or **-ras** Either of two lizardlike reptiles (*Sphenodon punctatus* or *S. guntheri*) of New Zealand, that are the only extant members of the Rhynchocephalia, an order that flourished during the Mesozoic Era. [Maori *tuatara* : *tua,* back + *tara,* spine.]

tub (tŭb) *n.* **1a.** An open flatbottom vessel, usu. round and typically wider than it is deep, used for washing, packing, or storing. **b.** The amount that such a vessel can hold. **c.** The contents of such a vessel. **2a.** A bathtub. **b.** *Informal* A bath taken in a bathtub. **3.** *Informal* A wide, clumsy, slow-moving boat. **4a.** A bucket used for conveying ore or coal up a mine shaft. **b.** A coal car used in a mine. ❖ *v.* **tubbed, tub·bing, tubs** —*tr.* **1.** To pack or store in a tub. **2.** To wash or bathe in a tub. —*intr.* To take a bath. [ME < MDu. or MLGer. *tubbe.*] —**tub′ba·ble** *adj.* —**tub′ber** *n.*

tu·ba (tōō′bə, tyōō′-) *n.* A large valved brass wind instrument with a bass pitch. [Ital. < Lat., trumpet; akin to *tubus,* tube.] —**tu′ba·ist, tu′bist** *n.*

tu·bal (tōō′bəl, tyōō′-) *adj.* Of, relating to, or occurring in a tube, such as the fallopian tube or the eustachian tube.

tubal ligation *n.* A method of sterilization in which the fallopian tubes are surgically tied.

tu·bate (tōō′bāt′, tyōō′-) *adj.* Forming or having a tube.

tub·by (tŭb′ē) *adj.* **-bi·er, -bi·est 1.** Short and fat. **2.** Having a dull sound; lacking resonance. —**tub′bi·ness** *n.*

tube (tōōb, tyōōb) *n.* **1a.** A hollow cylinder, esp. one that conveys a fluid or functions as a passage. **b.** An organic structure having the shape or function of a tube; a duct: *a bronchial tube.* **2.** A small flexible cylindrical container sealed at one end and having a screw cap at the other, for pigments, toothpaste, or other pastelike substances. **3.** *Music* The cylindrical part of a wind instrument. **4.** *Electronics* **a.** An electron tube. **b.** A vacuum tube. **5.** *Botany* The lower cylindrical part of a gamopetalous corolla or a gamosepalous calyx. **6.** *Chiefly British* An underground railroad system; a subway. **7.** A tunnel. **8a.** An inner tube. **b.** An inflatable tube or cushion used for recreational riding. **9.** *Informal* **a.** Television. **b.** A television set. **10. tubes** *Informal* The fallopian tubes. ❖ *v.* **tubed, tub·ing, tubes** —*tr.* **1.** To provide with a tube; insert a tube in. **2.** To place in or enclose in a tube. —*intr.* To ride or float on an inflated tube for recreation. —*idiom:* **down the tube** (or **tubes**) *Slang* Into a state of failure or ruin. [Fr. < OFr. < Lat. *tubus.*]

tube foot *n.* One of the numerous external fluid-filled muscular tubes of echinoderms, such as the starfish or sea urchin, serving as organs of locomotion, food handling, and respiration.

tube·less tire (tōōb′lĭs, tyōōb′-) *n.* A pneumatic vehicular tire in which the air is held in the assembly of casing and rim without an inner tube.

tube pan *n.* A round pan with a hollow projection in the middle, used for baking or molding foods in the shape of a ring.

tu·ber (tōō′bər, tyōō′-) *n.* **1.** A swollen, fleshy, usu. underground stem of a plant, such as the potato, bearing buds from which new plant shoots arise. **2.** A rounded projection or swelling; a tubercle. [Lat. *tūber,* lump.]

tu·ber·cle (tōō′bər-kəl, tyōō′-) *n.* **1.** A small rounded projecting part or outgrowth, such as a wartlike excrescence on the roots of some plants or a knoblike process on a bone. **2.** *Pathology* A nodule or swelling, esp. a mass of lymphocytes and epithelioid cells

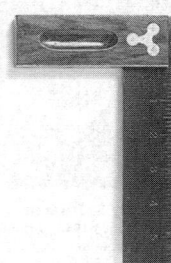

try square

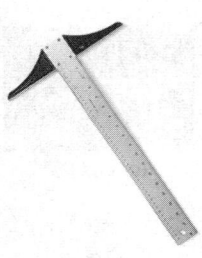

T-square

tuba

forming the characteristic lesion of tuberculosis. [Lat. *tūberculum*, dim. of *tūber*, lump. See TUBER.]

tubercle bacillus *n.* A rod-shaped aerobic bacterium *(Mycobacterium tuberculosis)* that causes tuberculosis.

tu•ber•cu•lar (to͞o-bûr′kyə-lər, tyo͞o-) *adj.* **1.** Of, relating to, or covered with tubercles; tuberculate. **2.** Of, relating to, or affected with tuberculosis. ❖ *n.* A person having tuberculosis.

tu•ber•cu•late (to͞o-bûr′kyə-lĭt, tyo͞o-) also **tu•ber•cu•lat•ed** (-lā′tĭd) *adj.* **1.** Having or affected with tubercles. **2.** Tubercular. —**tu•ber′cu•late•ly** *adv.* —**tu•ber′cu•la′tion** *n.*

tu•ber•cu•lin (to͞o-bûr′kyə-lĭn, tyo͞o-) *n.* A sterile liquid containing proteins extracted from cultures of tubercle bacilli and used in tests for tuberculosis. [Lat. *tūberculum*, tubercle; see TUBERCLE + –IN.]

tu•ber•cu•loid (to͞o-bûr′kyə-loid′, tyo͞o-) *adj.* **1.** Resembling tuberculosis. **2.** Resembling a tubercle.

tu•ber•cu•lo•sis (to͞o-bûr′kyə-lō′sĭs, tyo͞o-) *n.* **1.** An infectious disease of humans and animals caused by the tubercle bacillus and characterized by the formation of tubercles on the lungs and other tissues of the body, often developing long after the initial infection. **2.** Tuberculosis of the lungs, marked by fever and the coughing up of mucus and sputum. [Lat. *tūberculum*, tubercle; see TUBERCLE + –OSIS.]

tu•ber•cu•lous (to͞o-bûr′kyə-ləs, tyo͞o-) *adj.* **1.** Of, relating to, or having tuberculosis. **2.** Of, affected with, or caused by tubercles. —**tu•ber′cu•lous•ly** *adv.*

tube•rose[1] (to͞ob′rōz′, tyo͞ob′-, to͞o′bə-) *n.* A tuberous perennial Mexican herb *(Polianthes tuberosa)* having grasslike leaves and cultivated for its highly fragrant white flowers. [< NLat. *tūberōsa*, species name < fem. of Lat. *tūberōsus*, full of lumps < *tūber*, lump. See TUBER.]

tu•ber•ose[2] (to͞o′bə-rōs′, tyo͞o′-) *adj.* Variant of **tuberous.**

tu•ber•os•i•ty (to͞o′bə-rŏs′ĭ-tē, tyo͞o′-) *n., pl.* **-ties 1.** The quality or condition of being tuberous. **2.** A projection or protuberance, esp. one at the end of a bone for the attachment of a muscle or tendon.

tu•ber•ous (to͞o′bər-əs, tyo͞o′-) also **tu•ber•ose** (-bə-rōs′) *adj.* **1.** Producing or bearing tubers. **2.** Being or resembling a tuber: *a tuberous root.*

tube sock *n.* A sock that lacks a shaped heel.

tu•bi•fex (to͞o′bə-fĕks′, tyo͞o′-) *n., pl.* **tubifex** or **-fex•es** Any of various small slender reddish freshwater worms of the genus *Tubifex.* [NLat. *Tubifex*, genus name : Lat. *tubus*, tube + Lat. *-fex*, maker; see **dhē-** in App.]

tub•ing (to͞o′bĭng, tyo͞o′-) *n.* **1a.** Tubes considered as a group. **b.** A system of tubes. **c.** A piece or length of tube. **2.** Tubular fabric, such as that used for making pillowcases.

Tü•bing•en (to͞o′bĭng-ən, tü′-) A city of SW Germany on the Neckar R. S of Stuttgart. Pop. 75,333.

Tub•man (tŭb′mən), **Harriet** 1820?–1913. Amer. abolitionist who helped organize the Underground Railroad after 1849.

Tubman, William Vacanarat Shadrach 1895–1971. Liberian politician who served as president (1944–71).

tu•bo•cu•ra•rine (to͞o′bō-ko͞o-rä′rĭn, -rēn′, -kyo͞o-, tyo͞o′-) *n.* **1.** An alkaloid that is the active component of curare. **2.** The chloride of this alkaloid, $C_{38}H_{44}Cl_2N_2O_6$, used as a muscle relaxant. [Lat. *tubus*, tube (< the practice of shipping it in bamboo tubes) + *curarine* (CURARE + –INE[2]).]

tu•bo•plas•ty (to͞o′bō-plăs′tē, tyo͞o′-) *n., pl.* **-ties** Surgical repair of one or both fallopian tubes.

tub-thump (tŭb′thŭmp′) *intr.v.* **-thumped, -thump•ing, -thumps** *Slang* To argue for or promote something vigorously. —**tub′-thump′er** *n.*

tu•bu•lar (to͞o′byə-lər, tyo͞o′-) *adj.* **1.** Of or relating to a tube. **2.** Constituting or consisting of tubes or a tube. **3.** Shaped like a tube. —**tu′bu•lar′i•ty** (-lăr′ĭ-tē) *n.* —**tu′bu•lar•ly** *adv.*

tubular bell *n.* Any of a set of tuned metal pipes used as an orchestral instrument. Often used in the plural.

tu•bu•late (to͞o′byə-lĭt, -lāt′, tyo͞o′-) also **tu•bu•lat•ed** (-lā′tĭd) *adj.* **1.** Formed into or resembling a tube; tubular. **2.** Having a tube. [Lat. *tubulātus* < *tubulus*, dim. of *tubus*, tube.] —**tu′bu•la′tion** *n.* —**tu′bu•la′tor** *n.*

tu•bule (to͞o′byo͞ol, tyo͞o′-) *n.* A very small tube or tubular structure. [Lat. *tubulus*, dim. of *tubus*, tube.]

tu•bu•li•flo•rous (to͞o′byə-lə-flôr′əs, -flōr′-, tyo͞o′-) *adj.* Having flowers or florets with tubular corollas.

tu•bu•lin (to͞o′byə-lĭn, tyo͞o′-) *n.* A globular protein that is the basic structural constituent of microtubules.

tu•bu•lous (to͞o′byə-ləs, tyo͞o′-) *adj.* **1.** Shaped like a tube; tubular. **2a.** Composed of tubes. **b.** Having tubular parts.

Tu•ca•na (to͞o-kā′nə, -kä′-, tyo͞o-) *n.* A polar constellation in the Southern Hemisphere. [Tupi *tucana*, toucan.]

Tuch•man (tŭk′mən), **Barbara Wertheim** 1912–89. Amer. historian whose works include *The Guns of August* (1962).

tu•chun (to͞o′cho͞on′, do͞o′jün′) *n., pl.* **-chuns** or **tuchun** A Chinese provincial military governor. [Chin. (Mandarin) *dūjūn* : *dū*, to supervise + *jūn*, army.]

tuck[1] (tŭk) *v.* **tucked, tuck•ing, tucks** —*tr.* **1.** To make one or more folds in. **2.** To gather up and fold, thrust, or turn in so as to secure or confine. **3a.** To put in a snug spot. **b.** To put in an out-of-the-way, snug place. **c.** To store in a safe spot; save. **4a.** To draw in; contract. **b.** *Sports* To bring (a body part) into a tuck position. —*intr.* To make tucks. ❖ *n.* **1.** The act of tucking. **2.** A flattened pleat or fold, esp. a very narrow one stitched in place. **3.** *Nautical* The part of a ship's hull under the stern where the ends of the bottom planks come together. **4.** *Sports* **a.** A bodily position used in some sports, such as diving, in which the knees are bent and the thighs are drawn close to the chest, with the hands often clasped around the shins. **b.** A position in skiing in which the skier squats while holding the poles parallel to the ground and under the arms. **5.** *Chiefly British* Food, esp. sweets and pastry. ***—phrasal verbs:* tuck away** (or **into**) *Informal* To consume (food) heartily. **tuck in** To make secure in bed for sleep, esp. by tucking bedclothes into the bed. [ME *tukken*, poss. < MLGer. or MDu. *tocken, tucken.*]

tuck[2] (tŭk) *n.* A beat or tap, esp. on a drum. [< ME *tukken*, to beat a drum < ONFr. *toquer*, to strike < VLat. **toccāre.*]

tuck[3] (tŭk) *n. Archaic* A slender sword; a rapier. [Perh. < Fr. dialectal *étoc* < OFr. *estoc*, of Gmc. orig.]

tuck[4] (tŭk) *n.* Energy; vigor. [?]

tuck•a•hoe (tŭk′ə-hō′) *n.* Any of various plants or plant parts used by certain Native American peoples as food, esp. the edible root of certain arums or the sclerotium of certain fungi. [Of Virginia Algonquian orig.]

tuck•er[1] (tŭk′ər) *n.* **1.** One that tucks, esp. an attachment on a sewing machine for making tucks. **2.** A piece of linen or lace formerly worn by women around the neck and shoulders.

tuck•er[2] (tŭk′ər) *tr.v.* **-ered, -er•ing, -ers** *Informal* To make weary; exhaust. [Perh. < TUCK[1].]

tuck•et (tŭk′ĭt) *n.* A trumpet fanfare. [Prob. < obsolete *tuk* < ME < *tukken*, to beat a drum. See TUCK[2].]

tuck-point (tŭk′point′) *tr.v.* **-point•ed, -point•ing, -points** To point (grooved mortar joints) with a thin ridge of fine lime mortar or putty.

tuck-shop (tŭk′shŏp′) *n. Chiefly British* A shop where candy and other sweets are sold; a confectionery.

Tuc•son (to͞o′sŏn′) A city of SE AZ SSE of Phoenix; first settled permanently in 1775. Pop. 486,699.

–tude *suff.* Condition, state, or quality: *exactitude.* [Fr. < OFr. < Lat. *-tūdō, -tūdin-.*]

′tude (to͞od, tyo͞od) *n. Slang* An arrogant or hostile attitude or disposition. [Short for ATTITUDE.]

Tudj•man (to͞oj′mən), **Franjo** 1922–99. Croatian general who was president of Croatia (1990–99).

Tu•dor[1] (to͞o′dər, tyo͞o′-) English ruling dynasty (1485–1603).

Tu•dor[2] (to͞o′dər, tyo͞o′-) *adj.* **1.** Of or relating to the royal house of Tudor. **2.** Of, relating to, or characteristic of the Tudor period or of an architectural style derived from it, having exposed beams as a typical feature.

Tudor, Antony 1909–87. British-born Amer. dancer and choreographer whose ballets include *Undertow* (1945).

Tues•day (to͞oz′dē, -dā′, tyo͞oz′-) *n.* The third day of the week. [ME *Tuesdai* < OE *Tīwesdæg*, Tiu's day : *Tīwes*, genitive of *Tīw*, Tiu; see TIU + *dæg*, day (transl. of Lat. *diēs Mārtis*, Mars' day).] —**Tues′days** *adv.*

tu•fa (to͞o′fə, tyo͞o′-) *n.* **1.** The calcareous and siliceous rock deposits of springs, lakes, or ground water. **2.** See **tuff.** [Obsolete Ital. *tufa, tufo* < Lat. *tōfus.*] —**tu•fa′ceous** (-fā′shəs) *adj.*

tuff (tŭf) *n.* A rock composed of compacted volcanic ash varying in size from fine sand to coarse gravel. [Fr. *tuf* < OFr. < OItal. *tufo*, tufa. See TUFA.] —**tuff•a′ceous** (tŭ-fā′shəs) *adj.*

tuf•fet (tŭf′ĭt) *n.* **1.** A clump or tuft of grass. **2.** A low seat, such as a stool. [Alteration of TUFT.]

tuft (tŭft) *n.* **1.** A short cluster of elongated strands, as of yarn, hair, or grass, attached at the base or growing close together. **2.** A dense clump, esp. of trees or bushes. ❖ *v.* **tuft•ed, tuft•ing, tufts** —*tr.* **1.** To furnish or ornament with tufts or a tuft. **2.** To pass threads through the layers of (a quilt, a mattress, or upholstery), securing the thread ends with a knot or button. —*intr.* **1.** To separate or form into tufts. **2.** To grow in a tuft. [ME, prob. alteration of OFr. *tofe* < LLat. *tufa*, helmet crest, or of Gmc. orig.] —**tuft′er** *n.* —**tuft′y** *adj.*

tuft•ed duck (tŭf′tĭd) *n.* An Old World duck *(Aythya fuligula)* having a short plump body and a crest on its head.

tufted titmouse *n.* A bluish-gray titmouse *(Parus bicolor)* of the eastern and southern United States, having brown flanks and a crest on its head.

tug (tŭg) *v.* **tugged, tug•ging, tugs** —*tr.* **1.** To pull at vigorously or repeatedly. **2.** To move by pulling with great effort or exertion; drag. **3.** To tow by tugboat. —*intr.* **1.** To pull hard. See Syns at **pull. 2.** To toil or struggle; strain. **3.** To vie; contend. ❖ *n.* **1.** A strong pull or pulling force. **2.** A contest; a struggle. **3a.** A tugboat. **b.** A land, air, or space vehicle that moves or tows other vehicles. **4.** A rope, chain, or strap used in hauling, esp. a harness trace. [ME *tuggen* < OE *tēon.* See **deuk-** in App.] —**tug′ger** *n.*

tug•boat (tŭg′bōt′) *n.* A small powerful boat designed for towing or pushing larger vessels.

tug of war *n., pl.* **tugs of war 1.** *Games* A contest in which two teams tug on opposite ends of a rope, each trying to pull the other across a dividing line. **2.** A struggle for supremacy.

tu•grik (to͞o′grĭk) *n., pl.* **tugrik** See table at **currency.** [Mongolian *dughurik*, wheel, tugrik.]

tuberose[1]
Polianthes tuberosa

Harriet Tubman

tugboat
towing a sand barge

ă	pat	oi	boy
ā	pay	ou	out
âr	care	o͝o	took
ä	father	o͞o	boot
ĕ	pet	ŭ	cut
ē	be	ûr	urge
ĭ	pit	th	thin
ī	pie	*th*	this
îr	pier	hw	which
ŏ	pot	zh	vision
ō	toe	ə	about, item
ô	paw		

Stress marks:
′ (primary);
′ (secondary), as in
lexicon (lĕk′sĭ-kŏn′)

tu·i (tōō′ē) *n.*, *pl.* **-is** A honeyeater (*Prosthemadera novaesee-landiae*) of New Zealand having dark plumage with white feathers on the throat. [Maori *tūī*.]

tuille (twēl) *n.* A steel plate used in medieval armor for protecting the thigh. [ME *toile* < OFr. *teuille, tuille* < Lat. *tēgula*, tile. See **(s)teg-** in App.]

tu·i·tion (tōō-ĭsh′ən, tyōō-) *n.* **1.** A fee for instruction, esp. at a formal institution of learning. **2.** Instruction; teaching. **3.** *Archaic* Guardianship. [ME *tuicion*, protection < OFr. *tuition* < Lat. *tuitiō, tuitiōn-* < *tuitus*, p. part. of *tuērī*, to protect.] **—tu·i′tion·al, tu·i′tion·ar′y** (-ĭsh′ə-nĕr′ē) *adj.*

Tu·la (tōō′lə) A city of W Russia S of Moscow; first mentioned in 1146. Pop. 533,640.

tu·la·re·mi·a (tōō′lə-rē′mē-ə, tyōō′-) *n.* An infectious disease of rodents and humans caused by the bacterium *Francisella tularensis* that in humans is characterized by intermittent fever and swelling of the lymph nodes. [NLat., after *Tulare*, a county of south-central California.] **—tu′la·re′mic** *adj.*

tu·le (tōō′lē) *n.* **1.** Any of several bulrushes of the genus *Scirpus*, growing in marshy lowlands of the southwest United States. **2. tu·les** (tōō′lēz) *Northern California* Marshy or swampy land. [Am.Sp. < Nahuatl *tollin*, reed.]

tu·lip (tōō′lĭp, tyōō′-) *n.* **1.** Any of several bulbous plants of the genus *Tulipa*, native chiefly to Asia and having showy, variously colored flowers. **2.** The flower of any of these plants. [Fr. *tulipe*, alteration of *tulipan* < Ottoman Turk. *tülbend*, muslin, gauze, turban < Pers. *dulband*, turban.]

tulip tree *n.* A tall deciduous eastern North American tree (*Liriodendron tulipifera*) having large, tuliplike, green and orange flowers, aromatic twigs, and yellowish wood that is easily worked.

tu·lip·wood (tōō′lĭp-wŏŏd′, tyōō′-) *n.* **1.** The wood of the tulip tree. **2.** The irregularly striped ornamental wood of any of several related or similar trees.

tulle (tōōl) *n.* A fine, often starched net used esp. for veils, tutus, or gowns. [Fr., after *Tulle*, a city of south-central France.]

tul·li·bee (tŭl′ə-bē′) *n.* A large thick-backed cisco (*Coregonus artedi* or *Leucichthys artedi*) of the Great Lakes. [Canadian Fr. *toulibi* < Ojibwa dialectal **oto·lipi·*.]

Tul·sa (tŭl′sə) A city of NE OK on the Arkansas R. NE of Oklahoma City. Pop. 393,049.

tum·ble (tŭm′bəl) *v.* **-bled, -bling, -bles** *—intr.* **1.** To perform acrobatic feats such as somersaults, rolls, or twists. **2a.** To fall or roll end over end. **b.** To spill or roll out in confusion or disorder. **c.** To pitch headlong; fall. **d.** To proceed haphazardly. **3a.** To topple, as from power or a high position; fall. **b.** To collapse. **c.** To drop: *Prices tumbled.* **4.** To come upon accidentally; happen on. **5.** *Slang* To come to a sudden understanding; catch on. *—tr.* **1.** To cause to fall; bring down. **2.** To put, spill, or toss haphazardly. **3.** To toss or whirl in a drum, tumbler, or tumbling box. ❖ *n.* **1.** An act of tumbling; a fall. **2.** Confusion; disorder. [ME *tumblen*, freq. of *tumben*, to dance about < OE *tumbian*.]

tum·ble·bug (tŭm′bəl-bŭg′) *n.* Any of various dung beetles, esp. of the genera *Canthon* and *Phanaeus*, that roll up balls of fresh dung, inside which the female deposits her eggs.

tum·ble·down (tŭm′bəl-doun′) *adj.* Being in such bad repair as to seem in danger of collapsing; very dilapidated.

tum·ble·home (tŭm′bəl-hōm′) *n.* The inward curve of a ship's topsides. [< TUMBLE, to slope inward (obsolete).]

tum·bler (tŭm′blər) *n.* **1.** One that tumbles, esp. an acrobat or gymnast. **2a.** A drinking glass, originally with a rounded bottom. **b.** A flatbottom glass having no handle, foot, or stem. **c.** The contents of such a drinking glass. **3.** A toy made with a weighted rounded base so that it can rock over and then right itself. **4.** One of a breed of domestic pigeons characteristically tumbling or somersaulting in flight. **5.** A piece in a gunlock that forces the hammer forward by action of the mainspring. **6.** The part in a lock that releases the bolt when moved by a key. **7a.** The drum of a clothes dryer. **b.** A tumbling box. **8a.** A projecting piece on a revolving or rocking part in a mechanism that transmits motion to the part it engages. **b.** The rocking frame that moves a gear into place in a selective transmission. [Sense 2a < the fact that it would tumble if put down.]

tum·ble·set (tŭm′bəl-sĕt′) *n. Lower Southern US* See **somersault** 1. [Blend of TUMBLE and *somerset* (alteration of *somersaut*, var. of SOMERSAULT).]

REGIONAL NOTE In the Lower Southern word *tumbleset* for *somersault* *–set* at first glance seems not to have any relationship to *–sault* in *somersault*. However, *–set* is an old *l*-less variant of *–sault* (from Latin *saltus*, "a leap") that has been an alternative pronunciation throughout the word's history; hence, the variant *somerset*. *Somer–* is an alteration of Old French *sobre–*, from Latin *supra*, "over." In the word *tumbleset*, as in a folk etymology, *somer–*, part of a compound word that no longer bears any meaning for the speakers, has been replaced by *tumble*.

tum·ble·weed (tŭm′bəl-wēd′) *n.* Any of various densely branched annual plants, such as amaranth and Russian thistle, that break off from the roots at the end of the growing season and are rolled about by the wind.

tum·bling (tŭm′blĭng) *n.* Gymnastics, such as somersaults and rolls, performed without specialized apparatus.

tulip tree
Liriodendron tulipifera
a tulip tree flower

tumpline
woman picking tea leaves
in Kerala, India

tumbling box *n.* A revolving drum in which objects are dried, reduced in size, polished, or cleaned.

tum·brel or **tum·bril** (tŭm′brəl) *n.* **1.** A two-wheeled cart, esp. a farmer's cart that can be tilted to dump a load. **2.** A crude cart used to carry condemned prisoners to their place of execution, as during the French Revolution. [ME *tumberell* < OFr. *tomberel* < *tomber*, to let fall, perh. of Gmc. orig.]

tu·me·fa·cient (tōō′mə-fā′shənt, tyōō′-) *adj.* Producing or tending to produce swelling or tumefaction. [Lat. *tumefaciēns, tumefacient-*, pr. part. of *tumefacere*, to tumefy : *tumēre*, to swell + *facere*, to make; see **dhē-** in App.]

tu·me·fac·tion (tōō′mə-făk′shən, tyōō′-) *n.* **1a.** The act or process of puffing or swelling. **b.** A swollen condition. **2.** A puffy or swollen part. **—tu′me·fac′tive** (-tĭv) *adj.*

tu·me·fy (tōō′mə-fī′, tyōō′-) *intr & tr.v.* **-fied, -fy·ing, -fies** To swell or cause to swell. [Fr. *tuméfier* < Lat. *tumefacere*. See TUMEFACIENT.]

tu·mes·cence (tōō-mĕs′əns, tyōō-) *n.* **1a.** A swelling or enlarging. **b.** A swollen condition. **2.** A swollen part or organ.

tu·mes·cent (tōō-mĕs′ənt, tyōō-) *adj.* **1.** Somewhat tumid. **2.** Becoming swollen; swelling. [Lat. *tumēscēns, tumēscent-*, pr. part. of *tumēscere*, to begin to swell, inchoative of *tumēre*, to swell.]

tu·mid (tōō′mĭd, tyōō′-) *adj.* **1.** Swollen; distended. Used of a body part or organ. **2.** Of a bulging shape; protuberant. **3.** Overblown; bombastic. [Lat. *tumidus* < *tumēre*, to swell.] **—tu·mid′i·ty** *n.*

tumm·ler (tōōm′lər) *n.* **1.** One, such as a social director or entertainer, who encourages guest or audience participation. **2.** One who incites others to action. [Yiddish *tumler* < *tumlen*, to make a racket.]

tum·my (tŭm′ē) *n.*, *pl.* **-mies** *Informal* The human stomach or belly. [Baby-talk alteration of STOMACH.]

tummy tuck *n. Informal* Abdominoplasty.

tu·mor (tōō′mər, tyōō′-) *n.* **1.** An abnormal growth of tissue resulting from uncontrolled progressive multiplication of cells and serving no physiological function; a neoplasm. **2.** A swollen part; a swelling. [ME *tumour* < Lat. *tumor* < *tumēre*, to swell.] **—tu′mor·al, tu′mor·ous** *adj.*

tu·mor·i·gen·e·sis (tōō′mər-ə-jĕn′ĭ-sĭs, tyōō′-) *n.*, *pl.* **-ses** (-sēz′) Formation or production of tumors.

tu·mor·i·gen·ic (tōō′mər-ə-jĕn′ĭk, tyōō′-) *adj.* Capable of causing tumors. **—tu′mor·i·ge·nic′i·ty** (-jə-nĭs′ĭ-tē) *n.*

tumor necrosis factor *n.* A protein produced by macrophages in the presence of an endotoxin and shown experimentally to be capable of attacking and destroying cancerous tumors.

tump¹ (tŭmp) *v.* **tumped, tump·ing, tumps** *Chiefly Southern US —tr.* To overturn. Often used with *over*. *—intr.* To fall over. Often used with *over*. [Prob. akin to TUMBLE.]

tump² (tŭmp) *n.* **1.** A mound. **2.** A clump of trees, shrubs, or grass. [?]

tump·line (tŭmp′lĭn′) *n.* A strap slung across the forehead or the chest to support a load carried on the back. [*tump* (alteration of *mattump*, of Southern New England Algonquian orig.) + LINE¹.]

tu·mu·lar (tōō′myə-lər, tyōō′-) *adj.* Relating to or having the shape of a tumulus.

tu·mu·lose (tōō′myə-lōs′, tyōō′-) also **tu·mu·lous** (-ləs) *adj.* Having many mounds or small hills. [Lat. *tumulōsus* < *tumulus*. See TUMULUS.] **—tu′mu·los′i·ty** (-lŏs′ĭ-tē) *n.*

tu·mult (tōō′mŭlt′, tyōō′-) *n.* **1.** The din and commotion of a great crowd. **2a.** A disorderly commotion or disturbance. **b.** A tempestuous uprising; a riot. **3.** Agitation of the mind or emotions. [ME *tumulte* < Lat. *tumultus*.]

tu·mul·tu·ar·y (tōō-mŭl′chōō-ĕr′ē, tyōō′-) *adj.* Marked by haste, confusion, disorder, and irregularity. [Lat. *tumultuārius* < *tumultus*, commotion. See TUMULT.]

tu·mul·tu·ous (tōō-mŭl′chōō-əs, tyōō′-) *adj.* **1.** Characterized by tumult; noisy and disorderly: *tumultuous applause.* **2.** Tending to cause tumult. **3.** Confusedly or violently agitated. **—tu·mul′tu·ous·ly** *adv.* **—tu·mul′tu·ous·ness** *n.*

tu·mu·lus (tōō′myə-ləs, tyōō′-) *n.*, *pl.* **-li** (-lī′) An ancient grave mound; a barrow. [Lat.]

tun (tŭn) *n.* **1.** A large cask for liquids, esp. wine. **2.** A measure of liquid capacity, one equivalent to approx. 252 gallons (954 liters). [ME < OE *tunne*, poss. of Celt. orig.]

Tun. *abbr.* **1.** Tunisia **2.** Tunisian

tu·na¹ (tōō′nə, tyōō′-) *n.*, *pl.* **tuna** or **-nas 1a.** Any of various often large scombroid marine food and game fishes of the genus *Thunnus* and related genera, many of which, including *T. thynnus* and the albacore, are commercially important sources of canned fish. **b.** Any of several related fishes, such as the bonito. **2.** The edible flesh of tuna. [Am.Sp. < Sp. *atún* < Ar. *at-tūn*, the tuna < Lat. *thunnus*. See TUNNY.]

tu·na² (tōō′nə, tyōō′-) *n.* **1.** Any of several flat-jointed tropical American cacti of the genus *Opuntia*, esp. *O. tuna*, having yellow flowers and edible red fruit. **2.** The edible fruit of any of these cacti. [Am.Sp. < Taino.]

tun·a·ble also **tune·a·ble** (tōō′nə-bəl, tyōō′-) *adj.* **1.** That can be tuned: *a tunable wind instrument; a tunable radio.* **2.** *Archaic* Tuneful. **—tun′a·ble·ness** *n.* **—tun′a·bly** *adv.*

tuna fish *n.* See **tuna¹** 2.

tun·dra (tŭn′drə) *n.* A treeless area between the icecap and the tree line of Arctic regions, having a permanently frozen subsoil and supporting low-growing vegetation. [Russ. < Sami *tūndar*, flat-topped hill.]

tune (to͞on, tyo͞on) *n.* **1.** *Music* **a.** A melody, esp. a simple and easily remembered one. **b.** A song. **c.** Correct pitch. **d.** The state of being properly adjusted for pitch. **e.** Agreement in pitch. **f.** *Obsolete* A musical tone. **2a.** Concord or agreement; harmony. **b.** *Archaic* Frame of mind; disposition. **3.** *Electronics* Adjustment of a receiver or circuit for maximum response to a given signal or frequency. ❖ *v.* **tuned, tun•ing, tunes** —*tr.* **1a.** *Music* To put into proper pitch. **b.** *Archaic* To utter musically; sing. **2.** To adopt or adjust, esp. to bring into harmony. **3.** *Electronics* **a.** To adjust (a receiver) to a desired frequency. **b.** To adjust (a circuit) so as to make it resonant with a given input signal. **4.** To adjust (an engine, for example) for maximum usability or performance. —*intr.* To become attuned. ***—phrasal verbs:*** **tune in 1.** *Electronics* To adjust a receiver to receive signals at a particular frequency or a particular program. **2.** *Slang* To make or become aware or responsive. **tune out 1.** *Electronics* To adjust a receiver so as not to receive a particular signal. **2.** *Slang* **a.** To disassociate oneself from one's environment. **b.** To become unresponsive to; ignore. **tune up 1.** *Music* To adjust an instrument to a desired pitch or key. **2.** To adjust a machine so as to put it into proper condition. **3.** To prepare (oneself) for a specified activity. ***—idiom:*** **to the tune of** To the sum or extent of. [ME, var. of *tone*, tone. See TONE.]

tune•ful (to͞on′fəl, tyo͞on′-) *adj.* **1.** Full of tune; melodious. **2.** Producing musical sounds. **—tune′ful•ly** *adv.*

tune•less (to͞on′lĭs, tyo͞on′-) *adj.* **1.** Deficient in melody; not tuneful. **2.** Producing no music; silent. **—tune′less•ly** *adv.*

tun•er (to͞o′nər, tyo͞o′-) *n.* **1.** One that tunes: *a piano tuner.* **2.** A device for tuning, esp. an electronic circuit or device used to select signals at a specific radio frequency for amplification and conversion to sound.

tune•smith (to͞on′smĭth′, tyo͞on′-) *n.* One who composes melodies, esp. for popular songs.

tune-up (to͞on′ŭp′, tyo͞on′-) *n.* **1.** An adjustment, as of a motor, made to improve efficiency. **2.** A practice or preparatory session.

tung oil (tŭng) *n.* A yellow or brownish oil extracted from the seeds of the tung tree and used as a drying agent in varnishes and paints and for waterproofing.

tung•state (tŭng′stāt′) *n.* A salt of tungstic acid.

tung•sten (tŭng′stən) *n. Symbol* **W** A hard brittle corrosion-resistant metallic element extracted from wolframite, scheelite, and other minerals, having the highest melting point of any metal and used, along with its alloys, in high-temperature structural materials and in electrical elements, notably lamp filaments. Atomic number 74; atomic weight 183.84; melting point 3,410°C; boiling point 5,900°C; specific gravity 19.3 (20°C); valence 2, 3, 4, 5, 6. See table at **element.** [Swed. : *tung*, heavy (< ON *thungr*) + *sten*, stone (< ON *steinn*).] **—tung•sten′ic** (-stĕn′ĭk) *adj.*

tungsten carbide *n.* A very hard fine powder, WC, used in tools, dies, wear-resistant machine parts, and abrasives.

tungsten lamp *n.* An incandescent electric lamp with a tungsten filament.

tungsten steel *n.* A very hard heat-resistant steel containing tungsten.

tung•stic (tŭng′stĭk) *adj.* Of, relating to, or containing tungsten, esp. with valence 6. [TUNGST(EN) + -IC.]

tungstic acid *n.* A yellow powder, H_2WO_4, used in textiles and plastics.

tung tree *n.* Any of several eastern Asian trees of the genus *Aleurites*, esp. *A. montana* and *A. fordii*, whose seeds yield a commercially valuable drying oil. [Chin. (Mandarin) *tóng*.]

Tun•gus (to͝ong-go͞oz′, tŭn-) *n., pl.* **Tungus** or **-gus•es** See **Evenki.** [Russ. < East Turkic *tunguz*, wild pig, boar < O Turkic *tonguz*.]

Tun•gus•ic (to͝ong-go͞o′zĭk, tŭn-) *n.* A subfamily of the Altaic language family spoken in eastern Siberia and northern Manchuria including Evenki and Manchu. **—Tun•gus′ic** *adj.*

Tun•gus•ka (to͝ong-go͞o′skə, to͞on-) The name of three rivers of central Russia. The **Upper Tunguska** is the lower course of the Angara R. The **Lower Tunguska** flows c. 3,218 km (2,000 mi) N and W to the Yenisey R. The **Stony Tunguska,** c. 1,609 km (1,000 mi), flows WNW to the Yenisey.

tu•nic (to͞o′nĭk, tyo͞o′-) *n.* **1a.** A loose-fitting garment extending to the knees and worn esp. in ancient Greece and Rome. **b.** A medieval surcoat. **2a.** A long plain close-fitting jacket, usu. with a stiff high collar. **b.** A long, plain, sleeved or sleeveless blouse. **c.** A short pleated and belted dress worn by women for some sports. **3.** *Anatomy* A coat or layer enveloping an organ or part. **4.** *Botany* A loose membranous outer covering of a bulb or corm. **5.** See **tunicle.** [ME *tunik* < OFr. *tunique* < Lat. *tunica*, of Phoenician orig.; akin to Heb. *kuttōnet, kətōnet* < Central Semitic **kuttān, *kittān*. See CHITON.]

tu•ni•ca (to͞o′nĭ-kə, tyo͞o′-) *n., pl.* **-cae** (-kē′, -sē′) An enclosing membrane or layer of tissue. [Lat., tunic. See TUNIC.]

tu•ni•cate (to͞o′nĭ-kĭt, -kāt′, tyo͞o′-) *n.* Any of various chordate marine animals of the subphylum Tunicata or Urochordata, having a cylindrical or globular body enclosed in a tough outer covering and including the sea squirts and salps. ❖ *adj.* **1.** Of or relating to the tunicates. **2.** *Anatomy* Having a tunic. **3.** *Botany* Having a tunic. [Lat. *tunicātus*, p. part. of *tunicāre*, to clothe with a tunic < *tunica*, tunic. See TUNIC.]

tu•ni•cle (to͞o′nĭ-kəl, tyo͞o′-) *n. Ecclesiastical* A sleeved outer vestment reaching to the knees, worn over the alb by a subdeacon or sometimes under the dalmatic by a bishop or cardinal. [ME < Lat. *tunicula*, dim. of *tunica*, tunic. See TUNIC.]

tun•ing fork (to͞o′nĭng, tyo͞o′-) *n.* A small two-pronged metal device that when struck produces a sound of fixed pitch that is used as a reference, as in tuning musical instruments.

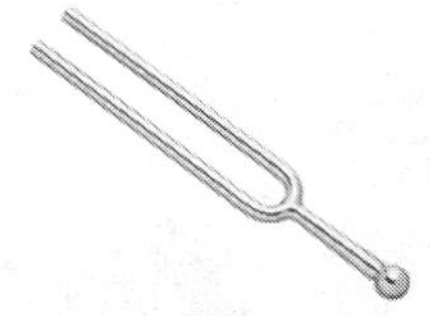

tuning fork

Tu•nis (to͞o′nĭs, tyo͞o′-) **1.** A former Barbary state on the N coast of Africa SW of Carthage; conquered by the Turks in 1575. **2.** The cap. of Tunisia, in the N part on the **Gulf of Tunis,** an inlet of the Mediterranean Sea. Pop. 596,654.

Tu•ni•sia (to͞o-nē′zhə, -shə, tyo͞o-) A country of N Africa bordering on the Mediterranean Sea; a French protectorate from 1881 to 1956. Cap. Tunis. Pop. 8,733,000.

Tu•ni•sian (to͞o-nē′zhən, -shən, tyo͞o-) *adj.* Of or relating to Tunisia or Tunis or their inhabitants. ❖ *n.* A native or inhabitant of Tunisia or Tunis.

tun•nel (tŭn′əl) *n.* **1.** An underground or underwater passage. **2.** A passage through or under a barrier. **3.** *Obsolete* The main flue on a chimney. ❖ *v.* **-neled, -nel•ing, -nels** or **-nelled, -nel•ling, -nels** —*tr.* **1.** To make a tunnel through or under. **2.** To produce, shape, or dig in the form of a tunnel. —*intr.* To make a tunnel. [ME *tonel*, tubular net < OFr. *tonnel*, dim. of *tonne*, tun, poss. of Celt. orig.] **—tun′nel•er, tun′nel•ler** *n.*

tunnel disease *n.* See **ancylostomiasis.**

tun•nel•ing (tŭn′ə-lĭng) *n.* In quantum mechanics, the passing of a particle through a seemingly impenetrable barrier without a cause that is explainable by classical physics.

tunnel vision *n.* **1.** Vision in which the visual field is severely constricted, as from within a tunnel looking out. **2.** An extremely narrow point of view; narrow-mindedness.

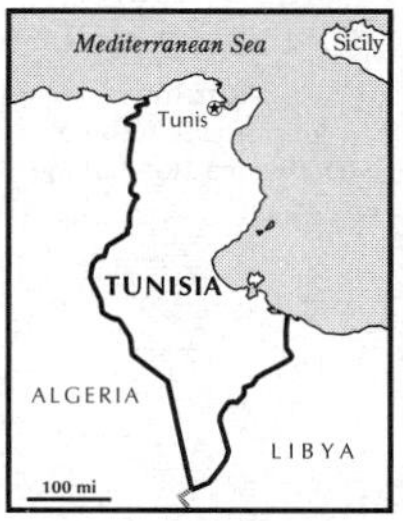

Tunisia

Tun•ney (tŭn′ē), **James Joseph** Known as "Gene." 1898–1978. Amer. prizefighter who won the world heavyweight championship in 1926 by defeating Jack Dempsey.

tun•ny (tŭn′ē) *n., pl.* **tunny** or **-nies** See **tuna**[1] 1a. [Ult. < O Provençal *ton* < Lat. *thynnus* < Gk. *thunnos*.]

tup (tŭp) *n.* **1.** *Chiefly British* A male sheep; a ram. **2.** A heavy metal body, esp. the head of a power hammer. ❖ *v.* **tupped, tup•ping, tups** —*tr.* To copulate with (a ewe). Used of a ram. —*intr.* To copulate with a ewe. [ME *tupe*.]

tu•pe•lo (to͞o′pə-lō′, tyo͞o′-) *n., pl.* **-los 1.** Any of several trees of the genus *Nyssa*, esp. *N. aquatica* of the southeast United States, having soft light wood. **2.** The wood of this tree. [Prob. Creek *'topilwa* : *ito*, tree + *opílwa*, swamp.]

Tupelo A city of NE MS S of Memphis TN; site of a Union victory (Jul. 1864). Pop. 34,211.

Tu•pi (to͞o′pē, to͞o-pē′) *n., pl.* **Tupi** or **-pis 1.** A member of any of a group of South American Indian peoples living along the coast of Brazil, in the Amazon River valley, and in Paraguay. **2.** The Tupian language of the Tupi.

Tu•pi•an (to͞o′pē-ən, to͞o-pē′-) *n.* **1.** A subdivision of Tupi-Guarani that includes Tupi. **2.** A member of a Tupian-speaking people. **—Tu′pi•an** *adj.*

Tu•pi-Gua•ra•ni (to͞o-pē′gwär-ə-nē′, to͞o′pē-) *n.* A language family widely spread throughout the Amazon River valley, coastal Brazil, and northeast South America. **—Tu•pi′-Gua•ra•ni′, Tu•pi′-Gua•ra•ni′an** *adj.*

tup•pence (tŭp′əns) *n. Chiefly British* Variant of **twopence.**

tup•pen•ny (tŭp′nē) *adj. Chiefly British* Variant of **twopenny.**

Tup•per (tŭp′ər), Sir **Charles** 1821–1915. Canadian politician who served as prime minister (1896).

turban

Tu•pun•ga•to (to͞o′po͝ong-gä′tō) A mountain, 6,804.6 m (22,310 ft), in the Andes on the Chile-Argentina border.

tuque (to͞ok, tyo͞ok) *n.* A knitted cap in the form of a cylindrical bag often with tapered ends, worn with one end tucked into the other. [Canadian Fr. < Fr. *toque*, toque. See TOQUE.]

tu quo•que (to͞o kwō′kwē, -kwā, tyo͞o) *n.* A retort accusing an accuser of a similar offense or similar behavior. [Lat. *tū quoque*, you also : *tū*, you + *quoque*, also.]

tu•ra•co (to͝or′ə-kō′) *n.* Variant of **touraco.**

Tu•ra•ni•an (to͞o-rā′nē-ən, -rä′-, tyo͞o-) *n.* **1.** See **Ural-Altaic. 2.** A member of any of the peoples who speak languages of the Ural-Altaic group. [< Pers. *Tūrān*, Turkistan.] **—Tu•ra′ni•an** *adj.*

tur•ban (tûr′bən) *n.* **1.** A traditionally Muslim headdress consisting of a long scarf wound around a small cap or directly around the head. **2.** A woman's close-fitting hat that consists of material wound around a small inner cap. [Fr. *turbant* < Ital. *turbante* < Ottoman Turk. *tülbend*, muslin, gauze, turban. See TULIP.]

tur•bel•lar•i•an (tûr′bə-lâr′ē-ən) *n.* Any of various free-living, chiefly aquatic ciliate flatworms of the class Turbellaria, which includes the common planarians of the genus *Dugesia*. [< NLat. *Turbellāria*, class name < Lat. *turbella*, bustle, dim. of *turba*, turmoil (< the motion of their cilia in the water). See TURBID.]

tur•bid (tûr′bĭd) *adj.* **1.** Having sediment or foreign particles stirred up or suspended; muddy. **2.** Heavy, dark, or dense, as smoke or fog. **3.** In a state of turmoil; muddled. [Lat. *turbidus*, disordered < *turba*, turmoil, prob. < Gk. *turbē*.] **—tur′bid•ly** *adv.* **—tur′bid•ness, tur•bid′i•ty** *n.*

ă	pat	oi	boy
ā	pay	ou	out
âr	care	o͝o	took
ä	father	o͞o	boot
ĕ	pet	ŭ	cut
ē	be	ûr	urge
ĭ	pit	th	thin
ī	pie	*th*	this
îr	pier	hw	which
ŏ	pot	zh	vision
ō	toe	ə	about,
ô	paw		item

Stress marks:
′ (primary);
′ (secondary), as in
lexicon (lĕk′sĭ-kŏn′)

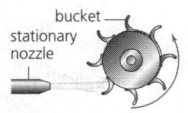

bucket
stationary
nozzle

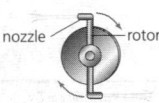

nozzle — rotor

turbine
top: impulse turbine
bottom: reaction turbine

tureen

Turkey

---

tur•bi•dim•e•ter (tûr′bĭ-dĭm′ĭ-tər) *n.* An instrument for measuring the loss in intensity of a light beam through a solution that contains suspended particulate matter. —**tur′bi•di•met′ric** (-də-mĕt′rĭk) *adj.* —**tur′bi•dim′e•try** *n.*

tur•bi•dite (tûr′bĭ-dīt′) *n.* A sedimentary deposit formed by a turbidity current.

turbidity current *n.* A swift downhill current in water, air, or other fluid, triggered by the weight of suspended material, such as silt in a current flowing down a continental shelf.

tur•bi•nate (tûr′bə-nĭt, -nāt′) also **tur•bi•nat•ed** (-nā′tĭd) *adj.* **1.** Shaped like a top. **2.** Spinning like a top. **3.** *Zoology* Spiral and decreasing sharply in diameter from base to apex. Used esp. of shells. **4.** *Anatomy* Of, relating to, or being a small curved bone that extends horizontally along the lateral wall of the nasal passage in higher vertebrates. [Lat. *turbinātus* < *turbō, turbin-*, spinning top. See TURBINE.]

tur•bi•na•tion (tûr′bə-nā′shən) *n.* A turbinate formation.

tur•bine (tûr′bĭn, -bīn′) *n.* Any of various machines in which the kinetic energy of a moving fluid is converted to rotary mechanical power. [Fr. < Lat. *turbō, turbin-*, spinning top, perh. < Gk. *turbē*, turmoil.]

tur•bit (tûr′bĭt) *n.* Any of a breed of domestic pigeons having a small crested head and a ruffled breast. [?]

turbo– *pref.* **1.** Turbine: *turbocharger.* **2.** Driven by a turbine: *turbojet.* [< TURBINE.]

tur•bo•charge (tûr′bō-chärj′) *tr.v.* **-charged, -charg•ing, -charg•es** **1.** To equip with a turbocharger. **2.** *Informal* To improve greatly the performance or quality of.

tur•bo•charg•er (tûr′bō-chär′jər) *n.* See **turbosupercharger.** —**tur′bo•charged′** *adj.*

tur•bo•fan (tûr′bō-făn′) *n.* **1.** A turbojet engine in which a fan supplements the total thrust by forcing air directly into the hot turbine exhaust. **2.** An aircraft using a turbofan.

tur•bo•jet (tûr′bō-jĕt′) *n.* **1.** A jet engine having a turbine-driven compressor and developing thrust from the exhaust of hot gases. **2.** An aircraft in which a turbojet is used.

tur•bo•prop (tûr′bō-prŏp′) *n.* **1.** A turbojet engine used to drive an external propeller. **2.** An aircraft using a turboprop.

tur•bo•shaft (tûr′bō-shăft′) *n.* A gas turbine engine that powers a rotating cylindrical shaft, as to a pump or a helicopter rotor.

tur•bo•su•per•charg•er (tûr′bō-sōō′pər-chär′jər) *n.* A supercharger that uses an exhaust-driven turbine to maintain air-intake pressure esp. in high-altitude aircraft. —**tur′bo•su′per•charged′** *adj.*

tur•bot (tûr′bət) *n., pl.* **turbot** or **-bots** **1.** A European flatfish, *Scophthalmus maximus,* that has a brown knobby upper side and is prized as food. **2.** Any of various flatfishes similar or related to this fish. [ME *turbut* < OFr. *tourbout*, prob. of Scand. orig.; akin to OSwed. *törnbut* : *törn*, thorn + *but*, flatfish.]

tur•bu•lence (tûr′byə-ləns) *n.* **1.** The state or quality of being turbulent. **2.** Turbulent flow. **3.** An eddying motion of the atmosphere that interrupts the flow of wind.

tur•bu•lent (tûr′byə-lənt) *adj.* **1.** Violently agitated or disturbed; tumultuous: *turbulent rapids.* **2.** Having a chaotic or restless character or tendency: *a turbulent period.* **3.** Causing unrest or disturbance; unruly. [ME < OFr. < Lat. *turbulentus* < *turba,* turmoil. See TURBID.] —**tur′bu•lent•ly** *adv.*

turbulent flow *n.* The motion of a fluid having local velocities and pressures that fluctuate randomly.

Tur•co•man (tûr′kə-mən) *n. & adj.* Variant of **Turkmen** 2, 3.

turd (tûrd) *n. Vulgar* **1.** A piece of excrement. **2.** *Slang* A contemptible person. [ME < OE *tord.*]

tu•reen (tōō-rēn′, tyōō-) *n.* A broad, deep, usu. covered dish used for serving foods such as soups or stews. [Fr. *terrine* < OFr. < *fem.* of *terrin,* earthen < VLat. **terrīnus* < Lat. *terra,* earth. See ters- in App.]

Tu•renne (tōō-rĕn′, tü-), Vicomte de. Title of Henri de La Tour d'Auvergne. 1611–75. French military leader noted for his campaigns (1635–42) during the Thirty Years' War.

turf (tûrf) *n., pl.* **turfs** also **turves** (tûrvz) **1a.** A surface layer of earth containing a dense growth of grass and its matted roots; sod. **b.** An artificial substitute for such a grassy layer, as on a playing field. **2.** A piece cut from a layer of earth or sod. **3.** Peat, esp. in the form of cut pieces, that is burned for fuel. **4.** *Slang* **a.** A range of authority or influence; a bailiwick. **b.** A geographical area; a territory. **c.** The area claimed by a gang as its personal territory. **5.** *Sports* **a.** A racetrack. **b.** The sport or business of racing horses. ❖ *tr.v.* **turfed, turf•ing, turfs** **1.** To spread with turf: *turfed the front yard.* **2.** *Chiefly British Slang* To discard or eject. [ME < OE.] —**turf′y** *adj.*

Tur•ge•nev (tōōr-gān′yəf, -gĕn′-, tōōr-gyĕ′nyĭf), Ivan Sergeevich. 1818–83. Russian writer whose works include stories, plays, and novels, most notably *Fathers and Sons* (1862).

tur•ges•cence (tûr-jĕs′əns) *n.* **1a.** The condition of being swollen. **b.** The process of swelling. **2.** Pomposity; self-importance. [< Lat. *turgēscere,* to begin to swell, inchoative of *turgēre,* to be swollen.] —**tur•ges′cent** *adj.*

tur•gid (tûr′jĭd) *adj.* **1.** Excessively ornate or complex in style or language; grandiloquent. **2.** Swollen or distended, as from a fluid; bloated. [Lat. *turgidus* < *turgēre,* to be swollen.] —**tur•gid′i•ty, tur′gid•ness** *n.* —**tur′gid•ly** *adv.*

tur•gor (tûr′gər, -gôr′) *n.* **1.** The state of being turgid. **2.** *Biology* The normal fullness or tension produced by the fluid content of blood vessels, capillaries, and plant or animal cells. [LLat. < Lat. *turgēre,* to be swollen.]

Tur•got (tōōr-gō′, tür-), Anne Robert Jacques. 1727–81. French economist and controller general (1774–76).

Tu•rin (tōōr′ĭn, tyōōr′-) also **To•ri•no** (tō-rē′nō) A city of NW Italy on the Po R. WSW of Milan; former cap. of the kingdom of Sardinia (1720–1861). Pop. 961,916.

Tur•ing (tōōr′ĭng), Alan Mathison. 1912–54. English mathematician who contributed to the allied victory in World War II by helping to decipher the German Enigma codes.

Turing machine *n.* A hypothetical computing device capable of storing information and responding to computational questions, used in mathematical studies of computability. [After Alan Mathison TURING, who conceived such a machine.]

tu•ri•on (tōōr′ē-ŏn′, tyōōr′-) *n. Botany* A thick fleshy young shoot or sucker. [Lat. *turiō, turiōn-.*]

Turk (tûrk) *n.* **1a.** A native or inhabitant of Turkey. **b.** A native or inhabitant of the Ottoman Empire. **2.** A member of the principal ethnic group of modern-day Turkey. **3.** A member of any of the Turkic-speaking peoples. **4.** *Obsolete* A Muslim. [ME < OFr. *Turc* < Turk. *Türk* < O Turkic *türk,* strong.]

Turk. *abbr.* **1a.** Turkey **b.** Turkish **2.** Turkmenistan

Tur•ka•na (tər-kän′ə, tōōr-kä′nə), **Lake** also **Lake Ru•dolf** (rōō′dŏlf′) A lake of NW Kenya in the Great Rift Valley.

Tur•ke•stan (tûr′kĭ-stăn′, -stän′) See **Turkistan.**

tur•key (tûr′kē) *n., pl.* **-keys** **1a.** A large North American bird (*Meleagris gallopavo*) that has brownish plumage and a bare wattled head and neck and is widely domesticated for food. **b.** A related bird (*Agriocharis ocellata*) of Mexico and Central America, brilliantly colored and having eyelike spots on its tail. **2.** *Slang* **a.** A person considered inept or undesirable. **b.** A failure, esp. a failed theatrical production or movie. **3.** *Sports* Three consecutive strikes in bowling. —*idiom:* **talk turkey** *Informal* To speak frankly and get down to the basic facts of a matter. [After TURKEY < a confusion with the guinea fowl, once believed to have a Turk. orig.]

Turkey A country of SW Asia and SE Europe between the Mediterranean and the Black seas; center of the Ottoman Empire for more than 600 years (until 1918) and a republic since 1923. Cap. Ankara. Pop. 61,183,000.

turkey buzzard *n.* See **turkey vulture.**

turkey cock *n.* **1.** A male turkey. **2.** A strutting and conceited person.

Turkey red *n.* A brilliant red. [< its use in cotton cloth manufactured in Turkey.]

turkey trot *n.* A ragtime dance marked by a springy walk with the feet well apart and a swinging up-and-down movement of the shoulders.

turkey vulture *n.* A New World vulture (*Cathartes aura*) having dark plumage and a bare red head and neck.

Tur•ki (tûr′kē) *adj.* Of or relating to the Turkic language subfamily, esp. the eastern Turkic languages. ❖ *n., pl.* **Turki** or **-kis** **1.** The Turkic language subfamily, esp. the eastern Turkic languages. **2.** A member of a Turkic-speaking people. [Pers. *turkī* < Turk, Turk < Turk. *Türk.* See TURK.]

Turk•ic (tûr′kĭk) *n.* A subfamily of the Altaic language family that includes Turkish. ❖ *adj.* **1.** Of or relating to Turkic or the peoples who speak Turkic. **2.** Turkish.

Turk•ish (tûr′kĭsh) *adj.* Of or relating to Turkey or its peoples, languages, or cultures. ❖ *n.* Ottoman Turkish.

Turkish bath *n.* A steam bath that induces heavy perspiration and is followed by a shower and massage.

Turkish coffee *n.* A sweetened brew of pulverized coffee.

Turkish delight *n.* A candy usu. consisting of jellylike cubes covered with powdered sugar.

Turkish Empire See **Ottoman Empire.**

Turkish towel *n.* A thick towel with a nap of uncut pile.

Turk•ism (tûr′kĭz′əm) *n.* The culture, religion, or social system of the Turks.

Tur•ki•stan also **Tur•ke•stan** (tûr′kĭ-stăn′, -stän′) A historical region of W-central Asia extending E from the Caspian Sea to the border of China.

Turk•men (tûrk′mĕn, -mən) *n., pl.* **Turkmen** or **-mens** **1.** A native or inhabitant of Turkmenistan. **2.** also **Tur•ko•man** or **Tur•co•man** (tûr′kə-mən), *pl.* **-ko•mans** or **-co•mans** A member of a traditionally nomadic Turkic people inhabiting Turkmenistan and neighboring areas in Iran and Afghanistan. **3.** also **Turkoman** or **Turcoman** The Turkic language of the Turkmen. [Med. Lat. *Turcomannus* < Pers. *Turkmān* < *turkmān,* like a Turk < Turk, Turk. See TURKI.] —**Turk′men, Tur′ko•man, Tur′co•man** *adj.*

Turk•men•i•stan (tûrk′mĕn-ĭ-stăn′, -stän′) A region and republic of W-central Asia E of the Caspian Sea; annexed by Russia in 1881 and a constituent republic from 1925 to 1991. Cap. Ashgabat. Pop. 4,010,000.

Turks and Caicos Islands (tûrks) Two island groups of the British West Indies in the SE Bahama Is.

Turk's-cap lily (tûrks′kăp′) *n.* **1.** Either of two North American lilies, *Lilium michauxii* or *L. superbum,* having spotted orange-red flowers with a reflexed perianth. **2.** See **martagon.** [< the rolled-back petals, resembling a turban.]

Turk's-head (tûrks′hĕd′) *n.* A turban-shaped knot made by winding a smaller rope around a larger one.

Tur•ku (to͝or′ko͞o′) A city of SW Finland on the Baltic Sea W of Helsinki; settled in the early 13th cent. Pop. 160,153.

tur•mer•ic (tûr′mər-ĭk, to͞o′-) *n.* **1.** A widely cultivated tropical plant *(Curcuma domestica)* of India having yellow flowers and an aromatic, somewhat fleshy rhizome. **2.** The powdered rhizome of this plant, used as a condiment and a yellow dye. **3.** Any of several other plants having similar rhizomes. [Alteration of ME *termeryte* < OFr. *terre-merite*, saffron < Med.Lat. *terra merita* : Lat. *terra*, earth; see **ters-** in App. + Lat. *merita*, fem. p. part. of *merēre*, to deserve.]

tur•moil (tûr′moil′) *n.* A state of extreme confusion or agitation; commotion or tumult. [?]

turn (tûrn) *v.* **turned, turn•ing, turns** —*tr.* **1.** To cause to move around an axis or center; cause to rotate or revolve. **2.** To cause to move around in order to achieve a result, such as opening, closing, or tightening. **3.** To alter or control the functioning of (a mechanical device, for example) by the use of a rotating or similar movement: *turn the iron to a hotter setting.* **4.** To perform or accomplish by rotating or revolving: *turn a somersault.* **5a.** To change the position of so that the underside becomes the upper side. **b.** To spade or plow (soil) to bring the undersoil to the surface. **c.** To reverse and resew the material of (a collar, for example). **6.** To revolve in the mind; meditate on; ponder. **7a.** To give a rounded form to (wood, for example) by rotating against a cutting tool. **b.** To give a rounded shape to (clay, for example) by rotating and shaping with the hands or tools. **c.** To give a rounded form to: *turn a heel in knitting a sock.* **d.** To give distinctive, artistic, or graceful form to: *knows how to turn a line.* **8a.** To change the position of by traversing an arc of a circle; pivot. **b.** To present in a specified direction by rotating or pivoting: *turn one's face to the wall.* **c.** To cause (a scale) to move up or down so as to register weight. **9a.** To fold, bend, or twist (something). **b.** To change the position or disposition of by folding, bending, or twisting: *Turn the hat inside out.* **c.** To make a bend or curve in: *turn steel.* **d.** To blunt or dull (the edge of a cutting instrument). **e.** To injure by twisting. **f.** To upset or make nauseated. **10.** To change the direction or course of. **11a.** To divert or deflect: *turn a stampede.* **b.** To reverse the course of; cause to retreat. **12.** To make a course around or about: *turn a corner.* **13.** To change the purpose, intention, or content of by persuasion or influence. **14.** To change the order or disposition of; unsettle: *turned my head.* **15a.** To aim or focus: *turned the camera on us.* **b.** To devote or apply (oneself, for example) to something. **16.** To cause to act or go against; make antagonistic. **17.** To cause to go in a specific direction; direct: *They turned their steps toward home.* **18.** To send, drive, or let go: *turned the dog loose.* **19.** To pour, let fall, or otherwise release (contents) from or into a receptacle. **20.** To cause to take on a specified character, nature, identity, or appearance; change or transform. Used with *to* or *into.* **21.** To make sour; ferment. **22.** To affect or change the color of. **23.** To exchange; convert. Used with *to* or *into.* **24.** To keep in circulation; sell and restock. **25a.** To make use of: *turn the situation to our advantage.* **b.** To bet by buying and selling: *turn a fair profit.* **26.** To perform successfully; complete: *turn a double play.* **27.** *Slang* To perform (an act of prostitution). —*intr.* **1.** To move around an axis or center; rotate or revolve. **2.** To have a sensation of revolving or whirling, esp. as a result of dizziness or giddiness. **3.** To change position from side to side or back and forth. **4.** To progress through pages so as to arrive at a given place. **5a.** To operate a lathe. **b.** To be formed on a lathe. **6.** To direct one's way or course. **7.** To change or reverse one's way, course, or direction. **8.** To have a specific reaction or effect, esp. when adverse. **9.** To change one's actions or attitudes adversely; become hostile or antagonistic. **10.** To attack suddenly and violently with no apparent motive: *The tiger turned on the trainer.* **11.** To channel one's attention, interest, or thought toward or away from something. **12.** To devote or apply oneself to something, as to a field of study. **13.** To convert to a religion. **14.** To switch one's loyalty from one side or party to another. **15.** To have recourse to a person or thing for help, support, or information. **16.** To depend on something for success or failure; hinge. **17a.** To change so as to be; become: *His hair turned gray.* **b.** To change; become transformed. Used with *to* or *into: The sky turned to pink at dawn.* **c.** To reach and pass (a certain age, for example). **18.** To become sour. **19.** To change color. **20.** To be stocked and sold: *goods that turned quickly.* **21.** To become dull or blunt by bending back. Used of the edge of a cutting instrument. ❖ *n.* **1.** The act of turning or the condition of being turned; rotation or revolution. **2.** A change of direction, motion, or position. **3.** A place, as in a road or path, where a change in direction occurs; a curve. **4.** A departure or deviation, as in a trend. **5.** A point marking the end of one period of time and the beginning of the next. **6a.** A chance or opportunity. **b.** One of a series of such opportunities accorded people in succession or in scheduled order. **7.** A period of participation. **8a.** An attack of illness or severe nervousness. **b.** *Informal* A momentary shock or scare. **9.** A characteristic mood, style, or habit; a natural inclination. **10.** A propensity or adeptness. **11.** A distinctive, graceful, or artistic expression or arrangement of words: *the poetic turn of a phrase.* **12a.** A movement or development in a particular direction: *a turn for the worse.* **b.** A variation of a given kind or type. **13.** A deed or action having a good or bad effect on another: *a good turn.* **14.** Advantage or purpose. **15.** A short walk or excursion out and back. **16.** A distortion in shape. **17.** The condition of being twisted or wound. **18a.** A winding of one thing about another. **b.** A single wind or convolution, as of wire on a spool. **19.** Something that winds or turns around a center axis. **20.** *Music* A figure or ornament, usually consisting of four or more notes in rapid succession and including the principal note, the one a degree above it, and the one a degree below it. **21.** A brief theatrical act or stage appearance. **22.** A transaction on the stock market involving both a sale and a purchase. **23.** *South Atlantic US* The amount that can be carried in the arms in one load. ***—phrasal verbs:*** **turn away 1.** To send away; dismiss. **2.** To repel. **3.** To avert; deflect. **turn back 1.** To reverse one's direction of motion. **2.** To drive back and away. **3.** To halt the advance of. **4.** To fold down. **turn down 1.** To diminish the speed, volume, intensity, or flow of. **2.** To reject or refuse, as a person, advice, or a suggestion. **3.** To fold or be capable of folding down. **turn in 1.** To hand in; give over. **2.** To inform on or deliver. **3.** To produce: *turned in a good performance.* **4.** *Informal* To go to bed. **turn off 1.** To stop the operation, activity, or flow of; shut off. **2.** *Slang* **a.** To affect with dislike, displeasure, or revulsion. **b.** To affect with boredom. **c.** To lose or cause to lose interest; withdraw. **d.** To cease paying attention to. **3.** To divert; deflect. **4.** *Chiefly British* To dismiss (an employee). **turn on 1.** To cause to begin the operation, activity, or flow of. **2.** To begin to display, employ, or exude. **3.** *Slang* **a.** To take or cause to take a mind-altering drug, esp. for the first time. **b.** To be or cause to become interested, pleasurably excited, or stimulated. Often used with *to.* **c.** To excite or become excited sexually. **turn out 1.** To shut off. **2.** To arrive or assemble, as for a public event or entertainment. **3.** To produce, as by a manufacturing process; make. **4.** To be found to be, as after experience or trial. **5.** To end up; result. **6.** To equip; outfit. **7.** *Informal* To get out of bed. **8.** To evict; expel. **turn over 1.** To bring the bottom to the top or vice versa; invert. **2a.** To shift the position of, as by rolling from one side to the other. **b.** To shift one's position by rolling from one side to the other. **3.** To rotate; cycle: *The engine turned over.* **4.** To think about; consider. **5.** To transfer to another; surrender. **6.** *Sports* To lose possession of (the ball). **7.** To do business to the extent or amount of. **8.** To seem to lurch or heave convulsively: *My stomach turned over.* **turn to** To begin work. **turn up 1.** To increase the speed, volume, intensity, or flow of. **2a.** To find. **b.** To be found. **3.** To make an appearance; arrive. **4.** To fold or be capable of folding up. **5.** To happen unexpectedly. **6.** To be evident. ***—idioms:*** **at every turn** In every place; at every moment. **by turns** One after another; alternately. **in turn** In the proper order or sequence. **out of turn 1.** Not in the proper order or sequence. **2.** At an inappropriate time or in an inappropriate manner. **to a turn** To a precise degree; perfectly. **turn a blind eye** To refuse to see or recognize something. **turn a deaf ear** To refuse to listen to or hear something. **turn a hair** To become afraid or upset. **turn (one's) back on 1.** To deny; reject. **2.** To abandon; forsake. **turn (one's) hand** To apply oneself, as to a task. **turn (one's) head 1.** To cause to become infatuated. **2.** To cause to become egotistical and conceited. **turn over a new leaf** To change, as one's attitude or conduct, for the better. **turn tail** To run away. **turn the** (or **a**) **corner** To reach and surpass a midpoint or milestone. **turn the other cheek** To respond to insult or injury by patiently eschewing retaliation. **turn the scales** To offset the balance of a situation. **turn the tables** To reverse a situation and gain the upper hand. **turn turtle** To capsize or turn upside-down. **turn up (one's) nose** To regard something with disdain or scorn. [ME *turnen* < OE *turnian, tyrnan* and OFr. *torner*, both < Lat. *tornāre*, to turn in a lathe < *tornus*, lathe < Gk. *tornos.* See **terə-**[1] in App.]

Turkmenistan

turn•a•bout (tûrn′ə-bout′) *n.* **1.** The act of turning about and facing or moving in the opposite direction. **2.** A shift or change in opinion, loyalty, or allegiance. **3.** A dance or party to which girls invite boys.

turn•a•round (tûrn′ə-round′) *n.* **1.** A space, as in a driveway, permitting the turning around of a vehicle. **2.** The act or an instance of turning about and facing or moving in the opposite direction; a reversal. **3.** A shift or change in opinion, loyalty, or allegiance. **4a.** The process of or time needed for loading, unloading, and servicing a vehicle. **b.** The process of or time needed for performing a task.

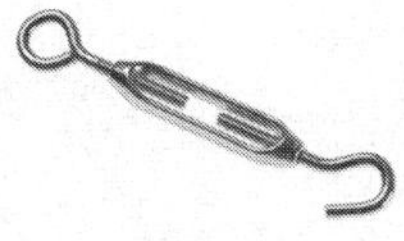

turnbuckle

turn•buck•le (tûrn′bŭk′əl) *n.* A metal coupling device consisting of an oblong piece internally threaded at both ends into which the corresponding sections of two threaded rods are screwed in order to form a unit that can be adjusted for tension or length.

turn•coat (tûrn′kōt′) *n.* One who traitorously switches allegiance.

turn•down (tûrn′doun′) *n.* **1.** A rejection. **2.** One who has been turned down or rejected. **3.** Something that is folded down, as on a garment. **4.** A downturn. ❖ *adj.* Being or capable of being turned or folded down: *a turndown collar.*

turned-on (tûrnd′ŏn′, -ôn′) *adj. Slang* **1.** Highly aware of and

ă	**pat**	oi	**boy**
ā	**pay**	ou	**out**
âr	**care**	o͝o	**took**
ä	**father**	o͞o	**boot**
ĕ	**pet**	ŭ	**cut**
ē	**be**	ûr	**urge**
ĭ	**pit**	th	**thin**
ī	**pie**	*th*	**this**
îr	**pier**	hw	**which**
ŏ	**pot**	zh	**vision**
ō	**toe**	ə	**about, item**
ô	**paw**		

Stress marks:
′ (primary);
′ (secondary), as in
lexicon (lĕk′sĭ-kŏn′)

responsive to what is fashionable and up-to-date. **2a.** Pleasantly excited or stimulated. **b.** Sexually aroused. **c.** Under the influence of a mind-altering drug.

turn·er¹ (tûr′nər) *n.* One that turns, esp. a person who operates a lathe or similar device.

turn·er² (tûr′nər) *n.* A gymnast or tumbler, esp. a member of a turnverein. [Ger. < *turnen,* to do gymnastics < OHGer. *turnēn,* to turn < Lat. *tornāre,* to turn in a lathe. See TURN.]

Turner, Frederick Jackson 1861–1932. Amer. historian who emphasized the importance of the frontier.

Turner, Joseph Mallord William 1775–1851. British painter who influenced the French impressionists.

Turner, Joseph Vernon Known as "Big Joe." 1911–85. Amer. jazz and blues singer who contributed greatly to the development of rhythm and blues.

Turner, Nat 1800–31. Amer. slave who led a rebellion against whites in VA (1831).

Tur·ner's syndrome (tûr′nərz) *n.* A congenital condition of females associated with a defect or absence of an X-chromosome, marked by short stature and sexual underdevelopment. [After Henry Hubert *Turner* (1892–1970), American endocrinologist.]

turn·er·y (tûr′nə-rē) *n., pl.* **-ies** The work or workshop of a lathe operator.

turn·ing (tûr′nĭng) *n.* **1.** A deviation from a straight course; a turn. **2a.** The shaping of metal or wood on a lathe. **b. turnings** Shavings produced in shaping metal on a lathe.

turning point *n.* **1.** The point at which a significant change occurs; a decisive moment. **2.** *Mathematics* A maximum or minimum point on a curve.

tur·nip (tûr′nĭp) *n.* **1.** A widely cultivated Eurasian plant (*Brassica rapa*) of the mustard family, having a large fleshy edible yellow or white root. **2.** The root of this plant, eaten as a vegetable. [*tur-,* of unknown meaning + dialectal *nepe,* turnip (< ME < OE *nǣp* < Lat. *nāpus.*)]

turn·key (tûrn′kē′) *n., pl.* **-keys** The keeper of the keys in a prison; a jailer. ❖ *adj.* **1.** Supplied, installed, or purchased in a condition ready for immediate use, occupation, or operation. **2.** Of or relating to something in this condition.

turn·off (tûrn′ôf′, -ŏf′) *n.* **1.** A branch of a road or path leading away from a main thoroughfare. **2.** The act or an instance of turning off. **3.** *Slang* **a.** One that is distasteful. **b.** Something that causes loss of interest.

turn-on (tûrn′ŏn′, -ôn′) *n. Slang* Something that causes pleasure or excitement.

turn·out (tûrn′out′) *n.* **1.** The number of people gathered for a particular event or purpose; attendance. **2.** A number of things produced; output. **3.** The act or an instance of turning out. **4.** *Chiefly British* **a.** A labor strike. **b.** A laborer on strike. **5.** An array of equipment; an outfit. **6.** An outfit of a carriage with its horse or horses; equipage. **7.** A railroad siding. **8.** A widening in a highway to allow vehicles to pass or park. **9.** The rotation of a dancer's legs from the hip sockets in classical ballet.

turn·o·ver (tûrn′ō′vər) *n.* **1.** The act of turning over; an upset or overthrow. **2.** An abrupt change; a reversal. **3.** A small pastry made by covering one half of a piece of dough with a filling, folding the other half on top, and sealing the edges. **4a.** The number of times a particular stock of goods is sold and restocked during a given period of time. **b.** The amount of business transacted during a given period of time. **c.** The number of shares of stock sold on the market during a given period of time. **5a.** The number of workers hired by an establishment to replace those who have left in a given period of time. **b.** The ratio of this number to the number of employed workers. **6.** *Sports* A loss of possession of the ball to the opposing team, as by a misplay. ❖ *adj.* Capable of being turned or folded down or over: *a turnover collar.*

turn·pike (tûrn′pīk′) *n.* **1.** A toll road, esp. an expressway. **2.** A tollgate. [ME *turnepike,* spiked barrier : *turnen,* to turn; see TURN + *pike,* point; see PIKE⁵.]

turn signal *n.* See **directional signal.**

turn·sole (tûrn′sōl′) *n.* **1.** Any of various plants that move or are believed to move in response to the sun. **2.** See **heliotrope** 1a. [ME *turnesole,* purple dye obtained from the plant < OFr. *tournesol* < OItal. *tornasole,* heliotrope : *tornare,* to turn (< Lat. *tornāre;* see TURN) + *sole,* sun (< Lat. *sōl;* see *sāwel-* in App.).]

turn·spit (tûrn′spĭt′) *n.* **1a.** One that turns a roasting spit. **b.** A roasting spit that can be turned. **2.** A dog formerly used in a treadmill to turn a roasting spit.

turn·stile (tûrn′stīl′) *n.* **1.** A mechanical device typically consisting of several horizontal arms supported by and radially projecting from a central post and allowing only the passage of individuals on foot. **2.** A similar structure that permits the passage of an individual once a charge has been paid or counts the number of individuals passing through.

turn·stone (tûrn′stōn′) *n.* Any of several wading birds of the genus *Arenaria,* esp. *A. interpres,* which is dark brown above with large areas of chestnut and black.

turn·ta·ble (tûrn′tā′bəl) *n.* **1a.** The rotating platform of a record player. **b.** The unit housing this platform. **2.** A rotating platform equipped with a railway track, used for turning locomotives. **3.** A rotating platform or disk.

turn·up (tûrn′ŭp′) *n.* Something, such as the cuff on a trouser

turnstone
ruddy turnstone
Arenaria interpres

leg, that is turned up or can be turned up. ❖ *adj.* Turned up or capable of being turned up.

turn·ver·ein (tûrn′və-rīn′, tŏŏrn′-) *n. Sports* A club of gymnasts or tumblers. [Ger. : *turnen,* to do gymnastics; see TURNER² + *Verein,* club (< obsolete *vereine,* back-formation < MHGer. *vereinen,* to unite : *ver-,* intensive pref. < OHGer. *far-;* see **per**¹ in App. + *einen,* to make one < *ein,* one < OHGer.; see **oi-no-** in App.).]

tur·pen·tine (tûr′pən-tīn′) *n.* **1.** A thin volatile essential oil, C₁₀H₁₆, distilled or extracted from the wood or exudate of certain pine trees and used as a paint thinner, solvent, and liniment. **2.** The sticky mixture of resin and volatile oil from which turpentine is distilled. **3.** A brownish-yellow resinous liquid obtained from the terebinth. ❖ *tr.v.* **-tined, -tin·ing, -tines 1.** To apply turpentine to or mix turpentine with. **2.** To extract turpentine from (a tree). [ME, resin of the terebinth < OFr. *terebentine* < Lat. *terebinthina* < *terebinthina* (resin) < Gk. *terebinthinē,* fem. of *terebenthinos* < *terebinthos,* terebinth tree.] **—tur′pen·tin′ic** (-tĭn′ĭk), **tur′pen·tin′ous** (-tĭn′əs) *adj.*

tur·pi·tude (tûr′pĭ-tōōd′, -tyōōd′) *n.* **1.** Depravity; baseness. **2.** A base act. [Ult. < Lat. *turpitūdō* < *turpis,* shameful.]

turps (tûrps) *pl.n.* (*used with a sing. verb*) *Informal* Turpentine.

tur·quoise (tûr′kwoiz′, -koiz′) *n.* **1.** A blue to blue-green mineral of aluminum and copper, mainly CuAl₆(PO₄)₄(OH)₈·4H₂O, prized as a gemstone in its polished blue form. **2.** A light to brilliant bluish green. [ME *turkeis* and Fr. *turquoise,* both < OFr. (*pierre*) *turqueise,* Turk. (stone), turquoise, fem. of *turqueis,* Turk. < *Turc,* Turk. See TURK.] **—tur′quoise′** *adj.*

tur·ret (tûr′ĭt, tŭr′-) *n.* **1.** A small tower or tower-shaped projection on a building. **2a.** A low, heavily armored structure, usu. rotating horizontally, containing mounted guns and their gunners, as on a warship or tank. **b.** A domelike gunner's enclosure of a combat aircraft. **3.** A tall wooden structure mounted on wheels and used in ancient warfare to scale an enemy fortress. **4.** An attachment for a lathe consisting of a rotating cylindrical block holding cutting tools. **5.** A rotating device holding various lenses, as for a microscope. [ME *turet* < OFr. *torete,* dim. of *tor,* tower. See TOWER.]

tur·ret·ed (tûr′ĭ-tĭd, tŭr′-) *adj.* **1.** Furnished with turrets or a turret. **2.** Having the shape or form of a turret.

tur·tle¹ (tûr′tl) *n.* **1.** Any of various aquatic or terrestrial reptiles of the order Testudines (or Chelonia), having horny toothless jaws and a bony or leathery shell into which the head, limbs, and tail can be withdrawn in most species. **2.** *Chiefly British* A sea turtle. ❖ *intr.v.* **-tled, -tling, -tles 1.** To hunt for turtles, esp. as an occupation. **2.** *Nautical* To capsize. [Perh. < Fr. *tortue,* perh. ult. < LLat. *tartarūchus,* of Tartarus < Gk. *tartaroukhos,* occupying Tartarus : *Tartaros,* Tartarus + *ekhein,* to hold; see EUNUCH.] **—tur′tler** *n.*

tur·tle² (tûr′tl) *n. Archaic* A turtledove. [ME < OE < Lat. *turtur,* prob. of imit. orig.]

tur·tle³ (tûr′tl) *n.* A turtleneck.

tur·tle·back (tûr′tl-băk′) *n.* Something shaped like the back of a turtle, esp.: **a.** *Nautical* An arched structure erected over the deck of a ship as protection from heavy seas. **b.** *Archaeology* A stone tool with a convex side. **—tur′tle·back′, tur′tle·backed′** *adj.*

turtle bean *n.* See **black bean.**

tur·tle·dove (tûr′tl-dŭv′) *n.* **1.** A small slender European dove (*Streptopelia turtur*) having a white-edged tail and a soft purring voice. **2.** See **mourning dove.**

tur·tle·head (tûr′tl-hĕd′) *n.* Any of several perennial North American herbs of the genus *Chelone,* esp. *C. glabra,* having white or pink flowers. [< the shape of its flowers.]

tur·tle·neck (tûr′tl-nĕk′) *n.* **1.** A high, tubular, often rolled-down collar that fits closely about the neck. **2.** A garment, such as a sweater, that has this type of collar.

turves (tûrvz) *n.* A plural of **turf.**

Tus·ca·loo·sa (tŭs′kə-lōō′sə) A city of W-central AL SW of Birmingham; pop. 77,906.

Tus·can (tŭs′kən) *adj.* **1.** Of or relating to Tuscany, its people, or their language. **2.** *Architecture* Of or relating to the Tuscan order. ❖ *n.* **1.** A native or inhabitant of Tuscany. **2a.** Any of the dialects of Italian spoken in Tuscany. **b.** The standard literary form of Italian. [ME < Lat. *Tuscānus,* Etruscan < *Tuscus,* an Etruscan.]

Tuscan order *n. Architecture* A classical order similar to Roman Doric but having columns with an unfluted shaft and a simplified base, capital, and entablature.

Tus·ca·ny (tŭs′kə-nē′) A region of W-central Italy between the N Apennines and the Ligurian and Tyrrhenian seas.

Tus·ca·ro·ra (tŭs′kə-rôr′ə, -rōr′ə) *n., pl.* **Tuscarora** or **-ras 1.** A member of a Native American people formerly inhabiting parts of North Carolina, with present-day populations in western New York and southeast Ontario, Canada. **2.** Their Iroquoian language.

tu·sche (tōōsh′ə) *n.* A black liquid used for drawing in lithography and as a resist in etching and silk-screen work. [Ger., back-formation < *tuschen,* to lay on colors < Fr. *toucher* < OFr. *tochier, touchier,* to touch. See TOUCH.]

tush¹ (tŭsh) *interj.* Used to express mild reproof, disapproval, or admonition.

tush² (tŭsh) *n.* **1.** A canine tooth, esp. of a horse. **2.** *Chiefly Southern US* See **tusk** 1. [ME *tusche* < OE *tūsc.* See TUSK.]

tush³ (tŏosh) *n. Slang* The buttocks. [Alteration of Yiddish *tokhes* < Heb. *tahat,* under, buttocks.]

tush•y also **tush•ie** (tŏosh′ē) *n., pl.* **-ies** *Slang* The buttocks.

tusk (tŭsk) *n.* **1.** An elongated pointed tooth extending outside the mouth in certain animals such as the walrus or elephant. **2.** A long projecting tooth or toothlike part. ❖ *tr. & intr.v.* **tusked, tusk•ing, tusks** To gore or dig with the tusks of a tusk. [ME *tux, tusce* < OE *tūx, tūsc,* canine tooth. See **dent-** in App.] —**tusked** *adj.*

Tus•ke•gee (tŭs-kē′gē) A city of E AL E of Montgomery; seat of the Tuskegee Institute (founded 1881). Pop. 11,846.

tusk•er (tŭs′kər) *n.* An animal that has tusks.

tusk shell *n.* See **tooth shell.**

tus•sah (tŭs′ə, tŭs′ô′) also **tus•sore** (tŭs′ôr′, -ōr′) *n.* **1.** An Asian silkworm, the larva of a large saturniid moth (*Antheraea paphia*), that produces a coarse brownish silk. **2.** This silk or a fabric woven from it. [Hindi *tasar* < Skt. *tasaram,* shuttle (prob. < the shape of its cocoon). See **ten-** in App.]

tus•sie-mus•sie (tŭs′ē-mŭs′ē) *n.* **1.** A small bouquet of flowers; a nosegay. **2.** A cone-shaped holder for such a bouquet. [ME *tussemose,* perh. redup. of **tusse.*]

tus•sis (tŭs′ĭs) *n., pl.* **-ses** (-sēz) A cough. [Lat.] —**tus′sive** *adj.*

tus•sle (tŭs′əl) *intr.v.* **-sled, -sling, -sles** To struggle roughly; scuffle. ❖ *n.* A rough or vigorous struggle; a scuffle. [ME *tussillen,* freq. of *-tousen,* to pull roughly.]

tus•sock (tŭs′ək) *n.* **1.** A clump or tuft, as of growing grass. **2.** A tuft of hair or feathers. [?] —**tus′sock•y** *adj.*

tussock moth *n.* Any of various dull-colored moths of the family Lymantriidae, the caterpillars of which have tufts of hair along the back and are often destructive to trees.

tut (*a t-like sound produced by suction rather than plosion; conventional spelling pronunciation,* tŭt) *interj.* Used to express annoyance, impatience, or mild reproof. —**tut** *n. & v.*

Tut•ankh•a•men (tŏot′ăng-kä′mən) fl. c. 1358 B.C. King of Egypt during the XVIII Dynasty whose tomb was found almost intact by Howard Carter in 1922.

tu•tee (tŏo-tē′, tyŏo-) *n.* One who is being tutored. [TUT(OR) + –EE¹.]

tu•te•lage (tŏot′l-ĭj, tyŏot′-) *n.* **1.** The capacity or activity of a guardian; guardianship. **2.** The capacity or activity of a tutor; instruction or teaching. **3.** The state of being under the direction of a guardian or tutor. [Lat. *tūtēla* (< *tūtus,* var. p. part. of *tuērī,* to guard) + –AGE.]

tu•te•lar•y (tŏot′l-ĕr′ē, tyŏot′-) also **tu•te•lar** (tŏot′l-ər, -är′, tyŏot′-) *adj.* **1.** Being or serving as a guardian or protector: *tutelary gods.* **2.** Of or relating to a guardian or guardianship. ❖ *n., pl.* **-lar•ies** also **-lars** One that serves as a guardian or protector.

tu•tor (tŏo′tər, tyŏo′-) *n.* **1a.** A private instructor. **b.** One that gives additional, special, or remedial instruction. **2.** A teacher or teaching assistant in some universities and colleges having a rank lower than that of an instructor. **3.** A graduate responsible for the supervision of an undergraduate at some British universities. ❖ *v.* **-tored, -tor•ing, -tors** —*tr.* **1.** To act as a tutor to; instruct or teach privately. **2.** To have the guardianship, tutelage, or care of. —*intr.* **1.** To function as a tutor. **2.** To be instructed by a tutor; study under a tutor. [Ult. < Lat. *tūtor < tūtus,* var. p. part. of *tuērī,* to guard.]

tu•to•ri•al (tŏo-tôr′ē-əl, -tōr′-, tyŏo-) *adj.* Of or relating to tutors or a tutor. ❖ *n.* Something that provides special, often individual instruction, esp.: **a.** A book or class that provides instruction in a particular area. **b.** A computer program that provides instruction for the use of a system or of software.

Tut•si (tŏot′sē) also **Wa•tu•si** (wä-) or **Wa•tu•si** (-tŏo′-) *n., pl.* **Tutsi** or **-sis** also **Watutsi** or **-sis** or **Watusi** or **-sis** A member of a Bantu-speaking people inhabiting Rwanda and Burundi.

tut•ti (tŏo′tē) *Music adv.* & *adj.* All. Used chiefly as a direction to indicate that all performers are to take part. ❖ *n., pl.* **-tis 1.** An ensemble of musicians in a concerto. **2.** A passage of ensemble music executed by all the performers simultaneously. [Ital., pl. of *tutto,* all < VLat. **tōttus,* var. of Lat. *tōtus.* See **teutā-** in App.]

tut•ti-frut•ti (tŏo′tē-frŏo′tē) *n., pl.* **-tis 1.** A confection, esp. ice cream, containing a variety of chopped and usu. candied fruits. **2.** A flavoring simulating the flavor of many fruits. [Ital. : *tutti,* pl. of *tutto,* all + *frutti,* pl. of *frutto,* fruit.]

tut-tut (*two t-like sounds produced by suction rather than plosion; conventional spelling pronunciation,* tŭt′tŭt′) *intr.v.* **-tut•ted, -tut•ting, -tuts** To express annoyance, impatience, or mild reproof. [Imit.]

tut•ty (tŭt′ē) *n., pl.* **-ties** An impure zinc oxide obtained as a sublimate from the flues of zinc-smelting furnaces and used as a polishing powder. [ME *tutie* < OFr. < Med.Lat. *tutia* < Ar. *tūtiyā* < Skt. *tuttham,* blue vitriol, prob. of Dravidian orig.; akin to Kannada *tutta.*]

tu•tu (tŏo′tŏo) *n.* A short skirt, usu. made up of layers of sheer fabric, worn by ballerinas. [Fr., perh. alteration of *cucu,* baby-talk redup. of *cul,* buttocks. See CULOTTE.]

Tu•tu (tŏo′tŏo), **Desmond** b. 1931. South African prelate who won the 1984 Nobel Peace Prize.

Tu•tu•i•la (tŏo′tŏo-ē′lä) An island of American Samoa in the SW-central Pacific Ocean.

Tu•va•lu (tŏo-vä′lŏo, tŏo′və-lŏo′) Formerly **El•lice Islands** (ĕl′ĭs) An island country of the W Pacific N of Fiji; organized as a British protectorate in 1892 and independent after 1978. Cap. Fongafale. Pop. 9,000.

tux (tŭks) *n. Informal* A tuxedo.

tux•e•do (tŭk-sē′dō) *n., pl.* **-dos** or **-does 1.** A man's dress jacket, usu. black with satin or grosgrain lapels, worn for formal or semiformal occasions. **2.** A complete outfit including this jacket, trousers usu. with a silken stripe down the side, a bow tie, and often a cummerbund. [Short for *Tuxedo coat,* after a country club at *Tuxedo* Park, a village of southeast New York.]

Tux•tla Gu•tiér•rez (tŏos′tlə gŏo-tyĕr′ĕs) A city of SE Mexico near the Isthmus of Tehuantepec. Pop. 131,096.

tu•yère (twē-yâr′) *n.* The pipe, nozzle, or other opening through which air is forced into a blast furnace or forge to facilitate combustion. [Fr. < OFr. < *tuyau,* pipe, prob. of Gmc. orig.]

TV (tē′vē′) *n.* Television.

TVA *abbr.* Tennessee Valley Authority

TV dinner *n.* A frozen prepared meal, usu. packaged in a disposable serving tray, that needs to be heated before serving.

Tver′ (tvĕr) Formerly **Ka•li•nin** (kə-lē′nĭn, kəl-yē′-) A city of W-central Russia on the Volga R. NW of Moscow. Pop. 449,461.

twa (twä, twô) *n., adj.,* & *pron. Scots* Two. [ME, var. of *two.* See TWO.]

twad•dle (twŏd′l) *intr.v.* **-dled, -dling, -dles** To talk foolishly; prate. ❖ *n.* Foolish, trivial, or idle talk or chatter. [Prob. var. of dialectal *twattle,* perh. alteration of TATTLE.] —**twad′dler** *n.*

twain (twān) *n., adj.,* & *pron.* Two. [ME *tweien, twaine* < OE *twēgen.* See **dwo-** in App.]

Twain, Mark See Samuel Langhorne **Clemens.**

twang (twăng) *v.* **twanged, twang•ing, twangs** —*intr.* **1.** To emit a twang. **2.** To resound with a twang. **3.** To speak in a twang. —*tr.* **1.** To cause to make a twang. **2.** To utter with a twang. ❖ *n.* **1.** A sharp vibrating sound, as that of a plucked string. **2.** A strongly nasal tone of voice, esp. as a peculiarity of certain regional dialects. [Imit.] —**twang′y** *adj.*

′twas (twŭz, twŏz, twəz *when unstressed*) Contraction of *it was.*

twat (twŏt) *n.* **1.** *Vulgar Slang* The vulva. **2.** *Offensive & Vulgar Slang* A woman or girl. [?]

tway•blade (twā′blād′) *n.* Any of numerous small terrestrial orchids of the genera *Liparis* and *Listera,* having usu. two basal leaves. [Obsolete *tway,* two (short for ME *twaine;* see TWAIN) + BLADE (transl. of Med.Lat. *bifolium,* two-leaf).]

tweak (twēk) *tr.v.* **tweaked, tweak•ing, tweaks 1.** To pinch, pluck, or twist sharply. **2.** To adjust; fine-tune. **3.** To make fun of; tease. ❖ *n.* **1.** A sharp twisting pinch. **2.** A teasing remark or action; a joke. [Prob. var. of dialectal *twick* < ME *twikken* < OE *twiccian.*] —**tweak′y** *adj.*

twee (twē) *adj. Chiefly British* Overly precious or nice. [Alteration of *tweet,* baby-talk alteration of SWEET.]

tweed (twēd) *n.* **1.** A coarse, rugged, often nubby woolen fabric made in any of various twill weaves and used chiefly for casual suits and coats. **2. tweeds** Clothing made of this fabric. [Alteration (poss. influenced by the river TWEED) of Sc. *tweel,* twill < ME *twile.* See TWILL.]

Tweed A river of SE Scotland flowing 156 km (97 mi) E to the North Sea.

Tweed, William Marcy Known as "Boss Tweed." 1823–78. Amer. politician who as the Democratic boss of New York City in the 1860s defrauded the city of millions of dollars.

twee•dle•dum and twee•dle•dee (twēd′l-dŭm′; twēd′l-dē′) *n.* Two people or two groups that are practically indistinguishable. [After *Tweedledum and Tweedledee,* names of two proverbial rival fiddlers, of imit. orig.]

tweed•y (twē′dē) *adj.* **-i•er, -i•est 1.** Made of tweed. **2.** Wearing tweeds. **3.** *Informal* Suggestive of casual, informal taste, habits, and lifestyle.

′tween (twēn) *prep.* Between.

tweet (twēt) *n.* A weak chirping sound. ❖ *intr.v.* **tweet•ed, tweet•ing, tweets** To utter a tweet. [Imit.]

tweet•er (twē′tər) *n.* A small loudspeaker designed to reproduce high-pitched sounds in a high-fidelity audio system.

tweeze (twēz) *tr.v.* **tweezed, tweez•ing, tweez•es** To handle or extract with tweezers. [Back-formation < TWEEZERS.]

tweez•er (twē′zər) *n.* Tweezers.

tweez•ers (twē′zərz) *pl.n.* (*used with a sing. or pl. verb*) Small pincers, usu. of metal, used for plucking or handling small objects. [< obsolete *tweezes,* pl. of *tweeze,* case for small instruments, alteration of *etweese* < Fr. *étuis,* pl. of *étui.* See ÉTUI.]

twelfth (twĕlfth) *n.* **1.** The ordinal number matching the number 12 in a series. **2.** One of 12 equal parts. [ME *twelfthe,* alteration of OE *twelfta.* See **dwo-** in App.] —**twelfth** *adv. & adj.*

Twelfth Day *n. Ecclesiastical* Epiphany.

Twelfth Night *n.* January 5, the eve of Epiphany, celebrated as a holiday in parts of Europe and the United States.

twelve (twĕlv) *n.* **1.** The cardinal number equal to the sum of 11 + 1. **2.** The twelfth in a set or sequence. **3. Twelve** *Bible* **a.** The twelve original disciples of Jesus. **b.** The books of the Minor Prophets in the Hebrew Scriptures. [ME < OE *twelf.* See **dwo-** in App.] —**twelve** *adj. & pron.*

twelve•mo (twĕlv′mō′) *n., pl.* **-mos** See **duodecimo.**

Tutankhamen

Desmond Tutu
photographed in 1984

Tuvalu

twelve·month (twĕlv′mŭnth′) *n.* A year.

twelve·pen·ny nail (twĕlv′pĕn′ē) *n.* A nail 3¼ inches (8.25 centimeters) long. [< the original price per hundred.]

twelve-step (twĕlv′stĕp′) *adj.* Of or being a program designed to assist in the recovery from addiction or compulsive behavior. [After the *Twelve Steps*, the twelve guiding concepts of the Alcoholics Anonymous program for curbing alcohol addiction.]

twelve-tone (twĕlv′tōn′) *adj. Music* Relating to, consisting of, or based on an arrangement of the 12 chromatic tones.

twen·ti·eth (twĕn′tē-ĭth, twŭn′-) *n.* **1.** The ordinal number matching the number 20 in a series. **2.** One of 20 equal parts. —**twen′ti·eth** *adv. & adj.*

twen·ty (twĕn′tē, twŭn′-) *n.* **1.** The cardinal number equal to 2 × 10. **2.** **twenties a.** A decade or the numbers from 20 to 29. **b.** often **Twenties** The decade from 20 to 29 in a century. **3.** A twenty-dollar bill. [ME < OE *twēntig.* See **dwo-** in App.] —**twen′ty** *adj. & pron.*

24-7 (twĕn′tē-fôr-sĕv′ən, -fôr-) *adv. Slang* Continuously; unceasingly. [Short for *24 hours a day, 7 days a week.*]

twen·ty-one (twĕn′tē-wŭn′, twŭn′-) *n.* See **blackjack** 3.

twen·ty-twen·ty or **20/20** (twĕn′tē-twĕn′tē, twŭn′tē-twŭn′tē) *adj.* Having normal visual acuity. [< a method of testing vision by reading charts at a distance of 20 feet.]

'twere (twûr) Contraction of *it were.*

twerp also **twirp** (twûrp) *n. Slang* A person regarded as insignificant and contemptible. [?]

Twi (chwē, chē) *n.* A variety of the Akan language spoken in Ghana.

twi·bill (twī′bĭl′) *n. Archaic* **1.** A battle-ax with two cutting edges. **2.** A mattock with one blade like an ax and the other like an adz. [ME < OE : *twi-*, two; see **dwo-** in App. + *bil,* billhook.]

twice (twīs) *adv.* **1.** In two cases or on two occasions; two times: *I rewrote the essay twice.* **2.** In doubled degree or amount: *twice as many.* [ME < OE *twiga.* See **dwo-** in App.]

twice-laid (twīs′lād′) *adj.* Made from strands of old or used rope. Used of rope.

twice-told (twīs′tōld′) *adj.* Very familiar because of repeated telling: *a twice-told tale.*

twid·dle (twĭd′l) *v.* **-dled, -dling, -dles** —*tr.* To turn over or around idly or lightly; fiddle with. —*intr.* **1.** To trifle with something. **2.** To be busy about trifles. **3.** To twirl or rotate without purpose. ❖ *n.* The act or an instance of twiddling. —*idiom:* **twiddle (one's) thumbs** To do little or nothing; be idle. [Poss. blend of TWIST and FIDDLE.] —**twid′dler** *n.*

twig¹ (twĭg) *n.* **1.** A young shoot representing the current season's growth of a woody plant. **2.** Any small leafless branch of a woody plant. [ME < OE *twigge.* See **dwo-** in App.]

twig² (twĭg) *v.* **twigged, twig·ging, twigs** *Chiefly British* —*tr.* **1.** To observe or notice. **2.** To understand or figure out. —*intr.* To be or become aware of the situation; understand. [Ir.Gael. *tuigim,* I understand < OIr. *tuicim.*]

twig³ (twĭg) *n. Chiefly British* The current style. [?]

twig·gy (twĭg′ē) *adj.* **-gi·er, -gi·est 1.** Resembling a twig or twigs, as in slenderness or fragility. **2.** Abounding in twigs.

twi·light (twī′līt′) *n.* **1a.** The diffused light from the sky during the early evening or early morning when the sun is below the horizon. **b.** The time of the day when the sun is just below the horizon, esp. the period between sunset and dark. **2.** Dim or diffused illumination. **3.** A period or condition of decline following growth, glory, or success: *in the twilight of his life.* **4.** A state of ambiguity or obscurity. [ME *twilighte* : OE *twi-,* two, half; see **dwo-** in App. + OE *līht,* light; see LIGHT¹.]

twilight zone *n.* An area of ambiguity between two distinct states or conditions.

twill (twĭl) *n.* **1.** A fabric with diagonal parallel ribs. **2.** The weave used to produce such a fabric. ❖ *tr.v.* **twilled, twill·ing, twills** To weave (cloth) so as to produce a pattern of diagonal parallel ribs. [ME *twile* < OE *twilic,* woven of double thread. See **dwo-** in App.]

twin (twĭn) *n.* **1.** One of two offspring born at the same birth. **2.** One of two identical or similar people, animals, or things; a counterpart. **3. twins** *Mineralogy* Two interwoven crystals that are mirror images of each other. **4.** A twin-size bed. ❖ *adj.* **1.** Being two or one of two offspring born at the same birth: *twin sisters.* **2.** Being two or one of two identical or similar people, animals, or things. **3.** Consisting of two identical or similar parts: *a twin lamp fixture.* **4.** *Botany* Of or relating to structures, such as flowers, that occur in pairs. ❖ *v.* **twinned, twin·ning, twins** —*intr.* **1a.** To give birth to twins. **b.** *Archaic* To be one of twin offspring. **2.** To be paired or coupled. —*tr.* **1.** To pair or couple. **2.** To provide a match or counterpart to. [ME < OE *twinn,* twofold. See **dwo-** in App.]

twin bed *n.* One of a matching pair of single beds.

twin·ber·ry (twĭn′bĕr′ē) *n.* **1.** See **partridgeberry. 2.** A deciduous North American shrub (*Lonicera involucrata*) having shiny purple-black berries.

twin bill *n.* **1.** A double feature. **2.** *Sports* A double-header.

twin·born (twĭn′bôrn′) *adj.* Born a twin or twins.

twine (twīn) *v.* **twined, twin·ing, twines** —*tr.* **1.** To twist together (threads, for example); intertwine. **2.** To form by twisting, intertwining, or interlacing. **3.** To encircle or coil about. **4.** To

wind, coil, or wrap around something. —*intr.* **1.** To become twisted, interlaced, or interwoven. **2.** To go in a winding course; twist about. ❖ *n.* **1.** A strong string or cord made of two or more threads twisted together. **2.** Something formed by twining. **3.** A tangle; a knot. [ME *twinen* < *twin,* twine < OE *twīn,* double thread. See **dwo-** in App.] —**twin′er** *n.*

twin-en·gine (twĭn′ĕn′jĭn) *adj.* Powered by two engines.

Twin Falls A city of S-central ID W of Pocatello near the **Twin Falls** of the Snake R. Pop. 34,469.

twin-flow·er (twĭn′flou′ər) *n.* A shrubby creeping evergreen plant (*Linnaea borealis*) of northern regions, having roundish opposite leaves and paired, bell-shaped pinkish flowers.

twinge (twĭnj) *n.* **1.** A sudden sharp physical pain. **2.** A mental or emotional pain: *a twinge of guilt.* ❖ *v.* **twinged, twing·ing, twing·es** —*tr.* **1.** To cause to feel a sharp pain. **2.** *Obsolete* To tweak; pinch. —*intr.* To feel a twinge or twinges. [< ME *twengen,* to pinch < OE *twengan.*]

twi·night (twī′nīt′) *adj. Baseball* Of or being a double-header in which the first game begins in late afternoon.

twin·kle (twĭng′kəl) *v.* **-kled, -kling, -kles** —*intr.* **1.** To shine with slight intermittent gleams, as stars; flicker; glimmer. **2.** To be bright or sparkling, as with merriment. **3.** To blink or wink the eyes. **4.** To move about or to and fro rapidly and gracefully; flit. —*tr.* To emit (light) in slight intermittent gleams. ❖ *n.* **1.** A slight intermittent gleam of light; a glimmer. **2.** A sparkle of merriment or delight in the eye. **3.** A brief interval; a twinkling. **4.** A rapid to-and-fro movement. [ME *twinklen* < OE *twinclian,* freq. of *twincan,* to blink.] —**twin′kler** *n.* —**twink′ly** *adj.*

twin·kling (twĭng′klĭng) *n.* **1.** The act of blinking. **2.** A blink or twinkle. **3.** The time it takes to blink once; an instant.

twin·ning (twĭn′ĭng) *n. Mineralogy* The formation of twin crystals. —**twinned** *adj.*

Twins (twĭnz) *pl.n.* (*used with a sing. verb*) See **Gemini** 1, 2a.

twin-screw (twĭn′skrōō′) *adj. Nautical* Having two propellers, one on either side of the keel, that usu. revolve in opposite directions.

twin·set or **twin set** (twĭn′sĕt) *n.* A sweater set consisting of a cardigan and a shell that match and are worn together.

twin-size (twĭn′sīz′) *adj.* **1.** Measuring about 39 by 75 inches (99 by 190 centimeters). Used of a bed. **2.** Being of a size that will fit such a bed. [< TWIN (BED).]

twirl (twûrl) *v.* **twirled, twirl·ing, twirls** —*tr.* **1.** To rotate or revolve briskly; swing in a circle; spin: *twirl a baton.* **2.** To twist or wind around. —*intr.* **1.** To move or spin around rapidly, suddenly, or repeatedly. **2.** To whirl or turn suddenly; make an about-face. **3.** *Baseball* To pitch. ❖ *n.* **1.** The act of twirling or the condition of being twirled. **2.** Something twirled; a twist. [?] —**twirl′er** *n.*

twirp (twûrp) *n. Slang* Variant of **twerp.**

twist (twĭst) *v.* **twist·ed, twist·ing, twists** —*tr.* **1a.** To wind together (threads, for example) so as to produce a single strand. **b.** To form in this manner. **2.** To wind or coil (rope, for example) about something. **3.** To interlock or interlace: *twist flowers in one's hair.* **4.** To make (one's) way in a tortuous manner. **5.** To turn so as to face another direction. **6.** To impart a spiral or coiling shape to. **7a.** To turn or open by turning. **b.** To pull, break, or snap by turning: *twist off a dead branch.* **8.** To wrench or sprain. **9.** To alter the normal aspect of; contort. **10.** To alter or distort the intended meaning of. **11.** To alter or distort the mental, moral, or emotional character of. —*intr.* **1.** To be or become twisted. **2.** To move or progress in a winding course; meander. **3.** To squirm; writhe. **4.** To rotate or revolve. **5.** To dance the twist. **6.** To move so as to face in another direction. ❖ *n.* **1.** Something twisted or formed by twisting, esp.: **a.** A length of yarn, cord, or thread, esp. a strong silk thread. **b.** Tobacco leaves processed into the form of a rope or roll. **c.** A loaf of bread or other bakery product made from pieces of dough twisted together. **d.** A sliver of citrus peel twisted over or dropped into a beverage for flavoring. **2.** The act of twisting or the condition of being twisted; a spin, twirl, or rotation. **3.** *Sports* **a.** A complete rotation of the body around its vertical axis, as in diving. **b.** A spinning motion given to a ball. **4a.** The state of being twisted spirally; torsional stress or strain. **b.** The degree or angle of torsional stress. **5a.** A contortion or distortion of the body, esp. the face. **b.** A distortion of meaning. **6.** A sprain or wrench, as of an ankle. **7.** A change in direction; a turn. **8.** An unexpected change in a process or a departure from a pattern, often producing a distortion or perversion. **9.** A personal inclination or eccentricity; a penchant or flaw. **10.** A dance characterized by vigorous gyrations of the hips and arms. —*idiom:* **twist (someone's) arm** *Slang* To coerce by or as if by physical force. [ME *twisten,* to squeeze, be divided < *twist,* a divided object, fork, rope < OE *-twist.* See **dwo-** in App.] —**twist′a·bil′i·ty** *n.* —**twist′a·ble** *adj.* —**twist′y** *adj.*

twist drill *n.* A drill having deep helical grooves along the shank from the point.

twist·er (twĭs′tər) *n.* **1.** One that twists, as in the manufacture of rope or yarn. **2.** *Informal* A tornado or cyclone.

twit (twĭt) *tr.v.* **twit·ted, twit·ting, twits** To taunt, ridicule, or tease, esp. for embarrassing mistakes or faults. See Syns at **ridicule.** ❖ *n.* **1.** The act or an instance of twitting. **2.** A reproach, gibe, or taunt. **3.** *Slang* A person regarded as foolishly annoying.

[Short for obsolete *atwite* < ME *atwiten* < OE *ætwītan* : *æt*, at + *wītan*, to reproach; see **weid-** in App.] —**twit′ter** *n.*

twitch (twĭch) *v.* **twitched, twitch•ing, twitch•es** —*tr.* To draw, pull, or move suddenly and sharply; jerk. —*intr.* **1.** To move jerkily or spasmodically. **2.** To ache sharply from time to time; twinge. ❖ *n.* **1.** A sudden involuntary or spasmodic muscular movement. **2.** A sudden pulling; a tug. **3.** A looped cord used to restrain a horse by tightening it around the animal's upper lip. [ME *twicchen*.] —**twitch′y** *adj.*

twitch•y (twĭch′ē) *adj.* **-i•er, -i•est 1.** Characterized by jerky or spasmodic motion: *the twitchy whiskers of a cat.* **2.** Nervous; jittery. —**twitch′i•ly** *adv.* —**twitch′i•ness** *n.*

twit•ter (twĭt′ər) *v.* **-tered, -ter•ing, -ters** —*intr.* **1.** To utter a succession of light chirping or tremulous sounds; chirrup. **2a.** To speak rapidly and in a tremulous manner. **b.** To giggle nervously; titter. **3.** To tremble with nervous agitation or excitement. —*tr.* To utter or say with a twitter. ❖ *n.* **1a.** The light chirping sound made by certain birds. **b.** A similar sound, esp. light tremulous speech or laughter. **2.** Agitation or excitement; flutter. [ME *twiteren*, ult. of imit. orig.] —**twit′ter•er** *n.* —**twit′ter•y** *adj.*

twixt also **′twixt** (twĭkst) *prep.* Betwixt.

two (to͞o) *n.* **1.** The cardinal number equal to the sum of 1 + 1. **2.** The second in a set or sequence. **3.** Something having two parts, units, or members, such as a playing card. **4.** A two-dollar bill. —***idiom:* in two** Into two separate parts; in half. [ME < OE *twā*. See **dwo-** in App.] —**two** *adj. & pron.*

two-bag•ger (to͞o′băg′ər) *n. Baseball* See **two-base hit.**

two-base hit (to͞o′bās′) *n. Baseball* A hit enabling the batter to reach second base.

two-bit (to͞o′bĭt′) *adj.* **1.** *Informal* Costing or worth 25 cents. **2.** *Slang* Worth very little; petty or insignificant.

two bits *pl.n.* **1.** *Informal* Twenty-five cents. **2.** *Slang* A petty sum.

two-by-four (to͞o′bī-fôr′, -fōr′, to͞o′bə-) *adj.* **1.** Measuring two units by four units, esp. inches. **2.** *Slang* Small in size; boxed in or cramped. ❖ *n.* A length of lumber that is 2 inches thick and 4 inches wide, or that is trimmed to slightly smaller dimensions.

two-di•men•sion•al (to͞o′dĭ-mĕn′shə-nəl, -dī-) *adj.* **1.** Having only two dimensions. **2.** Lacking range or depth.

two-edged (to͞o′ĕjd′) *adj.* **1.** Having two keen edges. **2.** Being such that two contrasting meanings, effects, or interpretations are possible: *a two-edged compliment.*

two-faced (to͞o′fāst′) *adj.* **1.** Having two faces or surfaces. **2.** Hypocritical or double-dealing; deceitful. —**two′-fac′ed•ly** (-fā′sĭd-lē, -fāst′lē) *adv.* —**two′-fac′ed•ness** *n.*

two•fer (to͞o′fər) *n. Informal* **1.** A coupon offering two items for the price of one. **2.** An offer, a deal, or an arrangement in which a single expense yields a dual return. [Alteration for *two for (the price of one).*]

two-fist•ed (to͞o′fĭs′tĭd) *adj.* **1.** Using or able to use two fists. **2.** *Informal* Marked by great vigor, energy, or enthusiasm.

two-grained spelt (to͞o′grānd′) *n.* See **emmer.**

two-hand•ed (to͞o′hăn′dĭd) *adj.* **1.** Requiring the use of two hands at once. **2.** Made to be operated by two people: *a two-handed crosscut saw.* **3.** Able to use both hands with equal facility; ambidextrous. **4.** Having two hands.

two-mast•er (to͞o′măs′tər) *n.* A sailing vessel having two masts.

twoo•nie (to͞o′nē) *n. Informal* Variant of **toonie.**

two•pence or **tup•pence** (tŭp′əns) *n.* **1.** *Chiefly British* **a.** Two pennies regarded as a monetary unit. **b.** A very small amount; a whit: *didn't care twopence about politics.* **2.** *pl.* **twopence** or **-penc•es** A British coin worth two pennies.

two•pen•ny (tŭp′ə-nē, to͞o′pĕn′ē) *adj.* **1.** Worth or costing two pennies: *twopenny candy.* **2.** Cheap; worthless.

two-phase (to͞o′fāz′) *adj. Electricity* Relating to two alternating currents with phases differing by 90°.

two-piece (to͞o′pēs′) *adj.* Made in or consisting of two parts or pieces. ❖ *n.* A garment consisting of two parts.

two-ply (to͞o′plī′) *adj.* **1.** Made of two interwoven layers. **2.** Consisting of two thicknesses or strands: *two-ply yarn.*

two-seat•er (to͞o′sē′tər) *n.* A vehicle for two people.

Two Sic•i•lies (sĭs′ə-lēz) A former kingdom comprising Sicily and Naples; annexed to Italy by Garibaldi in 1860.

two•some (to͞o′səm) *n.* **1.** Two people or things together; a pair or couple. **2.** *Sports* A round of golf played by two people.

two-spir•it (to͞o′spĭr′ĭt) *n.* A person, esp. a Native American man, who assumes the sexual identity and is granted the social status of the opposite sex. See Usage Note at **berdache.**

two-spot (to͞o′spŏt′) *n.* **1.** *Games* A playing card bearing two spots or pips; a deuce. **2.** *Slang* **a.** A two-dollar bill. **b.** Two dollars.

two-step (to͞o′stĕp′) *n.* **1.** A ballroom dance in 2/4 time, marked by long sliding steps. **2.** The music for this dance.

two-time (to͞o′tīm′) *tr.v.* **-timed, -tim•ing, -times** *Slang* **1.** To be unfaithful to (a spouse or lover). **2.** To deceive; double-cross. —**two′-tim′er** *n.*

two-tone (to͞o′tōn′) or **two-toned** (-tōnd′) *adj.* Having two colors or two shades of a single color.

two-way (to͞o′wā′) *adj.* **1a.** Affording passage in two directions: *a two-way street.* **b.** Moving in two directions: *two-way traffic.* **2a.** Permitting communication in two directions: *a two-way radio.* **b.** Permitting flow in two directions: *a two-way valve.* **3.** *Sports* Playing both offense and defense. **4a.** Expressive of or involving mutual action, relationship, or responsibility. **b.** Involving two participants.

two-way mirror *n.* See **one-way mirror.**

two-wheel•er (to͞o′hwē′lər, -wē′-) *n.* A vehicle with two wheels, esp. a bicycle.

twp. *abbr.* township

TX *abbr.* Texas

-ty *suff.* Condition; quality: *realty.* [ME *-te* < OFr. < Lat. *-tās.*]

ty•coon (tī-ko͞on′) *n.* **1.** A wealthy and powerful businessperson or industrialist; a magnate. **2.** Used formerly as a title for a Japanese shogun. [J. *taikun*, title of a shogun, of Chin. orig.]

ty•ing (tī′ĭng) *v.* Present participle of **tie.**

tyke also **tike** (tīk) *n.* **1.** A small child. **2.** A mongrel or cur. **3.** *Chiefly British* A man considered uncouth or mean; a boor. [ME, mongrel < ON *tīk*, bitch.]

Ty•le•nol (tī′lə-nôl′, -nŏl′) A trademark used for the drug acetaminophen.

Ty•ler (tī′lər) A city of NE TX ESE of Dallas. Pop. 83,650.

Tyler, John 1790–1862. The 10th President of the US (1841–45), whose administration was marked by the annexation of Texas (1845).

John Tyler
detail from a portrait by George Peter Alexander Healy (1813–94)

Tyler, Royall 1757–1826. Amer. jurist and writer whose plays include *The Contrast* (first produced 1787).

Tyler, Wat d. 1381. English revolutionary who led the Peasants' Revolt against Richard II's poll tax in June 1381.

tym•bal (tĭm′bəl) *n.* Variant of **timbal.**

tym•pan (tĭm′pən) *n.* **1.** *Printing* A padding, as of paper or cloth, placed over the platen of a press to regulate pressure. **2.** *Architecture* A tympanum. **3.** A tightly stretched sheet or membrane, as on a drum. [ME *timpan*, drum < OE *timpana* < Lat. *tympanum* < Gk. *tumpanon.*]

tym•pa•ni (tĭm′pə-nē) *pl.n.* Variant of **timpani.**

tym•pan•ic (tĭm-păn′ĭk) *adj.* **1.** Relating to or resembling a drum. **2.** *Anatomy* Of or relating to the middle ear or eardrum. [< Lat. *tympanum*, drum. See TYMPANUM.]

tympanic bone *n.* The part of the temporal bone that partially encloses the middle ear and supports the eardrum.

tympanic membrane *n.* See **eardrum.**

tym•pa•nist (tĭm′pə-nĭst) *n.* Variant of **timpanist.**

tym•pa•ni•tes (tĭm′pə-nī′tēz) *n.* A distention of the abdomen resulting from the accumulation of gas or air in the intestine or peritoneal cavity. [ME < LLat. *tympanītēs* < Gk. *tumpanītēs* < *tumpanon*, drum.] —**tym′pa•nit′ic** (-nĭt′ĭk) *adj.*

tym•pa•num also **tim•pa•num** (tĭm′pə-nəm) *n., pl.* **-na** (-nə) or **-nums 1a.** *Anatomy* See **middle ear. b.** See **eardrum. 2.** *Zoology* A membranous external auditory structure, as in certain insects. **3.** *Architecture* **a.** The ornamental recessed space or panel enclosed by the cornices of a triangular pediment. **b.** A similar space between an arch and the lintel of a portal or window. **4.** The diaphragm of a telephone. [Med.Lat. < Lat., drum < Gk. *tumpanon.*]

tympanum
east pediment of the Philadelphia Museum of Art

tym•pa•ny (tĭm′pə-nē) *n., pl.* **-nies 1.** *Archaic* Inflated manner or style; bombast. **2.** See **tympanites.** [Med.Lat. *tympanias*, tympanites < Gk. *tumpaniās* < *tumpanon*, drum.]

Tyn•dale also **Tin•dal** or **Tin•dale** (tĭn′dl), **William** 1494?–1536. English religious reformer whose translation of the New Testament was the basis of the King James Bible.

Tyn•dall (tĭn′dl), **Mount** A mountain, 4,275.8 m (14,019 ft), in the Sierra Nevada of S-central CA.

Tyn•dar•e•us (tĭn-dâr′ē-əs) *n. Greek Mythology* A king of Sparta and the husband of Leda.

Tyne (tīn) A river of N England flowing c. 129 km (80 mi) E to the North Sea.

typ•al (tī′pəl) *adj.* Of, relating to, or serving as a type; typical.

type (tīp) *n.* **1.** A number of people or things having in common traits or characteristics that distinguish them as a group or class. **2.** The general character or structure held in common by a number of people or things considered as a group or class. **3.** A person or thing having the features of a group or class. **4.** An example or a model having the ideal features of a group or class; an embodiment. **5.** A person regarded as exemplifying a particular profession, rank, or social group: *a group of executive types.* **6.** A figure, representation, or symbol of something to come, such as an event in the Old Testament that foreshadows another in the New Testament. **7a.** A taxonomic group, esp. a genus or species, chosen as the representative example of a larger taxonomic group. **b.** See **holotype. 8.** *Printing* **a.** A small block of metal or wood bearing a raised letter or character on the upper end that leaves a printed impression when inked. **b.** Such pieces considered as a group. **c.** Printed or typewritten characters; print. **d.** A size or style of printed or typewritten characters; a typeface: *a sans-serif type.* **9.** A pattern, a design, or an image impressed or stamped onto the face of a coin. ❖ *v.* **typed, typ•ing, types** —*tr.* **1.** To write (something) with a typewriter; typewrite. **2.** To determine the antigenic characteristics of (a blood or tissue sample). **3.** To typecast. **4.** To represent or typify. **5.** To prefigure. —*intr.* To write with a typewriter; typewrite. [ME, symbol < LLat. *typus*, type < Lat., image < Gk. *tupos*, impression.]

type A or **Type A** *adj.* Of or relating to a behavior pattern characterized by tenseness, impatience, and aggressiveness that

ă	**pat**	oi	**boy**
ā	**pay**	ou	**out**
âr	**care**	o͝o	**took**
ä	**father**	o͞o	**boot**
ĕ	**pet**	ŭ	**cut**
ē	**be**	ûr	**urge**
ĭ	**pit**	th	**thin**
ī	**pie**	*th*	**this**
îr	**pier**	hw	**which**
ŏ	**pot**	zh	**vision**
ō	**toe**	ə	**about, item**
ô	**paw**		

Stress marks:
′ (primary);
′ (secondary), as in
lexicon (lĕk′sĭ-kŏn′)

possibly increases one's risk of heart disease. ❖ *n.* One who exhibits this behavior pattern.

type B or **Type B** *adj.* Of or relating to a behavior pattern characterized by a relaxed manner, patience, and friendliness that possibly decreases one's risk of heart disease. ❖ *n.* One who exhibits this behavior pattern.

type·cast (tīp′kăst′) *tr.v.* **-cast, -cast·ing, -casts 1.** To cast in an acting role akin or natural to one's own personality or fitted to one's physical appearance. **2.** To assign (a performer) repeatedly to the same kind of part.

type·face (tīp′fās′) *n. Printing* **1a.** The surface of a block of type that makes the impression. **b.** The impression made by this surface. **2.** The size or style of the letter or character on a block of type. **3.** The full range of type of the same design.

type genus *n.* The taxonomic genus that is designated as representative of the family to which it belongs.

type-high (tīp′hī′) *adj. Printing* As high as the standard height of type, measured from the face to the foot, 23.3 millimeters (0.9186 inch).

type metal *n. Printing* An alloy used for making metal type, consisting mainly of lead, antimony, and tin.

type·script (tīp′skrĭpt′) *n.* **1.** A typewritten copy, as of a manuscript. **2.** Typewritten matter. [TYPE + (MANU)SCRIPT.]

type·set (tīp′sĕt′) *tr.v.* **-set, -set·ting, -sets** *Printing* To set (written material) into type; compose. —**type′set′ter** *n.*

type species *n.* A holotype.

type·style or **type style** (tīp′stīl′) *n. Printing* A specific style of type, as Roman.

type·write (tīp′rīt′) *tr. & intr.v.* **-wrote** (-rōt′), **-writ·ten** (-rĭt′n), **-writ·ing, -writes** To engage in writing or to write (matter) with a typewriter. [Back-formation < TYPEWRITER.]

type·writ·er (tīp′rī′tər) *n.* **1.** A writing machine that produces characters by a manually operated keyboard that actuates a set of raised types, which strike the paper through an inked ribbon. **2.** *Printing* A typestyle like that of typewritten copy.

type·writ·ing (tīp′rī′tĭng) *n.* **1.** The act, process, or skill of using a typewriter. **2.** Copy produced on a typewriter; typescript.

ty·phoid (tī′foid′) *n.* Typhoid fever. ❖ *adj.* also **ty·phoi·dal** (tī-foid′l) Of, relating to, or resembling typhoid fever. [N., short for TYPHOID FEVER. Adj., TYPH(US) + -OID (< its resemblance to typhus).]

typhoid fever *n.* An acute, highly infectious disease caused by a bacillus (*Salmonella typhi*) transmitted chiefly by contaminated food or water and marked by high fever, coughing, intestinal hemorrhaging, and red blood spots on the skin.

Typhoid Mary *n.* A person from whom something undesirable or deadly spreads to those nearby. [After *Typhoid Mary*, nickname of Mary Mallon (1870?–1938), Irish-born American cook and immune carrier of typhoid fever.]

Ty·phon (tī′fŏn′) *n. Greek Mythology* A monster with one hundred heads, thrown by Zeus into Tartarus. [Gk. *Tuphōn.* See **dheub-** in App.]

ty·phoon (tī-fōōn′) *n.* A tropical cyclone occurring in the western Pacific or Indian oceans. [Gk. *tuphōn,* whirlwind, and Ar. *ṭūfān,* deluge (< Gk. *tuphōn*), and Chin. (Cantonese) *taaîfung,* typhoon (equivalent to Chin. (Mandarin) *tái,* great + *fēng,* wind).]

WORD HISTORY Few words better illustrate the polyglot background of English than *typhoon,* with its Chinese, Arabic, East Indian, and Greek background. The Greek word *tuphōn,* both the name of the father of the winds and a common noun meaning "whirlwind, typhoon," was borrowed into Arabic as *ṭūfān.* This word passed into languages spoken in India, where Arabic-speaking Muslim invaders had settled in the 11th century, and where it referred specifically to a violent storm in India. From there it passed into English by 1588 as *touffon* or *tufan.* China, another great empire, gave us yet another word for a storm, in this case the hurricane that occurred in the waters around China. This Chinese word in its Cantonese form, *taaî fung,* was similar to our Arabic borrowing and is first recorded in English guise as *tuffoon* in 1699. The various forms coalesced and finally became *typhoon* by 1819.

Tzu Hsi

ty·phus (tī′fəs) *n.* Any of several forms of infectious disease caused by rickettsia, esp. those transmitted by fleas, lice, or mites, and marked by headache, high fever, and red rashes on the skin. [NLat. *typhus* < Gk. *tūphos,* stupor arising from a fever, vapor < *tūphein,* to smoke.] —**ty′phous** (-fəs) *adj.*

typ·i·cal (tīp′ĭ-kəl) *adj.* **1.** Exhibiting the qualities, traits, or characteristics that identify a kind, class, group, or category. **2.** Of or relating to a representative specimen; characteristic or distinctive. **3.** Conforming to a type: *typical of the baroque period.* **4.** also **typ·ic** (-ĭk) Of the nature of, constituting, or serving as a type; emblematic. [LLat. *typicālis < typicus* < Gk. *tupikos < tupos,* impression.] —**typ′i·cal·ly** *adv.* —**typ′i·cal·ness, typ′i·cal′i·ty** (-kăl′ĭ-tē) *n.*

typ·i·fy (tīp′ə-fī′) *tr.v.* **-fied, -fy·ing, -fies 1.** To serve as a typical example of; embody the essential characteristics of. **2.** To represent by an image, a form, or a model; symbolize or prefigure. —**typ′i·fi·ca′tion** (-fi-kā′shən) *n.* —**typ′i·fi′er** *n.*

typ·ist (tī′pĭst) *n.* One who operates a typewriter.

ty·po (tī′pō) *n., pl.* **-pos** *Informal* A typographical error.

ty·pog·ra·pher (tī-pŏg′rə-fər) *n.* One that sets written material into type; a compositor or printer.

typographical error *n.* A mistake in printing, typesetting, or typing, esp. one caused by striking an incorrect key on a keyboard.

ty·pog·ra·phy (tī-pŏg′rə-fē) *n., pl.* **-phies 1a.** The art and technique of printing with movable type. **b.** The composition of printed material from movable type. **2.** The arrangement and appearance of printed matter. [Fr. *typographie* < Med.Lat. *typographia* : Gk. *tupos,* impression + Lat. *-graphia,* -graphy.] —**ty′po·graph′i·cal** (tī′pə-grăf′ĭ-kəl), **ty′po·graph′ic** (-grăf′ĭk) *adj.* —**ty′po·graph′i·cal·ly** *adv.*

ty·pol·o·gy (tī-pŏl′ə-jē) *n., pl.* **-gies 1.** The study or systematic classification of types. **2.** A theory or doctrine of types, as in scriptural studies. —**ty′po·log′i·cal** (tī′pə-lŏj′ĭ-kəl), **ty′po·log′ic** (-lŏj′ĭk) *adj.* —**ty′po·log′i·cal·ly** *adv.* —**ty·pol′o·gist** *n.*

Tyr (tîr) *n. Mythology* A Norse god of war, son of Odin. [ON *Týr.* See **dyeu-** in App.]

ty·ra·mine (tī′rə-mēn′) *n.* A colorless crystalline amine, $C_8H_{11}NO$, used in medicine as a sympathomimetic agent. [TYR(OSINE) + AMINE.]

ty·ran·ni·cal (tĭ-răn′ĭ-kəl, tī-) also **ty·ran·nic** (-răn′ĭk) *adj.* **1.** Of or relating to a tyrant or tyranny. **2.** Characteristic of a tyrant or tyranny; despotic and oppressive. —**ty·ran′ni·cal·ly** *adv.* —**ty·ran′ni·cal·ness** *n.*

tyr·an·nize (tîr′ə-nīz′) *v.* **-nized, -niz·ing, -niz·es** —*tr.* To treat tyrannically; oppress. —*intr.* **1.** To exercise absolute power. **2.** To rule as a tyrant. [ME < OFr. *tyranniser < tyran,* tyrant. See TYRANT.] —**tyr′an·niz′er** *n.*

ty·ran·no·saur (tĭ-răn′ə-sôr′, tī-) also **ty·ran·no·saur·us** (tĭ-răn′ə-sôr′əs, tī-) *n.* A very large bipedal carnivorous dinosaur of the Upper Cretaceous Period of North America, having small forelimbs and a large head. [NLat. *Tyrannosaurus,* genus name : Gk. *turannos,* tyrant + Gk. *sauros,* lizard.]

tyr·an·nous (tîr′ə-nəs) *adj.* Characterized by tyranny; despotic. —**tyr′an·nous·ly** *adv.*

tyr·an·ny (tîr′ə-nē) *n., pl.* **-nies 1.** A government in which a single ruler is vested with absolute power. **2.** The office, authority, or jurisdiction of an absolute ruler. **3.** Absolute power, esp. when exercised unjustly or cruelly. **4a.** Use of absolute power. **b.** A tyrannical act. **5.** Extreme harshness or severity; rigor. [ME *tyrannie* < OFr. < LLat. *tyrannia* < Gk. *turanniā < turannos,* tyrant.]

ty·rant (tī′rənt) *n.* **1.** An absolute ruler who governs without restrictions. **2.** A ruler who exercises power in a harsh cruel manner. **3.** An oppressive, harsh, arbitrary person. [ME < OFr., alteration of *tyran* < Lat. *tyrannus* < Gk. *turannos.*]

tyrant flycatcher *n.* See **flycatcher** 2.

tyre (tîr) *n. Chiefly British* Variant of **tire**[1].

Tyre An ancient Phoenician city on the E Mediterranean Sea in S Lebanon; cap. of Phoenicia after the 11th cent. B.C.

Tyr·i·an purple (tîr′ē-ən) *n.* A reddish dyestuff obtained from the bodies of certain mollusks of the genus *Murex* and highly prized in ancient times. [After TYRE.]

ty·ro also **ti·ro** (tī′rō) *n., pl.* **-ros** A beginner in learning something. [Med.Lat. *tȳrō,* squire, var. of Lat. *tīrō,* recruit.]

Ty·rol or **Ti·rol** (tə-rōl′, tī-, tī′rōl′) A region of the E Alps in W Austria and N Italy. —**Ty·rol′le·an, Tyr′o·lese′** (tîr′ə-lēz′, -lēs′, tī′rə-) *adj. & n.*

ty·ros·i·nase (tī-rŏs′ə-nās′, -nāz′) *n.* A copper-containing enzyme of plant and animal tissues that catalyzes the production of melanin and other pigments from tyrosine.

ty·ro·sine (tī′rə-sēn′) *n.* A white crystalline amino acid, $C_9H_{11}NO_3$, that is obtained from the hydrolysis of proteins such as casein and is a precursor of epinephrine, thyroxine, and melanin. [Gk. *tūros,* cheese + -INE[2].]

Tyr·rhe·ni·an Sea (tə-rē′nē-ən) An arm of the Mediterranean Sea between the Italian peninsula and the islands of Corsica, Sardinia, and Sicily.

Tyu·men (tyōō-mĕn′) A city of W-central Russia E of Sverdlovsk; founded 1585. Pop. 490,857.

tzar (zär, tsär) *n.* Variant of **czar** 1. See Usage Note at **czar**.

Tze·kung (tsŭ′kŏong′, dzŭ′gŏong′) See **Zigong**.

Tze·po (tsŭ′pō′, dzŭ′bō′) See **Zibo**.

tzim·mes (tsĭm′ĭs) *n.* Variant of **tsimmes**.

Tzu Hsi (tsōō′ shē′) 1835–1908. The dowager empress of China (1861–1908), who was hostile to foreign influences.

tzu·ris (tsŏŏr′ĭs, tsûr′-) *n.* Variant of **tsuris**.

Uu

u¹ or **U** (yōō) *n., pl.* **u's** or **U's** also **us** or **Us** **1.** The 21st letter of the modern English alphabet. **2.** Any of the speech sounds represented by the letter *u.* **3.** The 21st in a series. **4.** Something shaped like the letter U.

u² *abbr.* up quark

U¹ (yōō) *adj. Chiefly British* Of or appropriate to the upper class, esp. in language usage. [U(PPER CLASS).]

U² (ōō) *n.* Used as a courtesy title before the name of a man in a Burmese-speaking area. [Burmese.]

U³ **1.** The symbol for the element **uranium. 2.** The symbol for **internal energy.**

U⁴ *abbr.* **1.** unsatisfactory **2.** uracil

UAE *abbr.* United Arab Emirates

UAR *abbr.* United Arab Republic

Uau·pés (wou-pĕs′) In its upper course **Vau·pés** (vou-pās′, -pĕs′) A river of NW South America rising in S-central Colombia and flowing c. 805 km (500 mi) to the Río Negro.

UAW *abbr.* United Automobile Workers (in full, United Automobile, Aerospace, and Agricultural Implement Workers)

U·ban·gi (yōō-băng′gē, ōō-bäng′-) A river of central Africa flowing c. 1,126 km (700 mi) along the NW border of Congo (formerly Zaire) to the Congo R.

U·ber·lân·di·a (ōō′bir-län′dē-ə, -dyä) A city of E Brazil WNW of Belo Horizonte. Pop. 366,729.

u·bi·e·ty (yōō-bī′ĭ-tē) *n.* The condition of being located in a particular place. [Lat. *ubī,* where; see UBIQUITY + –TY.]

u·bi·qui·none (yōō′bĭ-kwī-nōn′, -kĭn′ōn) *n.* A quinone compound that serves as an electron carrier between flavoproteins and in cellular respiration.

u·biq·ui·tous (yōō-bĭk′wĭ-təs) *adj.* Being or seeming to be everywhere at the same time; omnipresent. —**u·biq′ui·tous·ly** *adv.* —**u·biq′ui·tous·ness** *n.*

u·biq·ui·ty (yōō-bĭk′wĭ-tē) *n.* Existence or apparent existence everywhere at the same time; omnipresence. [NLat. *ubīquitās* < Lat. *ubīque,* everywhere : *ubī,* where; see k**ʷo**– in App. + –*que,* and, generalizing particle.]

U-boat (yōō′bōt′) *n.* A submarine of the German navy. [Transl. of Ger. *U-Boot,* short for *Unterseeboot* : *unter,* under (< MHGer. *under* < OHGer. *untar;* see **n̥dher**– in App.) + *See,* sea (< MHGer. *sē* < OHGer.) + *Boot,* boat.]

U-bolt (yōō′bōlt′) *n.* A bolt shaped like the letter U, fitted with threads and a nut at each end.

uc also **UC** *abbr.* uppercase

U·ca·ya·li (ōō′kä-yä′lē) A river of E Peru flowing c. 1,609 km (1,000 mi) to join the Marañón and form the Amazon R.

Uc·cel·lo (ōō-chĕl′lō), **Paolo** 1397–1475. Italian painter whose works include *The Battle of San Romano* (c. 1456).

UCMJ *abbr.* Uniform Code of Military Justice

UCS *abbr.* universal character set

UDC *abbr.* universal decimal system

ud·der (ŭd′ər) *n.* A baglike organ containing the mammary glands, characteristic of certain female mammals, such as cows, sheep, and goats. [ME < OE *ūder.*]

u·do (ōō′dō) *n., pl.* **u·dos** A perennial Japanese plant (*Aralia cordata*) having bipinnately compound leaves and young shoots that are cooked and eaten as a vegetable. [J.]

u·don (ōō′dŏn′) *n.* A thick Japanese noodle made with wheat flour, used in soup or broth. [J., wheat noodle.]

Ue·le (wĕl′ē, wĕl′ā) A river of N Congo (formerly Zaire) flowing c. 1,126 km (700 mi) W as a tributary of the Ubangi R.

U·fa (ōō-fä′) A city of SW Russia in the S Ural Mts. at the confluence of the **Ufa River** with the Belaya. The Ufa flows about 965 km (600 mi) NW and SW. Pop. 1,064,000.

UFO (yōō′ĕf-ō′) *n.* An unidentified flying object.

u·fol·o·gy (yōō-fŏl′ə-jē) *n.* The study of unidentified flying objects. [UFO + –LOGY.] —**u′fo·log′i·cal** (yōō′fə-lŏj′ĭ-kəl) *adj.* —**u·fol′o·gist** *n.*

UG *abbr.* universal grammar

U·gan·da (yōō-găn′də, ōō-gän′dä) A country of E-central Africa; gained independence from Great Britain in 1962. Cap. Kampala. Pop. 20,621,000. —**U·gan′dan** *adj. & n.*

U·ga·rit (ōō′gə-rēt′) An ancient city of W Syria on the Mediterranean Sea; flourished from c. 1450 to 1195 B.C.

U·ga·rit·ic (ōō′gə-rĭt′ĭk, yōō′-) *n.* The Semitic language of Ugarit.

ugh (ŭg, ŭk) *interj.* Used to express horror, disgust, or repugnance.

ug·li·fy (ŭg′lə-fī′) *tr.v.* **-fied, -fy·ing, -fies** To make ugly; disfigure. —**ug′li·fi·ca′tion** (-fĭ-kā′shən) *n.* —**ug′li·fi′er** *n.*

ug·ly (ŭg′lē) *adj.* **-li·er, -li·est 1.** Displeasing to the eye; unsightly. **2a.** Repulsive or offensive; objectionable: *an ugly remark.* **b.** *Chiefly Southern US* Rude: *Don't you be ugly to your grandparents.* **c.** *New England* Unmanageable. Used of animals, esp. cows or horses. **3.** Morally reprehensible; bad. **4.** Threatening or ominous: *ugly black clouds.* **5a.** Likely to cause embarrassment or trouble: *ugly rumors.* **b.** Marked by or inclined to anger or bad feelings; disagreeable: *an ugly scene.* ❖ *n., pl.* **-lies** *Informal* One that is ugly. [ME, frightful, repulsive < ON *uggligr* < *uggr,* fear.] —**ug′li·ly** *adv.* —**ug′li·ness** *n.*

ugly duckling *n.* One considered ugly or unpromising at first but having the potential to become beautiful or admirable in maturity. [After *The Ugly Duckling,* a story by Hans Christian Andersen.]

U·gri·an (ōō′grē-ən, yōō′-) *n.* **1.** A member of a group of Finno-Ugric peoples of western Siberia and Hungary, including the Magyars. **2.** Ugric. [< ORuss. *Ugre,* Hungarians, of Turkic orig.] —**U′gri·an** *adj.*

U·gric (ōō′grĭk, yōō′-) *n.* The branch of the Finno-Ugric subfamily of languages that includes Hungarian. —**U′gric** *adj.*

ug·some (ŭg′səm) *adj.* Disgusting; loathsome. [ME : *uggen,* to fear (< ON *ugga* < *uggr,* fear) + –*some,* characterized by; see –SOME¹.] —**ug′some·ness** *n.*

UGT *abbr.* urgent (telegram)

uh (ŭ) *interj.* Used to express hesitation or uncertainty.

UHF *abbr.* ultrahigh frequency

uh-huh (ŭn′hŭn′) *interj. Informal* Used to express agreement or an answer in the affirmative.

uh·lan also **u·lan** (ōō′län′, yōō′lən) *n.* One of a body of horse cavalry that formed part of the Polish, German, Austrian, and Russian armies. [Ger. < Pol. *ulan* < Turk. *oğlan,* youth < *oğul,* son.]

Uh·land (ōō′länt′), **Johann Ludwig** 1787–1862. German romantic poet known for his lyrical ballads and plays.

uh-oh (ŭ′ō′) *interj.* Used to express alarm, foreboding, or dismay.

uh-uh (ŭn′ŭn′, ŭn′ŭn′) *interj. Informal* Used to express disagreement or an answer in the negative.

Ui·gur also **Ui·ghur** (wē′gŏŏr) *n., pl.* **Uigur** or **-gurs** also **Uighur** or **-ghurs 1.** A member of a mainly agricultural Turkic people inhabiting the Xinjiang region in China. **2.** The Turkic language of the Uigurs. [Uigur.] —**Ui·gu′ri·an** (-gŏŏr′ē-ən), **Ui·gu′ric** (-gŏŏr′ĭk) *adj.*

uil·leann pipe also **uil·lean pipe** (ĭl′ən) *n.* A Celtic bagpipe whose air supply is produced by a bellows held under the arm and operated by the elbow. Often used in the plural. [Ir.Gael., genitive of *uillinn,* elbow < OIr. *uilenn.*]

U·in·ta Mountains (yōō-ĭn′tə) A range of the Rocky Mts. in NE UT and SW WY rising to 4,116.9 m (13,498 ft).

uit·land·er (oit′län′dər, ĭt′-) *n. South African* **1.** An outlander; a foreigner. **2.** **Uitlander** A native of Great Britain who resided in either of the former republics of the Orange Free State and Transvaal. [Afr. < MDu. *utelander* < *utelant,* foreign land : *ute,* out; see **ud**– in App. + *land,* land; see **lendh**– in App.]

Uj·jain (ōō′jīn′) A city of W-central India E of Ahmadabad; a Hindu pilgrimage site. Pop. 278,454.

U·jung Pan·dang (ōō-jŏŏng′ pän-däng′) Formerly **Ma·kas·sar** or **Ma·kas′sar** (mə-kăs′ər) A city of central Indonesia on SW Sulawesi I.; settled by the Dutch in 1607. Pop. 709,038.

UK *abbr.* United Kingdom

u·kase (yōō′kās′, -kāz′, ōōkās′, -kāz′) *n.* **1.** An authoritative order or decree; an edict. **2.** A proclamation of a czar having the force of law in imperial Russia. [Fr. < Russ. *ukaz,* decree < O Church Slavonic *ukazŭ,* a showing, proof : *u–,* at, to + *kazati,* to point out, show.]

uke (yōōk) *n. Informal* A ukulele.

U·kraine (yōō-krān′) A region and republic of E Europe; came under the control of Lithuania in the mid-14th cent. and was a constituent republic of the USSR from 1922 to 1991. Cap. Kiev. Pop. 51,910,000.

U·krain·i·an (yōō-krā′nē-ən) *n.* **1.** A native or inhabitant of the Ukraine. **2.** The Slavic language of the Ukrainians. —**U·krain′i·an** *adj.*

u·ku·le·le or **u·ke·le·le** (yōō′kə-lā′lē, ōō′kə-) *n.* A small four-stringed guitar popularized in Hawaii. [Hawaiian ′*ukulele* : ′*uku,* flea + *lele,* jumping.]

REGIONAL NOTE The word *ukulele* is one of a small stock of Polynesian borrowings into American English. Other Hawaiian words now common in American English are *aloha* (a greeting or farewell) and *luau* (an outdoor picnic usually featuring a whole

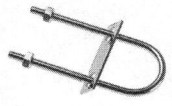

U-bolt

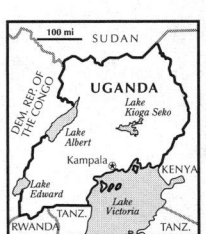

Uganda

Ukraine

ukulele

ă	pat	oi	boy
ā	pay	ou	out
âr	care	ŏŏ	took
ä	father	ōō	boot
ĕ	pet	ŭ	cut
ē	be	ûr	urge
ĭ	pit	th	thin
ī	pie	th	this
îr	pier	hw	which
ŏ	pot	zh	vision
ō	toe	ə	about,
ô	paw		item

Stress marks:
′ (primary);
′ (secondary), as in
lexicon (lĕk′sĭ-kŏn′)

barbecued pig). *Haole,* a word common in Hawaii itself but not well known on the American mainland, is the Hawaiian word for a white person.

U·laan·baa·tar (ōō'län-bä'tär') or **U·lan Ba·tor** (-tôr') The cap. of Mongolia, in the N-central part. Pop. 515,100.

u·lan (ōō'län', yōō'lən) *n.* Variant of uhlan.

U·la·no·va (ōō-lä'nə-və), **Galina** 1910–98. Russian-born dancer with the Bolshoi Ballet (1944–62).

U·lan-U·de (ōō'län-ōō-dā', ōō-län'ōō-dĕ') A city of S-central Russia near Lake Baikal and the Mongolian border; founded as a Cossack fortress in 1649. Pop. 363,967.

–ular *suff.* Of, relating to, or resembling: *tubular.* [Lat. *-ulāris* < *-ulus,* diminutive suff.]

Ul·bricht (ōōl'brĭkt, -brĭкнt), **Walter** 1893–1973. German politician who ordered the building of the Berlin Wall (1961).

ul·cer (ŭl'sər) *n.* **1.** A lesion of the skin or a mucous membrane such as the one lining the stomach that is accompanied by formation of pus and necrosis of surrounding tissue, usu. resulting from inflammation or ischemia. **2.** A corrupting condition or influence. [ME < OFr. *ulcere* < Lat. *ulcus, ulcer-.*]

ul·cer·ate (ŭl'sə-rāt') *v.* **-at·ed, -at·ing, -ates** *—intr.* To develop an ulcer; become ulcerous. *—tr.* To cause ulceration of. **—ul'cer·a·tive** (-sə-rā'tĭv, -sər-ə-tĭv) *adj.*

ul·cer·a·tion (ŭl'sə-rā'shən) *n.* **1.** Development of an ulcer. **2.** An ulcer or an ulcerous condition.

ul·cer·o·gen·ic (ŭl'sə-rō-jĕn'ĭk) *adj.* Tending to be the cause of an ulcer.

ul·cer·ous (ŭl'sər-əs) *adj.* **1.** Of the nature of ulcers or an ulcer. **2.** Having ulcers or an ulcer. **—ul'cer·ous·ly** *adv.*

–ule *suff.* Small one: *valvule.* [Fr. < Lat. *-ulus, -ula, -ulum,* diminutive suff.]

u·le·ma or **u·la·ma** (ōō'lə-mä') *pl.n.* Muslim scholars trained in Islam and Islamic law. [Turk. *'ulemā* < Ar. *'ulamā',* wise men, pl. of *'alim,* wise, learned, active part. of *'alima,* to know.]

u·lex·ite (yōō'lĭk-sīt', yōō-lĕk'-) *n.* A white mineral, $NaCaB_5O_9 \cdot 8H_2O$, that forms rounded masses of very fine needle-shaped crystals. [After Georg Ludwig *Ulex* (1811–83), German chemist.]

ULF *abbr.* ultralow frequency

ul·lage (ŭl'ĭj) *n.* **1.** The amount of liquid within a container that is lost during shipment or storage. **2.** The amount by which a container, such as a bottle, falls short of being full. [ME *ulage* < OFr. *ouillage < ouiller,* to fill up a cask < *ouil,* eye, bunghole < Lat. *oculus,* eye. See **okʷ-** in App.] **—ul'laged** *adj.*

Ulm (ōōlm) A city of S Germany on the Danube R. SE of Stuttgart; site of Napoleon's defeat of Austrian troops in Oct. 1805. Pop. 114,839.

ul·na (ŭl'nə) *n., pl.* **-nas** or **-nae** (-nē) **1.** The bone extending from the elbow to the wrist on the side opposite to the thumb in humans. **2.** A corresponding bone in the forelimb of other vertebrates. [Lat., elbow, forearm.] **—ul'nar** *adj.*

Ul·san (ōōl'sän') A city of SW South Korea on the Korea Strait NNE of Pusan. Pop. 682,411.

ul·ster (ŭl'stər) *n.* A long loose overcoat made of heavy rugged fabric and often belted. [After ULSTER.]

Ulster A historical region and ancient kingdom of N Ireland; now divided between Ireland and Northern Ireland, which is often called Ulster.

ult. *abbr.* **1.** ultimate **2.** ultimately **3.** ultimo

ul·te·ri·or (ŭl-tîr'ē-ər) *adj.* **1.** Lying beyond what is evident, revealed, or avowed, esp. being concealed intentionally so as to deceive: *an ulterior motive.* **2.** Lying beyond or outside the area of immediate interest. **3.** Occurring later; subsequent. [Lat., farther, comp. of **ulter,* on the other side. See **al-** in App.] **—ul·te'ri·or·ly** *adv.*

ul·ti·ma (ŭl'tə-mə) *n.* The last syllable of a word. [Lat., fem. of *ultimus,* last. See ULTIMATE.]

ul·ti·mate (ŭl'tə-mĭt) *adj.* **1.** Being last in a series, process, or progression. **2.** Fundamental; elemental: *an ultimate truth.* **3a.** Of the greatest possible size or significance; maximum. **b.** Representing or exhibiting the greatest possible development or sophistication: *the ultimate bicycle.* **c.** Utmost; extreme: *the ultimate insult.* **4.** Being most distant or remote; farthest. See Syns at last[1]. **5.** Eventual. ❖ *n.* **1.** The basic or fundamental fact, element, or principle. **2.** The final point; the conclusion. **3.** The greatest extreme; the maximum. [Lat. *ultimātus,* p. part. of *ultimāre,* to come to an end < *ultimus,* last, superl. of **ulter,* on the other side. See **al-** in App.]

ul·ti·mate·ly (ŭl'tə-mĭt-lē) *adv.* At last; in the end.

ultima Thu·le (thōō'lē) *n.* **1.** The northernmost region of the habitable world to ancient geographers. **2.** A distant territory or destination. **3.** A remote goal or ideal. [Lat. *ultima Thūlē : ultima,* fem. of *ultimus,* farthest + *Thūlē,* Thule.]

ul·ti·ma·tum (ŭl'tə-mā'təm, -mä'-) *n., pl.* **-tums** or **-ta** (-tə) **1.** A final statement of terms made by one party to another. **2.** A statement, esp. in diplomatic negotiations, that expresses or implies the threat of serious penalties if the terms are not accepted. [NLat. < neut. of Lat. *ultimātus,* last. See ULTIMATE.]

ul·ti·mo (ŭl'tə-mō') *adv.* In or of the month before the present one: *my letter of the 15th ultimo.* [Lat. *ultimō (mēnse),* in the last (month), ablative of *ultimus,* last. See ULTIMATE.]

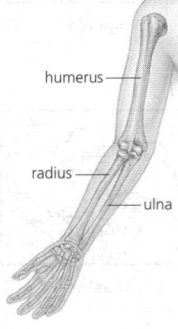

humerus

radius

ulna

ulna

ul·tra (ŭl'trə) *adj.* Immoderately adhering to a belief, fashion, or course of action; extreme. ❖ *n.* An extremist. [Fr. < Lat. *ultrā-,* ultra-.]

ultra– *pref.* **1.** Beyond; on the other side of: *ultraviolet.* **2.** Beyond the range, scope, or limit of: *ultrasonic.* **3.** Far beyond the normal or proper degree of: *ultraconservative.* [Lat. *ultrā- < ultrā,* beyond. See **al-** in App.]

ul·tra·ba·sic (ŭl'trə-bā'sĭk) *adj.* Containing magnesium and iron but poor in silica. Used of igneous rock.

ul·tra·cen·tri·fuge (ŭl'trə-sĕn'trə-fyōōj') *n.* A high-velocity centrifuge used in the separation of colloidal or submicroscopic particles.

ul·tra·con·ser·va·tive (ŭl'trə-kən-sûr'və-tĭv) *adj.* Conservative to an extreme, esp. in political beliefs; reactionary. ❖ *n.* One who is ultraconservative. **—ul'tra·con·ser'va·tism** *n.*

ul·tra·fiche (ŭl'trə-fēsh') *n.* A microfiche on which material is reduced by a factor of 100 or more. [*ultra(micro)fiche.*]

ul·tra·fil·tra·tion (ŭl'trə-fĭl-trā'shən) *n.* The filtration of a colloidal substance through a semipermeable medium that allows only the passage of small molecules.

ul·tra·high (ŭl'trə-hī') *adj.* Exceedingly high: *an ultrahigh vacuum.*

ultrahigh frequency *n.* A band of radio frequencies from 300 to 3,000 megahertz.

ul·tra·ism (ŭl'trə-ĭz'əm) *n.* Extremism, esp. in politics or government; radicalism. **—ul'tra·ist** *n.*

ul·tra·lib·er·al (ŭl'trə-lĭb'ər-əl, -lĭb'rəl) *adj.* Liberal to an extreme, esp. in political beliefs; radical. ❖ *n.* One who is extremely liberal.

ul·tra·light (ŭl'trə-līt', ŭl'trə-līt') *n.* A recreational aircraft constructed of lightweight materials such as aluminum, graphite compositions, or high-strength plastics, having an engine of 15 to 40 horsepower and resembling a motorized hang glider with wings. ❖ *adj.* Very light.

ul·tra·maf·ic (ŭl'trə-măf'ĭk) *adj.* Ultrabasic.

ul·tra·mar·a·thon (ŭl'trə-măr'ə-thŏn') *n.* A cross-country footrace with distances of 30 miles (48 kilometers) or more. **—ul'tra·mar'a·thon'er** *n.*

ul·tra·ma·rine (ŭl'trə-mə-rēn') *n.* **1a.** A blue pigment made from powdered lapis lazuli. **b.** A similar pigment made synthetically by heating clay, sodium carbonate, and sulfur together. **2.** A vivid or strong blue to purplish blue. ❖ *adj.* **1.** Of the color ultramarine. **2.** Of or from a place beyond the sea. [< Med.Lat. *ultrāmarīnus,* from beyond the sea : Lat. *ultrā,* ultra- + Lat. *marīnus,* of the sea (< *mare,* sea; see **mori-** in App.).]

ul·tra·mi·cro·fiche (ŭl'trə-mī'krō-fēsh', -krə-) *n.* See ultrafiche.

ul·tra·mi·cro·scope (ŭl'trə-mī'krə-skōp') *n.* A microscope with high-intensity illumination used to study very minute objects, such as colloidal particles that scatter the light and appear as bright spots against a dark background. **—ul'tra·mi·cros'co·py** (-krŏs'kə-pē) *n.*

ul·tra·mi·cro·scop·ic (ŭl'trə-mī'krə-skŏp'ĭk) *adj.* **1.** Too minute to be seen with an ordinary microscope. **2.** Of or relating to an ultramicroscope.

ul·tra·mi·cro·tome (ŭl'trə-mī'krə-tōm') *n.* A microtome for cutting very thin sections of material for use in electron microscopy. **—ul'tra·mi·crot'o·my** (-mī-krŏt'ə-mē) *n.*

ul·tra·mil·i·tant (ŭl'trə-mĭl'ĭ-tənt) *adj.* Militant to an extreme. ❖ *n.* One who is extremely militant.

ul·tra·min·i·a·ture (ŭl'trə-mĭn'ē-ə-chŏŏr', -chər, -mĭn'ə-) *adj.* Subminiature. **—ul'tra·min'i·a·tur·ize'** (-īz') *v.* **—ul'tra·min'i·a·tur·i·za'tion** (-chə-rĭ-zā'shən) *n.*

ul·tra·mod·ern (ŭl'trə-mŏd'ərn) *adj.* Extremely modern in ideas or style; completely up-to-date. **—ul'tra·mod'ern·ism** *n.* **—ul'tra·mod'ern·ist** *n.* **—ul'tra·mod'ern·is'tic** *adj.*

ul·tra·mon·tane (ŭl'trə-mŏn'tān', -mŏn-tān') *adj.* **1.** Of or relating to peoples or regions lying beyond the mountains, esp. the Alps. **2.** *Roman Catholic Church* **a.** Supporting the authority of the papal court over national or diocesan authority. **b.** Relating to or supporting the doctrine of papal supremacy. ❖ *n.* **1.** One who lives beyond the mountains, esp. south of the Alps. **2.** often **Ultramontane** *Roman Catholic Church* One who advocates support of papal policy in ecclesiastical and political matters. [Med. Lat. *ultrāmontānus : Lat. ultrā-,* ultra- + Lat. *montānus,* of mountains (< *mōns, mont-,* mountain).]

ul·tra·mon·ta·nism or **Ul·tra·mon·ta·nism** (ŭl'trə-mŏn'tə-nĭz'əm) *n. Roman Catholic Church* The policy that absolute authority in the Church should be vested in the pope. **—ul'tra·mon'ta·nist** *n.*

ul·tra·mun·dane (ŭl'trə-mŭn'dān', -mŭn-dān') *adj.* Extending or being beyond the world or the limits of the universe. [Lat. *ultrāmundānus : ultrā-,* ultra- + *mundānus,* of the world; see MUNDANE.]

ul·tra·na·tion·al·ism (ŭl'trə-năsh'ə-nə-lĭz'əm) *n.* Extreme nationalism, esp. when opposed to international cooperation. **—ul'tra·na'tion·al** *adj.* **—ul'tra·na'tion·al·ist** *n.* **—ul'tra·na'tion·al·is'tic** *adj.*

ul·tra·short (ŭl'trə-shôrt') *adj.* **1.** Of or relating to radio waves with a wavelength less than 10 meters (33 feet). **2.** Of extremely short duration. **3.** Extremely short.

ul·tra·son·ic (ŭl'trə-sŏn'ĭk) *adj.* **1.** Of or relating to acoustic frequencies above the range audible to the human ear, or above approx. 20,000 hertz. **2.** Of, relating to, or involving ultrasound. —**ul'tra·son'i·cal·ly** *adv.*

ul·tra·son·ics (ŭl'trə-sŏn'ĭks) *n.* (*used with a sing. verb*) **1.** The acoustics of ultrasonic sound. **2.** The science and technology that deals with the study and application of ultrasound.

ul·tra·son·o·gram (ŭl'trə-sŏn'ə-grăm', -sō'nə-) *n.* See **sono·gram**.

ul·tra·son·o·graph (ŭl'trə-sŏn'ə-grăf', -sō'nə-) *n.* An apparatus for producing images obtained by ultrasonography. [ULTRA- SON(IC) + -GRAPH.]

ul·tra·so·nog·ra·phy (ŭl'trə-sə-nŏg'rə-fē) *n.* **1.** Diagnostic imaging in which ultrasound is used to create visual representations of an internal body structure or a developing fetus. **2.** An imaging technique that uses high-frequency sound waves to create visual representations of underwater surfaces, boundaries, objects, and currents. —**ul'tra·so·nog'ra·pher** *n.* —**ul'tra·son'o·graph'ic** (-sə-nə-grăf'ĭk, -sō'nə-) *adj.*

ul·tra·so·phis·ti·cat·ed (ŭl'trə-sə-fĭs'tĭ-kā'tĭd) *adj.* Very sophisticated.

ul·tra·sound (ŭl'trə-sound') *n.* **1.** Ultrasonic sound. **2.** *Medicine* The use of ultrasonic waves for diagnostic or therapeutic purposes, esp. to image an internal body structure, monitor a fetus, or generate deep heat to the tissues.

ul·tra·struc·ture (ŭl'trə-strŭk'chər) *n.* The detailed structure of a biological specimen, such as a cell, tissue, or organ, that can be observed only by electron microscopy.

ul·tra·thin (ŭl'trə-thĭn') *adj.* Very thin.

ul·tra·vi·o·let (ŭl'trə-vī'ə-lĭt) *adj.* Of or relating to the range of invisible radiation wavelengths from about 4 nanometers, on the border of the x-ray region, to about 380 nanometers, just beyond the violet in the visible spectrum. ❖ *n.* Ultraviolet light or the ultraviolet part of the spectrum.

ul·tra·vi·rus (ŭl'trə-vī'rəs) *n., pl.* **-rus·es** See **filterable virus**.

U·lugh Muz·tagh (oō'lə məz-tä', -täg') A mountain, 7,729 m (25,341 ft), of the Kunlun Mts. in W China.

ul·u·late (ŭl'yə-lāt', yoōl'-) *intr.v.* **-lat·ed, -lat·ing, -lates** To howl, wail, or lament loudly. [Lat. *ululāre, ululāt-,* ult. of imit. orig.] —**ul'u·lant** (-lənt) *adj.* —**ul'u·la'tion** *n.*

Ul·ya·novsk (oōl-yä'nəfsk) See **Simbirsk**.

U·lys·ses (yoō-lĭs'ēz') *n. Mythology* Odysseus. [Lat. *Ulixēs, Ulyssēs* < Gk. dialectal *Olusseus,* var. of Gk. *Odusseus.*]

um also **umm** (ŭm, əm) *interj.* Used to express doubt or uncertainty or to fill a pause when hesitating in speaking.

u·ma·mi (oō-mä'mē) *n.* A taste characteristic of monosodium glutamate and associated with meats and other high-protein foods. It is sometimes considered to be a fifth basic taste along with sweet, sour, salty, and bitter. [J.]

U·ma·til·la (yoō'mə-tĭl'ə) *n., pl.* **Umatilla** or **-las 1.** A member of a Native American people of northeast Oregon. **2.** The dialect of Sahaptin spoken by the Umatilla.

U·may·yad (oō-mī'ăd) or **Om·mi·ad** also **O·may·yad** (ō-mī'ăd) *n.* The first dynasty of Arab caliphs (661–750).

um·bel (ŭm'bəl) *n.* A flower cluster in which the individual stalks arise from about the same point, as in the geranium. [NLat. *umbella* < Lat., parasol, dim. of *umbra,* shadow.]

um·bel·late (ŭm'bə-lāt', ŭm-bĕl'ĭt) also **um·bel·lat·ed** (-bə-lā'tĭd) *adj.* Having, forming, or of the nature of an umbel. —**um'bel·late'ly** *adv.*

um·bel·lif·er·ous (ŭm'bə-lĭf'ər-əs) *adj.* Bearing umbels.

um·bel·lule (ŭm'bəl-yoōl', ŭm-bĕl'-) *n.* A secondary umbel in a compound umbel, as in the carrot. [NLat. *umbellula,* dim. of *umbella,* umbel. See UMBEL.]

um·ber (ŭm'bər) *n.* **1.** A natural brown earth containing ferric oxide and manganese oxides, used as pigment. **2.** Any of the shades of brown produced by umber in its various states. ❖ *adj.* **1.** Of or related to umber. **2.** Having a brownish color. ❖ *tr.v.* **-bered, -ber·ing, -bers** To darken with or as if with umber. [Fr. *(terre d')ombre* or Ital. *(terra di) ombra,* shadow (earth), both poss. < alteration (influenced by Fr. *ombre* and Ital. *ombra,* shadow) of Lat. *Umbria,* a region of ancient Italy.]

um·bil·i·cal (ŭm-bĭl'ĭ-kəl) *adj.* **1.** Of, relating to, or resembling a navel or an umbilical cord. **2.** Located near the central area of the abdomen. ❖ *n. Aerospace* An umbilical cord. —**um·bil'i·cal·ly** *adv.*

umbilical cord *n.* **1a.** *Anatomy* The flexible cordlike structure that connects a fetus at the abdomen with the placenta and that transports nourishment to the fetus and removes its wastes. **b.** Something likened to this structure; a source or means of support or sustenance. **2.** *Aerospace* **a.** Any of the external electrical lines or fluid tubes that supply a rocket before launch. **b.** The line that supplies an astronaut with oxygen while outside the spacecraft.

um·bil·i·cate (ŭm-bĭl'ĭ-kĭt) also **um·bil·i·cat·ed** (-kā'tĭd) *adj.* **1.** Having a central mark or depression resembling a navel. **2.** Having a navel. —**um·bil'i·ca'tion** *n.*

um·bil·i·cus (ŭm-bĭl'ĭ-kəs, ŭm'bə-lī'kəs) *n., pl.* **-ci** (-sī') **1.** See **navel** 1. **2.** *Biology* A small opening or depression similar to a navel. [Lat. *umbilīcus.* See nobh- in App.]

um·bo (ŭm'bō) *n., pl.* **um·bo·nes** (ŭm-bō'nēz) or **um·bos 1.** The boss or knob at the center of a shield. **2a.** *Biology* A knoblike

protuberance, as the prominence near the hinge of a bivalve shell. **b.** *Anatomy* A small projection at the center of the outer surface of the eardrum. [Lat. *umbō, umbōn-.* See **nobh-** in App.]

um·bo·nal (ŭm'bə-nəl, ŭm-bō'nəl) *adj.*

um·bo·nate (ŭm'bə-nāt', ŭm-bō'nĭt) *adj.* Having or resembling a knob or knoblike protuberance.

um·bra (ŭm'brə) *n., pl.* **-bras** (-brəz) or **-brae** (-brē) **1.** A dark area, esp. the blackest part of a shadow from which all light is cut off. **2.** *Astronomy* **a.** The completely dark portion of the shadow cast by the earth, moon, or other body during an eclipse. **b.** The darkest region of a sunspot. [Lat., shadow.] —**um'bral** *adj.*

um·brage (ŭm'brĭj) *n.* **1.** Offense; resentment: *took umbrage at their rudeness.* **2a.** Something that affords shade. **b.** Shadow or shade. **3.** A vague or indistinct indication; a hint. [ME, shade < OFr. < Lat. *umbrāticum,* neut. of *umbrāticus,* of shade < *umbra,* shadow.]

um·bra·geous (ŭm-brā'jəs) *adj.* **1.** Affording or forming shade. **2.** Easily offended; irritable. —**um·bra'geous·ly** *adv.*

um·brel·la (ŭm-brĕl'ə) *n.* **1.** A device for protection from the weather consisting of a collapsible, usu. circular canopy mounted on a central rod. **2a.** Something that covers or protects. **b.** Air cover, esp. during a military operation. **3.** Something that encompasses or covers many different elements or groups. **4.** *Zoology* The gelatinous rounded mass that is the major part of the body of most jellyfish. [Ital. *ombrella* < LLat. *umbrella,* alteration (influenced by *umbra,* shade) of Lat. *umbella,* parasol; see UMBEL.]

umbrella bird *n.* Any of several tropical American birds of the genus *Cephalopterus,* esp. *C. ornatus,* having a retractile umbrellalike black crest and a long feathered wattle.

umbrella plant *n.* **1.** A widely cultivated ornamental robust sedge (*Cyperus alternifolius*) native to Madagascar and Mauritius and having a terminal umbrellalike cluster of grasslike leaves. **2.** *Midland US* The May apple.

umbrella tree *n.* **1.** Either of two trees (*Magnolia fraseri* or *M. tripetala*) of the southeast United States having large leaves clustered in an umbrellalike form at the ends of the branches. **2.** An Australian evergreen tree (*Brassaia actinophylla*) having palmately compound leaves. **3.** See **schefflera**.

um·brette (ŭm-brĕt') *n.* See **hammerhead** 3. [NLat. *umbretta,* species name < Fr. *ombrette,* shadow, dim. of *ombre,* shade < OFr. < Lat. *umbra.*]

Um·bri·a (ŭm'brē-ə, oōm'brē-ä) A region of central Italy in the Apennines; came under the control of the papacy in the 16th cent. and joined the kingdom of Sardinia in 1860.

Um·bri·an (ŭm'brē-ən) *n.* **1.** The Italic language of ancient Umbria. **2.** A native or inhabitant of Umbria. —**Um'bri·an** *adj.*

Um·bri·el (ŭm'brē-əl) *n.* A satellite of Uranus. [After *Umbriel,* a character in Pope's *Rape of the Lock.*]

Um·bun·du (oōm-boōn'doō, əm-) *n.* See **Mbundu** 2.

U·me (oō'mə, ü'mə) A river of northern Sweden flowing c. 459 km (285 mi) SE into the Gulf of Bothnia.

u·mi·ak also **oo·mi·ak** (oō'mē-ăk') *n.* A large open Inuit or Eskimo boat made of skins stretched on a wooden frame and usu. paddled. [Canadian and Inuit *umiaq.*]

um·laut (oōm'lout') *n.* **1. a.** A change in a vowel sound caused by partial assimilation esp. to a vowel or semivowel in the following syllable. **b.** A vowel sound changed in this manner. **2.** The diacritic mark (¨) over a vowel, indicating an umlaut, esp. in German. ❖ *tr.v.* **-laut·ed, -laut·ing, -lauts 1.** To modify by umlaut. **2.** To write or print (a vowel) with an umlaut. [Ger. : *um-,* around, alteration (< MHGer. *umb-* < *umbe* < OHGer. *umbi;* see **ambhi** in App.) + *Laut,* sound (< MHGer. *lūt* < OHGer. *hlūt;* see **kleu-** in App.).]

Um·nak Island (oōm'năk') An island of SW AK in the Aleutian Is. separated from Unalaska I. by **Umnak Pass**.

ump (ŭmp) *Sports n.* An umpire. ❖ *intr.v.* **umped, ump·ing, umps** To serve as an umpire.

um·pire (ŭm'pīr') *n.* **1.** *Sports* A person appointed to rule on plays, esp. in baseball. **2.** A person appointed to settle a dispute that arbitrators have been unable to resolve. ❖ *v.* **-pired, -pir·ing, -pires** —*tr.* To act as referee for; rule or judge. —*intr.* To be or act as a referee or an arbitrator. [ME *(an) oumpere,* (an) umpire, alteration of *(a) noumpere,* a mediator < OFr. *nonper : non-,* non- + *per,* equal, even, paired (< Lat. *pār;* see PAIR).]

ump·teen (ŭmp'tēn', ŭm'-) *adj. Informal* Being of a relatively large but unspecified number: *umpteen guests.* [Slang *ump(ty),* dash in Morse code (of imit. orig.) + *-teen* (as in THIRTEEN).] —**ump'teenth'** *adj.*

UMW *abbr.* United Mine Workers

UN *abbr.* United Nations

un-[1] *pref.* **1.** Not: *unhappy.* **2.** Opposite of; contrary to: *unrest.* [ME < OE. See **ne** in App.]

un-[2] *pref.* **1.** To reverse or undo the result of a specified action: *unbind.* **2a.** To deprive of or remove a specified thing: *unfrock.* **b.** To release, free, or remove from: *unyoke.* **3.** Used as an intensive: *unloose.* [ME < OE *on-,* alteration (influenced by *un-,* not) of *ond-, and-, an-,* against, opposing; see **ant-** in App.]

un·a·bashed (ŭn'ə-băsht') *adj.* **1.** Not disconcerted or embarrassed; poised. **2.** Not concealed or disguised; obvious.

un·a·bat·ed (ŭn'ə-bā'tĭd) *adj.* Sustaining an original intensity or maintaining full force with no decrease.

umbrella plant
Cyperus alternifolius

umiak

umpire

un·a·bridged (ŭn'ə-brĭjd') *adj.* Containing the original content; not condensed. Used of books, articles, and documents.

un·ac·cent·ed (ŭn-ăk'sĕn-tĭd) *adj.* **1.** Having no diacritical mark. Used of a word, syllable, or letter. **2.** Having weak stress or no stress, as in pronunciation or metrical rhythm.

un·ac·com·mo·dat·ed (ŭn'ə-kŏm'ə-dā'tĭd) *adj.* **1.** Not adapted or accommodated. **2.** Lacking accommodations.

un·ac·com·pa·nied (ŭn'ə-kŭm'pə-nēd) *adj.* **1.** Going or acting without companions or a companion. **2.** *Music* Performed or scored without accompaniment.

un·ac·count·ed-for (ŭn'ə-koun'tĭd-fôr') *adj.* **1.** Not explained, understood, or taken into account. **2.** Missing or absent without explanation, as from a roll call.

un·ac·cred·it·ed (ŭn'ə-krĕd'ĭ-tĭd) *adj.* **1.** Not having the proper credentials; unauthorized: *an unaccredited school.* **2.** Not ascribed or attributed to a source.

u·na cor·da (ōō'nə kôr'də) *adv.* & *adj.* With the soft pedal of the piano depressed. Used chiefly as a direction. [Ital. : *una,* one + *corda,* string (so called because depressing the soft pedal causes only one string to be struck of the two or three provided for each note).]

un·ad·dressed (ŭn-ə-drĕst') *adj.* **1.** Not brought up for discussion or solution: *questions that remain unaddressed.* **2.** Not containing the required address: *unaddressed letters.*

un·ad·just·ed (ŭn'ə-jŭs'tĭd) *adj.* **1.** Not having been adjusted to conform to new data or information. **2.** Not having adapted to new conditions. **3.** Needing to be made operable or accurate by adjusting or regulating.

un·a·dorned (ŭn'ə-dôrnd') *adj.* Without adornment or embellishment; simple or plain.

un·a·dul·ter·at·ed (ŭn'ə-dŭl'tə-rā'tĭd) *adj.* **1.** Not mingled or diluted with extraneous matter; pure. See Syns at **pure**. **2.** Out-and-out; utter: *the unadulterated truth.*

un·af·fect·ed (ŭn'ə-fĕk'tĭd) *adj.* **1.** Not changed or affected. **2.** Marked by lack of affectation; genuine. See Syns at **naive**. —**un'af·fect'ed·ly** *adv.* —**un'af·fect'ed·ness** *n.*

un·af·fil·i·at·ed (ŭn'ə-fĭl'ē-ā'tĭd) *adj.* Not associated with another or others as a subordinate, subsidiary, or member; independent.

Un·a·las·ka Island (ŭn'ə-lăs'kə, ōō'nə-) An island of SW AK in the E Aleutian Is. SW of Unimak I.

un·al·ien·a·ble (ŭn-āl'yə-nə-bəl, -ā'lē-ə-) *adj.* Not to be separated, given away, or taken away; inalienable.

un·a·ligned (ŭn'ə-līnd') *adj.* Nonaligned: *unaligned nations.*

un·al·loyed (ŭn'ə-loid') *adj.* **1.** Not in mixture with other metals; pure. **2.** Complete; unqualified: *unalloyed blessings; unalloyed relief.*

Miguel de Unamuno

un-A·mer·i·can (ŭn'ə-mĕr'ĭ-kən) *adj.* Considered contrary to the institutions or principles of the United States.

U·na·mi (ōō-nä'mē, yōō-näm'ē) *n., pl.* **Unami** or **-mis 1.** One of the two Algonquian languages of the Delaware peoples, originally spoken in central and southern New Jersey, eastern Pennsylvania, and northern Delaware. **2.** A member of the Unami-speaking branch of the Delaware peoples.

U·na·mu·no (ōō'nə-mōō'nō, -nä-), **Miguel de** 1864–1936. Spanish philosopher whose works include *The Tragic Sense of Life* (1913).

un·a·neled (ŭn'ə-nēld') *adj. Archaic* Not having received extreme unction. [UN–[1] + *aneled,* p. part. of *anele,* to anoint, administer extreme unction (< ME *anelen* : *an-,* on < OE *on-;* see ON + *elen,* to anoint < *ele,* oil < OE < Lat. *oleum;* see OIL).]

u·na·nim·i·ty (yōō'nə-nĭm'ĭ-tē) *n.* The condition of being unanimous.

u·nan·i·mous (yōō-năn'ə-məs) *adj.* **1.** Sharing the same opinions or views; being in complete harmony or accord. **2.** Based on or characterized by complete assent or agreement. [< Lat. *ūnanimus* : *ūnus,* one; see **oi-no-** in App. + *animus,* mind; see **ana-** in App.] —**u·nan'i·mous·ly** *adv.* —**u·nan'i·mous·ness** *n.*

un·an·swer·a·ble (ŭn-ăn'sər-ə-bəl) *adj.* Impossible to answer or refute; incontrovertible. —**un'an'swer·a·bil'i·ty, un·an'swer·a·ble·ness** *n.* —**un·an'swer·a·bly** *adv.*

un·an·tic·i·pat·ed (ŭn'ăn-tĭs'ə-pā'tĭd) *adj.* **1.** Not anticipated: *We had some unanticipated problems.* **2.** Not having been expected; unexpected. —**un'an·tic'i·pat'ed·ly** *adv.*

un·ap·peal·a·ble (ŭn'ə-pē'lə-bəl) *adj.* Not subject to appeal: *an unappealable grievance.* —**un'ap·peal'a·bly** *adv.*

un·ap·peal·ing (ŭn'ə-pē'lĭng) *adj.* Not appealing to the senses, as in taste or aroma. —**un'ap·peal'ing·ly** *adv.*

un·ap·pre·ci·at·ed (ŭn'ə-prē'shē-ā'tĭd) *adj.* **1.** Not recognized, as to quality or worth: *an unappreciated favor.* **2.** Not having risen in price or value: *an unappreciated investment.*

un·apt (ŭn-ăpt') *adj.* **1.** Not suitable or appropriate. **2.** Not likely or liable. —**un·apt'ly** *adv.* —**un·apt'ness** *n.*

un·armed (ŭn-ärmd') *adj.* **1a.** Lacking weapons or armor; defenseless. **b.** Not carrying, using, or displaying arms: *unarmed robbery.* **2.** *Biology* Having no thorns, spines, teeth, claws, or other protective parts.

un·ar·tic·u·lat·ed (ŭn'är-tĭk'yə-lā'tĭd) *adj.* **1a.** Not articulated: *our unarticulated fears.* **b.** Not carefully or thoroughly thought out. **2.** *Biology* Not having joints or segments.

u·na·ry operation (yōō'nə-rē) *n.* A mathematical operation, such as the square root function, that requires only one operand. [Blend of UNI– and BINARY.]

un·a·shamed (ŭn'ə-shāmd') *adj.* Feeling or showing no re-

---

morse, shame, or embarrassment: *lived in unashamed luxury.* —un·sham'ed·ly (-shā'mĭd-lē) *adv.*

un·as·sail·a·ble (ŭn'ə-sā'lə-bəl) *adj.* 1. Impossible to dispute or disprove; undeniable. 2. Not subject to attack or seizure; impregnable. —un'as·sail'a·bil'i·ty, un'as·sail'a·ble·ness *n.* —un'as·sail'a·bly *adv.*

un·as·sem·bled (ŭn'ə-sĕm'bəld) *adj.* Made with parts or sections ready to be joined or fitted together before use.

un·as·sist·ed (ŭn'ə-sĭs'tĭd) *adj.* 1. Not having assistance; unaided. 2. *Baseball* Of, relating to, or being a play handled by only one fielder.

un·at·tached (ŭn'ə-tăcht') *adj.* 1. Not joined, esp. to surrounding tissue. 2a. Not committed to or dependent on another person or group. b. Not engaged, married, or involved in a serious sexual or romantic relationship.

un·at·tend·ed (ŭn'ə-tĕn'dĭd) *adj.* 1. Not being attended to, looked after, or watched. 2. Having no attendants: *unattended counters.* 3. Not being paid attention to or listened to.

un·a·vail·ing (ŭn'ə-vā'lĭng) *adj.* Not availing; ineffectual or useless. See Syns at **futile.** —un'a·vail'ing·ly *adv.*

u·na vo·ce (yōō'nə vō'sē, ōō'nä vō'kā) *adv.* With one voice; unanimously. [Lat. *ūnā vōce* : *ūnā*, fem. ablative of *ūnus*, one + *vōce*, ablative of *vōx*, voice.]

un·a·void·a·ble (ŭn'ə-voi'də-bəl) *adj.* Impossible to avoid; inevitable. —un'a·void'a·bil'i·ty, un'a·void'a·ble·ness *n.* —un'a·void'a·bly *adv.*

un·a·ware (ŭn'ə-wâr') *adj.* Not aware or cognizant. ❖ *adv.* Unawares. —un'a·ware'ly *adv.* —un'a·ware'ness *n.*

USAGE NOTE *Unaware,* followed by a prepositional phrase with *of,* is the usual adjectival form: *Unaware of the difficulty, I went ahead. He was unaware of my presence. Unawares* is the usual adverbial form: *The rain caught them unawares.*

un·a·wares (ŭn'ə-wârz') *adv.* 1. By surprise; unexpectedly: *"Sorrow comes to all, and to the young it comes with bittered agony because it takes them unawares"* (Abraham Lincoln). 2. Without forethought or plan. See Usage Note at **unaware.**

un·backed (ŭn-băkt') *adj.* 1. Lacking backing or support. 2. Not having a back. 3. Never having been ridden.

un·bal·ance (ŭn-băl'əns) *tr.v.* -anced, -anc·ing, -anc·es 1. To upset the balance, stability, or equilibrium of. 2. To derange (the mind). ❖ *n.* The condition of being unbalanced. —un·bal'ance·a·ble *adj.*

un·bal·anced (ŭn-băl'ənst) *adj.* 1. Not in balance or in proper balance. 2a. Mentally deranged. b. Not exhibiting sound judgment; irrational. 3. *Accounting* Not satisfactorily adjusted so that debit and credit correspond.

un·bal·last·ed (ŭn-băl'ə-stĭd) *adj.* 1. Not stabilized or properly stabilized by ballast. 2. Unsteady; wavering.

un·bar (ŭn-bär') *tr. & intr.v.* -barred, -bar·ring, -bars To re-

move the bars from or become unbarred.

un·bat·ed (ŭn-bā'tĭd) *adj.* 1. Unabated. 2. *Archaic* Not blunted by a guard on the tip, as a sword or fencing foil.

un·bear·a·ble (ŭn-bâr'ə-bəl) *adj.* So unpleasant, distasteful, or painful as to be intolerable: *unbearable heat.* —un·bear'a·ble·ness *n.* —un·bear'a·bly *adv.*

un·beat·a·ble (ŭn-bē'tə-bəl) *adj.* Impossible to defeat or surpass: *an unbeatable team.* —un·beat'a·bly *adv.*

un·beat·en (ŭn-bēt'n) *adj.* 1. Not defeated: *an unbeaten team.* 2. Not traversed before; untrodden: *an unbeaten path.* 3. Not beaten or pounded, as in cooking: *unbeaten eggs.*

un·be·com·ing (ŭn'bĭ-kŭm'ĭng) *adj.* 1. Not appropriate, attractive, or flattering. 2. Not in accord with the standards implied by one's character or position. —un'be·com'ing·ly *adv.*

un·be·got·ten (ŭn'bĭ-gŏt'n) *adj.* 1. Not yet begotten; as yet unborn. 2. Self-existent; eternal.

un·be·known (ŭn'bĭ-nōn') *adj.* Occurring or existing without the knowledge of; unknown: *a crisis unbeknown to us.* [UN-¹ + obsolete *beknown*, known (< ME *beknowen*, p. part. of *beknowen*, to get to know < OE *becnāwan* : *be-*, *be-* + *cnāwan*, to know; see KNOW).]

un·be·knownst (ŭn'bĭ-nōnst') *adj.* Unbeknown. ❖ *adv.* Without the knowledge of a specified party. Used with *to.* [UNBEKNOWN + *-st* (as in AMONGST).]

un·be·lief (ŭn'bĭ-lēf') *n.* Lack of belief or faith, esp. in religious matters.

un·be·liev·er (ŭn'bĭ-lē'vər) *n.* One who lacks belief or faith, esp. in a particular religion; a nonbeliever.

un·belt·ed (ŭn-bĕl'tĭd) *adj.* 1. Made or designed to be worn without a belt. 2. Not having or using a seat belt.

un·bend (ŭn-bĕnd') *v.* -bent (-bĕnt'), -bend·ing, -bends —*tr.* 1. To release from mental tension, strain, or formality; relax. 2. To release (a bow, for example) from flexure or tension. 3. *Nautical* To untie or loosen (a knot or sail). 4. To straighten (something crooked or bent): *unbend a paper clip.* —*intr.* 1. To become less tense; relax. 2. To become less strict. 3. To become straight. —un·bend'a·ble *adj.*

un·bend·ing (ŭn-bĕn'dĭng) *adj.* 1. Not yielding; inflexible: *an unbending will.* 2. Aloof and often antisocial; extremely reserved: *an unbending manner.* —un·bend'ing·ly *adv.*

un·bi·ased also un·bi·assed (ŭn-bī'əst) *adj.* Without bias or prejudice; impartial. See Syns at **fair**¹. —un·bi'ased·ly *adv.* —un·bi'ased·ness *n.*

un·bid·den (ŭn-bĭd'n) also un·bid (-bĭd') *adj.* Not invited, asked, or requested; unasked: *unbidden guests.*

un·bind (ŭn-bīnd') *tr.v.* -bound (-bound'), -bind·ing, -binds 1. To untie or unfasten, as wrappings or bindings. 2. To release from restraints or bonds; free.

un·blessed also un·blest (ŭn-blĕst') *adj.* 1. Deprived of a blessing. 2. Evil. —un·bless'ed·ness (-blĕs'ĭd-nĭs) *n.*

---

un·friend'li·ness *n.*
un·friend'ly *adj.*
un·fund'ed *adj.*
un·fuss'y *adj.*
un·gen'er·ous *adj.*
un·gen'er·ous·ly *adv.*
un·grate'ful *adj.*
un·grate'ful·ly *adv.*
un·grate'ful·ness *n.*
un·hoped'-for' *adj.*
un·im·por'tance *n.*
un·im·por'tant *adj.*
un'in·form'a·tive *adj.*
un'in·form'a·tive·ly *adv.*
un'in·hab'it·a·ble *adj.*
un'in·hab'it·ed *adj.*
un·in'tel'li·gence *n.*
un·in'tel'li·gent *adj.*
un·in'tel'li·gent·ly *adv.*
un·in'tel'li·gi·bil'i·ty *n.*
un·in'tel'li·gi·ble *adj.*
un·in'tel'li·gi·bly *adv.*
un'in·ten'tion·al *adj.*
un'in·ten'tion·al·ly *adv.*
un'in·vit'ing *adj.*
un'in·vit'ing·ly *adv.*
un·latch' *tr. & intr.v.*
un·leav'ened *adj.*
un·link' *tr. & intr.v.*
un·man'age·a·ble *adj.*
un·man'age·a·bly *adv.*
un·man'ner·ly *adj. & adv.*
un·marked' *adj.*
un·mar'ried *adj. & n.*
un·mask' *tr. & intr.v.*
un·meet' *adj.*
un·mis·tak'a·ble *adj.*
un·mis·tak'a·bly *adv.*
un·mo·lest'ed *adj.*

un·muf'fle *tr. & intr.v.*
un·nec'es·sar'i·ly *adv.*
un·nec'es·sar'y *adj.*
un·ob·jec'tion·a·ble *adj.*
un·ob·struct'ed *adj.*
un·oc'cu·pied' *adj.*
un·of·fi'cial *adj.*
un·of·fi'cial·ly *adv.*
un·op·posed' *adj.*
un·o·rig'i·nal *adj.*
un·or'na·ment' *tr.v.*
un·or'nate' *adj.*
un·or'tho·dox' *adj.*
un·or'tho·dox'ly *adv.*
un·or'tho·dox'y *n.*
un·pack' *tr. & intr.v.*
un·pag'i·nat'ed *adj.*
un·pal'at·a·bil'i·ty *n.*
un·pal'at·a·ble *adj.*
un·pal'at·a·bly *adv.*
un·peo'ple *tr.v.*
un·peo'pled *adj.*
un·per·turbed' *adj.*
un·pile' *tr.v.*
un·planned' *adj.*
un·pleas'ant *adj.*
un·pleas'ant·ly *adv.*
un·pleas'ant·ness *n.*
un·po·lit'i·cal *adj.*
un·pop'u·lar *adj.*
un·pop'u·lar'i·ty *n.*
un·prec'e·dent'ed *adj.*
un·prec'e·dent'ed·ly *adv.*
un·pre·dict'a·bil'i·ty *n.*
un·pre·dict'a·ble *adj. & n.*
un·pre·dict'a·bly *adv.*
un·pre·pos·sess'ing *adj.*
un·priced' *adj.*
un·prin'ci·pled *adj.*

un·prof'it·a·bil'i·ty *n.*
un·prof'it·a·ble *adj.*
un·prof'it·a·bly *adv.*
un·pro·pi'tious *adj.*
un·pro·pi'tious·ly *adv.*
un·quench'a·ble *adj.*
un·quench'a·bly *adv.*
un·read'i·ly *adv.*
un·read'i·ness *n.*
un·read'y *adj.*
un·re·al'ized *adj.*
un·re·lent'ing *adj.*
un·re·lent'ing·ly *adv.*
un·re·li'a·bil'i·ty *n.*
un·re·li'a·ble *adj.*
un·re·li'a·bly *adv.*
un·re·mark'a·ble *adj.*
un·re·mark'a·bly *adv.*
un·re·marked' *adj.*
un·re·pent'ant *adj.*
un·re·pent'ant·ly *adv.*
un·re·proved' *adj.*
un·re·quit'ed *adj.*
un·re·quit'ed·ly *adv.*
un·re·spon'sive *adj.*
un·re·spon'sive·ly *adv.*
un·re·strained' *adj.*
un·re·straint' *n.*
un·ripe' *adj.*
un·roof' *tr.v.*
un·safe' *adj.*
un·sat'is·fac'to·ri·ly *adv.*
un·sat'is·fac'to·ri·ness *n.*
un·sat'is·fac'to·ry *adj.*
un·scathed' *adj.*
un·scru'pu·lous *adj.*
un·seal' *tr.v.*
un·seam' *tr.v.*

un·search'a·ble *adj.*
un·search'a·bly *adv.*
un·self'ish *adj.*
un·self'ish·ly *adv.*
un·shack'le *tr.v.*
un·sheathe' *tr.v.*
un·skilled' *adj.*
un·so·lic'it·ed *adj.*
un·sound' *adj.*
un·sound'ly *adv.*
un·stint'ing *adj.*
un·stint'ing·ly *adv.*
un·strap' *tr.v.*
un·strat'i·fied' *adj.*
un·stri'at'ed *adj.*
un·sub·stan'tial *adj.*
un·sub·stan'ti·al'i·ty *n.*
un·sub·stan'tial·ly *adv.*
un·suc·cess' *n.*
un·suc·cess'ful *adj.*
un·suc·cess'ful·ly *adv.*
un·suit'a·bil'i·ty *n.*
un·suit'a·ble *adj.*
un·suit'a·ble·ness *n.*
un·suit'a·bly *adv.*
un·swathe' *tr.v.*
un·sym·met'ri·cal *adj.*
un·sym·met'ri·cal·ly *adv.*
un·throne' *tr.v.*
un·trou'bled *adj.*
un·twine' *tr. & intr.v.*
un·twist' *tr.v.*
un·war'i·ly *adv.*
un·war'i·ness *n.*
un·war'y *adj.*
un·wed' *adj.*
un·work'a·ble *adj.*
un·work'a·bly *adv.*
un·worn' *adj.*

ă pat	oi boy		
ā pay	ou out		
âr care	ŏŏ took		
ä father	ōō boot		
ĕ pet	ŭ cut		
ē be	ûr urge		
ĭ pit	th thin		
ī pie	th this		
îr pier	hw which		
ŏ pot	zh vision		
ō toe	ə about,		
ô paw	item		

Stress marks:
' (primary);
' (secondary), as in
lexicon (lĕk'sĭ-kŏn')

un·blink·ing (ŭn-blĭng′kĭng) *adj.* **1.** Without blinking. **2.** Without visible emotion. **3.** Fearless in facing reality. —**un·blink′ing·ly** *adv.*

un·block (ŭn-blŏk′) *tr.v.* **-blocked, -block·ing, -blocks** To remove or clear an obstruction from: *unblock a road.*

un·blush·ing (ŭn-blŭsh′ĭng) *adj.* **1.** Lacking or exhibiting a lack of shame or embarrassment. **2.** Not blushing. —**un·blush′ing·ly** *adv.*

un·bod·ied (ŭn-bŏd′ēd) *adj.* **1.** Having no body or form; incorporeal. **2.** Being disembodied.

un·bolt (ŭn-bōlt′) *tr.v.* **-bolt·ed, -bolt·ing, -bolts** To release the bolts of (a door, for example); unlock.

un·bolt·ed¹ (ŭn-bōl′tĭd) *adj.* Not bolted or fastened; unlocked.

un·bolt·ed² (ŭn-bōl′tĭd) *adj.* Not sifted: *unbolted flour.*

un·born (ŭn-bôrn′) *adj.* **1.** Not yet born: *an unborn child.* **2.** Not yet appeared; future: *unborn inventions.*

un·bos·om (ŭn-bŏŏz′əm, -bōō′zəm) *v.* **-omed, -om·ing, -oms** —*tr.* **1.** To confide (one's thoughts or feelings). **2.** To relieve (oneself) of troublesome thoughts or feelings. —*intr.* To reveal one's thoughts or feelings. —**un·bos′om·er** *n.*

un·bound (ŭn-bound′) *v.* Past tense and past participle of **unbind.** ❖ *adj.* **1.** Not bound: *an unbound book.* **2.** Freed from bonds or restraints; released: *an unbound captive.*

un·bound·ed (ŭn-boun′dĭd) *adj.* **1.** Having no boundaries or limits: *unbounded space.* **2.** Not kept within bounds; unrestrained: *unbounded enthusiasm.* —**un·bound′ed·ly** *adv.* —**un·bound′ed·ness** *n.*

un·bowed (ŭn-boud′) *adj.* **1.** Not bowed; unbent. **2.** Not subdued; unyielding.

un·brace (ŭn-brās′) *tr.v.* **-braced, -brac·ing, -brac·es** **1.** To set free by removing bands or braces. **2.** To release from tension; relax. **3.** To make slack; weaken.

un·break·a·ble (ŭn-brā′kə-bəl) *adj.* **1.** Impossible to break; able to withstand rough usage: *unbreakable plates.* **2.** Able to withstand an attempt to break. Used of a horse. ❖ *n.* An article or object that is not easily broken. —**un·break′a·ble·ness** *n.* —**un·break′a·bly** *adv.*

un·bred (ŭn-brĕd′) *adj.* **1.** Not instructed; untaught. **2.** Not yet bred: *an unbred mare.* **3.** *Obsolete* Ill-bred; impolite.

un·bridge·a·ble (ŭn-brĭj′ə-bəl) *adj.* Impossible to span. —**un·bridge′a·bly** *adv.*

un·bri·dled (ŭn-brīd′ld) *adj.* **1.** Unrestrained; uncontrolled: *unbridled anger.* **2.** Not wearing or being fitted with a bridle: *an unbridled pony.* —**un·bri′dled·ly** *adv.*

un·bro·ken (ŭn-brō′kən) *adj.* **1.** Not tampered with; intact: *an unbroken dozen.* **2.** Not violated or breached: *unbroken promises.* **3.** Uninterrupted; continuous. **4.** Not tamed or broken to harness. **5.** Not disordered or disturbed: *unbroken family ties.* —**un·bro′ken·ly** *adv.* —**un·bro′ken·ness** *n.*

un·buck·le (ŭn-bŭk′əl) *v.* **-led, -ling, -les** —*tr.* To loosen or undo the buckle or buckles of. —*intr.* **1.** To undo buckles. **2.** *Informal* To relax.

un·budg·ing (ŭn-bŭj′ĭng) *adj.* Not moving or willing to move from a position or place.

un·build (ŭn-bĭld′) *v.* **-built** (-bĭlt′), **-build·ing, -builds** —*tr.* To dismantle, take apart, or demolish; raze. —*intr.* To dismantle something built.

un·build·a·ble (ŭn-bĭl′də-bəl) *adj.* **1.** That cannot be built: *an unbuildable house.* **2.** Unsuitable to be built upon.

un·bun·dling (ŭn-bŭn′dlĭng) *n.* The separate pricing of goods and services.

un·but·ton (ŭn-bŭt′n) *v.* **-toned, -ton·ing, -tons** —*tr.* **1.** To unfasten the buttons of. **2.** To free or remove (a button) from a buttonhole. **3.** To open as if by unbuttoning: *unbutton the hatches.* —*intr.* To undo buttons.

un·but·ton·ed (ŭn-bŭt′nd) *adj.* **1.** Not buttoned. **2.** Free and unrestrained in expression: *unbuttoned humor.*

un·cal·cu·lat·ed (ŭn-kăl′kyə-lā′tĭd) *adj.* Not thought out in advance; spontaneous.

un·cal·cu·lat·ing (ŭn-kăl′kyə-lā′tĭng) *adj.* Not using or involving calculation: *an uncalculating answer.*

un·called-for (ŭn-kôld′fôr′) *adj.* **1.** Not required or requested; unwanted: *uncalled-for suggestions.* **2.** Not justified or deserved; unwarranted: *uncalled-for rudeness.*

un·can·ny (ŭn-kăn′ē) *adj.* **-ni·er, -ni·est** **1.** Peculiarly unsettling, as if of supernatural origin or nature; eerie. **2.** So keen and perceptive as to seem preternatural. [UN-¹ + CANNY, fortunate, safe (obsolete).] —**un·can′ni·ly** *adv.* —**un·can′ni·ness** *n.*

un·cap (ŭn-kăp′) *v.* **-capped, -cap·ping, -caps** —*tr.* To remove the cap or covering of. —*intr.* To remove one's head covering as a sign of deference.

un·cared-for (ŭn-kârd′fôr′) *adj.* Not looked after; neglected.

un·car·ing (ŭn-kâr′ĭng) *adj.* Devoid of concern or sympathy.

Un·cas (ŭng′kəs) 1588?–1683? Native American leader who rebelled against his father's leadership of the Pequot and with his followers formed the Mohegan tribe.

un·caused (ŭn-kôzd′) *adj.* Existing without a perceptible cause; spontaneous.

un·cen·sored (ŭn-sĕn′sərd) *adj.* Not examined, expurgated, or given a rating for inclusion of improper or inappropriate material: *the uncensored version of a controversial film.*

un·cer·e·mo·ni·ous (ŭn-sĕr′ə-mō′nē-əs) *adj.* **1.** Without the due formalities; abrupt: *an unceremonious departure.* **2.** Not ceremonious; informal. —**un·cer′e·mo′ni·ous·ly** *adv.*

un·cer·tain (ŭn-sûr′tn) *adj.* **1.** Not known or established; questionable: *changes of uncertain consequences.* **2.** Not determined; undecided: *uncertain plans.* **3.** Not having sure knowledge: *an uncertain recollection of the events.* **4a.** Subject to change; variable. **b.** Unsteady; fitful: *uncertain light.* —**un·cer′tain·ly** *adv.*

un·cer·tain·ty (ŭn-sûr′tn-tē) *n., pl.* **-ties** **1.** The condition of being uncertain; doubt. **2.** Something uncertain: *the uncertainties of modern life.* **3.** *Statistics* The estimated amount or percentage by which an observed or calculated value may differ from the true value.

SYNONYMS *uncertainty, doubt, dubiety, skepticism, suspicion, mistrust* These nouns refer to the condition of being unsure about someone or something. *Uncertainty,* the least forceful, merely denotes a lack of assurance or conviction: *I regarded my decision with growing uncertainty. Doubt* and *dubiety* imply a questioning state of mind: *"Doubt is part of all religion"* (Isaac Bashevis Singer). *On this point there can be no dubiety. Skepticism* generally suggests an instinctive or habitual tendency to question and demand proof: *"A wise skepticism is the first attribute of a good critic"* (James Russell Lowell). *Suspicion* is doubt as to the innocence, truth, integrity, honesty, or soundness of someone or something: *His furtiveness aroused my suspicions. Mistrust* denotes lack of trust or confidence, as in a person's motives, arising from suspicion: *viewed the recommendations with mistrust.*

uncertainty principle *n.* A principle in quantum mechanics holding that it is impossible to determine simultaneously both the position and momentum of a very small particle, such as an electron, with a high degree of accuracy.

un·chain (ŭn-chān′) *tr.v.* **-chained, -chain·ing, -chains** To release from or as if from chains or bonds; set free. —**un·chain′a·ble** *adj.*

un·change·a·ble (ŭn-chān′jə-bəl) *adj.* Not to be altered; immutable: *the unchangeable seasons.* —**un·change′a·bil′i·ty, un·change′a·ble·ness** *n.* —**un·change′a·bly** *adv.*

un·chang·ing (ŭn-chān′jĭng) *adj.* Remaining the same; showing or undergoing no change: *unchanging friendliness.* —**un·chang′ing·ly** *adv.* —**un·chang′ing·ness** *n.*

un·charged (ŭn-chärjd′) *adj.* **1.** Not loaded. Used of a weapon. **2.** Lacking electric charge.

un·chart·ed (ŭn-chär′tĭd) *adj.* **1.** Not charted or recorded on a map or plan. **2.** Unknown.

un·chaste (ŭn-chāst′) *adj.* **-chast·er, -chast·est** Not chaste or modest. —**un·chaste′ly** *adv.* —**un·chas′ti·ty** (-chăs′tĭ-tē) *n.*

un·checked (ŭn-chĕkt′) *adj.* **1.** Not held in check; unrestrained: *an unchecked temper.* **2.** Not checked for accuracy, efficiency, or flaws: *an unchecked list.*

un·chris·tian (ŭn-krĭs′chən) *adj.* **1.** Not in accord with the spirit or principles of Christianity. **2.** Not Christian. **3.** *Informal* Very objectionable; dreadful: *woke me at an unchristian hour.*

un·church (ŭn-chûrch′) *tr.v.* **-churched, -church·ing, -church·es** **1.** To expel from a church or from church membership; excommunicate. **2.** To deprive (a congregation, sect, or building) of the status of a church.

un·churched (ŭn-chûrcht′) *adj.* Not belonging to or participating in a church. ❖ *n. (used with a pl. verb)* People who do not belong to or participate in a church considered as a group. Used with *the.*

un·ci (ŭn′sī) *n.* Plural of **uncus.**

un·cial also **Un·cial** (ŭn′shəl, -sē-əl) *adj.* Of or relating to a style of writing characterized by somewhat rounded capital letters and found esp. in Greek and Latin manuscripts of the fourth to the eighth century A.D. ❖ *n.* **1.** A style of writing characterized by such letters. **2.** A capital letter written in this style. [< LLat. *ūnciālēs (litterae),* inch-high (letters), uncials, pl. of Lat. *ūnciālis,* inch-high < *ūncia,* a twelfth part, ounce, inch. See **oi-no-** in App.]

un·ci·form (ŭn′sə-fôrm′) *adj.* Shaped like a hook. ❖ *n.* See **hamate.** [Lat. *uncus,* hook + –FORM.]

un·ci·nar·i·a (ŭn′sə-nâr′ē-ə) *n.* See **hookworm.** [NLat. *Uncīnāria,* hookworm genus < Lat. *uncīnus,* barb. See UNCINATE.]

un·ci·nate (ŭn′sə-nāt′, -nĭt) *adj.* Bent at the end like a hook; unciform. [Lat. *uncīnātus* < *uncīnus,* barb < *uncus,* hook.]

un·cir·cum·cised (ŭn-sûr′kəm-sīzd′) *adj.* **1.** Not circumcised. **2a.** Not Jewish; Gentile. **b.** Not Christian. —**un·cir′cum·ci′sion** (-sĭzh′ən) *n.*

un·civ·il (ŭn-sĭv′əl) *adj.* **1.** Discourteous; rude. **2.** *Archaic* Uncivilized. —**un·civ′il·ly** *adv.* —**un·civ′il·ness** *n.*

un·clad (ŭn-klăd′) *adj.* Not wearing clothes; naked.

un·claimed (ŭn-klāmd′) *adj.* Not claimed as property.

un·clasp (ŭn-klăsp′) *v.* **-clasped, -clasp·ing, -clasps** —*tr.* **1.** To release or loosen the clasp of. **2.** To release or loosen from a clasp or an embrace. —*intr.* **1.** To become unfastened. **2.** To release or relax a clasp or grasp; let go.

un·cle (ŭng′kəl) *n.* **1a.** The brother of one's mother or father. **b.** The husband of one's aunt. **2.** Used as a form of address for an older man, esp. by children. **3.** A kindly counselor. **4.** *Slang* A pawnbroker. **5. Uncle** Uncle Sam. —*idiom:* cry (or say) uncle

Informal To indicate a willingness to give up a fight or surrender. [ME < AN < Lat. *avunculus*, maternal uncle.]

un•clean (ŭn-klēn′) *adj.* **-clean•er, -clean•est 1.** Foul or dirty. **2.** Morally defiled; unchaste. **3.** Ceremonially impure. **—un•clean′ness** *n.*

un•clean•ly (ŭn-klēn′lē) *adj.* **-li•er, -li•est** Unclean. ❖ *adv.* (-klēn′-) In an unclean manner. **—un•clean′li•ness** *n.*

un•clear (ŭn-klîr′) *adj.* **-clear•er, -clear•est** Not clearly defined; not explicit.

Uncle Sam (săm) *n.* **1.** The government of the United States, often personified by a representation of a tall thin man having a white beard and wearing a blue tailcoat, red-and-white-striped trousers, and a tall hat with a band of stars. **2.** The American nation or its people. [< *US*, abbr. of UNITED STATES.]

Uncle Tom *n. Offensive* A Black person regarded as subservient or deferential to white people. [After *Uncle Tom*, a character in *Uncle Tom's Cabin* by Harriet Beecher Stowe.]

Uncle Tom•ism (tŏm′ĭz′əm) *n. Offensive* Deferential, subservient behavior and attitudes believed typical of an Uncle Tom.

un•clog (ŭn-klŏg′) *tr.v.* **-clogged, -clog•ging, -clogs** To clear a blockage from (a drain, for example).

un•close (ŭn-klōz′) *v.* **-closed, -clos•ing, -clos•es** —*tr.* **1.** To open. **2.** To disclose. —*intr.* **1.** To be opened. **2.** To undergo disclosure.

un•co (ŭng′kō) *Scots adj.* So unusual as to be surprising; uncanny. ❖ *n., pl.* **-cos 1.** An unusual or amazing person. **2.** A stranger. **3. uncos** News. ❖ *adv.* To an excessive degree; remarkably. [ME *unkow*, var. of *uncouth*, strange. See UNCOUTH.]

un•cod•ed (ŭn-kō′dĭd) *adj.* Not coded, esp. not having or not showing a Zip Code.

un•com•fort•a•ble (ŭn-kŭm′fər-tə-bəl, -kŭmf′tə-, -kŭmf′tər-) *adj.* **1.** Experiencing physical discomfort. **2.** Ill at ease; uneasy. **3.** Causing anxiety; disquieting. **—un•com′fort•a•ble•ness** *n.* **—un•com′fort•a•bly** *adv.*

un•com•mer•cial (ŭn′kə-mûr′shəl) *adj.* **1.** Not engaged in or involving trade or commerce. **2.** Not in accord with the spirit or methods of commerce. **3.** Uneconomical.

un•com•mit•ted (ŭn′kə-mĭt′ĭd) *adj.* Not pledged to a specific cause or course of action: *an uncommitted delegate.*

un•com•mon (ŭn-kŏm′ən) *adj.* **-er, -est 1.** Not common; rare. **2.** Wonderful; remarkable. **—un•com′mon•ly** *adv.*

un•com•mu•ni•ca•tive (ŭn′kə-myōō′nĭ-kā′tĭv, -kə-tĭv) *adj.* Not disposed to be communicative. **—un•com•mu′ni•ca′tive•ly** *adv.* **—un•com•mu′ni•ca′tive•ness** *n.*

Un•com•pah•gre Peak (ŭn′kəm-pä′grē) A mountain, 4,364.2 m (14,309 ft), in the San Juan Mts. of SW CO.

un•com•plet•ed (ŭn′kəm-plē′tĭd) *adj.* As yet unfinished.

un•com•pli•cat•ed (ŭn-kŏm′plĭ-kā′tĭd) *adj.* **1.** Not complex or involved; simple. **2.** Not involving medical complications.

un•com•pro•mis•a•ble (ŭn-kŏm′prə-mī′zə-bəl) *adj.* That cannot be compromised: *uncompromisable honesty.*

un•com•put•er•ized (ŭn′kəm-pyōō′tə-rīzd′) *adj.* Not equipped with or using computers.

un•con•cern (ŭn′kən-sûrn′) *n.* **1.** Lack of interest; indifference. **2.** Lack of worry or apprehensiveness. [Prob. back-formation < UNCONCERNED.]

un•con•cerned (ŭn′kən-sûrnd′) *adj.* **1.** Not interested; indifferent. **2.** Not worried or apprehensive. **—un′con•cern′ed•ly** (-sûr′nĭd-lē) *adv.* **—un′con•cern′ed•ness** *n.*

un•con•di•tioned (ŭn′kən-dĭsh′ənd) *adj.* **1.** Unconditional; unrestricted. **2.** *Psychology* Not dependent on or resulting from conditioning; unlearned or natural.

un•con•gen•ial (ŭn′kən-jēn′yəl) *adj.* **1.** Not compatible or sympathetic, as in character. **2.** Not appropriate; unsuitable. **3.** Not pleasing; disagreeable. **—un′con•ge′ni•al′i•ty** (-jē′nē-ăl′ĭ-tē) *n.*

un•con•scion•a•ble (ŭn-kŏn′shə-nə-bəl) *adj.* **1.** Not restrained by conscience; unscrupulous. **2.** Beyond prudence or reason; excessive: *unconscionable spending.* **—un•con′scion•a•ble•ness** *n.* **—un•con′scion•a•bly** *adv.*

un•con•scious (ŭn-kŏn′shəs) *adj.* **1.** Lacking awareness and the capacity for sensory perception; not conscious. **2.** Temporarily lacking consciousness. **3.** Occurring in the absence of conscious awareness or thought: *unconscious resentment.* **4.** Without conscious control; involuntary or unintended. ❖ *n.* The division of the mind in psychoanalytic theory containing elements of psychic makeup that are not subject to conscious perception or control but that often affect conscious thoughts and behavior. **—un•con′scious•ly** *adv.* **—un•con′scious•ness** *n.*

un•con•sid•ered (ŭn′kən-sĭd′ərd) *adj.* Not reasoned or considered; rash: *an unconsidered remark.*

un•con•sti•tu•tion•al (ŭn′kŏn-stĭ-tōō′shə-nəl, -tyōō′-) *adj.* Not in accord with the principles set forth in the constitution of a nation or state. **—un′con•sti•tu′tion•al′i•ty** (-shə-năl′ĭ-tē) *n.* **—un′con•sti•tu′tion•al•ly** *adv.*

un•con•struct•ed (ŭn′kən-strŭk′tĭd) *adj.* Designed or made with little or no interfacing, padding, or lining to produce a loose, soft shape. Used of apparel: *an unconstructed jacket.*

un•cool (ŭn-kōōl′) *adj. Slang* **1.** Lacking assurance, self-control, or sophistication. **2.** Not in accord with the standards or mores of a specified group.

un•co•or•di•nat•ed (ŭn′kō-ôr′dn-ā′tĭd) *adj.* **1.** Lacking physical or mental coordination. **2.** Lacking planning, method, or organization. **—un′co•or′di•nat′ed•ly** *adv.*

un•cork (ŭn-kôrk′) *tr.v.* **-corked, -cork•ing, -corks 1.** To draw the cork from. **2.** To free from a constrained or constrained condition.

un•count•a•ble (ŭn-koun′tə-bəl) *adj.* Too many to be counted; innumerable: *an uncountable number of tourists.*

un•count•ed (ŭn-koun′tĭd) *adj.* **1.** Not counted. **2.** Uncountable; innumerable.

un•cou•ple (ŭn-kŭp′əl) *v.* **-pled, -pling, -ples** —*tr.* **1.** To disconnect: *uncouple the trailer.* **2.** To set loose or release from a couple. —*intr.* To come or break loose. **—un•cou′pler** *n.*

un•couth (ŭn-kōōth′) *adj.* **1.** Crude; unrefined. **2.** Awkward or clumsy; ungraceful. **3.** *Archaic* Foreign; unfamiliar. [ME, unknown, strange < OE *uncūth* : *un-*, not; see UN-[1] + *cūth*, known; see *gnō-* in App.] **—un•couth′ly** *adv.* **—un•couth′ness** *n.*

un•cov•e•nant•ed (ŭn-kŭv′ə-nən-tĭd) *adj.* **1.** Not bound by a covenant. **2.** Not promised or guaranteed by a covenant.

un•cov•er (ŭn-kŭv′ər) *v.* **-ered, -er•ing, -ers** —*tr.* **1.** To remove the cover from: *uncovered the saucepan.* **2.** To manifest or disclose; reveal: *uncovered new evidence.* **3.** To remove the hat from, as in respect or reverence. —*intr.* **1.** To remove a cover. **2.** To bare the head in respect or reverence.

un•cov•ered (ŭn-kŭv′ərd) *adj.* **1.** Having no cover or protection. **2.** Lacking the protection of insurance or collateral security. **3.** Bareheaded.

un•cre•at•ed (ŭn′krē-ā′tĭd) *adj.* **1.** Not having been created; not yet in existence. **2.** Existing of itself; uncaused.

un•cred•it•ed (ŭn-krĕd′ĭ-tĭd) *adj.* **1.** Not having been credited, as on a ledger: *an uncredited deposit.* **2.** Not having been accorded due recognition: *an uncredited discovery.*

un•crewed (ŭn-krōōd′) *adj.* Not having a crew; crewless.

un•crit•i•cal (ŭn-krĭt′ĭ-kəl) *adj.* **1.** Not critical; undiscriminating or indulgent. **2.** Not using critical standards or methods, as in evaluation. **—un•crit′i•cal•ly** *adv.*

un•cross (ŭn-krôs′, -krŏs′) *tr.v.* **-crossed, -cross•ing, -cross•es** To move (one's legs, for example) from a crossed position.

un•crowned (ŭn-kround′) *adj.* **1.** Yet to be crowned. **2.** Having the authority of a monarch or a similar figure but not the title: *the uncrowned king of espionage.*

unc•tion (ŭngk′shən) *n.* **1.** The act of anointing as part of a religious, ceremonial, or healing ritual. **2.** An ointment or oil; a salve. **3.** Something that serves to soothe; a balm. **4.** Affected or exaggerated earnestness, esp. in choice and use of language. [ME < Lat. *ūnctiō, ūnctiōn-* < *ūnctus*, p. part. of *unguere*, to anoint.]

unc•tu•ous (ŭngk′chōō-əs) *adj.* **1.** Characterized by affected, exaggerated, or insincere earnestness. **2.** Having the quality or characteristics of oil or ointment; slippery. **3.** Containing or composed of oil or fat. **4.** Abundant in organic materials; soft and rich: *unctuous soil.* [ME < OFr. *unctueus* < Med.Lat. *ūnctuōsus* < Lat. *ūnctum*, ointment < neut. p. part. of *unguere*, to anoint.] **—unc′tu•ous•ly** *adv.* **—unc′tu•ous•ness, unc′tu•os′i•ty** (-ŏs′ĭ-tē) *n.*

un•cul•tured (ŭn-kŭl′chərd) *adj.* Not cultured or cultivated: *an uncultured village.*

un•cus (ŭng′kəs) *n., pl.* **un•ci** (ŭn′sī) *Biology* A hook-shaped part or process. [Lat., hook.]

un•cut (ŭn-kŭt′) *adj.* **1.** Not cut: *uncut hair.* **2.** *Printing* Having the page edge not slit or trimmed. Used of a book. **3.** Not cut or ground to a specific shape. Used of a gemstone. **4.** Not condensed, abridged, or shortened, as by an editor or a censor: *the uncut version of the scandal.* **5.** *Slang* Uncircumcised. Used of a man or boy. **—un•cut′ta•ble** *adj.*

un•damped (ŭn-dămpt′) *adj.* **1.** *Physics* Not tending toward a state of rest; not damped. Used of oscillations. **2.** Not stifled or discouraged; unchecked: *undamped ardor.*

un•daunt•a•ble (ŭn-dôn′tə-bəl, -dän′-) *adj.* Not admitting of discouragement: *undauntable optimism.*

un•daunt•ed (ŭn-dôn′tĭd, -dän′-) *adj.* Not discouraged or disheartened; resolutely courageous. See Syns at **brave**. **—un•daunt′ed•ly** *adv.* **—un•daunt′ed•ness** *n.*

un•dead (ŭn-dĕd′) *adj.* No longer living but supernaturally animated, as a zombie.

un•de•cil•lion (ŭn′dĭ-sĭl′yən) *n.* **1.** The cardinal number equal to 10[36]. **2.** *Chiefly British* The cardinal number equal to 10[66]. [Lat. *undecim, ūndecim* (ūnus, one; see **oi-no-** in App. + *decem*, ten; see **dekm̥** in App.) + (M)ILLION.] **—un′de•cil′lion** *adj.* **—un′de•cil′lionth** *adj., adv. & n.*

un•decked[1] (ŭn-dĕkt′) *adj.* Not decorated; unornamented.

un•decked[2] (ŭn-dĕkt′) *adj.* Having no deck. Used of a ship or boat.

un•de•mon•stra•tive (ŭn′dĭ-mŏn′strə-tĭv) *adj.* Not disposed

Uncle Sam
World War I poster by
James Montgomery Flagg
(1877–1960)

ă	pat	oi	boy
ā	pay	ou	out
âr	care	ōō	took
ä	father	ōō	boot
ĕ	pet	ŭ	cut
ē	be	ûr	urge
ĭ	pit	th	thin
ī	pie	th	this
îr	pier	hw	which
ŏ	pot	zh	vision
ō	toe	ə	about,
ô	paw		item

Stress marks: ′ (primary);
′ (secondary), as in
lexicon (lĕk′sĭ-kŏn′)

to expressions of feeling; reserved. —**un′de•mon′stra•tive•ly** *adv.*

un•der (ŭn′dər) *prep.* **1a.** In a lower position or place than: *a rug under a chair.* **b.** To or into a lower position or place than: *rolled the ball under the couch.* **2.** Beneath the surface of: *swam under water.* **3.** Beneath the assumed surface or guise of: *travel under a false name.* **4.** Less than; smaller than: *The jar's capacity is under three quarts.* **5.** Less than the required amount or degree of: *under voting age.* **6.** Inferior to in status or rank: *nine officers under me.* **7.** Subject to the authority, rule, or control of: *under a dictatorship.* **8.** Subject to the supervision, instruction, or influence of: *under parental guidance.* **9.** Undergoing or receiving the effects of: *under constant care.* **10.** Subject to the restraint or obligation of: *under contract.* **11.** Within the group or classification of: *listed under biology.* **12.** In the process of: *under discussion.* **13.** In view of; because of: *under these conditions.* **14.** With the authorization of. **15.** Sowed or planted with: *an acre under oats.* **16.** *Nautical* Powered or propelled by: *under sail.* **17.** During the time conventionally assigned to (a sign of the zodiac). ❖ *adv.* **1.** In or into a place below or beneath. **2.** In or into a subordinate or inferior condition or position. **3.** So as to be covered or enveloped. **4.** So as to be less than the required amount or degree. ❖ *adj.* **1.** Located or situated on a lower level or beneath something else. **2.** Lower in rank, power, or authority; subordinate. **3.** Less than is required or customary. [ME < OE. See n̥dher- in App.]

under– *pref.* **1.** Beneath or below in position: *underground.* **2.** Inferior or subordinate in rank or importance: *undersecretary.* **3.** Less in degree, rate, or quantity than normal or proper: *undersized.* [ME < OE. See n̥dher- in App.]

USAGE NOTE In forming compounds, *under–* is joined with the following element without a space or hyphen: *underrate; undergrow.* Note, however, that the preposition *under* may combine with other words as a hyphenated modifier: *an under-the-table deal.*

un•der•act (ŭn′dər-ăkt′) *v.* **-act•ed, -act•ing, -acts** —*tr.* **1.** To perform (a role) weakly or with insufficient expressiveness. **2.** To understate (a role) intentionally; underplay. —*intr.* To perform in an understated way.

un•der•age[1] (ŭn′dər-ĭj) *n.* **1.** An amount, as of money or goods actually on hand, that falls short of the listed amount in records or books of account. **2.** A deficient amount; a shortfall.

un•der•age[2] (ŭn′dər-āj′) also **un•der•aged** (-ājd′) *adj.* Below the customary or legal age, as for drinking or voting.

un•der•arm (ŭn′dər-ärm′) *adj.* **1.** Located, placed, or used under the arm. **2.** *Sports* Executed with the hand brought forward and up from below the level of the shoulder; underhand. ❖ *adv.* With an underarm motion or delivery. ❖ *n.* The armpit.

un•der•bel•ly (ŭn′dər-bĕl′ē) *n.*, *pl.* **-lies 1.** The soft belly or underside of the body of an animal. **2.** The vulnerable or weak part.

un•der•bid (ŭn′dər-bĭd′) *v.* **-bid, -bid•ding, -bids** —*tr.* To bid lower than (a competitor). —*intr.* **1.** To make an unnecessarily low bid. **2.** *Games* To bid less than the full value of one's hand in bridge. —**un′der•bid′** *n.* —**un′der•bid′der** *n.*

un•der•bite (ŭn′dər-bīt′) *n.* A malocclusion in which the lower teeth protrude beyond the upper teeth.

un•der•bod•y (ŭn′dər-bŏd′ē) *n.*, *pl.* **-ies 1.** See **underbelly** 1. **2.** The under parts of the body of a motor vehicle.

un•der•bred (ŭn′dər-brĕd′) *adj.* **1.** Poorly brought up; ill-bred. **2.** Of mixed breed; not thoroughbred.

un•der•brush (ŭn′dər-brŭsh′) *n.* Small trees, shrubs, or similar plants growing beneath the taller trees in a forest.

un•der•buy (ŭn′dər-bī′) *v.* **-bought** (-bôt′), **-buy•ing, -buys** —*tr.* **1.** To buy less (of something) than one wants or needs. **2.** To buy at a lower price than a competitor. **3.** To buy (something) at less than a proper or expected price. —*intr.* **1.** To buy less of something than what is wanted or needed. **2.** To buy something at less than a proper or expected price.

un•der•cap•i•tal•ize (ŭn′dər-kăp′ĭ-tl-īz′) *tr.v.* **-ized, -iz•ing, -iz•es** To supply (a business or government, for example) with so little capital that operations are hindered. —**un′der•cap′i•tal•i•za′tion** (-ĭ-zā′shən) *n.*

un•der•card (ŭn′dər-kärd′) *n.* The event or events coming before and supporting the main event, as of boxing matches.

un•der•car•riage (ŭn′dər-kăr′ĭj) *n.* **1.** A supporting framework or structure, as for the body of a motor vehicle. **2.** The landing gear of an aircraft.

un•der•charge (ŭn′dər-chärj′) *tr.v.* **-charged, -charg•ing, -charg•es 1.** To charge (a customer, for example) less than is customary or required. **2.** To load (a firearm) with an insufficient charge. ❖ *n.* (ŭn′dər-chärj′) An insufficient or improper charge.

un•der•class (ŭn′dər-klăs′) *n.* The lowest societal stratum, usu. composed of the disadvantaged.

un•der•class•man (ŭn′dər-klăs′mən) *n.* A student in the fresh-

man or sophomore class at a secondary school or college.

un•der•clothes (ŭn′dər-klōz′, -klōthz′) *pl.n.* See **underwear.**

un•der•cloth•ing (ŭn′dər-klō′thĭng) *n.* See **underwear.**

un•der•coat (ŭn′dər-kōt′) *n.* **1.** A coat worn beneath another coat. **2.** A covering of short hairs lying underneath the longer outer hairs of an animal's coat. **3.** also **un•der•coat•ing** (-kō′tĭng) **a.** A coat of sealing material applied to a surface before the outer coats, as of paint, are applied. **b.** The sealing material used for this purpose. **c.** A tarlike substance sprayed on the underside of a vehicle to prevent rusting. ❖ *tr.v.* **-coat•ed, -coat•ing, -coats** To apply an undercoat to.

un•der•cool (ŭn′dər-kōōl′) *tr.v.* **-cooled, -cool•ing, -cools** To supercool.

un•der•count (ŭn′dər-kount′) *tr.v.* **-count•ed, -count•ing, -counts** To record fewer than the actual number of (persons in a census, for example). —**un′der•count′** *n.*

un•der•cov•er (ŭn′dər-kŭv′ər) *adj.* **1.** Performed or occurring in secret: *an undercover investigation.* **2.** Engaged or employed in spying or secret investigation.

un•der•croft (ŭn′dər-krôft′, -krŏft′) *n.* A crypt, esp. for burial under a church. [ME : *under-*, under- + *croft*, crypt (< MDu. *crofte* < Med.Lat. *crupta* < Lat. *crypta*, crypt; see CRYPT).]

un•der•cur•rent (ŭn′dər-kûr′ənt, -kŭr′-) *n.* **1.** A current, as of air or water, below another current or beneath a surface. **2.** An underlying tendency, force, or influence often contrary to what is superficially evident; an intimation.

un•der•cut (ŭn′dər-kŭt′) *v.* **-cut, -cut•ting, -cuts** —*tr.* **1.** To diminish or destroy the province or effectiveness of; undermine. **2.** To sell at a lower price than or to work for lower wages or fees than (a competitor). **3.** To make a cut under or below. **4.** To create an overhang by cutting material away from, as in carving. **5.** *Sports* **a.** To impart backspin to (a ball) by striking downward as well as forward, as in golf. **b.** To cut or slice (a ball) with an underarm stroke, as in tennis. —*intr.* To engage in undercutting. ❖ *n.* (ŭn′dər-kŭt′) **1a.** A cut made in the under part to remove material. **b.** The material so removed. **2.** A notch cut in a tree to direct its fall and insure a clean break. **3.** *Chiefly British* The tenderloin of beef; the fillet. **4.** *Sports* **a.** A spin given to a ball opposite to its direction of flight; a backspin. **b.** A cut or slice imparting such a spin.

un•der•de•vel•oped (ŭn′dər-dĭ-vĕl′əpt) *adj.* **1.** Not adequately or normally developed; immature: *underdeveloped leaves and flowers.* **2.** Processed in too weak a developing solution, or for too short a time, or at too low a temperature to produce a normal degree of contrast. Used of film. **3.** Having a low level of economic productivity and technological sophistication; developing. —**un′der•de•vel′op•ment** *n.*

un•der•do (ŭn′dər-dōō′) *tr.v.* **-did** (-dĭd′), **-done** (-dŭn′), **-do•ing, -does** (-dŭz′) To do to an insufficient degree, esp. to cook for too short a time.

un•der•dog (ŭn′dər-dôg′, -dŏg′) *n.* **1.** One that is expected to lose a contest or struggle, as in sports or politics. **2.** One that is at a disadvantage.

un•der•done (ŭn′dər-dŭn′) *adj.* Not sufficiently cooked.

un•der•draw•ers (ŭn′dər-drôrz′) *pl.n.* Undershorts; underpants.

un•der•dress (ŭn′dər-drĕs′) *n.* **1.** Apparel worn beneath outer garments; underclothing. **2.** An outer garment, such as a dress beneath a tunic or coat, that serves as part of a costume or outfit. ❖ *intr.v.* (ŭn′dər-drĕs′) **-dressed, -dress•ing, -dress•es 1.** To dress too informally for the occasion. **2.** To dress without sufficient warmth.

un•der•drive (ŭn′dər-drīv′) *n.* A gearing device that causes the output drive shaft to rotate at a slower rate than the engine input shaft.

un•der•em•ployed (ŭn′dər-ĕm-ploid′) *adj.* **1.** Employed only part-time when needing and wanting full-time employment. **2.** Inadequately employed, esp. employed at a low-paying job that requires less skill or training than one possesses. **3.** Not fully or adequately used or employed. ❖ *n.* Underemployed persons considered as a group. —**un′der•em•ploy′ment** *n.*

un•der•es•ti•mate (ŭn′dər-ĕs′tə-māt′) *tr.v.* **-mat•ed, -mat•ing, -mates** To make too low an estimate of the quantity, degree, or worth of. ❖ *n.* (-ĕs′tə-mĭt) An estimate that is or proves to be too low. —**un′der•es′ti•ma′tion** *n.*

un•der•ex•pose (ŭn′dər-ĭk-spōz′) *tr.v.* **-posed, -pos•ing, -pos•es 1.** To expose (film) to light for too short a time or to light or radiation insufficient to produce normal image contrast. **2.** To provide with too little publicity. —**un′der•ex•po′sure** (-ĭk-spō′zhər) *n.*

un•der•feed (ŭn′dər-fēd′) *tr.v.* **-fed** (-fĕd′), **-feed•ing, -feeds 1.** To feed insufficiently. **2.** To supply (an engine) with fuel from the underside.

un•der•flow (ŭn′dər-flō′) *n.* A data-processing error arising

un′der•a•chieve′ *intr.v.*	**un′der•en•dow′** *tr.v.*	**un′der•priv′i•leged** *adj. & n.*	**un′der•re•act′** *intr.v.*
un′der•a•chieve′ment *n.*	**un′der•en•dow′ment** *n.*	**un′der•pro•duce′** *tr. & intr.v.*	**un′der•re•port′** *tr.v.*
un′der•ed′u•cat′ed *adj.*	**un′der•fund′** *tr.v.*	**un′der•pro•duc′tion** *n.*	**un′der•sup•ply′** *n. & tr.v.*
un′der•em′pha•sis *n.*	**un′der•pay′** *tr.v.*	**un′der•pro•duc′tive** *adj.*	**un′der•val′u•a′tion** *n.*
un′der•em′pha•size′ *tr.v.*	**un′der•pay′ment** *n.*	**un′der•rate′** *tr.v.*	**un′der•val′ue** *tr.v.*

when a computed quantity is smaller than the limits of precision of the computing device.

un·der·foot (ŭn′dər-fŏŏt′) *adv.* **1.** Below or under the foot or feet; against the ground: *trampled the beans underfoot.* **2.** At or under the foot or feet; on the ground. **3.** Hindering progress; in the way: *children underfoot.*

un·der·fur (ŭn′dər-fûr′) *n.* The soft fine undercoat of certain mammals, such as otters, beavers, and seals.

un·der·gar·ment (ŭn′dər-gär′mənt) *n.* A garment worn under outer garments, esp. one worn next to the skin.

un·der·gird (ŭn′dər-gûrd′) *tr.v.* **-gird·ed** or **-girt** (-gûrt′), **-gird·ing, -girds** To support or strengthen from beneath.

un·der·glaze (ŭn′dər-glāz′) *n.* Coloring or decoration applied to pottery before glazing.

un·der·go (ŭn′dər-gō′) *tr.v.* **-went** (-wĕnt′), **-gone** (-gôn′, -gŏn′), **-go·ing, -goes** (-gōz′) **1.** To pass through; experience. **2.** To endure; suffer: *undergo great hardship.*

un·der·grad (ŭn′dər-grăd′) *Informal adj.* Undergraduate. ❖ *n.* An undergraduate.

un·der·grad·u·ate (ŭn′dər-grăj′ŏŏ-ĭt) *n.* A college or university student who has not yet received a bachelor's or similar degree. ❖ *adj.* **1.** Of, relating to, or characteristic of undergraduates. **2.** Having the standing of an undergraduate.

un·der·ground (ŭn′dər-ground′) *adj.* **1.** Situated, occurring, or operating below the surface of the earth. **2a.** Hidden or concealed; clandestine. **b.** Of or relating to an organization involved in secret or illegal activity. **3.** Of or relating to an avant-garde movement or its films, publications, and art. ❖ *n.* **1.** A clandestine organization planning hostile activities against or the overthrow of a government. **2.** *Chiefly British* A subway system. **3.** An avant-garde movement or publication. ❖ *adv.* (ŭn′dər-ground′) **1.** Below the surface of the earth. **2.** In secret; stealthily.

Underground Railroad *n.* A secret cooperative network that aided fugitive slaves in reaching sanctuary in the free states or Canada in the years before the abolition of slavery in the United States.

un·der·grown (ŭn′dər-grōn′) *adj.* **1.** Not fully grown; puny. **2.** Covered with undergrowth.

un·der·growth (ŭn′dər-grōth′) *n.* **1.** Low-growing plants, saplings, and shrubs beneath trees in a forest. **2.** A growth of short fine hairs underlying the longer and thicker outer hairs of an animal's coat; underfur or underwool. **3.** The condition of being less than fully grown.

un·der·hair (ŭn′dər-hâr′) *n.* A covering of soft downy hairs lying underneath the outer hairs of an animal's coat.

un·der·hand (ŭn′dər-hănd′) also **un·der·hand·ed** (ŭn′dər-hăn′dĭd) *adj.* **1.** Marked by or done in a deceptive, secret, or sly manner; dishonest and sneaky. **2.** *Sports* Underarm: *an underhand pitch.* ❖ *adv.* **1.** With an underarm movement. **2.** In a sly and secret way. —**un′der·hand′** —**un′der·hand′ed·ly** *adv.* —**un′der·hand′ed·ness** *n.*

un·der·hung (ŭn′dər-hŭng′) *adj.* **1a.** Protruding from beneath. **b.** Supported by or lying over something that projects. **2.** Resting on or mounted along a supporting track, as a sliding door on rollers. **3.** Underslung, as a machine. **4.** Having the lower jaw projecting beyond the upper jaw.

un·der·in·sure (ŭn′dər-ĭn-shŏŏr′) *tr.v.* **-sured, -sur·ing, -sures** To insure under a policy that provides inadequate benefits. —**un′der·in·sur′ance** *n.*

un·der·kill (ŭn′dər-kĭl′) *n.* Insufficient force for the defeat of an enemy.

un·der·laid (ŭn′dər-lād′) *adj.* **1.** Placed or laid underneath. **2.** Supported or raised by something from beneath; having an underlay.

un·der·lay¹ (ŭn′dər-lā′) *tr.v.* **-laid** (-lād′), **-lay·ing, -lays** **1.** To put (one thing) under another. **2.** To provide with a base or support. **3.** *Printing* To raise or support (the level of a bed) by inserting a piece of paper or other material under the type. ❖ *n.* (ŭn′dər-lā′) **1.** Something, such as felt under a carpet, that is underlaid. **2.** *Printing* Paper or other material used to underlay the level of a bed.

un·der·lay² (ŭn′dər-lā′) *v.* Past tense of **underlie.**

un·der·let (ŭn′dər-lĕt′) *tr.v.* **-let, -let·ting, -lets** **1.** To lease for less than the proper value. **2.** To sublet.

un·der·lie (ŭn′dər-lī′) *tr.v.* **-lay** (-lā′), **-lain** (-lān′), **-ly·ing, -lies** **1.** To be located under or below. **2.** To be the support or basis of; account for. **3.** To constitute a prior financial claim over.

un·der·line (ŭn′dər-līn′, ŭn′dər-līn′) *tr.v.* **-lined, -lin·ing, -lines** **1.** To draw a line under; emphasize or cause to stand out; underscore. **2.** To emphasize; stress. ❖ *n.* (ŭn′dər-līn′) A line under something, such as a symbol, word, or phrase, used to indicate emphasis or italic type.

un·der·ling (ŭn′dər-lĭng) *n.* One of lesser rank or authority than another; a subordinate.

un·der·lin·ing (ŭn′dər-lī′nĭng) *n.* **1.** The act of drawing a line under; underscoring. **2.** Emphasis or stress, as in argument or rhetoric.

un·der·lip (ŭn′dər-lĭp′) *n.* The lower lip.

un·der·ly·ing (ŭn′dər-lī′ĭng) *adj.* **1.** Lying under or beneath something. **2.** Basic; fundamental. **3.** Present but not obvious; implicit: *an underlying meaning.* **4.** Taking precedence; prior.

un·der·mine (ŭn′dər-mīn′) *tr.v.* **-mined, -min·ing, -mines** **1.** To weaken by wearing away a base or foundation. **2.** To weaken, injure, or impair, often by degrees or imperceptibly; sap. **3.** To dig a mine or tunnel beneath.

un·der·most (ŭn′dər-mōst′) *adj.* Lowest in position, rank, or place; bottom. ❖ *adv.* In or to the lowest place.

un·der·neath (ŭn′dər-nēth′) *adv.* **1.** In or to a place beneath; below. **2.** On the lower face or underside. ❖ *prep.* **1.** Under; below; beneath. **2.** Under the power or control of. ❖ *adj.* Lower; under. ❖ *n.* The part or side below or under. [ME *underneth* < OE *underneothan* : *under*, under; see UNDER + *neothan*, below; see BENEATH.]

un·der·nour·ish (ŭn′dər-nûr′ĭsh, -nŭr′-) *tr.v.* **-ished, -ish·ing, -ish·es** To provide with insufficient quantity or quality of nourishment to sustain proper health and growth. —**un′der·nour′ish·ment** *n.*

un·der·pants (ŭn′dər-pănts′) *pl.n.* A lower undergarment, typically having short or no legs, worn next to the skin under other clothing.

un·der·part (ŭn′dər-pärt′) *n.* **1.** A lower part or a portion of a lower part or underside, esp. of an animal's body. **2.** A subordinate role, as in a play.

un·der·pass (ŭn′dər-păs′) *n.* **1.** A passage underneath something, esp. a section of road that passes under another road or a railroad. **2.** An intersection formed in this way.

un·der·per·form (ŭn′dər-pər-fôrm′) *v.* **-formed, -form·ing, -forms** —*tr.* **1.** To perform not as well as (something else): *stocks that underperformed the market.* **2.** To perform (a musical or theatrical work, for example) too seldom. —*intr.* To exhibit a level of performance that is below the standard. —**un′der·per·for′mance** *n.* —**un′der·per·form′er** *n.*

un·der·pin (ŭn′dər-pĭn′) *tr.v.* **-pinned, -pin·ning, -pins** **1.** To support from below, as with props, girders, or masonry. **2.** To give support or substance to.

un·der·pin·ning (ŭn′dər-pĭn′ĭng) *n.* **1.** Material or masonry used to support a structure, such as a wall. **2.** A support or foundation. Often used in the plural. **3.** *Informal* The human legs. Often used in the plural.

un·der·play (ŭn′dər-plā′, ŭn′dər-plā′) *v.* **-played, -play·ing, -plays** —*tr.* **1.** To act (a role) subtly or with restraint. **2.** To present or deal with subtly or with restraint; play down. —*intr.* **1.** To underplay a role. **2.** *Games* To play a low card while holding a higher card in the same suit.

un·der·plot (ŭn′dər-plŏt′) *n.* See **subplot** 1.

un·der·pop·u·lat·ed (ŭn′dər-pŏp′yə-lā′tĭd) *adj.* Lacking the normal or required population density. —**un′der·pop·u·la′tion** *n.*

un·der·price (ŭn′dər-prīs′) *tr.v.* **-priced, -pric·ing, -pric·es** **1.** To price lower than the real, normal, or appropriate value. **2.** To sell at a lower price than (a competitor).

un·der·proof (ŭn′dər-prŏŏf′) *adj.* Having a smaller proportion of alcohol than proof spirit.

un·der·prop (ŭn′dər-prŏp′) *tr.v.* **-propped, -prop·ping, -props** To prop (something) from below.

un·der·quote (ŭn′dər-kwōt′) *tr.v.* **-quot·ed, -quot·ing, -quotes** **1.** To offer (goods or services) for sale at a price lower than the official list or market price. **2.** To quote a lower price than that quoted by (another); undersell.

un·der·rep·re·sent (ŭn′dər-rĕp′rĭ-zĕnt′) *tr.v.* **-sent·ed, -sent·ing, -sents** To imply or suggest a lower amount, quantity, quality, or degree of than is actually present. —**un′der·rep′re·sen·ta′tion** *n.*

un·der·rep·re·sent·ed (ŭn′dər-rĕp′rĭ-zĕn′tĭd) *adj.* Insufficiently or inadequately represented: *the underrepresented voters in the younger segment of the population.*

un·der·run (ŭn′dər-rŭn′) *tr.v.* **-ran** (-răn′), **-run, -run·ning, -runs** To run, pass, or go beneath. ❖ *n.* **1.** Something that runs under, as: **a.** An amount or a quantity produced that is less than what has been estimated. **b.** The difference between this amount or quantity and what has been estimated. **2.** An undercurrent.

un·der·score (ŭn′dər-skôr′, -skōr′) *tr.v.* **-scored, -scor·ing, -scores** **1.** To underline. **2.** To emphasize; stress. ❖ *n.* An underline.

un·der·sea (ŭn′dər-sē′) *adj.* Existing, relating to, or created for use beneath the surface of the sea. ❖ *adv.* undersea (ŭn′dər-sē′) also **un·der·seas** (-sēz′) Beneath the surface of the sea.

un·der·sec·re·tar·y (ŭn′dər-sĕk′rə-tĕr′ē) *n., pl.* **-ies** An official directly subordinate to a member of a cabinet. —**un′der·sec′re·tar′i·at** (-târ′ē-ĭt) *n.*

un·der·sell (ŭn′dər-sĕl′) *tr.v.* **-sold** (-sōld′), **-sell·ing, -sells** **1.** To sell goods for a lower price than (another seller). **2.** To sell (something) at a price less than the actual value. **3.** To present (an idea, for example) with little enthusiasm. —**un′der·sell′er** *n.*

un·der·set (ŭn′dər-sĕt′) *n.* An ocean undercurrent.

un·der·sexed (ŭn′dər-sĕkst′) *adj.* Having less sexual desire or potency than what is regarded as normal.

un·der·shirt (ŭn′dər-shûrt′) *n.* An upper undergarment, usu. having short or no sleeves, that is worn next to the skin under a shirt.

un·der·shoot (ŭn′dər-shŏŏt′) *v.* **-shot** (-shŏt′), **-shoot·ing, -shoots** —*tr.* **1.** To shoot a projectile short of (a target). **2a.** To

underhand
underhand softball pitch

start the approach of an aircraft to (a landing area) too low or too soon. **b.** To land an aircraft short of (a landing area). —*intr.* **1.** To shoot short of a target. **2.** To land short of a landing area.

un·der·shorts (ŭn′dər-shôrts′) *pl.n.* Shorts or briefs worn as an undergarment, esp. those for a man; underpants.

un·der·shot (ŭn′dər-shŏt′) *adj.* **1.** Driven by water passing from below, as a water wheel. **2.** Having the lower jaw or teeth projecting beyond the upper; underhung.

un·der·shrub (ŭn′dər-shrŭb′) *n.* A very low-growing shrub.

un·der·side (ŭn′dər-sīd′) *n.* **1.** The side or surface that is underneath; the bottom side. **2.** The side that is less desirable, reputable, or noble than the obverse.

un·der·sign (ŭn′dər-sīn′) *tr.v.* **-signed, -sign·ing, -signs** To sign one's name at the bottom of (a letter or document).

un·der·signed (ŭn′dər-sīnd′) *adj.* **1.** Having signatures or a signature at the bottom or end. Used of documents. **2.** Signed or having signed at the bottom or end of a document: *the undersigned names; the undersigned people.* ❖ *n., pl.* **undersigned** A signer whose name appears at the bottom or end of a document.

un·der·sized (ŭn′dər-sīzd′) also **un·der·size** (-sīz′) *adj.* Of less than normal or sufficient size.

un·der·skirt (ŭn′dər-skûrt′) *n.* **1.** A skirt worn under another skirt; a petticoat. **2.** One skirt of a layered gown over which outer skirts are formed and draped.

un·der·sleeve (ŭn′dər-slēv′) *n.* **1.** A sleeve worn under another. **2.** An ornamental sleeve under another sleeve, extending below or showing through slashes in the outer sleeve.

un·der·slung (ŭn′dər-slŭng′) *adj.* **1.** Having springs attached to the axles from below. Used of a vehicle or its frame. **2.** Supported from above. **3.** Having a low center of gravity.

un·der·soil (ŭn′dər-soil′) *n.* Soil below the ground surface.

un·der·sold (ŭn′dər-sōld′) *v.* Past tense and past participle of **undersell.**

un·der·spin (ŭn′dər-spĭn′) *n.* A backspin.

un·der·staff (ŭn′dər-stăf′) *tr.v.* **-staffed, -staff·ing, -staffs** To supply with fewer employees than required.

un·der·stand (ŭn′dər-stănd′) *v.* **-stood** (-stŏŏd′), **-stand·ing, -stands** —*tr.* **1.** To perceive and comprehend the nature and significance of; grasp. See Syns at **apprehend. 2.** To know thoroughly by close contact or long experience with. **3a.** To grasp or comprehend the meaning intended or expressed by (another). **b.** To comprehend the language, sounds, form, or symbols of. **4.** To know and be tolerant or sympathetic toward. **5.** To learn indirectly, as by hearsay: *I understand his departure was unexpected.* **6.** To infer: *Am I to understand you are staying the night?* **7.** To accept (something) as an agreed fact: *It is understood that the fee will be 50 dollars.* **8.** To supply or add (words or a meaning, for example) mentally. —*intr.* **1a.** To have understanding, knowledge, or comprehension. **b.** To have sympathy or tolerance. **2.** To learn something indirectly or secondhand; gather. [ME *understanden* < OE *understandan* : *under-,* under- + *standan,* to stand; see **stā-** in App.] —**un′der·stand′a·bil′i·ty** *n.* —**un′der·stand′a·ble** *adj.* —**un′der·stand′a·bly** *adv.*

un·der·stand·ing (ŭn′dər-stăn′dĭng) *n.* **1.** The quality or condition of one who understands; comprehension. **2.** The faculty by which one understands; intelligence. **3.** Individual or specified judgment or outlook; opinion: *disagreed with the common understanding.* **4a.** A compact implicit between two or more people or groups. **b.** The matter implicit in such a compact. **5.** A reconciliation of differences; a state of agreement. **6.** A disposition to appreciate or share the feelings and thoughts of others; sympathy. ❖ *adj.* **1.** Marked by or having comprehension, good sense, or discernment. **2.** Compassionate; sympathetic. —**un′der·stand′ing·ly** *adv.*

un·der·state (ŭn′dər-stāt′) *v.* **-stat·ed, -stat·ing, -states** —*tr.* **1.** To state with less completeness or truth than seems warranted by the facts. **2.** To express with restraint or lack of emphasis, esp. ironically. **3.** To state (a quantity, for example) that is too low. —*intr.* To give an understatement.

un·der·stat·ed (ŭn′dər-stā′tĭd) *adj.* Exhibiting restrained good taste: *an understated décor.* —**un′der·stat′ed·ly** *adv.*

un·der·state·ment (ŭn′dər-stāt′mənt, ŭn′dər-stāt′-) *n.* **1.** A disclosure or statement that is less than complete. **2.** Restraint or lack of emphasis in expression, as for rhetorical effect. **3.** Restraint in artistic expression.

un·der·steer (ŭn′dər-stîr′) *intr.v.* **-steered, -steer·ing, -steers** To turn less sharply than the operator would expect. Used of vehicles. ❖ *n.* **1.** An instance of understeering. **2.** A tendency to understeer.

un·der·stood (ŭn′dər-stŏŏd′) *adj.* **1.** Agreed on; assumed: *the understood conditions of troop withdrawal.* **2.** Not expressed in writing; implied.

un·der·sto·ry (ŭn′dər-stôr′ē, -stōr′-) *n.* An underlying layer of vegetation, esp. the plants that grow beneath a forest's canopy.

un·der·stra·tum (ŭn′dər-strā′təm, -străt′əm) *n., pl.* **-stra·ta** (-strā′tə, -străt′ə) or **-stra·tums** A substratum.

un·der·stud·y (ŭn′dər-stŭd′ē) *v.* **-ied, -y·ing, -ies** —*tr.* **1.** To study or know (a role) so as to be able to replace the regular performer when required. **2.** To act as an understudy to. —*intr.* To be engaged in understudying a role. ❖ *n., pl.* **-ies 1.** A performer who understudies. **2.** A person trained to do the work of another.

un·der·sur·face (ŭn′dər-sûr′fəs) *n.* See **underside** 1.

un·der·take (ŭn′dər-tāk′) *v.* **-took** (-tŏŏk′), **-tak·en, -tak·ing, -takes** —*tr.* **1.** To take upon oneself; decide or agree to do. **2.** To pledge or commit oneself: *undertake to care for an elderly relative.* **3.** To set about; begin. **4.** *Obsolete* To accept combat with. —*intr.* *Archaic* To make oneself responsible. Used with *for.*

un·der·tak·er (ŭn′dər-tā′kər) *n.* **1.** (ŭn′dər-tā′kər) See **funeral director. 2.** One that undertakes a task or job.

un·der·tak·ing (ŭn′dər-tā′kĭng) *n.* **1.** A task or assignment undertaken; a venture. **2.** A guaranty, engagement, or promise. **3.** The profession or duties of a funeral director.

un·der-the-count·er (ŭn′dər-thə-koun′tər) *adv. & adj.* Transacted, given, or sold illicitly.

un·der-the-ta·ble (ŭn′dər-thə-tā′bəl) *adv. & adj.* Not straightforward; secret or underhand.

un·der·things (ŭn′dər-thĭngz′) *pl.n.* Underwear, esp. for women or girls.

un·der·tint (ŭn′dər-tĭnt′) *n.* A slight or subtle tint.

un·der·tone (ŭn′dər-tōn′) *n.* **1.** An underlying or implied tendency or meaning; an undercurrent. **2.** A tone of low pitch or volume, esp. of spoken sound. **3a.** A pale or subdued color. **b.** A color applied under or seen through another.

un·der·tow (ŭn′dər-tō′) *n.* The seaward pull of receding waves after they break on a shore.

un·der·trick (ŭn′dər-trĭk′) *n.* A trick in card games, the loss of which prevents a declarer from making a contract.

un·der·vest (ŭn′dər-vĕst′) *n.* *Chiefly British* An undershirt.

un·der·vote (ŭn′dər-vōt′) *n.* **1.** A ballot that has been cast but shows no selection in a given race or referendum. **2.** The number of such ballots cast in an election.

un·der·wa·ter (ŭn′dər-wô′tər, -wŏt′ər) *adj.* **1.** Relating to, occurring, used, or performed beneath the surface of water. **2.** *Nautical* Below a vessel's water line. —**un′der·wa′ter** *adv.*

under way or **un·der·way** (ŭn′dər-wā′) *adv. & adj.* **1.** In motion or operation. **2.** Already begun or initiated; in progress. **3.** *Nautical* Not anchored, aground, or moored to a fixed object.

un·der·wear (ŭn′dər-wâr′) *n.* Clothes worn next to the skin, beneath one's outer clothing.

un·der·weight (ŭn′dər-wāt′) *adj.* Weighing less than is normal, healthy, or required. ❖ *n.* Insufficiency of weight.

un·der·went (ŭn′dər-wĕnt′) *v.* Past tense of **undergo.**

un·der·whelm (ŭn′dər-hwĕlm′, -wĕlm′) *tr.v.* **-whelmed, -whelm·ing, -whelms** To fail to excite, stimulate, or impress. [UNDER– + (OVER)WHELM.]

un·der·wing (ŭn′dər-wĭng′) *n.* **1.** One of a pair of hind wings of an insect, such as a moth. **2.** Any of various noctuid moths of the genus *Calocala,* having brightly colored hind wings visible only during flight.

un·der·wire (ŭn′dər-wīr′) *n.* **1.** A semicircular wire support sewn into the underside of each cup of a brassiere. **2.** A brassiere with such a wire support.

un·der·wood (ŭn′dər-wŏŏd′) *n.* Shrubs and small trees growing beneath taller trees; underbrush.

un·der·wool (ŭn′dər-wŏŏl′) *n.* The soft woolly undercoat of certain animals, esp. sheep.

un·der·world (ŭn′dər-wûrld′) *n.* **1.** The part of society that is engaged in and organized for the purpose of crime and vice. **2.** A region, realm, or dwelling place conceived to be below the surface of the earth. **3.** The opposite side of the earth; the antipodes. **4.** *Greek & Roman Mythology* The world of the dead, located below the world of the living; Hades. **5.** *Archaic* The world beneath the heavens; the earth.

un·der·write (ŭn′dər-rīt′) *v.* **-wrote** (-rōt′), **-writ·ten** (-rĭt′n), **-writ·ing, -writes** —*tr.* **1.** To assume financial responsibility for; guarantee against failure. **2a.** To sign (an insurance policy) so as to assume liability in case of specified losses. **b.** To insure. **c.** To insure against losses totaling (a given amount). **3a.** To guarantee the purchase of (a full issue of stocks or bonds). **b.** To agree to buy the unsold part of (stock not yet sold publicly) at a fixed time and price. **4a.** To write under or at the end of something. **b.** To subscribe to, esp. to sign or endorse (a document). **5.** To support or agree to (a decision, for example). —*intr.* To act as an underwriter, esp. to issue an insurance policy.

un·der·writ·er (ŭn′dər-rī′tər) *n.* One that underwrites, esp.: **a.** A person or firm engaged in the insurance business. **b.** An insurance agent who assesses the risk of enrolling an applicant for coverage of a policy. **c.** One that guarantees the purchase of a full issue of stocks or bonds.

un·de·scend·ed testicle (ŭn′dĭ-sĕn′dĭd) *n.* A testicle that has remained within the inguinal canal and has not descended to the scrotum.

un·de·sign·ing (ŭn′dĭ-zī′nĭng) *adj.* Having no ulterior motives; straightforward.

un·de·sir·a·ble (ŭn′dĭ-zīr′ə-bəl) *adj.* **1.** Not likely to please; objectionable. **2.** Not wanted: *undesirable aliens.* ❖ *n.* A person regarded as undesirable. —**un′de·sir′a·bil′i·ty** —**un′de·sir′a·bly** *adv.*

un·de·ter·mined (ŭn′dĭ-tûr′mĭnd) *adj.* **1.** Not yet determined; undecided. **2.** Not specifically known or ascertained.

un·dies (ŭn′dēz) *pl.n. Informal* Underwear, esp. for women or girls.

un•dine (ŭn-dēn′, ŭn′dēn′) *n.* In the occult philosophy of Paracelsus, a being having water as its element. [NLat. *undīna* < Lat. *unda*, wave. See **wed-** in App.]

un•dip•lo•mat•ic (ŭn-dĭp′lə-măt′ĭk) *adj.* Not tactful or diplomatic. —**un•dip′lo•mat′i•cal•ly** *adv.*

un•di•rect•ed (ŭn′dĭ-rĕk′tĭd, -dī-) *adj.* **1.** Having no object or purpose; not guided. **2.** Having no prescribed destination. Used of mail.

un•dis•charged (ŭn′dĭs-chärjd′) *adj.* **1.** Not fulfilled: *an undischarged obligation.* **2.** Not paid: *an undischarged debt.* **3.** Not unloaded. Used of a ship's cargo.

un•dis•crim•i•nat•ing (ŭn′dĭ-skrĭm′ə-nā′tĭng) *adj.* **1.** Lacking sensitivity or judgment. **2.** Indiscriminate.

un•dis•posed (ŭn′dĭ-spōzd′) *adj.* **1.** Not settled, removed, or resolved: *undisposed assets.* **2.** Disinclined; unwilling.

un•dis•tin•guished (ŭn′dĭ-stĭng′gwĭsht) *adj.* **1a.** Marked by no peculiar quality; not distinguished; ordinary. **b.** Lacking particularly good qualities; mediocre. **2.** Not separated from others into categories. **3.** Unnoticed; obscure.

un•do (ŭn-dōō′) *v.* **-did** (-dĭd′), **-done** (-dŭn′), **-do•ing** (-dōō′ĭng), **-does** (-dŭz′) —*tr.* **1.** To reverse or erase; annul. **2.** To untie, disassemble, or loosen: *undo a shoelace.* **3.** To open (a parcel, for example); unwrap. **4a.** To cause the ruin or downfall of; destroy. **b.** To throw into confusion; unsettle. **5.** *Obsolete* To solve or interpret; unravel. —*intr.* To come open or unfastened. —**un•do′er** *n.*

un•dock (ŭn-dŏk′) *tr.v.* **-docked, -dock•ing, -docks 1.** *Nautical* To move (a ship) away from a dock. **2.** To uncouple (spacecraft).

un•doc•u•ment•ed (ŭn-dŏk′yə-mĕn′tĭd) *adj.* **1.** Not supported by written evidence: *undocumented accusations.* **2.** Not having the needed documents, as for permission to live or work in a foreign country. ❖ *n.* A person not having proper documentation, esp. for immigration.

un•do•ing (ŭn-dōō′ĭng) *n.* **1.** The act of unfastening or loosening. **2a.** Ruin; destruction. **b.** The act of bringing to ruin. **c.** A cause or source of ruin; downfall. **3.** The act of reversing or annulling something accomplished; a cancellation.

un•dou•ble (ŭn-dŭb′əl) *tr.v.* **-bled, -bling, -bles** To unfold, as a piece of paper money.

un•doubt•ed (ŭn-dou′tĭd) *adj.* Accepted as beyond question; undisputed. See Syns at **authentic.** —**un•doubt′ed•ly** *adv.*

un•draw (ŭn-drô′) *tr.v.* **-drew** (-drōō′), **-drawn** (-drôn′), **-draw•ing, -draws** To draw to one side, as a curtain.

un•dreamed (ŭn-drēmd′) *also* **un•dreamt** (-drĕmt′) *adj.* Beyond what could be imagined; unimaginable. Often used with *of: a peaceful settlement undreamed of a generation ago.*

un•dress (ŭn-drĕs′) *v.* **-dressed, -dress•ing, -dress•es** —*tr.* **1.** To remove the clothing of; disrobe. **2.** To remove the bandages from (a wound, for example). —*intr.* To take off one's clothing. ❖ *n.* **1.** Informal attire or uniform. **2a.** Nakedness or partial nakedness. **b.** Partial but incomplete dress.

un•dressed (ŭn-drĕst′) *adj.* **1a.** Naked. **b.** Partially but not fully dressed. **2.** Not specially treated or processed: *undressed leather.* **3a.** Not prepared for cooking or eating. Used of certain meats. **b.** Lacking sauce or dressing. Used of a salad. **4.** Not treated or bandaged: *an undressed wound.*

Und•set (ōōn′sĕt′), **Sigrid** 1882–1949. Danish-born Norwegian writer who won the 1928 Nobel Prize for literature.

un•due (ŭn-dōō′, -dyōō′) *adj.* **1.** Exceeding what is appropriate or normal; excessive. **2.** Not just, proper, or legal: *undue use of force.* **3.** Not yet payable or due: *an undue loan.*

un•du•lant (ŭn′jə-lənt, ŭn′dyə-, -də-) *adj.* Resembling waves in occurrence, appearance, or motion.

undulant fever *n.* See **brucellosis** 1.

un•du•late (ŭn′jə-lāt′, ŭn′dyə-, -də-) *v.* **-lat•ed, -lat•ing, -lates** —*tr.* **1.** To cause to move in a smooth wavelike motion. **2.** To give a wavelike appearance or form to. —*intr.* **1.** To move in waves or with a smooth wavelike motion. **2.** To have a wavelike appearance or form. **3.** To increase and decrease in volume or pitch as if in waves. ❖ *adj.* (-lĭt, -lāt′) Having a wavy outline or appearance: *leaves with undulate margins.* [< LLat. *undula*, small wave, dim. of Lat. *unda*, wave. See **wed-** in App.] —**un′du•la•to•ry** (-lə-tôr′ē, -tōr′ē) *adj.*

un•du•la•tion (ŭn′jə-lā′shən, ŭn′dyə-, -də-) *n.* **1.** A regular rising and falling or movement to alternating sides; movement in waves. **2.** A wavelike form, outline, or appearance. **3.** One of a series of waves or wavelike segments.

un•du•ly (ŭn-dōō′lē, -dyōō′-) *adv.* Excessively; immoderately: *unduly familiar with strangers.*

un•du•ti•ful (ŭn-dōō′tĭ-fəl, -dyōō′-) *adj.* Lacking a sense of duty. **2.** Unreliable or disobedient. —**un•du′ti•ful•ly** *adv.*

un•dy•ing (ŭn-dī′ĭng) *adj.* Endless; everlasting; immortal.

un•earned (ŭn-ûrnd′) *adj.* **1.** Not gained by work or service: *unearned income.* **2.** Not deserved: *unearned luck.* **3.** Paid in anticipation of goods or services not yet rendered.

unearned increment *n.* The increase in property value resulting from factors independent of the owner, such as a general rise in demand for land.

unearned run *n. Baseball* A run scored as a result of a fielding error, not counted in figuring a pitcher's earned run average.

un•earth (ŭn-ûrth′) *tr.v.* **-earthed, -earth•ing, -earths 1.** To bring up out of the earth; dig up. **2.** To bring to public notice; uncover.

un•earth•ly (ŭn-ûrth′lē) *adj.* **-li•er, -li•est 1.** Not of this earth; preternatural; supernatural. **2.** Unnaturally strange and frightening; eerie. **3.** Ridiculously unreasonable or uncustomary; absurd. —**un•earth′li•ness** *n.*

un•eas•y (ŭn-ē′zē) *adj.* **-i•er, -i•est 1.** Lacking a sense of security; anxious or apprehensive. **2.** Affording no ease or reassurance: *an uneasy calm.* **3a.** Awkward or unsure in manner; constrained: *uneasy with strangers.* **b.** Causing constraint or awkwardness: *an uneasy silence.* **4.** Not conducive to rest: *an uneasy sleep.* —**un•ease′, un•eas′i•ness** *n.* —**un•eas′i•ly** *adv.*

un•ed•it•ed (ŭn-ĕd′ĭ-tĭd) *adj.* **1.** Not edited or revised. **2.** Not adapted for a special audience or purpose.

un•ed•u•cat•ed (ŭn-ĕj′ə-kā′tĭd) *adj.* Not educated.

un•e•lect•a•ble (ŭn′ĭ-lĕk′tə-bəl) *adj.* Being such that election, as to high office, is difficult or impossible.

un•em•ploy•ment compensation (ŭn′ĕm-ploi′mənt) *n.* Financial compensation for unemployed workers, provided in the United States chiefly by state governments.

un-Eng•lish (ŭn-ĭng′glĭsh) *adj.* **1.** Not having the characteristics of English people or practices. **2.** Not in agreement with standard English usage.

un•e•qual (ŭn-ē′kwəl) *adj.* **1.** Not the same in any measurable aspect, such as extent or quantity. **2.** Not the same as another in rank or social position. **3.** Consisting of ill-matched opponents: *an unequal contest.* **4.** Having unbalanced sides or parts; asymmetrical. **5.** Not even or consistent; variable. **6.** Not having the required abilities; inadequate. **7.** Not fair. ❖ *n.* One that is not the equal of another. —**un•e′qual•ly** *adv.*

un•e•qualed *also* **un•e•qualled** (ŭn-ē′kwəld) *adj.* Not matched or paralleled by others of its kind; unrivaled.

un•e•quiv•o•cal (ŭn′ĭ-kwĭv′ə-kəl) *adj.* Admitting of no doubt or misunderstanding; clear and unambiguous: *an unequivocal success.* —**un′e•quiv′o•cal•ly** *adv.*

UNESCO *abbr.* United Nations Educational, Scientific, and Cultural Organization

un•es•sen•tial (ŭn′ĭ-sĕn′shəl) *adj.* Not necessary or important; dispensable. ❖ *n.* One that is unnecessary.

un•e•ven (ŭn-ē′vən) *adj.* **-er, -est 1a.** Not equal, as in size, length, or quality. **b.** Having ill-matched opponents: *an uneven contest.* **2.** Not consistent or uniform: *an uneven color.* **3.** Not smooth or level. **4.** Not straight or parallel. **5.** Of, relating to, or being an odd number. **6.** *Obsolete* Not fair or equitable. —**un•e′ven•ly** *adv.* —**un•e′ven•ness** *n.*

un•e•vent•ful (ŭn′ĭ-vĕnt′fəl) *adj.* **1.** Lacking in significant events. **2.** Occurring without disruption. —**un′e•vent′ful•ly** *adv.* —**un′e•vent′ful•ness** *n.*

un•ex•am•pled (ŭn′ĭg-zăm′pəld) *adj.* Without precedent; unparalleled.

un•ex•cep•tion•a•ble (ŭn′ĭk-sĕp′shə-nə-bəl) *adj.* Beyond any reasonable objection; irreproachable. —**un′ex•cep′tion•a•ble•ness** *n.* —**un′ex•cep′tion•a•bly** *adv.*

USAGE NOTE *Unexceptionable* and *unexceptional* are easily confused but actually have very different meanings. *Unexceptionable* means "not open to objection," while *unexceptional* means "not superior, ordinary." Thus *an unexceptionable work* is a work that one can find no fault with, while *an unexceptional work* is one that is run-of-the-mill.

un•ex•cep•tion•al (ŭn′ĭk-sĕp′shə-nəl) *adj.* **1.** Not varying from a norm; usual: *an unexceptional performance.* **2.** Not subject to exceptions; absolute. See Usage Note at **unexceptionable.** —**un′ex•cep′tion•al•ly** *adv.*

un•ex•pect•ed (ŭn′ĭk-spĕk′tĭd) *adj.* Coming without warning; unforeseen. —**un′ex•pect′ed•ly** *adv.* —**un′ex•pect′ed•ness** *n.*

un•ex•ploit•ed (ŭn′ĭk-sploi′tĭd) *adj.* Not exploited or developed: *unexploited oil reserves.*

un•ex•pressed (ŭn′ĭk-sprĕst′) *adj.* **1.** Not stated or conveyed: *unexpressed rage.* **2.** *Genetics* Not producing an effect or phenotype: *an unexpressed gene; an unexpressed trait.*

un•ex•pres•sive (ŭn′ĭk-sprĕs′ĭv) *adj.* **1.** Not conveying the meaning intended or the emotion felt. **2.** *Obsolete* Inexpressible. —**un′ex•pres′sive•ly** *adv.* —**un′ex•pres′sive•ness** *n.*

un•fail•ing (ŭn-fā′lĭng) *adj.* **1.** Always able to supply more; inexhaustible: *an unfailing source of good stories.* **2.** Constant; unflagging: *was pleased by their unfailing loyalty.* **3.** Incapable of error; infallible. —**un•fail′ing•ly** *adv.*

un•fair (ŭn-fâr′) *adj.* **-er, -est 1.** Not just or evenhanded; biased. **2.** Contrary to laws or conventions, esp. in commerce; unethical. —**un•fair′ly** *adv.* —**un•fair′ness** *n.*

un•faith (ŭn-fāth′) *n.* Absence of faith, esp. in religion.

un•faith•ful (ŭn-fāth′fəl) *adj.* **1.** Not adhering to promises, obligations, or allegiances; disloyal. **2.** Not true or constant to one's sexual partner. **b.** Not true to one's spouse; guilty of adultery. **3.** Not justly representing or reflecting the original; inaccurate. **4.** *Obsolete* Deficient in or lacking religious faith; unbelieving. —**un•faith′ful•ly** *adv.* —**un•faith′ful•ness** *n.*

un•fa•thered (ŭn-fä′thərd) *adj.* **1a.** Having no father; fatherless. **b.** Having no known father. **2.** Of uncertain origin or au-

Sigrid Undset

undulate
undulate leaf

ă	pat	oi	boy
ā	pay	ou	out
âr	care	ōō	took
ä	father	ōō	boot
ĕ	pet	ŭ	cut
ē	be	ûr	urge
ĭ	pit	th	thin
ī	pie	th	this
îr	pier	hw	which
ŏ	pot	zh	vision
ō	toe	ə	about,
ô	paw		item

Stress marks:
′ (primary);
′ (secondary), as in
lexicon (lĕk′sĭ-kŏn′)

thenticity: *denied the unfathered rumors.*

un·feel·ing (ŭn-fē′lĭng) *adj.* **1.** Having no physical feeling or sensation; insentient. **2.** Not sharing in the pleasures or pains of others; callous: *an unfeeling heart.* —**un·feel′ing·ly** *adv.* —**un·feel′ing·ness** *n.*

un·feigned (ŭn-fānd′) *adj.* Not feigned; genuine. —**un·feign′ed·ly** (ŭn-fā′nĭd-lē) *adv.*

un·fit (ŭn-fĭt′) *adj.* **1.** Not meant or adapted for a given purpose; inappropriate. **2.** Below the required standard; unqualified: *an unfit parent.* **3.** Not in good physical or mental health. **4.** *Biology* Unable to survive or produce viable offspring in a particular environment. ❖ *tr.v.* **-fit·ted, -fit·ting, -fits** To cause to be unsuited or unqualified. —**un·fit′ly** *adv.* —**un·fit′ness** *n.*

un·fix (ŭn-fĭks′) *tr.v.* **-fixed, -fix·ing, -fix·es 1.** To detach from what secures; unfasten. **2.** To cause to leave a tranquil condition; disturb.

un·flag·ging (ŭn-flăg′ĭng) *adj.* Not flagging; untiring.

un·flap·pa·ble (ŭn-flăp′ə-bəl) *adj.* Persistently calm; not easily upset or excited. —**un·flap′pa·bil′i·ty** *n.* —**un·flap′pa·bly** *adv.*

un·flapped (ŭn-flăpt′) *adj.* Not upset or excited; calm.

un·flat·ter·ing (ŭn-flăt′ər-ĭng) *adj.* Acknowledging few or no good aspects; unfavorable. —**un·flat′ter·ing·ly** *adv.*

un·fledged (ŭn-flĕjd′) *adj.* **1.** Not having the feathers necessary to fly. Used of a young bird. **2.** Inexperienced, immature, or untried.

un·flinch·ing (ŭn-flĭn′chĭng) *adj.* Showing neither fear nor indecision; resolute. —**un·flinch′ing·ly** *adv.* —**un·flinch′ing·ness** *n.*

un·fo·cused also **un·fo·cussed** (ŭn-fō′kəst) *adj.* **1.** Not brought into focus: *an unfocused lens.* **2.** Not centered on anything specific: *unfocused thoughts.*

un·fold (ŭn-fōld′) *v.* **-fold·ed, -fold·ing, -folds** —*tr.* **1.** To open and spread out (something folded); extend. **2.** To remove the coverings from; disclose to view. **3.** To reveal gradually by written or spoken explanation; make known. —*intr.* **1a.** To become spread out; open out: *Spring flowers unfolded.* **b.** To develop, as if by spreading out: *A brilliant career unfolded.* **2.** To be revealed gradually to the understanding. —**un·fold′ment** *n.*

un·fore·seen (ŭn′fôr-sēn′, -fôr-) *adj.* Not felt or realized beforehand; unexpected: *unforeseen difficulties.*

un·for·giv·ing (ŭn′fər-gĭv′ĭng) *adj.* **1.** Reluctant or refusing to forgive. **2.** Providing little or no opportunity to forestall undesired results or mistakes.

un·for·mat·ted (ŭn-fôr′măt′ĭd) *adj.* **1.** Not being in or having a proper format. **2.** *Computer Science* Not formatted into sectors, thus not allowing data to be stored.

un·formed (ŭn-fôrmd′) *adj.* **1.** Having no definite shape or structure; unorganized. **2.** Not yet developed to maturity. **3.** Not yet given a physical existence; uncreated.

un·for·tu·nate (ŭn-fôr′chə-nĭt) *adj.* **1.** Characterized by undeserved bad luck; unlucky. **2.** Causing misfortune; disastrous. **3.** Regrettable; deplorable. ❖ *n.* A victim of bad luck. —**un·for′tu·nate·ly** *adv.* —**un·for′tu·nate·ness** *n.*

un·found·ed (ŭn-foun′dĭd) *adj.* **1.** Not based on fact or sound evidence; groundless. **2.** Not yet established. —**un·found′ed·ly** *adv.* —**un·found′ed·ness** *n.*

un·fre·quent·ed (ŭn-frē′kwən-tĭd, ŭn′frē-kwĕn′tĭd) *adj.* Receiving few or no travelers or visitors: *unfrequented inns.*

un·frock (ŭn-frŏk′) *tr.v.* **-frocked, -frock·ing, -frocks** To defrock.

un·fruit·ful (ŭn-frōōt′fəl) *adj.* **1.** Not bearing fruit or offspring. **2.** Not productive of a good or useful result. —**un·fruit′ful·ly** *adv.*

un·furl (ŭn-fûrl′) *tr. & intr.v.* **-furled, -furl·ing, -furls** To spread or open (something) out or become spread or opened out: *The guard unfurled the flag. The flags unfurled in the breeze.*

un·gain·ly (ŭn-gān′lē) *adj.* **-li·er, -li·est 1.** Lacking grace or ease of movement or form; clumsy. **2.** Difficult to move or use; unwieldy. [UN–[1] + obsolete *gainly,* proper (< ME *gainli* < ME *gain, gainli* < ON *gegn,* direct).] —**un·gain′li·ness** *n.*

Un·ga·va Bay (ŭn-gä′və, -gä′-) An inlet of Hudson Strait in NE Quebec, Canada, between N Labrador and **Ungava Peninsula,** bordered on the W by Hudson Bay.

un·girt (ŭn-gûrt′) *adj.* **1.** Having the belt or girdle removed or loosened. **2.** Loose or free; slack.

un·glued (ŭn-glōōd′) *adj.* **1.** Loosened or separated; unfastened. **2.** *Informal* In confused distress; upset. —***idiom:* come unglued** *Informal* To lose one's composure.

un·god·ly (ŭn-gŏd′lē) *adj.* **-li·er, -li·est 1.** Not revering God; impious. **2.** Sinful; wicked. **3.** Outrageous: *had to leave for work at an ungodly hour.* —**un·god′li·ness** *n.*

un·gov·ern·a·ble (ŭn-gŭv′ər-nə-bəl) *adj.* Incapable of being governed, restrained, or controlled. —**un·gov′ern·a·bly** *adv.*

un·gra·cious (ŭn-grā′shəs) *adj.* **1.** Lacking social grace or graciousness; rude. **2.** Not welcome or acceptable; unattractive. **3.** *Archaic* Evil; wicked. —**un·gra′cious·ly** *adv.*

un·gram·mat·i·cal (ŭn′grə-măt′ĭ-kəl) *adj.* **1.** Not in accord with the rules of a grammar. **2.** Not in accord with standard or socially prestigious linguistic usage. —**un′gram·mat′i·cal′i·ty** (-kăl′ĭ-tē) *n.* —**un′gram·mat′i·cal·ly** *adv.*

un·gual (ŭng′gwəl) *adj.* **1.** Of, resembling, or bearing a hoof, nail, or claw. **2.** Of or relating to fingernails or toenails. [< Lat. *unguis,* nail. See UNGUIS.]

un·guard·ed (ŭn-gär′dĭd) *adj.* **1.** Lacking protection or a guard; vulnerable. **2.** Displaying, having, or feeling no wariness; incautious: *an unguarded remark.* —**un·guard′ed·ly** *adv.*

un·guent (ŭng′gwənt) *n.* A salve for soothing or healing; an ointment. [ME < Lat. *unguentum* < *unguere,* to anoint.] —**un·guen·tar′y** (-tĕr′ē) *adj.*

un·guic·u·late (ŭng-gwĭk′yə-lĭt, -lāt′) also **un·guic·u·lat·ed** (-lā′tĭd) *adj.* **1.** Having or resembling nails or claws. **2.** *Zoology* Having nails or claws, as opposed to hooves. Used of mammals. **3.** *Botany* Having a claw-shaped base: *an unguiculate petal.* ❖ *n.* *Zoology* A mammal having nails or claws. [NLat. *unguiculātus* < Lat. *unguiculus,* fingernail, dim. of *unguis.*]

un·guis (ŭng′gwĭs) *n., pl.* **-gues** (-gwēz) **1.** *Zoology* A nail, claw, or hoof. **2.** *Botany* The clawlike base of some petals. [Lat.]

un·gu·late (ŭng′gyə-lĭt, -lāt′) *adj.* **1a.** Having hooves. **b.** Resembling hooves; hooflike. **2.** Of or belonging to the former order Ungulata, now divided into the orders Perissodactyla and Artiodactyla and composed of the hoofed mammals such as horses, cattle, deer, and elephants. ❖ *n.* An ungulate mammal. [Lat. *ungulātus* < *ungula,* hoof, dim. of *unguis,* nail.]

un·hal·low (ŭn-hăl′ō) *tr.v.* **-lowed, -low·ing, -lows** *Archaic* To violate the holiness of; profane or desecrate.

un·hal·lowed (ŭn-hăl′ōd) *adj.* **1.** Not hallowed or consecrated. **2a.** Lacking reverence; impious or irreligious. **b.** Not conforming to accepted ethical standards; immoral.

un·hand (ŭn-hănd′) *tr.v.* **-hand·ed, -hand·ing, -hands** To remove one's hand from; let go.

un·hand·some (ŭn-hăn′səm) *adj.* **1.** Not attractive or beautiful; homely. **2.** Not courteous or in good taste; ungracious. —**un·hand′some·ly** *adv.* —**un·hand′some·ness** *n.*

un·hand·y (ŭn-hăn′dē) *adj.* **-i·er, -i·est 1.** Difficult to handle or manage; unwieldy. **2.** Lacking manual skill or dexterity. —**un·hand′i·ly** *adv.* —**un·hand′i·ness** *n.*

un·hap·py (ŭn-hăp′ē) *adj.* **-pi·er, -pi·est 1.** Not happy or joyful; sad or sorrowful. **2.** Not satisfied; displeased or discontented: *unhappy with her raise.* **3.** Not attended by or bringing good fortune; unlucky. **4.** Not suitable; inappropriate. —**un·hap′pi·ly** *adv.* —**un·hap′pi·ness** *n.*

un·har·ness (ŭn-här′nĭs) *tr.v.* **-nessed, -ness·ing, -ness·es 1.** To remove the harness or similar equipment from. **2.** To release or liberate (energy or passions, for example). **3.** To remove the armor from (a wearer).

un·health·y (ŭn-hĕl′thē) *adj.* **-i·er, -i·est 1a.** Being in a state of ill health; sick. **b.** Characterized by or symptomatic of ill health. **c.** Causing or conducive to poor health; unwholesome. **2.** Harmful to character or moral health; corruptive. **3.** Characterized by or symptomatic of disturbed mental health: *an unhealthy interest in violence.* **4.** Of a risky nature; dangerous. —**un′health′i·ly** *adv.* —**un·health′i·ness** *n.*

un·heard (ŭn-hûrd′) *adj.* **1.** Not heard: *unheard pleas for help.* **2.** Not given a hearing; not listened to: *unheard objections.* **3.** *Archaic* Not heard of; obscure.

un·heard-of (ŭn-hûrd′ŭv′, -ŏv′) *adj.* **1.** Not previously known; unknown. **2.** Without precedent; unparalleled. **3.** Highly offensive; outrageous or brazen.

un·hes·i·tat·ing (ŭn-hĕz′ĭ-tā′tĭng) *adj.* **1.** Prompt to act, move, or express oneself; ready: *I gave my unhesitating approval.* **2.** Unfaltering; steadfast. —**un·hes′i·tat′ing·ly** *adv.*

un·hinge (ŭn-hĭnj′) *tr.v.* **-hinged, -hing·ing, -hing·es 1.** To remove from hinges. **2.** To remove the hinges from. **3.** To confuse; disrupt. **4.** *Informal* To derange; unbalance.

un·his·tor·i·cal (ŭn′hĭ-stôr′ĭ-kəl, -stŏr′-) *adj.* Taking little or no account of history.

un·hitch (ŭn-hĭch′) *tr.v.* **-hitched, -hitch·ing, -hitch·es** To release from or as if from a hitch; unfasten.

un·ho·ly (ŭn-hō′lē) *adj.* **-li·er, -li·est 1.** Wicked; immoral. **2.** Not hallowed or consecrated. **3.** *Informal* Outrageous: *took unholy risks.* —**un·ho′li·ly** *adv.* —**un·ho′li·ness** *n.*

un·hook (ŭn-hŏŏk′) *tr.v.* **-hooked, -hook·ing, -hooks 1.** To release or remove from or as if from a hook. **2.** To unfasten the hooks of.

un·hoped (ŭn-hōpt′) *adj.* *Archaic* Not hoped or looked for.

un·horse (ŭn-hôrs′) *tr.v.* **-horsed, -hors·ing, -hors·es 1.** To cause to fall from a horse. **2.** To overthrow or dislodge; upset.

uni– *pref.* Single; one: *unicycle.* [Lat. *ūni–* < *ūnus,* one. See **oi-no-** in App.]

U·ni·at (yōō′nē-ăt′, -ĭt) also **U·ni·ate** (-ĭt, -āt′) *adj.* Of or relating to any of several Eastern Christian churches that are in communion with the Roman Catholic Church but retain their own languages, rites, and canon law. ❖ *n.* A member of any of these churches. [Russ. *uniyat* < Pol. *uniat,* the Union of Brest-Litovsk (1596) < *unija,* union < LLat. *ūniō.* See UNION.]

u·ni·ax·i·al (yōō′nē-ăk′sē-əl) *adj.* **1.** Of, relating to, or affecting one axis. **2.** *Botany* Of, relating to, or being a plant with one primary stem that has no branches and terminates in a flower. **3.** Having one direction along which double refraction of light does not take place. Used of a crystal.

u·ni·cam·er·al (yōō′nĭ-kăm′ər-əl) *adj.* Having or consisting of a single legislative chamber. [UNI- + Lat. *camera*, chamber; see CAMERA.] —**u′ni·cam′er·al·ly** *adv.*

UNICEF (yōō′nĭ-sĕf′) *abbr.* United Nations Children's Fund (formerly United Nations International Children's Emergency Fund)

u·ni·cel·lu·lar (yōō′nĭ-sĕl′yə-lər) *adj.* Having or consisting of one cell; one-celled: *unicellular organisms.* —**u′ni·cel′lu·lar′i·ty** (-lăr′ĭ-tē, -lär′-) *n.*

u·ni·col·or (yōō′nĭ-kŭl′ər) *adj.* Monochromatic.

u·ni·corn (yōō′nĭ-kôrn′) *n.* **1.** A fabled creature symbolic of virginity and usu. represented as a horse with a single straight spiraled horn projecting from its forehead. **2. Unicorn** *Astronomy* The constellation Monoceros. [ME *unicorne* < OFr. < LLat. *ūnicornis* < Lat., having one horn : *ūnus*, one; see **oi-no-** in App. + *cornū*, horn; see **ker-**[1] in App.]

u·ni·cos·tate (yōō′nĭ-kŏs′tāt′) *adj.* Having a single main costa, rib, or riblike part: *a unicostate leaf.*

u·ni·cy·cle (yōō′nĭ-sī′kəl) *n.* A vehicle consisting of a frame mounted over a single wheel, usu. propelled by pedals. [UNI- + -*cycle*, perh. on the model of BICYCLE.] —**u′ni·cy′clist** *n.*

un·i·den·ti·fied flying object (ŭn′ī-dĕn′tə-fīd′) *n.* A flying or apparently flying object of an unknown nature, esp. one suspected to have been sent by extraterrestrial beings.

u·ni·di·men·sion·al (yōō′nĭ-dĭ-mĕn′shə-nəl, -dī-) *adj.* One-dimensional.

u·ni·di·rec·tion·al (yōō′nĭ-dĭ-rĕk′shə-nəl, -dī-) *adj.* Having, operating, or moving in one direction only.

u·ni·fac·to·ri·al (yōō′nə-făk-tôr′ē-əl, -tōr′-) *adj.* Involving, dependent on, or controlled by a single gene.

U·ni·fi·ca·tion Church (yōō′nə-fĭ-kā′shən) *n.* A Christian church founded in 1954 by Sun Myung Moon and known for its communal activities.

u·ni·fied field theory (yōō′nə-fīd′) *n.* Any of various theories that combine two or more field theories, esp. one unifying the theories of nuclear, electromagnetic, and gravitational forces.

u·ni·fi·lar (yōō′nə-fī′lər) *adj.* Having or using only one filament, such as a thread or wire.

u·ni·fo·li·ate (yōō′nə-fō′lē-ĭt, -āt′) *adj. Botany* Having a single leaf.

u·ni·fo·li·o·late (yōō′nĭ-fō′lē-ə-lāt′) *adj. Botany* Compound in structure but having a single leaflet.

u·ni·form (yōō′nĭ-fôrm′) *adj.* **1.** Always the same, as in character or degree; unvarying. **2.** Conforming to one principle, standard, or rule; consistent. **3.** Being the same as or consonant with another or others. **4.** Unvaried in texture, color, or design. ❖ *n.* A distinctive outfit intended to identify those who wear it as members of a specific group. ❖ *tr.v.* **-formed, -form·ing, -forms 1.** To make (something) uniform. **2.** To provide or dress with a uniform. [Lat. *ūnifōrmis* : *ūni-*, uni- + *fōrma*, shape; see FORM.] —**u′ni·for′mi·ty, u′ni·form′ness** *n.* —**u′ni·form′ly** *adv.*

u·ni·for·mi·tar·i·an·ism (yōō′nə-fôr′mĭ-târ′ē-ə-nĭz′əm) *n.* The theory that geologic phenomena may be explained as the result of existing forces having operated uniformly from the origin of the earth to the present time. —**u′ni·for′mi·tar′i·an** *adj. & n.*

uniform resource locator *n.* See URL.

u·ni·fy (yōō′nə-fī′) *tr. & intr.v.* **-fied, -fy·ing, -fies** To make into or become a unit; consolidate. [Fr. *unifier* < OFr. < LLat. *ūnificāre* : Lat. *ūni-*, uni- + Lat. *-ficāre*, -fy.] —**u′ni·fi′a·ble** *adj.* —**u′ni·fi·ca′tion** (-fĭ-kā′shən) *n.* —**u′ni·fi′er** *n.*

u·ni·lat·er·al (yōō′nə-lăt′ər-əl) *adj.* **1.** Of, on, relating to, involving, or affecting only one side. **2.** Performed or undertaken by only one side: *unilateral disarmament.* **3.** Obligating only one of two or more parties, nations, or persons, as a contract or an agreement. **4.** Emphasizing or recognizing only one side of a subject. **5.** Having only one side. **6.** Tracing the lineage of one parent only: *a unilateral genealogy.* **7.** *Botany* Having leaves, flowers, or other parts on one side only. —**u′ni·lat′er·al·ism** *n.* —**u′ni·lat′er·a·list** *adj. & n.* —**u′ni·lat′er·al·ly** *adv.*

u·ni·lin·e·ar (yōō′nĭ-lĭn′ē-ər) *adj.* Of or developing in a progressive sequence usu. from the primitive to the advanced.

u·ni·lin·gual (yōō′nĭ-lĭng′gwəl) *adj.* Making use of or written in one language only.

u·ni·loc·u·lar (yōō′nĭ-lŏk′yə-lər) *adj. Botany* Having a single compartment in the ovary or fruit, as in a melon.

U·ni·mak Island (yōō′nə-măk′) An island of SW AK in the E Aleutian Is.

un·im·pas·sioned (ŭn′ĭm-păsh′ənd) *adj.* Not impassioned; devoid of emotional influence or appeal.

un·im·peach·a·ble (ŭn′ĭm-pē′chə-bəl) *adj.* **1.** Difficult or impossible to impeach: *an unimpeachable witness.* **2.** Beyond reproach; blameless. **3.** Beyond doubt; unquestionable. —**un′im·peach′a·bly** *adv.*

un·im·proved (ŭn′ĭm-prōōvd′) *adj.* **1.** Not improved; not made better. **2.** Not made use of or put to advantage. **3.** Not built on or cultivated so as to increase in value. Used of land.

un·in·formed (ŭn′ĭn-fôrmd′) *adj.* **1.** Not having, showing, or making use of information; not informed: *uninformed voters.*

un·in·hab·it·ed (ŭn′ĭn-hăb′ĭ-tĭd) *adj.* Having no residents.

un·in·hib·it·ed (ŭn′ĭn-hĭb′ĭ-tĭd) *adj.* **1.** Open and unrestrained: *uninhibited laughter.* **2.** Free from traditional social or

moral constraints. —**un′in·hib′it·ed·ly** *adv.*

un·i·ni·ti·ate (ŭn′ĭ-nĭsh′ē-ĭt) *adj.* Not experienced. —**un′i·ni′ti·ate** *n.*

un·i·ni·ti·at·ed (ŭn′ĭ-nĭsh′ē-ā′tĭd) *adj.* Not knowledgeable or skilled; inexperienced. ❖ *n.* An uninformed, unskilled, or inexperienced person or group of people.

un·in·spired (ŭn′ĭn-spīrd′) *adj.* Having no intellectual, emotional, or spiritual excitement; dull.

un·in·stall (ŭn′ĭn-stôl′) *tr.v.* **-stalled, -stall·ing, -stalls** *Computer Science* To remove completely from a system: *uninstalled the obsolete application.*

un·in·struct·ed (ŭn′ĭn-strŭk′tĭd) *adj.* Not educated or informed: *an uninstructed young mind.*

un·in·sured (ŭn′ĭn-shōord′) *adj.* Not covered by insurance. ❖ *n., pl.* **-sureds** A party that is not insured. Often used with *the.*

un·in·tend·ed (ŭn′ĭn-tĕn′dĭd) *adj.* Not deliberate or intentional; unplanned: *an unintended slight.*

un·in·ter·est (ŭn-ĭn′trĭst, -tər-ĭst, -trĕst′) *n.* Lack of interest or concern; indifference.

un·in·ter·est·ed (ŭn-ĭn′trĭ-stĭd, -tər-ĭ-stĭd, -tə-rĕs′tĭd) *adj.* **1a.** Without an interest: *uninterested parties.* **b.** Not having a financial interest. **2.** Marked by or exhibiting a lack of interest. See Usage Note at **disinterested.** —**un·in′ter·est·ed·ly** *adv.* —**un·in′ter·est·ed·ness** *n.*

un·in·ter·est·ing (ŭn-ĭn′trĭ-stĭng, -tər-ĭ-stĭng, -tə-rĕs′tĭng) *adj.* Boring. —**un·in′ter·est·ing·ly** *adv.*

u·ni·nu·cle·ate (yōō′nĭ-nōō′klē-ĭt, -nyōō′-) *adj.* Having one nucleus.

un·in·vit·ed (ŭn′ĭn-vī′tĭd) *adj.* Not welcome or wanted: *uninvited guests.*

un·in·volved (ŭn′ĭn-vŏlvd′) *adj.* Feeling or showing no interest or involvement; unconcerned: *an uninvolved bystander.*

un·ion (yōōn′yən) *n.* **1a.** The act of uniting or the state of being united. **b.** A combination so formed, esp. an alliance or confederation of people, parties, or political entities for mutual interest or benefit. **2.** *Mathematics* A set, every member of which is an element of one or another of two or more given sets. **3.** Agreement or harmony resulting from the uniting of individuals; concord. **4a.** The state of matrimony; marriage. **b.** Sexual intercourse. **5a.** A combination of parishes for joint administration of relief for the poor in Great Britain. **b.** A workhouse maintained by such a union. **6.** A labor union. **7.** A coupling device for connecting parts, such as rods. **8.** A device on a flag or ensign that signifies the union of two or more sovereignties. **9.** often **Union a.** An organization at a college or university that provides facilities for recreation; a student union. **b.** A building housing such facilities. **10. Union** The United States of America regarded as a national unit, esp. during the Civil War. ❖ *adj.* **1. Union** Of, relating to, or loyal to the United States of America during the Civil War. **2.** Of or relating to a labor union or labor union organizing: *union negotiations.* [ME < OFr. < LLat. *ūniō, ūniōn-* < Lat. *ūnus*, one. See **oi-no-** in App.]

union catalog *n.* A library catalog combining in alphabetical sequence the contents of more than one catalog or library.

union church *n.* A local interdenominational church bringing together worshipers of different denominational backgrounds.

un·ion·ism (yōōn′yə-nĭz′əm) *n.* **1.** The principle or theory of forming a union. **2.** The principles, theory, or system of a union, esp. a trade union. **3. Unionism** Loyalty to the federal government during the Civil War.

un·ion·ist (yōōn′yə-nĭst) *n.* **1.** One who believes in or supports a union or unionism. **2.** A member of a labor or trade union. **3. Unionist** One loyal to the federal government during the Civil War. —**un′ion·is′tic** *adj.*

un·ion·ize (yōōn′yə-nīz′) *v.* **-ized, -iz·ing, -iz·es** —*tr.* **1.** To organize into a labor union. **2.** To cause to join a labor union. —*intr.* To organize or join a labor union. —**un′ion·i·za′tion** (-yə-nĭ-zā′shən) *n.* —**un′ion·iz′er** *n.*

union jack *n.* **1.** A flag consisting entirely of a union. **2. Union Jack** The flag of the United Kingdom.

union label *n.* An identifying mark attached to a product indicating it has been produced by members of a trade union.

Union of Soviet Socialist Republics Commonly called **Soviet Union** or **Russia.** A former country of E Europe and N Asia with coastlines on the Baltic and Black seas and the Arctic and Pacific oceans; est. in Dec. 1922. In Dec. 1991 the Soviet Union was officially dissolved into a number of independent republics.

union shop *n.* A business or industrial establishment whose employees are required either to be union members or to join the union within a specified time after being hired.

union suit *n.* A one-piece undergarment combining shirt and long pants.

u·nip·a·rous (yōō-nĭp′ər-əs) *adj.* **1.** Producing only one egg or offspring at a time. **2.** *Botany* Forming a single axis at each branching, as certain flower clusters.

u·ni·per·son·al (yōō′nĭ-pûr′sə-nəl) *adj.* Manifested as or existent in the form of only one person: *a unipersonal spirit.*

u·ni·po·lar (yōō′nĭ-pō′lər) *adj.* **1.** Having, acting by means of, or produced by a single magnetic or electric pole. **2.** *Biology* Having a single fibrous process. Used of a neuron. —**u′ni·po·lar′i·ty** (-pō-lăr′ĭ-tē, -pə-) *n.*

unicorn
The Lady and the Unicorn
French tapestry, 1480–90

Union Jack

ă	pat	oi	boy
ā	pay	ou	out
âr	care	ōō	took
ä	father	ōō	boot
ĕ	pet	ŭ	cut
ē	be	ûr	urge
ĭ	pit	th	thin
ī	pie	*th*	this
îr	pier	hw	which
ŏ	pot	zh	vision
ō	toe	ə	about,
ô	paw		item

Stress marks:
′ (primary);
′ (secondary), as in
lexicon (lĕk′sĭ-kŏn′)

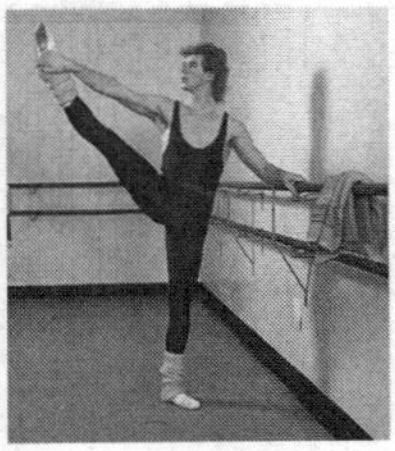

unitard

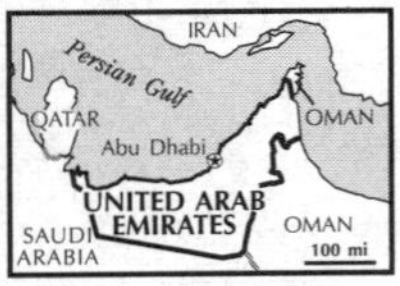

United Arab Emirates

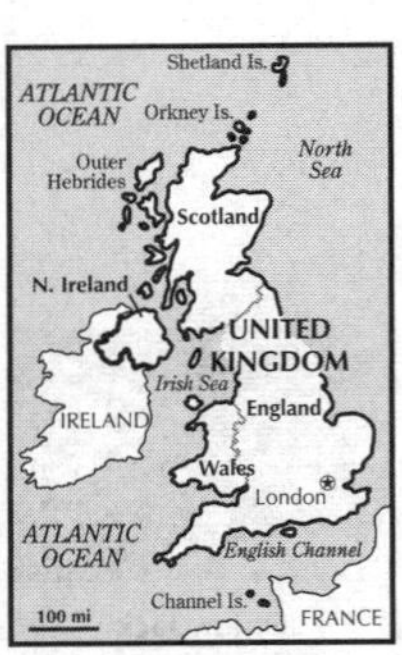

United Kingdom

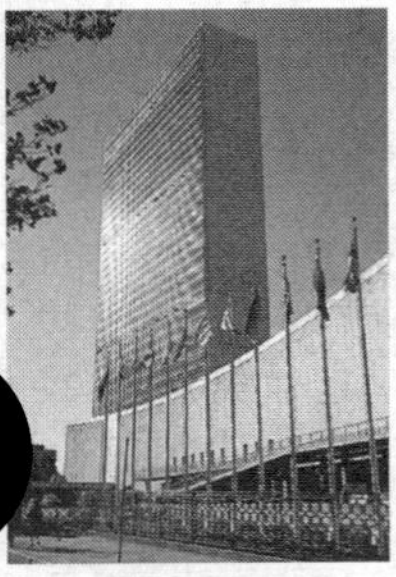

United Nations
United Nations headquarters in New York

u•ni•po•tent (yo͞o-nĭp′ə-tənt) *adj.* Capable of developing into only one type of cell or tissue.

u•nique (yo͞o-nēk′) *adj.* **1.** Being the only one of its kind. **2.** Without an equal or equivalent; unparalleled. **3a.** Characteristic of a particular category, condition, or locality: *a problem unique to coastal areas.* **b.** *Informal* Unusual; extraordinary. [Fr. < OFr. < Lat. *ūnicus.* See **oi-no-** in App.] —**u•nique′ly** *adv.* —**u•nique′ness** *n.*

USAGE NOTE Many grammarians regard *unique* as an absolute term, saying that a thing is either unique or not unique—it cannot be *very unique* or *more unique* than something else. Most of the Usage Panel supports this traditional view. Eighty percent disapprove of the sentence *Her designs are quite unique in today's fashions.* But as the language of advertising in particular attests, *unique* is widely used as a synonym for "extraordinary," and if so construed it may arguably be modified. Many reputable writers have in fact adopted this usage. Although the qualification of *unique* is defensible, writers should be aware that it is liable to incur the censure of some readers. See Usage Note at **infinite.**

u•ni•sex (yo͞o′nĭ-sĕks′) *adj.* **1.** Designed for or suitable to both sexes: *unisex clothing.* **2.** Not distinguished or distinguishable on the basis of sex: *a unisex look.* ❖ *n.* Elimination or absence of sexual distinctions, esp. in dress.

u•ni•sex•u•al (yo͞o′nĭ-sĕk′sho͞o-əl) *adj.* **1.** Of or relating to only one sex. **2.** Having only one type of sexual organ; not a hermaphrodite. **3.** *Botany* Having either stamens or pistils but not both. **4.** Unisex. —**u′ni•sex′u•al′i•ty** (-ăl′ĭ-tē) *n.* —**u′ni•sex′u•al•ly** *adv.*

u•ni•son (yo͞o′nĭ-sən, -zən) *n.* **1.** *Music* **a.** Identity of pitch; the interval of a perfect prime. **b.** The combination of parts at the same pitch or in octaves. **2.** The act or an instance of speaking the same words simultaneously by two or more speakers. **3.** An instance of agreement; concord. —***idiom:* in unison 1.** In complete agreement; harmonizing exactly. **2.** At the same time; at once. [ME < OFr. < Med.Lat. *ūnisonus,* in unison < LLat., monotonous : Lat. *ūni-,* uni- + Lat. *sonus,* sound.]

u•nit (yo͞o′nĭt) *n.* **1.** An individual, group, structure, or other entity regarded as an elementary constituent of a whole. **2.** A group regarded as a distinct entity within a larger group. **3a.** A mechanical part or module. **b.** An entire apparatus or the equipment that performs a specific function. **4.** A precise quantity in terms of which the magnitudes of other quantities of the same kind can be stated. **5.** *Medicine* The quantity of a drug or other agent necessary to produce a specific effect. **6a.** A fixed amount of scholastic study used in calculating academic credits, usu. measured in hours of formal instruction or laboratory work. **b.** A section of an academic course focusing on a selected theme: *a unit on Native Americans.* **7.** The number immediately to the left of the decimal point in the Arabic numeral system. **8.** *Mathematics* The lowest positive whole number; one. [Back-formation < UNITY.]

Unit. *abbr.* **1.** Unitarian **2.** Unitarianism

u•ni•tard (yo͞o′nĭ-tärd′) *n.* A one-piece tight-fitting leotard and tights combination, sometimes with foot straps. [UNI– + (LEO)TARD.]

U•ni•tar•i•an (yo͞o′nĭ-târ′ē-ən) *n.* **1.** An adherent of Unitarian Universalism. **2.** A monotheist who is not a Christian. **3.** A Christian who is not a Trinitarian. [< NLat. *ūnitārius,* monotheist < Lat. *ūnitās,* unity. See UNITY.] —**U′ni•tar′i•an** *adj.* —**U′ni•tar′i•an•ism** *n.*

Unitarian Universalism *n.* A religious association with no creed, derived from Christianity and seeing God as unipersonal, salvation universal, and reason and conscience the criteria for belief and practice. —**Unitarian Universalist** *adj. & n.*

u•ni•tar•y (yo͞o′nĭ-tĕr′ē) *adj.* **1.** Of or relating to a unit. **2.** Having the nature of a unit; whole. **3.** Based on or characterized by one or more units. —**u′ni•tar′i•ly** *adv.*

unit cell *n.* The smallest building block of a crystal, consisting of atoms, ions, or molecules, whose geometric arrangement defines a crystal's characteristic symmetry and whose repetition in space produces a crystal lattice.

unit character *n.* A trait inherited in accordance with Mendel's law of segregation.

unit cost *n.* The cost of a given unit of a product.

u•nite (yo͞o-nīt′) *v.* **u•nit•ed, u•nit•ing, u•nites** —*tr.* **1.** To bring together so as to form a whole. **2.** To combine (people) in interest, attitude, or action: *"the love that unites humanity"* (Germaine Greer). **3.** To join (a couple) in marriage. **4.** To cause to adhere. **5.** To have or demonstrate in combination: *She unites common sense with vision.* —*intr.* **1.** To become or seem to become joined, formed, or combined into a unit. **2.** To join and act together in a common purpose or endeavor. See Syns at **join. 3.** To be or become bound together by adhesion. [ME *uniten* < Lat. *ūnīre, ūnīt-* < *ūnus,* one. See **oi-no-** in App.]

u•nit•ed (yo͞o-nī′tĭd) *adj.* **1.** Combined into a single entity. **2.** Concerned with or resulting from mutual action. **3.** Being in harmony; agreed. —**u•nit′ed•ly** *adv.* —**u•nit′ed•ness** *n.*

United Arab Emirates Formerly **Tru•cial Oman** (tro͞o′shəl) A country of E Arabia, a federation of seven sheikdoms on the Persian Gulf and the Gulf of Oman; formed in 1971. Cap. Abu Dhabi. Pop. 1,861,000.

United Arab Republic 1. A former union of Egypt and Syria from 1958 to 1961. Yemen joined the union in 1958, thus creating the **United Arab States. 2.** See **Egypt.**

United Kingdom or **United Kingdom of Great Britain and Northern Ireland** Commonly called **Great Britain** or **Britain.** A country of W Europe comprising England, Scotland, Wales, and Northern Ireland. Beginning with the kingdom of England, it was created by three acts of union: with Wales (1536), Scotland (1707), and Ireland (1800). Cap. London. Pop. 58,091,000.

United Nations An international organization founded in 1945 to promote peace and economic development.

United States or **United States of America** A country of central and NW North America with coastlines on the Atlantic and Pacific oceans. It includes the noncontiguous states of AK and HI and various island territories in the Caribbean Sea and Pacific Ocean. Cap. Washington DC. Pop. 281,421,906.

u•ni•tive (yo͞o′nĭ-tĭv, yo͞o-nī′-) *adj.* Serving to unite.

u•nit•ize (yo͞o′nĭ-tīz′) *tr.v.* **-ized, -iz•ing, -iz•es 1.** To separate, classify, or package in discrete units. **2.** To make into a single unit. —**u′nit•i•za′tion** (yo͞o′nĭ-tĭ-zā′shən) *n.*

unit pricing *n.* The pricing of goods on the basis of cost per unit of measure.

unit rule *n.* A rule of procedure at a national political convention under which a state's entire vote must be cast for the candidate preferred by a majority of the state's delegates.

u•ni•ty (yo͞o′nĭ-tē) *n., pl.* **-ties 1.** The state or quality of being one; singleness. **2.** The state or quality of being in accord; harmony. **3a.** The combination or arrangement of parts into a whole; unification. **b.** A combination or union thus formed. **4.** Singleness or constancy of purpose or action; continuity. **5a.** An ordering of all elements in a work of art or literature so that each contributes to a unified aesthetic effect. **b.** The effect thus produced. **6.** One of the three principles of dramatic structure derived by French neoclassicists from Aristotle's *Poetics,* stating that a drama should have but one plot, which should take place in a single day and be confined to a single locale. **7.** *Mathematics* **a.** The number 1. **b.** See **identity element.** [ME *unite* < OFr. < Lat. *ūnitās* < *ūnus,* one. See **oi-no-** in App.]

univ. *abbr.* **1.** universal **2.** university

Univ. *abbr.* Universalist

u•ni•va•lent (yo͞o′nĭ-vā′lənt) *adj.* **1.** *Chemistry* **a.** Having valence 1. **b.** Having only one valence. **2.** *Genetics* Of or relating to an unpaired chromosome.

u•ni•valve (yo͞o′nĭ-vălv′) *adj.* **1.** Having a shell consisting of a single valve or piece. Used of a mollusk. **2.** Composed of a single valve or piece. Used of a shell. ❖ *n.* A univalve mollusk or shell.

u•ni•ver•sal (yo͞o′nə-vûr′səl) *adj.* **1.** Of, relating to, extending to, or affecting the entire world or all within the world; worldwide. **2.** Including, relating to, or affecting all members of the class or group under consideration: *the universal skepticism of philosophers.* See Syns at **general. 3.** Applicable or common to all purposes, conditions, or situations: *a universal remedy.* **4.** Of or relating to the universe or cosmos; cosmic. **5.** Knowledgeable about or constituting all or many subjects; comprehensively broad. **6.** Adapted or adjustable to many sizes or mechanical uses. **7.** *Logic* Encompassing all of the members of a class or group. Used of a proposition. ❖ *n.* **1.** *Logic* **a.** A universal proposition. **b.** A general or abstract concept or term considered absolute or axiomatic. **2.** A general or widely held principle, concept, or notion. **3.** A trait or pattern of behavior characteristic of all the members of a particular culture or of all humans. —**u′ni•ver′sal•ly** *adv.* —**u′ni•ver′sal•ness** *n.*

universal coupling *n.* See **universal joint.**

universal donor *n.* A person who has group O blood and is therefore able to serve as a donor to a person of any other blood group in the ABO system.

universal grammar *n.* A system of grammatical rules and constraints believed to underlie all natural languages.

u•ni•ver•sal•ism (yo͞o′nə-vûr′sə-lĭz′əm) *n.* **1. Universalism a.** *Theology* The doctrine of universal salvation. **b.** Unitarian Universalism. **2.** The condition of being universal; universality. **3.** A universal scope or range, as of knowledge.

U•ni•ver•sal•ist (yo͞o′nə-vûr′sə-lĭst) *n.* An adherent of Unitarian Universalism. —**U′ni•ver′sal•ist** *adj.*

u•ni•ver•sal•is•tic (yo͞o′nə-vûr′sə-lĭs′tĭk) *adj.* Universal in character or scope: *universalistic values.*

u•ni•ver•sal•i•ty (yo͞o′nə-vər-săl′ĭ-tē) *n., pl.* **-ties 1.** The quality, fact, or condition of being universal. **2.** Universal inclusiveness in scope or range, esp. great versatility of the mind.

u•ni•ver•sal•ize (yo͞o′nə-vûr′sə-līz′) *tr.v.* **-ized, -iz•ing, -iz•es** To make universal; generalize. —**u′ni•ver′sal•i•za′tion** (-sə-lĭ-zā′shən) *n.*

universal joint *n.* A joint or coupling that allows parts of a machine not in line with each other limited freedom of movement in any direction while transmitting rotary motion.

Universal Product Code *n.* A number and bar code that identify an individual consumer product.

universal recipient *n.* A person who has group AB blood and is therefore able to receive blood from any other group in the ABO system.

universal set *n.* *Mathematics* A set containing all elements of a problem that is under consideration.

universal time *n.* The mean solar time for the meridian at Greenwich, England, used as a basis for calculating time throughout most of the world.

u•ni•verse (yōō′nə-vûrs′) *n.* **1.** All matter and energy, including the earth, the galaxies, and the contents of intergalactic space, regarded as a whole. **2a.** The earth together with all its inhabitants and created things. **b.** The human race. **3.** The realm where something exists or takes place. **4.** *Logic* See **universe of discourse. 5.** *Statistics* See **population** 5. [ME < OFr. *univers* < Lat. *ūniversum* < neut. of *ūniversus,* whole : *ūnus,* one; see **oi-no-** in App. + *versus,* p. part. of *vertere,* to turn; see **wer-**[2] in App.]

universe of discourse *n. Logic* A class containing all the entities referred to in a discourse or argument.

u•ni•ver•si•ty (yōō′nə-vûr′sĭ-tē) *n., pl.* **-ties 1.** An institution for higher learning with teaching and research facilities constituting graduate and professional schools that award master's degrees and doctorates and an undergraduate division that awards bachelor's degrees. **2.** The buildings and grounds of a university. **3.** The body of students and faculty of such an institution. [ME *universite* < OFr. < Med.Lat. *ūniversitās* < Lat., the whole, a corporate body < *ūniversus,* whole. See UNIVERSE.]

u•niv•o•cal (yōō-nĭv′ə-kəl) *adj.* Having only one meaning; unambiguous. ❖ *n.* A word or term having only one meaning. [< LLat. *ūnivocus* : Lat. *ūni-,* uni- + Lat. *vocāre,* to say; see **wekʷ-** in App.] **—u•niv′o•cal•ly** *adv.*

Unix or **UNIX** (yōō′nĭks) A trademark used for a computer disk operating system.

un•joint (ŭn-joint′) *tr.v.* **-joint•ed, -joint•ing, -joints** To dislocate a joint of; disjoint.

un•just (ŭn-jŭst′) *adj.* **1.** Violating principles of justice or fairness; unfair. **2.** *Archaic* Faithless; dishonest. **—un•just′ly** *adv.* **—un•just′ness** *n.*

un•jus•ti•fi•a•ble (ŭn-jŭs′tə-fī′ə-bəl, ŭn′jŭs-tə-fī′-) *adj.* Impossible to excuse, pardon, or justify: *took an unjustifiable risk.* **—un•jus′ti•fi′a•bly** *adv.*

un•kempt (ŭn-kĕmpt′) *adj.* **1a.** Not combed: *unkempt hair.* **b.** Not properly maintained; disorderly or untidy: *an unkempt garden.* See Syns at **sloppy. 2.** Unpolished; rude. [ME *unkemd* : un-, not; see UN–[1] + *kembed,* p. part. of *kemben,* to comb (< OE *cemban;* see **gembh-** in App.).]

un•ken•nel (ŭn-kĕn′əl) *tr.v.* **-neled, -nel•ing, -nels** or **-nelled, -nel•ling, -nels 1a.** To drive from a lair or den. **b.** To loose from a kennel. **2.** To bring to light; uncover or disclose.

un•kept (ŭn-kĕpt′) *adj.* **1.** Unkempt: *an unkept cemetery plot.* **2.** Not kept or fulfilled: *an unkept promise.*

un•kind (ŭn-kīnd′) *adj.* **-er, -est 1.** Lacking kindness; inconsiderate or unsympathetic. **2.** Harsh; severe: *unkind winters.* **—un•kind′ness** *n.*

un•kind•ly (ŭn-kīnd′lē) *adj.* **-li•er, -li•est** Not kindly; unkind. ❖ *adv.* In an unkind manner. **—un•kind′li•ness** *n.*

un•kink (ŭn-kĭngk′) *v.* **-kinked, -kink•ing, -kinks** *—tr.* To remove kinks from; make straight. *—intr.* To become relaxed.

un•knit (ŭn-nĭt′) *tr. & intr.v.* **-knit** or **-knit•ted, -knit•ting, -knits** To unravel or undo (something knit or tied) or become unraveled or undone.

un•know•a•ble (ŭn-nō′ə-bəl) *adj.* Impossible to know, esp. being beyond human experience or understanding: *unknowable mysteries.* **—un•know′a•bil′i•ty, un•know′a•ble•ness** *n.* **—un•know′a•ble** *n.* **—un•know′a•bly** *adv.*

un•know•ing (ŭn-nō′ĭng) *adj.* Not knowing; unaware. **—un•know′ing•ly** *adv.*

un•known (ŭn-nōn′) *adj.* **1.** Not known; unfamiliar: *a problem unknown earlier.* **2a.** Not identified or ascertained: *flowers from an unknown admirer.* **b.** Not established or verified. **3.** Not well known or widely known: *an unknown artist.* ❖ *n.* **1a.** A person or thing that is unknown. **b.** A person who is not well known, as to the general public: *cast an unknown in the role.* **2.** *Mathematics* A quantity of unknown numerical value.

Unknown Soldier *n.* An unidentified soldier killed in war and chosen to be interred with national honors as a representative of all those who died in a war.

un•la•bored (ŭn-lā′bərd) *adj.* **1.** Done with or requiring little effort; effortless. **2.** Not tilled or cultivated.

un•lace (ŭn-lās′) *tr.v.* **-laced, -lac•ing, -lac•es 1a.** To loosen or undo the lacing or laces of. **b.** To loosen or remove the clothing of. **2.** *Obsolete* To disgrace.

un•lade (ŭn-lād′) *v.* **-lad•ed, -lad•ing, -lades** *Nautical —tr.* **1.** To unload (cargo) from a ship. **2.** To unload (a ship). *—intr.* To discharge a cargo.

un•lash (ŭn-lăsh′) *tr.v.* **-lashed, -lash•ing, -lash•es** To untie the lashing of; loose.

un•law•ful (ŭn-lô′fəl) *adj.* **1.** Not lawful; illegal. **2.** Contrary to accepted morality or convention; illicit. **3.** Of, relating to, or being a child or children born to parents not married to each other. **—un•law′ful•ly** *adv.* **—un•law′ful•ness** *n.*

un•lay (ŭn-lā′) *v.* **-laid** (-lād′), **-lay•ing, -lays** *Nautical —tr.* To untwist the strands of (a rope). *—intr.* To untwist.

un•lead (ŭn-lĕd′) *tr.v.* **-lead•ed, -lead•ing, -leads 1.** To remove the lead from. **2.** *Printing* To extricate the leads from between (lines of type).

un•lead•ed (ŭn-lĕd′ĭd) *adj.* **1.** Containing no lead or lead compounds. **2.** Not containing tetraethyl lead: *unleaded gasoline.* **3.** *Printing* Not spaced or separated with lead, as lines of type.

un•learn (ŭn-lûrn′) *tr.v.* **-learned** also **-learnt** (-lûrnt′), **-learn•ing, -learns 1.** To put (something learned) out of the mind; forget. **2.** To undo the effect of; put aside the practice of: *tried to unlearn his habit of nail-biting.*

un•learn•ed (ŭn-lûr′nĭd) *adj.* **1.** Not educated; ignorant or illiterate. **2.** Not skilled or versed in a specified discipline. **3.** (-lûrnd′) Not acquired by training or studying: *an unlearned response.*

un•leash (ŭn-lēsh′) *tr.v.* **-leashed, -leash•ing, -leash•es** To release or loose from or as if from a leash: *unleashed the dogs.*

un•less (ŭn-lĕs′) *conj.* Except on the condition that; except under the circumstances that. ❖ *prep.* Except for; except. [ME *unlesse,* alteration (influenced by *un-,* not) of *onlesse* : *on,* on; see ON + *lesse,* less; see LESS.]

un•let•tered (ŭn-lĕt′ərd) *adj.* **1a.** Not adept at reading and writing; deficient in the knowledge that can come from books. **b.** Illiterate. **2.** Having no lettering: *a plain, unlettered T-shirt.*

un•li•censed (ŭn-lī′sənst) *adj.* **1.** Having no official license. **2.** Done without permission; not authorized. **3.** Lacking moral restraint; unrestrained.

un•like (ŭn-līk′) *adj.* **1.** Not alike; different: *For twins, they are very unlike.* **2.** Not equal, as in amount. ❖ *prep.* **1.** Different from; not like: *She's unlike the rest of her family.* **2.** Not typical of: *It's unlike him not to call.*

un•like•li•hood (ŭn-līk′lē-hŏŏd′) *n.* **1.** The state of being unlikely or improbable; improbability. **2.** Something unlikely.

un•like•ly (ŭn-līk′lē) *adj.* **-li•er, -li•est 1.** Not likely; improbable. **2.** Not promising; likely to fail. **—un•like′li•ness** *n.*

un•like•ness (ŭn-līk′nĭs) *n.* The quality or condition of being unlike. See Syns at **difference.**

un•lim•ber (ŭn-lĭm′bər) *v.* **-bered, -ber•ing, -bers** *—tr.* **1.** To make ready for action. **2.** To detach (a gun or caisson) from its limber. *—intr.* To prepare something for action.

un•lim•it•ed (ŭn-lĭm′ĭ-tĭd) *adj.* **1.** Having no restrictions or controls: *an unlimited travel ticket.* **2.** Having or seeming to have no boundaries; infinite: *an unlimited horizon.* **3.** Without qualification or exception; absolute. **—un•lim′it•ed•ly** *adv.* **—un•lim′it•ed•ness** *n.*

un•list•ed (ŭn-lĭs′tĭd) *adj.* **1.** Not appearing on a list, esp. not listed in a telephone directory. **2.** Relating to or being stock or securities not listed on a stock exchange.

un•lis•ten•a•ble (ŭn-lĭs′ə-nə-bəl) *adj.* Being such that listening with comfort or pleasure is impossible.

un•liv•a•ble (ŭn-lĭv′ə-bəl) *adj.* Unfit for habitation.

un•live (ŭn-lĭv′) *tr.v.* **-lived, -liv•ing, -lives** To undo the effects of; annul.

un•load (ŭn-lōd′) *v.* **-load•ed, -load•ing, -loads** *—tr.* **1a.** To remove the load or cargo from. **b.** To discharge (cargo or a load). **2a.** To relieve of a burden; unburden: *unloaded the donkeys.* **b.** To give expression to (one's troubles or feelings); pour forth. **3.** To remove the charge from (a firearm). **4.** To dispose of, esp. by selling in great quantity; dump. *—intr.* To discharge a cargo or some other burden. **—un•load′er** *n.*

un•lock (ŭn-lŏk′) *v.* **-locked, -lock•ing, -locks** *—tr.* **1a.** To undo (a lock) by turning a key or corresponding part. **b.** To undo the lock of. **2.** To give access to; open. **3.** To set free; release: *The news unlocked a torrent of emotion.* **4.** To provide a key to; disclose or reveal: *unlock a mystery.* *—intr.* To become unfastened, loosened, or freed from something.

un•loose (ŭn-lōōs′) *tr.v.* **-loosed, -loos•ing, -loos•es 1.** To unfasten; untie. **2.** To set free from or as if from restraints. **3.** To relax: *unloosed my grip on the handlebars.*

un•loos•en (ŭn-lōō′sən) *tr.v.* **-ened, -en•ing, -ens** To unloose.

un•love•ly (ŭn-lŭv′lē) *adj.* **-li•er, -li•est 1.** Not deemed visually attractive. **2.** Not pleasant; disagreeable.

un•luck•y (ŭn-lŭk′ē) *adj.* **-i•er, -i•est 1.** Subjected to or marked by misfortune. **2.** Resulting or likely to result in misfortune; inauspicious. **3.** Not producing the desired outcome. **—un•luck′i•ly** *adv.* **—un•luck′i•ness** *n.*

un•made (ŭn-mād′) *adj.* Not made: *an unmade bed.*

un•make (ŭn-māk′) *tr.v.* **-made** (-mād′), **-mak•ing, -makes 1.** To deprive of position, rank, or authority; depose. **2.** To cause the ruin of; destroy. **3.** To alter the nature or characteristics of.

un•man (ŭn-măn′) *tr.v.* **-manned, -man•ning, -mans 1.** To cause to give up manly courage or spirit. **2.** To take away virility from; emasculate.

un•man•ly (ŭn-măn′lē) *adj.* **-li•er, -li•est 1a.** Dishonorable; degrading. **b.** Lacking courage; cowardly. **2.** Regarded as unbecoming to a man. **—un•man′li•ness** *n.*

un•manned (ŭn-mănd′) *adj.* **1.** Not crewed: *an unmanned spacecraft.* **2.** *Obsolete* Not trained. Used of a hawk.

un•man•nered (ŭn-măn′ərd) *adj.* **1.** Lacking good manners; rude. **2.** Natural and unaffected. **—un•man′nered•ly** *adv.*

un•matched (ŭn-mătcht′) *adj.* **1.** Not matched: *unmatched socks.* **2.** Without equal or rival; peerless: *unmatched skill.*

un•mean•ing (ŭn-mē′nĭng) *adj.* **1.** Devoid of meaning or sense; meaningless. **2.** Lacking intelligence or liveliness of expression; vacant. **—un•mean′ing•ly** *adv.*

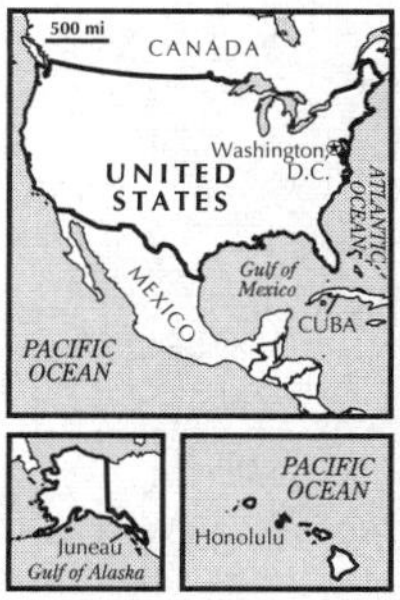

United States

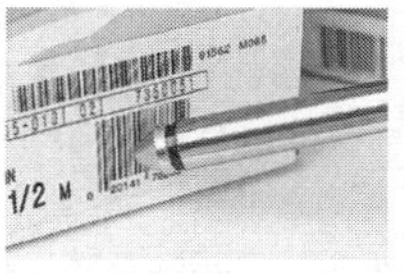

Universal Product Code

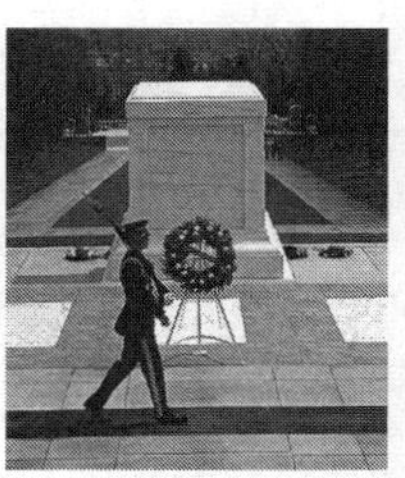

Unknown Soldier
Tomb of the Unknown Soldier, Arlington National Cemetery, Virginia

ă	pat	oi	boy
ā	pay	ou	out
âr	care	ŏŏ	took
ä	father	ōō	boot
ĕ	pet	ŭ	cut
ē	be	ûr	urge
ĭ	pit	th	thin
ī	pie	*th*	this
îr	pier	hw	which
ŏ	pot	zh	vision
ō	toe	ə	about, item
ô	paw		

Stress marks:
′ (primary);
′ (secondary), as in
lexicon (lĕk′sĭ-kŏn′)

un•meant (ŭn-mĕnt′) *adj.* Not intentional.

un•me•chan•i•cal (ŭn′mĭ-kăn′ĭ-kəl) *adj.* Lacking ability or skill with machinery and tools. —**un′me•chan′i•cal•ly** *adv.*

un•men•tion•a•ble (ŭn-mĕn′shə-nə-bəl) *adj.* Not fit to be mentioned or discussed; unspeakable. ❖ *n.* **1.** One that is not to be mentioned. **2. unmentionables** Underwear. —**un•men′tion•a•ble•ness** *n.* —**un•men′tion•a•bly** *adv.*

un•mer•ci•ful (ŭn-mûr′sĭ-fəl) *adj.* **1.** Having or exhibiting no mercy; merciless. **2.** Exceeding a normal or reasonable limit; excessive: *unmerciful heat.* —**un•mer′ci•ful•ly** *adv.* —**un•mer′ci•ful•ness** *n.*

un•met (ŭn-mĕt′) *adj.* Not satisfied or fulfilled.

un•mind•ful (ŭn-mīnd′fəl) *adj.* Failing to give due care or attention; inattentive. —**un•mind′ful•ly** *adv.* —**un•mind′ful•ness** *n.*

un•mit•i•gat•ed (ŭn-mĭt′ĭ-gā′tĭd) *adj.* **1.** Not diminished or moderated in intensity or severity; unrelieved: *unmitigated suffering.* **2.** Without qualification or exception; absolute. —**un•mit′i•gat′ed•ly** *adv.*

un•mixed (ŭn-mĭkst′) *adj.* Free from other elements; pure: *unmixed pleasure.* —**un•mix′ed•ly** (-mĭk′sĭd-lē) *adv.*

un•mold (ŭn-mōld′) *tr.v.* **-mold•ed, -mold•ing, -molds** To remove from a mold: *unmold a lemon mousse.*

un•moor (ŭn-mōōr′) *v.* **-moored, -moor•ing, -moors** —*tr.* **1.** To release from or as if from moorings. **2.** *Nautical* To release (a ship) from all but one anchor. —*intr.* To cast off moorings.

un•mor•al (ŭn-môr′əl, -mŏr′-) *adj.* **1.** Having no moral quality; amoral. **2.** Unrelated to moral or ethical considerations; nonmoral. —**un′mo•ral′i•ty** (-mə-răl′ĭ-tē, -mŏ-) *n.* —**un•mor′al•ly** *adv.*

un•mor•tise (ŭn-môr′tĭs) *tr.v.* **-tised, -tis•ing, -tis•es 1.** To loosen a mortised joint of. **2.** To separate.

un•mo•ti•vat•ed (ŭn-mō′tə-vā′tĭd) *adj.* Having no motive or incentive: *unmotivated students.*

un•moved (ŭn-mōōvd′) *adj.* Emotionally unaffected.

un•mov•ing (ŭn-mōō′vĭng) *adj.* **1.** Not moving; motionless. **2.** Not affecting the emotions.

un•mu•si•cal (ŭn-myōō′zĭ-kəl) *adj.* **1.** Lacking in musical qualities, such as melody or harmony. **2.** Sounding harsh to the ear; dissonant. **3.** Not skilled or interested in music. —**un•mu′si•cal•ly** *adv.*

un•muz•zle (ŭn-mŭz′əl) *tr.v.* **-zled, -zling, -zles 1.** To remove a muzzle from: *unmuzzle a dog.* **2.** *Informal* To free from restraint or censorship: *unmuzzle the press.*

un•my•e•lin•at•ed (ŭn-mī′ə-lĭ-nā′tĭd) *adj.* Lacking a myelin sheath. Used of a nerve fiber.

un•name•a•ble or **un•nam•a•ble** (ŭn-nā′mə-bəl) *adj.* Not to be named or identified: *unnameable fears.*

un•nat•u•ral (ŭn-năch′ər-əl) *adj.* **1.** In violation of a natural law. **2.** Inconsistent with an individual pattern or custom. **3.** Deviating from a behavioral or social norm: *an unnatural attachment.* **4.** Contrived or constrained; artificial: *smiled in an unnatural manner.* **5.** In violation of natural feelings; inhuman. —**un•nat′u•ral•ly** *adv.* —**un•nat′u•ral•ness** *n.*

un•nerve (ŭn-nûrv′) *tr.v.* **-nerved, -nerv•ing, -nerves 1.** To deprive of fortitude, strength, or firmness of purpose. **2.** To make nervous or upset. —**un•nerv′ing•ly** *adv.*

un•nil•en•ni•um (yōō′nĭl-ĕn′ē-əm) *n.* See meitnerium. [Lat. *ūnus,* one; see UNION + Lat. *nīl,* nothing; see NIL + Gk. *ennea,* nine; see ENNEAD + –IUM.]

un•nil•hex•i•um (yōō′nĭl-hĕk′sē-əm) *n.* See seaborgium. [Lat. *ūnus,* one; see UNION + Lat. *nīl,* nothing; see NIL + Gk. *hex,* six; see HEXA- + –IUM.]

un•nil•oc•ti•um (yōō′nə-lŏk′tē-əm) *n.* See hassium. [Lat. *ūnus,* one; see UNION + Lat. *nīl,* nothing; see NIL + Lat. *octō* or Gk. *oktō,* eight; see OCTO- + –IUM.]

un•nil•pen•ti•um (yōō′nĭl-pĕn′tē-əm) *n.* See dubnium. [Lat. *ūnus,* one; see UNION + Lat. *nīl,* nothing; see NIL + Gk. *pente,* five; see PENTAD + –IUM.]

un•nil•quad•i•um (yōō′nĭl-kwŏd′ē-əm) *n.* See rutherfordium. [Lat. *ūnus,* one; see UNION + *nīl,* nothing; see NIL + QUAD(RI)– + –IUM.]

un•nil•sep•ti•um (yōō′nĭl-sĕp′tē-əm) *n.* See bohrium. [Lat. *ūnus,* one; see UNION + Lat. *nīl,* nothing; see NIL + Lat. *septem,* seven; see SEPTET + –IUM.]

un•no•tice•a•ble (ŭn-nō′tĭ-sə-bəl) *adj.* Not readily noticeable. —**un•no′tice•a•bly** *adv.*

un•num•bered (ŭn-nŭm′bərd) *adj.* **1.** Innumerable; countless: *the unnumbered stars.* **2.** Not marked with an identifying number: *unnumbered pages.*

un•ob•tru•sive (ŭn′əb-trōō′sĭv) *adj.* Not undesirably noticeable or blatant; inconspicuous. —**un′ob•tru′sive•ly** *adv.* —**un′ob•tru′sive•ness** *n.*

un•or•gan•ized (ŭn-ôr′gə-nīzd′) *adj.* **1.** Lacking order, unity, or a system; disorganized. **2.** Having no organic qualities; inorganic. **3.** Not represented by a labor union.

un•os•ten•ta•tious (ŭn-ŏs′tĕn-tā′shəs, -tən-) *adj.* Not ostentatious; unpretentious. —**un′os•ten•ta′tious•ly** *adv.*

un•paid (ŭn-pād′) *adj.* **1.** Not yet paid: *unpaid bills.* **2.** Serving without pay; unsalaried: *unpaid research assistants.*

un•par•al•leled (ŭn-păr′ə-lĕld′) *adj.* Without parallel, equal, or match; unequaled: *unparalleled bravery.*

un•par•lia•men•ta•ry (ŭn′pär-lə-mĕn′tə-rē, -mĕn′trē) *adj.* Not in accord with parliamentary procedure.

un•per•fo•rat•ed (ŭn-pûr′fə-rā′tĭd) *adj.* **1.** Lacking perforations. **2.** Imperforate. Used of a postage stamp.

un•per•son (ŭn′pûr′sən) *n.* A nonperson.

un•pick (ŭn-pĭk′) *tr.v.* **-picked, -pick•ing, -picks** To undo (sewing) by removing stitches: *unpick a seam.*

un•pin (ŭn-pĭn′) *tr.v.* **-pinned, -pin•ning, -pins 1.** To remove pins or a pin from. **2a.** To open or unfasten by or as if by removing pins. **b.** To free.

un•pleas•ant•ry (ŭn-plĕz′ən-trē) *n., pl.* **-ries** A disagreeable remark, situation, or act.

un•plug (ŭn-plŭg′) *v.* **-plugged, -plug•ging, -plugs** —*tr.* **1a.** To remove a plug from. **b.** To free from an obstruction. **2a.** To remove (an electric plug) from an outlet. **b.** To disconnect (an electric appliance) by removing a plug from an outlet. —*intr.* To become unplugged.

un•plugged (ŭn-plŭgd′) *adj.* Of or involving the performance of music using acoustic instruments, sometimes amplified through microphones. —**un•plugged′** *adv.*

un•plumbed (ŭn-plŭmd′) *adj.* **1.** Not measured or sounded with a plumb: *unplumbed ocean depths.* **2.** Not fully examined or explored: *unplumbed ideas.*

un•pol•ished (ŭn-pŏl′ĭsht) *adj.* **1.** Not polished, as: **a.** Not smooth and shiny: *unpolished shoes.* **b.** Not elaborated, perfected, or completed: *an unpolished performance.* **c.** Not having attained a high degree of skill: *an unpolished tenor.* **2.** Lacking good manners, culture, or refinement. **3.** Natural and unsophisticated: *The service was friendly and unpolished.*

un•prac•ticed (ŭn-prăk′tĭst) *adj.* **1.** Not yet tested or tried. **2.** Lacking the benefit of experience; unskilled.

un•prej•u•diced (ŭn-prĕj′ə-dĭst) *adj.* Free from prejudice; impartial. See Syns at fair[1].

un•pre•med•i•tat•ed (ŭn′prĭ-mĕd′ĭ-tā′tĭd) *adj.* Not planned or thought out in advance. —**un′pre•med′i•tat′ed•ly** *adv.*

un•pre•pared (ŭn′prĭ-pârd′) *adj.* **1.** Having made no preparations. **2.** Not equipped to meet a contingency. **3.** Impromptu: *unprepared remarks.* —**un′pre•par′ed•ly** (-pâr′ĭd-lē) *adv.* —**un′pre•par′ed•ness** (-pâr′ĭd-nĭs, -pârd′nĭs) *n.*

un•pre•tend•ing (ŭn′prĭ-tĕn′dĭng) *adj.* Unpretentious.

un•pre•ten•tious (ŭn′prĭ-tĕn′shəs) *adj.* Lacking pretension or affectation; modest. —**un′pre•ten′tious•ly** *adv.*

un•print•a•ble (ŭn-prĭn′tə-bəl) *adj.* Not proper for publication for legal or social reasons: *unprintable remarks.*

un•pro•duc•tive (ŭn′prə-dŭk′tĭv) *adj.* **1.** Not productive; idle. **2.** *Economics* Adding nothing to exchangeable value. —**un′pro•duc′tive•ly** *adv.* —**un′pro•duc′tive•ness** *n.*

un•pro•fes•sion•al (ŭn′prə-fĕsh′ə-nəl) *adj.* **1a.** Not in a profession. **b.** Not a qualified member of a professional group. **2.** Not conforming to the standards of a profession. **3.** Characteristic of an amateur; inexpert. —**un′pro•fes′sion•al•ism** *n.* —**un′pro•fes′sion•al•ly** *adv.*

un•pro•nounce•a•ble (ŭn′prə-noun′sə-bəl) *adj.* **1.** Difficult or impossible to pronounce correctly: *an unpronounceable last name.* **2.** Not fit to be mentioned.

un•pro•vid•ed (ŭn′prə-vī′dĭd) *adj.* Not supplied, furnished, or equipped. —**un′pro•vid′ed•ly** *adv.*

un•pro•voked (ŭn′prə-vōkt′) *adj.* Not provoked or prompted: *an unprovoked attack.*

un•pub•lish•a•ble (ŭn-pŭb′lĭ-shə-bəl) *adj.* Unfit for publication: *an unpublishable manuscript.*

un•qual•i•fied (ŭn-kwŏl′ə-fīd′) *adj.* **1.** Lacking the proper or required qualifications: *unqualified for the job.* **2.** Not modified by conditions or reservations; absolute: *an unqualified refusal.* —**un•qual′i•fied′ly** *adv.*

un•ques•tion•a•ble (ŭn-kwĕs′chə-nə-bəl) *adj.* Beyond question or doubt; indisputable. See Syns at authentic. —**un•ques′tion•a•bil′i•ty** *n.* —**un•ques′tion•a•bly** *adv.*

un•ques•tioned (ŭn-kwĕs′chənd) *adj.* **1.** Not subjected to questioning; not interrogated. **2a.** Unquestionable; indisputable. **b.** Not called into question or examination; not doubted.

un•ques•tion•ing (ŭn-kwĕs′chə-nĭng) *adj.* Not marked by or exhibiting uncertainty or indecision: *unquestioning faith.* —**un•ques′tion•ing•ly** *adv.*

un•qui•et (ŭn-kwī′ĭt) *adj.* **-er, -est 1.** Emotionally or mentally restless or uneasy. **2.** Characterized by unrest or disorder; turbulent. —**un•qui′et•ly** *adv.* —**un•qui′et•ness** *n.*

un•quote (ŭn-kwōt′, ŭn′kwōt′) *n.* Used by a speaker to indicate the end of a quotation.

un•rav•el (ŭn-răv′əl) *v.* **-eled, -el•ing, -els** or **-elled, -el•ling, -els** —*tr.* **1a.** To undo or ravel the knitted fabric of. **b.** To separate (entangled threads). **2.** To separate and clarify the elements of (something mysterious or baffling); solve. See Syns at solve. —*intr.* To become unraveled.

un•reach•a•ble (ŭn-rē′chə-bəl) *adj.* Unable to be reached; inaccessible. —**un•reach′a•bil′i•ty** *n.* —**un•reach′a•bly** *adv.*

un•read (ŭn-rĕd′) *adj.* **1.** Not read, studied, or perused: *an unread book.* **2.** Having read little; lacking in knowledge acquired by reading. **3.** Not versed in a specified subject.

un•read•a•ble (ŭn-rē′də-bəl) *adj.* **1.** Not legible or decipherable; illegible: *unreadable handwriting.* **2.** Unsuitable for or not worth reading: *unreadable prose.* **3.** Not interesting; dull. **4.** Incomprehensible; opaque: *an unreadable facial expression.* —**un•read′a•bil′i•ty** *n.*

un•re•al (ŭn-rē′əl, -rēl′) *adj.* **1.** Not real or substantial; illusory. **2.** *Slang* So remarkable as to elicit disbelief; fantastic. **3.** Surreal.

un•re•al•is•tic (ŭn′rē-ə-lĭs′tĭk) *adj.* Not compatible with reality or fact; unreasonably idealistic: *unrealistic expectations.* —**un′re•al•is′ti•cal•ly** *adv.*

un•re•al•i•ty (ŭn′rē-ăl′ĭ-tē) *n., pl.* **-ties 1.** The quality or state of being unreal. **2.** Something unreal, insubstantial, or imaginary. **3.** A lack of ability to deal with reality.

un•rea•son (ŭn-rē′zən) *n.* **1.** Absence or lack of reason; irrationality. **2.** Nonsense; absurdity.

un•rea•son•a•ble (ŭn-rē′zə-nə-bəl) *adj.* **1.** Not governed by reason: *an unreasonable attitude.* **2.** Exceeding reasonable limits; immoderate. —**un•rea′son•a•ble•ness** *n.* —**un•rea′son•a•bly** *adv.*

un•rea•soned (ŭn-rē′zənd) *adj.* Not based on or guided by reason; unreasonable: *unreasoned prejudices.*

un•rea•son•ing (ŭn-rē′zə-nĭng) *adj.* Not governed or moderated by reason. —**un•rea′son•ing•ly** *adv.*

un•re•con•struct•ed (ŭn′rē-kən-strŭk′tĭd) *adj.* **1.** Not reconciled to social, political, or economic change; maintaining outdated attitudes, beliefs, and practices. **2.** Not reconciled to the outcome of the American Civil War.

un•reel (ŭn-rēl′) *tr. & intr.v.* **-reeled, -reel•ing, -reels** To unwind (something) from or as if from a reel or become unwound.

un•reeve (ŭn-rēv′) *v.* **-reeved** or **-rove** (-rōv′), **-reeved** or **-rove** or **-ro•ven** (-rō′vən), **-reev•ing, -reeves** *Nautical* —*tr.* To withdraw (a rope, for example) from an opening, such as a block or thimble. —*intr.* To become unreeved.

un•re•flect•ing (ŭn′rĭ-flĕk′tĭng) *adj.* Marked by or exhibiting a lack of serious thought or consideration: *unreflecting impulses.*

un•re•flec•tive (ŭn′rĭ-flĕk′tĭv) *adj.* Not reflective; unthinking. —**un′re•flec′tive•ly** *adv.*

un•re•gen•er•ate (ŭn′rĭ-jĕn′ər-ĭt) *adj.* **1a.** Not spiritually renewed or reformed; not repentant. **b.** Sinful; dissolute. **2a.** Not reconciled to change; unreconstructed. **b.** Stubborn; obstinate. —**un′re•gen′er•a•ble** *adj.* —**un′re•gen′er•a•cy** (-ə-sē) *n.* —**un′re•gen′er•ate•ly** *adv.*

un•re•hearsed (ŭn′rĭ-hûrst′) *adj.* Not rehearsed.

un•re•lieved (ŭn′rĭ-lēvd′) *adj.* Utter; complete: *unrelieved boredom.* —**un′re•liev′ed•ly** (-lē′vĭd-lē) *adv.*

un•re•mit•ting (ŭn′rĭ-mĭt′ĭng) *adj.* Never slackening; persistent: *an unremitting struggle for survival.* —**un′re•mit′ting•ly** *adv.*

un•re•serve (ŭn′rĭ-zûrv′) *n.* Frankness of manner; candor.

un•re•served (ŭn′rĭ-zûrvd′) *adj.* **1.** Not held back for a particular person: *an unreserved seat.* **2.** Given without reservation; unqualified: *unreserved praise.* **3.** Exhibiting no reserve: *unreserved behavior.* —**un′re•serv′ed•ly** (-zûr′vĭd-lē) *adv.*

un•rest (ŭn-rĕst′, ŭn′rĕst′) *n.* An uneasy or troubled condition: *social unrest.*

un•re•tire (ŭn′rĭ-tīr′) *intr.v.* **-tired, -tir•ing, -tires** To return to work after having taken retirement.

un•rid•dle (ŭn-rĭd′l) *tr.v.* **-dled, -dling, -dles** To solve or explain (a riddle or mystery). —**un•rid′dler** *n.*

un•rig (ŭn-rĭg′) *tr.v.* **-rigged, -rig•ging, -rigs** *Nautical* To strip (a vessel) of rigging.

un•right•eous (ŭn-rī′chəs) *adj.* **1.** Not righteous; wicked. **2.** Not right or fair; unjust. —**un•right′eous•ly** *adv.* —**un•right′eous•ness** *n.*

un•ri•valed or **un•ri•valled** (ŭn-rī′vəld) *adj.* Having no rival or equal; incomparable.

un•roll (ŭn-rōl′) *v.* **-rolled, -roll•ing, -rolls** —*tr.* **1.** To unwind and open (something rolled up). **2.** To unfold and present to view; reveal. —*intr.* To become unrolled.

un•root (ŭn-rōōt′, -rŏŏt′) *tr.v.* **-root•ed, -root•ing, -roots** To uproot.

un•round (ŭn-round′) *tr.v.* **-round•ed, -round•ing, -rounds** To pronounce (a sound) with the lips in a flattened or neutral position.

un•rove (ŭn-rōv′) *v.* A past tense and a past participle of **un•reeve.**

un•ro•ven (ŭn-rō′vən) *v.* A past participle of **unreeve.**

un•ruf•fled (ŭn-rŭf′əld) *adj.* **1.** Not agitated; calm. **2.** Regular and smooth, as the surface of water.

un•ru•ly (ŭn-rōō′lē) *adj.* **-li•er, -li•est** Difficult or impossible to discipline, control, or rule. [ME *unreuli* : *un-,* not; see UN-[1] + *reuli,* easy to govern (< *reule,* rule; see RULE).] —**un•ru′li•ness** *n.*

SYNONYMS *unruly, refractory, intractable, recalcitrant, headstrong, wayward* These adjectives mean resistant or marked by resistance to control. *Unruly* implies failure to submit to rule or discipline: *unruly behavior in class. Refractory* and *intractable* refer to what is obstinate and difficult to manage or control: "*the intractable ferocity of his captive*" (Edgar Allan Poe); "*The idea of ecclesiastical authority . . . woke all the refractory nerves of opposition inherited from five generations of Puritans*" (Harriet Beecher Stowe). One that is *recalcitrant* rebels against authority: *arrested*

the recalcitrant demonstrators. Headstrong describes one obstinately bent on having his or her own way: *The headstrong senator ignored his constituency.* One who is *wayward* willfully and often perversely departs from what is desired, advised, expected, or required: "*a lively child, who had been spoilt and indulged, and therefore was sometimes wayward*" (Charlotte Brontë).

un•sad•dle (ŭn-săd′l) *v.* **-dled, -dling, -dles** —*tr.* **1.** To remove a saddle from. **2.** To throw (a rider) from the saddle. Used of a horse. —*intr.* To remove a saddle from a horse.

un•said (ŭn-sĕd′) *adj.* Not said, esp. not uttered out loud.

un•san•i•tar•y (ŭn-săn′ĭ-tĕr′ē) *adj.* Not sanitary.

un•sat•u•rate (ŭn-săch′ər-ĭt) *n.* An unsaturated compound.

un•sat•u•rat•ed (ŭn-săch′ə-rā′tĭd) *adj.* **1.** Relating to or being a fat composed predominantly of fatty acids having one or more double bonds in the carbon chain. **2.** Capable of dissolving more of a solute at a given temperature. —**un′sat•u•ra′tion** *n.*

unsaturated fat *n.* A fat derived from plants and some animal sources, esp. fish, that contributes to reduced cholesterol levels in the blood.

un•sa•vor•y (ŭn-sā′və-rē) *adj.* **1.** Distasteful or disagreeable. **2.** Not savory: *an unsavory meal.* **3.** Morally offensive. —**un•sa′vor•i•ly** *adv.* —**un•sa′vor•i•ness** *n.*

un•say (ŭn-sā′) *tr.v.* **-said** (-sĕd′), **-say•ing, -says** To retract (something said).

un•say•a•ble (ŭn-sā′ə-bəl) *adj.* Not readily spoken or expressed: *unsayable fears.* ❖ *n.* **1.** Something not readily said. **2.** Something unfit to be said.

un•schooled (ŭn-skōōld′) *adj.* **1.** Not educated or instructed; having little or no formal schooling. **2.** Not the result of training; natural: *an artist of unschooled talents.*

un•sci•en•tif•ic (ŭn′sī-ən-tĭf′ĭk) *adj.* **1.** Not adhering to the principles of science. **2.** Not knowledgeable about science or the scientific method. —**un′sci•en•tif′i•cal•ly** *adv.*

un•scram•ble (ŭn-skrăm′bəl) *tr.v.* **-bled, -bling, -bles 1.** To straighten out or disentangle (a jumble or tangle); resolve. **2.** To restore (a scrambled message) to intelligible form. —**un•scram′bler** *n.*

un•screw (ŭn-skrōō′) *v.* **-screwed, -screw•ing, -screws** —*tr.* **1.** To take out the screw or screws from. **2.** To loosen, adjust, or remove by rotating. —*intr.* To become or allow to become unscrewed.

un•script•ed (ŭn-skrĭp′tĭd) *adj.* Not adhering to or in accordance with a script written beforehand: *an unscripted talk.*

un•sea•son•a•ble (ŭn-sē′zə-nə-bəl) *adj.* **1.** Not suitable to or appropriate for the season. **2.** Not characteristic of the time of year: *unseasonable weather.* **3.** Poorly timed; inopportune. —**un•sea′son•a•ble•ness** *n.* —**un•sea′son•a•bly** *adv.*

un•sea•soned (ŭn-sē′zənd) *adj.* **1.** Lacking experience and the knowledge gained from it; inexperienced. **2.** Inadequately aged or seasoned; not ripe or mature: *unseasoned wood.* **3.** Having no added seasoning: *unseasoned meat and carrots.*

un•seat (ŭn-sēt′) *tr.v.* **-seat•ed, -seat•ing, -seats 1.** To remove from a seat, esp. from a saddle. **2.** To dislodge from a location or position, esp. to remove from office.

un•seem•ly (ŭn-sēm′lē) *adj.* **-li•er, -li•est 1.** Not in accord with accepted standards of good taste; grossly improper. **2.** Not suited to the circumstances; inappropriate. ❖ *adv.* In an improper or inappropriate manner. —**un•seem′li•ness** *n.*

un•seen (ŭn-sēn′) *adj.* **1.** Not directly evident; invisible. **2.** Not previously read or studied: *an unseen translation.*

un•seg•re•gat•ed (ŭn-sĕg′rĭ-gā′tĭd) *adj.* Not segregated, esp. not racially segregated.

un•se•lec•tive (ŭn′sĭ-lĕk′tĭv) *adj.* **1.** Not selective; indiscriminate. **2.** Marked by random selection.

un•self•cons•cious or **un•self-cons•cious** (ŭn′sĕlf-kŏn′shəs) *adj.* Not self-conscious; natural and genuine. —**un′self•cons′cious•ly** *adv.* —**un′self•cons′cious•ness** *n.*

un•sell (ŭn-sĕl′) *tr.v.* **-sold** (-sōld′), **-sell•ing, -sells** To persuade not to believe in the advisability, worth, or truth of something.

un•set (ŭn-sĕt′) *adj.* **1.** Not yet firm or solidified: *unset cement.* **2.** Not mounted in a setting: *an unset gem.*

un•set•tle (ŭn-sĕt′l) *v.* **-tled, -tling, -tles** —*tr.* **1.** To displace from a settled condition; disrupt. **2.** To make uneasy; disturb. —*intr.* To become unsettled. —**un•set′tle•ment** *n.*

un•set•tled (ŭn-sĕt′ld) *adj.* **1.** Not in a state of order or calmness; disturbed: *these unsettled times.* **2.** Likely to change or vary; variable: *unsettled weather.* **3a.** Not determined or resolved: *an unsettled issue.* **b.** Uncertain or doubtful: *unsettled with respect to their future plans.* **4.** Not paid or adjusted; outstanding: *an unsettled bill.* **5.** Not populated; uninhabited. **6.** Not fixed or established: *an unsettled way of life.*

un•sex (ŭn-sĕks′) *tr.v.* **-sexed, -sex•ing, -sex•es 1.** To deprive of sexual capacity or sexual attributes. **2.** To castrate.

un•shak•a•ble (ŭn-shā′kə-bəl) *adj.* Incapable of being shaken: *unshakable faith.* —**un•shak′a•bly** *adv.*

un•shaped (ŭn-shāpt′) *adj.* **1.** Not shaped or formed. **2.** Imperfectly shaped or formed.

un•shap•en (ŭn-shā′pən) *adj.* Unshaped.

un•shell (ŭn-shĕl′) *tr.v.* **-shelled, -shell•ing, -shells** To remove from a shell.

ă	pat	oi	boy
ā	pay	ou	out
âr	care	ŏŏ	took
ä	father	ōō	boot
ĕ	pet	ŭ	cut
ē	be	ûr	urge
ĭ	pit	th	thin
ī	pie	*th*	this
îr	pier	hw	which
ŏ	pot	zh	vision
ō	toe	ə	about,
ô	paw		item

Stress marks:
′ (primary);
′ (secondary); as in
lexicon (lĕk′sĭ-kŏn′)

un•shift (ŭn-shĭft′) *intr.v.* **-shift•ed, -shift•ing, -shifts** To release the shift key on a typewriter or computer keyboard.

un•ship (ŭn-shĭp′) *v.* **-shipped, -ship•ping, -ships** —*tr.* **1.** To unload from a ship; discharge. **2.** To remove (a piece of gear) from its proper place; detach: *unship an oar.* —*intr.* To become or be capable of becoming removed or detached.

un•shod (ŭn-shŏd′) *adj.* Not having or wearing shoes or a shoe: *unshod horses.*

un•sight•ly (ŭn-sīt′lē) *adj.* **-li•er, -li•est** Unpleasant or offensive to look at; unattractive. —**un′sight′li•ness** *n.*

un•skill•ful (ŭn-skĭl′fəl) *adj.* **1.** Unskilled; inexpert. **2.** *Obsolete* Ignorant. —**un•skill′ful•ly** *adv.* —**un′skill′ful•ness** *n.*

un•sling (ŭn-slĭng′) *tr.v.* **-slung** (-slŭng′), **-sling•ing, -slings 1.** To remove from a sling or a slung position: *unsling a bag.* **2.** *Nautical* To remove the slings of (a yard, for example).

un•snag (ŭn-snăg′) *tr.v.* **-snagged, -snag•ging, -snags** To free of snags.

un•snap (ŭn-snăp′) *tr.v.* **-snapped, -snap•ping, -snaps** To loosen, unfasten, or free by or as if by undoing snaps.

un•snarl (ŭn-snärl′) *tr.v.* **-snarled, -snarl•ing, -snarls** To free of snarls; disentangle.

un•so•cia•ble (ŭn-sō′shə-bəl) *adj.* **1.** Not disposed to seek the company of others; reserved. **2.** Not congenial; incompatible. **3.** Not conducive to social exchange. —**un•so′cia•bil′i•ty, un•so′cia•ble•ness** *n.* —**un•so′cia•bly** *adv.*

un•so•cial (ŭn-sō′shəl) *adj.* Having or showing a lack of desire for the company of others. —**un•so′cial•ly** *adv.*

un•sold (ŭn-sōld′) *v.* Past tense of **unsell.**

un•so•phis•ti•cat•ed (ŭn′sə-fĭs′tĭ-kā′tĭd) *adj.* Not sophisticated. See Syns at **naive.** —**un′so•phis′ti•cat•ed•ly** *adv.* —**un′so•phis′ti•ca′tion** *n.*

un•sought (ŭn-sôt′, ŭn′sôt′) *adj.* Not looked or asked for: *received some unsought advice.*

un•spar•ing (ŭn-spâr′ĭng) *adj.* **1.** Unmerciful; severe: *unsparing criticism.* **2.** Not frugal; generous. —**un•spar′ing•ly** *adv.*

un•speak (ŭn-spēk′) *tr.v.* **-spoke** (-spōk′), **-spo•ken** (-spō′kən), **-speak•ing, -speaks** *Obsolete* To retract (something spoken); unsay.

un•speak•a•ble (ŭn-spē′kə-bəl) *adj.* **1.** Beyond description; inexpressible: *unspeakable joy.* **2.** Inexpressibly bad or objectionable: *unspeakable ills.* **3.** Not to be spoken: *unspeakable ideas.* —**un•speak′a•bly** *adv.*

un•spe•cial•ized (ŭn-spĕsh′ə-līzd′) *adj.* **1.** Without specialty or specialization. **2.** Having no special function: *unspecialized cells.*

un•sphere (ŭn-sfîr′) *tr.v.* **-sphered, -spher•ing, -spheres** To remove from a sphere or position in the heavens.

un•spo•ken (ŭn-spō′kən) *adj.* **1.** Not uttered or expressed: *unspoken resentment.* **2.** Understood without the need for words: *an unspoken pact.*

un•sports•man•like (ŭn-spôrts′mən-līk′, -spôrts′-) *adj.* Not displaying the qualities or behavior befitting a good sport.

un•spot•ted (ŭn-spŏt′ĭd) *adj.* **1.** Having no spots. **2.** Morally upright. —**un•spot′ted•ness** *n.*

un•sta•ble (ŭn-stā′bəl) *adj.* **-bler, -blest 1a.** Tending strongly to change: *unstable weather.* **b.** Not constant; fluctuating: *unstable vital signs.* **b.** Fickle. **b.** Lacking control of one's emotions; marked by unpredictable behavior. **3.** Not firmly placed; unsteady. **4.** *Chemistry* **a.** Decomposing readily. **b.** Highly or violently reactive. **5.** *Physics* **a.** Decaying relatively quickly. Used of subatomic particles. **b.** Radioactive. —**un•sta′ble•ness** *n.* —**un•sta′bly** *adv.*

un•stead•y (ŭn-stĕd′ē) *adj.* **-i•er, -i•est 1.** Not firm, solid, or securely in place; unstable. **2.** Fluctuating; changeable: *an unsteady market.* **3.** Not even or regular; wavering: *an unsteady voice.* ❖ *tr.v.* **-ied, -y•ing, -ies** To cause to become unsteady. —**un•stead′i•ly** *adv.* —**un•stead′i•ness** *n.*

un•step (ŭn-stĕp′) *tr.v.* **-stepped, -step•ping, -steps** *Nautical* To remove (a mast) from a step.

un•stick (ŭn-stĭk′) *tr.v.* **-stuck** (-stŭk′), **-stick•ing, -sticks** To free from a condition of adhesion: *couldn't unstick the door.*

un•stop (ŭn-stŏp′) *tr.v.* **-stopped, -stop•ping, -stops 1.** To remove a stopper from. **2.** To remove an obstruction from; open. **3.** *Music* To pull out the stops of (a pipe organ).

un•stop•pa•ble (ŭn-stŏp′ə-bəl) *adj.* Difficult or impossible to preclude or stop: "*This movement toward freedom is natural and unstoppable and good*" (Pauline Kael). —**un•stop′pa•bly** *adv.*

un•stopped (ŭn-stŏpt′) *adj.* **1.** Not stopped: *an era of unstopped progress in medicine.* **2.** Having no stopper or plug: *an unstopped bottle.* **3.** *Linguistics* Capable of being prolonged, as the consonants (z) and (l).

un•stressed (ŭn-strĕst′) *adj.* **1.** *Linguistics* Not stressed or accented: *an unstressed syllable.* **2.** Not subjected to stress.

un•string (ŭn-strĭng′) *tr.v.* **-strung** (-strŭng′), **-string•ing, -strings 1.** To remove from a string. **2.** To unfasten or loosen the strings of. **3.** *Informal* To deprive of composure or emotional stability; unnerve.

un•struc•tured (ŭn-strŭk′chərd) *adj.* **1.** Lacking a definite or formal structure or organization. **2.** Not regulated or regimented: *an unstructured environment.*

un•strung (ŭn-strŭng′) *adj.* **1.** Having a string or strings loosened or removed. **2.** *Informal* Emotionally upset.

un•stuck (ŭn-stŭk′) *adj.* Freed from being stuck. —*idiom:* **come** (or **become**) **unstuck** To break down or fall apart: *a marriage that came unstuck within a year.*

un•stud•ied (ŭn-stŭd′ēd) *adj.* **1.** Not contrived; natural: *unstudied grace.* **2.** Not gained by study or instruction; unschooled.

un•sub•scribe (ŭn′sŭb-skrīb′) *v.* **-scribed, -scrib•ing, -scribes** —*intr.* To cancel a subscription, esp. to an online publication, service, or mailing list. —*tr.* To cancel the subscription of (a subscriber): *Please unsubscribe me from your mailing list.*

un•sung (ŭn-sŭng′) *adj.* **1.** Not honored or praised; uncelebrated: *an unsung hero.* **2.** Not sung: *unsung hymns.*

un•sure (ŭn-shoor′, -shûr′) *adj.* **1.** Lacking confidence. **2.** Uncertain of the facts. **3.** Precarious; unstable; unreliable. —**un•sure′ly** *adv.*

un•sus•cep•ti•ble (ŭn′sə-sĕp′tə-bəl) *adj.* Not susceptible to or admitting of: *unsusceptible to illegal entry.*

un•sus•pect•ed (ŭn′sə-spĕk′tĭd) *adj.* **1.** Not under suspicion. **2.** Not known to exist: *an unsuspected disease.* —**un′sus•pect′ed•ly** *adv.*

un•sus•pect•ing (ŭn′sə-spĕk′tĭng) *adj.* Not suspicious; trusting. —**un′sus•pect′ing•ly** *adv.*

un•swear (ŭn-swâr′) *v.* **-swore** (-swôr′, -swōr′), **-sworn** (-swôrn′, -swōrn′), **-swear•ing, -swears** *Archaic* —*tr.* To retract (an oath), often by swearing another oath. —*intr.* To recant or retract something sworn.

un•swerv•ing (ŭn-swûr′vĭng) *adj.* **1.** Not veering or turning aside. **2.** Constant; steady: *unswerving devotion.* —**un•swerv′ing•ly** *adv.*

un•tan•gle (ŭn-tăng′gəl) *tr.v.* **-gled, -gling, -gles 1.** To free from a tangle; disentangle. **2.** To straighten out (something puzzling or complicated); clarify or resolve.

un•tapped (ŭn-tăpt′) *adj.* **1.** Not having been tapped: *an untapped cask of wine.* **2.** Not utilized: *untapped resources.*

un•taught (ŭn-tôt′) *adj.* **1.** Not instructed; ignorant. **2.** Not acquired by instruction; natural.

un•teach (ŭn-tēch′) *tr.v.* **-taught** (-tôt′), **-teach•ing, -teach•es 1.** To cause to forget or unlearn something. **2.** To teach the opposite or contrary of (something previously taught).

un•ten•a•ble (ŭn-tĕn′ə-bəl) *adj.* **1.** Being such that defense or maintenance is impossible: *an untenable position.* **2.** Being such that occupation or habitation is impossible. —**un•ten′a•bil′i•ty, un•ten′a•ble•ness** *n.* —**un•ten′a•bly** *adv.*

un•thank•ful (ŭn-thăngk′fəl) *adj.* **1.** Not thankful; ungrateful. **2.** Not drawing thanks; unwelcome. —**un•thank′ful•ly** *adv.*

un•think (ŭn-thĭngk′) *tr.v.* **-thought** (-thôt′), **-think•ing, -thinks** To dismiss from the mind; disregard.

un•think•a•ble (ŭn-thĭng′kə-bəl) *adj.* **1.** Impossible to imagine; inconceivable. **2.** Contrary to what is plausible or probable. **3.** Not to be thought of or considered. —**un•think′a•bil′i•ty, un•think′a•ble•ness** *n.* —**un•think′a•bly** *adv.*

un•think•ing (ŭn′thĭng′kĭng) *adj.* **1.** Not taking due thought; thoughtless or heedless. **2.** Exhibiting a lack of thought: *unthinking bravado.* **3.** Incapable of the power of thought. —**un•think′ing•ly** *adv.*

un•thread (ŭn-thrĕd′) *tr.v.* **-thread•ed, -thread•ing, -threads 1.** To draw out the thread from. **2.** To find one's way out of (a labyrinth, for example).

un•ti•dy (ŭn-tī′dē) *adj.* **-di•er, -di•est 1.** Not neat and tidy; sloppy. **2.** Disorderly and unorganized: *untidy financial affairs.* —**un•ti′di•ly** *adv.* —**un•ti′di•ness** *n.*

un•tie (ŭn-tī′) *v.* **-tied, -ty•ing** (-tī′ĭng), **-ties** —*tr.* **1.** To undo or loosen (a knot or something knotted). **2.** To free from something that binds or restrains. **3.** To straighten out (difficulties, for example); resolve. —*intr.* To become untied.

un•til (ŭn-tĭl′) *prep.* **1.** Up to the time of: *danced until dawn.* **2.** Before (a specified time): *can't leave until Friday.* **3.** *Scots* Unto; to. ❖ *conj.* **1.** Up to the time that: *walked until it got dark.* **2.** Before: *You cannot leave until you are finished.* **3.** To the point or extent that: *I talked until I was hoarse.* See Usage Note at **till**[2]. [ME : *un-*, up to (< ON *und*; see **ant-** in App.) + *til,* till; see TILL[2].]

un•time•ly (ŭn-tīm′lē) *adj.* **-li•er, -li•est 1.** Occurring or done at an inappropriate time; inopportune. **2.** Occurring too soon; premature: *an untimely death.* ❖ *adv.* **1.** Inopportunely. **2.** Prematurely. —**un•time′li•ness** *n.*

un•tir•ing (ŭn-tīr′ĭng) *adj.* **1.** Not tiring; tireless. **2.** Not ceasing despite fatigue or frustration; indefatigable: *untiring efforts.* —**un•tir′ing•ly** *adv.*

un•ti•tled (ŭn-tīt′ld) *adj.* **1.** Not named. **2.** Not holding a title, as of nobility. **3.** Having no right or claim.

un•to (ŭn′tōo) *prep.* **1.** To. **2.** *Used to death.* **3.** By: *a place unto itself.* [ME : *un-*, up to; see UNTIL + *to*, to; see TO.]

un•told (ŭn-tōld′) *adj.* **1.** Not told or revealed: *untold secrets.* **2.** Beyond description or enumeration: *untold suffering.*

un•touch•a•ble (ŭn-tŭch′ə-bəl) *adj.* **1.** Not to be touched. **2.** Out of reach; unobtainable. **3.** Being beyond the reach of criticism, impeachment, or attack. **4.** Loathsome or unpleasant to the touch. ❖ *n.* often **Untouchable** *Hinduism* A member of the class that is excluded from and considered unclean and defiling by the four Hindu castes. —**un•touch′a•bil′i•ty** *n.* —**un•touch′a•bly** *adv.*

un•to•ward (ŭn-tôrd′, -tōrd′) *adj.* **1.** Not favorable; unpropitious. **2.** Troublesome; adverse: *an untoward incident.* **3.** Hard to guide or control; unruly. **4.** Improper; unseemly. **5.** *Archaic* Awkward. —**un•to•ward′ly** *adv.* —**un•to•ward′ness** *n.*

un•tram•meled (ŭn-trăm′əld) *adj.* Not limited or restricted.

un•trav•eled (ŭn-trăv′əld) *adj.* **1.** Not traveled on. **2a.** Not having traveled. **b.** Provincial; narrow-minded.

un•tread (ŭn-trĕd′) *tr.v.* **-trod** (-trŏd′), **-trod•den** (-trŏd′n) or **-trod, -tread•ing, -treads** *Archaic* To go back over (one's course); retrace.

un•tried (ŭn-trīd′) *adj.* **1.** Not attempted, tested, or proved. **2.** *Law* Not tried in court.

un•true (ŭn-trōō′) *adj.* **-tru•er, -tru•est** **1.** Contrary to fact; false. **2.** Deviating from a standard; not straight, even, level, or exact. **3.** Disloyal; unfaithful. —**un•tru′ly** *adv.*

un•truss (ŭn-trŭs′) *v.* **-trussed, -truss•ing, -truss•es** *Archaic* —*tr.* **1.** To unfasten; undo. **2.** To undress. —*intr.* To remove one's clothes, esp. one's breeches.

un•truth (ŭn-trōōth′) *n.* **1.** Something untrue; a lie. **2.** The condition of being false; lack of truth. **3.** *Archaic* Unfaithfulness.

un•truth•ful (ŭn-trōōth′fəl) *adj.* **1.** Contrary to truth. **2.** Given to falsehood; mendacious. —**un•truth′ful•ly** *adv.* —**un•truth′-ful•ness** *n.*

un•tu•tored (ŭn-tōō′tərd, -tyōō′-) *adj.* **1.** Having had no formal education or instruction. **2.** Unsophisticated; unrefined.

un•ty•ing (ŭn-tī′ĭng) *v.* Present participle of **untie.**

un•un•bi•um (ə-nŭn′bē-əm) *n.* Element 112. [Lat. *ūnus,* one; see UNION + Lat. *ūnus* + Lat. *bi-,* bi- + –IUM.]

un•un•nil•i•um (ə-nə-nĭl′ē-əm) *n.* Element 110. [Lat. *ūnus,* one; see UNION + Lat. *ūnus* + Lat. *nīl,* nothing; see NIL + –IUM.]

un•un•un•i•um (ə-nə-nŭn′ē-əm) *n.* Element 111. [Lat. *ūnus,* one; see UNION + Lat. *ūnus* + Lat. *ūnus* + –IUM.]

un•used (ŭn-yōōzd′, ŭn-yōōst′) *adj.* **1.** Not in use or put to use. **2.** Never having been used. **3.** Not accustomed.

un•u•su•al (ŭn-yōō′zhōō-əl) *adj.* Not usual, common, or ordinary. —**un•u′su•al•ly** *adv.* —**un•u′su•al•ness** *n.*

un•ut•ter•a•ble (ŭn-ŭt′ər-ə-bəl) *adj.* **1.** That cannot or must not be uttered or expressed: *unutterable beauty.* **2.** Being such that pronunciation is impossible. —**un•ut′ter•a•bly** *adv.*

un•val•ued (ŭn-văl′yōōd) *adj.* **1.** Not prized or valued; unappreciated. **2.** Not appraised or assayed: *an unvalued gemstone.* **3.** *Obsolete* Inestimable; invaluable.

un•var•nished (ŭn-vär′nĭsht) *adj.* **1.** Not coated with varnish: *unvarnished floors.* **2.** Stated or otherwise presented without any effort to soften or disguise; plain.

un•veil (ŭn-vāl′) *v.* **-veiled, -veil•ing, -veils** —*tr.* **1.** To remove a veil or covering from. **2.** To disclose; reveal. —*intr.* **1.** To take off one's veil. **2.** To reveal oneself.

un•voice (ŭn-vois′) *tr.v.* **-voiced, -voic•ing, -voic•es** To devoice.

un•voiced (ŭn-voist′) *adj.* **1.** Not expressed or uttered: *unvoiced fears.* **2.** *Linguistics* Voiceless: *unvoiced consonants.*

un•war•rant•a•ble (ŭn-wôr′ən-tə-bəl, -wŏr′-) *adj.* Not justifiable; inexcusable. —**un′war′rant•a•bly** *adv.*

un•war•rant•ed (ŭn-wôr′ən-tĭd, -wŏr′-) *adj.* Having no justification; groundless.

un•washed (ŭn-wŏsht′, -wôsht′) *adj.* **1.** Not washed; unclean. **2.** Plebeian: *the unwashed masses.*

un•wea•ried (ŭn-wîr′ēd) *adj.* **1.** Not tired. **2.** Never wearying; tireless. —**un•wea′ried•ly** *adv.*

un•well (ŭn-wĕl′) *adj.* **1.** Being in poor health; sick. **2.** Menstruating.

un•wept (ŭn-wĕpt′) *adj.* **1.** Not mourned or wept for: *the unwept dead.* **2.** Not yet shed: *unwept tears.*

un•whole•some (ŭn-hōl′səm) *adj.* **1.** Injurious to physical, mental, or moral health; unhealthy. **2.** Suggestive of disease or degeneracy: *an unwholesome pallor.* **3.** Offensive or loathsome. —**un•whole′some•ly** *adv.* —**un•whole′some•ness** *n.*

un•wield•y (ŭn-wēl′dē) *adj.* **-i•er, -i•est** Difficult to carry or manage because of size, shape, weight, or complexity: *an unwieldy parcel.* —**un•wield′i•ly** *adv.* —**un•wield′i•ness** *n.*

un•willed (ŭn-wĭld′) *adj.* Involuntary; spontaneous.

un•will•ing (ŭn-wĭl′ĭng) *adj.* **1.** Not willing; hesitant or loath: *unwilling to face facts.* **2.** Done, given, or said reluctantly. —**un•will′ing•ly** *adv.* —**un•will′ing•ness** *n.*

un•wind (ŭn-wīnd′) *v.* **-wound** (-wound′), **-wind•ing, -winds** —*tr.* **1.** To reverse the winding or twisting of: *unwind a ball of yarn.* **2.** To separate the tangled parts of; disentangle. **3.** To free of nervous tension or pent-up energy. —*intr.* **1.** To become unwound. **2.** To become free of nervous tension; relax.

un•wis•dom (ŭn-wĭz′dəm) *n.* Lack of wisdom; imprudence or recklessness.

un•wise (ŭn-wīz′) *adj.* **-wis•er, -wis•est** Lacking or exhibiting a lack of wisdom; foolish or imprudent: *an unwise act.* —**un•wise′ly** *adv.*

un•wish (ŭn-wĭsh′) *tr.v.* **-wished, -wish•ing, -wish•es** **1.** To retract a wish for. **2.** *Obsolete* To wish out of existence.

un•wit•ting (ŭn-wĭt′ĭng) *adj.* **1.** Not knowing; unaware: *an unwitting dupe.* **2.** Not intended; unintentional: *an unwitting admission of guilt.* [ME *un-,* not; see UN–[1] + *witting,* pr. part. of *witten,* to know (< OE *witan;* see **weid-** in App.).] —**un•wit′ting•ly** *adv.*

un•wont•ed (ŭn-wôn′tĭd, -wōn′-, -wŭn′-) *adj.* **1.** Not habitual or ordinary; unusual: *"Her unwonted breach of delicacy . . . perplexed him"* (George Meredith). **2.** Not accustomed; unused. —**un•wont′ed•ly** *adv.*

un•world•ly (ŭn-wûrld′lē) *adj.* **-li•er, -li•est** **1.** Not of this world; spiritual. **2.** Concerned with matters of the spirit or soul. **3.** Not wise to the ways of the world; naive. —**un•world′li•ness** *n.*

un•wor•thy (ŭn-wûr′thē) *adj.* **-thi•er, -thi•est** **1a.** Insufficient in worth; undeserving: *a plan unworthy of consideration.* **b.** Lacking value or merit; worthless. **2.** Not suiting or befitting: *"The acquaintances she had already formed were unworthy of her"* (Jane Austen). **3.** Vile; despicable. —**un•wor′thi•ly** *adv.* —**un•wor′thi•ness** *n.*

un•wrap (ŭn-răp′) *tr. & intr.v.* **-wrapped, -wrap•ping, -wraps** To remove the wrapping or wrappings from or become unwrapped.

un•writ•ten (ŭn-rĭt′n) *adj.* **1.** Not written or recorded: *an unwritten agreement between friends.* **2.** Having authority based on custom, tradition, or usage rather than documentation. **3.** Not written on; blank.

un•yield•ing (ŭn-yēl′dĭng) *adj.* **1.** Not bending; inflexible. **2.** Not giving way to pressure or persuasion; obdurate: *an unyielding stance.* —**un•yield′ing•ly** *adv.*

un•yoke (ŭn-yōk′) *v.* **-yoked, -yok•ing, -yokes** —*tr.* **1.** To release from or as if from a yoke. **2.** To separate; disjoin. —*intr.* **1.** To remove a yoke. **2.** *Archaic* To stop working.

un•zip (ŭn-zĭp′) *tr. & intr.v.* **-zipped, -zip•ping, -zips** To open or unfasten by means of a zipper or become unzipped.

up (ŭp) *adv.* **1a.** In or to a higher position: *looking up.* **b.** In a direction opposite to the center of the earth or a comparable gravitational center: *up from the lunar surface.* **2.** In or to an upright position: *sat up in bed.* **3a.** Above a surface: *coming up for air.* **b.** So as to detach or unearth: *pulling up weeds.* **c.** Above the horizon: *as the sun came up.* **4.** Into view or existence: *draw up a will.* **5.** Into consideration: *take up a new topic.* **6.** In or toward a position conventionally regarded as higher, as on a scale, chart, or map: *up in Canada.* **7.** To or at a higher price: *Stocks are going up.* **8.** So as to advance, increase, or improve: *Our spirits went up.* **9.** With or to a greater intensity, pitch, or volume: *turn the sound up.* **10.** Into a state of excitement or turbulence: *rouse up.* **11.** Completely; entirely: *fastened up the coat.* **12.** Used as an intensifier of the action of a verb: *typed up a list.* **13.** So as to approach; near: *came up and kissed me.* **14.** To a stop: *pulled up to the curb.* **15.** Each; apiece: *The score was tied at 11 up.* **16.** Apart; into pieces: *tore it up.* **17.** *Nautical* To windward. ❖ *adj.* **1.** Being above a former position or level; higher: *My grades are up.* **2a.** Out of bed: *was up by seven.* **b.** Standing; erect. **c.** Facing upward: *the up side of a tossed coin.* **3.** Raised; lifted: *a switch in the up position.* **4.** Moving or directed upward: *an up elevator.* **5a.** Marked by increased excitement or agitation; aroused: *Our spirit was up.* **b.** *Informal* Cheerful; optimistic; upbeat. **c.** *Slang* Happily excited; euphoric: *I was really up after winning the award.* **6.** *Informal* Taking place; going on: *wondered what was up back home.* **7.** Being considered; under study: *a contract up for renewal.* **8.** Running as a candidate: *up for mayor.* **9.** On trial; charged: *The defendant is up for manslaughter.* **10.** Having been finished; over: *Your time is up.* **11.** *Informal* **a.** Prepared; ready: *up for the game.* **b.** Well informed; abreast: *not up on sports.* **12.** Functioning or capable of functioning normally; operational: *Their computers are now up.* **13.** *Sports* Being ahead of one's opponent: *up two strokes in golf.* **14.** *Baseball* At bat. **15.** As a bet; at stake. **16.** *Nautical* Bound; headed: *a freighter up for Panama.* ❖ *prep.* **1.** From a lower to or toward a higher point on: *up the hill.* **2.** Toward or at a point farther away: *two miles up the road.* **3.** In a direction toward the source of: *up the Mississippi.* **4.** *Nautical* Against: *up the wind.* ❖ *n.* **1.** An upward slope; a rise. **2.** An upward movement or trend. **3.** *Slang* A feeling of excitement or euphoria. ❖ *v.* **upped, up•ping, ups** —*tr.* **1.** To increase: *upped their fees.* **2.** To raise to a higher level, esp. to promote to a higher position. **3.** *Nautical* To raise: *up anchor.* —*intr.* **1.** To get up; rise. **2.** *Informal* To act suddenly or unexpectedly: *"She upped and perjured her immortal soul"* (Margery Allingham). —**idioms: on the up-and-up** (or **up and up**) *Informal* Open and honest. **up against** Confronted with; facing: *up against a strong opponent.* **up to 1.** Occupied with, esp. devising or scheming: *up to no good.* **2.** Able to do or deal with: *didn't feel up to a long drive.* **3.** Dependent on: *The success of this project is up to us.* **4a.** To the point of; as far as: *I'm up to page 100 in the book.* **b.** As long as: *allowed up to two hours for the test.* **c.** As many as: *seed that yields up to 300 bushels per acre.* [ME *up,* upward, and *uppe,* on high, both < OE *ūp.* See **upo** in App.]

UP *abbr.* **1.** underproof **2.** Upper Peninsula

up– *pref.* **1.** Up; upward: *upheave.* **2.** Upper: *upland.* [ME < OE *ūp-, upp-.* See **upo** in App.]

up-and-com•ing (ŭp′ən-kŭm′ĭng) *adj.* Showing signs of advancement and ambitious development. —**up′-and-com′er** *n.*

up-and-down (ŭp′ən-doun′) *adj.* **1.** Characterized by or exhibiting an alternating upward and downward movement. **2.** Variable; changeable. **3.** Vertical.

U•pan•i•shad (ōō-pän′ə-shäd′, ōō-pä′nĭ-shäd′) *n.* Any of a group of philosophical treatises that explicate the theology of the

John Updike

upland sandpiper
Bartramia longicauda

upright piano

Vedas. [Skt. *upaniṣad* : *upa*, under, near; see **upo** in App. + *ni-*, down + *sīdati, sad-*, he sits; see **sed-** in App.] —**U·pan'i·shad'ic** *adj.*

u·pas (yōō'pəs) *n.* **1.** A deciduous tree (*Antiaris toxicaria*) of tropical Africa and Asia that yields a latex used as an arrow poison. **2.** The poison obtained from this tree or from similar trees. [Malay (*pohun*) *upas*, poison (tree), of Javanese orig.]

up·beat (ŭp'bēt') *n.* **1.** *Music* An unaccented beat or beats that occur before the first beat of a measure. **2.** The upward stroke made by a conductor to indicate the beat that leads into a new measure. ❖ *adj. Informal* **1.** Optimistic: *an upbeat business forecast.* **2.** Happy; cheerful.

up·bow (ŭp'bō') *n.* A stroke on a stringed instrument in which the bow is moved across the strings from tip to heel.

up·braid (ŭp-brād') *tr.v.* **-braid·ed, -braid·ing, -braids** To reprove sharply; reproach. [ME *upbreiden* < OE *ūpbrēdan*, to bring forward as a ground for censure : *ūp-*, up- + *bregdan*, to turn, lay hold of.] —**up·braid'er** *n.*

up·bring·ing (ŭp'brĭng'ĭng) *n.* The rearing and training received during childhood.

UPC *abbr.* Universal Product Code

up·cast (ŭp'kăst') *adj.* Directed or thrown upward: *upcast volcanic ash.* ❖ *n.* **1.** Something cast upward. **2.** A ventilating shaft, as in a mine.

up·chuck (ŭp'chŭk') *tr. & intr.v.* **-chucked, -chuck·ing, -chucks** To vomit or experience vomiting.

up·com·ing (ŭp'kŭm'ĭng) *adj.* Occurring soon; forthcoming.

up·coun·try (ŭp'kŭn'trē) *n.* An inland or upland region of a country. ❖ *adj.* Of, located in, or coming from the upcountry. ❖ *adv.* (also ŭp-kŭn'trē) In, to, or toward the upcountry.

up·date (ŭp-dāt') *tr.v.* **-dat·ed, -dat·ing, -dates** To bring up to date: *update the files.* ❖ *n.* (ŭp'dāt') **1.** Information that updates something. **2.** The act or an instance of bringing up to date. **3.** An updated version of something.

Up·dike (ŭp'dīk'), **John Hoyer** b. 1932. Amer. writer noted for his tragicomic novels, such as *Rabbit, Run* (1960).

up·draft (ŭp'drăft') *n.* An upward current of air.

up·end (ŭp-ĕnd') *v.* **-end·ed, -end·ing, -ends** —*tr.* **1.** To stand, set, or turn on one end: *upend an oblong box.* **2.** To invalidate, destroy, or change completely; overthrow. **3.** To win victory over; defeat. —*intr.* To be upended.

up-front or **up·front** (ŭp'frŭnt') *Informal adj.* **1.** Straightforward; frank. **2.** Paid or due in advance: *up-front cash.* ❖ *adv.* also **up front** In advance; beforehand: *demanded to be paid up front.*

up·grade (ŭp'grād') *v.* **-grad·ed, -grad·ing, -grades** —*tr.* **1.** To raise to a higher grade or standard. **2.** To improve the quality of (livestock) by selective breeding. **3.** *Computer Science* To replace (a software program, for example) with an enhanced or improved version. —*intr.* **1.** To exchange a possession for one of greater value or quality; trade up. **2.** *Computer Science* To replace software or hardware with an upgrade. ❖ *n.* **1.** The act or an instance of upgrading. **2.** *Computer Science* An enhanced or improved software program or hardware device. **3.** An upward incline. ❖ *adv. & adj.* Uphill. —*idiom:* **on the upgrade** Improving or progressing.

up·growth (ŭp'grōth') *n.* **1.** The process of growing upward. **2.** Upward development.

up·heav·al (ŭp-hē'vəl) *n.* **1a.** The process of being heaved upward. **b.** An instance of being so heaved. **2.** A sudden violent disruption or upset. **3.** *Geology* A raising of a part of the earth's crust.

up·heave (ŭp-hēv') *v.* **-heaved, -heav·ing, -heaves** —*tr.* To lift forcefully from beneath; heave upward. —*intr.* To be lifted or thrust upward.

up·hill (ŭp'hĭl') *adj.* **1.** Located on high or higher ground: *an uphill mine entrance.* **2.** Going up a hill or slope. **3.** Marked by difficulty or strong resistance; laborious. ❖ *adv.* (ŭp'hĭl') **1.** To or toward higher ground; up a slope. **2.** Against adversity; with difficulty. ❖ *n.* An upward slope or incline.

up·hold (ŭp-hōld') *tr.v.* **-held** (-hĕld'), **-hold·ing, -holds 1.** To hold aloft; raise: *upheld the banner.* **2.** To prevent from falling or sinking; support. **3.** To maintain or affirm against opposition. See Syns at **support.** —**up·hold'er** *n.*

up·hol·ster (ŭp-hōl'stər, ə-pōl'-) *tr.v.* **-stered, -ster·ing, -sters** To supply (furniture) with stuffing, springs, cushions, and covering fabric. [Back-formation < UPHOLSTERER.]

up·hol·ster·er (ŭp-hōl'stər-ər, ə-pōl'-) *n.* One that upholsters furniture. [< obsolete *upholster* < ME *upholdester* : *upholden*, to repair (*up*, up; see UP + *holden*, to hold; see HOLD¹) + *-ster*, -ster.]

up·hol·ster·y (ŭp-hōl'stə-rē, -strē, ə-pōl'-) *n., pl.* **-ies 1.** Fabric, stuffing, and other materials used in upholstering. **2.** The craft, trade, or business of upholstering.

up·keep (ŭp'kēp') *n.* **1.** Maintenance in proper operation, condition, and repair. **2.** The cost of such maintenance.

up·land (ŭp'lənd, -lănd') *n.* **1.** Land or an area of land of high elevation, esp. when level. **2.** Land in the interior of a country. ❖ *adj.* Of, relating to, or located in an upland.

upland cotton *n.* A tropical American plant (*Gossypium hirsutum*) widely cultivated for the woolly lint around its seeds.

upland sandpiper *n.* A large brownish sandpiper (*Bartramia longicauda*) inhabiting the fields and uplands of eastern North America.

up·lift (ŭp-lĭft') *tr.v.* **-lift·ed, -lift·ing, -lifts 1.** To raise; elevate. **2.** To raise to a higher social, intellectual, or moral level or condition. **3.** To raise to spiritual or emotional heights; exalt: *Music uplifts the spirit.* ❖ *adj.* (ŭp'lĭft') Uplifted. ❖ *n.* (ŭp'lĭft') **1.** The act, process, or result of raising or lifting up. **2.** An effort or a movement to improve social, moral, or intellectual standards. **3.** *Geology* An upheaval.

up·link (ŭp'lĭngk') *n.* A transmission path by which radio or other signals are sent to an aircraft or a communications satellite.

up·load (ŭp'lōd') *v.* **-load·ed, -load·ing, -loads** —*tr.* To transfer (data or programs), usu. from a peripheral computer or device to a central computer or bulletin board. —*intr.* To upload data or programs.

up·man·ship (ŭp'mən-shĭp') *n.* One-upmanship.

up·mar·ket (ŭp'mär'kĭt) *adj.* Appealing to or designed for high-income consumers; upscale.

up·most (ŭp'mōst') *adj.* Uppermost.

U·po·lu (ōō-pō'lōō) A volcanic island of Samoa (formerly Western Samoa) in the S Pacific; site of Apia, the country's capital.

up·on (ə-pŏn', ə-pôn') *prep.* On. See Usage Note at **on.**

up·per (ŭp'ər) *adj.* **1.** Higher in place, position, or rank: *the upper bunk.* **2a.** Situated on higher ground: *upper regions.* **b.** also **Upper** Lying farther inland: *the upper Nile.* **c.** also **Upper** Northern: *the upper Midwest.* **3. Upper** *Geology & Archaeology* Of, relating to, or being a later division of the period named. **4.** Denoting the smaller and more. less broadly representative house of a bicameral legislature. ❖ *n.* **1.** The part of a shoe or boot above the sole. **2.** *Informal* An upper berth. **3. uppers** *Informal* The upper teeth or a set of upper dentures. **4.** *Slang* **a.** A drug, esp. an amphetamine, used as a stimulant. **b.** An exhilarating or euphoric experience. —*idiom:* **on (one's) uppers** *Informal* Impoverished; destitute.

upper atmosphere *n.* The part of the atmosphere above the troposphere.

Upper Avon See Avon.

upper bound *n.* A number that is greater than or equal to every number in a given set of real numbers.

Upper California See Alta California.

Upper Canada A historical region and province of British North America roughly coextensive with S Ontario; formed in 1791 and joined with Lower Canada in 1841.

Upper Carboniferous *n.* See Pennsylvanian 2.

up·per·case (ŭp'ər-kās') *Printing adj.* Of, written, formatted, or printed in capital letters: *an uppercase A.* ❖ *tr.v.* **-cased, -cas·ing, -cas·es 1.** To put (type or text) in uppercase letters. **2.** To begin a word with an uppercase letter.

upper class *n.* The highest socioeconomic class in a society. —**up'per-class'** (ŭp'ər-klăs') *adj.*

up·per·class·man (ŭp'ər-klăs'mən) *n.* A student in the junior or senior class of a secondary school or college.

upper crust *n. Informal* The highest social class or group. —**up'per-crust'** (ŭp'ər-krŭst') *adj.*

up·per·cut (ŭp'ər-kŭt') *n.* A swinging blow directed upward, as to a boxing opponent's chin.

Upper Egypt A region of ancient Egypt in the valley of the Nile R. S of the delta area, which was known as Lower Egypt. The two regions were united c. 3100 B.C.

upper hand *n.* A position of control or advantage.

up·per·most (ŭp'ər-mōst') *adv. & adj.* In the highest position, place, or rank.

Upper Palatinate See Palatinate.

Upper Peninsula The N part of MI between Lakes Superior and Michigan.

Upper Tunguska See Tunguska.

Upper Vol·ta (vŏl'tə, vōl'-) See Burkina Faso. —**Upper Vol·tan** *adj. & n.*

up·pish (ŭp'ĭsh) *adj. Informal* Uppity. —**up'pish·ly** *adv.*

up·pi·ty (ŭp'ĭ-tē) *adj. Informal* Taking liberties or assuming airs beyond one's station; presumptuous. [< UP.] —**up'pi·ti·ness, up'pi·ty·ness** *n.*

Upp·sa·la (ŭp'sə-lə, -sä'-, ōōp'sä'lä) A city of E Sweden NNW of Stockholm; cap. of a pre-Christian kingdom in the early Middle Ages. Pop. 174,554.

up quark *n.* A quark with a charge of $+\frac{2}{3}$, a mass about 607 times that of the electron, and an upward spin.

up·raise (ŭp-rāz') *tr.v.* **-raised, -rais·ing, -rais·es** To raise or lift up; elevate.

up·rear (ŭp-rîr') *v.* **-reared, -rear·ing, -rears** —*tr.* To raise or lift up. —*intr.* To rise up: *The stallion upreared.*

up·right (ŭp'rīt') *adj.* **1a.** Being in a vertical position or direction: *an upright post.* **b.** Erect in posture or carriage. **2.** Adhering strictly to moral principles; righteous. ❖ *adv.* Vertically: *walk upright.* ❖ *n.* **1.** A perpendicular position; verticality. **2.** Something, such as a goalpost, that stands upright. **3.** An upright piano. ❖ *tr.v.* **-right·ed, -right·ing, -rights** To restore to an upright position. —**up'right'ly** *adv.*

upright piano *n.* A piano having the strings mounted vertically in a rectangular case with the keyboard at a right angle to the case.

up•rise (ŭp-rīz′) *intr.v.* **-rose** (-rōz′), **-ris•en** (-rĭz′ən), **-ris•ing, -ris•es 1.** To get up or stand up; rise. **2.** To go, move, or incline upward; ascend. **3.** To rise into view, esp. from below the horizon. **4.** To increase in pitch or volume; swell. ❖ *n.* (ŭp′rīz′) **1.** The act or process of rising. **2.** An upward slope.

up•ris•ing (ŭp′rī′zĭng) *n.* **1.** A sometimes limited popular revolt against a government or its policies; a rebellion. **2.** The act or an instance of rising or rising up.

up•riv•er (ŭp′rĭv′ər) *adv. & adj.* Toward or near the source of a river; in the direction opposite to that of the current.

up•roar (ŭp′rôr′, -rōr′) *n.* **1.** A state of noisy excitement and confusion; tumult: *"The uproar of the street sounded violently and hideously cacophonous"* (Virginia Woolf). **2.** A heated controversy. [Prob. by folk ety. < MLGer. *uprōr* : *up-*, up (< *up*); see **upo** in App. + *rōr*, motion.]

up•roar•i•ous (ŭp-rôr′ē-əs, -rōr′-) *adj.* **1.** Causing or accompanied by an uproar. **2.** Loud and full; boisterous: *uproarious laughter.* **3.** Causing hearty laughter; hilarious: *uproarious tales.* —**up•roar′i•ous•ly** *adv.* —**up•roar′i•ous•ness** *n.*

up•root (ŭp-ro͞ot′, -ro͝ot′) *tr.v.* **-root•ed, -root•ing, -roots 1.** To pull up (a plant and its roots) from the ground. **2.** To destroy or remove completely. **3.** To force to leave an accustomed or native location. —**up•root′ed•ness** *n.* —**up•root′er** *n.*

up•rush (ŭp′rŭsh′) *n.* The swift advance of water from a breaking wave onto a beach.

up•scale (ŭp′skāl′) *adj.* Of, intended for, or relating to high-income consumers: *upscale fashions.* ❖ *tr.v.* (*also* ŭp-skāl′) **-scaled, -scal•ing, -scales 1.** To raise to a higher level; upgrade. **2.** To redesign or market for higher-income consumers.

up•set (ŭp-sĕt′) *v.* **-set, -set•ting, -sets** —*tr.* **1.** To cause to turn or tip over; capsize. **2.** To disturb the functioning, order, or course of: *upset the meeting by shouting.* **3.** To distress or perturb mentally or emotionally: *The bad news upset me.* **4.** To overthrow; overturn: *upset a will.* See Syns at **overthrow. 5.** (ŭp′sĕt′) To defeat unexpectedly (an opponent favored to win). **6.** To make (a heated metal bolt, for example) shorter and thicker by hammering on the end. —*intr.* **1.** To become overturned; capsize. **2.** To become disturbed. ❖ *n.* (ŭp′sĕt′) **1.** The act of upsetting or the condition of being upset. **2.** A disturbance, disorder, or state of agitation. **3.** A game or contest in which the favorite is defeated. **4a.** A tool used for upsetting; a swage. **b.** An upset part or piece. ❖ *adj.* **1.** Having been overturned; capsized. **2.** Exhibiting signs and symptoms of indigestion: *an upset stomach.* **3.** In a state of emotional or mental distress; distraught: *upset parents.* [ME *upsetten*, to set up : *up-*, up- + *setten*, to set; see SET[1].] —**up•set′ter** *n.* —**up•set′ting•ly** *adv.*

upset price *n.* The lowest price at which an item of property may be auctioned or sold at public sale. [P. part. of UPSET, to establish (obsolete).]

up•shift (ŭp′shĭft′) *intr.v.* **-shift•ed, -shift•ing, -shifts** To shift a motor vehicle into a higher gear. —**up′shift′** *n.*

up•shot (ŭp′shŏt′) *n.* **1.** The final result; the outcome. See Syns at **effect. 2.** The central idea or point; the gist. [Earlier *upshot*, the last shot in an archery contest.]

up•side (ŭp′sīd′) *n.* **1.** The upper side or portion. **2.** An advantageous aspect. **3.** An upward tendency, as in business profitability.

upside down *adv.* **1.** So that the upper or right side is down: *turned upside down.* **2.** In great disorder. [Alteration of ME *up so doun*, up as if down : *up*, up; see UP + *so*, as if; see SO[1] + *doun*, down; see DOWN[1].] —**up′side-down′** (ŭp′sīd-doun′) *adj.*

upside-down cake *n.* A single-layer cake baked with sliced fruit at the bottom, then served with the fruit side up.

up•si•lon (ŭp′sə-lŏn′, yo͞op′-) *n.* The 20th letter of the Greek alphabet. [L.Gk. *ū psīlon*, simple u (< the fact that *oi* was given the same pronunciation in L.Gk. as *u*) : *ū*, *hū*, u + *psīlon*, neut. of *psīlos*, simple (written with one letter as opposed to two).]

upsilon particle *n.* An electrically neutral meson having a mass 18,513 times that of the electron and a mean lifetime of approx. 8.0×10^{-20} seconds.

up•size (ŭp′sīz′) *tr. & intr.v.* **-sized, -siz•ing, -siz•es** To make or become greater or larger.

up•spring (ŭp-sprĭng′) *intr. v.* **-sprang** (-sprăng′) or **-sprung** (-sprŭng′), **-sprung, -spring•ing, -springs 1.** To spring up, as from the soil. **2.** To come into being; arise.

up•stage (ŭp′stāj′) *adv.* Toward, at, or on the rear part of a stage. ❖ *adj.* **1.** Of or relating to the rear part of a stage. **2.** *Informal* Haughty; aloof. ❖ *n.* (ŭp′stāj′) The rear part of a stage, away from the audience. ❖ *tr.v.* (ŭp-stāj′) **-staged, -stag•ing, -stag•es 1.** To distract attention from (another performer) by moving upstage, thus forcing the other performer to face away from the audience. **2.** To divert attention or praise from. **3.** To treat haughtily. —**up•stag′er** *n.*

up•stairs (ŭp′stârz′) *adv.* **1.** Up the stairs: *raced upstairs.* **2.** To or on a higher floor: *went upstairs.* **3.** To or at a higher level: *was promoted upstairs.* ❖ *adj.* Of or located on an upper floor. ❖ *n.* (ŭp′stârz′) (*used with a sing. verb*) The part of a building above the ground floor.

up•stand•ing (ŭp-stăn′dĭng, ŭp′stăn′-) *adj.* **1.** Standing erect or upright. **2.** Morally upright; honest.

up•start (ŭp′stärt′) *n.* A person of humble origin who attains sudden wealth, power, or importance, esp. one made immodest or presumptuous by the change; a parvenu. ❖ *adj.* **1.** Suddenly raised to a position of consequence. **2.** Self-important; presumptuous. ❖ *intr.v.* (ŭp-stärt′) **-start•ed, -start•ing, -starts** To spring or start up suddenly.

up•state (ŭp′stāt′) *n.* The northerly section of a state in the United States. ❖ *adv. & adj.* To, from, or in the northerly section of a state. —**up′stat′er** *n.*

up•stream (ŭp′strēm′) *adv. & adj.* In the direction opposite to the current of a stream.

up•stroke (ŭp′strōk′) *n.* An upward stroke, as of a brush.

up•surge (ŭp-sûrj′) *intr.v.* **-surged, -surg•ing, -surg•es** To surge up. ❖ *n.* (ŭp′sûrj′) A rapid or abrupt rise.

up•sweep (ŭp′swēp′) *n.* **1.** An upward curve or sweep. **2.** A hairdo that is smoothed upward in the back and piled on top of the head. ❖ *tr.v.* **-swept** (-swĕpt′), **-sweep•ing, -sweeps** To brush, curve, or sweep upward.

up•swing (ŭp′swĭng′) *n.* **1.** An upward swing or trend. **2.** An increase, as in movement or business activity.

up•take (ŭp′tāk′) *n.* **1.** A passage for drawing up smoke or air. **2.** Understanding; comprehension: *quick on the uptake.* **3.** An act of taking in or absorbing, esp. into a living organism.

up•talk (ŭp′tôk′) *n.* A manner of speaking in which declarative sentences are uttered with a rising intonation as though they were questions.

up-tem•po also **up•tem•po** (ŭp′tĕm′pō) *n., pl.* **-pos** A fast or lively tempo, as in jazz. —**up′-tem′po** *adj.*

up•throw (ŭp′thrō′) *n.* **1.** A throwing upward. **2.** *Geology* An upward displacement of rock on one side of a fault.

up•thrust (ŭp′thrŭst′) *n.* An upward thrust, esp. of part of the earth's crust. —**up′thrust′** *v.*

up•tick (ŭp′tĭk′) *n.* **1.** An increase, esp. a small or incremental one. **2.** A transaction in a stock market security above the price of the previous transaction. [< the indication of a rise in price of a stock by a plus sign on boards above stock market stations.]

up•tight (ŭp′tīt′) *adj. Slang* **1.** Tense; nervous. **2.** Financially pressed; destitute. **3.** Outraged; angry. **4.** Rigidly conventional, as in opinions. —**up′tight′ness** *n.*

up•time (ŭp′tīm′) *n.* The time during which a device, such as a computer, is functioning or available for use.

up-to-date (ŭp′tə-dāt′) *adj.* **1.** Informed of or reflecting the latest information or changes. **2.** Being in accord with the latest ideas, improvements, or styles. —**up′-to-date′ness** *n.*

up•town (ŭp′toun′) *n.* The upper part of a town or city. ❖ *adv.* (ŭp′toun′) To, toward, or in the upper part of a town or city. —**up′town′** *adj.* —**up′town′er** *n.*

up•trend (ŭp′trĕnd′) *n.* An upward trend; an upturn.

up•turn (ŭp′tûrn′, ŭp-tûrn′) *v.* **-turned, -turn•ing, -turns** —*tr.* **1.** To turn up or over: *upturn the soil.* **2.** To upset; overturn. **3.** To direct upward. —*intr.* To turn over or up. ❖ *n.* (ŭp′tûrn′) An upward movement, curve, or trend.

up•ward (ŭp′wərd) *adv.* or **up•wards** (-wərdz) **1.** In, to, or toward a higher place, level, or position: *flying upward.* **2.** Toward a higher position in a hierarchy or on a socioeconomic scale. **3.** To or toward the source, origin, or interior. **4.** Toward the head or upper parts. **5.** Toward a higher amount, degree, or rank: *Prices soared upward.* **6.** Toward a later time or age: *from adolescence upward.* ❖ *adj.* Directed toward a higher place or position. —***idiom:* upward** (or **upwards**) **of** More than; in excess of. —**up′ward•ly** *adv.*

upwardly mobile *adj.* Advancing or likely to advance in economic and social standing. —**upward mobility** *n.*

up•well (ŭp-wĕl′) *intr.v.* **-welled, -well•ing, -wells** To rise from a lower or inner source; well up.

up•well•ing (ŭp-wĕl′ĭng, ŭp′wĕl′-) *n.* **1.** The act or an instance of rising up from or as if from a lower source: *an upwelling of emotion.* **2.** The rising up of cold, often nutrient-rich waters, esp. from ocean depths or lake bottoms, toward the surface.

up•wind (ŭp′wĭnd′) *adv.* In or toward the direction from which the wind blows. —**up′wind′** *adj.*

Ur (ûr, o͝or) A city of ancient Sumer in S Mesopotamia on a site in present-day SE Iraq; an important center of Sumerian culture from c. 3000 B.C. until the 6th cent. B.C.

ur–[1] *pref.* Variant of **uro–**[1].

ur–[2] *pref.* Variant of **uro–**[2].

ur–[3] *pref.* Original; prototypical: *ur-language.* [Ger. See URSPRACHE.]

u•ra•cil (yo͝or′ə-sĭl) *n.* A pyrimidine base, $C_4H_4N_2O_2$, that is an essential constituent of RNA. [UR(EA) + AC(ETIC) + *-il*, substance relating to.]

u•rae•mi•a (yo͞o-rē′mē-ə) *n.* Variant of **uremia.**

u•rae•us (yo͞o-rē′əs) *n.* The figure of the sacred serpent depicted on the headdress of ancient Egyptian rulers and deities. [NLat. *ūraeus* < L.Gk. *ouraios*, cobra, perh. alteration (influenced by Gk. *ouraios*, of the tail) of Egypt. *y*ʿ*rt*.]

U•ral-Al•ta•ic (yo͝or′əl-ăl-tā′ĭk) *n.* A hypothetical language group that comprises the Uralic and Altaic language families. —**U′ral-Al•ta′ic** *adj.*

U•ral•ic (yo͞o-răl′ĭk) also **U•ra•li•an** (yo͞o-rā′lē-ən) *n.* A language family that comprises the Finno-Ugric and Samoyedic subfamilies. [After the URAL (MOUNTAINS).] —**U•ral′ic** *adj.*

U•ral Mountains (yo͝or′əl) A range of W Russia forming the tra-

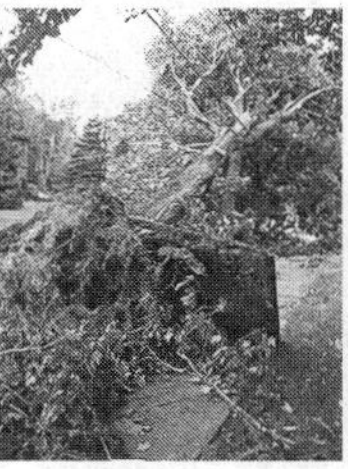

uproot

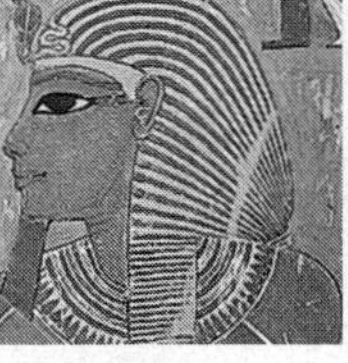

uraeus
depiction from the Tomb of Horemheb, the Valley of the Kings, Egypt

ă	pat	oi	boy
ā	pay	ou	out
âr	care	o͝o	took
ä	father	o͞o	boot
ĕ	pet	ŭ	cut
ē	be	ûr	urge
ĭ	pit	th	thin
ī	pie	*th*	this
îr	pier	hw	which
ŏ	pot	zh	vision
ō	toe	ə	about, item
ô	paw		

Stress marks:
′ (primary);
′ (secondary), as in
lexicon (lĕk′sĭ-kŏn′)

ditional boundary between Europe and Asia and extending c. 2,414 km (1,500 mi) from the Arctic Ocean to Kazakhstan.

Ural River A river of W Russia and W Kazakhstan rising in the S Ural Mts. and flowing c. 2,533 km (1,574 mi) to the Caspian Sea.

U·ralsk (yōō-rälsk′, ōō-rälsk′) See Oral.

U·ra·ni·a (yōō-rā′nē-ə, -rān′yə) n. Greek Mythology The muse of astronomy. [Lat. Ūrania < Gk. Ouraniā < ouranos, heaven.]

u·ran·ic[1] (yōō-răn′ĭk, -rā′nĭk) adj. Of or relating to the heavens; celestial. [< Gk. ouranos, heaven.]

u·ran·ic[2] (yōō-răn′ĭk, -rā′nĭk) adj. Of or relating to uranium, esp. with valence higher than in uranous compounds.

u·ra·ni·nite (yōō-rā′nə-nīt′) n. A brownish-black mineral, UO₂ that forms the chief ore of uranium and is isomorphous with thorianite. [Ger. Uranin (< NLat. ūranium, uranium; see URANIUM) + -ITE¹.]

u·ra·ni·um (yōō-rā′nē-əm) n. Symbol U An easily oxidized radioactive toxic metallic element having 14 known isotopes, of which U 238 is the most naturally abundant, occurring in several minerals, including uraninite and carnotite, and used in research, nuclear fuels, and nuclear weapons. Atomic number 92; atomic weight 238.03; melting point 1,132°C; boiling point 3,818°C; specific gravity 18.95; valence 2, 3, 4, 5, 6. See table at element. [After URANUS.]

uranium 235 n. A uranium isotope with mass number 235 and half-life 7.04 ×10⁸ years, fissionable with slow neutrons and capable in a critical mass of sustaining a chain reaction.

uranium 238 n. A uranium isotope with mass number 238 and half-life 4.46 ×10⁹ years, nonfissionable but irradiated with neutrons to produce fissionable plutonium 239.

urano– or **uran–** pref. Uranium: uranyl. [< URANIUM.]

u·ra·nous (yōō-rā′nəs, yōō-rā′nəs) adj. Of or relating to uranium, esp. with valence lower than in uranic compounds.

U·ra·nus (yōō′rə-nəs, yōō-rā′nəs) n. 1. Greek Mythology The earliest supreme god, who was the son and consort of Gaea and the father of the Cyclopes and Titans. 2. The seventh planet from the sun. [LLat. Ūranus < Gk. ouranos, heaven, Uranus.]

u·ra·nyl (yōōr′ə-nĭl, yōō-rā′nəl) n. The divalent radical UO₂²⁺.

u·rate (yōōr′āt′) n. A salt of uric acid. [UR(IC ACID) + -ATE².]

U·ra·wa (ōō-rä′wə, -wä) A city of E-central Honshu, Japan, a suburb of Tokyo. Pop. 442,381.

ur·ban (ûr′bən) adj. 1. Of or located in a city. 2. Characteristic of the city or city life. [Lat. urbānus < urbs, urb-, city.]

Urban II 1042?–99. Pope (1088–99) who promoted the First Crusade.

Ur·ban·a (ûr-băn′ə) A city of E-central IL adjoining Champaign. Pop. 36,395.

urban dance n. Any of various dances influenced by the rhythms and techniques of funk and hip-hop music.

urban district n. An administrative district of England, Wales, and Northern Ireland, usu. composed of several densely populated communities.

ur·bane (ûr-bān′) adj. **-ban·er, -ban·est** Polite, refined, and often elegant in manner. [Lat. urbānus, of a city. See URBAN.] —**ur·bane′ly** adv.

ur·ban·ism (ûr′bə-nĭz′əm) n. 1. The culture or way of life of city dwellers. 2. Urbanization.

ur·ban·ist (ûr′bə-nĭst) n. A specialist in the study and planning of cities. —**ur′ban·is′tic** adj.

ur·ban·ite (ûr′bə-nīt′) n. A city dweller.

ur·ban·i·ty (ûr-băn′ĭ-tē) n., pl. **-ties** 1. Refinement and elegance of manner; polished courtesy. 2. **urbanities** Courtesies; civilities.

ur·ban·ize (ûr′bə-nīz′) tr.v. **-ized, -iz·ing, -iz·es** To make urban in nature or character. —**ur′ban·i·za′tion** (-bə-nĭ-zā′shən) n.

urban legend n. An apocryphal story involving incidents of the recent past that spreads quickly and is popularly believed to be true.

ur·ban·ol·o·gist (ûr′bə-nŏl′ə-jĭst) n. A specialist in the problems of cities and urban life. —**ur′ban·ol′o·gy** n.

urban renewal n. Large-scale renovation or reconstruction of housing and public works in poor urban areas.

urban sprawl n. The unplanned, uncontrolled spreading of urban development into areas adjoining the edge of a city.

ur·ce·o·late (ûr-sē′ə-lĭt, ûr′sē-ə-lāt′) adj. Shaped like an urn: an urceolate corolla. [NLat. urceolātus < Lat. urceolus, dim. of urceus, jug.]

ur·chin (ûr′chĭn) n. 1. A playful or mischievous youngster; a scamp. 2. A sea urchin. 3. A hedgehog. [ME urchone, hedgehog < OFr. erichon < VLat. *ērīciō, ērīciōn- < Lat. ērīcius < ēr.]

Ur·du (ōōr′dōō, ûr′-) n. An Indic language, written in an Arabic alphabet, that is the official literary language of Pakistan and is also widely used in India. [Urdu urdū, short for zabān-i urdū, language of the camp < Pers. urdū, camp, court (< O Turkic ordu, residence, court).] —**Ur′du** adj.

–ure suff. 1. Act; process; condition: erasure. 2a. Function; office: judicature. b. Body performing a function: legislature. [ME < OFr. < Lat. -ūra.]

u·re·a (yōō-rē′ə) n. A water-soluble compound, CO(NH₂)₂, that is the major nitrogenous end product of protein metabolism and the chief nitrogenous component of the urine in mammals and

other organisms. [NLat. < Fr. urée < urine, urine < OFr. < Lat. ūrīna. See URINE.]

u·re·a-for·mal·de·hyde resin (yōō-rē′ə-fôr-măl′də-hīd′) n. Any of various thermosetting resins made by combining urea and formaldehyde, widely used to make molded objects.

u·re·ase (yōōr′ē-ās′, -āz′) n. An enzyme that promotes the hydrolysis of urea. [URE(A) + -ASE.]

u·re·din·i·um (yōōr′ĭ-dĭn′ē-əm) also **u·re·di·um** (yōō-rē′dē-əm) n., pl. **-din·i·a** (-dĭn′ē-ə) also **-di·a** (-dē-ə) A reddish pustulelike structure that is formed on the tissue of a plant infected by a rust fungus and produces uredospores. [NLat. ūrēdinium < Lat. ūrēdō, ūrēdin-, blight < ūrere, to burn.]

u·re·do·spore (yōō-rē′də-spôr′, -spōr′) also **u·re·din·i·o·spore** (yōōr′ĭ-dĭn′ē-ə-) n. A reddish spore that is produced in the uredinium of a rust fungus. [URED(INIUM) + SPORE.]

u·re·ide (yōōr′ē-īd′) n. Any of various derivatives of urea.

u·re·mi·a also **u·rae·mi·a** (yōō-rē′mē-ə) n. A toxic condition resulting from kidney disease in which waste products normally excreted in the urine are retained in the bloodstream. —**u·re′mic** adj.

u·re·o·tel·ic (yōōr′ē-ə-tĕl′ĭk, yōōr′ē-ō-) adj. Excreting urea as the chief component of nitrogenous waste. [URE(A) + TELIC.] —**u·re′o·tel′ism** (yōō-rē′ə-tĕl′ĭz′əm, yōōr′ē-ō-tĕl′ĭz′əm) n.

u·re·ter (yōō-rē′tər, yōōr′ĭ-tər) n. The long narrow duct that conveys urine from the kidney to the urinary bladder or cloaca. [NLat. ūrētēr < Gk. ourētēr < ourein, to urinate.] —**u·re′ter·al, u′re·ter′ic** (yōōr′ĭ-tĕr′ĭk) adj.

u·re·thane (yōōr′ĭ-thān′) also **u·re·than** (-thăn′) n. 1. A colorless or white crystalline compound, CO(NH₂)OC₂H₅, used in organic synthesis and formerly as a palliative treatment for leukemia. 2. Any of several esters, other than the ethyl ester, of carbamic acid. [UR(O)–¹ + ETH(YL) + -ANE.]

u·re·thra (yōō-rē′thrə) n., pl. **-thras** or **-thrae** (-thrē) The canal through which urine is discharged from the bladder in most mammals and through which semen is discharged in the male. [LLat. ūrēthra < Gk. ourēthra < ourein, to urinate.] —**u·re′thral** adj.

u·re·thri·tis (yōōr′ĭ-thrī′tĭs) n. Inflammation of the urethra.

u·re·thro·scope (yōō-rē′thrə-skōp′) n. An instrument for examining the interior of the urethra. —**u·re·thros′co·py** (yōōr′ə-thrŏs′kə-pē) n.

u·ret·ic (yōō-rĕt′ĭk) adj. Of or relating to urine; urinary. [LLat. ūrēticus < Gk. ourētikos < ourein, to urinate.]

U·rey (yōōr′ē), **Harold Clayton** 1893–1981. Amer. chemist who won a 1934 Nobel Prize.

Ur·fa (ōōr-fä′) A city of SE Turkey near the Syrian border. Pop. 357,900.

urge (ûrj) v. **urged, urg·ing, urg·es** —tr. 1. To force or drive forward or onward; impel. 2. To entreat earnestly and often repeatedly; exhort. 3. To advocate earnestly the doing, consideration, or approval of; press for: urge passage of the bill. 4. To stimulate; excite: "It urged him to an intensity like madness" (D.H. Lawrence). 5. To move or impel to action, effort, or speed; spur. —intr. 1. To exert an impelling force; push vigorously. 2. To present a forceful argument, claim, or case. ❖ n. 1. The act of urging. 2a. An impulse that prompts action or effort: an urge to laugh. b. An involuntary tendency to perform a given activity; an instinct. [Lat. urgēre.]

ur·gen·cy (ûr′jən-sē) n., pl. **-cies** 1. The quality or condition of being urgent; pressing importance: pleading with urgency. 2. A pressing necessity.

ur·gent (ûr′jənt) adj. 1. Compelling immediate action or attention; pressing. 2. Insistent or importunate: urgent words. 3. Conveying a sense of pressing importance: an urgent message. [ME < OFr. < Lat. urgēns, urgent-, pr. part. of urgēre, to urge.] —**ur′gent·ly** adv.

SYNONYMS urgent, exigent, pressing, imperative These adjectives mean compelling immediate attention. Urgent often implies that a matter takes precedence over others: "My business is too urgent to waste time on apologies" (John Buchan). Exigent and pressing suggest an urgency that requires prompt action: "When once disease was introduced into the rural districts, its effects appeared more horrible, more exigent, and more difficult to cure, than in towns" (Mary Shelley). "The danger now became too pressing to admit of longer delay" (James Fenimore Cooper). Imperative implies a need or demand whose fulfillment cannot be evaded or deferred: The necessity for preventing war has become imperative.

–urgy suff. Technique or process for working with: zymurgy. [NLat. -ūrgia < Gk. -ourgiā < -ourgos, working < ergon, work. See werg– in App.]

–uria suff. 1. The condition of having a specified substance in the urine: aciduria. 2. The condition of having a specified kind of urine: polyuria. [NLat. -ūria < Gk. -ouria < ouron, urine.]

U·ri·ah (yōō-rī′ə) In the Bible, the husband of Bathsheba who was sent to die in battle so that David could marry his wife.

u·ric (yōōr′ĭk) adj. Of, contained in, or obtained from urine.

uric acid n. A semisolid compound, C₅H₄N₄O₃, that is the chief nitrogenous component of the urine in birds, terrestrial reptiles, and insects.

u·ri·co·sur·ic (yōōr′ĭ-kə-sōōr′ĭk) adj. Promoting the excretion of uric acid in the urine. [< URIC + URIC.]

u·ri·co·tel·ic (yŏŏr′ĭ-kō-tĕl′ĭk) *adj.* Excreting uric acid as the chief component of nitrogenous waste. —**u′ri·co·tel′ism** (-kō-tĕl′ĭz′əm, -kŏt′l-) *n.*

u·ri·dine (yŏŏr′ĭ-dēn′) *n.* A white odorless powder, C₉H₁₂N₂O₆, that is the nucleoside of uracil, important in carbohydrate metabolism, and used in biochemical experiments.

U·ri·el (yŏŏr′ē-əl) *n.* One of the archangels named in the Apocrypha and in Hebrew tradition.

U·rim and Thum·mim (yŏŏr′ĭm, ōōr′ĭm; thŭm′ĭm, tōōm′ĭm) *pl.n.* Sacred objects carried inside the breastplate of the high priest of ancient Israel and used to divine the will of God. [Partial transl. of Heb. ′ûrîm wə-tummîm : ′ûrîm, perh. pl. of ′ûr, flame, light (< ′ôr, to be light) + wə-, and + tummîm, pl. of tōm, completion, integrity (< tam, to be complete).]

u·ri·nal (yŏŏr′ə-nəl) *n.* **1a.** A fixture, typically upright, used by men for urinating. **b.** A room or other place containing facilities for urinating. **2.** A portable receptacle for urine. [ME, chamber pot < OFr. < LLat. ūrīnāle < neut. of ūrīnālis, of urine < Lat. ūrīna, urine. See URINE.]

u·ri·nal·y·sis (yŏŏr′ə-nāl′ĭ-sĭs) *n., pl.* **-ses** (-sēz′) Laboratory analysis of urine, used to aid in the diagnosis of disease or detect the presence of a specific substance, such as an illegal drug. [URIN(O)- + (AN)ALYSIS.]

u·ri·nar·y (yŏŏr′ə-nĕr′ē) *adj.* **1.** Of or relating to urine, its production, function, or excretion. **2.** Of or relating to the organs involved in the formation and excretion of urine.

urinary bladder *n.* An elastic muscular sac, situated in the anterior part of the pelvic cavity, in which urine collects.

urinary calculus *n.* A hard mass of mineral salts in the urinary tract.

urinary tract *n.* A continuous anatomical tract, including the kidneys, ureters, and urethra, involved in the formation and excretion of urine.

u·ri·nate (yŏŏr′ə-nāt′) *intr.v.* **-nat·ed, -nat·ing, -nates** To excrete urine. [Med.Lat. ūrīnāre, ūrīnāt- < Lat. ūrīna, urine. See URINE.] —**u′ri·na′tion** *n.* —**u′ri·na′tive** *adj.* —**u′ri·na′tor** *n.*

u·rine (yŏŏr′ĭn) *n.* The waste product secreted by the kidneys that in mammals is a yellow to amber-colored, slightly acid fluid discharged from the body through the urethra. [ME < OFr. < Lat. ūrīna.]

u·ri·nif·er·ous (yŏŏr′ə-nĭf′ər-əs) *adj.* Conveying urine.

urino- or **urin-** *pref.* Urine: urinalysis. [< Lat. ūrīna, urine. See URINE.]

u·ri·no·gen·i·tal (yŏŏr′ə-nō-jĕn′ĭ-tl) *adj.* Variant of **urogenital**.

u·ri·nom·e·ter (yŏŏr′ə-nŏm′ĭ-tər) *n.* A hydrometer for measuring the specific gravity of urine.

u·ri·nous (yŏŏr′ə-nəs) also **u·ri·nose** (-nōs) *adj.* Of, resembling, or containing urine.

URL (yōō′är-ĕl′) *n.* An Internet address (for example, http://www.hmco.com/trade/), usu. consisting of the access protocol (http), the domain name (www.hmco.com), and optionally the path to a file or resource residing on that server (trade). [U(NIFORM) R(ESOURCE) L(OCATOR).]

Ur·mi·a (ŏŏr′mē-ə), **Lake** A shallow saline lake of NW Iran between Tabriz and the Turkish border. The city of **Urmia** is the reputed birthplace of Zoroaster. Pop. 300,746.

urn (ûrn) *n.* **1.** A vase of varying size and shape, usu. having a footed base or pedestal. **2.** A closed metal vessel that has a spigot and is used for warming or serving tea or coffee. **3.** *Botany* The spore-bearing part of a moss capsule. [ME urne < Lat. urna.]

uro-¹ or **ur-** *pref.* **1.** Urine: uric. **2.** Urinary tract: urology. **3.** Urea: urethane. [NLat. ūro- < Gk. ouro- < ouron, urine.]

uro-² or **ur-** *pref.* Tail: urochord. [NLat. ūro- < Gk. ouro- < ourā. See ors- in App.]

u·ro·chord (yŏŏr′ō-kôrd′) *n.* A notochord limited to the caudal region. [URO-² + CHORD².]

u·ro·chor·date (yŏŏr′ə-kôr′dāt) *n.* A chordate marine animal of the subphylum Urochordata; a tunicate. ❖ *adj.* Having a urochord.

u·ro·chrome (yŏŏr′ə-krōm′) *n.* The yellow pigment responsible for the color of urine.

u·ro·dele (yŏŏr′ə-dēl′) *n.* Any of various amphibians of the order Caudata, including the salamanders and newts, in which the larval tail persists in adult life. [< NLat. Ūrodēla, former order name : URO-² + Gk. dēlos, visible; see PSYCHEDELIC.]

u·ro·gen·i·tal (yŏŏr′ō-jĕn′ĭ-tl) also **u·ri·no·gen·i·tal** (yŏŏr′ə-nō-) *adj.* Of, relating to, or involving both the urinary and genital structures or functions.

u·ro·ki·nase (yŏŏr′ō-kī′nās, -nāz) *n.* An enzyme in human urine that catalyzes the conversion of plasminogen to plasmin and is used in medicine to dissolve blood clots.

u·ro·lith (yŏŏr′ə-lĭth′) *n.* See **urinary calculus**. —**u′ro·lith′ic** *adj.*

u·ro·lith·i·a·sis (yŏŏr′ə-lĭ-thī′ə-sĭs) *n.* A diseased condition resulting from the formation of urinary calculi.

u·rol·o·gy (yŏŏ-rŏl′ə-jē) *n.* The branch of medicine that deals with the diagnosis and treatment of diseases of the urinary tract and urogenital system. —**ur′o·log′ic** (yŏŏr′ə-lŏj′ĭk), **ur′o·log′i·cal** (-ĭ-kəl) *adj.* —**u·rol′o·gist** *n.*

–uronic *suff.* Connected with urine: hyaluronic acid. [< Gk. ouron, urine.]

u·ro·pod (yŏŏr′ə-pŏd′) *n.* One of the last pair of posterior abdominal appendages of certain crustaceans, such as the lobster or shrimp. [URO-² + -POD.]

uropygial gland *n.* A gland at the base of a bird's tail that secretes an oil used in preening.

u·ro·py·gi·um (yŏŏr′ō-pĭj′ē-əm, -pĭj′ē-) *n.* The posterior part of a bird's body, from which the tail feathers grow. [NLat. ūropȳgium < Gk. ouropugion : ouro-, tail; see URO-² + pugē, rump.] —**u′ro·py′gi·al** (-əl) *adj.*

u·ros·co·py (yŏŏ-rŏs′kə-pē) *n., pl.* **-pies** Examination of urine for diagnostic purposes.

–urous *suff.* Having a specified kind of tail: anurous. [< NLat. -ūrus < Gk. -ouros < ourā, tail. See ors- in App.]

urp (ûrp) *intr.v.* **urped, urp·ing, urps** *Mississippi River Delta* To vomit. [Imit.]

Ur·quhart (ûr′kərt, -kärt′), Sir **Thomas** 1611–60. Scottish writer and translator.

Ur·sa Major (ûr′sə) *n.* A constellation in the region of the north celestial pole near Draco and Leo, containing the seven stars that form the Big Dipper. [ME < Lat. Ursa Māior : ursa, bear + māior, comp. of magnus, great.]

Ursa Minor *n.* A constellation having the shape of a ladle with Polaris at the tip of its handle. [< LLat. minor Ursa : minor, lesser + ursa, bear.]

ur·sine (ûr′sīn′) *adj.* Of or characteristic of bears or a bear. [Lat. ursīnus < ursus, bear. See ṛtko- in App.]

Ur·spra·che (ŏŏr′shprä′кнə) *n.* See **protolanguage**. [Ger. : ur-, original (< MHGer., out of < OHGer.; see ud- in App.) + Sprache, language, speech (< MHGer. sprāche < OHGer. sprāhha).]

Ur·su·line (ûr′sə-lĭn, -līn′, -lēn′, ûr′syə-) *n.* A member of an order of nuns devoted to the education of girls. [After St. Ursula, legendary British princess and martyr.] —**Ur′su·line** *adj.*

ur·text (ûr′tĕkst′, ōōr′-) *n.* The original text, as of a musical score or literary work. [Ger. : ur-, original; see URSPRACHE + Text < MHGer. < LLat. textus.] See TEXT.]

ur·ti·cant (ûr′tĭ-kənt) *adj.* Causing itching or stinging. ❖ *n.* A substance that causes itching or stinging.

ur·ti·car·i·a (ûr′tĭ-kâr′ē-ə) *n.* See **hives**. [NLat. urticāria < Lat. urtica, nettle.] —**ur′ti·car′i·al** *adj.*

ur·ti·cate (ûr′tĭ-kāt′) *v.* **-cat·ed, -cat·ing, -cates** —*tr.* To sting or whip with or as if with nettles. —*intr.* To produce a stinging or itching sensation. ❖ *adj.* (-kĭt, -kāt′) Characterized by the presence of hives. [Med.Lat. urticāre, urticāt- < Lat. urtica, nettle.]

ur·ti·ca·tion (ûr′tĭ-kā′shən) *n.* **1.** The formation or development of hives. **2.** The sensation of having been stung by nettles. **3.** A lashing with nettles formerly used to treat a paralyzed part of the body.

U·ru·bam·ba (ōō′rōō-bäm′bə) A river of Peru rising in the Andes and flowing c. 724 km (450 mi) NNW to join the Apurímac R. and form the Ucayali R.

U·ru·guay (yŏŏr′ə-gwī′, -gwā′, ōō′rōō-gwī′) A country of SE South America on the Atlantic Ocean and the Río de la Plata; gained independence from Spain in 1814. Cap. Montevideo. Pop. 3,167,000. —**U′ru·guay′an** *adj. & n.*

Uruguay River A river of SE South America rising in S Brazil and flowing c. 1,609 km (1,000 mi) to the Río de la Plata.

Ü·rüm·qi also **U·rum·chi** (ōō-rōōm′chē, ū′rüm′chē′) A city of NW China in the Tian Shan. Pop. 1,160,775.

u·rus (yŏŏr′əs) *n., pl.* **u·rus·es** An extinct wild ox (Bos primigenius) of Europe, northern Africa, and western Asia, believed to be the ancestor of domestic cattle. [Lat. ūrus, of Gmc. orig.]

u·ru·shi·ol (ōō-rōō′shē-ôl′, -ōl′, -ŏl′) *n.* A toxic substance present in plants of the genus Rhus, including poison ivy and the lacquer tree. [J. urushi, lacquer + -OL¹.]

us (ŭs) *pron.* The objective case of **we**. **1.** Used as the direct object of a verb: She saw us. **2.** Used as the indirect object of a verb: offered us free tickets. **3.** Used as the object of a preposition: This letter is addressed to us. **4.** Informal Used as a predicate nominative: It's us. See Usage Note at **we**. **5.** Nonstandard Used reflexively as the indirect object of a verb: We bought us another car. See Note at **me**. [ME < OE ūs. See nes-² in App.]

US or **U.S.** abbr. **1.** Unit **2.** Uniform System (of lens aperture) **3.** United States **4.** United States highway

u.s. abbr. Latin **1.** ubi supra (where mentioned above) **2.** ut supra (as above)

USA abbr. **1.** United States Army **2.** or **U.S.A.** United States of America

us·a·ble also **use·a·ble** (yŏŏ′zə-bəl) *adj.* **1.** That can be used: usable byproducts. **2.** Fit for use; convenient to use: usable parts. —**us′a·bil′i·ty**, **us′a·ble·ness** *n.* —**us′a·bly** *adv.*

USAF abbr. United States Air Force

us·age (yŏŏ′sĭj, -zĭj) *n.* **1a.** The act, manner, or amount of using; use: water usage. **b.** The act or manner of treating; treatment. **2.** A usual, habitual, or accepted practice. See Syns at **habit**. **3.** The way in which words or phrases are actually used, spoken, or written in a speech community. **4.** A particular expression in speech

Uruguay

ă	pat	oi	boy
ā	pay	ou	out
âr	care	ŏŏ	took
ä	father	ōō	boot
ĕ	pet	ŭ	cut
ē	be	ûr	urge
ĭ	pit	th	thin
ī	pie	th	this
îr	pier	hw	which
ŏ	pot	zh	vision
ō	toe	ə	about,
ô	paw		item

Stress marks:
′ (primary);
′ (secondary), as in
lexicon (lĕk′sĭ-kŏn′)

or writing: *a nonce usage.* [ME < OFr. < *us* < Lat. *ūsus* < p. part. of *ūtī,* to use.]

us·ance (yōō′zəns) *n.* **1.** The length of time, established by custom and varying between countries, allowed for payment of a foreign bill of exchange. **2.** Use. **3.** Usage; custom. **4.** Interest paid on borrowed money. [ME, usage < OFr., prob. < VLat. *ūsantia* < *ūsāns, *ūsant-,* pr. part. of *ūsāre,* freq. of Lat. *ūtī.*]

USCG *abbr.* United States Coast Guard

USDA *abbr.* United States Department of Agriculture

use (yōōz) *v.* **used, us·ing, us·es** —*tr.* **1.** To put into service or apply for a purpose; employ. **2.** To avail oneself of; practice: *use caution.* **3.** To conduct oneself toward; treat or handle: *used his colleagues well.* **4.** To seek or achieve an end by means of; exploit: *felt he was being used.* **5.** To take or consume; partake of: *She rarely used alcohol.* —*intr.* (yōōs, yōōst) Used in the past tense followed by *to* in order to indicate a former state, habitual practice, or custom: *Mail service used to be faster.* ❖ *n.* (yōōs) **1a.** The act of using; the application or employment of something for a purpose: *with the use of a calculator.* **b.** The condition or fact of being used: *a chair in regular use.* **2.** The manner of using; usage: *learned the use of tools.* **3a.** The permission, privilege, or benefit of using something: *gave us the use of their summerhouse.* **b.** The power or ability to use something: *lost the use of one arm.* **4.** The need or occasion to use or employ: *no use for these old clothes.* **5.** The quality of being suitable or adaptable to an end; usefulness: *tried to be of use in the kitchen.* **6.** A purpose for which something is used: *a tool with several uses.* **7.** Gain or advantage; good: *There's no use in discussing it.* **8.** Accustomed or usual procedure or practice. **9.** *Law* **a.** Enjoyment of property, as by occupying or exercising it. **b.** The benefit or profit of lands and tenements of which the legal title and possession are vested in another. **c.** The arrangement establishing the equitable right to such benefits and profits. **10.** A liturgical form practiced in a particular church, ecclesiastical district, or community. **11.** *Obsolete* Usual occurrence or experience. —*phrasal verb:* **use up** To consume completely: *used up all our money.* [ME *usen* < OFr. *user* < VLat. *ūsāre,* freq. of Lat. *ūtī.* N., ME < OFr. *us* < Lat. *ūsus* < p. part. of *ūtī.*]

used (yōōzd) *adj.* **1.** Not new; secondhand: *a used car.* **2.** (*also* yōōst) Accustomed; habituated: *used to the weather.*

use·ful (yōōs′fəl) *adj.* **1.** Having a beneficial use; serviceable: *a useful gadget.* **2.** Being of practical use: *a useful job.* —**use′ful·ly** *adv.* —**use′ful·ness** *n.*

use·less (yōōs′lĭs) *adj.* **1.** Having or being of no beneficial use; futile or ineffective. **2.** Incapable of functioning or assisting; ineffectual. See Syns at **futile.** —**use′less·ly** *adv.* —**use′less·ness** *n.*

Use·net or **USE·NET** (yōōz′nĕt′) *n.* A messaging system that uses a computer network, esp. the Internet, to transfer messages organized in thematic groups.

us·er (yōō′zər) *n.* **1.** One that uses: *a user of public transportation.* **2.** *Law* The exercise or enjoyment of a right or property. **3.** One who uses addictive drugs.

us·er-friend·ly (yōō′zər-frĕnd′lē) *adj.* **-li·er, -li·est** Easy to use or learn to use. —**us′er-friend′li·ness** *n.*

us·er·name (yōō′zər-nām′) *n.* An identifying sequence of characters, distinct from a password, that is required when logging on to an online computer system.

ush·er (ŭsh′ər) *n.* **1.** One employed to escort people to their seats, as in a theater, church, or stadium. **2.** A man who attends a bridal party at a wedding. **3.** One who serves as official doorkeeper, as in a courtroom. **4.** An official whose duty is to make introductions between unacquainted persons or to precede persons of rank in a procession. **5.** *Archaic* An assistant teacher in a school. ❖ *v.* **-ered, -er·ing, -ers** —*tr.* **1.** To serve as an usher to; escort. **2.** To lead or conduct. **3.** To precede and introduce; inaugurate: *a celebration to usher in the new year.* —*intr.* To serve as an usher. [ME, doorkeeper < AN *usser* < VLat. *ūstiārius* < Lat. *ōstiārius* < *ōstium,* door. See **ōs-** in App.]

ush·er·ette (ŭsh′ə-rĕt′) *n.* A girl or woman employed to escort people to their seats, as in a theater or stadium.

USIA *abbr.* United States Information Agency

USM *abbr.* United States Mail

USMC *abbr.* United States Marine Corps

USN *abbr.* United States Navy

USNA *abbr.* United States Naval Academy

us·ne·a (ŭs′nē-ə, ŭz′-) *n.* Any of various common gray lichens of the genus *Usnea.* [< Ar. *'ušna,* moss; akin to Pers. *ušna.*]

USO *abbr.* United Service Organizations

USP *abbr.* United States Pharmacopoeia

Us·pal·la·ta Pass (ōō′spä-yä′tə, -tä) A pass, c. 3,813 m (12,500 ft), through the Andes between Mendoza, Argentina, and Santiago, Chile; site of a monumental sculpture of Christ.

USPO *abbr.* United States Post Office

USPS *abbr.* United States Postal Service

us·que·baugh (ŭs′kwĭ-bô′, -bä′) *n. Irish & Scots* Whiskey. [Sc. Gael. *uisge beatha* and Ir.Gael. *uisce beatha,* water of life, whiskey (transl. of Med.Lat. *aqua vitae*) : OIr. *uisce,* water; see **wed-** in App. + OIr. *bethad,* genitive of *bethu,* life; see **gʷeiə-** in App.]

USS *abbr.* **1.** United States Senate **2.** United States ship

Ussh·er (ŭsh′ər), **James** 1581–1656. Irish prelate and scholar who devised a scheme of biblical chronology.

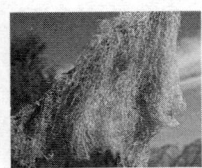

usnea

USSR *abbr.* Union of Soviet Socialist Republics

U·sti·nov (ōō-stĭn′ôf) See **Izhevsk.**

Ust-Ka·me·no·gorsk (ōōst′kə-mĕn′ə-gôrsk′) See **Öskemen.**

usu. *abbr.* usually

u·su·al (yōō′zhōō-əl) *adj.* **1.** Commonly encountered, experienced, or observed: *the usual summer heat.* **2.** Regularly or customarily used: *the usual expressions of thanks.* **3.** In conformity with regular practice or procedure: *Come at the usual time.* —*idiom:* **as usual** As commonly or habitually happens: *As usual, I slept late.* [ME < OFr. *usuel* < LLat. *ūsuālis* < Lat. *ūsus,* use < p. part. of *ūtī,* to use.] —**u′su·al·ly** *adv.* —**u′su·al·ness** *n.*

SYNONYMS usual, habitual, customary, accustomed These adjectives apply to what is expected or familiar because it occurs frequently or recurs regularly. *Usual* describes what accords with normal, common, or ordinary practice or procedure: *"The parson said the usual things about the sea—its blueness . . . its beauty"* (George du Maurier). *Habitual* implies repetition and force of habit: *a habitual liar. Customary* and *accustomed* refer to conformity with prevailing customs or conventions: *"It is the customary fate of new truths to begin as heresies and to end as superstitions"* (Thomas H. Huxley). *She resolved the difficulty with her accustomed resourcefulness.*

u·su·fruct (yōō′zə-frŭkt′, -sə-) *n.* The right to use and enjoy the profits and advantages of something belonging to another as long as the property is not damaged or altered in any way. [LLat. *ūsūfrūctus,* var. of Lat. *ūsusfrūctus* : *ūsus,* use; see USUAL + *frūctus,* enjoyment; see FRUIT.]

u·su·fruc·tu·ar·y (yōō′zə-frŭk′chōō-ĕr′ē, -sə-) *n., pl.* **-ies** One that holds property by usufruct. ❖ *adj.* Of or relating to the nature of a usufruct.

U·su·ma·cin·ta (ōō′sə-mə-sĭn′tə, -sōō-mä-sēn′tä) A river, c. 965 km (600 mi), of SE Mexico.

u·su·rer (yōō′zhər-ər) *n.* One who lends money at interest, esp. at an exorbitant or unlawfully high rate. [ME < AN < LLat. *ūsūrārius,* moneylender < Lat., interest-bearing < *ūsūra,* usury. See USURY.]

u·su·ri·ous (yōō-zhōōr′ē-əs) *adj.* **1.** Practicing usury. **2.** Of or constituting usury: *usurious interest rates.* —**u·su′ri·ous·ly** *adv.* —**u·su′ri·ous·ness** *n.*

u·surp (yōō-sûrp′, -zûrp′) *v.* **-surped, -surp·ing, -surps** —*tr.* **1.** To seize and hold (the power or rights of another, for example) by force and without legal authority. **2.** To take over or occupy without right: *usurp land.* —*intr.* To seize another's place, authority, or possession wrongfully. [ME *usurpen* < OFr. *usurper* < Lat. *ūsūrpāre,* to take into use, usurp. See **reup-** in App.] —**u·surp′er** *n.* —**u·surp′ing·ly** *adv.*

u·sur·pa·tion (yōō′sər-pā′shən, -zər-) *n.* **1.** The act of usurping, esp. the wrongful seizure of royal sovereignty. **2.** A wrongful seizure or exercise of authority or privilege belonging to another; an encroachment: *"in our own day, gross usurpations upon the liberty of private life"* (John Stuart Mill).

u·su·ry (yōō′zhə-rē) *n., pl.* **-ries 1.** The practice of lending money and charging interest, esp. at an exorbitant or illegally high rate. **2.** An excessive or illegally high rate of interest charged. **3.** *Archaic* Interest charged or paid on a loan. [ME < Med.Lat. *ūsūria,* alteration of Lat. *ūsūra* < *ūsus,* use. See USUAL.]

ut (ŭt, ōot) *n. Music* A syllable representing the tone C, otherwise represented by *do,* in the French system of solmization. [ME < Med.Lat. See GAMUT.]

UT *abbr.* **1.** universal time **2.** *or* **Ut.** Utah

U·tah (yōō′tô′, -tä′) A state of the W US; admitted as the 45th state in 1896. The area was settled in 1847 by Mormons led by Brigham Young. Cap. Salt Lake City. Pop. 2,233,169. —**U′tah·an, U′tahn** *adj. & n.*

UTC *abbr.* coordinated universal time

ut dict. *abbr. Latin* ut dictum (as directed)

Ute (yōōt) *n., pl.* **Ute** or **Utes 1.** A member of a Native American people formerly inhabiting a large area of Colorado, Utah, and northern New Mexico, with present-day populations in northeast Utah and along the Colorado–New Mexico border. **2.** The Uto-Aztecan language of the Ute. [< *Utah,* Ute Indian < Am.Sp. *Yuta;* akin to Southern Paiute *yuuttaci.*]

u·ten·sil (yōō-tĕn′səl) *n.* An instrument, implement, or container used domestically, esp. in a kitchen: *cooking utensils hung by the stove.* [ME < OFr. *utensile* < Lat. *ūtēnsilia,* utensils < neut. pl. of *ūtēnsilis,* fit for use < *ūtī,* to use.]

u·ter·ine (yōō′tər-ĭn, -tə-rīn′) *adj.* **1.** Of, relating to, or in the region of the uterus. **2.** Having the same mother but different fathers. **3.** Enclosed and dark; womblike. [ME < LLat. *uterīnus* < Lat. *uterus,* uterus.]

u·ter·us (yōō′tər-əs) *n., pl.* **u·ter·i** (yōō′tə-rī′) *or* **u·ter·us·es 1.** A hollow muscular organ located in the pelvic cavity of female mammals in which the fertilized egg implants and develops. **2.** A corresponding part in other animals. [ME < Lat.]

U Thant (ōō thänt′, thänt′) See **U Thant.**

U·ther Pen·dra·gon (yōō′thər pĕn-drăg′ən, ōō′-) *n.* In Arthurian legend, a king of Britain and the father of Arthur.

U·ti·ca (yōō′tĭ-kə) **1.** An ancient city of N Africa on the Mediterranean Sea NW of Carthage; destroyed by the Arabs c. A.D. 700. **2.** A city of central NY ENE of Syracuse. Pop. 60,651.

u·tile (yōōt′l, yōō′tīl′) *adj.* Useful. [ME < OFr. < Lat. *ūtilis.* See UTILITY.]

u·til·i·tar·i·an (yōō-tĭl′ĭ-târ′ē-ən) *adj.* **1.** Of, relating to, or in the interests of utility. **2.** Exhibiting or stressing utility over other values; practical. **3.** Of, characterized by, or advocating utilitarianism. ❖ *n.* One who advocates or practices utilitarianism. [UTILIT(Y) + −ARIAN.]

u·til·i·tar·i·an·ism (yōō-tĭl′ĭ-târ′ē-ə-nĭz′əm) *n.* **1.** The belief that the value of a thing or an action is determined by its utility. **2.** The ethical theory that all action should be directed toward achieving the greatest happiness for the greatest number of people. **3.** The quality of being utilitarian: *housing of bleak utilitarianism.*

u·til·i·ty (yōō-tĭl′ĭ-tē) *n., pl.* **-ties 1.** The quality or condition of being useful; usefulness. **2.** A useful article or device. **3a.** A public utility. **b.** A commodity or service, such as electricity or water, provided by a public utility. **4.** *Computer Science* A utility program. ❖ *adj.* **1.** Used, serving, or working in several capacities as needed, esp.: **a.** Prepared to play any of the smaller theatrical roles on short notice: *a utility cast member.* **b.** Capable of playing as a substitute in any of several positions: *a utility infielder.* **2.** Designed for various often heavy-duty practical uses: *a utility knife.* **3.** Raised or kept for the production of a farm product rather than for show or as pets: *utility livestock.* **4.** Of the lowest US Government grade: *utility beef.* [ME *utilite* < OFr. < Lat. *ūtilitās* < *ūtilis,* useful < *ūtī,* to use.]

utility program *n.* A program that performs a specific task related to the management of computer functions, resources, or files, as password protection or file compression.

utility room *n.* A room used for the placement of large appliances, such as a washing machine, or for the storage of cleaning items, such as a mop and pail.

utilization review *n.* A process for monitoring the use and delivery of services, esp. one used by a managed care provider to control health care costs.

u·til·ize (yōōt′l-īz′) *tr.v.* **-ized, -iz·ing, -iz·es** To put to use, esp. to find a profitable or practical use for. [Fr. *utiliser* < Ital. *utilizzare* < *utile,* useful < Lat. *ūtilis* < *ūtī,* to use.] **—u′til·iz′a·ble** *adj.* **—u′til·i·za′tion** (-ĭ-zā′shən) *n.* **—u′til·iz′er** *n.*

USAGE NOTE Many critics regard *utilize* as an unnecessary and pretentious substitute for *use.* But this is not true in all cases. *Utilize* can mean "to find a profitable or practical use for." Thus the sentence *The teachers were unable to use the new computers* might mean only that the teachers were unable to operate the computers, whereas *The teachers were unable to utilize the new computers* suggests that the teachers could not find ways to employ the computers in instruction.

---

ut·most (ŭt′mōst′) *adj.* **1.** Being or situated at the most distant limit or point; farthest: *the utmost tip of the peninsula.* **2.** Of the highest or greatest degree, amount, or intensity; most extreme: *of the utmost importance.* ❖ *n.* The greatest possible amount, degree, or extent; the maximum: *worked to the utmost of her abilities.* [ME < OE *ūtmest : ūt,* out; see **ud-** in App. + *-mest,* -most.]

U·to-Az·tec·an (yōō′tō-ăz′tĕk′ən) *n.* **1.** A language phylum of North and Central America that includes Ute, Hopi, Nahuatl, and Shoshone. **2.** A member of a tribe speaking a Uto-Aztecan language. ❖ *adj.* Of or relating to the Uto-Aztecans or to the languages spoken by them. [< UTE + AZTEC.]

u·to·pi·a (yōō-tō′pē-ə) *n.* **1a.** often **Utopia** An ideally perfect place, esp. in its social, political, and moral aspects. **b.** A work of fiction describing a utopia. **2.** An impractical idealistic scheme for reform. [NLat. *Ūtopia,* imaginary island in *Utopia* (1516) by Sir Thomas More : Gk. *ou,* not, no; see **aiw-** in App. + Gk. *topos,* place.]

u·to·pi·an (yōō-tō′pē-ən) *adj.* **1.** often **Utopian** Of, relating to, describing or having the characteristics of a Utopia: *a Utopian island.* **2a.** Excellent or ideal but impracticable; visionary. **b.** Proposing impractically ideal schemes. ❖ *n.* A zealous but impractical reformer of human society.

u·to·pi·an·ism also **U·to·pi·an·ism** (yōō-tō′pē-ə-nĭz′əm) *n.* The ideals or principles of a utopian; idealistic and impractical social theory.

U·trecht (yōō′trĕkt′, ü′trĕкнt) A city of central Netherlands SSE of Amsterdam. The Treaty of Utrecht ended the War of the Spanish Succession (1701–13). Pop. 234,139.

u·tri·cle¹ (yōō′trĭ-kəl) *n.* **1.** A membranous sac contained within the labyrinth of the inner ear and connected with the semicircu-lar canals. **2.** *Botany* A small bladderlike one-seeded indehiscent fruit, as in the amaranth. [Lat. *utriculus,* dim. of *uter, utr-,* leather bottle, poss. < Gk. *hudriā,* water vessel < *hudōr,* water. See **wed-** in App.]

u·tri·cle² (yōō′trĭ-kəl) *n.* A small vestigial blind pouch of the prostate gland. [Lat. *utriculus,* sac, dim. of *uterus,* uterus.]

u·tric·u·lar¹ (yōō-trĭk′yə-lər) *adj.* **1.** Of, relating to, or resembling a utricle. **2.** Having one or more utricles.

u·tric·u·lar² (yōō-trĭk′yə-lər) *adj.* Relating to the uterus.

u·tric·u·lus (yōō-trĭk′yə-ləs) *n., pl.* **-li** (-lī′) A utricular sac.

U·tril·lo (yōō-trĭl′ō, ü-trē-ō′), **Maurice** 1883–1955. French painter known esp. for his street scenes of Paris.

U·tsu·no·mi·ya (ōōt′sə-nō′mē-ə, ōō-tsōō′nô-mē′yä) A city of central Honshu, Japan, N of Tokyo. Pop. 434,029.

ut·ter¹ (ŭt′ər) *tr.v.* **-tered, -ter·ing, -ters 1.** To send forth with the voice: *uttered a cry.* **2.** To articulate (words); pronounce or speak. See Syns at **vent¹**. **3.** *Law* To circulate (counterfeit money, for example). **4.** To publish (a book, for example). **5.** *Obsolete* To sell or deliver (merchandise) in trading. [ME *utteren,* partly < MLGer. *uteren* (< *uter,* outer, comp. of *ūt,* out; see **ud-** in App.), and partly alteration (influenced by *utter,* outer) of ME *outen,* to disclose (< *out,* out; see OUT).] **—ut′ter·a·ble** *adj.* **—ut′ter·er** *n.*

ut·ter² (ŭt′ər) *adj.* Complete; absolute; entire: *utter darkness.* [ME < OE *ūtera,* outer. See **ud-** in App.]

ut·ter·ance¹ (ŭt′ər-əns) *n.* **1a.** The act of uttering; vocal expression. **b.** The power of speaking; speech. **c.** A manner of speaking. **2.** Something uttered or expressed; a statement.

ut·ter·ance² (ŭt′ər-əns) *n.* The uttermost end or extremity; the bitter end. [ME < OFr. *outrance < outrer,* to go beyond limits < VLat. **ultrāre* < Lat. *ultrā,* beyond. See **al-** in App.]

ut·ter·ly (ŭt′ər-lē) *adv.* Completely; absolutely; entirely.

ut·ter·most (ŭt′ər-mōst′) *adj.* **1.** Utmost. **2.** Outermost. ❖ *n.* The greatest amount or degree possible; the utmost. [ME : *utter,* outer; see UTTER² + -most, -most.]

U-turn (yōō′tûrn′) *n.* A turn, as by a vehicle, completely reversing the direction of travel.

UV *abbr.* ultraviolet

u·va·rov·ite (yōō-vär′ə-vīt′, ōō-) *n.* An emerald-green variety of garnet, $Ca_3Cr_2(SiO_4)_3$, found in chromium deposits. [After Count Sergei Semenovitch *Uvarov* (1785–1855), president of the St. Petersburg Academy.]

u·ve·a (yōō′vē-ə) *n.* The vascular middle layer of the eye constituting the iris, ciliary body, and choroid. [Med.Lat. *ūvea* < Lat. *ūva,* grape.] **—u′ve·al** *adj.*

u·ve·i·tis (yōō′vē-ī′tĭs) *n.* Inflammation of the uvea.

UV index (yōō′vē′) *n.* A scale ranging from zero to ten, used to estimate the risk for sunburn in midday sunlight under conditions that account for cloud cover, ozone, and location.

u·vu·la (yōō′vyə-lə) *n.* A small conical fleshy mass of tissue suspended from the center of the soft palate. [ME < Med.Lat. *ūvula,* swollen uvula, dim. of Lat. *ūva,* grape, swollen uvula.]

u·vu·lar (yōō′vyə-lər) *adj.* **1.** Of, relating to, or associated with the uvula. **2.** *Linguistics* Articulated by vibration of the uvula or with the back of the tongue near or touching the uvula.

UW *abbr.* underwriter

ux. *abbr.* Latin *uxor* (wife)

Ux·mal (ōōs-mäl′) An ancient ruined Mayan city of Yucatán in SE Mexico; flourished from 600 to 900.

ux·o·ri·al (ŭk-sôr′ē-əl, -sôr′-, ŭg-zôr′-, -zôr′-) *adj.* Of a wife; regarded as befitting a wife. [< Lat. *uxōrius.* See UXORIOUS.] **—ux·o′ri·al·ly** *adv.*

ux·o·ri·cide (ŭk-sôr′ĭ-sīd′, -sôr′-, ŭg-zôr′-, -zôr′-) *n.* **1.** The killing of a wife by her husband. **2.** A man who kills his wife. [Med.Lat. *uxōricīdium :* Lat. *uxor,* wife + Lat. -*cīdium,* -cide.]

ux·o·ri·ous (ŭk-sôr′ē-əs, -sôr′-, ŭg-zôr′-, -zôr′-) *adj.* Excessively submissive or devoted to one's wife. [< Lat. *uxōrius < uxor,* wife.] **—ux·o′ri·ous·ly** *adv.* **—ux·o′ri·ous·ness** *n.*

Uz·bek (ōōz′bĕk′, ŭz′-) *n., pl.* **Uzbek** or **-beks 1.** A member of a Turkic people inhabiting Uzbekistan and neighboring areas. **2.** The Turkic language of the Uzbeks. [Russ. < Uzbek *ŭzbek.*]

Uz·bek·i·stan (ōōz-bĕk′ĭ-stän′, -stän′, ŭz-) A region and republic of W-central Asia; conquered by Alexander the Great, Genghis Khan, and Tamerlane and finally overrun by Uzbek peoples in the early 16th cent. It was a constituent republic of the USSR from 1924 to 1991. Cap. Tashkent. Pop. 22,349,000.

U·zi or **U·ZI** (ōō′zē) *n., pl.* **U·zis** or **U·ZIs** Any of various compact submachine guns having a caliber of 9 millimeters, originally designed in Israel in the 1950s. [After *Uzi* el-Gal, 20th-cent. Israeli army officer and weapons designer.]

Maurice Utrillo
c. 1921 portrait by his mother, Suzanne Valadon (1865–1938)

Uzbekistan

V v

v or **V** (vē) *n., pl.* **v's** or **V's** also **vs** or **Vs 1.** The 22nd letter of the modern English alphabet. **2.** Any of the speech sounds represented by the letter *v*. **3.** The 22nd in a series. **4.** Something shaped like the letter V.

V¹ 1. The symbol for the element **vanadium. 2.** *Electricity* The symbol for **potential difference. 3.** also **v** The symbol for the Roman numeral 5.

V² ** *abbr.* **1. velocity **2.** victory **3.** vocative **4.** volt **5.** volume **6.** vowel

V-1 (vē′wŭn′) *n.* A robot bomb deployed by the Germans in World War II. [Ger. *Vergeltungswaffe eins*, retaliation weapon (number) one.]

V-2 (vē′tōō′) *n.* A long-range liquid-fuel rocket used by the Germans as a ballistic missile in World War II. [Ger. *Vergeltungs-waffe zwei*, retaliation weapon (number) two.]

V-6 (vē′sĭks′) *n.* A V-engine having six cylinders.

V-8 (vē′āt′) *n.* A V-engine having eight cylinders.

v. *abbr.* **1.** verb **2.** verse **3.** version **4.** verso **5.** versus **6.** vide **7.** volume (book)

V. *abbr.* **1.** venerable (in titles) **2.** very (in titles)

VA *abbr.* **1.** Veterans Administration **2.** vicar apostolic **3.** also **Va.** Virginia **4.** volt-ampere

Vaal (väl) A river rising in E South Africa and flowing c. 1,207 km (750 mi) to the Orange R.

VAB *abbr.* voice answer back

va•can•cy (vā′kən-sē) *n., pl.* **-cies 1.** The condition of being vacant or unoccupied. **2.** An empty or unoccupied space. **3.** A position, office, or place of accommodation that is unfilled or unoccupied. **4.** Emptiness of mind; inanity. **5.** A crystal defect caused by the absence of an atom, ion, or molecule in a crystal lattice. **6.** *Archaic* A period of leisure; idleness.

va•cant (vā′kənt) *adj.* **1.** Containing nothing; empty. **2.** Without an incumbent or occupant; unfilled: *a vacant position.* **3.** Not occupied or put to use: *a vacant lot.* **4a.** Lacking intelligence or knowledge. **b.** Lacking expression; blank. **5.** Not filled with any activity. [ME < OFr. < Lat. *vacāns, vacant-,* pr. part. of *vacāre,* to be empty.] —**va′cant•ly** *adv.* —**va′cant•ness** *n.*

va•cate (vā′kāt′, vā-kāt′) *v.* **-cat•ed, -cat•ing, -cates** —*tr.* **1a.** To cease to occupy or hold; give up. **b.** To empty of occupants or incumbents. **2.** *Law* To make void or annul; countermand: *vacate a death sentence.* —*intr.* To leave a job, office, or lodging. [Lat. *vacāre, vacāt-,* to be empty.]

va•ca•tion (vā-kā′shən, və-) *n.* **1.** A period of time devoted to pleasure, rest, or relaxation, esp. one with pay granted to an employee. **2a.** A holiday. **b.** A fixed period of holidays, esp. one during which a school, court, or business suspends activities. **3.** *Archaic* The act or an instance of vacating. ✦ *intr.v.* **-tioned, -tion•ing, -tions** To take or spend a vacation. [Ult. < Lat. *vacātiō, vacātiōn-,* freedom from occupation < *vacātus,* p. part. of *vacāre,* to be empty, at leisure.] —**va•ca′tion•er, va•ca′tion•eer′** (-shə-nîr′) *n.*

va•ca•tion•ist (vā-kā′shə-nĭst, və-) *n.* One on vacation.

va•ca•tion•land (vā-kā′shən-lănd′) *n.* A place with special attractions for those on vacation.

Vac•a•ville (văk′ə-vĭl′) A city of central CA WSW of Sacramento. Pop. 88,625.

vac•ci•nal (văk′sə-nəl, văk-sē′-) *adj.* **1.** Of or relating to vaccination or a vaccine. **2.** Induced by vaccination.

vac•ci•nate (văk′sə-nāt′) *v.* **-nat•ed, -nat•ing, -nates** —*tr.* To inoculate with a vaccine in order to produce immunity to an infectious disease, such as diphtheria or typhus. —*intr.* To perform vaccinations or a vaccination. —**vac′ci•na′tor** *n.*

vac•ci•na•tion (văk′sə-nā′shən) *n.* **1.** Inoculation with a vaccine in order to protect against a particular disease. **2.** A scar left on the skin by vaccinating.

vac•cine (văk-sēn′, văk′sēn′) *n.* **1a.** A preparation of a weakened or killed pathogen, such as a bacterium or virus, or of a portion of the pathogen's structure that upon administration stimulates antibody production against the pathogen but is incapable of causing severe infection. **b.** A vaccine prepared from the cowpox virus that protects against smallpox. **2.** *Computer Science* A software program designed to detect and stop the progress of computer viruses. [< Lat. *vaccīnus,* of cows < *vacca,* cow.]

vac•ci•nee (văk′sə-nē′) *n.* One that has been vaccinated.

vac•cin•i•a (văk-sĭn′ē-ə) *n.* **1.** The cowpox virus or a virus derived from it. **2.** A usu. mild illness that occurs as a reaction to inoculation with smallpox vaccine. [NLat. *vaccīnia* < Lat. *vaccīnus,* of cows. See VACCINE.] —**vac•cin′i•al** *adj.*

vac•il•lant (văs′ə-lənt) *adj.* Undergoing vacillation; wavering.

vac•il•late (văs′ə-lāt′) *intr.v.* **-lat•ed, -lat•ing, -lates 1.** To sway from one side to the other; oscillate. **2.** To swing indecisively from one course of action or opinion to another. [Lat. *vacillāre, vacillāt-,* to waver.] —**vac′il•la′tion** *n.* —**vac′il•la′tor** *n.*

vac•il•la•to•ry (văs′ə-lə-tôr′ē, -tōr′ē) *adj.* Inclined to waver; irresolute.

va•cu•i•ty (vă-kyōō′ĭ-tē, və-) *n., pl.* **-ties 1.** Total absence of matter; emptiness. **2.** An empty space; a vacuum. **3.** Total lack of ideas; emptiness of mind. **4.** Absence of meaningful occupation; idleness. **5.** The quality or fact of being devoid of something specified: *a vacuity of taste.* **6.** Something, esp. a remark, that is pointless or inane. [ME *vacuite* < OFr. < Lat. *vacuitās* < *vacuus,* empty. See VACUUM.]

vacuolar membrane *n.* See **tonoplast.**

vac•u•o•lat•ed (văk′yōō-ō-lā′tĭd) also **vac•u•o•late** (-lāt′, -lĭt) *adj.* Containing vacuoles or a vacuole.

vac•u•ole (văk′yōō-ōl′) *n.* A small cavity in cell cytoplasm, bound by a single membrane and containing water, food, or metabolic waste. [Fr. < Lat. *vacuus,* empty. See VACUUM.] —**vac′u•o′lar** (-ō′lər, -lär′) *adj.* —**vac′u•o•la′tion** *n.*

vac•u•ous (văk′yōō-əs) *adj.* **1.** Devoid of matter; empty. **2a.** Lacking intelligence; stupid. **b.** Devoid of substance or meaning; inane: *a vacuous comment.* **c.** Devoid of expression; vacant. **3.** Lacking serious purpose or occupation; idle. [< Lat. *vacuus,* empty. See VACUUM.] —**vac′u•ous•ly** *adv.* —**vac′u•ous•ness** *n.*

vac•u•um (văk′yōō-əm, -yōōm, -yəm) *n., pl.* **-u•ums** or **-u•a** (-yōō-ə) **1a.** Absence of matter. **b.** A space empty of matter. **c.** A space relatively empty of matter. **d.** A space in which the pressure is significantly lower than atmospheric pressure. **2.** A state of emptiness; a void. **3.** A state of being sealed off from external or environmental influences; isolation. **4.** *pl.* **-uums** A vacuum cleaner. ✦ *adj.* **1.** Of, relating to, or used to create a vacuum. **2.** Containing air or other gas at a reduced pressure. **3.** Operating by means of suction or by maintaining a partial vacuum. ✦ *tr. & intr.v.* **-umed, -um•ing, -ums** To clean with or use a vacuum cleaner. [Lat., empty space < neut. of *vacuus,* empty < *vacāre,* to be empty.]

vacuum bottle *n.* A bottle or flask having a vacuum between its inner and outer walls, designed to maintain the desired temperature of the contents.

vacuum cleaner *n.* An electrical appliance that cleans surfaces by suction.

vacuum gauge *n.* A device for measuring pressures below atmospheric pressure.

vac•u•um-packed (văk′yōō-əm-păkt′, -yōōm-, văk′yəm-) *adj.* **1.** Packed in an airtight container. **2.** Sealed under low pressure or a partial vacuum.

vacuum pump *n.* **1.** A pump used to evacuate an enclosure. **2.** See **pulsometer.**

vacuum tube *n.* An electron tube from which all or most of the gas has been removed, permitting electrons to move with low interaction with any remaining gas molecules.

va•de me•cum (vā′dē mē′kəm, vä′dē mā′-) *n., pl.* **va•de me•cums 1.** A useful thing that one constantly carries about. **2.** A book, such as a guidebook, for ready reference. [Lat. *vāde mēcum,* go with me : *vāde,* sing. imper. of *vādere,* to go + *mē,* ablative sing. of *egō,* I + *cum,* with.]

VADM *abbr.* vice admiral

Va•do•da•ra (və-dō′də-rä′) or **Ba•ro•da** (bə-rō′də) A city of W-central India SE of Ahmadabad; former cap. of the princely state of **Baroda.** Pop. 1,031,346.

va•dose (vā′dōs′) *adj.* Of, relating to, or being water located in the zone of aeration in the earth's crust above the ground water level. [Lat. *vadōsus,* shallow < *vadum,* a shallow, ford.]

Va•duz (vä-dōōts′, fä-) The cap. of Liechtenstein, in the W part on the Rhine R. Pop. 4,927.

vag•a•bond (văg′ə-bŏnd′) *n.* **1.** A person without a permanent home who moves from place to place. **2.** A vagrant; a tramp. **3.** A wanderer; a rover. ✦ *adj.* **1.** Of, relating to, or characteristic of a wanderer; nomadic. **2.** Aimless; drifting. **3.** Irregular in course or behavior; unpredictable. ✦ *intr.v.* **-bond•ed, -bond•ing, -bonds** To lead the life of a vagabond; roam about. [ME *vaga-bonde* < OFr. *vagabond* < LLat. *vagābundus,* wandering < Lat. *vagārī,* to wander < *vagus,* wandering.] —**vag′a•bond′age, vag′a•bond′ism** *n.*

va•gal (vā′gəl) *adj.* Of or relating to the vagus nerve.

va•ga•ry (vā′gə-rē, və-gâr′ē) *n., pl.* **-ries** An extravagant or erratic notion or action. [< Lat. *vagārī,* to wander < *vagus,* wandering.]

va•gi (vā′gī, -jī) *n.* Plural of **vagus.**

vag·ile (văj′əl, -īl) *adj.* Able to move about or disperse in a given environment: *a vagile animal species.* [Lat. *vagus,* wandering + –ILE¹.] —**va·gil′i·ty** (və-jĭl′ĭ-tē, vă-) *n.*

va·gi·na (və-jī′nə) *n., pl.* **-nas** or **-nae** (-nē) **1.** *Anatomy* **a.** The passage leading from the opening of the vulva to the cervix of the uterus in female mammals. **b.** A similar part in some invertebrates. **2.** *Botany* A sheathlike structure, such as the leaf of a grass that surrounds a stem. [Lat. *vāgīna,* sheath.]

vag·i·nal (văj′ə-nəl) *adj.* **1.** Of or relating to the vagina. **2.** Relating to or resembling a sheath. —**vag′i·nal·ly** *adv.*

vag·i·nate (văj′ə-nĭt, -nāt′) also **vag·i·nat·ed** (-nā′tĭd) *adj.* **1.** Forming or enclosed in a sheath. **2.** Resembling a sheath.

vag·i·nis·mus (văj′ə-nĭz′məs) *n.* A painful spasm of the vagina. [NLat. *vāgīnismus :* VAGIN(A) + Lat. *-ismus,* -ism.]

vag·i·ni·tis (văj′ə-nī′tĭs) *n.* Inflammation of the vagina.

vag·i·no·sis (văj′ə-nō′sĭs) *n.* A disease of the vagina.

va·got·o·my (vā-gŏt′ə-mē) *n., pl.* **-mies** Surgical division of fibers of the vagus nerve, used to diminish acid secretion of the stomach and control a duodenal ulcer. [VAG(US) + –TOMY.]

va·go·to·ni·a (vā′gə-tō′nē-ə) *n.* Overactivity or irritability of the vagus nerve, adversely affecting function of the blood vessels, stomach, and muscles. [VAG(US) + –TONIA.] —**va′go·ton′ic** (-tŏn′ĭk) *adj.*

va·go·tro·pic (vā′gə-trō′pĭk, -trŏp′ĭk) *adj.* Affecting or acting on the vagus nerve. Used chiefly of a drug.

va·gran·cy (vā′grən-sē) *n., pl.* **-cies 1a.** The state of being a vagrant. **b.** The conduct or mode of existence of a vagrant. **c.** The offense of being a vagrant. **2.** A wandering in mind.

va·grant (vā′grənt) *n.* **1.** One who wanders from place to place without a permanent home or a means of livelihood. **2.** A wanderer; a rover. **3.** One who lives on the streets and constitutes a public nuisance. ❖ *adj.* **1.** Wandering from place to place and lacking any means of support. **2.** Wayward; unrestrained: *a vagrant impulse.* **3.** Moving in a random fashion; not fixed in place. [ME *vagraunt,* prob. alteration of OFr. *wacrer,* to wander, of Gmc. orig.] —**va′grant·ly** *adv.*

vague (vāg) *adj.* **vagu·er, vagu·est 1.** Not clearly expressed; inexplicit. **2.** Not thinking or expressing oneself clearly. **3.** Lacking definite shape, form, or character; indistinct: *a vague outline.* **4.** Not clear in meaning or application. **5.** Indistinctly felt, perceived, understood, or recalled; hazy. [Fr. < OFr., wandering < Lat. *vagus.*] —**vague′ly** *adv.* —**vague′ness** *n.*

va·gus (vā′gəs) *n., pl.* **-gi** (-gī, -jī) The vagus nerve.

vagus nerve *n.* Either of the tenth and longest of the cranial nerves that innervate the neck, thorax, and abdomen with sensory and motor nerve fibers. [NLat. *(nervus) vagus,* wandering (nerve) < Lat.]

Váh (vä, väкн) A river of W Slovakia flowing c. 394 km (245 mi) W and S to the Danube R.

va·hi·ne (vä-hē′nē, -nā) *n.* Variant of **wahine.**

vail¹ (vāl) *v.* **vailed, vail·ing, vails** *Archaic* —*tr.* **1.** To lower (a banner, for example). **2.** To doff (one's hat) as a token of respect or submission. —*intr.* **1.** To descend; lower. **2.** To doff one's hat. [ME *valen,* short for *avalen* < OFr. *avaler* < *aval,* downward < Lat. *ad vallem,* to the valley : *ad,* ad- + *vallem,* accusative of *vallēs,* valley; see **wel-** in App.]

vail² (vāl) *n. Obsolete* Variant of **veil.**

vain (vān) *adj.* **vain·er, vain·est 1.** Not yielding the desired outcome; fruitless: *a vain attempt.* **2.** Lacking substance or worth: *vain talk.* See Syns at **futile. 3.** Excessively proud of one's appearance or accomplishments; conceited. **4.** *Archaic* Foolish. —*idiom:* **in vain 1.** To no avail; without success. **2.** In an irreverent or disrespectful manner. [ME < OFr. < Lat. *vānus,* empty.] —**vain′ly** *adv.* —**vain′ness** *n.*

vain·glo·ri·ous (vān-glôr′ē-əs, -glōr′-) *adj.* **1.** Marked by or showing excessive vanity; boastful. **2.** Proceeding from vainglory. —**vain·glo′ri·ous·ly** *adv.* —**vain·glo′ri·ous·ness** *n.*

vain·glo·ry (vān′glôr′ē, -glōr′ē, vān-glôr′ē, -glōr′ē) *n., pl.* **-ries 1.** Boastful, unwarranted pride in one's accomplishments or qualities. **2.** Vain, ostentatious display. [ME *vein glory* < OFr. *vaine gloire* < Lat. *vāna glōria,* empty pride : *vāna,* fem. of *vānus,* empty; see VAIN + *glōria,* glory, pride.]

vair (vâr) *n.* **1.** A fur, probably squirrel, much used in medieval times to line and trim robes. **2.** *Heraldry* A representation of fur. [ME < OFr., variegated, vair < Lat. *varius,* variegated.]

Vaish·na·va (vīsh′nə-və) *n. Hinduism* One who worships Vishnu. [< Skt. *vaiṣṇava-,* relating to Vishnu < *Viṣṇuḥ,* Vishnu.] —**Vaish′na·vism** (-vĭz′əm) *n.*

Vais·ya (vī′shə, vīsh′yə) *n.* A member of the second-lowest of the four major castes of traditional Indian society, comprising farmers, herders, merchants, and businessmen. [Skt. *vaiśyaḥ,* settler, homesteader < *viśaḥ,* house. See **weik-** in App.]

Val. *abbr.* valley

val·ance (văl′əns, vā′ləns) *n.* **1.** An ornamental drapery hung across a top edge, as of a bed. **2.** A short drapery, decorative board, or metal strip mounted esp. across the top of a window to hide structural fixtures. ❖ *tr.v.* **-anced, -anc·ing, -anc·es** To supply with valances or a valance. [ME.]

Val·dai Hills also **Val·day Hills** (văl-dī′) An upland region of W Russia between St. Petersburg and Moscow.

Val·de·mar I (văl′də-mär′) See **Waldemar I.**

Val·dez (văl-dēz′) A city of S AK on an inlet of Prince William Sound; S terminus of the oil pipeline from Prudhoe Bay. Pop. 4,036.

Val·do (văl′dō, väl′-), Peter See Peter **Waldo.**

vale¹ (vāl) *n.* A valley, often coursed by a stream; a dale. [ME < OFr. *val* < Lat. *vallēs.* See **wel-** in App.]

va·le² (vā′lē, wä′lā) *interj.* Used to express leave-taking or farewell. ❖ *n.* A farewell. [Lat. *valē,* sing. imper. of *valēre,* to be strong or well.]

val·e·dic·tion (văl′ĭ-dĭk′shən) *n.* **1.** An act of bidding farewell; a leave-taking. **2.** A speech or statement made as a farewell. **3.** A word or phrase of farewell used to end a letter or message. [< Lat. *valedictus,* p. part. of *valedīcere,* to say farewell : *valē,* farewell; see VALE² + *dīcere,* to say; see **deik-** in App.]

val·e·dic·to·ri·an (văl′ĭ-dĭk-tôr′ē-ən, -tōr′-) *n.* The student with the highest academic rank in a class who delivers the valedictory at graduation.

val·e·dic·to·ry (văl′ĭ-dĭk′tə-rē) *n., pl.* **-ries** A closing or farewell statement or address, esp. one delivered at graduation exercises. ❖ *adj.* Of, relating to, or expressing a valedictory.

va·lence (vā′ləns) also **va·len·cy** (-lən-sē) *n., pl.* **-lenc·es** also **-len·cies 1.** *Chemistry* **a.** The combining capacity of an atom or radical determined by the number of electrons that it will lose, add, or share when it reacts with other atoms. **b.** A positive or negative integer used to represent this capacity. **2.** *Biochemistry* The number of binding sites of a molecule, such as an antibody or antigen. **3.** *Psychology* The attraction or aversion that one feels toward a specific object or event. [Lat. *valentia,* capacity < *valēns, valent-,* pr. part. of *valēre,* to be strong.]

valence electron *n.* An electron in an outer shell of an atom that can join in forming chemical bonds with other atoms.

valence shell *n.* The outermost shell of an atom consisting of the valence electrons.

Va·len·ci·a (və-lĕn′shē-ə, -chə, -sē-ə) **1.** (*also* bä-lĕn′thyä) A region and former kingdom of E Spain on the Mediterranean coast S of Catalonia; inhabited by Iberian peoples in early times and later colonized by Greek and Carthaginian traders. **2.** (*also* bä-lĕn′thyä) A city of E Spain on the **Gulf of Valencia,** a wide inlet of the Mediterranean Sea; captured by the Moors in 714. Pop. 749,361. **3.** (*also* bä-lĕn′syä) A city of N Venezuela WSW of Caracas on the W shore of **Lake Valencia.** Pop. 1,034,033.

Va·len·ci·ennes¹ (və-lĕn′sē-ĕnz′, vă-län-syĕn′) A city of N France near the Belgian border SE of Lille; noted for its lace industry since the 15th century. Pop. 40,275.

Va·len·ci·ennes² (və-lĕn′sē-ĕn′, -ĕnz′, văl′ən-sē-) *n.* A fine lace with a floral pattern.

Va·lens (vā′lənz, -lĕnz′) A.D. 328?–378. Emperor of Rome in the East (364–378) who ruled jointly with his brother Valentinian I in the West.

–valent *suff.* Having a specified valence or valences: *polyvalent.* [< VALENCE.]

val·en·tine (văl′ən-tīn) *n.* **1a.** A sentimental or humorous greeting card sent, as to a sweetheart, on Saint Valentine's Day. **b.** A gift sent as a token of love to one's sweetheart on Saint Valentine's Day. **2.** A person singled out esp. as one's sweetheart on Saint Valentine's Day. [After St. VALENTINE.]

Valentine, Saint. fl. 3rd cent. A.D. Roman Christian who according to tradition was martyred during the persecution of Christians by Emperor Claudius II.

Val·en·tine's Day or **Val·en·tines Day** (văl′ən-tīnz′) *n.* See **Saint Valentine's Day.**

Val·en·tin·i·an I (văl′ən-tĭn′ē-ən, -tĭn′yən) A.D. 321–375. Emperor of Rome in the West (364–375) who ruled jointly with his brother Valens in the East.

Valentinian II A.D. 371?–392. Emperor of Rome (375–392) who ruled jointly with Gratian in the East (375–383).

Valentinian III A.D. 419–455. Emperor of Rome in the West (425–455) whose reign was marked by numerous raids by Germanic tribes.

Val·en·ti·no (văl′ĭn-tē′nō), **Rudolph** 1895–1926. Italian-born Amer. actor known for his romantic leading roles in silent films.

va·le·ri·an (və-lîr′ē-ən) *n.* **1.** A plant of the genus *Valeriana,* esp. *V. officinalis* of Eurasia, widely cultivated for its small fragrant white to pink or lavender flowers and for use in medicine. **2.** The dried rhizomes of this plant, used as a sedative. [ME < OFr. *valeriane* < Med.Lat. *valeriāna,* prob. < fem. of Lat. *Valeriānus,* of Valeria, Roman province.]

Valerian Originally Publius Licinius Valerianus d. c. A.D. 260. Emperor of Rome (253–260) who was defeated by Persian forces (260) and died in captivity.

va·le·ric acid (və-lîr′ĭk, -lĕr′-) *n.* A colorless liquid, $C_5H_{10}O_2$, used in flavorings, perfumes, plasticizers, and pharmaceuticals. [VALERIAN(?) its occurrence in the plant's root) + -IC.]

Va·lé·ry (văl′ə-rē′, vä-lä-rē′), **Paul Ambroise** 1871–1945. French poet known for *Le Cimitière Marin* (1932).

val·et (vă-lā′, văl′ā, văl′ĭt) *n.* **1.** A man's male servant, who takes care of his clothes and performs other personal services. **2.** An employee, as in a hotel or on a ship, who performs personal services for guests or passengers. **3.** A rack or stand for holding clothes. ❖ *v.* **-et·ed, -et·ing, -ets** —*tr.* To act as a personal servant to; attend. —*intr.* To work as a valet. [ME *valette* < OFr. *vas-*

ă	pat	oi	boy
ā	pay	ou	out
âr	care	ŏŏ	took
ä	father	ōō	boot
ĕ	pet	ŭ	cut
ē	be	ûr	urge
ĭ	pit	th	thin
ī	pie	*th*	*th*is
îr	pier	hw	which
ŏ	pot	zh	vision
ō	toe	ə	about,
ô	paw		item

Stress marks:
′ (primary);
′ (secondary), as in
lexicon (lĕk′sĭ-kŏn′)

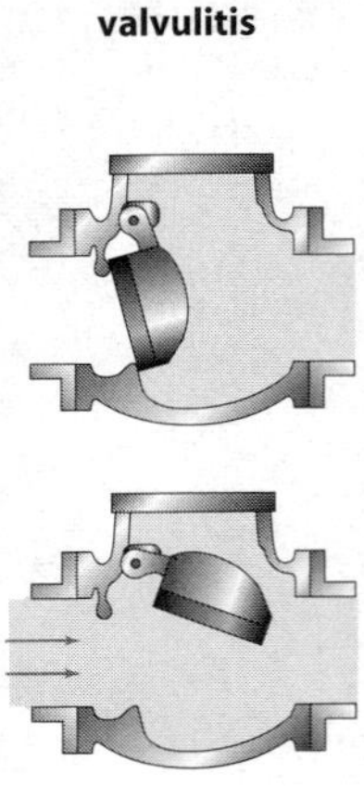

valve
top: closed check valve
bottom: open check valve

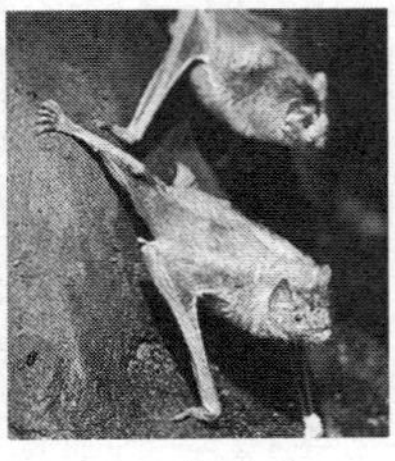

vampire bat

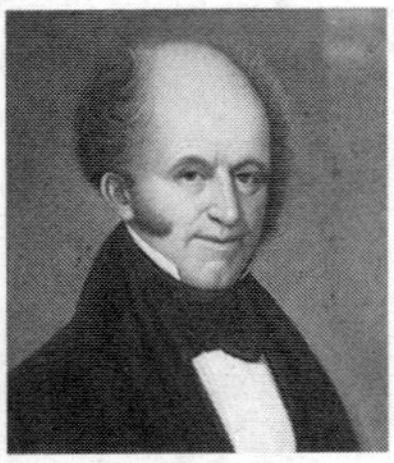

Martin Van Buren
detail from an 1838 portrait by John Langendoerffer (active 1830–38)

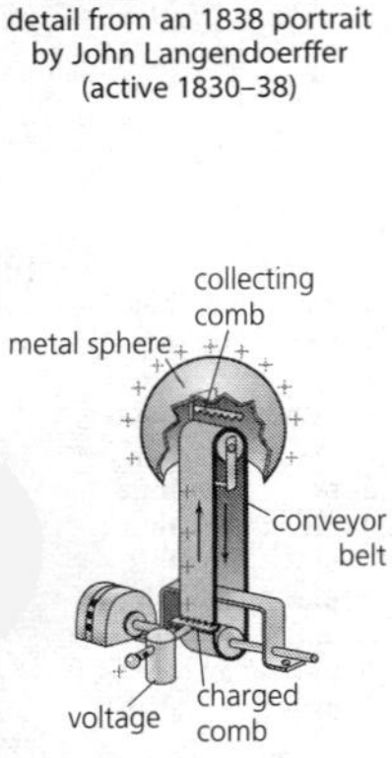
collecting comb
metal sphere
conveyor belt
charged comb
voltage

Van de Graaff generator

let, valet, servant, squire < VLat. **vassellitus,* dim. of **vassus,* vassal. See VASSAL.]

valet parking *n.* Parking provided to and done for patrons, as of a restaurant.

val•e•tu•di•nar•i•an (văl′ĭ-to͞od′n-âr′ē-ən, -tyo͞od′-) *n.* A sickly or weak person, esp. one constantly and morbidly concerned with his or her health. ❖ *adj.* **1.** Chronically ailing; sickly. **2.** Constantly and morbidly concerned with one's health. [< Lat. *valētūdinārius* < *valētūdō, valētūdin-,* state of health < *valēre,* to be strong or well.] **—val′e•tu′di•nar′i•an•ism** *n.*

val•e•tu•di•nar•y (văl′ĭ-to͞od′n-ĕr′ē, -tyo͞od′-) *adj.* Of, relating to, or typical of a valetudinarian. **—valetudinary** *n.*

val•gus (văl′gəs) *adj.* **1.** Characterized by an abnormal outward turning of a bone, esp. of the hip, knee, or foot. **2.** Knock-kneed. ❖ *n.* A valgus bone. [Lat., bowlegged.] **—val′goid′** (-goid′) *adj.*

Val•hal•la (văl-hăl′ə, văl-hä′lə) also **Wal•hal•la** (wăl-hăl′ə, văl-, wäl-hä′lə, väl-) *n. Mythology* The hall in which Odin received the souls of slain heroes. [NLat. < ON *Valhöll* : *valr,* the slain in battle; see **welə-** in App. + *höll, hall,* hall; see **kel-** in App.]

val•iant (văl′yənt) *adj.* **1.** Possessing valor; brave. **2.** Marked by or done with valor. See Syns at **brave.** ❖ *n.* A brave person. [ME < OFr. *vaillant* < Lat. *valēns, valent-,* pr. part. of *valēre,* to be strong.] **—val′ian•cy, val′iance** *n.* **—val′iant•ly** *adv.*

val•id (văl′ĭd) *adj.* **1.** Well grounded; just: *a valid objection.* **2.** Producing the desired results; efficacious: *valid methods.* **3.** Having legal force; effective or binding: *a valid title.* **4.** *Logic* **a.** Containing premises from which the conclusion may logically be derived. **b.** Correctly inferred or deduced from a premise. **5.** *Archaic* Of sound health; robust. [Fr. *valide* < OFr. < Lat. *validus,* strong < *valēre,* to be strong.] **—va•lid′i•ty, val′id•ness** *n.* **—val′id•ly** *adv.*

SYNONYMS *valid, sound, cogent, convincing* These adjectives describe assertions, arguments, conclusions, reasons, or intellectual processes that are persuasive because they are well founded. What is *valid* is based on or borne out by truth or fact or has legal force: *a valid excuse; a valid claim.* What is *sound* is free from logical flaws or is based on valid reasoning: *sound principles.* Something *cogent* is both sound and compelling: *cogent testimony; a cogent explanation. Convincing* implies the power to dispel doubt or overcome resistance or opposition: *convincing proof.*

val•i•date (văl′ĭ-dāt′) *tr.v.* **-dat•ed, -dat•ing, -dates 1.** To declare or make legally valid. **2.** To mark with an indication of official sanction. **3.** To establish the soundness of; corroborate. **—val′i•da′tion** *n.*

val•ine (văl′ēn′, vā′lēn′) *n.* An essential amino acid, $C_5H_{11}NO_2$. [VAL(ERIC ACID) + -INE².]

va•lise (və-lēs′) *n.* A small piece of hand luggage. [Fr. < Ital. *valigia.*]

Val•i•um (văl′ē-əm) A trademark used for the drug diazepam.

Val•kyr•ie (văl-kîr′ē, -kī′rē, văl′kə-rē) also **Wal•kyr•ie** (wăl-kîr′ē, -kī′rē, väl-, wăl′kə-rē, väl′-) *n. Mythology* Any of Odin's handmaidens who conducted the souls of the slain to Valhalla. [ON *Valkyrja.* See **welə-** in App.]

Val•la•do•lid (văl′ə-də-lĭd′, bä′lyä-thō-lēth′) A city of NW-central Spain NNW of Madrid. Pop. 331,885.

val•la•tion (vă-lā′shən) *n.* **1.** An earthwork wall used for military defense; a rampart. **2.** The process of planning or erecting earth fortifications. [LLat. *vallātiō, vallātiōn-* < Lat. *vallātus,* p. part. of *vallāre,* to surround with a rampart < *vallum,* rampart < *vallus,* stake.]

val•lec•u•la (vă-lĕk′yə-lə, və-) *n., pl.* **-lae** (-lē′) A shallow groove, depression, or furrow, as between the hemispheres of the brain. [LLat., dim. of Lat. *vallēs,* valley.] **—val•lec′u•lar, val•lec′u•late** (-lĭt, -lāt′) *adj.*

Val•le d'A•os•ta (vä′lā dä-ō′stə, -stä) A region of NW Italy bordering on France and Switzerland.

Val•le•jo (və-lā′ō, -hō) A city of W CA on San Pablo Bay N of Oakland. Pop. 116,760.

Val•let•ta (və-lĕt′ə) The cap. of Malta, on the NE coast of the main island; founded in the 16th cent. Pop. 9,149.

val•ley (văl′ē) *n., pl.* **-leys 1.** An elongated lowland between ranges of mountains, hills, or other uplands, often having a river or stream. **2.** An extensive area of land drained or irrigated by a river system. **3.** A depression or hollow resembling or suggesting a valley, as the point at which the two slopes of a roof meet. [ME *valey* < OFr. *valee* < VLat. **vallāta* < Lat. *vallēs.* See **wel-** in App.] **—val′leyed** *adj.*

valley fever *n.* See **coccidioidomycosis.**

Valley Forge A village of SE PA on the Schuylkill R. NW of Philadelphia; site of the Continental Army headquarters (Dec. 1777–Jun. 1778).

Valley of Ten Thousand Smokes A volcanic region of SW AK at the upper end of the Alaska Peninsula; formed by the eruption of Mt. Katmai in 1912.

Valley of the Kings A narrow valley of E-central Egypt surrounding the site of ancient Thebes between Karnak and Luxor. The valley contains the tombs of numerous pharaohs of the XVIII, XIX, and XX Dynasties.

Val•mi•ki (väl-mē′kē) fl. 4th century B.C. Indian epic poet, traditionally considered the author of the *Ramayana.*

Va•lois¹ (văl′wä, väl-wä′) A French ruling dynasty (1328–1589) that succeeded the Capetian line.

Va•lois² (văl′wä′, väl-wä′) A historical region and former duchy of N France; an appanage of the royal house of Valois after 1285.

va•lo•ni•a (və-lō′nē-ə, -lŏn′yə) *n.* The dried acorn cups of an oak tree *(Quercus aegilops)* of the eastern Mediterranean, used chiefly in tanning and dyeing. [Ital. *vallonia* < Mod.Gk. *balania,* pl. of *balani,* acorn < Gk. *balanos.*]

val•or (văl′ər) *n.* Courage and boldness, as in battle; bravery. [ME *valour* < OFr. < LLat. *valor* < Lat. *valēre,* to be strong.]

val•or•ize (văl′ə-rīz′) *tr.v.* **-ized, -iz•ing, -iz•es 1.** To establish and maintain the price of (a commodity) by governmental action. **2.** To give or assign a value to. [Port. *valorizar* < *valor,* value < LLat. See VALOR.] **—val′or•i•za′tion** (-ər-ĭ-zā′shən) *n.*

val•or•ous (văl′ər-əs) *adj.* Marked by or possessing great personal bravery; valiant. **—val′or•ous•ly** *adv.*

val•our (văl′ər) *n. Chiefly British* Variant of **valor.**

Val•pa•ra•í•so (văl′pə-rī′zō, bäl′pä-rä-ē′sō) A city of central Chile on the Pacific Ocean WNW of Santiago. Pop. 276,756.

Val•sal•va maneuver (văl-săl′və) *n.* Expiratory effort when the mouth is closed and the nostrils are pinched shut, which forces air into the eustachian tubes and increases pressure on the inside of the eardrum. [After Antonio Maria *Valsalva* (1666–1723), Italian anatomist.]

val•u•a•ble (văl′yo͞o-ə-bəl, văl′yə-) *adj.* **1.** Having considerable monetary or material value for use or exchange: *a valuable diamond.* **2.** Of great importance, use, or service: *valuable advice.* **3.** Having admirable or esteemed qualities or characteristics: *a valuable friend.* ❖ *n.* A personal possession with a relatively high monetary value. Often used in the plural. **—val′u•a•bly** *adv.*

val•u•ate (văl′yo͞o-āt′) *tr.v.* **-at•ed, -at•ing, -ates** To set a value for; appraise. [Back-formation < VALUATION.]

val•u•a•tion (văl′yo͞o-ā′shən) *n.* **1.** The act or process of assessing value or price; an appraisal. **2.** Assessed value or price. **3.** An estimation or appreciation of worth, merit, or character. **—val′u•a′tion•al** *adj.*

val•u•a•tor (văl′yo͞o-ā′tər) *n.* One that estimates values.

val•ue (văl′yo͞o) *n.* **1.** An amount, as of goods, services, or money, considered to be a fair and suitable equivalent for something else; a fair price or return. **2.** Monetary or material worth: *the value of gold.* **3.** Worth in usefulness or importance to the possessor; utility or merit: *the value of an education.* **4.** A principle, standard, or quality considered worthwhile or desirable. **5.** Precise meaning or import, as of a word. **6.** *Mathematics* An assigned or calculated numerical quantity. **7.** *Music* The relative duration of a tone or rest. **8.** The relative darkness or lightness of a color. **9.** *Linguistics* The sound quality of a letter or diphthong. **10.** One of a series of specified values: *issued a stamp of new value.* ❖ *tr.v.* **-ued, -u•ing, -ues 1.** To determine or estimate the worth or value of; appraise. **2.** To regard highly; esteem. See Syns at **appreciate. 3.** To rate according to relative estimate of worth or desirability; evaluate. **4.** To assign a value to (a unit of currency, for example). [ME < OFr. < fem. p. part. of *valoir,* to be strong, be worth < Lat. *valēre.*] **—val′u•er** *n.*

val•ue-add•ed tax (văl′yo͞o-ăd′ĭd) *n.* A tax on the estimated market value added to a product or material at each stage of its manufacture or distribution, ultimately passed on to the consumer.

value judgment *n.* A judgment that assigns a value, as to an object or action; a subjective evaluation.

val•var (văl′vər) *adj.* Valvular.

val•vate (văl′vāt′) *adj.* **1.** Having valvelike parts. **2.** *Botany* **a.** Meeting at the edges without overlapping, as some petals. **b.** Opening by valves, as the capsule of a lily or iris.

valve (vălv) *n.* **1.** *Anatomy* A membranous structure in a hollow organ or passage, as in an artery or vein, that folds or closes to prevent the return flow of the body fluid passing through it. **2a.** Any of various devices that regulate the flow of gases, liquids, or loose materials through piping or apertures by opening, closing, or obstructing ports or passageways. **b.** The movable control element of such a device. **c.** *Music* A device in a brass wind instrument that permits change in pitch by a rapid varying of the air column in a tube. **3.** *Biology* **a.** One of the paired hinged shells of certain mollusks and of brachiopods. **b.** One of the two silicified halves of the cell wall of a diatom. **c.** The entire one-piece shell of certain mollusks. **4.** *Botany* **a.** One of the sections into which the wall of a seedpod or other dehiscent fruit splits. **b.** A lidlike covering of an anther. **5.** *Chiefly British* An electron tube or a vacuum tube. **6.** *Archaic* Either half of a double or folding door. ❖ *tr.v.* **valved, valv•ing, valves 1.** To provide with a valve. **2.** To control by means of a valve. [ME, leaf of a door < Lat. *valva.* See **wel-** in App.] **—valve′less** *adj.*

valve-in-head engine (vălv′ĭn-hĕd′) *n.* An internal-combustion engine that has the inlet and exhaust valves in the cylinder head instead of in the engine block.

val•vu•lar (văl′vyə-lər) *adj.* Relating to, having, or operating by means of valves or valvelike parts.

val•vule (văl′vyo͞ol′) also **val•vu•la** (-vyə-lə) *n., pl.* **-vules** also **-vu•lae** (-vyə-lē′) A small valve or valvelike structure.

val•vu•li•tis (văl′vyə-lī′tĭs) *n.* Inflammation of a valve, esp. a cardiac valve.

vam·brace (văm′brās′) *n.* Armor used to protect the forearm. [ME *vambras* < AN *vauntbras* : *vaunt* (var. of OFr. *avaunt*, before; see VANGUARD) + *bras*, arm; see BRACER².]

va·moose (vă-mōōs′, vǝ-) *intr.v.* **-moosed, -moos·ing, -moos·es** *Slang* To leave hurriedly. [< Sp. *vamos*, let's go < Lat. *vādāmus*, first pers. pl. pr. subjunctive of *vādere*, to go.]

vamp¹ (vămp) *n.* **1.** The upper part of a boot or shoe covering the instep and sometimes extending over the toe. **2a.** Something patched up or refurbished. **b.** Something rehashed, as a book based on old material. **3.** *Music* An improvised accompaniment. ❖ *v.* **vamped, vamp·ing, vamps** —*tr.* **1.** To provide (a shoe) with a new vamp. **2.** To patch up (something old); refurbish. **3.** To put together; fabricate or improvise: *Reporters vamped up questions.* **4.** *Music* To improvise (an accompaniment, for example) for a solo. —*intr. Music* To improvise simple accompaniment or variation of a tune. [ME *vampe*, sock < OFr. *avanpie* : *avaunt*, see VANGUARD + *pie*, foot (< Lat. *pēs*; see **ped-** in App.).] —**vamp′er** *n.*

vamp² (vămp) *Informal n.* A woman who uses her sex appeal to entrap and exploit men. ❖ *v.* **vamped, vamp·ing, vamps** —*tr.* To seduce or exploit (someone) in the manner of a vamp. —*intr.* To play the part of a vamp. [Short for VAMPIRE.] —**vamp′ish** *adj.* —**vamp′ish·ly** *adv.* —**vamp′y** *adj.*

vam·pire (văm′pīr′) *n.* **1.** A reanimated corpse that is believed to rise from the grave at night to suck blood from people in their sleep. **2.** A person who preys upon others. **3.** A vampire bat. [Fr. < Ger. *Vampir*, of Slav. orig.] —**vam·pir′ic** (văm-pĭr′ĭk), **vam·pir′i·cal** (-ĭ-kǝl), **vam′pir′ish** (-ĭsh) *adj.*

vampire bat *n.* **1.** Any of various tropical American bats of the family Desmodontidae that bite mammals and birds to feed on their blood and often carry diseases such as rabies. **2.** Any of various other bats, as those of the family Megadermatidae, erroneously believed to feed on blood.

vam·pir·ism (văm′pīr-ĭz′ǝm) *n.* **1.** Belief in vampires. **2.** The behavior of a vampire.

van¹ (văn) *n.* **1a.** A boxlike motor vehicle having rear or side doors and side panels that is used esp. for transporting people. **b.** A covered or enclosed truck or wagon that is often used for transporting goods or livestock. **2.** *Chiefly British* A closed railroad car that is used for carrying baggage or freight. ❖ *v.* **vanned, van·ning, vans** —*tr.* To transport by van: *vanned the horses to the racetrack.* —*intr.* To drive or travel in a van: *vanned around the country.* [Short for CARAVAN.]

van² (văn) *n.* The vanguard; the forefront. [Short for VANGUARD.]

van³ (văn) *n.* **1.** A wing. **2.** *Archaic* A winnowing device, such as a fan. [ME < OE *fann* and OFr. *van*, both < Lat. *vannus*. See **wet-¹** in App.]

Van (văn, vän), **Lake** A salt lake of E Turkey having no known outlet.

van·a·date (văn′ǝ-dāt′) *n.* Any of three anions, VO₃, VO₄, or V₂O₇, containing pentavalent vanadium.

va·na·dic acid (vǝ-nā′dĭk, -nă′dĭk) *n.* An acid containing a vanadate group, esp. HVO₃, H₃VO₄, or H₄V₂O₇, not existing in a pure state.

va·na·di·nite (vǝ-năd′n-īt′, -năd′-, văn′ǝ-dē′nīt′) *n.* A red, yellow, or brown mineral that is an ore of vanadium and lead.

va·na·di·um (vǝ-nā′dē-ǝm) *n. Symbol* **V** A soft ductile metallic element found in several minerals, usually vanadinite and carnotite, and used in rust-resistant high-speed tools, as a carbon stabilizer in some steels, and as a catalyst. Atomic number 23; atomic weight 50.942; melting point 1,890°C; boiling point 3,000°C; specific gravity 6.11; valence 2, 3, 4, 5. See table at **element.** [< ON *Vanadīs*, the goddess Freya. See **wen-** in App.]

Van Al·len belt (văn ăl′ǝn) *n.* Either of two zones of high-intensity particulate radiation trapped in Earth's magnetic field and surrounding the planet, beginning at an altitude of about 800 kilometers (500 miles) and extending into space. [After James Alfred *Van Allen* (born 1914), American physicist.]

Van Bu·ren (văn byŏŏr′ǝn), **Martin** 1782–1862. The 8th President of the US (1837–41), who also served in the US Senate (1821–28) and as Vice President (1833–37).

van·co·my·cin (văng′kǝ-mī′sĭn, văn′kǝ-) *n.* An antibiotic, C₆₆H₇₅Cl₂N₉O₂₄, obtained from the actinomycete *Amycolatopsis orientalis* and used to treat staphylococcal and spirochetal infections.

Van·cou·ver (văn-kōō′vǝr) **1.** A city of SW British Columbia, Canada, on the Strait of Georgia opposite Vancouver I. Pop. 514,008. **2.** A city of SW WA on the Columbia R. opposite Portland, OR. Pop. 143,560.

Vancouver, George 1757–98. British navigator who led expeditions to Australia, New Zealand, and the Hawaiian Is. (1791–92) and the coast of North America (1792–94).

Vancouver, Mount A peak, 4,873.6 m (15,979 ft), in the St. Elias Mts. of SW Yukon Terr., Canada.

Vancouver Island An island of SW British Columbia, Canada, in the Pacific Ocean separated from the mainland by the Strait of Georgia and Queen Charlotte Strait.

Van·dal (văn′dl) *n.* **1. vandal** One who willfully or maliciously defaces or destroys public or private property. **2.** A member of a Germanic people that overran Gaul, Spain, and northern Africa in the fourth and fifth centuries A.D. and sacked Rome in 455.

[Lat. *Vandalus*, a Vandal, prob. of Gmc. orig.] —**Van·dal′ic** (văn-dăl′ĭk) *adj.*

van·dal·ism (văn′dl-ĭz′ǝm) *n.* Willful or malicious destruction of public or private property. —**van′dal·is′tic** *adj.*

van·dal·ize (văn′dl-īz′) *tr.v.* **-ized, -iz·ing, -iz·es** To destroy or deface (public or private property) willfully or maliciously. —**van′dal·i·za′tion** (-ĭ-zā′shǝn) *n.*

Van de Graaff generator (văn′ dǝ grăf′) *n.* An electrostatic generator in which an electric charge is transferred to a large hollow spherical electrode by a rapidly moving belt, producing potentials of millions of volts. [After Robert Jemison *Van de Graaff* (1901–67), American physicist.]

Van·der·bilt (văn′dǝr-bĭlt′), **Cornelius** 1794–1877. Amer. transportation promoter and financier who amassed a great fortune through railroad and shipping interests.

Van Der Ro·he (văn dǝr rō′ǝ, fän) See Ludwig **Mies Van Der Rohe.**

van der Waals force (văn′ dǝr wôlz′, wälz′) *n.* A weak attractive force between atoms or nonpolar molecules caused by a temporary change in dipole moment of one atom or molecule, inducing a similar change in adjacent atoms or molecules. [After Johannes Diderik *van der Waals* (1837–1923), Dutch physicist.]

Van Die·men's Land (văn dē′mǝnz, vän) See **Tasmania.**

Van Dor·en (văn dôr′ǝn, dōr′-), **Carl Clinton** 1885–1950. Amer. literary critic, editor, and biographer. His brother **Mark** (1894–1972), a writer and critic, is best known for his poetry.

Van·dyke (văn-dīk′) *n.* **1.** A Vandyke beard. **2.** A Vandyke collar. **3a.** A V-shaped point that is part of a decorative border or edging. **b.** A border made up of such points.

Vandyke or **Van Dyck** (văn dīk′), Sir **Anthony** 1599–1641. Flemish painter known for his idealized portraits.

Vandyke beard *n.* A short pointed beard.

Vandyke brown *n.* A moderate to grayish brown.

Vandyke collar *n.* A large collar of linen or lace having a deeply indented or scalloped edge. [After Sir Anthony VANDYKE.]

vane (văn) *n.* **1.** A weathervane. **2.** Any of several usu. relatively thin, rigid, flat, or sometimes curved surfaces radially mounted along an axis, as a sail on a windmill, that is turned by or used to turn a fluid. **3.** The flattened weblike part of a feather, consisting of a series of barbs on either side of the shaft. **4a.** The movable target on a leveling rod. **b.** A sight on a quadrant or compass. **5.** One of the metal guidance or stabilizing fins attached to the tail of a bomb or other missile. [ME *fane, vane* < OE *fana*, flag.]

Vane, Sir **Henry** or **Harry** 1613–62. English politician and leading Parliamentarian during the English Civil War.

Vä·nern (vâ′nǝrn, vě′-) A lake of SW Sweden; navigable for small oceangoing ships via the Göta Canal.

van Eyck (văn īk′), **Jan** 1390?–1441. Flemish painter whose works include the *Altarpiece of the Lamb* (1432), begun by his brother **Hubert** (1366?–1426).

vang (văng) *n.* A rope running from the peak of a gaff to a ship's rail or mast, used to steady the gaff. [Du., a catch < *vangen*, to catch.]

van Gogh (văn gō′, gôкн′, vän кнôкн′), **Vincent** 1853–90. Dutch postimpressionist painter whose works include numerous self-portraits and a series of sunflower paintings (1888).

Vincent van Gogh
1889 self-portrait

van·guard (văn′gärd) *n.* **1.** The foremost position in an army or fleet advancing into battle. **2a.** The foremost or leading position in a trend or movement. **b.** Those occupying a foremost position. [ME *vandgard* < *avaunt garde* < OFr. : *avaunt*, before (< Lat. *abante*; see ADVANCE) + *garde*, guard (< *garder*, to guard; see GUARD).] —**van′guard·ism** *n.* —**van′guard·ist** *n.*

va·nil·la (vǝ-nĭl′ǝ) *n.* **1.** Any of various tropical American vines of the genus *Vanilla* in the orchid family, esp. *V. planifolia*, cultivated for their long narrow seedpods from which a flavoring agent is obtained. **2.** This seedpod. **3.** A flavoring extract prepared from the cured seedpods of this plant or produced synthetically. ❖ *adj.* **1.** Flavored with vanilla. **2.** Lacking adornments or special features; basic or ordinary. [Obsolete Sp. *vainilla*, dim. of *vaina*, sheath < Lat. *vāgīna*.]

vanilla
Vanilla planifolia
vanilla beans

vanilla bean *n.* See **vanilla** 2.

vanilla plant *n.* A fragrant perennial herb (*Carphephorus odoratissimus*) of the southeast United States having numerous lavender to purple flower heads.

va·nil·lic (vǝ-nĭl′ĭk) *adj.* Of, relating to, or derived from vanilla or vanillin.

va·nil·lin (vǝ-nĭl′ĭn, văn′ǝ-lĭn) *n.* A white or yellowish crystalline compound, C₈H₈O₃, found in vanilla beans and certain balsams and resins and used in perfumes, flavorings, and pharmaceuticals.

Va·nir (vä′nîr′) *pl.n. Mythology* An early race of Norse gods who dwelt with the Aesir in Asgard. [ON. See **wen-** in App.]

van·ish (văn′ĭsh) *intr.v.* **-ished, -ish·ing, -ish·es 1.** To pass out of sight, esp. quickly; disappear. See Syns at **disappear. b.** To pass out of existence. **2.** *Mathematics* To become zero. Used of a function or variable. [ME *vanisshen*, alteration of OFr. *esvanir, esvaniss-* < VLat. **exvanīre*, alteration of Lat. *ēvānēscere* : *ē-, ex-, ex-* + *vānēscere*, to vanish (< *vānus*, empty).] —**van′ish·er** *n.* —**van′ish·ment** *n.*

van·ish·ing point (văn′ī-shĭng) *n.* **1a.** The point at which parallel lines receding from an observer seem to converge. **b.** The

vanishing point
Texas highway

point at which a thing disappears or ceases to exist. **2.** The point at which a thing disappears or ceases to exist.

van·i·ty (văn′ĭ-tē) *n., pl.* **-ties 1.** The quality or condition of being vain. **2.** Excessive pride in one's appearance or accomplishments; conceit. **3.** Lack of usefulness, worth, or effect; worthlessness. **4a.** Something that is vain, futile, or worthless. **b.** Something about which one is vain or conceited. **5.** A vanity case. **6.** See **dressing table**. **7.** A bathroom cabinet with storage space that encloses a basin and its water lines and drain. [ME *vanite* < OFr. < Lat. *vānitās* < *vānus*, empty.]

vanity case *n.* **1.** A small handbag or case used by women for carrying cosmetics or toiletries. **2.** A woman's compact.

Vanity Fair also **vanity fair** *n.* A place or scene of ostentation or empty, idle amusement and frivolity. [From *Vanity Fair*, the fair in *Pilgrim's Progress* by John Bunyan.]

vanity plate *n.* A license plate for a motor vehicle bearing a combination of letters or numbers selected by the purchaser.

vanity press *n.* A publisher that publishes a book at the expense of the author.

van·load (văn′lōd′) *n.* The quantity, as of passengers or goods, that a van can carry.

van·quish (văng′kwĭsh, văn′-) *tr.v.* **-quished, -quish·ing, -quish·es 1a.** To defeat or conquer in battle; subjugate. **b.** To defeat in a contest, conflict, or competition. **2.** To overcome or subdue (an emotion, for example); suppress. See Syns at **defeat.** [ME *vaynquisshen* < OFr. *vainquir*, *vainquiss-* < Lat. *vincere*.] —**van′quish·er** *n.* —**van′quish·ment** *n.*

Van Rens·se·laer (văn rĕn′sə-lîr′, rĕn′sə-lər, văn rĕn′sə-lär′), **Killian** or **Kiliaen** 1595–1644. Dutch merchant who established Rensselaerswyck (1635), the only successful privately held colony in America, in present-day upstate NY.

Van Rensselaer, Stephen 1764–1839. Amer. army officer and politician who was an early advocate of the Erie Canal project.

van·tage (văn′tĭj) *n.* **1a.** An advantage in a competition or conflict; superiority. **b.** A position, condition, or opportunity that is likely to provide superiority or an advantage. **2.** A position that affords a broad overall view or perspective, as of a place. **3.** A vantage point. **4.** *Sports* An advantage. [ME < AN, short for OFr. *avantage*, advantage. See ADVANTAGE.]

vantage point *n.* A position that affords a broad overall view or perspective, as of a place or situation.

Va·nu·a Le·vu (və-nōō′ə lĕv′ōō) A volcanic island of Fiji in the S Pacific NE of Viti Levu.

Va·nu·a·tu (vä′nōō-ä′tōō) Formerly **New Hebrides.** An island country of the S Pacific E of N Australia; under joint French and British control after 1906 and independent since 1980. Cap. Port-Vila. Pop. 165,000. —**Va′nu·a′tu·an** *adj. & n.*

Vanuatu

Van Vleck (văn vlĕk′), **John Hasbrouck** 1899–1980. Amer. physicist who shared a 1977 Nobel Prize.

Van·zet·ti (văn-zĕt′ē, vän-dzĕt′tē), **Bartolomeo** 1888–1927. Italian-born Amer. anarchist who with Nicola Sacco was convicted of murder and sentenced to death (1921). Despite the circumstantial nature of the evidence against them, the two were executed in 1927.

vap·id (văp′ĭd, vā′pĭd) *adj.* **1.** Lacking liveliness, animation, or interest; dull. **2.** Lacking taste, zest, or flavor; flat. [Lat. *vapidus.*] —**va·pid′i·ty, vap′id·ness** *n.* —**vap′id·ly** *adv.*

va·por (vā′pər) *n.* **1.** Barely visible or cloudy diffused matter, such as mist or smoke, suspended in the air. **2a.** A gas that is below its critical temperature and can be liquefied by pressure. **b.** The gaseous state of a substance that is liquid or solid under ordinary conditions. **3a.** The vaporized form of a substance for use in industrial, military, or medical processes. **b.** A mixture of a vapor and air, as the explosive gasoline-air mixture burned in an internal-combustion engine. **4.** *Archaic* **a.** Something insubstantial, worthless, or fleeting. **b.** A fantastic or foolish idea. **5.** **vapors** *Archaic* **a.** Exhalations within a bodily organ, esp. the stomach, supposed to affect one's condition. **b.** A nervous disorder such as depression or hysteria. ❖ *v.* **-pored, -por·ing, -pors** —*tr.* To vaporize. —*intr.* **1.** To give off vapor. **2.** To evaporate. **3.** To engage in idle, boastful talk. [ME *vapour* < AN < Lat. *vapor.*] —**va′por·er** *n.*

vapor density *n.* The ratio of the weight of a given volume of one gas to the weight of an equal volume of another gas, typically hydrogen, at the same temperature and pressure.

va·por·es·cence (vā′pə-rĕs′əns) *n.* Formation of vapor.

va·por·if·ic (vā′pə-rĭf′ĭk) *adj.* **1.** Producing or turning to vapor. **2.** Having the nature of vapor; vaporous.

va·por·ing (vā′pər-ĭng) *n.* Boastful or bombastic talk or behavior. —**va′por·ing** *adj.* —**va′por·ing·ly** *adv.*

va·por·ish (vā′pər-ĭsh) *adj.* **1.** Suggestive of or resembling vapor. **2.** *Archaic* Affected by the vapors; given to spells of hysteria or low spirits. —**va′por·ish·ness** *n.*

va·por·ize (vā′pə-rīz′) *tr. & intr.v.* **-ized, -iz·ing, -iz·es** To convert or be converted into vapor. —**va′por·iz′a·ble** *adj.* —**va′por·i·za′tion** (-ĭ-zā′shən) *n.*

va·por·iz·er (vā′pə-rī′zər) *n.* One that vaporizes, esp. a device used to vaporize medicine for inhalation.

vapor lock *n.* A pocket of vaporized gasoline in the fuel line of an internal-combustion engine that obstructs the normal flow of fuel. —**va′por-lock′** (vā′pər-lŏk′) *v.*

va·por·ous (vā′pər-əs) *adj.* **1.** Of or resembling vapor. **2a.** Producing vapors; volatile. **b.** Full of vapors. **3.** Insubstantial, vague, or ethereal. See Syns at **airy. 4.** Extravagantly fanciful; highflown. —**va′por·os′i·ty** (vā′pə-rŏs′ĭ-tē), **va′por·ous·ness** (-pər-əs-nĭs) *n.* —**va′por·ous·ly** *adv.*

vapor pressure *n.* The pressure exerted by a vapor in equilibrium with its solid or liquid phase.

vapor trail *n.* See **contrail.**

va·por·ware (vā′pər-wâr′) *n.* New software that has been announced or marketed but has not been produced.

va·por·y (vā′pə-rē) *adj.* Vaporous.

va·pour (vā′pər) *n. & v. Chiefly British* Variant of **vapor.**

va·que·ro (vä-kâr′ō) *n., pl.* **-ros** *Chiefly Texas* See **cowboy** 1. [Sp. < *vaca*, cow < Lat. *vacca.*]

REGIONAL NOTE Used chiefly in southwest and central Texas to mean a ranch hand or cowboy, the word *vaquero* is a direct loan from Spanish. In California, however, the same word was Anglicized to *buckaroo.* Craig M. Carver, author of *American Regional Dialects,* points out that the two words reflect cultural differences between cattlemen in Texas and California. The Texas vaquero was typically a bachelor who hired on with different outfits, while the California buckaroo usually married and stayed on the same ranch where he was born or had grown up.

var. *abbr.* **1.** variable **2.** variant **3.** variation **4.** variety **5.** various

va·ra (vär′ə) *n.* **1.** A Spanish, Portuguese, and Latin-American unit of linear measure varying from about 81 to 109 centimeters (32 to 43 inches). **2.** A square vara. [Sp. and Port., rod, both < Lat. *vāra*, forked pole < *vārus*, bent.]

va·rac·tor (və-răk′tər, vä-) *n.* A semiconductor device in which the capacitance varies with the applied voltage. [VAR(IABLE) + (RE)ACT(ANCE) + −OR[1].]

Va·ra·na·si (və-rä′nə-sē) also **Be·na·res** (bə-när′əs, -ēz) or **Ba·na·ras** (bə-när′əs) A city of NE-central India on the Ganges R. SE of Lucknow. Pop. 929,270.

Var·dar (vär′där′) A river rising in NW Macedonia and flowing c. 386 km (240 mi) to an arm of the Aegean Sea.

Va·rèse (və-räz′, vä-rĕz′), **Edgard** 1883–1965. French-born Amer. composer of arrhythmic and atonal works.

Var·gas (vär′gəs), **Getulio Dornelles** 1883–1954. Brazilian politician who led a successful revolution (1930) and served as president (1930–45 and 1951–54).

Var·gas Llo·sa (vär′gəs yō′sə, bär′gäs yō′sä), **Mario** b. 1936. Peruvian writer whose novels include *The Green House* (1966).

vari– *pref.* Variant of **vario-.**

var·i·a (vâr′ē-ə, văr′-) *n.* A miscellany, esp. of literary works. [Lat. < neut. pl. of *varius*, various.]

var·i·a·bil·i·ty (vâr′ē-ə-bĭl′ĭ-tē, văr′-) *n., pl.* **-ties** The quality, state, or degree of being variable or changeable.

var·i·a·ble (vâr′ē-ə-bəl, văr′-) *adj.* **1.** Likely to change or vary; subject to variation. **b.** Inconstant; fickle. **2.** *Biology* Tending to deviate, as from a normal or recognized type; aberrant. **3.** *Mathematics* Having no fixed quantitative value. ❖ *n.* **1.** Something that varies or is prone to variation. **2.** *Astronomy* A variable star. **3.** *Mathematics* **a.** A quantity capable of assuming any of a set of values. **b.** A symbol representing such a quantity. —**var′i·a·ble·ness** *n.* —**var′i·a·bly** *adv.*

variable annuity *n.* An annuity in which payments to the annuitant vary according to the changing market value of the underlying investment.

var·i·a·ble-rate mortgage (vâr′ē-ə-bəl-rāt′, văr′-) *n.* See **adjustable-rate mortgage.**

variable star *n.* A star whose brightness varies because of internal changes or periodic eclipsing by a mutually revolving star.

var·i·ance (vâr′ē-əns, văr′-) *n.* **1a.** The act of varying. **b.** The state or quality of being variant or variable. **c.** A difference between what is expected and what actually occurs. **2.** The state or fact of differing or of being in conflict. **3.** *Law* A discrepancy between two statements or documents in a proceeding. **b.** License to engage in an act contrary to a usual rule: *a zoning variance.* **4.** *Statistics* The square of the standard deviation. **5.** *Chemistry* The number of thermodynamic variables, such as temperature and pressure, required to specify a state of equilibrium of a system. —*idiom:* **at variance** In a state of discrepancy; differing.

var·i·ant (vâr′ē-ənt, văr′-) *adj.* **1.** Having or exhibiting variation; differing. **2.** Tending or liable to vary; variable. **3.** Deviating from a standard, usu. by only a slight difference. ❖ *n.* Something that differs in form only slightly from something else, as a different spelling of the same word. [ME < OFr. < Lat. *variāns, var.-,* pr. part. of *variāre*, to vary. See VARY.]

var·i·ate (vâr′ē-ĭt, -āt′, văr′-) *n. Statistics* A random variable with a numerical value defined for a given sample. [< Lat. *variāta,* p. part. of *variāre*, to vary. See VARY.]

var·i·a·tion (vâr′ē-ā′shən, văr′-) *n.* **1a.** The act, process, or result of varying. **b.** The state or fact of being varied. See Syns at **difference. 2.** The extent or degree to which something varies. **3.** Magnetic declination. **4.** Something slightly different from another of the same type. **5.** *Biology* **a.** Marked difference or deviation from the normal or recognized form, function, or structure. **b.** An organism or plant exhibiting such difference or deviation. **6.** *Mathematics* A function that relates the values of one variable to those of other variables. **7.** *Music* **a.** A form that is an altered version of a given theme. **b.** One of a series of forms based on a single theme. **8.** A solo dance, esp. as part of a larger work. —**var′i•a′tion•al** *adj.*

var•i•cel•la (văr′ĭ-sĕl′ə) *n.* See **chickenpox.** [NLat., dim. of *variola,* variola. See VARIOLA.]

var•i•cel•late (văr′ĭ-sĕl′īt, -āt) *adj.* Having small varices, as certain gastropod shells.

var•i•cel•la-zos•ter virus (văr′ĭ-sĕl′ə-zŏs′tər) *n.* A herpesvirus that causes chickenpox and shingles.

var•i•ces (văr′ĭ-sēz′) *n.* Plural of **varix.**

varico– or **varic–** *pref.* Varix; varicose vein: *varicosis.* [< Lat. *varix, varic-,* varix.]

var•i•co•cele (văr′ĭ-kō-sēl′) *n.* A varicose condition of veins of the spermatic cord or the ovaries, forming a soft tumor.

var•i•col•ored (văr′ĭ-kŭl′ərd, văr′-) *adj.* Having a variety of colors; variegated.

var•i•cose (văr′ĭ-kōs′) *adj.* **1.** Abnormally swollen or knotted: *varicose veins.* **2.** Relating to or causing unusual swelling. **3.** Resembling a varix on the surface of a shell. [Lat. *varicōsus < varix, varic-,* swollen vein.]

var•i•co•sis (văr′ĭ-kō′sĭs) *n., pl.* **-ses** (-sēz) **1.** The condition of being varicose. **2.** Formation of varices.

var•i•cos•i•ty (văr′ĭ-kŏs′ĭ-tē) *n., pl.* **-ties 1.** Varicosis. **2.** A varicose enlargement or swelling. **3.** The condition of having varicose veins.

var•i•cot•o•my (văr′ĭ-kŏt′ə-mē) *n., pl.* **-mies** Surgical removal of varicose veins.

var•ied (văr′ēd, văr′-) *adj.* **1.** Having or consisting of various kinds or forms; diverse. See Syns at **miscellaneous. 2.** Having been modified or altered. **3.** Of several colors; varicolored or variegated. —**var′ied•ly** *adv.*

var•i•e•gate (văr′ē-ĭ-gāt′, văr′ĭ-gāt′, văr′-) *tr.v.* **-gat•ed, -gat•ing, -gates 1.** To change the appearance of, esp. by marking with different colors; streak. **2.** To give variety to; make varied. [< LLat. *variegātus,* p. part. of *variegāre* : Lat. *varius,* various + Lat. *agere,* to do, drive; see **ag–** in App.] —**var′i•e•ga′tor** *n.*

var•i•e•gat•ed (văr′ē-ĭ-gā′tĭd, văr′ĭ-gā′-, văr′-) *adj.* **1.** Having streaks, marks, or patches of a different color or colors; varicolored. **2.** Distinguished or characterized by variety.

var•i•e•ga•tion (văr′ē-ĭ-gā′shən, văr′ĭ-gā′-, văr′-) *n.* The state of being variegated; diversified coloration.

va•ri•e•tal (və-rī′ĭ-tl) *adj.* Of, indicating, or characterizing a variety, esp. a biological variety. ❖ *n.* A wine made principally from one variety of grape and carrying the name of that grape. [< VARIETY.] —**va•ri′e•tal•ly** *adv.*

va•ri•e•ty (və-rī′ĭ-tē) *n., pl.* **-ties 1.** The quality or condition of being various or varied; diversity. **2.** A number or collection of varied things, esp. of a particular group; an assortment. **3.** A group distinguished from other groups by a specific characteristic or set of characteristics. **4.** *Biology* **a.** A taxonomic subdivision of a species consisting of groups or individuals that differ from the remainder of the species in certain minor characteristics. **b.** An organism, esp. a plant, belonging to such a subdivision. **5.** A variety show. [Fr. *variété* < OFr. < Lat. *varietās, varietāt-* < *varius,* various.]

variety meat *n.* **1.** Meat taken from a part other than skeletal muscles. **2.** Meat, such as sausage, that has been processed.

variety show *n.* A theatrical entertainment consisting of successive unrelated acts, such as songs and comedy skits.

variety store *n.* A retail store that carries a large variety of usu. inexpensive merchandise.

var•i•form (văr′ə-fôrm′, văr′-) *adj.* Having a variety of forms; diversiform.

vario– or **vari–** *pref.* Variety; difference; variation: *variometer.* [< Lat. *varius,* speckled.]

va•ri•o•la (və-rī′ə-lə, văr′ē-ō′lə, văr′-) *n.* See **smallpox.** [NLat. < Med.Lat., pustule < Lat. *varius,* speckled.]

var•i•o•late (văr′ē-ə-lāt′, văr′-) *adj.* Having pustules or marks like those of smallpox. ❖ *tr.v.* **-lat•ed, -lat•ing, -lates** To inoculate with the smallpox virus.

var•i•ole (văr′ē-ōl′) *n.* A small pocklike mark, as on an insect.

var•i•o•lite (văr′ē-ə-līt′, văr′-) *n.* A basic rock whose pockmarked appearance is caused by the presence of numerous white rounded embedded spherules. —**var′i•o•lit′ic** (-lĭt′ĭk) *adj.*

var•i•o•loid (văr′ē-ə-loid′, văr′-, və-rī′ə-loid′) *n.* A mild form of smallpox occurring in people who have been previously vaccinated or who have had the disease.

va•ri•o•lous (və-rī′ə-ləs, văr′ē-ō′-, văr′-) *adj.* Of, relating to, or affected with smallpox.

var•i•om•e•ter (văr′ē-ŏm′ĭ-tər, văr′-) *n.* A variable inductor used to measure variations in terrestrial magnetism.

var•i•o•rum (văr′ē-ôr′əm, -ōr′-) *n.* **1.** An edition of the works of an author with notes by various scholars or editors. **2.** An edition containing various versions of a text. ❖ *adj.* Of or relating to a variorum edition or text. [Lat. *(editiōcum notīs)* variōrum, (edition with the notes) of various persons, genitive pl. of *varius,* various.]

var•i•ous (văr′ē-əs, văr′-) *adj.* **1a.** Of diverse kinds: *for various reasons.* **b.** Unlike; different. **2.** Being more than one; several. **3.** Many-sided; versatile: *a person of various skills.* **4.** Having a varie-

gated nature or appearance. **5.** Being an individual or separate member of a class or group: *The various reports all agreed.* **6.** *Archaic* Changeable; variable. ❖ *pron.* (used with a pl. verb) *Usage Problem* Several different individuals. [< Lat. *varius.*] —**var′i•ous•ly** *adv.* —**var′i•ous•ness** *n.*

var•i•sized (văr′ĭ-sīzd′, văr′-) *adj.* Of different sizes.

var•ix (văr′ĭks) *n., pl.* **-i•ces** (-ĭ-sēz′) **1.** An abnormally dilated or swollen vein, artery, or lymph vessel. **2.** One of the longitudinal ridges on a gastropod shell. [Lat., swollen vein.]

var•let (văr′lĭt) *n.* **1.** An attendant or servant. **2.** A knight's page. **3.** A rascal; a knave. [ME < OFr., var. of *vaslet.* See VALET.]

var•let•ry (văr′lĭ-trē) *n., pl.* **-tries** *Archaic* **1.** A crowd of attendants or menials. **2.** A disorderly crowd; a rabble.

var•mint (văr′mĭnt) *n. Informal* One that is considered undesirable, obnoxious, or troublesome. [Variant of VERMIN.]

Var•na (văr′nə) A city of E Bulgaria on the Black Sea NNE of Burgas; founded in the 6th cent. B.C. Pop. 308,600.

var•nish (văr′nĭsh) *n.* **1a.** A paint containing a solvent and an oxidizing or evaporating binder, used to coat a surface with a hard, glossy transparent film. **b.** The smooth coating or gloss resulting from the application of this paint. **2a.** Something suggestive of or resembling varnish. **b.** A deceptively attractive external appearance; an outward show. ❖ *tr.v.* **-nished, -nish•ing, -nish•es 1.** To cover with varnish. **2.** To give a smooth and glossy finish to. **3.** To give a deceptively attractive appearance to; gloss over. [ME *vernisshe* < OFr. *vernis* < Med.Lat. *veronix, vernix,* sandarac resin < Med.Gk. *verenikē* < Gk. *Berenikē,* Berenice (Benghazi), an ancient city of Cyrenaica.] —**var′nish•er** *n.*

varnish tree *n.* Any of several trees having milky juice used to make varnish.

var•si•ty (văr′sĭ-tē) *n., pl.* **-ties 1.** The principal team representing a university, college, or school in competitions. **2.** *Chiefly British* A university. [Shortening and alteration of UNIVERSITY.]

Va•ru•na (văr′rōō-nə, vŭl′-) *n. Hinduism* The god of the ocean, often considered king of the gods. [Skt. *Varunah.*]

var•us (văr′əs, văr′-) *n.* An abnormal position of a bone of the leg or foot. [< Lat. *vārus,* crooked.]

varve (värv) *n.* A layer or series of layers of sediment deposited in a body of still water in one year. [Swed. *varv,* layer < *varva,* to bend < ON *hverfa.*]

var•y (văr′ē, văr′ē) *v.* **-ied** (-ēd), **-y•ing, -ies** (-ēz) —*tr.* **1.** To make or cause changes in the characteristics or attributes of; modify or alter. **2.** To give variety to; make diverse: *vary one's diet.* **3.** To introduce under new aspects; express in a different manner: *vary a tempo.* —*intr.* **1.** To undergo or show change. **2.** To be different; deviate. **3.** To undergo successive or alternate changes in attributes or qualities. [ME *varien,* to undergo change < OFr. *varier* < Lat. *variāre < varius,* various.]

var•y•ing hare (văr′ē-ĭng, văr′-) *n.* See **snowshoe hare.**

vas (văs) *n., pl.* **va•sa** (vā′zə) *Anatomy* A vessel or duct. [Lat. *vās,* vessel.]

vas– *pref.* Variant of **vaso–.**

va•sal (vā′səl, -zəl) *adj.* Of, relating to, or connected with a vessel or duct of the body.

Va•sa•ri (və-zär′ē, -sär′ē, vä-zä′rē), **Giorgio** 1511–74. Italian painter and architect known for his history of Italian Renaissance art (1550).

vas•cu•lar (văs′kyə-lər) *adj.* Of, characterized by, or containing vessels that carry or circulate fluids, such as blood or sap, through the body of an animal or plant. [< Lat. *vāsculum,* dim. of *vās,* vessel.] —**vas′cu•lar′i•ty** (-lăr′ĭ-tē) *n.*

vascular bundle *n.* A strand of primary conductive plant tissue consisting essentially of xylem and phloem.

vascular cambium *n.* A lateral meristem that produces secondary xylem to the inside and secondary phloem to the outside.

vas•cu•lar•i•za•tion (văs′kyə-lər-ĭ-zā′shən) *n.* **1.** The process of making or becoming vascular; the formation of vessels. **2.** An abnormal or pathological formation of blood vessels.

vascular plant *n.* Any of various plants, such as the ferns and seed-bearing plants, in which the phloem transports sugar and the xylem transports water and salts.

vascular tissue *n.* The supportive and conductive tissue in plants, consisting of xylem and phloem.

vas•cu•lum (văs′kyə-ləm) *n., pl.* **-la** (-lə) A small box or case used for carrying collected plant specimens. [Lat. *vāsculum,* small vessel. See VASCULAR.]

vas def•er•ens (dĕf′ər-ənz, -ə-rĕnz′) *n., pl.* **vasa def•er•en•ti•a** (dĕf′ə-rĕn′shē-ə) The main duct through which semen is carried from the epididymis to the ejaculatory duct. [NLat. *vās dēferēns* : *vās,* duct + Lat. *dēferēns,* pr. part. of *dēferre,* to carry away.]

vase (vās, vāz, väz) *n.* An open container used for holding flowers or for ornamentation. [Fr. < Lat. *vās,* vessel.]

va•sec•to•my (və-sĕk′tə-mē, vā-zĕk′-) *n., pl.* **-mies** Surgical removal of all or part of the vas deferens, usu. as a means of ster-

vase
Chinese porcelain vase from the Qianlong period (1735–96) of the Qing dynasty

ă	pat	oi	boy
ā	pay	ou	out
âr	care	ŏŏ	took
ä	father	ōō	boot
ĕ	pet	ŭ	cut
ē	be	ûr	urge
ĭ	pit	th	thin
ī	pie	*th*	this
îr	pier	hw	which
ŏ	pot	zh	vision
ō	toe	ə	about,
ô	paw		item

Stress marks:
′ (primary);
′ (secondary), as in
lexicon (lĕk′sĭ-kŏn′)

Vatican City

Sarah Vaughan
photographed in 1960

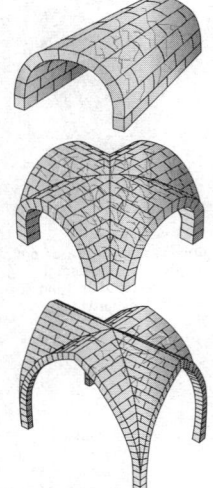

vault¹
*top to bottom: barrel, groin,
and rib vaults*

ilization. —**va·sec′to·mize′** *v.*

vas ef·fer·ens (ĕf′ər-ənz, -ə-rĕnz′) *n., pl.* **vasa ef·fer·en·ti·a** (ĕf′ə-rĕn′shē-ə) Any of a number of small ducts that carry semen from the testis to the epididymis. [NLat. *vās efferēns* : *vās*, duct + Lat. *efferēns*, pr. part. of *efferre*, to carry out.]

Vas·e·line (văs′ə-lēn′, văs′ə-lēn′) A trademark used for a brand of petroleum jelly.

vaso– *or* **vas–** *pref.* **1.** Blood vessel: *vasoconstriction.* **2.** Vas deferens: *vasectomy.* [< Lat. *vās*, vessel.]

va·so·ac·tive (vā′zō-ăk′tĭv) *adj.* Causing constriction or dilation of blood vessels. —**va′so·ac·tiv′i·ty** *n.*

va·so·con·stric·tion (vā′zō-kən-strĭk′shən) *n.* Constriction of a blood vessel. —**vas′o·con·stric′tive** *adj.*

va·so·con·stric·tor (vā′zō-kən-strĭk′tər) *n.* Something, such as a nerve or drug, that causes vasoconstriction.

va·so·di·la·tion (vā′zō-dī-lā′shən, -dī-) *also* **va·so·dil·a·ta·tion** (-dĭl′ə-tā′shən, -dī′lə-) *n.* Dilation of a blood vessel, as by the action of a nerve or drug.

va·so·di·la·tor (vā′zō-dī-lā′tər, -dī-, -dĭl′ā-) *n.* Something, such as a nerve or drug, that causes vasodilation.

va·so·mo·tor (vā′zō-mō′tər) *adj.* Relating to, causing, or regulating constriction or dilation of blood vessels.

va·so·pres·sin (vā′zō-prĕs′ĭn) *n.* A hormone secreted by the posterior lobe of the pituitary gland that constricts blood vessels, raises blood pressure, and reduces excretion of urine.

va·so·pres·sor (vā′zō-prĕs′ər) *adj.* Of or causing constriction of blood vessels. ❖ *n.* A vasopressor agent.

va·so·spasm (vā′zō-spăz′əm) *n.* A sudden constriction of a blood vessel. —**va′so·spas′tic** (-spăs′tĭk) *adj.*

va·so·va·gal (vā′zō-vā′gəl) *adj.* Relating to or involving blood vessels and the vagus nerve.

vas·sal (văs′əl) *n.* **1.** A person who held land from a feudal lord and received protection in return for homage and allegiance. **2.** A bondman; a slave. **3.** A subordinate or dependent. [ME < OFr. < VLat. *vassallus* < *vassus*, of Celt. orig. See **upo** in App.]

vas·sal·age (văs′ə-lĭj) *n.* **1.** The condition of being a vassal. **2.** The service, homage, and fealty required of a vassal. **3.** A position of subordination or subjection; servitude. **4.** The land held by a vassal; a fief. **5.** Vassals, esp. those of a particular lord, considered as a group.

vast (văst) *adj.* **vast·er, vast·est 1.** Very great in size, number, amount, or quantity. **2.** Very great in area or extent. **3.** Very great in degree or intensity. ❖ *n. Archaic* An immense space. [Lat. *vāstus.*] —**vast′ly** *adv.* —**vast′ness** *n.*

Väs·ter·ås (vĕs′tə-rōs′) A city of E Sweden WNW of Stockholm. Pop. 120,889.

vas·ti·tude (văs′tĭ-tōōd′, -tyōōd′) *also* **vas·ti·ty** (-tē) *n.* Immensity. [Lat. *vāstitūdō < vāstus*, vast.]

vast·y (văs′tē) *adj.* **-i·er, -i·est** *Archaic* Vast.

vat (văt) *n.* A large vessel, such as a tub or barrel, used to hold or store liquids. ❖ *tr.v.* **vat·ted, vat·ting, vats** To put into or treat in a vat. [ME, var. of *fat* < OE *fæt.*]

VAT *abbr.* value-added tax

Vat. *abbr.* Vatican

vat dye *n.* A dye, such as indigo, that produces a fast color by impregnating fiber with a reduced soluble form that is then oxidized to an insoluble form. —**vat′-dyed′** (văt′dīd′) *adj.*

vat·ic (văt′ĭk) *also* **vat·i·cal** (-ĭ-kəl) *adj.* Of or characteristic of a prophet; oracular. [< Lat. *vātēs*, seer, of Celt. orig. See **wet-¹** in App.]

Vat·i·can (văt′ĭ-kən) *n.* **1.** The official residence of the pope in Vatican City. **2.** The papal government; the papacy. [Lat. *Vatīcānus (mōns)*, the Vatican (Hill).]

Vatican City An independent papal state on the Tiber R. within Rome, Italy; created by the Lateran Treaty signed by Pope Pius XI and Victor Emmanuel III of Italy in 1929. Pop. 766.

Vatican Council *n.* Either of two ecumenical councils of the Roman Catholic Church, the **First Vatican Council** (1869–70) and the **Second Vatican Council** (1962–65), convoked by Pius IX and John XXIII, respectively. The First is noted for its affirmation of papal infallibility, and the Second resulted in the revision of most of the liturgy.

Vat·i·can·ism (văt′ĭ-kə-nĭz′əm) *n.* The policies and authority of the papacy.

va·tic·i·nal (və-tĭs′ə-nəl, və-) *adj.* Prophetic.

va·tic·i·nate (və-tĭs′ə-nāt′, vā-) *v.* **-nat·ed, -nat·ing, -nates** —*tr.* To prophesy; foretell. —*intr.* To be a prophet. [Lat. *vāticinārī, vāticināt- < vātēs*, seer. See **VATIC**.] —**va·tic′i·na′tor** *n.*

va·tic·i·na·tion (və-tĭs′ə-nā′shən, vā-) *n.* **1.** The act of prophesying. **2.** A prediction; a prophecy.

Vät·tern (vĕt′ərn) A lake of S-central Sweden SE of Lake Vänern; connected with the Baltic Sea by the Göta Canal.

va·tu (vä′tōō) *n.* See table at **currency**. [Native word in Vanuatu.]

vau (väv, vôv) *n.* Variant of **vav**.

vaude·ville (vôd′vĭl′, vôd′ə-, vōd′ə-) *n.* **1a.** Stage entertainment offering a variety of short acts such as song-and-dance routines and juggling performances. **b.** A theatrical performance of this kind; a variety show. **2.** A light comic play that often includes songs and pantomime. **3.** A popular, often satirical song. [Fr., alteration of OFr. *vaudevire*, occasional or topical light popular

song, poss. short for *chanson du Vau de Vire*, song of Vau de Vire, a valley of NW France, or perh. dialectal *vauder*, to go + *virer*, to turn; see **VEER¹**.]

vaude·vil·lian (vôd-vĭl′yən, vōd-, vô′də-) *n.* One, esp. a performer, who works in vaudeville. —**vaude·vil′lian** *adj.*

Vau·dois (vō-dwä′) *pl.n.* See **Waldenses.** [Fr. < OFr. *vaudeis* < Med.Lat. *Waldēnsēs*. See **WALDENSES**.]

Vaughan (vôn), **Henry** Known as "the Silurist." 1622–95. Welsh poet whose works include *Silex Scintillans* (1650–55).

Vaughan, Sarah 1924–90. Amer. jazz singer known for her complex bebop phrasing and her scat-singing virtuosity.

Vaughan Williams, Ralph 1872–1958. British composer whose works include the ballet *Job* (1930).

vault¹ (vôlt) *n.* **1a.** An arched structure, usu. of masonry or concrete, serving to cover a space. **b.** An arched overhead covering, such as the sky, that resembles a vault in form. **2.** A room or space, such as a cellar or storeroom, with arched walls and ceiling, esp. when underground. **3.** A room or compartment, often built of steel, for the safekeeping of valuables. **4.** A burial chamber, esp. when underground. **5.** *Anatomy* An arched part of the body, esp. the top part of the skull. ❖ *tr.v.* **vault·ed, vault·ing, vaults 1.** To construct or supply with an arched ceiling; cover with a vault. **2.** To build or make in the shape of a vault; arch. [ME *vaute* < OFr. < VLat. *volvita, *volta* < fem. of *volvitus*, arched, alteration of Lat. *volūtus*, p. part. of *volvere*, to roll. See **wel-** in App.]

vault² (vôlt) *v.* **vault·ed, vault·ing, vaults** —*tr.* To vault over. —*intr.* **1.** To jump or leap, esp. with the use of the hands or a pole. **2.** To do something as if by leaping suddenly or vigorously. ❖ *n.* The act of vaulting; a jump. [Obsolete Fr. *volter* < OFr. < OItal. *voltare* < VLat. *volvitāre*, freq. of Lat. *volvere*, to turn, roll. See **wel-** in App.] —**vault′er** *n.*

vault·ing¹ (vôl′tĭng) *n.* **1.** The act, practice, or method of constructing vaults. **2.** A vault or vaulted structure.

vault·ing² (vôl′tĭng) *adj.* **1.** Leaping upward or over. **2.** Reaching too far; exaggerated: *his vaulting ambition.* **3.** Employed in leaping over: *a vaulting pole.*

vaulting horse *n.* A piece of gymnastic equipment with an upholstered body used esp. for vaulting.

vaunt (vônt, vänt) *v.* **vaunt·ed, vaunt·ing, vaunts** —*tr.* To speak boastfully of; brag about. —*intr.* To speak boastfully; brag. ❖ *n.* **1.** A boastful remark. **2.** Speech of extravagant self-praise. [ME *vaunten* < OFr. *vanter* < LLat. *vānitāre*, to talk frivolously, freq. of Lat. *vānāre* < *vānus*, empty.] —**vaunt′er** *n.*

vaunt-cour·i·er (vônt′kŏŏr′ē-ər, -kûr′-, kŭr′-, vônt′-) *n. Archaic* A person, such as a herald, sent in advance. [Short for obsolete Fr. *avaunt-courier* : OFr. *avaunt*, in front; see **VANGUARD** + OFr. *courrier*, messenger; see **COURIER**.]

Vau·pés (vou-pās′, -pĕs′) See **Uaupés**.

vav *also* **vau** *or* **waw** (väv, vôv) *n.* The sixth letter of the Hebrew alphabet. [Heb. *wāw* < Phoenician *wāw, *wō*, pin (sense uncertain), sixth letter of the Phoenician alphabet.]

vav·a·sor *also* **vav·a·sour** (văv′ə-sôr′, -sôr′, -sōōr′) *n.* A feudal tenant ranking directly below a baron or peer. [ME *vavasour* < OFr. < Med.Lat. *vavassor*, poss. contraction of *vassus vassōrum*, vassal of vassals : *vassus*, vassal (< VLat. *vassus*; see **VASSAL**) + *vassōrum*, genitive pl. of *vassus*, vassal.]

vb. *abbr.* **1.** verb **2.** verbal

VC *abbr.* **1.** venture capitalist **2.** vice chancellor **3.** vice consul **4.** Victoria Cross **5.** Vietcong

V-chip (vē′chĭp′) *n.* A computer chip installed in a television to allow the user to control the certain programs, esp. of sexual or violent content. [V(IEWER) and V(IOLENCE) + CHIP¹.]

VCR (vē′sē-är′) *n.* An electronic device for recording and playing back video images and sound on a videocassette. [V(IDEO)C(ASSETTE) R(ECORDER).]

VD *abbr.* **1.** vapor density **2.** venereal disease

V-day (vē′dā′) *n.* A day of victory, as at war's end.

VDT *abbr.* video display terminal

've Contraction of *have*: *I've been invited.*

veal (vēl) *n.* **1.** The meat of a calf. **2.** *also* **veal·er** (vē′lər) A calf raised to be slaughtered for food. [ME *veel* < OFr. < Lat. *vitellus*, dim. of *vitulus*, calf. See **wet-²** in App.]

Veb·len (vĕb′lən), **Thorstein Bunde** 1857–1929. Amer. economist who described a fundamental conflict between the provision of goods and the making of money.

vec·tor (vĕk′tər) *n.* **1.** *Mathematics* **a.** A quantity, such as velocity, completely specified by a magnitude and a direction. **b.** A one-dimensional array. **c.** An element of a vector space. **2.** *Pathology* An organism, such as a tick, that carries disease-causing microorganisms from one host to another. **3.** *Genetics* A bacteriophage, plasmid, or other agent that transfers genetic material from one cell to another. **4.** A force or influence. **5.** A course or direction, as of an airplane. ❖ *tr.v.* **-tored, -tor·ing, -tors** To guide (a pilot or aircraft, for example) by means of radio communication according to vectors. [Lat., carrier < *vehere, vect-*, to carry. See **wegh-** in App.] —**vec·to′ri·al** (vĕk-tôr′ē-əl, -tōr′-) *adj.*

vector boson *n.* Any of the elementary particles that mediate one of the four fundamental forces. The particles and their corresponding forces are the photon and the electromagnetic force, the graviton and the gravitational force, the intermediate vector boson and the weak interaction, and the gluon and the strong interaction.

vector graphic *n.* A computer image that is stored and displayed in terms of vectors rather than points, allowing for easier scaling and storage.

vector product *n.* A vector ***c***, depending on two other vectors ***a*** and ***b***, whose magnitude is the product of the magnitude of ***a***, the magnitude of ***b***, and the sine of the angle between ***a*** and ***b***. Its direction is perpendicular to the plane through ***a*** and ***b*** and oriented so that a right-handed rotation about it carries ***a*** into ***b*** through an angle not greater than 180°.

vector space *n.* A set of generalized vectors and a field of scalars, having the same rules for vector addition and scalar multiplication as physical vectors and scalars.

Ve•da (vā′də, vē′-) *n.* Any of the oldest and most authoritative Hindu sacred texts, composed in Sanskrit and gathered into four collections. [Skt. *vedaḥ*, sacred lore, knowledge, Veda. See **weid-** in App.]

Ve•dan•ta (vĭ-dän′tə, -dăn′-) *n. Hinduism* The philosophy that further develops the implications in the Upanishads that all reality is a single principle, Brahman, and teaches that the believer's goal is to transcend the limitations of self-identity and realize one's unity with Brahman. [Skt. *vedāntaḥ*, complete knowledge of the Veda : *vedaḥ*, Veda; see VEDA + *antaḥ*, end; see **ant-** in App.] **—Ve•dan′tic** *adj.* **—Ve•dan′tism** *n.* **—Ve•dan′tist** *n.*

V-E Day (vē′ē′) *n.* May 8, 1945, on which the Allies announced the surrender of German forces in Europe. [*V(ictory in) E(urope) Day.*]

Ved•da also **Ved•dah** (vĕd′ə) *n., pl.* **Vedda** or **-das** also **Veddah** or **-dahs** A member of the earliest people of Sri Lanka, originally forest-dwelling hunters but now almost completely assimilated into the Sinhalese population. [Sinhalese, hunter.]

ve•dette also **vi•dette** (vĭ-dĕt′) *n.* A mounted sentinel stationed in advance of an outpost. [Fr. < Ital. *vedetta*, alteration of *veletta*, prob. < Sp. *vela*, watch < *velar*, to watch < Lat. *vigilāre*, to watch by night < *vigil*, awake.]

Ve•dic (vā′dĭk, vē′-) *adj.* Of or relating to the Veda or Vedas, the variety of Sanskrit in which they are written, or the Hindu culture that produced them. ❖ *n.* This early Sanskrit.

vee (vē) *n.* The letter *v.*

vee•jay (vē′jā′) *n.* A video jockey. [V(IDEO) + (D)EEJAY.]

vee•na (vē′nə) *n.* Variant of **vina.**

veep (vēp) *n. Slang* A vice president. [Pronunciation of VP.]

veer¹ (vîr) *v.* **veered, veer•ing, veers** *—intr.* **1.** To turn aside from a course, direction, or purpose; swerve. See Syns at **swerve. 2.** To shift clockwise in direction, as from north to northeast. Used of the wind. **3.** *Nautical* To veer a ship. *—tr.* **1.** To alter the direction of; turn. **2.** *Nautical* To change the course of (a ship) upwind by turning the stern through the wind. ❖ *n.* A change in direction; a swerve. [Fr. *virer* < OFr.]

veer² (vîr) *tr.v.* **veered, veer•ing, veers** *Nautical* To let out or release (a line or an anchor chain). [ME *veren* < MDu. *vieren*. See **per¹** in App.]

vee•ry (vîr′ē) *n., pl.* **-ries** A New World thrush *(Hylocichla fuscescens)* having a reddish-brown head, back, and tail and an indistinctly spotted breast. [Poss. imit. of its song.]

veg (vĕj) *intr.v.* **vegged, veg•ging, veg•es** *Informal* To engage in relaxing or passive activities. Often used with *out.* [Short for VEGETATE.]

Ve•ga (vē′gə, vā′-) *n.* The brightest star in Lyra. [Med.Lat. < Ar. *(an-nasr) al-wāqi'*, the falling (eagle), Vega : *al-*, the, *wāqi'*, falling, active part. of *waqa'a*, to fall.]

Ve•ga (vā′gə, bĕ′gä), **Lope de** 1562–1635. Spanish playwright whose works include *Fuenteovejuna* (c. 1619).

ve•gan (vē′gən, vĕj′ən) *n.* A vegetarian who eats only plant products, esp. one who uses no products derived from animals, such as leather or fur. [Short for VEGETARIAN.] **—veg′an•ism** *n.*

veg•e•ta•ble (vĕj′tə-bəl, vĕj′ĭ-tə-) *n.* **1a.** A plant cultivated for an edible part, such as the leaf of spinach. **b.** This edible part. **c.** A member of the vegetable kingdom; a plant. **2.** *Offensive Slang* One who is severely impaired mentally and physically, as by brain injury or disease. **3.** One who is regarded as dull, passive, or unresponsive. ❖ *adj.* **1.** Of or derived from plants or a plant. **2.** Suggestive of or resembling a plant. **3.** Growing or multiplying like plants. [< ME, living and growing as plants do < OFr. < Med.Lat. *vegetābilis* < LLat., enlivening < Lat. *vegetāre*, to enliven < *vegetus*, lively < *vegēre*, to be lively.]

WORD HISTORY When the speaker in Andrew Marvell's "To His Coy Mistress" tells his mistress that "Had we but world enough, and time . . . /My vegetable love should grow/Vaster than empires and more slow," he uses *vegetable* figuratively to mean "having the property of life and growth, as does a plant." This use is based on the ancient religious and philosophical notion of the tripartite soul as interpreted by the Scholastics: the *vegetative* soul common to plants, animals, and humans; the *sensitive* soul common to animals and humans; and the *rational* soul, found only in humans. "Vegetable love" in Marvell's poem is thus a love that grows, takes nourishment, and reproduces, although it grows slowly. Marvell's use illustrates the original sense of *vegetable*, first recorded in the 15th century. In a work published in 1582 we first find the adjective use "having to do with plants." In a work of the same date appears the noun, meaning "a plant."

vegetable ivory *n.* A hard ivorylike material obtained from the ivory nut, used for small objects such as buttons.

vegetable kingdom *n.* See **plant kingdom.**

vegetable marrow *n. Chiefly British* Marrow squash.

vegetable oil *n.* Any of various oils obtained from plants and used in food products and industrially.

vegetable oyster *n.* See **salsify.**

vegetable silk *n.* Any of several silky fibers from the seedpods of certain plants, such as the kapok.

vegetable sponge *n.* See **loofa** 2.

vegetable tallow *n.* **1.** Any of various waxy fats obtained from certain plants, such as the bayberry, and used in making soap and candles. **2.** See **Chinese tallow tree.**

vegetable wax *n.* A waxy substance of plant origin.

veg•e•tal (vĕj′ĭ-tl) *adj.* **1.** Of, relating to, or characteristic of plants. **2.** Relating to growth rather than to sexual reproduction; vegetative. [ME < Med.Lat. *vegetālis* < Lat. *vegetāre*, to enliven. See VEGETABLE.] **—veg′e•tal•ly** *adv.*

vegetal pole *n. Embryology* The portion of an egg that is opposite the animal pole that contains most of the yolk.

veg•e•tar•i•an (vĕj′ĭ-târ′ē-ən) *n.* **1.** One who practices vegetarianism. **2.** A herbivore. ❖ *adj.* **1.** Of or relating to vegetarianism or vegetarians. **2.** Consisting primarily or wholly of vegetables and vegetable products. [VEGET(ABLE) + -ARIAN.]

veg•e•tar•i•an•ism (vĕj′ĭ-târ′ē-ə-nĭz′əm) *n.* The practice of subsisting on a diet composed of vegetables, grains, fruits, nuts, and seeds, with or without eggs and dairy products.

veg•e•tate (vĕj′ĭ-tāt′) *intr.v.* **-tat•ed, -tat•ing, -tates 1.** To grow or sprout as a plant does. **2.** *Pathology* To grow in size or spread abnormally. **3.** To exist in a state of inactivity or insensibility. **4.** *Informal* To engage in relaxing or passive activities, such as watching television. [Lat. *vegetāre, vegetāt-*, to enliven. See VEGETABLE.]

veg•e•ta•tion (vĕj′ĭ-tā′shən) *n.* **1.** The act or process of vegetating. **2.** The plants of an area or a region; plant life: *lush vegetation.* **3.** *Pathology* An abnormal growth on the body. **—veg′e•ta′tion•al** *adj.*

veg•e•ta•tive (vĕj′ĭ-tā′tĭv) also **veg•e•tive** (-ĭ-tĭv) *adj.* **1.** Of or characteristic of plants or their growth. **2.** *Biology* **a.** Of or capable of growth. **b.** Of or functioning in processes such as growth or nutrition rather than sexual reproduction. **c.** Of or relating to asexual reproduction, such as fission. **3.** *Medicine* Of or relating to an impaired level of brain function in which there is response to certain sensory stimuli but no demonstrable cognitive function. **4.** Spending much time sitting or lying down; physically inactive.

veg•gie also **veg•ie** (vĕj′ē) *n. Informal* A vegetable.

ve•he•ment (vē′ə-mənt) *adj.* **1.** Forceful or intense in expression, emotion, or conviction; fervid. **2.** Vigorous or energetic; strong: *a vehement storm.* [ME < OFr. < Lat. *vehemēns, vehement-*, perh. < *vehere*, to carry. See **wegh-** in App.] **—ve′he•mence, ve′he•men•cy** *n.* **—ve′he•ment•ly** *adv.*

ve•hi•cle (vē′ĭ-kəl) *n.* **1a.** A device or structure for transporting persons or things; a conveyance: *a space vehicle.* **b.** A self-propelled conveyance that runs on tires; a motor vehicle. **2.** A medium through which something is transmitted, expressed, or accomplished. **3.** The concrete or specific word or phrase that is applied to the tenor of a metaphor and gives the metaphor its figurative power, as *walking shadow* in *"Life's but a walking shadow"* (Shakespeare). **4.** A play, role, or piece of music used to display the special talents of one performer or company. **5.** A substance of no therapeutic value used to convey an active medicine. **6.** A substance in which paint pigments are mixed for application. [Lat. *vehiculum* < *vehere*, to carry. See **wegh-** in App.]

ve•hic•u•lar (vē-hĭk′yə-lər) *adj.* **1.** Of, relating to, or intended for vehicles, esp. motor vehicles. **2.** Serving as a vehicle.

Ve•ii (vē′ī) An ancient city of Etruria N of modern-day Rome, Italy; conquered by Rome in 396 B.C.

veil (vāl) *n.* **1.** A cloth worn, usu. by women, over the head, shoulders, and often the face. **2.** A length of netting attached to a woman's hat or headdress, worn for decoration or to protect the head and face. **3a.** The part of a nun's headdress that frames the face and falls over the shoulders. **b.** The life or vows of a nun. **4a.** A piece of light fabric hung to serve as a curtain. **b.** Something that conceals, separates, or screens like a curtain: *a veil of secrecy.* **5.** *Biology* A membranous covering or part; a velum. ❖ *tr.v.* **veiled, veil•ing, veils 1.** To cover with or as if with a veil. **2.** To conceal or disguise. [ME < ONFr. < Lat. *vēla*, pl. of *vēlum*, a covering.]

veiled (vāld) *adj.* **1.** Covered with a veil. **2.** Concealed or disguised as if with a veil.

veil•ing (vā′lĭng) *n.* **1.** A veil. **2.** Sheer material used for veils.

vein (vān) *n.* **1a.** *Anatomy* Any of the membranous tubes that form a branching system and carry blood to the heart. **b.** A blood vessel. **2.** *Botany* One of the vascular bundles or ribs that form the branching framework of conducting and supporting tissues in a leaf. **3.** *Zoology* One of the horny ribs that stiffen and support the wing of an insect. **4.** *Geology* A regularly shaped and lengthy

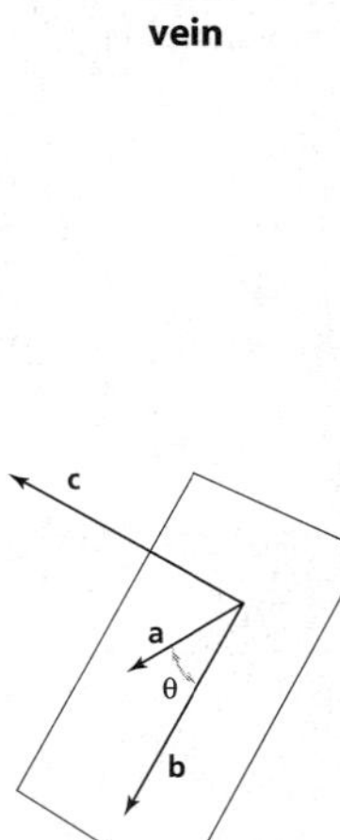

vector product
$c = a \times b$

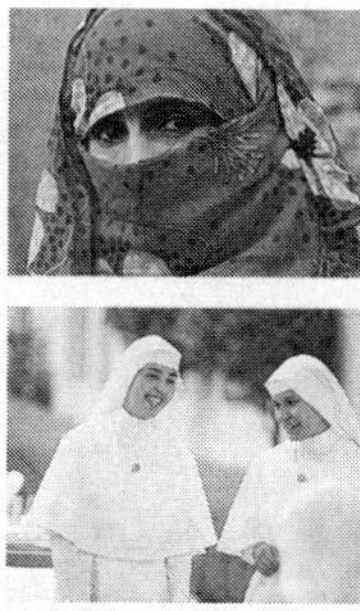

veil
top: Muslim woman
bottom: Christian nuns

ă	pat	oi	boy
ā	pay	ou	out
âr	care	o͝o	took
ä	father	o͞o	boot
ĕ	pet	ŭ	cut
ē	be	ûr	urge
ĭ	pit	th	thin
ī	pie	*th*	this
îr	pier	hw	which
ŏ	pot	zh	vision
ō	toe	ə	about, item
ô	paw		

Stress marks:
′ (primary);
′ (secondary), as in
lexicon (lĕk′sĭ-kŏn′)

occurrence of an ore; a lode. **5.** A long wavy strip of a different shade or color, as in marble. **6.** A fissure, crack, or cleft. **7.** A pervading character or quality; a streak. **8a.** A transient attitude or mood. **b.** A particular turn of mind: *in a serious vein.* ❖ *tr.v.* **veined, vein·ing, veins 1.** To supply or fill with veins. **2.** To mark or decorate with veins. [ME *veine* < OFr. < Lat. *vēna*.] —**vein′al** *adj.*

veined (vānd) *adj.* Having veins or showing veinlike markings.

vein·ing (vā′nĭng) *n.* Distribution or arrangement of veins or veinlike markings.

vein·let (vān′lĭt) *n.* A small or secondary vein, as on the wing of an insect.

vein·stone (vān′stōn′) *n.* Mineral matter in a vein exclusive of the ore; gangue.

vein·ule (vān′yōōl) *n.* A small vein.

vein·y (vā′nē) *adj.* **-i·er, -i·est** Full of or exhibiting veins; veined.

vel. *abbr.* **1.** vellum **2.** velocity

ve·la (vē′lə) *n.* Plural of **velum.**

Ve·la (vē′lə, vā′-) A Southern constellation near Pyxis and Carina. [Lat. *vēla,* pl. of *vēlum,* a covering.]

ve·la·men (və-lā′mən) *n.,* pl. **-lam·i·na** (-lăm′ə-nə) **1.** *Anatomy* A membranous covering or partition; velum. **2.** *Botany* The spongy multiple epidermis that covers the aerial roots of certain plants and is capable of absorbing atmospheric moisture. [Lat., covering < *vēlāre,* to cover < *vēlum,* a covering.] —**vel′a·men′tous** (vĕl′ə-mĕn′təs) *adj.*

ve·lar (vē′lər) *adj.* **1a.** Of or relating to a velum. **b.** Of or using the soft palate. **2.** Articulated with the back of the tongue touching or near the velum, as (g) in *good.* ❖ *n.* A velar sound. —**ve′lar·ize′** *v.* —**ve′lar·i·za′tion** *n.*

ve·lar·i·um (və-lâr′ē-əm) *n.,* pl. **-i·a** (-ē-ə) A large awning, esp. one suspended over a Roman theater or amphitheater. [Lat. *vēlārium* < *vēlum,* sail, sheet, curtain.]

ve·late (vē′lāt′, -lĭt) *adj. Biology* Having or covered by a velum or veil.

Ve·láz·quez (və-läs′kĕs, bĕ-läth′kĕth), **Diego Rodríguez de Silva y** 1599–1660. Spanish painter whose works include *The Surrender of Breda* (1635).

Vel·cro (vĕl′krō) A trademark used for a fastening tape consisting of a strip of nylon with a surface of minute hooks that fasten to a corresponding strip with a surface of uncut pile.

veldt also **veld** (vĕlt, fĕlt) *n.* Any of the open grazing areas of southern Africa. [Afr. *veld* < MDu., field. See **pelə-²** in App.]

Ve·li·a (vē′lē-ə) See **Elea.**

ve·li·ger (vē′lĭ-jər, vĕl′ĭ-) *n.* A larval stage of a mollusk characterized by the presence of a velum. [NLat. *vēliger : vēlum,* velum; see VELUM + Lat. *gerere,* to bear.]

vel·le·i·ty (vĕ-lē′ĭ-tē, və-) *n.,* pl. **-ties 1.** Volition at its lowest level. **2.** A mere wish or inclination. [NLat. *velleitās* < Lat. *velle,* to wish.]

vel·lum (vĕl′əm) *n.* **1a.** A fine parchment made from calfskin, lambskin, or kidskin and used for the pages and binding of books. **b.** A work written or printed on this parchment. **2.** A heavy off-white fine-quality paper resembling this parchment. [ME *velim* < OFr. *velin* < *veel,* calf. See VEAL.]

ve·lo·ce (və-lō′chə) *adv. Music* Rapidly. [Ital. < Lat. *vēlōx, vēlōc-,* rapid. See VELOCITY.]

ve·lo·cim·e·ter (vē′lō-sĭm′ĭ-tər, vĕl′ō-) *n.* A device for measuring the speed of sound in water. [VELOCI(TY) + -METER.]

ve·loc·i·pede (və-lŏs′ə-pēd′) *n.* **1.** A tricycle. **2a.** Any of several early bicycles with pedals on the front wheel. **b.** An early bicycle propelled by the feet. [Fr. *vélocipède* : Lat. *vēlōx, vēlōc-,* fast; see VELOCITY + Lat. *pēs, ped-,* foot; see -PED.]

ve·loc·i·ty (və-lŏs′ĭ-tē) *n.,* pl. **-ties 1.** Rapidity or speed of motion; swiftness. **2.** *Physics* A vector quantity whose magnitude is a body's speed and whose direction is the body's direction of motion. **3.** The rate of speed of action or occurrence. [ME *velocite* < OFr. < Lat. *vēlōcitās* < *vēlōx, vēlōc-,* fast.]

ve·lo·drome (vē′lə-drōm′, vĕl′ə-) *n.* A sports arena with a banked oval track for bicycle and motorcycle racing. [Fr. *vélodrome* : *vélo*(cipède), velocipede; see VELOCIPEDE + -drome, racecourse (< Lat. -*dromus;* see -DROME).]

ve·lour or **ve·lours** (və-lōor′) *n.,* pl. **-lours** (-lōorz′) **1.** A closely napped fabric resembling velvet. **2.** A felt resembling velvet, used in making hats. [Alteration of Fr. *velours,* velvet < OFr. *velour,* alteration of *velous* < O Provençal *velos* < Lat. *villōsus,* hairy < *villus,* shaggy hair.]

ve·lou·té (və-lōō-tā′) *n.* A white sauce made of chicken, veal, or fish stock thickened with a roux of flour and butter. [Fr. < OFr. *vellute,* velvety < *velous,* velvet. See VELOUR.]

ve·lum (vē′ləm) *n.,* pl. **-la** (-lə) **1.** *Biology* A covering or partition of thin membranous tissue, such as the veil of a mushroom or a membrane of the brain. **2.** *Anatomy* The soft palate. **3.** *Zoology* A ciliated swimming organ that develops in certain larval stages of most marine gastropod mollusks. [Lat. *vēlum,* veil.]

ve·lure (vĕ-lōor′, vĕl′yər) *n. Obsolete* Velvet or a velvetlike fabric. [Alteration of Fr. *velours.* See VELOUR.]

ve·lu·ti·nous (və-lōōt′n-əs) *adj.* Covered with dense soft silky hairs. [< NLat. *velūtīnus* < Med.Lat. *velūtum,* velvet < VLat. **villūtus.* See VELVET.]

vel·vet (vĕl′vĭt) *n.* **1.** A soft fabric, such as silk, rayon, or nylon, having a smooth dense pile and a plain underside. **2.** Something suggesting the smooth surface of velvet. **3.** The soft furry covering on the developing antlers of deer. **4.** *Informal* **a.** The winnings of a gambler. **b.** A profit or gain beyond what is expected or due. **5.** *New England* See **milk shake** 1. See Regional Note at **milk shake.** [ME *veluet,* prob. < O Provençal < VLat. **villūtittus,* dim. of **villūtus* < Lat. *villus,* shaggy hair, nap.]

velvet ant *n.* Any of various wasps of the family Mutillidae, the females of which are wingless and have a coat of velvety hair.

vel·vet·een (vĕl′vĭ-tēn′) *n.* A cotton pile fabric resembling velvet. [< VELVET.]

velvet plant *n.* See **mullein.** [< its dense, velvety hairs.]

vel·vet·y (vĕl′vĭ-tē) *adj.* **-i·er, -i·est 1.** Suggestive of the texture of velvet; soft and smooth: *velvety skin.* **2.** Smooth-tasting; mellow: *a velvety sherry.*

Ven. *abbr.* **1.** venerable **2.** Venezuela

ven– *pref.* Variant of **veno–.**

ve·na (vē′nə) *n.,* pl. **-nae** (-nē) *Anatomy* A vein. [ME < Lat. *vēna.*]

vena ca·va (kā′və) *n.,* pl. **venae ca·vae** (kā′vē) Either of two large veins that drain blood from the upper body and the lower body and empty into the right atrium of the heart. [NLat. *vēna cava* : Lat. *vēna,* vein + Lat. *cava,* hollow.]

ve·nal (vē′nəl) *adj.* **1a.** Open to bribery; mercenary: *a venal police officer.* **b.** Capable of betraying honor, duty, or scruples for a price; corruptible. **2.** Marked by corrupt dealings, esp. bribery: *a venal administration.* **3.** Obtainable for a price. [Lat. *vēnālis* < *vēnum,* sale. See **wes-³** in App.] —**ve′nal·ly** *adv.*

ve·nal·i·ty (vē-năl′ĭ-tē) *n.,* pl. **-ties 1.** The condition of being susceptible to bribery or corruption. **2.** The use of a position of trust for dishonest gain.

ve·na·tion (vē-nā′shən, vĕ-) *n.* **1.** Distribution or arrangement of a system of veins, as in a leaf blade. **2.** The veins of such a system considered as a group. —**ve·na′tion·al** *adj.*

vend (vĕnd) *v.* **vend·ed, vend·ing, vends** —*tr.* **1a.** To sell by means of a vending machine. **b.** To sell, esp. by peddling. **2.** To offer (an idea, for example) for public consideration. —*intr.* To sell. [Lat. *vēndere,* shortening of *vēnumdare : vēnum,* sale; see **wes-³** in App. + *dare,* to give; see **dō-** in App.]

Ven·da¹ (vĕn′də) **1.** A member of a people of northeast South Africa constituting the principal inhabitants of the former homeland of Venda. **2.** The Bantu language of the Venda.

Ven·da² (vĕn′də) A former internally self-governing Black African homeland in NE South Africa; granted nominal independence in 1979, dissolved and reintegrated into South Africa by the 1993 interim constitution.

vend·ee (vĕn-dē′) *n.* One to whom something is sold; a buyer.

ven·det·ta (vĕn-dĕt′ə) *n.* **1.** A feud between two families or clans that arises out of a slaying and is perpetuated by retaliatory acts of revenge; a blood feud. **2.** A bitter, destructive feud. [Ital. < Lat. *vindicta,* revenge. See VINDICTIVE.]

vend·i·ble also **vend·a·ble** (vĕn′də-bəl) *adj.* **1.** Suitable or fit for sale; salable: *vendible items of food.* **2.** *Obsolete* Venal. ❖ *n.* Something that can be sold.

vend·ing machine (vĕn′dĭng) *n.* A coin-operated machine that dispenses merchandise.

Ven·dôme (vän-dōm′), **Duc de.** Title of Louis Joseph de Bourbon. 1654–1712. French general who commanded Spanish troops in Italy (1710) during the War of the Spanish Succession.

ven·dor or **ven·der** (vĕn′dər) *n.* **1.** One that sells or vends: *a street vendor.* **2.** A vending machine.

ven·due (vĕn′dōō, -dyōō, vĕn-dōō′, -dyōō′) *n.* A public sale; an auction. [Du. *vendu* < obsolete Fr. *vendue,* sale < OFr., fem. p. part. of *vendre,* to sell < Lat. *vēndere.* See VEND.]

ve·neer (və-nîr′) *n.* **1.** A thin surface layer, as of wood, glued to a base of inferior material. **2.** Any of the thin layers glued together to make plywood. **3.** A decorative facing, as of brick. **4.** A deceptive superficial show; a façade. ❖ *tr.v.* **-neered, -neer·ing, -neers 1.** To overlay (a surface) with a thin layer of a fine or decorative material. **2.** To glue together (layers of wood) to make plywood. **3.** To conceal, as something crude, with a deceptively attractive outward show. [Alteration of obsolete *faneering* < Ger. *Furnierung* < *furnieren,* to furnish, veneer < Fr. *fournir,* to furnish < OFr. *furnir,* of Gmc. orig. See **per¹** in App.] —**ve·neer′er** *n.*

ven·e·na·tion (vĕn′ə-nā′shən) *n.* **1.** Introduction of a venom into animal tissue. **2.** The poisoned condition produced by a venom. [< Lat. *venēnātus,* p. part. of *venēnāre,* to poison < *venēnum,* venom. See VENOM.]

ven·ene (və-nēn′, vĕn′ēn) *n.* **1.** A preparation of snake venoms used in medicine, esp. in the treatment of epilepsy. **2.** Variant of **venin.** [Lat. *venēnum,* venom. See VENOM.]

ve·ne·punc·ture (vē′nĭ-pŭngk′chər, vĕn′ĭ-) *n.* Variant of **venipuncture.**

ven·er·a·ble (vĕn′ər-ə-bəl) *adj.* **1.** Commanding respect by virtue of age, dignity, character, or position. **2.** Worthy of reverence, esp. by religious or historical association. **3. Venerable a.** *Roman Catholic Church* Used as a form of address for a person who has reached the first stage of canonization. **b.** Used as a form of address for an archdeacon in the Anglican Church or the Episcopal

Church. —ven′er•a•ble•ness, ven′er•a•bil′i•ty n. —ven′er•a•bly adv.

ven•er•ate (věn′ə-rāt′) tr.v. -at•ed, -at•ing, -ates To regard with respect, reverence, or heartfelt deference. See Syns at revere[1]. [Lat. venerārī, venerāt-, to venerate < venus, vener-, love, desire. See wen- in App.] —ven′er•a′tor n.

ven•er•a•tion (věn′ə-rā′shən) n. 1. The act of venerating. 2. Profound respect or reverence. 3. The condition or status of one who is venerated. —ven′er•a′tion•al adj.

ve•ne•re•al (və-nîr′ē-əl) adj. 1a. Transmitted by sexual intercourse. b. Of or relating to a sexually transmitted disease. 2. Of or relating to sexual intercourse. 3. Of or relating to the genitals. [ME venerealle < Lat. venereus < venus, vener-, desire, love. See wen- in App.]

venereal disease n. A sexually transmitted disease.

venereal wart n. See genital wart.

ven•er•y[1] (věn′ə-rē) n., pl. -ies Archaic 1. Indulgence in or pursuit of sexual activity. 2. The act of sexual intercourse. [ME venerie < OFr. < Med.Lat. veneria < Lat. venus, vener-, desire, love. See wen- in App.]

ven•er•y[2] (věn′ə-rē) n., pl. -ies Archaic The act or sport of hunting; the chase. [ME venerie < OFr. < vener, to hunt < Lat. vēnārī. See wen- in App.]

ven•e•sec•tion (věn′ĭ-sěk′shən, vē′nĭ-) n. See phlebotomy. [NLat. vēnae sectiō < Lat. vēna, genitive sing. of vēna, vein + Lat. sectiō, section-, cutting; see SECTION.]

Ve•ne•ti•a (və-nē′shē-ə, -shə) A historical region of NE Italy including Istria and the lands between the Po R. and the Alps.

Ve•ne•tian (və-nē′shən) adj. Of or relating to Venice, Italy, or its people, language, or culture. ❖ n. 1. A native or inhabitant of Venice. 2. The variety of Italian spoken in Venice. [Med.Lat. Venetiānus < Lat. Venetia, region of NE Italy.]

venetian blind or Venetian blind n. A window blind consisting of a number of thin horizontal adjustable slats that overlap when closed.

venetian blue n. A strong blue to greenish blue.

Venetian glass n. A fine, often colored and ornamented glassware made in or near Venice.

venetian red n. A deep to strong reddish brown.

Ve•net•ic (və-nět′ĭk) n. An extinct Indo-European language known from short inscriptions in Veneto dating from the 6th to the 1st centuries B.C.

Ve•ne•to (věn′ĭ-tō′) A region of NE Italy bordering the Adriatic Sea; passed to Austria in 1797 and became part of Italy in 1866.

Ven•e•zue•la (věn′ə-zwā′lə) A country of N South America on the Caribbean Sea; liberated from Spain in 1821 but not formally separated from Colombia until 1830. Cap. Caracas. Pop. 21,177,000. —Ven′e•zue′lan adj. & n.

Venezuela, Gulf of An inlet of the Caribbean Sea between NW Venezuela and N Colombia.

venge (věnj) tr.v. venged, veng•ing, veng•es Archaic To avenge. [ME vengen < OFr. vengier. See VENGEANCE.]

ven•geance (věn′jəns) n. Infliction of punishment in return for a wrong; retribution. —idiom: with a vengeance 1. With great violence or force. 2. To an extreme degree. [ME < OFr. < vengier, to avenge < Lat. vindicāre. See VINDICATE.]

venge•ful (věnj′fəl) adj. 1. Desiring vengeance; vindictive. 2. Indicating or proceeding from a desire for revenge. 3. Serving to exact vengeance. —venge′ful•ly adv. —venge′ful•ness n.

V-en•gine (vē′ěn′jən) n. An internal-combustion engine having cylinders arranged so that pairs form V shapes.

ve•ni•al (vē′nē-əl, věn′yəl) adj. Easily excused or forgiven; pardonable: a venial offense. [ME < OFr. < LLat. veniālis < Lat. venia, forgiveness. See wen- in App.] —ve′ni•al′i•ty (vē′nē-ăl′ĭ-tē, věn-yăl′-), ve′ni•al•ness n. —ve′ni•al•ly adv.

Ven•ice (věn′ĭs) A city of NE Italy on islets within a lagoon in the Gulf of Venice, a wide inlet of the N Adriatic Sea. Founded in the 5th cent. A.D., it became a major maritime power by the 13th cent. and was ceded to Italy in 1866. Pop. 308,717.

ven•in (věn′ĭn, vē′nĭn) also ve•nene (və-nēn′, věn′ēn) n. Any of various toxic substances found in the venom of snakes.

ve•ni•punc•ture also ve•ne•punc•ture (vē′nĭ-pŭngk′chər, věn′ĭ-) n. Puncture of a vein, as for drawing blood, intravenous feeding, or administration of medicine.

ven•i•son (věn′ĭ-sən, -zən) n. 1. The flesh of a deer used as food. 2. Archaic The flesh of a game animal used as food. [ME veneson < OFr. < Lat. vēnātiō, vēnātiōn-, hunting < vēnātus, p. part. of vēnārī, to hunt. See wen- in App.]

Venn diagram (věn) n. A diagram using circles to represent sets, with the position and overlap of the circles indicating the relationships between the sets. [After John Venn (1834–1923), British logician.]

veno- or veni- or ven- pref. Vein: venipuncture. [< Lat. vēna.]

ve•no•gram (vē′nə-grăm′) n. A radiograph of a vein after injection of a radiopaque substance.

ve•nog•ra•phy (vī-nŏg′rə-fē) n. Radiography of veins or a vein after injection of a radiopaque substance.

ven•om (věn′əm) n. 1. A poisonous secretion of an animal, such as a snake, spider, or scorpion, usu. transmitted by a bite or sting. 2. A poison. 3. Malice; spite. [ME venim < OFr. < VLat. *venīmen

ven•om•ous (věn′ə-məs) adj. 1a. Secreting and transmitting venom: a venomous snake. b. Full of or containing venom. 2. Malicious; spiteful: a venomous remark. —ven′om•ous•ly adv. —ven′om•ous•ness n.

ve•nose (vē′nōs′) adj. 1. Having noticeable veins or veinlike markings. 2. Venous. [Lat. vēnōsus < vēna, vein.]

ve•nos•i•ty (vē-nŏs′ĭ-tē) n. The quality or condition of being venous or venose.

ve•nous (vē′nəs) adj. 1. Of, relating to, or contained in the veins: venous blood. 2. Having numerous veins, as a leaf or the wings of an insect. [< Lat. vēnōsus < vēna, vein.] —ve′nous•ly adv. —ve′nous•ness n.

vent[1] (věnt) n. 1. A means of escape or release from confinement; an outlet: give vent to anger. 2. An opening permitting the escape of fumes, a liquid, a gas, or steam. 3. The small hole at the breech of a gun through which the charge is ignited. 4. Zoology The external opening of the cloaca. 5. Geology a. The opening of a volcano in the earth's crust. b. An opening on the ocean floor that emits hot water and dissolved minerals. ❖ v. vent•ed, vent•ing, vents —tr. 1. To express (one's thoughts or feelings, for example), esp. forcefully. 2. To release or discharge (steam, for example) through an opening. 3. To provide with a vent. —intr. 1. To vent one's feelings or opinions. 2. To be released or discharged through an opening. 3. To rise to the surface of water to breathe. Used of a marine mammal. [Partly < Fr. vent (< Lat.) and partly alteration of Fr. évent (< OFr. esvent < esventer, to let out air < VLat. *exventāre : Lat. ex-; see EX– + Lat. ventus, wind; see wē- in App.).] —vent′er n.

SYNONYMS vent, express, utter, voice, air These verbs mean to give outlet to thoughts or emotions. To vent is to unburden oneself of a strong pent-up emotion: "She was jealous . . . and glad of any excuse to vent her pique" (Edward G.E.L. Bulwer-Lytton). Express refers to both verbal and nonverbal communication: "expressing emotion in the form of art" (T.S. Eliot). Utter involves vocal expression: "The words were uttered in the hearing of Montezuma" (William Hickling Prescott). Voice denotes the expression of an outlook or viewpoint: voiced her satisfaction with the verdict. To air is to show off one's feelings, beliefs, or ideas: They aired their differences during dinner.

vent[2] (věnt) n. A slit in a garment, as in the back seam of a jacket. [ME vente, alteration of fente < OFr., slit < fendre, to split open < Lat. findere. See FISSION.]

vent•age (věn′tĭj) n. A small opening; a vent.

ven•tail (věn′tāl′) n. The lower movable part of the front of a medieval helmet, fitting over the mouth or neck. [ME < OFr. vantail < vent, wind < Lat. ventus. See wē- in App.]

ven•ter (věn′tər) n. 1. Anatomy a. The abdomen. b. The prominent fleshy portion of a muscle. c. A cavity or hollowed surface, esp. of a bone. 2. Zoology A part in lower forms of animal life corresponding to the abdomen of mammals. 3. Botany The swollen lower portion of an archegonium containing the egg. [AN < Lat.]

ven•ti•fact (věn′tə-făkt′) n. A stone that has been shaped, polished, or faceted by wind-driven sand. [Lat. ventus, wind; see VENT[1] + (ARTI)FACT.]

ven•ti•late (věn′tl-āt′) tr.v. -lat•ed, -lat•ing, -lates 1. To admit fresh air into (a mine, for example) to replace stale or noxious air. 2. To circulate through and freshen. 3. To provide with a vent, as for airing. 4. To expose (a substance) to fresh air, as to retard spoilage. 5. To expose to public discussion or examination: ventilated their grievances. 6. To aerate or oxygenate (blood). [ME ventilaten, to blow away < Lat. ventilāre, ventilāt-, to fan < ventulus, dim. of ventus, wind. See wē- in App.] —ven′ti•la′tion n.

ven•ti•la•tor (věn′tl-ā′tər) n. 1. A device that circulates fresh air and expels stale or foul air. 2. Medicine A respirator. —ven′ti•la•to′ry (věn′tl-ə-tôr′ē, -tōr′ē) adj.

ven•tral (věn′trəl) adj. 1. Anatomy a. Of or situated on or close to the abdomen; abdominal. b. Of or situated on or close to the anterior aspect of the human body or the lower surface of the body of an animal. 2. Botany Of or on the inner or lower surface of an organ that faces the axis. ❖ n. 1. A ventral fin. 2. The abdominal segment of an insect. [LLat. ventrālis < Lat. venter, ventr-, belly.] —ven′tral•ly adv.

ventral fin n. A fin, such as a pelvic fin or an anal fin, that is found on the ventral side of a fish.

ven•tri•cle (věn′trĭ-kəl) n. A small cavity or chamber within a body or organ, esp.: a. The chamber on the left side of the heart that receives arterial blood from the left atrium and contracts to force it into the aorta. b. The chamber on the right side of the heart that receives venous blood from the right atrium and forces it into the pulmonary artery. c. Any of the interconnecting cavities of the brain. [ME < OFr. ventricule < Lat. ventriculus, dim. of venter, belly.]

ven•tri•cose (věn′trĭ-kōs′) also ven•tri•cous (-kəs) adj. Inflated, swollen, or distended, esp. on one side: an insect's ventricose gullet. [NLat. ventricōsus < Lat. venter, ventr-, belly.] —ven′tri•cos′i•ty (-kŏs′ĭ-tē) n.

ven•tric•u•lar (věn-trĭk′yə-lər) adj. Of or relating to a ventricle

Venezuela

ă	pat	oi	boy
ā	pay	ou	out
âr	care	oͦo	took
ä	father	oͦo	boot
ě	pet	ŭ	cut
ē	be	ûr	urge
ĭ	pit	th	thin
ī	pie	th	this
îr	pier	hw	which
ŏ	pot	zh	vision
ō	toe	ə	about,
ô	paw		item

Stress marks:
′ (primary);
′ (secondary), as in
lexicon (lěk′sĭ-kŏn′)

or ventriculus: *ventricular fibrillation.*

ven·tric·u·lus (věn-trĭk′yə-ləs) *n., pl.* **-li** (-lī′) **1.** A hollow digestive organ, esp. the stomach of certain insects or the gizzard of a bird. **2.** The digestive cavity in the body of a sponge. [Lat., dim. of *venter, ventr-,* belly.]

ven·tril·o·quism (věn-trĭl′ə-kwĭz′əm) also **ven·tril·o·quy** (-kwē) *n.* The art of projecting one's voice so that it seems to come from another source, as from a wooden figure. [< Lat. *ventriloquus,* speaking from the belly : *venter, ventr-,* belly + *loquī,* to speak.] —**ven′tri·lo′qui·al** (-trə-lō′kwē-əl) *adj.* —**ven·tril′o·quize′** (-kwīz′) *v.*

ven·tril·o·quist (věn-trĭl′ə-kwĭst) *n.* One, esp. an entertainer, who is adept at ventriloquism. —**ven·tril′o·quis′tic** *adj.*

ventro– or **ventr–** *pref.* Ventral: *ventrolateral.* [< Lat. *venter, ventr-,* belly.]

ven·tro·dor·sal (věn′trō-dôr′səl) *adj.* Both ventral and dorsal; extending from a ventral to a dorsal surface. —**ven′tro·dor′sal·ly** *adv.*

ven·tro·lat·er·al (věn′trō-lăt′ər-əl) *adj.* Both ventral and lateral; extending from a ventral to a lateral surface. —**ven′tro·lat′er·al·ly** *adv.*

ven·tro·me·di·al (věn′trō-mē′dē-əl) *adj.* Both ventral and medial; extending toward the median line of the ventral surface. —**ven′tro·me′di·al·ly** *adv.*

Ven·tu·ra (věn-tŏŏr′ə) A city of S CA on the Pacific Ocean W of Los Angeles; founded 1782. Pop. 100,916.

ven·ture (věn′chər) *n.* **1.** A dangerous, daring, or dubious undertaking. **2.** A business enterprise involving some risk in expectation of gain. **3.** Something, such as cargo, at hazard in a risky enterprise. ❖ *v.* **-tured, -tur·ing, -tures** —*tr.* **1.** To expose to danger or risk. **2.** To brave the dangers of. **3.** To express at the risk of denial, criticism, or censure. —*intr.* **1.** To take a risk; dare. **2.** To proceed despite possible danger or risk. —**idiom: at a venture** By mere chance or fortune; at random. [ME, chance, short for *aventure,* adventure. See ADVENTURE.] —**ven′tur·er** *n.*

venture capital *n.* Money for investment in innovative enterprises or research in which both the risk of loss and the potential for profit may be considerable. —**venture capitalist** *n.*

ven·ture·some (věn′chər-səm) *adj.* **1.** Disposed to venture or to take risks; daring. **2.** Involving risk or danger; hazardous. —**ven′ture·some·ness** *n.*

ven·tu·ri (věn-tŏŏr′ē) *n., pl.* **-ris 1.** A short tube with a constricted throat used to determine fluid pressures and velocities by measurement of differential pressures generated at the throat as a fluid traverses the tube. **2.** A constricted throat in the air passage of a carburetor, causing a reduction in pressure that results in fuel vapor being drawn out of the carburetor bowl. [After Giovanni Battista *Venturi* (1746–1822), Italian physicist.]

ven·tur·ous (věn′chər-əs) *adj.* Venturesome. —**ven′tur·ous·ly** *adv.* —**ven′tur·ous·ness** *n.*

ven·ue (věn′yōō) *n.* **1.** *Law* **a.** The locality where a crime is committed or a cause of action occurs. **b.** The locality or political division from which a jury is called and in which a trial is held. **c.** The clause within a declaration naming the locality in which a trial will be held. **d.** The clause in an affidavit naming the place where it was sworn to. **2.** The scene or setting in which something takes place; a locale. [ME, attack < OFr., a coming, attack < fem. p. part. of *venir,* to come < Lat. *venīre.* See gʷā- in App.]

ven·ule (věn′yōōl, vēn′-) *n.* A small vein, esp. one joining capillaries to larger veins. [Lat. *vēnula,* dim. of *vēna,* vein.] —**ven′u·lar** (-yə-lər) *adj.*

Ve·nus (vē′nəs) *n.* **1.** *Roman Mythology* The goddess of love and beauty. **2.** The second planet from the sun. See table at **planet.** [ME < OE < Lat., love, Venus. See wen- in App.]

Venus flytrap or **Ve·nus flytrap** (vē′nəs, vē′nə-sĭz) also **Venus's flytrap** (-nə-sĭz) *n.* An insectivorous plant (*Dionaea muscipula*) of the Carolinas having sensitive, hinged, marginally bristled two-lobed leaf blades that close and entrap insects.

Venus hair or **Venus' hair** also **Venus's hair** *n.* A maidenhair fern (*Adiantum capillus-veneris*) of warm moist regions having slender blackish stalks, bipinnately compound fronds, and marginal sori.

Venus flytrap
Dionaea muscipula

Ve·nu·sian (vĭ-nōō′zhən, -shē-ən, -nyōō′-) *adj.* Of, relating to, or characteristic of the planet Venus. ❖ *n.* A hypothetical inhabitant of the planet Venus.

ver. *abbr.* **1.** verse **2.** version

ve·ra·cious (və-rā′shəs) *adj.* **1.** Honest; truthful. **2.** Accurate; precise. [< Lat. *vērāx, vērāc-* < *vērus,* true. See wērə-o- in App.] —**ve·ra′cious·ly** *adv.* —**ve·ra′cious·ness** *n.*

ve·rac·i·ty (və-răs′ĭ-tē) *n., pl.* **-ties 1.** Adherence to the truth; truthfulness. **2.** Conformity to fact or truth; accuracy or precision. **3.** Something that is true. [Med.Lat. *vērācitās* < Lat. *vērāx, vērāc-,* true. See VERACIOUS.]

Ve·ra·cruz (věr′ə-krōōz′, bā′rä-krōōs′) A city of E-central Mexico on the Gulf of Mexico E of Puebla. Pop. 284,822.

ve·ran·da or **ve·ran·dah** (və-răn′də) *n.* A porch or balcony, usu. roofed and often partly enclosed, extending along the outside of a building. [Hindi *varaṇḍā,* prob. < Port. *varanda,* perh. ult. < VLat. *barra,* barrier, bar.]

ve·rap·a·mil (və-răp′ə-mĭl′) *n.* A vasodilator, $C_{27}H_{38}N_2O_4$, that inhibits calcium activity, used in the treatment of hypertension,

angina pectoris, and certain cardiac arrythmias. [*vera-* (shortening and alteration of VALERIC ACID) + *-pamil,* vasodilating drug suff. (perh. P(ROPYL) + AM(INO) + (NITR)IL(E)).]

ve·rat·ri·dine (və-rǎt′rĭ-dēn′) *n.* A yellowish-white amorphous powdered alkaloid, $C_{36}H_{51}NO_{11}$, obtained from sabadilla seeds and the rhizome of hellebore. [VERATR(INE) + –ID(E) + –INE².]

ver·a·trine (věr′ə-trēn′, -trĭn) *n.* A poisonous mixture of colorless crystalline alkaloids extracted from sabadilla seeds and formerly used medicinally as a counterirritant. [NLat. *Vērātrum,* hellebore genus (< Lat. *vērātrum,* hellebore) + –INE².]

verb (vûrb) *n.* **1a.** The part of speech that expresses existence, action, or occurrence in most languages. **b.** Any of the words belonging to this part of speech, as *be, run,* or *conceive.* **2.** A phrase or other construction used as a verb. [ME *verbe* < OFr. < Lat. *verbum,* word, verb (transl. of Gk. *rhēma,* word, verb). See wer-¹ in App.]

ver·bal (vûr′bəl) *adj.* **1.** Of, relating to, or associated with words. **2a.** Concerned with words only rather than with content or ideas. **b.** Consisting of words alone without action. **3.** Spoken rather than written; oral: *a verbal contract.* **4.** Corresponding word for word; literal. **5.** *Grammar* **a.** Relating to, having the nature or function of, or derived from a verb. **b.** Used to form verbs: *a verbal suffix.* **6.** Of or relating to proficiency in the use and understanding of words: *verbal aptitude.* ❖ *n. Grammar* A verbal noun or adjective. [ME < OFr. < LLat. *verbālis* < Lat. *verbum,* word. See VERB.] —**ver′bal·ly** *adv.*

verbal adjective *n.* An adjective that is derived from a verb and that in some constructions preserves the verb's syntactic features, such as transitivity.

ver·bal·ism (vûr′bə-lĭz′əm) *n.* **1a.** An expression in words; a word or phrase. **b.** The manner in which something is phrased; wording. **2.** A wordy phrase or sentence with little meaning. **3.** Abundant use of words without conveying much meaning.

ver·bal·ist (vûr′bə-lĭst) *n.* **1.** One skilled in the use of words. **2.** One who favors words over ideas or substance. —**ver′bal·is′tic** *adj.*

ver·bal·ize (vûr′bə-līz′) *v.* **-ized, -iz·ing, -iz·es** —*tr.* **1.** To express in words. **2.** *Grammar* To convert to use as a verb: *verbalized the noun contact.* —*intr.* **1.** To express oneself in words. **2.** To be verbose. —**ver′bal·i·za′tion** (-bə-lĭ-zā′shən) *n.* —**ver′bal·iz′er** *n.*

verbal noun *n.* A noun that is derived from a verb and usu. preserves the verb's syntactic features, such as transitivity.

ver·ba·tim (vər-bā′tĭm) *adj.* Using exactly the same words; corresponding word for word: *a verbatim report of the conversation.* ❖ *adv.* In exactly the same words; word for word. [ME < Med.Lat. *verbātim* < Lat. *verbum,* word. See VERB.]

ver·be·na (vər-bē′nə) *n.* **1.** Any of various New World plants of the genus *Verbena,* esp. one of several species having spikes of showy flowers. **2.** Any of several similar plants, such as the lemon verbena. [Lat. *verbēna,* sacred foliage. See wer-² in App.]

ver·bi·age (vûr′bē-ĭj, -bĭj) *n.* **1.** An excess of words for the purpose; wordiness. **2.** The manner in which something is expressed in words: *software verbiage.* [Fr. < OFr. *verbier,* to chatter < *verbe,* word < Lat. *verbum.* See VERB.]

ver·big·er·a·tion (vər-bĭj′ə-rā′shən) *n.* Obsessive repetition of meaningless words and phrases, esp. due to mental illness. [< Lat. *verbigerātus,* p. part. of *verbigerāre,* to chat, dispute < *verbiger,* carrying words : *verbum,* word; see VERB + *gerere,* to carry.]

ver·bose (vər-bōs′) *adj.* Using or containing a great and usu. an excessive number of words; wordy. [ME *verbous* < Lat. *verbōsus* < *verbum,* word. See VERB.] —**ver·bose′ly** *adv.* —**ver·bose′ness, ver·bos′i·ty** (-bŏs′ĭ-tē) *n.*

ver·bo·ten (vər-bōt′n, fĕr-) *adj.* Forbidden; prohibited. [Ger., p. part. of *verbieten,* to forbid < MHGer. < OHGer. *farbiotan.* See bheudh- in App.]

verb phrase *n.* **1.** A phrase consisting of a verb and its auxiliaries, as *should be done.* **2.** A phrase whose head is a verb, and including the verb's auxiliaries, complements, and other modifiers, as *should be done with the exam by noon* in the sentence *The students should be done with the exam by noon.*

ver·dant (vûr′dnt) *adj.* **1.** Green with vegetation; covered with green growth. **2.** Green in hue. **3.** Lacking experience or sophistication; naive. [Fr. *verdoyant* < OFr., pr. part. of *verdoyer,* to become green < VLat. **viridiāre* < Lat. *viridis,* green.] —**ver′dan·cy** *n.* —**ver′dant·ly** *adv.*

verd antique also **verde antique** (vûrd) *n.* A dull green mottled or veined serpentine used in interior decoration. [Obsolete Fr. < Ital. *verde antico : verde,* green + *antico,* antique.]

Verde (vûrd), **Cape** A peninsula of W Senegal projecting into the

Atlantic Ocean; the westernmost point of Africa.

ver•der•er also **ver•der•or** (vûr′dər-ər) *n.* A man serving as an official in charge of the royal forests of medieval England. [AN < *verd*, green < Lat. *viridis*.]

Ver•di (vâr′dē), **Giuseppe** 1813–1901. Italian composer whose operas include *La Traviata* (1853).

ver•dict (vûr′dĭkt) *n.* **1.** *Law* The finding of a jury in a trial. **2.** An expressed conclusion; a judgment or opinion: *the verdict of history.* [ME *verdit* < AN : *ver*, true (< Lat. *vērus*; see **wērə-o-** in App.) + *dit*, speech (< Lat. *dictum* < neut. p. part. of *dīcere*, to say; see **deik-** in App.).]

ver•di•gris (vûr′dĭ-grēs′, -grĭs′, -grē′) *n.* **1.** A blue or green powder consisting of basic cupric acetate used as a paint pigment and fungicide. **2.** A green patina or crust of copper sulfate or copper chloride formed on copper, brass, and bronze exposed to air or seawater for long periods of time. [ME *vertegrez* < OFr. *verte grez*, alteration of *vert-de-Grice* : *verd*, green; see VERDURE + *de*, of (< Lat. *dē*; see DE–) + *Grice*, Greece.]

Ver•di•gris (vûr′dĭ-grĭs) A river, c. 451 km (280 mi), of SE KS and NE OK flowing generally S to the Arkansas R.

ver•din (vûr′dn) *n.* A small grayish bird *(Auriparus flaviceps)* of Mexico and the southwest United States having a yellowish head and throat. [Fr., bunting < *vert*, green < OFr. *verd*. See VERDURE.]

ver•di•ter (vûr′dĭ-tər) *n.* Either of two basic carbonates of copper, used as a blue or green pigment. [ME, alteration of OFr. *verd de terre*, green of earth : *verd*, green; see VERDURE + *de*, of; see VERDIGRIS + *terre*, earth (< Lat. *terra*; see **ters-** in App.).]

Ver•dun (vər-dŭn′, vĕr-dœn′) A city of NE France on the Meuse R. W of Metz; site of a prolonged World War I battle (Feb.–Dec. 1916). Pop. 21,516.

ver•dure (vûr′jər) *n.* **1a.** The lush greenness of flourishing vegetation. **b.** Vigorous greenery. **2.** A fresh or flourishing condition. [ME < OFr. < *verd*, green < Lat. *viridis*.] **—ver′dur•ous** *adj.*

verge[1] (vûrj) *n.* **1.** The extreme edge or margin; a border. See Syns at **border. 2a.** An enclosing boundary. **b.** The space enclosed by such a boundary. **3.** The point beyond which an action, state, or condition is likely to begin or occur; the brink: *on the verge of prosperity.* **4.** *Architecture* The edge of the tiling that projects over a roof gable. **5.** *Chiefly British* The shoulder of a road. **6.** A rod, wand, or staff carried as an emblem of authority or office. **7.** *Obsolete* The rod held by a feudal tenant while swearing fealty to a lord. **8.** The spindle of a balance wheel in a clock or watch, esp. such a spindle in a clock with vertical escapement. **9.** The male organ of copulation in certain invertebrates. ❖ *intr.v.* **verged, verg•ing, verg•es 1.** To approach the nature or condition of something specified; come close. Used with *on*: *a brilliance verging on genius.* **2.** To be on the edge or border: *Her land verges on state forest.* [ME < OFr., rod, ring < Lat. *virga*, rod, strip.]

verge[2] (vûrj) *intr.v.* **verged, verg•ing, verg•es 1.** To slope or incline. **2.** To tend to move in a particular direction. **3.** To pass or merge gradually. [Lat. *vergere*. See **wer-**[2] in App.]

verg•er (vûr′jər) *n.* *Chiefly British* **1.** One who carries the verge or other emblem of authority before a scholastic, legal, or religious dignitary in a procession. **2.** One who takes care of the interior of a church and acts as an attendant during ceremonies.

Ver•gil (vûr′jəl) See **Virgil.**

ve•rid•i•cal (və-rĭd′ĭ-kəl) also **ve•rid•ic** (-rĭd′ĭk) *adj.* **1.** Truthful; veracious. **2.** Coinciding with future events or apparently unknowable present realities. [< Lat. *vēridicus* : *vērus*, true; see **wērə-o-** in App. + *dīcere*, to say; see **deik-** in App.] **—ve•rid′i•cal′i•ty** (-kăl′ĭ-tē) *n.*

ver•i•fi•a•ble (vĕr′ə-fī′ə-bəl) *adj.* Possible to verify. **—ver′i•fi′a•bil′i•ty, ver′i•fi′a•ble•ness** *n.* **—ver′i•fi′a•bly** *adv.*

ver•i•fi•ca•tion (vĕr′ə-fĭ-kā′shən) *n.* **1.** The act of verifying or the state of being verified. **2a.** A confirmation of truth or authority. **b.** The evidence for such a confirmation. **c.** A formal assertion of validity. **3.** *Law* An affidavit that attests to the truth of a pleading. **—ver′i•fi•ca′tive** *adj.*

ver•i•fy (vĕr′ə-fī′) *tr.v.* **-fied, -fy•ing, -fies 1.** To prove the truth of with evidence or testimony; substantiate. **2.** To determine or test the truth or accuracy of, as by comparison or investigation. **3.** *Law* **a.** To affirm formally or under oath. **b.** To append a verification to (a pleading); conclude with a verification. [ME *verifien* < OFr. *verifier* < Med.Lat. *vērificāre* : Lat. *vērus*, true; see **wērə-o-** in App. + Lat. *-ficāre*, -fy.] **—ver′i•fi′er** *n.*

ver•i•ly (vĕr′ə-lē) *adv.* **1.** In truth; in fact. **2.** With confidence; assuredly. [ME *verraily* < *verrai*, true. See VERY.]

ver•i•sim•i•lar (vĕr′ə-sĭm′ə-lər) *adj.* Appearing to be true or real; probable. [< Lat. *vērisimilis* : *vērī*, genitive of *vērum*, truth < neut. sing. of *vērus*, true; see **wērə-o-** in App. + *similis*, similar; see SIMILAR.] **—ver′i•sim′i•lar•ly** *adv.*

ver•i•si•mil•i•tude (vĕr′ə-sĭ-mĭl′ĭ-to͞od′, -tyo͞od′) *n.* **1.** The quality of appearing to be true or real. **2.** Something that has the appearance of being true or real. [Lat. *vērisimilitūdō* < *vērisimilis*, verisimilar. See VERISIMILAR.] **—ver′i•si•mil′i•tu′di•nous** (-to͞od′n-əs, -tyo͞od′-) *adj.*

ver•ism (vĕr′ĭz′əm) *n.* Realism in art and literature. [Ital. *verismo* < *vero*, true < Lat. *vērus*. See **wērə-o-** in App.] **—ver′ist** *n.* **—ve•ris′tic** (və-rĭs′tĭk) *adj.*

ve•ris•mo (və-rĭz′mō) *n.* **1.** Verism. **2.** An artistic movement of the late 19th century, originating in Italy and influential esp. in grand opera, marked by the use of rural characters and common themes often treated in a melodramatic manner. [Ital. See VERISM.]

ver•i•ta•ble (vĕr′ĭ-tə-bəl) *adj.* Being truly so called; real or genuine. [ME < OFr. < *verite*, truth. See VERITY.] **—ver′i•ta•ble•ness** *n.* **—ver′i•ta•bly** *adv.*

vé•ri•té (vā-rē-tā′, vâr′ĭ-tā′) *n.* Cinéma vérité.

ver•i•ty (vĕr′ĭ-tē) *n., pl.* **-ties 1.** The quality or state of being true, factual, or real. **2.** Something, such as a statement or principle, that is true, esp. an enduring truth. [ME *verite*, truth < OFr. < Lat. *vēritās* < *vērus*, true. See **wērə-o-** in App.]

ver•juice (vûr′jo͞os′) *n.* **1.** The acidic juice of crab apples or other sour fruit. **2.** Sourness, as of disposition. [ME *verjus* < OFr. *vertjus* : *verd*, unripe; see VERDURE + *jus*, juice; see JUICE.]

Ver•kho•yansk Range (vĕr′kə-yänsk′, vĭr-KHô-) A mountain chain of NE Russia parallel to and E of the lower Lena R.

Ver•laine (vĕr-lān′, -lĕn′), **Paul** 1844–96. French symbolist poet whose works include *Romances sans Paroles* (1874).

Ver•meer (vər-mîr′, -mâr′), **Jan** 1632–75. Dutch painter noted for the masterful use of lighting in his interior genre scenes.

ver•meil (vûr′məl, -māl′) *n.* **1.** Vermilion or a similar bright red color. **2.** (vĕr-mā′) Gilded silver, bronze, or copper. ❖ *adj.* Bright red in color. [ME *vermail* < OFr. *vermeil* < LLat. *vermiculus*, a kind of red worm < Lat., grub, dim. of *vermis*, worm. See **wer-**[2] in App.]

vermi– *pref.* Worm: *vermicide.* [< Lat. *vermis*, worm. See **wer-**[2] in App.]

ver•mi•cel•li (vûr′mĭ-chĕl′ē, -sĕl′ē) *n.* Pasta in long, very thin strands. [Ital., pl. of *vermicello*, dim. of *verme*, worm < Lat. *vermis.* See **wer-**[2] in App.]

ver•mi•cide (vûr′mĭ-sīd′) *n.* A substance used to kill worms. **—ver′mi•cid′al** (-sīd′l) *adj.*

ver•mic•u•lar (vər-mĭk′yə-lər) *adj.* **1.** Having the shape or motion of a worm. **2.** Having wormlike markings; vermiculate. **3.** Caused by or relating to worms. [Med.Lat. *vermiculāris* < Lat. *vermiculus*, dim. of *vermis*, worm. See **wer-**[2] in App.] **—ver•mic′u•lar•ly** *adv.*

ver•mic•u•late (vər-mĭk′yə-lāt′) *tr.v.* **-lat•ed, -lat•ing, -lates** To adorn with wavy or winding lines. ❖ *adj.* (-lĭt, -lāt′) **1.** Bearing wavy wormlike lines. **2.** Wormlike in motion; twisting or wriggling. **3.** Sinuous; tortuous. **4.** Infested with worms; worm-eaten. [Lat. *vermiculārī*, *vermiculāt-* < *vermiculus*, dim. of *vermis*, worm. See VERMICULAR.]

ver•mic•u•la•tion (vər-mĭk′yə-lā′shən) *n.* **1.** Motion resembling that of a worm, esp. the wavelike contractions of the intestine; peristalsis. **2.** Wormlike marks or carvings, as in a mosaic or masonry. **3.** The condition of being worm-eaten.

ver•mic•u•lite (vər-mĭk′yə-līt′) *n.* Any of a group of micaceous hydrated silicate minerals related to the chlorites and used in heat-expanded form as insulation and as a planting medium.

ver•mi•form (vûr′mə-fôrm′) *adj.* Resembling or having the long, thin, cylindrical shape of a worm.

vermiform appendix *n.* A narrow vestigial process projecting from the cecum in the lower right-hand part of the abdomen of some mammals, including humans.

ver•mi•fuge (vûr′mə-fyo͞oj′) *n.* A medicine that expels intestinal worms. ❖ *adj.* Causing expulsion of intestinal worms.

ver•mil•ion also **ver•mil•lion** (vər-mĭl′yən) *n.* **1.** A bright red mercuric sulfide used as a pigment. **2.** A vivid red to reddish orange. ❖ *adj.* Of the color vermilion. ❖ *tr.v.* **-ioned, -ion•ing, -ions** also **-lioned, -lion•ing, -lions** To color or dye (something) in the hue vermilion. [ME *vermelion* < OFr. *vermeillon* < *vermeil*. See VERMEIL.]

ver•min (vûr′mĭn) *n., pl.* **vermin 1.** Various small animals or insects, such as rats or cockroaches, that are destructive, annoying, or injurious to health. **2.** Animals that prey on game, such as foxes. **3a.** A person considered loathsome or highly offensive. **b.** Such people considered as a group. [ME < OFr. < VLat. **vermīnum* < Lat. *vermis*, worm. See **wer-**[2] in App.]

ver•mi•na•tion (vûr′mə-nā′shən) *n.* Infestation by vermin, esp. parasitic vermin.

ver•min•ous (vûr′mə-nəs) *adj.* **1.** Of, relating to, or caused by vermin: *verminous diseases.* **2.** Infested with vermin. **3.** Of the nature of vermin; repulsive. **—ver′min•ous•ly** *adv.*

ver•mis (vûr′mĭs) *n., pl.* **-mes** (-mēz) The region of the cerebellum lying between and connecting the two hemispheres. [NLat. < Lat., worm. See **wer-**[2] in App.]

ver•miv•o•rous (vər-mĭv′ər-əs) *adj.* Feeding on worms or insect vermin. Used of a bird.

Ver•mont (vər-mŏnt′) A state of the NE US bordering on Canada; admitted as the 14th state in 1791. Cap. Montpelier. Pop. 608,827. **—Ver•mont′er** *n.*

ver•mouth (vər-mo͞oth′) *n.* A sweet or dry fortified wine flavored with aromatic herbs and often used in mixed drinks. [Fr. *vermout* < Ger. *Wermut* < MHGer. *wermuot*, wormwood < OHGer. *wermuota.*]

ver•nac•u•lar (vər-năk′yə-lər) *n.* **1.** The standard native language of a country or locality. **2a.** The everyday language spoken by a people as distinguished from the literary language. **b.** A variety of such everyday language specific to a social group or region: *the vernaculars of New York City.* **3.** The idiom of a particular

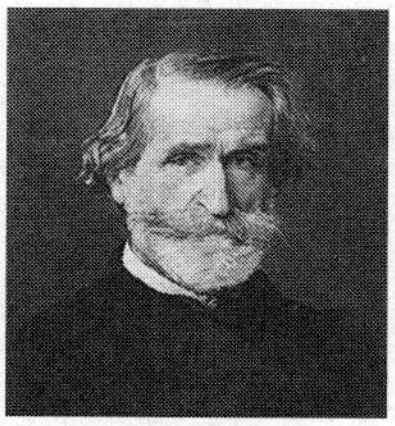

Giuseppe Verdi
detail from an 1886 portrait
by Giovanni Boldini
(1845–1931)

ă	pat	oi	boy
ā	pay	ou	out
âr	care	o͝o	took
ä	father	o͞o	boot
ĕ	pet	ŭ	cut
ē	be	ûr	urge
ĭ	pit	th	thin
ī	pie	*th*	this
îr	pier	hw	which
ŏ	pot	zh	vision
ō	toe	ə	about, item
ô	paw		

Stress marks:
′ (primary);
′ (secondary), as in
lexicon (lĕk′sĭ-kŏn′)

trade or profession. **4.** An idiomatic word, phrase, or expression. **5.** The common nonscientific name of a plant or an animal. ❖ *adj.* **1.** Native to or commonly spoken by the members of a particular country or region. **2.** Using the native language of a region, esp. as distinct from the literary language. **3.** Relating to or expressed in the native language or dialect. **4.** Of or being an indigenous building style using local materials and traditional methods of construction and ornament. **5.** Occurring or existing in a particular locality; endemic. **6.** Relating to or being the common nonscientific name of a plant or animal. [< Lat. *vernaculus,* native < *verna,* native slave, perh. of Etruscan orig.] —**ver·nac′u·lar·ly** *adv.*

ver·nac·u·lar·ism (vər-năk′yə-lə-rĭz′əm) *n.* A vernacular word or expression.

ver·nac·u·lar·ize (vər-năk′yə-lə-rīz′) *tr.v.* **-ized, -iz·ing, -iz·es** To translate into everyday language.

ver·nal (vûr′nəl) *adj.* **1.** Of, relating to, or occurring in the spring. **2.** Characteristic of or resembling spring. **3.** Fresh and young; youthful. [Lat. *vērnālis < vērnus < vēr,* spring. See **wesr** in App.] —**ver′nal·ly** *adv.*

vernal equinox *n.* **1.** The point at which the ecliptic intersects the celestial equator, the sun having a northerly motion. **2.** The moment at which the sun passes through the vernal equinox, marking the beginning of spring in the Northern Hemisphere.

ver·nal·i·za·tion (vûr′nə-lĭ-zā′shən) *n.* Subjection of seeds or seedlings to low temperature to hasten plant development. —**ver′nal·ize′** *v.*

ver·na·tion (vər-nā′shən) *n.* The arrangement of the young leaves within a bud. [NLat. *vērnātiō, vērnātiōn-* < Lat. *vērnātus,* p. part. of *vērnāre,* to flourish < *vērnus,* vernal. See VERNAL.]

Verne (vûrn, vĕrn), **Jules** 1828–1905. French writer whose novels include *Journey to the Center of the Earth* (1864).

Ver·ner's Law (vûr′nərz, vĕr′-) *n. Linguistics* The voicing of Proto-Germanic noninitial fricatives in voiced environments when the previous syllable was unstressed in Proto-Indo-European. [After Karl Adolph *Verner* (1846–96), Danish philologist.]

ver·ni·er (vûr′nē-ər) *n.* **1.** A small movable auxiliary graduated scale attached parallel to a main graduated scale, calibrated to indicate fractional parts of the subdivisions of the larger scale and used to increase accuracy in measurement. **2.** An auxiliary device designed to facilitate fine adjustments or measurements on precision instruments. ❖ *adj.* Of, relating to, or having a vernier. [After Pierre *Vernier* (1580?–1637), French mathematician.]

vernier caliper *n.* A measuring instrument that consists of an L-shaped frame with a linear scale along its longer arm and an L-shaped sliding attachment with a vernier scale, used to read directly the thickness or diameter of an object.

vernier scale *n.* See **vernier** 1.

ver·nis·sage (vĕr′nĭ-säzh′) *n.* A private showing before an art exhibition opens. [Fr. < *vernis,* varnish < OFr. See VARNISH.]

ver·nix (vûr′nĭks) *n.* A waxy white protective substance covering the skin of a fetus. [Short for VERNIX CASEOSA.]

vernix ca·se·o·sa (kā′sē-ō′sə) *n.* Vernix. [NLat. *vernix cāseōsa : vernix,* varnish + *cāseōsa,* cheeselike.]

Ve·ro·na (və-rō′nə) A city of N Italy on the Adige R. W of Venice; became an independent republic in A.D. 1107 and formed the powerful Veronese League in 1164. Pop. 252,689. —**Ve′ro·nese′** (vĕr′ə-nēz′, -nēs′) *adj. & n.*

Ve·ro·ne·se (vĕr′ə-nā′sĕ, -zĕ, vĕ′rō-nĕ′zĕ), **Paolo** 1528–88. Italian painter whose works include *Rape of Europa* (1576).

ve·ron·i·ca¹ (və-rŏn′ĭ-kə) *n.* Any of various plants of the genus *Veronica,* which includes the speedwells. [NLat. *Veronica,* genus name.]

ve·ron·i·ca² (və-rŏn′ĭ-kə) *n.* **1a.** According to legend, an image of the face of Jesus impressed on the handkerchief offered to him by Saint Veronica on his way to Calvary. **b.** The handkerchief itself. **2.** A cloth bearing an image of Jesus's face. [Med.Lat., perh. alteration of *vēra īconica,* true image : Lat. *vēra,* fem. of *vērus,* true; see VERY + Lat. *īconica,* fem. of *īconicus,* of an image (< Gk. *eikonikos < eikōn,* image; see ICON).]

ve·ron·i·ca³ (və-rŏn′ĭ-kə) *n.* A maneuver in bullfighting in which the matador stands with both feet fixed in position and swings the cape slowly away from the charging bull. [Sp. < *veronica,* the veronica (< the gesture Saint Veronica made) < Med.Lat. See VERONICA².]

Veronica, Saint. A woman of Jerusalem who gave Jesus her headcloth to wipe his face as he bore the cross to Calvary.

Ver·ra·za·no or **Ver·raz·za·no** (vĕr′ə-zä′nō, -rä-tsä′-), **Giovanni da** 1485?–1528? Italian explorer of the Atlantic coast of North America.

Ver·roc·chio (və-rō′kē-ō, vĕr-rōk′kyō), **Andrea del** 1435–88. Florentine artist who tutored Leonardo da Vinci.

ver·ru·ca (və-rōō′kə) *n., pl.* **-cae** (-kē) A wart or wartlike projection. [Lat. *verrūca.*]

ver·ru·cose (və-rōō′kōs′) also **ver·ru·cous** (-kəs) *adj.* Covered with warts or wartlike projections. [Lat. *verrūcōsus < verrūca,* wart.]

vers *abbr.* versed sine

Ver·sailles (vər-sī′, vĕr-) A city of N-central France WSW of Paris; known for its magnificent palace, built by Louis XIV in the mid-17th cent. Pop. 91,494.

ver·sant (vûr′sənt) *n.* **1.** The slope of a side of a mountain or mountain range. **2.** The general slope of a region. [Fr., pr. part. of *verser,* to turn < OFr. < Lat. *versāre,* to turn frequently. See VERSATILE.]

ver·sa·tile (vûr′sə-təl, -tīl′) *adj.* **1.** Capable of doing many things competently. **2.** Having varied uses or serving many functions. **3.** Variable or inconstant; changeable. **4.** *Biology* Capable of moving freely in all directions, as the toe of an owl. [Lat. *versātilis < versātus,* p. part. of *versāre,* to turn. See **wer-²** in App.] —**ver′sa·tile·ly** *adv.* —**ver·sa·til′i·ty** (-tĭl′ĭ-tē), **ver′sa·tile·ness** (-təl-nĭs, -tīl′-) *n.*

verse¹ (vûrs) *n.* **1a.** A single metrical line in a poetic composition; one line of poetry. **b.** A division of a metrical composition, such as a stanza of a poem. **c.** A poem. **2.** Metrical or rhymed composition as distinct from prose; poetry. **3a.** The art or work of a poet. **b.** A group of poems: *a book of verse.* **4.** Metrical writing that lacks depth or artistic merit. **5.** A particular type of metrical composition, such as blank verse. **6.** One of the numbered subdivisions of a chapter in the Bible. ❖ *tr. & intr.v.* **versed, vers·ing, vers·es** To versify. [ME *vers* < OE *fers* and < OFr. *vers,* both < Lat. *versus* < p. part. of *vertere,* to turn. See **wer-²** in App.]

verse² (vûrs) *tr.v.* **versed, vers·ing, vers·es** To familiarize by study or experience. [Lat. *versāre.* See VERSATILE.]

versed (vûrst) *adj.* Acquainted through study or experience; knowledgeable or skilled: *She is well versed in languages.*

versed cosine *n.* A trigonometric function of an angle equal to one minus the sine of that angle. [VERSED (SINE) + COSINE.]

versed sine *n.* A trigonometric function of an angle equal to one minus the cosine of that angle. [Transl. of NLat. *sinus versus : sinus,* sine + Lat. *versus,* p. part. of *vertere,* to turn.]

ver·si·cle (vûr′sĭ-kəl) *n.* A short verse. **2.** A short sentence spoken or chanted in a Christian liturgy. [ME < Lat. *versiculus,* dim. of *versus,* verse. See VERSE¹.]

ver·si·col·or (vûr′sĭ-kŭl′ər) also **ver·si·col·ored** (-kŭl′ərd) *adj.* **1.** Having a variety of colors; variegated. **2.** Changing in color; iridescent. [Lat. : *versus,* p. part. of *vertere,* to turn; see VERSE¹ + *color,* color; see COLOR.]

ver·si·fy (vûr′sə-fī′) *v.* **-fied, -fy·ing, -fies** —*tr.* **1.** To change from prose into metrical form. **2.** To treat or tell in verse. —*intr.* To write verses. [ME *versifien* < OFr. *versifier* < Lat. *versificāre : versus,* verse; see VERSE¹ + *-ficāre,* -fy.] —**ver′si·fi·ca′tion** (-fĭ-kā′shən) *n.* —**ver′si·fi′er** *n.*

ver·sine (vûr′sīn′) *n.* See **versed sine.** [Contraction of VERSED SINE.]

ver·sion (vûr′zhən, -shən) *n.* **1.** An account from one point of view, esp. as opposed to another. **2a.** A translation from another language. **b.** often **Version** A translation of the entire Bible or a part of it. **3.** A particular form or variation of an earlier or original type. **4.** An adaptation of a work of art or literature into another medium or style. **5.** *Medicine* **a.** Manipulation of a fetus in the uterus to bring it into a desirable position for delivery. **b.** Deflection of an organ, such as the uterus, from its normal position. [Fr. < OFr., act of turning < Med.Lat. *versiō, versiōn-* < Lat. *versus,* p. part. of *vertere,* to turn. See **wer-²** in App.] —**ver′sion·al** *adj.*

vers li·bre (vĕr lē′brə) *n.* Free verse. [Fr.]

ver·so (vûr′sō) *n., pl.* **-sos 1.** A left-hand page of a book or the reverse side of a leaf, as opposed to the recto. **2.** The back of a coin or medal. [NLat. *versō (foliō),* (with the page) turned, verso < Lat. *versō,* ablative of *versus,* p. part. of *vertere,* to turn. See VERSION.]

verst (vûrst) *n.* A Russian measure of linear distance equivalent to about two thirds of a mile. [Fr. *verste* or Ger. *Werst,* both < Russ. *versta.* See **wer-²** in App.]

ver·sus (vûr′səs, -səz) *prep.* **1.** Against: *the plaintiff versus the defendant.* **2.** As the alternative to or in contrast with. [ME < Med.Lat. < Lat., turned, toward < p. part. of *vertere,* to turn. See **wer-²** in App.]

vert (vûrt) *n.* **1.** *Heraldry* The color green. **2a.** Green vegetation that can serve as cover for deer. **b.** The right to cut such vegetation. [ME *verte* < AN, fem. of *verd.* See VERDERER.]

vert. *abbr.* **1.** vertebrate **2.** vertical

ver·te·bra (vûr′tə-brə) *n., pl.* **-brae** (-brā′, -brē′) or **-bras** Any of the bones or cartilaginous segments forming the spinal column. [ME < Lat. < *vertere,* to turn. See **wer-²** in App.]

ver·te·bral (vûr′tə-brəl, vər-tē′brəl) *adj.* **1.** Of, relating to, or of the nature of a vertebra. **2.** Having or consisting of vertebrae. **3.** Having a spinal column. —**ver′te·bral·ly** *adv.*

vertebral canal *n.* See **spinal canal.**

vertebral column *n.* See **spinal column.**

ver·te·brate (vûr′tə-brĭt, -brāt′) *adj.* **1.** Having a backbone or spinal column. **2.** Of or characteristic of vertebrates or a vertebrate. ❖ *n.* A member of the subphylum Vertebrata, a primary division of the phylum Chordata that includes the fishes, amphibians, reptiles, birds, and mammals, all of which are characterized by a segmented spinal column and a distinct, well-differentiated head. [Lat. *vertebrātus,* having joints < *vertebra,* vertebra. See VERTEBRA.]

ver·te·bra·tion (vûr′tə-brā′shən) *n.* Division into segments like those of the spinal column; vertebral formation.

ver·tex (vûr′tĕks′) *n., pl.* **-ti·ces** (-tĭ-sēz′) also **-tex·es 1.** The highest point; the apex or summit. **2.** *Anatomy* **a.** The highest point of the skull. **b.** The top of the head. **3.** *Astronomy* The highest point reached in the apparent motion of a celestial body. **4.** *Mathematics* **a.** The point at which the sides of an angle intersect. **b.** The point on a triangle or pyramid opposite to and farthest away from its base. **c.** A point on a polyhedron common to three or more sides. [Lat., whirlpool, crown of the head (where the hair forms a whorl), vertex < *vertere*, to turn. See **wer-²** in App.]

ver·ti·cal (vûr′tĭ-kəl) *adj.* **1.** Being or situated at right angles to the horizon; upright. **2.** Situated at the vertex or highest point; directly overhead. **3.** *Anatomy* Of or relating to the vertex of the head. **4.** *Economics* Relating to or involving all stages from production to sale: *vertical integration.* **5.** Relating to or composed of elements at different levels, as of society. ❖ *n.* **1.** Something vertical, as a line, plane, or circle. **2.** A vertical position. [LLat. *verticālis*, overhead < Lat. *vertex, vertic-*, highest point. See VERTEX.] —**ver′ti·cal′i·ty** (-kăl′ĭ-tē), **ver′ti·cal·ness** (-kəl-nĭs) *n.* —**ver′ti·cal·ly** *adv.*

vertical angle *n.* Either of two angles formed by two intersecting lines and lying on opposite sides of the point of intersection.

vertical circle *n.* A great circle on the celestial sphere that passes through the zenith and the nadir and thus is perpendicular to the horizon.

vertical file *n.* A collection of resource materials, such as pamphlets and photographs, for ready reference, as in a library.

vertical union *n.* An industrial union.

ver·ti·cil (vûr′tĭ-sĭl′) *n.* A circular arrangement, as of flowers, leaves, or hairs, growing about a central point; a whorl. [Lat. *verticillus*, the whorl of a spindle, dim. of *vertex, vertic-*, highest point. See VERTEX.]

ver·ti·cil·las·ter (vûr′tĭ-sə-lăs′tər) *n.* A cymose inflorescence resembling a whorl but actually arising in the axils of opposite bracts, as in most mints. [NLat. *verticillastēr* : Lat. *verticillus*, whorl; see VERTICIL + Lat. *astēr*, star; see ASTER.]

ver·ti·cil·late (vûr′tĭ-sĭl′ĭt, -āt′) *also* **ver·ti·cil·lat·ed** (-sĭl′ā′tĭd) *adj.* Arranged in or forming whorls or a whorl.

ver·tig·i·nous (vər-tĭj′ə-nəs) *adj.* **1.** Turning about an axis; revolving or whirling. **2.** Affected by vertigo; dizzy. **3.** Tending to produce vertigo. **4.** Inclined to change quickly. [< Lat. *vertīgō, vertīgin-*, a whirling < *vertere*, to turn. See VERSION.] —**ver·tig′i·nous·ly** *adv.* —**ver·tig′i·nous·ness** *n.*

ver·ti·go (vûr′tĭ-gō′) *n., pl.* **-goes** *or* **-gos** **1a.** The sensation of dizziness. **b.** An instance of such a sensation. **2.** A confused, disoriented state of mind. [ME < Lat. *vertīgō* < *vertere*, to turn. See **wer-²** in App.]

ver·tu (vər-tōō′) *n.* Variant of virtu.

ver·vain (vûr′vān′) *n.* See verbena 1. [ME *verveine* < OFr. < Lat. *verbēna*, leafage. See VERBENA.]

verve (vûrv) *n.* **1.** Energy and enthusiasm in the expression of ideas, esp. in artistic performance or composition. **2.** Vitality; liveliness. **3.** *Archaic* Aptitude; talent. [Fr. < OFr., fanciful expression, prob. < VLat. *verva* < Lat. *verba*, pl. of *verbum*, word. See **wer-¹** in App.]

ver·vet (vûr′vĭt) *n.* A small long-tailed African monkey (*Cercopithecus aethiops*) having a yellowish-brown or greenish coat. [Fr. : *vert*, green (< OFr. *verd*; see VERDANT) + (*gri*)*vet*, grivet.]

ver·y (vĕr′ē) *adv.* **1.** In a high degree; extremely: *very happy.* **2.** Truly; absolutely: *the very best advice.* **3.** Very Used in titles: *the Very Reverend Jane Smith.* ❖ *adj.* **-i·er, -i·est** **1.** Complete; absolute: *the very opposite.* **2.** Being the same one; identical: *the very question she asked.* **3.** Being particularly suitable or appropriate: *the very item needed.* **4.** Being precisely as stated: *the very center of town.* **5.** Mere: *The very thought is frightening.* **6.** Actual: *caught in the very act.* **7.** Genuine; true. [ME *verrai* < OFr. *verai*, true < VLat. **vērācus* < Lat. *vērāx, vērāc-*, truthful < *vērus*, true. See **wērə-o-** in App.]

very high frequency *n.* A band of radio frequencies falling between 30 and 300 megahertz.

very low frequency *n.* A band of radio frequencies falling between 3 and 30 kilohertz.

Ver·y pistol (vĕr′ē, vîr′ē) *n.* A pistol used for firing colored signal flares. [After Edward Wilson *Very* (1847–1910), Amer. naval officer.]

Ve·sa·li·us (vĭ-sā′lē-əs, -zā′-), **Andreas** 1514–64. Flemish anatomist considered the founder of modern anatomy.

ve·si·ca (və-sī′kə, -sē′-) *n., pl.* **-cae** (-kē, -sē) A bladder, esp. the urinary bladder or the gallbladder. [Lat. *vēsīca.*] —**ves′i·cal** (vĕs′ĭ-kəl) *adj.*

ves·i·cant (vĕs′ĭ-kənt) *n.* A blistering agent, esp. mustard gas, used in chemical warfare. ❖ *adj.* Causing blisters.

ves·i·cate (vĕs′ĭ-kāt′) *tr. & intr.v.* **-cat·ed, -cat·ing, -cates** To blister or become blistered. [NLat. *vēsīcāre, vēsīcāt-* < Lat. *vēsīca*, bladder, blister.] —**ves′i·ca′tion** *n.*

ves·i·ca·to·ry (vĕs′ĭ-kə-tôr′ē, -tōr′ē) *adj.* Vesicant. ❖ *n., pl.* **-ries** A vesicant.

ves·i·cle (vĕs′ĭ-kəl) *n.* **1.** A small bladderlike cell or cavity. **2.** *Anatomy* A small sac or cyst, esp. one containing fluid. **3.** *Pathology* A serum-filled blister formed in or beneath the skin. **4.** *Geology* A small cavity formed in volcanic rock by entrapment of a gas bubble during solidification. [ME < OFr. *vesicule* < Lat. *vēsīcula*, dim. of *vēsīca*, bladder, blister.]

ve·sic·u·lar (vĕ-sĭk′yə-lər, və-) *adj.* **1.** Of or relating to vesicles. **2.** Composed of or containing vesicles. **3.** Having the form of a vesicle. —**ve·sic′u·lar·ly** *adv.*

vesicular stomatitis *n.* An acute viral disease of cattle, swine, and horses, transmitted by insects and having symptoms resembling those of vesicular exanthema.

ve·sic·u·late (vĕ-sĭk′yə-lāt′, və-) *tr. & intr.v.* **-lat·ed, -lat·ing, -lates** To make or become vesicular. ❖ *adj.* (-lĭt, -lāt′) Full of or bearing vesicles; vesicular. —**ve·sic′u·la′tion** *n.*

Ves·pa·sian (vĕs-pā′zhən, -zhē-ən) Originally Titus Flavius Vespasianus A.D. 9–79. Emperor of Rome (69–79) who reformed the army.

ves·per (vĕs′pər) *n.* **1.** A bell that summons worshipers to vespers. **2.** Vesper The evening star, esp. Venus. **3.** *Archaic* Evening. [ME, evening star < Lat., evening. See **wes-pero-** in App.]

ves·per·al (vĕs′pər-əl) *Ecclesiastical* *n.* **1.** A book concerning the vespers liturgy. **2.** A covering used to protect an altar cloth. ❖ *adj.* Of or relating to vesper or vespers.

ves·pers *also* **Ves·pers** (vĕs′pərz) *pl.n.* (used with a sing. or pl. verb) **1.** *Ecclesiastical* **a.** The sixth of the seven canonical hours. **b.** The evening office of many Western Christian churches. **c.** The time of day appointed for this service. **2.** Evensong. [Obsolete Fr. *vespres* < OFr. < Med.Lat. *vesperās*, evening service < Lat., accusative pl. of *vespera*, evening, var. of *vesper*. See VESPER.]

vesper sparrow *n.* A North American sparrow (*Pooecetes gramineus*) having white markings on its outer tail feathers.

ves·per·til·i·o·nid (vĕs′pər-tĭl′ē-ə-nĭd) *n.* Any of various widely distributed insect-eating bats of the family Vespertilionidae, characterized by a long tail. [< NLat. *Vespertiliōnidae*, family name < *Vespertiliō, Vespertiliōn-*, type genus < Lat. *vespertiliō*, bat < *vesper*, evening. See **wes-pero-** in App.]

ves·per·tine (vĕs′pər-tīn′) *also* **ves·per·ti·nal** (vĕs′pər-tī′nəl) *adj.* **1.** Of, relating to, or occurring in the evening. **2.** *Botany* Opening or blooming in the evening. **3.** *Zoology* Becoming active in the evening, as bats and owls; crepuscular. [Lat. *vespertīnus* < *vesper*, evening. See VESPER.]

ves·pi·ar·y (vĕs′pē-ĕr′ē) *n., pl.* **-ies** A nest or colony of wasps or hornets. [Lat. *vespa*, wasp + (AP)IARY.]

ves·pid (vĕs′pĭd) *n.* Any of various widely distributed social insects of the family Vespidae, which includes certain wasps and yellow jackets. [< NLat. *Vespidae*, family name < *Vespa*, type genus < Lat. *vespa*, wasp.] —**ves′pid** *adj.*

ves·pine (vĕs′pīn′) *adj.* Of, relating to, or resembling a wasp. [< Lat. *vespa*, wasp.]

Ves·puc·ci (vĕs-pōō′chē, -pyōō′-), **Amerigo** Latin name Americus Vespucius. 1454–1512. Italian explorer of the South American coast. America was named in his honor.

ves·sel (vĕs′əl) *n.* **1.** A hollow utensil, such as a cup, vase, or pitcher, used as a container, esp. for liquids. **2a.** *Nautical* A craft, esp. one larger than a rowboat, designed to navigate on water. **b.** An airship. **3.** *Anatomy* A duct, canal, or other tube that contains or conveys a body fluid: *a blood vessel.* **4.** *Botany* One of the tubular conductive structures of xylem, consisting of dead cylindrical cells attached end to end and connected by perforations. **5.** A person seen as the agent or embodiment, as of a quality: *a vessel of mercy.* [ME < OFr. < LLat. *vāscellum*, dim. of Lat. *vāsculum*, dim. of *vās*, vessel.]

vest (vĕst) *n.* **1.** A sleeveless garment, often having buttons down the front, worn usu. over a shirt or blouse. **2.** A waist-length sleeveless garment worn for protection: *a warm down vest.* **3.** A fabric trim worn to fill in the neckline of a woman's garment; a vestee. **4.** *Chiefly British* An undershirt. **5a.** *Archaic* Clothing; raiment. **b.** *Obsolete* An ecclesiastical vestment. ❖ *v.* **vest·ed, vest·ing, vests** —*tr.* **1.** To place (authority, property, or rights, for example) in the control of a person or group, esp. to give someone an immediate right to present or future possession or enjoyment of (an estate, for example). Used with *in*: *vested his estate in his daughter.* **2.** To invest or endow (a person or group) with something, such as power or rights. Used with *with*: *vested the council with broad powers.* **3.** To clothe or robe, as in ecclesiastical vestments. —*intr.* **1.** To become legally vested. **2.** To dress oneself, esp. in ecclesiastical vestments. [Fr. *veste*, robe < Ital. *vesta* < Lat. *vestis*, garment. See **wes-²** in App.]

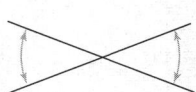

vertical angle

vervet
Cercopithecus aethiops

ă	pat	oi	boy
ā	pay	ou	out
âr	care	ŏŏ	took
ä	father	ōō	boot
ĕ	pet	ŭ	cut
ē	be	ûr	urge
ĭ	pit	th	thin
ī	pie	th	this
îr	pier	hw	which
ŏ	pot	zh	vision
ō	toe	ə	about,
ô	paw		item

Stress marks:
′ (primary);
′ (secondary), as in
lexicon (lĕk′sĭ-kŏn′)

Ves·ta (vĕs′tə) n. **1.** *Roman Mythology* The goddess of the hearth, worshiped in a temple containing the sacred fire tended by the vestal virgins. **2.** The brightest asteroid. [Lat. See **wes-**[1] in App.]

ves·tal (vĕs′təl) adj. **1.** *Roman Mythology* **a.** Of or relating to Vesta. **b.** Relating to or characteristic of the vestal virgins. **2.** Chaste; pure. ❖ n. **1.** *Roman Mythology* A vestal virgin. **2.** A woman who is a virgin. **3.** A nun.

vestal virgin n. *Roman Mythology* One of the priestesses who tended the sacred fire in the temple of Vesta in ancient Rome and remained celibate during their servitude.

vest·ed (vĕs′tĭd) adj. **1.** *Law* Settled, fixed, or absolute; being without contingency: *a vested right*. **2.** Dressed or clothed, esp. in ecclesiastical vestments.

vested interest n. **1.** *Law* A right or title, as to present or future possession of an estate, that can be conveyed to another. **2.** A fixed right granted to an employee under a pension plan. **3.** A special interest in protecting or promoting that which is to one's own personal advantage. **4. vested interests** Those groups that seek to maintain or control an existing system or activity from which they derive private benefit.

vest·ee (vĕ-stē′) n. A garment worn by women as a blouse front under a sweater or jacket. [< VEST.]

ves·ti·ar·y (vĕs′tē-ĕr′ē, -chē-) adj. Of or relating to clothes. ❖ n., pl. **-ies** A dressing room, cloakroom, or vestry. [Lat. *vestiārius* < *vestis*, garment. See VEST.]

ves·tib·u·lar (vĕ-stĭb′yə-lər) adj. Of or serving as a vestibule.

vestibular nerve n. A division of the auditory nerve that conducts impulses related to maintaining balance to the brain. [< the role of the vestibule to the ear in maintaining balance.]

ves·ti·bule (vĕs′tə-byōōl′) n. **1.** A small entrance hall or passage between the outer door and the interior of a house or building. **2.** An enclosed area at the end of a passenger car on a railroad train. **3.** *Anatomy* A cavity, chamber, or channel that leads to or is an entrance to another cavity. [Lat. *vestibulum.*]

ves·tige (vĕs′tĭj) n. **1.** A visible trace, evidence, or sign of something that exists or appears no longer. **2.** *Biology* A rudimentary or degenerate, usu. nonfunctioning structure that is the remnant of a formerly fully developed or functioning organ or part. [Fr. < OFr. < Lat. *vestīgium*.]

ves·tig·i·al (vĕ-stĭj′ē-əl, -stĭj′əl) adj. **1.** Of, relating to, or constituting a vestige. **2.** *Biology* Occurring or persisting as a rudimentary or degenerate structure. —**ves·tig′i·al·ly** adv.

ves·tig·i·um (vĕ-stĭj′ē-əm) n., pl. **-i·a** (-ē-ə) *Biology* A vestige. [Lat. *vestīgium*, footprint.]

ves·ti·men·tif·er·an (vĕs′tə-mĕn-tĭf′ər-ən) n. Any of various marine tubeworms of the phylum Vestimentifera, including the giant tubeworms, which inhabit areas close to deep sea hydrothermal vents. [NLat. *Vestīmentifera*, phylum name : Lat. *vestīmentum*, outer garment; see VESTMENT + Lat. *-fera*, neut. pl. of *-fer*, -fera.]

vest·ing (vĕs′tĭng) n. The granting to an employee of credits toward a pension even if separated from the job before retirement.

vest·ment (vĕst′mənt) n. **1.** A garment, esp. a robe or gown of office or state. **2.** *Ecclesiastical* Any of the liturgical robes worn by celebrants or assistants, esp. at the celebration of the Eucharist. [ME *vestement* < OFr. *vestment* < Lat. *vestīmentum* < *vestīre*, to clothe < *vestis*, garment. See VEST.] —**vest·men′tal** (-mĕn′tl) adj.

vest-pock·et (vĕst′pŏk′ĭt) adj. **1.** Small enough to fit into a vest pocket: *a vest-pocket book.* **2.** Very small; diminutive: *a vest-pocket park.*

ves·try (vĕs′trē) n., pl. **-tries 1.** A room in or attached to a church where clergy put on their vestments and where sacred objects are stored; a sacristy. **2.** A room in a church used for meetings and classes. **3.** A committee of members elected to administer the temporal affairs of a parish. **4.** A business meeting of parishioners in a parish. [ME *vestrie*, ult. < Lat. *vestiārius*, of clothes.]

ves·try·man (vĕs′trē-mən) n. A man who is a member of a vestry.

ves·try·wom·an (vĕs′trē-wōōm′ən) n. A woman who is a member of a vestry.

ves·ture (vĕs′chər) n. **1.** Clothing; apparel. **2.** Something that covers or cloaks: *hills in a vesture of mist.* ❖ tr.v. **-tured, -tur·ing, -tures** To cover with vesture; clothe. [ME < OFr. < VLat. *vestītūra* < Lat. *vestītus*, p. part. of *vestīre*, to clothe < *vestis*, garment. See VEST.]

ve·su·vi·an (vĭ-sōō′vē-ən) n. A friction match with a phosphorus tip. ❖ adj. Marked by sudden or violent outbursts. [After Mt. VESUVIUS.]

ve·su·vi·an·ite (vĭ-sōō′vē-ə-nīt′) n. A green, brown, or yellow, metamorphic silicate mineral, $Ca_{10}Mg_2Al_4Si_9O_{34}(OH)_4$. [First found in old lava on Mt. VESUVIUS.]

Ve·su·vi·us (vĭ-sōō′vē-əs), **Mount** A volcano, 1,281 m (4,200 ft), of S Italy on the E shore of the Bay of Naples. A violent eruption in A.D. 79 destroyed the nearby city of Pompeii. —**Ve·su′vi·an** adj.

vet[1] (vĕt) *Informal* n. A veterinarian. ❖ v. **vet·ted, vet·ting, vets** —tr. **1.** To subject to veterinary evaluation, examination, medication, or surgery. **2.** To subject to thorough examination or evaluation: *vet a manuscript.* —intr. To engage in the practice of veterinary medicine.

vet[2] (vĕt) n. *Informal* A veteran.

vetch (vĕch) n. Any of various herbs of the genus *Vicia,* having pinnately compound leaves that terminate in tendrils and small, variously colored flowers. [ME *vetche* < ONFr. *veche* < Lat. *vicia.* See **weik-**[2] in App.]

vetch·ling (vĕch′lĭng) n. Any of several plants of the genus *Lathyrus,* having pinnately compound leaves, slender tendrils, and variously colored flowers.

vet·er·an (vĕt′ər-ən, vĕt′rən) n. **1.** A person who is long experienced or practiced in an activity or capacity. **2.** One who has served in the armed forces. **3.** An old soldier who has seen long service. ❖ adj. **1.** Having had long experience or practice. **2.** Of or relating to former members of the armed forces. [Lat. *veterānus* < *vetus, veter-,* old. See **wet-**[2] in App.]

Vet·er·ans Day (vĕt′ər-ənz, vĕt′rənz) n. November 11, observed in honor of veterans of the armed services and in commemoration of the armistice that ended World War I in 1918.

vet·er·i·nar·i·an (vĕt′ər-ə-nâr′ē-ən, vĕt′rə-) n. A person who practices veterinary medicine.

vet·er·i·nar·y (vĕt′ər-ə-nĕr′ē, vĕt′rə-) adj. Of or relating to veterinary medicine; concerned or connected with the medical or surgical treatment of animals, esp. domestic animals. ❖ n., pl. **-ies** A veterinarian. [Lat. *veterīnārius,* ult. < *veterīnus,* of beasts of burden. See **wet-**[2] in App.]

veterinary medicine n. The branch of medicine that deals with the causes, diagnosis, and treatment of diseases and injuries of animals, esp. domestic animals.

veterinary surgeon n. A veterinarian.

vet·i·ver (vĕt′ə-vər) n. **1.** A grass (*Vetiveria zizanioides*) of tropical India cultivated for its aromatic roots that yield an oil used in perfumery. **2.** The root of this plant. [Fr. *vétiver* < Tamil *veṭṭivēr* : *veṭṭi,* worthless + *vēru,* useless.]

vet·i·vert (vĕt′ə-vûrt′) n. The essential oil of the vetiver.

Vet·lu·ga (vĕt-lōō′gə) A river of W Russia flowing c. 850 km (528 mi) generally S to the Volga R.

ve·to (vē′tō) n., pl. **-toes 1a.** The vested power or constitutional right of one branch or department of government to refuse approval of measures proposed by another branch, esp. the power of a chief executive to reject a bill passed by the legislature and thus prevent or delay its enactment into law. **b.** Exercise of this right. **c.** An official document or message from a chief executive stating the reasons for rejection of a bill. **2.** An authoritative prohibition or rejection of a proposed or intended act. ❖ tr.v. **-toed, -to·ing, -toes 1.** To prevent (a legislative bill) from becoming law by exercising the power of veto. **2.** To forbid or prohibit authoritatively. [< Lat. *vetō,* first pers. sing. pr. t. of *vetāre,* to forbid.] —**ve′to·er** n.

vex (vĕks) tr.v. **vexed, vex·ing, vex·es 1.** To annoy, as with petty importunities; bother. **2.** To cause perplexity in; puzzle. **3.** To bring distress or suffering to; plague or afflict. **4.** To debate or discuss (a question, for example) at length. **5.** To toss about or shake up. [ME *vexen* < OFr. *vexer* < Lat. *vexāre.* See **wegh-** in App.] —**vex′ed·ly** (vĕk′sĭd-lē) adv. —**vex′er** n. —**vex′ing·ly** adv.

vex·a·tion (vĕk-sā′shən) n. **1.** The act of annoying, irritating, or vexing. **2.** The quality or condition of being vexed; annoyance. **3.** A source of irritation or annoyance.

vex·a·tious (vĕk-sā′shəs) adj. **1.** Causing or creating vexation; annoying. **2.** Full of annoyance or distress; harassed. **3.** Intended to vex or annoy. —**vex·a′tious·ly** adv. —**vex·a′tious·ness** n.

vexed (vĕkst) adj. **1.** Irritated, distressed, or annoyed. **2.** Much discussed or debated: *a vexed question.*

vex·il·lar·y (vĕk′sə-lĕr′ē) n., pl. **-ies 1.** A member of the oldest class of army veterans who served under a special standard in ancient Rome. **2.** A standard-bearer. ❖ adj. Of or relating to a vexillum. [Lat. *vexillārius* < *vexillum,* flag. See VEXILLUM.]

vex·il·late (vĕk′sə-lĭt, -lāt′) adj. Having a vexillum.

vex·il·lol·o·gy (vĕk′sə-lŏl′ə-jē) n. The study of flags. —**vex·il·lo·log′i·cal** (vĕk-sĭl′ə-lŏj′ĭ-kəl) adj. —**vex·il·lol′o·gist** n.

vex·il·lum (vĕk-sĭl′əm) n., pl. **vex·il·la** (vĕk-sĭl′ə) **1.** *Botany* See standard 9. **2.** *Zoology* The weblike part of a feather; the vane. [Lat., flag, dim. of *vēlum,* a covering.]

VF abbr. **1.** video frequency **2.** visual field

VFD abbr. volunteer fire department

VFR abbr. visual flight rules

VFW abbr. Veterans of Foreign Wars

VG abbr. *Roman Catholic Church* vicar general

VGA abbr. video graphics array

VHF abbr. very high frequency

VHS (vē′āch-ĕs′) A trademark used for a videotape format.

VI or **V.I.** abbr. Virgin Islands

v.i. abbr. *Latin* **1.** verbum intransitum (verb intransitive) **2.** vide infra (see below)

vi·a (vī′ə, vē′ə) prep. **1.** By way of: *to Pittsburgh via Philadelphia.* **2.** By means of: *sent the letter via airmail.* [Lat. *viā,* ablative of *via,* road. See **wegh-** in App.]

vi·a·ble (vī′ə-bəl) adj. **1.** Able to live, develop, or germinate under favorable conditions. **2.** Able to live outside the uterus. Used of a fetus or newborn. **3.** Capable of success or continuing effectiveness; practicable. [Fr. < *vie,* life < OFr. < Lat. *vīta.* See **gʷeiə-** in App.] —**vi′a·bil′i·ty** n. —**vi′a·bly** adv.

vi·a·duct (vī′ə-dŭkt′) *n.* A series of spans or arches used to carry a road or railroad over a wide valley or over other roads or railroads. [Lat. *via,* road; see VIA + (AQUE)DUCT.]

Vi·ag·ra (vī-ăg′rə) *n.* A trademark for the drug sildenafil citrate.

vi·al (vī′əl) *n.* A small container, usu. with a closure, esp. for liquids. ❖ *tr.v.* **-aled, -al·ing, -als** or **-alled, -al·ling, -als** To put or keep in or as if in a vial. [ME *viole,* var. of *fiol.* See PHIAL.]

via me·di·a (mē′dē-ə, mĕd′ē-ə, mä′dē-ə) *n.* The middle course or way. [Lat. : *via,* way + *media,* fem. of *medius,* middle.]

vi·and (vī′ənd) *n.* **1a.** An item of food. **b.** A very choice or delicious dish. **2.** **viands** Provisions; victuals. [ME *viaunde* < OFr. *viande* < VLat. **vivanda,* alteration of Lat. *vivenda,* neut. pl. gerundive of *vivere,* to live. See g^wei- in App.]

vi·at·i·cal (vī-ăt′ĭ-kəl) *adj.* **1.** or **vi·at·ic** (vī-ăt′ĭk) Of or relating to traveling, a road, or a way. **2.** Of or relating to a contractual arrangement in which a business buys life insurance policies from terminally ill patients for a percentage of the face value. [< Lat. *viaticus,* relating to a journey < *via,* road. See VIA. Sense 2 < VIATICUM.]

vi·at·i·cum (vī-ăt′ĭ-kəm, vē-) *n., pl.* **-ca** (-kə) or **-cums** **1.** *Ecclesiastical* The Eucharist given to a dying person or one in danger of death. **2.** Journey supplies. [LLat. *viaticum* < Lat., traveling provisions < neut. of *viaticus,* viatic. See VIATICAL.]

vibe (vīb) *n. Slang* A vibration. Often used in the plural: *a nostalgic vibe to the decor; a stranger who gave off bad vibes.* [Short for VIBRATION.]

vibes (vībz) *pl.n.* A vibraphone. **—vib′ist** (vī′bĭst) *n.*

vi·brac·u·lum (vī-brăk′yə-ləm) *n., pl.* **-la** (-lə) One of the long, whiplike, modified zooids on the surface of certain bryozoan colonies. [NLat. *vibraculum* < Lat. *vibrare,* to shake. See VIBRATE.] **—vi·brac′u·lar** (-lər) *adj.*

vi·bra·harp (vī′brə-härp′) *n.* See vibraphone. **—vi′bra·harp·ist** *n.*

vi·brant (vī′brənt) *adj.* **1a.** Pulsing or throbbing with energy or activity: *vibrant city streets.* **b.** Vigorous, lively, and vital. **2.** Exhibiting or characterized by rapid, rhythmic movement back and forth or to and fro; vibrating. **3.** Produced as a result of vibration; resonant or resounding: *vibrant voices.* **4.** Relatively high on the scale of brightness: *a vibrant hue.* **—vi′bran·cy, vi′brance** *n.* **—vi′brant·ly** *adv.*

vi·bra·phone (vī′brə-fōn′) *n.* A percussion instrument similar to a marimba but having metal bars and rotating disks in the resonators to produce a vibrato. [Lat. *vibrare,* to shake; see VIBRATE + –PHONE.] **—vi′bra·phon′ist** *n.*

vi·brate (vī′brāt′) *v.* **-brat·ed, -brat·ing, -brates** **—***intr.* **1.** To move back and forth or to and fro, esp. rhythmically and rapidly. **2.** To feel a quiver of emotion. **3.** To shake or move with or as if with a slight quivering or trembling motion. **4.** To produce a sound; resonate. **5.** To fluctuate or waver in making choices; vacillate. **—***tr.* **1.** To cause to tremble or quiver. **2.** To cause to move back and forth rapidly. **3.** To produce (sound) by vibration. [Lat. *vibrare, vibrat-.*] **—vi′bra·tive** (-brə-tôr′ē, -tōr′ē) *adj.*

vi·bra·tile (vī′brə-tl, -tīl′) *adj.* **1.** Characterized by vibration. **2.** Capable of or adapted to vibratory motion. [Fr. < Lat. *vibratus,* p. part. of *vibrare,* to vibrate. See VIBRATE.] **—vi′bra·til′i·ty** (-tĭl′ĭ-tē) *n.*

vi·bra·tion (vī-brā′shən) *n.* **1a.** The act of vibrating. **b.** The condition of being vibrated. **2.** *Physics* **a.** A rapid linear motion of a particle or of an elastic solid about an equilibrium position. **b.** An oscillation. **3.** A single complete vibrating motion; a quiver. **4.** *Slang* A distinctive aura or atmosphere held to be instinctively sensed. Often used in the plural. **—vi·bra′tion·al** *adj.*

vi·bra·to (və-brä′tō, vī-) *n., pl.* **-tos** A tremulous or pulsating effect produced in an instrumental or vocal tone by minute and rapid variations in pitch. [Ital. < LLat. *vibratus,* a quivering < Lat., p. part. of *vibrare,* to vibrate. See VIBRATE.]

vi·bra·tor (vī′brā′tər) *n.* **1.** Something that vibrates. **2.** An electrically operated massage device. **3.** An electrical device consisting of a vibrating conductor interrupting a current.

vib·ri·o (vĭb′rē-ō′) *n., pl.* **-os** Any of various short motile S-shaped or comma-shaped bacteria of the genus *Vibrio,* esp. *V. cholerae,* which causes cholera. [NLat. *Vibrio,* genus name < Lat. *vibrare,* to vibrate (< their vibratory motion). See VIBRATE.] **—vib′ri·oid′** (-oid′) *adj.*

vib·ri·o·sis (vĭb′rē-ō′sĭs) *n., pl.* **-ses** (-sēz) **1.** Infection with the bacterium *Vibrio parahaemolyticus,* often from eating undercooked seafood from contaminated waters. **2.** A venereal infection in cattle and sheep caused by the bacterium *Vibrio fetus,* often producing infertility or spontaneous abortion.

vi·bris·sa (vī-brĭs′ə, və-) *n., pl.* **-bris·sae** (-brĭs′ē) **1.** Any of the long stiff hairs that project from the snout or brow of most mammals, as the whiskers of a cat. **2.** One of several long modified feathers that grow along the gape of the mouth of insect-eating birds. [< LLat. *vibrissae,* nostril hairs < Lat. *vibrissae,* to vibrate. See VIBRATE.]

vi·bron·ic (vī-brŏn′ĭk) *adj.* Of or relating to changes in molecular energy states associated with the vibrational energy of atoms. [VIBR(ATION) + (ELECTR)ONIC.]

vi·bur·num (vī-bûr′nəm) *n.* Any of various shrubs or trees of the genus *Viburnum,* having opposite leaves, white or pink flow-ers, and red or black drupes. [NLat. *Viburnum,* genus name < Lat. *viburnum,* a shrub.]

vic·ar (vĭk′ər) *n.* **1a.** A parish priest in the Church of England who receives a stipend or salary but no tithes. **b.** A cleric in charge of a chapel in the Episcopal Church. **c.** A cleric acting in the place of a rector or bishop in the Anglican Communion. **2.** *Roman Catholic Church* A priest who acts for or represents another cleric. [ME < OFr. *vicaire* < Lat. *vicarius,* vicarious, a substitute < *vicis,* genitive of **vix,* change.] **—vic′ar·ship′** *n.*

vic·ar·age (vĭk′ər-ĭj) *n.* **1.** The residence of a vicar. **2.** The benefice of a vicar. **3.** The duties or office of a vicar; a vicariate.

vicar apostolic *n., pl.* **vicars apostolic** *Roman Catholic Church* A titular bishop who administers a region that is not yet a diocese or in which the ordinary episcopal jurisdiction is impeded.

vicar general *n., pl.* **vicars general** **1.** *Roman Catholic Church* **a.** A priest acting as deputy to a bishop. **b.** The head of a religious order. **2.** An official in the Church of England, usu. a layperson, who assists a bishop.

vi·car·i·al (vī-kâr′ē-əl, -kăr′-, vĭ-) *adj.* **1.** Of or relating to a vicar. **2.** Acting as or having the position of a vicar. **3.** Serving in the place of someone or something else.

vi·car·i·ate (vī-kâr′ē-ĭt, -āt′, -kăr′-, vĭ-) *n.* **1.** The office or authority of a vicar. **2.** The district under a vicar.

vi·car·i·ous (vī-kâr′ē-əs, -kăr′-, vĭ-) *adj.* **1.** Felt or undergone as if one were taking part in the experience or feelings of another. **2.** Endured or done by one person substituting for another: *vicarious punishment.* **3a.** Acting or serving in place of someone or something else; substituted. **b.** Committed or entrusted to another, as powers or authority; delegated. **4.** *Physiology* Occurring in or performed by a part of the body not normally associated with a certain function. [< Lat. *vicarius.* See VICAR.] **—vi·car′i·ous·ly** *adv.* **—vi·car′i·ous·ness** *n.*

Vicar of Christ *n. Roman Catholic Church* The pope.

vice[1] (vīs) *n.* **1a.** An evil, degrading, or immoral practice or habit. **b.** A serious moral failing. **c.** Wicked or evil conduct or habits; corruption. **2.** Sexual immorality, esp. prostitution. **3a.** A slight personal failing; a foible. **b.** A flaw; a defect. **4.** A physical defect or weakness. **5.** An undesirable habit in a domestic animal. **6a.** **Vice** A character representing generalized or particular vice in English morality plays. **b.** A jester or buffoon. [ME < OFr. < Lat. *vitium.*]

vice[2] (vīs) *n. & v.* Variant of *vise.*

vi·ce[3] (vī′sē, -sə) *prep.* In place of; replacing. [Latin, ablative of **vix,* change. See VICE–.]

vice– *pref.* One who acts in the place of another; deputy: *vice-chairman.* [ME < OFr. *vis-, vice-* < LLat. *vice-* < Lat. *vice,* ablative of **vix,* change.]

vice admiral (vīs) *n.* A commissioned officer in the US Navy or Coast Guard ranking above rear admiral and below admiral.

vice-ad·mir·al·ty (vīs-ăd′mər-əl-tē) *n., pl.* **-ties** The office, rank, or command of a vice admiral.

vice chancellor (vīs) *n.* **1.** A deputy or an assistant chancellor in a university. **2.** A deputy to or a substitute for a head of state or an official bearing the title chancellor. **3.** *Law* A judge in equity courts ranking below a chancellor. **—vice-chan′cel·lor·ship′** (vīs-chăn′sə-lər-shĭp′, -chăns′lər-) *n.*

vice consul (vīs) *n.* A consular officer who is subordinate to and a deputy of a consul or consul general. **—vice-con′su·lar** (vīs-kŏn′sə-lər) *adj.* **—vice-con′su·late** (-sə-lĭt), **vice-con′sul·ship′** (-səl-shĭp′) *n.*

vice·ge·ren·cy (vīs-jîr′ən-sē) *n., pl.* **-cies** **1.** The position, function, or authority of a vicegerent. **2.** A district under a vicegerent's jurisdiction.

vice·ge·rent (vīs-jîr′ənt) *n.* A person appointed by a ruler or head of state to act as an administrative deputy. [Med.Lat. *vicegerens, vicegerent-* : Lat. *vice,* ablative of **vix,* change. See VICE[3] + Lat. *gerēns,* governing; see GERENT.] **—vice·ge′ral** (-jîr′əl) *adj.*

vic·e·nar·y (vīs′ə-nĕr′ē) *adj.* Consisting of, relating to, or based on 20. [Lat. *vīcēnārius* < *vīcēnī,* twenty each < *vīgintī,* twenty. See wīkm̥tī in App.]

vi·cen·ni·al (vī-sĕn′ē-əl) *adj.* **1.** Happening once every 20 years. **2.** Existing or lasting for 20 years. [< LLat. *vīcennium,* period of twenty years : Lat. *vīciens,* twenty times (< *vīgintī,* twenty; see VICENARY) + Lat. *annus,* year.]

Vi·cen·za (vĭ-chĕn′zä, vē-chĕn′dzä) A city of NE Italy W of Venice; founded by Ligurians c. 1st cent. B.C. Pop. 107,076.

vice president or **vice-pres·i·dent** (vīs′prĕz′ĭ-dənt, -dĕnt′) *n.* **1.** An officer ranking next below a president, usu. empowered to assume the president's duties under conditions such as absence or death. **2.** A deputy to a president, esp. in a corporation, in charge of a specific department or location: *vice president of sales.* **—vice-pres′i·den·cy** (vīs-prĕz′ĭ-dən-sē, -dĕn′-) *n.* **—vice-pres′i·den′tial** (-dĕn′shəl) *adj.*

vice·re·gal (vīs-rē′gəl) *adj.* Of or relating to a viceroy. **—vice·re′gal·ly** *adv.*

vice regent (vīs) *n.* One who acts as a regent's deputy. **—vice·re′gen·cy** (vīs-rē′gən-sē) *n.*

vice·reine (vīs′rān′) *n.* **1.** The wife of a viceroy. **2.** A woman who governs a country, province, or colony as the representative of a sovereign. [Fr. : *vice-,* vice (< OFr.; see VICE[3]) + *reine,* queen (< Lat. *rēgīna,* fem. of *rēx, rēg-,* king; see reg- in App.).]

viaduct
Tunkhannock Creek Viaduct, Nicholson, Pennsylvania

vibraphone

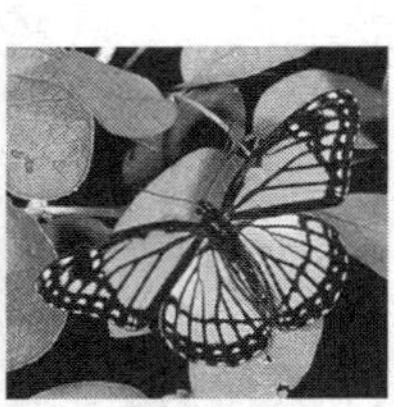

viceroy
Limenitis archippus

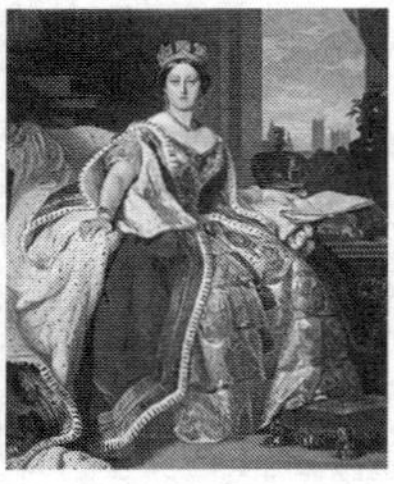

Victoria[1]
detail from *Queen Victoria in Her Coronation Robes,* c. 1838, by Franz Xaver Winterhalter (1806–73)

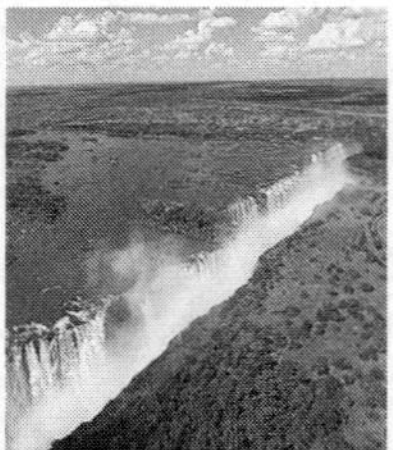

Victoria Falls
aerial view of a section of the falls

vice•roy (vīs′roi′) *n.* **1.** A man who governs a country, province, or colony as the representative of a sovereign. **2.** An orange and black North American butterfly *(Limenitis archippus)* resembling the monarch. [Fr. : *vice-*, vice; see VICEREINE + *roi*, king (< Lat. *rēx, rēg-*; see **reg-** in App.).]

vice•roy•al•ty (vīs′roi′əl-tē, vīs-roi′-) *n., pl.* **-ties 1.** The office, authority, or term of service of a viceroy. **2.** A district or province governed by a viceroy.

vice•roy•ship (vīs′roi-shĭp′) *n.* Viceroyalty.

vice squad (vīs) *n.* A police division charged with law enforcement in areas such as gambling and prostitution.

vi•ce ver•sa (vī′sə vûr′sə, vīs′) *adv.* With the order or meaning reversed; conversely. [Lat. *vice versā* : *vice*, ablative of **vix*, position + *versā*, fem. ablative of *versus*, p. part. of *vertere*, to turn.]

Vi•chy (vĭsh′ē, vē′shē) A city of central France SSE of Paris; cap. of unoccupied France from Jul. 1940 until Nov. 1942 during World War II. Pop. 30,527.

vi•chys•soise (vĭsh′ē-swäz′, vē′shē-) *n.* A thick creamy potato soup flavored with leeks or onions, usu. served cold. [Fr. < fem. of *vichyssois*, of Vichy.]

Vichy water *n.* **1.** A naturally effervescent mineral water from the springs at Vichy. **2.** A sparkling mineral water resembling this effervescent beverage.

vic•i•nage (vĭs′ə-nĭj) *n.* **1a.** A limited region around a particular area; a vicinity. **b.** A number of places near each other, considered as a group. **2.** The residents of a given neighborhood. **3.** The state of living in a neighborhood; proximity. [ME *vesinage* < OFr. < *vesin*, neighboring < Lat. *vīcīnus*. See VICINITY.]

vic•i•nal (vĭs′ə-nəl) *adj.* **1.** Of, belonging to, or restricted to a limited area or neighborhood; local. **2.** Relating to or being a local road. **3.** *Mineralogy* Approximating, resembling, or taking the place of a fundamental crystalline form or face. **4.** *Chemistry* Of or relating to consecutive positions on a benzene ring. [Lat. *vīcīnālis* < *vīcīnus*, neighboring. See VICINITY.]

vi•cin•i•ty (vĭ-sĭn′ĭ-tē) *n., pl.* **-ties 1.** The state of being near in space or relationship; proximity. **2.** A nearby, surrounding, or adjoining region; a neighborhood. **3.** An approximate degree or amount. [Lat. *vīcīnitās* < *vīcīnus*, neighboring < *vīcus*, neighborhood. See **weik-** in App.]

vi•cious (vĭsh′əs) *adj.* **1.** Having the nature of vice; evil, immoral, or depraved. **2.** Given to vice, immorality, or depravity. **3.** Spiteful; malicious. **4.** Disposed to or characterized by violent or destructive behavior. See Syns at **cruel. 5.** Marked by an aggressive disposition; savage. Used chiefly of animals. **6.** Severe or intense; fierce: *a vicious storm.* **7.** Faulty, imperfect, or otherwise impaired by defects or a defect. **8.** Impure; foul. [ME < OFr. *vicieus* < Lat. *vitiōsus* < *vitium*, vice.] **—vi′cious•ly** *adv.* **—vi′cious•ness** *n.*

vicious circle *n.* **1.** A situation in which the apparent solution of one problem in a chain of circumstances creates a new problem. **2.** A condition in which a disorder or disease gives rise to another. **3.** *Logic* A fallacy in reasoning in which the premise is used to prove the conclusion and the conclusion used to prove the premise. [Transl. of NLat. *circulus vitiōsus*, circular argument : Med. Lat. *circulus*, circular argument + Lat. *vitiōsus*, flawed, faulty.]

vi•cis•si•tude (vĭ-sĭs′ĭ-to͞od′, -tyo͞od′) *n.* **1a.** A change or variation. **b.** The quality of being changeable; mutability. **2.** One of the sudden or unexpected changes or shifts often encountered in one's life, activities, or surroundings. Often used in the plural. See Syns at **difficulty.** [Lat. *vicissitūdō* < *vicissim*, in turn, prob. < *vicēs*, pl. of **vix*, change.]

vi•cis•si•tu•di•nar•y (vĭ-sĭs′ĭ-to͞od′n-ĕr′ē, -tyo͞od′-) also **vi•cis•si•tu•di•nous** (-to͞od′n-əs, -tyo͞od′-) *adj.* Characterized by, full of, or subject to vicissitudes.

Vicks•burg (vĭks′bûrg′) A city of W MS on bluffs above the Mississippi R. W of Jackson; besieged and captured (1862–63) by Union troops in the Civil War. Pop. 26,407.

vic•tim (vĭk′tĭm) *n.* **1.** One who is harmed or killed by another. **2.** A living creature slain and offered as a sacrifice during a religious rite. **3.** One harmed by or made to suffer from an act, circumstance, agency, or condition. **4.** One who suffers injury, loss, or death as a result of a voluntary undertaking. **5.** One who is tricked, swindled, or taken advantage of. [Lat. *victima.*] **—vic′tim•hood′** (-ho͝od′) *n.*

vic•tim•ize (vĭk′tə-mīz′) *tr.v.* **-ized, -iz•ing, -iz•es 1.** To subject to swindle or fraud. **2.** To make a victim of. **—vic′tim•i•za′tion** (-tə-mĭ-zā′shən) *n.* **—vic′tim•iz′er** *n.*

vic•tim•less crime (vĭk′tĭm-lĭs) *n.* An illegal act that is felt to have no direct or identifiable victim.

vic•tor (vĭk′tər) *n.* One who defeats an adversary; the winner in a fight, contest, or struggle. [Ult. < Lat. < *victus*, p. part. of *vincere*, to conquer.]

Victor Em•man•u•el II (ĭ-măn′yo͞o-əl) 1820–78. Italian king (1861–78) who completed the unification of Italy by acquiring Venice (1866) and Rome (1870).

Victor Emmanuel III 1869–1947. Italian king (1900–46) who appointed Benito Mussolini prime minister in 1922 and abdicated in 1946.

vic•to•ri•a (vĭk-tôr′ē-ə, -tōr′-) *n.* **1.** A low light four-wheeled carriage for two with a folding top and an elevated driver's seat in front. **2.** A touring car with a folding top usu. covering only the rear seat. [After VICTORIA[1].]

Victoria[1] 1819–1901. Queen of Great Britain and Ireland (1837–1901) and empress of India (1876–1901).

Victoria[2] **1.** The cap. of British Columbia, Canada, on SE Vancouver I. at the E end of the Strait of Juan de Fuca; founded in 1843 as a Hudson's Bay Company outpost. Pop. 73,504. **2.** The cap. of Hong Kong, on the NW coast of Hong Kong I. Pop. 1,183,621. **3.** The cap. of Seychelles, on the NE coast of Mahé I. on the Indian Ocean. Pop. 23,000.

Victoria, Lake also **Victoria Ny•an•za** (nī-ăn′zə, nyän′-) A lake of E-central Africa bordered by Uganda, Kenya, and Tanzania.

Victoria Cross *n.* A bronze Maltese cross, Britain's highest military award for conspicuous valor. [After VICTORIA[1].]

Victoria Day *n.* The last Monday before May 25, observed in Canada in commemoration of the birthday of Queen Victoria.

Victoria Falls A waterfall, 108.3 m (355 ft), of S-central Africa in the Zambezi R. between SW Zambia and NW Zimbabwe.

Victoria Island An island of N Canada, in the Arctic Archipelago E of Banks I.

Victoria Land A region of Antarctica bounded by Ross Sea and Wilkes Land; discovered by Sir James Clark Ross during his 1839–43 expedition.

Vic•to•ri•an (vĭk-tôr′ē-ən, -tōr′-) *adj.* **1.** Of or relating to the period of the reign of Queen Victoria. **2.** Relating to or displaying the standards of morality regarded as characteristic of the time of Queen Victoria. **3.** Being in the highly ornamented style of architecture, decor, and furnishings popular in 19th-century England. ❖ *n.* One belonging to or exhibiting characteristics typical of the Victorian period. **—Vic•to′ri•an•ism** *n.* **—Vic•to′ri•an•ize′** *v.*

Vic•to•ri•an•a (vĭk-tôr′ē-ăn′ə, -ä′nə, -tōr′-) *n.* Material or a collection of materials from or relating to the Victorian era.

Victoria Nile A section of the Nile R., c. 418 km (260 mi), between Lake Victoria and Lake Albert in central Uganda.

vic•to•ri•ous (vĭk-tôr′ē-əs, -tōr′-) *adj.* **1.** Being the winner in a contest or struggle: *the victorious army.* **2.** Characteristic of or expressing a sense of victory or fulfillment: *a victorious cheer.* **—vic•to′ri•ous•ly** *adv.* **—vic•to′ri•ous•ness** *n.*

vic•to•ry (vĭk′tə-rē) *n., pl.* **-ries 1.** Defeat of an enemy or opponent. **2.** Success in a struggle against difficulties or an obstacle. **3.** The state of having triumphed. [ME < OFr. *victorie* < Lat. *victōria* < *victor*, victor. See VICTOR.]

vict•ual (vĭt′l) *n.* **1.** Food fit for human consumption. **2. victuals** Food supplies; provisions. ❖ *v.* **-ualed, -ual•ing, -uals** or **-ualled, -ual•ling, -uals** *—tr.* To provide with food. *—intr.* **1.** To lay in food supplies. **2.** To eat. [Alteration of ME *vitaille* < OFr. < LLat. *vīctuālia*, provisions < neut. pl. of Lat. *vīctuālis*, of nourishment < *vīctus*, nourishment < p. part. of *vīvere*, to live. See **gʷeiə-** in App.]

vict•ual•er also **vict•ual•ler** (vĭt′l-ər) *n.* **1.** A supplier of victuals; a sutler. **2.** *Chiefly British* An innkeeper. **3.** *Nautical* A supply ship.

vi•cu•ña also **vi•cu•na** (vī-ko͞o′nyə, vĭ-, vī-ko͞o′nə, -kyo͞o′-, vĭ-) *n.* **1.** A llamalike ruminant mammal *(Vicugna vicugna)* of the central Andes having fine silky fleece. **2.** This fleece. **3.** Fabric made from vicuña fleece. [Sp. < Quechua *wikuña.*]

Vi•dal (vĭ-däl′), **(Eugene Luther) Gore** b. 1925. Amer. writer whose works include the novel *Myra Breckinridge* (1968).

vi•de (vī′dē, vē′dā′, wē′-) *v.* See. Used to direct a reader's attention. [Lat. *vidē*, sing. imper. of *vidēre*, to see. See **weid-** in App.]

vi•del•i•cet (vĭ-dĕl′ĭ-sĕt′, vī-, wĭ-dā′lĭ-kĕt′) *adv.* That is; namely. Used to introduce examples, lists, or items. [Lat. *vidēlicet*, contraction of *vidēre licet*, it is permitted to see : *vidēre*, to see; see VIDE + *licet*, third pers. sing. pr. t. of *licēre*, to be permitted.]

vid•e•o (vĭd′ē-ō′) *adj.* **1.** Of or relating to television, esp. televised images. **2.** Of or relating to videotaped productions or videotape equipment and technology. **3.** *Computer Science* Of or relating to the production of images on video displays. ❖ *n., pl.* **-os 1.** The visual portion of a televised broadcast. **2.** Television: *a star of video.* **3.** A videocassette or videotape, esp. one containing a recording for playback on a television set. **4.** A music video. **5.** The appearance of text and graphics on a video display. [< Lat. *videō*, first pers. sing. pr. t. of *vidēre*, to see. See VIDE.]

video camera *n.* A portable camera that records on videocassettes for playback on a television set.

vid•e•o•cas•sette (vĭd′ē-ō-kə-sĕt′, -kă-) *n.* A cassette containing blank or prerecorded videotape.

videocassette recorder *n.* A VCR.

vid•e•o•con•fer•ence (vĭd′ē-ō-kŏn′fər-əns, -frəns) *n.* A teleconference using video technology, such as closed-circuit television. **—vid′e•o•con′fer•enc•ing** *n.*

vid•e•o•disc also **vid•e•o•disk** (vĭd′ē-ō-dĭsk′) *n.* A recording on an optical disk, esp. of a movie, that can be played on a television. See Usage Note at **compact disk.** [Orig. a Ger. trademark.]

video display *n.* See **display** 6a.

video display terminal *n.* A computer terminal having a video display that uses a cathode-ray tube.

video game *n.* An electronic or computerized game played by manipulating images on a display screen.

vid•e•og•ra•phy (vĭd′ē-ŏg′rə-fē) *n.* The art or practice of using a video camera. **—vid′e•og′ra•pher** *n.*

video jockey *n.* One who announces, plays, and provides commentary on videotaped programs, esp. music videos.

vid•e•o•phone (vĭd′ē-ō-fōn′) *n.* A telephone equipped for both audio and video transmission.

vid•e•o•tape (vĭd′ē-ō-tāp′) *n.* **1.** A magnetic tape used to record visual images and associated sound for playback or broadcasting. **2.** A recording made on such a tape. ❖ *tr.v.* **-taped, -tap•ing, -tapes** To make a videotape recording of.

vid•e•o•tex (vĭd′ē-ō-tĕks′) also **vid•e•o•text** (-tĕkst′) *n.* An information service in which data is transmitted over television cables or telephone lines and displayed on a television or computer screen in the home.

video vérité *n.* A documentary television filming or videotaping technique in which the subjects are portrayed with frank, unbiased realism. [VIDEO + (CINÉMA) VÉRITÉ.]

vi•dette (vĭ-dĕt′) *n.* Variant of **vedette.**

vid•i•con (vĭd′ĭ-kŏn′) *n.* A small television camera tube that forms a charge-density image on a photoconductive surface for subsequent electron-beam scanning. [VID(EO) + ICON(OSCOPE).]

Vi•dor (vē′dôr), **King Wallis** 1894–1982. Amer. director whose films include *The Big Parade* (1925).

vie (vī) *v.* **vied, vy•ing** (vī′ĭng), **vies** —*intr.* To strive for victory or superiority; contend. —*tr.* **1.** *Archaic* To offer in competition; match. **2.** *Obsolete* To wager or bet. [Short for ME *envien* < OFr. *envier* < Lat. *invītāre*, to invite, give occasion for. See INVITE.]

Vi•en•na (vē-ĕn′ə) The cap. of Austria, in the NE part of the country on the Danube R.; became the official residence of the house of Hapsburg in 1278. Pop. 1,560,471.

Vienna sausage *n.* A small sausage resembling a frankfurter, often served as an hors d'oeuvre. [After VIENNA.]

Vienne (vyĕn) A river of SW-central France flowing c. 349 km (217 mi) generally NW to the Loire R.

Vi•en•nese (vē′ə-nēz′, -nēs′) *adj.* Relating to or characteristic of Vienna. ❖ *n., pl.* **Viennese 1.** A native or inhabitant of Vienna. **2.** The variety of German spoken in Vienna.

Vien•tiane (vyĕn-tyän′) The cap. of Laos, in the N-central part of the country on the Mekong R. Pop. 210,000.

Viet. *abbr.* **1.** Vietnam **2.** Vietnamese

Vi•et•cong also **Viet Cong** (vē-ĕt′kŏng′, -kông′, vē′ĭt-, vyĕt′-) *n., pl.* **Vietcong** also **Viet Cong** A Vietnamese belonging to or supporting the National Liberation Front of South Vietnam. [Vietnamese, short for *Cong San Viet Nam*, Vietnamese Communist.]

Vi•et•minh also **Viet Minh** (vē-ĕt′mĭn′, vyĕt′-, vē′ĭt-) *n., pl.* **Vietminh** also **Viet Minh** A member of the Vietnamese political and military movement that challenged the Japanese and defeated the French between 1941 and 1954. [Vietnamese, short for *Viet Nam Doc Lap Dong Minh Hoi*, Vietnam Federation of Independence.]

Vi•et•nam (vē-ĕt′näm′, -năm′, vē′ĭt-, vyĕt′-) A country of SE Asia in E Indochina on the South China Sea. Occupied by the French in the 19th cent., it was partitioned into **North Vietnam** and **South Vietnam** after 1954 and reunited in Jul. 1976 after the end of the Vietnam War (1954–75). Cap. Hanoi. Pop. 72,510,000.

Vi•et•nam•ese (vē-ĕt′nə-mēz′, -mēs′, vē′ĭt-, vyĕt′-) *adj.* Of or relating to Vietnam or its people, language, or culture. ❖ *n., pl.* **Vietnamese 1.** A native or inhabitant of Vietnam. **2.** The language of the largest ethnic group in Vietnam and the official language of the nation.

Vietnam War *n.* A protracted military conflict (1954–75) between the Communist forces of North Vietnam supported by China and the Soviet Union and the non-Communist forces of South Vietnam supported by the United States.

view (vyo͞o) *n.* **1a.** An examination or inspection. **b.** A sight; a look. **2.** A systematic survey; coverage. **3.** An individual and personal perception, judgment, or interpretation; an opinion. **4.** Field of vision. **5.** A scene or vista. **6.** A picture of a landscape. **7.** A way of showing or seeing something, as from a particular angle. **8.** Something kept in sight as an aim or intention. **9.** Expectation; chance. ❖ *tr.v.* **viewed, view•ing, views 1.** To look at; watch. **2a.** To examine or inspect. **b.** To survey or study mentally; consider. **3.** To think of in a particular way; regard. See Syns at **see**[1]. —***idioms:* in view of** Taking into account; in consideration of. **on view** Placed so as to be seen; exhibited. [ME *vewe* < AN < fem. p. part. of *veoir*, to see < Lat. *vidēre*. See **weid-** in App.] —**view′a•ble** *adj.*

view•da•ta (vyo͞o′dā′tə, -dăt′ə, -dä′tə) *n.* An interactive videotex system.

view•er (vyo͞o′ər) *n.* **1.** One that views, esp. an onlooker or spectator. **2.** Any of various optical devices used to facilitate the viewing of photographic transparencies. **3.** One who watches television or movies: *viewers of prime-time shows.*

view•er•ship (vyo͞o′ər-shĭp′) *n.* The people who watch a television program or motion picture.

view•find•er (vyo͞o′fīn′dər) *n.* A device on a camera that indicates what will appear in the field of view of the lens.

view•ing (vyo͞o′ĭng) *n.* **1.** The act of seeing, watching, or examining. **2.** The act or an instance of watching a movie or television. **3.** *Pennsylvania* See **wake**[1] 2. ❖ *adj.* Engaged in watching a movie or television.

view•less (vyo͞o′lĭs) *adj.* **1.** Providing no view. **2.** Not having or expressing opinions or views. —**view′less•ly** *adv.*

view•point (vyo͞o′point′) *n.* A position from which something is observed or considered; a point of view.

view•y (vyo͞o′ē) *adj.* **-i•er, -i•est 1.** Exhibiting extravagant or visionary opinions. **2.** Conspicuous or striking; showy.

vi•ga (vē′gə) *n. Southwestern US* A rafter or roofbeam, esp. a trimmed and peeled tree trunk whose end projects from an outside adobe wall. [Am.Sp. < Sp., perh. < Lat. *bīga*, team of horses, cart (< the long pole between the two horses). See **yeug-** in App.]

Vi•gée-Le•brun (vē-zhā′lə-brœN′), **(Marie Louise) Élisabeth** 1755–1842. French painter noted for her portraits.

vi•ges•i•mal (vī-jĕs′ə-məl) *adj.* **1.** Twentieth. **2.** Proceeding or occurring in intervals of 20. **3.** Based on or relating to 20. [< Lat. *vīgēsimus*, var. of *vīcēsimus*, twentieth < *vīgintī*, twenty. See **wīkm̥tī** in App.]

vi•gi•a (vĭ-jē′ə, -hē′-) *n.* A warning on a navigational chart indicating a possible rock, shoal, or other hazard, the exact position of which is unknown. [Sp. *vigía* < Port. *vigia* < *vigiar*, to look out < Lat. *vigilāre*. See VIGILANTE.]

vig•il (vĭj′əl) *n.* **1a.** A watch kept during normal sleeping hours. **b.** The act or a period of observing; surveillance. **2.** The eve of a religious festival observed by staying awake as a devotional exercise. **3.** Ritual devotions observed on the eve of a holy day. Often used in the plural. [ME *vigile*, a devotional watching < OFr. < Lat. *vigilia*, wakefulness, watch < *vigil*, awake.]

vig•i•lance (vĭj′ə-ləns) *n.* Alert watchfulness.

vigilance committee *n.* A group that without authority assumes powers such as punishing those suspected of crime.

vig•i•lant (vĭj′ə-lənt) *adj.* On the alert; watchful. See Syns at **aware.** [ME < OFr. < Lat. *vigilāns*, *vigilant-*, pr. part. of *vigilāre*, to be watchful. See VIGILANTE.] —**vig′i•lant•ly** *adv.*

vig•i•lan•te (vĭj′ə-lăn′tē) *n.* **1.** One who takes or advocates the taking of law enforcement into one's own hands. **2.** A member of a vigilance committee. [Sp., watchman, vigilante < Lat. *vigilāns*, *vigilant-*, pr. part. of *vigilāre*, to be watchful < *vigil*, watchful.] —**vig′i•lan′tism** (-lăn′tĭz-əm), **vig′i•lan′te•ism** (-tē-ĭz′əm) *n.*

vigil light *n.* **1.** A candle kept burning in the chancel of Christian churches to symbolize the Holy Sacrament; an altar light. **2.** A candle lit by a worshiper for a devotional purpose. **3.** A light or candle kept burning at a shrine or before an icon.

vi•gin•til•lion (vī′jĭn-tĭl′yən) *n.* **1.** The cardinal number equal to 10^{63}. **2.** *Chiefly British* The cardinal number equal to 10^{120}. [Lat. *vīgintī*, twenty; see **wīkm̥tī** in App. + (M)ILLION.] —**vi′gin•til′lion** *adj.* —**vi′gin•til′lionth** *adj., adv. & n.*

vi•gnette (vĭn-yĕt′) *n.* **1.** A decorative design placed at the beginning or end of a book or chapter or along the border of a page. **2.** An unbordered picture that shades off into the surrounding color at the edges. **3a.** A short, usu. descriptive literary sketch. **b.** A short scene or incident, as from a movie. ❖ *tr.v.* **-gnet•ted, -gnet•ting, -gnettes 1.** To soften the edges of (a picture) in vignette style. **2.** To describe in a brief way. [Fr. < OFr., dim. of *vigne*, vine (< the use of vine tendrils in decorative borders). See VINE.]

vi•gnet•ter (vĭn-yĕt′ər) *n.* **1.** A device used to print photographs and illustrations with borders that fade gradually into the background. **2.** also **vi•gnet•tist** (-ĭst) One who makes or specializes in the making of vignettes.

Vi•gny (vēn-yē′), Comte **Alfred Victor de** 1797–1863. French writer whose works include *Les Destinées* (1864).

Vi•go (vē′gō, bē′-) A city of NW Spain on the **Bay of Vigo,** an inlet of the Atlantic Ocean. Pop. 276,109.

vig•or (vĭg′ər) *n.* **1.** Physical or mental strength, energy, or force. **2.** The capacity for natural growth and survival, as of plants or animals. **3.** Strong feeling; enthusiasm or intensity. **4.** Legal effectiveness or validity. [ME < OFr. < Lat. < *vigēre*, to be lively.]

vig•o•rish (vĭg′ər-ĭsh) *n. Slang* **1a.** A charge taken on bets, as by a bookie or gambling establishment. **b.** The rate or amount of such a charge. **2.** Interest, esp. excessive interest, paid to a moneylender. [Yiddish slang < Russ. *vyigrysh*, winnings : *vy-*, out; see **ud-** in App. + *igrat'*, to play.]

vig•o•ro•so (vĭg′ə-rō′sō, -zō, vē′gə-) *adv. & adj. Music* With emphasis and spirit. [Ital. < Med.Lat. *vigōrōsus* < Lat. *vigor*, vigor. See VIGOR.]

vig•or•ous (vĭg′ər-əs) *adj.* **1.** Strong, energetic, and active in mind or body; robust. See Syns at **healthy. 2.** Marked by or done with force and energy. —**vig′or•ous•ly** *adv.* —**vig′or•ous•ness** *n.*

vig•our (vĭg′ər) *n. Chiefly British* Variant of **vigor.**

Vi•ja•ya•wa•da (vĭj′ə-yə-wä′də, vē′jə-) Formerly **Bez•wa•da** (bĕz-wä′də) A city of SE India ESE of Hyderabad. Pop. 454,577.

Vi•king (vī′kĭng) *n.* **1.** One of a seafaring Scandinavian people who raided the coasts of northern and western Europe from the eighth through the tenth century. **2.** A Scandinavian. [ON *víkingr*, perh. < *vík*, creek, inlet.]

vil. *abbr.* village

Vi•la (vē′lə, vē-lä′) See **Port-Vila.**

vi•la•yet (vē′lä-yĕt′) *n.* An administrative division of Turkey. [Turk. *vilâyet*, administrative district < Ar. *wilāya*, province < *waliya*, to administer.]

vile (vīl) *adj.* **vil•er, vil•est 1.** Loathsome; disgusting: *vile language.* **2.** Unpleasant or objectionable. **3a.** Contemptibly low in worth or account; second-rate. **b.** Of mean or low condition. **4.** Miserably poor and degrading; wretched: *a vile existence.* **5.** Mor-

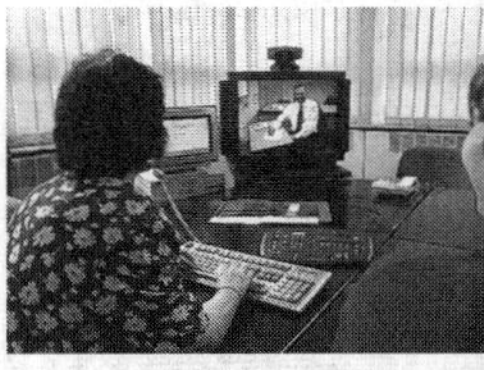

videoconference

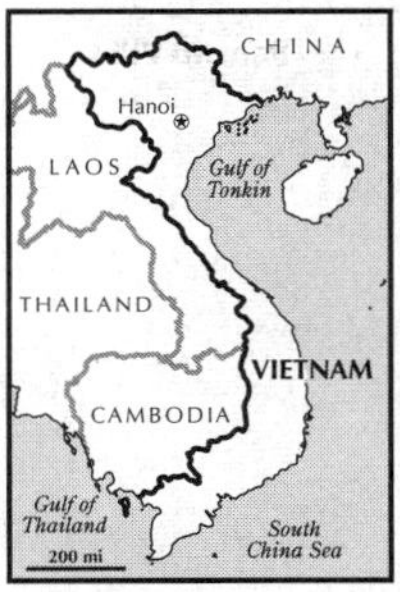

Vietnam

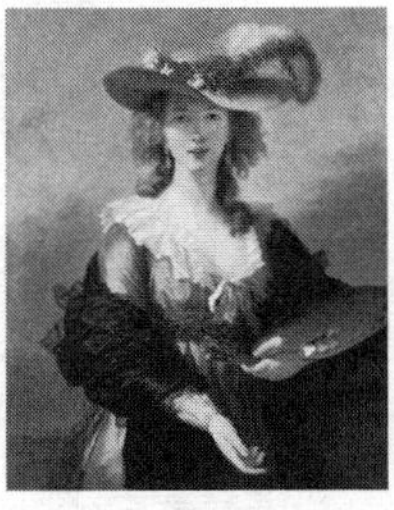

Élisabeth Vigée-Lebrun
Self-portrait in Straw Hat, 1782

ă	pat	oi	boy
ā	pay	ou	out
âr	care	o͝o	took
ä	father	o͞o	boot
ĕ	pet	ŭ	cut
ē	be	ûr	urge
ĭ	pit	th	thin
ī	pie	*th*	this
îr	pier	hw	which
ŏ	pot	zh	vision
ō	toe	ə	about, item
ô	paw		

Stress marks:
′ (primary);
′ (secondary), as in
lexicon (lĕk′sĭ-kŏn′)

Pancho Villa

ally depraved; ignoble or wicked. [ME < OFr. < Lat. *vīlis*. See **wes-**³ in App.] —**vile′ly** *adv.* —**vile′ness** *n.*

vil•i•fy (vĭl′ə-fī′) *tr.v.* **-fied, -fy•ing, -fies** To make vicious and defamatory statements about. [ME *vilifien* < LLat. *vīlificāre*, to hold cheap : Lat. *vīlis*, worthless; see **wes-**³ in App. + Lat. *-ficāre*, -fy.] —**vil′i•fi•ca′tion** (-fĭ-kā′shən) *n.* —**vil′i•fi′er** *n.*

vil•i•pend (vĭl′ə-pĕnd′) *tr.v.* **-pend•ed, -pend•ing, -pends** 1. To view or treat with contempt; despise. 2. To speak ill of; disparage. [Ult. < Lat. *vīlipendere* : *vīlis*, worthless; see **wes-**³ in App. + *pendere*, to consider, weigh.]

vil•la (vĭl′ə) *n.* 1. The often large, luxurious country house of a well-to-do person. 2. A country estate with a substantial house. 3. *Chiefly British* A house in a middle-class suburb. [Ital. < Lat. *villa*. See **weik-** in App.]

Vil•la (vē′ə, bē′yä), **Francisco** Known as "Pancho." 1877?–1923. Mexican revolutionary leader who ran unsuccessfully for the presidency after the Mexican Revolution (1910).

vil•lage (vĭl′ĭj) *n.* 1. A small group of dwellings in a rural area, usu. ranking in size between a hamlet and a town. 2. In some US states, an incorporated community smaller in population than a town. 3. The inhabitants of a village. 4. A group of bird or animal habitations suggesting a village. [ME < OFr. < Lat. *villāticum*, farmstead < neut. of *villāticus*, of a farmstead < *villa*, country house, farm. See **weik-** in App.]

vil•lag•er (vĭl′ə-jər) *n.* An inhabitant of a village.

Vil•la•her•mo•sa (vē′ə-ĕr-mō′sə, bē′yä-) A city of SE Mexico E of the Isthmus of Tehuantepec. Pop. 158,216.

vil•lain (vĭl′ən) *n.* 1. A wicked or evil person; a scoundrel. 2. A dramatic or fictional character typically at odds with the hero. 3. (*also* vĭl′ān′, vĭ-lān′) Variant of **villein**. 4. Something said to be the cause of particular trouble or an evil. 5. *Obsolete* A peasant regarded as vile and brutish. [ME *vilein*, person of coarse feelings < OFr. < VLat. **villānus*, feudal serf < Lat. *villa*, country house. See **weik-** in App.]

vil•lain•age (vĭl′ə-nĭj) *n.* Variant of **villeinage**.

vil•lain•ess (vĭl′ə-nĭs) *n.* A woman who is a villain. See Usage Note at **-ess**.

vil•lain•ous (vĭl′ə-nəs) *adj.* **1a.** Appropriate to a villain, as in wickedness or depravity. **b.** Being or manifesting the nature of a villain. 2. Highly undesirable or offensive; obnoxious. —**vil′-lain•ous•ly** *adv.* —**vil′lain•ous•ness** *n.*

vil•lain•y (vĭl′ə-nē) *n., pl.* **-ies** 1. Baseness of mind or character. 2. Viciousness of conduct or action. 3. A treacherous or vicious act.

Vil•la-Lo•bos (vē′lə-lō′bŏs, vē′lä-lô′bŏŏs), **Heitor** 1887–1959. Brazilian composer influenced by folk traditions.

vil•la•nelle (vĭl′ə-nĕl′) *n.* A 19-line poem of fixed form consisting of five tercets and a final quatrain on two rhymes, with the first and third lines of the first tercet repeated alternately to close the succeeding tercets and joined as the final couplet of the quatrain. [Fr. < Ital. *villanella* < fem. of *villanello*, rustic < *villano*, peasant < VLat. **villānus* < Lat. *villa*, country house. See **weik-** in App.]

Vil•lard (vĭ-lär′, -lärd′), **Oswald Garrison** 1872–1949. Amer. journalist who was president of the *New York Evening Post* (1900–18) and owner of *The Nation* (1918–35).

vil•lat•ic (vĭ-lăt′ĭk) *adj.* Rustic; rural. [Lat. *villāticus*, of a farmstead. See **VILLAGE**.]

Vil•la•vi•cen•ci•o (vē′ə-vĭ-sĕn′sē-ō′, bē′yä-vē-sĕn′syō) A city of central Colombia SE of Bogotá. Pop. 162,556.

-ville *suff.* Quality; condition: *dullsville*. [< place names ending in -*ville* (as JACKSONVILLE) < Fr., town < OFr. *vile* < Lat. *villa*, country house, farm. See **weik-** in App.]

vil•lein (vĭl′ən, -ān′, vĭ-lān′) *n.* One of a class of feudal serfs who held the legal status of freemen in their dealings with all people except their lord. [ME *vilein*. See **VILLAIN**.]

vil•lein•age *also* **vil•lain•age** (vĭl′ə-nĭj) *n.* 1. The legal status or condition of a villein. 2. The legal tenure by which a villein held land.

Vil•liers (vĭl′ərz, -yərz), **George** See **Buckingham**.

vil•li•form (vĭl′ə-fôrm′) *adj.* Having the form of villi.

Vil•lon (vē-yôN′), **François** 1431–63? French poet whose satirical works include *Le Testament* (c. 1461).

vil•los•i•ty (vĭ-lŏs′ĭ-tē) *n., pl.* **-ties** 1. The condition of being villous. 2. A villous surface or coating. 3. A villus.

vil•lous (vĭl′əs) *also* **vil•lose** (-ōs′) *adj.* 1. *Biology* Of, resembling, or covered with villi. 2. *Botany* Covered with villi. [< Lat. *villōsus*, hairy < *villus*, shaggy hair.] —**vil′lous•ly** *adv.*

vil•lus (vĭl′əs) *n., pl.* **vil•li** (vĭl′ī) 1. *Biology* A minute projection arising from a mucous membrane, esp.: **a.** One of the numerous vascular projections of the small intestine. **b.** One of the finger-like projections of the chorion that forms the placenta in mammals. 2. *Botany* A fine hairlike epidermal outgrowth. [Lat., shaggy hair.]

Vil•ni•us (vĭl′nē-əs) *or* **Vil•na** (-nə) The cap. of Lithuania, in the SE part ESE of Kaunas; founded in the 10th cent. Pop. 581,500.

Vil•yu•i (vĭl-yŏŏ′ē) A river of E Russia flowing c. 2,446 km (1,520 mi) to the Lena R.

vim (vĭm) *n.* Ebullient vitality and energy. [Lat., accusative of *vīs*. See **weiə-** in App.]

Vim•i•nal (vĭm′ə-nəl) One of the seven hills of ancient Rome.

vin– *pref.* Variant of **vini–**.

vi•na *also* **vee•na** (vē′nə) *n.* A stringed instrument of India that has a long fretted fingerboard with resonating gourds at each end. [Hindi *vīnā* < Skt.]

vi•na•ceous (vī-nā′shəs, vĭ-) *adj.* Having the color of red wine. [< Lat. *vīnāceus*, refuse from wine pressing < *vīnum*, wine.]

Vi•ña del Mar (vēn′yə dĕl mär′, bē′nyä) A city of central Chile, a suburb of Valparaíso. Pop. 281,063.

vin•ai•grette (vĭn′ī-grĕt′) *n.* 1. A small decorative bottle or container with a perforated top, used for holding an aromatic preparation such as smelling salts. 2. A cold sauce or dressing made of vinegar or lemon juice and oil, often flavored with seasonings. [Fr. < OFr., dim. of *vinaigre*, vinegar. See **VINEGAR**.]

vi•nasse (vī-năs′, vĭ-) *n.* The residue left in a still after the process of distillation. [Fr. < Provençal *vinassa* < Lat. *vīnācea* < fem. of *vīnāceus*. See **VINACEOUS**.]

vin•blas•tine (vĭn-blăs′tēn′) *n.* An alkaloid, $C_{46}H_{58}N_4O_9$, obtained from the Madagascar periwinkle and used as an antineoplastic drug. [Short for *vincaleukoblastine* : NLat. *Vinca*, periwinkle genus; see **VINCA** + E. *leukoblast*, a developing leukocyte (LEUKO- + –BLAST) + –INE².]

vin•ca (vĭng′kə) *n.* Any of the shrubby, evergreen plants of the genus *Vinca*, which includes the periwinkle. [NLat. *Vinca*, genus name < Lat. *vinca* (*pervinca*), periwinkle. See **PERIWINKLE²**.]

Vin•cent de Paul (vĭn′sənt də pôl′), **Saint.** 1581–1660. French ecclesiastic who founded the Congregation of the Mission (1625) and the Daughters of Charity (1633).

Vin•cent's angina (vĭn′sənts) *n.* See **trench mouth**. [After Jean Hyacinthe *Vincent* (1862–1950), French physician.]

vin•ci•ble (vĭn′sə-bəl) *adj.* Capable of being overcome or defeated: *a vincible army.* [Lat. *vincibilis* < *vincere*, to conquer.] —**vin′ci•bil′i•ty** *n.* —**vin′ci•bly** *adv.*

vin•cris•tine (vĭn-krĭs′tēn′) *n.* An alkaloid, $C_{46}H_{56}N_4O_{10}$, obtained from the Madagascar periwinkle and used as an antineoplastic drug. [NLat. *Vinca*, periwinkle genus; see **VINCA** + Lat. *crista*, crest; see **CREST** + –INE².]

vin•cu•lum (vĭng′kyə-ləm) *n., pl.* **-lums** *or* **-la** (-lə) 1. *Mathematics* A bar drawn over two or more algebraic terms to indicate that they are to be treated as a single term. 2. *Anatomy* A ligament that limits the movement of an organ or part. 3. A bond or tie. [Lat., bond, tie < *vincīre*, to tie.]

vin•da•loo (vĭn′də-lōō) *n., pl.* **-loos** 1. A blend of red chilis, tamarind, and other spices, such as ginger, cumin, and mustard seeds. 2. Any of various dishes of southern and central India made with this spice blend. [Prob. Konkani (Indic language of western India) *vindalu* < Port. *vin d'alho* : *vinho*, wine (< Lat. *vīnum*) + *de*, of (< Lat. *dē*; see DE–) + *alho*, garlic (< Lat. *alium*).]

Vin•dhya Range (vĭn′dyə) A chain of hills in central India rising to c. 915 m (3,000 ft).

vin•di•ca•ble (vĭn′dĭ-kə-bəl) *adj.* Possible to vindicate.

vin•di•cate (vĭn′dĭ-kāt′) *tr.v.* **-cat•ed, -cat•ing, -cates** 1. To clear of accusation, blame, suspicion, or doubt with supporting arguments or proof: *He vindicated himself of the charges.* 2. To provide justification or support for: *vindicate one's claim.* 3. To justify or prove the worth of, esp. in light of later developments. 4. To defend, maintain, or insist on the recognition of (one's rights, for example). 5. To exact revenge for; avenge. [Lat. *vindicāre, vindicāt-* < *vindex, vindic-*, surety, avenger. See **deik-** in App.] —**vin′di•ca′tor** *n.*

vin•di•ca•tion (vĭn′dĭ-kā′shən) *n.* 1. The act of vindicating or condition of being vindicated. 2. The defense, such as evidence or argument, that serves to justify a claim or deed.

vin•di•ca•to•ry (vĭn′dĭ-kə-tôr′ē, -tōr′ē) *adj.* 1. Affording vindication; justifying. 2. Exacting retribution; punitive.

vin•dic•tive (vĭn-dĭk′tĭv) *adj.* 1. Disposed to seek revenge. 2. Marked by or resulting from a desire to hurt; spiteful. [< Lat. *vindicta*, vengeance < *vindex, vindic-*, surety, avenger. See **VINDICATE**.] —**vin•dic′tive•ly** *adv.* —**vin•dic′tive•ness** *n.*

vine (vīn) *n.* **1a.** A weak-stemmed plant that derives its support from climbing, twining, or creeping along a surface. **b.** The stem of such a plant. **2a.** A grapevine. **b.** Grapevines considered as a group: *products of the vine.* ❖ *intr.v.* **vined, vin•ing, vines** To form or develop like a vine. [ME < OFr. *vigne* < Lat. *vīnea* < fem. of *vīneus*, of wine < *vīnum*, wine.]

vine•dress•er (vīn′drĕs′ər) *n.* One that cultivates and prunes grapevines.

vin•e•gar (vĭn′ĭ-gər) *n.* 1. An impure dilute solution of acetic acid obtained by fermentation beyond the alcohol stage and used as a condiment and preservative. 2. Sourness of speech or mood; ill temper. 3. Liveliness and enthusiasm; vim. [ME *vinegre* < OFr. *vinaigre* : *vin*, wine (< Lat. *vīnum*) + *aigre*, sour (< VLat. **acrus* < Lat. *ācer*; see **ak-** in App.).]

vinegar eel *n.* A minute nematode worm (*Anguillula aceti*) that feeds on the organisms causing fermentation in vinegar.

vinegar fly *n.* See **fruit fly** 1.

vin•e•gar•roon (vĭn′ĭ-gə-rōōn′) *also* **vin•e•ga•rone** (-rōn′) *n.* A large whip scorpion (*Mastigoproctus giganteus*) of the southern United States and Mexico that emits a strong odor of vinegar when disturbed. [Am.Sp. *vinagrón* < Sp. *vinagre*, vinegar < OSpan. < OFr. *vinaigre*. See **VINEGAR**.]

vinegar worm *n.* See **vinegar eel**.

vin•e•gar•y (vĭn′ĭ-gə-rē, -grē) *adj.* **1.** Having the taste, smell, or nature of vinegar. **2.** Unpleasant and irascible.

vin•er•y (vī′nə-rē) *n., pl.* **-ies** An area or greenhouse for growing vines.

vine•yard (vĭn′yərd) *n.* **1.** Ground planted with cultivated grapevines. **2.** A sphere of spiritual, mental, or physical endeavor. —**vine′yard•ist** *n.*

vingt-et-un (văn′tā-œN′) *n. Games* See **blackjack** 3. [Fr., twenty-one : *vingt,* twenty + *et,* and + *un,* one.]

vini– or **vino–** or **vin–** *pref.* Wine. [< Lat. *vīni–* < *vīnum.*]

vi•nic (vī′nĭk) *adj.* Of, contained in, or derived from wine.

vin•i•cul•ture (vĭn′ĭ-kŭl′chər, vī′nĭ-) *n.* Cultivation of grapes. —**vin′i•cul′tur•al** *adj.* —**vin′i•cul′tur•ist** *n.*

vin•i•fy (vĭn′ə-fī′) *tr.v.* **-fied, -fy•ing, -fies** To convert (the juice of grapes, for example) into wine by the process of fermentation. —**vin′i•fi•ca′tion** (-fĭ-kā′shən) *n.*

Vin•land (vĭn′lənd) An unidentified coastal region of NE North America visited by Norse voyagers as early as c. 1000.

Vin•ny•tsya or **Vin•ni•tsa** (vĭn′ĭ-tsə, vē′nĭ-) A city of W Ukraine SW of Kiev; founded in the 14th cent. Pop. 367,000.

vi•no (vē′nō) *n., pl.* **-nos** Wine. [Ital. and Sp., both < Lat. *vīnum.*]

vin or•di•naire (văn′ ôr-dē-nâr′, vēN) *n.* **vins or•di•naires** (văNz′ ôr-dē-nâr′) An inexpensive red table wine. [Fr.]

vi•nos•i•ty (vī-nŏs′ĭ-tē) *n., pl.* **-ties** The distinctive body, color, and taste of wine. [LLat. *vīnōsitās* < Lat. *vīnōsus,* vinous. See VI-NOUS.]

vi•nous (vī′nəs) *adj.* **1.** Of or made with wine. **2.** Affected or caused by the consumption of wine. **3.** Of the color of wine. [Lat. *vīnōsus* < *vīnum,* wine.] —**vi′nous•ly** *adv.*

Vin•son (vĭn′sən), Frederick Moore 1890–1953. Amer. jurist; chief justice of the US Supreme Court (1946–53).

vin•tage (vĭn′tĭj) *n.* **1.** The yield of wine or grapes from a vineyard or district during one season. **2.** Wine, usu. of high quality, identified as to year and vineyard or district of origin. **3.** The year or place in which a wine is bottled. **4a.** The harvesting of a grape crop. **b.** The initial stage of winemaking. **5.** *Informal* **a.** A group of people or things sharing certain characteristics. **b.** A year or period of origin. **c.** Length of existence; age. ❖ *adj.* **1.** Of or relating to a vintage. **2.** Characterized by excellence, maturity, and enduring appeal; classic. **3.** Old or outmoded. **4a.** Of the best: *played songs that were vintage Cole Porter.* **b.** Of the most distinctive. [ME < AN, alteration of OFr. *vendange* < Lat. *vīndēmia* : *vīnum,* grapes + *dēmere,* to take off (*dē,* de- + *emere,* to obtain).]

vin•tag•er (vĭn′tə-jər) *n.* A producer or harvester of wine grapes.

vintage year *n.* **1.** The year in which a vintage wine is produced. **2.** A year of outstanding achievement or success.

vint•ner (vĭnt′nər) *n.* **1.** A wine merchant. **2.** One who makes wine. [ME *vineter* < OFr. *vinetier* < Med.Lat. *vīnētārius* < Lat. *vīnētum,* vineyard < *vīnum,* wine.]

vin•y (vī′nē) *adj.* **-i•er, -i•est** **1.** Of, relating to, or having the nature of vines. **2.** Overgrown with or abounding in vines.

vi•nyl (vī′nəl) *n.* **1.** The univalent chemical radical CH_2CH. **2.** Any of various easily polymerized compounds containing the vinyl radical, used as basic materials for plastics. **3.** Any of various tough flexible shiny plastics used for coverings and clothing. **4.** Phonograph records considered as a group. [VIN(I)– + –YL.] —**vi•nyl′ic** (-nĭl′ĭk) *adj.*

vinyl chloride *n.* A flammable gas, CH_2:$CHCl$, used as a monomer for polyvinyl chloride.

vi•ol (vī′əl) *n.* Any of a family of stringed instruments, chiefly of the 16th and 17th centuries, having a fretted fingerboard, usu. six strings, and a flat back and played with a curved bow. See **viola da gamba.** [Alteration of ME *viel* < OFr. *viole, vielle* < O Provençal *viola.* See VIOLA[1].]

vi•o•la[1] (vē-ō′lə) *n.* A stringed instrument of the violin family, slightly larger than a violin, tuned a fifth lower, and having a deeper, more sonorous tone. [Ital. < O Provençal, *viola,* prob. of imit. orig.] —**vi′o′list** *n.*

vi•o•la[2] (vī-ō′lə, vē-, vī′ə-lə) *n.* A plant of the genus *Viola,* which includes the violets and pansies. [ME < Lat.]

vi•o•la•ble (vī′ə-lə-bəl) *adj.* That can be violated. —**vi′o•la•bil′i•ty, vi′o•la•ble•ness** *n.* —**vi′o•la•bly** *adv.*

vi•o•la da brac•cio (vē-ō′lə də brä′chō) *n., pl.* **viola da braccios** A stringed instrument of the violin family with approximately the range of the viola. [Ital. : *viola,* viol + *da,* of, for + *braccio,* arm.]

viola da gam•ba (găm′bə, gäm′-) *n.* A stringed instrument, the bass of the viol family, with approximately the cello's range. [Ital. : *viola,* viol + *da,* of, for + *gamba,* leg.]

viola d'a•mo•re (dä-môr′ā, -môr′ē, -môr′ē, -môr′ē) *n.* A stringed instrument, the tenor of the violin family, having six or seven stopped strings and an equal number of sympathetic strings. [Ital. : *viola,* viol + *da,* of + *amore,* love.]

vi•o•late (vī′ə-lāt′) *tr.v.* **-lat•ed, -lat•ing, -lates** **1.** To break or disregard (a law, for example). **2.** To assault (a person) sexually. **3.** To do harm to (property or qualities seen as sacred); desecrate or defile. **4.** To disturb rudely or improperly; interrupt. [ME *violaten* < Lat. *violāre, violāt–* < *vīs, vi–,* force. See **weiə-** in App.] —**vi′o•la′tive** *adj.* —**vi′o•la′tor** *n.*

vi•o•la•tion (vī′ə-lā′shən) *n.* The act or an instance of violating or the condition of being violated. See Syns at **breach.**

vi•o•lence (vī′ə-ləns) *n.* **1.** Physical force exerted for the purpose of violating, damaging, or abusing: *crimes of violence.* **2.** The act or an instance of violent action or behavior. **3.** Intensity or severity, as in natural phenomena; untamed force. **4.** Abusive or unjust exercise of power. **5.** Abuse or injury to meaning, content, or intent. **6.** Vehemence of feeling or expression; fervor.

vi•o•lent (vī′ə-lənt) *adj.* **1.** Marked by, acting with, or resulting from great force: *a violent attack.* **2.** Having or showing great emotional force. **3.** Marked by intensity; extreme. **4.** Caused by unexpected force or injury rather than by natural causes: *a violent death.* **5.** Tending to distort or injure meaning, phrasing, or intent. [ME < OFr. < Lat. *violentus* < *vīs, vi–,* force. See **weiə-** in App.] —**vi′o•lent•ly** *adv.*

vi•o•let (vī′ə-lĭt) *n.* **1a.** Any of various low-growing herbs of the genus *Viola,* having short-spurred irregular flowers that are typically purplish-blue. **b.** Any of several similar plants, such as the African violet. **2.** The hue of the short-wave end of the visible spectrum, evoked in the human observer by radiant energy with wavelengths of approx. 380 to 420 nanometers; any of a group of colors that are reddish-blue in hue. [ME < OFr. *violete,* dim. of *viole* < Lat. *viola.*]

vi•o•lin (vī′ə-lĭn′) *n.* A stringed instrument that is played with a bow, having four strings that are tuned at intervals of a fifth, an unfretted fingerboard, a shallower body than the viol, and a flexible range, tone, and dynamics. [Ital. *violino,* dim. of *viola,* viola. See VIOLA[1].] —**vi′o•lin′ist** *n.* —**vi′o•lin′is′tic** *adj.*

Viol•let-le-Duc (vē′ə-lĕt′lə-dōōk′, -dyōōk′, vyô-lĕ′lə-dük′), Eugène Emmanuel 1814–79. French architect who was a leader of the Gothic revival in France.

vi•o•lon•cel•lo (vē′ə-lən-chĕl′ō, vī′ə-) *n., pl.* **-los** A cello. [Ital., dim. of *violone,* a very low-pitched viol, augmentative of *viola,* viola. See VIOLA[1].] —**vi′o•lon•cel′list** *n.*

VIP (vē′ī-pē′) *n. Informal* A person of great importance or influence, esp. a dignitary who commands special treatment. [*v(ery) i(mportant) p(erson).*]

vi•per (vī′pər) *n.* **1.** Any of several venomous Old World snakes of the family Viperidae, having a pair of long hollow fangs and a thick heavy body. **2.** A pit viper. **3.** A venomous or supposedly venomous snake. **4.** A person regarded as malicious or treacherous. [ME *vipere* < OFr. < Lat. *vīpera,* snake, contraction of **vīvipera* < *vīvus,* alive; see **g**[w]**eiə-** in App. + *parere,* to give birth.]

violin

vi•per•fish (vī′pər-fĭsh′) *n., pl.* **viperfish** or **-fish•es** Any of various small deep-sea fish of the family Chauliodontidae, having fanglike teeth and a long first ray of the dorsal fin.

vi•per•ine (vī′pə-rīn′) *adj.* Of, resembling, or characteristic of a viper.

vi•per•ish (vī′pər-ĭsh) *adj.* Spiteful or malicious; venomous.

vi•per•ous (vī′pər-əs) *adj.* **1.** Suggestive of or related to a viper. **2.** Venomous; malicious. —**vi′per•ous•ly** *adv.*

vi•per's bugloss (vī′pərz) *n.* Any of various Eurasian plants of the genus *Echium,* including the blueweed, having bright blue to white flowers, bristly foliage, and a dense scorpioid inflorescence.

vir– *pref.* Variant of viro–.

Vi•ra•co•cha (vē′rə-kō′chə) *n. Mythology* The creator god of the Incas.

vi•ra•go (və-rä′gō, -rā′-, vîr′ə-gō′) *n., pl.* **-goes** or **-gos** **1.** A woman regarded as noisy, scolding, or domineering. **2.** A large, strong, courageous woman. [Lat. *virāgō* < *vir,* man. See **wī-ro-** in App.] —**vi•rag′i•nous** (və-răj′ə-nəs) *adj.*

vi•ral (vī′rəl) *adj.* Of, relating to, or caused by a virus. —**vi′ral•ly** *adv.*

viral load *n.* The concentration of a virus in the blood.

vir•e•lay or **vir•e•lai** (vîr′ə-lā′) *n., pl.* **-lays** or **-lais** Any of several medieval French verse and song forms, esp. one in which each stanza has two rhymes, the end rhyme recurring as the first rhyme of the following stanza. [ME *virelai* < OFr., alteration (influenced by *lai,* lay) of *vireli,* song refrain.]

vi•re•mi•a (vī-rē′mē-ə) *n.* The presence of viruses in the bloodstream. —**vi•re′mic** (-mĭk) *adj.*

vir•e•o (vîr′ē-ō′) *n., pl.* **-os** Any of various small insect-eating New World songbirds of the genus *Vireo,* having grayish or greenish plumage. [Lat. *vireō,* a bird < *virēre,* to be green.]

vi•res•cence (və-rĕs′əns, vī-) *n.* The state or process of becoming green, esp. the abnormal development of green coloration in plant parts normally not green.

vi•res•cent (və-rĕs′ənt, vī-) *adj.* **1.** Becoming green. **2.** Somewhat green; greenish. [Lat. *virēscēns, virēscent–,* pr. part. of *virēscere,* to become green, inchoative of *virēre,* to be green.]

vir•ga (vûr′gə) *n.* Wisps of precipitation streaming from a cloud but evaporating before reaching the ground. [Lat., twig, virga.]

vir•gate[1] (vûr′gāt′) *adj.* Shaped like a wand or rod. [Lat. *virgātus,* made of twigs < *virga,* twig.]

vir•gate[2] (vûr′gāt) *n.* An early English measure of land area of varying value, often equal to about 30 acres (12 hectares). [Med. Lat. *virgāta* < fem. of Lat. *virgātus,* relating to a rod. See VIRGATE[1].]

Vir•gil also **Ver•gil** (vûr′jəl) Originally Publius Vergilius Maro 70–19 B.C. Roman poet best known for the epic poem *Aeneid.* —**Vir•gil′i•an** (vûr-jĭl′ē-ən, -jĭl′yən) *adj.*

vir•gin (vûr′jĭn) *n.* **1.** A person who has not experienced sexual

viperfish
head of a viperfish

intercourse. **2.** A chaste or unmarried woman; a maiden. **3.** An unmarried woman who has taken religious vows of chastity. **4. Virgin** The Virgin Mary. **5.** *Zoology* **a.** A female animal that has not copulated. **b.** A female insect or other arthropod that produces fertile eggs without copulating. **6. Virgin** See **Virgo.** ❖ *adj.* **1.** Of, relating to, or being a virgin; chaste. **2.** Being in a pure or natural state; unsullied: *virgin snow.* **3.** Unused, uncultivated, or unexplored. **4.** Existing in native or raw form; not processed or refined. **5.** Happening for the first time; initial. **6.** Obtained directly from the first pressing: *virgin olive oil.* **7.** *Zoology* Producing fertile eggs without copulating. [ME < OFr. *virgine* < Lat. *virgō, virgin-.*]

vir•gin•al[1] (vûr′jə-nəl) *adj.* **1.** Relating to, characteristic of, or befitting a virgin; chaste. **2.** Remaining in a state of virginity. **3.** Untouched or unsullied; fresh. **4.** *Zoology* Virgin. —**vir′gin•al•ly** *adv.*

vir•gin•al[2] (vûr′jə-nəl) *n.* A small legless rectangular harpsichord popular in the 16th and 17th centuries. Often used in the plural. [< VIRGIN (perh. < its being associated with female performers).]

Virgin Birth or **virgin birth** *n. Christianity* The doctrine that Jesus was born of Mary, whose virginity remained intact.

Vir•gin•ia (vər-jĭn′yə) A state of the E US on Chesapeake Bay and the Atlantic Ocean; admitted as one of the original Thirteen Colonies in 1788. The first permanent settlement in the region was at Jamestown in 1607. Cap. Richmond. Pop. 7,078,515. —**Vir•gin′ian** *adj.* & *n.*

Virginia Algonquian *n.* The extinct Eastern Algonquian language of eastern Virginia.

Virginia Beach An independent city of SE VA on the Atlantic Ocean E of Norfolk. Pop. 425,257.

Virginia bluebell *n.* See **Virginia cowslip.**

Virginia cowslip *n.* An eastern North American plant (*Mertensia virginica*) having clusters of nodding blue flowers.

Virginia creeper *n.* A North American climbing vine (*Parthenocissus quinquefolia*) having palmately compound leaves with five leaflets and bluish-black berries.

Virginia fence *n.* See **worm fence.**

Virginia ham *n.* A lean hickory-smoked ham.

Virginia rail *n.* A small reddish-brown American rail (*Rallus limicola*) having a long slender bill.

Virginia reel *n.* An American country-dance in which couples perform various steps together to the instructions of a caller.

Virgin Islands **1.** A group of islands of the NE West Indies E of Puerto Rico divided into the **British Virgin Islands** to the NE and the Virgin Islands of the US to the SW. **2.** Officially **Virgin Islands of the United States.** A US territory constituting the SW group of the Virgin Is.; purchased from Denmark in 1917. Cap. Charlotte Amalie. Pop. 104,000.

vir•gin•i•ty (vər-jĭn′ĭ-tē) *n., pl.* **-ties** **1.** The quality or condition of being a virgin. **2.** The state of being pure, unsullied, or untouched.

Virgin Mary *n.* **1.** The mother of Jesus. **2.** A bloody mary made without alcohol.

vir•gin's bower (vûr′jĭnz) *n.* Any of several climbing plants of the genus *Clematis,* esp. *C. virginiana* of eastern North America, having white flowers and a cluster of seedlike fruits, each with a feathery persistent style.

virgin wool *n.* Wool not previously used in manufacture.

Vir•go (vûr′gō) *n.* **1.** A constellation in the region of the celestial equator between Leo and Libra. **2a.** The sixth sign of the zodiac in astrology. **b.** *pl.* **-gos** One who is born under this sign. [ME < Lat., virgin, the constellation Virgo < *virgō,* virgin.]

vir•gu•late (vûr′gyə-lĭt, -lāt′) *adj.* Shaped like a small rod. [< Lat. *virgula,* small rod < *virga,* rod.]

vir•gule (vûr′gyōōl) *n. Printing* A diagonal mark (/) used esp. to separate alternatives, as in *and/or,* to represent the word *per,* as in *miles/hour,* and to indicate the ends of verse lines printed continuously, as in *Old King Cole/Was a merry old soul.* [Fr., comma, obelus < LLat. *virgula,* accentual mark < Lat., obelus, dim. of *virga,* rod.]

vi•ri•cide (vī′rĭ-sīd′) also **vi•ru•cide** (vī′rə-) *n.* A substance that inhibits or destroys viruses. —**vi′ri•cid′al** (-sīd′l) *adj.*

vir•id (vîr′ĭd) *adj.* Bright green with or as if with vegetation; verdant. [Lat. *viridis* < *virēre,* to be green.]

vir•i•des•cent (vîr′ĭ-dĕs′ənt) *adj.* Green or slightly green. [LLat. *viridēscēns, viridēscent-,* pr. part. of *viridēscere,* to become green < Lat. *viridis,* green. See VIRID.] —**vir′i•des′cence** *n.*

vi•rid•i•an (və-rĭd′ē-ən) *n.* A durable bluish-green pigment.

vi•rid•i•ty (və-rĭd′ĭ-tē) *n.* **1a.** The quality or condition of being green; greenness. **b.** The green color of vegetation or leaves. **2.** Innocence or inexperience.

vir•ile (vîr′əl, -īl′) *adj.* **1.** Of, relating to, or having the characteristics of an adult male. **2.** Having or showing masculine spirit, strength, vigor, or power. **3.** Capable of performing sexually as a male; potent. [ME < OFr. *viril* < Lat. *virīlis* < *vir,* man. See wī-ro- in App.]

vir•il•ism (vîr′ə-lĭz′əm) *n.* The presence of male secondary sexual characteristics in a female.

vi•ril•i•ty (və-rĭl′ĭ-tē) *n.* **1.** The quality or state of being virile; manly character. **2.** Masculine vigor; potency.

Virginia creeper
Parthenocissus quinquefolia

vir•il•i•za•tion (vîr′ə-lĭ-zā′shən) *n.* Development of male secondary sexual characteristics. —**vir′il•ize′** (-ə-līz′) *v.*

vi•ri•on (vī′rē-ŏn′, vîr′ē-) *n.* A complete viral particle, consisting of RNA or DNA surrounded by a protein shell and constituting the infective form of a virus. [VIR(US) + -ON[1].]

viro- or **vir-** *pref.* Virus: *virology.* [< VIRUS.]

vi•roid (vī′roid′) *n.* A viruslike infectious particle that consists solely of a strand of RNA and causes disease in plants.

vi•rol•o•gy (vī-rŏl′ə-jē) *n.* The study of viruses and viral diseases. —**vi′ro•log′i•cal** (vī′rə-lŏj′ĭ-kəl), **vi′ro•log′ic** (-ĭk) *adj.* —**vi•rol′o•gist** *n.*

vir•tu (vər-tōō′, vîr-) also **ver•tu** (vər-) *n.* **1.** A knowledge of or taste for the fine arts. **2.** The quality of being beautiful, rare, or collectible. **3.** Objects of art, esp. fine antique objets d'art, considered as a group. [Ital. *virtù,* virtue, virtu < Lat. *virtūs,* excellence, virtue. See VIRTUE.]

vir•tu•al (vûr′chōō-əl) *adj.* **1.** Existing or resulting in essence or effect though not in actual fact, form, or name. **2.** Created, simulated, or carried on by means of a computer or computer network: *virtual conversations in a chatroom.* [ME *virtuall,* effective < Med.Lat. *virtuālis* < Lat. *virtūs,* excellence. See VIRTUE.] —**vir′tu•al′i•ty** (-ăl′ĭ-tē) *n.*

> **USAGE NOTE** The adjectives *virtual* and *digital* and the prefixes *e-* and *cyber-* refer to things carried out chiefly in an electronic medium. *Digital* can be used for most devices or activities that make use of computer technology: *a digital network. Virtual* often refers to things that mimic their physical equivalents: *a virtual tour of a cathedral.* The prefix *e-* is often used in speaking of the Web's commercial applications (*e-commerce*), whereas *cyber-* tends to be used when speaking of computer networks from a broader cultural point of view (*cyberspace*).

virtual focus *n.* The point from which divergent rays of reflected or refracted light seem to have emanated.

virtual image *n.* An image from which rays of reflected or refracted light appear to diverge.

vir•tu•al•ly (vûr′chōō-ə-lē) *adv.* **1.** In fact or to all purposes; practically. **2.** Almost but not quite; nearly.

virtual memory *n.* Memory, often as simulated on a hard disk, that emulates RAM, allowing an application to operate as though the computer has more memory than it actually does.

virtual particle *n.* A subatomic particle whose existence violates the principles of conservation of mass and conservation of energy but is allowed to exist for a short time within the limits of the uncertainty principle.

virtual reality *n.* A computer simulation of a real or imaginary system that enables a user to perform operations on the simulated system and shows the effects in real time.

vir•tue (vûr′chōō) *n.* **1a.** Moral excellence and righteousness; goodness. **b.** An example or kind of moral excellence: *the virtue of patience.* **2.** Chastity, esp. in a woman. **3.** A particularly efficacious, good, or beneficial quality; advantage. **4.** Effective force or power. **5. virtues** *Christianity* The fifth of the nine orders of angels. **6.** *Obsolete* Manly courage; valor. —**idiom: by** (or **in**) **virtue of** On the grounds or basis of; by reason of. [ME *vertu* < OFr. < Lat. *virtūs,* manliness, excellence, goodness < *vir,* man. See wī-ro- in App.]

vir•tu•o•sa (vûr′chōō-ō′sə, -zə) *n.* A woman who is a virtuoso. [Ital., fem. of virtuoso, virtuoso. See VIRTUOSO.]

vir•tu•os•i•ty (vûr′chōō-ŏs′ĭ-tē) *n., pl.* **-ties** **1.** The technical skill, fluency, or style exhibited by a virtuoso. **2.** An appreciation for or interest in fine objects of art.

vir•tu•o•so (vûr′chōō-ō′sō, -zō) *n., pl.* **-sos** or **-si** (-sē) **1.** A musician with masterly ability, technique, or personal style. **2.** A person with masterly skill or technique, esp. in the arts. **3.** *Archaic* A very learned person. ❖ *adj.* Exhibiting the ability, technique, or personal style of a virtuoso: *a virtuoso performance.* [Ital., skilled, of great worth, virtuoso < LLat. *virtuōsus,* virtuous < Lat. *virtūs,* excellence. See VIRTUE.] —**vir′tu•o′sic** (-ō′sĭk, -zĭk) *adj.* —**vir′tu•o′si•cal•ly** *adv.*

vir•tu•ous (vûr′chōō-əs) *adj.* **1.** Having or showing virtue, esp. moral excellence: *led a virtuous life.* **2.** Possessing or characterized by chastity; pure. See Syns at **moral.** —**vir′tu•ous•ly** *adv.* —**vir′tu•ous•ness** *n.*

virtuous circle *n.* A condition in which a favorable circumstance or result gives rise to another that subsequently supports the first. [Modeled on VICIOUS CIRCLE.]

vi•ru•cide (vī′rə-sīd′) *n.* Variant of **viricide.**

vir•u•lent (vîr′yə-lənt, vîr′ə-) *adj.* **1a.** Extremely infectious, malignant, or poisonous. Used of a disease or toxin. **b.** Capable of causing disease by breaking down protective mechanisms of the host. Used of a pathogen. **2.** Bitterly hostile or antagonistic; hateful: *virulent criticism.* **3.** Intensely irritating, obnoxious, or harsh. [ME < Lat. *vīrulentus* < *vīrus,* poison.] —**vir′u•lence, vir′u•len•cy** *n.* —**vir′u•lent•ly** *adv.*

vir•u•lif•er•ous (vîr′yə-lĭf′ər-əs, vîr′ə-) *adj.* Carrying or containing a virus: *viruliferous aphids.* [VIRUL(ENCE) + -FEROUS.]

vi•rus (vī′rəs) *n., pl.* **-rus•es** **1a.** Any of various noncellular, submicroscopic entities capable of causing disease that are unable to replicate without a host cell, consist of a core of RNA or DNA surrounded by a protein coat, and are typically not considered living organisms. **b.** A disease caused by a virus. **2.** Something that poisons one's soul or mind: *the virus of racism.* **3.** *Computer Science* A computer virus. [Lat. *vīrus*, poison.]

vi•sa (vē′zə) *n.* An official authorization appended to a passport, permitting entry into and travel within a particular country or region. ❖ *tr.v.* **-saed, -sa•ing, -sas 1.** To endorse or ratify (a passport). **2.** To give a visa to. [Fr., short for Lat. *(carta) vīsa*, (the document has been) seen < fem. p. part. of *vidēre*, to see. See **weid-** in App.]

vis•age (vĭz′ĭj) *n.* **1.** The face or facial expression of a person; countenance. **2.** Appearance; aspect: *the bleak visage of winter.* [ME < OFr. < *vis* < Lat. *vīsus*, appearance < p. part. of *vidēre*, to see. See **weid-** in App.]

Vi•sa•kha•pat•nam (vĭ-sä′kə-pŭt′nəm) also **Vi•za•ga•pa•tam** (vĭ-zä′gə-pŭt′əm) A city of E India on the Bay of Bengal NE of Chennai (Madras). Pop. 752,037.

Vi•sa•lia (vī-sāl′yə) A city of S-central CA SE of Fresno. Pop. 91,565.

vis•ard (vĭz′ərd, -ärd′) *n.* Variant of **vizard.**

vis-à-vis (vē′zə-vē′) *prep.* **1.** Face to face with; opposite to. **2.** Compared with. **3.** In relation to. ❖ *adv.* Face to face. ❖ *n., pl.* **vis-à-vis** (-vēz′, -vē′) **1.** One that is face to face with or opposite to another. **2.** A date or an escort. **3.** One that has the same functions and characteristics as another; a counterpart. [Fr. : *vis*, face + *à*, to.] **—vis′-à-vis′** *adj.*

Vi•sa•yan (vĭ-sī′ən) also **Bi•sa•yan** (bĭ-) *n.* **1.** A member of the largest ethnic group indigenous to the Philippines, found in the Visayan Islands. **2.** Their Austronesian language. **—Vi•sa′yan** *adj.*

Visayan Islands An island group of the central Philippines in and around the **Visayan Sea** between Luzon and Mindanao.

vis•ca•cha (vĭ-skä′chə) *n.* Any of several gregarious burrowing South American rodents of the genera *Lagostomus* and *Lagidium*, related to and resembling the chinchilla. [Sp. *vizcacha* < Quechua *wiskácha*.]

vis•cer•a (vĭs′ər-ə) *pl.n.* **1.** The soft internal organs of the body, esp. those contained within the abdominal and thoracic cavities. **2.** The intestines. [Lat. *vīscera*, pl. of *vīscus*.]

vis•cer•al (vĭs′ər-əl) *adj.* **1.** Relating to, situated in, or affecting the viscera. **2.** Perceived in or as if in the viscera; profound. **3.** Instinctive: *visceral needs.* **—vis′cer•al•ly** *adv.*

vis•cer•o•mo•tor (vĭs′ər-ə-mō′tər) *adj.* Producing or related to movements of the viscera.

vis•cid (vĭs′ĭd) *adj.* **1.** Thick and adhesive. Used of a fluid. **2.** Covered with a sticky or clammy coating. [LLat. *viscidus* < Lat. *viscum*, mistletoe, birdlime made from mistletoe berries.] **—vis•cid′i•ty, vis′cid•ness** *n.* **—vis′cid•ly** *adv.*

vis•com•e•ter (vĭ-skŏm′ĭ-tər) *n.* An instrument used to measure viscosity. [Short for VISCOSIMETER.] **—vis′co•met′ric** (vĭs′kə-mĕt′rĭk) *adj.* **—vis•com′e•try** *n.*

vis•cose (vĭs′kōs′) *n.* **1.** A thick golden-brown viscous solution of cellulose xanthate, used in making rayon and cellophane. **2.** Viscose rayon. ❖ *adj.* **1.** Viscous. **2.** Of, relating to, or made from viscose. [VISC(OUS) + -OSE[2]. Adj., sense 1, ME, viscous < LLat. *viscōsus* < Lat. *viscum*, mistletoe, birdlime made from mistletoe berries.]

viscose rayon *n.* A rayon made by reconverting cellulose from a soluble xanthate form to tough fibers by washing in acid.

vis•co•sim•e•ter (vĭs′kə-sĭm′ĭ-tər) *n.* See **viscometer.** **—vis•cos′i•met′ric** (vĭ-skŏs′ə-mĕt′rĭk) *adj.*

vis•cos•i•ty (vĭ-skŏs′ĭ-tē) *n., pl.* **-ties 1.** The condition or property of being viscous. **2.** *Physics* A numerical measure of the degree to which a fluid resists flow under an applied force.

vis•count (vī′kount′) *n.* **1.** A nobleman ranking below an earl or count and above a baron. **2.** Used as a title for such a nobleman. [ME < OFr. *visconte* < Med.Lat. *vicecomes, vicecomit-* : LLat. *vice-*, vice- + LLat. *comes*, occupant of any state office; see COUNT[2].]

vis•count•cy (vī′kount′sē) *n., pl.* **-cies** The rank, title, or dignity of a viscount.

vis•count•ess (vī′koun′tĭs) *n.* **1.** The wife or widow of a viscount. **2.** A noblewoman holding a viscountcy in her own right. **3.** Used as a title for such a noblewoman.

Viscount Melville Sound An arm of the Arctic Ocean between Victoria and Melville islands in N Canada.

vis•count•y (vī′koun′tē) *n., pl.* **-ies** See **viscountcy.**

vis•cous (vĭs′kəs) *adj.* **1.** Having relatively high resistance to flow. **2.** Viscid; sticky. [ME < OFr. < LLat. *viscōsus*. See VISCOSE.] **—vis′cous•ly** *adv.* **—vis′cous•ness** *n.*

vis•cus (vĭs′kəs) *n.* Singular of **viscera.**

vise also **vice** (vīs) *n.* A clamping device, usu. consisting of two jaws closed or opened by a screw or lever and used in carpentry or metalworking to hold a piece in position. ❖ *tr.v.* **vised, vis•ing, vis•es** also **viced, vic•ing, vic•es** To hold or compress in or as if in a vise. [ME *vis*, screwlike device < OFr., screw < Lat. *vītis*, vine (< its spiral wrappings).]

Vish•nu (vĭsh′no͞o) *n.* *Hinduism* One of the principal Hindu deities, a member of the triad including also Brahma and Shiva and worshiped as the protector and preserver of worlds. [Skt. *Viṣṇuḥ*.]

vis•i•bil•i•ty (vĭz′ə-bĭl′ĭ-tē) *n., pl.* **-ties 1.** The fact, state, or degree of being visible. **2.** The greatest distance under given weather conditions to which it is possible to see without instrumental assistance. **3a.** The capability of being easily observed. **b.** The capability of providing a clear unobstructed view: *a windshield with good visibility.*

vis•i•ble (vĭz′ə-bəl) *adj.* **1.** Possible to see; perceptible to the eye. **2a.** Obvious to the eye: *a visible change of expression.* **b.** Being often in the public view; conspicuous. **3.** Manifest; apparent: *no visible solution.* **4.** On hand; available. **5.** Constructed or designed to keep important parts in easily accessible view: *a visible file.* **6.** Represented visually, as by symbols. [ME < OFr. < Lat. *vīsibilis* < *vīsus*, p. part. of *vidēre*, to see. See VISION.] **—vis′i•ble•ness** *n.* **—vis′i•bly** *adv.*

visible speech *n.* A system of phonetic notation used in teaching speech to hearing-impaired people and consisting of diagrams of the speech organs in the positions required to articulate sounds.

Vis•i•goth (vĭz′ĭ-gŏth′) *n.* A member of the western Goths that invaded the Roman Empire in the fourth century A.D. and settled in France and Spain, establishing a monarchy that lasted until the early eighth century. [LLat. *Visigothī*, the Visigoths. See **wes-pero-** in App.] **—Vis′i•goth′ic** *adj.*

vi•sion (vĭzh′ən) *n.* **1a.** The faculty of sight; eyesight: *poor vision.* **b.** Something that is or has been seen. **2.** Unusual competence in discernment or perception; intelligent foresight. **3.** The manner in which one sees or conceives of something. **4.** A mental image produced by the imagination. **5.** The mystical experience of seeing as if with the eyes the supernatural or a supernatural being. **6.** A person or thing of extraordinary beauty. ❖ *tr.v.* **-sioned, -sion•ing, -sions** To see in or as if in a vision; envision. [ME < OFr. < Lat. *vīsiō, vīsiōn-* < *vīsus* < p. part. of *vidēre*, to see. See **weid-** in App.] **—vi′sion•al** *adj.* **—vi′sion•al•ly** *adv.*

vi•sion•ar•y (vĭzh′ə-nĕr′ē) *adj.* **1.** Characterized by vision or foresight. **2a.** Having the nature of fantasies or dreams; illusory. **b.** Existing in imagination only; imaginary. **3a.** Characterized by or given to apparitions, prophecies, or revelations. **b.** Given to daydreams or reverie; dreamy. **4a.** Not practicable or realizable; utopian. **b.** Tending to envision things in perfect but unrealistic form; idealistic. ❖ *n., pl.* **-ies 1.** One who is given to impractical or speculative ideas; a dreamer. **2.** One who has visions; a seer. **—vi′sion•ar′i•ness** *n.*

vi•sion•less (vĭzh′ən-lĭs) *adj.* **1.** Lacking the faculty of sight; blind. **2.** Lacking intelligent foresight or imagination.

vis•it (vĭz′ĭt) *v.* **-it•ed, -it•ing, -its** —*tr.* **1a.** To call on socially. **b.** To go to see or spend time at (a place) with a certain intent. **c.** To stay with as a guest. **d.** To go to see in an official or professional capacity: *visited the dentist.* **2.** To go or come to: *visits the bank on Fridays.* **3.** To go to see in order to aid or console. **4.** To make itself known to or seize fleetingly: *visited by a bizarre thought.* **5a.** To afflict or assail: *A plague visited the village.* **b.** To inflict punishment on or for; avenge. —*intr.* **1.** To make a visit. **2.** *Informal* To converse or chat. ❖ *n.* **1.** The act or an instance of visiting a person, place, or thing. **2.** A stay or sojourn as a guest. **3.** The act of visiting in a professional capacity. **4.** The act of visiting in an official capacity, such as an inspection. [ME *visiten* < OFr. *visiter* < Lat. *vīsitāre*, freq. of *vīsere*, to want to see, go to see < *vidēre*, to see. See **weid-** in App.]

vis•it•a•ble (vĭz′ĭ-tə-bəl) *adj.* **1.** Subject to inspection or visitation. **2.** Accessible or open.

vis•i•tant (vĭz′ĭ-tənt) *n.* **1.** A visitor; a guest. **2.** A supernatural being; a ghost. **3.** A migratory bird that stops in a particular place for a limited period of time. ❖ *adj.* Visiting.

vis•i•ta•tion (vĭz′ĭ-tā′shən) *n.* **1.** The act or an instance of visiting or an instance of being visited. **2.** An official visit for the purpose of inspection or examination. **3.** The right of a parent to visit a child as specified in a divorce or separation order. **4a.** A visit of punishment or affliction or of comfort and blessing regarded as ordained by God. **b.** A calamitous event or experience; a grave misfortune. **5.** The appearance or arrival of a supernatural being. **6. Visitation** *Roman Catholic Church* **a.** The visit of the Virgin Mary to her cousin Elizabeth. **b.** May 31, observed in commemoration of this event. **—vis′i•ta′tion•al** *adj.*

vis•i•ta•to•ri•al (vĭz′ĭ-tə-tôr′ē-əl, -tōr′-) *adj.* **1.** Of or relating to an official visitor or visit. **2.** Having the right or power of visitation.

vis•it•ing card (vĭz′ĭ-tĭng) *n.* See **calling card** 1.

visiting fireman *n.* *Informal* **1.** An important visitor who is entertained impressively. **2.** A visitor, esp. a tourist or conventioneer, thought to be a free spender.

visiting nurse *n.* A registered nurse employed by a public health agency or hospital to promote community health and esp. to visit and treat sick people in their homes.

visiting professor *n.* A professor invited to serve on the faculty of another college or university for a limited period of time.

visiting teacher *n.* A teacher who visits and instructs sick or disabled children in a public school system.

vis•i•tor (vĭz′ĭ-tər) *n.* One that visits: *evening visitors.*

vi•sor also **vi•zor** (vī′zər) *n.* **1.** A piece projecting from the front of a cap or an elastic headband to shade or protect the eyes. **2.** A shield against glare attached above the windshield of an automotive vehicle. **3.** The front piece of the helmet of a suit of armor, capable of being raised and lowered and designed to protect the eyes, nose, and forehead. **4.** A means of concealment or disguise;

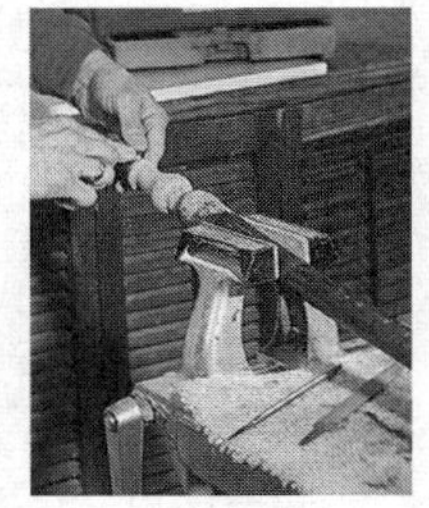

vise

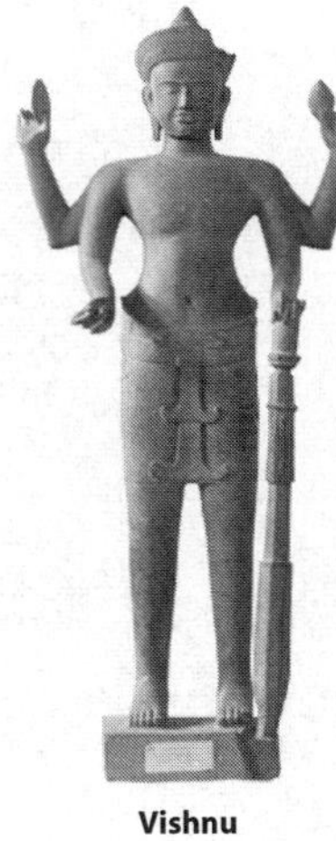

Vishnu
Khmer sculpture in sandstone

ă	pat	oi	boy
ā	pay	ou	out
âr	care	o͝o	took
ä	father	o͞o	boot
ĕ	pet	ŭ	cut
ē	be	ûr	urge
ĭ	pit	th	thin
ī	pie	*th*	this
îr	pier	hw	which
ŏ	pot	zh	vision
ō	toe	ə	about, item
ô	paw		

Stress marks:
′ (primary);
′ (secondary), as in
lexicon (lĕk′sĭ-kŏn′)

a mask. ❖ *tr.v.* **-sored, -sor•ing, -sors** also **-zored, -zor•ing, -zors** To provide or protect with a visor. [Alteration of ME *viser* < AN < *vis,* face < Lat. *vīsus,* appearance. See VISAGE.]

vis•ta (vĭs′tə) *n.* **1a.** A distant view or prospect, esp. one seen through an opening, as between rows of trees. **b.** An avenue or other passage affording such a view. **2.** An awareness of a range of time, events, or subjects; a broad mental view. [Ital. < fem. p. part. of *vedere,* to see < Lat. *vidēre.* See **weid-** in App.] —**vis′taed** (-təd) *adj.*

VISTA *abbr.* Volunteers In Service To America

Vis•tu•la (vĭs′chə-lə, -choŏ-) A river of Poland rising near the border of the Czech Republic and flowing c. 1,091 km (678 mi) in an arc to the Gulf of Gdańsk.

vi•su•al (vĭzh′ōō-əl) *adj.* **1.** Of or relating to the sense of sight. **2.** Seen or able to be seen by the eye; visible. **3.** Optical. **4.** Done, maintained, or executed by sight only. **5.** Having the nature of or producing an image in the mind: *a visual memory.* **6.** Of or relating to a method of instruction involving sight. **7.** Of or relating to art work, such as painting or sculpture, that appeals primarily to the sense of sight. ❖ *n.* A picture, chart, or other presentation that appeals to the sense of sight, used in promotion or for illustration or narration. Often used in the plural: *an ad campaign with striking visuals.* [ME < LLat. *vīsuālis* < Lat. *vīsus,* sight < p. part. of *vidēre,* to see. See VISION.] —**vi′su•al•ly** *adv.* —**vi′su•al•ness, vi′su•al′i•ty** (-ăl′ĭ-tē) *n.*

visual acuity *n.* Sharpness of vision, esp. as tested with a Snellen chart, according to which normal visual acuity is 20/20.

visual aid *n.* An instructional aid, such as a scale model, poster, or videotape, that presents information visually.

visual field *n.* The space or range within which objects are visible to the immobile eyes at a given time.

vi•su•al•ize (vĭzh′ōō-ə-līz′) *v.* **-ized, -iz•ing, -iz•es** —*tr.* **1.** To form a mental image of. **2.** To make visible. —*intr.* To form a mental image. —**vi′su•al•i•za′tion** (-ə-lĭ-zā′shən) *n.* —**vi′su•al•iz′er** *n.*

visually impaired *adj.* **1.** Having impaired vision; partially sighted. **2.** Incapable of sight; blind. ❖ *n.* (*used with a pl. verb*) Visually impaired people considered as a group.

visual purple *n.* See **rhodopsin.**

vi•su•o•spa•tial (vĭsh′ōō-ō-spā′shəl) *adj.* Of or relating to visual perception of spatial relationships among objects.

vi•ta (vī′tə, vē′-) *n., pl.* **vi•tae** (vī′tē, vē′tī) **1.** A curriculum vitae. **2.** A short account of a person's life. [Lat. *vīta,* life. See VITAL.]

vi•tal (vīt′l) *adj.* **1.** Of, relating to, or characteristic of life. **2.** Necessary to the continuation of life; life-sustaining: *a vital organ.* **3.** Full of life; animated. **4.** Imparting life or animation; invigorating: *the sun's vital rays.* **5.** Necessary to continued existence or effectiveness; essential. **6.** Concerned with or recording data pertinent to lives. **7.** *Biology* Used or done on a living cell or tissue. **8.** Destructive to life; fatal: *a vital injury.* [ME < OFr. < Lat. *vītālis* < *vīta,* life. See *g*ʷ**ei**ə- in App.] —**vi′tal•ly** *adv.* —**vi′tal•ness** *n.*

vital capacity *n.* The amount of air that can be forcibly expelled from the lungs after breathing in as deeply as possible.

vi•tal•ism (vīt′l-ĭz′əm) *n.* The theory or doctrine that life processes arise from or contain a nonmaterial vital principle and cannot be explained entirely as physical and chemical phenomena. —**vi′tal•ist** *adj. & n.* —**vi′tal•is′tic** *adj.*

vi•tal•i•ty (vī-tăl′ĭ-tē) *n., pl.* **-ties 1.** The capacity to live, grow, or develop. **2.** Physical or intellectual vigor; energy. **3.** The characteristic, principle, or force that distinguishes living things from nonliving things. **4.** Power to survive.

vi•tal•ize (vīt′l-īz′) *tr.v.* **-ized, -iz•ing, -iz•es 1.** To endow with life; animate. **2.** To make more lively or vigorous; invigorate. —**vi′tal•i•za′tion** (-ĭ-zā′shən) *n.* —**vi′tal•iz′er** *n.*

vi•tals (vīt′lz) *pl.n.* **1.** The vital body organs. **2.** The parts essential to continued functioning, as of a system.

vital signs *pl.n.* The pulse rate, temperature, and respiratory rate of an individual.

vital statistics *pl.n.* Statistics concerning the important events in human life, such as births, deaths, and marriages.

vi•ta•min (vī′tə-mĭn) *n.* Any of various fat-soluble or water-soluble organic substances essential in minute amounts for normal growth and activity of the body and obtained naturally from plant and animal foods. [Alteration of *vitamine* : Lat. *vīta,* life; see *g*ʷ**ei**ə- in App. + AMINE (so called because they were orig. thought to be amines).] —**vi′ta•min′ic** *adj.*

vitamin A *n.* A fat-soluble vitamin or a mixture of vitamins, esp. vitamin A_1 or a mixture of vitamins A_1 and A_2, occurring principally in fish-liver oils, milk, and some yellow and dark green vegetables and functioning in normal cell growth, the maintenance of epithelial tissue, and the prevention of night blindness.

vitamin A_1 *n.* A yellow crystalline compound, $C_{20}H_{30}O$, extracted from egg yolks, milk, and cod-liver oil.

vitamin A_2 *n.* A golden yellow oil, $C_{20}H_{28}O$, occurring chiefly in the livers of freshwater fish.

vitamin B *n.* **1.** Vitamin B complex. **2.** A member of the vitamin B complex, esp. thiamine.

vitamin B_1 *n.* See **thiamine.**

vitamin B_2 *n.* See **riboflavin.**

vitamin B_6 *n.* See **pyridoxine.**

vitamin B_{12} *n.* A complex compound containing cobalt, found

esp. in liver and widely used to treat pernicious anemia.

vitamin B_c *n.* See **folic acid.**

vitamin B complex *n.* A group of water-soluble vitamins including thiamine, riboflavin, niacin, pantothenic acid, biotin, pyridoxine, folic acid, inositol, and vitamin B_{12} and occurring chiefly in yeast, liver, eggs, and some vegetables.

vitamin C *n.* See **ascorbic acid.**

vitamin D *n.* A fat-soluble vitamin occurring in several forms, esp. vitamin D_2 or vitamin D_3, required for normal growth of teeth and bones and produced in general by ultraviolet irradiation of sterols in milk, fish, and eggs.

vitamin D_2 *n.* A white crystalline compound, $C_{28}H_{44}O$, produced by ultraviolet irradiation of ergosterol.

vitamin D_3 *n.* A colorless crystalline compound, $C_{27}H_{44}O$, found in fish-liver oils.

vitamin E *n.* Any of several fat-soluble vitamins consisting of tocopherols, esp. alpha-tocopherol, that are found chiefly in plant leaves, wheat germ oil, and milk and that act as antioxidants in the body.

vitamin G *n.* Riboflavin.

vitamin H *n.* Biotin.

vitamin K *n.* A fat-soluble vitamin existing in several related forms, occurring in leafy green vegetables, tomatoes, and egg yolks and functioning to promote blood clotting and prevent hemorrhaging.

vitamin K_1 *n.* A yellow viscous oil, $C_{31}H_{46}O_2$, found in leafy green vegetables or made synthetically, used by the body in the synthesis of prothrombin.

vitamin K_2 *n.* A crystalline compound, $C_{41}H_{56}O_2$, found in various intestinal bacteria and used to stop hemorrhaging.

vitamin P *n.* A water-soluble vitamin found as a crystalline substance esp. in citrus juices and functioning as a bioflavonoid in promoting capillary resistance to hemorrhaging.

Vi•tebsk (vē′tĭpsk) See **Vitsyebsk.**

vi•tel•lin (vī-tĕl′ĭn, vĭ-) *n.* A protein found in egg yolk.

vi•tel•line (vī-tĕl′ĭn, -ēn′, vĭ-) *adj.* **1.** Of, relating to, or associated with the yolk of an egg. **2.** Having the yellow hue of an egg yolk; dull yellow. ❖ *n.* The yolk of an egg. [VITELL(US) + −INE[1].]

vitelline membrane *n.* **1.** The membrane that develops around an oocyte in insects, mollusks, amphibians, and birds. **2.** The zona pellucida.

vi•tel•lo•gen•e•sis (vī-tĕl′ō-jĕn′ĭ-sĭs, vĭt′-) *n.* Formation of the yolk of an egg. [VITELL(US) + −GENESIS.] —**vi′tel•lo•ge•net′ic** (-jə-nĕt′ĭk), **vi′tel•lo•gen′ic** (-jĕn′ĭk) *adj.*

vi•tel•lus (vī-tĕl′əs, vĭ-) *n., pl.* **-lus•es** The yolk of an egg. [Lat., prob. dim. of *vitulus,* calf. See **wet-**[2] in App.]

vi•ti•ate (vĭsh′ē-āt′) *tr.v.* **-at•ed, -at•ing, -ates 1.** To reduce the value or impair the quality of. **2.** To corrupt morally; debase. **3.** To make ineffective; invalidate. [Lat. *vitiāre, vitiāt-* < *vitium,* fault.] —**vi′ti•a•ble** (vĭsh′ē-ə-bəl) *adj.* —**vi′ti•a′tion** *n.* —**vi′ti•a′tor** *n.*

vit•i•cul•ture (vĭt′ĭ-kŭl′chər, vī′tĭ-) *n.* The cultivation of grapes. [Lat. *vītis,* vine + CULTURE.] —**vit′i•cul′tur•al** *adj.* —**vit′i•cul′tur•ist** *n.*

Vi•ti Le•vu (vē′tē lĕv′ōō) The largest of the Fiji Is., in the SW Pacific Ocean.

vit•i•li•go (vĭt′l-ī′gō, -ē′gō) *n., pl.* **-gos** See **leukoderma.** [Lat. *vitilīgō,* tetter.]

Vi•tim (vĭ-tēm′) A river of SE Russia flowing c. 1,834 km (1,140 mi) generally NE and N to the Lena R.

Vi•to•ri•a (vĭ-tôr′ē-ə, -tōr′-, bĕ-tō′ryä) A city of N-central Spain SSE of Bilbao; probably founded by the Visigoths in the 6th cent. A.D. Pop. 208,755.

Vi•tó•ri•a (vĭ-tôr′ē-ə, -tōr′-, -tō′ryä) A city of E Brazil on the Atlantic Ocean NE of Rio de Janeiro. Pop. 258,243.

vit•rec•to•my (vĭ-trĕk′tə-mē) *n., pl.* **-mies** Surgical removal of the vitreous humor from the eyeball.

vit•re•ous (vĭt′rē-əs) *adj.* **1.** Of, relating to, resembling, or having the nature of glass; glassy. **2.** Obtained or made from glass. **3.** Of or relating to the vitreous humor. ❖ *n.* The vitreous humor. [< Lat. *vitreus* < *vitrum,* glass.] —**vit′re•os′i•ty** (-ŏs′ĭ-tē), **vit′re•ous•ness** (-əs-nĭs) *n.*

vitreous humor *n.* The clear gelatinous substance that fills the eyeball between the retina and the lens.

vit•ri•fy (vĭt′rə-fī′) *v.* **-fied, -fy•ing, -fies** —*tr.* To change or make into glass or a glassy substance, esp. through heat fusion. —*intr.* To become vitreous. [Fr. *vitrifier* < Med.Lat. *vitrificāre* : Lat. *vitrum,* glass + Lat. *-ficāre, -fy.*] —**vit′ri•fi′a•bil′i•ty** *n.* —**vit′ri•fi′a•ble** *adj.* —**vit′ri•fi•ca′tion** (-fĭ-kā′shən) *n.*

vi•trine (vĕ-trēn′) *n.* A glass-paneled cabinet or case for displaying articles such as china, objects d'art, or fine merchandise. [Fr. < *vitre,* pane of glass < OFr., glass, window with multiple lights < Lat. *vitrum.*]

vit•ri•ol (vĭt′rē-ōl′, -əl) *n.* **1a.** See **sulfuric acid. b.** Any of various sulfates of metals, such as zinc sulfate. **2.** Bitterly abusive feeling or expression. ❖ *tr.v.* **-oled, -ol•ing, -ols** or **-olled, -ol•ling, -ols** To expose or subject to vitriol. [ME < OFr. < Med.Lat. *vitriolum* < LLat. *vitreolum,* neut. of *vitreolus,* of glass < Lat. *vitreus.* See VITREOUS.]

vit•ri•ol•ic (vĭt′rē-ōl′ĭk) *adj.* **1.** Of, similar to, or derived from vitriol. **2.** Bitterly scathing; caustic: *vitriolic criticism.*

Vi·tru·vi·us (vĭ-trōō′vē-əs) fl. 1st cent. B.C. Roman architect known for the text *De Architectura*.

Vit·syebsk (vĭt′syĭpsk) or **Vi·tebsk** (vē′tĭpsk) A city of NE Belarus on the Western Dvina R. NE of Minsk. Pop. 365,100.

vit·ta (vĭt′ə) *n., pl.* **vit·tae** (vĭt′ē) **1.** *Zoology* A streak or band of color, as on the bill of a bird. **2.** *Botany* An oil tube in the fruit of certain plants, such as the carrot or parsley. [Lat., headband, ribbon.] —**vit′tate′** (vĭt′āt′) *adj.*

vit·tle (vĭt′əl) *n. & v.* Nonstandard Variant of **victual** 2.

vi·tu·per·ate (vī-tōō′pə-rāt′, -tyōō′-, vĭ-) *v.* **-at·ed, -at·ing, -ates** —*tr.* To rebuke or criticize harshly or abusively; berate. —*intr.* To use harshly abusive language; rail. [Lat. *vituperāre, vituperāt-.*] —**vi·tu′per·a·tor** *n.*

vi·tu·per·a·tion (vī-tōō′pə-rā′shən, -tyōō′-, vĭ-) *n.* **1.** The act or an instance of vituperating; abusive censure. **2.** Sustained, harshly abusive language; invective.

vi·tu·per·a·tive (vī-tōō′pər-ə-tĭv, -tyōō′-, -pə-rā′-, vĭ-) *adj.* Using, containing, or marked by harshly abusive language. —**vi·tu′per·a·tive·ly** *adv.* —**vi·tu′per·a·tive·ness** *n.*

vi·va (vē′və, -vä′) *interj.* Used to express acclamation, salute, or applause. [Ital. and Sp., (long) live, both < Lat. *vīvat,* third pers. sing. pr. subjunctive of *vīvere,* to live. See **gʷeiə-** in App.]

vi·va·ce (vē-vä′chā) *adv. & adj. Music* In a vivacious manner. [Ital. < Lat. *vīvāx, vīvāc-,* vivacious. See VIVACIOUS.]

vi·va·cious (vĭ-vā′shəs, vī-) *adj.* Full of animation and spirit; lively. [< Lat. *vīvāx, vīvāc-* < *vīvere,* to live. See **gʷei-** in App.] —**vi·va′cious·ly** *adv.* —**vi·va′cious·ness** *n.*

vi·vac·i·ty (vĭ-văs′ĭ-tē, vī-) *n.* The quality or condition of being vivacious; liveliness.

Vi·val·di (vĭ-väl′dē), **Antonio Lucio** 1675?–1741. Italian composer whose works include *The Four Seasons* (1725).

vi·var·i·um (vī-vâr′ē-əm) *n., pl.* **-i·ums** or **-i·a** (-ē-ə) A place, esp. an indoor enclosure, for keeping and raising living animals and plants under natural conditions for observation or research. [Lat. *vīvārium* < neut. of *vīvārius,* of living creatures < *vīvus,* alive. See VIVIFY.]

vi·va vo·ce (vī′və vō′sē, vē′və) *adv. & adj.* By word of mouth: *a report submitted viva voce.* [Med.Lat. *vīvā vōce,* with the living voice : Lat. *vīvā,* fem. ablative sing. of *vīvus,* living + Lat. *vōce,* ablative of *vōx,* voice.]

vi·ver·rine (vī-vĕr′īn, -ĭn′) also **vi·ver·rid** (-ĭd) *adj.* Of or belonging to the family Viverridae, which includes small carnivorous mammals such as the civets and mongooses. [NLat. *Vīverra,* type genus (< Lat. *vīverra,* ferret) + -INE, 1.] —**viverrine** *n.*

viv·id (vĭv′ĭd) *adj.* **-er, -est 1.** Perceived as bright and distinct; brilliant. **2a.** Having intensely bright colors: *a vivid tapestry.* **b.** Having a very high degree of saturation: *a vivid purple.* **3.** Presented in clear and striking manner: *a vivid account of the incident.* See Syns at **graphic. 4.** Perceived or felt with the freshness of immediate experience: *a vivid recollection.* **5.** Active in forming lifelike images: *a vivid imagination.* [Lat. *vividus* < *vīvere,* to live. See **gʷeiə-** in App.] —**viv′id·ly** *adv.* —**viv′id·ness** *n.*

viv·i·fy (vĭv′ə-fī′) *tr.v.* **-fied, -fy·ing, -fies 1.** To give or bring life to; animate. **2.** To make more lively, intense, or striking; enliven. [ME *vivifien* < OFr. *vivifier* < LLat. *vīvificāre* : Lat. *vīvus,* alive; see **gʷeiə-** in App. + Lat. *-ficāre,* -fy.] —**viv′i·fi·ca′tion** (-fĭ-kā′shən) *n.* —**viv′i·fi′er** *n.*

vi·vip·a·rous (vī-vĭp′ər-əs, vĭ-) *adj.* **1.** *Zoology* Giving birth to living offspring that develop within the mother's body. **2.** *Botany* **a.** Germinating or producing seeds that germinate before becoming detached from the parent plant. **b.** Producing bulbils or new plants rather than seeds. [< Lat. *vīviparus* : *vīvus,* alive; see **gʷeiə-** in App. + *-parus,* -parous.] —**vi·vi·par′i·ty** (vī′və-păr′ĭ-tē, vĭv′ə-) *n.* —**vi·vip′a·rous·ly** *adv.*

viv·i·sect (vĭv′ĭ-sĕkt′) *v.* **-sect·ed, -sect·ing, -sects** —*tr.* To perform vivisection on (an animal). —*intr.* To practice vivisection. [Back-formation < VIVISECTION.] —**viv′i·sec′tor** *n.*

viv·i·sec·tion (vĭv′ĭ-sĕk′shən, vĭv′ĭ-sĕk′-) *n.* The act or practice of cutting into or otherwise injuring living animals, esp. for the purpose of scientific research. [Lat. *vīvus,* alive; see VIVIFY + (DIS)SECTION.] —**viv′i·sec′tion·al** *adj.* —**viv′i·sec′tion·al·ly** *adv.* —**viv′i·sec′tion·ist** *n.*

vix·en (vĭk′sən) *n.* **1.** A female fox. **2.** A woman regarded as quarrelsome, shrewish, or malicious. [< dialectal alteration of ME *fixen* < OE *fyxe.*] —**vix′en·ish** *adj.*

viz. *abbr.* videlicet

Vi·za·ga·pa·tam (vĭ-zä′gə-pŭt′əm) See Visakhapatnam.

viz·ard also **vis·ard** (vĭz′ərd, -ärd′) *n.* **1.** A visor or mask. **2.** A disguise. [Alteration of obsolete *vizar* < ME *viser.* See VISOR.]

vi·zier (vĭ-zîr′, vĭz′yər) *n.* A high officer in a Muslim government, esp. in the Ottoman Empire. [Turk. *vezir* < Ar. *wazīr,* burdened, minister < *'azara,* to help, derived form of *'azara,* to surround, derived form of *wazara,* to carry a burden.] —**vi·zier′ate** (vĭ-zîr′ĭt, -āt′, vĭz′yər-ĭt, -yə-rāt′) *n.* —**vi·zier′i·al** *adj.*

vi·zor (vī′zər) *n. & v.* Variant of **visor.**

vizs·la (vĭzh′lä) *n.* Any of a Hungarian breed of shorthaired medium-sized hunting dogs having a deep rust-gold coat and a docked tail. [Hung.]

VJ *abbr.* video jockey

V-J Day (vē′jā′) *n.* August 15, 1945, the day on which the Allies announced the surrender of Japanese forces during World War II. [*V(ictory in) J(apan) Day.*]

VL *abbr.* Vulgar Latin

Vla·di·kav·kaz (vlăd′ĭ-kăf′kăz′, vlə-dyĭ-kəf-käs′) A city of SW Russia at the foot of the Caucasus Mts. NNW of Tbilisi; founded 1784. Pop. 307,575.

Vla·di·mir (vlăd′ə-mîr′, vlə-dyē′mîr′) A city of W-central Russia E of Moscow; founded c. 10th cent. Pop. 335,352.

Vla·di·vos·tok (vlăd′ə-və-stŏk′, -vŏs′tŏk′, vlə-dyə-və-stôk′) A city of extreme SE Russia on an arm of the Sea of Japan; a naval base since 1872. Pop. 637,351.

Vla·minck (vlä-măNk′), **Maurice de** 1876–1958. French artist who was a leading exponent of fauvism.

VLBI *abbr.* very long baseline interferometry

VLF *abbr.* very low frequency

Vlis·sing·en (vlĭs′ĭng-ən) also **Flush·ing** (flŭsh′ĭng) A city of SW Netherlands on an island in the Scheldt estuary and the North Sea; chartered 1247. Pop. 26,500.

Vlo·rë (vlôr′ə, vlŏr′ə) also **Vlo·ne** (vlō′nə) A city of SW Albania on **Vlorë Bay,** an inlet of the Adriatic Sea; site of the proclamation of Albania's independence in 1912. Pop. 61,100.

VLSI *abbr. Electronics* very-large-scale integration

Vl·ta·va (vŭl′tə-və) A river of W Czech Republic flowing c. 434 km (270 mi) to the Elbe R.

VMD *abbr. Latin* Veterinariae Medicinae Doctor (Doctor of Veterinary Medicine)

V-neck (vē′nĕk′) *n.* A V-shaped neckline, as of a sweater.

VO *abbr.* voice-over

vo. *abbr.* verso

VOA *abbr.* Voice of America

voc. *abbr.* **1.** vocational **2.** vocative

vo·ca·ble (vō′kə-bəl) *n.* A word considered only as a sequence of sounds or letters rather than as a unit of meaning. ❖ *adj.* Capable of being voiced or spoken. [Fr. < OFr. < Lat. *vocābulum,* name < *vocāre,* to call. See **wekʷ-** in App.]

vo·cab·u·lar·y (vō-kăb′yə-lĕr′ē) *n., pl.* **-ies 1.** All the words of a language. **2.** The sum of words used by, understood by, or at the command of a particular person or group. **3.** A list of words and often phrases, usu. arranged alphabetically and defined or translated; a lexicon or glossary. **4.** A supply of expressive means; a repertoire of communication: *a dancer's vocabulary of movement.* [Fr. *vocabulaire* < OFr. < Med.Lat. *vocābulārium* < neut. of *vocābulārius,* of words < Lat. *vocābulum,* name. See VOCABLE.]

vo·cal (vō′kəl) *adj.* **1.** Of or relating to the voice: *vocal organs.* **2.** Uttered or produced by the voice. **3.** Having a voice; capable of emitting sound or speech. **4.** Full of voices; resounding. **5.** Tending to express oneself often or freely; outspoken: *a vocal critic.* **6.** *Linguistics* **a.** Of or resembling vowels; vocalic. **b.** Voiced. **7.** *Music* Of, relating to, or performed by singing: *vocal music.* ❖ *n.* **1.** A vocal sound. **2.** *Music* A popular composition for a singer, often with instrumental accompaniment. [ME < OFr. < Lat. *vocālis* < *vōx, vōc-,* voice. See **wekʷ-** in App.] —**vo′cal·ly** *adv.* —**vo′cal·ness** *n.*

vocal cords *pl.n.* Either of two pairs of bands or folds of mucous membrane in the throat that project into the larynx, the lower pair of which produces sound when air is passed up from the lungs.

vocal folds *pl.n.* Vocal cords.

vo·cal·ic (vō-kăl′ĭk) *adj.* **1.** Containing, marked by, or consisting of vowels. **2.** Of, relating to, or having the nature of a vowel. —**vo·cal′i·cal·ly** *adv.*

vo·cal·ise¹ (vō′kə-lēz′) *n.* An exercise, composition, or arrangement in which a performer sings solmization syllables or other meaningless vocal sounds rather than a text. [Fr. < *vocaliser,* to vocalize < *vocal,* vocal < OFr. See VOCAL.]

vo·cal·ise² (vō′kə-līz′) *v. Chiefly British* Variant of **vocalize.**

vo·cal·ism (vō′kə-lĭz′əm) *n.* **1.** Use of the voice in speaking or singing. **2.** *Music* The act, technique, or art of singing. **3.** *Linguistics* **a.** A vowel sound. **b.** A system of vowels used in a language or dialect. —**vo′cal·is′tic** *adj.*

vo·cal·ist (vō′kə-lĭst) *n.* A singer.

vo·cal·ize (vō′kə-līz′) *v.* **-ized, -iz·ing, -iz·es** —*tr.* **1.** To produce with the voice. **2.** To give voice to; articulate. **3.** To mark (a vowelless Hebrew text, for example) with vowel points. **4.** *Linguistics* **a.** To change (a consonant) into a vowel during articulation. **b.** To voice. —*intr.* **1a.** To use the voice. **b.** *Music* To sing. **2.** *Linguistics* To be changed into a vowel. —**vo′cal·i·za′tion** (-kə-lĭ-zā′shən) *n.* —**vo′cal·iz′er** *n.*

vocal tract *n.* The airway used in the production of speech, esp. the passage above the larynx, including the mouth, pharynx, and nasal cavities.

vo·ca·tion (vō-kā′shən) *n.* **1.** A regular occupation, esp. one for which a person is particularly suited or qualified. **2.** An inclination, as if in response to a summons, to undertake a certain kind of work, esp. a religious career; a calling. [Ult. < Lat. *vocātiō, vocātiōn-,* a calling < *vocātus,* p. part. of *vocāre,* to call. See **wekʷ-** in App.]

vo·ca·tion·al (vō-kā′shə-nəl) *adj.* **1.** Of or relating to a vocation or vocations: *vocational counseling.* **2.** Relating to, providing, or undergoing training in a special skill to be pursued in a trade: *vocational students.* —**vo·ca′tion·al·ly** *adv.*

vo·ca·tion·al·ism (vō-kā′shə-nə-lĭz′əm) *n.* The stressing of

vizsla

vocational training in education. —**vo•ca′tion•al•ist** *n.*

vocational school *n.* A school, esp. one on a secondary level, that offers instruction and practical introductory experience in skilled trades such as mechanics, carpentry, and plumbing.

voc•a•tive (vŏk′ə-tĭv) *adj.* **1.** Relating to, characteristic of, or used in calling. **2.** Relating to or being a grammatical case that indicates the person or thing being addressed. ❖ *n.* **1.** The vocative case. **2.** A word in the vocative case. [ME *vocatif* < OFr. < Lat. *vocātīvus* (*cāsus*), vocative (case) < *vocātus,* p. part. of *vocāre,* to call. See VOCATION.] —**voc′a•tive•ly** *adv.*

vo•cif•er•ant (vō-sĭf′ər-ənt) *adj.* Vociferous.

vo•cif•er•ate (vō-sĭf′ə-rāt′) *tr. & intr.v.* **-at•ed, -at•ing, -ates** To utter (something) or cry out loudly and vehemently, esp. in protest. [Lat. *vōciferārī, vōciferāt-* < *vōcifer,* carrying the voice : *vōx, vōc-,* voice; see VOICE + *ferre,* to carry; see **bher-¹** in App.] —**vo•cif′er•a′tion** *n.* —**vo•cif′er•a′tor** *n.*

vo•cif•er•ous (vō-sĭf′ər-əs) *adj.* Making, given to, or marked by noisy and vehement outcry. —**vo•cif′er•ous•ly** *adv.* —**vo•cif′er•ous•ness** *n.*

vo•cod•er (vō′kō′dər) *n.* An electronic device or system for synthesizing speech. [VO(ICE) + COD(E) + -ER¹.]

vod•ka (vŏd′kə) *n.* An alcoholic liquor originally distilled from fermented wheat mash but now also made from a mash of rye, corn, or potatoes. [Russ., dim. of *voda,* water. See **wed-** in App.]

vo•doun or **vo•dun** (vō-dōōn′) *n.* See **voodoo** 1. [Haitian Creole < Ewe *vodu* or Fon *vodun.*]

vogue (vōg) *n.* **1.** The prevailing fashion, practice, or style: *Hoop skirts were once the vogue.* **2.** Popular acceptance or favor; popularity: *a game no longer in vogue.* ❖ *intr.v.* **vogued, vogue•ing** or **vogu•ing, vogues** To dance by striking a series of rigid, stylized poses evocative of fashion models during photograph shoots. [Fr. < OFr., prob. < *voguer,* to sail, row, of Gmc. orig.; see **wegh-** in App. V., after the fashion magazine *Vogue.*]

vogu•ish (vō′gĭsh) *adj.* **1.** Fashionable; chic: *a suit of voguish cut.* **2.** Temporarily in frequent use; faddish: *voguish terminology.* —**vogu′ish•ly** *adv.* —**vogu′ish•ness** *n.*

Vo•gul (vō′gōōl) *n., pl.* **Vogul** or **-guls** **1.** A member of a people inhabiting the region of the Ob River in western Siberia, related to the Ostyak. **2.** Their Ugric language.

voice (vois) *n.* **1a.** The sound produced by the vocal organs of a vertebrate, esp. a human. **b.** The ability to produce such sounds. **2.** A specified quality, condition, or pitch of vocal sound. **3.** *Linguistics* Expiration of air through vibrating vocal cords, used in the production of vowels and voiced consonants. **4.** A sound resembling or reminiscent of vocal utterance. **5.** *Music* **a.** Musical sound produced by vibration of the human vocal cords and resonated within the throat and head cavities. **b.** The quality or condition of a person's singing. **c.** A singer. **d.** One of the individual parts or strands in a composition. **6a.** Expression; utterance. **b.** A medium or agency of expression. **c.** The right or opportunity to express a choice or opinion. **7.** *Grammar* A property of verbs or a set of verb inflections indicating the relation between the subject and the action expressed by the verb: *"Birds build nests" uses the active voice; "nests built by birds" uses the passive voice.* **8.** The distinctive style or manner of expression of an author or of a character in a book. ❖ *tr.v.* **voiced, voic•ing, voic•es** **1.** To give voice to; utter. See Syns at **vent¹**. **2.** *Linguistics* To pronounce with vibration of the vocal cords. **3.** *Music* **a.** To provide (a composition) with voice parts. **b.** To regulate the tone of (the pipes of an organ, for example). **4.** To provide the voice for (a cartoon character, for example). —*idiom:* **with one voice** In complete agreement; unanimously. [ME < OFr. *vois* < Lat. *vōx, vōc-.* See **wek*-** in App.]

voice box *n.* The larynx.

voiced (voist) *adj.* **1.** Having a voice or a specified kind of voice. Often used in combination: *harsh-voiced.* **2.** *Linguistics* Uttered with vibration of the vocal cords, as the sounds (b) and (d). —**voiced′ness** (voist′nĭs, voi′sĭd-) *n.*

voice•ful (vois′fəl) *adj.* Having a voice, esp. a loud voice; resounding. —**voice′ful•ness** *n.*

voice•less (vois′lĭs) *adj.* **1.** Having no voice; mute. **2.** *Linguistics* Uttered without vibration of the vocal cords, as the sounds (t) and (p). —**voice′less•ly** *adv.* —**voice′less•ness** *n.*

voice mail or **voice•mail** (vois′māl′) *n.* An interactive computerized system for answering and routing telephone calls, for recording, saving, and relaying messages, and sometimes for paging the user.

voice-o•ver or **voice•o•ver** (vois′ō′vər) *n.* **1.** The voice of an unseen narrator or of an onscreen character not seen speaking in a movie or a television broadcast. **2.** A film or videotape recording narrated by a voice-over.

voice part *n.* **1.** A part or strand of a musical composition written for the human voice. **2.** See **voice** 5d.

voice•print (vois′prĭnt′) *n.* An electronically recorded graphic representation of a person's voice, uniquely characteristic of the individual speaker.

voic•er (voi′sər) *n.* **1.** One that voices: *a voicer of criticism.* **2.** *Music* A specialist in regulating the tone of organ pipes.

voice vote *n.* A parliamentary vote that is determined by the relative volume of noise of those shouting "aye" and "no" or "nay."

voic•ing (voi′sĭng) *n.* **1.** The act, practice, or process of one

that voices. **2.** *Music* Tonal quality of an instrument in an ensemble, esp. a jazz ensemble, or of the ensemble as a whole. **3.** The vibration of the vocal cords during the production of speech or a speech sound.

void (void) *adj.* **1.** Containing no matter; empty. **2.** Not occupied; unfilled. **3.** Completely lacking; devoid: *void of understanding.* **4.** Ineffective; useless. **5.** Having no legal force or validity; null: *a contract rendered void.* **6.** *Games* Lacking cards of a particular suit in a hand. ❖ *n.* **1a.** An empty space. **b.** A vacuum. **2.** An open space or a break in continuity; a gap. **3.** A feeling or state of emptiness, loneliness, or loss. **4.** *Games* Absence of cards of a particular suit in a hand. ❖ *v.* **void•ed, void•ing, voids** —*tr.* **1.** To take out (the contents of something); empty. **2.** To excrete (body wastes). **3.** To leave; vacate. **4.** To make void; invalidate. —*intr.* To excrete body wastes. [ME < OFr. *voide,* fem. of *voit* < VLat. **vocitus,* alteration of Lat. *vacīvus, vocīvus,* var. of *vacuus* < *vacāre,* to be empty.] —**void′er** *n.*

void•a•ble (voi′də-bəl) *adj.* That can be voided or esp. annulled: *voidable contracts.* —**void′a•ble•ness** *n.*

void•ance (void′ns) *n.* **1.** The act of voiding. **2.** The condition of being vacant; emptiness.

void•ed (voi′dĭd) *adj. Heraldry* Having the central area cut out or left vacant, leaving an outline or narrow border.

voi•là (vwä-lä′) *interj.* Used to call attention to or express satisfaction with a thing shown or accomplished. [Fr. : *voi,* sing. imper. of *voir,* to see (< OFr.) + *là,* there (< OFr. *la, lai,* prob. < Lat. *illāc,* by that way : *illā,* ablative sing. fem. of *ille,* that; see **al-** in App. + *-ce,* deictic particle).]

voile (voil) *n.* A light plain-weave sheer fabric of cotton, rayon, silk, or wool used esp. for making dresses and curtains. [Fr. < OFr. *veile,* veil < Lat. *vēla,* neut. pl. of *vēlum,* covering.]

voir dire (vwär dîr′) *n.* A preliminary examination of prospective jurors or witnesses under oath to determine their competence or suitability. [AN, to speak the truth : Lat. *vērus,* true; see **wērə-o-** in App. + Lat. *dīcere,* to say; see **deik-** in App.]

Voj•vo•di•na (voi′və-dē′nə) A region of N Serbia; formerly part of Hungary and an autonomous region of Yugoslavia after 1946.

vol. *abbr.* **1.** volcano **2.** volume **3.** volunteer

Vo•lans (vō′lănz′) *n.* A constellation in the polar region of the celestial Southern Hemisphere near Carina and Dorado. [Lat. *volāns,* pr. part. of *volāre,* to fly.]

vo•lant (vō′lənt) *adj.* **1.** Flying or capable of flying. **2.** Moving quickly or nimbly. **3.** *Heraldry* Depicted with the wings extended as in flying. [Lat. *volāns, volant-,* pr. part. of *volāre,* to fly. Sense 3 < Fr. < OFr., pr. part. of *voler,* to fly < Lat. *volāre.*]

Vo•la•pük (vō′lə-pook′, vŏl′ə-, vōl′ə-) *n.* An artificial international language based on English. [Volapük : *vola,* genitive sing. of *vol,* world (alteration of E. WORLD) + *pük,* speech (alteration of E. SPEECH).]

vo•lar (vō′lər) *adj.* Of or relating to the sole of the foot or the palm of the hand. [< Lat. *vola,* sole, palm.]

vol•a•tile (vŏl′ə-tl, -tīl′) *adj.* **1.** *Chemistry* **a.** Evaporating readily at normal temperatures and pressures. **b.** That can be readily vaporized. **2a.** Tending to vary often or widely, as in price. **b.** Inconstant; fickle. **c.** Lighthearted; flighty. **d.** Ephemeral; fleeting. **3.** Tending to violence; explosive. **4.** Flying or capable of flying; volant. [Fr. < OFr. < Lat. *volātilis,* flying < *volātus,* p. part. of *volāre,* to fly.] —**vol′a•tile** *n.* —**vol′a•til′i•ty** (-tĭl′ĭ-tē), **vol′a•tile•ness** (-tl-nĭs, -tīl′-) *n.*

volatile oil *n.* A rapidly evaporating oil, esp. an essential oil.

vol•a•til•ize (vŏl′ə-tl-īz′) *intr. & tr.v.* **-ized, -iz•ing, -iz•es** **1.** To become or make volatile. **2.** To evaporate or cause to evaporate. —**vol′a•til•iz′a•ble** *adj.* —**vol′a•til•i•za′tion** (-ĭ-zā′shən) *n.* —**vol′a•til•iz′er** *n.*

vol-au-vent (vô′lō-vän′) *n.* A light pastry shell filled with a ragout. [Fr. : *vol,* flight + *au,* with the + *vent,* wind.]

vol•can•ic (vŏl-kăn′ĭk, vôl-) *adj.* **1.** Of, resembling, or caused by a volcano or volcanoes. **2.** Produced by or discharged from a volcano. **3.** Characterized by the presence of volcanoes. **4.** Powerfully explosive. —**vol•can′i•cal•ly** *adv.*

volcanic arc *n.* A usu. arc-shaped chain of volcanoes located on the margin of the overriding plate at a convergent plate boundary.

volcanic glass *n.* Natural glass produced by the cooling of molten lava too quickly to permit crystallization.

vol•ca•nism (vŏl′kə-nĭz′əm) also **vul•ca•nism** (vŭl′-) *n.* **1.** Volcanic force or activity. **2.** The phenomena associated with volcanic activity.

vol•ca•nize (vŏl′kə-nīz′) *tr.v.* **-nized, -niz•ing, -niz•es** To subject to or change by the effects of volcanic heat. —**vol′ca•ni•za′tion** (-nĭ-zā′shən) *n.*

vol•ca•no (vŏl-kā′nō) *n., pl.* **-noes** or **-nos** **1a.** An opening in the earth's crust through which molten lava, ash, and gases are ejected. **b.** A similar opening on the surface of another planet. **2.** A mountain formed by the materials ejected from a volcano. [Ital. < Sp. *volcán* or Port. *volcão,* both prob. < Lat. *volcānus,* fire, flames < *Volcānus,* Vulcan.]

Volcano Islands A group of Japanese islands in the NW Pacific N of the Mariana Is.

vol•ca•nol•o•gy (vŏl′kə-nŏl′ə-jē, vôl′-) also **vul•ca•nol•o•gy**

(vŭl′-) *n.* The scientific study of volcanoes. —**vol′ca•no•log′i•cal** (-nə-lŏj′ĭ-kəl) *adj.* —**vol′ca•nol′o•gist** *n.*

vole[1] (vōl) *n.* Any of various rodents of the genus *Microtus* and related genera, resembling rats or mice but having a shorter tail and limbs and a heavier body. [Short for obsolete *volemouse,* perh. < Norw. **vollmus* : ON *vǫllr,* field + ON *mūs,* mouse.]

vole[2] (vōl) *n. Games* The winning of all the tricks during the play of one hand; a grand slam. [Fr., prob. < *voler,* to fly < OFr. < Lat. *volāre,* to fly.]

Vol•ga (vŏl′gə, vôl′-, vōl′-) A river of W Russia rising in the Valdai Hills NW of Moscow and flowing c. 3,701 km (2,300 mi) to the Caspian Sea.

Vol•go•grad (vŏl′gə-grăd′, vōl′-, vəl-gə-grät′) Formerly **Sta•lin•grad** (stä′lĭn-grăd′, stə-lyĭn-grät′) A city of SW Russia on the Volga R. NE of Rostov; founded 1589. The city was besieged and severely damaged during a prolonged battle in World War II, with extensive casualties of both German and Soviet troops. Pop. 996,992.

vol•i•tant (vŏl′ĭ-tnt) *adj.* **1.** Flying or capable of flying. **2.** Moving about rapidly. [Lat. *volitāns, volitant-,* pr. part. of *volitāre,* to fly to and fro, freq. of *volāre,* to fly.]

vol•i•ta•tion (vŏl′ĭ-tā′shən) *n.* **1.** The act of flying; flight. **2.** The ability to fly. —**vol′i•ta′tion•al** *adj.*

vo•li•tion (və-lĭsh′ən) *n.* **1.** The act or an instance of making a conscious choice or decision. **2.** A conscious choice or decision. **3.** The power or faculty of choosing; the will. [Fr. < Med.Lat. *volitiō, volitiōn-* < Lat. *velle, vol-,* to wish.] —**vo•li′tion•al** *adj.* —**vo•li′tion•al•ly** *adv.*

vol•i•tive (vŏl′ĭ-tĭv) *adj.* **1.** Of, relating to, or originating in the will. **2.** Expressing a wish or permission.

volks•lied (fōks′lēt′, fôlks′-) *n., pl.* **-lie•der** (-lē′dər) A folk song. [Ger. : *Volks,* genitive of *Volk,* people (< MHGer. *volc* < OHGer. *folc;* see **pelə-**[1] in App.) + *Lied,* song; see LIED.]

vol•ley (vŏl′ē) *n., pl.* **-leys 1a.** A simultaneous discharge of a number of missiles. **b.** The missiles thus discharged. **2.** A bursting forth of many things together: *a volley of oaths.* **3.** *Sports* **a.** The flight of a ball before it touches the ground. **b.** A shot, esp. in tennis, made by striking the ball before it touches the ground. ❖ *v.* **-leyed, -ley•ing, -leys** —*tr.* **1.** To discharge in or as if in a volley. **2.** *Sports* To strike (a tennis ball, for example) before it touches the ground. —*intr.* **1.** To be discharged in or as if in a volley. **2.** *Sports* To make a volley, esp. in tennis. **3.** To move rapidly, forcefully, or loudly like missiles: *The hailstones volleyed down.* [Fr. *volée* < OFr. < *voler,* to fly < Lat. *volāre,* to fly.] —**vol′ley•er** *n.*

vol•ley•ball (vŏl′ē-bôl′) *n.* **1.** A game played on a rectangular court divided by a high net, in which each of two teams tries to ground the ball on the other team's side of the net. **2.** The inflated, spherical ball used in this game. —**vol′ley•ball′er** *n.*

Vo•log•da (vô′ləg-də) A city of W Russia NNE of Moscow; founded in the mid-12th cent. Pop. 289,537.

Vó•los (vō′lŏs′, vô′lôs) A city of E Greece in Thessaly on the **Gulf of Vólos,** an inlet of the Aegean Sea. Pop. 71,378.

vol•plane (vŏl′plān′, vôl′-) *intr.v.* **-planed, -plan•ing, -planes 1a.** To glide toward the earth in an airplane with the engine cut off. **b.** To glide toward the earth with the engine cut off. Used of an airplane. **2.** To make one's way or go by gliding. ❖ *n.* The act or an instance of volplaning. [< Fr. *vol plané,* gliding flight : *vol,* flight (< OFr. < *voler,* to fly; see VOLLEY) + *plané,* gliding, p. part. of *planer,* to glide; see PLANE[3].]

Vol•sci (vôl′skē, vŏl′sī, -sē, -shē) *pl.n.* A people of ancient Italy whose land was conquered by Rome in the fourth century B.C.

Vol•scian (vŏl′shən, vôl′skē-ən) *adj.* Of or relating to the Volsci or their language. ❖ *n.* **1.** The Italic language of the Volsci. **2.** A member of the Volsci.

Vol•stead (vŏl′stĕd′, vôl′-, vōl′-), **Andrew John** 1860–1947. Amer. legislator who sponsored the Volstead Act (1919), prohibiting the sale, manufacture, and transportation of alcoholic beverages.

volt[1] (vōlt) *n.* The International System unit of electric potential and electromotive force, equal to the difference of electric potential between two points on a conducting wire carrying a constant current of one ampere when the power dissipated between the points is one watt. [After Count Alessandro VOLTA.]

volt[2] (vōlt, vôlt) *n. Sports* A sudden movement made in avoiding a thrust in fencing. [Fr. *volte* < Ital. *volta,* turn < *voltare,* to turn, leap. See VAULT[2].]

Vol•ta (vŏl′tə, vōl′-, vôl′-) A river formed in central Ghana by the confluence of the White Volta and the Black Volta and flowing c. 467 km (290 mi) through artificial **Lake Volta** to the Bight of Benin in the Gulf of Guinea.

Vol•ta (vōl′tə, -tä), Count **Alessandro** 1745–1827. Italian physicist who invented the first electric battery (1800).

volt•age (vōl′tĭj) *n.* Electromotive force or potential difference, usu. expressed in volts.

voltage divider *n.* A number of resistors in series provided with taps at certain points to make available a fixed or variable fraction of the applied voltage.

vol•ta•ic (vŏl-tā′ĭk, vōl-, vôl-) *adj.* **1.** Of, relating to, or being electricity or electric current produced by chemical action; galvanic. **2.** Producing electricity by chemical action. [After Count Alessandro VOLTA.]

voltaic cell *n.* See **primary cell.**

voltaic pile *n.* A source of electricity consisting of a number of alternating disks of two different metals separated by acid-moistened pads, forming primary cells connected in series.

Vol•taire (vōl-târ′, vŏl-, vôl-tĕr′) Pen name of François Marie Arouet. 1694–1778. French philosopher and writer whose works include *Candide* (1759).

vol•ta•ism (vŏl′tə-ĭz′əm, vōl′-, vôl′-) *n.* See **galvanism** 1.

volt•am•me•ter (vōl-tăm′mē′tər, vōlt′ăm′-) *n.* An instrument for measuring electrical current or potential.

volt-am•pere (vōlt′ăm′pîr′) *n.* A unit of electric power in an alternating current circuit, equivalent to one watt.

volte-face (vôlt-fäs′, vôl′tə-) *n.* A reversal, as in policy; an about-face. [Fr. < Ital. *voltafaccia* : *volta* (< *voltare,* to turn; see VAULT[2]) + *faccia,* face (< VLat. **facia;* see FACE).]

volt•me•ter (vōlt′mē′tər) *n.* An instrument for measuring potential differences in volts.

vol•u•ble (vŏl′yə-bəl) *adj.* **1.** Marked by a ready flow of speech; fluent. **2a.** Turning easily on an axis; rotating. **b.** *Botany* Twining or twisting. [ME, moving easily < OFr. < Lat. *volūbilis,* revolving, fluent < *volvere,* to roll. See **wel-** in App.] —**vol′u•bil′i•ty, vol′u•ble•ness** *n.* —**vol′u•bly** *adv.*

vol•ume (vŏl′yo͞om, -yəm) *n.* **1a.** A collection of written or printed sheets bound together; a book. **b.** One of the books of a work printed and bound in more than one book. **c.** A series of issues of a periodical, usu. covering one calendar year. **d.** A unit of written material assembled together and cataloged in a library. **2.** A roll of parchment; a scroll. **3a.** The amount of space occupied by a three-dimensional object or region of space, expressed in cubic units. **b.** The capacity of such a region or of a specified container, expressed in cubic units. **4a.** Amount; quantity: *a low volume of business.* **b.** A large amount. Often used in the plural: *volumes of praise.* **5a.** The amplitude or loudness of a sound. **b.** A control, as on a radio, for adjusting amplitude or loudness. [ME < OFr. < Lat. *volūmen,* roll of writing < *volvere,* to roll. See **wel-** in App.]

vol•umed (vŏl′yo͞omd, -yəmd) *adj.* **1.** Consisting of a volume or volumes. Often used in combination: *a large-volumed edition.* **2.** Formed or moving in rolling or rounded masses.

vol•u•me•ter (vŏl′yo͞o-mē′tər) *n.* Any of several instruments for measuring volume.

vol•u•met•ric (vŏl′yo͞o-mĕt′rĭk) *adj.* Of or relating to measurement by volume. —**vol′u•met′ri•cal•ly** *adv.*

volumetric analysis *n.* **1.** Quantitative analysis using accurately measured titrated volumes of standard chemical solutions. **2.** Analysis of a gas by volume.

vo•lu•mi•nous (və-lo͞o′mə-nəs) *adj.* **1.** Having great volume, fullness, size, or number. **2.** Filling or capable of filling a large volume or many volumes. **3.** Ample or lengthy in speech or writing. **4.** Having many coils; winding. [LLat. *volūminōsus,* having many folds < Lat. *volūmen, volūmin-,* roll of writing. See VOLUME.] —**vo•lu′mi•nos′i•ty** (-nŏs′ĭ-tē), **vo•lu′mi•nous•ness** *n.* —**vo•lu′mi•nous•ly** *adv.*

vol•un•ta•rism (vŏl′ən-tə-rĭz′əm) *n.* **1.** The use of or reliance on voluntary action. **2.** A theory or doctrine that regards the will as the fundamental principle of the individual or of the universe. —**vol′un•ta•rist** *n.* —**vol′un•ta•ris′tic** *adj.*

vol•un•tar•y (vŏl′ən-tĕr′ē) *adj.* **1.** Done or undertaken of one's own free will. **2.** Acting or done willingly and without constraint or expectation of reward: *voluntary community work.* **3.** Normally controlled by or subject to individual volition: *voluntary muscle contractions.* **4.** Capable of making choices; having the faculty of will. **5.** Supported by contributions or charitable donations rather than by government appropriations. ❖ *n., pl.* **-ies 1.** *Music* **a.** A short piece of music played as an introduction to a larger work. **b.** A piece for solo organ played before, during, or after a religious service. **2.** A volunteer. [ME < Lat. *voluntārius* < *voluntās,* choice < *velle, vol-,* to wish.] —**vol′un•tar′i•ly** (-târ′ə-lē) *adv.* —**vol′un•tar′i•ness** *n.*

SYNONYMS *voluntary, intentional, deliberate, willful, willing* These adjectives mean being or resulting from one's own free will. *Voluntary* implies the operation of unforced choice: *"Ignorance, when it is voluntary, is criminal"* (Samuel Johnson). *Intentional* applies to something undertaken to further a plan or realize an aim: *"I will abstain from all intentional wrongdoing and harm"* (Hippocratic Oath). *Deliberate* stresses premeditation and full awareness of the character and consequences of one's acts: *taking deliberate and decisive action. Willful* implies deliberate, headstrong persistence in a self-determined course of action: *a willful waste of time. Willing* suggests ready or cheerful acquiescence in the proposals or requirements of another: *"The first requisite of a good citizen . . . is that he shall be able and willing to pull his weight"* (Theodore Roosevelt).

vol•un•tar•y•ism (vŏl′ən-tĕr′ē-ĭz′əm) *n.* Reliance on voluntary contributions rather than government funds, as for churches or schools; voluntarism. —**vol′un•tar′y•ist** *n.*

voluntary muscle *n.* Muscle normally controlled by individual volition.

vol•un•teer (vŏl′ən-tîr′) *n.* **1.** A person who performs or offers to perform a service voluntarily. **2.** *Botany* A cultivated plant

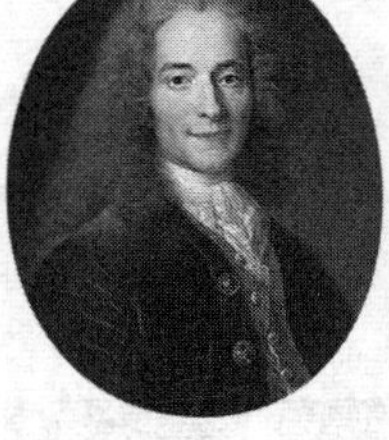

Voltaire
detail from *Voltaire in 1718,* after a portrait by Nicolas de Largillière (1656?–1746)

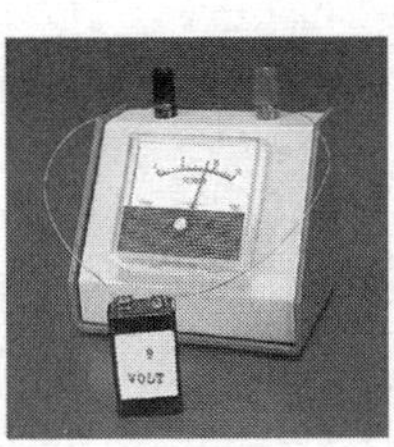

voltmeter
checking the voltage of a nine-volt battery

ă	pat	oi	boy
ā	pay	ou	out
âr	care	o͝o	took
ä	father	o͞o	boot
ĕ	pet	ŭ	cut
ē	be	ûr	urge
ĭ	pit	th	thin
ī	pie	*th*	this
îr	pier	hw	which
ŏ	pot	zh	vision
ō	toe	ə	about, item
ô	paw		

Stress marks:
′ (primary);
′ (secondary), as in
lexicon (lĕk′sĭ-kŏn′)

growing from self-sown or accidentally dropped seed. ❖ *adj.* **1.** Being, consisting of, or done by volunteers. **2.** *Botany* Growing from self-sown or accidentally dropped seed. Used of a cultivated plant or crop. ❖ *v.* **-teered, -teer·ing, -teers** —*tr.* To give or offer to give voluntarily: *volunteer to give blood.* —*intr.* **1.** To perform or offer to perform a service of one's own free will. **2.** To do charitable or helpful work without pay. [Obsolete Fr. *voluntaire* < OFr., voluntary < Lat. *voluntārius.* See VOLUNTARY.]

vol·un·teer·ism (vŏl′ən-tîr′ĭz′əm) *n.* Use of or reliance on volunteers, esp. to perform social or educational work.

vo·lup·tu·ar·y (və-lŭp′chōō-ĕr′ē) *n., pl.* **-ies** A person whose life is given over to luxury and sensual pleasures; a sensualist. [Fr. *voluptuaire* < OFr. < LLat. *voluptuārius,* var. of Lat. *voluptārius,* devoted to pleasure < *voluptās,* pleasure < *volup,* with pleasure.] —**vo·lup′tu·ar′y** *adj.*

vo·lup·tu·ous (və-lŭp′chōō-əs) *adj.* **1.** Giving, characterized by, or suggesting ample, unrestrained pleasure to the senses: *a voluptuous ripe fruit.* **2a.** Devoted to or indulging in sensual pleasures. **b.** Directed toward or anticipating sensual pleasure: *voluptuous thoughts.* **c.** Arising from or contributing to the satisfaction of sensuous or sensual desires. [ME < OFr. *voluptueux* < Lat. *voluptuōsus,* full of pleasure < *voluptās,* pleasure. See VOLUPTUARY.] —**vo·lup′tu·ous·ly** *adv.* —**vo·lup′tu·ous·ness** *n.*

vo·lute (və-lōōt′) *n.* **1.** A spiral scroll-like ornament such as that on an Ionic capital. **2a.** A spiral formation, such as a whorl of a gastropod shell. **b.** Any of various marine gastropod mollusks of the family Volutidae, having a spiral, often colorfully marked shell. [Fr. < Ital. *voluta* < Lat. *volūta* < fem. p. part. of *volvere,* to turn, roll. See **wel-** in App.] —**vo·lut′ed** (-lōō′tĭd) *adj.*

vo·lu·tion (və-lōō′shən) *n.* **1.** A turn or twist about a center; a spiral. **2.** *Zoology* One of the whorls of a spiral gastropod shell. [< Lat. *volūtus,* p. part. of *volvere,* to turn. See VOLUTE.]

vol·va (vŏl′və, vôl′-) *n.* A cuplike structure around the base of the stalk of certain fungi. [Lat., a covering. See **wel-** in App.] —**vol′vate′** (-vāt′) *adj.*

vol·vox (vŏl′vŏks′, vôl′-) *n.* Any of various freshwater algae of the genus *Volvox* that form spherical multicellular colonies. [NLat. *Volvox,* genus name < Lat. *volvere,* to roll. See **wel-** in App.]

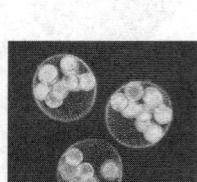

volvox

vol·vu·lus (vŏl′vyə-ləs, vôl′-) *n.* Abnormal twisting of the intestine causing obstruction. [NLat. < Lat. *volvere,* to turn. See VOLVOX.]

Volzh·skiy (vôlzh′skē, vôlsh′-) A city of SW Russia on the Volga R., a suburb of Volgograd. Pop. 281,947.

vo·mer (vō′mər) *n.* A thin flat bone forming the inferior and posterior part of the nasal septum and dividing the nostrils in most vertebrates. [Lat. *vōmer,* plowshare.] —**vo′mer·ine′** (-mə-rīn′) *adj.*

vom·it (vŏm′ĭt) *v.* **-it·ed, -it·ing, -its** —*intr.* **1.** To eject part or all of the contents of the stomach through the mouth, usu. in a series of involuntary spasmic movements. **2.** To be discharged forcefully and abundantly; spew or gush. —*tr.* **1.** To eject (contents of the stomach) through the mouth. **2.** To eject or discharge in a gush; spew out. ❖ *n.* **1.** The act or an instance of vomiting from the stomach. **2.** Matter ejected in vomiting. **3.** An emetic. [ME *vomiten* < Lat. *vomitāre,* freq. of *vomere.* See **wemə-** in App.] —**vom′it·er** *n.* —**vom′i·tive** *adj. & n.*

vom·i·to·ry (vŏm′ĭ-tôr′ē, -tōr′ē) *adj.* Relating to or inducing vomiting. ❖ *n., pl.* **-ries** **1.** Something that induces vomiting. **2.** An aperture through which matter is discharged. **3.** One of the tunnellike passages of an amphitheater or stadium between the seats and the outside wall or passageway.

vom·i·tus (vŏm′ĭ-təs) *n.* Vomited matter. [Lat. < p. part. of *vomere,* to vomit. See VOMIT.]

Von·ne·gut (vŏn′ĭ-gət), **Kurt, Jr.** b. 1922. Amer. writer whose novels include *Slaughterhouse Five* (1969).

von Wil·le·brand's disease (vŏn wĭl′ə-brăndz′, fôn vĭl′ə-bränts′) *n.* A hereditary disease characterized by a tendency to hemorrhage, caused by a deficiency or abnormality of the blood proteins that control platelet activity. [After Erik Adolf *von Willebrand* (1870–1949), Finnish physician.]

voo·doo (vōō′dōō) *n., pl.* **-doos** **1.** A religion practiced chiefly in Caribbean countries, esp. Haiti, combining Roman Catholic ritual elements and West African animism, in which a supreme God rules a large pantheon of deities, deified ancestors, and saints, who communicate with believers in dreams, trances, and ritual possessions. **2.** A charm, fetish, spell, or curse holding magic power for adherents of voodoo. **3.** A practitioner, priest, or priestess of voodoo. **4.** Deceptive or delusive nonsense. ❖ *t.v.* **-dooed, -doo·ing, -doos** To place under the influence of a spell or curse; bewitch. ❖ *adj.* **1.** Of or relating to the beliefs or practices of voodoo. **2.** Based on unrealistic or delusive assumptions: *voodoo economics.* [Louisiana Fr. *voudou* < Ewe *vodu* and Fon *vodun.*]

voo·doo·ism (vōō′dōō-ĭz′əm) *n.* **1.** The practice and doctrines of voodoo. **2.** The practice of sorcery or witchcraft. —**voo′doo·ist** *n.* —**voo′doo·is′tic** *adj.*

vo·ra·cious (vô-rā′shəs, və-) *adj.* **1.** Consuming or eager to consume great amounts of food; ravenous. **2.** Having or marked by an insatiable appetite for an activity or pursuit; greedy: *a voracious reader.* [< Lat. *vorāx, vorāc-* < *vorāre,* to swallow, devour.]

—**vo·ra′cious·ly** *adv.* —**vo·rac′i·ty** (-răs′ĭ-tē), **vo·ra′cious·ness** *n.*

vor·la·ge (fôr′lä′gə, fōr′-) *n.* A posture in skiing in which the skier leans forward from the ankles, usu. without lifting the heels. [Ger. : *vor,* forward, before (< MHGer. < OHGer. *fora;* see **per**[1] in App.) + *Lage,* stance (< MHGer. *lāge* < OHGer. *lāga,* act of laying; see **legh-** in App.).]

Vo·ro·nezh (və-rô′nĭsh) A city of W Russia on the Don R. S of Lipetsk; founded 1586. Pop. 898,854.

Vo·ro·shi·lov (vôr′ə-shē′lôf′, -ləf), **Kliment Efremovich** 1881–1969. Soviet commissar for defense (1925–40).

Vo·ro·shi·lov·grad (vôr′ə-shē′ləf-grăd′, və-rə-shē-ləf-grät′) See **Luhans′k.**

–vorous *suff.* Eating; feeding on: *vermivorous.* [< Lat. *-vorus* < *vorāre,* to swallow, devour.]

Vor·ster (fôr′stər), **Balthazar Johannes** 1915–83. South African prime minister (1966–78).

vor·tex (vôr′tĕks′) *n., pl.* **-tex·es** or **-ti·ces** (-tĭ-sēz′) **1.** A spiral motion of fluid within a limited area, esp. a whirling mass of water or air that sucks everything near it toward its center. **2.** A place or situation regarded as drawing into its center all that surrounds it. [Lat. *vortex, vortic-,* var. of *vertex* < *vertere,* to turn. See **wer-**[2] in App.]

vor·ti·cal (vôr′tĭ-kəl) *adj.* Of, relating to, or moving in a vortex; whirling. —**vor′ti·cal·ly** *adv.*

vor·ti·cel·la (vôr′tĭ-sĕl′ə) *n., pl.* **-cel·lae** (-sĕl′ē) or **-cel·las** Any of various stalked bell-shaped ciliate protozoans of the genus *Vorticella,* living underwater often attached to a plant or other object. [NLat. *Vorticella,* genus name < Lat. *vortex, vortic-,* vortex. See VORTEX.]

vor·ti·cism (vôr′tĭ-sĭz′əm) *n.* A short-lived English movement in art and literature that arose in 1914 and was heavily influenced by cubism and futurism.

vor·tic·i·ty (vôr-tĭs′ĭ-tē) *n., pl.* **-ties** **1.** *Physics* A measure of the rate of rotational spin in a fluid. **2.** *Meteorology* A measure of the spin of an air mass such as a low- or high-pressure weather system.

vor·ti·cose (vôr′tĭ-kōs′) *adj.* Vortical.

vor·tig·i·nous (vôr-tĭj′ə-nəs) *adj.* Vortical. [Blend of VORTEX and VERTIGINOUS.]

Vosges (vōzh) A mountain range of NE France extending c. 193 km (120 mi) parallel to the Rhine R.

vo·ta·ry (vō′tə-rē) *n., pl.* **-ries** **1a.** One bound by vows to a life of religious worship or service. **b.** A devout adherent of a cult or religion; a committed worshiper: *the votaries of Isis.* **2.** One who is fervently devoted, as to a leader or ideal; a faithful follower. **3.** One who is filled with enthusiasm, as for a pursuit; an enthusiast. [< Lat. *vōtum,* vow. See VOTE.]

vote (vōt) *n.* **1a.** A formal expression of preference for a candidate for office or a proposed resolution of an issue. **b.** A means by which such a preference is made known, such as a marked ballot. **2.** The number of votes cast in an election or to resolve an issue: *a heavy vote.* **3.** A group of voters alike in some way. **4.** The act or process of voting: *took a vote.* **5.** The result of an election or referendum. **6.** The right to participate as a voter; suffrage. ❖ *v.* **vot·ed, vot·ing, votes** —*intr.* **1.** To express one's preference for a candidate or a proposed resolution of an issue; cast a vote. **2.** To express a choice or opinion. —*tr.* **1.** To express one's preference for by vote. **2.** To decide the disposition of by vote, as by electing or defeating: *vote in a new mayor.* **3.** To bring into existence or make available by vote. **4.** To be guided by in voting: *vote one's conscience.* **5.** To declare or pronounce by general consent. **6.** *Informal* To state as a preference or opinion. [ME, vow < Lat. *vōtum* < neut. p. part. of *vovēre,* to vow.] —**vot′a·ble, vote′a·ble** *adj.* —**vot′er** *n.*

vote·less (vōt′lĭs) *adj.* Having no vote; denied a vote or the right to vote.

vot·ing machine (vō′tĭng) *n.* An apparatus for use in polling places that mechanically records and counts votes.

vo·tive (vō′tĭv) *adj.* **1.** Given or dedicated in fulfillment of a vow or pledge: *a votive offering.* **2.** Expressing or symbolizing a wish, desire, or vow: *a votive prayer.* [Lat. *vōtīvus* < *vōtum,* vow. See VOTE.] —**vo′tive·ly** *adv.*

votive Mass *n. Roman Catholic Church* A Mass differing from the one prescribed for the day, said for a special intention.

vouch (vouch) *v.* **vouched, vouch·ing, vouch·es** —*intr.* **1.** To give personal assurances; give a guarantee. **2.** To constitute supporting evidence; substantiate. —*tr.* **1.** To substantiate by supplying evidence; prove. **2.** To refer to (an authority, for example) in support or corroboration; cite. **3.** To assert; declare. ❖ *n. Obsolete* A declaration of opinion; an assertion. [ME *vouchen,* to summon to court, warrant < AN *voucher,* prob. < VLat. **voticāre,* alteration of Lat. *vocitāre,* freq. of *vocāre,* to call. See **wekʷ-** in App.]

vouch·er (vou′chər) *n.* **1.** A piece of substantiating evidence; a proof. **2.** A written record of an expenditure, disbursement, or completed transaction. **3.** A written authorization or certificate, esp. one exchangeable for cash or representing a credit against future expenditures. ❖ *tr.v.* **-ered, -er·ing, -ers** **1.** To substantiate or authenticate with evidence. **2.** To prepare a voucher for. **3.** To issue a voucher to.

vouch·safe (vouch-sāf′, vouch′sāf′) *tr.v.* **-safed, -saf·ing,**

-safes To condescend to grant or bestow (a privilege, for example); deign. [ME *vouchen sauf*, to warrant as safe : *vouchen*, to warrant; see VOUCH + *sauf*, safe; see SAFE.] —**vouch·safe′·ment** *n.*

vous·soir (vōō-swär′) *n.* One of the wedge-shaped stones forming the curved parts of an arch or vaulted ceiling. [Fr. < OFr. *vossoir* < VLat. *volsōrium* < *volsus*, p. part. of Lat. *volvere*, to turn, roll. See **wel-** in App.]

Vou·vray (vōō-vrā′) *n.* A dry white table wine from central France, made of Chenin Blanc grapes. [After *Vouvray*, a village of W-central France.]

vow¹ (vou) *n.* **1.** An earnest promise to perform a specified act or behave in a certain manner, esp. a promise to live by the rules of a religious order: *take the vows of a nun.* **2.** A declaration or assertion. ❖ *v.* **vowed, vow·ing, vows** —*tr.* **1.** To promise solemnly; pledge. **2.** To make a pledge or threat to undertake: *vowing revenge.* —*intr.* To vow; promise. [ME *vou* < OFr. < Lat. *vōtum.* See VOTE.] —**vow′er** *n.*

vow² (vou) *tr.v.* To declare or assert. [Short for AVOW.]

vow·el (vou′əl) *n.* **1.** A speech sound, such as (ē) or (ĭ), created by the relatively free passage of breath through the larynx and oral cavity, usu. forming the most prominent and central sound of a syllable. **2.** A letter, such as *a* or *e* in the English alphabet, that represents a vowel. [ME *vowelle* < OFr. *vouel* < Lat. *(littera) vōcālis*, sounding (letter) < *vōx, vōc-*, voice. See **wekʷ-** in App.]

vow·el·ize (vou′ə-līz′) *tr.v.* **-ized, -iz·ing, -iz·es** To provide with vowel points. —**vow′el·i·za′tion** (-ə-lĭ-zā′shən) *n.*

vowel mutation *n.* See **umlaut** 1.

vowel point *n.* Any of a number of diacritical marks written above or below consonants to indicate a vowel in languages usu. written without vowel letters, as in Hebrew and Arabic.

vox po·pu·li (vŏks′ pŏp′yə-lī′, -lē) Popular opinion. [Lat. *vōx populī* : *vōx*, voice + *populī*, genitive of *populus*, people.]

voy·age (voi′ĭj) *n.* **1.** A long journey to a foreign or distant place, esp. by sea. **2a.** The events of a journey of exploration or discovery considered as material for a narrative. **b.** Such a narrative. In both senses often used in the plural. ❖ *v.* **-aged, -ag·ing, -ages** —*intr.* To make a voyage. —*tr.* To sail across; traverse: *voyaged the western ocean.* [ME < OFr. *veyage* < LLat. *viāticum*, a journey < Lat., provisions for a journey < neut. of *viāticus*, of a journey < *via*, road. See **wegh-** in App.] —**voy′ag·er** *n.*

voy·a·geur (voi′ə-zhûr′, vwä′yä-zhœr′) *n., pl.* **-geurs** (-zhûr′, -zhœr′) A workman, boatman, or guide employed by a fur company to transport goods and supplies between remote stations in Canada or the US Northwest. [Fr., traveler < *voyager*, to travel < *voyage*, journey < OFr. *veyage*. See VOYAGE.]

voy·eur (voi-yûr′) *n.* **1.** A person who derives sexual gratification from observing the naked bodies or sexual acts of others, esp. secretly. **2.** An obsessive observer of sordid or sensational subjects. [Fr. < OFr., one who lies in wait < *voir*, to see < Lat. *vidēre*, to see. See **weid-** in App.] —**voy′eur·ism** *n.* —**voy′eur·is′tic** *adj.* —**voy′eur·is′ti·cal·ly** *adv.*

Voz·ne·sen·ski (vŏz′nə-sĕn′skē), **Andrei** b. 1933. Russian poet whose collections of verse include *Parabola* (1960).

VP *abbr.* **1.** variable pitch **2.** verb phrase **3.** vice president

VR *abbr.* virtual reality

Vree·land (vrē′lənd), **Diana Dalziel** 1903–89. French-born Amer. editor of *Vogue* (1963–71).

VRML *abbr.* Virtual Reality Modeling Language

vroom (vrōōm, vrŏŏm) *n.* The loud, roaring noise of an engine operating at high speed. ❖ *intr.v.* **vroomed, vroom·ing, vrooms** To move noisily at high speed in or as if in a motor vehicle. [Imit.]

VS *abbr.* veterinary surgeon

vs. *abbr.* versus

v.s. *abbr.* Latin *vide supra* (see above)

V sign *n.* A hand sign indicating victory, solidarity, or approval, formed by the raised index and middle fingers in the shape of a V.

vss. *abbr.* **1.** verses **2.** versions

V/STOL (vē′stôl′) *n.* A convertiplane that can take off and land vertically or on a short runway. [*v(ertical) s(hort) t(ake)o(ff and) l(anding).*]

VT *abbr.* **1.** vacuum tube **2.** variable time **3.** also **Vt.** Vermont

VTOL (vē′tôl′) *n.* A convertiplane that can take off and land vertically. [*v(ertical) t(ake)o(ff and) l(anding).*]

VTR *abbr.* videotape recorder

vug (vŭg, vōŏg) *n.* A small cavity in a rock or vein, often with a mineral lining of different composition from that of the surrounding rock. [Cornish *vooga.*] —**vug′gy** *adj.*

Vuil·lard (vwē-yär′), **(Jean) Édouard** 1868–1940. French painter whose works include *Public Gardens* (1894).

Vul. *abbr.* Vulgate

Vul·can (vŭl′kən) *n.* Roman Mythology The god of fire and metalworking. [Lat. *Volcānus, Vulcānus.*]

vul·ca·ni·an (vŭl-kā′nē-ən) *adj.* **1.** Of, relating to, or originating from an explosive volcanic eruption. **2. Vulcanian** *Roman Mythology* Of or relating to Vulcan. **3.** Of or relating to metalworking or craft.

vul·ca·nism (vŭl′kə-nĭz′əm) *n.* Variant of **volcanism**.

vul·ca·nite (vŭl′kə-nīt′) *n.* A hard vulcanized rubber.

vul·ca·nize (vŭl′kə-nīz′) *tr.v.* **-nized, -niz·ing, -niz·es** To improve the strength, resiliency, and freedom from stickiness of (rubber, for example) by combining with sulfur or other additives under heat and pressure. —**vul′ca·niz′a·ble** *adj.* —**vul′ca·ni·za′tion** (-nĭ-zā′shən) *n.* —**vul′ca·niz′er** *n.*

vul·ca·nol·o·gy (vŭl′kə-nŏl′ə-jē) *n.* Variant of **volcanology**.

vulg. *abbr.* vulgar

Vulg. *abbr.* Vulgate

vul·gar (vŭl′gər) *adj.* **1.** Crudely indecent. **2a.** Deficient in taste, delicacy, or refinement. **b.** Marked by a lack of good breeding; boorish. **c.** Offensively excessive in self-display or expenditure; ostentatious. **3.** Spoken by or expressed in language spoken by the common people; vernacular: *technical and vulgar names for an animal.* **4.** Of or associated with the great masses of people; common. [ME < Lat. *vulgāris < vulgus*, the common people.] —**vul′gar·ly** *adv.* —**vul′gar·ness** *n.*

vul·gar·i·an (vŭl-gâr′ē-ən) *n.* A vulgar person, esp. one who makes a conspicuous display of wealth.

vul·gar·ism (vŭl′gə-rĭz′əm) *n.* **1.** Vulgarity. **2a.** A crudely indecent word or phrase; an obscenity. **b.** A word, phrase, or manner of expression used chiefly by uneducated people.

vul·gar·i·ty (vŭl-găr′ĭ-tē) *n., pl.* **-ties 1.** The quality or condition of being vulgar. **2.** Something, such as an act or expression, that offends good taste or propriety.

vul·gar·ize (vŭl′gə-rīz′) *tr.v.* **-ized, -iz·ing, -iz·es 1.** To make vulgar; debase. **2.** To disseminate widely; popularize. —**vul′gar·i·za′tion** (-gər-ĭ-zā′shən) *n.* —**vul′gar·iz′er** *n.*

Vulgar Latin *n.* The common speech of the ancient Romans, which is distinguished from standard literary Latin and is the ancestor of the Romance languages.

vul·gate (vŭl′gāt′, -gĭt) *n.* **1.** The common speech of a people; the vernacular. **2.** A widely accepted text or version of a work. **3. Vulgate** The Latin edition of the Bible made by Saint Jerome at the end of the fourth century A.D. [Med.Lat. *Vulgāta < LLat. vulgāta (ēditiō)*, popular (edition) < Lat., fem. p. part. of *vulgāre*, to make known to all < *vulgus*, the common people.]

vul·ner·a·ble (vŭl′nər-ə-bəl) *adj.* **1a.** Susceptible to physical or emotional injury. **b.** Susceptible to attack. **c.** Open to censure or criticism. **2a.** Liable to succumb, as to persuasion or temptation. **b.** *Games* In a position to receive greater penalties or bonuses in a hand of bridge. [LLat. *vulnerābilis*, wounding < Lat. *vulnerāre*, to wound < *vulnus, vulner-*, wound. See **welə-** in App.] —**vul′ner·a·bil′i·ty, vul′ner·a·ble·ness** *n.* —**vul′ner·a·bly** *adv.*

vul·ner·ar·y (vŭl′nə-rĕr′ē) *adj.* Used in the healing or treating of wounds. ❖ *n., pl.* **-ies** A remedy used in healing or treating wounds. [Lat. *vulnerārius < vulnus, vulner-*, wound. See VULNERABLE.]

Vul·pec·u·la (vŭl-pĕk′yə-lə) *n.* A constellation in the celestial Northern Hemisphere near Cygnus and Sagitta. [NLat. < Lat. *vulpēcula*, dim. of *vulpēs*, fox. See VULPINE.]

vul·pec·u·lar (vŭl-pĕk′yə-lər) *adj.* Vulpine.

vul·pine (vŭl′pīn′) *n.* **1.** Of, resembling, or characteristic of a fox. **2.** Cunning; clever. [Lat. *vulpīnus < vulpēs*, fox. See **wl̥p-ē-** in App.]

vul·ture (vŭl′chər) *n.* **1.** Any of various large birds of prey of the New World family Cathartidae or the Old World family Accipitridae, characteristically having dark plumage and a featherless head and neck and generally feeding on carrion. **2.** A person of a rapacious, predatory, or profiteering nature. [ME < OFr. *voltour* < Lat. *vultur.*]

vul·tur·ine (vŭl′chə-rīn′) also **vul·tur·ous** (-chər-əs) *adj.* **1.** Of or characteristic of a vulture. **2.** Predatory.

vul·va (vŭl′və) *n., pl.* **-vae** (-vē) The external genital organs of the female, including the mons pubis, labia majora, labia minora, clitoris, and vestibule of the vagina. [Lat., womb, covering. See **wel-** in App.] —**vul′val, vul′var** (-vər, -vär′) *adj.* —**vul′vate** (-vāt′, -vĭt) *adj.* —**vul′vi·form** (-və-fôrm′) *adj.*

vul·vi·tis (vŭl-vī′tĭs) *n.* Inflammation of the vulva.

vul·vo·vag·i·nal (vŭl′vō-văj′ə-nəl) *adj.* Of or relating to the vulva and the vagina.

vul·vo·vag·i·ni·tis (vŭl′vō-văj′ə-nī′tĭs) *n.* Inflammation of the vulva and vagina.

vum (vŭm) *interj.* New England Used to express surprise. [Alteration of VOW².]

vv. *abbr.* verses

v.v. *abbr.* vice versa

Vyat·ka (vyät′kə) A river of W Russia rising in the Ural Mts. and flowing c. 1,368 km (850 mi) to the Kama R.

Vy·cheg·da (vĭch′ĭg-də) A river of NW Russia flowing c. 1,126 km (700 mi) to the Northern Dvina R.

vy·ing (vī′ĭng) *v.* Present participle of **vie.**

V sign
British Prime Minister
Winston Churchill,
photographed in 1954

vulture
lappet-faced vulture
Torgos tracheliotus

ă	pat	oi	boy
ā	pay	ou	out
âr	care	ōō	took
ä	father	ōō	boot
ĕ	pet	ŭ	cut
ē	be	ûr	urge
ĭ	pit	th	thin
ī	pie	th	this
îr	pier	hw	which
ŏ	pot	zh	vision
ō	toe	ə	about,
ô	paw		item

Stress marks:
′ (primary);
′ (secondary), as in
lexicon (lĕk′sĭ-kŏn′)

w¹ or **W** (dŭb′əl-yŏō, -yŏō) *n., pl.* **w's** or **W's** also **ws** or **Ws 1.** The 23rd letter of the modern English alphabet. **2.** Any of the speech sounds represented by the letter *w.* **3.** The 23rd in a series. **4.** Something shaped like the letter W.

w² *abbr.* **1.** weight **2.** width **3.** *Physics* work

W¹ The symbol for the element **tungsten.** [< Ger. *Wolfram.* See WOLFRAM.]

W² *abbr.* **1.** watt **2.** Wednesday **3.** week **4a.** west **b.** western

w. *abbr.* **1.** wife **2.** also **w/** with

W. *abbr.* Welsh

WA *abbr.* **1.** Washington **2.** with average

Waal (väl) The S branch of the Lower Rhine R. in S Netherlands flowing c. 84 km (52 mi) to the Maas R.

Wa·ba·na·ki (wä′bə-nä′kē) *n., pl.* **Wabanaki** or **-kis** See Abenaki.

Wa·bash (wô′băsh′) A river of the E-central US rising in W OH and flowing c. 764 km (475 mi) to the Ohio R.

wab·ble (wŏb′əl) *v. & n.* Variant of **wobble.**

wack (wăk) *Slang n.* A person regarded as eccentric. ❖ *adj.* **wack·er, wack·est** Very bad.

wack·o (wăk′ō) also **whack·o** (hwăk′ō, wăk′ō) *Slang n., pl.* **-os** A person regarded as eccentric or irrational. ❖ *adj.* Wacky.

wack·y (wăk′ē) also **whack·y** (hwăk′ē, wăk′ē) *adj.* **-i·er, -i·est** *Slang* **1.** Eccentric or irrational: *a wacky person.* **2.** Crazy; silly: *a wacky outfit.* [Variant of *whacky,* prob. < the phrase *out of whack.* See WHACK.] —**wack′i·ly** *adv.* —**wack′i·ness** *n.*

Wa·co (wā′kō) A city of E-central TX S of Dallas–Fort Worth. Pop. 113,726.

wad (wŏd) *n.* **1.** A small mass of soft material, often folded or rolled, used for padding, stuffing, or packing. **2.** A compressed ball, roll, or lump, as of tobacco or chewing gum. **3a.** A plug, as of cloth or paper, used to retain a powder charge in a muzzleloading gun or cannon. **b.** A disk, as of felt or paper, used to keep the powder and shot in place in a shotgun cartridge. **4.** *Informal* A large amount: *a wad of troubles.* **5.** *Informal* **a.** A sizable roll of paper money. **b.** A considerable amount of money. ❖ *v.* **wad·ded, wad·ding, wads** —*tr.* **1.** To compress into a wad. **2.** To pad, pack, line, or plug with wadding. **3a.** To hold (shot or powder) in place with a wad. **b.** To insert a wad into (a firearm). —*intr.* To form into a wad. [?]

Wad·den·zee (wäd′n-zā′) An inlet of the North Sea off N Netherlands between the Ijsselmeer and the West Frisian Is.

wad·ding (wŏd′ĭng) *n.* **1a.** A wad. **b.** Wads considered as a group. **2.** A soft layer of fibrous cotton or wool used for padding or stuffing. **3.** Material for gun wads.

wad·dle (wŏd′l) *intr.v.* **-dled, -dling, -dles 1.** To walk with short steps that tilt the body from side to side. **2.** To walk heavily and clumsily with a pronounced sway. ❖ *n.* A swaying gait. [Frequentative of WADE.] —**wad′dler** *n.*

wad·dy¹ (wŏd′ē) *Australian n., pl.* **-dies** A heavy stick, esp. a war club. ❖ *tr.v.* **-died** (wŏd′ēd), **-dy·ing, -dies** (wŏd′ēz) To strike with a waddy. [Dharuk *wadi.*]

wad·dy² also **wad·die** (wŏd′ē) *n., pl.* **-dies** *Western US* **1.** See **cowboy** 1. **2.** A cattle rustler. [?]

wade (wād) *v.* **wad·ed, wad·ing, wades** —*intr.* **1.** To walk in or through water or something else that similarly impedes normal movement. **2.** To make one's way arduously. —*tr.* To cross or pass through (water, for example) with difficulty. ❖ *n.* The act or an instance of wading. —*phrasal verb:* **wade in** (or **into**) To plunge into, begin, or attack resolutely and energetically. [ME *waden* < OE *wadan.*]

wad·er (wā′dər) *n.* **1.** See **wading bird. 2. waders** Waterproof hip boots or trousers worn esp. while fishing.

wa·di also **wa·dy** (wä′dē) *n., pl.* **-dis** also **-dies 1a.** A valley, gully, or streambed in northern Africa and southwest Asia that remains dry except during the rainy season. **b.** A stream that flows through such a channel. **2.** An oasis. [Ar. *wādi.*]

wad·ing bird (wā′dĭng) *n.* A long-legged bird, such as a crane or stork, that frequents shallow water in search of food.

wa·fer (wā′fər) *n.* **1.** A small thin crisp cake, biscuit, or candy. **2.** *Ecclesiastical* A small thin disk of unleavened bread used in the Eucharist. **3.** A small disk of adhesive material used as a seal for papers. **4.** *Electronics* A small thin circular slice of a semiconducting material, such as pure silicon, on which an integrated circuit can be formed. ❖ *tr.v.* **-fered, -fer·ing, -fers 1.** To seal or fasten together with a wafer. **2.** *Electronics* To divide into wafers. [ME *wafre* < AN, var. of ONFr. *waufre,* of Gmc. orig. See **webh-** in App.]

waff (wăf, wäf) *Scots intr. & tr.v.* **waffed, waff·ing, waffs** To

waders

wave or flutter or cause to do so. ❖ *n.* **1.** A waving or fluttering motion. **2.** A gust of air; a waft. [ME *waffen,* to wave, alteration of *waven.* See WAVE.]

waf·fle¹ (wŏf′əl) *n.* A light crisp battercake baked in a waffle iron. [Du. *wafel* < MDu. *wāfel.* See **webh-** in App.]

waf·fle² (wŏf′əl) *Informal v.* **-fled, -fling, -fles** —*intr.* To speak or write evasively. —*tr.* To speak, write, or act evasively about. ❖ *n.* Evasive or vague speech or writing. [Prob. freq. of obsolete *waff,* to yelp, prob. of imit. orig.] —**waf′fler** *n.* —**waf′fling·ly** *adv.* —**waf′fly** *adj.*

waffle iron *n.* An appliance having hinged indented plates that impress a grid pattern into waffle batter as it bakes.

waft (wăft, wäft) *v.* **waft·ed, waft·ing, wafts** —*tr.* **1.** To cause to go gently and smoothly through the air or over water. **2.** To convey or send floating through the air or over water. —*intr.* To float gently; drift. ❖ *n.* **1.** Something, such as an odor, carried through the air. **2.** A light breeze; a rush of air. **3.** The act of fluttering or waving. **4.** *Nautical* A flag used for signaling or indicating wind direction. [Back-formation < *wafter,* convoy ship, alteration of ME *waughter* < MDu. or MLGer. *wachter,* a guard < *wachten,* to guard.] —**waft′er** *n.*

wag¹ (wăg) *v.* **wagged, wag·ging, wags** —*intr.* **1.** To move briskly and repeatedly from side to side, to and fro, or up and down. **2.** To move rapidly in talking. Used of the tongue. **3.** To walk with a clumsy sway; waddle. **4.** *Archaic* To be on one's way; depart. —*tr.* To move (a body part) rapidly from side to side or up and down, as in playfulness, admonition, or chatter. ❖ *n.* The act or motion of wagging: *a wag of the hand.* [ME *waggen.* See **wegh-** in App.] —**wag′ger** *n.*

wag² (wăg) *n.* A humorous or droll person; a wit. [Perh. < WAG¹.]

wage (wāj) *n.* **1.** Payment for labor or services to a worker, esp. remuneration on an hourly, daily, or weekly basis or by the piece. **2. wages** *Economics* The portion of the national product that represents the aggregate paid for all contributing labor and services. **3.** A fitting return; a recompense. Often used in the plural with a singular or plural verb: *the wages of sin.* ❖ *tr.v.* **waged, wag·ing, wag·es** To engage in (a war or campaign, for example). [ME < ONFr., of Gmc. orig.]

wage earner *n.* **1.** One who works for wages. **2.** One whose earnings support or help support a household.

wa·ger (wā′jər) *n.* **1a.** An agreement under which each bettor pledges something against the outcome of an unsettled matter. **b.** A matter bet on; a gamble. **2.** Something staked on an uncertain outcome; a bet. See Syns at **bet. 3.** *Archaic* A pledge of personal combat to resolve an issue or case. ❖ *v.* **-gered, -ger·ing, -gers** —*tr.* To risk or stake (an amount or possession) on an uncertain outcome; bet. —*intr.* To make a bet. [ME < AN *wageure* < ONFr. *wagier,* to pledge < *wage,* pledge. See WAGE.] —**wa′ger·er** *n.*

wage scale *n.* The scale of wages paid to employees for the various jobs within an industry, factory, or company.

wage slave *n.* A wage earner whose livelihood is completely dependent on the wages earned.

wage·work·er (wāj′wûr′kər) *n.* A wage earner.

wag·ger·y (wăg′ə-rē) *n., pl.* **-ies 1.** Waggish behavior or spirit; drollery. **2.** A droll remark or act.

wag·gish (wăg′ĭsh) *adj.* Characteristic of or resembling a wag; jocular or witty. —**wag′gish·ly** *adv.* —**wag′gish·ness** *n.*

wag·gle (wăg′əl) *v.* **-gled, -gling, -gles** —*tr.* To move (an attached part, for example) with short quick motions. —*intr.* To move shakily; wobble. ❖ *n.* A wobbling motion. [ME *wagelen,* freq. of *waggen.* See WAG¹.] —**wag′gly** *adj.*

Wag·ner (väg′nər), **Richard** 1813–83. German composer known esp. for *Der Ring des Nibelungen* (1853–74). —**Wag′ner′i·an** (-nîr′ē-ən) *adj. & n.*

wag·on (wăg′ən) *n.* **1.** A four-wheeled, usu. horse-drawn vehicle with a large rectangular body, used to transport loads. **2a.** A light automotive transport or delivery vehicle. **b.** A station wagon. **c.** A police patrol wagon. **3.** A child's low four-wheeled cart pulled by a long handle. **4.** A small table or tray on wheels used for serving drinks or food. **5. Wagon** The Big Dipper. **6.** *Chiefly British* An open railway freight car. ❖ *tr. & intr.v.* **-oned, -on·ing, -ons** To transport or undergo transportation by wagon. —*idioms:* **off the wagon** *Slang* No longer abstaining from alcoholic beverages. **on the wagon** *Slang* Abstaining from alcoholic beverages. [ME *waggin* < MDu. *wagen.* See **wegh-** in App.]

wag·on·er (wăg′ə-nər) *n.* **1.** One who drives a wagon. **2.** **Wagoner** Auriga.

wa·gon-lit (vä′gôn-lē′) *n., pl.* **wa·gons-lits** or **wa·gon-lits** (vä′gôn-lē′) A sleeping car on a European railroad train. [Fr.

wagon, railroad car (< E. WAGON) + *lit*, bed (< OFr. < Lat. *lēctus*; see **legh-** in App.).]

wag•on•load (wăg′ən-lōd′) *n.* The amount a wagon holds.

wagon train *n.* A line or train of wagons that are traveling cross-country.

Wa•gram (vä′gräm′) A town of NE Austria NE of Vienna; site of Napoleon's defeat of the Austrians in Jul. 1809.

wag•tail (wăg′tāl′) *n.* Any of various chiefly Old World birds of the family Motacillidae, having a slender body with a long tail that constantly wags.

Wah•ha•bi or **Wa•ha•bi** (wä-hä′bē) *n., pl.* **-bis** A member of a Muslim sect founded by Abdul Wahhab (1703–92), known for its strict observance of the Koran. **—Wah•ha′bism** (-bĭz′əm) *n.*

wa•hi•ne (wä-hē′nē, -nā′) also **va•hi•ne** (vä-) *n.* **1.** *Hawaii* A Polynesian woman. **2.** *Slang* A woman surfer. [Hawaiian < Proto-Polynesian *fafine*.]

wa•hoo[1] (wä-hōō′, wä′hōō′) *n., pl.* **-hoos** A deciduous shrub or small tree (*Euonymus atropurpurea*) of eastern North America having purplish flowers. [Dakota *wáhu*.]

wa•hoo[2] (wä-hōō′, wä′hōō′) *n., pl.* **-hoos 1.** An elm tree (*Ulmus alata*) of the southeast United States having twigs with winged corky edges. **2.** Any of several similar trees. [?]

wa•hoo[3] (wä-hōō′, wä′hōō′) *n., pl.* **wahoo** or **-hoos** A tropical marine food and game fish (*Acanthocybium solanderi*) of the mackerel family, having a pointed snout, narrow body, and long dorsal fin. [Perh. of West Indian orig.]

wa•hoo[4] (wä′hōō′) *Chiefly Western US interj.* Used to express exuberance. ❖ *n., pl.* **-hoos** An exuberant cry.

Wah•pe•ku•te (wä′pə-kōō′tē) *n., pl.* **Wahpekute** or **-tes** A member of a Native American people of the Santee branch of the Sioux.

Wah•pe•ton (wä′pĭ-tn) *n., pl.* **Wahpeton** or **-tons** A member of a Native American people of the Santee branch of the Sioux.

wah-wah also **wa-wa** (wä′wä′) *n.* A wavering sound produced by an instrument, as by alternately muting and uncovering a trumpet or trombone. [Imit.] **—wah′-wah′** *adj.*

waif[1] (wāf) *n.* **1a.** A homeless person, esp. a forsaken or orphaned child. **b.** An abandoned young animal. **2.** Something found and unclaimed, as an object cast up by the sea. [ME, stray animal < AN, prob. of Scand. orig.]

waif[2] (wāf) *n. Nautical* See **waft** 4. [Prob. of Scand. orig.]

Wai•ki•ki (wī′kē-kē′) A beach and resort district of Oahu, HI, SE of Honolulu.

wail (wāl) *v.* **wailed, wail•ing, wails** —*intr.* **1.** To grieve or protest loudly and bitterly; lament. See Syns at **cry. 2.** To make a prolonged high-pitched sound suggestive of a cry: *The wind wailed through the trees.* —*tr.* To lament over; bewail. ❖ *n.* **1.** A long loud high-pitched cry, as of grief or pain. **2.** A long loud high-pitched sound. **3.** A loud bitter protest. [ME *wailen*, prob. of Scand. orig.] **—wail′er** *n.* **—wail′ing•ly** *adv.*

wail•ful (wāl′fəl) *adj.* **1.** Resembling a wail; mournful. **2.** Issuing a sound resembling a wail. **—wail′ful•ly** *adv.*

Wail•ing Wall (wā′lĭng) See **Western Wall.**

wain (wān) *n.* **1.** A large open farm wagon. **2. Wain** The Big Dipper. [ME < OE *wǣn, wægn.* See **wegh-** in App.]

wain•scot (wān′skət, -skŏt′, -skōt′) *n.* **1.** A facing or paneling, usu. of wood, applied to the walls of a room. **2.** The lower part of an interior wall when finished in a material different from that of the upper part. ❖ *tr.v.* **-scot•ed, -scot•ing, -scots** or **-scot•ted, -scot•ting, -scots** To line or panel (a room or wall) with wainscoting. [ME < MDu. *waghenscot* : perh. *waghen, wagen,* wagon (< the quality of wood used for carriagework); see WAGON + *scot,* partition.]

wain•scot•ing or **wain•scot•ting** (wān′skə-tĭng, -skŏt′ĭng, -skō′tĭng) *n.* **1.** A wainscoted wall or walls; paneling. **2.** Material, such as wood, used for wainscoting.

wain•wright (wān′rīt′) *n.* A wagon builder and repairer.

Wai•pa•hu (wī-pä′hōō) A city of S Oahu, HI, on the NW shore of Pearl Harbor. Pop. 33,108.

waist (wāst) *n.* **1a.** The part of the human trunk between the bottom of the rib cage and the pelvis. **b.** The narrow part of the abdomen of an insect. **2a.** The part of a garment that encircles the waist of the body. **b.** The upper part of a garment, extending from the shoulders to the waistline, esp. the bodice of a dress. **c.** A blouse. **d.** A child's undershirt. **3.** The middle section or part of an object, esp. when narrower than the rest. **4.** *Nautical* The middle part of the upper deck of a ship between the forecastle and the quarterdeck. [ME *wast,* perh. < OE **wǣst,* growth, size.] **—waist′less** *adj.*

waist•band (wāst′bănd′) *n.* A band of material encircling and fitting the waist of a garment, such as trousers or a skirt.

waist•cloth (wāst′klôth′, -klŏth′) *n.* A loincloth.

waist•coat (wĕs′kĭt, wāst′kōt′) *n.* **1.** A garment formerly worn by men under a doublet. **2.** *Chiefly British* A short sleeveless collarless garment worn esp. over a shirt and often under a suit jacket; a vest. **—waist′coat′ed** *adj.*

waist•line (wāst′līn′) *n.* **1a.** A line thought of as encircling the body at the waist. **b.** The measurement of this line. **2a.** The line at which the skirt and bodice of a dress join. **b.** The part of a garment that lies at or according to fashion above or below the narrowest part of the waist.

waist pack *n.* A small, usu. zippered pack or pouch attached to a belt and worn around the waist.

wait (wāt) *v.* **wait•ed, wait•ing, waits** —*intr.* **1a.** To remain or rest in expectation: *waiting for the guests to arrive.* See Syns at **stay**[1]. **b.** To tarry until another catches up. **2.** To remain or be in readiness. **3.** To remain temporarily neglected, unattended to, or postponed. **4.** To work as a waiter or waitress. —*tr.* **1.** To remain or stay in expectation of; await. **2.** *Informal* To delay (a meal or an event); postpone. **3.** To be a waiter or waitress at. ❖ *n.* **1.** The act of waiting or the time spent waiting. **2.** *Chiefly British* **a.** One of a group of musicians employed to play in parades or public ceremonies. **b.** One of a group of musicians or carolers who perform in the streets at Christmastime. **—phrasal verbs: wait on** (or **upon**) **1.** To serve the needs of; be in attendance on. **2.** To make a formal call on; visit. **3.** To follow as a result; depend on. **4.** To await. **wait out** To delay until the termination of. **wait up 1.** To postpone going to bed in anticipation of something or someone. **2.** *Informal* To stop or pause so that another can catch up. [ME *waiten* < ONFr. *waitier,* to watch, of Gmc. orig.]

wait-a-bit (wāt′ə-bĭt′) *n.* Any of several plants having sharp, often hooked thorns. [Transl. of Afr. *wag-'n-bietjie*.]

Waite (wāt), **Morrison Remick** 1816–88. Amer. jurist; chief justice of the US Supreme Court (1874–88).

wait•er (wā′tər) *n.* **1.** One who serves at a table, as in a restaurant. **2.** A tray or salver.

wait•ing (wā′tĭng) *n.* **1.** The act of remaining inactive or stationary. **2.** A period of time spent waiting. **—idiom: in waiting** In attendance, esp. at a royal court.

waiting game *n.* The stratagem of deferring action and allowing the passage of time to work in one's favor.

waiting list *n.* A list of persons waiting, as for an appointment.

waiting room *n.* A room for the use of people waiting.

wait•list (wāt′lĭst′) *n.* A waiting list. ❖ *tr.v.* also **wait-list -list•ed, -list•ing, -lists** To put on a waiting list.

wait•per•son (wāt′pûr′sən) *n.* A waiter or waitress.

wait•ress (wā′trĭs) *n.* A woman who serves at a table, as in a restaurant. See Usage Note at **–ess.**

wait•ron (wā′trŏn′, -trən) *n.* A waiter or waitress.

wait staff or **wait•staff** (wāt′stăf′) *n.* Personnel employed to serve at tables, as in a restaurant.

waive (wāv) *tr.v.* **waived, waiv•ing, waives 1.** To give up (a claim or right) voluntarily; relinquish. See Syns at **relinquish. 2.** To refrain from insisting on or enforcing (a rule, for example); dispense with. **3.** To put aside or off temporarily; defer. [ME *weiven,* to abandon < AN *weyver* < *waif,* ownerless property. See WAIF[1].]

waiv•er (wā′vər) *n.* **1a.** Intentional relinquishment of a right, claim, or privilege. **b.** The document that evidences such relinquishment. **2.** A dispensation, as from a rule. **3.** A deferment. **4.** Permission for a professional athletic club to assign a player to the minor leagues or release a player from the club, granted only after all other clubs have been given the opportunity to claim the player and have not done so. **—idiom: on waivers** In a state of being available for claiming by other professional clubs. [AN *weyver* < *weyver,* to abandon. See WAIVE.]

Wa•kash•an (wä-kăsh′ən, wô′kə-shăn′) *n.* A family of North American Indian languages spoken by the Nootka and other peoples of Washington and British Columbia. [Ult. < Nootka *waakaash,* bravo!] **—Wa•kash′an** *adj.*

Wa•ka•ya•ma (wä′kə-yä′mə) A city of S Honshu, Japan, SSW of Osaka on the Inland Sea. Pop. 395,496.

wake[1] (wāk) *v.* **woke** (wōk) or **waked** (wākt), **waked** or **wok•en** (wō′kən), **wak•ing, wakes** —*intr.* **1a.** To cease to sleep; become awake: *overslept and woke late.* **b.** To stay awake. **c.** To be brought into a state of awareness or alertness. **2.** To keep watch or guard, esp. over a corpse. —*tr.* **1.** To rouse from sleep; awaken. **2.** To stir, as from a dormant or inactive condition; rouse. **3.** To make aware of; alert. **4a.** To keep a vigil over. **b.** To hold a wake over. ❖ *n.* **1.** A watch; a vigil. **2.** A watch over a corpse before burial. **3. wakes** (*used with a sing. or pl. verb*) *Chiefly British* **a.** A parish festival, often in honor of a patron saint. **b.** An annual vacation. [ME *wakien, waken* < OE *wacan,* to wake up, and *wacian,* to be awake, keep watch.] **—wak′er** *n.*

USAGE NOTE The pairs *wake, waken* and *awake, awaken* have formed a bewildering array since the Middle English period. All four words have similar meanings, though there are some differences in use. Only *wake* is used in the sense "to be awake," as in expressions such as *waking* (not *wakening*) *and sleeping, every waking hour. Wake* is also more common than *waken* when used together with *up,* and *awake* and *awaken* never occur in this context: *She woke up* (rarely *wakened up*; never *awakened up* or *awoke up*). Some writers have suggested that *waken* should be used only transitively and *awaken* only intransitively, but there is ample literary precedent for usages such as *He wakened early* and *They did not awaken her.* In figurative senses *awake* and *awaken* are more prevalent: *awoke to the danger; awakened my memory.*

REGIONAL NOTE Regional American dialects vary in the way that certain verbs form their principal parts. Northern dialects seem to favor forms that change the internal vowel in the verb—hence *dove* for the past tense of *dive,* and *woke* for *wake: They*

ă pat	oi boy
ā pay	ou out
âr care	oo took
ä father	oo boot
ĕ pet	ŭ cut
ē be	ûr urge
ĭ pit	th thin
ī pie	th this
îr pier	hw which
ŏ pot	zh vision
ō toe	ə about,
ô paw	item

Stress marks:
′ (primary);
′ (secondary), as in
lexicon (lĕk′sĭ-kŏn′)

wake²

wakeboard

Lech Walesa

Alice Walker

woke up with a start. Southern dialects, on the other hand, tend to prefer forms that add an *–ed* to form the past tense and the past participle of these same verbs: *The children dived into the pool. The baby waked up early.*

wake² (wāk) *n.* **1.** The visible track of turbulence left by something moving through water: *the wake of a ship.* **2.** A track, course, or condition left behind. —*idiom:* **in the wake of 1.** Following directly on. **2.** In the aftermath of; as a consequence of. [Poss. < MLGer., hole in the ice, of Scand. orig.]

wake·board (wāk′bôrd′, -bōrd′) *n.* A short, very broad water ski ridden in the manner of a surfboard by a person towed by a motorboat. —**wake′board′er** *n.* —**wake′board′ing** *n.*

Wake·field (wāk′fēld′) A borough of N-central England ENE of Manchester; site of the Battle of Wakefield (1460), in which Richard Plantagenet, the 3rd duke of York (1411–60), was slain by Lancastrian forces in the Wars of the Roses.

wake·ful (wāk′fəl) *adj.* **1a.** Not sleeping or not able to sleep. **b.** Without sleep; sleepless. **2.** Watchful; alert. —**wake′ful·ly** *adv.* —**wake′ful·ness** *n.*

Wake Island An island of the W Pacific Ocean between HI and Guam; annexed by the US in 1898.

wake·less (wāk′lĭs) *adj.* Unbroken. Used of sleep.

wak·en (wā′kən) *v.* **-ened, -en·ing, -ens** —*tr.* **1.** To rouse from sleep; awake: *The noise wakened me.* **2.** To rouse from a quiescent or inactive state; stir. —*intr.* To become awake; wake up: *I plan to waken at 6:00 tomorrow.* See Usage Note at **wake¹**. [ME *wakenen* < OE *wæcnan.*] —**wak′en·er** *n.*

wake-rob·in (wāk′rŏb′ĭn) *n.* **1.** See **trillium. 2.** Any of various North American aroid plants that bloom early in the spring.

wake-up call *n.* **1.** A telephone call that one requests to occur at a specific time in order to be woken up, esp. in a hotel. **2.** A sign or warning that alerts one to negative or dangerous behavior or circumstances.

wak·ing (wā′kĭng) *adj.* Marked by full consciousness, awareness, and alertness: *worked all of my waking hours.*

Waks·man (wäks′mən), **Selman Abraham** 1888–1973. Russian-born microbiologist who won a 1952 Nobel Prize.

Wa·la·chi·a (wə-lā′kē-ə, wō-) See **Wallachia.**

Wa·la·pai (wä′lə-pī′) *n.* Variant of **Hualapai.**

Wal·cott (wôl′kŏt′, wŏl′-), **Derek** b. 1930. West Indian writer known esp. for his epic poem *Omeros* (1990). He won the 1992 Nobel Prize for literature.

Wal·de·mar I (wôl′də-mär′, väl′-) or **Val·de·mar I** (väl′-) 1131–82. Danish king (1157–82) who gained recognition for the hereditary rule of his family.

Wal·den Pond (wôl′dən) A pond of NE MA near Concord. Henry David Thoreau lived in a cabin near the pond from 1845 to 1847.

Wal·den·ses (wŏl-dĕn′sēz, wôl-) *pl.n.* A Christian schismatic sect that originated in southern France in the late 12th century and adopted Calvinist doctrines in the 16th century. [Med.Lat. *Waldēnsēs,* after Peter **WALDO.**] —**Wal·den′sian** (-shən) *adj. & n.*

Wald·heim (wôld′hīm′, vält′-), **Kurt** b. 1918. Austrian diplomat who served as secretary-general of the United Nations (1972–81) and president of Austria (1986–92).

Wal·do (wôl′dō, wäl′-) or **Val·do** (väl′-, väl′-), **Peter** fl. 12th cent. French religious leader who founded the Waldenses and was excommunicated in 1184.

Wal·dorf salad (wôl′dôrf′) *n.* A salad of diced raw apples, celery, and walnuts mixed with mayonnaise. [After the *Waldorf*-Astoria Hotel in New York City.]

wale (wāl) *n.* **1.** A mark raised on the skin, as by a whip; a weal or welt. **2a.** One of the parallel ribs or ridges in the surface of a fabric such as corduroy. **b.** The texture or weave of such a fabric: *a wide wale.* **3.** *Nautical* **a.** A gunwale. **b.** One of the heavy planks or strakes extending along the sides of a wooden ship. ❖ *tr.v.* **waled, wal·ing, wales** To raise marks on (the skin), as by whipping. [ME < OE, var. of *walu.* See **wel-** in App.]

Wal·er also **wal·er** (wā′lər) *n.* A saddle horse developed in Australia and formerly exported to the British military forces in India. [After New South *Wales* in Australia.]

Wales (wālz) A principality of the United Kingdom on the W peninsula of Great Britain; incorporated with England since the Act of Union of 1536. Cap. Cardiff. Pop. 2,790,462.

Wa·le·sa (wä-lĕn′sə, vä-wĕn′sä), **Lech** b. 1943. Polish politician who won the 1983 Nobel Peace Prize and served as president of Poland (1990–95).

Wal·hal·la (wäl-häl′ə, väl-, wäl-hä′lə, väl-) *n.* Variant of **Valhalla.**

walk (wôk) *v.* **walked, walk·ing, walks** —*intr.* **1.** To move over a surface by taking steps with the feet at a pace slower than a run. **2a.** To go or travel on foot. **b.** To go on foot for pleasure or exercise; stroll. **c.** To move in a manner suggestive of walking: *a woodpecker walking up a tree.* **3.** To conduct oneself or behave in a particular manner; live: *walks in seriousness and dignity.* **4.** *Slang* **a.** To go out on strike. **b.** To resign from one's job abruptly; quit. **c.** To be acquitted. **5a.** *Baseball* To go to first base after the pitcher has thrown four balls. **b.** *Basketball* To move illegally while holding the ball; travel. **6.** *Obsolete* To be in constant motion. —*tr.* **1.**

To go or pass over, on, or through by walking. **2.** To bring to a specified condition by walking: *walked himself into exhaustion.* **3.** To cause to walk or proceed at a walk. **4.** To accompany in walking; escort on foot. **5.** To traverse on foot in order to survey or measure; pace off. **6.** To move (a heavy or cumbersome object) in a manner suggestive of walking. **7.** *Baseball* **a.** To allow (a batter) to go to first base by pitching four balls. **b.** To cause (a run) to score by walking a batter. Often used with *in.* ❖ *n.* **1a.** The gait of a human or other biped in which the feet are lifted alternately with one foot always on the ground. **b.** The gait of a quadruped in which at least two feet are always touching the ground, esp. this gait in a horse. **c.** The extravehicular movement of an astronaut in space **2.** The act or an instance of walking, esp. a stroll for pleasure or exercise. **3a.** The rate at which one walks; a walking pace. **b.** The characteristic way in which one walks. **4.** The distance covered or to be covered in walking. **5.** A place, such as a sidewalk, on which one may walk. **6.** A route or circuit particularly suitable for walking. **7a.** *Baseball* A base on balls. **b.** *Basketball* The act or an instance of moving illegally with the ball; traveling. **8.** *Sports* **a.** A track event in which contestants compete in walking a specified distance. **b.** Racewalking. **9.** An enclosed area designated for the exercise or pasture of livestock. **10a.** An arrangement of trees or shrubs planted in widely spaced rows. **b.** The space between such rows. —*phrasal verbs:* **walk out 1.** To go on strike. **2.** To leave suddenly, often as a signal of disapproval. **walk over** *Informal* **1.** To treat badly or contemptuously. **2.** To gain an easy or uncontested victory over. **walk through 1.** To perform (a play, for example) in a perfunctory fashion, as at a first rehearsal. **2.** To guide (someone) deliberately through (a process), one step at a time. —*idioms:* **walk away from 1.** To outdo, outrun, or defeat with little difficulty. **2.** To survive (an accident) with very little injury. **walk away with 1.** To win easily or unexpectedly. **2.** To steal. **walk on air** To feel elated. **walk out on** To desert or abandon. **walk the plank** To be forced, as by pirates, to walk off a plank extended over the side of a ship so as to drown. [ME *walken* < OE *wealcan,* to roll. See **wel-** in App.] —**walk′a·bil′i·ty** *n.* —**walk′a·ble** *adj.*

walk·a·bout (wôk′ə-bout′) *n.* **1.** *Australian* A temporary return to traditional Aboriginal life, usu. involving time spent in the bush. **2.** A walking trip. **3.** *Chiefly British* A public stroll taken by an important person, such as a monarch.

walk·a·way (wôk′ə-wā′) *n.* Something that is easy and presents no difficulties, esp. an easily won sports contest; a walkover.

walk·er (wô′kər) *n.* **1.** One that walks, esp. a contestant in a footrace. **2.** A frame device used to support someone walking, such as an infant or convalescent. **3.** A shoe designed for walking comfortably. Often used in the plural.

Walker, Alice b. 1944. Amer. writer whose works include the novel *The Color Purple* (1982).

Walker, James John ("Jimmy") 1881–1946. Amer. politician who was the mayor of New York City (1926–32).

Walker, Sarah Breedlove Known as "Madam C.J. Walker." 1867–1919. Amer. businesswoman who developed a straightening agent for hair (1905) and built the most successful Black-owned company of her day.

walk·ie-talk·ie also **walk·y-talk·y** (wô′kē-tô′kē) *n., pl.* **-ies** A hand-held, battery-powered radio transceiver.

walk-in (wôk′ĭn′) *adj.* **1.** Large enough to admit entrance. **2.** Located so as to be entered directly from the street. ❖ *n.* **1.** A room, such as a closet, large enough to admit entrance. **2.** An easily won victory, esp. in an election. **3.** *Informal* One who walks in without having an appointment.

walk·ing (wô′kĭng) *adj.* **1.** Able to walk despite injury or illness. **2.** Regarded as having the capabilities or qualities of a specified object: *He's a walking rule book.* **3.** Used, intended, or suitable for walking. **4.** Marked by the act of walking: *a walking tour.* **5.** Guided by a person who walks alongside. Used of a machine or farming tool. ❖ *n.* **1.** The action of one that walks. **2.** The state of the surface on which one walks: *The walking is slippery after the ice storm.*

walking bass (bās) *n.* A bass line composed of nonsyncopated notes of equal value, used in jazz and baroque music, for example.

walking catfish *n.* A freshwater catfish (*Clarius batrachus*) of southeast Asia that is able to travel short distances on land.

walking delegate *n.* A trade union official appointed to inspect and confer with local unions or to serve as a representative of a union in dealings with an employer.

walking fern *n.* An eastern North American fern (*Camptosorus rhizophyllus*) having fronds that often take root at the tip.

walking leaf *n.* **1.** A walking fern. **2.** See **leaf insect.**

walking papers *pl.n. Slang* A notice of discharge or dismissal.

walking stick *n.* **1.** A cane or staff used as an aid in walking. **2.** A stick insect, esp. the widely distributed, brown to green North American species *Diapheromera femorata.*

Walk·man (wôk′măn′, -mən) A trademark used for a pocket-sized cassette player, compact disk player, radio, or combined unit with lightweight earphones.

walk of life *n., pl.* **walks of life** An occupation, profession, or social class: *people from all walks of life.*

walk-on (wôk′ŏn′, -ôn′) *n.* **1.** A minor role in a theatrical production. **2.** A performer playing such a role.

walk·out (wôk′out′) *n.* **1.** A labor strike. **2.** The act of leaving or quitting a meeting or organization, esp. in protest.

walk·o·ver (wôk′ō′vər) *n.* **1.** Something that is easy and presents no difficulties, esp. an easily won sports contest. **2.** A horserace with only one horse entered. **3.** A gymnastic feat in which the body is bent forward or backward from an upright position, the hands are placed on the floor, and the legs are arced one after the other over the hands to finish in a standing position

walk-through (wôk′thrōō′) *n.* **1.** A brief rehearsal, as of a play or role, performed usu. in an early stage of production. **2.** A television rehearsal during which no cameras are used. **3.** A thorough demonstration or explanation that details each step of a process.

walk·up also **walk-up** (wôk′ŭp′) *n.* **1.** An apartment house or office building with no elevator. **2.** An apartment or office in a building with no elevator.

walk·way (wôk′wā′) *n.* A passage or path for walking.

Wal·kyr·ie (wăl-kîr′ē, -kī′rē, văl-, wăl′kə-rē, văl′-) *n.* Variant of **Valkyrie.**

walk·y-talk·y (wô′kē-tô′kē) *n.* Variant of **walkie-talkie.**

wall (wôl) *n.* **1.** An upright structure, as of masonry, serving to enclose, divide, or protect an area, esp. a vertical construction forming an inner partition or exterior siding of a building. **2.** A continuous structure, as of masonry, forming a rampart and built for defensive purposes. Often used in the plural. **3.** A structure of stonework, cement, or other material built to retain a flow of water. **4a.** Something resembling a wall in appearance, function, or construction, as the surface of a body organ. **b.** Something resembling a wall in impenetrability or strength. **c.** An extreme or desperate condition or position, such as defeat or ruin. **5.** *Sports* The vertical surface of an ocean wave in surfing. ❖ *tr.v.* **walled, wall·ing, walls 1.** To enclose, surround, or fortify with or as if with a wall. **2.** To divide or separate with or as if with a wall. Often used with *off: wall off half a room.* **3.** To confine or seal behind a wall; immure. **4.** To block or close (an opening or a passage, for example) with or as if with a wall. —**idioms: off the wall** *Slang* **1.** Extremely unconventional. **2.** Without foundation; ridiculous. **up the wall** *Slang* Into a state of extreme frustration, anger, or distress. **writing (or handwriting) on the wall** An ominous indication of the course of future events. [ME < OE *weall* < Lat. *vallum,* palisade < *vallus,* stake.]

wal·la·by (wôl′ə-bē) *n., pl.* **-bies** or **wallaby** Any of various marsupials of the genus *Wallabia* and related genera of Australia and adjacent islands, related to the kangaroos but generally smaller and often having a colorful coat. [Dharuk *walaba.*]

Wal·lace (wôl′ĭs), **Alfred Russel** 1823–1913. British naturalist whose concept of evolution paralleled that of Darwin.

Wallace, George Corley 1919–98. Amer. politician who ran unsuccessfully for the presidency in 1968 and 1972.

Wallace, Henry Agard 1888–1965. Vice President of the US (1941–45) who ran unsuccessfully for President in 1948.

Wallace, Lew(is) 1827–1905. Amer. general, diplomat, and writer known esp. for his novel *Ben Hur* (1880).

Wallace, Sir **William** 1272?–1305. Scottish patriot who led resistance against the English and briefly gained control of Scotland in 1298.

Wal·lace's line (wôl′ĭ-sĭz) *n.* A hypothetical line demarcating the distribution of Asian and Australian fauna, passing between the islands of Bali and Lombok to the south and Borneo and Sulawesi to the north, used esp. in biogeographic studies of evolution. [After Alfred Russel WALLACE.]

Wal·la·chi·a also **Wa·la·chi·a** (wo-lā′kē-ə, wŏ-) A historical region of SE Romania between the Transylvanian Alps and the Danube R.; united with Moldavia to form Romania in 1861. —**Wal·la′chi·an** *adj. & n.*

wal·lah also **wal·la** (wä′lä, wä′lə) *n.* One employed or engaged in a particular occupation or activity. [< Hindi -*vālā,* connected with.]

wal·la·roo (wôl′ə-rōō′) *n., pl.* **-roos** or **wallaroo** A large kangaroo (*Macropus robustus*) having reddish or gray fur. [Dharuk *walaru.*]

wall·board (wôl′bôrd′, -bōrd′) *n.* See **plasterboard.**

wall creeper *n.* A long-billed crimson and gray Old World bird (*Tichodroma muraria*) of alpine regions that feeds on insects.

Wal·len·stein (wôl′ən-stīn′, väl′ən-shtīn′), **Albrecht Eusebius Wenzel von** 1583–1634. Austrian military leader who fought for the Hapsburgs during the Thirty Years' War (1618–48).

Wal·ler (wôl′ər), **Edmund** 1606–87. English poet known for his love lyrics, including "Go, Lovely Rose" (1645).

Waller, Thomas Wright Known as **"Fats."** 1904–43. Amer. jazz musician whose songs include "Ain't Misbehavin'" (1929).

wal·let (wôl′ĭt) *n.* A flat pocket-sized folding case, usu. made of leather, for holding paper money, cards, or photographs; a billfold. [ME *walet,* knapsack, poss. < ONFr. **walet,* roll, knapsack. See **wel-** in App.]

wall·eye (wôl′ī′) *n.* **1.** *pl.* **walleye** or **-eyes** A freshwater food and game fish (*Stizostedium vitreum*) of North America having large staring eyes. **2a.** Exotropia. **b.** An eye affected with exotropia. [Back-formation < WALLEYED.]

wall·eyed (wôl′īd′) *adj.* **1.** Affected with exotropia. **2a.** Having large bulging eyes, as some fish. **b.** Having eyes wide-open and

glaring, as in anger. **3.** *Slang* Intoxicated; drunk. [ME *wawileyed* < ON *vagl-eygr* : *vagl,* film over the eye; see **wegh-** in App. + *auga,* eye; see **ok**ʷ- in App.]

walleyed pike *n.* See **walleye 1.**

wall fern *n.* A low-growing Eurasian fern (*Polypodium vulgare*) characterized by creeping stems that form dense mats.

wall·flow·er (wôl′flou′ər) *n.* **1a.** Any of numerous herbs of the genus *Erysimum* of the mustard family, having fragrant yellow, orange, or brownish flowers. **b.** Any of several perennial herbs of the genus *Cheiranthus,* esp. *C. cheiri.* **2.** One whose shyness or unpopularity prevents participation at a social event.

wall hanging *n.* A flat decorative object, such as a tapestry, hung against a wall.

Wal·lis and Fu·tu·na Islands (wôl′ĭs; fōō-tōō′nə) A French overseas territory in the SW Pacific Ocean W of Samoa.

Wal·lo·ni·a (wä-lō′nē-ə) A French-speaking region of S Belgium; granted limited autonomy in 1980.

Wal·loon (wŏ-lōōn′) *n.* **1.** One of a French-speaking people of Celtic descent inhabiting southern and southeast Belgium and adjacent regions of France. **2.** The dialect of French spoken by this people. [Fr. *Wallon* < OFr., of Gmc. orig.]

wal·lop (wôl′əp) *Informal v.* **-loped, -lop·ing, -lops** —*tr.* **1.** To beat soundly; thrash. **2.** To strike with a hard blow. **3.** To defeat thoroughly. —*intr.* **1.** To move in a rolling, clumsy manner; waddle. **2.** To boil noisily. Used of a liquid. ❖ *n.* **1.** A hard or severe blow. **2a.** The ability to strike a powerful blow. **b.** The capacity to create a forceful effect. [ME *walopen,* to gallop < ONFr. **waloper.*] —**wal′lop·er** *n.*

wal·lop·ing (wôl′ə-pĭng) *Informal adj.* **1.** Very large; huge. **2.** Very fine; impressive. ❖ *adv.* Used as an intensive: *a walloping huge lie.* ❖ *n.* A sound thrashing or defeat.

wal·low (wôl′ō) *intr.v.* **-lowed, -low·ing, -lows 1.** To roll the body about indolently or clumsily in or as if in water, snow, or mud. **2.** To luxuriate; revel. **3.** To be plentifully supplied. **4.** To move with difficulty in a clumsy or rolling manner; flounder. **5.** To swell or surge forth; billow. ❖ *n.* **1.** The act or an instance of wallowing. **2a.** A pool of water or mud where animals go to wallow. **b.** The depression, pool, or pit produced by wallowing animals. **3.** A condition of degradation or baseness. [ME *walowen* < OE *wealwian.* See **wel-** in App.] —**wal′low·er** *n.*

wall·pa·per (wôl′pā′pər) *n.* **1.** Paper often printed with designs that is pasted to a wall as a decorative covering. **2.** A picture or design displayed as the background of a computer screen. ❖ *v.* **-pered, -per·ing, -pers** —*tr.* To cover with or as if with wallpaper. —*intr.* To decorate a wall or room with wallpaper.

wall plate *n.* **1.** A timber situated along the top of a wall at the level of the eaves for bearing the ends of joists or rafters. **2.** A plate used to attach a bracket or similar device to a wall.

wall plug *n.* An electric socket, usu. located in a wall.

wall rock *n.* The rock that forms the walls of a vein or lode.

wall rue *n.* A small delicate fern (*Asplenium ruta-muraria*) that grows on rocks or in rocky crevices.

Wall Street *n.* The controlling financial interests of the United States. [After *Wall Street* in New York City.] —**Wall′-Street′er** (wôl′strē′tər) *n.*

wall-to-wall (wôl′tə-wôl′) *adj.* **1.** Completely covering a floor. **2.** *Informal* **a.** Present or spreading throughout an entire area. **b.** Found everywhere or including everything; pervasive. ❖ *n.* A carpet that completely covers a floor.

wal·ly·ball (wôl′ē-bôl′) *n.* A game similar to volleyball played on a four-walled court with a ball that is allowed to bounce once off the ceiling or once off the walls before being returned over the net. [Blend of WALL and VOLLEYBALL.]

wal·nut (wôl′nŭt′, -nət) *n.* **1a.** Any of several deciduous trees of the genus *Juglans,* having pinnately compound leaves and a round sticky outer fruit wall that encloses a nutlike stone with an edible seed. **b.** The stone or the ridged or corrugated seed of such a tree. **2.** The hard, dark brown wood of any of these trees. [ME *walnot* < OE *wealhhnutu*: *wealh,* Celt, foreigner + *hnutu,* nut.] —**wal′nut** *adj.*

Walnut Creek A city of W CA NE of Oakland. Pop. 64,296.

Wal·pole (wôl′pōl′, wŏl′-), **Horace** or **Horatio** 4th Earl of Orford. 1717–97. British writer and historian noted for his correspondence and memoirs and the Gothic novel *The Castle of Otranto* (1764).

Walpole, Sir **Robert.** 1st Earl of Orford. 1676–1745. English politician who as first lord of the treasury and Chancellor of the Exchequer (1715–17 and 1721–42) was regarded as Britain's first prime minister.

Wal·pur·gis Night (väl-pŏŏr′gĭs) *n.* **1a.** The eve of May Day, observed in some areas in celebration of spring. **b.** The eve of Beltane, believed by medieval Christians to be the occasion of a witches' Sabbath. **2.** An episode or a situation having the quality of nightmarish wildness. [Partial transl. of Ger. *Walpurgisnacht*: *Walpurgis,* Saint Walpurga (died 779) + *Nacht,* night.]

wal·rus (wôl′rəs, wŏl′-) *n., pl.* **walrus** or **-rus·es** A large marine mammal (*Odobenus rosmarus*) of Arctic regions, related to the seals and having two long tusks, tough wrinkled skin, and four flippers. [Du., of Scand. orig.]

walrus mustache *n.* A bushy, drooping mustache.

Wal·sall (wôl′sôl′, -səl) A borough of west-central England

wallaby
wallaby with joey in pouch

walnut
black walnut
Juglans nigra

NW of Birmingham. Pop. 264,716.

Wal·ter (väl′tər), **Bruno** 1876–1962. German conductor noted for his interpretations of Mozart and Mahler.

Wal·ter Mit·ty (wôl′tər mĭt′ē) *n.* An ordinary, often ineffectual person who daydreams of fantastic personal triumphs. [After "The Secret Life of *Walter Mitty*" (1939) by James Thurber.]

Wal·ters (wôl′tərz), **Barbara** b. 1931. Amer. newscaster and reporter who was the first woman to anchor the nightly news on network television.

Wal·ther von der Vo·gel·wei·de (väl′tər fôn dər fō′gəl-vī′də) 1170?–1230? German minnesinger. The German national anthem is based on one of his songs.

Wal·ton (wôl′tən), **Ernest Thomas Sinton** 1903–95. Irish physicist who shared a 1951 Nobel Prize.

Walton, Izaak 1593–1683. English writer primarily known for *The Compleat Angler* (1653), a literary treatise on fishing.

Walton, Sir William Turner 1902–83. British composer of orchestral works and chamber music, including *Façade* (1923).

waltz (wôlts, wôls) *n.* **1a.** A ballroom dance in triple time with a strong accent on the first beat. **b.** A piece of music for this dance. **c.** An instrumental or vocal composition in triple time. **2.** *Informal* Something that can be accomplished with little effort. ❖ *v.* **waltzed, waltz·ing, waltz·es** —*intr.* **1.** To dance the waltz. **2.** *Slang* To move unhesitantly, briskly, and with aplomb. **3.** *Informal* To accomplish a task with little effort. —*tr.* **1.** To dance the waltz with. **2.** *Slang* To lead or force to move briskly and purposefully; march. —*idiom:* **waltz Matilda** *Australian* To travel about, esp. on foot, carrying a swag. [Ger. *Walzer* < *walzen*, to turn about < MHGer., to roll < OHGer. *walzan*. See **wel-** in App.] —**waltz′er** *n.*

Wal·vis Bay (wôl′vĭs) An inlet of the Atlantic Ocean on the W coast of Namibia.

wam·ble (wŏm′bəl, wăm′-) *intr.v.* **-bled, -bling, -bles 1.** To move in a weaving, wobbling, or rolling manner. **2.** To turn or roll. Used of the stomach. ❖ *n.* **1.** A wobble or roll. **2.** An upset stomach. [ME *wamelen*, to feel nausea. See **wemə-** in App.] —**wam′bli·ness** *n.* —**wam′bling·ly** *adv.* —**wam′bly** *adj.*

Wam·pa·no·ag (wăm′pə-nō′ăg) *n., pl.* **Wampanoag** or **-ags 1.** A member of a Native American people formerly inhabiting Rhode Island and Massachusetts, with present-day descendants in this same area. **2.** The Algonquian language of the Wampanoag. [Narragansett, those of the east.]

wam·pum (wŏm′pəm, wôm′-) *n.* **1.** Small cylindrical beads made from polished shells, formerly used by certain Native American peoples as currency and jewelry or for ceremonial purposes. **2.** *Informal* Money. [Short for WAMPUMPEAG.]

wam·pum·peag (wŏm′pəm-pēg′, wôm′-) *n.* White shell beads used as wampum. [Massachusett.]

wan (wŏn) *adj.* **wan·ner, wan·nest 1.** Unnaturally pale, as from distress. **2.** Suggestive or indicative of weariness, illness, or unhappiness; melancholy. ❖ *intr.v.* **wanned, wan·ning, wans** To become pale. [ME, pale, gloomy < OE *wann*, gloomy, dark.] —**wan′ly** *adv.* —**wan′ness** *n.*

WAN (wăn) *n.* A communications network that uses such devices as telephone lines, satellite dishes, or radio waves to span a larger geographic area than can be covered by a LAN. [W(IDE) A(REA) N(ETWORK).]

Wan·a·ma·ker (wŏn′ə-mā′kər), **John** 1838–1922. Amer. merchant who founded one of the first department stores.

wand (wŏnd) *n.* **1.** A thin supple rod, twig, or stick. **2.** A slender rod carried as a symbol of office; a scepter. **3.** *Music* A conductor's baton. **4.** A stick or baton used by a magician, conjurer, or diviner. **5.** A pipelike attachment that lengthens the handle of a device or tool. **6.** A hand-held electronic device, often rod-shaped, that is used for security purposes to detect metal. **7.** A six-foot by two-foot slat used as an archery target. [ME < ON *vöndr.*]

wan·der (wŏn′dər) *v.* **-dered, -der·ing, -ders** —*intr.* **1.** To move about without a definite destination or purpose. **2.** To go by an indirect route or at no set pace; amble: *wander toward town.* **3.** To proceed in an irregular course; meander. **4.** To go astray. **5.** To lose clarity or coherence of thought or expression. —*tr.* To wander across or through. ❖ *n.* The act or an instance of wandering; a stroll. [ME *wanderen* < OE *wandrian.*] —**wan′der·er** *n.*

wampum
Washington Covenant Belt,
from the Onondaga Nation
of the Iroquois Confederacy

SYNONYMS *wander, ramble, roam, rove, range, meander, stray, gallivant, gad* These verbs mean to move about at random or without destination or purpose. *Wander* and *ramble* stress the absence of a fixed course or goal: *She wandered into the room.* "*They would go off together, rambling along the river*" (John Galsworthy). *Roam* and *rove* emphasize freedom of movement, often over a wide area: "*Herds of horses and cattle roamed at will over the plain*" (George W. Cable). "*For ten long years I roved about, living first in one capital, then another*" (Charlotte Brontë). *Range* suggests wandering in all directions: "*a large hunting party known to be ranging the prairie*" (Francis Parkman). *Meander* suggests leisurely wandering over an irregular or winding course: "*He meandered to and fro . . . observing the manners and customs of Hillport society*" (Arnold Bennett). *Stray* refers to deviation from a proper course: "*I ask pardon, I am straying from the question*" (Oliver Goldsmith). *Gallivant* refers to wandering in search of pleasure: *gallivanted all over the city during the class trip. Gad*

---

suggests restless, pointless wandering: *gadded about unaccompanied in foreign places.*

wan·der·ing albatross (wŏn′dər-ĭng) *n.* A large, mostly white albatross (*Diomedea exulans*) of southern seas.

wandering Jew *n.* Any of three trailing plants, *Tradescantia albiflora, T. fluminensis,* or *Zebrina pendula,* native to tropical America and having usu. variegated foliage.

Wandering Jew *n.* A Jew of medieval legend condemned to wander until the Day of Judgment for having mocked Jesus on the day of the Crucifixion.

wan·der·lust (wŏn′dər-lŭst′) *n.* A very strong or irresistible impulse to travel. [Ger. : *wandern,* to wander (< MHGer.) + *Lust,* desire (< MHGer. < OHGer.).]

wane (wān) *intr.v.* **waned, wan·ing, wanes 1.** To decrease gradually in size, amount, intensity, or degree; decline. **2.** To exhibit a decreasing illuminated area from full moon to new moon. **3.** To approach an end. ❖ *n.* **1.** The act or process of gradually declining or diminishing. **2a.** A time or phase of gradual decrease. **b.** The period of the decrease of the moon's illuminated visible surface. **3.** A defective edge of a board caused by remaining bark or a beveled end. —*idiom:* **on the wane** In a period of decline or decrease. [ME *wanen* < OE *wanian.*]

wan·gle (wăng′gəl) *v.* **-gled, -gling, -gles** *Informal* —*tr.* **1.** To make, achieve, or get by contrivance. **2.** To manipulate or juggle, esp. fraudulently. **3.** To extricate (oneself) from difficulty. —*intr.* **1.** To use indirect, tricky, or fraudulent methods. **2.** To extricate oneself by subtle or indirect means, as from difficulty; wriggle. [?] —**wang′le** *n.* —**wang′ler** *n.*

wan·i·gan or **wan·ni·gan** (wŏn′ĭ-gən) also **wan·gun** (wŏn′gən, wăng′-) *n.* **1.** *New England & Upper Northern US* **a.** A boat or small chest equipped with supplies for a lumber camp. **b.** Provisions for a camp or cabin. **2.** *Alaska* **a.** A small building mounted on skids and towed behind a tractor train as eating and sleeping quarters for a work crew. **b.** An addition built onto a trailer house for extra living or storage space. [Ojibwa *waanikaan,* storage pit.]

wank (wăngk) *Chiefly British Vulgar Slang tr. & intr.v.* **wanked, wank·ing, wanks** To masturbate. Often used with *off.* ❖ *n.* **1.** An act of masturbation. **2.** A detestable person. [?]

Wan·kel engine (văng′kəl, wăng′-, wäng′-) *n.* A rotary internal-combustion engine in which a triangular rotor performs the functions allotted to the pistons of a conventional engine. [After Felix *Wankel* (1902–88), German engineer.]

wank·er (wăng′kər) *n. Chiefly British Vulgar Slang* **1.** A person who masturbates. **2.** A detestable person.

wan·na (wä′nə) *Informal* **1.** Contraction of *want to: You wanna go now?* **2.** Contraction of *want a: You wanna slice of pie?*

wan·na·be also **wan·na·bee** (wŏn′ə-bē′, wôn′-) *Informal n.* **1.** One who aspires to a role or position. **2.** One who imitates the behavior, customs, or dress of an admired person or group. **3.** A product designed to imitate the qualities or characteristics of something. ❖ *adj.* Wishing or aspiring to be; would-be. [Alteration of *want to be.*]

want (wŏnt, wônt) *v.* **want·ed, want·ing, wants** —*tr.* **1a.** To desire greatly; wish for: *She wants a glass of water.* See Syns at **desire.** **b.** To desire (someone to do something): *I want you to clean your room.* **2a.** To request the presence or assistance of: *You are wanted by your office.* **b.** To seek with intent to capture: *The fugitive is wanted by the police.* **3.** To have an inclination toward; like: *Say what you want, but be tactful.* **4.** *Informal* To be obliged (to do something): *You want to be careful on the ice.* **5.** To be without; lack. See Syns at **lack. 6.** To be in need of; require. —*intr.* **1.** To have need: *wants for nothing.* **2.** To be destitute or needy. **3.** To be disposed; wish. ❖ *n.* **1.** The condition or quality of lacking something usual or necessary. **2.** Pressing need; destitution: *lives in want.* **3.** Something desired: *a person of few wants.* **4.** A defect of character; a fault. —*phrasal verbs:* **want in** *Slang* **1.** To desire greatly to enter. **2.** To wish to join a project, business, or other undertaking. **want out** *Slang* **1.** To desire greatly to leave: *The cat wants out.* **2.** To wish to leave a project, a business, or other undertaking. [ME *wanten,* to be lacking < ON *vanta.*] —**want′er** *n.*

USAGE NOTE When *want* is followed immediately by an infinitive construction, it does not take *for: I want you to go* (not *want for you to go*). When *want* and the infinitive phrase are separated in the sentence, however, *for* is used: *What I want is for you to go. Want* in its meaning of "have need" normally takes *for: They'll not want for anything now that they've inherited his estate.* See Usage Note at **wish.**

---

want ad *n. Informal* A classified advertisement.

want·ing (wŏn′tĭng, wôn′-) *adj.* **1.** Absent; lacking. **2.** Not measuring up to standards or expectations. ❖ *prep.* **1.** Without. **2.** Minus; less: *an hour wanting 15 minutes.*

wan·ton (wŏn′tən) *adj.* **1.** Immoral or unchaste; lewd. **2a.** Gratuitously cruel; merciless. **b.** Marked by unprovoked, gratuitous maliciousness; capricious and unjust. **3.** Unrestrainedly excessive. **4.** Luxuriant; overabundant. **5.** Frolicsome; playful. **6.** Undisciplined; spoiled. **7.** *Obsolete* Rebellious; refractory. ❖ *v.* **-toned, -ton·ing, -tons** —*intr.* **1.** To act, grow, or move in a wanton manner; be wanton. —*tr.* To waste or squander extravagantly. ❖ *n.* **1.** One who is immoral, lewd, or licentious. **2.** One that is playful or frolicsome. **3.** One that is undisciplined or spoiled. [ME *wanto-wen* : *wan-*, not, lacking (< OE; akin to *wana*, lack) + *towen*, p. part. of *teen*, to bring up (< OE *tēon*, to lead, draw; see **deuk-** in App.).] —**wan′ton•ly** *adv.* —**wan′ton•ness** *n.*

wap•en•take (wŏp′ən-tāk′, wăp′-) *n.* A historical subdivision of some northern counties in England, corresponding roughly to the hundred. [ME < OE *wǣpengetæc* (transl. of ON *vápnatak*, act of taking weapons to indicate assent in an assembly) : *wǣpen*, weapon + *-getæc*, act of taking (< *tacan*, to take; see TAKE).]

wap•i•ti (wŏp′ĭ-tē) *n., pl.* **wapiti** or **-tis** A large light brown or grayish-brown North American deer (*Cervus canadensis*) having long branching antlers. [Shawnee *waapiti*.]

Wap•pin•ger (wä′pĭn-jər) *n., pl.* **Wappinger** or **-gers** A member of a Native American people formerly inhabiting the lower east bank of the Hudson River. [Of Algonquian orig.]

Wap•si•pin•i•con (wŏp′sə-pĭn′ĭ-kən) A river rising in S MN and flowing c. 410 km (255 mi) to the Mississippi R.

war (wôr) *n.* **1a.** A state of open, armed conflict between nations, states, or parties. **b.** The period of such conflict. **c.** The techniques and procedures of war; military science. **2a.** A condition of active antagonism or contention. **b.** A concerted effort to combat something injurious. ❖ *intr.v.* **warred, war•ring, wars** **1.** To wage or carry on warfare. **2.** To be in a state of hostility or rivalry; contend. —*idiom:* **at war** In an active state of conflict or contention. [ME *warre* < ONFr. *werre*, of Gmc. orig.]

Wa•ran•gal (wə-rŭng′gəl, wôr′əng-) A city of SE India NE of Hyderabad. Pop. 447,657.

war baby *n.* A child born during wartime, esp. during World War I or World War II.

War Between the States *n.* See **civil war** 3.

war•ble¹ (wôr′bəl) *v.* **-bled, -bling, -bles** —*tr.* To sing (a note, for example) with trills or other melodic embellishments. —*intr.* **1.** To sing with trills, runs, or quavers. **2.** To be sounded in a trilling or quavering manner. ❖ *n.* The act or an instance of warbling. [ME *werbelen* < ONFr. *werbler*, of Gmc. orig.]

war•ble² (wôr′bəl) *n.* **1a.** An abscessed boillike swelling on the back of cattle, deer, and certain other animals, caused by the larva of a warble fly. **b.** The warble fly, esp. in its larval stage. **2.** A hard lump of tissue on a riding horse's back caused by the saddle. [Prob. of Scand. orig.]

warble fly *n.* Any of several large hairy flies of the family Oestridae, having larvae that form warbles.

war•bler (wôr′blər) *n.* **1.** Any of various small New World songbirds of the family Parulidae, such as the redstart, many of which are brightly colored. **2.** Any of various small, often brownish or grayish Old World songbirds of the family Silviidae, such as the blackcap. **3.** One that warbles; a singer.

war bonnet *n.* A ceremonial headdress used by some Plains Indians consisting of a cap or band and a trailing extension and decorated with erect feathers.

war bride *n.* A woman who marries a serviceman during war.

War•burg (wôr′bərg, vär′bŏŏrk′), **Otto Heinrich** 1883–1970. German biochemist who won a 1931 Nobel Prize.

war chest *n.* **1.** An accumulation of funds to finance a war effort. **2.** A fund reserved for a particular purpose.

war correspondent *n.* A journalist, reporter, or commentator assigned to report directly from a war or combat zone.

war crime *n.* Any of various crimes, such as genocide or the mistreatment of prisoners of war, considered in violation of the conventions of warfare. —**war criminal** *n.*

war cry *n.* **1.** A cry uttered by combatants as they attack; a battle cry. **2.** A phrase used to rally people to a cause.

ward (wôrd) *n.* **1.** A division of a city or town, esp. an electoral district, for administrative and representative purposes. **2.** A district of some English and Scottish counties corresponding roughly to the hundred or the wapentake. **3a.** A room in a hospital usu. holding six or more patients. **b.** A division in a hospital for the care of a particular group of patients: *a maternity ward.* **4.** One of the divisions of a penal institution, such as a prison. **5.** An open court or area of a castle or fortification enclosed by walls. **6a.** *Law* A minor or incompetent person placed under the care or protection of a guardian or court. **b.** A person under the protection or care of another. **7.** The state of being under guard; custody. **8.** The act of guarding or protecting; guardianship. **9.** A means of protection; a defense. **10.** A defensive movement or attitude, esp. in fencing; a guard. **11a.** The projecting ridge of a lock or keyhole that prevents the turning of a key other than the proper one. **b.** The notch cut into a key that corresponds to such a ridge. ❖ *tr.v.* **ward•ed, ward•ing, wards** To guard; protect. —*phrasal verb:* **ward off** **1.** To turn aside; parry: *ward off blows.* **2.** To try to prevent; avert. [ME, action of guarding < OE *weard*, a watching, protection.]

Ward¹, Artemus 1727–1800. Amer. Revolutionary general who directed the siege of Boston until 1776.

Ward², Artemus See **Charles Farrar Browne.**

Ward, Mary Augusta Arnold Known as "Mrs. Humphry Ward." 1851–1920. British writer whose works include *Robert Elsmere* (1888).

–ward or **–wards** *suff.* **1a.** In a specified direction in time or space: *downward.* **b.** Toward a specified place or position: *skyward.* **2a.** Occurring or situated in a specified direction: *leftward.* **b.** Having a direction toward a specified place or position: *landward.* [ME < OE *-weard.* See **wer-²** in App.]

ward•ed (wôr′dĭd) *adj.* Having notches or ridges. Used of a key or lock.

war•den (wôrd′n) *n.* **1.** The chief administrative official of a prison. **2.** An official charged with enforcing certain laws and regulations. **3.** *Chiefly British* **a.** The chief executive official in charge of a port or market. **b.** Any of various crown officers having administrative duties. **c.** One of the governing officials of certain schools, guilds, or hospitals; a trustee. **4.** The chief executive of a borough in certain states. **5.** A churchwarden. [ME *wardein* < ONFr.: < *warder*, to guard, of Gmc. orig.] —**war′den•ship′** *n.*

war•den•ry (wôrd′n-rē) *n., pl.* **-ries** The office, duties, or jurisdiction of a warden.

ward•er¹ (wôr′dər) *n.* **1.** A guard, porter, or watcher of a gate or tower. **2.** *Chiefly British* A prison guard. [ME < AN *wardere* < ONFr. *warder*, to guard. See WARDEN.] —**war′der•ship′** *n.*

ward•er² (wôr′dər) *n.* A baton formerly used by a ruler or commander as a symbol of authority and to signal orders. [ME, poss. < *warden*, to ward < OE *weardian.*]

ward heeler *n.* *Informal* A worker for the ward organization of a political machine.

ward•robe (wôr′drōb′) *n.* **1.** A tall cabinet, closet, or small room built to hold clothes. **2.** Garments considered as a group, esp. all the clothing belonging to one person. **3a.** The costumes belonging to a theater or theatrical troupe. **b.** The place in which theatrical costumes are kept. **4.** The department in charge of wearing apparel, jewelry, and accessories in a royal or noble household. [ME *warderobe* < ONFr.: *warder*, to guard + *robe*, garment; see ROBE.]

ward•room (wôrd′rōōm′, -rŏŏm′) *n.* **1.** The common recreation area and dining room for the commissioned officers on a warship. **2.** The commissioned officers on a warship.

–wards *suff.* Variant of **-ward.**

ward•ship (wôrd′shĭp′) *n.* **1.** The state of being in the charge of a guardian. **2.** Custody; guardianship.

ware¹ (wâr) *n.* **1.** An article of commerce. **2.** An immaterial asset or benefit regarded as an article of commerce. [ME < OE *waru*, goods.]

ware² (wâr) *tr.v.* **wared, war•ing, wares** *Archaic* To beware of. ❖ *adj. Obsolete* **1.** Watchful; wary. **2.** Aware. [ME *waren* < OE *warian.* Adj., ME; see WARY.]

–ware *suff.* **1.** Articles of the same general kind, specified material, or use: *hardware; silverware.* **2.** Software: *groupware; shareware.* [< WARE¹. Sense 2 < SOFTWARE.]

ware•house (wâr′hous′) *n.* **1.** A place in which goods or merchandise are stored; a storehouse. **2.** A large, usu. wholesale shop. ❖ *tr.v.* (*also* -houz′) **-housed, -hous•ing, -hous•es** **1.** To place or store in a warehouse, esp. in a bonded or government warehouse. **2.** To institutionalize (people) in usu. deficient housing and in substandard conditions. —**ware′hous′er** (-hou′zər) *n.*

ware•room (wâr′rōōm′, -rŏŏm′) *n.* A room used for the storage or display of goods or wares.

war•fare (wôr′fâr′) *n.* **1a.** The waging of war against an enemy; armed conflict. **b.** Military operations marked by a specific characteristic: *guerrilla warfare.* **2.** A state of disharmony or conflict; strife. **3.** Acts undertaken to destroy or undermine the strength of another. [ME : *warre*, war; see WAR + *fare*, journey (< OE *faru* < *faran*, to journey; see FARE).]

war•fa•rin (wôr′fər-ĭn) *n.* A white crystalline compound, $C_{19}H_{16}O_4$, used as a rodenticide and as an anticoagulant. [*W(isconsin) A(lumni) R(esearch) F(oundation)* + (COUM)ARIN.]

war game *n.* **1.** A simulation of a military operation. **2.** A simulation of a proposed plan of action or strategy to test its validity. —**war′-game′** *v.*

war hawk *n.* **1.** A member of the 12th US Congress (1811–13) who advocated war with Great Britain. **2.** One who advocates war; a hawk.

war•head (wôr′hĕd′) *n.* A part of the armament system usu. in the forward part of a projectile that contains the explosive or other agent intended to inflict damage on a target.

War•hol (wôr′hôl′, -hōl′), **Andy** 1930?–87. Amer. artist who was a leader of the pop art movement.

war•horse also **war-horse** (wôr′hôrs′) *n.* **1.** A horse used in combat; a charger. **2.** *Informal* One who has been through many battles or struggles. **3.** *Informal* A musical or dramatic work that has been performed so often that it has become widely familiar.

war•like (wôr′līk′) *adj.* **1.** Belligerent; hostile. **2a.** Of or relating to war; martial. **b.** Indicative of or threatening war.

war•lock (wôr′lŏk′) *n.* A male witch, sorcerer, or demon. [ME *warloghe* < OE *wǣrloga*, oath-breaker : *wǣr*, pledge; see *wēra-o-* in App. + *-loga*, liar (< *lēogan*, to lie).]

war•lord (wôr′lôrd′) *n.* A military commander exercising civil power in a region, whether in nominal allegiance to the national government or in defiance of it. —**war′lord•ism** *n.*

Warl•pi•ri (wäl′bə-rē) *n., pl.* **Warlpiri** or **-ris** **1.** A member of a traditionally nomadic Aboriginal people of north-central and central Australia. **2.** Their Pama-Nyungan language.

warm (wôrm) *adj.* **warm•er, warm•est** **1.** Somewhat hotter than

wapiti
Cervus canadensis

Andy Warhol
photographed in 1978

warming pan

wart hog
Phacochoerus aethiopicus

Booker T. Washington
photographed c. 1895

temperate; moderately, often comfortably hot. **2.** Having the natural heat of living beings: *a warm body*. **3.** Preserving or imparting heat: *a warm overcoat*. **4.** Having or causing a sensation of unusually high body heat, as from exercise; overheated. **5.** Marked by enthusiasm; ardent. **6.** Marked by liveliness, excitement, or disagreement; heated: *a warm debate*. **7.** Marked by or revealing friendliness or sincerity; cordial: *warm greetings*. **8.** Loving; passionate. **9.** Excitable, impetuous, or quick to be aroused. **10.** Predominantly red or yellow in tone. **11.** Recently made; fresh: *a warm trail*. **12.** Close to guessing or finding something, as in certain games. **13.** *Informal* Uncomfortable because of danger or annoyance. ❖ *v.* **warmed, warm•ing, warms** —*tr.* **1.** To raise slightly in temperature; make warm: *warm up the house*. **2.** To make zealous or ardent; enliven. **3.** To fill with pleasant emotions. —*intr.* **1.** To become warm. **2.** To become ardent, enthusiastic, or animated. **3.** To become kindly disposed or friendly. ❖ *n. Informal* A warming or heating. —*phrasal verb:* **warm up 1.** *Sports* To prepare for an athletic event by exercising, stretching, or practicing. **2.** To make or become ready for an event or operation. **3.** To make more enthusiastic, excited, or animated. **4.** To approach a state of confrontation or violence. [ME < OE *wearm*.] —**warm′er** *n.* —**warm′ish** *adj.* —**warm′ly** *adv.* —**warm′ness** *n.*

warm-blood•ed (wôrm′blŭd′ĭd) *adj.* **1.** *Zoology* Maintaining a relatively constant and warm body temperature independent of environmental temperature; homeothermic. **2.** Ardent; passionate. —**warm′-blood′ed•ness** *n.*

warm boot *n.* The act or process of restarting a computer without turning off the power.

warmed-o•ver (wôrmd′ō′vər) *adj.* **1.** Warmed up; reheated. **2.** Not new, fresh, or spontaneous; stale.

warm front *n.* A front along which an advancing mass of warm air rises over a mass of cold air.

warm-heart•ed (wôrm′här′tĭd) *adj.* Marked by kindness, sympathy, and generosity. —**warm′heart′ed•ness** *n.*

warm•ing pan (wôr′mĭng) *n.* A metal pan with a cover and a long handle, designed to hold hot liquids or coals and used to warm a bed.

war•mon•ger (wôr′mŭng′gər, -mŏng′-) *n.* One who advocates or tries to stir up war. —**war′mon′ger•ing** *adj. & n.*

war•mouth (wôr′mouth′) *n., pl.* **-mouths** (-mouthz′, -mouths′) or **warmouth** A freshwater sunfish (*Lepomis gulosus*) of the eastern and Midwestern United States having a large mouth and minute teeth on its tongue. [?]

warmth (wôrmth) *n.* **1.** The state, sensation, or quality of producing or having a moderate degree of heat. **2a.** Friendliness, kindness, or affection. **b.** Excitement or intensity, as of love; ardor. **3.** The glowing effect produced by using warm hues. [ME *warmeth* < *warm*, warm. See WARM.]

warm-up or **warm up** (wôrm′ŭp′) *n.* **1a.** The act or procedure of warming up. **b.** A period spent in warming up. **2.** Clothing, such as a sweatsuit, designed to be worn before or after an athletic event. Often used in the plural.

warn (wôrn) *v.* **warned, warn•ing, warns** —*tr.* **1.** To make aware in advance of actual or potential harm, danger, or evil. **2.** To admonish as to action or manners. **3.** To notify (a person) to go or stay away: *warned them off the property*. **4.** To notify or apprise in advance. —*intr.* To give a warning. [ME *warnen* < OE *warnian*.] —**warn′er** *n.*

War•ner (wôr′nər), **Harry Morris** 1881–1958. Amer. filmmaker who with his brothers **Albert** (1884–1967), **Samuel Louis** (1887–1927), and **Jack** (1892–1978) founded Warner Brothers Pictures.

warn•ing (wôr′nĭng) *n.* **1.** An intimation, threat, or sign of impending danger or evil. **2a.** Advice to beware. **b.** Counsel to desist from a specified course of action. **3.** A cautionary or deterrent example. **4.** Something, such as a signal, that warns. ❖ *adj.* Acting or serving to warn.

warning coloration *n.* The conspicuous markings of an animal, such as a skunk, that serve to warn off predators.

warning track *n. Baseball* A strip of dirt or gravel along the outfield wall, designed to warn outfielders when they are approaching the wall.

war of nerves *n., pl.* **wars of nerves** A conflict marked by psychological tactics, such as intimidation and threats, that are intended to confuse, exhaust, and demoralize an enemy.

War of the Roses *n., pl.* **Wars of the Roses** A series of intermittent civil wars in the 15th century between the English royal houses of York and Lancaster and their supporters, ending in victory for the Lancastrians in 1485. Often used in the plural. [< the symbols of the two houses.]

warp (wôrp) *v.* **warped, warp•ing, warps** —*tr.* **1.** To turn or twist (wood, for example) out of shape. **2.** To turn from a correct or proper course; deflect. **3.** To affect unfavorably, unfairly, or wrongly; bias. **4.** To arrange (strands of yarn or thread) so that they run lengthwise in weaving. **5.** *Nautical* To move (a vessel) by hauling on a line that is fastened to or around a piling, anchor, or pier. —*intr.* **1.** To become bent or twisted out of shape. **2.** To turn aside from a true, correct, or natural course; go astray. **3.** *Nautical* To warp a vessel. ❖ *n.* **1.** The state of being twisted or bent out of shape. **2.** A distortion or twist, esp. in a piece of wood.

3. A mental or moral twist, aberration, or deviation. **4.** The threads that run lengthwise in a woven fabric, crossed at right angles to the weft. **5.** Warp and weft. **6.** *Nautical* A towline used in warping a vessel. [ME *werpen* < OE *weorpan*, to throw away. See **wer-²** in App.] —**warp′er** *n.*

war paint *n.* **1.** Pigments applied to the face or body in preparation for battle, as in certain tribal societies. **2.** *Informal* Cosmetics such as lipstick, rouge, or mascara.

warp and woof *n.* The underlying structure on which something is built; a base or foundation.

war party *n.* **1.** A band of warriors engaged in fighting or raiding an enemy. Used esp. of Native Americans. **2.** A usu. blatantly patriotic political party supporting a war.

war•path (wôr′păth′, -päth′) *n.* **1.** A course that leads to warfare or battle. **2.** A hostile course or mood.

war•plane (wôr′plān′) *n.* A combat aircraft.

warp speed *n. Informal* An extremely rapid speed or state of activity. [< *warp speed*, speed used for interstellar travel in the science-fiction television series *Star Trek*, referring to the use of time or space warps.]

war•rant (wôr′ənt, wŏr′-) *n.* **1.** Authorization or certification; sanction, as given by a superior. **2.** Justification for an action or belief; grounds. **3.** Something that provides assurance or confirmation; a guarantee or proof: *a warrant of authenticity*. **4.** An order that serves as authorization, esp.: **a.** A voucher authorizing payment or receipt of money. **b.** *Law* A judicial writ authorizing an officer to make a search, seizure, or arrest or to execute a judgment. **5a.** A warrant officer. **b.** A certificate of appointment given to a warrant officer. ❖ *tr.v.* **-rant•ed, -rant•ing, -rants 1.** To guarantee or attest to the quality, accuracy, or condition of. **2.** To guarantee or attest to the character or reliability of; vouch for. **3a.** To guarantee (a product). **b.** To guarantee (a purchaser) indemnification against damage or loss. **4.** To guarantee the immunity or security of. **5.** To provide adequate grounds for; justify. **6.** To grant authorization or sanction to (someone); authorize or empower. **7.** *Law* To guarantee clear title to (real property). [ME *warant* < ONFr., of Gmc. orig.] —**war′rant•a•bil′i•ty** *n.* —**war′rant•a•ble** *adj.* —**war′rant•a•bly** *adv.*

war•ran•tee (wôr′ən-tē′, wŏr′-) *n.* One to whom a warranty is made or a warrant is given.

warrant officer *n.* A military officer, usu. a skilled technician or a helicopter pilot, intermediate in rank between a noncommissioned officer and a commissioned officer and having authority by virtue of a warrant.

war•ran•tor (wôr′ən-tər, -tôr′, wŏr′-) also **war•rant•er** (-tər) *n.* One that makes a warrant or gives a warranty.

war•ran•ty (wôr′ən-tē, wŏr′-) *n., pl.* **-ties 1.** Official authorization, sanction, or warrant. **2.** Justification or valid grounds for an act or a course of action. **3.** *Law* **a.** An assurance by the seller of property that the goods or property are as represented or will be as promised. **b.** The insured's guarantee that the facts are as stated in reference to an insurance risk or that specified conditions will be fulfilled to keep the contract effective. **c.** A covenant by which the seller of land binds himself or herself and his or her heirs to defend the security of the estate conveyed. **d.** A judicial writ; a warrant. **4.** A guarantee given to a purchaser stating that a product is reliable and free from known defects and that the seller will repair or replace defective parts. [ME *warantie* < ONFr. < fem. p. part. of *warantir*, to guarantee < *warant*, warrant.]

war•ren (wôr′ən, wŏr′-) *n.* **1a.** An area where rabbits live in burrows. **b.** A colony of rabbits. **2.** An enclosure for small game animals. **3a.** An overcrowded living area. **b.** A mazelike place where one may easily become lost. [ME *warenne* < ONFr., enclosure.]

Warren A city of SE MI, a suburb of Detroit. Pop. 138,247.

Warren, Earl 1891–1974. Amer. jurist; chief justice of the US Supreme Court (1953–69).

Warren, Robert Penn 1905–89. Amer. writer and critic known for his novel *All the King's Men* (1946).

war•ren•er (wôr′ə-nər, wŏr′-) *n.* **1.** One who owns or keeps a rabbit warren. **2.** A gamekeeper.

War•ring•ton (wôr′ĭng-tən, wŏr′-) A borough of W-central England E of Liverpool on the Mersey R. Pop. 185,005.

war•ri•or (wôr′ē-ər, wŏr′-) *n.* **1.** One who is engaged in or experienced in battle. **2.** One who is engaged aggressively or energetically in an activity, cause, or conflict. [ME *werreour* < ONFr. *werrieur* < *werreier*, to make war < *werre*, war. See WAR.]

war room *n.* A room in which strategic decisions, esp. for a military or political campaign, are made.

war•saw (wôr′sô) *n.* A large Caribbean grouper (*Epinephelus nigritus*). [Perh. alteration of Am.Sp. *guasa*, a sea bass.]

Warsaw The cap. of Poland, in the E-central part of the country on the Vistula R.; founded in the 13th cent. Pop. 1,654,491.

war•ship (wôr′shĭp′) *n.* A combat ship.

wart (wôrt) *n.* **1a.** A hard rough skin growth caused by viral infection, typically on the hands or feet. **b.** A similar growth or protuberance, as on a plant. **2.** A genital wart. **3a.** One that resembles or is likened to a wart, esp. in unattractiveness. **b.** An imperfection; a flaw. —*idiom:* **warts and all** *Slang* All defects and imperfections notwithstanding. [ME < OE *wearte*.] —**wart′ed,** **wart′y** *adj.*

War•ta (vär′tə, -tä) A river rising in S-central Poland NW of Kra-

wart hog also **wart·hog** (wôrt′hôg′, -hŏg′) *n.* A wild African hog (*Phacochoerus aethiopicus*) that has a pair of prominent tusks and wartlike growths on the face.

war·time (wôr′tīm′) *n.* A period during a war.

War·wick (wôr′wĭk) A city of E-central RI on Narragansett Bay S of Providence; settled in 1643. Pop. 85,808.

War·wick (wôr′ĭk), Earl of. Title of Richard Neville. Known as "the Kingmaker." 1428–71. English military and political leader who fought for the Yorkists during the Wars of the Roses and secured the throne for Edward IV (1461). He then changed allegiance and restored Henry VI to the throne (1470).

war·y (wâr′ē) *adj.* **-i·er, -i·est 1.** On guard; watchful. **2.** Characterized by caution. [ME *ware* < OE *wær*.] —**war′i·ly** *adv.* —**war′i·ness** *n.*

was (wŭz, wŏz) *wəz when unstressed) v.* First and third person singular past indicative of **be**. [ME < OE *wæs*. See **wes-**[1] in App.]

wa·sa·bi (wä′sä-bē) *n.* A very pungent green Japanese condiment made from the root of the herb *Eutrema wasabi*. [J.]

Wa·satch Range (wô′săch′) A range of the Rocky Mts. in SE ID and central UT rising to 3,662.4 m (12,008 ft).

wash (wŏsh, wôsh) *v.* **washed, wash·ing, wash·es** *—tr.* **1a.** To cleanse, using water or other liquid, usu. with soap, detergent, or bleach, by immersing, dipping, rubbing, or scrubbing: *wash one's hands; wash windows.* **b.** To soak, rinse out, and remove (dirt or stain) with or as if with water: *wash grease out of overalls.* **2.** To make moist or wet; drench. **3.** To flow over, against, or past. **4.** To carry, erode, remove, or destroy by the action of moving water: *Heavy rains washed the topsoil away.* **5.** To rid of corruption or guilt; cleanse or purify. **6.** To cover or coat with a watery layer of paint or other coloring substance. **7.** *Chemistry* **a.** To purify (a gas) by passing through or over a liquid, as to remove soluble matter. **b.** To pass a solvent through (a precipitate). **8.** To separate constituents of (an ore) by immersion in or agitation with water. **9.** To cause to undergo a swirling action. *—intr.* **1.** To cleanse something in or by means of water or other liquid. **2a.** To undergo washing without fading or other damage. **b.** *Informal* To hold up under examination; be convincing. **3.** To flow, sweep, or beat with a characteristic lapping sound. **4.** To be carried away, removed, or drawn by the action of water. ❖ *n.* **1.** The act or process of washing or cleansing. **2.** A quantity of articles washed or intended for washing. **3.** Waste liquid; swill. **4.** Fermented liquid from which liquor is distilled. **5.** A preparation or product used in washing or coating. **6.** A cosmetic or medicinal liquid, such as a mouthwash. **7a.** A thin layer of water color or India ink spread on a drawing. **b.** A light tint or hue. **8a.** A rush or surge of water or waves. **b.** The sound of this rush or surge. **9a.** Removal or erosion of soil by the action of moving water. **b.** A deposit of recently eroded debris. **10a.** Low or marshy ground washed by tidal waters. **b.** A stretch of shallow water. **11.** *Western US* The dry bed of a stream. **12.** Turbulence in air or water caused by the motion or action of an oar, propeller, jet, or airfoil. **13.** *Informal* An activity, action, or enterprise that yields neither marked gain nor marked loss. ❖ *adj.* **1.** Used for washing. **2.** Being such that washing is possible; washable. **—phrasal verbs: wash down 1.** To clean by washing with water from top to bottom. **2.** To follow the ingestion of (food, for example) with the ingestion of a liquid. **wash out 1a.** To remove or be removed by washing. **b.** To cause to fade by laundering. **2.** To carry or wear away or be carried or worn away by the action of moving water. **3.** To deplete or become depleted of vitality. **4.** To eliminate or be eliminated as unsatisfactory. **5.** To cause (an event) to be rained out. **wash up 1.** To wash one's hands and face. **2.** *Chiefly British* To wash dishes after a meal. **3.** To bring about the end or ruin of; finish. **—idioms: come out in the wash** *Slang* **1.** To be revealed eventually. **2.** To turn out well in the end. **wash (one's) hands of 1.** To refuse to accept responsibility for. **2.** To abandon; renounce. [ME *washen* < OE *wacsan, wæscan*. See **wed-** in App.]

Wash An inlet of the North Sea off E-central England.

Wash. *abbr.* Washington

wash·a·ble (wŏsh′ə-bəl, wôsh′-) *adj.* Capable of being washed without injury. —**wash′a·bil′i·ty** *n.*

wash-and-wear (wŏsh′ən-wâr′, wôsh′-) *adj.* Treated so as to be easily or quickly washed or rinsed clean and to require little or no ironing. Used of clothes and linens.

wash·ba·sin (wŏsh′bā′sən, wôsh′-) *n.* See **washbowl**.

wash·board (wŏsh′bôrd′, -bōrd′, wôsh′-) *n.* **1a.** A board having a corrugated surface on which clothes can be rubbed in the process of laundering. **b.** *Music* A similar board used as a percussion instrument. **2.** A board fastened to a wall at the floor; a baseboard. **3.** *Nautical* A thin plank fastened to the side of a boat or the sill of a port to keep out the sea.

wash·bowl (wŏsh′bōl′, wôsh′-) *n.* A basin that can be filled with water for use in washing oneself.

wash·cloth (wŏsh′klôth′, -klŏth′, wôsh′-) *n.* A small, usu. square cloth used for washing the face or body.

wash·day (wŏsh′dā′, wôsh′-) *n.* A day set aside for doing household washing.

wash drawing *n.* A drawing or painting in which washes of color are used.

washed-out (wŏsht′out′, wôsht′-) *adj.* **1.** Lacking color or inten-

sity; faded. **2.** Exhausted or tired-looking. **3.** Having dropped an enterprise or having been dropped from one.

washed-up (wŏsht′ŭp′, wôsht′-) *adj.* **1.** No longer successful or needed; finished. **2.** Ready to give up in disgust.

wash·er (wŏsh′ər, wô′shər) *n.* **1.** One who washes. **2.** An appliance used for washing, esp.: **a.** A washing machine. **b.** An automatic dishwasher. **3.** A flat disk, as of metal, placed beneath a nut or at an axle bearing or a joint to relieve friction, prevent leakage, or distribute pressure.

wash·er·wom·an (wŏsh′ər-woŏm′ən, wô′shər-) also **wash·wom·an** (wŏsh′woŏm′ən, wôsh′-) *n.* A woman who washes clothes and linens for a living.

wash·e·teria (wŏsh′ĭ-tîr′ē-ə, wô′shĭ-) *n.* A laundromat. [WASH + (CAF)ETERIA.]

wash·ing (wŏsh′ĭng, wô′shĭng) *n.* **1.** The act or process of one that washes. **2.** Articles washed or intended to be washed at one time. **3.** The residue after an ore or other material has been washed. **4.** The liquid used to wash something. Often used in the plural.

washing machine *n.* A usu. automatic machine for washing clothes and linens.

washing soda *n.* A hydrated sodium carbonate used as a general cleanser.

Wash·ing·ton (wŏsh′ĭng-tən, wô′shĭng-) **1.** A state of the NW US on the Pacific Ocean; admitted as the 42nd state in 1889. Cap. Olympia. Pop. 5,894,121. **2.** The cap. of the US, on the Potomac R. between VA and MD and coextensive with the District of Columbia; designated as cap. in 1800. Pop. 572,059. —**Wash′ing·to′ni·an** (wŏsh′ĭng-tō′nē-ən, wô′shĭng-) *adj. & n.*

Washington, Booker T(aliaferro) 1856–1915. Amer. educator and principal of Tuskegee Institute from 1881 to 1915.

Washington, George 1732–99. Amer. military leader and the first President of the US (1789–97).

Washington, Lake A lake in W-central WA on the E boundary of Seattle.

Washington, Martha Dandridge Custis 1731–1802. First Lady of the US (1789–97).

Washington, Mount A mountain, 1,917.8 m (6,288 ft), in the White Mts. of E NH.

Wash·ing·ton's Birthday (wŏsh′ĭng-tənz, wô′shĭng-) *n.* February 22, formerly observed to commemorate the birth of George Washington in 1732.

Wash·i·ta (wŏsh′ĭ-tô′, wô′shĭ-) A river rising in NW TX and flowing c. 724 km (450 mi) across OK to the Red R.

wash·out (wŏsh′out′, wôsh′-) *n.* **1a.** Erosion of a relatively soft surface by a sudden gush of water, as from a downpour. **b.** A channel thus produced. **2a.** A total failure or disappointment. **b.** One who fails to measure up to a standard, as by failing a course of training or study.

wash·rag (wŏsh′răg′, wôsh′-) *n.* See **washcloth**.

wash·room (wŏsh′roōm′, -roŏm′, wôsh′-) *n.* A bathroom.

wash·stand (wŏsh′stănd′, wôsh′-) *n.* **1.** A stand designed to hold a basin and pitcher of water for washing. **2.** A stationary bathroom sink.

wash·tub (wŏsh′tŭb′, wôsh′-) *n.* A tub used for washing clothes.

wash·wom·an (wŏsh′woŏm′ən, wôsh′-) *n.* Variant of **washerwoman**.

wash·y (wŏsh′ē, wô′shē) *adj.* **-i·er, -i·est 1.** Watery; diluted. **2.** Lacking strength or intensity. —**wash′i·ness** *n.*

was·n't (wŭz′ənt, wŏz′-) Contraction of *was not*.

wasp (wŏsp, wôsp) *n.* Any of numerous social or solitary insects, chiefly of the superfamilies Vespoidea and Sphecoidea, having two pairs of membranous wings, mouths adapted for biting or sucking, and in the females an ovipositor often modified as a sting. [ME *waspe* < OE *wæps, wæsp*.] —**wasp′y** *adj.*

WASP or **Wasp** *n.* **1.** A white Protestant of Anglo-Saxon ancestry. **2.** A white, usu. Protestant member of the American upper social class. [W(hite) A(nglo-)S(axon) P(rotestant).]

wasp·ish (wŏs′pĭsh) *adj.* **1.** Of, relating to, or suggestive of a wasp. **2.** Easily irritated or annoyed; irascible. **3.** Indicative of irritation, annoyance, or spite: *a waspish remark.* —**wasp′ish·ly** *adv.* —**wasp′ish·ness** *n.*

wasp waist *n.* A very slender waist or one that is tightly corseted. —**wasp′-waist′ed** (wŏs′wās′tĭd, wôsp′-) *adj.*

was·sail (wŏs′əl, wŏ-sāl′) *n.* **1a.** A salutation or toast given in drinking someone's health or as an expression of goodwill. **b.** The drink used in such toasting, commonly ale or wine spiced with roasted apples and sugar. **2.** A festivity characterized by much drinking. ❖ *v.* **-sailed, -sail·ing, -sails** *—tr.* To drink to the health of; toast. *—intr.* To engage in or drink a wassail. [ME, contraction of *wæshæil*, be healthy < ON *ves heill* : *ves*, imper. sing. of *vera*, to be; see **wes-**[1] in App. + *heill*, healthy; see **kailo-** in App.] —**was′sail·er** *n.*

Was·ser·mann reaction (wä′sər-mən) *n.* A complement-fixing reaction to the Wassermann test.

Wassermann test *n.* A diagnostic test for syphilis involving the fixation or inactivation of a complement by an antibody in a blood serum sample. [After August von *Wassermann* (1866–1925), German bacteriologist.]

wast (wŏst; wəst *when unstressed) v. Archaic* A second person singular past tense of **be**.

George Washington
detail from a portrait by Thomas Sully

Martha Washington
detail from an early 19th-century portrait by an unidentified artist

wast•age (wā′stĭj) *n.* **1.** Loss by deterioration, wear, or destruction. **2.** The gradual process of wasting. **3.** An amount that is wasted or lost by wear.

waste (wāst) *v.* **wast•ed, wast•ing, wastes** —*tr.* **1.** To use, consume, spend, or expend thoughtlessly or carelessly. **2.** To cause to lose energy, strength, or vigor; enervate, tire, or enfeeble. **3.** To fail to take advantage of or use for profit; lose. **4a.** To destroy completely. **b.** *Slang* To kill; murder. —*intr.* **1.** To lose energy, strength, weight, or vigor; become weak or enfeebled: *wasting away.* **2.** To pass without being put to use. ❖ *n.* **1.** The act or an instance of wasting or the condition of being wasted. **2.** A place, region, or land that is uninhabited or uncultivated; a desert or wilderness. **3.** A devastated or destroyed region, town, or building; a ruin. **4a.** An unusable or unwanted substance or material. **b.** Something, such as steam, that escapes without being used. **5.** Garbage; trash. **6.** The undigested residue of food eliminated from the body; excrement. ❖ *adj.* **1.** Regarded or discarded as worthless or useless. **2.** Used as a conveyance or container for refuse. **3.** Excreted from the body. —*idiom:* **waste (one's) breath** To gain or accomplish nothing by speaking. [ME *wasten* < ONFr. *waster* < Lat. *vāstāre*, to make empty < *vāstus*, empty.]

waste•bas•ket (wāst′băs′kĭt) *n.* A relatively small, open-topped container for discarding trash.

wast•ed (wā′stĭd) *adj.* **1.** Not profitably used or maintained. **2.** Needless or superfluous. **3.** Deteriorated; ravaged. **4.** Frail and enfeebled, as from prolonged illness; emaciated. **5.** *Slang* Drunk or intoxicated. **6.** *Archaic* Having elapsed.

waste•ful (wāst′fəl) *adj.* Marked by or inclined to waste; extravagant. —**waste′ful•ly** *adv.* —**waste′ful•ness** *n.*

waste•land (wāst′lănd′) *n.* **1.** Land that is desolate, barren, or ravaged. **2.** A place, era, or aspect of life considered as lacking in spiritual, aesthetic, or other humanizing qualities.

waste•pa•per (wāst′pā′pər) *n.* Discarded paper.

waste pipe *n.* A pipe that carries off liquid waste.

wast•er (wā′stər) *n.* **1.** One that wastes. **2.** One that destroys.

waste•wa•ter (wāst′wô′tər, -wŏt′ər) *n.* Water that has been used, as for washing or flushing or in a manufacturing process, and so contains waste products; sewage.

wast•ing (wā′stĭng) *adj.* **1.** Gradually deteriorating; declining. **2.** Sapping the strength, energy, or substance of the body; emaciating: *a wasting disease.* —**wast′ing•ly** *adv.*

wast•rel (wā′strəl) *n.* **1.** One who wastes, esp. one who wastes money; a profligate. **2.** An idler or a loafer. [WAST(E) + -*rel* (as in SCOUNDREL).]

wat (wät) *n.* A Buddhist temple in Thailand or Cambodia. [Thai < Skt. *vāṭaḥ*, enclosure.]

watch (wŏch) *v.* **watched, watch•ing, watch•es** —*intr.* **1.** To look or observe attentively or carefully; be closely observant. **2.** To look and wait expectantly or in anticipation. **3.** To act as a spectator; look on. **4.** To stay awake at night while serving as a guard, sentinel, or watcher. **5.** To stay alert as a devotional or religious exercise; keep vigil. —*tr.* **1.** To look at steadily; observe carefully or continuously. **2.** To keep a watchful eye on; guard. **3.** To observe the course of mentally; keep informed about. **4.** To tend (a flock, for example). See Syns at **tend**[2]. ❖ *n.* **1.** The act or process of keeping awake or mentally alert, esp. for the purpose of guarding. **2a.** The act of observing closely or the condition of being closely observed; surveillance. **b.** A period of close observation. **3.** A person or group of people serving to guard or protect. **4.** The post or period of duty of a guard, sentinel, or watcher. **5.** Any of the periods into which the night is divided; a part of the night. **6.** *Nautical* **a.** Any of the periods of time, usu. four hours, aboard ship into which the day is divided and during which the crew is assigned to duty. **b.** The members of a ship's crew on duty during a specific watch. **c.** A chronometer on a ship. **7a.** A period of wakefulness, esp. one observed as a religious vigil. **b.** A funeral wake. **8.** A small portable timepiece, esp. one worn on the wrist or carried in the pocket. **9.** A flock of nightingales. —*phrasal verbs:* **watch out** To be careful or on the alert; take care. **watch over** To be in charge of; superintend. —*idioms:* **watch it** To be careful. **watch (one's) step** **1.** To act or proceed with care and caution. **2.** To behave as is demanded, required, or appropriate. [ME *wacchen* < OE *wæccan*, to watch, be awake.]

watch•a•ble (wŏch′ə-bəl) *adj.* **1.** Capable of being watched; viewable. **2.** Good enough to watch.

watch•band (wŏch′bănd′) *n.* A band, as of leather, that holds a wristwatch in place.

watch cap *n.* A dark blue knitted cap worn in cold weather, esp. by enlisted naval personnel.

watch•case (wŏch′kās′) *n.* The casing for the mechanism of a watch.

watch•dog (wŏch′dôg′, -dŏg′) *n.* **1.** A dog trained to guard people or property. **2.** A guardian or protector against waste, loss, or illegal practices. —**watch′dog′** *v.*

watch•er (wŏch′ər) *n.* **1.** One that watches or observes. **2.** One who keeps vigil, as at a sick person's bedside.

watch•eye (wŏch′ī′) *n.* Walleye, esp. in dogs.

watch fire *n.* A fire kept burning at night, as for a signal.

watch•ful (wŏch′fəl) *adj.* **1.** Closely observant or alert; vigilant. See Syns at **aware, careful**. **2.** *Archaic* Not sleeping; awake. —**watch′ful•ly** *adv.* —**watch′ful•ness** *n.*

watch glass *n.* **1.** A shallow glass dish used as a beaker cover or evaporating surface. **2.** A concavo-convex glass or plastic disk used to cover the face of a watch.

watch•mak•er (wŏch′mā′kər) *n.* One that makes or repairs watches.

watch•man (wŏch′mən) *n.* A man who is employed to stand guard or keep watch.

watch night *n.* **1.** New Year's Eve. **2.** A religious service held on New Year's Eve.

watch•tow•er (wŏch′tou′ər) *n.* An observation tower on which a guard or lookout is stationed to keep watch.

watch•word (wŏch′wûrd′) *n.* **1.** A prearranged reply to a challenge, as from a guard; a password. **2.** A rallying cry.

wa•ter (wô′tər, wŏt′ər) *n.* **1.** A clear, colorless, odorless, and tasteless liquid, H_2O, essential for most plant and animal life and the most widely used of all solvents. Freezing point 0°C (32°F); boiling point 100°C (212°F); specific gravity (4°C) 1.0. **2a.** Any of various forms of water. **b.** Naturally occurring mineral water, as at a spa. Often used in the plural. **3a.** A body of water such as a sea, lake, river, or stream. **b. waters** A particular stretch of sea or ocean, esp. that of a state or country. **4a.** A supply of water. **b.** A water supply system. **5a.** Any of the fluids normally secreted by the body, such as urine, perspiration, or saliva. **b.** A fluid present in a body part in abnormal quantities as a result of injury or disease. **c.** The fluid surrounding a fetus in the uterus; amniotic fluid. **6.** An aqueous solution of a substance, esp. a gas: *ammonia water.* **7.** A wavy finish or sheen, as of a fabric. **8a.** The valuation of the assets of a business firm beyond their real value. **b.** Stock issued in excess of paid-in capital. **9a.** The transparency and luster of a gem. **b.** A level of excellence. ❖ *v.* **-tered, -ter•ing, -ters** —*tr.* **1.** To pour or sprinkle water on; make wet: *watered the garden.* **2a.** To give drinking water to. **b.** To lead (an animal) to drinking water. **3.** To dilute or weaken by adding water. **4.** To give a sheen to the surface of (silk, linen, or metal). **5.** To increase (the number of shares of stock) without increasing the value of the assets represented. **6.** To irrigate (land). —*intr.* **1.** To produce or discharge fluid, as from the eyes. **2.** To salivate in anticipation of food. **3.** To take on a supply of water, as a ship. **4.** To drink water, as an animal. —*phrasal verb:* **water down** To reduce the strength or effectiveness of. —*idioms:* **above water** Out of difficulty or trouble. **water under the bridge** A past occurrence that cannot be undone or rectified. [ME < OE *wæter.* See **wed-** in App.] —**wa′ter•er** *n.*

water bag *n.* The membranous sac filled with amniotic fluid that protects a fetus during pregnancy.

water ballet *n.* **1.** Dancelike movement in water; synchronized swimming. **2.** A performance or competition of this.

water bear *n.* See **tardigrade**.

Water Bearer *n.* See **Aquarius**.

wa•ter•bed (wô′tər-bĕd′, wŏt′ər-) *n.* A bed with a mattress made of a tough plastic that is filled with water.

water beetle *n.* Any of various aquatic beetles, esp. of the family Dytiscidae, having a smooth oval body and flattened and fringed hind legs adapted for swimming.

water bird *n.* A swimming or wading bird.

water biscuit *n.* A biscuit made of flour and water.

water blister *n.* A blister having watery contents without blood or pus.

water bloom *n.* A growth of algae at or near the surface of a body of water, such as a pond.

water boatman *n.* Any of various aquatic insects of the families Corixidae and Notonectidae, having long oarlike hind legs adapted for swimming.

wa•ter•borne (wô′tər-bôrn′, -bōrn′, wŏt′ər-) *adj.* **1.** Floating on or supported by water; afloat. **2.** Transported by water. **3.** Transmitted in water: *waterborne disease.*

wa•ter•buck (wô′tər-bŭk′, wŏt′ər-) *n., pl.* **waterbuck** or **-bucks** Any of several African antelopes of the genus *Kobus*, having curved ridged horns and frequenting swamps, rivers, and other bodies of water. [Transl. of Afr. *waterbok*.]

water buffalo *n.* A widely domesticated buffalo (*Bubalus bubalis*) of Asia having large spreading horns.

water buffalo
Bubalus bubalis

water bug *n.* **1.** Any of various aquatic insects, esp. the water boatman and certain backswimmers. **2.** A large cockroach.

Wa•ter•bur•y (wô′tər-bĕr′ē, wŏt′ər-) A city of W-central CT NNW of New Haven. Pop. 107,271.

wa•ter•bus (wô′tər-bŭs′, wŏt′ər-) *n., pl.* **-bus•es** or **-bus•ses** A large motorboat used for carrying passengers on rivers or canals.

water caltrop *n.* See **water chestnut** 1.

water cannon *n.* A truck-mounted apparatus that fires water at high pressure, used esp. to control crowds.

water chestnut *n.* **1.** A floating aquatic plant (*Trapa natans*) native to Eurasia and Africa and bearing four-pronged nutlike fruit. **2a.** A tropical Asian aquatic sedge (*Eleocharis dulcis*) having an edible corm and cylindrical leaves. **b.** This corm.

water chinquapin *n.* A North American aquatic plant (*Nelumbo lutea*) related to the lotus and having shield-shaped aerial leaves, pale-yellow flowers, and edible nutlike seeds.

water clock *n.* A clepsydra.

water closet *n.* A room or booth containing a toilet and often a washbowl.

wa·ter·col·or (wô′tər-kŭl′ər, wŏt′ər-) *n*. **1a.** A paint composed of a water-soluble pigment. **b.** A work that is executed through the use of this paint. **2.** The art of using watercolors. —**wa′ter·col′or** *adj*. —**wa′ter·col′or·ist** *n*.

wa·ter-cool (wô′tər-kōōl′, wŏt′ər-) *tr.v.* **-cooled, -cool·ing, -cools** To cool (an engine) with water, esp. circulating water.

water cooler *n*. A device for cooling and dispensing drinking water.

wa·ter·course (wô′tər-kôrs′, -kōrs′, wŏt′ər-) *n*. **1.** A natural or artificial channel for flowing water. **2.** A stream or river.

wa·ter·craft (wô′tər-krăft′, wŏt′ər-) *n*. **1.** Skill in boating, swimming, or other water-related sports. **2a.** A boat or ship. **b.** (*used with a pl. verb*) Water vehicles considered as a group.

wa·ter·cress (wô′tər-krĕs′, wŏt′ər-) *n*. **1.** A pungent perennial Eurasian herb (*Rorippa nasturtium-aquaticum*) of the mustard family, growing in ponds and streams and often used as a garnish. **2.** Any of several related aquatic plants.

water cure *n*. Hydropathy or hydrotherapy.

water cycle *n*. The cycle that controls the distribution of the earth's water as it evaporates from bodies of water, condenses, precipitates, and returns to those bodies of water.

water dog *n*. **1.** A dog that takes easily to the water, esp. one trained for hunting waterfowl. **2.** *Informal* A person who feels at home in or on the water. **3.** often **wa·ter·dog** (wô′tər-dôg′, -dŏg′, wŏt′ər-) See **mudpuppy** 1. **4.** *Western US* Any of several large salamanders.

wa·tered-down (wô′tərd-doun′, wŏt′ərd-) *adj*. Diminished in force or effect.

Wa·ter·ee (wô′tə-rē, wŏt′ə-) A river of central SC flowing c. 233 km (145 mi) S to form the Santee R. Its upper course in NC is called the Catawba R.

water elm *n*. See **planer tree**.

wa·ter·fall (wô′tər-fôl′, wŏt′ər-) *n*. A steep descent of water from a height; a cascade.

wa·ter·find·er (wô′tər-fīn′dər, wŏt′ər-) *n*. A dowser.

water flea *n*. Any of various small active aquatic crustaceans of the order Cladocera, esp. the daphnia.

Wa·ter·ford (wô′tər-fərd, wŏt′ər-) A borough of SE Ireland SSW of Dublin. Pop. 38,473.

wa·ter·fowl (wô′tər-foul′, wŏt′ər-) *n., pl.* **waterfowl** or **-fowls** **1.** A water bird, esp. a swimming bird. **2.** Swimming game birds, such as ducks and geese, considered as a group.

wa·ter·front (wô′tər-frŭnt′, wŏt′ər-) *n*. **1.** Land abutting a body of water. **2.** The part of a town or city that abuts water, esp. a district of wharves where ships dock.

water gap *n*. A transverse cleft in a mountain ridge through which a stream flows.

water gas *n*. A fuel gas, chiefly carbon monoxide and with some hydrogen, methane, carbon dioxide, and nitrogen, made from coke, air, and steam.

water gate *n*. **1.** See **floodgate** 1. **2.** A gate that provides access to a body of water.

Wa·ter·gate (wô′tĕr-gāt′, wŏt′ər-) *n*. A series of scandals occurring during the Nixon administration in which members of the executive branch organized illegal political espionage and were charged with bribery, contempt of Congress, and attempted obstruction of justice. [After *Watergate*, a building complex in Washington DC, the site of a burglary (1972) that gave rise to the scandals.]

water gauge *n*. An instrument indicating the level of water, as in a boiler, tank, reservoir, or stream.

water glass *n*. **1.** A drinking glass or goblet. **2.** An open tube or box having a glass bottom for making observations below the surface of the water. **3.** See **sodium silicate**. **4.** A water gauge made of glass. **5.** See **clepsydra**.

water gun *n*. See **squirt gun**.

water hammer *n*. **1.** A banging noise heard in a water pipe following an abrupt alteration of the flow with resultant pressure surges. **2.** A banging noise in steam pipes, caused by steam bubbles entering a cold pipe partially filled with water.

water hemlock *n*. Any of several poisonous perennial herbs of the genus *Cicuta*, esp. *C. maculata* of marshy areas of North America, having bipinnately compound leaves.

water hen *n*. Any of various water birds of the family Rallidae, as the gallinule, rail, or coot, that inhabit marshland.

water hole *n*. See **watering hole**.

water hyacinth *n*. An aquatic tropical American herb (*Eichhornia crassipes*) forming dense floating masses and having bluish-purple flowers.

water ice *n*. A dessert made of finely crushed ice that has been sweetened and flavored.

wa·ter·ing can (wô′tər-ĭng, wŏt′ər-) *n*. A vessel, usu. having a long spout with a perforated nozzle, used to water plants.

watering hole *n*. **1.** A small natural depression in which water collects, esp. a pool where animals come to drink. **2.** *Informal* A social gathering place, such as a bar or saloon, where drinks are served.

watering place *n*. **1.** A place where animals find water to drink. **2.** A health resort with mineral springs; a spa. **3.** *Informal* A watering hole.

watering pot *n*. See **watering can**.

wa·ter·ish (wô′tər-ĭsh, wŏt′ər-) *adj*. Resembling water; watery.

water jacket *n*. A casing containing water circulated by a pump, used around a part to be cooled, esp. in water-cooled internal-combustion engines. —**wa′ter-jack′et** *v*.

water key *n*. A lever covering a small hole on certain brass instruments, such as the trombone, that is pressed to drain saliva that has accumulated in the instrument.

wa·ter·leaf (wô′tər-lēf′, wŏt′ər-) *n., pl.* **-leafs** Any of various North American herbs of the genus *Hydrophyllum*, having pinnately lobed leaves and white or purplish flowers.

wa·ter·less (wô′tər-lĭs, wŏt′ər-) *adj*. **1.** Lacking water; dry. **2.** Not requiring water, as a cooling system.

water level *n*. **1.** The level of the surface of a body of water. **2.** *Geology* See **water table** 2. **3.** The water line of a ship.

water lily *n*. Any of various cosmopolitan aquatic herbs of the genus *Nymphaea*, having floating leaves and showy, variously colored flowers, esp. *N. odorata*.

water line or **wa·ter·line** (wô′tər-līn′, wŏt′ər-) *n*. **1a.** The line on the hull of a ship to which the surface of the water rises. **b.** Any of several lines parallel to this line, marked on the hull of a ship to indicate the depth at which the ship is submerged under various loads. **2.** A line or stain, as one left on a seawall, indicating the height to which water has risen or may rise; a watermark.

wa·ter·log (wô′tər-lôg′, -lŏg′, wŏt′ər-) *tr.v.* **-logged, -log·ging, -logs** **1.** To make (a boat, for example) heavy and unwieldy by flooding with water. **2.** To saturate with water and make soggy or unusable. [Back-formation < WATERLOGGED.]

wa·ter·logged (wô′tər-lôgd′, -lŏgd′, wŏt′ər-) *adj*. **1.** *Nautical* Heavy and sluggish in the water because of flooding, as in the hold. **2.** Soaked or saturated with water. [WATER + *logged*, p. part. of LOG¹, to accumulate (water) in a ship.]

wa·ter·loo (wô′tər-lōō′, wŏt′ər-, wô′tər-lōō′) *n., pl.* **-loos** A final, crushing defeat. [After WATERLOO, Belgium.]

Waterloo 1. A town of central Belgium near Brussels; site of Napoleon's final defeat (Jun. 18, 1815). **2.** A city of NE IA NW of Cedar Rapids; first settled in 1845. Pop. 68,747.

wa·ter·man (wô′tər-mən, wŏt′ər-) *n*. A boatman.

wa·ter·mark (wô′tər-märk′, wŏt′ər-) *n*. **1a.** A mark showing the greatest height to which water has risen. **b.** A line showing the heights of high and low tide. **2a.** A translucent design impressed on paper during manufacture and visible when the paper is held to the light. **b.** The metal pattern that produces this design. —*tr.* **-marked, -mark·ing, -marks** **1.** To mark (paper) with a watermark. **2.** To impress (a design) as a watermark.

wa·ter·mel·on (wô′tər-mĕl′ən, wŏt′ər-) *n*. **1.** An African vine (*Citrullus lanatus*) cultivated for its large edible fruit. **2.** The fruit of this plant, having a hard green rind and sweet watery pink or reddish flesh.

water milfoil *n*. Any of various aquatic herbs of the genus *Myriophyllum*, having finely dissected submersed leaves and entire or toothed emersed leaves.

water mill *n*. A mill with machinery that is driven by water.

water moccasin *n*. **1.** A semiaquatic pit viper (*Agkistrodon piscivorus*) of the southern United States. **2.** Any of various similar but harmless water snakes.

water mold *n*. Any of various parasitic or saprobic fungi of the phylum Oomycota, living chiefly in fresh water or moist soil.

water nymph *n*. *Mythology* A nymph, such as a naiad or Nereid, living in or near water.

water oak *n*. Any of various oak trees that grow in wetlands, esp. *Quercus nigra* of eastern North America.

water of crystallization *n*. Water in chemical combination with a crystal, capable of being removed by sufficient heat.

water of hydration *n*. Water combined with a substance in such a way that it can be removed without substantially changing the chemical composition of the substance.

water ouzel *n*. See **dipper** 2.

water park *n*. An amusement park whose attractions include slides, fountains, and other recreational settings involving water.

water parting *n*. See **watershed** 1.

water pepper *n*. A North American perennial herb (*Polygonum hydropiperoides*) of marshes and bogs, having reddish stems, small greenish flowers, and acrid-tasting leaves.

water pipe *n*. **1.** A pipe that is a conduit for water. **2.** An apparatus for smoking in which the smoke is drawn through a container of water or ice and cooled before inhaling.

water pistol *n*. See **squirt gun**.

water plantain *n*. Any of various aquatic herbs of the genus *Alisma*, having small, three-petaled, white or pinkish flowers.

water polo *n*. A water sport with two teams of swimmers each of which tries to pass a ball into the other's goal.

wa·ter·pow·er (wô′tər-pou′ər, wŏt′ər-) *n*. **1a.** The energy produced by running or falling water that is used for driving machinery, esp. for generating electricity. **b.** A source of such energy, as a waterfall. **2.** A water right owned by a mill.

wa·ter·proof (wô′tər-prōōf′, wŏt′ər-) *adj*. **1.** Impervious to or unaffected by water. **2.** Made of or coated or treated with rubber, plastic, or a sealing agent to prevent penetration by water. ❖ *n.* **1.** A material or fabric impervious to water. **2.** *Chiefly British* A raincoat or other such garment. ❖ *tr.v.* **-proofed, -proof·ing, -proofs** To make impervious to water.

watercolor
Woman with a Rose,
c. 1879, by Winslow Homer

water polo

water rat *n.* **1a.** Any of various semiaquatic rodents, esp. *Neofiber alleni* of Florida and southern Georgia, closely related to and resembling the muskrat. **b.** See **muskrat** 1. **2.** *Slang* A petty thief or ruffian who frequents waterfronts.

wa•ter•re•pel•lent (wô′tər-rĭ-pĕl′ənt, wŏt′ər-) *adj.* Resistant to penetration by water but not entirely waterproof.

wa•ter•re•sis•tant (wô′tər-rĭ-zĭs′tənt, wŏt′ər-) *adj.* Water-repellent.

water right *n.* **1.** The right to draw water from a particular source, such as a lake, canal, or stream. Often used in the plural. **2.** *Nautical* The right to navigate on particular waters.

Wa•ters (wô′tərz, wŏt′ərz), **Ethel** 1896–1977. Amer. actress and singer who appeared on Broadway and in films such as *The Sound and the Fury* (1959).

Waters, Muddy Orig. McKinley Morganfield. 1915–83. Amer. blues singer and musician whose many blues classics include "Mannish Boy."

water sapphire *n.* A clear blue cordierite often used as a gemstone.

wa•ter•scape (wô′tər-skāp′, wŏt′ər-) *n.* A seascape.

water scorpion *n.* Any of various aquatic insects of the family Nepidae, having a large breathing tube projecting from the posterior part of the abdomen and inflicting a painful sting.

wa•ter•shed (wô′tər-shĕd′, wŏt′ər-) *n.* **1.** A ridge of high land dividing two areas that are drained by different river systems. **2.** The region draining into a river, river system, or other body of water. **3.** A critical point that marks a division or a change of course; a turning point. [Prob. transl. of Ger. *Wasserscheide* : *Wasser*, water + *Scheide*, divide, parting.]

water shield *n.* **1.** A cosmopolitan aquatic herb (*Brasenia schreberi*) having floating elliptic or ovate leaves and purplish flowers. **2.** Any of several New World aquatic herbs of the genus *Cabomba*, having alternate floating leaves and finely divided opposite or whorled submersed leaves.

wa•ter•sick (wô′tər-sĭk′, wŏt′ər-) *adj.* Unproductive because of excessive irrigation: *water-sick soil.*

wa•ter•side (wô′tər-sīd′, wŏt′ər-) *n.* Land bordering a body of water; a bank or shore. ❖ *adj.* **1.** Of or situated at the waterside. **2.** Living or working along the waterside.

water ski or **wa•ter•ski** (wô′tər-skē′, wŏt′ər-) *n.* A broad ski for skiing on water.

wa•ter•ski (wô′tər-skē′, wŏt′ər-) *intr.v.* **-skied, -ski•ing, -skis** To ski on water while being towed by a motorboat. **—wa′ter•ski′er** *n.* **—wa′ter•ski′ing** *n.*

water snake *n.* **1.** Any of various nonvenomous snakes of the genus *Natrix*, living in or frequenting freshwater streams and ponds. **2.** Any of various aquatic or semiaquatic snakes.

water softener *n.* **1.** A substance used to reduce the hardness of water. **2.** A device that monitors and reduces the hardness of the water.

water spaniel *n.* A large spaniel having a curly water-resistant coat, often used in hunting to retrieve waterfowl.

wa•ter•sport (wô′tər-spôrt′, -spōrt′, wŏt′ər-) *n.* A sport played or undertaken on or in the water, as swimming, snorkeling, or surfing.

wa•ter•spout (wô′tər-spout′, wŏt′ər-) *n.* **1.** A tornado or lesser whirlwind occurring over water. **2.** A hole or pipe from which water is discharged.

water sprite *n.* A sprite or nymph that inhabits or haunts a body of water.

water strider *n.* Any of various insects of the family Gerridae, having long slender legs to support themselves on water.

water supply *n.* **1.** The water available for a community or region. **2.** The source and delivery system of such water.

water system *n.* **1.** A river and all its tributaries. **2.** A water supply.

water table *n.* **1.** A projecting ledge, molding, or stringcourse along the side of a building, designed to divert rainwater. **2.** The level below which the ground is completely saturated with water.

water taxi *n.* A ferryboat that takes passengers to a variety of possible destinations instead of operating over a fixed route.

water thrush *n.* Either of two New World warblers (*Seiurus noveboracensis* or *S. motacilla*) living near streams and ponds.

wa•ter•tight (wô′tər-tīt′, wŏt′ər-) *adj.* **1.** Made so that water cannot enter or escape. **2.** Having no flaws or loopholes; impossible to fault, refute, or evade.

water tower *n.* **1.** A standpipe or elevated tank used as a reservoir or for keeping equal pressure in a water system. **2.** A firefighting apparatus for lifting hoses to high levels.

water turkey *n.* See **anhinga.**

water vapor *n.* Water in a gaseous state, esp. diffused in the atmosphere and at a temperature below boiling point.

wa•ter•vas•cu•lar system (wô′tər-văs′kyə-lər, wŏt′ər-) *n.* A system of water-filled canals derived from the coelom that connects the tube feet of echinoderms.

wa•ter•way (wô′tər-wā′, wŏt′ər-) *n.* **1.** A navigable body of water, such as a river, channel, or canal. **2.** A channel at the edge of a ship's deck to drain away water.

wa•ter•weed (wô′tər-wēd′, wŏt′ər-) *n.* Any of various submersed aquatic herbs of the genus *Elodea*, native to the New World and having narrow leaves and small axillary flowers.

water wheel
at Mabry Mill, Blue Ridge
Parkway, Virginia

wattle
close-up of a rooster

water wheel also **water•wheel** (wô′tər-hwēl, -wēl, wŏt′ər-) *n.* **1.** A wheel propelled by falling or running water and used to power machinery. **2.** A wheel with buckets attached to its rim for raising water.

water wings *pl.n.* A pair of inflatable waterproof bags designed so that one can be attached to each arm to provide buoyancy.

water witch *n.* One who claims to be able to find underground water by means of a divining rod; a dowser.

wa•ter•works (wô′tər-wûrks′, wŏt′ər-) *pl.n.* **1a.** (*used with a sing. or pl. verb*) The water system, including reservoirs, pumps, and pipes, that supplies water to a municipality. **b.** (*used with a sing. verb*) A single unit, such as a pumping station, within such a system. **2.** (*used with a sing. verb*) An exhibition of moving water, such as a fountain.

wa•ter•y (wô′tə-rē, wŏt′ə-) *adj.* **-i•er, -i•est 1.** Filled with, consisting of, or soaked with water; wet or soggy: *watery soil.* **2.** Containing too much water; diluted: *watery soup.* **3.** Suggestive of water, as in being thin, pale, or liquid: *watery sunshine.* **4.** Lacking force or substance; weak or insipid: *watery prose.* **5.** Secreting or discharging water or watery fluid, esp. as a symptom of disease. **6.** Accompanied by tears; tearful: *a watery goodbye.* **—wa′ter•i•ness** *n.*

Wat•lings Island (wät′lĭngz) See **San Salvador**[1].

WATS *abbr.* Wide-Area Telecommunications Service

Wat•son (wŏt′sən), **James Dewey** b. 1928. Amer. biologist who with Francis Crick proposed the double helix for the molecular structure of DNA and shared a 1962 Nobel Prize.

Wat•son-Crick model (wät′sən-krĭk′) *n.* A three-dimensional model of the DNA molecule, consisting of two polynucleotide strands wound in the form of a double helix and joined in a ladderlike fashion by hydrogen bonds between the purine and pyrimidine bases. [After James WATSON and Francis CRICK.]

watt (wŏt) *n.* An International System unit of power equal to one joule per second. [After James WATT.]

Watt, James 1736–1819. British engineer and inventor who made fundamental improvements in the steam engine.

watt•age (wŏt′ĭj) *n.* **1.** An amount of power, esp. electric power, expressed in watts or kilowatts. **2.** The electric power required by an appliance or device.

Wat•teau (wŏ-tō′, vä-), **Jean Antoine** 1684–1721. French painter noted for his scenes of festive gatherings.

watt-hour (wŏt′our′) *n.* A unit of energy, esp. electrical energy, equal to the work done by one watt acting for one hour and equivalent to 3,600 joules.

wat•tle (wŏt′l) *n.* **1a.** A construction of poles intertwined with twigs, reeds, or branches, used for walls, fences, and roofs. **b.** Material used for such construction. **2.** A fleshy, wrinkled, often brightly colored fold of skin hanging from the neck or throat, characteristic of certain birds, such as chickens or turkeys, and some lizards. **3.** *Botany* Any of various Australian trees or shrubs of the genus *Acacia.* ❖ *tr.v.* **-tled, -tling, -tles 1.** To construct from wattle. **2.** To weave into wattle. [ME *wattel* < OE *watel*, hurdle.] **—wat′tled** *adj.*

wattle and daub *n.* A building material consisting of interwoven rods and laths or twigs plastered with mud or clay, used esp. in the construction of simple dwellings or as an infill between members of a timber-framed wall.

wat•tle•bird (wŏt′l-bûrd′) *n.* Any of several honeyeaters of the genus *Anthochaera*, having wattles on either side.

watt•me•ter (wŏt′mē′tər) *n.* An instrument for measuring in watts the power flowing in a circuit.

Watts (wŏts), **Isaac** 1674–1748. English poet and theologian whose poems include *The Psalms of David Imitated* (1719).

Wa•tut•si (wä-tŏŏt′sē) also **Wa•tu•si** (wä-tŏŏ′sē) *n., pl.* **Wa•tutsi** or **-sis** also **Watusi** or **-sis** Variants of *Tutsi.* [Kinyarwanda : *wa-*, pl. human pref. + *-tutsi*, Tutsi.]

Waugh (wô), **Evelyn (Arthur Saint John)** 1903–66. British writer whose satirical novels include *Decline and Fall* (1928).

Wau•ke•gan (wô-kē′gən) A city of NE IL on Lake Michigan N of Chicago. Pop. 87,901.

wave (wāv) *v.* **waved, wav•ing, waves** *—intr.* **1.** To move freely back and forth or up and down in the air, as branches in the wind. **2.** To make a signal with an up-and-down or back-and-forth hand movement or hand-held object. **3.** To have an undulating or wavy form; curve or curl. *—tr.* **1.** To cause to move back and forth or up and down, either once or repeatedly. **2a.** To move or swing as in giving a signal: *He waved his hand.* **b.** To signal or express by waving the hand or an object held in the hand: *waved goodbye.* **c.** To signal (a person) to move in a specified direction. **3.** To arrange into curves, curls, or undulations. ❖ *n.* **1a.** A ridge or swell moving through or along the surface of a large body of water. **b.** A small ridge or swell moving across the interface of two fluids and dependent on surface tension. **2.** The sea. Often used in the plural. **3.** Something that suggests the form and motion of a wave in the sea, esp.: **a.** A moving curve or succession of curves in or on a surface; an undulation. **b.** A curve or succession of curves, as in the hair. **c.** A curved shape, outline, or pattern. **4.** A movement up and down or back and forth. **5a.** A surge or rush, as of sensation. **b.** A sudden great rise, as in activity or intensity. **c.** A rising trend that involves large numbers of individuals. **d.** One of a succession of mass movements: *the first wave of settlers.*

e. A maneuver in which fans at a sports event simulate an ocean wave by rising quickly in sequence with arms upraised and then quickly sitting down again in a continuous rolling motion. **6.** A widespread persistent meteorological condition, esp. of temperature: *a heat wave.* **7.** *Physics* **a.** A disturbance traveling through a medium by which energy is transferred from one particle of the medium to another without causing any permanent displacement of the medium itself. **b.** A graphic representation of the variation of such a disturbance with time. **c.** A single cycle of such a disturbance. —*phrasal verb:* **wave off 1.** To dismiss or refuse by waving the hand or arm. **2.** *Sports* To cancel or nullify by waving the arms, usu. from a crossed position: *waved off a goal because time had run out.* [ME **waven** < OE **wafian.** See **webh-** in App.] —**wav′er** *n.*

wave•band (wāv′bănd′) *n.* A range of frequencies, esp. radio frequencies, such as those assigned to broadcasting.

wave equation *n.* **1.** A partial differential equation used to represent wave motion. **2.** The fundamental equation of wave mechanics.

wave•form (wāv′fôrm′) *n.* The mathematical representation of a wave, esp. a graph obtained by plotting a characteristic of the wave against time.

wave front *n.* The continuous line or surface including all the points in space reached by a wave or vibration at the same instant as it travels through a medium.

wave function *n.* A mathematical function used in quantum mechanics to describe the propagation of the wave associated with any particle or group of particles.

wave•guide (wāv′gīd′) *n.* A solid dielectric rod or dielectric-filled tubular conductor capable of guiding high-frequency electromagnetic waves.

wave•length (wāv′lĕngkth′, -lĕngth′) *n.* The distance between one peak or crest of a wave and the next corresponding peak or crest. —*idiom:* **on the same wavelength** *Informal* In complete accord.

wave•let (wāv′lĭt) *n.* A small wave; a ripple.

Wa•vell (wā′vəl), **Archibald Percival.** 1st Earl Wavell. 1883–1950. British field marshal in North Africa (1940–41) and viceroy of India (1943–47).

wa•vel•lite (wā′və-līt′) *n.* A colorless to greenish yellow or black mineral, $Al_3(PO_4)_2(OH)_3 \cdot 5H_2O$, having finely acicular, radiating crystals. [After William *Wavell* (died 1829), British physician.]

wave mechanics *n.* (*used with a sing. or pl. verb*) A theory that ascribes characteristics of waves to subatomic particles and attempts to interpret these characteristics on this basis.

wave number *n.* The reciprocal of the wavelength of a wave.

wa•ver (wā′vər) *intr.v.* **-vered, -ver•ing, -vers 1.** To move unsteadily back and forth. **2a.** To exhibit irresolution or indecision; vacillate. **b.** To become unsteady or unsure; falter. **3.** To tremble or quaver in sound, as of the voice. **4.** To flicker or glimmer, as light. ❖ *n.* The act of wavering. [ME **waveren.** See **webh-** in App.] —**wa′ver•er** *n.*

wave train *n.* *Physics* A succession of similar wave pulses.

wav•y (wā′vē) *adj.* **-i•er, -i•est 1.** Abounding or rising in waves: *a wavy sea.* **2.** Marked by or moving in a wavelike form or motion; sinuous. **3.** Having curls, curves, or undulations: *wavy hair.* **4.** Characteristic or suggestive of waves. **5.** Wavering; unstable. —**wav′i•ly** *adv.* —**wav′i•ness** *n.*

waw (väv, vôv) *n.* Variant of **vav.**

wa-wa (wä′wä′) *n.* Variant of **wah-wah.**

wax¹ (wăks) *n.* **1a.** Any of various natural, oily or greasy heat-sensitive substances, consisting of hydrocarbons or esters of fatty acids. **b.** Beeswax. **c.** Cerumen. **2a.** A plastic solid or semisolid, such as paraffin, originating from petroleum and used in coatings, as insulation, and in crayons. **b.** A preparation containing wax used for polishing floors and other surfaces. **3.** A resinous mixture used by shoemakers to rub on thread. **4.** A phonograph record. **5.** Something suggestive of wax in being impressionable or readily molded. ❖ *adj.* Made of wax. ❖ *tr.v.* **waxed, wax•ing, wax•es 1.** To coat, treat, or polish with wax. **2.** *Informal* To make a phonograph record of. —*idiom:* **on wax** In the medium of phonograph recordings. [ME < OE **weax.**]

wax² (wăks) *intr.v.* **waxed, wax•ing, wax•es 1.** To increase gradually in size, number, strength, or intensity. **2.** To show a progressively larger illuminated area, as the moon does in passing from new to full. **3.** To grow or become as specified: *waxed poetic.* [ME **waxen** < OE **weaxan.**]

wax bean *n.* A variety of string bean having yellow pods.

wax•ber•ry (wăks′bĕr′ē) *n.* The waxy fruit of the wax myrtle or the snowberry.

wax•bill (wăks′bĭl′) *n.* Any of various tropical Old World birds of the genus *Estrilda* and related genera, having a short, often brightly colored waxy beak.

waxed paper (wăkst) *n.* Wax paper.

wax•en (wăk′sən) *adj.* **1.** Made of or covered with wax. **2.** Pale or smooth as wax: *waxen skin.* **3.** Weak, pliable, or impressionable.

wax•er (wăk′sər) *n.* One that polishes with or applies wax.

wax moth *n.* See **bee moth.**

wax museum *n.* A place where life-size wax figures, usu. of famous people, are exhibited.

wax myrtle *n.* An evergreen shrub (*Myrica cerifera*) of the south-

east United States having usu. serrate leaves and small berrylike fruit with a waxy coating.

wax palm *n.* Any of several palm trees that yield wax, as *Copernica prunifera,* the source of carnauba wax, or *Ceroxylon alpinum* of South America.

wax paper *n.* Paper that has been made moistureproof by treatment with wax, used esp. in cooking and in food storage.

wax•wing (wăks′wĭng′) *n.* Any of several birds of the genus *Bombycilla,* having crested heads, grayish-brown plumage, and waxy red tips on the wing feathers.

wax•work (wăks′wûrk′) *n.* **1.** The art of modeling in wax. **2.** A figure made of wax, esp. a life-size wax effigy of a famous person. **3. waxworks** (*used with a sing. or pl. verb*) An exhibition of wax figures in a museum.

wax•y (wăk′sē) *adj.* **-i•er, -i•est 1.** Resembling wax, esp.: **a.** Pale. **b.** Smooth and lustrous. **c.** Pliable or impressionable. **2.** Consisting of, abounding in, or covered with wax. **3.** *Pathology* Containing amyloid deposits, as an organ.

way (wā) *n.* **1a.** A road, path, or highway affording passage from one place to another. **b.** An opening affording passage: *the only way into the attic.* **2a.** Space to proceed. **b.** Opportunity to advance: *the way to peace.* **3.** A course that is or may be used in going from one place to another: *the shortest way home.* **4.** Progress or travel along a certain route or in a specific direction. **5.** A course of conduct or action. **6.** A manner or method of doing: *no way to reach her.* **7.** A usual or habitual manner or mode of being, living, or acting. **8.** An individual or personal manner of behaving, acting, or doing. **9.** also **ways** (wāz) (*used with a sing. verb*) *Informal* Distance: *a long way.* **10a.** A specific direction: *He glanced my way.* **b.** A participant. Often used in combination: *a three-way conversation.* **11a.** An aspect, particular, or feature: *in no way comparable.* **b.** Nature or category: *not much in the way of a plot.* **12.** Freedom to do as one wishes. **13.** An aptitude or a facility: *a way with words.* **14.** A state or condition. **15.** Vicinity. **16.** A longitudinal strip on a surface that serves to guide a moving machine part. Often used in the plural. **17. ways** (*used with a sing. or pl. verb*) *Nautical* The structure on which a ship is built and from which it slides when launched. **18.** *Nautical* Motion through the water: *The ship had too much way on.* ❖ *adv. Informal* **1.** By a great distance or to a great degree; far. **2.** *Slang* Very; extremely: *way cool.* **3.** From this place; away: *Go way.* —*idioms:* **all the way** From beginning to end; completely. **by the way** Incidentally. **by way of 1.** Through; via. **2.** As a means of. **go out of one's (or the) way** To inconvenience oneself in doing something beyond what is required. **in a way 1.** To a certain extent; with reservations. **2.** From one point of view. **in the way** In a position to obstruct, hinder, or interfere. **no way** *Informal* Certainly not. **on one's (or the) way** In the process of coming, going, or traveling. **on the way** On the route of a journey. **out of the way 1.** In such a position as not to obstruct, hinder, or interfere. **2.** Taken care of. **3.** In a remote location. **4.** Of an unusual character; remarkable. **5.** Improper; amiss. [ME < OE **weg.** See **wegh-** in App.]

SYNONYMS *way, route, course, passage, pass, artery* These nouns refer to paths leading from one place or point to another. *Way* is the least specific: "*Many ways meet in one town*" (Shakespeare). *Route* refers to a planned, well-established, or regularly traveled way: "*Their one purpose of speed over the great ocean routes was achieved by perfect balance of spars and sails to the curving lines of the . . . hull*" (Samuel Eliot Morison). *Course* suggests the path or channel taken by something that moves: "*earth's diurnal course*" (William Wordsworth). *Passage* denotes a traversal over, across, or through something: *The shortcut was a passage between the buildings. Pass* usually refers to a way affording passage around, over, or through a barrier: "*They had reached one of those very narrow passes between two tall stones*" (George Eliot). An *artery* is a main route for the circulation of traffic: *An accident on the central artery backed up traffic.* See also Syns at **method.**

way•bill (wā′bĭl′) *n.* A document giving details and instructions relating to a shipment of goods.

way•far•er (wā′fâr′ər) *n.* One who travels, esp. on foot. [ME *weifarere* : *wei,* way; see WAY + *faren,* to go on a journey (< OE *faran*; see **per-²** in App.).]

way•far•ing (wā′fâr′ĭng) *n.* Traveling, esp. on foot. [< ME *waifaringe,* journeying < OE *wegfarende* : *weg,* way; see WAY + *farende,* pr. part. of *faran,* to go on a journey; see **per-²** in App.] —**way′far′ing** *adj.*

way•lay (wā′lā′) *tr.v.* **-laid** (-lād′), **-lay•ing, -lays 1.** To lie in wait for and attack from ambush. **2.** To accost or intercept unexpectedly. —**way′lay′er** *n.*

Wayne (wān), **Anthony** Known as "Mad Anthony." 1745–96. Amer. Revolutionary general at Brandywine (1777) and Monmouth (1778).

Wayne, John 1907–79. Amer. film actor who played tough heroes in Westerns such as *Red River* (1948).

way-out (wā′out′) *adj. Slang* Very unconventional, unusual, or strange.

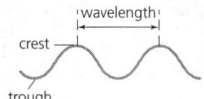

crest — wavelength

trough

wavelength

waxwing
cedar waxwing
Bombycilla cedrorum

ă	pat	oi	boy
ā	pay	ou	out
âr	care	ŏŏ	took
ä	father	ōō	boot
ĕ	pet	ŭ	cut
ē	be	ûr	urge
ĭ	pit	th	thin
ī	pie	th	this
îr	pier	hw	which
ŏ	pot	zh	vision
ō	toe	ə	about,
ô	paw		item

Stress marks:
′ (primary);
′ (secondary), as in
lexicon (lĕk′sĭ-kŏn′)

way·point (wā′point′) *n.* A point between major points on a route, as along a track.

ways (wāz) *n.* (*used with a sing. verb*) *Informal* Variant of **way** 9. See Usage Note at **way.**

–ways *suff.* In a specified way, manner, direction, or position: *sideways.* [ME < *weies, wais,* in such a way < OE *weges : weg,* way; see WAY + *-es,* gen. sing. suff.; see *–s*³.]

ways and means *pl.n.* **1.** Methods and resources available to accomplish an end, esp. to meet expenses. **2.** Methods and means, esp. legislation, for raising government revenue.

way·side (wā′sīd′) *n.* The side or edge of a road, way, path, or highway. ❖ *adj.* Situated at or near a wayside. **—idioms: fall by the wayside** To fail to continue; give up. **go by the wayside** To be set aside or discarded because of other considerations.

way station *n.* A station between principal stations on a route.

way·ward (wā′wərd) *adj.* **1.** Given to or marked by willful, often perverse deviation from what is desired, expected, or required in order to gratify one's own impulses or inclinations. See Syns at **unruly. 2.** Swayed or prompted by caprice; unpredictable. [ME, short for *awaiward,* turned away, perverse : *awai,* away; see AWAY + *-ward,* -ward.] **—way′ward·ly** *adv.* **—way′ward·ness** *n.*

way·worn (wā′wôrn′, -wōrn′) *adj.* Wearied by traveling.

Wa·zir·i·stan (wo-zîr′ĭ-stăn′, -stän′) A mountainous region of NW Pakistan on the Afghanistan border, divided into **North Waziristan** and **South Waziristan.**

Wb *abbr.* weber

WBC *abbr.* white blood cell

WbN *abbr.* west by north

W boson *n.* An elementary particle that has a mass approx. 160,000 times that of the electron, exists in positively and negatively charged forms, and constitutes the quantum of weak interactions in which the charges of participating particles change.

WbS *abbr.* west by south

WC *abbr.* **1.** water closet **2.** wind chill **3.** worker's compensation

WD *abbr.* War Department

we (wē) *pron.* **1.** Used by the speaker or writer to indicate the speaker or writer along with another or others as the subject: *We made it on time.* **2.** Used to refer to people in general, including the speaker or writer. **3.** Used instead of *I,* esp. by a writer wishing to reduce or avoid a subjective tone. **4.** Used instead of *I,* esp. by an editorialist, in expressing the opinion or point of view of a publication's management. **5.** Used instead of *I* by a sovereign in formal address to refer to himself or herself. **6.** Used instead of *you* in direct address, esp. to imply a patronizing camaraderie with the addressee: *How are we feeling today?* [ME < OE *wē.* See **we-** in App.]

weathercock

USAGE NOTE Appositive nouns or noun phrases sometimes lead writers and speakers to choose incorrect pronoun forms. Thus *us* is frequently found in constructions such as *Us owners will have something to say about the contract,* where *we* is required as the subject of the sentence. Less frequently, *we* is substituted in positions where *us* should be used, as in *For we students, it's a no-win situation.* In all cases, the function of the pronoun within the sentence should determine its form, whether or not it is followed by a noun or noun phrase. See Usage Notes at **be, I**¹.

weak (wēk) *adj.* **weak·er, weak·est 1.** Lacking physical strength, energy, or vigor; feeble. **2.** Likely to fail under pressure, stress, or strain; lacking resistance: *a weak link in a chain.* **3.** Lacking firmness of character or strength of will. **4.** Lacking the proper strength or amount of ingredients: *weak coffee.* **5.** Lacking the ability to function normally or fully: *a weak heart.* **6.** Lacking aptitude or skill. **7.** Lacking or resulting from a lack of intelligence. **8.** Lacking persuasiveness; unconvincing: *a weak argument.* **9.** Lacking authority or the power to govern. **10.** Lacking potency or intensity: *weak sunlight.* **11.** *Linguistics* **a.** Of or relating to those verbs in Germanic languages that form a past tense and past participle with a dental suffix, as *start, started; bring, brought.* **b.** Of or relating to the inflection of nouns or adjectives in Germanic languages with a declensional suffix that historically contained an *n.* **12.** Unstressed or unaccented in pronunciation or poetic meter. Used of a word or syllable. **13.** Being a verse ending in which the metrical stress falls on a word or syllable that is unstressed in normal speech, such as a preposition. **14.** Tending downward in price. [ME *weike* < ON *veikr,* pliant.]

weak·en (wē′kən) *tr. & intr.v.* **-ened, -en·ing, -ens** To make or become weak or weaker. **—weak′en·er** *n.*

weak·fish (wēk′fĭsh′) *n., pl.* **weakfish** or **-fish·es** A marine food and game fish (*Cynoscion regalis*) of North American Atlantic waters. [Obsolete Du. *weekvis : week,* soft (< MDu. *weec*) + Du. *vis,* fish (< MDu.).]

weak interaction *n.* A fundamental interaction between elementary particles that is several orders of magnitude weaker than the electromagnetic interaction and is responsible for nuclear beta decay and neutrino interaction. Also called *weak force.*

weak-kneed (wēk′nēd′) *adj.* Lacking strength of character or purpose.

weak·ling (wēk′lĭng) *n.* One of weak constitution or character.

weak·ly (wēk′lē) *adj.* **-li·er, -li·est** Delicate in constitution; frail or sickly. ❖ *adv.* **1.** With little physical strength or force. **2.** With little strength of character. **—weak′li·ness** *n.*

weak-mind·ed (wēk′mīn′dĭd) *adj.* **1.** Having or exhibiting a lack of judgment or conviction. **2.** Foolish; silly. **3.** Of less than normal intellect. Not in scientific use. **—weak′-mind′ed·ness** *n.*

weak·ness (wēk′nĭs) *n.* **1.** The condition or quality of being weak. **2.** A personal defect or failing. **3a.** A special fondness or inclination: *has a weakness for fast cars.* **b.** Something of which one is excessively fond or desirous.

weak·on (wē′kŏn′) *n.* Either of two bosons, the W particle or the Z particle, that are quanta of the weak interaction.

weak sister *n. Slang* **1.** A weak or undependable member of a group. **2.** A person regarded as timid or indecisive.

weal¹ (wēl) *n.* **1.** Prosperity; happiness: *in weal and woe.* **2.** The welfare of the community; the general good: *the public weal.* [ME *wele* < OE *wela.*]

weal² (wēl) *n.* A ridge on the flesh raised by a blow; a welt. [Alteration (influenced by WHEAL) of WALE.]

weald (wēld) *n. Chiefly British* **1.** A woodland. **2.** An area of open rolling upland. [< *Weald,* a once-forested area in SE England < OE *wald, weald,* forest.]

wealth (wĕlth) *n.* **1a.** An abundance of valuable material possessions or resources; riches. **b.** The state of being rich; affluence. **2.** All goods and resources having value in terms of exchange or use. **3.** A great amount; a profusion: *a wealth of advice.* [ME *welthe < wele* < OE *wela.*]

wealth·y (wĕl′thē) *adj.* **-i·er, -i·est 1.** Having wealth; rich. **2.** Marked by abundance: *a wealthy land.* **3.** Well supplied: *wealthy in love.* ❖ *n.* (*used with a pl. verb*) Rich people considered as a group. Often used with *the.* **—wealth′i·ly** *adv.* **—wealth′i·ness** *n.*

wean (wēn) *tr.v.* **weaned, wean·ing, weans 1.** To accustom (the young of a mammal) to take nourishment other than by suckling. **2.** To detach from that to which one is strongly habituated or devoted: *She weaned herself from cigarettes.* **3.** To accustom to something from an early age. Often used with *on: hardy folk weaned on a harsh environment.* [ME *wenen* < OE *wenian.* See **wen-** in App.]

wean·ling (wēn′lĭng) *n.* A newly weaned child or young animal. ❖ *adj.* Newly weaned.

weap·on (wĕp′ən) *n.* **1.** An instrument of attack or defense in combat, as a gun or sword. **2.** *Zoology* A part or organ, such as a claw, used by an animal in attack or defense. **3.** A means used to defend against or defeat another: *Logic was her weapon.* ❖ *tr.v.* **-oned, -on·ing, -ons** To supply with weapons or a weapon; arm. [ME *wepen* < OE *wǣpen.*]

weap·on·eer (wĕp′ə-nîr′) *n.* **1.** One who prepares a nuclear weapon for release. **2.** One who designs weapons, esp. nuclear weapons. **—weap′on·eer′ing** *n.*

weap·on·ize (wĕp′ə-nīz′) *tr.v.* **-ized, iz·ing, iz·es 1.** To supply with weapons or deploy weapons in: *weaponize outer space.* **2a.** To place or mount (an explosive, for example) on a missile or other delivery system. **b.** To equip (a missile, for example) with an explosive or other weapon. **3.** To produce or refine (a substance) for use as a weapon.

weap·on·ry (wĕp′ən-rē) *n.* **1.** Weapons considered as a group. **2.** The design and production of weapons.

wear (wâr) *v.* **wore** (wôr, wōr), **worn** (wôrn, wōrn), **wear·ing, wears** —*tr.* **1.** To carry or have on the person as covering, adornment, or protection: *wearing a seat belt.* **2.** To carry or have habitually on the person, esp. as an aid: *wears glasses.* **3.** To display in one's appearance: *always wears a smile.* **4.** To bear, carry, or maintain in a particular manner: *wears her hair long.* **5.** To fly or display (colors). Used of a ship, jockey, or knight. **6.** To damage, diminish, erode, or consume by long or hard use, attrition, or exposure. Often used with *away, down,* or *off.* **7.** To produce by constant use, attrition, or exposure: *wore hollows in the stone steps.* **8.** To bring to a specified condition by long use or attrition: *pebbles worn smooth.* **9.** To fatigue, weary, or exhaust. **10.** *Nautical* To make (a sailing ship) change course from close-hauled on one tack to close-hauled on the other by turning the stern to windward. —*intr.* **1a.** To last under continual or hard use. **b.** To last through the passage of time. **2.** To break down or diminish through use or attrition. **3.** To pass gradually or tediously: *The hours wore on.* **4.** *Nautical* To wear a sailing ship. ❖ *n.* **1.** The act of wearing or the state of being worn; use. **2.** Clothing, esp. of a particular kind or for a particular use. Often used in combination: *footwear.* **3.** Gradual impairment or diminution resulting from use or attrition. **4.** The ability to withstand impairment from use or attrition. **—phrasal verbs: wear down** To break down or exhaust by relentless pressure or resistance. **wear off** To diminish gradually in effect. **wear out 1.** To make or become unusable through long or heavy use. **2.** To use up or consume gradually. **3.** To exhaust; tire. **4.** *Chiefly Southern US* To punish by spanking. **—idioms: wear the pants (or trousers)** *Informal* To exercise controlling authority in a household. **wear thin 1.** To be weakened or eroded gradually. **2.** To become less convincing, acceptable, or popular, as through repeated use. [ME *weren* < OE *werian.* See **wes-**² in App.] **—wear′er** *n.*

wear·a·bil·i·ty (wâr′ə-bĭl′ĭ-tē) *n.* The ability of a garment to withstand prolonged wear.

wear·a·ble (wâr′ə-bəl) *adj.* **1.** Suitable for wear. **2.** Suitable for easy wear: *wearable evening clothes.* ❖ *n.* Something that can be worn, esp. a garment. Often used in the plural.

wear and tear (târ) *n.* Loss, damage, or depreciation resulting from ordinary use and exposure.

wea·ri·ful (wîr′ē-fəl) *adj.* 1. Causing weariness; tedious. 2. Fatigued; exhausted. —**wea′ri·ful·ly** *adv.* —**wea′ri·ful·ness** *n.*

wea·ri·less (wîr′ē-lĭs) *adj.* Displaying or feeling no fatigue; tireless. —**wea′ri·less·ly** *adv.*

wear·ing (wâr′ĭng) *adj.* 1. Intended to be worn. 2. Causing fatigue; tiring. 3. Causing wear; eroding. 4. Subject to or showing indication of wear.

wea·ri·some (wîr′ē-səm) *adj.* Causing physical or mental fatigue; tedious or tiresome. —**wea′ri·some·ly** *adv.*

wea·ry (wîr′ē) *adj.* **-ri·er, -ri·est** 1. Physically or mentally fatigued. 2. Expressive of or prompted by fatigue: *a weary smile.* 3. Having one's interest, forbearance, or indulgence worn out: *weary of delays.* 4. Causing fatigue; tiresome: *a weary wait.* ❖ *tr. & intr.v.* **wea·ried** (wîr′ēd), **wea·ry·ing, wea·ries** (wîr′ēz) To make or become weary. [ME *weri* < OE *wērig.*] —**wea′ri·ly** *adv.* —**wea′ri·ness** *n.*

wea·sand (wē′zənd) *n.* The gullet or throat. [ME *wesand,* perh. < OE **wāsend,* var. of *wāsand.*]

wea·sel (wē′zəl) *n.* 1. Any of various carnivorous mammals of the genus *Mustela,* having a long slender body, a long tail, short legs, and brownish fur that in many species turns white in winter. 2. A person regarded as sneaky or treacherous. ❖ *intr.v.* **-seled, -sel·ing, -sels** also **-selled, -sel·ling, -sels** To be evasive; equivocate. —*phrasal verb:* **weasel out** *Informal* To back out of a situation or commitment in a sneaky or cowardly manner. [ME *wesele* < OE *wesle.*]

weasel word *n.* An equivocal word used to deprive a statement of its force or evade a direct commitment. [< the weasel's habit of sucking the contents out of an egg without breaking the shell.]

weath·er (wĕth′ər) *n.* 1. The state of the atmosphere at a given time and place, with respect to variables such as temperature, humidity, and wind velocity. 2a. Adverse or destructive atmospheric conditions, such as high winds or heavy rain. b. The unpleasant or destructive effects of such atmospheric conditions. 3. **weathers** Changes of fortune. ❖ *v.* **-ered, -er·ing, -ers** —*tr.* 1. To expose to the action of the elements, as for drying, seasoning, or coloring. 2. To discolor, disintegrate, wear, or otherwise affect adversely by exposure. 3. To come through (something) safely; survive. 4. To slope (a roof, for example) so as to shed water. 5. *Nautical* To pass to windward of. —*intr.* 1. To show the effects, such as discoloration, of exposure to the elements. 2. To withstand the effects of weather. ❖ *adj.* 1. *Nautical* Of or relating to the windward side of a ship; windward. 2. Relating to or used in weather forecasting. —*phrasal verb:* **weather in** To experience or cause to experience weather conditions that prevent movement: *a fleet weathered in by a typhoon.* —*idioms:* **make heavy weather of** To exaggerate the difficulty of something to be done. **under the weather 1.** Somewhat indisposed; slightly ill. 2. *Slang* **a.** Intoxicated; drunk. **b.** Suffering from a hangover. [ME *weder, wether* < OE *weder.* See **wē-** in App.]

weather balloon *n.* A balloon used to carry instruments aloft to gather meteorological data, either in the process of manufacture or as it is in the atmosphere.

weath·er-beat·en (wĕth′ər-bēt′n) *adj.* 1. Worn by exposure to weather. 2. Lined or coarsened from being outdoors: *a weatherbeaten face.*

weath·er·board (wĕth′ər-bôrd′, -bōrd′) *n.* See **clapboard.**

weath·er·board·ing (wĕth′ər-bôr′dĭng, -bōr′-) *n.* Clapboards considered as a group; siding.

weath·er-bound (wĕth′ər-bound′) *adj.* Delayed, halted, or kept indoors by bad weather.

weather bureau *n.* An agency that gathers and interprets meteorological data for weather study and forecasts.

weath·er·cast (wĕth′ər-kăst′) *n.* A broadcast of weather conditions. [WEATHER + (FORE)CAST.] —**weath′er·cast′er** *n.*

weath·er·cock (wĕth′ər-kŏk′) *n.* 1. A weathervane, esp. one in the form of a rooster. 2. One that is very changeable or fickle. ❖ *intr.v.* **-cocked, -cock·ing, -cocks** To have a tendency to veer in the direction of the wind. Used of an aircraft or a missile.

weather deck *n.* A ship's deck that is open to the sky and exposed to the weather.

weath·ered (wĕth′ərd) *adj.* 1. Worn, stained, or warped by or as if by exposure to weather; seasoned. 2. *Architecture* Sloped to shed water.

weather eye *n.* An ability to recognize quickly signs of changes in the weather. —*idiom:* **keep a (or one's) weather eye open** To keep watch; stay alert.

weath·er·glass (wĕth′ər-glăs′) *n.* An instrument, such as a barometer, that indicates changes in atmospheric conditions.

weath·er·ing (wĕth′ər-ĭng) *n.* Any of the chemical or mechanical processes by which rocks exposed to the weather undergo changes in character and break down.

weath·er·ize (wĕth′ə-rīz′) *tr.v.* **-ized, -iz·ing, -iz·es** To protect (a structure) against cold weather, as with insulation.

weath·er·ly (wĕth′ər-lē) *adj.* Able to sail close to the leeward with little drift to leeward. —**weath′er·li·ness** *n.*

weath·er·man (wĕth′ər-măn′) *n.* A man who reports and forecasts the weather.

weather map *n.* A map or chart depicting the meteorological

conditions over a specific geographic area at a specific time.

weath·er·proof (wĕth′ər-prōōf′) *adj.* Capable of withstanding exposure to weather without damage. ❖ *tr.v.* **-proofed, -proof·ing, -proofs** To make weatherproof.

weather ship *n.* An oceangoing vessel equipped to make meteorological observations.

weather station *n.* A facility or location where meteorological data is gathered, recorded, and released.

weath·er-strip (wĕth′ər-strĭp′) *tr.v.* **-stripped, -strip·ping, -strips** To fit or equip with weather stripping.

weather stripping *n.* 1. A narrow piece of material, such as plastic, rubber, felt, or metal, installed around doors and windows to protect an interior from external extremes in temperature. 2. This material considered as a unit.

weath·er·vane (wĕth′ər-vān′) *n.* A wind direction indicator.

weath·er-wise (wĕth′ər-wīz′) *adj.* Skilled in predicting shifts, as in the weather or public opinion.

weath·er·worn (wĕth′ər-wôrn′, -wōrn′) *adj.* Weather-beaten.

weave (wēv) *v.* **wove** (wōv), **wo·ven** (wō′vən), **weav·ing, weaves** —*tr.* **1a.** To make (cloth) by interlacing the threads of the weft and the warp on a loom. **b.** To interlace (threads, for example) into cloth. 2. To construct by interlacing or interweaving strips or strands of material. **3a.** To interweave or combine (elements) into a complex whole. **b.** To contrive (something complex or elaborate) in this way. 4. To introduce (another element) into a complex whole; work in. 5. To spin (a web, for example). **6.** *past tense* **weaved** To make (a path or way) by winding in and out or from side to side. —*intr.* **1a.** To engage in weaving; make cloth. **b.** To work at a loom. **2.** *past tense* **weaved** To move in and out or sway from side to side. ❖ *n.* The pattern, method of weaving, or construction of a fabric: *a loose weave.* [ME *weven* < OE *wefan.* See **webh-** in App.]

weav·er (wē′vər) *n.* 1. One that weaves. 2. A weaverbird.

weav·er·bird (wē′vər-bûrd′) *n.* Any of various chiefly tropical Old World birds of the family Ploceidae, marked by the ability to build complex woven communal nests.

wea·ver's knot (wē′vərz) *n.* See **sheet bend.**

web (wĕb) *n.* **1a.** A woven fabric, esp. one on a loom or just removed from it. **b.** The structural part of cloth. 2. A latticed or woven structure: *a web of palm branches.* 3. A structure of delicate threadlike filaments characteristically spun by spiders or certain insect larvae. 4. Something intricately contrived, esp. something that ensnares or entangles: *a web of lies.* 5. A complex interconnected structure or arrangement: *a web of telephone wires.* 6. often **Web** The World Wide Web. 7. A radio or television network. 8. A membrane or fold of skin connecting the toes, as of certain amphibians, birds, and mammals. 9. The barbs on each side of the shaft of a bird's feather; a vane. 10. *Baseball* A piece of leather or leather mesh that fills the space between the thumb and forefinger of a baseball glove. 11. *Architecture* A space or compartment between the ribs or groins of a vault. 12. A metal sheet or plate connecting the heavier sections, ribs, or flanges of a structural element. 13. A thin metal plate or strip, as the bit of a key or the blade of a saw. 14. A large continuous roll of paper, such as newsprint, either in the process of manufacture or as it is fed into a web press. ❖ *tr.v.* **webbed, web·bing, webs** 1. To provide with a web. 2. To cover or envelop with a web. 3. To ensnare in a web. [ME < OE. See **webh-** in App.]

USAGE NOTE The word *Web* is usually capitalized when referring to the World Wide Web: *Many sites on the Web have information about used cars.* In this use, however, the word is increasingly found lowercase, and this usage may become dominant. In any event, the word *web* need not be capitalized when it applies to technologies that are typically but not exclusively used with the World Wide Web. A *web authoring tool,* for example, might be a tool that is used for the creation of documents using the HTML markup language, for whatever purpose.

Webb (wĕb), **Sidney James.** 1st Baron Passfield. 1859–1947. British sociologist and a founder of the London School of Economics (1895). He and his wife, **Beatrice Potter Webb** (1858–1943), were key members of the Fabian Society.

webbed (wĕbd) *adj.* 1. Having or connected by a web. 2. Linked or related to the World Wide Web.

web·bing (wĕb′ĭng) *n.* 1. A strong, narrow, closely woven fabric used esp. for seat belts and harnesses or in upholstery. 2. Something forming a web. 3. *Baseball* See **web** 10.

web·by (wĕb′ē) *adj.* **-bi·er, -bi·est** Consisting of, resembling, or having webs or a web.

web·cam (wĕb′kăm′) *n.* A digital camera capable of downloading images to a computer for transmission over the Internet or other network. [WEB + CAM(ERA).]

web·cast (wĕb′kăst′) *n.* A broadcast of an event or a recording of an event over the World Wide Web. [WEB + (BROAD)CAST.]

web·er (wĕb′ər, vā′bər) *n.* The unit of magnetic flux in the meter-kilogram-second system equal to the flux that produces in a circuit of one turn an electromotive force of one volt, when the flux is uniformly reduced to zero within one second. [After Wilhelm Eduard *Weber* (1804–91), German physicist.]

We·ber (vā′bər), **Ernst Heinrich** 1795–1878. German physiologist considered a founder of experimental psychology.

weathering
weathered sandstone of Balanced Rock, Arches National Park, Utah

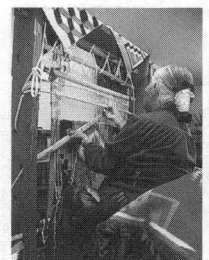

weave
weaving a Navajo blanket

We·ber (vā′bər), Baron Karl Maria Friedrich Ernst von 1786–1826. German composer of *Der Freischütz* (1821).

We·ber[1] (vā′bər), Max 1864–1920. German sociologist and a pioneer of the modern analytical method of sociology.

We·ber[2] (wĕb′ər), Max 1881–1961. Russian-born Amer. painter known for his avant-garde abstract works.

We·bern (vā′bərn), Anton Friedrich Wilhelm von 1883–1945. Austrian composer whose works are characterized by brevity and tonal dissonance.

web·foot (wĕb′fŏŏt′) *n., pl.* **-feet** (-fēt′) **1.** A foot with webbed toes. **2.** An animal with webbed feet.

web-foot·ed (wĕb′fŏŏt′ĭd) *adj.* Having webbed toes.

web·log (wĕb′lôg′, -lŏg′) *n.* A website that displays in chronological order the postings by one or more individuals and usu. has links to comments on specific postings.

web·mas·ter (wĕb′măs′tər) *n.* A person whose occupation is designing, developing, marketing, or maintaining websites.

web member *n.* One of the structural elements connecting the top and bottom flanges of a lattice girder or the outside members of a truss.

web·page or **Web page** (wĕb′pāj′) *n.* A document on the World Wide Web, consisting of an HTML file and any related files, usu. hyperlinked to other such documents.

web press *n.* A rotary press that prints on a web.

web·site or **Web site** (wĕb′sīt′) *n.* A set of interconnected webpages prepared and maintained as a collection of information by a person or organization.

web spinner *n.* Any of various social insects of the order Embioptera, producing silk from glands in the front legs.

web·ster (wĕb′stər) *n. Obsolete* A weaver of cloth. [ME < OE *webbestre*, fem. of *webba*, weaver < *webb*, web. See **webh-** in App.]

Webster, Daniel 1782–1852. Amer. legislator and public official noted for his oratory.

Webster, John 1580?–1625? English playwright whose works include *The White Devil* (published 1612).

Webster, Noah 1758–1843. Amer. lexicographer whose *American Dictionary of the English Language* was first published in 1828.

web-toed (wĕb′tōd′) *adj.* Web-footed.

web·worm (wĕb′wûrm′) *n.* Any of various usu. destructive caterpillars that construct webs.

wed (wĕd) *v.* **wed·ded, wed** or **wed·ded, wed·ding, weds** —*tr.* **1.** To take as a spouse; marry. **2.** To perform the marriage ceremony for. **3.** To unite closely. **4.** To cause to adhere devotedly or stubbornly: *be wedded to an idea.* —*intr.* To take a spouse; marry. [ME *wedden* < OE *weddian.*]

Wed. *abbr.* Wednesday

we'd (wĕd) **1.** Contraction of *we had.* **2.** Contraction of *we would.*

wed·ded (wĕd′ĭd) *adj.* **1.** Joined in marriage. **2.** Of or relating to marriage. **3.** Closely attached or devoted.

Wed·dell Sea (wĭ-dĕl′, wĕd′l) A sea of the S Atlantic Ocean off W Antarctica E of the Antarctic Peninsula.

wed·ding (wĕd′ĭng) *n.* **1a.** The act of marrying. **b.** The ceremony or celebration of a marriage. **2.** The anniversary of a marriage. **3.** The act or an instance of joining closely.

wedding band *n.* See **wedding ring.**

wed·ding-cake (wĕd′ĭng-kāk′) *adj.* Of or being a highly ornate architectural style. [< the detailed decoration typical of wedding cakes.]

wedding ring *n.* A ring, often one of a pair of plain gold or platinum bands, given during the wedding ceremony by the groom or bride to his or her future spouse.

we·del (vād′l) *intr.v.* **-deled, -del·ing, -dels** To ski on snow by means of wedeln. [Back-formation < WEDELN.]

we·deln (vād′ln) *n.* A snow-skiing style in which the skier executes a series of short quick parallel turns by moving the backs of the skis from side to side at a constant speed. [Ger. < *wedeln,* to wag the tail, fan < MHGer. *wadelen, wedelen < wadel, wedel,* fan, tuft of hair < OHGer. *wadal, wedil.* See **wet-**[1] in App.]

wedge (wĕj) *n.* **1.** A piece of material, such as metal, thick at one edge and tapered to a thin edge at the other for insertion in a narrow crevice, used for splitting, tightening, securing, or levering. **2a.** Something shaped like a wedge. **b.** *Downstate New York* See **submarine** 2. See Regional Note at **submarine. c.** A wedge-shaped formation, as in ground warfare. **3a.** Something that intrudes and causes division or disruption. **b.** Something that forces an opening or a beginning. **4.** *Sports* An iron golf club with a very slanted face, used to lift the ball, as from sand. **5.** One of the triangular characters of cuneiform writing. ❖ *v.* **wedged, wedg·ing, wedg·es** —*tr.* **1.** To split or force apart with or as if with a wedge. **2.** To fix in place or tighten with a wedge. **3.** To crowd or squeeze into a limited space. —*intr.* To become lodged or jammed. [ME *wegge* < OE *wecg.*]

wedge tomb *n.* A Neolithic chamber tomb found chiefly in the British Isles that narrows from the entrance to the back.

wedg·ie (wĕj′ē) *n.* **1.** A shoe having a wedge-shaped heel joined to a half sole so as to form a continuous undersurface. **2.** The condition of having one's clothing stuck between the buttocks, often from having had one's pants or underwear pulled up as a prank. [Orig. a trademark. Sense 2 < WEDGE.]

Wedg·wood (wĕj′wŏŏd′) A trademark used for a type of pot-

weeping willow
Salix babylonica

weevil
black vine weevil
Otiorhynchus sulcatus

tery made by Josiah Wedgwood and his successors.

Wedgwood, Josiah 1730–95. British potter who produced some of the finest examples of British earthenware.

wed·lock (wĕd′lŏk′) *n.* The state of being married; matrimony. —*idiom:* **out of wedlock** Of parents not legally married to each other: *born out of wedlock.* [ME *wedlocke* < OE *wedlāc* : *wedd,* pledge + *-lāc,* n. suff. expressing activity.]

Wednes·day (wĕnz′dē, -dā′) *n.* The fourth day of the week. [ME < OE *Wōdnesdæg,* Woden's day : *Wōdnes,* genitive of *Wōden,* Woden; see **wet-**[1] in App. + *dæg,* day; see DAY.] —**Wednes′days** *adv.*

WORD HISTORY The practice of dividing the year into seven-day units is based on the ancient astrological notion that the seven celestial bodies (the sun, the moon, Mars, Mercury, Jupiter, Venus, and Saturn) influence what happens on Earth and that each controls the first hour of the day named for it. This system was brought into Hellenistic Egypt from Mesopotamia, where astrology had been practiced for millennia and where seven had always been a propitious number. In A.D. 321 Constantine the Great grafted the Hellenistic astrological system onto the Roman calendar, making the first day of the week a day of rest and worship and imposing the following sequence of names on the days: *Diēs Sōlis,* "Sun's Day"; *Diēs Lūnae,* "Moon's Day"; *Diēs Martis,* "Mars's Day"; *Diēs Mercuriī,* "Mercury's Day"; *Diēs Jovis,* "Jove's Day" or "Jupiter's Day"; *Diēs Veneris,* "Venus's Day"; and *Diēs Saturnī,* "Saturn's Day." This new Roman system was adopted with modifications throughout most of western Europe. In the Germanic languages, such as Old English, the names of four of the Germanic gods were converted into those of the corresponding Germanic gods. Therefore in Old English we have the following names (with their Modern English developments): *Sunnandæg,* Sunday; *Mōnandæg,* Monday; *Tiwesdæg,* Tuesday (Tiu, like Mars, was a god of war); *Wōdnesdæg,* Wednesday (Woden, like Mercury, was quick and eloquent); *Thunresdæg,* Thursday (Thunor in Old English or Thor in Old Norse, like Jupiter, was lord of the sky; Old Norse *Thōrsdagr* influenced the English form); *Frīgedæg,* Friday (Frigg, like Venus, was the goddess of love); and *Saeternesdæg,* Saturday.

wee (wē) *adj.* **we·er, we·est 1.** Very small; tiny. **2.** Very early: *the wee hours of the morning.* ❖ *n. Scots* A short time; a little bit. [ME *wei, we,* a small amount, small < OE *wæge, wēg,* weight. See **wegh-** in App.]

weed[1] (wēd) *n.* **1a.** A plant considered undesirable, unattractive, or troublesome, esp. one growing where it is not wanted, as in a garden. **b.** Rank growth of such plants. **2.** A water plant, esp. seaweed. **3.** The leaves or stems of a plant as distinguished from the seeds: *dill weed.* **4.** Something useless, detrimental, or worthless, esp. an animal unfit for breeding. **5.** *Slang* **a.** Tobacco. **b.** A cigarette. **c.** Marijuana. ❖ *v.* **weed·ed, weed·ing, weeds** —*tr.* **1.** To clear of weeds. **2.** To remove (weeds). Often used with *out.* **3.** To eliminate as unsuitable or unwanted. Often used with *out.* —*intr.* To remove weeds. [ME < OE *wēod,* herb, grass, weed.]

weed[2] (wēd) *n.* **1.** A token of mourning, as a black band worn on a man's hat or sleeve. **2. weeds** The black mourning clothes of a widow. **3.** An article of clothing; a garment. Often used in the plural. [ME *wede,* garment < OE *wǣd.*]

weed·er (wē′dər) *n.* One that removes weeds.

weed·y (wē′dē) *adj.* **-i·er, -i·est 1.** Full of or consisting of weeds: *a weedy lawn.* **2.** Resembling or characteristic of a weed: *a weedy plant.* **3.** Of a scrawny build; spindly or gawky. —**weed′i·ly** *adv.* —**weed′i·ness** *n.*

week (wēk) *n.* **1a.** A period of seven days: *a week of rain.* **b.** A seven-day calendar period, esp. one starting with Sunday and continuing through Saturday: *this week.* **2a.** A week designated by an event or holiday occurring within it. **b.** A week dedicated to a particular cause or institution. **3.** The part of a calendar week devoted to work, school, or business: *working a three-day week.* **4a.** One week from a specified day: *I'll see you Friday week.* **b.** One week ago from a specified day: *It was Friday week that we last met.* [ME *weke* < OE *wicu.*]

week·day (wēk′dā′) *n.* Any of the days of the week exclusive of Sunday and often Saturday. —**week′days′** *adv.*

week·end (wēk′ĕnd′) *n.* The last part of the week, normally spent away from work, esp. the period from Friday evening through Sunday evening. ❖ *intr.v.* **-end·ed, -end·ing, -ends** To spend weekends or a weekend. —**week′ends′** *adv.*

week·end·er (wēk′ĕn′dər) *n.* **1.** One who vacations or visits on a weekend. **2.** A small suitcase or bag for carrying clothing and toiletries for a weekend.

week·long (wēk′lông′, -lŏng′) *adj.* Continuing through the week: *a weeklong conference.*

week·ly (wēk′lē) *adv.* **1.** Once a week. **2.** Every week. **3.** By the week. ❖ *adj.* **1.** Of or relating to a week. **2.** Occurring, appearing, or done once a week or every week. **3.** Computed by the week. ❖ *n., pl.* **-lies** A weekly publication.

week·night (wēk′nīt′) *n.* Any of the nights of the week other than weekend nights. —**week′nights′** *adv.*

ween (wēn) *tr.v.* **weened, ween·ing, weens** *Archaic* To think; suppose. [ME *wenen* < OE *wēnan.* See **wen-** in App.]

ween·ie (wē′nē) *n.* **1.** *Informal* A wiener. **2.** *Slang* A person, esp.

a man, who is regarded as being weak and ineffectual.

wee·ny (wē′nē) also **ween·sy** (wēn′sē) *adj.* **-ni·er, -ni·est** also **-si·er, -si·est** *Informal* Tiny. [Perh. blend of WEE and TINY.]

weep (wēp) *v.* **wept** (wĕpt), **weep·ing, weeps** —*tr.* **1.** To shed (tears) as an expression of emotion. **2.** To express grief or anguish for; lament. **3.** To bring to a specified condition by weeping. **4.** To exude or let fall (drops of liquid). —*intr.* **1.** To express emotion, such as grief or sadness, by shedding tears. See Syns at **cry. 2.** To mourn or grieve. **3.** To emit or run with drops of liquid. ❖ *n.* A period or fit of weeping. Often used in the plural. [ME *wepen* < OE *wēpan.*]

weep·er (wē′pər) *n.* **1.** One that weeps. **2.** A hired mourner. **3.** A badge of mourning, such as a black veil. **4.** A hole or pipe in a wall to allow water to run off. **5.** *Informal* A highly sentimental artistic, cinematic, or dramatic work.

weep·ie (wē′pē) *n. Informal* A work, esp. a film or play, that is excessively sentimental.

weep·ing (wē′pĭng) *adj.* **1.** Shedding tears; tearful. **2.** Dropping rain. **3.** Having slender drooping branches.

weeping willow *n.* A widely cultivated deciduous tree *(Salix babylonica)* native to China and having long slender drooping branches and narrow leaves.

weep·y (wē′pē) *adj.* **-i·er, -i·est** Weeping or inclined to weep.

wee·vil (wē′vəl) *n.* Any of numerous beetles of the superfamily Curculionoidea, esp. the snout beetle, that have a downward-curving snout and are destructive to nuts, fruits, stems, and roots. [ME *wevel* < OE *wifel.* See **webh-** in App.]

weft (wĕft) *n.* **1a.** The horizontal threads interlaced through the warp in a woven fabric; woof. **b.** Yarn used for the weft. **2.** Woven fabric. [ME < OE *wefta.* See **webh-** in App.]

Wei (wā) Name of several Chinese dynasties ruling from A.D. 220 to 265 and 386 to 556.

Wei·er·strass (vī′ər-sträs′, -shträs′), **Karl Theodor Wilhelm** 1815–97. German mathematician noted for his contributions to real and complex analysis.

wei·ge·la (wī-gē′lə, -jē′-, wī′jə-) *n.* Any of various deciduous shrubs of the genus *Weigela* of Asia, esp. *W. florida,* widely cultivated for its pink, white, or red flowers. [NLat. *Weigela,* genus name, after Christian Ehrenfried *Weigel* (1748–1831), German physician.]

weigh[1] (wā) *v.* **weighed, weigh·ing, weighs** —*tr.* **1.** To determine the weight of by or as if by using a scale or balance. **2.** To measure or apportion (a certain quantity) by or as if by weight. Often used with *out.* **3a.** To balance in the mind in order to make a choice; ponder or evaluate. **b.** To choose carefully or deliberately. **4.** *Nautical* To raise (anchor). —*intr.* **1.** To be of a specified weight. **2.** To have consequence or importance. See Syns at **count[1]. 3a.** To cause to bend heavily by or as if by added weight. Used with *on* or *upon: Wet snow weighed upon the branches.* **b.** To burden or oppress: *His guilty conscience weighed on him.* **4.** *Nautical* To raise anchor. ***—phrasal verbs:* weigh down 1.** To cause to bend down with added weight. **2.** To burden or oppress. **weigh in 1.** *Sports* To be weighed at a weigh-in. **2.** To have one's baggage weighed, as at an airport. **3.** To be of a specified weight: *The new book weighs in at 7 pounds.* **4.** *Slang* To join in a discussion; utter a remark. [ME *weien* < OE *wegan.* See **wegh-** in App.] **—weigh′er** *n.*

weigh[2] (wā) *n. Nautical* Way. Used in the phrase *under weigh.* [Variant of WAY (influenced by WEIGH[1]).]

weigh-in (wā′ĭn′) *n.* An official weighing of the participants in an athletic contest, such as in a wrestling match, in order to ensure that they weigh within the limits stipulated for the event.

weight (wāt) *n.* **1.** The relative heaviness of an object. **2.** The force with which a body is attracted to Earth or another celestial body, equal to the product of the object's mass and the acceleration of gravity. **3a.** A unit measure of gravitational force: *a table of weights and measures.* **b.** A system of such measures: *avoirdupois weight.* **4.** The measured heaviness of a specific object: *a two-pound weight.* **5.** An object used principally to exert a force by virtue of its gravitational attraction to Earth, esp.: **a.** A metallic solid used as a standard of comparison in weighing. **b.** An object used to hold something else down. **c.** A counterbalance in a machine. **d.** *Sports* A heavy object, such as a dumbbell, lifted for exercise or in athletic competition. **6.** Excessive fat; corpulence: *reduce weight.* **7.** *Statistics* A factor assigned to a number in a computation, as in determining an average, to make the number's effect on the computation reflect its importance. **8.** Oppressiveness; pressure: *the weight of responsibility.* **9.** The greater part; preponderance: *The weight of the evidence is against us.* **10a.** Influence, importance, or authority: *Her opinion carries great weight.* **b.** Ponderous quality; unwieldiness. **11.** *Sports* A classification according to comparative lightness or heaviness. Often used in combination: *a heavyweight boxer.* **12.** The heaviness or thickness of a fabric in relation to a particular season or use. Often used in combination: *wore a summerweight jacket.* ❖ *tr.v.* **weight·ed, weight·ing, weights 1.** To add to by or as if by attaching a weight; make heavy or heavier. **2.** To load down, burden, or oppress. **3.** To increase the weight or body of (fabrics) by treating with chemicals. **4.** *Statistics* To assign weights or a weight to. **5.** To cause to have a slant or bias. **6.** *Sports* To assign to (a horse) the weight it must carry as a handicap in a race. ***—idioms:* by weight** According to weight rather than volume or other measure. **make weight** *Sports* To weigh within the limits stipulated for an athletic contest. [ME *wight* < OE *wiht.* See **wegh-** in App.]

weight·ed (wā′tĭd) *adj.* **1.** Made heavy or heavier by the addition of something. **2.** *Statistics* Adjusted to reflect value or proportion: *a weighted average.*

weight·less (wāt′lĭs) *adj.* **1.** Having little or no weight. **2.** Not experiencing the effects of gravity. **—weight′less·ly** *adv.* **—weight′less·ness** *n.*

weight·lift·er or **weight lift·er** (wāt′lĭf′tər) *n.* One who engages in weightlifting.

weight·lift·ing (wāt′lĭf′tĭng) *n.* The lifting of weights in a prescribed manner as an exercise or in athletic competition.

weight training *n.* Weightlifting done as a training program for improving or maintaining overall fitness, strength, or endurance.

weight·y (wā′tē) *adj.* **-i·er, -i·est 1.** Having considerable weight; heavy. **2.** Burdensome; oppressive: *coped with weighty problems.* **3.** Of great consequence; momentous: *weighty matters before the delegates.* **4.** Having great power or influence: *a weighty argument.* **5.** Solemn; serious: *weighty music.* **—weight′i·ly** *adv.* **—weight′i·ness** *n.*

Wei He (wā′ hŭ′) A river of central China flowing c. 724 km (450 mi) to the Huang He (Yellow R.).

Weil (vā), **André** 1906–98. French mathematician who influenced the development of modern number theory and algebraic geometry.

Weil, Simone 1909–43. French philosopher and mystic whose works include *Waiting for God.*

Weill (wīl, vīl), **Kurt** 1900–50. German-born composer who collaborated with Brecht on *The Threepenny Opera* (1928).

Wei·mar (wī′mär′, vī′-) A city of central Germany SW of Leipzig. The **Weimar Republic,** established here, lasted from 1919 to 1933. Pop. 64,007.

Weimaraner

Wei·mar·an·er (vī′mə-rä′nər, wī′-) *n.* Any of a large breed of hunting dog that originated in Germany, having a smooth grayish coat. [Ger., after WEIMAR.]

weir (wîr) *n.* **1.** A fence or wattle placed in a stream to catch or retain fish. **2.** A dam placed across a river or canal to raise or divert the water, as for a millrace, or regulate or measure the flow. [ME *were* < OE *wer.*]

weird (wîrd) *adj.* **weird·er, weird·est 1.** Of, relating to, or suggestive of the preternatural or supernatural. **2.** Of a strikingly odd or unusual character; strange. **3.** *Archaic* Of or relating to fate or the Fates. ❖ *n.* **1a.** Fate; destiny. **b.** One's assigned lot or fortune, esp. when evil. **2.** often **Weird** *Greek & Roman Mythology* One of the Fates. ❖ *tr. & intr.v.* **weird·ed, weird·ing, weirds** *Slang* To experience or cause to experience an odd, unusual, and sometimes uneasy sensation. Often used with *out.* [ME *werde,* fate, having power to control fate < OE *wyrd,* fate. See **wer-[2]** in App.] **—weird′ly** *adv.* **—weird′ness** *n.*

Chaim Weizmann

weird·ie also **weird·y** (wîr′dē) *n., pl.* **-ies** *Slang* A strange person, event, or thing.

weird·o (wîr′dō) *n., pl.* **-oes** *Slang* **1.** A very strange or eccentric person. **2.** A deranged, potentially dangerous person.

weis·en·hei·mer (wīz′ən-hī′mər) *n. Informal* Variant of **wisenheimer.**

Weis·mann (vīs′män′), **August Friedrich Leopold** 1834–1914. German biologist who asserted that hereditary characteristics are transmitted by a germinal plasm.

Weis·mann·ism (wīs′mə-nĭz′əm, vīs′män-ĭz′əm) *n.* The theory that all heritable characteristics arise in the germ plasm and that acquired characteristics cannot be inherited. [After August Friedrich Leopold WEISMANN.]

Weiz·mann (wīts′mən, vīts′män), **Chaim Azriel** 1874–1952. Polish-born chemist and first president of Israel (1948–52).

we·ka (wē′kə, wā′-) *n.* A flightless bird *(Gallirallus australis)* of New Zealand having mottled brown plumage. [Maori.]

welch (wĕlch) *v.* Variant of **welsh.**

wel·come (wĕl′kəm) *adj.* **1.** Received with pleasure and hospitality into one's company or home: *a welcome guest.* **2.** Giving pleasure or satisfaction; agreeable or gratifying: *a welcome respite from hard work.* **3.** Cordially or willingly permitted or invited. **4.** Used in the expression *you're welcome* to acknowledge an expression of gratitude. ❖ *n.* **1.** A cordial greeting or hospitable reception given to an arriving person. **2.** A reception upon arrival. **3.** The state of being welcome. ❖ *tr.v.* **-comed, -com·ing, -comes 1.** To greet, receive, or entertain (another or others) cordially or hospitably. **2.** To receive or accept gladly. ❖ *interj.* Used to greet cordially a visitor or recent arrival. ***—idiom:* wear out (one's) welcome** To visit so often or stay so long as to become a nuisance. [ME, alteration (influenced by *wel,* well) of OE *wilcuma,* welcome guest, welcome. See **gʷā-** in App.] **—wel′come·ly** *adv.* **—wel′come·ness** *n.* **—wel′com·er** *n.*

welcome mat *n.* **1.** A mat placed in front of a door to welcome visitors and to allow them a place to wipe their feet before entering. **2.** Warm hospitality accorded to a guest.

weld[1] (wĕld) *v.* **weld·ed, weld·ing, welds** —*tr.* **1.** To join (metals) by applying heat and pressure. **2.** To bring into close association or union. —*intr.* To be capable of being welded. ❖ *n.* **1.** The union of two metal parts by welding. **2.** The joint formed by welding. [Alteration (prob. influenced by *welled,* p. part. of

ă	pat	oi	boy
ā	pay	ou	out
âr	care	ŏŏ	took
ä	father	ōō	boot
ĕ	pet	ŭ	cut
ē	be	ûr	urge
ĭ	pit	th	thin
ī	pie	*th*	this
îr	pier	hw	which
ŏ	pot	zh	vision
ō	toe	ə	about, item
ô	paw		

Stress marks:
′ (primary);
′ (secondary), as in
lexicon (lĕk′sĭ-kŏn′)

WELL¹) of WELL¹, to weld (obsolete and dialectal).] —**weld′er,** **wel′dor** n.

weld² (wĕld) also **wold** (wōld) n. **1.** See **dyer's rocket. 2.** The yellow dye obtained from dyer's rocket. [ME *welde.*]

weld·ment (wĕld′mənt) n. A unit composed of an assemblage of pieces welded together.

wel·fare (wĕl′fâr′) n. **1a.** Health, happiness, and good fortune; well-being. **b.** Prosperity. **2.** Welfare work. **3a.** Financial or other aid provided, esp. by the government, to people in need. **b.** Corporate welfare. —*idiom:* **on welfare** Receiving regular assistance from the government or private agencies because of need. [ME < *wel faren,* to fare well < OE *wel faran* : *wel,* well; see WELL² + *faran,* to get along; see FARE.]

Welfare Island See **Roosevelt Island** 1.

welfare state n. **1.** A social system whereby the state assumes primary responsibility for the welfare of its citizens, as in matters of health care, education, employment, and social security. **2.** A nation in which such a system operates.

welfare work n. Organized efforts by a community, organization, or agency to improve the socioeconomic conditions of disadvantaged groups in society. —**welfare worker** n.

wel·kin (wĕl′kĭn) n. *Archaic* **1.** The vault of heaven; the sky. **2.** The upper air. [ME *welken* < OE *wolcen, weolcen,* cloud.]

well¹ (wĕl) n. **1.** A deep hole or shaft sunk into the earth to obtain water, oil, gas, or brine. **2.** A container or reservoir for a liquid, such as ink. **3a.** A place where water issues from the earth; a spring or fountain. **b.** A mineral spring. **c. wells** A watering place; a spa. **4.** An abundant source. **5.** An open space extending vertically through the floors of a building, as for stairs or ventilation. **6.** *Nautical* **a.** An enclosure in a ship's hold for the pumps. **b.** A compartment or recessed area in a ship, used for stowage. **7.** A cistern with a perforated bottom in the hold of a fishing vessel for keeping fish alive. **8.** An enclosed space for receiving and holding something, such as the wheels of an airplane when retracted. **9.** *Chiefly British* The central space in a law court, directly in front of the judge's bench, where the counsel or solicitor sits. ❖ v. **welled, well·ing, wells** —*intr.* **1.** To rise to the surface, ready to flow. **2.** To rise or surge from an inner source: *Anger welled up.* —*tr.* To pour forth. [ME *welle* < OE. See **wel-** in App.]

well² (wĕl) adv. **bet·ter** (bĕt′ər), **best** (bĕst) **1.** In a good or proper manner. **2.** Skillfully or proficiently. **3.** Satisfactorily or sufficiently: *slept well.* **4.** Successfully or effectively: *gets along well with others.* **5.** In a comfortable or affluent manner. **6.** In a manner affording benefit or gain; advantageously: *married well.* **7.** With reason or propriety; reasonably: *can't very well say no.* **8.** In all likelihood; indeed: *You very well might regret that remark.* **9.** In a prudent or sensible manner: *You would do well to say no more.* **10.** In a close or familiar manner: *knew them well.* **11.** In a favorable or approving manner: *spoke well of them.* **12.** Thoroughly; completely: *was cooked well.* **13.** Perfectly; clearly: *I well understand.* **14.** To a suitable or appropriate degree: *This product performs equally well.* **15.** To a considerable extent or degree: *well over the estimate.* **16.** With care or attention: *listened well.* **17.** Entirely; fully: *well worth seeing.* ❖ adj. **better, best 1.** In a satisfactory condition; right or proper. **2a.** Not ailing, infirm, or diseased; healthy. See Syns at **healthy. b.** Cured or healed, as a wound. **c.** Of or characterized by the maintenance of good health practices. Often used in combination: *a well-baby clinic.* **3a.** Advisable; prudent. **b.** Fortunate; good: *It is well that you stayed.* ❖ interj. **1.** Used to introduce a remark, resume a narrative, or fill a pause during conversation. **2.** Used to express surprise. —*idioms:* **as well 1.** In addition; also. **2.** With equal effect: *I might as well go.* **in well with** *Informal* In a position to influence or be favored by. [ME *wel* < OE.]

USAGE NOTE English speakers have used *well* both as an adjective and as an adverb since Old English times. When applied to people, the adjective *well* usually refers to a state of health and is normally restricted to the predicate, as in *He hasn't been well lately. Good,* among its many other senses, can also mean "healthy," but can be subtly different from *well* in not referring to a general state of well-being. Thus a patient suffering from a chronic disease might say *I feel good today* when referring to a relative lack of physical discomfort, but might say *I feel well today* if he believes his ailment has disappeared. See Usage Note at **good.**

we'll (wēl) Contraction of *we will.*

Wel·land (wĕl′ənd) A city of SE Ontario, Canada, on the **Welland Ship Canal,** 44.4 km (27.6 mi), which connects Lake Erie with Lake Ontario. Pop. 48,411.

well-ap·point·ed (wĕl′ə-poin′tĭd) adj. Having a full array of suitable equipment or furnishings: *a well-appointed kitchen.*

well-bal·anced (wĕl′băl′ənst) adj. **1.** Evenly proportioned, balanced, or regulated. **2.** Mentally stable; sensible or sound.

well-be·ing (wĕl′bē′ĭng) n. The state of being healthy, happy, or prosperous; welfare.

well-born (wĕl′bôrn′) adj. Of good lineage or stock.

well-bred (wĕl′brĕd′) adj. **1.** Of good upbringing; well-mannered and refined. **2.** Of good breed. Used of animals.

well-de·fined (wĕl′dĭ-fīnd′) adj. **1.** Having definite and distinct lines or features: *a well-defined silhouette.* **2.** Accurately and un-

Ida B. Wells

Welsh corgi

ambiguously stated or described: *a well-defined argument.*

well-dis·posed (wĕl′dĭ-spōzd′) adj. Disposed to be kindly, friendly, or sympathetic.

well-done (wĕl′dŭn′) adj. Cooked all the way through.

Welles (wĕlz), **(George) Orson** 1915–85. Amer. filmmaker and actor who directed and starred in *Citizen Kane* (1941).

well-fa·vored (wĕl′fā′vərd) adj. Handsome; attractive.

well-fed (wĕl′fĕd′) adj. **1.** Adequately or properly nourished. **2.** Overfed; fat.

well-fixed (wĕl′fĭkst′) adj. *Informal* Financially secure; well-to-do; well-off.

well-found (wĕl′found′) adj. Properly furnished or equipped.

well-found·ed (wĕl′foun′dĭd) adj. Based on sound judgment, reasoning, or evidence; adequately substantiated.

well-groomed (wĕl′grōōmd′) adj. **1.** Attentive to details of dress; meticulously neat. **2.** Carefully tended or curried: *a well-groomed horse.* **3.** Trim and tidy: *a well-groomed lawn.*

well-ground·ed (wĕl′groun′dĭd) adj. **1.** Adequately versed in a subject. **2.** Having a sound basis; justified.

well-han·dled (wĕl′hăn′dəld) adj. **1.** Managed well. **2.** Showing signs of much handling.

well·head (wĕl′hĕd′) n. **1.** The source of a well or stream. **2.** A principal source. **3.** The structure built over a well.

well-heeled (wĕl′hēld′) adj. Having plenty of money; prosperous; well-to-do.

Wel·ling·ton (wĕl′ĭng-tən) The cap. of New Zealand, on an inlet of Cook Strait in extreme S North I.; founded in 1840 and supplanted Auckland as the cap. in 1865. Pop. 133,200.

Wellington, 1st Duke of. Title of Arthur Wellesley. Known as "the Iron Duke." 1769–1852. British general who defeated Napoleon at Waterloo (1815) and served as prime minister (1828–30).

Wellington boot n. **1.** A boot extending to the top of the knee in front but cut low in back. **2.** *Chiefly British* A waterproof rubber or leather boot reaching to below the knee. [After the Duke of WELLINGTON.]

well-in·ten·tioned (wĕl′ĭn-tĕn′shənd) adj. Marked by or having good intentions.

well-knit (wĕl′nĭt′) adj. Strongly knit, esp. strongly and firmly constructed: *a well-knit body; a well-knit plot.*

well-known (wĕl′nōn′) adj. **1.** Widely known; familiar or famous. **2.** Fully known.

well-man·nered (wĕl′măn′ərd) adj. Polite; courteous.

well-mean·ing (wĕl′mē′nĭng) adj. Well-intentioned.

well-meant (wĕl′mĕnt′) adj. Kindly or honestly intended.

well·ness (wĕl′nĭs) n. The condition of good physical and mental health, esp. when properly maintained.

well-nigh (wĕl′nī′) adv. Nearly; almost.

well-off (wĕl′ôf′, -ŏf′) adj. **1.** Well-to-do. **2.** In fortunate circumstances. [OFF, circumstanced, prob. < the phrase *to come well off,* to emerge from in good circumstances.]

well-read (wĕl′rĕd′) adj. Knowledgeable through having read extensively.

well-round·ed (wĕl′roun′dĭd) adj. **1.** Comprehensively developed and well-balanced in a range or variety of aspects. **2.** Having a fully developed or shapely figure.

Wells (wĕlz), **H(erbert) G(eorge)** 1866–1946. British writer whose novels include *The War of the Worlds* (1898).

Wells, Ida Bell 1862–1931. Amer. journalist and reformer who founded the Negro Fellowship League in 1910.

well-spo·ken (wĕl′spō′kən) adj. **1.** Chosen or expressed with aptness or propriety. **2.** Courteous in speech.

well·spring (wĕl′sprĭng′) n. **1.** The source of a stream or spring. **2.** A source: *a wellspring of ideas.*

well-tak·en (wĕl′tā′kən) adj. Based on valid reasoning; sound or convincing.

well-thought-of (wĕl-thôt′ŭv′, -ŏv′) adj. Regarded with respect; esteemed.

well-tim·bered (wĕl′tĭm′bərd) adj. **1.** Having a good framework or structure. **2.** Covered with a good growth of timber.

well-timed (wĕl′tīmd′) adj. Occurring or done opportunely.

well-to-do (wĕl′tə-dōō′) adj. Prosperous; affluent; well-off. [< the phrase *well to do in the world* : WELL², prosperous, affluent + TO, for + DO¹, doing.]

well-turned (wĕl′tûrnd′) adj. **1.** Shapely: *a well-turned ankle.* **2.** Concisely or aptly expressed: *a well-turned phrase.* **3.** Expertly rounded or turned: *a well-turned bedpost.*

well-wish·er (wĕl′wĭsh′ər) n. One who extends good wishes to another. —**well′-wish′ing** adj. & n.

well-worn (wĕl′wôrn′) adj. **1.** Showing signs of much wear or use. **2.** Repeated too often; trite or hackneyed. **3.** Carried or worn in a becoming manner: *well-worn fame.*

welsh (wĕlsh) also **welch** (wĕlch) *intr.v.* **welshed, welsh·ing, welsh·es** also **welched, welch·ing, welch·es** *Informal* **1.** To swindle a person by not paying a debt or wager: *He welshed on his debts.* **2.** To fail to fulfill an obligation. [?] —**welsh′er** n.

Welsh (wĕlsh, wĕlch) adj. Of or relating to Wales or its people, language, or culture. ❖ n. **1.** The people of Wales. **2.** The Celtic language of Wales. [ME *Walisce* < OE *Wælisc* < *Wealh,* foreigner, Welshman, Celt, perh. of Celt. orig.]

Welsh corgi n. **-gis** Either of two breeds of dog originating in Wales and having a long body, short legs, and a foxlike head.

Welsh·man (wĕlsh′mən, wĕlch′-) *n.* A man who is a native or inhabitant of Wales.

Welsh rabbit *n.* A dish made of cheese, milk or cream, seasonings, and sometimes ale, served hot over toast or crackers.

Welsh rare·bit (râr′bĭt) *n.* Welsh rabbit.

Welsh springer spaniel *n.* Any of a breed of medium-sized hunting dog of Welsh origin, having a red and white coat.

Welsh terrier *n.* Any of a breed of terrier originating in Wales and having a wiry, black and tan coat.

Welsh·wom·an (wĕlsh′wŏom′ən, wĕlch′-) *n.* A woman who is a native or inhabitant of Wales.

welt (wĕlt) *n.* **1.** A strip, as of leather, stitched into a shoe between the sole and the upper. **2.** A tape or covered cord sewn into a seam as reinforcement or trimming. **3a.** A ridge or bump on the skin, esp. one caused by a lash or blow. **b.** A lash or blow producing such a mark. ❖ *tr.v.* **welt·ed, welt·ing, welts 1.** To reinforce or trim with a welt. **2.** To beat severely; flog. **3.** To raise welts or a welt on. [ME *welte.*]

Welt·an·schau·ung (vĕlt′än′shou′ŏong) *n., pl.* **-ungs** or **-ung·en** (-ŏong-ən) See **worldview.** [Ger. : *Welt,* world (< MHGer. *wĕrlt* < OHGer. *weralt;* see **wī-ro-** in App.) + *Anschauung,* view (< MHGer. *anschouwunge,* observation, mystical contemplation : *an-,* on, at < OHGer. *ana-;* see ANLAGE + *schouwunge,* look < *schouwen,* to look at < OHGer. *scouwōn*).]

wel·ter (wĕl′tər) *n.* **1.** A confused mass; a jumble. **2.** Confusion; turmoil. ❖ *intr.v.* **-tered, -ter·ing, -ters 1.** To wallow, roll, or toss about, as in mud or high seas. **2.** To lie soaked in a liquid. **3.** To roll and surge, as the sea. [< ME *welteren,* to toss about < MLGer. or MDu., to roll; see **wel-** in App.]

wel·ter·weight (wĕl′tər-wāt′) *n.* **1.** A professional boxer weighing more than 135 and not more than 147 pounds (approx. 61–66.5 kilograms), heavier than a lightweight and lighter than a middleweight. **2.** A contestant in various other sports in a similar weight class. [< *welter,* heavyweight boxer, perh. < WELT.]

Welt·schmerz (vĕlt′shmĕrts′) *n.* Sadness over the evils of the world, esp. as an expression of romantic pessimism. [Ger. : *Welt,* world; see WELTANSCHAUUNG + *Schmerz,* pain (< MHGer. *smërze* < OHGer. *smerzo*).]

Wel·ty (wĕl′tē), **Eudora** 1909–2001. Amer. writer known esp. for her tales of rural Southern life.

wen¹ (wĕn) *n.* **1.** A harmless cyst containing the fatty secretion of a sebaceous gland. [ME < OE.]

wen² (wĕn) *n.* Variant of **wynn.**

Wen·ces·las also **Wen·ce·slaus** (wĕn′sĭ-slôs′), Saint. In German **Wen·zel** (vĕn′tsəl) c. 907–929. Duke of Bohemia who encouraged Christianization and was martyred by his brother Boleslav. He is the patron saint of Bohemia.

Wen·ces·laus (wĕn′sĭ-slôs′) In German **Wen·zel** (vĕn′tsəl) 1361–1419. Holy Roman emperor and king of Germany (1378–1400) and Bohemia (1378–1419).

wench (wĕnch) *n.* **1.** A young woman or girl, esp. a peasant girl. **2.** A woman servant. **3.** A wanton woman. ❖ *intr.v.* **wenched, wench·ing, wench·es** To consort or engage in sex with wanton women. Used of a man. [ME, short for *wenchel,* child < OE *wencel.*] —**wench′er** *n.*

wend (wĕnd) *v.* **wend·ed, wend·ing, wends** —*tr.* To proceed on or along; go: *wend one's way home.* —*intr.* To go one's way; proceed. [ME *wenden* < OE *wendan.*]

Wend *n.* See **Sorb.** [Ger. *Wende* < MHGer. *Winde, Wende* < OHGer. *Winid.* See **wen-** in App.] —**Wend** *adj.*

Wend·ish (wĕn′dĭsh) *n.* See **Sorbian 2.** —**Wend′ish** *adj.*

went (wĕnt) *v.* **1.** Past tense of **go**¹. **2.** *Archaic* A past tense and a past participle of **wend.** [ME < OE *wende,* p. t. and p. part. of *wendan,* to go.]

wen·tle·trap (wĕn′tl-trăp′) *n.* Any of various marine snails of the family Epitoniidae, having a tapering, usu. white spiral shell. [Du. *wenteltrap,* spiral staircase, wentletrap < MDu. *wendeltrappe* : *wendel,* winding (< *wenden,* to wind) + *trappe,* stairs.]

wept (wĕpt) *v.* Past tense and past participle of **weep.**

were (wûr) *v.* **1.** Second person singular and plural and first and third person plural past indicative of **be.** **2.** Past subjunctive of **be.** See Usage Notes at **if, wish.** [ME *were, weren* < OE *wǣre, wǣron;* see **wes-**¹ in App.]

we're (wîr) Contraction of *we are.*

were·n't (wûr′ənt, wûr′nt) Contraction of *were not.*

were·wolf also **wer·wolf** (wâr′wŏolf′, wîr′-, wûr′-) *n.* A person transformed into a wolf or capable of assuming the form of a wolf. [ME < OE *werewulf* : *wer,* man; see **wī-ro-** in App. + *wulf,* wolf; see WOLF.]

wer·geld (wûr′gĕld′) also **wer·gild** or **were·gild** (-gĭld′) *n.* In Anglo-Saxon and Germanic law, a price set upon a person's life on the basis of rank and paid by the family of a slayer to the kindred or lord of a slain person. [ME *wargeld* < OE *wergeld* : *wer,* man; see **wī-ro-** in App. + *geld,* payment.]

wer·ner·ite (wûr′nə-rīt′) *n.* See **scapolite.** [After Abraham Gottlob *Werner* (1750–1817), German mineralogist.]

Wer·nick·e's encephalopathy (vĕr′nĭ-kĕz, -kəz) *n.* An acute disease of the brain caused by a deficiency of thiamine, usu. associated with alcoholism and marked by loss of muscular coordination, abnormal eye movements, and confusion. [After Karl *Wernicke* (1848–1905), German neurologist.]

wert (wûrt) *v. Archaic* A second person singular past indicative and past subjunctive of **be.** [WERE + *-t,* archaic second person sing. ending (as in ART² and WAST).]

We·ser (vā′zər) A river of central and NW Germany flowing c. 483 km (300 mi) to the North Sea.

wes·kit (wĕs′kĭt) *n.* A waistcoat; a vest. [Variant of WAISTCOAT.]

Wes·ley (wĕs′lē, wĕz′-), **John** 1703–91. British cleric who founded Methodism (1738). His brother **Charles** (1707–88) wrote the hymn "Hark, the Herald Angels Sing."

Wes·ley·an (wĕs′lē-ən, wĕz′-) *adj.* Of or relating to John or Charles Wesley or to Methodism. ❖ *n.* A Methodist. —**Wes′ley·an·ism** *n.*

Wes·sex (wĕs′ĭks) A region and ancient Anglo-Saxon kingdom of S England; traditionally founded by the Saxon conquerors of Britain.

west (wĕst) *n.* **1a.** The cardinal point on the compass 270° clockwise from due north and directly opposite east. **b.** The direction opposite to the direction of the earth's axial rotation. **2.** An area or region lying in the west. **3.** often **West a.** The western part of the earth, esp. Europe and the Western Hemisphere. **b.** The western part of a region or country. **4.** often **West a.** A historical region of the United States west of the Allegheny Mountains. **b.** The region of the United States west of the Mississippi River. **5.** often **West a.** The United States, Canada, and the noncommunist nations of Europe, esp. during the Cold War. **b.** The nations of North America and Europe with developed capitalist economies, esp. in contrast to less-developed nations. ❖ *adj.* **1.** To, toward, of, facing, or in the west. **2.** Originating in or coming from the west: *a west wind.* ❖ *adv.* In, from, or toward the west. [ME < OE. See **wes-pero-** in App.]

West, Benjamin 1738–1820. Amer. painter who was the first American to study art in Italy (1760–63).

West, Mae 1892?–1980. Amer. actress whose films include *I'm No Angel* (1933).

West, Nathanael 1903–40. Amer. writer known for his novels of dark comedy, such as *Miss Lonelyhearts* (1933).

West, Dame Rebecca Pen name of Cicily Isabel Fairfield Andrews. 1892–1983. British writer and critic whose works include psychological novels, such as *The Judge* (1922).

West Africa A region of W Africa between the Sahara and the Gulf of Guinea. —**West African** *adj. & n.*

West Atlantic *n.* The westernmost branch of the Niger-Congo language family.

West Bank A disputed territory of SW Asia between Israel and Jordan W of the Jordan R.

West Berlin See **Berlin.**

west·bound (wĕst′bound′) *adj.* Going toward the west.

west by north *n.* The direction or point on the compass halfway between due west and west-northwest, or 78°45′ west of due north. ❖ *adv. & adj.* Toward or from west by north.

west by south *n.* The direction or point on the compass halfway between due west and west-southwest, or 101°15′ west of due north. ❖ *adv. & adj.* Toward or from west by south.

West Coast A region of the W US bordering on the Pacific Ocean and including WA, OR, and CA.

West End The W section of central London, England, noted for its fashionable districts and its shops and theaters.

west·er (wĕs′tər) *n.* A strong wind coming from the west. ❖ *intr.v.* **-ered, -er·ing, -ers** To move westward. Used of the sun, the moon, or a star. [ME *westren* < *west,* west. See WEST.]

west·er·ly (wĕs′tər-lē) *adj.* **1.** Situated toward the west. **2.** Coming or being from the west: *westerly winds.* ❖ *n., pl.* **-lies** A storm or wind coming from the west. [ME < *wester,* western < OE *westra.* See **wes-pero-** in App.] —**west′er·ly** *adv.*

west·ern (wĕs′tərn) *adj.* **1.** Situated in, toward, or facing the west. **2.** Coming from the west: *western breezes.* **3.** Native to or growing in the west. **4.** often **Western** Of, relating to, or characteristic of western regions or the West. **5. Western** Of, relating to, or descended from those Christian churches that use or formerly used Latin as their liturgical language. ❖ *n.* often **Western** A novel or dramatic work including themes, characters, or settings characteristic of the American West, esp. of the later 1800s. [ME < OE *westerne.* See **wes-pero-** in App.] —**west′ern·ness** *n.*

Western Bug (bŏog, bŏok) See **Bug 1.**

Western Dvina See **Dvina 2.**

Western Empire or **Western Roman Empire** The W section of the Roman Empire, set apart in A.D. 286 by Emperor Diocletian and lasting until 476.

west·ern·er also **West·ern·er** (wĕs′tər-nər) *n.* A native or inhabitant of the west, esp. the western United States.

Western Europe The countries of W Europe, esp. those allied with the US and Canada in the North Atlantic Treaty Organization (NATO).

Western Ghats See **Ghats.**

Western Hemisphere The half of the earth comprising North America, Central America, and South America.

Western Isles See **Hebrides.**

west·ern·ize (wĕs′tər-nīz′) *tr.v.* **-ized, -iz·ing, -iz·es** To convert to the customs of Western civilization. —**west′ern·i·za′tion** (wĕs′tər-nĭ-zā′shən) *n.*

west·ern·most (wĕs′tərn-mōst′) *adj.* Farthest west.

ă	pat	oi	boy
ā	pay	ou	out
âr	care	ŏŏ	took
ä	father	ōō	boot
ĕ	pet	ŭ	cut
ē	be	ûr	urge
ĭ	pit	th	thin
ī	pie	th	this
îr	pier	hw	which
ŏ	pot	zh	vision
ō	toe	ə	about,
ô	paw		item

Stress marks:
′ (primary);
′ (secondary), as in
lexicon (lĕk′sĭ-kŏn′)

western omelet *n.* An omelet cooked with diced ham, chopped green pepper, and onion.

Western Reserve A historical region of NE OH bordering on Lake Erie.

Western Roman Empire See **Western Empire.**

western saddle *n.* See **stock saddle.**

Western Sahara also **Spanish Sahara** A region of NW Africa on the Atlantic coast; claimed as a protectorate by Spain in 1884 and partly annexed (1976) and occupied (1979) by Morocco.

Western Samoa See **Samoa².**

Western Shoshone *n.* See **Shoshone** 1b.

western tanager *n.* A tanager (*Piranga ludoviciana*) of western North America, the male of which is yellow with a red head and a black back.

Western Wall also **Wail•ing Wall** (wā′lĭng) A remnant of the wall of the second Temple in Jerusalem; a site of pilgrimage, lamentation, and prayer.

West Frisian Islands See **Frisian Islands.**

West Germanic *n.* A subdivision of the Germanic languages that includes High German, Low German, Yiddish, Dutch, Afrikaans, Flemish, Frisian, and English.

West Germany A former country of central Europe bordering on the North Sea; part of Germany until 1945, when the country was divided into US, French, British, and Soviet zones of occupation. In 1949 the three W zones were reconstituted as West Germany; the Soviet zone became East Germany. The two countries were reunified in Oct. 1990. —**West German** *adj. & n.*

West Highland white terrier *n.* A small white terrier with upright ears and tail, developed in Scotland.

West In•dies (ĭn′dēz) An archipelago between SE North America and N South America, separating the Caribbean Sea from the Atlantic Ocean and including the Greater Antilles, the Lesser Antilles, and the Bahama Is. —**West Indian** *adj. & n.*

West Indies Federation A group of ten former British colonies in the West Indies, including Jamaica, Trinidad and Tobago, and Barbados, that lasted from 1958 to 1962. Some of the islands later formed the British-sponsored **West Indies Associated States,** which was gradually disbanded as the islands achieved independence in the 1970s and 1980s.

west•ing (wĕs′tĭng) *n.* **1.** The difference in longitude between two positions as a result of a movement to the west. **2.** Progress toward the west. [< WEST.]

West•ing•house (wĕs′tĭng-hous′), **George** 1846–1914. Amer. engineer who received more than 400 patents for his inventions, including the air brake (1869).

West•land (wĕst′lănd) A city of SE MI, a suburb of Detroit. Pop. 86,602.

West•min•ster (wĕst′mĭn′stər) **1.** Officially **City of Westminster.** A borough of Greater London in SE England on the Thames R.; site of Buckingham Palace. **2.** A city of N-central CO, a suburb of Denver. Pop. 100,940.

West Nile virus *n.* A viral disease of varying severity occurring in Africa, Asia, the Mediterranean, and parts of North America that is transmitted by a culex mosquito.

west-north•west (wĕst′nôrth′wĕst′, -nôr-wĕst′) *n.* The direction or point on the compass halfway between due west and northwest, or 67°30′ west of due north. ❖ *adj.* To, toward, of, facing, or in the west-northwest. ❖ *adv.* In, from, or toward the west-northwest.

Wes•ton (wĕs′tən), **Edward** 1886–1958. Amer. photographer known esp. for his stark images of landscapes.

West Pakistan A former region of Pakistan (after 1947) separated by c. 1,609 km (1,000 mi) from East Pakistan, formerly East Bengal. In 1971 East Pakistan declared its independence as Bangladesh, and West Pakistan became the sole territory governed by Pakistan.

West Palm Beach A city of SE FL opposite Palm Beach. Pop. 82,103.

West•pha•lia (wĕst-fāl′yə, -fā′lē-ə) A historical region and former duchy of W-central Germany E of the Rhine R. The Peace of Westphalia (1648) marked the end of the Thirty Years' War. —**West•pha′lian** *adj. & n.*

West Point A US military installation in SE NY on the W bank of the Hudson R. N of New York City.

West Prussia A historical region of NE Germany between Pomerania and East Prussia S of the Baltic Sea.

West Saxon *n.* **1.** The dialect of Old English used in southern England that was the chief literary dialect of England before the Norman Conquest. **2.** One of the Saxons inhabiting Wessex before the Norman Conquest.

West Slavic *n.* A subdivision of the Slavic languages that includes Czech, Polish, Slovak, and Sorbian.

west-south•west (wĕst′south′wĕst′, -sou-wĕst′) *n.* The direction or point on the compass halfway between due west and southwest, or 112°30′ west of due north. ❖ *adj.* To, toward, of, facing, or in the west-southwest. ❖ *adv.* In, from, or toward the west-southwest.

West Virginia A state of the E-central US; admitted as the 35th state in 1863. It was part of VA until the area refused to endorse secession in 1861. Cap. Charleston. Pop. 1,808,344. —**West Virginia** *adj. & n.*

Western Wall

wetsuit

west•ward (wĕst′wərd) *adv. & adj.* Toward, to, or in the west. ❖ *n.* A westward direction, point, or region. —**west′ward•ly** *adv. & adj.* —**west′wards** *adv.*

wet (wĕt) *adj.* **wet•ter, wet•test 1.** Covered or soaked with a liquid, such as water. **2.** Not yet dry or firm: *wet paint.* **3.** Stored or preserved in liquid. **4.** Used or prepared with water or other liquids. **5a.** Rainy, humid, or foggy: *wet climate.* **b.** Marked by frequent or heavy precipitation: *a wet climate.* **6.** *Informal* Allowing the sale of alcoholic beverages: *a wet county.* **7.** Characterized by the presence of liquid reagents: *wet chemistry.* ❖ *n.* **1.** Something that wets; moisture. **2.** Rainy or snowy weather. **3.** *Informal* One who supports the legality of alcoholic beverages. ❖ *v.* **wet** or **wet•ted, wet•ting, wets** —*tr.* **1.** To make wet; dampen. **2.** To make (a bed or one's clothes) wet by urinating. —*intr.* **1.** To become wet. **2.** To urinate. —*idioms:* **all wet** *Slang* Entirely mistaken. **wet behind the ears** Inexperienced; green. **wet (one's) whistle** *Informal* To take a drink. [ME < OE *wǣt.* See **wed-** in App.]

SYNONYMS *wet, damp, moist, dank, humid* These adjectives mean covered with or saturated with liquid. *Wet* describes not only what is covered or soaked (*a wet sponge*) but also what is not yet dry (*wet paint*). *Damp* and *moist* both mean slightly wet, but *damp* often implies an unpleasant clamminess: *a cold, damp cellar; a moist breeze.* *Dank* emphasizes disagreeable, often unhealthful wetness: *a dank cave.* *Humid* refers to an unpleasantly high degree of moisture in the atmosphere: *hot, humid weather.*

---

wet•back (wĕt′băk′) *n. Offensive Slang* Used as a disparaging term for a Mexican, esp. one who enters the US illegally. [< the fact that the Rio Grande is a common entry point.]

wet bar *n.* A small bar or counter for making alcoholic drinks that is equipped with a sink and running water.

wet blanket *n. Informal* One that discourages enjoyment or enthusiasm.

wet cell *n. Electricity* A primary cell with a liquid electrolyte.

wet dream *n.* An erotic dream accompanied by ejaculation.

wet fly *n.* An artificial fly used in fishing that sinks below the surface of the water.

weth•er (wĕth′ər) *n.* A castrated ram. [ME < OE. See **wet-²** in App.]

wet•land (wĕt′lănd′) *n.* A lowland area, such as a marsh or swamp, that is saturated with moisture.

wet•ness (wĕt′nĭs) *n.* **1.** The condition of being wet. **2.** Moisture. **3.** Rainy or persistently damp weather.

wet nurse *n.* **1.** A woman who suckles another woman's child. **2.** One who treats another with excessive care or solicitude. —**wet′nurse′** (wĕt′nûrs′) *v.*

wet•suit also **wet suit** (wĕt′sōōt′) *n.* A tight-fitting permeable suit worn in cold water, as by skin divers, to retain body heat.

wet•ter (wĕt′ər) *n.* One that wets.

Wet•ter•horn Peak (vĕt′ər-hôrn′) A mountain, 4,274.6 m (14,015 ft), in the San Juan Mts. of SW CO.

wet•ting agent (wĕt′ĭng) *n.* A substance that reduces the surface tension of a liquid, causing the liquid to spread across or penetrate more easily the surface of a solid.

we've (wēv) Contraction of *we have.*

Wey•den (wīd′n, vīd′n), **Rogier van der** 1400?–64. Flemish painter whose works include *The Deposition* (c. 1435).

wf *abbr.* wrong font

WFTU *abbr.* World Federation of Trade Unions

WH *abbr.* watt-hour

whack (hwăk, wăk) *v.* **whacked, whack•ing, whacks** —*tr.* **1.** To strike with a sharp blow; slap. **2.** *Slang* To kill deliberately; murder. —*intr.* To deal a sharp resounding blow. ❖ *n.* **1.** A sharp swift blow. **2.** The sound made by a sharp swift blow. —*phrasal verb:* **whack off** *Vulgar Slang* To masturbate. —*idioms:* **have (or take) a whack at** *Informal* To try out; attempt. **out of whack** *Informal* Improperly ordered or balanced; not functioning correctly. **whacked out** *Slang* **1.** Exhausted. **2.** Crazy. **3.** Under the influence of a mind-altering drug. [Prob. imit.]

whack•ing (hwăk′ĭng, wăk′-) *Chiefly British Slang adj.* Very large; huge. ❖ *adv.* Very; extremely.

whack•o (hwăk′ō, wăk′ō) *n.* Variant of **wacko.**

whack•y (hwăk′ē, wăk′ē) *adj. Slang* Variant of **wacky.**

whale¹ (hwāl, wāl) *n.* **1.** Any of various marine mammals of the order Cetacea, having the general shape of a fish with forelimbs modified to form flippers, a tail with horizontal flukes, and one or two blowholes for breathing, esp. one of the very large species. **2.** *Informal* An impressive example: *a whale of a story.* ❖ *intr.v.* **whaled, whal•ing, whales** To engage in the hunting of whales. [ME < OE *hwæl.*]

whale² (hwāl, wāl) *v.* **whaled, whal•ing, whales** —*tr.* To strike or hit repeatedly and forcefully; thrash. —*intr.* To attack vehemently. [?]

whale•back (hwāl′băk′, wāl′-) *n.* A steamship with the bow and upper deck rounded so as to shed water.

whale•boat (hwāl′bōt′, wāl′-) *n.* **1.** A long rowboat, pointed at both ends and designed to move and turn swiftly, formerly used in the pursuit and harpooning of whales. **2.** A boat similar to such a rowboat in size and shape; a whaler.

whale•bone (hwāl′bōn′, wāl′-) *n.* **1.** The elastic horny material forming the fringed plates that hang from the upper jaw of baleen whales and strain plankton from the water. **2.** An object made of this material.

whalebone whale *n.* See **baleen whale.**

whale oil *n.* An oil obtained from whale blubber, formerly used in making soap and candles and as a lubricating oil and a fuel for lamps.

whal·er (hwā′lər, wā′-) *n.* **1.** One that hunts or processes whales. **2.** A whaling ship. **3.** A whaleboat.

Whales (hwălz, wălz), **Bay of** An inlet of the Ross Sea in the Ross Ice Shelf of Antarctica.

whale shark *n.* A very large shark (*Rhincodon typus*) of warm marine waters having a network of rakelike sieves extending from its gills for straining plankton from the water.

whal·ing (hwā′lĭng, wāl′-) *n.* The business or practice of hunting, killing, and processing whales.

wham (hwăm, wăm) *n.* **1.** A forceful, resounding blow. **2.** The sound of such a blow; a thud. ❖ *v.* **whammed, wham·ming, whams** —*tr.* To strike or smash into with resounding impact. —*intr.* To smash with great force. [Imit.]

wham·mo (hwăm′ō, wăm′ō) *interj. Slang* Used to indicate the startling abruptness of a sound, action, or event.

wham·my (hwăm′ē, wăm′ē) *n., pl.* **-mies** *Slang* **1.** A supernatural spell for subduing an adversary; a hex. **2.** A serious or devastating setback. [Perh. < WHAM.]

whang¹ (hwăng, wăng) *n.* **1.** A thong or whip of hide or leather. **2a.** A lashing blow, as of a whip. **b.** The sound of such a blow. **3.** *Vulgar Slang* The penis. ❖ *tr.v.* **whanged, whang·ing, whangs 1.** To beat or whip with a thong. **2.** To beat with a sharp blow or blows. [Dialectal var. of ME *thong, thwang, thong.* See THONG.]

whang² (hwăng, wăng) *Informal v.* **whanged, whang·ing, whangs** —*tr.* To strike so as to produce a loud reverberant noise. —*intr.* To produce a loud reverberant noise. ❖ *n.* A loud reverberant noise. [Imit.]

whang·ee (hwăng-gē′, wăng′-) *n.* **1.** Any of several Asian bamboos of the genus *Phyllostachys.* **2.** A walking stick made from the woody stem of any of these bamboos. [Chin. (Mandarin) *huáng lí.*]

wharf (hwôrf, wôrf) *n., pl.* **wharves** (hwôrvz, wôrvz) or **wharfs 1.** A landing place or pier where ships may tie up and load or unload. **2.** *Obsolete* A shore or riverbank. ❖ *v.* **wharfed, wharf·ing, wharfs** —*tr.* **1.** To moor (a vessel) at a wharf. **2.** To take to or store on a wharf. **3.** To furnish, equip, or protect with wharves or a wharf. —*intr.* To berth at a wharf. [ME < OE *hwearf.*]

wharf·age (hwôr′fĭj, wôr′fĭj) *n.* **1a.** The use of wharves or a wharf. **b.** The charges for this usage. **2.** A group of wharves.

wharf·in·ger (hwôr′fĭn-jər, wôr′-) *n.* One who owns or manages a wharf. [Alteration of WHARFAGE + -ER¹.]

wharf rat *n.* **1.** A rat that infests wharves and ships. **2.** *Slang* A person who frequents wharves.

Whar·ton (hwôr′tn, wôr′-), **Edith Newbold Jones** 1862–1937. Amer. writer whose novels include *Ethan Frome* (1911).

what (hwŏt, hwŭt, wŏt, wŭt; hwət, wət *when unstressed*) *pron.* **1.** Which thing or which particular one of many: *What do you want?* See Usage Note at **which. b.** Which kind, character, or designation: *What are these objects?* **c.** Which kind, character, or significance: *What are possessions to a dying man?* **2a.** That which; the thing that: *Listen to what I tell you.* **b.** Whatever thing that: *come what may.* **3.** *Informal* Something: *I'll tell you what.* **4.** *Nonstandard* Which, who, or that: *It's the poor what gets the blame.* ❖ *adj.* **1.** Which one or ones of several or many: *What musical is that song from?* **2.** Whatever: *Repair what damage has been done.* **3.** How great; how astonishing: *What a fool!* ❖ *adv.* How much; in what respect; how: *What does it matter?* ❖ *conj.* That: *I don't know but what I'll go.* ❖ *interj.* **1.** Used to express surprise, incredulity, or other strong or sudden excitement. **2.** *Chiefly British* Used as a tag question, often to solicit agreement. —*idioms:* **what for** *Informal* A scolding or strong reprimand. **what have you** What remains and need not be mentioned. **what if 1.** What would occur if; suppose that. **2.** What does it matter if. **what it takes** The necessary expertise or qualities for success. **what's what** *Informal* The fundamentals and details of a situation or process; the true state. **what with** Taking into consideration; because of. [ME < OE *hwæt.* See kʷo- in App.]

what·cha·ma·call·it (hwŏch′ə-mə-kôl′ĭt, hwŭch′-, wŏch′-, wŭch′-) also **what·cha·ma·call·um** (-əm) *n.* Something whose name has been forgotten or is not known. [Alteration of *what you may call it.*]

what·ev·er (hwŏt-ĕv′ər, hwŭt-, wŏt-, wŭt-) *pron.* **1.** Everything or anything that: *Do whatever you please.* **2.** What amount that; the whole of what: *Whatever is left is yours.* **3.** No matter what: *Whatever happens, we'll meet tonight.* **4.** *Informal* Which thing or things; what: *Whatever does he mean?* **5.** *Informal* What remains and need not be mentioned; what have you: *Please bring something to the party—pretzels, crackers, whatever.* ❖ *adj.* **1.** Of any number or kind; any: *whatever requests you make.* **2.** All of; the whole of: *whatever strength she had.* **3.** Of any kind at all: *no campers whatever.* ❖ *interj.* Used to indicate indifference to or scorn for something, such as a remark or suggestion: *We're having pizza tonight.*—*Whatever. I don't care.*

USAGE NOTE Both *whatever* and *what ever* can be used in sentences such as *Whatever* (or *What ever*) *made her say that?* Critics have occasionally objected to the one-word form, but many respected writers have used it. The same is true of the forms *whoever, whenever, wherever,* and *however.* In adjectival uses, only the one-word form is used: *Take whatever books you need.* • It is regarded as incorrect to use *that* before relative clauses following adjectives like *whatever,* as in *whatever book that you want to look at.* Instead, one should write *Whatever book you want to look at will be sent to your office* or *Whichever book costs less is fine with us.* See Usage Notes at **however, that.**

what·not (hwŏt′nŏt′, hwŭt′-, wŏt′-, wŭt′-) *n.* **1.** A minor or unspecified object or article. **2.** A set of light, open shelves for ornaments. ❖ *pron.* Any of various additional or unspecified things or items.

what·sit (hwŏt′sĭt, hwŭt′-, wŏt′-, wŭt′-) or **what·sis** (-sĭs) *n. Informal* Something or someone whose name has been forgotten or is not known. [< *What's it (called)?*]

what·so·ev·er (hwŏt′sō-ĕv′ər, hwŭt′-, wŏt′-, wŭt′-) *pron.* Whatever. ❖ *adj.* Whatever: *no power whatsoever.*

wheal (hwēl, wēl) *n.* A small swelling on the skin that usu. itches or burns. [Prob. alteration of WALE.]

wheat (hwēt, wēt) *n.* **1.** Any of various annual cereal grasses of the genus *Triticum* of the Mediterranean region and southwest Asia, esp. *T. aestivum,* widely cultivated in temperate regions for their edible grain. **2.** The grain of any of these grasses, ground to produce flour used in breadstuffs and pasta. [ME *whete* < OE *hwǣte.*]

wheat bread *n.* A bread made from a mixture of white and whole-wheat flours.

wheat·ear (hwēt′ĭr′, wēt′-) *n.* A small thrush (*Oenanthe oenanthe*) of northern regions having a gray back, buff breast, and white rump. [Back-formation < earlier *wheatears* (taken as pl.), prob. by folk ety. < WHITE + ARSE.]

wheat·en (hwēt′n, wēt′n) *adj.* Of or derived from wheat.

wheat germ *n.* The vitamin-rich embryo of the wheat kernel separated in milling for use as a cereal or food supplement.

wheat·grass (hwēt′grăs′, wēt′-) *n.* Any of certain wheat plants, esp. crested wheatgrass, whose sprouted berries are used for pasture and may have health benefits for humans.

Wheat·ley (hwēt′lē, wēt′-), **Phillis** 1753?–84. African-born Amer. poet whose works include *Poems on Various Subjects, Religious and Moral* (1773).

wheat rust *n.* **1.** A destructive disease of wheat caused by a rust fungus. **2.** Any of several rust fungi of the genus *Puccinia* that cause this disease.

Wheat·stone bridge (hwēt′stōn′, wēt′-) also **Wheat·stone's bridge** (-stōnz′) *n.* An instrument or circuit used to determine the value of an unknown resistance in terms of three known resistances. [After Sir Charles *Wheatstone* (1802–75), British physicist.]

wheat·worm (hwēt′wûrm′, wēt′-) *n.* A small nematode worm (*Anguina tritici*) that is destructive to wheat.

whee (hwē, wē) *interj.* Used to express extreme pleasure or enthusiasm.

whee·dle (hwēd′l, wēd′l) *v.* **-dled, -dling, -dles** —*tr.* **1.** To persuade or attempt to persuade by flattery or guile; cajole. **2.** To obtain through the use of flattery or guile. —*intr.* To use flattery or cajolery for one's ends. [?] —**whee′dler** *n.*

wheel (hwēl, wēl) *n.* **1.** A solid disk or a rigid circular frame, designed to turn around a central axle. **2.** Something resembling such a wheel in appearance or movement or having a wheel as its principal part or characteristic, as: **a.** The steering device on a vehicle. **b.** A potter's wheel. **c.** A water wheel. **d.** A spinning wheel. **e.** *Games* A device used in roulette and other games of chance. **f.** A firework that rotates while burning. **g.** *Informal* A bicycle. **h.** An instrument to which a victim was bound for torture during the Middle Ages. **3. wheels** Forces that provide energy, movement, or direction. **4.** The act or process of turning; revolution or rotation. **5. wheels** *Slang* A motor vehicle or access thereto. **6.** *Slang* A person with a great deal of power or influence. ❖ *v.* **wheeled, wheel·ing, wheels** —*tr.* **1.** To roll, move, or transport on wheels or a wheel. **2.** To cause to turn around or as if around a central axis; revolve or rotate. **3.** To provide with wheels or a wheel. —*intr.* **1.** To turn around or as if around a central axis; revolve or rotate. **2.** To roll or move on or as if on wheels or a wheel. **3.** To fly in a curving or circular course. **4.** To turn or whirl around in place; pivot. **5.** To reverse one's opinion or practice: *wheel about on a subject.* —*idioms:* **at** (or **behind**) **the wheel 1.** Operating the steering mechanism of a vehicle; driving. **2.** Directing or controlling; in charge. **wheel and deal** *Informal* To engage in the advancement of one's own interests, esp. in a canny, aggressive, or unscrupulous way. [ME < OE *hwēol.* See kʷel-¹ in App.]

wheel and axle *n.* A machine consisting of an axle to which a wheel is fastened so that torque applied to the wheel winds a rope or chain onto the axle.

wheel·bar·row (hwēl′băr′ō, wēl′-) *n.* A one- or two-wheeled vehicle with handles at the rear, used for small loads.

wheel·base (hwēl′bās′, wēl′-) *n.* The distance between front

Edith Wharton

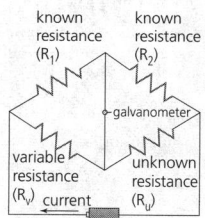

Wheatstone bridge
to calculate the unknown resistance:

$$R_u = \left(\frac{R_2}{R_1}\right) R_v$$

ă pat	oi boy
ā pay	ou out
âr care	ŏŏ took
ä father	ōō boot
ĕ pet	ŭ cut
ē be	ûr urge
ĭ pit	th thin
ī pie	th this
îr pier	hw which
ŏ toe	zh vision
ō toe	ə about,
ô paw	item

Stress marks:
′ (primary);
′ (secondary), as in
lexicon (lĕk′sĭ-kŏn′)

wheel and rear wheel centers in a motor vehicle.

wheel bug *n.* A large assassin bug (*Arilus cristatus*) of North America that has a notched wheellike projection on the back of the thorax and preys on other insects.

wheel·chair (hwēl′châr′, wēl′-) *n.* A chair with large wheels for a sick or disabled person.

wheeled (hwēld, wēld) *adj.* Having wheels or a wheel. Often used in combination: *a three-wheeled bike.*

wheel·er (hwē′lər, wē′-) *n.* **1.** One that wheels. **2.** A thing that moves on or is equipped with wheels or a wheel. Often used in combination: *a three-wheeler.* **3.** A wheel horse.

wheel·er-deal·er (hwē′lər-dē′lər, wē′-) *n. Informal* One who advances his or her own interests by canny, aggressive, or unscrupulous behavior.

wheel horse *n.* **1.** The horse in a team that follows the leader and is harnessed nearest the front wheels. **2.** A diligent dependable worker, esp. in a political organization.

wheel·house (hwēl′hous′, wēl′-) *n.* See **pilothouse.**

wheel·ie (hwē′lē, wē′-) *n.* A stunt in which the front wheel or wheels of a vehicle, such as a bicycle, are raised so that the vehicle is balanced momentarily on its rear wheel or wheels.

Wheel·ing (hwē′lĭng, wē′-) A city of NW WV in the Panhandle SW of Pittsburgh PA; settled in 1769. Pop. 31,419.

wheel lock *n.* **1.** A firing mechanism in certain obsolete small arms, in which a small wheel produces sparks by revolving against a flint. **2.** A firearm using such a mechanism.

wheel·man (hwēl′mən, wēl′-) *n.* **1.** *Nautical* One who steers a ship; a helmsman. **2.** The driver of an automobile, esp. of a getaway car. **3.** A bicyclist.

wheels·man (hwēlz′mən, wēlz′-) *n.* A wheelman.

wheel·work (hwēl′wûrk′, wēl′-) *n.* An arrangement of gears or wheels in a mechanical device.

wheel·wright (hwēl′rīt′, wēl′-) *n.* One who builds and repairs wheels.

wheeze (hwēz, wēz) *v.* **wheezed, wheez·ing, wheez·es** —*intr.* **1.** To breathe with difficulty, producing a hoarse whistling sound. **2.** To make a sound resembling wheezing. —*tr.* To produce or utter with a hoarse whistling sound. ❖ *n.* **1.** A wheezing sound. **2.** *Informal* An old joke. [ME *whesen,* prob. < ON *hvæsa,* to hiss.] —**wheez′er** *n.*

wheez·y (hwē′zē, wē′-) *adj.* **-i·er, -i·est 1.** Given to wheezing. **2.** Producing a wheezing sound. —**wheez′i·ly** *adv.* —**wheez′i·ness** *n.*

whelk[1] (hwělk, wělk) *n.* Any of various large, mostly edible marine snails of the family Buccinidae, esp. *Buccinum undatum,* having a pointed spiral shell. [ME *welke, whelke* < OE *weoloc.* See **wel-** in App.]

whelk[2] (hwělk, wělk) *n.* An inflamed swelling, such as a pimple or pustule. [ME *whelke* < OE *hwylca.*] —**whelk′y** *adj.*

whelm (hwělm, wělm) *tr.v.* **whelmed, whelm·ing, whelms 1.** To cover with water; submerge. **2.** To overwhelm. [ME *whelmen,* to overturn, prob. alteration of *whelven* < OE *-hwelfan* (as in *āhwelfan,* to cover over).]

whelp (hwělp, wělp) *n.* **1.** A young offspring of a mammal, such as a dog or wolf. **2a.** A child; a youth. **b.** An impudent young fellow. See Usage Note at **adage. 3a.** A tooth of a sprocket wheel. **b.** *Nautical* Any of the ridges on the barrel of a windlass or capstan. ❖ *v.* **whelped, whelp·ing, whelps** —*intr.* To give birth to whelps or a whelp. —*tr.* To give birth to (whelps or a whelp). [ME < OE *hwelp.*]

when (hwěn, wěn) *adv.* At what time: *When will we leave?* ❖ *conj.* **1.** At the time that: *in the spring when the snow melts.* **2.** As soon as: *I'll call when I arrive.* **3.** Whenever: *When the wind blows, the doors rattle.* **4.** During the time at which; while: *When I was young, I was happy.* **5.** Whereas; although: *She stopped when she should have continued.* **6.** Considering that; if: *How can he get paid when he won't work?* ❖ *pron.* What or which time: *Since when has this been going on?* ❖ *n.* The time or date: *Have they decided the where and when?* [ME < OE *hwenne.* See **kʷo-** in App.]

USAGE NOTE In informal style *when* is often used after *be* in definitions: *A dilemma is when you don't know which way to turn.* Although useful, this construction is widely regarded as incorrect or unsuitable for formal discourse. In formal style rephrase such definitions to avoid is *when: A dilemma is a situation in which you don't know which way to turn. You are in a dilemma when you don't know which way to turn.*

when·as (hwěn-ăz′, wěn-) *conj. Archaic* **1.** When. **2.** Whereas.

whence (hwěns, wěns) *adv.* **1.** From where; from what place: *Whence came you?* **2.** From what origin or source. ❖ *conj.* **1.** Out of which place; or from or out of which. **2.** By reason of which; from which: *The dog was black, whence the name Shadow.* [ME *whennes : whenne,* whence (< OE *hwanon;* see **kʷo-** in App.) + *-es,* genitive sing. suff.; see **-s**[3].]

USAGE NOTE The construction *from whence* has been criticized as redundant since the 18th century. It is true that *whence* incorporates the sense of *from: a remote village, whence little news reached the wider world.* But *from whence* has been used steadily by reputable writers since the 14th century. Still, *whence* (like *thence*) is most often used nowadays to impart an archaic or

wheelchair

highly formal tone to a passage, an effect better realized if the archaic syntax of the word—without *from*—is preserved as well.

whence·so·ev·er (hwěns′sō-ěv′ər, wěns′-) *adv.* From whatever place or source. ❖ *conj.* From any place or source that.

when·ev·er (hwěn-ěv′ər, wěn-) *adv.* **1.** At whatever time. **2.** When. See Usage Note at **whatever.** ❖ *conj.* **1.** At whatever time that: *We'll leave whenever you're ready.* **2.** Every time that: *He smiles whenever the puppy appears.*

when·so·ev·er (hwěn′sō-ěv′ər, wěn′-) *adv.* At whatever time at all; whenever. ❖ *conj.* Whenever.

where (hwâr, wâr) *adv.* **1.** At or in what place: *Where is the phone?* **2.** In what situation or position: *Where would we be without you?* **3.** From what place or source: *Where did you get this idea?* **4.** To what place; toward what end: *Where is this argument leading?* ❖ *conj.* **1.** At what or which place: *She moved to the city, where jobs are available.* **2a.** In a place in which: *He lives where the climate is mild.* **b.** In any place or situation in which; wherever: *Where there's smoke, there's fire.* **3a.** To a place in which: *Go where it is quieter.* **b.** To a place or situation in which: *Go where you are happy.* ❖ *n.* **1.** The place or occasion: *We know the when but not the where of it.* **2.** What place, source, or cause: *Where are you from?* [ME < OE *hwǣr.* See **kʷo-** in App.]

USAGE NOTE When *where* is used to refer to a point of origin, the preposition *from* is required: *Where did she come from?* When it is used to refer to a point of destination, the preposition *to* is generally superfluous: *Where is she going?* (rather than *Where is she going to?*). When it is used to refer to the location of something, the use of *at* is widely regarded as regional or colloquial: *Where is the station?* (not *Where is the station at?*). See Usage Note at **why.**

where·a·bouts (hwâr′ə-bouts′, wâr′-) *adv.* About where; in, at, or near what location: *Whereabouts do you live?* ❖ *n.* (used with a sing. or pl. verb) Approximate location.

where·as (hwâr-ăz′, wâr′-) *conj.* **1.** It being the fact that; inasmuch as. **2.** While at the same time. **3.** While on the contrary. ❖ *n.* **1.** An introductory statement to a formal document; a preamble. **2.** A conditional statement.

where·at (hwâr-ăt′, wâr′-) *conj.* **1.** Toward or at which. **2.** As a result or consequence of; whereupon.

where·by (hwâr-bī′, wâr′-) *conj.* In accordance with which; by or through which.

where·fore (hwâr′fôr′, -fōr′, wâr′-) *adv.* **1.** For what purpose or reason; why. **2.** Therefore. ❖ *n.* A purpose or cause.

where·from (hwâr′frŭm′, -frŏm′, wâr′-) *conj.* From which.

where·in (hwâr-ĭn′, wâr′-) *adv.* In what way; how: *Wherein have we sinned?* ❖ *conj.* **1.** In which location; where. **2.** During which. **3.** In what way; how.

where·in·to (hwâr-ĭn′tōō, wâr-) *conj.* Into which.

where·of (hwâr-ŏv′, -ŭv′, wâr-) *conj.* **1.** Of what: *I know whereof I speak.* **2a.** Of which: *pottery whereof many examples are lost.* **b.** Of whom. ❖ *adv. Archaic* Of what.

where·on (hwâr-ŏn′, -ôn′, wâr-) *adv. Archaic* On which or what: *"the ground whereon she trod"* (John Milton).

where·so·ev·er (hwâr′sō-ěv′ər, wâr′-) *conj.* In, to, or from whatever place at all; wherever.

where·through (hwâr′thrōō′, wâr′-) *conj.* Through, because of, or during which.

where·to (hwâr′tōō′, wâr′-) *adv.* To what place; toward what end. ❖ *conj.* To which.

where·un·to (hwâr-ŭn′tōō, wâr-) *adv. & conj.* Whereto.

where·up·on (hwâr′ə-pŏn′, -pôn′, wâr′-) *conj.* **1.** On which. **2.** In close consequence of which.

wher·ev·er (hwâr-ěv′ər, wâr-) *adv.* **1.** In or to whatever place: *used red pencil wherever needed.* **2.** Where: *Wherever have you been so long?* See Usage Note at **whatever.** ❖ *conj.* In or to whichever place or situation.

where·with (hwâr′wĭth′, -wĭth′, wâr′-) *pron.* The thing or things with which. ❖ *conj.* By means of which. ❖ *adv. Obsolete* With what or which.

where·with·al (hwâr′wĭth-ôl′, -wĭth-, wâr′-) *n.* The necessary means, esp. financial means: *the wherewithal to survive.* ❖ *conj.* Wherewith. ❖ *pron.* Wherewith.

wher·ry (hwěr′ē, wěr′ē) *n., pl.* **-ries 1.** A light, swift rowboat built for one person and often used in racing. **2.** A sailing barge used in East Anglia. [ME *whery.*]

whet (hwět, wět) *tr.v.* **whet·ted, whet·ting, whets 1.** To sharpen (a knife, for example); hone. **2.** To make more keen; stimulate: *The smell whetted my appetite.* ❖ *n.* **1.** The act of whetting. **2.** Something that whets. **3.** *Informal* An appetizer. [ME *whetten* < OE *hwettan.*]

wheth·er (hwěth′ər, wěth′-) *conj.* **1.** Used in indirect questions to introduce one alternative: *Find out whether the museum is open.* See Usage Note at **if. 2.** Used to introduce alternative possibilities: *whether she wins or whether she loses.* **3.** Either: *He passed the test, whether by skill or luck.* ❖ *pron. Archaic* Which. —*idiom:* **whether or no** Regardless of circumstances. [ME < OE *hwether.* See **kʷo-** in App.]

whet·stone (hwět′stōn′, wět′-) *n.* A hard, fine-grained stone for honing tools.

whew (hwyōō, hwōō) *interj.* Used to express strong emotion, such as relief or amazement.

whey (hwā, wā) *n.* The watery part of milk that separates from the curds, as in the process of making cheese. [ME < OE *hwæg.*] —**whey′ey** *adj.*

whey-face (hwā′fās′, wā′-) *n.* A person with a pallid face.

which (hwĭch, wĭch) *pron.* **1.** What particular one or ones: *Which is yours?* **2.** The one or ones previously mentioned or implied, specifically: **a.** Used as a relative pronoun in a clause that provides additional information about the antecedent: *my house, which is old.* **b.** Used as a relative pronoun preceded by *that* or a preposition in a clause that defines or restricts the antecedent: *that which he needed.* **c.** Used instead of *that* as a relative pronoun in a clause that defines or restricts the antecedent: *The movie which was shown later was better.* **3.** Any of the things, events, or people designated or implied; whichever: *Choose which you like best.* **4.** A thing or circumstance that: *He left early, which was wise.* ❖ *adj.* **1.** What particular one or ones of a number of things or people: *Which part of town is it?* **2.** Any one or any number of; whichever: *Use which door you please.* **3.** Being the one or ones previously mentioned or implied: *It blew up, at which point we ran.* [ME < OE *hwilc.* See **kʷo-** in App.]

USAGE NOTE The antecedent of *which* can sometimes be a sentence or clause, as in *She ignored him, which proved to be unwise.* Care should be taken that this usage does not cause ambiguities. The sentence *It emerged that Edna made the complaint, which surprised everybody* may mean either that the complaint was surprising or that it was surprising that Edna made it. The ambiguity can be avoided with paraphrases such as *It emerged that Edna made the complaint, a revelation that surprised everybody.* • In its use to refer to the contents of sentences and clauses, *which* should be used only when it is preceded by its antecedent. When the antecedent follows, *what* should be used, particularly in formal style: *Still, what is more surprising, he has not said he will withdraw.* See Usage Notes at **that, whose.**

which·ev·er (hwĭch-ĕv′ər, wĭch-) *pron.* Whatever one or ones. ❖ *adj.* Being any one or any number of a group: *Read whichever books you please.* See Usage Note at **whatever.**

which·so·ev·er (hwĭch′sō-ĕv′ər, wĭch′-) *pron. & adj.* Whichever.

whick·er (hwĭk′ər, wĭk′-) *intr.v.* **-ered, -er·ing, -ers** To whinny. ❖ *n.* A whinny. [Imit.]

whid·ah (hwĭd′ə, wĭd′ə) *n.* Variant of **whydah.**

Whid·bey Island (hwĭd′bē, wĭd′-) An island of NW WA in Puget Sound NW of Everett.

whiff (hwĭf, wĭf) *n.* **1.** A slight, gentle gust of air; a waft. **2a.** A brief passing odor carried in the air. **b.** A minute trace. **3.** An inhalation, as of air or smoke. **4.** *Baseball* A strikeout. ❖ *v.* **whiffed, whiff·ing, whiffs** —*intr.* **1.** To be carried in brief gusts; waft. **2.** *Sports* To swing at and miss a ball or puck. **3.** *Baseball* To strike out. —*tr.* **1.** To blow or convey in whiffs. **2.** To inhale through the nose; sniff. **3.** *Baseball* To strike out (a batter). [Perh. alteration of ME *weffe,* offensive smell.] —**whiff′er** *n.*

whif·fle (hwĭf′əl, wĭf′-) *v.* **-fled, -fling, -fles** —*intr.* **1.** To move or think erratically; vacillate. **2.** To blow in fitful gusts; puff. **3.** To whistle lightly. —*tr.* To blow, displace, or scatter with gusts of air. [Perh. freq. of WHIFF.]

whif·fle·tree (hwĭf′əl-trē, wĭf′-) *n. Northeastern US* The pivoted horizontal crossbar to which the harness traces of a draft animal are attached and which is in turn attached to a vehicle or an implement. [Variant of WHIPPLETREE.]

Whig (hwĭg, wĭg) *n.* **1.** A member of an 18th- and 19th-century British political party opposed to the Tories. **2.** A supporter of the war against England during the American Revolution. **3.** A 19th-century American political party formed to oppose the Democratic Party and favoring high tariffs and a loose interpretation of the Constitution. [Probably short for *Whiggamore,* a member of a body of 17th-cent. Scottish Presbyterian rebels.] —**Whig′ger·y** *n.* —**Whig′gish** *adj.* —**Whig′gism** *n.*

while (hwīl, wīl) *n.* **1.** A period of time: *stayed for a while.* See Usage Note at **awhile.** **2.** The time, effort, or trouble taken in doing something: *The project wasn't worth my while.* ❖ *conj.* **1.** As long as; during the time that: *It was lovely while it lasted.* **2.** At the same time that; although: *While we love the children, we are strict with them.* **3.** Whereas; and: *While the soles are leather, while the uppers are canvas.* ❖ *tr.v.* **whiled, whil·ing, whiles** To spend (time) idly or pleasantly: *while the hours away.* [ME < OE *hwīl.*]

whiles (hwīlz, wīlz) *conj. Archaic* While. [ME : *while,* while; see WHILE + *-es,* genitive sing. suff.; see −s³.]

whi·lom (hwī′ləm, wī′-) *adj.* Having once been; former. ❖ *adv. Archaic* At a past time; formerly. [ME, at times < OE *hwīlum,* dative pl. of *hwīl,* time, while.]

whilst (hwīlst, wīlst) *conj. Chiefly British* While. [ME *whilest,* alteration of *whiles,* while. See WHILES.]

whim (hwĭm, wĭm) *n.* **1.** A sudden or capricious idea; a fancy. **2.** Arbitrary thought or impulse: *governed by whim.* **3.** A vertical horse-powered drum used as a hoist in a mine. [Short for *whim-wham,* fanciful object.]

whim·brel (hwĭm′brəl, wĭm′-) *n.* A grayish-brown wading bird (*Numenius phaeopus*) having a white, heavily streaked breast.

[Perh. alteration of WHIMPER (< its cry).]

whim·per (hwĭm′pər, wĭm′-) *v.* **-pered, -per·ing, -pers** —*intr.* **1.** To cry or sob with soft intermittent sounds; whine. See Syns at **cry.** **2.** To complain. —*tr.* To utter in a whimper. ❖ *n.* A low, broken, sobbing sound; a whine. [Prob. imit.] —**whim′per·er** *n.* —**whim′per·ing·ly** *adv.*

whim·si·cal (hwĭm′zĭ-kəl, wĭm′-) *adj.* **1.** Determined by, arising from, or marked by whim or caprice. **2.** Erratic in behavior or degree of unpredictability. [< WHIMSY.]

whim·si·cal·i·ty (hwĭm′zĭ-kăl′ĭ-tē, wĭm′-) *n., pl.* **-ties 1.** The quality or state of being whimsical. **2.** A whimsical idea or its expression; a caprice.

whim·sy also **whim·sey** (hwĭm′zē, wĭm′-) *n., pl.* **-sies** also **-seys 1.** An odd or fanciful idea; a whim. **2.** A quaint or fanciful quality. [Prob. < *whim-wham,* fanciful object.]

whin¹ (hwĭn, wĭn) *n.* See **gorse.** [ME *whinne,* prob. of Scand. orig.]

whin² (hwĭn, wĭn) *n.* A whinstone. [ME *quin.*]

whin·chat (hwĭn′chăt′, wĭn′-) *n.* A small brownish Old World songbird (*Saxicola rubetra*) found in open country.

whine (hwīn, wīn) *v.* **whined, whin·ing, whines** —*intr.* **1.** To utter a plaintive, high-pitched, protracted sound, as in pain or complaint. **2.** To complain or protest in a childish fashion. **3.** To produce a sustained noise of relatively high pitch. —*tr.* To utter with a whine. ❖ *n.* **1.** The act of whining. **2.** A whining sound. **3.** A complaint uttered in a plaintive tone. [ME *whinen* < OE *hwīnan,* to make a whizzing sound.] —**whin′er** *n.* —**whin′ing·ly** *adv.* —**whin′y, whin′ey** *adj.*

whinge (hwĭnj, wĭnj) *intr.v.* **whinged, whing·ing, whing·es** *Chiefly British* To complain or protest, esp. in an annoying or persistent manner. [Dialectal alteration of ME *whinsen* < OE *hwinsian.*] —**whing′er** *n.* —**whing′ing·ly** *adv.*

whin·ny (hwĭn′ē, wĭn′ē) *v.* **whin·nied** (hwĭn′ēd, wĭn′-), **whin·ny·ing, whin·nies** (hwĭn′ēz, wĭn′-) —*intr.* To neigh, esp. in a gentle tone. —*tr.* To express in a whinny. ❖ *n., pl.* **-nies** The sound made in whinnying; a neigh. [Prob. akin to WHINE, to whinny.]

whip (hwĭp, wĭp) *v.* **whipped** or **whipt** (hwĭpt, wĭpt), **whip·ping, whips** —*tr.* **1.** To strike with repeated strokes, as with a strap; lash. **2a.** To punish or chastise by repeated striking with a strap or rod; flog. **b.** To afflict, castigate, or reprove severely. **3.** To drive, force, or compel by flogging, lashing, or other means. **4.** To strike or affect in a manner similar to whipping or lashing. **5.** To beat (eggs, for example) into a froth or foam. **6.** *Informal* To snatch, pull, or remove in a sudden manner. **7.** To sew with a loose overcast or overhand stitch. **8.** To wrap or bind (a rope, for example) with thread or twine to prevent unlaying; seize. **9.** *Nautical* To hoist by means of a rope passing through a single block. **10.** *Informal* To defeat; outdo. —*intr.* **1.** To move in a sudden quick manner; dart. **2.** To move in a manner similar to a whip; thrash or snap about. ❖ *n.* **1.** An instrument, either a flexible rod or a flexible thong or lash attached to a handle, used for whipping. **2.** A whipping or lashing motion or stroke; a whiplash. **3.** A blow, wound, or cut made by or as if by whipping. **4.** Something similar to a whip in form or flexibility. **5.** *Sports* Flexibility, as in the shaft of a golf club. **6a.** A member of a legislative body in charge of enforcing party discipline and ensuring attendance. **b.** A call issued to party members in a lawmaking body to ensure attendance at a particular time. **7.** A dessert made of sugar and stiffly beaten egg whites or cream, often with fruit: *prune whip.* **8.** An arm on a windmill. **9.** *Nautical* A hoist consisting of a single rope passing through an overhead block. **10.** A ride in an amusement park, consisting of small cars that move in a rapid, whipping motion along an oval track. —*phrasal verbs:* **whip in** To keep together, as members of a political party or hounds in a pack. **whip up 1.** To arouse; excite. **2.** *Informal* To prepare quickly. —*idiom:* **whip into shape** *Informal* To bring to a specified state or condition, vigorously and often forcefully. [ME *wippen, whippen.*] —**whip′per** *n.*

whip·cord (hwĭp′kôrd′, wĭp′-) *n.* **1.** A worsted fabric with a distinct diagonal rib. **2.** A strong twisted or braided cord sometimes used in making whiplashes. **3.** Catgut.

whip hand *n.* **1.** A dominating position; an advantage. **2.** The hand in which a whip is held.

whip·lash (hwĭp′lăsh′, wĭp′-) *n.* **1.** The lash of a whip. **2.** An injury to the cervical spine caused by an abrupt jerking motion of the head, either backward or forward.

whip·per·snap·per (hwĭp′ər-snăp′ər, wĭp′-) *n.* A person regarded as insignificant and pretentious. [Alteration (influenced by WHIP) of dialectal *snippersnapper.*]

whip·pet (hwĭp′ĭt, wĭp′-) *n.* Any of a breed of swift short-haired dog developed in England for racing, resembling the greyhound but smaller. [Prob. < WHIP.]

whip·ping (hwĭp′ĭng, wĭp′-) *n.* **1.** The act of one that whips. **2.** A thrashing administered esp. as punishment. **3.** Material, such as cord or thread, used to lash or bind parts.

whipping boy *n.* **1.** A scapegoat. **2.** A boy formerly raised with a nobleman and whipped for the latter's misdeeds.

Whip·ple (hwĭp′əl, wĭp′-), **George Hoyt** 1878–1976. Amer. pathologist who shared a 1934 Nobel Prize.

whip·ple·tree (hwĭp′əl-trē′, wĭp′-) *n. Upper Northern US* See whiffletree. [Perh. blend of dialectal *whippin*, whippletree, and SWINGLETREE.]

whip•poor•will (hwĭp′ər-wĭl′, wĭp′-, hwĭp′ər-wĭl′, wĭp′-) *n.* A nocturnal North American bird *(Caprimulgus vociferus)* of the goatsucker family, having spotted brown feathers that blend with its woodland habitat. [Imit. of its call.]

whip•saw (hwĭp′sô′, wĭp′-) *n.* A narrow two-person crosscut saw. ❖ *tr.v.* **-sawed, -sawed** or **-sawn** (-sôn′), **-saw•ing, -saws 1.** To cut with a whipsaw. **2.** *Games* To win two bets from (a person) at one time, as in faro. **3.** To cause to move or alternate rapidly in contrasting directions. **4.** To defeat or best in two ways at once.

whip scorpion *n.* Any of various arachnids of the order Pedipalpi that resemble scorpions but have a whiplike process on the abdomen and no poisonous sting.

whip snake *n.* **1.** Any of several slender nonvenomous New World snakes of the genus *Masticophis*, having a long tail that resembles a whip. **2.** Any of several similar or related snakes.

whip•stall (hwĭp′stôl′, wĭp′-) *n.* A usu. intentional stall in which a small aircraft enters a vertical climb, pauses, slips backward momentarily, then drops nose downward.

whip•stitch (hwĭp′stĭch′, wĭp′-) *tr.v.* **-stitched, -stitch•ing, -stitch•es** To sew with overcast stitches, as in finishing or binding fabric. ❖ *n.* A stitch made in this manner.

whipt (hwĭpt, wĭpt) *v.* A past tense and a past participle of **whip.**

whip•tail (hwĭp′tāl′) *n.* Any of various New World lizards of the genus *Cnemidophorus*, having a long slender tail.

whippoorwill
Caprimulgus vociferus

whip•worm (hwĭp′wûrm′, wĭp′-) *n.* A slender whip-shaped parasitic nematode worm *(Trichuris trichiura)* that often infests the intestine of humans.

whir (hwûr, wûr) *v.* **whirred, whir•ring, whirs** —*intr.* To move so as to produce a vibrating or buzzing sound. —*tr.* To cause to make a vibratory sound. ❖ *n.* **1.** A sound of buzzing or vibration. **2.** Excited noisy activity. [ME *whirren*, prob. of Scand. orig.]

whirl (hwûrl, wûrl) *v.* **whirled, whirl•ing, whirls** —*intr.* **1.** To revolve rapidly about a center or an axis. **2.** To rotate or spin rapidly. **3.** To turn rapidly, changing direction; wheel. **4.** To have the sensation of spinning; reel. **5.** To move circularly and rapidly in varied, random directions. —*tr.* **1.** To cause to rotate or turn rapidly. **2.** To move or drive in a circular or curving course. **3.** To drive at high speed. **4.** *Obsolete* To hurl. ❖ *n.* **1.** The act of rotating or revolving rapidly. **2.** Something, such as a cloud of dust, that whirls or is whirled. **3.** A state of confusion. **4.** A swift succession of events. **5.** A state of mental confusion or dizziness. **6.** *Informal* A short trip or ride. **7.** *Informal* A brief or experimental try. [ME *whirlen*, prob. < ON *hvirfla.*] —**whirl′er** *n.*

whirl•i•gig (hwûr′lĭ-gĭg′, wûr′-) *n.* **1.** Any of various spinning toys. **2.** A carousel; a merry-go-round. **3.** Something that continuously whirls. **4.** The whirligig beetle. [ME *whirlegigge* : *whirlen*, whirl; see WHIRL + *-gigge*, something that rotates, poss. of Scand. orig.; akin to GIG[1].]

whisker
walrus whiskers

whirligig beetle *n.* Any of various gregarious beetles of the family Gyrinidae that circle about rapidly on water.

whirl•pool (hwûrl′po͞ol′, wûrl′-) *n.* **1.** A rapidly rotating current of water; a vortex. **2a.** Turmoil; whirl. **b.** A magnetic impelling force into which one may be pulled. **3.** A bathtub or pool having jets of warm water.

whirl•wind (hwûrl′wĭnd′, wûrl′-) *n.* **1.** A rapidly rotating, generally vertical column of air, such as a tornado. **2a.** A tumultuous confused rush. **b.** A destructive force or thing. ❖ *adj.* Tumultuous or rapid: *a whirlwind political campaign.*

whirl•y•bird (hwûr′lē-bûrd′, wûr′-) *n. Informal* A helicopter.

whirr (hwûr, wûr) *v. & n. Chiefly British* Variant of **whir.**

whisk (hwĭsk, wĭsk) *v.* **whisked, whisk•ing, whisks** —*tr.* **1.** To move or cause to move with quick light sweeping motions. **2.** To whip (eggs or cream). —*intr.* To move lightly, nimbly, and rapidly. ❖ *n.* **1.** A quick light sweeping motion. **2.** A whiskbroom. **3.** A small bunch, as of twigs or hair, attached to a handle and used in brushing. **4.** A kitchen utensil, usu. in the form of stiff, thin wire loops attached to a handle, used for whipping foodstuffs. [ME *wisken*, of Scand. orig.]

whisk•broom (hwĭsk′bro͞om′, -bro͝om′, wĭsk′-) *n.* A small short-handled broom used esp. to brush clothes.

whisk•er (hwĭs′kər, wĭs′-) *n.* **1a. whiskers** The hair on the cheeks and chin. **b.** A single hair of a beard or mustache. **2.** One of the long stiff tactile bristles or hairs that grow near the mouth and elsewhere on the head of most mammals; a vibrissa. **3.** *Informal* A narrow margin; a hairsbreadth. **4.** *Nautical* One of two spars or booms projecting from the side of a bowsprit for spreading the jib or flying-jib guys. **5.** *Chemistry* An extremely fine filamentary crystal with extraordinary shear strength and unusual electrical or surface properties. [ME *wisker*, anything that whisks < *wisken*, to whisk. See WHISK.] —**whisk′ered, whisk′er•y** *adj.*

whis•key also **whis•ky** (hwĭs′kē, wĭs′-) *n., pl.* **-keys** also **whis•kies 1.** An alcoholic liquor distilled from grain, such as corn, rye, or barley. **2.** A drink of such liquor. [Shortening and alteration of USQUEBAUGH.]

whiskey jack *n.* See **gray jay.** [Alteration of *whiskey-john*, by folk ety. < Cree dialectal *wiiskachaan.*]

whiskey sour *n.* A cocktail made with whiskey, lemon juice, and sugar.

whis•per (hwĭs′pər, wĭs′-) *n.* **1.** Soft speech produced without full voice. **2.** Something uttered very softly. **3.** A secretly or surreptitiously expressed belief, rumor, or hint: *whispers of scandal.* **4.** A low rustling sound. ❖ *v.* **-pered, -per•ing, -pers** —*intr.* **1.** To speak softly. **2.** To speak quietly and privately, as by way of gossip or intrigue. **3.** To make a soft rustling sound. —*tr.* **1.** To utter very softly. **2.** To say or tell privately or secretly. [< ME *whisperen*, to whisper < OE *hwisprian.*] —**whis′per•er** *n.* —**whis′per•y** *adj.*

whist (hwĭst, wĭst) *n.* A card game played with a full deck by two teams of two players, in which the last card dealt indicates trump and the object of play is to win the majority of the tricks. [Alteration of dialectal *whisk*, perh. < WHISK.]

whis•tle (hwĭs′əl, wĭs′-) *v.* **-tled, -tling, -tles** —*intr.* **1.** To produce a clear musical sound by forcing air through the teeth or through an aperture formed by pursing the lips. **2.** To produce a clear, shrill, sharp musical sound by blowing on or through a device. **3a.** To produce a high-pitched sound when moving swiftly through the air. **b.** To produce a high-pitched sound by the rapid movement of air through an opening or past an obstruction. **4.** To emit a shrill, sharp, high-pitched cry, as some birds and other animals. —*tr.* **1.** To produce by whistling. **2.** To summon, signal, or direct by whistling. **3.** To cause to move with a whistling noise. ❖ *n.* **1a.** A small wind instrument for making whistling sounds by means of the breath. **b.** A device for making whistling sounds by means of forced air or steam. **2.** A sound produced by a whistling device or by whistling through the lips. **3.** A whistling sound, as of an animal or a projectile. **4.** The act of whistling. **5.** A whistling sound used to summon or command. ***—idioms:* blow the whistle** *Slang* To expose a wrongdoing in the hope of bringing it to a halt. **whistle in the dark** To attempt to keep one's courage up. [ME *whistlen* < OE *hwistlian.*]

whis•tle•blow•er or **whis•tle-blow•er** (hwĭs′əl-blō′ər, wĭs′-) *n.* One who brings wrongdoing within an organization to light. —**whis′tle-blow′ing** *n.*

whistle pig *n. Appalachian Mountains* See **woodchuck.** See Regional Note at **woodchuck.**

whis•tler (hwĭs′lər, wĭs′-) *n.* **1.** One that whistles. **2a.** A marmot *(Marmota caligata)* of the mountains of northwest North America having a grayish coat and a shrill whistling cry. **b.** Any of various birds that produce a whistling sound. **c.** A horse having a respiratory disease characterized by wheezing. **3.** *Physics* An electromagnetic wave of audio frequency produced by atmospheric disturbances such as lightning, having a characteristic whistling sound in detection equipment.

Whistler, James Abbott McNeill 1834–1903. Amer. painter whose subtle coloring and tonal harmony were influenced by musical aesthetics and Japanese art.

whistle stop *n.* **1.** A town or station at which a train stops only if signaled. **2.** A brief appearance of a political candidate in a small town, traditionally on a train observation platform.

whis•tle-stop (hwĭs′əl-stŏp′, wĭs′-) *intr.v.* **-stopped, -stop•ping, -stops** To conduct a political campaign by making brief appearances or speeches in a series of small towns.

whis•tling swan (hwĭs′lĭng, wĭs′-) *n.* A white North American swan *(Olor columbianus)* having a soft, musical trumpeting voice and a black beak with a yellow spot at the base.

whit (hwĭt, wĭt) *n.* The least bit; an iota: *not a whit afraid.* [ME, amount < OE *wiht.*]

white (hwīt, wīt) *n.* **1.** The achromatic color of maximum lightness; the color of objects that reflect nearly all light of all visible wavelengths; the complement or antagonist of black. **2.** The white or nearly white part, as: **a.** The albumen of an egg. **b.** The white part of an eyeball. **c.** A blank unprinted area, as of an advertisement. **3.** One that is white or nearly white, as: **a. whites** White trousers or a white outfit of a special nature. **b. whites** The white dress uniform of the US Navy or Coast Guard. **c.** A white wine. **d.** A white pigment. **e.** A white breed, species, or variety of animal. **f.** also **White** A member of a racial group of people having light skin coloration, esp. one of European origin. See Usage Note at **black. g.** A product of a white color, such as flour, salt, and sugar. Often used in the plural. **4.** *Games* **a.** The white or light-colored pieces, as in chess. **b.** The player using these pieces. **5a.** The outermost ring of an archery target. **b.** A hit in this ring. **6. whites** *Pathology* Leukorrhea. **7.** A politically ultraconservative or reactionary person. ❖ *adj.* **whit•er, whit•est 1.** Being of the color white; devoid of hue, as new snow. **2.** Approaching the color white, as: **a.** Weakly colored; almost colorless; pale: *white wine.* **b.** Pale gray; silvery and lustrous: *white hair.* **c.** Bloodless; blanched. **3.** Light or whitish in color or having light or whitish parts. Used with animal and plant names. **4.** also **White** Of or belonging to a racial group having light skin coloration, esp. one of European origin. **5.** Not written or printed on; blank. **6.** Unsullied; pure. **7.** Habited in white. **8.** Accompanied by or mantled with snow: *a white Christmas.* **9a.** Incandescent: *white flames.* **b.** Intensely heated; impassioned: *white with fury.* **10.** Ultraconservative or reactionary. **11.** With milk added. Used of tea or coffee. ❖ *tr.v.* **whit•ed, whit•ing, whites 1.** *Printing* To create or leave blank spaces in (printed or illustrated matter). Often used with *out.* **2.** *Archaic* **a.** To whiten; whitewash. **b.** To blanch. [ME < OE *hwīt.*] —**white′ness** *n.*

White, Byron Raymond b. 1917. Amer. jurist; associate justice of the US Supreme Court (1962–93).

White, Edward Douglass 1845–1921. Amer. jurist; associate justice (1894–1910) and chief justice (1910–21) of the US Supreme Court.

White, E(lwyn) B(rooks) 1899–1985. Amer. writer known for his children's books, such as *Charlotte's Web* (1952), and his revision of a 1918 writing manual, *The Elements of Style* (1959).

White, Patrick 1912–90. Australian writer who won the 1973 Nobel Prize for literature.

White, Stanford 1853–1906. Amer. architect particularly noted for his interior designs and ornate eclectic buildings.

White, T(erence) H(anbury) 1906–64. British writer best known for the novel *The Once and Future King* (1958).

White, William Allen 1868–1944. Amer. newspaper editor and writer noted for his politically influential editorials.

white admiral *n.* A nymphalid butterfly (*Limenitis arthemis*) of eastern North America having a broad white band on blue-black wings.

white ant *n.* See **termite**.

white·bait (hwīt′bāt′, wīt′-) *n.* **1.** The young of various fishes, esp. the herring, considered a delicacy when fried. **2.** Any of various similar or related small edible fishes.

white bass (băs) *n.* A North American freshwater food fish (*Morone chrysops*) having a silvery color and blackish stripes.

white birch *n.* Any of several birch trees having white bark, as the paper birch of North America.

white blood cell *n.* Any of various blood cells, containing both cytoplasm and a nucleus, that help protect the body from infection and disease and include neutrophils, lymphocytes, and monocytes.

white·board (hwīt′bôrd′, -bōrd′, wīt′-) *n.* A panel covered with white, glossy plastic for writing on with erasable markers. [WHITE + (BLACK)BOARD.]

white book *n.* An official publication of a national government. [< its formerly being bound in white.]

white bread *n.* Bread made from finely ground, usu. bleached wheat flour.

white-bread (hwīt′brĕd′, wīt′-) *adj.* Blandly conventional, esp. when considered as typical of white middle-class America.

white·cap (hwīt′kăp′, wīt′-) *n.* A wave with a crest of foam.

white cedar *n.* Either of two North American evergreen trees (*Thuja occidentalis* or *Chamaecyparis thyoides*) having light-colored wood.

white cell *n.* See **white blood cell**.

white chip *n.* **1.** *Games* A white disk used in poker as a betting token of minimal value. **2.** Something of minimal value.

white chocolate *n.* Cocoa butter combined with milk and a sweetener, often flavored with vanilla.

white cloud *n.* A small, brightly colored freshwater fish (*Tanichthys albonubes*) native to China and popular in aquariums.

white clover *n.* A common European clover (*Trifolium repens*) having rounded white flower heads.

white-col·lar (hwīt′kŏl′ər, wīt′-) *adj.* Of or relating to workers whose work usu. does not involve manual labor.

white corpuscle *n.* See **white blood cell**.

white crappie *n.* A silvery edible North American freshwater fish (*Pomoxis annularis*) related to the sunfish.

whit·ed sepulcher (hwī′tĭd, wī′-) *n.* An evil person who pretends to be holy or good; a hypocrite. [< the simile applied by Jesus to hypocrites (Matthew 23:27).]

white dwarf *n.* The remnant of a star that has collapsed, having an extremely dense state with no empty space between its atoms, but not reaching the extreme density of a neutron star or black hole.

white elephant *n.* **1a.** A rare expensive possession that is a financial burden to maintain. **b.** Something of dubious or limited value. **2.** An article no longer wanted by its owner. **3.** An endeavor or venture that fails conspicuously. **4.** A rare whitish or light-gray form of the Asian elephant, venerated in regions of southeast Asia and India.

white-eye (hwīt′ī′, wīt′ī′) *n.* Any of various small, greenish, chiefly tropical Old World birds of the genus *Zosterops*, having a narrow ring of white feathers around each eye.

white·face (hwīt′fās′, wīt′-) *n.* **1.** White facial makeup. **2.** A white-faced animal, esp. a Hereford.

white-faced (hwīt′fāst′, wīt′-) *adj.* **1.** Having a pale face; pallid. **2.** Having a white face or a white patch extending from the muzzle to the forehead: *a white-faced antelope.*

white feather *n.* A sign of cowardice. **—idiom: show the white feather** To act like a coward. [< the belief that a gamecock with a white feather in its tail was a poor fighter.]

White·field (hwīt′fēld′, wīt′-, hwĭt′-, wĭt′-), **George** 1714–70. British religious leader who was a central figure in the establishment of Methodism in America.

white·fish (hwīt′fĭsh′, wīt′-) *n.*, *pl.* **whitefish** or **-fish·es 1a.** Any of various chiefly North American freshwater food fishes of the genus *Coregonus*, having a generally white or silvery color. **b.** Any of various similar or related fishes, such as the lake herring, whiting, or menhaden. **2.** See **beluga** 2.

white flag *n.* A white cloth or flag signaling truce or surrender.

white·fly (hwīt′flī′, wīt′-) *n.* Any of various small whitish homopterous insects of the family Aleyrodidae, having long wings and a white waxy body and often injurious to plants.

white-foot·ed mouse (hwīt′foot′ĭd, wīt′-) *n.* A semidesert mouse (*Peromyscus leucopus*) of New Mexico that feeds on crop-damaging insects.

white fox *n.* The arctic fox in its winter color phase.

White Friar *n.* See **Carmelite** 1. [< the color of the habit.]

white frost *n.* See **hoarfrost**.

white gasoline *n.* Gasoline containing no tetraethyl lead.

white gold *n.* An alloy of gold and nickel, sometimes also containing palladium or zinc, having a pale platinumlike color.

white goods *pl.n.* **1.** White fabrics, usu. of cotton or linen. **2.** Household merchandise made of fabric, such as bed sheets and curtains. **3.** Large household appliances, such as ovens and refrigerators. [Senses 2 and 3, because orig. they were typically white.]

White·hall¹ (hwīt′hôl′, wīt′-) *n.* A wide thoroughfare in London, England, running N and S between Trafalgar Square and the Houses of Parliament; site of many government offices.

White·hall² (hwīt′hôl′, wīt′-) *n.* The British civil service. [After WHITEHALL¹.]

white·head (hwīt′hĕd′, wīt′-) *n.* See **milium**.

Whitehead, Alfred North 1861–1947. British philosopher and a founder of mathematical logic.

white-head·ed (hwīt′hĕd′ĭd, wīt′-) *adj.* **1.** Having white hair, fur, or plumage on the head. **2.** *Irish* Favorite; darling.

white heat *n.* **1.** The temperature or physical condition of a white-hot substance. **2.** Intense emotion or excitement.

white hole *n.* A hypothetical hole in outer space from which energy and matter emerge. [WHITE + (BLACK) HOLE.]

white hope *n.* **1.** Someone, esp. a beginning competitor, whom supporters hope will gain success. **2.** A white prizefighter believed to have a chance of defeating a Black champion.

White·horse (hwīt′hôrs′, wīt′-) The cap. of Yukon Terr., Canada, in the S part on the Yukon R. Pop. 21,808.

white-hot (hwīt′hŏt′, wīt′-) *adj.* **1.** So hot as to glow with a bright white light. **2.** Zealous; fervid.

White House *n.* **1.** The executive branch of the US government. **2.** The executive mansion of the President of the United States.

white iron pyrites *n.* See **marcasite** 1.

white knight *n.* One that comes to the rescue; a savior.

white-knuck·le (hwīt′nŭk′əl, wīt′-) also **white-knuck·led** (-əld) *adj.* *Slang* Characterized by tense nervousness or apprehension.

white lead (lĕd) *n.* A heavy white poisonous powder, essentially basic lead carbonate, formerly used in paint pigments.

white leather also **whit·leath·er** (hwīt′lĕth′ər, wīt′-) *n.* A soft leather specially treated with salt and alum.

white lie *n.* An often trivial, diplomatic or well-intentioned untruth.

white lightning *n.* *Chiefly Southern US* See **moonshine** 3.

white-liv·ered (hwīt′lĭv′ərd, wīt′-) *adj.* Cowardly. [< the notion that a deficiency of bile caused a pale liver and lack of vigor or courage.]

white magic *n.* Magic or incantation practiced for good purposes or as a counter to evil.

white mahogany *n.* See **primavera¹** 2.

white man's burden *n.* The supposed or presumed responsibility of white people to govern and impart their culture to non-white people, often advanced as a justification for European colonialism. [From *"The White Man's Burden"* by Kipling.]

white marlin *n.* A small marlin (*Tetrapturus albidus*) of the western Atlantic Ocean, having silvery underparts.

white marriage *n.* A marriage without sexual relations. [Prob. transl. of Fr. *mariage blanc* : *mariage*, marriage + *blanc*, white.]

white matter *n.* Whitish nerve tissue, esp. of the brain and spinal cord, consisting chiefly of myelinated nerve fibers.

white meat *n.* Light-colored meat, esp. of poultry.

white metal *n.* Any of various whitish alloys, such as pewter, that contain high percentages of tin or lead.

white mica *n.* See **muscovite**.

White Mountain A peak, 4,345 m (14,246 ft), in the Sierra Nevada of E-central CA.

White Mountains A section of the Appalachian Mts. in N NH rising to 1,917.8 m (6,288 ft).

whit·en (hwīt′n, wīt′n) *tr. & intr.v.* **-ened, -en·ing, -ens** To make or become white or whiter, esp. by bleaching. **—whit·en·er** *n.*

white night *n.* **1.** A night without sleep. **2.** A night without full darkness, as during the summer in high latitudes.

White Nile A section of the Nile R. in E Africa flowing to Khartoum, where it joins the Blue Nile to form the Nile R. proper.

white noise *n.* Acoustical or electrical noise with equal intensity at all frequencies within a given band. [< white light, which contains all visible spectrum frequencies.]

white oak *n.* **1.** A large oak (*Quercus alba*) of eastern North America, having light-colored wood. **2.** See **roble** 1.

white·out (hwīt′out′, wīt′-) *n.* **1.** A polar weather condition caused by a heavy cloud cover over the snow, characterized by absence of shadow, invisibility of the horizon, and discernibility of only very dark objects. **2.** A usu. white fluid that dries quickly and

White House
top: North Portico, facing Pennsylvania Avenue
bottom: South Portico

white oak
Quercus alba

ă	pat	oi	boy
ā	pay	ou	out
âr	care	ŏŏ	took
ä	father	ōŏ	boot
ĕ	pet	ŭ	cut
ē	be	ûr	urge
ĭ	pit	th	thin
ī	pie	*th*	this
îr	pier	hw	which
ŏ	pot	zh	vision
ō	toe	ə	about,
ô	paw		item

Stress marks:
′ (primary);
′ (secondary), as in
lexicon (lĕk′sĭ-kŏn′)

is applied to printed or written matter to cover mistakes.

white pages *pl.n.* A volume or section of a telephone directory that alphabetically lists the names of people and sometimes businesses.

white paper *n.* **1.** A government report. **2.** An authoritative report on a major issue, as by a team of journalists.

white pepper *n.* Pepper ground from peppercorns from which the outer black layer has been removed.

white perch *n.* A small silvery food fish (*Roccus americanus*) native to the Atlantic coast and freshwater streams of eastern North America.

white pine *n.* **1.** A timber tree (*Pinus strobus*) of eastern North America having needles in clusters of five and durable, easily worked wood. **2.** The wood of this tree. **3.** Any of several other pines having needles in clusters of five.

white poplar *n.* A deciduous Eurasian tree (*Populus alba*) having palmately lobed leaves with whitish undersides.

white potato *n.* The edible tuber of the common potato.

white·print (hwīt′prĭnt′, wīt′-) *n.* A photomechanical copy, usu. of a line drawing, in which black or colored lines appear on a white background.

White River 1. A river of N AR and S MO flowing c. 1,110 km (690 mi) to the Mississippi R. **2.** A river of NW NE and S SD flowing c. 523 km (325 mi) to the Missouri R.

white room *n.* See **clean room.**

White Russia See **Belarus.**

White Russian *n.* **1a.** A Belarusian. **b.** The Belarusian language. **2.** A cocktail consisting of vodka, a coffee liqueur, and milk or cream. [Transl. of Russ. *belorusskiĭ* : *belyĭ*, white + *russkiĭ*, Russian.]

white sale *n.* A sale of household items, esp. white goods.

white sauce *n.* A sauce made with butter, flour, and milk, cream, or stock, used as a base for other sauces.

White Sea A sea of NW Russia, an inlet of the Barents Sea.

white separatist *n.* One who advocates the creation of a society in which whites live separately from other races or from which nonwhite races are excluded. —**white separatism** *n.*

white shark *n.* The great white shark.

white-shoe (hwīt′shōō′) *adj.* Of or being a long-established business known for reputable service and a wealthy clientele.

white slave *n.* A woman held unwillingly for prostitution.

white slaver *n.* A procurer of or trafficker in white slaves.

white slavery *n.* Forced prostitution.

white·smith (hwīt′smĭth′, wīt′-) *n.* **1.** One who works white metal. **2.** One who does finish work, such as polishing, on iron. [WHITE + (BLACK)SMITH.]

white snakeroot *n.* A poisonous eastern North American plant (*Eupatorium rugosum*) having opposite, heart-shaped leaves and flat-topped clusters of small white flower heads.

white space *n.* Space on a page or poster not covered by print or graphic matter.

white squall *n.* A sudden squall occurring in tropical or subtropical waters, characterized by the absence of a dark cloud and the presence of white-capped waves or broken water.

white stork *n.* The common stork (*Ciconia ciconia*) of Europe and Asia, having black and white plumage, a dark red bill, and pinkish-red legs.

white supremacy *n.* The belief that white people are superior to other races and should therefore dominate society. —**white supremacist** *n.*

white·tail (hwīt′tāl′, wīt′-) *n.* See **white-tailed deer.**

white-tailed deer (hwīt′tāld′, wīt′-) *n.* A common North American deer (*Odocoileus virginianus*) having a tail that is white on the underside.

white·throat (hwīt′thrōt′, wīt′-) *n.* **1.** Either of two Old World songbirds (*Sylvia communis* or *S. curruca*) having a white throat and belly. **2.** See **white-throated sparrow.**

white-throat·ed sparrow (hwīt′thrō′tĭd, wīt′-) *n.* A large North American sparrow (*Zonotrichia albicollis*) having a white patch on the throat and a striped crown.

white tie *n.* **1.** A white bow tie worn as a part of men's formal evening dress. **2.** Men's formal evening dress. —**white′-tie′** (hwīt′tī′, wīt′-) *adj.*

white trash *n. Offensive Slang* **1.** Used as a disparaging term for a poor white person or poor white people. **2.** Used as a disparaging term for a white person or white people perceived as being lazy and ignorant.

white vitriol *n.* See **zinc sulfate.**

White Vol·ta (vŏl′tə, vōl′-, vôl′-) A river of Burkina Faso and N Ghana flowing c. 885 km (550 mi) to join the Black Volta and form the Volta R.

white·wall tire (hwīt′wôl′, wīt′-) *n.* A vehicular tire having a white sidewall.

white walnut *n.* See **butternut** 1a.

white·wash (hwīt′wŏsh′, -wôsh′, wīt′-) *n.* **1.** A mixture of lime and water, often with whiting, size, or glue added, that is used to whiten walls, fences, or other structures. **2.** Concealment or palliation of flaws or failures. **3.** A defeat in a game in which the loser scores no points. ❖ *tr.v.* **-washed, -wash·ing, -wash·es 1.** To paint or coat with or as if with whitewash. **2.** To conceal or gloss over (wrongdoing, for example). —**white′wash′er** *n.*

white-tailed deer
Odocoileus virginianus

whitewall tire
whitewall tires on an antique car

whittle
whittling a wooden figure

white water *n.* Turbulent or frothy water, as in rapids or surf.

white-wa·ter (hwīt′wô′tər, -wŏt′ər, wīt′-) *adj.* Of, intended for, or taking place on white water, esp. in river rapids.

white whale *n.* A small toothed whale (*Delphinapterus leucas*), chiefly of northern waters, that is white when full-grown.

white·wood (hwīt′wŏod′, wīt′-) *n.* **1.** Any of various deciduous trees such as the tulip tree, basswood, or cottonwood. **2.** The soft light-colored wood of any of these trees.

whit·ey also **Whit·ey** (hwī′tē, wī′-) *n., pl.* **-eys** *Offensive Slang* Used as a disparaging term for a white person or white people.

whith·er (hwĭth′ər, wĭth′-) *adv.* To what place, result, or condition: *Whither are we wandering?* ❖ *conj.* **1.** To which specified place or position. **2.** To whatever place, result, or condition. [ME < OE *hwider.* See **kʷo-** in App.]

whith·er·so·ev·er (hwĭth′ər-sō-ĕv′ər, wĭth′-) *adv.* To whatever place; to any place whatsoever.

whit·ing[1] (hwī′tĭng, wī′-) *n.* A pure white grade of chalk that has been ground and washed for use in paints, ink, and putty. [ME *whityng* < *whiten,* to whiten < *white,* white. See WHITE.]

whit·ing[2] (hwī′tĭng, wī′-) *n., pl.* **whiting** or **-ings 1.** A food fish (*Merlangus merlangus*) of European Atlantic waters, related to the cod. **2.** Any of several marine food fishes of the genera *Menticirrhus* and *Merluccius* of North American coastal waters, including the corbina and the silver hake. [ME *whitynge* < MDu. *wijting.*]

whit·ish (hwī′tĭsh, wī′-) *adj.* Somewhat white.

whit·leath·er (hwīt′lĕth′ər, wīt′-) *n.* Variant of **white leather.**

whit·low (hwīt′lō, wīt′-) *n.* See **felon**[2]. [Alteration of ME *whitflawe* : perh. alteration (influenced by *whit,* white) of MDu. *vijt,* abscess (ult. < Lat. *ficus,* fig, fig-shaped swelling, piles) + *flaue,* splinter, flaw; see FLAW[1].]

Whit·man (hwīt′mən, wīt′-), **Marcus** 1802–47. Amer. missionary who with his wife **Narcissa Prentiss** (1808–47) established a post in the Oregon region (1836).

Whitman, Walt 1819–92. Amer. poet known esp. for his collection *Leaves of Grass* (1855).

Whit·mon·day also **Whit-Mon·day** (hwīt′mŭn′dē, -dā′, wīt′-) *n.* The day after Whitsunday.

Whit·ney (hwīt′nē, wīt′-), **Eli** 1765–1825. Amer. inventor and manufacturer who invented the cotton gin (1793) and developed the first factory to use mass-production techniques.

Whitney, Mount A peak, 4,420.7 m (14,494 ft), in the Sierra Nevada of E-central CA.

Whit·sun (hwīt′sən, wīt′-) *adj.* Of, relating to, or observed on Whitsunday or at Whitsuntide.

Whit·sun·day (hwīt′sən-dē, -dā′, wīt′-) *n.* See **Pentecost**[1]. [ME *whitsonday* < OE *hwīta sunnandæg,* White Sunday (< the white vestments worn on this day).]

Whit·sun·tide also **Whit·sun Tide** (hwīt′sən-tīd′, wīt′-) *n.* The week starting on Whitsunday, esp. its first three days.

Whit·ti·er (hwĭt′ē-ər, wĭt′-) A city of S CA ESE of Los Angeles; founded by Quakers in 1887. Pop. 83,680.

Whittier, John Greenleaf 1807–92. Amer. poet whose poems about New England include *Snow-Bound* (1866).

Whit·ting·ton (hwĭt′ĭng-tən, wĭt′-), **Richard** 1358?–1423. English merchant and mayor of London who loaned large sums of money to Henry IV and Henry V.

whit·tle (hwĭt′l, wĭt′l) *v.* **-tled, -tling, -tles** —*tr.* **1a.** To cut small bits or pare shavings from (a piece of wood). **b.** To fashion or shape in this way: *whittle a toy boat.* **2.** To reduce or eliminate gradually, as if by whittling with a knife: *whittled down the debt.* —*intr.* To cut or shape wood with a knife. [< ME *whyttel,* knife, var. of *thwitel < thwiten,* to whittle < OE *thwītan,* to strike, whittle down.] —**whit′tler** *n.*

Whit·worth (hwīt′wûrth′, wīt′-), **Kathrynne Ann ("Kathy")** b. 1939. Amer. golfer who had 88 career wins and was the LPGA Player of the Year seven times (1966–69 and 1971–73).

whiz also **whizz** (hwĭz, wĭz) *v.* **whizzed, whiz·zing, whiz·zes** —*intr.* **1.** To make a whirring or hissing sound, as of an object speeding through air. **2.** To move swiftly with or as if with such a sound; rush. —*tr.* To throw or spin rapidly. ❖ *n., pl.* **whiz·zes 1.** A whirring or hissing sound. **2.** A rapid passage or journey. **3.** *Informal* One who has remarkable skill. —*idiom:* **take a whiz** *Vulgar Slang* To urinate. [Imit.]

whiz-bang also **whizz-bang** (hwĭz′băng′, wĭz′-) *Informal n.* One that is conspicuously effective, successful, or skillful. ❖ *adj.* **1.** Conspicuously effective, successful, or skillful. **2.** Very rapid and eventful; rushed. [< *whizzbang,* a shell heard only an instant before landing and exploding.]

whiz kid *n. Informal* A young person who is exceptionally intelligent, innovatively clever, or precociously successful. [Alteration of *Quiz Kid,* a panelist on an early game show.]

who (hōō) *pron.* **1.** What or which person or persons: *Who left?* **2.** Used as a relative pronoun to introduce a clause when the antecedent is a person or persons or one to whom personality is attributed: *the visitor who came yesterday.* **3.** The person or persons that; whoever: *Who believes that will believe anything.* [ME < OE *hwā.* See **kʷo-** in App.]

USAGE NOTE The traditional rules for choosing between *who* and *whom* are relatively simple but not always easy to apply. *Who* is used for a grammatical subject, where a nominative pronoun such as *I* or *he* would be appropriate, and *whom* is used elsewhere. Thus, we write *the actor who played Hamlet*, since *who* is the subject of *played*; *Whom do you like best?* because *whom* is the object of the verb *like*, and *To whom did you give the letter?* because *whom* is the object of the preposition *to*. • It is more difficult, however, to apply these rules in complicated sentences, particularly when *who* or *whom* is separated from the verb or preposition that determines its form. Thus a sentence like *Who do you think is the best candidate?* requires *who* as the subject of the verb *is* (not *whom*; it is not the object of *think*) and *The man whom the papers criticized did not show up* requires *whom* as the object of the verb *criticized*. It is thus not surprising that writers from Shakespeare onward have often interchanged *who* and *whom*. Nevertheless, the distinction remains a hallmark of formal style. • In speech and informal writing, *who* may sound more natural than *whom* in a sentence such as *Who did John say he was going to support?*—though it is incorrect according to the traditional rules. *Whom* may sound stuffy even when correctly used, and to use it where *who* would be correct may betray grammatical ignorance, as in *Whom shall I say is calling?* Similarly, though traditionalists will insist on *whom* when the relative pronoun is the object of a preposition that ends a sentence, grammarians since Noah Webster have argued that the excessive formality of *whom* is at odds with the relative informality associated with this construction; thus they contend that a sentence such as *Who did you give it to?* should be regarded as entirely acceptable. • Some grammarians have argued that only *who* and not *that* should be used to introduce a restrictive relative clause that identifies a person. This restriction has no basis either in logic or in the usage of the best writers; it is entirely acceptable to write either *the woman that wanted to talk to you* or *the woman who wanted to talk to you*. • The grammatical rules governing the use of *who* and *whom* in formal writing apply equally to *whoever* and *whomever* and are similarly often ignored in speech and informal writing. See Usage Notes at **that, whose.**

WHO *abbr.* World Health Organization
whoa (hwō, wō) *interj.* Used to order a halt, as by a horse.
who'd (hōod) **1.** Contraction of *who would*. **2.** Contraction of *who had*.
who·dun·it or **who·dun·nit** (hōo-dŭn′ĭt) *n. Informal* A detective story.
who·ev·er (hōo-ĕv′ər) *pron.* **1.** Whatever person or persons: *Whoever comes will be welcomed.* **2.** Who: *Whoever could have dreamed of it?* See Usage Notes at **whatever, who.**
whole (hōl) *adj.* **1.** Containing all components; complete. **2.** Not divided or disjoined; in one unit: *a whole loaf.* **3.** Constituting the full amount, extent, or duration: *ran the whole way home.* **4a.** Not wounded, injured, or impaired; sound or unhurt. **b.** Having been restored; healed. **5.** Having the same parents. ❖ *n.* **1.** A number, group, set, or thing lacking no part or element; a complete thing. **2.** An entity or a system made up of interrelated parts. ❖ *adv. Informal* Entirely; wholly. —*idioms:* **as a whole** All parts or aspects considered; altogether. **on the whole 1.** Considering everything. **2.** In most instances or cases; as a rule. [ME *hole*, unharmed < OE *hāl*. See **kailo-** in App.] —**whole′ness** *n.*

SYNONYMS *whole, all, entire, gross, total* These adjectives mean including every constituent or individual: *a whole town devastated by an earthquake; all the class going on a field trip; the entire group; gross income; the total cost.* **ANTONYM** *partial*

whole blood *n.* Blood drawn from the body from which no constituent, such as plasma or platelets, has been removed.
whole-cell vaccine (hōl′sĕl′) *n.* A vaccine composed of suspensions of whole bacterial cells that have been killed.
whole cloth *n.* Pure fabrication or fiction. [< the fabrication of garments out of new full-sized pieces of cloth.]
whole·heart·ed (hōl′här′tĭd) *adj.* Marked by unconditional commitment, unstinting devotion, or unreserved enthusiasm. —**whole′heart′ed·ly** *adv.* —**whole′heart′ed·ness** *n.*
whole hog *Slang n.* The whole way; the fullest extent. ❖ *adv.* Completely; unreservedly.
whole language *n.* A method of teaching children to read by emphasizing the use and recognition of words in everyday contexts. —**whole′-lan′guage** (hōl′lăng′gwĭj) *adj.*
whole life insurance *n.* Life insurance that provides protection for the entire lifetime of the insured in return for constant premiums as long as the insured owns the policy.
whole milk *n.* Milk from which no constituent, such as fat, has been removed.
whole note *n. Music* A note having, in common time, the value of four beats.
whole number *n.* **1.** A member of the set of positive integers and zero. **2.** A positive integer. **3.** An integer.
whole rest *n. Music* A rest having the value of four beats in common time.
whole·sale (hōl′sāl′) *n.* The sale of goods in large quantities, as for resale by a retailer. ❖ *adj.* **1.** Of, relating to, or engaged in the sale of goods in large quantities for resale. **2.** Made or accomplished extensively and indiscriminately; blanket. ❖ *adv.* **1.** In

large bulk or quantity. **2.** Extensively; indiscriminately. ❖ *v.* **-saled, -sal·ing, -sales** —*tr.* To sell in large quantities for resale. —*intr.* **1.** To engage in wholesale selling. **2.** To be sold wholesale. —**whole′sal′er** *n.*
whole·some (hōl′səm) *adj.* **-som·er, -som·est 1.** Conducive to sound health or well-being; salutary. **2.** Promoting mental, moral, or social health. **3.** Sound; healthy. See Syns at **healthy.** [ME *holsom* < OE **hālsum.* See **kailo-** in App.] —**whole′some·ly** *adv.* —**whole′some·ness** *n.*
whole-wheat (hōl′hwēt′, -wēt′) *adj.* **1.** Made from the entire grain of wheat, including the bran: *whole-wheat flour.* **2.** Made with whole-wheat flour: *whole-wheat bread.*
who'll (hōol) Contraction of *who will.*
whol·ly (hō′lē, hōl′lē) *adv.* **1.** Completely; entirely. **2.** Exclusively; solely.
whom (hōom) *pron.* The objective case of **who.** See Usage Note at **who.** [ME < OE *hwǣm, hwām.* See **k***ʷ***o-** in App.]
whom·ev·er (hōom-ĕv′ər) *pron.* The objective case of **whoever.** See Usage Note at **who.**
whomp (hwŏmp, wŏmp) *Informal n.* A loud, heavy blow or thud. ❖ *v.* **whomped, whomp·ing, whomps** —*tr.* **1.** To hit or strike. **2.** To defeat soundly; trounce. **3.** To prepare or make, esp. with little effort. Often used with *up: "Meanwhile, you whomp up yams and spuds and bake your pies"* (Garrison Keillor). —*intr.* To hit or strike with a whomp.
whom·so·ev·er (hōom′sō-ĕv′ər) *pron.* The objective case of **whosoever.**
whoop (hōop, hwōop, wōop) *n.* **1a.** A loud cry of exultation or excitement. **b.** A shout uttered by a hunter or warrior. **2.** A hooting cry, as of a bird. **3.** The paroxysmal gasp characteristic of whooping cough. ❖ *v.* **whooped, whoop·ing, whoops** —*intr.* **1.** To utter a loud shout or cry. See Syns at **shout. 2.** To utter a hooting cry. **3.** To make the paroxysmal gasp characteristic of whooping cough. —*tr.* **1.** To utter a whoop. **2.** To chase, call, urge on, or drive with a whoop. —*idiom:* **whoop it up** *Slang* **1.** To have a jolly, noisy celebration. **2.** To express or arouse enthusiasm; cheer. [< ME *whopen*, to whoop, var. of *hopen* < OFr. *hopper*, of imit. orig.]
whoop·ee (hwōop′ē, wōop′ē, hwōo′pē, wōo′-) *interj. Slang* Used to express jubilance. —*idiom:* **make whoopee** *Slang* **1.** To engage in a noisy boisterous celebration. **2.** To make love. [Alteration of WHOOP.]
whoop·er (hōo′pər, hwōo′-, wōo′-) *n.* A whooping crane.
whoop·ing cough (hōo′pĭng, hwōo′-, wōo′-, hōop′ĭng) *n.* A highly contagious disease, usu. affecting children, that is caused by the bacterium *Bordetella pertussis* and marked by spasms of coughing interspersed with deep noisy inhalations.
whooping crane *n.* A large, long-legged North American bird (*Grus americana*), now very rare, having predominantly white plumage and a loud trumpeting cry.
whoops (hwōops, wōops, hwōops, wōops) also **woops** (wōops, wōops) *interj.* Used to express apology or mild surprise.
whoosh (hwōosh, wōosh, hwōosh, wōosh) also **woosh** (wōosh, wōosh) *n.* **1.** A sibilant or swift rushing sound. **2.** A swift movement or flow; a rush or spurt. ❖ *intr.v.* **whooshed, whoosh·ing, whoosh·es** also **wooshed, woosh·ing, woosh·es 1.** To make a swift rushing sound. **2.** To move or flow swiftly with or as if with such a sound. [Imit.]
whop (hwŏp, wŏp) *tr.v.* **whopped, whop·ping, whops 1.** To strike with a heavy blow. **2.** To defeat soundly; thrash. ❖ *n.* A heavy blow; a sharp thud. [ME *whappen*, var. of *wappen*, to throw violently.]
whop·per (hwŏp′ər, wŏp′-) *n. Slang* **1.** Something exceptionally big or remarkable. **2.** A gross untruth. [< WHOPPING.]
whop·ping (hwŏp′ĭng, wŏp′-) *Slang adj.* Exceptionally large. ❖ *adv.* Used as an intensive: *a whopping good joke.* [Pr. part. of WHOP.]
whore (hôr, hōr) *n.* **1.** A prostitute. **2.** A person considered sexually promiscuous. **3.** A person considered as having compromised principles for personal gain. ❖ *intr.v.* **whored, whor·ing, whores 1.** To associate or have sexual relations with prostitutes or a prostitute. **2.** To accept payment in exchange for sexual relations. **3.** To compromise one's principles for personal gain. [ME *hore* < OE *hōre.* See **kā-** in App.]
whore·dom (hôr′dəm, hōr′-) *n.* **1.** Prostitution. **2a.** Unlawful sexual relations. **b.** Promiscuous sex. **3.** *Bible* Unfaithfulness to God; idolatry. [ME *hordom* < ON *hórdōmr.* See **kā-** in App.]
whore·house (hôr′hous′, hōr′-) *n.* A house of prostitution.
whore·mas·ter (hôr′măs′tər, hōr′-) *n.* **1.** A man who associates with or pays for sexual relations with prostitutes or a prostitute. **2.** A pimp.
whore·mong·er (hôr′mŭng′gər, -mŏng′-, hōr′-) *n.* A whoremaster.
whore·son (hôr′sən, hōr′-) *n.* A contemptible or detestable person. ❖ *adj.* Abominable; detestable.
Whorf (wôrf, hwôrf), **Benjamin Lee** 1897–1941. Amer. linguist who developed what came to be known as the Sapir-Whorf hypothesis in collaboration with his teacher Edward Sapir.
whor·ish (hôr′ĭsh, hōr′-) *adj.* Of or characteristic of whores or a whore; lewd. —**whor′ish·ly** *adv.* —**whor′ish·ness** *n.*
whorl (hwôrl, wôrl, hwûrl, wûrl) *n.* **1.** A form that coils or spirals;

whooping crane
Grus americana

whorl
whorled leaves

ă	pat	oi	boy
ā	pay	ou	out
âr	care	ōo	took
ä	father	ōo	boot
ĕ	pet	ŭ	cut
ē	be	ûr	urge
ĭ	pit	th	thin
ī	pie	th	this
îr	pier	hw	which
ŏ	pot	zh	vision
ō	toe	ə	about,
ô	paw		item

Stress marks:
′ (primary);
′ (secondary); as in
lexicon (lĕk′sĭ-kŏn′)

a curl or swirl. **2.** *Botany* An arrangement of three or more leaves, petals, or other organs radiating from a single node. **3.** *Zoology* A single turn or volution of a spiral shell. **4.** One of the circular ridges or convolutions of a fingerprint. **5.** *Architecture* An ornamental device, as in stonework or weaving, consisting of stylized vine leaves and tendrils. **6.** A small flywheel that regulates the speed of a spinning wheel. [ME *whorle*, alteration of *whirle*, whirl < *whirlen*, to whirl. See WHIRL.]

whorled (hwôrld, wôrld, hwûrld, wûrld) *adj.* Having or forming whorls or a whorl: *whorled flower parts.*

whort (hwûrt, wûrt) also **whor•tle** (hwûr′tl, wûr′tl) *n.* The whortleberry or its fruit. [Variant of dialectal *hurt.*]

whor•tle•ber•ry (hwûrt′l-bĕr′ē, wûrt′-) *n.* **1.** Either of two deciduous shrubs, *Vaccinium myrtillus* of Eurasia or *V. corymbosum* of eastern North America, having edible blackish berries. **2.** Their fruit. [Dialectal var. of *hurtleberry* < ME *hurtilberi* : perh. alteration of *hurt*, an azure-colored ball (< OFr. *heurte*) + *berye, beri,* berry; see BERRY.]

who's (hōōz) **1.** Contraction of *who is.* **2.** Contraction of *who has.*

whose (hōōz) *adj.* **1.** The possessive form of **who. 2.** The possessive form of **which.** [ME *whos* < OE *hwæs.* See **kʷo-** in App.]

USAGE NOTE It has sometimes been claimed that *whose* is properly used only as the possessive form of *who* and thus should be restricted to animate antecedents. But there is extensive literary precedent for the use of *whose* with inanimate antecedents, as in *The play, whose style is rigidly formal, is typical of the period.* In an earlier survey this example was acceptable to a large majority of the Usage Panel. Those who avoid this usage employ *of which: The play, the style of which is rigidly formal, is typical of the period.* But, as this example shows, substituting *of which* for *whose* often results in a stilted sentence. See Usage Notes at **which, who.**

who•so (hōō′sō) *pron.* Who; whoever; whatever person.

who•so•ev•er (hōō′sō-ĕv′ər) *pron.* Whoever.

W-hr *abbr.* watt-hour

whs. *abbr.* warehouse

whsle. *abbr.* wholesale

whump (hwŭmp, wŭmp) *n.* A thump; a thud. [Imit.]

whup (hwŭp, wŭp, hwōōp, wōōp) *v.* Chiefly Southern US Variant of **whip.** [Sc., var. of WHIP.]

why (hwī, wī) *adv.* For what purpose, reason, or cause; with what intention, justification, or motive: *Why do birds sing?* ❖ *conj.* **1.** The reason, cause, or purpose for which: *I know why you left.* **2.** *Usage Problem* On account of which; for which: *The reason why he failed the exam is unclear.* ❖ *n., pl.* **whys 1.** The cause or intention underlying a given action or situation. **2.** A difficult problem or question. ❖ *interj.* Used to express mild surprise, indignation, or impatience. [ME < OE *hwȳ.* See **kʷo-** in App.]

USAGE NOTE Many language critics have noticed that *why* could be eliminated in sentences such as *The reason why he accepted the nomination is not clear* with no loss to the sense. For that matter, *the reason* could just as easily be eliminated instead. But the phrase *the reason why* has been used by reputable English writers since the Renaissance, and the redundancy of this longstanding construction is similarly idiomatic to that of set phrases such as *old adage* and *young whelp.* See Usage Note at **where.**

whyd•ah also **whid•ah** (hwĭd′ə, wĭd′ə) *n.* Any of several African weaverbirds of the genus *Vidua,* the male of which grows long, drooping, predominantly black tail feathers during the breeding season. [Prob. alteration of WIDOW (BIRD).]

WI *abbr.* Wisconsin

w.i. *abbr.* when issued (financial stock)

W.I. *abbr.* **1.** West Indian **2.** West Indies

WIA *abbr.* wounded in action

Wic•ca (wĭk′ə) *n.* **1.** A polytheistic Neo-Pagan nature religion inspired by various pre-Christian western European beliefs, whose central deity is a mother goddess and which includes the use of herbal magic and benign witchcraft. **2.** A group or community of believers or followers of this religion. [OE *wicca,* necromancer.] —**Wic′can** *adj. & n.*

Wich•i•ta¹ (wĭch′ĭ-tô′) *n., pl.* **Wichita** or **-tas 1.** A member of a Native American confederacy formerly inhabiting Kansas, Oklahoma, and Texas, with a present-day population in southwest Oklahoma. **2.** Their Caddoan language. [Caddo *wíic′ita.*]

Wich•i•ta² (wĭch′ĭ-tô′) A city of S-central KS SW of Kansas City; founded in the 1860s. Pop. 344,284.

Wichita Falls A city of N-central TX near the OK border NW of Fort Worth. Pop. 104,197.

wick (wĭk) *n.* **1.** A cord or strand of loosely woven, twisted, or braided fibers, as on a candle or oil lamp, that draws up fuel to the flame by capillary action. **2.** A piece of material that conveys liquid by capillary action. ❖ *tr. & intr.v.* **wicked** (wĭkt), **wick•ing, wicks** To convey or be conveyed by capillary action. [ME *wike* < OE *wēoce.*]

wick•ed (wĭk′ĭd) *adj.* **-er, -est 1.** Evil by nature and in practice. **2.** Playfully malicious or mischievous. **3.** Severe and distressing. **4.** Highly offensive; obnoxious. **5.** *Slang* Strikingly good, effective, or skillful. ❖ *adv. Slang* Used as an intensive. [ME, alteration of *wicke,* ult. < OE *wicca,* sorcerer.] —**wick′ed•ly** *adv.* —**wick′ed•ness** *n.*

wick•er (wĭk′ər) *n.* **1.** A flexible plant branch or twig, as of a willow, used in weaving baskets or furniture. **2.** Wickerwork. [ME *wiker,* of Scand. orig.]

wick•er•work (wĭk′ər-wûrk′) *n.* Work made of interlaced plant branches or twigs.

wick•et (wĭk′ĭt) *n.* **1.** A small door or gate, esp. one built into or near a larger one. **2.** A small window or opening, often fitted with glass or a grating. **3.** A sluice gate for regulating the amount of water in a millrace or canal or for emptying a lock. **4.** *Sports* In cricket: **a.** Either of the two sets of three stumps, topped by bails, that forms the target of the bowler and is defended by the batsman. **b.** A batsman's innings, which may be terminated by the ball knocking the bails off the stumps. **c.** The termination of a batsman's innings. **d.** The period during which two batsmen are in together. **e.** See **pitch²** 3. **5.** *Games* Any of the small arches, usu. made of wire, through which players try to drive their ball in croquet. [ME < ONFr. *wiket,* nook, wicket.]

wick•i•up also **wik•i•up** (wĭk′ē-ŭp′) *n.* A frame hut covered with matting, as of bark or brush, used by nomadic Native Americans of North America. [Fox *wiikiyaapi,* wigwam.]

Wick•liffe or **Wic•lif** (wĭk′lĭf), **John** See John **Wycliffe.**

wic•o•py (wĭk′ə-pē) *n., pl.* **-pies** See **leatherwood** 1. [Eastern Abenaki *wikapi,* inner bark for cordage.]

wid. *abbr.* **1.** widow **2.** widower

wid•der•shins (wĭd′ər-shĭnz′) or **with•er•shins** (wĭth′-) *adv.* In a contrary or counterclockwise direction. [MLGer. *weddersinnes* < MHGer. *widersinnes* : *wider,* back (< OHGer. *widar*) + *sinnes,* in the direction of (< *sin,* direction < OHGer.).]

wide (wīd) *adj.* **wid•er, wid•est 1a.** Having a specified extent from side to side: *a ribbon two inches wide.* **b.** Extending over a great distance from side to side; broad: *a wide road.* **2.** Having great extent or range; including much or many: *a wide selection.* **3.** Fully open or extended: *wide eyes.* **4a.** Being at a distance from a desired goal or point. **b.** *Baseball* Outside. **c.** *Sports* Being near one of the side boundaries of a playing area, such as a sideline on a football field. **5.** *Linguistics* Lax. ❖ *adv.* **wider, widest 1.** Over a great distance; extensively: *traveled far and wide.* **2.** To the full extent; completely. **3.** To the side of or at a distance from a given boundary, limit, or goal. **4.** *Sports* Toward or near one of the sides of a playing area. ❖ *n. Sports* A ball bowled outside of the batsman's reach, counting as a run for the batting team in cricket. [ME < OE *wīd.*] —**wide′ly** *adv.* —**wide′ness** *n.*

-wide *suff.* Extending or effective throughout a specified area or region: *statewide.* [< WIDE.]

wide-an•gle (wīd′ăng′gəl) *adj.* Of, having, or being a camera lens with a relatively short focal length that permits an angle of view wider than approx. 70°.

wide area network *n.* See WAN.

wide-a•wake (wīd′ə-wāk′) *adj.* **1.** Completely awake. **2.** Alert; watchful. ❖ *n.* See **sooty tern.** —**wide′a•wake′ness** *n.*

wide-bod•y or **wide•bod•y** (wīd′bŏd′ē) *n., pl.* **-bod•ies** A jet aircraft having a wide fuselage with passenger seats divided by two lengthwise aisles.

wide-eyed (wīd′īd′) *adj.* **1.** Having the eyes completely opened, as in wonder. **2.** Innocent; credulous.

wid•en (wīd′n) *tr. & intr.v.* **wid•ened, wid•en•ing, wid•ens** To make or become wide or wider. —**wid′en•er** *n.*

wide-o•pen (wīd′ō′pən) *adj.* **1.** Completely open: *a wide-open door.* **2.** Being without laws or law enforcement.

wide receiver *n. Football* A receiver who usu. lines up several yards to the side of the offensive formation.

wide•spread (wīd′sprĕd′) *adj.* **1.** Spread or scattered over a considerable extent. **2.** Occurring or accepted widely.

wid•geon (wĭj′ən) also **wi•geon** (wĭj′ən) *n., pl.* **widgeon** also **wigeon** or **-geons** Either of two wild freshwater ducks (*Anas americana* of North America or *A. penelope* of Europe) having a grayish or brownish back and a white belly. [?]

widg•et (wĭj′ĭt) *n.* **1.** A small mechanical device or control; a gadget. **2.** An unnamed or hypothetical manufactured article. [Perh. alteration of GADGET.]

wid•ow (wĭd′ō) *n.* **1.** A woman whose husband has died and who has not remarried. **2.** *Informal* A woman whose husband is often away pursuing a sport or hobby. **3.** An additional hand of cards dealt face down in some card games, to be used by the highest bidder. **4.** A single, usu. short line of type, as one at the end of a paragraph or at the top of a page or column. ❖ *tr.v.* **-owed, -ow•ing, -ows** To make a widow or widower of. [ME *widewe* < OE *widuwe.*] —**wid′ow•hood′** *n.*

widow bird *n.* See **whydah.** [< its black plumage.]

wid•ow•er (wĭd′ō-ər) *n.* A man whose wife has died and who has not remarried. [ME *widewer* < *widewe,* widow. See WIDOW.] —**wid′ow•er•hood′** *n.*

wid•ow's mite (wĭd′ōz) *n.* A small contribution made by one who has little. [< the widow who gave two small coins to the Temple treasury (Mark 12:43).]

widow's peak *n.* A V-shaped point formed by the hair near the top of the human forehead. [< the superstition that it is a sign of early widowhood.]

widow's walk *n.* A railed rooftop platform typically on a coastal house, originally designed to observe vessels at sea.

width (wĭdth, wĭth, wĭtth) *n.* **1.** The state, quality, or fact of being

wickiup

wide. 2. The measurement of the extent of something from side to side. **3.** A piece of material measured along its smaller dimension or its crosswise grain, esp. a piece of fabric measured from selvage to selvage. [WIDE + -TH².]

width·wise (wĭdth′wīz′, wĭth′-, wĭtth-) *adv.* From side to side; in terms of width.

wield (wēld) *tr.v.* **wield·ed, wield·ing, wields** **1.** To handle (a weapon or tool, for example) with skill and ease. **2.** To exercise (authority or influence, for example) effectively. [ME *welden* < OE *wealdan*, to rule, and *wieldan*, to govern.] —**wield′a·ble** *adj.* —**wield′er** *n.*

wield·y (wēl′dē) *adj.* **-i·er, -i·est** Easily wielded or managed.

wie·ner (wē′nər) *n.* **1.** Wienerwurst. **2.** A frankfurter. **3.** *Vulgar Slang* A penis. [Ger., short for *Wienerwurst*. See WIENERWURST.]

Wie·ner (wē′nər), **Norbert** 1894–1964. Amer. mathematician who founded cybernetics.

Wie·ner schnit·zel (vē′nər shnĭt′səl) *n.* A breaded veal cutlet. [Ger. : *Wiener*, of Vienna, Austria + *Schnitzel*, cutlet.]

wie·ner·wurst (wē′nər-wûrst′, -wŏorst′) *n.* A smoked pork or beef sausage similar to a frankfurter. [Ger. : *Wiener*, of Vienna, Austria + *Wurst*, sausage; see WURST.]

Wies·ba·den (vēs′bäd′n) A city of W-central Germany on the Rhine R. W of Frankfurt; founded as a Celtic settlement in the 3rd cent. B.C. Pop. 270,873.

Wie·schaus (wē′shous′, vē′-), **Eric** b. 1947. German-born biologist. He shared a 1995 Nobel Prize in medicine.

Wie·sel (vē′səl), **Elie(zer)** b. 1928. Romanian-born writer and lecturer who won the 1986 Nobel Peace Prize.

Wie·sen·thal (wē′sən-thäl′, vē′zən-täl′), **Simon** b. 1908. Ukrainian-born Holocaust survivor who, as founder (1961) and head of the Jewish Documentation Center, has tracked down more than 1,000 Nazi war criminals.

wife (wīf) *n., pl.* **wives** (wīvz) A woman joined to a man in marriage; a female spouse. [ME *wif* < OE *wīf.* See **ghwībh-** in App.] —**wife′hood′** *n.*

wife·ly (wīf′lē) *adj.* Of or befitting a wife. —**wife′li·ness** *n.*

wig (wĭg) *n.* A covering of human or synthetic hair worn on the head for adornment, as part of a costume, or to conceal baldness. ❖ *tr.v.* **wigged, wig·ging, wigs** To scold or censure. —**phrasal verb: wig out** *Slang* To make or become wildly excited, enthusiastic, or crazy. [Short for PERIWIG.]

wig·an (wĭg′ən) *n.* A stiff fabric used for stiffening.

Wigan A borough of NW England NE of Liverpool. Pop. 313,196.

wi·geon (wĭj′ən) *n.* Variant of widgeon.

Wig·gin (wĭg′ĭn), **Kate Douglas Smith** 1856–1923. Amer. writer of *Rebecca of Sunnybrook Farm* (1903).

wig·gle (wĭg′əl) *v.* **-gled, -gling, -gles** —*intr.* **1.** To move back and forth with quick irregular motions. **2a.** To move or proceed with a twisting or turning motion; wriggle. **b.** To insinuate or extricate oneself by sly or subtle means: *wiggled out of the appointment.* —*tr.* **1.** To cause to move back and forth with quick irregular motions: *wiggle a loose tooth.* **2.** To make (one's way, for example) by or as if by wiggling: *wiggled his way out of a jam.* ❖ *n.* A wiggling movement or course. —**idiom: get a wiggle on** *Slang* To hurry or hurry up. [ME *wiglen*, prob. < MLGer. *wigelen*, to totter. See **wegh-** in App.] —**wig′gly** *adj.*

wig·gler (wĭg′lər) *n.* **1.** One that wiggles, such as a worm or a restless child. **2.** The larva or pupa of a mosquito.

wiggle room *n.* Flexibility, as of options or interpretation.

Wig·gles·worth (wĭg′əlz-wûrth′), **Michael** 1631–1705. English-born Amer. cleric and poet whose works include the poem *The Day of Doom* (1662).

wig·gy (wĭg′ē) *adj.* **-gi·er, -gi·est** *Slang* Excited, eccentric, or crazy, esp. in reaction to something.

wight¹ (wīt) *n. Obsolete* A living being; a creature. [ME < OE *wiht.*]

wight² (wīt) *adj. Archaic* Valorous; brave. [ME < ON *vīgt,* neut. of *vīgr,* able to fight.]

Wight, Isle of An island in the English Channel off S-central England.

Wig·ner (wĭg′nər), **Eugene Paul** 1902–95. Hungarian-born Amer. physicist who shared a 1963 Nobel Prize.

wig·wag (wĭg′wăg′) *v.* **-wagged, -wag·ging, -wags** —*intr.* **1.** To move back and forth; wag steadily or rhythmically. **2.** To signal by waving a flag, light, or an upraised arm esp. in accordance with a code. —*tr.* **1.** To move (something) back and forth steadily or rhythmically. **2.** To convey (a message or signal) by waving a flag, light, or an upraised arm. ❖ *n.* **1.** The act or practice of wigwagging. **2.** A message thus sent. [Dialectal *wig*, to move + WAG¹.] —**wig′wag′ger** *n.*

wig·wam (wĭg′wŏm′) *n.* A Native American dwelling commonly having an arched or conical framework overlaid with bark, hides, or mats. [Eastern Abenaki *wikəwɑm.*]

wik·i·up (wĭk′ē-ŭp′) *n.* Variant of wickiup.

Wil·ber·force (wĭl′bər-fôrs′, -fōrs′), **William** 1759–1833. British politician who as a member of Parliament (1780–1825) campaigned for the British abolition of slavery.

Wil·bur (wĭl′bər), **Richard Purdy** b. 1921. Amer. poet whose works include *Things of This World* (1956).

wil·co (wĭl′kō) *interj.* Used esp. in radio communications to indicate agreement or compliance. [< *wil(l) co(mply).*]

wild (wīld) *adj.* **wild·er, wild·est** **1.** Occurring, growing, or living in a natural state; not domesticated, cultivated, or tamed: *wild geese; edible wild plants.* **2.** Not inhabited or farmed. **3.** Uncivilized or barbarous; savage. **4a.** Lacking supervision or restraint. **b.** Disorderly; unruly. **c.** Characterized by a lack of moral restraint; dissolute or licentious. **5.** Lacking regular order or management; disarranged. **6.** Full of, marked by, or suggestive of strong, uncontrolled emotion. **7.** Extravagant; fantastic. **8.** Furiously disturbed or turbulent; stormy. **9.** Risky; imprudent. **10a.** Impatiently eager. **b.** *Informal* Highly enthusiastic. **11.** Based on little or no evidence or probability; unfounded. **12.** Deviating greatly from an intended course; erratic. **13.** *Games* Having an equivalence or value determined by the cardholder's choice. ❖ *adv.* In a wild manner. ❖ *n.* **1.** A natural or undomesticated state. **2.** An uninhabited or uncultivated region. ❖ *intr.v.* **wild·ed, wild·ing, wilds** *Slang* To go about in a group threatening, robbing, or attacking others. [ME *wilde* < OE.] —**wild′ly** *adv.* —**wild′ness** *n.*

wild bergamot *n.* See horsemint 1.

wild boar *n.* An Old World wild pig (*Sus scrofa*) with dark dense bristles that is the ancestor of the domestic hog.

wild card *n.* **1.** *Games* A playing card whose value can vary as determined by its holder. **2.** *Sports* An athlete or team selected to compete in a tournament or playoff from among those not meeting the regular requirements. **3.** *Computer Science* A symbol that stands for one or more unspecified characters. **4.** *Slang* An unpredictable or unforeseeable factor.

wild carrot *n.* See Queen Anne's lace.

wild·cat (wīld′kăt′) *n.* **1.** Any of various wild felines of small to medium size, esp. of the genus *Lynx,* including the bobcat and the caracal. **2.** Either of two small felines (*Felis silvestris* subsp. *silvestris* or subsp. *lybica*) of Europe, Asia, and Africa, often regarded as being the ancestor of the domestic cat. **3a.** A quick-tempered person. **b.** A fierce person. **4.** A wildcat oil or natural-gas well. **5.** A wildcat strike. ❖ *adj.* **1a.** Risky or unsound, esp. financially. **b.** Issued by a financially irresponsible bank. **c.** Operating or accomplished outside business procedural and ethical norms. **2.** Of or being an oil or natural-gas well drilled speculatively in a supposedly unproductive area. **3.** Undertaken by workers without approval of union officials. ❖ *v.* **-cat·ted, -cat·ting, -cats** —*tr.* To prospect for (oil, for example) as a wildcatter. —*intr.* **1.** To wildcat for oil or other minerals. **2.** To go out on a wildcat strike.

wild·cat·ter (wīld′kăt′ər) *n.* **1.** One who is engaged in speculative mining or well drilling in areas not known to be productive. **2.** A promoter of speculative or fraudulent business enterprises. **3.** A worker who participates in a wildcat strike.

Wilde (wīld), **Oscar** Orig. Fingal O'Flahertie Wills. 1854–1900. Irish-born writer whose works include *The Picture of Dorian Gray* (1891) and *The Importance of Being Earnest* (1895).

wil·de·beest (wĭl′də-bēst′, vĭl′-) *n., pl.* **-beests** or **wildebeest** See gnu. [Obsolete Afr. : MDu. *wild,* wild + MDu. *beeste,* beast (< OFr. *beste;* see BEAST).]

wil·der (wĭl′dər) *v.* **-dered, -der·ing, -ders** *Archaic* —*tr.* **1.** To lead astray; mislead. **2.** To bewilder; perplex. —*intr.* **1.** To lose one's way. **2.** To become bewildered. [Perh. ME **wildren,* blend of *wilden,* to be wild (< *wilde,* wild; see WILD) and *wanderen,* to wander; see WANDER.] —**wil′der·ment** *n.*

Wilder, Billy b. 1906. Austrian-born Amer. filmmaker whose works include *Some Like It Hot* (1959).

Wilder, Laura Ingalls 1867–1957. Amer. writer whose novels include *Little House on the Prairie* (1935).

Wilder, Thornton (Niven) 1897–1975. Amer. writer best known for the drama *Our Town* (1938).

wil·der·ness (wĭl′dər-nĭs) *n.* **1.** An unsettled, uncultivated region left in its natural condition, esp.: **a.** A large wild tract of land covered with dense vegetation or forests. **b.** An extensive area, such as a desert or ocean, that is barren or empty; a waste. **c.** A piece of land set aside to grow wild. **2.** Something characterized by bewildering vastness, perilousness, or unchecked profusion. [ME < OE **wilddēornes,* prob. < *wilddēor,* wild beast : *wilde,* wild + *dēor,* wild animal.]

Wilderness Road The principal route for westward migration in the US from c. 1790 to 1840, stretching from VA to the Ohio R.

wild-eyed (wīld′īd′) *adj.* **1.** Glaring in or as if in anger, terror, or madness. **2.** Extreme and passionate in belief or advocacy.

wild·fire (wīld′fīr′) *n.* **1.** A raging, rapidly spreading fire. **2.** Something that acts very quickly and intensely. **3.** Lightning occurring without audible thunder. **4.** A luminosity that appears over swamps or marshes at night; ignis fatuus. **5.** A highly flammable material once used in warfare. —**idiom: like wildfire** Rapidly and intensely.

wild·flow·er also **wild flow·er** (wīld′flou′ər) *n.* **1.** A flowering plant that grows in a natural uncultivated state. **2.** The flower of such a plant.

wild·fowl (wīld′foul′) *n., pl.* **wildfowl** or **-fowls** A wild game bird, such as a duck, goose, or quail.

wild geranium *n.* A North American woodland plant (*Geranium maculatum*) having rose-purple flowers.

wild ginger *n.* Any of various plants of the genus *Asarum,* esp. *A. canadense* of North America, having broad leaves, a solitary brownish flower, and an aromatic root.

wild-goose chase (wīld′goos′) *n.* A futile pursuit or search.

Elie Wiesel
photographed in 1986

ă	pat	oi	boy
ā	pay	ou	out
âr	care	ŏŏ	took
ä	father	ōō	boot
ĕ	pet	ŭ	cut
ē	be	ûr	urge
ĭ	pit	th	thin
ī	pie	*th*	this
îr	pier	hw	which
ŏ	pot	zh	vision
ō	toe	ə	about,
ô	paw		item

Stress marks:
′ (primary);
′ (secondary), as in
lexicon (lĕk′sĭ-kŏn′)

wild turkey
male wild turkey displaying

Ted Williams

Woodrow Wilson
detail from a 1921 portrait
by Edmund Charles Tarbell
(1862–1938)

wild indigo *n.* Any of several North American plants of the genus *Baptisia*, esp. *B. tinctoria*, having bright yellow flowers.

wild•ing (wīl′dĭng) *n.* **1.** A plant that grows wild or has escaped from cultivation, esp. a wild apple tree or its fruit. **2.** A wild animal. **3.** *Slang* The act or practice of going about in a group threatening, robbing, or attacking others. ❖ *adj.* **1.** Growing wild; not cultivated. **2.** Undomesticated. [< WILD.]

wild•life (wīld′līf′) *n.* Wild animals and vegetation, esp. animals living in a natural undomesticated state.

wild•ling (wīld′lĭng) *n.* A wild plant or animal, esp. a wild plant transplanted to a cultivated spot.

wild oat *n.* **1.** An annual Eurasian grass (*Avena fatua*) related to the cultivated oat. Often used in the plural. **2. wild oats** Misdeeds and indiscretions committed when young.

wild olive *n.* See **devilwood**.

wild pansy *n.* The heartsease.

wild pink *n.* A perennial herb (*Silene caroliniana*) of eastern North America having pink or white flowers.

wild pitch *n.* *Baseball* An erratic pitch that the catcher cannot be expected to catch and that enables a base runner to advance.

wild rice *n.* **1.** A tall aquatic annual grass (*Zizania aquatica*) of North America bearing edible grain. **2.** This grain.

wild rye *n.* Any of various grasses of the genus *Elymus* of the Northern Hemisphere.

wild turkey *n.* A wild variety of turkey, esp. the ancestor of the common domesticated North American turkey.

wild type *n.* The typical form of an organism, strain, gene, or characteristic as it occurs in nature, as distinguished from mutant forms that may result from selective breeding.

Wild West *n.* The western United States during the period of its settlement, esp. with reference to its lawlessness.

wild•wood (wīld′wŏŏd′) *n.* A forest or wooded area in its natural state.

wile (wīl) *n.* **1.** A stratagem or trick intended to deceive or ensnare. **2.** A disarming or seductive manner, device, or procedure. **3.** Trickery; cunning. ❖ *tr.v.* **wiled, wil•ing, wiles 1.** To influence or lead by means of wiles; entice. **2.** To pass (time) agreeably: *wile away an afternoon.* [ME *wil* < ONFr. < ON *vél*, trick, or of LGer. orig.]

wil•ful (wĭl′fəl) *adj.* Variant of **willful**.

Wil•helm (wĭl′hĕlm) See **William**.

Wil•hel•mi•na (wĭl′ə-mē′nə, vĭl′hĕl-) 1880–1962. Queen of the Netherlands (1890–1948) who sought refuge in England during World War II.

Wil•helms•ha•ven (vĭl′hĕlmz-hä′fən) A city of NW Germany on an inlet of the North Sea; a major naval base during World Wars I and II. Pop. 97,495.

Wilkes (wĭlks), **Charles** 1798–1877. Amer. naval officer who explored Antarctica and the W coast of North America.

Wilkes, John 1727–97. British political reformer noted for his support of the rights of American colonists.

Wilkes Land A coastal region of Antarctica S of Australia; mainly claimed by Australia.

Wil•kins (wĭl′kĭnz), **Sir George Hubert** 1888–1958. Australian explorer and aviator who was the first to explore the Arctic by air (1928).

Wilkins, Maurice Hugh Frederick b. 1916. British biophysicist who shared a 1962 Nobel Prize.

Wilkins, Roy 1901–81. Amer. civil rights leader who asserted that racial equality should be achieved through the democratic process.

will[1] (wĭl) *n.* **1a.** The mental faculty by which one deliberately chooses or decides upon a course of action. **b.** The act of exercising the will. **2a.** Diligent purposefulness; determination. **b.** Self-control; self-discipline. **3.** A desire, purpose, or determination, esp. of one in authority. **4.** Deliberate intention or wish: *against my will.* **5.** Free discretion; inclination or pleasure. **6.** Bearing or attitude toward others; disposition. **7a.** A legal declaration of how a person wishes his or her possessions to be disposed of after death. **b.** A legally executed document containing this declaration. ❖ *v.* **willed, will•ing, wills** —*tr.* **1.** To decide on; choose. **2.** To yearn for; desire. **3.** To decree, dictate, or order. **4.** To resolve with a forceful will; determine. **5.** To induce or try to induce by sheer force of will. **6.** To grant in a legal will; bequeath. —*intr.* **1.** To exercise the will. **2.** To make a choice; choose. —*idiom:* **at will** Just as or when one wishes. [ME < OE *willa.*]

will[2] (wĭl) *aux.v.* Past tense **would** (wŏŏd). **1.** Used to indicate simple futurity: *They will appear later.* **2.** Used to indicate likelihood or certainty: *You will regret this.* **3.** Used to indicate willingness: *Will you help me?* **4.** Used to indicate requirement or command: *You will report to me.* **5.** Used to indicate intention: *I will go if I feel like it.* **6.** Used to indicate customary or habitual action: *People will talk.* **7.** Used to indicate capacity or ability: *This metal will not crack.* **8.** Used to indicate probability or expectation: *That will be the dog.* ❖ *tr. & intr.v.* To wish; desire: *Sit here if you will.* See Usage Note at **shall**. [ME *willen*, to intend to < OE *willan.*]

Wil•lam•ette (wə-lăm′ĭt) A river of NW OR flowing c. 473 km (294 mi) to the Columbia R. near Portland.

Wil•lard (wĭl′ərd), **Emma Hart** 1787–1870. Amer. educator who was an early proponent of higher education for women.

Willard, Frances Elizabeth Caroline 1839–98. Amer. reformer who was president of the Woman's Christian Temperance Union (1879–98).

willed (wĭld) *adj.* **1.** Having a will of a specified kind. Often used in combination: *weak-willed.* **2.** Determined by or proceeding from the will; deliberate.

wil•lem•ite (wĭl′ə-mīt′) *n.* A colorless often fluorescent mineral, Zn_2SiO_4, a minor ore of zinc. [Du. *willemit*, after *Willem* I (1772–1843), king of the Netherlands.]

Wil•lem•stad (vĭl′əm-stät′) The cap. of the Netherlands Antilles, on the S coast of Curaçao; founded 1634. Pop. 43,547.

wil•let (wĭl′ĭt) *n.* A large grayish shore bird (*Catoptrophorus semipalmatus*) of North America having black wings with a broad white stripe. [Imit. of its call.]

will•ful also **wil•ful** (wĭl′fəl) *adj.* **1.** Said or done on purpose; deliberate. See Syns at **voluntary**. **2.** Obstinately bent on having one's own way. —**will′ful•ly** *adv.* —**will′ful•ness** *n.*

Wil•liam (wĭl′yəm) also **Wil•helm** (vĭl′hĕlm) 1882–1951. German crown prince who renounced the crown at the close of World War I.

William I[1] Known as "William the Conqueror." 1027?–87. King of England (1066–87) and duke of Normandy (1035–87) who led the Norman invasion of England (1066) and defeated Harold at the Battle of Hastings.

William I[2] Prince of Orange. Known as "William the Silent." 1533–84. Dutch stadholder (1579–84) who was made governor of Holland, Zeeland, and Utrecht (1559) by Phillip II of Spain and later led a revolt (1568–76) against Spanish rule.

William I[3] also **Wilhelm I** 1797–1888. King of Prussia (1861–88) and emperor of Germany (1871–88) whose reign was marked by the Franco-Prussian War (1870–71).

William II[1] Known as "William Rufus." 1056?–1100. King of England (1087–1100) who was the second son of William the Conqueror, on whose death he succeeded to the throne.

William II[2] also **Wilhelm II** 1859–1941. Emperor of Germany and king of Prussia (1888–1918).

William III Known as "William of Orange." 1650–1702. King of England, Scotland, and Ireland (1689–1702), Dutch stadholder (1672–1702), and prince of Orange. Married to Mary, daughter of James II, he invaded England (1688) and was proclaimed joint monarch with Mary (1689) after James fled.

William IV 1765–1837. King of Great Britain and Ireland (1830–37). Son of George III and brother of George IV, he was succeeded by his niece Victoria.

William of Malmes•bur•y (mämz′bĕr′ē, -bə-rē, -brē) 1090?–1143? English monk and historian whose works include *Chronicle of the Kings of England* (1120).

Wil•liams (wĭl′yəmz), **Elizabeth ("Betty")** b. 1943. Irish peace activist who shared the 1976 Nobel Peace Prize.

Williams, Eric 1911–81. Trinidadian politician and historian who led his country to independence from Britain and became its first prime minister (1962–81). His works include *Capitalism and Slavery* (1944).

Williams, (Hiram) Hank 1923–53. Amer. singer and songwriter whose influential hit songs include "Your Cheatin' Heart."

Williams, Roger 1603?–83. English cleric in America who founded Providence (1636) and obtained a royal charter for Rhode Island (1663).

Williams, Tennessee Orig. Thomas Lanier Williams. 1911–83. Amer. playwright whose works include *A Streetcar Named Desire* (1947).

Williams, Theodore Samuel ("Ted") b. 1918. Amer. baseball player who hit 521 home runs and had a .344 batting average as left fielder for the Boston Red Sox (1939–60).

Williams, William Carlos 1883–1963. Amer. poet whose verse is marked by a lucid spare style.

Wil•liams•burg (wĭl′yəmz-bûrg′) A city of SE VA NW of Newport News; settled c. 1632 and site of a large-scale restoration project begun in 1926. Pop. 11,998.

Wil•liam•son (wĭl′yəm-sən), **Mount** A peak, 4,382.9 m (14,370 ft), in the Sierra Nevada of E-central CA.

William the Conqueror See **William I**[1].

wil•lies (wĭl′ēz) *pl.n. Slang* Feelings of uneasiness. Often used with *the: They gave me the willies.* [Perh. < dialectal *will*, desolate, gone astray, bewildered < ON *villr* or *villi*-, wild, bewildering; akin to OE *wilde*, wild.]

will•ing (wĭl′ĭng) *adj.* **1.** Disposed or inclined; prepared. **2.** Acting or ready to act gladly; eagerly compliant. **3.** Done, given, accepted, or borne voluntarily or ungrudgingly. See Syns at **voluntary**. **4.** Of or relating to exercise of the will; volitional. —**will′ing•ly** *adv.* —**will′ing•ness** *n.*

wil•li•waw (wĭl′ē-wô′) *n.* **1.** A violent gust of cold wind blowing seaward from a mountainous coast, esp. in the Straits of Magellan. **2.** A sudden gust of wind; a squall. [?]

Will•kie (wĭl′kē), **Wendell Lewis** 1892–1944. Amer. politician who was the Republican nominee for President in 1940.

will-o'-the-wisp (wĭl′ə-thə-wĭsp′) *n.* **1.** See **ignis fatuus** 1. **2.** A delusive or misleading hope. [< the name *Will.*]

wil•low (wĭl′ō) *n.* **1a.** Any of various deciduous trees or shrubs of the genus *Salix*, having usu. narrow leaves and strong lightweight wood. **b.** The wood of any of these trees. **2.** Something, such as a cricket bat, that is made from willow. **3.** A textile machine con-

consisting of a spiked drum revolving inside a chamber fitted internally with spikes, used to open and clean unprocessed cotton or wool. ❖ *tr.v.* **-lowed, -low•ing, -lows** To open and clean (textile fibers) with a willow. [ME *wilowe* < OE *welig.* See **wel-** in App.]

willow herb *n.* See **fireweed** 1.

willow oak *n.* A deciduous timber tree (*Quercus phellos*) of southern and central North America having willowlike leaves.

wil•low•ware (wĭl′ō-wâr′) *n.* Household china with a blue-on-white design depicting a willow tree and often a river.

wil•low•y (wĭl′ō-ē) *adj.* **-i•er, -i•est 1.** Planted with or abounding in willows. **2.** Resembling a willow tree, esp.: **a.** Flexible; pliant. **b.** Tall, slender, and graceful.

will•pow•er or **will pow•er** (wĭl′pou′ər) *n.* The strength of will to carry out one's decisions, wishes, or plans.

wil•ly-nil•ly (wĭl′ē-nĭl′ē) *adv.* **1.** Whether desired or not. **2.** Without order or plan; haphazardly. ❖ *adj.* **1.** Being or occurring whether desired or not. **2.** Disordered; haphazard. [Alteration of *will ye* (or *he*), *nill ye* (or *he*), be you (or *he*) willing, be you (or he) unwilling.]

Wil•ming•ton (wĭl′mĭng-tən) **1.** A city of NE DE on the Delaware R. SW of Philadelphia PA; founded as Fort Christina by Swedish settlers in 1638. Pop. 72,664. **2.** A city of SE NC on the Cape Fear R. SSE of Raleigh; settled c. 1730. Pop. 75,838.

Wil•son (wĭl′sən), **August** b. 1945. Amer. playwright whose works include *Fences* (1985).

Wilson, Charles Thomson Rees 1869–1959. British physicist who shared a 1927 Nobel Prize.

Wilson, Edith Bolling 1872–1961. First Lady of the US (1915–21) as the second wife of President Woodrow Wilson.

Wilson, Edmund 1895–1972. Amer. literary critic whose works include *Axel's Castle* (1931) and *Patriotic Gore* (1962).

Wilson, Ellen Louise Axson 1860–1914. First Lady of the US (1913–14) as the first wife of President Woodrow Wilson.

Wilson, Harriet 1808–70? Amer. author whose work *Our Nig* (1859) was the first novel by an African American published in the US.

Wilson, James 1742–98. Amer. jurist who signed the Declaration of Independence and later served as an associate justice of the US Supreme Court (1789–98).

Wilson, (James) Harold. Baron Wilson of Rievaulx. 1916–95. British prime minister (1964–70 and 1974–76).

Wilson, Mount 1. A mountain, 1,741.6 m (5,710 ft), in the San Gabriel Mts. of SW CA NE of Pasadena; site of an observatory (est. 1904). **2.** A peak, 4,345 m (14,246 ft), in the San Juan Mts. of SW CO.

Wilson, (Thomas) Woodrow 1856–1924. The 28th President of the US (1913–21), who won the 1919 Nobel Peace Prize. —**Wil•so′ni•an** (-sō′nē-ən) *adj.*

Wilson cycle *n.* The cyclical opening and closing of ocean basins caused by movement of the earth's plates. [After John Tuzo *Wilson* (1908–93), Canadian geophysicist.]

Wil•son's disease (wĭl′sənz) *n.* A rare hereditary disease marked by an accumulation of copper deposits in organs such as the brain, liver, and kidneys. [After Samuel Alexander Kinnier *Wilson* (1878–1937), British neurologist.]

Wilson's phalarope *n.* A grayish American wading bird (*Phalaropus tricolor*) with white underparts and a needlelike bill. [After Alexander *Wilson* (1766–1813), Scottish-born American ornithologist.]

Wilson's snipe *n.* A common North American snipe (*Capella gallinago* subsp. *delicata*).

Wilson's thrush *n.* See **veery.**

Wilson's warbler *n.* A North American warbler (*Wilsonia pusilla*) with olive-green plumage, yellow underparts, and a black patch on top of the head.

wilt¹ (wĭlt) *v.* **wilt•ed, wilt•ing, wilts** —*intr.* **1.** To become limp or flaccid; droop. **2.** To feel or exhibit the effects of fatigue or exhaustion; weaken markedly. —*tr.* **1.** To cause to droop or lose freshness. **2.** To deprive of energy or vigor; fatigue or exhaust. ❖ *n.* **1.** The act of wilting or the state of being wilted. **2.** Any of various plant diseases characterized by slow or rapid collapse of terminal shoots, branches, or entire plants. [Poss. alteration of dialectal *welk* < ME *welken.*]

wilt² (wĭlt) *aux.v. Archaic* A second person singular present tense of **will²**.

Wil•ton (wĭl′tən) *n.* A carpet woven on a jacquard loom and having a velvety surface formed by the cut loops of a pile. [After *Wilton,* a municipal borough of south-central England.]

Wilt•shire (wĭlt′shîr, -shər) *n.* A white sheep of a breed originating in England, characterized by a long head with spiraling horns. [After *Wiltshire,* a county of S-central England.]

wi•ly (wī′lē) *adj.* **-li•er, -li•est** Full of wiles; cunning. —**wil′i•ly** *adv.* —**wil′i•ness** *n.*

wim•ble (wĭm′bəl) *n.* Any of numerous hand tools for boring holes. [ME < AN, *gimble* < MDu. *wimmel.*] —**wim′ble** *v.*

Wim•ble•don (wĭm′bəl-dən) A district of S Greater London, England; site of a major annual tennis tournament.

wimp (wĭmp) *Slang n.* A weak or ineffectual person. ❖ *intr.v.* **wimped, wimp•ing, wimps** To be timid or cowardly. Usually used with *out.* [Perh. < WHIMPER.] —**wimp′ish, wimp′y** *adj.*

WIMP (wĭmp) *n.* A subatomic particle that has a large mass and interacts with other matter primarily through gravitation. [*w(eakly) i(nteracting) m(assive) p(article).*]

wim•ple (wĭm′pəl) *n.* **1.** A cloth wound around the head, framing the face, and drawn into folds beneath the chin, worn by women in medieval times and as part of the habit of certain orders of nuns. **2a.** A fold or pleat in cloth. **b.** A ripple, as on the surface of water. **c.** A curve or bend. ❖ *v.* **-pled, -pling, -ples** —*tr.* **1.** To cover with or dress in a wimple. **2.** To cause to form folds, pleats, or ripples. —*intr.* **1.** *Archaic* To form or lie in folds. **2.** To ripple. [ME *wimpel* < OE.]

win (wĭn) *v.* **won** (wŭn), **win•ning, wins** —*intr.* **1.** To achieve victory or finish first in a competition. **2.** To achieve success in an effort or venture. —*tr.* **1.** To achieve victory or finish first in. **2.** To receive as a prize or reward for performance. **3a.** To achieve or attain by effort. **b.** To obtain or earn (a livelihood, for example). See Syns at **earn¹.** **4.** To make (one's way) with effort. **5.** To reach with difficulty. **6.** To take in battle; capture. **7.** To succeed in gaining the favor or support of; prevail on. **8a.** To gain the affection or loyalty of. **b.** To appeal successfully to (someone's sympathy, for example). **c.** To persuade (another) to marry one. **9a.** To discover and open (a vein or deposit) in mining. **b.** To extract from a mine or from mined ore. ❖ *n.* **1a.** A victory, esp. in a competition. **b.** First place in a competition. **2.** An amount won or earned. —*phrasal verbs:* **win out** To succeed or prevail. **win through** To overcome difficulties and attain a desired goal or end. —*idiom:* **win the day** To be successful. [ME *winnen* < OE *winnan,* to fight, strive. See **wen-** in App.] —**win′less** *adj.*

wince (wĭns) *intr.v.* **winced, winc•ing, winc•es** To shrink or start involuntarily, as in pain or distress; flinch. ❖ *n.* A shrinking or startled movement or gesture. [ME *wincen,* to kick < ONFr. *wencier,* var. of O French *guencir,* of Gmc. orig.] —**winc′er** *n.*

winch (wĭnch) *n.* **1.** A stationary motor-driven or hand-powered machine used for hoisting or hauling, having a drum around which is wound a rope or chain attached to the load being moved. **2.** The crank used to give motion to a grindstone or similar device. ❖ *tr.v.* **winched, winch•ing, winch•es** To move with or as if with a winch. [ME *winche,* pulley < OE *wince,* reel, roller.] —**winch′er** *n.*

Win•ches•ter (wĭn′chĕs′tər, -chĭ-stər) A trademark used for a shoulder firearm.

Winck•el•mann (vĭng′kəl-män′), **Johann Joachim** 1717–68. German archaeologist and art historian who was the first to study ancient art as history.

wind¹ (wĭnd) *n.* **1a.** Moving air, esp. a natural and perceptible movement of air parallel to or along the ground. **b.** A movement of air generated artificially, as by bellows or a fan. **2a.** The direction from which a movement of air comes. **b.** A movement of air coming from one of the four cardinal points of the compass. **3.** Moving air carrying sound, an odor, or a scent. **4a.** Breath, esp. normal or adequate breathing; respiration. **b.** Gas produced in the stomach or intestines during digestion; flatulence. **5.** *Music* **a.** The brass and woodwinds sections of a band or orchestra. **b.** Wind instruments or their players considered as a group. **c.** Woodwinds. In all three senses, often used in the plural. **6a.** Something that disrupts or destroys. **b.** A tendency; a trend. **7.** Information, esp. of something concealed; intimation. **8a.** Speech or writing empty of meaning; verbiage. **b.** Vain self-importance; pomposity. ❖ *tr.v.* **wind•ed, wind•ing, winds 1.** To expose to free movement of air; ventilate or dry. **2a.** To detect the smell of; catch a scent of. **b.** To pursue by following a scent. **3.** To cause to be out of or short of breath. **4.** To afford a recovery of breath. —*idioms:* **before the wind** *Nautical* In the same direction as the wind. **close to the wind** *Nautical* As close as possible to the direction from which the wind is blowing. **in the wind** Likely to occur; in the offing. **near the wind 1.** *Nautical* Close to the wind. **2.** Close to danger. **off the wind** *Nautical* In a direction away from the wind. **on** (or **into** or **down**) **the wind** *Nautical* In the same or nearly the same direction as the wind. **under the wind 1.** *Nautical* To the leeward. **2.** In a location protected from the wind. **up the wind** *Nautical* In a direction opposite or nearly opposite the wind. [ME < OE. See **wē-** in App.]

wind² (wīnd) *v.* **wound** (wound), **wind•ing, winds** —*tr.* **1.** To wrap (something) around a center or another object once or repeatedly. **2.** To wrap or encircle (an object) in a series of coils; entwine. **3a.** To go along (a curving or twisting course). **b.** To proceed on (one's way) with a curving or twisting course. **4.** To introduce in a disguised or devious manner; insinuate. **5.** To turn (a crank, for example) in a series of circular motions. **6.** To coil the spring of (a mechanism) by turning a stem or cord, for example. **b.** To coil (thread, for example), as onto a spool or into a ball. **c.** To remove or unwind (thread, for example), as from a spool. **7.** To lift or haul by means of a windlass or winch. —*intr.* **1.** To move in or have a curving or twisting course. **2a.** To move in or have a spiral or circular course. **b.** To be coiled or spiraled. **3.** To be twisted or whorled into curved forms. **4.** To proceed misleadingly or insidiously in discourse or conduct. **5.** To become wound. ❖ *n.* **1.** The act of winding. **2.** A single turn, twist, or curve. —*phrasal verbs:* **wind down** *Informal* **1.** To diminish gradually in energy, intensity, or scope. **2.** To relax; unwind. **wind up 1.** To come or bring to a finish; end. **2.** To put in order;

wimple
detail from *Portrait of a Woman* by Rogier van der Weyden

winch

settle. **3.** *Informal* To arrive in a place or situation after or because of a course of action. **4.** *Baseball* To swing back the arm and raise the foot in preparation for pitching the ball. [ME *winden* < OE *windan.*]

wind³ (wīnd, wĭnd) *tr.v.* **wind·ed** (wīn′dĭd, wĭn′-) or **wound** (wound), **wind·ing, winds** *Music* **1.** To blow (a wind instrument). **2.** To sound by blowing. [< WIND¹.] —**wind′er** *n.*

wind·age (wĭn′dĭj) *n.* **1a.** The effect of wind on the course of a projectile. **b.** The point or degree at which the wind gauge or sight of a rifle or gun must be set to compensate for the effect of the wind. **c.** The difference in a given firearm between the diameter of the projectile fired and the diameter of the bore of the firearm. **2.** The disturbance of air caused by the passage of a fast-moving object. **3.** *Nautical* The part of the surface of a ship exposed to the wind.

Win·daus (vĭn′dous′), **Adolf** 1876–1959. German chemist who won a 1928 Nobel Prize.

wind·bag (wĭnd′băg′) *n.* **1.** The flexible air-filled chamber of a bagpipe or similar instrument. **2.** *Slang* A talkative person who communicates nothing of substance or interest.

wind-bell (wĭnd′bĕl′) *n.* **1.** A light bell that can be sounded by the wind. **2. wind-bells** See **wind chimes.**

wind-blast (wĭnd′blăst′) *n.* **1.** An exceedingly strong gust of wind. **2.** The damaging effect of air friction on a pilot ejected from a high-speed aircraft.

wind·blown (wĭnd′blōn′) *adj.* **1.** Blown or dispersed by the wind: *windblown pollen.* **2.** Growing or shaped in a manner governed by the prevailing winds: *windblown pines.* **3.** Cut short and curled or combed toward the front of the head.

wind·break (wĭnd′brāk′) *n.* A hedge, fence, or row of trees serving to lessen or break the force of the wind.

Wind·break·er (wĭnd′brā′kər) A trademark used for a warm outer jacket having close-fitting cuffs and waistband.

wind-bro·ken (wĭnd′brō′kən) *adj.* Suffering from the heaves or other impairment of breathing. Used of a horse.

wind·burn (wĭnd′bûrn′) *n.* An irritation or chafing of the skin caused by long exposure to the wind. —**wind′burned′** *adj.*

wind-chill factor (wĭnd′chĭl′) *n.* The temperature of windless air that would have the same effect on exposed human skin as a given combination of wind speed and air temperature.

wind chimes (wĭnd) *pl.n.* An arrangement of small suspended pieces, as of glass, metal, or ceramic, hung loosely together so that they tinkle pleasingly when blown by the wind.

wind cone (wĭnd) *n.* See **windsock.**

wind·ed (wĭn′dĭd) *adj.* **1.** Having breath or respiratory power of a specified kind. Often used in combination: *short-winded.* **2.** Out of breath: *a winded runner.*

wind·er¹ (wīn′dər) *n.* **1.** One that winds, esp. a textile worker or machine that winds cloth or materials. **2.** An object, such as a spool or barrel, around which material is wound. **3.** A device, such as a key, for winding up a spring-driven mechanism. **4.** One of the steps of a winding staircase.

win·der² (wĭn′dər) *n. Upper Southern US* Variant of **window.** See Regional Note at **holler².**

Win·der·mere (wĭn′dər-mîr′), **Lake** A lake of NW England.

wind·fall (wĭnd′fôl′) *n.* **1.** A sudden unexpected piece of good fortune or personal gain. **2.** Something, such as a ripened fruit, that has been blown down by the wind.

wind farm (wĭnd) *n.* A power plant that uses windmills or wind turbines to generate electricity.

wind·flaw (wĭnd′flô′) *n.* A sudden gust or blast of wind.

wind·flow·er (wĭnd′flou′ər) *n.* See **anemone** 1.

wind gap (wĭnd) *n.* A shallow notch in the crest of a mountain ridge.

wind harp (wĭnd) *n.* See **Aeolian harp.**

Wind·hoek (vĭnt′hŏŏk′) The cap. of Namibia, in the central part of the country. Pop. 88,700.

wind·hov·er (wĭnd′hŭv′ər, -hŏv′-) *n. Chiefly British* A kestrel.

wind·ing (wīn′dĭng) *n.* **1a.** Something wound about a center or an object. **b.** The way in which something is wound. **c.** One complete turn of something wound. **2.** A curve or bend, as of a road. ❖ *adj.* **1.** Twisting or turning; sinuous. **2.** Spiral. —**wind′ing·ly** *adv.*

wind·ing-sheet (wīn′dĭng-shēt′) *n.* A sheet for wrapping a corpse; a shroud.

wind instrument (wĭnd) *n.* **1.** A musical instrument, such as a clarinet, trumpet, or harmonica, in which sound is produced by the movement of an enclosed column of air, esp. the breath, and excluding keyboard instruments such as the organ or accordion. Woodwind and brass instruments are both types of wind instruments. **2.** A woodwind instrument, as opposed to a brass instrument.

wind·jam·mer (wĭnd′jăm′ər) *n.* A large sailing ship.

wind·lass (wĭnd′ləs) *n.* Any of numerous hauling or lifting machines consisting essentially of a horizontal cylinder turned by a crank or a motor so that a line attached to the load is wound around the cylinder. ❖ *tr.v.* **-lassed, -lass·ing, -lass·es** To raise with a windlass. [ME *wyndlas,* alteration of *windas* < ON *vindāss* : *vinda,* to wind + *āss,* pole.]

win·dle·straw (wĭn′dl-strô′) *n. Chiefly British* A thin, dried stalk of grass. [OE *windelstrēaw* : *windel,* basket (< *windan,* to

windmill
La Mancha, Spain

Windsor chair
yew-wood Windsor armchair

wind) + *strēaw,* straw; see STRAW.]

wind·mill (wĭnd′mĭl′) *n.* **1.** A machine that runs on the energy generated by a wheel of adjustable blades or slats rotated by the wind. **2.** Something, such as a toy pinwheel, similar to a windmill in appearance or operation. ❖ *intr. & tr.v.* **-milled, -mill·ing, -mills** To move or cause to move like the wheel of a windmill. —*idiom:* **tilt at windmills** To confront and engage in conflict with an imagined opponent or threat.

Win·dom Peak (wĭn′dəm) A mountain, 4,295 m (14,082 ft), in the San Juan Mts. of SW CO.

win·dow (wĭn′dō) *n.* **1a.** An opening constructed in a wall or roof that admits light or air to an enclosure and is often framed and spanned with glass mounted to permit opening and closing. **b.** A framework enclosing a pane of glass for such an opening; a sash. **c.** A pane of glass or similar material in such a framework. **2a.** An opening that resembles a window in function or appearance. **b.** The transparent panel on a window envelope. **3.** The area or space behind a window, esp. at the front of a shop. **4.** A means of access or observation. **5.** An interval of time during which an activity can or must take place. **6.** Strips of foil dropped from an aircraft to confuse enemy radar; chaff. **7.** A range of electromagnetic frequencies that pass unobstructed through a planetary atmosphere. **8.** *Computer Science* A rectangular area on a screen in which a document, database, or application can be viewed independently of the other such areas. **9.** *Aerospace* A launch window. [ME < ON *vindauga* : *vindr,* air, wind; see **wē-** in App. + *auga,* eye; see **okʷ-** in App.]

window box *n.* **1.** A usu. long narrow box for growing plants, placed on a windowsill or ledge. **2.** One of the vertical grooves on the inner sides of a window frame for the weights that counterbalance the sash.

win·dow-dress·ing also **win·dow dress·ing** (wĭn′dō-drĕs′ĭng) *n.* **1a.** Decorative exhibition of retail merchandise in store windows. **b.** Goods and trimmings used in such displays. **2.** A means of improving appearances or creating a falsely favorable impression. —**win′dow-dress′er** *n.*

win·dow·pane (wĭn′dō-pān′) *n.* **1.** A piece of glass filling a window or a section of a window. **2.** A pattern of thin lines forming large squares on a background of a different color. **3.** *Slang* LSD.

Win·dows (wĭn′dōz) A trademark for any of a series of GUIs or GUI-based computer operating systems.

window shade *n.* An opaque fabric mounted to cover or expose a window.

win·dow-shop (wĭn′dō-shŏp′) *intr.v.* **-shopped, -shop·ping, -shops** To look at merchandise in store windows or showcases without making purchases. —**win′dow-shop′per** *n.*

win·dow·sill (wĭn′dō-sĭl′) *n.* The horizontal member at the base of a window opening.

wind·pipe (wĭnd′pīp′) *n.* See **trachea** 1.

Wind River Range (wĭnd) A section of the Rocky Mts. in W-central WY rising to 4,210.2 m (13,804 ft).

Wind River Shoshone (wĭnd) *n.* See **Shoshone** 1c.

wind rose (wĭnd) *n.* A meteorological diagram depicting the distribution of wind direction and speed at a location over a period of time. [Transl. of Ger. *Windrose,* compass card : *Wind,* wind, air + *Rose,* rose.]

wind·row (wĭnd′rō′) *n.* **1.** A row, as of snow, heaped up by the wind. **2.** A long row of cut hay or grain left to dry in a field before bundling. ❖ *tr.v.* **-rowed, -row·ing, -rows** To shape or arrange into a windrow. —**wind′row′er** *n.*

wind·screen (wĭnd′skrēn′) *n.* **1.** A screen for protection against the wind. **2.** *Chiefly British* The windshield of a motor vehicle.

wind shake (wĭnd) *n.* A crack or separation between growth rings in timber, attributed to the straining of tree trunks in high winds.

wind shear (wĭnd) *n.* A change in wind direction and speed between slightly different altitudes, esp. a sudden downdraft.

wind·shield (wĭnd′shēld′) *n.* **1.** A framed pane of usu. curved glass or other transparent shielding located in front of the occupants of a vehicle to protect them from the wind. **2.** A shield placed to protect an object from the wind.

wind·sock (wĭnd′sŏk′) *n.* A tapered open-ended sleeve pivotally attached to a standard to indicate wind direction.

Wind·sor¹ (wĭn′zər) Ruling house of Great Britain (since 1917), including George V, who adopted the name.

Wind·sor² (wĭn′zər) **1.** A city of SE Ontario, Canada, on the Detroit R. opposite Detroit MI; settled by the French after 1701. Pop. 197,694. **2.** A municipal borough of S-central England on the Thames R. SW of London; site of Windsor Castle, a royal residence since the time of William the Conqueror. Pop. 28,700.

Windsor, Duke of. See **Edward VIII.**

Windsor, Wallis Warfield. Duchess of Windsor. 1896–1986. Amer. divorcée who married the Duke of Windsor in 1937.

Windsor chair *n.* A wooden chair having a high spoked back, outward-slanting legs connected by crossbars, and a saddle seat. [After WINDSOR², England.]

Windsor knot *n.* A wide triangular slipknot used to tie a four-in-hand necktie. [Perh. after the Duke of WINDSOR.]

Windsor tie *n.* A wide silk necktie tied in a loose bow.

wind sprint (wĭnd) *n.* One of a series of sprints that are run to

develop breath and physical endurance.

wind·storm (wĭnd′stôrm′) *n.* A storm with high winds or violent gusts but little or no rain.

wind·suck·ing (wĭnd′sŭk′ĭng) *n.* The injurious habit of horses of drawing in and swallowing air. —**wind′suck′er** *n.*

wind·surf (wĭnd′sûrf′) *intr.v.* **-surfed, -surf·ing, -surfs** To engage in windsurfing.

Wind·surf·er (wĭnd′sûr′fər) A trademark used for a brand of sailboard.

wind·surf·ing (wĭnd′sûr′fĭng) *n.* The sport of sailing while standing on a sailboard.

wind·swept (wĭnd′swĕpt′) *adj.* Exposed to or swept by winds: *windswept moors.*

wind tee (wĭnd) *n.* A large weathervane with a horizontal T-shaped wind indicator, commonly found at airfields.

wind tunnel (wĭnd) *n.* A chamber through which air is forced at controlled velocities in order to study the effects of aerodynamic flow around airfoils, scale models, or other objects.

wind-up or **wind·up** (wĭnd′ŭp′) *n.* **1a.** The act of bringing something to an end. **b.** A concluding part; a conclusion. **2.** *Baseball* The movements of a pitcher, including the swinging back of the arm and the raising of the forward foot, preparatory to pitching the ball. ❖ *adj.* Operated by a manually wound spring.

wind·ward (wĭnd′wərd) *adj.* **1.** Of or moving toward the quarter from which the wind blows. **2.** Of or on the side exposed to the wind or to prevailing winds. ❖ *adv.* In a direction from which the wind blows; against the wind. ❖ *n.* The direction from which the wind blows. —**idiom: to windward** Into or to an advantageous posture or position.

Windward Islands An island group of the SE West Indies, including the S group of the Lesser Antilles from Martinique S to Grenada.

Windward Passage A channel between E Cuba and NW Haiti connecting the Atlantic Ocean with the Caribbean Sea.

wind·y (wĭn′dē) *adj.* **-i·er, -i·est 1.** Characterized by or abounding in wind. **2.** Open to the wind; unsheltered. **3.** Resembling the wind in speed, force, or variability. **4a.** Lacking substance; empty. **b.** Given to or characterized by wearisome verbosity. **5.** Flatulent. —**wind′i·ly** *adv.* —**wind′i·ness** *n.*

wine (wīn) *n.* **1a.** A beverage made of the fermented juice of any of various kinds of grapes, usu. containing from 10 to 15 percent alcohol by volume. **b.** A beverage made of the fermented juice of any of various other fruits or plants. **2.** Something that intoxicates or exhilarates. **3.** The color of red wine. ❖ *v.* **wined, win·ing, wines** —*tr.* To provide or entertain with wine. —*intr.* To drink wine. [ME < OE *wīn* < Lat. *vīnum*.]

wine·bib·bing (wīn′bĭb′ĭng) *adj.* Given to much drinking of wine. ❖ *n.* Habitual drinking of wine. —**wine′bib′ber** *n.*

wine cellar *n.* **1.** A place for storing wine. **2.** A stock of wines.

wine cooler *n.* **1.** A container, such as an ice-filled bucket or chest, for cooling wine. **2.** A bottled mixture of wine, fruit juice, and sometimes soda water.

wine·glass (wīn′glăs′) *n.* A glass, usu. with a stem, from which wine is drunk.

wine·grow·er (wīn′grō′ər) *n.* One that owns a vineyard and produces wine.

wine·mak·ing (wīn′mā′kĭng) *n.* The art and science of making wine. —**wine′mak′er** *n.* —**wine′mak′ing** *adj.*

wine palm *n.* Any of various palm trees having sap or juice from which wine is made.

wine·press (wīn′prĕs′) *n.* **1.** A vat in which the juice is pressed from grapes. **2.** A machine or device that presses the juice from grapes.

win·er·y (wī′nə-rē) *n., pl.* **-ies** An establishment at which wine is made.

Wine·sap (wīn′săp′) *n.* A variety of apple having dark red skin.

wine·skin (wīn′skĭn′) *n.* A bag, as of goatskin, used for holding and dispensing wine.

wine taster *n.* **1.** One who evaluates the quality of wine by tasting it, esp. on a professional basis. **2.** A small bowl used to hold wine for tasting.

wine·tast·ing (wīn′tā′stĭng) *n.* A gathering of people to taste and compare a number of wines.

win·ey (wī′nē) *adj.* Variant of **winy.**

Win·frey (wĭn′frē), **Oprah** b. 1954. Amer. host and producer of television's *The Oprah Winfrey Show* (1986–present).

wing (wĭng) *n.* **1.** One of a pair of movable organs for flying, as the feather-covered modified forelimb of a bird. **2.** Any of usu. four membranous organs for flying that extend from the thorax of an insect. **3.** A winglike organ or structure used for flying, as the folds of skin of a flying squirrel. **4.** *Botany* **a.** A thin or membranous extension, as of the fruit of the elm. **b.** One of the lateral petals of the flower of a pea or of most plants in the pea family. **5.** *Informal* A person's arm. **6.** An airfoil whose principal function is providing lift, esp. either of two such airfoils symmetrically positioned on each side of the fuselage of an aircraft. **7.** Something that resembles a wing in appearance, function, or position relative to a main body. **8a.** The act or manner of flying. **b.** A means of flight or rapid movement. **9a.** Something, such as a weathervane, that is moved by or moves against the air. **b.** The sail of a ship. **10.** *Chiefly British* The fender of a motor vehicle. **11.** A

folding section, as of a double door. **12.** Either of the two side projections on the back of a wing chair. **13a.** A flat of theatrical scenery projecting onto the stage from the side. **b. wings** The unseen backstage area on either side of the stage of a proscenium theater. **14.** A structure attached to and connected internally with the side of a main building. **15.** A section of a large building devoted to a specific purpose. **16.** A group affiliated with or subordinate to an older or larger organization. **17a.** Either of two groups with opposing views within a larger group; a faction. **b.** A section of a party, legislature, or community holding distinct, esp. dissenting, political views. **18a.** Either the left or right flank of an army or a naval fleet. **b.** An air force unit larger than a group but smaller than a division. **19.** *Sports* Either of two players in forward positions near the sides of the playing area, esp. in hockey. **20. wings** An outspread pair of stylized bird's wings worn as insignia by qualified pilots or air crew members. ❖ *v.* **winged, wing·ing, wings** —*intr.* To move on or as if on wings; fly. —*tr.* **1a.** To furnish with wings. **b.** To cause or enable to fly or speed swiftly along. **2.** To feather (an arrow). **3a.** To pass over or through with or as if with wings. **b.** To carry or transport by or as if by flying. **c.** To effect by flying. **4.** To throw or dispatch (a ball, for example). **5a.** To wound the wing of (a game bird, for example). **b.** To wound superficially. **6.** To furnish with side or subordinate extensions, as a building. —**idioms: in the wings 1.** In the stage wings, unseen by the audience. **2.** Close by in the background; available at short notice. **on the wing** In flight; flying. **take wing** To fly off; soar away. **under (one's) wing** Under one's protection; in one's care. **wing it** *Informal* To improvise. [ME *wenge, wenge*, of Scand. orig. See **wē-** in App.]

wing and wing *adv. Nautical* With sails extended on both sides.

wing·back (wĭng′băk′) *n. Football* **1.** A back positioned on offense behind or outside of an end. **2.** This position.

wing·bow (wĭng′bō′) *n.* A distinctive mark of color on the bend of a bird's wing, esp. in domestic fowl.

wing case *n.* See **elytron.**

wing chair also **wing-chair** (wĭng′châr′) *n.* An armchair with a high back from which large enclosing side pieces project.

wing·ding (wĭng′dĭng′) *n. Informal* A lavish or lively party or celebration. [?]

winged (wĭngd, wĭng′ĭd) *adj.* **1a.** Having wings or winglike appendages. **b.** Having wings of a specified kind. Often used in combination: *large-winged.* **2.** Moving on or as if on wings; flying. **3.** Soaring as if with wings; elevated or sublime. **4.** Swift; fleet.

wing·er (wĭng′gər) *n. Sports* A player who plays wing, as in hockey.

wing-foot·ed (wĭng′fŏot′ĭd) *adj.* **1.** Having winged feet. **2.** Swift; fleet.

wing·less (wĭng′lĭs) *adj.* Having no wings or only rudimentary wings. —**wing′less·ness** *n.*

wing·let (wĭng′lĭt) *n.* **1.** A small or rudimentary wing. **2.** A short, almost vertical stabilizing fin projecting from the tip of an aircraft wing.

wing loading *n.* The gross weight of an airplane divided by the wing area. Used in stress analysis.

wing·man (wĭng′mən) *n.* A pilot whose plane is positioned behind and outside the leader in a formation of flying aircraft.

wing nut *n.* A nut with winglike projections for thumb and forefinger leverage in turning.

wing nut

wing·o·ver (wĭng′ō′vər) *n.* A flight maneuver or stunt in which an airplane enters a climbing turn until almost stalled and is allowed to fall while the turn is continued until normal flight is attained in a direction opposite the original heading.

wing·span (wĭng′spăn′) *n.* **1.** The linear distance between the extremities of an airfoil. **2.** Wingspread.

wing·spread (wĭng′sprĕd′) *n.* The distance between the tips of the wings, as of a bird or insect, when fully extended.

wing·tip also **wing tip** (wĭng′tĭp′) *n.* **1a.** An often perforated shoe part that covers the toe and extends backward along the sides of the shoe from a point at the center. **b.** A style of shoe having such a tip. **2.** The tip of the wing of a bird or other animal. **3.** The extreme edge of a wing, as of an aircraft.

wink (wĭngk) *v.* **winked, wink·ing, winks** —*intr.* **1.** To close and open the eyelid of one eye deliberately, as to convey a message, signal, or suggestion. **2.** To close and open the eyelids of both eyes; blink. **3.** To shine fitfully; twinkle: *Harbor lights winked in the distance.* —*tr.* **1.** To close and open (an eye or the eyes) rapidly. **2.** To signal or express by winking. ❖ *n.* **1a.** The act of winking. **b.** A signal or hint conveyed by winking. **2.** The very brief time required for a wink; an instant. **3.** A quick closing and opening of the eyelids; a blink. **4.** A gleam or twinkle. **5.** *Informal* A brief period of sleep. —**phrasal verb: wink at** To pretend not to see. [ME *winken*, to close one's eyes < OE *wincian*.]

wink·er (wĭng′kər) *n.* One that winks, as: **a.** A blinder for a horse. **b.** *Informal* An eye. **c.** *Informal* An eyelash.

win·kle¹ (wĭng′kəl) *n. Zoology* A periwinkle.

win·kle² (wĭng′kəl) *tr.v.* **-kled, -kling, -kles** *Chiefly British* To pry, extract, or force from a place or position. Often used with *out.* [< WINKLE¹ (< extracting periwinkles).]

win·na·ble (wĭn′ə-bəl) *adj.* Possible to win or achieve. —**win′na·bil′i·ty** *n.*

wingtip
pair of wingtips

Oprah Winfrey

ă	pat	oi	boy
ā	pay	ou	out
âr	care	ŏŏ	took
ä	father	ōō	boot
ĕ	pet	ŭ	cut
ē	be	ûr	urge
ĭ	pit	th	thin
ī	pie	*th*	this
îr	pier	hw	which
ŏ	pot	zh	vision
ō	toe	ə	about,
ô	paw		item

Stress marks:
′ (primary);
′ (secondary); as in
lexicon (lĕk′sĭ-kŏn′)

Win•ne•ba•go (wĭn'ə-bā'gō) *n., pl.* **Winnebago** or **-gos** or **-goes 1.** A member of a Native American people formerly inhabiting the Green Bay area of Wisconsin, with present-day populations in Wisconsin and Nebraska. **2.** Their Siouan language. [Fox *wiinepyeekooha*, those of the dirty water.]

Winnebago, Lake A lake of E WI traversed by the Fox R.

win•ner (wĭn'ər) *n.* One that wins, esp. a victor in sports or a notably successful person.

win•ner's circle (wĭn'ərz) *n., pl.* **winners' circles** An enclosed area at a racetrack where the winning horse and jockey are brought for awards and publicity.

win•ning (wĭn'ĭng) *adj.* **1a.** Of or relating to the act of winning. **b.** Successful; victorious. **2.** Attractive; charming. ❖ *n.* **1.** The act of one that wins; victory. **2.** Something won, esp. money. Often used in the plural. **3.** A section of a mine that has been recently prepared or opened for working. —**win'ning•ly** *adv.* —**win'ning•ness** *n.*

Win•ni•peg (wĭn'ə-pĕg') The cap. of Manitoba, Canada, in the SE part at the confluence of the Red and Assiniboine rivers. Pop. 618,477.

Winnipeg, Lake A lake of S-central Manitoba, Canada; a remnant of the glacial Lake Agassiz.

Win•ni•pe•go•sis (wĭn'ə-pĭ-gō'sĭs), **Lake** A lake of SW Manitoba, Canada, W of Lake Winnipeg.

Winnipeg River A river of SW Ontario and SE Manitoba, Canada, flowing c. 322 km (200 mi) to Lake Winnipeg.

Win•ni•pe•sau•kee (wĭn'ə-pĭ-sô'kē), **Lake** A lake of E-central NH.

win•now (wĭn'ō) *v.* **-nowed, -now•ing, -nows** —*tr.* **1a.** To separate the chaff from (grain) by means of a current of air. **b.** To rid of undesirable parts. **2.** To blow (chaff) off or away. **3.** To blow away; scatter. **4.** To blow on; fan: *A breeze winnowed the grass.* **5.** To examine closely in order to separate the good from the bad; sift. **6a.** To separate or get rid of (an undesirable part); eliminate: *winnowing out errors.* **b.** To sort or select (a desirable part); extract. —*intr.* **1.** To separate grain from chaff. **2.** To separate the good from the bad. ❖ *n.* **1.** A device for winnowing grain. **2.** An act of winnowing. [ME *winnewen*, alteration of *windwen* < OE *windwian* < *wind*, wind. See WIND¹.] —**win'now•er** *n.*

win•o (wī'nō) *n., pl.* **-os** *Slang* An indigent wine-drinking alcoholic.

Win•slow (wĭnz'lō), **Edward** 1595–1655. English colonial administrator who served as governor of Plymouth Colony (1633, 1636, and 1644).

win•some (wĭn'səm) *adj.* Charming, often in a childlike or naive way. [ME *winsum* < OE *wynsum* : < *wynn*, joy; see **wen-** in App. + *-sum*, characterized by; see —SOME¹.] —**win'some•ly** *adv.*

Win•ston-Sa•lem (wĭn'stən-sā'ləm) A city of N-central NC NNE of Charlotte. Salem was founded by Moravians in 1766, and Winston was est. in 1849; the cities were consolidated in 1913. Pop. 185,776.

win•ter (wĭn'tər) *n.* **1.** The usu. coldest season of the year, occurring between autumn and spring and comprising December, January, and February in the Northern Hemisphere or, as calculated astronomically, extending from the winter solstice to the vernal equinox. **2.** A year as expressed through the recurrence of the winter season. **3.** A period of time characterized by coldness, misery, barrenness, or death. ❖ *adj.* **1.** Of, relating to, occurring in, or appropriate to the season of winter. **2.** Grown during the season of winter. ❖ *v.* **-tered, -ter•ing, -ters** —*intr.* **1.** To spend the winter. **2.** To feed in winter. Used with *on: deer wintering on cedar bark.* —*tr.* To lodge, keep, or care for during the winter. [ME < OE. See **wed-** in App.] —**win'ter•ish** *adj.*

winter aconite *n.* Any of various Eurasian herbs of the genus *Eranthis*, esp. *E. hyemalis*, having palmately dissected leaves and a yellow flower that blooms in winter or early spring.

win•ter•ber•ry (wĭn'tər-bĕr'ē) *n.* **1.** Any of several North American shrubs of the genus *Ilex*, having showy red berries. See **black alder** 1.

win•ter-feed (wĭn'tər-fēd') *tr.v.* **-fed** (-fĕd'), **-feed•ing, -feeds** To feed (livestock) when grazing is not possible.

winter flounder *n.* A dark rusty-brown flounder (*Pseudopleuronectes americanus*) of the North American Atlantic coast, prized esp. in winter as a food fish.

win•ter•green (wĭn'tər-grēn') *n.* **1a.** A low-growing creeping evergreen plant (*Gaultheria procumbens*) of North America having solitary nodding white flowers, aromatic leaves, and spicy edible scarlet berries. **b.** An oil or flavoring obtained from this plant. **2.** Any of several similar or related plants, such as the pipsissewa. [Transl. of Du. *wintergroen*.]

win•ter•ize (wĭn'tə-rīz') *tr.v.* **-ized, -iz•ing, -iz•es** To prepare or equip (an automobile or house, for example) for winter weather. —**win'ter•i•za'tion** (-tĕr-ĭ-zā'shən) *n.*

win•ter•kill (wĭn'tər-kĭl') *v.* **-killed, -kill•ing, -kills** —*tr.* To kill (plants, for example) by exposing to extremely cold winter weather. —*intr.* To die from exposure to cold winter weather. Used esp. of plants. ❖ *n.* Death, as of plants, resulting from exposure to winter weather.

winter melon *n.* See **honeydew melon**. [Transl. of Chin. (Mandarin) *dōngguā : dōng*, winter + *guā*, melon.]

winter savory *n.* See **savory² 2.**

winter solstice *n.* In the Northern Hemisphere, the solstice that occurs on or about December 22.

winter squash *n.* Any of several thick-rinded varieties of squash that can be stored for long periods.

Win•ter•thur (vĭn'tər-tŏŏr') A city of N Switzerland NE of Zurich; became a free imperial city in 1415. Pop. 84,600.

win•ter•time (wĭn'tər-tīm') *n.* The season of winter.

winter wheat *n.* Wheat planted in the autumn and harvested the following spring or early summer.

Win•throp (wĭn'thrəp), **John** 1588–1649. English colonial administrator who was the first governor of Massachusetts Bay Colony, serving seven terms between 1629 and 1649. His son **John** (1606–76) was governor of Connecticut (1636, 1657, and 1659–76).

win•try (wĭn'trē) also **win•ter•y** (wĭn'tə-rē) *adj.* **-tri•er, -tri•est** also **-ter•i•er, -ter•i•est 1.** Belonging to or characteristic of winter; cold. **2.** Suggestive of winter, as in cheerlessness. —**win'tri•ly** *adv.* —**win'tri•ness** *n.*

win-win (wĭn'wĭn') *adj.* Of or being a situation in which the outcome benefits each of two often opposing groups.

win•y or **wine•y** (wī'nē) *adj.* **win•i•er, win•i•est** Having the qualities or taste of wine; heady or intoxicating.

winze (wĭnz) *n.* An inclined or vertical shaft or passage between levels in a mine. [Alteration of obsolete *winds*, prob. < WIND², apparatus for winding.]

wipe (wīp) *tr.v.* **wiped, wip•ing, wipes 1a.** To subject to light rubbing or friction, as with a cloth, in order to clean or dry. **b.** To clean or dry by rubbing. **c.** To rub, move, or pass (a cloth, for example) over a surface. **2a.** To remove by or as if by rubbing. **b.** To blot out completely, as from the memory. **3a.** To spread or apply by or as if by wiping. **b.** To form (a joint) in plumbing by spreading solder with a piece of cloth or leather. ❖ *n.* **1.** The act or an instance of wiping. **2.** Something used for wiping. **3.** A cam that activates another part; a wiper. **4a.** A blow or swipe. **b.** *Informal* A jeer; a gibe. **5.** A transition from one scene in a film to another, effected by means of a line passing across the screen. —*phrasal verb:* **wipe out 1.** To destroy or be destroyed completely. **2.** *Slang* To murder. **3.** *Sports* To lose one's balance and fall, as when skiing or surfing. [ME *wipen* < OE *wīpian*.]

wiped-out (wīpt'out') *adj. Slang* Totally exhausted.

wipe•out (wīp'out') *n.* **1a.** The act or an instance of wiping out. **b.** Complete destruction. **2.** *Sports* A fall, as from a surfboard or bicycle.

wip•er (wī'pər) *n.* **1.** One that wipes. **2.** Something, such as a towel, used for wiping. **3.** A device designed for wiping, as on an automobile windshield. **4.** A projecting cam that activates another machine part. **5.** A movable electrical contact.

wire (wīr) *n.* **1.** A usu. pliable metallic strand or rod made in many lengths and diameters and often electrically insulated, used chiefly for structural support or to conduct electricity. **2.** A group of wire strands bundled or twisted together as a functional unit; a cable. **3.** Something resembling a wire, as in slenderness. **4.** An open telephone connection. **5.** *Slang* A hidden microphone, as on a person's body. **6a.** A telegraph service. **b.** A telegram or cablegram. **7.** A wire service. **8.** The screen on which sheets of paper are formed in a papermaking machine. **9.** *Sports* The finish line of a racetrack. **10.** **wires a.** The system of strings for manipulating puppets in a show. **b.** Hidden controlling influences. **11.** *Slang* A pickpocket. **12.** Fencing usu. made of barbed wire. ❖ *v.* **wired, wir•ing, wires** —*tr.* **1.** To bind, connect, or attach with wires or a wire. **2.** To string (beads, for example) on wire. **3.** To equip with a system of electrical wires. **4.** *Slang* To install electronic eavesdropping equipment in (a room, for example). **5.** To send by telegraph. **6.** To send a telegram to. **7.** *Computer Science* To implement (a capability) through logic circuitry that is permanently connected in the hardware. **8.** To determine or put into effect by physiological or neurological mechanisms; hard-wire: *an ability that is wired in the brain.* —*intr.* To send a telegram. —*idioms:* **down to the wire** *Informal* To the very end, as in a contest. **under the wire 1.** *Sports* At the finish line. **2.** *Informal* Just in the nick of time. [ME < OE *wīr*.] —**wir'a•ble** *adj.*

wired (wīrd) *adj.* **1.** Equipped with a system of wires, as for electric, telephone, cable television, or computer network connections. **2.** *Slang* Equipped with hidden electronic eavesdropping devices. **3a.** Reinforced or supported by wires. **b.** Tied or bound up with wire. **4.** *Slang* Having influential connections, as with high-ranking members of an organization. **5.** *Slang* Very stimulated or excited, as from a stimulant.

wire•draw (wīr'drô') *tr.v.* **-drew** (-drōō'), **-drawn** (-drôn'), **-draw•ing, -draws 1.** To draw (metal) into wire. **2.** To treat (a subject, for example) with great length, excessive detail, or over-refinement; spin out. —**wire'draw'er** *n.*

wire•drawn (wīr'drôn') *adj.* Overly subtle and particularized.

wire fox terrier *n.* Any of a breed of small fox terrier developed in northern England and having a rough wiry coat.

wire fraud *n.* Fraud committed by means of electronic communication, as by telephone or modem.

wire gauge *n.* **1.** A gauge for measuring the diameter of wire, usu. consisting of a disk having variously sized slots in its periphery or a long graduated plate with similar slots along its edge. **2.**

A standardized system of wire sizes.

wire glass *n.* Sheet glass reinforced with wire netting.

wire·grass (wīr'grăs') *n.* Any of various grasses, such as Bermuda grass, having tough wiry roots or rootstocks.

wire·hair (wīr'hâr') *n.* See **wire fox terrier.**

wire·haired (wīr'hârd') *adj.* Having a coat of stiff wiry hair. Used esp. of breeds of dogs.

wirehaired pointing griffon *n.* Any of a breed of medium-sized hunting dog originating in the Netherlands and having a rough steel-gray coat with patches of chestnut.

wirehaired terrier *n.* See **wire fox terrier.**

wire·less (wīr'lĭs) *adj.* **1.** Having no wires: *a wireless security system.* **2.** *Chiefly British* Of or relating to radio communication. ❖ *n. Chiefly British* **1.** A message transmitted by wireless telegraph or telephone. **2.** Radio. ❖ *tr. & intr.v.* **-lessed, -less·ing, -less·es** *Chiefly British* To communicate with or send communications by wireless.

wireless telegraphy *n.* Telegraphy by radio rather than by long-distance transmission lines.

wireless telephone *n.* See **radiotelephone.**

wire·man (wīr'mən) *n.* **1.** One who works with electric wiring. **2.** *Slang* One who taps telephone lines; a wiretapper.

Wire·pho·to (wīr'fō'tō) A trademark used for a photograph electrically transmitted over telephone wires.

wire·pull·er (wīr'pŏŏl'ər) *n.* **1.** *Slang* One who uses private influence or underhand means to reach a goal. **2.** One who pulls wires or strings, as of puppets. —**wire'pull'ing** *n.*

wire rope *n.* Rope made of twisted strands of wire.

wire service *n.* A news-gathering organization that distributes syndicated copy electronically, as by teletype or the Internet, usu. to subscribers.

wire·tap (wīr'tăp') *n.* **1.** A concealed listening or recording device connected to a communications circuit. **2.** The act of installing such a device. ❖ *v.* **-tapped, -tap·ping, -taps** —*tr.* **1.** To connect a wiretap to. **2.** To monitor (a telephone line) with a wiretap. —*intr.* To install a wiretap or use it to monitor communications. —**wire'tap'per** *n.*

wire·worm (wīr'wûrm') *n.* **1.** The yellowish hard-bodied larva of various click beetles that feeds on the roots and seedlings of many crop plants. **2.** Any of various millipedes.

wir·ing (wīr'ĭng) *n.* **1.** The act of attaching, connecting, or installing electric wires. **2.** A system of electric wires.

wir·ra (wĭr'ə) *interj. Irish* Used to express sorrow or anxious concern. [< Ir.Gael. *a Mhuire,* Virgin Mary : *a,* O (< OIr. *á*) + *Muire,* Mary.]

wir·y (wīr'ē) *adj.* **-i·er, -i·est** **1.** Of or relating to wire. **2.** Resembling wire in form or quality, esp. in stiffness: *wiry red hair.* **3.** Sinewy and lean. **4.** Produced by or as if by wire being vibrated. Used of sounds. —**wir'i·ly** *adv.* —**wir'i·ness** *n.*

Wis. *abbr.* **1.** Wisconsin **2.** *Bible* Wisdom of Solomon

Wis·con·sin¹ (wĭs-kŏn'sĭn) A state of the N-central US; admitted as the 30th state in 1848. The region became part of the Northwest Terr. in 1787. Cap. Madison. Pop. 5,363,675. —**Wis·con'sin·ite'** *n.*

Wis·con·sin² (wĭs-kŏn'sĭn) *adj.* Of the fourth glacial stage of the Pleistocene Epoch in North America.

Wisconsin River A river of central and SW WI flowing c. 692 km (430 mi) to the Mississippi R.

wis·dom (wĭz'dəm) *n.* **1.** The ability to discern or judge what is true, right, or lasting; insight. **2.** Common sense; good judgment. **3a.** The sum of learning through the ages; knowledge. **b.** Wise teachings of the ancient sages. **4.** A wise outlook, plan, or course of action. **5.** Wisdom Wisdom of Solomon. [ME < OE *wīsdōm.* See **weid-** in App.]

Wisdom of Jesus, the Son of Si·rach (sī'răk') *n.* Ecclesiasticus.

Wisdom of Solomon *n.* See table at **Bible.**

wisdom tooth *n.* One of four rearmost molars on each side of both jaws in humans.

wise¹ (wīz) *adj.* **wis·er, wis·est** **1.** Having the ability to discern or judge what is true, right, or lasting; sagacious: *a wise leader.* **2.** Exhibiting common sense; prudent: *a wise decision.* **b.** Shrewd; crafty. **3.** Having great learning; erudite. **4.** Provided with information; informed. Used with *to.* **5.** *Slang* Rude and disrespectful; impudent. —*phrasal verb:* **wise up** *Slang* To make or become aware, informed, or sophisticated. [ME < OE *wīs.* See **weid-** in App.] —**wise'ly** *adv.* —**wise'ness** *n.*

wise² (wīz) *n.* Method or manner of doing; way: *in no wise; in any wise.* [ME < OE *wīse.* See **weid-** in App.]

Wise, Stephen Samuel 1874–1949. Hungarian-born Amer. founder of the World Jewish Congress (1936).

-wise *suff.* **1.** In a specified manner, direction, or position: *clockwise.* **2.** With reference to; in regard to: *profitwise.* [ME < OE *-wīsan < -wīse,* manner. See **WISE²**.]

USAGE NOTE The suffix *–wise* has a long history of use to mean "in the manner or direction of," as in *clockwise, otherwise,* and *slantwise.* Since the 1930s, however, the suffix has been widely used in the vaguer sense of "with reference to," as in *This has not been a good year saleswise.* This usage has always been associated with informal prose and is still considered by many to be awk-

ward. It can be avoided by using paraphrases: *This has not been a good year with respect to sales.*

wise·a·cre (wīz'ā'kər) *n. Slang* A person regarded as disagreeably egotistical and self-assured. [Alteration (by folk ety.) of MDu. *wijssegger,* soothsayer, transl. of MHGer. *wīssage* < OHGer. *wīssago,* seer, alteration of *wīzago < wīzag,* knowledgeable. See **weid-** in App.]

wise·ass also **wise-ass** (wīz'ăs') *n. Vulgar Slang* A smart aleck.

wise·crack (wīz'krăk') *Slang n.* A flippant, usu. sardonic remark. ❖ *intr.v.* **-cracked, -crack·ing, -cracks** To make or utter a wisecrack. —**wise'crack'er** *n.*

wise guy *n. Slang* A smart aleck.

wise man *n.* **1.** One of the magi who paid homage to the baby Jesus; a magus. **2.** A sage.

wis·en·heim·er also **weis·en·heim·er** (wī'zən-hī'mər) *n. Informal* A smart aleck. [WISE + Ger. *-enheimer* (in such surnames as *Oppenheimer*).]

wi·sent (vē'zənt) *n.* The European bison *(Bison bonasus)* having a smaller and higher head than the North American bison. [Ger. < MHGer. < OHGer. *wisunt.*]

wish (wĭsh) *n.* **1.** A desire, longing, or strong inclination for a specific thing. **2.** An expression of a wish; a petition. **3.** Something desired or longed for. ❖ *v.* **wished, wish·ing, wish·es** —*tr.* **1.** To long for; want. See Syns at **desire.** **2.** To entertain or express wishes for; bid: *He wished her good night.* **3.** To call or invoke upon: *I wish them luck.* **4.** To order or entreat: *I wish you to go.* **5.** To impose or force; foist. —*intr.* **1.** To have or feel a desire. **2.** To express a wish. [ME *wissh < wisshen,* to wish < OE *wȳscan.* See **wen-** in App.] —**wish'er** *n.*

USAGE NOTE When *wish* precedes a subordinate clause containing a contrary-to-fact statement, strict grammatical correctness requires that one use *were* rather than *was: I wish I were lighter on my feet.* However, precedent for using the indicative *was* in such clauses can be found in the works of many good writers. See Usage Notes at **if, want.**

wish·bone (wĭsh'bōn') *n.* **1.** The forked bone anterior to the breastbone of most birds, formed by the fusion of the clavicles. **2.** *Football* An offensive formation in which the halfbacks are positioned behind and to the left and right of the fullback. [< the superstition that when two people pull the bone apart, the one with the longer part will get a wish.]

wish·ful (wĭsh'fəl) *adj.* Having or expressing a wish or longing. —**wish'ful·ly** *adv.* —**wish'ful·ness** *n.*

wish fulfillment *n.* **1.** Gratification of a desire. **2.** In psychoanalytic theory, the satisfaction of a desire, need, or impulse through a dream or other exercise of the imagination.

wishful thinking *n.* Identification of one's wishes or desires with reality.

wish list *n.* An often mental list of things wanted.

wish-wash (wĭsh'wŏsh', -wôsh') *n. Informal* **1.** Speech or writing deemed banal or foolish. **2.** A thin watery drink. [Reduplication of WASH.]

wish·y-wash·y (wĭsh'ē-wŏsh'ē, -wô'shē) *adj.* **-i·er, -i·est** *Informal* **1.** Thin and watery, as tea or soup; insipid. **2.** Lacking in strength of character or purpose; ineffective. [Reduplication of *washy,* thin, watery < WASH.] —**wish'y-wash'i·ness** *n.*

wisp (wĭsp) *n.* **1.** A small bunch or bundle, as of straw, hair, or grass. **2a.** One that is thin, frail, or slight. **b.** A thin or faint streak or fragment, as of smoke or clouds. **3.** A fleeting trace or indication; a hint. **4.** A flock of birds, esp. snipe. **5.** See **ignis fatuus** 1. ❖ *v.* **wisped, wisp·ing, wisps** —*tr.* To twist into wisps or a wisp. —*intr.* To drift in wisps. [ME.] —**wisp'i·ly** *adv.* —**wisp'i·ness** (wĭs'pē-nĭs) *n.* —**wisp'y** *adj.*

wist (wĭst) *v. Archaic* Past tense and past participle of **wit²**.

Wis·ter (wĭs'tər), **Owen** 1860–1938. Amer. writer known esp. for his novel *The Virginian* (1902).

wis·te·ri·a (wĭ-stîr'ē-ə) also **wis·tar·i·a** (wĭ-stâr'-) *n.* Any of several climbing vines of the genus *Wisteria* in the pea family, having pinnately compound leaves and drooping racemes of purplish or white flowers. [NLat. *Wisteria,* genus name, after Caspar Wistar (1761–1818), American physician.]

wist·ful (wĭst'fəl) *adj.* **1.** Full of wishful yearning. **2.** Pensively sad; melancholy. [< obsolete *wistly,* intently.] —**wist'ful·ly** *adv.* —**wist'ful·ness** *n.*

wit¹ (wĭt) *n.* **1.** The natural ability to perceive and understand; intelligence. **2a.** Keenness and quickness of perception or discernment; ingenuity. Often used in the plural. **b. wits** Sound mental faculties; sanity. **3a.** The ability to perceive and express in an ingeniously humorous manner the relationship between seemingly incongruous or disparate things. **b.** One noted for this ability, esp. one skilled in repartee. **c.** A person of exceptional intelligence. —*idioms:* **at (one's) wits' end** At the limit of one's mental resources; utterly at a loss. **have (or keep) (one's) wits about (one)** To remain alert or calm, esp. in a crisis. [ME < OE. See **weid-** in App.]

wit² (wĭt) *v.* **wist** (wĭst), **wit·ting** (wĭt'ĭng), *first and third person singular present tense* **wot** (wŏt) *Archaic* —*tr.* To be or become aware of; learn. —*intr.* To know. —*idiom:* **to wit** That is to say; namely. [ME < OE *witan.* See **weid-** in App.]

wisent
Bison bonasus

wit·an (wĭt′ăn) *pl.n.* **1.** The members of the witenagemot in Anglo-Saxon England. **2.** The witenagemot. [OE, pl. of *wita,* councilor. See WITENAGEMOT.]

witch (wĭch) *n.* **1.** A woman claiming or popularly believed to possess magical powers and practice sorcery. **2.** A believer or follower of Wicca. **3.** A hag. **4.** A woman considered to be spiteful or overbearing. **5.** *Informal* A woman or girl considered bewitching. **6.** One particularly skilled or competent at one's craft. ❖ *v.* **witched, witch·ing, witch·es** —*tr.* **1.** To work or cast a spell on; bewitch. **2.** To cause, bring, or effect by witchcraft. —*intr.* To dowse. [ME *wicche* < OE *wicce,* witch, and *wicca,* wizard, sorcerer.] —**witch′er·y** (-ə-rē) *n.* —**witch′y** *adj.*

witch·craft (wĭch′krăft′) *n.* **1.** Magic; sorcery. **2.** Wicca. **3.** A magical or irresistible influence, attraction, or charm.

witch doctor *n. Anthropology* A sorcerer, prophet, or shamanistic healer, esp. among African peoples. Not in scientific use.

witch elm *n.* Variant of **wych elm.** [Alteration of WYCH ELM.]

witch·es′ brew (wĭch′ĭz) *n.* A powerful or terrifying concoction.

witches′ broom *n.* An abnormal brushlike growth of shoots or branches on a tree, caused by fungi or viruses.

witches′ Sabbath *n.* A meeting of witches, supposed by medieval Christians to be a demonic orgy.

witch grass *n.* **1.** An annual North American grass (*Panicum capillare*) having branching purplish panicles. **2.** See **couch grass.** [Prob. alteration of QUITCH GRASS.]

witch hazel *n.* **1.** Any of several deciduous shrubs or small trees of the genus *Hamamelis,* esp. *H. virginiana* of eastern North America, having yellow flowers. **2.** An alcoholic solution containing an extract of the bark and leaves of this plant, used as a mild astringent. [Alteration of obsolete *wych,* wych elm; see WYCH ELM + HAZEL.]

witch-hunt also **witch hunt** (wĭch′hŭnt′) *n.* An investigation carried out ostensibly to uncover subversive activities but actually used to harass and undermine those with differing views. —**witch′-hunt′er** *n.* —**witch′-hunt′ing** *adj.* & *n.*

witch·ing (wĭch′ĭng) *adj.* **1.** Of or characteristic of witchcraft. **2.** Having the power to charm or enchant; bewitching. ❖ *n.* Witchcraft; sorcery. —**witch′ing·ly** *adv.*

witch moth *n.* Any of several large noctuid moths of the genus *Erebus* of the southern United States and tropical America.

wite (wīt) *n. Scots* Blame; fault. [ME < OE *wīte,* penalty. See **weid-** in App.]

wit·e·na·ge·mot (wĭt′n-ə-gə-mōt′) *n.* An Anglo-Saxon advisory council to the king, convened at intervals to discuss administrative and judicial affairs. [OE *witena gemōt,* meeting of councilors : *witena,* genitive pl. of *wita,* councilor; see **weid-** in App. + *gemōt,* meeting (*ge-,* collective pref.; see **kom** in App. + *mōt,* meeting).]

with (wĭth, wĭth) *prep.* **1.** In the company of; accompanying: *Did you go with her?* **2.** Next to; alongside of: *sat with them.* **3.** Having as a possession, an attribute, or a characteristic: *a man with a moustache.* **b.** Used as a function word to indicate accompanying detail or condition: *sat with his mouth open.* **4a.** In a manner characterized by: *performed with skill.* **b.** In the performance, use, or operation of: *trouble with the car.* **5.** In the charge or keeping of: *left the cat with the neighbors.* **6.** In the opinion or estimation of: *if it's all right with you.* **7a.** In support of; on the side of: *I'm with you.* **b.** Of the same opinion or belief as: *with us on that issue.* **8.** In the same group or mixture as; among: *planted onions with the carrots.* **9.** In the membership or employment of: *is with a small company.* **10a.** By the means or agency of: *eat with a fork.* **b.** By the presence or use of: *a pillow stuffed with feathers.* **11.** In spite of: *With all her experience, she failed.* **12.** In the same direction as: *sail with the wind.* **13.** At the same time as: *gets up with the birds.* **14a.** In regard to: *pleased with her decision.* **b.** Used as a function word to indicate a party to an action, a communicative activity, or an informal agreement or settlement: *lives with an aunt.* **15.** In comparison or contrast to: *pants identical with her sister's.* **16.** Having received: *With her permission, he left.* **17a.** And; plus: *My books, with my brother's, are here.* **b.** Inclusive of; including: *$29.95 with postage.* **18.** In opposition to; against: *wrestling with him.* **19.** As a result or consequence of: *sick with the flu.* **20.** So as to be touching or joined to: *linked arms with their partners.* **21.** So as to be free of or separated from: *parted with them.* **22.** In the course of: *We grow older with the hours.* **23.** In proportion to: *improves with age.* **24.** In relationship to: *at ease with my peers.* **25.** As well as; in favorable comparison to: *sang with the best.* **26.** According to the experience or practice of: *With me, it is all the same.* **27.** Used as a function word to indicate close association: *With the advent of the rockets, the Space Age began.* —**idioms: in with** *Informal* In league or association with. **with it** *Informal* **1.** Interested in and sensitive to the latest styles and trends; up-to-date. **2.** Streetwise and knowing; savvy. **3.** Mentally competent. [ME, with, against, from < OE.]

> **USAGE NOTE** When the subject of a sentence is followed by a noun or noun phrase introduced by *with* rather than *and,* the verb remains singular: *The governor, with his aides, is here.* See Usage Notes at **and, together.**

with·al (wĭth-ôl′, wĭth-) *adv.* **1.** In addition; besides. **2.** Despite that; nevertheless. **3.** *Archaic* Therewith. ❖ *prep. Archaic* With.

Used after its object at the end of a sentence or clause. [ME : *with,* with; see WITH + *al,* all; see ALL.]

with·draw (wĭth-drô′, wĭth-) *v.* **-drew** (-drōō′), **-drawn** (-drôn′), **-draw·ing, -draws** —*tr.* **1a.** To take back or away; remove. **b.** To remove (money) from an account. **c.** To turn away (one's gaze, for example). **d.** To draw aside. **2a.** To remove from consideration or participation. **b.** To recall or retract. —*intr.* **1a.** To move or draw back; retire. **b.** To retreat from a battlefield. **2a.** To remove oneself from active participation. **b.** To become detached from social or emotional involvement. **3.** To recall or remove a motion from consideration in parliamentary procedure. **4.** To discontinue the use of an addictive substance. [ME *withdrawen* : *with,* away from; see WITH + *drawen,* to pull; see DRAW.] —**with·draw′a·ble** *adj.* —**with·draw′er** *n.*

with·draw·al (wĭth-drô′əl, wĭth-) *n.* **1.** The act or process of withdrawing, as: **a.** A retreat or retirement. **b.** Retreat of a military force in the face of enemy attack or after a defeat. **c.** Detachment, as from emotional involvement. **d.** A removal from a place or position of something that has been deposited. **2a.** Discontinuation of the use of an addictive substance. **b.** The physiological and mental readjustment that accompanies such discontinuation. **3.** The act or an instance of retracting or revoking.

with·drawn (wĭth-drôn′, wĭth-) *adj.* **1.** Not readily approached; remote. **2a.** Not friendly or sociable; aloof. **b.** Emotionally unresponsive and detached; introverted. —**with·drawn′ness** *n.*

withe (wĭth, wĭth, wĭth) *n.* A tough supple twig, esp. of willow, used to bind things together. [ME < OE *withthe.*]

with·er (wĭth′ər) *v.* **-ered, -er·ing, -ers** —*intr.* **1.** To dry up or shrivel from or as if from loss of moisture. **2.** To lose freshness; droop. —*tr.* **1.** To cause to shrivel or fade. **2.** To render speechless or incapable of action; stun. [Alteration of ME *widderen,* perh. var. of *wederen,* to weather < *weder,* weather. See WEATHER.]

with·ered (wĭth′ərd) *adj.* Shriveled, shrunken, or faded from or as if from loss of moisture or sustenance.

with·er·ing (wĭth′ər-ĭng) *adj.* Tending to overwhelm or destroy; devastating: *withering sarcasm.* —**with′er·ing·ly** *adv.*

with·er·ite (wĭth′ə-rīt′) *n.* A white, yellow, or gray mineral, chiefly BaCO₃. [Ger. *Witherit,* after William *Withering* (1741–99), British physician.]

withe·rod (wĭth′rŏd′, wĭth′-, wĭth′-) *n.* An eastern North American deciduous shrub (*Viburnum cassinoides*) having clusters of small white flowers and bluish-black edible fruit. [WITHE + ROD.]

with·ers (wĭth′ərz) *pl.n.* The high part of the back of a horse or similar animal, located between the shoulder blades. [Poss. < obsolete *wither-,* against (< the strain exerted on them when a horse draws a load) < ME < OE.]

with·er·shins (wĭth′ər-shĭnz′) *adv.* Variant of **widdershins.**

With·er·spoon (wĭth′ər-spōōn′), **John** 1723–94. Scottish-born Amer. cleric and Revolutionary leader who was a signer of the Declaration of Independence.

with·hold (wĭth-hōld′, wĭth-) *v.* **-held** (-hĕld′), **-hold·ing, -holds** —*tr.* **1.** To keep in check; restrain. **2.** To refrain from giving, granting, or permitting. See Syns at **keep. 3.** To deduct (withholding tax) from an employee's salary. —*intr.* To refrain or forbear. [ME *witholden* : *with,* away from; see WITH + *holden,* to hold; see HOLD¹.] —**with·hold′er** *n.*

with·hold·ing tax (wĭth-hōl′dĭng, wĭth-) *n.* A portion of an employee's wages or salary withheld by the employer as partial payment of the employee's income tax.

with·in (wĭth-ĭn′, wĭth-) *adv.* **1.** In or into the inner part; inside. **2.** Inside the mind, heart, or soul; inwardly. ❖ *prep.* **1.** In the inner part or parts of; inside. **2a.** Inside the limits or extent of in time or distance. **b.** Inside the fixed limits of; not beyond. **c.** In the scope or sphere of. **d.** Inside a specified amount or degree. ❖ *n.* An inner position, place, or area. [ME *withinne* < OE *withinnan* : *with,* with; see WITH + *innan,* from within (< *in,* in; see IN¹).]

with·in·doors (wĭth-ĭn′dôrz′, -dōrz′, wĭth-) *adv.* Into or inside a house or other building; indoors.

with·out (wĭth-out′, wĭth-) *adv.* **1.** On the outside. **2.** With something absent or lacking. ❖ *prep.* **1a.** Not having; lacking. **b.** Not accompanied by; in the absence of. **2.** At, on, to, or toward the outside or exterior of: *standing without the door.* ❖ *n.* An outer position, place, or area: *a security threat that came from without.* ❖ *conj. Regional* Unless. [ME *withoute* < OE *withūtan* : *with,* with; see WITH + *ūtan,* from without (< *ūt,* out; see OUT).]

with·out·doors (wĭth-out′dôrz′, -dōrz′, wĭth-) *adv.* Outside a house or other building; outdoors.

with·stand (wĭth-stănd′, wĭth-) *v.* **-stood** (-stōōd′), **-stand·ing, -stands** —*tr.* **1.** To resist or oppose with determined effort: *The soldiers withstood the attack.* **2.** To be undamaged or unaffected by: *The house withstood the storm.* —*intr.* To resist or endure successfully. [ME *withstanden* < OE *withstandan* : *with,* against; see WITH + *standan,* to stand; see STAND.]

with·y (wĭth′ē, wĭth′ē) *adj.* **1.** Made of or as flexible as withes; tough. **2.** Wiry and agile. ❖ *n., pl.* **-ies 1.** A rope or band made of withes. **2a.** A long flexible twig, as that of an osier. **b.** A tree or shrub having such twigs. [WITHE + -Y¹. N., ME *withye,* willow branch < OE *wīthig,* willow.]

wit·less (wĭt′lĭs) *adj.* Lacking intelligence or wit; foolish. —**wit′less·ly** *adv.* —**wit′less·ness** *n.*

wit·ling (wĭt′lĭng) *n.* **1.** One who aspires to wittiness. **2.** One who has little wit.

wit·loof (wĭt′lōf′) *n.* See **endive** 2. [Du. dialectal : *wit,* white (< MDu.) + *loof,* leaf (< MDu.).]

wit·ness (wĭt′nĭs) *n.* **1a.** One who can give a firsthand account of something. **b.** One who furnishes evidence. **2.** Something that serves as evidence; a sign. **3.** *Law* **a.** One who is called on to testify before a court. **b.** One who is called on to attest to what takes place at a transaction. **c.** One who signs one's name to a document to attest to its authenticity. **4.** An attestation to a fact, statement, or event; testimony. **5a.** One who publicly affirms religious faith. **b.** **Witness** A member of the Jehovah's Witnesses. ❖ *v.* **-nessed, -ness·ing, -ness·es** —*tr.* **1a.** To be present at or have personal knowledge of. **b.** To take note of; observe. **2.** To provide or serve as evidence of. **3.** To testify to; bear witness. **4.** To be the setting or site of. **5.** To attest to the legality or authenticity of by signing one's name to. —*intr.* **1.** To furnish or serve as evidence; testify. **2.** To testify to one's religious beliefs. [ME < OE < *wit,* knowledge. See WIT¹.] —**wit′ness·er** *n.*

witness box *n. Chiefly British* A witness stand.

witness stand *n.* A stand or enclosed area in a courtroom from which a witness presents testimony.

wit·ted (wĭt′ĭd) *adj.* Having wit or intellectual comprehension. Often used in combination: *keen-witted.* —**wit′ted·ness** *n.*

Wit·ten·berg (wĭt′n-bûrg′, vĭt′n-bĕrk′) A city of E-central Germany E of Dessau; center of the Protestant Reformation after Martin Luther nailed his 95 theses to the door of the Schlosskirche in 1517. Pop. 54,306.

Witt·gen·stein (vĭt′gən-shtīn′, -stīn′), **Ludwig** 1889–1951. Austrian-born philosopher whose major works, *Tractatus Logico-Philosophicus* (1921) and *Philosophical Investigations* (1953), explore the relation between language and the world.

wit·ti·cism (wĭt′ĭ-sĭz′əm) *n.* A witty remark. [Blend of WITTY and CRITICISM.]

wit·ting (wĭt′ĭng) *adj.* **1.** Aware or conscious of something. **2.** Done intentionally or with premeditation; deliberate. ❖ *v. Archaic* Present participle of **wit²**. ❖ *n. Chiefly British* **1.** Knowledge or awareness; cognizance. **2.** Information obtained and passed on; news. —**wit′ting·ly** *adv.*

wit·tol (wĭt′l) *n. Archaic* A man who knows of and tolerates his wife's infidelity. [ME *wetewold* : *weten,* to know (< OE *witan;* see WIT²) + *(coke)wold,* cuckold; see CUCKOLD.]

wit·ty (wĭt′ē) *adj.* **-ti·er, -ti·est 1.** Possessing or demonstrating wit in speech or writing; very clever and humorous. **2.** Marked by or having the nature of wit; funny. **3.** Quick to discern and express amusing insights or relationships. **4.** Entertainingly and strikingly clever or original in concept, design, or performance. —**wit′ti·ly** *adv.* —**wit′ti·ness** *n.*

Wit·wa·ters·rand (wĭt-wô′tərz-rănd′, -ränd′, -wŏt′ərz-rănt′) **Rand** (rănd) A region of NE South Africa between the Vaal R. and Johannesburg; one of the richest gold-mining areas in the world since the discovery of gold in 1886.

wive (wīv) *v.* **wived, wiv·ing, wives** —*tr.* **1.** To marry (a woman). **2.** To provide a wife for. —*intr.* To marry a woman. [ME *wiven* < OE *wīfian* < *wīf,* woman.]

wi·vern (wī′vərn) *n.* Variant of **wyvern**.

wives (wīvz) *n.* Plural of **wife**.

wiz (wĭz) *n. Informal* A person considered exceptionally gifted or skilled. [Short for WIZARD.]

wiz·ard (wĭz′ərd) *n.* **1.** One who practices magic; a sorcerer or magician. **2.** A skilled or clever person: *a wizard at math.* **3.** *Archaic* A sage. ❖ *adj.* **1.** *Chiefly British Slang* Excellent. **2.** *Archaic* Of or relating to wizards or wizardry. [ME *wisard* : *wise,* wise; see WISE¹ + *-ard,* pejorative suffix; see -ARD.]

wiz·ard·ly (wĭz′ərd-lē) *adj.* **1.** Having the qualities or attributes of a wizard. **2.** Astonishing in design, performance, or execution; fabulous: *wizardly lighting.*

wiz·ard·ry (wĭz′ər-drē) *n., pl.* **-ries 1.** The art, skill, or practice of a wizard; sorcery. **2.** A power or effect that appears magical by its capacity to transform: *computer wizardry.* **3.** Great ability or adroitness in a pursuit: *artistic wizardry.*

wiz·en (wĭz′ən) *v.* **-ened, -en·ing, -ens** —*intr.* To dry up; wither or shrivel. —*tr.* To cause to wither or shrivel. ❖ *adj.* Shriveled or dried up; withered. [ME *wisenen* < OE *wisnian.*]

wiz·ened (wĭz′ənd) *adj.* Withered; wizen.

wk. *abbr.* week

WL *abbr.* **1.** water line **2.** wavelength

WNW *abbr.* west-northwest

wo (wō) *n. Archaic* Variant of **woe**.

w/o *abbr.* without

woad (wōd) *n.* **1.** An annual Old World plant (*Isatis tinctoria*) in the mustard family, having leaves that yield a blue dye. **2.** The dye obtained from this plant. [ME *wode* < OE *wād.*]

woad·wax·en (wōd′wăk′sən) *n.* See **dyer's greenweed.** [Alteration of WOODWAXEN.]

wob·ble also **wab·ble** (wŏb′əl) *v.* **-bled, -bling, -bles** —*intr.* **1.** To move or rotate with an uneven or rocking motion from side to side. **2.** To tremble or quaver: *a voice that wobbled with emotion.* **3.** To waver in one's views or feelings. —*tr.* To cause to wobble. ❖ *n.* **1.** The act or an instance of wobbling; unsteady motion. **2.** A tremulous, uncertain tone or sound: *a vocal wobble.* [Prob.

< LGer. *wabbeln.* See **webh-** in App.] —**wob′bler** *n.*

wob·bly (wŏb′lē) *adj.* **-bli·er, -bli·est** Tending to wobble; unsteady. —**wob′bli·ness** *n.*

Wobbly *n., pl.* **-blies** A member of the Industrial Workers of the World, a chiefly US labor organization dedicated to the overthrow of capitalism, active esp. in the early 1900s. [< *I Wobbly Wobbly,* humorous alteration of *I(ndustrial) W(orkers of the) W(orld).)*]

w.o.c. *abbr.* without compensation

Wode·house (wŏŏd′hous′), **P(elham) G(renville)** 1881–1975. British writer known for his humorous works featuring the aristocrat Bertie Wooster and his butler Jeeves.

Wo·den also **Wo·dan** (wōd′n) *n. Mythology* An Anglo-Saxon god identified with Odin. [ME < OE *Wōden.* See **wet-¹** in App.]

woe (wō) *n.* **1.** Deep distress or misery, as from grief. **2.** Misfortune; calamity. ❖ *interj.* Used to express sorrow or dismay. [ME *wa,* *wo* < OE *wā,* *woe!*]

woe·be·gone (wō′bĭ-gôn′, -gŏn′) *adj.* **1.** Affected with or marked by deep sorrow, grief, or wretchedness. See Syns at **sad. 2.** Of an inferior or deplorable condition: *a woebegone old shack.* [ME *wo begon,* beset with woe : *wo,* woe; see WOE + *begon,* p. part. of *begon,* to beset (< OE *begān* : *be-,* be- + *gān,* to go; see GO¹).] —**woe′be·gone′ness** *n.*

woe·ful also **wo·ful** (wō′fəl) *adj.* **1.** Affected by or full of woe. **2.** Causing or involving woe. **3.** Deplorably bad or wretched. —**woe′ful·ly** *adv.* —**woe′ful·ness** *n.*

wog (wŏg) *n. Chiefly British Offensive Slang* Used as a disparaging term for a person of color, esp. a person from northern Africa or western or southern Asia. [Prob. short for GOLLIWOG.]

wok (wŏk) *n.* A metal pan having a rounded bottom, used esp. in Asian cooking. [Chin. (Cantonese) *wōk,* equivalent to Chin. (Mandarin) *hù, huò.*]

woke (wōk) *v.* A past tense of **wake¹**. See Regional Note at **wake¹**.

wok·en (wō′kən) *v.* A past participle of **wake¹**.

wold¹ (wōld) *n.* An unforested rolling plain; a moor. [ME < OE *weald,* forest.]

wold² (wōld) *n.* Variant of **weld²**.

Wolds (wōldz) A range of chalk hills in NE England along both banks of the Humber R.

wolf (wŏŏlf) *n., pl.* **wolves** (wŏŏlvz) **1a.** Either of two carnivorous mammals of the family Canidae, esp. the gray wolf of northern regions, that typically live and hunt in hierarchical packs. **b.** The fur of such an animal. **c.** Any of various similar or related mammals, such as the hyena. **2.** The destructive larva of any of various moths, beetles, or flies. **3.** One that is regarded as predatory, rapacious, and fierce. **4.** *Slang* A man given to paying unwanted sexual attention to women. **5.** *Music* **a.** A harshness in some tones of a bowed stringed instrument due to defective vibration. **b.** Dissonance in perfect fifths on a keyboard instrument tuned to a system of unequal temperament. ❖ *tr.v.* **wolfed, wolf·ing, wolfs** To eat greedily or voraciously: *wolfing down food.* —*idioms:* **wolf at the door** Creditors or a creditor. **wolf in sheep's clothing** One with malevolent intentions who feigns congeniality. [ME < OE *wulf.* See **wl̥k**ʷ**o-** in App.]

Wolf (vôlf), **Hugo** 1860–1903. Austrian composer known esp. for his lieder.

wolf·ber·ry (wŏŏlf′bĕr′ē) *n.* A deciduous shrub (*Symphoricarpos occidentalis*) of western North America having white berries and pinkish bell-shaped flowers.

wolf dog (wŏŏlf) *n.* **1.** A dog trained to hunt wolves. **2.** The hybrid offspring of a dog and a wolf.

Wolfe (wŏŏlf), **James** 1727–59. British general who defeated the French at Quebec (1759) but was mortally wounded in the battle.

Wolfe, Thomas (Clayton) 1900–38. Amer. writer best known for his autobiographical novels, including *Look Homeward, Angel* (1929) and *You Can't Go Home Again* (1940).

Wolff (vôlf), **Kaspar Friedrich** 1733–94. German anatomist noted for his pioneering work in embryology.

Wolff·i·an body (wŏŏl′fē-ən) *n.* See **mesonephros.**

wolf·fish (wŏŏlf′fĭsh′) *n.* Any of several northern marine fishes of the genus *Anarhichas,* having sharp teeth and a voracious appetite.

wolf·hound (wŏŏlf′hound′) *n.* Any of various large dogs, such as the borzoi, trained to hunt wolves or other large game.

wolf·ish (wŏŏl′fĭsh) *adj.* **1.** Of or relating to wolves. **2a.** Suggestive of or resembling a wolf. **b.** Fierce or rapacious. —**wolf′ish·ly** *adv.* —**wolf′ish·ness** *n.*

wolf·ram (wŏŏl′frəm) *n.* See **tungsten.** [Ger. *wolframite, tungsten* : prob. *Wolf,* wolf (< MHGer. < OHGer.; see **wl̥k**ʷ**o-** in App.) + *-ram* (< MHGer. *rām,* dirt).]

wolf·ram·ite (wŏŏl′frə-mīt′) *n.* Any of several red-brown to black minerals with the general formula $(Fe,Mn)WO_4$, constituting a major source of tungsten.

wolfs·bane (wŏŏlfs′bān′) *n.* **1.** See **aconite.** **2.** Any of several poisonous perennial herbs of the genus *Aconitum,* esp. *A. lycoctonum,* having rounded leaves and purplish flowers.

wolf spider *n.* Any of various spiders of the family Lycosidae that stalk prey on the ground and do not spin webs, esp. a common small species (*Lycosa tarentula*) of southern Europe.

wolf whistle *n.* A typically two-note whistle made as an often un-

wolf
gray wolf
Canis lupus

solicited expression of sexual attention. —**wolf whistle** *v.*

Wol·las·ton (wŏol′ə-stən), **William Hyde** 1766–1828. British chemist who discovered palladium (1803) and rhodium (1804).

wol·las·ton·ite (wŏol′ə-stə-nīt′) *n.* A white to gray mineral, essentially CaSiO₃, found in metamorphic rocks and used in ceramics, paints, plastics, and cements.

Wol·lon·gong (wŏol′ən-gŏng′, -gông′) A city of SE Australia on the Tasman Sea SSW of Sydney. Pop. 176,500.

Woll·stone·craft (wŏol′stən-krăft′, -krăft′), **Mary** In full Mary Wollstonecraft Godwin. 1759–97. British writer and reformer noted for *A Vindication of the Rights of Woman* (1792).

Wo·lof (wō′lôf′) *n.* **1.** A member of a West African people primarily inhabiting coastal Senegal. **2.** Their West Atlantic language, widely used as a lingua franca in Senegal.

Wol·sey (wŏol′zē), **Thomas** 1475?–1530. English prelate who fell from favor after failing to secure papal approval for Henry VIII's divorce from Catherine of Aragon (1529).

Wol·ver·hamp·ton (wŏol′vər-hămp′tən, -hăm′-) A borough of W-central England NW of Birmingham. Pop. 246,439.

wol·ver·ine (wŏol′və-rēn′, wŏol′və-rēn′) *n.* A solitary burrowing carnivorous mammal (*Gulo gulo*) of northern forest regions, related to the weasel and having a heavyset body, short legs, dark fur, and a bushy tail. [Prob. < WOLF.]

wolves (wŏolvz) *n.* Plural of **wolf**.

wom·an (wŏom′ən) *n., pl.* **wom·en** (wĭm′ĭn) **1.** An adult female human. **2.** Women considered as a group; womankind. **3.** An adult female human belonging to a specified occupation, group, nationality, or other category. Often used in combination: *congresswoman.* **4.** Feminine quality or aspect; womanliness. **5.** A female servant or subordinate. **6.** *Informal* **a.** A wife. **b.** A female lover or sweetheart. See Usage Notes at **lady, man, person.** —*idiom:* **(one's) own woman** Independent in judgment or action. [ME < OE *wimman,* var. of *wīfmann* : *wīf,* woman; see **ghwibh-** in App. + *man,* person; see MAN.]

woman about town *n., pl.* **women about town** A sophisticated and socially active woman who frequents fashionable places.

wom·an·ful·ly (wŏom′ən-fŭl′ē) *adv.* With the characteristic grace, strength, or purposefulness of a woman.

wom·an·hood (wŏom′ən-hŏod′) *n.* **1.** The state of being a woman. **2.** The composite of qualities deemed appropriate to or representative of women. **3.** Women considered as a group.

wom·an·ish (wŏom′ə-nĭsh) *adj.* **1.** Of, characteristic of, or natural to a woman. **2.** Resembling or suggestive of a woman. —**wom′an·ish·ly** *adv.* —**wom′an·ish·ness** *n.*

wom·an·ist (wŏom′ə-nĭst) *adj.* Having or expressing a belief in or respect for women that is not limited by issues of race and class. —**wom′an·ism** *n.* —**wom′an·ist** *n.*

wom·an·ize (wŏom′ə-nīz′) *v.* **-ized, -iz·ing, -iz·es** —*intr.* To pursue women lecherously. —*tr.* To give female characteristics to; feminize. —**wom′an·iz′er** *n.*

wom·an·kind (wŏom′ən-kīnd′) *n.* Women considered as a group.

wom·an·like (wŏom′ən-līk′) *adj.* **1.** Resembling a woman: *a womanlike image.* **2.** Belonging to or befitting a woman.

wom·an·ly (wŏom′ən-lē) *adj.* **-li·er, -li·est 1.** Having qualities generally attributed to a woman. **2.** Of or representative of a woman; feminine. —**wom′an·li·ness** *n.*

woman of letters *n., pl.* **women of letters** A woman who is devoted to literary or scholarly pursuits.

woman of the hour *n., pl.* **women of the hour 1.** A woman in whose honor a gathering is held. **2.** A woman who is currently an object of public attention.

woman of the house *n., pl.* **women of the house** The primary woman of a household.

woman of the world *n., pl.* **women of the world** A sophisticated, worldly woman.

wom·an·pow·er (wŏom′ən-pou′ər) *n.* Power in terms of the women available to a particular group or required for a particular task.

woman suffrage *n.* **1.** The right of women to vote. **2.** A movement to promote and secure such rights.

wom·an·to·wom·an (wŏom′ən-tə-wŏom′ən) *adj.* Characterized by direct interaction between or among women.

womb (wŏom) *n.* **1.** See **uterus** 1. **2a.** A place where something is generated. **b.** An encompassing, protective hollow or space. **3.** *Obsolete* The belly. [ME < OE *wamb.*]

wom·bat (wŏm′băt′) *n.* Any of several small bear-like burrowing Australian marsupials of the family Vombatidae. [Dharuk *wambad.*]

wom·en (wĭm′ĭn) *n.* Plural of **woman**.

wom·en·folk (wĭm′ĭn-fōk′) also **wom·en·folks** (-fōks′) *pl.n.* **1.** Women considered as a group. **2.** The women of a community or family.

wom·en·kind (wĭm′ən-kīnd′) *n.* Womankind.

wom·en's movement (wĭm′ĭnz) *n.* A movement in support of women's rights, esp. the mid-twentieth century movement in North America and Europe.

women's rights *pl.n.* **1.** Socioeconomic, political, and legal rights for women equal to those of men. **2.** A movement in support of these rights.

women's room *n.* A restroom for women.

women's studies *pl.n.* (*used with a sing. or pl. verb*) An academic curriculum focusing on the roles and contributions of women in fields such as literature, history, and the social sciences.

women's wear *n.* Clothing for women.

wom·er·a (wŏm′ər-ə) *n.* Variant of **woomera**.

won¹ (wŭn, wŏn) *intr.v.* **wonned, won·ning, wons** *Archaic* To dwell or abide. [ME *wonen* < OE *wunian.* See **wen-** in App.]

won² (wŏn) *n., pl.* **won** See table at **currency**. [Korean.]

won³ (wŭn) *v.* Past tense and past participle of **win**.

won·der (wŭn′dər) *n.* **1a.** One that arouses awe, astonishment, surprise, or admiration; a marvel. **b.** The emotion aroused by a wonder. **2.** An event inexplicable by the laws of nature; a miracle. **3.** A feeling of puzzlement or doubt. **4.** often **Wonder** A monumental human creation regarded with awe, esp. one of seven monuments of the ancient world that appeared on various lists of late antiquity. ❖ *v.* **-dered, -der·ing, -ders** —*intr.* **1a.** To have a feeling of awe or admiration; marvel. **b.** To have a feeling of surprise. **2.** To be filled with curiosity or doubt. —*tr.* To feel curiosity or be in doubt about. ❖ *adj.* **1a.** Arousing awe or admiration. **b.** Wonderful. **2.** Far superior to anything formerly recognized or foreseen. —*idiom:* **for a wonder** As a cause for surprise; surprisingly. [ME < OE *wundor.*] —**won′der·er** *n.*

SYNONYMS *wonder, marvel, miracle, phenomenon, prodigy, sensation* These nouns denote one that evokes amazement or admiration: *the wonders of Paris; a marvel of technology; a miracle of culinary art; a phenomenon of science; a musical prodigy; a theatrical sensation.*

wonder drug *n.* See **miracle drug**.

won·der·ful (wŭn′dər-fəl) *adj.* **1.** Capable of eliciting wonder; astonishing. **2.** Admirable; excellent. —**won′der·ful·ly** *adv.* —**won′der·ful·ness** *n.*

won·der·ing (wŭn′dər-ĭng) *adj.* Feeling or expressing awe, admiration, amazement, or surprise. —**won′der·ing·ly** *adv.*

won·der·land (wŭn′dər-lănd′) *n.* **1.** A marvelous imaginary realm. **2.** A marvelous real place or scene.

won·der·ment (wŭn′dər-mənt) *n.* **1.** Astonishment, awe, or surprise. **2.** Something that produces wonder; a marvel. **3.** Puzzlement or curiosity.

won·der·work (wŭn′dər-wûrk′) *n.* A marvelous or miraculous act, work, or achievement; a marvel. —**won′der·work′er** *n.* —**won′der·work′ing** *adj.*

won·drous (wŭn′drəs) *adj.* Remarkable or extraordinary; wonderful. ❖ *adv. Archaic* To a wonderful or remarkable extent. —**won′drous·ly** *adv.* —**won′drous·ness** *n.*

wonk (wŏngk) *n. Slang* **1.** A student who studies excessively. **2.** One who studies an issue or topic thoroughly or excessively. [?]

won·ky (wŏng′kē) *adj.* **-ki·er, -ki·est** *Chiefly British* **1.** Shaky; feeble. **2.** Wrong; awry. [Prob. alteration of dialectal *wanky,* alteration of *wankle* < ME *wankel* < OE *wancol,* unsteady.]

Won·san (wŭn′sän′) A city of SE North Korea on the Sea of Japan E of Pyongyang. Pop. 350,000.

wont (wônt, wŏnt, wŭnt) *adj.* **1.** Accustomed or used. **2.** Likely. ❖ *n.* Customary practice; usage. ❖ *v.* **wont** or **wont·ed, wont·ing, wonts** —*tr.* To make accustomed to. —*intr.* To be in the habit of doing something. [ME, p. part. of *wonen,* to be used to, dwell. See WON¹.]

won't (wōnt) Contraction of *will not.*

wont·ed (wôn′tĭd, wōn′-, wŭn′-) *adj.* Accustomed; usual. —**wont′ed·ly** *adv.*

won ton or **won·ton** (wŏn′tŏn′) *n.* A noodle-dough dumpling filled typically with spiced minced pork or other ground meat. [Chin. (Cantonese) *wān t'ān,* equivalent to Chin. (Mandarin) *húntun.*]

woo (wŏo) *v.* **wooed, woo·ing, woos** —*tr.* **1.** To seek the affection of with romantic intentions. **2a.** To seek to achieve; try to gain. **b.** To tempt or invite. **3.** To entreat, solicit, or importune. —*intr.* To court a woman. [ME *wowen* < OE *wōgian.*] —**woo′er** *n.*

wood¹ (wŏod) *n.* **1a.** The secondary xylem of trees and shrubs, lying beneath the bark and consisting largely of cellulose and lignin. **b.** This tissue, often cut and dried esp. for use as building material and fuel. **2a.** A dense growth of trees. Often used in the plural. **b.** A forest. Often used in the plural. **3.** An object made of wood, esp. a woodwind. **4.** *Sports* A golf club used to hit long shots, having a bulbous head made of wood, metal, or graphite, and numbered one to five in order of increasing loft. ❖ *v.* **wood·ed, wood·ing, woods** —*tr.* **1.** To fuel with wood. **2.** To cover with trees; forest. —*intr.* To gather or be supplied with wood. ❖ *adj.* **1.** Made of or consisting of wood; wooden. **2.** Used or suitable for cutting, storing, or working with wood. **3. woods** Living, growing, or present in forests. —*idiom:* **out of the woods** *Informal* Free of a difficult or hazardous situation; safe or secure. [ME *wode* < OE *wudu.*]

wood² (wŏod) *adj. Archaic* Mentally unbalanced; insane. [ME < OE *wōd.* See **wet-¹** in App.]

Wood, Grant 1892–1942. Amer. artist whose paintings include *American Gothic* (1930).

Wood, Leonard 1860–1927. Amer. military leader who was governor-general of the Philippines (1921–27).

wood alcohol *n.* See **methanol**.

wombat
common wombat
Vombatus ursinus

wood anemone
Anemone quinquefolia

woodpecker
male red-bellied
woodpecker
Melanerpes carolinus

wood anemone *n.* Either of two plants, *Anemone quinquefolia* of eastern North America or *A. nemorosa* of Eurasia, with deeply divided leaves and a solitary white to crimson flower.

wood betony *n.* See **lousewort**.

wood·bin (wŏŏd′bĭn′) *n.* A box for holding firewood.

wood·bine (wŏŏd′bīn′) *n.* **1.** Any of various climbing vines, esp. a Mediterranean honeysuckle (*Lonicera periclymenum*) having yellowish flowers. **2.** See **Virginia creeper**. [ME *wodebinde* < OE *wudubinde* : *wudu*, wood + *binde*, wreath (< *bindan*, to bind; see **bhendh-** in App.).]

wood·block (wŏŏd′blŏk′) *n.* **1.** See **woodcut**. **2.** also **wood block** *Music* A hollow block of wood struck with a drumstick to produce percussive effects in an orchestra.

wood·bor·er (wŏŏd′bôr′ər, -bōr′ər) *n.* Any of various insects, insect larvae, or mollusks that bore into wood. —**wood′bor′ing** *adj.*

Wood·bridge (wŏŏd′brĭj′) A city of NE NJ SSW of Elizabeth; settled in 1665. Pop. 97,203.

wood·carv·ing (wŏŏd′kär′vĭng) *n.* **1.** The art or process of creating or decorating objects of wood by carving with a sharp hand-held tool. **2.** A carved wood object. —**wood′carv′er** *n.*

wood·chat (wŏŏd′chăt′) *n.* An Old World shrike (*Lanius senator*) having black and white plumage with a reddish crown.

wood·chip·per (wŏŏd′chĭp′ər) *n.* A power-driven machine for cutting wood into chips.

wood·chuck (wŏŏd′chŭk′) *n.* A common burrowing rodent (*Marmota monax*) of northern and eastern North America having a short-legged, heavy-set body and grizzled brownish fur. [By folk ety., prob. of New England Algonquian orig.]

REGIONAL NOTE The woodchuck goes by several names in the United States. The most famous of these is *groundhog*, under which name all the legends about the animal's hibernation have accrued. In the Appalachian Mountains the woodchuck is known as a *whistle pig*.

wood coal *n.* **1.** Charcoal. **2.** Lignite.

wood·cock (wŏŏd′kŏk′) *n., pl.* **woodcock** or **-cocks** Either of two related game birds, *Scolopax rusticola* of the Old World or *Philohela minor* of North America, having brownish plumage, short legs, and a long bill.

wood·craft (wŏŏd′krăft′) *n.* **1.** Skill and experience in matters relating to the woods, as hunting or fishing. **2.** The act, process, or art of carving or fashioning objects from wood.

wood·cut (wŏŏd′kŭt′) *n.* **1.** A block of wood on which a design for printing is engraved. **2.** A print made from a woodcut.

wood·cut·ting (wŏŏd′kŭt′ĭng) *n.* **1.** The act, activity, or job of cutting wood. **2.** The art or process of making woodcuts.

wood duck *n.* A brightly colored American duck (*Aix sponsa*) that nests in hollow trees, the male of which has a large crest.

wood·ed (wŏŏd′ĭd) *adj.* Covered with trees or woods.

wood·en (wŏŏd′n) *adj.* **1.** Made or consisting of wood. **2.** Stiff and unnatural; without spirit: *a wooden smile*. **3.** Clumsy and awkward; ungainly. —**wood′en·ly** *adv.* —**wood′en·ness** *n.*

wood engraving *n.* **1a.** A block of wood on whose surface a design for printing is engraved across the end grain. **b.** A print made from a wood engraving. **2.** The art or process of making wood engravings.

wood·en·head (wŏŏd′n-hĕd′) *n.* A stupid person.

wood·en·ware (wŏŏd′n-wâr′) *n.* Articles made of wood.

Wood·hull (wŏŏd′hŭl′), **Victoria Clafin** 1838–1927. Amer. reformer who ran for the US presidency (1872).

wood ibis *n.* Any of several large, mainly white wading birds of the subfamily Mycteriinae, related to the storks.

wood·ie (wŏŏd′ē) *n.* Variant of **woody**.

wood·land (wŏŏd′lənd, -lănd′) *n.* Land having a cover of trees and shrubs. ❖ *adj.* **1.** Of, relating to, or constituting woodland. **2.** Living, growing, or present in woodland: *woodland flowers*. —**wood′land·er** (-lən-dər) *n.*

wood lot or **wood·lot** (wŏŏd′lŏt′) *n.* A usu. private area restricted to the growing of forest trees, esp. for building material or fuel.

wood louse *n.* **1.** See **pill bug**. **2.** See **sow bug**.

wood·man (wŏŏd′mən) *n.* A woodsman.

wood·note (wŏŏd′nōt′) *n.* **1.** A song or call characteristic of a woodland bird. **2.** Natural spontaneous verbal utterance.

wood nymph *n.* **1.** A nymph of the forest; a dryad. **2.** Any of several tropical hummingbirds of the genera *Thalurania* and *Cyanophaia*. **3.** Any of various butterflies of the family Satyridae, esp. *Cercyonis pegala*, having brownish wings with dark eyespots.

wood·peck·er (wŏŏd′pĕk′ər) *n.* Any of various usu. brightly colored birds of the family Picidae, having strong claws and a stiff tail for climbing trees and a chisellike bill for drilling into bark and wood.

wood pigeon *n.* A large pigeon (*Columba palumbus*) of Europe and Asia having a white band on each wing.

wood·pile (wŏŏd′pīl′) *n.* A pile of wood, esp. for fuel.

wood pulp *n.* Pulp made from wood, used esp. to make paper.

wood pussy *n. Slang* A skunk.

wood rat *n.* See **pack rat** 1.

wood·ruff (wŏŏd′rəf, -rŭf′) *n.* **1.** A perennial herb (*Galium odoratum*) of Eurasia and North Africa having small white flow-

---

ers and narrow leaves used for flavoring wine and in sachets. **2.** Any of various plants of the genus *Asperula*, having whorled leaves and small funnel-shaped flowers. [ME *woderofe* < OE *wudurofe* : *wudu*, wood + *-rofe*.]

Woods, Lake of the A lake of SW Ontario and SW Manitoba, Canada, and N MN.

woods colt *n. Chiefly Southern US* See **old-field colt**.

wood·shed (wŏŏd′shĕd′) *n.* A shed in which firewood is stored. ❖ *intr.v.* **-shed·ded, -shed·ding, -sheds** *Slang* To practice on a musical instrument.

woods·man (wŏŏdz′mən) *n.* A man who works or lives in the woods or is versed in woodcraft; a forester.

wood sorrel *n.* See **oxalis**.

wood spirits *pl.n.* (*used with a sing. or pl. verb*) See **methanol**.

wood sugar *n.* See **xylose**.

woods·y (wŏŏd′zē) *adj.* **-i·er, -i·est** Of, relating to, characteristic of, or suggestive of the woods.

wood tar *n.* A viscous black fluid that is a byproduct of the destructive distillation of wood and is used in pitch, preservatives, and medicines.

wood thrush *n.* A large plump thrush (*Hylocichla mustelina*) of wooded areas of eastern North America having a reddish-brown head and a spotted cream-colored breast.

wood tick *n.* Any of various ticks of the genus *Dermacentor* that live in or on wood and transmit the microorganism causing Rocky Mountain spotted fever and tularemia in humans.

wood·turn·ing (wŏŏd′tûr′nĭng) *n.* The art or process of shaping wood into forms on a lathe. —**wood′turn′er** *n.*

wood vinegar *n.* See **pyroligneous acid**.

wood warbler *n.* See **warbler** 1.

Wood·ward (wŏŏd′wərd), **Robert Burns** 1917–79. Amer. chemist who won a 1965 Nobel Prize.

wood·wax·en (wŏŏd′wăk′sən) *n.* See **dyer's greenweed**. [ME *wodewaxen* < OE *wuduweaxe* : *wudu*, wood + *weaxan*, to grow; see WAX².]

wood·wind (wŏŏd′wĭnd′) *n.* **1.** A wind instrument in which sound is produced by the vibration of reeds in the mouthpiece, as a clarinet or oboe, or by the passing of air across the mouthpiece, as a flute. **2. woodwinds a.** The section of a band or orchestra composed of woodwinds. **b.** Woodwind instruments or their players considered as a group.

wood·work (wŏŏd′wûrk′) *n.* Objects made of or work done in wood, esp. wooden interior fittings in a house, as moldings, doors, staircases, or windowsills. —**idiom: out of the woodwork** Out of obscurity or a place of seclusion.

wood·work·ing (wŏŏd′wûr′kĭng) *n.* The act, art, or trade of working with wood. —**wood′work′er** *n.*

wood·y (wŏŏd′ē) *adj.* **-i·er, -i·est** **1.** Forming or consisting of wood; ligneous. **2.** Marked by the presence of wood or xylem: *woody plants*. **3.** Characteristic or suggestive of wood. **4.** Abounding in trees; wooded. ❖ *n.* also **wood·ie** (wŏŏd′ē) *pl.* **wood·ies** **1.** A station wagon with exterior wood paneling. **2.** *Vulgar Slang* An erection of the penis. —**wood′y·ness** *n.*

woof¹ (wŏŏf, wŏŏf) *n.* **1.** The threads that run crosswise in a woven fabric, at right angles to the warp threads. **2.** The texture of a fabric. [Alteration (influenced by WARP) of ME *oof* < OE *ōwef* : *ō-, on-*, on; see ON + *wefan*, to weave; see **webh-** in App.]

woof² (wŏŏf) *n.* **1.** The characteristically deep gruff bark of a dog. **2.** A sound similar to a woof. ❖ *intr.v.* **woofed, woof·ing, woofs** To make this sound. [Imit.]

woof·er (wŏŏf′ər) *n.* A loudspeaker designed to reproduce bass frequencies. [< WOOF².]

wool (wŏŏl) *n.* **1a.** The dense, soft, often curly hair forming the coat of sheep and certain other mammals, consisting of cylindrical fibers of keratin covered by minute overlapping scales and used as a textile fabric. **b.** A material or garment of wool. **2.** The furry hair of some insect larvae. **3.** A filamentous or fibrous covering or substance suggestive of the texture of true wool. [ME *wolle* < OE *wull*.] —**wool** *adj.*

wool·en also **wool·len** (wŏŏl′ən) *adj.* **1.** Made or consisting of wool. **2.** Of or relating to the production or marketing of woolen goods. ❖ *n.* Fabric or clothing made from wool. Often used in the plural.

Woolf (wŏŏlf), **(Adeline) Virginia (Stephen)** 1882–1941. British writer whose works include *To the Lighthouse* (1927) and *A Room of One's Own* (1929).

wool fat *n.* **1.** See **wool grease**. **2.** See **lanolin**.

wool·gath·er (wŏŏl′găth′ər) *intr.v.* **-ered, -er·ing, -ers** To engage in fanciful daydreaming. —**wool′gath′er·er** *n.*

wool grease *n.* A fatty, pale yellow wax that coats the fibers of sheep's wool and yields lanolin.

wool·grow·er (wŏŏl′grō′ər) *n.* One that raises sheep or other animals for the production of wool. —**wool′grow′ing** *n.*

wool·ly also **wool·y** (wŏŏl′ē) *adj.* **-li·er, -li·est** also **-i·er, -i·est** **1a.** Of, relating to, or covered with wool. **b.** Resembling wool. **2a.** Lacking sharp detail or clarity. **b.** Mentally or intellectually disorganized or unclear. **3.** Having the characteristics of the rough, generally lawless atmosphere of the American frontier. ❖ *n., pl.* **-lies** also **-ies 1.** A garment made of wool, esp. a knitted undergarment. **2.** *Australian* A sheep. —**wool′li·ness** *n.*

woolly bear *n.* The hairy caterpillar of any of various moths, esp.

wood tick
American dog tick
Dermacentor variabilis

Virginia Woolf

woolly bear
Isia isabella

ă	pat	oi boy
ā	pay	ou out
âr	care	ŏŏ took
ä	father	ōō boot
ĕ	pet	ŭ cut
ē	be	ûr urge
ĭ	pit	th thin
ī	pie	th this
îr	pier	hw which
ŏ	pot	zh vision
ō	toe	ə about,
ô	paw	item

Stress marks:
′ (primary);
′ (secondary), as in
lexicon (lĕk′sĭ-kŏn′)

that of the North American tiger moth *Isia isabella.*

wool·ly-head·ed (wŏŏl′ē-hĕd′ĭd) *adj.* **1.** Having hair that looks or feels like wool. **2.** Vague or muddled.

woolly mammoth *n.* A Pleistocene mammoth (*Mammuthus primigenius*) once widespread in the cold regions of the Northern Hemisphere.

wool·sack (wŏŏl′săk′) *n.* **1.** A sack for wool. **2.** The official seat of the Lord Chancellor in the House of Lords.

wool shed *n.* A building or buildings in which sheep are sheared and wool is prepared for shipment to market.

wool·skin (wŏŏl′skĭn′) *n.* A sheepskin with the wool attached.

wool-sort·er's disease (wŏŏl′sôr′tərz) *n.* A pulmonary form of anthrax that results from the inhalation of spores of the bacterium *Bacillus anthracis,* found in the wool of contaminated sheep.

wool-sta·pler (wŏŏl′stā′plər) *n.* **1.** A dealer in wool. **2.** One who sorts wool by the quality of the staple or fiber. —**wool′-sta′pling** *adj. & n.*

Wool·worth (wŏŏl′wûrth′), **Frank Winfield** 1852–1919. Amer. merchant who built a successful national chain of five-and-tens after 1879.

woom·er·a (wŏŏm′ər-ə) also **wom·er·a** (wŏm′-) *n.* A hooked wooden stick used by Aboriginal peoples of Australia for hurling a spear or dart. [Dharuk *wamara.*]

woops (wŏŏps, wŏŏps) *interj.* Variant of **whoops.**

wooz·y (wŏŏ′zē, wŏŏz′ē) *adj.* **-i·er, -i·est 1.** Dazed or confused. **2.** Dizzy or queasy. [Poss. < alteration of *boozy,* drunken < BOOZE.] —**wooz′i·ly** *adv.* —**wooz′i·ness** *n.*

wop (wŏp) *n. Offensive Slang* Used as a disparaging term for a person of Italian birth or descent. [Ital. dialectal *guappo,* thug < Sp. *guapo,* handsome, dashing, braggart, bully < Fr. dialectal *wape,* rogue < Lat. *vappa,* rogue, scoundrel.]

Worces·ter[1] (wŏŏs′tər) **1.** A borough of W-central England on the Severn River SSW of Birmingham; site of Cromwell's final victory over Charles II and the Scottish army (Sep. 3, 1651). Pop. 73,900. **2.** A city of central MA W of Boston. Pop. 172,648.

Worces·ter[2] (wŏŏs′tər) A trademark used for a fine porcelain made in Worcester, England.

Worcester, Joseph Emerson 1784–1865. Amer. lexicographer noted for his *Comprehensive Pronouncing and Explanatory Dictionary of the English Language* (1830).

Worces·ter·shire (wŏŏs′tər-shîr, -shər) *n.* A piquant sauce of soy, vinegar, and spices.

word (wûrd) *n.* **1.** A sound or a combination of sounds, or its representation in writing or printing, that symbolizes and communicates a meaning and may consist of a single morpheme or of a combination of morphemes. **2.** Something said; an utterance, remark, or comment: *said a word about taxes.* **3.** *Computer Science* A set of bits constituting the smallest unit of addressable memory. **4. words** Discourse or talk; speech. **5. words** *Music* The text of a vocal composition; lyrics. **6.** An assurance or promise; sworn intention. **7a.** A command or direction; an order. **b.** A verbal signal; a password or watchword. **8a.** News. **b.** Rumor. **9. words** Hostile or angry remarks made back and forth. **10.** Used euphemistically in combination with the initial letter of a term that is considered offensive or taboo or that one does not want to utter. **11. Word a.** See **Logos** 3. **b.** The Scriptures; the Bible. ❖ *tr.v.* **word·ed, word·ing, words** To express in words. —*idioms:* **at a word** In immediate response. **good word 1.** A favorable comment. **2.** Favorable news. **have no words for** To be unable to describe or talk about. **in a word** In short; in summary. **in so many words 1.** In precisely those words; exactly. **2.** Speaking candidly and straightforwardly. **of few words** Not conversational or loquacious; laconic. **of (one's) word** Displaying personal dependability. **take at (one's) word** To be convinced of another's sincerity and act in accord with his or her statement. **upon my word** Indeed; really. [ME < OE. See **wer-**[1] in App.]

word·age (wûr′dĭj) *n.* **1.** Words considered as a group. **2.** The use of an excessive number of words; verbiage. **3.** The number of words used, as in a novel. **4.** Wording.

word association test *n. Psychology* A test in which the subject is asked to respond to a given word with the first word that comes to mind or with a certain kind of word, such as an antonym.

word blindness *n.* See **alexia.** —**word′-blind′** (wûrd′blīnd′) *adj.*

word·book (wûrd′bŏŏk′) *n.* A lexicon, vocabulary, or dictionary.

word deafness *n.* A form of aphasia in which the meaning of ordinary spoken words becomes incomprehensible.

word for word *adv.* In exactly the same words; verbatim. —**word′-for-word′** (wûrd′fər-wûrd′) *adj.*

word-hoard (wûrd′hôrd′, -hōrd′) *n.* The sum of words one uses or understands; a vocabulary. [Transl. of OE *wordhord.*]

word·ing (wûr′dĭng) *n.* The act or style of expressing in words.

word·less (wûrd′lĭs) *adj.* **1.** Not expressed in words; unspoken: *wordless animosity.* **2.** Inarticulate; silent: *wordless spectators.* —**word′less·ly** *adv.* —**word′less·ness** *n.*

word·mon·ger (wûrd′mŭng′gər, -mŏng′-) *n.* A writer or speaker who uses language pretentiously or carelessly.

word of mouth *n.* Spoken communication. —**word′-of-mouth′** (wûrd′əv-mouth′) *adj.*

word order *n.* The syntactic arrangement of words in a sentence, clause, or phrase.

word·play (wûrd′plā′) *n.* **1.** Witty or clever verbal exchange; repartee. **2.** The act or an instance such exchange.

word proc·ess·ing (prŏs′ĕs′ĭng, prō′sĕs′-) *n.* The creation, editing, and production of documents and texts using a computer. —**word′-proc′ess** (wûrd′prŏs′ĕs, -prō′sĕs) *v.*

word processor *n.* **1.** A computer or computer program that is designed primarily for word processing. **2.** One who uses a word processor.

word·smith (wûrd′smĭth′) *n.* **1.** A fluent and prolific writer, esp. one who writes professionally. **2.** An expert on words.

word square *n. Games* A set of words arranged in a square such that they read the same horizontally and vertically.

Words·worth (wûrdz′wûrth′), **William** 1770–1850. British poet whose most important collection, *Lyrical Ballads* (1798), published jointly with Samuel Taylor Coleridge, helped establish romanticism in England. —**Words·worth′i·an** *adj.*

word·y (wûr′dē) *adj.* **-i·er, -i·est 1.** Relating to or consisting of words; verbal. **2.** Tending to use, using, or expressed in more words than are necessary to convey meaning. —**word′i·ly** *adv.* —**word′i·ness** *n.*

wore (wôr, wōr) *v.* Past tense of **wear.**

work (wûrk) *n.* **1.** Physical or mental effort or activity directed toward the production or accomplishment of something. **2a.** A job; employment. **b.** A trade, profession, or other means of livelihood. **3a.** Something that one is doing, making, or performing, esp. as an occupation or undertaking; a duty or task. **b.** An amount of such activity either done or required. **4a.** The part of a day devoted to an occupation or undertaking. **b.** One's place of employment. **5a.** Something produced or accomplished through the effort, activity, or agency of a person or thing. **b.** Full action or effect of an agency. **c.** An act; a deed. **6a.** An artistic creation, such as a painting or musical composition; a work of art. **b. works** The output of a writer, artist, or musician considered or collected as a whole. **7a. works** Engineering structures, such as bridges or dams. **b.** A fortified structure, such as a trench or fortress. **8a.** Needlework, weaving, lacemaking, or a similar textile art. **b.** A piece of such textile art. **9.** A material or piece of material being processed in a machine during manufacture. **10. works** (*used with a sing. or pl. verb*) A factory or similar building or complex of buildings where a specific type of business or industry is carried on. Often used in combination: *a steelworks.* **11. works** Internal mechanism. **12.** The manner, style, or quality of working or treatment; workmanship. **13.** *Physics* The transfer of energy from one physical system to another, esp. the transfer of energy to a body by the application of a force that moves the body in the direction of the force. **14. works** *Theology* Moral or righteous acts or deeds. **15. works a.** *Informal* The full range of possibilities; everything. Used with *the: a pizza with the works.* **b.** *Slang* A thorough beating or other severe treatment. Used with *the.* ❖ *adj.* Of, relating to, designed for, or engaged in work. ❖ *v.* **worked** also **wrought** (rôt), **work·ing, works** —*intr.* **1.** To exert oneself physically or mentally to do, make, or accomplish something. **2.** To be employed; have a job. **3a.** To function; operate: *How does this latch work?* **b.** To function or operate in the desired or required way: *My watch hasn't worked since I dropped it.* **4a.** To have a given effect or outcome. **b.** To have the desired effect or outcome; prove successful. **5.** To exert an influence. Used with *on* or *upon.* **6.** To arrive at a specified condition through gradual or repeated movement: *The stitches worked loose.* **7.** To proceed or progress slowly and laboriously. **8.** To move in an agitated manner, as with emotion: *Her mouth worked with fear.* **9.** To behave in a specified way when handled or processed: *Not all metals work easily.* **10.** To ferment. **11.** *Nautical* **a.** To strain in heavy seas so that the joints give slightly and the fastenings become slack. Used of a boat or ship. **b.** To sail against the wind. **12.** To undergo small motions that result in friction and wear: *The gears work against each other.* —*tr.* **1.** To cause or effect; bring about. **2.** To cause to operate or function; actuate, use, or manage: *worked the controls.* **3.** To shape or forge. **4.** To make or decorate by needlework. **5.** To solve (a problem) by calculation and reasoning. **6.** To knead, stir, or otherwise manipulate in preparation. **7.** To bring to a specified condition by gradual or repeated effort. **8.** To make, achieve, or pay for by work or effort: *worked her way to the top.* **9.** *Informal* To arrange or contrive. Often used with *it.* **10.** To make productive; cultivate: *work a farm.* **11.** To cause to work: *works his laborers hard.* **12.** To excite or provoke: *worked the mob into a frenzy.* **13.** *Informal* **a.** To gratify, cajole, or enchant artfully, esp. for influencing: *The politician worked the crowd.* **b.** To use or manipulate to one's own advantage; exploit. **14.** To carry on an operation or function in or through. **15.** To ferment (liquor, for example). —*phrasal verbs:* **work in 1.** To insert or introduce. **2.** To make an opening for, as in a schedule. **3.** To cause to be inserted by repeated or continuous effort. **work into 1.** To insert or introduce into. **2.** To make an opening for (someone or something) in. **3.** To cause to be inserted in by repeated or continuous effort. **work off** To get rid of by work or effort. **work out 1.** To accomplish by work or effort. **2.** To find a solution for; solve. **3.** To formulate or develop. **4.** To discharge (an obligation or debt) with labor in place of money. **5.** To prove successful, ef-

William Wordsworth
19th-century engraving

fective, or satisfactory: *The new strategy may not work out.* **6.** To have a specified result. **7.** To engage in strenuous exercise for physical conditioning. **8.** To exhaust (a mine, for example). **work over 1.** To do for a second time; rework. **2.** *Slang* To inflict severe physical damage on; beat up. **work up 1.** To arouse the emotions of; excite. **2a.** To increase one's skill, responsibility, efficiency, or status through work. **b.** To intensify gradually. **3.** To develop or produce by mental or physical effort. —*idioms:* **at work 1.** Engaged in labor; working. **2.** In operation. **in the works** In preparation; under development. **out of work** Without a job; unemployed. **put in work** To perform labor or duties, as on a specified project. **work both sides of the street** To engage in double-dealing; be duplicitous. **work like a charm** To function very well or have a very good effect or outcome. **work (one's) fingers to the bone** To labor extremely hard; toil or travail. [ME < OE *weorc.* See **werg-** in App.]

work·a·ble (wûr′kə-bəl) *adj.* **1.** Capable of being worked, dealt with, or handled. **2.** Capable of being put into effective operation; practicable or feasible. —**work′a·bil′i·ty, work′a·ble·ness** *n.* —**work′a·bly** *adv.*

work·a·day (wûr′kə-dā′) *adj.* **1.** Relating to or suited for working days; everyday. **2.** Mundane; commonplace. [< ME *werkeday,* workday : *werke* (alteration of *work;* see WORK) + *day,* day; see DAY.]

work·a·hol·ic (wûr′kə-hô′lĭk, -hŏl′ĭk) *n.* One who compulsively needs to work. —**work′a·hol′ism** *n.*

work·bag (wûrk′băg′) *n.* A bag to hold implements needed for work or material, such as needlework, that one is working on.

work·bench (wûrk′bĕnch′) *n.* A sturdy table or bench at which manual work is done, as by a machinist or a jeweler.

work·book (wûrk′bŏŏk′) *n.* **1.** A booklet containing problems and exercises with space included for written answers. **2.** A manual containing operating instructions, as for an appliance or machine. **3.** A book in which a record is kept of work proposed or accomplished.

work camp *n.* **1.** See **prison camp** 3. **2.** A camp where volunteers work together on community service projects.

work·day (wûrk′dā′) *n.* **1.** A day on which work is usu. done. **2.** The part of the day during which one works: *an eight-hour work-day.* ❖ *adj.* Workaday.

work·er (wûr′kər) *n.* **1a.** One who works at a particular occupation or activity. **b.** One who does manual or industrial labor. **2.** A member of the working class. **3.** A member of a colony of social insects such as ants, usu. a sterile female, that performs specialized work such as building the nest.

work·ers' compensation (wûr′kərz) *n.* Payments required by law to be made to an employee who is injured or disabled in connection with work.

work ethic *n.* A set of values based on the moral virtues of hard work and diligence.

work·fare (wûrk′fâr′) *n.* A form of welfare in which capable adults are required to perform work, often in public-service jobs, as a condition of receiving aid. [WORK + (WEL)FARE.]

work farm *n.* A correctional facility that operates as a farm worked by prisoners.

work·flow (wûrk′flō′) *n.* **1.** The flow or progress of work done by a company, industry, department, or person. **2.** The rate at which such flow or progress takes place.

work·folk (wûrk′fōk′) also **work·folks** (-fōks′) *pl.n.* Laborers, esp. farm workers.

work force or **work·force** (wûrk′fôrs′, -fōrs′) *n.* **1.** The workers employed in a specific project or activity. **2.** All the people working or available to work, as in a nation or company.

work function *n.* The minimum amount of energy required to remove an electron from the surface of a metal.

work hardening *n.* The increase in strength that accompanies plastic deformation of a metal.

work·horse (wûrk′hôrs′) *n.* **1.** Something, such as a machine, that performs dependably under heavy or prolonged use. **2.** A horse used for labor rather than for racing or riding. **3.** *Informal* A person who works tirelessly.

work·house (wûrk′hous′) *n.* **1.** A prison in which limited sentences are served at manual labor. **2.** *Chiefly British* A poorhouse.

work·ing (wûr′kĭng) *adj.* **1a.** Performing work: *a working committee.* **b.** Operating or functioning as required. **2.** Having a paying job; employed. **3a.** Spent at work. **b.** Taken while continuing to work: *a working vacation.* **4a.** Sufficient to allow action: *a working majority.* **b.** Adequate for practical use. **5.** Serving as a basis or guide for further work. ❖ *n.* **1.** The manner in which something operates or functions. Often used in the plural: *the workings of the mind.* **2.** The parts of a mine or quarry that have been or are being excavated. Often used in the plural.

working capital *n.* **1.** The assets of a business that can be applied to its operation. **2.** The amount of current assets that exceeds current liabilities.

working class *n.* The socioeconomic class consisting of people who work for wages, esp. low wages, including unskilled and semiskilled laborers and their families. —**work′ing-class′** (wûr′kĭng-klăs′) *adj.*

working dog *n.* Any of various breeds of dogs developed or trained to do useful work, such as herding animals.

working girl *n.* **1.** A young woman who works. **2.** *Slang* A woman prostitute.

work·ing·man (wûr′kĭng-măn′) *n.* **1.** A man who works for wages. **2.** A man who performs heavy manual or industrial labor.

working papers *pl.n.* Legal documents certifying the right to employment of a minor or alien.

working storage *n.* The section of computer storage reserved for data to be temporarily stored while a program runs.

working substance *n.* A substance, such as a fluid, used to effect a thermodynamic or other change in a system.

work·ing·wom·an (wûr′kĭng-wŏŏm′ən) *n.* A woman who works for wages.

work in progress *n., pl.* **works in progress** A yet incomplete artistic, theatrical, or musical work, often made available for public viewing or listening.

work·load (wûrk′lōd′) *n.* **1.** The amount of work assigned to or expected from a worker in a specified time period. **2.** The amount of work that a machine produces or can produce in a specified time period.

work·man (wûrk′mən) *n.* **1.** A man who performs manual or industrial labor for wages. **2.** A craftsman or artisan.

work·man·like (wûrk′mən-līk′) *adj.* Befitting a skilled artisan or craftsperson; skillfully done.

work·man·ship (wûrk′mən-shĭp′) *n.* **1.** The skill of a craftsperson or artisan. **2.** The quality of something made, as by an artisan. **3.** Something made or produced by a workman. **4.** The product of effort or endeavor.

work·men's compensation (wûrk′mənz) *n.* Workers' compensation.

work of art *n., pl.* **works of art 1.** A product of the fine arts, esp. a painting or sculpture. **2.** Something likened to a fine artistic work, as by a measure of beauty or craft.

work·out (wûrk′out′) *n.* **1.** A session of exercise or practice to improve fitness, as for athletic competition. **2.** A strenuous test of ability and endurance.

work·peo·ple (wûrk′pē′pəl) *n. Chiefly British* Those who work for wages; workers.

work·place (wûrk′plās′) *n.* **1.** A place where people are employed. **2.** The work setting in general.

work release *n.* A correctional program under which prisoners are permitted employment outside a prison while serving their sentences. —**work′-re·lease′** (wûrk′rĭ-lēs′) *adj.*

work·room (wûrk′rŏŏm′, -rŏŏm′) *n.* A room for work.

work sheet or **work·sheet** (wûrk′shēt′) *n.* **1.** A sheet of paper on which work records are kept. **2.** A sheet of paper on which preliminary notes or computations are set down.

work·shop (wûrk′shŏp′) *n.* **1.** A room, area, or small establishment where manual or light industrial work is done. **2.** An educational seminar or series of meetings, usu. for a small group, emphasizing interaction.

work song *n.* A song sung to accompany work, typically having a steady rhythm.

work·space (wûrk′spās′) *n.* An area for one's work.

work·sta·tion (wûrk′stā′shən) *n.* An area, as in an office, outfitted with equipment and furnishings for one worker and usu. including a computer.

work stoppage *n.* A cessation of work by a group of employees as a means of protest.

work-stud·y (wûrk′stŭd′ē) *adj.* Of, relating to, or being an academic program that enables students to gain work experience and make money while continuing their studies.

work·ta·ble (wûrk′tā′bəl) *n.* A table designed for a specific kind of task or activity, such as needlework.

work to rule *n.* A job action in which employees do no more than the minimum required by the rules of a workplace in order to cause a slowdown. —**work′-to-rule′** (wûrk′-tə-rŏŏl′) *adj.*

work·up (wûrk′ŭp′) *n.* A thorough medical examination for diagnostic purposes.

work·week (wûrk′wēk′) *n.* The hours or days worked in a week: *a four-day workweek.*

work·wom·an (wûrk′wŏŏm′ən) *n.* A woman who performs manual or industrial labor for wages.

world (wûrld) *n.* **1.** The earth. **2.** The universe. **3.** The earth with its inhabitants. **4.** The inhabitants of the earth; the human race. **5a.** Humankind considered as social beings; human society. **b.** People as a whole; the public. **6.** often **World** A specified part of the earth. **7.** A part of the earth and its inhabitants as known at a given period in history: *the ancient world.* **8.** A realm or domain: *the animal world.* **9a.** A sphere of human activity or interest. **b.** A class or group of people with common characteristics or pursuits. **10.** A particular way of life. **11.** All that relates to or affects the life of a person: *He saw his world collapse.* **12.** Secular life and its concerns. **13a.** Human existence; life: *brought a child into the world.* **b.** A state of existence: *the next world.* **14.** A large amount; much. Often used in the plural: *worlds of good.* **15.** A celestial body such as a planet. ❖ *adj.* **1.** Of or relating to the world: *a world champion.* **2.** Involving or extending throughout the entire world. —*idioms:* **for all the world** In all respects; precisely. **in the world** Used as an intensive: *How in the world did they manage?* **out of this world** *Informal* Extraordinary; superb. **the world over** Throughout the world. **world without end** Forever.

ă pat	oi boy
ā pay	ou out
âr care	ŏŏ took
ä father	ŏŏ boot
ĕ pet	ŭ cut
ē be	ûr urge
ĭ pit	th thin
ī pie	th this
îr pier	hw which
ŏ pot	zh vision
ō toe	ə about,
ô paw	item

Stress marks:
′ (primary);
′ (secondary), as in
lexicon (lĕk′sĭ-kŏn′)

[ME < OE *weorold*. See **wī-ro-** in App.]
world·beat (wûrld′bēt′) *n.* World music.

world-class (wûrld′klăs′) *adj.* Ranking among the foremost in the world; of an international standard of excellence; of the highest order: *a world-class figure skater.*

World Cup *n.* A soccer tournament held every four years in which qualifying national teams compete to determine a world champion.

world line *n.* The path in space-time traveled by an elementary particle for the time and distance that it retains its identity.

world·ling (wûrld′lĭng) *n.* One who is absorbed by worldly pursuits and pleasures.

world·ly (wûrld′lē) *adj.* **-li·er, -li·est 1.** Of, relating to, or devoted to the temporal world; earthly. **2.** Experienced in human affairs; sophisticated or worldly-wise. —**world′li·ness** *n.* —**world′ly** *adv.*

world·ly-mind·ed (wûrld′lē-mīn′dĭd) *adj.* Absorbed in the affairs of this world. —**world′ly-mind′ed·ness** *n.*

world·ly-wise (wûrld′lē-wīz′) *adj.* Experienced in the ways of the world.

world music *n.* Music from cultures other than those of Western Europe and English-speaking North America, esp. popular music from Latin America, Africa, and Asia.

World Series *n.* A series of baseball games played each fall between the winning teams of the American League and the National League for the major-league championship.

world's fair (wûrldz) *n.* A large exposition featuring exhibits, of arts and crafts, scientific discoveries, and industrial products, provided by countries from around the world.

world soul *n.* A spiritual principle having the same relation to the physical world as the human soul does to the body; the animating force of the world.

world·view (wûrld′vyōo′) *n.* **1.** The overall perspective from which one sees and interprets the world. **2.** A collection of beliefs about life and the universe held by an individual or group. [Transl. of Ger. *Weltanschauung* : *Welt*, world + *Anschauung*, view.]

World War I *n.* A war fought from 1914 to 1918, in which Great Britain, France, Russia, Belgium, Italy, Japan, the United States, and other allies defeated Germany, Austria-Hungary, Turkey, and Bulgaria.

World War II *n.* A war fought from 1939 to 1945, in which Great Britain, France, the Soviet Union, the United States, China, and other allies defeated Germany, Italy, and Japan.

world-wea·ry (wûrld′wîr′ē) *adj.* **-ri·er, -ri·est** Tired of the world; bored with life. —**world′-wea′ri·ness** *n.*

world·wide (wûrld′wīd′) *adj.* Involving or extending throughout the entire world; universal. —**world′wide′** *adv.*

World Wide Web *n.* The complete set of documents residing on all Internet servers that use the HTTP protocol, accessible to users via a simple point-and-click system.

worm (wûrm) *n.* **1.** Any of various invertebrates, as those of the phyla Annelida, Nematoda, Nemertea, or Platyhelminthes, having a long flexible rounded or flattened body, often without obvious appendages. **2.** Any of various crawling insect larvae, such as a grub or a caterpillar, having a soft elongated body. **3.** Any of various unrelated animals, such as the shipworm, resembling a worm in habit or appearance. **4a.** Something, such as the thread of a screw, that resembles a worm in form or appearance. **b.** The spirally threaded shaft of a worm gear. **5.** An insidiously tormenting or devouring force. **6.** A person regarded as pitiable or contemptible. **7.** **worms** *Pathology* Infestation of the intestines or other parts of the body with worms or wormlike parasites; helminthiasis. **8.** *Computer Science* A malicious program that replicates itself until it fills all of the storage space on a drive or network. ❖ *v.* **wormed, worm·ing, worms** —*tr.* **1.** To make (one's way) with or as if with the sinuous crawling motion of a worm. **2.** To work (one's way or oneself) subtly or gradually; insinuate. **3.** To elicit by artful or devious means. Usually used with *out of*. **4.** To cure of intestinal worms. **5.** *Nautical* To wrap yarn or twine spirally around (rope). —*intr.* **1.** To move in a manner suggestive of a worm. **2.** To make one's way by artful or devious means. [ME < OE *wurm*, var. of *wyrm*. See **wer-²** in App.]

worm-eat·en (wûrm′ēt′n) *adj.* **1.** Bored through or gnawed by worms. **2.** Decayed; rotten. **3.** Antiquated; decrepit.

worm fence *n.* A fence of crossed rails supporting one another and forming a zigzag pattern.

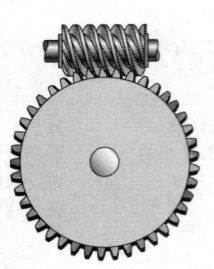

worm gear
worm gear assembly

worm gear *n.* **1.** A gear consisting of a spirally threaded shaft and a wheel with marginal teeth that mesh into it. **2.** The toothed wheel of this gear; a worm wheel.

worm·hole (wûrm′hōl′) *n.* **1.** A hole made by a worm. **2.** *Physics* A theoretical distortion of space-time in a region of the universe that would link one location or time with another through a path that is shorter in distance or duration than would otherwise be expected.

Worms (wûrmz, vôrms) A city of SW Germany on the Rhine R. NNW of Mannheim; site of the Diet of Worms (1521) in which Martin Luther refused to recant his beliefs and was outlawed by the Roman Catholic Church. Pop. 72,610.

worm·seed (wûrm′sēd′) *n.* **1.** A tropical American plant (*Chenopodium ambrosioides*) yielding an oil used as an anthelmintic.

2. Any of several other plants used thus.

worm's-eye view (wûrmz′ī′) *n.* A view from below or from an inferior position.

worm snake *n.* A small harmless burrowing snake (*Carphophis amoena*) of the central and eastern United States, usu. living under stones or logs and feeding chiefly on earthworms.

worm wheel *n.* The toothed wheel of a worm gear.

worm·wood (wûrm′wood′) *n.* **1.** Any of several aromatic plants of the genus *Artemisia*, esp. *A. absinthium* of Europe, yielding a bitter extract used in making absinthe and in flavoring certain wines. **2.** Something harsh or embittering. [ME, alteration of *wermod* < OE *wermōd*.]

worm·y (wûr′mē) *adj.* **-i·er, -i·est 1.** Infested with or damaged by worms. **2.** Suggestive of a worm. —**worm′i·ness** *n.*

worn (wôrn, wōrn) *v.* Past participle of **wear.** ❖ *adj.* **1.** Affected by wear or use. **2.** Impaired or damaged by wear or use. **3.** Showing the wearing effects of overwork, care, worry, or suffering. [ME, p. part. of *weren*, to wear. See **WEAR.**]

worn-out (wôrn′out′, wōrn′-) *adj.* **1.** Worn or used until no longer usable or effective. **2.** Thoroughly exhausted; spent.

wor·ri·ment (wûr′ē-mənt, wŭr′-) *n.* **1.** The act or an instance of worrying. **2.** A source of anxiety; a worry.

wor·ri·some (wûr′ē-səm, wŭr′-) *adj.* **1.** Causing worry or anxiety. **2.** Tending to worry. —**wor′ri·some·ly** *adv.*

wor·ry (wûr′ē, wŭr′ē) *v.* **wor·ried, wor·ry·ing, wor·ries** —*intr.* **1.** To feel uneasy or concerned about something; be troubled. See Syns at **brood. 2.** To pull or tear at something with or as if with the teeth. **3.** To proceed doggedly in the face of difficulty or hardship; struggle. —*tr.* **1.** To cause to feel anxious, distressed, or troubled. See Syns at **trouble. 2.** To bother or annoy, as with petty complaints. **3a.** To seize with the teeth and shake or tug at repeatedly. **b.** To attack roughly and repeatedly; harass. **c.** To touch, move, or handle idly; toy with. ❖ *n.*, *pl.* **-ries 1.** The act of worrying or the condition of being worried; persistent mental uneasiness. See Syns at **anxiety. 2.** A source of nagging concern or uneasiness. —*idiom:* **not to worry** *Informal* There is nothing to worry about. [ME *werien, worien*, to strangle < OE *wyrgan*. See **wer-²** in App.] —**wor′ri·er** *n.*

worry beads *pl.n.* A string of beads for fingering in times of worry, boredom, or tension.

wor·ry·wart (wûr′ē-wôrt′, wŭr′-) *n.* One who worries excessively and needlessly.

worse (wûrs) *adj.* Comparative of **bad¹, ill. 1.** More inferior, as in quality, condition, or effect. **2.** More severe or unfavorable. **3.** Being further from a standard; less desirable or satisfactory. **4.** Being in poorer health; more ill. ❖ *n.* Something that is worse. ❖ *adv.* Comparative of **badly, ill.** In a worse manner; to a worse degree. —*idiom:* **for better or (for) worse** Whether the situation or consequences are good or ill. [ME < OE *wyrsa*.]

wors·en (wûr′sən) *tr. & intr.v.* **-ened, -en·ing, -ens** To make or become worse.

wors·er (wûr′sər) *adv. & adj.* Nonstandard Worse.

wor·ship (wûr′shĭp) *n.* **1a.** The reverent love and devotion accorded a deity, an idol, or a sacred object. **b.** The ceremonies, prayers, or other religious forms by which this love is expressed. **2.** Ardent devotion; adoration. **3.** often **Worship** *Chiefly British* Used as a form of address for magistrates, mayors, and certain other dignitaries: *Your Worship.* ❖ *v.* **-shiped, -ship·ing, -ships** or **-shipped, -ship·ping, -ships** —*tr.* **1.** To honor and love as a deity. **2.** To regard with ardent or adoring esteem or devotion. See Syns at **revere¹.** —*intr.* **1.** To participate in religious rites of worship. **2.** To perform an act of worship. [ME *worshipe*, worthiness, honor < OE *weorthscipe* : *weorth*, worth; see **WORTH¹** + *-scipe*, -ship.] —**wor′ship·er, wor′ship·per** *n.*

wor·ship·ful (wûr′shĭp-fəl) *adj.* **1.** Given to or expressive of worship; reverent or adoring. **2.** *Chiefly British* Used as a respectful form of address. —**wor′ship·ful·ly** *adv.* —**wor′ship·ful·ness** *n.*

worst (wûrst) *adj.* Superlative of **bad¹, ill. 1.** Most inferior, as in quality, condition, or effect. **2.** Most severe or unfavorable. **3.** Being furthest from an ideal or a standard; least desirable or satisfactory. ❖ *adv.* Superlative of **badly, ill.** In the worst manner or degree. ❖ *tr.v.* **worst·ed, worst·ing, worsts** To gain the advantage over; defeat. ❖ *n.* Something that is worst. —*idioms:* **at (the) worst** Under the most negative circumstances, estimation, or interpretation. **get (or have) the worst of it** To suffer a defeat or disadvantage. **if (the) worst comes to (the) worst** If the very worst thing happens. **in the worst way** *Informal* Very much; a great deal. [ME < OE *wyrsta*.]

worst-case (wûrst′kās′) *adj.* Most unfavorable; being or involving the worst possibility.

wor·sted (woos′tĭd, wûr′stĭd) *n.* **1.** Firm-textured, compactly twisted woolen yarn made from long-staple fibers. **2.** Fabric made from such yarn. [ME, var. of *worthstede*, after Worthstede (Worstead) in E England.] —**wor′sted** *adj.*

wort¹ (wûrt, wôrt) *n.* A plant. Often used in combination: *liverwort; milkwort.* [ME < OE *wyrt.* See **wrād-** in App.]

wort² (wûrt, wôrt) *n.* An infusion of malt that is fermented to make beer. [ME < OE *wyrt.* See **wrād-** in App.]

worth¹ (wûrth) *n.* **1.** The quality that renders something desirable, useful, or valuable. **2.** Material or market value. **3.** A quantity of something that may be purchased for a specified sum or by a specified means: *wanted their money's worth.* **4.** Wealth; riches: *her net worth.* **5.** Quality that commands esteem or respect; merit. ❖ *adj.* **1.** Equal in value to something specified. **2.** Deserving of; meriting. **3.** Having wealth or riches amounting to. **—idioms: for all (one) is worth** To the utmost of one's powers or ability. **for what it's worth** Even though it may not be important or valuable. [ME < OE *weorth.* See **wer-²** in App.]

worth² (wûrth) *intr.v.* **worthed, worth·ing, worths** *Archaic* To befall; betide. [ME *worthen* < OE *weorthan.* See **wer-²** in App.]

worth·less (wûrth′lĭs) *adj.* **1.** Lacking worth; of no use or value. **2.** Low; despicable. **—worth′less·ly** *adv.* **—worth′less·ness** *n.*

worth·while (wûrth′hwīl′, -wīl′) *adj.* Sufficiently valuable or important to be worth one's time, effort, or interest. **—worth′-while′ness** *n.*

wor·thy (wûr′thē) *adj.* **-thi·er, -thi·est 1.** Having worth, merit, or value; useful or valuable. **2.** Honorable; admirable: *a worthy fellow.* **3.** Having sufficient worth; deserving: *worthy of acclaim.* ❖ *n., pl.* **-thies** An eminent or distinguished person. **—wor′thi·ly** *adv.* **—wor′thi·ness** *n.*

-worthy *suff.* **1.** Of sufficient worth for: *creditworthy.* **2.** Suitable or safe for: *crashworthy.* [< WORTHY.]

wot (wŏt) *v. Archaic* First and third person singular present tense of **wit².** [ME *wat* < OE *wāt.* See **weid-** in App.]

Wo·tan (vō′tän′) *n. Mythology* A German god identified with Odin. [Ger. < OHGer. *Wuotan.* See **wet-¹** in App.]

Wouk (wōk), **Herman** b. 1915. Amer. writer whose novels include *The Caine Mutiny* (1951).

would (wŏŏd) *aux.v.* Past tense of **will².** **1.** Used to express desire or intent: *She said she would meet us at the corner.* **2.** Used to express a wish: *Would that we had gone with you!* **3.** Used after a statement of desire, request, or advice: *I wish you would stay.* **4.** Used to make a polite request: *Would you go with me?* **5.** Used in the main clause of a conditional statement to express a possibility or likelihood: *If I had enough money, I would buy a car.* See Usage Note at **if.** **6.** Used to express presumption or expectation: *That would be Steve at the door.* **7.** Used to indicate uncertainty: *He would seem to be getting better.* **8.** Used to express repeated or habitual action in the past: *Every day we would walk in the garden.*

would-be (wŏŏd′bē′) *adj.* Desiring, attempting, or professing to be: *a would-be pilot.*

would·n't (wŏŏd′nt) Contraction of *would not.*

wouldst (wŏŏdst) or **would·est** (wŏŏd′ĭst) *v. Archaic* Second person singular past tense of **will².**

wound¹ (wŏŏnd) *n.* **1.** An injury, esp. one in which the skin or another external surface is torn, pierced, cut, or otherwise broken. **2.** An injury to the feelings. ❖ *v.* **wound·ed, wound·ing, wounds** *—tr.* To inflict wounds or a wound on. *—intr.* To inflict wounds or a wound. [ME < OE *wund.*] **—wound′ed·ly** *adv.* **—wound′ing·ly** *adv.*

wound² (wound) *v.* Past tense and past participle of **wind².**

wound³ (wound) *v. Music* A past tense and a past participle of **wind³.**

Wound·ed Knee (wŏŏn′dĭd) A creek of SW SD. Almost 200 Native Americans were massacred here by US troops on Dec. 29, 1890.

wound·wort (wŏŏnd′wûrt′, -wôrt′) *n.* **1.** See **betony** 1. **2.** Any of several plants formerly used to treat wounds.

wove (wōv) *v.* Past tense of **weave.**

wo·ven (wō′vən) *v.* Past participle of **weave.** ❖ *adj.* Made by weaving. ❖ *n.* Material or a fabric made by weaving.

wove paper *n.* Paper made on a closely woven wire roller or mold and having a faint mesh pattern. [Variant p. part. of WEAVE.]

Wo·vo·ka (wō-vō′kə) 1858?–1932. Paiute religious leader who founded the Ghost Dance movement.

wow¹ (wou) *Informal interj.* Used to express wonder, amazement, or great pleasure. ❖ *n.* An outstanding success. ❖ *tr.v.* **wowed, wow·ing, wows** To have a strong, usu. pleasurable effect on.

wow² (wou) *n.* Slow variation in the pitch of a sound reproduction resulting from variations in the speed of the recording or reproducing equipment. [Imit.]

wow·ser (wou′zər) *n. Australia & New Zealand* A person regarded as obnoxiously puritanical. [Poss. < dialectal *wow,* to howl, complain, of imit. orig.]

Woz·ni·ak (wŏz′nē-ăk′), **Stephen** b. 1950. Amer. computer engineer who cofounded Apple Computers (1975).

WP *abbr.* **1.** weather permitting **2a.** word processing **b.** word processessor

WPA *abbr.* Work Projects Administration

W particle *n.* See **W boson.**

wpm *abbr.* words per minute

wrack¹ also **rack** (răk) *n.* **1.** Destruction or ruin. **2.** A remnant or vestige of something destroyed. [ME < OE *wræc,* punishment (influenced by MDu. *wrak,* shipwreck).]

wrack² also **rack** (răk) *n.* **1a.** Wreckage, esp. of a ship cast ashore. **b.** *Chiefly British* Violent destruction of a building or vehicle. **2a.** Dried seaweed. **b.** Marine vegetation, esp. kelp. ❖ *v.* **wracked, wrack·ing, wracks** also **racked, rack·ing, racks** —*tr.* To cause the ruin of; wreck. *—intr.* To be wrecked. [ME *wrak* < MDu.]

wraith (rāth) *n.* **1.** An apparition of a living person that appears

as a portent just before that person's death. **2.** The ghost of a dead person. **3.** Something shadowy and insubstantial. [?]

Wran·gel Island (răng′gəl, vrän′gyĭl) An island of NE Russia in the Arctic Ocean NW of the Bering Strait.

Wran·gell (răng′gəl), **Mount** A peak, 4,319.7 m (14,163 ft), of the central Wrangell Mts. in S AK.

Wrangell Mountains A mountain range of S AK extending c. 161 km (100 mi) and rising to 5,032.5 m (16,500 ft).

wran·gle (răng′gəl) *v.* **-gled, -gling, -gles** *—intr.* To quarrel noisily or angrily; bicker. *—tr.* **1.** To win or obtain by argument. **2.** To herd (horses or other livestock). ❖ *n.* **1.** The act of wrangling. **2.** An angry noisy argument or dispute. [ME *wranglen,* of MLGer. orig. See **wer-²** in App.]

wran·gler (răng′glər) *n.* **1.** One who wrangles or quarrels. **2.** A cowboy or cowgirl, esp. one who tends saddle horses.

wrap (răp) *v.* **wrapped** or **wrapt** (răpt), **wrap·ping, wraps** —*tr.* **1.** To arrange or fold (something) about as cover or protection. **2.** To cover, envelop, or encase, as by folding or coiling something about. **3.** To enclose, esp. in paper, and fasten: *wrapped the package.* **4.** To clasp, fold, or coil about something. **5.** To move (text that will not fit on a line) automatically to the following line. **6.** To envelop and obscure. **7.** To surround or involve in a specified quality or atmosphere: *wrapped in secrecy.* **8.** To engross: *wrapped in thought.* —*intr.* **1.** To coil or twist about or around something. **2.** To be moved automatically to the following line upon reaching a margin. Used of text. **3.** To put on warm clothing. Usu. used with *up.* **4.** To conclude filming. ❖ *n.* **1.** A garment to be wrapped or folded about a person, esp. an outer garment such as a robe or coat. **2.** A blanket. **3.** A wrapping or wrapper. **4.** A flatbread, such as a tortilla or lavash, rolled around a filling. **5.** The completion of filming on a movie. **—phrasal verb: wrap up 1.** To bring to a conclusion; settle finally or successfully. **2.** To summarize; recapitulate. **—idioms: under wraps** *Informal* Secret or concealed. **wrapped up in 1.** Completely immersed or absorbed in. **2.** Involved in. [ME *wrappen.* See **wer-²** in App.]

wrap·a·round (răp′ə-round′) *adj.* **1.** Designed to be wrapped around the body and fastened: *a wraparound skirt.* **2.** Shaped to curve around the sides: *a wraparound windshield.* ❖ *n.* **1.** A garment open to the side and wrapped around the body. **2.** Something that encompasses or laps over something else. **3.** A text placement feature, as of a word processing program, that automatically moves text that will not fit on one line to the following line.

wrap·per (răp′ər) *n.* **1.** That in which an object is wrapped or covered, as: **a.** The material, such as paper, in which something is wrapped. **b.** The material encircling a magazine or newspaper sent by mail. **c.** A book jacket. **d.** The tobacco leaf covering a cigar. **2.** A loose dressing gown or negligee. **3.** One that wraps, as a store employee who wraps parcels.

wrap·ping (răp′ĭng) also **wrap·pings** (-ĭngz) *n.* The material in which something is wrapped.

wrap-up (răp′ŭp′) *n.* **1.** A brief final summary, as of the news. **2.** A concluding or final action: *the wrap-up of a campaign.*

wrasse (răs) *n.* Any of numerous chiefly tropical, often brightly colored marine fishes of the family Labridae, having spiny fins, thick lips, and powerful jaws and often valued for food. [Cornish *gwragh* and Welsh *gwrach,* old woman.]

wrath (răth, räth) *n.* **1.** Forceful, often vindictive anger. See Syns at **anger. 2a.** Punishment or vengeance as a manifestation of anger. **b.** Divine retribution for sin. ❖ *adj. Archaic* Wrathful. [ME < OE *wrǣththu* < *wrāth,* angry. See **wer-²** in App.]

wrath·ful (răth′fəl, räth′-) *adj.* **1.** Full of wrath; fiercely angry. **2.** Proceeding from or expressing wrath. **—wrath′ful·ly** *adv.* **—wrath′ful·ness** *n.*

wreak (rēk) *tr.v.* **wreaked, wreak·ing, wreaks 1.** To inflict (vengeance or punishment) upon a person. **2.** To express or gratify (anger, malevolence, or resentment); vent. **3.** To bring about; cause: *wreak havoc.* **4.** *Archaic* To take vengeance for; avenge. [ME *wreken* < OE *wrecan.*]

USAGE NOTE *Wreak* is sometimes confused with *wreck,* perhaps because the wreaking of damage may leave a wreck: *The storm wreaked* (not *wrecked*) *havoc along the coast.* The past tense and past participle of *wreak* is *wreaked,* not *wrought,* which is an alternative past tense and past participle of *work.*

wreath (rēth) *n., pl.* **wreaths** (rēthz, rēths) **1a.** A ring or circlet of flowers, boughs, or leaves worn on the head, placed on a memorial, or hung as a decoration. **b.** A representation of this ring or circlet, as in woodwork. **2.** A curling or circular form. [ME *wrethe* < OE *writha,* band. See **wer-²** in App.]

wreathe (rēth) *v.* **wreathed, wreath·ing, wreathes** —*tr.* **1.** To twist or entwine into a wreath. **2.** To twist or curl into a wreathlike shape. **3.** To crown, decorate, or encircle with or as if with a wreath. **4.** To coil or curl. **5.** To form a wreath or wreathlike shape around. —*intr.* **1.** To assume the form of a wreath. **2.** To curl, writhe, or spiral. [< WREATH.]

wreck (rĕk) *n.* **1.** The act of wrecking or the state of being wrecked; destruction. **2.** Accidental destruction of a ship; a shipwreck. **3a.** The stranded hulk of a severely damaged ship. **b.** Fragments of a ship or its cargo cast ashore by the sea after a ship-

ă	pat	oi	boy
ā	pay	ou	out
âr	care	ŏŏ	took
ä	father	ōō	boot
ĕ	pet	ŭ	cut
ē	be	ûr	urge
ĭ	pit	th	thin
ī	pie	th	this
îr	pier	hw	which
ŏ	pot	zh	vision
ō	toe	ə	about,
ô	paw		item

Stress marks:
′ (primary);
′ (secondary), as in
lexicon (lĕk′sĭ-kŏn′)

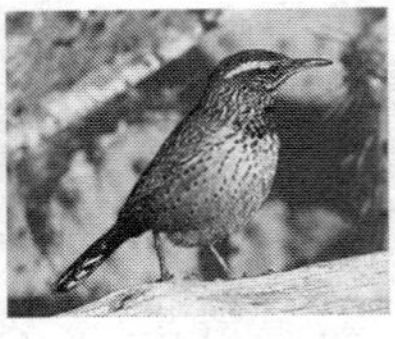

wren
cactus wren
Campylorhynchus brunneicapillus

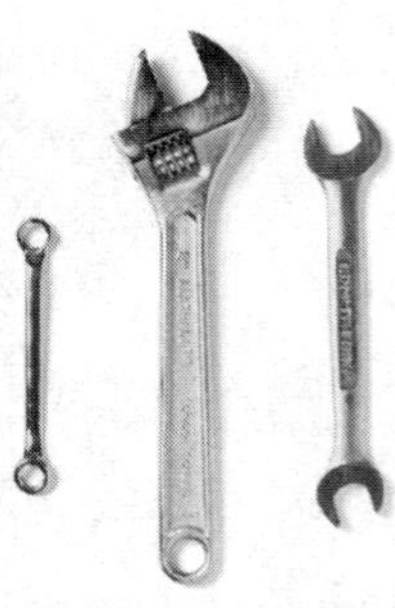

wrench
left to right: ratcheting box, adjustable, and open end wrenches

wreck. **4.** The remains of something wrecked or ruined. **5.** Something shattered or dilapidated. **6.** One who is broken down or worn out. ❖ *v.* **wrecked, wreck•ing, wrecks** —*tr.* **1.** To cause the destruction of in or as if in a collision. **2.** To dismantle or raze; tear down. **3.** To cause to undergo ruin or disaster. See Syns at **ruin.** See Usage Note at **wreak.** —*intr.* **1.** To suffer destruction or ruin; become wrecked. **2.** To work as a wrecker. [ME *wrek* < AN *wrec*, of Scand. orig.; akin to ON *rec*, wreckage.]

wreck•age (rĕk′ĭj) *n.* **1.** The act of wrecking or the state of being wrecked. **2.** Something wrecked. **3.** The debris of something wrecked.

wrecked (rĕkt) *adj. Slang* Drunk or intoxicated.

wreck•er (rĕk′ər) *n.* **1.** One that wrecks or destroys: *a wrecker of dreams.* **2a.** One who is in the business of demolishing old buildings. **b.** One who dismantles cars for salvage. **3a.** A person, vehicle, or piece of equipment employed in recovering or removing wrecks. **b.** One that salvages wrecked cargo or parts. **4a.** One who lures a vessel to destruction, as by a display of lights on a rocky coastline, in order to plunder it. **b.** A plunderer.

wreck•ing bar (rĕk′ĭng) *n.* A small crowbar with a claw at one end and a slight curve at the other end.

wren (rĕn) *n.* **1.** Any of various small brownish songbirds of the family Troglodytidae, having rounded wings, a slender bill, and a short, often erect tail. **2.** Any of various similar unrelated songbirds. [ME *wrenne* < OE *wrenna.*]

Wren, Sir **Christopher** 1632–1723. English architect who designed more than 50 London churches, most notably Saint Paul's Cathedral (1675–1710), and many secular works.

wrench (rĕnch) *n.* **1.** A sudden sharp, forcible twist or turn. **2.** An injury produced by twisting or straining. **3.** A sudden tug at one's emotions; a surge of compassion, sorrow, or anguish. **4a.** A break or parting that causes emotional distress. **b.** The pain so associated. **5.** A distortion in the original form or meaning of something written or spoken; twisted interpretation. **6.** Any of various hand or power tools, often having fixed or adjustable jaws, used for gripping, turning, or twisting objects such as nuts, bolts, or pipes. ❖ *v.* **wrenched, wrench•ing, wrench•es** —*tr.* **1a.** To twist or turn suddenly and forcibly. **b.** To twist and sprain. **2.** To move, extract, or force free by pulling violently; yank. **3.** To pull at the feelings or emotions of; distress. **4.** To distort or twist the original character or import of. —*intr.* To give a wrench, twist, or turn. [< ME *wrenchen*, to twist < OE *wrencan.* See **wer-**[2] in App.] —**wrench′ing•ly** *adv.*

wrest (rĕst) *tr.v.* **wrest•ed, wrest•ing, wrests 1.** To obtain by or as if by pulling with violent twisting movements. **2.** To usurp forcefully. **3.** To extract by or as if by force, twisting, or persistent effort; wring. **4a.** To distort or twist the nature or meaning of. **b.** To divert to an improper use; misapply. ❖ *n.* **1.** The act of wresting. **2.** *Music* A small tuning key for the wrest pins of a stringed instrument. [ME *wresten* < OE *wrǣstan*, to twist. See **wer-**[2] in App.] —**wrest′er** *n.*

wres•tle (rĕs′əl) *v.* **-tled, -tling, -tles** —*intr.* **1.** To contend by grappling and attempting to throw or immobilize one's opponent, esp. under contest rules. **2.** To contend or struggle. **3.** To strive in an effort to master something. —*tr.* **1a.** To take part in (a wrestling match). **b.** To take part in a wrestling match with. **2.** To move or lift with great effort and force. **3.** To throw (a calf or other animal) for branding. ❖ *n.* **1.** The act or a bout of wrestling. **2.** A struggle. [ME *wrestlen* < OE **wrǣstlian*, freq. of *wrǣstan*, to twist. See **wer-**[2] in App.] —**wres′tler** *n.*

wres•tling (rĕs′lĭng) *n.* A sport in which two competitors attempt to throw or immobilize each other by grappling.

wrest pin *n.* One of the pins to which the strings of a musical instrument, esp. of a keyboard instrument, are attached and by turning which they are tuned.

wretch (rĕch) *n.* **1.** A miserable, unfortunate, or unhappy person. **2.** A person regarded as base, mean, or despicable. [ME *wrecche* < OE *wrecca*, exile, wretch.]

wretch•ed (rĕch′ĭd) *adj.* **-er, -est 1.** In a deplorable state of distress or misfortune; miserable. **2.** Characterized by or attended with misery or woe. **3.** Of a poor or mean character; dismal. **4.** Contemptible; despicable. **5.** Of very inferior quality. [ME *wrecched* < *wrecche*, wretch. See WRETCH.] —**wretch′ed•ly** *adv.* —**wretch′ed•ness** *n.*

wri•er (rī′ər) *adj.* A comparative of **wry.**

wri•est (rī′ĭst) *adj.* A superlative of **wry.**

wrig•gle (rĭg′əl) *v.* **-gled, -gling, -gles** —*intr.* **1.** To turn or twist the body with sinuous writhing motions; squirm. **2.** To proceed with writhing motions. **3.** To worm one's way into or out of a situation; insinuate or extricate oneself by sly or subtle means. —*tr.* **1.** To move with a wriggling motion. **2.** To make (one's way, for example) by or as if by wriggling. ❖ *n.* **1.** A wriggling movement. **2.** A sinuous path, line, or marking. [ME *wrigglen*, perh. < MLGer. *wriggeln.* See **wer-**[2] in App.] —**wrig′gly** *adj.*

wrig•gler (rĭg′lər) *n.* **1.** The larva of a mosquito. **2.** One that wriggles or squirms.

wright (rīt) *n.* One that constructs or repairs something. Often used in combination: *a playwright; a shipwright.* [ME < OE *wryhta.* See **werg-** in App.]

Wright, Frank Lloyd 1869–1959. Amer. architect whose distinctive style was based on natural forms.

Wright, James Arlington 1927–80. Amer. poet who won a Pulitzer Prize for his *Collected Poems* (1971).

Wright, Orville 1871–1948. Amer. aviation pioneer who with his brother **Wilbur** (1867–1912) made the first controlled sustained flights in a powered heavier-than-air vehicle on Dec. 17, 1903, near Kitty Hawk NC.

Wright, Richard 1908–60. Amer. writer whose works include *Native Son* (1940) and *Black Boy* (1945).

wring (rĭng) *v.* **wrung** (rŭng), **wring•ing, wrings** —*tr.* **1.** To twist, squeeze, or compress, esp. to extract liquid. Often used with *out.* **2.** To extract (liquid) by twisting or compressing. Often used with *out.* **3.** To wrench or twist forcibly or painfully. **4.** To clasp and twist or squeeze (one's hands), as in distress. **5.** To clasp firmly and shake (another's hand), as in congratulation. **6.** To cause distress to; affect with painful emotion. **7.** To obtain or extract by applying force or pressure. —*intr.* To writhe or squirm, as in pain. ❖ *n.* The act or an instance of wringing; a squeeze or twist. [ME *wringen* < OE *wringan.* See **wer-**[2] in App.]

wring•er (rĭng′ər) *n.* One that wrings, esp. a device in which laundry is pressed between rollers to extract water. ***—idiom:* put (someone) through the wringer** *Slang* To subject to a severe trial or ordeal.

wrin•kle (rĭng′kəl) *n.* **1.** A small furrow, ridge, or crease on a normally smooth surface, caused by crumpling, folding, or shrinking. **2.** A line or crease in the skin, as from age. **3.** A clever trick, method, or device, esp. one that is new and different; an innovation. **4.** A problem or imperfection; a fault. ❖ *v.* **-kled, -kling, -kles** —*tr.* **1.** To make wrinkles or a wrinkle in. **2.** To draw up into wrinkles; pucker: *wrinkled her nose.* —*intr.* To form wrinkles. [ME, back-formation < *wrinkled*, wrinkled, prob. < OE *gewrinclod*, p. part. of *gewrinclian*, to wind, crease. See **wer-**[2] in App.] —**wrin′kly** *adj.*

wrist (rĭst) *n.* **1a.** The joint between the hand and the forearm. **b.** See **carpus** 1. **2.** The part of a sleeve or glove that encircles the wrist. [ME < OE. See **wer-**[2] in App.]

wrist•band (rĭst′bănd′) *n.* A band, as on a long sleeve or a wristwatch, that encircles the wrist.

wrist•let (rĭst′lĭt) *n.* **1.** A band of material worn round the wrist for warmth or support. **2.** A bracelet.

wrist•lock (rĭst′lŏk′) *n.* A wrestling hold in which an opponent's wrist is gripped and twisted to immobilize the opponent.

wrist pin *n.* A pin that attaches one end of a connecting rod to a wheel, crank, or piston.

wrist shot *n.* A quick shot made in hockey by snapping the wrists forward when the puck is against the stick blade.

wrist•watch (rĭst′wŏch′) *n.* A watch worn on a band that fastens about the wrist.

writ[1] (rĭt) *n.* **1.** *Law* A written order issued by a court, commanding the party to whom it is addressed to perform or cease performing a specified act. **2.** Writings. [ME < OE.]

writ[2] (rĭt) *v.* A past tense and a past participle of **write.**

writ•a•ble also **write•a•ble** (rī′tə-bəl) *adj. Computer Science* Capable of recording data. Used of a storage medium.

write (rīt) *v.* **wrote** (rōt), **writ•ten** (rĭt′n) also **writ** (rĭt), **writ•ing, writes** —*tr.* **1a.** To form (letters, words, or symbols) on a surface such as paper with an instrument such as a pen. **b.** To spell. **2.** To form (letters or words) in cursive style. **3.** To compose and set down, esp. in literary or musical form. **4.** To draw up in legal form; draft. **5.** To fill in or cover with writing. **6.** To express in writing; set down. **7.** To communicate by correspondence. **8.** To underwrite, as an insurance policy. **9.** To indicate; mark: *sadness written on his face.* **10.** To ordain or prophesy. **11.** *Computer Science* To transfer or copy (information) from memory to a storage device or output device. —*intr.* **1.** To trace or form letters, words, or symbols on paper or another surface. **2.** To produce written material, such as articles or books. **3.** To compose a letter; communicate by mail. ***—phrasal verbs:* write down 1.** To set down in writing. **2.** To reduce in rank, value, or price. **3.** To disparage in writing. **4.** To write in a conspicuously simple or condescending style. **write in 1.** To cast a vote by inserting (a name not listed on a ballot). **2.** To insert in a text or document. **3.** To communicate with an organization by mail. **write off 1.** To reduce to zero the book value of (an asset that has become worthless). **2.** To cancel from accounts as a loss. **3.** To consider as a loss or failure. **write out 1.** To express or compose in writing. **2.** To write in full or expanded form. **write up 1.** To write a report or description of, as for publication. **2.** To bring (a journal, for example) up to date. **3.** To overstate the value of (assets). **4.** To report (someone) in writing, as for breaking the law. ***—idioms:* write (one's) own ticket** To set one's own terms or course of action entirely according to one's own needs or wishes. **writ large** Signified, expressed, or embodied in a greater or more prominent magnitude or degree. [ME *writen* < OE *wrītan.*]

write-down (rīt′doun′) *n. Accounting* A reduction of the entered value of an asset.

write-in (rīt′ĭn′) *n.* **1.** A vote cast by writing in the name of a candidate not on the ballot. **2.** A candidate thus voted for.

write-off (rīt′ôf′, -ŏf′) *n. Accounting* **1a.** A cancellation of an item in account books. **b.** The amount canceled or lost. **2.** A reduction to zero of the entered value of an item.

write-pro•tect (rīt′prə-tĕkt′) *tr.v.* **-tect•ed, -tect•ing, -tects**

Computer Science To modify (a file or disk) so that its data cannot be edited or erased.

writ·er (rī′tər) *n.* One who writes, esp. as an occupation.

writer's block (rī′tərz) *n.* A usu. temporary psychological inability to begin or continue work on a piece of writing.

writer's cramp *n., pl.* **writers' cramps** A cramp or spasm of the muscles of the fingers, hand, and forearm during writing.

write-up (rīt′ŭp′) *n.* **1.** A published account, review, or notice, esp. a favorable one. **2.** *Accounting* An intentional overevaluation of a corporation's assets.

writhe (rīth) *v.* **writhed, with·ing, writhes** —*intr.* **1.** To twist, as in pain or embarrassment. **2.** To move with a twisting or contorted motion. **3.** To suffer acutely. —*tr.* To cause to twist or squirm; contort. ❖ *n.* The act or an instance of writhing; a contortion. [ME *writhen* < OE *wrīthan.* See **wer-²** in App.] —**with′er** *n.*

writ·ing (rī′tĭng) *n.* **1.** The act of one who writes. **2.** Written form. **3.** Handwriting; penmanship. **4.** Something written, esp.: **a.** Meaningful letters or characters that constitute readable matter. **b.** A written work, esp. a literary composition. **5.** The occupation or style of a writer. **6. Writings** (*used with a sing. or pl. verb*) The third of the three divisions of the Hebrew Scriptures, composed of Psalms, Proverbs, Job, Song of Solomon, Ruth, Lamentations, Ecclesiastes, Esther, Daniel, Ezra, Nehemiah, and Chronicles. See table at **Bible.**

writ of election *n., pl.* **writs of election** A writ issued by a governor or other executive authority requiring that an election be held, esp. a special election to fill a vacancy.

writ of error *n., pl.* **writs of error** A writ commissioning an appellate court to review the proceedings of another court and correct the judgment given if deemed necessary.

writ of prohibition *n., pl.* **writs of prohibition** An order issued by a higher court commanding a lower court to cease from proceeding in some matter not within its jurisdiction.

writ of summons *n., pl.* **writs of summons** A writ directing a person to appear in court to answer a complaint.

writ·ten (rĭt′n) *v.* Past participle of **write.**

Wro·cław (vrôt′släf′, -swäf′) *also* **Bres·lau** (brĕs′lou) A city of SW Poland on the Oder R.; assigned to Poland by the Potsdam Conference (1945). Pop. 643,071.

wrong (rông, rŏng) *adj.* **1.** Not in conformity with fact or truth; incorrect or erroneous. **2a.** Contrary to conscience, morality, or law; immoral or wicked. **b.** Unfair; unjust. **3.** Not required, intended, or wanted: *took a wrong turn.* **4.** Not fitting or suitable; inappropriate or improper. **5.** Not in accord with established usage, method, or procedure. **6.** Not functioning properly; out of order. **7.** Unacceptable or undesirable according to social convention. **8.** Being the side, as of a garment, that is less finished and not intended to show. ❖ *adv.* **1.** In a wrong manner; mistakenly or erroneously. **2.** In a wrong course or direction. **3.** Immorally or unjustly. **4.** In an unfavorable way. See Syns at **amiss.** ❖ *n.* **1a.** An unjust or injurious act. **b.** Something contrary to ethics or morality. **2a.** An invasion or violation of another's legal rights. **b.** *Law* A tort. **3.** The condition of being in error or at fault: *in the wrong.* ❖ *tr.v.* **wronged, wrong·ing, wrongs 1.** To treat unjustly or injuriously. **2.** To discredit unjustly; malign. **3.** To treat dishonorably; violate. —*idioms:* **do (someone) wrong** *Informal* To be unfaithful or disloyal to. **go wrong 1.** To take a wrong turn or make a wrong move. **2.** To go astray morally. **3.** To go amiss; turn out badly. [ME, of Scand. orig. See **wer-²** in App.] —**wrong′er** *n.* —**wrong′ly** *adv.* —**wrong′ness** *n.*

wrong·do·er (rông′do͞o′ər, rŏng′-) *n.* One who does wrong, esp. morally or ethically. —**wrong′do′ing** *n.*

wrong·ful (rông′fəl, rŏng′-) *adj.* **1.** Wrong; unjust. **2.** Unlawful. —**wrong′ful·ly** *adv.* —**wrong′ful·ness** *n.*

wrongful death *n.* A death that is caused by the wrongful act or negligence of another and that serves as the basis for a civil action for damages on behalf of the decedent's heirs.

wrong-head·ed (rông′hĕd′ĭd, rŏng′-) *adj.* Stubbornly defiant of what is right or reasonable; obstinately perverse in judgment or opinion. —**wrong′-head′ed·ly** *adv.* —**wrong′-head′ed·ness** *n.*

wrote (rōt) *v.* Past tense of **write.**

wroth (rôth) *adj.* Wrathful; angry. [ME < OE *wrāth.* See **wer-²** in App.]

wrought (rôt) *v.* A past tense and a past participle of **work.** ❖ *adj.* **1.** Put together; created: *a carefully wrought plan.* **2.** Shaped by hammering with tools. Used chiefly of metals or metalwork. **3.** Made delicately or elaborately. [ME *wroght,* p. part. of *wyrcan,* to work. See **werg-** in App.]

wrought iron *n.* An easily worked iron that is a mixture of refined metallic iron with 1 to 3 percent siliceous slag.

wrought-up *also* **wrought up** (rôt′ŭp′) *adj.* Agitated; excited.

wrung (rŭng) *v.* Past tense and past participle of **wring.**

wry (rī) *adj.* **wri·er** (rī′ər), **wri·est** (rī′ĭst) *or* **wry·er, wry·est 1.** Dryly humorous, often with a touch of irony. **2.** Temporarily twisted in an expression of distaste or displeasure: *a wry face.* **3.** Abnormally twisted or bent to one side; crooked: *a wry nose.* **4.** Being at variance with what is right, proper, or suitable; perverse. [< ME *wrien,* to turn < OE *wrīgian.* See **wer-²** in App.] —**wry′ly** *adv.* —**wry′ness** *n.*

wry·neck (rī′nĕk′) *n.* **1.** Either of two small Old World woodpeckers, *Jynx torquilla* or *J. ruficollis,* having a sharply pointed bill and the habit of twisting the head and neck into contortions. **2a.** *See* **torticollis. b.** A person with torticollis.

WSW *abbr.* west-southwest

wt. *abbr.* weight

WTO *abbr.* World Trade Organization

Wu·han (wo͞o′hän′) A city of E-central China on the Chang Jiang (Yangtze R.); cap. of Hubei province. Pop. 3,832,536.

Wu·hu (wo͞o′ho͞o′) A city of E-central China on the Chang Jiang (Yangtze R.) SSW of Nanjing. Pop. 552,932.

Wu Jiang (wo͞o′ jyäng′) A river rising in S-central China and flowing c. 805 km (500 mi) to the Chang Jiang (Yangtze R.).

wul·fen·ite (wo͝ol′fə-nīt′) *n.* A usu. yellow to orange-brown mineral, PbMoO₄, a molybdenum ore. [Ger. *Wulfenit,* after Franz Xavier von *Wulfen* (1728–1805), Austrian mineralogist.]

wun·der·kind (vo͝on′dər-kĭnd′, wŭn′-) *n., pl.* **-kin·der** (-kĭn′dər) **1.** A child prodigy. **2.** A person of remarkable talent or ability who achieves great success or acclaim at an early age. [Ger. : *Wunder,* wonder, prodigy (< MHGer. < OHGer. *wuntar*) + *Kind,* child; see KINDERGARTEN.]

Wup·per·tal (vo͝op′ər-täl′) A city of W-central Germany NNE of Düsseldorf. Pop. 386,625.

wurst (wûrst, wo͝orst) *n.* Sausage. [Ger. < MHGer. < OHGer.]

Würt·tem·berg (wûr′təm-bûrg′, vür′təm-bĕrk′) A historical region and kingdom (1806–1918) of SW Germany.

wurt·zite (wûrt′sīt′) *n.* A light to dark brown mineral, (Zn,Fe)S, that is a polymorph of sphalerite. [Fr., after Charles *Wurtz* (1817–84), French chemist.]

Würz·burg (wûrts′bûrg′, vürts′bo͝ork′) A city of S-central Germany on the Main R. Pop. 128,875.

wu·shu *also* **wu shu** (wo͞o′sho͞o′) *n.* The Chinese martial arts. [Chin. (Mandarin) *wǔshù* : *wǔ,* martial + *shù,* skill, art.]

wuss (wo͝os) *n. Slang* A person regarded as weak or timid and esp. as unmanly. [Prob. blend of WIMP and PUSSY¹.] —**wuss′y** *adj.*

Wu·xi *also* **Wu·sih** (wo͞o′shē′) A city of E China between Shanghai and Nanjing. Pop. 3,181,895.

WV *or* **W.Va.** *abbr.* West Virginia

WWI *abbr.* World War I

WWII *abbr.* World War II

WWW *abbr.* World Wide Web

WY *abbr.* Wyoming

Wy·an·dot *also* **Wy·an·dotte** (wī′ən-dŏt′) *n., pl.* **Wyandot** *or* **-dots** *also* **Wyandotte** *or* **-dottes 1.** A member of a Native American people formerly located in Ohio and the upper Midwest and now living in northeast Oklahoma. **2.** Their Iroquoian language. [Wyandot *wädát,* tribal name.]

Wy·an·dotte (wī′ən-dŏt′) *n.* **1.** A medium-sized domestic chicken of a breed developed in North America for its eggs and meat. **2.** Variant of **Wyandot.**

Wy·att *or* **Wy·at** (wī′ət), Sir **Thomas** 1503–42. English poet noted for introducing the sonnet form into English literature.

wych elm *also* **witch elm** (wĭch) *n.* A Eurasian elm (*Ulmus glabra*) often planted as a shade tree. [< ME *wiche* < OE *wice.*]

Wych·er·ley (wĭch′ər-lē), **William** 1640?–1716. English satirist whose plays include *The Country Wife* (1675).

Wyc·liffe *also* **Wick·liffe** *or* **Wyc·lif** *or* **Wic·lif** (wĭk′lĭf), **John** 1328?–84. English theologian and religious reformer whose rejection of the biblical basis of papal power and dispute with the doctrine of the transubstantiation of the host anticipated the Protestant Reformation.

wye (wī) *n.* **1.** The letter *y.* **2.** An object shaped like a Y.

Wy·eth (wī′ĭth), **Andrew** b. 1917. Amer. artist whose realistic paintings, such as *Christina's World* (1948), depict stark rural scenes. His father, **Newell Convers Wyeth** (1882–1945), was also a painter and a book illustrator.

Wy·lie (wī′lē), **Elinor Morton Hoyt** 1885–1928. Amer. writer whose works include *Nets to Catch the Wind* (1921).

wynn (wĭn) *or* **wen** (wĕn) *n.* An Old English rune (ƿ) having the sound (w) and used in Old English and Middle English writing. [OE. See **wen-** in App.]

Wyo. *abbr.* Wyoming

Wy·o·ming (wī-ō′mĭng) A state of the W US; admitted as the 44th state in 1890. Cap. Cheyenne. Pop. 493,782.

WYSIWYG (wĭz′ē-wĭg′) *adj.* Relating to or being a word processing or desktop publishing system in which the screen displays text exactly as it will be printed. ❖ *n.* A WYSIWYG system, effect, or screen display. [w(hat) y(ou) s(ee) i(s) w(hat) y(ou) g(et).]

wy·vern *also* **wi·vern** (wī′vərn) *n. Heraldry* A two-legged dragon having wings and a barbed tail. [Alteration of ME *wyvere,* viper < ONFr. *wivre* < Lat. *vīpera.* See VIPER.]

Orville and Wilbur Wright

Wyandotte
Silver Laced Wyandotte

Xx

x¹ or **X** (ĕks) *n.*, *pl.* **x's** or **X's** also **xs** or **Xs 1.** The 24th letter of the modern English alphabet. **2.** Any of the speech sounds represented by the letter *x*. **3.** The 24th in a series. **4.** Something shaped like the letter X. **5.** A mark inscribed in lieu of the signature of one who is unable to sign one's name. **6.** An unknown or unnamed factor, thing, or person. ❖ *tr.v.* **x'd, x'ing, x's** or **X'd, X'ing, X's 1.** To mark or sign with an X. **2.** To delete, cancel, or obliterate with a series of X's. Often used with *out.*

x² The symbol for **abscissa.**

X¹ *n.* A movie rating indicating that admission will not be granted to anyone under the age of 17.

X² 1. The symbol for **reactance. 2.** also **x** The symbol for the Roman numeral 10.

X³ *abbr.* **1.** Christ (Greek Χριστος, *Khristos*) **2.** Christian **3.** or **x** experimental **4.** extra

x. *abbr. Business* ex

Xan·a·du (zăn′ə-dōō′, -dyōō′) *n.* An idyllic beautiful place. [After *Xanadu* in "Kubla Khan" by Samuel Taylor Coleridge.]

xan·than gum (zăn′thən) *n.* A natural gum produced by culture fermentation of glucose and used as a stabilizer in commercial food preparation. [< NLat. *Xanthomonas (campestris)*, name of the bacterium used to produce it : Gk. *xanthos*, yellow (< its color) + Gk. *monas*, monad; see MONAD.]

xan·thate (zăn′thāt′) *n.* A salt of a xanthic acid, esp. a simple xanthic acid salt, as of sodium or potassium, used as a flotation collector for copper, silver, and gold.

xan·thene (zăn′thēn′) *n.* A yellow crystalline compound, CH₂(C₆H₄)₂O, used as a fungicide and in organic synthesis.

xan·thic acid (zăn′thĭk) *n.* Any of various unstable acids of the form ROC(S)SH, in which R is usu. an alkyl radical.

xan·thine (zăn′thēn′, -thĭn) *n.* **1.** A yellowish-white crystalline purine base, C₅H₄N₄O₂, that is a precursor of uric acid and is found in blood, urine, muscle tissue, and certain plants. **2.** Any of several derivatives of this compound.

Xan·thip·pe (zăn-thĭp′ē, -tĭp′ē) or **Xan·tip·pe** (-tĭp′ē) 5th cent. B.C. The wife of Socrates, traditionally described as shrewish.

xantho– or **xanth–** *pref.* **1.** Yellow: *xanthine.* **2.** Xanthic acid: *xanthate.* [Gk., yellow < *xanthos.*]

xan·tho·chroid (zăn′thə-kroid′) *adj.* Having a light complexion and light hair. ❖ *n.* A person having a light complexion and light hair. [NLat. *Xanthōchroi*, yellow-haired, fair-skinned people (a subdivision in a classification of varieties of humans by Thomas H. Huxley : Gk. *xantho-*, xantho- + Gk. *ōkhroi*, pl. of *ōkhros*, pale) + –OID.] **—xan·tho·chro′ic** (-krō′ĭk) *adj.*

xan·tho·ma (zăn-thō′mə) *n.*, *pl.* **-mas** or **-ma·ta** (-mə-tə) A yellowish-orange lipid-filled nodule or papule in the skin, often on an eyelid or over a joint.

xan·tho·phyll (zăn′thə-fĭl′) *n.* **1.** A yellow carotenoid pigment, C₄₀H₅₆O₂, found with chlorophyll in green plants and identical with lutein. **2.** Any of various related yellow pigments. **—xan′·tho·phyl′lic, xan′tho·phyl′lous** *adj.*

xan·thous (zăn′thəs) *adj.* **1.** Yellow. **2.** Having light brown or yellowish skin.

Xan·thus (zăn′thəs) An ancient city of Lycia in present-day SW Turkey; besieged and taken by the Persians (c. 546 B.C.) and the Romans (c. 42 B.C.).

Xa·vi·er (zā′vē-ər, zăv′ē-), Saint **Francis** 1506–52. Spanish missionary who was a cofounder of the Jesuit order (1534).

x-ax·is (ĕks′ăk′sĭs) *n.*, *pl.* **x-ax·es** (-ăk′sēz) **1.** The horizontal axis of a two-dimensional Cartesian coordinate system. **2.** One of three axes in a three-dimensional Cartesian coordinate system.

XC or **X-C** *abbr.* cross-country

X-chro·mo·some or **X chromosome** (ĕks′krō′mə-sōm′) *n.* The sex chromosome associated with female characteristics in mammals, occurring paired in the female and single in the male.

XD or **x-div** *abbr.* ex dividend

Xe The symbol for the element **xenon.**

xe·bec also **ze·bec** or **ze·beck** (zē′bĕk′) *n.* A small three-masted Mediterranean vessel with both square and lateen sails. [Fr. *chebec*, prob. < Catalan *xabec* < Ar. dialectal *šabbāk* < *šabaka*, to entwine, fasten.]

xe·ni·a (zē′nē-ə, zēn′yə) *n.* The direct effect on a hybrid plant produced by the transfer of pollen from one strain to the endosperm of a different strain. [NLat. < Gk. *xeniā*, hospitality < *xenos*, guest, stranger. See XENO–.]

xeno– or **xen–** *pref.* **1.** Stranger; foreigner: *xenophobia.* **2.** Strange; foreign; different: *xenolith.* [NLat. < Gk. < *xenos*, stranger. See **ghos-ti-** in App.]

xen·o·bi·ot·ic (zĕn′ə-bī-ŏt′ĭk, zē′nə-) *adj.* Foreign to the body or to living organisms. Used of chemical compounds. ❖ *n.* A xenobiotic chemical, such as a pesticide.

xen·o·blast (zĕn′ə-blăst′, zē′nə-) *n.* A mineral deposit that has developed during metamorphism without developing crystalline faces.

xen·o·cryst (zĕn′ə-krĭst′, zē′nə-) *n.* A crystal foreign to the igneous rock in which it occurs. [XENO– + CRYST(AL).]

xen·o·gen·e·sis (zĕn′ə-jĕn′ĭ-sĭs, zē′nə-) *n.* **1.** The production of offspring markedly different from either parent. **2.** See **alternation of generations. —xen′o·ge·net′ic** (-jə-nĕt′ĭk), **xen′o·gen′ic** (-jĕn′ĭk) *adj.*

xen·o·graft (zĕn′ə-grăft′, zē′nə-) *n.* See **heterograft.**

xen·o·lith (zĕn′ə-lĭth′, zē′nə-) *n.* A rock fragment foreign to the igneous mass in which it occurs.

xe·non (zē′nŏn′) *n. Symbol* **Xe** A colorless, odorless, highly unreactive gaseous element found in minute quantities in the atmosphere, extracted commercially from liquefied air and used in stroboscopic, bactericidal, and laser-pumping lamps. Atomic number 54; atomic weight 131.29; melting point –111.9°C; boiling point –107.1°C; density (gas) 5.887 grams per liter; specific gravity (liquid) 3.52 (–109°C). See table at **element.** [< Gk., neut. of *xenos*, foreign, strange. See XENO–.]

Xe·noph·a·nes (zə-nŏf′ə-nēz′) 560?–478? B.C. Greek philosopher whose rationalism is often regarded as a major influence on the Eleatic tradition.

xen·o·phile (zĕn′ə-fīl′, zē′nə-) *n.* A person attracted to that which is foreign, esp. to foreign peoples, manners, or cultures. **—xen′o·phil′i·a** (-fĭl′ē-ə) *n.* **—xe·noph′i·lous** (zē-nŏf′ə-ləs, zē-) *adj.*

xen·o·phobe (zĕn′ə-fōb′, zē′nə-) *n.* A person unduly fearful or contemptuous of that which is foreign, esp. of strangers or foreign peoples. **—xen′o·pho′bi·a** *n.* **—xen′o·pho′bic** *adj.*

Xen·o·phon (zĕn′ə-fən, -fŏn′) 430?–355? B.C. Greek soldier who after a failed attack on Persia (401 B.C.) led Greek troops to the Black Sea, an ordeal recounted in *Anabasis.*

xen·o·pus (zĕn′ə-pəs) *n.* Any of various aquatic, tongueless frogs of the genus *Xenopus*, native to southern Africa, esp. *X. laevis*, used to study vertebrate development. [NLat. *Xenopūs*, genus name : XENO– + Gk. *pous*, foot; see OCTOPUS.]

xen·o·trans·plan·ta·tion (zĕn′ə-trăns′plăn-tā′shən, zē′nə-) *n.* The surgical transfer of cells, tissues, or esp. whole organs from one species to another.

Xer (ĕk′sər) *n.* A member of Generation X.

xer·ic (zĕr′ĭk, zîr′-) *adj.* Of, characterized by, or adapted to an extremely dry habitat. **—xer′i·cal·ly** *adv.*

Xer·i·scape (zîr′ĭ-skāp′) A trademark used for a landscaping method that employs drought-resistant plants in an effort to conserve resources, esp. water.

xero– or **xer–** *pref.* Dry; dryness: *xeroderma.* [Gk. *xēro- < xēros.*]

xer·o·der·ma (zîr′ō-dûr′mə) also **xe·ro·der·mi·a** (-mē-ə) *n.* Excessive or abnormal dryness of the skin, as in ichthyosis.

xe·rog·ra·phy (zĭ-rŏg′rə-fē) *n.* A dry photographic or photocopying process in which a negative image formed by a resinous powder on an electrically charged plate is electrically transferred to and thermally fixed as positive on a paper or other copying surface. **—xe·rog′ra·pher** *n.* **—xer′o·graph′ic** (zîr′ə-grăf′ĭk) *adj.* **—xer′o·graph′i·cal·ly** *adv.*

xe·roph·i·lous (zĭ-rŏf′ə-ləs) *adj.* Flourishing in or adapted to a dry hot environment. **—xe·roph′i·ly** *n.*

xer·oph·thal·mi·a (zîr′ŏf-thăl′mē-ə) *n.* Extreme dryness and thickening of the conjunctiva, often resulting from a deficiency of vitamin A. **—xer′oph·thal′mic** *adj.*

xer·o·phyte (zîr′ə-fīt′) *n.* A plant adapted to living in an arid habitat; a desert plant. **—xer′o·phyt′ic** (-fĭt′ĭk) *adj.* **—xer′o·phyt′ism** (-fī′tĭz-əm, -fī-tīz′-) *n.*

xe·ro·sis (zĭ-rō′sĭs) *n., pl.* **-ses** (-sēz) **1.** Abnormal dryness, esp. of the skin, eyes, or mucous membranes. **2.** The normal hardening of aging tissue.

xer·o·sto·mi·a (zîr′ə-stō′mē-ə) *n.* Abnormal dryness of the mouth. [NLat. *xērostomia* : XERO– + Gk. *stoma*, mouth.]

xer·o·ther·mic (zîr′ə-thûr′mĭk) *adj.* **1.** Both dry and hot: *a xerothermic climate.* **2.** Adapted to or flourishing in an environment that is both dry and hot: *xerothermic organisms.*

Xer·ox (zîr′ŏks) A trademark used for a photocopying process or machine employing xerography.

Xer·xes I (zûrk′sēz) Known as "Xerxes the Great." 519?–465 B.C. King of Persia (486–465) who organized a vast army that defeated the Greeks at Thermopylae and destroyed Athens (480).

Xerxes I
relief sculpture from
Persepolis, fifth century B.C.

x-height (ĕks′hīt′) *n. Printing* The height of a lowercase x.

Xho·sa also **Xo·sa** (kō′sä, -zə) *n., pl.* **Xhosa** or **-sas** also **Xosa** or **-sas 1.** A member of a Bantu people inhabiting the eastern part of Cape Province, South Africa. **2.** The Nguni language of this people, closely related to Zulu.

xi (zī, sī, ksē) *n.* **1.** The 14th letter of the Greek alphabet. **2.** See **xi baryon.** [Gk. *xei, xī.*]

XI *abbr. Business* ex interest

Xia·men (shyä′mən) also **A·moy** (ä-moi′) A city of E China ENE of Guangzhou. Pop. 639,436.

Xi′an (shē′än′, shyän) also **Si·an** (sē′än′, shē′-) or **Hsian** (shyän) A city of central China SW of Beijing; cap. (221–206 B.C.) of the Qin dynasty. Pop. 2,872,539.

Xiang Jiang (shyäng′ jyäng′) also **Siang Kiang** (syäng′ kyäng′, shyäng′) or **Hsiang Kiang** (shyäng′) A river, c. 1,150 km (715 mi), flowing generally N from SE China.

Xiang·tan (shyäng′tän′) also **Siang·tan** (syäng′-, shyäng′-) A city of S-central China on the Xiang Jiang SSW of Changsha. Pop. 1,531,117.

xi baryon *n.* Either of two subatomic particles in the baryon family, one neutral and one negatively charged, with masses of 2,630 and 2,643 times that of the electron.

xi-c baryon (zī′sē′, sī′-, ksē′-) *n.* Either of two subatomic particles in the baryon family, one neutral and one positively charged, with masses of 4,826 and 4,834 times that of an electron.

Xi Jiang (shē′ jyäng′) also **Si Kiang** (sē′ kyäng′, shē′) A river rising in SE China and flowing c. 2,011 km (1,250 mi) generally E to the South China Sea near Guangzhou.

Xin·gu (shēng-gōō′) A river of central and N Brazil flowing c. 1,979 km (1,230 mi) to the Amazon R.

Xi·ning (shē′nĭng′) A city of central China NNE of Chengdu; cap. of Qinghai province. Pop. 697,780.

Xin·jiang Uy·gur (shĭn′jyäng′ wē′gər) also **Sin·kiang Ui·ghur** or **Sin·kiang Ui·gur** (sĭn′kyäng′, shĭn′jyäng′) An autonomous region of extreme W China; came under Chinese control in the 16th cent. Cap. Ürümqi. Pop. 15,155,778.

Xin·xiang (shĭn′shyäng′) A city of E China SSE of Taiyuan. Pop. 1,770,370.

xiph·i·ster·num (zĭf′ĭ-stûr′nəm) *n., pl.* **-na** (-nə) The posterior and smallest of the three divisions of the sternum, below the gladiolus and the manubrium. [< Gk. *xiphos,* sword.]

xiph·oid (zĭf′oid′) *adj.* **1.** Shaped like a sword. **2.** Of or relating to the xiphisternum. ❖ *n.* See **xiphisternum.** [Gk. *xiphoeidēs : xiphos,* sword + *-oeidēs, -oid.*]

xiphoid process *n.* See **xiphisternum.**

xiph·o·su·ran (zĭf′ə-sŏŏr′ən) *n.* An arthropod of the order Xiphosura, which includes the horseshoe crab and many extinct forms. [< NLat. *Xiphosūra,* order name : Gk. *xiphos,* sword + Gk. *ourā.*] **—xiph′o·su′ran** *adj.*

Xi·zang (shē′dzäng′) or **Ti·bet** (tə-bĕt′) An autonomous region of SW China N and W of the Himalaya Mts.; controlled by China since 1720 and formally proclaimed an autonomous region in 1965. Cap. Lhasa. Pop. 2,196,010.

XL *abbr.* **1.** extra large **2.** extra long

X-linked (ĕks′lĭngkt′) *adj.* **1.** Of or relating to an inherited trait produced by a gene on an X-chromosome. **2.** Of or relating to a gene on an X-chromosome.

X·mas (krĭs′məs) *n.* Christmas. [< *X,* the Greek letter chi, first letter of Gk. *Khrīstos,* Christ. See CHRIST.]

USAGE NOTE *Xmas* has been used for hundreds of years in religious writing, where the *X* represents a Greek chi, the first letter of Χριστος, *Khristos,* "Christ." In this use it is parallel to other forms like *Xtian,* "Christian." But people unaware of the Greek origin of this *X* often mistakenly interpret *Xmas* as an informal shortening pronounced (ĕks′məs). Many believe frown upon the term *Xmas* because it seems to them a commercial convenience that omits Christ from Christmas.

XML (ĕks′ĕm-ĕl′) *n.* A metalanguage written in SGML that allows one to design a markup language and facilitates the exchange of data. [*Ex(tensible) M(arkup) L(anguage).*]

XOR (ĕks′ôr′) *n.* A logical operator that returns a true value if one, but not both, of its operands is true. [Short for EXCLUSIVE OR.]

Xo·sa (kō′sä, -zə) *n.* Variant of **Xhosa.**

x-ra·di·a·tion (ĕks′rā′dē-ā′shən) *n.* **1.** Treatment with or exposure to x-rays. **2.** Radiation composed of x-rays.

X-rat·ed (ĕks′rā′tĭd) *adj.* **1.** Having the rating X: *an X-rated movie.* **2.** Vulgar, obscene, or explicit in the treatment of sex.

x-ray also **X-ray** (ĕks′rā′) *n.* also **x ray** or **X ray 1a.** A relatively high-energy photon with wavelength in the approximate range from 0.01 to 10 nanometers. **b.** A stream of such photons, used for their penetrating power in radiography, radiology, radiotherapy, and scientific research. Often used in the plural. **2.** A photograph taken with x-rays. ❖ *tr.v.* **x-rayed, x-ray·ing, x-rays** also **X-rayed, X-ray·ing, X-rays 1.** To irradiate with x-rays. **2.** To photograph with x-rays. [< the fact that it was a previously unknown form of radiation when first discovered.]

x-ray astronomy *n.* The branch of astronomy that deals with the origin and nature of emissions from extraterrestrial sources in the x-ray range of electromagnetic radiation rather than in the visible range.

x-ray diffraction *n.* The scattering of x-rays by crystal atoms, producing a diffraction pattern that yields information about the structure of the crystal.

x-ray spectrometer *n.* A spectrometer that uses x-rays to trigger the release of energy from the chemical constituents of a substance so that the resultant spectral lines can be identified and the concentrations of the various constituents can be determined.

x-ray star *n.* A celestial object, esp. a star, that emits a major portion of its radiation in x-rays.

x-ray therapy *n.* Medical treatment using controlled doses of x-ray radiation.

x-ray tube *n.* A vacuum tube containing electrodes that accelerate electrons and direct them to a metal anode, where their impacts produce x-rays.

Xu·zhou (shōō′jō′) also **Sü·chow** (sōō′chou′, sü′jō′) A city of E China NNW of Nanjing. Pop. 841,000.

xy·lan (zī′lən) *n.* A yellow water-soluble gummy polysaccharide found in plant cell walls and yielding xylose upon hydrolysis.

xy·lem (zī′ləm) *n.* The supporting and water-conducting tissue of vascular plants, consisting primarily of tracheids and vessels; woody tissue. [Ger. < Gk. *xulon,* wood.]

xy·lene (zī-lēn′, zī′lēn′) also **xy·lol** (zī′lôl′, -lŏl′) *n.* **1.** Any of three flammable isomeric hydrocarbons, $C_6H_4(CH_3)_2$, obtained from wood and coal tar. **2.** A mixture of xylene isomers used as a solvent in making lacquers and rubber cement.

xy·li·dine (zī′lĭ-dēn′, -dĭn, zĭl′ĭ-) *n.* **1.** Any of six isomers, $(CH_3)_2C_6H_3NH_2$, derived from xylene and used as dye intermediates. **2.** Any of various mixtures of xylidine isomers.

xy·li·tol (zī′lĭ-tôl′, -tōl′, -tŏl′) *n.* A sweet white crystalline alcohol, $C_5H_{12}O_5$, derived from xylose and used esp. as a sugar substitute in oral health products. [XYL(OSE) + (SORB)ITOL.]

xylo– or **xyl–** *pref.* **1.** Wood: *xylograph.* **2.** Xylene: *xylidine.* [Gk. *xulo-* < *xulon,* wood.]

xy·lo·graph (zī′lə-grăf′) *n.* **1.** An engraving on wood. **2.** An impression from a woodblock. ❖ *tr.v.* **-graphed, -graph·ing, -graphs** To print from a wood engraving. **—xy′log′ra·pher** (-lŏg′rə-fər) *n.*

xy·log·ra·phy (zī-lŏg′rə-fē) *n.* **1.** Wood engraving, esp. of an early period. **2.** The art of printing texts or illustrations, sometimes with color, from woodblocks, as distinct from typography. **—xy′lo·graph′ic** (-lə-grăf′ĭk), **xy′lo·graph′i·cal** (-ĭ-kəl) *adj.* **—xy′lo·graph′i·cal·ly** *adv.*

xy·loid (zī′loid′) *adj.* Of or similar to wood.

xy·loph·a·gous (zī-lŏf′ə-gəs) *adj.* **1.** Feeding on wood, as certain insects or insect larvae. **2.** Destructive to wood, as certain crustaceans or fungi. **—xy′lo·phage′** (zī′lə-fāj′) *n.*

xy·loph·i·lous (zī-lŏf′ə-ləs) *adj.* Growing or living on or in wood.

xy·lo·phone (zī′lə-fōn′) *n.* A percussion instrument consisting of a mounted row of wooden bars graduated in length to sound a chromatic scale, played with two small mallets. **—xy′lo·phon′ist** *n.*

WORD HISTORY Alphabet books for children frequently feature the word *xylophone* because it is one of the few words beginning with *x* that a child (or most adults, for that matter) would know. The majority of English words beginning with *x,* including many obscure scientific terms, are of Greek origin, the *x,* pronounced (z), representing the Greek letter xi. In the case of *xylophone, xylo–* is a form meaning "wood," derived from Greek *xulon,* "wood," and *–phone* represents Greek *phōnē,* "voice, sound," the same element found in words such as *telephone, microphone,* and *megaphone.* Our famous *x* word is first recorded in the April 7, 1866, edition of the *Athenaeum:* "A prodigy . . . who does wonderful things with little drumsticks on a machine of wooden keys, called the 'xylophone.'"

xy·lose (zī′lōs′) *n.* A white crystalline sugar, $C_5H_{10}O_5$, used in dyeing and tanning and as a sugar substitute in foods.

XYZ (ĕks′wī-zē′) *interj. Informal* Used to indicate to someone that the zipper of his or her pants is open. [*ex(amine) y(our) z(ipper).*]

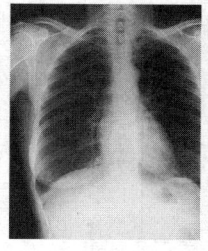

x-ray
x-ray of a healthy human chest

xylophone

y¹ or **Y** (wī) *n.*, *pl.* **y's** or **Y's** also **ys** or **Ys** **1.** The 25th letter of the modern English alphabet. **2.** Any of the speech sounds represented by the letter *y.* **3.** The 25th in a series. **4.** Something shaped like the letter Y.

y² The symbol for **ordinate**.

Y¹ *n.* The Young Men's Christian Association, the Young Women's Christian Association, the Young Men's Hebrew Association, the Young Women's Hebrew Association, or one of their facilities. Used with *the.*

Y² **1.** The symbol for the element **yttrium**. **2.** The symbol for **admittance** 3. **3.** The symbol for **hypercharge**.

Y³ *abbr.* year

–y¹ or **–ey** *suff.* **1.** Characterized by; consisting of: *clayey.* **2a.** Like: *summery.* **b.** To some degree; somewhat: *chilly.* **3.** Tending toward; inclined toward: *sleepy.* [ME < OE *-ig.*]

–y² *suff.* **1.** Condition; state; quality: *jealousy.* **2a.** Activity: *cookery.* **b.** Instance of a specified action: *entreaty.* **3a.** Place for an activity: *cannery.* **b.** Result or product of an activity: *laundry.* **4.** Collection; body; group: *soldiery.* [ME *-ie* < OFr. < Lat. *-ia.* Sense 2b, ult. < Lat. *-ium.*]

–y³ or **–ie** *suff.* **1.** Small one: *doggy.* **2.** Dear one: *sweetie.* **3.** One having to do with or characterized by: *townie.* [ME *-ie, -y.*]

Y2K (wī′tōō-kā′) *adj.* **1.** Of or relating to the year 2000. **2.** Of or relating to the Y2K bug: *Y2K testing.* [Alteration of *y(ear) 2000 < K,* symbol for 1000.]

Y2K bug *n.* A defect in the code of a computer program caused when a year is represented by its last two digits only and the program interprets that year as falling inclusively between 1900 and 1999 instead of between 2000 and 2099.

yab•ber (yăb′ər) *Australian n.* Jabber. ❖ *tr.* & *intr.v.* **-bered, -ber•ing, -bers** To jabber (something) or engage in jabbering. [< Australian pidgin, perh. < Wuywurung (Aboriginal language of SE Australia) *yaba,* to talk.]

Ya•blo•no•vy Range (yä′blə-nə-vē′) A mountain chain of SE Russia extending NE from near the Mongolian border.

yacht (yät) *n.* Any of various relatively small sailing or motor-driven vessels, used for pleasure cruises or racing. ❖ *intr.v.* **yacht•ed, yacht•ing, yachts** To sail, cruise, or race in a yacht. [Prob. obsolete Norw. *jagt* < MLGer. *jacht,* short for *jachtschip : jagen,* to chase (< OHGer. *jagōn*) + *schip,* ship.]

yachts•man (yäts′mən) *n.* A man who owns or sails a yacht.

yachts•wom•an (yäts′wŏŏm′ən) *n.* A woman who owns or sails a yacht.

yack (yăk) *v.* & *n. Slang* Variant of **yak²**.

yack•e•ty-yak (yăk′ĭ-tē-yăk′) *n. Slang* Prolonged, sometimes senseless talk. [Imit.]

Ya•fo (yä′fō) or **Jaf•fa** (jäf′ə, yä′fə) A former city of W-central Israel on the Mediterranean Sea; now part of Tel Aviv–Yafo.

YAG (yăg) *n.* A hard synthetic yttrium aluminum garnet used in laser technology.

ya•gi (yä′gē, yäg′ē) *n.*, *pl.* **-gis** A directional radio and television antenna consisting of a horizontal conductor with several insulated dipoles parallel to and in the plane of the conductor. [After Hidetsugu *Yagi* (1886–1976), Japanese electrical engineer.]

ya•hoo (yä′hōō, yä′-) *n.*, *pl.* **-hoos** A crude or brutish person. [From *Yahoo,* member of a race of brutes in *Gulliver's Travels* by Jonathan Swift.] **—ya′hoo•ism** *n.*

Yahr•zeit (yär′tsīt, -zīt′) *n. Judaism* The anniversary of the death of a relative, observed with mourning and the recitation of religious texts. [Yiddish, anniversary < MHGer. *jārzīt : jār,* year (< OHGer.; see **yēr-** in App.) + *zīt,* time (< OHGer.; see **dā-** in App.).]

Yah•weh (yä′wā, -wĕ) also **Yah•veh** (-vā, -vĕ) or **Jah•veh** (yä′vā, -vĕ) or **Jah•weh** (yä′wä, -wĕ) A name for God assumed by modern scholars to be a convention for pronouncing the Tetragrammaton. [Heb.]

Yah•wist (yä′wĭst) also **Yah•vist** (-vĭst) *n.* The putative author of the earliest sources of the Hexateuch in which God is consistently referred to by the Tetragrammaton. **—Yah•wis′tic** *adj.*

yak¹ (yăk) *n.* **1.** A wild shaggy-haired ox (*Bos grunniens*) of the mountains of central Asia. **2.** A domesticated yak, used as a work animal or raised for meat and milk. [Tibetan *gyag.*]

yak² also **yack** (yăk) *Slang intr.v.* **yakked, yak•king, yaks** also **yacked, yack•ing, yacks** To talk persistently and meaninglessly; chatter. ❖ *n.* Prolonged, sometimes senseless talk; chatter. [Imit.]

Ya•ka•ma (yä′kə-mə) or **Ya•ki•ma** (yăk′ə-mə, -mô) *n.*, *pl.* **-ma** or **-mas** also **Yakima** or **-mas 1.** A member of a Native American people inhabiting south-central Washington. **2.** Their dialect of Sahaptin.

yak¹
Bos grunniens

Ya•ki•ma (yăk′ə-mə, -mô′) A city of S-central WA SE of Seattle. Pop. 71,845.

Yakima River A river of central and SE WA flowing c. 327 km (203 mi) to the Columbia R.

ya•ki•to•ri (yä′kĭ-tôr′ē, -tōr′ē) *n.* A dish of bite-sized marinated chicken pieces grilled on skewers. [J. : *yaki,* roasting + *tori,* bird.]

Ya•kut (yä-kōōt′) *n.*, *pl.* **Yakut** or **-kuts 1.** A member of a people inhabiting the region of the Lena River in eastern Siberia. **2.** The Turkic language of the Yakut. **—Ya•kut′** *adj.*

Ya•kutsk (yə-kōōtsk′) A city of E-central Russia on the Lena R.; founded as a fort in 1632. Pop. 196,341.

ya•ku•za (yä′kōō-zä′) *n.*, *pl.* **yakuza 1.** A loose alliance of Japanese criminal organizations and illegal enterprises. **2.** A Japanese gangster. [J., good-for-nothing, gambler, racketeer.]

Yale (yāl), **Elihu** 1649–1721. Colonial-born English merchant who made a series of contributions to the Collegiate School, which was renamed in his honor (1718).

Yale, Mount A peak, 4,329.8 m (14,196 ft), in the Sawatch Range of the Rocky Mts. in central CO.

y'all (yôl) *pron. Chiefly Southern US* Variant of **you-all**. See Regional Note at **you-all**.

Ya•long Jiang (yä′lōōng′ jyäng′) A river of S-central China flowing c. 1,287 km (800 mi) to the Chang Jiang (Yangtze R.).

Yal•ow (yăl′ō), **Rosalyn Sussman** b. 1921. Amer. medical physicist who shared a 1977 Nobel Prize.

Yal•ta (yôl′tə) A city of SE Ukraine in the S Crimea; site of an Allied conference in Feb. 1945. Pop. 86,000.

Ya•lu Jiang (yä′lōō′ jyäng′) A river, c. 805 km (500 mi), forming part of the North Korea–China border.

yam (yăm) *n.* **1.** Any of numerous chiefly tropical vines of the genus *Dioscorea,* many of which have edible tuberous roots. **2.** The starchy root of any of these plants, used as food. **3.** *Chiefly Southern US* See **sweet potato 1.** See Regional Note at **goober**. [Port. *inhame* or obsolete Sp. *igname, iñame,* both < Port. and E. Creole *nyam,* to eat, of West African orig.; akin to Wolof *ñam,* food, to eat, or Bambara *ñambu,* manioc.]

Ya•ma•see (yä′mə-sē′) *n.*, *pl.* **Yamasee** or **-sees** A member of a Native American people formerly inhabiting parts of coastal Georgia and South Carolina.

Yam•bol (yäm′bôl′) A city of SE Bulgaria E of Stara Zagora; under Turkish rule from the 15th to the 19th cent. Pop. 91,000.

ya•men (yä′mən) *n.* The office or residence of an official in the Chinese Empire. [Chin. (Mandarin) *yámen : yá,* magistracy (< *yá,* tooth, flag with a serrated edge planted outside an official's hut) + *mén,* gate.]

yam•mer (yăm′ər) *Informal v.* **-mered, -mer•ing, -mers** *—intr.* **1.** To complain peevishly or whimperingly; whine. **2.** To talk volubly and loudly. *—tr.* To utter or say in a complaining or clamorous tone. ❖ *n.* The act of yammering. [ME *yameren,* to lament, prob. < MFlem. *jammeren,* to be sorrowful.] **—yam′mer•er** *n.*

Ya•mous•sou•kro (yä′mōō-sōō′krō) The cap. of Côte d'Ivoire, in the S-central part N of Abidjan. Pop. 120,000.

Yam•pa (yăm′pə) A river of NW CO flowing c. 402 km (250 mi) to the Green R. near the UT border.

Ya•mu•na (yŭm′ə-nə) or **Jum•na** (jŭm′nə) A river of N India rising in the Himalaya Mts. and flowing c. 1,384 km (860 mi) to the Ganges R.

Ya•na (yä′nə) A river of NE Russia flowing c. 1,207 km (750 mi) to the Laptev Sea.

yang (yäng) *n.* The active, male cosmic principle in Chinese dualistic philosophy. [Chin. (Mandarin) *yáng,* sun, light, male element.]

Yan•gon (yän′gôn′) Formerly **Ran•goon** (răn-gōōn′, răng-) The cap. of Myanmar (Burma), in the S part near the Irrawaddy R. delta. Pop. 2,458,712.

Yang•tze River (yăng′sĕ′, -tsĕ′, yäng′dzŭ′) See **Chang Jiang**.

Yang•zhou also **Yang•chow** (yäng′jō′) A city of E-central China on the Grand Canal; a cap. of China in the 6th cent. A.D. Pop. 2,769,300.

yank (yăngk) *v.* **yanked, yank•ing, yanks** *—tr.* **1.** To pull with a quick, strong movement; jerk. **2.** *Slang* To extract or remove abruptly. *—intr.* To pull on something suddenly. ❖ *n.* A sudden vigorous pull; a jerk. [?]

Yank *n. Informal* A Yankee.

Yan•kee (yăng′kē) *n.* **1.** A native or inhabitant of New England. **2.** A native or inhabitant of a northern US state, esp. a Union soldier during the Civil War. **3.** A native or inhabitant of the United States. [Prob. < Du. *Janke,* nickname of *Jan,* John.]

Yankee Doodle *n.* A Yankee. [< the title of a song that was popular during the Revolutionary War.]

Yan·kee·ism (yăng′kē-ĭz′əm) *n.* A Yankee custom, characteristic, usage, or pronunciation.

Yank·ton (yăngk′tən) *n., pl.* **Yankton** or **-tons** A member of a division of the Sioux people formerly inhabiting northern Minnesota, now located mainly in the eastern Dakotas.

Yank·to·nai (yăngk′tə-nī′) *n., pl.* **Yanktonai** or **-nais** A member of a division of the Sioux people formerly inhabiting northern Minnesota, now located in the Dakotas and eastern Montana.

Ya·no·ma·mi (yä′no-mä′mē) or **Ya·no·ma·mo** (-mō′) *n., pl.* **Yanomami** or **-mis** or **Yanomamo** or **-mos** 1. A member of a South American Indian people living in widely scattered villages along the Brazil-Venezuela border. 2. Their language.

Yao[1] (you) *n., pl.* **Yao** or **Yaos** 1. A member of a people related to the Hmong and inhabiting southern China, Laos, Thailand, and Vietnam. 2. The Miao-Yao language of the Yao.

Yao[2] (you) A city of S Honshu, Japan, a suburb of Osaka. Pop. 276,324.

Ya·oun·dé (yä-ōōn-dā′) The cap. of Cameroon, in the S-central part; founded 1888. Pop. 653,670.

yap (yăp) *v.* **yapped, yap·ping, yaps** *—intr.* 1. To bark sharply or shrilly; yelp. 2. *Slang* To talk noisily or stupidly; jabber. *—tr.* To utter by yapping. ❖ *n.* 1. A sharp, shrill bark; a yelp. 2. *Slang* Noisy stupid talk; jabber. 3. *Slang* The mouth: *Shut your yap.* 4. *Slang* A stupid, crude, or loud person. [Prob. imit.] **—yap′per** *n.*

Yap (yăp, yäp) An island group and state of the Federated States of Micronesia in the W Caroline Is. of the W Pacific Ocean.

ya·pok (yə-pŏk′) *n.* An aquatic opossum (*Chironectes minimus*) of tropical America having webbed hind feet and a long tail. [After the *Oyapock*, a river of northern South America.]

Ya·qui (yä′kē) *n., pl.* **Yaqui** or **-quis** 1. A member of a Native American people of Sonora, a state of northwest Mexico, now also located in southern Arizona. 2. The Uto-Aztecan language of the Yaqui. [Sp. < Yaqui *hiaki.*]

yar·bor·ough (yär′bûr′ō, -bûr′ō, -bər-ə) *n. Games* A bridge or whist hand containing no honor cards. [After Charles Anderson Worsley, 2nd Earl of *Yarborough* (1809–97), said to have bet 1,000 to 1 that such a hand would not occur.]

yard[1] (yärd) *n.* 1. A fundamental unit of length in both the US Customary System and the British Imperial System, equal to 3 feet, or 36 inches (0.9144 meter). See table at **measurement.** 2. *Nautical* A long tapering spar slung to a mast to support and spread the head of a square sail, lugsail, or lateen. [ME *yerde,* stick, unit of measure < OE *gerd.*]

yard[2] (yärd) *n.* 1. A tract of ground next to, surrounding, or surrounded by a building or buildings. 2. A tract of ground, often enclosed, used for a specific business or activity. 3. An area where railroad trains are made up and cars are switched, stored, and serviced on tracks and sidings. **4a.** A winter pasture for deer or other grazing animals. **b.** An enclosed tract of ground in which animals are kept. ❖ *v.* **yarded, yard·ing, yards** *—tr.* To enclose, collect, or put into or as if into a yard. *—intr.* To be gathered into or as if into a yard. [ME < OE *geard.* See **gher-** in App.]

yard·age[1] (yär′dĭj) *n.* 1. An amount or length measured in yards. 2. Cloth sold by the yard.

yard·age[2] (yär′dĭj) *n.* 1. The use of a livestock yard at a station in transporting cattle by railroad. 2. A fee paid for such usage.

yard·arm (yärd′ärm′) *n. Nautical* Either end of a yard of a square sail.

yard bird *n. Slang* **1a.** An untrained military recruit. **b.** A soldier confined to a restricted area or assigned menial tasks as a punishment. 2. A convict; a prisoner.

yard goods *pl.n.* See **piece goods.**

yard·man (yärd′mən) *n.* A man employed in a yard, esp. a railroad yard.

yard·mas·ter (yärd′măs′tər) *n.* A railroad employee in charge of a yard.

yard sale *n.* A sale of used household belongings, typically held outdoors at the home of the seller.

yard·stick (yärd′stĭk′) *n.* 1. A graduated measuring stick one yard in length. 2. A test or standard used in measurement, comparison, or judgment.

yare (yâr) *adj.* 1. Agile; lively. 2. *Nautical* Responding easily; maneuverable. Used of a vessel. 3. *Archaic* Ready; prepared. [ME < OE *gearo,* ready.] **—yare′ly** *adv.*

Yar·kant He (yär′känt′ hŭ′, -känt′) also **Yar·kand River** (-känd′, -känd′) A river of NW China flowing c. 805 km (500 mi) to the Tarim He.

yar·mul·ke also **yar·mel·ke** (yär′məl-kə, yä′məl-) *n.* A skullcap worn by Jewish men and boys, esp. those adhering to Orthodox or Conservative Judaism. [Yiddish < Pol. and Ukrainian *yarmulka,* poss. < Turk. *yağmurluk,* rain clothing < *yağmur,* rain.]

yarn (yärn) *n.* 1. A continuous strand of twisted threads of natural or synthetic material, such as wool or nylon, used in weaving or knitting. 2. *Informal* A narrative of real or fictitious adventures; an entertaining tale. ❖ *intr.v.* **yarned, yarn·ing, yarns** *Informal* To tell a yarn or series of yarns. [ME < OE *gearn.*]

Ya·ro·slavl (yär′ə-slä′vəl, yə-ro-) A city of W-central Russia on the Volga R. NE of Moscow; annexed by Moscow in 1463. Pop. 628,302.

yar·row (yăr′ō) *n.* Any of several plants of the genus *Achillea* of the composite family, esp. *A. millefolium,* native to Eurasia, having finely dissected foliage and flat, usu. white flower heads. [ME *yarowe* < OE *gearwe.*]

yash·mak also **yash·mac** (yäsh-mäk′, yäsh′mäk) *n.* A veil worn by Muslim women to cover the face in public. [Turk. *yaçmak.*]

Yat (yăt) *n. New Orleans* 1. A member of a lower- and middle-class segment of the white population of New Orleans. 2. The variety of English spoken by these people, derived from Irish English. [< *Where you at?, Whe'yat?,* How are you? (local greeting).]

yat·a·ghan (yăt′ə-găn′, -gən) *n.* A Turkish sword or scimitar having a double-curved blade but lacking a handle guard. [Turk. *yatağan.*]

yau·pon (yô′pən) *n.* An evergreen holly (*Ilex vomitoria*) of the southeast United States having dried leaves used to make a bitter tea. [Catawba *yā′pā.*]

Ya·va·pai (yăv′ə-pī′, yä′və-) *n., pl.* **Yavapai** or **-pais** 1. A member of a Native American people inhabiting western Arizona. 2. The Yuman language of the Yavapai.

yaw (yô) *v.* **yawed, yaw·ing, yaws** *—intr.* 1. *Nautical* To swerve off course momentarily or temporarily. 2. To turn about the vertical axis. Used of an aircraft, spacecraft, or projectile. 3. To move unsteadily; weave. *—tr.* To cause to yaw. ❖ *n.* 1. The act of yawing. 2. Extent of yawing, measured in degrees. [Perhaps of Scand. orig.]

yawl (yôl) *n.* 1. A two-masted fore-and-aft-rigged sailing vessel similar to the ketch but having a smaller jigger- or mizzenmast stepped abaft the rudder. 2. A ship's small boat, crewed by rowers. [Du. *jol,* poss. < LGer. *jolle.*]

yawn (yôn) *v.* **yawned, yawn·ing, yawns** *—intr.* 1. To open the mouth wide with a deep inhalation, usu. involuntarily from drowsiness, fatigue, or boredom. 2. To open wide; gape. *—tr.* To utter wearily, while or as if while yawning. ❖ *n.* 1. The act of yawning. 2. A fatigued or bored response. 3. *Informal* One that provokes yawns; a bore. [ME *yanen,* alteration of *yonen, yenen* < OE *geonian.*] **—yawn′er** *n.*

yawn·ing (yô′nĭng) *adj.* Gaping open; cavernous.

yawp (yôp) *intr.v.* **yawped, yawp·ing, yawps** 1. To utter a sharp cry; yelp. 2. To talk loudly, raucously, or coarsely. ❖ *n.* 1. A bark; a yelp. 2. Loud or coarse talk or utterance. [ME *yolpen,* poss. var. of *yelpen.* See YELP.] **—yawp′er** *n.*

yaws (yôz) *pl.n.* (*used with a sing. or pl. verb*) A highly contagious tropical disease that chiefly affects children, caused by the spirochete *Treponema pertenue* and characterized by raspberrylike sores. [< Am.Sp. *yaya,* sore < Carib *yaya,* disease.]

y-ax·is (wī′ăk′sĭs) *n., pl.* **y-ax·es** (wī′ăk′sēz) 1. The vertical axis of a two-dimensional Cartesian coordinate system. 2. One of three axes in a three-dimensional Cartesian coordinate system.

yay (yā) *interj.* Used as an exclamation of pleasure, approval, elation, or victory. [Alteration of YEA.]

Ya·zoo (yə-zōō′, yăz′ōō) A river of W-central MS flowing 302.5 km (188 mi) to the Mississippi R. above Vicksburg.

Yb The symbol for the element **ytterbium.**

Y-chro·mo·some or **Y chromosome** (wī′krō′mə-sōm′) *n.* The sex chromosome associated with male characteristics in mammals, not occurring in females and occurring with one X-chromosome in the male sex-chromosome pair.

y·clept (ĭ-klĕpt′) or **y·cleped** (ĭ-klĕpt′, ĭ-klĕp′) *v.* A past participle of **clepe.** [ME *icleped* < OE *geclepod,* p. part. of *gecleopian,* to call : *ge-,* v. pref.; see **kom** in App. + *cleopian,* to call.]

yd. *abbr.* yard (measurement)

ye[1] (yē) *pron.* 1. (*used with a pl. verb*) *Archaic* You. 2. (*used with a sing. verb*) *Archaic* You. [ME < OE *gē.* See **yu-** in App.]

ye[2] (thē, yē) *def.art. Archaic* The. [Alteration of ME *þe* (< use of *y* to represent thorn (*þ*) in early English printing).]

yea (yā) *adv.* 1. Yes; aye. 2. Indeed; truly. ❖ *n.* 1. An affirmative statement or vote. 2. One who votes affirmatively. [ME < OE *gēa.* See **i-** in App.]

yeah (yĕ′ə, yă′ə, yā′ə) *adv. Informal* Yes. [Variant of YEA.]

yean (yēn) *v.* **yeaned, yean·ing, yeans** *—intr.* To bear young. Used of sheep and goats. *—tr.* To give birth to; bear. Used of sheep and goats. [ME *iyenen, yenen* < OE **geēanian : ge-,* v. pref.; see **kom** in App. + *ēanian,* to bear young.]

yean·ling (yēn′lĭng) *n.* The young of a sheep or goat; a lamb or kid. ❖ *adj.* Newly born; infant.

year (yîr) *n.* **1a.** The period of time during which Earth completes a single revolution around the sun, consisting of 365 days, 5 hours, 49 minutes, and 12 seconds of mean solar time, beginning in the Gregorian calendar on January 1 and ending on December 31. **b.** A period approximately equal to a year in other calendars. **c.** A period of approximately the duration of a calendar year: *We were married a year ago.* 2. A sidereal year. 3. A solar year. 4. A period equal to the calendar year but beginning on a different date: *a fiscal year.* 5. A specific period of time, usu. shorter than 12 months, devoted to a special activity: *the academic year.* **6.** **years** Age, esp. old age. 7. **years** An indefinitely long period of time: *years since we saw her.* [ME *yere* < OE *gēar.* See **yēr-** in App.]

year·book (yîr′bŏŏk′) *n.* 1. A documentary, memorial, or historical book published every year, containing information about the previous year. 2. A publication compiled by the graduating class of a school or college, recording the year's events and typically containing photographs of students.

yarmulke

year-end also **year·end** (yîr′ĕnd′) *n.* The end of a year. ❖ *adj.* Occurring or done at the end of the year.

year·ling (yîr′lĭng) *n.* **1.** An animal that is one year old or has not completed its second year. **2.** A thoroughbred racehorse one year old dating from January 1 of the year in which it was foaled. ❖ *adj.* Being one year old.

year·long (yîr′lông′, -lŏng′) *adj.* Lasting one year.

year·ly (yîr′lē) *adj.* Occurring once a year or every year. ❖ *adv.* Once a year; annually. ❖ *n., pl.* **-lies** A publication issued once a year.

yearn (yûrn) *intr.v.* **yearned, yearn·ing, yearns 1.** To have a strong, often melancholy desire. **2.** To feel deep pity, sympathy, or tenderness. [ME *yernen* < OE *geornan, giernan.*] —**yearn′er** *n.*

yearn·ing (yûr′nĭng) *n.* A persistent, often wistful or melancholy desire; a longing.

year-round (yîr′round′) *adj.* Existing, active, or continuous throughout the year: *a year-round resort.*

yea-say·er (yā′sā′ər) *n.* **1.** One who is confidently affirmative in attitude. **2.** One who uncritically agrees.

yeast (yēst) *n.* **1a.** Any of various unicellular fungi of the genus *Saccharomyces,* esp. *S. cerevisiae,* reproducing by budding and from ascospores and capable of fermenting carbohydrates. **b.** Any of various similar fungi. **2.** Froth consisting of yeast cells together with the carbon dioxide they produce in the process of fermentation, present in or added to fruit juices and other substances in the production of alcoholic beverages. **3.** A powdered or compressed commercial preparation, having yeast cells and inert material such as meal and used chiefly as a leavening agent or as a dietary supplement. **4.** Foam; froth. **5.** An agent of ferment or activity. ❖ *intr.v.* **yeast·ed, yeast·ing, yeasts 1.** To ferment. **2.** To froth or foam. [ME *yeest* < OE *gist.*]

yeast·y (yē′stē) *adj.* **-i·er, -i·est 1.** Of, similar to, or containing yeast. **2.** Causing or characterized by unrest or agitation; turbulent. **3.** Frothy; frivolous: *a yeasty comedy.* **4.** Full of productivity or vitality; exuberantly creative. —**yeast′i·ly** *adv.* —**yeast′i·ness** *n.*

Yeats (yāts), **William Butler** 1865–1939. Irish poet who won the 1923 Nobel Prize for literature. —**Yeats′i·an** *adj.*

William Butler Yeats

yech or **yecch** (yĕкн, yŭкн, yĕk) *interj.* Used to express contempt or disgust. [Imit.]

yegg (yĕg) *n. Slang* A thief, esp. a burglar or safecracker. [?]

Ye·ka·te·rin·burg (yi-kăt′ər-ĭn-bûrg′) Formerly **Sverd·lovsk** (sfĕrd-lôfsk′) a city of W-central Russia in the E foothills of the Ural Mts. Pop. 1,350,861.

yell (yĕl) *v.* **yelled, yell·ing, yells** —*intr.* To cry out loudly, as in pain, fright, surprise, or enthusiasm. —*tr.* To utter or express with a loud cry. See Syns at **shout.** ❖ *n.* **1.** A loud cry; a shout. **2.** A rhythmic cheer uttered or chanted in unison. [ME *yellen* < OE *giellan, gellan.*] —**yell′er** *n.*

yellow jacket

yel·low (yĕl′ō) *n.* **1a.** The hue of that portion of the visible spectrum lying between orange and green, evoked in the human observer by radiant energy with wavelengths of approx. 570 to 590 nanometers; any of a group of colors of a hue resembling that of ripe lemons; one of the subtractive primaries; one of the psychological primary hues. **b.** A pigment or dye having this hue. **c.** Something that has this hue. **2.** *Chiefly Southern US* The yolk of an egg. **3.** *Western US* Gold. Used formerly by prospectors. **4.** **yellows** Any of various plant diseases usu. caused by fungi of the genus *Fusarium* or viruses of the genus *Chlorogenus* and characterized by yellow or yellowish discoloration. ❖ *adj.* **-er, -est 1.** Of the color yellow. **2a.** Having a yellow-brown skin color. **b.** *Often Offensive* Of or being a person of East Asian origin. **3.** *Slang* Cowardly. ❖ *tr. & intr.v.* **-lowed, -low·ing, -lows** To make or become yellow. [ME *yelow* < OE *geolu.* See **ghel-** in App.] —**yel′low·ness** *n.*

yel·low-bel·lied (yĕl′ō-bĕl′ĕd) *adj.* **1.** Having a belly that is yellow or yellowish. Used of certain birds, for example. **2.** *Slang* Cowardly. —**yel′low-bel′ly** *n.*

yellow-bellied sapsucker *n.* A sapsucker (*Sphyrapicus varius*) having a yellowish belly and in the male a scarlet crown and throat.

yellow bile *n.* One of the four humors of ancient and medieval physiology, thought to cause anger and bad temper when present in excess; choler.

yellow birch *n.* A North American deciduous tree (*Betula alleghaniensis*) having aromatic twigs, yellowish bark, and hard light-colored wood used for furniture and flooring.

yel·low·bird (yĕl′ō-bûrd′) *n.* Any of various yellow or mostly yellow birds, such as the yellow warbler.

yel·low·cake (yĕl′ō-kāk′) *n.* The concentrated oxide of uranium formed in the milling of uranium ore.

yellow card *n.* A yellow-colored card shown by a referee to a player, esp. in soccer, to indicate that the player has committed a flagrant foul. Being shown two yellow cards results in ejection from the game. —**yel′low-card′** *v.*

yel·low-dog contract (yĕl′ō-dôg′, -dŏg′) *n.* An employer-employee contract, no longer legal, by which the employee agrees not to join a union while employed.

yellow fever *n.* An infectious tropical disease caused by an arbovirus transmitted by the mosquitoes of the genera *Aedes,* esp. *A. aegypti,* and *Haemagogus,* characterized by high fever and jaundice.

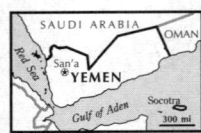

Yemen

yel·low-fe·ver mosquito (yĕl′ō-fē′vər) *n.* See **aedes.**

yel·low·fin tuna (yĕl′ō-fĭn′) *n.* A commercially important tuna (*Thunnus albacares*) with yellow fins, found in warm seas.

yellow-green alga (yĕl′ō-grēn′) *n.* An alga of the division Chrysophyta, plastids of which contain golden yellow pigments that mask the chlorophyll.

yel·low·ham·mer (yĕl′ō-hăm′ər) *n.* **1.** A small bunting (*Emberiza citrinella*) of Europe and western Asia having bright yellow plumage on the head, neck, and breast. **2.** See **yellow-shafted flicker.** [By folk ety. < earlier *yelambre,* perh. < ME **yelwambre* : *yelow,* yellow; see YELLOW + OE *amore,* a kind of bird.]

yel·low·ish (yĕl′ō-ĭsh) *adj.* Somewhat yellow; tinged with yellow.

yellow jack *n.* **1.** A yellowish-silver carangid food fish (*Caranx bartholomaei*) of western Atlantic and Caribbean waters. **2.** *Nautical* A yellow flag hoisted on a ship to request pratique or warn of disease on board. **3.** See **yellow fever.**

yellow jacket *n.* Any of several small social wasps of the family Vespidae that have yellow and black markings.

yellow jessamine *n.* See **Carolina jasmine.**

yellow journalism *n.* Journalism that exploits, distorts, or exaggerates the news to create sensations. [< the use of yellow ink in printing "Yellow Kid," a cartoon strip in the *New York World,* a newspaper noted for sensationalism.]

Yel·low·knife (yĕl′ō-nīf′) The cap. of Northwest Terrs., Canada, on the N shore of Great Slave Lake; founded in 1935 and the provincial cap. since 1967. Pop. 17,275.

yel·low·legs (yĕl′ō-lĕgz′) *n., pl.* **yellowlegs** Either of two North American wading birds (*Tringa melanoleuca* or *T. flavipes*) having yellow legs and a long narrow bill.

yellow ocher *n.* **1.** A yellow pigment, usu. containing limonite. **2.** A moderate orange with yellow overtones.

yellow pages or **Yellow Pages** *pl.n.* A volume or section of a telephone directory listing businesses, services, or products alphabetically by field. [Usu. printed on yellow paper.]

yellow perch *n.* A North American perch (*Perca flavescens*) having yellowish sides with dark vertical bars.

yellow peril or **Yellow Peril** *n. Offensive* Threatened expansion of Asian populations as imagined in the West.

yellow pine *n.* **1.** See **shortleaf pine. 2.** See **longleaf pine. 3.** The wood of either of these pines.

yellow poplar *n.* The tulip tree.

yellow rain *n.* A powdery poisonous yellow substance reported as dropping from the air in southeast Asia and found to be the excrement of wild honeybees contaminated with a fungal toxin.

Yellow River See **Huang He.**

Yellow Sea An arm of the Pacific Ocean between the Chinese mainland and the Korean Peninsula.

yel·low-shaft·ed flicker (yĕl′ō-shăf′tĭd) *n.* A large woodpecker (*Colaptes auratus*) of eastern North America having a black crescent on the breast, a conspicuous white rump, and yellow shafts in the wing and tail feathers.

yellow spot *n.* See **macula lutea.**

Yel·low·stone (yĕl′ō-stōn′) A river, c. 1,080 km (671 mi), of NW WY and S and E MT flowing through **Yellowstone Lake** and **Yellowstone National Park** to the Missouri R.

yel·low·tail (yĕl′ō-tāl′) *n.* **1.** Any of several large marine game fishes of the genus *Seriola,* having a yellow or yellowish tail. **2.** Any of several other fishes having a yellowish tail, as the silver perch.

yel·low·throat (yĕl′ō-thrōt′) *n.* Any of several small New World warblers of the genus *Geothlypis,* esp. *G. trichas,* having a yellow throat and a black facial mask in the male.

yel·low-throat·ed warbler (yĕl′ō-thrō′tĭd) *n.* A warbler (*Dendroica dominica*) of the southern United States, having a yellow throat and breast.

yellow warbler *n.* A small New World warbler (*Dendroica petechia*) having mostly yellow plumage with chestnut streaks along the sides.

yel·low·wood (yĕl′ō-wŏŏd′) *n.* **1a.** A deciduous tree (*Cladrastis lutea*) of the southeast United States having drooping clusters of white flowers and wood yielding a yellow dye. **b.** This wood. **2.** Any of various trees having yellow wood.

yel·low·y (yĕl′ō-ē) *adj.* Somewhat yellow; yellowish.

yelp (yĕlp) *v.* **yelped, yelp·ing, yelps** —*intr.* To utter a short sharp bark or cry. —*tr.* To utter by yelping. ❖ *n.* A short sharp bark or cry. [ME *yelpen,* to cry aloud < OE *gelpan, gielpan,* to boast.] —**yelp′er** *n.*

Yel·tsin (yĕlt′sĭn), **Boris Nikolaevich** b. 1931. Russian politician who was president of the republic of Russia from 1991 until his resignation in 1999.

Yem·en (yĕm′ən, yä′mən) A country of SW Asia at the S tip of Arabia; formed when Yemen (or North Yemen) merged with Southern Yemen in May 1990. Cap. Sana. Pop. 12,672,000. —**Yem′en·ite′, Yem′e·ni** (-ə-nē) *adj. & n.*

yen¹ (yĕn) *n.* A strong desire or inclination; a yearning or craving. ❖ *intr.v.* **yenned, yen·ning, yens** To have a yen. [Chin. (Cantonese) *uên,* hope, wish, equivalent to Chin. (Mandarin) *yuàn.*]

yen² (yĕn) *n., pl.* **yen** See table at **currency.** [J. *en* < Chin. (Mandarin) *yuán,* dollar.]

Ye·ni·sey (yĕn′ĭ-sā′, yĭ-nĭ-syä′) A river of central Russia flowing c. 4,023 km (2,500 mi) to the Kara Sea through **Yenisey Bay,** a long estuary.

yen·ta (yĕn′tə) *n. Slang* A person, esp. a woman, who is meddlesome or gossipy. [Yiddish *yente*, back-formation < the woman's name *Yente*, alteration of *Yentl* < OItal. *Gentile* < *gentile,* amiable, highborn < Lat. *gentīlis,* of the same clan. See GENTLE.]

yeo. *abbr.* **1.** yeoman **2.** yeomanry

yeo·man (yō′mən) *n.* **1a.** An attendant, servant, or lesser official in a royal or noble household. **b.** A yeoman of the guard. **2.** A petty officer performing chiefly clerical duties in the US Navy. **3.** An assistant or other subordinate, as of a sheriff. **4.** A diligent, dependable worker. **5.** A farmer who cultivates his own land, esp. a member of a former class of small freeholders in England. [ME *yoman,* perh. < OE *gēaman < O Frisian *gāman,* villager : *gā,* region, district, *man,* man. See man- in App.]

yeoman of the guard *n., pl.* **yeomen of the guard** A member of a ceremonial guard attending the British sovereign and royal family and also guarding the Tower of London.

yeo·man·ry (yō′mən-rē) *n., pl.* **-ries 1.** The class of yeomen; small freeholding farmers. **2.** A British volunteer cavalry force organized in 1761 to serve as a home guard and later incorporated into the Territorial Army.

yep (yĕp) *adv. Informal* Yes. [Alteration of YES.]

yer·ba ma·te (yûr′bə mä′tā, yâr′bə mä-tā′) *n.* See maté 2. [Am.Sp. *yerba mate : yerba,* herb + *mate,* maté.]

Ye·re·van also **E·re·van** or **E·ri·van** (yĕ′rĭ-vän′) The cap. of Armenia, in the W-central part. Pop. 1,254,000.

Yer·kes (yûr′kēz), **Robert Mearns** 1876–1956. Amer. psychologist who studied the intelligence of humans and primates.

yes (yĕs) *adv.* It is so; as you say or ask. Used to express affirmation, agreement, positive confirmation, or consent. ❖ *n., pl.* **yes·es** also **yes·ses 1.** An affirmative or consenting reply. **2.** An affirmative vote or voter. ❖ *tr.v.* **yessed, yes·sing, yes·ses** also **yes·es** To give an affirmative reply to. ❖ *interj.* Used to express great satisfaction, approval, or happiness. [ME < OE *gēse,* so be it! : prob. *gēa,* so) yes + *sīe,* may it be so; see **es-** in App.]

ye·shi·va or **ye·shi·vah** (yə-shē′və) *n. Judaism* **1.** An institute of learning where students study sacred texts, primarily the Talmud. **2.** An elementary or secondary school with a curriculum that includes religion and culture. [Heb. *yašîbâ < yāšab,* to sit down.]

yes man *n. Informal* One who slavishly agrees with a superior.

yester– *pref.* Yesterday: *yesternight.* [ME < OE *geostran.* See **dhgh(y)es-** in App.]

yes·ter·day (yĕs′tər-dā′, -dē) *n.* **1.** The day before the present day. **2.** also **yesterdays** Time in the past, esp. the recent past. ❖ *adv.* **1.** On the day before the present day. **2.** A short while ago. [ME < OE *geostran dæg : geostran,* yesterday; see YESTER– + *dæg,* day.]

yes·ter·night (yĕs′tər-nīt′) *n.* Last night. **—yes′ter·night′** *adv.*

yes·ter·year (yĕs′tər-yîr′) *n.* **1.** The year before the present year. **2.** Time past; yore. **—yes′ter·year′** *adv.*

yes·treen (yĕs-trēn′) *n. Scots* Yesterday evening.

yet (yĕt) *adv.* **1.** At this time; for the present: *isn't ready yet.* **2.** Up to a specified time; thus far: *The end had not yet come.* **3.** At a future time; eventually: *may yet change his mind.* **4.** Besides; in addition: *returned for yet another helping.* **5.** Still more; even: *a yet sadder tale.* **6.** Nevertheless: *young yet wise.* ❖ *conj.* And despite this; nevertheless: *She said she would be late, yet she arrived on time.* **—idiom: as yet** Up to the present time; up to now. [ME < OE *gīet.* See **i–** in App.]

> **USAGE NOTE** In formal style, *yet* in the sense "up to now" requires that the accompanying verb be in the present perfect, rather than in the simple past: *He hasn't started yet,* not *He didn't start yet.*

ye·ti (yĕt′ē) *n., pl.* **-tis** See abominable snowman. [Alteration of Tibetan *miti : mi,* person + *ti,* a kind of animal.]

Yev·tu·shen·ko (yĕv′tə-shĕng′kō, yĭf-tōō-shĕn′kə), **Yevgeny Aleksandrovich** b. 1933. Russian poet whose works include "Babi Yar" (1961).

yew (yōō) *n.* **1.** Any of several evergreen trees or shrubs of the genus *Taxus,* having scarlet cup-shaped arils and flat needles. **2.** Their wood. [ME *iw* < OE *īw.*]

Ygg·dra·sil also **Yg·dra·sil** (ĭg′drə-sĭl, ūg′-) *n. Mythology* In Norse mythology, the great ash tree that holds together earth, heaven, and hell by its roots and branches.

YHWH also **YHVH** or **JHVH** or **JHWH** (yōōd′hä′väv′hä′, yä′wä, yä′wĕ) *n.* A transliteration of the Tetragrammaton.

yid (yĭd) *n. Offensive Slang* Used as a disparaging term for a Jew. [Yiddish < MHGer. *jüde.* See YIDDISH.]

Yid·dish (yĭd′ĭsh) *n.* The language historically of Ashkenazic Jews of Central and Eastern Europe, resulting from a fusion of elements derived principally from medieval German dialects and secondarily from Hebrew and Aramaic, various Slavic languages, and Old French and Old Italian. [Yiddish *yidish,* Jewish, Yiddish < MHGer. *jüdisch,* Jewish < *jude, jüde,* Jew < OHGer. *judo < Lat. *Iūdaeus.* See JEW.] **—Yid′dish** *adj.* **—Yid′dish·ism** *n.*

yield (yēld) *v.* **yield·ed, yield·ing, yields** —*tr.* **1a.** To give forth by or as if by a natural process, esp. by cultivation. **b.** To furnish as return for effort or investment; be productive of. **2a.** To give over possession of, as in deference or defeat; surrender. **b.** To give up (an advantage, for example) to another; concede. —*intr.* **1a.** To give forth a natural product; be productive. **b.** To produce a return for effort or investment. **2a.** To give up, as in defeat; surrender or submit. **b.** To give way to pressure or force: *The door yielded to a gentle push.* **c.** To give way to argument, persuasion, influence, or entreaty. **d.** To give up one's place, as to one that is superior. ❖ *n.* **1a.** An amount yielded or produced; a product. **b.** A profit obtained from an investment; a return. **2.** The energy released by a nuclear explosion, expressed in units of weight of TNT required to produce an equivalent release. [ME *yielden < OE *geldan,* to pay.] **—yield′er** *n.*

SYNONYMS *yield, bow, defer, submit, succumb* These verbs mean to give in to what one can no longer oppose or resist. *Yield* has the widest application: "The child . . . soon yielded to the drowsiness" (Charles Dickens). *Bow* suggests giving way in defeat or through courtesy: "Bow and accept the end/Of a love" (Robert Frost). To *defer* is to yield out of respect for or in recognition of another's authority, knowledge, or judgment: "Philip . . . had the good sense to defer to the . . . wisdom of his father" (William Hickling Prescott). *Submit* implies giving way out of necessity, as after futile or unsuccessful resistance: "obliged to submit to those laws which are imposed upon us" (Abigail Adams). *Succumb* strongly suggests submission to something overpowering or overwhelming: "I didn't succumb without a struggle to my uncle's allurements" (H.G. Wells). See also Syns at **produce, relinquish.**

yield·ing (yēl′dĭng) *adj.* Inclined to give way to pressure, argument, or influence; docile. **—yield′ing·ness** *n.*

yikes (yīks) *interj.* Used to express mild fear or surprise. [?]

yin (yĭn) *n.* The passive, female cosmic principle in Chinese dualistic philosophy. [Chin. (Mandarin) *yīn,* moon, shade, female element.]

yin
yin-yang symbol

Yin·chuan also **Yin·chwan** (yĭn′chwän′) A city of N-central China WSW of Beijing; cap. of Ningxia Hiuzu province. Pop. 502,030.

yip (yĭp) *n.* A sharp high-pitched bark; a yelp. ❖ *intr.v.* **yipped, yip·ping, yips** To emit a yip; yelp. [Perh. ME *yippe,* a cheeping sound < *yippen,* to cheep, of imit. orig.]

yipe (yīp) also **yipes** (yīps) *interj. Informal* Used to express surprise, fear, or dismay.

yip·pee (yĭp′ē) *interj. Informal* Used to express joy or elation.

yip·pie (yĭp′ē) *n.* A member of a group of politically radical hippies, active esp. during the late 1960s. [< Y(outh) I(nternational) P(arty) (influenced by HIPPIE).]

-yl *suff.* An organic acid radical: *carbonyl.* [Fr. *-yle < Gk. *hūlē,* wood, matter.]

y·lang-y·lang or **i·lang-i·lang** (ē′läng-ē′läng) *n.* **1.** An Asian tree (*Cananga odorata*) having fragrant greenish-yellow flowers that yield an oil used in perfumery. **2.** An oil or a perfume obtained from the flowers of this tree. [Tagalog *ilang-ilang.*]

y·lem (ī′ləm) *n.* A form of matter hypothesized by proponents of the big bang theory to have existed before the formation of the chemical elements. [ME, universal matter < OFr. *ilem < Med.Lat. *hȳlem,* accusative of *hȳlē,* matter < Gk. *hūlē.*]

YMCA *abbr.* Young Men's Christian Association

YMHA *abbr.* Young Men's Hebrew Association

–yne *suff.* An unsaturated organic compound containing a triple bond between carbon atoms: *ethyne.* [Variant of –INE².]

yo (yō) *interj. Slang* Used as a greeting or to attract someone's attention.

yob (yŏb) *n. Chiefly British Slang* A rowdy, aggressive, or violent young man. [Alteration of BOY (spelled backward).]

yock (yŏk, yŭk) *Slang intr.v.* **yocked, yock·ing, yocks** To laugh or joke, esp. loudly. ❖ *n.* A loud laugh or joke. [Imit.]

yocto– *pref.* One septillionth (10⁻²⁴): *yoctosecond.* [Alteration of OCTO– (< its representing the eighth power of a thousand).]

yoc·to·sec·ond (yŏk′tə-sĕk′ənd) *n.* One septillionth (10⁻²⁴) of a second.

yo·del (yōd′l) *v.* **-deled, -del·ing, -dels** or **-delled, -del·ling, -dels** —*intr.* To sing so that the voice fluctuates rapidly between the normal chest voice and a falsetto. —*tr.* To sing (a song) by yodeling. ❖ *n.* A song or cry that is yodeled. [Ger. *jodeln < Ger. dialectal *jo,* exclamation of delight, of imit. orig.] **—yo′del·er** *n.*

yodh (yōōd, yōd) *n.* The tenth letter of the Hebrew alphabet. [Heb. *yôd* < Phoenician **yōd,* hand, tenth letter of the Phoenician alphabet.]

yo·ga (yō′gə) *n.* **1.** also **Yoga** A Hindu discipline aimed at training the consciousness for a state of perfect spiritual insight and tranquillity. **2.** A system of exercises practiced as part of this discipline to promote control of the body and mind. [Skt. *yogaḥ,* union, joining. See **yeug–** in App.] **—yo′gic** (-gĭk) *adj.*

yogh (yōкн) *n.* The Middle English letter ȝ, used to represent the sound (y) and the voiced and voiceless velar fricatives. [ME, poss. < OE *īw, ēoh,* yew.]

yo·gi (yō′gē) *n., pl.* **-gis** One who practices yoga. [Hindi *yogī* < Skt. < *yogaḥ,* union. See YOGA.]

yo·gurt also **yo·ghurt** or **yo·ghourt** (yō′gərt) *n.* A custardlike tart-flavored food prepared from milk curdled by bacteria, esp. *Lactobacillus bulgaricus* and *Streptococcus thermophilus,* often

yoga

sweetened or flavored. [Turk. *yoğurt* < *yoğur*, to knead.]

Yog·ya·kar·ta (yŏg′yə-kär′tə, jŏk′jä-, jŏk′yə-) or **Jog·ja·kar·ta** (jŏg′yə-kär′tə, jŏk′jä-) A city of S Java, Indonesia, ESE of Jakarta; founded 1749. Pop. 398,727.

yo·him·bine (yō-hĭm′bēn′) *n.* A poisonous alkaloid, $C_{21}H_{26}N_2O_3$, derived from the bark of a tree, *Corynanthe yohimbe,* and formerly used as an aphrodisiac, a local anesthetic, and a mydriatic. [NLat. *yohimbe,* specific epithet of *Corynanthe yohimbe,* species of tree from which it is derived (of Cameroonian Bantu orig.; akin to Douala *djombe*) + −INE².]

yoicks (yoiks) also **hoicks** (hoiks) *interj.* Used as a hunting cry to urge hounds after a fox.

yoke (yōk) *n.* **1a.** A crossbar with two U-shaped pieces that encircle the necks of a pair of oxen or other draft animals working together. **b.** *pl.* **yoke** or **yokes** A pair of draft animals, such as oxen, joined by a yoke. **c.** A bar used with a double harness to connect the collar of each horse to the pole of a wagon or coach. **2.** A frame designed to be carried across a person's shoulders with equal loads suspended from each end. **3.** *Nautical* A crossbar on a ship's rudder to which the steering cables are connected. **4.** A clamp or vise that holds a machine part in place or controls its movement or that holds two such parts together. **5.** A piece of a garment that is closely fitted, either around the neck and shoulders or at the hips, and from which an unfitted or gathered part of the garment is hung. **6.** Something that connects or joins together; a bond or tie. **7.** *Electronics* A series of two or more magnetic recording heads fastened securely together for playing or recording on more than one track simultaneously. **8a.** Any of various emblems of subjugation, such as a structure made of two upright spears with a third laid across them, under which conquered enemies of ancient Rome were forced to march. **b.** The condition of being subjugated by or as if by a conqueror; subjugation or bondage. ❖ *v.* **yoked, yok·ing, yokes** —*tr.* **1.** To fit or join with a yoke. **2a.** To harness a draft animal to. **b.** To harness (a draft animal) to a vehicle or an implement. **3.** To join securely as if with a yoke; bind. **4.** To force into heavy labor, bondage, or subjugation. —*intr.* To become joined securely. [ME < OE *geoc.* See **yeug-** in App.]

yo·kel (yō′kəl) *n.* A rustic; a bumpkin. [?]

Yo·ko·ha·ma (yō′kə-hä′mə, yō′kô-hä′mä) A city of SE Honshu, Japan, on the W Tokyo Bay. Pop. 3,288,464.

Yo·ko·su·ka (yō′kə-soō′kə, yō′kô-soō′kä) A city of SE Honshu, Japan, on Tokyo Bay. Pop. 435,383.

Yo·kuts (yō′kŭts) *n., pl.* **Yokuts 1.** A member of a group of Native American peoples inhabiting the southern San Joaquin Valley and adjacent foothills of the Sierra Nevada. **2.** Any or all of the languages of the Yokuts peoples.

yolk (yōk) *n.* **1a.** The yellow, usu. spherical portion of an egg of a bird or reptile, surrounded by the albumen and serving as nutriment for the developing young. **b.** A corresponding portion of the egg of other animals, consisting of protein and fat that serve as the primary source of nourishment for the early embryo. **2.** A greasy substance found in unprocessed sheep's wool. [ME *yolke* < OE *geolca* < *geolu,* yellow. See YELLOW.] —**yolk′y** *adj.*

yolk sac *n.* A membranous sac attached to an embryo, enclosing yolk in bony fishes, sharks, reptiles, birds, and primitive mammals and functioning as the circulatory system of the human embryo before internal circulation begins.

yolk stalk *n.* A narrow ductlike part that connects the yolk sac to the middle of the digestive tract of an embryo.

Yom Kip·pur (yŏm′ kĭp′ər, yŏm′, yŏm′, yŏm′ kē-poōr′) *n.* Judaism A holy day observed on the tenth day of Tishri and marked by fasting and prayer for the atonement of sins. [Heb. *yôm kippûr* : *yôm,* day + *kippûr,* atonement (< *kippēr,* to cover, atone).]

yon (yŏn) *adv. & adj.* Yonder. ❖ *pron. Regional* That one or those yonder. [ME, short for *yond,* yond; see YOND, and *yonder,* yonder; see YONDER. Pron., ME < OE *geon.* See **i-** in App.]

yond (yŏnd) *adv. & adj. Archaic* Yonder. [ME < OE *geond.* See **i-** in App.]

yon·der (yŏn′dər) *adv.* In or at that indicated place: *the house over yonder.* ❖ *adj.* Being at an indicated distance, usu. within sight. ❖ *pron.* One that is at an indicated place, usu. within sight. [ME < *yond,* yond. See YOND.]

yo·ni (yō′nē) *n., pl.* **-nis** *Hinduism* A stylized representation of a vulva worshiped as a symbol of a goddess or Shakti. [Skt. *yoniḥ,* womb, abode, source.]

Yon·kers (yŏng′kərz) A city of SE NY N of New York City; settled by the Dutch in the mid-1600s. Pop. 196,086.

yoo-hoo (yoō′hoō′) *interj.* Used to call someone at a distance or to gain someone's attention.

Yoo·per (yoō′pər) *n. Michigan & Northern Wisconsin* A native or inhabitant of the Upper Peninsula of Michigan. [< UP.]

yore (yôr, yōr) *n.* Time long past: *days of yore.* [ME, long ago, time long past < OE *gēara, gēara,* long ago < genitive pl. of *gēar,* year. See YEAR.]

York¹ (yôrk) Ruling house of England (1461–85), including Edward IV, Edward V, and Richard III. During the Wars of the Roses its symbol was a white rose.

York² A borough of N England on the Ouse R. ENE of Leeds; orig. a Celtic settlement. Pop. 101,600.

York, Alvin Cullum 1887–1964. Amer. World War I hero famed

Yorkshire terrier

Cy Young

for his single-handed attack on a German post.

York, Cape 1. The northernmost point of Australia, on Torres Strait at the tip of Cape York Peninsula. **2.** A cape of NW Greenland in N Baffin Bay; used as a base by Robert E. Peary.

Yorke Peninsula (yôrk) A narrow peninsula of S Australia bounded by Spencer Gulf.

York River An estuary, c. 64 km (40 mi), of E VA flowing SE into Chesapeake Bay.

York·shire (yôrk′shĭr, -shər) A historical region and former county of N England; an important area during Roman times and later part of the kingdom of Northumbria.

Yorkshire pudding *n.* A popoverlike quick bread served with roast beef, baked in the drippings of the beef. [After YORKSHIRE.]

Yorkshire terrier *n.* Any of a breed of toy terrier developed in Yorkshire and having a long silky bluish-gray coat.

York·town (yôrk′toun′) A village of SE VA on the York R. N of Newport News; site of important battles during the American Revolution and the Civil War.

Yo·ru·ba (yôr′ə-bə, yōr′-, yō-roō-bä′) *n., pl.* **Yoruba** or **-bas 1.** A member of a West African people living chiefly in southwest Nigeria. **2.** The Benue-Congo language of this people. —**Yo′ru·ban** *adj.*

Yo·sem·i·te Valley (yō-sĕm′ĭ-tē) A valley of E-central CA along the Merced R. It is surrounded by **Yosemite National Park** and includes many noted waterfalls, such as **Yosemite Falls,** with a total drop of 739.6 m (2,425 ft).

Yo·shi·hi·to (yō′shĭ-hē′tō, yô′shē-hē′tô) 1879–1926. Emperor of Japan (1912–26).

yotta– *pref.* One septillion (10^{24}): *yottahertz.* [Alteration of OCTO– (< its representing the eighth power of a thousand).]

yot·ta·hertz (yŏt′tə-hûrts′) *n.* One septillion (10^{24}) hertz.

you (yoō) *pron.* **1.** Used to refer to the one or ones being addressed: *I'll lend you the book.* See Regional Note at **you-all. 2.** Used to refer to an indefinitely specified person; one: *You can't win them all.* **3.** *Nonstandard* Used reflexively as the indirect object of a verb: *You might want to get you another hat.* See Note at **me.** [ME < OE *ēow,* dative and accusative of *gē,* ye, you. See **yu-** in App.]

you-all (yoō′ôl′) also **y'all** (yôl) *pron. Chiefly Southern US* You. Used in addressing two or more people or referring to two or more people, one of whom is addressed.

REGIONAL NOTE The single most famous feature of southern United States dialects is the pronoun *you-all,* often heard in its variant *y'all.* This plural form of *you* allows speakers to make the singular/plural distinction that English used to have in *thou/you.* When a single person is addressed as *you-all,* the speaker is not just referring to the person present, but to people associated with that person, such as relatives: *Did you-all* (that is, you and the others) *have dinner yet?* Other regions have their own plural forms of *you.* Some speakers in the Northeast and in Ireland say *youse,* while speakers in western Pennsylvania and the Appalachians say *you-uns.* Broadly in the northern US, the form *you guys* has arisen to serve this same function, and it appears to be spreading throughout the nation.

you'd (yoōd) **1.** Contraction of *you had.* **2.** Contraction of *you would.*

you'll (yoōl, yoōl; yəl *when unstressed*) Contraction of *you will.*

young (yŭng) *adj.* **young·er, young·est 1.** Being in an early period of life, development, or growth. **2.** Newly begun or formed; not advanced: *The evening is still young.* **3.** Of, belonging to, or suggestive of youth or early life. **4.** Vigorous or fresh; youthful. **5.** Lacking experience; immature. **6.** Being the junior of two people having the same name. **7.** *Geology* Being of an early stage in a geologic cycle. Used of bodies of water and land formations. ❖ *n.* **1.** Young persons considered as a group; youth. **2.** Offspring; brood. —*idiom:* **with young** Pregnant. [ME *yong* < OE *geong.* See **yeu-** in App.] —**young′ness** *n.*

Young, Andrew Jackson, Jr. b. 1932. Amer. politician who was US ambassador to the United Nations (1977–79) and mayor of Atlanta (1981–89).

Young, Brigham 1801–77. Amer. religious leader who directed the Mormon Church after the assassination (1844) of its founder, Joseph Smith, and led an exodus of the Mormons from IL to the west of present-day Salt Lake City UT.

Young, Denton True Known as "Cy." 1867–1955. Amer. baseball player who pitched the first perfect game (1904).

Young, Edward 1683–1765. English poet known for *Night Thoughts on Life, Death, and Immortality* (1742–45).

Young, Lester Willis Known as "Pres." 1909–59. Amer. jazz musician who greatly influenced jazz improvisation.

Young, Thomas 1773–1829. British physician, physicist, and Egyptologist who helped decipher the Rosetta Stone.

young·ber·ry (yŭng′bĕr′ē) *n.* **1.** A trailing prickly hybrid between a blackberry and a dewberry (*Rubus ursinus* cv. *Young*) of the rose family. **2.** The edible dark red berry of this plant. [After B.M. *Young* (fl. 1905), American fruit grower.]

young·ish (yŭng′ĭsh) *adj.* Somewhat young.

young·ling (yŭng′lĭng) *n.* A young person, animal, or plant.

young·ster (yŭng′stər) *n.* **1.** A young person; a child or youth. **2.** A young animal. **3.** A person who is a member of the second-year class in the US Naval Academy.

Youngs·town (yŭngz′toun′) A city of NE OH E of Akron. Pop. 82,026.

Young Turk n. 1. A member of a Turkish reformist and nationalist political party active in the early 20th century. 2. also **young Turk a.** A young progressive or insurgent member of a collective enterprise, such as a political party. b. A young person who rebels against authority.

young·'un (yŭng′ən) n. Informal A young one; a child.

youn·ker (yŭng′kər) n. 1. A young man. 2. A child. [Obsolete Du. jonchere, young nobleman < MDu. : jonc, young; see **yeu-** in App. + here, lord.]

your (yŏŏr, yŏr, yôr; yər when unstressed) adj. The possessive form of **you.** 1. Used as a modifier before a noun: your boots. 2. A person's; one's: The light switch is on your right. 3. Informal Used with little or no sense of possession to indicate a type familiar to the listener: your basic frame house. [ME < OE ēower, genitive of gē, ye. See **YOU.**]

you're (yŏŏr; yər when unstressed) Contraction of you are.

yours (yŏŏrz, yôrz, yŏrz) pron. (used with a sing. or pl. verb) 1. Used to indicate the one or ones belonging to you: The larger boots are yours. 2. Used often with an adverbial modifier in the complimentary close of a letter: Sincerely yours. —**idiom: yours truly** I, myself, or me. [ME < your, your. See **YOUR.**]

your·self (yŏŏr-sĕlf′, yôr-, yŏr-, yər-) pron. 1. That one identical with you. a. Used reflexively as the direct or indirect object of a verb or as the object of a preposition: Did you buy yourself a gift? b. Used for emphasis: You yourself were certain of the facts. c. Used in an absolute construction: In office yourself, you helped push the bill along. 2. Your normal or healthy condition: Are you feeling yourself again? See Usage Note at **myself.**

your·selves (yŏŏr-sĕlvz′, yôr-, yŏr-, yər-) pron. Plural of **yourself.** See Usage Note at **myself.**

youse (yŏŏz) pron. Chiefly Northern US You. Used in addressing two or more people or referring to two or more people, one of whom is addressed. See Regional Note at **you-all.** [YOU + -s[1].]

youth (yŏŏth) n., pl. **youths** (yŏŏthz, yŏŏthz) 1a. The condition or quality of being young. b. An early period of development or existence. 2. The time of life between childhood and maturity. 3a. A young person, esp. a young male in late adolescence. b. (used with a pl. verb) Young people considered as a group. 4. Geology The first stage in the erosion cycle. [ME youthe < OE geoguth. See **yeu-** in App.]

youth·ful (yŏŏth′fəl) adj. 1. Characterized by youth; young. 2. Of, relating to, or suggesting youth. 3. In an early stage of development; new. 4. Geology Young: a youthful streambed. —**youth′ful·ly** adv. —**youth′ful·ness** n.

youth hostel n. A supervised inexpensive lodging place for young travelers.

you-uns (yŏŏ′ənz) pron. Upper Southern US You. Used in addressing two or more people. [YOU + dialectal uns, people (var. of ones, pl. of ONE).]

you've (yŏŏv) Contraction of you have.

yow (you) interj. Used to express alarm, pain, or surprise.

yowl (youl) v. **yowled, yowl·ing, yowls** —intr. To utter a yowl. —tr. To say or utter with a yowl. ❖ n. A long loud mournful cry; a wail. [ME yowlen, prob. of imit. orig.]

yo-yo (yō′yō′) n., pl. **-yos** 1. A toy consisting of a flattened spool wound with string that is spun down from and reeled up to the hand by motions of the wrist. 2. Informal One that undergoes frequent shifts or reversals, as of opinion; a vacillator. 3. Slang A stupid or objectionable person. ❖ intr.v. **-yoed, -yo·ing, -yos** Informal To undergo frequent shifts or reversals, as of opinion; vacillate. [Orig. a trademark.]

Y·pres (ē′prə) See **Ieper.**

yr. abbr. 1. year 2. your

ys or **ysec** abbr. yoctosecond

Y.T. abbr. Yukon Territory

yt·ter·bi·um (ĭ-tûr′bē-əm) n. Symbol **Yb** A soft bright allotropic rare-earth element used as an x-ray source, in some laser materials, and in some special alloys. Atomic number 70; atomic weight 173.04; melting point 824°C; boiling point 1,196°C; specific gravity 6.972 or 6.54 (25°C) depending on allotropic form; valence 2, 3. See table at **element.** [After Ytterby, a town in Sweden.] —**yt·ter′bic** (-bĭk) adj.

yt·tri·a (ĭt′rē-ə) n. Symbol **yttrium oxide.** [NLat., after Ytterby, a town in Sweden.]

yt·tri·um (ĭt′rē-əm) n. Symbol **Y** A metallic element, not a rare earth but occurring in nearly all rare-earth minerals, used in various alloys, esp. to strengthen magnesium and aluminum alloys. Atomic number 39; atomic weight 88.906; melting point 1,522°C; boiling point 3,338°C; specific gravity 4.45 (25°C); valence 3. See table at **element.** [< YTTRIA.] —**yt′tric** (ĭt′rĭk) adj.

yttrium oxide n. A yellowish powder, Y₂O₃, used in optical glasses, ceramics, and color-television tubes.

yu·an (yŏŏ-än′, yü-) n., pl. **yuan** or **-ans** See table at **currency.** [Chin. (Mandarin) yuán, dollar.]

Yuan A Chinese dynasty (1279–1368) founded by Kublai Khan at

Peking (Beijing). [Chin. (Mandarin) Yuán < the phrase dà zāi qián yuán, how large the heaven is < yuán, primary, first.]

Yuan Jiang (jyäng′) See **Red River** 1.

yu·ca (yŏŏ′kə) n. See **cassava.** [Am.Sp. < Taino.]

Yu·ca·tán (yŏŏ′kə-tăn′, -tän′) A peninsula mostly in SE Mexico between the Caribbean Sea and the Gulf of Mexico and separated from W Cuba by the **Yucatán Channel.**

Yuc·a·tec (yŏŏ′kə-tĕk′) n., pl. **Yucatec** or **-tecs** 1. A member of a Mayan people inhabiting the Yucatán Peninsula. 2. The Mayan language of the Yucatec.

yuc·ca (yŭk′ə) n. Any of various evergreen plants of the genus Yucca, native to the warmer regions of North America and having often tall stout stems and white flowers. [< NLat. Iucca, genus name < Sp. yuca, cassava < Taino.]

Yu·chi (yŏŏ′chē) n., pl. **Yuchi** or **-chis** 1. A member of a Native American people formerly inhabiting northern Georgia and eastern Tennessee. 2. Their language. [Prob. Cherokee yutsi.]

yuck also **yuk** (yŭk) interj. Slang Used to express rejection or strong disgust.

yuck·y (yŭk′ē) adj. **-i·er, -i·est** Slang Repugnant; disgusting. —**yuck′i·ness** n.

Yu·ga (yŏŏg′ə) n. Hinduism One of the four ages constituting a cycle of history. [Skt. yugam, yoke, pair, era. See **yeug-** in App.]

Yugo. abbr. Yugoslavia

Yu·go·sla·vi·a (yŏŏ′gō-slä′vē-ə) A country (since 1992) of SE Europe comprising Serbia and Montenegro. It was orig. formed in 1918 as the Kingdom of Serbs, Croats, and Slovenes and renamed Yugoslavia in 1929. After 1946 the country included six constituent republics, four of which declared independence in 1991. Cap. Belgrade. Pop. 12,098,779. —**Yu′go·sla′vi·an** adj. & n.

yuk¹ (yŭk) Informal n. 1. An exuberant laugh. 2. One, such as a joke, that causes such a laugh. ❖ tr. & intr.v. **yukked, yuk·king, yuks** To joke or laugh exuberantly: yukked it up at the party. [Imit.]

yuk² (yŭk) interj. Slang Variant of **yuck.**

Yu·ka·wa (yŏŏ-kä′wä), **Hideki** 1907–81. Japanese physicist who won a 1949 Nobel Prize.

Yu·kon River (yŏŏ′kŏn′) A river flowing c. 3,218 km (2,000 mi) from S Yukon Terr., Canada, through AK to the Bering Sea; a major route to the Klondike during the gold rush of 1897–98.

Yukon Territory A territory of NW Canada E of AK; joined the Confederacy in 1898. Cap. Whitehorse. Pop. 30,766.

Yukon Time n. Alaska Standard Time.

Yule (yŏŏl) n. Christmas, or the season or feast celebrating Christmas. [ME yole < OE geōl.]

yule log n. A large log traditionally burned in a fireplace at Christmas.

Yule·tide (yŏŏl′tīd′) n. The Christmas season.

Yu·ma¹ (yŏŏ′mə) n., pl. **Yuma** or **-mas** 1. A member of a Native American people inhabiting an area along the lower Colorado River. 2. Their Yuman language. [Sp. < Papago yuumi.]

Yu·ma² (yŏŏ′mə) A city of SW AZ on the Colorado R. and the CA border. Pop. 77,515.

Yu·man (yŏŏ′mən) n. A language family constituting the languages of the Yuma and Mohave peoples and other Native American languages of western Arizona and adjacent parts of California and Mexico. —**Yu′man** adj.

yum·my (yŭm′ē) adj. **-mi·er, -mi·est** 1. Very pleasing to the taste or smell; delicious. 2. Delightful; pleasing. [< yum, the sound of smacking the lips.] —**yum′mi·ness** n.

Yun·nan (yŏŏ′nän′) A province of S-central China bordering on Vietnam, Laos, and Myanmar (Burma); became part of China in the 17th cent. Cap. Kunming. Pop. 36,972,610.

yup (yŭp) adv. Slang Yes. [Alteration of YEP.]

Yu·pik (yŏŏ′pĭk) n., pl. **Yupik** or **-piks** 1. A member of a group of Eskimoan peoples inhabiting the southwest coastal areas of Alaska and extreme northeastern Siberia, particularly the central part of this range. 2a. The family of languages spoken by the Yupik. b. Any of the languages spoken by the Yupik. See Usage Note at **Eskimo.** [Yupik Yup'ik, real person : yuk, human being + -pik, real.]

yup·pie (yŭp′ē) n. Informal A young city or suburban resident with a well-paid professional job and an affluent lifestyle. [Y(OUNG) + U(RBAN) + P(ROFESSIONAL), influenced by YIPPIE.]

yuppie flu n. Informal Chronic fatigue syndrome. [< the perception of it as a psychosomatic illness restricted to members of the young middle and upper classes.]

yup·pi·fy (yŭp′ə-fī′) tr.v. **-fied, -fy·ing, -fies** To make (an urban area, for example) attractive to young affluent residents or consumers. [YUPPIE + -FY.] —**yup′pi·fi·ca′tion** (-fĭ-kə′shən) n.

Yu·rok (yŏŏr′ŏk) n., pl. **Yurok** or **-roks** 1. A member of a Native American people inhabiting northwest California along the Pacific coast and lower Klamath River. 2. The language of this people. [Karok yúruk, downstream.]

yurt (yŏŏrt) n. A circular domed portable tent used by nomadic peoples of central Asia. [Russ. yurta, of Turkic orig.]

YWCA abbr. Young Women's Christian Association

YWHA abbr. Young Women's Hebrew Association

y·wis (ĭ-wĭs′) adv. Variant of **iwis.**

yucca
Mojave yucca
Yucca schidigera

Yugoslavia

yurt

ă pat	oi boy	
ā pay	ou out	
âr care	ŏŏ took	
ä father	ōō boot	
ĕ pet	ŭ cut	
ē be	ûr urge	
ĭ pit	th thin	
ī pie	th this	
îr pier	hw which	
ŏ pot	zh vision	
ō toe	ə about,	
ô paw	item	

Stress marks:
′ (primary);
′ (secondary), as in
lexicon (lĕk′sĭ-kŏn′)

Zz

z or **Z** (zē) *n., pl.* **z's** or **Z's** also **zs** or **Zs** **1.** The 26th letter of the modern English alphabet. **2.** Any of the speech sounds represented by the letter z. **3.** The 26th in a series. **4.** Something shaped like the letter Z. **5. z's** *Slang* Sleep.

Z 1. The symbol for **atomic number. 2.** The symbol for **impedance.**

za (zä) *n. Slang* Pizza. [Shortening and alteration of PIZZA.]

OUR LIVING LANGUAGE When young people today speak casually of ordering a *za*, "pizza," they are unwittingly producing an expression that is quite interesting to language historians. *Za* derives from the full form *pizza* by a process known as *clipping*. Two types of clipping are common in English: dropping the unstressed syllables or syllables not receiving the primary word stress, as in *fridge* from *refrigerator*; and dropping all syllables after the first syllable, as in *ab, dis,* and *vibe,* whether or not the first syllable was originally stressed. In the case of *za,* the syllable that was dropped was originally stressed *and* was the first syllable, which is unusual. *Rents* for "parents" is another recent example of the same kind of clipping. Interestingly, we don't need to stay in the realm of contemporary youth slang to see the results of this unusual process. The words *phone, bus,* and *wig* (from *telephone, omnibus, periwig*) belong to Standard English but had their start as slangy or catchy neologisms formed by clipping stressed syllables, just like *za.* Who knows whether in fifty years *za* and *rents* will be as widely accepted as *phone* and *wig* are now? See Note at **rent³.**

---

za·ba·glio·ne (zä′bəl-yō′nē, -bäl-yō′nē) *n.* A dessert or sauce consisting of egg yolks, sugar, and wine beaten until thick. [Ital., var. of *zabaione,* ult. < Illyrian *sabaium,* beer.]

Zab·rze (zäb′zhě) A city of S-central Poland W of Katowice; founded in the 13th cent. Pop. 205,544.

Zach·a·rias (zăk′ə-rī′əs) also **Zech·a·ri·ah** (zěk′ə-rī′ə) In the Bible, the husband of Elizabeth and the father of John the Baptist.

zaf·fer also **zaf·fre** (zăf′ər) *n.* An impure oxide of cobalt, used to produce a blue color in enamel and in the making of smalt. [Ital. *zaffera* < OFr. *safre,* perh. alteration of *safir,* sapphire; see SAPPHIRE, or < Ar. *ṣufr,* yellow copper, brass (< *'aṣfar,* yellow).]

zaf·tig or **zof·tig** (zäf′tĭk, -tĭg) *adj.* **1.** Full-bosomed. **2.** Having a full shapely figure. [Yiddish *zaftik,* juicy < MHGer. *saftec* < *saft,* juice < OHGer. *saf.*]

zag (zăg) *n.* One of a series of sharp turns or reversals: *zigs and zags.* ❖ *intr.v.* **zagged, zag·ging, zags 1.** To turn or change direction suddenly. Usu. used in contrast to *zig: The runner zigged when he should have zagged.* **2.** To behave erratically or indecisively. Usu. used with *zig.* [< ZIGZAG.]

Za·greb (zä′grěb) The cap. of Croatia, in the N part on the Sava R. Pop. 867,717.

Zag·ros Mountains (zăg′rəs) A range of W Iran forming the W and S borders of the central Iranian plateau and rising to 4,550.6 m (14,920 ft).

Za·har·i·as (zə-här′ē-əs), **Mildred Ella Didrikson** Known as "Babe." 1914–56. Amer. athlete who excelled in golf and track and won two gold medals at the 1932 Olympics.

zai·bat·su (zī′bät-sōō′) *n., pl.* **zaibatsu 1.** A powerful family-controlled commercial combine of Japan. **2.** A Japanese conglomerate or cartel. [J. : *zai,* wealth (< M Chin. *dzəi*) + *batsu,* powerful person or family (< M Chin. *buat*).]

Za·ire (zī′îr, zä-îr′) See **Congo** 2. —**Za·ir′e·an, Za·ir′i·an** *adj. & n.*

Zaire River See **Congo River.**

zal·ci·ta·bine (zăl′sī-tə-bīn′) *n.* See **DDC.** [*zal-* (perh. (de)s-, var. of DE- + AL(COHOL)) + alteration of CYTIDINE.]

Za·ma (zā′mə, zä′mä) An ancient town of N Africa SW of Carthage in present-day N Tunisia; site of the Roman defeat of Hannibal, which ended the Second Punic War (202 B.C.).

Zam·be·zi (zăm-bē′zē) A river of central and S Africa rising in NW Zambia and flowing c. 2,735 km (1,700 mi) to the Mozambique Channel.

Zam·bi·a (zăm′bē-ə) A country of S-central Africa; gained independence from Great Britain in 1964. Cap. Lusaka. Pop. 9,160,000. —**Zam′bi·an** *adj. & n.*

Zam·bo·ni (zăm-bō′nē) A trademark used for a machine that resurfaces the ice in an ice rink.

za·mi·a (zā′mē-ə) *n.* Any of various chiefly tropical American cycads of the genus *Zamia,* having a thick trunk, palmlike terminal leaves, and seeds borne in woody cones. [NLat. *Zamia,* genus name < misreading of *(nucēs) azāniae,* pine cone (nuts), prob.

< Gk. *azainein,* to dry up < *azein,* to dry. See **as-** in App.]

zam·in·dar also **zem·in·dar** (zăm′ən-där′, zěm′-, zə-měn-där′) *n.* **1.** An official in precolonial India assigned to collect the land taxes of his district. **2.** A landholder in British colonial India responsible for collecting and paying to the government the taxes on the land under his jurisdiction. [Hindi *zamīndār* < Pers. : *zamīn,* earth; see **dhghem-** in App. + *-dār,* -holder.]

zan·der (zăn′dər) *n., pl.* **zander** or **-ders** A common European pikeperch (*Stizostedion lucioperca*) valued as a food fish. [Ger. < LGer. *Sander* < MLGer. *sandāt,* perh. of Slav. orig.]

za·ny (zā′nē) *n., pl.* **-nies 1.** A comic performer who assists or imitates a clown, acrobat, or mountebank. **2.** A comical person given to extravagant or outlandish behavior. ❖ *adj.* **-ni·er, -ni·est 1.** Ludicrously comical; clownish. **2.** Comical because of incongruity or strangeness; bizarre. [Fr. *zani* < Ital. dialectal *zanni* < *Zanni,* var. of Ital. *Gianni,* nickname for *Giovanni,* John, the name of servants who act as clowns in commedia dell'arte.] —**za′ni·ly** *adv.* —**za′ni·ness** *n.*

Zan·zi·bar (zăn′zə-bär′) **1.** A region of E Africa, comprising Zanzibar Island and several adjacent islands; became an independent sultanate in 1963 and in 1964 joined Tanganyika to form Tanzania. **2.** A city of Tanzania on the W coast of Zanzibar I.; founded in the 16th cent. Pop. 133,000.

zap (zăp) *Slang v.* **zapped, zap·ping, zaps** —*tr.* **1a.** To destroy or kill with a burst of gunfire, flame, or electric current. **b.** To kill or destroy as if by shooting. **c.** To strike suddenly and forcefully as if with a projectile or weapon. **d.** To expose to radiation; irradiate. **2.** To attack (an enemy) with heavy firepower; strafe or bombard. **3.** To use a remote control device to switch (channels on a television) or to turn off (a television set). —*intr.* To move swiftly; zoom. ❖ *n.* Something that imparts excitement or great interest. ❖ *interj.* **1.** Used to imitate a sound made by a gun when fired. **2.** Used to indicate a sudden occurrence. [Imit.]

Za·pa·ta (zə-pä′tə, sä-pä′tä), **Emiliano** 1879?–1919. Mexican revolutionary who led an agrarian revolt (1910–19).

za·pa·te·a·do (zä′pə-tā-ä′dō, sä′pä-tě-) *n., pl.* **-dos** A Spanish flamenco dance in which the performer stamps and taps rhythmically with the heels. [Sp. < *zapatear,* to tap with the shoe < *zapato,* shoe.]

Za·po·pan (zä′pō-pän′, sä′-) A city of SW Mexico W of Guadalajara. Pop. 345,390.

Za·po·rizh·zhya (zä′pō-rězh′zhyä) or **Za·po·ro·zhe** (zä′pō-rō′zhě) Formerly **A·lek·san·drovsk** (äl′ĭk-sän′drəfsk, ə-lĭk-sän′-) A city of S Ukraine W of Donetsk; founded 1770. Pop. 897,600.

Za·po·tec (zä′pə-těk′, sä′pō-) *n., pl.* **Zapotec** or **-tecs 1a.** A member of a Mesoamerican Indian people of southern Mexico, whose civilization reached its height around A.D. 300–900. **b.** A modern-day descendant of this people. **2.** Any of a group of related languages spoken in southern Mexico. [Sp. *Zapoteco* < Nahuatl *tzapotēcah,* pl. of *tzapotēcatl,* person from Tzapotlan < *Tzapotlan,* place name : *tzapotl,* sapodilla + *tlān,* place.] —**Za′po·tec′** *adj.*

zap·py (zăp′ē) *adj.* **-pi·er, -pi·est** *Slang* Lively: *a zappy tune.*

Za·ra·go·za (zär′ə-gō′zə, thä′rä-gō′thä) See **Saragossa.**

Zar·a·thu·stra (zär′ə-thōō′strə) See **Zoroaster.**

za·re·ba also **za·ree·ba** (zə-rē′bə) *n.* **1.** An enclosure of bushes or stakes protecting a campsite or village in northeast Africa. **2.** A campsite or village protected by such an enclosure. [Ar. *zarība,* cattle pen.]

zarf (zärf) *n.* A chalicelike holder for a hot coffee cup, typically made of ornamented metal, used in the Middle East. [Ar. *ẓarf,* container.]

zas·tru·ga (ză-strōō′gə, zä-) *n.* Variant of **sastruga.**

z-ax·is (zē′ăk′sĭs) *n., pl.* **z-ax·es** (zē′ăk′sēz) One of three axes in a three-dimensional Cartesian coordinate system.

za·yin (zä′yĭn) *n.* The seventh letter of the Hebrew alphabet. [Heb. < Phoenician **zēn,* seventh letter of the Phoenician alphabet.]

Z boson *n.* An elementary particle that has a mass 182,000 times that of the electron, is electrically neutral, and constitutes the quantum of weak interactions in which the charges of participating particles do not change.

Zc *abbr. Bible* Zechariah

zeal (zēl) *n.* Enthusiastic devotion to a cause, ideal, or goal and tireless diligence in its furtherance. [ME *zele* < OFr. *zel* < LLat. *zēlus* < Gk. *zēlos.*]

Zea·land (zē′lənd) See **Sjaelland.**

zeal·ot (zěl′ət) *n.* **1a.** One who is zealous, esp. excessively so. **b.**

**Babe Didrikson
Zaharias**

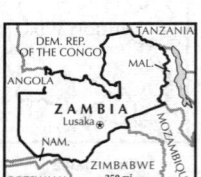

Zambia

Emiliano Zapata

A fanatically committed person. **2. Zealot** A member of a Jewish movement of the first century A.D. that fought against Roman rule in Palestine as incompatible with strict monotheism. [ME *zelote* < Lat. *zēlōtēs* < Gk. < *zēlos*, zeal.]

zeal•ot•ry (zĕl′ə-trē) *n.* Excessive zeal; fanaticism.

zeal•ous (zĕl′əs) *adj.* Filled with or motivated by zeal; fervent. **—zeal′ous•ly** *adv.* **—zeal′ous•ness** *n.*

ze•a•tin (zē′ə-tĭn) *n.* A cytokinin originally isolated from young corn kernels. [NLat. *Zēa*, corn genus; see ZEIN + –IN.]

ze•bec or **ze•beck** (zē′bĕk′) *n.* Variant of xebec.

Zeb•e•dee (zĕb′ĭ-dē′) In the Bible, a fisherman whose sons James and John became disciples of Jesus.

ze•bra (zē′brə) *n.* Any of several swift, wild, horselike African mammals of the genus *Equus*, having distinctive overall markings of alternating white and black or brown stripes. [Ital. < OPort. *zevro, zevra*, wild ass.] **—ze′brine′** (zē′brīn′) *adj.*

zebra crossing *n. Chiefly British* A pedestrian crosswalk.

zebra danio *n.* See zebra fish.

zebra finch *n.* A small Australian bird (*Poephila guttata*) having black and white markings and popular as a cage bird.

zebra fish *n.* A small freshwater tropical fish (*Brachydanio rerio*) of India having horizontal dark blue and silvery stripes.

zebra mussel *n.* A small freshwater mussel (*Dreissena polymorpha*) with a usu. striped shell, native to Eurasia but now widely established in the Great Lakes and other North American waterways.

ze•bra•wood (zē′brə-wo͝od′) *n.* **1.** Any of several African or tropical American trees having striped wood. **2.** The wood of any of these trees, used in cabinetmaking.

ze•bu (zē′bo͞o, -byo͞o) *n.* A domesticated ox (*Bos indicus*) of Asia and eastern Africa having a prominent hump on the back and a large dewlap. [Fr. *zébu*.]

Zeb•u•lon also **Zeb•u•lun** (zĕb′yə-lən) In the Bible, a son of Jacob and Leah and the forebear of one of the tribes of Israel.

zec•chi•no (zĕ-kē′nō) also **zec•chin** or **zech•in** (zĕk′ĭn) *n., pl.* **-ni** (-nē) or **-nos** also **-chins** or **-ins** See sequin 2. [Ital. See SEQUIN.]

Zech. *abbr. Bible* Zechariah

Zech•a•ri•ah[1] (zĕk′ə-rī′ə) A Hebrew prophet of the 6th cent. B.C. [Heb. *Zəkaryāh*, Yahweh has remembered : *zākar, zakar*, he remembered + *yāh*, Yahweh.]

Zech•a•ri•ah[2] (zĕk′ə-rī′ə) See Zacharias.

Zech•a•ri•ah[3] (zĕk′ə-rī′ə) *n.* See table at Bible. [After ZECHARIAH[1].]

zed (zĕd) *n. Chiefly British* The letter z. [ME < OFr. *zede* < LLat. *zēta*, zeta < Gk. See ZETA.]

Zed•e•ki•ah (zĕd′ĭ-kī′ə) 6th cent. B.C. The last king of Judah (597–586 B.C.), who led an unsuccessful uprising (588–586) against Nebuchadnezzar II and died in captivity in Babylon.

zed•o•ar•y (zĕd′ō-ĕr′ē) *n., pl.* **-ies 1.** An Indian plant (*Curcuma zedoaria*) having yellow flowers and starchy tuberous rhizomes. **2.** The dried rhizomes of this plant, used as a condiment and in perfumes, medicines, and cosmetics. [ME *zeduarie* < Med.Lat. *zeduāria* < Ar. *zadwār* < Pers.]

zee (zē) *n.* The letter z.

Zee•land (zē′lənd, zā′länt) A historical region of SW Netherlands bordering on Belgium and the North Sea; part of Holland after the 10th cent.

Zee•man (zā′män′), **Pieter** 1865–1943. Dutch physicist who shared a 1902 Nobel Prize.

Zeeman effect *n.* The splitting of single spectral lines of an emission spectrum into three or more polarized components when the radiation source is in a magnetic field.

ze•in (zē′ĭn) *n.* A prolamine protein derived from corn, used in the manufacture of various plastics, coatings, and lacquers. [NLat. *Zēa*, corn genus (< Lat. *zēa*, emmer < Gk. *zeia*, one-seeded wheat, barley) + –IN.]

Zeit•geist (tsīt′gīst′, zīt′-) *n.* The spirit of the time; the taste and outlook characteristic of a period or generation. [Ger. : *Zeit*, time (< MHGer. *zīt* < OHGer.; see dā– in App.) + *Geist*, spirit; see POLTERGEIST.]

zem•in•dar (zăm′ən-där′, zĕm′-, zə-mēn-där′) *n.* Variant of zamindar.

zemst•vo (zĕmst′vō, zyĕm′stvə) *n., pl.* **-vos** An elective council responsible for the local administration of a provincial district in czarist Russia. [Russ. < ORuss. *zemĭ*, land. See dhghem- in App.]

Zen (zĕn) *n.* A school of Mahayana Buddhism, practiced mainly in China, Japan, Korea, and Vietnam, asserting that enlightenment can be attained through meditation, self-contemplation, and intuition. [J. *zen* < Chin. (Mandarin) *chán*, meditation < Pali *jhānam*, meditation < Skt. *dhyānam, < dhyāti*, he meditates.]

ze•na•na (zə-nä′nə) *n.* The part of a house in Asian countries such as India and Pakistan reserved for the women of the household. [Hindi *zenāna* < Pers. < *zan*, woman. See gʷen- in App.]

Zen Buddhism *n.* See Zen. **—Zen Buddhist** *n.*

Zend (zĕnd) *n.* **1.** The Avesta. No longer in scholarly use. **2.** Avestan. No longer in scholarly use. [Short for ZEND-AVESTA.]

Zend-A•ves•ta (zĕn′də-vĕs′tə) *n.* The Avesta. [Fr. < Pers. *zandavastā* < transposition of *Avestā-va-zend*, text and commentary < MPers. *Abestāg u zand* : *abestāg*, text (sense uncertain, poss. < Avestan **upastāvaka-*, praise < *upastaoiti*, he praises : *upa-*, up

to, at; see upo in App. + *staoiti*, he praises) + *u*, with + *zand*, explanation (< Avestan *zainti-*, knowledge, interpretation; see gnō- in App.).] **—Zend′-A•ves′ta•ric** (-vĕs-tä′rĭk) *adj.*

ze•ner diode or **Ze•ner diode** (zē′nər) *n.* A silicon semiconductor device used as a voltage regulator because of its ability to maintain an almost constant voltage with a wide range of currents. [After Clarence Melvin Zener (1905–93), American physicist.]

Zeng•er (zĕng′gər, -ər), **John Peter** 1697–1746. German-born colonial printer and journalist whose acquittal (1735) of libel charges set a legal precedent for freedom of the press.

ze•nith (zē′nĭth) *n.* **1.** The point on the celestial sphere that is directly above the observer. **2.** The upper region of the sky. **3.** The highest point above the observer's horizon attained by a celestial body. **4.** The point of culmination; the peak: *the zenith of her career.* [ME *senith* < OFr. *cenith* < Med.Lat. < Ar. *samt (ar-ra's)*, path (over the head) < Lat. *sēmita*, path.]

Ze•no of Cit•i•um (zē′nō, sĭt′ē-əm) 335?–263? B.C. Greek philosopher who founded the Stoic school.

Zeno of E•le•a (ē-lē′ə) 495?–430? B.C. Greek philosopher who formulated numerous paradoxes that challenged the ideas of pluralism and the existence of motion and change.

ze•o•lite (zē′ə-līt′) *n.* Any one of a family of hydrous aluminum silicate minerals, whose molecules enclose cations of sodium, potassium, calcium, strontium, or barium, or a corresponding synthetic compound, used as molecular filters and ion-exchange agents. [Swed. *zeolit* < Gk. *zein*, to boil (< swelling and boiling under the blowpipe). See yes– in App.]

zep (zĕp) *n. Chiefly New Jersey* See submarine 2. See Regional Note at **submarine.** [Poss. short for ZEPPELIN (< its shape).]

Zep or **Zeph.** *abbr. Bible* Zephaniah

Zeph•a•ni•ah[1] (zĕf′ə-nī′ə) A Hebrew prophet of the 7th cent. B.C. [Heb. *ṣəpanyāh*, Yahweh has treasured : *šāpan, sapan*, he has hidden, he has treasured + *yāh*, Yahweh.]

Zeph•a•ni•ah[2] (zĕf′ə-nī′ə) *n.* See table at Bible. [After ZEPHANIAH[1].]

zeph•yr (zĕf′ər) *n.* **1.** The west wind. **2.** A gentle breeze. **3.** Any of various soft light fabrics, yarns, or garments. **4.** Something that is airy, insubstantial, or passing. [ME *Zephirus, Zephyrus* < Lat. *Zephyrus* < Gk. *Zephuros*.]

Zeph•y•rus (zĕf′ər-əs) *n. Greek Mythology* A god personifying the west wind.

zep•pe•lin also **Zep•pe•lin** (zĕp′ə-lĭn) *n.* A rigid airship having a long cylindrical body supported by internal gas cells.

Zep•pe•lin (zĕp′ə-lĭn, zĕp′lĭn, tsĕp′ə-lēn′), Count **Ferdinand von** 1838–1917. German inventor who designed the first motorized rigid-frame dirigible balloon (1900).

zepto– *pref.* One sextillionth (10^{-21}): *zeptosecond.* [< alteration of Lat. *septem*, seven (< its representing the seventh power of a thousandth). See SEPTET.]

zep•to•sec•ond (zĕp′tō-sĕk′ənd) *n.* One sextillionth (10^{-21}) of a second.

ze•ro (zîr′ō, zē′rō) *n., pl.* **-ros** or **-roes 1.** The numerical symbol 0; a cipher. **2.** *Mathematics* **a.** The identity element for addition. **b.** A cardinal number indicating the absence of any or all units under consideration. **c.** An ordinal number indicating an initial point or origin. **d.** An argument at which the value of a function vanishes. **3.** The temperature indicated by the numeral 0 on a thermometer. **4.** A sight setting that enables a firearm to shoot on target. **5.** *Informal* One having no influence or importance; a nonentity. **6.** The lowest point: *Prospects approached zero.* **7.** A zero-coupon bond. **8.** *Informal* Nothing; nil. ❖ *adj.* **1.** Of, relating to, or being zero. **2a.** Having no determinable value. **b.** *Informal* Absent, inoperative, or irrelevant in specified circumstances. **3.** *Meteorology* **a.** Being a ceiling not more than 16 meters (52 feet) high. **b.** Limited in horizontal visibility to no more than 55 meters (180 feet). **4.** *Linguistics* Of or relating to a morpheme that is expected by an established, regular paradigm but has no spoken or written form. *Moose* has a zero plural; that is, its plural is *moose.* ❖ *tr.v.* **-roed, -ro•ing, -roes** To adjust (an instrument or a device) to zero value. **—phrasal verb: zero in 1a.** To aim or concentrate firepower on an exact target location. **b.** To adjust the aim or sight of by repeated firings. **2.** To converge intently; close in: *The children zeroed in on the toys.* [Ital. < alteration of Med.Lat. *zephirum* < Ar. *ṣifr*, nothing, cipher. See CIPHER.]

ze•ro-base (zîr′ō-bās′, zē′rō-) or **ze•ro-based** (-bāst′) *adj.* Having each expenditure or item justified as to need or cost.

zero copula *n.* The absence of an overt copula, esp. when meaning "is" or "are."

OUR LIVING LANGUAGE A widely known feature of African American Vernacular English (AAVE) and some varieties of Southern American English spoken by working-class white people is the absence of a form of *be* in situations where Standard English would normally require one. In these varieties of English, one can say *He working,* where Standard English has *He is working,* meaning "He is working right now." Linguists frequently describe this zero usage as *zero copula,* although strictly speaking it should be described as *zero auxiliary* before progressive verb forms, as in *He working,* and before *going to* or *gon(na),* as in *He gon do it.* For some AAVE speakers, zero copula occurs 80 to 90 percent of the time where Standard English requires *is* or *are.* No other varieties of American English use zero copula as often. • In the late 1960s, linguist William Labov described the use of zero copula by stating that wherever Standard English can contract *is* or *are,* AAVE can delete it. Thus, in AAVE, *was* and *were* are never deleted. Equally systematic are the quantitative regularities of the zero copula. Throughout the United States, zero copula is less frequent when followed by a noun (*He a man*) than when followed by an adjective (*He happy*). It is most frequent when followed by progressives and *gon(na),* as exemplified above. • This pattern of *be*-deletion is also found in Gullah and Caribbean creole varieties of English. Since zero copula is not a feature of the British dialects of English that colonial settlers brought to the United States, it is one of the strongest indicators that the development of AAVE may have been influenced by Caribbean English creoles or that AAVE itself may have evolved from an American Creole-like ancestor. See Note at **be.**

ze·ro-cou·pon (zîr'ō-koō'pŏn, -kyō'-, zē'rō-) *adj.* Paying no interest until maturity or sale: *a zero-coupon bond.*

zero gravity *n.* The condition of apparent weightlessness occurring when the centrifugal force on a body exactly counterbalances the gravitational attraction on it.

zero hour *n.* The scheduled time for the start of an operation or action, esp. a combat operation of great size.

ze·ro-point energy (zîr'ō-point', zē'rō-) *n.* The irreducible minimum energy possessed by a substance at absolute zero temperature.

zero population growth *n.* The limiting of population increase to the number of live births needed to replace the existing population.

ze·ro-sum (zîr'ō-sŭm', zē'rō-) *adj.* Of or relating to a situation in which a gain is offset by an equal loss.

zero-sum game *n.* A situation in which a gain by one must be matched by a loss by another.

ze·roth (zē'rōth, zē'rōth) *adj.* The ordinal number matching the number 0 in a series: *the zeroth power of 10.*

zero tolerance *n.* The policy or practice of not tolerating undesirable behavior, such as illegal drug use, esp. in the automatic imposition of severe penalties for first offenses.

zest (zĕst) *n.* **1a.** Flavor or interest; piquancy. **b.** The outermost part of the rind of an orange, lemon, or other citrus fruit, used as flavoring. **2.** Spirited enjoyment; gusto. ❖ *tr.v.* **zest·ed, zest·ing, zests** To give zest, charm, or spirit to. [Obsolete Fr., orange or lemon peel.] —**zest'ful** *adj.* —**zest'ful·ly** *adv.*

ze·ta (zā'tə, zē'-) *n.* The sixth letter of the Greek alphabet. [Gk. *zēta* < Phoenician **zēn,* seventh letter of the Phoenician alphabet (influenced by the following letter *ēta,* eta).]

Ze·thus also **Ze·thos** (zē'thəs) *n. Greek Mythology* The twin brother of Amphion.

zetta– *pref.* One sextillion (10²¹): *zettahertz.* [< alteration of Lat. *septem,* seven (< its representing the seventh power of a thousand). See SEPTET.]

zet·ta·hertz (zĕt'ə-hûrts') *n.* One sextillion (10²¹) hertz.

zeug·ma (zoōg'mə) *n.* **1.** A construction in which a single word, esp. a verb or an adjective, is applied to two or more nouns when its sense is appropriate to only one of them or to both in different ways, as in *He took my advice and my wallet.* **2.** Syllepsis. [Lat. < Gk., a joining, bond. See yeug- in App.]

Zeus (zoōs) *n. Greek Mythology* The principal god of the Greek pantheon, ruler of the heavens and father of other gods and mortal heroes. [Gk. See dyeu- in App.]

WORD HISTORY Homer's *Iliad* calls him "*Zeus who thunders on high,*" and Milton's *Paradise Lost, "the Thunderer,"* so it is surprising to learn that the Indo-European ancestor of *Zeus* was a god of the bright daytime sky. In the *Iliad,* prayers to Zeus begin with the vocative form *Zeu pater,* "o father Zeus"; Father Zeus was the head of the Greek pantheon. Another ancient Indo-European society, the Romans, called the head of their pantheon *Iūpiter* or *Iuppiter,* "Jupiter." His name means "father Jove" (*-piter* is just a reduced form of *pater,* "father," and *Iū-* is from *Iov-,* "Jove"). In fact, *Iūpiter* corresponds precisely to *Zeu pater* in Greek. A third exact parallel is found in the early Hindu god addressed in Sanskrit as *Dyauṣ pitar. Pitar* means "father," and *dyauṣ* means "sky." We can equate Greek *Zeu pater,* Latin *Iūpiter,* and Sanskrit *Dyauṣ pitar* and reconstruct an Indo-European deity, **Dyēus pater,* who was associated with the sky and addressed as "father." Comparative philology has revealed that the "sky" word refers specifically to the bright daytime sky, as it is derived from the root meaning "to shine." • Closely related to these words is Indo-European **deiwos,* "god," which shows up, among other places, in the name of the Old English god *Tīw* in Modern English *Tuesday,* "Tiw's day."

Zeux·is (zoōk'sĭs) 5th cent. B.C. Greek artist who was among the first Athenians to use shading.

Ze·ya (zā'yə, zyē'-) A river of SE Russia flowing c. 1,287 km (800 mi) to the Amur R.

Zham·byl (jäm-bĭl') or **Dzham·bul** (-boōl') A city of S-central Kazakhstan near the border with Kyrgyzstan; founded in the 7th cent. Pop. 317,000.

Zeus
c. 455 B.C. bronze statue recovered from the sea off Cape Artemision, Greece

Zimbabwe²

Zhang·jia·kou (jäng'jyä'kō') also **Kal·gan** (käl'gän') A city of NE China NW of Beijing. Pop. 719,672.

Zhan·jiang also **Chan·chiang** (jän'jyäng') or **Chan·kiang** (chän'kyäng') A city of SE China SW of Guangzhou on an inlet of the South China Sea. Pop. 1,800,720.

Zhao Kuang·yin or **Chao K'uang-yin** (jou' kwäng'yĭn') 927–976. Emperor of China (960–976) who founded the Song dynasty and unified much of China.

Zhao Zi·yang (jou' dzē-yäng') or **Chao Tzu-yang** (jou' dzoō-yäng') b. 1919. Chinese premier (1980–87) and general secretary of the Communist Party (1987–89).

Zhda·nov (zhdä'nəf) See **Mariupol'.**

Zhe·jiang (jŭ'jyäng') also **Che·kiang** (chŭ'kyäng', jŭ'gyäng') A province of E China on the East China Sea. Cap. Hangzhou. Pop. 41,445,930.

Zheng·zhou also **Cheng·chow** (jŭng'jō') A city of E-central China SSW of Beijing; cap. of Henan province. Pop. 1,752,374.

Zhen·jiang (jĕn'jyäng') also **Chin·kiang** (chĭn'kyäng', jĭn'gyäng') A city of E China on the Grand Canal E of Nanjing. Pop. 1,280,027.

Zhou or **Chou** or **Chow** (jō) A Chinese dynasty (traditionally dated 1122–221 B.C.) characterized by great intellectual achievements, including the rise of Confucianism and Taoism.

Zhou En·lai or **Chou En-lai** (jō' ĕn-lī') 1898–1976. Chinese revolutionary who was the first prime minister (1949–76) and foreign minister (1949–58) of China.

Zhu Jiang (joō' jyäng') or **Pearl River** A river of SE China flowing 771 km (110 mi) to the South China Sea.

Zhu·kov (zhoō'kəf), **Georgi Konstantinovich** 1896–1974. Soviet army officer who relieved the siege of Leningrad (1942–43) and captured Berlin (1945).

Zhy·to·myr (zhĭ-tô'mîr) A city of W Ukraine W of Kiev; first mentioned in 1240. Pop. 299,400.

ZHz *abbr.* zettahertz

Zi·a ul-Haq (zē'ə oōl-häk', -häk') , **Mohammad** 1924–88. Pakistani politician who overthrew Ali Bhutto (1977) and as president (1978–88) introduced strict Islamic law.

zib·e·line or **zib·el·line** (zĭb'ə-lēn', -lĭn') *n.* **1.** A thick lustrous soft fabric of wool and other animal hair, having a silky nap. **2.** The sable or its fur. [Fr., sable < Ital. *zibellino,* of Slav. orig.]

Zi·bo (dzē'bō') also **Tze·po** (tsŭ'pō', dzü'bō') A city of E China E of Jinan. Pop. 2,484,206.

zi·do·vu·dine (zī-dō'vyoō-dēn') *n.* See **AZT.** [Alteration of (A)ZIDO(THYMI)DINE (with -*vu*- < ANTIVIRAL).]

Zieg·feld (zĭg'fĕld', -fĕld', zēg'-), **Florenz** 1869–1932. Amer. theatrical producer famed for his extravagant revues known as the *Ziegfeld Follies* (1907–31).

Zie·gler (zē'glər, tsē'-), **Karl Waldemar** 1898–1973. German chemist who shared a 1963 Nobel Prize.

zig (zĭg) *n.* One of a series of sharp turns or reversals. ❖ *intr.v.* **zigged, zig·ging, zigs 1.** To turn or change direction suddenly. Usu. used in contrast to *zag: When your opponent zigs, zag!* **2.** To behave erratically or indecisively. Usu. used with *zag.* [< ZIGZAG.]

zig·gu·rat (zĭg'ə-răt') *n.* A temple tower of the ancient Assyrians and Babylonians, having the form of a terraced pyramid of successively receding stories. [Akkadian *ziqqurratu,* temple tower < *zaqāru,* to build high.]

Zi·gong (dzē'gŏng') also **Tze·kung** (tsŭ'koōng', dzü'goōng') A city of S-central China W of Chongqing. Pop. 977,147.

zig·zag (zĭg'zăg') *n.* **1a.** A line or course that proceeds by sharp turns in alternating directions. **b.** One of a series of zigzags. **2.** Something that exhibits one or a series of sharp turns. ❖ *adj.* Moving in or having a zigzag. ❖ *adv.* In a zigzag manner or pattern. ❖ *v.* **-zagged, -zag·ging, -zags** —*intr.* To move in or form a zigzag. —*tr.* To cause to zigzag. [Fr., alteration of *zic-zac* < Ger. *Zickzack,* perh. redup. of *Zacke,* tooth, cog < MHGer. *zacke,* point, nail.]

zilch (zĭlch) *Slang n.* **1.** Zero; nothing. **2.** A person regarded as insignificant; a nonentity. ❖ *adj.* Amounting to nothing; nil. [Perh. < alteration of Z(ERO) + (N)ILCH.]

zill (zĭl) *n.* One of a pair of round metal cymbals attached to the fingers and struck together for rhythm and percussion in belly dancing. [Turk. *zil,* cymbals.]

zil·lion (zĭl'yən) *n. Informal* An indeterminately huge number. [On the model of MILLION, BILLION, etc.]

Zim·bab·we¹ (zĭm-bäb'wē, -wā) A ruined city of SE Zimbabwe S of Harare; first occupied in the 3rd cent. A.D.

Zim·bab·we² (zĭm-bäb'wē, -wā) Formerly **Rho·de·sia** (rō-dē'zhə) A country of S Africa. Administered by the British South Africa Company (1889–1923), it declared itself independent in 1965, although independence was not formally granted by Great Britain until 1980. Cap. Harare. Pop. 11,150,000. —**Zim·bab'we·an** *adj. & n.*

zinc (zĭngk) *n. Symbol* **Zn** A lustrous metallic element that is brittle at room temperature but malleable with heating, used to form a wide variety of alloys including brass, bronze, and nickel silver, in galvanizing metals, for electric fuses and meter cases, and in roofing, gutters, and various household objects. Atomic number 30; atomic weight 65.39; melting point 419.4°C; boiling point 907°C; specific gravity 7.133 (25°C); valence 2. See table at **element.** ❖ *tr.v.* **zinced, zinc·ing, zincs** or **zincked, zinck·ing,**

zincks To coat or treat with zinc; galvanize. [Ger. *Zink*, poss. < *Zinke*, spike (< becoming jagged in the furnace) < MHGer. *zinke* < OHGer. *zinko*.]

zinc•ate (zĭng′kāt′) *n.* A salt of zinc hydroxide.

zinc blende *n.* See **sphalerite**.

zinc chloride *n.* A white, water-soluble crystalline compound, ZnCl₂, used as a wood preservative, as a soldering flux, and for a variety of industrial purposes, including the manufacture of cements and paper parchment.

zinc•ite (zĭng′kīt′) *n.* A red to yellow-orange zinc ore, ZnO.

zinc•og•ra•phy (zĭng-kŏg′rə-fē) *n.* The process of engraving zinc printing plates. —**zinc′og′ra•pher** *n.* —**zinc′o•graph′ic** (zĭng′kə-grăf′ĭk), **zinc′o•graph′i•cal** (-ĭ-kəl) *adj.*

zinc ointment *n.* A salve consisting of about 20 percent zinc oxide with beeswax or paraffin and petrolatum, used in the treatment of skin disorders.

zinc oxide *n.* An amorphous white or yellowish powder, ZnO, used as a pigment, in compounding rubber, in the manufacture of plastics, and in pharmaceuticals and cosmetics.

zinc spinel *n.* See **gahnite**.

zinc sulfate *n.* A crystalline compound, ZnSO₄·7H₂O, used medicinally as an emetic and astringent, as a fungicide, and in wood and skin preservatives.

zinc white *n.* See **zinc oxide**.

zine also **'zine** (zēn) *n.* **1.** An inexpensively produced, self-published, underground publication. **2.** An e-zine. [Short for MAGAZINE.]

Zin•fan•del (zĭn′fən-dĕl′) *n.* **1.** A variety of red grape grown extensively in California. **2.** A dry red wine made from this grape. [?]

zing (zĭng) *n.* A brief high-pitched humming or buzzing sound, such as that made by a swiftly passing object or a taut vibrating string. ❖ *v.* **zinged, zing•ing, zings** —*intr.* **1.** To make a zing. **2.** To move swiftly with or as if with a zing: *an arrow zinging toward its target.* **3.** *Informal* To be vivacious or lively: *a conversation zinging along.* —*tr. Informal* **1.** To attack verbally; criticize sharply. **2.** To strike suddenly. [Imit.]

zing•er (zĭng′ər) *n. Informal* **1.** A witty, often caustic remark. **2.** A sudden shock, revelation, or turn of events.

zing•y (zĭng′ē) *adj.* -**i•er, -i•est** *Informal* **1.** Pleasantly stimulating. **2.** Exceptionally attractive or appealing.

zin•ni•a (zĭn′ē-ə) *n.* Any of various plants of the genus *Zinnia* of tropical America, esp. *Z. elegans,* widely cultivated for their showy, rayed, variously colored flower heads. [NLat. *Zinnia,* genus name, after J.G. Zinn (1727–59), German botanist.]

Zi•nov•iev (zĭ-nôf′ē-ĕf′, zyĭ-nôf′yĭf), **Grigori Evseyevich** 1883–1936. Soviet politician who briefly shared power with Kamenev and Stalin after Lenin's death (1924).

Zins•ser (zĭn′sər), **Hans** 1878–1940. Amer. bacteriologist and pioneer immunologist who helped develop immunization against varieties of typhus fever (1930).

Zin•zen•dorf (zĭn′zən-dôrf′, tsĭn′tsən-), Count **Nikolaus Ludwig von** 1700–60. German theologian who founded the Moravian Church (1722).

Zi•on (zī′ən) also **Si•on** (sī′ən) *n.* **1a.** The historic land of Israel as a symbol of the Jewish people. **b.** The Jewish people; Israel. **2.** A place or religious community regarded as sacredly devoted to God. **3.** An idealized harmonious community; utopia. [ME *Sion* < OE < LLat. *Siōn* < Gk. *Seiōn* < Heb. *ṣiyyôn.*]

Zi•on•ism (zī′ə-nĭz′əm) *n.* A Jewish movement that arose in the late 19th century in response to growing anti-Semitism and sought to reestablish a Jewish homeland in Palestine and that is now concerned with the support and development of the state of Israel. —**Zi′on•ist** *adj. & n.* —**Zi′on•is′tic** *adj.*

zip (zĭp) *n.* **1.** A brief sharp hissing sound. **2.** Energy; vim. **3.** A zipper. **4.** *Slang* Nothing; nil; zero. ❖ *v.* **zipped, zip•ping, zips** —*intr.* **1a.** To move with a sharp hissing sound. **b.** To move or act with a speed that suggests such a sound. **2.** To act or proceed swiftly and energetically: *zipped through her homework.* **3.** To become fastened or unfastened by a zipper. —*tr.* **1.** To give speed and force to. **2.** To impart life or zest to. **3.** To fasten or unfasten with a zipper. [Imit.]

Zip Code A trademark used for a system designed to expedite the sorting and delivery of mail by assigning a series of numbers to each delivery area in the United States.

zip gun *n. Slang* A crude homemade pistol.

zip•per (zĭp′ər) *n.* A fastening device consisting of parallel rows of metal, plastic, or nylon teeth on adjacent edges of an opening that are interlocked by a sliding tab. ❖ *tr. & intr.v.* -**pered, -per•ing, -pers** To fasten or unfasten or become fastened or unfastened with a zipper; zip. [Orig. a trademark.]

WORD HISTORY Trademark laws exist to prevent the appropriation of words like *zipper.* Registered in 1925, *zipper* was originally a B.F. Goodrich trademark for overshoes with fasteners. A Goodrich executive is said to have slid the fastener up and down on the boot and exclaimed, "Zip 'er up," echoing the sound made by this clever device. *Zip* already existed as both a noun and verb referring to a light sharp sound or to motion accompanied by that kind of sound (*zip* was first recorded as a noun in 1875; as a verb, in 1852). Both words were imitations of the sound made by

a rapidly moving object. As the fastener that "zipped" came to be used in other articles, its name was used as well. B.F. Goodrich sued to protect its trademark but was allowed to retain proprietary rights only over *Zipper Boots. Zipper* itself had moved into the world of common nouns.

zip•py (zĭp′ē) *adj.* -**pi•er, -pi•est** Full of energy; lively.

zir•ca•loy (zûr′kə-loi′) *n.* A stable corrosion-resistant zirconium alloy. [ZIRC(ONIUM) + AL(L)OY.]

zir•con (zûr′kŏn′) *n.* A brown to colorless mineral, ZrSiO₄, that is heated, cut, and polished to form a brilliant blue-white gem. [Ger. *Zirkon* < Ar. *siriqun* < Gk. *surikon* < Pers. *āzargūn,* fire color : *āzar,* fire (ult. < OPers. **ātar*) + -*gūn,* color (< MPers.; akin to Avestan *gaonam,* hair).]

zir•co•ni•a (zûr-kō′nē-ə) *n.* Cubic zirconia. [NLat. < ZIRCON.]

zir•co•ni•um (zûr-kō′nē-əm) *n. Symbol* **Zr** A lustrous strong ductile metallic element obtained primarily from zircon and used chiefly in ceramic and refractory compounds, as an alloying agent, and in nuclear reactors as a highly corrosion-resistant alloy. Atomic number 40; atomic weight 91.22; melting point 1,852°C; boiling point 4,377°C; specific gravity 6.56 (20°C); valence 2, 3, 4. See table at **element**.

zirconium oxide *n.* A hard white amorphous powder, ZrO₂, derived from zirconium and also found naturally, used chiefly in pigments, refractories, and ceramics and as an abrasive.

zit (zĭt) *n. Slang* A pimple. [?]

zith•er (zĭth′ər, zĭth′-) also **zith•ern** (-ərn) *n.* A musical instrument composed of a flat sound box with about 30 to 40 strings stretched over it and played horizontally with the fingertips, a plectrum, or a bow, or set into vibration by the wind, as in the Aeolian harp. [Ger. < MHGer. **zitter* < OHGer. *zitera* < Lat. *cithara,* cithara < Gk. *kitharā.*] —**zith′er•ist** *n.*

zi•ti (zē′tē) *n.* Pasta in medium-sized, often ridged tubes. [Ital. < pl. of *zito,* boy, var. of obsolete *citto.*]

zi•zith (tsē-tsēt′, tsĭt′sĭs) *pl.n. Judaism* The 613 fringes of thread, symbolizing the 613 commandments in the Hebrew Scriptures, attached to the corners of a garment, esp. a tallith. [Heb. *ṣiṣīt.*]

zlo•ty (zlô′tē) *n., pl.* **zloty** or **-tys** See table at **currency**. [Pol. *złoty,* golden, zloty < *złoto,* gold. See **ghel-** in App.]

Zn The symbol for the element **zinc**.

zo– *pref.* Variant of **zoo–**.

zo•a (zō′ə) *n.* A plural of **zoon¹**.

zo•ca•lo (sō′kä-lō′) *n., pl.* -**los** A town square or plaza, esp. in Mexico. [Am.Sp. *zócalo* < Sp. *socle* < Ital. *zoccolo.* See SOCLE.]

zo•di•ac (zō′dē-ăk′) *n.* **1a.** *Astronomy* A band of the celestial sphere extending about 8° to either side of the ecliptic that represents the path of the principal planets, the moon, and the sun. **b.** In astrology, this band divided into 12 equal parts called signs, each 30° wide, bearing the name of a constellation for which it was originally named but with which it no longer coincides owing to the precession of the equinoxes. **c.** A diagram or figure representing the zodiac. **2.** A complete circuit; a circle. [ME < OFr. *zodiaque* < Lat. *zōdiacus* < Gk. *zōidiakos (kuklos),* (circle) of the zodiac < *zōidion,* small represented figure, zodiacal sign, dim. of *zōion,* living being. See ZOON¹.] —**zo•di′a•cal** (-dī′ə-kəl) *adj.*

zodiacal light *n.* A faint hazy cone of light, apparently caused by the reflection of sunlight from meteoric particles in the plane of the ecliptic.

zo•e•a (zō-ē′ə) *n., pl.* -**e•ae** (-ē′ē) or -**e•as** A larval form of crabs and other decapod crustaceans, characterized by one or more spines on the carapace and rudimentary limbs on the abdomen and thorax. [NLat. < Gk. *zōē,* life. See AZO–.]

zof•tig (zäf′tĭk, -tĭg) *adj.* Variant of **zaftig**.

–zoic *suff.* **1.** Relating to a specified manner of animal existence: *holozoic.* **2.** Of or relating to a specified geologic era: *Archeozoic.* [< Gk. *zōikos,* of animals < *zōion,* living being. See gʷeiə- in App.]

zoi•site (zoi′sīt′) *n.* A gray, brown, or pink mineral, Ca₂Al₃(SiO₄)₃(OH), used in ornamental stonework. [Ger. *Zoisit,* after Baron Sigismund *Zois* von Edelstein (1747–1819), Slovenian noble.]

Zo•la (zō′lə, zō-lä′), **Émile** 1840–1902. French writer and critic whose works include *Nana* (1880) and "J'Accuse" (1898), a letter in defense of Alfred Dreyfus.

zom•bie also **zom•bi** (zŏm′bē) *n., pl.* **zom•bies** also **zom•bis** **1.** A voodoo snake spirit. **2a.** A supernatural power or spell that according to voodoo can enter into and reanimate a corpse. **b.** A corpse revived in this way. **3.** One who looks or behaves like an automaton. **4.** A tall mixed drink made of various rums, liqueur, and fruit juice. [Caribbean Fr. and E. Creole < Kimbundu *-zumbi,* ghost, departed spirit.]

zon•al (zō′nəl) *adj.* **1.** Of or associated with a zone. **2.** Divided into zones. **3.** *Geology* Of or relating to soil characterized by well developed horizons, reflecting the type of vegetation the soil supports and the climate to which it is exposed. —**zon′al•ly** *adv.*

zo•na pel•lu•ci•da (zō′nə pə-loo′sĭ-də, pĕl-yoo′-) *n.* The thick solid transparent outer membrane of a developed mammalian ovum. [NLat. *zōna pellūcida* : Lat. *zōna,* belt, girdle + Lat. *pellūcida,* fem. of *pellūcidus,* transparent.]

zo•nate (zō′nāt′) also **zo•nat•ed** (-nā′tĭd) *adj.* Having zones; belted, striped, or ringed.

zinnia
Zinnia elegans

ă	pat	oi	boy
ā	pay	ou	out
âr	care	ŏŏ	took
ä	father	ōō	boot
ĕ	pet	ŭ	cut
ē	be	ûr	urge
ĭ	pit	th	thin
ī	pie	*th*	this
îr	pier	hw	which
ŏ	pot	zh	vision
ō	toe	ə	about,
ô	paw		item

Stress marks:
′ (primary);
′ (secondary), as in
lexicon (lĕk′sĭ-kŏn′)

zo·na·tion (zō-nā′shən) *n.* **1.** Arrangement or formation in zones; zonate structure. **2.** *Ecology* The distribution of organisms in biogeographic zones.

zone (zōn) *n.* **1.** An area distinguished from adjacent parts by a distinctive feature or characteristic. **2a.** Any of the five regions of the surface of the earth that are loosely divided according to prevailing climate and latitude, including the Torrid Zone, the North and South Temperate zones, and the North and South Frigid zones. **b.** A similar division on any other planet. **c.** *Mathematics* A portion of a sphere bounded by the intersections of two parallel planes with the sphere. **3.** *Ecology* An area characterized by distinct physical conditions and populated by communities of certain kinds of organisms. **4.** *Anatomy* A ringlike or cylindrical growth or structure. **5.** *Geology* A region or stratum distinguished by composition or content. **6.** A section of an area or territory established for a specific purpose, as a section of a city restricted to a particular type of building, enterprise, or activity: *a residential zone.* **7.** An area of a given radius within which a uniform rate is charged, as for shipping. **8.** *Computer Science* **a.** A region on a punch card or on magnetic tape in which nondigital information is recorded. **b.** A section of storage to be used for a particular purpose. **9.** *Archaic* A belt or girdle. ❖ *tr.v.* **zoned, zon·ing, zones** **1.** To divide into zones. **2.** To designate or mark off into zones. **3.** To surround or encircle with or as if with a belt or girdle. ❖ *adj.* **1.** Of, relating to, associated with, or divided into zones; zonal. **2.** *Sports* Of or relating to a system of defense, as in basketball, in which each defender guards a part of the playing area instead of a specific player. —**phrasal verb: zone out** *Informal* To lose concentration or become inattentive. —**idiom: in the zone** In a state of focused attention or energy so that one's performance is enhanced. [ME, one of the encircling regions of the earth < Lat. *zōna*, girdle, celestial zone < Gk. *zōnē*.]

zone melting *n.* A purification technique for crystalline substances in which a heating system passes slowly over a bar of the material to be refined, creating a molten region that carries impurities with it across the bar.

zone of accumulation *n.* See B horizon.

zone of illuviation *n.* See B horizon.

zone of leaching *n.* See A horizon.

zone refining *n.* See zone melting.

zone·time (zōn′tīm′) *n. Nautical* The standard time throughout a time zone that is the actual time at the meridian on which the time zone is based.

zonk (zôngk, zŏngk) *v.* **zonked, zonk·ing, zonks** *Slang* —*tr.* **1.** To stupefy; stun. **2.** To intoxicate with drugs or alcohol. —*intr.* To become intoxicated with drugs or alcohol. [?]

zon·ule (zōn′yool) *n.* A small zone, as of a ligament.

zoo (zoo) *n., pl.* **zoos** **1.** A park or institution in which living animals are kept and usu. exhibited to the public. **2.** *Slang* A place or situation marked by confusion or disorder. [Short for ZOOLOGICAL GARDEN.]

zoo– or **zo–** *pref.* **1.** Animal; animal kingdom: *zoography.* **2.** Motile: *zoospore.* [Gk. *zōo-, zōio-* < *zōion*, living being. See **gʷeiə–** in App.]

zo·o·chore (zō′ə-kôr′, -kōr′) *n.* A plant dispersed by animals.

zo·o·flag·el·late (zō′ə-flăj′ə-lĭt, -lāt′) *n.* A flagellated protist that ingests food and lacks chlorophyll.

zo·o·gen·ic (zō′ə-jĕn′ĭk) also **zo·og·e·nous** (zō-ŏj′ə-nəs) *adj.* Originating in or produced by animals.

zo·o·ge·og·ra·phy (zō′ə-jē-ŏg′rə-fē) *n.* The biological study of the geographic distribution of animals, esp. its causes and effects. —**zo′o·ge·og′ra·pher** *n.* —**zo′o·ge′o·graph′ic** (-ə-grăf′ĭk), **zo′o·ge′o·graph′i·cal** (-ĭ-kəl) *adj.*

zo·o·gle·a also **zo·o·gloe·a** (zō′ə-glē′ə) *n., pl.* **-gle·ae** (-glē′ē′) or **-gle·as** also **-gloe·ae** (-glē′ē′) or **-gloe·as** An aggregate of bacteria forming a jellylike mass. [ZOO– + NLat. *gloea*, gum (< Med.Gk. *gloia, glia*, gum, glue < Gk. *gloios*).]

zo·og·ra·phy (zō-ŏg′rə-fē) *n.* The biological description of animals and their habitats. —**zo′o·graph′ic** (-ə-grăf′ĭk), **zo′o·graph′i·cal** (-ĭ-kəl) *adj.*

zo·oid (zō′oid′) *n.* **1a.** An organic cell or organized body that has independent movement within a living organism, esp. a motile gamete such as a spermatozoon. **b.** An independent animallike organism produced asexually. **2.** One of the distinct individuals forming a colonial animal such as a bryozoan or hydrozoan. —**zo·oid′al** (-oid′l) *adj.*

zoo·keep·er (zoo′kē′pər) *n.* One who takes care of animals in a zoo.

zo·ol·a·try (zō-ŏl′ə-trē) *n.* Worship of animals. —**zo·ol′a·ter** *n.* —**zo·ol′a·trous** *adj.*

zo·o·log·i·cal (zō′ə-lŏj′ĭ-kəl) also **zo·o·log·ic** (-lŏj′ĭk) *adj.* **1.** Of or relating to animals or animal life. **2.** Of or relating to the science of zoology. —**zo′o·log′i·cal·ly** *adv.*

zoological garden *n.* See zoo 1.

zo·ol·o·gy (zō-ŏl′ə-jē, zoo-) *n., pl.* **-gies** **1.** The branch of biology that deals with the study of the structure, physiology, development, and classification of animals. **2.** The animal life of a particular area or period: *the zoology of the Pleistocene.* **3.** The characteristics of a particular animal group or category: *the zoology of mammals.* —**zo·ol′o·gist** *n.*

USAGE NOTE Traditionally, the first syllable of *zoology* has been pronounced as (zō), rhyming with *toe.* However, most likely due to the familiarity of the word *zoo* (which is merely a shortened form of *zoological garden*), the pronunciation of the first syllable as (zoo) is also commonly made. In 1999, 88 percent of the Panelists found the (zō-) pronunciation acceptable, and 60 percent found the (zoo-) pronunciation acceptable, with 68 percent using the (zō-) pronunciation and 32 percent using the (zoo-) pronunciation in their own speech. Thus, while both pronunciations can be considered acceptable, the (zō-) pronunciation may be perceived as more correct.

zoom (zoom) *v.* **zoomed, zoom·ing, zooms** —*intr.* **1a.** To buzz or hum at a continuous low pitch. **b.** To move while making such a sound. **2.** To climb suddenly and sharply. Used of an airplane. **3.** To move about rapidly; swoop. **4.** To simulate movement rapidly away from or toward a subject using a zoom lens. **5.** *Computer Science* To cause text or other graphics in a window or frame to appear larger on the screen. —*tr.* To cause to zoom. ❖ *n.* **1.** The act or sound of zooming. **2.** A zoom lens. [Imit.]

zoom lens *n.* A camera lens whose focal length can be rapidly changed, allowing rapid change in the size of an image or the illusion of camera movement.

zo·o·mor·phism (zō′ə-môr′fĭz′əm) *n.* **1.** Attribution of animal traits or qualities to a god. **2.** Use of animal forms in symbolism, literature, or graphics. —**zo′o·mor′phic** *adj.*

zo·on¹ (zō′ŏn′) *n., pl.* **zo·ons** or **zo·a** (zō′ə) **1.** An animal developed from a fertilized egg. **2.** One of the distinct individuals that join to form a compound or colonial animal; a zooid. [NLat. *zōon* < Gk. *zōion, zōon*, living being. See **gʷeiə–** in App.]

zoon² (zoon) *intr.v.* **zooned, zoon·ing, zoons** *Chiefly Southern US* To fly with a humming or buzzing sound. [Prob. imit.]

–zoon *suff.* Animal; independently moving organic unit: *spermatozoon.* [NLat. *-zōon* < Gk. *zōion, zōon*, living being. See **gʷeiə–** in App.]

zo·o·no·sis (zō-ŏn′ə-sĭs) *n., pl.* **-ses** (-sēz′) A disease of animals, such as rabies or psittacosis, that can be transmitted to humans. [NLat. : ZOO– + *-nosis*, alteration (influenced by –OSIS) of Gk. *nosos*, disease.] —**zo′o·not′ic** (-ə-nŏt′ĭk) *adj.*

zo·o·oph·a·gous (zō-ŏf′ə-gəs) *adj.* Feeding on animal matter.

zo·o·phil·i·a (zō′ə-fĭl′ē-ə) also **zo·oph·i·lism** (zō-ŏf′ə-lĭz′əm) *n.* **1.** Affection or affinity for animals. **2.** A tendency to feed or grow on animal tissue. **3.** Erotic attraction to animals. —**zo′o·phile′** (-fīl′) *n.* —**zo′o·phil′ic** (zō′ə-fĭl′ĭk) *adj.*

zo·oph·i·lous (zō-ŏf′ə-ləs) *adj. Botany* Pollinated by animals.

zo·o·pho·bi·a (zō′ə-fō′bē-ə) *n.* An abnormal fear of animals. —**zo′o·phobe′** (-fōb′) *n.*

zo·o·phyte (zō′ə-fīt′) *n.* Any of various invertebrate animals, such as a sea anemone or sponge, that attach to surfaces and superficially resemble plants. —**zo′o·phyt′ic** (-fĭt′ĭk), **zo′o·phyt′i·cal** (-ĭ-kəl) *adj.*

zo·o·plank·ton (zō′ə-plăngk′tən) *n.* Plankton that consists of animals, including the corals, rotifers, sea anemones, and jellyfish. —**zo′o·plank·ton′ic** (-tŏn′ĭk) *adj.*

zo·o·spo·ran·gi·um (zō′ə-spə-răn′jē-əm) *n., pl.* **-gi·a** (-jē-ə) A sporangium in which zoospores develop.

zo·o·spore (zō′ə-spôr′, -spōr′) *n.* A motile flagellated asexual spore, as of certain algae and fungi. —**zo′o·spor′ic** (-spôr′ĭk, -spōr′-), **zo′o·spor′ous** (zō′ə-spôr′əs, -spōr′-, zō-ŏs′pər-əs) *adj.*

zo·os·ter·ol (zō-ŏs′tə-rôl′, -rōl′) *n.* A sterol, such as cholesterol, that is produced by animals rather than plants.

zo·ot·o·my (zō-ŏt′ə-mē) *n., pl.* **-mies** **1.** The anatomy of animals. **2.** Dissection of animals. —**zo′o·tom′ic** (zō′ə-tŏm′ĭk), **zo′o·tom′i·cal** (-ĭ-kəl) *adj.* —**zo·ot′o·mist** *n.*

zoot suit (zoot) *n. Slang* A man's suit popular during the early 1940s, marked by full-legged, tight-cuffed trousers and a long coat with wide lapels and padded shoulders. [Prob. < an alteration of SUIT.] —**zoot′-suit′er** (zoot′soo′tər) *n.*

zo·ri (zôr′ē, zō′rē) *n., pl.* **zori** or **-ris** A flat sandal with thongs, usu. made of straw or leather. [J. *zōri* : *sō*, grass, straw (< M Chin. *tsaw*) + *ri*, sole (< M Chin. *li*).]

zor·ille also **zor·il** (zôr′ĭl, zôr′-) or **zo·ril·la** (zə-rĭl′ə) *n.* A skunklike carnivorous African mammal (*Ictonyx striatus*) related to the weasel. [Fr. < Sp. *zorrillo*, skunk, dim. of *zorro*, fox < OSpan., idler, vagabond, fox.]

Zo·ro·as·ter (zôr′ō-ăs′tər, zōr′-) also **Zar·a·thu·stra** (zăr′ə-thoo′strə) 6th cent. B.C. Persian prophet who founded Zoroastrianism.

Zo·ro·as·tri·an·ism (zôr′ō-ăs′trē-ə-nĭz′əm) *n.* The religious system founded by Zoroaster and set forth in the Avesta, teaching the worship of Ahura Mazda in the context of a universal struggle between the forces of light and of darkness. —**Zo′ro·as′tri·an** *adj. & n.*

Zor·ril·la y Mo·ral (zə-rē′ə ē mə-räl′, thō-rē′lyä ē mō-räl′), **José** 1817–93. Spanish writer whose works include the play *Don Juan Tenorio* (1844).

zos·ter (zŏs′tər) *n.* **1.** A belt or girdle worn by men in ancient Greece. **2.** Herpes zoster. [Gk. *zōstēr*, girdle.]

Zou·ave (zoo-äv′, zwäv) *n.* **1.** A member of a French infantry unit, originally composed of Algerian recruits. **2.** A member of a group patterned after the French Zouaves, esp. a member of such a unit of the Union Army during the US Civil War. [Fr. < Berber *Zwāwa,* an Algerian tribe.]

zouk (zōōk) *n.* A popular dance music of the French West Indies that incorporates African drumming styles. [Antillean Fr. Creole, party; prob. akin to JUKE[1].]

zounds (zoundz) *interj.* Used to express anger, surprise, or indignation. [Shortening and alteration of *God's wounds!*]

zoy·sia (zoi′shə, -zhə, -sē-ə, -zē-ə) *n.* Any of several creeping lawn grasses of the genus *Zoysia,* native to southeast Asia and New Zealand. [NLat. *Zoysia,* genus name, after Karl von *Zoys* zu Laubach (1756–1800?), Austrian botanist.]

Zp *abbr. Bible* Zephaniah

Z particle *n.* See **Z boson.**

ZPG *abbr.* zero population growth

Zr The symbol for the element **zirconium.**

zs or **zsec** *abbr.* zeptosecond

Z score *n. Statistics* A measure of the distance in standard deviations of a sample from the mean.

zuc·chet·to (zōō-kĕt′ō, tsōōk-kĕt′tō) *n., pl.* **-tos** or **-ti** (-tē) A skullcap worn by certain Roman Catholic clerics, varying in color according to rank. [Ital., var. of *zucchetta,* dim. of *zucca,* gourd, head. See ZUCCHINI.]

zuc·chi·ni (zōō-kē′nē) *n., pl.* **zucchini** or **-nis** A variety of squash having an elongated shape and a smooth thin green rind. [Ital., pl. of *zucchino,* dim. of *zucca,* gourd < LLat. *cucutia.*]

Zug·un·ru·he (tsōōk′ŏōn-rōō′hə) *n.* The migratory drive in animals, esp. birds. [Ger. : *Zug,* a pulling, move, migration; see ZUGZWANG + *Unruhe,* restlessness (< MHGer. *unruowe* < OHGer. *unruowa* < -*un,* not; see **ne** in App. + *ruowa,* rest).]

zug·zwang (tsōōk′tsväng′) *n.* A situation in a chess game in which a player is forced to make an undesirable or disadvantageous move. [Ger. *Zugzwang* : *Zug,* pull, move (< MHGer. *zuc,* pull < OHGer. < *ziohan,* to pull; see **deuk-** in App.) + *Zwang,* compulsion (< MHGer. *twanc* < OHGer. *twanc*).]

Zui·der Zee (zī′dər zē′, zā′, zoi′dər zā′) A former shallow inlet of the North Sea in NE Netherlands.

Zu·kor (zōō′kər), **Adolph** 1873–1976. Hungarian-born Amer. film producer and executive who helped found Paramount Studios (1933).

Zu·kov·sky (zōō-kôv′skē), **Louis** 1904–1978. American poet and translator noted for his book-length poem *A,* which he wrote over the course of his life.

Zu·lu (zōō′lōō) *n., pl.* **Zulu** or **-lus 1.** A member of a Bantu people of southeast Africa, primarily inhabiting northeast Natal province in South Africa. **2.** The Nguni language of this people, closely related to Xhosa.

Zu·lu·land (zōō′lōō-lănd′) A historical region of NE Natal Province in South Africa. Settled by Zulu clans, it was annexed by the British in 1887.

Zulu time *n.* See **universal time.** [< *Zulu,* spoken representation of the letter *Z* in *z-time,* military designation of this time zone.]

Zu·ni (zōō′nē) also **Zu·ñi** (-nyē, -nē) *n., pl.* **Zuni** or **-nis** also **Zuñi** or **-ñis 1.** A member of a Pueblo people located in western New Mexico. **2.** Their language, of no known linguistic affiliation.

Zur·ba·rán (zōōr′bä-rän′, thōōr′-), **Francisco de** 1598–1664. Spanish painter whose works include *The Adoration of the Shepherds* (1638).

Zu·rich (zōōr′ĭk) A city of NE Switzerland on the **Lake of Zurich;** joined the Swiss Confederation in 1351. Pop. 343,981.

Zu·se (tsōō′zĕ), **Konrad** 1910–95. German engineer who developed the first general-purpose program-controlled calculator (1941) and the first transistorized calculator (1958).

zuz (zōōz) *n.* An ancient Hebrew silver coin. [Mishnaic Heb. *zûz* < Aram. < Akkadian *zūzu,* half, division, unit of weight < *zâzu,* to divide.]

Zweig (zwīg, swīg, tsvīk), **Arnold** 1887–1968. German-born writer best known for *The Case of Sergeant Grischa* (1927).

Zweig, Stefan 1881–1942. Austrian writer whose works include *Three Masters* (1920).

zwie·back (swē′băk′, -bäk′, swī′-, zwē′-, zwī′-) *n.* A usu. sweetened bread baked first as a loaf and later cut into slices and toasted. [Ger. : *zwie-,* twice (< MHGer. *zwi-* < OHGer.; see **dwo-** in App.) + *backen,* to bake (< MHGer. < OHGer. *bahhan, backan*).]

Zwing·li (zwĭng′lē, swĭng′-, tsvĭng′-), **Ulrich** or **Huldreich** 1484–1531. Swiss religious reformer whose sermons on the absolute authority of the Bible (1519) marked the beginning of the Reformation in Switzerland.

Zwing·li·an (zwĭng′lē-ən, swĭng′-, tsvĭng′-) *adj.* Of or relating

to Ulrich Zwingli or to his theology, esp. that Jesus is not physically present in the Eucharist. ❖ *n.* A follower of Zwingli. —**Zwing′li·an·ism** *n.*

zwit·ter·i·on (zwĭt′ər-ī′ən, swĭt′-, tsvĭt′-) *n.* A molecule carrying both a positive and a negative charge. [Ger. : *Zwitter,* hybrid (< MHGer. *zwitarn* < OHGer. < *zwi-,* twice; see **dwo-** in App.) + *Ion,* ion (< Gk.; see ION).] —**zwit′ter·i·on′ic** (-ī-ŏn′ĭk) *adj.*

Zwor·y·kin (zwôr′ĭ-kĭn, zvôr′yə-), **Vladimir Kosma** 1889–1982. Russian-born Amer. physicist and inventor of the iconoscope (1923), the first practical television camera.

zy·de·co (zī′dĭ-kō′) *n.* Popular music of southern Louisiana that combines elements of French and Caribbean music and the blues, featuring the guitar, the accordion, and a washboard. [< Louisiana Fr., poss. alteration of *Les haricots (sont pas salé),* name of a song, pl. of Fr. *haricot,* bean. See HARICOT.]

zyg·a·poph·y·sis (zĭg′ə-pŏf′ĭ-sĭs, zī′gə-) *n., pl.* **-ses** (-sēz′) One of two usu. paired processes of the neural arch of a vertebra that articulates with corresponding parts of adjacent vertebrae.

zygo- or **zyg-** *pref.* **1.** Yoke; pair: *zygodactyl.* **2.** Union: *zygospore.* [NLat. < Gk. *zugo-* < *zugon,* yoke. See **yeug-** in App.]

zy·go·dac·tyl (zī′gə-dăk′tĭl, zĭg′ə-) *adj.* Having two toes projecting forward and two projecting backward, as certain climbing birds. ❖ *n.* A zygodactyl bird, such as a parrot.

zy·go·gen·e·sis (zī′gō-jĕn′ĭ-sĭs) *n., pl.* **-ses** (-sēz′) Reproduction involving the formation of a zygote. —**zy′go·ge·net′ic** (-jə-nĕt′ĭk) *adj.*

zy·go·ma (zī-gō′mə, zĭ-) *n., pl.* **-ma·ta** (-mə-tə) or **-mas 1.** The zygomatic bone. **2.** The zygomatic arch. **3.** The zygomatic process. [NLat. *zygōma, zygōmat-* < Gk. *zugōma,* bolt < *zugoun,* to join. See **yeug-** in App.]

zy·go·mat·ic (zī′gə-măt′ĭk) *adj.* Of, relating to, or located in the area of the zygoma: *a zygomatic muscle.*

zygomatic arch *n.* The bony arch in vertebrates that extends along the side or front of the skull beneath the eye socket and that is formed by the zygomatic bone and the zygomatic process of the temporal bone.

zygomatic bone *n.* A small bone in vertebrates on each side of the face socket, forming the prominence of the cheek.

zygomatic process *n.* Any of three processes that articulate with the zygomatic bone, esp. the process from the temporal bone that articulates to form the zygomatic arch.

zy·go·mor·phic (zī′gə-môr′fĭk, zĭg′ə-) also **zy·go·mor·phous** (-fəs) *adj.* Bilaterally symmetrical. Used of organisms or parts. —**zy′go·mor′phism** *n.*

zy·gos·i·ty (zī-gŏs′ĭ-tē) *n.* The genetic condition of a zygote, esp. with respect to its being a homozygote or a heterozygote.

zy·go·spore (zī′gə-spôr′, -spōr′, zĭg′ə-) *n.* A large multinucleate spore formed by union of similar gametes, as in algae.

zy·gote (zī′gōt′) *n.* **1.** The cell formed by the union of two gametes, esp. a fertilized ovum before cleavage. **2.** The organism that develops from a zygote. [< Gk. *zugotos,* yoked < *zugoun,* to yoke. See **yeug-** in App.] —**zy·got′ic** (-gŏt′ĭk) *adj.* —**zy·got′i·cal·ly** *adv.*

zy·go·tene (zī′gə-tēn′) *n.* The stage in prophase of meiosis during which homologous chromosomes become paired. [Fr. *zygotène* : *zygo-,* pair (< NLat.; see ZYGO–) + *-tène,* ribbon (< Lat. *taenia;* see TAENIA).]

–zygous *suff.* Having a zygotic constitution of a specified kind: *heterozygous.* [< Gk. *-zugos,* yoked < *zugon,* yoke. See **yeug-** in App.]

zy·mase (zī′mās′, -māz′) *n.* The enzyme complex in yeasts that catalyzes the breakdown of sugar into alcohol and carbon dioxide.

–zyme *suff.* Enzyme: *lysozyme.* [< Gk. *zūmē,* leaven.]

zymo- or **zym-** *pref.* **1.** Fermentation: *zymurgy.* **2.** Enzyme: *zymase.* [NLat. *zȳmo-* < Gk. *zūmē,* leaven.]

zy·mo·gen (zī′mə-jən) *n.* See **proenzyme.**

zy·mol·o·gy (zī-mŏl′ə-jē) *n.* The chemistry of fermentation. —**zy′mo·log′ic** (-mə-lŏj′ĭk) *adj.* —**zy·mol′o·gist** *n.*

zy·mol·y·sis (zī-mŏl′ĭ-sĭs) *n.* Fermentation. —**zy′mo·lyt′ic** (-mə-lĭt′ĭk) *adj.*

zy·mom·e·ter (zī-mŏm′ĭ-tər) *n.* An instrument used to determine fermentation efficiency.

zy·mo·sis (zī-mō′sĭs) *n., pl.* **-ses** (-sēz) **1.** Fermentation. **2.** *Medicine* **a.** The process of infection. **b.** An infectious disease, esp. one caused by a fungus. [Gk. *zūmōsis* < *zūmoun,* to leaven < *zūmē,* leaven.] —**zy·mot′ic** (-mŏt′ĭk) *adj.*

zy·mur·gy (zī′mûr′jē) *n.* The branch of chemistry that deals with fermentation processes, as in brewing.

zyz·zy·va (zĭz′ə-və) *n.* Any of various tropical American weevils of the genus *Zyzzyva,* often destructive to plants. [NLat. *Zyzzyva,* genus name, prob. < *Zyzza,* former genus of leafhoppers.]

zucchetto
Roman Catholic archbishop

zucchini

ă	pat	oi	boy
ā	pay	ou	out
âr	care	ŏō	took
ä	father	ōō	boot
ĕ	pet	ŭ	cut
ē	be	ûr	urge
ĭ	pit	th	thin
ī	pie	*th*	this
îr	pier	hw	which
ŏ	pot	zh	vision
ō	toe	ə	about,
ô	paw		item

Stress marks:
′ (primary);
′ (secondary), as in
lexicon (lĕk′sĭ-kŏn′)

Indo-European and the Indo-Europeans

CALVERT WATKINS

The Appendix of Indo-European Roots that follows this essay is designed to allow the reader to trace English words derived from Indo-European languages back to their fundamental components in Proto-Indo-European, the parent language of all ancient and modern Indo-European languages. This essay provides some basic information about the structure and grammar of Proto-Indo-European as an aid to understanding the etymologies of these English words. In the text below, terms in boldface are Indo-European roots and words that appear as entries in the Appendix. Words in small capitals are Modern English derivatives of Indo-European roots. An asterisk (*) is used to signal a word or form that is not preserved in any written documents but that can be reconstructed on the basis of other evidence.

The Comparative Method

Indo-European is the name given for geographic reasons to the large and well-defined linguistic family that includes most of the languages of Europe, past and present, as well as those found in a vast area extending across Iran and Afghanistan to the northern half of the Indian subcontinent. In modern times the family has spread by colonization throughout the Western Hemisphere.

A curious byproduct of the age of colonialism and mercantilism was the introduction of Sanskrit in the 18th century to European intellectuals and scholars long familiar with Latin and Greek and with the European languages of culture—Romance, Germanic, and Slavic. The comparison of the classical language of India with the two classical languages of Europe revolutionized the perception of linguistic relationships.

Speaking to the Asiatick Society in Calcutta on February 2, 1786, the English Orientalist and jurist Sir William Jones (1746–94) observed of the Sanskrit, Greek, and Latin languages that

> no philologer could examine them all three, without believing them to have sprung from some common source, which, perhaps, no longer exists.

It has been rightly said that the comparatist has one fact and one hypothesis. The one fact is that certain languages present similarities among themselves so numerous and so precise that they cannot be attributed to chance and of such a kind that they cannot be explained as borrowings or as universal features. The one hypothesis is that these languages must then be the result of descent from a common original.

In the early part of the 19th century, scholars set about systematically exploring the similarities observable among the principal languages spoken now or formerly in the regions from Iceland and Ireland in the west to India in the east and from Scandinavia in the north to Italy and Greece in the south. They were able to group these languages into a family that they called *Indo-European*.

The dialects or branches of Indo-European still represented today by one or more languages are Indic and Iranian, Greek, Armenian, Slavic, Baltic, Albanian, Celtic, Italic, and Germanic. The present century has seen the addition of two branches to the family, both of which are extinct: Hittite and other Anatolian languages, the earliest attested in the Indo-European family, spoken in what is now Turkey in the second and first millennia B.C.; and the two Tocharian languages, the easternmost of Indo-European dialects, spoken in Chinese Turkistan (modern Xinjiang Uygur) in the first millennium A.D.

English is the most prevalent member of the Indo-European family, the native language of nearly 350 million people and the most important second language in the world. It is one of many direct descendants of Indo-European, one of whose dialects became prehistoric Common Germanic, which subdivided into dialects of which one was West Germanic; this in turn broke up into further dialects, one of which emerged into documentary attestation as Old English. From Old English we can follow the development of the language directly, in texts, down to the present day.

This history is our linguistic heritage; our ancestors, in a real cultural sense, are our linguistic ancestors. But it must be stressed that linguistic heritage, while it may tend to correspond with cultural continuity, does not imply genetic or biological descent. Linguists use the phrase "genetically related" to refer simply to languages descended from a common ancestor. The transmission of language by conquest, assimilation, migration, or any other ethnic movement is a complex and enigmatic process that this discussion does not propose to examine—beyond the gen-

Viking runes. Carved in stone in the form of a snake. The stone is located in front of Gripsholm Castle in Mariefred, Sweden. 11th century.

eral proposition that in the case of Indo-European no genetic conclusions can or should be drawn.

The comparative method—what we have called the comparatist's "one fact and one hypothesis"—remains today the most powerful device for elucidating linguistic history. When it is carried to a successful conclusion, the comparative method leads not merely to the assumption of the previous existence of an antecedent common language but to a reconstruction of all the salient features of that language. In the best circumstances, as with Indo-European, we can reconstruct the sounds, forms, words, even the structure of sentences—in short, both grammar and lexicon—of a language spoken before the human race had invented the art of writing. It is worth reflecting on this accomplishment. A reconstructed grammar and dictionary cannot claim any sort of completeness, to be sure, and the reconstruction may always be changed because of new data or better analysis. But it remains true, as one distinguished scholar has put it, that a reconstructed protolanguage is "a glorious artifact, one which is far more precious than anything an archaeologist can ever hope to unearth."

Proto-Indo-European Grammar: Sounds and Forms

A large part of the success of the comparative method with the Indo-European family is due to both the number and the precision of the agreements among the languages, not only in the regular sound correspondences of the roots but even more strikingly in the particulars of morphology, the forms of language in their grammatical function. Consider the partial paradigms of the words for "dog" (**kwon-**) and "to kill" (**gʷhen-**):

	Hittite	Greek	Vedic Sanskrit
nominative	kuwas	kúōn	ś(u)vá̄
accusative	kuwanan	kúna	śvánam
genitive	kūnas	kunós	śúnas

	Lithuanian	Old Irish	Proto-Indo-European
nominative	šuõ	cú	*k(u)wō(n)
accusative	šùni	coin	*kwónṃ
genitive	šuñs	con	*kunés

	Hittite	Vedic Sanskrit	Proto-Indo-European
third singular present indicative	kuenzi	hánti	*gʷhén-ti
third plural present indicative	kunanzi	ghnánti	*gʷhn-énti

The agreement of detail in sound correspondences (see the chart on pages 1606–07), in vowel alternations and their distribution, in the accent, in the grammatical forms (endings), and in the syntactic functions is little short of astounding.

Speech Sounds and Their Alternations. The system of *sounds* in Proto-Indo-European was rich in stop consonants. There was an unvoiced series, *p, t, k, kʷ* (like the *qu* of *quick*), a voiced series, *b, d, g, gʷ*, and a voiced aspirate or

"murmured" series, *bh, dh, gh, gʷh*, pronounced like the voiced series but followed by a puff of breath. The language had a single continuant *s*, which was voiced to *z* before voiced stop consonants. It had as well three so-called *laryngeals* or *h*-like sounds, $\partial_1, \partial_2, \partial_3$, of disputed phonetic value, all of which are written here as schwa, or ∂ (equivalent notations are *H* or *h*).

Proto-Indo-European had two nasals, *m* and *n*, two liquids, *r* and *l*, and the glides *w* and *y*. A salient characteristic of Indo-European was that these sounds could function both as consonants and as vowels. Their consonantal value was as in English. As vowels, symbolized *ṃ, ṇ, ḷ,* and *ṛ*, the liquids and nasals sounded much like the final syllables of English *bottom, button, bottle,* and *butter*. The vocalic counterparts of *w* and *y* were the vowels *u* and *i*. The laryngeals too could function both as consonants and as vowels: their consonantal value was that of *h*-like sounds, while as vowels they were varieties of schwa, much like the final syllable of English *sofa;* hence the choice of schwa to represent laryngeals in the Appendix.

The other vowels of Indo-European were *e, o,* and *a*. These, as well as *i* and *u*, occurred both long and short, as did the diphthongs *ei, oi, ai, eu, ou, au*. (All vowels are pronounced as in Latin or Italian.) Since we can distinguish chronological layers in Proto-Indo-European, it can be said that a number of the long vowels of later Indo-European resulted from the contraction of early Indo-European short vowels with a following ∂. Already in Proto-Indo-European itself, two of the three laryngeals had the property of "coloring" an adjacent fundamental vowel *e* to *a* and *o*, respectively, before the contractions took place. Thus the root **pā-**, "to protect," is contracted from older **paə₂-*, with "a-coloring" from **peə₂-*; the root **dō-**, "to give," is contracted from older **doə₃-*, with "o-coloring" from **deə₃-*; and the root **dhē-**, "to set, put," is contracted from older **dheə₁-*, without coloring. The basic or fundamental vowel in each of these roots, as in most Indo-European roots, was originally *e*. In scholarly usage it is now customary to write the noncoloring laryngeal as ∂_1 (or h_1); the a-coloring laryngeal as ∂_2 (or h_2); and the o-coloring laryngeal as ∂_3 (or h_3). This typographically cumbersome notation has been simplified in the Appendix, since the vowel before the schwa is sufficient to distinguish the three in the cases of contraction to a long vowel, and in other positions in most languages other than Greek the three merge to one. No systematic notice has been taken in this Appendix of word-initial laryngeals before vowels (amply attested in Hittite), since the root forms with initial vowel are readily convertible by the reader. Thus **ant-**, "front, forehead," is from earlier **ə₂ent-, *əant-* (Hittite *ḫant-*, "front, forehead"); **op-**, "to work, produce in abundance," from **ə₃ep-, *əop-* (Hittite *ḫapp-in-ant-*, "rich"); and **ed-**, "to eat," is from earlier **ə₁ed-, *əed-*, without coloring (Hittite *ed-*, "to eat").

A characteristic feature of Indo-European was the system of vocalic *alternations* termed *apophony* or *ablaut*. This was a set of internal vowel changes expressing different morphological functions. A clear reflex of this feature is preserved in the English strong verbs, where, for example, the vocalic alternations between *write* and *wrote*, *give* and *gave*, express the present and past tenses. Ablaut in Indo-European affected the vowels *e* and *o*. The fundamental form was *e*; this *e* could appear as *o* under certain conditions, and in other conditions both *e* and *o* could disappear entirely. On this basis we speak of given forms in Indo-European as exhibiting, respectively, the *e-grade* (or *full grade*), the *o-grade*, or the *zero grade*. The *e* and the *o* might furthermore occur as long *ē* or *ō*, termed the *lengthened grade*.

To illustrate: the Indo-European root **ped-**, "foot," appears in the e-grade in Latin *ped-* (PEDAL), but in the o-grade in Greek *pod-* (PODIATRIST). Germanic **fōtuz* (FOOT) reflects the lengthened o-grade **pōd-*. The zero grade of the same root shows no vowel at all: **pd-*, **bd-*, a form attested in Sanskrit.

When the zero grade involved a root with one of the sounds *m, n, r, l, w,* or *y* (collectively termed *resonants*), the resonant would regularly appear in its vocalic function, forming a syllable. We have the e-grade root **senkʷ-* in English SINK, the o-grade form **sonkʷ-* in SANK, and the zero-grade form **sṇkʷ-* in SUNK.

In the paradigms cited earlier, the word for "dog," **kwon-**, appears in the o-grade in the accusative case **kwón-(ṃ)*, in the zero grade in the genitive case **kun-(és)*, and in the lengthened o-grade in the nominative case **kwō(n)*. Note that the nonsyllabic resonant *w* appears as the vowel *u* when it becomes syllabic.

In the case of roots with long vowels arising from contraction with *ə*, the ablaut can be most clearly understood by referring to the older, uncolored and uncontracted forms. Thus **pā-**, "to protect," contracted from **peə₂-* colored to **paə-*, has a zero grade **pə-*; **dō-**, "to give," contracted from **deə₃-* colored to **doə-*, has a zero grade **də-*; **dhē-**, "to place," contracted from **dheə₁-*, has a zero grade **dhə-*. The fundamental vowel of the full grade disappears in the zero grade, and only the *ə* remains. Long *ū* and long *ī* could also arise from contraction: full grade **peuə-**, "to purify," has a zero grade **puə-* contracted to **pū-* (PURE).

Grammatical Forms and Syntax. Proto-Indo-European was a highly inflected language. Grammatical relationships and the syntactic function of words in the sentence were indicated primarily by variations in the endings of the words.

With the exception of the numbers five to ten and a group of particles including certain conjunctions and quasi-adverbial forms, all Indo-European words underwent inflection. The structure of all inflected words, regardless of part of speech, was the same: *root* plus one or more *suffixes* plus *ending*. Thus the word **ker-wo-s*, "a stag," is composed of the root **ker-¹**, "horn," plus the noun suffix **-u-*, plus the possessive adjective suffix **-o-*, plus the nominative singular ending **-s*: "the horned one." The root contained the basic semantic kernel, the underlying notion, which the suffix could modify in various ways. It was primarily the suffix that determined the part of speech of the word. Thus a single root like **prek-**, "to ask," could, depending on the suffix, form a verb **pṛk-sko-*, "to ask" (Latin *poscere*), a noun **prek-*, "prayer" (Latin *precēs*), and an adjective **prok-o-*, "asking" (underlying Latin *procus*, "suitor"). Note that **prek-*, **prok-*, and **pṛk-* have, respectively, e-grade, o-grade, and zero grade.

The root plus the suffix or suffixes constituted the *stem*. The stems represented the basic lexical stock of Indo-European, the separate words of its dictionary. Yet a single root would commonly furnish a large number of derivative stems with different suffixes, both nominal and verbal, much as English *love* is both noun and verb as well as the base of such derivatives as *lovely, lover,* and *beloved*. For this reason it is customary to group such collections of derivatives, in a variety of Indo-European languages, under the root on which they are built. The root entries of the Appendix are arranged in this way, with derivatives that exhibit similar suffixes forming subgroups consisting of Indo-European stems or words.

An important technique of word formation in Indo-European was *composition*, the combining of two separate words or notions into a single word. Such forms were and continue to be built on underlying simple sentences; an example in English would be "He is someone who *cuts wood*," whence "He is a *woodcutter*." It is in the area of composition that English has most faithfully preserved the ancient Indo-European patterns of word formation, by continuously forming them anew, re-creating them.

Lexicon and Culture

The reconstruction of a *protolanguage*—the common ancestor of a family of spoken or attested languages—has a further implication. Language is a social fact; languages are not spoken in a vacuum but by human beings living in a society. When we have reconstructed a protolanguage, we have also necessarily established the existence of a prehistoric society, a speech community that used that protolanguage. The existence of Proto-Indo-European presupposes the existence, in some fashion, of a society of Indo-Europeans.

Though by no means a perfect mirror, the lexicon of a language remains the single most effective way of approaching and understanding the culture of its speakers. As such, the contents of the Indo-European lexicon provide a remarkably clear view of the whole culture of an otherwise unknown prehistoric society.

We may examine the contents of this Indo-European lexicon, which aside from its inherent interest permits us to ascertain many characteristics of Indo-European society. It is remarkable that by far the greater part of this reconstructed vocabulary is preserved in native or borrowed derivatives in Modern English.

General Terms. It is appropriate to begin with a sampling of basic terms that have no special cultural value but attest to the richness of the tradition. All are widespread in the family. There are two verbs expressing existence, **es-** and **bheuə-**, found in English IS, Latin *esse*, and English BE, Latin *fu-tūrus* (FUTURE), respectively.

A number of qualitative adjectives are attested that go back to the protolanguage. Some come in semantic pairs: **sen-*, "old," and **newo-**, "new"; also **sen-*, "old," and **yeu-**, "youthful vigor"; **tenu-*, "thin" (under **ten-**), and **tegu-*, "thick"; **gʷerə-**, "heavy," and **legʷh-*, "light." There are also the two prefixes **(e)su-*, "good, well-," and **dus-*, "bad, ill-," in the Greek forms borrowed as EU- and DYS-.

The personal pronouns belong to the very earliest layer of Indo-European that can be reached by reconstruction. The lack of any formal resemblance in English between the subject case (nominative) I and the object case (accusative) ME is a direct and faithful reflection of the same disparity in Proto-Indo-European, respectively **eg** (**egō*) and **me-¹**. The other pronouns are **tu-** (**te-*), "thou," **nes-²** or **we-**, "we," and **yu-**, "you." No pronouns for the third person were in use.

The most persistent and widespread pronominal stems are **to-** and **kʷo-**, which are preserved in the English demonstrative and interrogative-relative pronouns and adverbs beginning with *th-* (THIS, THEN) and *wh-* (WHO, WHICH, WHEN).

All the languages of the family show some or all of the Indo-European numerals. The language had a decimal system. There is complete agreement on the numerals from two to ten: **dwo-** (**duwō*), **trei-** (**treyes*), **kʷetwer-** (**kʷetwores*), **penkʷe**, **s(w)eks**, **septṃ**, **oktō(u)**, **newṇ**, **dekṃ**. For the numeral "one" the dialects vary. We have a root **sem-¹** in

Chariot of the sun. Fourteenth-century B.C. bronze and gold-leaf statue from the Trundholm region of Denmark.

some derivatives, while the western Indo-European languages Germanic, Celtic, and Latin share the form **oi-no-**. The word for "hundred," formed from **dekm̥**, "ten," was *(d)km̥tom*. No common form for "thousand" or any other higher number can be reconstructed for the protolanguage.

Nature and the Physical Environment. In Indo-European, "moon/month" is a derivitive of the verb "to measure," **mē-**. The adjective *sen-*, "old," was also used for the waning of the moon, on the evidence of several languages.

The other celestial bodies recognized were the sun, **saəwel-**, and the stars, **ster-**. There is evidence from several traditions for similar designations of the constellation Ursa Major, though these may not go back to the earliest Indo-European times. The movement of the sun dictated the names for the points of the compass. The word EAST is derived from the verbal root **aus-**, "to shine," as is the word for "dawn" (Latin *Aurora*), deified since Indo-European times on the evidence of Greek, Lithuanian, and Sanskrit. The setting sun furnished the word for "evening" and "west": **wes-pero-**. The most widespread of the words for "night" was **nekʷ-t-**.

The Indo-Europeans knew snow in their homeland; the word **sneigʷh-** is nearly ubiquitous. Curiously enough, however, the word for "rain" varies among the different branches; we have words of differing distribution such as *seuə-*.

The root **dyeu-** occurs widely as the divine bright sky, but certain languages viewed the heavens as basically cloudy; **nebh-** is "sky" in Balto-Slavic and Iranian, but "cloud" elsewhere. Another divine natural phenomenon is illustrated by the root **(s)tenə-**, "thunder," and the name of the Germanic god THOR.

A word for the earth can be reconstructed as **dhghem-** (*dheghom*). The root **mori-**, "sea," is attested dialectally (MERE²), but it may well have referred to a lake or other smaller body of water. Transportation by or across water was, however, known to the Indo-Europeans, since most of the languages attest an old word for "boat" or "ship," *nāu-*, probably propelled by oars or a pole (*erə-*, "to row").

The names for a number of different trees are widely enough attested to be viewed as Proto-Indo-European in date. The general term for "tree" and "wood" was **deru-**. The original meaning of the root was doubtless "to be firm, solid," and from it is derived not only the family of English TREE but also that of English TRUE.

Indo-European had a generic term for "wild animal," **ghwer-** (FERAL). The wolf was known and evidently feared; its name is subject to taboo deformation (the conscious alteration of the form of a tabooed word, as in English *gol-derned, dad-burned*). The variant forms **wl̥kʷo-**, *lupo-*, and **wl̥p-ē-** (also "fox") are all found. The name of the bear was likewise subject to a hunter's taboo: the animal could not be mentioned by its real name on the hunt. The southern Indo-European languages have the original form, **r̥tko-** (Latin *ursus*, Greek *arktos*), but all the northern languages have a substitute term. In Slavic the bear is known as the "honey-eater," in Germanic the "brown one" (BEAR², and note also BRUIN).

A generic term for "fish" existed, *dhghū-* (also *peisk-* in Europe). The salmon (**laks-**) and the eel (*angʷhi-*) were known, the latter also in the meaning "snake." Several birds were known, including the crane (*gerə-*) and the eagle (*or-*).

The names for a number of insects can be reconstructed in the protolanguage, including the wasp (*wopsā*), the hornet (*kr̥s-ro-*, a derivative of **ker-¹**, "head," from the shape of the insect), and the fly (*mū-*). The bee (**bhei-**) was particularly important as the producer of honey, for which we have the common Indo-European name *melit-* (MILDEW). Honey was the only source of sugar and sweetness (**swād-**, "sweet," is ancient), and notably was the base of the only certain Indo-European alcoholic beverage, **medhu-**, which in different dialects meant both MEAD ("wine" in Greece and Anatolia) and "honey."

People and Society. For human beings themselves, a number of terms were employed, with different nuances of meaning. The usual terms for "man" and "woman" are **wī-ro-** (VIRILE) and *gʷenā-* from **gʷen-** (GYNECOLOGY). For "person" in general, the oldest word was apparently *manu-* (MAN-¹), as preserved in English MAN (nominative plural *manw-es*, becoming Germanic *mann-iz*, becoming Old English *menn, men*) and in Slavic and Sanskrit. A word for "woman" recently identified in Anatolian Luvian, *esōr*, combining form *-s(o)r-*, formed the feminine of the numbers "three" and "four," as well as appearing in **swesor-**, SISTER, and the Latin word for "wife." The Germanic word for "woman" (WIFE) was completely isolated until a cognate was recently identified in Tocharian. For its curious semantic history, see **ghwībh-**. In other dialects we find interesting metaphorical expressions that attest a set of religious concepts opposing the gods as immortal and celestial to humankind as mortal and terrestrial. Humans are either *mr̥tos*, "mortal" (**mer-**, "to die"), or *dhghomyo-*, "earthling" (**dhghem-**, "earth").

The parts of the body belong to the basic layer of vocabulary and are for the most part faithfully preserved in Indo-European languages. Such are **ker-¹**, "head" (also *kaput-* in dialects, doubtless a more colloquial word), **genu-²**, "chin, jaw," **dent-**, "tooth," **okʷ-**, "to see," whence "eye," **ous-**, "ear," **nas-**, "nose," **leb-**, "lip," **bhrū-**, "brow," **os-**, "mouth," and **dn̥ghū-**, "tongue." The word for "foot" is attested everywhere (**ped-**), while that for "hand" differs according to dialect; the most widespread is *ghes-or* (**ghes-**, CHIRO-).

Internal organs were also named in Indo-European times, including the heart (**kerd-**), womb (*gʷelbh-*), gall (**ghel-**), and liver (**yēkʷr̥**). The male sexual organs, *pes-* and *ergh-*, are common patrimony, as is **ors-**, "backside."

A large number of kinship terms have been reconstructed. They are agreed in pointing to a society that was patriarchal, patrilocal (the bride leaving her household to join that of her husband's family), and patrilineal (descent reckoned by the male line). "Father" and "head of the household" are one: **pəter-**, with his spouse, the **māter-**. These terms are ultimately derived from the baby-talk syllables *pa(pa)* and *ma(ma)*, but the kinship-term suffix -ter- shows that they had a sociological significance over and above this in the Indo-European family. Related terms are found for the grandfather (**awo-*) and the maternal uncle (**awon-*), and correspondingly the term **nepōt-** (feminine **neptī-*) applied to both grandson (perhaps originally "daughter's son") and NEPHEW ("sister's son"). English SON and DAUGHTER clearly reflect Indo-European **sūnu-* (from **seuə-**) and **dhugəter-**.

Male blood relations were designated as **bhrāter-** (BROTHER), which doubtless extended beyond those with a common father or mother; the Greek cognate means "fellow member of a clanlike group." The female counterpart was **swesor-** (SISTER), probably literally "female member of the kin group," with a word for woman (**esōr*) and the root **s(w)e-**, designating the self, one's own group.

The root **dem-** denoted both the house (Latin *domus*) and the household as a social unit. The father of the family (Latin *pater familiās*) was the "master of the house" (Greek *despotēs*) or simply "he of the house" (Latin *dominus*). A larger unit was the village, designated by the word **weik-**. Human settlements were frequently built on the top of high places fortified for defense, a practice taken by Indo-European migrants into central and western Europe and into Italy and Greece, as confirmed by archaeological finds. Words for such fortified high places vary; there are **pelə-*, variant **poli-* (ACROPOLIS), the Celtic word for "ring fort," **dhū-no-* (TOWN), and **bhergh-** (*-burg* in place names).

Economic Life and Technology.

A characteristic of Indo-European and other archaic societies was the principle of exchange and reciprocal gift-giving. The presentation of a gift entailed the obligation of a countergift, and the acts of giving and receiving were equivalent. They were simply facets of a single process of generalized exchange, which assured the circulation of wealth throughout the society.

This principle has left clear traces in the Indo-European vocabulary. The root **dō-** of Latin *dōnāre* means "to give" in most dialects but in Hittite means "to take." The root **nem-** is "to distribute" in Greek (NEMESIS), but in German it means "to take," and the cognate of English GIVE (**ghabh-**) has the meaning "to take" in Irish. The notion of exchange predominates in the roots **mei-¹** and **gher-²**. The GUEST (**ghos-ti-**) in Indo-European times was the person with whom one had mutual obligations of hospitality. But he was also the stranger, and the stranger in an uncertain and warring tribal society may well be hostile: the Latin cognate *hostis* means "enemy."

The Indo-Europeans practiced agriculture and the cultivation of cereals. We have several terms of Indo-European antiquity for grain: **grə-no-** (CORN), **yewo-*, and **pūro-*, which may have designated wheat or spelt. Of more restricted distribution is **bhares-*, "barley." Such terms for cereals could originally have designated the wild rather than cultivated varieties. A root for grinding is attested, **melə-** (MEAL², MILL). Another Indo-European term is **sē-**, "to sow," not found in Greek, Armenian, or Indo-Iranian. The verb "to plow" is **arə-*, again a common European term, with the name of the plow, **arə-trom*.

Stockbreeding and animal husbandry were an important part of Indo-European economic life. The names for all the familiar domesticated animals are present throughout the family: **gʷou-**, "cow" and "bull," **owi-**, "sheep," **agʷh-no-*,

Iberian hut. Restored dwelling and foundation ruins of a village on Mount Santa Tecla near La Guardia, Spain.

"lamb," **sū-**, "swine," and **porko-**, "farrow." The domestic dog was ancient (**kwon-**). The common Indo-European name of the horse, **ekwo-**, is probably derived from the adjective **ōku-*, "swift." The expansion and migration of the Indo-European-speaking peoples in the later third and early second millennia B.C. is intimately bound up with the diffusion of the horse. The verbal root **demə-*, "to force," acquired the special sense of "to tame horses," whence English TAME.

Stock was a source and measure of wealth; the original sense of **peku-** was probably "wealth, riches," as in Latin *pecūnia*, which came to mean "wealth in cattle" and finally "cattle" proper.

The verbal roots **pā-**, "to protect," and **kʷel-**, "to revolve, move around," are widely used for the notion of herding or watching over stock.

Roots indicating a number of technical operations are attested in most of the languages of the family. One such is **teks-*, which in some dialects means "to fabricate, especially by working with an ax," but in others means "to weave" (TEXTILE). The root **dheigh-**, meaning "to mold, shape," is applied both to bread (DOUGH) and to mud or clay, whence words for both pottery and mud walls (Iranian **pari-daiza-*, "walled around," borrowed into Greek as the word that became English PARADISE.)

The house (**dem-**) included a **dhwer-** (DOOR), which probably referred originally to the gateway into the enclosure of the household. The house would have had a central hearth, denoted in some languages by **as-** (properly a verb, "to burn"). Fire itself was known by two words, one of animate gender (**egni-*, Latin *ignis*) and one neuter (**paəwr̥**, Greek *pūr*).

The Indo-Europeans knew metal and metallurgy, to judge from the presence of the word **ayes-* in Sanskrit, Germanic, and Latin. The term designated copper and perhaps bronze. Iron is a latecomer, technologically, and the terms for it vary from dialect to dialect. Latin has *ferrum*, while the Germanic and Celtic term was **isarno-*, properly "holy (metal)," from **eis-**, perhaps so called because the first iron was derived from small meteorites. Gold, **ghel-**, also dialectally **aus-o-*, probably "yellow (metal)" or "shining," was known from ancient times, though the names for it vary. Silver was **arg-**, with various suffixes, doubtless meaning "white (metal)."

It was probably not long before the dispersal of the Proto-Indo-European community that the use of the wheel and wheeled transport was adopted. Despite the existence of widespread word families, most terms relating to wheeled vehicles seem to be metaphors formed from already existing words, rather than original, unanalyzable ones. So NAVE, or hub of the wheel (**nobh-**), is the same word as NAVEL. This is clearly the case with WHEEL itself, where the widespread *$k^w(e)$-k^wl-o-* is an expressive derivative of a verb (**k^wel-**) meaning "to revolve or go around." Other words for "wheel" are dialectal and again derivative, such as Latin *rota* from a verbal root *ret-*, "to run." The root **wegh-**, "to go, transport in a vehicle" (WAGON), is attested throughout the family, including now Hieroglyphic Luvian. This evidence for the late appearance of the wheel agrees with archaeological findings that date the distribution of the wheel in Europe to the latter part of the fifth millennium B.C., the latest possible date for the community of Proto-Indo-European proper.

Ideology. A number of verbs denoting mental activity are found. The most widespread is **men-**[1], preserved in English MIND. Other derivatives refer to remembering, warning (putting in mind), and thinking in general.

The notions of government and sovereignty were well represented. The presence of the old word for tribal king, *reg-* (**reg-**), only in the extreme east (RAJAH) and the extreme west (Latin *rēx*, Celtic *-rīx*) virtually guarantees its presence in the earliest Indo-European society. Another aspect of the function of sovereignty is the sphere of the law. There is an old word, *yewes-*, probably for "religious law," in Latin *iūs*. Latin *lēx* is also ancient (**leg-** or **legh-**), though the details of its etymology are uncertain. In a society that emphasized the principle of exchange and reciprocity, it is scarcely surprising that the notion of contractual obligation should be well represented. Several roots specify the notion of "bond": **bhendh-**, *ned-*, and *leig-*, all of which have derivatives with technical legal meanings in various languages.

Indo-European is particularly rich in religious vocabulary. An important form, which is also found only in the peripheral languages Sanskrit, Latin, and Celtic, is the two-word metaphoric phrase *kred-dhē-*, literally "to put (**dhē-**) heart (**kerd-**)." The two words have been joined together in the western languages, as in Latin *crēdo*, "I believe."

Oral prayers, requests of the deity, and other ritual utterances must have played a significant role in Indo-European religion. We have already seen **prek-** (PRAY), and note also the roots *wegh-* (in Latin *vovēre*, to VOW), **sengh-** (SING), and *g^werə-*, which in Latin *grātia* (GRACE) has had a new life in Christianity. The root **spend-** has the basic meaning of "to make an offering or perform a rite," whence "to engage oneself by a ritual act." Its Latin derivative *spondēre* means "to promise" (SPOUSE).

It is noteworthy that the idea of "holy" is intimately bound up with that of "whole, healthy," in a number of forms: **kailo-** (WHOLE and HOLY) and **solə-**, whence Latin *salvus* (SALVATION). An ancient root relating solely to religion is **sak-** (SACRED).

Finally we may add that poetry and a tradition of poetics are also common patrimony in most of the Indo-European traditions. The hymns of the Rig-Veda are composed in meters related to those used by the Greek poets, and the earliest verse forms found among the Celts and the Slavs go back to the same Indo-European source. Furthermore, one securely reconstructible Indo-European place name rests squarely on a metaphor: *Pīwer-iā* in Greek *Pīeriā* (PIERIAN SPRING) and *Īwer-ion-*, the prehistoric Celtic name for Ireland (Gaelic *Éire*, *Érin*); both continue an Indo-European feminine adjective *pīwer-iə*, "fat," metaphorically "fertile," from **peiə-**, the same root that gives English FAT.

Most interesting are the cases where it is possible to reconstruct from two or more traditions (usually including Homer and the Rig-Veda) a poetic phrase or formula consisting of two members. Such are the expressions "imperishable fame," *klewos ņdhg^whitom* (**kleu-**, *dhg^whei-*); "holy (mental) force," *isərom menos* (**eis-**, **men-**[1]); and the "weaver (or crafter) of words," the Indo-European poet himself, *wek^wōm teks-on* (**wek^w-**, **teks-**). The immortality of the gods (*ņ-mŗto-*, from **mer-**) is emphasized anew by the vivid verb phrase **nek- terə-**[2], "to overcome death," appearing in the Greek word *nektar*, the drink of the gods. And at least one three-member formula (in the sense of the word in traditional oral poetry) can be reconstructed for the poetic language of prayer, on the combined evidence of four languages, Latin, Umbrian, Avestan, and Sanskrit: "Protect, keep safe, man and cattle!" (**pā- wī-ro- peku**).

Conclusion

This survey has touched on only a representative sample of the available reconstructed Indo-European lexicon and has made no attempt to cite the mass of evidence in all the languages of the family, ancient and modern, for these reconstructions.

For this essay, we have given only the information about Indo-European culture that could be derived from language and lexicon alone. Other disciplines serve to fill out and complete the picture to be gathered from the study of vocabulary: archaeology, prehistory, comparative religion, and the history of institutions.

Archaeologists have not in fact succeeded in locating the Indo-Europeans. The so-called Kurgan peoples, named after the Russian word for their characteristic "barrow" or "tumulus" grave structure, may well have spoken an Indo-European language. The correlation between the Kurgan cultural features described by archaeologists and the Indo-European lexicon are striking, down to architectural features such as a small subterranean or aboveground rectangular hut (*dom-*, **dem-**) of timber uprights (*kli-t-*, **klei-**, and *stu-t-*, **stā-**, still with us in English STUD).

Sometime around the middle of the fifth millennium B.C., these people expanded from the steppe zone north of the Black Sea and beyond the Volga into the Balkans and adjacent areas. These Kurgan peoples bore a new mobile and aggressive culture into Neolithic Europe, and it is not unreasonable to associate them with the coming of the Indo-Europeans. But we should perhaps be content to recognize the Kurgan peoples as speakers of certain Indo-European languages and as sharing a common Indo-European patrimony. The ultimate "cradle" of the Indo-Europeans may well never be known, and language remains the best and fullest evidence for prehistoric Indo-European society. It is the comparative method in historical linguistics that can illumine not only ancient ways of life but also ancient modes of thought.

Guide to the Appendix

This Dictionary carries the etymology of the English language to its logical and natural conclusion, for if the documentary history of words is of interest and value, so is their reconstructed prehistory. The historical component is given in the etymologies, after the definitions in the main body of the Dictionary. This Appendix supplies the prehistoric component, tracing the ultimate Indo-European derivations of those English words that are descended from a selected group of Indo-European roots.

In the Appendix, the form given in **boldface** type at the head of each entry is, unless otherwise identified, an Indo-European root in its basic form. The basic root form is followed in some cases by one or more variants, also in boldface type. Then the basic reconstructed meaning or meanings of the root are given. Meanings that are different parts of speech are separated by a semicolon:

> **kei-** To lie; bed, couch; beloved, dear.
>
> **pelə-²** Flat; to spread.
>
> **leg-** To collect; with derivatives meaning "to speak."

After the basic meaning there may appear further information about the phonological shape or nature of the root:

> **skrībh-** To cut, separate, sift. Extension of **(s)ker-¹**.
>
> **kʷr̥mi-** Worm. Rhyme word to *wr̥mi-, worm (see **wer-**).
>
> **pā-** To protect, feed. Contracted from *paə-.
>
> **dyeu-** To shine (and in many derivatives, "sky, heaven, god"). Zero-grades *dyu- (before consonants) and *diw- (before vowels).

Most, but not all, of the additional information is self-explanatory. In the first two examples, the boldface forms **(s)ker-¹** and **wer-** are cross-references to those roots, which are main entries in this Appendix. Every boldface form appearing in the text of an entry is such a cross-reference. In the example **pā-** the form *paə- represents an older root form; the nature of these contractions is explained in the preceding essay under "Speech Sounds and Their Alternations" (page 1599). In the last example (**dyeu-**) the meaning is followed by morphological information designed to clarify the relationship among various forms later in the entry.

The text of each entry describes in detail the development of Modern English words from the root. Each numbered section of an entry begins with a list, in SMALL CAPITALS, of the Modern English words derived from a particular form of the root. (This list may be preceded by an intermediate step; see further below.) The simple (uncompounded) derivatives are given first; the compounds follow, separated from them by a semicolon. In some cases no further semantic or morphological development needs to be explained, and the *lemma*, the historically attested representative of the root, is given next, as *avis* at the entry **awi-**:

> **awi-** Bird. I. 1. AVIAN . . . from Latin *avis*, bird.

Much more commonly, however, intermediate developments require explanation. These intermediate stages are reconstructions representing a word stem in Indo-European that is necessary to explain the lemma following it (see the section "Grammatical Forms and Syntax" in the preceding essay, page 1600). The reconstructed forms are not historically attested; they are preceded by an asterisk (*) to denote this fact. Sometimes earlier or later developments of the intermediate forms are given in parentheses, as in the example of **stā-** below. In these cases the symbol < is used to mean "derived from" and the symbol > is used to mean "developed into." Intermediate stages that are in fact attested (such as the stages between Latin *avis* and English BUSTARD in the example above) are usually not given in the Appendix, but in the etymology of the word in the main vocabulary of the Dictionary. The following terms are used to describe typical morphological processes of Indo-European:

Full-grade form: A form with e-vocalism (the basic form); so identified for descriptive contrast.

O-grade form: A form with o-vocalism:

> **dhers-** . . . O-grade form *dhors- . . .

Zero-grade form: A form with zero-vocalism:

> **men-¹** . . . I. Zero-grade form *mn̥-.

Lengthened-grade form: A form with lengthened vocalism:

> **sed-** . . . IV. Lengthened-grade form *sēd-.

Secondary full-grade form: A new full-grade form created by inserting the fundamental vowel e in the zero-grade form of an extended root:

> **stā-** . . . V. Zero-grade extended root *stū- (< *stuə-). . . . VI. Secondary full-grade form *steuə-.

Basic form: The unchanged root; so identified for descriptive contrast.

Suffixed form: A form with one or more suffixes, written with an internal hyphen:

> **laks-** . . . Suffixed form *laks-o-.
> **pet-** . . . 1. Suffixed form *pet-rā-.

Prefixed form: A form with a prefix, written with an internal hyphen:

> **dhē-** . . . III. Zero-grade form *dhə-. 1a. Prefixed form *kom-dhə-.

Extended form: A form with an extension or enlargement, written without internal hyphens:

> **pel-²** . . . II. Extended form *pelə-.

Nasalized form: A form with a nasal infix, written with internal hyphens:

> **tag-** . . . 1. Nasalized form *ta-n-g-.

Reduplicated form: A form prefixed by its own initial consonant followed by a vowel:

> **segh-** . . . **5.** Reduplicated form *si-sgh-.

Expressive form: A form with "expressive gemination" (doubling of the final consonant), written without internal hyphens:

> **nas-** . . . **3.** Lengthened-grade form *nās-. . . . **b.** expressive form *nāss-.

Compound form: A form compounded with a form of another root, written with internal hyphens:

> **dem-** . . . **3.** Compound *dems-pot- . . .

Shortened form: A form with shortened vocalism:

> **syū-** . . . **III.** Suffixed shortened form *syu-men-.

Reduced form: A form with loss of one or more sounds:

> **ambhi** . . . **1.** Reduced form *bhi.

Variant form: A form altered in any way other than those described in the above categories:

> **deru-** . . . **2.** Variant form *dreu-.

Inflected Form: A form having an inflectional ending:

> **ant-** . . . **I.** Inflected form (locative singular) *anti, "against" . . .

These terms can be combined freely to describe in as much detail as necessary the development from the root to the lemma.

> **(s)keu-** . . . **4.** Extended zero-grade form *kus-.
> **kap-** . . . **III.** Lengthened-grade variant form *kōp-.
> **ker-¹** . . . **VI.** Suffixed further extended form *kr̥as-no-.
> **wed-** . . . **6.** Suffixed nasalized zero-grade form *u-n-d-ā-.

In order to emphasize the fact that English belongs to the Germanic branch of Indo-European and give precedence to directly inherited words in contrast to words borrowed from other branches, the intermediate stages in Germanic etymologies are covered in fuller detail. The Common or Proto-Germanic (here called simply Germanic) forms underlying English words are always given. Where no other considerations intervene, Germanic is given first of the Indo-European groups, and Old English is given first within Germanic, although this order of precedence is not rigidly applied.

The final item in most entries is an abbreviated reference, in brackets, to Julius Pokorny's *Indogermanisches Etymologisches Wörterbuch* [*Indo-European Etymological Dictionary*] (Bern, 1959). This, the standard work of reference and synthesis in the Indo-European field, carries a full range of the actual comparative material on which the roots are reconstructed. Our Appendix presents only those aspects of the material that are directly relevant to English. For example, the English word DAUGHTER is found at the root **dhugəter-**, "daughter." This entry describes the transition of the Indo-European form through Germanic *dohtar-* to Old English *dohtor*, "daughter." It does not cite the comparative evidence from outside English and Germanic on which this assertion is based, but it refers to "Pokorny *dhug(h)əter-* 277." The entry *dhug(h)əter-* on page 277 in Pokorny's dictionary cites, in addition to the Old English word, the forms attested in Sanskrit, Avestan, Armenian, Oscan, Gothic, Old High German, Old Norse, Slavic, Lithuanian, and Tocharian from which the reconstruction of the root was made. These references should serve as a reminder that the information given in this Appendix is assertive rather than expository and that the evidence and evaluation upon which its assertions are based are not presented here.

Symbols: * unattested
< derived from
> developed into

Parentheses within a form enclose sound(s) or letter(s) sometimes or optionally present.

INDO-EUROPEAN SOUND CORRESPONDENCES

Probably the most basic element of language change is a gradual shift in the way individual speech sounds are pronounced. As the Indo-European speech community expanded over the centuries into new territories, local dialectal variations gave rise to increasingly divergent language families. This table shows the historical development of sounds from Proto-Indo-European to the principal older Indo-European languages. For example, reading down the first column, it can be seen that Proto-Indo-European initial p remains p in Latin, but it is lost entirely in Old Irish and becomes f in Germanic and consequently in Old English: thus Indo-European *pəter-, meaning "father,"

becomes Latin *pater*, Old Irish *athir*, and Common Germanic *fadar, Old English *fæder*. A more precise way of describing this relationship is to say that initial p in Proto-Indo-European corresponds to p in Latin, to f in Germanic and Old English, and to zero in Old Irish. The correspondences shown in the table are regular: they always occur as stated unless specific factors intervene. This table shows only the initial consonants and vowels in initial syllables, which are generally the simplest elements involved in sound change. All other phonetic elements including stress and environment also show regular correspondences, but often with considerable complexity.

LANGUAGE	CONSONANTS												CONTINUANT	LARYNGEALS		
	STOPS															
	Unvoiced				Voiced				Voiced Aspirate							
Indo-European	p	t	k	kʷ	b	d	g	gʷ	bh	dh	gh	gʷh	s	$ə_1$	$ə_2$	$ə_3$
Hittite	p	t	k	ku	p	t	k	ku	p	t	k	ku	s	–	h	h
Tocharian	p	t/c/ts	k/ś	k/ś	p	t/c/ts	k/ś	k/ś	p	t/c/ts	k/ś	k/ś	s/ṣ	–	–	–
Sanskrit	p	t	ś	k/c	b	d	j	g/j	bh	dh	h	gh/h	s/ṣ	–	–	–
Avestan	p	t	s	k/c	b	d	z	g/j	b	d	z	g/j	h	–	–	–
Old Persian	p	t	th	k	b	d	d	g/j	b	d	d	g/j	h	–	–	–
Old Church Slavonic	p	t	s	k/č/c	b	d	z	g/ž/z	b	d	z	g/ž/z	s	–	–	–
Lithuanian	p	t	š	k	b	d	ž	g	b	d	ž	g	s	–	–	–
Armenian	h	th	s	kh	p	t	c	k	b	d	j	g	h	–	–	–
Greek	p	t	k	p/t/k	b	d	g	b/d/g	ph	th	kh	ph/th/kh	h	–/e	–/a	–/o
Latin	p	t	c	qu	b	d	g	v	f	f	h	f	s	–	–	–
Old Irish	–	t	c	c	b	d	g	b	b	d	g	g	s	–	–	–
Common Germanic	f	th	h	hw	p	t	k	kw/k	b	d	g	b/g	s	–	–	–
Gothic	f	th	h	hw/w	p	t	k	q	b	d	g	b/g	s	–	–	–
Old Norse†	f	th	h	hv	p	t	k	kv	b	d	g	b/g	s	–	–	–
Old High German†	f	d	h	hw/w	p/pf	z	k	qu	b	t/d	g	b/g	s	–	–	–
Middle Dutch†	v	th/d	h	w	p	t	k	qu	b	d	g	b/g	s	–	–	–
Old English†	f	th	h	hw	p	t	c	cw/c	b	d	g	b/g	s	–	–	–

NOTES: – means lacking: p was lost in Old Irish.
         w was lost in Greek.
         y was lost in Old Irish, Old Norse.
         Initial laryngeals are preserved only in Hittite.

A slash (/) differentiates reflexes of the same sound in different environments.
†The effects of umlaut are not considered.
‡Common Greek ā, whence ē in Attic-Ionic dialect, source of most Greek words in English.

Nasals		Liquids		Glides		Short					Long					Syllabic Sonorants			
m	n	r	l	y	w	e	o	a	i	u	ē(eə)	ō(oə)	ā(aə)	ī(iə)	ū(uə)	m̥	n̥	r̥	l̥
m	n	r	l	y	w	e/i	a	a	i	u	e/i	a	a/ah	i	u/uh	am	an	ar	al
m	n	r	l	y	w	ä	e	ā	ä/i	ä/u	e	o/ā	o/ā	i	u	ām	ān	är	äl
m	n	r/l	r/l	y	v	a	a/ā	a	i	u	ā	ā	ā	ī	ū	a	a	r̥	r̥
m	n	r	r	y	v	a	a/ā	a	i	u	ā	ā	ā	ī	ū	a	a	ərə	ərə
m	n	r	r	y	v	a	a/ā	a	i	u	ā	ā	ā	ī	ū	a	a	(a)r	(a)r
m	n	r	l	j	v	e	o	o	ĭ	ŭ	e	a	a	i	u	ę	e	rŭ	lŭ
m	n	r	l	j	v	e	a	a	i	u	ė	uo	o	y	u	im	in	ir	il
m	n	r	l	y	g/v	e	o	a	i	u	i	u	a	ĭ	u	am	an	ar	ał
m	n	r	l	h/z	–	e	o	a	i	u	ē	ō	ā/ē‡	ī	ū	a	a	ar/ra	al/la
m	n	r	l	i	v	e	o	a	i	u	ē	ō	ā	ī	ū	em	en	or	ul
m	n	r	l	–	f	e/i	o/u	a	i/e	u/o	ī	ā	ā	ī	ū	(*am)ē	(*an)ē	ri	li
m	n	r	l	j	w	e	a	a	i	u	ē	ō	ō	ī	ū	um	un	ur	ul
m	n	r	l	j	w	i/ai	a	a	i/e	u	ē	ō	ō	ī	ū	um	un	aur	ul
m	n	r	l	–	v/–	e	a	a	i/e	u/o	ā	ō	ō	ī	ū	um	un	ur/or	ul/ol
m	n	r	l	j	w	e	a	a	i/e	u/o	ā	uo	uo	ī	ū	um	un	ur/or	ul/ol
m	n	r	l	g	w	e	a	a	i/e	u/o	ē	ō	ō	ī	ū	um	un	ur/or	ul/ol
m	n	r	l	g/y	w	e	æ/a	æ/a	i/e	u/o	ǣ	ō	ō	ī	ū	um	un	ur/or	ul/ol

Indo-European Roots

ag- To drive, draw, move. **1.** ACT, ACTIVE, ACTOR, ACTUAL, ACTUARY, ACTUATE, AGENDUM, AGENT, AGILE, AGITATE; ALLEGE, AMBAGE, AMBIGUOUS, ASSAY, CACHE, COAGULUM, COGENT, ESSAY, EXACT, EXACTA, EXAMINE, EXIGENT, EXIGUOUS, FUMIGATE, FUSTIGATE, INTRANSIGENT, LEVIGATE, LITIGATE, NAVIGATE, OBJURGATE, PRODIGALITY, REDACT, RETROACTIVE, SQUAT, TRANSACT, VARIEGATE, from Latin *agere,* to do, act, drive, conduct, lead, weigh. **2.** -AGOGUE, AGONY; ANAGOGE, ANTAGONIZE, CHORAGUS, DEMAGOGUE, EPACT, GLUCAGON, HYPNAGOGIC, MYSTAGOGUE, PEDAGOGUE, PROTAGONIST, STRATAGEM, SYNAGOGUE, from Greek *agein,* to drive, lead, weigh. **3.** Suffixed form **ag-to-*. AMBASSADOR, EMBASSAGE, EMBASSY, from Latin *ambactus,* servant, from Celtic **amb(i)-ag-to-*, "one who goes around" (**ambi,* around; see **ambhi**). **4.** Suffixed form **ag-ti-*, whence adjective **ag-ty-o-*, "weighty." AXIOM; AXIOLOGY, CHRONAXIE, from Greek *axios,* worth, worthy, of like value, weighing as much. **5.** Possibly suffixed form **ag-ro-*, driving, pursuing, grabbing. PELLAGRA, PODAGRA, from Greek *agrā,* a seizing. **6.** O-grade suffixed form **og-mo-*, furrow, track, metaphorically "incised line." OGHAM, from Old Irish *Ogma* (from Celtic **Ogmios*), name of a Celtic god and traditional inventor of the ogham alphabet. [Pokorny *aĝ-* 4.] See also derivative **agro-**.

agro- Field. Probably originally a derivative of **ag-**. **1.** ACRE, from Old English *æcer,* field, acre, from Germanic **akraz.* **2.** AGRARIAN; AGRICULTURE, PEREGRINE, PILGRIM, from Latin *ager* (genitive *agrī*), earlier **agros,* district, property, field. **3.** AGRO-; AGROSTOLOGY, ONAGER, STAVESACRE, from Greek *agros,* field, and *agrios,* wild. [In Pokorny *aĝ-* 4.]

aim- Copy. **1.** Suffixed full-grade form **aim-olo-*. EMULATE, EMULOUS, from Latin *aemulus,* emulous. **2.** Zero-grade form **im-*. **a.** IMITATE; INIMITABLE, from Latin *imitārī,* to imitate, from suffixed form **im-eto-;* **b.** IMAGE, IMAGO, IMAGINE, from Latin *imāgō,* image. [Not in Pokorny; compare Hittite *ḫimma-*, ritual substitute.]

aiw- Also **ayu-**. Vital force, life, long life, eternity; also "endowed with the acme of vital force, young." **1a.** NO[1], from Old English *ā,* ever; **b.** AUGHT[1], from Old English *āwiht, āuht,* anything, "ever a creature"; **c.** EVER; EVERY, NEVER, from Old English *ǣfre* (second element obscure), ever; **d.** AYE[2]; NAY, from Old Norse *ei,* ever. **a, c,** and **d** all from extended Germanic form **aiwi;* **b** from Germanic **aiwi* + **wihti,* "ever a thing, anything" (**wihti-*, thing). **2a.** Suffixed form **aiw-o-*. COEVAL, LONGEVITY, MEDIEVAL, PRIMEVAL, from Latin *aevum,* age, eternity; **b.** further suffixed form **aiwo-tā(ti)-*. AGE; COETANEOUS, from Latin *aetās* (stem *aetāti-*), age; **c.** further suffixed form **aiwo-t-erno-*. ETERNAL, ETERNE, ETERNITY; SEMPITERNAL, from Latin *aeternus,* eternal. **3.** Suffixed form **aiw-en-*. EON, from Greek *aiōn,* age, vital force. **4.** Zero-grade form **yu-* (earlier **əyu-*) in compound **yu-gʷiə-es-*, "having a vigorous life" (**gʷiə-es-*, life; see **gʷeiə-**). HYGIENE, from Greek *hugiēs,* healthy. **5.** O-grade form **oyu-*. **a.** UTOPIA, from Greek *ou,* not, variant of *ouk,* probably from a pre-Greek phrase **(ne) oyu (kʷid),* "(not on your) life" (**ne,* not, and **kʷid,* indefinite pronoun used as emphasizing particle; see **ne** and **kʷo-**); **b.** AYURVEDA, from Sanskrit *āyuḥ,* life, health, from suffixed form **oyu-s-*. [Pokorny *aiu̯-* 17.] See also derivative **yeu-**.

ak- Sharp. **1.** Suffixed form **ak-yā-*. **a.** EDGE; SELVAGE, from Old English *ecg,* sharp side, from Germanic **agjō;* **b.** EGG[2], from Old Norse *eggja,* to incite, goad, from Germanic **agjan.* **2.** Suffixed form **ak-u-*. **a.** EAR[2], from Old English *æhher, ēar,* spike, ear of grain, from Germanic **ahuz-;* **b.** ACICULA, ACUITY, ACULEATE, ACUMEN, ACUPUNCTURE, ACUTE, AGLET, AGUE, EGLANTINE, from Latin *acus,* needle; **c.** ACEROSE, from Latin *acus,* chaff. **3.** Suffixed form **ak-i-*. ACIDANTHERA, from Greek *akis,* needle. **4.** Suffixed form **ak-men-*, stone, sharp stone used as a tool, with metathetic variant **ka-men-*, with variants: **a.** **ka-mer-*. HAMMER, from Old English *hamor,* hammer, from Germanic **hamaraz;* **b.** **ke-men-* (probable variant). HEAVEN, from Old English *heofon, hefn,* heaven, from Germanic **hibin-*, "the stony vault of heaven," dissimilated form of **himin-*. **5.** Suffixed form **ak-onā-*, independently created in: **a.** AWN, from Old Norse *ögn,* ear of grain, and Old English *agen,* ear of grain, from Germanic **aganō;* and **b.** PARAGON, from Greek *akonē,* whetstone. **6.** Suffixed lengthened form **āk-ri-*. ACERATE, ACRID, ACRIMONY, EAGER[1]; CARVACROL, VINEGAR, from Latin *ācer,* sharp, bitter. **7.** Suffixed form **ak-ri-bhwo-*. ACERBIC, EXACERBATE, from Latin *acerbus,* bitter, sharp, tart. **8.** Suffixed (stative) form **ak-ē-*. ACID, from Latin *acēre,* to be sharp. **9.** Suffixed form **ak-ēto-*. ACETABULUM, ACETIC, ACETUM; ESTER, from Latin *acētum,* vinegar. **10.** Suffixed form **ak-mā-*. ACME, ACNE, from Greek *akmē,* point. **11.** Suffixed form **ak-ro-*. ACRO-; ACROBAT, ACROMION, from Greek *akros,* topmost. **12.** O-grade form **ok-* (from earlier **əok-*) in suffixed form **ok-ri-*. MEDIOCRE, from Latin *ocris,* rugged mountain. **13.** Suffixed o-grade form **ok-su-*. AMPHIOXUS, OXALIS, OXYGEN, OXYTONE, OXYURIASIS, PAROXYSM, from Greek *oxus,* sharp, sour. [Pokorny 2. *ak̂-* 18, 3. *k̂em-* 556.]

akʷ-ā- Water. **1.** AIT; ISLAND, from Old English *īg, īeg,* island, from Germanic **aujō,* "thing on the water," from **agwjō.* **2.** AQUA, AQUARELLE, AQUARIUM, AQUATIC, AQUI-, EWER, GOUACHE; AQUAMARINE, AQUATINT, AQUAVIT, AQUEDUCT, SEWER[1], from Latin *aqua,* water. [Pokorny *aku̯ā-* 23.]

al- Beyond. **1.** O-grade form **ol-*, "beyond." **a.** Compound forms **ol-se-, *ol-so-* (**so-*, pronominal stem; see **so-**). ALARM, ALERT, ALFRESCO, ALLIGATOR, EL NIÑO, HOOPLA, LAGNIAPPE, LANGUE D'OÏL, LARIAT, VOILÀ, from Latin *ille* (feminine *illa,* neuter *illud*), "yonder," that, from Archaic Latin *ollus;* **b.** suffixed forms **ol-s, *ol-tero-*. OUTRÉ, ULTERIOR, ULTIMATE, ULTRA-, UTTERANCE[2], from Latin *uls, *ulter, ultrā,* beyond. **2.** Suffixed form **al-tero-*, "other of two." **a.** ALTER, ALTERCATE, ALTERNATE, ALTRUISM; SUBALTERN, from Latin *alter,* other, other of two; **b.** ADULTERATE, ADULTERINE, ADULTERY, from Latin *adulterāre,* to commit adultery with, pollute, probably from the phrase *ad alterum,* "(approaching) another (unlawfully)" (*ad,* to); **c.** variant suffixed form **an-tero-*, "other (of two)." OTHER, from Old English *ōther,* from Germanic **anthara-*. **3.** Suffixed form **al-eno-*. ARANYAKA, from Sanskrit *araṇa-*, foreign. **4.** Extended form **alyo-*, "other of more than two." **a.** ELSE; ELDRITCH, from Old English *el-, elles,* else, otherwise, from Germanic **aljaz* (with adverbial suffix); **b.** ALIAS, ALIEN; ALIBI, ALIQUOT, HIDALGO, from Latin *alius,* other of more than two; **c.** ALLO-; ALLEGORY, ALLELOMORPH, ALLELOPATHY, MORPHALLAXIS, PARALLAX, PARALLEL, TROPHALLAXIS, from Greek *allos,* other. [Pokorny 1. *al-* 24, 2. *an* 37.]

albho- White. **1.** Possibly Germanic **albiz, *albaz,* elf, if meaning "white ghostly apparition." **a.** ELF, from Old English *ælf,* elf; **b.** OAF, from Old Norse *alfr,* elf; **c.** OBERON, from Old French *Auberon,* from a source akin to Old High German *Alberich,* "ruler of elves," from Old High German **alb,* elf. **2.** ELFIN, from Old English *-elfen,* elf, possibly from Germanic **albinjō.* **3.** ABELE, ALB, ALBEDO, ALBESCENT, ALBINO, ALBITE, ALBUM, ALBUMEN, AUBADE, AUBURN; DAUB, from Latin *albus,* white. [Pokorny *albho-* 30.]

alu- In words related to sorcery, magic, possession, and intoxication. Suffixed form **alu-t-*. ALE, from Old English *ealu,* from Germanic **aluth-*. [Pokorny *alu-* 33.]

ambhi Also **m̥bhi.** Around. Probably derived from **ant-bhi,* "from both sides" (see **ant-**). **1.** Reduced form **bhi.* **a.** BY[1]; ABAFT, BUT, from Old English *bi, bī, be,* by; **b.** BE-, from Old English *be-*, on all sides, be-, also intensive prefix; **c.** BELEAGUER, from Middle Dutch *bie,* by; **d.** BIVOUAC, from Old High German *bi,* by, at. **a–d** all from Germanic **bi, *bi-* (intensive prefix). **2a.** EMBER DAY, from Old English *ymbe,* around; **b.** OMBUDSMAN, from Old Norse *um(b),* about, around; **c.** UMLAUT, from Old High German *umbi,* around. **a–c** all from Germanic **umbi.* **3a.** AMBI-, from Latin *ambi-*, around, about; **b.** ALLEY[1], ALLEY-OOP, AMBULANCE, AMBULATE, ANDANTE, FUNAMBULIST, PERAMBULATE, PREAMBLE, from Latin *ambulāre,* to go about, walk (**ambh(i)-al-ā-; *-al-*, to wander, go). **4.** AMPHI-, from Greek *amphi,* around, about. **5.** Celtic **ambi,* around, in compound **amb(i)-ag-to-* (see **ag-**). [Pokorny *ambhi* 34.]

anə- To breathe. Suffixed form **anə-mo-*. **1.** ANIMA, ANIMADVERT, ANIMAL, ANIMATE, ANIMATO, ANIMISM, ANIMOSITY, ANIMUS; EQUANIMITY, LONGANIMITY, MAGNANIMOUS, PUSILLANIMOUS, UNANIMOUS, from Latin *animus,* reason, mind, spirit, and *anima,* soul, spirit, life, breath. **2.** ANEMO-, ANEMONE, from Greek *anemos,* wind. [Pokorny 3. *an(ə)-* 38.]

ant- Front, forehead.

I. Inflected form (locative singular) **anti,* "against," with derivatives meaning "in front of," "before"; also "end." **1.** UN-[2]; ALONG, from Old English *and-*, indicating opposition, from Germanic **andi-* and **anda-*. **2.** END, from Old English *ende,* end, from Germanic **andjaz.* **3.** ANCIENT[1], ANTE, ANTE-, ANTERIOR; ADVANCE, ADVANTAGE, VANGUARD, from Latin *ante,* before, in front of, against. **4.** ANTI-; ENANTIOMER, ENANTIOMORPH, from Greek *anti,* against, and *enantios,* opposite. **5.** Compound form **anti-əkʷo-*, "appearing before, having prior aspect" (**əkʷ-*, appearance; see **okʷ-**). ANTIC, ANTIQUE, from Latin *antīquus,* former, antique. **6.** Reduced form **n̥ti-*. **a.** UNTIL, from Old Norse *und,* until, unto; **b.** ELOPE, from Middle Dutch *ont-*, away from. Both **a** and **b** from Germanic **und-*. **7.** Variant form **anto-*. VEDANTA, from Sanskrit *antaḥ,* end.

II. Probable inflected form (ablative plural) **ant-bhi,* "from both sides," whence **ambhi,* around. See **ambhi-**. [Pokorny *ant-s* 48.]

apo- Also **ap-**. Off, away. **1a.** OF, OFF, OFFAL, from Old English *of, æf,* off; **b.** EBB, from Old English *ebba,* low tide; **c.** ABLAUT, from Old High German *aba,* off, away from; **d.** AFT; ABAFT, from Old English *æftan,* behind, from Germanic **aftan-*. **a–d** all from Germanic **af.* **2.** AB-[1], from Latin *ab, ab-*, away from. **3.** APO-, from Greek *apo,* away from, from. **4.** Suffixed (comparative) form **ap(o)-tero-*. AFTER, from Old English *æfter,* after, behind, from Germanic **aftar-*. **5.** Suffixed form **ap-t-is-*. EFTSOONS, from Old English *eft,* again, from Germanic **aftiz.* **6.** Suffixed form **apu-ko-*. AWKWARD, from Old Norse *öfugr,* turned backward, from Germanic **afuga-*. **7.** Possible variant root form **po(s),* on, in. **a.** POGROM, from Russian *po,* at, by, next to; **b.** POST-, POSTERIOR; POSTMORTEM, PREPOSTEROUS, PUISNE, PUNY, from Latin *post,* behind, back, afterward; **c.** APPOSITE, APPOSITION, APROPOS, COMPONENT, COMPOSE, COMPOSITE, COMPOSITION, COMPOST, COMPOTE, COMPOUND[1], CONTRAPPOSTO, DEPONE, DEPOSIT, DISPOSE, EXPONENT, EXPOSE, EXPOUND, IMPOSE, IMPOST[1], IMPOST[2], INTERPOSE, JUXTAPOSE, OPPOSE, POSITION, POSITIVE, POST[2], POST[3], POSTICHE, POSTURE, PREPOSITION[1], PROPOSE, PROVOST, PUNT[3], REPOSIT, SUPPOSE, TRANSPOSE, from Latin *pōnere,* to put, place, from **po-s(i)nere* (*sinere,* to leave, let). [Pokorny *apo-* 53.]

arg- To shine; white; the shining or white metal, silver. **1.** Suffixed form **arg-ent-*. ARGENT, ARGENTINE, from Latin *argentum,* silver. **2.** Suffixed form **arg-i-l(l)-*. ARGIL, from Greek *argillos,* white clay. **3.** Suffixed form **arg-u-ro-*. LITHARGE, PYRARGYRITE, from Greek *arguros,* silver. **4.** Suffixed form **arg-i-n-*. ARGININE, from Greek *arginoeis,* brilliant, bright-shining. **5.** Suffixed form **arg-u-*, brilliant, clear. ARGUE, from Latin denominative *arguere,* to make clear, demonstrate (< **argu-yo-*). **6.** Suffixed zero-grade form **ər̥g-ro-*, becoming **arg-ro-*. AGRI-

MONY, possibly from Greek _argos,_ white (< _*argros_). [Pokorny _ar(e)-ĝ-_ 64.]

as- To burn, glow. **1.** Extended form _*asg-_. ASH[1], from Old English _æsce, asce,_ ash, from Germanic _*askōn-_. **2.** Suffixed form _*ās-ā-_. ARA, from Latin _āra,_ altar, hearth. **3.** Suffixed (stative) form _*ās-ē-_. **a.** ARID, from Latin _āridus,_ dry, parched, from _ārēre,_ to be dry; **b.** ARDENT, ARDOR, ARSON, from Latin _ārdēre,_ to burn, be on fire, from _āridus,_ parched. **4.** Extended form _*asd-_. **a.** ZAMIA, from Greek _azein,_ to dry; **b.** AZALEA, from Greek _azaleos,_ dry. [Pokorny _ăs-_ 68.]

aus- To shine (said especially of the dawn). **1a.** EAST, from Old English _ēast,_ east (< "the direction of the sunrise"); **b.** OSTMARK, from Old High German _ōstan,_ east. Both **a** and **b** from Germanic _*aust-_. **2a.** EASTERN, from Old English _ēasterne,_ eastern; **b.** OSTROGOTH, from Late Latin _ostro-,_ eastern. Both **a** and **b** from Germanic _*austra-_. **3.** EASTER, from Old English _ēastre,_ Easter, from Germanic _*austrōn-,_ dawn. **4.** Possibly in Latin _auster,_ the south wind, formally identical to the Germanic forms in **2** and **3,** but the semantics are unclear: AUSTRO-[1]. **5.** Probably suffixed form _*ausōs-,_ dawn, also Indo-European goddess of the dawn. **a.** AURORA, from Latin _aurōra,_ dawn; **b.** EO-, EOS; EOSIN, from Greek _ēōs_ (< _*āwōs_ < _*ausōs_), dawn. [Pokorny _au̯es-_ 86.]

awi- Bird.

I. 1. AVIAN, AVIARY, AVIATION; AVICULTURE, AVIFAUNA, BUSTARD, OCARINA, OSPREY, OSTRICH, from Latin _avis,_ bird. **2.** Compound _*awi-spek-,_ "observer of birds" (_*spek-,_ to see; see **spek-**). AUSPICE, from Latin _auspex,_ augur.

II. A possible derivative is the Indo-European word for egg, _*ōwyo-, *ōyyo-_. **1a.** COCKNEY, from Old English _ǣg,_ egg; **b.** EGG[1], from Old Norse _egg,_ egg. Both **a** and **b** from Germanic _*ajja(m)_. **2.** OVAL, OVARY, OVATE, OVI-, OVOLO, OVULE, OVUM, from Latin _ōvum,_ egg. **3.** OO-, from Greek _ōion,_ egg. **4.** CAVIAR, from a source akin to Middle Persian _khāyak,_ egg, from Old Iranian _*āvyaka-,_ diminutive of _*āvya-,_ egg. [Pokorny _au̯ei-_ 86, _ō(u̯)i̯-om_ 783.]

bel- Strong. **1.** Suffixed o-grade form _*bol-iyo-_. BOLSHEVIK, from Russian _bol'shoĭ,_ large. **2.** Prefixed form _*dē-bel-i-,_ "without strength" (_dē-,_ privative prefix). DEBILITATE, DEBILITY, from Latin _dēbilis,_ weak. [Pokorny 2. _bel-_ 96.]

bhā- To speak. Contracted from _*bhaə-_. **1.** FABLE, FABLIAU, FABULOUS, FADO, FAIRY, FANDANGO, FATE, FAY[2]; AFFABLE, FANTOCCINI, INEFFABLE, INFANT, INFANTRY, PREFACE, from Latin _fārī,_ to speak. **2.** -PHASIA; APOPHASIS, PROPHET, from Greek _phanai,_ to speak. **3a.** BAN, from Old English _bannan,_ to summon, proclaim, and Old Norse _banna,_ to prohibit, curse; **b.** BANAL, BANNS; ABANDON, from Old French _ban,_ feudal jurisdiction, summons to military service, proclamation, Old French _bandon,_ power, and Old English _gebann,_ proclamation; **c.** BANISH, from Old French _banir,_ to banish; **d.** CONTRABAND, from Late Latin _bannus, bannum,_ proclamation; **e.** BANDIT, from Italian _bandire,_ to muster, band together (< "to have been summoned"). **a–e** all from Germanic suffixed form _*ban-wan, *bannan,_ to speak publicly (used of particular kinds of proclamation in feudal or prefeudal custom; "to proclaim under penalty, summon to the levy, declare outlaw"). **4.** Suffixed form _*bhā-ni-_. **a.** BOON[1], from Old Norse _bōn,_ prayer, request; **b.** BEE[1], perhaps from Old English _bēn,_ prayer, from a Scandinavian source akin to Old Norse _bōn,_ prayer. Both **a** and **b** from Germanic _*bōni-_. **5.** Suffixed form _*bhā-mā-_. **a.** FAME, FAMOUS; DEFAME, INFAMOUS, from Latin _fāma,_ talk, reputation, fame; **b.** EUPHEMISM, POLYPHEMUS, from Greek _phēmē,_ saying, speech. **6.** Suffixed o-grade form _*bhō-nā-_. PHONE[2], -PHONE, PHONEME, PHONETIC, PHONO-, -PHONY; ANTHEM, ANTIPHON, APHONIA, CACOPHONOUS, EUPHONY, SYMPHONY, from Greek _phōnē,_ voice, sound, and (denominative) _phōnein,_ to speak. **7.** Suffixed zero-grade form _*bhə-to-_. CONFESS, PROFESS, from Latin _fatērī,_ to acknowledge, admit. **8.** BLAME, BLASPHEME, from Greek _blasphēmos,_ blasphemous, perhaps from _*ml̥s-bhā-mo-,_ "speaking evil" (_*ml̥s-,_ evil; see **mel-**). [Pokorny 2. _bhā-_ 105.]

bha-bhā- Broad bean. **1.** FAVA BEAN, FAVELA, from Latin _faba,_ broad bean. **2.** Variant form _*bha-un-_. BEAN, from Old English _bēan,_ broad bean, bean of any kind, from Germanic _*baunō_. **3.** Possible suffixed form _*bha-ko-_. PHACOEMULSIFICATION, from Greek _phakos,_ lentil. [Pokorny _bhabhā_ 106.]

bhag- To share out, apportion, also to get a share. **1.** -PHAGE, -PHAGIA, PHAGO-, -PHAGOUS; ESOPHAGUS, from Greek _phagein,_ to eat (< "to have a share of food"). **2.** PORGY, from Greek _phagros,_ whetstone ("eater, that eats metal"), also a name for the sea bream, from Greek suffixed form _*phag-ro-_. **3.** NEBBISH, from a Slavic source akin to Czech _neboh,_ poor, unfortunate, from Common Slavic _*ne-bogŭ,_ poor ("un-endowed"). **4.** PAGODA; BHAGAVAD-GITA, from Sanskrit _bhagaḥ,_ good fortune. **5.** BHAKTI, from Sanskrit _bhajati,_ he apportions. **6.** Extended form _*bhags-_. BAKSHEESH, BUCKSHEE, from Persian _bakhshīdan,_ to give, from Avestan _bakhsh-_. [Pokorny 1. _bhag-_ 107.]

bhāgo- Beech tree. **1a.** BOOK, from Old English _bōc,_ written document, composition; **b.** BUCKWHEAT, from Middle Dutch _boek,_ beech; **c.** BOKMÅL, from Norwegian _bok,_ book. **a–c** all from Germanic _*bōkō,_ beech, also "beech staff for carving runes on" (an early Germanic writing device). **2.** BEECH, from Old English _bēce,_ beech, from Germanic _*bōkjōn-_. [Pokorny _bhāgó-s_ 107.]

bhardh-ā- Beard. **1.** BEARD, from Old English _beard,_ beard, from Germanic _*bardaz_. **2.** HALBERD, from Old High German _barta,_ beard, ax, from Germanic _*bardō,_ beard, also hatchet, broadax. **3.** BARB[1], BARBEL[1], BARBELLATE, BARBER, BARBETTE, BARBICEL, BARBULE; REBARBATIVE, from Latin _barba,_ beard. [Pokorny _bhardhā_ 110.]

bhei- A bee. BEE[1], from Old English _bēo,_ a bee, from Germanic suffixed form _*bīōn-_. [Pokorny _bhei-_ 116.]

bheid- To split; with Germanic derivatives referring to biting (hence also to eating and to hunting) and woodworking. **1a.** BEETLE[1], BITE, from Old English _bītan,_ to bite; **b.** TSIMMES, from Old High German _bīzan, bizzan,_ to bite. Both **a** and **b** from Germanic _*bītan_. **2.** Zero-grade form _*bhid-_. **a.** BIT[2], from Old English _bite,_ a bite, sting, from Germanic _*bitiz;_ **b.** _(i)_ BIT[1], from Old English _bita,_ a piece bitten off, morsel; _(ii)_ BITT, from a Germanic source akin to Old Norse _biti,_ bit, crossbeam. Both _(i)_ and _(ii)_ from Germanic _*bitōn-;_ **c.** suffixed form _*bhid-ro-_. BITTER, from Old English _bit(t)er,_ "biting," sharp, bitter. **3.** O-grade form _*bhoid-_. **a.** BAIT[1], from Old Norse _beita_ (verb), to hunt with dogs, and _beita_ (noun), pasture, food; **b.** ABET, from Old French _beter,_ to harass with dogs. Both **a** and **b** from Germanic _*baitjan_. **4.** BATEAU, BOAT; BOATSWAIN, from Old English _bāt,_ boat, from Germanic _*bait-,_ a boat (< "dugout canoe" or "split planking"). **5.** Nasalized zero-grade form _*bhi-n-d-_. -FID, FISSI-, FISSILE, FISSION, FISSURE, VENT[2], from Latin _findere,_ to split (past participle _fissus_ < suffixed zero-grade form _*bhid-to-_). [Pokorny _bheid-_ 116.]

bheidh- To trust. **1.** Probably Germanic _*bīdan,_ to await (< "to await trustingly, expect, trust"). ABIDE, ABODE, from Old English _bīdan,_ to wait, stay. **2.** FIANCÉ, FIDUCIAL, FIDUCIARY; AFFIANCE, AFFIANT, AFFIDAVIT, CONFIDANT, CONFIDE, CONFIDENT, DEFIANCE, DEFY, DIFFIDENT, from Latin _fīdere,_ to trust, confide, and _fīdus,_ faithful. **3.** Suffixed o-grade form _*bhoidh-es-_. FEDERAL, FEDERATE; CONFEDERATE, from Latin _foedus_ (stem _foeder-_), treaty, league. **4.** Zero-grade form _*bhidh-_. FAITH, FAY[3], FEALTY, FIDEISM, FIDELITY; INFIDEL, PERFIDY, from Latin _fidēs,_ faith, trust. [Pokorny 1. _bheidh-_ 117.]

bhel- To thrive, bloom.

I. Suffixed o-grade form _*bhol-yo-,_ leaf. **1.** FOIL[2], FOLIAGE, FOLIO, FOLIUM; CINQUEFOIL, DEFOLIATE, EXFOLIATE, FEUILLETON, MILFOIL, PERFOLIATE, PORTFOLIO, TREFOIL, from Latin _folium,_ leaf. **2.** -PHYLL, PHYLLO-, -PHYLLOUS; CHERVIL, GILLYFLOWER, PODOPHYLLIN, from Greek _phullon,_ leaf.

II. Extended form _*bhlē-_ (contracted from earlier _*bhleə-_). **1.** O-grade form _*bhlō-_. **a.** Suffixed form _*bhlō-w-_. BLOW[3], from Old English _blōwan,_ to flower, from Germanic _*blō-w-;_ **b.** _(i)_ BLOOM[1], from Old Norse _blōm, blōmi,_ flower, blossom; _(ii)_ BLOOM[2], from Old English _blōma,_ a hammered ingot of iron (semantic development obscure). Both _(i)_ and _(ii)_ from Germanic suffixed form _*blō-mōn-;_ **c.** BLOSSOM, from Old English _blōstm, blōstma,_ flower, blossom, from Germanic suffixed form _*blō-s-;_ **d.** FERRET[2], FLORA, FLORA, FLORAL, FLORET, FLORIATED, FLORID, FLORIN, FLORIST, -FLOROUS, FLOUR, FLOURISH, FLOWER; CAULIFLOWER, DEFLOWER, EFFLORESCE, ENFLEURAGE, FLORIGEN, MILLEFLEUR, from Latin _flōs_ (stem _flōr-_), flower, from Italic suffixed form _*flō-s-;_ **e.** suffixed form _*bhlō-to-,_ possibly in the meaning "swell, gush, spurt" in Germanic _*blōdam,_ blood. _(i)_ BLOOD, from Old English _blōd,_ blood; _(ii)_ BLEED, from Old English _*blēdan,_ to bleed, from Germanic denominative _*blōdjan; (iii)_ BLESS, from Old English _bloedsian, blētsian,_ to consecrate, from Germanic _*blōdisōn,_ to treat or hallow with blood. **2.** EMBLEMENTS, from Medieval Latin _blādum, bladium,_ produce of the land, grain, from Germanic suffixed form _*blē-da-_. **3.** Suffixed zero-grade form _*bhlə-to-_. BLADE, from Old English _blæd,_ leaf, blade, from Germanic _*bladaz_. [Pokorny 4. _bhel-_ 122.]

bhendh- To bind. **1a.** BIND; WOODBINE, from Old English _bindan,_ to bind; **b.** BINDLESTIFF, from Old High German _binten,_ to bind. Both **a** and **b** from Germanic _*bindan_. **2.** BANDANNA, from Sanskrit _bandhati,_ he ties. **3.** O-grade form _*bhondh-_. **a.** BEND[2], from Old English _bend,_ band, and Old French _bende,_ band, from Germanic _*bandjō;_ **b.** BEND[1], from Old English _bendan,_ to bend, from Germanic _*bandjan;_ **c.** _(i)_ BAND[1], BOND, from Old Norse _band,_ band, fetter; _(ii)_ GUM BAND, from Old High German _band,_ band; _(iii)_ BAND[1], from Old French _bande,_ bond, tie, link. _(i)–(iii)_ all from Germanic _*bandam; (iv)_ RIBBON, from Old French _ruban,_ ribbon, perhaps from Germanic _*bandam_ (first element unclear). **a–c** all from Germanic _*band-_. **4.** Suffixed form _*bhond-o-_. BUND[1]; CUMMERBUND, from Avestan _banda-,_ bond, fetter. **5.** Zero-grade form _*bhn̥dh-_. **a.** BUND[2], from Middle High German _bunt,_ league; **b.** BUNDLE, from Middle Dutch _bondel,_ sheaf of papers, bundle. Both **a** and **b** from Germanic _*bund-_. [Pokorny _bhendh-_ 127.]

bher-[1] To carry; also to bear children. **1a.** _(i)_ BEAR[1], from Old English _beran, to carry; (ii)_ FORBEAR[1], from Old English _forberan,_ to bear, endure (_for-,_ for-; see **per[1]**). Both _(i)_ and _(ii)_ from Germanic _*beran;_ **b.** BIER, from Old English _bēr, bǣr,_ bier, and Old French _biere,_ bier, both from Germanic _*bērō;_ **c.** BORE[3], from Old Norse _bāra,_ wave, billow, from Germanic _*bēr-_. **2a.** BAIRN, from Old English _bearn,_ child, from Germanic _*barnam;_ **b.** BARROW[1], from Old English _bearwe,_ basket, wheelbarrow, from Germanic _*barwōn-_. **3.** Zero-grade form _*bhr̥-,_ becoming Germanic _*bur-_. **a.** BURLY, from Old English _*borlic,_ excellent, exalted (< "borne up"); **b.** BURDEN[1], from Old English _byrthen,_ burden, from Germanic _*burthinja-;_ **c.** BIRTH, from a source akin to Old Norse _burdhr,_ birth, from Germanic _*burthiz;_ **d.** BIRR[1], from Old Norse _byrr,_ favorable wind, perhaps from Germanic _*burja-_. **4.** Compound root _*bhrenk-,_ to bring (< _*bher-_ + _*enk-,_ to bring). BRING, from Old English _bringan,_ to bring, from Germanic _*brengan_. **5.** -FER, FERTILE; AFFERENT, CIRCUMFERENCE, CONFER, DEFER[1], DEFER[2], DIFFER, EFFERENT, INFER, OFFER, PREFER, PROFFER, REFER, SUFFER, TRANSFER, VOCIFERATE, from Latin _ferre,_ to carry. **6.** Prefixed and suffixed zero-grade form _*pro-bhr-o-,_ "something brought before one" (_*pro-,_ before; see **per[1]**). OPPROBRIUM, from Latin _probrum,_ a reproach. **7.** Possibly suffixed zero-grade form _*bhr̥-tu-_ in Latin words having to do with chance (? < "a bringing, that which is brought"). **a.** FORTUITOUS, from Latin _fortuītus,_ happening by chance; **b.** FORTUNA, FORTUNE, from Latin _fortūna,_ chance, good luck, fortune, and _Fortūna,_ goddess of good fortune. **8.** Probably lengthened o-grade form _*bhōr-_. FERRET[1], FURTIVE, FURUNCLE; FURUNCULOSIS, from Latin _fūr,_ thief. **9.** -PHORE, -PHORESIS, -PHOROUS; AMPHORA, ANAPHORA, DIAPHORESIS, EUPHORIA, METAPHOR, PERIPHERY, PHEROMONE, TELPHER, TOCOPHEROL, from Greek _pherein,_ to carry, with o-grade noun _phoros,_ a carrying. **10.** PARAPHERNALIA, from Greek _phernē,_ dowry ("something brought by a bride"). **11.** SAMBAL, from Sanskrit _bharati,_ he carries, brings. [Pokorny 1. _bher-_ 128.]

bher-[2] Bright, brown. **1.** Suffixed variant form _*bhrū-no-_. **a.** BROWN, from Old English _brūn,_ brown; **b.** BRUIN, from Middle Dutch _bruun;_ **c.** BRUNET, BURNET, BURNISH, from Old French _brun,_ shining, brown. **a–c** all from Germanic _*brūna-,_ brown. **2.** Reduplicated form _*bhibhru-, *bhebhru-,_ "the brown animal," beaver. BEAVER[1], from Old English _be(o)for,_ beaver, from Germanic _*bebruz_. **3.** BEAR[2], from Old English _bera,_ bear, from Germanic _*berō,_ "the brown animal," bear. **4.** BERSERKER, from Old Norse _björn,_ bear, from Germanic _*bernuz._ [Pokorny 5. _bher-_ 136.]

bhergh- High; with derivatives referring to hills and hill-forts. **1a.** BARROW[2], from Old English _beorg,_ hill; **b.** ICEBERG, from Middle Dutch _bergh,_ mountain; **c.** INSELBERG, from Old High German _berg,_ mountain; **d.** Germanic compound _*harja-bergaz_ (see **koro-**). **a–d** all from Germanic _*bergaz,_ hill, mountain. **2.** BELFRY, from Old French _berfroi,_ tower, from Germanic compound _*berg-frithu-,_ "high place of safety," tower (_*frithu-,_ peace, safety; see **prī-**). **3.** Zero-grade form _*bhr̥gh-._ **a.** BOROUGH, BURG, from Old English _burg, burh, byrig,_ (fortified) town; **b.** BURGOMASTER, from Middle Dutch _burch,_ town; **c.** BOURG, BOURGEOIS, BURGESS, BURGLAR; FAUBOURG, from Late Latin _burgus,_ fortified place, and Old French _burg,_ borough; **d.** BURGHER, from Old High German _burgāri,_ townsman, from Germanic compound _*burg-warōn-,_ "city protector" (_*warōn-,_ protector). **a–d** all from Germanic _*burgs,_ hill-fort. **4.** Possibly suffixed zero-grade form _*bhr̥gh-to-._ FORCE, FORT, FORTALICE, FORTE[1], FORTE[2], FORTIS, FORTISSIMO, FORTITUDE, FORTRESS; COMFORT, DEFORCE, EFFORT, ENFORCE, FORTIFY, PIANOFORTE, REINFORCE, from Latin _fortis,_ strong (but this is also possibly from **dher-**[2]). [Pokorny _bhereĝh-_ 140.]

bheudh- To be aware, to make aware. **1a.** BID, from Old English _bēodan,_ to offer, proclaim; **b.** FORBID, from Old English _forbēodan,_ to forbid; **c.** VERBOTEN, from Old High German _farbiotan,_ to forbid. **a–c** all from Germanic _*(for)beudan_ (_*for,_ before; see **per**[1]). **2.** BODE[1], from Old English _bodian,_ to announce, from _boda,_ messenger, from Germanic _*budōn-._ **3.** BEADLE, from Old English _bydel,_ herald, messenger, and Old High German _butil,_ herald, both from Germanic _*budilaz,_ herald. **4.** OMBUDSMAN, from Old Norse _bodh,_ command, from Germanic _*budam._ **5.** BUDDHA[2]; BODHISATTVA, BO TREE, from Sanskrit _bodhati,_ he awakes, is enlightened, becomes aware, and _bodhiḥ,_ perfect knowledge. [Pokorny _bheudh-_ 150.]

bheuə- Also **bheu-.** To be, exist, grow.

I. Extended forms _*bhwiy(o)-, *bhwī-._ **1.** BE; FOREBEAR, from Old English _bēon,_ to be, from Germanic _*biju,_ I am, will be. **2.** FIAT, from Latin _fierī,_ to become. **3.** Possibly suffixed form _*bhwī-lyo-,_ seen by some as the source of Latin _fīlius,_ son, but this is more likely from a different root.

II. Lengthened o-grade form _*bhōw-._ **1.** BONDAGE, BOUND[4]; BUSTLE[1], HUSBAND, from Old Norse _būa,_ to live, prepare, and _būask,_ to make oneself ready (_-sk,_ reflexive suffix; see **s(w)e-**). **2.** BAUHAUS, from Old High German _būan,_ to dwell. **3.** BOOTH, from Middle English _bothe,_ market stall, from a Scandinavian source akin to Old Danish _bōth,_ dwelling, stall. **1–3** all from Germanic _*bōwan._

III. Zero-grade form _*bhu-._ **1a.** BUILD, from Old English _byldan,_ to build, from _bold,_ dwelling, house, from Germanic _*buthlam;_ **b.** BOODLE, from Middle Dutch _bōdel,_ riches, property, from alternate Germanic form _*bōthlam._ **2.** PHYSIC, PHYSICS, PHYSIO-, PHYSIQUE, -PHYTE, PHYTO-, PHYTON; APOPHYSIS, DIAPHYSIS, DIPHYODONT, EPIPHYSIS, EUPHUISM, HYPOPHYSIS, IMP, MONOPHYSITE, NEOPHYTE, PERIPHYTON, SYMPHYSIS, TRACHEOPHYTE, from Greek _phuein,_ to bring forth, make grow, _phutos, phuton,_ a plant, and _phusis,_ growth, nature. **3.** Suffixed form _*bhu-tā-._ EISTEDDFOD, from Welsh _bod,_ to be. **4.** Suffixed form _*bhu-tu-._ FUTURE, from Latin _futūrus,_ "that is to be," future.

IV. Zero-grade form _*bhū-_ (< _*bhuə-_). **1a.** BOWER[1], from Old English _būr,_ "dwelling space," bower, room; **b.** NEIGHBOR, from Old English _gebūr,_ dweller (_ge-,_ collective prefix; see **kom**); **c.** BOER, BOOR, from Middle Dutch _gheboer, ghebuer,_ peasant. **a–c** all from Germanic _*būram,_ dweller, especially farmer. **2.** BYRE, from Old English _byre,_ stall, hut, from Germanic _*būrjam,_ dwelling. **3.** BYLAW, from a Scandinavian source akin to Old Norse _bȳr,_ settlement, from Germanic _*būwi-._ **4.** Suffixed form _*bhū-lo-._ PHYLE, PHYLETIC, PHYLUM; PHYLOGENY, from Greek _phūlon,_ tribe, class, race, and _phūlē,_ tribe, clan.

V. Zero-grade reduced suffixal form _*-bhw-,_ in Latin compounds. **1.** Latin _dubius,_ doubtful, and _dubitāre,_ to doubt, from _*du-bhw-io-_ (see **dwo-**). **2.** Latin _probus,_ upright, from _*pro-bhw-o-,_ "growing well or straightforward" (see **per**[1]). **3.** Latin _superbus,_ superior, proud, from _*super-bhw-o-,_ "being above" (see **uper**).

VI. Possibly Germanic _*baumaz_ (and _*bagmaz_), tree (? < "growing thing"). **1.** BEAM, from Old English _bēam,_ tree, beam. **2.** BOOM[2], from Middle Dutch _boom,_ tree. **3.** BUMPKIN[1], BUMPKIN[2], from Flemish _boom,_ tree. [Pokorny _bheu-_ 146.]

bhrāter- Brother, male agnate. **1a.** BROTHER, from Old English _brōthor,_ brother; **b.** BULLY[1], from Middle Dutch _broeder,_ brother. Both **a** and **b** from Germanic _*brōthar._ **2.** FRA, FRATERNAL, FRATERNITY, FRATERNIZE, FRIAR; CONFRERE, FRATRICIDE, from Latin _frāter,_ brother. **3.** PHRATRY, from Greek _phrātēr,_ fellow member of a clan. **4.** PAL, from Sanskrit _bhrātā_ (stem _bhrātar-_), brother. [Pokorny _bhrāter-_ 163.]

bhreg- To break. **1a.** BREAK, from Old English _brecan,_ to break; **b.** BREACH, from Old English _brēc,_ a breaking; **c.** BRASH[2], BRECCIA, from Italian _breccia,_ breccia, rubble, breach in a wall, from Old High German _*brehha,_ from _brehhan,_ to break; **d.** BRAY[2], from Old French _breier,_ to break; **e.** BRIOCHE, from Old French _brier,_ dialectal variant of _broyer,_ to knead. **a–e** all from Germanic _*brekan._ **2.** BRACKEN, BRAKE[4], from Middle English _brake(n),_ bracken, probably from a Scandinavian source akin to Old Norse _*brakni,_ undergrowth; **b.** BRAKE[5], from Middle Low German _brake,_ thicket. Both **a** and **b** from Germanic _*brak-,_ bushes (< "that which impedes motion"). **3.** BRAKE[2], from Middle Low German _brake,_ flax brake, from Germanic _*brāk-,_ crushing instruments. **4.** Nasalized zero-grade form _*bhr̥-n-g-._ FRACTAL, FRACTED, FRACTION, FRACTIOUS, FRACTURE, FRAGILE, FRAGMENT, FRAIL[1], FRANGIBLE; ANFRACTUOUS, CHAMFER, DEFRAY, DIFFRACTION, INFRACT, INFRANGIBLE, INFRINGE, IRREFRANGIBLE, OSSIFRAGE, REFRACT, REFRAIN[2], REFRINGENT, SASSAFRAS, SAXIFRAGE, SEPTIFRAGAL, from Latin _frangere,_ to break. **5a.** SUFFRAGAN, SUFFRAGE, from Latin _suffrāgium,_ the right to vote, from _suffrāgārī,_ to vote for (? < "to use a broken piece of tile as a ballot"); **b.** IRREFRAGABLE, from Latin _refrāgārī,_ to vote against. [Pokorny 1. _bhreĝ-_ 165.]

bhrū- Eyebrow. Contracted from _*bhruə-._ **1.** BROW, from Old English _brū-,_ eyebrow, eyelid, eyelash, from Germanic _*brūs._ **2.** Possibly in the sense of a beam of wood, and perhaps a log bridge. BRIDGE[1], from Old English _brycg(e),_ bridge, from Germanic _*brugjō_ (with cognates in Celtic and Slavic). [Pokorny 1. _bhrū-_ 172, 2. _bhrū-_ 173.]

dā- To divide. Contracted from _*daə-._

I. Suffixed form _*dā-mo-,_ perhaps "division of society." DEME, DEMOS, DEMOTIC; DEMAGOGUE, DEMIURGE, DEMOCRACY, DEMOGRAPHY, ENDEMIC, EPIDEMIC, PANDEMIC, from Greek _dēmos,_ people, land.

II. Extended form _*dai-_ (contracted from _*daəi-_), with zero-grade _*dī-_ (< _*diə-,_ metathesized from _*dəi-_). **1.** Root form _*dai-._ GEODESY, from Greek _daiesthai,_ to divide. **2.** Suffixed form _*dai-mon-,_ divider, provider. DAIMON, DEMON, from Greek _daimōn,_ divinity. **3.** Suffixed zero-grade form _*dī-ti-._ **a.** TIDE[1]; EVENTIDE, from Old English _tīd,_ time, season; **b.** TIDE[2], from Old English denominative _tīdan,_ to happen (< "to occur in time"); **c.** TIDING, from Old Norse _tīdhr,_ occurring; **d.** YAHRZEIT, ZEITGEIST, from Old High German _zīt,_ time. **a–d** all from Germanic _*tīdiz,_ division of time. **4.** Suffixed zero-grade form _*dī-mon-._ TIME, from Old English _tīma,_ time, period, from Germanic _*tīmōn-._ [Pokorny _dā : də-_ 175.]

dakru- Tear. **1a.** TEAR[2], from Old English _tēar, tehher,_ tear; **b.** TRAIN OIL, from Middle Dutch _trane,_ tear, drop. Both **a** and **b** from Germanic _*tahr-, *tagr-._ **2.** Suffixed form _*dakru-mā-._ LACHRYMAL, from Latin _lacrima_ (Archaic Latin _dacruma_), tear. [Pokorny _dak̂ru-_ 179.]

deik- Also **deig-.** To show, pronounce solemnly; also in derivatives referring to the directing of words or objects.

I. Variant _*deig-._ **1.** O-grade form _*doig-._ **a.** TEACH, from Old English _tǣcan,_ to show, instruct, from Germanic _*taikjan,_ to show; **b.** _(i)_ TOKEN, from Old Eng- lish _tācen, tācn,_ sign, mark; _(ii)_ BETOKEN, from Old English _tācnian,_ to signify; _(iii)_ TETCHY, from Gothic _taikns,_ sign; _(iv)_ TACHISME, from Old French _tache, teche,_ mark, stain. _(i)–(iv)_ all from Germanic _*taiknam._ **2.** Zero-grade form _*dig-._ DIGIT, from Latin _digitus,_ finger (< "pointer," "indicator").

II. Basic form _*deik-._ **1.** Possibly o-grade form _*doik-._ TOE, from Old English _tā, tahe,_ toe, from Germanic _*taihwō._ **2.** Basic form _*deik-._ DICTATE, DICTION, DICTUM, DITTO, DITTY; ADDICT, BENEDICTION, CONDITION, CONTRADICT, EDICT, FATIDIC, HERB BENNET, INDICT, INDICTION, INDITE, INTERDICT, JURIDICAL, JURISDICTION, MALEDICT, MALISON, PREDICT, VALEDICTION, VERDICT, VERIDICAL, VOIR DIRE, from Latin _dīcere,_ to say, tell. **3.** Suffixed zero-grade form _*dik-ā-._ ABDICATE, DEDICATE, PREACH, PREDICAMENT, PREDICATE, from Latin _dicāre,_ to proclaim. **4.** Agential suffix _*-dik-._ **a.** INDEX, INDICATE, from Latin _index,_ indicator, forefinger (_in-,_ toward; see **en**); **b.** JUDGE, JUDICIAL; PREJUDICE, from Latin _iūdex_ (< _*yewes-dik-_), judge, "one who shows or pronounces the law" (_iūs,_ law); **c.** VENDETTA, VINDICATE; AVENGE, REVENGE, from Latin _vindex_ (first element obscure), surety, claimant, avenger. **5.** DEICTIC, DEIXIS; APODICTIC, PARADIGM, POLICY[2], from Greek _deiknunai,_ to show, and noun _deigma_ (_*deik-mn̥_), sample, pattern. **6.** Zero-grade form _*dik-._ DISK; DICTYOSOME, from suffixed form _*dik-skos,_ from Greek _dikein,_ to throw (< "to direct an object"). **7.** Form _*dikā-._ DICAST; SYNDIC, THEODICY, from Greek _dikē,_ justice, right, court case. [Pokorny _deik̂-_ 188.]

dekm̥ Ten.

I. Basic form _*dekm̥._ **1a.** TEN, from Old English _tīen,_ ten; **b.** Old Norse _tjan,_ ten, in compound _āttjān_ (see **oktō(u)**). Both **a** and **b** from Germanic _*tehun._ **2.** EIGHTEEN, FIFTEEN, FOURTEEN, NINETEEN, SEVENTEEN, SIXTEEN, THIRTEEN, from Old English suffix _-tēne, -tīne, -tȳne,_ ten, -teen, from Germanic _*tehan._ **3.** DECI-, DECIMAL, DECIMATE, DECUPLE, DECURION, DICKER, DIME; DECEMBER, DECEMVIR, DECENNARY, DECENNIUM, DECUSSATE, DOZEN, DUODECIMAL, OCTODECIMO, SEXTODECIMO, from Latin _decem,_ ten. **4.** DENARIUS, DENARY, DENIER[2], DINAR, from irregular Latin distributive _dēnī,_ by tens, ten each (formed by analogy with _nōnī,_ nine each). **5.** DEAN, DECA-, DECADE, DOYEN; DECAGON, DECALOGUE, DODECAGON, from Greek _deka,_ ten.

II. Germanic _*tigu-,_ ten, decad (of uncertain formation, as though < _*deku-_), in compound _*twēgentig_ (see **dwo-**).

III. Ordinal number _*dekm̥to-._ TENTH, TITHE, from Old English _teogotha, tēotha,_ tenth, from Germanic _*teguntha-._

IV. Suffixed zero-grade form _*-dkm̥-tā,_ reduced to _*-km̥tā,_ and lengthened o-grade form _*-dkōm-tā,_ reduced to _*-kontā._ **1.** NONAGENARIAN, OCTOGENARIAN, SEPTUAGINT, SEXAGENARY, from Latin _-gintā,_ ten times. **2.** PENTECOST, from Greek _*-konta,_ ten times.

V. Suffixed zero-grade form _*dkm̥-tom,_ hundred, reduced to _*km̥tom._ **1.** HUNDRED, from Old English _hundred,_ from dialectal North and West Germanic _*hund(a)-rada-_ (_*-rada-,_ from Germanic _*radam,_ number), from Germanic _*hundam,_ hundred. **2.** Germanic compound _*thūs-hundi,_ "swollen hundred," thousand (_*thūs-,_ swollen). THOUSAND, from Old English _thūsend._ **3.** CENT, CENTAL, CENTAVO, CENTENARIAN, CENTENARY, CENTESIMAL, CENTI-, CENTIME, CENTNER, CENTUM, CENTURY; CENTENNIAL, CINQUECENTO, PERCENT, QUATTROCENTO, SEICENTO, SEXCENTENARY, TRECENTO, from Latin _centum,_ hundred. **4.** HECATOMB, HECTO-, from Greek _hekaton,_ a hundred (? dissimilated from _*hem-katon,_ one hundred; _*hem-,_ one; see **sem-**[1]). **5.** SATEM, from Avestan _satəm,_ hundred. [Pokorny _dek̂m̥_ 191.] See also compound root **wīkm̥tī.**

deks- Right (opposite left); hence, south (from the viewpoint of one facing east). Suffixed form _*deks(i)-tero-._ DESTRIER, DEXTER, DEXTERITY, DEXTRO-; AMBIDEXTROUS, from Latin _dexter,_ right, on the right side. [In Pokorny 1. _dek̂-_ 189.]

del- Long.

I. Probably extended and suffixed zero-grade form _*dlon-gho-._ **1a.** LONG[1]; ALONG, LONGSHORE, from Old English _lang, long,_ long; **b.** LANGLAUF, from Old High German _lang,_ long; **c.** BELONG, from Old English _gelang,_ along; **d.** LONG[2], from Old English denominative _langian,_ to grow longer, yearn for, from Germanic _*langōn;_ **e.** LINGER, from Old English _lengan,_ to prolong (possibly influenced by Old Norse _lengja,_ to lengthen), from Germanic _*langjan,_ to make long; **f.** LOMBARD, from Latin compound _Longobardus, Langobardus_ (with Germanic ethnic name _*Bardi_). **a–f** all from Germanic _*langaz,_ long. **2a.** LENGTH, from Old English _lengthu,_ length; **b.** LENT, from Old English _lengten, lencten,_ spring, Lent, from West Germanic _*langitinaz,_ lengthening of day. Both **a**

and **b** from Germanic abstract noun **langithō*. **3.** LING[1], from Middle English *lenge,* ling, from a Low German source akin to Dutch *lenghe, linghe,* "long one," from Germanic **langīn-*. **4.** LINGUIÇA, LONGERON, LONGITUDE, LOUNGE; ELOIGN, ELONGATE, LONGEVITY, LUNGE, OBLONG, PROLONG, PURLOIN, from Latin *longus,* long.

II. Possibly suffixed variant form **dḷə-gho-*. DOLICHOCEPHALIC, DOLICHOCRANIAL, from Greek *dolikhos,* long. [Pokorny 5. *del-* 196.]

dem- House, household. **1.** Suffixed o-grade form **dom-o-, *dom-u-,* house. **a.** DOME, DOMESTIC, DOMICILE; MAJOR-DOMO, from Latin *domus,* house; **b.** suffixed form **dom-o-no-*. DAME, DAN[2], DANGER, DOM, DOMAIN, DOMINATE, DOMINICAL, DOMINIE, DOMINION, DOMINO[1], DOMINO[2], DON[1], DONNA, DUNGEON; BELLADONNA, DUENDE, MADAM, MADAME, MADEMOISELLE, MADONNA, PREDOMINATE, from Latin *dominus,* master of a household (feminine *domina).* **2.** Possibly suffixed lengthened-grade form **dōm-ṇ*. DOME, from Greek *dōma,* house. **3.** Compound **dems-pot-,* "house-master" (**-pot-,* powerful; see **poti-**). DESPINA, DESPOT, from Greek *despotēs,* master, lord, and feminine *despoina,* lady, queen, mistress (< **dems-pot-nya*). **4.** Root form **dem(ə)-,* to build (possibly a separate root). **a.** TIMBER, from Old English *timber,* building material, lumber, from Germanic **timram;* **b.** TOFT, from Old Norse *topt,* homestead, from Germanic **tumftō*. [Pokorny *dem-* 198.]

dent- Tooth. (Originally **əd-ent-,* "biting," present participle of **əed-,* to eat, in the earlier meaning "to bite"; see **ed-**.) **1.** O-grade form **(ə)dont-*. **a.** TOOTH, from Old English *tōth,* tooth, from Germanic **tanthuz;* **b.** -ODON, -ODONT, ODONTO-; CERATODUS, MASTODON, from Greek *odōn, odous,* tooth. **2.** Zero-grade form **dṇt-*. TUSK, from Old English *tūsc, tūx,* canine tooth, from Germanic **tunth-sk-*. **3.** Full-grade form **dent-*. DENTAL, DENTATE, DENTI-, DENTICLE, DENTIST; DANDELION, EDENTATE, EDENTULOUS, INDENT[1], INDENTURE, TRIDENT, from Latin *dēns* (stem *dent-*), tooth. [In Pokorny *ed-* 287.]

deru- Also **dreu-**. To be firm, solid, steadfast; hence specialized senses "wood," "tree," and derivatives referring to objects made of wood. **1.** Suffixed variant form **drew-o-*. **a.** TREE, from Old English *trēow,* tree, from Germanic **trewam;* **b.** TRUCE, from Old English *trēow,* pledge, from Germanic **treuwō*. **2.** Variant form *dreu-*. **a.** TRUE, from Old English *trēowe,* firm, true; **b.** TROW, from Old English *trēowian, trūwian,* to trust; **c.** TRIG[1], from Old Norse *tryggr,* firm, true; **d.** TROTH, TRUTH; BETROTH, from Old English *trēowth,* faith, loyalty, truth, from Germanic abstract noun **treuwithō;* **e.** TRUST, from Old Norse *traust,* confidence, firmness, from Germanic abstract noun **traustam;* **f.** TRYST, from Old French *triste,* waiting place (< "place where one waits trustingly"), probably from a source akin to Old Norse denominative *treysta,* to trust, make firm. **a–f** all from Germanic **treuwaz*. **3.** Variant form **drou-*. TRAY, from Old English *trēg, trīg,* wooden board, from Germanic **traujam*. **4.** Suffixed zero-grade form **dru-ko-*. **a.** TROUGH, from Old English *trog,* wooden vessel, tray; **b.** TRUG, from Old Norse *trog,* trough. Both **a** and **b** from Germanic **trugaz*. **5.** Suffixed zero-grade form **dru-mo-*. **a.** TRIM, from Old English *trum,* firm, strong; **b.** SHELTER, from Old English *truma,* troop. Both **a** and **b** from Germanic **trum-*. **6.** Variant form **derw-*. TAR[1], from Old English *te(o)ru,* resin, pitch (obtained from the pine tree), from Germanic **terw-*. **7.** Suffixed variant form **drū-ro-*. DOUR, DURAMEN, DURESS, DURUM; DURA MATER, ENDURE, INDURATE, OBDURATE, from Latin *dūrus,* hard (many of whose English derivatives represent a semantic cross with the unrelated Latin verb *dūrāre,* to last long). **8.** Lengthened zero-grade form **drū-*. DRUPE, DRYAD; DRYOPITHECINE, GERMANDER, HAMADRYAD, from Greek *drūs,* oak. **9.** Reduplicated form **der-drew-,* dissimilated with suffix in **der-drew-on*. DENDRO-, DENDRON; PHILODENDRON, RHODODENDRON, from Greek *dendron,* tree. **10.** DRUID, from Latin *druides,* druids, probably from Celtic compound **dru-wid-,* "strong seer" (**wid-,* seeing; see **weid-**), the Celtic priestly caste. **11.** O-grade form **doru-*. DEODAR, from Sanskrit *dāru,* wood, timber. [Pokorny *deru-* 214.]

deu- To do, perform, show favor, revere. **1.** Suffixed zero-grade form **dw-eno-*. **a.** BONBON, BONITO, BONNY, BONUS, BOON[2], BOUNTY; BONANZA, BONHOMIE, DEBONAIR, from Latin *bonus,* good (< "useful, efficient, working"); **b.** adverbial form **dw-enē*. BENEDICTION, BENEFACTION, BENEFACTOR, BENEFIC, BENEFICENCE, BENEFIT, BENEVOLENT, BENIGN, HERB BENNET, from Latin *bene,* well; **c.** diminutive form **dw-en-elo-*. BEAU, BEAUTY, BELLE; BELDAM, BELLADONNA, BELVEDERE, EMBELLISH, from Latin *bellus,* handsome, pretty, fine. **2.** Possibly suffixed zero-grade form **dw-eye-*. BEATITUDE; BEATIFIC, BEATIFY, from Latin *beāre,* to make blessed. **3.** Possible (but unlikely for formal and semantic reasons) suffixed zero-grade form **du-nə-*. DYNAMIC, DYNAMITE, DYNAST, DYNASTY; AERODYNE, from Greek *dunasthai,* to be able. [Pokorny 2. *(deu-)* 218.]

deuk- To lead. **1a.** TUG; WANTON, from Old English *tēon,* to pull, draw, lead; **b.** ZUGUNRUHE, ZUGZWANG, from Old High German *ziohan,* to pull. Both **a** and **b** from Germanic **teuhan*. **2.** Suffixed zero-grade form **duk-ā-*. TOW[1], TAUT, from Old English *togian,* to draw, drag, from Germanic **tugōn*. **3.** Suffixed o-grade form **douk-eyo-*. TIE, from Old English **tīegan, tīgan,* to bind. **4.** Suffixed o-grade form **douk-mo-*. TEAM, from Old English *tēam,* descendant, family, race, brood, team, from Germanic **tau(h)maz*. **5.** TEEM[1], from Old English *tēman, tīeman,* to beget, from Germanic denominative **tau(h)mjan*. **6.** Basic form **deuk-*. DOGE, DOUCHE, DUCAL, DUCAT, DUCE, DUCHESS, DUCHY, DUCT, DUCTILE, DUKE; ABDUCENS, ABDUCT, ADDUCE, AQUEDUCT, CIRCUMDUCTION, CON[3], CONDOTTIERE, CONDUCE, CONDUCT, DEDUCE, DEDUCT, EDUCE, ENDUE, INDUCE, INTRODUCE, PRODUCE, REDOUBT, REDUCE, SEDUCTION, SUBDUCTION, SUBDUE, TRADUCE, TRANSDUCER, from Latin *dūcere,* to lead (past participle *ductus* < suffixed zero-grade form **duk-to-*). **7.** Suffixed zero-grade form **duk-ā-*. EDUCATE, from Latin *ēducāre,* to lead out, bring up (*ē-* < *ex-,* out; see **eghs**). [Po- korny *deuk-* 220.]

dhē- To set, put. (Contracted from earlier **dheə-*.)

I. Basic form **dhē-*. **1.** Suffixed form **dhē-ti-,* "thing laid down or done, law, deed." DEED; INDEED, from Old English *dǣd,* doing, deed, from Germanic **dēdiz*. **2.** Suffixed form **dhē-k-*. THECA, TICK[3]; AMPHITHECIUM, APOTHECARY, APOTHECIUM, BIBLIOTHECA, BODEGA, BOUTIQUE, CLEISTOTHECIUM, ENDOTHECIUM, PERITHECIUM, from Greek *thēkē,* receptacle. **3.** Basic form **dhē-*. BARD[2], PURDAH, from Old Persian *dā-,* to place. **4.** Suffixed form **dhē-to-,* set down, created, in Old Iranian compound **khvatō-dāta-* (see **s(w)e-**). **5.** Reduplicated form **dhe-dhē-*. SANDHI, from Sanskrit *dadhāti,* he places.

II. O-grade form **dhō-*. **1.** DO[1]; FORDO, from Old English *dōn,* to do, from Germanic **dōn*. **2.** Suffixed o-grade form **dhō-men-*. ABDOMEN, from Latin *abdōmen,* belly, abdomen, perhaps "part placed away, concealed part" (*ab-,* away; see **apo**). **3.** Suffixed o-grade form **dhō-mo-*. **a.** DOOM, from Old English *dōm,* judgment (< "thing set or put down"); **b.** -DOM, from Old English *-dōm,* abstract suffix indicating state, condition, or power; **c.** Old Norse *-dōmr,* condition, in compound *hōrdōmr* (see **kā-**); **d.** DUMA, DUMKA, from Russian *Duma,* Duma, from a Germanic source akin to Gothic *dōms,* judgment; **e.** DEEM, from Old English *dēman,* to judge, from Germanic denominative *dōmjan*. **a–e** all from Germanic *dōmaz*. **4.** Suffixed o-grade form **dhō-t-* in compound **sakro-dhōt-* (see **sak-**).

III. Zero-grade form **dhə-*. **1a.** Prefixed form **kom-dhə-*. ABSCOND, INCONDITE, RECONDITE, SCONCE[2], from Latin *condere,* to put together, establish, preserve (**kom,* together; see **kom**); **b.** prefixed and suffixed form **kom-dh(ə)-yo-*. CONDIMENT, SALMAGUNDI, from Latin *condīre,* to season, flavor; **c.** compound **kred-dhə-* (see **kerd-**); **d.** compound suffixed form **gʷṛə-dh(ə)-o-,* "he who makes praises" (**gʷ(e)rə-,* praise, favor). BARD[1], from Welsh *bardd* and Scottish and Irish Gaelic *bard,* bard, from Celtic *bardo-*. **2.** Suffixed zero-grade form **dhə-k-* (perhaps zero-grade of **dhē-k-* in **I. 2.** above). **a.** -FACIENT, FACT, FACTION[1], -FACTION, FACTITIOUS, FACTITIVE, FACTOR, FACTORY, FAENA, FASHION, FEASIBLE, FEAT[1], FEATURE, FETISH, -FIC, -FY, HACIENDA; AFFAIR, AFFECT[1], AFFECT[2], AFFECTION, AMPLIFY, ARTIFACT, ARTIFICE, BEATIFIC, BENEFACTION, BENEFIC, BENEFICE, BENEFICENCE, BENEFIT, CHAFE, COMFIT, CONFECT, CONFETTI, COUNTERFEIT, DEFEASANCE, DEFEAT, DEFECT, DEFICIENT, DISCOMFIT, EDIFICE, EDIFY, EFFECT, EFFICACIOUS, EFFICIENT, FACSIMILE, FACTOTUM, FECKLESS, FORFEIT, INFECT, JUSTIFY, MALEFACTOR, MALFEASANCE, MANUFACTURE, MISFEASANCE, MODIFY, MOLLIFY, NIDIFY, NOTIFY, NULLIFY, OFFICINAL, ORIFICE, PERFECT, PETRIFY, PLUPERFECT, PONTIFEX, PREFECT, PROFICIENT, PROFIT, PUTREFY, QUALIFY, RAREFY, RECTIFY, REFECT, REFECTORY, RUBEFACIENT, SACRIFICE, SATISFY, SPINIFEX, SUFFICE, SUFFICIENT, SURFEIT, TUBIFEX, TUMEFACIENT, VIVIFY, from Latin *facere* (< **fak-yo-*), to do, make, and Latin combining form *-fex* (< **-fak-s*), "maker"; **b.** FAÇADE, FACE, FACET, FACIAL, FACIES; DEFACE, EFFACE, SURFACE, from Latin derivative *faciēs,* shape, face (< "form imposed on something"); **c.** OFFICE, from Latin compound *officium* (< **opi-fici-om*), service, duty, business, performance of work (**opi-,* work); **d.** further suffixed form **dhə-k-li-*. FACILE, FACILITATE, FACULTY, DIFFICULTY, from Latin *facilis* (< Archaic Latin *facul*), feasible, easy. **3.** Suffixed zero-grade form **dhə-s-* (probably identical with zero-grade of **dhēs-**). NEFARIOUS, from Latin *fās,* divine law, right. **4.** MULTIFARIOUS, OMNIFARIOUS, from Latin *-fāriam,* adverbial suffix, as in *bifāriam,* in two places, parts, double, from **dwi-dh(ə)-,* "making two" (**dwi-,* two; see **dwo-**). **5.** Reduplicated form **dhi-dhə-*. THESIS, THETIC; ANATHEMA, ANTITHESIS, DIATHESIS, EPENTHESIS, EPITHET, HYPOTHECATE, HYPOTHESIS, METATHESIS, PARENTHESIS, PROSTHESIS, PROTHESIS, SYNTHESIS, from Greek *tithenai,* to put, with zero-grade noun *thesis* (**dhə-ti-*), a placing, and verbal adjective *thetos* (**dhə-to-*), placed. **6.** Suffixed zero-grade form **dhə-mṇ*. THEMATIC, THEME, from Greek *thema,* "thing placed," proposition. **7.** Reduced form **dh-* in compound forms **awis-dh-* or **au-dh-,* "to place perception" (**au-,* to perceive). **a.** AUDIBLE, AUDIENCE, AUDILE, AUDIO-, AUDIT, AUDITION, AUDITOR, AUDITORIUM, AUDITORY, OYEZ; OBEY, SUBAUDITION, from Latin *audīre,* to hear; **b.** AESTHETIC; ANAESTHESIA, from Greek *aisthanesthai,* to feel. [Pokorny 2. *dhē-* 235.]

dheigh- To form, build. **1.** DAIRY, from Old English *dǣge,* bread kneader, from Germanic **daigjōn-*. **2.** Zero-grade form **dhigh-*. LADY, from Old English compound *hlǣfdige,* mistress of a household (< "bread kneader"; *hlāf,* bread, loaf), from Germanic **dig-*. **3.** Suffixed o-grade form **dhoigh-o-*. **a.** DOUGH, from Old English *dāg,* dough, from Germanic **daigaz;* **b.** PARADISE, from Avestan *daēza-,* wall (originally made of clay or mud bricks). **4.** Suffixed zero-grade form **dhigh-ūrā-*. FIGURE, FIGURINE; CONFIGURE, DISFIGURE, PREFIGURE, TRANSFIGURE, from Latin *figūra,* form, shape. **5.** Nasalized zero-grade form **dhi-n-gh-*. FAINÉANT, FAINT, FEIGN, FEINT, FICTILE, FICTION, FIGMENT; EFFIGY, from Latin *fingere,* to shape. **6.** Probable nasalized zero-grade form **dhi-n-g(h)-*. THIGMOTAXIS, THIXOTROPY, from Greek *thinganein,* to touch. [Pokorny *dheiĝh-* 244.]

dhers- To venture, be bold. O-grade form **dhors-* and zero-grade form **dhṛs-*. DARE, DURST, from Old English *dearr* and *durst,* first and third person singular present and past indicative of *durran,* to venture, respectively from Germanic **dars-* and **durz-*. [Pokorny *dhers-* 259.]

dhēs- Root of words in religious concepts. Possibly an extension of **dhē-**. **1.** Suffixed form **dhēs-yā-*. FAIR[2], FERIA, from Latin *fēriae* (< Archaic Latin *fēsiae*), holidays. **2.** Suffixed form **dhēs-to-*. FEAST, FEST, FESTAL, FESTIVAL, FESTIVE, FESTOON, FETE, FIESTA; OKTOBERFEST, from Latin *fēstus,* festive. **3.** Suffixed zero-grade form **dhəs-no-*. FANATIC; PROFANE, from Latin *fānum,* temple. **4.** Suffixed zero-grade form **dhəs-o-*. THEO-; APOTHEOSIS, ATHEISM, ENTHUSIASM, HENOTHEISM, PANTHEON, POLYTHEISM, TIFFANY, from Greek *theos* (< **thes-os*), god. [Pokorny *dhēs-* 259.]

dheu- Also **dheuə-**. To die. **1.** Suffixed o-grade form **dhou-to-*. DEAD, from Old English *dēad,* dead, from Germanic **dauda-*. **2.** Suffixed o-grade form **dhou-tu-*. DEATH, from Old English *dēath,* death, from Germanic **dauthuz*. **3.** Suffixed o-grade form **dhow-yo-*. DIE[1], from Old Norse *deyja,* to die. **4.** Extended zero-grade form **dhuəi-,* metathesized to **dhwiə-,* contracted to **dhwī-,* whence suffixed form **dhwī-no-*. DWINDLE, from Old English *dwīnan,* to diminish, languish, from Germanic **dwīnan*. [Pokorny 2. *dheu-* 260.]

dheub- Also **dheubh-**. Deep, hollow. **1.** DEEP, DEPTH, from Old English *dēop,* deep, from Germanic **deupa-*. **2.** DIP, from Old English *dyppan,* to immerse, dip, from Germanic expressive denominative **duppjan*. **3.** Parallel root form **dheubh-*. DIVE[1], from Old

English *dȳfan,* to dip, and *dūfan,* to sink, dive, from Germanic verb **dūbjan,* from **deub-*, **dub-*. **4.** Suffixed parallel root form **dhŭbh-(o)n-*, with expressive variants. PYTHON, PYTHON, TYPHON, from Greek *Pūthōn* and *Tuphōn,* mythical monsters, from **dhub(h)-n-* and **b(h)ud(h)-n-*, which already in Indo-European were doublets by inversion, referring to "bottom," "foundation," "depths," and the mythological monsters that inhabited them. [Pokorny *dheu-b-* 267.]

dhghem- Earth. **1.** Suffixed zero-grade form **(dh)ghm̥-on-*, "earthling." BRIDEGROOM, from Old English *guma,* man, from Germanic **gumōn-*. **2.** O-grade form **dh(e)ghom-*. CHTHONIC; AUTOCHTHON, from Greek *khthōn,* earth. **3.** Zero-grade form **(dh)ghm̥-*. CHAMAEPHYTE, CHAMELEON, CHAMOMILE, GERMANDER, from Greek *khamai,* on the ground. **4.** Suffixed o-grade form **(dh)ghom-o-*. HUMBLE, HUMILIATE, HUMILITY, HUMUS[1], OMERTA; EXHUME, INHUME, TRANSHUMANCE, from Latin *humus,* earth. **5.** Suffixed o-grade form **(dh)ghom-on-*, "earthling." **a.** HOMAGE, HOMBRE[1], HOMINID, HOMO[1], HOMUNCULUS, OMBRE; BONHOMIE, HOMICIDE, from Latin *homō,* human being, man; **b.** HUMAN, HUMANE, from Latin *hūmānus,* human, kind, humane (in part from **dhghem-**). **6.** Suffixed form **(dh)ghem-yā-*. CHERNOZEM, ZEMSTVO, from Old Russian *zemĭ,* land, earth. **7.** Full-grade form **(dh)ghem-*. ZAMINDAR, from Persian *zamīn,* earth, land. [Pokorny *ĝhđem-* 414.]

dhgh(y)es- Yesterday. Suffixed (comparative) form **(dh)ghes-ter-*. YESTER-, YESTERDAY, from Old English *geostran, giestran,* "yester-," from Germanic **ges-ter-*. [Pokorny *ĝhđi̯és* 416.]

dhreg- To draw, glide. **1.** DRINK, from Old English *drincan,* to drink, from nasalized Germanic form **drenkan,* to draw into the mouth, drink. **2.** DRENCH, from Old English *drencan,* to soak, from nasalized o-grade Germanic causative form **drankjan,* "to cause to drink." **3.** DROWN, from a Scandinavian or late Old English source similar to Old Norse *drukkna,* to drown, from Germanic zero-grade suffixed form **drunk-nōn.* [Pokorny *dhreĝ-* 273.]

dhugəter- Daughter. DAUGHTER, from Old English *dohtor,* daughter, from Germanic **dohtar.* [Pokorny *dhug(h)əter-* 277.]

dhwer- Door, doorway (usually in plural). Originally an ablauting noun **dhwor, *dhur-*, in the plural, designating the entrance to the enclosure (**dhwor-o-*) surrounding the house proper. **1.** Zero-grade form **dhur-* in suffixed forms **dhur-n̥s* (accusative plural) and **dhur-o-* (neuter). DOOR, from Old English *duru,* door (feminine, originally plural), and *dor,* door (neuter), respectively from Germanic **durunz* and **duram.* **2.** Suffixed o-grade form **dhwor-āns* (accusative plural). FAROUCHE, FOREIGN, from Latin *forās,* (toward) out of doors, outside. **3.** Suffixed o-grade form **dhwor-ois* (locative plural). FOREST; AFFOREST, FAUBOURG, FORECLOSE, FORFEIT, from Latin *forīs,* (being) out of doors. **4.** Suffixed o-grade form **dhwor-o-*. FORENSIC, FORUM, from Latin *forum,* marketplace (originally the enclosed space around a home). **5.** DURBAR, from Old Persian *duvara-*, door, gate. **6.** Zero-grade form **dhur-*. THYROID, from Greek *thurā,* door. [Pokorny *dhu̯ĕr-* 278.]

dlegh- To engage oneself. European root found in Celtic, Germanic, Slavic, and possibly Latin. **1a.** PLAY, from Old English *plegian,* to exercise oneself, play; **b.** PLEDGE; FRANKPLEDGE, REPLEVIN, from Late Latin *plevium* (> Old French *plevir,* to pledge), pledge, guarantee; **c.** PLIGHT[2], from Old English *pliht,* danger, peril, from Germanic derivative noun **plehtiz.* **a–c** from Germanic **plegan,* probably altered (by dissimilation) from **tlegan.* **2.** Zero-grade form **dl̥gh-*. INDULGE, from Latin *indulgēre,* to indulge, explained by some as from prefixed and suffixed stative form **en-dl̥gh-ē-* (**en-*, in; see **en**). [Pokorny *dhl̥gh-* 271.]

dn̥ghū- Tongue. **1a.** TONGUE, from Old English *tunge,* tongue; **b.** BILTONG, from Middle Dutch *tonghe,* tongue. Both **a** and **b** from Germanic **tungōn-*. **2.** LANGUAGE, LANGUET, LIGULA, LIGULE, LINGO, LINGUA, LINGUINE, LINGUIST; BILINGUAL, from Latin *lingua* (< Archaic Latin *dingua*), tongue, language. [Pokorny *dn̥ĝhū* 223.]

dō- To give. Contracted from **doə-*. **1.** Zero-grade form **də-*. DADO, DATE[1], DATIVE, DATUM, DIE[2]; ADD, BETRAY, EDITION, PERDITION, RENDER, RENT[1], SURRENDER, TRADITION, TRAITOR, TREASON, VEND, from Latin *dare,* to give. **2.** Suffixed form **dō-no-*. DONATION, DONATIVE, DONOR; CONDONE, PARDON, from Latin *dōnum,* gift. **3.** Suffixed form **dō-t(i)-*. **a.** DOT[2], DOWAGER, DOWER, DOWRY; ENDOW, from Latin *dōs* (genitive *dōtis*), dowry; **b.** DACHA, from Russian *dacha,* gift, dacha, from Slavic **datja;* **c.** SAMIZDAT, from Russian *samizdat,* samizdat, from *dat',* to give. **4.** Suffixed form **dō-ro-*. LOBSTER THERMIDOR, PANDORA, from Greek *dōron,* gift. **5.** Reduplicated form **di-dō-*. DOSE; ANECDOTE, ANTIDOTE, APODOSIS, EPIDOTE, from Greek *didonai,* to give, with zero-grade noun *dosis* (< **də-ti-*), something given. [Pokorny *dō-* 223.]

dwo- Two.

I. Variant form **duwo.* **1a.** TWO, from Old English *twā,* two (nominative feminine and neuter); **b.** TWAIN; TWAYBLADE, from Old English *twēgen,* two (nominative and accusative masculine). Both **a** and **b** from Germanic **twa,* two. **2.** TWELFTH, TWELVE, from Old English *twelf,* twelve, and *twelfta,* twelfth, from Germanic compound **twa-lif-*, "two left (over from ten)," twelve (**-lif-*, left; see **leikʷ-**).

II. Adverbial form **dwis* and combining form **dwi-*. **1a.** TWIBILL, TWILIGHT, from Old English *twi-*, two; **b.** ZWIEBACK, ZWITTERION, from Old High German *zwi-*, twice; **c.** TWILL, from Old English *twilic,* double, woven of double thread, partial translation of Latin *bilīx,* woven of double thread. **a–c** all from Germanic **twi-*. **2.** BI-[1], BIS; BALANCE, BAROUCHE, BEZEL, BISCUIT, BISTORT, from Latin *bis* (combining form *bi-*), twice. **3.** DI-[1], from Greek *dis* (combining form *di-*), twice. **4.** TWIST, from Old English *-twist,* divided object, fork, rope, from Germanic **twis.* **5.** TWICE, from Old English *twige, twiga,* twice, from Germanic **twiyes.* **6.** TWENTY, from Old English *twēntig,* twenty, from Germanic compound **twēgentig,* "twice ten" (**-tig,* ten; see **dekm̥**). **7.** TWINE, from Old English *twīn,* double thread, from Germanic **twiznaz,* double thread, twisted thread. **8.** BETWEEN, BETWIXT, TWIXT, from Old English *betwēonum* and *betweox, betwix,* between, from Germanic compounds **bi-twīhna* and **bi-twisk,* "at the middle point of two" (*bi,* at, by; see **ambhi**). **9.** Suffixed form **dwis-no-*. **a.** TWIN, from Old English *twinn, getwinn,* two by two, twin, from Germanic **twisnaz,* double; **b.** BI-[1], BINAL, BINARY; COMBINE, PINOCHLE, from Latin *bīnī,* two by two, two each. **10.** Suffixed form **dwi-ko-*. TWIG[1], from Old English *twigge,* a branch, from Germanic **twig(g)a,* a fork. **11.** Compound **dwi-plo-*, twofold (**-plo-*, -fold). DIPLO-, DIPLOE, DIPLOID, DIPLOMA; ANADIPLOSIS, DIPLODOCUS, from Greek *diploos, diplous,* twofold. **12.** Suffixed reduplicated form **dwi-du-mo-*. DIDYMIUM, DIDYMOUS; EPIDIDYMIS, from Greek *didumos,* double, the testicles. **13.** Suffixed form **dwi-gha.* DICHASIUM, DICHO-, from Greek *dikha,* in two.

III. Inflected form **duwō.* **1.** DEUCE[1], DOZEN, DUAL, DUET, DUO, DUO-; DUODECIMAL, DUUMVIR, from Latin *duo,* two. **2.** DUAD, DYAD; DODECAGON, HENDIADYS, from Greek *duo, duō,* two.

IV. Variant form **du-*. **1.** Compound **du-plo-*, twofold (**-plo-*, -fold). DOUBLE, DOUBLET, DOUBLOON, DUPLE, from Latin *duplus,* double. **2.** Compound **du-plek-*, twofold (**-plek-*, -fold; see **plek-**). DUPLEX, DUPLICATE, DUPLICITY; CONDUPLICATE, from Latin *duplex,* double. **3.** Suffixed form **du-bhw-io-* in Latin *dubius,* doubtful (< "hesitating between two alternatives"; **-bhw-*, being; see **bheuə-**), and *dubitāre,* to be in doubt: DOUBT, DUBIOUS; REDOUBTABLE [Pokorny *du̯ō(u)* 228.]

dyeu- To shine (and in many derivatives, "sky, heaven, god"). Zero-grades **dyu-* (before consonants) and **diw-* (before vowels).

I. Basic form **dyeu-*, Jove, the name of the god of the bright sky, head of the Indo-European pantheon. **1.** JOVE, JOVIAL, from Latin *Iovis,* Jupiter, or *Iov-*, stem of *Iuppiter,* Jupiter. **2.** JULY, from Latin *Iūlius,* "descended from Jupiter" (name of a Roman gens), from derivative **iou-il-*. **3.** Vocative compound **dyeu-pəter,* "O father Jove" (**pəter-*, father; see **pəter-**). JUPITER, from Latin *Iuppiter, Iūpiter,* head of the Roman pantheon. **4.** DIONE, ZEUS; DIANTHUS, DIOSCURI, from Greek *Zeus* (genitive *Dios* < *Diwos*), Zeus.

II. Noun **deiwos,* god, formed by *e*-insertion to the zero-grade **diw-* and suffixation of (accented) *-o-*. **1a.** TIU, TUESDAY, from Old English *Tīw* (genitive *Tīwes*), god of war and sky; **b.** TYR, from Old Norse *Tȳr,* sky god. Both **a** and **b** from Germanic **Tīwaz.* **2.** DEISM, DEITY, JOSS; ADIEU, DEIFIC, from Latin *deus,* god. **3.** DIVA, DIVINE, from Latin *dīvus,* divine, god. **4.** DIS, DIVES, from Latin *dīves,* rich (< "fortunate, blessed, divine"). **5.** Suffixed zero-grade form **diw-yo-*, heavenly. DIANA, from Latin *Diāna,* moon goddess. **6.** DEVI; DEODAR, DEVANAGARI, from Sanskrit *devaḥ,* god, and *deva-*, divine. **7.** ASMODEUS, from Avestan *daēva-*, spirit, demon.

III. Variant form **dyē-* (< earlier **dyeə-*). DIAL, DIARY, DISMAL, DIURNAL, JOURNAL, JOURNEY; ADJOURN, CIRCADIAN, MERIDIAN, POSTMERIDIAN,

IV. Variant form **deiə-* (earlier **deia-*). PSYCHEDELIC, from Greek *dēlos* (< **deyalos*), clear. [Pokorny 1. *dei-* 183.]

ed- To eat; original meaning "to bite." **1a.** EAT, from Old English *etan,* to eat; **b.** ETCH, from Old High German *ezzen,* to feed on, eat; **c.** ORT, from Middle Dutch *eten,* to eat; **d.** *(i)* FRET[1], from Old English *fretan,* to devour; *(ii)* FRASS, from Old High German *frezzan,* to devour. Both *(i)* and *(ii)* from Germanic compound **fra-etan,* to eat up (**fra-*, completely; see **per**[1]). **a–d** all from Germanic **etan.* **2.** EDACIOUS, EDIBLE, ESCAROLE, ESCULENT, ESURIENT; COMEDO, COMESTIBLE, OBESE, from Latin *edere,* to eat. **3.** PRANDIAL, from Latin compound *prandium,* lunch, probably from **prām-(e)d-yo-*, "first meal" (**prām-*, first; see **per**[1]). **4.** Suffixed form **ed-un-ā-*. ANODYNE, PLEURODYNIA, from Greek *odunē,* pain (< "gnawing care"). **5.** SAMOYED, from Russian *-ed,* eater. **6.** Suffixed zero-grade (participial) form **əd-ent-*, "biting, the biting one, tooth," from earliest root form **əed-* (see **dent-**). [Pokorny *ed-* 287.]

eg I. Nominative form of the personal pronoun of the first person singular. For oblique forms see **me-**[1]. **1.** I[1], from Old English *ic,* I, from Germanic **ek.* **2.** Extended form **egō.* EGO, EGOIST, EGOTISM, from Latin *ego,* I. [Pokorny *eĝ-* 291.]

eghs Out. **1.** Variant **eks.* **a.** EX[1], EX-, from Latin *ex, ex-*, out of, away from; **b.** ECTO-, EX-, EXO-, EXOTERIC, EXOTIC; ELECTUARY, LEKVAR, SYNECDOCHE, from Greek *ex, ek,* out of, from. **2.** Suffixed (comparative) variant form **eks-tero-*. **a.** ESTRANGE, EXTERIOR, EXTERNAL, EXTRA-, STRANGE, from Latin *exter,* outward (feminine ablative *exterā, extrā,* on the outside); **b.** further suffixed (superlative) form **eks-t(e)r-ēmo-*. EXTREME, from Latin *extrēmus,* outermost (**-mo-*, superlative suffix). **3.** Suffixed form **eghs-ko-*. ESCHATOLOGY, from Greek *eskhatos,* outermost, last. **4.** Celtic **eks-*, out (of), in compound **eks-dī-sedo-* (see **sed-**). **5.** SAMIZDAT, from Russian *iz,* from, out of, from Balto-Slavic **iz.* [Pokorny *eĝhs* 292.]

ei-[1] To go. **1.** Full-grade form **ei-*. **a.** ADIT, AMBIENT, AMBITION, CIRCUIT, COITUS, COMITIA, EXIT, INTROIT, ISSUE, OBITUARY, PERISH, PRAETOR, PRETERIT, SEDITION, SUBITO, SUDDEN, TRANCE, TRANSIENT, TRANSIT, TRANSITIVE, from Latin *īre,* to go (past participle *itus* < suffixed zero-grade form **i-to-*); **b.** ION; ANION, CATION, DYSPROSIUM, from Greek *ienai,* to go; **c.** RAMAYANA, from Sanskrit *eti,* he goes (< Indo-Iranian **ai-ti*), and abstract noun *ayanam,* a going, way. **2.** Suffixed zero-grade form **i-t-*. **a.** Further suffixed form **i-t-yo-*. COMMENCE, INITIAL, INITIATE, from Latin *initium,* entrance, beginning (*in-*, in; see **en**); **b.** COUNT[2], COUNTY; CONCOMITANT, CONSTABLE, VISCOUNT, from Latin *comes* (stem *comit-*), companion (< "one who goes with another"; *com-*, with; see **kom**). **3.** Suffixed form **i-ter.* ERRANT, EYRE, ITINERANT, ITINERARY, from Latin *iter,* journey. **4.** Extended form **yā-*. Suffixed forms **yā-no-*, **yā-nu-*. **a.** JANITOR, JANUARY, JANUS, from Latin *iānus,* archway, and *Iānus,* god of doors and of the beginning of a year; **b.** HINAYANA, MAHAYANA, from Sanskrit *yānam,* way (in Buddhism, "mode of knowledge," "vehicle"). [Pokorny 1. *ei-* 293.]

eis- In words denoting passion. **1.** Suffixed form **eis-ā-*. IRASCIBLE, IRATE, IRE, from Latin *īra,* anger. **2.** Suffixed zero-grade form **is-(ə)ro-*, powerful, holy. HIERATIC, HIERO-; HIERARCH, HIERARCHY, HIERODULE, HIEROGLYPHIC, HIEROPHANT, from Greek *hieros,* "filled with the divine," holy. **3a.** IRON, from Old English *īse(r)n, īren,* iron; **b.** GISARME, SPIEGELEISEN, from Old High German *īsarn, īsan,* iron. Both **a** and

b from Germanic **īsarno-*, "holy metal" (possibly from Celtic). **4.** Suffixed o-grade form **ois-tro-*, madness. ESTRUS; ESTROGEN, ESTRONE, from Greek *oistros*, gadfly, goad, anything causing madness. **5.** Suffixed form **eis-mo-*. ASMODEUS, from Avestan *aēšma-*, anger. [Pokorny 1. *eis-* 299.]

ekwo- Horse. Probably to be segmented **ekw-o-*, a suffixed form akin to the lengthened o-grade adjective **ōku-*, swift. **1.** EQUESTRIAN, EQUINE, EQUITANT, EQUITATION; EQUISETUM, from Latin *equus*, horse. **2.** EOHIPPUS, HIPPOCAMPUS, HIPPOCRENE, HIPPODROME, HIPPOGRIFF, HIPPOPOTAMUS, from Greek *hippos*, horse. [Pokorny *ek̂u̯o-s* 301.]

en In. **1a.** IN[1] (preposition), from Old English *in*, in; **b.** IN[1] (adverb), from Old English *inn*, into, *inne*, inside; **c.** INN, from Old English *inn*, habitation, inn; **d.** TSIMMES, from Old High German *in*, in; **e.** INNER, from Old English *innera*, farther in, inner, from Germanic (comparative) **inn(e)ra*; **f.** BEN, from Old English *binnan*, within, contracted from **be innan* (*be*, by; see **ambhi**), from Germanic **innan*. **a–f** all from Germanic **in*. **2.** EN-[1], IN-[2], from Latin *in*, *in-*, in, into. **3.** EN-[2]; ENKEPHALIN, PARENCHYMA, PARENTHESIS, from Greek *en*, *en-*, in. **4.** Suffixed form **en-t(e)ro-*. **a.** INTRO-; INTRODUCE, INTROIT, INTROMIT, INTRORSE, INTROSPECT, from Latin *intrō*, inward, within; **b.** ENTER, INTRA-; INTRADOS, from Latin *intrā*, inside, within; **c.** INTERIM, INTRINSIC, from Latin *interim*, meanwhile, with ablative suffix *-im*, and *intrīnsecus*, on the inside, from *int(e)rim* + *secus*, alongside (see **sek^w-[1]**). **5.** Suffixed form **en-ter*. ENTRAILS, INTER-, INTERIOR, INTERN, INTERNAL, from Latin *inter*, *inter-*, between, among. **6.** INTIMA, INTIMATE[2], from Latin (superlative) *intimus*, innermost (**-mo-*, superlative suffix). **7.** Extended form **en-do*. **a.** INDUSTRY, from Latin *industrius*, diligent (Archaic Latin *indostruus*; **stru-*, to construct); **b.** INDIGENT, from Latin *indigēre*, to be in need (*egēre*, to be in need). Both **a** and **b** from Latin *indu-*, within, from Archaic Latin *endo*; **c.** ENDO-, from Greek *endon*, *endo-*, within. **8.** Suffixed form **en-tos*. **a.** DEDANS, INTESTINE, INTINE, INTUSSUSCEPTION, from Latin *intus*, within, inside; **b.** ENTO-, from Greek *entos*, within. **9.** Suffixed form **en-tero-*. **a.** ENTERIC, ENTERO-, ENTERON; DYSENTERY, EXENTERATE, MESENTERY, from Greek *enteron*, intestine; **b.** ATOLL, perhaps ultimately from Sanskrit *antara-*, interior. **10.** Extended form **ens*. **a.** EPISODE, from Greek *eis*, into; **b.** suffixed form **ens-ō*. ESOTERIC, ESOTROPIA, from Greek *esō*, within. **11.** Possibly suffixed zero-grade form **n̥-dha*. AND, from Old English *and*, and, from Germanic **anda*, **unda*. [Pokorny 1. *en* 311.]

epi Also **opi**. Near, at, against. **1.** OB-, from Latin *ob*, *ob-*, before, to, against. **2.** EPI-, from Greek *epi*, on, over, at. **3.** OPISTHOBRANCH, OPISTHOGNATHOUS, from Greek *opisthen*, behind, at the back. **4.** Zero-grade form **pi*, on, in Greek *piezein* (see **sed-**). **5.** OBLAST, from Russian *oblast'*, oblast, from Old Church Slavonic *ob*, on. **6.** Reduced prefixal form **op-* in **op-wer-yo-*, "cover over" (**wer-*, to cover). COVER, OPERCULUM; KERCHIEF, from Latin *operīre*, to cover. **7.** OPSONIN, from Greek **ops*, extra on the side, with, in noun *opson*, condiment, cooked food. [Pokorny *epi* 323.]

er- To move, set in motion.

I. Basic form **er-*. **1.** Probably Germanic **ar-*, **or-*, to be, exist. ARE[1], ART[2], from Old English *eart* and *aron*, second person singular and plural present of *bēon*, to be. **2.** Perhaps Germanic suffixed form **er-n-os-ti-*. EARNEST[1], from Old English *eornoste*, zealous, serious. **3.** Uncertain o-grade suffixed form **ori-yo-*. ORIENT, ORIGIN, ORIGINAL; ABORT, from Latin *orīrī*, to arise, appear, be born. **4.** Suffixed o-grade form **or-smā-*. HORMONE, from Greek *hormē*, impulse, onrush.

II. Enlarged extended form **ərei-s-*. **1.** RISE; ARISE, from Old English *rīsan*, from Germanic **rīsan*. **2.** Suffixed o-grade (causative) form **rois-ye-*. **a.** REAR[2], from Old English *rǣran*, to rear, raise, lift up; **b.** RAISE, from Old Norse *reisa*, to raise. Both **a** and **b** from Germanic **raizjan*. [Pokorny 3. *er-* 326; *ergh-* 339.]

es- To be. **1.** Athematic first person singular form **es-mi*. AM, from Old English *eam*, *eom*, am, from Germanic **izm(i)*. **2.** Athematic third person singular form **es-ti*. IS, from Old English *is*, is, from Germanic **ist(i)*. **3.** Zero-grade form **əs-*, from earliest full-grade root form **əes-*. **a.** Optative stem **sī-* (< **əs-iə-*). YES, from Old English *gēse*, yes, from *sīe*, may it be (so) (*gēa*, yea; see **i-**), from Germanic **si-jai-*; **b.** participial form **sont-* (< **əs-ont-*), being, existing, hence real, true. *(i)* SOOTH, SOOTHE, from Old English *sōth*, true, from Germanic **santhaz*; *(ii)* suffixed (collective) zero-grade form **sn̥t-yā-*, "that which is." SIN[1], from Old English *synn*, sin, from Germanic **sun(d)jō*, sin (< "it is true," "the sin is real"); *(iii)* SUTTEE; BODHISATTVA, SATYAGRAHA, from Sanskrit *sat-*, *sant-*, existing, true, virtuous. **4.** Basic form **es-*. ENTITY, ESSENCE; ABSENT, IMPROVE, INTEREST, OSSIA, PRESENT[1], PRESENT[2], PROUD, QUINTESSENCE, REPRESENT, STOVER, from Latin *esse*, to be. **5.** Basic form **es-*. -ONT, ONTO-; -BIONT, HOMOIOUSIAN, PAROUSIA, SCHIZONT, from Greek *einai* (present participle *ont-*, being), to be. **6.** Suffixed form **es-ti-*. SWASTIKA, from Sanskrit *asti*, being (*su-*, well, good). [Pokorny *es-* 340.]

gel- Cold; to freeze. **1.** CHILL, from Old English *c(i)ele*, chill, from Germanic **kaliz*, coldness. **2.** COLD, from Old English *ceald*, cold, from Germanic **kalda-*, cold. **3a.** COOL, from Old English *cōl*, cold, cool; **b.** KEEL[3], from Old English *cēlan*, to cool, from Germanic **kōljan*, to cool. Both **a** and **b** from Germanic **kōl-*, cool. **4.** Suffixed form **gel-ā-*. GELATIN, GELATION, JELLY; CONGEAL, from Latin *gelāre*, to freeze. **5.** Suffixed form **gel-u-*. GELID, from Latin *gelū*, frost, cold. **6.** Probably suffixed zero-grade form **gl̥-k-*. GLACÉ, GLACIAL, GLACIATE, GLACIER, GLACIS, from Latin *glaciēs*, ice. [Pokorny 3. *gel(ə)-* 365.]

gembh- Tooth, nail. **1.** Suffixed o-grade form **gombh-o-*. **a.** COMB, KAME, from Old English *comb*, *camb*, comb; **b.** CAM, from Dutch *kam*, cog, comb; **c.** UNKEMPT, from Old English *cemban*, to comb, from Germanic denominative **kambjan*, to comb. **a–c** all from Germanic **kambaz*, comb. **2.** Suffixed zero-grade form **gm̥bh-ōn-*. OAKUM, from Old English *ā-cumba*, part of flax separated in hackling, oakum ("stuff combed off"; *ā-*, away, off). **3.** Perhaps Germanic **kimb-*. CHIME[2], from Old English *cim-*, *cimb-*, rim (only in compounds). **4.** Possibly suffixed form **gembh-mā-*. GEM, GEMMA, GEMMATE, GEMMULE, from Latin *gemma*, bud, hence gem. [Pokorny *ĝembh-* 369.]

genə- Also **gen-**. To give birth, beget; with derivatives referring to aspects and results of procreation and to familial and tribal groups.

I. Basic form **genə-*. **1.** Suffixed form **genə-es-*. **a.** GENDER, GENERAL, GENERATE, GENERATION, GENERIC, GENEROUS, GENRE, GENUS; CONGENER, DEGENERATE, ENGENDER, MISCEGENATION, from Latin *genus*, race, kind; **b.** GENE; ALLOGENEIC, GENEALOGY, GENOCIDE, GENOTYPE, HETEROGENEOUS, from Greek *genos* and *geneā*, race, family; **c.** -GEN, -GENY; EPIGENE, from Greek suffix *-genēs*, "-born." **2.** Suffixed form **gen(ə)-yo-*. **a.** GENIAL[1], GENIUS; CONGENIAL, from Latin *genius*, procreative divinity, inborn tutelary spirit, innate quality; **b.** ENGINE, INGENIOUS, from Latin *ingenium*, inborn character (*in-*, in; see **en**). **3.** Suffixed form **genə-ā-*. INDIGEN, INDIGENOUS, from Latin *indigena*, born in (a place), indigenous (*indu-*, within; see **en**). **4.** Suffixed form **genə-wo-*. GENUINE, INGENUOUS, from Latin *ingenuus*, born in (a place), native, natural, freeborn (*in-*, in; see **en**). **5.** Suffixed form **gen(ə)-men-*. GERM, GERMAN[2], GERMANE, GERMINAL, GERMINATE, from dissimilated Latin *germen*, shoot, bud, embryo, germ.

II. O-grade form **gonə-*, reduced to **gon-* in suffixed form **gon-o-*. **1.** GONAD, GONO-, -GONY; ARCHEGONIUM, EPIGONE, from Greek *gonos*, child, procreation, seed. **2.** HARIJAN, from Sanskrit *janaḥ*, offspring, child, person.

III. Zero-grade form **gn̥ə-*. **1.** Suffixed form **gn̥ə-yo-*. **a.** KIN; KINDRED, from Old English *cyn(n)*, race, family, kin; **b.** KING, from Old English *cyning*, king, from Germanic **kuningaz*, king. Both **a** and **b** from Germanic **kunjam*, family. **2.** Suffixed form **gn̥ə-t-*. **a.** KIND[2], from Old English *cynd*, *gecynd(e)*, origin, birth, race, family, kind, from Germanic **kundjaz*, family, race; **b.** KIND[1], from Old English *gecynde*, natural, native, fitting (*ge-*, collective prefix; see **kom**), from Germanic **kundi-*, natural, native; **c.** suffixed form **gn̥ə-ti-*. *(i)* GENS, GENTEEL, GENTILE, GENTLE, GENTRY, JAUNTY; GENDARME, from Latin *gēns* (stem *genti-*), race, clan; *(ii)* GENESIS, -GENESIS, from Greek *genesis*, birth, beginning; **d.** KINDERGARTEN, KRISS KRINGLE, WUNDERKIND, from Old High German *kind*, child, from Germanic secondary full-grade variant **kentham*. **3.** Reduplicated form **gi-gn(ə)-*. GENITAL, GENITIVE, GENITOR, GENITURE, GENT[1], GINGERLY; CONGENITAL, PRIMOGENITOR, PRIMOGENITURE, PROGENITOR, PROGENY, from Latin *gignere* (past participle *genitus*), to beget. **4.** Reduced form **gn-* in suffixed form **-gn-o-*. BENIGN, MALIGN, from Latin *benignus*, good-natured, kindly (*bene*, well; see **deu-**), and *malignus*, evil-natured, malevolent (*male*, ill; see **mel-**). **5.** Zero-grade form **gn̥ə-* becoming **gnā-*. PREGNANT[1]; IMPREGNATE, from Latin *praegnās*, pregnant (*prae-*, before; see **per[1]**). **6.** Suffixed form **gn̥ə-sko-* becoming **gnā-sko-*. NAIVE, NASCENT, NATAL, NATION, NATIVE, NATURE, NÉE, NOËL; ADNATE, AGNATE, COGNATE, CONNATE, ENATE, INNATE, NEONATE, PUISNE, PUNY, RENAISSANCE, from Latin *gnāscī*, *nāscī* (past participle *gnātus*, *nātus*), to be born. **7.** Reduced form **gn̥-* in Sanskrit compound *kr̥mi-ja-* (see **k^wr̥mi-**). [Pokorny 1. *ĝen-* 373.]

genu- Knee; also angle. **1.** Variant form **gneu-*. **a.** KNEE, from Old English *cnēo*, knee, from Germanic **knewam*; **b.** KNEEL, from Old English *cnēowlian*, to kneel, from Germanic **knewljan*. **2.** Basic form **genu-*. GENICULATE, GENUFLECT, from Latin *genū*, knee. **3.** O-grade form **gonu*. POLYGONUM, PYCNOGONID, from Greek *gonu*, knee. **4.** Suffixed variant form **gōnw-yā-*. -GON, GONION; AMBLYGONITE, DIAGONAL, GONIOMETER, ORTHOGONAL, from Greek *gōniā*, angle, corner. [Pokorny 1. *ĝenu-* 380.]

gerbh- To scratch. **1.** CARVE, from Old English *ceorfan*, to cut, from Germanic **kerban*. **2.** KERF, from Old English *cyrf*, a cutting (off), from zero-grade Germanic form **kurbiz*. **3.** Variant form **grebh-*. **a.** CRAB[1], from Old English *crabba*, a crab, from Germanic **krab(b)-*; **b.** CRAYFISH, from Old High German *kerbiz*, edible crustacean, from Germanic **krabiz-*; **c.** perhaps Germanic **krab-*. CRAWL[1], from Old Norse *krafla*, to crawl. **4.** Zero-grade form **gr̥bh-*. **a.** GLAMOUR, GRAFFITO, GRAFT[1], GRAM[1], -GRAM, GRAMMAR, -GRAPH, -GRAPHER, GRAPHIC, -GRAPHY; AGRAPHA, AGRAPHIA, ANAGRAM, DIAGRAM, EPIGRAM, EPIGRAPH, GRAPHITE, ICONOGRAPHY, PARAGRAPH, PARALLELOGRAM, PROGRAM, PSEUDEPIGRAPHA, TETRAGRAMMATON, TOPOGRAPHY, from Greek *graphein*, to scratch, draw, write, *gramma* (< **gr̥bh-mn̥*), a picture, written letter, piece of writing, and *grammē*, a line; **b.** LANDGRAVE, MARGRAVE, PALSGRAVE, from Middle Dutch *grāve* and Middle Low German *grave*, count, from West Germanic **grafa*, a designation of rank, possibly borrowed from Greek *grapheus*, scribe. [Pokorny *gerebh-* 392.]

geus- To taste, choose. **1a.** CHOOSE, from Old English *cēosan*, *ceōsan*, to choose, from Germanic **keusan*; **b.** CHOICE, from a Germanic source akin to Gothic *kausjan*, to test, taste, from Germanic causative **kausjan*. **2.** Zero-grade form **gus-*. VALKYRIE, from Old Norse *Valkyrja*, "chooser of the slain," Valkyrie (*valr*, the slain; see **welə-**), from Germanic **kuz-*. **3.** Suffixed zero-grade form **gus-tu-*. GUST[2], GUSTO; RAGOUT, from Latin *gustus*, taste. **4.** Suffixed zero-grade form **gus-to-*, whence further suffixed (frequentative) form **gus-t-ā-*. GUSTATION; DEGUST, DISGUST, from Latin *gustāre*, to taste. [Pokorny *ĝeus-* 399.]

ghabh- Also **ghebh-**. To give or receive. **1.** Form **ghebh-*. **a.** GIVE, from Old English *giefan*, to give, and Old Norse *gefa*, to give; **b.** FORGIVE, from Old English *forgi(e)fan*, to give, give up, leave off (anger), remit, forgive, from Germanic compound **far-geban*, to give away (**far-*, away; see **per[1]**). Both **a** and **b** from Germanic **geban*. **2.** Suffixed form **ghebh-ti-*, something given (or received). GIFT, from Old Norse *gipt*, *gift*, a gift, from Germanic **giftiz*. **3.** O-grade form **ghobh-*. GAVEL[2], from Old English *gafol*, tribute, tax, debt, from Germanic **gab-ulam*, something paid (or received). **4.** Form **ghabh-ē-*. **a.** ABLE, BINNACLE, HABILE, HABIT, HABITABLE, HABITANT, HABITAT; AVOIRDUPOIS, COHABIT, EXHIBIT, INHABIT, INHIBIT, MALADY, PREBEND, PROHIBIT, PROVENDER, from Latin *habēre*, to hold, possess, have, handle (> *habitāre*, to dwell); **b.** DEBENTURE, DEBIT, DEBT, DEVOIR, DUE, DUTY; ENDEAVOR, from Latin *dēbēre*, to owe (*dē-*, away from). [Pokorny *ghabh-* 407.] Compare **kap-**.

ghans- Goose. **1a.** GOOSE; GOSHAWK, from Old English *gōs* (nominative plural *gēs*), goose; **b.** GOSLING, from Old Norse *gās*, goose; **c.** GUNSEL, from Old High German *gans*, goose; **d.** GONZO, from Spanish *ganso,* goose, from a Germanic source akin to Old High German *gans,* goose. **a–d** all from Germanic **gans-* (nominative plural **gansiz*). **2.** GANDER, from Old English *ganra, gandra,* gander, from Germanic **gan(d)rōn-*. **3.** GANNET, from Old English *ganot,* gannet, from Germanic **ganōtōn-*. **4.** Suffixed form **ghans-er-*. ANSERINE; MERGANSER, from Latin *ānser* (< **hanser*), goose. **5.** Basic form **ghans-*. CHENOPOD, from Greek *khēn,* goose. [Pokorny *ĝhan-s-* 412.]

ghē- To release, let go; (in the middle voice) to be released, go. Contracted from **gheə-*. **1.** GO[1]; AGO, FOREGO[1], FORGO, from Old English *gān,* to go, from Germanic variant form **gaian.* **2.** Suffixed form **ghē-ro-*. HEIR, HEREDITAMENT, HEREDITY, HERITAGE; INHERIT, from Latin *hērēs,* heir (? < "orphan" < "bereft"). **3.** Possibly suffixed o-grade form **ghō-ro-,* "empty space." **a.** -CHORE; ANCHORITE, CHOROGRAPHY, from Greek *khōros,* place, country, particular spot; **b.** CHORIPETALOUS, from Greek *khōris, khōri,* apart, separate. **4.** Possible suffixed zero-grade form **ghət(w)ā-*. **a.** GAIT, GATE[2], from Old Norse *gata,* path, street; **b.** GANTLET[1], GAUNTLET[2], from Old Swedish *gata,* lane. Both **a** and **b** from Germanic **gatwōn-,* a going. **5.** Suffixed zero-grade form **ghə-no-*. HINAYANA, from Sanskrit *hīna-,* inferior, verbal adjective of *jahāti,* he leaves, lets go (< reduplicated **ghe-ghē-ti*). [Pokorny 1. *ĝhē-* 418.]

ghebh-el- Head. **1.** GABLE, from Old Norse *gafl,* gable, from Germanic **gablaz,* top of a pitched roof. **2.** Form **kephal-,* dissimilated from **khephal-*. CEPHALIC, CEPHALO-, -CEPHALOUS; ENCEPHALO-, ENKEPHALIN, HYDROCEPHALUS, PACHYCEPHALOSAUR, from Greek *kephalē,* head. [Pokorny *ghebh-el-* 423.]

ghei- Theoretical base of **ghyem-, *ghiem-,* winter. **1.** Form **ghiem-*. HIEMAL, from Latin *hiems,* winter. **2.** Suffixed variant form **gheim-ri-no-*. HIBERNACULUM, HIBERNATE, from Latin *hībernus,* pertaining to winter. **3.** Suffixed zero-grade form **ghim-r̥-yə,* "female animal one year (winter) old." CHIMERA, from Greek *khimaira,* she-goat. [Pokorny 2. *ĝhei-* 425.]

ghel- To shine; with derivatives referring to colors, bright materials, gold (probably "yellow metal"), and bile or gall.

I. Words denoting colors. **1.** Suffixed form **ghel-wo-*. YELLOW, from Old English *geolu,* yellow, from Germanic **gelwa-*. **2.** Suffixed variant form **ghlō-ro-*. CHLORO-; CHLORITE[1], from Greek *khlōros,* green, greenish yellow. **3.** Suffixed variant form **ghlo-wo-*. CHLOASMA, from Greek *khloos* (< **khlowo-s*), greenish color. **4.** O-grade form **ghol-*. PODZOL, from Russian *zola,* ashes (from their color). **5.** Suffixed form **ghel-i-*. HARE KRISHNA, HARIJAN, from Sanskrit *hari-,* tawny yellow. **6.** Possibly suffixed zero-grade form **ghl̥-wo-* in Latin *fulvus,* tawny (with dialectal *f-* as in *fel,* gall; see **III. 3.** below): GRISEOFULVIN.

II. Words denoting gold. **1.** Suffixed zero-grade form **ghl̥-to-*. **a.** GOLD, from Old English *gold,* gold; **b.** GILD[1], from Old English *gyldan,* to gild, from Germanic denominative verb **gulthjan;* **c.** GUILDER, GULDEN, from Middle Dutch *gulden,* golden; **d.** GOWAN, from Middle English *gollan,* yellow flower, possibly from a source akin to Old Norse *gullinn,* golden. **a–d** all from Germanic **gultham,* gold. **2.** Suffixed o-grade form **ghol-to-*. ZLOTY, from Polish *złoto,* gold. **3.** Suffixed full-grade form **ghel-no-*. ARSENIC, from Syriac *zarnīkā,* orpiment, from Middle Iranian **zarnik-,* from Old Iranian **zarna-,* golden.

III. Words denoting bile. **1.** Suffixed o-grade form **ghol-no-*. GALL[1], from Old English *gealla,* gall, from Germanic **gallōn-,* bile. **2.** Suffixed o-grade form **ghol-ā-*. CHOLE-, CHOLER, CHOLERA; ACHOLIA, MELANCHOLY, from Greek *kholē,* bile. **3.** Suffixed full-grade form **ghel-n-*. FELON[2], from Latin *fel,* bile (with dialectal *f-*).

IV. A range of Germanic words with initial *gl-* (where no preforms are given, the words are late creations). **1.** GLEAM, from Old English *glǣm,* bright light, gleam, from Germanic **glaimiz.* **2.** GLIMPSE, from Middle English *glimsen,* to glimpse, from a source akin to Middle High German *glimsen,* to gleam. **3.** GLINT, from Middle English *glent,* a glint, and *glenten,* to shine, from a source akin to Swedish dialectal *glinta,* to shine. **4.** GLIMMER, from Middle English *glimeren,* to glimmer, from a source akin to Swedish *glimra,* glimmer. **5.** GLITTER, from Old Norse *glitra,* to shine. **6.** GLITZ, from Old High German *glīzan,* to sparkle. **7.** GLISTEN, from Old English *glisnian,* to shine. **8.** GLISTER, from Middle Dutch *glinsteren* or Middle Low German *glisteren,* to shine. **9.** GLASS, GLAZE, GLAZIER, from Old English *glæs,* glass, from Germanic **glasam,* glass. **10.** GLARE[1], from Middle English *glaren,* to glitter, stare, from a source akin to Middle Low German *glaren,* to glisten, from Germanic **glaz-*. **11.** GLOSS[1], from a source perhaps akin to Icelandic *glossi,* a spark. **12.** GLANCE[2], from Old High German *glanz,* bright. **13.** GLEG, from Old Norse *glöggr,* clear-sighted. **14.** GLAD[1], from Old Eng- lish *glæd,* shining, joyful, from Germanic **glada-*. **15.** GLEE; GLEEMAN, from Old English *glēo,* sport, merriment, from Germanic **gleujam.* **16a.** GLEED, from Old English *glēd,* ember; **b.** GLOGG, from Old Norse *glodh,* ember. Both **a** and **b** from Germanic **glō-di-*. **17a.** GLOW, from Old English *glōwan,* to glow; **b.** GLOWER, from Middle English *gloren,* to gleam, stare, probably from a source akin to Norwegian dialectal *glora,* to gleam, stare; **c.** GLOAT, from a source perhaps akin to Old Norse *glotta,* to smile (scornfully). **a–c** all from Germanic **glō-*. **18.** GLOAMING, from Old English *glōm,* twilight, from Germanic **glō-m-*. **19.** Possibly distantly related to this root is Germanic **glīdan,* to glide. **a.** GLIDE, from Old English *glīdan,* to slip, glide; **b.** GLISSADE, from Old French *glier,* to glide; **c.** GLITCH, from Old High German *glītan,* to glide; **d.** GLEDE, from Old English *glida,* kite (< "gliding, hovering bird"), from derivative Germanic **glidōn-*. **20.** GLIB, from a source possibly akin to Middle Low German *glibberich,* slippery. [Pokorny 1. *ĝhel-* 429.]

ghend- Also **ghed-**. To seize, take. **1a.** GET, from Old Norse *geta,* to get; **b.** BEGET, from Old English *beg(i)etan,* to get, beget, from Germanic compound **bigetan,* to acquire (**bi-,* intensive prefix; see **ambhi**); **c.** FORGET, from Old English *forg(i)etan,* to forget, from Germanic compound **fer-getan,* "to lose one's hold," forget (**fer-,* prefix denoting rejection; see **per[1]**). **a–c** all from Germanic **getan.* **2.** GUESS, from Middle English *gessen,* to guess, from a Scandinavian source akin to Old Swedish *gissa,* to guess, from Germanic **getisōn,* "to try to get," aim at. **3.** Basic form **ghend-*. PREHENSILE, PREHENSION, PRISON, PRIZE[2], PRIZE[3], PRY[2]; APPREHEND, APPRENTICE, APPRISE, COMPREHEND, COMPRISE, EMPRISE, ENTERPRISE, ENTREPRENEUR, IMPRESARIO, MISPRISION[1], PREGNABLE, PREG- NANT[1], REPREHEND, REPRIEVE, REPRISE, SURPRISE, from Latin *prehendere, prēndere,* seize, grasp (*pre-, prae-,* before; see **per[1]**). **4.** Form **ghed-*. PREDATORY, PREY, SPREE; DEPREDATE, OSPREY, from Latin *praeda,* booty (< **prai-hedā,* "something seized before"; *prai-,* before; see **per[1]**). [Pokorny *ghend-* 437.]

gher- To grasp, enclose; with derivatives meaning "enclosure." **1.** Suffixed zero-grade form **ghr̥-dh-*. **a.** GIRD[1], GIRT[1], from Old English *gyrdan,* to gird, from Germanic **gurdjan;* **b.** GIRDLE, from Old English *gyrdel,* girdle; **c.** GIRTH, from Old Norse *gjördh,* girdle, girth. **2.** Suffixed o-grade forms **ghor-to-, *ghor-dho-,* an enclosure. **a.** Form **ghor-to-*. HORTICULTURE, ORTOLAN, from Latin *hortus,* garden; **b.** form **ghor-to-* or **ghor-dho-*. *(i)* YARD[2]; ORCHARD, from Old English *geard,* enclosure, garden, yard; *(ii)* GARTH; ASGARD, from Old Norse *gardhr,* enclosure, garden, yard; *(iii)* KINDERGARTEN, from Old High German *garto,* garden; *(iv)* GARDEN, JARDINIÈRE, from Old North French *gart,* garden; *(v)* HANGAR, from Old French *hangard,* shelter, possibly from Germanic **haimgardaz* (**haimaz,* home; see **tkei-**); *(vi)* Germanic compound **midja-gardaz* (see **medhyo-**). *(i)–(vi)* all from Germanic **gardaz.* **3.** Prefixed and suffixed zero-grade form **ko(m)-ghr̥-ti-* (**ko(m)-,* collective prefix, "together"; see **kom**). COHORT, CORTEGE, COURT, COURTEOUS, COURTESAN, COURTESY, COURTIER, CURTILAGE, CURTSY, from Latin *cohors* (stem *cohort-*), enclosed yard, company of soldiers, multitude. **4.** Perhaps suffixed o-grade form **ghor-o-*. CAROL, CHOIR, CHORAL, CHORALE, CHORIC, CHORISTER, CHORUS, HORA; CHORAGUS, TERPSICHORE, from Greek *khoros,* dancing ground (? perhaps originally a special enclosure for dancing), dance, dramatic chorus. **5.** Suffixed zero-grade form **ghr̥-dh-o-*. GADJO, from Sanskrit *gr̥haḥ,* house (< "enclosure"). [Pokorny 4. *ĝher-* 442, *ĝherdh-* 444.]

ghes- Hand. **1.** Suffixed form **ghes-ōr,* stem **ghes-(e)r-*. CHIRO-; CHIRURGEON, ENCHIRIDION, SURGEON, SURGERY, from Greek *kheir,* hand. **2.** Suffixed form **ghes-to-*. PRESS[2], PRESTO; IMPREST, from Latin *praestō,* at hand, perhaps from prefixed form **prai-ghes-to-* (**prai-,* before; see **per[1]**). [Pokorny 1. *ĝhesor-* 447.]

gheu- To pour, pour a libation.

I. Extended form **gheud-*. **1.** Zero-grade form **ghud-*. GUT, from Old English *guttas,* intestines, from Germanic **gut-*. **2.** Nasalized zero-grade form **ghu-n-d-*. FOISON, FONDANT, FONDUE, FONT[2], FOUND[2], FUNNEL, FUSE[2], FUSILE, FUSION; AFFUSION, CIRCUMFUSE, CONFOUND, CONFUSE, DIFFUSE, EFFUSE, INFUSE, PERFUSE, PROFUSE, REFUND, REFUSE[1], REFUSE[2], SUFFUSE, TRANSFUSE, from Latin *fundere,* to melt, pour out.

II. Extended form **gheus-*. **1a.** GUST[1], from Old Norse *gustr,* a cold blast of wind, from Germanic suffixed form **gustiz;* **b.** GUSH, from Middle English *gushen,* to gush, perhaps akin to Icelandic *gusa,* to gush. Both **a** and **b** from Germanic zero-grade form **gus-*. **2.** GEYSER, from Old Norse *geysa,* to gush, from Germanic suffixed o-grade form **gausjan.* **3a.** Suffixed zero-grade form **ghus-mo-*. CHYME; ECCHYMOSIS, from Greek *khūmos,* juice; **b.** suffixed zero-grade form **ghus-lo-*. CHYLE, from Greek *khūlos,* juice.

III. Suffixed form **gheu-ti-*. FUTILE, from Latin *fūtilis,* "(of a vessel) easily emptied, leaky," hence untrustworthy, useless.

IV. Basic form **gheu-*. CHOANOCYTE, PARENCHYMA, from Greek *khein,* to pour, with o-grade noun *khoanē,* funnel.

V. Suffixed form **ghu-to-,* "poured," perhaps in Germanic **gudam,* god (but this is traditionally referred to **gheu(ə)-**). [Pokorny *ĝheu-* 447.]

gheu(ə)- To call, invoke. Suffixed zero-grade form **ghu-to-,* "the invoked," god. **1.** GOD, from Old English *god,* god. **2.** GIDDY, from Old English *gydig, gidig,* possessed, insane, from Germanic **gud-iga-,* possessed by a god. **3.** GÖTTERDÄMMERUNG, from Old High German *got,* god. **1–3** all from Germanic **gudam,* god (but this is perhaps better referred to **gheu-**). [Pokorny *ĝhau-* 413.]

ghos-ti- Stranger, guest, host; properly "someone with whom one has reciprocal duties of hospitality." **1.** Basic form **ghos-ti-*. **a.** *(i)* GUEST, from Old Norse *gestr,* guest; *(ii)* GASTARBEITER, from Old High German *gast,* guest. Both *(i)* and *(ii)* from Germanic **gastiz;* **b.** HOST[2], HOSTILE, from Latin *hostis,* enemy (< "stranger"). **2.** Compound **ghos-pot-, *ghos-po(d)-,* "guest-master," one who symbolizes the relationship of reciprocal obligation (**pot-,* master; see **poti-**). HOSPICE, HOSPITABLE, HOSPITAL, HOSPITALITY, HOST[1], HOSTAGE, HOSTEL, HOSTLER, from Latin *hospes* (stem *hospit-*), host, guest, stranger. **3.** Suffixed zero-grade form **ghs-en-wo-*. XENIA, XENO-, XENON; AXENIC, PYROXENE, from Greek *xenos,* guest, host, stranger. [Pokorny *ghosti-s* 453.]

ghredh- To walk, go. Suffixed zero-grade form **ghr̥dh-yo-*. **1.** GRESSORIAL; AGGRESS, CONGRESS, DEGRESSION, DIGRESS, EGRESS, INGREDIENT, INGRESS, INTROGRESSION, PLANTIGRADE, PROGRESS, REGRESS, RETROGRADE, RETROGRESS, TARDIGRADE, TRANSGRESS, from Latin *gradī* (past participle *gressus*), to walk, go. **2.** GRADE, GRADUAL, GRADUATE, GREE; CENTIGRADE, DEGRADE, DEGREE, from Latin *gradus* (< deverbative **grad-u-*), step, stage, rank. [Pokorny *ghredh-* 456.]

ghrendh- To grind. **1.** GRIND, from Old English *grindan,* to grind, from Germanic **grindan.* **2.** GRIST, from Old English *grīst,* the action of grinding, from Germanic **grinst-,* a grinding. **3.** FRAISE, FRENULUM, FRENUM; REFRAIN[1], from Latin *frendere,* to grind. **4.** Sometimes but improbably regarded as from this root (in variant form **ghrend-*) is Greek *khondros,* granule, groats, hence cartilage: CHONDRO-; HYPOCHONDRIA, MITOCHONDRION. [Pokorny *ghren-* 459.]

ghwer- Wild beast. **1.** Suffixed form **ghwer-o-*. FERAL, FERINE, FIERCE, from Latin *ferus,* wild. **2.** Compound **ghwero-əkʷ-,* "of wild aspect" (**-əkʷ-,* "-looking"; see **okʷ-**). FEROCIOUS, from Latin *ferōx* (stem *ferōc-*), fierce. **3.** Lengthened-grade form **ghwēr-*. TREACLE; CHALICOTHERE, DINOTHERE, EUTHERIAN, INDRICOTHERE, MEGATHERE, THEROPOD, from Greek *thēr,* wild beast. [Pokorny *ĝhu̯ēr-* 493.]

ghwībh- Shame, also pudenda. Expressive root, found only in Tocharian (in the literal meaning) and Germanic. WIFE; HUSSY, MIDWIFE, WOMAN, from Old English *wīf,* woman, from Germanic **wībam,* woman (with semantic weakening from the original meaning; for the semantics, compare the histories of *pudendum* and *cunt*), and from Old English compound *wīf-man(n),* "woman-person, wife person," female (as opposed to *wæpen-man(n),* "weapon-person," male, with clear sexual overtones). [Not in Pokorny; compare Tocharian B *kwīpe* and Tocharian A *kip,* female pudenda.]

gnō- To know. Contracted from **gnoə-*. **1.** Lengthened-grade form **gnē-* (contracted from **gnēə-*). KNOW; KNOWLEDGE, ACKNOWLEDGE, from Old English *cnāwan,* to know, from Germanic **knē(w)-*. **2.** Zero-grade form **gn̥ə-*. **a.** CAN[1], CON[2], CUNNING, from Old English *cunnan,* to know, know how to, be able to, from Germanic **kunnan* (Old English first and third singular *can* from Germanic **kann,* from o-grade **gonə-*); **b.** KEN, KENNING, from Old English *cennan,* to declare, and Old Norse *kenna,* to know, name (in a formal poetic metaphor), from Germanic causative verb **kannjan,* to make known; **c.** COUTH; UNCOUTH, from Old English *cūth,* known, well-known, usual, excellent, familiar, from Germanic **kuntha-;* **d.** KITH AND KIN, from Old English *cȳth(the), cȳththu,* knowledge, acquaintance, friendship, kinfolk, from Germanic **kunthithō.* **3.** Suffixed form **gnō-sko-*. NOTICE, NOTIFY, NOTION, NOTORIOUS; ACQUAINT, COGNITION, COGNIZANCE, CONNOISSEUR, INCOGNITO, QUAINT, RECOGNIZE, RECONNAISSANCE, RECONNOITER, from Latin *(g)nōscere, cognōscere,* to get to know, get acquainted with. **4.** Suffixed form **gnō-ro-*. IGNORANT, IGNORE, from Latin *ignōrāre,* not to know, to disregard (*i-* for *in-*, not; see **ne**). **5.** Suffixed form **gnō-dhli-*. NOBLE, from Latin *nōbilis,* knowable, known, famous, noble. **6.** Reduplicated and suffixed form **gi-gnō-sko-*. GNOME[2], GNOMON, GNOSIS, GNOSTIC; AGNOSIA, DIAGNOSIS, PATHOGNOMONIC, PHYSIOGNOMY, PROGNOSIS, from Greek *gignōskein,* to know, think, judge (verbal adjective *gnōtos,* known), with *gnōsis* (< **gnō-ti-*), knowledge, inquiry, and *gnōmōn,* judge, interpreter. **7.** Suffixed zero-grade form **gn̥ə-ro-*. NARRATE, from Latin *narrāre* (< **gnarrāre*), to tell, relate, from *gnārus,* knowing, expert. **8.** Suffixed zero-grade form **gn̥ə-ti-*. ZEND-AVESTA, from Avestan *zainti-*, knowledge (remade from earlier **zāti-* after *zan-*, to know). **9.** Traditionally but improbably referred here are: **a.** NOTE; ANNOTATE, CONNOTE, PROTHONOTARY, from Latin *nota,* a mark, note, sign, cipher, shorthand character; **b.** NORM, NORMAL; ABNORMAL, ENORMOUS, from Latin *norma,* carpenter's square, rule, pattern, precept, possibly from an Etruscan borrowing of Greek *gnōmōn,* carpenter's square, rule. [Pokorny 2. *ĝen-* 376.]

grə-no- Grain. **1a.** CORN[1], from Old English *corn,* grain; **b.** KERNEL, from Old English derivative noun *cyrnel,* seed, pip; **c.** EINKORN, from Old High German *korn,* grain. **a–c** all from Germanic **kornam.* **2.** GARNER, GARNET[1], GRAIN, GRAM[2], GRANADILLA, GRANARY, GRANGE, GRANI-, GRANITA, GRANITE, GRANULE, GRENADE, GRENADINE; FILIGREE, GROSGRAIN, POMEGRANATE, from Latin *grānum,* grain. [In Pokorny *ĝer-* 390.]

g^wā- Also **g^wem-**. To go, come. Contracted from **g^waə-*. **1a.** COME, from Old English *cuman,* to come; **b.** WELCOME, from Old English *wilcuma,* a welcome guest, and *wilcume,* the greeting of welcome, from Germanic compound **wil-kumōn-*, a desirable guest (**wil-*, desirable), from **kumōn-*, he who comes, a guest; **c.** BECOME, from Old English *becuman,* to become, from Germanic compound **bi-kuman,* to arrive, come to be (**bi-*, intensive prefix; see **ambhi**). **a–c** all from Germanic **kuman.* **2.** Suffixed variant form **g^w(e)m-yo-*. VENUE; ADVENT, ADVENTITIOUS, ADVENTURE, AVENUE, CIRCUMVENT, CONTRAVENE, CONVENE, CONVENIENT, CONVENT, CONVENTICLE, CONVENTION, COVEN, COVENANT, EVENT, EVENTUAL, INTERVENE, INVENT, INVENTORY, MISADVENTURE, PARVENU, PREVENIENT, PREVENT, PROVENANCE, PROVENIENCE, REVENANT, REVENUE, SOUVENIR, SUBVENTION, SUPERVENE, from Latin *venīre,* to come. **3.** Suffixed zero-grade variant form **g^wm̥-yo-*. BASE[1], BASIS; ABASIA, ACROBAT, ADIABATIC, AMPHISBAENA, ANABAENA, ANABASIS, DIABASE, DIABETES, HYPERBATON, KATABATIC, STEREOBATE, STYLOBATE, from Greek *bainein,* to go, walk, step, with *basis* (< **g^wə-ti-*, suffixed zero-grade form of **g^wā-*), a stepping, tread, base, *-batos* (< **g^wə-to-*), going, and *-batēs* (< **g^wə-tā-*), agential suffix, "one that goes or treads, one that is based." **4.** Suffixed zero-grade form **g^w(ə)-u-* in compound **pres-g^wu-* (see **per**[1]). **5.** Basic form **g^wā-*. BEMA, from Greek *bēma,* step, seat, raised platform. **6.** Reduplicated form **g^we-g^wā-*. JUGGERNAUT, from Sanskrit *jagat,* moving, the world, originally present participle of **jagāti* (remade as *jigāti*), he goes. [Pokorny *g^uā-* 463.]

g^weiə- Also **g^wei-**. To live.

I. Suffixed zero-grade form **g^wi-wo-*, **g^wī-wo-* (< **g^wi(ə)-wo-*), living. **1a.** QUICK; QUICKSILVER, from Old English *cwic, cwicu,* living, alive; **b.** COUCH GRASS, QUITCH GRASS, from Old English *cwice,* couch grass (so named from its rapid growth). Both **a** and **b** from Germanic **kwi(k)waz.* **2a.** *(i)* VIVIFY, VIVIPAROUS, from Latin *vīvus,* living, alive; *(ii)* VIPER, WYVERN, from Latin *vīpera,* viper, contracted from **vī-vipera,* "bearing live young" (from the belief that it hatches its eggs inside its body), from feminine of earlier **vīvo-paros* (*-paros,* bearing); **b.** VIAND, VICTUAL, VIVA, VIVACIOUS, VIVID; CONVIVIAL, REVIVE, SURVIVE, from Latin denominative *vīvere,* to live. **3.** AZOTH, from Middle Persian **zhīwak,* alive, from Old Persian **jīvaka-*, extension of *jīva-*, alive. **4.** Further suffixed form **g^wī-wo-tā-*. VIABLE, VITAL; VITAMIN, from Latin *vīta,* life. **5.** Further suffixed form **g^wi-wo-tūt-*. USQUEBAUGH, WHISKEY, from Old Irish *bethu,* life.

II. Suffixed zero-grade form **g^wiə-o-*. BIO-, BIOTA, BIOTIC; AEROBE, AMPHIBIAN, ANABIOSIS, CENOBITE, MICROBE, RHIZOBIUM, SAPROBE, SYMBIOSIS, from Greek *bios,* life (> *biotē,* way of life).

III. Variant form **g^wyō-*. **1.** AZO-; DIAZO, HYLOZOISM, from Greek *zoē,* life. **2.** Suffixed form **g^wyō-yo-*. ZODIAC, -ZOIC, ZOO-, ZOON[1], -ZOON, from Greek *zōon, zōion,* living being, animal.

IV. Compound suffixed zero-grade form **yu-g^wiə-es-* (see **aiw-**).

V. Possibly Old English *cwifer-*, nimble: QUIVER[1]. [Pokorny 3. *g^uei-* 467.]

g^welə- Also **g^wel-**. To throw, reach, with further meaning to pierce.

I. Words denoting to throw, reach. Variant form **g^wlē-*, contracted from **g^wleə-*. **1.** Nasalized zero-grade form **g^wl̥-n-ə-*. **a.** BALLISTA; AMPHIBOLE, ARBALEST, ASTROBLEME, BOLIDE, DEVIL, DIABOLICAL, EMBOLISM, EMBOLY, EPIBOLY, HYPERBOLA, HYPERBOLE, METABOLISM, PALAVER, PARABLE, PARABOLA, PARLEY, PARLIAMENT, PARLOR, PAROL, PAROLE, PROBLEM, SYMBOL, from Greek *ballein,* to throw (with o-grade **bol-* and variant **blē-*); **b.** BALL[2], BALLAD, BALLET, BAYADERE, from Greek *ballizein,* to dance. **2.** Suffixed o-grade form **g^wol(ə)-ā-*. BOLOMETER, from Greek *bolē,* beam, ray. **3.** Possible suffixed o-grade form **g^wol(ə)-sā-*. BOULE[1], ABULIA, from Greek *boulē,* determination, will (< "throwing forward of the mind"), council. **4.** Suffixed full-grade form **g^welə-mno-*. BELEMNITE, from Greek *belemnon,* dart, javelin.

II. Words denoting to pierce. **1.** Suffixed o-grade form **g^wol-eyo-*. **a.** QUELL, from Old English *cwellan,* to kill, destroy; **b.** QUAIL[2], from Middle Dutch *quelen,* to be ill, suffer. Both **a** and **b** from Germanic **kwaljan.* **2.** Suffixed zero-grade form **g^wl̥-yo-*. KILL[1], from Middle English *killen,* to kill, perhaps from Old English **cyllan,* to kill, from Germanic **kuljan.* [Pokorny 2. *g^uel-* 471, 1. *g^uel-* 470.]

g^wen- Woman. **1.** Suffixed form **g^wen-ā-*. **a.** QUEAN, from Old English *cwene,* woman, prostitute, wife, from Germanic **kwenōn-;* **b.** BANSHEE, from Old Irish *ben,* woman; **c.** ZENANA, from Persian *zan,* woman. **2.** Suffixed lengthened-grade form **g^wēn-i-*. QUEEN, from Old English *cwēn,* woman, wife, queen, from Germanic **kwēniz.* **3.** Suffixed zero-grade form **g^wn̥-ā-*. -GYNE, GYNO-, -GYNOUS, -GYNY; GYNECOCRACY, GYNECOLOGY, GYNOECIUM, from Greek *gunē,* woman. [Pokorny *g^uĕnā* 473.]

g^werə- Heavy.

I. Zero-grade form **g^wr̥ə-*. **1.** Suffixed form **g^wr̥ə-wi-*. GRAVE[2], GRAVID, GRAVIMETER, GRAVITATE, GRAVITY, GRIEF, GRIEVE; AGGRAVATE, AGGRIEVE, from Latin *gravis,* heavy, weighty. **2.** Suffixed form **g^wr̥ə-u-*. **a.** BARITE, BARIUM, BARYON, BARYTA; BARITONE, BARYCENTER, BARYSPHERE, CHARIVARI, from Greek *barus,* heavy; **b.** GURU, from Sanskrit *guru-*, heavy, venerable. **3.** Suffixed form **g^wr̥ə-es-*. BAR[2], BARO-; CENTROBARIC, ISALLOBAR, ISOBAR, from Greek *baros,* weight. **4.** Possibly **g^wrī-* in Greek compound **u(d)-bri-* (see **ud-**).

II. Suffixed extended form **g^wrū-to-*. BRUT, BRUTE, from Latin *brūtus,* heavy, unwieldy, dull, stupid, brutish.

III. Suffixed extended form **g^wrī-g-*. **1.** BRIO, from Spanish *brio* or Provençal *briu,* vigor, from Celtic **brīg-o-*, strength. **2.** BRIG, BRIGADE, BRIGAND, BRIGANTINE, from Old Italian *briga,* strife, from Celtic **brīg-ā-*, strife. **3.** BLITZKRIEG, from Old High German *krēg, chrēg,* stubbornness, from Germanic **krīg-*.

IV. Suffixed full-grade form **g^werə-nā-*, millstone. QUERN, from Old English *cweorn,* quern. [Pokorny 2. *g^uer-* 476.]

g^when- To strike, kill. **1.** O-grade form **g^whon-*. **a.** BANE, from Old English *bana,* slayer, cause of ruin or destruction; **b.** AUTOBAHN, from Middle High German *ban, bane,* way, road (< "strike" in a technical sense like "swath"). Both **a** and **b** from Germanic suffixed form **ban-ōn-*. **2.** Suffixed zero-grade form **g^whn̥-tyā-*. **a.** GUN, from Old Norse *gunnr,* war; **b.** GONFALON, from Italian *gonfalone,* standard, from Germanic compound **gund-fanōn-*, "battle flag" (**fanōn-*, flag). Both **a** and **b** from Germanic **gunthjō,* war, battle. **3.** Suffixed form **g^when-do-*. **a.** DEFEND, DEFENSE, FENCE, FEND, from Latin *dēfendere,* to ward off (*dē-*, away); **b.** OFFEND, OFFENSE, from Latin *offendere,* to strike against, be offensive, offend (*ob-*, against; see **epi**). **4.** Suffixed zero-grade form **g^whn̥-tro-*. BEZOAR, from Persian *zahr,* poison, from Old Iranian **jathra-*. **5.** Full-grade form **g^when-*. BONZE, from Sanskrit *hanti,* he strikes. [Pokorny 2. *g^{uh}en-(ə)-* 491, *bhen-* 126.]

g^wher- To heat, warm. **1.** Zero-grade form **g^whr̥-*. **a.** BURN[1], from Old English *beornan, byrnan* (intransitive) and *bærnan* (transitive), to burn; **b.** BRIMSTONE, from late Old English *brynstān,* "burning mineral," sulfur (*stān,* stone); **c.** BRINDLED, from Old Norse *brenna,* to burn. **a–c** all from Germanic **brennan* (intransitive) and *brannjan* (transitive), formed from **brenw-* with nasal suffix and analogical vocalism. **2a.** BRAND, from Old English *brand,* piece of burning wood, sword; **b.** BRANDY, from Dutch *branden,* to burn, distill; **c.** BRANDISH, from Old French *brand,* sword. **a–c** all from Germanic **brandaz,* a burning, a flaming torch, hence also a sword. **3.** Suffixed form **g^wher-m(n)o-*. THERM, -THERM, THERMO-, -THERMY; HYPOTHERMIA, LOBSTER THERMIDOR, from Greek *thermos,* warm, hot, and *thermē,* heat. **4.** O-grade form **g^whor-*. FORCEPS, from Latin *forceps,* pincers, fire tongs (< "that which holds hot things"; *-ceps,* agential suffix, "-taker"; see **kap-**). **5.** Suffixed o-grade form **g^whor-no-*. **a.** FORNAX, FURNACE, HORNITO, from Latin *furnus, fornus, fornāx,* oven; **b.** probably Latin *fornix,* arch, vault (< "vaulted brick oven"): FORNICATE, FORNIX. **6.** Suffixed zero-grade form **g^whr̥-to-*, heated, likely source of Sanskrit *ghr̥tam,* ghee, clarified butter: GHEE. [Pokorny *g^{uh}er-* 493, *bh(e)reu-* 143.]

g^wou- Ox, bull, cow. Nominative singular form **g^wōu-s.* **1.** COW[1], KINE; COWSLIP, from Old English *cū, cȳ, cȳe,* cow, from Germanic **kōuz* (> **kūz*). **2a.** BEEF, BOVINE, BUGLE[1], from Latin *bōs* (stem *bov-*), ox, bull, cow; **b.** BUCCINATOR, from Latin *būcina,* horn, trumpet, from **bou-kanā-*, "bellower" (**-kanā-*, singer; see **kan-**). **3a.** BOÖTES, BOUSTROPHEDON, BUCOLIC, BUGLOSS, BULIMIA, BUMELIA, BUPRESTID, BUTTER, BUTYRIC, from Greek *bous,* ox, bull, cow; **b.** BUFFALO, from Greek *boubalos,* buffalo, perhaps from *bous.* **4.** GAYAL; GUAR, GURKHA, NILGAI, from Sanskrit *gauḥ, go-*, cow. **5.** Suffixed form **g^wou-no-*. GUNNY, from Pali *goṇa-*, ox. **6.** Suffixed form **g^wōu-ro-*. GAUR, from Sanskrit *gauraḥ,* wild ox. **7.** Zero-grade suffixed form **g^ww-ā-*. HECATOMB, from Greek *hekatombē,* sacrifice of a hundred oxen (*hekaton,* hundred; see **dekm̥**). [Pokorny *g^uōu-* 482.]

i- Pronominal stem. **1.** ILK[1], from Old English *ilca,* same, from Germanic **is-līk-* (**līk-*, like). **2.** YON, from Old English *geon,* that, from Germanic **jaino-, *jeno-*. **3a.** YOND, YONDER, from Old English *geond,* as far as, yonder, from Germanic **jend-;* **b.** BEYOND, from Old English *geondan,* beyond, from Germanic **jendana-*. **4.** Extended forms **yām, *yāi.* YEA, YES, from Old English *gēa,* affirmative particle, and *gēse,* yes (< **gēa-sīe,* "may it be so"; *sīe,* may it be; see **es-**), from Germanic **jā, *jai.* **5.** YET, from Old English *gīet, gīeta,* still (preform uncertain). **6.** Relative stem **yo-* plus particle. IF, from Old English *gif,* if, from Germanic **ja-ba.* **7.** Basic form **i-*, with neuter **id-em.* ID, IDEM, IDENTICAL, IDENTITY; IDENTIFY, from Latin *is,* he (neuter *id,* it), and *īdem,* same. **8.** Suffixed form **i-tero-*. ITERATE; REITERATE, from Latin *iterum,* again. **9.** Suffixed and extended form **it(ə)-em.* ITEM, from Latin *item,* thus, also. **10.** Stem **i-* plus locatival particle **-dha-i.* IBIDEM, from Latin *ibīdem,* in the same place. **11.** Suffixed variant form **e-tero-* in compound **ke-e-tero-* (see **ko-**). [Pokorny 3. *e-* 281.]

kā- To like, desire. Contracted from **kaə-.* **1.** Suffixed form **kā-ro-.* **a.** *(i)* WHORE, from Old English *hōre;* *(ii)* WHOREDOM, from Old Norse compound *hōrdōmr* (*-dōmr,* "condition"; see **dhē-**). Both *(i)* and *(ii)* from Germanic **hōraz* (feminine **hōrōn-*), "one who desires," adulterer; **b.** CARESS, CHARITY, CHERISH; MOTHER CAREY'S CHICKEN, from Latin *cārus,* dear. **2.** Suffixed form **kā-mo-.* KAMA[1]; KAMASUTRA, from Sanskrit *kāmaḥ,* love, desire. [Pokorny *kā-* 515.]

kailo- Whole, uninjured, of good omen. **1a.** HALE[1], WHOLE, from Old English *hāl,* hale, whole; **b.** WHOLESOME, from Old English **hālsum* (> Middle English *holsom*), wholesome; **c.** HAIL[2]; WASSAIL, from Old Norse *heill,* healthy. **a–c** all from Germanic **haila-.* **2.** HEALTH, from Old English *hǣlth,* health, from Germanic **hailithō.* **3.** HEAL, from Old English *hǣlan,* to heal, from Germanic **hailjan.* **4a.** HOLY; HALIBUT, HALIDOM, HOLIDAY, HOLLYHOCK, from Old English *hālig,* holy, sacred; **b.** HALLOW; ALLHALLOWMAS, HALLOWEEN, from Old English *hālgian,* to consecrate, bless, from Germanic derivative verb **hailagōn.* Both **a** and **b** from Germanic **hailaga-.* [Pokorny *kai-lo-* 520.]

kan- To sing. **1.** HEN, from Old English *hen(n),* hen, from Germanic **han(e)nī.* **2a.** CANOROUS, CANT[2], CANTABILE, CANTATA, CANTICLE, CANTILLATE, CANTO, CANTOR, CANZONE, CHANT, CHANTEUSE, CHANTEY, CHANTRY; ACCENT, CHANTICLEER, DESCANT, ENCHANT, INCANTATION, INCENTIVE, PRECENTOR, RECANT, from Latin *canere,* to sing (> *cantāre,* to sing, frequentative of *canere*); **b.** suffixed form **kan-ā-,* "singer," in Latin compound **bou-kanā* (see **gʷou-**). **3.** OSCINE, from Latin *oscen,* a singing bird used in divination (< **obs-cen,* "one that sings before [the augurs]"; *ob-,* before; see **epi**). **4.** Suffixed form **kan-men-.* CHARM, from Latin *carmen,* song, poem. [Pokorny *kan-* 525.]

kap- To grasp.

I. Basic form **kap-.* **1.** HEDDLE, from Old English *hefeld,* thread used for weaving, heddle (a device which grasps the thread), from Germanic **haf-.* **2.** HAFT, from Old English *hæft,* handle, from Germanic **haftjam.* **3.** Form **kap-o-.* HAVE; BEHAVE, from Old English *habban,* to have, hold, from Germanic **habai-, *habēn.* **4.** HEAVY, from Old English *hefig,* heavy, from Germanic **hafiga-,* "containing something," having weight. **5.** HAVEN, from Old English *hæfen,* a haven, from Germanic **hafnō-,* perhaps "place that holds ships." **6.** HAWK[1], from Old English *h(e)afoc,* hawk, from Germanic **habukaz.* **7.** Latin combining form *-ceps* (< **kap-s*), "taker" (see **gʷher-, man-[2], per[1]**). **8.** Probably from this root is Germanic **gaf-,* the source of Provençal *gafar,* to seize: GAFF[1].

II. Suffixed form **kap-yo-.* **1.** HEAVE, HEFT, from Old English *hebban,* to lift, from Germanic **hafjan.* **2.** CABLE, CACCIATORE, CAITIFF, CAPABLE, CAPACIOUS, CAPIAS, CAPSTAN, CAPTION, CAPTIOUS, CAPTIVATE, CAPTIVE, CAPTOR, CAPTURE, CATCH, CATER, CHASE[1], COP[2], COPPER[2]; ACCEPT, ANTICIPATE, CATCHPOLE, CONCEIVE, DECEIVE, EXCEPT, INCEPTION, INCIPIENT, INTERCEPT, INTUSSUSCEPTION, MUNICIPAL, NUNCUPATIVE, OCCUPY, PARTICIPATE, PERCEIVE, PRECEPT, RECEIVE, RECIPE, RECOVER, RECUPERATE, SUSCEPTIBLE, from Latin *capere,* to take, seize, catch.

III. Lengthened-grade variant form **kōp-.* **1a.** BEHOOF, from Old English *behōf,* use, profit, need; **b.** BEHOOVE, from Old English *behōfian,* to have need of. Both **a** and **b** from Germanic compound **bi-hōf,* "that which binds," requirement, obligation (**bi-,* intensive prefix; see **ambhi**), from **hōf-.* **2.** COPEPOD, from Greek *kōpē,* oar, handle. [Pokorny *kap-* 527.] Compare **ghabh-**.

kaput- Head. **1a.** HEAD; BEHEAD, FOREHEAD, from Old English *hēafod,* head; **b.** HETMAN, from Old High German *houbit,* head. Both **a** and **b** from Germanic **haubudam, *haubidam.* **2.** CADDIE, CADET, CAPE[2], CAPITAL[1], CAPITAL[2], CAPITATE, CAPITATION, CAPITELLUM, CAPITULATE, CAPITULUM, CAPO[1], CAPO[2], CAPRICE, CAPTAIN, CATTLE, CAUDILLO, CHAPITER, CHAPTER, CHEF, CHIEF, CHIEFTAIN, CORPORAL[2]; ACHIEVE, BICEPS, DECAPITATE, KERCHIEF, MISCHIEF, OCCIPUT, PRECIPITATE, RECAPITULATE, SINCIPUT, TRICEPS, from Latin *caput,* head [Pokorny *kap-ut-* 529.]

kei- To lie; bed, couch; beloved, dear.

I. Basic form **kei-.* **1.** Suffixed form **kei-wo-.* **a.** HIND[3], from Old English *hīwan,* members of a household, from Germanic **hīwa-;* **b.** HIDE[3], from Old English *hīgid, hīd,* a measure of land (< "household"), from suffixed Germanic form **hīwidō.* **2.** Suffixed form **kei-wi-.* CITY, CIVIC, CIVIL, from Latin *cīvis,* citizen (< "member of a household").

II. O-grade form **koi-.* **1.** Suffixed form **koi-nā-.* INCUNABULUM, from Latin *cūnae,* a cradle. **2.** Suffixed form **koi-m-ā-.* CEMETERY, from Greek *koimān,* to put to sleep.

III. Suffixed zero-grade form **ki-wo-.* SHIVA, from Sanskrit *śiva-,* auspicious, dear. [Pokorny 1. *k̑ei-* 539.]

keiə- To set in motion.

I. Possibly extended o-grade variant from **koid-* in Germanic **hait-,* to call, summon (but this may be from a separate Indo-European root **kaid-*). **1.** HIGHT, from Old English *hātan,* to call, summon, order, from Germanic **haitan.* **2.** Suffixed form **koid-ti-.* **a.** HEST, from Old English *hǣs,* a command, bidding; **b.** BEHEST, from Old English compound *behǣs,* a vow, promise, command (*be-,* intensive prefix; see **ambhi**). Both **a** and **b** from Germanic **haissiz,* from **hait-ti-.*

II. Zero-grade form **kiə-.* **1.** Suffixed iterative form **kiə-eyo-.* CITE; EXCITE, INCITE, OSCITANCY, RESUSCITATE, SOLICITOUS, from Latin *ciēre* (past participle *citus*), with its frequentative *citāre,* to set in motion, summon. **2.** Suffixed form **kiə-neu-.* KINEMATICS, KINESICS, -KINESIS, KINETIC; BRADYKININ, CINEMATOGRAPH, HYPERKINESIA, KINESIOLOGY, KINESTHESIA, TELEKINESIS, from Greek *kīnein,* to move. [Pokorny *k̑ēi-* 538.]

kel- To cover, conceal, save.

I. O-grade form **kol-.* **1a.** HELL, from Old English *hell;* **b.** HEL, from Old Norse *Hel,* the underworld, goddess of death. Both **a** and **b** from Germanic **haljō,* the underworld (< "concealed place"). **2a.** HALL, from Old English *heall,* hall; **b.** VALHALLA, from Old Norse *höll,* hall. Both **a** and **b** from Germanic **hallō,* covered place, hall. **3.** Suffixed form **kol-eyo-.* COLEUS; COLEOPTERAN, COLEOPTILE, COLEORHIZA, from Greek *koleon, koleos,* sheath.

II. Zero-grade form **kl̥-.* **1a.** HOLD[2], HULL, from Old English *hulu,* husk, pod (< "that which covers"); **b.** HOLE, from Old English *hol,* a hollow; **c.** HOLLOW, from Old English *holh,* hole, hollow. **a–c** all from Germanic **hul-.* **2a.** HOLSTER, from Old High German *hulft,* covering; **b.** HOUSING[2], from Medieval Latin *hultia,* protective covering. Both **a** and **b** from suffixed Germanic form **hulftī-.* **3.** Extended form **kl̥ə-* becoming **klā-.* CLANDESTINE, from Latin *clam,* in secret. **4.** Suffixed variant form **kal-up-yo-.* CALYPSO[1], CALYPTRA; APOCALYPSE, EUCALYPTUS, from Greek *kaluptein,* to cover, conceal.

III. Full-grade form **kel-.* **1a.** HELM[2], from Old English *helm,* protection, covering; **b.** HELMET, from Middle English *helmet,* helmet, from a source akin to Frankish **helm,* helmet. Both **a** and **b** from Germanic **helmaz,* "protective covering." **2.** OCCULT, from Latin *occulere* < **ob-kel-* (past participle *occultus*), to cover over (*ob-,* over; see **epi**). **3.** Suffixed form **kel-os-.* COLOR, from Latin *color,* color, hue (< "that which covers"). **4.** Suffixed form **kel-nā-.* CELL, CELLA, CELLAR, CELLARER; RATHSKELLER, from Latin *cella,* storeroom, chamber. **5.** Suffixed form **kel-yo-.* CILIUM, SEEL; SUPERCILIOUS, from Latin *cilium,* lower eyelid.

IV. Lengthened-grade form **kēl-.* CONCEAL, from Latin *cēlāre,* to hide, from suffixed form **kēl-ā-.* [Pokorny 4. *k̑el-* 553.]

kelə- To shout.

I. Variant form **klā-,* contracted from **klaə-.* **1.** LOW[2], from Old English *hlōwan,* to roar, low, from Germanic **hlō-.* **2.** Suffixed form **klā-mā-.* CLAIM, CLAMANT, CLAMOR; ACCLAIM, DECLAIM, EXCLAIM, PROCLAIM, RECLAIM, from Latin *clāmāre,* to call, cry out.

II. O-grade form **kolə-.* **1.** KEELHAUL, from Middle Dutch *halen,* to haul, pull (? < "to call together, summon"). **2.** HALE[2], HAUL; HALYARD, from Old French *haler,* to haul. Both **1** and **2** from Germanic **halōn,* to call.

III. Zero-grade form **kl̥ə-* (> **kal-*). **1.** Suffixed form **kal-yo-.* CONCILIATE, COUNCIL; RECONCILE, from Latin *concilium,* a meeting, gathering (< "a calling together"; *con-,* together; see **kom**). **2.** Suffixed form **kal-end-.* CALENDAR, CALENDS, from Latin *kalendae,* the calends, the first day of the month, when it was publicly announced on which days the nones and ides of that month would fall. **3.** Suffixed form **kal-e-.* ECCLESIA, PARACLETE, from Greek *kalein* (variant *klē-*), to call. **4.** Suffixed form **kal-ā-.* INTERCALATE, NOMENCLATOR, from Latin *calāre,* to call, call out. **5.** Suffixed form **kl̥ə-ro-* or suffixed variant form **klaə-ro-* contracted to **klā-ro-.* CLEAR, GLAIR; AUFKLÄRUNG, CHIAROSCURO, CLAIRVOYANT, DECLARE, ÉCLAIR, from Latin *clārus,* bright, clear.

IV. Possibly extended zero-grade form **kl̥(ə)d-,* becoming **klad-* in suffixed form **klad-ti-.* CLASS, from Latin *classis,* summons, division of citizens for military draft, hence army, fleet, also class in general. [Pokorny 6. *kel-* 548.]

ker-[1] Horn, head; with derivatives referring to horned animals, horn-shaped objects, and projecting parts.

I. Zero-grade form **kr̥-.* **1.** Suffixed form **kr̥-no-.* **a.** *(i)* HORN, HORNBEAM, from Old English *horn,* horn; *(ii)* ALPENHORN, ALTHORN, FLÜGELHORN, HORNBLENDE, from Old High German *horn,* horn. Both *(i)* and *(ii)* from Germanic **hurnaz.*

II. Extended o-grade form **koru-.* **1.** CORYMB, from Greek *korumbos,* uppermost point (< "head"). **2.** CORYPHAEUS, from Greek *koruphē,* head. **3.** Suffixed form **koru-do-.* CORYDALIS, from Greek *korudos,* crested lark. **4.** Suffixed form **koru-nā-.* CORYNEBACTERIUM, from Greek *korunē,* club, mace.

III. Italic and Celtic blend of (**I**) **kr̥-no-* and (**II**) **koru-* yielding **kor-nu-.* CORN[2], CORNEA, CORNEOUS, CORNER, CORNET, CORNICULATE, CORNU; BICORNUATE, CAPRICORN, CORNIFICATION, LAMELLICORN, LONGICORN, TRICORN, UNICORN, from Latin *cornū,* horn.

IV. Extended e-grade form **keru-.* **1.** Suffixed form **kerw-o-,* "having horns." **a.** CERVINE, SERVAL, from Latin *cervus,* deer; **b.** CERVIX, from Latin *cervīx,* neck. **2.** Suffixed form **keru-do-.* **a.** HART, from Old English *heorot,* hart, stag; **b.** HARTEBEEST, from Middle Dutch *hert,* deer, hart. Both **a** and **b** from Germanic **herutaz.*

V. Extended zero-grade form **kr̥ə-.* **1.** CHARIVARI; CHEER, from Greek *karē, karā,* head. **2.** CAROTID, from Greek *karoun,* to stupefy, be stupefied (< "to feel heavy-headed"). **3.** CARROT, CAROTENE, from Greek *karōton,* carrot (from its hornlike shape).

VI. Suffixed further extended form **kr̥əs-no-.* **1.** CRANIUM; MIGRAINE, OLECRANON, from Greek *krānion,* skull, upper part of the head. **2.** HORNET, from Old English *hyrnet,* hornet, from Germanic **hurznuta-.*

VII. E-grade further extended form **kerəs-.* **1.** CARAT, CERASTES, KERATO-; CERATODUS, CERATOPSIAN, CHELICERA, CLADOCERAN, KERATIN, MONOCEROS, RHINOCEROS, TRICERATOPS, from Greek *keras,* horn. **2.** SIRDAR, TARBOOSH, from Persian *sar,* head, from Avestan *sarah-,* head. **3.** Suffixed form **kerəs-ro.* CEREBELLUM, CEREBRUM, SAVELOY, from Latin *cerebrum,* brain.

VIII. Extended form **krei-.* **1.** REINDEER, from Old Norse *hreinn,* reindeer, from Germanic **hraina-.* **2.** RINDERPEST, from Old High German *hrind,* ox, from Germanic **hrinda-.* [Pokorny 1. *k̑er-* 574.]

ker-[2] To grow. **1.** Suffixed form **ker-es-.* CEREAL, CERES, from Latin *Cerēs,* goddess of agriculture, especially the growth of grain. **2.** Extended form **krē-.* **a.** Suffixed form **krē-yā-.* CREATE, CREATURE, CREOLE, GRIOT; PROCREATE, from Latin *creāre,* to bring forth, create, produce (< "to cause to grow"); **b.** suffixed form **krē-sko-.* CRESCENDO, CRESCENT, CREW[1]; ACCRUE, CONCRESCENCE, CONCRETE, DECREASE, EXCRESCENCE, INCREASE, RECRUIT, from Latin *crēscere,* to grow, increase. **3.** Suffixed o-grade form **kor-wo-,* "growing," adolescent. KORE, KOUROS; DIOSCURI, HYPOCORISM, from Greek *kouros, koros,* boy, son, and *korē,* girl. **4.** Compound **sm̥-kēro-,* "of one growth" (**sm̥-,* same, one; see **sem-[1]**). SINCERE, from Latin *sincērus,* pure, clean. [Pokorny 2. *k̑er-* 577.]

kerd- Heart. **1.** Suffixed form **kerd-en-.* HEART, from Old English *heorte,* heart, from Germanic **hertōn-.* **2.** Zero-grade form **kr̥d-.* **a.** CORDATE, CORDIAL, COURAGE, QUARRY[1]; ACCORD, CONCORD, CORDIFORM, DISCORD, MISERICORD, RECORD, from Latin *cor* (stem _cord-_), heart; **b.** suffixed form *kr̥d-yā-. CARDIA, CARDIAC, CARDIO-; ENDOCARDIUM, EPICARDIUM, MYOCARDIUM, PERICARDIUM, from Greek _kardiā_, heart, stomach, orifice. **3.** Possibly *kred-dhə-, "to place trust" (an old religious term; *dhə-, to do, place; see **dhē-**). CREDENCE, CREDIBLE, CREDIT, CREDO, CREDULOUS, GRANT; MISCREANT, RECREANT, from Latin _crēdere_, to believe. [Pokorny _(k̂ered-)_ 579.]

kerp- To gather, pluck, harvest. Variant *karp-. **1.** HARVEST, from Old English _hærfest_, harvest, from Germanic *harbistaz. **2.** CARPET; EXCERPT, SCARCE, from Latin _carpere_, to pluck. **3.** -CARP, CARPEL, CARPO-, -CARPOUS, from Greek _karpos_, fruit. [In Pokorny 4. _sker-_ 938.]

klei- To lean.

I. Full-grade form *klei-. **1.** Suffixed form *klei-n-. DECLINE, INCLINE, RECLINE, from Latin _-clīnāre_, to lean, bend. **2.** Suffixed form *klei-tro-. CLITELLUM, from Latin _clītellae_, packsaddle, from diminutive of *clītra, litter. **3.** Suffixed form *klei-wo-. ACCLIVITY, DECLIVITY, PROCLIVITY, from Latin _clīvus_, a slope. **4.** Suffixed form *klei-tor-, "incline, hill." CLITORIS, from Greek diminutive _kleitoris_, clitoris.

II. Zero grade form *kli-. **1.** LID, from Old English _hlid_, cover, from Germanic *hlid-, "that which bends over," cover. **2.** Suffixed form *kli-n-. LEAN[1], from Old English _hlinian_ and _hleonian_, to lean, from Germanic *hlinēn. **3.** Suffixed form *kli-ent-. CLIENT, from Latin _cliēns_, dependent, follower. **4.** Suffixed form *kli-to- in compound *aus-klit-ā- (see **ous-**). **5.** Suffixed form *kli-n-yo-. -CLINAL, CLINE, -CLINE, -CLINIC, CLINO-; ACLINIC LINE, ANACLISIS, CLINANDRIUM, ENCLITIC, PROCLITIC, from Greek _klīnein_, to lean. **6.** Suffixed form *kli-mn̥. CLIMATE, from Greek _klima_, sloping surface of the earth. **7.** Lengthened zero-grade form *klī-, with lengthening of obscure origin. **a.** Suffixed form *klī-n-ā-. CLINIC; DICLINOUS, MONOCLINOUS, TRICLINIUM, from Greek _klīnē_, bed; **b.** suffixed form *klī-m-. CLIMAX, from Greek _klīmax_, ladder.

III. Suffixed o-grade form *kloi-tr-. LADDER, from Old English _hlǣd(d)er_, ladder, from Germanic *hlaidri-. [Pokorny _k̂lei-_ 600.]

kleu- To hear.

I. Extended form *kleus-. LEER, from Old English _hlēor_, cheek (< "side of the face" < "ear"), from Germanic *hleuza-.

II. Zero-grade form *klu-. **1.** LIST[4], from Old English _hlystan_, to listen, from Germanic *hlustjan. **2.** LISTEN, from Old English _hlysnan_, to listen, from Germanic *hlusinōn. **3.** Suffixed lengthened form *klū-to-. **a.** LOUD, from Old English _hlūd_, loud; **b.** ABLAUT, UMLAUT, from Old High German _hlūt_, sound. Both **a** and **b** from Germanic *hlūdaz, "heard," loud.

III. Full-grade form *kleu-. **1.** Suffixed form *klew-yo-. CLIO, from Greek _kleiein_, to praise, tell. **2.** Suffixed form *klew-es-, "fame," in Greek personal names ending in _-klēs_ (earlier _-kleēs_). HERCULES, from Latin _Herculēs_, from Greek _Hēraklēs, Hērakleēs_, "having Hera's fame" (_Hērā_, Hera). **3.** Suffixed form *kleu-to-. SAROD, from Middle Persian _srōd_, sarod, akin to Avestan _sraota-_, hearing, sound, from Iranian *srauta-. [Pokorny 1. _k̂leu-_ 605.]

ko- Stem of demonstrative pronoun meaning "this."

I. Variant form *ki-. **1a.** HE[1], from Old English _hē_, he; **b.** HIM, from Old English _him_, him (dative of _hē_); **c.** HIS, from Old English _his_, his (genitive of _hē_); **d.** HER, from Old English _hire_, her (dative and genitive of _heo_, she); **e.** IT, from Old English _hit_, it (neuter of _hē_); **f.** HERE, from Old English _hēr_, here; **g.** HENCE, from Old English _heonane, heonon_, from here. **a–g** all from Germanic *hi-. **2.** Suffixed form *ki-tro-. HITHER, from Old English _hider_, hither, from Germanic *hi-thra-. **3.** Suffixed form *ki-s. CIS-, from Latin _cis_, on this side of.

II. Variant form *ke-. **1.** Preposed in *ke-etero- (*e-tero-, a second time, again; see **i-**). ET CETERA, from Latin _cēterus_ (neuter plural _cētera_), the other part, that which remains. **2.** Postposed in Latin _-ce_ (see **nu-**).

III. Attributed by some to this root (but more likely of obscure origin) is Germanic *hind-, behind. **1.** BEHIND, HIND[1], from Old English _behindan_, in the rear, behind (_bi_, at; see **ambhi**). **2.** HINTERLAND, from Old High German _hintar_, behind. **3.** HINDER[1], HINDRANCE, from Old English _hindrian_, to check, hinder, from Germanic derivative verb *hindrōn, to keep back. [Pokorny 1. _ko-_ 609.]

kom Beside, near, by, with. **1a.** ENOUGH, GEMOT, HANDIWORK, WITANAGEMOT, YCLEPT, YEAN, from Old English _ge-_, with, also participial, collective, and intensive prefix; **b.** GEMÜTLICH, GEMÜTLICHKEIT, from Old High German _gi-_, abstract and collective prefix. Both **a** and **b** from Germanic *ga-, together, with (collective and intensive prefix and marker of the past participle). **2.** CUM; COONCAN, from Latin _cum, co-_, with. **3.** CO-, COM-, from Latin _com-_, with (collective and intensive prefix). **4.** British Celtic *kom-, collective prefix, in compound *kombrogos (see **merg-**). **5.** Suffixed form *kom-trā-. CON[1], CONTRA-, CONTRARY, COUNTER[1], COUNTER-, COUNTRY; ENCOUNTER, from Latin _contrā_, against, opposite. **6.** Suffixed form *kom-yo-. COENO-; CENOBITE, EPICENE, KOINE, from Greek _koinos_, common, shared. **7.** Reduced form *ko- in compounds (see **gher-**). [Pokorny _kom_ 612.]

koro- War; also war-band, host, army. **1.** HERIOT, from Old English _here_, army. **2.** ARRIÈRE-BAN, from Old French _herban_, a summoning to military service (_ban_, proclamation, summons; see **bhā-**). **3a.** HARBOR, from Old English _herebeorg_, lodging; **b.** HARBINGER, from Old French _herberge_, lodging. Both **a** and **b** from Germanic compound *harja-bergaz, "army hill," hill-fort, later shelter, lodging, army quarters (*bergaz, hill; see **bhergh-**). **4.** HERALD, from Anglo-Norman _herald_, herald, from Germanic compound *harja-waldaz, "army commander" (*wald-, rule, power). **5.** HARNESS, from Old French _harneis_, harness, from Germanic compound *harja-nestam, "army provisions" (*nestam, food for a journey; see **nes-[1]**). **6.** HARRY, HURRY, from Old English _hergian_, to ravage, plunder, raid, from Germanic denominative *harjōn. **7.** HARANGUE, from Old Italian _aringo, arringa_, public square, from Germanic compound *harihring, assembly, "host-ring" (*hringaz, ring). **1–7** all from Germanic *harjaz, army. [Pokorny _koro-s_ 615.]

kous- To hear. **1a.** HEAR, from Old English _hīeran_, to hear; **b.** HEARKEN, from Old English _he(o)rcnian_, to hearken. Both **a** and **b** from Germanic *hauzjan. **2.** Suffixed form *əkous-yo-. ACOUSTIC, from Greek _akouein_, to hear. [Pokorny 1. _keu-_ 587.]

krei- To sieve, discriminate, distinguish. **1.** Basic form with variant instrumental suffixes. **a.** Suffixed form *krei-tro-. RIDDLE[1], from Old English _hridder, hriddel_, sieve, from Germanic *hridra-; **b.** suffixed form *krei-dhro-. CRIBRIFORM, GARBLE, from Latin _crībrum_, sieve. **2.** Suffixed form *krei-men-. **a.** CRIME, CRIMINAL; RECRIMINATE, from Latin _crīmen_, judgment, crime; **b.** DISCRIMINATE, from Latin _discrīmen_, distinction (_dis-_, apart). **3.** Suffixed zero-grade form *kri-no-. CERTAIN; ASCERTAIN, CONCERN, CONCERT, DECREE, DISCERN, DISCONCERT, EXCREMENT, EXCRETE, INCERTITUDE, RECREMENT, SECERN, SECRET, SECRETARY, from Latin _cernere_ (past participle _crētus_), to sift, separate, decide. **4.** Suffixed zero-grade form *kri-n-yo-. CRISIS, CRITIC, CRITERION; APOCRINE, DIACRITIC, ECCRINE, ENDOCRINE, EPICRITIC, EXOCRINE, HEMATOCRIT, HYPOCRISY, from Greek _krīnein_, to separate, decide, judge, and _krīnesthai_, to explain. [Pokorny 4. _sker-_, Section II. 945.]

kreuə- Raw flesh. **1.** Suffixed o-grade form *krowə-o-. RAW, from Old English _hrēaw_, raw, from Germanic *hrawaz. **2.** Suffixed form *krewə-s-. CREATINE, CREODONT, CREOSOTE, PANCREAS, from Greek _kreas_, flesh. **3.** Suffixed zero-grade form *krū-do- (< *kruə-do-). **a.** CRUDE; ECRU, RECRUDESCE, from Latin _crūdus_, bloody, raw; **b.** CRUEL, from Latin _crūdēlis_, cruel. [Pokorny 1. A. _kreu-_ 621.]

ksun Preposition and preverb meaning "with." **1.** SYN-, from Greek _sun, xun_, together, with. **2.** Reduced form *su(n)-. **a.** SOVIET, from Old Russian compound _sŭvětŭ_, assembly; **b.** SPUTNIK, from Russian _so-, s-_, with, together. **a** and **b** from Old Russian _sŭ(n)-_, with, together. [In Pokorny 2. _sem-_ 902.]

kʷei- To pay, atone, compensate. Suffixed o-grade form *kʷoi-nā-. PAIN, PENAL, PENALTY, PINE[2], PUNISH; IMPUNITY, PENOLOGY, PUNITORY, REPINE, SUBPOENA, from Greek _poinē_, fine, penalty. [Pokorny 1. _kᵘ̯ei-(t-)_ 636.]

kʷel- Also **kʷelə-**.

I. Basic form *kʷel-. COLONY, CULT, CULTIVATE, CULTURE, KULTUR; INCULT, INQUILINE, SILVICULTURE, from Latin _colere_, to till, cultivate, inhabit (< *kʷel-o-).

II. Suffixed form *kʷel-es-. TELIC, TELIUM, TELO-, TELOS; ENTELECHY, TALISMAN, TELEOLOGY, TELEOST, TELEUTOSPORE, from Greek _telos_, "completion of a cycle," consummation, perfection, end, result.

III. Suffixed reduplicated form *kʷ(e)-kʷl-o-, wheel, circle. **1.** WHEEL, from Old English _hwēol, hweogol_, wheel, from Germanic *hwewlaz. **2.** CYCLE, CYCLO-, CYCLOID, CYCLONE, CYCLOSIS; BICYCLE, ENCYCLICAL, EPICYCLE, from Greek _kuklos_, circle, wheel. **3.** CHAKRA, CHUKKER, from Sanskrit _cakram_, circle, wheel. **4.** Metathesized form *kʷe-lkʷ-o-. CHARKHA, from Old Persian *carka-, wheel.

IV. O-grade form *kʷol-. **1.** Suffixed form *kʷol-so-, "that on which the head turns," neck. **a.** _(i)_ HAWSE, from Old Norse _hāls_, neck, ship's bow; _(ii)_ RINGHALS, from Middle Dutch _hals_, neck; _(iii)_ HABERGEON, HAUBERK, from Old French _hauberc_, hauberk, from Germanic compound *h(w)als-berg-, "neck-protector," gorget (*bergan, to protect). _(i)–(iii)_ all from Germanic *h(w)alsaz; **b.** COL, COLLAR, COLLET, CULLET; ACCOLADE, DECOLLATE[1], DÉCOLLETÉ, MACHICOLATE, TORTICOLLIS, from Latin _collum_, neck. **2.** Suffixed form *kʷol-ā-. -COLOUS; PRATINCOLE, from Latin _-cola_ and _incola_, inhabitant (_in-_, in; see **en**). **3.** Suffixed form *kʷol-o-. **a.** ANCILLARY, from Latin _anculus_, "he who bustles about," servant (_an-_, short for _ambi-_, around, about; see **ambhi**); **b.** POLE[1], PULLEY, from Greek _polos_, axis of a sphere; **c.** BUCOLIC, from Greek _boukolos_, cowherd, from _-kolos_, herdsman. **4.** Suffixed form *kʷol-es- (probably a blend of o-grade *kʷol-o- and expected e-grade *kʷel-es-). CALASH, from Slavic _kolo, koles-_, wheel. **5.** Suffixed o-grade form *kʷol-eno- in Old Iranian compound *vahā-carana- (see **wes-[3]**).

V. Suffixed zero-grade variant form *kʷl̥ə-i-. PALIMPSEST, PALINDROME, PALINGENESIS, PALINODE, from Greek _palin_, again (< "revolving"). [Pokorny 1. _kᵘ̯el-_ 639.]

kʷetwer- Four.

I. O-grade form *kʷetwor-. **1.** Probably Germanic *fe(d)wor- (with _f-_ from following numeral *fimf, five; see **penkʷe**). **a.** FOUR, from Old English _fēower_, four; **b.** FORTY, from Old English _fēowertig_, forty; **c.** FOURTEEN; FORTNIGHT, from Old English _fēowertēne_, fourteen (_-tēne_, ten; see **dekm̥**). **2.** QUATRAIN; CATER-CORNERED, QUATTROCENTO, from Latin _quattuor_, four. **3.** CZARDAS, from Old Iranian _cathwārō_, four.

II. Multiplicatives *kʷeturs, *kʷetrus, and combining forms *kʷetur-, *kʷetru-. **1.** CAHIER, CARILLON, CARNET, CASERN, QUATERNARY, QUATERNION, QUIRE[1], from Latin _quater_, four times. **2.** CADRE, QUADRATE, QUADRILLE[1], QUARREL[2], QUARRY[2]; ESCADRILLE, SQUAD, SQUARE, TROCAR, from Latin _quadrum_, square. **3.** QUADRI-, from Latin _quadri-_, four. **4.** QUADRANT, from Latin _quadrāns_, a fourth part. **5.** QUARANTINE, from Latin _quadrāgintā_, forty (_-gintā_, ten times; see **dekm̥**). **6.** QUADRICENTENARY, from Latin _quadri(n)gentī_, four hundred. **7.** Variant form *kʷet(w)r̥-. **a.** TETRA-, from Greek _tetra-_, four; **b.** TESSERA; DIATESSARON, from Greek _tessares, tettares_, four; **c.** TETRAD, from Greek _tetras_, group of four; **d.** zero-grade form *kʷt(w)r̥-. TRAPEZIUM, from Greek _tra-_, four.

III. Ordinal adjective *kʷetur-to-. **1a.** FOURTH, from Old English _fēortha, fēowertha_, fourth; **b.** FIRKIN, from Middle Dutch _veerde_, fourth; **c.** FARTHING, from Old English _fēorthing, fēorthung_, fourth part of a penny. **a–c** all from Germanic *fe(d)worthōn-. **2.** QUADRILLE[2], QUADROON, QUART, QUARTAN, QUARTER, QUARTO, from Latin _quārtus_, fourth, quarter. [Pokorny _kᵘ̯etu̯er-_ 642.]

kʷo- Also **kʷi-**. Stem of relative and interrogative pronouns.**1a.** WHO, WHOSE, WHOM, from Old English _hwā, hwæs, hwǣm_, who, whose, whom, from Germanic personal pronouns *hwas, *hwasa, *hwam; **b.** WHAT, from Old English _hwæt_, what, from Germanic pronoun *hwat; **c.** WHY, from Old English _hwȳ_, why, from Germanic adverb *hwī; **d.** WHICH, from Old English _hwilc, hwelc_, which, from Germanic relative pronoun *hwa-līk- (*līk-, body, form); **e.** HOW, from Old English _hū_, how, from Germanic adverb *hwō; **f.** _(i)_ WHEN, from Old English _hwenne, hwanne_, when; _(ii)_ WHENCE, from Old English _hwanon_, whence. Both _(i)_ and _(ii)_ from Germanic adverb *hwan-; **g.** WHITHER, from Old English _hwider_, whither, from Germanic adverb *hwithrē; **h.** WHERE, from Old English _hwǣr_, where, from Germanic adverb *hwar-. **a–h** all from Germanic *hwa-, *hwi-. **2a.** WHETHER; NEITHER, from Old English _hwæther_, *hwether,* which of two, whether; **b.** EITHER, from Old English *ǣghwæther, ǣther,* either, from Germanic phrase **aiwo gihwatharaz,* "ever each of two" (**aiwo, *aiwi,* ever, and **gi-* from **ga-,* collective prefix; see **aiw-** and **kom**). Both **a** and **b** from Germanic **hwatharaz.* **3.** QUA, QUIBBLE, QUORUM, from Latin *quī,* who. **4.** HIDALGO, QUIDDITY, QUIDNUNC, QUIP; KICKSHAW, from Latin *quid,* what, something. **5.** QUASI, from Latin *quasi,* as if (< *quam* + *sī,* if; see **swo-**), from *quam,* as, than, how. **6.** QUODLIBET, from Latin *quod,* what. **7.** Suffixed form **kʷo-ti.* **a.** QUOTE, QUOTIDIAN, QUOTIENT; ALIQUOT, from Latin *quot,* how many; **b.** further suffixed form **kʷo-ty-o-.* POSOLOGY, from Greek *posos,* how much. **8.** QUONDAM, from Latin *quom,* when. **9.** COONCAN, from Latin *quem,* whom. **10.** QUANTITY, from Latin *quantus,* how great. **11.** QUALITY; KICKSHAW, from Latin *quālis,* of what kind. **12.** CUE[2], from Latin *quandō,* when (from **kʷām* + *-dō,* to, till). **13.** NEUTER, from Latin *uter,* either of two, ultimately from **kʷo-tero-* (becoming *-cuter* in such compounds as *necuter,* neither, from which *uter* was abstracted out by false segmentation). **14.** UBIQUITY, from Latin *ubi,* where, ultimately from locative case **kʷo-bhi* (becoming *-cubi* in such compounds as *alicubi,* somewhere, from which *ubi* was abstracted out by false segmentation, perhaps under the influence of *ibi,* there). **15.** CHEESE[3], from Old Persian **ciš-ciy,* something (< **kʷid-kʷid*). [Pokorny *k̯ʷo-* 644.]

kwon- Dog. **1.** CYNIC; CYNOSURE, PROCYON, QUINSY, from Greek *kuōn,* dog. **2.** Suffixed zero-grade form **kwn̥-to-.* **a.** HOUND, from Old English *hund,* dog; **b.** DACHSHUND, from Old High German *hunt,* dog; **c.** KEESHOND, from Middle Dutch *hond,* dog. **a–c** all from Germanic **hundaz.* **3.** Nominative form **kwō.* CORGI, from Welsh *ci,* dog. **4.** Variant **kan-i-.* CANAILLE, CANARY, CANICULAR, CANINE, CHENILLE, KENNEL[1], from Latin *canis,* dog. [Pokorny *k̑uon-* 632.]

kʷrep- Body, form, appearance. Probably a verbal root meaning "to appear." **1.** Suffixed form **kʷrep-es-.* MIDRIFF, from Old English *hrif,* belly from Germanic **hrefiz-.* **2.** Suffixed zero-grade form **kʷr̥p-es-.* CORPORAL[1], CORPORAL[3], CORPORATE, CORPOREAL, CORPOSANT, CORPS, CORPSE, CORPULENCE, CORPUS, CORPUSCLE, CORSAGE, CORSE, CORSET; LEPRECHAUN, from Latin *corpus,* body, substance. [Pokorny 1. *krep-* 620.]

kʷr̥mi- Worm. Rhyme word to **wr̥mi-,* worm (see **wer-**). CARMINE, CRIMSON, KERMES, from Arabic *qirmiz,* kermes, borrowed from Sanskrit compound *kr̥mi-ja-,* "(red dye) produced by worms" (*-ja-,* produced; see **genə-**), from *kr̥mi-,* worm. [Pokorny *k̯ʷr̥mi-* 649.]

laks- Salmon. Suffixed form **laks-o-.* **1.** LOX[1], from Old High German *lahs,* salmon. **2.** GRAVLAX, from Swedish *lax,* salmon. Both **1** and **2** from Germanic **lahsaz.* [In Pokorny *lak̑-* 653.]

leg- To collect; with derivatives meaning "to speak." **1.** Perhaps Germanic **lēkjaz,* enchanter, one who speaks magic words. LEECH[1], from Old English *lǣce,* physician. **2.** LECTERN, LECTION, LECTURE, LEGEND, LEGIBLE, LEGION, LESSON; COIL[1], COLLECT[1], DILIGENT, ELECT, FLORILEGIUM, INTELLIGENT, NEGLECT, PRELECT, SACRILEGE, SELECT, SORTILEGE, from Latin *legere,* to gather, choose, pluck, read. **3.** LEXICON, LOGION, -LOGUE, -LOGY; ALEXIA, ANALECTS, ANTHOLOGY, CATALOG, DIALECT, DIALOGUE, DYSLEXIA, ECLECTIC, ECLOGITE, ECLOGUE, HOROLOGE, LECTOTYPE, PROLEGOMENON, from Greek *legein,* to gather, speak, with o-grade derivative *logos,* a gathering, speech (see also **6** below for derivatives independently built to *logos*). **4.** Suffixed form **leg-no-.* LIGNEOUS, LIGNI-, from Latin *lignum,* wood, firewood (< "that which is gathered"). **5.** Possibly lengthened-grade form **lēg-.* **a.** LEGAL, LEGIST, LEGITIMATE, LEX, LOYAL; LEGISLATOR, PRIVILEGE, from Latin *lēx,* law (? < "collection of rules"); **b.** LEGACY, LEGATE; COLLEAGUE, COLLEGIAL, DELEGATE, RELEGATE, from Latin denominative *lēgāre,* to depute, commission, charge (< "to engage by contract"). (It is also possible, but uncertain, that Latin *lēx* comes, like English *law,* from a form meaning "that which is set or laid down," from **legh-**.) **6.** Suffixed o-grade form **log-o-.* LOGIC, LOGISTIC, LOGO-, LOGOS, -LOGY; ANALOGOUS, APOLOGUE, APOLOGY, DECALOGUE, EPILOGUE, HOMOLOGOUS, LOGARITHM, PARALOGISM, PROLOGUE, SYLLOGISM, from Greek *logos,* speech, word, reason. [Pokorny *leĝ-* 658.]

legh- To lie, lay. **1.** Suffixed form **legh-yo-.* **a.** LIE[1], from Old English *licgan,* to lie, from Germanic **ligjan;* **b.** *(i)* LAY[1], LEDGE, LEDGER, from Old English *lecgan,* to lay; *(ii)* BELAY, from Old English *belecgan,* to cover, surround (*be-,* over; see **ambhi**). Both *(i)* and *(ii)* from Germanic **lagjan.* **2.** Suffixed form **legh-ro-.* **a.** LAIR, from Old English *leger,* lair; **b.** LEAGUER[1]; BELEAGUER, from Middle Dutch *leger,* lair, camp; **c.** LAAGER, LAGER; STALAG, from Old High German *legar,* bed, lair. **a–c** all from Germanic **legraz.* **3.** LEES, from Medieval Latin *lia,* sediment, from Celtic **leg-yā-.* **4.** Lengthened-grade form **lēgh-.* LOW[1], from Old Norse *lāgr,* low, from Germanic **lēga-,* "lying flat," low. **5.** Suffixed form **legh-to-.* COVERLET, LITTER; WAGON-LIT, from Latin *lectus,* bed. **6.** Suffixed o-grade form **logh-o-.* **a.** LAW; BYLAW, DANELAW, from Old Norse **lagu, lag-,* law, "that which is set down"; **b.** FELLOW, from Old Norse *lag,* a laying down; **c.** OUTLAW, from Old Norse *lög,* law; **d.** ANLAGE, VORLAGE, from Old High German *lāga,* act of laying. **a–d** all from Germanic **lagam.* **7.** LAGAN, from Old Norse *lögn,* dragnet (< "that which is laid down"), from Germanic **lag-īnō-.* **8.** Suffixed o-grade form **logh-o-.* LOCHIA, from Greek *lokhos,* childbirth, place for lying in wait. [Pokorny *legh-* 658, 2. *leĝh-* 660.]

leigh- To lick. **1.** ELECTUARY, LEKVAR, LICHEN, from Greek *leikhein,* to lick. **2.** Zero-grade form **ligh-.* **a.** LICK, from Old English *liccian,* to lick; **b.** LECHER, from Old French *lechier,* to live in debauchery. Both **a** and **b** from Germanic **likkōn.* **3.** Nasalized zero-grade form **li-n-gh-.* ANILINGUS, CUNNILINGUS, from Latin *lingere,* to lick. [Pokorny *leiĝh-* 668.]

leikʷ- To leave. **1.** Basic form **leikʷ-.* ECLIPSE, ELLIPSIS, from Greek *leipein,* to leave. **2.** O-grade form **loikʷ-.* **a.** Suffixed form **loikʷ-nes-.* LOAN, from Old Norse *lān,* loan, from Germanic **laihwniz;* **b.** LEND, from Old English *lǣnan,* to lend, loan from Germanic denominative **laihwnjan.* **3.** Zero-grade form **likʷ-.* **a.** Germanic compound **ain-lif-* (see **oi-no-**); **b.** Germanic compound **twa-lif-* (see **dwo-**). Both **a** and **b** from Germanic **-lif-,* left. **4.** Nasalized zero-grade form **li-n-kʷ-.* DELINQUENT, DERELICT, RELIC, RELINQUISH, from Latin *linquere,* to leave. [Pokorny *leik̯ʷ-* 669.]

leu- To loosen, divide, cut apart.

I. Extended Germanic root **leus-.* **1a.** LORN, LOSEL, from Old English *-lēosan,* to lose; **b.** *(i)* FORLORN, from Old English *forlēosan,* to forfeit, lose; *(ii)* FORLORN HOPE, from Dutch *verliezen* (past participle *verloren*), to lose. Both *(i)* and *(ii)* from Germanic **fer-leusan, *far-leusan* (**fer-, *far-,* prefix denoting rejection or exclusion; see **per**[1]). Both **a** and **b** from Germanic **leusan* (with Old English and Dutch past participle *loren* from Germanic **luzana-,* from Indo-European suffixed zero-grade form **lus-ono-*). **2a.** LEASING, -LESS, from Old English *lēas,* "loose," free from, without, untrue, lacking; **b.** LOSE, LOSS, from Old English *los,* loss; **c.** LOOSE, from Old Norse *lauss, louss,* loose; **d.** LOESS, from German dialectal *lösch,* loose. **a–d** all from Germanic **lausa-.* **3.** LEISTER, from Old Norse *ljōsta,* to strike, perhaps from Germanic **leustan.*

II. Basic form **leu-.* **1.** LAG[2], probably from a source akin to Swedish *lagg,* barrel stave (< "split piece of wood"), from Germanic **lawwō.* **2.** Zero-grade form **lu-.* **a.** LYO-, LYSIS, LYSO-, -LYTE, LYTIC, -LYTIC; ANALYSIS, CATALYSIS, DIALYSIS, LYASE, PALSY, PARALYSIS, TACHYLYTE, from Greek *lūein,* to loosen, release, untie; **b.** LUES, from Latin *luēs,* plague, pestilence (< "dissolution, putrefaction"); **c.** prefixed form **se-lu-* (**se-,* apart; see **s(w)e-**). SOLUBLE, SOLUTE, SOLVE; ABSOLUTE, ABSOLVE, ASSOIL, DISSOLVE, RESOLUTE, RESOLVE, from Latin *solvere,* to loosen, untie. [Pokorny 2. *leu-* 681.]

leudh- To mount up, grow. **1.** Basic form **leudh-.* LANDSLEIT, from Old High German *liut,* person, people, from Germanic **liud-i-.* **2.** Suffixed form **leudh-ero-.* LIBERAL, LIBERATE, LIBERTINE, LIBERTY, LIVERY; DELIVER, from Latin *līber,* free (the precise semantic development is obscure). [Pokorny 1. *leudh-* 684.]

leu(ə)- To wash. **1.** Suffixed form **lou-kā-.* LYE, from Old English *lēag,* lye, from Germanic **laugō.* **2.** Suffixed form **lou-tro-.* **a.** LATHER, from Old English *lēthran, līthran,* to lather; **b.** LUTEFISK, from Old Norse *laudhr,* soap, foam. **3.** Variant form **law-.* **a.** LOMENT, LOTION; ABLUTION, ALLUVION, COLLUVIUM, DELUGE, DILUTE, ELUENT, ELUTE, ELUVIUM, from Latin *lavere,* to wash (in compounds, *-luere*); **b.** suffixed form **law-ā-.* LAUNDER, LAVABO, LAVAGE, LAVATORY, LAVE, LAVISH, from Latin *lavāre,* to wash; **c.** LATRINE, from Latin *lavātrīna, lātrīna,* a bath, privy. **4.** O-grade form **lou-.* PYROLUSITE, from Greek *louein,* to wash. [Pokorny *lou-* 692.]

leuk- Light, brightness.

I. Basic form **leuk-.* **1.** Suffixed form **leuk-to-.* **a.** LIGHT[1], from Old English *lēoht, līht,* light; **b.** LIGHTNING, from Old English *līhtan,* to shine, from Germanic **leuhtjan,* to make light. Both **a** and **b** from Germanic **leuhtam.* **2.** Basic form **leuk-.* LUCINA, LUCULENT, LUX; LUCIFER, LUCIFERIN, from Latin *lūx,* light. **3.** Suffixed form **leuk-smen-.* LIMBERS, LIMN, LUMEN, LUMINARY, LUMINOUS; ILLUMINATE, PHILLUMENIST, from Latin *lūmen,* light, opening. **4.** Suffixed form **leuk-snā-.* LUNA, LUNAR, LUNATE, LUNATIC, LUNE, LUNULA; MEZZALUNA, SUBLUNARY, from Latin *lūna,* moon. **5.** Suffixed form **leuk-stro-.* **a.** LUSTER, LUSTRUM, from Latin *lūstrum,* purification; **b.** ILLUSTRATE, from Latin *lūstrāre,* to purify, illuminate. **6.** Suffixed form **leuko-dhro-.* LUCUBRATE; ELUCUBRATION, from Latin *lūcubrāre,* to work by lamplight. **7.** Suffixed form **leuk-o-.* LEUKO-, from Greek *leukos,* clear, white.

II. O-grade form **louk-.* **1.** Suffixed form **louk-o-.* **a.** LEA, from Old English *lēah,* meadow (< "place where light shines"), from Germanic **lauhaz;* **b.** LEVIN, from Middle English *levin,* lightning, from Germanic **lauh-ubni-.* **2.** Suffixed (iterative) form **louk-eyo-.* LUCENT, LUCID; ELUCIDATE, NOCTILUCA, PELLUCID, RELUCENT, TRANSLUCENT, from Latin *lūcēre,* to shine.

III. Zero-grade form **luk-.* **1.** Suffixed form **luk-sno-.* LINK[2], LYCHNIS, from Greek *lukhnos,* lamp. **2.** Attributed by some to this root (but more likely of obscure origin) is Greek *lunx,* lynx (as if from its shining eyes): LYNX, OUNCE[2]. [Pokorny *leuk-* 687.]

lūs- Louse. LOUSE, from Old English *lūs,* louse, from Germanic **lūs-.* [Pokorny *lūs-* 692.]

man-¹ Also **mon-.** Man. **1.** Extended forms **manu-, *manw-.* **a.** MAN; LEMAN, NORMAN[1], from Old English *man(n)* (plural *menn*), man; **b.** FUGLEMAN, LANDSMAN[2], from Old High German *man,* man; **c.** MANIKIN, MANNEQUIN, from Middle Dutch *man,* man; **d.** YEOMAN, from Old Frisian *man,* man; **e.** NORMAN[1], OMBUDSMAN, from Old Norse *madhr, mannr,* man; **f.** ALEMANNI, possibly from Germanic **Ala-manniz,* tribal name (< "all men"; **ala-,* all). **a–f** all from Germanic **manna-* (plural **manniz*); **g.** MANU, from Sanskrit *manuḥ,* man, from Indo-Iranian **manu-.* **2.** MENSCH, from Old High German *mennisco,* human, from Germanic adjective **manniska-,* human, from **manna-* (see **1**). **3.** MUZHIK, from Russian *muzh,* man, male, from Slavic suffixed form **mon-gyo-.* [Pokorny *manu-s* 700.]

man-² Hand. **1a.** MANACLE, MANAGE, MANÈGE, MANNER, MANUAL, MANUBRIUM, MANUS; AMANUENSIS, MAINTAIN, MANEUVER, MANICOTTI, MANICURE, MANIFEST, MANSUETUDE, MANUFACTURE, MANUMIT, MANURE, MANUSCRIPT, MASTIFF, MORTMAIN, QUADRUMANOUS, from Latin *manus,* hand; **b.** MANIPLE, MANIPULATION, from Latin *manipulus,* handful (*-pulus,* perhaps -ful; see **pelə-**[1]). **2.** Suffixed form **man-ko-,* maimed in the hand. MANQUÉ, from Latin *mancus,* maimed, defective. **3.** EMANCIPATE, from Latin compound *manceps,* "he who takes by the hand," purchaser (*-ceps,* agential suffix, "taker"; see **kap-**). **4.** MANDAMUS, MANDATE, MAUNDY THURSDAY; COMMAND, COMMANDO, COMMEND, COUNTERMAND, DEMAND, RECOMMEND, REMAND, from Latin compound *mandāre,* "to put into someone's hand," entrust, order (*-dere,* to put; see **dhē-**). [Pokorny *mə-r* 740.]

me-¹ Oblique form of the personal pronoun of the first person singular. For the nominative see **eg. 1.** ME, MYSELF, from Old English *mē̆* (dative and accusative), from Germanic **mē̆-.* **2.** Possessive adjective **mei-no-.* **a.** MINE[2], MY, from Old English *mīn,* my; **b.** MYNHEER, from Middle Dutch *mijn,* my. Both **a** and **b** from Germanic **mīn-.* **3.** Possessive adjective **me-yo-.* MADAME, MADONNA, MONSIEUR, from Latin *meus,* mine. **4.** Genitive form **me-wo.* MAVOURNEEN, from Old Irish *mo,* my. [Pokorny 1. *me-* 702.]

me-² In the middle of. **1.** Suffixed form **me-dhi.* MIDWIFE, from Old English *mid,* among, with, from Germanic **mid-.* **2.** Suffixed form **me-ta.* META-, from Greek _meta,_ between, with, beside, after. [Pokorny 2. _me-_ 702.] See also **medhyo-**.

mē-^{1} To measure. Contracted from earlier _*meə-_.
I. Basic form _mē-_. **1.** Suffixed form _*mē-lo-_. MEAL^{2}; PIECEMEAL, from Old English _mǣl,_ "measure, mark, appointed time, time for eating, meal," from Germanic _*mēlaz_. **2.** Suffixed form _*mē-ti-_. **a.** MEASURE, MENSURAL; COMMENSURATE, DIMENSION, IMMENSE, from Latin _mētīrī,_ to measure; **b.** METIS, from Greek _mētis,_ wisdom, skill. **3.** Possibly Greek _metron,_ measure, rule, length, proportion, poetic meter (but referred by some to **med-**): METER^{1}, METER^{2}, METER^{3}, -METER, METRICAL, -METRY; DIAMETER, GEOMETRY, ISOMETRIC, METROLOGY, METRONOME, SYMMETRY. **4.** Reduplicated zero-grade form _*mi-mə-_. MAHOUT, MAUND, from Sanskrit _mimīte,_ he measures.
II. Extended and suffixed forms _*mēn-, *mēn-en-, *mēn-ōt-, *mēn-s-_, moon, month (an ancient and universal unit of time measured by the moon). **1.** MOON; MONDAY, from Old English _mōna,_ moon, from Germanic _*mēnōn-_. **2.** MONTH, from Old English _mōnath,_ month, from Germanic _*mēnōth-_. **3.** MENO-; AMENORRHEA, CATAMENIA, DYSMENORRHEA, EMMENAGOGUE, MENARCHE, MENISCUS, MENOPAUSE, from Greek _mēn, mēnē,_ month. **4.** MENSES, MENSTRUAL, MENSTRUATE; BIMESTRIAL, SEMESTER, TRIMESTER, from Latin _mēnsis,_ month. [Pokorny 3. _mē-_ 703, _mēnōt_ 731.]

mē-^{2} To cut down grass or grain with a sickle or scythe. Contracted from _*(ə)meə-_. **1.** MOW^{2}, from Old English _māwan,_ to mow, from Germanic _*mē-_. **2.** Suffixed form _*mē-ti-_. AFTERMATH, from Old English _mǣth,_ a mowing, a mown crop, from Germanic _*mēthiz_. **3.** Suffixed form _*mē-twā-_, a mown field. MEAD^{2}, MEADOW, from Old English _mǣd,_ meadow, from Germanic _*mēdwō_. [Pokorny 2. _mē-_ 703.]

med- To take appropriate measures. **1a.** METE^{1}, from Old English _metan,_ to measure (out), from Germanic _*metan;_ **b.** MEET^{2}, from Old English _gemǣte,_ "commensurate," fit (_ge-_, with; see **kom**), from Germanic derivative _*mǣtō,_ measure. **2a.** MEDICAL, MEDICATE, MEDICINE, MEDICO; METHEGLIN, REMEDY, from Latin _medērī,_ to look after, heal, cure; **b.** MEDITATE, from Latin _meditārī,_ to think about, consider, reflect. **3.** Suffixed form _*med-es-_. **a.** MODEST; IMMODEST, from Latin _modestus,_ "keeping to the appropriate measure," moderate; **b.** MODERATE; IMMODERATE, from Latin _moderārī,_ "to keep within measure," to moderate, control. Both **a** and **b** from Latin _*modes-_, replacing _*medes-_ by influence of _modus_ (see **5** below). **4.** MEDUSA, from Greek _medein,_ to rule (feminine participle _medousa_ < _*med-ont-ya_). **5.** Suffixed o-grade form _*mod-o-_. MODAL, MODE, MODEL, MODERN, MODICUM, MODIFY, MODULATE, MODULE, MODULUS, MOLD^{1}, MOOD^{2}, MOULAGE; ACCOMMODATE, COMMODE, COMMODIOUS, COMMODITY, from Latin _modus,_ measure, size, limit, manner, harmony, melody. **6.** Suffixed o-grade form _*mod-yo-_. MODIOLUS, MUTCHKIN, from Latin _modius,_ a measure of grain. **7.** Possibly lengthened o-grade form _*mōd-_. **a.** MOTE^{2}, MUST^{1}, from Old English _mōtan,_ to have occasion, to be permitted or obliged; **b.** EMPTY, from Old English _ǣmetta,_ rest, leisure, from Germanic compound _*ē-mōt-ja-_ (prefix _*ē-_, meaning uncertain). Both **a** and **b** from Germanic _*mōt-_, ability, leisure. [Pokorny 1. _med-_ 705.]

medhu- Honey; also mead. **1.** MEAD^{1}, from Old English _meodu,_ mead, from Germanic _*medu_. **2.** AMETHYST, METHYLENE, from Greek _methu,_ wine. [Pokorny _médhu-_ 707.]

medhyo- Middle. **1a.** MID^{1}, MIDST; AMID, from Old English _midd(e),_ middle; **b.** MIDDLE, from Old English _middel,_ middle, from West Germanic diminutive form _*middila-;_ **c.** MIDGARD, from Old Norse _Midhgardhr,_ Midgard, from Germanic compound _*midja-gardaz,_ "middle zone," name of the earth conceived as an intermediate zone lying between heaven and hell (_*gardaz,_ enclosure, yard; see **gher-**). **a–c** all from Germanic _*midja-_. **2.** MEAN^{3}, MEDAL, MEDIAL, MEDIAN, MEDIASTINUM, MEDIATE, MEDIUM, MEZZANINE, MIZZEN, MOIETY, MULLION; INTERMEDIATE, MEDIEVAL, MEDIOCRE, MEDITERRANEAN; MERIDIAN, MEZZALUNA, MEZZOTINT, MILIEU, from Latin _medius,_ middle, half. **3.** MESO-, from Greek _mesos,_ middle. [Pokorny _medhi-_ 706.] See also **me-^{2}**.

meg- Great. **1a.** MICKLE, MUCH, from Old English _micel, mycel,_ great; **b.** MICKLE, from Old Norse _mikill_. Both **a** and **b** from Germanic suffixed form _*mik-ila-_. **2.** Suffixed form _*mag-no-_. MAGNATE, MAGNITUDE, MAGNUM; MAGNANIMOUS, MAGNIFIC, MAGNIFICENT, MAGNIFICO, MAGNIFY, MAGNILOQUENT, from Latin _magnus,_ great. **3.** Suffixed (comparative) form _*mag-yos-_. **a.** MAJOR, MAJOR-DOMO, MAJORITY, MAJUSCULE, MAYOR, from Latin _māior,_ greater; **b.** MAESTOSO, MAJESTY, from Latin _māiestās,_ greatness, authority; **c.** MAESTRO, MAGISTERIAL, MAGISTRAL, MAGISTRATE, MASTER, MISTER, MISTRAL, MISTRESS, from Latin _magister,_ master, high official (< "he who is greater"). **4.** Suffixed (superlative) form _*mag-samo-_. MAXIM, MAXIMUM, from Latin _maximus,_ greatest. **5.** Suffixed (feminine) form _*mag-ya-_, "she who is great." MAY^{2}, MAY, from Latin _Maia,_ name of a goddess. **6.** Suffixed form _*meg-ə-(l-)_. MEGA-, MEGALO-; ACROMEGALY, OMEGA, from Greek _megas_ (stem _megal-_), great. **7.** Suffixed (superlative) form _*meg-(ə)-isto-_. ALMAGEST, HERMES TRISMEGISTUS, from Greek _megistos,_ greatest. **8.** Variant (Indo-Iranian) form _*megh-_. MAHABHARATA, MAHARAJAH, MAHARANI, MAHARISHI, MAHATMA, MAHAYANA, MAHOUT, from Sanskrit _mahā-, mahat-,_ great. [Pokorny _meĝ(h)-_ 708.]

meik- Also **meig-**. To mix. **1.** Zero-grade variant form _*mig-_. AMPHIMIXIS, APOMIXIS, PANMIXIA, from Greek _mignunai,_ to mix, and noun _mixis_ (< _*mig-ti-_), a mingling. **2.** Suffixed zero-grade form _*mik-sk-_. MEDDLE, MEDLEY, MÉLANGE, MELEE, MESCLUN, MESTIZO, MISCELLANEOUS, MISCIBLE, MIX, MIXTURE, MUSTANG; ADMIX, COMMIX, IMMIX, MISCEGENATION, PELL-MELL, PROMISCUOUS, from Latin _miscēre_ (past participle _mixtus_), to mix. **3.** Possibly Germanic _*maisk-_ (phonological details unclear). MASH, from Old English _*māsc, *mācs, māx-,_ mashed malt. [Pokorny _mei-ḱ-_ 714.]

mel- False, bad, wrong. **1.** MAL-, MALICE, MALIGN; DISMAL, MALADY, MALARIA, MALEDICT, MALEFACTOR, MALEFIC, MALENTENDU, MALEVOLENCE, MALISON, MALVERSATION, from Latin _malus,_ bad, and _male,_ ill (> _malignus,_ harmful). **2.** Perhaps suffixed zero-grade form _*ml̥-s-_. BLAME, BLASPHEME, from Greek _blasphēmos,_ blasphemous, perhaps from _*ml̥s-bhā-mo-_, "speaking evil" (_*bhā-_, to speak; see **bhā-**). **3.** Suffixed form _*mel-yo-_. MARKHOR, from Avestan _mairiia-,_ treacherous. [Pokorny 2. _mel-_ 719, _mēlo-_ 724.]

melə- Also **mel-**. To crush, grind; with derivatives referring to various ground or crumbling substances (such as flour) and to instruments for grinding or crushing (such as millstones). **1.** O-grade form _*mol-_. MAELSTROM, from Middle Dutch _malen,_ to whirl, from Germanic _*mal-_. **2.** Full-grade form _*mel-_. MEAL^{1}, from Old English _melu,_ flour, meal, from Germanic suffixed form _*mel-wa-_. **3.** Zero-grade form _*ml̥-_. MOLD^{3}, MOLDER, from Old English _molde,_ soil, from Germanic suffixed form _*mul-dō_. **4.** Full-grade form _*mel-_. **a.** MEUNIÈRE, MILL^{1}, MOLA^{2}, MOLAR^{2}, MOLE^{4}, MOULIN; EMOLUMENT, IMMOLATE, ORMOLU, from Latin _molere,_ to grind (grain), and its derivative _mola,_ a millstone, mill, coarse meal customarily sprinkled on sacrificial animals; **b.** possible suffixed form _*mel-iyo-_. MEALIE, MILIARY, MILIUM, MILLET; GROMWELL, from Latin _milium,_ millet. **5.** Suffixed variant form _*mal-ni-_. MALLEABLE, MALLEOLUS, MALLET, MALLEUS, MAUL; PALL-MALL, from Latin _malleus,_ hammer, mallet. **6.** Zero-grade form _*ml̥-_. AMYLUM, MYLONITE, from Greek _mulē, mulos,_ millstone, mill. **7.** Possibly extended form _*mlī-_. BLINTZ, from Old Russian _blinŭ,_ pancake. [Pokorny 1. _mel-_ 716.]

melg- To rub off; also to milk.
I. 1. Zero-grade form _*ml̥g-_. EMULSION, from Latin _mulgēre,_ to milk. **2.** Full-grade form _*melg-_. **a.** MILK, from Old English _meolc, milc;_ **b.** MILCH, from Old English _-milce,_ milch, from Germanic suffixed form _*meluk-ja-_, giving milk; **c.** MILCHIG, from Old High German _miluh,_ milk. **a–c** all from Germanic _*melkan,_ to milk, contaminated with an unrelated noun for milk, cognate with the Greek and Latin forms given in **II** below, to form the blend _*meluk-_.
II. Included here to mark the unexplained fact that no common Indo-European noun for milk can be reconstructed is another root _*g(a)lag-, *g(a)lakt-,_ milk, found only in: **a.** GALACTIC, GALACTO-, GALAXY; AGALACTIA, POLYGALA, from Greek _gala_ (stem _galakt-_), milk; **b.** LACTATE^{1}, LACTEAL, LACTESCENT, LACTO-, LETTUCE, from Latin _lac,_ milk; **c.** the blended Germanic form cited in **I. 2.** above. [Pokorny _melĝ-_ 722, _glag-_ 400.]

melit- Honey. **1.** HYDROMEL, MARMALADE, MELILOT, OENOMEL, from Greek _meli_ (stem _melit-_), honey. **2a.** MELLIFEROUS, MELLIFLUOUS, MOLASSES, from Latin _mel_ (stem _mell-_), honey, from _*meld-_, syncopated from _*melid-;_ **b.** suffixed zero-grade form _*ml̥d-to-_, "honied." MOUSSE, from Latin _mulsus,_ honey-sweet. **3.** MILDEW, from Old English _mildēaw,_ honeydew, nectar, from Germanic compound _*melith-dauwaz,_ honeydew (a substance secreted by aphids on leaves; it was formerly imagined to be distilled from the air like dew; _*dauwaz,_ dew), from _*melith-_. [Pokorny _meli-t_ 723.]

men-^{1} To think; with derivatives referring to various qualities and states of mind and thought.
I. Zero-grade form _*mn̥-_. **1.** Suffixed form _*mn̥-ti-_. **a.** MIND, from Old English _gemynd,_ memory, mind, from Germanic _*ga-mundi-_ (_*ga-_, intensive prefix; see **kom**); **b.** MENTAL^{1}; AMENT^{2}, DEMENT, from Latin _mēns_ (stem _ment-_), mind; **c.** MENTION, from Latin _mentiō,_ remembrance, mention. **2.** Suffixed form _*mn̥-to-_. AUTOMATIC, from Greek _-matos,_ "willing." **3.** Suffixed form _*mn̥-yo-_. **a.** MAENAD, from Greek _mainesthai,_ to be mad; **b.** AHRIMAN, from Avestan _mainiiuš,_ spirit. **4a.** MANIA, MANIAC, MANIC, from Greek _maniā,_ madness; **b.** BALLETOMANE, from Greek _-manēs,_ ardent admirer.
II. Full-grade form _*men-_. **1.** Suffixed form _*men-ti-_. **a.** MINNESINGER, from Old High German _minna,_ love; **b.** MINIKIN, from Middle Dutch _minne,_ love. Both **a** and **b** from Germanic _*minthjō_. **2a.** MEMENTO, from Latin reduplicated form _meminisse,_ to remember; **b.** COMMENT, from Latin _comminīscī,_ to contrive by thought (_com-_, intensive prefix; see **kom**); **c.** REMINISCENT, from Latin _reminīscī,_ to recall, recollect (_re-_, again, back); **d.** possibly Latin _Minerva,_ name of the goddess of wisdom: MINERVA. **3a.** MENTOR, from Greek _Mentōr,_ Mentor, man's name (probably meaning "adviser"); **b.** -MANCY, MANTIC, MANTIS, from Greek _mantis,_ seer (vocalism obscure). **4.** MANDARIN, MANTRA, from Sanskrit _mantraḥ,_ counsel, prayer, hymn. **5.** Suffixed form _men-es-_. EUMENIDES, from Greek _menos,_ spirit.
III. O-grade form _*mon-_. **1.** Suffixed (causative) form _*mon-eyo-_. MONISH, MONITION, MONITOR, MONSTER, MONUMENT, MUSTER; ADMONISH, DEMONSTRATE, PREMONITION, SUMMON, from Latin _monēre,_ to remind, warn, advise. **2.** Suffixed o-grade form _*mon-twa_. MOSAIC, MUSE, MUSEUM, MUSIC, from Greek _Mousa,_ a Muse.
IV. Extended form _*mnā-_, contracted from _*mnaə-_. **1.** AMNESIA, AMNESTY, ANAMNESIS, from Greek reduplicated form _mimnēskein,_ to remember. **2.** MNEMONIC, from Greek _mnēmōn,_ mindful. **3.** MNEMOSYNE, from Greek _mnēmē,_ memory.
V. Suffixed form _*men-s_ (zero-grade _*mn̥-s_), mind, in Indo-European verb phrase _*mens dhē-_, "to set mind" (_*dhē-_, to put; see **dhē-**), underlying compound noun _*mn̥s-dhē-_. AHURA MAZDA, MAZDAISM, ORMAZD, from Avestan _mazdā-,_ wise. [Pokorny 3. _men-_ 726, _mendh-_ 730.]

men-^{2} Small, isolated. **1.** MANOMETER, from Greek _manos,_ rare, sparse. **2.** Suffixed o-grade form _*mon-wo-_. MONAD, MONASTERY, MONK, MONO-; PSEUDOMONAD, from Greek _monos,_ alone, single, sole. **3.** Possibly also suffixed form _*men-i-_, a small fish. MINNOW, from Middle English _meneu,_ a small fish, from a source akin to Old English _myne, mynwe,_ minnow. [Pokorny 4. _men-_ 728, $m_{e}ni$- 731.]

mer- To rub away, harm.
I. 1. NIGHTMARE, from Old English _mare, mære,_ goblin, incubus, from Germanic _*marōn-_, goblin. **2.** MARASMUS; AMARANTH, from Greek _marainein,_ to waste away, wither. **3.** Probably suffixed zero-grade form _*mr̥-to-_, "ground down." MORTAR, from Latin _mortārium,_ mortar. **4.** Possibly extended root _*merd-_. MORDACIOUS, MORDANT, MORDENT, MORSEL; PREMORSE, REMORSE, from Latin _mordēre,_ to bite. **5.** Possibly suffixed form _*mor-bho-_. MORBID, from Latin _morbus,_ disease (but this is more likely of unknown origin).
II. Possibly the same root is _*mer-_, "to die," with derivatives referring to death and to human beings as subject to death. **1.** Zero-grade form _*mr̥-_. **a.** Suffixed form _*mr̥-tro-_. MURDER, from Old English _morthor,_ murder, from Germanic suffixed form _*mur-thra-;_ **b.** suffixed form _*mr̥-ti-_. MORT^{1}, MOR-

TAL; AMORTIZE, MORTIFY, POSTMORTEM, from Latin *mors* (stem *mort-*), death; **c.** suffixed form **mr̥-yo-*. MORIBUND, MORTGAGE, MORTMAIN, MORTUARY, MURRAIN, from Latin *morī,* to die, with irregular past participle *mortuus* (< **mr̥-two-*), replacing older **mr̥-to-* (for which see **d**); **d.** prefixed and suffixed form **n̥-mr̥-to-*, "undying, immortal." (**n̥-*, negative prefix; see **ne**). *(i)* IMMORTAL, from Latin *immortālis;* *(ii)* AMBROSIA, from Greek *ambrotos,* immortal, divine (*a-* + *-mbrotos, brotos,* mortal); *(iii)* AMRITA, from Sanskrit *amṛtam,* immortality (*a-* + *mṛta-*, dead). **2.** Suffixed o-grade form **mor-t-yo-*. MANTICORE, from Greek *mantikhōras* (corrupted from *marti(o)khōras*), manticore, probably from Iranian compound **martiya-khvāra-*, "man-eater" (**khvāra-*, eating), from Old Persian *martiya-*, a mortal man. [Pokorny 4. *mer-*, 5. *mer-* 735.]

merg- Boundary, border. **1a.** MARK[1], from Old English *mearc,* boundary, landmark, sign, trace; **b.** MARGRAVE, from Middle Dutch *marc,* border; **c.** MARCH[2], MARQUEE, MARQUIS, MARQUISE, from Old French *marc, marche,* border country; **d.** MARCHESE, MARCHIONESS, from Medieval Latin *marca,* boundary, border; **e.** DEMARCATION, from Old Italian *marcare,* to mark out; **f.** MARK[2], from Old English *marc,* a mark of weight or money; **g.** MARKKA, from Swedish *mark,* a mark of money; **h.** MARKA, from Middle High German *marke,* mark of money. **a–h** all from Germanic **mark-*, boundary, border territory; also to mark out a boundary by walking around it (ceremonially "beating the bounds"); also a landmark, boundary marker, and a mark in general (and in particular a mark on a metal currency bar, hence a unit of currency); these various meanings are widely represented in Germanic descendants and in Romance borrowings. **2.** LETTERS OF MARQUE, MARQUETRY; REMARK, from Old Norse *merki,* a mark, from Germanic **markja-*, mark, border. **3.** MARC, MARCH[1], from Frankish **markōn,* to mark out, from Germanic denominative verb **markōn.* **4.** MARGIN; EMARGINATE, from Latin *margō,* border, edge. **5.** Celtic variant form **mrog-*, territory, land. CYMRY, from Welsh *Cymro,* Wales, from British Celtic **kom-brogos,* fellow countryman (**kom-*, collective prefix; see **kom**), from **brogos,* district. [Pokorny *mereĝ-* 738.]

mori- Body of water; lake (?), sea (?). **1a.** MERE[2]; MERMAID, from Old English *mere,* sea, lake, pond; **b.** MARRAM, from a Scandinavian source akin to Old Norse *marr,* sea; **c.** MEERSCHAUM, from Old High German *mari,* sea; **d.** MEERKAT, from Middle Dutch *meer,* sea. **a–d** all from Germanic **mari-*. **2a.** MARSH, from Old English *mersc, merisc,* marsh; **b.** MORASS, from Old French *maresc, mareis,* marsh. Both **a** and **b** from Germanic **mariska-*, water-logged land. **3.** MAAR, MARE[2], MARINARA, MARINE, MARITIME; BÊCHE-DE-MER, CORMORANT, MARICULTURE, ORMER, ULTRAMARINE, from Latin *mare,* sea. [Pokorny *mori* 748.]

mūs- A mouse; also a muscle (from the resemblance of a flexing muscle to the movements of a mouse). **1.** MOUSE, from Old English *mūs* (plural *mȳs*), mouse, from Germanic **mūs-* (plural **mūsiz*). **2.** MURINE, MUSCLE, MUSSEL, MUSTELINE, from Latin *mūs,* mouse. **3.** MYELO-, MYO-; EPIMYSIUM, MYOSOTIS, MYSTICETE, PERIMYSIUM, SYRINGOMYELIA, from Greek *mūs,* mouse, muscle. **4.** Perhaps suffixed shortened form **mus-ko-*. MUSCADET, MUSCAT, MUSCATEL, MUSK, MUST[5]; NUTMEG, from Sanskrit *muṣkaḥ,* testicle, scrotum (? < "little mouse"). [Pokorny *mūs* 752.]

nas- Nose. **1.** NOSE, NUZZLE; NOSTRIL, from Old English *nosu,* nose, from Germanic zero-grade form **nusō.* **2.** NESS, from Old English *næss,* headland, from Germanic **nasjaz.* **3.** Lengthened-grade form **nās-*. **a.** NARIS, from Latin *nāris,* nostril; **b.** expressive form **nāss-*. NASAL, NASO-; NASTURTIUM, PINCE-NEZ, from Latin *nāsus,* nose. **4.** NARK[2], from Romany *nāk,* nose, from expressive Indo-Aryan form **nakka-*. [Pokorny *nas-* 755, *neu-ks-* 768.]

n̥dher- Under. **1a.** UNDER, UNDER-, from Old English *under,* under; **b.** U-BOAT, from Old High German *untar,* under. Both **a** and **b** from Germanic **under-*. **2.** INFERIOR, from Latin *īnferus,* lower. **3.** INFERNAL, INFERNO, from Latin *īnfernus,* lower. **4.** INFRA-, from Latin *īnfrā,* below. [Pokorny *n̥dhos* 771.]

ne Not. **1a.** NAUGHT, NAUGHTY, NEITHER, NEVER, NILL, NO[1], NO[2], NONE, NOR[1], NOT, NOTHING, from Old English *ne,* not, and *nā,* no; **b.** NAY, from Old Norse *ne,* not; **c.** NIX[2], from Old High German *ne, ni,* not. **a–c** all from Germanic **ne-*, **na-*. **2.** ANNUL, NEFARIOUS, NESCIENCE, NEUTER, NICE, NULL, NULLIFY, NULLIPARA, from Latin *ne-*, not, and *nūllus,* none (*ne-* + *ūllus,* any; see **oi-no-**). **3.** NIMIETY, from Latin *nimis,* too much, excessively, very (< **ne-mi-s,* "not little"; **mi-*, little). **4.** NIHILISM, NIHILITY, NIL; ANNIHILATE, from Latin *nihil, nīl,* nothing, contracted from *nihilum,* nothing (< **ne-hīlum,* "not a whit, nothing at all"; *hīlum,* a thing, trifle; origin unknown). **5.** NON-; NONPLUS, NONSUIT, from Latin *nōn,* not (< **ne-oinom,* not one thing"; **oino-*, one; see **oi-no-**). **6.** NISI, from Latin *nisi,* unless, from Archaic Latin *nesei* (*sei,* if; see **swo-**). **7a.** NEGLECT, NEGLIGEE, NEGOTIATE, from Latin prefix *neg-*, not; **b.** NEGATE; ABNEGATE, DENY, RENEGADE, RENEGE, from Latin *negāre,* to deny. Both **a** and **b** from Italic **nek,* not. **8.** NEPENTHE, from Greek *nē-*, not. **9.** Zero-grade combining form **n̥-*. **a.** *(i)* UN-[1], from Old English *un-*, not; *(ii)* ZUGUNRUHE, from Old High German *un-*, not. Both *(i)* and *(ii)* from Germanic **un-;* **b.** IN-[1], from Latin *in-*, not; **c.** A-[1], AN-, from Greek *a-*, *an-*, not; **d.** AHIMSA, from Sanskrit *a-*, *an-*, not; **e.** compound **n̥-mr̥-to-* (see **mer-**). [Pokorny 1. *nĕ* 756.]

nebh- Cloud. **1.** Suffixed form **nebh-(e)lo-*. **a.** NIFLHEIM, from Old Norse *nifl-*, "mist" or "dark," probably from Germanic **nibilaz;* **b.** NIBELUNG, from Old High German *Nibulunc, Nibilung,* from Germanic suffixed patronymic form **nibul-unga-*, beside Old High German *nebul,* mist, fog, from Germanic **neblaz.* **2.** Suffixed form **nebh-elā-*. **a.** NEBULA, NEBULOUS, from Latin *nebula,* cloud; **b.** NEPHELINE; NEPHELOMETER, from Greek *nephelē,* cloud. **3.** Nasalized form **ne-m-bh-*. NIMBUS, from Latin *nimbus,* rain, cloud, aura. [Pokorny 2. *(enebh-)* 315.]

nek- Death. **1.** INTERNECINE, PERNICIOUS, from Latin *nex* (stem *nec-*), death. **2.** Suffixed (causative) o-grade form **nok-eyo-*. NOCENT, NOCUOUS, NUISANCE; INNOCENT, INNOCUOUS, from Latin *nocēre,* to injure, harm. **3.** Suffixed o-grade form **nok-s-*. NOXIOUS; OBNOXIOUS, from Latin *noxa,* injury, hurt, damage entailing liability. **4.** Suffixed full-grade form **nek-ro-*. NECRO-, NECROSIS; NECROMANCY, from Greek *nekros,* corpse. **5.** NECTAR, NECTARINE, from Greek *nektar,* the drink of the gods, "overcoming death" (**tar-*, overcoming; see **terə-[2]**). [Pokorny *neḱ-* 762.]

nekʷ-t- Night. Probably from a verbal root **negʷ-*, to be dark, be night. O-grade form **nokʷ-t-*. **1a.** NIGHT; FORTNIGHT, from Old English *niht, neaht,* night; **b.** KRISTALLNACHT, from Old High German *naht,* night. Both **a** and **b** from Germanic **naht-*. **2.** NOCTI-, NOCTURN, NOCTURNAL, EQUINOX, from Latin *nox* (stem *noct-*), night. **3.** NOCTUID, NOCTULE, from Latin *noctua,* night owl. **4.** NYCTALOPIA, NYCTITROPISM, from Greek *nux* (stem *nukt-*), night. **5.** Suffixed plain verbal root **negʷ-ro-*, dark. NEGRO, NIELLO, NIGRESCENCE, NIGROSINE; DENIGRATE, from Latin *niger,* black. [Pokorny *neku̯-(t-)* 762.]

nem- To assign, allot; also to take. **1a.** NIM[1], NUMB; BENUMB, from Old English *niman,* to take, seize; **b.** NIMBLE, from Old English *nǣmel,* quick to seize, and *numol,* quick at learning, seizing; **c.** NIM[2], from Old High German *nëman,* to take. **a–c** all from Germanic **neman,* to take. **2.** NEMESIS; ECONOMY, from Greek *nemein,* to allot. **3.** O-grade form **nom-*. **a.** NOME, -NOMY; ANOMIE, ANTINOMIAN, ANTINOMY, ASTRONOMER, ASTRONOMY, AUTONOMOUS, DEUTERONOMY, METRONOME, NOMOGRAPH, NOMOLOGY, NOMOTHETIC, NUMISMATIC, from Greek *nomos,* portion, usage, custom, law, division, district; **b.** NOMA, from Greek *nomē,* pasturage, grazing, hence a spreading, a spreading ulcer; **c.** NOMAD, from Greek *nomas,* wandering in search of pasture; **d.** NUMMULAR, NUMMULITE, from Greek *nomimos,* legal. **4.** Perhaps suffixed o-grade form **nom-eso-*. NUMBER, NUMERAL; ENUMERATE, INNUMERABLE, SUPERNUMERARY, from Latin *numerus,* number, division. [Pokorny 1. *nem-* 763.]

nepōt- Grandson, nephew. Feminine **neptī-*. NEPHEW, NEPOTISM, NIECE, from Latin *nepōs,* grandson, nephew, and *neptis,* granddaughter, niece. [Pokorny *nepōt-* 764.]

ner- Man; basic sense "vital, strong." Oldest form **əner-*. ANDRO-, -ANDROUS, -ANDRY; PHILANDER, from Greek *anēr* (stem *andr-*, from zero-grade form **ənr-*), man. [Pokorny 1. *ner-(t-)* 765.]

nes-[1] To return safely home. **1.** HARNESS, from Old French *harneis,* harness, possibly from a Germanic source akin to Old English, Old High German (in composition), and Old Norse *nest,* food for a journey, from Germanic **nes-tam.* **2.** Suffixed o-grade form **nos-to-*. NOSTALGIA, from Greek *nostos,* a return home. [Pokorny *nes-* 766.]

nes-[2] Oblique cases of the personal pronoun of the first person plural. For the nominative see **we-**. **1.** Zero-grade form **n̥s-*. US, from Old English *ūs,* us (accusative), from Germanic **uns.* **2.** Suffixed (possessive) zero-grade form **n̥s-ero-*. OUR, OURS, from Old English *ūser, ūre,* our, from Germanic **unsara-*. **3.** O-grade form **nos-*, with suffixed (possessive) form **nos-t(e)ro-*. NOSTRATIC, NOSTRUM; PATERNOSTER, from Latin *nōs,* we, and *noster,* our. [Pokorny 3. *ne-* 758.]

newn̥ Nine. **1.** NINE, NINETEEN, NINETY, NINTH, from Old English *nigon,* nine, with derivatives *nigontig,* ninety, and *nigontēne,* nineteen (*-tēne,* ten; see **dekm̥**), from Germanic **nigun,* variant of **niwun.* **2.** NOVEMBER, NOVENA; NONAGENARIAN, from Latin *novem,* nine (< **noven,* with *m* for *n* by analogy with the *m* of *septem,* seven, and *decem,* ten). **3.** Ordinal form **neweno-*. NONA-, NONES, NOON; NONAGON, NONANOIC ACID, from Latin *nōnus,* ninth. **4.** Prothetic or prefixed forms **ənewn̥, *ənwn̥.* ENNEAD, from Greek *ennea,* nine (< **ennewa, *enwa-*). [Pokorny *e-neu̯en* 318.]

newo- New. Related to **nu-**. **1.** Suffixed form **new-yo-*. **a.** NEW, from Old English *nēowe, nīwe,* new; **b.** NYNORSK, SPAN-NEW, from Old Norse *nȳr,* new. Both **a** and **b** from Germanic **neuja-*. **2.** Basic form **newo-*. NEO-, NEON, NEOTERIC; MISONEISM, from Greek *newos, neos,* new. **3.** Suffixed form **new-aro-*. ANEROID, from Greek *nēron,* water, from *nēros,* fresh (used of fish and of water), contracted from *nearos,* young, fresh. **4.** Basic form **newo-*. NOVA, NOVATION, NOVEL[1], NOVEL[2], NOVELTY, NOVICE; INNOVATE, RENOVATE, from Latin *novus,* new. **5.** Suffixed form **new-er-ko-*. NOVERCAL, from Latin *noverca,* stepmother (< "she who is new"). [Pokorny *neu̯os* 769.]

nobh- Also **ombh-**. Navel; later also "central knob," boss of a shield, hub of a wheel. **1a.** NAVE[2], from Old English *nafu, nafa,* hub of a wheel; **b.** AUGER, from Old English *nafogār,* auger, from Germanic compound **nabō-gaizaz,* tool for piercing wheel hubs (**gaizaz,* spear, piercing tool). Both **a** and **b** from Germanic **nabō.* **2.** Variant form **ombh-*. UMBO, from Latin *umbō,* boss of a shield. **3.** Suffixed form **nobh-alo-*. NAVEL, from Old English *nafela,* navel, from Germanic **nabalō.* **4.** Suffixed variant form **ombh-alo-*. **a.** UMBILICUS; NOMBRIL, from Latin *umbilīcus,* navel; **b.** OMPHALOS, from Greek *omphalos,* navel. [Pokorny 1. *(enebh-)* 314.]

nō̆-mn̥ Name. **1.** NAME, from Old English *nama,* name, from Germanic **namōn-*. **2.** NOMINAL, NOMINATE, NOUN; AGNOMEN, BINOMIAL, COGNOMEN, DENOMINATE, IGNOMINY, MISNOMER, NOMENCLATOR, NUNCUPATIVE, PRAENOMEN, PRONOUN, RENOWN, from Latin *nōmen,* name, reputation. **3.** ONOMASTIC, -ONYM, -ONYMY; ALLONYM, ANONYMOUS, ANTONOMASIA, EPONYM, EPONYMOUS, EUONYMUS, HETERONYMOUS, HOMONYMOUS, MATRONYMIC, METONYMY, ONOMATOPOEIA, PARONOMASIA, PARONYMOUS, PATRONYMIC, PSEUDONYM, SYNONYMOUS, from Greek *onoma, onuma,* name (assimilated from *enuma,* preserved in proper names in Laconian). **4.** MONIKER, from Old Irish *ainm,* name. [Pokorny *en(o)mn̥-* 321.]

nu- Now. Related to **newo-**. **1.** NOW, from Old English *nū,* now. **2.** QUIDNUNC, from Latin *nunc,* now (< **nun-ce; -ce,* a particle meaning "this," "here"; see **ko-**). [Pokorny *nu-* 770.]

oi-no- One, unique.

I. Basic form **oi-no-*. **1a.** A[1], AN[1], ONCE, ONE; ALONE, ANON, ATONE, LONE, LONELY, NONCE, NONE, from Old English *ān,* one; **b.** ELEVEN, from Old English *endleofan,* eleven, from Germanic compound **ain-lif-*, "one left (beyond ten)," eleven (**lif-*, left over; see **leikʷ-**); **c.** EINKORN, TURNVEREIN, from Old High German *ein,* one. **a–c** all from Germanic **aina-*. **2.** UNI-, UNION, UNITE, UNITY; COADUNATE, TRIUNE, UNANIMOUS, UNICORN, UNIVERSE, from Latin *ūnus,* one. **3.** INDRICOTHERE, from Old Russian *inŭ,* one. **4.** Latin compound **ne-oinom* (see **ne**).

II. Suffixed form **oino-ko-*. **1.** ANY, from Old English *ǣnig,* one, anyone, from Germanic **ainiga-*. **2.** UNIQUE, from Latin *ūnicus,* sole, single. **3.** INCH[1],

OUNCE[1], UNCIAL; QUINCUNX, from Latin *ūncia,* one twelfth of a unit.

III. Suffixed form **oino-lo-.* Latin *ūllus,* any, in compound **ne-ūllus, nūllus* (see **ne**). [Pokorny 3. D. *e-* 281.]

oktō(u) Eight. **1a.** EIGHT, EIGHTEEN, EIGHTY, from Old English *eahta,* eight, with derivatives *eahtatig,* eighty, and *eahtatēne,* eighteen (-*tēne,* ten; see **dekm̥**); **b.** ATTO-, from Old Norse *āttjān,* eighteen (*tjān,* ten; see **dekm̥**). Both **a** and **b** from Germanic **ahtō.* **2.** OC-TANS, OCTANT, OCTAVE, OCTAVO, OCTET, OCTO-, OCTO-BER, OCTONARY; OCTODECIMO, OCTOGENARIAN, from Latin *octō,* eight. **3.** OCTAD, OCTO-; OCTOPUS, from Greek *oktō,* eight. [Pokorny *oktō(u)* 775.]

okʷ- To see. **1a.** EYE; DAISY, from Old English *ēage,* eye; **b.** WALLEYED, WINDOW, from Old Norse *auga,* eye; **c.** OGLE, from Low German *oog, oge,* eye. **a–c** all from Germanic **augōn-* (perhaps with taboo deformation). **2.** Suffixed form **okʷ-olo-.* **a.** EYELET, OCEL-LUS, OCULAR, OCULIST, OCULUS, ULLAGE; ANTLER, INOC-ULATE, MONOCLE, OCULOMOTOR, PINOCHLE, from Latin *oculus,* eye; **b.** INVEIGLE, from French *aveugle,* blind, from Gallo-Latin compound **ab-oculus,* blind, calqued on Gaulish *exs-ops,* blind ("with eyes out": *exs-,* out + *ops,* eye). **3.** Form **okʷ-s.* CERATOPSIAN, METOPIC, MYOPIA, NYCTALOPIA, Pelops, PHLOGOPITE, PROSOPOGRAPHY, PROSOPOPEIA, PYROPE, TRICERATOPS, from Greek *ōps,* eye (and stem **op-,* to see). **4.** Suffixed form **okʷ-ti-.* OPSIN, -OPSIS, -OPSY; AUTOPSY, DROPSY, IODOPSIN, RHODOPSIN, SYNOPSIS, from Greek *opsis,* sight, appearance. **5.** Suffixed form **okʷ-to-.* OPTIC; DIOPTER, OPTOELECTRONICS, OPTOMETRY, PAN-OPTIC, from Greek *optos,* seen, visible. **6.** Suffixed form **okʷ-ā-.* METOPE, from Greek *opē,* opening. **7.** Suffixed form **okʷ-mn̥.* OMMATIDIUM, from Greek *omma* (< **opma*), eye. **8.** Suffixed form **okʷ-tro-.* CATOPTRIC, from Greek *katoptron,* "back-looker," mirror (*kata-,* down, back). **9.** OPHTHALMO-; EXOPH-THALMOS, from Greek *ophthalmos,* eye (with taboo deformation). **10.** Zero-grade form **ək̄ʷ-* (from oldest full-grade root form **aokʷ-*), in compounds (see **ant-, ghwer-**). [Pokorny *okʷ-* 775.]

orbh- To change allegiance, pass from one status to another. Suffixed form **orbh-o-,* "bereft of father," also "deprived of free status." **1.** ORPHAN, from Greek *orphanos,* orphaned. **2.** ROBOT, from Czech *robota,* compulsory labor, drudgery, from Old Church Slavonic *rabota,* servitude, from *rabŭ,* slave, from Old Slavic **orbŭ.* **3.** GASTARBEITER, from Old High German *arabeit(i),* labor, from Germanic **arb-aithi-* (source of suffix uncertain). [Pokorny *orbho-* 781.]

ors- Buttocks, backside. **1.** Suffixed form **ors-o-.* **a.** ARSE, ASS[2], from Old English *ærs, ears,* backside; **b.** DODO, from Middle Dutch *ærs,* backside, tail. Both **a** and **b** from Germanic **arsaz.* **2.** Suffixed form **ors-ā-.* **a.** URO-[2], -UROUS; ANTHURIUM, ANURAN, COE-NURUS, CYNOSURE, DASYURE, EREMURUS, OXYURIASIS, SQUIRREL, from Greek *ourā,* tail; **b.** SILURID, from Greek *silouros,* sheatfish, probably from *ourā,* tail (with an obscure first element). [Pokorny *ers-* 340.]

ōs- Mouth. **1.** ORAL, OS[1], OSCILLATE, OSCULATE, OSCU-LUM, OSTIUM, USHER; INOSCULATE, ORIFICE, ORINASAL, OROTUND, OSCITANCY, PERORAL, from Latin *ōs* (stem *ōr-*), mouth, face, orifice, and derivative *ōstium* (< suffixed form **ōs-to-*), door. **2.** Possibly Latin *aurīga,* charioteer (< **ōr-īg-,* "he who manages the (horse's) bit"; *-īg-,* lengthened from *-ig-,* driving, from **ag-;* see **ag-**): AURIGA. [Pokorny 1. *ōus-* 784.]

ost- Bone. **1.** OS[2], OSSEOUS, OSSICLE, OSSUARY; OSSI-FRAGE, OSSIFY, from Latin *os* (stem *oss-*), bone. **2.** OS-TEO-; ENDOSTEUM, EXOSTOSIS, PERIOSTEUM, SYNOSTOSIS, TELEOST, from Greek *osteon,* bone. **3.** Suffixed form **ost-r-.* **a.** OSTRACIZE, OSTRACOD, OSTRACON; OSTRACO-DERM, from Greek *ostrakon,* shell, potsherd; **b.** from **ast-.* OYSTER, from Greek *ostreon,* oyster; **c.** AS-TRAGAL, ASTRAGALUS, from Greek *astragalos,* vertebra, ball of the ankle joint, knucklebone, Ionic molding. [Pokorny *ost(h)-* 783.]

ous- Ear. **1.** Suffixed form **ous-en-.* EAR[1], from Old English *ēare,* ear, from Germanic **auzōn-.* **2.** Suffixed form **aus-i-.* **a.** AURAL, AURICLE; AURIFORM, ORMER, from Latin *auris,* ear. **3.** AUSCULTATION, SCOUT[1], from Latin *auscultāre,* to listen to (< **aus-klit-ā-; *aus-* + **kli-to-,* inclined; see **klei-**[1]). **4.** Suffixed basic form **ous-os-.* OTIC, OTO-[1]; MYOSITIS, PAROTID GLAND, from Greek *ous* (stem *ōt-*), ear. **5.**

Basic form **ous-* in Greek compound **lag-ous-* (see **slēg-**). [Pokorny 2. *ōus-* 785.]

owi- Sheep. **1.** EWE, from Old English *ēowe, eōwu,* ewe, from Germanic **awiz.* **2.** OVINE, from Latin *ovis,* sheep. [Pokorny *óu̯i-s* 784.]

pā- To protect, feed. Contracted from **paə-.* **1.** Suffixed form **pā-trom.* **a.** FODDER, from Old English *fōdor,* fodder; **b.** FORAGE, FORAY, FOURRAGÈRE, from Old French *feurre,* fodder; **c.** FUR, FURRIER, from Old French *forre, fuerre,* trimming made from animal skin, fur (< *"*sheath, case, lining*"*). **a–c** all from Germanic **fōdram.* **2.** Suffixed form **pā-dhlom* (doublet of **pā-trom*). PABULUM, from Latin *pābulum,* food, fodder. **3.** Extended form **pāt-.* **a.** FOOD, from Old English *fōda,* food, from Germanic **fōd-;* food; **b.** FEED, from Old English *fēdan,* to feed, from Germanic denominative **fōdjan,* to give food to; **c.** suffixed form **pāt-tro-.* FOSTER, from Old English *fōstor,* food, nourishment, from Germanic **fōstra-.* **4.** Extended form **pās-.* **a.** Suffixed form **pās-sko-.* PAS-TURE; ANTIPASTO, REPAST, from Latin *pāscere,* to feed; **b.** suffixed form **pās-tor-.* PASTERN, PASTOR, PESTER, from Latin *pāstor,* shepherd; **c.** suffixed form **pās-t-ni-.* PANADA, PANATELA, PANIC GRASS, PANNIER, PANOCHA, PANTRY, PASTILLE, PENUCHE; APPANAGE, COMPANION[1], COMPANY, from Latin *pānis,* bread. **5.** Suffixed form **pā-tor-.* BEZOAR, from Persian *pād,* protecting and from Iranian **pātar-* (Avestan *pātar-*). **6.** Suffixed form **pā-won-,* protector. SA-TRAP, from Old Persian *khshathra-pāvā,* protector of the province. [Pokorny *pā-* 787, 1. *pō(i)-* 839.]

peiə- To be fat, swell. **I.** Zero-grade form **pī-* (< **piə-*). **1.** Possibly suffixed form **pī-tu-t̄-.* PITUITARY, from Latin *pītuīta,* moisture exuded from trees, gum, phlegm. **2.** Possibly suffixed form **pī-nu-.* PINE[1], PINEAL, PIN-NACE, PIÑON, PINOT; PIÑA CLOTH, from Latin *pīnus,* pine tree (yielding a resin). **3.** Suffixed form **pī-won-.* PROPIONIC ACID, from Greek *pīōn,* fat. **4.**

Suffixed form **pī-wer-,* "fat, fertile." **a.** ERSE, IRISH, from **Ī̆wer-iū,* the prehistoric Celtic name for Ireland, whence Latin *Hibernia,* Ireland, Old Irish *Ériu,* Ireland, and Old English *Īras,* the Irish; **b.** PIERIAN SPRING, from Greek *Pieriā,* a region of Macedonia, from **Pīwer-iā-.* **II.** Extended o-grade form **poid-.* FAT, from Old English *fæt(t),* fat, from Germanic past participle **faitida,* fattened, from derivative verb **faitjan,* to fatten, from **faita-,* plump, fat. [Pokorny *pei̯(ə)-* 793.]

peku- Wealth, movable property, livestock. **1a.** FEL-LOW, from Old Norse *fē,* property, cattle; **b.** FEE, FIEF, ENFEOFF, FEOFFMENT, from Old French *fie,* fief, and Old English *feoh,* cattle, goods, money; **c.** FEUD[2], from Medieval Latin *feudum,* feudal estate. **a–c** all from Germanic **fehu-.* **2.** PECORINO, from Latin *pecus,* cattle. **3.** Suffixed form **peku-n-.* PECUNIARY; IMPECUNIOUS, from Latin *pecūnia,* property, wealth. **4.** Suffixed form **peku-l-.* PECULATE, PECULIAR, from Latin *pecūlium,* riches in cattle, private property. [In Pokorny 2. *pek̑-* 797.]

pekʷ- To cook, ripen. **1.** Assimilated form (in Italic and Celtic) **kʷekʷ-.* **a.** COOK, CUISINE, KITCHEN, QUIT-TOR; APRICOT, BISCOTTO, BISCUIT, CHARCUTERIE, CON-COCT, DECOCT, PRECOCIOUS, RICOTTA, TERRA COTTA, from Latin *coquere,* to cook; **b.** CULINARY, KILN, from Latin *culīna,* kitchen, deformed from *coquīna.* **2.** PEPO; PUMPKIN, from Greek *pepōn,* ripe. **3.** PEPTIC, PEPTIZE; DRUPE, EUPEPTIC, PEPSIN, PEPTONE, from Greek *peptein,* to cook, ripen, digest (> *peptos,* cooked). **4.** DYSPEPSIA, from Greek *-pepsiā,* digestion. **5.** PUKKA, from Sanskrit *pakva-,* ripe. [Pokorny *pekʷ-* 798.]

pel-[1] Skin, hide. **1.** Suffixed form **pel-no-.* FELL[3], from Old English *fell,* skin, hide, from Germanic **felnam.* **2.** FILM, from Old English *filmen,* membrane, from Germanic suffixed form **fel-man-ja-.* **3.** Suffixed form **pel-ni-.* PELISSE, PELLICLE, PELT[1], PELTRY, PILLION; PELLAGRA, SURPLICE, from Latin *pellis,* skin. **4.** ERYSIPELAS, from Greek *-pelas,* skin. **5.** Suffixed form **pel-to-.* PELTATE, from Greek *peltē,* a shield (made of hide). [Pokorny 3b. *pel-* 803.]

pel-[2] To thrust, strike, drive. **I.** Suffixed form **pel-de-.* **1a.** ANVIL, from Old English *anfilt(e), anfealt,* anvil ("something beaten on"); **b.** (i) FELT[1], from Old English *felt,* felt; (ii) FILTER, FIL-TRATE, from Medieval Latin *filtrum,* filter, piece of felt. Both (i) and (ii) from Germanic **feltaz, *filtiz,* compressed wool. Both **a** and **b** from Germanic **felt-, *falt-,* to beat. **2.** PELT[2], POUSSETTE, PULSATE, PULSE[1], PUSH; COMPEL, DISPEL, EXPEL, IMPEL, IMPULSE, PROPEL, REPEL, from Latin *pellere* (past participle *pul-sus*), to push, drive, strike. **3a.** Suffixed o-grade form **pol-o-,* fuller of cloth. POLISH, from Latin *polīre,* to make smooth, polish (< "to full cloth"); **b.** suffixed o-grade form **pol-o-* (with different accentuation from the preceding), fulled (of cloth). INTERPOLATE, from Latin compound adjective *interpolis* (also *interpolus*), refurbished (*inter-,* between; see **en**). **II.** Extended form **pelə-.* **1.** Present stem **pelnā-.* **a.** APPEAL, PEAL, RAPPEL, REPEAL, from Latin *appellāre,* "to drive to," address, entreat, appeal, call (*ad-,* to); **b.** COMPELLATION, from Latin *compellāre,* to accost, address (*com-,* intensive prefix; see **kom**). **2.** Possible suffixed zero-grade extended adverbial form **plə-ti-,* or locative plural **plə-si.* PLESIOSAUR, from Greek *plē-sios,* near (< "pushed toward"), from pre-Greek **plāti* or **plāsi.* [Pokorny 2a. *pel-* 801.]

pelə-[1] To fill; with derivatives referring to abundance and multitude. **I.** Zero-grade form **plə-.* **1.** Suffixed form **plə-no-.* FULL[1], from Old English *full,* full, from Germanic **fulla-* (< **fulna-*), full. **2.** FILL, from Old English *fyllan,* to fill (from Germanic derivative verb **fulljan,* to fill), and *fyllu,* full amount (from Germanic abstract noun **fullīnō-,* fullness). **3.** PLENARY, PLENI-TUDE, PLENTY, PLENUM, PLENIPOTENTIARY, REPLENISH, TERREPLEIN, from Latin *plēnus,* full, from Latin stem **plēno-,* replacing **plāno-* (influenced by Latin verb *plēre,* to fill; see **IV.** 1. below). **4.** Suffixed form **plə-go-.* **a.** FOLK, from Old English *folc,* people; **b.** VOLKSLIED, from Old High German *folc,* people. Both **a** and **b** from Germanic **folkam.* **II.** Suffixed form **p(e)lə-u-.* **1.** Obscure comparative form. PIÙ, PLURAL, PLUS, NONPLUS, PLUPERFECT, SUR-PLUS, from Latin *plūs,* more (Archaic Latin *plous*). See also **IV.** 5. below. **2.** O-grade form **pol(ə)-u-.*

POLY-; HOI POLLOI, from Greek _polus,_ much, many. **3.** Possibly from this root (but probably rather from **pel-^{1}**) is Latin _palūs,_ marsh (? < "inundated"): PALUDAL.

III. Suffixed form _*p(e)lə-o-._ Latin compound _manipulus_ (see **man-^{2}**).

IV. Variant form _*plē-._ **1.** ACCOMPLISH, COMPLEMENT, COMPLETE, COMPLIMENT, COMPLY, DEPLETE, EXPLETIVE, IMPLEMENT, REPLETE, SUPPLETION, SUPPLY, from Latin _plēre,_ to fill. **2.** Possibly suffixed form _*plē-dhw-._ PLEBE, PLEBEIAN, PLEBS; PLEBISCITE, from Latin _plēbs, plēbēs,_ the people, multitude. **3.** Suffixed form _*plē-dhwo-._ PLETHORA; PLETHYSMOGRAPH, from Greek derivative verb _plēthein,_ to be full. **4.** Suffixed adjective (positive) form _*plē-ro-._ PLEROCERCOID, from Greek _plērēs,_ full. **5.** Suffixed (comparative) form _*plē-i(s)on-._ PLEO-, PLEONASM; PLEIOTAXY, PLEIOTROPISM, PLIOCENE, from Greek _pleōn, pleiōn,_ more. **6.** Suffixed (superlative) form _*plē-isto-._ PLEISTOCENE, from Greek _pleistos,_ most.

V. Possibly Sanskrit _pūraḥ,_ cake (< "that which fills or satisfies"): POORI. [Pokorny 1. _pel-_ 798.]

pelə-^{2} Flat; to spread. **1.** Suffixed form _*pel(ə)-tu-._ FIELD, from Old English _feld,_ open field, from Germanic _*felthuz,_ flat land. **2.** Suffixed form _*pel(ə)-t-es-_ (by-form of _*pel(ə)-tu-_). **a.** FELDSPAR, from Old High German _feld,_ field; **b.** VELDT, from Middle Dutch _veld, velt,_ field. Both **a** and **b** from Germanic _*feltha-,_ flat land. **3.** Variant form _*plā-._ **a.** Suffixed form _*plā-ru-._ FLOOR, from Old English _flōr,_ floor, from Germanic _*flōruz,_ floor; **b.** suffixed form _*plā-no-._ LLANO, PIANO^{2}, PLAIN, PLANARIAN, PLANE^{1}, PLANE^{2}, PLANE^{3}, PLANISH, PLANO-, PLANULA; ESPLANADE, EXPLAIN, PIANOFORTE, from Latin _plānus,_ flat, level, even, plain, clear. **4.** Suffixed zero-grade form _*pl̥ə-mā-._ PALM^{1}, PALM^{2}, PALMARY, from Latin _palma_ (< _*palama_), palm of the hand. **5.** Possibly extended variant form _*plan-._ **a.** PLANET; APLANATIC, from Greek _planāsthai,_ to wander (< "to spread out"); **b.** perhaps Germanic _*flan-._ FLÂNEUR, from French _flâner,_ to walk the streets idly, from a source akin to Old Norse _flana,_ to wander aimlessly. **6.** Suffixed zero-grade form _*plə-dh-._ -PLASIA, PLASMA, -PLAST, PLASTER, PLASTIC, PLASTID, -PLASTY; DYSPLASIA, METAPLASM^{1}, TOXOPLASMA, from Greek _plassein_ (< _*plath-yein_), to mold, "spread out." **7.** O-grade form _*polə-._ **a.** POLYNYA, from Russian _polyĭ,_ open; **b.** POLACK, POLKA, from Slavic _*polje,_ broad flat land, field. [Pokorny _pelə-_ 805.]

penkʷe Five.

I. Basic form _*penkʷe._ **1.** Assimilated form _*pempe._ **a.** _(i)_ FIVE; FIFTY, from Old English _fīf,_ five, with derivative _fīftig,_ fifty (_-tēne,_ ten; see **dekm̥**); _(ii)_ FIN^{2}, from Old High German _finf, funf,_ five. Both _(i)_ and _(ii)_ from Germanic _*fimf;_ **b.** _(i)_ FIFTEEN, from Old English _fīftēne,_ fifteen; _(ii)_ FEMTO-, from Old Norse _fimmtān,_ fifteen. Both _(i)_ and _(ii)_ from Germanic compound _*fimftehun,_ fifteen (_*tehun,_ ten; see **dekm̥**). **2.** Assimilated form (in Italic and Celtic) _*kʷenkʷe._ **a.** CINQUAIN, CINQUE, QUINQUE-; CINQUECENTO, CINQUEFOIL, QUINCUNX, from Latin _quīnque,_ five; **b.** KENO, QUINATE, from Latin distributive _quīnī,_ five each; **c.** QUINDECENNIAL, from Latin compound _quīndecim,_ fifteen (_decem,_ ten; see **dekm̥**). **3.** PENTA-, PENTAD; PENSTEMON, PENTAGON, PENTAMETER, PENTATHLON, from Greek _pente,_ five. **4.** PUNCH^{3}; PACHISI, from Sanskrit _pañca,_ five, from Indo-Iranian _*panca._

II. Compound _*penkʷe-(d)konta,_ "five tens," fifty (_*-(d)konta,_ group of ten; see **dekm̥**). **1.** QUINQUAGENARIAN, from Latin _quīnquāgintā,_ fifty. **2.** PENTECOST, from Greek _pentēkonta,_ fifty.

III. Ordinal adjective _*penkʷ-to-._ **1.** FIFTH, from Old English _fīfta,_ fifth, from Germanic _*fimftōn-._ **2.** QUINT^{1}, QUINTAIN, QUINTET, QUINTILE; QUINTESSENCE, QUINTILLION, QUINTUPLE, from Latin _quīntus_ (< _*quinc-tos_), feminine _quīnta,_ fifth.

IV. Suffixed form _*penkʷ-ro-._ FINGER, from Old English _finger,_ finger, from Germanic _*fingwraz,_ finger (< "one of five").

V. Suffixed reduced zero-grade form _*pn̥k-sti-._ **1.** FIST, from Old English _fȳst,_ fist. **2.** FOIST, from Dutch _vuist,_ fist. Both **1** and **2** from Germanic _*funhstiz._ [Pokorny _penkʷe_ 808, _pn̥ksti-_ 839.]

pent- To tread, go. **1.** FIND, from Old English _findan,_ to find, from Germanic _*finthan,_ to come upon, discover. **2.** Suffixed o-grade form _*pont-i-._ **a.** PONS, PONTIFEX, PONTIFF, PONTINE, PONTOON, PUNT^{1}; TRANSPONTINE, from Latin _pōns_ (stem _pont-_), bridge (earliest meaning, "way, passage," preserved in the priestly title _pontifex,_ "he who prepares the way"; _-fex,_ maker; see **dhē-**); **b.** SPUTNIK, from Russian _sputnik,_ fellow traveler, sputnik, from _put',_ path, way, from Slavic _*potĭ._ **3.** Zero-grade form _*pn̥t-._ PERIPATETIC, from Greek _patein,_ to tread, walk. **4.** Suffixed zero-grade form _*pn̥t-ə-._ **a.** PATH, from Old English _pæth,_ path; **b.** PAD^{2}; FOOTPAD^{1}, from Middle Dutch _pad,_ way, path. Both **a** and **b** from Germanic _*patha-,_ way, path, probably borrowed (? via Scythian) from Iranian _*path-._ [Pokorny _pent-_ 808.]

per^{1} Base of prepositions and preverbs with the basic meanings of "forward," "through," and a wide range of extended senses such as "in front of," "before," "early," "first," "chief," "toward," "against," "near," "at," "around."

I. Basic form _*per_ and extended form _*peri._ **1a.** TURNVEREIN, from Middle High German _vereinen,_ to unite, from Old High German _far-;_ **b.** VEER^{2}, from Middle Dutch _vieren,_ to let out, slacken; **c.** Germanic compound _*fer-getan_ (see **ghend-**); **d.** FRUMP, from Middle Dutch _verrompelen,_ to wrinkle. **a–d** all from Germanic _*fer-, *far-,_ used chiefly as an intensive prefix denoting destruction, reversal, or completion. **2.** Suffixed (comparative) form _*per-ero-,_ farther away. FAR, from Old English _feor(r),_ far, from Germanic _*fer(e)ra._ **3.** PER, PER-; PARAMOUNT, PARAMOUR, PARGET, PARTERRE, PARVENU, from Latin _per,_ through, for, by. **4.** PERI-; PERISSODACTYL, from Greek _peri,_ around, near, beyond. **5a.** PALANQUIN, from Sanskrit _pari-,_ around; **b.** PARADISE, from Avestan _pairi-,_ around; **c.** BARD^{2}, PURDAH, from Old Persian _pari,_ around, over; **d.** BARBICAN, from Old Iranian compound _*pari-vāraka-,_ protective (_*vāraka-,_ covering). **a–d** all from Indo-Iranian _*pari-,_ around. **6.** PERESTROIKA, from Old Russian _pere-,_ around, again, from Slavic _*per-._

II. Zero-grade form _*pr̥-._ **1a.** FOR, from Old English _for,_ before, instead of, on account of; **b.** FOR-, from Old English _for-,_ prefix denoting destruction, pejoration, exclusion, or completion. Both **a** and **b** from Germanic _*fur,_ before, in. **2.** Extended form _*pr̥t-._ FORTH; AFFORD, from Old English _forth,_ from Germanic _*furth-,_ forward. **3.** Suffixed (comparative) form _*pr̥-tero-._ FURTHER, from Old English _furthra, furthor,_ farther away, from Germanic _*furthera-._ **4a.** Compound _*pr̥-st-i-_ or _*por-st-i-,_ with o-grade form _*por-_ (see **stā-**); **b.** PORRECT, from Latin _por-,_ forth, forward. Both **a** and **b** from Latin _por-_ from _*pr̥-._ **5.** Suffixed form _*pr̥-sōd._ PARGET, from Latin _porrō,_ forward.

III. Extended zero-grade form _*pr̥ə-._ **1.** Suffixed (superlative) form _*pr̥ə-mo-._ **a.** FORMER^{2}, from Old English _forma,_ first, from Germanic _*fruma-, *furma-;_ **b.** FOREMOST, from Old English _formest,_ first, from Germanic _*frumista-, *furmista-;_ **c.** Latin compound _prandium,_ "first meal," late breakfast, lunch (probably < _*prām-d-ium_ < _*pr̥əm-(e)d-yo-;_ second element _*-(e)d-,_ to eat; see **ed-**). **2.** Suffixed (superlative) form _*pr̥ə-isto-._ FIRST, from Old English _fyrst, fyrest,_ first, from Germanic _*furista-,_ foremost. **3.** Suffixed form _*pr̥ə-wo-._ **a.** PROW, from Greek _prōira,_ forward part of a ship, from analogically suffixed form _*prōw-arya;_ **b.** PROTEIN, PROTIST, PROTO-, PROTON, from Greek _prōtos,_ first, foremost, from suffixed (superlative) form _*prōw-ato-._ Both **a** and **b** from Greek _*prōwo-,_ first, foremost. **4.** Suffixed form _*pr̥ə-i._ ARPENT, from Latin _arepennis,_ half-acre (second element obscure), from Gaulish _ari_ (combining form _are-_), before, from Celtic _*(p)ari, *are._

IV. Extended form _*pr̥ə̆._ **1a.** FORE, FORE-; FOREFATHER, from Old English _fore, for,_ before; **b.** VORLAGE, from Old High German _fora,_ before; **c.** BEFORE, from Old English _beforan,_ before, from Germanic prefixed and suffixed form _*bi-fora-na,_ in the front (_*bi-,_ at, by; see **ambhi**). **a–c** all from Germanic _*fura,_ before. **2.** PARA-^{1}; PALFREY, from Greek _para,_ beside, alongside of, beyond.

V. Extended form _*prŏ._ **1a.** FRAE, FRO; FROWARD, from Old Norse _frā,_ from, from Germanic _*fra,_ forward, away from; **b.** Germanic _*fra-,_ completely, in compounds (see **ed-**). **2.** Suffixed form _*prŏ-mo-._ **a.** FRAME, FROM, from Old English _fram,_ forward, from, from Germanic _*fram,_ from; **b.** FURNISH, FURNITURE, VENEER, from Old French _f(o)urnir,_ to supply, provide, from Germanic derivative verb _*frumjan,_ to further, from Germanic _*frum,_ forward; **c.** PRAM^{2}, from Czech _prám,_ raft. **3.** Suffixed form _*prō-wo-._ **a.** _(i)_ FRAU, FRÄULEIN, from Old High German _frouwa,_ lady; _(ii)_ FREYA, from Old Norse _freyja,_ lady. Both _(i)_ and _(ii)_ from Germanic _*frōwō,_ lady, lengthened-grade feminine of _*frawan-;_ lord; **b.** FREY, from Old Norse _Freyr,_ from Germanic _*frawaz,_ alteration of _*frawan-._ lord. **4.** PRIDE, PRO^{1}, PRO-^{1}, PRODIGALITY, PROUD, PROWESS; IMPROVE, PURCHASE, from Latin _prō, prŏ-,_ before, for, instead of. **5.** Suffixed form _*prō-no-._ PRONE, from Latin _prōnus,_ leaning forward. **6.** Possible suffixed form _*pro-ko-._ RECIPROCAL, from Latin compound _reciprocus,_ alternating, "backward and forward" (_*re-ko-,_ backward; see **re-**). **7.** Suffixed adverb _*pro-kʷe._ **a.** APPROACH, RAPPROCHEMENT, REPROACH, from Latin _prope,_ near; **b.** suffixed form _*prokʷ-inkʷo-._ PROPINQUITY, from Latin _propinquus,_ near; **c.** suffixed (superlative) form _*prokʷ-isamo-._ PROXIMATE; APPROXIMATE, from Latin _proximus,_ nearest. **8.** Compound _*pro-bhw-o-,_ growing well or straightforward (_*bhw-o-,_ to grow; see **bheuə-**). PROBABLE, PROBE, PROBITY, PROOF, PROVE; APPROVE, IMPROBITY, REPROVE, from Latin _probus,_ upright, good, virtuous. **9.** PRO-^{2}, from Greek _pro,_ before, in front, forward. **10.** Suffixed (comparative) form _*pro-tero-._ HYSTERON PROTERON, PROTEROZOIC, from Greek _proteros,_ before, former. **11.** PRAKRIT, from Sanskrit _pra-,_ before, forth. **12.** Celtic _*ro-,_ intensive prefix. GALORE, from Old Irish _roar,_ enough, from Celtic compound _*ro-wero-,_ sufficiency (_*-wero-,_ see **wērə-o-**).

VI. Extended forms _*prai-, *prei-._ **1a.** PRE-; PRETERIT, from Latin _prae,_ before; **b.** compound _*prai-ghes-to-_ (see **ghes-**). **2.** Suffixed (comparative) form _*prei-yos-._ PRIOR^{2}, from Latin _prior,_ former, higher, superior. **3.** Suffixed form _*prei-wo-._ **a.** PRIVATE, PRIVILEGE, PRIVITY, PRIVY; DEPRIVE, from Latin _prīvus,_ single, alone (< "standing in front," "isolated from others"); **b.** PROPER, PROPERTY; APPROPRIATE, EXPROPRIATE, PROPRIOCEPTION, PROPRIOCEPTOR, PROPRIUM, from Latin _proprius,_ one's own, particular (< _prō prīvō,_ in particular, from the ablative of _prīvus,_ single; _prō,_ for; see **V. 4.**). **4.** Extended form _*preis-._ **a.** Suffixed (superlative) form _*preis-mo-._ _(i)_ PREMIER, PRIMAL, PRIMARY, PRIMATE, PRIME, PRIMITIVE, PRIMO, PRIMUS; IMPRIMIS, PRIMAVERA^{1}, PRIMEVAL, PRIMIPARA, PRIMOGENITOR, PRIMOGENITURE, PRIMORDIAL, from Latin _prīmus_ (< _*prīsmus_), first, foremost; _(ii)_ PRINCE, PRINCIPAL, PRINCIPLE, from Latin compound _prīnceps,_ "he who takes first place," leader, chief, emperor (_-ceps,_ "-taker"; see **kap-**); **b.** suffixed form _*preis-tano-._ PRISTINE, from Latin _prīstinus,_ former, earlier, original.

VII. Extended form _*pres-_ in compound _*pres-gʷu-,_ "going before" (_*gʷ-u-,_ going; see **gʷā-**). PRESBYTER, PRESTER JOHN, PRIEST; PRESBYOPIA, from Greek _presbus,_ old, old man, elder.

VIII. Extended form _*proti._ PROS-, from Greek _pros,_ against, toward, near, at. [Pokorny 2. A. _per_ 810.] Other possibly related forms are grouped under **per-^{2}**.

per-^{2} To lead, pass over. A verbal root belonging to the group of **per^{1}**.

I. Full-grade form _*per-._ **1.** Suffixed form _*per-tu-._ FIRTH, FJORD, from Old Norse _fjördhr,_ an inlet, estuary, from Germanic _*ferthuz,_ place for crossing over, ford. **2.** Suffixed form _*per-onā-._ PERONEAL, from Greek _peronē,_ pin of a brooch, buckle (< "that which pierces through"). **3.** Suffixed form _*per-yo-._ DIAPIR, from Greek _peirein,_ to pierce. **4.** Suffixed form _*per-trā-._ PETRO-, PETROUS, PIER; PARSLEY, PETRIFY, PETROLEUM, SALTPETER, from Greek _petrā,_ cliff, rock (dissimilated from _*pertrā-_), with possible earlier meaning "bedrock" (< "what one comes through to").

II. O-grade form _*por-._ **1a.** _(i)_ FARE; WARFARE, WAYFARER, WAYFARING, WELFARE, from Old English _faran,_ to go on a journey, get along; _(ii)_ FIELDFARE, from Old English _feldeware,_ possibly altered by folk etymology in Old English from an earlier _*feldefare,_ from _*fare,_ a goer, from _faran_ (see _(i)_ above); **b.** GABERDINE, from Old High German _faran,_ to go, travel; **c.** FARTLEK, from Old Norse _fara,_ to go, move. **a–c** all from Germanic _*faran,_ to go. **2.** Suffixed form _*por-o-,_ passage, journey. PORE^{2}; APORIA, EMPORIUM, from Greek _poros,_ journey, passage. **3.** Suffixed (causative) form _*por-eyo-,_ to cause to go, lead, conduct. **a.** FERRY, from Old English _ferian,_ to transport, from Germanic _*farjan,_ to ferry; **b.** GUAR, from Sanskrit _pārayati, pālayati,_ he leads across, brings to safety. **4.** Lengthened-grade form *pōr-. **a.** FERE, from Old English _(ge)fēra,_ "fellow-traveler," companion (_ge-_, together, with; see **kom**), from Germanic suffixed form *fōr-ja-; **b.** FÜHRER, from Old High German _fuoren,_ to lead, from Germanic suffixed (causative) form *fōr-jan. **5.** Possibly suffixed form *por-no-, feather, wing (< "that which carries a bird in flight"). **a.** FERN, from Old English _fearn,_ fern (having feathery fronds), from Germanic *farnō, feather, leaf; **b.** PAN[2], from Sanskrit _parṇam,_ leaf, feather.

III. Zero-grade form *pr̥-. **1.** Suffixed form *pr̥-tu-, passage. **a.** FORD, from Old English _ford,_ shallow place where one may cross a river, from Germanic *furduz; **b.** PORT[1]; IMPORTUNE, OPPORTUNE, PASSPORT, from Latin _portus,_ harbor (< "passage"). **2.** Suffixed form *pr̥-tā-. PORCH, PORT[3], PORTAL, PORTCULLIS, PORTER[2], PORTICO, PORTIÈRE, PORTULACA, PURSLANE, from Latin _porta,_ gate. **3.** Suffixed (denominative) form *pr̥-to-. PORT[5], PORTABLE, PORTAGE, PORTAMENTO, PORTATIVE, PORTER[1]; COMPORT, DEPORT, EXPORT, IMPORT, IMPORTANT, PORTFOLIO, PURPORT, RAPPORT, REPORT, SPORT, SUPPORT, TRANSPORT, from Latin _portāre,_ to carry. [Pokorny 2. B. _per_ 816.]

perd- To fart. **1.** FART, from Old English *feortan, to fart, from Germanic *fertan, *fartōn. **2.** PARTRIDGE, from Greek _perdix,_ partridge (which makes a sharp whirring sound when suddenly flushed). [Pokorny _perd-_ 819.]

perə- To grant, allot (reciprocally, to get in return). Zero-grade form *pr̥ə- (becoming *par- in Latin). **1.** Suffixed form *par-ti-. **a.** PARCEL, PARCENER, PARSE, PART, PARTICLE, PARTISAN[1], PARTITA, PARTY; BIPARTITE, COMPART, IMPART, PARTICIPATE, REPARTEE, from Latin _pars_ (stem _part-_), a share, part; **b.** possibly suffixed form *par-tiōn-. PORTION, PROPORTION, from Latin _portiō,_ a part (first attested in the phrase _prō portiōne,_ in proportion, according to each part, perhaps assimilated from *prō partiōne). **2.** Perhaps Latin _pār,_ equal: PAIR, PAR, PARITY[1], PEER[2]; COMPARE, IMPARITY, NONPAREIL, PARI-MUTUEL. [Pokorny 2. C. _per_ 817.]

perkʷu- Oak. **1.** Zero-grade form *pr̥kʷ-. FIR, probably from a Scandinavian source akin to Old Icelandic _fȳri,_ fir, from Germanic *furh-jōn-. **2.** Assimilated form *kʷerkʷu-. CORK, QUERCETIN; QUERCITRON, from Latin _quercus,_ oak. [Pokorny _perkʷu-s_ 822.]

pet- To rush, fly. Also **petə-**. **1.** Suffixed form *pet-rā-. FEATHER, from Old English _fether,_ feather, from Germanic *fethrō, feather. **2.** -PETAL, PETITION, PETULANT; APPETITE, COMPETE, IMPETIGO, IMPETUOUS, IMPETUS, PERPETUAL, REPEAT, from Latin _petere,_ to go toward, seek. **3.** Suffixed form *pet-nā-. PANACHE, PEN[1], PENNA, PENNATE, PENNON, PIN, PINNA, PINNACLE, PINNATE, PINNATI-, PINNULE; EMPENNAGE, from Latin _penna, pinna,_ feather, wing. **4.** Suffixed form *pet-ro- in compound *aku-petro-, "swift-flying" (*aku-, swift). ACCIPITER, from Latin _accipiter,_ hawk. **5.** Suffixed form *pet-yo-. PROPITIOUS, from Latin _propitius,_ favorable, gracious, originally a religious term meaning "falling or rushing forward," hence "eager," "well-disposed" (said of the gods; _prō-,_ forward; see **per[1]**). **6.** Suffixed zero-grade form *pt-ero-. -PTER; ACANTHOPTERYGIAN, APTERYX, ARCHAEOPTERYX, COLEOPTERAN, DIPTERAL, MECOPTERAN, METHOTREXATE, ORTHOPTERAN, PERIPTERAL, PLECOPTERAN, PTERIDOLOGY, PTERYGOID, SAUROPTERYGIAN, from Greek _pteron,_ feather, wing, and _pterux,_ wing. **7.** Suffixed zero-grade form *pt-ilo-. COLEOPTILE, from Greek _ptilon,_ soft feathers, down, plume. **8.** Reduplicated form *pi-pt-. PTOMAINE, PTOSIS; ASYMPTOTE, PERIPETEIA, PROPTOSIS, SYMPTOM, from Greek _piptein,_ to fall, with verbal adjective _ptōtos_ (< *ptō-to-), falling, fallen, and nominal derivatives _ptōsis_ (< *ptō-ti-), a fall, and _ptōma_ (< *ptō-mn̥), a fall, fallen body, corpse. **9.** O-grade form *pot-. HIPPOPOTAMUS, POTAMOLOGY, from Greek _potamos_ "rushing water," river (_-amo-,_ Greek suffix). **10.** Suffixed form *pet-tro-. TALIPOT, from Sanskrit _pattram,_ feather, leaf. [Pokorny 2. _pet-_ 825.]

pəter- Father. **1.** FATHER; FOREFATHER, from Old English _fæder,_ father, from Germanic *fadar. **2.** PADRE, PATER, PATERNAL, PATRI-, PATRICIAN, PATRIMONY, PATRON, PÈRE; COMPADRE, EXPATRIATE, GOOMBAH, PERPETRATE, from Latin _pater,_ father. **3.** PATRI-, PATRIOT; ALLOPATRIC, EUPATRID, PATRIARCH, SYMPATRIC, from Greek _patēr,_ father. [Pokorny _pətē(r)_ 829.]

plāk- To strike. Contracted from *plaək-. **1.** Nasalized variant forms *pla-n-k-, *pla-n-g-. **a.** FLING, from Middle English _flingen,_ to fling, from a Scandinavian source akin to Old Norse _flengja,_ to flog, whip, from Germanic *flang-; **b.** PLAINT, PLANGENT; COMPLAIN, from Latin _plangere,_ to strike (one's own breast), lament; **c.** suffixed form *plang-yo-. PLANKTON, from Greek _plazein,_ to drive away, turn aside. **2.** Variant form *plāg-. PLAGUE, from Latin _plāga,_ a blow, stroke. **3.** Suffixed form *plāk-yo-. PLECTRUM, -PLEGIA, PLEXOR; APOPLEXY, PARAPLEGIA, from Greek _plēssein,_ to beat, strike. [Pokorny 2. _plāk-_ 832.]

plek- To plait. **1.** Suffixed o-grade form *plok-so-. FLAX, from Old English _fleax,_ flax, from Germanic *flahsam, flax. **2.** Full-grade form *plek-. MULTIPLEX, from Latin _-plex,_ -fold (in compounds such as _duplex,_ twofold; see **dwo-**). **3.** PLAIT, PLEAT, PLIANT, PLICA, PLICATE, PLIGHT[1], PLISSÉ, PLY[1]; APPLY, COMPLICATE, COMPLICE, DEPLOY, DISPLAY, EMPLOY, EXPLICATE, EXPLICIT, EXPLOIT, IMPLICATE, IMPLICIT, REPLICATE, REPLY, SPLAY, from Latin _plicāre,_ to fold (also in compounds used as denominatives of words in _-plex,_ genitive _-plicis_). **4.** Suffixed forms *plek-to- and *plek-t-to-. PLEACH, PLEXUS; AMPLEXICAUL, COMPLECT, COMPLEX, PERPLEXED, from Latin _plectere_ (past participle _plexus_), to weave, plait, entwine. **5.** PLECOPTERAN, PLECTOGNATH, from Greek _plekein,_ to plait, twine, and _plektos,_ twisted. [Pokorny _plek̂-_ 834.]

pleu- To flow.

I. Basic form *pleu-. **1.** PLOVER, PLUVIAL, PLUVIOUS, from Latin _pluere,_ to rain. **2.** PLEUSTON, from Greek _pleusis,_ sailing. **3.** Suffixed zero-grade form *plu-elos. PYELITIS, from Greek dissimilated _puelos,_ trough, basin. **4.** Suffixed form *pl(e)u-mon-, "floater," lung(s). **a.** PULMONARY, PULMONOLOGY, from Latin _pulmō_ (< *plumonēs), lung(s); **b.** PNEUMO-, PNEUMONIA, PNEUMONIC, from Greek _pleumōn, pneumōn_ (influenced by _pneuma,_ breath), lung. **5.** Suffixed o-grade form *plou-to-. PLUTO; PLUTOCRACY, from Greek _ploutos,_ wealth, riches (< "overflowing"). **6.** Lengthened o-grade form *plō(u)-. **a.** _(i)_ FLOW, from Old English _flōwan,_ to flow; _(ii)_ perhaps Middle Dutch _vluwe,_ fishnet: FLUE[2]. Both _(i)_ and _(ii)_ from Germanic *flōwan, to flow; **b.** suffixed form *plō-tu-. FLOOD, from Old English _flōd,_ flood, from Germanic *flōduz, flowing water, deluge.

II. Extended form *pleuk-. **1.** FLY[1], from Old English _flēogan,_ to fly, from Germanic *fleugan, to fly. **2.** FLY[2], from Old English _flēoge,_ a fly, from Germanic *fleugōn-, flying insect, fly. **3.** Probably Germanic *fleuhan, to run away. FLEE, from Old English _flēon,_ to flee. **4.** FLEY, from Old English _flȳgan, flēgan,_ to put to flight, from Germanic causative *flaugjan. **5.** FLÈCHE, FLETCHER, from Old French _fleche,_ arrow, from Germanic suffixed form *fleug-ika-. **6.** Zero-grade form *pluk-. **a.** FLEDGE, from Old English *flycge, with feathers (only in _unfligge,_ featherless), from Germanic *flugja-, ready to fly; **b.** FLIGHT[1], FLIGHT[2], from Old English _flyht,_ act of flying, and *flyht, act of fleeing, escape, from Germanic suffixed form *flug-ti-; **c.** FOWL, from Old English _fugol,_ bird, from Germanic *fuglaz, bird, dissimilated from possible (but unlikely) suffixed form *flug-laz; **d.** FLUGELHORN, FUGLEMAN, from Middle High German _vlügel,_ wing, from Germanic suffixed form *flugilaz.

III. Extended form *pleud-. **1.** FLEET[1], FLEET[2], from Old English _flēotan,_ to float, swim (from Germanic *fleutan), and Old Norse _fljótr,_ fleet, swift (from Germanic *fleuta-). **2.** Zero-grade form *plud-. **a.** _(i)_ FLOAT, from Old English _flotian,_ to float; _(ii)_ FLOTSAM, from Old French _floter,_ to float. Both _(i)_ and _(ii)_ from Germanic derivative *flotōn, to float; **b.** FLOTILLA, from Old Norse _floti,_ raft, fleet; **c.** FLUTTER, from Old English _floterian, flotorian,_ to float back and forth (_-erian,_ iterative and frequentative suffix); **d.** FLIT, from Old Norse _flytja,_ to further, convey, from Germanic *flutjan, to float. **a–d** all from Germanic *flut-, *flot-. **3.** FLUSTER, probably from a Scandinavian source akin to Icelandic _flaustr,_ hurry, and _flaustra,_ to bustle, from Germanic *flausta-, contracted from suffixed form *flaut-stā-, probably from *pleud-, o-grade *ploud-. [Pokorny _pleu-_ 835, _pl(e)u-mon-_ 837.]

pō(i)- To drink. Contracted from *poə(i)-.

I. Unextended form *pō-. **1.** Suffixed form *pō-to-. POTABLE, POTATION, POTATORY, from Latin _pōtus,_ drunk; a drink (whence _pōtāre,_ to drink). **2.** Suffixed form *pō-ti-. POISON, POTION, from Latin _pōtiō,_ a drink. **3.** Suffixed form *pō-tlo-, drinking vessel. HIBACHI, from Sanskrit _pātram,_ cup, bowl. **4.** Suffixed reduplicated zero-grade form *pi-pə-o-, whence *pi-bo-, assimilated to *bi-bo-. BEER, BEVERAGE, BIB, BIBULOUS; IMBIBE, IMBRUE, from Latin _bibere,_ to drink. **5.** Suffixed zero-grade form *pə-ti-, *po-ti-. SYMPOSIUM, from Greek _posis,_ drink, drinking.

II. Zero-grade form *pī- (< *piə-, contracted from *pəi-). **1.** Suffixed form *pī-ro-. PIROGI, from Old Church Slavonic _pirŭ,_ feast. **2.** Suffixed (nasal present) form *pī-no-. PINOCYTOSIS, from Greek _pīnein,_ to drink. [Pokorny 2. _pō(i)-_ 839.]

porko- Young pig. **1a.** FARROW[1], from Old English _fearh,_ little pig; **b.** AARDVARK, from Middle Dutch diminutive form _varken,_ small pig. Both **a** and **b** from Germanic *farhaz. **2.** PORCELAIN, PORCINE, PORK; PORCUPINE, PORPOISE, from Latin _porcus,_ pig. [Pokorny _pork̂o-s_ 841.]

poti- Powerful; lord. **1.** PODESTA, POSSESS, POWER, from Latin _potis,_ powerful, able, and compound _possidēre_ (_pos-_ < *pots), to hold in one's control, possess. **2.** POSSIBLE, POTENT; IMPOTENT, OMNIPOTENT, PREPOTENT, from Latin compound _posse,_ to be able (contracted from _potis,_ able + _esse,_ to be; see **es-**). **3.** BASHAW, PADISHAH, PASHA, from Old Persian _pati-,_ master. **4.** Form *pot-. **a.** Compound *ghos-pot- (see **ghos-ti-**); **b.** compound *dems-pot- (see **dem-**). [Pokorny _poti-s_ 842.]

prek- To ask, entreat. **1.** Basic form *prek-. PRAY, PRAYER[1], PRECARIOUS; DEPRECATE, IMPRECATE, PRIE-DIEU, from *prex, prayer (attested only in the plural _precēs_), with Latin denominative _precārī,_ to entreat, pray. **2.** Suffixed zero-grade form *pr̥(k)-sk- becoming *por(k)-sk- in Italic, contracted to *posk- in suffixed form *posk-to-, contracted to *posto-. POSTULATE; EXPOSTULATE, from Latin _postulāre,_ to ask, request. [Pokorny 4. _perk̂-_ 821.]

prī- To love. Contracted from *priə-, becoming *priy- before vowels. **1.** Suffixed form *priy-o-. **a.** FREE, from Old English _frēo,_ free, and _frēon, freogan,_ to love, set free; **b.** FILIBUSTER, FREEBOOTER, from Dutch _vrij,_ free. Both **a** and **b** from Germanic *frija-, beloved, belonging to the loved ones, not in bondage, free, and *frijōn, to love. **2.** Suffixed (participial) form *priy-ont-, loving. FRIEND, from Old English _frīond, frēond,_ friend, from Germanic *frijand-, lover, friend. **3.** Suffixed shortened form *pri-tu-. **a.** AFFRAY, AFRAID, from Old French _esfreer,_ to disturb, from Vulgar Latin *exfredāre, to break the peace, from _ex-,_ out, away (see **eghs**) + *fridāre, to make peace, from Germanic *frithu-, peace; **b.** Germanic compound *berg-frithu- (see **bhergh-**). Both **a** and **b** from Germanic *frithuz, peace. **4.** Suffixed feminine form *priy-ā-, beloved. **a.** FRIGG, from Old Norse _Frigg,_ goddess of the heavens, wife of Odin; **b.** FRIDAY, from Old English _Frīgedæg,_ Friday, from Germanic compound *frije-dagaz, "day of Frigg" (translation of Latin _Veneris diēs,_ "Venus's day"). Both **a** and **b** from Germanic *frijjō, beloved, wife. [Pokorny _prāi-_ 844.]

pū̆- To rot, decay. (Oldest form probably *puə-, becoming *puw- before vowels.) **1.** Suffixed form *pū-lo-. **a.** FOUL, from Old English _fūl,_ unclean, rotten; **b.** FULMAR, from Old Norse _fūll,_ foul; **c.** FILTH, from Old English _fȳlth,_ foulness, from Germanic abstract noun *fūlithō; **d.** FILE[3], FOIL[1]; DEFILE[1], from Old English _fȳlan,_ to sully, from Germanic denominative *fūljan, to soil, dirty. **a–d** all from Germanic *fūla-, rotten, filthy. **2.** Extended form *pug-. FOG[2], from Middle English _fog, fogge,_ aftermath grass, from a Scandinavian source probably akin to Icelandic _fūki,_ rotten sea grass, and Norwegian _fogg,_ rank grass, from Germanic *fuk-. **3.** Extended variant form *pous-. FUZZY, from Low German _fussig,_ spongy, from Germanic *fausa-. **4.** Suffixed form *pu-tri-. PUTRESCENT, PUTRID; OLLA PODRIDA, POTPOURRI, PUTREFY, from Latin _puter_ (stem _putri-_), rotten. **5.** Suffixed form *puw-os-. **a.** PURULENT, PUS; SUPPURATE, from Latin _pūs,_ pus; **b.** PYO-, from Greek _puon, puos,_ pus. **6.** EMPYEMA, from Greek compound _empuein,_ to suppurate (_en-,_ in; see **en**). [Pokorny 2. _pū̆-_ 848.]

reg- To move in a straight line, with derivatives meaning "to direct in a straight line, lead, rule."

I. Basic form *reg-. **1.** Suffixed form *reg-to-. RIGHT, from Old English _riht,_ right, just, correct, straight, from Germanic *rehta-. **2.** REALM, RECTITUDE, RECTO,

RECTOR, RECTUM, RECTUS, REGENT, REGIME, REGIMEN, REGIMENT, REGION; ADDRESS, ADROIT, ALERT, CORRECT, DIRECT, ERECT, INCORRIGIBLE, PORRECT, RECTANGLE, RECTIFY, RECTILINEAR, RESURGE, RISORGIMENTO, SOURCE, SURGE, from Latin *regere,* to lead straight, guide, rule (past participle *rēctus,* whence adjective *rēctus,* right, straight). **3.** ANORECTIC, ANOREXIA, from Greek *oregein,* to stretch out, reach out for (with *o-* from oldest root form **ǝreg-*).
II. Lengthened-grade form **rēg-,* Indo-European word for a tribal king.
1a. BISHOPRIC, ELDRITCH, from Old English *rīce,* realm; **b.** RIKSMÅL, from Old Norse *rīki,* realm; **c.** REICH; REICHSMARK, from Old High German *rīchi,* realm; **d.** RICH, from Old English *rīce,* strong, powerful, and Old French *riche,* wealthy. **a–d** all from Germanic **rīkja-,* from Celtic suffixed form **rīg-yo-.* **2.** REAL[2], REGAL, REGULUS, REIGN, RIAL[1], RIYAL, ROYAL; REGICIDE, REGIUS PROFESSOR, VICEREINE, VICEROY, from Latin *rēx,* king (royal and priestly title). **3.** Suffixed form **rēg-en-.* RAJ, RAJAH, RANI, RYE[2]; MAHARAJAH, MAHARANI, from Sanskrit *rājā, rājan-,* king, rajah (feminine *rājñī,* queen, rani), and *rājati,* he rules.
III. Suffixed lengthened-grade form **rēg-olā-.* RAIL[1], REGLET, REGULAR, REGULATE, RULE, from Latin *rēgula,* straight piece of wood, rod.
IV. O-grade form **rog-.* **1.** RAKE[1], from Old English *raca, racu,* rake (implement with straight pieces of wood), from Germanic **rakō.* **2.** RACK[1], from Middle Dutch *rec,* framework, from Germanic **rak-.* **3.** Possibly Germanic **ranka-* (with nasal infix). RANK[2], from Old English *ranc,* straight, strong, hence haughty, overbearing. **4.** RECKON, from Old English *gerecenian,* to arrange in order, recount (*ge-,* collective prefix; see **kom**), from Germanic **rakina-,* ready, straightforward. **5.** Suffixed form **rog-ā-.* ROGATION, ROGATORY; ABROGATE, ARROGATE, CORVÉE, DEROGATE, INTERROGATE, PREROGATIVE, PROROGUE, SUBROGATE, SUPEREROGATE, from Latin *rogāre,* to ask (< "stretch out the hand"). **6.** Suffixed form **rog-o-.* ERGO, from Latin *ergō,* therefore, in consequence of, perhaps contracted from a Latin phrase **ē rogō,* "from the direction of" (*ē* < *ex,* out of; see **eghs**), from a possible Latin noun **rogus,* "extension, direction."
V. Lengthened o-grade form **rōg-.* **1.** RECK, from Old English *rec(c)an,* to pay attention to, take care (formally influenced by Old English *reccan,* to extend, stretch out, from Germanic **rakjan*), from Germanic **rōkjan.* **2.** RECKLESS, from Old English *rēcelēas,* careless (*-lēas,* lacking; see **leu-**), from Germanic **rōkja-.*
VI. Suffixed zero-grade form **r̥g-yo-.* RAITA, from Sanskrit *r̥jyati,* he stretches out. [Pokorny 1. *reĝ-* 854.]

reudh- Red, ruddy.
I. O-grade form **roudh-.* **1a.** RED, from Old English *rēad,* red; **b.** RORQUAL, from Old Norse *raudhr,* red. Both **a** and **b** from Germanic **raudaz.* **2.** ROWAN, from a source akin to Old Norse *reynir,* mountain ash, rowan (from its red berries), from Germanic **raudnia-.* **3.** RUFESCENT, RUFOUS, from Latin *rūfus* (of dialectal Italic origin), reddish. **4.** RUBIGINOUS, from Latin *rōbus,* red. **5.** ROBLE, ROBORANT, ROBUST; CORROBORATE, RAMBUNCTIOUS, from Latin *rōbur, rōbus,* red oak, hardness, and *rōbustus,* strong.
II. Zero-grade form **rudh-.* **1.** Suffixed form **rudh-ā-.* **a.** RUDDLE, from Old English *rudu,* red color; **b.** RUDDOCK, from Old English *rudduc,* robin; **c.** RUDDY, from Old English *rudig,* ruddy. **a–c** all from Germanic **rudō.* **2.** Suffixed form **rudh-sto-.* RUST, from Old English *rūst* (and perhaps also **rust*), rust, from Germanic **rustaz.* **3.** ROUGE, RUBEOLA, RUBY; RUBEFACIENT, from Latin *rubeus,* red. **4.** RUBICUND, from Latin *rubicundus,* red, ruddy. **5.** RUBIDIUM, from Latin *rūbidus,* red. **6.** Suffixed (stative) form **rudh-ē-.* RUBESCENT, from Latin *rubēre,* to be red. **7.** Suffixed form **(ǝ)rudh-ro-.* **a.** RUBELLA, RUBRIC; BILIRUBIN, from Latin *ruber,* red; **b.** RUTILANT, RUTILE, from Latin *rutilus,* reddish; **c.** ERYTHEMA, ERYTHRO-, from Greek *eruthros,* red; **d.** ERYSIPELAS, from possibly remade Greek *erusi-,* red, reddening. **8.** Suffixed form **rudh-to-.* ROUX, RUSSET, from Latin *russus,* red. [Pokorny *reudh-* 872.]

reup- Also **reub-.** To snatch.
I. Basic form **reub-.* RIP[1], from Flemish *rippen,* to rip, from Germanic **rupjan.*
II. O-grade form **roup-.* **1a.** REAVE[1], from Old English *rēafian,* to plunder; **b.** BEREAVE, from Old English *berēafian,* to take away (*be-, bi-,* intensive prefix; see **ambhi**); **c.** ROVER[2], from Middle Dutch and Middle Low German *roven,* to rob. **a–c** all from Germanic **(bi-)raubōn.* **2a.** ROB, from Old French *rober,* to rob; **b.** RUBATO, from Italian *rubare,* to rob. Both **a** and **b** from a Romance borrowing from Germanic **raubōn,* to rob. **3.** ROBE; GARDEROBE, from Old French *robe,* robe (< "clothes taken as booty"), from Germanic **raubō,* booty. **4.** Suffixed form **roup-tro-.* LOOT, from Sanskrit *loptram,* booty. **5.** RUBLE, from Old Russian *rubiti,* to chop, hew, from Slavic **rub-.*
III. Zero-grade form **rup-.* **1.** USURP, from Latin *ūsūrpāre* (< **ūsu-rup-; ūsus,* use, usage, from *ūtī,* to use), originally "to interrupt the orderly acquisition of something by the act of using," whence to take into use, usurp. **2.** Nasalized zero-grade form **ru-m-p-.* ROUT[1], RUPTURE; ABRUPT, BANKRUPT, CORRUPT, DISRUPT, ERUPT, INTERRUPT, IRRUPT, RUPICOLOUS, from Latin *rumpere,* to break. [In Pokorny 2. *reu-* 868.]

r̥tko- Bear. **1.** URSINE, from Latin *ursus,* bear (< **orcsos*). **2.** ARCTIC, ARCTURUS, from Greek *arktos,* bear. [Pokorny *r̂k̂þo-s* 875.]

sāǝwel- The sun. **1.** Variant forms **swen-, *sun-.* **a.** *(i)* SUN, from Old English *sunne,* sun; *(ii)* SUNDEW, from Middle Dutch *sonne,* sun. Both *(i)* and *(ii)* from Germanic **sunnōn-;* **b.** SUNDAY, from Old English *sunnandæg,* Sunday, from Germanic compound **sunnōn-dagaz,* "day of the sun" (translation of Latin *diēs sōlis*); **c.** SOUTH, SOUTHERN, from Old English *sūth,* south, and *sūtherne,* southern, from Germanic derivative **sunthaz,* "sun-side," south. **2.** Variant form **s(ǝ)wōl-.* SOL[3], SOL, SOLAR, SOLARIUM; GIRASOL, INSOLATE, PARASOL, SOLANACEOUS, SOLANINE, SOLSTICE, TURNSOLE, from Latin *sōl,* the sun. **3.** Suffixed form **sāwel-yo-.* HELIACAL, HELIO-, HELIUM; ANTHELION, APHELION, ISOHEL, PARHELION, PERIHELION, from Greek *hēlios,* sun. [Pokorny *sâu̯el-* 881.]

sak- To sanctify. **1.** Suffixed form **sak-ro-.* **a.** SACRED, SACRISTAN, SEXTON; CONSECRATE, EXECRATE, from Latin *sacer,* holy, sacred, dedicated; **b.** compound **sakro-dhōt-,* "performer of sacred rites" (**-dhōt-,* doer; see **dhē-**). SACERDOTAL, from Latin *sacerdōs,* priest. **2.** Nasalized form **sa-n-k-.* SAINT, SANCTUM; CORPOSANT, SACROSANCT, SANCTIFY, from Latin *sancīre* (past participle *sānctus*), to make sacred, consecrate. [Pokorny *sak-* 878.]

sal- Salt. **1.** Extended form **sald-.* **a.** Suffixed form **sald-o-.* SALT, from Old English *sealt,* salt, from Germanic **saltam;* **b.** *(i)* SOUSE[1], from Old French *sous,* pickled meat; *(ii)* SILT, from Middle English *cylte,* fine sand, from a source probably akin to Danish and Norwegian *sylt,* salt marsh. Both *(i)* and *(ii)* from Germanic zero-grade suffixed extended form **sult-jō;* **c.** SALSA, SAUCE, SAUSAGE, from Latin *sallere* (past participle *salsus* < **sald-to-*), to salt. **2.** SAL, SALAD, SALAMI, SALARY, SALI-, SALINE; SALMAGUNDI, SALTCELLAR, SALTPETER, from Latin *sāl* (genitive *salis*), salt. **3.** HALO-, from Greek *hals* (stem *hal-*), salt, sea. [Pokorny 1. *sal-* 878.]

sed- To sit.
I. Basic form **sed-.* **1.** Suffixed form **sed-yo-.* **a.** SIT, from Old English *sittan,* to sit; **b.** SITZ BATH, SITZMARK, from Old High German *sizzen,* to sit. Both **a** and **b** from Germanic **sitjan.* **2.** Suffixed form **sed-lo-,* seat. SETTLE, from Old English *setl,* seat, from Germanic **setlaz.* **3.** Suffixed (stative) form **sed-ē-.* SÉANCE, SEDENTARY, SEDILE, SEDIMENT, SESSILE, SESSION, SEWER[2], SIEGE; ASSESS, ASSIDUOUS, ASSIZE, DISSIDENT, INSESSORIAL, INSIDIOUS, OBSESS, POSSESS, PRESIDE, RESIDE, SUBSIDY, SUPERSEDE, SURCEASE, from Latin *sedēre,* to sit. **4.** Suffixed form **sed-rā-.* -HEDRON; CATHEDRA, CATHEDRAL, CHAIR, EPHEDRINE, EXEDRA, SANHEDRIN, TETRAHEDRON, from Greek *hedrā,* seat, chair, face of a geometric solid. **5.** Prefixed and suffixed form **pi-sed-yo-,* to sit upon (**pi,* on; see **epi**). PIEZO-; ISOPIESTIC, from Greek *piezein,* to press tight. **6.** Basic form **sed-.* **a.** EDAPHIC, from Greek *edaphos,* ground, foundation (with Greek suffix *-aphos*); **b.** UPANISHAD, from Sanskrit *upaniṣad,* Upanishad, from *-sad,* sitting; **c.** TANIST, from Old Irish *tānaise,* designated successor, from Celtic **tānihessio-,* "one who is waited for," from **to-ad-ni-sed-tio-,* from **to-ad-ni-sed-,* to wait for (**to-,* to; **ad-,* to; **ni-,* down). **7.** Suffixed form **sed-o-,* sitting. EISTEDDFOD, from Welsh *eistedd,* sitting, from Celtic **eks-dī-sedo-* (**eks-,* out, and **dī-,* out, from; see **eghs**).
II. O-grade form **sod-.* **1.** Perhaps suffixed form **sod-dhlo-.* SADDLE, from Old English *sadol,* saddle, from Germanic **sadulaz,* seat, saddle. **2.** Suffixed (causative) form **sod-eyo-.* **a.** SET[1], from Old English *settan,* to place; **b.** BESET, from Old English *besettan,* to set near; **c.** ERSATZ, from Old High German *irsezzan,* to replace, from *sezzan,* to set. **a–c** all from Germanic **(bi-)satjan,* to cause to sit, set. **3.** Suffixed form **sod-yo-.* SOIL[1], from Latin *solium,* throne, seat.
III. Zero-grade form **-sd-* (in compounds), assimilated to **-zd-.* **1.** Reduplicated form **si-sd-* becoming **si-zd-.* **a.** SUBSIDE, from Latin *sīdere,* to sit down, settle; **b.** SYNIZESIS, from Greek *hizein,* to sit down, settle down. **2.** Compound suffixed form **ni-zd-o-,* nest, literally "(bird's place of) sitting down" (**ni-,* down). **a.** NEST, from Old English *nest,* from Germanic **nistaz;* **b.** NICHE, NICK, NIDE, NIDUS; EYAS, NIDICOLOUS, NIDIFUGOUS, NIDIFY, from Latin *nīdus.* nest. **3.** Compound suffixed form **kuzdho-zd-,* "sitting over a treasure" (**kuzdho-,* treasure; see **(s)keu-**). CUSTODY, from Latin *custōs,* guard.
IV. Lengthened-grade form **sēd-.* **1.** SEE[2], from Latin *sēdēs,* seat, residence. **2.** Suffixed form **sēd-i-,* settler. COSSET, possibly from Old English *-sǣta, -sǣte,* inhabitant(s), from Germanic **sētōn-, *sāti-.* **3.** Suffixed form **sēd-yo-.* SEAT, from Old Norse *sæti,* seat, from Germanic **(ge)sētjam,* seat (**ge-, *ga-,* collective prefix; see **kom**). **4.** Suffixed form **sēd-ā-.* SEDATE[1], from Latin *sēdāre,* to settle, calm down. **5.** Suffixed form **sēd-es-,* seat. BANSHEE, from Old Irish *síd,* fairy mound.
V. Lengthened o-grade form **sōd-.* SOOT, from Old English *sōt,* soot (< "that which settles"), from Germanic **sōtam,* from suffixed form **sōd-o-.* [Pokorny *sed-* 884.]

segh- To hold. **1.** HECTIC; CACHEXIA, CATHEXIS, ENTELECHY, EUNUCH, OPHIUCHUS, from Greek *ekhein,* to hold, possess, be in a certain condition, and *hexis,* habit, condition. **2.** Possible suffixed (abstract noun) form **segh-wēr,* toughness, steadfastness, with derivative **segh-wēr-o-,* tough, stern. SEVERE; ASSEVERATE, PERSEVERE, from Latin *sevērus,* stern; **b.** STHENIA; ASTHENIA, CALISTHENICS, HYPERSTHENE, MYASTHENIA, from Greek *sthenos,* physical strength, from a possible related abstract noun form **sgh-wen-es-* (with zero-grade of the root). **3.** O-grade form **sogh-.* EPOCH, from Greek *epokhē,* "a holding back," pause, cessation, position in time (*epi-,* on, at; see **epi**). **4.** Zero-grade form **sgh-.* **a.** SCHEME, from Greek *skhēma,* "a holding," form, figure; **b.** SCHOLAR, SCHOLASTIC, SCHOLIUM, SCHOOL[1], from Greek *skholē,* "a holding back," stop, rest, leisure, employment of leisure in disputation, school. **5.** Reduplicated form **si-sgh-.* ISCHEMIA, from Greek *iskhein,* to keep back. [Pokorny *seĝh-* 888.]

sek- To cut. **1.** SCYTHE, from Old English *sīthe, sigthe,* sickle, from Germanic **segithō,* sickle. **2.** Suffixed o-grade form **sok-ā-.* SAW[1]; HACKSAW, from Old English *sagu, sage,* saw, from Germanic **sagō,* a cutting tool, saw. **3.** Suffixed o-grade form **sok-yo-.* SEDGE, from Old English *secg,* sedge, from Germanic **sagjaz,* "sword," plant with a cutting edge. **4.** Suffixed o-grade form **sok-so-* in Germanic **sahsam,* knife. Traditionally (but doubtfully) regarded as from Germanic **sahsam* is the West Germanic tribal name **Saxon-,* Saxon (as if "warrior with knives"). SAXON, from Late Latin *Saxō* (plural *Saxonēs*), a Saxon. **5.** Extended root **skend-,* to peel off, flay. SKIN, from Old Norse *skinn,* skin, from Germanic **skinth-.* **6.** Basic form **sek-.* SECANT, -SECT, SECTILE, SECTION, SECTOR, SEGMENT; DISSECT, INSECT, INTERSECT, RESECT, TRANSECT, from Latin *secāre,* to cut. **7.** Lengthened-grade form **sēk-.* SICKLE, from Latin *sēcula,* sickle. **8.** Possible suffixed variant form **sak-so-.* SASSAFRAS, SAXATILE; SAXIFRAGE, from Latin *saxum,* stone (< "broken-off piece"?). [Pokorny 2. *sĕk-* 895, *sken-(d-)* 929.] See also extended root **(s)ker-[1]**.

sek^w-[1] To follow. **1.** SECT, SEGUE, SEGUIDILLA, SEQUACIOUS, SEQUEL, SEQUENCE, SUE, SUIT, SUITE, SUITOR; CONSEQUENT, ENSUE, EXECUTE, OBSEQUIOUS, PERSECUTE, PROSECUTE, PURSUE, SUBSEQUENT, from Latin *sequī,* to follow. **2.** SEQUESTER, SEQUESTRUM, from Latin *sequester,* "follower," mediator, depositary. **3.** Suffixed (participial) form **sek^w-ondo-.* SECOND[2], SECONDO, SECUND, from Latin *secundus,* following, coming next, second. **4.** Suffixed form **sek^{w}-os,* following. EXTRINSIC, INTRINSIC, from Latin *secus,* along, alongside of. **5.** Suffixed form **sek^{w}-no-.* SCARLET, SCARLATINA, SEAL[1], SEGNO, SIGIL, SIGN; ASSIGN, CONSIGN, DESIGNATE, INSIGNIA, RESIGN, from Latin *signum,* identifying mark, sign (< "standard that one follows"). **6.** Suffixed o-grade form **sok^{w}-yo-.* SOCIABLE, SOCIAL, SOCIETY, SOCIO-; ASSOCIATE, CONSOCIATE, DISSOCIATE, from Latin *socius,* ally, companion (< "follower"). [Pokorny 1. *sek^{u}-* 896.]

sek^{w}-[2] To perceive, see. **1.** SEE[1], from Old English *sēon,* to see, from Germanic **sehwan,* to see. **2.** SIGHT, from Old English *sihth, gesiht,* vision, spectacle, from Germanic abstract noun **sih-tiz.* [Pokorny 2. *sek^{u}-* 897.]

sek^{w}-[3] To say, utter. **1.** O-grade form **sok^{w}-.* **a.** Suffixed form **sok^{w}-yo-.* SAY; GAINSAY, from Old English *secgan,* to say, from Germanic **sagjan;* **b.** suffixed form **sok^{w}-ā-.* *(i)* SAW[2], from Old English *sagu,* a saying, speech; *(ii)* SAGA, from Old Norse *saga,* a saying, narrative. Both *(i)* and *(ii)* from Germanic **sagō,* a saying. **2.** Perhaps suffixed zero-grade form **sk^{w}-e-tlo-,* narration. **a.** SKALD, from Old Norse *skāld,* poet, "satirist"; **b.** SCOLD, from Middle English *scolde,* an abusive person, from a Scandinavian source akin to Old Norse *skāld* (see above). Both **a** and **b** from North Germanic **skathla.* [In Pokorny 2. *sek^{u}-* 897.]

sem-[1] One; also adverbially "as one," together with.

I. Full-grade form **sem-.* **1a.** HENDECASYLLABIC, HENDIADYS, HENOTHEISM, HYPHEN, from Greek *heis* (< nominative singular masculine **hen-s* < **hem-s*), one; **b.** Greek *he-* in *hekaton,* one hundred (? dissimilated from **hem-katon;* see **dekm̥**). Both **a** and **b** from Greek **hem-.* **2.** Suffixed form **sem-el-.* SIMULTANEOUS; ASSEMBLE, ENSEMBLE, from Latin *simul,* at the same time. **3.** Suffixed form **sem-golo-.* SINGLE, from Latin *singulus,* alone, single. **4.** Compound **sem-per-* (**per,* during, for; see **per[1]**). SEMPRE; SEMPITERNAL, from Latin *semper,* always, ever (< "once for all").

II. O-grade form **som-.* **1.** BONZE, SAMBAL, SAMSARA, SANDHI, SANKHYA, SANNYASI, SANSKRIT, from Sanskrit *sam,* together. **2.** Suffixed form **som-o-.* **a.** SAME, from Old Norse *samr,* same, from Germanic **sama-,* same; **b.** HOMEO-, HOMO-; ANOMALOUS, from Greek *homos,* same; **c.** HOMILY, from Greek *homīlos,* crowd. **3.** Suffixed form **som-alo-.* HOMOLOGRAPHIC, from Greek *homalos,* like, even, level.

III. Lengthened o-grade form **sōm-.* **1.** Suffixed form **sōm-i-.* SEEM, SEEMLY, from Old Norse *sœmr,* fitting, agreeable (< "making one," "reconciling"), from Germanic **sōmi-.* **2.** Suffixed lengthened o-grade form **sōm-o-.* SAMIZDAT, SAMOVAR, from Russian *sam(o)-,* self.

IV. Zero-grade form **sm̥-.* **1.** ACOLYTE, ANACOLUTHON, from Greek compound *akolouthos,* accompanying (*-kolouthos,* from o-grade of *keleuthos,* way, path), from *ha-, a-,* together. **2.** Compound form **sm̥-plo-* (**-plo-,* -fold). **a.** SIMPLE, from Latin *simplus,* simple; **b.** HAPLOID, from Greek *haploos, haplous,* single, simple. **3.** Suffixed form **sm̥m-o-.* **a.** SOME, from Old English *sum,* one, a certain one; **b.** -SOME[1], from Old English *-sum,* -like. Both **a** and **b** from Germanic **suma-.* **4.** Suffixed form **sm̥m-alo-.* SIMILAR; ASSIMILATE, RESEMBLE, from Latin *similis,* of the same kind, like. **5.** Compound **sm̥-kēro-,* of one growing (see **ker-[2]**). **6.** Suffixed form **sm̥-tero-.* HETERO-, from Greek *heteros* (earlier *hateros*), one of two, other. **7.** Compound **sm̥-plek-,* "one-fold," simple (**-plek-,* -fold; see **plek-**). SEMPLICE, SIMPLEX, SIMPLICITY, from Latin *simplex,* simple. **8.** Suffixed compound form **sm̥-g^{w}elbh-(e)yo-,* "of one womb" (**g^{w}elbh-,* womb). DIADELPHOUS, MONADELPHOUS, from Greek *adelph(e)os,* brother, originally adjective meaning "of the same womb" in the phrase **phrātēr adelpheos,* uterine brother. **9.** Extended form **sm̥ma.* HAMADRYAD, from Greek *hama,* together with, at the same time. [Pokorny 2. *sem-* 902.]

sem-[2] Summer. Also **semə-.** Suffixed zero-grade form **sm̥ə-aro-.* SUMMER[1], from Old English *sumor,* summer, from Germanic **sumaraz.* [Pokorny 3. *sem-* 905.]

seng^{w}h- To sing, make an incantation. **1a.** SING, from Old English *singan,* to sing; **b.** MEISTERSINGER, MINNESINGER, SINGSPIEL, from Old High German *singan,* to sing. Both **a** and **b** from Germanic **singan.* **2.** Suffixed o-grade form **song^{w}h-o-,* singing, song. SONG, from Old English *sang, song,* song, from Germanic **sangwaz.* [Pokorny *seng^{u}h-* 906.]

septm̥ Seven. **1.** SEVEN; SEVENTEEN, SEVENTY, from Old English *seofon,* seven, with derivatives *(hund)seofontig,* seventy, and *seofontīne,* seventeen (*-tīne,* ten; see **dekm̥**), from Germanic **sebun.* **2.** SEPTEMBER, SEPTENNIAL, SEPTET, SEPTUAGINT, SEPTUPLE; SEPTENTRION, from Latin *septem,* seven. **3.** HEBDOMAD, HEPTA-, HEPTAD, from Greek *hepta,* seven. [Pokorny *septm̥* 909.]

ser- To protect. **1.** Extended form **serw-.* CONSERVE, OBSERVE, PRESERVE, RESERVE, RESERVOIR, from Latin *servāre,* to keep, preserve. **2.** Perhaps suffixed lengthened-grade form **sēr-ōs-.* HERO, from Greek *hērōs,* "protector," hero. [Pokorny 2. *ser-* 910.]

seuə- To give birth. Suffixed zero-grade form in derivative noun **su(ə)-nu-,* son. SON, from Old English *sunu,* son, from Germanic **sunuz.* [Pokorny 2. *seu-* 913.] See also **sū-.**

(s)ker-[1] To cut.

I. Basic form **sker-, *ker-.* **1a.** SHEAR, from Old English *scieran, sceran,* to cut; **b.** SHEER[1], from Low German *scheren,* to move to and fro, and Dutch *scheren,* to withdraw, depart. Both **a** and **b** from Germanic **skeran.* **2a.** SHARE[2], from Old English *scēar,* plowshare; **b.** SHARE[1], from Old English *scearu, scaru,* portion, division (but recorded only in the sense of "fork of the body," "tonsure"). Both **a** and **b** from Germanic **skeraz.* **3a.** SHEAR, from Old English *scēar,* scissors, from Germanic **skēr-ō* and **sker-iz-;* **b.** compound **skēr-berg-,* "sword protector," scabbard (**berg-,* protector). SCABBARD, from Old French *escauberc,* scabbard, possibly from a Germanic source akin to Old High German *scarberc,* scabbard. Both **a** and **b** from Germanic **skēr-.* **4.** SCORE, from Old Norse *skor,* notch, tally, twenty, from Germanic **skur-.* **5.** SCAR[2], SKERRY, from Old Norse *sker,* low reef (< "something cut off"), from Germanic suffixed form **skar-jam.* **6.** Suffixed o-grade extended form **skorp-o-.* SCARF[2], from Old Norse *skarfr,* diagonally-cut end of a board, from Germanic **skarfaz.* **7.** Suffixed o-grade extended form **skord-o-.* SHARD, from Old English *sceard,* a cut, notch, from Germanic **skardaz.* **8.** Extended form **skerd-* in suffixed zero-grade form **skr̥d-o-.* **a.** SHORT, from Old English *scort, sceort,* "cut," short; **b.** SHIRT, from Old English *scyrte,* skirt (< "cut piece"); **c.** SKIRT, from Old Norse *skyrta,* shirt. **a–c** all from Germanic **skurtaz.* **9a.** SCRIMMAGE, SKIRMISH, from Old French *eskermir,* to fight with a sword, fence, and Old Italian *scaramuccia,* skirmish, from a source akin to Old High German *skirmen,* to protect; **b.** SCREEN, from Middle Dutch *scherm,* shield. Both **a** and **b** from Germanic extended form **skerm-.* **10.** Variant form **kar-.* CARNAGE, CARNAL, CARNASSIAL, CARNATION, CARNIVAL, CARRION, CARUNCLE, CHARNEL, CRONE; CARNIVOROUS, CHARCUTERIE, INCARNATE, from Latin *carō* (stem *carn-*), flesh. **11.** Suffixed o-grade form **kor-yo-.* CORIACEOUS, CORIUM, CUIRASS, CURRIER; EXCORIATE, from Latin *corium,* leather (originally "piece of hide"). **12.** Suffixed zero-grade form **kr̥-to-.* CURT, CURTAL, KIRTLE, from Latin *curtus,* short. **13.** Suffixed o-grade form **kor-mo-.* CORM, from Greek *kormos,* a trimmed tree trunk. **14.** Suffixed o-grade form **kor-i-.* COREOPSIS, from Greek *koris,* bedbug (< "cutter"). **15.** Suffixed zero-grade form **skr̥-ā-.* SHORE[1], from Old English *scora,* shore, from Germanic **skur-ō.*

II. Extended roots **skert-, *kert-.* **1.** Zero-grade form **kr̥t-* or o-grade form **kort-.* CORTEX; DECORTICATE, from Latin *cortex,* bark (< "that which can be cut off"). **2.** Suffixed form **kert-snā-.* CENACLE, from Latin *cēna,* meal (< "portion of food").

III. Extended root **skerp-.* SCURF, probably from a Scandinavian source akin to Old English *sceorf,* scab, scurf, from Germanic **skerf-.*

IV. Extended root **skerb(h)-, *skreb(h)-.* **1a.** SHARP, from Old English *scearp,* sharp; **b.** SCARP, from Italian *scarpa,* embankment, possibly from a Germanic source akin to Gothic *skarpō,* pointed object. Both **a** and **b** from Germanic **skarpa-,* cutting, sharp. **2a.** SCRAP[1], from Old Norse *skrap,* "pieces," remains; **b.** SCRAPE, from Old Norse *skrapa,* to scratch. Both **a** and **b** from Germanic **skrap-.* **3a.** SCRABBLE, from Middle Dutch *schrabben,* to scrape; **b.** SCRUB[1], from Middle Dutch *schrobben,* to scrape. Both **a** and **b** from Germanic **skrab-.* **4.** SHRUB[1], from Old English *scrybb,* shrub (< "rough plant"), from Germanic **skrub-.* **5.** SCROBICULATE, from Latin *scrobis,* trench, ditch. **6.** SCREW, SCROFULA, from Latin *scrōfa,* a sow (< "rooter, digger").

V. Extended root **(s)kers-.* BIAS, from Greek *epikarsios,* at an angle (*epi-,* at; see **epi**), from suffixed zero-grade form **kr̥s-yo-.* [Pokorny 4. *(s)ker-,* Section I. 938.] See also extended root **skrībh-.**

sker-[2] Excrement, dung. **1.** Noun form **sk-ōr, *sk-n-.* SCATO-, SCORIA, SKATOLE, from Greek *skōr* (stem *skat-* < **sk-n̥-t-*), dung. **2.** Form **sker-.* Extended form **skert-* in taboo metathesis **sterk-os-.* **a.** STERCORACEOUS, from Latin *stercus,* dung; **b.** variant forms **(s)terg-, *(s)treg-.* DRECK, from Middle High German *drëc,* dung, from Germanic **threkka-.* [Pokorny *sk̑er-(d-)* 947, 8. *(s)ter-* 1031.]

(s)keu- To cover, conceal. Zero-grade form **(s)ku-.* Variant **(s)keuə-,* zero-grade form **(s)kuə-,* contracted to **(s)kū-.* **1.** Suffixed basic form. **a.** SKY, from Old Norse *skȳ,* cloud; **b.** SKEWBALD, from a Scandinavian source akin to Old Norse *skȳ,* cloud. Both **a** and **b** from Germanic **skeu-jam,* cloud ("cloud cover"). **2.** Zero-grade form **skū-.* **a.** Suffixed form **skū-mo-.* *(i)* SKIM, from Old French *escume,* scum; *(ii)* MEERSCHAUM, from Old High German *scūm,* scum; *(iii)* SCUM, from Middle Dutch *schūm,* scum. *(i)–(iii)* all from Germanic **skūmaz,* foam, scum (< "that which covers the water"); **b.** suffixed form **skū-ro-.* OBSCURE; CHIAROSCURO, from Latin *obscūrus,* "covered," dark (*ob-,* away from; see **epi**). **3.** Zero-grade form **ku̥-.* **a.** Suffixed form **kū-ti-.* HIDE[2], from Old English *hȳd,* skin, hide, from Germanic **hūdiz;* **b.** suffixed form **ku-ti-.* CUTANEOUS, CUTICLE, CUTIS; CUTIN, from Latin *cutis* skin; **c.** possibly suffixed form **kū-lo-.* CULET, CULOTTE; BASCULE, RECOIL, from Latin *cūlus,* the rump, backside; **d.** suffixed form **ku-to-.* -CYTE, CYTO-, from Greek *kutos,* a hollow, vessel. **4.** Extended zero-grade form **kus-.* **a.** *(i)* HOSE, HOSEL, from Old English *hosa, hose,* covering for the leg; *(ii)* LEDERHOSEN, from Old High German *hosa,* leg covering. Both *(i)* and *(ii)* from Germanic **husōn-;* **b.** suffixed form **kuz-dho-* (or suffixed extended form **kudh-to-*). *(i)* HOARD, from Old English *hord,* stock, store, treasure (< "thing hidden away"), from Germanic **huzdam;* *(ii)* compound **kuzdho-zd-,* "sitting (over) a treasure" (**-zd-,* sitting; see **sed-**); **c.** KISHKE, from Russian *kishka,* gut (< "sheath"). **5.** Suffixed extended zero-grade form **kut-no-.* CUNNILINGUS, from Latin *cunnus,* vulva (< "sheath"). **6.** Extended root **keudh-.* **a.** HIDE[1], from Old English *hȳdan,* to hide, cover up, from Germanic suffixed lengthened zero-grade form **hūd-jan;* **b.** HUT, from French *hutte,* hut, from Germanic suffixed zero-grade form **hūd-jōn-;* **c.** HUDDLE, from Low German *hudeln,* to crowd together, probably from Germanic **hŭd-.* **7.** SHIELING, from a Scandinavian source akin to Old Norse *skāli,* hut, from Germanic suffixed o-grade form **skaw-ala-.* [Pokorny 2. *(s)keu-* 951.]

skrībh- To cut, separate, sift. Extension of **(s)ker-[1].** **1.** SCRIBBLE, SCRIBE, SCRIPT, SCRIPTORIUM, SCRIPTURE, SERIF, SHRIVE; ASCRIBE, CIRCUMSCRIBE, CONSCRIPT, DESCRIBE, FESTSCHRIFT, INSCRIBE, MANUSCRIPT, POSTSCRIPT, PRESCRIBE, PROSCRIBE, RESCRIPT, SUBSCRIBE, SUPERSCRIBE, TRANSCRIBE, from Latin *scrībere,* to scratch, incise, write. **2.** SCARIFY[1], from Greek *skarīphos,* scratching, sketch, pencil. [Pokorny 4. *(s)ker-,* Section II. 945.]

sleiə- Bluish. **1.** O-grade form **sloi(ə)-.* SLOE, from Old English *slāh, slā,* sloe (< "bluish fruit"), from Germanic **slaihwōn.* **2.** Zero-grade form **slī-* (< **sliə-*). **a.** Suffixed form **slī-wo-.* LAVENDER, LIVID, from Latin *līvēre,* to be bluish; **b.** suffixed form **slī-wā-.* SLIVOVITZ, from Serbo-Croatian *šljìva,* plum. [Pokorny *(s)lī-* 965.]

(s)mer- To remember. **1.** Suffixed zero-grade form **mr̥-no-.* MOURN, from Old English *murnan,* to mourn, from Germanic **murnan,* to remember sorrowfully. **2.** Reduplicated form **me-mor-.* **a.** MIMIR, from Old Norse *Mímir,* a giant who guards the well of wisdom, from Germanic **mi-mer-;* **b.** MEMORABLE, MEMORANDUM, MEMORY; COMMEMORATE, REMEMBER, from Latin *memor,* mindful. [Pokorny *(s)mer-* 969.]

snā- To swim. Contracted from **snaə-.* **1.** Extended form **snāgh-.* NEKTON, from Greek *nēkhein,* to swim. **2.** Suffixed zero-grade form **(s)nə-to-.* NATANT, NATATION, NATATORIAL, NATATORIUM; SUPERNATANT, from Latin *nāre,* to swim, and frequentative *natāre,* to swim. **3.** Attributed by some to this root (but more likely obscure) is Greek *nēsos,* island: CHERSONESE. [Pokorny *snā-* 971.] See also extended root **(s)nāu-**.

(s)nāu- To swim, flow, let flow, whence suckle. Contracted from **(s)naəu-;* extension of **snā-**. **1.** Suffixed basic form **nāw-yo-*. NAIAD, from Greek *Naias,* fountain nymph, probably from *nān,* to flow. **2.** Variant (metathesized) root form **(s)neu(ə)-*. NEUSTON, from Greek *nein,* to swim. **3.** Zero-grade form **(s)nū-* (< **snuə-*) in suffixed form **nū-trī* (with feminine agent suffix). NOURISH, NURSE, NURTURE, NUTRIENT, NUTRIMENT, NUTRITION, NUTRITIOUS, NUTRITIVE, from Latin *nūtrīx,* nurse, and *nūtrīre,* to suckle, nourish. [In Pokorny *snā-* 971.]

so- This, that (nominative). For other cases see **to-**. **1.** THE[1], from Late Old English *the,* masculine demonstrative pronoun, replacing *se* (with *th-* from oblique forms; see **to-**). **2.** HOI POLLOI, from Greek *ho,* the. **3.** Feminine form **syā-*. SHE, from Old English *sēo, sīe,* she, from Germanic **sjō.* **4.** Compound variant form **sei-ke* (**-ke,* "this"; see **ko-**). SIC[1], from Latin *sīc,* thus, so, in that manner. [Pokorny *so(s)* 978.]

sol- Whole. Also **solə-**.
I. Basic form **sol-*. **1.** Suffixed form **sol-ido-*. SOLDER, SOLDIER, SOLID, SOU; CONSOLIDATE, from Latin *solidus,* solid. **2.** Suffixed form **sol-wo-*. HOLO-; CATHOLIC, from Greek *holos,* whole. **3.** Dialectal geminated form **soll-o-*. **a.** SOLICIT, SOLICITOUS; INSOUCIANT, from Latin *sollus,* whole, entire, unbroken; **b.** SOLEMN, from Latin *sollemnis* (second element obscure), celebrated at fixed dates (said of religious rites), established, religious, solemn.
II. Variant form **solə-*. **1.** Suffixed zero-grade form **sḷə-u-* giving **sal-u-*. SALUBRIOUS, SALUTARY, SALUTE, from Latin *salūs,* health, a whole or sound condition. **2.** Suffixed zero-grade form **sḷə-wo-* giving **sala-wo-*. SAFE, SAGE[2], SALVAGE, SALVO[1], SALVO[2], SAVE[1], SAVE[2], from Latin *salvus,* whole, safe, healthy, uninjured. [Pokorny *solo-* 979.]

spek- To observe.
I. Basic form **spek-*. **1a.** ESPY, SPY, from Old French *espier,* to watch; **b.** ESPIONAGE, from Old Italian *spione,* spy, from Germanic derivative **speh-ōn-,* watcher. Both **a** and **b** from Germanic **spehōn.* **2.** Suffixed form **spek-yo-*. SPECIMEN, SPECTACLE, SPECTRUM, SPECULATE, SPECULUM, SPICE; ASPECT, CIRCUMSPECT, CONSPICUOUS, DESPISE, EXPECT, FRONTISPIECE, INSPECT, INTROSPECT, PERSPECTIVE, PERSPICACIOUS, PROSPECT, RESPECT, RESPITE, RETROSPECT, SPIEGELEISEN, SUSPECT, TRANSPICUOUS, from Latin *specere,* to look at. **3.** SPECIES, SPECIOUS; ESPECIAL, from Latin *speciēs,* a seeing, sight, form. **4.** Suffixed form **spek-s,* "he who sees." **a.** Latin *auspex,* diviner (see **awi-**); **b.** possibly Latin *haruspex,* diviner (if < **ghṛəu-speks,* "he who inspects entrails," but perhaps borrowed from Etruscan): HARUSPEX. **5.** Suffixed form **spek-ā-*. DESPICABLE, from Latin (denominative) *dēspicārī,* to despise, look down on (*dē-,* down). **6.** Suffixed metathetical form **skep-yo-*. SKEPTIC, from Greek *skeptesthai,* to examine, consider.
II. Extended o-grade form **spoko-*. SCOPE, -SCOPE, -SCOPY; BISHOP, EPISCOPAL, HOROSCOPE, TELESCOPE, from metathesized Greek *skopos,* one who watches, also object of attention, goal, and its denominative *skopein* (< **skop-eyo-*), to see. [Pokorny *spek-* 984.]

spend- To make an offering, perform a rite, hence to engage oneself by a ritual act. O-grade from **spond-*. **1.** Suffixed form **spond-eyo-*. SPONSOR, SPOUSE; DESPOND, ESPOUSE, RESPOND, from Latin *spondēre,* to make a solemn promise, pledge, betroth. **2.** Suffixed form **spond-ā-*. SPONDEE, from Greek *spondē,* libation, offering. [Pokorny *spend-* 989.]

sperə- Ankle. Zero-grade form **spṛ(ə)-*. **1.** SPUR, from Old English *spura, spora,* spur, from Germanic suffixed form **spur-ōn-*. **2.** Nasalized zero-grade form **spṛ-n-ə-*. SPURN, from Old English *spurnan, spornan,* to kick, strike against, from Germanic **spurnōn.* **3.** SPOOR, from Middle Dutch *spor, spoor,* track of an animal, from Germanic suffixed form **spur-am.* [Pokorny 1. *sp(h)er-* 992.]

sreu- To flow. **1.** Suffixed o-grade form **srou-mo-*. **a.** STREAM, from Old English *strēam,* stream; **b.** MAELSTROM, from Middle Dutch *stroom,* stream. Both **a** and **b** from Germanic **straumaz,* stream. **2.** Basic form **sreu-*. **a.** RHEO-, -RRHEA; CATARRH, DIARRHEA, HEMORRHOID, RHYOLITE, from Greek *rhein,* to flow, with o-grade *rhoos,* flowing, a flowing; **b.** suffixed form **sreu-mṇ.* RHEUM, from Greek *rheuma,* stream, humor of the body. **3.** Suffixed zero-grade form **sru-dhmo-*. RHYTHM, from Greek *rhuthmos,* measure, recurring motion, rhythm. **4.** Suffixed zero-grade form **sru-to-*. RHYTON, from Greek *rhutos,* fluid, liquid. **5.** Perhaps zero-grade extended form **srug-*. SASTRUGA, from Russian *struga,* deep place. [Pokorny *sreu-* 1003.]

stā- To stand; with derivatives meaning "place or thing that is standing." Contracted from **staə-*.
I. Basic form **stā-*. **1.** Extended form **stādh-*. **a.** STEED, from Old English *stēda,* stallion, studhorse (< "place for breeding horses"), from Germanic **stōd-jōn-;* **b.** STUD[2], from Old English *stōd,* establishment for breeding horses, from Germanic **stōdō.* **2.** Suffixed form **stā-lo-*. **a.** STOOL, from Old English *stōl,* stool; **b.** Germanic compound **faldistōlaz* (see **pel-**[3]). Both **a** and **b** from Germanic **stōlaz.* **3.** ESTANCIA, STAGE, STANCE, STANCH[1], STANCHION, STANZA, STATIVE, STATOR, STAY[1], STET; ARREST, CIRCUMSTANCE, CONSTANT, CONTRAST, COST, DISTANT, EXTANT, INSTANT, OBSTACLE, OBSTETRIC, OUST, REST[2], RESTHARROW, RESTIVE, SUBSTANCE, from Latin *stāre,* to stand. **4.** Suffixed form **stā-men-*. ETAMINE, STAMEN, STAMMEL, from Latin *stāmen,* thread of the warp (a technical term). **5.** Suffixed form **stā-mon-*. PENSTEMON, from Greek *stēmōn,* thread. **6.** Suffixed form **stā-ro-*. STARETS, from Old Church Slavonic *starŭ,* old ("long-standing").
II. Zero-grade form **stə-* (before consonants). **1.** Nasalized extended form **stə-n-t-*. **a.** STAND, from Old English *standan,* to stand; **b.** UNDERSTAND, from Old English *understandan,* to know, stand under (*under-,* under-; see **ṇdher-**); **c.** STANDARD, from Frankish **standan,* to stand; **d.** STOUND, from Old English *stund,* a fixed time, while, from secondary zero-grade form in Germanic **stund-ō.* **a–d** all from Germanic **standan.* **2.** Suffixed form **stə-tyo-*. STITHY, from Old Norse *stedhi,* anvil, from Germanic **stathjōn-*. **3.** Suffixed form **stə-tlo-*. STADDLE, STALL[2], STARLING[2]; STALWART, from Old English *stathol,* foundation, from Germanic **stathlaz.* **4.** Suffixed form **stə-mno-*. **a.** *(i)* STEM[1], from Old English *stefn,* stem, tree trunk; *(ii)* STALAG, from Old High German *stam,* stem. Both *(i)* and *(ii)* from Germanic **stamniz;* **b.** ESTAMINET, probably from Walloon *stamen,* post to which a cow is tied at the feeding-trough, from a source derived from or akin to Germanic **stamniz.* **5.** Suffixed form **stə-ti-*. **a.** *(i)* STEAD, from Old English *stede,* place; *(ii)* SHTETL, from Old High German *stat,* place. Both *(i)* and *(ii)* from Germanic **stadiz;* **b.** STAT[2], from Latin *statim,* at once; **c.** STATION, from Latin *statiō,* a standing still; **d.** ARMISTICE, SOLSTICE, from Latin *-stitium,* a stoppage; **e.** STASIS, from Greek *stasis* (see **III. 1. b.**), a standing, a standstill. **6.** Suffixed form **stə-to-*. **a.** BESTEAD, from Old Norse *stadhr,* place, from Germanic **stadaz,* placed; **b.** -STAT, STATIC, STATICE, STATO-; ASTASIA, ASTATINE, from Greek *statos,* placed, standing. **7.** Suffixed form **stə-no-*. **a.** DESTINE, from Latin *dēstināre,* to make firm, establish (*dē-,* thoroughly); **b.** OBSTINATE, from Latin *obstināre,* to set one's mind on, persist (*ob-,* on; see **epi**). **8.** Suffixed form **stə-tu-*. ESTATE, ÉTAGÈRE, STAGE, STATE, STATISTICS, STATUE, STATURE, STATUS, STATUTE; CONSTITUTE, DESTITUTE, INSTITUTE, PROSTITUTE, RESTITUTE, SUBSTITUTE, SUPERSTITION, from Latin *status,* manner, position, condition, attitude, with derivatives *statūra,* height, stature, *statuere,* to set up, erect, cause to stand, and *superstes* (< **-stə-t-*), witness ("who stands beyond"). **9.** Suffixed form **stə-dhlo-*. STABLE[2]; CONSTABLE, from Latin *stabulum,* "standing place," stable. **10.** Suffixed form **stə-dhli-*. ESTABLISH, STABLE[1], from Latin *stabilis,* standing firm. **11.** Suffixed form **stə-tā.* -STAT; ENSTATITE, from Greek *-statēs,* one that causes to stand, a standing.
III. Zero-grade form **st-, *st(ə)-* (before vowels). **1.** Reduplicated form **si-st(ə)-*. **a.** ASSIST, CONSIST, DESIST, EXIST, INSIST, INTERSTICE, PERSIST, RESIST, SUBSIST, from Latin *sistere,* to set, place, stop, stand; **b.** APOSTASY, CATASTASIS, DIASTASE, ECSTASY, EPISTASIS, EPISTEMOLOGY, HYPOSTASIS, ICONOSTASIS, ISOSTASY, METASTASIS, PROSTATE, SYSTEM, from Greek *histanai* (aorist *stanai*), to set, place, with *stasis* (**stə-ti-*), a standing (see **II. 5. e.**); **c.** HISTO-; HISTIOCYTE, HISTOGRAM, from Greek *histos,* web, tissue (< "that which is set up"). **2.** Compound form **tri-st-i-* (see **trei-**). **3.** Compound form **por-st-i-* (see **per**[1]). POST[1], from Latin *postis,* post. **4.** Suffixed form **st-o-* in compound **upo-st-o-* (see **upo**).
IV. Extended root **stāu-,* basic meaning "stout-standing, strong." **1.** Suffixed extended form **stāw-ā-*. STOW, from Old English *stōw,* place, from Germanic **stōwō.* **2.** Probable o-grade suffixed extended form **stōw-yā-*. STOA, STOIC, from Greek *stoā* (also *stoiā, stōiā*), porch. **3.** Suffixed extended form **stau-ro-*. **a.** *(i)* STORE; INSTAURATION, from Latin *īnstaurāre,* to restore, set upright again (*in-,* on; see **en**); *(ii)* RESTORE, from Latin *restaurāre,* to restore, rebuild (*re-,* anew, again); **b.** STAUROLITE, from Greek *stauros,* cross, post, stake. **4.** Variant **tau-ro-,* bull (see **tauro-**).
V. Zero-grade extended root **stū-* (< **stuə-,* metathesized from **stəu-*). **1.** Suffixed form **stū-lo-*. STYLITE; AMPHISTYLAR, ASTYLAR, EPISTYLE, HYPOSTYLE, PERISTYLE, PROSTYLE, STYLOBATE, from Greek *stūlos,* pillar. **2.** Secondary full-grade form **steuə-*. Suffixed form **steuə-ro-*. THERAVADA, from Sanskrit *sthavira-,* thick, stout, old. **3.** Variant zero-grade extended root **stu-*. Suffixed form **stu-t-*. STUD[1], from Old English *stuthu, studu,* post, prop.
VI. Secondary full-grade form **steu-*. **1.** Suffixed form **steu-rā-*. STARBOARD, from Old English *stēor-,* a steering, from Germanic **steurō,* "a steering." **2a.** STEER[1], from Old English *stīeran, stēran,* to steer; **b.** STERN[2], from Middle English *sterne,* stern of a boat, possibly from a source akin to Old Norse *stjōrn,* a rudder, a steering, derivative of *stȳra,* to steer. Both **a** and **b** from Germanic denominative **steurjan.* **3.** Suffixed form **steu-ro-,* a larger domestic animal. STEER[2], from Old English *stēor,* steer, from Germanic **steuraz,* ox. **4.** Probably Germanic diminutive **steur-ika-*. STIRK, from Old English *stīrc, stierc,* calf. [Pokorny *stā-* 1004.]

(s)teg- To cover.
I. O-grade form **tog-*. **1a.** THATCH, from Old English *theccan,* to cover; **b.** DECK[2], from Middle Dutch *decken,* to cover; **c.** DECKLE, from Old High German *decchen,* to cover. **a–c** all from Germanic **thakjan.* **2a.** THATCH, from Old English *thæc,* thatch; **b.** DECK[1], from Middle Dutch *dec, decke,* roof, covering. Both **a** and **b** from Germanic **thakam.* **3.** Suffixed form **tog-ā-,* covering. TOGA, from Latin *toga,* toga. **4.** Possibly Sanskrit *sthagayati,* he covers: THUG.
II. Basic form **steg-*. STEGODON, STEGOSAUR, from Greek *stegein,* to cover.
III. Basic form **teg-*. TECTRIX, TECTUM, TEGMEN, TEGMENTUM, TEGULAR, TEGUMENT, TILE, TUILLE; DETECT, INTEGUMENT, OBTECT, PROTECT, from Latin *tegere,* to cover, and *tēgula,* tile (with lengthened-grade root). [Pokorny 1. *(s)teg-* 1013.]

steigh- To stride, step, rise. **1.** Basic form **steigh-*. STY[2]; STIRRUP, from Old English *stīgan,* to go up, rise, from Germanic **stīgan.* **2.** Zero-grade form **stigh-*. **a.** STILE[1], from Old English *stigel,* series of steps, from Germanic **stigila-;* **b.** suffixed form **stigh-to-*. STICKLE, from Old English *stiht(i)an,* to settle, arrange, from Germanic **stihtan,* "to place on a step or base"; **c.** suffixed form **stigh-o-*. STICH; ACROSTIC, CADASTRE, DISTICH, HEMISTICH, PENTASTICH, STICHOMETRY, STICHOMYTHIA, from Greek *stikhos,* row, line, line of verse. **3.** O-grade form **stoigh-*. **a.** Suffixed form **stoigh-ri-*. STAIR, from Old English *stǣger,* stair, step, from Germanic **staigrī;* **b.** STOICHIOMETRY, from Greek *stoikheion,* shadow line, element. [Pokorny *steigh-* 1017.]

stel- To put, stand; with derivatives referring to a standing object or place.
I. Basic form **stel-*. **1.** Suffixed form **stel-ni-*. STILL[1], from Old English *stille,* quiet, fixed, from Germanic **stilli-*. **2.** Suffixed form **stel-yo-*. APOSTLE, DIASTOLE, EPISTLE, PERISTALSIS, SYSTALTIC, from Greek *stellein,* to put in order, prepare, send, make compact (with o-grade and zero-grade forms *stol-* and *stal-*).
II. O-grade form **stol-*. **1.** Suffixed form **stol-no-*. **a.** STALL[1]; FORESTALL, from Old English *steall,* standing place, stable; **b.** STALE[1]; INSTALLMENT[1], from Old French *estal,* place; **c.** STALLION, from Anglo-Norman *estaloun,* stallion; **d.** PEDESTAL, from Old Italian *stallo,* stall; **e.** INSTALL, from Medieval Latin *stallum,* stall; **f.** GESTALT, from Old High German *stellen,* to set, place, from Germanic denominative **stalljan.* **a–f** all from Germanic **stalla-*. **2.** Suffixed form **stol-ōn-*. STO-

LON, from Latin *stolō,* branch, shoot. **3.** Suffixed form **stol-ido-.* STOLID, from Latin *stolidus,* "firm-standing," stupid. **4.** Suffixed form **stol-ā-.* **a.** STALK[1], from Old English *stalu,* upright piece, stalk, from Germanic **stalō;* **b.** STOLE[1], from Greek *stolē,* garment, array, equipment.

III. Zero-grade form **stl̥-.* **1.** Suffixed form **stl̥-to-.* STULTIFY, from Latin *stultus,* foolish (< "unmovable, uneducated"). **2.** Suffixed zero-grade form **stl̥-no-.* STULL, STOLLEN, from Old High German *stollo,* post, support, from Germanic **stullōn-.* **3.** Suffixed zero-grade form **stal-nā-.* STELE, from Greek *stēlē,* pillar.

IV. Extended form **steld-.* **1.** STILT, from Middle English *stilte,* crutch, stilt, from a source akin to Low German and Flemish *stilte,* stick, from Germanic **stiltjōn-.* **2.** Zero-grade form **stl̥d-.* STOUT, from Old French *estout,* stout, from Germanic **stult-,* "walking on stilts," strutting. [Pokorny 3. *stel-* 1019.]

(s)tenə- To thunder. **1.** Zero-grade form **stn̥ə-.* **a.** THUNDER; THURSDAY, from Old English *thunor,* thunder, Thor; **b.** BLUNDERBUSS, DUNDERHEAD, from Middle Dutch *doner, donder,* thunder; **c.** THOR, from Old Norse *Thōrr* (older form *Thunarr*), "thunder," thunder god. **a–c** all from Germanic **thunaraz.* **2.** O-grade form **tonə-.* TORNADO; ASTONISH, DETONATE, STUN, from Latin *tonāre,* to thunder. [Pokorny 1. *(s)ten-* 1021.]

ster- Star. **1.** Suffixed form **ster-s-.* STAR, from Old English *steorra,* star, from Germanic **sterzōn-.* **2.** Suffixed lengthened-grade form **stēr-lā-.* STELLAR, STELLATE; CONSTELLATION, from Latin *stēlla,* star. **3.** Basic form **əster-.* ASTER, ASTERIATED, ASTERISK, ASTERISM, ASTEROID, ASTRAL, ASTRO-; DISASTER, from Greek *astēr,* star, with its derivative *astron,* star, and possible compound *astrapē, asteropē,* lightning, twinkling (< "looking like a star"; *ōps, op-,* eye, appearance; see **ok^{w}-**). **4.** ESTHER[1], perhaps from Persian *sitareh,* star, from Iranian stem **stăr-* (or perhaps of Semitic origin). [Pokorny 2. *stĕr-* 1027.]

sū- Pig. (Contracted from earlier **suə-;* probably a derivative of **seuə-**.) **1.** Suffixed form **suə-īno-.* **a.** SWINE, from Old English *swīn,* swine; **b.** KEELSON, from Old Norse *svīn,* swine. Both **a** and **b** from Germanic **swīnam.* **2.** Suffixed reduced form **su-kā-.* **a.** *(i)* HOG, from Old English *hogg,* hog, from British Celtic **hukk-,* from Celtic expressive form **sukko-,* swine, snout of a swine; *(ii)* SOCKET, from Anglo-Norman *soc,* plowshare, perhaps from Celtic **sukko-;* **b.** SOW[2], from Old English *sugu,* sow, from Germanic **sugō.* **3.** Basic form **sū-.* SOW[2], from Old English *sū,* from Germanic **sū-.* **4.** SOIL[2], from Latin *sūs,* pig. **5.** HYADES, HYENA; HYOSCINE, from Greek *hūs,* swine. [Pokorny *sŭ-s* 1038.]

swād- Sweet, pleasant. **1.** SWEET, from Old English *swēte,* sweet, from Germanic **swōtja-.* **2.** Suffixed form **swād-ē-.* SUASION; ASSUASIVE, DISSUADE, PERSUADE, from Latin *suādēre,* to advise, urge (< "recommend as good"). **3.** Suffixed form **swād-wi-.* SOAVE, SUAVE; ASSUAGE, from Latin *suāvis,* delightful. **4.** Suffixed form **swād-es-.* AEDES, from Greek *ēdos,* pleasure. **5.** Suffixed form **swād-onā.* HEDONIC, HEDONISM, from Greek *hēdonē,* pleasure. [Pokorny *su̯ād-* 1039.]

s(w)e- Pronoun of the third person and reflexive (referring back to the subject of the sentence); further appearing in various forms referring to the social group as an entity, "(we our)selves." **1.** Suffixed extended form **sel-bho-.* SELF, from Old English *self, sylf,* self, same, from Germanic **selbaz,* self. **2.** Suffixed form **s(w)e-bh(o)-.* SIB; GOSSIP, from Old English *sibb,* relative, from Germanic **sibja-,* "one's own," blood relation, relative. **3.** Suffixed form **se-ge.* BUSTLE[1], from Old Norse *-sk,* reflexive suffix (as in *būask,* to make oneself ready), from *sik,* oneself (reflexive pronoun), from Germanic **sik,* self. **4.** Suffixed form **swoi-no-.* SWAIN; BOATSWAIN, from Old Norse *sveinn,* herdsman, boy, from Germanic **swainaz,* "one's own (man)," attendant, servant. **5.** Suffixed form **s(u)w-o-,* one's own. **a.** SUICIDE, from Latin *suī* (genitive), of oneself; **b.** SWAMI, from Sanskrit *svāmī,* "one's own master," owner, prince, from *sva-* (< **swo-*), one's own. **6.** Extended form **sed.* SECEDE, SECERN, SECLUDE, SECRET, SECURE, SEDITION, SEDUCTION, SEDULOUS, SEGREGATE, SELECT, SEPARATE, SEVER, SURE, from Latin *sēd, sē, sē(d)-,* without, apart (< "on one's own"); **c.** SOBER, from Latin compound *sōbrius,* not drunk (*ēbrius,* drunk). **7.** Possibly suffixed lengthened o-grade form **sō-lo-.* SOLE[2], SOLITARY, SOLITUDE, SOLO, SULLEN; DESOLATE, SOLILOQUY, SOLIPSISM, from Latin *sōlus,* by oneself alone. **8.** Extended root **swĕdh-,* "that which is one's own," peculiarity, custom. **a.** SODALITY, from Latin *sodālis* (Archaic Latin *suodāl-*), companion (< "one's own," "relative"); **b.** suffixed form **swēdh-sko-.* CONSUETUDE, CUSTOM, DESUETUDE, MANSUETUDE, MASTIFF, from Latin *suēscere,* to accustom, get accustomed; **c.** ETHIC, ETHOS; CACOËTHES, from Greek *ēthos,* custom, disposition, trait; **d.** suffixed form **swedh-no-.* ETHNIC, ETHNO-, from Greek *ethnos,* band of people living together, nation, people (< "people of one's own kind"). **9.** Suffixed extended form **swet-aro-.* HETAERA, from Greek *hetairos,* comrade, companion, earlier *hetaros.* **10.** Suffixed extended form **swed-yo-.* IDIO-, IDIOM, IDIOT; IDIOPATHY, IDIOSYNCRASY, from Greek *idios,* personal, private ("particular to oneself"). **11.** Suffixed form **swei-no-.* SINN FEIN, from Old Irish *féin,* self. **12.** Suffixed (ablatival) form **swe-tos,* from oneself. KHEDIVE, from Old Iranian *khvadāta-,* lord, by haplology from compound form **khvatō-dāta-,* created from oneself (*dāta-,* created; see **dhē-**). **13.** Perhaps suffixed form **swe-tono-.* KHOTANESE, from Khotanese *Hvatana-,* perhaps "those holding their own (power), masters." [Pokorny *se-* 882.] See also derivative **swo-**.

sweid- Sweat; to sweat.

I. O-grade form **swoid-.* **1.** SWEAT, from Old English *swǣtan,* to sweat, from Germanic **swaitaz,* sweat, with its denominative **swaitjan,* to sweat. **2.** Suffixed form **swoid-os-.* SUDORIFIC; SUDORIFEROUS, from Latin *sūdor,* sweat. **3.** O-grade form **swoid-ā-.* SUDATORIUM, SUINT; EXUDE, TRANSUDE, from Latin *sūdāre,* to sweat.

II. Suffixed zero-grade form **swid-r-os-.* HIDROSIS, from Greek *hidrōs,* sweat. [Pokorny 2. *su̯eid-* 1043.]

s(w)eks Six.

I. Form **seks.* **1.** SIX; SIXTEEN, SIXTY, from Old English *s(i)ex, six,* with derivatives *sixtig,* sixty, and *sixtȳne,* sixteen (*-tȳne,* ten; see **dekm̥**), from Germanic **seks.* **2.** SENARY, SEX-; SEICENTO, SEMESTER, from Latin *sex,* six. **3.** Suffixed form **seks-to-.* SESTET, SESTINA, SEXT, SEXTANT, SEXTILE; SEXTODECIMO, SIESTA, SISTINE, from Latin *sextus,* sixth.

II. Form **sweks.* HEXA-, HEXAD, from Greek *hex,* six. [Pokorny *su̯eḱs* 1044.]

swep- To sleep. **1.** Suffixed form **swep-os-.* SOPOR; SOPORIFIC, from Latin *sopor,* a deep sleep. **2.** Suffixed form **swep-no-.* SOMNI-, SOMNOLENT; INSOMNIA, from Latin *somnus,* sleep. **3.** Suffixed zero-grade form **sup-no-.* HYPNO-, HYPNOSIS, HYPNOTIC, from Greek *hupnos,* sleep. [Pokorny 1. *su̯ep-* 1048.]

swesor- Sister. Perhaps originally a compound of **s(w)e-** and **esōr,* woman, so literally "woman of one's own kin group" in an exogamous society. **1.** Zero-grade form **swesr-.* **a.** SISTER, from Old English *sweostor,* sister, and Old Norse *systir,* sister, both from Germanic **swestar* (with *-t-* from stem **swestr-* < **swesr-*); **b.** suffixed form **swesr-īno-.* COUSIN, from Latin *sobrīnus,* maternal cousin. **2.** SORORAL, SORORITY; SORORICIDE, from Latin *soror,* sister. [Pokorny *su̯esor-* 1051.]

swo- Pronominal stem; so. Derivative of **s(w)e-**. **1a.** SO[1], from Old English *swā,* so; **b.** SUCH, from Old English *swylc,* such, from Germanic compound **swa-līk-,* "so like," of the same kind (**līk-,* same). **2.** Adverbial form **swai.* NISI, QUASI, from Latin *sī* (Archaic Latin *sei*), if, in *nisi,* unless (Archaic Latin *nesei; ne,* not; see **ne**), and *quasi,* as if (*quam,* as; see **k^{w}o-**). [In Pokorny *se-* 882.]

syū- Also **sū-**. To bind, sew. Contracted from **syuə-.*

I. Basic form **syū-.* SEW, from Old English *seowian, siowan,* to sew, from Germanic **siwjan.*

II. Variant form **sū-.* **1.** SEAM, from Old English *sēam,* seam, from Germanic **saumaz.* **2.** SUTURE; ACCOUTER, COUTURE, from Latin *suere* (past participle *sūtus*), to sew. **3.** Suffixed form **sū-dhlā-.* SUBULATE, from Latin *sūbula,* awl (< "sewing instrument"). **4.** Suffixed form **sū-tro-.* SUTRA; KAMASUTRA, from Sanskrit *sūtram,* thread, string.

III. Suffixed shortened form **syu-men-.* HYMEN, from Greek *humēn,* thin skin, membrane. [Pokorny *si̯ū-* 915.]

tag- To touch, handle. **1.** Nasalized form **ta-n-g-.* TACT, TANGENT, TANGIBLE, TASK, TASTE, TAX; ATTAIN, CONTACT, INTACT, from Latin *tangere,* to touch, with derivatives *taxāre,* to touch, assess (possibly a frequentative of *tangere,* but probably influenced by Greek *tassein, taxai,* to arrange, assess), and *tāctus,* touch. **2.** Compound form **n̥-tag-ro-,* "untouched, intact" (**n̥-,* negative prefix; see **ne**). ENTIRE, INTEGER, INTEGRATE, INTEGRITY, from Latin *integer,* intact, whole, complete, perfect, honest. **3.** Suffixed form **tag-smen-.* CONTAMINATE, from Latin *contāmināre,* to corrupt by mixing or contact (< **con-tāmen-,* "bringing into contact with"; *con-, com-,* with; see **kom**). [Pokorny *tag-* 1054.]

tauro- Bull. Derivative of **stā-**, but an independent word in Indo-European. **1.** TAURINE[1], TAURUS, TOREADOR, TORERO; BITTERN[1], from Latin *taurus,* bull. **2.** TAURINE[2]; TAUROCHOLIC ACID, from Greek *tauros,* bull. [In Pokorny *tēu-* 1080.]

tek- To beget, give birth to. **1.** Suffixed form **tek-no-,* child. THANE, from Old English *thegn,* freeman, nobleman, military vassal, warrior, from Germanic **thegnaz,* boy, man, servant, warrior. **2.** Suffixed o-grade form **tok-o-.* OXYTOCIC, POLYTOCOUS, TOCOLOGY, from Greek *tokos,* birth. [Pokorny 1. *tek-* 1057.]

telə- To lift, support, weigh; with derivatives referring to measured weights and thence to money and payment. **1.** Suffixed form **telə-mon-.* TELAMON, from Greek *telamōn,* supporter, bearer. **2.** Suffixed form **tel(ə)-es-.* **a.** TOLL[1]; PHILATELY, from Greek *telos,* tax, charge; **b.** TOLERATE, from Latin *tolerāre,* to bear, endure. **3.** Suffixed zero-grade form **tl̥ə-i-.* TALION; RETALIATE, from Latin *tāliō,* reciprocal punishment in kind, possibly "something paid out," from **tali-* (influenced by *tālis,* such). **4.** Suffixed variant zero-grade form **tala-nt-.* TALENT, from Greek *talanton,* balance, weight, any of several specific weights of gold or silver, hence the sum of money represented by such a weight. **5.** Perhaps (but unlikely) intensive reduplicated form **tantal-.* TANTALIZE, TANTALUS, from Greek *Tantalos,* name of a legendary king, "the sufferer." **6.** Perhaps (but unlikely) zero-grade form **tl̥ə-.* ATLANTIC, ATLAS, from Greek *Atlās* (stem *Atlant-*), name of the Titan supporting the world. **7.** Suffixed zero-grade form **tl̥ə-to-.* ABLATION, ABLATIVE, COLLATE, DILATORY, ELATE, ILLATION, ILLATIVE, LEGISLATOR, OBLATE[1], PRELATE, PROLATE, RELATE, SUBLATE, SUPERLATIVE, TRANSLATE, from Latin *lātus,* "carried, borne," used as the suppletive past participle of *ferre,* to bear (see **bher-**[1]), with its compounds. **8.** Suffixed zero-grade form **tl̥ə-ā-.* TOLA, from Sanskrit *tulā,* scales, balance, weight. **9.** Nasalized zero-grade form **tl̥-n-ə-.* EXTOL, from Latin *tollere,* to lift. [Pokorny 1. *tel-* 1060.]

ten- To stretch.

I. Derivatives with the basic meaning. **1.** Suffixed form **ten-do-.* **a.** TEND[1], TENDER[2], TENSE[1], TENT[1]; ATTEND, CONTEND, DETENT, DÉTENTE, DISTEND, EXTEND, INTEND, OSTENSIBLE, PRETEND, SUBTEND, from Latin *tendere,* to stretch, extend; **b.** PORTEND, from Latin *portendere,* "to stretch out before" (*por-,* variant of *pro-,* before; see **per**[1]), a technical term in augury, "to indicate, presage, foretell." **2.** Suffixed form **ten-yo-.* TENESMUS; ANATASE, BRONCHIECTASIS, CATATONIA, ENTASIS, EPITASIS, HYPOTENUSE, NEOTENY, PERITONEUM, PROTASIS, TELANGIECTASIA, from Greek *teinein,* to stretch, with o-grade form *ton-* and zero-grade noun *tasis* (< **tn̥-ti-*), a stretching, tension, intensity. **3.** Reduplicated zero-grade form **te-tn̥-o-.* TETANUS, from Greek *tetanos,* stiff, rigid. **4.** Suffixed full-grade form **ten-tro-.* **a.** TANTRA, from Sanskrit *tantram,* loom; **b.** SITAR, from Persian *tār,* string. **5.** Basic form (with stative suffix) **ten-ē-.* TENABLE, TENACIOUS, TENACULUM, TENANT, TENEMENT, TENET, TENON, TENOR, TENURE, TENUTO; ABSTAIN, CONTAIN, CONTINUE, DETAIN, ENTERTAIN, LIEUTENANT, MAINTAIN, OBTAIN, PERTAIN, PERTINACIOUS, REIN, RETAIN, RETINACULUM, RETINUE, SUSTAIN, from Latin *tenēre,* to hold, keep, maintain (< "to cause to endure or continue, hold on to").

II. Derivatives meaning "stretched," hence "thin." **1.** Suffixed zero-grade form **tn̥-u-.* THIN, from Old English *thynne,* thin, from Germanic **thunni-,* from **thunw-.* **2.** Suffixed full-grade form **ten-u-.* TENUOUS; ATTENUATE, EXTENUATE, from Latin *tenuis,* thin, rare, fine. **3.** Suffixed full-grade form **ten-ero-.* TENDER[1], TENDRIL; INTENERATE, from Latin *tener,* tender, delicate.

III. Derivatives meaning "something stretched or capable of being stretched, a string." **1.** Suffixed form **ten-ōn-*. TENDON, TENO-, from Greek *tenōn,* tendon. **2.** Suffixed o-grade form **ton-o-*. TONE; BARITONE, TONOPLAST, from Greek *tonos,* string, hence sound, pitch. **3.** Suffixed zero-grade form **tn̥-yā-*. TAENIA, from Greek *tainiā,* band, ribbon. [Pokorny 1. *ten-* 1065.]

terə-[1] To rub, turn; with some derivatives referring to twisting, boring, drilling, and piercing; and others referring to the rubbing of cereal grain to remove the husks, and thence to the process of threshing either by the trampling of oxen or by flailing with flails.
I. Full-grade form **ter(ə)-*. **1a.** TRITE, TRITURATE; ATTRITION, CONTRITE, DETRIMENT, from Latin *terere* (past participle *trītus*), to rub away, thresh, tread, wear out; **b.** TEREDO, from Greek *terēdōn,* a kind of biting worm. **2.** Suffixed form **ter-et-*. TERETE, from Latin *teres* (stem *teret-*), rounded, smooth. **3.** Suffixed form **ter-sko-*. **a.** THRASH, THRESH, from Old English *therscan,* to thresh; **b.** THRESHOLD, from Old English *therscold, threscold,* sill of a door (over which one treads; second element obscure). Both **a** and **b** from Germanic **therskan, *threskan,* to thresh, tread.
II. O-grade form **tor(ə)-*. **1.** TOREUTICS, from Greek *toreus,* a boring tool. **2.** Suffixed form **tor(ə)-mo-*, hole. DERMA[2], from Old High German *darm,* gut, from Germanic **tharma-*. **3.** Suffixed form **tor(ə)-no-*. TURN; ATTORN, ATTORNEY, CONTOUR, DETOUR, RETURN, from Greek *tornos,* tool for drawing a circle, circle, lathe.
III. Zero-grade form **tr(ə)-*. DRILL[1], from Middle Dutch *drillen,* to drill, from Germanic **thr-*.
IV. Variant form **trē-* (< **treə-*). **1.** THROW, from Old English *thrāwan,* to turn, twist, from Germanic **thrēw-*. **2.** Suffixed form **trē-tu-*. THREAD, from Old English *thrǣd,* thread, from Germanic **thrēdu-*, twisted yarn. **3.** Suffixed form **trē-mn̥* (< **treə-* or **tr̥ə-*). MONOTREME, TREMATODE, from Greek *trēma,* perforation. **4.** Suffixed form **trē-ti-* (< **treə-* or **tr̥ə-*). ATRESIA, from Greek *trēsis,* perforation.
V. Form **trī-* (< **triə-*, metathesized from **trəi-*, zero-grade of extended form **treəi-*). **1.** Probably suffixed form **trī-ōn-*. SEPTENTRION, from Latin *triō,* plow ox. **2.** Suffixed form **trī-dhlo-*. TRIBULATION, from Latin *trībulum,* a threshing sledge.
VI. Various extended forms **1.** Forms **trō-*, **trau-*. TRAUMA, from Greek *trauma,* hurt, wound. **2.** Form **trīb-*. DIATRIBE, TRIBOELECTRICITY, TRIBOLOGY, TRYPSIN, from Greek *trībein,* to rub, thresh, pound, wear out. **3.** Form **trōg-*, **trag-*. **a.** TROGON, TROUT, from Greek *trōgein,* to gnaw; **b.** DREDGE[2], from Greek *tragēma,* sweetmeat. **4.** Form **trup-*. TREPAN[1]; TRYPANOSOME, from Greek *trupē,* hole. **5.** Possible form **trūg-*. TRUANT, from Old French *truant,* beggar. [Pokorny 3. *ter-* 1071.]

terə-[2] To cross over, pass through, overcome.
I. Zero-grade form **tr̥(ə)-*. **1.** THRILL; NOSTRIL, from Old English *thyr(e)l, thȳrel,* a hole (< "a boring through"), from Germanic suffixed form **thur-ila-*. **2.** Suffixed form **tr̥ə-kʷe*. THOROUGH, THROUGH, from Old English *thurh, thuruh,* through, from Germanic **thurh.* **3.** Combining zero-grade form **-tr̥(ə)* in Greek *nektar* (see **nek-**). **4.** Zero-grade form **tr̥ə-* and full-grade form **ter(ə)-*. AVATAR, from Sanskrit *tirati, tarati,* he crosses over.
II. Variant form **trā-*. **1.** TRANS-, TRANSIENT, TRANSOM, from Latin *trāns,* across, over, beyond, through (perhaps originally the present participle of a verb **trāre,* to cross over). **2.** Suffixed form **trā-yo-*. SERAGLIO, SERAI; CARAVANSARY, LAMASERY, from Persian *sarāy,* inn, palace, from Iranian **thrāya-*, to protect.
III. Possible extended form **tru-*. **1.** Suffixed form **tru-k-*. TRUCULENT, from Latin *trux* (stem *truc-*), savage, fierce, grim (< "overcoming," "powerful," "penetrating"). **2.** Suffixed nasalized zero-grade form **tru-n-k-o-*. TRENCH, TRUNCATE, TRUNK, from Latin *truncus,* deprived of branches or limbs, mutilated, hence trunk (? < "overcome, maimed"). [Pokorny 5. *ter-* 1075.]

ters- To dry. **1.** Suffixed zero-grade form **tr̥s-*. **a.** THIRST, from Old English *thurst,* dryness, thirst, from Germanic suffixed form **thurs-tu-;* **b.** CUSK, from Old Norse *thorskr,* cod (< "dried fish"). Both **a** and **b** from Germanic **thurs-*. **2.** Suffixed basic form **ters-ā-*. TERRACE, TERRAIN, TERRENE, TERRESTRIAL, TERRIER, TERRITORY, TUREEN; FUMITORY, INTER, MEDITERRANEAN, PARTERRE, SUBTERRANEAN, TERRAQUEOUS, TERREPLEIN, TERRE-VERTE, TERRICOLOUS, TERRIGENOUS, TURMERIC, VERDITER, from Latin *terra,* "dry land," earth. **3.** Suffixed o-grade form **tors-eyo-*. TOAST[1], TORRENT, TORRID, from Latin *torrēre,* to dry, parch, burn. **4.** Suffixed zero-grade form **tr̥s-o-*. TARSUS, from Greek *tarsos,* frame of wickerwork (originally for drying cheese), hence a flat surface, sole of the foot, ankle. [Pokorny *ters-* 1078.]

teutā- Tribe. **1a.** DUTCH, from Middle Dutch *duutsch,* German, of the Germans or Teutons; **b.** PLATTDEUTSCH, from Old High German *diutisc,* of the people. Both **a** and **b** from Germanic **theudiskaz,* of the people. Both **a** and **b** from Germanic **theudō,* people. **2.** Suffixed form **teut-onōs,* "they of the tribe." TEUTON, from Latin *Teutonī,* the Teutons, borrowed via Celtic from Germanic tribal name **theudanōz.* **3.** Possibly Latin *tōtus,* all, whole (? < "of the whole tribe"): TOTAL, TUTTI; FACTOTUM, TEETOTUM. [In Pokorny *tēu-* 1080.]

tkei- To settle, dwell, be home. **1.** Suffixed o-grade form **(t)koi-mo-*. **a.** HOME, from Old English *hām,* home; **b.** NIFLHEIM, from Old Norse *heimr,* home; **c.** HAIMISH, from Old High German *heim,* home; **d.** HAME, from Middle Dutch *hame,* hame (< "covering"); **e.** HAMLET, from Old French *ham,* village, home; **f.** HAUNT, from Old French *hanter,* to frequent, haunt, from Germanic **haimatjan,* to go or bring home; **g.** HANGAR, from Old French *hangard,* shelter, possibly from Germanic **haimgardaz* (**gardaz,* enclosure; see **gher-**). **a–g** all from Germanic **haimaz,* home. **2.** Zero-grade form **tki-*. **a.** AMPHICTYONY, PROTOCTIST, from Greek *ktizein,* to found, settle, from metathesized **kti-;* **b.** probably Italic **si-*. SITUATE, SITUS, from Latin *situs,* location, from suffixed form **si-tu-*. [Pokorny 1. *k̑ei-* 539, *k̑pei-* 626.]

to- Demonstrative pronoun. For the nominative singular see **so-**. **1a.** THE[2]; NATHELESS, from Old English *thē, thȳ* (instrumental case), by the; **b.** DECOY, from Middle Dutch *de,* the; **c.** LEST, from Old English *the,* a conjunction. **a–c** from Germanic **thē,* from Indo-European instrumental form **tē.* **2.** THOUGH, from Middle English *though,* from a Scandinavian source akin to Old Norse *thō,* though, from Germanic **thauh,* "for all that." **3.** THESE, THIS, THOSE, from Old English *thes, this,* this, from Germanic **thasi-*. **4.** THAN, THEN, from Old English *thanne, thænne, thenne,* than, then, from Germanic **thana-*. **5.** THENCE, from Old English *thanon,* thence, from Germanic **thanana-*. **6.** THERE, from Old English *thǣr, thēr,* there, from Germanic **thēr.* **7.** THITHER, from Old English *thæder, thider,* thither, from Germanic **thathro.* **8a.** THEY, from Old Norse *their,* they; **b.** BOTH, from Old Norse *bādhir,* both, from Germanic **bai thaiz,* "both the" (**bai,* both; see **ambhō**). Both **a** and **b** from Germanic nominative plural **thai.* **9.** THEIR, from Old Norse *their(r)a,* theirs, from Germanic genitive plural **thaira.* **10a.** THEM, from Old Norse *theim* and Old English *thām, thǣm,* them; **b.** NONCE, from Middle English *for then anes, for the nonce,* for the occasion, from *then,* dative singular article, from Old English *thām, thǣm,* dative singular article, originally dative plural used as singular. Both **a** and **b** from Germanic dative plural **thaimiz.* **11.** Extended neuter form **tod-*. **a.** THAT, from Old English *thæt,* that, from Germanic **that;* **b.** MYSTICETE, from Greek *to,* the. **12.** THUS, from Old English *thus,* thus, from Germanic **thus-*. **13.** Adverbial (originally accusative) form **tam.* TANDEM, TANTAMOUNT, from Latin *tandem,* at last, so much, and *tantus,* so much. **14.** Suffixed reduced form **t-āli-*. TALES, from Latin *tālis,* such. **15.** TAUTO-, from Greek *to,* the. [Pokorny 1. *to-* 1086.]

trei- Three.
I. Nominative plural form **treyes.* **1a.** THREE, THRICE; THIRTEEN, THIRTY, from Old English *thrīe, thrēo, thrī,* three, with its derivatives *thrīga, thrīwa,* thrice, *thrītig,* thirty, and *thrēotīne,* thirteen (*-tīne,* ten; see **dekm̥**); **b.** TRILLIUM, from Old Swedish *thrīr,* three. Both **a** and **b** from Germanic **thrijiz.* **2.** TREY; TRAMMEL, TRECENTO, TREPHINE, TRIUMVIR, TROCAR, from Latin *trēs,* three. **3.** TRISKAIDEKAPHOBIA, from Greek *treis, tris,* three.
II. Zero-grade form **tri-*. **1.** Suffixed form **tri-tyo-*. **a.** *(i)* THIRD, from Old English *thrid(d)a, thirdda,* third; *(ii)* RIDING[2], from Old Norse *thridhi,* third. Both *(i)* and *(ii)* from Germanic **thridja-*, third; **b.** TERCEL, TERCET, TERTIAN, TERTIARY, TIERCE; SESTERCE, from Latin *tertius,* third. **2.** Combining form **tri-*. **a.** TRI-, TRIBE, TRIO, TRIPLE, from Latin *tri-,* three; **b.** TRI-; TRICLINIUM, TRICROTIC, TRIDACTYL, TRIGLYPH, TRITONE, from Greek *tri-,* three; **c.** TRIMURTI, from Sanskrit *tri-,* three. **3.** TRIAD, from Greek *trias,* the number three. **4.** TRICHOTOMY, from Greek *trikha,* in three parts. **5.** TRIERARCH, from Greek compound *triērēs,* galley with three banks of oars, trireme (*-ērēs,* oar). **6.** Suffixed form **tri-to-*. TRITIUM, from Greek *tritos,* third. **7.** Compound form **tri-pl-*, "threefold" (**-pl-* < combining form **-plo-*, -fold). TRIPLOBLASTIC, from Greek *triploos,* triple. **8.** Compound form **tri-plek-*, "threefold" (**-plek-*, -fold; see **plek-**). TRIPLEX, from Latin *triplex,* triple. **9.** Compound form **tri-st-i-*, "third person standing by" (**-st-*, standing; see **stā-**). TESTAMENT, TESTIMONY, TESTICLE, TESTIS; ATTEST, CONTEST, DETEST, OBTEST, PROTEST, TESTIFY, from Latin *testis,* a witness. **10.** SITAR, TEAPOY, from Persian *si,* three.
III. Extended zero-grade form **tris,* "thrice." **1.** TERN[2]; TERPOLYMER, from Latin *ter,* thrice. **2.** TRISOCTAHEDRON, HERMES TRISMEGISTUS, from Greek *tris,* thrice. **3.** Suffixed form **tris-no-*. TRINE, TRINITY, from Latin *trīnī,* three each.
IV. Suffixed o-grade form **troy-o-*. TROIKA, from Russian *troje,* group of three. [Pokorny *trei-* 1090.]

tu- Second person singular pronoun; you, thou. **1.** Lengthened form **tū* (accusative **te,* **tege*). THEE, THOU[1], from Old English *thū* (accusative *thec, thē*), thou, from Germanic **thū* (accusative **theke*). **2.** Suffixed extended form **t(w)ei-no-*. THINE, THY, from Old English *thīn,* thine, from Germanic **thīna-*. [Pokorny *tū̆* 1097.]

ud- Also **ūd-**. Up, out. **1a.** OUT; UTMOST, from Old English *ūt,* out; **b.** CAROUSE; AUSLANDER, from Old High German *ūz,* out; **c.** OUTLAW, from Old Norse *ūt,* out; **d.** UITLANDER, from Middle Dutch *ute, uut,* out; **e.** UTTER[1], from Middle Low German *ūt,* out; **f.** UTTER[2], from Old English *ūtera,* outer, from Germanic suffixed (comparative) form **ūt-era-;* **g.** BUT; ABOUT, from Old English *būtan, būte,* outside (adverb), from Germanic compound **bi-ūtana,* "at the outside" (**bi-,* by, at; see **ambhi**). **a–g** all from Germanic **ūt-*, out. **2.** Extended form **uds.* **a.** ERSATZ, from Old High German *irsezzan,* to replace, from *ir-,* out; **b.** ORT, from Middle Dutch *oor,* out; **c.** Germanic compound **uz-dailjam,* "a portioning out," judgment (**dailjam,* portioning). ORDEAL, from Old Eng- lish *ordāl,* trial by ordeal; **d.** URSPRACHE, from Old High German *ur-,* out of, original. **a–d** all from Germanic **uz,* **uz-*, out. **3.** Suffixed (comparative) form **ud-tero-*. HYSTERESIS, HYSTERON PROTERON, from Greek *husteros,* later, second, after. **4.** HUBRIS, from Greek compound *hubris,* violence, outrage, insolence (*bri-,* perhaps "heavy," "violent"; see **gʷerə-**), from *hu-*. **5.** VIGORISH, from Russian *vy-,* out. [Pokorny *ud-* 1103.]

uper Over. **1.** Extended form **uperi.* **a.** OVER, OVER-, from Old English *ofer,* over; **b.** ORLOP, from Middle Low German *over,* over. Both **a** and **b** from Germanic **uberi.* **2.** Variant form **(s)uper.* **a.** SOUBRETTE, SOVEREIGN, SUPER-, SUPERABLE, SUPERIOR, SUPREME, SUPREMO, SUR-; SIRLOIN, from Latin *super, super-,* above, over; **b.** suffixed form **(s)uper-no-*. SUPERNAL, from Latin *supernus,* above, upper, top; **c.** suffixed form **super-bhw-o-*, "being above" (**bhw-o-*, being; see **bheuə-**). SUPERB, from Latin *superbus,* superior, excellent, arrogant; **d.** suffixed (superlative) reduced form **sup-mo-*. SUM, SUMMIT, from Latin *summus,* highest, topmost; **e.** suffixed form **super-o-*. SOPRANINO, SOPRANO, SUPRA-; SOMERSAULT, from Latin *suprā* (feminine ablative singular), above, beyond. **3.** Basic form **uper.* HYPER-, from Greek *huper,* over. [Pokorny *upér* 1105.]

upo Under, up from under, over. **1a.** UP, from Old English *up, uppe,* up; **b.** UP-, from Old English *ūp-, upp-,* up; **c.** UPROAR, from Middle Low German *up,* up; **d.** AUFKLÄRUNG, from Old High German *ūf,* up. **a–d** all from Germanic **upp-*, up. **2.** OPEN, from Old English *open,* open, from Germanic **upana-*, "put or set up," open. **3.** ABOVE, from Old English *būfan,* above, over, from Germanic compound **bi-ufana,* "on, above" (**bi-,* by, at; see **ambhi**). **4.** Possibly suffixed form **up-t-*. OFT, OFTEN, from Old English *oft,* often, from Germanic **ufta,* frequently. **5.** Extended form **upes-*. **a.** EAVES, from Old English *efes,* eaves; **b.** EAVESDROP, from Old English *yfesdrype,* water from the eaves, from Germanic **obisdrup-*, dripping water from the eaves (**drup-*, to drip). Both **a** and **b** from Germanic **ubaswō*, **ubizwō*, vestibule, porch, eaves (< "that which is above or in front"). **6.** Variant form **(s)up-*. **a.** SOUTANE, SUB-, from Latin *sub,* under; **b.** SUPINE; RESUPINATE, from Latin *supīnus,* lying on the back (< "thrown backward or under"); **c.** suffixed form **sup-ter.* SUBTERFUGE, from Latin *subter,* secretly; **d.** Latin compound *supplex* (< **sub-plak-;* see **plāk-**). **7.** Basic form **upo.* HYPO-, from Greek *hupo,* under. **8.** Suffixed variant form **ups-o-.* HYPSO-, from Greek *hupsos,* height, top. **9.** Basic form **upo-.* Celtic **wo-,* under, in compound **wo-rēd-,* type of horse (**rēd-,* to ride). PALFREY, from Latin *verēdus,* post horse. **10.** Probably compound **upo-st-o-.* VALET, VARLET, VASSAL, from Vulgar Latin **vassus,* vassal, from Celtic **wasso-,* "one who stands under," servant, young man (**sto-,* standing; see **stā-**). **11a.** OPAL, UPANISHAD, from Sanskrit *upa,* near to, under; **b.** ZEND-AVESTA, from Avestan *upa,* up to, at (in **upastāvaka-,* praise). Both **a** and **b** from Indo-Iranian **upa.* [Pokorny *upo* 1106.]

we- We. For oblique cases of the pronoun see **nes-**[2]. Suffixed variant form **wey-es.* WE, from Old English *wē, we,* we, from Germanic **wīz.* [Pokorny *u̯ĕ-* 1114.]

wē- To blow. Contracted from **(ə)weə-.* **1.** Suffixed shortened form **we-dhro-.* WEATHER, from Old English *weder,* weather, storm, wind, from Germanic **wedram* wind, weather. **2.** Suffixed (participial) form **wē-nt-o-,* blowing. **a.** *(i)* WIND[1], from Old English *wind,* wind; *(ii)* WINDOW, from Old Norse *vindr,* wind. Both *(i)* and *(ii)* from Germanic **windaz;* **b.** VENT[1], VENTAIL, VENTILATE, from Latin *ventus,* wind. **3.** WING, from Middle English *wenge,* wing, from a Scandinavian source akin to Old Norse *vængr,* wing, from suffixed Germanic form **wē-ing-jaz.* **4.** Basic form **wē-.* NIRVANA, from Sanskrit *vāti* (stem *vā-*), it blows. [Pokorny 10. *au̯(e)-* 81.]

webh- To weave, also to move quickly. **1.** WEAVE, WOOF[1], from Old English *wefan,* to weave, from Germanic **weban.* **2.** WEFT, from Old English *wefta, weft,* cross thread, from Germanic **weftaz.* **3.** Suffixed o-grade form **wobh-yo-.* WEB, WEBSTER, from Old English *web(b),* web, from Germanic **wabjam,* fabric, web. **4.** WEEVIL, from Old English *wifel,* weevil (< "that which moves briskly"), from suffixed Germanic form **webilaz.* **5a.** *(i)* GOFFER, from Old French *gaufre,* honeycomb, waffle; *(ii)* WAFER, from Old North French *waufre,* wafer. Both *(i)* and *(ii)* from a source akin to Middle Low German *wāfel,* honeycomb; **b.** WAFFLE[1], from Middle Dutch *wāfel,* waffle. Both **a** and **b** from suffixed Germanic form **wabila-,* web, honeycomb. **6.** Possibly Germanic **wab-,* to move back and forth as in weaving. **a.** WAVE, from Old English *wafian,* to move (the hand) up and down; **b.** WAVER, from Middle English *waveren,* to waver; **c.** WOBBLE, from Low German *wabbeln,* to move from side to side, sway. **7.** Suffixed zero-grade form **ubh-ā-.* HYPHA, from Greek *huphē,* web. [Pokorny *u̯ebh-* 1114.]

wed- Water; wet. **1.** Suffixed o-grade form **wod-ōr.* **a.** WATER, from Old English *wæter,* water; **b.** KIRSCHWASSER, from Old High German *wassar,* water. Both **a** and **b** from Germanic **watar.* **2.** Suffixed lengthened-grade form **wēd-o-.* WET, from Old English *wǣt, wēt,* wet, from Germanic **wēta-.* **3.** O-grade form **wod-.* WASH, from Old English *wæscan, wacsan,* to wash, from Germanic suffixed form **wat-skan,* to wash. **4.** Nasalized form **we-n-d-.* WINTER, from Old English *winter,* winter, from Germanic **wintruz,* winter, "wet season." **5.** Suffixed zero-grade form **ud-ōr.* HYDRANT, HYDRO-, HYDROUS, UTRICLE[1]; ANHYDROUS, CLEPSYDRA, DROPSY, HYDATHODE, HYDATID, from Greek *hudōr,* water. **6.** Suffixed nasalized zero-grade form **u-n-d-ā-.* UNDINE, UNDULATE; ABOUND, INUNDATE, REDOUND, REDUNDANT, SURROUND, from Latin *unda,* wave. **7.** Suffixed zero-grade form **ud-ro-, *ud-rā-,* water animal. **a.** OTTER, from Old English *otor,* otter, from Germanic **otraz,* otter; **b.** NUTRIA, from Latin *lutra,* otter (with obscure *l-*); **c.** HYDRUS, from Greek *hudros,* a water snake; **d.** HYDRA, from Greek *hudrā,* a water serpent, Hydra. **8.** Suffixed zero-grade form **ud-skio-.* USQUEBAUGH, WHISKEY, from Old Irish *uisce,* water. **9.** Suffixed o-grade form **wod-ā-.* VODKA, from Russian *voda,* water. [Pokorny 9. *au̯(e)-* 78.]

wegh- To go, transport in a vehicle. **1.** WEIGH[1], from Old English *wegan,* to carry, balance in a scale, from Germanic **wegan.* **2.** WEE, from Old English *wǣg(e),* weight, unit of weight, from Germanic lengthened-grade form **wēgō.* **3.** Suffixed form **wegh-ti-.* WEIGHT, from Old English *wiht, gewiht,* weight, from Germanic **wihti-.* **4a.** WAY; ALWAYS, AWAY, from Old English *weg,* way; **b.** NORWEGIAN, from Old Norse *vegr,* way; **c.** THALWEG, from Old High German *weg,* way. **a–c** all from Germanic **wegaz,* course of travel, way. **5.** Suffixed o-grade form **wogh-no-.* **a.** WAIN, from Old English *wæ(g)n,* wagon; **b.** WAGON, from Middle Dutch *wagen,* wagon. Both **a** and **b** from Germanic **wagnaz.* **6.** Suffixed o-grade form **wogh-lo-.* **a.** WALLEYED, from Old Norse *vagl,* chicken roost, perch, beam, eye disease, from Germanic **waglaz;* **b.** OCHLOCRACY, OCHLOPHOBIA, from Greek *okhlos,* populace, mob (< "moving mass"). **7.** Distantly related to this root are: **a.** *(i)* GRAYWACKE, from Old High German *waggo, wacko,* boulder rolling on a riverbed, from Germanic **wag-,* "to move about"; *(ii)* WAG[1], from Middle English *waggen,* to wag, possibly from Germanic **wag-;* **b.** VOGUE, from Old French *voguer,* to row, sail, from Old Saxon **wogōn,* to rock, sway, from Germanic **wēga-,* water in motion; **c.** *(i)* EARWIG, from Old English *wicga,* insect (< "thing that moves quickly"); *(ii)* WIGGLE, from Middle Dutch and Middle Low German *wiggelen,* to move back and forth, wag. Both *(i)* and *(ii)* from Germanic **wig-.* **8.** Basic form **wegh-.* VECTOR, VEHEMENT, VEHICLE; ADVECTION, CONVECTION, EVECTION, INVECTIVE, INVEIGH, from Latin *vehere* (past participle *vectus*), to carry. **9.** Suffixed basic form **wegh-yā-.* FOY, VIA, VIATICAL, VOYAGE; CONVEY, CONVOY, DEVIATE, DEVIOUS, ENVOY[1], INVOICE, OBVIATE, OBVIOUS, OGEE, OGIVE, PERVIOUS, PREVIOUS, TRIVIAL, TRIVIUM, VIADUCT, from Latin *via,* way, road. **10.** Suffixed form **wegh-s-.* VEX, from Latin *vexāre,* to agitate (< "to set in motion"). **11.** Probably suffixed form **wegh-so-.* CONVEX, from Latin *convexus,* "carried or drawn together (to a point)," convex (*com-,* together; see **kom**). [Pokorny *u̯eg̑h-* 1118.]

weid- To see.

I. Full-grade form **weid-.* **1a.** TWIT, from Old English *wītan,* to reproach; **b.** GUIDE, GUIDON, from Old Provençal *guidar,* to guide; **c.** GUY[1], from Old French *guier,* to guide; **d.** WITE, from Old English *wīte,* fine, penalty, from Germanic derivative noun **wīti-.* **a–d** all from Germanic **wītan,* to look after, guard, ascribe to, reproach. **2.** Suffixed form **weid-to-.* **a.** WISE[1], from Old English *wīs,* wise; **b.** WISDOM, from Old English *wīsdōm,* learning, wisdom (*-dōm,* abstract suffix; see **dhē-**); **c.** WISEACRE, from Old High German *wīzag,* knowledgeable; **d.** *(i)* WISE[2], from Old English *wīse, wīs,* manner; *(ii)* GUISE, from Old French *guise,* manner. Both *(i)* and *(ii)* from Germanic **wīssōn-,* appearance, form, manner. **a–d** all from Germanic **wīssaz.* **3.** Suffixed form **weid-es-.* EIDETIC, EIDOLON, IDOL, IDYLL, -OID; IDOCRASE, KALEIDOSCOPE, from Greek *eidos,* form, shape.

II. Zero-grade form **wid-.* **1a.** WIT[1], from Old English *wit, witt,* knowledge, intelligence; **b.** WITENAGEMOT, from Old English *wita,* wise man, councilor. Both **a** and **b** from Germanic **wit-.* **2.** WIT[2], WOT; UNWITTING, from Old English *witan,* to know, from Germanic **witan* (Old English first and third person singular *wāt,* from Germanic **wait,* from Indo-European o-grade form **woid-*). **3.** Suffixed form **wid-to-.* IWIS, from Old English *gewis, gewiss,* certain, sure, from Germanic **(ga)wissa-,* known (**ga-,* past participial prefix; see **kom-**). **4.** Form **wid-ē-* (with the participial form **weid-to-*). VIDE, VIEW, VISA, VISAGE, VISION, VISIT, VISOR, VISTA, VOYEUR; ADVICE, ADVISE, BELVEDERE, CLAIRVOYANT, ENVY, EVIDENT, IMPROVISE, INTERVIEW, INVIDIOUS, PREVISE, PROVIDE, PRUDENT, PURVEY, PURVIEW, REVIEW, REVISE, SUPERVISE, SURVEY, from Latin *vidēre,* to see, look. **5.** Suffixed form **wid-es-yā-.* IDEA, IDEO-, from Greek *ideā,* appearance, form, idea. **6.** Suffixed form **wid-tor-.* HISTORY, STORY[1]; POLYHISTOR, from Greek *histōr,* wise, learned, learned man. **7.** HADAL, HADES, from Greek *Haidēs* (also *Aidēs*), the underworld, perhaps "the invisible," and from **wid-.* **8.** Suffixed nasalized zero-grade form **wi-n-d-o-.* **a.** COLCANNON, from Old Irish *find,* white (< "clearly visible"); **b.** PENGUIN, from Welsh *gwyn, gwynn,* white. **9.** Celtic **wid-,* seer, in compound **dru-wid-* (see **deru-**).

III. Suffixed o-grade form **woid-o-.* VEDA; RIG-VEDA, from Sanskrit *vedaḥ,* knowledge. [Pokorny 2. *u̯(e)di-* (misprint for *u̯(e)id-*) 1125.]

weiə- To go after someting, pursue with vigor, desire, with noun forms meaning force, power. Related to **wī-ro-**. **1.** Zero-grade form **wī-* (< **wiə-*). VIM, VIOLATE, VIOLENT, from Latin *vīs,* force, with irregular derivatives *violāre,* to treat with force, and *violentus,* vehement. **2.** Suffixed o-grade form **woi(ə)-tyā-.* GAIN[1]; ROWEN, from Old French *gaaignier, gaignier,* to obtain, from Germanic **waithanjan,* to hunt, plunder, denominative verb from **wai-thjō,* "pursuit," hunting. **3.** Suffixed zero-grade form **wiə-to-* becoming **wī-to-.* INVITE, from Latin *invītāre,* to invite (*in-,* in; see **en**). [Pokorny 3. *u̯ei-* 1123.]

weik- Clan (social unit above the household). **1.** Suffixed form **weik-slā-.* VILLA, VILLAGE, VILLAIN, VILLANELLE, VILLEIN; BIDONVILLE, NASTY, from Latin *vīlla,* country house, farm. **2.** Suffixed o-grade form **woik-o-.* **a.** VICINAGE, VICINITY; BAILIWICK, from Latin *vīcus,* quarter or district of a town, neighborhood; **b.** ANDROECIUM, AUTOECIOUS, DIOCESE, DIOECIOUS, ECESIS, ECOLOGY, ECONOMY, ECUMENICAL, HETEROECIOUS, MONOECIOUS, PARISH, PAROCHIAL, from Greek *oikos,* house, and its derivatives *oikiā,* a dwelling, and *oikēsis,* dwelling, administration. **3.** Zero-grade form **wik-.* VAISYA, from Sanskrit *viśaḥ,* dwelling, house. [Pokorny *u̯eik̑-* 1131.]

wek^w- To speak. **1.** O-grade form **wōk^w-.* **a.** VOCAL, VOICE, VOWEL, from Latin *vōx,* voice; **b.** CALLIOPE, from Greek *ops,* voice. **2.** Suffixed o-grade form **wok^w-ā-.* VOCABLE, VOCATION, VOUCH; ADVOCATE, AVOCATION, CONVOKE, EQUIVOCAL, EVOKE, INVOKE, PROVOKE, REVOKE, UNIVOCAL, from Latin *vocāre,* to call. **3.** Suffixed form **wek^w-es-.* EPIC, EPOS; EPOPEE, ORTHOEPY, from Greek *epos,* song, word. [Pokorny *u̯ek$^u̯$-* 1135.]

wel- To turn, roll; with derivatives referring to curved, enclosing objects.**1a.** WALTZ, from Old High German *walzan,* to roll, waltz; **b.** WELTER, from Middle Low German or Middle Dutch *welteren,* to roll. Both **a** and **b** from Germanic **walt-.* **2.** WHELK[1], from Old English *weoluc, weoloc,* mollusk (having a spiral shell), whelk, from Germanic **weluka-.* **3.** Perhaps Germanic **wel-.* WILLOW, from Old English *welig,* willow (with flexible twigs). **4.** Perhaps Germanic **welk-.* WALK, from Old English *wealcan,* to roll, toss, and *wealcian,* to muffle up. **5.** O-grade form **wol-.* **a.** WELL[1], from Old English *wiella, wælla, welle,* a well (< "rolling or bubbling water," "spring"); **b.** GABERDINE, from Old High German *wallōn,* to roam; **c.** WALLET, possibly from Old North French **walet,* roll, knapsack. **a–c** all from Germanic **wall-.* **6.** Perhaps suffixed o-grade form **wol-ā-.* **a.** WALE, from Old English *walu,* streak on the skin, weal, welt; **b.** Old High German **-walu,* a roll, round stem, in compound **wurzwalu* (see **wrād-**). Both **a** and **b** from Germanic **walō.* **7.** Extended form **welw-.* **a.** WALLOW, from Old English *wealwian,* to roll (in mud), from Germanic **walwōn;* **b.** VAULT[1], VAULT[2], VOLT[2], VOLUBLE, VOLUME, VOLUTE, VOLVOX, VOUSSOIR; ARCHIVOLT, CIRCUMVOLVE, CONVOLVE, DEVOLVE, EVOLVE, INVOLUCRUM, INVOLVE, REVOLVE, from Latin *volvere,* to roll; **c.** suffixed o-grade form **wolw-ā-.* VOLVA, VULVA, from Latin *vulva, volva,* covering, womb; **d.** suffixed zero-grade form **wl̥w-ā-.* VALVE, VALVULE, from Latin *valva,* leaf of a door (< "that which turns"); **e.** suffixed zero-grade form **wl̥u-ti-.* ALYCE CLOVER, from Greek *halusis,* chain; **f.** suffixed form **welu-tro-.* ELYTRON, from Greek *elutron,* sheath, cover. **8.** Suffixed form **wel-n-.* ILEUS; NEURILEMMA, from Greek *eilein* (< **welnein*), to turn, squeeze. **9.** Perhaps variant **wall-.* VAIL[1], VALE[1], VALLEY, from Latin *vallēs, vallis,* valley (< "that which is surrounded by hills"). **10.** Possibly suffixed form **wel-enā-.* ELECAMPANE, INULIN, from the Greek name *Helenē* (oldest form *Welenā*), Helen. **11.** Suffixed form **wel-ik-.* HELICON, HELIX; HELICOPTER, from Greek *helix,* spiral object. **12.** Suffixed form **wel-mi-nth-.* HELMINTH; ANTHELMINTIC, PLATYHELMINTH, from Greek *helmis, helmins* (stem *helminth-*), parasitic worm. [Pokorny 7. *u̯el-* 1140.]

welə- To strike, wound. **1.** Suffixed o-grade form **wol(ə)-o-.* **a.** VALHALLA, from Old Norse *Valhöll,* Valhalla; **b.** VALKYRIE, from Old Norse *Valkyrja,* "chooser of the slain," name of one of the twelve war goddesses (*-kyrja,* chooser; see **geus-**). Both **a** and **b** from Old Norse *valr,* the slain in battle, from Germanic **walaz.* **2.** Suffixed basic form **welə-nes-.* VULNERABLE, from Latin *vulnus* (stem *vulner-*), a wound. **3.** Suffixed zero-grade form **wl̥ə-to-.* BERDACHE, from Old Iranian **varta-* (Avestan *varəta-*), seized, prisoner. [In Pokorny 8. *u̯el-* 1144.]

wemə- To vomit. **1.** WAMBLE, from Middle English *wam(e)len,* to feel nausea, stagger, from a Scandinavian source probably akin to Old Norse *vamla,* qualm, and Danish *vamle,* to become sick, from Germanic **wam-.* **2.** VOMIT; NUX VOMICA, from Latin *vomere,* to vomit. **3.** EMESIS, EMETIC, from Greek *emein,* to vomit. [Pokorny *u̯em-* 1146.]

wen- To desire, strive for. **1.** Suffixed form **wen-w-.* WIN, from Old English *winnan,* to win, from Germanic **winn(w)an,* to seek to gain. **2.** Suffixed zero-grade form **wn̥-yā-.* WYNN, WINSOME, from Old English *wynn, wen,* pleasure, joy, from Germanic **wunjō.* **3.** Suffixed (stative) zero-grade form **wn̥-ē-,* to be contented. WON[1], WONT, from Old English *wunian,* to become accustomed to, dwell, from Germanic **wunēn.* **4.** Suffixed (causative) o-grade form **won-eyo-.* WEAN, from Old English *wenian,* to accustom, train, wean, from Germanic **wanjan.* **5.** WEEN, from Old English *wēnan,* to expect, imagine, think, from Germanic denominative **wēnjan,* to hope, from **wēniz,* hope. **6.** Suffixed zero-grade form **wn̥-sko-.* WISH, from Old English *wȳscan,* to desire, wish, from Germanic **wunsk-.* **7.** Perhaps o-grade form **won-.* **a.** VANIR, from Old Norse *Vanir,* the Vanir; **b.** VANADIUM, from Old Norse *Vanadīs,* name of the goddess Freya. Both **a** and **b** from Germanic **wana-.* **8.** Suffixed form **wen-es-.* **a.** VENERATE, VENEREAL, VENERY[1], VENUS, from Latin *venus,* love; **b.** suffixed form **wen-es-no-.* VENOM, from Latin *venēnum,* love potion, poison. **9.** Possibly suffixed form **wen-eto-,* "beloved." WEND, from Old High German *Winid,* Wend, from Germanic **Weneda-,* a Slavic people. **10.** Suffixed form **wen-yā-.* VENIAL, from Latin *venia,* favor, forgiveness. **11.** Lengthened-grade form **wēn-ā-.* VENERY[2], VENISON, from Latin *vēnārī,* to hunt. **12.** Possibly zero-grade suffixed form **wn̥-ig-.* BANYAN, from Sanskrit *vaṇik, vāṇijaḥ,* merchant (? < "seeking to gain"). [Pokorny 1. *u̯en-* 1146.]

wer- Conventional base of various Indo-European roots; to turn, bend.

I. Root **wert-,* to turn, wind. **1.** Germanic **werth-.* **a.** *(i)* -WARD, from Old English *-weard,* toward (< "turned toward"); *(ii)* INWARD, from Old English *inweard,* inward, from Germanic **inwarth,* inward (**in,* in; see **en**). Both *(i)* and *(ii)* from Germanic variant **warth;* **b.** perhaps Germanic derivative **wertha-,* "toward, opposite," hence "equivalent, worth." WORTH[1]; STALWART, from Old English *weorth,* worth, valuable, and derivative noun *weorth, wierth,* value. **2.** WORTH[2], from Old English *weorthan,* to befall, from Germanic **werthan,* to become (< "to turn into"). **3.** Zero-grade form **wr̥t-.* WEIRD, from Old English *wyrd,* fate, destiny (< "that which befalls one"), from Germanic **wurthiz.* **4.** VERSATILE, VERSE[1], VERSION, VERSUS, VERTEBRA, VERTEX, VERTIGO, VORTEX; ADVERSE, ANNIVERSARY, AVERT, BOULEVERSEMENT, CONTROVERSY, CONVERSE[1], CONVERT, DEXTRORSE, DIVERT, EVERT, EXTRORSE, EXTROVERSION, EXTROVERT, INTRORSE, INTROVERT, INVERT, MALVERSATION, OBVERT, PEEVISH, PERVERT, PROSE, RETRORSE, REVERT, SINISTRORSE, SUBVERT, TERGIVERSATE, TRANSVERSE, UNIVERSE, from Latin *vertere,* to turn, with its frequentative *versāre,* to turn, and passive *versārī,* to stay, behave (< "to move around a place, frequent"). **5.** VERST, from Russian *versta,* line, from Balto-Slavic **wirstā-,* a turn, bend.

II. Root **wreit-,* to turn. **a.** WREATH, from Old English *writha,* band (< "that which is wound around"); **b.** WRITHE, from Old English *wrīthan,* to twist, torture; **c.** WRATH, WROTH, from Old English *wrāth,* angry (< "tormented, twisted"). **a–c** all from Germanic **wrīth-, *wraith-.*

III. Root **wergh-,* to turn. **1.** WORRY, from Old English *wyrgan,* to strangle, from Germanic **wurgjan.* **2.** Nasalized variant **wrengh-.* **a.** WRING, from Old English *wringan,* to twist, from Germanic **wreng-;* **b.** *(i)* WRONG, from Middle English *wrong,* wrong, from a Scandinavian source akin to Old Norse **vrangr, rangr,* curved, crooked, wrong; *(ii)* WRANGLE, from Middle English *wranglen,* to wrangle, from a Low German source akin to *wrangeln,* to wrestle. Both *(i)* and *(ii)* from Germanic **wrang-.*

IV. Root **werg-,* to turn. **1.** Nasalized variant form **wreng-.* **a.** WRENCH, from Old English *wrencan,* to twist; **b.** WRINKLE, from Old English *gewrinclian,* to wind (*ge-,* collective prefix; see **kom**). Both **a** and **b** from Germanic **wrankjan.* **2.** VERGE[2]; CONVERGE, DIVERGE, from Latin *vergere,* to turn, tend toward.

V. Root **wreik-,* to turn. **1a.** WRY, from Old English *wrīgian,* to turn, bend, go; **b.** WRIGGLE, from Middle Low German *wriggeln,* to wriggle. Both **a** and **b** from Germanic **wrīg-.* **2a.** WRIST, from Old English *wrist,* wrist; **b.** GAITER, from Old French *guietre,* gaiter, from Frankish **wrist-.* Both **a** and **b** from Germanic **wristiz,* from **wrihst-.* **3.** WREST, WRESTLE, from Old English *wrǣstan,* to twist, from secondary Germanic derivative **wraistjan.* **4.** Possibly o-grade form **wroik-.* BRIAR[1], BRUSQUE, from Late Latin *brūcus,* heather, from Gaulish **brūko-.*

VI. RIBALD, from Old French *riber,* to be wanton, from Germanic root **wrib-.*

VII. Root **werb-,* also **werbh-,* to turn, bend. **1.** WARP, from Old English *weorpan,* to throw away, from Germanic **werpan,* "to fling by turning the arm." **2.** REVERBERATE, from Latin *verber,* whip, rod. **3.** VERBENA, VERVAIN, from Latin *verbēna,* sacred foliage. **4.** Zero-grade form **wr̥b-.* RHABDOMANCY, RHABDOVIRUS, from Greek *rhabdos,* rod. **5.** Nasalized variant form **wrembh-.* RHOMBUS, from Greek *rhombos,* magic wheel, rhombus.

VIII. Root **werp-,* to turn, wind. **1.** Metathesized form **wrep-.* WRAP, from Middle English *wrappen,* to wrap, from a source akin to Danish dialectal *vravle,* to wind, from Germanic **wrap-.* **2.** Zero-grade form **wr̥p-.* RAPHE, RHAPSODY, TENORRHAPHY, from Greek *rhaptein,* to sew.

IX. Root **wr̥mi-,* worm; rhyme word to **kʷr̥mi-**. **1.** WORM, from Old English *wyrm,* worm, from Germanic **wurmiz.* **2.** VERMEIL, VERMI-, VERMICELLI, VERMICULAR, VERMIN, from Latin *vermis,* worm. [Pokorny 3. *u̯er-* 1152.]

werə- Also **wer-**. To speak. **1.** Suffixed zero-grade form **wr̥-dho-.* WORD, from Old English *word,* word, from Germanic **wurdam.* **2.** Suffixed form **wer-dho-.* VERB, VERVE; ADVERB, PROVERB, from Latin *verbum,* word. **3.** Suffixed form **wer-yo-.* IRONY, from Greek *eirein,* to say, speak. **4.** Variant form **wrē-.* **a.** Suffixed form **wrē-tor-.* RHETOR, from Greek *rhētōr,* public speaker; **b.** suffixed form **wrē-mn̥.* RHEME, from Greek *rhēma,* word. [Pokorny 6. *u̯er-* 1162.]

wērə-o- True, trustworthy. **1.** WARLOCK, from Old English *wǣr,* faith, pledge, from Germanic **wēra-.* **2.** VERACIOUS, VERISM, VERITY, VERY; AVER, VERDICT, VERIDICAL, VERIFY, VERISIMILAR, VOIR DIRE, from Latin *vērus,* true. **3.** Normal grade **wero-,* from **werə-o-,* in Celtic compound **ro-wero-* (see **per**[1]). [Pokorny 11. *u̯er-* 1165.]

werg- To do.

I. Suffixed form **werg-o-.* **1a.** WORK; HANDIWORK, from Old English *weorc, werc,* work; **b.** BOULEVARD, BULWARK, from Old High German *werc,* work. Both **a** and **b** from Germanic **werkam,* work. **2.** ERG, ERGATIVE, -URGY; ADRENERGIC, ALLERGY, ARGON, CHOLINERGIC, DEMIURGE, DRAMATURGE, ENDERGONIC, ENDOERGIC, ENERGY, ERGOGRAPH, ERGOMETER, ERGONOMICS, EXERGONIC, EXERGUE, EXOERGIC, GEORGIC, HYPERGOLIC, LETHARGY, LITURGY, METALLURGY, SURGERY, SYNERGID, SYNERGISM, THAUMATURGE, from Greek *ergon,* work, action, and o-grade agent noun (in composition) *-orgos* (< **worgos*), doer, worker.

II. Zero-grade form **wr̥g-.* **1.** Suffixed forms **wr̥g-yo-, *wr̥g-to-.* **a.** WROUGHT, from Old English *wyrcan,* to work; **b.** IRK, from Old Norse *yrkja,* to work. Both **a** and **b** from Germanic **wurkjan,* to work, participle **wurhta-.* **2.** Suffixed form **wr̥g-t-.* WRIGHT, from Old English *wryhta,* maker, wright, from Germanic **wurhtjō-.*

III. O-grade form **worg-.* **1.** ORGAN, ORGANON, from Greek *organon* (with suffix *-ano-*), tool. **2.** ORGY, from Greek *orgia,* secret rites, worship (< "service"). [Pokorny 2. *u̯erĝ-* 1168.]

wes-[1] To live, dwell, pass the night, with derivatives meaning "to be." **1.** O-grade (perfect tense) form **wos-.* WAS, from Old English *wæs,* was, from Germanic **was-.* **2.** Lengthened-grade form **wēs-.* WERE, from Old English *wǣre* (subjunctive), *wǣron* (plural), were, from Germanic **wēz-.* **3.** WASSAIL, from Old Norse *vesa, vera,* to be, from Germanic **wesan.* **4.** Perhaps suffixed form **wes-tā-.* VESTA, from Latin *Vesta,* household goddess. **5.** Possibly suffixed variant form **was-tu-.* ASTUTE, from Latin *astus,* skill, craft (practiced in a town), from Greek *astu,* town (< "place where one dwells"). **6.** Suffixed form **wes-eno-.* DIVAN, from Old Persian *vahanam,* house. [Pokorny 1. *u̯es-* 1170.]

wes-[2] To clothe. **1.** Suffixed o-grade (causative) form **wos-eyo-.* WEAR, from Old English *werian,* to wear, carry, from Germanic **wazjan.* **2.** Suffixed form **wes-ti-.* VEST; DEVEST, INVEST, REVET, TRAVESTY, from Latin *vestis,* garment. **3.** Suffixed form **wes-nu-.* HIMATION, from Greek *hennunai,* to clothe, with nominal derivative *heima, hīma* (< **wes-mn̥*), garment. [Pokorny 5. *u̯es-* 1172.]

wes-[3] To buy, sell. **1.** Suffixed form **wes-no-.* VENAL, VEND, from Latin *vēnum,* sale. **2.** Suffixed o-grade form **wos-no-.* MONOPSONY, from Greek *ōneisthai,* to buy. **3.** Suffixed form **wes-ā-.* BAZAAR, from Persian *bāzār,* from Old Iranian **vahā-cārana-,* "sale-traffic." **4.** Perhaps suffixed form **wes-li-.* VILE; REVILE, VILIFY, VILIPEND, from Latin *vīlis,* cheap, base. [Pokorny 8. *u̯es-* 1173.]

wes-pero- Evening, night.

I. Reduced form **wes-.* **1.** Suffixed form **wes-to-.* **a.** WEST, from Old English *west,* west; **b.** WESTERN, from Old English *westerne,* western; **c.** WESTERLY, from Old English *westra,* more westerly. **a–c** all from Germanic **west-.* **2.** Possibly Germanic **wis-,* west, in Late Latin *Visigothī,* "West Goths" (*Gothī,* the Goths): VISIGOTH.

II. Basic form **wespero-.* **1.** PIPISTRELLE, VESPER, VESPERTILIONID, from Latin *vesper,* evening. **2.** HESPERIAN, HESPERIDES, HESPERUS, from Greek *hesperos,* evening. [Pokorny *u̯esperos* 1173.]

wesr̥ Spring. VERNAL; PRIMAVERA[1], from Latin *vēr,* spring (phonologically irregular). [Pokorny *u̯es-r̥* 1174.]

wet-[1] To blow, inspire, spiritually arouse. **1.** Lengthened-grade form **wōt-.* **a.** WODEN; WEDNESDAY, from Old English *Wōden,* Woden; **b.** ODIN, from Old Norse *Ōdhinn,* Odin; **c.** WOTAN, from Old High German *Wuotan.* **a–c** all from Germanic suffixed form **wōd-eno-, *wōd-ono-,* "raging," "mad," "inspired," hence "spirit," name of the chief Teutonic god **Wōd-enaz;* **d.** WOOD[2], from Old English *wōd,* mad, insane, from Germanic **wōda-;* **e.** Celtic **wāt-.* VATIC, from Latin *vātēs,* prophet, poet, from a Celtic source akin to Old Irish *fáith,* seer. **2.** O-grade form **wot-.* WEDELN, from Old High German *wedil,* fan, from Germanic suffixed form **wath-ilaz.* **3.** Suffixed variant form **wat-no-.* FAN[1], VAN[3], from Latin *vannus,* a winnowing fan. **4.** Oldest basic form **əwet-* becoming Greek **awet-* in suffixed form **awet-mo-.* ATMOSPHERE, from Greek *atmos* (< **aetmos*), breath, vapor. [Pokorny 1. *u̯ăt-* 1113.]

wet-[2] Year. **1.** Suffixed form **wet-ru-.* WETHER; BELLWETHER, from Old English *wether,* wether, from Germanic **wethruz,* perhaps "yearling." **2.** Suffixed form **wet-es-.* **a.** VETERAN; INVETERATE, from Latin *vetus,* old (< "having many years"); **b.** VETERINARY, from Latin *veterīnus,* of beasts of burden, of cattle (perhaps chiefly old cattle); **c.** ETESIAN, from Greek *etos,* year. **3.** Suffixed form **wet-olo-.* VEAL, VITELLUS, from Latin *vitulus,* calf, yearling. [Pokorny *u̯et-* 1175.]

wīkm̥tī- Twenty. Compound of *wi-,* in half, hence two, and **(d)km̥t-ī* (nominative dual), decade, reduced zero-grade form of **dekm̥**.) **1.** VICENARY, VIGESIMAL, VIGINTILLION, from Latin *vīgintī,* twenty. **2.** EICOSAPENTAENOIC ACID, ICOSAHEDRON, from Greek *eikosi,* twenty. **3.** PACHISI, from Sanskrit *viṁśatiḥ,* twenty. [Pokorny *u̯ī-km̥t-ī* 1177.]

wī̆-ro- Man. Contracted from **wiə-ro-;* derivative of **weiə-**. **1a.** WEREWOLF, WERGELD, from Old English *wer,* man; **b.** *(i)* WORLD, from Old English *weorold,* world; *(ii)* WELTANSCHAUUNG, WELTSCHMERZ, from Old High German *weralt,* world. Both *(i)* and *(ii)* from Germanic compound **wer-ald-,* "life or age of man" (**-ald-,* age); **c.** LOUP-GAROU, from Old French *garoul,* werewolf, from Frankish **wer-wulf,* "man-wolf" (**wulf,* wolf; see **wl̥kʷo-**). Both **a** and **b** from Germanic **weraz,* from shortened form **wiraz.* **2.** VIRAGO, VIRILE, VIRTUE, VIRTUOSA, VIRTUOSO; DECEMVIR, DECURION, DUUMVIR, TRIUMVIR, from Latin *vir,* man. **3.** CURIA, from Latin *cūria,* curia, court, possibly from **co-vir-ia*, "men together" (**co-*, together; see **kom**). [Pokorny *u̯ı̄ro-s* 1177.]

w̥l̥kʷo- Wolf. **1a.** WOLF, from Old English *wulf*, wolf; **b.** AARDWOLF, from Middle Dutch *wolf*, *wulf*, wolf; **c.** WOLFRAM, from Old High German *wolf*, wolf; **d.** Frankish **wulf*, wolf, in compound **wer-wulf* (see **wī-ro-**). **a–d** all from Germanic **wulfaz*. **2.** Taboo variant **lupo-*. LOBO, LUPINE¹, LUPINE², LUPUS, ROBALO; LOUP-GAROU, from Latin *lupus*, wolf. **3.** Taboo variant **lukʷo-*. **a.** LYCANTHROPE, LYCOPODIUM, from Greek *lukos*, wolf; **b.** suffixed form **lukʷ-ya*. ALYSSUM, from Greek *lussa*, martial rage, madness, rabies ("wolf-ness"). [Pokorny *u̯l̥kʷos* 1178.]

w̥l̥p-ē- Fox. **1.** VULPINE, from Latin *vulpēs*, fox. **2.** Taboo variant **əlōpĕk-*. ALOPECIA, from Greek *alōpēx*, fox. [Pokorny *u̯l̥p-* 1179.]

wŏs You (plural). RENDEZVOUS, from Latin *vōs*, you. [In Pokorny 1. *i̯u-* 513.]

wrād- Branch, root. Contracted from **wraəd-*.
I. Basic form **wrād-*. ROOT¹; RUTABAGA, from Old Norse *rōt*, root, from Germanic **wrōt-*.
II. Zero-grade form **wrəd-*. **1a.** WORT¹, from Old English *wyrt*, plant, herb; **b.** GEWÜRZTRAMINER, from Old High German *wurz*, plant, root; **c.** MANGEL-WURZEL, from German *Wurzel*, root (< **wurzwala*, rootstock; **-wala*, a roll, round stem; see **wel-**). **a–c** all from Germanic **wurtiz*. **2.** Suffixed form **wrəd-yā-*. WORT², from Old English *wyrt*, brewer's wort, from Germanic **wurtjō*. **3.** Suffixed form **wr̥d-ī-*. RADICAL, RADICLE, RADISH, RADIX; DERACINATE, ERADICATE,

IRRADICABLE, from Latin *rādīx*, root. **4.** Suffixed form **wrəd-mo-*. RAMOSE, RAMUS; RAMIFY, from Latin *rāmus*, branch. **5.** Perhaps suffixed reduced form **wr̥(ə)d-ya*. RHIZO-, RHIZOME; COLEORHIZA, LICORICE, MYCORRHIZA, from Greek *rhiza*, root. [Pokorny *u̯(e)rād-* 1167.]

yeg- Ice. ICICLE, from Old English *gicel*, icicle, ice, from Germanic **jakilaz, *jekilaz.* [Pokorny *i̯eg-* 503.]

yĕkʷr̥ Liver. **1.** HEPATIC, HEPATO-; HEPARIN, HEPATITIS, from Greek *hēpar*, liver (stem *hēpat-* < **yĕkʷn̥-t-* < Indo-European oblique stem **yĕkʷn-*). **2.** GIZZARD, from Persian *jigar*, liver. [Pokorny *i̯eku̯-r̥(t-)* 504.]

yēr- Year, season. Contracted from **year-*. **1.** Suffixed basic form **yēr-o-*. **a.** YEAR, from Old English *gēar*, year; **b.** YAHRZEIT, from Old High German *jār*, year. Both **a** and **b** from Germanic **jēram*, year. **2.** Suffixed o-grade form **yōr-ā-*. HORARY, HOUR; HOROLOGE, HOROLOGY, HOROSCOPE, from Greek *hōrā*, season. [In Pokorny 1. *ei-* 293.]

yeu- Vital force, youthful vigor. Derivative of **aiw-**. Suffixed zero-grade form **yuwen-* (< **yu-əen-*), "possessing youthful vigor," young. **1.** Further suffixed form **yuwn̥-ti-*. YOUTH, from Old English *geoguth*, youth, from Germanic **jugunthi-, *jugunthō.* **2.** Further suffixed form **yuwn̥ko-*. **a.** YOUNG, from Old English *geong*, young; **b.** JUNKER, from Old High German *junc*, young; **c.** YOUNKER, from Middle Dutch *jonc*, young. **a–c** all from Germanic **junga-*, from **juwunga-*. **3a.** JUVENILE; REJU-

VENATE, from Latin *iuvenis*, young; **b.** zero-grade form **yūn-* (< **yu-ən-*). (*i*) JUNIOR, from Latin comparative *iūnior*, younger; (*ii*) JUNE, JUNO, from Latin *Iūnō*, Juno (probably "the young one," perhaps because she was the goddess of the new moon), and Latin month name *Iūnius*, traditionally derived from *Iūnō*. [Pokorny 3. *i̯eu-* 510.]

yeug- To join.
I. Zero-grade form **yug-*. **1.** Suffixed form **yug-o-*. **a.** YOKE, from Old English *geoc*, yoke, from Germanic **yukam*; **b.** JUGATE, JUGULAR, JUGUM; CONJUGATE, SUBJUGATE, from Latin *iugum*, yoke; **c.** ZYGO-, ZYGOMA, ZYGOTE, -ZYGOUS; AZYGOUS, SYZYGY, from Greek *zugon*, yoke, and *zugoun*, to join; **d.** YUGA, from Sanskrit *yugam*, yoke. **2.** Suffixed (superlative) form **yug-isto-*. JOSTLE, JOUST; ADJUST, JUXTAPOSITION, from Latin *iūxtā*, close by, perhaps from **iugistā (viā)*, "on a nearby (road)." **3.** Nasalized zero-grade form **yu-n-g-*. JOIN, JOINDER, JOINT, JOINTURE, JUNCTION, JUNCTURE, JUNTA; ADJOIN, CONJOIN, CONJUGAL, CONJUNCT, ENJOIN, INJUNCTION, REJOIN¹, REJOINDER, SUBJOIN, from Latin *iungere*, to join.
II. Suffixed form **yeug-mn̥*. ZEUGMA, from Greek *zeugma*, a bond.
III. Suffixed o-grade form **youg-o-*. YOGA, from Sanskrit *yogaḥ*, union. [Pokorny 2. *i̯eu-* 508.]

yu- You. Second person (plural) pronoun. YE¹, YOU, from Old English *gē* and *ēow*, you, from Germanic **jūz* (nominative) and **iwwiz* (oblique). [Pokorny 1. *i̯u-* 513.]

Picture Credits

The editorial and production staff wishes to thank the many individuals, organizations, and agencies that have contributed to the art program of this dictionary.

Credits on the following pages are arranged alphabetically by boldface entry word. At entries for which there are two or more picture sources, the sources follow the order of the illustrations.

Locator maps were rendered by Mapping Specialists Limited of Madison, Wisconsin.

Photographs that accompany the essay by Calvert Watkins were provided by the following sources: Viking runes–Corbis/Kevin Schafer; sun chariot–Corbis/Archivo Iconografico, S.A.; Iberian hut–Corbis/Archivo Iconografico, S.A.

The following source abbreviations are used throughout the credits: AA\Academy Artworks; AA-ES\Animals Animals-Earth Scenes; AP-WWP\AP-Wide World Photos; AR\Art Resource; AW\Alan Witschonke; CI\Carlyn Iverson; COR\Corbis; EM\Elizabeth Morales; FPG\FPG International; GC\The Granger Collection, New York; GH\Grant Heilman Photography, Inc.; GP\Globe Photos, Inc.; HAR\H. Armstrong Roberts, Inc.; HM\© School Division, Houghton Mifflin Company; ISI\Index Stock Imagery; LA\Liaison Agency, Inc.; LOC\Library of Congress; PDI\© 2001 PhotoDisc, Inc.; PE\PhotoEdit; PI\Positive Images; PG\Precision Graphics; PR\Photo Researchers, Inc.; SB\Stock, Boston; SS\SuperStock, Inc.; ST\ Stone; WS\Wendy Smith.

Hank Aaron FPG\Hy Peskin **abacus** HM **abbey** PDI **Ralph Abernathy** COR\Flip Schulke **abomasum** EM **abscissa** AA **Abu Simbel** SB\Dallas & John Heaton ST\Sylvain Grandadam **acanthus** PE\Bill Aron **Acapulco** SS\Steve Vidler **acciaccatura** Tech-Graphics **accordion** HM **acerose** EM **acetabulum** CI **achene** EM **acorn squash** HM **acropolis** ST\George Grigoriou **action painting** AR\Tate Gallery, London. ©2000 Pollock-Krasner Foundation/Artists Rights Society (ARS), New York **acute angle** AA **John Adams** AR\National Portrait Gallery, Smithsonian Institution **John Quincy Adams** AR\National Portrait Gallery, Smithsonian Institution **Adam's-needle** COR\Hal Horwitz **Jane Addams** GC **addax** COR\Steve Kaufman **Adélie penguin** SB\Leonard Rue **Adirondack chair** SB\William Johnson **adit** ISI\Stephen Saks **adjacent angle** AA **admiral** PR\Michael Lustbader **adobe** HAR\R. Krubner **adrenal gland** CI **adsorption** AA **adz** HM **aerobics** FPG\Jeff Kaufman **aerodynamics** AA **A-frame** ISI\Camerique **African buffalo** PDI **agouti** PR\Jany Sauvanet **aiguille** FPG\Jean Kugler **aileron** PG **air-cushion vehicle** PG **air dam** HAR **Akbar the Great** SS\Bridgeman Art Library, London **akee** PR\Kjell B. Sandved **Akhenaton** PR\Explorer **alabaster** SS\Egyptian Museum, Cairo, Egypt & Giraudon, Paris **Madeleine Albright** COR\Wally McNamee **alcazar** HAR\A. Tovy **Louisa May Alcott** GC **alder** WS **alembic** HAR\E.R. Degginger **Alexander the Great** AR\Scala **alfalfa** GH\Runk & Schoenberger **Alhambra** SS\Steve Vidler **Muhammad Ali** COR\Lynn Goldsmith **alpaca** AA-ES\Mickey Gibson **alpenhorn** COR\Paul Almasy **altar** FPG\Gary A. Conner COR\Richard Cummins **alternate angle** AA **altocumulus** PR\G.R. Roberts **amaryllis** HM **American elm** WS **ammeter** PR\Charles D. Winters **ammonite** PDI **amoeba** GH\Runk & Schoenberger **amphibian** HAR\L. Smith **amphora** AR\Scala **ampoule** SS\Robert Llewellyn **anaconda** AA-ES\Zigmund Leszczynski **anchor** PG **Marian Anderson** LOC **anemone** GH\Lefever & Grushow COR\Brandon D. Cole **aneroid barometer** PG **Angel Fall** SS\James A. Martin **Maya Angelou** AP-WWP\Chuck Burton **angioplasty** PG **Angora cat** AA-ES\Ulrike Schanz **ankh** HM **annual ring** PR\Gilbert S. Grant **anole** PR\A. Cosmos Blank **anorak** COR\Paul Almasy **antefix** AW **antenna** GH\Runk & Schoenberger **Susan B. Anthony** COR **anticipation** Tech-Graphics **anticline** PG **antler** EM **anvil** ISI\Stephen Saks **ao dai** PE\Michael Newman **aoudad** SS **aphelion** AA **Appaloosa** AA-ES\Robert Maier **aquacade** GP\NBC **aqueduct** SS\Steve Vidler **Saint Thomas Aquinas** GC **arabesque** PE\Felicia Martinez SB\Richard Pasley **Arabian horse** COR\Amos Nachoum **arch** ST\Arne Hodalic GP\James M. Kelly **arborvitae** WS **arch[1]** PG **archaic smile** SS\Acropolis Museum, Athens, Greece & Spiros Tselentis **archivolt** SS\Chigmaroff & Davidson **arctic fox** HAR\John Patton **area** AA **argyle** HM **Jean-Bertrand Aristide** SB\Rob Crandall **Aristotle** AR\Scala **armadillo** COR\Eric & David Hosking **Neil Armstrong** COR **arrowhead** AA-ES\Richard Kolar **art deco** AR\The Newark Museum **artesian well** PG **Chester A. Arthur** GC **art nouveau** GC\©2000 Artists Rights Society (ARS), New York/ADAGP, Paris FPG\Fergus O'Brien **ascender** PG **ash[2]** EM **Arthur Ashe** COR\Hulton-Deutsch Collection **Isaac Asimov** Archive Photos\Saga, Frank Capri **aspen** GH\Grant Heilman **assemblage** ISI\Jaye R. Phillips. ©2000 Artists Rights Society (ARS), New York/ADAGP, Paris **aster** AA-ES\Patti Murray **astragal** AW **astrobleme** PR\SPL, David Parker **astrolabe** GC **asymptote** AA **Atahualpa** GC **Athena** GC **Atlantic salmon** PR\Jeffrey L. Rotman **atom** AA **attitude** HAR\Adamsmith Productions **auger** PDI **Augustus** AR\Erich Lessing **Aung San Suu Kyi** LA\Daniel Simon **aurora borealis** AA-ES\Norbert Rosing **aviator glasses** PE\Gary Conner **avocado** HM **avocet** AA-ES\Phyllis Greenberg **axolotl** PR\Stephen Dalton **Johann Sebastian Bach** SS\Vienna Society for the Friends of Music & ET Archive, London **back dive** PG **backhand** PR\Will & Deni McIntyre **backhoe** HAR\D. Logan **bacterium** PR\Biophoto Associates PR\David M. Phillips PR\SPL, CNRI **Josephine Baker** COR\Bettmann **bald eagle** AA-ES\Don Skillman **James Baldwin** LOC\Carl Van Vechten Collection **ball-peen hammer** HM **balsam fir** WS **balustrade** ISI\Eric Roth **bamboo** HAR\M. Thonig **band shell** HAR\J. Messerschmidt **banjo** PR\Mandolin Bros., Stan Jay **baobab** PR\Tierbild Okapia **barbel[1]** AA-ES\Robert Lubeck **barge** SS **bar graph** AA **barn swallow** SS **baroque** SS **barrel cactus** PR\Gerald C. Kelley **bartizan** HAR\H. Sutton **Clara Barton** LOC **bascule** HAR\D. Logan **basil** PDI **basilica** AA **basketry** PR\Leonard Lee Rue III **bass clef** Tech-Graphics **basset hound** AA-ES\Gerard Lacz **battlement** PG **Bauhaus** COR\Robert Holmes **bay window** COR\Ric Ergenbright **beagle** AA-ES\Ralph

Reinhold **beak** EM **bearded iris** HAR\H. Abernathy **bearskin** HAR\J. Messerschmidt **Pierre G.T. Beauregard** AP-WWP **beech** WS **beefeater** PI\Candace Cochrane **Menachem Begin** LA\Benami Neumann **begonia** HM **belfry** HAR\R. Kord **Alexander Graham Bell** LOC **bellows** HM **David Ben Gurion** LA\Hulton Getty Picture Library **benzene ring** AA **Bermuda shorts** ISI\Barry Winiker **Bernese mountain dog** PR\Tierbild Okapia **Sarah Bernhardt** LOC **Chuck Berry** COR\Neal Preston **Mary McLeod Bethune** GC\National Portrait Gallery, Smithsonian Institution; Gift of the Harmon Foundation **bevel gear** AA **biconcave** PG **biconvex** PG **bighorn** PR\James Zipp **binnacle** PDI **biplane** PR\Jerry Irwin **birch** WS **bird of paradise** PDI **Otto von Bismarck** SS\A.K.G., Berlin **bison** GH\Arthur C. Smith III **bit[2]** AA **Black Hawk** SS\Private Collection, Pablo Prints **black knot** PR\Noble Proctor **black letter** Chris Costello **Tony Blair** COR\Peter Turnley **Mont Blanc** ST **blaze[2]** SS **blazing star** PR\John M. Coffman **blinders** HAR\K. Wyle **block and tackle** Gail Piazza **blockhouse** ST\James P. Rowan **bloomer[2]** GC **blowhole** PR\Tim Davis **blue whale** CI **bobbin lace** PR\Explorer **bobcat** PR\Tom Leeson **bobsled** PR\Bernard Asset, Agence Vandystadt **Humphrey Bogart** AP-WWP **boiler** PG **bok choy** HM **Simón Bolívar** SS\Explorer **boll weevil** GH\Grant Heilman **bongo[1]** PR\R. Van Nostrand **bonsai** HM **boom[2]** ISI\George Goodwin **Daniel Boone** Courtesy of the Massachusetts Historical Society **John Wilkes Booth** LOC **borzoi** ©Houghton Mifflin Company - Photograph by Evelyn Shafer **boss[2]** Chris Costello **Margaret Bourke-White** COR\Bettmann **bouzouki** PE\Spencer Grant **bowhead** CI **bowknot** HM **bow saw** HM **brace** FPG\Ron Chapple HM **bracer[2]** SB\Bob Daemmrich **Mathew Brady** LOC **Braille** AA **brain** Laurel Cook Lhowe **brain coral** PR\Greg Ochocki **Joseph Brant** National Gallery of Canada, Ottawa, Purchased 1951 **breadfruit** GH\Alan Pitcairn **breakfront** COR\Peter Harholdt **bridge[1]** SB\Bob Daemmrich AR\Scala **brisket** Ka Botzis **bristlecone pine** HAR\E. Cooper **brittle star** COR\Jeffrey L. Rotman **brocade** HM **bromeliad** SB\Thomas Fletcher **Brontë** SS\National Portrait Gallery, London **brooch** FPG\Paul Markow **John Brown** COR\The National Archives **Brown Swiss** ISI\Lynn Stone **Blanche Kelso Bruce** GC **James Buchanan** SS **Pearl S. Buck** GP\NBC **Buddha[1]** FPG\Josef Beck **bugle[1]** PDI **bullfinch** AA-ES\Robert Maier **bullfrog** PR\Michael P. Gadomski **bundt cake** PDI **bungee jumping** SB\Peter Southwick **Bunraku** COR\Michael S. Yamashita **burette** PE\David Kelly Crow **burl** PR\Ken Brate **Barbara Bush** LOC **George Bush** LOC **George W. Bush** COR\Jim Bourg, Reuters NewMedia Inc. **Laura Bush** COR\Larry Downing, Reuters NewMedia Inc. **bustard** COR\S. Charles Brown, Frank Lane Picture Agency **butterfly valve** PG **butt hinge** Gail Piazza **Byzantine** SS\Leonid Bogdanov **cable car** FPG\Bill Losh **cable stitch** HM **cabochon** HM **Mother Cabrini** LOC **caduceus** AA **Julius Caesar** SS\Christie's Images **cairn** COR\Richard Cummins **Sarah Caldwell** GP\Dennis Barna **calico** PDI **California condor** PR\Tom McHugh **caliper** PG **calla lily** COR\Tania Midgley **calligraphy** COR\Arne Hodalic **camera** PG **campanile** COR\Kevin Schafer **canal** ISI\David Ball **candelabrum** HM **cane toad** AA-ES\Breck P. Kent **cannoli** HM **canopy** HAR\K. Rice **cantaloupe** HM **cant hook** PG **canvasback** PR\Jeffrey Lepore **caparison** COR\Gianni Dagli Orti **cape[2]** PR\SPL, Earth Satellite Corp. **Cape Cod cottage** COR\Philippa Lewis **Capitol** ST\Doug Armand **capo[1]** HM **capybara** FPG\Luis Rosendo **carabiner** HM **carambola** AA-ES\Patti Murray **caravan** SB\Michele Burgess **card[2]** SB\Jay Syverson **cardinal** PDI **cardioid** AA **caricature** AR\National Portrait Gallery, Smithsonian Institution; Gift of the family of Mr. Charles Dunn **Carlsbad Caverns** HAR\Camerique **carnauba** PR\Jacques Jangoux **carrel** SB\Richard Pasley **carrion flower** PR\V. Weinland **Rachel Carson** COR\Underwood & Underwood **Jimmy Carter** LOC **Rosalynn Carter** LOC **Cartesian coordinate system** AA **cartouche** PR\Brian Brake **George Washington Carver** AP-WWP **caryatid** PR\Carl Purcell **cashew** AA-ES\Patti Murray **Mary Cassatt** AR\National Portrait Gallery, Smithsonian Institution **Cassini division** PR\Science Source, NASA **Fidel Castro** COR\Jacques M. Chenet **catalpa** WS **catenary** AA **Catherine the Great** AR\Scala **catkin** GH\Runk & Schoenberger **CAT scanner** ISI\Larry Lawfer **Carrie Chapman Catt** AR\National Portrait Gallery, Smithsonian Institution; Transfer from the National Museum of American History, Gift of the National American Woman Suffrage Association through Mrs. Carrie Chapman Catt, 1939 **cauldron** PC\Franz Kraus **causeway** PE\Jeff Greenberg **C clef** Tech-Graphics **cecropia moth** SS **cell** Laurel Cook Lhowe **Celtic cross** COR\Tom

Bean **centrifuge** PR\Charles D. Winters **centripetal force** PG **cereal leaf beetle** PR\Holt Studios **chain** AA **chairlift** PR\Jan Halaska **chalet** PR\Explorer **chameleon** AA-ES\Marian Bacon **chamois** COR\Maurizio Lanini **chanoyu** SB\Charles Gupton **chanterelle** PR\Tom Martin **Charlie Chaplin** SS **Charlemagne** SS\Stadtmuseum, Aachen & ET Archive, London **chasuble** PE\Tony Freeman **César Chávez** LA\Bob Riha **checkers** HM **cheetah** GP\Angelo Cozzi, Imapress **cheongsam** ISI\Dorian Weber **cherry picker** AA-ES\Donald Specker **Chiang Kai-shek** WWP **Chicago School** COR\Angelo Hornak **Chichén Itzá** AR\SEF **Chimera** SS\Archaeological Museum, Florence, Italy & A.K.G., Berlin **chimpanzee** ST\Tim Davis **Chincoteague pony** AA-ES\Bertram G. Murray **Chinese lantern** HM **Jacques Chirac** AP\Popperfoto **Chi-Rho** Gail Piazza **cholla** GH\Runk & Schoenberger **chopstick** PDI **Agatha Christie** AP-WWP **chromosome** ST\Adrian T. Sumner **chukar** COR\D. Robert Franz **Sir Winston Churchill** SS\Bridgeman Art Library, London **cinder block** PDI **circle** AA **circuit** AA **circular saw** SB\Bill Gallery **cirrus** PR\SPL **cittern** SS\Christie's Images **civet** AA-ES\Dale & Marian Zimmerman **clamp** HM **clamshell** COR\Tim Wright **clarinet** SB\Bob Daemmrich **Claudius I** GC **claw hammer** PDI **clean room** ISI\Ed Lallo **Samuel L. Clemens** GC **clerestory** PG **Grover Cleveland** SS\Culver Pictures, Inc. **clevis** AA **Patsy Cline** COR\Bettmann **Hillary Rodham Clinton** Courtesy of the White House Photo Office **Bill Clinton** Archive Photos\CNP **clipper** SS\Bridgeman Art Library, London **cloister** AR\Scala **clotheshorse** HM **Clovis I** AR\Giraudon **Clydesdale** AA-ES\Robert Maier **Ty Cobb** AP-WWP **cobblestone** ST\Kindra Clineff **cobra** PR\Tom McHugh **coccyx** CI **cockatiel** AA-ES\Robert Pearcy **cocker spaniel** GP\Anton Thau **cock-of-the-rock** PR\Kenneth W. Fink **coconut palm** WS **Buffalo Bill Cody** SS **coelacanth** EM **coffee** COR\Kennan Ward **coffer** SS **cog railway** SB\Robert B. Henderson **colander** HM **coliseum** SB\Grant LeDuc **collie** ISI\Ralph Reinhold **colonnade** HAR\Larry Lee **Colorado potato beetle** PR\Tierbild Okapia, K.G. Vock **color guard** GP\Daniel Teboul **Christopher Columbus** LOC **column** PG **combine** GH\Arthur C. Smith III **comet** PR\John Chumack **command module** SS **commode** SS\Peter Harholdt **common grackle** AA-ES\Alan G. Nelson **compass** HM PD **Composite order** AW **compound**[1] EM **compound eye** SS **concave** PG **conch** PDI **condyle** CI **cone** AA **coneflower** FPG\Buddy Mays **Conestoga wagon** ISI\Stephen Saks **Confucius** GC **conic section** AA **conning tower** COR\Yogi, Inc. **console**[2] PE\Novastock **John Constable** SS\National Portrait Gallery, London **Constantine the Great** AR\Scala **continental shelf** PG **contrail** PDI\ **control tower** HAR\K. Scholz **convex** PG **Captain Cook** GC **Calvin Coolidge** SS **cop**[3] HM **coping saw** PDI **coquina** AA-ES\Jim Doran **corbel arch** AW **corbie-step** SB\Dallas & John Heaton **Corinthian order** AW **cormorant** PR\Craig K. Lorenz **corncrib** HAR\W.J. Scott **corset** SS\Musee des Augustins, Toulouse, France & Giraudon, Paris **Hernando Cortés** AR\Giraudon **Bill Cosby** COR\Lynn Goldsmith **cosecant** AA **cosine** AA **costume** SS\Steve Vidler **cotangent** AA **cotton** ISI\Inga Spence **cottonwood** WS **Coulter pine** WS **countersink** AA **coupler** ISI\O.G.S. Inc. **Jacques Cousteau** LA\Alain Benainous **covered bridge** ST\Tom Mackie **cowboy boot** PDI **cowcatcher** SB\John Elk III **coyote** AA-ES\Alan G. Nelson **crampon** ISI\Camerique **crappie** AA-ES\Breck P. Kent **Crazy Horse** SS **crazy quilt** AR\The Newark Museum **crenate** EM **crescent** SS\Larry Chiger **crevasse** ISI\David Trask **cricket**[2] COR\Tony Arruza **crocus** GH\Stanley Schoenberger **crop-dusting** COR\George Lepp **cross** AA **cross-country skiing** PR\James McCann **crosscut saw** PDI **cross-stitch** HM **crostino** HM **croustade** HM **crowbar** HM **crow's-nest** ISI\Phyllis Picardi **cruet** HM **crutch** PG **cube** AA **cubism** AR\Scala. ©2000 Estate of Pablo Picasso/Artists Rights Society (ARS), New York **cuckoopint** COR\Ken Wilson, Papilio **cummerbund** PE\Richard Hutchings **cupola** HAR\J. McGrail **Marie Curie** GC **curlew** PR\David Weintraub **curling** PR\Bernard Asset, Agence Vandystadt **currant** PR\Antony B. Joyce **currycomb** HM **George Armstrong Custer** LOC **cutter** SB\Rick Browne **cuttlefish** CI **cycad** PR\Gary Retherford **cylinder** AA **cyma** AW **cypress** WS **dachshund** AA-ES\Ralph Reinhold **Dalai Lama** GP\Andrea Renault **Salvador Dalí** COR\Photo B.D.V. **Dall sheep** PR\Ken M. Johns **dalmatian** FPG\Ken Reid **damascene** HM **dandelion** EM **Dante Alighieri** AR\Scala **dapple-gray** PR\Elisabeth Weiland **Darius I** AR\SEF **Clarence Darrow** COR\Bettman **date palm** PR\Paolo Koch **Jefferson Davis** AR\National Portrait Gallery, Smithsonian Institution **Miles Davis** COR\Lynn Goldsmith **davit** HAR\P. Buddle **deadeye** ISI\Susan Van Etten **decagon** AA **decahedron** AA **décolletage** SS\The Huntington Library, Art Collections, and Botanical Gardens, San Marino, California **decoy** PDI **deer mouse** PR\Rod Planck **deer tick** HAR\E.R. Degginger **Charles de Gaulle** AP-WWP **delft** HM **delta wing** COR\NASA **demijohn** HM **Cecil B. De Mille** AP-WWP **demoiselle crane** PR\Kenneth W. Fink **dendrite** HM **dentate** EM **Denver boot** FPG\Joachim Messerschmidt **deodar** PR\Geoffrey Bryant **depot** SB\Martin Rogers **derby** SB\Hansen Lightworks, Inc. **derrick** FPG\Joe Robbins **dervish** COR\Hans Georg Roth **desalinize** PG **Descartes** AR\Erich Lessing **descender** PG **desert 1** COR\Gordon Whitten **detector** COR\Adam Woolfitt **Eamon De Valera** Archive Photos\Illustrated London News **Devi** AR\Erich Lessing **dewlap** PR\Tom McHugh **diagonal** AA **diamondback terrapin** SS\David A. Northcott **Diamond Head** COR\Douglas Peebles **diatom** PR\SPL, Jan Hinsch **dibble** HM **dickcissel** PR\G. Ronald Austing **Charles Dickens** GC **differential windlass** AA **digestive system** CI **digger wasp** AA-ES\James H. Robinson **Joe DiMaggio** COR\Underwood & Underwood **dimorphism** PR\James H. Robinson **dingo** PR\James Steinberg **dinoflagellate** AA-ES\Oxford Scientific Films **diorama** COR\Lowell Georgia **dipteral** AA **director's chair** HM **dirndl** HAR **dirt bike** HAR\A. Hubrich **discus** SS **dish antenna** SB\Bill Gallery **disk harrow** ISI\Larsh Bristol **Walt Disney** GP **Benjamin Disraeli** SS\National Portrait Gallery, London **distaff** PI\Patricia J. Bruno **diverticulosis** CI **divi-divi** FPG\Barbara Peacock **Dorothea Dix** GC **DNA** Laurel Cook Lhowe **Doberman pinscher** ISI\Camerique **dodecagon** AA **dodecahedron** AA **dogsled** ISI\Inga Spence **dogtooth** AW **dogwood** PR\Jane Latta **dolphin** AA-ES\James Watt **dome** COR\Dave Bartruff **MC>Donatello** AR\Scala **donkey** AA-ES\Robert Maier **door** AA **Doric order** AW **dormer** SB\Peter Vandermark **double bass** PDI **double-decker** ISI\Jeffrey Greenberg **Douglas fir** WS **Frederick Douglass** COR\Bettmann **dovetail** AA **dowitcher** AA-ES\Mark Chappell **downspout** PE\Felicia Martinez **downy woodpecker** PR\Steve Maslowski **dowser** SS\David Harvey **dragon** SB\Lawrence Migdale **dragonfly** PR\Rod Planck **drawbridge** GH\Alan Pitcairn **drawknife** HM **dredge**[1] ISI\Arnie Feinberg COR\James L. Amos **dreidel** PDI **drill press** SB\John Coletti **drive-through** PR\J. Gerard Smith **drogue parachute** HAR **drought** FPG\Ken Ross **dry dock** HAR\L. Smith **dry wall** COR\Jennie Woodcock, Reflections Photolibrary **W.E.B. Du Bois** AR\National Portrait Gallery, Smithsonian Institution; Gift of Walter Waring in memory of his wife, Laura Wheeler Waring, through the Harmond Foundation **dugong** EM **duiker** COR\Michael Gore, Frank Lane Picture Agency **dump truck** ISI\Phil Moughmer **dung beetle** PR **Dungeness crab** PR\Tom McHugh, Steinhart Aquarium **dunk shot** FPG\Jim Cummins **duomo** AR\Scala **Albrecht Dürer** AR\Giraudon **dust storm** AA-ES\M. Coe, Oxford Scientific Films **Dutch door** ISI\Glasheen Graphics **Dutchman's breeches** PR\Rod Planck **Dutch oven** PI\Karen Bussolini **Mary Dyer** Courtesy of the Social Law Library, Boston **Bob Dylan** GP\Corkery News **eagle ray** AA-ES\Zigmund Leszczynski **Eames chair** PE\Bill Aron **Amelia Earhart** GC **earth** PDI **earwig** AA-ES\James Robinson **Easter Island** PDI **Ebola virus** PR\SPL, Barry Dowset **echidna** PR\Tom McHugh **echinacea** PI\Jerry Howard **eclosion** GH\Runk & Schoenberger **Mary Baker Eddy** LOC **edelweiss** AA-ES\Leonard Rue Enterprises **Gertrude Ederle** AP-WWP **Thomas Edison** GC **egg-and-dart** AW **eggplant** PD **egret** COR\Eric & David Hosking **Albert Einstein** GC **Dwight D. Eisenhower** COR **Mamie Eisenhower** The White House Collection, © White House Historical Association **eland** SS **elbow** AA **El Capitan** ISI\Glasheen Graphics **electrocardiogram** SS\Robert Llewellyn **electrostatic generator** GH\Runk & Schoenberger **elephant** ISI\Stephen Maka FPG\Khalid Ghani **elevon** PG **T.S. Eliot** GC **Elizabeth II** GP\©Alpha **Duke Ellington** AP-WWP **ellipse** AA **elytron** EM **emarginate** EM **emblem** PI\Martin Miller **embroidery** SB\Bob Daemmrich **Ralph Waldo Emerson** AR\National Portrait Gallery, Smithsonian Institution **empennage** PR\Dale Boyer **emperor penguin** AA-ES\Johnny Johnson **Empire** AR\Giraudon SS\Peter Harholdt **emu** ST\Paul Hurd **enamel** GC **endive** HM **ensign** FPG\Peter Gridley **entablature** PG **entasis** AW **epaulet** SB\Robert Fried **Ephesus** ISI\Rick Strange **epicycloid** AA **equestrian** HAR\R. Krubner **Erasmus** AR\Scala **erosion** COR\Chinch Gryniewicz, Ecoscene **eruption** COR **Julius Erving** LA\Michael Abramson **escapement** PG **escarpment** SB\Dallas & John Heaton **Escorial** PR\Ronny Jacques **escutcheon** PG **espadrille** HM **Etruscan** COR\Gianni Dagli Orti **eucalyptus** WS **Euripides** SS\ET Archive, London **Mount Everest** AA-ES\Martyn Colbeck, Oxford Scientific Films **Chris Evert** COR\Hulton-Deutsch Collection **ewer** COR\Royal Ontario Museum **excurrent** EM **exercise bicycle** PDI **exposure meter** HM **expressionism** AR\Nimatallah **exterior angle** CL/AA **extinguisher** PDI **extravehicular activity** ISI\Scott Berner **eyeblack** COR\AFP **eye chart** PDI **eyespot** AA-ES\R.F. Head **eyestalk** GH\Runk & Schoenberger **facemask** ISI\William Meyer **faceplate** COR\Craig Lovell **faience** COR\Austrian Archives **falcon** ISI\Ralph Reinhold **falls** COR\Buddy Mays **fallow deer** AA-ES\Robert Maier **fanlight** HAR\C.S. Bauer **fan vaulting** PDI **Fannie Farmer** GC **fasces** GC **fastigiate** PI\Karen Bussolini **fault** PG **featherstitch** AA **fedora** HM **felucca** PDI **femur** CI **fencing** SB\Bob Daemmrich **fennel** AA-ES\Fritz Prenzel **fermata** PG **ferryboat** COR\Natalie Fobes **feverfew** AA-ES\Richard Shiell **fez** SS **fibula** CI **fiddlehead** PI\Jacob Mosser **fiddler crab** COR\Brandon D. Cole **field hockey** PE\Tony Freeman **fife** PI\Jim Kahnweiler **figurehead** COR\Adam Woolfitt **Millard Fillmore** COR\Bettmann **fin**[1] EM **finch** ISI\Gregory Scott **fingerboard** HAR\D. Logan **finial** PI\Margaret Hensel **fire escape** PE\Rudi Von Briel **fire tower** GH\Fred Habegger **fisheye** PI\Dennis Frates **fish ladder** GH\Lou Jacobs Jr. **fissipalmate** EM **Ella Fitzgerald** COR\Bettmann **F. Scott Fitzgerald** AR\National Portrait Gallery, Smithsonian Institution **fjord** ISI\J. Messerschmidt **flake**[2] ISI\J. Messerschmidt **flamenco** PE\Bonnie Kamin **flamingo** AA-ES\Charles Palek **flattop** PDI **flatworm** AA-ES\Peter Parks, Oxford Scientific Films **flèche** ISI\Rick Strange **fleur-de-lis** HM **flipper** SS\Alan Briere HM **flounder**[2] AA-ES\Herb Segars **flower** EM **flute** SB\Richard Pasley **fly agaric** ST\Laurie Campbell **flycatcher** AA-ES\McDonald Wildlife Photography **flying boat** SS\Ping Amranand **flying buttress** SB\John Elk III **flying fox** AA-ES\Studio Carlo Dani **focaccia** HM **fold**[1] PG **folium** AA **folk art** AR\National Museum of American Art, Washington, DC **Margot Fonteyn** GP\Richard Corkery **food chain** PG **foot** CI\ **footrope** PC\James Lemass **Forbidden City** SS\Hidekazu Nishibata **Betty Ford** GP\Michael Ferguson **Gerald Ford** GP\James M. Kelly **Henry Ford** COR\Bettmann **forehand** PDI **forelock**[1] PR\Tierbild Okapia **forge**[1] GH\John Colwell **forklift** PR\Benelux Press BV **forsythia** SB\Bela Kalman **fortune cookie** PDI **foul line** HAR\Camerique **fountain** PDI **four-o'clock** COR\Scott T. Smith **fox** ST\Darrell Gulin **fractal** ST\Stephen Johnson **Francis of Assisi** SS\ET Archive, London **Francisco Franco** GC **frangipani** AA-ES\Fritz Prenzel **Anne Frank** COR\Bettman, UPI **Benjamin Franklin** COR\North Carolina Museum of Art **Frederick II** SS **freesia** PDI **French curve** HM **French horn** SB\Lawrence Migdale **French knot** AA **fret**[3] AW **Sigmund Freud** GC **frigate** SB\C.J. Allen **frilled lizard** AA-ES\Klaus Uhlenhut **Robert Frost** LA\Hulton Getty Picture Library **f-stop** AA **Carlos Fuentes** GP\James M. Kelly **Mount Fuji** SB\Dallas & John Heaton **furrow** PI\Jerry Howard **fur seal** AA-ES\Patti Murray **fuse**[2] PG **futurism** AR\Tate Gallery, London **gable** HAR\D. Lada **Yuri Gagarin** COR\Bettmann **Galileo Galilei** GC **gall**[3] PDI **galleon** COR\Steve Lindridge, Eye Ubiquitous **galosh** HM **gambrel roof** SB\Thomas Fletcher **gamelan** COR\Wolfgang Kaehler **Indira Gandhi** GP\Brad Markel **Mahatma Gandhi** LA\Hulton Getty Picture Library **gantry** PE\Susan Van Etten Lawson **Jerry Garcia** LA\Iovino **James A. Garfield** PR\Tom McHugh **gargoyle** PDI **William Lloyd Garrison** GC **gas turbine** PG **gatehouse** COR\Jack Fields **Bill Gates** FPG\Mark Reinstein **gazebo** SB\William Johnson **gecko** AA-ES\Color-Pic **geisha** SS\Culver Pictures, Inc. **gemsbok** COR\Peter Johnson **generator** PDI **genet**[1] SS\Holton Collection **geodesic dome** SS\Mia & Klaus Matthes **George III** SS\National Portrait Gallery, London **gerenuk** HAR\B. von Hoffmann **German shepherd** AA-ES\Phil Degginger **Geronimo** COR\Hulton-Deutsch Collection **giant sequoia** SB\Roy C. Bishop **Gibraltar**[1] ISI\Rick Strange **Althea Gibson** COR\Bettmann **Dizzy Gillespie** PR\Brock May **gimbal** PG **ginger** PDI **ginkgo** WS **giraffe** AA-ES\Leonard Rue Enterprises **girdle** PG **glacier** AA-ES\Johnny Johnson **glass blowing** SB\John Coletti **John Glenn** Archive Photos/ Reuters, NASA **gloxinia** AA-ES\Richard Shiell **glyph** SB\Michael Dwyer **gnu** AA-ES\D. Allen Photography **goggles** PI\Mikki Ansin **golden retriever** ST\Chip Henderson **goldenseal** PR\Jeffrey Lepore **goldfinch** PR\Gregory K. Scott **gondola** SS AA-ES\Bertram G. Murray **goose** AA-ES\Robert Maier **gooseberry** GH\Runk & Schoenberger **Mikhail Gorbachev** AP-WWP **Berry Gordy, Jr.** COR\Neal Preston **gorilla** ST\Art Wolfe **Gothic** SS **Gothic revival** COR\Paul Seheult, Eye Ubiquitous **Francisco Goya** AR\Scala **gradin** PDI **Martha Graham** COR\Bettmann **Grand Canal** FPG\VCG **Grand Canyon** FPG\Gerald French **grandfather clock** PE\Tony Freeman **Ulysses S. Grant** GC **grasshopper** GH\Runk & Schoenberger **grate**[2] FPG\Suzanne Murphy-Larronde **great blue heron** ISI\Ralph Reinhold **Great Dane** PR\Jacana **great seal** ISI\Russ Lappa **Great Wall of China** ISI\Bill Bachman **greenhouse effect** PG **Alan Greenspan** COR\Matt Mendelsohn **grindstone** PE\Tony Freeman **Walter Gropius** WWP **grouse**[1] AA-ES\Dale & Marian Zimmerman **gueridon** GC **Guernsey**[2] GH\Larry Lefever **Che Guevara** LA\Hulton Getty Picture Library **guide dog** AA-ES\Ralph Reinhold **guinea fowl** AA-ES\Trevor Barrett **gullwing** HAR\E. Masterson **Johann Gutenberg** GC **Hadrian** AR\Alinari **haku** HAR\E. Masterson **Alex Haley** GP\Michael Ferguson **half note** PG **Halley's comet** PDI **hamadryas** PR\Gerald C. Kelley **hamantasch** HM **Alexander Hamilton** AR\National Portrait Gallery, Smithsonian Institution **hand** CI **handcar** SS\William Hamilton **hand organ**

ISI\Gil Fahey **Panama Canal** COR\The National Archives **pancreas** CI **panda** PR\George Holton **Pangaea** Jerry Malone **pangolin** COR\Nigel J. Dennis, ABPL **panpipe** PDI **papaya** PR\Holt Studios **papyrus** AA-ES\Richard Shiell **parabola** AA **paraboloid** AA **parachute** PI\Les Campbell **parallel bars** SB\Bob Daemmrich **parallelipiped** AA **parallelogram** AA **paramecium** ST\Robert Brons, BPS **parasail** PE\Myrleen Ferguson Cate **parasol** ST\Yann Layma **parka** PR\P. Chickering **Rosa Parks** AR\National Portrait Gallery, Smithsonian Institution; Gift of the Anheuser-Busch Companies and Artis Lane **parsley** HM **parsnip** PR\Antony B. Joyce **parterre** COR\Tony Arruza **Parthenon** HAR\Key-Color, Zefa **Blaise Pascal** AR\Giraudon **pasqueflower** AA-ES\Charles Palek **passionflower** PI\Harry Haralambou **pastel** AR\Giraudon **Louis Pasteur** GC **patchwork** HM **pattypan squash** GH\John Colwell **Alice Paul** LOC **Linus Pauling** AP-WWP **Luciano Pavarotti** FPG\Kozlowski Productions **pavilion** PG **Anna Pavlova** COR\Bettmann **peacock** ISI\Jerry Koontz **pearl[1]** HM **Robert E. Peary** COR\Hulton-Deutsch Collection **pedicab** PR\Will & Deni McIntyre **pediment** ISI\Henry Kaiser **I.M. Pei** COR\Owen Franken **pelican** PR\Tierbild Okapia **pendant[1]** HM **pendentive** PG **penguin** GH\George H. Harrison **pentagon** AA PR **peony** PI\Albert Squillace **Percheron** COR\Kit Houghton Photography **peregrine falcon** PR\George Galicz **perfoliate** EM **perihelion** AA **peristyle** COR\Massimo Listri **periwinkle[1]** AA-ES\Patti Murray **Frances Perkins** COR\Bettmann, UPI **Eva and Juan Perón** LA\Hulton Getty Picture Library **Perpendicular** COR\Brian Harding, Eye Ubiquitous **Persepolis** SS\Kurt Scholz **Perseus** AR\Scala **Persian cat** SS **persimmon** AA-ES\Richard Shiell **personal watercraft** SB\Spencer Grant **pestle** HM **Peter the Great** AR\Lauros - Giraudon **petri dish** SS\Charles Orrico **petroglyph** HAR\Wendell Metzen **peyote** PR\Jacana **Philae** COR\Stephanie Colasanti **Phillip II[3]** PR\AKG **philodendron** HM **phoebe** HAR\T. Ulrich **phonograph** PDI **phylactery** COR\Neil Beer **physical therapy** SB\Bill Horsman **Edith Piaf** AP-WWP **Pablo Picasso** COR\Bettmann **Piccadilly Circus** FPG\VCG **pickax** HM **picket fence** SS\George Schaub **pier** ISI\Mark Gibson **Franklin Pierce** GC **pietà** SS\Canali PhotoBank, Milan **pike[2]** PR\Tom McHugh, Steinhart Aquarium **pileated woodpecker** AA-ES\McDonald Wildlife Photography **piñata** PDI **pinkroot** PR\Richard J. Green **pinnacle** SS\Steve Vidler **pinnate** EM **pintail** PI\Les Campbell **pinto** FPG\Clyde H. Smith **pipeline** PR\Tom Leeson **pipkin** HM **pitcher plant** PR\Scott Camazine **pitchfork** COR\Dean Conger **pitta** PR\Tom McHugh **plaid** HM **plane[2]** PDI **plantain lily** ISI\Kindrea Clineff **plastron** SB\Bob Daemmrich **platypus** SS **plein air** Photograph © 1999, The Art Institute of Chicago. All rights reserved. John Singer Sargent, American, 1856–1925, *The Fountain, Villa Torlonia, Frascati, Italy,* oil on canvas, 1907, 71.4 ˘ 56.5 cm, Friends of American Art Collection, 1914.57. **plexor** PDI **plover** SS **plume** PE\Myrleen Ferguson Cate **plus fours** COR\Tony Roberts **Plymouth Rock** COR\James Marshall **Pocahontas** AR\National Portrait Gallery, Smithsonian Institution **podium** PE\Jonathan Nourok **Edgar Allan Poe** COR\Bettmann **poinsettia** PDI **pointe** PR\Blair Seitz **pointillism** AR\Erich Lessing. ©2000 Artists Rights Society (ARS), New York/ADAGP, Paris **poison ivy** PI\Jerry Howard **polar bear** PI\Jacob Mosser III **polar coordinate** AA **pole vault** PR\Gerard Vandystadt **Polish Corridor** Jerry Malone **James K. Polk** COR\The Corcoran Gallery of Art **polo** ST\Richard Francis **Marco Polo** GC **polyhedral angle** AA **Pomeranian** AA-ES\Daphne Godfrey Trust **pommel horse** FPG\Darryl Zimmerman **pontoon** ISI\J & S Austin **pontoon bridge** COR\Enzo Ragazzini **poodle** ISI\Ralph Reinhold **pop art** AR\©2000 Andy Warhold Foundation/ARS, NY. TM Licensed by Campbell's Soup Co. All Rights Reserved. **poplar** WS **porcupine** HAR\T. Ulrich **porcupine fish** AA-ES\Zigmund Leszczynski **porringer** HM **portal** ISI\Jim & Bonnie McGrath **Cole Porter** COR\Hulton-Deutsch Collection **portico** COR\Angelo Hornak **postimpressionism** AR\Erich Lessing **potbelly stove** COR\Gunter Marx **potter's wheel** PR\Joseph Nettis **pouch** PR\Michael James **powder horn** ISI\Glasheen Graphics **Colin Powell** SB\Bob Daemmrich **prairie dog** PR\Tim Davis **prayer rug** AR **prayer wheel** PDI **praying mantis** PR\Michael Lustbader **precipice** HAR\H. Abernathy **precisionism** AR\National Museum of American Art, Smithsonian Institution, Washington, DC **pre-Columbian** SS\Jacksonville Museum of Contemporary Art, Florida **prefab** HAR\R. J. Bennett **Pre-Raphaelite** AR\Tate Gallery, London **present arms** PE\Jeff Greenberg **Elvis Presley** GP\NBC **press[1]** COR\Michael Boys **pricket** HM **primitive** SS\Barnes Foundation, Merion, Pennsylvania **printed circuit** PR\SPL, Rosenfeld Images Ltd. **proboscis** FPG\Lee Kuhn **profile** SS\Städelsches Art Institute, Frankfurt, Germany **prominence** PR\Science Source, Hale Observatories **pronghorn** SS\Maurice Carlisle **propeller** PE\Michael Newman **prosthesis** PR\Catherine Ursillo **prostyle** AA **Marcel Proust** AR\Erich Lessing. ©2000 Artists Rights Society (ARS), New York/ADAGP, Paris **prow** PI\Jerry Howard **ptarmigan** AA-ES\Ruth Cole **Giacomo Puccini** GC **pueblo[1]** SB\Donald Dietz **puffball** AA-ES\Michael Fogden **puffin** ST\Tom Tietz **pug[1]** FPG\Jeffrey Sylvester **pump[1]** PG **pumpkinseed** AA-ES\Gerard Lacz **punching bag** PR\Jerry Wachter **punt[1]** COR\Michael S. Yamashita **punty** COR\Paul A. Souders **pupa** GH\Runk & Schoenberger **Purple Heart** PDI **Aleksandr S. Pushkin** SS\A.K.G., Berlin **pussy willow** AA-ES\Patti Murray **putt** COR\Deborah Ortiz **putto** SS\Canali PhotoBank, Milan **pygmy hippopotamus** AA-ES\Zigmund Leszczynski **pylon** SS\Michelle Burgess **pyramid** SB\Dallas & John Heaton **pyrrhuloxia** SS **Pythagoras** SS\Museo Capitolino, Rome & ET Archive, London **Pythagorean theorem** AA **Muammar al-Qaddafi** COR\Peter Turnley **quadrilateral** AA **quadripartite** HAR\Roger Miller **quail[1]** SB\John Cancalosi **quarry[2]** ST\Grilly Bernard **quartet** SB\Randall Hyman **quatrefoil** COR\Paul Almasy **Queen Anne's lace** ISI\Steve Solum **Manuel Quezon y Molina** AP-WWP **quillwork** PR\Tom McHugh **quilt** COR\Jacqui Hurst **quipu** ST\Robert Frerck **quiver[2]** HM **quoin** AW **Ra[1]** GC **rabbet** AA **raccoon** HAR\T. Ulrich **racket[1]** HM **radar** FPG\VCG **radio telescope** HAR\A. Tovy **radius** CI **rafflesia** PR\W.K. Fletcher **ragged robin** COR\Michael Maconachie, Papilio **raglan** HM **ragwort** COR\Niall Benvie **rail fence** PR\Adam Jones **rainbow trout** PR\Tom Leeson **ramada** COR\Greg Probst **Rameses II** FPG\Josef Beck **ranch house** ISI\Camerique **Jeannette Rankin** GC **Raphael[2]** SS\Galleria degli Uffizi, Florence, Italy **raspberry** AA-ES\Robert Maier **rat** GH\Runk & Schoenberger **ratel** AA-ES\ABPL Image Library **rattlesnake** AA-ES\John Gerlach **ravioli** Eye Wire **razor wire** COR\Mark L. Stephenson **Nancy Reagan** SB\Michael Grecco **Ronald Reagan** GC **reamer** HM **rebozo** SS **receiver** PG **recorder** Eye Wire **Red Cloud** COR\Library of Congress **Red Cross** COR\Leif Skoogfors **red fox** ST\Lewis Kemper **red oak** WS **red-tailed hawk** FPG\Lee Kuhn **reel[1]** PDI **reentrant angle** AA **reflecting telescope** CL/AA **reflection** HAR\M. Miller **reflex angle** AA **refracting telescope** AA **regardant** PG **Regency** SS\Christie's Images **William H. Rehnquist** GP **reindeer** PR\Eric Hosking **reliquary** GC **Rembrandt van Rijn** COR\Francis G. Mayer **Renaissance** AR\Scala COR\Francis G. Mayer **reniform** EM **Janet Reno** FPG\Mark Reinstein **repoussé** AR\The Jewish Museum, New York **respiratory system** Laurel Cook Lhowe **rest[1]** Tech-Graphics **restoration** PR\Robin Laurance **retable** HAR\R. Waldkirch **retriever** ISI\Jay Vergenz **Paul Revere** GC **revolving door** PDI **rheumatoid arthritis** PG **rhinoceros** HAR\E.R. Degginger **rhinoceros beetle** GH\Runk & Schoenberger **Rhodesian ridgeback** AA-ES\Gerard Lacz **rhombohedron** AA **rhombus** AA **rhyton** COR\Gianni Dagli Orti **ribbing** HAR\M. Loken **Sally Ride** COR\Bettmann, UPI **rigging** SS\Kurt Scholz **right angle** AA **Jacob August Riis** COR\Library of Congress **Ring Nebula** FPG\Finley-Holiday **ring-necked pheasant** PI\Roger & Donna Aitkenhead **Diego Rivera** FPG\Bernard Silberstein **roadrunner** HAR\T. Ulrich **roadster** HAR\F. Sieb **Paul Robeson** COR\Hulton-Deutsch Collection **robin** PR\William A. Dyer **Jackie Robinson** COR\Bettmann, UPI **robot** PR\SPL, Volker Steger **John D. Rockefeller** SS **rocking chair** PDI **Knute Rockne** AP-WWP **Richard Rodgers** COR\Bettmann, UPI **Ginger Rogers** SS\Culver Pictures, Inc. **rolamite** PG **Romanesque** COR\John Heseltine **rood screen** COR\Dave Bartruff **rookery** AA-ES\Gerald L. Kooyman **Eleanor Roosevelt** The White House Collection, © White House Historical Association **Franklin Delano Roosevelt** GC **Theodore Roosevelt** GC **roseate spoonbill** ST\Darrell Gulin **rose window** HAR\R. Kord **rotifer** GH\Runk & Schoenberger **rottweiler** AA-ES\Ralph Reinhold **rotunda** FPG\Peter Gridley **Jean Jacques Rousseau** AR\Giraudon **row house** COR\Philippa Lewis, Edifice **Manuel Roxas y Acuña** AP-WWP **royal lily** COR\Eric Crichton **royal palm** PR\Geoffrey Bryant **rubber plant** HM **Peter Paul Rubens** AR\Erich Lessing **ruff[1]** AR\Scala **Rugby[2]** ST\David Davies **runcinate** EM **Salman Rushdie** FPG\Mark Reinstein **Mount Rushmore** HAR\R. Kord **Babe Ruth** GP **Albert Sabin** PR\Will & Deni McIntyre **sabot** HM **Sacagawea** GC **sacrum** CI **Anwar el-Sadat** AP-WWP **safflower** ISI\Priscilla Connell **sagittate** EM **saguaro** HAR\D. Lada **saiga** SS **sailboat** PG **Andrei Sakharov** FPG\Mark Reinstein **salamander** ST\James P. Rowan **Jonas Salk** FPG\Steve Kahn **salsify** COR\Hal Horwitz **saltbox** PI\Candace Cochrane **saluki** PR\Jeanne White **samara** EM **Samoyed** PR\Kent Dannen **sampan** SB\John Elk III **samurai** GC **George Sand** LOC **sand painting** FPG\Buddy Mays **Margaret Sanger** COR\Bettmann, UPI **sansevieria** PI\Patricia J. Bruno **sans serif** PG **santoor** AR\SEF **Sappho** SS **Saqqara** FPG\Ulf Sjostedt **sarcophagus** AR\Erich Lessing **John Singer Sargent** SS\Bridgeman Art Library, London **sari** COR\Barnabas Bosshart **sarong** SS\Ping Amranand **Saturn** GH **Savonarola** AR\Nicolo Orsi Battaglini **saw[1]** AA **saxophone** PDI **scalene** AA **scallop** COR\Douglas P. Wilson, Frank Lane Picture Agency **scalpel** PR\SPL, Claire Paxton & Jacqui Farrow **scarecrow** ST\Philip H. Coblentz **Elsa Schiaparelli** FPG\Keystone Color **schipperke** HM\The Evelyn Shafer Collection **schnauzer** AA-ES\Ralph Reinhold **schooner** FPG\M. Corsetti **Albert Schweitzer** FPG\Eddy Vanderveen **scolex** GH\Runk & Schoenberger **scoliosis** COR\Lester V. Bergman **sconce[2]** COR\Adam Woolfitt **scoreboard** PE\Brian Haimer **Dred Scott** GC **scree** COR\Chinch Gryniewicz, Ecoscene **screen** COR\Sakamoto Photo Research Laboratory **screw** AA **scrimshaw** ISI\Danny Daniels **scroll** FPG\Ulf Sjostedt **scuffle[2]** HM **sea lion** AA-ES\Patti Murray **Elizabeth Seaman** COR\Bettmann **Seattle[1]** Washington State Historical Society, Tacoma **secant** AA **Second Empire** COR\Adam Woolfitt **secretary** COR\Philadelphia Museum of Art **secretary bird** FPG\Stan Osolinski **Pete Seeger** AP-WWP **sego lily** AA-ES\David Welling **seine** GH\Alan Pitcairn **seismograph** PR\Tom McHugh **selvage** HM **semé** PG **semisubmersible** HAR\Larry Lee **Léopold Senghor** COR\Bettmann **sensitive plant** SS **sentry box** PDI **Sequoya** AR\National Portrait Gallery, Smithsonian Institution **sergeant major** AA-ES\Herb Segars **series circuit** AA **serif** PG **serpent** GC **Junípero Serra** GC **serval** AA-ES\Patti Murray **sesame** EM **Elizabeth Seton** GC **Georges Seurat** GC **Sèvres** SS\Private Collection-Peter Harholdt **sextant** PDI **shadow play** PDI **shagbark** PI\Jerry Howard **Shah Jahan** AR\Victoria & Albert Museum, London **Shaker** GC **shamisen** PE\David Young-Wolff **Ravi Shankar** COR\Ted Streshinsky **Shar-Pei** AA-ES\Ralph Reinhold **shear** ISI\Frank Siteman AA **Mary Wollstonecraft Shelley** SS\National Portrait Gallery, London **William Tecumseh Sherman** GC **Shetland pony** AA-ES\John A.L. Cooke **Eduard Shevardnadze** FPG\Mark Reinstein **shield** SS\The Lowe Art Museum, The University of Miami **Shih Tzu** AA-ES\Renee Stockdale **shiitake** HM **Shire horse** AA-ES\Robert Maier **Shiva** AR\Victoria & Albert Museum, London **shock[2]** GH\Larry Lefever **shock absorber** AA **shoebill** COR\David A. Northcott **shoetree** HM **shofar** HAR\Zefa **shot[1]** PDI **shot put** PE\David Young-Wolff **shovel** AA **shrimp** AA-ES\Zigmund Leszczynski **Shropshire[2]** GH\John Colwell **shuttlecock** PDI **Siamese cat** SS **Siamese fighting fish** EM **sickle cell** PR\Meckes-Ottawa **signpost** ST\Paul Hurd **silhouette** GC **silk-cotton tree** PR\Van D. Bucher **silk-screen** HAR\Pelton & Associates **silo** ISI\Aneal Vohra **silverbell tree** WS **Sinai Peninsula** HAR\NASA **sine** AA **sine curve** AA **sisal** GH\Lou Jacobs, Jr. **sitar** SB\Miro Vintoniv **Sitting Bull** GC **skate[2]** PR\Neil McDaniel **sketch** SS\Galleria Degli Uffizi, Florence, Joseph D. Barnell **skewback** PG **skimmer** HM **skort** HM **skull** CI **skunk** PDI **skysurfing** ISI\Benelux Press **slalom** ISI\Joan Eaton **sledge** HAR\M. Rogers, Camerique **sledgehammer** PDI **sling[1]** PDI **slingback** HM **slipknot** HM **sloop** COR\Paul A. Souders **sloth** COR\Michael Fogden & Patricia Fogden **slug[2]** GH\Runk & Schoenberger **sluice** COR\Dorothy Burrows, Eye Ubiquitous **smelter** ST\Paul Chesley **Bessie Smith** LOC\Carl Van Vechten Collection **Joseph Smith** PR\Tom McHugh **smocking** HM **smudge pot** COR\Michael Boys **smudge stick** Courtesy David R. Kurtz of American Treasures, Lafayette, IN **snaffle** HM **snapdragon** PDI **snapping turtle** AA-ES\C.C. Lockwood **snare drum** PDI **snowboard** GP\Paul Savin **snowmobile** GP\Mark E. Gibson **snowshoe** AA-ES\Michael Gadomski **socket wrench** HM **sockeye salmon** ST\Stuart Westmorland **solar panel** ST\Bruce Hands **solenoid** AA **sombrero** PE\Jonathan Nourok **Stephen Sondheim** GP\R. Henry McGee **Sophocles** AR\Scala **souk** SS **Wole Soyinka** LA\Frederic Reglain **spadix** EM **spandrel** AW **Spanish moss** AA-ES\Stephen Ingram **spark plug** AA **sparrow** COR\Michael Callan, Frank Lane Picture Agency **Special Olympics** SB\Bob Daemmrich **spherical angle** AA **sphinx** SS\Kurt Scholz **sphygmomanometer** PE\Merritt Vincent **spicebush swallowtail** HAR\H. Abernathy **spider monkey** FPG\John Giustina **Steven Spielberg** GP\Sylvia Norris **spinal column** CI **spinnaker** SB\Frank Siteman **spinning wheel** SB\John Eastcott & Yva Momatiuk **spiral galaxy** COR\NASA **spirillum** PR\Michael Abbey **spittlebug** PI\Les Campbell **splay** ISI\John Coletti **sponge** SS\Deborah Meeks **sporran** ISI\Don B. Stevenson **spotted owl** ST\Tim Davis **springer spaniel** AA-ES\Robert Pearcy **spruce[1]** GH **spur** PDI COR\Karen Tweedy-Holmes **spur gear** AA **square knot** HM **squash[1]** GH\Jane Grushow **squinch[1]** PG **squirrel monkey** HAR\B. von Hoffmann **stag beetle** HAR\Lanks **stalactite** GH\Runk & Schoenberger **Joseph Stalin** GC **standing stone** COR\Gianni Dagli Orti **Elizabeth Cady Stanton** AR\National Portrait Gallery, Smithsonian Institution; Transfer from the National Museum of Amercian History; Gift of the National American Woman Suffrage Association through Mrs. Harriet Stanton Blatch **star-nosed mole** AA-ES\Michael Habicht **steamboat** ISI\Dennis MacDonald **steel drum** COR\Wolfgang Kaehler steeple FPG\Gary Randall **stele** SS\ET Archive, London **stencil** HM **stentor** PR\Eric Grave **stereoscope** HM **stethoscope** SB\Charles Gupton **stevedore's knot** HM **stile**[1] ST\John Beatty **stingray** AA-ES\Mickey Gibson **stirrup** AA **stockinette stitch** AA **stoma** COR\Ron Boardman, Frank Lane Picture Agency **stomach** CI **Lucy Stone** COR\Bettmann **stopwatch** PDI **stork** AA-ES\Austin J. Stevens **Harriet Beecher Stowe** AR\National Portrait Gallery, Smithsonian Institution **strainer** HM **stratiform** ST\Robert E. Daemmrich **streetcar** PDI **strip-cropping** GH\Larry Lefever **stroller** ST\David Young-Wolff **strophoid** AA **stuccowork** COR\Massimo Listri **stupa** COR\Richard Bickel **submarine** COR\U.S. Department of Defense **subway** COR\Colin Garratt, Milepost 92 ¹/, **Antonio José de Sucre** GC **Suez Canal** SS **Suffolk**[2] PDI **suffragist** LOC **sugar maple** WS **Suleiman I** COR\Ali Meyer **sulky**[2] ISI\Dennis Macdonald **sumo** SS **sun** AA **sunburst** SB\Robert Fried **sunflower** PDI **Sun Yat-sen** COR\Bettmann **supertanker** SS\Malcolm Fife **supplement** AA **supporter** PDI **surfbird** PR\Anthony Mercieca **surfing** COR\Neil Rabinowitz **suricate** SS **surrealism** AR\Giraudon. ©2000 Artists Rights Society (ARS), New York **surrey** GC **suspension** Tech-Graphics **suspension bridge** HAR\G.L. French **swallowtail** ST\Gary Vestal **swamp boat** SB\Greig Cranna **swan** GH\Runk & Schoenberger **swan dive** ST\Bob Torrez **sweet gum** WS **Swiss Guard** HAR\J. Messerschmidt **sycamore** WS **syncopation** Tech-Graphics **Tabriz**[2] SS\Peter Harholdt **tadpole** EM **William Howard Taft** AR\National Portrait Gallery, Smithsonian Institution; Gift of William E. Schevill **Sir Rabindranath Tagore** GC **tail fin** HAR\Camerique **tallith** SB\David Austen **tandem bicycle** FPG\Arthur Tilley **tandoor** COR\Michael Freeman **tangent** AA **tanka**[2] AR\Erich Lessing **tapa**[1] AA-ES\Paddy Ryan **tapir** AA-ES\Zigmunt Leszczynski **tarantula** AA-ES\Allen Blake Sheldon **Ida Tarbell** GC **tarot** HM **tarsier** PR\Tom McHugh **Tasmanian devil** AA-ES\Gary Lewis, Photo Library-Sydney **tatami** HAR\K. Scholz **Zachary Taylor** AR\National Portrait Gallery, Smithsonian Institution **teasel** AA-ES\John Anderson **Renata Tebaldi** COR\Studio Patellani **teething ring** COR\Laura Dwight **Kiri Te Kanawa** COR\Hulton-Deutsch Collection **temple**[1] SS **Alfred, Lord Tennyson** AP-WWP **tent**[1] AA **tent caterpillar** AA-ES\Charles Palek **tepee** COR\Tom Bean **Mother Teresa** GP\Adam Scull **Valentina Tereshkova** PR\SPL **termitarium** PR\Gregory G. Dimijian, MD **terrace** HAR\A. Tovy **tesseract** AA **test tube** ISI\Jacob Halaska **tetrahedron** AA **thatch** ST\John Lawrence **Margaret Thatcher** PR\Mark Reinstein **theodolite** SB\Bob Daemmrich **Theresa of Ávila** AR\Erich Lessing **thistle** AA-ES\Color-Pic **Henry David Thoreau** GC **Jim Thorpe** COR\Bettmann **Three Mile Island** GH\Larry Lefever **thunderbird** COR\Gunter Marx **Thutmose III** COR\Gianni Dagli Orti **thyme** PDI **tiara** PE\Gary Conner **tibia** CI **tide**[1] SB\John Elk III **titmouse** PI\Les Campbell **Tito** COR\Bettmann **toad** AA-ES\Brent P. Kent **tobacco mosaic virus** GH\Runk & Schoenberger **toboggan** ISI\Bob Winsett **toby** HM **toggle bolt** HM **Leo Tolstoy** AR\Scala **tomato hornworm** GH\Denny Eilers **tondo** AR\Scala **tongs** HM **tooth** Laurel Cook Lhowe **topiary** FPG\Peter Gridley **Torah** SB\Miro Vintoniv **torii** SB\Dallas & John Heaton **tornado** COR\Bettmann, UPI **tortoise** GH\Runk & Schoenberger **torus** AW **totem pole** GH\Grant Heilman **toucan** FPG\Gail Shumway **Toussaint L'Ouverture** GC **tracery** AR\Scala **Trajan** AR\SEF **transformer** PG **transom** PE\Mary Steinbacher **transversal** AA **trapezoid** AA **travois** LOC **treble clef** Tech-Graphics **tree frog** PR\Dr. Paul A. Zahl **trefoil** AW **trellis** GH\Larry Lefever **tricorn** ISI\Barry Winiker **trident** COR\Gary Braasch **triglyph** PG **trilithon** HAR\R. Kord **trilobite** PR\SPL **Trimurti** AR\SEF **triplane** COR\George Hall **triple-decker** PI\Jerry Howard **triptych** SS\Church Parish, Cascia di Reggello, Florence, Italy **trisoctahedron** AA **Triton** COR\John Heseltine **trombone** PDI **Leon Trotsky** GC **trowel** AA **trug** HM **Bess Truman** The White House Collection, © White House Historical Association **Harry S. Truman** AR\National Portrait Gallery, Smithsonian Institution; Gift of Dean Acheson, Thomas C. Clark, John W. Snyder, Robert A. Lovett, Clinton P. Anderson, Charles F. Brannan, Charles Sawyer, W. Averell Harriman, David K.E. Bruce, Edward H. Foley, Stuart Symington, William McChesney Martin, Clark Clifford, Charles S. Murphy, Ward M. Canaday, and Joseph Stack. **truss bridge** GP **Sojourner Truth** LOC **try square** HM **T-square** HM **tuba** SB\Bob Daemmrich **tuberose**[1] PR\Geoffrey Bryant **Harriet Tubman** LOC **tugboat** SS **tulip tree** PR\Larry Richardson **tumpline** SS\AGE FotoStock **tuning fork** PDI **turban** ISI\Bill Bachman **turbine** AA **tureen** HM **turnbuckle** PDI **turnstone** AA-ES\Robert Maier **Tutankhamen** FPG\Jean Kugler **Desmond Tutu** FPG\Mark Reinstein **John Tyler** AR\National Portrait Gallery, Smithsonian Institution **tympanum** HAR\Ralph Krubner **Tzu Hsi** GC **U-bolt** PDI **ukulele** PDI **ulna** CI **umbrella**

plant PI\Ben Phillips **umiak** AA-ES\Doug Allan, Oxford Scientific Films **umpire** PE\Tom Prettyman **Miguel de Unamuno** AP-WWP **Uncle Sam** LOC **underhand** PE\David Young-Wolff **Sigrid Undset** AP-WWP **undulate** EM **unicorn** AR\Erich Lessing **Union Jack** GP\©1997 Imapress **unitard** HAR\B. Taylor **United Nations** HAR\Camerique **Universal Product Code** PR\Alan L. Detrick **Unknown Soldier** FPG\Jeffrey Sylvester **John Updike** AP-WWP **upland sandpiper** PR\Steve Maslowski **upright piano** SB\Bob Daemmrich **uproot** SB\Eric Neurath **uraeus** SB\Robert Caputo **usnea** AA-ES\Leonard Rue Enterprises **Maurice Utrillo** AR\Giraudon. ©2000 Artists Rights Society (ARS), New York/ADAGP, Paris **valve** AA **vampire bat** PR\Tom McHugh **Martin Van Buren** AR\National Portrait Gallery, Smithsonian Institution **Van de Graaff generator** AA **Vincent van Gogh** AR\Erich Lessing **vanilla** AA-ES\Patti Murray **vanishing point** SB\Bob Daemmrich **vase** COR\Royal Ontario Museum **Sarah Vaughan** COR\Hulton-Deutsch Collection **vault**[1] AA **vector product** AA **veil** SS\Holton Collection PE\Mark Richards **velocipede** COR\Museum of the City of New York **Venus flytrap** AA-ES\Oxford Scientific Films **Giuseppe Verdi** AR\Scala. ©2000 Artists Rights Society (ARS), New York/ADAGP, Paris **vernier caliper** GH\Runk & Schoenberger **veronica**[2] AR\Nimatallah **Versailles** GP\Cris Haigh Photography **vertical angle** AA **vervet** AA-ES\Johnny Johnson **viaduct** AA-ES\Michael P. Gadomski **vibraphone** PDI **viceroy** AA-ES\Breck P. Kent **Victoria**[1] SS\Stock Montage **Victoria Falls** AA-ES\D. Allen Photography **videoconference** PR\SPL **Élisabeth Vigée-Lebrun** COR\The National Gallery, London **Pancho Villa** COR\Hulton-Deutsch Collection **violin** PDI **viperfish** PR\Gregory Ochocki **Virginia creeper** PR\Alan L. Detrick **vise** HAR\T. Del Amo **Vishnu** COR\Kevin R. Morris **vizsla** HM\The Evelyn Shafer Collection **Voltaire** AR\Giraudon **voltmeter** GH\Runk & Schoenberger **volvox** PR\Hermann Eisenbeiss **V sign** COR\Bettmann **vulture** SS **waders** ST\David Epperson **wake**[2] PR\Bill Bachman **wakeboard** COR\Neil Rabinowitz **Lech Walesa** COR\Peter Turnley **Alice Walker** GP\Andrea Renault **wallaby** ST\Art Wolfe **walnut** WS **wampum** SB\Lawrence Migdale **wapiti** GH\Arthur C. Smith III **Andy Warhol** FPG\Alex Wasinski **warming pan** PE\Susan Van Etten Lawson **wart hog** HAR\Leonard Lee Rue III **Booker T. Washington** AR\National Portrait Gallery, Smithsonian Institution **George Washington** SS\David David Gallery, Philadelphia **Martha Washington** AR\National Portrait Gallery, Smithsonian Institution **water buffalo** ST\Kevin R. Morris **watercolor** SS\San Diego Museum of Art, California (Bequest of Mrs. Eda Hurd Lord) **water polo** HAR\A. Hubrich **water wheel** SS\Roy King **wattle** HAR\W. Metzen **wavelength** AA **waxwing** HAR\T. Ulrich **weathercock** GH **weathering** PI\Dennis Frates **weave** PE\Paul Conklin **weeping willow** PI\Jerry Howard **weevil** PI\Holt Studios **Weimaraner** PR\Tim Davis **Chaim Weizmann** COR\Bettmann **Ida B. Wells** GC **Welsh corgi** HAR\Camerique **Western Wall** HAR\C. Ursillo **wetsuit** COR\Rick Doyle **Edith Wharton** COR\Bettmann **Wheatstone bridge** AA **wheelchair** FPG\Mark Scott ISI\Kindra Clineff **whippoorwill** PR\Adam Jones **whisker** GP\Shawn M. Lowe **White House** PR\Vanessa Vick ISI\David Ball **white oak** WS **white-tailed deer** AA-ES\Don Enger **whitewall tire** HAR\R. Downs **whittle** FPG\Jim Cummins **whooping crane** AA-ES\Ruth Cole **whorl** EM **wickiup** FPG\Jim Mejuto **Elie Wiesel** COR\Owen Franken **wild turkey** FPG\Adolf Schmidecker **Ted Williams** FPG\Evan Peskin **Woodrow Wilson** PR\Tom McHugh, The National Portrait Gallery, Smithsonian Institution; Transfer from the National Museum of American Art; Gift of the city of New York through the National Art Committee, 1923 **wimple** SS\Fratelli Alinari **winch** COR\Nigel Rolstone, Cordaiy Photo Library **windmill** PDI **Windsor chair** SS\Christie's Images **Oprah Winfrey** GP\Evie Sullivan **wing nut** HM **wingtip** HM **wisent** AA-ES\Studio Carlo Dani **wolf** HAR\Len Rue, Jr. **wombat** SB\John Cancalosi **wood anemone** GH\Runk & Schoenberger **woodpecker** PI\Scott Leonhart **wood tick** AA-ES\James Robinson **Virginia Woolf** GC **woolly bear** GH\Runk & Schoenberger **William Wordsworth** GC **worm gear** AA **wren** AA-ES\Paul Berquist **wrench** HM **Orville and Wilbur Wright** FPG\Library of Congress **Wyandotte** AA-ES\Richard Kolar **Xerxes I** COR\Roger Wood **x-ray** ST\Med. Illus. SBHA **xylophone** PDI **yak**[1] AA-ES\Peter Weimann **yarmulke** ISI\Jeff Greenberg **William Butler Yeats** COR\Bettmann **yellow jacket** GH\Runk & Schoenberger **yin** PG **yoga** SB\Bob Daemmrich **Yorkshire terrier** PR\Jeanne White **Cy Young** COR\Bettmann **yucca** PR\Mark Newman **yurt** PR\Eagy Landau **Babe Didrikson Zaharias** COR\Bettmann **Emiliano Zapata** GC **Zeus** AR\Nimatallah **zinnia** PI\Ben Phillips **zucchetto** SB\Bob Daemmrich **zucchini** ST\Agriculture File

THE INDO-EUROPEAN FAMILY OF LANGUAGES

The Indo-European family of languages, of which English is one member, is descended from the prehistoric Proto-Indo-European language, which was spoken in an as yet unidentified area between eastern Europe and the Aral Sea around the fifth millennium B.C. This chart displays the genetic relationships among the principal languages of the Indo-European family and

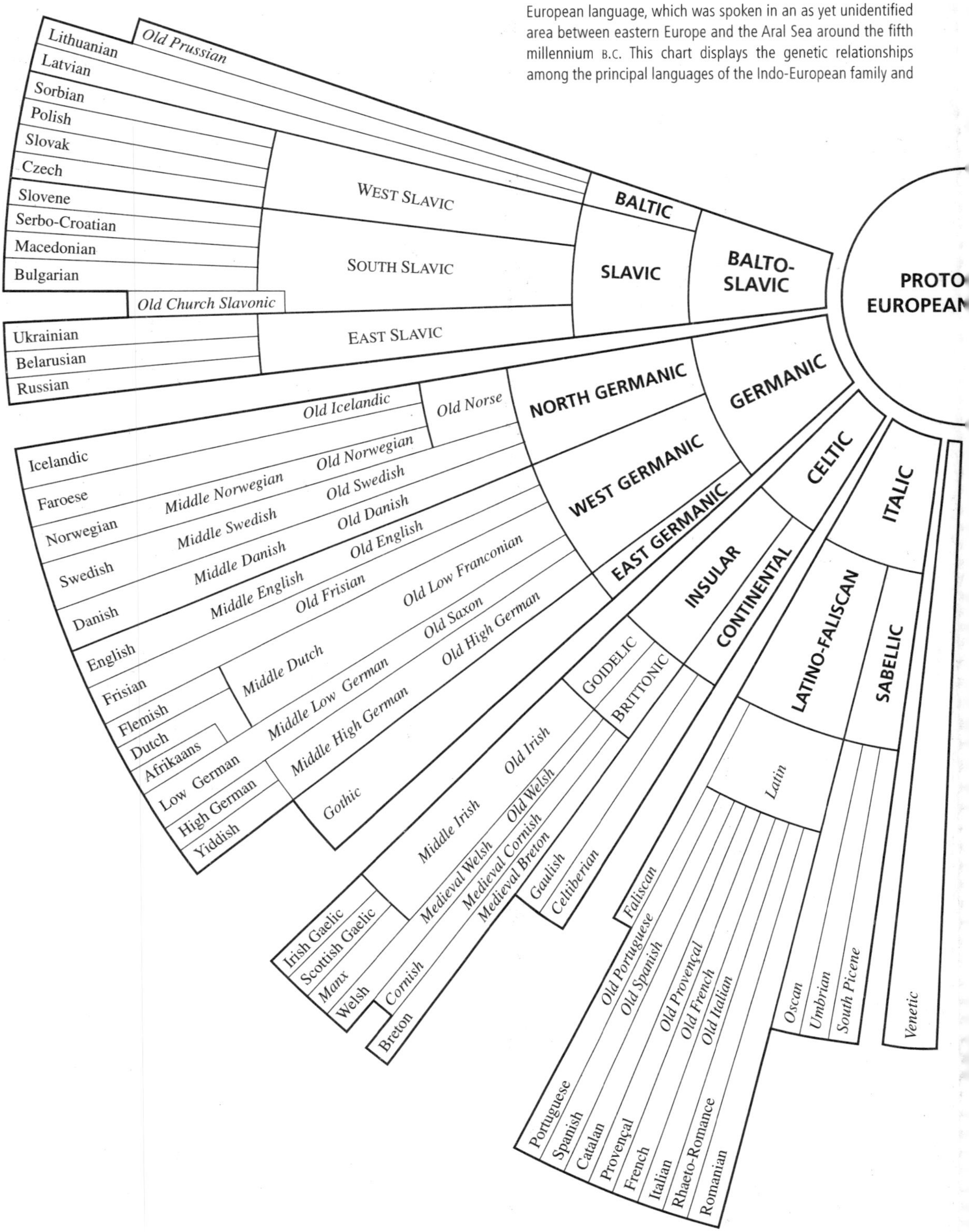

PROTO
EUROPEAN

BALTO-SLAVIC

BALTIC

Lithuanian
Old Prussian

SLAVIC

WEST SLAVIC

Latvian
Sorbian
Polish
Slovak
Czech
Slovene
Serbo-Croatian
Macedonian
Bulgarian

SOUTH SLAVIC

Old Church Slavonic

EAST SLAVIC

Ukrainian
Belarusian
Russian

GERMANIC

NORTH GERMANIC

Old Icelandic
Old Norse

Icelandic
Faroese
Norwegian
Swedish
Danish

Middle Norwegian
Middle Swedish
Middle Danish

Old Norwegian
Old Swedish
Old Danish

WEST GERMANIC

Old English
Middle English
Old Frisian

English
Frisian
Flemish
Dutch
Afrikaans
Low German
High German
Yiddish

Middle Dutch
Middle Low German
Middle High German

Old Low Franconian
Old Saxon
Old High German

EAST GERMANIC

Gothic

CELTIC

INSULAR

GOIDELIC

BRITTONIC

Old Irish
Middle Irish
Medieval Welsh
Old Welsh
Medieval Cornish
Medieval Breton

Irish Gaelic
Scottish Gaelic
Manx
Welsh
Cornish
Breton

CONTINENTAL

Gaulish
Celtiberian

ITALIC

LATINO-FALISCAN

Latin

Faliscan
Old Portuguese
Old Spanish
Old Provençal
Old French
Old Italian

Portuguese
Spanish
Catalan
Provençal
French
Italian
Rhaeto-Romance
Romanian

SABELLIC

Oscan
Umbrian
South Picene

Venetic